Who's Who in Finance and Industry

Biographical Titles Currently Published by Marquis Who's Who

Who's Who in America
Who's Who in America derivatives:
   Geographic/Professional Index
   Supplement to Who's Who in America
   Who's Who in America Classroom Project Book
Who Was Who in America
   Historical Volume (1607-1896)
   Volume I (1897-1942)
   Volume II (1943-1950)
   Volume III (1951-1960)
   Volume IV (1961-1968)
   Volume V (1969-1973)
   Volume VI (1974-1976)
   Volume VII (1977-1981)
   Volume VIII (1982-1985)
   Volume IX (1985-1989)
   Index Volume (1607-1989)
Who's Who in the World
Who's Who in the East
Who's Who in the Midwest
Who's Who in the South and Southwest
Who's Who in the West
Who's Who in Advertising
Who's Who in American Law
Who's Who of American Women
Who's Who of Emerging Leaders in America
Who's Who in Entertainment
Who's Who in Finance and Industry
Index to Who's Who Books
Directory of Medical Specialists
Supplement to Directory of Medical Specialists

Who's Who
in Finance
and Industry ®

26th edition
1989-90

MARQUIS
Who's Who

Macmillan Directory Division
3002 Glenview Road
Wilmette, Illinois 60091 U.S.A.

James J. Pfister—President
Paul E. Rose—Executive Vice President
Timothy J. Sullivan—Vice President, Finance
A. Robert Weicherding—Vice President, Publisher
Sandra S. Barnes—Group Vice President, Product Management
Jill E. Lazar—Product Manager

WHO'S WHO IN FINANCE AND INDUSTRY is a registered trademark of
Macmillan Information Company, Inc.

Library of Congress Catalog Card Number 70–616550
International Standard Book Number 0–8379–0326–2
Product Code Number 030543

Distributed in Asia by
United Publishers Services Ltd.
Kenkyu-Sha Bldg.
9, Kanda Surugadai 2-Chome
Chiyoda-ku, Tokyo, Japan

Manufactured in the United States of America

Table of Contents

Preface

For the twenty-sixth edition of *Who's Who in Finance and Industry*, the editors present comprehensive coverage of approximately 23,500 North American and international professionals who are of current business reference interest.

This volume includes executives from important companies in the following areas: accounting, advertising, banking and finance, communications, construction and engineering, industrial and commercial firms, insurance, investment companies, retail trade, transportation, utilities, as well as other sectors of the business community. In addition, the directory covers professionals in business-related fields, such as selected government officials, heads of stock exchanges, business educators and researchers, directors of professional and trade associations in business, and labor union officers. Also included are professionals in smaller businesses important or prominent in their home regions.

Each candidate for inclusion in *Who's Who in Finance and Industry* is invited to submit biographical data about his or her life and business career. This information is reviewed by the Marquis editorial staff before being written into sketch form. A prepublication proof of the sketch is sent to the biographee for verification. The verified sketch, when returned and accepted by Marquis Who's Who, is rechecked and put into final Who's Who format.

In the event that a reference-worthy individual fails to submit biographical data, the Marquis staff compiles the information through independent research. Such sketches are denoted by an asterisk. Brief key information is provided in the sketches of selected individuals, new to this edition, who did not submit data.

Marquis Who's Who editors exercise the utmost care in preparing each biographical sketch for publication. Occasionally, however, errors do appear, despite all precautions taken to minimize such occurrences. Users of this directory are requested to draw to the attention of the publisher any errors found so that corrections can be made in a subsequent edition.

Board of Advisors

Marquis Who's Who gratefully acknowledges the following distinguished individuals who have made themselves available for review, evaluation, and general comment with regard to the publication of the twenty-sixth edition of *Who's Who in Finance and Industry*. The advisors have enhanced the reference value of this edition by the nomination of outstanding individuals for inclusion. However, the Board of Advisors, either collectively or individually, is in no way responsible for the selection of names or for the accuracy of the information in this volume.

William M.H. Hammett
President
Manhattan Institute for
  Policy Research

Thomas R. Horton
President and Chief Executive Officer
American Management Association

Russell E. Palmer
Dean
Wharton School of Business
University of Pennsylvania

Louis Rukeyser
Economic Commentator
Host, *Wall Street Week*
  with Louis Rukeyser

Alexander B. Trowbridge
President
National Association of Manufacturers

Julia M. Walsh
Managing Director
Tucker Anthony

Standards of Admission

In the process of compiling names for inclusion in *Who's Who in Finance and Industry*, the aim has been to select qualified men and women in all lines of useful and reputable financial endeavor. The standards of admission provide for the selection of those individuals who, because of prominence in particular branches of business, have become subjects of interest, inquiry, or discussion in the business world. Others are chosen because of positions held in financial and industrial concerns defined by size based on assets or sales, or by other specialized rating criteria.

The first group includes persons who have accomplished conspicuous achievements that distinguish them from the majority of their business contemporaries. Frequently appearing are individuals who are prominent in some special fields, but who may be little known in their own communities. On the other hand, some of the biographees may be known in their own communities, but may not be widely recognized in their particular fields of endeavor.

The second group consists of incumbents in specified positions: principals of financial and industrial concerns capitalized at or above a certain figure; principals of business organizations of the type not readily judged on capitalization alone, but of high commercial rating; principals of leading firms engaged in international industry or finance; principals of a select list of highly specialized concerns; and holders of specific positions in business-related organizations.

Key to Information

[1] **BURKE, GEORGE ALLEN,** [2] engineering design company executive; [3] b. Highland Park, Ill., Mar. 23, 1926; [4] s. Miles Benjamin and Thelma Ruth (Allen) B.; [5] m. Leota Gruber, Jan. 28, 1946; [6] children: Evangeline Marie Burke Rossett, Joseph Paul, Harvey Edwin, Suzanne Claire. [7] BS, U. Ill., 1948, MS, 1951. [8] Registered profl. engr., Ill. [9] With Nat. Engring. Corp., Peoria, Ill., 1954—, mem. tech. staff, 1956-60, rsch. engr., 1960-65, sr. rsch. engr., 1965-72, sr. v.p., 1972-80, exec. v.p., 1980-85, pres., 1985—; cons. GATX Corp., Chgo.; lectr. Peoria Community Coll., 1982-84. [10] Contbr. articles to profl. jours. [11] Active Boy Scouts Am.; sec. Ill. Gov.'s Commn. on Pub. Safety, 1982-86; mem. Peoria Heights Bd. Edn., 1970-76. [12] Served USN, 1943-45, PTO. [13] Decorated Purple Heart; recipient Silver Beaver award Boys Scouts Am., 1969. [14] Fellow ASME; mem. Nat. Soc. Profl. Engrs., Am. Phys. Soc., ASTM, Sigma Xi. [15] Democrat. [16] Presbyterian. [17] Clubs: Peoria Lake Country, Chgo. Athletic. [18] Lodges: Masons, Shriners. [19] Home: 903 Spring Dr Peoria Heights IL 61613 [20] Office: Nat Engring Corp 1912 Main St Peoria IL 61606

KEY

[1]	Name
[2]	Occupation
[3]	Vital statistics
[4]	Parents
[5]	Marriage
[6]	Children
[7]	Education
[8]	Professional certifications
[9]	Career
[10]	Writings and creative works
[11]	Civic and political activities
[12]	Military
[13]	Awards and fellowships
[14]	Professional and association memberships
[15]	Political affiliation
[16]	Religion
[17]	Clubs
[18]	Lodges
[19]	Home Address
[20]	Office Address

Table of Abbreviations

The following abbreviations and symbols are frequently used in this book

*An asterisk following a sketch indicates that it was researched by the Marquis Who's Who editorial staff and has not been verified by the biographee.

AA, A.A. Associate in Arts, Associate of Arts
AAAL American Academy of Arts and Letters
AAAS American Association for the Advancement of Science
AAHPER Alliance for Health, Physical Education and Recreation
AAU Amateur Athletic Union
AAUP American Association of University Professors
AAUW American Association of University Women
AB, A.B. Arts, Bachelor of
AB Alberta
ABA American Bar Association
ABC American Broadcasting Company
AC Air Corps
acad. academy, academic
acct. accountant
acctg. accounting
ACDA Arms Control and Disarmament Agency
ACLU American Civil Liberties Union
ACP American College of Physicians
ACS American College of Surgeons
ADA American Dental Association
a.d.c. aide-de-camp
adj. adjunct, adjutant
adj. gen. adjutant general
adm. admiral
adminstr. administrator
adminstrn. administration
adminstrv. administrative
ADP Automatic Data Processing
adv. advocate, advisory
advt. advertising
AE, A.E. Agricultural Engineer
A.E. and P. Ambassador Extraordinary and Plenipotentiary
AEC Atomic Energy Commission
aero. aeronautical, aeronautic
aerodyn. aerodynamic
AFB Air Force Base
AFL-CIO American Federation of Labor and Congress of Industrial Organizations
AFTRA American Federation of TV and Radio Artists
AFSCME American Federation of State, County and Municipal Employees
agr. agriculture
agrl. agricultural
agt. agent
AGVA American Guild of Variety Artists
agy. agency

A&I Agricultural and Industrial
AIA American Institute of Architects
AIAA American Institute of Aeronautics and Astronautics
AICPA American Institute of Certified Public Accountants
AID Agency for International Development
AIDS Acquired Immune Deficiency Syndrome
AIEE American Institute of Electrical Engineers
AIM American Institute of Management
AIME American Institute of Mining, Metallurgy, and Petroleum Engineers
AK Alaska
AL Alabama
ALA American Library Association
Ala. Alabama
alt. alternate
Alta. Alberta
A&M Agricultural and Mechanical
AM, A.M. Arts, Master of
Am. American, America
AMA American Medical Association
amb. ambassador
A.M.E. African Methodist Episcopal
Amtrak National Railroad Passenger Corporation
AMVETS American Veterans of World War II, Korea, Vietnam
anat. anatomical
ann. annual
ANTA American National Theatre and Academy
anthrop. anthropological
AP Associated Press
APO Army Post Office
apptd. appointed
Apr. April
apt. apartment
AR Arkansas
ARC American Red Cross
archeol. archeological
archtl. architectural
Ariz. Arizona
Ark. Arkansas
ArtsD, ArtsD. Arts, Doctor of
arty. artillery
AS American Samoa
AS Associate in Science
AS Associate of Applied Science
ASCAP American Society of Composers, Authors and Publishers
ASCE American Society of Civil Engineers
ASHRAE American Society of Heating, Refrigeration, and Air Conditioning Engineers

ASME American Society of Mechanical Engineers
ASPCA American Society for the Prevention of Cruelty to Animals
assn. association
assoc. associate
asst. assistant
ASTM American Society for Testing and Materials
astron. astronomical
astrophys. astrophysical
ATSC Air Technical Service Command
AT&T American Telephone & Telegraph Company
atty. attorney
Aug. August
AUS Army of the United States
aux. auxiliary
Ave. Avenue
AVMA American Veterinary Medical Association
AZ Arizona

B. Bachelor
b. born
BA, B.A. Bachelor of Arts
BAgr, B.Agr. Bachelor of Agriculture
Balt. Baltimore
Bapt. Baptist
BArch, B.Arch. Bachelor of Architecture
BAS, B.A.S. Bachelor of Agricultural Science
BBA, B.B.A. Bachelor of Business Administration
BBC British Broadcasting Corporation
BC, B.C. British Columbia
BCE, B.C.E. Bachelor of Civil Engineering
BChir, B.Chir. Bachelor of Surgery
BCL, B.C.L. Bachelor of Civil Law
BCS, B.C.S. Bachelor of Commercial Science
BD, B.D. Bachelor of Divinity
bd. board
BE, B.E. Bachelor of Education
BEE, B.E.E. Bachelor of Electrical Engineering
BFA, B.F.A. Bachelor of Fine Arts
bibl. biblical
bibliog. bibliographical
biog. biographical
biol. biological
BJ, B.J. Bachelor of Journalism
Bklyn. Brooklyn
BL, B.L. Bachelor of Letters
bldg. building
BLS, B.L.S. Bachelor of Library Science
Blvd. Boulevard

BMW Bavarian Motor Works (Bayerische Motoren Werke)
bn. batallion
B.& O.R.R. Baltimore & Ohio Railroad
bot. botanical
BPE, B.P.E. Bachelor of Physical Education
BPhil, B.Phil. Bachelor of Philosophy
br. branch
BRE, B.R.E. Bachelor of Religious Education
brig. gen. brigadier general
Brit. British, Brittanica
Bros. Brothers
BS, B.S. Bachelor of Science
BSA, B.S.A. Bachelor of Agricultural Science
BSBA Bachelor of Science in Business Administration
BSChemE Bachelor of Science in Chemical Engineering
BSD, B.S.D. Bachelor of Didactic Science
BST, B.S.T. Bachelor of Sacred Theology
BTh, B.Th. Bachelor of Theology
bull. bulletin
bur. bureau
bus. business
B.W.I. British West Indies

CA California
CAA Civil Aeronautics Administration
CAB Civil Aeronautics Board
CAD-CAM Computer Aided Design-Computer Aided Model
Calif. California
C.Am. Central America
Can. Canada, Canadian
CAP Civil Air Patrol
capt. captain
CARE Cooperative American Relief Everywhere
Cath. Catholic
cav. cavalry
CBC Canadian Broadcasting Company
CBI China, Burma, India Theatre of Operations
CBS Columbia Broadcasting Company
CCC Commodity Credit Corporation
CCNY City College of New York
CCU Cardiac Care Unit
CD Civil Defense
CE, C.E. Corps of Engineers, Civil Engineer
cen. central
CENTO Central Treaty Organization
CERN European Organization of Nuclear Research
cert. certificate, certification, certified
CETA Comprehensive Employment Training Act
CFL Canadian Football League
ch. church
ChD, Ch.D. Doctor of Chemistry
chem. chemical
ChemE, Chem.E. Chemical Engineer
Chgo. Chicago

chirurg. chirurgical
chmn. chairman
chpt. chapter
CIA Central Intelligence Agency
Cin. Cincinnati
cir. circuit
Cleve. Cleveland
climatol. climatological
clin. clinical
clk. clerk
C.L.U. Chartered Life Underwriter
CM, C.M. Master in Surgery
CM Northern Mariana Islands
C.&N.W.Ry. Chicago & North Western Railway
CO Colorado
Co. Company
COF Catholic Order of Foresters
C. of C. Chamber of Commerce
col. colonel
coll. college
Colo. Colorado
com. committee
comd. commanded
comdg. commanding
comdr. commander
comdt. commandant
commd. commissioned
comml. commercial
commn. commission
commr. commissioner
compt. comptroller
condr. conductor
Conf. Conference
Congl. Congregational, Congressional
Conglist. Congregationalist
Conn. Connecticut
cons. consultant, consulting
consol. consolidated
constl. constitutional
constn. constitution
constrn. construction
contbd. contributed
contbg. contributing
contbn. contribution
contbr. contributor
contr. controller
Conv. Convention
coop. cooperative
coord. coordinator
CORDS Civil Operations and Revolutionary Development Support
CORE Congress of Racial Equality
corp. corporation, corporate
corr. correspondent, corresponding, correspondence
C.&O.Ry. Chesapeake & Ohio Railway
coun. council
C.P.A. Certified Public Accountant
C.P.C.U. Chartered Property and Casualty Underwriter
CPH, C.P.H. Certificate of Public Health
cpl. corporal
C.P.R. Cardio-Pulmonary Resuscitation
C.P.Ry. Canadian Pacific Railway
CRT Cathode Ray Terminal

C.S. Christian Science
CSB, C.S.B. Bachelor of Christian Science
C.S.C. Civil Service Commission
CT Connecticut
ct. court
ctr. center
CWS Chemical Warfare Service
C.Z. Canal Zone

D. Doctor
d. daughter
DAgr, D.Agr. Doctor of Agriculture
DAR Daughters of the American Revolution
dau. daughter
DAV Disabled American Veterans
DC, D.C. District of Columbia
DCL, D.C.L. Doctor of Civil Law
DCS, D.C.S. Doctor of Commercial Science
DD, D.D. Doctor of Divinity
DDS, D.D.S. Doctor of Dental Surgery
DE Delaware
Dec. December
dec. deceased
def. defense
Del. Delaware
del. delegate, delegation
Dem. Democrat, Democratic
DEng, D.Eng. Doctor of Engineering
denom. denomination, denominational
dep. deputy
dept. department
dermatol. dermatological
desc. descendant
devel. development, developmental
DFA, D.F.A. Doctor of Fine Arts
D.F.C. Distinguished Flying Cross
DHL, D.H.L. Doctor of Hebrew Literature
dir. director
dist. district
distbg. distributing
distbn. distribution
distbr. distributor
disting. distinguished
div. division, divinity, divorce
DLitt, D.Litt. Doctor of Literature
DMD, D.M.D. Doctor of Medical Dentistry
DMS, D.M.S. Doctor of Medical Science
DO, D.O. Doctor of Osteopathy
DPH, D.P.H. Diploma in Public Health
DPhil, D.Phil. Doctor of Philosophy
D.R. Daughters of the Revolution
Dr. Drive, Doctor
DRE, D.R.E. Doctor of Religious Education
DrPH, Dr.P.H. Doctor of Public Health, Doctor of Public Hygiene
D.S.C. Distinguished Service Cross
DSc, D.Sc. Doctor of Science
D.S.M. Distinguished Service Medal
DST, D.S.T. Doctor of Sacred Theology
DTM, D.T.M. Doctor of Tropical Medicine
DVM, D.V.M. Doctor of Veterinary Medicine
DVS, D.V.S. Doctor of Veterinary Surgery

E, E. East
ea. eastern

E. and P. Extraordinary and Plenipotentiary
Eccles. Ecclesiastical
ecol. ecological
econ. economic
ECOSOC Economic and Social Council (of the UN)
ED, E.D. Doctor of Engineering
ed. educated
EdB, Ed.B. Bachelor of Education
EdD, Ed.D. Doctor of Education
edit. edition
EdM, Ed.M. Master of Education
edn. education
ednl. educational
EDP Electronic Data Processing
EdS, Ed.S. Specialist in Education
EE, E.E. Electrical Engineer
E.E. and M.P. Envoy Extraordinary and Minister Plenipotentiary
EEC European Economic Community
EEG Electroencephalogram
EEO Equal Employment Opportunity
EEOC Equal Employment Opportunity Commission
E.Ger. German Democratic Republic
EKG Electrocardiogram
elec. electrical
electrochem. electrochemical
electrophys. electrophysical
elem. elementary
EM, E.M. Engineer of Mines
ency. encyclopedia
Eng. England
engr. engineer
engring. engineering
entomol. entomological
environ. environmental
EPA Environmental Protection Agency
epidemiol. epidemiological
Episc. Episcopalian
ERA Equal Rights Amendment
ERDA Energy Research and Development Administration
ESEA Elementary and Secondary Education Act
ESL English as Second Language
ESPN Entertainment and Sports Programming Network
ESSA Environmental Science Services Administration
ethnol. ethnological
ETO European Theatre of Operations
Evang. Evangelical
exam. examination, examining
Exch. Exchange
exec. executive
exhbn. exhibition
expdn. expedition
expn. exposition
expt. experiment
exptl. experimental
Expwy. Expressway

F.A. Field Artillery
FAA Federal Aviation Administration

FAO Food and Agriculture Organization (of the UN)
FBI Federal Bureau of Investigation
FCA Farm Credit Administration
FCC Federal Communications Commission
FCDA Federal Civil Defense Administration
FDA Food and Drug Administration
FDIA Federal Deposit Insurance Administration
FDIC Federal Deposit Insurance Corporation
FE, F.E. Forest Engineer
FEA Federal Energy Administration
Feb. February
fed. federal
fedn. federation
FERC Federal Energy Regulatory Commission
fgn. foreign
FHA Federal Housing Administration
fin. financial, finance
FL Florida
Fl. Floor
Fla. Florida
FMC Federal Maritime Commission
FOA Foreign Operations Administration
found. foundation
FPC Federal Power Commission
FPO Fleet Post Office
frat. fraternity
FRS Federal Reserve System
Frwy. Freeway
FSA Federal Security Agency
Ft. Fort
FTC Federal Trade Commission

G-1 (or other number) Division of General Staff
GA, Ga. Georgia
GAO General Accounting Office
gastroent. gastroenterological
GATT General Agreement of Tariff and Trades
GE General Electric Company
gen. general
geneal. genealogical
geod. geodetic
geog. geographic, geographical
geol. geological
geophys. geophysical
gerontol. gerontological
G.H.Q. General Headquarters
GM General Motors Corporation
GMAC General Motors Acceptance Corporation
G.N.Ry. Great Northern Railway
gov. governor
govt. government
govtl. governmental
GPO Government Printing Office
grad. graduate, graduated
GSA General Services Administration
Gt. Great
GTE General Telephone and Electric Company

GU Guam
gynecol. gynecological

HBO Home Box Office
hdqrs. headquarters
HEW Department of Health, Education and Welfare
HHD, H.H.D. Doctor of Humanities
HHFA Housing and Home Finance Agency
HHS Department of Health and Human Services
HI Hawaii
hist. historical, historic
HM, H.M. Master of Humanics
HMO Health Maintenance Organization
homeo. homeopathic
hon. honorary, honorable
Ho. of Dels. House of Delegates
Ho. of Reps. House of Representatives
hort. horticultural
hosp. hospital
HUD Department of Housing and Urban Development
Hwy. Highway
hydrog. hydrographic

IA Iowa
IAEA International Atomic Energy Agency
IBM International Business Machines Corporation
IBRD International Bank for Reconstruction and Development
ICA International Cooperation Administration
ICC Interstate Commerce Commission
ICU Intensive Care Unit
ID Idaho
IEEE Institute of Electrical and Electronics Engineers
IFC International Finance Corporation
IGY International Geophysical Year
IL Illinois
Ill. Illinois
illus. illustrated
ILO International Labor Organization
IMF International Monetary Fund
IN Indiana
Inc. Incorporated
Ind. Indiana
ind. independent
Indpls. Indianapolis
indsl. industrial
inf. infantry
info. information
ins. insurance
insp. inspector
insp. gen. inspector general
inst. institute
instl. institutional
instn. institution
instr. instructor
instrn. instruction
internat. international
intro. introduction
IRE Institute of Radio Engineers

IRS Internal Revenue Service
ITT International Telephone & Telegraph Corporation

JAG Judge Advocate General
JAGC Judge Advocate General Corps
Jan. January
Jaycees Junior Chamber of Commerce
JB, J.B. Jurum Baccalaureus
JCB, J.C.B. Juris Canoni Baccalaureus
JCD, J.C.D. Juris Canonici Doctor, Juris Civilis Doctor
JCL, J.C.L. Juris Canonici Licentiatus
JD, J.D. Juris Doctor
jg. junior grade
jour. journal
jr. junior
JSD, J.S.D. Juris Scientiae Doctor
JUD, J.U.D. Juris Utriusque Doctor
jud. judicial

Kans. Kansas
K.C. Knights of Columbus
K.P. Knights of Pythias
KS Kansas
K.T. Knight Templar
KY, Ky. Kentucky

LA, La. Louisiana
L.A. Los Angeles
lab. laboratory
lang. language
laryngol. laryngological
LB Labrador
LDS Church Church of Jesus Christ of Latter Day Saints
lectr. lecturer
legis. legislation, legislative
LHD, L.H.D. Doctor of Humane Letters
L.I. Long Island
libr. librarian, library
lic. licensed, license
L.I.R.R. Long Island Railroad
lit. literature
LittB, Litt.B. Bachelor of Letters
LittD, Litt.D. Doctor of Letters
LLB, LL.B. Bachelor of Laws
LLD, L.L.D. Doctor of Laws
LLM, L.L.M. Master of Laws
Ln. Lane
L.&N.R.R. Louisville & Nashville Railroad
LPGA Ladies Professional Golf Association
LS, L.S. Library Science (in degree)
lt. lieutenant
Ltd. Limited
Luth. Lutheran
LWV League of Women Voters

M. Master
m. married
MA, M.A. Master of Arts
MA Massachusetts
MADD Mothers Against Drunk Driving
mag. magazine
Man. Manitoba
Mar. March

MArch, M.Arch. Master in Architecture
Mass. Massachusetts
math. mathematics, mathematical
MATS Military Air Transport Service
MB, M.B. Bachelor of Medicine
MB Manitoba
MBA, M.B.A. Master of Business Administration
MBS Mutual Broadcasting System
M.C. Medical Corps
MCE, M.C.E. Master of Civil Engineering
mcht. merchant
mcpl. municipal
MCS, M.C.S. Master of Commercial Science
MD, M.D. Doctor of Medicine
MD, Md. Maryland
MDiv Master of Divinity
MDip, M.Dip. Master in Diplomacy
mdse. merchandise
MDV, M.D.V. Doctor of Veterinary Medicine
ME, M.E. Mechanical Engineer
ME Maine
M.E.Ch. Methodist Episcopal Church
mech. mechanical
MEd., M.Ed. Master of Education
med. medical
MEE, M.E.E. Master of Electrical Engineering
mem. member
meml. memorial
merc. mercantile
met. metropolitan
metall. metallurgical
MetE, Met.E. Metallurgical Engineer
meteorol. meteorological
Meth. Methodist
Mex. Mexico
MF, M.F. Master of Forestry
MFA, M.F.A. Master of Fine Arts
mfg. manufacturing
mfr. manufacturer
mgmt. management
mgr. manager
MHA, MH.A. Master of Hospital Administration
M.I. Military Intelligence
MI Michigan
Mich. Michigan
micros. microscopic, microscopical
mid. middle
mil. military
Milw. Milwaukee
Min. Minister
mineral. mineralogical
Minn. Minnesota
MIS Management Information Systems
Miss. Mississippi
MIT Massachusetts Institute of Technology
mktg. marketing
ML, M.L. Master of Laws
MLA Modern Language Association
M.L.D. Magister Legnum Diplomatic
MLitt, M.Litt. Master of Literature
MLS, M.L.S. Master of Library Science

MME, M.M.E. Master of Mechanical Engineering
MN Minnesota
mng. managing
MO, Mo. Missouri
moblzn. mobilization
Mont. Montana
MP Northern Mariana Islands
M.P. Member of Parliament
MPA Master of Public Administration
MPE, M.P.E. Master of Physical Education
MPH, M.P.H. Master of Public Health
MPhil, M.Phil. Master of Philosophy
MPL, M.P.L. Master of Patent Law
Mpls. Minneapolis
MRE, M.R.E. Master of Religious Education
MS, M.S. Master of Science
MS, Ms. Mississippi
MSc, M.Sc. Master of Science
MSChemE Master of Science in Chemical Engineering
MSF, M.S.F. Master of Science of Forestry
MST, M.S.T. Master of Sacred Theology
MSW, M.S.W. Master of Social Work
MT Montana
Mt. Mount
MTO Mediterranean Theatre of Operation
MTV Music Television
mus. museum, musical
MusB, Mus.B. Bachelor of Music
MusD, Mus.D. Doctor of Music
MusM, Mus.M. Master of Music
mut. mutual
mycol. mycological

N. North
NAACP National Association for the Advancement of Colored People
NACA National Advisory Committee for Aeronautics
NAD National Academy of Design
NAE National Academy of Engineering
NAFE National Association of Female Executives
N.Am. North America
NAM National Association of Manufacturers
NAPA National Association of Performing Artists
NARAS National Academy of Recording Arts and Sciences
NAREB National Association of Real Estate Boards
NARS National Archives and Record Service
NAS National Academy of Sciences
NASA National Aeronautics and Space Administration
nat. national
NATAS National Academy of Television Arts and Sciences
NATO North Atlantic Treaty Organization
NATOUSA North African Theatre of Operations
nav. navigation

NB, N.B. New Brunswick
NBA National Basketball Association
NBC National Broadcasting Company
NC, N.C. North Carolina
NCAA National College Athletic Association
NCCJ National Conference of Christians and Jews
ND, N.D. North Dakota
NDEA National Defense Education Act
NE Nebraska
NE, N.E. Northeast
NEA National Education Association
Nebr. Nebraska
NEH National Endowment for Humanities
neurol. neurological
Nev. Nevada
NF Newfoundland
NFL National Football League
Nfld. Newfoundland
NG National Guard
NH, N.H. New Hampshire
NHL National Hockey League
NIH National Institutes of Health
NIMH National Institute of Mental Health
NJ, N.J. New Jersey
NLRB National Labor Relations Board
NM New Mexico
N.Mex. New Mexico
No. Northern
NOAA National Oceanographic and Atmospheric Administration
NORAD North America Air Defense
Nov. November
NOW National Organization for Women
N.P.Ry. Northern Pacific Railway
nr. near
NRA National Rifle Association
NRC National Research Council
NS, N.S. Nova Scotia
NSC National Security Council
NSF National Science Foundation
NSW New South Wales
N.T. New Testament
NT Northwest Territories
numis. numismatic
NV Nevada

NW, N.W. Northwest
N.W.T. Northwest Territories
NY, N.Y. New York
N.Y.C. New York City
NYU New York University
N.Z. New Zealand

OAS Organization of American States
ob-gyn obstetrics-gynecology
obs. observatory
obstet. obstetrical
Oct. October
OD. O.D. Doctor of Optometry
OECD Organization of European Cooperation and Development
OEEC Organization of European Economic Cooperation
OEO Office of Economic Opportunity
ofcl. official

OH Ohio
OK Oklahoma
Okla. Oklahoma
ON Ontario
Ont. Ontario
oper. operating
ophthal. ophthalmological
ops. operations
OR Oregon
orch. orchestra
Oreg. Oregon
orgn. organization
ornithol. ornithological
OSHA Occupational Safety and Health Administration
OSRD Office of Scientific Research and Development
OSS Office of Strategic Services
osteo. osteopathic
otol. otological
otolaryn. otolaryngological

PA, Pa. Pennsylvania
P.A. Professional Association
paleontol. paleontological
path. pathological
PBS Public Broadcasting System
P.C. Professional Corporation
PE Prince Edward Island
P.E.I. Prince Edward Island
PEN Poets, Playwrights, Editors, Essayists and Novelists (international association)
penol. penological
P.E.O. women's organization (full name not disclosed)
pers. personnel
pfc. private first class
PGA Professional Golfers' Association of America
PHA Public Housing Administration
pharm. pharmaceutical
PharmD, Pharm.D. Doctor of Pharmacy
PharmM, Pharm.M. Master of Pharmacy
PhB, Ph.B. Bachelor of Philosophy
PhD, Ph.D. Doctor of Philosophy
PhDChemE Doctor of Science in Chemical Engineering
PhM, Ph.M. Master of Philosophy
Phila. Philadelphia
philharm. philharmonic
philol. philological
philos. philosophical
photog. photographic
phys. physical
physiol. physiological
Pitts. Pittsburgh
Pk. Park
Pkwy. Parkway
Pl. Place
Pla. Plaza
P.&L.E.R.R. Pittsburgh & Lake Erie Railroad
P.O. Post Office
PO Box Post Office Box
polit. political
poly. polytechnic, polytechnical

PQ Province of Quebec
PR. P.R. Puerto Rico
prep. preparatory
pres. president
Presbyn. Presbyterian
presdl. presidential
prin. principal
proc. proceedings
prod. produced (play production)
prodn. production
prof. professor
profl. professional
prog. progressive
propr. proprietor
pros. atty. prosecuting attorney
pro tem pro tempore
PSRO Professional Services Review Organization
psychiat. psychiatric
psychol. psychological
PTA Parent-Teachers Association
ptnr. partner
PTO Pacific Theatre of Operations, Parent Teacher Organization
pub. publisher, publishing, published
pub. public
publ. publication
pvt. private

quar. quarterly
qm. quartermaster
Q.M.C. Quartermaster Corps
Que. Quebec

radiol. radiological
RAF Royal Air Force
RCA Radio Corporation of America
RCAF Royal Canadian Air Force
RD Rural Delivery
Rd. Road
R&D Research & Development
REA Rural Electrification Administration
rec. recording
ref. reformed
regt. regiment
regtl. regimental
rehab. rehabilitation
rels. relations
Rep. Republican
rep. representative
Res. Reserve
ret. retired
Rev. Reverend
rev. review, revised
RFC Reconstruction Finance Corporation
RFD Rural Free Delivery
rhinol. rhinological
RI, R.I. Rhode Island
RISD Rhode Island School of Design
Rm. Room
RN, R.N. Registered Nurse
roentgenol. roentgenological
ROTC Reserve Officers Training Corps
RR Rural Route
R.R. Railroad

rsch. research
Rte. Route
Ry. Railway

S. South
s. son
SAC Strategic Air Command
SAG Screen Actors Guild
SALT Strategic Arms Limitation Talks
S.Am. South America
san. sanitary
SAR Sons of the American Revolution
Sask. Saskatchewan
savs. savings
SB, S.B. Bachelor of Science
SBA Small Business Administration
SC, S.C. South Carolina
SCAP Supreme Command Allies Pacific
ScB, Sc.B. Bachelor of Science
SCD, S.C.D. Doctor of Commercial Science
ScD, Sc.D. Doctor of Science
sch. school
sci. science, scientific
SCLC Southern Christian Leadership
    Conference
SCV Sons of Confederate Veterans
SD, S.D. South Dakota
SE, S.E. Southeast
SEATO Southeast Asia Treaty Organization
SEC Securities and Exchange Commission
sec. secretary
sect. section
seismol. seismological
sem. seminary
Sept. September
s.g. senior grade
sgt. sergeant
SHAEF Supreme Headquarters Allied
    Expeditionary Forces
SHAPE Supreme Headquarters Allied
    Powers in Europe
S.I. Staten Island
S.J. Society of Jesus (Jesuit)
SJD Scientiae Juridicae Doctor
SK Saskatchewan
SM, S.M. Master of Science
So. Southern
soc. society
sociol. sociological
S.P. Co. Southern Pacific Company
spl. special
splty. specialty
Sq. Square
S.R. Sons of the Revolution
sr. senior
SS Steamship
SSS Selective Service System
St. Saint, Street
sta. station
stats. statistics
statis. statistical
STB, S.T.B. Bachelor of Sacred Theology
stblzn. stabilization
STD, S.T.D. Doctor of Sacred Theology
Ste. Suite
subs. subsidiary

SUNY State University of New York
supr. supervisor
supt. superintendent
surg. surgical
svc. service
SW, S.W. Southwest

TAPPI Technical Association of the Pulp
    and Paper Industry
Tb. Tuberculosis
tchr. teacher
tech. technical, technology
technol. technological
Tel. & Tel. Telephone & Telegraph
temp. temporary
Tenn. Tennessee
Ter. Territory
Terr. Terrace
Tex. Texas
ThD, Th.D. Doctor of Theology
theol. theological
ThM, Th.M. Master of Theology
TN Tennessee
tng. training
topog. topographical
trans. transaction, transferred
transl. translation, translated
transp. transportation
treas. treasurer
TT Trust Territory
TV television
TVA Tennessee Valley Authority
TWA Trans World Airlines
twp. township
TX Texas
typog. typographical

U. University
UAW United Auto Workers
UCLA University of California at Los
    Angeles
UDC United Daughters of the Confederacy
U.K. United Kingdom
UN United Nations
UNESCO United Nations Educational,
    Scientific and Cultural Organization
UNICEF United Nations International
    Children's Emergency Fund
univ. university
UNRRA United Nations Relief and
    Rehabilitation Administration
UPI United Press International
U.P.R.R. United Pacific Railroad
urol. urological
U.S. United States
U.S.A. United States of America
USAAF United States Army Air Force
USAF United States Air Force
USAFR United States Air Force Reserve
USAR United States Army Reserve
USCG United States Coast Guard
USCGR United States Coast Guard Reserve
USES United States Employment Service
USIA United States Information Agency
USMC United States Marine Corps
USMCR United States Marine Corps
    Reserve

USN United States Navy
USNG United States National Guard
USNR United States Naval Reserve
USO United Service Organizations
USPHS United States Public Health Service
USS United States Ship
USSR Union of the Soviet Socialist
    Republics
USTA United States Tennis Association
USV United States Volunteers
UT Utah

VA Veterans' Administration
VA, Va. Virginia
vet. veteran, veterinary
VFW Veterans of Foreign Wars
VI, V.I. Virgin Islands
vice pres. vice president
vis. visiting
VISTA Volunteers in Service to America
VITA Volunteers in Technical Service
vocat. vocational
vol. volunteer, volume
v.p. vice president
vs. versus
VT, Vt. Vermont

W, W. West
WA Washington (state)
WAC Women's Army Corps
Wash. Washington (state)
WAVES Women's Reserve, US Naval
    Reserve
WCTU Women's Christian Temperance
    Union
we. western
W. Ger. Germany, Federal Republic of
WHO World Health Organization
WI Wisconsin
W.I. West Indies
Wis. Wisconsin
WSB Wage Stabilization Board
WV West Virginia
W.Va. West Virginia
WY Wyoming
Wyo. Wyoming

YK Yukon Territory
YMCA Young Men's Christian Association
YMHA Young Men's Hebrew Association
YM & YWHA Young Men's and Young
    Women's Hebrew Association
yr. year
YT, Y.T. Yukon Territory
YWCA Young Women's Christian
    Association

zool. zoological

Alphabetical Practices

Names are arranged alphabetically according to the surnames, and under identical surnames according to the first given name. If both surname and first given name are identical, names are arranged alphabetically according to the second given name. Where full names are identical, they are arranged in order of age—with the elder listed first.

Surnames beginning with De, Des, Du, however capitalized or spaced, are recorded with the prefix preceding the surname and arranged alphabetically under the letter D.

Surnames beginning with Mac and Mc are arranged alphabetically under M.

Surnames beginning with Saint or St. appear after names that begin Sains, and are arranged according to the second part of the name, e.g. St. Clair before Saint Dennis.

Surnames beginning with Van, Von or von are arranged alphabetically under letter V.

Compound hyphenated surnames are arranged according to the first member of the compound. Compound unhyphenated surnames are treated as hyphenated names.

Parentheses used in connection with a name indicate which part of the full name is usually deleted in common usage. Hence Abbott, W(illiam) Lewis indicates that the usual form of the given name is W. Lewis. In such a case, the parentheses are ignored in alphabetizing. However, if the name is recorded Abbott, (William) Lewis, signifying that the entire name William is not commonly used, the alphabetizing would be arranged as though the name were Abbott, Lewis.

Who'sWho in Finance and Industry

AADAHL, JORG, business executive; b. Trondheim, Norway, June 16, 1937; came to U.S., 1966; s. Ottar P. and Gurli (Lockra) A.; MS in Mech. Engring., Tech. U. Norway, 1961; MBA, U. San Francisco, 1973; m. Inger R. Holst, July 13, 1973; children: Erik, Nina. Research fellow Tech. U. Norway, Trondheim, 1961-62; mgr. arc welding devel. NAG, Oslo, 1964-66; mfg. engr. Varian Assocs., Palo Alto, Calif., 1966-67; bus. mgr. United Airlines, San Francisco, 1974-75, sr. systems analyst, 1977-81; strategic planning specialist Magnex Corp., San Jose, 1981-82; cons. in mgmt., 1982-84; founder, pres. Safeware, Inc., Santa Clara, Calif., 1984—. Developer Safechem Hazardous Chem. Mgmt. System. Recipient Certificate of Honor, San Francisco Bd. Suprs., 1973. Mem. Leif Erikson League (pres. 1973), Norwegian Soc. Profl. Engrs. Club: Young Scandinavians (v.p. 1971). Author: Strength Analysis, Welded Structures, 1967; contbr. articles in various fields to profl. jours.; editor Nordic Highlights, 1972. Office: Safeware Inc 4677 Old Ironsides Dr Santa Clara CA 95054

AAGARD, TODD ALLEN, transportation executive; b. Seattle, Mar. 31, 1961; s. Ken Jullian and Rosalie Sue (Otis) A.; m. Kathleen Anastasia May 2, 1987. BBA, Seattle U., 1984. CPA, Wash. Controller Martha Lake Electronics, Lynwood, Wash., 1980-84; staff auditor Laventhol & Horwath, Seattle, 1984-85; controller Gordon Trucking, Sumner, Wash., 1986—; bd. dirs., cons. Martha Lake Electronics, Lynwood, Wash. Bd. dirs. United Way, Youth Advocates. Mem. Wash. State CPA'S, Nat. Acctg. and Fin. Council, Am. Trucking Assn. Home: 25010 98th Pl S Ste B305 Kent WA 98031

AALSETH, JACK ELDON, marketing executive; b. Clark, S.D., Nov. 25, 1932; s. Norman Oliver and Margaret Ella (Blackman) A.; m. Lois M. Gutherie, Oct. 15, 1952 (div. July 1978); m. Marie A. Young, June 26, 1984. BS in Physics, San Diego State U., 1958. Engr. Gen. Dynamics, San Diego, 1956-58, Lockheed Missile and Space, Sunnyvale, Calif., 1958-62; mgr., engr., cons. services officer United Testing Labs., Los Angeles, 1962-63; pres. PRC Tech. Applications, Los Angeles, 1963-70; pvt. practice fin., mgmt., tech. cons. San Diego, 1971-75; pres., chief exec. officer Evaluation Research Corp., Vienna, Va., 1976-85; chmn., chief exec. officer ERC Internat., Vienna, 1985—; bd. dirs. ESI Industries, Dallas, Washington Technology; bd. dirs., past pres. Profl. Services Council, Washington. Bd. dirs. USO-Washington, 1983—. Served to staff sgt. USMC, 1950-54. Clubs: City Club of Washington, Tower Club. Office: ERC Internat 3211 Jermantown Rd PO Box 10107 Fairfax VA 22030

AAMOT, KRIS L., financial systems analyst; b. Bellingham, Wash., Sept. 19, 1962; s. Arnold Wesley and Charlotte June (Reeck) A. BA in Acctg. and Fin. magna cum laude, Western Wash. U., 1985. With Rentals Inc., Bellingham, 1979-85; fin. systems analyst Boeing Co., Seattle, 1985—; Bd. dirs. Mobile Crew Svcs., Inc. Youth adviser Jr. Achievement. Elks scholar, 1980-81, Western Wash. U. scholar, 1984-85. Mem. Nat. Assn. Accts. Home: 4023 45th Ave SW Seattle WA 98116 Office: Boeing Co P31-31 Seattle WA 98124

AARON, BERTRAM DONALD, corporation executive; b. Newport News, Va., Jan. 10, 1922; s. Harry and Lillian (Blackman) A.; B.S. in Elec. Engring., Va. Poly. Inst., 1943; children—Harry, Cynthia, Jill; m. Judith Goldstein, Dec. 28, 1985. Aero. research scientist Nat. Adv. Com. for Aeros., Langley AFB, Va., 1946-50; pres. Aaron Investors, Inc., 1948-80; elec. engr. Signal Corps Supply Agy., Phila., 1950-53; propr. Bertram D. Aaron and Co., Los Angeles, 1953-58, pres., Plainview, N.Y., 1958—; pres. Microwave Instrumentation Labs., 1959-80, HAL Antenna Products, Inc., Aaron Tech. Market, Inc. Served to capt., Signal Corps, U.S. Army, 1943-46. Registered profl. engr., N.Y., Pa., Va. Mem. IEEE (various offices), Electronic Reps. Assn. (pres., chmn. bd.), Assn. of Old Crows. Jewish. Author: Hydrogen Thyratron Circuitry Considerations, 1953; Surveillance Under Low Light Level Conditions, 1971; editor Procs. of Integration Com. on Hydrogen Thyratrons, 1951-53; patentee antenna. Home: 65 Cedarfield Rd Laurel Hollow NY 11791 Office: BD Aaron Co Inc 88 Sunnyside Blvd Ste 203 Plainview NY 11803

AARON, MERIK ROY, educator, financial executive; b. N.Y.C., May 22, 1947; s. Harry and Gertrude S. (Scherl) A.; m. Karen M. Snyder, 1984; 1 child, Stacey Lynn. BA, L.I. U., 1969, MA, 1971; profl. diploma Hofstra U., 1975; EdD, Nova U., 1982; postgrad. Touro Coll. Dist. sci. supr. Carle Place (N.Y.) Pub. Schs., 1969-80; dist. sci. supr. Lawrence (N.Y.) Pub. Schs., 1980-84; adminstr. Bellmore-Merrick Cen. High Sch. Dist., Merrick, N.Y., 1984-86. dir. curriculum, Bellmore-Merrick Cen. High Sch. Dist., 1986—; pres. G.N.S. Investment Fund, N.Y.C., 1971—; v.p. Mervic Enterprises, Smithtown, N.Y., 1980— ; adj. prof. Nassau Community Coll., 1975—, Syracuse (N.Y.) U., 1974-80. Trustee, Carle Place Bd. Edn., 1981-86 . Recipient Outstanding Contbns. to Edn., Nassau County, 1981, Outstanding Sci. Supr. State N.Y., 1986. Mem. ABA, Nat. Assn. Investment Clubs, Nat. Sci. Tchrs. Assn. (exec. bd. 1986), Nat. Sci. Suprs. Assn. (exec. bd. 1983-88, pres. 1986-87), N.Y. State Sci. Suprs. Assn. (pres. 1982-83), N.Y. Acad. Scis., Nassau County Sci. Suprs. Assn. (pres. 1979), Am. Assn. Sex Educators, Bar Assn. Nassau County, Counselors and Therapists (cert.), Phi Delta Kappa (exec. bd. 1988). Republican. Club: Civic. Lodges: Kiwanis (pres. Westbury, N.Y. club 1982-83), (Merrick club), Masons, Shriners. Home: 544 Green Pl Woodmere NY 11598

AARON, SHIRLEY MAE, tax consultant; b. Covington, La., Feb. 28, 1935; d. Morgan and Pearl (Jenkins) King; m. Richard L. King, Feb. 16, 1952 (div. Feb. 1965); children: Deborah, Richard, Roberta, Keely; m. Michael A. Aaron, Nov. 27, 1976 (dec. July 1987). Adminstrv. asst. South Central Bell, Covington, La., 1954-62; acct. Brown & Root, Inc., Houston, 1962-75; timekeeper Alyeska Pipeline Co., Fairbanks, Alaska, 1975-77; adminstrv. asst. Boeing Co., Seattle, 1979—; pres. Aaron Enterprises, Seattle, 1977—. Bd. dirs. Burien 146 Homeowners Assn., Seattle, 1979—, pres., 1980-83. Mem. NAFE. Avocation: singing.

AARON, SUSAN SANDRA, financial executive; b. Bronx, N.Y., July 16, 1949; d. George and Sylvia (Einbinder) A. BS, CCNY, 1971; MEd, Springfield (Mass.) Coll., 1972; MBA, Fordham U., 1985. Tchr. John F. Kennedy High Sch., Bronx, N.Y., 1972-78; writer, editor N.Y.C. Bd. Edn., 1978-80, adminstr. purchasing and payables, 1980-85, dir. budget, 1985-88; dir. patient accounts The Bronx Lebanon Hosp. Ctr., 1988—. Author: Horizons in Health, 1978, Fire Prevention, 1982, Be a Water Watcher, 1983, Take Aim Against Guns, 1984. Mem. N.Y. State Assn. Sch. Bus. Ofcls., Nat. Assn. Female Execs., Healthcare Fin. Mgmt. Assn., Beta Gamma Sigma. Democrat. Office: Bronx Lebanon Hosp 1276 Fulton Ave Doctor's Dorm Rm 202 Bronx NY 10456

AARS, RALLIN JAMES, communications executive; b. Clifton, Tex., Sept. 28, 1941; s. C. Pernell and Rosalie (Rueter) A.; m. Barbara Ann Zuehlke, June 13, 1964; children: Christian, James, Michael. BA, Baylor U., 1964; MA, Mich. State U., 1970; Grad. with honors, Indsl. Coll. of the Armed Forces, 1980. Commd. USAF, 1964, advanced through grades to col., 1980; chief of pub. affairs Bergstrom AFB USAF, Austin, Tex., 1970-72; chief of info. and liaison armed forces radio and TV USAF, L.A., 1972-76; exec. officer joint casulty resolution ctr. USAF, U'Tapao, Thailand, 1976-77; dir. pub. affairs electronic security command USAF, San Antonio, Tex., 1977-80; dir. plans and resources, office of pub. affairs, sec. of the Air Force USAF, Washington, 1980-82; dir. pub. affairsUN command USAF, Seoul, Korea, 1982-84; retired USAF, 1984; v.p. Gurasich, Spence, Darilek & McClure, Dallas, 1984-86, The Oakley Co., Dallas, 1986-87; v.p. communications PTNRS. Nat. Health Plans, Irving, Tex., 1987—. Producer (TV documentary) Berlin: Freedom's Island, 1968 (George Washington honor medal 1968), Airlift Anniversary, 1969 (George Washington honor medal 1969), Money Box, 1988 (Golden Tops award 1988), Perfect Health Plan (Silver Tops award 1989, Bronze Tops award 1989). Pres. Internat. Luth. Ch., Seoul, 1983; v.p. New Life In Christ Luth. Ch., Dallas, 1986-88. Decorated Nat. Order of Mil. Merit, Republic of Korea, 1984, Legion of Merit U.S. Govt., 1984. Mem. Pub. Rels. Soc. of Am. (v.p. San Antonio chpt. 1979-80), Tex. Pub. Rels. Soc., Aviation and Space Writers Assn., Nat. Assn. Govt. Communicators, Air Force Assn., Assn. of the U.S. Army, LaCima Club (Irving). Home: 1254 Whispering Oaks De Soto TX 75115 Office: PTNRS Nat Health Plans 5215 N O'Connor Rd Irving TX 75039

ABADIE, ROBELYNN HOOD, insurance executive; b. Denham Springs, La., Nov. 11, 1950; d. Robin Sr. and Ernestine Aubrey (Facundus) Hood; children: Melissa Anne, Jason Matthew. Grad., St. Louis Inst. Music, 1969. Clk. bank card dept. La. Nat. Bank, Baton Rouge, 1970-71, analyst real estate, 1976-77; owner, mgr. Water Bros., Inc., Baton Rouge, 1971-73; owner, distbr. Seyforth Labs., Inc., Dallas, 1977-79; sales agt. Southwestern Life Ins. Co., Baton Rouge, 1979-82; mgr. sales Mut. Security Life Ins. Co., Baton Rouge, 1982-84; mgr. agy. Am. Gen. Life Ins. Co., Baton Rouge, 1984-86; gen. agt. Fidelity Union Life Ins. Co., Baton Rouge, 1986-88, New Eng. Mut., Baton Rouge, 1987—; mem. task force on credit life State of La., Baton Rouge, 1985; speaker in field. Contbr. articles to profl. jours. Dir. tng. union Parkview Bapt. Ch., Baton Rouge, 1980-81, tchr. Sunday sch., leader Bible study, 1982-83, chmn. ins. com., 1982-84, mem. fin. com., 1985-86, outreach dir., 1986-89; mem. leadership com. local chpt. YWCA, 1987-88. Named Rookie of Yr. Baton Rouge Gen. Agts. and Mgrs. Assn., 1980. Fellow Life Underwriters Tng. Coun.; mem. Nat. Assn. Life Underwriters (Nat. Quality award 1979-81, 87-88), La. Assn. Life Underwriters, Baton Rouge Assn. Life Underwriters (chmn. pub. svc. 1979-80, chmn. house com. 1980-83, chmn. legis. com. 1983-86, 88-89, bd. dirs. 1980-86, 88—), Baton Rouge Gen. Agts. and Mgrs. Assn. (sec., treas. 1988—, Rookie of Yr. 1980), Women Life Underwriters Conf. (bd. dirs. 1983-85, charter chmn., parliamentarian 1986, treas. 1986-87), Women Life Underwriters Confederation (v.p. 1987-88, pres.-elect 1988—), Baton Rouge C. of C. Clubs: Century (Baton Rouge) (polit. action com. 1979—), Ambassador. Office: Abadie Fin Svcs 8748 Quarters Lake Rd Baton Rouge LA 70809

ABALOS, ROBERT JOSEPH, investor, lawyer; b. Bronx, N.Y., Apr. 28, 1960; s. Aurelio Ambrose and Agnes (Wagner) A. BS, Boston U., 1982; JD, Boston Coll., 1985. Prin., sr. ptnr. Abalos & Assocs., Washington, 1985—; pres., chief exec. officer Commonwealth Realty & Investment Corp., Vienna, Va., 1988—; chief staff atty., USA Investments, Falls Church, Va., 1986-87; chief exec. officer, chmn. bd. Global Holdings, Ltd. (formerly Abalos Investments, Ltd.), Alexandria, Va., 1984—; bd. dirs. Internat. Mercantile and Marine Co. Ltd., Phoenix Fin., Ltd., Vencap Internat., Ltd., Investment Properties Internat., Ltd. Author: Investing in Second Mortgages and TDs, 1985, Yes, You Can Own Your Own Home, 1986, The LBO: Theory and Practice, 1987; editor Boston Coll. Third World Law Jour., 1984-85. Dir. Chantilly (Va.) High Sch. Debate Team, 1986—. Republican. Roman Catholic. Office: Global Holdings Ltd 2800 Evelyn Court Vienna VA 22180

ABATE, FRANK J., consulting firm executive; b. San Martino, Avellino, Italy, Nov. 7, 1928; came to U.S., 1937; s. Giusseppe and Carmella (Simeone) A; m. Rosemary Lo Dolce, Dec. 16, 1950; children: Nicolette Frances Schindler, Camille Marie, Francis Eugene, Jeanne René Allen. BEE, NYU, 1956. Engr., draftsman NYU, N.Y.C., 1950-52; test engr. W.L. Maxson Corp., N.Y.C., 1952-54; gen. mgr. Kearfott Singer Corp., Little Falls, N.J., 1954-64; mgr. Bowmar Instruments Corp., Ft. Wayne, Ind., 1964-68; pres. Hybrid Data Systems, Inc., Ridgewood, N.J., 1968-71; mgr. I.T.T. avioncs div., Nutley, N.J., 1971-74; dir. mktg. Republic Electronics, Melville, N.Y., 1974-78; pres. Frank Abate & Assocs., Inc., Bethesda, Md., 1978—; cons. LTV-Sierra Research div., Buffalo, 1982-88. Mem. Armed Forces Communications and Electronics Assn., Capitol Marines, Navy League of U.S.A., Air Force Assn., Order of the Sons of Italy (treas. 1986-87). Republican. Roman Catholic. Club: Exchange (Washington). Home: 7555 Pepperell Dr Bethesda MD 20817

ABBE, COLMAN, investment banker; b. N.Y.C., Sept. 24, 1932; s. Leo Theodore and Beatrice (Shiff) A.; m. Nancy Adele Hyams, June 23, 1963; children—Elizabeth, Leo, Richard. BS in Acctg., Bucknell U., 1953; MBA, NYU, 1962. CPA, N.Y. Ptnr. Belsky & Abbe CPA's, N.Y.C., 1960-70; stockbroker Loeb Rhoades, N.Y.C., 1971-72; pres. Sagittarius Fund, N.Y.C., 1973, OCG Technology Inc., N.Y.C., Profl. Mediquip Inc., Scarsdale, N.Y., Abbe & Co. Inc., 1984-85; mng. dir. corp. fin. Evans & Co. Inc., N.Y.C., 1985-87; mng. dir. corp. fin. Reich & Co., Inc., 1988—. Trustee Heart Rsch. Found., N.Y.C., 1982—, pres. 1986; Am. Friends of HAIFA Med. Ctr., 1989. Mem. N.Y. State Soc. CPA's, Am. Inst. CPA's. Democrat. Jewish. Office: Reich & Co Inc 50 Broadway New York NY 10004

ABBEY, G(EORGE) MARSHALL, health care company executive, general counsel; b. Dunkirk, N.Y., July 24, 1933; s. Ralph Ambrose and Grace A. (Fisher) A.; m. Sue Carroll, July 13, 1974; children—Mark, Steven, Michael, Lincoln. B.A. with high distinction, U. Rochester, 1954; J.D. with distinction, Cornell U., 1957. Bar: N.H. 1957, Ill. 1969. Atty. McLane, Carleton, Graf, Greene & Brown, Manchester, N.H., 1957-65; atty. Baxter Travenol Labs. Inc., Deerfield, Ill., 1965-69, gen. counsel, 1969-72, sec., gen. counsel, 1972-75, v.p., sec., gen. counsel, 1975-82, sr. v.p., sec., gen. counsel, 1982-85, sr. v.p., gen. counsel, 1985—; bd. dirs. Deerfield State Bank. Editor Cornell Law Rev., 1956-57. Mem. vis. com. Law Sch., U. Chgo., 1978-81; mem. indsl. adv. com. U. P.R., Northwestern U. Sch. Law Corp. Counsel Ctr.; dir., v.p., PRUSA Found., B.U.I.L.D., Chgo., 1980-84; bd. dirs., sec. Hundred Club of Lake County, Ill., 1976-86; bd. dirs. Evanston Inventure, 1986-88; former trustee Winnetka Congl. Ch.; dir. Nat. Com. for Quality Health Care; mem. adv. bd. Corp. Counsel Ctr., Northwestern U.; mem. adv. com. P.R. Community Found., also dir. Mem. ABA, Food & Drug Law Inst. (bd. dirs.), Health Industry Mfrs. Assn. (chmn. legal/regional affairs 1976-78, bd. dirs., mem. govt. affairs com. 1978-81), Chgo. Bar Assn., N.H. Bar Assn., University Club, Exmoor Country Club, Capitol Hill Club, Order of Coif, Phi Beta Kappa. Clubs: Bankers (P.R.); University (Chgo.); Exmoor Country (Highland Park, Ill.); Capitol Hill (Washington); Mission Hills Country (Northbrook, Ill.). Office: Baxter Healthcare Corp 1 Baxter Pkwy Deerfield IL 60015

ABBOT, QUINCY SEWALL, insurance executive; b. Wilkes-Barre, Pa., Apr. 24, 1932; s. Theodore S. and Alice (Howell) A.; m. Zelia Gillam, Jan. 12, 1957; children: Elizabeth, Susan, Rebecca, Jane. A.B., Williams Coll., 1954. Actuarial student Conn. Gen. Life Ins. Co., Hartford, 1954-55, 59-64, asst. actuary, 1964-67, assoc. actuary, 1967-70, dir. taxes, 1970-75, v.p., 1975-82; v.p. CIGNA, Hartford, Conn., 1982-85; sr. v.p. CIGNA, 1985—. Pres. Hartford Assn. Retarded Citizens, 1975-76; pres. Conn. Assn. Retarded Citizens, 1981-83, Corp. Ind. Living, Hartford, 1980-81, Corp. Supported Employment, 1985-88; bd. dirs. Conn. Community Care, Inc., 1987—, Nat. Assn. Retarded Citizens, 1977-80; chmn. Inst. for Human Resources Devel. 1st lt. U.S. Army, 1955-58. Fellow Soc. Actuaries; mem. Am. Ins. Assn. (chmn. tax com. 1986-87), Tax Execs. Inst. (chpt. pres. 1970-71), Ins. Assn. Conn. (chmn. tax com. 1975-83), Am. Council Life Ins. (chmn. tax com. 1975-77, 88—). Republican. Mem. United Ch. of Christ. Home: 52 Sunrise Hill Dr West Hartford CT 06107 Office: Cigna Corp 750 Bloomfield Ave Hartford CT 06152 also: Cigna Corp 1 Logan Sq Philadelphia PA 19103

ABBOTT, C. WEBSTER, real estate executive; b. Balt., Mar. 3, 1922; s. John Mengel Abbott and Mary Wilson (Mish) Hakes; m. Caroline Gaubert Collis, 1953 (div. 1962); children: Aline Abbott Ybarra (by previous marriage), John C., Jesse F.H., Carrie Abbott Moore; m. Margaret Hawkins, Dec. 27, 1965. BS in Econs., Haverford Coll., 1943. Security analyst Merrill, Lynch, Pierce, Fenner & Beane, N.Y.C., 1946-47; credit analyst William H. Hamilton & Co., N.Y.C., 1947-48; chief credit investigator Irving Trust Co., N.Y.C., 1949-51; credit asst. Hanover Bank, N.Y.C., 1951-54; asst. v.p. Citizens Fidelity Bank & Trust, Louisville, 1954-59; gen. mgr. Francis Co., Louisville, 1959-61; assoc. broker Palermo & Co., Lanham, Md., 1962-64; salesman Sigler & Co., Balt., 1965-68; pres. Abbott Assocs. Inc., Balt., 1968—. Sgt.-at-arms Rep. Nat. Conv., Chgo., 1952. Ensign USNR, 1943-46. Mem. Greater Balt. Bd. Realtors, Md. Assn. Realtors, Nat. Assn. Realtors, Charles Village Bus. Assn. (pres. 1981-82), Exchange Club (pres. Mason-Dixon Dist. 1974-75), Rotary (pres. 1988-89). Episcopalian. Home and Office: 1900 Indian Head Rd Baltimore MD 21204

ABBOTT, CHARLES DENNIS, office equipment company executive; b. Dayton, Ohio, Oct. 19, 1939; s. Wilbur Hollis and Bertha Elizabeth (Herbert) A.; B.S. in Bus. Adminstrn., Ohio State U., 1962; m. Anne Louise Maciorowski, Aug. 17, 1968; children—Elizabeth Anne, Steven Charles. With Ernst & Whinney, N.Y.C., 1963-72, supervising sr. auditor, 1970-72; treas., sec. Comart Assos., Inc., N.Y.C., 1972-74; with Hawker Siddeley Inc., N.Y.C. (changed to Lister Diesels Inc., Olathe, Kans. 1976), 1974-86, v.p. fin., sec., dir., 1974-86; sr. v.p. fin., bd. dirs. Lister-Petter, Inc., 1986-87; dir. H.S. Investments Inc.; v.p., chief fin. officer Electronic Bus. Equipment Inc., Kansas City, Mo., 1987—. Bd. dirs., sec. Pinehurst Estates Homes Assn., 1977-78; chmn. bd. Cultural Arts Center, 1980-82. Served with Army N.G., 1963. Mem. Am. Inst. C.P.A.'s, N.Y. State Soc. C.P.A.'s, Am. Mgmt. Assn. Roman Catholic. Clubs: Brookridge Country, Indian Creek Ctr. for Fitness. Office: Electronic Bus Equipment Inc 1500 Grand Ave Kansas City MO 64108

ABBOTT, CHARLES FAVOUR, JR., lawyer; b. Sedro-Woolley, Wash., Oct. 12, 1937; s. Charles Favour and Violette Doris (Boulter) A.; m. Oranee Harward Sept. 19, 1958; children: Patricia, Stephen, Nelson, Cynthia, Lisa, Alyson. BA in Econs., U. Wash., 1959, JD, 1962. Bar: Calif. 1962, Utah 1981. Law clk. Judge M. Oliver Koelsch, U.S. Ct. Appeals (9th cir.), San Francisco, 1963; assoc. Jones, Hatfield & Abbott, Escondido, Calif., 1964; sole practice, Escondido, 1964-77; of counsel Meuller & Abbott, Escondido, 1977—; ptnr. Abbott, Thorn & Hill, Provo, Utah, 1981-83; sole practice, Provo, Utah, 1983—. Mem. Utah Bar Assn., Calif. Bar Assn., Assn. Trial Lawyers Am. Mem. Ch. of Jesus Christ of Latter Day Saints. Editorial bd. Wash. Law Rev. and State Bar Assn. Jour., 1961-62; author: How to Do Your Own Legal Work, 1976, 2d edit., 1981, How to Win in Small Claims Court, 1981, How to be Free of Debt in 24 Hours, 1981, How to Hire the Best Lawyer at the Lowest Fee, 1981, The Lawyers' Inside Method of Making Money, 1979, The Millionaire Mindset, 1987, How to Make Big Money in the Next 30 Days, 1989; contbr. articles to profl. jours. Home: 3737 Foothill Dr Provo UT 84604

ABBOTT, CRIS PYE, apparel executive; b. Dallas, Sept. 29, 1951; d. Jimmie Edwin and Maie Marie (Fountain) F.; m. Kenneth G. Abbott, Nov. 12, 1988. Student, U. Tex., Arlington, 1969-71, cert., 1984. V.p. sales and mktg. Eidelberg & Assocs., Inc., Dallas, 1974-82; regional v.p. Uniforms to You & Co., Chgo., 1982—. Mem. Amarillo Symphony Guild, Lone Star Ballet, Art Alliance; bd. dirs. Airport Assistance Ctr., Dallas/Ft. Worth Airport, 1986—. Named one of Outstanding Young Women of Am., 1985. Mem. NAFE, Nat. Assn. Accts., Sales and Mktg. Execs., Dallas Bapt. Univ. Women (exec. bd. 1986—), Jr. Women's Club (chmn. and dir. 1981-83), Delta Delta Delta (advisor). Home and Office: 4405 Tiffani Ln Amarillo TX 79109

ABBOTT, JAMES AYRE, airline executive; b. St. Paul, June 11, 1928; s. Cecil Ayre and Helen Caroline (Martens) A.; m. Patricia Agene Grieb, Dec. 9, 1953; children—Martha, Michael, Jane, William. B.A., U. Minn., 1954, LL.B., 1957. Bar: Minn. 1957, U.S. Dist. Ct. Minn. 1966, U.S. Ct. Appeals (D.C. cir.) 1974. Asst. dir. employee and labor relations Gould Nat. Batteries, St. Paul, 1958-59; mgr. ground labor relations Northwest Airlines, Inc., St. Paul, 1959-64, corp. counsel, 1964-67, corp. sec., gen. counsel, 1967; v.p. Orient region Northwest Airlines, Inc., Tokyo, 1967-70; v.p. law, gen. counsel Northwest Airlines, Inc., St. Paul, 1970-83, sr. v.p. law, gen. counsel, 1983-84, exec. v.p. fin. and adminstrn., gen. counsel, 1985-86, vice chmn., gen. counsel, 1986—, also dir.; dir. NWA Inc., St. Paul, Gatwick Handling, London, Compass 315, London, Northwest Aircraft, Inc. Served to cpl. U.S. Army, 1950-52. Club: Minnesota (St. Paul). Office: Northwest Airlines Inc Mpls-St Paul Internat Airport Saint Paul MN 55111

ABBOTT, KENNETH COLIN, healthcare and consumer products company executive; b. N.Y.C., Oct. 10, 1945; s. Colin Cedric and Mary Frances (Griglack) A.; children: Christine, Carolyn, Colin. BS in Acctg., Fairleigh Dickinson U., 1974, MBA, 1987. With Warner-Lambert Co., Morris Plains, N.J., 1965—, mgr. domestic banking, 1978-81, mgr. cash mgmt., 1981-83, dir. domestic treasury svcs., 1983-86, asst. treas. domestic, 1986—. Mem. N.J. Cash Mgmt. Assn. (membership com. 1979-80, v.p.-treas. 1980-81, pres. 1981-82, chmn. 1982-83), Antique Automobile Club Am.. Republican. Home: 41 Corey Rd Flanders NJ 07836 Office: Warner-Lambert Co 201 Tabor Rd Morris Plains NJ 07950

ABBOTT, NANCY LEE, lawyer, nurse; b. Bklyn., Apr. 27, 1952; d. Michael and Louise Emma (Eklund) Abbott; m. Robert Andrew Feinschreiber, July 21, 1979 (div. 1984). BA in Econs., Rutgers U., Newark, 1978; MBA in Acctg., NYU, 1981; JD, U. Miami, 1982. Bar: Fla., N.J.; RN. Sec., treas. Interstate Tax Press Inc., Key Biscayne, Fla.; dir. Corp. Tax Press Inc., Key Biscayne, 1981-83; treas. Internat. Bus. Conf. Inc., Key Biscayne, 1982-83; tax cons. Feinschreiber & Assocs., N.Y.C., Key Biscayne, 1976-83; sole practice, Miami, Fla., 1983-87; assoc. Voorhees & Acciavatti, Morristown, N.J., 1987—; lectr. bus. orgns., others. Mng. editor: Internat. Tax Jour., 1982-83, asst. editor, 1976-82; contbr. chpts. to books, tax articles to profl. jours. Mem. ABA (tax sect.), N.J. Bar Assn., Am. Assn. Critical Care Nurses, Fla. Bar Assn., Dade County Bar Assn., Nat. Assn. Female Execs., Omicron Delta Epsilon. Home: 187 Stirling Rd Warren NJ 07060

ABBOTT, RALPH EDWIN, product development executive; b. Boston, Aug. 4, 1940; s. Howard Hanscom and Lois (Swett) A.; m. Mary Louise Davis, June 17, 1967; children: Jennifer Lynn, Jeffrey Davis. BS in Mech. Engring., Bucknell U., 1962; postgrad., U. San Francisco Sch. Bus., 1965-66. Registered profl. engr., Can. Market mgr. Adcole Corp., Waltham, Mass., 1970-73; v.p. mktg. Am. Sci. and Engring., Inc., Cambridge, Mass., 1973-80; gen. mgr. Vedette Energy Research, Los Angeles, 1980-82; v.p. Dynatrend, Inc., Woburn, Mass., 1982-84; pres. Plexus Research, Inc., Acton, Mass., 1984—, Protection Systems, Inc., Acton, Mass., 1984—; cons. Harris Corp., Melbourne, Fla., 1983—, Brown Boveri, Switzerland, 1985—, Electric Power Research Inst., Palo Alto, Calif., 1983—, Allmanna Svenska Electriska Aktiebolaget, Sweden, 1985-86, Matsushita Electric Works, Japan, 1986—, So.

Calif. Edison Co., 1987—. Contbr. numerous articles to profl. jours.; patentee in process control and security systems. Mem. bd. of Appeals, Acton, Mass., 1978-80; mem. Mass. Prison Adv. Com., Concord, Mass., 1985-86. Served with U.S. Army, 1963-64. Decorated D.S.M. Mem. IEEE, Assn. Profl. Engrs. Ont., Delta Upsilon of New Eng. Republican. Office: Plexus Rsch Inc Strawberry Hill Bldg 287 Great Rd Acton MA 01720

ABBOUD, ALFRED ROBERT, banker, consultant and investor; b. Boston, May 29, 1929; s. Alfred and Victoria (Karam) A.; m. Joan Grover, June 11, 1955; children: Robert G., Jeanne Frances, Katherine Jane. B.S. cum laude, Harvard U., 1951, LL.B., 1956, M.B.A., 1958. Bar: Mass. 1957, Ill. 1959. Asst. cashier First Nat. Bank of Chgo., 1960-62, asst. v.p., 1962-64, v.p., 1964-69, sr. v.p., 1969-72, exec. v.p., 1972-73, vice chmn. bd., 1973-74, dep. chmn. bd., 1974-75, chmn. bd., chief exec. officer, 1975-80; pres., chief operating officer Occidental Petroleum Corp., L.A., 1980-84; pres. A. Robert Abboud and Co., Fox River Grove, Ill., 1984—, Braeburn Capital, Inc., Fox River Grove, 1984—; chmn., chief exec. officer First City Bancorp. of Tex. Inc., Houston, 1988—, First City Nat. Bank of Houston, 1988—; chmn. Houston Internat. Bus. Expo; bd. dirs. Hartmarx Corp., Chgo., Inland Steel Co., Chgo., ICN Pharm., Inc., Costa Mesa, Calif., AAR Corp., Elk Grove Village, Greater Houston Partnership. Author: Money in the Bank: How Safe Is It?, 1988. Capt. USMC, 1951-53. Baker scholar. 1958. Mem. Econ. Comml. Club (Chgo.), Barrington Hills Country Club, Ramada Club, Petroleum Club, Forum Club. Home: 101 Westcott Unit #603 Bldg 1-B Houston TX 77007 Office: First City Bancorp 1001 Main St 2d Fl Houston TX 77002

ABBRUZZESE, ALBERT VINCENT, JR., investment executive, educator; b. Boston, May 14, 1950; s. Albert Vincent Sr. and Angelina (Guerrerio) A. BS, Boston Coll., 1972; postgrad., N.Y. Inst. Fin., 1977. Account executive Prudential-Bache Securities, New Orleans, 1976-77; investment exec. Shearson Am. Express, New Orleans, 1977-82; portfolio mgr. E.F. Hutton, Inc., New Orleans, 1982-87; v.p. investments Prudential-Bache Securities, New Orleans, 1987-88; pres. investments Dean Witter Reynolds, New Orleans, 1988—; adj. prof. fin. Tulane U., New Orleans, 1980—. Bd. dirs. ACLU, New Orleans, 1985-88, Mental Health Assn. of Greater New Orleans, 1985-88, Mental Health Assn. in La., 1985—; pres. Park Timbers Homeowners Assn., New Orleans, 1984-86. Mem. Internat. Assn. Fin. Planners (assoc.). Democrat. Roman Catholic. *Died March 3, 1989.*

ABDELNOUR, ZIAD KHALIL, investment banker; b. Beirut, Jan. 8, 1961; came to U.S., 1981; s. Khalil I. and Rose S (Salha) A.; m. Nada S Sahyoun, Dec. 23, 1983; 1 child, Karl. BA, Am. U. of Beirut, 1981; MBA, U. Pa., 1984. Fin. cons. Am. Express Bank, N.Y.C., 1984-86; asst. v.p. Drexel Burnham Lambert, N.Y.C., 1986-88, v.p., 1988—. Contbr. articles to profl. jours. Mem. Rep. Senatorial Inner Circle, Washington. Mem. Arab Bankers Assn. N.Am. (dir.), Arab Bankers Assn., Pres.'s Club, Arab Am. Inst., N.Y.C. Council on Fgn. Relations, U.S.-Arab C. of C. Roman Catholic. Clubs: Metropolitan, Century (N.Y.C.), Jr. Internat. Home: 245 E 44th St Apt N 8E New York NY 10017 Office: Drexel Burnham Lambert 60 Broad St 5th Fl New York NY 10004

ABDNOR, JAMES, former senator, government agency administrator; b. Kennebec, S.D., Feb. 13, 1923; s. Samuel J. and Mary (Wehby) A. B.A. in Bus. Adminstrn., U. Nebr., 1945. Tchr., coach Presho, S.D., 1946-48; farmer, rancher Kennebec, 1945—; mem. 93d-96th Congresses from S.D., 1973-81; U.S. senator 1981-87; adminstr. SBA, Washington, 1987-89; Chmn. S.D. Young Republicans, 1953-55; mem. S.D. Senate, 1956-69, pres. pro-tem, 1967-68; lt. gov. S.D., 1969-70. Served with AUS. Mem. Kennebec Jr. C. of C. (past pres.), Am. Legion, S.D. Wheat Producers, S.D. Stockgrowers, S.D. Farmers Union, S.D. Farm Bur., Isaak Walton League, Sigma Chi. Lodges: Masons, Elks, Lions. Home: Kennebec SD 57544 Office: Small Business Adminstrn Office of the Administrator 1441 L Street NW Washington DC 20416 *

ABEL, ALLAN BERNARD, management consultant; b. Williams, Calif., Dec. 22, 1924; s. Allen and Consuelo (Benham) A.; student U. Calif., Berkeley, 1943-50, Golden Gate Coll., 1947, Instituto Cultural Mexicano-Americano, Guadalajara, Mexico, 1961; m. Maria Socorro; children—Allan Bernard, Allen Raymond, Sonya. Practice in Reno, 1954-69, Las Vegas, 1969—; investment adviser, tax cons., rare coinbroker, 1963-67; asso., bus. cons. Bus. Consultants, Inc., bus. and mgmt. cons. in 11 Western states and Mexico, 1967—; pres. SUMCO, Inc.; officer, dir. Centro de Vivienda para Retirados, S.A., Abel de Mexico., S.A.; sec.-treas. Magic Valley Enterprises, Inc.; sec.-treas. Central Devel. Co., Las Vegas, also dir.; sec. Gastrox Constrn. Co., Las Vegas. Agt., Nev. Gaming Control Bd., Nev. Gaming Commn., 1956; dir. So. Nev. conf. Pop Warner Jr. Football, 1st v.p., 1981—; mem. nat. com. Young Democrats Clubs Am., 1955-57, bd. dirs., 1957-59; mem. exec. bd. Clark County Dem. Central Com., 1970—; mem. Nev. State Dem. State Central Com., 1970—, vice chmn., 1957-58; gen. mgr. retirement housing project, Mexico, 1965-67; pres. chpt. 15 Mother Earth News; state chmn. com. select del. Humphrey; chmn. Lucy Branch Kidney Fund; counselor Family Abuse Center; pres. Flame Soccer Club; dir. Las. Las Vegas Under 23 Select Soccer Team; Lic. pub. accountant, Nev. Mem. Nat. Soc. Pub. Accountants, U. Calif. Alumni Assn. (life), Inst. Indsl. Relations Alumni Assn., Internat. Platform Assn., Am. Numis. Assn. Democrat. Spaceite. Clubs: Calif. 23 (Berkeley); Tower and Flame, Daily Californian, Am. Soc. Jalisco. Pub.: Nev. Report. Research on problems of aged living in fgn. country, 1963-64. Home: 900 Antonio Dr Las Vegas NV 89107 Office: 3540 W Sahara Ste 298 Las Vegas NV 89104

ABEL, CHARLES GERALD, management, sales consultant; b. Monroe, Iowa, Dec. 19, 1920; s. Robert Carl and Margaret (Dotts) A.; m. Lucie W. Morris, June 4, 1963; children: Margaret, Steve, Tamara, Bryan. V.p. Brickell Inst., Memphis, 1950-58; exec. v.p. Nat. Investors Life Ins., Little Rock, 1958-71; pres. Charles G. Abel, Inc., Jonesboro, Ark., 1971—; lectr. various univs. Author: Profitable Prospecting, 1985, How to Work Payroll Accounts, 1979. Past vice chmn. Pioneer dist. Boy Scouts Am.; past mem. exec. bd. Quapaw Area council Boy Scouts Am.; past dir. Ark. Arthritis Found.; former tng. chmn. United Fund. Served to capt. USAF, 1942-46. Mem. Assn. Life Underwriters Speakers Bur., Sales and Mktg. Exec. Clubs Speakers Bur. Republican. Methodist. Club: Rotary. Home: 1110 Robin Rd Jonesboro AR 72401 Office: 1720 S Caraway Jonesboro AR 72401

ABEL, GENE PAUL, educational business officer; b. Allentown, Pa., Feb. 5, 1941; s. Paul John and Lorraine Charlotte (Hoffner) A.; m. Lucy Diane Brinker, Oct. 15, 1960 (div. June 1977); children: Robert, Paul, Jonathan; m. Carol Lynne Kallenbach, Dec. 11, 1977. BS in Fin. and Econs., Pa. State U., 1963; MBA in Mgmt., Lehigh U., 1964; grad. internat. relations, Army War Coll., 1985. Fin. analyst, space div. Gen. Electric Co., King of Prussia, Pa., 1968-69; bus. mgr. Dept. Biology U. Pa., Phila., 1969-72; dir. communications and materials mgmt. Hahnemann U., Phila., 1972-81; data processing project mgr. U.S. Army Fin. Ctr., Ft. Harrison, Ind., 1981-83; dir. facilities mgmt. Mchts. Nat. Bank, Allentown, 1983-84; chief fin. and bus. officer Reading (Pa.) Area Community Coll., 1984-86; bus. mgr., treas. Cen. Bucks Sch. Dist., Doylestown, Pa., 1986—. Contbr. articles to profl. jours. Mem. Adminstrv. Assembly, U. Pa., chmn. 1971-72; active Pa. Rep. campaigns, Valley Forge, 1974, 76; chmn. Cub Scout pack King of Prussia, 1970, 71. Served as col. USAR. Named Disting. Mil. Grad., Pa. State U.; recipient Commendation and Meritorious Service medals, U.S. Army. Mem. Nat. Assn. College and Univ. Bus. Officers. Republican. Lutheran. Lodge: Masons. Office: Cen Bucks Sch Dist Adminstrn Ctr 315 W State St Doylestown PA 18901

ABELLA, MARISELA CARLOTA, business executive; b. Havana, Cuba, Feb. 5, 1943; d. Carlos and Angela (Acosta) Abella; m. Alberto Herrera Nogueira, Apr. 6, 1968 (div. Apr. 1986); 1 child, Carlos Alberto Herrera Abella. Asst. to v.p. and gen. mgr. bonding dept. Manuel San Juan (P.R.) Co. Inc., 1962-64; asst. corp. sec. and exec. sec. to pres. and stockholder Interstate Gen. Corp., Hato Rey, P.R., 1964-72, corp. sec. and pvt. sec. to corp. pres., 1972-79; sec.-treas., dir. A. H. Enterprises Inc., Caparra Heights, P.R., 1979-86; v.p., sec., bd. dirs. El Viajero Inc.; bd. dirs. A. H. Enterprises Inc., San Juan; pres. Marisela Abella Mktg. and Selling Promotional Items and Ideas, Caparra Heights, 1986—. Roman Catholic. Clubs: Caribe Hilton Swimming and Tennis, Barry U. Alumnae Assn. Home: 909 Borinquen Towers 2 Caparra Heights PR 00920 Office: PO Box 10510 Caparra Heights PR 00922

ABELOV, STEPHEN LAWRENCE, clothing company executive; b. N.Y.C., Apr. 1, 1923; s. Saul S. and Ethel (Esterman) A.; B.S., NYU, 1945, M.B.A., 1950; m. Phyllis S. Lichtenson, Nov. 18, 1945; children—Patricia C. (Mrs. Marvin Demoff), Gary M. Asst. div. mgr. Nat. Silver Co., N.Y., 1945; sales rep. Angelica Uniform Co., N.Y., 1945-50; asst. sales mgr., 1950-56, western regional mgr., Los Angeles, 1956-66, v.p. Angelica Uniform Co. of Calif., 1958-66, nat. v.p. sales, 1966-72, v.p. Angelica Corp. 1968—group v.p. mktg., 1972-80, exec. v.p., chief mktg. officer Angelica Uniform Group, 1980—; vis. lectr. mktg. NYU Grad. Sch. Bus. Adminstrn. Vice comdr. Am. Legion; mem. vocational adv. bd. VA.; adv. bd. Woodcraft Rangers; bd. dirs. Univ. Temple. Served with USAF, 1942-44. Mem. Am. Assn. Contamination Control (dir.), Am. Soc. for Advancement Mgmt. (chpt. pres.), Am. Mktg. Assn., Health Industries Assn. Am. (dir.), Inst. Environ. Scis., various trade assns., St. Louis Council on World Affairs, Sales Execs. Club (bd. dirs.), NYU Alumni Assn., Phi Epsilon Pi (treas.). Mem. B'nai B'rith (past pres.). Clubs: Men's (exec. v.p.); Town Hall, NYU, Aqua Sierra Sportsmen, Clayton. Contbr. articles to profl. jours. Home: 9821 Log Cabin Ct Ladue MO 63124 Office: Angelica Corp 10176 Corporate Square Dr Saint Louis MO 63132

ABELSON, ALAN, editor, columnist; b. N.Y.C., Oct. 12, 1925; s. Harry Carl and Vivian (Finkelstein) A.; m. Virginia Eloise Peterson, Sept. 1, 1951; children—Justin Adams, Reed Vivian. B.S. in Chemistry and English, Coll. City N.Y., 1946; M.A. in Creative Writing, U. Iowa, 1947. Reporter N.Y. Jour. Am., N.Y.C., 1949-56; stock market columnist N.Y. Jour. Am., 1952-56; with Barron's Mag., N.Y.C., 1956—; mng. editor Barron's Mag., 1965-81, editor, 1981—; columnist Up & Down Wall St., 1966—. Office: Barron's Mag 200 Liberty St New York NY 10281

ABER, JOHN WILLIAM, educator; b. Canonsburg, Pa., Sept. 9, 1937; s. John William and Rose (Lauda) A.; S.B., Pa. State U., 1959; M.B.A. (McKinsey scholar), Columbia U., 1965; D.B.A. (Bus. Sch. leadership fellow, Div. of Research fellow), Harvard U., 1972; m. Cynthia Louise Sousa, Nov. 24, 1962; children—John, Valerie, Alexander. Cons., Univ. Affiliates, Inc., Boston, 1969-71; asst. prof. fin. Ga. State U., Atlanta, 1971-72; asst. prof. Boston U., 1972-78, asso. prof. fin., 1978—, dir. mgmt. devel. program, 1978-82, dir. advanced mgmt. devel. program, 1983—; fin. and bank mgmt. cons. Served with USN, 1959-64. Mem. Am. Fin. Assn., Eastern Fin. Assn., Fin. Mgmt. Assn. Club: Harvard of Boston. Author: Beta Coefficients and Models of Security Return, 1973. Home: 51 Columbia St Brookline MA 02146 Office: Boston U 704 Commonwealth Ave Boston MA 02215

ABERCROMBIE, VALERIA CAROL, exercise club executive; b. Atlanta, July 12, 1957; d. Joseph William and Ella Marie (Andersen) Bauer; m. Bruce Willis Abercrombie, June 9, 1978; children: Caroline Leigh and Brigette Marie (twins). Student, North Ga. Tech. and Vocat. Sch., 1975-76; AA cum laude, Truett McConnell Coll., 1978; student, Gainesville (Ga.) Jr. Coll., 1978; diploma, Inst. Children's Literature, 1988. Asst. mgr. Smith's Soda Shop, Cleveland, Ga., 1976-78, 80-87; underwriting clk. Liberty Mut. Ins. Co., Gainesville, 1978-80; owner, mgr. Bodyworks, Dahlonega, Ga., 1987—. Tchr. Bible sch. St. Paul United Meth. Ch., Dahlonega, 1986-88, Sunday sch. tchr., 1987—, mem. adminstrv. coun., 1988. Whitehead Found. scholar, 1976. Mem. Nat. Mothers of Twins. Lutheran. Home: Rt 2 Box 580 Dahlonega GA 30533

ABERE, ANDREW EVAN, economist; b. N.Y.C., June 16, 1961; s. Frank Joseph and Ruth (Mofenson) A. BA, Columbia U., 1983, MA in Econs., 1986, M of Philosophy in Econs., 1987. Economist Skadden, Arps, N.Y.C., 1984—; instr. dept. econs. Columbia U., N.Y.C., 1987—. Columbia fellow, 1985-87. Mem. ABA, Am. Econ. Assn. Office: Skadden Arps 919 Third Ave New York NY 10022

ABERNATHY, JAMES LOGAN, public relations executive; b. Kansas City, Mo., Jan. 23, 1941; s. James Logan and Caryl (Nicolson) A. ; m. Kevin Kearns McLean, Sept. 12, 1981; 1 child, Nell Logan. Student, Brown U., 1959-64. Assoc. dir. investor relations CBS Inc., N.Y.C., 1967-72; v.p. investor relations Warner Communications Inc., N.Y.C., 1972-74; v.p. investor relations ABC Inc., N.Y.C., 1974-79, v.p. corp. affairs, 1979-84; chmn. Abernathy/MacGregor Group Inc., N.Y.C., 1984—. Trustee Caron Found., Wernersville, Pa. (chmn.), 1983—, Hackley Sch., Tarrytown, N.Y., 1982—. Cpl. USMCR, 1959-65. Mem. Investor Relations Assn. (pres. 1979-80), Nat. Investor Relations Inst. Clubs: Knickerbocker, N.Y.C., Doubles, N.Y.C., Lawrence Beach, Long Island. Home: 130 East End Ave New York NY 10028 Office: Abernathy/MacGregor Group Inc 501 Madison Ave New York NY 10022

ABI-ALI, RICKY SALIM, aerospace corporation executive; b. Dakar, Senegal, Sept. 14, 1940; s. Salim Salman and Zahia (Khazzou) A.; m. Elizabeth Winter; 1 child, Richard. BS in Aeros., Calif. Poly. State U., San Luis Obispo, 1962; BA in Mgmt., Addis Ababa U., Ethiopia, 1976. Sr. systems engr. Middle East Airlines, Beirut, 1962-69; mgr. engring. Ethiopian Airlines, Addis Ababa, 1970-76; regional dir. Sundstrand Aerospace Corp., Dubai, United Arab Emirates, 1977—. Office: Sundstrand Aerospace, PO Box 3880, Dubai United Arab Emirates

ABLON, ARNOLD NORMAN, accountant; b. Ft. Worth, July 12, 1921; s. Esir R. and Hazel (Dreeben) A.; B.S., La. State U., 1941; M.B.A., Northwestern U., 1942; m. Carol Sarbin, July 25, 1962; children—Jan Ellen, Elizabeth Jane, William Neal, Robert Jack. Lectr. acctg. So. Meth. U., 1946-47; auditor Levine's Dept. Stores, 1947-49; acct. Peat, Marwick, Mitchell & Co., 1946-47; sr. partner Arnold N. Ablon and Co., C.P.A.s; owner ANA Properties, Dallas; pres., dir. Ablon Enterprises, Inc.; dir. 1st Continental Enterprises, Inc., Hunsaker Truck Lease, Inc. Bd. trustees St. Mark's Sch. of Tex., Lamplighter Sch., mem. exec. com.; past trustee Spl. Care Sch., Greenhill Sch., June Shelton Sch.; co-chmn. Parents Annual Fund Georgetown U., past v.p. Temple Emanuel; past vice chmn. Greenhill Sch.; mem. Parents Council, Georgetown U. Served to capt. AUS, 1942-45. Mem. Am. Inst. C.P.A.s, Tex. Soc. C.P.A.s, Nat. Assn. Cost Accts. Mason (Shriner). Clubs: Columbian, Dallas, City (Dallas). Home: 9129 Clearlake Dallas TX 75225 Office: NCNB Ctr-I Dallas TX 75201

ABLON, BENJAMIN MANUEL, accountant; b. Dallas, Feb. 12, 1929; s. Esir R. and Hazel (Dreeben) A.; B.B.A., So. Meth. U., 1948; M.B.A., Northwestern, 1949; LL.B., Harvard, 1956; m. Renee Angrist, Jan. 6, 1962 (div. Oct. 1969); 1 son, Edward Lawrence. Lic. real estate broker. Admitted to Tex. bar, 1956, D.C. bar, 1957; with tax rulings div. IRS, Washington, 1956-60; asso. law firm, N.Y.C., 1960-62; accountant, tax mgr. Price Waterhouse & Co., N.Y.C., 1963-68; accountant, partner Arnold N. Ablon & Co., C.P.A.'s, Dallas, 1968—. Served to lt. USAF, 1951-53. Mem. Am. Inst. C.P.A.'s, Tex. Soc. C.P.A.'s, State Bar Tex., Am. Assn. Attys.-C.P.A.'s, Dallas Estate Planning Council, Beta Gamma Sigma. Contbr. articles to profl. jours. Office: 3100 NCNB Ctr Tower I 310 N Ervay Dallas TX 75201

ABLON, RALPH E., manufacturing company executive; b. 1916. Student, Ohio State U., 1939. With Luria Bros. & Co., 1939-62, exec. v.p., 1948-55, pres., 1955-62, dir., 1962—; chmn., chief exec. officer Ogden Corp., N.Y.C., 1962—, pres., dir., 1972-86. Served with USNR, World War II. Office: Ogden Corp 2 Pennsylvania Pla New York NY 10121 *

ABOFF, SHELDON JAY, publishing company executive; b. N.Y.C., 1947. Grad., Bernard M. Baruch Coll. CUNY, 1970. Vice chmn. fin. and ops., treas., bd. dirs. Pergamon Press Inc., Elmsford, N.Y.; vice chmn. Pergamon Holding Corp.; vice chmn., sec., treas., dir. Pergamon Info Line Inc., Info. On Demand Inc., Pergamon Press Can. Ltd.; vice chmn. Cedibra Editora Brasileira Ltd.; sec., treas., dir. Maxwell Communication Info. Corp.; bd. dirs. Anco Engrs. Inc.; sec., treas., bd. dirs. PergaBase Inc.; vice chmn., sec., treas., bd. dirs. Maxwell Sci. Internat.; v.p. spl. projects Macmillan Inc., N.Y.C. Mem. AICPA, Nat. Assn. Accts., Am. Mgmt. Assn. Office: Pergamon Press Inc Fairview Pk Elmsford NY 10523 *

ABORN, FOSTER LITCHFIELD, insurance company executive; b. Providence, July 8, 1934; s. John Russell and Helene Cecile (Hesse) A.; m. Sara Holbrook; children: Justin, Hilary. BA, Dartmouth Coll., 1956; MBA, 1957. Asst. v.p. Mellon Bank, N.A., Pitts., 1957-68; pres. investment and pension sector John Hankcock Mut. Life Ins. Co., Boston, 1968—;bd. dir. John Hancock Capital Corp., John Hancock Venture Capital Mgmt., Inc., Boston, John Hancock Subs., Inc., Independence Investment Assocs., 1987—, John Hancock Freedom Securities Corp., 1988—, John Hancock Mut. Life Ins. Co. Trustee Boston U. Community Tech. Found., 1974—, New England Deaconess Hosp., Boston, 1976. Republican. Unitarian. Home: 121 Main St Hingham MA 02043 Office: John Hancock Mut Life Ins PO Box 1111 Boston MA 02117

ABRAHAM, MARIAN FAY, financial planner; b. South Bend, Ind., Oct. 10, 1961; d. Hassen Jacob and Lulu (Fayz) A. BBA in Mktg. and Mgmt., Ind. U., 1987. Fin. planner IDS-Am. Express. Co., South Bend, 1988—. Republican. Moslem. Home: 1959 Thornhill Dr South Bend IN 46614 Office: IDS/Am Express Co 401 E Colfax St Ste 107 South Bend IN 46617

ABRAMIS, DAVID JOSEPH, psychology educator, researcher, consultant; b. Fontana, Calif., Feb. 19, 1955; s. Dov and Pearl (Lein) A. BA, U. Calif., Santa Cruz, 1979; MA, U. Mich., 1981, PhD, 1985. Rsch. assoc. inst. for social rsch. U. Mich., Ann Arbor, 1980-85; prof. psychology sch. bus. adminstrn. Calif. State U., Long Beach, 1985—; sr. cons. Abramis & Assoc., L.A., 1980—; lectr. in field; conductor seminars in field. Contbr. articles to profl. jours. Grantee Calif. State U., 1986-88, NIMH fellow, 1980, 83, 84; recipient Meritorious Performance and Profl. Promise award, 1986, 87, 89. Mem. Acad. Mgmt., Am. Psychol. Assn., Soc. for Psychol. Study of Social Issues. Home: 944 19th St Ste E Santa Monica CA 90403 Office: Calif State U. Dept Mgmt Sch Bus Adminstrn Long Beach CA 90804

ABRAMOVITCH, SAM, business executive. Chmn., dir. United Westburne Industries, Ltd., Montreal, Que., Can. Office: United Westburne Industries Ltd, 6333 Decarie Blvd, Montreal, PQ Canada H3W 3E1 *

ABRAMS, JULIUS, construction executive; b. Butrimantzi, Lithuania, Oct. 27, 1902; brought to U.S., 1903; s. Harry Isaac and Etta (Ginsberg) A.; B.C.E., Northeastern U., 1925, D.Eng. (hon.), 1973; m. Eva Hodess, June 2, 1926; children—Fay Rosalind Abrams Wilgoren, Benjamin Emanuel, Phillip. Civil and constrn. engr. Gleason Engring. Corp., Wellesley, Mass., 1932-36; chief engr. B.A. Gardett Corp., 1936-40; civil engr., supt. J. Slotnik Co., Boston, 1940-43; engr. Joseph Bennett Co., Boston, 1943-45; pres. Poley-Abrams Corp., Brookline, Mass., 1945—; pres. J. Abrams Constrn. Co. Inc., 1975—, chmn. bd., 1978—. Dir., past pres. Asso. Gen. Contractors of Mass. Past chmn. Greater Boston Hillel Com., mem., chmn. bd. of examiners Brookline Bldg. Dept.; mem. designer selection bd. Commonwealth of Mass., 1972-76, cons. to spl. commn. on state and county bldgs., 1979; chmn. adv. com. Northeastern U. Hillel; bd. advs. U. Indsl. Mgmt.; mem. corp. Northeastern U., Lesley Coll. Named Outstanding Civil Engr. Alumnus, Northeastern U., 1981; registered profl. engr., Mass. Fellow Am. Inst. Constructors; mem. Nat. Soc. Profl. Engrs., Am. Arbitration Assn., Am. Soc. Engring. Edn., Am. Council Constrn. Edn., Assn. Engrs. and Architects Israel (speaker 4th World Congress, Israel 1976), Alpha Epsilon Pi. Republican. Clubs: Masons, B'nai B'rith (past pres. Architects-Engrs. lodge). Home: 210 Nahanton St Newton MA 02159 Office: P O Box 900 Brookline MA 02167

ABRAMS, ROBERTA BUSKY, nurse, hospital administrator; b. Bklyn., Feb. 16, 1937; d. Albert H. and Gladys Busky; m. Robert L. Abrams, June 28, 1959 (div. 1977); children: Susan Abrams Federman, David B. BSN, U. Rochester, 1959; MA, Fairfield U., 1977. Asst. head nurse Jewish Hosp., Bklyn., 1959-60; instr. medicine/surgery Bklyn. Hosp., 1960-62, U. Rochester, N.Y., 1963-64; instr. ob-gyn Malden (Mass.) Hosp. Sch. Nursing, 1965-66; instr. prospective parents ARC, San Rafael, Calif., 1968-69; instr. ob-gyn SUNY, Farmingdale, 1970-71; instr. maternal/child health Stamford (Conn.) Hosp., 1971-75; clinician maternal/child health Lawrence Hosp., Bronxville, N.Y., 1975-78; asst. prof. nursing Ohio Wesleyan U., Delaware, 1981-84; dir. Elizabeth Blackwell Hosp. at Riverside Meth., Columbus, Ohio, 1978-86; dir. nursing Henry Ford Hosp., Detroit, 1986-87, assoc. adminstr. nursing, 1988—; cons. maternal/child nursing currents Ross Labs., 1984-88; lectr. in field. Contbr. articles to profl. jours. Mem. LWV, Nurses Assn. Am. Coll. Obstreticians and Gynocologists (vice-chmn. Ohio chpt. 1984-87), Am. Soc. Psychoprophylaxsis, Greater Detroit Orgn. Nurse Execs., Sigma Theta Tau. Home: 32478 Dunford Farmington Hills MI 48018 Office: Henry Ford Hosp 2799 W Grand Blvd Detroit MI 48202

ABRAMSON, NORMAN, retail executive; b. N.Y.C., Oct. 13, 1939; s. Morris and Rose (Gayer) A.; m. Carreen Etta Fields, Apr. 25, 1962; children: Pamela Sue, Russell Jay. BBA, CCNY, 1962; MBA, NYU, 1972. CPA, N.Y., N.J. Staff acct. Peat, Marwick, Mitchell & Co., N.Y.C., 1962-65; chief fin. officer Golding Bros. div. W.R. Grace Co., N.Y.C., 1965-71; chief fin. and adminstrv. officer Merchandise Products Group, N.Y.C., 1971-75; exec. v.p. Herman World of Sporting Goods, 1975-79; pres., chief exec. officer Herman's World of Sporting Goods, Carteret, N.J., 1979-81; exec. v.p., chief fin. officer United Dept. Stores Inc., N.Y.C., 1981-82; v.p. fin. Izod Ltd., N.Y.C., 1982-83; sr. exec. v.p. ops. and fin. Lerner Stores Corp., N.Y.C., 1983-86; pres., chief operating officer Clothestime Inc., Anaheim, Calif., 1986—. Office: The Clothestime Inc 5325 E Hunter Ave Anaheim CA 92807

ABRAMSON, ROBERT MARTIN, entrepreneur; b. Boston, Jan. 9, 1943; s. Albert David and Janet (Koopetz) A.; m. Elizabeth L. Lewis, June 20, 1976; children: David, Daniel. B in Polit. Sci., U. Mich., 1964; MBA, Harvard U., 1968. Vol. U.S. Peace Corp., Mahabad, Iran, 1964-66; cons. Fry Cons., Chgo., 1968-69; sr. cons. Arthur D. Little Inc., Cambridge, Mass., 1969-72, v.p., dean. sch. mgmt., 1973-80; gen. mgr. Alco Tire Co., Boston, 1972-73; sr. v.p. Primerica Corp., Greenwich, Conn., 1980-87; pvt. practice investment brokerage Westport, Conn., 1987—; bd. dirs. Southeast Asia Venture Investment Co., Singapore, Advent-Technoventure Fund., Tokyo, Primerica Found., Greenwich. Home: 14 Broad St Westport CT 06880

ABSHER, JANET S., banker; b. Fairfield, Ala., July 17, 1955; d. Farris R. and Martha L. (Edmonds) A. BS in Acctg., U. Ala., 1976. Cert. internal auditor. Auditor AmSouth Bank, Birmingham, Ala., 1976-78; sr. auditor Fed. Res. Bank, Birmingham, 1978-81; supervising auditor Fed. Res. Bank, Atlanta, 1981, mgr. auditing, 1981-83, mgr. acctg., 1983-85, mgr. electronic payments, 1985—; instr. Fed. Res. Audit Tng., various U.S. cities, 1981-85. Mem. Young Careers, Atlanta, 1985, Atlanta Landmarks, 1986, Smithsonian Instn., Washington, Zoo Atlanta, 1987, Atlanta Bot. Gardens, 1988, High Mus. Art, Historic Preservation Soc. Mem. Inst. Internal Auditors (gov. 1980—, instr. Atlanta chpt. 1983), Am. Inst. Bankers and Acctg. Instrs. Republican. Baptist. Home: 1130 Willivee Dr Decatur GA 30033 Office: Fed Res Bank Atlanta 104 Marietta St Atlanta GA 30303

ABU-HAJAR, ABDUL-WAHAB ABDUL-RAHMAN (BOU HADJAR), airlines executive; b. Jeddah, Saudi Arabia, Jan. 1, 1934; s. Abdul-Rahman Mohammed and Habibah Mohammed (El Gharraz) Abu-H.; B.A. in Sociology and Econs., Cairo U., 1957; m. Elham Ibrahim El-Gharrz, Mar. 22, 1972; children—Ahmed, Alaa, Amal. Clk., Arab Bank, Ltd., Jeddah, 1951-53; tutor, supr. Ministry of Edn., Jeddah, 1957-58; head office mgr. Riyadh Bank Ltd., Jeddah, 1958-62; dir. gen. Printing, Press & Publ. Corp., Jeddah, 1963-64; corp. sec. gen., dir. Saudi Arabian Airlines, Jeddah, 1964—. Mem. Am. Assn. Individual Investors, Internat. Airline Passengers Assn., Inst. of Dirs., London (assoc.). Moslem. Club: Sport Club of Saudi Arabian Airlines (Jeddah). Office: care Saudi Arabian Airlines Corp, Cost Centre III, PO Box 620, Jeddah Saudi Arabia 21231

ACCOLA, HARLAN J., photographer; b. Wisconsin Rapids, Wis., Apr. 26, 1960; s. Donald Laverne and Laverne Norma (Kleinstick) A.; m. Brenda Lee Schill, June 15, 1985. Grad. high sch. Ins. adjuster U.S. Govt., Wis., 1978-79; with Fed. Crop Ins., Mpls., 1979-80; mktg. rep. AgriView Newspaper, 1979-80; owner Skypix, Inc., Marshfield, Wis., 1980-85, Am. Images, Inc., Marshfield, 1986—. Mem. Profl. Aerial Photographers Assn., Optimists. Home: 200 Westview Dr Marshfield WI 54449 Office: Am Images Inc PO Box 1203 Marshfield WI 54449

ACCORDINO, FRANK JOSEPH, architect, car rental company executive; b. Bklyn., July 14, 1946; s. Carmine Anthony and Elvira Helen (Saccone) A.; m. Sheila May Lloyd, Sept. 6, 1969. BS, SUNY, N.Y. Inst. Tech., 1969; MArch, U. N.Mex., 1971. Registered architect, N.Y., Ill.; cert. Nat. Council Archtl. Registration Bds. Project architect Gencorelli & Salo Architects, Mineola, N.Y., 1971-74, Grove Haack & Assocs., P.C., Architects, Engrs., Planners, Ft. Lauderdale, Fla., 1974-76; v.p., dir. Cashin Assocs., P.C., Architects, Engrs., Planners, Mineola, 1976-79; prin. Frank Accordino, AIA, Merrick, N.Y., 1979-80; sr. architect, facilities devel. Eastern Airlines, Inc., Miami, Fla., 1980-83; sr. architect Dean Witter Reynolds, Inc., N.Y., 1983-84; v.p. corp. facilities Avis Rent-A-Car-System, Inc., Garden City, N.Y., 1984—. Mem. AIA (continuing edn. cert. of achievement 1979), Soc. Am. Registered Architects. Republican. Roman Catholic. Office: Avis Rent-A-Car System Inc 900 Old Country Rd Garden City NY 11530

ACERRA, MICHELE (MIKE), engineering and construction company executive; b. Messina, Italy, Apr. 15, 1937; came to U.S., 1978; s. Luigi and Matilde Mazzullo A.; m. Elena Fino, May 31, 1975; children—Marco Eugenio, Matilde Enrica, Jennifer. Dr. Chem. Engring., Politecnico, Milan, Italy, 1962. Vessels designer Foster Wheeler Italiana, Milan, 1962, asst. mgr. drawing office, 1963, project mgr., 1963-70, project engr., 1970-74; pres. Glitsch Italiana, Rome, 1974-78; pres. Glitsch Inc., Dallas, 1978-85, dir. eight subs. cos.; pres., chief exec. officer Foster Wheeler USA Corp., Perryville, N.J., 1986-89; group v.p. Faster Wheeler Corp. Roman Catholic. Office: Foster Wheeler USA Corp Perryville Corp Park Clinton NJ 08809-4000

ACHIWA, NAOKI (NICKY), economic development company executive; b. Nishio, Aichi, Japan, Sept. 15, 1944; s. Iwao and Saki A.; m. Reiko Ozawa Achiwa, Mar. 10, 1976; children: Ryo, Takeshi, Keiko. BS in Econs., Hitotsubashi U., 1964-68; PMD (hon.), Harvard U., 1981. Asst. trainee Mitsui & Co., Ltd., Tokyo, 1968-70, U. Birmingham, U.K., 1970-71; trainee asst. Mitsui & Co. (London) Ltd., 1971-72, Mitsui & Co., Ltd., Tokyo, 1972-78; asst. gen. mgr. Mitsui & Co. (USA) Inc., New York, 1978-85; mgr. Mitsui & Co., Ltd., Tokyo, 1985-87; gen. mgr. chem. dept. Mitsui & Co. (USA) Inc., New York, 1987—. Home: 22 Mimosa Dr Cos Cob CT 06807 Office: Mitsui & Co (USA) Inc 200 Park Ave New York NY 10166

ACKERMAN, DAVID BRUCE, actuary, consultant; b. Peoria, Ill., Nov. 21, 1952; s. Bruce Merle and Florence E. (Vinje) A.; m. Donna Lynn Alber, June 8, 1974; children: Joel, Katie. BA, U. Iowa, 1974. Actuary Bus. Men's Assurance, Kansas City, Mo., 1974-78; employee benefits cons. Towers, Perrin, Overland Park, Kans., 1978—; pres. St. Louis Actuaries Club, 1983-84. Fellow Soc. Actuaries; mem. Am. Acad. Actuaries. Methodist. Lodge: Rotary. Home: 2405 W 123d Leawood KS 66211 Office: Towers Perrin 6900 College Blvd Suite 700 Overland Park KS 66211

ACKERMAN, DON EUGENE, venture capital executive; b. Gothenburg, Nebr., Dec. 30, 1933; s. Herman Eilert and Fern Helene (Witte) A.; m. Joan Mason, June 17, 1956 (div. Sept. 1985); children: Cherilyn Kay, Michael Alan, Steven Jay; m. Janet Lorain Norman, Sept. 19, 1987. BS, U.S. Mil. Acad., 1956; MBA with honors, Harvard U., 1963. Commd. 2d lt. USAF, 1956, advanced through grades to maj., 1966, pilot trainee, 1956-58, pilot 492 Tact. Fighter Squadron, France and Eng., 1958-61; instr. dept. econs. USAF Acad., 1963-66; systems analyst tactical air div. Dept. Def., Washington, 1966-67, resigned, 1967; assoc. J.H. Whitney & Co., N.Y.C., 1967-69, ptnr., 1969—; chmn. bd. Genigraphics Corp., 1982—, Genicom Corp., 1984—, Decision Data Inc., 1988—, Decision Data Inc., 1988—; dir. Chem. Bank Adv. Bd., 1986—; bd. dirs. Schlumberger, Ltd., Kraftware-Morgan, Walden Lakes, Inc., Inc., Numonics Corp. Bd. dirs. Sun City Ctr., 1986—. Mem. Nat. Venture Capital Assn. (bd. dirs. 1983-88). Clubs: Univ. (N.Y.C.); New Canaan (Conn.) Field. Avocations: tennis, skiing. Office: J H Whitney & Co 630 Fifth Ave Ste 3200 New York NY 10111 also: Genicom Corp One General Electric Dr Waynesboro VA 22980

ACKERMAN, GEORGE SMITH, manufacturing company executive; b. Plainfield, N.J., Apr. 30, 1920; s. Marion S. and Martha (Smith) A.; m. Patricia Buller, June 23, 1957; children—George S., Christopher B., Allison Ackerman Mayfield. B.A., Babson Coll., 1942. Vice-pres. edn./govt. sales Virco Mfg. Corp., Los Angeles. Bd. dirs. Coalition for Adequate Sch. Housing, Calif. Office and Ednl. Dealers, moderator Presbytery of the Pacific, Los Angeles and Hawaii, 1984—; trustee Synod So. Calif. and Hawaii. Served to capt. USMCR, 1942-46; PTO. Mem. Calif. Assn. Sch. Bus. Officials (chmn.). Republican. Presbyterian.

ACKERMAN, JOHN CYRIL, plyproducts company executive; b. Jasper, Ind.; s. John O. and Teresa (Burger) A.; children—Jeffrey, John. B.S., Purdue U., 1962. Exec. v.p. Kimball Internat. Inc., Jasper, Ind., 1963—. Served with U.S. Army, 1956-58. Republican. Roman Catholic. Office: Kimball Internat Inc 1600 Royal St Jasper IN 47546

ACKERMAN, LEOPOLD (LEE), II, real estate broker and investor; b. Clayton, Mo., Oct. 29, 1921; s. Melville and Ruth (Corday) A.; m. Leslie Rogers, Dec. 22, 1943; children: Mary, Byron, Carl, Elizabeth; m. 2d, Celia Franco Meyer, Feb. 10, 1962; children: Doug, Paul; m. 3d, Carol Dianne Webb, Nov. 27, 1982; children: Becky, Kris, Erica, Adriane. AB in Govt., Harvard U., 1947; MS in Criminal Justice, Ariz. State U., 1975. CLU. Pilot Pan-Am. Airways, 1942; reporter Aviation Editor, 1947-48; pub. relations dir. Phoenix Newspapers, Inc., 1947-48; v.p., King, Ackerman, Deckard & Burch, 1948-53; mem. Ariz. Ho. of Reps., 1950-52; pres. Lee Ackerman Investment Co. (merged with Western Equities, Inc. 1961), Phoenix, 1953-61, Western Growth Capital Corp., 1965-67; with N.Y. Life Ins. Co., 1967-75; pres. Developers Service Corp. (named changed to Lee Ackerman Investment Co. 1983), Phoenix, 1969—, also chmn. bd.; former v.p., pres. SW Savs. and Loan Assn.; pres. Lee Ackerman Real Estate, Inc., W.-Coast Printing Co., W.-Coast Investment Co., Lee Ackerman Mgmt. Co., Inc., Phoenix Indsl. Ctr., Inc., CBV Apts., Inc., 2d Devel. Corp., A Bar R Ranches, Inc., also others. Democratic nominee for Ariz. Gov., 1960; state chmn. Ariz. Soc. for Crippled Children, 1960 (Bronze Plaque award 1960); chmn. bd. Ariz. Heart Assn. (Silver Heart award 1960), 1958-60; dir. Boys Club Phoenix, Inc., 1961-66; state chmn. Nat. Fund for Med. Edn., 1963-64; co-chmn. Johnson-Humphrey Campaign for Ariz., 1965; Democratic nat. committeeman for Ariz., 1964-68. Recipient Alumni Achievement award Gov. Dummer Acad., 1961; nat. media recognition, 1957-61. Served with USAF, 1942-45; maj. Res. (ret.). Club: One Hundred (1st chmn. 1965). Home: 6333 E Mariposa Scottsdale AZ 85251 Office: Lee Ackerman Investments 6710 E Camelback Ste 234 Scottsdale AZ 85251

ACKERMAN, PHILIP CHARLES, utility executive, lawyer; b. Kenmore, N.Y., Feb. 14, 1944; s. Harold Lewis and Marion (Ehrhardt) A.; m. Nancy Margaret Weig, Sept. 11, 1967; children—David Philip, Kathryn Elizabeth. BS in Acctg., SUNY, Buffalo, 1965; LLB, Harvard U., 1968. Bar: N.Y. 1968. Atty. Iroquois Gas Corp., Buffalo, 1968-72; asst. sec. Nat. Fuel Gas Distbn. Corp., Buffalo, 1974-75, sec., 1975-84; gen. counsel Nat. Fuel Gas Distbn. Corp., 1978-84, sr. v.p., 1983-84, also bd. dirs.; sr. v.p. Nat. Fuel Gas Supply Corp., Buffalo, 1984-88; exec. v.p. Nat. Fuel Gas Supply Corp., 1988—; v.p. Nat. Fuel Gas Co., Buffalo, 1980—; bd. dirs., sec. Empire Exploration, Inc., 1983—; treas. Penn-York Energy Corp., 1976-81; bd. dirs. Enerop Corp., 1981—, sec. 1981-84. Mem. Orchard Park (N.Y.) Planning Bd., 1972-78, chmn., 1977-78; adv. sch. bus. adminstrn. coun. Canisius Coll., Buffalo, 1982, Buffalo Regional Bd., Chase Lincoln First Bank, 1985. Mem. ABA, N.Y. State Bar Assn. (vice chmn. com. on pub. utility law 1983-87), Erie County Bar Assn., Niagara Frontier Corp. Counsel Assn. (chmn. audit com. 1979-81), Am. Gas Assn. (chmn. ins. com. 1974-76, mem. legal sect. mng. com.), Audubon Soc., Sierra Club., Buffalo Soc. Natural Scis. (bd. mgrs. 1982). Republican. Club: Sitzmarker Ski (dir.). Office: Nat. Fuel Gas Co 10 Lafayette Sq Buffalo NY 14203

ACKERMAN, ROY ALAN, research and development executive; b. Bklyn., Sept. 9, 1951; s. Jack A. and Estelle (Kuchlik) A.; m. Janet Sharon Ostrow, July 4, 1974 (div. 1984); children: Shanna Avrah, Shira Batya. BSChemE, Poly. Inst. of N.Y., 1972; MSChemE, MIT, 1974; PhD, U. Va., 1986. Chem. engr. Tri-Flo Research Labs., Bellmore, N.Y., 1972-74; sr. project engr. Thetford Corp., Ann Arbor, Mich., 1975; dir. research and devel. Applied Sci. Through Research and Engring. (now ASTRE), Ann Arbor, 1976-77, ASTRE Cons. Corp., Charlottesville, Va., 1978-81; tech. dir. ASTRE Corp. Group, Charlottesville, 1981-89, Alexandria, Va., 1989—; bd. dirs. Indsl. Microgenics Ltd., Charlottesville; chmn. Bicarbolyte Corp., Charlottesville. Author: Water Reuse and Recycle, 1981; patentee in field. Lay leader Congregation Beth Israel, Charlottesville, 1979-89. Scholar Samuel Ruben Found., 1968-72. Fellow Am. Inst. Chemists; mem. Water Pollution Control Fedn., Am. Soc. Artificial Internal Organs, Am. Assn. Research Cos., Sigma Xi, Tau Beta Pi. Office: ASTRE Corp Group 1228 Prince St Alexandria VA 22302

ACKLEY, EVERETT LOSEY, business executive, educator, consultant; b. Cohocton, N.Y., Feb. 18, 1914; s. William Rawlings and Ella (Hurlbert) A.; m. E. Bernice Collier, Mar. 27, 1937; children: Kenneth, Linda Gaston, Stephen, Christopher. Cert. in bus. adminstrn., U. Rochester, 1948; BS in Liberal Arts, U. of State of N.Y., Albany, 1983; postgrad., Calif. State U., 1985-86, U. Fla., 1987. Registered real estate broker; lisc. real estate instr. Traffic and prodn. asst. Blum Shoe Mfg. Co., Dansville, N.Y., 1934-42; product supr. Gen. Cable Corp., Perth Amboy, N.J., 1942-45; prodn. mgr., personnel dir. Ann Page Foods, Inc., Brockport, N.Y., 1945-50; mfg. coordinator Ann Page Foods, Inc., N.Y.C., 1950-54; dir. quality control, mktg. Duncan Hines Inst., Ithaca, N.Y., 1954-58; pres. Gemex Precision Metals, Inc., Union, N.J., 1958-64, C M Worldwide Personnel Cons. Inc., N.Y.C., 1964-70; chief operating officer AFC Assocs. Inc., Sanford, Fla., 1970—; also bd. dirs. AFC Assocs. Inc., Sanford; adj. instr. Seminole Community Coll., Sanford, Fla., 1975—; bd. dirs. Standard Savs. Loan Assn., Gaithersburg, Md., Harley Buckle Corp., N.Y., Domino Industries, Wilmington, Del., I.P.S. Inc., Tampa, Fla., C M Worldwide Personnel Cons. Inc., N.Y.C. Author: Professional Career Placement, 1968; inventor of completely adjustable metal watch band. Commr. Boy Scouts Am., Westchester, 1954-79; bd. dirs. Community Chest Orgn., Westchester, 1952-56, 100 Club Tottenville S.I., 1943-45; elder Presbyn. Ch., 1954—. Mem. Cert. Personnel Cons., Internat. Cons. Assn., Fla. Watercolor Soc., KADY DIAR (pres. 1984), Mason, Phi Theta Kappa, Psi Upsilon. Home: 118 Lake Dot Dr Sanford FL 32773

ACKMANN, LOWELL EUGENE, electrical engineer; b. Elgin, Ill., July 2, 1923; s. Henry C. and Matilda (Rineck) A.; m. Dorothy Collier, July 26, 1948; children: Robert, Lee, Barbara. B.S.E.E., U. Ill., 1944. Engr. Allis-Chalmers Mfg. Co., Milw., 1946-48; sales engr. Allis-Chalmers Mfg. Co., Chgo., 1948-52, Peoria, Ill., 1952-54; v.p. Roland Constrn. Co., Dallas, 1954-56; elec. engr. Sargent & Lundy, Chgo., 1956-68, ptnr., 1966, mgr. electric dept., 1968-76, dir. services, 1976-84, sr. ptnr., 1984-87, ret., 1987. Served with USN, 1943-46. Recipient Disting. Alumnus award Elec. Engring. Alumni Assn., U. Ill., 1979. Mem. Western Soc. Engrs., Ill. Soc. Profl. Engrs., IEEE, Nat. Soc. Profl. Engrs. Clubs: Inverness Golf, Chgo. Athletic Assn. Home: 200 Dover Circle Inverness IL 60067 Office: Sargent & Lundy 55 E Monroe St Chicago IL 60603

ACS, GABRIEL ALEXANDER, venture capitalist, real estate investor, financier, writer; b. Budapest, Hungary, Apr. 24, 1956; came to U.S., 1967; s. John and Marie (Stumpf) A.; m. Kenny Lynne Tiger; 1 child, Diadon Gabriel. Grad., Granton Inst. Tech. Tng. dir. Bridge Publs., Inc., Los Angeles, 1977-80; v.p. Webber Internat., Seattle, 1980-82; pres. ACS, Inc., Kirkland, Wash., 1982—, A.C.S. Venture Corp. (USA) Ltd., Dover, Del., 1983—; chmn., chief exec. officer Washington Acquisition and Disposition Assocs., Inc., Kirkland, 1986—; bd. dirs. Gabor Industries, Inc., Dover; bd. dirs., advisor Advance Capital Services, Victoria, B.C., Can., 1983-87; bd. dirs., treas. DMT Fin. Corp., Dover, 1983-86; atty.-in-fact First Republic Bank Ltd., Majuro, Marshall Island, Micronesia, 1983-85; registered agt. Ametex Inc., Spokane, Wash., 1986—; pres., bd. dirs. ACS Mining Ventures, Inc., Dover, 1987—, AM-CAP Services, Inc., Kirkland, 1988—; cons. New West Mining and Prospecting, Woodinville, Wash., 1987—; dir., distbr. Sunrider Internat., Torrence, Calif., advisor Tesla, Inc., Leadville, Colo., 1988—. Author: The Death of Barbarism, 1983, Going From A to B, 1985, 21st Century Banking, 1986. Office: ACS Venture Corp 9805 NE 116th Ste 7115 Kirkland WA 98034

ACUFF, THOMAS ALDRICH, corporate executive; b. Bklyn., July 26, 1936; s. Fieldon Harpe and Doris (Gray) A.; children: Mark Thomas, Elizabeth Guilliams; m. Veronica Yvette Packham. BS in Indsl. Engring., Iowa State U., 1961; postgrad., U. Louisville, 1970. Advanced mfg. engr. Gen. Electric Co., Louisville, 1961-66; indsl. engring. mgr. Allis Chalmers Corp., Louisville, 1966-68, supt. mfg., 1968-71; gen. mgr. Famco-Asia, Allis Chalmers Corp., Singapore, 1971-75; mfg. dir. internat. Allis Chalmers Corp., Louisville, 1975-78; regional dir. Far East and Pacific, Allis Chalmers Corp., Singapore, 1978-80; dir. advanced ops. ITT Europe, Brussels, 1980-84, dir. bus. ops., 1984-88; v.p. Andlinger & Co. Inc., Brussels, 1988—; bd. dirs. Famco-Asia, Singapore, Japan Air Filter, Tokyo, AAF Famco B.V., The Netherlands, G3 Ferrari Spa, Gaggia Finanziaria Spa, Gruppo Saeco Finanziaria Spa, Daniel Finanziaria Spa, Italy. Contbr. articles to profl. jours. Chmn. Am. Cancer Soc., Louisville, 1971. Served to lt. comdr. USNR, 1954-57. Mem. Inst. Indsl. Engrs. (sr., bd. dirs. 1970), Am. Bus. Council (Singapore), Am. Mgmt. Assn. (div. council), Armed Forces Communications and Electronics Assn. (bd. dirs., pres. 1987). Club: Tanglin (Singapore), Am. (Singapore), Internat. Club (Brussels). Office: Andlinger & Co Inc, 475 Ave Louise Bte 10, B1050 Brussels Belgium

ADACHI, SUEO, trading company executive; b. Tokyo, Aug. 24, 1926; s. Tadashi and Kohko Adachi; m. Yoko Kabashima, Oct. 6, 1960; children: Akiko Sugiyama, Sachiko. BA, Keio U., Tokyo, 1947. Gen. mgr. plant export dept. Marubeni Corp., Tokyo, 1971-78, gen. mgr. machinery IV div., 1979-83, mng. dir., gen. mgr. plant div., 1983-85; pres., chief exec. officer Marubeni Am. Corp., N.Y.C., 1985-87, chmn., chief exec. officer, 1987-88. Mem. Japanese C. of C. (bd. dirs. N.Y. chpt. 1985—). Clubs: The Nippon (bd. dirs.), Met. (N.Y.C.); Scarsdale (N.Y.) Golf. Office: Marubeni Am Corp 200 Park Ave New York NY 10016 *

ADAIR, GLENDA R., accountant; b. Haleyville, Ala., May 18, 1962; d. Albert Price and Rebie Virginia (Hobbs) A. Student, Wallace State Community Coll., 1980-82; BS in Acctg., U. Ala., 1985, postgrad. Sec., receptionist Wallace State Community Coll., Hanceville, Ala., 1981-82; clk. U. Ala., University, 1982-85; staff acct. Durr Fillauer Med. Supply, Inc., Montgomery, Ala., 1985-86; examiner Dept. Revenue, Tuscaloosa, Ala., 1986—. J. Hubert Scruggs Jr. scholar U. Ala., Hohenburg Trust scholar U. Ala., Isabella Hummel Graham scholar U. Ala., Upperclassman scholar U. Ala. Fellow NAFE, Nat. Assn. Accts., Ala. Acctg. Soc., Beta Alpha Psi. Baptist. Home: Star Rte PO Box 425 Double Springs AL 35553 Office: State Ala Dept Revenue 518 19th Ave Tuscaloosa AL 35403

ADAM, ORVAL MICHAEL, transportation company financial executive, lawyer; b. Detroit, Apr. 25, 1930; s. Edgar Michael and Beatrice Rose (White) A.; m. Mary P. Knowles, Dec. 29, 1956; children: Margaret, Celine, Sarah, Mary Katherine, Charles, Bridget. BBA, Canisius Coll., 1953; LLB, Georgetown U., 1956. Atty. IRS, Washington, 1956-60, Atchison, Topeka & Santa Fe Ry. Co., Chgo., 1960-73; asst. v.p. law Santa Fe Industries, Chgo., 1970-75, asst. v.p., tax counsel, 1975-76, v.p., tax counsel, 1977-83, sr. v.p. fin., tax counsel, 1983-84; v.p., treas., chief fin. officer Santa Fe So. Pacific Corp., Chgo., 1984-87, sr. v.p., chief fin. officer, 1988—; dir. Santa Fe Industries, So. Pacific Co., Atchison, Topeka & Santa Fe Ry. Co. Bd. editors Georgetown Law Jour., 1955-56. Bd. dirs., pres. Homeowner's Civic Assn., Flossmoor, Ill., 1966-71; mem. zoning bd. appeals Village of Flossmoor, 1967-73, trustee, 1973-79; mem. fiscal bd. Infant Jesus of Prague Catholic Ch., Flossmoor, 1973-74; mem. exec. com. Taxpayers Fedn. Ill. Mem. ABA, Tax Fund (mem. adv. bd.), Taxpayer's Fedn. Ill. (trustee), Fin. Execs. Inst., Fed. Bar Assn., Tax Coun. (bd. dirs., chmn. fin. exec. com.), Olympia Fields Country Club, Chgo. Athletic Club, The Chgo. Club. Republican.

ADAMO, MARILYN H(ANK), information specialist; b. Queens, N.Y., July 20, 1953; d. Vincent J. and Evelyn F. (Ingerling) Hank; m. Ernest J. Adamo, June 21, 1975. BA, CUNY, 1975; MS, Pratt Inst., 1978. Reference librarian Citibank N.A., N.Y.C., 1973-81; asst. dir. library svcs. Cravath, Swaine and Moore, N.Y.C., 1981-87; v.p., mgr. info. ctr. Oppenheimer and Co. Inc., N.Y.C., 1987—. Mem. Law Librarians Assn. Greater N.Y., Spl. Libraries Assn., Am. Assn. Law Librarians. Office: Oppenheimer & Co Inc World Financial Ctr New York NY 10281

ADAMS, BEEJAY (MEREDITH ELISABETH JANE J.), sales executive; b. Jefferson Banks, Mo., June 9, 1920; d. Alden Humphrey and Louise Marion (Banta) Seabury; m. Merlin Francis Adams, July 10, 1948 (dec. 1977); children: S(tephen) Kent, Mark Francis. AB, Bradley U., 1942. Svc. editor Peoria (Ill.) Jour. Star, 1942-46; women's program dir. Sta. WEEK-AM, Peoria, 1946-47; on air personality Sta. KSD-AM, St. Louis, 1948; lectr. Sch. Assembly Svc., Chgo., 1948-49; pres. M.F. Adams, Inc., Quincy, Ill., 1977-85; commodities broker Quincy, 1985-87; pres. MarKent, Inc., Quincy, 1975—; sec., treas. Miss. Belle Distbn. Co., Inc., Quincy, 1976—, v.p., treas., 1979—. Active Quincy Svc. League, 1949—, local polit. campaigns, co-chmn. local presdl. campaigns, 1952-77; founder, past pres. Quincy Jr. Theatre, 1953-78; charter mem. Quincy Community Theatre. Mem. Quincy C. of C., Sales and Mktg. Execs. Club, Quincy Art Club, Atlantis Study Club, Quincy Country Club, Phi Beta Phi. Home: 2303 Jersey St Quincy IL 62301 Office: Miss Belle Distbn Co Inc PO Box 768 Quincy IL 62306

ADAMS, BUEL THOMAS, construction company executive; b. Mansfield, Ohio, Feb. 8, 1933; s. Oliver Buel and Marion Elizabeth (Kinney) A.; m. Phyllis Joan Flahive, Apr. 23, 1960; children: Thomas, Kenneth, Gary, Timothy, Christopher. BS in Acctg., St. Joseph's Coll., Rensselaer, Ind., 1954; MBA in Acctg., U. Pa., 1960. CPA. Mgr. Arthur Andersen and Co., Pitts., 1959-69; sr. v.p. adminstrn. Blue Cross Blue Shield of Ill., Chgo., 1969-75; v.p., treas. Playboy Enterprises, Chgo., 1975-76; controller Bell & Howell, Lincolnwood, Ill., 1976-78, Blount, Inc., Montgomery, Ala., 1978-81; v.p. fin. The Richardson Co., Des Plaines, Ill., 1981-83; v.p., treas. CBI Industries, Oak Brook, Ill., 1983—. Elijah Watts Sells award Am. Inst. CPAs., 1962. Mem. Fin. Execs. Inst. (pres. Chgo. chpt. 1986-87, nat. bd. 1988—), The Chgo. Forum, 1975-76, Machinery and Allied Products Inst.(fin. council). Roman Catholic. Home: 233 Meadowbrook Ln Hinsdale IL 60521 Office: CBI Industries Inc 800 Jorie Blvd Oak Brook IL 60521

ADAMS, C. LEE, marketing executive; b. Houston, Dec. 5, 1940; s. Carl Adams and Ruth (Carroll) Adams McGraw; BBA, Tex. A&M U., 1963; m. Betty Leatherwood, June 1, 1963; children: Diana, Carroll Ann. Export sales service asst. Comet Rice Mills, Inc., Houston, 1963-64, asst. export sales mgr., 1964-67, export sales mgr., 1967-68; gen. mgr. Country Cupboard Foods Div., Comet Rice Mills, 1968-71; sales mgr. Childers Mfg. Co., Houston, 1971-75; export sales mgr. Am. Rice, Inc., Houston, 1975-76, v.p. internat. mktg., 1976-80, group v.p. mktg., 1980-85, group v.p. internat. mktg., 1986—; mem. rice com. New Orleans Commodity Exchange, 1981-84. Bd. dirs. Harris County Water Control and Improvement Dist. 93, 1974-76; mem. Chelford One Mcpl. Utility Dist. Appraisal Rev. Bd., 1982-85. Served with USMCR, 1960-66. Mem. Am. Arab C. of C. (dir. 1978-81), TAMU 12th Man Found. (bd. dirs. 1987—), Rice Council for Market Devel., Rice Millers Assn. (dir. 1983—, pres. 1986-87), Assn. Former Students Tex. A&M U. Roman Catholic. Clubs: Elsik High Sch. Ram Rods (pres. 1984-85), Sweetwater Country. Lodge: K.C. Office: Am Rice Inc PO Box 2587 Houston TX 77252

ADAMS, CHARLES ARTHUR, municipal financial analyst; b. Caldwell, Idaho, July 25, 1933; s. John Woodrow and Eileen (Vail) A.; BA, Coll. Idaho, 1962; m. Susan Rae Donovan, Jan. 30, 1960; children: Michael C., Teresa M. Sales mgr. Hoppins Ins. Agy., Nampa, Idaho, 1961-63; auditor Indsl. Indemnity Ins. Co., Boise, Idaho, 1964-65, Argonaut Ins. Co., Portland, 1966-67; br. mgr. Am. Mut. Ins. Co., Portland, 1968-70; underwriting mgr. Alaska Pacific Assurance Co., Juneau, 1970-73; pres. A.I.M. Ins. Inc., Anchorage, 1973-78, pres. parent co. A.I.M. Corp., 1977-78, also sr. v.p. A.I.M. Internat., Tokyo, 1975-78; fin. officer City of Petersburg (Alaska), 1978, City of Homer (Alaska), 1979; fin. analyst Municipality of Anchorage, 1980—; community adv. bd. KSKA, 1983— . Vol. in corrections, State of Alaska, 1981; mem. central com. Libertarian Party of Alaska, 1981-84, vice chmn., 1985—, chmn., Anchorage, 1982-83. Sgt. maj. AUS, USARSF 1952-76, ret. Mem. Resource Devel. Council Alaska, Homebuilders Alaska (dir. 1974-78), Homeowners Warranty Council Alaska (v.p. 1977), Porsche Club Am., Airborne Assn., VFW, Am. Legion, Spl. Forces Decade Assn., Alaska Council Sports Car Clubs (dir. 1976-78), Alaska World Affairs Council (chmn. fin. and devel. com. 1983-84, dir. 1984—, univ. and coll. liaison com. 1985—). Clubs: Toastmasters (named Summit Club Speaker of Yr. 1969), Wednesday Club, Captain Cook Athletic. Lodge: KC. Author: fin. procedures and master policy to insure constrn. of Alaska pipeline. Home: 3258 Montpelier Ct Anchorage AK 99503 Office: Pouch 6-650 Anchorage AK 99502

ADAMS, DOUGLAS FLETCHER, banker; b. Bklyn., May 18, 1937; s. Gordon D. and Blanche (Fletcher) A.; m. Judith S. Adams, Dec. 18, 1965; children—Douglas Jr., Sally Carlyle, Annie Laurie. A.B. in History, Dartmouth Coll., 1959; M.B.A. in Fin. NYU, 1965; J.D., St. Johns U., 1969. Asst. sr. adminstr. Bank of N.Y., 1962-66, asst. trust officer, 1966-68, asst. v.p., 1968-71, v.p., 1971-77, sr. v.p., 1977-81, exec. v.p., 1981—; dir. Bank of N.Y. Internat. Trust Group, Trust Co. of Fla., NA, Miami, Bank N.Y. Trust Co. Calif. Trustee Winterthur Swiss Ins. Co. Trust; bd. dirs. Nova Arts Found. Served to lt. (j.g.) USN, 1959-62. Mem. N.Y. State Bar Assn., Fin. Analyst Fedn., N.Y. Soc. of Security Analysts, Am. Bankers Assn. (exec. com. trust div.). Republican. Methodist. Clubs: Fairfield Beach (Conn.), Laurel Beach (Conn.). Office: Bank NY 48 Wall St New York NY 10286

ADAMS, EDMUND JOHN, lawyer; b. Lansing, Mich., June 6, 1938; s. John Edmund and Helen Kathryn (Pavlick) A.; m. Mary Louise Riegler, Aug. 11, 1962. BA, Xavier U., 1960; LLB, U. Notre Dame, 1963. Bar: Ohio 1963. Assoc. Paxton & Seasongood, Cin., 1965-70; assoc. Frost & Jacobs, 1970-71, ptnr., 1971—, exec. com., 1985-88. Author: Catholic Trails West, The Founding Catholic Families of Pennsylvania, 1988. Trustee, Southwest Ohio Regional Transit Authority, 1980—, pres. 1988; chmn. Sister Cities Assn. of Greater Cin., 1984—; mem. Hamilton County Republican Exec. Com., 1982—. 1st lt. U.S. Army, 1963-65. Mem. ABA, Ohio Bar Assn., Cin. Bar Assn. Roman Catholic. Clubs: Cin. Tennis, Hyde Park Country. Home: 3210 Columbia Pkwy Cincinnati OH 45226 Office: Frost & Jacobs 2500 Cen Trust Ctr 201 E 5th St Cincinnati OH 45202

ADAMS, F. GERARD, economist, educator; b. Apr. 28, 1929; s. Walter and Margot Adams; m. Courtney Sherbrooke, June 13, 1953; children: Leslie, Colin, Loren, Mark. B.A., U. Mich., 1949, M.A., 1951, Ph.D., 1956. Instr. dept. econs. U. Mich., Ann Arbor, 1952-56; economist Calif. Tex. Oil Corp., N.Y.C., 1956-59; cons. economist, mgr. gen. econs. dept. Compagnie Française des Petroles, N.Y.C. and Paris, 1959-61; mem. faculty U. Pa., Phila., 1961—; prof. econs. and fin. U. Pa., 1971—; dir. Econs. Research Unit, 1961—, chmn. Faculty Senate, 1987—; chmn. profl. bd. WEFA Group, Phila., 1969—. Author: (with others) An Econometric Analysis of International Trade, 1969, (with J.R. Behrman) Econometric Models of World Agricultural Commodity Markets, 1976, Commodity Exports and Economic Development, 1982, (with L.R. Klein) Industrial Policies for Growth and Competitiveness, 1983, The Business Forecasting Revolution, 1986; editor: (with S.A. Klein) Stabilizing World Commodity Markets - Analysis, Practice and Policy, 1978. Home: 105 W Ivywood Ln Radnor PA 19087 Office: U Pa Econs Rsch Unit 3718 Locust Walk Philadelphia PA 19104-6297

ADAMS, HALL, JR. (CAP ADAMS), advertising agency executive; b. Chicago, July 28, 1933. B.A., Williams Coll., 1954. Asst. account exec. Leo Burnett Co. Inc., Chicago, 1960-62, account exec., 1962-66, brand supervisor, 1966-68, v.p., account supr., 1968-69, sr. v.p., from 1969, now chmn., chief exec. officer. Served with U.S. Army, 1954-56. Office: Leo Burnett Co Inc Prudential Pla Chicago IL 60601 *

ADAMS, HERBERT JOHN, oil company executive; b. Oak Park, Ill., Dec. 2, 1952; s. Herbert Loren and Donna (Rae) A.; m. Mary Dean Edwards, Oct. 7, 1978 (div. Nov. 1982); one child, Joshua; m. Karen Ruth Bernard, Dec. 17, 1984; children: Samuel, David. BA in Theology, Oral Robert U., 1975. Lic. real estate broker, Okla. Sales assoc. Mike Coulter Realtors, Tulsa, 1976-77; v.p. brokers Ron Minkler and Assocs., Tulsa, 1977-80; acct. exec. W&W Explorations, Tulsa, 1980-81; broker Real Estate Cons., Tulsa, 1981-82; v.p. Torrent Petroleum Corp., Tulsa, 1983-84; chief exec. officer Wolfen Energy Corp., Tulsa, 1984-87; chmn. Joshua Inc., Tulsa, 1983—; pres. JSD Energy Inc., Tulsa, 1987—. Lay pastor First Meth. Ch., Tulsa, mem. spiritual life commn. Republican. Methodist. Office: JSD Energy Inc 2431 E 51 Suite 602 Tulsa OK 74105

ADAMS, JACK, film company executive, screenwriter, educator; b. Lakehurst, N.J., Sept. 15, 1952; s. John Carey and Dorothy Jeanne (Conover) A.; m. Shirley Janulewicz, June 28, 1975; children: Carey Miller, Chanine Angelina, Mikael Walter. MusB in Music Edn., U. Del., 1974. Pres. Koala Studio, Valencia, Calif., 1977—; v.p. Unifilms, Inc., North Hollywood, Calif., 1984—; tchr. film, TV writing Coll. of the Canyons, Valencia, 1988—. Composer (film) EAT, 1980 (Filmex award 1981, Best Short Film award Cinemagic mag. 1981); columnist Hollywood Scriptwriter, 1987—. Mem. Am. Film Inst., (alumni assn. writers workshop), Scriptwriters Network, Film Artists Network, NBC Writers Workshop (pres.), Ind. Writers So. Calif. Scriptwriters Caucus, Assn. Info. Systems Profls. (dir. 1983), Larry Wilson Devel. Workshop (Paramount Studios), L.A. Filmmakers Workshop, Ind. Feature Project West. Home: 22931 Sycamore Creek Dr Valencia CA 91354-2050 Office: Unifilms Inc 6748 Clybourn Ave Ste 124 North Hollywood CA 91606

ADAMS, JOHN BRETT, investment banker; b. Tiverton, U.K., Dec. 6, 1940; came to U.S., 1972; s. Harold Coates and Mildred B. (Jones) A.; m. Laura Marie Schneider, July 15, 1970; children—Alexa, Caroline. B.A., Oxford U., Eng., 1962; M.B.A., Stanford U., 1964. Exec. dir. S.G. Warburg & Co., Ltd., London, 1964-72; dir. Singer & Friedlander, Ltd., London, 1972-74; sr. v.p. White, Weld & Co., Inc., N.Y.C., 1974-78; mng. dir. Merrill Lynch Capital Markets, N.Y.C., 1978-85; ptnr. M.J.H. Nightingale & Co., N.Y.C., 1986—; dir. Am. Swiss Assn., N.Y.C.; mem. internat. com. Securities Industry Assn., N.Y.C. Bd. dirs. Brit. Schs. and Univs. Found., Inc., N.Y.C., 1982—. Clubs: Racquet and Tennis (N.Y.C.); Maidstone (East Hampton, N.Y.); Nat. Golf Links (Southampton, N.Y.). Avocations: golf, skiing, racquet sports. Home: 63 E 93d St New York NY 10128

ADAMS, JOHN CARTER, JR., insurance executive; b. Williston, Fla., June 13, 1936; s. John Carter and Katharine Anna (Beall) A.; B.S. in Bus. Adminstrn., U. Fla., 1958; m. Leila Nora Johnson, Nov. 28, 1958; children—Julia Katharine, Ruth Anne. Agt., Pan Am. Ins. Co. 1958-59; acct. exec. Guy B. Odum & Co., Inc. 1959-63, v.p. 1963-66, exec. v.p. 1966-71, pres. 1971-76; pres. Jay Adams & Assocs., Inc. Daytona Beach, Fla., 1976-85, pres. Hilb Rogal & Hamilton Co., Daytona Beach, 1986—; mem. exec. com. Hilb Rogal & Hamilton Co., Richmond, Va., 1988—, chmn. operating com., 1987—, sr. v.p. ops., 1989—, also bd. dirs.; pres. Futures, Inc., 1987-88; chmn. adv. bd. Datona Beach region Am. Pioneer Savs. Bank, Orlando, Fla., 1983-86, also bd. dirs.; bd.dirs. Consolidated-Tomoka Land Co. Bd. visitors Embry-Riddle Aero. U., Daytona Beach, 1967-69, trustee, 1969—, mem. exec. com., 1972—, vice chmn. bd., 1981-87, chmn. exec. com., 1983—, devel. council chmn. fund drive Hunt Meml. Library Embry-Riddle Aero U., 1985; campaign chmn. Easter Seal Soc. 1969, trustee 1970-73, pres. 1972-73; bd. dirs. YMCA, Daytona Beach 1968-76, 1978—, treas. 1970, v.p. 1971-82, pres., 1983; dir. Futures, Inc., 1985—, Nat. Intercollegiate Sports Festival, 1985-87; gen. campaign chmn. United Way of Volusia County, Fla. 1977, pres. 1979, dir. 1976-82, trustee, 1985—; chmn. Civic League of Halifax Area, 1983-84, exec. com., 1977—, vice chmn., 1981-82; mem. Tourist Devel. Council Volusia County, 1983-85, Halifax Advt. Authority, 1985; bd. dirs. Volusia County Bus. Devel. Council, 1984—; bd. dirs. Daytona Beach Community Found., 1984-87. Served with USNR 1953-61. Recipient Disting. Service award Bd. visitors Embry-Riddle Aero. U. 1975; CHIEF award (Champion Higher Ind. Edn. in Fla.), Ind. Colls. and Univs. of Fla., 1973. Mem. Daytona Beach C. of C. (bd. govs. 1968-70, v.p. bus. and govt. 1970, pres. 1975, gen. campaign chmn. devel. fund drive 1984, Louis Fuchs Man of Yr. award, 1985), Volusia County Insurors Assn., Fla. Assn. Ins. Agts. (bd. dirs. 1978-81), Nat. Assn. Casualty & Surety Agts. Republican. Episcopalian. Home: 1616 S Penisula Dr Daytona Beach FL 32015 Office: 121 N Ridgewood Ave Daytona Beach FL 32014

ADAMS, JOHN DAVID VESSOT, manufacturing company executive; b. Ottawa, Ont., Can., Jan. 7, 1934; s. Albert Oliver and Estelle Priscilla (Vessot) A.; m. Dorothy Marion Blyth, June 27, 1959; children: Nancy, Joel, Louis. Student Carleton U., 1950-51; B in Engring., McGill U., 1955; MBA, U. Western Ont., 1958. Registered profl. engr., Ont. Project engr. Abitibi Paper Co., Toronto, Ont., 1962-63, Cockshutt Farm Equipment Co. Ltd., Brantford, Ont., 1958-62, Can. Industries Ltd., Kingston, Ont., 1955-58; mgr. fin. analysis and planning Rio Tinto Zinc Group, London, 1963-66; mgr. adminstrn. and planning Can. Gypsum Co. Ltd., Toronto, 1966-72; mgr. logistics and fin. Massey Ferguson Co. Ltd., Toronto, 1972-79; pres. Can. Spool & Bobbin Co. Ltd., Walkerton, Ont., 1979-88, pres. Quality Performance Engring., Inc., 1989—; consulting, mfg., Owen Sound, Ont., Can. Mem. Assn. Profl. Engrs. Province Ont. Mem. United Ch. of Can. Clubs: Walkerton Golf and Curling, Rotary. Home: 386 14th Ave, Hanover, ON Canada N4N 2Y1 Office: Quality Performance Engring Inc, 3195 3rd Ave E, PO Box 759, Owen Sound, ON Canada N4K 5N9

ADAMS, JOHN LAURENCE, casino executive; b. Reading, Pa., Feb. 24, 1943; s. Charles Anthony and Edith May (Frame) A.; B.S., Lehigh U., 1965, M.B.A., 1978. Data processing trainee IBM, Bethlehem, Pa., 1966-67, mktg. rep. data processing div., 1967-72, adv. mktg. rep., 1973-76, internat. account mgr., 1976-84; v.p. info. systems Caesars Atlantic City Casino/Hotel, 1984—. Bd. dirs., mem. fin. com., chmn. mgmt. assistance program, v.p. long range planning United Way of Atlantic County. Served with U.S. Army, 1965-71. Mem. Am. Mgmt. Assn., Data Processing Mgmt. Assn., Pa. Soc., EDP Auditors Assn. Republican. Roman Catholic. Home: 4038 4th Ave Avalon NJ 08202 Office: Caesars Atlantic City On the Boardwalk at Ark Ave Atlantic City NJ 08401

ADAMS, JOHN WAYNE, real estate executive; b. Roanoke, Va., Nov. 15, 1947; s. John Douglas and Ruth Mildred (Watson) A.; m. Linda Marie Webb, Feb. 1, 1969; 1 child, David Wayne. A in Acctg., Nat. Bus. Coll., Roanoke, 1969; completed various seminars, VPI and State U., U. Va., James Madison U.; completed Dale Carnegie Course, 1977. From acctg. clerk to gen. acct. mgr. Continental Homes, Boones Mill, Va., 1969-73; acct. mgr. Nationwide Homes, Martinsville, Va., 1973-77, asst. corp. sec., 1977—. Mem. Ridgeway (Va.) Fire Dept., 1973—, lt. capt., 1975—, pres. 1982-85, bd. dirs., 1982—; mem. bd. adminstrn., audit com., budget com., Clearview Wesleyan Ch., Martinsville, 1977-79. Mem. Henry County Firemens' Assn. (v.p. 1981-87, trustee 1984—, treas. 1987—). Lodge: Woodmen of World. Home: Rt #3 Box 7 Ridgeway VA 24148 Office: Nationwide Homes Inc Div Insilco Corp 1100 Rives Rd Martinsville VA 24112

ADAMS, KATHARINE ODELL, accountant; b. New Delhi, Jan. 8, 1954; d. J. Wesley and Frances Elizabeth (McStay) A. BBA magna cum laude, U. D.C., 1985. Acct. HUD, Washington, 1986—. Contbr. to numerous charities.

ADAMS, KENNETH FRANCIS, automobile manufacturing company executive; b. Danbury, Conn., Feb. 4, 1946; s. Donald and Evelyn Trocola (Mulvihill) A.; m. Annette Talarico, Sept. 28, 1968; children—Amy, Ella Louise, Elizabeth. Student Mt. St. Mary's Coll., 1964-68. C.P.A., Conn. Mgr., Price Waterhouse & Co., Bridgeport, Conn., 1968-74; v.p. fin., treas. Saab-Scania Am., Inc., Orange, Conn., 1974—. Served with USAR, 1968-74. Mem. AICPA, Conn. Soc. CPA's. Democrat. Roman Catholic. Office: Saab-Scania Am Inc PO Box 697 Orange CT 06477

ADAMS, LEONARD JOSEPH, recruiting executive, personnel consultant; b. N.Y.C., Feb. 3, 1954; s. Melvin and Angela (Francese) Eidlen; m. Marie Ann Cicero, June 6, 1976; children: Heather, Matthew. BBA, Pace U., 1981. Cert. personnel cons. V.p., mgr. KPA/Kling Assocs. Inc., N.Y.C., 1969—. Contbr. articles in field to profl. jours. Treas. A.E. Smith Dem. Orgn., N.Y.C., 1978. Mem. Assn. Personnel Cons. (bd. dirs.). Roman Catholic. Office: KPA/Kling Assocs 180 Broadway Ste 501 New York NY 10038

ADAMS, MICHAEL THOMAS, retail executive; b. Chgo., Nov. 17, 1948; s. William Thomas and Loretta Virginia (Penn) A.; m. Margaret Mary Comella, July 3, 1971; children: Thomas James, Michele Marie, Kimberly Ann, Nicole Marie. BS in Acctg., St. Joseph's Coll., Rensselaer, Ind., 1970; MBA, U. Chgo., 1984. Sr. auditor George S. Olive & Co., CPA's, Indpls., 1970-78; asst. controller W.F. Hall Printing Co., Chgo., 1978-80; mgr. internal audit Pullman, Inc., Chgo., 1980; mgr. internal audit IC Industries, Inc., Chgo., 1980-83, dir. internal audit, 1983-86; controller U.S. ops. Midas Internat. Corp., Chgo., 1986-88, v.p., controller U.S. ops., 1988—. Lectr. St. Margaret Mary Lectrs. and Commentators, Naperville, Ill., 1984—; fundraiser Benet Acad. Annual Fund, Lisle, Ill., 1987-88. Served with USAR, 1971-77. Mem. AICPA, Ind. CPA Soc., U. Chgo. Grad. Sch. Bus. Alumni Assn. Roman Catholic. Club: U. Chgo. Exec. Program. Office: Midas Internat Corp 225 N Michigan Ave Chicago IL 60601-7601

ADAMS, ROBERT HUGO, business news publisher, English teacher; b. Washington, Dec. 6, 1943; s. Gerald Hugo and Ella Mary (Hodge) A.; m. Elaine Louise Lassiter, Dec. 24, 1968 (div. 1976); 1 child, Tiffany K. BS, D.C. Tchrs. Coll., 1967; postgrad., U. Hawaii, 1972-73. Tchr. English D.C. Pub. Schs., 1967-68; salesman Xerox Corp., Hawaii, 1974-75; account exec. Sta. KGMB and Sta. KHON, Hawaii, 1975-76; mgr. King Furniture Stores, Hawaii, 1976-77; owner, mgr. R.H. Adams and Assocs., Hawaii, 1977-78; salesman Levitz Furniture, Garden City, N.Y., 1978-79; bus. editor N.Y. Amsterdam News, N.Y.C., 1979-81; editor, owner, pub. Minority Bus. Rev., N.Y.C., 1981—; guest news commentator various TV stas., N.Y., 1983—. Author: Little Black Book of Business Inspirations, 1987; contbr. articles to newspapers. V.p. African-Am. Heritage Assn., 1982-84; publicity N.Y. Council Black Reps., 1987—. Capt. U.S. Army, 1968-72. Recipient 1st Pl. Essay award Advt. Club N.Y., 1980; Cert. of Appreciation African-Am. Heritage Assn., 1983; named Regional Minority Adv. of Yr. U.S. Dept. Commerce, 1987. Mem. NAACP, Assn. Minority Enterprises of N.Y. (service award 1983), Nat. Minority Bus. Council, Nat. Assn. Minority Contractors (chmn. publicity 1984—), Minority Bus. Enterprise Legal Def. Edn. Fund, Omega Psi Phi. Republican. Episcopalian. Office: Minority Bus Rev PO Box 2132 Hempstead NY 11551

ADAMS, ROY, building materials company executive, rancher; b. Anna, Tex., Mar. 25, 1933; s. Leroy F. and Buelah B. (Bryan) A.; m. Dana G. Rattan, Apr. 18, 1957; children—Dawn, Darja, Adam, Alicia. B.B.A., N. Tex. State U., 1959, M.B.A., 1960. C.P.A., Tex. With Price Waterhouse & Co., Dallas, 1960-62; treas., Capital Wire & Cable Corp., Plano, Tex., 1962-72; v.p. fin. Delwood Furniture Co., Dallas, 1972-74; group v.p. fin. Bldg. and Materials group U.S. Industries, Dallas, 1974-80; v.p. fin. Summit Oilfield Corp., Dallas, 1980-86; sr. v.p., chief fin. officer, Dallas Corp., Dallas, 1986—; dir. Republic Bank, Plano, Served with U.S. Army, 1953-55. Mem. Am. Inst. C.P.A.s. Democrat. Baptist. Lodge: Masons. Office: Dallas Corp 6750 LBJ Frwy Dallas TX 75240

ADAMS, SALVATORE CHARLES, attorney, financial consultant; b. Bklyn., July 10, 1934; s. Charles Joseph and Rose (Scala) A.; m. Ann Shepherdson, Aug. 3, 1957 (div. Feb. 1973); children: Mark, Scott, David, Christopher; m. Linda Lewis Pollock, Mar. 31, 1973 (div. May 1980). BCE, Rensselaer Poly. Inst., 1955; MS, U. Conn., 1961; JD, U. Miami, 1968. Bar: Fla., U.S. Dist. Ct. (so. dist.) Fla., U.S. Ct. Appeals (5th cir.), U.S. Supreme Ct.; Registered profl. engr., N.Y., Conn. Pres. Motivation Cons., Miami, Fla., 1965-68; v.p. Exposition Corp., Miami, 1968-72; corp. counsel City of Pompano Beach, Fla., 1972-76, Five Star Industries, Hialeah, Fla., 1976-80; chmn., chief exec. officer Atlantic Services Group, Ft. Lauderdale, Fla., 1977-86; fin. cons. Merrill Lynch Price Fenner & Smith, Ft. Lauderdale, 1987—; bd. dirs. Atlantic Services Group, Inc., Ft. Lauderdale. Candidate Fla. Ho. of Reps., Miami, 1967, Dade County Commn., Miami, 1968; del. White House Conf. on Small Bus., Washington, 1986; appointed to joint Presdl.-Congl. Com. by Pres. Reagan, 1984. Served to lt. (j.g.) USN, 1955-57. Recipient Pres.'s award Broward County Bar Assn., 1975. Mem. North Broward Bar Assn. (treas., bd. dirs.), Broward County Mcpl. Judges Assn. (pres.), Nat. Inst. Mcpl. Law Officers (chmn. ethics com.), Rensselaer Poly. Inst. Alumni Assn. (pres. South Fla. chpt.). Republican. Office: The Adams Group PO Box 11339 Fort Lauderdale FL 33339-1339

ADAMS, SCOTT LESLIE, accountant; b. Seattle, Nov. 23, 1955; s. Brock and Mary Elizabeth (Scott) A.; m. Crystal Hood, Aug. 7, 1978; children: Brock, Justin, Margie Elizabeth. BS in Acctg. magna cum laude, Jones Coll., 1984. Dist. dir. The Scott Co., Washington, 1972-75; pres. Slade Corp., Greenbelt, Md., 1977-80; shift supr. U.S. Ho. Reps., Washington, 1977-82; acct. Comprehensive Bus. Services, Jacksonville, Fla., 1984-85; prin. Contemporary Bus. Services, Jacksonville, 1985—; pres. Scott Investment Inc., Jacksonville, 1980—; v.p. Scoco, Bebo, Atlantic Blvd. Land, Jacksonville, 1982—. Deacon St. John's Park Bapt. Ch., Jacksonville, 1987—; pres. Jacksonville West Camp, Gideons U.S.A., 1987—. Mem. Am. Inst. CPAs, Nat. Soc. Pub. Accts., Nat. Soc. Tax Practitioners, Nat. Assn. Accts., Jacksonville C. of C. Democrat. Home: 1311 Windsor Pl Jacksonville FL 32205 Office: Contemporary Bus Svcs 4070 Herschel St Jacksonville FL 32210

ADAMS, STEPHEN M., publishing company executive. Sr. v.p. fin. and adminstrn. Macmillan Pub. Office: Macmillan Pub Co 866 3rd Ave New York NY 10022 *

ADAMS, SUSAN VIRGINIA, appliance distributor executive; b. Detroit, Apr. 30, 1948; d. Robert Edwin and Virginia Grace (Houghton) A. BA in Elem. Edn., Elmira Coll., 1970; MA in Teaching Spanish, The Experiment's Sch. Internat. Tng., Brattleboro, Vt., 1971. Tchr. Am. Sch. Found., Mexico City, 1971-73; travel cons. Bradford Travel, Columbus, Ohio, 1973-76; dir. ops. Excursions Unltd., Columbus, 1976-80; dist. mgr. Top Brands Inc., Columbus, 1980-86; v.p., majority stockholder Top Brands Inc., Cleve., 1986—. Vol. Jr. League, Columbus, 1983-87, Jr. League, Cleve., 1987—, Jr. Com. Cleve. Orch., 1987—; mem. auction com. Project Friendship, Cleve., 1987—. Mem. Nat. Kitchen and Bath Assn., Nat. Assn. Profl. Saleswomen (sec. 1983), Play House Club, Shaker Country Club (Shaker Hts., Ohio). Republican. Prebyterian. Office: Top Brands Inc 16485 Rockside Rd Cleveland OH 44137

ADAMS, WALTER HOLLAND, III, manufacturing executive; b. Tyler, Tex., Sept. 11, 1952; s. Walter Holland Jr. and Grace Pearl (Pierce) A.; m. Linda Yvonne Beck, May 25. 1975 (div. 1981); m. Sabine Maria Klose, Oct. 10, 1982; children: Seth Holland, Silas L. BBA, Tex. A&M U., 1976. Foreman Norton Chem. Co., College Station, Tex., 1976-78; prodn. mgr. Power Systems, Lancaster, Tex., 1976-78; br. mgr. div. NCH, Aqua Terr Brochem, Lancaster, 1982-86; ops. mgr. Partsmaster U.S.A., Irving, Tex., 1986—. Mem. adv. bd. Cedar Valley Coll., Lancaster, 1982—. Episcopalian. Home: Rte 1 340 Apple Ct Midlothian TX 76065 Office: Partsmaster USA 1400 E Northgate Irving TX 75012

ADAMS, WAYNE W., university dean. BS in Chem. Engring., Vanderbilt U., 1965; MBA, Harvard U., 1967; MA, Columbia U., 1981; diploma Advanced Healthcare Mgmt. Program, Yale U., 1984; postgrad., Luther Rice Seminary, Jacksonville, Fla., 1989. Mgmt. cons. McKinsey and Co., 1970-71; govt. appointee specializing in mgmt. Washington, 1971-75; pres. Witness Art, 1975-79; v.p. computer companies 1979-83; v.p. planning and mktg. major med. ctr., 1983-84; pres. Adams and Assocs., Tampa Bay, Fla., 1984—; dean Grad. Sch. Bus. CBN Univ., Virginia Beach, Va., 1989—; speaker in field. Author: What I Wish They Had Taught Me At Harvard Business School: The Bible and Business Success. Mem. Gov.'s Healthcare Commn. Tenn., 1983; co-founder, bd. dirs. Leadership Knoxville (Tenn.), 1984; tchr. adult Sunday Sch.; founder Wayside Christian Ctr., Washington, Christian Bus. Inst. Served to capt. USMC, 1967-70. Mem. Harvard Bus. Sch. Club (pres., chmn. bd. dirs.), Phi Beta Kappa. Baptist. Address: 501 Park Ave Clearwater FL 34616

ADAMS, WILLIAM JOHNSTON, accounting firm executive; b. Detroit, Nov. 24, 1934; s. William Montgomery and Sara Emogene (Johnston) A.; m. Lynn Laviolette, Aug. 24, 1957 (div. Sept. 1976); 1 child, William David; m. Donna Wolcott, Apr. 24, 1977. BBA, U. Mich., 1957, MBA, 1958. CPA, Mich. Staff acct. Arthur Andersen & Co., Detroit, 1958-62, tax mgr., 1962-70, tax ptnr., 1970—. Trustee, sec., treas., pres. Grosse Pointe (Mich.) Pub. Schs., 1969-72; chmn. Greater Detroit Fgn. Trade Zone, Inc., 1983—; mem. adv. bd. Paton Fund, 1988; bd. dirs. Civic Searchlight, Detroit, 1985-88, 2d v.p., 1989. Named Outstanding Young Man of Yr. Grosse Pointe Jaycees, 1970; named to Pres.' Club U. Mich., Ann Arbor, 1975. Mem. Mich. Assn. CPA's, AICPA, Tappan Soc. Congregationalist. Clubs: Detroit, Detroit Boat (bd. dirs., treas. 1985-87, com. 1986), Indian Village Tennis (Detroit). Home: 1453 Iroquois Detroit MI 48214

ADAMS, WILLIAM WHITE, manufacturing company executive; b. Dubuque, Iowa, May 14, 1934; s. Waldo and Therese (White) A.; m. Susan Joanne Cole, Dec. 29, 1956; children: Nancy, Sara, Mark, Catherine. B.S. in Indsl. Adminstrn., Iowa State U., 1956. With Armstrong World Industries, Inc., Lancaster, Pa., 1956—, gen. sales mgr. residential ceiling systems div., 1975-80, group v.p. bldg. products ops., 1981, exec. v.p., 1982-88, chmn., pres., chief exec. officer, 1988—; dir. Bell Telephone Co. of Pa., 1986—. Chmn. adv. bd. Lancaster-Lebanon council Boy Scouts Am., 1970—; bd. dirs. United Way Lancaster County, (Pa.), 1977-82, WITF Pub. Broadcasting, 1986-88; bd. dirs. Lancaster Symphony Assn., 1978-87, pres., 1983-84. Recipient Silver Beaver award Boy Scouts Am., 1979. Mem. Pa. C. of C. (dir.), Pa. Bus. Roundtable (dir.), Nat. Assn. Mfgrs. (dir.), Bus. Roundtable. Club: Lancaster Country (dir. 1978-84). Office: Armstrong World Industries Inc PO Box 3001 333 W Liberty St Lancaster PA 17604

ADCOX, STEPHEN I., telecommunications company executive; b. Fayetteville, N.C., Oct. 20, 1946; s. Maness and V. Juanita (Livingston) A.; m. Jeanne E. Brabant, June 10, 1967 (div. 1977). BBA, Pa. State U., 1976, M of Telecommunications, 1979. Staff announcer Sta. WFAI, Fayetteville, 1965-68; program dir. Sta. WEEO, Waynesboro, Pa., 1971-74; from mktg. analyst to mgr. mktg. adminstrn. No. Telecom, Inc., Raleigh, N.C., 1979-86; mgr. mktg. rsch. and product planning No. Telecom, Inc., Research Triangle Park, N.C., 1986-87, mgr. account mktg. Can., 1989—. Loaned exec. Wake County United Way, 1987; bus. simulation dir. Fuqua Sch. Bus., Duke U., Durham, 1987. With U.S. Army, 1968-71. Mem. Soc. Computer Simulation, Am. Mktg. Assn. Home: 5622 Hamstead Crossing Raleigh NC 27612 Office: No Telecom Inc PO Box 12646 Research Triangle Park NC 27709

ADDERLEY, TERENCE E., corporate executive; b. 1933; married. BBA, U. Mich., 1951, BMA, 1956. Former fin. analyst Standard Oil Co. of N.J., 1956-57; with Kelly Services, Inc., Troy, Mich., 1957—, v.p., 1961-65, exec. v.p., 1965-67, pres., chief operating officer, 1967—, also dir. Office: Kelly Services Inc 999 W Big Beaver Rd Troy MI 48084 *

ADDINGTON, CONLEY RICHMOND, JR., marketing consulting company executive; b. Dallas, Apr. 26, 1945; m. Barbara J. Blesedell, May 13, 1972 (div. Nov. 1985); children: Tara, Tricia, Elizabeth. BBA, U. Miami, 1968; A in Securities Industry (hon.), U. Pa., 1986. Founder Dact Assocs., Miami, Fla., 1968-72; stockbroker Dean Witter Reynolds Co., Phila., 1972-82; sr. v.p. Van Kampen Merrit Co., Phila., 1982-87; chmn. MarkTech Systems, Inc., Phila., 1987—. Mem. Pub. Secs. Assn. (mem. mktg. bd. 1985—). Republican. Office: MarkTech Systems Inc 4630 Trevose Corporate Ctr Trevose PA 19047

ADDIS, SARA ALLEN, franchise executive; b. El Paso, Tex., May 15, 1930; d. Waldo Rufus and Cordelia Dean (Kerr) Allen; m. Bobby Joe Addis, June 5, 1949; children—Craig Dell, Alan Blake, Neil Clark, Sara Kathleen. Sec. to adminstr. Southwestern Gen. Hosp., El Paso, 1948-49; sec. to dir. of personnel U. Tex., El Paso, 1964-65; pres., founder Sara Care Franchise Corp., El Paso, 1978—. Named Small Bus. Person of Yr., Small Bus. Adminstrn., 1986, 87. Mem. Internat. Franchise Assn., Nat. Fedn. Ind. Businesses, Presidents Assn. Am. Mgmt. Assn., El Paso Better Bus. Bur., El Paso C. of C., Assn. Pioneer Women. (Entrepreneur of Yr.), Bus. and Profl. Women El Paso (Small Bus. Person of Yr. 1983, 85, 86, 87), Exec. Forum, Profl. Women's Network U. Tex. El Paso. Republican. Club: Lower Valley Women's. Lodge: Order Eastern Star. Avocations: oil painting; music; travel. Home: 8417 Parkland St El Paso TX 79925 Office: Sara Care Franchise Corp 1200 Golden Key Cir Ste 368 El Paso TX 79925

ADDISON, CAROLE BRACKEN, financial analyst; b. Indpls., June 26, 1960; d. John Robert and Mary Ann (Kascha) Bracken; m. Leonard Ross Addison, Nov. 11, 1984. BBA, Drake U., 1982; MBA, Rutgers U., 1989. Dist. agt. Prudential Ins. Co. Am., Palisades Park, N.J., 1982-83; equity analyst Vickersda Costa Sec. Inc., N.Y.C., 1983-86; internat. equity analyst Baring Securities Inc., N.Y.C., 1986-88. Mem. Soc. Automobile Analysts, Jr. League. Republican. Presbyterian.

ADDISON, CHARLES HENRY, insurance company executive; b. McAlester, Okla., Apr. 11, 1941; s. Cecil L. and Mable L. (Davis) A.; m. Margaret A. Barbee, Sept. 26, 1970; children: Lynne Paige, Lisa Carol, Garrik Charles, Brene Charles. BA in Econs. and Physics, U. Okla., 1970. Supr. acctg. unit Southwestern Bell Telephone Co., Oklahoma City, Okla., 1963-68; asst. dir. computing svcs. U. Okla., Norman, 1968-72; asst. dir. computing div. Am. Nat. Ins., Galveston, Tex., 1972-75, asst. v.p., dir., 1975-78; sr. v.p. systems planning and computing Am. Nat. Ins. Co., Galveston, 1978—; bd. dirs. Am. Nat. Property & Casualty Co., Springfield, Mo. Trustee Galveston United Way, 1987—, Trinity Episc. Sch., Galveston, 1986—; troop com. chmn. council Boy Scouts Am., Galveston. Served with USAF, 1959-63. Mem. Life Office Mgmt. Assn. (system research com.), Assn. Computing Machinery. Methodist. Office: Am Nat Ins Co 1 Moody Pla Galveston TX 77550

ADDISON, EDWARD L., utility holding company executive; b. 1930; married. B.E.E., U. S.C., 1950. Pres., chief exec. officer So. Co. Services, Inc., Atlanta, 1983—, also bd. dirs.; dir., chmn. exec. com. So. Co. Services Inc. subs. So. Co., Birmingham, Ala.; bd. dirs. Ala. Power Co., Ga. Power Co., Gulf Power Co., Miss. Power Co., So. Electric Internat. Inc., So. Investments Group, So. Electric Generating Co., SW Forest Industries. Served with U.S. Army, 1951-53. Office: So Co Svcs Inc care Buddy Eller 64 Perimeter Ctr E Atlanta GA 30346 *

ADDY, FREDERICK SEALE, oil company executive; b. Boston, Jan. 1, 1932; s. William R. and Edith (Seale) A.; m. Joyce Marilyn Marshall, Mar. 26, 1954; children: Deborah, William, Brian. B.A., Mich. State U., 1953, M.B.A., 1957. With Amoco Corp.; (and its subsidiaries), 1957—, fin. analyst, 1957-61; econs. supr. Amoco Prodn. Co., 1962-67, acquisition mgr., 1968-71; treas. Am. Oil Co., Chgo., 1971-72; mgr. financial planning Amoco Corp. (formerly Standard Oil), 1972-73; v.p. adminstrn. Amoco Prodn. Co., 1973-75; gen. mgr. corp. planning Amoco Corp. (Formerly Standard Oil), 1975-77, treas., 1978-81; v.p. fin. ops. Standard Oil, 1981-83, v.p. fin., 1983—. Served with USAF, 1954-56. Mem. Soc. Petroleum Engrs. Home: 1230 Loch Ln Lake Forest IL 60045 Office: Amoco Corp 200 E Randolph Dr Chicago IL 60601

ADEGBOLA, SIKIRU KOLAWOLE, aerospace engineer, educator; b. Ibadan, Nigeria, Jan. 21, 1949; came to U.S., 1971; s. Lasisi and Moriamo Abeke (Akinyemi) A. BSME, Calif. State U., Fullerton, 1974; MBA, Calif. State U., Dominguez Hills, 1988; MSME, U. Ariz., 1975; MS in Applied Mechanics, U. So. Calif., 1977; PhD in Engring., Calif. Coast U., 1983. Registered profl. mech. engr., Calif., Ariz. Research engr. Jet Propulsion Lab., Pasadena, Calif., 1976-78; stress analyst Bechtel Power Corp., Norwalk, Calif., 1978-87; engring. mem. tech. staff Structural Analysis dept. Space Transp. Systems div. Rockwell Internat., Downey, Calif., 1987—; prof. engring. Calif. State U., Fullerton, 1984—. Leopold Schepp Found. fellowship, 1972-74. Mem. ASME (assoc.), NSPE, Calif. Soc. Profl. Engrs., Nat. Mgmt. Assn. Home: PO Box 345 Downey CA 90241 Office: Rockwell Internat Corp Space Transp Systems Div Structural Analysis Dept 12214 Lakewood Blvd Downey CA 90241

ADELBERG, ARTHUR WILLIAM, lawyer; b. Oakland, Calif., Aug. 18, 1951; s. Edward Allen and Mary (Sanders) A.; m. Janet Herkomer, May 9, 1976; children: Jeffrey, Sarah. BA, Yale U., 1973; JD, U. N.C., 1976. Bar: Conn. 1976, D.C. 1977, Maine 1985. Gen. atty. FTC, Washington, 1976-80; assoc. Pepper Hamilton & Scheetz, Washington, 1980-84, ptnr., 1984-85; gen. counsel Cen. Maine Power Co., Augusta, Maine, 1985—; v.p., gen. counsel Cen. Maine Power Co., Augusta, 1988—; lectr. U. Maine Law Sch., Portland, 1987—. Mem. ABA, Fed. Energy Bar Assn., Maine Milk Commn., Fed. Bar Assn. (chmn. 1986-87, officer, bd. mem. 1984-86). Home: RR 5 PO Box 640 Augusta ME 04330 Office: Cen Maine Power Co Edison Dr Augusta ME 04330

ADELI, HOJJAT, civil engineer, educator; b. Langrood, Iran, June 3, 1950; came to U.S., 1974; s. Jafar and Mokarram (Soofi) A.; m. Nahid Dadmehr, Mar., 1979; children—Amir, Anahita. MS in Civil Engring., U. Teheran, Iran, 1973; Ph.D. in Civil Engring., Stanford U., 1976. Asst. prof.

Northwestern U., Evanston, Ill., 1977; asst. prof. U. Teheran, 1978-81, assoc. prof., 1981-82; assoc. prof. U. Utah, Salt Lake City, 1982-83; assoc. prof. Ohio State U., Columbus, 1983-88, prof., chmn. structures faculty, 1988—; cons. Atomic Orgn. of Iran, Teheran, 1978-79, Iran Ministry of Housing, Teheran, 1979-82. Co-author: Expert Systems for Structural Design-A New Generation, 1988; author: Computer-Aided Design of Steel Structures, 1990, Interactive Microcomputer-Aided Structural Steel Design, 1988; editor: Expert Systems in Construction and Structural Engineering, 1988, Microcomputer Knowledge-Based Expert Systems in Civil Engineering, 1988, Parallel and Distributed Processing in Structural Engineering, 1988, Knowledge Engineering Vol. 1 and 2, 1989; contbr. more than 170 publs. to profl. jours.; editor-in-chief Internat. Jour. Microcomputers in Civil Engring and four other jours.; editor-at-large Computer Sci. Applications, Marcel Dekker. Recipient First Degree Medal of Knowledge, Iran Ministry of Higher Edn., 1973, Medal of Honor Am. Biog. Inst. 1987, Rsch award U.S. Nat. Sci. found. USAF Flight Dynamics Lab., Craig Rsch., Inc., Bethlehem Steel Corp., Ohio Thomas Edison Program. Mem. ASCE, IEEE, Earthquake Engring. Research Inst. Home: 1131 Fifth Ave Worthington OH 43085

ADELIZZI, ROBERT FREDERICK, financial institution executive; b. Phila., Feb. 9, 1935; s. Alfred Frederick and Natalie Marie (Vilotti) A.; m. Thomasine Starr Lane, Dec. 22, 1959; children: Mary Lee, Judith Anne, James Frederick. A.B., Dartmouth, 1957; J.D., U. San Diego, 1963. Bar: Calif. 1964. Pres., dir. Home Fed. Savs. & Loan Assn., San Diego, 1981—, also chief operating officer; bd. dirs. Pioneer Fed. Savs. & Loan Assn., Honolulu. Chmn. bd. trustees Children's Hosp. and Health Ctr.; gen. campaign chmn. United Way San Diego County. Served to capt. USMC, 1957-61. Mem. ABA, Calif. Bar Assn., San Diego County Bar Assn. Republican. Roman Catholic. Clubs: Kona Kai, San Diego Tennis and Racquet, San Diego Yacht. Office: Home Fed Savs & Loan Assn 625 Broadway Suite 1400 San Diego CA 92101

ADELSON, MERVYN LEE, entertainment and communication industry executive; b. Los Angeles, Oct. 23, 1929; s. Nathan and Pearl (Schwarzman) A.; m. Barbara Walters, May 10, 1986; children from previous marriage: Ellen, Gary, Andrew. Student, Menlo Park Jr. Coll. Pres. Markettown Supermarket and Builders Emporium, Las Vegas, 1953-63; mng. ptnr. Paradise Devel., Las Vegas, 1958—; pres. Realty Holdings, 1962—, La Costa, Inc., 1963-87; chmn. bd. dirs. Lorimar Inc., Culver City, Calif., 1969-86; chmn. bd. dirs., chief exec. officer Lorimar Telepictures Corp., Culver City, 1986—. Co-founder Nathan Adelson Hospice Found. Recipient Sherill Corwin Human Relations award Am. Jewish Com., 1987. Mem. Am. Film Inst. (trustee), Am. Mus. of Moving Images (trustee), Entertainment Industries Council (trustee), Acad. Motion Pictures Arts and Scis., Acad. TV Arts and Sciences, Nat. Acad. Cable Programming, Alliance for Capital Access (bd. dirs.), Com. Publicly Owned Cos. (bd. dirs.).

ADER, RICHARD ALAN, marketing executive; b. Chgo., Dec. 20, 1951; s. Milton and Catherine (Hope) A.; m. Carol L. Weinman, Feb. 16, 1986. BS, U. Ill., 1973; MD, Albert Einstein U., 1977. Med. intern Michael Reese Hosp., Chgo., 1977-78; resident Montefiore Med. Ctr., Bronx, N.Y., 1978-79; dir. proprietary systems Seaboard Industries, Inc., New Rochelle, N.Y., 1979-81, mktg. dir., 1981-83, v.p. sales, 1983-85; nat. product mgr. Radionics, Inc., Salinas, Calif., 1985—. Com. mem. Security Equipment Industry Assn. Office: Radionics Inc 1800 Abbott St Salinas CA 93901

ADERTON, JANE REYNOLDS, lawyer; b. Riverside, Calif., Dec. 22, 1913; d. Charles Low and Verna Mae (Marshall) Reynolds; m. Robert Granville Johnson (div. 1959); children: Marshall Fallon, Jeannette Townsend; m. Thomas Radcliffe Aderton, Oct. 18, 1964. BS in Merchandising, U. So. Calif., 1935; JD, Southwestern U., Los Angeles, 1965. Bar: Calif. 1968. Jud. sec. Dist. Ct. Appeals, Los Angeles, 1960-65; sole practice Beverly Hills, Calif., 1968-79, Riverside, 1979—; assoc. Wyman, Bautzer, Rothman & Kuchel, 1970-79; del. Calif. Bar Conf., 1976, 77, 78. Mem. Founders' Club, Riverside Community Hosp., 1980—; mem. women's aux. Salvation Army, 1981-83, pres., adv. bd., 1983, sec., 1985-87; mem. World Affairs Council Inland So. Calif., 1981—, Affiliates U. Calif., Riverside, 1984—, Mus. Photography, 1985—; v.p., pres.-elect Art Alliance of the Riverside Art Mus., 1984-85, pres. 1985-86, mem., 1982—; mem. Riverside Hospice, 1983—, Riverside Opera Guild; bd. dirs. Friends of Mission Inn, 1986—, sec., 1987—; bd. dirs. San Gorgonio Girl Scout Council, 1987—. Mem. ABA, Calif. Bar Assn., Riverside Bar Assn., Beverly Hills Bar Assn. (bd. govs. 1976-79, chmn. probate and trust com. 1975-77, chmn. del. to calif. bar conf. 1978), Calif. Mus. Photography, Phi Alpha Delta, Pi Beta Phi (pres. Riverside Alumni Club 1981-83, 88—). Clubs: Victoria Country (Riverside); Newport Harbor Yacht (Newport Beach, Calif.). Lodge: Soroptimist Internat. Home: 5190 Stonewood Dr Riverside CA 92506 Office: Riverside CA

ADKINS, CRAIG IVAN, educational supply company executive; b. Chgo., Feb. 12, 1963; s. Leon Adkins and Ruth (Anderson) A. BBA, Ill. Inst. Tech., 1985; postgrad., U. Chgo., 1989—. Corp. staff acct. Union Carbide Co., Chgo., 1985-87; corp. fin. analyst Ideal Sch. Supply Corp., Chgo., 1987-89, mgr. corp. acctg., 1989—. Bus. Sch. scholar Ill. Inst. Tech., 1984-85, Ill. State scholar, 1981-85, Ill. Inst. Tech. scholar, 1983-85. Home: 721 W 107th St Chicago IL 60628-3103 Office: Ideal Sch Supply Corp 11000 S Lavergne Oak Lawn IL 60453

ADKINS, JOHN ROCKWOOD, retail executive; b. N.Y.C., May 1, 1944; s. John Clemens and Judy Margaret (Cramer) A. BS, U. Utah, 1967. With Argonne Cancer Rsch. Lab., U. Chgo., 1971-72; emergency lab. technologist Cottonwood Hosp., Salt Lake City, 1972-80, nuclear medicine cons., 1972-76; owner, mgr. Viking Sewing Machine Co., Salt Lake City, 1977-86; owner, mgr. Gateweigh Weight Loss Ctr., Salt Lake City, San Diego, and Las Vegas, Nev., 1985—; owner, dir. skydiving Cedar Valley Airport, Cedar Fort, Utah, 1973—. Contbr. articles to med. publs. Co-organizer Vietnam Moratorium Marches, Washington, 1969. With U.S. Army, 1967-71. Mem. Am. Soc. Clin. Pathologists, Am. Soc. Med. Technologists, Kappa Sigma. Republican. Home: 770 E Kensington Ave Salt Lake City UT 84105 Office: Gateweigh Weight Loss Ctrs 3761 South 700 East Salt Lake City UT 84106

ADKINS-HUNT, KATHY L., closing supervisor; b. Atlanta, May 29, 1962; d. James D. an Shelby (Poole) A.; m. DuRee DuPree Hunt III, Dec. 2, 1986. Student, Gainesville Jr. Coll., 1980, 89—, Ga. Southwestern Coll., 1980. From receptionist to adminstrv. asst. Shearson Lehman Am. Express, Atlanta, 1983, mortgage bankers adminstrv. asst., 1983-85; owner Cricket's Records & Tapes, Cumming, Ga., 1985-87; from loan analyst to closing supr. CTX Mortgage Co., Roswell, Ga., 1987—. Office: CTX Mortgage Co 11111 Houze Rd Ste 204 Roswell GA 30076

ADKINSON, BRIAN LEE, sales executive; b. Lebanon, Ind., July 10, 1959; s. Marion Leroy and Edith Marie (Shonkwiler) A.; m. Pamela Lea Dinkins, June 12, 1982; children: Katherin Elizabeth, Anna Mary Josephine. BS in Fin., Ind. U., 1982. Asst. bank examiner FDIC, Chgo., 1980-81; acctg. assoc.battery prodn. Union Carbide Co., Bennington, Vt., 1982-83; sr. ptnr. AC Sales Assocs., Murfreesboro, Tenn., 1983—; spl. examiner-in-charge Union Carbide Credit Union, Bennington, 1982-83, acctg. adv. co. store, 1982-83. Vol. Zionsville (Ind.) Christian Ch., 1975-82, Cen. Christian Ch., Murfreesboro, 1983-87; mem. edn. com. Trinity United Meth. Ch., Murfreesboro, 1987—, chmn. fin. com., 1988—, adminstrv. bd., 1988—; mem. Rutherford Co. Humane Soc., Beasley, 1987—; bd. dirs. Wesley Found. Mid. Tenn. State U., 1989—. Mem. Ind. U. Alumni Membership Assn. (Nashville chpt.), Sigma Pi (mem. alumni assn.). Republican. Methodist. Home and Office: 719 Woodhill Dr Murfreesboro TN 37129

ADLER, ERWIN ELLERY, lawyer; b. Flint, Mich., July 22, 1941; s. Ben and Helen M. (Schwartz) A.; m. Stephanie Ruskin, June 8, 1967; children—Lauren, Michael, Jonathan. B.A., U. Mich., 1963, LL.M., 1967; J.D., Harvard U., 1966. Bar: Mich. 1966, Calif. 1967. Assoc. Pillsbury, Madison & Sutro, San Francisco, 1967-73; assoc. Lawler, Felix & Hall, Los Angeles, 1973-76, ptnr., 1977-82; ptnr. Rogers & Wells, Los Angeles, 1982-84, Richards, Watson & Gershon, Los Angeles, 1984—. Bd. dirs. Hollywood Civic Opera Assn., 1975-76, Children's Scholarships Inc., 1979-80. Mem. ABA (vice chmn. appellate advocacy com. 1982-87), Calif. Bar Assn., Phi Beta Kappa, Phi Kappa Phi. Jewish. Office: Richards Watson & Gershon 333 S Hope St 38th Fl Los Angeles CA 90071

ADLER, JEFFREY ALAN, real estate development executive; b. Cleve., May 10, 1952; s. Richard S. and Joan R. (Rothschild) A.; m. Rita Nussbaum, Feb. 8, 1975; children: Danielle, Alexandra. BA in Polit. Sci., Ohio State U., 1974; MBA in Fin., Mgmt., Northwestern U., 1977. With sales staff Viking Steel Co., Elk Grove Village, Ill., 1974-78; real estate loan assoc., officer Continental Nat. Bank & Trust Co. Chgo., 1979-82, 2d v.p., 1983—; exec. v.p., chief operating officer Vistana Resort Devel., Inc., Orlando, Fla., 1983—. Bd. dirs., mem. exec. com., mem. fin. com. Jewish Fedn. Greater Orlando, 1988—; chmn. Orlando Community Alliance Project, 1988. Home: 625 Sweetwater Cove Blvd S Longwood FL 32779 Office: Vistana Resort Devel Inc State Rt 535 Orlando FL 32821

ADLER, SAMUEL IRWIN, real estate executive; b. N.Y.C., Feb. 4, 1924; s. Morris and Esther (Koenig) A.; m. Bernyce Shinensky, Dec. 29, 1946; children: Karen Greenwald, Michael, Sara Raiffe. Student, U. So. Ill., 1943. Cert. gen. contractor, Fla. Owner Adco Bldg. Co., Westchester, N.Y., 1947-58; pres. So. Gen. Builders, Miami, Fla., 1958—; mng. ptnr. Adler Assn., Miami, 1969—; sec.-treas. Am. Capital Corp., Miami, 1983—, also bd. dirs.; chmn. bd. dirs. Adler Group, Inc., Miami., Regency Ins. Co., Miami, Regency Fin. Co., Miami, Regency Life Ins. Co., Miami; bd. dirs. Oriole Homes Corp., Pompano Beach, Fla., TransCapital Fin. Corp., Cleve., TransOhio Savs. & Loan Corp., Cleve., Carnival Cruise Lines, Miami. Pres. Greater Miami Jewish Fedn., 1984-86; vice chmn. nat. bd. United Jewish Appeal, N.Y.C.; pres. Mt. Sinai Hosp. Found., Miami, 1987—; v.p. Temple Emanuel, Miami, 1980—; bd. dirs. Nat. Found. Advancement Arts, Miami, 1983—, New World Symphony, Miami, 1980—. Served to 1st lt. USAAF, 1942-46, PTO. Democrat. Clubs: Westview Country (Miami); Grand Champions (Aspen, Colo.), Brickell City. Home: 3 Grove Isle Miami FL 32901

ADLER, WILLIAM JAY, JR., writer; b. N.Y.C., Dec. 1, 1956; s. William Jay and Gloria G. A. BA, Wesleyan U., 1978; M in INternat. Affairs, Columbia U. Congl. lobbyist Ams. for Dem. Action, Washington, 1981-82; dir. Nuclear Control Inst., Washington, 1982-83, ind. polit. cons., 1983-86, ind. writer book packager, 1986—. Authors: The Home Buyer's Guide, 1984, The Student's Memory Book, 1988, The Lottery Book, 1986; editor: The Wit and Wisdom of Wall Street, 1985. Mem. Author's Guild, Washington Ind. Writers (pres. 1989—). Democrat. Home: 3021 Macomb St NW Washington DC 20008 Office: 2900Connecticut AveNW Ste 345 Washington DC 20008

ADOLF, RAMOND ROMER, marketing executive; b. American Falls, Idaho, June 9, 1932; s. Eric Frederick and Frances Clara (Wuebbenhorst) A.; m. Imogene Love, Aug. 23, 1983; 1 child, Derek S. BSChemE, Oreg. State U., 1961. With GE, Oakland, Calif., 1961, Dow Chem. Co., 1964—; mgr. product sales Dow Chem. Co., Walnut Creek, Calif., 1966-70, mgr. dist. sales, 1970-75; mgr. group mktg. Dow Chem. Co., Midland, Mich., 1975-79, mgr. mktg. resources, 1980-85, mgr. comml. resources, 1985—. Active Little League Football and Baseball, Midland; chmn. Music Parent Assn., Midland, 1980-84. 1st lt. U.S. Army, 1962-63. Mem. Am. Mgmt. Assn., Masons (Shriner). Republican. Lutheran. Home: 4404 Brambleridge Ln Midland MI 48640 Office: Dow Chem Co 2020 Dow Ctr Midland MI 48674

ADOLPH, MARY ROSENQUIST, financial company executive; b. Springfield, Mass., Oct. 7, 1949; d. Jesse Woodson and Doris May (Marquette) Rosenquist; m. Earl Anthony Soares, Mar. 18, 1972 (div. 1982); m. Joseph Edward Adolph, Oct. 3, 1986. Student San Domenico Sch., 1966-68, Dominican Coll., San Rafael, 1967-69, Calif., San Francisco Conservatory of Music, 1968-70; A.A., Coll. of Marin, 1969. Asst. v.p. Western Travelers Life Ins. Co./Putnam Fin. Services, San Rafael, 1970-80; v.p. Unimarc, Ltd., Novato, Calif., 1980-83; v.p. mktg. Western States Monetary Planning Services, Inc., Newhall, Calif., 1983—. Mem. exec. com. San Marin Valley Homeowners Assn., 1979-81. Mem. Internat. Assn. Fin. Planners, Life Underwriters Assn. Democrat. Roman Catholic. Home: 14710 Burbank Blvd #102 Van Nuys CA 91411 Office: Western States Monetary Planning Svcs Inc 23030 Lyons Ave Ste 209 Newhall CA 91321

ADVANI, CHANDERBAN GHANSHAMDAS (G. A. CHANDRU), merchant; b. Hyderabad, India, July 23, 1924; s. Ghanshamdas Gobindux and Rukibai Advani; m. Devi K. Jagtiani, Nov. 30, 1958; children: Meera, Nalin. BA, Sind U., 1947. Mgr. V.H. Advani & Co., Karachi, 1941-48, French Drug Co., Karachi, 1941-48, Paragon Products Co., Karachi, 1941-48; pres. Nephew's Internat. Comml. Corp., Karachi, 1949-51; mgr. Indo French Traders, Pondichary, India, 1951-52, Ms. L. Mohnani, 1953-59; pres. G.A. Chandru, Shokai, Yokohama, Japan, 1959—, Nephew's Internat., Inc., Yokohama, 1985—; cons. in field. Recipient medal Mayor of Bombay, letter of Appreciation Mayor of Yokohama. Mem. Indian Mchts. Assn. (hon. past pres.), Indian C. of C. Japan (hon. joint sec.), Propeller Club U.S.-Yokohama-Tokyo (past bd. govs.), Fgn. Corrs., Yokohama Fgn. Trade Inst., Yokohama Bombay Sister-City Assn. (vice chmn.), Yokohama C. of C. and Industry (dir. internat. div.). Lodges: Masons, Shriners. Home: 502 NewPort Bldg 25-6, Yamashita-cho, Naka-ku, Yokohama 231, Japan

AFFAN, ALI OSMAN, agricultural company executive, agricultural development consultant; b. Medani, Gezira, Sudan, Jan. 1, 1934; s. Osman Affan Mohamed and Fatma Ahmed Dawood; m. Afaf Ahmed Abdel Ber, July 23, 1963; children—Mayada, Amjad, Ashraf, Howayda. Diploma in Gen. Agr., U. Khartoum, Sudan, 1957, M.Sc. in Agrl. Engring., 1960. Mng. dir. Affan Agrl. Co., Khartoum, 1960-69, 1973-79, 1981-87; state minister agr., natural resources (Sudan), 1987—; dep. mng. dir. and chief engr. Girba Agrl. Project, Sudan, 1969-71; gen. mgr. Nat. Agr. Orgn., Khartoum, 1972-73; farm power expert FAO, UN, Tripoli, Libya, 1979-81; cons. Arab Sugar Fed., Khartoum, 1978—, Gulf Group, Geneve, Switzerland, 1983-84, Harrington Mfg. Co., Lewiston, N.C., 1975-76; mem. Tech. com. for cotton mechanization, Rahad, Sudan, 1978-79; dir. feasibility study on farm mechanization in the Gezira, 1976. Mem. The First Nat. Econ. Conf., Khartoum, 1981; mem. high polit. council UMMA Nat. Party, Khartoum, 1985. Fellow The Econ. Devel. Inst. of the World Bank in Agro Indsl. Projects; mem. Sudanese Soc. Agrl. Engrs., Sudan-U.S. Bus. Council. Moslem. Avocation: photography. Office: Affan Agrl Co, PO Box 1719, Khartoum Sudan

AFFELDT, JOHN FREDERICK, management consultant; b. Endwell, N.Y., June 25, 1947; s. John Robert and Marion (Brink) A.; m. Mary Beth Mullock, June 7, 1969; children: Christopher, Rebeccah, Gregory, Todd. BS in Physics, U. Scranton, 1969; MS in Ops. Rsch., Naval Postgrad. Sch., 1980. Assoc. Booz, Allen and Hamilton, Arlington, Va., 1985-87, sr. assoc., 1987—. Cub scout leader Boy Scouts Am., Newport, R.I., 1980-81, Dale City, Va., 1984-86, council pres., 1986—; dir. edn. local ch., Dale City, 1984-86, council pres., 1986—. Major U.S. Army, 1969-85. Mem. Am. Radio Relay League, Soc. for Computer Simulation, Am. Def. Preparedness Assn., Soc. Wireless Pioneers. Republican. Lutheran. Home: 12805 Kerrydale Rd Woodbridge VA 22193

AGATHER, MAX DAVID, financial planner; b. Libby, Mont., Nov. 26, 1948; s. Alfons Julius and Isabel Brinton (Kienitz) A.; m. Linda Helen Henrickson, Aug. 24, 1979; 1 child, Adrienne L. B in Bus. Fin., Seattle U., 1974. Cert. fin. planner. Yard foreman United Bldg. Supply, Anchorage, Alaska, 1975-76; salesman Spenard Bldg. Supply, Anchorage, 1977-79, head of mktg., 1980-82; owner, pres. Glacier Life & Health, Kalispell, Mont., 1983—. Chmn. spl. events Am. Cancer Soc., 1985-86. Republican. Lutheran. Home: 87 Konley Dr Kalispell MT 59901 Office: Glacier Life & Health 6 Sunset Pla Kalispell MT 59901

AGBETTOR, EMMANUEL OFOE, engineer; b. Ghana, Nov. 5, 1927; s. Isaac Tetteh and Agnes Doe (Bannerman) A.; m. Hilda Alba Pratt, 1960 (dec.); m. 2d Doris Ocansey, 1970; children—Eva, Vincent, Eunice, Isaac, Emmanuel, Deborah, Michella. Student U. Coll. Gold Coast, Accra, Ghana, 1948-50; B.S. in Engring., U. London, 1953; postgrad. Manchester U. (Eng.), 1953-54, Tech. U. Copenhagen, 1954-55. With Shell Co. of West Africa, Accra, Lagos, Kano, Freetown, 1956-67; chief engr. Shell Ghana Ltd., 1965-67; mng. dir. ACME Engring. & Constrn. Co., road contractors, Accra, 1967-71; chief cons. Engring. & Indsl. Cons., Accra, 1972—; chmn. Acme Fin. & Investment Trust Ltd., Accra; dir. Ballast Nedam (Ghana) Ltd., Ghana Internat. Devel. Co., Eurometal Works Ltd., Ada Rural Bank, Paramount Ins. Co.; chmn. tech. com. investigation into Electricity Corp. of Ghana, 1980, coordinator for early implementation tech. com. report, 1981. Candidate for Nat. Assembly Ghana, 1969; bd. dirs. Ada Secondary Sch. (Ghana), 1973-79, Ghana Investment Centre, 1985—; chmn. Ada Citizens Congress, 1980—, mem. nat. energy bd., 1985—. Danish Govt. fellow, 1954-55. Fellow Ghana Inst. Engrs.; mem. Brit. Instn. Elec. Engrs., Brit. Inst. Mech. Engrs., Boston Soc. Civil Engrs., AFIT Nationwide Bldg. Soc. Presbyterian. Clubs: Achimota Golf, Accra-Tema Yacht. Lodges: Academic, Unity, Research (Accra); Ada (primus). Office: Acme Fin & Investment Trust Ltd, Investment House, PO Box 2547, Accra Ghana

AGERBEK, SVEN, mechanical engineer; b. Soerabaya, Dutch Indies, Aug. 2, 1926; came to U.S., 1958, naturalized, 1964; s. Niels Magnus and Else Heidam (Nielsen) Agerbek-Poulsen; m. Helen Hadsbjerg Gerup, May 30, 1963; 1 child, Jesper. MSME, Tech. U., Denmark, 1952; LLB, LaSalle Estension U., 1967; postgrad., UCLA, 1969. Registered profl. engr., Calif., Ohio, Fla. With Danish Refrigeration Research Inst., Copenhagen, 1952; engr. B.P. Oil Co., Copenhagen, 1952-54; refrigeration insp. J. Lauritzen, Copenhagen, 1954-56; engr. Danish-Am. Gulf Oil Co., Copenhagen, 1956-58; instr. Ohio U., Athens, 1958-60; asst. prof. Calif. State Poly. U., San Luis Obispo, 1960-62; prin. engr., environment dept. Ralph M. Parsons Co., Los Angeles, 1962-73; engring. supr. Bechtel Power Co., Norwalk, Calif., 1973-85; pres., owner Woodcraft Cabinets, Inc., Rancho Cordova, Calif., 1985—. Past mem. Luth. Ch. council, pres. Luth. Sch. bd. Served with Danish underground movement, World War II. Mem. ASHRAE (author Guide on Air Conditioning of Nuclear Power Plants), Danish Engring. Soc. Home: 5201 Vista del Oro Way Fair Oaks CA 95628 Office: Woodcraft Cabinets Inc 11386 Amalgam Way Rancho Cordova CA 95670

AGGELER, JOHN HARVEY, financial executive, real estate developer, consultant; b. Jefferson City, Mo., July 17, 1945; s. Leroy B. and Virginia C. (Ager) A.; m. Carol F. Pulwicz, June 26, 1970; children: Christopher, Matthew, Nicholas. Cert. in bus., Grand Rapids Jr. Coll., 1978. Gen. mgr. John's Lumber and Hardware, Mt. Clemens, Mich., 1968-73; mgr. sales and purchasing Monument Forest Products, Grand Rapids, 1973-77; pres. Surewood Founds., Inc., Grand Rapids, 1978-80, Century Capital Corp., Grand Rapids, 1981—; pres. Evergreen Forest Products, Grand Rapids, 1977-82, All Am. Mortgage Corp., 1987—. Mem. Nat. Assn. Mortgage Brokers, Internat. Soc. Financiers, Grand Rapids C. of C., Mich. C. and C., Better Bus. Bur., Home Builders Assn. Republican. Roman Catholic. Office: Century Capital Corp 1444 Michigan St NE Grand Rapids MI 49503

AGGER, JAMES H., lawyer; b. 1936; married. A.B., St. Joseph's U., 1958; J.D., U. Pa., 1961. Mem. Krusen, Evans & Byrne, 1965-69; gen. counsel Catalytic Inc., Air Products and Chems. Inc., 1969-77; asst. gen. counsel Air Products and Chems. Inc., Trexlertown, Pa., 1977-80, gen. counsel, 1980—, v.p., 1982—. Capt., USNR (ret.). Office: Air Products & Chems Inc Box 538 Allentown PA 18105

AGINIAN, RICHARD DICRAN, communications company executive; b. N.Y.C., Sept. 13, 1941; s. Hrant and Virginia (Solakian) A.; m. Diana Carol Tashjian, July 31, 1966; children: Dawn, Marla. B in Philosophy, Wayne State U., 1963; MBA, Rutgers U., 1964. CPA, Mich. Audit mgr. Arthur Andersen, Detroit, 1964-75; asst. to pres. Falvey Motors, Troy, Mich., 1975-76; treas. Suburban Communications, Livonia, Mich., 1976-77; pres., chief exec. officer Suburban Communications Corp., Livonia, Mich., 1977—. Bd. dirs., chmn. Henry Ford Hosp., West Bloomfield, Mich., 1978-84; bd. dirs. Community House of Birmingham , Mich., 1985, v.p., 1987—; bd. dirs. Walsh Coll.,Troy, 1985. Mem. Mich. Press Assn. (bd. dirs. 1982-89), Suburban Newspapers of Am. (pres. 1985-86), Young Pres. Orgn. Clubs: Oakland Hills Country, Econ. Club. Home: 835 Westwood Birmingham MI 48009 Office: Suburban Communications Corp 36251 Schoolcraft Rd Livonia MI 48150

AGNEW, FRANKLIN ERNEST, III, former food company executive; b. St. Louis, Apr. 13, 1934; s. Frank Ernest, Jr. and Susanne (Kohlsaat) A.; m. Dorothy Powning, Feb. 17, 1962; children—Carolyn W., Timothy S., Jennifer S. A.B. in Econs, Princeton, 1956; M.B.A., Harvard, 1958. C.P.A., 1961. With First Nat. Bank Chgo., 1958-62, loan officer, 1960-62; with Rockwell Mfg. Co., 1963-71, controller, 1963-66, v.p. mfg. power tool div., 1967-68, v.p. mfg. valve div., 1968-69, v.p. finance, 1969-71; sr. v.p., dir. H.J. Heinz Co., Pitts., 1971-86; chief fin. officer H.J. Heinz Co., 1971-73, group exec., 1973-86, resigned, 1986; pvt. practice cons. Pitts., 1986—; trustee Sharon Steel Corp.; bd. dirs. Bausch & Lomb Inc. Bd. dirs. St. Margaret Meml. Hosp., Pitts.; charter trustee emeritus Princeton U. Served with AUS, 1959. Mem. Duquesne Club, Fox Chapel Golf Club. Home: 170 Forest Dr Pittsburgh PA 15238 Office: One Mellon Bank Ctr Ste 2120 Pittsburgh PA 15219

AGNEW, JAMES KEMPER, advertising agency executive; b. Parkersburg, W.Va., May 10, 1939; s. James Pugh and Elinor Mary (Kemper) A.; m. Ann Haughey, Sept. 15, 1962; children: Scott Kemper, Steven James, Derek John. B.B.A., U. Mich., 1961; M.B.A., U. Calif., Berkeley, 1962; postgrad. spl. bus. studies, U. Oslo. With J. Walter Thompson, N.Y.C. and Paris, 1962-73; account exec. J. Walter Thompson, 1962-67; chmn. mgmt. com. J. Walter Thompson, Paris, 1967-70; v.p., mgmt. supr J. Walter Thompson, N.Y.C., 1970-73; exec. v.p. J. Walter Thompson Co., Los Angeles, 1982—; head JWT/West, Los Angeles and San Francisco, 1982—; sr. v.p., group account dir. McCann Erickson, Inc., N.Y.C., 1973-76; exec. v.p., gen. mgr. McCann Erickson, Inc., Los Angeles, 1976-79; pres., chief exec. officer McCann Erickson, Inc., N.Y.C., 1979-81. Bd. advisors Pacific Crest Outward Bound Sch. Mem. Am. Assn. Advt. Agencies (sec., treas., bd. govs. we. coun.), Los Angeles Natural History Mus. (bd. dirs.), U. Mich. Alumnae Club N.Y., U. Calif. Berkeley Alumnae Club. Office: J Walter Thompson Co 10100 Santa Monica Blvd Los Angeles CA 90067

AGNEW, PETER TOMLIN, employee benefit consultant; b. Orange, N.J., Nov. 20, 1948; s. William Harold and Janet Elisabeth (Gittinger) A.; children: Jonathan, Stephan, Douglas, Karen. BA cum laude, Amherst Coll., 1971; MBA, NYU, 1976. CLU. Asst. investment officer Mutual Benefit Life, Newark, 1971-78; exec. v.p., bd. dir., prin. Post & Kurtz, Inc., N.Y.C., 1978-85; exec. v.p., sr. regional dir. Minet, Post & Kurtz, Inc., N.Y.C., 1985—; pres. P. Tomlin Agnew Assocs., 1982—. Capt. United Way, Newark, 1978; assoc. class agt. Amherst Coll. Alumni Fund, 1980—; mem. troop com. Boy Scouts Am., Morristown; mem. steering com. N.J. New Phil. Orch. Mem. Chartered Life Underwriters (N.Y. chpt. com. chmn. 1984), Nat. Assn. Life Underwriters, Nat. Assn. Platform Speakers, Yale Ins. Group, Downtown Assn. N.Y., Williams Club, Mendham Racquet Club. Republican. Presbyterian. Home: 69 Hampshire Dr Mendham NJ 07945

AGNICH, RICHARD JOHN, electronics company executive, lawyer; b. Eveleth, Minn., Aug. 24, 1943; s. Frederick J. and Ruth H. (Welton) A.; m. Victoria Webb Trescher, Apr. 19, 1969; children: Robert Frederick, Michael McCord, Jonathon Welton. A.B. in Econs., Stanford U., 1965; J.D., U. Tex., 1969. Bar: Tex. 1969. Legis. asst., legal counsel to John G. Tower U.S. Senate, 1969-70, adminstrv. asst. to John G. Tower, 1971-72; asst. counsel Tex. Instruments Inc., Dallas, 1973-78, asst. gen. counsel, 1978-82, v.p., sec., gen. counsel, 1982—, sr v.p., sec. gen. counsel, 1988—. Mem. adv. council Sch. Social Scis., U. Tex.-Dallas, Dallas Assembly. Fellow Tex. State Bar; mem. ABA (com. corporate law depts.), Tex. Bar Assn. (corp. counsel sect.), Dallas Bar Assn., Am. Soc. Corp. Secs., Southwestern Legal Found. (adv. bd. Internat. and Comparative Law Ctr.), Assn. Gen. Counsel. Republican. Presbyterian. Home: 9446 Hathaway Dallas TX 75220 Office: Tex Instruments Inc PO Box 655474 MS 236 Dallas TX 75265 also: Tex Instruments Inc 13500 N Central Expwy Dallas TX 75243

AGRAWAL, HARI MOHAN, construction equipment manufacturing company executive; b. Allahabad, U.P., India, Jan. 3, 1935; came to U.S., 1963, naturalized, 1974; s. Brij Kishore and Suryamukhi Devi A.; B.S. in Agrl. Engring., U. Allahabad, 1954; M.S. in Agrl. Engring., U. Mass., 1965; M.S. in Mech. Engring., W.Va. U., 1967. Asst. prof., mech. engr. Govt. of Madhya Pradesh, India, 1954-63; research asst., design engr. U. Mass., Amherst, 1963-65; instr. indsl. engring. dept. W.Va. U., Morgantown, part-time, 1965-67; design engr. Allis Chalmers, Springfield, Ill., summer 1966; devel. engr. Barber Greene, Aurora, Ill., 1967-69, sr. design engr., 1969-73; project mgr. Stephens-Adamson, Inc., div. Allis-Chalmers, Aurora, 1973-78, contracts adminstrn., 1978—. Recipient engring. achievement award Barber

Greene 1973; registered profl. engr., Ill. Hindu. Home: 565 High St Aurora IL 60505 Office: Stephens-Adamson Inc Div Allis-Chalmers Ridgeway Ave Aurora IL 60507

AGUINSKY, RICHARD DANIEL, electronic engineer; b. Buenos Aires, Dec. 26, 1958; s. Elias Lorenzo and Rosa Isabel (Grille) A. Electronics Engr., Univ. Tech. Nacional, Avellaneda, 1984. Serial prodn. technician Norman S.A., Buenos Aires, 1978-80; electronics lab. technician Univ. Technologica Nacional, Avellaneda, 1980-84; engring. sub mgr. Northern Telecom, Buenos Aires, 1983-86; design engr. No. Telecom, Santa Clara, Calif., 1986—. Instr. digital technics Univ. Tech. Nacional, Avellaneda, 1985. Contbr. articles to Revista Telegrafica Electronica, No. Telecom, Am. Nat. Standard Telecommunications. Lodge: Kiwanis Internat. Avocations: travel, camping, windsurfing, skiing, sky diving. Office: No Telecom 2305 Mission College Blvd Santa Clara CA 95035

AHEARN, MATTHEW JOSEPH, financial services corporation president; b. N.Y.C., Mar. 15, 1936; s. Joseph Edward and Agatha Josephine (McNamara) A.; m. Kay Frances Phelps, June 2, 1957; children: Neal Francis, Paul Eugene, Eileen Cecelia Ahearn Staples. BS, USCG Acad., 1957; AAS, Coll. of the Albemarle, 1985. Cert. CLU, chartered fin. cons. Pres. Rivershore Enterprises Inc., Elizabeth City, N.C., 1981—, City Enterprises, Inc., Elizabeth City, N.C., 1981-82; gen. agt. GPM Life Ins. Agy., Elizabeth City, N.C., 1977—; cons. Jones & McDaniels Co., Elizabeth City, 1986—, City Motor Parts, Inc. Elizabeth City, 1986—. Dir. St. Elizabeth's Found., Elizabeth City, N.C., 1983—. With USCG, 1953-77. Mem. Am. Soc. of CLU and Chartered Fin. Cons., Northeastern Assn. of Life Underwriters (pres. 1985-86), Nat. Assn. of Life Underwriters, Ret. Officers Assn., Nat. Geog. Soc., Lions, VFW, KC, Ancient Order of Pterodactyl. Democrat. Roman Catholic. Home: 2078 Rivershore Rd Elizabeth City NC 27909 Office: Rivershore Enterprise Inc PO Box 1886 Elizabeth City NC 27906

AHERN, FRANK J., computer executive; b. New Orleans, June 25, 1925; s. James William Ahern and Ethel (Kleyle) Abadie; divorced; children: Kenneth, Patrick, Cathlyn, Terry. BBA, Tulane U., 1949, MBA, 1956. Field tech. rep. IBM, New Orleans, 1956, systems analyst, 1957; sr. systems analyst IBM, Miami, Fla., 1958-60; program systems rep. IBM, N.Y.C., 1960, product mktg. rep., 1961-65; pres. Computer Assocs., Inc., New Orleans, 1965—. Author 7 books; co-inventor input output control systems, 1956-60; patentee various computer programsn and concepts. Candidate for gov. State of La., 1968, for supt. edn., 1972, for Pres. U.S., 1976, 88; organizer Am. Reform Movement. With USMC, 1943-46, capt., 1950-56. Decorated Bronze Star with combat V., Purple Heart with star. Mem. Data Processors Mgmt. Assn. Democrat. Roman Catholic. Home and Office: 2762 Palmyra St New Orleans LA 70119

AHLUVALIA, JASJIT T., management consultant; b. Ajmer, India, Nov. 17, 1938; came to U.S., 1973, naturalized, 1979; s. Tara and Beyant Kaur (Ahluwalia) Singh; m. Jyoti Balbirsingh Ahluwalia, Jan. 19, 1969; children: Taruna, Vineeta. Grad. Brit. Inst. Mgmt., London, 1966; DSM, Jamnalal Bajaj Inst. Mgmt. Studies, U. Bombay, 1972; BS in Ops. Mgmt., SUNY, Albany, 1977; MS in Computer Sci., Fairleigh Dickinson U., 1978. Cert. systems profl. Materials asst. Kaiser Engrs., Jamshedpur, India, 1956-58; adminstr. New Activity Sch., Bombay, 1958-59; chief of cardex Brown & Root, Inc., Bombay, 1959-61; sr. systems analyst Union Carbide India Ltd., Bombay, 1961-73; v.p. mgmt. info. systems Indsl. Acoustics Co., Inc., Bronx, N.Y., 1973—; pres. Data Processing Solutions, Inc., Westwood, N.J. Mem. Assn. Computing Machinery, Computer and Automated Systems Assn. SME, Assn. Systems Mgmt. (cert. systems profl.), COMMON Users Group.

AHMED, S. BASHEER, research company executive, educator; b. Kurnool, Andhra, India, Jan. 1, 1934; s. S. M. and K.A. (Bee) H.; m. Alice Cordelia Pearce; 1 child, Ivy Amina. BA, Osmania Coll., Kurnool, 1955; MA, Osmania U., Hyderabad, India, 1957; MS, Tex. A&M U., 1963, PhD, 1966. Asst. prof. Tenn. Tech. U., Cookeville, 1966-68, Ohio U., Athens, 1968-70; vis. fellow Princeton U., N.J., 1977-78; prof. Western Ky. U., Bowling Green, 1970-80; prof. Mgmt. Scis. Lubin Grad. Sch. Bus., dir. doctoral program Pace U., N.Y.C., 1982—; pres. Princeton Econ. Rsch., Inc., 1980—; cons. Oak Ridge (Tenn.) Nat. Lab., 1969-77, Inst. for Energy Analysis, Oak Ridge, 1975, Honeywell Corp., Mpls., 1985—; bd. dir. doctoral programs Lubin Grad. Sch. Bus. Pace U., N.Y.C. Author: Quantitative Methods for Business, 1974, Nuclear Fuel and Energy Policy, 1979; author, editor: Technology, International Stability, and Growth, 1984. Recipient Achievement award Oak Ridge Nat. Lab., 1977, IEEE Centennial Medal, 1983. Fellow AAAS, Systems, Man, and Cybernetics Soc. (pres. 1980-82). Republican. Moslem. Home: 401 Knoll Way Rocky Hill NJ 08553

AHN, SUHN YUNG, brokerage executive; b. Seoul, Republic of Korea, Jan. 27, 1934; came to U.S., 1955; d. Taek Sung and Hae Song; m. Kyung Jin Ahn, Aug. 24, 1957; children: Maureen, Jennifer, James. BA, Seoul Nat. U., 1956, Skidmore Coll., 1957; MA, NYU, 1962. Cert. fin. planner. Lectr. Calumet Coll., Whiting, Ind., 1976-79; account exec. Eldon-Emmor, Munster, Ind., 1980-81; account exec. Drexel Burnham Lambert, Chgo., 1981, v.p. investment, 1983—. Home: 1901 Mirmar Rd Munster IN 46321

AHR, PAUL ROBERT, clinical psychologist, management consultant; b. Irvington, N.J., Jan. 4, 1945; s. Wilbur Frederick and Marcella Elizabeth (Brady) A.; m. Kathryn Danielle Cramer; children by previous marriage—Thomas Brady, Andrew Travers. A.B., U. Notre Dame, 1966; Ph.D., Cath. U. Am., 1971; M.P.A., U. So. Calif., 1977. Postdoctoral fellow Harvard Med. Sch., Boston, 1972-73; dir. children's program Va. Dept. Mental Health and Mental Retardation, Richmond, 1973-74, dir. program analysis planning, 1974-75, asst. commr., 1975-79; dir. Mo. Dept. Mental Health, Jefferson City, 1979-86; pres. The Altenahr Group, Ltd., 1986—; sec. The Corp. Psychology Ctr., Inc., 1986—; lectr. U. Mo. Sch. Health Related Professions, Columbia, 1980, clin. assoc. prof. U. Mo. Sch. Medicine, 1980—; clin. assoc. prof. dept. psychiatry U. Mo., Kansas City, 1980—; assoc. clin. prof. St. Louis U. Sch. Medicine, 1982—. Served with USN, 1969-72. NIMH fellow, 1972-73, Vocat. Rehab. Adminstrn. fellow, 1966-69. Fellow Am. Coll. Mental Health Adminstrs.; mem. Am. Psychol. Assn., Am. Soc. Pub. Adminstrn. Roman Catholic. Office: The Altenahr Group Ltd 225 S Meramec Ste 1032 Saint Louis MO 63105

AHRENS, GILBERT POMEROY, banker; b. Hartford, Conn., June 24, 1938; s. Bernhard John August and Mary Weston (Bissell) A.; m. Christine von der Schulenburg, Dec. 30, 1961; children—Gilbert von der Schulenburg, Margot Hatheway. B.S. in Econs., U. Pa., 1962. Security analyst Phoenix Ins. Co., Hartford, 1962-67; asst. investment officer First Bank and Trust, Springfield, Mass., 1967-69; trust officer Hartford Nat. Bank and Trust Co., 1969-74; v.p. Conn. Nat. Bank, Hartford, 1974—; dir. Brookside Drive Co., Suffield, Conn. Treas. Wildwood Property Owners Assn. Tolland (Mass.), 1982—; bd. dirs. YMCA Camp Jewel, Colebrook, Conn., 1979—, Am. Baptist Chs. of Conn., 1978—; mem. Hist. Dist. commn., Suffield (Conn.), 1980—; pres. John Bissell 1628 Assn., Windsor, Conn., 1968—. Fellow Fin. Analysts Feds.; mem. Hartford Soc. Fin. Analysts. Republican. Club: Suffield Country. Lodge: Rotary (treas. 1985). Avocations: tennis; fishing; photography; travel; jazz music. Home: 391 S Main St Suffield CT 06078 Office: Conn Nat Bank 777 Main St Hartford CT 06115

AHRENSFELD, THOMAS FREDERICK, lawyer; b. Bklyn., June 30, 1923; s. Frederick Herman and Madeline Florence (Moffett) A.; m. Joan Ann McGowan, Mar. 17, 1944; 1 child, Thomas Frederick. A.B., Bklyn. Coll., 1948; LL.B., Columbia U., 1948. Bar: N.Y. 1948. Assoc., then ptnr. Conboy, Hewitt, O'Brien & Boardman, N.Y.C., 1948-58; sec., assoc. gen. counsel Philip Morris Inc., N.Y.C., 1959-70, v.p., gen. counsel, 1970-76, sr. v.p., gen. counsel, 1976-85; sr. v.p., gen. counsel Philip Morris Cos., Inc., N.Y.C., 1985-88, cons., 1988—. Trustee Trinity-Pawling Sch. Corp., 1976—; mem. exec. com. Ctr. Pub. Resources; bd. visitors Columbia U. 1st lt. USAAF, 1942-45. Decorated D.F.C., Air medal with oak leaf clusters. Mem. ABA, N.Y.C. Bar Assn., N.Y. Athletic Club. Presbyn. (elder). Home: 85 Nannahagan Rd Pleasantville NY 10570 Office: Philip Morris Cos Inc 120 Park Ave New York NY 10017

AIBEL, HOWARD JAMES, diversified industry executive, lawyer; b. N.Y.C., Mar. 24, 1929; m. Katherine Walter Webster, June 6, 1952; children: David Webster, Daniel Walter, Jonathan Brown. AB magna cum laude, 1950; LLB cum laude, Harvard U., 1951. Bar: N.Y. 1952. Assoc. White & Case, N.Y.C., 1952-57; with GE, 1957-64, litigation counsel, 1960-64; with ITT Corp., N.Y.C., 1964—, sr. v.p., gen. counsel, 1968-87, exec. v.p., gen. counsel, 1987—; bd. dirs. Internat. Standard Electric Co., The Sheraton Corp.; vice chmn. Fund for Modern Cts. Mem. vis. com. Northwestern U., 1984—, vice chmn. 1987—; mem. adv. com. Corp. Counsel Ctr., chmn. 1986-87; chmn. Alliance of Resident Theatres, N.Y., vice chmn., 1988—; chmn. adv. com. U. Bridgeport, 1987—. Fellow Am. Bar Found. (sr., life); mem. ABA (coun. internat. law and practice sect. 1986—), Am. Law Inst., Assn. of Bar of City of N.Y. (chmn. fed. legis. com. 1987—), N.Y. State Bar Assn., Fed. Bar Assn., Am. Arbitration Assn. (bd. dirs.), Harvard Club (N.Y.C.). Home: 183 Steep Hill Rd Weston CT 06883 Office: ITT Corp 320 Park Ave New York NY 10022

AIELLO, GENNARO C., insurance company executive; b. Ridgway, Pa., Dec. 16, 1953; s. Victor C. and Victoria I. (Bevacqua) A.; m. Cynthia K. Medvid, Sept. 20, 1975; children: Erin M., Kathryn T. BS, Gannon U., 1975; postgrad., Pa. State U, 1974-76. Lic. ins. agt., real estate agt. Sales rep. Met. Ins. Co., DuBois, Pa., 1975-80; owner, agt. Ins. Mktg. Assocs., Ridgway, 1980-86; acct. exec. The Pa. Mfrs. Assn. Group, Ridgway, 1986—; gen. mgr. Wolf Run Marina, Warren, Pa., 1978-79; controller U.S. Coal, Inc., Ridgway, 1981-83; realtor Anderson and Kime, St. Marys, Pa., 1983—. V.p., dir. Ridgway Action for Community Enhancement, 1986—; chmn. St. Leo's Home and Sch. Assn., Ridgway, 1989—; bd. dirs. St. Leo's Parish Council, 1986—, pres. sports assn., 1988-89; bd. dirs. Elk County Council on the Arts, 1989—. Mem. Johnsonburg C. of C. (dir., pres. 1989—), Elk-Cameron Bd. Realtors, Jaycees (pres. local chpt. 1986-87). Lodge: Rotary (pres. Johnsonburg 1980-81), Ducks Unltd. (spons. chmn. 1987-88). Home: 220 Montmorenci Ave Ridgway PA 15853 Office: The PMA Group PO Box I Mfr's Bldg Ridgway PA 15853

AIKEN, ROBERT MCCUTCHEN, chemical company executive; b. Washington, Pa., Nov. 8, 1930; s. Robert Wilson and Helen (McCutchen) A.; m. Brenda Jean Ashton, Nov. 6, 1957; children: Jennifer Ann, Robert Ashton. B.S. in M.E., Case Inst. Tech., cleve. With E.I. duPont Co., 1952—; planning mgr. plastics dept. E.I. duPont Co., Wilmington, Del., 1967-69; dist. sales mgr. E.I. duPont Co., Atlanta, 1969-70; asst. plant mgr. E.I. duPont Co., Victoria, Tex., 1970-71; mgr. polymer intermediates ops. E.I. duPont Co., Cape Fear, N.C., 1971-74; dir. Caustic-Chlorine div. E.I. duPont Co., Wilmington, 1974-75; asst. dir. Latin Am. div. E.I. duPont, Wilmington, 1975-81; dir. E.I. duPont Co., Wilmington, 1975-78; gen. mgr. internat. dept. E.I. duPont Co., 1978-81; v.p. internat. E.I. du Pont Co., Wilmington, 1981—, now group v.p. Served to lt. j.g. USN, 1955-58. Mem. World Affairs Council, Am. Chem. Soc. (group v.p.). Republican. Clubs: Palmeto Country (Aiken, S.C.); Wilmington, Wilmington Country. Home: 1225 Birmingham Rd West Chester PA 19380 Office: E I du Pont de Nemours & Co 1007 Market St Wilmington DE 19898 *

AIKMAN, ALBERT EDWARD, lawyer; b. Norman, Okla., Mar. 11, 1922; s. Albert Edwin and Thelma Annette (Brooke) A.; m. Shirley Barnes, June 24, 1944; children—Anita Gayle, Priscilla June, Rebecca Brooke. B.S., Tex. A&M U., 1947; J.D. cum laude, So. Meth. U., 1948, LL.M., 1954. Bar: Tex. 1948, U.S. Supreme Ct. 1956. Staff atty. Phillips Petroleum Co., Amarillo, Tex., 1948-49; sole practice, Amarillo, 1949-53; tax counsel Magnolia Petroleum Co., Dallas, 1953-56; ptnr. Locke, Purnell, Boren, Laney & Neely, Dallas, 1956-71; sole practice, Dallas, 1973-81; of counsel Pickens Energy Corp., Dallas, 1981—. Served with inf. U.S. Army, 1943-45. Mem. ABA, Tex. Bar Assn., Dallas Bar Assn. Methodist. Contbr. articles in field to profl. jours.

AIMONE, MICHAEL DENNIS, financial executive; b. St. Louis, June 24, 1943; s. Bartholomew and Mildred V. (Hargett) A.; m. H. Eileen Decker, Dec. 18, 1965; children: Michael S., Steven D. BBA, U. Mo., 1967, MA in Acctg., 1968. CPA, Mo. Audit mgr. Ernst & Whinney, St. Louis, 1968-73; asst. treas. Miss. Lime Co., Alton, Ill., 1973-83, treas., 1984—; mem. corp. assembly Blue Cross Health Services, Inc., St. Louis, 1984—. dir. Alton Wood River Jr. Achievement Dist. Bd., 1983—, River Bend United Way, 1987—; exec. bd. Piasa Bird coun. Boy Scouts Am., 1987—. Mem. Am. Inst CPA's, Mo. Soc. CPA's, Am. Assn. Indsl. Mgmt. (exec. roundtable), Future Bus. Leaders Am. (adv. counsil 1984—). Home: 5210 Dover Dr Godfrey IL 62035 Office: Miss Lime Co 7 Alby St Alton IL 62002

AINSLIE, MICHAEL LEWIS, organization executive; b. Johnson City, Tenn., May 12, 1943; s. George Lewis and Jean Clare (Waddell) A.; m. Lucy Scardino, Dec. 11, 1971 (div.); 1 son, Michael Loren; m. Suzanne H. Braga, Dec. 13, 1986; stepchildren: Katherine, Robbie Ann, Liza. B.A., Vanderbilt U., 1965; M.B.A., Harvard U., 1968. Assoc. McKinsey & Co., N.Y.C., 1968-71; pres. Palmas Del Mar, P.R., 1971-75; sr. v.p., chief operating officer N-Ren Corp., Cin., 1975-80; pres. Nat. Trust for Historic Preservation, Washington, 1980-84; pres., chief exec. officer Sotheby's Holdings, Inc., N.Y.C., 1984—. Bd. overseers U. Pa. Grad. Sch. Fine Arts, Phila., 1982—; mem. exec. council Harvard Bus. Sch., 1982-85; bd. dirs. N.Y. Landmarks Conservancy, 1985—, The Wexner Ctr. for Visual Arts, 1986—, The Markle Found., 1986—, Graham Windham, 1986—; bd. dirs. Jefferson Restoration; mem. alumni bd. Vanderbilt U., 1983—; adv. bd. U. Va., 1984—, Friends of Vieilles Maisons Francaises. Corning Found. fellow, 1965-66. Mem. Young Pres.'s Orgn. (bd. dirs. 1986—). Clubs: Metropolitan (D.C.), River, Meadow (Southampton); Buck's (N.Y.); Queen's (London). Office: Sotheby's Holding Inc 1334 York Ave New York NY 10021

AIRES, RANDOLF H., retail company executive; b. Lancaster, Pa., Mar. 2, 1935; s. Ray G. and Anna H. Aires; m. Virginia P. Peters; children: John, Juliet, Kevin, Katherine. AB, Dartmouth Coll., 1957; JD, U. Mich., 1962; postgrad., Dartmouth Coll., U. Colo. Bar: Colo., Calif., D.C. Atty. Colo. Nat. Bank, Denver, 1962-64; assoc. Montgomery and Little, Denver, 1964-68; atty. Sears, Roebuck and Co., Los Angeles, 1968-72; atty. Sears, Roebuck and Co., Washington, 1972-80, v.p., 1981—. Chmn. bd. dirs. Bryce Harlow Found., Washington, 1984—, Am. Retail Fedn., 1983—, Fed. City Council, Congl. Charity Tennis Tournament; bd. dirs., sec. Bus.-Govt. Relations Council of Washington Bus. Group on Health, 1983—; bd. dirs., pres. Bus.-Govt. Relations Council; bd. dirs. Am. Assembly Collegiate Schs. Bus., St. Louis, 1986—; bd. dirs., mem. exec. com. Fed. City Council, Washington, 1985—. Served as capt. USNR, 1957-81. Mem. ABA, D.C. Bar Assn., Calif. Bar Assn. Clubs: Carlton (bd. dirs.); Dartmouth of Washington (bd. dirs.), Econ. of Washington (bd. dirs.), City, Capitol Hill. Office: Sears Roebuck & Co 633 Pennsylvania Ave NW 600 Washington DC 20004

AIRINGTON, HAROLD L., forest products company executive; b. Rockingham, N.C., Nov. 30, 1927; s. Clarence L. and Etta (Ross) A.; m. Joyce M. Pendergast, June 6, 1950; children: Karen, Deborah, Russell, James. Student, Balt. City Coll. Salesman Ga. Pacific Corp., Charlotte, N.C., 1954-60; br. mgr. distbn. div. G-P Corp., Richmond, Va., 1960-70; regional mgr. distbn. div. G-P Corp., Landover, Md., 1970-78; v.p. wood products sales Ga.-Pacific Corp., Atlanta, 1978, exec. v.p. bldg. products, 1978-88, pres., chief oper. officer, 1988-89, now vice chmn., 1989—.

AITKIN, W. ROY, mining company executive; b. Glasgow, Scotland, Apr. 5, 1932; m. Pamela Mary Evans, 1958; children: Neil, Richard. BS, Glasgow U., 1953; postgrad., U. Western Ontario, Can., 1973. With Inco Ltd., 1970—, exec. v.p., 1984—. Mem. Ontario Mining Assn. (bd. dirs.), Can. Mfrs. Assn. (bd. dirs., Can. com.). Office: Inco Ltd, Ste 2200, Royal Trust Tower, PO Box 44, Toronto Dominion Ctr, Toronto, ON Canada M5K 1N4 *

AIUVALASIT, ANTHONY GEORGE, JR., lawyer, drug company administrator; b. New Orleans, Sept. 3, 1949; s. Anthony George and Clare Rosaria (Monjure) A.; m. Marcie Ann Nebenzahl, Aug. 26, 1971; children: Sharon Lynn, Tony III. BA, Rice U., 1971; JD, New Eng. Sch. Law, 1974. Bar: N.J. 1978, Mass. 1979. Trial atty. antitrust div. U.S. Dept. Justice, Washington, 1974-78; corp. counsel BOC Group, Inc., Montvale, N.J., 1978-85; dir. product assurance Ohmeda div., Murray Hill, N.J., 1985-88, Block Drug Co., Inc., Jersey City, N.J., 1988—. Mem. Health Industry Mfrs. Assn. (chmn. good mfg. practices com. 1987-88). Office: Block Drug Co Inc 257 Cornelison Ave Jersey City NJ 07302

AKASAKI, TOSHIRO, machinery manufacturing executive; b. Tokyo, Sept. 14, 1925; s. Toshifumi and Ine (Kawanabe) A.; BS in Engring., Keio U., Tokyo, 1948; m. Yoshiko, Mar. 23, 1954; children: Shoko, Sayuri. Engr., Ministry Internat. Trade and Industry, Tokyo, 1948-50; asst. comml. sec. Japanese embassy, Ottawa, Ont., Can., 1950-53; dir. Japan Trade Center, Cairo, 1953-58; mgr. research sect. JETRO, Tokyo, 1958-60; mgr. plastic sect. Marubeni Co. Ltd., 1960-61; v.p. Sekisui Plastic Corp., Hazelton, Pa., 1962-67; pres. Danfoss Japan Mfg. Co., Tokyo, 1968-72, Toyo Carrier Engring. Co., Tokyo, 1972-78; v.p. Nordson Corp., Amherst, Ohio, 1978-87, cons., advisor, 1987—; pres., chmn. bd. Nordson K.K., Tokyo, 1978-87. Home: 5-2-18-1403 Mita, Minato-ku, 108 Tokyo Japan Office: Nordson KK, 3-32-36 Higashi-Shinagawa, 140, Shinagawa-ku Tokyo Japan also: Nordson Corp 28601 Clemens Rd Westlake OH 44145

AKERS, CATHAYANNE MARIE, manufacturing executive, chemist; b. San Jose, Calif., Aug. 13, 1952; d. Charles Marshall Sr. and Georgia Irene (Miller) A.; m. James Floyd Dorris, Jan. 4, 1969 (dec. Nov. 1974); 1 child, Cindy Lee Anne Dorris. Diploma in gen. edn., Clackamas Community Coll.; AAS, Lower Columbia Coll., 1977; student, Monroe County (Mich.) Community Coll., 1986, U. Toledo, 1987—. Inventory clk., receptionist Hood River County Abundant Food Stores, Dalles, Oreg., 1970; guard Lawrence Security, Portland, Oreg., 1971-72; store detective Lipman & Wolfe, Portland, Oreg., 1972-74; exptl. technician I Weyerhaeuser Paper Co., Longview, Wash., 1977-79; water shed technician Wash. State Dept. Agri., Kelso, 1979; chemist Indsl. Chems. div. Am. Cyanamid Co., Longview, 1979-82; lab. technician City of Monroe (Mich.) Wastewater Treatment Plant, 1984-85; electrician apprentice Geal Electric, Monroe, 1985; product engr. intern Monroe Auto Equipment Div. of Tenneco Automatic, 1986; pres., chief exec. officer Gap Plumbing, Inc., Monroe, 1987—, bd. dirs.; lab. analyst Lower Columbia Coll., 1976; plumber's apprentice Plumbers, Pipe Fitters and Refrigeration Joint Apprenticeship and Tng. Com., Tacoma, 1982-84. Participant Hands Across Am., Toledo, 1986; team leader March of Dimes-Walk Am., Monroe, 1988. Pell grantee U. Toledo, 1987-88. Mem. Soc. Women Engrs. (student), VFW Aux., Nat. Safety Council (defensive driving campaign 1977). Democrat. Roman Catholic. Home: 237 White Oak Ct Monroe MI 48161 Office: Gap Plumbing Inc 121 N Roessler St Monroe MI 48161

AKERS, JOHN FELLOWS, information processing company executive; b. Boston, Dec. 28, 1934; s. Kenneth Fellows and Mary Joan (Reed) A.; m. Susan Davis, Apr. 16, 1960; children: Scott, Pamela, Anne. B.S., Yale U., 1956. With IBM Corp., Armonk, N.Y., 1960—, v.p., asst. group exec., 1976-78, v.p., group exec., 1978-82, sr. v.p., group exec., 1982-83, pres., dir., 1983—, chief exec. officer, 1985—, chmn. bd., 1986—; dir. N.Y. Times Co. Mem. adv. bd. Yale Sch. Orgn. and Mgmt.; co-chmn. Bus. Roundtable; trustee Met. Mus. Art, Calif. Inst. Tech.; bd. govs. United Way Am. Served to lt. USNR, 1956-60. Office: IBM Corp Old Orchard Rd Armonk NY 10504

AKERS, LYNN WILLSON, controller; b. Knoxville, Tenn., Oct. 14, 1956; d. Ivan Matson and Nancy Evelyn (Veal) Willson; m. Ray Field Akers, Jr., Oct. 6, 1984; 1 child, Willson Tyler. BS in Acctg., U. Tenn., 1977, MBA in Fin. and Mgmt., 1979. Staff acct. Park Nat. Bank, Knoxville, 1979-80, chief acct., 1982-83; controller Aztex Energy Corp., Knoxville, 1980-82; asst. controller First Am. Nat. Bank, Knoxville, 1982-84, controller, 1984—. Team capt. C. of C. Membership Drive, 1987, Jr. Achievement Bowl-A-Thon, 1988. Mem. Nat. Assn. Accts. Republican. Methodist. Office: First Am Nat Bank 505 S Gay St PO Box 511 Knoxville TN 37901

AKERS, SHARON LYNN, public relations, marketing executive; b. Cheverly, Md., May 10, 1956; d. Shirley Ross and Helen Frances (Triplett) A. BS in Journalism, U. Md., 1978. Specialty cert. govt. and urban pub. rels., Md. Asst. dir. pub. rels. Providence Hosp., Washington, 1978-79, dir. mktg. devel., 1979-81; dir. pub. rels., mktg. and devel. Montgomery Gen. Hosp., Olney, Md., 1981-84; dir. bus. and found. rels. George Washington U., Washington, 1984-87; dir. pub. rels. mid Atlantic area Touche Ross, Washington, 1987-88; dir. spl. projects, liason with co. & fin. orgns. Mark Vogel Cos., 1988—; cons. fed. govt., pvt. orgns., partnerships, Md., Washington, 1984—. Active Greater Washington Bd. Trade; mem. pub. rels. com. Bd. Trade, 1987—. Cert. of Esteem Dept. Def., 1978. Mem. Am. Mgmt. Assn. Republican. Methodist. Home: 5802 Nicholson Ln #205 Rockville MD 20852

AKIN, RALPH HARDIE, JR., oil company executive; b. Decatur, Ill., Oct. 18, 1938; s. Ralph Hardie and Darla (Sutterfield) A.; m. Joan Clements, Dec. 30, 1960 (div. 1972); children—Laura Elizabeth, Michael Hardie; m. Elaine Fleming, June 28, 1974; children—Jennifer Aimee, Julie Alicia. B.S., Centenary Coll., 1960; M.S., U. Tulsa, 1966. Computer opr. Western Geophys. Co., Shreveport, La., 1960-62, geologist Apache Corp., Tulsa and Houston, 1963-67; geologist, exploration mgr. Ada Exco, Houston, 1967-70; v.p. T.C. Bartling and Assocs., Houston, 1971-76; pres. Akin Energy Corp., Houston, 1977—. Mem. Am. Assn. Petroleum Geologists, Am. Assn. Petroleum Landmen, Houston Geol. Soc. Republican. Methodist. Home: 11611 Windy Ln Houston TX 77024 Office: Akin Energy Corp Americana Bldg Room 1417 Houston TX 77002

AKINS, GEORGE CHARLES, accountant; b. Willits, Calif., Feb. 22, 1917; s. Guy Brookins and Eugenie (Swan) A.; A.A., Sacramento City Coll., 1941; m. Jane Babcock, Mar. 27, 1945. Accountant, auditor Calif. Bd. Equalization, Dept. Finance, Sacramento, 1940-44; controller-treas. DeVons Jewelers, Sacramento, 1944-73, v.p., controller, 1973-80, v.p., chief fin. officer, dir., 1980-84; individual accounting and tax practice, Sacramento, 1944—. Accountant, cons. Mercy Children's Hosp. Guild, Sacramento, 1957-77. Served with USAAF, 1942. Mem. Soc. Calif. Pioneers, Nat. Soc. Pub. Accountants, U.S. Navy League, Calif. Hist. Soc., English Speaking Union, Drake Navigators Guild, Internat. Platform Assn., Mendocino County Hist. Soc., Sacramento County Hist. Soc. Republican. Roman Catholic. Clubs: Commonwealth of Calif., Comstock. Contbg. author: Portfolio of Accounting Systems for Small and Medium-Sized Business, 1968, rev., 1977. Home and Office: 96 S Humboldt St Willits CA 95490

AKINS, VAUGHN EDWARD, engineering company executive; b. Gowanda, N.Y., Sept. 28, 1934; s. Elsworth D. and Alice (Carlton) A.; grad. pub. schs.; student U.S. Naval Schs., 1956-57, IBM Engring. Sch., 1961-65; m. Muriel M. Hoglund, May 15, 1960; children—Sonja L., Coleen R., Joseph E. Lab. specialist IBM, Poughkeepsie, N.Y., Boulder, Colo. and East Fishkill, N.Y., 1959-69; test engr. Semi, Phoenix, 1969-74; mgr. computer-aided mfg. and test engring. semiconductor process research and devel. Motorola Corp., Mesa, Ariz., 1974-84; applications mgr. (CIM) Motorola Corp. New Enterprises Group, Mesa, Ariz., 1984-86, mgr. computer integrated mfg. semiconductor products sector, Phoenix, 1986-87; with start-up team SEMATECH, Inc., Austin, Tex., 1988—. Precinct committeeman N.Y. State Conservative Party, 1963; instr. first aid Am. Red Cross, 1971-78. Served with USNR, 1956-59. Mem. IEEE (sr.), Nat. Rifle Assn. (life), Am. Mgmt. Assn., Electrochem. Soc. (cons. to exec. bd.; founding com. chmn. Automation in Mfg. chpt., exec. com. electronics div.), Semiconductor Equipment Mfrs. Internat. (co-chair). Republican. Fundamentalist. Patentee in field. Home: 11419 Sundown Trail Austin TX 78749 Office: Sematech Inc 2706 Montopolis Dr Austin TX 78741

AKIVA, ISAAC SHOUKET, pharmacist, executive; b. Baghdad, Feb. 11, 1947; came to U.S., 1970; s. Heskel and Julie (Irani) A.; m. Evelyn Finkelstein, Nov. 25, 1971; children: Ann Claire, Nathaniel E. BS in Pharmacy, Howard U., 1975; DSC, Irvine Inst. for Med. Scis., 1979. Lic. pharmacist, Calif., Nev. V.p. ops. Biomerica Inc. subs. NMS Pharmaceauthicals Inc., Newport Beach, Calif., 1976-84; pres. IMI Scientific Inc., Newport Beach, 1984—, bd. dirs. Served with Israeli Air Force, 1964-69. Mem. Calif. Employee Pharmacists Assn. Club: U. Calif. at Irvine Soccer. Home: 3305 Grey Dolphin Dr Las Vegas NV 89117

AKSELRAD, DAVID MARTIN, lawyer, consultant; b. Bklyn., July 31, 1959; s. Ralph and Rachel (Elbirt) A. BA in Econs., NYU, 1981, MBA,

1986; JD, Cardozo Sch. Law, N.Y.C., 1985. Pvt. practice real estate cons. Bklyn., 1983—. Author: The Housing Crisis of World War I, 1980, Improving Rent-Regulated Housing in New York City, 1985. Exec. v.p., treas. NYU Entrepreneurs Assn., N.Y.C., 1979. N.Y. State Regents scholar, 1977. Mem. Community Housing Improvement Program, Am. Sailing Assn. Home: Hamilton House 10031 4th Ave Brooklyn NY 11209 Office: 50 Ocean Pkwy Brooklyn NY 11218

AKYÜZ, RINT, trading company executive, consultant; b. Ankara, Turkey, Jan. 3, 1949; s. Kenan and Emel (Iliris) A.; m. Ayfer Caycizade, June 1, 1978; 1 child, Iren Akyuz. BSc, Middle East Tech. U., Ankara, Turkey, 1971. Asst. Teknim Co. Ltd., Ankara, 1971-75, mgr. export, 1975-80, v.p., 1980-82; v.p. Karat Corp., Istanbul, Turkey, 1982-83; pres. Karat Corp., Istanbul, 1983-85; cons. Diler Corp., Istanbul, 1985-86, Cukurova Corp., Istanbul, 1985-86; chmn. Rotel Corp., Istanbul, 1985—; cons. Cukurova Fgn. Trade Corp., Istanbul, 1985-86, Diler Fgn. Trade Corp., Istanbul, 1985-86; bd. dirs. Rom Gida Corp. Contbr. articles to profl. jours. Mem. Clothing Mgrs. Assn., Union Chambers, Chamber of Industry (pres. 1975-82), Turkish Am. Businessmen Assn. (mem., gen. sec.), Am. C. of C. in Turkey. Moslem. Clubs: Büyük Kulüp, Bizim Tepe (Istanbul). Home: Cemil Topuzlu cad 143-6, 81060 Istanbul Turkey Office: Rotel Corp, Nisantasi Ihlamur Yolu 27, 80200 Istanbul Turkey

ALAFOUZO, ANTONIA, marketing professional; b. Cairo, Egypt, Oct. 13, 1952; came to U.S., 1982; d. Pano Antony and Agni-Maria (Ranos) A.; m. Thomas D'Ambola, Jr., May 29, 1988. BSC in Econs., Brunel U., London, 1975; Diploma in Econs. and Politics, Oxford (Eng.) U., 1977, M of Philosophy, PhD, 1980. Staff reporter The Economist, London, 1973-75, contbg. writer, 1975-82; communications exec. Rubenstein, Wolfson Co., N.Y.C., 1982-87; founder, pres. Markcom Ltd., N.Y.C., 1987—; contbg. writer Fin. Report, London, 1975-82; cons. writer Fin. Times, London, 1980-82; cons. communications and econs. World Gold Council, N.Y.C., 1982—. Contbr. reports to fin. publs. Mem. Inst. Journalism, Internat. Precious Metals Inst. (mem. internat. publicity com. 1987-89), Oxford Union Soc. Office: Markcom Ltd 185 Madison Ave Ste 1101 New York NY 10016

ALBAN, ROGER CHARLES, construction equipment distribution executive; b. Columbus, Ohio, Aug. 3, 1948; s. Charles Ellis and Alice Jacqueline (Hosfeld) A.; student pub. schs.; m. 2d Rebecca Lynn Gallicchio, Aug. 12, 1978; children: Roger Charles II, Charles Michael; 1 dau. by previous marriage, Allison Ann. With Alban Equipment Co., Columbus, 1963—, sales mgr., 1972-75, gen. mgr., 1975-85, treas., 1978-85, v.p., 1980-85, pres. 1985—. Mem. Grandview Heights Bd. Edn., Columbus, 1978-85, pres., 1979, v.p., 1982, legis. liaison, 1978-79, 83-84; elected Grandview Heights City Council, 1986; mem. Met. Ednl. Council, Columbus Area Leadership Program, 1982-83. Mem. Assoc. Equipment Distbrs. (lt. dir. region 6 1980, 85, 86, 88, dir. 1989-91, chmn. light equipment dist. com. 1985, chmn. sales and mktg. com. 198, elected dir. region 6 1989—), Ohio Sch. Bds. Assn. (all-cen. region bd. 1984), Bldg. Industry Assn. Cen. Ohio, Internat. Platform Assn., Am. Rental Assn., Builders Exchange Cen. Ohio (trustee 1987—), Am. Mgmt. Assn., Nat. Right To Work Com., Nat. Fedn. Ind. Bus., Ohio Equipment Distbrs. Assn. (dir. 1982, 84—, pres. 1983), Roundtable, Mensa (chpt. exec. com. 1979-80). Roman Catholic. Clubs: Rotary, Downtown Columbus. Home: 1430 Cambridge Blvd Columbus OH 43212-3207 Office: 1825 McKinley Ave Columbus OH 43222

ALBANESE, VINCENT GANDOLFO, banker; b. Bklyn., May 23, 1949; s. Gandolfo V. and Jennie J. (Pizzarelli) A.; m. Andrea J. Pellito, Aug. 19, 1972; children: Vanessa, Vincent Jr., Valerie. BA, L.I. Univ., 1972; MBA, Pace U., 1983. Analyst cost and methods Chase Manhattan Bank N.A., N.Y.C., 1972-76, mgr. bus. analysis, 1976-81, dir. productivity analysis, 1981-88, bus. exec. collection svcs., 1988—. Bd. dirs. Great Kills Little League, S.I., N.Y., 1986-88. Mem. Assn. Internal Mgmt. Cons., Productivity Coun. N.Y. Banks. Republican. Roman Catholic. Office: Chase Manhattan Bank NA 1 New York Pla 4th Fl New York NY 10081

ALBANI, THOMAS J., manufacturing company executive; b. Hartford, Conn., May 3, 1942; s. Charles A. and Marie F. Albani; m. Suzanne Beardsley, Sept. 3, 1966; children: Karin, Steven. B.A., Amherst Coll., 1964; M.B.A., Wharton Sch. U. Pa., 1967. Asst. product mgr. Gen. Mills, Inc., Mpls., 1967-69; dir. mktg. Am. Can Co., Greenwich, Conn., 1969-73; mgmt. cons. McKinsey and Co., Inc., N.Y.C., 1973-78; gen. mgr. Gen. Electric Corp., Bridgeport, Conn., 1978-84; group v.p. Black & Decker, Inc., Bridgeport, 1984; corp. v.p. Sunbeam No. Am. Appliance Div. Allegheny Internat., Oak Brook, Ill., 1984-86; pres. appliance bus. Allegheny Internat. Inc., Pitts., 1986, exec. v.p., chief operating officer, 1986-89. Mem. Nat. Housewares Mfrs. Assn. (bd. dirs. 1985—), Assn. Home Appliance Mfrs. (bd. dirs. 1985-87), Chgo. Assn. Commerce and Industry (bd. dirs. 1986). Office: Allegheny Internat Inc PO Box 456 Pittsburgh PA 15230

ALBEE, DON DALE, insurance company executive; b. Binghamton, N.Y., Feb. 10, 1935; s. Donald Lorenzo and Kathryn Mary (Kohler) A.; m. Lucille Frances Hayes, Jan. 3, 1960; 1 child: Donald Hayes. BS in Fin., Bucknell U., 1956; student, Am. Coll., 1964. CLU. Agt. New Eng. Mutual Ins. Co., N.Y.C., 1958-62; dir. region Safaco Ins. Co., River Edge, N.J., 1962-67; v.p. region Am. Internat. Assurance Co., Bangkok, Thailand, 1967-72; dir. region Paul Revere Life Ins. Co., Dallas, 1972-75; sr. v.p. mktg. Ga. Life Ins. Co., Atlanta, 1975-78; exec. v.p. Nat. Sav. Life, Murfreesboro, Tenn., 1978-80; mgr. area Am. Nat. Ins. Co., Mobile, Ala., 1980—. Served to col., U.S. Army, 1956-87. Mem. Nat. Assn. Life Underwriters. Republican. Home: PO Box 884 Point Clear AL 36564 Office: Am Nat Ins Co PO Box 199 Point Clear AL 36564

ALBERDA VAN EKENSTEIN, EISO WILLEM ANTON, chemical company executive; b. Eelde, Drenthe, The Netherlands, Mar. 24, 1951; came to U.S., 1984; s. Jacob and Louisa (Veenhuis) A.v.E; m. Ingrid Dykstra, Apr. 7, 1976; children: Onno, Janneke. Degree in Econs., Royal U. Groningen, 1974. With mgmt. devel. dept. Akzo N.V., Arnhem, The Netherlands, 1974-77; asst. treas. Akzo N.Y., Arhem, The Netherlands, 1982-84; economist Akzo Chemie, Amersfoort, The Netherlands, 1977-82; asst. treas. Arzona/Akzo Am., Asheville, N.C., 1984-85; treas. Akzo Am., Asheville, 1985-86; v.p., treas. Akzo Am., N.Y.C., 1986—. Presbyterian. Home: 282 Mariomi Rd New Canaan CT 06840 Office: Akzo Am Inc 111 W 40th St New York NY 10018

ALBERS, JOHN RICHARD, soft drink company executive; b. Mpls., Oct. 5, 1931; s. Raymond A. and Lillian (Sharp) A.; m. Carol Jean Heines; children: Scott Alan, Wendy Jean. B.A. in Econs., U. Minn., 1957; postgrad. exec. program, Stanford U., 1980. Sales rep. Minn. Mining, Chgo., 1957-59; account exec. Campbell-Mithun, Mpls., 1959-64; v.p. Grant Advt., Dallas, 1965; account supr. Knox-Reeves, Mpls., 1966-69; co-founder Zapata Foods, Mpls., 1969-71; v.p. Dr. Pepper, Dallas, 1971-81; pres. Dr. Pepper Co., Dallas, 1983-84, pres., chief operating officer, 1984-86, pres., chief exec. officer, 1986—; pres., chief exec. officer Seven-Up Co., Dallas, 1986—; dir. Central Life Assurance Co., Des Moines, Dallas Acad., Zebbie's, Inc. Mem. adv. bd. U. Dallas, 1981-83. Served to 1st. U.S. Army, 1954-56. Mem. Dallas Citizens Council, Gtr. Dallas C. of C. Clubs: Tower, Bent Tree ,DAC County, Chaparral (Dallas). Home: 5519 Bent Trail Dallas TX 75248 Office: Dr Pepper/Seven-Up Cos Inc 8144 Walnut Hill Ln Dallas TX 75231

ALBERS, ROBERT JOHN, service executive; b. Lindner, N.Y., May 4, 1941; s. William Henry and Rose Marie (Linder) A.; m. Randy Ann Abbruzzese, Sept. 15, 1963; children: Robert Joseph, Glenn Matthew, Cynthia Marie. BS in Mining Engring., Lehigh U., 1963. Various operational positions Chevron Corp., Can. and U.S., 1963-81; mgr. data processing Houston, 1982; chief geophysicist Geosource Inc., Houston, 1982, pres. tech. group, 1982, pres. ops. and tech. group, 1986-88; chmn. bd. dirs. Knowledge Systems Inc., Houston, 1987—. Mem. Soc. Exploration Geophysicists, U. Club (Houston). Office: Geosources Inc 6909 SW Frwy Houston TX 77236-6306

ALBERT, JANYCE LOUISE, banker; b. Toledo, July 27, 1932; d. Howard C. and Glenola Mae (Masters) Blessing; m. John R. Albert, Aug. 7, 1954; children: John R., James H. Student Ohio Wesleyan U., 1949-51; BA, Mich. State U., 1953; MS, Iowa State U., 1980. Asst. personnel mgr./tng. supr. Sears, Roebuck & Co., Toledo, 1953-56; tchr. adult edn. Tenafly Pub. Schs. (N.J.), 1966-70; personnel officer, tng. officer, tng. and edn. mgr. Iowa Dept. Transp., Ames, 1974-77; coll. recruiting coordinator Rockwell Internat., Cedar Rapids, Iowa, 1977-79, engring. adminstrn. mgr., 1979-80; employee relations and job evaluation analyst Phillips Petroleum Co., Bartlesville, Okla., 1980-81; v.p., dir. personnel Republic Bancorp, Tulsa, 1981-83; v.p. and dir. human resources First Nat. Bank, Rockford, Ill., 1983—; advisor to Nat. Profl. Secs. Assn. Mem. employee services com. Rockford Bd. Edn.; v.p. bd. dirs. Rocvale Children's Home; bd. dirs. Rockford Community Action Program, 1988—, chairperson legis. com., 1989; bd. dirs. United Way of Ames, 1976-77; mem. employee service comm. Rockford Pub. Schs., 1988—; bd. dirs. Rockford Human Resources Community Action Program; 2d chairperson Rockford br. State of Ill. Job Services Employers Coun., 1989; publicity chmn. Tenafly 300th Ann. Celebration, 1969; bd. deacons Presbyn. Ch., Ames, 1972-75; mem. adv. council Rockford YWCA, bd. dirs., 1986; co-chmn. YWCA Leader Luncheon, 1985; advisor Rockford chpt. ARC; mem. Mayor's Task Force for Rockford Project Self-Sufficiency. Pres.'s scholar, 1951-53; recipient YWCA Kate O'Connor award for Women in Labor Force 1984. Mem. Rockford Network (past chairperson 1985, pres. 1986), Rockford C. of C. (transp. com.), Rockford Personnel Assn. (co-chmn. programs 1985-86, adv. council), Am. Soc. Personnel Adminstrn., Rockford Personnel Assn., Employee Benefits Assn. No. Ill. (membership chmn.), Rockford Council Affordable Health Care, Rockford Personal and Profl. Power Coalition, P.E.O., Sigma Epsilon, Alpha Gamma Delta, Phi Kappa Phi. Home: 5587 Thunderidge Dr Rockford IL 61107 Office: First Nat Bank Rockford 401 E State St Rockford IL 61110

ALBERT, ROGER CHARLES, trade association and financial service executive; b. Berwyn, Ill., Aug. 23, 1944; m. Cheryl Jean Hamilton Sept. 23, 1967; children: Colleen Joy, Ryan Colin. BS Acctg., No. Ill. U., 1966. CPA, Ill. Audit mgr. Peat, Marwick, Main & Co., Chgo., 1966-76; from v.p., contr., treas. to sr. v.p., chief fin. officer U.S. League Savs. Insts. and Affiliates, Chgo., 1976—. Mem. Am. Inst. CPA's, Ill. SOc. CPA's, Beta Alpha Psi (hon.). Home: 1105 Honest Pleasure Naperville IL 60540 Office: US League Savs Inst & Affiliates 111 E Wacker Dr Chicago IL 60601

ALBERTHAL, LESTER M., JR., electronic systems company executive; b. 1944; married. BBA, U. Tex., 1967. With Electronic Data Systems Corp. subs. Gen. Motors Corp., Dallas, 1968—, v.p. ins. group, 1979-84, v.p. bus. ops., from 1984, pres., 1986—, chief exec. officer, 1987—, also dir. Office: Electronic Data Systems Corp 7171 Forest Ln Dallas TX 75230 *

ALBERTI, JOSEPH ALVIN, sales and marketing executive; b. Mils., Nov. 17, 1943; s. Joseph Nick and Lauretta (Keller) A.; m. Patricia Anne Opitz, Oct. 3, 1964; children: Joell Lee, Jennifer Anne, Jane. Student, Marquette U.; grad. in consumer banking, U. Va., 1975. Collection mgr. First Wis. Nat. Bank, Milw., 1967-69, credit mgr., 1969-72, asst. sales mgr., 1972-75, v.p. risk mgmt., 1975-83; v.p. First Ins. Mgmt. subs. First Wis. Corp., Milw., 1983-85, 1st v.p. sales and mktg. Elan Fin./Ins. Svcs. subs., 1985-89; 1st v.p. Elan Life Ins. Co., Phoenix, 1986-89, Elan Title Ins. Svcs., Milw., 1989—. Mem. Italian Community Ctr., Milw., 1987. Mem. Ind. Ins. Agts. Wis., Profl. Ins. Agts. Wis., Lions. Republican. Roman Catholic. Home: 5804 Glenhaven Dr Green Oak WI 53129 Office: Elan Fin Svcs 8ll E Wisconsin St Milwaukee WI 53202

ALBERTS, IRWIN N., publishing company executive. Pres., chief exec. officer Panini USA, N.Y.C.; also sr. v.p. adminstrn. and devel. Macmillan Pub., N.Y.C. Office: Macmillan Pub Co 866 3rd Ave New York NY 10022 *

ALBIN, JOHN SANFORD, farmer, banker; b. Newman, Ill., Oct. 28, 1928; s. Leonard Bruce and Grace Nettie (Herrington) A.; m. Marjorie Ann Martin, Sept. 10, 1949; children: Perry A.,david. A. BS with honors, U. Ill., 1950; Farmer, Newman, 1951—; operator Albin Farm; pres. Albin Pork Farm, Inc.; chmn. bd. dirs. Longview State Bank (Ill.); pres. Longview Capital Corp., 1977—, chmn. bd. dirs. State Bank Charisman (Ill.). Pres., Newman Community Unit 303 Sch. Bd., 1958-66; trustee Parkland Coll., Champaign, Ill., 1968—, v.p., 1977-88; chmn. bd. 1st Nat. Bank of Ogden (Ill.). Recipient Ill. 4H Alumni award, 1968, Master Farmer award Prairie Farmer mag., 1970, award of merit U. Ill. Coll. Agr. Alumni Assn., 1977. Mem. Am. Shropshire Registry Assn. (pres. 1962-65), Ill. Farm Bus. Farm Mgrs. Assn. (pres. 1968-83), E. Central Farm Bus. Farm Mgrs. Assn. (pres. 1965-72), Douglas County Farm Bur. (bd. dirs. 1968—), Top Farmers Assn. Am., Tri-City Country Club (Villa Grove), Sycamore Hills Country Club (Paris, Ill.), Champaign Country Club, Lions, Masons, Farm House, Alpha Zeta.. Republican. Home: PO Box 377 Newman IL 61942 Office: Longview State Bank 237 Logan Longview IL 61942

ALBIN, WILLIAM FRANCIS, III, computer-based training executive; b. Cambridge, Mass., May 15, 1947; s. William Francis and Ruth Kathleen (Sabine) A.; m. Marilyn Jones, Dec. 14, 1968. BA, U. Conn., 1972, MSW, 1974. Youth services coordinator Town of Wethersfield (Conn.), 1974-75; assoc. exec. dir. Ednl. Resources, Inc., West Hartford, Conn., 1975-80; pres., staff cons. Assocs. for Human Devel., West Hartford, 1980-81; instr. St. Joseph Coll., West Hartford, 1981-83; pres., chief exec. officer Micro Training Assocs., Canton, Conn., 1983—. Served with USAF, 1967-71. Mem. Am. Soc. Tng. and Devel., Soc. Applied Learning Tech. Office: 320 Albany Turnpike Canton CT 06019

ALBRECHT, ARTHUR JOHN, advertising agency executive; b. Woodhaven, N.Y., June 11, 1931; s. Charles Arthur and Anna (Klingner) A.; m. Sandi Edith Roberson, May 14, 1952; 1 child, Sherylyn. BA cum laude, Fla. State U., 1957. Salesman, sales promotion mgr., product mgr. Vick Chem. Co., N.Y.C., 1958-63; group product mgr. Whitehall Labs., N.Y.C., 1963-65; v.p. mktg. J.B. Williams Inc., N.Y.C., 1965-66; sr. v.p. mktg. Mitchum-Thayer div. Revlon, N.Y.C., 1966-71; sr. v.p., mgmt. supr. William Esty Co. Inc., N.Y.C., 1971-81; pres. Petersen Albrecht Co., N.Y.C., 1981-85, Albrecht Advt., Inc., Boca Raton, Fla., 1985—; adj. asst. prof. Pace U., 1976-85; bd. dirs. Brand Acceleration, Inc., N.Y.C., Damon Therepeutics, Inc., N.Y.C.; cons./lectr., 1985—. Author: Magic Town, U.S.A, 1978; contbr.: articles to profl. jours. Ency. Advt. Pres. Villard Hill Assn., 1973-74. With USMC, 1950-55. Mem. Pharm. Advt. Club, Nat. Writers Club, Fla. State U. Alumni Assn., Internat. Platform Assn., Phi Beta Kappa, Phi Kappa Phi, Phi Eta Sigma, Alpha Delta Sigma (past chpt. pres., Outstanding Service award 1957), Indian Spring Country Club, Century Club. Republican. Unitarian. Home: 1148 Parkside Cir N Boca Raton FL 33486

ALBRECHT, FREDERICK IVAN, food products executive; b. Akron, Ohio, June 11, 1917; s. Ivan Willard and Fern Louella (Heathman) A.; m. Francia Adelaide Holliday, Dec. 11, 1941; children: Heather, Ivan Holliday, Frederick Steven, Gwyneth, Tatiana, Monica. BA, Colgate U., 1940; LLB, U. Akron, 1951. Bar: Ohio 1951. With Fred W. Albrecht Grocery Co., Akron, 1939-59, pres., 1959-82; pres. Albrecht, Inc., Akron, 1976—, chmn. bd. dirs.; bd. dirs. Bank One Akron, 1976—, Ruhlin Constrn. Co., 1969-83, Akron Savs. and Loan Co. 1959-75; chmn. Fred W. Albrecht Grocery Co., Akron, 1982—. Chmn. Acme-Zip Commn. 1953—, Akron Area Devel. Com., 1964-65, Community Improvement Corp. for Summit, Medina, Portage Counties, 1966-74, Little Hoover Commn., 1967-69, Akron Sesquicentennial, 1974-75; bd. dirs. Children's Hosp., 1960-83, U. Akron, 1961-67; bd. trustees local United Way; chmn. bd. dirs. U. Akron, 1967-70; vice chmn. USA Bicentennial Akron Co., 1976; 1st vice chmn. Akron Small Bus. Devel. Corp., 1981-83; pres. devel. found. U. Akron, 1967-88, chmn. bd. dirs., 1967-70, pres. Hilltoppers Club, 1970-71; gen. campaign chmn. Akron United Way and ARC, 1977; mem. Weathervane Theatre Million Dollar Captital Campaign, 1988, YMCA. 1st lt. U.S. Army, 1941-46, World War II. Recipient U. Akron Alumni Hon. award, 1972, Disting. Exec. of Yr. award, 1975, Citizen of Yr. award local realtors, 1978, Meritorious Svc. award Varsity Assn. U. Akron, 1980, Bert A. Polsky Humanitarian award, 1987, A.G.M.R. Cert. of Recognition, 1980, Ace adn Click 40-yr. Club award, 1980. Mem. Exec. Assn. Akron (Sales and Mktg. award 1976), U. Club Akron (chmn. 1983-87), Cascade Club (dir. 1971-78), Portage Country Club, Rotary. Office: Fred W Albrecht Grocery Co 2700 Gilchrist Rd Akron OH 44309

ALBRECHT, RICHARD RAYMOND, airplane manufacturing company executive, lawyer; b. Storm Lake, Iowa, Aug. 29, 1932; s. Arnold Louis and Catherine Dorothea (Boettcher) A.; m. Constance Marie Berg, June 16, 1957; children: John Justin, Carl Arnold, Richard Louis, Henry Berg. B.A., U. Iowa, 1958, J.D. with highest honors, 1961. Bar: Wash. 1961. Assoc. firm Perkins, Coie, Stone, Olsen & Williams, Seattle, 1961-67; ptnr. Perkins, Coie, Stone, Olsen & Williams, 1968-74; gen. counsel U.S. Dept. Treasury, Washington, 1974-76; v.p., gen. counsel, sec. Boeing Co., Seattle, 1976-81, v.p. fin., contracts and internat. bus., 1981-83, v.p., gen. mgr. Everett div., 1983-84; exec. v.p. Boeing Comml. Airplanes, 1984—; bd. dirs. Security Pacific Bank, Washington. Bd. regents Wash. State U., 1987. Served with AUS, 1955-58. Recipient Outstanding Citizen of Yr. award Seattle-King County Municipal League, 1968-69. Mem. Am., Wash. State, Seattle-King County bar assns., Am. Judicature Soc., Order of Coif, Sigma Nu, Omicron Delta Kappa, Phi Delta Phi. Club: Rainier (Seattle). Home: 1940 Shenandoah Dr E Seattle WA 98112 Office: Boeing Comml Airplane PO Box 3707 M/S 75-17 Seattle WA 98124

ALBRECHT, RONALD LEWIS, financial services executive; b. Derby, Conn., Dec. 30, 1935; s. Lewis Davis and Gladys Imogene (Spear) A.; m. Mikyong Kim, Dec. 28, 1968; children: Rondi Kim, Kathryn Lynn, Karen Ann. BS in Agr., U. Vt., 1957; BBA in Bus. Mgmt., Baylor U., 1966; MA in Bus. Mgmt., Cen. Mich. U., 1975. Commd. 2d lt. USAF, 1957, advanced through grades to lt. col., 1973; comdr. detachment USAF, Sioux City AB, Iowa, 1957-60; air traffic control officer USAF, Cheveston, Eng., 1960-62; dir. air traffic control HQ12 USAF, Waco, Tex., 1962-66; comdr. detachment USAF, Kimpo AB, Korea, 1967-68; comdr. squadron Sewart AFB USAF, Tenn., 1969-70; comdr. squadron Holloman AFB USAF, N.Mex., 1970-73; staff officer, air traffic control HQ air force systems command USAF, Andrews AFB, 1973-75; dep. comdr. group USAF, Pentagon, 1975-77; staff officer electronics HQ joint staff USAF, Yongson, Korea, 1977-79; staff officer air traffic control communications area USAF, Rome, N.Y., 1979-80; retired USAF, 1980; real estate broker Bangor, Maine, 1980—; retirement, investment and fin. planning exec. Bangor (Maine) Savs. Bank, 1981-87; pres. Maine Fin. Services Inc., Bangor, 1987—; instr. Los Angeles Community Coll., Seoul, Korea, 1977-79, Husson Coll. Bangor, 1981-84. Mem. loaned exec. bd. div. planning com. United Way of Penobscot Valley, Bangor, 1981—, Rep. Party, Bangor, 1981—. Hood Dairy scholar U. Vt., 1955. Mem. Internat. Assn. Fin. Planning (v.p. programs, co-founder 1985, pres. Maine chpt. 1988—), Inst. Cert. Fin. Planners, Internat. Cert. Fin. Planners (mem. Bd. Standards and Practices), Retired Officers Assn., Am. Assn. Retired Persons, Air Traffic Control Assn., Armed Forces Communications Electronics Assn., Kiwanis (2d and 1st v.p. Bangor club, pres. 1987-88), Masons, Anah Temple, Valley of Tokyo, Orient of Japan and Korea. Home: 98 Judson Blvd Bangor ME 04401

ALBRIGHT, ARCHIE EARL, JR., investment banker; b. Akron, Ohio, Aug. 21, 1920; s. Archie E. and Hazel (Beard) A.; m. Elizabeth Bell, June 19, 1988; children: John, Anne, Catherine. AB magna cum laude, Wittenberg Coll., 1942; LLB, JD, Yale U., 1948. Bar: N.Y. 1948. Mem. firm Patterson, Belknap & Webb, 1948-53; asst. to pres. Stauffer Chem. Co., N.Y.C., 1953; v.p. Stauffer Chem. Co., 1958-65, exec. v.p., 1965-68; partner Kuhn Loeb & Co., N.Y.C., 1968-69; pres., chief exec. officer Glore Forgan Staats, Inc., 1969-70, Loeb Rhoades & Co., 1971; chmn. bd., chief exec. officer Drexel Firestone, Inc., 1972-73; vice chmn. bd., chmn. fin. com. Drexel Burnham Lambert Inc., 1973-78; chmn. bd., dir. Transp. Equipment Corp., 1978-80; chmn. bd. GVC Corp., 1980—; sr. advisor First Chgo. Corp., 1987-88; chmn. Ecogen, Inc., 1987—; pres., chief exec. officer Internat. Process Systems, Inc., Glastonbury, Conn., 1988—; bd. dirs. Grumman Corp.; vis. prof., mem. adv. council Johns Hopkins U. Sch. Advanced Internat. Studies. Trustee Legal Aid Soc., Nat. Repertory Theater; mem. adv. council Hampshire Coll.; bd. dirs. Fgn. Policy Assn., Police Athletic League, Yale U. Law Sch. Fund; mem. N.Y. Philharmonic Soc.; mem. pres.'s council Kirkland Coll. Served to lt. USNR, 1942-46. Woodrow Wilson vis. fellow. Mem. Assn. Bar City N.Y., Council on Fgn. Relations, Pilgrims Soc. Clubs: Yale (N.Y.C.), Links (N.Y.C.); Pine Valley Golf; Nat. Golf (Southampton). Home: 46 Mountain Spring Rd Farmington CT 06032 Office: Internat Process Systems Inc 655 Winding Brook Dr Glastonbury CT 06033

ALBRIGHT, CARL WAYNE, JR., banker; b. Birmingham, Ala., Apr. 27, 1944; s. Carl Wayne Sr. and Grace Charlotte (Teas) A.; m. Sally Rainer Lamar, Sept. 7, 1968; children: Sally, Carl W. III. BS in Aerospace Engring., U. Ala., 1967, JD, 1970. Bar: Ala. 1970, U.S. Dist. Ct. (no. dist.) Ala. 1973m U.S. Dist. Ct. (so. dist) Ala. 1978, U.S. Ct. Appeals (11th cir.) 1981. Ptnr. Rosen, Wright, Harwood, Albright & Cook P.A., Tuscaloosa, Ala., 1970-80; sr. v.p., gen. counsel 1st Nat. Bank Tuskaloosa, 1981-83, exec. v.p., 1984-88, also bd. dirs.; pres., chief exec. officer AmSouth Bank of Tuskaloosa, 1988—; v.p. 1st Tuskaloosa Corp., 1983-87, bd. dirs.; judge Northport Mcpl. Ct., Ala., 1975-80; exec. v.p. AmSouth N.A., 1987—. V.p., treas. bd. dirs. Family Counseling Service; coordinator regional campaign Am. Heart Fund, Ala; mem. United Way, YMCA, Boy Scouts Am., DCH Found.; pres. Stillman Found., 1985—; chmn. Tuscaloosa Port Authority, 1985—; chmn. Tuscaloosa County Industrial Devel. Authority, 1989; trustee Stillman Coll., 1984—; bd. dirs. Indian Rivers Community Mental Health Ctr.; pres. West Ala. Chamber Found., Inc., 1987. 150th Anniversary Disting. Engring. fellow U. Ala. Coll. Engring., 1988. Mem. Tuscaloosa County Bar Assn. (pres. 1981-82), U. Ala. Law Sch. Alumni Assn. (pres. 1985), West Ala. C. of C. (chmn. 1986, vice chmn. 1985). Presbyterian. Clubs: NorthRiver Yacht, Indian Hills Country (Tuscaloosa). Office: AmSouth Bank of Tuscaloosa 2330 University Blvd Tuscaloosa AL 35401

ALBRIGHT, HARRY WESLEY, JR., banker; b. Albany, N.Y., Mar. 19, 1925; s. Harry Wesley and Ruth Agnes (Kerwin) A.; m. Joan Diekman, June 27, 1953; children: Mary Kimberly, Deborah V., Harry Wesley, III, Peter D., Joan Kerwin, John D. B.A., Yale U., 1949; LL.B., Cornell U., 1952. Bar: N.Y. State bar 1954. With firm DeGraff, Foy, Conway & Holt-Harris, Albany, 1964-67; dep. sec. to gov. N.Y. State, 1967-68, dep. sec., appointments officer, 1968-70, exec. asst. to gov., 1970-72, supt. banks, 1972-74; spl. counsel to Vice Pres. Nelson A. Rockefeller, 1974-75; pres.; chief operating officer, trustee Dime Savs. Bank N.Y., Bklyn., 1975-81, chmn., chief exec. officer, 1981—; pres. Thrift Instns. Adv. Council Fed. Res. Bd., 1983—. Bd. editors: N.Y. Law Jour, 1974. Bd. dirs. Bodman Found., Pratt Inst., Bklyn.; mem. regional panel selection White House Fellows; chmn. bd. Marymount Coll.; greater N.Y. adv. bd. Salvation Army. Served with AUS, 1943-46. Mem. Am., N.Y. State bar assns. Clubs: University (N.Y.C.); Sleepy Hollow Country (Scarborough-on-Hudson, N.Y.); Stockbridge (Mass.) Golf. Home: 567 Bedford Rd North Tarrytown NY 10591 Office: Dime Savs Bank 1225 Franklin Ave Garden City NY 11530 *

ALBRIGHT, LOVELIA FRIED, art importing executive; b. N.Y.C., Dec. 13, 1934; d. George and Hilda (Lazanov) Fried; m. Lee Albright, Nov. 30, 1958; children: Gregre Scott, Glenn Keith, Todd Cameron. Student, Bennington Coll., 1952-55, Grad. Sch. Internat. Studies, Geneva, 1955-56. Publicist Doubleday & Co., N.Y.C., 1960-63; pres., owner Design Cons. for Industry, N.Y.C., 1964-72, Lovelia Enterprises, Inc., N.Y.C., 1972—. Monthly columnist home furnishings N.Y. Antique Guide, 1972. Office: Lovelia Enterprises Inc 356 E 41st Pl New York NY 10017

ALBRIGHT, WARREN EDWARD, advertising executive; b. Camden, N.J., Nov. 27, 1937; s. Warren Edward and Adele (Barr) A. B.S., U. Notre Dame, 1959. Product mgr. Gen. Foods Corp., White Plains, N.Y., 1959-64; account exec. Grey Advt., N.Y.C., 1964-65; account supr. Cunningham & Walsh, N.Y.C., 1965-69, v.p., mgmt. supr., 1969-78, sr. v.p., dir. account mgmt., 1978-84, exec. v.p., gen. mgr., 1984-87; exec. v.p., account dir. N.W. Ayer, Inc., N.Y.C., 1987—, also bd. dirs. Republican. Roman Catholic. Office: NW Ayer Inc 1345 Ave of the Americas New York NY 10105

ALCORN, SAMUEL, insurance brokerage executive; b. Phila., May 31, 1927; s. David and Emily Sarah (Stewart) A.; children—Janet Elaine, Shelia Ann. Student Temple U., 1948-52; B.S. in Bus. Adminstrn., Washington U., St. Louis, 1955. Underwriter Wasau Ins. Cos., Phila., 1947-52, br. underwriting mgr., St. Louis, 1952-57, Los Angeles, 1957-59; mktg. mgr. Kuhrts, Cox & Brander, Los Angeles, 1959-63; v.p. mktg. Bayly, Martin & Fay, Los Angeles, 1963-73, v.p. then sr. v.p. Corp. Staff, 1973—, now sr. v.p. ops. and internat. devels. Cpl. USAAF, 1945-47. Mem. Soc. Chartered Property & Casualty Underwriters (publs. com.), Ins. Ednl. Assn (chmn. 1981-82), Am. Inst. for Liability & Property (trustee), Ins. Inst. Am. (trustee). Presbyterian. Lodge: Masons. Contbr. articles to ins. trade publs. Office: Bayly Martin & Fay Internat Inc 201 Main St Suite 1990 Fort Worth TX 76102

ALDEA, PATRICIA, architect; b. Bucharest, Romania, Mar. 18, 1947; came to U.S., 1976; d. Dan Jasmin Negreanu and Sonia (Friedgant) Philip-Negreanu; m. Val O. Aldea, Feb. 17, 1971; 1 child, Donna-Dana. MArch, Ion Mincu, Bucharest, 1970. Registered architect, N.Y. Architect, project. mgr. The Landmark Preservation Inst., Bucharest, 1971-76; architect Edward Durell Stone Assn., N.Y.C., 1977-79; assoc. architect, project mgr. Alan Lapidus P.C., N.Y.C., 1980—. Columnist Contemporanul art jour., 1969-73. Hist. landmarks study fellow Internationes Fed. Republic of Germany, 1974. Office: Alan Lapidus PC 2112 Broadway New York NY 11023

ALDEN, VERNON ROGER, financial executive; b. Chgo., Apr. 7, 1923; s. Arvid W. and Hildur Pauline (Johnson) A.; m. Marion Frances Parson, Aug. 18, 1951; children: Robert Parson, Anne Elizabeth, James Malcolm, David Douglas. AB magna cum laude, Brown U., 1945; MBA, Harvard, 1950; LL.D. (hon.), Brown U., 1964, Emerson Coll., 1957, Ohio Wesleyan U., 1964, R.I. Coll., 1965, William Jewell Coll., 1965, Loyola U., 1966, Wilberforce U., 1970, Ottawa U., 1970, Babson Coll., 1972; L.H.D., North Park Coll., 1965; Lit.D., Ohio U., 1969; D.P.S., Bowling Green U., 1969; Litt.D., Bethany Coll., 1970. Admission officer Brown U., 1946-48; asst. dir. admissions Northwestern U., 1950-51; dir. fin. aid Harvard Grad. Sch. Bus. Adminstrn., assoc. dean, faculty, 1951-61; pres. Ohio U., Athens, 1962-69; chmn. bd., chmn. exec. com. Boston Co. and subsidiary Boston Safe Deposit & Trust Co., 1969-78; Ednl. dir. U. Hawaii Advanced Mgmt. Program, summer 1960, Keio U. Advanced Mgmt. Program, Tokyo, summers 1960-61; bd. dirs. Augat Inc., Colgate-Palmolive Co., Digital Equipment Corp., Intermet Corp., McGraw-Hill Inc., Sonesta Internat. Hotels Corp. Chmn. Pres.'s Task Force to plan Job Corps program; chmn. com. Future U. of U. Mass., 1971; chmn. Mass. Coun. on Arts and Humanities, 1972-84; chmn. Mass. Bus. Devel. Coun. and Fgn. Bus. Coun., 1978-83; trustee Boston Symphony Orch.; chmn. arts facilities com. M.I.T.; bd. visitors Fletcher Sch. Law and Diplomacy; trustee Brown U., Lewis and Clark Coll., Mus. Sci., Boston, Northfield-Mt. Hermon Sch.; chmn. exec. com., trustee French Lib., Boston; overseer Mus. Fine Arts, Boston; mem. adv. coun. Harvard Program on Japan-U.S. Rels. Served to lt. USNR, 1943-46. Recipient Gov.'s award State Ohio, 1969; Founder's citation Ohio U., 1969; Bus. Statesman award Harvard Grad. Sch. Bus., 1975; decorated Order Rising Sun, Star, Disting. Civilian Svc. medal U.S. Army, 1969. Mem. Assn. Japan-Am. Socs (chmn.), Japan Soc. of Boston (pres.), Phi Beta Kappa, Phi Kappa Phi, Phi Delta Theta, Beta Gamma Sigma, Omicron Delta Kappa. Episcopalian. Clubs: Somerset (Boston); Edgartown Yacht (Martha's Vineyard); Country (Brookline); Farm Neck Golf (Martha's Vineyard); Mariner Sands Country (Fla.). Home: 37 Warren St Brookline MA 02146 Office: 20 Park Pla Ste 1028 Boston MA 02116

ALDERMAN, MINNIS AMELIA, psychologist, educator, small business owner; b. Douglas, Ga., Oct. 14, 1928; d. Louis Cleveland Sr. and Minnis Amelia (Wooten) A. AB in Music, Speech and Drama, Ga. State Coll., Milledgeville, 1949; MA in Supervision and Counseling Psychology, Murray State U., 1960; postgrad. Columbia Pacific U., 1987—. Tchr. music Lake County Sch. Dist., Umatilla, Fla., 1949-50; instr. vocal and instrumental music, dir. band, orch. and choral Fulton County Sch. Dist., Atlanta, 1950-54; instr. English, speech, debate, vocal and instrumental music, dir. drama, band, choral and orch. Elko County Sch. Dist., Wells, Nev., 1954-59; tchr. English and social studies Christian County Sch. Dist., Hopkinsville, Ky., 1960; instr. psychology, guidance counselor Murray (Ky.) State U., 1961-63, U. Nev., Reno, 1963-67; owner Minisizer Exercising Salon, Ely, Nev., 1969-71, Knit Knook, Ely, 1969—, Minimimeo, Ely, 1969—, Gift Gamut, Ely, 1977—; prof. dept. fine arts Wassuk Coll., Ely, 1986—, assoc. dean, 1986-87, dean, 1987—; counselor White Pine County Sch. Dist., Ely, 1960-68; dir. Child and Family Ctr., Ely Indian Colony, 1988—; supr. testing Ednl. Testing Svc., Princeton, N.J., 1960-68, Am. Coll. Testing Program, Iowa, 1960-68, U. Nev., Reno, 1960-68; chmn. bd. White Pine Sch. Dist. Employees Fed. Credit Union, Ely, 1961-69; psychologist mental hygiene div. Nev. Personnel, Ely, 1969-75, dept. employment security, 1975-80; sec.-treas. bd. dirs. Great Basin Enterprises, Ely, 1969-71; pvt. instr. piano, violin, voice and organ, Ely, 1981—; dir. band Sacred Heart Sch., Ely, 1982—. Author various news articles, feature stories, pamphlets, handbooks and grants in field. Pres. White Pine County Mental Health Assn., 1960-63, 78—; mem. Gov.'s Mental Health State Commn., 1963-65; bd. dirs. White Pine County Sch. Employees Fed. Credit Union, 1961-68, pres., 1963-68; 2d v.p. White Pine Community Concert Assn., 1965-67, pres., 1967, 85—, treas., 1975—, dr. chmn., 1981—; dir. Community Choir, 1975—; bd. dirs. White Pine chpt. ARC, 1978-82; mem. Nev. Hwy. Safety Leaders Bd., 1979-82; mem. Gov.'s Commn. on Status Women, 1968-74; sec.-treas. White Pine Rehab. Tng. Ctr. for Retarded Persons, 1973-75; mem. Gov.'s Commn. on Hwy. Safety, 1979-81; dir. Ret. Sr. Vol. Program, 1973-74; vice chmn. Great Basin Health Council, 1973-75, Home Extension Adv. Bd., 1977-80; sec.-treas. Great Basin chpt. Nev. Employees Assn.; bd. dirs. United Way, 1970-76; vice chmn. White Pine Council on Alcoholism and Drug Abuse, 1975-76, chmn., 1976-77; grants author, originator Community Tng. Center for Retarded People, 1972, Ret. Sr. Vol. Program, 1974, Nutrition Program for Sr. Citizens, 1974, Sr. Citizens Ctr., 1974, Home Repairs for Sr. Citizens, 1974, Sr. Citizens Home Assistance Program, 1977, Creative Crafters Assos., 1976, Inst. Current World Affairs, 1989—; bd. dirs. Sacred Heart Parochial Sch., 1982—, dir. band, 1982—; candidate for diaconal ministry, 1982—. Precinct reporter ABC News 1966. Fellow Am. Coll. Musicians, Nat. Guild Piano Tchrs.; mem. NEA (life), Nat. Fedn. Ind. Bus. (dist. chair 1971-85, nat. guardian council 1985—, state guardian council 1987—), AAUW (pres. Wells br. 1957-58, pres. White Pine br. 1965-66, 86-87, bd. dirs. 1965-87, rep. edn. 1965-67, implementation chair 1967-69, area advisor 1969-73), Nat. Fedn. Bus. and Profl. Women (1st v.p. Ely chpt. 1965-66, pres. Ely chpt. 1966-68, 74-76, 85—, bd. dirs. Nev. chpt. 1966—, 1st v.p. Nev. chpt. 1970-71, pres. Nev. chpt. 1972-73, nat. bd. dirs. 1972-73), Mensa (supr. testing 1965—), Delta Kappa Gamma (chpt. pres. 1968-72, state bd. 1967—, chpt. parliamentarian 1974-78, state 1st v.p. 1967-69, state pres. 1969-71, nat. bd. 1969-71, state parliamentarian 1971-73), White Pine Knife and Fork Club (1st v.p. 1969-70, pres. 1970-71, bd. dirs. 1979—). Home: 945 Ave H PO Box 457 East Ely NV 89315 Office: 16 Shoshone Cir Ely NV 89301 also: 13 Shoshone Circle Ely NV 89301

ALDERMAN, WALTER ARTHUR, JR., computer company, corporate rescue executive; b. Stoneham, Mass., July 29, 1945; s. Walter Arthur and Ida Ellen (Patchett) A.; m. Sandra May Johnston, Aug. 23, 1969; children: Walter Arthur III, Deborah Ellen. BSBA with honors, Northeastern U., 1968; MBA, Harvard U., 1971. Divisional controller Anken Industries, Williamstown, Mass., 1971-73; treas., controller James Hunter Machine Co., North Adams, Mass., 1973-78; gen. mgr. Petricca Industries, Pittsfield, Mass., 1978-80; chmn., pres. Alderman Assocs. Inc., Coral Springs, Fla., 1980-85, Bedford Computer Corp., Londonderry, N.H., 1985—; bd. dirs. Mahoney and Assocs., Inc., Springfield, Mass.; instr., mem. adv. bd. North Adams (Mass.) State Coll., 1976-78; registered rep. First New England Securities, Stockbridge, Mass., 1968-74. Bd. dirs., pres. Mass. C. of C., 1976-78, YMCA, 1976-78; commr. Indsl. Devel. Commn., Mass., 1976-78; section leader United Fund, Mass., 1977. Served to lt. U.S. Army Res., 1968-74. Named Entrepreneur of the Yr., Arthur Young/Venture Mag., Boston, 1987; recipient Outstanding Service award C. of C., 1978, Community Service award United Fund, 1977. Mem. Beta Gamma Sigma, Phi Kappa Phi. Office: Bedford Computer Corp 37 Indsl Dr Londonderry NH 03053

ALDERSON, CREED FLANARY, JR., financial services executive; b. Norton, Va., Nov. 21, 1933; s. Creed Flanary and Mary (Ford) A.; B.S. in Commerce, U. Va., 1959; m. Nicola DeChurch, July 16, 1983; children: Robert Barney, Mary Anne. Vice pres., resident mgr. Dean Witter Reynolds, Ft. Lauderdale, Fla., 1974-79; sr. v.p., resident mgr. Smith Barney, Ft. Lauderdale, 1979—. Served to 1st lt. C.E., U.S. Army, 1952-55. Clubs: University (Miami, Fla.); Boca Raton Hotel and Club. Home: 4900 N Ocean Blvd Ste 1516 Fort Lauderdale FL 33308 Office: Smith Barney 3696 N Federal Hwy Fort Lauderdale FL 33308

ALDERSON, GERALD ROBERT, finance company executive; b. San Jose, Calif., Aug. 28, 1946; s. Raymond Charles and Phyllis Laverne (Boston) A.; m. Roberta Gail Bradbury, Aug. 24, 1970; children: Alison, Anne, Katie, Kory. BS, Occidental Coll., 1968; MBA, Harvard U., 1970. Staff acct. Arthur Andersen & Co., San Francisco, 1970-71; dir. acctg. Itel Corp., San Francisco, 1972-74, controller, 1974-75, v.p., controller, 1975-76, v.p. planning and control, 1976-78, pres. lease fin. div., 1978-80; pres., chief exec. officer Kennetech Corp., San Francisco, 1980—; bd. dirs. RMR Corp., Energy Fin. Corp., San Francisco, Property Resources Equity Trust, Los Gatos, Calif. Republican. Club: Bankers (San Francisco). Office: Kenetech Corp 500 Sansome St Ste 600 San Francisco CA 94111

ALDRICH, FRANK NATHAN, banker; b. Jackson, Mich., June 8, 1923; s. Frank Nathan and Marion (Butterfield) A.; m. Edna Dora DeJan, Nov. 21, 1956; children: Marion Dolores, Clinton Pershing. Student, U. Md., summer 1943; A.B. in Govt, Dartmouth Coll., 1948; postgrad., Harvard U., summer 1948. Sub-mgr. First Nat. Bank of Boston, Havana, Cuba, 1949-60, Rio de Janeiro, Brazil, 1961-62; sub-mgr. Rio de Janeiro, Sao Paulo, Brazil, 1963-64; mgr. Rio de Janeiro, 1965, exec. mgr., 1966; v.p. Latin Am.-Asia-Africa-Middle East div., Boston, 1970-73; sr. v.p. Latin Am. div., Boston, 1973-88; pres., chief exec. officer McLaughlin Bank N.V., Netherlands Antilles, 1989—. Trustee Pan Am. Devel. Program, Washington. Served with USAAF, 1943-46. Decorated Air medal with 4 oak leaf clusters, D.F.C. U.S.; Medalha Marechal Candido Mariano da Silva Rondon (Brazil); Ordem Nacional do Cruzeiro do Sul (Brazil). Fellow Brit. Interplanetary Soc.; mem. Air Force Assn., Res. Officers Assn., Confederate Air Force, Inst. Nav., Royal Astron. Soc. Canada, Md. Hist. Soc., Am. C. of C. Rio de Janeiro, Am. C. of C. Sao Paulo, Sphinx Soc., Vets. of the Battle of the Bulge, Beta Theta Pi. Clubs: Harvard (Boston), Dartmouth College, Yale (N.Y.C.), Army and Navy (Washington), American (Miami, Fla.), Wellesley (Mass.) Country, Wellesley Coll. Lodges: Masons, Shriners. Home: 3 Indian Spring Rd Dover MA 02030 Office: Wilhelminaplein 14/16, Willemstad Netherlands Antilles

ALDRICH, FREDERIC DELONG, historian, educator; b. Port Huron, Mich., Nov. 2, 1899; s. Horace Nathan and Helen Grace (Champlain) A.; m. Dorothy May Lindquist, June 19, 1937; children: Frederic DeLong, John L., William J., Andrew L. AB, Willamette U., 1921; postgrad. U. Oreg., summer 1923; MA, Western Res. U., 1931, EdD, 1953. Tchr. history and English, coach Cleve. Sr. High Sch., 1921-40, 47-53; lectr. Western Res. U. Grad. Sch., Cleve., 1953-56; prof. edn., head edn. dept. Alderson-Broaddus Coll., Philippi, W.Va., 1956-57; dir. audio-visual center, chmn. edn. dept. Chatham Coll., Pitts., 1957-61; lectr. U. Vt., Burlington, 1962—; edn. specialist Vt. State Dept. Edn., 1966; cons. Gifted Children's Workshop, Kent State U., 1954; lectr. Pa. State U., 1958. Author: A Brief Outline of Church History, 1927, rev., 1977, The School Library in Ohio, 1959, History of Calvary Episcopal Church, Underhill, Vermont, 1978. Mem. Cuyahoga County Republican Exec. Com., 1934-38; chmn. finances Richmond (Vt.) Town Rep. Com., 1963-65, town chmn., 1965—; member Chittenden County Rep. Committee, 1965—; del. Vt. Rep. Conv., 1964, 66, Rep. Platform Conv., 1968—, Oreg. Rep. Nat. Conv., Cleve., 1924; justice of peace, mem. Bd. Civil Authority, Richmond, 1983—. Served to lt. col. AUS, 1941-46. Mem. Am. Hist. Assn., Orgn. Am. Historians, Medieval Acad. Am., North Central, Middle States Assns. Colls. and Secondary schs., Pitts. C. of C. (colls. and univs. com. 1957-61), Burlington-Lake Champlain C. of C. (legis. affairs and edn. coms. 1962—), Delta Theta Phi, Phi Delta Kappa. Episcopalian. Club: Barbour Country (Philippi, W.Va.); Univ. (Cleve.). Home: RD 1 PO Box 293 Richmond VT 05477

ALDRIDGE, CHARLES RAY, brokerage house executive, trade director; b. Jefferson City, Mo., July 23, 1946; s. Ray and Helen Frances (Fowler) A.; m. Jeannine Frances Holtmeier, May 11, 1974; children: Kimberly Rae, Steven Charles. BSBA in Fin., U. Mo., 1969, MA in Polit. Sci., 1973. Mktg. specialist Mo. Dept. Agr., Jefferson City, 1973-74; commodities broker Clayton Brokerage Co. St. Louis Inc., 1974-82; v.p. Stock Index Futures Co. Inc., St. Louis, 1982-87, pres., 1987—; v.p., dir. trading Alvery Bartlett Brokerage Co., St. Louis, 1982-87, pres., 1987—; cons. dir. Lehman Venture Capital, N.Y.C., 1984—. Contbr. articles to profl. jours. Served with U.S. Army, 1969-71, Vietnam. Decorated Bronze Star. Mem. Nat. Futures Assn., Phi Delta Theta (pres. Alumni Club 1984-85). Republican. Home: 11868 Shallowbrook Dr Saint Louis MO 63146 Office: Alvery Bartlett Brokerage Co 8182 Maryland Ave Saint Louis MO 63105

ALDRIDGE, DANNY WAYNE, limousine company executive; b. Little Rock, July 14, 1947; s. James Henry and Lillian Genoah (Franks) A.; divorced; 1 child, Christopher Patrick. BA, U. Ark., Little Rock, 1969. Sales rep. Xerox Corp., Little Rock, 1969-71; v.p. Ouachita Marine, Arkadelphia, Ark., 1971-76; v.p. sales and mktg. Vivian (La.) Indsl. Plastics, 1976-81, Armbruster Stageway, Ft. Smith, Ark., 1981-87; pres. Aldridge Internat. Coach Sales Inc., Plano, Tex., 1987—. Sec. Jaycees, Hot Springs, Ark., 1971; v.p. Young Dems. Ark., Little Rock, 1970; bd. dirs. Fulfill A Dream, Ft. Smith, 1981—. Republican. Baptist. Office: Aldridge Internat Coach Sales Inc 4101 West Plano Pkwy Plano TX 75075

ALDRIDGE, JAMES RAY, utility executive; b. Jackson, Miss., Mar. 23, 1930; s. Drew Weeks and Caroline (Talbert) A.; m. Lucie Jay Atkinson, June 26, 1952; children: Lucie Kathryn, James Drew. BA, Millsaps Coll., 1952; MA, Peabody U., 1955; PhD, U. Houston, 1987. Mgr. employee rels. GE, Houston, Detroit,, and Bridgeport, Conn., 1956-78; v.p. indsl. rels. and personnel Am. Standard, Inc., N.Y.C., 1978-80; v.p. human resources Gulf States Utilities Co., Beaumont, Tex., 1980—. Lt. (j.g.) USN, 1952-54. Carnegie Found. fellow, 1954-55. Mem. Kappa Delta Pi, Phi Delta Kappa. Home: 2490 Long Ave Beaumont TX 77702 Office: Gulf States Utilities Co PO Box 2951 350 Pine St Beaumont TX 77704

ALDRIDGE, ROGER MERLE, systems analyst, applications development consultant; b. Kansas City, Mo., Sept. 18, 1946; s. Merle R. and Juana M. (Rogers) A.; m. Peggy A. Sigler, Mar. 7, 1979; children: Angelle, Jheremy. BA, McKendree Coll., 1973; MA, N. Mex. Highlands U., 1974. Instr. music Fontbonne Coll., St. Louis, 1974-77; programmer, analyst Southwestern Bell, St. Louis, 1977-83; project leader Bell Atlantic, Silver Spring, Md., 1983-88; sr. application analyst Fannie Mae, Washington, 1988—; cons. Bell Atlantic, Silver Spring, 1988—; lectr.in computer sci. Montgomery Coll., Rockville, Md., 1988—. Mem. community action team Southwestern Bell, St. Louis, 1982-83, ch. coms. Sandy Spring Friends Meeting, Sandy Springs, Md., 1984-88; scoutmaster Boy Scouts Am., Silver Spring, 1987-88. Inst. for Sci. Studies grantee, 1973. Mem. Inst. for Cert. Computer Profls. (asst. area gov. 1979—), Soc. of Friends. Democrat. Clubs: Toastmasters; Friends of Earth (Sandy Spring). Office: Fannie Mae 3900 Wisconsin Ave NW Washington DC 20016

ALEDORT, PAUL JEFFREY, financial planner; b. N.Y.C., Feb. 16, 1954; s. David and Bernice (Vallon) A.; m. Kathy Kliegman, June 21, 1981; children: Diana Rachel, Brian Matthew. BBA, Eastern Mich. U., 1978; MBA, Adelphi U., 1987. Sr. actuarial asst. George Buck Cons., N.Y.C., 1979-83; pension analyst ITT Corp., N.Y.C., 1983-85; pres. Cert. Fin. Planning Corp., Hicksville, N.Y., 1985-87; fin. cons. New Eng. Fin. Advisors, N.Y.C., 1987—. Mem. Internat. Assn. for Fin. Planning (v.p. programs L.I. chpt. 1987—), Inst. Cert. Fin. Planners, Am. Pension Conf., Nat. Assn. Life Underwriters. Office: New Eng Fin Advisors 1230 Ave of the Americas New York NY 10020

ALESCHUS, JUSTINE LAWRENCE, land broker; b. New Brunswick, N.J., Aug. 13, 1925; d. Walter and Mildred Lawrence; student Rutgers U.; m. John Aleschus, Jan. 23, 1949; children—Verdene Jan, Janine Kimberley, Joanna Lauren. Dept. sec. Am. Baptist Home Mission Soc., N.Y.C., 1947-49; claims examiner Republic Ins. Co., Dallas, 1950-52; broker Damon Homes, L.I., 1960-72; exclusive broker estate of Kenneth H. Leeds, L.I., 1980—; pres. Justine Aleschus Real Estate. Past-pres. Nassau-Suffolk Council of Hosp. Aux., 1981-82; hon. mem. aux. of St. John's Episcopal Hosp., Smithtown, N.Y., past pres., hosp. adv. bd.; pres. L.I. Coalition for Sensible Growth, Inc.; mem. Smithtown Industry Adv. Bd.; exec. bd. dirs. Suffolk County council Boy Scouts Am.; mem. adv. bd. Suffolk County council Girl Scouts U.S. With Suffolk County Real Estate Bd. (pres.), L.I. Mid-Suffolk Businessmen's Assn., Eastern L.I. Execs. (v.p., sponsor-trustee), Smithtown Bus. and Profl. Women's Network, L.I. Assn., JEI Com., Hauppauge Indsl. Assn. Advancement Commerce & Industry. Republican. Lutheran. Club: Sky Island (gov.). Office: Kenneth H Leeds 300 Hawkins Ave Lake Ronkonkoma NY 11779

ALEXANDER, BEVERLY MOORE, mechanical engineer; b. Portsmouth, Va., Apr. 11, 1947; d. Julian Morgan and Ezefferlee (Griffin) Moore; m. Ronald Lee Rutherford, Dec. 21, 1969 (div. Dec. 1977); m. Larry Ray Alexander, Mar. 4, 1978. BS, Aero. Engring., Va. Poly. Inst. and State U., 1969; postgrad., U. New Orleans. Registered profl. engr., La. Assoc. engr. McDonnell Douglas Corp., St. Louis, 1969-74; design engr. Bell Aerospace Textron, New Orleans, 1974-81; supr. systems integration, New Orleans, 1981-83, chief interface activities, 1983-84; chief engr. Bell Aerospace Textron, New Orleans, 1984-85, dir. engring. planning and control, 1985-86, chief engr. engring. services, 1986—. Mem. La. Engring. Soc., Nat. Assn. Female Execs., ASNE, SNAME. Republican. Episcopalian. Home: 313 Margon CT Slidell LA 70458 Office: Textron Marine Systems 6800 Plaza Dr New Orleans LA 70127

ALEXANDER, BRUCE DONALD, real estate executive; b. Hartford, Conn., May 11, 1943. BA, Yale U., 1965; JD, Duke U., 1968. With Rouse Co., Balt., 1969—, sr. v.p., dir. comml. devel. div., 1978—; bd. dirs. Balt. Equitable Ins. Co. Trustee Goucher Coll., Balt., 1984—; trustee Columbia (Md.) Found., 1981-86, pres., 1983-85; bd. dirs. Balt. Symphony Orch., 1986—. Office: Rouse Co 10275 Little Patuxent Pkwy Columbia MD 21044

ALEXANDER, CHERYL LEE, executive search and consulting firm executive; b. Mpls., Feb. 22, 1946; d. Wallace Einar and Dorothy Florence (Abrahamson) Arneson; m. Douglas Joel Hawkinson, Mar. 5, 1966; children: Tamara Lee, Alexander Lowell. Student, Gustavus Adolphus Coll., 1964-66, Nan Yang U., Singapore, 1971; BA summa cum laude, U. Minn., 1972. Personnel recruiter Nat. Recruiters, Mpls., 1972; pres. Alexander Recruiters, Mpls., 1973-79, Alexander Cos., (formerly Alexander Recruiters), Mpls., 1979—; former dir. Micro Application Systems, Inc., Proto Circuits, Inc.; lectr. numerous univs.; faculty, adv. Master Class, Inc. Author: Up The Typewriter, 1977; Transition Management, 1980; subject of interviews by profl. jours, TV and radio. Advisor Hennepin County Pvt. Industry Council, Mpls., 1981-83; mem. St. Paul Set-Aside Adv. Com., 1981-82, Mpls. Tech. Enterprise Ctr., 1984—; participant White House Conf. on Small Bus., 1980; judge Internat. Sci. and Engring. Fair, 1980; bd. dirs. Children's Communication Exchange, 1981-82. Mem. Soc. Women Engrs. (founder, bd. dirs., sec.), Assn. Women in Computing (founder, bd. dirs., v.p. 1978-79), Nat. Assn. Women Bus. Owners (founder, bd. dirs. v.p., nat. sec. 1978-81). Avocations: tennis, public speaking, skiing, sailing. Office: Alexander Cos 3205 Casco Cir Wayzata MN 55391

ALEXANDER, DIANE MARIE, telemarketing and sales executive; b. Clinton, Okla., Aug. 31, 1945; d. Edwin Michael Jr. and Gloria Louise (McCray) Drass; m. Larry Edward Allen, Dec. 18, 1965 (div. Aug. 1972); children: Larry Dean, Lynn Edward; m. Nicol Brandon Alexander, June 28, 1980 (div. Jan. 1988); children: Danielle Nicole, Derek Brandon. Student, Lindenwood Coll., 1963-64, Abilene Christian Coll., 1964-65. Cert. neurolinguistic programming practioner, 1989. Telesales rep. GTE Corp., Irving, Tex., 1974-77, dist. telesales mgr., 1977-78; v.p. Brandon and Assocs., Inc., Grand Prairie, Tex., 1980-81; v.p. TeleMktg. Enterprises, Inc., Grand Prairie, 1982-88, pres., owner, 1988—; v.p. mktg. Barakel Corp., Arlington, Tex., 1981-82; pub. speaker various civic and trade orgns., IRA Summit Conv., New Orleans, 1986, TBT Conv., Atlanta, 1988, Orland, 1989; cons., tchr. Internat. Aviation and Travel Acad./Frontier Airlines, Arlington, Tex., 1983-84. Author: Advanced Communications Technology, 1980, Telemarketing Series, 1982-87, Professional TeleAppointments, 1985; contbr. articles to profl. jours. Jr. Achievement scholar Lindenwood Coll., 1963. Mem. Am. Soc. Tng. and Devel., Assn. Women Entrepreneurs of Dallas, Internat. Customer Svc. Assn. (conv. speaker Orlando chpt. 1989). Republican. Episcopalian. Office: Telemktg Enterprises Inc 2307 Oak Ln Ste 115 Grand Prairie TX 75051

ALEXANDER, FRANK LYON, corporate executive; b. Parkersburg, W.Va., May 9, 1939; s. Edward Eugene and Sarah Beerits (Lyon) A.; m. Grace Delano Tyler, Sept. 10, 1966; children: Frank Lyon, Priscilla Brooke. BS, Princeton U., 1961; MBA, Harvard U., 1967. Fin. and bus. mgr. Union Carbide Corp., N.Y.C., 1967-79; v.p. fin. Oxirane Internat., Princeton, N.J., 1979-81; dir. internat. planning and devel. ARCO Chem. Co., Phila., 1981-83; treas. Dun & Bradstreet Corp., N.Y.C., 1983-86, v.p. investor services, 1986—. Served to lt. USN, 1961-65. Schepp scholar, 1965-67. Mem. Princeton Univ. Rowing Assn. (trustee 1980-86), Nat. Investor Relations Inst. Republican. Episcopalian. Clubs: Princeton (N.Y.), Bedens Brook (Princeton). Home: 21 Nelson Ridge Rd Princeton NJ 08540 Office: Dun & Bradstreet Corp 299 Park Ave New York NY 10171

ALEXANDER, HAROLD CAMPBELL, insurance consultant; b. Houston, Dec. 11, 1920; s. Henry Campbell and Essie Mae (Gilbert) A.; m. Dorothy Emma Schraub, Aug. 21, 1925; children: Linda Carol, Beverly Lynn Whitworth, Daniel James Alexander, William Campbell. BS, Miss. State U., 1938-42; postgrad., South Tex. Sch. Law, 1954-56, Harvard U., 1943, Navy Fin. and Supply Sch., 1942-43. Asst. div. credit mgr. Continental Emsco Co., Houston, 1953-56; gen. agt. and mgr. United Founders Life Ins. Co., 1956-69; mgr. Holt & Bridges Ins., Houston, 1960-69; owner, pres. Holt & Alexander Ins. Agy., Inc., Houston, 1969-85; ins. cons. Lawrence Ilfrey & Co., Houston, 1985—. Mem. Houston Adv. Council Bd., 1985; bd. dirs. 500 Club Ltd., Houston, 1984—. Served as lt. commdr. USN, 1942-46, 1950-52. Mem. Profl. Ins. Agts. Tex. (state bd. dirs. 1973-74), Soc. Cert. Ins. Counselors. Republican. Presbyterian. Club: Pine Forest Country, Club of Houston. Home: 8727 Manhattan Houston TX 77096 Office: Lawrence Ilfrey & Co 5200 San Felipe Houston TX 77056

ALEXANDER, JUDD HARRIS, paper company executive; b. Owatonna, Minn., Mar. 23, 1925; s. Mark Hastings and Veta Enola (Harris) A.; m. Theo Mary Paltzer, May 19, 1956; children: Morah Lee, Duncan McIndoe, Todd Stewart. B.A., Carleton Coll., 1949; postgrad. in bus, Harvard U., 1967. Co-founder Nu-Bilt Co., Owatonna; dir. Nu-Bilt Co., 1942-71; sec. in pres.'s office, salesman Marathon Corp., Rothschild, Wis., 1949-57; with Am. Can Co., Greenwich, Conn., 1957—, v.p., gen. mgr. spl. products packaging, 1972-73, sr. v.p. group exec. packaging, 1974-75, sr. v.p. office of chmn., 1975-81, exec. v.p. paper sector, 1981-82; exec. v.p. James River Corp., Norwalk, Conn., 1982—; chmn. Paperboard Packaging Council, 1976-78, Can Mfrs. Inst., 1978-80, Solid Waste Council of Paper Industry, 1977—; adj. prof. environ. sci. SUNY, Syracuse, 1979-84. Contbr. articles to profl. and bus. jours., including Wall Street Jour., N.Y. Times, Industry Week. Trustee Carleton Coll., 1973—, Am. Shakespeare Theater, 1980-82; bd. dirs. New Eng. Legal Found., 1979-82, Norwalk (Conn.) Hosp., 1985—; chmn. bd. trustees Keep Am. Beautiful, 1986—. Served with U.S. Army, 1943-46. Decorated Combat Inf. badge; Woodrow Wilson vis. fellow, 1975-82. Mem. Conn. Bus. and Industry Assn. (dir. 1976-80). Republican. Congregationalist. Clubs: Country (Darien, Conn.); North Shore Golf (Menasha, Wis.); Quechee (Vt.). Home: 2 Woods End Rd Darien CT 06820 Office: James River Corp Tredegar St Richmond VA 23219

ALEXANDER, NORMAN E., diversified manufacturing company executive; b. N.Y.C., 1914; m. Marjorie Wulf; four children. AB, Columbia U., 1934, LLB, 1936. Chmn. bd., chief exec. officer Sequa Corp., N.Y.C., 1957—; chmn. bd. Chromalloy Am. Corp., St. Louis, 1980-86; bd. dirs. Chock Full o' Nuts, N.Y.C., 1982—, Interim Systems Corp., N.Y.C., 1987. Past chmn. bd. trustees N.Y. Med. Coll./Flower-Fifth Ave. Hosps.; trustee Rockefeller U. Coun. Mem. NAM (trustee), Conf. Bd., Chief Execs. Forum (bd. dir.). Office: Sequa Corp 200 Park Ave New York NY 10106 also: Ampacet Corp 250 S Terrace Ave Mount Vernon NY 10550

ALEXANDER, PETER ALBERT, banker; b. Shreveport, Feb. 24, 1942; s. Edward P. and Nicole M. (Ducrot) A.; m. Margaret Hickman Powell; children: Corinne Eve Nicole, Marc Edward Drake. B.A., Hautes Etudes Commerciales, Paris, 1964; M.B.A., Wharton Sch., U. Pa., 1966. With Chem. Bank, N.Y.C., 1971—; regional v.p. N. Asia Chem. Bank, Tokyo, 1977; sr. v.p. multinat. group Chem. Bank, N.Y.C., 1981-83; sr. v.p., div. head-Europe London, 1983-87; sr. bus. bus. mgr. banking and corp. fin. group N.Y.C., 1987—. Home: 80 Prospect Hill Ave Summit NJ 07901 Office: Chem Bank House, 180 Strand, London WC2R 1ET, England

ALEXANDER, SAMUEL ALLEN, JR., electronics company executive; b. Washington, Oct. 9, 1938; s. Samuel Allen and Mary Pearl (Last) A.; B.S. and B.A., Tufts U., 1962; postgrad. in biochemistry George Washington U., 1963; m. Susan Karinch, Aug. 25, 1973; children—Carolyn, Samuel Allen, Emily, Jonathan, David, Susan M. Investment banker, registered rep. Ferris & Co., Washington, 1966-69; pres. Command Fin., Washington, 1969-72, Potomac Fed. Corp., Washington, 1973-75; v.p. adminstrn. and ops. officer

Potter Instrument Co., Gonic, N.H., 1975-78, pres., chief exec. officer, 1978-83; pres. successor firm Precision Magnetics and Ceramics, 1984-86; chmn. bd., chief exec. officer ETI Techs., 1986—; participant investment banking seminar Wharton Sch. Bus., U. Pa., 1968-69. Mem. Delta Tau Delta. Roman Catholic. Clubs: Chevy Chase (Md.); Army Navy (Washington); Lake Sunapee Yacht (Sunapee, N.H.).

ALEXANDERSON, ALVIN, financial executive; b. Detroit, May 26, 1947; s. Eldon and Emily Pauline Alexanderson; m. Mary Jo Lackey; children: Lindsay, Bryan. BS in Bus., Hillsdale Coll., 1969; JD, U. Mich., 1971. Mgmt. trainee Bank of Commonwealth, Detroit, 1969; asst. atty. gen. Dept. Justice, State of Oreg., Salem, 1972-78; asst. gen. counsel Portland (Oreg.) Gen. Electric Co., 1979-86; v.p. fin., treas. Portland Gen. Corp., 1986-88; pres. Portland Gen. Exch., Inc., 1988—. Mem. Fin. Execs. Inst., Oreg. State Bar. Club: Univ. (Portland). Office: Portland Gen Corp 121 SW Salmon St Portland OR 97204

ALEXIOU, MARINA S., business management company executive; b. N.Y.C., Feb. 12, 1940; d. Stanley and Mary S. (Couloumbi) A. Cert. in bus. mgmt. U. N.C., 1959; student bus. mgmt. Ctr. for Degree Studies, Scranton, Pa. Legal sec. Jordan, Wright, Henson & Nichols, attys., Greensboro, N.C., 1959-60; with North Am. Philips Co., 1961— (company mergered with Consol. Electronics 1969 then became North Am. Philips Corp.), adminstrv. asst. to pres. and dir., 1965-69, adminstrv. asst. to chmn., chief exec. officer, pres. and dir., 1969-77, adminstrv. asst to chmn., chief exec. officer and dir., 1978-80, adminstrv. asst. to chmn. and dir., chmn. governing com. U.S. Philips Trust, 1981-84, adminstrv. asst. to dir., chmn. governing com. U.S. Philips Trust, 1985-86, mgr. corp. purchasing, 1985—. Mem. U.S. Senatorial Bus. Adv. Bd. and Steering Com., Washington; adv. bd. Am. Security Council, Washington. Asst. chmn. fund raising Am. Cancer Soc., 1978—, mem. exec. com., 1985—. Dep. chmn. exec. Republican Com. of Bronxville (N.Y.), 1980—; mem. Rep. Presdl. Task Force, Washington, Rep. Senatorial Inner Circle. Mem. Nat. Assn. Exec. Sec., Nat. Assn. Female Execs., Am. Soc. Profl. and Exec. Women, Internat. Platform Assn., UN We Believe (exec. planning com.), Smithsonian Nat. Assocs., N.Y. Philharm. Soc. Republican. Greek Orthodox. Lodge: Toastmasters (charter). Home: Northgate Alger Ct Bronxville NY 10708 Office: NAm Philips Corp 100 E 42nd St New York NY 10017

ALEXY, R. JAMES, manufacturing company executive; b. Washington, Pa., Oct. 24, 1940; s. Robert J. and Julia S. (Stevens) A.; m. Sue Anne Snyder, Sept. 1, 1962; children: Brooke Elizabeth, Jennifer Paige. B.A., Cornell U., 1962, M.B.A., 1964. Indsl. sales mgr. Scott Paper Co., Phila., 1964-67; div. mktg./sales mgr. Brown Co., Gulf & Western Industries, Kalamazoo, 1968-71; div. gen. mgr. Brown Co., Gulf & Western Industries, N.Y.C., 1971-73; group v.p., gen. mgr. Brown Co., Gulf & Western Industries, Eau Claire, Wis., 1973-79; exec. v.p. Pope & Talbot, Inc., Eau Claire, 1980-81, Ft. Howard Corp., Green Bay, Wis., 1981—; pres. Md. Cup Corp. subs. Ft. Howard Corp., 1984—; dir. First Wis. Nat. Bank, Eau Claire. Chmn. United Way, Eau Claire, 1981; bd. dirs. Eau Claire YMCA; bd. advisers U. Wis., Stout, U. Wis.-Eau Claire Found. Mem. Am. Paper Inst. (past pres. tissue div.). Republican. Clubs: N.Y. Athletic (N.Y.C.); Oneida Country (Green Bay); Greenspring Valley Hunt (Garrison, Md.). Home: 2071 Trissino Way Green Bay WI 54304 Office: Fort Howard Corp PO Box 19130 Green Bay WI 54307

AL-FADHLY, WALLEED S. See WEST, JAMES

ALFORD, JOAN FRANZ, entrepreneur; b. St. Louis, Sept. 16, 1940; d. Henry Reisch and Florence Mary (Shaughnessy) Franz; m. Charles Hebert Alford, Dec. 28, 1978; stepchildren: Terry, David, Paul. BS, St. Louis U., 1962; postgrad. Consortium of State Univ., Calif., 1975-77; MBA, Pepperdine U., 1987, postgrad., Fielding Inst. Head user services Lawrence Berkeley Lab., Calif., 1977-78, head software support and devel. Computer Ctr., 1978-82, dep. head, 1980-81; regional site analyst mgr. Cray Research, Inc., Pleasanton, Calif., 1982-83; owner, pres. Innovative Leadership, Oakland, Calif., 1983—. Contbr. articles to profl. jours. Bd. dirs., sec. Vol. Ctrs. of Alameda, Oakland, 1985, bd. dirs., 1984—; campaign mem. Marge Gibson for County Supr., Oakland, 1984; mem. Oakland Piedmont Rep. Orgn., Alameda County Apt. Owners Assn., 1982. Mem. Assn. Computing Machinery, Spl. Interest Group on Computer Personnel Research. (past chmn.), Internat. Platform Assn., Small Owners for Fair Treatment. Republican. Clubs: Claremont Pool and Tennis, Lakeview, San Francisco Opera Guild. Avocations: swimming, skiing, opera, horseback riding, gardening. Home: 2605 Beaconsfield Pl Oakland CA 94611 Office: Innovative Leadership 2605 Beaconsfield Pl Oakland CA 94611

ALFORD, LIONEL DEVON, manufacturing company executive; b. Winnsboro, La., Mar. 1, 1925; s. Columbus F. and Jennie A. (Lee) A.; m. Sallie Julia Bryan, Feb. 2, 1951; children: Lionel Devon Jr., Scott Franklin. B.S. in M.E, La. Tech. U., 1951; postgrad. (Sloan fellow), Stanford U., 1966. Test pilot Boeing Co., Seattle, 1955-59; mgr. various missile test ops. Boeing Co., 1959-65; pres. Boeing Mil. Airplane Co., Seattle and Wichita, Kans., 1977-84; corp. sr. v.p. The Boeing Co., Seattle and Wichita, Kans., 1984—; bd. dirs. Fourth Fin. Corp., Wichita. Kans. vol. state chmn. U.S. Savs. Bonds, 1980—; bd. dirs. St. Francis Regional Med. Ctr., Wichita, Kans. Foodbank Warehouse, Inc. With USAF, 1943-46, 51-54. Decorated D.F.C., Air medal with 3 oak leaf clusters. Mem. Mil. Airlift Commn., Nat. Def. Transp. Assn., Stanford U. Alumni Assn. Republican. Baptist. Office: Boeing Co PO Box 7730 Wichita KS 67277-7730

ALFORD, SYLVIA ELENA, human resources executive; b. Coral Gables, Fla., Nov. 22, 1954; d. Peter and Norma (Viera) Guarisco; m. Randall Lynn Alford, Aug. 27, 1983. BS, Samford U., 1976. Asst. in personnel Fla. Dept. Banking and Fin., Tallahassee, 1978-80; dir. Fla. Realtors Polit. Action Com., Tallahassee, 1980-83; adminstrv. asst. Marine Resources Council East Cen. Fla., Melbourne, 1984-85; spl. asst. Brevard County Bd. of County Commrs., Melbourne, 1985-88; assoc. Devel. Strategies Inc., Satellite Beach, Fla., 1988; personnel officer Brevard County Bd. County Commrs., Merritt Island, Fla., 1988—. Coord. Fla. Senatorial Campaigns, Leon and Brevard Counties, 1976, 84; vol. coord. Haven for Children Inc., Satellite Beach, 1987-88; bd. dirs. Jr. League S. Brevard, Melbourne, 1986-88, ARC of Brevard County, 1987—; mem. distbn. bd. United Way Brevard County, 1986-87; chair community council com. Fla. Inst. Tech., Melbourne, 1988—; mem. lang. com. Space Coast Council Internat. Visitors, Melbourne, 1986-88. Mem. South Brevard Profl. Women's Network, Fla.-Colombia Ptnrs. (mem. bus. and industry com. 1984-85), Am. Bus. Women's Assn., Am. Assn. U. Women (v.p. 1986-87, parliamentarian 1987-88, recording sec. 1988—), Toastmasters (v.p. 1986-88), Circulo Cultural Hispano (treas. 1984-86) Rotary Ann, Phi Chi Theta. Republican. Southern Baptist. Home: 630 Hunan St NE Palm Bay FL 32907 Office: Brevard County Bd County Commrs 2575 N Courtenay Pkwy Merritt Island FL 32953

ALI, NAWAB, electrical engineering company executive; b. Nakodar, Punjab, India, Mar. 2, 1937; s. Haji Rahmat and June Ali; m. Bertha Ali, Aug. 4, 1962; children: Raza, Linda, Rahmat David. BS in Agr., Punjab U., Lahore, Pakistan, 1952; BSEE, U. Calif., Berkeley, 1959; MSEE, West Coast U., 1965; Phd in Elec. Engring., Century U., 1984. Program dir. Sera Lab, San Carlos, Calif., 1974-78; engring. supr. Tech. Devel. Corp., Santa Clara, Calif., 1978-82; engring. mgr. Nicolet, Fremont, Calif., 1982-85; project mgr. E.M. Systems, Fremont, 1985—; cons. Frontier Corp., Santa Ana, Calif., 1972-74. Author: Topology & Placement of Semicustom Gate-Arrays, 1984; inventor. Mem. AAAS, IEEE, Assn. for Computer Engrs. Machinery, Wescon Exhibit, Assn. Old Crows. Home: 20034 Wheaton Dr Cupertino CA 95014 Office: EM Systems 45757 W Northport Loop Fremont CA 94539

ALIBER, JAMES A., bank executive; b. 1925; married. BA, U. Mich., 1947. Asst. buyer J.L. Hudson Co., Detroit, 1947-49; with advt. sales dept. R.L. Polk & Co., Detroit, 1949-54; asst. cashier Nat. Bank Detroit, 1954-57; exec. asst. First Fed. Mich., Detroit, 1957-58, v.p., 1958-65, treas., 1960-66, exec. v.p., 1965-69, pres., 1969-79, chief exec. officer, 1977—, chmn., 1979—, also bd. dirs. Served to lt. (j.g.) USN, 1943-46. Office: 1st Fed Mich 1001 Woodward Detroit MI 48226 *

ALIBRANDI, JOSEPH FRANCIS, diversified industrial company executive; b. Boston, Nov. 9, 1928; s. Paul and Anna (Amendolia) A.; m. Lambertha A. Araskiewicz, May 12, 1957; children: Paul, Ann-Marie, Carolyn. B.S.M.E., MIT, 1952. With Fairchild Engring. & Airplane Corp., 1951; mgr. indsl. engring. dept. Raytheon Co., Lexington, Mass., 1952-56; asst. plant mgr. Raytheon Co., Lowell, Mass., 1956-58, plant mgr., 1958-62, ops. mgr., 1962-65, v.p., gen. mgr., 1965-68, sr. v.p., gen. mgr., 1968-70; exec. v.p., dir. Whittaker Corp., Los Angeles, 1970, pres., 1970-86, chief exec. officer, 1974—, chmn., 1986—; dir. Fed. Res. Bank of San Francisco, 1973-76, chmn., 1977-79; dir. Daniel, Mann, Johnson & Mendenhall, Los Angeles, from 1979; mem. Western region adv. bd. Arkwright-Boston Ins., San Francisco, from 1978. Mem. corp. vis. com. Sloan Sch. Mgmt., MIT, from 1972, corp. vis. com. dept. biology, from 1979, mem. corp. devel. com., from 1973, mem. nat. bus. com., from 1977; chmn. bus. adv. council UCLA, from 1976, exec. com. bd. visitors Grad. Sch. Mgmt., from 1979; bd. councilors Sch. Bus. Adminstrn., U. So. Calif., from 1977; bd. dirs. Los Angeles World Affairs Council, from 1980. Served with U.S. Army, 1946-48. Mem. U.S. C. of C. (internat. policy com. from 1978). Office: Whittaker Corp 10880 Wilshire Blvd Los Angeles CA 90024 *

ALIG, FRANK DOUGLAS STALNAKER, construction company executive; b. Indpls., Oct. 10, 1921; s. Clarence Schirmer and Marjory (Stalnaker) A.; m. Ann Bobbs, Oct. 22, 1949; children: Douglas, Helen, Barbara. Student U. Mich., 1939-41; BS, Purdue U., 1948. Registered profl. engr., Ind. Project engr. Ind. State Hwy. Commn., Indpls., 1948; pres. Alig-Stark Constrn. Co., Inc., 1949-57, Frank S. Alig, Inc., 1957—; chmn. bd. Concrete Structures Corp., Indpls.; v.p., dir. Bo-Wit Products Corp., Edinburg, Ind.; pres. dir. Home Stove Realty Co.; pres, dir. Home Land Investment Co., Inc. Served with AUS, 1943-46. Mem. U.S. Soc. Profl. Engrs., Ind. Soc. Profl. Engrs., Indpls. C. of C., Woodstock Club, Dramatic Club, Lambs Club. Republican. Presbyterian.

ALLAIRE, PAUL ARTHUR, office equipment company executive; b. Worcester, Mass., July 21, 1938; s. Arthur E. Allaire and Elodie (LePrade) Murphy; m. Kathleen Buckley, Jan. 26, 1963; children—Brian, Christiana. B.S.E.E., Worcester Poly. Inst., 1960; M.S.I.A., Carnegie-Mellon U., 1966. Fin. analyst Xerox Corp., Rochester, N.Y., 1966-70; dir. fin. analysis Rank Xerox Ltd., London, 1970-73; dir. internat. ops. fin. Xerox Corp., Stamford, Conn., 1973-75; chief staff officer Rank Xerox Ltd., London, 1975-79, mng. dir., 1979-83; sr. v.p., chief staff officer Xerox Corp., Stamford, 1983-86, pres., 1986—, also bd. dirs.; mem. investment policy adv. com. U.S. Trade Rep.; dir. Rank Xerox Ltd., Crum & Forster, Morristown, N.J. Patron, Am. European Community Assn., London, 1982; bd. dirs. Nat. Planning Assn., Washington, 1986, chmn. Com. on New Am. Realities, 1986; bd. dirs. Waveny Care Ctr., New Canaan, Conn., 1984; bus. adv. council Grad. Sch. Indsl. Adminstrn. Carnegie Mellon U., also univ. trustee; trustee Worchester Poly. Inst. Mem. Tau Beta Pi, Eta Kappa Nu. Democrat. Office: Xerox Corp PO Box 1600 Stamford CT 06904 *

ALLARD, JAMES EDWARD, oil company executive; b. Rockville, Conn., Dec. 10, 1942; s. Napoleon G. and Dorothea A. (Barbero) A.; m. Vicky Sanford, Oct. 3, 1964; children: Valerie, Marjorie, Jessica. BS, U. Conn., 1964; postgrad., Cornell U., 1976, Harvard U., 1984. Mgr. fin. Amoco Internat. Oil Co., London, 1977-79; div. controller Standard Oil Co. of Ind., Chgo., 1980-81, treas., 1981-82, controller, 1981-86; v.p. and treas. Amoco Corp., Chgo., from 1986; sr. v.p. fin. and adminstrn. Amoco Corp., Calgary, Alta., Can. Office: Amoco Corp, 240 4th Ave SW, Calgary, AB Canada T2P 4H4 *

ALLBRITTON, JOE LEWIS, business executive; b. D'Lo, Miss., Dec. 29, 1924; s. Lewis A. and Ada (Carpenter) A.; m. Barbara Jean Balfanz, Feb. 23, 1967; 1 son, Robert Lewis. LL.B., Baylor U., 1949, LL.D. (hon.), 1964, J.D., 1969; L.H.D., Calif. Bapt. Coll., 1973. Bar: Tex. 1949. Dir. Perpetual Corp., Houston, 1958—; pres. Perpetual Corp., 1965-76, 78-81, chmn. bd., 1973—; chmn. bd. Pierce Nat. Life Ins. Co., Los Angeles, 1958-72, 75—, dir., 1958—; chmn. bd. Univ. Bancshares, Inc., Houston, 1975—, Allbritton Communications Co., 1974—, Houston Fin. Svcs., Ltd., London, 1977—, Riggs Nat. Corp., Washington, 1981—; dir. Riggs Nat. Bank, Washington, 1981—, chmn., 1983—; mem. Greater Washington Bd. Trade, 1983-88. Trustee Fed. City Council, Washington, 1975—, Jonh F. Kennedy Ctr. Performing Arts, Washington, 1985—, trustee Nat. Geographic Soc., 1986—, The Mitre Corp. Bedofrd, Mass., 1987—. Served with USN, 1943-46. Mem. State Bar Tex., Assn. Res. City Bankers, Nat. Geographic Soc. (trustee 1986—). Office: Perpetual Corp 5615 Kirby Dr Ste 310 Houston TX 77005

ALLDREDGE, ROBERT LOUIS, manufacturing company executive; b. Johnston City, Ill., Feb. 11, 1922; s. Samuel and Mary Elizabeth (Kreie) A.; B.S. in Chem. Engring., U. Denver, 1942; m. Shirley Alice Harrod, Dec. 15, 1944; children—Alice Louise, Mark Harrod. Research assoc. E.I. DuPont de Nemours & Co., Eastern Lab., Gibbstown, N.J., 1942-44; engring. research assoc. Manhattan Project, Los Alamos (N.Mex.) Sci. Lab., 1944-46; chem. engr. Denver Research Inst., U. Denver, 1946-50; pres. Alldredge & McCabe, Denver, 1950-81, exec., 1981—; pres. Serpentix Conveyor Corp., Denver, 1969—, Serpentix, Inc., Denver, 1969—; dir. Beryl Ores Co., Broomfield, Colo. Served with C.E., U.S. Army, 1944-46. Mem. Nat. Soc. profl. Engrs. (founding mem. Colo. div.), U. Denver Alumni Assn. (dir. 1965-72), Am. Chem. Soc., Profl. Engrs. Colo., AAAS, Sigma Alpha Epsilon. Methodist. Contbr. articles to profl. jours. Home: 130 Pearl St 1108 Denver CO 80203 Office: Alldredge & McCabe 9085 Marshall Ct Westminster CO 80030

ALLEGRA, PETER ALEXANDER, lawyer; b. N.Y.C., Nov. 19, 1953; s. Edward Colombo and Frances Paula (Masella) A.; m. Karen Lloyd Middleton, July 16, 1983; children: Francesca Paula, Edward Christopher. BA, Boston Coll., 1975; JD, Seton Hall, 1979. Law sec. N.J. Superior Ct., Freehold, 1979-80; atty. Allegra, Paley & Forsman, Red Bank, N.J., 1980—; lectr. Am. Inst. Banking, Long Branch, N.J., 1982-84; mock trial coordinator N.J. State Bar Assn., Jersey City, 1985—; adv. trustee Ocean-Monmouth Legal Services, Freehold, N.J., 1986—. Mem. ABA, N.J. Bar, Fla. Bar, U.S. Supreme Ct. Bar, Assn. Trial Lawyers Am. Roman Catholic. Clubs: Dante Alighieri (N.J.), Figli di Colombo (N.J.). Office: Allegra Paley & Forsman 286 Broad St Red Bank NJ 07701

ALLEN, BELLE, management consulting firm executive, communications company executive; b. Chgo.; d. Isaac and Clara (Friedman) A. Ed., U. Chgo. Cons., v.p., treas., dir. William Karp Cons. Co. Inc., Chgo., 1961-79, chmn. bd., pres., treas., 1979—; pres. Belle Allen Communications, Chgo., 1961—; v.p., treas., bd. dirs. Cultural Arts Survey Inc., Chgo., 1965-79; cons., bd. dirs. Am. Diversified Rsch. Corp., Chgo., 1967-70; v.p., sec., bd. dirs. Mgmt. Performance Systems Inc., 1976-77; cons. City Club Chgo., 1962-65, Ill. Commn. on Tech. Progress, 1965-67; mem. Ill. Gov.'s Grievance Panel for State Employees, 1979—; mem. grievance panel Ill. Dept. Transp., 1985—; mem. adv. governing bd. Ill. Coalition on Employment of Women, 1980—; spl. program advisor President's Project Partnership, 1980—; mem. consumer adv. coun. FRS, 1979—. Editor: Operations Research and the Management of Mental Health Systems, 1968; contbr. articles to profl. jours. Mem. campaign staff Adlai E. Stevenson II, 1952, 56, John F. Kennedy, 1960; founding mem. women's bd. United Cerebral Palsy Assn., Chgo., 1954, bd. dirs., 1954-58; pres. Dem. Fedn. Ill., 1958-61; pres. conf. staff Eleanor Roosevelt, 1960; mem. Welfare Pub. Rels. Forum, 1960-61; bd. dirs., mem. exec. com., chmn. pub. rels. com. Regional Ballet Ensemble, Chgo., 1961-63; bd. dirs. Soc. Chgo. Strings, 1963-64; mem. Ind. Dem. Coalition, 1968-69; bd. dirs. Citizens for Polit. Change, 1969; campaign mgr. aldermanic election 42d ward Chgo. City Coun., 1969. Recipient Outstanding Service award United Cerebral Palsy Assn., Chgo., 1954, 55, Chgo. Lighthouse for Blind, 1986; Spl. Communications award The White House, 1961; cert. of appreciation Ill. Dept. Human Rights, 1985, Internat. Assn. Ofcl. Human Rights Agys., 1985; selected as reference source Am. Bicentennial Research Inst. Library Human Resources, 1973; named Hon. Citizen, City of Alexandria, Va., 1985. Mem. Affirmative Action Assn. (bd. dirs. 1981—, chmn. mem. and program coms. 1981—, pres. 1983—), Fashion Group (bd. dirs. 1981-83, chmn. Retrospective View of An Hist. Decade 1960-70, editor The Bull. 1981), Indsl. Rels. Rsch. Assn. (bd. dirs., chmn. personnel placement com. 1960-61), AAAS, NOW, Sarah Siddons Soc., Soc. Personnel Adminstrs., Women's Equity Action League, Nat. Assn. Inter-Group Rels. Ofcls. (nat. conf. program 1959), Publicity Club Chgo. (chmn. inter-city rels. com. 1960-61, Disting. Svc. award 1968), Ill. C. of C. (community rels. com., alt. mem. labor rels. com. 1971-74), Chgo. C. of C. and Industry (merit employment com. 1961-63). Club: Chgo. Press (chmn. women's activities 1969-71). Office: 111 E Chestnut St Chicago IL 60611

ALLEN, CARLTON BARRINGTON, financial analyst, consultant; b. Kingston, Jamaica, Mar. 23, 1959; came to U.S., 1986; s. Dodriddge Wesley Allen and Bertlin (McFee) Thompson; m. Cheryl Corner, Nov. 28, 1986; children: Kelly Ann, Carlton Jr., Fabion, Malcom. BSC, U. W.I., 1983; diploma mktg., Inst. Mgmt., 1983, cert. sales, 1984. Mgr. Sea-View Food Processing, Kingston, Jamaica, 1981-83; mng. dir. Choice Travel and Car Rental, Kingston, Jamaica, 1982-84, Tropicana Enterprises, Kingston, Jamaica, 1983-85; pres. Barry Allen Merchandising, Melbourne, Fla., 1985—, Allen Bus. Services, Bklyn., 1986—, Allen & Allen Assocs., Bklyn., 1987—; cons. Welt-View Tower, Inc., Reciprocal Traden, Inc., 1986—. Mem. Am. Entrepreneurs Assn., West State Mortgage Assn., Am. Fin. Coordinators. Mem. Pentacostal Ch. Home and Office: Allen & Allen Assocs 784 St Johns Pl 3RT Brooklyn NY 11216

ALLEN, CAROLYN JUNE, corporate executive; b. Maplewood, Ohio, June 29, 1935; d. Tyra Franklin and Julia Anna (Yeager) Weber; m. Leebern Kash Allen, May 12, 1956; children: Rebecca Ann, Deborah Lynn. Grad., Miami-Jacobs Bus. Coll., Dayton, Ohio, 1955. Asst. sec. United Aircraft Products, Inc., Dayton, 1969-86, corp. sec., 1986—. Mem. Soc. Corp. Secs. Lutheran. Home: 532 Hialeah Ct Vandalia OH 45377 Office: United Aircraft Products PO Box 90007 Dayton OH 45490-0007

ALLEN, CHARLES RICHARD, retired financial executive; b. Cleve., Mar. 10, 1926; s. Charles Ross and Jennie (Harmon) A.; m. Marion Elizabeth Taylor, Aug. 17, 1946; children: Kathleen Allen Templin, Jeanne Allen Duffy, Kenneth. Student, Occidental Coll., 1942-43; BS, UCLA, 1945. Acctg. supr. N.Am. Aviation, Inc., Los Angeles, 1946-55; div. controller TRW, Inc., Los Angeles, 1955-61, dir. fin., 1961-64; assoc. controller TRW, Inc., Cleve., 1964-66, controller, 1966-67, v.p., 1967-77, exec. v.p., 1977-86, chief fin. officer, 1967-86; advisor New Court Ptnrs., N.Y.C. Trustee Maritime Mus. San Diego; mem. San Diego World Affairs Coun. Served with USNR, 1943-46. Mem. Fin. Execs. Inst., Am. Fin. Assn. Club: Wall Street (N.Y.C.). Home: 1730 Avenida del Mundo Coronado CA 92118

ALLEN, CLIVE VICTOR, lawyer, communications company executive; b. Montreal, Que., Can., June 11, 1935; s. John Arthur and Norah (Barnett) A.; m. Barbara Mary Kantor, Feb. 22, 1964; children—Drew, Blair. B.A., McGill U., 1956, B.C.L., 1959. Called to bar 1960. Mem. firm Hackett, Mulvena, & Drummond & Fiske, 1960-63, Fiske, Emery, Allen & Lauzon, 1964-66; v.p., sec. Allied Chem. Can. Ltd., 1966-74; sr. v.p., gen. counsel Northern Telecom Ltd., 1974—; mem. Can. adv. bd. Allendale Ins., Can.-U.S. Law Inst.; mem. adv. com. internat. bus. and trade law program, U. Toronto. Mem. editorial bd. Trade Law Topics Newsletter. Mem. Can. Bar Assn., Barreau du Quebec, Internat. Bar Assn. (chmn. corp. law depts. com.), Assn. Can. Gen. Counsel, Can. Tax Found. Clubs: Montreal Badminton & Squash, St. James's (Montreal); Granite (Toronto). Home: 18A Deer Park, Crescent, Toronto, ON Canada M4V 2C2 Office: No Telecom Ltd, 3 Robert Speck Pkwy, Mississauga, ON Canada L4Z 3C8

ALLEN, DARRYL FRANK, industrial company executive; b. Detroit, Sept. 7, 1943; s. Hairston Ulysses and Frances (Akers) A.; m. Sharon Mae Baines, Aug. 27, 1966; children: Richard Baines, James Bretten, Michael Jeffery. B.A., Mich. State U., 1965; M.B.A., U. Mich., 1966. Mgr. Arthur Andersen & Co., Detroit, 1965-72; corporate controller Aeroquip Corp., Jackson, Mich., 1972-76, v.p. finance, 1976-78, v.p. fin. and adminstrn., 1978-79; v.p. fin. services Libbey-Owens-Ford Co., Toledo, 1980-81, chief fin. officer, 1981-83, group v.p., 1983-84, pres., 1984-86, chief operating officer; pres., chief exec. officer Trinova Corp. (formerly Libbey-Owens-Ford Co.), Toledo, 1986—; bd. dirs. First Ohio Bancshares. Mem. Am. Inst. C.P.A.s, Mich. Assn. C.P.A.s. Home: 2808 Westchester Toledo OH 43615 Office: Trinova Corp 1705 Indian Wood Cir Maumee OH 43537 *

ALLEN, DAVID DONALD, insurance company executive; b. Scranton, Pa., Feb. 17, 1931; s. Robert William and Muriel Joan (Malia) A.; m. Eleanor M. Corwin, May 17, 1952; children—Lisa and Laura (twins), Joan. B.A., Harpur Coll., 1956. With IBM Corp., 1956-69; Eastern region mgr. systems IBM Corp., N.Y.C., 1965-67; data processing div. mgr. comml. analysis IBM Corp., White Plains, N.Y., 1967-69; v.p. operations Computer Tech. East, N.Y.C., 1969-70; v.p. mgmt. information systems CBS, N.Y.C., 1970-76; v.p. Lincoln Nat. Life Ins. Co., 1976-79; v.p. Lincoln Nat. Corp., 1979-86, exec. v.p., 1986—. Served with AUS, 1950-53. Home: 12204 Covington Rd Fort Wayne IN 46804 Office: Lincoln Nat Corp 1300 S Clinton St PO Box 1110 Fort Wayne IN 46801

ALLEN, DAVID RATCLIFF, management consultant; b. Jonesboro, La., Dec. 28, 1945; s. Gordon Emmet Allen and Miriam (Foster) Allen Drummond. BA, New Coll., 1968. Gen. mgr. Natural Landscape Co., L.A., 1977-80; pres. Allen Assocs., L.A., 1980-83; v.p. Insight Consulting Group, Santa Monica, Calif., 1983—. Author cassette program on productivity mgmt. Home: 16641 Merivale Ln Pacific Palisades CA 90272 Office: Insight Cons Group 2103 Wilshire St Santa Monica CA 90403

ALLEN, DONALD VAIL, investment executive; b. South Bend, Ind., Aug. 1, 1928; s. Frank Eugene and Vera Irene (Vail) A.; m. Betty Dunn, Nov. 17, 1956. BA magna cum laude, UCLA, 1972, MA, 1973. Editor Times-Herald, Washington, 1947-56; adminstrv. engr. Bendix Corp., Detroit, 1956-58; exec. mgr. Englander Corp., Detroit, 1958-69; with City Products, Los Angeles, 1969-72; v.p. real property devel., holding and syndication Cambridge Investments, Pasadena, Calif., 1972-75; pres. Cambridge Investments, Pasadena, 1975—, also chmn. bd. dirs., 1979—; guest lectr. George Washington and Am. Univs., Washington, Pasadena City Colls. Contbr. several hundred articles to various publs. including L.A. Times, N.Y. Herald Tribune, Washington, D.C. Times-Herald, others, 1947—; translated works of Ezra Pound from Italian into English; performing musician (pianist, organist) Steinway roster of artists, specialist in works of Chopin, Debussy, Beethoven and Liszt; first performance of works by Am. composers Paul Creston, Norman dello Joio, Ross Lee Finney, appearances in N.Y., Washington (Nat. Gallery of Arts, Phillips Art Gallery). Pres. Funds for Needy Children, 1974-76. Mem. Am. Mgmt. Assn., Calif. Assn. Realtors, Am. Guild of Organists, Chamber Music Soc. Republican. Episcopalian. Home: 3371 Celinda Dr Carlsbad CA 92008 Office: Cambridge Investments 2940 Sombrosa St Carlsbad CA 92009

ALLEN, EDDIE D., corporate professional. MA in Bus. Finance and Econs., Air U.; cert. pilot, USAF Jet Pilot Sch. Lic. fin. prin. SEC. Commd. 2d lt. USAF, 1955, advance through grades to col., 1966; v.p. Calvin Bullock, Ltd., N.Y.C., 1966-71; pres., chief exec. officer Am. Life Underwriters, Newport Beach, Calif., 1979—, Nat. Assn. for Employee Benefits, Newport Beach, Calif., 1971—; coachbaseball Kamehameha Schs., Hawaii, U. So. Calif. Appointed by v.p. Bush to the Nat. Steering Com.of the Bush for pres. coun., appointed pres. prestigious Nat. Coun. Bus. Advisors, 1984; cons. adminstrn., congress, state and local govts., corps., charitable orgns.; mem. adv. coun. Big Bros. Am., Drug Rehab. Program Boys Town. U. So. Calif. scholar, Inst. Tech. scholar Harvard U. Mem. Air Force Assn., Nat. Assn. Security Dealers (adv. coun.), Nat. Assn. Profl. Baseball Players, KC. Home: 19 Tiburon Bay Corona Del Mar CA 92660 Office: Nat Assn. Employee Benefits 610 Newport Ctr Dr Ste 1200 Newport Beach CA 92660

ALLEN, FRANKLIN GLENN, corporation executive, lawyer; b. Athens, Ohio, Sept. 12, 1925; s. George Samuel and Lola Elma (Davis) A. BA in Physics, Ohio State U., 1950, JD, 1952; LL.M, NYU, 1959; MBA, U. Chgo., 1963. Bar: Ill., Ohio, 1952, N.Y., 1956. Assoc. Vedder, Price, Kaufman & Kammholz, Chgo., 1952-53, Byron, Hume, Groen & Clement, Chgo., 1953-55, Davis, Polk, Wardwell, Sunderland & Kiendl, N.Y.C., 1955-57; corp. counsel Hubbard & Co., Chgo. and Pitts., 1957-64, Dyson-Kissner Corp., N.Y.C., 1960-64, The Marmon Group, Inc., Chgo., 1964-69, Pritzker & Pritzker, Chgo., 1965-69; ptnr., of counsel Sachnoff, Weaver, Rubenstein Ltd., Chgo., 1969—; chmn. bd., pres. Pantera's Corp., St. Louis, 1978—. Served to Sgt. U.S. Army, 1943-46. Mem. ABA, Ill. Bar Assn., Chgo. Bar

Assn., Delta Theta Phi. Republican. Presbyterian. Club: Chicago. Home: 1321 W Berwyn Ave Chicago IL 60640 Office: Pantera's Corp 30 S Wacker Dr 29th Fl Chicago IL 60606

ALLEN, GORDON PHILLIP, insurance company executive; b. Roxboro, N.C., Apr. 29, 1929; s. George Lemnel Sr. and Sallie (Wilkerson) A.; m. Betsy Harris, July 12, 1952; children: Phillip, Kassie, Betsy, George, Page. AA in Bus., Mars Hill Coll., 1949. Br. mgr. Reynolds Tobacco Co., Springfield, Tenn., 1950-51; sales exec. Thompson Ins. Agy., Roxboro, 1954-57; pres. Thompson-Allen, Inc., Roxboro, 1957—; chmn. Home Savs. and Loan Assn., Durham, N.C., 1986—. Pres. Roxboro Kiwanis Club, 1959, Roxboro Area C. of C., 1961; senator State of N.C., 1969-74, chmn. dept. local affairs, 1969-71, pres. pro tem, majority leader, 1971-74; past chmn. bd. steards, trustee, bldg. and fin. coms. Long Meml. United Meth. Ch. Served with U.S. Army, 1951-53, Korea. Democrat. Methodist. Home: 223 Crestwood Roxboro NC 27573 Office: Thompson-Allen Inc 107 N Main Box 100 Roxboro NC 27573

ALLEN, HERBERT, investment banker; b. N.Y.C., Feb. 13, 1908; s. Charles and Francis (Mayer) A.; m. Kathleen Heffernan (dec.); children—Herbert Anthony, Susan Kathleen Wilson; m. Ethel Strong. D.C.S. (hon.), Ithaca Coll. Ptnr. Allen & Co., N.Y.C., 1927—; dir. emeritus Irvine Co., Newport Beach, Calif. Trustee, v.p. Hackley Sch., Tarrytown, N.Y. Clubs: Deepdale Golf; Indian Creek Golf (Fla.); Mark's (London); Saratoga Golf and Polo; Bal Harbour. Office: Allen & Co 711 Fifth Ave New York NY 10022

ALLEN, HOWARD D., insurance company executive; b. Boston, Apr. 1, 1930; s. Elmer F. and Bessie D. (Dyer) A.; children: April, May, Mark, June, Juliette. BA, Harvard U., 1950. Asst. actuary Pan Am Life, New Orleans, 1955-57; asst. actuary John Hancock Mut. Life Ins. Co., Boston, 1957-61, assoc. actuary, 1961-66, 2d v.p., 1966-68, v.p., 1968-78, sr. v.p., 1978-87; v.p. Boston Mut. Life Ins. Co., 1988—; chmn. research planning com. Life Ins. Mgmt. Assn., Hartford, Conn., 1976-78; chmn. N.Y. Exp. Lim. subcom. Am. Council of Life Ins., Washington, 1978-80, 84-86; dir. J.H. Casualty Holding Co., chmn. dirs.' compensation com. Chmn. sch. survey com. Westwood, Mass., 1968; chmn. EDP study com. Stoughton. Served to 1st lt. USAF, 1950-52. Fellow Soc. of Actuaries, Am. Acad. Actuaries. Clubs: Harvard (Boston); Braeburn Country (Newton, Mass.). Home: 68 Village St South Easton MA 02375 Office: Boston Mut Life Ins Co 120 Royall St Canton MA 02021

ALLEN, HOWARD PFEIFFER, electric utility executive, lawyer; b. Upland, Calif., Oct. 7, 1925; s. Howard Clinton and Emma Maud (Pfeiffer) A.; m. Dixie Mae Illa, May 14, 1948; 1 child, Alisa Cary. AA, Chaffey Jr. Coll., 1946; BA in Econs. cum laude, Pomona Coll., 1948; JD, Stanford U., 1951. Bar: Calif. 1951, U.S. Supreme Ct. Asst. prof. law, asst. dean law sch. Stanford (Calif.) U., 1951-54; with So. Calif. Edison Co., Rosemead, Calif., 1954—; v.p. So. Calif. Edison Co., Rosemead, 1962-71, sr. v.p., 1971-73, exec. v.p., 1973-80, pres., dir., 1980-84; chmn., chief exec. officer So. Calif. Edison Co., Rosemead, Calif., 1984—, also bd. dirs.; chmn. bd., chief exec. officer SCEcorp, 1988—, also bd. dirs.; bd. dirs. Cal Fed Inc., Calif. Fed. Savs. and Loan, Computer Scis. Corp., MCA Inc., Northrop Corp., PS Group Inc., Trust Co. West; vice chmn. bd., founding bd. mem. mayor's select com. on 1984 Olympics. Mem. exec. com. Bus. Coun., exec. com., policy com. Bus. Roundtable, commdr. coun. Salvation Army, bd. overseers Rand/UCLA Ctr. for Study Soviet Internat. Behavior; trustee, mem. nominating com. Conf. Bd.; trustee Com. Econ. Devel.; trustee, mem. exec. com. L.A. County Mus. Art, Pomona Coll.; bd. dirs., mem. exec. com. Calif. Econ. Devel. Corp.; bd. dirs. Edison Electric Inst., L.A. County Fair Assn; bd. dirs. LAOC Amateur Athletic Found.; dir. Calif. Civic Light Opera Assn., 1980-84; fin. chmn. Watts Summer Games, 1982. Recipient Whitney M. Young, Jr. award L.A. Urban League, 1985, Outstanding Pub. Svc. Recognition awards State of Calif., County of L.A., City of L.A., Carrie Chapman Catt award LWV, 1985, Human Rels. award Am. Jewish Com., 1986, Am. Spirit award Coun. Energy Resource Tribes, 1987, Spl. award Improvment for Sci. Edn. Calif. State Dept. Edn., 1988. Mem. ABA, NCCJ (nat. Protestant co-chmn. 1983-87, Brotherhood award 1988), Am. Judicature Soc., Pacific Coast Elec. Assn. (pres. 1984-85, bd. dirs.), Inst. for Resource Mgmt. (chmn. bd.), Assn. Edison Illuminating Cos. (bd. dirs.), Electric Power Rsch. Inst. (bd. dirs.), Calif. C. of C. (Outstanding Community Svc. Merit award 1982, bd. dirs.), Calif. Club (L.A.), Pacific Union Club (San Francisco), Bohemian Club (San Francisco), L.A. Country Club, La Quinta Hotel Golf Club, PGA West Golf Club, Mission Hills Country Club, 100 Club (exec. com.). Office: So Calif Edison Co 2244 Walnut Grove Ave Rosemead CA 91770

ALLEN, JESSE OWEN, III, management development and organizational behavior administrator; b. Albany, Ga., Apr. 7, 1938; s. Jesse Owen Jr. and Erma Hazel (Pearson) A.; m. Alva Juanita Inabinet, Jan. 26, 1960 (div. Jan. 1985); children: Charlotte Renee Butner, Garrett Owen, Cheryl Hazel; m. Barbara Joanna Smith Ozment, May 23, 1987; 1 child, Pamela Ozment Price. LLB, LaSalle Law Sch., 1967; AS, SUNY, Albany, 1978, BA in History, Lit., and Bus., 1986; MA in Philosophy, Calif. State U., 1987; doctoral studies, Union Grad Sch. Cin. Ohio, 1988—. Ordained pastor, Evang. Ch. Alliance, 1985. Sales engr. Ingersoll-Rand Corp., St. Louis, 1962-64; dir. mktg. Coin Acceptors, Inc., St. Louis, 1964-67; mkt. analyst McDonnell Douglas Corp., St. Louis, 1967-68; exec. v.p. Data Base, Inc., St. Louis, 1968-71; founder, pres. Specific Action Corp., Greensboro, N.C., 1971—; dir. Inst. Christian Studies div. Specific Action Corp., Greensboro, N.C., 1987—; lectr. in field internat. Author book, manual, course: Weatherization Production Control, 1978, Personal Profile Labs, 1980, Management Power: The Specific Action Way, 1985, Personality Power: The Specific Action Way, 1988; patentee Allen Valve, 1967; contbr. articles to profl. jours. Missionary, Evang. Ch. Alliance, El Salvador, 1985—. Named to Hon. Order of Ky. Cols., Commonwealth of Ky., 1978, Hon. Adm. State of Nebr., 1978, one of Sons of Confederacy Order of Stars and Bars State of Miss., 1976. Mem. Am. Soc. Tng. and Devel. (pres. 1976, Best Chpt. award 1976), Nat. Speakers Assn. (cert. speaking profl. 1988), Internat. Platform Assn., Inst. Mgmt. Cons. (cert. 1989). Republican. Club: Toastmasters Internat. Lodge: Lions Internat. Home: 520 Lindley Rd Greensboro NC 27410 Office: Specific Action Corp Guilford Coll Sta Lockbox 19125 Greensboro NC 27419-9125

ALLEN, JOHN THOMAS, JR., lawyer; b. St. Petersburg, Fla., Aug. 23, 1935; s. John Thomas and Mary Lita (Shields) A.; m. Joyce Ann Lindsey, June 16, 1958 (div. 1985); children—John Thomas, III, Linda Joyce, Catherine Lee (dec.); m. Janice Dearmin Hudson, Mar. 16, 1988. BS in Bus. Adminstrn. with honors, U. Fla., 1958; JD, Stetson U., 1961. Bar: Fla. 1961, U.S. Dist. Ct. (mid. dist.) Fla. 1962, U.S. Ct. Appeals (5th cir.) 1963, U.S. Supreme Ct. 1970. Assoc. Mann, Harrison, Mann & Rowe and successor Greene, Mann, Rowe, Stanton, Mastry & Burton, St. Petersburg, 1961-67, ptnr., 1967-74; sole practice, St. Petersburg, 1974; counsel Pinellas County Legis. Del., 1974; counsel for Pinellas County as spl. counsel on water matters, 1975—. Mem. Com. of 100, St. Petersburg, 1975—. Mem. ABA, Fla. Bar Assn., St. Petersburg Bar Assn., St. Petersburg C. of C., Beta Gamma Sigma. Democrat. Methodist. Club: Lions (St. Petersburg). Office: County of Pinellas 4508 Central Ave Saint Petersburg FL 33711

ALLEN, JOHN WHITLOCK, SR., insurance company executive; b. Enfield, Conn., Feb. 25, 1930; s. Herbert Walden and Evalene Loueza (Smith) A.; m. Marilyn Joan Holland, Aug. 25, 1956; children: Barbara Gordon Allen Simpson, John Whitlock Jr. BBA, Am. Internat. Coll., 1951; JD, Boston U., 1957. Bar: Conn. 1958, Ill. 1969, U.S. Supreme Ct. 1969, Mass. 1972. Claims atty. Phoenix of Hartford (Conn.) Ins. Group, 1957-59; trial atty. Law Offices of George A. Downing, East Hartford, Conn., 1959-69; mng. atty. Law Offices of John W. Allen, Chgo., 1969-71; regional mng. atty. Liberty Mut. Ins. Co., Boston, 1971-82, v.p., gen. atty., 1982—; bd. dirs. E.C. Allen's Sons Inc., Enfield, 1966—. Chmn. Rep. Town. Com., Coventry, Conn., 1965-69, Town Charter Commn., Coventry, 1966-67; mem. Coventry Bd. Fin., 1967-69. Served with counter intelligence corps U.S. Army, 1951-54. Recipient Cert. of Merit, Conn. Legislature, Hartford, 1969. Mem. ABA, Internat. Assn. Def. Counsel (v.p., mem. exec. com. 1986—). Republican. Office: Liberty Mut Ins Co 175 Berkeley St Boston MA 02117

ALLEN, JULIAN MYRICK, JR., industrial engineer; b. Mobile, Ala., Mar. 29, 1956; s. Julian Myrick Sr. and Sarah Jane (Scanlon) A.; m. Betty Jo Culpepper; children: Kiesha Monique, Jaron Myrick. AA, Jones County Jr. Coll., 1976; BSBA, U. So. Miss., 1980; MBA, Miss. State U., 1985. Store mgr. Burger King Inc., Slidell, La., 1976-78; indsl. engr. Howard Industries, Laurel, Miss., 1978-80; plant indsl. engr. Fairbanks Scale div. Colt Industries, Meridian, Miss., 1980-86; sr. indsl. engr. COMM/TEC div. Reliance Electric, Greenville, Miss., 1986-88; indsl. engr. William L. Bonnell div. Ethyl Corp., Newnan, Ga., 1988—. Author: Welding Robotics Handbook, 1986; contbr. articles to profl. jours. Tchr. United Pentecostal Ch., Meridian, 1983-86. Mem. Soc. Mfg. Engrs. (speaker confs. 1984-86, Pres. Club 1985, Outstanding Paper Robotics Internat. 1985-86, sr. mem.), Inst. Indsl. Engrs. (sr. mem.), Am. Welding Soc., Assn. MBA Execs. Republican. Office: Ethyl Aluminum Group PO Box 428 Newnan GA 30263

ALLEN, KENNETH DALE, insurance executive, corporate counsel; b. Carthage, Mo., Apr. 5, 1939; s. Herbert Herman and Viola Elizabeth (Woodley) A.; m. Donna Sue Viator, Aug. 26, 1961; children: Jeffrey Scott, Kristin Michelle, Timothy Brian, Bradley Todd. A.B., Central Mo. State U., 1960; LL.B., George Washington U., 1963; A.M.P., Harvard Sch. Bus., 1983. Legis. and research asst. Office Sen. Stuart Symington, Washington, 1960-65; asst. Washington counsel Health Ins. Assn., 1965-72; exec. v.p. Am. Nat. Ins. Co., Galveston, Tex., 1972-78; sr. exec. v.p., gen. counsel, dir. Southwestern Life Ins. Co., Dallas, 1978-84, pres., 1986; exec. v.p. Tenneco Ins. Co., Houston, 1984-86; pres. Southwestern Life, Dallas, 1986; vice pres., dep. gen. counsel Tenneco Inc., Houston, 1987—. Mem. D.C. Bar Assn., Assn. Life Ins. Counsel. Democrat. Episcopalian. Office: Tenneco Inc PO Box 2511 Houston TX 77252

ALLEN, LAWRENCE DAVID JR., banker; b. Americus, Ga., Feb. 15, 1952; s. Lawrence David and Dorothy Virginia (Linton) A.; m. Jennifer Lynn Harrison, Oct. 3, 1981; children: Lawrence David III, Benjamin Harrison. AA, Wingate Coll., 1972; BA, U. N.C., 1974. Loan supr. Comml. Credit Bus. Loans, Charlotte, N.C., 1974-77; ter. mgr. Comml. Credit Bus. Loans, West Palm Beach, Fla., 1977-80; v.p. Union Planters Nat. Bank, Memphis, 1980-82; v.p., mgr. 1st Tenn. Nat. Bank, Memphis, 1982-88; v.p., regional mgr. Exchange Nat. Bank, Memphis, 1988—. Team leader Memphis United Way, 1980-82; active Boy Scouts Am., 1980—, dist. commr., Memphis, 1986, 87, scouting coord., 1988. Recipient Scouters Key, Boy Scouts Am., 1986, Dist. Merit award, Memphis, 1987. Mem. Am. Inst. Banking, Nat. Comml. Fin. Assn., Nat. Assn. Accts., Nat. Exch. Club. Republican. Methodist. Lodge: Order of Arrow. Home: 8352 Stavenger Cove Cordova TN 38018 Office: Exch Nat Bank 6055 Primary Pkwy Ste 401 Memphis TN 38119

ALLEN, LEE HARRISON, wholesale company executive; b. Cleve., Oct. 12, 1924; s. Horace Joseph and Eleanor Quayle (Malone) A.; B.Engring. Metallurgy, Yale U., 1948; m. Marieke Sellenraad, Sept. 18, 1954; children—Horace, Jan, Adrian, Carel, Eleanor. With Hickman, Williams & Co., supplier raw materials to iron and steel industry, Detroit, 1948—, metallurgist, 1951-70, div. mgr., 1970—, v.p., dir., 1971-76, pres., 1976-84, chmn. bd., chief exec. officer, 1984—; chmn. bd., chief exec. officer Hickman, Williams Can. Inc., 1980—; owner L.H. Allen & Sons, wholesale tree nursery, Frankenmuth, Mich., 1969—; chmn. bd. Mich. Shelf Distbrs. Inc., 1985—. Trustee Grosse Pointe Bd. Edn., 1968-76. Mem. Am. Arbitration Assn., Am. Coal and Coke Chem. Inst., Am. Inst. of Mining and Metall. Engrs., Am. Iron and Steel Inst., Am. Foundrymen's Soc. Clubs: Yale of N.Y.C.; Country of Detroit, Economic of Detroit, Detroit Athletic. Home: 71 Moross Rd Grosse Pointe Farms MI 48236 Office: Hickman Williams & Co 100 Renaissance Ctr Ste 1976 Detroit MI 48243 also: Hickman Williams & Co Columbia Pla Cincinnati OH 45201

ALLEN, PAUL HOWARD, management consultant; b. Aldershot, Eng., Apr. 5, 1954; came to U.S., 1979; s. William and Frances Elva (Mason) A.; m. Marissa Celeste Wesely, Sept. 17, 1983; 1 child, Emma Elizabeth Wesely Allen. BA in Jurisprudence, Oxford (Eng.) U., 1976; MA in Jurisprudence, Oxford U., 1988; MBA, Harvard U., 1981. Bar: solicitor Eng. and Wales 1977. Solicitor of Supreme Ct. London, Freshfields, Eng., 1977-79; lectr. law Exeter Coll. Oxford U., 1978-79; assoc. McKinsey and Co. Inc., London, 1981-84; assoc. McKinsey and Co. Inc., N.Y.C., 1984-87, ptnr., 1987—; bd. dirs. Runfold Investments, London. Contbr. articles to profl. publs. Cons. CARE, N.Y.C., 1987—. McKinnon scholar Magdalen Coll. Oxford U., 1976; Harkness Fellow Commonwealth Fund N.Y., 1979-81; Baker scholar Harvard U., 1981. Mem. Brit. Inst. Mgmt. Office: McKinsey & Co Inc 55 E 52d St New York NY 10022

ALLEN, PHILLIP STEPHEN, lawyer; b. Washington, Nov. 20, 1952; s. Robert Mitchell and Edna Beverly (Feldman) A. BA with honors, U. Md., 1974; JD, George Washington U., 1978; LLM in Taxation, Georgetown U., 1982. Bar: D.C. Ct. Appeals, U.S. Dist. Ct., U.S. Tax Ct., U.S. Ct. Claims, U.S. Supreme Ct. Atty. office assoc. chief counsel IRS, Washington, 1978-84; asst. v.p. Met. Life Ins. Co., N.Y.C., 1984—; lectr. World Trade Inst., N.Y.C., 1987—. Mem. ABA (tax sect.), Fed. Bar Assn. (tax sect.), Union League N.Y. Republican. Jewish. Home: 329 Franklin Turnpike Ridgewood NJ 07450 Office: Met Life Ins Co One Madison Ave New York NY 10010

ALLEN, REUBEN ARTHUR, JR., financial executive, management consultant; b. Emporia, Va., July 28, 1941; s. Reuben Arthur and Hazel Gwendolyn (Mitchell) A.; m. Janice Roach, Sept. 2, 1961; children: Tammala R., Reuben A. III. BS in Acctg., Southeastern U., 1965; postgrad., U. Richmond, 1968-71. Acct. Washington Gas & Light Co., 1960-65; chief acct. Stuart T. Devell & Co., Centreville, Va., 1965-66; asst. to controller Marriott Corp., Washington, 1966-68; mgr. legis. and exec. info. systems State of Va., Richmond, 1968-70; pres. Data Systems Corp., Richmond, 1970-79; prin. The Allen Co., Richmond, 1979-85; dir. mgmt. adv. svcs. Goodman & Co., Norfolk, Va., 1985-88; prin. Allen Consulting Group, Virginia Beach, 1988—. Contbr. articles to profl. publs. Mem. Va. Soc. CPAs, Fairfax Jaycees, Rotary. Presbyterian. Home: 224 43d St Virginia Beach VA 23451

ALLEN, RICHARD DOUGLAS, management educator; b. Tulsa, Oct. 27, 1938; s. Peter George and Eva Lynn (Cunningham) A.; m. Charlessa Weber, Aug. 5, 1967; children: Beth Denise, Gregory Douglas. BS in Indsl. Engring., Okla. State U., 1964, MBA, 1971, PhD in Bus. Adminstrn., 1980. Registered profl. engr., Okla. Indsl. engr. USAF, Oklahoma City, 1964-69; grad. asst. Okla. State U., Stillwater, 1969-71; rsch. assoc. Okla. Vo-tech Edn. Dept., Okla. State U., Stillwater, 1971-72, instr., 1973-76; mgmt. analyst FAA, Oklahoma City, 1972-73; prof. mgmt., dir. MBA program Cen. State U., Edmond, Okla., 1976—; program chmn. SW Bus. Symposium, Edmond, 1983, 86; mem. adv. bd. Dushkin Pub. Group, Inc., Guilford, Conn., 1987—; cons. reviewer Richard D. Irwin, Inc., Homewood, Ill., 1988. Author booklet: Selected Readings in Business, 1986; contbr. articles to profl. publs. Vol. Edmond and Sulphur, Okla. counsels Boy Scouts Am., 1986-87, 4th of July Festival, Edmond, 1987, Alzheimer's Disease and Disorders, Oklahoma City, 1987. Mem. Nat. Acad. Mgmt., So. Mgmt. Assn., Midwest Acad. Mgmt., SW Acad. Mgmt., Edmond Mgmt. Club, Beta Gamma Sigma. Home: 1412 Cedar Ridge Rd Edmond OK 73013 Office: Cen State U Mgmt Dept 100 N University Dr Edmond OK 73060-0115

ALLEN, RICHARD HOOPES, lawyer; b. Wilmington, Del., May 16, 1932; s. John William and Mildred Sample (Hoopes) A.; m. Mary Eller Allen, Sept. 8, 1962; 1 child, Christopher. AB, Bowdoin Coll., 1954; JD, U. Chgo., 1959. Bar: Del., Pa. Assoc. Morris, Nichols, Arsht & Tunnell, Wilmington, Del., 1959-63, Atlas Chem. Corp., Wilmington, 1963-66; asst. gen. counsel Rockwell Internat., Pitts., 1966-76; sec., gen. counsel Incom Internat. Inc., Pitts., 1976-85, pres., chief exec. officer, 1985-88, also bd. dirs.; of counsel Phillips & Snyder P.A., Pitts., 1988—. Cons. Del. Human Relations Commn., Wilmington, 1964-66; bd. dirs. Del. Dept. Welfare, Dover, 1964-65; pres. bd. dirs. Fox Chapel Country Day Sch., Pitts., 1968-72. Served to 1st lt. U.S. Army, 1954-56. Mem. ABA, Allegheny County Bar Assn., Del. Bar Assn., Pa. Bar Assn., Order of Coif, Phi Beta Kappa. Home: 12 Deer Park Ln Chadds Ford PA 19317 Office: Phillips & Snyder 300 Delavan Ave Ste 800 Wilmington DE 19899

ALLEN, RICHARD JAMES, electrical engineer; b. Long Beach, Calif., Aug. 1, 1943; s. Richard James and Mary Veronica (Cote) A.; m. Nancy L. Fletcher, June 17, 1967 (div. Nov. 1984); children: Richard, Christopher, Michael. BSEE, Calif. State U., Long Beach, 1967, MSEE, 1974. Design engr. TRW, Redondo Beach, Calif., 1967-71, project mgr., 1972—; project mgr. Honeywell Marine Systems, Seattle, 1971-72. Coach Am. Youth Soccer Orgn., Huntington Beach, Calif.

ALLEN, ROBERT ENGLISH, management consultant, business broker; b. Mt. Pleasant, Tenn., Mar. 31, 1945; s. Robert English and Ruth Faye (Hill) A.; m. Patricia Ann Gifford, June 12, 1968 (div. 1982); children: George Clayton, Paedra Thais; m. Robin Ann Enscore, May 26, 1984. BS in Chemistry, U. Tenn., 1968; PhD, Iowa State U., 1974. Resch. scientist Celanese Fibers Co., Charlotte, N.C., 1974-78; tech. mgr. Celanese Fibers Mktg. Co., Charlotte, 1978-82; mgr. new bus. devel. Celanese Fibers Ops. Co., Charlotte, 1982-85; dir. ops. Chardon Labs, Charlotte, 1985; pres., chief exec. officer Allen Cons. Group Inc., Charlotte, 1985—; cons. Jordan Constrn. Co., Charlotte, 1984—, Ord Mfg. Co., Monroe, N.C., 1986—, also numerous others, 1985—; chief exec. officer Allen-Marshall Inc., Charlotte, 1987-88; pres. Rosegate Internat. Inc., Charlotte, 1988—. Contbr. articles to profl. jours. Mem. pub. relations and strategic planning coms. Jr. Achievement Charlotte, 1986—. With U.S. Army, 1969-70. Mem. Charlotte C. of C. (small bus. action coun. 1987-88, pub. affairs com. 1988—), Execs. Club (v.p. 1987-88, pres. 1988—), Tips Club (v.p. 1986-88), Phi Kappa Phi, Phi Lambda Upsilon, Alpha Chi Sigma. Republican. Home and Office: 5835 Winburn Ln Charlotte NC 28226

ALLEN, ROBERT EUGENE, communications company executive; b. Joplin, Mo., Jan. 25, 1935; s. Walter Clark and Frances (Patton) A.; m. Elizabeth Terese Pfeffer, Aug. 4, 1956; children: Jay Robert, Daniel Scott, Katherine Louise, Ann Elizabeth, Amy Susan. B.A., Wabash Coll., 1957, LL.D (hon.), 1984; postgrad., Harvard Bus. Sch., 1965. With Ind. Bell Telephone Co. Inc., Indpls., 1957-74, traffic student, 1957-61; dist. traffic supr. Ind. Bell Telephone Co. Inc., Bloomington, 1961-62, dist. comml. mgr., 1962-66; div. comml. mgr. Ind. Bell Telephone Co. Inc., Bloomington, Indpls., 1966-68, asst. to operations v.p., 1968, gen. comml. mgr., 1968-72, v.p., sec., treas., 1972-74; v.p., gen. mgr. Bell Telephone Co. of Pa., Phila., 1974-76; v.p., chief operating officer, dir. Ill. Bell Telephone Co., Phila., 1976-78; v.p. AT&T, Basking Ridge, N.J., 1978-81; pres., chmn. bd. C&P Telephone Cos., Washington, 1981-83, exec. v.p. corp. adminstrn. and fin., 1983-84; chmn., chief exec. officer AT&T Info. Systems, Morristown, N.J., 1985; pres., chief operating officer AT&T, N.Y.C., 1986-88, chmn., chief exec. officer, 1988—, also bd. dirs.; bd. dirs. Bristol Myers Co., Mfrs. Hanover Trust, Mfrs. Hanover Corp., Bus. Council N.Y. State Inc., Ing. C. Olivetti & c.S.p.A., Japan Soc. Trustee Wabash Coll., Columbia U.; mem. leadership com. for Lincoln Ctr. Consol. Corp. Fund., United Way of Am. Mem. Nat. Assn. Wabash Men, Conf. Bd., Bus. Roundtable (policy com.), Bus. Coun. Presbyterian. Clubs: Short Hills, Baltusrol Golf, Burning Tree, Congressional Country; Bay Head Yacht; Country of Fla. Home: 60 Stewart Rd Short Hills NJ 07078 Office: AT&T 550 Madison Ave New York NY 10022

ALLEN, ROBERT EUGENE BARTON, lawyer; b. Bloomington, Ind., Mar. 16, 1940; s. Robert Eugene Barton and Berth R. A.; m. Cecelia Ward Dooley, Sept. 23, 1960 (div. 1971); children—Victoria, Elizabeth, Robert; m. Judith Elaine Hecht, May 27, 1979 (div. 1989). B.S., Columbia U., 1962; LL.B., Harvard U., 1965. Bar: Ariz. 1965, U.S. Dist. Ct. Ariz. 1965, U.S. Tax Ct., 1965, U.S. Supreme Ct. 1970, U.S. Ct. Customs and Patent Appeals 1971, U.S. Dist. Ct. D.C. 1972, U.S. Ct. Appeals (9th cir.) 1974, U.S. Ct. Appeals (10th and D.C. cirs.) 1984, Ptnr., dir. Streich, Lang, Weeks and Cardon, Phoenix, 1965-83; ptnr., dir. Brown & Bain, Phoenix, Palo Alto (Calif.), 1983—. Nat. pres. Young Democrat Clubs Am., 1971-73; mem. exec. com. Dem. Nat. Com., 1972-73; mem. Ariz. Gov.'s Kitchen Cabinet working on wide range of state projects; bd. dirs. Phoenix Baptist Hosp. and Health Systems, Phoenix and Valley of the Sun Conv. and Visitors Bur., United Cerebral Palsy Ariz., 1984—, Planned Parenthood of Cen. and No. Ariz., 1984—; mem. Ariz. Aviation Futures Task Force; chmn. Ariz. Airport Devel. Criteria. Subcom.; mem. Apache Junction Airport Rev. Com., former mem Vestry and Sunday Sch. Tchr. Trinity Episcopal Cathedral; Am. rep. exec. bd. Atlantic Alliance of Young Polit. Leaders, 1973-77, 1977-80; trustee Am. Counsel of Young Polit. Leaders, 1971-76, 1981-85, mem. Am. delegations to Germany, 1971, 72, 76, 79, USSR, 1971, 76, 88, France, 1974, 79, Belgium, 1974, 77, Can., 1974, Eng., 1975, 79, Norway, 1975, Denmark, 1976, Yugoslavia and Hungary, 1985; Am.observer European Parliamentary elections, Eng., France, Germany, Belgium, 1979. Mem. ABA, Ariz. Bar Assn., Maricopa County Bar Assn., N. Mex. State Bar, D.C. Bar Assn., Am. Judicature Soc., Fed. Bar Assn., Am. Arbitration Assn., Phi Beta Kappa. Democrat. Episcopalian (lay reader). Club: Harvard (Phoenix). Contbr. articles on comml. litigation to profl. jours.

ALLEN, RONALD ALFRED, association executive; b. Ellicott City, Md., Apr. 8, 1940; s. Alfred Lafayette and Anne Laura (Sloan) A.; m. Susan Colstead Goodwin, Aug. 21, 1965; children: Warren Scott, Kari Goodwin. BS in Acctg., U. Balt., 1969; cert. in computer tech., U. Del., 1970. Sr. acct. Crown Zellerbach Corp., Newark, Del., 1966-68; data processing mgr. Am. Hoechst Corp., Delaware City, Del., 1969-71; dir. fin. and adminstrn. Internat. Reading Assn., Newark, 1971-84; exec. dir., chief exec. officer Assn. Sch. Bus. Ofcls. Internat., Reston, 1984—; trustee Trust for Insuring Educators, Kansas City, 1980—; dir. Ednl. Rsch. Svcs, Arlington, Va., 1984—; sec., dir. Ednl. leadership Consortium, Washington, 1984—; mem. nat. adv. bd. Eric Clearinghouse on Ednl. Mgmt., 1988—. Contbr. articles, commentaries to numerous profl. jours. Recipient Recognition of Excellence award Internat. Reading Assn., 1980; named hon. mayor, San Antonio, Tex., 1987. Mem. Am. Soc. Assn. Execs., Greater Washington Soc. Assn. Execs., Del. Valley Soc. Assn. Execs. (bd. dirs. 1981-83). Home: 11822 Blue Spruce Rd Reston VA 22091 Office: Assn Sch Business Ofcls Internat 11401 N Shore Dr Reston VA 22090

ALLEN, RONALD W., airline company executive; b. 1941; married. B.S.I.E., Ga. Inst. Tech. With Delta Air Lines, Inc., Atlanta, 1963—, asst. v.p. adminstrn., 1967-69, v.p. adminstrn., 1969-70, sr. v.p. personnel, 1970-79, sr. v.p. adminstrv. personnel, 1979-83, pres., chief operating officer, 1983-87, chmn., chief exec. officer, 1987—, also dir. Office: Delta Air Lines Inc Hartsfield Atlanta Internat Airport Atlanta GA 30320 *

ALLEN, STUART (STUART ALLEN SUP), film and TV company executive; b. N.Y.C., July 24, 1943; s. Rudolph and Rita Geraldine (Tellez) Sup; m. Carol Ann Terminelli, June 30, 1982. A in Engring., NYU, 1961; BA in Communications, Pace U., 1963. Free-lance photographer, photojournalist N.Y.C., 1963—; producer, dir. Stuart Allen Assocs., Iselin, N.J., 1967-76; pres., chief exec. officer Internat. Media Services, Inc., Plainfield, N.J., 1976—. Spl. producer ABC-TV Evil Knievel Snake River Canyon Jump, 1974; author, producer Counterattack, 1978 (One to One Media award 1979), producer, dir. Eagle in the Wind, 1980 (Best Film award 1984). Chmn. Plainfield, N.J. Cultural and Heritage Commn., 1982—; mcpl. liaison Union County, N.J. Cultural and Heritage Adv. Bd., 1982—; trustee Drake House Mus., Plainfield Hist. Soc., 1982—; dir. Plainfield Econ. Devel. Corp., 1984—. N.J. State Council Arts grantee, 1979, 86. Mem. Indsl. Photographers Assn. N.J. (pres. 1976-77, award of Excellence), Internat. TV Assn., Am. Film Inst., Cen. Jersey C. of C. Club: Marco Polo (Chgo.). Home and Office: 718 Sherman Ave Plainfield NJ 07060

ALLEN, WELLS PRESTON, JR., utility executive; b. Scranton, Pa., Apr. 6, 1921; s. Wells P. and Marguerite (Allen) A.; m. Jessie Jobson, June 23, 1946; children: James, Carolyn, Barbara. B.E.E., Rensselaer Poly. Inst., 1949. Registered profl. engr., N.Y. Cadet engr. N.Y. State Electric & Gas Corp., Binghamton, 1949-51; jr. engr. N.Y. State Electric & Gas Corp., 1951-54, engr., 1954-58, chief power supply engr., 1958-63, asst. to pres., 1963-65, v.p., 1965-71, sr. v.p., 1971-73, exec. v.p., 1974-76, pres., 1976-83, chmn., chief exec. officer, 1983-88, also dir., chmn. exec. fin. com., 1988—; dir. Utilities Mut. Ins. Co.; regional adv. bd. dirs. First City div. Chase Lincoln First Bank, N.A.; dir. Chase Lincoln First Bank, N.A., Columbian Mut. Life Ins. Co. Past pres. Broome-Tioga chpt. N.Y. State Assn. for Retarded Children; council Rensselaer Poly. Inst.; mem. SUNY at Binghamton Found., 1973—; bd. dirs. Pathfinder Village. Served with AUS, 1942-45. Mem. IEEE, Am. Legion. Presbyterian. Lodge: Masons (33 degree). Office: NY State Electric & Gas Corp 4500 Vestal Pkwy E Binghamton NY 13903

ALLENDER, PATRICK W., manufacturing company executive; b. Balt., Nov. 13, 1946; s. John J. and Anne (Kehl) A.; m. Deborah Keadle, Oct. 3, 1981; 1 child, John W. BS in Acctg. cum laude, Loyola Coll., Balt., 1968. CPA, Md. Audit mgr., mem. staff Arthur Andersen & Co., Balt., 1968-80, ptnr., 1981-85; treas., fin. officer Easco Corp., Balt., 1986, also bd. dirs.; chief fin. officer Danaher Corp., Washington, 1987—. Bd. dirs. treas. Nat. Aquarium Balt., 1978-85, Nat. Aquarium Found., Balt., 1983—; mem. Mayor's Bus. Roundtable, Balt., 1981-83; bd. dirs., treas. Babe Ruth Birthplace Found., Balt., 1982-87. Served to capt. USAF, 1969-75. Recipient Cert. Recognition Mayor City Balt., 1985. Mem. Am. Inst. CPA's, Md. Assn. CPA's. Office: Danaher Corp 3524 Water St NW Washington DC 20007

ALLENDER, ROBERT MICHAEL, accountant; b. Ottamwa, Iowa, June 12, 1953; s. Kenneth Wayne and Delores Marie (Garland) A. BSBA in Acctg., N.E. Mo. State U., 1976. CPA, Iowa. Staff acct. Anderson, Larkin & Co., P.C., Ottumwa, 1976-80; in-charge auditor Internat. Multifoods Corp., Mpls., 1980-81, supervising sr. auditor, 1982-83, mgr. corp. fin. reporting, 1983—. Mem. AICPA, Minn. Soc. CPA's. Home: 7320 York Ave S #2-112 Edina MN 55435 Office: Internat Multifoods Corp Multifoods Tower Box 2942 Minneapolis MN 55402

ALLER, ROBERT LUNDEEN, financial executive; b. Omaha, Jan. 14, 1934; s. Dudley Ogden and Agnes Marie (Lundeen) A.; m. Susan Jeanette Bivin, July 2, 1955; children: Hugh Bivin, Benjamin Dudley. BA, Antioch Coll., 1956; MS, Columbia U., 1958. Fin. analyst Bendix Corp., N.Y.C., 1959-65; fin. dir. Bendibérica, Barcelona, Spain, 1965-72, sub-dir. gen., 1972-74; v.p. fin. Bendix Europe, Paris, 1974-77; asst. treas. internat. div. Bendix Corp., Southfield, Mich., 1977-79; treas. Loctite Corp., Newington, Conn., 1979-85, v.p., chief fin. officer, treas., 1985—. Trustee Conn. Hist. Soc. Republican. Mem. United Ch. Christ. Office: Loctite Corp 10 Columbus Blvd Hartford CT 06106

ALLERHEILIGEN, ROBERT PAUL, marketing educator; b. Denver, Dec. 23, 1944; s. Paul William and Helen Idris (Hodges) A.; m. Sandra Jeanne Lee, June 17, 1967 (div. 1982); children: Laura, Brad. BA, Colo. State U., 1967, MBA, 1974; PhD, U. So. Calif., 1986. Asst. prof. U. No. Colo., Greeley, 1974-75; coordinator spl. programs Colo. State U., Ft. Collins, 1975-79, asst. prof. mktg., 1985—; instr. U. So. Calif., L.A., 1979-85; officer JMN Enterprises, Inc., L.A., 1980—; prof. Exec. Devel. Inst., Ft. Collins, 1985—; cons. in field. Contbr. articles to profl. jours. Capt. USMC, 1967-70. Mem. Internat. Trade Assn. Colo., Colo. Internat. Edn. Assn., Am. Mktg. Assn., Internat. Bus. Assn. Rockies (bd. dirs. no. Colo.-Wyo. chpt.), Sertoma (bd. dirs.). Republican. Home: 1201 Solstice Ln Fort Collins CO 80525 Office: Colo State U Mktg Dept Clark Bldg Fort Collins CO 80523

ALLERS, MARLENE ELAINE, law office business manager; b. Crosby, Minn., Dec. 29, 1931; d. Robert Prudent and Tressa Ida May (Hiller) Huard; m. Herbert Dodge Allers, Aug. 29, 1950 (dec. Aug. 1977); children—Melanie Lynn, Geoffrey Brian. B.S. in Math., U. Minn.-Mpls., 1966, B.A. in Acctg., 1968, M.B.A. in Personnel and Fin. Mgmt., 1972. Bus. mgr., Earl Clinic, St. Paul, 1959-68, Lindquist & Vennum, Mpls., 1968-79, Stacker, Ravich & Simon, Mpls., 1979-82, Wagner, Johston & Falconer, Ltd., Mpls., 1983—; lectr. Inst. of Continuing Legal Edn., Mpls., 1977. Recipient Outstanding Achievement award in Bus. Young Women's Christian Assn., Mpls., 1978. Mem. Minn. Legal Adminstrs. Assn., Mensa. Avocations: bridge; reading. Home: 608 Queen Ave S Minneapolis MN 55405

ALLEY, WILLIAM JACK, holding company executive; b. Vernon, Tex., Dec. 27, 1929; s. W. H. and Opal M. (Cater) A.; m. Deborah Bunn, Dec. 28, 1979; children: Susan Jane, Pamela Jean, Patricia Ann, Sarah Elizabeth, Brayton. AA, Northeastern A. and M. Coll., 1949; BBA, U. Okla., 1951, JD, 1954. Bar: Okla. 1954; CLU. Atty. State Ins. Bd. Okla., 1956-57; asst. v.p. Pioneer Am. Ins. Co., 1957-59, v.p., 1959-60, v.p., agy. dir., 1960-66, dir., 1961, sr. v.p. mktg., 1966; v.p. Franklin Life Ins. Co., 1967-69, sr. v.p. agy., 1969-74, exec. v.p., 1974-75, pres., chief exec. officer, 1976-85, chmn. bd., 1977-87; dir. Am. Brands Inc., 1979, sr. v.p. strategic planning, 1983-85; sr. v.p., chief fin. officer Am. Brands, Inc., Old Greenwich, Conn., 1985-86, vice chmn., 1986-87, chmn., chief exec. officer, 1987—; bd. dirs. subs. cos.; bd. dirs. Cen. Ill. Pub. Service Co., Bunn-o-matic Corp., Southwestern Area Commerce and Industry Assn. Conn.; bd. govs. Internat. Ins. Seminars Inc., Ins. Hall of Fame. Bd. dirs. Co-operation Ireland, United Way Tri-State, U. Okla.'s Centennial Commn.; bd. advisors U. Olka.'s Coll. Bus. Administrn., Coun. Competitiveness; bd. overseers Exec. Coun. Fgn. Diplomats. Capt. USAF, 1954-56. Mem. Okla. Bar. Assn., Delta Sigma Pi, Phi Kappa Sigma, Phi Alpha Delta. Clubs: Illini Country, Sangamo, Tavern (Chgo.); New Canaan Field, Northport Point, New Canaan Country; Economic (N.Y.C.) (bd. govs.). Lodges: Masons, Shriners. Office: Am Brands Inc 1700 E Putnam Ave PO Box 819 Old Greenwich CT 06870-0819

ALLIA, DARLENE MARY, accountant; b. Phila., Jan. 30, 1950; d. Rosario and Angelina (Nicosia) A. Student, Community Coll., Phila., LaSalle Coll., Phila. Adminstrv. asst. regional counsel IRS, Phila., 1973; taxpayer service rep. IRS, Phila. and Bensalem, Pa., 1973-77; instr. taxpayer services IRS, Bensalem, 1976-77; tax auditor IRS, Jenkintown, Pa., 1977-83; instr. auditing IRS, Phila. and Jenkintown, Pa., 1981-83; enrolled agt., tax acct. Allia & Assocs., Phila., 1983—; realtor assoc. V.H. Pasquarella Co., 1987—. Recipient Sustained Superior Performance award Army Electronics Command Phila., 1970, cert. of Appreciation IRS, 1974, 82, cert. of Recognition IRS, 1974. Mem. Nat. Assn. Enrolled Agts., Pa. Soc. Pub. Accts. (bd. dirs.), Nat. Assn. Realtors, Pa. Soc. Realtors, Bus. Women's Network. Office: Allia & Assocs 3257 Disston St Philadelphia PA 19149 also: Allia & Assocs 3257 Disston St Philadelphia PA 19149

ALLIGOOD, DAVID LAMAR, manufacturing company executive; b. Thomas County, Ga., Mar. 1, 1934; s. Oscar Linton and Katie Mae (Stanaland) A.; m. Edna Price, Sept. 3, 1954; children—Laura Melissa, Candace Lynn, Matthew David. Student U. Ga., 1957-59, UCLA, 1959-60, Los Angeles S.W. Coll., 1961-63. Mgr. engring. Welded Tube Co., Chgo., 1969-78, mgr. ops., 1978-79, asst. v.p. ops., 1979-80, v.p. engring. and planning, 1980-88, dir. tech. devel., 1988—; pres. Lake Calumet Sanitary Assn., Chgo., 1983—. Served to sgt. USAF, 1955-59. Mem. Assn. Iron and Steel Engrs., Lake Calumet Sanitary Assn. (pres., chmn. bd. 1983—). Democrat. Home: 806 Carnation Ln Matteson IL 60443 Office: Welded Tube Co Am 1855 E 122d St Chicago IL 60633

ALLINGHAM, JOHN PAUL, manufacturing executive; b. Hamilton, Ont., Can., July 9, 1944; m. Joanne Allingham, Aug. 27, 1966; children: Tara Lynn, Kerri Leigh, Paul Mark. B in Engring., McMaster U., Hamilton, 1966, MBA, 1969. Process engr. Union Carbide Can. Ltd., Montreal, 1966-67; various positions Ford Motor Co. Can., Oakville, 1969-72; controller gen. parts and svc. div. Ford Motor Co. Can., Oakville, 1979; successively treas., sec.-treas., dir. fin., v.p. fin. Reed, Inc., Toronto, 1980-88, exec. v.p., 1988—. Home: 329 Shoreacres Rd, Burlington, ON Canada L7L 5P3 Office: Daishowa Forest Products Ltd, 207 Queens Quay W Ste 880, Toronto, ON Canada M5J 1A7

ALLIO, ROBERT JOHN, management consultant executive; b. N.Y.C., Sept. 1, 1931; s. Albert Joseph and Helen (Gerbereux) A.; m. Barbara Maria Littauer, Oct. 3, 1953; children: Mark, Paul, David, Michael. B.Metal. Engring., Rensselaer Poly. Inst., 1952, Ph.D., 1957; M.S., Ohio State U., 1954. Mgr. advanced materials Gen. Electric Co., Schenectady, 1957-60; sr. staff AEC, Washington, 1962; engring. mgr. atomic power div. Westinghouse Corp., Pitts., 1962-68; dir. corp. planning Babcock & Wilcox, N.Y., 1968-75; v.p. Can. Wire Co., Toronto, Ont., 1975-78; pres. Canstar Communications, Toronto, 1976-78; sr. staff mem. Arthur D. Little Co., Cambridge, Mass., 1978-79; dean Rensselaer Poly. Inst. Sch. Mgmt., Troy, N.Y., 1981-83; pres. Robert J. Allio and Assoc., Duxbury, Mass., 1979—; prof. mgmt. Babson Coll., 1985—; bd. dirs. Springboard Software Inc., Microtech. Sources Ltd. Author: Corporate Planning: Techniques and Applications, 1979, Corporate Planning, 1985, The Practical Strategist, 1988; editor: Planning Rev. Jour., 1972-86. Mem. Planning Forum (pres. 1976-77). Club: Union League (N.Y.C.). Home: 21 Prior Farm Rd Duxbury MA 02332 Office: Robert J Allio & Assocs 24 Bay Rd PO Box 2831 Duxbury MA 02331

ALLISH, RICHARD EUGENE, JR., trucking company executive; b. Saginaw, Mich., Aug. 8, 1958; s. Richard Eugene and Marie Ann (Russell) A.; m. Susan Marion Grey, Feb. 19, 1983; 1 stepchild, Jason Michael Rhodes. AA, Fla. Jr. Coll., 1978; BBA in transp. and logistics, U. North Fla., 1981. Sales rep. Smalley Transp., Jacksonville, Fla., 1981-82; dispatcher Kee Transp., Jacksonville, 1982-85; dispatcher, terminal mgr. Taylor-Maid Transp., Jacksonville, 1985; terminal mgr. Bicentennial Transport, Jacksonville, 1985-86, dir. SE ops., 1986—. Mem. Eagle Scout, 1973. Republican. Methodist. Home: 2530 Kershaw Dr W Jacksonville FL 32211

ALLISON, GRACE, lawyer; b. Chgo., Aug. 25, 1946; d. Daniel J. and Vivian Allison (Futter) Pachman; m. David J. White, Sept. 12, 1985; 1 child, Daniel Andrew; 1 stepchild, David G. AB, Wellesley Coll., 1967; MA in Teaching, U. Chgo., 1969, JD, 1979. Bar: Ill. 1979; cert. English tchr., N.Y. Instr. English Peru (N.Y.) Cen. High Sch., 1969-70, SUNY, Plattsburgh, 1970-72; writer, producer SVE, Inc., Chgo., 1974-76; assoc. McDermott, Will & Emery, Chgo., 1979-84; from assoc. to ptnr. Friedman & Koven, Chgo., 1984-86; ptnr. Altheimer & Gray, Chgo., 1986-89, Katten Muchin & Zavis, Chgo., 1989—; sec., founding bd. dirs. Lawyers Trust Fund Ill., 1983-85; bd. dirs. Chgo. Fin. Exch. Writer/producer filmstrip series: Citizenship Adventures of the Lollipop Dragon, 1975; author chpt. to book; contbr. articles to profl. jours. Mem. ABA (taxation sect. 1983—), Ill. Bar Assn. (sect. on fed. taxation coun. 1982-83), Chgo. Bar Assn. (fed. tax com. 1980—, chmn. legal aid com. 1982-83), Nat. Assn. Bond Lawyers. Home: 2322 Schiller Wilmette IL 60091-2330 Office: Katten Muchin & Zavis 525 W Monroe Chicago IL 60606

ALLISON, HERBERT MONROE, JR., human resources executive; b. Pitts., Aug. 24, 1943; s. Herbert M. Sr. and Mary B. (Boardman) A.; m. Simin N. Nazemi, May 9, 1974; children: John, Andrew. BA, Yale U., 1965; MBA, Stanford U., 1971. With Merrill Lynch & Co., Inc., N.Y.C., Paris, London and Tehran, Iran, 1971-78; asst. to pres. Merrill Lynch & Co., Inc., N.Y.C., 1978-80, mgr. market planning, 1980-83, treas., 1983-86, sr. v.p., dir. human resources, 1986—. Bd. dirs. N.Y. Infirmary-Beekman Downtown Hosp., 1986. With USN, 1965-69, Vietnam. Mem. Wall Street Personnel Mgmt. Assn. Office: Merrill Lynch & Co Inc 250 Vesey St 31st Fl New York NY 10281-1219

ALLISON, JOHN ANDREW, IV, banker; b. Charlotte, N.C., Aug. 14, 1948; s. John Andrew III and Anne Allison; m. Elizabeth Mc Donald, Aug. 19, 1973; 1 child, Eric Andrew. BBA, U. N.C., 1971; M in Mgmt., Duke U., 1973; grad. Stonier Sch. Banking, Rutgers U., 1981. Mgr. fin. analysis Br. Banking & Trust Co., Wilson, N.C., 1971-72, mgr. loan officer devel. program, 1972-73, regional loan adminstr., 1973-80, mgr. bus. loan adminstrn., 1980-81, mgr. banking div. (now Br. Banking Group), 1981—, pres., 1987—, also bd. dirs.; vice chmn. BB&T Fin. Corp., Wilson, 1987—, also bd. dirs.; bd. dirs. Br. Banking and Trust S.C. (name formerly Community Bank), Greenville, S.C. Bd. dirs., capital campaign chmn. Children's Services of Eastern N.C., Greenville , 1985—; bd. dirs. Diversified Opportunities, Inc., Wilson, 1980-87; mem. exec. com. state fin. Com. to Re-elect Gov. Martin, Raleigh, N.C., 1988; adv. bd., alumni coun. Fuqua Sch. Bus. Duke U.; bd. dirs. Med. Found. East Carolina U., Brody Found.; bd. regents comml. loan workshop East Carolina U. Mem. Am. Bankers Assn., N.C. Bankers Assn., Robert Morris Assocs. (past bd. regents comml. loan workshop E. Carolina U.), N.C. Citizens for Bus. and Industry, Phi Beta Kappa. Office: Branch Banking & Trust Co 223 W Nash St PO Box 1847 Wilson NC 27893

ALLISON, JOHN R., management consultant; b. Peterborough, Ont., Can., 1913; student Northwestern U., Am. Inst. Banking, Sophia U.; Dir. fin., econ. and sci. sect. Staff of Supreme Comdr. Allied Powers, Japan, 1945-51; treas. Norton Co., Norton Internat., Inc., 1957-58; v.p. internat., controller Richardson-Merrell, Inc., 1955-63; v.p., treas. PepsiCo Inc., 1963-65, v.p., controller, chief accounting officer, 1965-67; pres., chief exec. officer PepsiCo Service Industries, 1967-70; sr. v.p., treas. Raytheon Co., Lexington, Mass., 1970-73; mgmt. cons. 1973—; cons., profl. Bd. visitors Boston U. Sch. Bus., 1970-72; mem. N.Y. Bus. and Adv. Council, 1965-70; mem. Pacific Basin Econ. Council, 1968-72. dir. Served to 1st lt. U.S. Army, 1943-45. Home and Office: 143 Chestnut Cir Lincoln MA 01773

ALLISON, LAIRD BURL, business educator; b. St. Marys, W.Va., Nov. 7, 1917; s. Joseph Alexander and Opal Marie (Robinson) A.; m. Katherine Louise Hunt, Nov. 25, 1943 (div. 1947); 1 child, William Lee; m. Genevieve Nora Elmore, Feb. 1, 1957. BS in Personnel and Indsl. Relations magna cum laude, U. So. Calif., 1956; MBA, UCLA, 1958. Chief petty officer USN, 1936-51, PTO; asst. prof. to prof. mgmt. Calif. State U., L.A., 1956-83; asst. dean Calif. State U. Sch. Bus. and Econs., L.A., 1971-72, assoc. dean, 1973-83, emeritus prof. mgmt., 1983—; vis. asst. prof. mgmt. Calif. State U., Fullerton, 1970. Co-authored the Bachelors degree program in mgmt. sci. at Calif. State U., 1963. Mem. U.S. Naval Inst., Navy League U.S. Ford Found. fellow, 1960. Mem. Acad. Mgmt., Inst. Mgmt. Sci., Western Econs. Assn. Internat., World Future Soc., Am. Acad. Polit. Social Sci., Calif. State U. Assn. Emeriti Profs., Calif. State U. L.A. Emeriti Assn. (v.p. programs 1986-87, v.p. administrn. 1987-88, pres. 1988-89), Am. Assn. Individual Investors, Am. Assn. Retired Persons, Alpha Kappa Psi. Club: Retired Pub. Employees Assn. of Calif. (sec. Calif. State U. L.A. 1984-88, v.p. 1989). Home: 1615 S El Molino Alhambra CA 91801 Office: Calif State U Dept of Mgmt 5151 State University Dr Los Angeles CA 90032

ALLISON, LATHAM LEE, corporate strategic planning executive; b. Cleve., Dec. 2, 1933; s. Latham Lee and Celia (Fisher) A.; m. Margot Louise Rusch, Apr. 28, 1956; children—Michael, Jennifer, Peter, Nancy. B.A., Wesleyan U., 1955; M.B.A., Harvard U., 1957. Comptroller and other positions, aerospace div. Kaman Corp., Bloomfield, Conn., 1960-68; asst. controller Hamilton Standard div. United Techs. Corp., Windsor Locks, Conn., 1968-71, controller, 1971-76; corp. dir. fin. planning United Techs. Corp., Hartford, Conn., 1976-80; sr. v.p. fin. and adminstrn. Sikorsky Aircraft div. United Techs. Corp., Stratford, Conn., 1981-83; corp. v.p. strategic planning United Techs. Corp., Hartford, Conn., 1983-88; exec. v.p. Norden Systems Inc. sub. United Techs. Corp., Norwalk, Conn., 1988—. Served to 1st lt. USAR, 1957-60.

ALLISON, ROBERT J., JR., oil and gas company executive; b. Evanston, Ill., Jan. 29, 1939; s. Robert James and Mary Susan (Rohrer) A.; m. Carolyn J. Grother, June 17, 1961; children—Amy, Ann Stanislaw, Jane. B.S. in Petroleum Engring., Kans. U., 1960. Engring. mgmt. Amoco Prodn. Co., U.S., Trinidad and Iran, 1960-73; v.p. ops., chmn., chief exec. officer Anadarko Petroleum Corp., Ft. Worth and Houston, 1973-76, 86—; pres. Anadarko Petroleum Co., Ft. Worth and Houston, 1976—, chief exec. officer, 1979—; group v.p. Panhandle Eastern Corp., Houston, 1980, chmn., chief exec. officer, 1986—; bd. dirs. Panhandle Eastern Corp. Bd. dirs. Sam Houston Area Council Boy Scouts Am., Houston, 1985—; adv. council U. Tex. Engring. Found. Mem. Am. Petroleum Inst. (Mem. gen. com.), Ind. Petroleum Assn. Am. (bd. dirs.), Tex. Mid-Continent Oil and Gas Assn. (bd. dirs.), AIME. Republican. Presbyterian. Club: Lochinvar Golf (pres. 1982-85), The Houston, Petroleum, Champions Golf (Houston). Home: 5618 Green Springs Houston TX 77066 Office: Anadarko Petroleum Corp PO Box 1330 Houston TX 77251-1330

ALLISON, STEPHEN GALENDER, radio station executive; b. Springfield, Mo., Dec. 11, 1952; s. Edgbert and Naomi Louise (Chamless) A.; m. Linda Katherine Lavelle, Apr. 6, 1978 (div. Dec. 1983); children: Julie Ann, Jennifer Erin; m. Tara Rae Foster, Aug. 20, 1986. Personality Sta. WSBB, New Smyrna, Fla., 1971-72, Sta. WMFJ-AM-FM, Daytona Beach, Fla., 1972-75, Sta. KADI-FM, St. Louis, 1975-76, Sta. KAUM-FM, Houston, 1976-79, Sta. WKYS-FM, Washington, 1979-81; gen mgr. Sta. KSTM-FM, Phoenix, 1981-85; pres. Allison Broadcasting Co., Inc. (merged with The Dayton Group), Phoenix, 1985-87, The Daytona Group, Phoenix, 1987—, Allison Broadcast Group, Inc., Dallas, Del Mar, Calif., 1987—; owner Stas. KGRX-FM/KIKO, Phoenix, 1987—, Sta. KDGE-FM, Dallas; mktg. cons. St. Louis Post-Dispatch, 1975-76, Houston Chronicle, 1976-79, Washington Star, 1980-81; advt. cons. Celebrity Theatre, Phoenix, 1985-86. Bd. dirs. Desert-Mountain Foothills Assn., Scottsdale, Ariz., 1981—, Alwun House Cultural Ctr., Phoenix, 1982—, Film in Ariz., Phoenix, 1985—, Ariz. Commn. on the Arts, Phoenix, 1986—; mem. Nat. Rep. Congl. Com., 1988—. Mem. Nat. Assn. Broadcasters, Ariz. Broadcasters Assn. Republican. Club: Phoenix Active 20-30. Home: 7507 Summitview Dr Irving TX 75063 Office: 1320 Greenway Dr Irving TX 75038

ALLMAN, JAMES MALCOLM, chemical engineer; b. Longview, Tex., Jan. 8, 1956; s. Samuel Herbert and Sarah Curtis (Aldridge) A.; m. Lucia Leigh Williams, May 26, 1979 (div. 1984). BS in Chemistry and Chem. Engring., U. Tex., 1977; MA in Process Control, U. Houston, 1980. Process engr. Monsanto Corp., Texas City, Tex., 1978-82; rsch. engr. Monsanto Corp., St. Louis, 1982—. Mem. Am. Chem. Soc., Am. Inst. Chem. Engrs., Internat. Folk Dance (University City, Mo.). Republican. Baptist. Home: 1833 Seven Pines Dr Saint Louis MO 63146 Office: Monsanto Corp 800 Lindbergh St Saint Louis MO 63167

ALLMAN, WILLIAM BERTHOLD, musician, engineer, consultant; b. Phila., Feb. 16, 1927; s. Drue Nunez and Blanche (Oppenheimer) A.; m. Margo Hutz, Feb. 19, 1954; children: Avis Louise, David Drue. BSEE, Drexel U., 1949; MBA, U. Pa., 1951. Registered profl. engr., Pa. Contract engr. Atlantic Refining, Phila., 1951-55, E.I. DuPont de Nemours & Co., Inc., Wilmington, Del., 1955-58; constrn. engr. Niagra Falls, N.Y., 1958-59; cons. engr. Wilmington, 1959-82, Allman Assocs., West Grove, Pa., 1982—; owner, mgr. Allman Bldgs., Phila., 1965-87. Contbr. numerous articles on plastic pipe to profl. mags.; drummer, washboard player with Allman, Melton and Co. band; performed with various musicians including Lionel Hampton, Brownie McGhee, Mississippi Fred McDowell, Sonny Terry. Mem. Bi-racial com. City of Newark, Del., 1963-71, chmn. 1965, London Grove Township Mcpl. Authority, Chester County, Pa., 1985—, chmn. 1986; Dem. committeeman, Del., 1964-71, chmn., 1968; candidate Mayor, City of Newark, 1970. Served with USNR, 1945-46, ETO. Mem. Am. Assn. Individual Investors, Del. Ctr. Contemporary Arts, Del. Art Mus. Democrat. Unitarian. Home and Office: 202 E State Rd West Grove PA 19390

ALLMENDINGER, PAUL FLORIN, retired engineering association executive; b. Moline, Ill., Mar. 2, 1922; s. Andrew Louis A. and Nellie L. (Florin) Inman; m. Sara Jo Breazeale, Aug. 31, 1947; children: James, Glen, John. Student, Augustana Coll., Rock Island., Ill., 1940-41; B.S., U.S. Naval Acad., 1944. Dir. engring. Prestolite Co.-Eltra Corp., Toledo, Ohio, 1961-67; dir. engring. Power Tool div. Rockwell Internat., Pitts., 1967-68, v.p. engring. Power Tool div., 1968-77; v.p. tech. affairs Motor Vehicle Mfrs. Assn., Detroit, 1977-81; dep. exec. dir. ASME, N.Y.C., 1981-82, exec. dir., 1982-87. Served to lt (j.g.) USN, 1941-47. Fellow Inst. Mech. Engrs.; mem. ASME (Centennial award 1980), Soc. Automotive Engrs. (bd. dirs. 1963-66), Am. Soc. Engring. Edn., Soc. Mfg. Engrs., Engrs. Council for Profl. Devel. (bd. dirs. 1973-80, pres. 1976-78, Grinter Disting. Service award 1986), Am. Nat. Standards Inst. (bd. dirs. 1977-82), Tau Beta Pi. Republican. Presbyterian. Clubs: University (Washington and N.Y.C.). Office: Am Soc Mech Engrs 345 E 47th St New York NY 10017

ALLMON, MICHAEL BRYAN, accountant; b. Oceanside, Calif., July 14, 1951; s. William Bryan and Cecelia Audrey (Wright) A.; m. Monika Ann Arth, Sept. 15, 1979; 1 child, Stefanie Michelle. BBA, U. Tex., 1975; MBT U. So. Calif., 1986. CPA, Calif. Staff acct. Alexander Grant & Co., L.A., 1976-77; acct. Laventhol & Horwath, CPAs, L.A., 1977-85; dir. tax, fin. planning services Zusman, Cameron and Allmon, CPAs, 1985-88; chief exec. officer, dir. Essential Profl. Svcs., Inc., 1985-86; owner Michael B. Allmon & Co. CPAs, Marina Del Rey, 1988—. Contbr. articles to profl. jours. Mem. AICPAs (fed. tax div.), Calif. Soc. CPAs (fin. planning com.), Internat. Assn. for Fin. Planning, Acctg. Circle U. So. Calif., Am. Assn. Profl. Fin. Planners (L.A. chpt. pres.), Walnut Track Club (pres. team) (L.A.), Manhattan (Calif.) Country Club.

ALLPORT, WILLIAM WILKENS, lawyer; b. Cleve., May 31, 1944; s. H. Burnham and Vernes Sophia (Wilkens) A.; m. Roberta Charlotte Warfield, Dec. 17, 1966; children—Christine Anne, Laura Warfield. A.B., Gettysburg Coll., 1966; J.D., Case Western Res. U., 1969. Bar: Ohio 1969, U.S. Ct. Appeals (6th cir.) 1971, U.S. Supreme Ct. 1973, U.S. Ct. Appeals (8th cir.) 1976, U.S. Ct. Appeals (7th cir.) 1978, U.S. Ct. Appeals (1st cir.) 1980, N.Y. 1981, U.S. Ct. Appeals (5th, 3d, 4th cirs.) 1981, U.S. Ct. Appeals (11th cir.) 1982, U.S. Ct. Appeals (2d cir.) 1983. Assoc. Baker & Hostetler, Cleve., 1969-75; chief labor counsel Leaseway Transp. Corp., Cleve., 1975-84, v.p., chief labor counsel, 1984—. Ward chmn. Rep. Com.; trustee Soap Box Derby Assn.; explorer advisor Boy Scouts Am.; mem. Citizens League of Greater Cleve.; bd. govs. Case Western Res. Law Sch., 1983—, trustee Jr. Achievement of Greater Cleve., N.E. Ohio Soap Box Derby Assn. Mem. ABA, Ohio Bar Assn., N.Y. State Bar Assn., Cleve. Bar Assn., Internat. Law Soc., Case Western Res. Law Sch. Alumni Assn. (pres. 1985—), Eagle Scout Assn., Phi Delta Phi, Theta Chi, Pi Lambda Sigma. Editor: Case Western Res. U. Law Rev., 1968-69. Republican. Presbyterian (elder). Club: Smoker's (pres. 1969-73). Avocations: sailing, motorcycling. Home: 3337 Thomson Cir Rocky River OH 44116 Office: Leaseway Transp Corp 3700 Park East Blvd Cleveland OH 44122

ALLY, ARTHUR D., investment firm executive; b. Cleve., Apr. 17, 1942; s. Arthur and Virginia (Jacobs) A.; m. Bonnie Jean Danielson, July 3, 1961; children: Douglas, Stephen, Cheryl. BBA in Acctg., Cleve. State U., 1973. CPA; cert. fin. planner. Br. mgr. Capital Fin. corp., Sherman, Tex., 1961-69; credit mgr. Montgomery Ward, Cuyanoga Falls, Ohio, 1969-71; owner Ally Recovery Svc., Cleve., 1971-73; internal auditor Gulf Oil Corp., Houston, 1973-76; contr. Tex. Pipe & Supply Co., Houston, 1976-78; account exec., br. mgr. Prudential Bache Securities, Orlando, Fla., 1978-83; fin. cons., br. mgr. Shearson Lehman Hutton Inc., Boca Raton, Fla., 1983—. Contbr. articles to profl. pubs. Mem. standing com. Why We Stand, Boca Raton, 1987-88, adv. bd. United Way Volusia County, Daytona Beach, Fla., 1985-86, Estate Planning Coun., Boca Raton, 1987—, adv. bd. Fla. Hosp. Group, Orlando, 1984-85; chmn. gifts com., exec. com., bd. dirs. United Way South Palm Beach County, Fla.; sponsor Spl. Olympics-Palm Beach County, 1988; maj. sponsor Drug Abuse Coun. South Palm Beach, 1987. Mem. AICPA, Fla. Inst. CPA's, Bankers Club. Republican. Presbyterian. Home: 1677 NW 48th St Boca Raton FL 33434 Office: Shearson Lehman Hutton 1200 N Federal Hwy Boca Raton FL 33432

ALM, JAMES, human resource development executive; b. Hubbard Woods, Ill., May 6, 1937; s. Carl W. and Berith J. A. (Lundstrom) A.; BA in English, Cornell Coll., Mt. Vernon, Iowa, 1959. Claim negotiator Continental Nat. Am., Chgo., 1962-64; tng. evaluator Allstate Ins. Cos., Northbrook, Ill., 1964-80; dir. corp. tng. and human resource devel. Midas Internat., Chgo., 1980—; part-time lectr. Mus. Contemporary Art, 1984-89; adviser human resources ARC, 1983. Spl. adv. Crusade of Mercy, Chgo., 1964-65; mem. adv. bd. Broader Urban Involvement and Leadership Devel., Chgo., 1965; mem. U.S.S. Nautilus Nat. Landmark Com., 1982-88. Served with Submarine Service, USN, 1960-62. Mem. Am. Soc. Tng. and Devel., Am. Soc. Personnel Adminstrn., Human Resources Planning Soc., Orgn. Devel. Inst., Chgo. Orgn. Devel. Assn., Ill. Tng. Dirs. Assn., Nat. Soc. Performance and Instrn. Methodist. Author: Intrinsic Programming: A Primer, 1964; contbr. articles to profl. publs.; subject of profl. articles. Office: care Midas Internat 225 N Michigan Ave Chicago IL 60606

AL-MANSOUR, KHALID ABDULLAH, lawyer, banker; b. Pitts., Jan. 29, 1936; s. George Jamil and Arma (Jackson) Warden. B.A., Howard U., 1958; J.D., U. Calif., Berkeley, 1962. Bar: Calif. 1962. Sr. ptnr., co-founder firm Al-Talal, Al-Waleed and Al-Mansour, San Francisco, N.Y.C., Africa, Saudi Arabia and Qatar, 1964—; dir. Al-Bakah Corp., Kapital Bank, Zurich, TranSyt Internat. Ltd., J.B. Broadcasting Corp., African ArabianIslamic Bank Ltd., Nassau, Bahamas. Mem. ABA, African Am. Assn., Internat. Bar Assn., Phi Beta Kappa. Islamic. Author: Legal and Business Aspects of Conducting Business in the Middle East, 1976; Islamic Economics, 1982. Office: African Arabian Islamic Bank Ltd 601 California St Suite 300 San Francisco CA 94108

ALMOND, JOAN, chemistry instructor; b. Bklyn., May 19, 1934; d. Harry Christian Nintzel and Helen Pauline (Diviak) Levesen; m. Randall Leroy Field Sr., Nov. 15, 1952 (div. Feb. 1972); children: Randall Leroy Jr., Roland, Gary, Brian, Lorraine, Thomas; m. Bransford Wayne Almond, Dec. 9,

1986. Grad. high sch., Bklyn. Sec. Fulton Savs. Bank, Bklyn., 1952-53; mgr. reprodn. Air Pre-heater Corp., Wellsville, N.Y., 1958; chemistry technician fibers div. Allied Chem., Hopewell, Va., 1963-76; chemistry technician Va. Power Co.-North Anna Power Sta., Mineral, 1976-86, assoc. instr., 1987—. Recipient Cert. Achievement Nat. Acad. for Nuclear Tng., 1988. Mem. Women of Moose (chair Moosehart Hopewell com. chpt. 1971). Roman Catholic. Office: Va Power Co-North Anna Power Sta Box 402 Mineral VA 23114

ALONZO, RONALD THOMAS, manufacturing executive; b. Mexico City, June 12, 1942; came to U.S., 1957; s. Rosendo and Alice Jane (Ratcliff) A.; m. Denise Angèle Rufin, Feb. 10, 1968; children: Rodrigo, Micaela. BA in Polit. Sci., Tulane U., 1965. Adminstrv. asst. Humble Oil & Refinery Co., New Orleans, 1965-67; advt. and sales promotion mgr. internat. div. Whirlpool Corp., Benton Harbor, Mich., 1968-72; regional mgr. Europe and Latin Am. internat. div. Whirlpool Corp., Benton Harbor, 1972-78; internat. sales mgr. Kohler (Wis.) Co., 1978-83; internat. v.p. Vollrath Co., Sheboygan, Wis., 1983-84; v.p., chief mktg. and internat. officer Jet Spray Corp., Norwood, Mass., 1984—. Mem. Nat. Assn. Food Equipment Mfrs. (vice. chmn. internat. com., steering com. mem. 1987—, chmn. internat. com. 1989-80), Nat. Council U.S. China Trade, Internat. Bus. Ctr., Internat. Food Mfrs. Assn., Am. Mktg. Assn., Nat. Assn. Food Mfrs. (vice chmn. internat. com. and mem. of steering com. 1987—, chmn. internat. com.), U.S. Arab C. of C., Sales and Mktg. Execs. Greater Boston, Inc. Avocations: gastronomy, oenology, photography. Home: PO Box 2452 Duxbury MA 02331 Office: Jet Spray Corp 825 University Ave Norwood MA 02062

ALPERIN, IRWIN EPHRAIM, clothing company executive; b. Scranton, Pa., Apr. 29, 1925; s. Louis I. and Bessie (Wickner) A.; m. Francine Leah Friedman, Dec. 5, 1948; children: Barbara Joy, Jane Leslie. BS in Indsl. Engring., Lehigh U., 1947; cert. mech. engring. Pa. State U., 1945. Mgmt. trainee Mayflower Mfg. Co., Scranton, Pa., 1947-49, sec., 1952-79, pres., 1980—; with Triple A Trouser Mfg. Co., Inc., Scranton, 1952, v.p., treas., 1958-79, pres., 1980—; with Gold Star Mfg. Co., Inc., Scranton, 1956, pres., 1956—; sec. Astro Warehousing, Inc., Scranton, 1962—; sec.-treas. Bondeal, Inc., Scranton, 1978—; vice chmn. Montage Inc., 1979—; sec. Alperin, Inc., 1982—; bd. dirs. Sacquoit Industries Inc., Scranton. Bd. dirs. Econ. Devel. Council N.E. Pa., Avoca, 1974—, v.p., 1978-83; bd. dirs. ARC, Scranton, 1968—; bd. dirs. Jewish Home Eastern Pa., Scranton, 1970—, treas., 1981—; bd. dirs. Jewish Community Ctr., Scranton, 1971-86, Pa. United Way, Harrisburg, Pa., 1973-78, Scranton Mental Health-Mental Retardation Ctr., 1975-78; pres. Planning Council Social Services Lackawanna County, 1972-74, now life mem.; pres. Jewish Family Service of Lackawanna County, 1967-70, now life bd. mem.; v.p. United Way Lackawanna County, 1974-78, exec. com., 1978-86; pres. Alperin Found., Scranton, 1962—; treas. Scranton-Lackawanna Jewish Fedn., 1973-75, life mem. bd. dirs.; trustee Amos Lodge Found., 1982—, Found. Jewish Elderly, 1984—, v.p. 1985—; trustee Pocono N.E. Devel. Fund, 1983-86, sec. 1986—. Temple Hesed pres., 1969-71, life mem., bd. dirs., Scranton, Pa.; mem. Lackawanna County Library Bd., 1983-85; treas. Community Arts Project, Lackawanna County, 19876—; bd. dirs. Broadway Theatre League Lakawanna County, 1989—. Served with C.E., AUS, 1944-46. Recipient Americanism award, 1982; named Man of Year, Jewish Community Ctr., 1973, Disting. Pennsylvanian, Phila. C. of C., 1982. Mem. Am. Inst. Indsl. Engrs. (sr.). Club: Glen Oak Country (Clarks Summit, Pa.). Lodges: Masons, Shriners, Elks, B'nai B'rith (trustee; Man of Yr. 1982). Home: 600 Colfax Ave Scranton PA 18510 Office: Penn and Vine Sts PO Box 470 Scranton PA 18503

ALPERIN, STANLEY I., publisher, writer, editor, consultant; b. Boston, Jan. 3, 1931; s. Herman and Esther (Gorovitz) A.; m. Sondra Price, Sept. 8, 1957; children: Lisa Alperin Rose, Marlene Alperin Hochman, Hillary Price. Editor U.S. Directory Service, Miami, Fla., 1966—. Author: Careers in the Health Care Field, Careers in Nursing; editor, researcher numerous medical directories. Home: 7960 SW 89th Terr Miami FL 33156 Office: US Directory Svc Pubs 655 NW 128 St Miami FL 33168

ALPERT, BARRY MARK, insurance company and banking executive; b. Chgo., Apr. 17, 1941; s. Isadore Daniel and Betty Shane A.; m. Judith Rae Schwartz, Dec. 24, 1969; children: Daniel Ian, Jason Bradley, Stephanie Ann. Student, Ind. U., 1958-60; BBA, Roosevelt U., 1961; MBA in Banking, U. Wis., 1965. V.p. Exchange Nat. Bank, Chgo., 1961-72; pres., chief exec. officer Belleair Bluffs Corp., Largo, Fla., 1973-77; chmn., chief exec. officer Orange State Life and Health Ins. Co., Largo, 1977—; pres., chief exec. officer United Ins. Cos., Inc., Largo, 1988—; chmn. bd., founder Life Savs. and Loan Assn., Clearwater, Fla., 1979-83; asst. prof. fin. Roosevelt U., Chgo., 1965-69; host radio program Ask a Banker, Sta. WBBM/CBS, Chgo., 1966-67. Founding dir., treas. Ruth Eckerd Hall-Pact Inc., Clearwater, 1980-86; founder North Suncoast Symphony Guild, Clearwater, 1974; bd. dirs. Fla. Orch., Clearwater, 1974-80, St. Petersburg (Fla.) chpt. United Way, 1975. Served with USAFR, 1961-65. Home: 14123 85th Ave N Seminole FL 34646 Office: Orange State Life & Health Ins Co 2400 W Bay Dr Largo FL 34640

ALPERT, WARREN, oil company executive; b. Chelsea, Dec. 2, 1920; s. Goodman and Tena (Horowitz) A. B.S. Boston U, 1942; M.B.A., Harvard U., 1947. Mgmt. trainee Standard Oil Co. of Calif., 1947-48; financial specialist The Calif. Oil Co., 1948-52; pres. Warren Petroleum Co., 1952-54; now chmn. bd.; founder, pres., chmn. bd. Warren Equities, Inc., from 1954; chmn. Ritz Tower Hotel; chmn. bd. Kenyon Oil Co., Inc., Mid-Valley Petroleum Corp., Puritan Oil Co., Inc., Drake Petroleum Co., Inc.; Mem. of U.S. Com. for UN, 1958; exec. com. Small Bus. Adminstrn., 1958; adminstr. for adminstrn. U.S. AID, 1962; Former trustee, mem. exec. com. Boston U.; trustee Emerson Coll.; former v.p. Petroleum Marketing Edn. Found.; bd. dirs. Assocs. of Harvard Bus. Sch.; mem. com. for resource and devel. Harvard Med. Sch. Served with Signal Intelligence AUS, 1943-45. Andrew Wellington Cordier fellow Sch. Internat. Affairs, Columbia U. Mem. Am. Petroleum Industry 25 Year Club, Young Presidents Orgn. (past dir.), Am. Petroleum Inst. (dir. mktg. div.), Harvard Bus. Sch. Club (exec. com., dir., bd. govs., pres. 1960-61), Harvard Club (N.Y.C., Boston), Marco Polo Club, Met. Club. Home: 465 Park Ave New York NY 10022 Office: Waren Equities Inc 10 E 53rd St New York NY 10022

ALPERT, WESLEY SIMON, wholesale candy and tobacco corporation executive; b. Fall River, Mass., Mar. 14, 1926; s. Jacob and Bertha Lillian (Cohen) A.; m. Grace M. Kennison, May 10, 1968. A.B., Harvard U., 1947. Warehouse mgr. Alpert Bros., Inc., Fall River, 1948-69, pres., chief exec. officer, 1969—. Bd. dirs. Temple Beth-El Men's Club, Providence. Served with USNR, 1945-46. Mem. Nat. Candy Wholesalers Assn. (Candy Merchandiser of Yr. 1974), Mass. Candy and Tobacco Distbrs. (pres. 1979-81, chmn. bd., 1981-83, R.J. Reynolds Leadership award 1981), Nat. Assn. Tobacco Distbrs. (trustee 1986—), Fall River C. of C. Jewish. Clubs: Ledgemont Country (Seekonk, Mass.); Harvard (R.I.). Lodges: Masons, B'nai B'rith (bd. dirs. Boston). Home: 53 Wingate Rd Providence RI 02906 Office: Alpert Bros Inc 185 Riverside Ave Somerset MA 02726

AL-SARI, AHMAD MOHAMMAD, data processing executive; b. Al-Mukalla, South Yemen, Feb. 22, 1947; s. Mohammad Salem and Fatima Daoud (Al-Jilani) Al-S.; student U. Petroleum and Minerals, Dhahran, Saudi Arabia, 1965-67; B.Sc. in Chem. Engring., U. Tex., Austin, 1970. Lab. asst. Center Hwy. Research, Austin, 1969-70; programmer/analyst Data Processing Center, U. Petroleum and Minerals, 1970-76, dir. data processing center, 1976-80; chmn. Al-Khaleej Computers & Electronic Systems, Al-Khobar, Saudi Arabia, 1980—; dir. Internat. Systems Engring. Co.; co-founder Al-Falak Electronic Equipment and Supplies Co., United Computer Services Co., United Systems Engring. Co.; cons. various Saudi Arabian ministries; chmn. 1st Nat. Computer Conf., 1974. Mem. Assn. Computing Machinery U.S. (asso.), Saudi Computer Soc. (founding mem., treas.). Editor Procs. Symposium on Arabic Code Standards, Saudi Arabian Standards Orgn., 1981, The DPC Bull., 1972-76. Office: PO Box 16091, Riyadh 11464, Saudi Arabia

ALSPACH, HOWARD JOSEPH, JR., publisher, entrpreneur; b. Lancaster, Ohio, Sept. 13, 1944; s. Howard J. Sr. and Anna May (Noice) A. BS in Journalism, Ohio U., 1972. Sec., treas. Achor/Alspac, Inc., Lockwood, Inc., Alspach Varga Communications, Inc.; pub. Cen. Ohio Advts., Inc. Mem. planning commn. City of Lancaster. Home: 1099 Granville Park Lancaster OH 43130

ALSPACH, PHILIP HALLIDAY, manufacturing company executive; b. Buffalo, Apr. 19, 1923; s. Walter L. and Jean E. (Halliday) A.; m. Jean Edwards, Dec. 20, 1947; children—Philip Clough, Bruce Edwards, David Christopher; m. Loretta M. Hildebrand, Aug. 1982. B.Engring. in Mech. Engring, Tulane U., 1944. Registered profl. engr., Mass., Wis., La. With Gen. Electric Co., 1945-64, mgr. indsl. electronics div. planning, 1961-64; v.p., gen. mgr. constrn. machinery div. Allis Chalmers Mfg. Co., Milw., 1964-68; exec. v.p., dir., mem. exec. com. Jeffrey Galion, Inc., 1968-69; v.p. I.T.E. Imperial Corp., Springhouse, Pa., 1969-75; pres. E.W. Bliss div. Gulf & Western Mfg. Co., Southfield, Mich., 1975-79; group v.p. Katy Industries, Inc., Elgin, Ill., 1979-85; pres. Intercon Inc., Irvine, Calif., 1985—; bd. dirs. Winnebago Industries, Inc., Coen Co., Inc., A.J. Gerrard & Co., Advanced Computer Communications, Jandy Industries, Inc., Data-Design Labs., Pansini Corp. Author papers in field. Mem. pres.'s council Tulane U. Mem. Soc. Automotive Engrs. (sr.), IEEE, Soc. Mfg. Engrs., Nat. Assn. Corp. Dirs., Inst. Dirs. (U.K.), Am. Mgmt. Assn. Clubs: Canadian (N.Y.C.), Met. (N.Y.C.). Home: 23 Alejo Irvine CA 92715 Office: Intercon Inc 2500 Michelson Dr Suite 410 Irvine CA 92715

ALSTON, PENNY KAYE, realtor, educator; b. Salt Lake City, Nov. 17, 1950; d. James Darwin and Shirley Faye (Norris) Pitchford; M. James A. Alston, July 25, 1970; children: Amy, Matthew. BS in Bus. Edn., U. W. Fla., 1981. Cert. secondary tchr., Fla.; lic. real estate agt. Substitute tchr. Choctawhatchee High Sch., Ft. Walton Beach, Fla., 1981-83; realtor Reca/Better Homes and Gardens, Albuquerque, 1984-87; realtor, assoc. Realty One Svcs., Inc., Ft. Walton Beach, 1987—; instr. Realty One Sch. Real Estate, Ft. Walton Beach, 1988—. Active Realtors Polit. Action Com., 1988; mem. Eldorado High Sch. Cheerleading Prents Assn., Albuquerque, 1985-86; chaperone chmn. Choctawhatchee Choral Parents, Ft. Walton Beach, 1987-88. Mem. Nat. Assn. Realtors, Eglin Officers' Wives Club. Home: 18 Poquito Rd Shalimar FL 32579 Office: Realty One Svcs Inc 16 Ferry Rd SE Fort Walton Beach FL 32548

AL-SUWAIDI, SALEM MOHAMMED, management professional; b. Dareen, Ea. Province, Saudi Arabia, Jan. 15, 1956; s. Mohammed Salem Al-Suwaidi and Sarah (Rashid) Al-Sopai; m. May Sayegh Al-Suwaidi, Feb. 14, 1983; children: Nadia and Sarah (twins). BS in Bus., William Carey Coll., Hattiesburg, Miss., 1984; MBA, Century U., Beverly Hills, Calif., 1986. V.p. comml. M.S. Al-Suwaidi Orgn., Rahima, Saudi Arabia, 1984—. Author: Joint-venture in Saudi Arabia, 1986. Recipient Mgmt. Challenge cert. Bensen and Hedges Co. and Ashridge Coll. of London, Bahrain, 1985. Home and Office: Al-Suwaidi Orgn, PO Box 12, Rahima 31941, Saudi Arabia

ALT, CHRISTOPHER BOYDEN, financial executive; b. Balt., Dec. 23, 1948; s. Richard Melton and Martha (Boyden) A.; m. Barbara DiVitto, Sept. 15, 1979; children: Lily, Zachary. BA, Bowdoin Coll., 1971; MPA in Info. Systems, U. Pa., 1973; PhD in Mgmt., MIT, 1982. Cons. Data Resources, Inc., Washington, 1973-74; systems analyst FEA, Washington, 1974-76; asst. prof. sch. of mgmt. Boston U., 1980-82; corp. planner Conoco, Inc., Stamford, Conn., 1982-83; mgr. fin. planning and analysis Wang Labs., Inc., Lowell, Mass., 1983-85; dir., treas. planning and ops. Lotus Devel. Corp., Cambridge, Mass., 1985-88; chief exec. officer, treas. MedChem Products Inc., Woburn, Mass., 1988—. Office: MedChem Products Inc 444 Washington St Woburn MA 01801

ALTER, GERALD L., real estate executive; b. Rensselaer, Ind., Aug. 24, 1910; s. Leslie and Lettie (Willis) A.; m. Margaret A. Davis, Sept. 15, 1939; children: Judith Ann (dec.), John Edward. Student Bus. Coll., 1927-28. Clk. and office mgr., 1929-35; bldg. contractor, 1936-45; real estate broker and ins. agt., 1946—; pres. Alter Realty & Ins., Leads, Inc., investments, Alter Ins. Agy., Inc., REMCO Real Estate Mgmt. Co., Alter Devel. Co.; pres. Developers & Builders. Planning commr. City of Torrance, 1966-83, chmn. Torrance Planning Commn. 1982-83; water commr. City of Torrance, 1984—, chmn. 1987-88; former bd. dirs. Harbor Area United Way. Mem. Torrance-Lomita-Carson Bd. Realtors (pres. 1978, v.p. 1980-81), Calif. Assn. Realtors (dir. 1978-81), Nat. Assn. Realtors, Torrance C. of C. (past dir.), Am. Legion. Republican. Clubs: OX-5 (pioneer airman). Lodge: Rotary. Home: 1337 Engracia Ave Torrance CA 90501 Office: 2305 Torrance Blvd Torrance CA 90501

ALTFEST, LEWIS JAY, financial and investment advisor; b. N.Y.C., Oct. 14, 1940; s. Sam and Ruth (Zwang) A.; m. Karen Caplan, Dec. 25, 1966; children: Ellen Wendy, Andrew Gamer. BBA with honors, CCNY, 1962; MBA, NYU, 1970; PhD, CUNY, 1978. CPA, N.Y.; chartered fin. analyst. Sr. investment analyst Wertheim and Co., N.Y.C., 1969-75, Lehman Bros., N.Y.C., 1975-76; dir. research, gen. ptnr. Lord Abbett and Co., N.Y.C., 1976-82; pres. L.J. Altfest and Co., Inc., N.Y.C., 1982—; assoc. prof. fin. Pace U. Grad. Sch. Bus., N.Y.C., 1984—; dir. fin. planning and investments program New Sch. for Socical Research, N.Y.C., 1988—; arbitrator Nat. Assn. Securities Dealers, Am. Arbitration Assn. Author: (with others) Introduction to Business, 1978, Capital Budgeting Handbook, 1986; Author: Risk-Return and Mutual Fund Performance in The New York Planner, 1987-88. Pres. 240 E. 79th Coop. Bd., N.Y.C., 1983-86. Served with U.S. Army, 1962-63. Named one of best fin. planners in U.S. Money mag., 1987. Mem. Nat. Assn. Personal Fin. Advisors (bd. dirs. 1985—), Am. Inst. CPA's, Internat. Assn. for Fin. Planning (bd. dirs. N.Y. chpt. 1987—), Inst. Chartered Fin. Analysts, Am. Fin. Assn., Fin. Analysts Fedn., Fin. Mgmt. Assn., N.Y. Soc. Security Analysts, Registry Fin. Planning Practitioners, CCNY Bus. Alumni Assn. (bd. dirs. 1983-87), Acad. of Fin. Svcs. Office: LJ Altfest & Co Inc Penthouse 140 William St New York NY 10038

ALTHAUS, DAVID STEVEN, research company executive; b. Massilon, Ohio, Dec. 25, 1945; s. James Horace and Mary Jane (Horan) A.; m. Joan Elizabeth Wrenn, Aug. 4, 1973; children: D. Steven Jr., Matthew, Beth Anne. BA, Miami U., Oxford, Ohio, 1967; cert., Def. Lang. Inst., Monterey, Calif., 1969; MBA, Miami U., Oxford, Ohio, 1976. CPA; Cert. profl. in human resources. Internal auditor Harris Corp., Cleve., 1976-77; sr. staff acct. Harris Corp., Rochester, N.Y., 1977-78; acctg. supr. Imperial Group Ltd., Wilson, N.C., 1978-80; dir. planning Am. Mortgage Ins. Cos., Raleigh, N.C., 1980-83; asst. v.p., budget mgr. Gen. Electric Mortgage Ins. Cos., Raleigh, 1983-84; controller Chem. Industry Inst. Toxicology, Research Triangle Park, N.C., 1984—. Served as capt. USMC, 1968-74, Vietnam. Decorated Cross of Galantry, Rep. of Vietnam, Da Nang, 1970. Mem. Nat. Assn. Accts., Am. Soc. for Personnel Adminstrn., Am. Compensation Assn., Controller's Council, Bus. Planning Bd., Am. Inst. CPA's, U.S. Naval Inst. Baptist. Office: Chem Industry Inst Toxicology PO Box 12137 Research Triangle Park NC 27709

ALTHAVER, LAMBERT EWING, manufacturing company executive; b. Kansas City, Mo., May 18, 1931; s. Edward William and Dorothy Lambert (Ewing) A.; m. Holly Elizabeth Walpole, Feb. 28, 1953; children: Brian, Lauren. BA, Principia Coll, 1952. Account exec. Walbro Corp., Cass City, Mich., 1954-58, asst. to pres., 1958-65, v.p. fin., 1965-70, exec. v.p., 1970-77, pres., chief ops. officer, 1977-82, pres., chief exec. officer, 1982-87, chmn., pres., chief exec. officer, 1987—. Councilman Village of Cass City, 1963-65; pres. Village of Cass City, 1965-84, 87—; commr. Tuscola County Planning Commn., Caro, Mich, 1966—; chmn. Cass City Econ. Devel. Corp., 1983—; bd. dirs. Tuscola County Econ. Devel. Corp., 1985—; vice-chmn., sec., dir. Artrain, Inc., 1975—; v.p., bd. dirs. Lake Huron area Boy Scouts Am., 1988—; v.p., dir. Village Bach Festival, 1979—. With U.S. Army, 1952-54. Named Citizen of Yr. Cass City C. of C., 1978; Paul Harris fellow Rotary Internat., Evanston, Ill., 1979. Mem. Mich. State C. of C. (bd. dirs.), Detroit Athletic Club. Republican. Mem. Ch. Christian Sci. Office: Walbro Corp 6242 Garfield St Cass City MI 48726

ALTHERR, JACK RICHARD, accountant; b. Indpls., Apr. 1, 1949; s. Jack Richard and Mary Virginia (Branch) A.; m. Lucy Carolyn Jordan, June 4, 1971; children: Carrie Alison, Jonathan. BS, U. Ala., 1971, MBA, 1976. CPA, Ala. Auditor, cons. Arthur Young & Co., Birmingham, Ala., 1976-81; corp. controller Birmingham Bolt Co., 1981-82; div., cost and budgets Avondale Mills, Sylacauga, Ala., 1982—, dir. internal auditing, 1983-84, controller fabrics div., 1985-86, v.p. and controller, 1986-87, v.p. adminstr. and sec., 1987-89, v.p., chief fin. officer, sec., 1989—. Served as lt. USNR, 1971-74. Mem. Ala. Soc. CPA's, Am. Inst. CPA's, Sylacauga C. of C. (bd. dirs. 1987—). Club: Coosa Valley Country (Sylacauga). Lodge: Rotary (pres. elect Sylacauga). Home: 1834 Pleasant Ridge Sylacauga AL 35150 Office: Avondale Mills Inc Avondale Ave Sylacauga AL 35150

ALTIER, WILLIAM JOHN, management consultant; b. Drexel Hill, Pa., July 22, 1935; s. William John and Gertrude (Soule) A.; BA, Lafayette Coll., 1958; MBA, Pa. State U., 1962; m. Mileen Rishel Bower, June 21, 1958; children—William Clark, Dwight Douglas. Assoc., Kepner-Tregoe Inc., Princeton, N.J., 1964-68; gen. mgr. div. Princeton Research Press, 1970-75, sr. assoc., 1975-76; assoc. Applied Synergetics Ctr., Waltham, Mass., 1968-69; dir. mktg. Comstock & Wescott Inc., Cambridge, Mass., 1969-70; pres. Princeton Assocs. Inc., Buckingham, Pa., 1976—; grad. asst. Dale Carnegie Courses; lectr. Assn. for Media-Based Continuing Edn. for Engrs.; guest lectr. Grad. Sch. Mgmt., New Sch. for Social Research, bd. dirs. Inst. Mgmt. Cons. Co-chmn. indsl. div. United Community Fund, Carlisle, Pa., 1963; elder Doylestown Presbyn. Ch.; exec. v.p. Bucks County br. ARC, also mem. planning com. Southeastern Pa. chpt.; vol. worker civic orgns. Cert. mgmt. cons. Mem. Acad. Mgmt., Am. Chem. Soc., Am. Vacuum Soc., Armed Forces Communications and Electronics Assn., Am. Mgmt. Assn., Product Devel. and Mgmt. Assn. (v.p.), Indsl. Mgmt. Club, Inst. Mgmt. Cons. (participative process cons. spl. interest group), Am. Arbitration Assn. (panel arbitrators), U. So. Calif. Ctr. for Futures Research, Assn. Mng. Cons. (trustee), Mensa, Kappa Sigma Alumni Corp. (chpt. pres.). Clubs: Exchange (bd. control 1960-64) (Carlisle); 1000. Research and devel. fundamental analytical thinking processes relative to change; patentee, author articles in field. Home: RD 4 Doylestown PA 18901 Office: PO Box 820 Buckingham PA 18912

ALTMAN, ROBERT A., lawyer; b. Washington, Feb. 23, 1947; s. Norman S. and Sophie B. (Robinson) A.; m. Lynda J. Carter, Jan. 29, 1984; 1 child, James Clifford. BA, U. Wis., 1968; JD, George Washington U., 1971. Bar: D.C. Ptnr. Clifford & Warnke, Washington, 1971—; pres. 1st Am. Corp., Washington, 1982—; bd. dirs. 1st Am. Bankshares Inc., Washington, 1st Am. Bank N.Y., N.Y.C., 1st Am. Bank of Ga., Atlanta. Office: Clifford & Warnke 815 Connecticut Ave NW Washington DC 20006

ALTMAN, WILLIAM KEAN, lawyer; b. San Antonio, Feb. 18, 1944; s. Marion K. and Ruth (Nunnelee) A.; m. Doris E. Johnson, May 29, 1964; children: Brian, Brad, Blake. BBA, Tex. A&M U., 1965, MBA, 1967; JD, U. Tex., 1979. Bar: Tex., U.S. Dist. ct. (no. and ea. dists.) Tex., U.S. Ct. Appeals (5th and 11th cirs.), U.S. Supreme Ct. Prin., owner William K. Altman P.C., Wichita Falls, Tex., 1970—. Mem. ABA, Tex. Bar Assn., Assn. Trial Lawyers Am. (bd. of govs. 1980-83, active coms. and sects.), Tex. Trial Lawyers Assn. (assoc. bd. dirs. 1977-78, bd. dirs. 1978—, active various coms. and sect.). Democrat. Baptist. Office: 500 Oil & Gas Bldg Wichita Falls TX 70301

ALTOBELLO, DANIEL JOSEPH, service executive; b. Westfield, Mass., Feb. 28, 1941; s. Henry Daniel and Josephine (LaMontagne) A.; m. Maureen Ann Cahill, July 27, 1963; children: Mark D., David A. AB, Georgetown U., 1963; MBA, Loyola Coll., Balt., 1978. Alumni staff asst. for admissions and programs Georgetown U. Alumni Assn., Washington, 1963-64, asst. exec. dir., 1964-66; asst. to pres. Georgetown U., Washington, 1966-74, sec., 1968-74, v.p. adminstrv. svcs., 1974-79; v.p. food svc. mgmt. Marriott Corp., Washington, 1979-82, v.p. Marriott in-flight svcs., 1982-84, exec. v.p., 1984-86, exec. v.p., pres. airport ops. group, 1988—. Trustee The Loyola Found., Inc., Washington, 1978—; bd. sponsors Loyola Coll., Balt., 1986—; bd. visitors Georgetown U., Washington, 1986—, bd. regents, 1980—. Mem. Internat. Flight Catering Assn., Inflight Food Svcs. Assn., Nat. Restaurant Assn., The Wings Club Inc. (bd. dirs.), Burning Tree Club, TPC at Avenel Club. Office: Marriott Corp Marriott Dr Washington DC 20058

ALTOBELLO, MILDRED FRANCES, realtor; b. West Palm Beach, Fla., Mar. 3, 1953; d. Francis Anthony and Ethel Hamner (Martin) A. BA, U. Ala., 1975; MBA, Samford U., 1977. Ter. mgr. Burroughs Corp., Miami, Fla., 1978-80; mgmt. trainee Coral Gables Fed. Savs. and Loan (Fla.), 1981; realtor-assoc. Keyes Co., Coral Gables, 1981-88; mem. Keyes Million Dollar Sales Club, Keyes Inner Circle, 1986; active Coral Gables Bd. of Realtors (realtor-lawyer com. 1985—, communications com. 1985-88, realtors polit. action com. 1987—, govtl. affairs com. 1988—), Civic Opera of Palm Beaches, 1969—; chmn. liturgical com. U. of Ala., Tuscaloosa, 1973. Recipient Spl. award for Outstanding Dedication and Successful Achievement in the 1988 RPAC Goal. Mem. Soc. Profl. Journalists, Women in Communications, Inc., Sunset Jaycees, Coral Gables C. of C. Democrat. Roman Catholic.

ALTON, ANN LESLIE, judge, lawyer, educator; b. Pipestone, Minn., Sept. 10, 1945; d. Howard Robert, Jr. and Camilla Ann (DeMong) Alton; m. Gerald Russell Freeman Sr.; children: Matthew Alton-Freeman (dec.), Brady Michael Alton-Freeman. BA Smith Coll., 1967; JD U. Minn., 1970. Bar: Minn. 1970, U.S. Dist. Ct. Minn. 1972, U.S. Supreme Ct. 1981. Asst. county atty., Hennepin County, Mpls., 1970-89, felony prosecutor, criminal div., 1970-75, acting chief citizen protection div., 1975-76, chief citizen protection/econ. crime div., 1976-79, chief econ. crime unit, 1979-85, sr. atty. civil div. handling labor and employment law, 1985-89, judge Dist. Ct. 4th Jud. Dist., Hennepin County, Minn., 1989—; instr. Hamline U. Law Sch., St. Paul, 1973-76; adj. prof. law William Mitchell Coll. Law, St. Paul, 1977—; adj. prof. U. Minn. Law Sch., 1978-82; lectr. in field, 1970—; mem. faculty Minn. Advocacy Inst., 1988—. Vice-chmn. bd. dirs. Minn. Realty Co., 1987—, Minn. Program on Victims of Sexual Assault, 1974-76; bd. dirs. Physician's Health Plan, Health Maintenance Orgn., 1976-80, exec. com. 1977-80; mem. legal drug abuse subcom. Gov. Minn. Adv. Com. Drug Abuse, 1972-74; bd. visitors U. Minn. Law Sch., 1979-85; mem. child abuse project coordinating com. Hennepin County Med. Soc., 1982-83, chmn. corp., labor, ins. subcom. 1982. Mem. ABA (criminal law, labor and employment law, civil litigation sects.), Hennepin County Bar Assn. (ethics com. 1973-76, criminal law com. 1973—, vice chmn. 1979-80, 83-84, unauthorized practice law com. 1977-78, individual rights and responsibilities com. 1977-78, labor and employment law com. 1985—, civil litigation com. 1985—), Nat. Dist. Attys. Assn. (office liaison econ. crime project assn. 1975-83), Nat. Assn. Women Judges, Minn. County Attys. Assn., Minn. Trial Lawyers Assn., Minn. Women Lawyers, U. Minn. Law Sch. Alumni Assn. (dir. 1979-85). Author articles, pamphlet, manual. Home: 2105 Xanthus Ln Plymouth MN 55447 Office: 1251C Hennepin County Govt Center Minneapolis MN 55487

ALTORFER, H(ANS) JOHN, management consultant; b. Hartford, Conn., Apr. 19, 1936; s. Hans A. and Martha M. (Meyer) A.; m. Suzanna L. Bradbrook, May 11, 1955 (div. 1975); children: David C., Suzanne L. BSBA, U. Calif., Berkeley, 1962; MS in Indsl. Adminstrn., Carnegie-Mellon U., 1964. Asst. to mgr. corp. planning Kaiser Aluminum & Chem. Corp., Oakland, Calif., 1964-66; assoc. Booz Allen & Hamilton, Chgo., 1966-70; dir. corp. devel. Chemetron Corp., Chgo., 1970-76; pres. Chemetron Indsl. Gases, Chgo., 1976-79; v.p. Union Camp Corp., Wayne, N.J., 1979-83; exec. v.p. TLB Plastics Corp., Brewster, N.Y., 1983-85; pres. H.J. Altorfer & Co., Inc., Franklin Lakes, N.J., 1985—; v.p. Spl. Metals Corp., New Hartford, N.Y., 1986-87. Served as sgt. USMC, 1954-57. Mem. Ctr. for Entrepreneurial Mgmt., Phi Beta Kappa. Republican. Home: 578 Huckleberry Ln Franlin Lakes NJ 07417 Office: 637 Wyckoff Ave Ste 107 Wyckoff NJ 07481

ALTSCHUL, ALFRED SAMUEL, airline executive; b. Chgo., Oct. 16, 1939; s. Herman and Lillian (Ginsburg) A.; m. Lynn Silverman, Sept. 8, 1968; children: Howard, Steven, Mark. B.S., U. Wis., 1961; M.B.A., U. Chgo., 1963. C.P.A., Ill. With G.A.T.X. Corp., Chgo., 1965-69; asst. treas. G.A.T.X. Corp., 1967-70, treas., 1970-81; v.p. fin., chief fin. officer Midway Airlines, Chgo., 1981—; lectr. in field. Lectr. fin. mgmt. Active Talent Assistance Program. Served with AUS, 1963-69. Mem. Financial Mgrs. Assn. (pres.) Am. Inst. CPA's, Fin. Execs. Inst., Alpha Epsilon Pi. Jewish religion. Club: Standard (Chgo.). Home: 8824 N Lowell Skokie IL 60076 Office: Midway Airlines Inc 5959 S Cicero Chicago IL 60638

ALTSCHULER, DAVID EDWARD, financial planner; b. Kew Gardens, N.Y., Nov. 4, 1952; s. Julius and Edith A.; m. Karen Schonberg Burros, Sept. 1, 1986; children: Dina Burros, Max. BS, Quinnipiac Coll., 1973.

Cert. fin. planner. Salesman Ruth Cohen Real Estate, Flushing, N.Y., 1978-80; with First Investors Corp., N.Y.C., 1979-80; fin. planner Investors Planning Services, Melville, N.Y., 1980-81; br. mgr. Cardell & Assocs., Morris Plains, N.J., 1981-83; pres. founder Iras & Keoghs Inc., Garden City, N.Y., 1981—; chief exec. officer Global Capital Group, Inc. (formerly Life Group, Inc.), Garden City, N.Y., 1985—; adj. prof. corp. fin. C.W. Post Coll., Greenvale, N.Y., 1980-82; pres.sec. prin. Sterling Diversified Services, Great Neck, N.Y., 1982; instr. Inst. Fin. Planning, Adelphi U., Garden City, N.Y., 1982-83; lectr. in field. Contbr. articles to profl. jours. Recipient Fin. Writers award Fin. Planner Mag. Mem. Internat. Assn. Fin. Plannnig, Nat.Speakers Assn., N.Y. Educators Assn. Office: Global Capital Group Inc 100 Garden City Pla Ste 100 Garden City NY 11530

ALTUCH, PETER MARK, personnel consultant; b. Newark, Sept. 30, 1952; s. Francis and Jeanne V. (Mark) A. BS, U. Hartford, 1974, MBA, 1977; MA, NYU, 1987. Mgr. labor relations Western Union, Upper Saddle River, N.J., 1977-81; mgr. employee relations Western Union, N.Y.C., 1981-85; mgr. devel., internal cons. Orange and Rockland Utilities, Pearl River, N.Y., 1985-87; dir. personnel Samsung Electronics, Saddle Brook, N.Y., 1987—. Mem. Am. Soc. Personnel Adminstrn. (treas. Bergen Rockland chpt. 1985-87, v.p. 1988), N.J. Utilities Assn. (chmn. compensation com. 1987). Republican. Home: 230 E 79th St New York NY 10021 Office: Samsung Electronics 301 Mayhill St Saddle Brook NJ 07662

ALTUNIAN, GARY E., retail executive; b. Pasadena, Calif., July 21, 1951; s. Igor and Elizabeth (Leaf) A.; m. Eleanor D., Aug. 28, 1976; 1 child, Jason. Store mgr. Audio Assocs., Pasadena, 1971-73, Stereo E., Los Angeles, 1973-76; store mgr. Federated Group, L.A., 1976-78, mgr. tng., 1978-81, dist. mgr., 1981-84, dir. tng., 1984—; nat. tng. mgr. Audio, Yamaha Electronic, Buena Park, Calif., 1988—.

ALVARADO, JOSE ANTONIO, investment banker; b. Granada, Nicaragua, Sept. 1, 1951; s. Jose Antonio and Esmeralda Alvarado; married; children: Jose Antonio, Isabel Victoria, Francisco-Jose. JD, Universidad Catolica, Nicaragua, 1973; MA in Econs., U. Rome, 1975; LLM, Harvard U., 1979, D of Juridical Sci., 1980. Minister plenipotentiary UN, Geneva, 1975-76; amb. UN, N.Y.C., 1976-78; ptnr., prin. Cambridge (Mass.) Analitica, 1978-81; fin. cons. Am. Express Corp., N.Y.C., 1981-83; dir., prin. First Equity Corp., Miami, Fla., 1983-85; chmn. Am. Investment Banking Corp., Miami, 1985—. Contbr. articles to profl. jours. Bd. dirs. Coun. for Internat. Visitors, Miami, 1983—, Internat. Ctr. of Fla., Miami, 1983-86, United Way, Miami, 1984—; bd. gov's. Hispanic Heritage Found., Miami; trustee Miami Dade County Community Coll.; bd. dirs. Miami Childrens Hosp. Recipient Lincoln prize, Lincoln Inst. Land Policy, Cambridge, 1979. Club: Harvard Faculty, Bankers. Office: AIBC Fin Corp 1390 Brickell Ave Miami FL 33131

ALVARADO, RICARDO RAPHAEL, corporate executive, lawyer; b. Washington, Mar. 29, 1927; s. Alfonso and Beatrice (Raphael) A.; m. Rita Logue, Feb. 14, 1948; children—Donna, Bonita, Ricardo R. (dec.) Rita, Susan, Peter, Christina. B.S., U.S. Mcht. Marine Acad., 1948; J.D., Am. U., 1953; LL.M., Georgetown U., 1963; M.A., George Washington U., 1976. Bar: Va. 1953. Commd. 2d lt. U.S. Air Force, 1951, advanced through grades to col., 1969, dep. dir. Congl. liason Office Sec. Def., 1970-72; mgr. govt. relations Lockheed Corp., Washington, 1972-73, corp. dir. govt. affairs, 1973-82; corp. v.p. The Signal Cos., Washington, 1982-85, Allied-Signal Inc., 1985—. Decorated Legion of Merit with cluster; recipient Outstanding Alumnus Profl. Achievement award U.S. Merchant Marine Acad., 1983, Meritorious Alumni Service award U.S. Mcht. Marine Acad., 1988. Mem. Air Force Assn. (life), Bus.-Govt. Relations Council, Washington Indsl. Round Table. Clubs: Aero; Army Navy (bd. dirs. 1975-76), International, City (Washington); Army Navy Country (Arlington, Va.). Home: 6108 Fort Hunt Rd Alexandria VA 22307 Office: 1001 Pennsylvania Ave NW Ste 700 Washington DC 20004 also: Allied-Signal Inc Columbia Rd & Park Ave Morristown NJ 07960

ALVARES, JOSEPH, business executive; b. Bombay, Dec. 19, 1935; came to U.S., 1970; BBA, Baruch Coll., 1975, MBA, 1977. Cert. Cost and Works Acct. Gen. mgr. Blue Skies Travel and Tours, Bombay, 1964-70; fin. mgr. Drake Am., N.Y.C., 1970-73; v.p., fin. controller Youngland Industries, E. Newark, N.J., 1973-84; pres. Budget Bus. Services, Inc., Floral Park, N.Y., 1984—. Mem. Brit. Inst. Mgmt. Office: Budget Bus Svcs 2 Brokaw Ave Floral Park NY 11001

ALVAREZ, PAUL HUBERT, public relations consultant; b. Glen Ridge, N.J., Jan. 16, 1942; s. Hugh Peter and Emilie (Stock) A.; m. Annette E. Kluss, Feb. 5, 1986; 1 child, Amy Elizabeth. B.A., Muskingum Coll., 1963. Editor Rockwell Internat., Pitts., 1964-65, PPG Industries, Pitts., 1965-68; account exec. Burson-Marsteller, Pitts., 1968-71; v.p. Ketchum Pub. Relations, Pitts., 1971-81, chmn., chief exec. officer, 1981-88; pres. Ketchum Specialized Svcs. Group, N.Y.C., 1988—; bd. dirs. Ketchum Communications, Pitts.; chmn. Counselor's Acad., N.Y.C., 1985; bd. advisors Sch. Journalism, U. Fla., Gainesville, 1981—; co-chmn. Am. Educators in Journalism Study on Grad. Edn. in Pub. Relations, Brimingham, Ala., 1982-84; pres., bd. dirs. Pub. Relations Found. Research and Edn. Author, editor: What Happens in Public Relations, 1980. Mem. exec. com., bd. dirs. Civic Light Opera Assn., Pitts., 1979-83; bd. dirs. Arthritis Found. Western Pa., 1981-82; v.p., dir. Pub. Relations Found., N.Y.C., 1985—. Served as sgt., USNG, 1963-69. Mem. Pub. Relations Soc. Am. Democrat. Presbyterian. Club: Siwanoy Country (Bronxville, N.Y.); Larchmont (N.Y.) Yacht; Dusquense (Pitts.). Home: 175 Riverside Dr New York NY 10024 Office: Ketchum Pub Communications Inc 1133 Ave of the Americas New York NY 10036

ALVERNAZ, RODRIGO, insurance company executive; b. Faial, Azores, Dec. 28, 1936; came to U.S., 1954; ; s. Frank P. and Ana (Leal) A.; m. Jean Bettencourt, May 31, 1958; children: Roderick, Mario, Anina, Gina. Gen. edn., Liceu Passos Manuel, Lisbon, Portugal, 1954; BBA in Acctg., Heald Coll., 1958; cert. bus. mgmt., Calif. State U., Hayward, 1980. Acct. United Nat. Life Ins. Soc., Oakland, Calif., 1958-62, asst. sec., agy. supr., 1962-64, asst. sec., treas., 1964-81, asst. v.p., 1970-81, sec., treas., 1981-83, sec. Luso-Am. Fraternal Fedn., 1981-88, v.p., sec., 1983-88; exec. v.p., chief exec. officer, Luso-Am. Fraternal Fedn. United Nat. Life Ins. Soc., Oakland, 1988—; v.p. Luso-Am. Edn. Found., 1979—. Pres. League Portugese Fraternal Socs. of Calif., 1986; co-chmn. Portugese-Ams. for Statue of Liberty, 1985-86. Recipient Commendation Order of Merit, Portugal, 1987. Mem. No. Calif. Life Ins. Assn., No. Calif. Policyowners' Svc. Assn. Republican. Roman Catholic. Lodge: Lions (local pres. 1980-81, local treas. 1981-86).

ALVINE, ROBERT, industrialist, entrepreneur, manufacturing company executive; b. Newark, Aug. 25, 1938; s. James C. and Marie Alvine; m. Diane C. Marzulli, May 6, 1961; children: Robert James, Laurie Anne. BS, Rutgers U., 1960; postgrad., Syracuse U., 1968-69, Harvard U., 1972. With Celanese Corp., 1960-77; bus. mgr. Celanese Plastics Co., Newark, 1969-72; dir. mktg. and ops. Celanese Piping Systems and Fabricated Products Co., Hilliard, Ohio, 1972-75; v.p. comml. Celanese Polymer Spltys. Co., Louisville, 1975-77, Uniroyal Inc., 1977-87; dir. strategy planning and bus. devel. Uniroyal-Chem., Naugatuck, Conn., 1977; v.p. corp. planning and devel. Uniroyal Inc., Middlebury, Conn., 1978-79; v.p., gen. mgr. Uniroyal Tire Co., 1979-80; pres. Uniroyal Merchandising Co., 1979-82, Uniroyal Devel. Co., 1980-82; sr. v.p. mergers and acquisitions Uniroyal Inc., 1980-87; chief exec., group v.p. Engineered Products, Worldwide, 1983-87; pres. Uniroyal Plastics & Power Transmission Cos., 1983-87; also corp. sr. officer responsible for mergers and acquisitions Uniroyal, Inc., 1982-87; and sr. corp. officer and major prin. in mgmt. leverage buy-out of Uniroyal, Inc. 1985; founder, chmn., chief exec. officer i-Ten Mgmt. Corp., Woodbridge, Conn., 1987—; chmn., chief exec. officer Aim Capital Group, Woodbridge, 1987—; chmn. Charter Power Systems, Plymouth Meeting, Pa., 1988—; prin. Charter House Group Internat., 1988—; founder, chief exec. officer, chmn. bd. dirs. i-Ten Cap. Corp., i-Ten Capital Corp., founder Aim Capital Group, Woodbridge, Conn., 1987; chmn. Charter Power Systems, Plymouth Meeting, Pa., 1988—; prin. Charter House Internat., N.Y.C., 1988—, Uniroyal Holdings, Waterbury, Conn., 1985—; bd. dirs. Wedge Computer, Boston, 1987—, A.P. Parts Co., Toledo. Served with AUS, 1962-68. Honor grad. Southeastern Signal Sch.; named Ky. Col., 1976. Mem. Nat. Assoc. Corp. Dirs., Pres.'s Assn., Am. Inst. Mgmt., Nat. Planning Inst., Assn. for Corp. Growth, N.Am. Planning Soc., Nat. Assn. Corp. Growth, Rubber Mfrs. Assn., Battery Coun. Internat., Newcomen Soc. Am., Soc. Plastics Industry, Soc. Plastics Engrs. (past dir.), Mfg. Chemists Assn., Nat. Paint and Coatings Assn., Council of Americas. Mem. Ch. of Christ. Clubs: Oaklane Country, Renaissance. Home: 55 N Racebrook Rd Woodbridge CT 06525

ALVORD, JOEL BARNES, bank executive; b. Manchester, Conn., Nov. 29, 1938; s. Martin Earl and Elizabeth (Barnes) A.; m. Anne Stilson, June 23, 1962; children: Sarah, Seth. A.B., Dartmouth Coll., 1960, M.B.A., 1961. With Hartford Nat. Corp., Conn., 1963—; exec. v.p. investments and exec. v.p. Hartford Nat. Corp., 1976-78, pres., 1978-88, chief exec. officer, 1986-88, chmn., 1988—, also bd. dirs.; chmn. Conn. Nat. Bank subs. Shawmut Nat. Corp., 1986—; chmn., chief exec. officer Shawmut Nat. Corp., 1988—; dir. Hartford Steam Boiler Inspection and Ins. Co. Bd. dirs. Inst. of Living, Hartford; trustee Wadsworth Atheneum. Served with Ordnance Corps U.S. Army, 1961-62. Mem. Res. City Bankers Assn. Congregationalist.

AL-ZAMIL, FAISAL SALEH, retail stores executive; b. Alkhobar, Saudi Arabia, Feb. 6, 1955; s. Saleh Abdulaziz Al-Zamil and Taibah (Abhullah) Al-Omran; m. Fawzia Al-Mousa, May 5, 1961; children: Abdullah, Maan. BS, U. Bridgeport, 1977; MBA, U. Petroleum and Minerals, Dhahran, Saudi Arabia, 1979. Gen. mgr. Zamil Internat., Aklhobar, 1981-85; pres. Al-Zamil Stores, Aklhobar, 1985—. Office: Al-Zamil Stores Corp, PO Box 217, Alkhobar 31952, Saudi Arabia

AMANN, DAVID WILLIAM, financial executive; b. Erie, Pa., Feb. 18, 1958; s. E.G. and M.E. (Motsch) A.; m. Susan Douglas, Aug. 21, 1982; childern: Amanda,Nathan. BS in Fin., Pa. State U., 1979. Asst. controller J. Milton Newton, Tampa, Fla., 1979-81; controller Mercury Enterprises, Tampa, 1981-82; mgr. Price Waterhouse, Tampa, 1982-86; chief fin. officer Century Group, Inc., Lakeland, Fla., 1986—. Home: 1258 Scottsland Dr Lakeland FL 33813 Office: Century Group Inc 4935 Southfork Dr Lakeland FL 33813

AMAREL, JOHN ANTHONY, optical instrument company executive; b. Massena, N.Y., May 12, 1931; s. John Cordeiro and Angeline Marie (Glovanonne) A.; m. Joyce Ann Carbone, Nov. 29, 1958; children: Anthony, Suzanne, Sherry. BS in Math., Optics, U. Rochester, 1969; postgrad., Rochester Inst. Tech., 1971. Engr. quality assurance Bausch & Lomb, Rochester, N.Y., 1961-65, mgr. quality engring., 1965-67, dir. quality assurance, 1967-71, v.p. sales and mktg., 1971-77, v.p.internat. sales and div. services, 1977-80; pres. Amarel Precision Instruments Inc., Rochester, 1980—, also chmn. bd. Bd. dirs. Perinton Vol. Ambulance Corps, Fairport, N.Y., 1984—. Served with U.S. Army, 1952-54. Mem. Optical Soc. Am. Republican. Roman Catholic. Lodge: Lions (officer 1976-82). Home: 42 Squirrels Heath Dr Fairport NY 14450 Office: Amarel Precision Instruments Inc Perinton Industrial Estates Fairport NY 14450

AMARILIOS, JOHN ALEXANDER, lawyer, consultant; b. Jamaica, N.Y., Apr. 18, 1958; s. Alexander Arthur and Amalia (Tomazinou) A. BS, LeHigh U., 1980, MBA, 1981; JD, U. Bridgeport, 1987. Bar: Conn., 1987, U.S. Dist. Ct., Conn. 1987. Ops. mgr. Bavarian Precision Products, New Canaan, Conn., 1981-84; import mgr. Omega Svc. Parts Corp., New Canaan, 1984-85; cons. Union Carbide Corp., Danbury, Conn., 1985-88; assoc. Tate, Capasse, Johnson, Westport, Conn., 1988, Law Offices Bruce L. Lev. P.C., Rowayton, Conn., 1988—; real estate cons. Union Carbide Corp., Danbury, Conn., 1985-88. Vol. counsel Am. Radio League, Newington, Conn., 1988; v.p Greek Orthodox Youth Assn., Stamford, Conn., 1984. Mem. ABA, Conn. Bar Assn., Westchester/Fairfield Bar Assn., Amatuer Radio Club (Stamford). Home: PO Box 28 New Canaan CT 06840 Office: Law Office Bruce L Lev PC 105 Rowayton Ave Rowayton CT 06856

AMATANGELO, NICHOLAS S., financial printing company executive; b. Monessen, Pa., Feb. 12, 1935; s. Sylvester and Lucy Amatangelo; m. Kathleen Driscoll, May 3, 1964; children: Amy Kathleen, Holly Megan. BA, Duquesne U., 1957; MBA, U. Pitts., 1958. Indsl. engr. U.S. Steel Co., Pitts., 1959-61; indsl. engr. mgr. Anaconda Co., N.Y.C., 1961-63; product mktg. mgr., Xerox Corp., N.Y.C., 1965-68; dir. mktg. Macmillan Co., N.Y.C., 1968-70; dir. product planning Philco-Ford Corp., Phila., 1970-72; pres. Bowne of San Francisco, Inc., 1972-79; pres. Bowne of Houston, Inc., 1979-86, Bowne of Chgo., Inc., 1983—, Bowne of Detroit, Inc., 1987—; instr. U. Pitts., 1959-61; asst. prof. Westchester Community Coll., N.Y.C., 1961-64, 70-72. Contbr. articles in field to profl. jours. Bd. dirs. San Francisco Boys Club, 1974-79, Boys Towns Italy, 1973-79, Alley Theatre, Houston, 1982-86; mem. pres. council Houston Grand Opera, 1980-86. Served with U.S. Army, 1958-59, 61-62. Mem. Printing Industries Am. (bd. dirs.), Am. Soc. Corp. Secs., Am. Mgmt. Assn.-Pres. Assn., Am. Inst. Indsl. Engrs., Am. Soc. Tng. and Devel. Clubs: Forest, Houston, University (Houston); Executive (bd. mem.), Economics (Chgo., Detroit); Olympic (San Francisco). Lodge: Kiwanis. Office: Bowne of Chgo 325 W Ohio St Chicago IL 60610

AMATO, CAROL JOY, anthropologist, technical publications consulting company executive, writer; b. Portland, Oreg., Apr. 9, 1944; d. Sam Lawrence and Lena Dorothy (Dindia) A.; m. Neville Stanley Motts, Aug. 26, 1967 (div. 1978); children: Tracy, Damon. BA, U. Portland, 1966; MA, Calif. State U., 1986. Freelance writer, Westminster, Calif., 1969—; human factor cons. Design Sci. Corp., Los Angeles, 1979—; dir. software documentation Trans-Ed Communications, Westminster, 1980-84, pres. Advanced Profl. Software, Inc., Westminster, 1984-86, Systems Rsch. Analysis, Inc., Westminster, 1986—. Editor, Cultural Futuristics, 1975-80; author numerous articles and short stories, 1973—; participant in numerous radio and TV interviews. Sec. bd. dirs. Am. Space Meml. Found., L.A., 1986—; bd. dirs. Coalition Concerned for Adolescent Pregnancy, Santa Ana, Calif., 1986—; bd. dirs. Orange County Acad. Decathalon. Mem. Am. Anthrop. Assn., Orange County C. of C., Anthropology Assn., Ind. Writers of So. Calif., Human Factor Soc., Writers' Club of Whittier, Inc. Home: 10151 Heather Ct Westminster CA 92683

AMATO, LARRY, financial executive; b. Boston, Jan. 14, 1953; s. Salvatore Vincent and Ethal (Weiner) A.; m. Ellen J. (Baillie) Amato, Sept., 1988; children: Suzanne Gayle, Michelle Toby. BS, Northeastern U., 1975. CPA. Sr. supr. Coopers & Lybrand, Boston, 1976-78; regional mgr. Nat. Med. Care Inc., Waltham, Mass., 1978-85; v.p., chief operating officer Am. Scott Bus. Products Inc., Quincy, Mass., 1985; treas., chief fin. officer Elkay Products Inc., Shrewsbury, Mass., 1985—. Mem. adv. com. Town of Easton, Mass, 1984-85, mem. fin. com., 1985. Fellow Am. Inst. CPAs, Mass. Soc. CPAs. Home: 11 Gibbs C-34 Worcester MA 01607 Office: Elkay Products Inc 800 Boston Turnpike Shrewsbury MA 01545

AMBERG, RICHARD HILLER, JR., newspaper executive; b. Phila., Oct. 26, 1942; s. Richard Hiller and Janet Katharine (Law) A.; m. Virginia Beverley Sharp, Aug. 27, 1966; children—Elizabeth Law, Richard Hiller. BA, Harvard U., 1964; LLD (hon.), Troy State U., s1988. Mgmt. trainee S.I. Advance, N.Y., 1966-71; asst. editor Post Standard, Syracuse, N.Y., 1971-72; editor Globe Democrat, St. Louis, 1972-84, v.p., gen. mgr., exec. editor, 1984-86; pres., pub. Advertiser, Ala. Jour., Montgomery, 1986—; chmn. nat. schs. and scholarship com. Harvard U., 1982-84; bd. dirs. Mo. Press-Bar Commn., 1985-86. Treas., bd. dirs. Mo. Perinatal Assn., 1980-84; pres., bd. dirs. Conway Day Sch., 1979-80, Harvard Club St. Louis, 1983-84; sec., bd. dirs. devel. bd. St. Louis Children's Hosp., 1976-77; bd. dirs. Greater St. Louis Health Systems Agy., 1981, Mo. Vets. Found., 1984-86, Mental Health Assn. St. Louis, 1985-86, Downtown St. Louis Inc., 1984-86, Ptnrs. in Edn., Landmarks Found., United Way of Montgomery, Goodwill Industries of Montgomery, Downtown Unlimited, Gift of Life Found.; v.p. Montgomery Ballet, Brantwood Children's Home; adv. bd. Child Protect;, bd. dirs. Montgomery chpt. Am. Cancer Soc., Montgomery Mental Health Assn., Montgomery Area chpt. ARC, Blue-Gray Patrons Tennis Found., Davis Theatre for Performing Arts, Scott and Zelda Fitzgerald Mus., Montgomery Bus. Com. for Arts; v.p. Tukabatchee coun.Boy Scouts Am.; pres. Ala. Sr. Olympics, Ala. Shakespeare Festival; sec. Mark Twain Summer Inst., 1985-86, St. Louis Regional Maternal and Child Health Coun., 1974-86, Old Newsboys Fund for Children, 1984-86; founder, bd. dirs. Ala. World Affairs Coun.; mem. One Montgomery, Montgomery Area Com. of 100; area chmn. United Way Campaign; mem. long-range planning com. Montgomery Sch. Bd.; mem. strategic planning com. Mental Health Assn. in Ala.; vice chmn. capital fund drive Montgomery YMCA; mem. Gov.'s Task Force on Infant Mortality, Auburn U. Coll. Bus. Adv. Coun., Opportunities Industrialization Ctrs. Adv. Bd., Harvard Class Com., Montgomery Coun. Navy League (co-founder), Jimmy Hitchcock Meml. Award Com. Served to lt. (j.g.), USN, 1964-66, capt. Res. Mem. Harvard Alumni Assn. (bd. dirs. 1980-83), Ala. Press Assn. (bd. dirs.), So. Newspaper Pubs. Assn. (editorial com.), Montgomery Area C. of C. (bd. dirs.). Presbyterian. Clubs: Montgomery Rotary; English-Speaking Union; The Thirteen; Harvard of Birmingham. Home: 845 Felder Ave Montgomery AL 36106-1930 Office: The Advertiser Co 200 Washington Ave Montgomery AL 36104

AMBIELLI, ROBERT JOHN, insurance company executive; b. Newark, May 28, 1951; s. Robert and Anne (Angerame) A.; m. Patricia Marian Roesch, Feb. 15, 1975; children: Steven, Eric. BSBA, Montclair State Coll., 1973; MBA, Seton Hall U., 1979. Career trainee Electronic Data Systems, N.Y.C., 1973-74; sr. dir. Automatic Data Processing, Clifton, N.J., 1974-83; v.p. Crum & Forster Comml. Ins., Parsippany, N.J., 1983—. Roman Catholic. Home: 217 Ledden Terr South Plainfield NJ 07080 Office: Crum & Forster Comml Ins 6 Sylvan Way Parsippany NJ 07054

AMBLER, DAVID SAMUEL, account manager; b. Danbury, Conn., Apr. 24, 1954; s. DeAlton St. John (dec.) and Barbara Jane (Blodgett) A.; m. Beverly Lynn Dunn, May 29, 1976; children: Nicole Marie, Jennifer Rebekah, Peter James. BA in Religion and Bus. Adminstrn., Lebanon Valley Coll., Annville, Pa., 1976; postgrad., U. New Haven, Conn., 1983-84; student, Phila. Coll. Textiles and Sci., 1987-89. Lic. realtor N.J. Mgr. Jack's Religious Gift Shop, Salisbury, Md., 1976-78, The Living Word, Danbury, 1978; controller Conn. Appliance Distbrs., Danbury, 1978-82; sr. credit rep. Union Carbide Corp., Danbury, 1982-85; mgr. fin. services accounts Union Carbide Corp., Chgo., 1985-86, Moorestown, N.J., 1986—; fin. analyst Waste Site Rev. Bd. Union Carbide Corp., 1987-89; fin. analyst waste site rev. bd. Union Carbide Corp., 1987-89, Waste Site Inspection Consortium, 1987-89. Treas. Bible Study Fellowship, Ridgefield, Conn., 1983-85, Cornerstone Evangelical Free Ch. Washington Twp., 1987-88, Indian Princesses Cree Tribe, 1987-88; asst. treas. Grace Community Ch., Brookfield, Conn., 1984-85; trustee Glen Ellyn (Ill.) Bible Ch., 1986; treas. Washington Twp. Young Life, 1988-89.. Republican. Fundamental Evang. Christian. Home: 804 Richmond Dr Washington Twp Sicklerville NJ 08081 Office: Union Carbide Corp 308 Harper Dr Moorestown NJ 08057

AMBLER, ERNEST, government official; b. Bradford, Eng., Nov. 20, 1923; came to U.S., 1953, naturalized, 1958; s. William and Sarah Alice (Binns) A.; m. Alice Virginia Seiler, Nov. 19, 1955; children: Christopher William, Jonathan Ernest. B.A., New Coll., Oxford U., 1945, M.A., 1949, Ph.D., 1953. With Armstrong Siddeley Motors, Ltd., Coventry, Eng., 1944-48; Nuffield Research fellow Oxford U., 1953; with Nat. Inst. Standards and Tech. (formerly Nat. Bur. Standards), Commerce Dept., 1953-89; div. chief inorganic materials div. Nat. Inst. Standards and Tech. (formerly Nat. Bur. Standards), Commerce Dept., Washington, 1965-68, dep. dir., 1973, acting dir., 1975-78, dir. bur., 1978-89; dir. Inst. for Basic Standards, Washington, 1968-73; Liaison rep. to div. phys. scis. Nat. Acad. Sci.-NRC, 1968-69; Sponsor's del. Nat. Conf. Standards Lab., 1968; U.S. rep. Internat. Com. on Weights and Measures, 1972—; acting under sec. for tech. U.S. Dept. Commerce. Patentee low temperature refrigeration apparatus. D.C. mem. bd. govs. Israel/U.S. Binat. Indsl. Research and Devel. Found.; mem. Md. High Tech. Roundtable. Recipient Arthur S. Flemming award Washington Jr. C. of C., 1961; John Simon Guggenheim Meml. Found. fellow, 1963; recipient William A. Wildhack award in metrology, 1976, Pres.'s award for Distinguished Fed. Civilian Service, 1977. Fellow AAAS; mem. Am. Phys. Soc. (editor Rev. Modern Physics 1966-69), Washington Acad. Scis. Home: 1600 N Oak St #626 Arlington MD 22209 Office: Nat Inst Standards & Tech Bldg 101 Rte 270 Gaithersburg MD 20899

AMBROSINO, CARMEN FELICE, drug abuse facility administrator, educator; b. Kingston, Pa., Dec. 21, 1948; s. Carmen C. and Rose (Aufiero) A.; m. Bernice C. Szumski, Nov. 20, 1971; 1 child, Carmen F. Jr. BA in English, King's Coll., 1970; M in Health Adminstrn., Wilkes Coll., 1986. Cert. addiction counselor, Pa., employee assistance profl., Pa. Caseworker Luzerne County Child Welfare, Wilkes-Barre, Pa., 1971-73; chief exec. officer Wyo. Valley Alcohol and Drug Services, Inc., Kingston, Pa., 1973—; adj. prof. Wilkes Coll., Wilkes-Barre, 1986—; instr. Luzerne Intermediate Unit, Kingston, 1987—; cons. Nesbitt Care Unit, Kingston, 1987—. Author: A Student Handbook on Drug/Alcohol Abuse, 1984, Slugger, 1984. Served with Pa. NG, 1970-76. Named to Chapel of 4 Chaplains, one of Outstanding Young Men Pa., Pa. Jaycees, 1979. Mem. Am. Coll. Addiction Treatment Adminstrs. Democrat. Roman Catholic. Home: 9 East Ln Stauffer Heights Hughestown PA 18640 Office: Wyoming Valley Alcohol/Drug Services Inc 383 Wyoming Ave Kingston PA 18704

AMBROSIO, FRANCESCO VITTORIO, food products company executive; b. St. Gennariello di Ottaviano, Naples, Italy, Sept. 18, 1932; came to U.S., 1962; s. Domenico and Speranza (Catapano) A.; m. Giovanna Sacco, Oct. 29, 1960; children—Massimo, Mauro. Degree (hon.), Istituto Agrario, Naples, Italy, 1958. Mills mgr. Fratelli Ambrosio Mills, Castellammare di Stabia, Naples, 1954-58; owner, pres. Italgrani di F. Ambrosio, Naples, 1958-79; pres. Italgrani S.P.A., Naples, 1979—, Italgrani USA Inc., St. Louis, 1979—; also owner two durum wheat mills, Boston, St. Louis. Contbr. articles to profl. jours. Named hon. citizen City of Duluth, Minn., 1981. Mem. Associazione Nazionale Cerealisti Roma Italy (pres. 1980-85), Associazione Italiana Pastai e Mugnai Roma Italy (exec. com. 1979-85), Naples C. of C., Rome C. of C. Clubs: Canottiera Napoli; Jockey (Buenos Aires, Argentina).

AMBRUSTER, JOHN REA, manufacturing company executive; b. Sturgis, Mich., Aug. 27, 1931; s. John R. and Dorothy A. (Stoops) A.; m. Joyce Bok, Dec. 22, 1953; children: Sara, Jeanne, David. BA, Swarthmore Coll., 1953; MBA, U. Pa., 1955. With S.C. Johnson & Son, Inc., Racine, Wis., 1955-79, v.p., 1979-86; v.p. Johnson Worldwide Assocs., Racine, 1986—; pres. Plastimo, S.A., Lorient, France, 1984—. Bd. dirs. Women's Resource Ctr., Racine, 1982-84. Democrat. Home: 56260 Larmor, PO Box 32, 56850 Plege France Office: Johnson Worldwide Assocs 4041 N Main St Racine WI 53402

AMDAHL, GENE MYRON, computer company executive; b. Flandreau, S.D., Nov. 16, 1922; s. Anton E. and Inga (Brendsel) A.; m. Marian Quissell, June 23, 1946; children: Carlton Gene, Beth Delaine, Andrea Leigh. BSEE, S.D. State U., 1948, DEng (hon.), 1974; PhD, U. Wis., 1952, DSc (hon.), 1979; D.Sc. (hon.), Luther Coll., 1980, Augustana Coll., 1984. Project mgr. IBM Corp., Poughkeepsie, N.Y., 1952-55; group head Ramo-Wooldridge Corp., L.A., 1956; mgr. systems design Aeronutronics, L.A., 1956-60; mgr. systems design advanced data processing systems IBM Corp., N.Y.C., Los Gatos, Calif., Menlo Park, Calif., 1960-70; founder, chmn. Amdahl Corp., Sunnyvale, Calif., 1970-80, Trilogy Systems Corp., Cupertino, Calif., 1980-87; chmn. bd. Elxsi (name changed from Trilogy Systems Corp.), San Jose, Calif., 1987-89; founder, chmn. pres., chief exec. officer Andor Systems, Inc., Cupertino, 1987—; bd. dirs. Modular Power, Andor Systems Internat., Western Tech. Investments. Patentee in field. With USN, 1942-44. Recipient Disting. Alumnus award S.D. State U., 1973, Data Processing Man of Yr. award Data Processing Mgmt. Assn., 1976, Disting. Svc. citation U. Wis., 1976, Michelson-Morley award Case-Western Res. U., 1977, Harry Goode Meml. award for outstanding contbns. to design and manufacture of large, high-performance computers, 1983 and Eckert-Mauchly award, 1987, Am. Fedn. Info. Processing Socs., Centennial Alumnus award S.D. State U., 1987; named to Info. Processing Hall of Fame, Infomart, Tex., 1985; IBM fellow, 1965. Fellow IEEE, Brit. Computer Soc. (disting.); mem. Nat. Acad. Engring., IEEE (profl. group, W.W. McDowell award 1976), Quadrato della Radio, Pontecchio Marcon. Presbyterian. Club: Los Altos (Calif.) Country. Home: 165 Patricia Dr Atherton CA 94025 Office: Andor Systems Inc 20380 Town Center Ln Ste 250 Cupertino CA 95014

AMDALL, WILLIAM JOHN, energy company executive, accountant; b. Texas City, Tex., Nov. 1, 1953; s. Roger and Lenore (Crum) A.; m. Brenda J. Upchurch, Aug. 3, 1974; children: Jonathan, Jessica. BBA in Acctg., North Tex. State U., 1977. CPA, Tex. Mem. audit staff Peat Marwick Mitchell and Co., Dallas, 1977-80; treas., chief fin. officer Targa Oil and Gas

Inc., Dallas, 1980—; v.p., chief fin. officer Chapman Energy Inc., Dallas, 1983—. Mem. AICPA, Nat. Assn. Securities Dealers (fin. communications and investor rels. com. 1985—), Gleneagles Country Club (Plano, Tex.). Office: Chapman Energy Inc 9400 N Central Expwy Ste 500 Dallas TX 75231

AMELIO, GILBERT FRANK, semiconductor company executive; b. N.Y.C., Mar. 1, 1943; s. Anthony and Elizabeth (DeAngelis) A.; m. Glenda Charlene Amelio; children: Anthony Todd, Tracy Elizabeth, Andrew Ryan. B.S. in Physics, Ga. Inst. Tech., 1965, M.S. in Physics, 1967, Ph.D. in Physics, 1968. Tech. dir., co-founder Info. Sci., Atlanta, 1962-65; mem. tech. staff Bell Telephone Labs., Murray Hill, N.J., 1968-71; div. v.p., gen. mgr. Fairchild, Mountain View, Calif., 1971-83; pres. semiconductor products div. Rockwell Internat., Newport Beach, Calif., 1983-88, pres. communication systems, 1988—; dir. Ga. Inst. Tech. Nat. Adv. Bd., Atlanta, 1981-87, Ga. Inst. Tech. Research Inst., Atlanta, 1982—, Sematech; dir., chmn. Recticon, Pottstown, Pa., 1983—. Patentee in field. Mem. chief exec. roundtable Univ. Calif. at Irvine. Fellow IEEE (chmn. subcom. 1974-81); mem. Semiconductor Industry Assn. (dir. 1983—). Republican. Roman Catholic. Home: 38 Rockingham Dr Newport Beach CA 92660 Office: Rockwell Communication Systems PO Box C Newport Beach CA 92660

AMENTA, MICHAEL JOSEPH, accountant; b. N.Y.C., Apr. 21, 1933; s. Angelo and Jessie Catherine (Purpura) A.; m. Antoinette M. Florio, Feb. 20, 1955; children: Michael, Marie, Theresa. BBA, CUNY, 1955. CPA, N.Y.; cert. specialist in real estate securities. Nat. real estate ptnr. Laventhol & Horwath, N.Y.C., 1958—. Editor: (newsletters) Real Estate Insight, 1984—, Laventhol & Horwath Real Estate Newsletter, 1978—; mem. editorial bd. Real Estate Securities Jour., 1980—, Real Estate Fin., 1983—, Perspective, 1978—. Mem. bd. appeals and zoning Village of Port Washington North, 1960-70; pres. Cath. League Nassau County, N.Y., 1980-82; assoc. trustee North Shore U. Hosp., N.Y., 1975—. Served with U.S. Army, 1955-57. Mem. Real Estate Securities and Syndication Inst. (pres. N.Y. state chpt. 1982-84), Urban Land Inst., Internat. Council Shopping Ctrs., Nat. Assn. Home Builders. Club: Plandome (N.Y.) Country. Home: 102 Boulder Rd Manhasset NY 11030 Office: Laventhol & Horwath 919 3rd Ave New York NY 10022

AMENTAS, GEORGE JAMES, bank executive; b. N.Y.C., July 14, 1949; S. James John and Despina (Hionas) A.; m. Kathleen Frances, Aug. 26, 1972. BBA, Baruch Coll., 1974; MBA, Fordham U., 1979. Asst. v.p. Lincoln Savs. Bank, N.Y.C., 1974-82; sr. v.p., chief investment officer, treas. Village Savs. Bank, N.Y.C., 1982-88, Port Chester, N.Y., 1988—. Mem. Savs. Banks Assn. N.Y. (treas. group 7, 1985-86, pres. 1986-87), Investment Officers Assn. of N.Y. Home: 40 Coulter Ave Pawling NY 12564 Office: Village Savs Bank One Gateway Pla Port Chester NY 10573

AMERINE, ANNE FOLLETTE, aerospace engineer; b. San Francisco, Sept. 27, 1950; d. William T. and Wilma (Carlson) F.; m. Jorge Armando Verdi D'Eguia, July 4, 1970 (div.); m. Donald Amerine, Dec. 18, 1983. AA, Coll. Marin, 1977; BA in Math. with honors, Mills Coll., 1979. Sr. computer operator Bank of Am. Internat. Services, San Francisco, 1972-74; mathematician Pacific Missile Test Ctr., Pt. Mugu, Calif., 1979-80; engr. Grumman Aerospace Corp., Pt. Mugu, 1979-83; engr. Litton Guidance and Control Systems, 1984-86, product support and assurance dept. project mgr., 1986—. Chmn. Marina West Neighborhood Council, 1982-84; mem. NOW; chmn. subcom. Ventura County Community Coll. Dist. Citizen's Adv. Com. on Status of Women, 1983-84. Aurelia Henry Reinhart scholar, 1978-79; recipient Project Sterling award Grumman Aerospace Corp., 1982. Mem. Nat. Assn. Female Execs., Soc. Women Engrs. (chmn. career guidance com. and speaker Ventura County sect.), Litton Women's Enhancement Orgn. (founder, v.p. and chmn. info. and edn. com. 1985-86, editor newsletter 1986-87), Assn. Old Crows, Mills Coll. Alumni, Alpha Gamma Sigma (life). Office: Litton Guidance & Control Systems 5500 Canoga Ave MS 80 Woodland Hills CA 91367-6698

AMERMAN, JOHN W., toy company executive; b. 1932; married. BA, Dartmouth Coll., 1953, MBA, 1954. With Colgate-Palmolive Co., 1958-64, Warner-Lambert Co., 1965-80; v.p. Du Barry Cosmetics, 1971-72, v.p. internat. group, 1972-77, v.p. Am. Chicle div., 1977-79, pres. Am. Chicle div., 1979-80; pres. Mattel Internat., from 1980, exec. v.p. worldwide ops., from 1985; exec. v.p. Mattel Inc., Hawthorne, Calif., until 1987, chmn., chief exec. officer, 1987—, also bd. dirs. Served with U.S. Army, 1954-57. Office: Mattel Inc 5150 Rosecrans Ave Hawthorne CA 90250

AMES, CRAIG L., lawyer; b. Eldora, Iowa, Nov. 25, 1944; s. Stanley J. Stacknik and Helen J. (Hobson) Fortner; m. Mary M. Fisher, Feb. 3, 1968; children: Steven, Zachary. BS, Loyola U., Chgo., 1967; JD, De Paul U., 1969. Bar: Ill. 1970; cert. assoc. in risk mgmt., 1980. Atty. Walgreen Co., Deerfield, Ill., 1970-76, dir. ins. and risk mgmt., 1976—; sec., dir. Employer's Group on Health, Lake County, Ill., 1985-87; active membership adv. bd. PruCare Ill., 1983-86. Mem. editorial bd. Cash Flow Mag., 1986-87. Sgt. USMC, 1969-76. Mem. Ill. Bar Assn., Am. Mgmt. Assn., Risk Ins. Mgmt. Soc. (pres., dir. 1981-82), Lions Club (treas., dir. Elk Grove Village, Ill. chpt. 1977, sec. Mt. Prospect, Ill. chpt. 1978), Toastmasters-Speakers Unltd. (treas. 1982-84), Phi Alpha Delta. Republican. Roman Catholic. Office: Walgreen Co 200 Wilmot Rd Deerfield IL 60015

AMES, DAMARIS, publishing executive; b. Cin., Jan. 31, 1944; d. Van Meter and Betty (Breneman) A. BA, Radcliffe Coll., 1965; MA, Harvard U., 1967. Editing asst. coll. div. Houghton Mifflin Co., Boston, 1969-71, editing mgr. coll. div., 1971-76, sr. editing mgr. coll. div., 1976-77, editing dir. coll. div., 1977-78, corp. analyst for chief exec. officer, 1978-81, communications dir., 1981-86, v.p., dir. pub. and communications, 1986, v.p., pub., 1986-87, sr. v.p., pub., 1987-88, exec. v.p., pub., 1988—. Office: Houghton Mifflin Co 1 Beacon St Boston MA 02108

AMES, JOHN HERSH, food products executive; b. Harrisburg, Pa., July 9, 1943; s. John Hersh Sr. and Savilla Kathryn (Nedimyer) A.; m. Linda Jayne Castro, Aug. 23, 1969; 1 child, Jennifer Jane. BS in Chemistry, Lafayette Coll., 1965. Quality auditor Hershey (Pa.) Chocolate Co., 1972-75, sect. leader, 1975-78, supr. quality assurance, 1978-84; mgr. quality assurance Hershey Chocolate U.S.A., 1984—. Mem. Swatara (Pa.) Twp. Recreation Bd., 1981—, Leadership Harrisburg Area, 1986-87, Cen. Atlantic States Assn. Food and Drug Ofcls., Am. Soc. Quality Control, Fraternal Order Police, Rutherford Youth Club (v.p. 1977, pres. 1978), Moose Lodge, Lions Club. Home: 6226 Lehigh Ave Harrisburg PA 17111 Office: Hershey Chocolate USA 19 E Chocolate Ave Hershey PA 17033

AMES, MARC L., lawyer; b. Bklyn., Mar. 14, 1943; s. Arthur L. and Ray (Sardas) A.; m. Eileen, July 12, 1970; J.D., Bklyn. Law Sch., 1967; LL.M., NYU, 1968. Bar: N.Y. 1967, U.S. Dist. Ct. (ea. and so. dist.) N.Y. 1973, U.S. Ct. Appeals (2nd cir.) 1973, U.S. Supreme Ct. 1973, U.S. Ct. Appeals (3rd cir.) 1982; cert. arbitrator U.S. Dist. Ct. (ea. dist.) N.Y., 1986. Mem. faculty L.I. U., 1968-69, N.Y.C. Community Coll., 1969-70; practice, 1967—, now pvt. practice, N.Y.C.; cons. disability retirement and pensions; arbitrator Am. Arbitration Assn.; chmn., chief exec. officer A.J. Enterprises, Inc.; bd. dirs. Internat. Communications Concepts, Inc., Recipient cert. appreciation N.Y. State Trial Lawyers, commendation for disting. service as arbitrator. Mem. N.Y. State Trial Lawyers Assn., N.Y. County Lawyers, N.Y. State Bar Assn., Electronic Technol. Soc. N.J. Inc. Contbr. articles to various publs.; inventor bridge for billiards, storage materials for sport cards collections; patentee auto mirror. Office: 225 Broadway Suite 3005 New York NY 10007

AMES, RAYMOND GARDNER, financial planner; b. Natick, Mass., July 4, 1932; s. Raymond Guy Ames and Muriel (Griffin) Ames Vargus; m. Clare Howard, 1982; children: Maureen, Brendan, Stephen, Allison, Michael. BBA, Northeastern U., 1960; MS, Am. Coll., Bryn Mawr, Pa., 1982. CLU; cert. fin. planner. Field underwriter Home Life Ins. Co. N.Y., Boston, 1962-83; registered rep. 1st New England Securities Corp., 1979-86, Commonwealth Equity Svcs., Inc., Newton, 1986—; owner, prin. Ames Fin. Svcs., Franklin, 1983—; pres. Ames Ins. Agy., Inc., 1984—, Am. Heritage Investment Svcs., Inc., Franklin, Mass., 1985—; ptnr. Ames and McClay Fin. Svcs.,, 1987—. Recipient Leadership award Physicians Planning Svc. Corp., 1971, 78. Mem. Internat. Assn. Fin. Planning (dir. greater Boston chpt.), Am. Soc. CLU's and Chartered Fin. Cons., Inst. Cert. Fin. Planners, Million Dollar Round Table, Registry of Fin. Planning Practitioners. Office: Am Heritage Investment Svcs Inc 29 Dean Ave PO Box 611 Franklin MA 02038

AMES, ROBERT SAN, retired manufacturing company executive; b. N.Y.C., Jan. 23, 1919; s. Leonard and Felicia (San) A.; m. Margaret Grossman, Oct. 14, 1945; children: Linda (Mrs. K.J. Cassady), David, Elizabeth. B.A., Columbia U., 1940, B.S. in Mech. Engring., 1941; M.S. in Mech. Engring., 1942; M.S. in Indsl. Mgmt. (Sloan fellow), Mass. Inst. Tech., 1954. With Goodyear Aircraft Corp., Akron, Ohio, 1942-60; v.p. Aeroprojects, Inc., West Chester, Pa., 1960-62; mgr. planning RCA Def. Elec. Products, Camden, N.J., 1962-64; v.p. mfg. Bell Aerospace Co., Buffalo, 1964-68; group v.p. Textron, Inc., Providence, 1968-71; sr. v.p. ops. Textron, Inc., 1971-79, mem. adminstrv. and investment coms., exec. v.p.-aerospace, 1979-84; Pres., dir. Am. Research and Devel. Corp., Boston, 1972-73; dir. Criton Corp., Precision Castparts, Pneumo-Abex Corp., Esterline Corp. Bd. dirs. Providence Athenaeum, 1972-75; bd. dirs. Lincoln Sch. Mem. Nat. Security Indsl. Assn. (chmn. bd. dirs. 1982), Aerospace Industries Assn. (chmn. bd. govs. 1983). Home: 626 Angell St Providence RI 02906 Office: RI Hosp Trust Nat Bank Bldg Rm 1103 15 Westminster St Providence RI 02903

AMES, SANDRA PATIENCE, sales office executive; b. Quincy, Calif., May 23, 1947; d. Bruce Ray Richards and Margaret Elizabeth (Steiner) Richards Johnson; m. Martin P.M. Bettenhausen, Dec. 10, 1965 (div. 1972); m. Thomas William Ames, Nov. 28, 1975. Student Yuba City Jr. Coll., 1965-66. Sales corr. Nat. Can Corp. (now known as Am. Nat. Can Co.), Seattle, 1974-76, Lehigh Valley, Pa., 1976-79, nat. account sales corr., Chgo., 1979-81, dist. sales office mgr., 1981-82, sales analyst I, Oakbrook, Ill., 1982-84, regional sales office mgr., 1984-86; mgr. regional sales office, Oakbrook, 1987—. Mem. Nat. Assn. Female Execs. Republican. Office: Am Nat Can Co 915 Harger Rd Oak Brook IL 60521

AMES, STEVEN REEDE, financial planner; b. Washington, Aug. 15, 1951; s. Reede Maughan and Mary (Soderberg) A.; m. Rozalia Collins, Apr. 1, 1978. BS in Bus. Adminstrn., U. Md., 1973; MPA, Am. U., 1976. Specialist bus. financing Gov.'s Office State Del., Dover, 1978-83; exec. v.p. Econ. and Bus. Devel. Corp. Montgomery County, Rockville, Md., 1983-85; owner, operator Scarborough Ames and Assocs., Annapolis, Md., 1986—; instr. Anne Arundel Community Coll., Annapolis, 1987—. Mem. Anne Arundel County Trade Coun., Annapolis, 1987—. Mem. Internat. Assn. Fin. Planners, Inst. Cert. Fin. Planners, Annapolis C. of C. (ambassador 1987—), Kiwanis (bd. dirs. 1986—). Office: Scarborough Ames & Assocs 2083 West St Penthouse Ste Annapolis MD 21401

AMHAUS, GORDON ARTHUR, sales and marketing executive; b. Milw., Nov. 22, 1946; s. Elroy and Armella (Nottling) A.; m. Sharon Enrico, June 21, 1969; children: Eric, Craig,. BS, U. Wis., Menomonie, 1968. Tchr. Minnetonka (Minn.) High Sch., 1968-69; dir. chpt. svcs. P.S.E. Frat., Indpls., 1969-72; salesman Tremco div. B.F.G., Cleve., 1972-75, dist. sales mgr., 1975-78, reg. sales mgr., 1979-82, div. mktg. specialist, 1982-85; v.p. sales and mktg. Tarmac Roof Systems, Wilmington, Del., 1985—. Contbr. articles to profl. jours. Mem. Constrn. Specifiers Inst., Roof Cons. Inst. Office: Tarmac Roofing Systems 1401 Silverside Rd Wilmington DE 19810

AMICO, CHARLES WILLIAM, management consultant; b. Boston, May 6, 1942; s. William Charles and Marie Josephine (Nicholas) A. Assoc. in Engring., Franklin Inst., 1962; BS, Suffolk U., 1968. Jr. chem. technician Avco Corp., Lowell, Mass., 1963-64; advanced vacuum tech. technician Nat. Rsch. Corp., Newton, Mass., 1964-68; semicondr. engr. IBM, Essex Junction, Vt., 1968-72, semicondr. mfg. engring. mgr., 1972-76, mgmt. devel. cons., 1976-86; founder, pres., chief exec. officer Creative Directions, Inc., Charlotte, Vt., 1982—; bd. dirs. Holiday Project, 1987-88. State chmn. Vt. Hugh O'Brian Youth Leadership Seminar; bd. dirs. Vt. Hugh O'Brian Youth Seminars, Inc., chief exec officer, 1984-85; mem. Bay Area O.D. Network. Recipient Hugh O'Brian Outstanding State Chmn. in Nation award, 1984. Mem. San Francisco C. of C. Office: Creative Directions Inc 2932 Pierce St San Francisco CA 94123

AMICO, RICHARD JOSEPH, sales executive; b. Rochester, N.Y., Mar. 26, 1953; s. Sam c. and Rosemary L. (Steo) A.; m. Cynthia Lawson, Sept. 20, 1980 (div. 1985); m. Judith Anne Winegar, Apr. 24, 1986; 1 adopted child, Kristopher W. Student, Monroe Community Coll., 1971-72. Regional mgr. Cons. & Designers, Inc., Dallas, 1983-86; regional sales rep. Sci. Calculations, Inc., Dallas, 1984-85; dir. mktg., sales and N.Am. ops. Scan Group Internat., Inc., Englewood, Colo., 1986-89; sr. sales rep. Alliant Computer Systems Corp., Englewood, Colo., 1989—; cons. in field. Mem. Nat. Computer Graphics Assn., Am. Inst. Design Draftsman. Republican. Roman Catholic. Home: 4183 W Radcliff Ave Denver CO 80236 Office: Alliant Computer Systems Corp 5445 DTC Parkway P-4 Englewood CO 80111

AMIEVA, MARTA Z(ENAIDA), investment banker; b. Havana, Cuba, Oct. 11, 1945; came to U.S., 1961, naturalized, 1969; d. Jose and Alsina (Felipe) Ferreira; m. Carlos Amieva, Nov. 25, 1961. Grad., Corazon de Maria, Havana, 1961; student, N.Y. Inst. Tech., Commack, 1973—. Clk. Phoenix of London, N.Y.C., 1963-65; mgr. A.M.C., N.Y.C., 1965-70, Gambit Mgmt., N.Y.C., 1970-75; v.p. Republic Bank N.Y., N.Y.C., 1975-81; pres. AMK Systems, Inc., N.Y.C., 1981-88; v.p. Investment Bank, 1988—; cons. to fin. insts. Active Thirteen, N.Y.C., Nat. Cancer Inst. and Ptnrs. in Courage. Named Woman of Yr., N.Y.C. YMCA, 1980. Mem. AAAS, Women in Communications, N.Y. Acad. Scis., Women in Computing, Nat. Assn. Female Execs., Smithsonian Assocs., Nat. Mus. Women in Arts (charter), NOW (charter).

AMINI, BIJAN KHAJEHNOURI, technology company executive; b. Nice, France, Oct. 3, 1943; came to U.S., 1946; s. Ahmad and Georgianna Amini. B.S. in Physics, Carnegie Mellon U., 1962; M.S. in Aerospace Physics, Pa. State U., 1963, Ph.D., 1968. Lectr. UCLA, NASA, Pa. State U., 1968-73; sr. scientist Northrop Corp., 1968-71; pres., chief operating officer Armstrong Cork Co., Iran, 1976-79; sr. v.p. Gulf Interstate Corp., Houston, from 1981; pres. Gulf Applied Research; dir. Gulf Applied Techs.; lectr. in field; lectr. Rice U., 1984; mem. Adv. Bd. Miss. Inst. for Tech. Devel., 1985—; co-chmn. Mitsui Ocean Devel. Engring Gen. Techs., Houston and Tokyo, 1985—; chmn. Gen. Techs., 1985—. Bd. dirs. Nat. Inst. Tech. and Applied Scis., Washington, 1978-81, Nat. Commn. on Indsl. Innovation, Inst. Tech. Devel. Mem. AIAA, ASME, AAAS, Sigma Xi.

AMIOKA, WALLACE SHUZO, retired petroleum company executive, public affairs consultant; b. Honolulu, June 28, 1914; s. Tsurumatsu and Reye (Yoshimura) A.; B.A., U. Hawaii, 1966, M.B.A., 1968; m. Ellen Misao Honda, Aug. 9, 1942; children—Carol L. Amioka Price, Joanne M. Amioka Chikuma. With Shell Oil Co., 1931-77, fin. svcs. mgr., Honolulu, 1973-77; pub. affairs cons., Honolulu, 1977-87; gen. ptnr. Pub. Affairs Cons. Hawaii, 1988—; lectr. econs. U. Hawaii, 1969-79. Mem. Honolulu Police Commn., 1965-73, vice chmn., 1966, 68, chmn., 1971; U.S. civil adm. Ryuku Islands, 1950-52. Mem. City and County of Honolulu Charter Commn., 1981-82; bd. dirs. Honolulu Symphony Soc., 1968. Served with M.I., AUS, 1944-48. Mem. M.I. Service Vets. (pres. 1981-82), Hawaii C. of C. (chmn. edn. com. 1963-64, chmn. pub. health com. 1966-67), Hui 31 Club, Hui Aikene Club, Honolulu Police Old Timers Club, Phi Beta Kappa, Phi Kappa Phi. Home: 4844 Matsonia Dr Honolulu HI 96816 Office: Pub Affairs Cons-Hawaii 711 Keeaumoku St Honolulu HI 96814

AMLADI, PRASAD GANESH, management consulting executive, health care consultant, researcher; b. Mudhol, India, Sept. 12, 1941; came to U.S., 1967, naturalized, 1968; s. Ganesh L. and Sundari G. Amladi; m. Chitra G. Panje, Dec. 20, 1970; children—Amita, Amol. B.Tech. with honors, Indian Inst. Tech., Bombay, 1963; M.S., Stanford U., 1968; M.B.A. with high distinction U. Mich., 1975. Sr. research engr. Ford Motor Co., Dearborn, Mich., 1968-75; mgr. strategic planning Mich. Consol. Gas Co., Detroit, 1975-78; mgr. planning services The Resources Group, Bloomfield Hills, Mich., 1978-80; project mgr., sr. cons. Mediflex Systems Corp., Bloomfield Hills, 1980-85; mgr. strategic planning services Mersco Corp., Bloomfield Hills, 1985-86, mgr. corp. planning and research Diversified Techs., Inc., New Hudson, Mich., 1986—. Author numerous research papers. Recipient Kodama Meml. Gold medal, 1957; India Merit scholar Govt. of India, 1959-63, K.C. Mahindra scholar, 1967, R.D. Sethna Grad. scholar, 1968. Mem. Inst. Indsl. Engrs. (sr.), N.Am. Soc. Corp. Planning, Economic Club Detroit, Beta Gamma Sigma. Office: Blue Cross & Blue Shield of Mich 600 E Lafayette Detroit MI 48226

AMMANN, LILLIAN ANN NICHOLSON, interior landscape executive; b. Pearsall, Tex., June 20, 1946; d. Harvey Franklin and Annie Laura (Matthews) Nicholson; m. Jack Jordan Ammann Jr., May 31, 1967; 1 child, William Erik. BA magna cum laude, Southwestern U., 1968. Mgr. inventory Kelly AFB, San Antonio, 1967-70; employment counselor Tex. Employment Commn., San Antonio, 1970-75; owner, operator Lillie's Lovely Little Gardens, San Antonio, 1975-77; owner, operator Lillie's Interior Landscapes, San Antonio, 1980-82, pres., 1983—; sec. Jack Ammann Inc., 1983-87; pres. Lillie's & Sherry's Plants & Pottery, San Antonio, 1977-80. Author: Lillie's Lovely Little Gardening Book, 1976. Mem. Women in Bus., Nat. Council Interior Hort. Cert. (charter cert. interior horticulturist), San Antonio Interior Landscape Assn. (founder, 1st pres.), Associated Landscape Contractors of Am., North San Antonio C. of C., Greater San Antonio C. of C. Episcopalian. Home: 603 Mauze San Antonio TX 78216 Office: Lillie's Interior Landscapes 17585 Blanco Rd #16-1 San Antonio TX 78232

AMMERMAN, DAN SHERIDAN, electronic media training school administrator; b. Tyrone, Pa., June 10, 1932; s. Eugene Harry and Helen L. (Morrow) A.; m. Mary T. Graca, Jan. 10, 1953; children—Terri L., Mark Alan. Broadcast journalist Sta. WVAM, Altoona, Pa., 1950-59, Sta. KGNC-AM-TV, Amarillo, Tex., 1959-66, Sta. KTRH, Houston, 1966-67; contbg. corr. CBS Radio Network, 1967-68; anchorman KTRK-TV, Houston, 1968-72; with ABC Radio Network, 1972-73; founder, pres. Ammerman Enterprises Inc., Houston, 1973—, Ammerman Broadcasting; owner Kani, Wharton, Tex.; nat. speaker in field. Nat. bd. dirs. Vols. of Am. Served to 2d lt. U.S. Army, 1947-52; Korea. Named Big Bro. of Yr., Amarillo, 1965. Mem. Pub. Relations Soc. Am. (Tex. dir.), Internat. Platform Assn. Republican. Roman Catholic. Clubs: Press, Sugar Creek Country (Houston). Home: 214 E Sutton Sq Stafford TX 77477 Office: Ammerman Enterprises 4800 Sugar Grove Blvd Suite 400 Stafford TX 77477

AMMON, JAMES E., retail executive; b. Carmi, Ill., May 17, 1935; s. Otis Elwell and Katherine Bernice (Lairmer) A.; m. Patricia Carol Kucera, Aug. 30, 1958; children—Lynn Allison, Scott Anderson. B.B.A., Tulane U., 1959. C.P.A., La. Sr. acct. Haskins & Sells, New Orleans, 1959-63; sr. acct. Mid. South Services, Inc., New Orleans, 1963-67, asst. sec., asst. treas., 1968, treas., 1968-78, v.p., 1975-78; treas. Mid. South Utilities, Inc., New Orleans, 1970-78, v.p., 1978-86; sr. v.p. fin. D.H. Holmes Co. Ltd., New Orleans, 1986, exec. v.p. fin., 1986—, also bd. dirs.; Bd. dirs. Sizeler Properties Investors, Inc. Served with USMC, 1954-56. Mem. Fin. Exec. Inst., Am. Inst. C.P.A.s, Nat. Retail Mchts. Assn., New Orleans C. of C. Democrat. Clubs: Metairie (La.) Country, Internat. House. Home: 462 Homestead Ave Metairie LA 70005 Office: D H Holmes Co Ltd 819 Canal St New Orleans LA 70112

AMORUSO, VICTOR ANTHONY, banker; b. Bronx, N.Y., Apr. 27, 1945; s. Anthony Joseph and Marge (D'Esposito) A.; ABA, Suffolk Community Coll., 1974; BBA, Dowling Coll., 1976, MBA, 1982; m. Shawn E. McLaughlin, Feb. 19, 1966; children: Victor Anthony, Donna Marie, William Michael, Denise, Melissa, Sean Patrick, Amanda. Investment asst. Bank of N.Y., N.Y.C., 1968-73; investment officer Chem. Bank, N.Y.C., 1973-76; v.p. Treasury Americas, Australia and N.Z. Banking Group, Ltd., N.Y.C., 1976—. Mem. Selden (N.Y.) Vol. Fire Dept., 1969-75, treas., 1973-74; mem. exec. bd. Patchogue (N.Y.) Regional Cath. Sch., 1979-82. Served with USN, 1963-65. Republican. Club: World Trade (N.Y.C.). Home: 437 Hopper Ave Ridgewood NJ 07450 Office: 120 Wall St New York NY 10005

AMOS, ALAN SCOTT, food company executive; b. Parkersburg, W.Va., July 19, 1956; s. Dewey Harold and Dora C. (Ames) A.; m. Elisa A. Crouse, May 14, 1977; 1 child, Geoffrey Bryant. BS in Chem. Engring., Purdue U., 1978; MBA, Tenn. State U., 1980. Process engr. Stauffer Chem. Co., Nashville, 1978-79; buyer III Air Products and Chems., Inc., Allentown, Pa., 1980-83; procurement specialist Air Products and Chems., Inc., Calvert City, Ky., 1983-85; mgr. engring. procurement Ralston Purina Co., St. Louis, 1985—. V.p., bd. dirs. Edwardsville Montessori Sch., Granite City, Ill., 1988. Mem. Nat. Assn. Purchasing Mgmt., Am. Inst. Chem. Engrs., Am. Mgmt. Assn. Republican. Home: 33 Spring Brook Ln Edwardsville IL 62025 Office: Ralston Purina Co Checkerboard Sq Saint Louis MO 63164

AMOS, CHARLES CLINTON, insurance company executive; b. Tucson, Sept. 3, 1940; s. Charles Cliff and Lucille Elizabeth (Pierce) A.; m. Joan Marie LaBelle, Feb.2, 1962; 1 child, Jonathan Ashley. Student, N.Mex. Mil. Inst., 1955-58, Boston U., 1969-70. CPCU. Salesman and field sales mgr. Employers Ins. Co. of Wausau, Pitts. and Belmont, Mass., 1965-69; pres., chief exec. officer Henry J. LeBianc Ins. Agy., Inc., Fitchburg, Mass., 1969-74, Aanco Underwriters, Inc., St. Petersburg, Fla., 1972-88; chmn., chief fin. officer Aanco Underwriters, Inc., 1988—; pres., chief exec. officer Aanco Ins. Svcs., Inc., Culver City, Calif., 1983-87; pres., chief exec. officer Pass-A-Grille Fishery, Inc., St. Petersburg, Fla., 1981—, Countryside Insurors, Inc., St. Petersburg, 1983-85; pres. Latat Devel. Corp., 1985-88, Lanax Constrn., Inc., 1985—, Gulfport Mini-storage Inc., 1986—; chmn. Flagship Mortgage Corp., Culver City, 1985-87; sec. treas. Blue Marlin Inc., Clearwater, Fla., 1982-85, Cruising World Inc., St. Petersburg, 1983-85; v.p., treas. Ins. Premium Acceptance Corp. Active Pinellas Assn. Retarded Children, Pinellas County Com. of 100, Fla. Gulf Coast Symphony; commr., chmn. Pinellas County Housing Authority, 1975-79, 89—. With U.S. Army, 1960-63. Named Agt. of Yr. Travelers Ins. Co., 1981, Nat. Sales Leader Aetna Life Ins. Co., 1978; recipient other sales awards. Mem. Soc. CPCU's, CPCU's (fgn. ins. com. 1986—), Ind. Agts. Assn., Sales and Mktg. Execs., Rotary, Kappa Alpha, Hon. Order Ky. Cols. Republican. Baptist. Home: 300 Rafael Blvd NE Saint Petersburg FL 33704 Office: Aanco Underwriters Inc 10033 9th St N Saint Petersburg FL 33702

ANAGNOSTOPOULOS, MADELAINE LYNCH, financial consultant; b. N.Y.C., Dec. 30, 1941; d. George Philip and Gertrude (Low) Lynch; m. Peter A. K. Reese, Dec. 10, 1966 (dec. July 1978); m. Constantine Efthymios Anagnostopoulos, Mar. 19, 1983; children: Peter Reese, Anne Reese, Anne-Marie. BA, U. Ill., Chgo., 1971; MBA, Loyola U., Chgo., 1980. Econ. analyst Amoco Internat. Oil Co., Chgo., 1979-83; cons. fin. planning Design Capital Planning Group Inc., Hauppauge, N.Y., 1984-86; fin. cons. Roberts Loucks and Co. Inc., Locust Valley, N.Y., 1986—. Treas., bd. dirs. Am. Lung Assn. Nassau-Suffolk, N.Y., Hauppauge, 1986—. Mem. Assn. MBA Execs., Inst. Cert. Fin. Planners (cert.), Internat. Assn. Fin. Planning. Home: 7 The Courtyard Locust Valley NY 11560

ANAST, NICK JAMES, lawyer; b. Gary, Ind., Apr. 20, 1947; s. James Terry and Kiki (Pappas) A.; m. Linda K. Skirvin, Oct. 28, 1972; children: Jason, Nicole. AB, Ind. U., 1969, JD, 1972. Bar: Ind. 1972, U.S. Dist. Ct. (no. and so. dists.) Ind. 1972, U.S Ct. Appeals (7th cir.) 1975, U.S. Supreme Ct. 1976. Ptnr. Pappas, Tokarski & Anast, Gary, 1972-74; ptnr. Tokarski & Anast, Gary, 1974-85, Schererville, Ind., 1985—; dep. pros. atty. Lake County Prosecutors Office, Crown Point, Ind., 1973-74; pub. defender Lake County Superior Ct., Gary, 1974-78; atty. Town of Schererville, 1982, 88, 89, Lowell, 1983, City of Lake Station, Ind., 1978. Pres. St. John (Ind.) Twp. Young Dems., 1980. Recipient Service to Youth award YMCA, 1980, Outstanding Service award Schererville Soccer Club, 1985. Fellow Ind. Bar Found.; mem. ABA, Ind. Bar Assn., Lake County Bar Assn. (bd. dirs.) 1983-85, Outstanding Service award 1985). Democrat. Greek Orthodox. Lodge: Lions (pres. Schererville chpt. 1985-86). Office: Tokarski & Anast 7803 W 75th Ave Ste 1 Schererville IN 46375

ANASTASIO, JAMES, insurance company executive; b. N.Y.C., Sept. 28, 1930; s. Alphonse and Clara (Santangini) A.; m. Lucy Di Staulo, Feb. 14, 1953; children—Michael, Janis. Student, Pace Coll., 1959. With Union Reinsurance Co., N.Y.C., 1955-62; with Am. Re-Ins. Co., N.Y.C., 1962—; now v.p., treas. Am. Re-Ins. Co.; faculty Coll. of Ins., 1977. Served with USN, 1951-55. Mem. Soc. Ins. Accountants (exec. com.), Ins. Accounting and Statis. Assn. Club: K.C. (past grand knight). Home: 39 Nottingham

Rd Manalapan NJ 07726 Office: Am Re-Ins Co One Liberty Pla New York NY 10006

ANAWATY, MARK ANTHONY, real estate company executive; b. Port Arthur, Tex., Dec. 27, 1950; s. Henry Anthony and Bernadine (Siragusa) A.; m. Gail Ann Edelen, Nov. 17, 1979; children: Colin Anthony, Tyler Anthony. BA in Communications, U. Houston, 1972. Pres., owner Anmark Devel. Co. and Anmark Co., Houston, 1978—; bd. dirs. Anari Tex. Inc., Houston. Dir. Harris County Health Facilities Devel. Corp.; life mem. Houston Livestock Show and Rodeo, 1978—; chmn. Harris County Toll Rd. Com., Houston, 1987—; state conv. dir., organizer, chmn. press and media com. ARC, Houston, 1988—. Recipient Prism award Greater Houston Builders Assn., 1979. Mem. USCG Capt.'s Assn. Republican. Methodist. Home: 5407 Holly Valley Richmond TX 77469

ANCELL, ROBERT M., publisher; b. Phoenix, Oct. 16, 1942; s. Robert M. and Alice (Lovett) A.; m. Janet C. Neuber, Dec. 21, 1966 (div. 1984); children: Kevin, Kristin; m. Christine Marie Miller, Mar. 30, 1985. BA, U. N.Mex., 1971. Announcer KDEF Radio, Albuquerque, 1966-67; reporter Sta. KOB-TV, Albuquerque, 1967-72; sr. sales representative Xerox Corp., Albuquerque, 1972-78; gen. sales mgr. Sta. KRDO-TV, Colorado Springs, Colo., 1978-79; publisher Titsch Pub., Denver, 1979-82; publ. dir. Denver Bus. Mag., 1982-83; advt. mgr. U.S. Naval Res. (recalled to active duty), New Orleans, 1984-85; publisher Endless Vacation Pubs., Indpls., 1985—; cons. Media Masters, Denver, 1983-84. Contbr. articles to mags., profl. jours., newspapers, 1960—. Served to lt. comdr. USNR, 1980. Recipient First Place award N.Mex. Broadcasters, 1970; First Place award UPI, 1970, Pres. Club award Xerox Corp., 1973, 75-76. Mem. Reserve Officers Assn. of U.S. (tng. officer 1980-81, Cert. of Appreciation 1981), U.S. Naval. Inst., Air Force Assn., Manuscript Soc. Republican. Presbyterian. Avocations: private pilot, bicycling, bridge, writing, photography. Office: Endless Vacation Pubs One RCI Pla 3502 Woodview Indianapolis IN 46268

ANCETTI, CARLO GUIDO, construction company executive; b. Udine, Italy, Oct. 7, 1933; s. Carlo C. and Laura Maria Luisa (Bozzola) A.; m. Nicoletta M. Menzaghi, Oct. 7, 1961; children: Barbara, Giancarlo, Claudio. Degree in Geometry, Antonio Zanon U., Udine, Italy, 1953. Job site supr. Italscavi Udine, San Quirino, Italy, 1953-54; mgr. rock drilling and blasting Italscavi Udine, Val Frera, Italy, 1954-55; mgr. job site Italscavi Udine, Val di Non, Italy, 1956-57; mgr. excavation Farsura Milano, Pertusillo, Italy, 1958; mgr. project research Farsura Milano, Milan, 1958-59; mgr. sales Acesa Milano, Milan, 1959-66; chmn. Anbel SpA, Milan, 1966—; pres. Tamrock Italiana SpA, San Donato Milanes, Italy, 1971—. Named Cavaliere di Santo Sepolcro di Gerusalemme, 1988. Mem. Fogolar Furlan Assn. Roman Catholic. Club: Malaspina Sporting (Milan, San Felice). Office: Tamrock Italiana SpA, Via A Grandi 18, 20097 San Donato Milanese Italy

ANCHEL, EDWARD, manufacturing executive; b. Port Jervis, N.Y., June 19, 1939; s. Jonas H. and Claire Beatrice (Krawitz) A.; m. Sandra Zeldin, May 5, 1961 (div. 1973); children: Michael, David, Jennifer; m. Judith Gail Kaplan, Oct. 2, 1975. BSBA, Pa. State U., 1960. V.p. Sparkomatic Corp., Milford, Pa., 1960-70, pres., 1970—, chmn., 1980—; bd. dirs. Westport Ltd. Hong Kong, S.P.C.S. Ltd. Crewe, England, Pa. State Coll. Bus.; mem. exec. com. Pa. State. Named Man of Yr., United Jewish Appeal Fedn., 1981, Alumni fellow Pa. State U., 1984. Jewish. Office: Sparkomatic Corp Rt 6 and 209 Milford PA 18337

ANCKER-JOHNSON, BETSY, physicist, automotive company executive; b. St. Louis, Apr. 29, 1927; d. Clinton James and Fern (Lalan) A.; m. Harold Hunt Johnson, Mar. 15, 1958; children: Ruth P. Johnson, David H. Johnson, Paul A. Johnson, Martha H. Johnson. B.A. in Physics with high honors (Pendleton scholar), Wellesley Coll., 1949; Ph.D. magna cum laude, U. Tuebingen, Germany, 1953; D.Sc. (hon.), Poly. Inst. N.Y., 1979, Trinity Coll., 1981, U. So. Calif., 1984, Alverno Coll., 1984; LL.D. (hon.), Bates Coll., 1980. Instr., jr. research physist U. Calif., 1953-54; physicist Sylvania Microwave Physics Lab., 1956-58; mem. tech. staff RCA Labs., 1958-61; research specialist Boeing Co., 1961-70, exec., 1970-73; asst. sec. commerce for sci. and tech. 1973-77; dir. phys. research Argonne Nat. Lab., Ill., 1977-79; v.p. environ. activities staff Gen. Motors Tech. Center, Warren, Mich., 1979—; affiliate prof. elec. engring. U. Wash., 1964-73; dir. Gen. Mills; mem. Energy Research Adv. Bd. Dept. Energy, U.S Safety Rev. Panel Nat. Sci. Found. Author over 70 sci. papers; patentee in field. Mem. staff Inter-Varsity Christian Fellowship, 1954-56; mem. visiting com. elec. and computer div. MIT, U. Wash.; mem. bd. visitors Oakland U., Dept. Def. Sci. Bd.; mem. adv. bd. Stanford U. Sch. Engring., Fla. State U., Fla. A&M U., Congrl. Caucus for Sci. and Tech.; trustee Wellesley Coll., 1972-77. AAUW fellow, 1950-51; Horton Hollowell fellow, 1951-52; NSF grantee, 1967-72. Fellow Am. Phys. Soc. (councillor-at-large 1973-76), IEEE, AAAS; mem. Nat. Acad. Engring., World Environ. Ctr. (chmn., bd. dirs. 1988—), Air Pollution Control Assn., NSF (U.S. Safety Rev. Panel), Soc. Automotive Engrs. (bd. dirs. 1979-81), Phi Beta Kappa, Sigma Xi. Office: GM Environ Activities Staff 30400 Mound Rd Warren MI 48090-9015

ANCTIL, MATTHEW J., financial analyst, consultant; b. San Bernardino, Calif., Jan. 17, 1956; s. Ralph J. and Elsbeth (Roeder) A. BS in Bus., U. Colo., 1978; MBA, U. Mich., 1985. CPA, Tex. Acct. Hamilton Bros. Oil Co., Denver, 1978-81; mgr. acctg. Ladd & Lukowicz, Inc., Denver, 1981-82; controller Francarep U.S.A., Denver, 1982-83; sr. fin. analyst Am. Airlines, Dallas, 1985—; bd. dirs. Inland Gold Inc., Denver. Mem. Am. Inst. CPA's. Home: 4009 Pin Oak Terr 210 Euless TX 76040

ANDERLUH, JOHN R., office equipment company executive; b. Niagara Falls, N.Y., Aug. 31, 1934; s. John R. Sr. and Rose (Barone) A.; m. Patricia Bewll, Apr. 27, 1957; 4 children. BA, Cornell U., 1956. Internal sales rep. Moore Bus. Forms, Buffalo, 1956-63; field sales rep. Moore Bus. Forms, Glenview, Ill., 1969-73, regional mgr., 1969-73; mgr. Response Graphics, Libertyville, Ill., 1973-79, gen. mgr., 1979-80, v.p., gen. mgr., 1980-83; v.p. sales and mktg. Moore, U.S. Bus. Forms & Systems Div., Glenview, 1983-86, pres., 1986-88; group pres. Moore, U.S. Ops., Glenview, 1988—. With U.S. Army, 1957-59. Named. Mktg. Exec. of Yr. Nat. Accounts Mktg. Assn., 1987. Office: Moore US Ops 1205 Milwaukee Ave Glenview IL 60025 Also: Moore Bus Forms & Systems 1205 Milwaukee Ave Glenview IL 60025

ANDERS, WILLIAM ALISON, aerospace and diversified manufacturing company executive, former astronaut, former U.S. Ambassador; b. Hong Kong, Oct. 17, 1933; s. Arthur Ferdinand and Muriel Florence (Adams) A.; m. Valerie Elizabeth Hoard, June 26, 1955; children: Alan Frank, Glen Thomas, Gayle Alison, Gregory Michael, Eric William, Diana Elizabeth. B.S., U.S. Naval Acad., Annapolis, 1955; M.S., U.S. Inst. Tech., Wright-Patterson AFB, 1962. Commnd. 2d lt. U.S. Air Force, 1955, pilot, engr., 1955-69; astronaut NASA-Johnson Space Ctr., Houston, 1963-69, Apollo 8, 1st lunar flight, 1968; exec. sec. Nat. Aero. and Space Council, Washington, 1963-72; commr. AEC, Washington, 1973-74; chmn. Nuclear Regulatory Commn., Washington, 1975-76; U.S. Ambassador to Norway 1976-77; v.p., gen. mgr. nuclear energy products div. Gen. Electric Co., 1977-80; v.p., gen. mgr. aircraft equipment div. Gen. Electric Co., DeWitt, N.Y., 1980-84; sr. exec., v.p. ops. Textron Inc., Providence, R.I., 1984—; major-gen. U.S. Air Force Res., 1983-88, Nat. Acad. Engring. Decorated various mil. awards; recipient Wright, Collier, Goddard and Arnold flight awards; co-holder several world flight records. Mem. Soc. Exptl. Test Pilots (holder several world speed and altitude records), Def. Sci. Bd., Tau Beta Pi. Office: Textron Inc 40 Westminster St Providence RI 02903

ANDERSEN, DORIS EVELYN, real estate broker; b. Christian County, Ky., Oct. 30, 1923; d. William Earl and Blanche Elma (Withers) Johnston; m. Roger Lewis Shirk, July 9, 1944 (div. 1946); 1 child, Vicki Lee Shirk Sanderson; m. DeLaire Andersen, July 6, 1946; children: Craig Bryant, Karen Rae, Kent DeLaire, Chris Jay, Mardi Lynn. Diploma, South Bend Coll. Commerce, 1942; diploma in banking Notre Dame U., 1946; student Ind. U., 1942-44. Tng. dir. First Nat. Bank, Portland, Oreg., 1963-69; assoc. broker Stan Wiley, Inc., Portland, 1969-79; prin. Doris Andersen & Assocs., Portland, 1979—; speaker at seminars; mem. Gov.'s Task Force Council on Housing, Salem, Oreg., 1985-86. Contbr. articles to profl. jours. Mem. task force Oreg. Dept. Energy, Salem, 1984-85. Mem. Nat. Assn. Realtors (dir. 1983—, regional v.p. Northwest region 1988), Oreg. Assn. Realtors (dir. 1979—, pres. 1986—), Portland Bd. Realtors (pres. 1982), Women's Council Realtors (local pres. 1977, state pres. 1978, gov. nat. orgn. 1979), Internat. Platform Assn., Internat. Biog. Assn. Avocations: reading, travel. Home and Office: PO Box 1169 Shady Cove OR 97539

ANDERSEN, ELMER L., manufacturing executive, former governor of Minnesota; b. Chgo., June 17, 1909; s. Arne and Jennie (Johnson) A.; m. Eleanor Johnson, 1932; children: Anthony L., Julian L., Emily E. BBA, U. Minn., 1931; LLD (hon.), Macalester College, St. Paul, 1965; LHD, Carleton Coll., 1972; D of Mgmt. (hon.), U. Minn., 1984. With H.B. Fuller Co. (mfrs. indsl. adhesives), 1934—, sales mgr., 1937-41, pres., 1941-61, 63-71, chmn., 1961-63, 71—, chief exec. officer, 1971-74, chmn. bd., 1974—; dir. Davis Consol. Industries, Sydney, Australia, Prenor Group Ltd., Montreal, Que., 1972-76, Geo. A. Hormel & Co., Austin, 1971-75, First Trust Co., St. Paul, 1969-74; mem. Minn. Senate, 1949-58; gov. of Minn. 1961-63; pub. Princeton (Minn.) Union Eagle, 1976—, Sun Newspapers, 1978-84; chmn. bd. ECM Publishers, Princeton, Minn., 1987—. Campaign chmn. St. Paul Community Chest, 1959—; exec. com. Boy Scouts Am.; mem. Nat. Parks Centennial Commn., 1971, Gov.'s Voyageurs Nat. Park Adv. Commn., Select Com. on Minn. Jud. System; chmn. Minn. Constl. Study Commn.; Bd. dirs., pres. Child Welfare League Am., 1965-67; past pres. St. Paul Gallery and Sch. of Art; past trustee Augsburg Coll., Mpls.; pres. Charles A. Lindbergh Meml. Fund, 1978-88, chmn. 1986-88; regent U. Minn., 1967-75; chmn. bd., 1971-75; chmn. Bush Found., St. Paul; bd. dirs. Council on Founds., N.Y.C; chmn. U. Minn. Found.; chmn. bd. Alliss Found., 1982-88; mem. exec. council Minn. Hist. Soc. Decorated Order of Lion Finland; recipient Outstanding Achievement award U. Minn., 1959; award of merit Izaak Walton League; Silver Beaver award; Silver Antelope award Boy Scouts Am.; Conservation award Mpls. C. of C.; Taconite award Minn. chpt. Am. Inst. Mining Engrs., 1976; Nat. Phi Kappa Phi award U. Minn., 1977; Minn. Bus. Hall Fame award, 1977; Greatest Living St. Paulite award St. Paul C. of C., 1980; award Adhesive and Sealant Council, 1980; others. Fellow Morgan Library (N.Y.C); Mem. Adhesive Mfrs. Assn. Am. (past pres.), Voyageurs Nat. Park Assn. (past pres.), Minn. Hist. Soc. (exec. com., pres. 1966-70), Am. Antiquarian Soc. Republican. Lutheran. Clubs: Rotarian (St. Paul) (past pres. St. Paul, past dist. gov.), Grolier, Univ. (N.Y.C.); St. Paul Gavel (past pres.). Home: 1483 Bussard Ct Arden Hills MN 55112

ANDERSEN, HARRY EDWARD, oil equipment co. exec.; b. Omaha, Apr. 25, 1906; s. John Anton and Caroline (Ebbensgaard) A.; student pub. schs. and spl. courses, including Ohio State U., 1957, U. Okla., 1959; Ph.D. in Bus. Adminstrn. (hon.), Colo. State Christian Coll., 1972; m. Alma Theora Vawter, June 12, 1931; children—Jeanenne Dee (Mrs. Gaylord Fernstrom) and Maureen Lee (Mrs. Roger Podany) (twins), John Harry. Founder N.W. Service Sta. Equipment Co., Mpls., 1934, pres., treas., 1956—; owner Joint Ops. Co., real estate mgmt.; dir. Franklin Nat. Bank, Mpls. Spl. dep. sheriff Hennepin County, 1951—; hon. fire chief of Mpls., 1951—; pres. Washington Lake Improvement Assn., 1955. Mem. Shrine Directors Assn. (N.W. gov.), Nat. Assn. Oil Equipment Jobbers (pres. 1957-58, dir. 1954-56), C. of C., Upper Midwest Oil Mans Club. Lutheran. Mason (32deg., K.T., Shriner), Jester. Clubs: Viking (pres.), Engineers, Toastmasters, Minneapolis Athletic, Golden Valley Golf, Le Mirador Country (Lake Geneva, Switzerland). Home: 2766 W River Pkwy Minneapolis MN 55406 Office: 1121 Jackson St NE Minneapolis MN 55413

ANDERSEN, K(ENT) TUCKER, investment executive; b. Manchester Conn., June 5, 1942; s. Alfred Hans and Dorothy Emily (Ray) A.; m. Karen Ann Kirchofer, Oct. 11, 1963; children: Heather Michele, Kristen Eileen. Student, Phillips Exeter Acad., N.H., 1957-59; BA, Wesleyan U., 1963. Chartered fin. analyst. Actuarial student Travelers Ins. Co., Hartford, Conn., 1963-66; security analyst Smith Barney & Co., N.Y.C., 1968-69; ptnr. Rudman Assocs., N.Y.C., 1969-72; ptnr. Cumberland Assocs., N.Y.C., 1972—, mng. ptnr., 1982—. Bd. dirs. Cato Inst., Washington, 1987—; trustee YWCA of Montclair, North Essex, N.J., 1980—, 1st United Meth. Ch. of Montclair, 1976—; admission rep. for N.J. area Phillips Exeter Acad., N.H., 1983—. Served with USPHS, 1966-68. Recipient Distinguished Alumni award Wesleyan U., 1988. Mem. Soc. Actuaries, N.Y. Soc. Security Analysts, Inst. Chartered Fin. Analysts, Polit. Club for Growth (mem. exec. com. 1984—), Kappa Nu Kappa (pres. 1963). Republican. Avocation: marathons. Office: Cumberland Assocs 1114 Ave of Americas New York NY 10036

ANDERSON, A. RICHARD, food products executive; b. Staten Island, N.Y., Aug. 30, 1942; s. Albert Vincent and Helen (Sarakun) A.; m. Sandra Lee Cooper, Aug. 27, 1966; children: Heather, Lance. BS, Cornell U., 1965; MS, Purdue U., 1967. Assoc. product mgr. Gen. Foods Corp., White Plains, N.Y., 1967-71; mktg. mgr. Pillsbury Co., Mpls., 1971-76; dir. new products Internat. Multifoods, Mpls., 1976-79; v.p. mktg. and sales Savannah Foods, Birmingham, Ala., 1980-82; dir. mktg. frozen pizza div. Pillsbury Co., Mpls., 1982-87, dir. mktg. vegetable side dishes div., 1987—; guest lectr. U. Mich., Ann Arbor, Cornell U., Ithaca, N.Y. Recipient Clio award, 1979; named to Hon. Order Ky. Cols., 1986. Mem. Frozen Pizza Inst. (chmn. retail com. 1985-87, pres. 1987). Republican. Roman Catholic. Clubs: Cornell of Minn. (v.p. 1988), Tower (Ithaca). Office: Pillsbury Co Pillsbury Ctr Minneapolis MN 55402

ANDERSON, ANNELISE GRAEBNER, economist; b. Oklahoma City, Nov. 19, 1938; d. Elmer and Dorothy (Zilisch) Graebner; m. Martin Anderson, Sept. 25, 1965. B.A., Wellesley Coll., 1960; M.A., Columbia U., 1965, Ph.D., 1974. Assoc. editor McKinsey and Co., Inc., 1963-65; researcher Nixon Campaign Staff, 1968-69; project mgr. Dept. Justice, 1970-71; from asst. prof. bus. adminstrn. to assoc. prof. Calif. State U.-Hayward, 1975-80; sr. policy adviser Reagan Presdl. campaign and transition, Washington, 1980; assoc. dir. econs. and govt. Office Mgmt. and Budget, Washington, 1981-83; sr. research fellow Hoover Instn., Stanford U., Calif., 1983—; mem. Nat. Sci. Bd., 1985—; Author: The Business of Organized Crime: A Cosa Nostra Family, 1979, Illegal Alins and Employer Sanctions: Solving the Wrong Problem, 1986; co-editor: Thinking About America: The United States in the 1990's, 1988; contbr. articles to profl. jours., chpts. to books. Mem. bd. overseers Rand/UCLA Ctr. for Study Soviet Internat. Behavior, Los Angeles, 1987—. Mem. Am. Econ. Assn., Western Econ. Assn., Beta Gamma Sigma. Office: Stanford U Hoover Instn Stanford CA 94305-6010

ANDERSON, ARNOLD STUART, lawyer; b. N.Y.C., June 4, 1934; s. David and Mary (Bilgoray) A.; m. Barbara Sapkowitz, Oct. 1, 1955; children: David Jay, Randi Lee. B.A., CCNY, 1956; J.D., Columbia U., 1959. Bar: N.Y. 1959, U.S. Supreme Ct. 1971. Gen. atty., office gen. counsel FAA, Washington, 1960-61; assoc. Fly, Shuebruck, Blume & Gaguine, N.Y.C., 1962-63; asst. counsel N.Y. Moreland Commn. on Alcoholic Beverage Control Law, N.Y.C., 1963-64; assoc. Winthrop, Stimson, Putnam & Roberts, N.Y.C., 1964-79; v.p., gen. counsel F.W. Woolworth Co., N.Y.C., 1979-80; sr. v.p., gen. counsel F.W. Woolworth Co., 1980-82, exec. v.p. adminstrn., gen. counsel, 1982—; asst. counsel investigation into jud. conduct Supreme Ct. Appellate Div. 2d Dept., 1970; bd. dirs. F.W. Woolworth Ltd. (Can.), Woolworth Mexicana S.A. de C.V. (Mex.), Kinney Shoe Corp., Kinney Can., Inc., Richman Bros. Co., Saltzman's Little Folk Shops Inc. Author: (with R.S. Taft) N.Y. Practice Series, Personal Taxation, Vol. I, 1975; contbr. (with R.S. Taft) articles to profl. jours. Asst. counsel investigation jud. conduct Supreme Ct. Appelatte. Mem. Am. Bar Assn., Fed. Bar Assn., N.Y. Bar Assn., N.Y.C. Bar Assn. Office: F W Woolworth Co Woolworth Bldg 233 Broadway New York NY 10279

ANDERSON, BARRY STANLEY, health care executive; b. Atlanta, Sept. 6, 1942; s. Rex and Virginia A.; m. Katherine Krupp, Dec. 26, 1966 (div. 1973); 1 child, Jon Robert; m. Patricia Ann O'Neil, May 25, 1974; children: Russell Barry, Robert Bruce. AA, Foothill Coll., 1968; BA, San Francisco State U., 1976; MBA, U. N.D., 1984. V.p. Ventilation Assocs., Inc., Houston, 1971-74; program dir. Inst. Med. Studies, Berkeley, Calif., 1976-78; program dir. Sch. Respiratory Care, St. Alexius Med. Ctr., Bismarck, N.D., 1978-84, health care cons., dir. edn., 1984-87; mgr. respiratory care ops. Medisys Mgmt. System, 1988; program dir. Loma Vista Adult Ctr., Concord, Calif., 1988—; instr. Entrepreneurial Mgmt. Bus. Tng. Internat., Sacramento, 1988—. chmn. bd. dirs., pres. Creative Mktg., Inc., Bismarck (N.D.), Vacaville (Calif.), 1982—; v.p. Baby Products Ltd., 1987—; asst. prof. U. of Mary, 1982-85; instr. bus. edn. div. Solano Community Coll., Suisun, Calif., 1988—. Author: (with D. Quesinberry) Blood Gas Interpretations, 1974; mem. editorial adv. bd. Respiratory Mgmt.; contbr. articles to profl. jours. Nominee Am. Coll. Healthcare Execs. Mem. Am. Mktg. Assn., Am. Mgmt. Assn., Am. Hosp. Assn., Acad. for Health Svcs. Mktg., Assn. MBA Execs., Ctr. for Entrepreneurial Mgmt., U. N.D. Alumni Assn., Elks. Avocations: computer programming, writing, reading, lecturing, sailing. Office: Loma Vista Adult Ctr 1266 San Carlos Ave Concord CA 94518

ANDERSON, (WILLIAM) BRIAN, bank executive; b. Cleburne, Tex., July 20, 1958; s. William Roy and Betty (Vaughan) A. BBA in Acctg., Baylor U., 1980. CPA Tex. Staff acct. Deloitte, Haskins & Sells, Ft. Worth, 1980-82; bank analyst Tex. Am. Bancshares, Inc., Ft. Worth, 1982-86; mgr. fin. reporting and planning Tex. Am. Bancshares, Inc., Dallas, 1986—. Mem. Am. Inst. CPA's, Tex. Soc. CPA's, Dallas Soc. CPA's. Democrat. Methodist. Home: 5641 Wembley Downs Arlington TX 76017 Office: Tex Am Bank Dallas 100 Exchange Park N Dallas TX 75235

ANDERSON, CAROLE LEWIS, investment banker; b. East Stroudsburg, Pa., Oct. 7, 1944; d. William A. and Rosamonde (Lewis) A.; m. John Mason Lee Sweet, Apr. 9, 1983; children: John Mason Lee Anderson-Sweet, Dunn Lewis Anderson-Sweet. B.A. in Polit. Sci., Pa State U., 1966; M.B.A. in Fin., NYU, 1976. Securities analyst PaineWebber, Jackson & Curtis, N.Y.C., 1971-73, assoc. v.p., 1973-75, v.p. research, 1975-77; v.p. PaineWebber, Inc., N.Y.C., 1977-82, mng. dir., 1982-85; sr. v.p. corp. devel. Hasbro, Inc., N.Y.C., 1985-87; also dir. Hasbro, Inc., Pawtucket, R.I., 1985-87; mng. dir. Md. Nat. Investment Banking Co., Washington, 1987-88, pres., chief exec. officer, 1988—; bd. dirs. Master Media Ltd., Forum for Women Dirs., N.Y.C. County com. person Democratic Party, Manhattan, N.Y., 1975-82; chmn. Hasbro Children's Found., 1985-88, mem. exec. com. and trustee, 1988—; mem. N.Y. com. U.S. Commn. on Civil Rights, 1980-84; trustee Mary Baldwin Coll., Staunton, Va., 1987—, Penn State Alumni Council, 1987—. Named to Acad. Women Achievers, YWCA, N.Y.C., 1982; recipient Disting. Alumna award Pa. State U., 1987. Mem. Pa. State U. Alumni Council. Office: Md Nat Investment Banking Co 7474 Greenway Center Dr Greenbelt MD 20770

ANDERSON, CATHERINE AGNES, manufacturing executive; b. Crosby, Minn., Nov. 19, 1946; d. Charles Francis and Mary Flora (Middleton); m. Stephen Thomas Anderson, Dec. 5, 1970; children: Amy Lynn, S. Carver. BS, Coll. of St. Scholastica, 1968. Lic. med. technologist. Med. technologist supr. U. Minn. Hosps., Mpls., 1968-72, assoc. scientist, 1972-76; v.p. Med. Graphics Corp., St. Paul, Minn., 1976-81; exec. v.p. Med. Graphics Corp., St. Paul, 1981-86, pres., chief operating officer, 1986-88, chmn., chief exec. officer, 1988—. Patentee high tech. med. equipment. Named to Men and Women Under 40 Who are Changing Am. Esquire Mag., 1984; recipient 100 award Inc. Mag.,1983, 84. Mem. Am. Coll. Clinical Pathol. (award 1968), Am. Mgmt. Assn. (award recipient 1986). Roman Catholic. Office: Medical Graphics Corp 350 Oak Grove Pkwy Saint Paul MN 55127-8599

ANDERSON, CHARLES ROBERT, marketing professional; b. Joliet, Ill., Feb. 4, 1942; s. Harold Charles and Hazel Irene (McKnight) A. BSEE, Carnegie-Mellon U., 1964, MSEE, 1965. Staff scientist Los Alamos (N.Mex.) Sci. Lab., 1967-73; design engr. Gen. Dynamics Corp., Pomona, Calif., 1973-75; mgr. research and development Nicolet Instrument Corp., Madison, Wis., 1975-83, mgr. sales and mktg., 1984-86, mgr. internat. ops., 1986—; mem. adv. com. EPA, Nat. Bur. Standards, Washington, 1985—. Author: (with others) Aldrich Library of Infrared Spectra, 1983, Sigma Library of Infrared Spectra, 1985; contbr. articles to profl. jours.; patentee in field. Joint com. for Atomic and Molecular Properties. Mem. Coblentz Soc., Optical Soc. Am., Wis. Assn. Research Mgrs. Home: N11W31812 Phyllis Pkwy Delafield WI 53018 Office: Nicolet Instrument Corp 5225-1 Verona Rd Madison WI 53711

ANDERSON, CHARLES ROSS, civil engineer; b. N.Y.C., Oct. 4, 1937; s. Biard Eclare and Melva (Smith) A.; m. Susan Breinholt, Aug. 29, 1961; children: Loralee, Brian, Craig, Thomas, David. BSCE, U. Utah, 1961; MBA, Harvard U., 1963. Registered profl. engr.; cert. land surveyor. Owner, operator AAA Engring. and Drafting, Inc., Salt Lake City, 1960—. Mayoral appointee Housing Devel. com., Salt Lake City, 1981-86; bd. dirs., cons. Met. Water Dist., Salt Lake City, 1985—; bd. dirs., v.p., sec. bd. dirs. Utah Mus. Natural History, Salt Lake City, 1980—; asst. dist. commr. Sunrise Dist. Boy Scouts Am., Salt Lake City, 1985-86; fund raising coord. architects and engrs. United Fund; mem. Sunstone Nat. Adv. Bd., 1980—; bd. dirs. Provo River Water Users Assn., 1986—. Fellow Am. Gen. Contractors, Salt Lake City, 1960; recipient Hamilton Watch award, 1961. Mem. ASCE, Am. Congress on Surveying and Mapping, Harvard U. Bus. Sch. Club (pres. 1970-72), Pres. Club U. Utah, U. Utah Alumni Assn. (bd. dirs. 1989), The Country Club, Bonneville Knife and Fork Club, Rotary (chmn. election com. 1980-81, vice chmn. membership com. 1988-89), Pi Kappa Alpha (internat. pres. 1972-74, trustee endowment fund 1974-80, Oustanding Alumnus 1967, 72), Phi Eta Sigma, Chi Epsilon, Tau Beta Pi. Home: 2689 Comanche Dr Salt Lake City UT 84108 Office: AAA Engring & Drafting Inc 1865 S Main St Salt Lake City UT 84115

ANDERSON, DALE, film production executive; b. Houston, Aug. 15, 1933; s. Elwin Dale Sr. and Thelma Ilene (Phillips) A.; m. Patricia Ann Lawrence, Aug. 29, 1952; children: Roxann, Ross, Eleceann. Student, Welch Sch. Music, Houston, 1952-57, U. Houston, 1956-59. Owner Dale Anderson Prodns. Internat., Houston, 1963—. Producer over 500 corp. films and 15 TV spls. in numerous langs. worldwide; over 300 guest appearances TV travel mus. shows and various programs. Home and Office: 123 N Rushwing Circle The Woodlands TX 77381

ANDERSON, DANIEL ODIN, leasing company executive; b. Hebron, Nebr., Mar. 31, 1941; s. Clark Odin and Kathryn Ann (Dahlstedt) A.; m. Marilyn Lorraine Lortz, July 29, 1961; children: Jeffrey, Erica. BS, U. So. Calif., 1966, MBA, 1969. Fin. analyst McDonnell Douglas Corp., Long Beach, Calif., 1967-70; mgr. spl. airline credits McDonnell Douglas Fin. Corp., Long Beach, 1970-72, mgr. credit dept., 1972-74, mgr. comml. fin., 1974-77, midwest regional mgr., 1977-81, dir. mktg., 1981-84, asst. v.p., 1984-85, v.p., 1985—. Mem. Alpha Gamma Sigma, Beta Gamma Sigma. Office: McDonnell Douglas Fin Corp 340 Golden Shore St Long Beach CA 90801

ANDERSON, DAREL BURTON, paper company executive; b. North Branch, Minn., Dec. 6, 1927; s. Axel C. and Verna (Johnson) A.; m. Lois Maxine Olson, June 30, 1929; children: Gregory, Gayle, Gretchen. Sales trainee Leslie Paper Co., Mpls., 1947-50; sales rep. Leslie Paper Co., Fargo, N.D., 1950-60; br. mgr. Leslie Paper Co., Sioux Falls, S.D., 1960-65; sales mgr. Leslie Paper Co., Mpls., 1965-72, v.p. sales, 1972-77, exec. v.p., 1977-82, pres., chief operating officer, 1982—. Republican. Lutheran. Clubs: Mpls. Athletic, Mpls. Golf. Home: 15000 Cherry Ln Minnetonka MN 55345 Office: Leslie Paper Co PO Box 1351 Minneapolis MN 55440

ANDERSON, DAVID BOYD, lawyer, steel company executive; b. Moorhead, Minn., Mar. 10, 1942; children: Kimberly, Erik, Jonathan, Caroline J. BA, U. Minn., 1964, JD, 1967; LLM, DePaul U., 1983. Bar: Ill. Labor relations supr. Continental Can Co., N.Y.C., 1970-72; asst. gen. counsel Am. Hosp. Supply Co., Evanston, Ill., 1972-83; v.p. planning and gen. counsel Inland Steel Industries, Inc., Chgo., 1983—. Bd. dirs. Evang. Health Systems, Community Equity Assistance corp.; active adv. com. LISC, planning com. Northwestern U. Corp. Counsel Inst. Served as capt. U.S. Army, 1967-70. Mem. ABA, Ill. Bar Assn., Minn. Bar Assn. Home: 845 Moseley Rd Highland Park IL 60035 Office: Inland Steel Industries Inc 30 W Monroe St Chicago IL 60603

ANDERSON, DAVID LANGLEY, management consultant; b. Southbridge, Mass., Nov. 16, 1944; s. Arthur Godfrey and Gertrude Mary Langley; m. Melinda Marshman, June 17, 1967; children: Joy, Scott. BA in Econs., U. Conn., 1966; PhD in Econs., Boston Coll., 1972. Chief industry analysis U.S. Dept. Transp., Cambridge, Mass., 1972-75; v.p. Data Resources Inc., Lexington, Mass., 1975-82, Temple, Barker and Sloane Inc., Lexington, Mass., 1982—. Contbr. articles to profl. jours. Bd. dirs. Boston Lyric

Opera, 1987—. Fellow Internat. Soc. Physical Distbrn. Mgmt.; mem. Am. Econs. Assn., Council Logistics Mgmt. Home: 19 Glenridge Dr Bedford MA 01730 Office: Temple Barker & Sloane 33 Hayden Ave Lexington MA 02173

ANDERSON, DAVID NEWTON, banker; b. Spartanburg, S.C., May 13, 1955; s. James Newton and Betty Jean (Hill) A.; m. Brenda Gail Gunter; children: Michael David, Krista Marie. BA in Econs., Wofford Coll., 1977; grad., S.C. Banker's Sch., 1985. Mgmt. assoc. C&S Nat. Bank, Columbia, S.C., 1978-79; supr. C&S Nat. Bank, Columbia, 1979-80, asst. ops. officer, 1980-82, ops. officer, 1982-84, corp. banking officer, 1984-86, asst. v.p., 1986—. Mem. Cash Mgmt. Assn. S.C. (cert.), Am. Inst. Banking (cert. 1979, 81). Baptist.

ANDERSON, DAVID OSBORNE, electronics company executive; b. Buffalo, Mar. 31, 1955; s. Charles William and Dorothy Lee (Osborne) A. BS in Indsl. Arts, Millersville U., 1977; BS in Electronic Physics, LaSalle U., 1986. Electronics tchr. Oxford (Pa.) Area High Sch., 1978-79; with SGS Thomson Microelectronics, Montgomeryville, Pa., 1979-83, test engring. mgr., 1983-85, mfg. engring. mgr., 1985—. Home: 416 Shearer St North Wales PA 19454 Office: SGS Thomson Microelectronics Co Commerce Dr Montgomeryville PA 18936

ANDERSON, DONALD GEORGE, marketing educator; b. Burlington, Iowa, Oct. 11, 1930; s. George H. and Esther (McCaleb) A.; m. Beulah Esther Fargo, June 6, 1959; children: David A., Susan R. AA, Burlington Jr. Coll., 1950; BS, U. Iowa, 1956, MA, 1957, PhD, 1962. Instr. U. S.D., 1957-59; instr. mktg. U. Iowa, 1959-61; asst. prof. mktg. U. N.D., 1961-62, prof., 1963-88, chmn. dept. mktg., 1963-75, 78-87; Harvey Jones prof. bus. and transp. studies Ouachita Bapt. U., Arkadelphia, Ark., 1988—; asst. prof. mktg. U. South Fla., 1962-63; vis. prof. bus. adminstrn. Moorhead State Coll., 1972. Contbg. editor Small Bus. Mgmt, 1973; contbr. articles on mktg. and small bus. to profl. jours. Chmn. New Indsl. Devel. Subcom. N.D. Economic Devel. Commn., 1967. Served with USN, 1951-54. Recipient B.H. Gamble award for disting. teaching and service. Mem. Am., So. mktg. assns., So., Midwest econ. assns., Small Bus. Inst. Dirs. Assn., Gideons Internat., VFW, Beta Gamma Sigma, Order Artus, Delta Sigma Pi. Home: 1703 Cordova Cir Arkadelphia AR 71923 Office: Ouachita Bapt U PO Box 3710 Arkadelphia AR 71923

ANDERSON, DOUGLAS SCRANTON HESLEY, investment banker; b. Springfield, Mass., Aug. 23, 1929; s. Lloyd Douglas Hesley and Alice Scranton (Eastman) Anderson. grad. Deerfield Acad., 1947; A.B., Harvard U., 1951; cert. investment banking Northwestern U., 1959; m. Elizabeth Bartram Radley, Sept. 20, 1969; 1 dau., Katherine Scranton. Gen. partner The Anderson Co., Greenwich, Conn., 1953—, MAH Co., Greenwich, 1979—; investment banker Lehman Bros., Salomon Bros. & Hutzler, Legg & Co. and Sterling, Grace & Co., Inc., N.Y.C., 1960-81. Pres., Pecksland Rd. Assn., 1977-78; bd. dirs. Indian Harbor Assn., 1979—, treas., 1986— ; rep. Greenwich Town Meeting, 1979—, legis. com., 1979—, vice chmn., 1986-87, chmn., 1988—, founder, mem. spl. cost containment com., 1984-86, sec., 1986; assoc. Rep. town com., 1984-87, mem., 1988—; trustee Round Hill Community Ch., Greenwich, 1980-85, treas., 1982-85 ; sec. Greenwich Selectman's Utility Watch Com., 1982—. Served to lt. USNR, 1951-53. Mem. Assn. Former Intelligence Officers, Conn. Police Chiefs Assn., Soc. Colonial Wars (council 1984—, gov. 1988—), Mayflower Descs., Order Founders and Patriots, Soc. Cincinnati. Clubs: Round Hill, Fox, Harvard Varsity, Harvard of Boston; Army and Navy (Washington); West Palm Beach Fishing; Edgartown (Mass.) Yacht, Chappaquiddick Beach. Home: 39 Vista Dr Greenwich CT 06830-7128

ANDERSON, EDWARD MARSHALL, manufacturing company executive; b. Nyack, N.Y., Jan. 19, 1931; s. Edward Martin and Hulda Bertina (Hanson) A.; m. Gloria Waterfield, June 15, 1962 (div. July 1971); m. Patricia Lee Stamper, July 21, 1971; children: Merritt, Catherine. AB, Gettysburg (Pa.) Coll. Owner Anderson Co., Phila., 1956-60; pres. Micronics Corp., Phila., 1960-63, Edwards-Roberts, Phila., 1963-70, Lil' Orbits, Inc., Mpls., 1974—, Anderson-Stepwell Inc., Mpls., 1974—. Inventor automatic donut machine, automatic oil/water separator. Mem. Nat. Sanitation Found., Spill Control Assn. Am. Republican. Lutheran. Office: Lil' Orbits 8851 Research Ctr Minneapolis MN 55428

ANDERSON, ERIC HALL, human resources development specialist; b. N.Y.C., Dec. 19, 1936; s. Carl Magnus and Ida (Johnson) A. BA, Hobart Coll., 1959; postgrad. Law Sch., U. Minn., 1959-60. Instr., Sly Park Job Corps Ctr., Pollock Pines, Calif., 1965-67; basic edn. cons. McGraw-Hill Book Co., N.Y.C., 1967-68; regional coordinator Ednl. Systems Corp., Washington, 1968-71; cons. for adminstrn. Internat. Tng. Consultants, Burbank, Calif., 1971-75; program dir. Care About Now, Inc., Chelsea, Mass., 1977-79; mgmt. devel. specialist Honeywell Info. Systems, Billerica, Mass., 1980-85, orgn. devel. specialist Honeywell Electro-Optics div., Wilmington, Mass., 1985-86, sr. human resources devel. specialist, 1986—. Author: A Program of Instruction in Reading, 1971; A Program of Instruction in Preparation for a Job, 1971. Treas. Mystic River Watershed Assn., Arlington, Mass., 1976—. Served to lt. USN, 1960-64. Mem. Am. Soc. Tng. and Devel., New Eng. Soc. Applied Psychologists, Am.-Scandinavian Found., Experiment in Internat. Living Pres.'s Assocs., Ancient Order of Deep, Theta Delta Chi. Democrat. Lutheran. Home: 34 Hamilton Rd Arlington MA 02174 Office: Honeywell Electro-Optics Div 2 Forbes Rd Lexington MA 02173

ANDERSON, ETHEL AVARA, retail executive; b. Meridian, Miss.; d. Thomas Franklin and Annie Ethel (Jones) Avara.; m. Theron Young Anderson, Aug. 2, 1940 (dec. Aug. 1964); 1 child, Brenda Anderson Jackson. Grad. high sch., Meridian. Owner, mgr. Med. and Mchts. Collections, Meridian, 1977—. Mem. exec. bd., sec. United Way of Meridian, 1983-87; mem. exec. bd., dir. Miss. Industries for Developmentally Disabled, Meridian, 1984-87, Lauderdale Assn. Retarded Children, Meridian, 1983-87. Mem. Meridian C. of C. (liaison 1985-87), Xi Gamma, Beta Sigma Phi. Methodist. Lodge: Civitan (bd. dirs. Meridian club 1984-87). Home: 3400 20th St Meridian MS 39301 Office: Med and Mchts Collection 906 20th Ave Ste 205 Meridian MS 39301

ANDERSON, FLETCHER NEAL, chemical executive; b. Kansas City, Mo., Nov. 5, 1930; s. Chester Gustav and Astrid Cecilia (Crone) A.; m. Marilyn Lucille Henke; children: Karl C., Keith F., Susan L. BSChemE, U. Mo., Columbia, 1951; MSChemE, Washington U., St. Louis, 1956; grad. exec. program, Stanford U., 1972. Registered profl. engr., Mo., Pa. With Mallinckrodt, Inc., St. Louis, 1951-81; group v.p. food, drug and cosmetic chems. div. Mallinckrodt, Inc., 1974-76, group v.p. chem. group, 1976-78, sr. v.p. chem. group, 1978-81, also dir.; pres., dir. Chomerics, Inc., Woburn, Mass., 1981-85; pres., chief exec. officer, dir. Chemtech Industries, St. Louis, 1986—. Adv. council Engring. Sch., U. Mo., Columbia, 1978—; Mem. Florissant (Mo.) Charter Commn., 1961-63. Recipient Disting. Service to Engring. award U. Mo., Columbia, 1978. Mem. Am. Inst. Chem. Engrs. Lutheran. Clubs: Algonquin Golf, University. Office: Chemtech Industries 1655 Des Peres Rd Saint Louis MO 63131

ANDERSON, FRANCES LEE, accounts payable coordinator; b. N.Y.C., Mar. 28; d. James Benjamin Anderson and Mattie Jane Moats. A in Occupational Sci., Monroe Bus. Inst., 1985. Cashier H.G.S. Supermkt., N.Y.C., 1980-85; data entry operator Riom Trucking & Messenger, N.Y.C., 1985-86; coordinator accts. payable Paul, Weiss, Rifkind, Wharton & Garrison, N.Y.C., 1986—. Mem. NAFE. Home: 67 Knapp Pl 1st Floor Englewood NJ 07631

ANDERSON, GEOFFREY ALLEN, lawyer; b. Chgo., Aug. 3, 1947; s. Roger Allen and Ruth (Teninga) A.; B.A. cum laude, Yale U., 1969; J.D., Columbia U., 1972. Bar: Ill. 1972. Assoc., Isham, Lincoln & Beale, Chgo., 1972-79, ptnr., 1980-81; ptnr. Reuben & Proctor, Chgo., 1981-85; dep. gen. counsel Tribune Co., Chgo., 1985—; gen. counsel Chgo. Cubs, 1986—. Elder Fourth Presbyn Ch., Chgo. Recipient Citizenship award Am. Legion, 1965. Mem. Chgo. Bar Assn. (chmn. entertainment com. 1981-82, best performance award, 1977), Phi Delta Phi. Clubs: Yale (N.Y.C.); Attic (Chgo.). Office: Tribune Co 435 N Michigan Ave Chicago IL 60611

ANDERSON, GEORGE MCCULLOUGH, III, banking executive; b. Balt., Oct. 16, 1935; s. George McCullough and Sophie (Miller) A.; m. Joanna Anderson, Nov. 21, 1960 (div. 1978); children: Kristina, Susan, George IV; m. Phoebe Matthews, June 14, 1980. BA in Econs., Yale U., 1958; MBA in Fin., U. Pa., 1960. Asst. v.p. Mellon Bank, Pitts., 1960-68; v.p., corp. sec. Equitable Trust Co., Balt., 1968-78; v.p., sec. Equitable Bancorp., Balt., 1972-78; pres., bd. dirs. First Nat. Bank of Georgetown, Del., 1978-81; prin. P&G Anderson, Inc., Phila., 1982—; bd. dirs. Nat. Bank of the Main Line, Wayne Pa., Bank of the Brandywine Valley, West Chester, Pa.; founder Chestnut Hill Nat. Bank, Phila. Club: Md., L'Hirondell. Home: PO Box 14 Bethel DE 19931 Office: P&G Anderson Inc PO Box 27564 Philadelphia PA 19118

ANDERSON, GEORGE WILLIAM, II, controller; b. Zanesville, Ohio, May 8, 1954; s. George William Jr. and Mildred Pauline (Buker) A.; m. Diana Lynn Ritchie, June 14, 1980; children: Timothy Joseph, Stephanie Michelle. BS in Bus. Adminstrn., Ohio State U., 1976; MBA in Fin., U. Calif., Berkeley, 1983. CPA, Ohio, Calif. Sr. auditor Peat Marwich, Columbus, Ohio, 1976-79; sr. auditor Memorex, Santa Clara, Calif., 1979-80, mgr. gen. acctg., 1980-82; mgr. fin. Tandy Corp., Santa Clara, 1982-83; div. controller Spectra Physics, San Jose, Calif., 1984-85; controller Distek, Westerville, Ohio, 1986—. Mem. Am. Inst. CPAs, Fin. Exec. Inst. Methodist. Club: Del. Golf (Ohio) (treas. 1987—).

ANDERSON, GERALD EDWIN, utilities executive; b. Boston, Apr. 9, 1931; s. Clarence Gustav and Lela Pauline (Kelley) A.; m. Mary Elizabeth Iverson, May 21, 1955; children: Todd K., Timothy J., Kristin E. A.A., Worthington (Minn.) Jr. Coll., 1950; B.B.A., U. Minn., 1952. C.P.A., Minn. Staff accountant, audit mgr. Arthur Andersen & Co., Mpls., 1953-65; asst. comptroller Commonwealth Energy System (formerly New Eng. Gas & Electric Assn.), Cambridge, Mass., 1966, system comptroller, 1967-71, v.p., comptroller, 1971-72, treas. parent co., financial v.p. system, 1972-74, pres., 1974—, chief exec. officer, 1975—; trustee parent co.; also dir. operating subs. Commonwealth Energy System; dir. Algonquin Energy, Inc. and subs., 1975-86, Bay Bank Harvard Trust Co., Liberty Mut. Ins. Co., Liberty Mut. Fire Ins. Co., Liberty Life Assurance Co. of Boston, Edison Electric Inst., 1983-86. Vice chmn. United Ways Eastern New England, 1986, dir., 1988—; mem. town fin. com., Carlisle, Mass., 1968-73, chmn., 1972-73; dir. Swedish Coun. Am., 1987—; mem. Corp. of Mass. Gen. Hosp., 1988—. 1st lt. USAF, 1952-53. Mem. AICPA, Mass. Soc. CPAs, Minn. Soc. CPAs, Fin. Execs. Inst., Beta Alpha Psi, Beta Gamma Sigma. Episcopalian. Clubs: Algonquin, Oyster Harbors, Commercial Club of Boston. Home: 75 Hornbeam Ln Centerville MA 02632 Office: Commonwealth Energy System 1 Main St PO Box 9150 Cambridge MA 02142-9150

ANDERSON, GERALD RAY, sales executive; b. Virginia, Minn., Nov. 11, 1955; s. Raymond Fred Anderson and Shirley Jacquelyn (Peterson) Charles; m. Cheryl Rae Johnson, July 24, 1976; children: Paul Raymond, Adam Ray. BS in Mech. Engring., U. Minn., 1985. With King of Owatonna, Minn. Mem. Internat. Inst. Ammonia Refrigeration, ASHRAE (student treas. 1984-85). Democrat. Lutheran. Home: 445 Kim Ln Owatonna MN 55060 Office: King of Owatonna 1001 21st Ave NW Owatonna MN 55060

ANDERSON, HOWARD, corporate executive. BA, U. Pa., 1966; MBA, Harvard U., 1968. Pres. Yankee Group, Boston, 1970—; mng. dir. Battery Ventures, Boston.

ANDERSON, IAIN MAIR, automobile manufacturing company executive; b. Calcutta, India, May 11, 1931; came to U.S., 1963; s. Ian Hoyle and Elizabeth (Wilson) A.; m. Joan Gordon Sutherland, Oct. 30, 1954; children—Ian Gordon, Kenneth Sutherland, Joan Elizabeth. Chartered accountant, Glasgow (Scotland) U., 1953. Chartered accountant 1948-53; asst. treas. Boynton Acceptance Co., Toronto, Can., 1954-55; financial, mfg. and purchasing positions with Ford Motor Co. Cn., 1955-63; with Am. Motors Co., 1963-78, ops. control dir., 1965-66, controller, 1966—, v.p. finance, 1967-75, group v.p. fin. and govt. affairs, 1975-77, exec. v.p., 1977; exec. v.p. fin. and adminstrn., treas. Volkswagen of Am., 1978—. Office: Volkswagen Am Inc 888 W Big Beaver Rd Troy MI 48084

ANDERSON, JAMES ARTHUR, mining company executive; b. Aurelia, Iowa, Mar. 25, 1935; s. Vernon L. and Agnes (Weiland) A.; m. Ann Charlene Sutherland, Sept. 9, 1956. BS in Geol. Engring., U. Utah, 1957; MS in Mining Geology, Harvard U., 1960, PhD in Econ. Geology, 1965; MBA, Stanford U., 1978, exec. program, 1978. From staff geologist, sr. exploration geologist to exploration researcher Kennecott Copper Corp., Salt Lake City, 1960-68; v.p. U.S. metal exploration, U.S. exploration mgr. Occidental Minerals Corp., Denver, 1968-75; exec. v.p., dir. Homestake Mining Co., San Francisco, 1975-87; exec. v.p. Fulcrum Mgmt. Inc., Lakewood, Colo., 1987—; pres., chief exec. officer MinVen Gold Corp. (amalgamation MFC Mining Fin. Corp. and Brohm Resources), Lakewood, 1988—, also bd. dirs.; pres., dir. MFC Mining Fin. Corp., 1987-88; exec. v.p., dir., Brohm Resources, 1987-88; chmn., dir. Blackdome Mining Corp., 1987—; chmn. Calif. State Mining and Geology Bd., Sacramento, 1985—. Contbg. author: Advances in Geology of the Porphyry Copper Deposits, Southwest NA, 1982; contbr. articles in tech. jour. Mem. Soc. Mining Engrs., AIME, Geol. Soc. Am., Soc. Econ. Geologists, World Affairs Council Calif., Mining and Metall. Soc. Am., Colo. Mining Assn. Republican. Methodist. Clubs: Commonwealth Calif. (San Francisco); Banker San Francisco. Office: MinVen Gold Corp 7596 W Jewell Ave Ste 303 Lakewood CO 80226

ANDERSON, JAMES AYLOR, construction company executive; b. Lexington, Va., Oct. 24, 1921; s. James Aylor and Isabelle (Bronsen) A.; m. Mary Louise Heel, Aug. 31, 1946; children: James Aylor III, Alston Anderson Griffin. BS, Va. Mil. Inst., 1943; MBA, Harvard U., 1948. Registered profl. engr. Va., Ga., surveyor, Ga.; lic. gen. contractor, Fla., Ga. Office engr. Bowers Constrn. Co., Raleigh, N.C., 1950-52; engr. estimator, exec. v.p. H & H Constrn. & Supply Co., Inc., Thomasville, Ga., 1952—; bd. dirs., v.p. Thomas County Fed. Savs. & Loan Assn., Thomasville, Ga. Pres. Community Chest Thomasville, 1962; chmn. Thomasville-Thomas County Planning and Zoning Bd. 1967-85. Served to capt. U.S. Army, 1945. Fellow ASCE. Republican. Episcopalian. Club: Duckhayen Gun (sec.-treas. 1966—), Glen Aryen Country (Thomasville). Lodge: Rotary (pres. 1958, Paul Harris fellow 1985). Office: H & H Constrn Co 500 W Jefferson St PO Box 1076 Thomasville GA 31799

ANDERSON, JAMES BURTON, financial planner; b. Bklyn., Jan. 28, 1943. B of Chem. Engring., Poly. Inst., 1962; MBA, CCNY, 1966. Registered investment advisor. Mgr. standard products Graver Winter Conditioning, N.Y.C., 1962-65; sales mgr. Chgo. Heater Co., Mineola, N.Y., 1965-70, Century 21 Real Estate USA, N.Y.C., 1975-77; dir. spl. projects Apollo Techs., Whippany, N.J., 1970-75; pres. JBA Assocs., Boonton, N.J., 1977-81, Anderson Cons., Boonton, 1977-81; acct. exec. Dean Witter Reynolds, Morristown, N.J., 1981-84; 2d v.p. sales Smith Barney Harris Upshaw, Morristown, 1984-86; v.p. investments Advest, Inc., Bernardsville, N.J., 1986-87; owner The Investment Ctr, Flemington, N.J., 1987—; salesman N.J. Real Estate Community, Trenton, 1975—, N.J. Ins. Community, 1981—. Author: The Golf Bible, 1985; author poetry book; contbr. articles to profl. jours.; inventor in field. Served to capt. U.S. Army, 1971-73, Vietnam. Mem. Inst. Registered Fin. Planners, Coll. Fin. Planners, Nat. Assn. Environ. Profls., Hunterdon County C. of C., Mensa. Republican. Home and Office: PO Box 688 Flemington NJ 08822

ANDERSON, JAMES MILTON, lawyer; b. Chgo., Dec. 29, 1941; s. Milton H. and Eunice (Carlson) A.; BA, Yale U., 1963; JD, Vanderbilt U., 1966; m. Marjorie Henry Caldwell, Jan. 22, 1966; children: James Milton II, Joseph, Hilding F., Marjorie Caldwell II. Admitted to Ohio bar, 1967; assoc. law firm Taft, Stettinius & Hollister, Cin., 1968-75, ptnr., 1975-77, 82—; pres. U.S. ops., dir. Xomox Corp., Cin., 1977-81; sec. Access Corp., 1984—; asst. sec. Carlisle Cos., 1985—; dir., chmn. Cin. Stock Exchange, 1980—; dir. Lebanon Steel Foundry, 1979-83. Mem. Indian Hill Council, 1981—, vice-mayer, 1985-87, mayor, 1987—; mem. Hamilton County Airport Authority, 1980-85. Trustee, Children's Hosp. Med. Center, also mem. exec. com., 1977—, chmn. personnel com., mem. fin. com. ; trustee Cin. Center for Developmental Disorders, pres., 1974-80; trustee Dan Beard council Boy Scouts Am., 1982-87, chmn., 1984-87; trustee Cin. Mus. Natural History, 1984-87. Served to capt. AUS, 1966-68. Decorated Bronze Star with two oak leaf clusters; Air medal. Mem. Ohio Bar Assn., Cin. Bar Assn., Am. Bar Assn., Valve Mfrs. Assn., Young Presidents Orgn., Order of Coif. Republican. Clubs: Cin. Country, Queen City. Avocation: sailing. Office: Cin Stock Exch 205 Dixie Terminal Bldg Cincinnati OH 45202

ANDERSON, JANELLE MARIE, account executive; b. Beloit, Wis., Mar. 28, 1954; d. Lyle Kenneth Anderson and Helen Catherine (Hammer) Hughes; adopted d. Hilary William Hughes. AA, U. Wis., Fond du Lac, 1976; postgrad., Arnie DeLuca Sem., Chgo., 1983, Women's Bus. Inst., Neenah, Wis., 1986. Legal sec. Nugent & Nugent, Attys., Waupun, Wis., 1976-80; salesman Modern Motors, Fond du Lac, 1980-82; clk., technician Old World Stained Glass, Fond du Lac, 1982-83; mgr. classifieds Pub.'s Devel. Services Inc., Fond du Lac, 1983-86, account mgr. nat. sales, 1985—; cons. Decra-Led Corp. Am., Portage, Wis., 1985. Mem. Milw. Advt. Club, Wis. Advt. Pubs. Assn. (chmn. bd. 1987-88), Milw. Grocery Mfrs. Reps. (bd. dirs. 1988—), Milw. Food Brokers Assn., Fond du Lac Jaycees (bd. dirs. 1984-85, 88—, chmn. bd. 1987-88, v.p. individual devel. 1985-86, 1st woman pres. 1986-87, Wis. program dir. Outstanding Wisconsinite and Young Adult awards 1987-88, numerous awards). Roman Catholic. Home: 136 1/2 E Merrill Ave Fond du Lac WI 54935 Office: Pubs Devel Svcs Inc 101 S Main St Fond du Lac WI 54935

ANDERSON, JANICE LINN, real estate broker; b. Paris, Tenn., Sept. 2, 1943; d. Orel Vernon and Rosie Elizabeth (Brockwell) L.; m. David James Anderson, June 11, 1965 (div. Oct. 1973). Entertainer, recording artist 4-Sons Record Co., Paris, Tenn., 1958-73; med. transcriptionist The Paris Clinic, 1965-73; computer operator, asst. to v.p. Medicare Adminstrn./Equitable, Nashville, 1973-74; property mgmt. asst. Dobson & Johnson, Inc., Nashville, 1974-76; dir. leasing and mgmt. Fortune-Nashville Co., 1976-78; real estate brokerage asst. J.G. Martin, Jr./Caudill Properties, Inc., Nashville, 1978—; pvt. practice resume preparation, Nashville, 1982—. Active Girl Scouts U.S., Paris, 1967-69; mem. ARC, Nashville, 1978, Am. Inst. for Cancer Research, Washington, D.C., 1985, Christian Appalachian Project, Lancaster, Ky., 1986. Mem. Nat. Assn. Female Execs., Bus. and Profl. Womens Club (Pres. 1965-73), Profl. Musicians Union, Womens Missionary Union (bd. dirs. Paris chpt. 1970-71), Internat. Platform Assn., Realtors' Secs. Assn., Am. Biog. Inst., Inc. Baptist. Home: 812 Elissa Dr Nashville TN 37217 Office: J G Martin Jr/Caudill Properties Inc American Trust Bldg 15th Fl Nashville TN 37201

ANDERSON, JAY NORMAN, account representative; b. Langdale, Ala., Dec. 10, 1965; s. William Thomas and Joan (Edwards) Pinson. BS, Jacksonville State U., Ala., 1988; postgrad., Auburn U. Account rep. NCR Corp., Montgomery, Ala., 1988—. Recipient Nat. Coll. Bus. Merit award; Jacksonville State U. football scholar, 1984. Mem. Montgomery Jaycees, Omicron Delta Kappa, Phi Beta Lambda. Home: 201 Gunn Rd Montgomery AL 36117 Office: NCR Corp 201 Gunn Rd Montgomery AL 36117

ANDERSON, JEFFREY PAUL, banker; b. Long Beach, Calif., July 18, 1950; s. Roy Lewis Anderson and Jeanne M. (Burke) Whitcomb; m. Gwynne Allyn Jenkins, Mar. 30, 1973; children: Kimberly, Ryan, Kaitlyn. BS, U. So. Calif., 1972; MBA, Calif. State U., 1978. V.p. Security Pacific Nat. Bank, L.A., 1972-79; v.p., mgr. Rainier Nat. Bank, Seattle, 1979-82; v.p., mng. dir. Security Pacific Southwest, Inc., Houston, 1982-86; mng. dir. Security Pacific Mcht. Bank, L.A., 1986—. Bd. dirs. Cy-Champ P.U.D., Houston, 1984-86, Calif. Mus. Sci. and Industry, L.A., 1987. Republican. Roman Catholic. Office: Security Pacific Mcht Bank 333 S Hope St H14 55 Los Angeles CA 90071

ANDERSON, JERRY ALLEN, operations analysis manager; b. Ashland, Wis., Feb. 10, 1947; s. Elmer and Thelma Louise (Fallis) A.; m. Anne Marie Brown, June 7, 1975; 1 child, Kristen Marie. BBA, Temple U., 1969, MBA, 1975. Sr. investment officer Girard Bank, Phila., 1970-80; sr. investment analyst Sanford C. Bernstein, N.Y.C., 1980-83; dir. planning Sperry New Holland (Pa.), Inc., 1983-85, mgr. ops. analysis, 1985-87, fin. mgr. spl. markets, 1987—; cons. in fin.; instr. sch. bus. Temple U., 1976-79, Sch. Bus. and Govt. Svcs., 1979-80. Recipient Cert. of Recognition Am. Mktg. Assn., 1968, 69, Outstanding Performance award Ford New Holland, 1987. Fellow Fin. Analysts Fedn.; mem. Fin. Analysts of Phila., N.Y. Soc. Security Analysts, Model A Ford Club Am., Beta Gamma Sigma, Theta Chi. Avocations: Model A restoration, numismatics, fishing, scuba diving, hunting. Home: 544 Norwyck Dr King of Prussia PA 19406 Office: Ford New Holland Inc 500 Diller Ave New Holland PA 17557

ANDERSON, JERRY WILLIAM, JR., electronics company executive; b. Stow, Mass., Jan. 14, 1926; s. Jerry William and Heda Charlotte (Petersen) A.; B.S. in Physics, U. Cin., 1949, Ph.D. in Econs., 1976; M.B.A., Xavier U., 1959; m. Joan Hukill Balyeat, Sept. 13, 1947; children—Katheleen, Diane. Research and test project engr. meteorol. equipment, Wright-Patterson AFB, Ohio, 1949-53; project engr., electronics div. AVCO Corp., Cin., 1953-70, program mgr., 1970-73; program mgr. Cin. Electronics Corp. (successor to electronics div. AVCO Corp.), 1973-78; pres. Anderson Industries Unltd., 1978; chmn. dept. mgmt. and mgmt. info. services Xavier U., 1980—; lectr. No. Ky. U., 1977-78; tech. adviser Cin. Tech. Coll., 1971—. Served with USNR, 1943-46. Mem. Madeira (Ohio) City Planning Commn., 1962—; founder, pres. Grassroots, Inc., 1964; active United Appeal, Heart Fund, Multiple Sclerosis Fund; co-founder, tech. Presbyterian Ch., Cin., 1964. Named Man of Year, City of Madeira, 1964. Mem. Assn. Energy Engrs. (charter), Soc. Non-Destructive Testing, Nat. Wood Carvers Assn., Am. Legion (past comdr.), Acad. Mgmt., Madeira Civic Assn. (past v.p.), Omicron Delta Epsilon. Republican. Contbr. articles on lasers, infrared detection equipment, air pollution to govt. publs. and profl. jours. Home and Office: 7208 Sycamorehill Ln Cincinnati OH 45243

ANDERSON, JOHN LEONARD, chemical company executive; b. Chgo., July 27, 1927; s. Elmer G. and Florence (Peterson) A.; m. Patricia Ann Burtwell, Oct. 30, 1954 (div. Jan. 1986); children—Bryan John, Kimberly Sconce; m. Leslie Wallace, Apr. 26, 1986. B.S. in Chem. Engring., Northwestern U., 1951, M.B.A., 1960. Tech. developer Diversey Corp., Chgo., 1951-53; salesman George C. Peterson Co., Chgo., 1955-57, Am. Potash & Chem., Chgo., N.Y.C., 1957-66; sales mgr. Cominco Am., Spokane, Wash., 1966-73, v.p. mktg., 1973-82, pres., chief exec. officer, 1982-85, also bd. dirs.; pres. Chemicals and Fertilizers div., Cominco Ltd., Calgary, Alta., Can., 1986—, also bd. dirs. Served to cpl. U.S. Army, 1953-55. Mem. Potash Phosphate Inst. (dir.), The Fertilizer Inst. (dir.). Republican. Episcopalian. Clubs: Union League (Chgo.); Calgary Golf and Country. Avocations: tennis, golf, skiing, fishing, gardening. Office: Cominco Ltd, 10333 Southport Rd, Calgary, AB Canada 2TW 3X6

ANDERSON, JOHN ROBERT, tire and rubber manufacturing executive; b. Boston, June 26, 1936; s. Robert Elmer and Alma Evelyn (Webster) A.; m. Carole Kilgore, Jan. 5, 1980; 1 child, Christine Anne; m. Sherry Floe, June 4, 1958 (div. 1979); children—Robin Evelyn, Douglas Carl, Dana Katharine, Judith Carol. AB, U. S.C., 1958; MBA, Stanford U., 1963. Asst. contr. Ford Motor Co., Dearborn, Mich., 1972-73; dir. diversified products analysis Ford Motor Co., Dearborn, 1973-74, asst. treas., 1974-77, fin. ops. planning dir., 1977-78; pres. Ford Motor Land Devel. Corp., Dearborn, 1978-83; sr. v.p., chief fin. officer Firestone Tire & Rubber Co., Chgo., 1983—, also bd. dirs.; bd. dirs. OMAC, Inc., Akron Priority Group. Bd. dirs., mem. exec. com. Mich. Statewide Health Coordinating Coun., 1975-77. Lt. USN, 1958-61. Mem. Fin. Execs. Inst. (trustee), Nat. Planning Assn. (com. on changing internat. realities). Republican. Methodist. Clubs: Chgo., Chgo. Yacht. Office: Firestone Tire & Rubber Co 205 N Michigan Ave Chicago IL 60601

ANDERSON, KARL RICHARD, aerospace engineer, consultant; b. Vinita, Okla., Sept. 27, 1917; s. Axel Richard and Hildred Audrey (Marshall) A.; B.S., Calif. Western U., 1964, M.A., 1966; Ph.D., U.S. Internat. U., 1970; m. Jane Shigeko Hiratsuka, June 20, 1953; 1 son, Karl Richard. Engr. personnel subsystems Atlas Missile Program, Gen. Dynamics, San Diego, 1960-63; design engr. Solar div. Internat. Harvester, San Diego, 1964-66, sr. design engr., 1967-69, project engr., 1970-74, product safety specialist, 1975-78; aerospace engring. cons., 1979-86; cons. engring., 1979—; lectr. Am. Indian Sci. and Engring. Soc. Served to maj. USAF, 1936-60. Recipient Spl. Commendation San Diego County Bd. Supervisors, 1985, Spl. Commendation

San Diego City Council, 1985. Registered profl. engr., Calif. Republican. Episcopalian. Home: 5886 Scripps St San Diego CA 92122

ANDERSON, KELLY ELIZABETH, marketing professional; b. Oakland, Calif., June 7, 1957; d. Frank Stoakes Anderson and Emily Elizabeth (Wright) Kimlinger. BA in Math., BA in Environ. Studies, U. Calif., Santa Cruz, 1979, BA in Sci. Communications, 1980. Staff writer Charlotte (N.C.) Observer, 1980; sci. writer, editor Frank Porter Graham Child Devel Ctr., U. N.C., Chapel Hill, 1980-81; coordinator communications Sea Grant Coll. Program, U. Calif., San Diego, 1981-84; mgr. tech. publs. Loral Instrumentation, San Diego, 1984-87, mgr. mktg. communications, 1987—; acting dir. tech. services, Loral Instrumentation, San Diego, 1986. Contbr. more than 200 articles to profl. jours. Mem. Desktop Pub. Adv. Com. Grossmont Coll., San Diego, 1986—. AAAS fellow, 1980; recipient Excellence in Writing award Internat. Assn. Bus. Communicators, 1981, Council for Advancement and Support of Edn., 1984. Mem. Nat. Mgmt. Assn. (v.p. 1986), Soc. for Tech. Communication (awards of Excellence and Achievement 1981-84), Computer and Electronics Mktg. Assn. (officer 1987—). Office: Loral Instrumentation 8401 Aero Dr San Diego CA 92123

ANDERSON, KENT TAYLOR, corporate lawyer; b. Salt Lake City, June 24, 1953; s. Neldon Leroy and Vera Minnie (Taylor) A.; m. Ellis Anderson (div. June 1979); m. Tara Dayle, Apr. 30, 1982; 1 child, Claire Marie. BA, U. Utah, 1975; JD, Georgetown U., 1978. Bar: Utah 1978, Calif. 1987. Assoc. Jones, Waldo, Holbrook & McDonough, Salt Lake City, 1978-83, ptnr., 1983-84; v.p., gen. counsel Am. Stores Properties, Inc., Salt Lake City, 1984-86; v.p., gen. counsel, asst. sec. Am. Stores Co., Salt Lake City, 1987—; sr. v.p., gen. counsel, sec. Alpha Beta Stores, Inc., Anaheim, Calif., 1986-89; exec. v.p., gen. counsel, asst. sec. Am. Stores Co., Salt Lake City, 1989—; Mem. staff Georgetown Law Jour., 1976-78. Mem. Utah Bar Assn., Calif. Bar Assn., Phi Beta Kappa. Office: Am Stores Co PO Box 27447 Salt Lake City UT 84127

ANDERSON, LAFE F., financial executive; b. Park City, Utah, Apr. 5, 1931; s. Lafayette F. and Rhoda (Workman) A.; m. Betty Alice Kazebeer, Aug. 20, 1950; children: Steve, Linda, Mark. BS, hastings Coll., 1954. With Morrison Enterprises, Hastings, Nebr., 1953-86, chief fin. officer, 1986—; bd. dirs. Am. Charter S&L, Lincoln, Nebr. Mem. Rotary, Elks. Republican. Mormon. Office: Morrison Enterprises PO Box 609 Hastings NE 68902

ANDERSON, LYLE ARTHUR, manufacturing company executive; b. Jewell, Kans., Dec. 29, 1931; s. Arvid Herman and Clara Vera (Herman) A.; m. Harriet Virginia Robson, June 12, 1953; children—Brian, Karen, Eric. B.S., U. Kans., 1953; M.S., Butler U., 1961. C.P.A., Mo., Kans. Mgmt. trainee, internal auditor RCA, Camden, N.J. and Indpls., 1955-59; auditor Ernst & Ernst (C.P.A.'s), Kansas City, Mo., 1959-63; v.p. fin. and adminstrn., treas., dir. Affiliated Hosp. Products, Inc., St. Louis, 1963-71; sr. v.p. Consol. Foods Corp., Deerfield, Ill., 1971-74; exec. v.p. fin. Consol. Foods Corp., Chgo., 1974-76; chmn. bd. Valley Electromagnetics Corp., Spring Valley, Ill.; pres. Happy Baby, Inc., Crystal Lake. Bd. dirs. Meml. Hosp. of McHenry County, Crystal Lake Civic Ctr. Authority. Served with AUS, 1953-55. Mem. Am. Inst. C.P.A.'s, Ill. Mfrs. Assn. (bd. dirs.), Omicron Delta Kappa. Republican. Methodist. Home: 9804 Partridge Ln Crystal Lake IL 60014 Office: Valley Electromagnetics Corp 365 E Prairie St Crystal Lake IL 60014

ANDERSON, MARK JAMES, manufacturing company executive; b. Austin, Minn., July 16, 1953; s. James Joseph and Karen Ann (LaPlant) A.; m. Karen Ann Koenig, Aug. 17, 1974; children: Benjamin, Henry, Emily, Carolyn. BSChemE with high distinction, U. Minn., 1975, MBA, 1980. Registered profl. engr., Minn. Rsch. engr. Union Oil Co., Brea, Calif., 1975-77; dir. strategic materials Henkel Corp., Mpls., 1977-86; pres. MD Therapy Systems Inc., Stillwater, Mpls., 1986—; dir. Stat-Ease Inc., Mpls. Patentee coal desulfurization. Pres. Stockyard Days Inc., New Brighton, Minn., 1983; mem. Long Lake Regional Park Bd., Ramsey County, Minn., 1985. Mem. Am. Inst. Chem. Engrs., Toastmasters, Rotary, Optimists, Beta Gamma Sigma. Roman Catholic. Office: Stat Ease Inc 3801 Nicollet Ave S Minneapolis MN 55409

ANDERSON, MARK T., business developer, entrepreneur; b. Provo, Utah, Jan. 28, 1953; s. Billy Joe and Norma (Tucker) A.; m. Aleca Alleman, May 5, 1976; children: John Tucker, Amy, Megan. BS finance, Brigham Young U., 1984. Pres., dir. G.B. Mark T. Inc., Orem, Utah, 1975—, Mark Anderson & Assocs., Provo, 1979—, R&D Connections Inc., Salt Lake City, 1983-85; dir., exec. v.p. Kara Signature Chocolates Inc., Salt Lake City, 1985-88; pres., mng. dir. Network Capital LTD., Salt Lake City, 1986—; pres. Mark Anderson Mgmt. Co., 1988—. Named Eagle Scout Boy Scouts Am. Republican. Mormon. Clubs: Riverside Country (Provo), Ridge Athel (Provo). Lodge: Elks. Home: 4101 N Timpview Dr Provo UT 86404 Office: NetWork Capital Ltd 46 W Broadway Ste 250 Salt Lake City UT 84101

ANDERSON, MICHAEL L., financial economist; b. Topeka, May 6, 1958. BA in Econs. with honors, U. Colo., 1980. Economist Colo. Dept. Labor, Colorado Springs, 1980-81; labor market analyst Pueblo (Colo.) County, 1981-83; regional economist Pikes Peak Govts. Council, Colorado Springs; financial economist City of Colorado Springs, 1984—; bd. dirs. Pikes Peak Area Govts. Council socioecon. adv. com. Author: 1983 Housing Market Analysis, Colorado Springs, 1984; also contbr. to profl. jours. Mem. Enrollment Dist. II Com., Colorado Springs, 1985-88. U. Colo. scholar, 1977-80. Mem. Govt. Fin. Officers Assn., Phi Beta Kappa. Office: City Colorado Springs Office Budget Mgmt 30 S Nevado Colorado Springs CO 80903

ANDERSON, MILADA FILKO, manufacturing company executive; b. Chgo., Nov. 17, 1922; s. John and Anna (Sianta) Filko; m. George Richard Anderson, Aug. 29, 1945 (div. Sept. 1974); children: Mark, Renee, Teri. BS, Northwestern U., 1944, MS in Mgmt., 1979. Tchr. history Evanston (Ill.) Township High Sch., 1946; tchr. social studies Mt. Prospect (Ill.) Jr. High Sch., 1947-48; dir. F&B Mfg. Co., Chgo., 1965—, pres., chmn. bd., 1972—. Mem. Northwestern U. Profl. Womens Assn., Nat. Assn. Investment Clubs, Zeta Tau Alpha. Republican. Lutheran. Office: F&B Mfg Co 5480 Northwest Hwy Chicago IL 60630

ANDERSON, OLIVER DUNCAN, consulting statistician, educator; b. Bournemouth, Eng., July 31, 1940; s. Edward William and Mary Barbara (Weller) A.; m. Luisa Ros-Montfort, Aug. 28, 1967; children: Edward, John. BA in Engring., Caius Coll., Cambridge U., 1962, MA, 1966, PhD, 1985; BS in Natural Scis., U. London, 1966, BS with 1st class honours in Math., 1973, BS with 1st class honours in Econs., 1977; MS in Stats., U. Birmingham, 1968; MS in Math., U. Nottingham, 1974. Engr. Mott, Hay & Anderson, London, 1962; schoolmaster Lancing Coll., Sussex, 1963-64; lectr. Southampton Coll. Tech., Hampshire, 1965-66; sr. lectr. Rugby Coll. Engring. Tech., Warwickshire, 1968-73; course dir. Civil Service Coll., London, 1974-76; tech. dir. Statis. Applications Ltd., Nottingham, 1977-79; chmn. Oliver Anderson Cons., Nottingham, 1980-85; prof. mgmt. sci. Pa. State U., 1986-87; prof. stats. Temple U., Phila., 1987-88, U. Western Ont., 1989—; lectr.; vis. prof. various univs.; organizer internat. confs.; chmn. internat. confs. Author: Time Series Analysis and Forecasting: The Box-Jenkins Approach, 1975; contbr. tech., ednl. and sci. articles to jours. and encys.; editor: Forecasting 1979, Time Series, 1980, Analysing Time Series, 1980, Forecasting Public Utilities, 1980, Time Series Analysis, 1981, Time Series Analysis: Theory and Practice 1, 1982, Applied Time Series Analysis, 1982, Time Series Analysis: Theory and Practice 2, 1982, Time Series Analysis: Theory and Practice 3, 1983, Time Series Analysis: Theory and Practice 4, 1983, Time Series Analysis: Theory and Practice 5, 1984, Time Series Analysis: Theory and Practice 6, 1985, Time Series Analysis: Theory and Practice 7, 1985, Time Series Analysis: Theory and Practice 8, 1986, TSA&F News, 1979-86, TSA&F Flyer, 1980-86; acting editor: Statistician, 1975-77; mng. editor: Jour. of Time Series Analysis, 1980-82; assoc. editor: internat. jours. State scholar, 1959-62; State Studentship, 1967; Royal Soc. vis. fellow, 1980. Fellow Am. Statis. Assn., Royal Statis. Soc., Inst. Math. and Its Applications, Inst. of Statisticians (mem. council 1976-79, 79-82), Brit. Inst. Mgmt., Inst. Tng. and Devel., Am. Statis. Assn.; mem. Operational Research Soc. Am., Brit. Computer Soc., Inst. Word Processing, Math. Assn., Soc. Indsl. and Applied Math., Nat. Council Tchrs. Math. (U.S.), Econometric Soc., Inst. Math. Stats., Royal Inst. Navigation, Royal Econ. Soc., Statis. Soc. Can., Statis. Soc. Australia, Internat. Inst. Forecasters, Inst. Mgmt. Scis., SE Asian Math. Soc. (corr.), Internat. Statis. Inst., Time Series Analysis and Forecasting Soc. (bd. dirs. 1981-86, chmn. 1982-86). Anglican. Office: U Western Ont Stats Dept, Rm 3005 EMSc, London, ON Canada N6A 5B9

ANDERSON, OLIVER JOHN, financial consultant, educator; b. Clayton, Mo., Sept. 16, 1928; s. Oliver John and Jane Thomas (Bemis) A.; m. Mary Creed Davis, Sept. 9, 1951; children—Peter Howard, Mary Randolph. B.A., Yale U., 1950; M.B.A., Harvard U., 1956. Chartered fin. analyst. Bus. cons. A&H Kroeger, N.Y.C., 1956-60; research aalyst DLJ Inc., N.Y.C., 1960-64, co-dir. research, 1964-68, cons., 1980—, also dir.; founder, chief operating officer Alliance Capital Mgmt., N.Y.C., 1969-76, vice chmn., 1976-80, cons., 1980—, also dir.; cons. dir., chmn. bd. Quasar Assocs.; trustee St. Edwards Sch. 1988; chmn. bd. trustees Alliance Convertible Fund, Alliance Counterpoint Fund, Fiduciary Mgmt. Assocs., N.Y.C.; dir. Fishers Island Utility Co. (N.Y.); instr. econs. St. Edwards Sch., Vero Beach, Fla., 1980—, trustee 1986— . Served to lt. (j.g.), USN, 1951-54; Europe. Republican. Episcopalian. Clubs: Yale N.Y.C., ; Fishers Island (pres. 1982-86); Bent Pine Golf (Vero Beach, Fla.); Links (N.Y.C.). Home: 380 Island Creek Dr Vero Beach FL 32963 Office: care Wood Struthers & Winthrop 140 Broadway St 42d Floor New York NY 10005

ANDERSON, PAUL IRVING, management executive; b. Portland, Oreg., Mar. 23, 1935; s. William F. and Ruth M. (Sundquist) A.; m. Lorraine A. Franz, Nov. 21, 1959; children: Todd, Susan, Cheryl, Cynthia. B.S., Oreg. State U., 1956. Various positions in mktg., sales and engring. mgmt. 3M Co., St. Paul and Boston, 1956-74; product dir. 3M Co., Brussels, Belgium, 1974-77; group bus. planning mgr. 3M Co., St. Paul, 1977-79; sr. v.p., gen. mgr. Rayovac Corp., Madison, Wis., 1979-82; pres. Anderson Cons. Co., Madison, 1982-83; div. v.p. RCA Corp., Indpls., 1983-84; pres. Anderson & Assocs., La Costa, Calif., 1984-87; pres., chief exec. officer Electro-Imaging Advisors, Inc., La Jolla, Calif., 1987—. Mem. Am. Mgmt. Assn., Tau Beta Pi, Pi Tau Sigma, Sigma Tau. Republican. Presbyterian. Clubs: Columbia (Indpls.); Madison; Nakoma Golf (Madison). Home: 6418 Cayenne Ln Carlsbad CA 92009

ANDERSON, PAUL MILTON, energy company executive; b. Richland, Wash., Apr. 1, 1945; s. Paul Milton and Elfrieda (Blehm) A.; m. Kathleen Sue Kinzel, Feb. 25, 1984; children: Wendy Christine, Heather Colleen. BSME, U. Wash., 1967; MBA, Stanford U., 1969. Mgr. product planning Ford Motor Co., Dearborn, 1969-77; various positions Tex. Eastern Corp., Houston, 1977-85, v.p., 1985-87, sr. v.p., 1987—. Office: Tex Ea Corp PO Box 2521 Houston TX 77001

ANDERSON, PETER SCOTT, data systems executive; b. Cambridge, Mass., Oct. 22, 1942; s. Edwin Julius and Margaret (Doig) A.; student Coll. William and Mary, 1960-61; B.A. cum laude, Boston U., 1964; m. Mary Jeanne McKenna, Aug. 5, 1972; children—Mark Brian, Jonathan Scott, David Taylor, Marie Louise Therese. Mktg. rep. IBM Corp., Waltham, Mass., 1964-68, dist. staff, 1968-70; Eastern regional mgr. Raytheon Co., Norwood, Mass., 1970-71, mgr. product mktg., 1971-72; v.p. info. systems div. Bunker Ramo Corp., Trumbull, Conn., 1972-75; v.p., gen. mgr. bus. systems div. Gen. Instrument Corp., N.Y.C., 1972-75, gen. mgr. comml. data systems , 1975-77, v.p. mktg. devel., 1978-79; pres. N.Am. group Mohawk Data Scis. Corp., Parsippany, N.J., 1979-80, sr. v.p. mktg., 1980-81, pres. MDS Systems div., 1981-83; pres., chief exec.officer Ztel, Inc., Wilmington, Mass., 1983-84; pres. DASA Corp., Andover, Mass., 1984—. Mem. Mass. High Tech. Council, Am. Electronic Assn., Am. Mgmt. Assn. Republican. Episcopalian. Home: 18 Atlantic Ave North Hampton NH 03862 Office: 138 Old River Rd Andover MA 01810 Office: 84 Upper Richmond Rd, London SW15 Z5T, England

ANDERSON, R. QUINTUS, diversified company executive; b. Jamestown, N.Y., Nov. 27, 1930; s. Paul N. and Cecille (Ogren) A.; m. Sondra Rumsey, June 5, 1954; children: Heidi, Kristin, Gerrit, Mitchell, Tracy, Brooks. Grad., Phillips Acad., Andover, Mass., 1949; BS in Engring., Princeton U., 1953; postgrad., Grad. Sch. Indsl. Mgmt., MIT. With Dahlstrom Corp., Jamestown, 1957-76, exec. v.p., 1965, pres., 1968-76; founder, pres. Aarque Steel Corp., Jamestown, 1976-78, Aarque Mgmt. Corp., Jamestown, 1978—; founder, chmn. Aarque Cos., Jamestown, 1980—; bd. dirs. Chase Lincoln 1st Bank, N.A., Bus. Council N.Y. State, Inc.; chmn. Aarque Office Systems, Inc., Aarque Holdings Ltd., Cold Metal Products Co., Inc., Aarque Steel Group, Kardex Systems, Inc.; trustee Northwestern Mut. Life Ins. Co. Patentee in field. Chmn. Jamestown United Fund drive, 1964, 74; bd. dirs. N.Y. State Dept. Environ. Conservation. Served with USNR, 1954-57. Mem. Mfrs. Assn. Jamestown Area (pres. 1967-68), Empire State C. of C. (pres. 1974-76), Tau Beta Pi. Republican. Episcopalian. Clubs: Moon Brook Country (Jamestown); Sportsmen's (Chautaqua, N.Y.); Union League Met. (N.Y.C.). Office: Aarque Cos 111 W 2nd St Jamestown NY 14701

ANDERSON, REX HERBERT, JR., finance executive; b. Greenwich, Conn., Apr. 20, 1954; s. Rex Herbert and Martha Jean A. BA, Emory U., 1976; MBA, U. Pa., 1978. Asst. to exec. v.p. Phoenix Steel Corp., Claymont, Del., 1978-79; pvt. practice in cons. Villanova, Pa., 1980-83; dir. spl. projects Lease Fin. Corp. (now called LFC Fin. Corp.), Radnor, Pa., 1984-86, v.p., 1987—. Mem. Phi Beta Kappa. Republican. Presbyterian. Club: Phila. Country. Office: LFC Fin Corp 3 Radnor Corp Ctr Suite 400 Radnor PA 19087

ANDERSON, RICHARD BRADFORD, economist; b. Mpls., July 31, 1931; s. Francis Xavier and Evelyn (Hanson) A.; BBA magna cum laude, Nat. U., 1977, MBA, 1978; DBA, U.S. Internat. U., 1981; m. Mary Kathryn Schwenn; children: Jacquelyn Sue, Marta Jean, Richard Bradford, Ariana M. Asst. cashier First Nat. Bank San Diego, 1949-62; v.p., cashier Bank La Jolla (Calif.), 1962-64; broker Hayden-Stone & Co., Inc., San Diego, 1965-71; v.p., ptnr. Roberts-Scott & Co., Inc., San Diego, 1971-73; asst. to pres., sec.-treas. Commodore Resources, Inc., San Diego, 1974-75; sr. ptnr. Bradford Anderson Assocs., Salt Lake City, 1976-77; ptnr. Schwennco, Ltd., Carson City, Nev., 1978—; mem. faculty U.S. Internat. U., San Diego, 1980-81; domestic and internat. cons., 1976—. Pres., San Diego County Young Reps., 1958; bd. dirs. Mother Goose Parade Assn., 1955-62; chmn. Reps. of La Jolla, 1973-74; maj. U.S. Mormon Bn., 1978—, nat. donations officer, nat. liaison officer, gen. staff, 1981—; mem. nat. adv. bd. Am. Security Coun., 1979-83. Mem. Am. Enterprise Inst. (assoc.), Nat. Geog. Soc., Smithsonian Instn. Publs. Executive Attitudes Toward Federal Regulations in Banking, Trucking and Airlines, 1981.

ANDERSON, RICHARD CARL, banker; b. Chgo., Apr. 14, 1932; s. Wallace Hubert and Adelaide Sabina (Kusmerz) A.; m. Barbara Ann Farmer, June 2, 1956; children: James Wallace, Jeffrey Richard, Susan Elizabeth. BA, Oberlin Coll., 1954; MBA, Northwestern U., 1955. V.p., mgr. Cen. Nat. Bank, Cleve., 1959-81; v.p. Clark Consol. Industries, Rocky River, Ohio, 1981-84; exec. v.p. Lorain County Bank, Elyria, Ohio, 1984-88; fin. cons. 1989—; bd. dirs. Gorman-Lavelle Corp., Cleve., Target Stamped Products Corp., Kinsman, Ohio. Trustee, vice-chmn. Commerce and Industry Assn. Greater Elyria, Ohio, 1986-88; trustee Credit Bur. Services N.E. Ohio, Cleve., 1986—, Elyria United Meth. Home,1987—. Republican. Club: Lakewood Country (Westlake, Ohio) (pres. 1983). Home: 377 Hamilton Circle Elyria OH 44035

ANDERSON, RICHARD GORDON, real estate developer; b. Kansas City, Kans., Apr. 7, 1949; s. Bernard M. and Jeanette (Tweedie) A.; m. Karen J. Wishnick, Aug. 2, 1980; children: Kendra, Linzy. BS in Econs., U. Pa., 1971; MBA, George Washington U., Washington, D.C., 1977. CPA, N.J., Va. Tax cons. Arthur Andersen & Co., Washington, 1977-83; chief fin. officer Union Valley Corp., Howell, N.J., 1983—, also bd. dirs. Lt. USNR, 1972-75. Mem. AICPA, N.J. Soc. CPA's, Nat. Assn. Homebuilders, Cen. Jersey Builders Assn., Urban Land Inst. (assoc.). Office: Union Valley Corp 2209 Rte 9 Howell NJ 07731

ANDERSON, ROBERT, manufacturing company executive; b. Columbus, Nebr., Nov. 2, 1920; s. Robert and Lillian (Devlin) A.; m. Constance Dahlun Severy, Oct. 2, 1942 (div.); children: Robert, Kathleen D.; m. Diane Clark Lowe, Nov. 2, 1973. BS in Mech. Engring, Colo. State U., 1943, LLD (hon.), 1966; M Automotive Engring., Chrysler Inst. Engring., 1948; DHL (hon.), U. Neb., 1985; JD (hon.), Pepperdine U., 1986; D of Engring. (hon.), Milw. Sch. Engring., 1987. With Chrysler Corp., 1946-68, v.p. corp., gen. mgr. Chrysler-Plymouth div., 1965-67; with Rockwell International Corp., 1968—, pres. comml. products group, 1968-69, v.p. corp., 1968-69, exec. v.p., 1969-70, pres., chief operating officer, 1970-74, pres., 1974-79, chief exec. officer, 1974-88, chmn., 1979-88, dir., 1968—, chmn. exec. com., 1988—; bd. dirs. Security Pacific Corp. and subs. Security Pacific Nat. Bank, Los Angeles, Hosp. Corp. Am., Optical Data Systems, Doheny Eye Clinic, L.A. Trustee Calif. Inst. Tech., bd. of overseers Exec. Council Fgn. Diplomats; chmn. bus.-higher edn. forum Am. Council on Edn., 1982-84; chmn. Western Hwy. Inst., 1983-84. Served to capt. F.A. AUS, 1943-46. Named Exec. of Yr. Nat. Mgmt. Assn., 1980. Mem. Soc. Automotive Engrs., Phi Kappa Phi, Tau Beta Pi, Sigma Nu. Clubs: Rolling Rock (Ligonier, Pa.), Laurel Valley Golf (Ligonier, Pa.); Fox Chapel (Pa.) Golf, Vintage Country, Desert Horizons (Calif.), Country; Duquesne (Pitts.); Los Angeles Country. Office: Rockwell Internat Corp 2230 E Imperial Hwy El Segundo CA 90245-2899

ANDERSON, ROBERT MORRIS, JR., electrical engineer; b. Crookston, Minn., Feb. 15, 1939; s. Robert Morris and Eleanor Elaine (Huotte) A.; m. Janice Ilene Pendell, Sept. 3, 1960; children—Erik Martin, Kristi Lynn. B.E.E., U. Mich., 1961, M.E.E., 1963, M.S. in Physics, 1965, Ph.D. in Elec. Engring, 1967. Asst. research engr. U. Mich., Ann Arbor, 1963-67; research engr. Conductron Corp., Ann Arbor, summer 1967; asst. prof. elec. engring. Purdue U., West Lafayette, Ind., 1967-71; assoc. prof. Purdue U., 1971-79, prof., 1979, engring. coordinator for continuing edn., 1973-79, Ball Bros. prof., 1976-79; mgr. engring. edn. and tng., corp. cons. services Gen. Electric Co., Bridgeport, Conn., 1979-82, mgr. tech. edn. operation, corp. engring. and mfg., 1982-88, mgr. tech. edn., corp. mgmt. devel., 1988—. Author: multi-media learning package Fundamentals of Vacuum Technology, 1973, (with others) Divided Loyalties, 1980; contbr. (with others) articles to profl. jours. Named Best Tchr. Elec. Engring. Purdue U., 1974; recipient Dow Outstanding Young Faculty award, 1974. Fellow Am. Soc. Engring. Edn. (cert. of merit 1977, Joseph M. Biedenbach Disting. Svc. award, 1986); mem IEEE (sr. mem., Meritorious Achievement award in continuing edn. activities 1987), Am. Mgmt. Assn., Am. Soc. Tng. and Devel. Lutheran. Home: 128 Hurd Rd Trumbull CT 06611 Office: GE Bldg 27DW 1285 Boston Ave Bridgeport CT 06602

ANDERSON, RONALD HOWARD, consumer packaged goods company marketing executive; b. Worcester, Mass., Aug. 12, 1935; s. Carl Howard and Evelyn (Johnson) A.; BA, Middlebury Coll., 1959; MBA (Scott Paper Co. fellow), Mich. State U., 1967; MDP, Harvard U., 1972; m. Jo Ann Witmer, Aug. 22, 1959; children: David Gordon, Carol Lynn. Mktg. mgr. Scott Paper Co., Phila., 1959-67, sales and mktg. positions, product mgr. Gen. Foods Corp., White Plains, N.Y., 1967-72; group product mgr. Am. Can Co., Greenwich, Conn., 1972-74; v.p. sales and mktg. Cadbury Schweppes, Stamford, Conn., 1974-76, Tetley Inc., Shelton, Conn., 1976-85; sr. v.p. mktg. Penn Mut. Life Ins. Co., Phila., 1985-86; gen. mgr. Chock Full O' Nuts Corp., 1986—; instr. in mktg. Pace U. Officer N.Y. State Republican Com., 1967—; bd. dirs. Bedford (N.Y.) Presbyterian Ch., 1974-78, Bedford Assn., 1975-80; trustee Low-Heywood Sch., Stamford, Conn. Served with U.S. Army, 1953-55. Mem. Am. Mgmt. Assn., Assn. Nat. Advertisers, Nat. Coffee Assn. (chmn. pub. relations com.), Nat. Tea Assn. (chmn. pub. relations com.). Republican. Clubs: Princeton (N.Y.); Bedford Golf and Tennis. Office: 370 Lexington Ave New York NY 10017

ANDERSON, ROSS BARRETT, health science facility administrator; b. Toronto, Ont., Aug. 25, 1951; came to U.S., 1956; s. John Ross and Constance (Nielson) A.; m. Gladys Jeanette Vincent, Aug. 26, 1972; children: Christopher Matthew, John Ross II, Josiah Dan. Student, Boston U., 1970-73. Housekeeping supr. Parker Hill Med. Ctr., Roxbury, Mass., 1973-76; housekeeping mgr. Union Hosp., Lynn, Mass., 1976-77, Quincy (Mass.) City Hosp., 1977-78, St. Joseph's Hosp., Lowell, Mass., 1978-79; housekeeping mgr. Waltham Weston Hosp. and Med. Ctr., Waltham, Mass., 1979-86, support services mgr., 1986—. Active Boston Latin Sch. Assn., 1985—, Scots Charitable Soc. Boston, 1989—; trustee Cochesett United Meth. Ch., 1988—, coach basketball team, 1988—. Home: 389 Crescent St West Bridgewater MA 02379 Office: Waltham Weston Hosp & Med Ctr Hope Ave Waltham MA 02254

ANDERSON, ROYAL J., advertising agency executive; b. Portland, Oreg., Sept. 12, 1914; s. John Alfred and Martha Marie (Jacobsen) A.; B.A., Albany Coll., 1939; postgrad. U. Oreg., summers 1939-41, Oreg. Inst. Tech., 1940-41; m. Leticia G. Anderson; children: Michael, Johnny, Dora Kay, Mark Roy, Stan Ray, Ruth Gay, Janelle A., Jennifer T., Joseph, Daisy, Dina; 1 adopted dau., Muoi-Muoi. Corp. cons. Dupont Corp., Beverly Hills, Calif., 1967-68; editor-pub. Nev. State Democrat, Carson City, Nev. State Pub. Observer, Nev. State Congl. Assn., Carson City, 1962-78; pres. Allied-Western Produce Co., Yuma, Ariz., Nev. Dem. Corp., 1966-78; pres. Western Restaurant Corp., 1978-81, Nev. State Sage Co., 1979—, Midway Advt. Co., Environ. Research Corp., 1983—, Mid-City Advt. Agy., 1983—, Nat. Newspaper Found., 1969, 71-76, The Gt. North Banks Seafood Co., 1984—, Food Services Corp., 1985—, Sterling Cruise Lines, 1986—, No-Tow Mfg. Inc.; dir. plant research safari cen. Amazon Gador Expdn., 1988-89; chmn. bd. Press/Register Daily Newspapers, Foster Mortgage Co., 1983—. Inventor No-Tow, 1988 worldwide. Bishop, Ch. of Palms, Mexico. Dep. registrar voters, Washoe County, Nev., 1966. Recipient Heroism award for rescue, 1933. Research fellow, Alaska, 1936. Mem. Am. Hort. Soc., Sparks (pres. 1970-81), Nev. chambers commerce, C. of C. of U.S., Chatso Farm Assn. (pres. 1962-88), Smithsonian Assos., N.Am. C. of C. Execs., Nat. Geog. Soc., Am. Newspaper Alliance (v.p. 1976), Club: Millionare. Lodges: Kiwanis, Elks, Lions. Designer prefabricated milk carton container, 1933, well water locating under-stream device, 1938. Home: PO Box 4349 North Las Vegas NV 89030 Home: 5600 E Sundance Ave Las Vegas NV 89110

ANDERSON, STANLEY WILLARD, manufacturers representative company owner; b. Upsala, Minn., Aug. 6, 1923; s. Gustav Adolph and Katherine Elsie (Melby) A.; m. Jacqueline Naomi Johnson, Mar. 26, 1955. Student, Coll. Commerce, 1941-42. Acct. Standard Oil Ind., Mpls., 1946-47; sales rep. Foley Mfg. Co., Mpls., 1947-53; founder, pres. Stan Anderson Co., Mpls., 1953—; co-founder Innovative Industries, Inc., Chanhassen, Minn., 1973; bd. dirs., cons. Innovative Industries, Chanhassen. Past mem. Jr. C. of C., St. Paul. Served with U.S. Army, 1944-46, PTO. Recipient Hall of Fame Eagle award The Foley Co., 1982. Mem. Northwest Hardware/Housewares Club, Chgo. Housewares Club. Republican. Lutheran. Clubs: Decathalon Athletic (Mpls.); Town and Country (St. Paul). Home: 2148 Juno Ave Saint Paul MN 55116 Office: Stan Anderson Co 1701 E 79th St Minneapolis MN 55420

ANDERSON, STEFAN STOLEN, banker; b. Madison, Wis., Apr. 15, 1934; s. Theodore M. and Siri (Stolen) A.; m. Joan Timmermann, Sept. 19, 1959; children—Sharon Jill, Theodore Peter. A.B. magna cum laude, Harvard, 1956; M.B.A., U. Chgo., 1960. With Am. Nat. Bank & Trust Co. of Chgo., 1960-74, v.p., 1966-68, group v.p., 1968, exec. v.p., 1969-74; exec. v.p., dir. Mchts. Nat. Bank, Muncie, Ind., 1974-79, pres., dir., 1979—, chmn. bd. dirs., 1987—; pres., dir. First Mchts. Corp., Muncie, 1983-87, chmn. bd. dirs., pres., 1987—; bd. dirs. Maxon Corp., Del. Advancement Corp., Community Found. of Muncie and Del. County. Past pres. Delaware County United Way; past pres. Muncie Symphony Orch.; trustee Roosevelt U., 1970-74, George Francis Ball Found., 1987—, Muncie Family YMCA, 1987—, Community Found.; nat. chmn. ann. fund Ball State U., 1985-86. Served with USNR, 1956-58. Mem. Independent Bankers Assn. Ind. (past dir.), Ind. Bankers Assn. (past dir.), Ind. State C. of C. (dir.), Phi Beta Kappa, Beta Gamma Sigma. Clubs: Delaware Country (Muncie), Skyline (Indpls.), Rotary (past pres.) (Muncie). Home: 2705 W Twickingham Dr Muncie IN 47304 Office: Mchts Nat Bank 200 E Jackson St Muncie IN 47305

ANDERSON, STEPHEN MILLS, investment broker; b. Portland, Maine, Jan. 12, 1946; s. Stuart Mills and Elaine (Crommett) A.; BA, Ohio U., 1969; m. Mary Elizabeth Carter, Aug. 23, 1969; children—Melissa Carter, Hope Stuart. Dir. admissions, dir. devel., dir. alumni affairs Gould Acad., Bethel, Maine, 1973-76; investment broker Burbank & Co., Portland, Maine, 1976-82, office mgr., 1978-82; investment broker, office mgr., v.p. A.G. Edwards

& Sons, Portland, 1982—; pres. Stroudwater Corp. Bd. dirs. North Yarmouth Acad., Stroudwater Improvement Assn.; mem. adv. bd. Baxter State Park. Mem. Nat. Assn. Accts., Nat. Assn. Registered Reps. Clubs: Cumberland, Severance, The Woodlands. Lodge: Masons. Office: AG Edwards & Sons 185 Middle St PO Box 7041 Portland ME 04112

ANDERSON, STEVEN LANE, financial analyst; b. Springfield, Mo., May 7, 1958; s. Jerry Rex and Mary Ann (Barr) A.; m. Julia Kathryn North, Feb. 10, 1979; children: Steven Lucas, Jameson Ross. BS in Banking and Fin., SW Mo. State U., 1981. Teller, bancard 1st Nat. Bank and Trust, Oklahoma City, 1979-80; witn new accounts dept. Systematic Savs. and Loan, Springfield, 1981; mgr. asset/liability Penn Sq. Bank, Oklahoma City, 1982, Citizens Nat. Bank, Oklahoma City, 1982-84; fin. analyst Local Fed. Savs. and Loan, Oklahoma City, 1984—. Cons. Okla. Christian Coll., Okalhoma City, 1985—, v.p. booster club, 1986—, alumni rep. budget and recruitment coms., 1986—; fin. cons. Coll. Ch. Christ, Oklahoma City, 1986—; v.p. Young Dems., Springfield and Oklahoma City, 1976. Named one of Outstanding Young Men Am., 1984. Mem. Fin. Mgrs. Soc., Kiwanis (Kiwanian of Yr. 1976), Rotary (award Springfield club 1976). Home: 1102 W Neptune Edmond OK 73034

ANDERSON, THOMAS RALPH, financial services company executive; b. Aurora, Ill., Feb. 12, 1938; s. Ralph A. and Jeannette C. (Malmer) A.; m. Carol Tremaine, Oct. 6, 1962; children: Brian, Rodney, Nicole. BS, U. Ill., 1961. CPA, Ill. Auditor Arthur Young & Co., Chgo., 1961-66; compt. Kemper Fin. Svcs., Inc., Chgo., 1966-71, v.p., compt., 1971-75, exec. v.p., 1975-77, pres., chief exec. officer, bd. dirs., 1977-83, chmn., chief exec. officer, bd. dirs., 1983—; chmn., treas. Kemper Investors Life Ins. Co., Chgo., 1976-78, chmn., chief exec. officer, treas., 1978-79, chmn., chief exec. officer, 1979—, mgr., dir. separate accounts, 1983—; sr. v.p., bd. dirs. Kemper Corp., Long Grove, Ill., 1983-86, exec. v.p., bd. dirs., 1986—; sr. v.p., bd. dirs. Lumbermens Mut. Casualty Co., Chgo., 1983-86, exec. v.p., bd. dirs., 1986—; sr. v.p., bd. dirs. Am. Motorists Ins. Co., Long Grove, 1983-86, exec. v.p., bd. dirs., 1986; sr. v.p., bd. dirs. Am. Mfrs. Mut. Ins. Co., Long Grove, 1983-86, now exec. v.p., bd. dirs., 1986—; chmn. bd. dirs. Kemper/Cymrot, Inc., Chgo., 1983—; chmn. bd. dirs., pres. and chief exec. officer Kemper Fin. Cos., Inc., Chgo., 1986—; v.p., trustees Kemper Multi-Market Income Trust, Kemper Strategic Mcpl. Income Trust, Kemper Tech. Fund, Kemper Growth Fund, Kemper Summit Fund, Kemper Total Return Fund, Kemper Income & Capital Preservation Fund, Kemper Money Market Fund, Kemper Mcpl. Bond Fund, Kemper Option Income Fund, Kemper U.S. Govt. Securities Fund, Kemper High Yield Fund, Cash Equivalent Fund, Kemper Internat. Fund, Kemper Govt. Money Market Fund, Tax-Exempt Money Market Fund, Kemper Calif. Tax-Free Income Fund, Kemper High Income Trust, kemper Intermediate Govt. Trust, Kemper Mcpl. Income Trust, Kemmper Blue Chip Fund, Kemper Enhanced Govt. Fund, Kemper Gold Fund, Investment Portfolios, Inc.; bd. dirs. Fin. Guaranty Ins. Co., Bateman Eichler Hill Richards, Inc., Blunt, Ellis & Loewi, Inc., Prescott, Ball & Turben, Inc., Lovett Mitchell Webb & Garrison, Inc., Boettcher & Co., Inc., Peers & Co., FGIC Corp., Gulfstream Fin. Assocs. Inc., Kemper Currency Inc., Kemper Clearing Corp. Trustee, chmn. fin. com. Ill. chpt. Leukemia Soc. Am., 1980-86; trustee James S. Kemper Found., 1983—; bd. dirs. Robert Crown Ctr. Health Edn., 1986—, Plymouth Pl., Inc., 1986—. Mem. Am. Inst. CPA's, Ill. Soc. CPA's, Am. Inst. Corp. Contrs., Alpha Tau Omega. Congregationalist. Clubs: Economics, LaGrange (Ill.) Country; University, Attic, Whitehall (Chgo.); Chgo. Golf (Wheaton, Ill.); Wynstone Country Club (North Barrington, Ill.). Lodge: Masons. Home: 209 S Blackstone Ave LaGrange IL 60525 Office: Kemper Fin Svcs 120 S LaSalle St Chicago IL 60603

ANDERSON, TONI-RENEE, lawyer; b. Johnstown, Pa.; d. Stephen and Rita Mae (Bellavia) Hnatkovich; m. Mark Edward Anderson, Aug. 2, 1986. BS in Edn., Indiana U. of Pa., 1976, MS in Edn., 1976; JD, U. Pitts., 1979. Bar: Pa. 1980, U.S. Dist. Ct. (we. dist.) Pa. 1980, U.S. Supreme Ct. 1984. Sole practice Ebensburg, Pa., 1983—; master Orphans' Ct. Cambria County Ct. Common Pleas, Ebensburg, 1984—; mcpl. solicitor Cambria Twp., Ebensburg, 1984—, Tunnelhill, 1987—, Gallitzin, 1988—. Jud. Legal asst. Ct. Common Pleas Cambria County, Ebensburg, 1981-86, asst. dist. atty., 1986-88, ct. adminstr., 1988—; speaker Jud. Retention Campaign, Cambria County, 1981, Jud. Superior Ct. Campaign, Cambria County, 1983, YWCA, Johnstown, Pa., 1981-83; coordinator legal div. Law Day/Red Mass, Cambria County, 1981-88. Mem. ABA, Pa. Bar Assn. (Cambria County young lawyers' rep. 1986-87), Cambria County Bar Assn. (young lawyers' liason 1986-88), Cambria County Young Lawyers' Div. (sec., treas. 1981-83, v.p. 1983-84, pres. 1984-85), Am. Assn. Profl. Women (speaker 1982), Kappa Delta Phi. Office: Courthouse Ct Adminstrs Office Center St Ebensburg PA 15931

ANDERSON, WILLIAM CLYDE, controller; b. Nashville, Tenn., Apr. 4, 1959; s. William Clyde and Katherine Sue (Horner) A.; m. Debra Ann Lenane, May 21, 1983; 1 child, Melissa. BBA, Emory U., 1980. CPA, Ga. Auditor Touche Ross & Co., Atlanta, 1980-82; sr. internal auditor Cluett Peabody & Co., Atlanta, 1982-83; controller Grizzard Advt., Atlanta, 1983—. Pres. Singles Group, St. Thomas the Apostle Ch., Smyrna, Ga., 1981. Mem. Am. Inst. CPA's, Ga. Soc. CPA's. Roman Catholic. Home: 4322 Crestridge Ln Stone Mountain GA 30083 Office: Grizzard Advt 1144 Mailing Ave SE Atlanta GA 30315

ANDERSON, WILLIAM PIKE, financial consultant, securities trader; b. Proctor, Vt., Aug. 4, 1948; s. Stuart James and Lucie (Pike) A.; m. Margaret Ann Dicesare, Mar. 25, 1972; children: Matthew David, Kathryn Joyce. BA, U. Vt., 1971. Lab technician components div. IBM, Essex Junction, Vt., 1969-70; surveillance officer smallpox eradication program WHO, Addis Ababa, Ethiopia, 1971-73; supr. ops. Social Security Adminstrn. HEW, Manchester, N.H. and Rutland, Vt., 1973-78; fin. cons. Shearson Lehman Hutton, Rutland, 1978—. Columnist Rutland Bus. Jour., 1986-87. Bd. dirs. Am. Cancer Soc., Rutland, 1984—; asst. treas. Rutland County Dem. Com., 1986—; class agt. U. Vt., 1986—; chmn. Dem. Town Com., Brandon, Vt., 1986; county chmn. Am. Cancer Soc., Rutland, 1987; vice-chmn. Rutland County Dem. Com., 1987—; mem. Gov.'s Commn. Higher Edn., 1988—. Mem. Rotary (pres. 1984, sec. Brandon chpt. 1985—). Congregationalist. Home: 67 Park St Brandon VT 05733 Office: Shearson Lehman Hutton 74 Merchants Row Rutland VT 05701

ANDERSSON, CRAIG REMINGTON, chemical company executive; b. Winnipeg, Man., Can., June 16, 1937; came to U.S., 1937; s. Anders Einar and Doris (Pearson) A.; m. Dawn Marie Traver, June 13, 1959; children—Lee Erik, Karin Ingrid, Jon Kristien, Jenni Kate. B.S. in Chem. Engring., U. Minn., 1960; postgrad., U. Del., 1960-66. Researcher Sun Oil, 1960-67; v.p. ops. Custom Chems., Inc., 1967-68; Engr., supr. U.S. Steel Chems., Haverhill, Ohio, 1968-76; product mgr. U.S. Steel Chems., Pitts., 1976-80; gen. mgr. U.S. Steel Chems., Cin., 1980-82; v.p. U.S. Steel Chems., Pitts., 1982-85, pres., 1985-86; pres., chief operating officer Aristech Chem. Corp., Pitts., 1986—. Contbr. articles to profl. jours.; patentee in field. Mem. Am. Inst. Chem. Engrs., Soc. Chem. Industry, Chem. Mfrs. Assn., Soc. Plastics Industry, Alpha Chi Sigma. Lutheran. Office: Aristech Chem Corp 600 Grant St Pittsburgh PA 15230 •

ANDERTON, JAMES FRANKLIN, IV, finance company executive; b. Lansing, Mich., Aug. 2, 1943; s. James Franklin III and Florence Ethel (Bear) A.; m. Deborah Anne Garlock, Apr. 2, 1966 (div. 1985); 1 child, James Franklin V.; m. Denise Marie Thelen, July 6, 1985. BA, Hobart Coll., Geneva, N.Y., 1965; MBA, Cornell U, 1967. Controller Summit Steel Processing Corp., Lansing, 1967-69; exec. v.p. Summit Steel processing Corp., Lansing, 1970; pres. Summit Steel Processing Corp., Lansing, 1971—, Processed Plastics Co., Ionia, Mich., 1986—, Universal Steel Co. of Mich., Lansing, 1988—; chmn., pres., chief exec. officer Summit Holdings Corp., Lansing, 1986—; pres. Inst. of Scrap Recycling Industries, Washington, 1982-83, bd. dirs. 1976—; v.p. Bur. Internat. de la Recuperation, Brussels, Belgium, 1984-85; dir. Alpena (Mich.) Power Co., 1977—, First of Am. Bank Cen., Lansing, 1977—. Pres. Lansing Met. Devel. Authority, 1971-72, Delta Twp. Econ. Devel. Authority, 1975-76; campaign chmn. United Way Capital Area, Lansing, 1976; chmn. Montessori Children's House, Lansing, 1982-85, St. Lawrence Hosp., Lansing, 1985-86; dir. Capital Region Community Found., Lansing, 1989—. Staff sgt. NG, 1968-74. Mem. Young Pres. Organ. (local chpt. chmn. 1977-78), Country Club of Lansing. Republican. Episcopal. Home: 1700 Old Mill Rd East Lansing MI 48823 Office: Summit Holdings Corp 1900 W Willow St Lansing MI 48917

ANDRASICK, JAMES STEPHEN, agribusiness company executive; b. Passaic, N.J., Mar. 27, 1944; s. Stephen Adam and Emily (Spolnik) A.; m. Kathleen Hancock Dudden, Mar. 5, 1966; children: Christopher J., Gregory O. B.S., U.S. Coast Guard Acad., 1965; M.S., MIT, 1971. Systems analyst Jamesbury Corp., 1970; mem. corp. fin. and product devel. staffs Ford Motor Co., 1971-74; mgr. corp. devel. IU Internat. Corp., Phila., 1974-78; v.p. planning, controller C. Brewer & Co., Ltd., Honolulu, 1978-81, sr. v.p. fin., chief fin. officer, 1981-83, exec. v.p., 1983—; chmn. bd., mng. gen. ptnr. Mauna Loa Macadamia Ptnrs., 1986-88; chmn. bd. HCPC, Olokele Sugar Co., 1989—; bd. dirs. C&H Sugar. bd. dirs. Aloha United Way, Honolulu, 1983—; treas., bd. dirs. ARC, Hawaii, 1983—; trustee UH Found., 1988—. Lt. USCG, 1965-69, Vietnam. Mem. Fin. Execs. Inst. Home: 609 Ahakea St Honolulu HI 96816 Office: C Brewer & Co Ltd 827 Fort St Honolulu HI 96813

ANDRASZ, NICHOLAS, oil company official; b. Carteret, N.J., Sept. 14, 1931; s. Stephen and Adela (Chaplinski) A.; m. Helen Mitroka, June 9, 1962; children: Steven Nicholas, Michael Stanley. BBA, Fairleigh Dickinson U., 1964. Acct. U.S. Metals Refining Co., Carteret, 1956-61; adminstr. Vulcan Materials Co., Sewaren-Clark, N.J., 1962-66; supr. lubricants Shell Oil Co., Sewaren, 1970-71, supr. stock acctg., 1971-75, supr. communicators, 1975-77; sr. analyst mktg. Shell Oil Co., West Orange, N.J., 1977-83; fin. services analyst Shell Oil Co., Sewaren, 1983—; chmn. supervisory com. Sewaren Employees Fed. Credit Union, 1977—. Mem. Carteret Rep. Com., 1976, Carteret Mayor's Adv. Council, 1977—. With USAF, 1951-55, Korea. Mem. VFW (honor guard Carteret 1983—, state honor guard 1988—, All State Commdr. award 1986, 87), Internat. Mgmt. Council (bd. control 1983—, chmn. 1984-88, 2d v.p. 1984-85, 1st v.p. 1986-88), Ukranian Citizens Club (v.p. 1980-85), Holy Name Soc. (sec. 1975-84, also pres. 1985-88), Ukranian Cath. Youth League (membership dir. 1956-61), K.C. Home: 62 Daniel St Carteret NJ 07008 Office: Shell Oil Co 111 State St Sewaren NJ 07077

ANDREAS, DAVID LOWELL, banker; b. St. Paul, Minn., Mar. 1, 1949; s. Lowell Willard and Nadine B. (Hamilton) A.; m. Debra Kelley, June 20, 1985; 1 child, Genevieve Nadine. BA, U. Denver, 1971; MA, Mankato State U., 1976. Credit mgmt. trainee United Calif. Bank, Los Angeles, 1976-77; comml. loan officer Nat. City Bank of Mpls., 1977-80; from v.p., sr. vp., to chmn., chief exec. officer Nat. City Bancorp., Mpls., 1980—; chmn. ADAPA, Inc., Mpls., 1986—. Mem. exec. com., dir. Children's Heart Fund., 1988—; dir. Mankato U. Found. Bd.; mem. The Hunger Project, Mankato U. Coll. Bus. Adv. Council. With U.S. Army, 1971-73. Mem. Mpls. Club, Mpls. Athletic Club. Office: Nat City Bancorp 75 S 5th St Minneapolis MN 55402

ANDREAS, DWAYNE ORVILLE, corporation executive; b. Worthington, Minn., Mar. 4, 1918; s. Reuben P. and Lydia (Stoltz) A.; m. Bertha Benedict, 1938 (div.); 1 dau., Sandra Ann Andreas McMurtie; m. Dorothy Inez Snyder, Dec. 21, 1947; children: TerryLynn, Michael D. Student, Wheaton (Ill.) Coll., 1935-36; hon. degree, Barry U. V.p., dir. Honeymead Products Co., Cedar Rapids, Iowa, 1936-46; chmn. bd., chief exec. officer Honeymead Products Co. (now Nat. City Bancorp.), Mankato, Minn., 1952-72; v.p. Cargill, Inc., Mpls., 1946-52; exec. v.p. Farmers Union Grain Terminal Assn., St. Paul, 1960-66; chmn. bd., chief exec. officer Archer-Daniels-Midland Co., Decatur, Ill., 1970—, also mem. exec. com., dir.; pres. Seaview Hotel Corp., 1958—; bd. dirs. Salomon, Inc., Lone Star Industries, Inc., Greenwich, Conn.; mem. Pres.'s Gen. Adv. Commn. on Fgn. Assistance Programs, 1965-68, Pres.'s Adv. Coun. on Mgmt. Improvement, 1969-73; chmn. Pres.'s Task Force on Internat. Pvt. Enterprise. Pres. Andreas Found.; trustee U.S. Naval Acad. Found., Freedom from Hunger Found.; nat. bd. dirs. Boys' Club Am.; chmn. U.S.-USSR Trade and Econ. Coun.; chmn. Exec. Coun. on Fgn. Diplomats; trustee Hoover Inst. on War, Revolution and Peace, Woodrow Wilson Internat. Ctr. for Scholars; mem. Trilateral Commn.; chmn. Found. for Commemoration of the U.S. Constitution, 1986. Mem. Fgn. Policy Assn. N.Y. (dir.). Clubs: Union League (Chgo.); Indian Creek Country (Miami Beach, Fla.); Mpls., Minikahda (Mpls.); Blind Brook Country (Purchase, N.Y.); Economic of N.Y. (chmn.), Links, Knickerbocker, Friars (N.Y.C.).

ANDREAS, MICHAEL DWAYNE, agricultural business executive; b. Coral Gables, Fla., Dec. 30, 1948; s. Dwayne Orville and Inez (Snyder) A.; m. Sally Ann Whitley, Sept. 26, 1981; children: Eric Michael, Regan Inez, Melissa Ann, Benjamin Michael. B.A., Northwestern U., 1970. Grain trader Archer Daniels Midland, Decatur, Ill., 1970-79, exec., 1979—, also bd. dirs.; bd. dirs. Toepfer Internat., Hamburg, Fed. Republic Germany; chmn. bd. Golden Peanut Co., Atlanta., 1986—. Mem. Chgo. Bd. Trade (dir.), Decatur C. of C. (dir. 1980). Episcopalian. Clubs: Decatur Country, Southside Country; Indian Creek (Miami, Fla.). Home: 83 N Country Club Dr Decatur IL 62521 Office: Archer-Daniels-Midland Co 4666 Faries Pkwy Decatur IL 62525

ANDREOFF, CHRISTOPHER ANDON, lawyer; b. Detroit, July 15, 1947; s. Andon Anastas and Mildred Dimitry (Kolinoff) A.; m. Nancy Anne Krochmal, Jan. 12, 1980; children: Alison Brianne, Lauren Kathleen. BA, Wayne State U., 1969; postgrad. in law Washington U., St. Louis, 1969-70; JD, U. Detroit, 1972. Bar: Mich. 1972, U.S. Dist. Ct. (ea. dist.) Mich. 1972, U.S. Ct. Appeals (6th cir.) 1974, Fla. 1978, U.S. Supreme Ct. 1980. Legal intern Wayne County Prosecutor's Office, Detroit, 1970-72; law clk. Wayne County Cir. Ct., Detroit, 1972-73; asst. U.S. atty. U.S. Dept. Justice, Detroit, 1973-80, asst. chief Criminal Div., U.S. Atty.'s Office, 1977-80, spl. atty. Organized Crime and Racketeering sect. U.S. Dept. Justice, 1980-84, dep. chief Detroit Organized Crime Strike Force, 1982-85, mem. narcotics adv. com. U.S. Dept. Justice, 1979-80; ptnr. Evans & Luptak, Detroit, 1985—; lectr. U.S. Atty. Gen. Advocacy Inst., 1984. Recipient numerous spl. commendations FBI, U.S. Drug Enforcement Adminstrn., U.S. Dept. Justice, U.S. Atty. Gen. Mem. ABA, Fed. Bar Assn. (speaker criminal law sect. Detroit 1983—), Mich. Bar Assn., Fla. Bar Assn., Nat Assn. Criminal Def. Lawyers, Detroit Bar Assn. Greek Orthodox. Home: 4661 Rivers Edge Dr Troy MI 48098 Office: Evans & Luptak 2500 Buhl Bldg Detroit MI 48226

ANDRESEN, FINN OLE, liquid filtration and mining equipment company executive; b. Lillestrom, Norway, Nov. 7, 1932; s. Erik and Marie (Magnussen) A.; Examen Artium, Lillestrom Interkommunale Hogere Almenskole, 1952; student Molstad and Moen U., 1952-54; m. Kari von Krogh, July 14, 1957; children—Erik Johan, Elisabeth. Prodn. planning mgr. Aanonsen Fabrikker Co., Oslo, 1954-58, adminstrv. asst., 1958-60, sales adminstrn. mgr., 1960-68; v.p. mktg. IBM, Oslo, 1968-71; pres. Polyclon Inc., Woburn, Mass., 1971—; founder, pres., owner Euro-Trade, Inc., export-import co., Weston, Mass., 1978—. Trustee, Waltham (Mass.) Hosp., 1979—, exec. com., 1982-85 . Served with Royal Guard, Norway, 1951-52. Mem. ASME, Filtration Soc. New Eng. Clubs: Royal Norwegian Yacht, Royal Norwegian Automobil (Oslo); Newton (Mass.) Yacht; Charles River Yacht. (commodore 1987-88), Commodores of Am. Home: 15 Pond Brook Circle Weston MA 02193 Office: 39 Industrial Pkwy Woburn MA 01801

ANDREUZZI, DENIS, chemical company executive; b. N.Y.C., Apr. 15, 1931; s. Mario and Lina (Beltrame) A.; m. Catherine Rappa, Sept. 7, 1963; children—Carol, Jean, Thomas. B.A., Columbia Coll., 1953; M.B.A., NYU, 1958. Adminstrv. asst. sales dept. Witco Corp., N.Y.C., 1957-60, mgr. wholesale sales, 1960-65, mgr. midwest sales, 1966-67, v.p. mktg., 1967-75, gen. mgr., group v.p., 1975-83, dep. exec. v.p., 1983-84, exec. v.p., 1984—; dir. Witco Corp., Witco BV, Amsterdam, Netherlands, Witco Corp., N.Y.C. Served with U.S. Army, 1953-55. Mem. Nat. Petroleum Refiners Assn., Chem. Mfrs. Assn., Ind. Lubricants Mfrs. Assn. Roman Catholic.

ANDREW, LLOYD B., JR., chemical company executive; b. Joliet, Ill., Nov. 30, 1923; s. Lloyd Brummond and Elizabeth (Frick) A.; m. Frances Burdett, Dec. 31, 1948; children: Joyce, Cindy, Lloyd B. III. Student, Ill. Inst. Tech., 1944-46; B.S.M.E. with distinction, Purdue U., 1948; M.S.M.E., La. State U., 1956. Process engr. Phillips Petroleum, Oklahoma City, 1948-50, Borger, Tex., 1950-51; with Ethyl Corp., 1951—; gen. mgr. VisQueen div. Ethyl Corp., Baton Rouge, 1963-68; dir. fin. relations parent co. Ethyl Corp., Richmond, Va., 1968-74; v.p. fin. relations Ethyl Corp., 1974-81, v.p., treas., 1981-83, sr. v.p., treas., 1983-84, exec. v.p., chief fin. officer, 1984—, mem exec. com. bd. dirs., 1985—. Served with USAAC, 1942-44, ETO. Decorated D.F.C., Air medal with 4 oak leaf clusters. Republican. Methodist. Clubs: Wall St. (N.Y.C.). Lodge: Kiwanis. Home: 103 Roslyn Hills Dr Richmond VA 23229 Office: Ethyl Corp 330 S 4th St PO Box 2189 Richmond VA 23219

ANDREW, LUCIUS ARCHIBALD DAVID, III, corporate executive; b. Highland Park, Ill., Mar. 5, 1938; s. Lucius Archibald David Jr. and Victoria (Rollins) A.; m. Susan Ott, June 1, 1963 (div. 1973); children—Ashley W., L.A. David IV; m. Phoebe Haffner Kellogg, Dec. 21, 1974; children—Gaylord M., Charles H., Matthew K., Louise M. Kellogg. B.S., U. Pa., 1962; M.B.A., NYU, 1965. Asst. treas. The Bank of N.Y., N.Y.C., 1962-68; instl. salesman Drexel, Harriman, Ripley, N.Y.C., 1968-70; v.p., br. mgr. Drexel, Firestone, Inc., Chgo., 1970-72; ptnr., br. mgr. Fahnestock & Co., Chgo., 1972-74; vice chmn. Viner's, Ltd., Sheffield, Eng., 1981-82; pres. N.E.A., Inc., 1975-85; chmn. exec. com. Cert. Mfg. Co., Shelton, Wash., 1975-85; bd. dirs. First Am. Bank, Skokie, Ill., 1965—, chmn., 1982—; dir. First Am. Bank Corp., 1985—, First Am. Data Corp., 1982—; chmn. FGI, Inc., Forest Grove, Oreg., 1985-86, Union St. Capital Corp., Seattle, Wash., 1986-87, Brudi Inc., Seattle, 1988—. Trustee Brooks Sch. Past trustee Seattle Repertory Theatre. Clubs: The Brook, Racquet and Tennis (N.Y.C.); Racquet (Chgo.); Rainier, University, Golf, Tennis, (Seattle). Home: The Highlands Seattle WA 98177 Office: 1001 4th Ave Pla Ste 4300 Seattle WA 98154

ANDREWS, ALEXIS ATHENA, marketing and sales executive; b. Newburgh, N.Y., Feb. 10, 1957; d. Angelo and Margaret (Kokarakis) A. Grad. high sch., Newburgh. Sales rep., mktg. analyst Ajayem Lumber Corp., Walden, N.Y., 1981—. Camp asst. mentally retarded YMCA, Newburgh, 1974—. Home: 317 Butternut Dr New Windsor NY 12550 Office: Ajayem Lumber Corp Wholesale Distbn Ctr Rt 208 PO Box 399 Walden NY 12550

ANDREWS, CRAIG ALAN, accountant; b. Bryan, Ohio, Jan. 6, 1948; s. James Frederick and Wanda Lavina (Mack) A.; m. Christine Ruth Hilbert, Nov. 1, 1969 (div. Oct. 1971); 1 child, Shaun David. BS, Ind. U., Fort Wayne, 1971. CPA. Mgr., treas. Midwest Tool, Inc., Hicksville, Ohio, 1969-79; machinist Manville, Waterville, Ohio, 1979-81; mgr. Bleckner Weber & Co., Toledo, 1981-85; ptnr. Weber Haessler & Andrews, Toledo, 1985-87; owner Craig Andrews CPA, Sylvania, Ohio, 1987—; treas. Creative Photo Crafts, Toledo, 1987—. Mem. Am. Inst. CPAs, Ohio Soc. CPAs, Kiwanis (dir. Toledo chpt., 1987—), Sylvania Country Club. Office: 5800 Monroe Bldg D Sylvania OH 43560

ANDREWS, FRANCES BARBARA, communications executive; b. Phila., Feb. 7, 1936; d. John Thomas and Claire Eunice (Carr) Loftus; 1 child, Michael Douglas. BA in Geology, Geography, San Diego State U., 1961; MBA, Pepperdine U., 1978. Flight test engr. Gen. Dynamics/Astronautics, San Diego, 1961-73; program mgr. Hughes Aircraft Co., Los Angeles, 1973-77; quality assurance mgr. GTE Govt. Systems, Mt. View, Calif., 1977-79; mgr. quality assurance subcontracts HBH Consortium, Roslyn, Va., 1979-80; dir. corp. telecommunications GTE Svc. Corp., Stamford, Conn., 1980—; advisor office info. and tech. State of Conn., Hartford, 1986—. Mem. bd. taxation and apportionment Shelton (Conn.) City Govt., 1987-89. Mem. Soc. Info. Mgmt., Women in Mgmt., Good Govt. Club, Mensa, Appalachian Mountain Club. Home: 13 Red Oak Cir Shelton CT 06484 Office: GTE Svc Corp One Stamford Forum Stamford CT 06904

ANDREWS, HAROLD WAYNE, cafeteria chain company executive; b. Olney, Tex., Jan. 8, 1938; s. Sam and Grace (Welch) A.; m. Betty Lou Phelps, Apr. 2, 1958; children: Cynthia Waters, Sherry Martinez, Harold Jr. Grad. high sch., Olney, 1958. Mgr. trainee Furr's Cafeterias Inc., Odessa, Tex., 1958; asst. mgr. 1958-59, mgr., 1959-61; mgr. and dist. mgr. Albuquerque, 1961-64; dist. mgr. 1964-72; v.p. Albuquerque and Lubbock, Tex., 1972-75; exec. v.p. ops. 1975-82; pres., chief operating officer Lubbock, 1982—. Mem. Nat. Restaurant Assn. Republican. Office: Furr's Cafeterias Inc 6901 Quaker Ave Lubbock TX 79413

ANDREWS, HOLDT, investment banker; b. N.Y.C., May 2, 1946; s. William Lloyd and Edna (Faulconer) A.; m. Nina Lawrence, Sept. 16, 1982; 1 child, Kelli. BS, U. Fla., 1968; MBA, Fla. Atlantic U., 1971. Asst. to v.p. mktg. Eltra Corp., Wilmington, Mass., 1972-74; v.p. Bank of Am., N.Y.C., 1974-81; group v.p. Amrobank, N.Y.C., 1981-84; exec. v.p. CenTrust Savs. Bank, Miami, Fla., 1984, KMC Group, Miami, 1985-86; sr. mng. dir. J.W. Charles Capital Corp.-Bush Securities, Boca Raton, Fla., 1986—; mem. adv. bd. Tucker State Bank, Jacksonville, Fla., 1987—. 1st lt. U.S. Army, 1968-70. Mem. Blue Key. Christian Scientist. Office: JW Charles Capital Corp Bush Securities Inc 980 N Federal Hwy Boca Raton FL 33432

ANDREWS, JEFFREY JOEL, service company executive; b. Littleton, N.H., July 14, 1961; s. William A. and Vera B. (Young) A. Diploma, Plymouth Area H.S., 1979. Lic. master electrician, N.H. Field electrician Thompson Electric, Plymouth, N.H., 1979-81; elec. foreman Pan Am Electric Corp., Nashville, 1981-82; maintenance elctrician Pike Industries Inc, Tilton, N.H., 1982-84; pres., owner Custom Crushing Co., Ashland, N.H., 1984—. Republican. Home and Office: Route 3 Ashland NH 03217

ANDREWS, STEPHEN CRANDALL, development agency executive; b. Decatur, Ill., May 7, 1941; s. Kenneth Crandall and Irma Isabell (Tibbetts) A.; m. Patricia Ann Kruse, Sept. 7, 1968. BA, Mich. Tech. U., 1970; postgrad., U. N.D., 1970-72; student, Mich. State U., 1971. Cert. soil tester. Scientist A.E. Staley Mfg. Co., Decatur, Ill., 1963-66; program mgr. ARC, Rockford, Ill., 1966-68; mgr. facility plan Ill. EPA, Springfield, 1972-74; project dir. N.W. Regional Planning Commn., Superior, Wis., 1974-78, sr. planner, 1978-86, deputy dir., 1987—; mem. Duluth (Minn.)-Superior Harbor Adv., 1976—, Gov.'s Water Quality Task Force, Madison, Wis., 1976-81; tech. advisor Internat. Joint Commn., Washington, 1976-82; dir. Douglas County Housing Authority, Superior, 1980—. Contbr. articles to profl. publs. Active Northland chpt. ARC, Duluth, 1986—. Recipient scholarship Nat. Science Found., 1971, Disting. Performance award State Wis., 1974, 76, Exceptional Performance award State Wis., 1975, Pub. Svc. award N.W. Regional Planning, 1984. Mem. Am. Planning Assn. Lutheran. Home: Rte 2 PO Box 60 Iron River WI 54847 Office: NW Regional Planning Douglas County Courthouse Rm 204 Superior WI 54880

ANDREWS, WILLIAM EUGENE, construction and services company executive; b. Augusta, Ga., May 9, 1943; s. William D. and Mildred (Aldridge) A.; m. Marilynn Knox, Mar. 21, 1975. BS, Miss. State U., State College, 1964, MBA, 1980. CPA, Ala., Miss., Ill. Auditor Coopers & Lybrand, Birmingham, Ala., 1964-69; div. controller Ceco Bldg. div. Ceco Corp., Columbus, Miss., 1969-81; controller The Ceco Corp., Oak Brook, Ill., 1981-86, v.p., controller, 1986—. Named One of Outstanding Young Leaders, State Miss. Econ. Council, 1974. Mem. Am. Inst. CPA's, Miss. Soc. CPA's. Republican. Presbyterian. Office: The CECO Corp One Tower Ln Oakbrook Terrace IL 60181

ANDREWS, WILLIAM FREDERICK, manufacturing executive; b. Easton, Pa., Oct. 7, 1931; s. William Frederick and Lydia Nielson (Cross) A.; m. Carol Beaman, Feb. 8, 1962; children: William Frederick III, Whitney, Carter, Clayton, Sloane. B.S., U. Md., 1953; M.B.A., Seton Hall U., 1961. Product mgr. Scovill Mfg. Co., Waterbury, Conn., 1965-68; v.p., gen. mgr. Scovill Mfg. Co., Raleigh, N.C., 1968-73; group v.p. Scovill Mfg. Co., Nashville, 1973-79; pres. Scovill Mfg. Co., Waterbury, 1979-81; chmn. Scovill Mfg. Co., 1981-86; chmn., chief exec. officer SSMC Inc., 1986—; bd. dirs. Burndy Corp., So. New Eng. Telephone Co., Corrections Corp. Am., Navistar Internat. Co. Bd. dirs. Nat. ARC, Litchfield Jr. Republic. With USAF, 1953-56. Recipient Silver Beaver award Boy Scouts Am., 1979. Mem. Nat. Assn. Mfrs. (bd. dirs., exec. com.), Machinery Allied Products Inst. (dir., exec. com.), Nat. Fluid Power Assn. (past pres.), Brit. N.Am. Soc., Conn. Bus. and Indsl. Assn. Republican. Episcopalian. Clubs: Bellemeade Country (Nashville); Waterbury, Waterbury Country, Highfield Country. Office: SSMC Inc PO Box 875 Shelton CT 06484

ANDRISANI, PAUL J(OSEPH), business educator, personnel consultant; b. Wilmington, Del., Oct. 19, 1946; s. Paul and Mary (Tavani) A.; B.S., U. Del., 1968, M.B.A., 1970; Ph.D., Ohio State U., 1973, postgrad., 1973-74; m. Barbra Lee Frank, Nov. 23, 1968; children—Nathan, Damian, Danielle. Sr. research assoc. Center for Human Resource Research, Ohio State U., Columbus, 1973-74, vis. research assoc., 1979; asst. prof. Sch. Bus., Temple U., Phila., 1974-76, assoc. prof., 1977-83, prof., 1983—, dir. Bur. Econ. Research, 1977-78, dir. Ctr. for Labor and Human Resource Studies, 1985—, assoc. dean 1989—; pres. St. Anthony's Edn. Fund, 1986—; pres. Paul J. Andrisani Personnel Cons. Services, Wilmington, Del., 1977—; cons. Price Waterhouse, U.S. EEOC, Acme Markets, CBS, City of Tucson, Chevron, La. Power and Light, La. Land and Exploration, PanAm, Smith Kline, Carpenter Tech., The Aerospace Corp. of Am., Dynalectron Corp., Lukens Steel, Traveler's Ins., Suffolk County Police Dept., Internat. Communications Agy., N.Y. Times, U.S. Steel, Lukens Steel, Travelers Ins. Cos., Readers Digest, K-Mart, Ins. of N.Am., Suffolk County Police Dept., Russell Sage Found., Del. Econ. Forecasting Adv. Com., New Orleans Public Service Inc., Del. Disability and Pension Rev., Rockwell Internat., ARCO, Nationwide Ins., ICI Ams., DuPont, GTE, Inco, U.S. Army Recruiting Command, govt. agys., others; lectr. Internat. Communications Agy., Japan and Portugal, Brandeis U., Pa. State U., Columbia U., William and Mary Coll., U. So. Calif., Nat. Employment Law Inst., San Francisco and Washington. Salzburg fellow; Roosevelt Youth Policy fellow. Served to capt. U.S. Army, 1972-73. Grantee, U.S. Dept. Labor, 1974-77, Nat. Commn. for Employment Policy, 1979-83, Adminstrn. on Aging, 1981-82, U.S. Dept. Army, 1986. Mem. Am. Econs. Assn., Indsl. Relations Research Assn., Am. Sociol. Assn., Am. Acad. Polit. and Social Sci., Gerontol. Soc. Am. Author: Work Attitudes and Labor Market Experience, 1978, Pre-Retirement Years, 1974; editorial bd. Jour. Econs. and Bus., 1979-83; contbr. over 40 articles to profl. jours. Office: Temple U Sch Bus & Mgmt Philadelphia PA 19122

ANDRUS, BRET R., insurance agency executive; b. Salt Lake City, Feb. 17, 1958; s. Ray B. and Delfa (Hand) A.; m. Joyce Tagge, Mar. 20, 1981; children: Timothy Bret, Brittany, Stephanie. BS in Fin., U. Utah, 1983. Agt. C.M. Alliance, Salt Lake City, 1983—; agy. supr. C.M. Alliance/Intermountain Fin. Group, Salt Lake City, 1987—. Mem. Salt Lake Assn. Life Underwriters (bd. dirs. 1987—, Nat. Quality award 1983, 86). Republican. Mormon. Home: 1787 E 7020 S Salt Lake City UT 84121 Office: Intermountain Fin Group 139 E South Temple Ste 5000 Salt Lake City UT 84121

ANDRZEJAK, MARILYN KATHLEEN, sales and marketing management company executive; b. Detroit, Sept. 19, 1960; d. Serge and Pauline Mary (Pawlas) A. Cert., Wayne County Community Coll., Detroit, 1980, Golden Gate U., 1983; student, Ga. State U., 1987—. Prodn. mgr. Prudential Bldg. Maintenance Co., Detroit, 1978-82; sales rep. SP Communications Sprint, Birmingham, Mich., 1981-82; sales supr. Communications Sprint, Birmingham, Mich., 1982; dist. sales mgr. GTE Sprint Communications, Birmingham, 1982-85; regional sales mgr. U.S. Sprint Communications, Sacramento, 1985-87; prin. IMS Increase Market Share, Atlanta, 1987—; cons. in field. Mem. Am. Mgmt. Assn., Am. Telemktg. Assn., Atlanta C. of C. Roman Catholic. Office: IMS Integrated Mktg Solutions 8 Piedmont Ctr Ste 110 Atlanta GA 30305

ANDRZEJAK-ANDRE, MARILYN KATHLEEN, sales and marketing company executive; b. Detroit, Sept. 19, 1960; d. Serge and Pauline Mary (Pawlas) A. Cert., Wayne County Community Coll., Detroit, 1980, Golden Gate U., 1983; student, Ga. State U., 1987—. Prodn. mgr. Prudential Bldg. Maintenance Co., Detroit, 1978-82; sales rep. SP Communications Sprint, Birmingham, Mich., 1981-82, sales supr., 1982; dist. sales mgr. GTE Sprint Communications, Birmingham, 1982-85, regional sales mgr., 1982-85; regional sales mgr. US Sprint Communications, Sacramento, Calif., 1985-87; prin. IMS Increase Market Share, Atlanta, 1987—; cons. in field. Mem. Atlanta C. of C., Am. Mgmt. Assn., Am. Telemktg. Assn. Roman Catholic. Office: IMS Integrated Mktg. Solutions 8 Piedmont Ctr Ste 110 Atlanta GA 30305

ANDUJAR, RAFAEL, sales executive; b. Melilla, Spain, Dec. 20, 1946; s. Antonio and Ines (Vilches) A.; m. Montserrat Murcia; children: Emmanuel, Valerie, Delphine, Xavier. MBA, N.W. London, 1985; PhD Internat. Commerce, U. London, 1985; MBA, CESEM, Barcelona, Spain, 1986, CESEM, Barcelona, Spain, 1986. Salesman RUMASA, Madrid, 1970-72, sales mgr., 1972-76; area rep. C.R. Bard, Inc.-USCI Int. Div., Billerica, Mass., 1977-80, mng. dir., 1981-88; v.p., mng. dir. for South Europe C.R. Bard, Inc., 1988—; gen. mgr. Bard de España, S.A., Barcelona, gen. mgr. Bard Belgium N.V., Louvin, Belgium; exec. v.p. BARD Italia S.R.L., Rome. Office: Bard de España SA Bard Europe, Avda Diagonal 429 S Europe Div Office, Barcelona 08036, Spain

ANGE, JEAN-PAUL, investment banking company executive; b. Paris, Aug. 29, 1943; came to U.S., 1980; s. Jean Charles Ange and Genevieve (Rouffy) Pelanne; m. Julia Ann Holmes, Dec. 21, 1981; 1 child, Alexandre. Degree in Engring., Ecole Polytechnique, Paris, 1966. Commd. officer French Navy, 1969, advanced through grades to capt., resigned, 1980; diplomat French Embassy, N.Y.C., 1980-86; sr. v.p. C.L. Global Ptnrs. Securities Corp., N.Y.C., 1986—. Mem. French Am. C. of C. (v.p. 1986). Office: CL Global Ptnrs Securities Corp 95 Wall St New York NY 10005

ANGEL, ALLEN ROBERT, mathematics educator, author, consultant; b. N.Y.C., Oct. 13, 1942; s. Isaac and Sylvia (Budnick) A.; m. Kathryn Mary Pollinger, Feb. 14, 1966; children: Robert Allen, Steven Scott. AAS in Electrical Tech., N.Y.C. Community Coll., 1962; BS in Physics, SUNY, New Paltz, 1965; MS in Math., SUNY, 1967; postgrad., Rutgers U., 1969. Tchr. physics Rhineback (N.Y.) Cen. Sch., 1965-66; instr. physics, math. Sullivan County Community Coll., Loch Sheldrake, N.Y., 1967-70; prof. math. Monroe Community Coll., Rochester, N.Y., 1970—; chmn. math./computer sci. Monroe Community Coll., Rochester, 1988—; asst. dir. nat. sci. found., math. summer insts. Rutgers U., New Brunswick, N.J., 1970-72; cons. reviewer various pub. cos. including Prentice-Hall Pub. Co., Englewood Cliffs, N.J., 1983—, Addison-Wesley Pub. Co., Reading, Mass., 1978—. Author: (textbooks) A Survey of Mathematics 3d Edit., 1985, Elementary Algebra-A Practical Approach, 1985, Intermediate Algebra-A Practical Approach, 1986, Elementary Algebra for College Students 2nd Edit., 1988, 3d Edit., 1989, Intermediate Algebra for College Students, 2d edit., 1988, Algebra for College Student's, 1988. Mem. Am. Math. Assn. of Two Yr. Colls. (v.p. 1985—, chmn. conv. 1984, Pres.'s award), N.Y. State Math. Assn. of Two Yr. Colls. (pres. 1978-80, chmn. summer inst. 1976-78, Outstanding Contributions award), Math. Assn. of Am., Nat. Council of Tchrs. of Math., Assn. Math. Tchrs. of N.Y. State, New England Math. Assn. of Two Yr. Colls. Home: 125 Holley Ridge Cir Rochester NY 14625 Office: Monroe Community Coll 1000 E Henrietta Rd Rochester NY 14623

ANGELL, WAYNE D., economist, banker; b. Liberal, Kans., June 28, 1939; s. Charlie Francis and Adele Thelma (Edwards) A.; children: Patrice, Wynne, Ryan, Wiley. BA, Ottawa U., 1952; MA, U. Kans., 1953, PhD, 1957. Instr. econs. U. Kans., Lawrence, 1954-56; prof. econs. Ottawa (Kans.) U., 1956-85, dean, 1969-72; pres., bd. dirs. Hume (Mo.) Bancshares, Inc., 1972-85; bd. dirs. Fed. Res. Bank, Kansas City, Mo., 1979-86; mem. bd. govs. FRS, Washington, 1986—; econ. cons. Franklin Savs. Assn., Ottawa, 1981-86, First Nat. Bank, Manhattan, Kans., 1984-86, Adams Bus. Forms, Inc., Topeka, 1981-85; chmn. bd. dirs. First State Bank, Pleasanton, 1975-76. Rep. Kans Ho. of Reps., Topeka, 1961-67; exec. com. State C. of C., Topeka, 1967-70; vice chmn. Rep. State Legis. Campaign Com., Topeka, 1964; chmn. Rep. Congl. Conv. 3d Dist., Overland Park, Kans., 1964. Mem. Am. Econ. Assn., Phi Beta Kappa. Republican. Baptist. Home: 1600 N Oak St Arlington VA 22209 Office: FRS 20th & C Sts NW Washington DC 20551

ANGELO, IAN JAMES, industrial engineer, banker; b. Bklyn., June 27, 1938; s. Charles James and Frances (Beloff) A.; div.; children: Joseph James, James Vincent. BS in Indsl. Engring., N.J. Inst. Tech., 1969; postgrad., L.I. U., 1985—. Asst. engr. Air Reduction Co, Union, N.J., 1964-66; sr. project indsl. engr. Burroughs Corp., Warren, N.J., 1966-71; mgr. indsl. engring. North Am. Phillips, Morristown, N.J., 1971-75; internal cons. Chase Manhattan Bank, N.Y.C., 1975-77; supr. indsl. engring. Rowe Internat., Whippany, N.J., 1977-82; sr. indsl. engr. Sperry Flight Systems, Boonton, N.J., 1983-84; asst. sec. Mfrs. Hanover Trust, N.Y.C., 1984—. Dir. Pub. Relations Friends Parsippany (N.J.) Library, 1984. Served with U.S. Army, 1962-64. Mem. Inst. Indsl. Engrs. (sr., dris. facilities 1970—, sec. 1979, 81, treas. 1980, 82), Am. Legion. Democrat. Office: Mfrs Hanover Trust 140 E 45th St New York NY 10017

ANGELO, MARGARET IDA, stock broker, correspondent liaison; b. Elizabeth, N.J., June 21, 1960; d. Ernest James and Margaret P. (Falcetano) A. BA in History, Seton Hall U., 1982. Sr. option prin., asst. v.p., correspondent liaison Richardson Greenshields Securities Inc., N.Y.C., 1984—. Mem. Met. Mus. Art, N.Y.C., 1986—, Mus. of Natural History, N.Y.C., 1986—. Mem. Securities Traders Assn., Phi Alpha Theta. Roman Catholic. Office: Richardson Greenshields 4 World Trade Ctr New York NY 10048

ANGELO, RONALD JOHN, municipal official; b. Newark, Feb. 2, 1952; s. Samuel James and Dolores (Deluca) A.; m. Judith Anne Springer, Sept. 14, 1975; children: Ronald Jr., Richard. BSBA, Seton Hall U., 1974. Staff acct. Sammuel Klein & Co., Newark, 1974-80; asst. treas. City of Summit, N.J., 1980-85, city treas., 1985—. Mem. Mcpl. Fin. Officers Assn. N.J. (exec. bd. 1985—), Govtl. Purchasing Assn. N.J., Tax Collector's and Treas.' Assn. N.J., Govt. Fin. Officers Assn. Republican. Roman Catholic. Office: City of Summit 512 Springfield Ave Summit NJ 07901

ANGELONE, ALFRED C., business executive; b. Providence, Mar. 19, 1939; m. Sheila H. Pfister, Sept. 4, 1963; children: A. Douglas, Matthew F. BS cum laude, Providence Coll., 1962; MBA, Columbia U., 1964. Mgr. Arthur Anderson & Co., Boston, 1964-69; chief exec. officer ASA Internat., Ltd., Westborough, Mass., 1969—; plater Tanury Industries, Inc., Lincoln, R.I., 1985—; investemnt adv. Emerson Mgmt. Inc., Boston, 1986—; ins. agy. Feingold & Feingold, Worcester, 1987—. Fund raiser Kennedy Meml. Hosp. Assocs., Brighton, Mass., 1979-83. Mem. Aurora Civic Assn., Ship and Scales Honor Soc., Tryall Golf and Beach Club (pres.), Charles River Country Club, East Greenwich Yacht Club, Delta Epsilon Sigma. Roman Catholic. Home: 303 Hillside St Milton MA 02186 Office: ASA Internat Ltd 1700 W Park Dr Westborough MA 01581

ANGELOTTI, RICHARD H., banker; b. Erie, Pa., Dec. 12, 1944; s. Henry and Ann (DiPlacido) A.; m. Carol A. Flaherty, Feb. 14, 1944; children: Kimberly, Nicole. BA, U. Notre Dame, 1966; JD, Loyola U., Chgo., 1969. Assoc. Brown Fox and Blumberg, Chgo., 1972-75, Angelotti and Cesario, Hinsdale, Ill., 1975-82; dir. mktg., v.p. Northern Trust Bank of Fla., Sarasota, 1983—, also bd. dirs. Author: Estate Planning Techniques, 1975. Trustee, treas. Mote Marine Lab., Sarasota, 1987—; bd. dirs. United Way of Sarasota, 1985—, Suncoast Heart Assn., 1986—, Sarasota Family YMCA, 1988; pres., bd. dirs. Asolo Theater, Sarasota, 1986—. Mem. Am. Inst. Bank Marketers. Republican. Roman Catholic. Office: Northern Trust Bank 1515 Ringling Blvd Sarasota FL 34236

ANGERMUELLER, HANS H., banker; b. 1924; married. B.A., Harvard U., 1946, M.S. in Engring., 1947, LL.B., 1950. Ptnr. Shearman & Sterling, N.Y.C., 1950-72; with Citicorp, 1972—, sr. v.p., gen. counsel, then sr. exec. v.p., then vice chmn., 1982—; also vice chmn. Citibank N.A.; dir. Citicorp. Served with USN. Office: Citibank 399 Park Ave New York NY 10043

ANGIOLI, RENATA MARIA, sports publicist, realtor; b. N.Y.C., Dec. 14, 1962; d. Peter and Lidia Dahlia (Temoczko) Jacynicz; m. Carmine Enrico Angioli, July 18, 1987. BA, Fordham Coll., 1984; MBA, Wagner Coll., 1986. Lic. realtor, N.Y. Mem. coll. basketball pub. relations staff Madison Square Garden, N.Y.C., 1987-88; real estate salesperson VIP/Better Homes & Gardens, S.I., N.Y., 1988—; dir. rules Met. Collegiate Hockey Conf., S.I., 1984-87; exec. cons. Fordham Ice Hockey Yr. Book, 1985—. Troupleader Plast, N.Y.C., 1976-80. Mem. Coll. Sports Info. Dirs. Am., Fordham Ice Hockey Club (pres. 1980-84). Republican. Roman Catholic. Home: 2 Elmwood Park Dr #710 Staten Island NY 10314 Office: VIP/Better Homes & Gardens 1787 Victory Blvd Staten Island NY 10314

ANGLE, JOHN CHARLES, life insurance company executive; b. N.Y.C., Aug. 22, 1923; s. Everett Edward and Catharine Elizabeth (Dodge) A.; m. Catherine Anne Sellers, Oct. 4, 1945; children: Margaret Susan, James Sellers. S.B., U. Chgo., 1944. With Union Nat. Life Ins. Co., Lincoln, Nebr., 1948-51; v.p., actuary Woodmen Accident and Life Co., Lincoln, 1953-73; dir. Woodmen Accident and Life Co., 1969-73; sr. v.p., chief actuary Guardian Life Ins. Co. Am., N.Y.C., 1973-77; exec. v.p. Guardian Life Ins. Co. Am., 1977-80, pres., 1980-84, chmn. bd., chief exec. officer, 1985-88, also dir.; chmn. Guardian Ins. & Annuity Co.; bd. dir. Guardian Park Ave. Fund, Guardian Cash Fund, Guardian Investor Svcs. Corp. Consulting editor: Life and Health Insurance Handbook, 2d edit., 1964. Pres. Lincoln Community Chest, 1965, Lincoln Community Coun., 1966-68, 14th St-Union Sq. Bus. Improvement Dist., 1985; trustee Am. Coll., 1987—; bd. dirs. Lincoln Gen. Hosp., 1970-73. 1st lt. USAF, 1943-46, capt. USAF, 1951-52. Fellow Soc. Actuaries (dir. publs. 1975-79, bd. govs. 1980-83, 84-87); mem. Am. Acad. Actuaries (bd. dirs. 1977-79), Internat. Actuarial Assn. (v.p. U.S. sect.), Health Ins. Assn. Am. (bd. dirs. 1985-88), Life Office Mgmt. Assn. (bd. dirs. 1983—, chmn. 1987), Am. Coun. Life Ins. (bd. dirs. 1986-88), Life Ins. Coun. N.Y. (bd. dirs. 1985-88). Clubs: Union League, Lincoln Country. Office: Guardian Life Ins Co 201 Park Ave S New York NY 10003

ANGLE, MARGARET SUSAN, lawyer; b. Lincoln, Nebr., Feb. 20, 1948; d. John Charles and Catherine (Sellers) A. BA with distinction in Polit. Sci., U. Wis., Madison, 1970, MA in Scandinavian Studies (scholarship, NDEA fellow), 1972, JD cum laude, 1976. Bar: Wis. 1977, Minn. 1978. Law clk., Madison, Mpls., Chgo., 1974-76; law clk. U.S. Dist. Ct., Mpls., 1977-78; mem. firm Faegre & Bensen, Mpls., 1978-84; sr. atty., asst. gen. counsel, asst. sec. Nat. Car Rental System, Inc., Mpls., 1984—, corp. sec. car rental claims. Note and comment editor U. Wis. Law Rev.; contbr. articles to profl. publs. Mem. ABA, Am. Car Rental Assn. (bd. dirs.), Minn. Bar Assn., Wis. Bar Assn., Hennepin County Bar Assn., Order of Coif. Home: 4340 Fox Ridge Ct Eagan MN 55122 Office: Nat Car Rental System Inc 7700 France Ave S Minneapolis MN 55435

ANGULO, CHARLES BONIN, foreign service officer, lawyer; b. N.Y.C., Aug. 6, 1943; s. Manuel R. and Carolyn C. (Bonin) A.; m. Penelope Snare, June 28, 1986. BA, U. Va., 1966; cert., U. Madrid, 1966; J.D., Tulane U., 1969. Bar: Va. 1969. Assoc., Michael & Dent, Charlottesville, Va., 1969-73; assoc. editor The Michie Pub. Co., Charlottesville, 1973; fgn. svc. officer U.S. Dept. State, Washington, 1973-75, Am. Embassy, Brussels, 1976-78, Legal Advisor's Office, Dept. State, Washington, 1978-81, Am. Embassy, Santo Domingo, 1981-85; exec. dir. office of insp. gen. Dept. State, Washington, 1985-86, asst. chief protocol for U.S. Dept. State, Washington, 1986-88; Am. consulate gen. Jeddah, Saudi Arabia, 1988—. Mem. Coun. Fgn. Rels. Home: 200 N Pickett St Apt 1107 Alexandria VA 22304

ANGULO, GERARD ANTONIO, financial executive, investor, consultant; b. Havana, Cuba, Sept. 24, 1956; came to U.S., 1960; s. Ricardo A. and Rosario (Mestas) A. Arabic cert., Yale U., 1977; BA, Princeton U., 1978; MBA, Harvard U., 1980. With office of pres. Consol. Mining & Industries, N.Y.C., 1980-83; pvt. practice as financier, N.Y.C., 1982-83; fin. exec. IFB Mng. Ptnrship, N.Y.C., 1984-86; fin. exec. First City Fin., N.Y.C., 1987; gen. ptnr. First Capital Ptrns., N.Y.C., 1988—; cons. in field; prof. grad. bus. sch. Columbia U., 1988—, NYU, 1989—. Author: Multinational Corporate Investment, 1978, Anaconda's Chilean Investment, 1980; contbr. articles to profl. jours. Fund raiser Princeton U., 1978-83, Harvard U., 1980-83, Univ. Hosp. NYU Med. Ctr., 1983—. Mem. New Eng. Soc. (bd. dirs. 1986—, Achievement award 1979-80). Republican. Roman Catholic. Clubs: Harvard, Princeton (N.Y.C.). Office: First Capital Ptnrs 730 Fifth Ave 21st Fl New York NY 10019

ANISHI, AKIRA, economics educator, academic administrator; b. Tokyo, Jan. 5, 1929; s. Tatsunosuke and Tomi (Fusegawa) O.; m. Noriko Shimizu, Sept. 27, 1963; children: Kimihiro, Masahiro. BA in Econs., Keio U., Tokyo, 1954, MA in Econs., 1958, PhD in Econs., 1963. Rsch. officer Inst. Developing Economies, Tokyo, 1963-65; assoc. prof. Chuo U., Tokyo, 1965-67; econ. affairs officer UN Econ. Commn. for Asia and Far East, Bangkok, Thailand, 1967-68; econ. affairs officer ILO, Geneva, 1968-70; chief economist Japan Econ. Research Ctr., Tokyo, 1970-71; prof. econs. Soka U., Tokyo, 1971—, dir. Inst. Applied Econ. Research, 1976—, dean Grad. Sch. Econs., 1978—, v.p., 1989—. Author: Japanese Economy in Global Age, 1974; numerous articles on global econ. modeling, 1977—. Grantee Japan Found., 1958-60, Japan Econ. Research Found., 1974-75, Australia-Japan Found., 1981-82; recipient SGI Culture award, 1985. Fellow Japan Soc. Internat. Econs., Japan Soc. Econ. Policy, Japan Assn. Simulation and Gaming (v.p. 1989—). Buddhist. FUGI global model used by UN, 1982—. Home: 4-9-4 Seijyo, Setagaya-Ku, Tokyo 157, Japan Office: Soka U, 1-236 Tangi-cho, Hachiji-shi, Tokyo 192, Japan

ANIXTER, EDWARD FRANKLIN, retired electronics company executive; b. Chgo., Dec. 11, 1917; s. Arthur Nathanial and Sadie (Novey) A.; B.S., U. Pa., 1939; m. Edith Pearl, Nov. 19, 1941; children—Barbara, Steven, Jo Ann (Mrs. Luis Silva). With Englewood Elec. Supply Co., Chgo., 1939-67, v.p., 1958-67; v.p. Potter-Englewood Corp., Chgo., 1967-71; pres. Pemcor, Inc., Westchester, Ill., 1971-78; pres. Internat. Jensen, Inc., subs. Esmark, Inc., 1979-80; pres. Estronics, Inc., subs. Esmark, Inc., from 1980-84, chmn., dir., vice pres. Schwab Rehab. Hosp., Chgo., 1953-62. Served with AUS, 1941-45. Decorated Bronze Star medal. Mem. Nat. Assn. Elec. Distbrs. (pres. 1972), Electric Assn. Chgo. (pres. 1962-63). Clubs: Standard (Chgo.), Idlewild Country (pres. Flossmoor, Ill. 1969-70), Tamarisk Country (Rancho Mirage, Calif.).

ANJARD, RONALD PAUL, SR, business and industry executive, consultant, educator, technologist; b. Chgo., July 31, 1935; s. Auguste L. and Florence M. (Byrne) A.; m. Marie B. Sampler; children: Ronald Paul Jr., Michael P., Michele M., John R. BS in Metall. Engring., Carnegie Mellon U., 1957; MS/MBA in Indsl. Adminstrn., Purdue U., 1968; AS in Supervision, Ind. U., 1973; BBA, USNY, 1978; BA in Humanities, T.A. Edison Coll., 1979; PhD in Edn., Columbia Pacific U., 1981, PhD in Metall. Engring., 1982; postgrad., Ind. U. Law Sch., 1975, La. State U., 1978, U. Calif., 1978. Metallurgist U.S. Steel Corp., Braddock, Pa., 1956-57; metall. engr. Crucible Steel Co., Pitts., 1957-58; process engr. Raytheon Mfg. Co., Newton, Mass., 1958-59; program mgmt. engr. Delco Electronics div. GM, Kokomo, Ind., 1959-81; div. quality mgr. Aux. Materials Div. Delco Electronics div. GM, Kokomo, 1981-82, div. quality mgr., JMI Electronic Materials div., 1982-83; v.p. engring. AG Tech, 1983—; pres. Anjard Internat. Cons., 1983, 86—, Anjard Solder Paste Tech., 1983—, Anjard Solder and Mfg. Tech., 1987—; corp. dir. Gen. Dynamics-Convair-Quality, 1987; corp. dir. quality Kaypro Corp., 1983-87; pres. Anjard Imports, 1965-80; sr. bank officer Mission Viejo (Calif.) Nat. Bank, 1986-87; v.p. mktg. Alpha Cast Products, 1987—; v.p. adminstrn. Triage Network, 1988—; sr. exec. broker Futures Investment Firm, 1983; quality cons. Gen. Dynamics, Convair, 1987; distributor Vertical Computer System, 1987; free-lance writer, photographer, 1966—; retail salesman Nurseryland, 1987-88; instr. Ball State U., 1970-71, 75-76, Kokomo Apprentice Program, 1971-81, Ind. Vocat. Tech. Coll., 1978-81, U. Phoenix, 1983, U. So. Calif., 1985—, U. La Verne, 1985—, Ala. A&M U., 1983, Chapman Coll., 1983—, Nat. U., 1982-83, San Diego Community Coll., 1984—, U. Calif. San Diego, 1986—, Golden State U., 1986—, U. La Jolla, San Diego Job Corps, Union of Experimental Colls. and Univs., 1987—, Karanovich Counseling Ctr., Cen. Tex. Coll., 1987—, numerous others; thesis mentor Columbia Pacific U., 1981—. writer in tech. and non-tech. pubs.; rev. editor: Solid State Technology, rev. edit., Microelectronics and Reliability, 1982—, Ceram, 1985—, IEEE Circuits and Devices, 1985—. Pres. Greater Kokomo Assn. Chs., 1972-74; chmn. Diocesan Pastoral Council, Diocese Layfayette, Ind., 1977-78, diocesan ecumenical officer, 1972-78, diocesan impact coordinator, 1972-81; mem. Ascension Council, 1984—; active Ind. Council Chs., 1971-81; mem. Tierra Santa Town Council, 1988—; councilman Howard County Council, Ind., 1981; trustee Clay Twp., 1970-75; dir. 5th dist. Ind. Twp. Trustees Assn.; vice chmn. Ind. State U. Young Republicans; del. Rep. State Conv., 1970, 74, 78, 80, dep. registration officer, 1970, 72, 74, 76, 80; mem. Rep. Nat. Com., 1970-75, mem. San Diego Rep. Cen. Com.; resolutions chmn. Young Reps. Conv., 1969; state minority chmn., dir. Howard County Young Reps.; regional dir. Leadership Tng. Sch.; chmn. 5th Dist. Young Reps.; mem. San Diego Rep. Cen. Com., 1985—; mem. Ind. State Com. for Med. Assistance, Ind. Citizens Adv. Council on Alcoholism, Ind. Citizens Council on Addictions, Mayor's Human Rights Com.; active Meshingomesia council Boy Scouts Am.; chmn. Clay Twp. Bicentennial Com., 1974-76; mem. exec. com. Kokomo Bicentennial Com., 1974-76; govt. agys. chmn. Howard County Bicentennial Com., 1974-76; capt. capital fund drive Sangralea Valley Boys Home Campaign, 1968; mem. San Diego Rep. Cen. Com., 1985—; regional bd. dirs. Drug Abuse Council, Howard County; bd. dirs., membership chmn. Mental Health Assn.; lector Ascension, San Diego, 1984—, mem. council, 1985—, also numerous other civic activities. Served to capt., Ordnance Corps U.S. Army, 1957-66. Recipient Ind. Mental Health citations, 1969, 70, Howard County Mental Health citations, 1969, 70, Nat. Young Rep. Hard Charger award, 1970, Gen. Motors Community Service award, 1970, Jaycee Disting. Service award, 1970, Disting. Service award InYoung Reps., 1971, Layman of Year award K.C., 1971, Ind. Mental Health award, 1971-72, Heart Fund award, 1973, Ind. Gov.'s Vol. Action commendation, 1975, 78, award Greater Kokomo Council of Chs., 1975; named Outstanding Ind. Young Rep., 1970; fellow Harry S. Truman Library, 1974—. Mem. Internat. Soc. for Hybrid Microelectronics (Midwest regional dir., charter state pres., treas., v.p., publicity chmn., program chmn., others 1970), Semicondr. Materials Soc., Am. Soc. Quality Control (editor non-periodic publs., electronics div.), Am. Soc. Metals, Am. Bar Assn., ASTM (chmn. subcoms. 1963-68), AIME, Kokomo Engring. Soc., Internat. Platform Assn., Internat. Brick Collector's Assn. (pres., gov. bd. 1983—), Am. Indian Assn., Ind. Chess Assn., Nat. Hist. Soc., Ind. Hist. Soc., Howard County Hist. Soc. (bd. dirs.), Tippecanoe County Hist. Assn., Found. Ill. Archeology, Epigraphic Soc., Nat., Fla., Clearwater Audubon socs., N.Am. Acad. Ecumenists, Soc. Investigation of Unexplained, Ancient Astronaut Soc., Internat. Assn. for Investigation Ancient Civilizations (internat. dir. 1980—), Internat. UFO Registry, Kokomo Fine Arts Assn., Nat. Wilderness Soc., Whitewater Valley R.R. Assn., Kokomo Mgmt. Club (auditor 1970), Am. Hort. Soc., Nat. Greentown Glass Assn., San Diego Hist. Soc., San Diego Archeol. Soc., Calif. Archeol. Soc., San Diego Zool. Soc., Soc. for Hist. Archaeology, Soc. for Calif. Archaeology, San Diego Cymbidium Soc., San Diego Orch. and Soc., Nat. Acad. Ecumenists, Internat. Order St. Luke the Physician, Sigma Xi, numerous other organizations. Clubs: Kokomo Photo Guild, Ind. Chess, Donora Sportsman, Sycamore Racquet, Kokomo Rose Soc, Kokomo Astronomy, Kokomo Poetry, Kokomo Swim, East County Rep. Home: 10942 Montego Dr San Diego CA 92124

ANKENY, DEWALT HOSMER, JR., bank executive; b. Mpls., Dec. 29, 1932; s. DeWalt and Marie Josephine (Hamm) A.; BA. summa cum laude, Dartmouth Coll., 1954, M.B.A., Amos Tuck Sch. Bus. Adminstrn., 1955; M.S. in Mech. Engring., Thayer Sch. Engring., 1955; m. Margaret Dayton, June 24, 1955; children: Donald, Harriett, Sarah, Charles, Phillip. With Theo. Hamm Brewing Co., 1955-66; with 1st Nat. Bank Mpls., 1967-82, pres., 1976-82, chmn., 1980-82, also dir.; vice chmn. 1st Bank System, 1983, pres., 1984-85, chmn., chief exec. officer, 1985—. Bd. dirs. United Way Mpls., Greater Mpls. Met. Housing Corp. Mem. Minn. Bankers Assn., Assn. Reserve City Bankers, Am. Bankers Assn. Clubs: Woodhill Country, Mpls. Office: 1st Bank System Inc 1200 First Bank Pl E PO Box A512 Minneapolis MN 55480 *

ANKER, PETER LOUIS, investment banker, security analyst; b. Germany, May 14, 1935; s. Hans and Dorothea (Nadel) A.; divorced 1977; children: Philip A., Kent K. AB, Columbia U., 1957; MBA, U. Pa., 1961. Security analyst Shields & Co., N.Y.C., 1960-65; 1st v.p. Smith Barney & Co., N.Y.C., 1965-76; mng. dir. First Boston Corp., N.Y.C., 1976—. Served with USAF, 1958-61. Mem. Steel Analysts Group (pres.), Non-Ferrous Metals Analysts Group (pres.), N.Y. Metals and Mining Analysts Group (pres.), N.Y. Soc. Security Analysts (bd. dirs. 1983-87). Clubs: India House (N.Y.C.). Avocations: woodworking, tennis, skiing.

ANNECHINI, WILLIAM, JR., insurance company executive; b. Trenton, N.J., Mar. 12, 1950; s. William Sr. and Dorothy (Hartshorn) A. BA, Marietta Coll., 1972; MBA, U. Hartford, 1976. Mgr., fin. analyst Conn. Gen. Ins. Co., Hartford, 1972-77; dir. acctg., non-ins. ops. Colonial Penn Group, Phila., 1977-81; dir. acctg. controls, expense mgmt. CIGNA Corp., Phila., 1981-87; v.p. fin., adminstrn. YMCA of Phila. & Vicinity, Inc., 1987—; coll. level instr., Phila. and suburbs, 1982—; lectr. Ins. Soc. Phila., 1981—. Vol., asst. Devon Horse Show, Bryn Mawr, Pa., 1978-82. Recipient Outstanding Educator award Ins. Soc. Phila., 1986. Mem. Nat. Assn.

Accts., Assn. MBA Execs., Leadership, Inc., Brant Beach Yacht Club (trustee N.J. chpt.). Republican. Roman Catholic.

ANNEKEN, WILLIAM B., apparel company executive; b. Erlanger, Ky., 1933; s. William H. and Ann C. (Domaschko) A.; m. Corol Marie Menke, Aug. 21, 1954; children: William Gerard, Steven Michael, James Gregory, Cynthia Marie, Lisa Michelle. BSBA, Xavier U., 1956, MBA, 1964. With Palm Beach Inc., 1956-88, controller, 1963-72, sec., 1965-76, v.p., treas., controller, 1969-75, chief fin. officer, 1972-76, exec. v.p., chief fin. officer, 1975-88, also bd. dirs.; v.p. fin. Crystal Brands Inc., 1988—. Trustee Coll. Mt. St. Joseph. Served with U.S. Army, 1953-55. Mem. Fin. Execs. Inst., Soc. for Advancement of Mgmt., Am. Mgmt. Assn. Office: Palm Beach Inc 400 Pike St Cincinnati OH 45202

ANNENBERG, WALTER H., foundation administrator, former ambassador; b. Milw., 1908; m. Veronica Dunkelman (div.); 1 child, Wallis; m. Leonore Cohn. Ed., The Peddie Sch., Wharton Sch., U. Pa.; ed. hon. degrees; D.Journalism, Mt. Sinai Med. Coll., Temple U.; L.H.D., Widener Coll.; LL.D., La Salle Coll., U. Pa., Dropsie Coll., U. So. Calif., 1977; L.H.D., Albert Einstein Coll. Medicine, Elizabethtown Coll., Coll. Podiatric Medicine, Phila., 1977; L.H.D. (hon.), U. Notre Dame. Former pres. Triangle Publs., Inc., pubs. Seventeen mag., TV Guide, Daily Racing Form, Phila.; chmn., chief exec. officer Triangle Publs., Inc., pubs. Seventeen mag., TV Guide, Daily Racing Form, 1984-88; former U.S. ambassador to Great Britain and No. Ireland.; Pres. M.L. Annenberg Found., Annenberg Fund; founder, pres. Annenberg Sch. Communications, Grad. Sch. U. Pa., U. S.C. Trustee Dermatology Found.; trustee Met. Mus. Art, United Fund Phila. Area, U. Pa., Nat. Trust for Historic Preservation; trustee-at-large Found. for Ind. Colls., Inc.; bd. dirs., trustee emeritus Eisenhower Med. Center, Rancho Mirage, Calif.; bd. govs. Acad. Food Mktg. of St. Joseph's Coll.; trustee emeritus Peddie Sch.; adv. bd. lay trustees Villanova U.; donor Walter H. Annenberg Library and The Masters' House to the Peddie Sch., Hightstown, N.J.; mem. Nat. Neiman Fund Com., Navy nat. com. Army-Navy Mus. Former comdr. USNR. Decorated officer French Legion of Honor; comdr. Order of the Lion Finland, Order of Crown of Italy, comdr. Order of Merit, Italy; knight comdr. Order Brit. Empire; recipient Russell H. Conwell award Temple U.; Gold medal award Freedoms Found.; Pa. Meritorious Service medal; Man of Year award Del. Valley Council, 1964; gold medal award Phila. Club of Printing House Craftsmen; Samuel S. Fels medal award, 1968; Ralph Lowell award Corp. Pub. Broadcasting, 1983; Presdl. Medal of Freedom, 1986; Presdl. Gold Medallion for Humanitarianism, B'nai B'rith Internat., 1986; named Pub. of Yr., Mag. Pubs. Assn., 1984. Fellow Pa. Acad. Fine Arts; mem. Navy League, Newcomen Soc., Alliance Francaise de Phila., Am. Soc. Newspaper Editors, Internat. Press Inst., Inter Am. Press Assn., Friars Sr. Soc., Cum Laude Soc., English-Speaking Union, Am. Swedish Hist. Found., Am. Newspaper Pubs. Assn., Explorers Club, Phi Sigma Delta, Sigma Delta Chi. Clubs: Rittenhouse, Racquet, Poor Richard, Faculty U. Pa. (Phila.); Tamarisk Country (Palm Springs); Lyford Cay (Nassau, Bahamas); Overseas Press (N.Y.C.); Nat. Press (Washington); Century Country (White Plains, N.Y.); White's (London); Swinley Forest (Ascot, Eng.); California (Los Angeles); Pilgrims; Castle Pines (Denver). *

ANNS, PHILIP HAROLD, pharmaceutical company executive; b. London, Eng., June 24, 1925; came to U.S., 1950; s. Harold Falkner and Dorothy Louise (Torckler) A.; m. Jacqueline Estelle Wyrtzen, Dec. 27, 1952 (div. 1975); 1 child, Jean Anns Lozyniak; m. Arlene Claire Eiserman, Apr. 1, 1978. BA in Econs., Christ Coll., Cambridge, Eng., 1948, MA in Econs., 1950. Asst. to pres. BASF Inc., N.Y.C., 1954-58; gen. mgr. Squibb Australia E.R. Squibb and Sons, Princeton, N.J., 1958-68; dir. animal health E.R. Squibb and Sons, New Brunswick, N.J.; gen. mgr. animal health Am. Hoechst, Kansas City, Mo., 1968-72; exec. v.p. Lakeside Labs., Milw., 1972-75; sr. v.p., gen. mgr. internat. ops. A.H. Robins Co., Inc., Richmond, Va., 1975-85; sr. v.p. corp. govt. relations A.H. Robins Co., Inc., Washington, 1986—; chmn. Va. Dist. Export Council. Served to lt. Brit. Royal Navy, 1943-46, ETO. Republican. Episcopalian. Lodge: Rotary. Home: 101 Brianwood Ct Quinton VA 23142 Office: A H Robins Co Inc 1101 Vermont NW Ste 405 Washington DC 20005

ANSARDI, PATRICIA ADAM, bank executive; b. New Orleans, Aug. 27, 1941; d. Charles Joseph and Thelma (Grob) Adam; m. Edward Ansardi Jr., Feb. 17, 1962 (div. 1981); 1 child, Christopher Edward. Student, Southwestern La. U., 1981; cert., Leonard's Sch., Dallas, 1984; diploma, La. State Sch. Banking, 1983. Sec. Freeport Sulphur Co., Port Sulphur, La., 1960-63; proof operator Delta Bank & Trust Co., Buras, La., 1967-69; teller Delta Bank & Trust Co., Port Sulphur, 1969-71, loan teller, 1971-73, sec., 1973-79; sec. Delta Bank & Trust Co., Belle Chasse, La., 1979-80, adminstrv. asst., 1980-81, asst. cashier, 1981-87, asst. v.p., 1988—; pvt. practice fin. planning, Belle Chasse, 1985—. Mem. Am. Inst. Banking, Am. Bankers Assn., La. Bankers Assn., Nat. Fin. Planners, Nat. Assn. Bank Women, Bank Adminstrs. Inst., Plaq Parish Fair Club. Republican. Roman Catholic. Office: Delta Bank & Trust Co 611 BC Hwy N Belle Chasse LA 70037

ANSARY, CYRUS A., lawyer, investor; b. Shoraz, Oram, Nov. 20, 1933; s. Adbul and Jamali (Mostmand) A.; m. Janet C. Hodges, Aug. 1, 1970; children: Douglas, Pary Ann, Jeffrey C., Bradley C. BS, Am. U., 1955; LLB, Columbia U., 1958. Bar: Md. 1959, D.C. 1960, Va. 1961. Practiced law Washington, 1959-72; sr. ptnr. firm Ansary, Kirkpatrick and Rosse, 1964-72; chmn. bd. Industry Reports, Inc., Washington, 1960-72; organizer, 1st chmn. bd., pres. Woodland Nat. Bank, Alexandria, Va., 1963-67; lectr. Sch. Bus. Adminstrn., Am. U., 1967-71; chmn. bd. Fin. Dynamics Corp., Washington, 1967-72, Campbell Music Co., Washington, 1968-72, John L. Lindstrom and Assocs., Inc., Washington, 1962-86; pres. IK Investment A.G., Zurich, Switzerland, 1974-79, Investment Services Internat. Co., Washington, 1973-88; chmn. MACO Bancorp Md., 1989—; chmn. bd. dirs. Elizabeth Broadcasting Co., John Hanson Savs. Bank, Beltsville, Md.; bd. dirs. 1st Am. Bank Md., Silver Springs, Washington Mut. Investors Fund, Potomac Asset Mgmt. Co., Washington, Accumetric, Inc., Elizabethtown, Ky., Caspian Enterprises, 1st Fed.Savs. Bank Ind., Merrillville; trustee Internat. Law Inst., 1976-86. Trustee Am. U., 1968—, chmn. bd., 1982—; trustee Internat. Law Inst., Wolf Trap Found., Vienna, Va., 1978-81, Krupp Found., Esen, 1977-79, Washington Opera Soc., 1982—; pres. Ansary Found., Washington, 1983—; dir. Growth Fund Washington, 1985—, Am. Funds Tax-Exempt Series I, Washington, 1986—. Served with USMCR, 1959-63. Mem. Washington Soc. Investment Analysts. Clubs: Nat. Press (Washington), Metropolitan (Washington), Congl. Country (Bethesda), Econ. Club Washington. Lodge: Rotary. Office: 1725 K St NW Washington DC 20005

ANSCHER, BERNARD, plastics manufacturing executive; b. Bklyn., June 9, 1922; s. Abraham and Esther (Draznin) A.; student Sch. Tech., CCNY, 1939-42; B in Mech. Engring., NYU, 1948, MBA, 1953, postgrad., 1953-65; m. Marcia Daniel, Mar. 7, 1942; children—William, Marlene, Joseph. Chief, metall. and fabrication devel. reactor materials br. AEC, N.Y.C., 1946-50; devel., mgr., gen. sales mgr. domestic sales, asst. to v.p. Loewy-Hydropress, Inc., N.Y.C., 1950-55; cons., mfrs.' rep. Mercury Engring. Co., N.Y.C., 1955-65; founder, pres. Nat. Molding Corp., Farmingdale, N.Y., 1965-87; pres. Custom Molds, Opa Locka, Fla., 1975—; founder, pres. Nat. Indsl. Robotic Controls, 1983—; founder, instr. mktg. program in community coll., N.Y.C., 1962-65; mem. industry adv. group Underwriters Labs., robotics standards com. Robot Inst. Mem. Met. Opera Guild, Am. Queens County committeeman Rep. Party, 1960-68. With AUS, 1943-46; PTO. Recipient Spl. award Manhattan Dist., 1946; cert. mfg. engr. Mem. N.Y. State Mktg. Educators (chmn. curriculum research com. 1964), Soc. Mfg. Engrs., Soc. Plastics Engrs., Am. Mgmt. Assn., Robotics Internat., U. Miami Pres.'s Club, NYU Alumni Assn. Reviewing editor Die Design Handbook, 1954-55; patentee; contbr. publs. in field. Office: Custom Molds 3970 NW 132d St Bldg I Opa Locka FL 33054

ANSELMINI, JEAN-PIERRE, communication corporation executive; b. Cours, Rhone, France, Sept. 26, 1940; s. Jean and Simonne (Desalles) A.; m. Anne-Marie Ollivier, Nov. 17, 1965; children: Jean-Christophe, Laure, Juliette. Student, Ecole Centrale des Arts et Manufactures de Paris, 1964; MSc, MIT, 1965. Scientist-ingénieur L'Air Liquide, Paris, 1967-70; head mktg. div., with corp. planning br., with corp. banking Credit Lyonnais, 1970-88; dep. chmn. Maxwell Communication Corp., London, 1988; bd. dirs. London and Bishopsgate Holdings, 1988—, London and Bishopsgate Internat., 1988—.

ANTHONY, BETTY ARLENE, medical center executive; b. Jacksonville, Fla., July 14, 1926; d. Glessner Earl and Florence Claudine (Smyth) Pratt; m. Yancey Lamar Anthony, II, Sept. 13, 1983. Student Jones Bus. Coll., Jacksonville, 1944, New Orleans Bapt. Theol. Sem., 1952, U. Fla., 1953-54, Tampa U., 1956. Promotion sec. Fla. Bapt. Conv., Jacksonville, 1945-53; sec. First Bapt. Ch., Tampa, 1955-59; sec. to asst. adminstr. Bapt. Med. Ctr., Jacksonville, 1960-65, sec. to exec. dir., 1966-80, corp. sec., 1980—; asst. sec., treas. Bapt. Health, Inc., Jacksonville, 1983—; sec. Bapt. Health Found., Inc., Jacksonville, 1983—; Bapt. Health Properties, Inc., Jacksonville, 1983—, Bapt. Med. Ctr. of Port St., Inc., Jacksonville, 1981—; sec. and treas. Bapt. Med. Ctr. of Ga., Inc., Jacksonville, 1980—; asst. sec. N.E. Fla. Breast Ctr., Inc., Jacksonville, 1984—; sec. Healthcare Mgmt. Services, Inc., Jacksonville, 1980—; asst. sec., treas. So. Bapt. Hosp. of Fla. Inc., Jacksonville, 1985—; sec.-treas. Southbank Advt. Inc., 1987; asst. sec. The Pavilion Developer Inc., 1987; asst. sec., treas. Lakewood Apothecary, Inc., 1988—; Dame of Grace Mil. and Hosp. Order St. Lazarus of Jerusalem, 1983. Mem. Fla. Hosp. Exec. Secs. Assn. (dir. 1973-76, pres. 1975-76, program chmn. 1974-75), Am. Soc. Corp. Secs. Avocations: jogging, creative writing, church activities, oil painting/drawing, gardening. Office: Baptist Health Inc 1300 Gulf Life Dr Ste 303 Jacksonville FL 32207

ANTHONY, EDWARD LOVELL, II, investments executive; b. Boston, Sept. 24, 1921; s. DeForest and Dorothy (Dodge) A.; m. Constance Foss, Oct. 2, 1954; children: Edward Lovell, Victoria Noble, Richard Geoffrey David. A.B., Harvard U., 1943, M.B.A., 1952; postgrad., Boston U., 1943. Asst. to pres. Daltry Opera Co., Middletown, Conn., 1938-40; asst. to headmaster Manter Hall Sch., Cambridge and Wianno, Mass., 1941; assoc. editor Pub. Affairs Press, Washington, 1945-46; asst. chief photog. intelligence tng. U.S. Navy, 1946-50; dir. publs SBA, 1952-62; editor Harvard Bus. Sch. Bull., Boston, 1962-80, Exec. Letter, Boston, 1964-70; prin. E.L. Anthony & Co., 1980—; treas., dir. Lomel Corp., 1979—. Editor: Management Aids for Small Business Annual, 5 vols., 1955-59, Equity Capital for Small Business, 1960. Vice chmn. Community Fund, Washington, 1960; trustee, pres. Dr. Franklin Perkins Sch., Lancaster, Mass., 1977-87; trustee Pine Manor Coll., Chestnut Hill, Mass., 1978-87. Served with U.S. Army, 1942-45. Mem. English Speaking Union, Friends of Boston Symphony Orch., Nat. Assn. Retarded Citizens, Internat. Council Small Bus., Harvard Bus. Sch. Assn. Boston, Navy League U.S. (Boston council; life), USO Council New England (life), Order of Lafayette. Episcopalian (vestryman, warden). Clubs: Country (Brookline, Mass.); University (Washington); Harvard (Boston); Harvard (N.Y.C.); Hundred of Mass. Home: 68 Woodcliff Rd Wellesley Hills MA 02181

ANTHONY, ROBERT HOLLAND, department store chain executive; b. Oklahoma City, May 15, 1948; s. Guy Mauldin and Christine (Holland) A.; m. Nancy Bargo, May 25, 1975; children: Elizabeth Bargo, Christine Holland, Suzanne Mauldin, Katherine Beeler. BS in Econs., U. Pa., 1970; MSc in Econs., London Sch. Econs., 1971; MA, Yale U., 1973; MPA, Harvard U., 1977. Dir. employee benefit plans C.R. Anthony Co., Oklahoma City, 1974-80, chmn. pension and profit sharing trust, 1976-85, asst. to pres., 1978-80, v.p., 1979-80, pres., chmn. exec. com., 1980-87, chmn. bd. dirs., 1986—, also bd. dirs.; commr. Okla. Corp. Commn. State of Okla., 1989—; staff economist U.S. Ho. of Reps. Com. on Interior and Insular Affairs, 1972; asst. to adminstr., staff economist Okla. Gov.'s Office of Community Affairs and Planning, 1973-74; econ. cons. U.S. Library of Congress, 1975; bd. dirs. Banks of Mid-Am., Liberty Nat. Bank, Oklahoma City; trustee Casady Sch., 1987—. Author: Energy Demand Studies: An Analysis and Appraisal, 1972. Councilman City of Oklahoma City, 1979-80, vice mayor, 1980; bd. dirs. Oklahoma County Council for Mentally Retarded Children, 1974-79, Cen. br., YMCA, Oklahoma City, 1977-79, East Side br. YMCA, 1981—, Leadership Oklahoma City, 1982—, Port Authority of Oklahoma City, 1987—, Okla. Hist. Soc., 1988—; mem. adminstrv. bd. 1st Meth. Ch., Edmond, Okla., 1976-77, Crown Heights Meth. Ch., Oklahoma City, 1978—; trustee Okla. Sci. and Arts Mus., 1978-81, Okla. City Zoo, 1979-80, Oklahoma City U., 1981—, Oklahoma City Econ. Devel. Fund, 1982—; commr. Oklahoma City Convs. and Tourism Commn., 1979-80; mem. Gov.'s Adv. Bd. on Productivity, 1982-84; mem. undergrad. exec. bd. Wharton Sch. U. Pa. Served as capt. U.S. Army, 1966-78. Mem. Oklahoma City C. of C. (bd. dirs. 1984—), Okla. State C. of C. (bd. dirs. 1987—), Beta Gamma Sigma. Clubs: Oklahoma City Men's Dinner, Econ. of Okla. (bd. dirs. 1981—). Home: 3605 N McKinley Oklahoma City OK 73118 Office: C R Anthony Co 701 N Broadway Oklahoma City OK 73102

ANTHONY, ROSALYN MECHELLE, accountant, bank examiner; b. West Point, Miss., Dec. 15, 1961; d. Elton Franklin and Ruby Lee (Caldwell) Deanes; m. Walker S. Anthony, May 31, 1986. BS, Jackson State U., 1983. CPA, Tenn. Nat. bank examiner, compt. currency Treasury Dept., Memphis, 1983—. V.p. Sunday sch. class Middle Bapt. Ch., Memphis, 1988—. Mem. Nat. Assn. Black Accts., Tenn. Soc. CPAs. Democrat. Home: 324 Dreger Rd Memphis TN 38109 Office: Compt Currency Treasury Dept 80 Monroe St Ste 500 Memphis TN 38103

ANTIA, KERSEY H., industrial and clinical psychologist, consultant; b. Surat, Gujarat, India, Jan. 7, 1936; came to U.S. 1965; s. Hormasji and Dinsi R. (Mistry) A.; m. Dilshad K. Khambalta, Dec. 18, 1966; children: Anahita, Mazda, Jimmy. AB with honors, U. Bombay, 1958; MS, Tata Inst. Social Scis., Bombay, 1960, N.C. State U., 1969; PhD, Ind. No. U., 1976. Lic. psychologist, Ill.; cert. social worker, Ill. Personnel mgr., welfare officer Tata Steel and Tata Chem., 1960-65; research asst. psychology dept. N.C. State U., 1966-67, U. N.C., 1967-69; project dir. Behavior Systems, Inc., Raleigh, N.C., 1969-70; dir. Midwest Inst. Human Resources, Tinley Park, Ill., 1972—. Lang. scholar U. Bombay, 1954-56. Mem. Chgo. Psychol. Assn., Ill. Psychol. Assn. (health service adv. bd.), N.Y. Acad. Sci., Nat. Forensic Ctr., Orland Park C. of C., Am. Jaycees. Zoroastrian. Lodge: Masons. Home: 8318 W 138th Pl Orland Park IL 60462 Office: Tinley Ctr 17730B S Oak Park Ave Tinley Park IL 60477

ANTILA, DAVID ERIC, software engineer, software developer; b. Pitts., May 10, 1960; s. Eric Matthew and Orla Diane (Ringman) A. AB, Kenyon Coll., 1982. Ptnr., gen. mgr. Pierce Shoppes Restaurant, Gambier, Ohio, 1981-82; food and beverage supr. Four Seasons Hotel, Ltd., Toronto, Ont., Can., 1982-83; v.p., chief oper. officer Three R Group Advt., Chgo., 1983-86; pres., chief exec. officer Specialty Bus. Software Solutions, Inc., Chgo., 1983—; pres., chief exec. officer, chmn. Profit Pathway, Inc., Chgo., 1988—; mng. dir. Sumerian Holdings Ltd., Chgo., R & D Unltd. Inc.; cons. NORCOM Internat., Inc., Chgo., Am. Computer Svcs., Chgo., 1987—. Developer application software. Vice chmn., sec. Latino Art Fest Com., Chgo., 1985-87; vice chmn., treas. Little Village Book Fair Com., Chgo., 1985-87; mem. Rep. Nat. Com., 1984; bd. dirs. Westside Bus.-Econ. Devel. Com. City Colls., Chgo., 1985. Mem. Chgo. Area Relational Database Soc. (treas., mem. exec. com. 1988—). Lutheran. Home: 6158 Knollway Dr Willowbrook IL 60514 Office: Profit Pathway Inc 208 S LaSalle St Chicago IL 60604

ANTILLA, SUSAN, journalist; b. New Rochelle, N.Y., May 18, 1954; d. Oscar E. Antilla and Gloria (Jennings) Claudet; m. James Harlan Burdsall, Sept. 26, 1981. BA, Manhattanville Coll., 1976; MA, NYU, 1981. Reporter Dun's Bus. Month, N.Y.C., 1978-81, asst. editor, 1981-82; contbg. editor Working Woman Mag., N.Y.C., 1980-86; stock market reporter, Washington editorial writer USA Today, N.Y.C., 1982-85, bur. mgr., money bur. chief, 1986—; fin. bur. chief Balt. Sun, N.Y.C., 1985-86; guest lectr. Marymount Manhattan Coll., 1984, 85, NYU, 1985; adj. prof. NYU, 1987-88. Regular contbr. Savvy mag., 1986—; contbr. articles to other mags. and profl. jours. Cons. Girls Club Am., N.Y.C., 1983. Mem. N.Y. Fin. Writers Assn., N.Y. Women in Communications. Office: USA Today 535 Madison Ave New York NY 10022

ANTOCI, MARIO, financial services company executive; b. 1934; married. With Southern Calif. Savs. & Loan Assn., Los Angeles, 1964-66; with Home Savs. & Loan Assn. (now Home Savs. Am.), Irwindale, Calif., 1962-64, 67—, exec. v.p. fin., now pres., chief operating officer; pres., chief operating officer H.F. Ahmanson and Co., until 1988; chmn., chief exec. officer Am. Savs. Bank S.A., 1988—. Office: Am Savs Bank 18401 Von Karman Ave Irvine CA 92715 other: H F Ahmanson & Co 3731 Wilshire Blvd Los Angeles CA 90010 *

ANTON, ALBERT JOSEPH, JR., investment analyst; b. N.Y.C., Jan. 6, 1936; s. Albert Joseph and Helen (Cichoski) A.; m. Sara Jane Lembcke, Sept. 6, 1958; children: Claire Elizabeth, Christopher Paul, Thomas Robert. AB, Columnbia U., 1957; MBA, U. Pa., 1958. Chartered fin. analyst. V.p. div. exec. Chase Manhattan Bank, N.Y.C., 1959-69; ptnr. Carl H. Pfozheimer, N.Y.C., 1970—; mem. investment com. Petroleum and Trading Corp., N.Y.C., 1970—, dir., 1978—; dir. Burnwood Corp., N.Y.C. Vice chmn. South Orange-Maplewood YMCA, 1973-77, chmn., 1977-78; bd. dirs. YMCA of the Oranges, Maplewood and West Essex, N.J., 1975—, treas. 1977-85, trustee, 1979-85, vice chmn. 1985—; trustee Village South Orange, 1971-73, also chmn. fin. com., 1971-73; mem. bd. sch. estimate South Orange-Maplewood, 1971-73; mem. bd. St. Benedict's Prep. Sch., Newark, 1978—, mem. exec. com. Lackawamma Coalition, 1987—. Served with USAF, 1961-62. Mem. Inst. Chartered Fin. Analysts, N.Y. Soc. Security Analysts, Ind. Petroleum Assn. Am., Nat. Assn. Petroleum Investment Analysts (dir. 1976-81, treas. 1976-78, sec. 1978-79, pres. 1979-80), Oil Analysts Group N.Y., Internat. Assn. Energy Economists, Soc. Mining Engrs., Delta Upsilon. Roman Catholic. Club: City Midday. Home: 332 Beech Spring Rd South Orange NJ 07079 Office: 70 Pine St New York NY 10270

ANTON, HARVEY, textile company executive; b. N.Y.C., Nov. 10, 1923; s. Abraham J. and Byrdie (Casin) A.; student Western State Coll. Colo., 1941, Savage Sch. Edn., 1941-42; B.S., N.Y. U., 1949; m. Betty L. Weintraub, Dec. 18, 1949; children—Bruce Norman, Lynne Beth. Pres., Anton Yarn Corp. (merged with Robison Textile Co. to form Robison-Anton Textile Co. 1959), N.J., 1949-50, pres., 1973—; v.p. Arrow Spinning, Susquehanna, Pa.; adv. bd. 1st Jersey Nat. Bank; v.p.Mid-Valley Textile; sec. Bloomsburg Dye; chmn. bd. Robison-Anton Textile Co. Trustee Erza Charitable Found.; pres. Anton Found. Served to 1st lt. AUS, 1943-46. Clubs: Masons, KP; Leonia Tennis; N.Y. Univ. Letter (N.Y.C.). Home: 41 Longview Dr Emerson NJ 07630 Office: Robison Anton Textile Co 175 Bergen Blvd Fairview NJ 07022

ANTON, MARK J., energy corporation executive; b. Newark, Feb. 12, 1926; s. Mark and Adele (Buecke) A.; m. Elizabeth Flower, Oct. 31, 1953. B.A., Bowdoin Coll., 1951. Various mgmt. positions Suburban Propane Gas Corp., Whippany, N.J., 1951-58, v.p., 1958-61, exec. v.p., 1961-63, pres., chief exec. officer, 1963-79, chmn., pres., chief exec. officer, 1979-83, chmn., pres., 1983-88; exec. v.p. Quantum Chem. Corp. (acquired Suburban Propane Gas Corp., 1983), Whippany, N.J., 1987-89; bd. dirs. Chem. Bank N.J., Morristown, Home Life Ins. Co., N.Y.C., Pittston Co., Greenwich, Conn. Lt. USN, 1944-46. Mem. Nat. Propane Gas Assn. (bd. dirs.), Nat. Assn. Corp. Dirs., 25-Yr. Club Petroleum Industry, Baltusrol Golf Club (Springfield, N.J.), Short Hills Club (N.J.), Mill Reef Club (Antiqua, W.I.), Bay Head Yacht Club (N.J.). Office: Suburban Propane Div Quantum Chem Corp 240 Rte 10 Whippany NJ 07981

ANTON, NICHOLAS GUY, consulting physicist, engineer; b. Trieste, Austria, Dec. 14, 1906; came to U.S., 1926, naturalized, 1943; s. Joseph and Ann (Mandle) A.; m. Bernice Irene Skripsky, June 19, 1932; children—Joan Carol Anton Pearlman, Linda Elaine Anton Kincaid, Nancy Helen Anton Bobrow. Grad., Tech. Inst. Leonardo da Vinci, 1926; student, Columbia U., 1926-28. Various engring. positions Duovac Radio Tube Corp., Bklyn., 1928-31; pres., chmn. bd. Electronic Labs., Inc., Bklyn., 1931-32; founder, gen partner in charge mfg., factory engring. Amperex Electronics Products, 1932-48; pres., dir. research, devel., engring. Anton Electronic Labs., Bklyn., 1948-61; chmn. bd. Anton Imco Corp., 1959-61; founder, pres., dir. research, devel. EON Corp., Bklyn., 1961-78; cons., lectr. N.Y.C., 1978-79; pres., chmn. Dosimeter Corp., 1963-75; lectr. L.I. U., 1969-78; indsl. tech. cons. AEC for UN Internat. Conf. on Peaceful Uses of Atomic Energy, Geneva, 1955; Mem. Pres.'s Conf. on Indsl. Safety, 1967—, Albert Gallatin Assos.-N.Y. U., 1951-54; Centennary com. Poly. Inst. Bklyn., 1963-64, U.S. Nat. UN Day Com., 1972-74, 76. Patentee in field; contbr. numerous articles, papers to profl. lit. Recipient cert. of appreciation Office of Pres., Wisdom award Wisdom Soc. Fellow IEEE, Am. Phys. Soc., N.Y. Acad. Scis., N.Y. Acad. Medicine (asso.), AAAS, Am. Philos. Soc.; mem. ASME, Am. Math. Soc., Am. Soc. for Nondestructive Testing, Electronic Industries Assn. (past chmn. various coms.), Am. Standard Assn. Jewish. Clubs: Unity, Engineers. Home: 2501 Antigua Terr A3 Coconut Creek FL 33066

ANTON, THOMAS, temporary help company executive; b. Grosse Pointe Park, Mich., Mar. 8, 1931; s. Pando and Stephanie (Andreeff) A.; m. Arlene Carol Zick, Sept. 1, 1951; children—Thomas L., Scott G. BBA, U. Mich., 1953, MBA, 1956. CPA La., Mich. Staff auditor White, Bower & Prevo, CPAs, Detroit, 1956-61; controller Gordon Baking Co., Detroit, 1961-64; controller Kelly Svcs., Inc., Troy, Mich., 1964-68, br. mgr., 1968-71, group dir., 1972-75, v.p., 1975-81, sr. v.p., 1981-84, exec. v.p., 1984—. Served with USN, 1952-53. Republican. Lutheran. Mem. Pine Lake Country Club, La Quinta Country Club. Office: Kelly Svcs Inc 999 W Big Beaver Rd Troy MI 48084

ANTONACCI, ANTHONY EUGENE, food corporation engineer; b. Sept. 21, 1949; s. Salvatore Natali and Odile Estella (Stanton) A.; m. Sherry Lee Kessler, Mar. 6, 1971; children—Don Warren, Lance Anthony. Student U.S. Air Force Acad., 1968-69; Assocs. in Sci., Forest Park Coll., St. Louis, 1971. Lic. stationary engr. Asst. supr. data processing ops. 1st Nat. Bank, St. Louis, 1969-71; engr. Installation and Service Engring. (Mech. and Nuclear) div. Gen. Electric Corp., St. Louis, 1971-76; engr. Anheuser-Busch Corp., St. Louis, 1976—; software author. Trustee, treas. Antonette Hills Trusteeship, Affton, Mo., 1976-80. Recipient Spl. Performance awards Gen. Electric Co., 1972, 74. Mem. Brewers and Maltsters Local 6 (del. 1982, 83), Nat. Aerospace Edn. Council, Apple Programmers and Developers Assn. Republican. Roman Catholic. Avocations: classic auto restoration, music (trumpet). Home: 8971 Antonette Hills Saint Louis MO 63123

ANTONIC, JAMES PAUL, international marketing consultant; b. Milw., Mar. 29, 1943; s. George Paul and Betti Ware (Littler) A.; m. Irene Robson, Dec. 26, 1970; 1 child, Glenn. BS in Metallurgy, U. Wis., 1964; MBA, Boston U., 1976. Owner JPA Supply and Warehouse Co., Milw., 1966-68; product mgr., market mgr. Delta Oil Products, Milw., 1968-74; v.p. internat. ops., Brussels, 1974—; pres. Internat. Market Devel. Group, Barrington, Ill., 1976—; exec. v.p. J & M, Ltd., Okazaki, Japan; lectr. Cast Metals Inst., Am. Mgmt. Assn., various colls. Served with U.S. Army, 1964-66. Mem. Licensing Execs. Soc., Internat. Trade Club Chgo. Episcopalian. Home: 655 Plum Tree Rd Barrington Hills IL 60010 Office: PO Box 751 Barrington IL 60011-0751 also: 76-4 Kanayama, Ikegane, Okazaki, Aichi 444-35, Japan

ANTONINI, JOSEPH E., apparel company executive; b. Morgantown, W.Va., July 13, 1941. Grad., W.Va. U. With K Mart Corp., Troy, Mich., 1964—, pres., dir., K Mart Apparel Corp., North Bergen, N.J., 1984-86, chief operating officer, 1986-87, pres., 1986—, chmn., chief exec. officer, 1987—, pres., 1988—; bd. dirs. Mich. Bell Telephone Co. Office: K-Mart Corp 3100 W Big Beaver Rd Troy MI 48084 also: K Mart Apparel Corp 7373 Westside Ave N North Bergen NJ 07047 *

ANTONINI, MARION HUGH, diversified manufacturing company executive; b. Clinton, Ind., June 7, 1930; s. Valentine and Josephine (Dal Sasso) A.; B.S. in Mech. Engring., U. Toledo, 1952; m. Penelope Sue Fromong, Dec. 20, 1971; children—Caryn Marie, John Marius. Gen. foreman on spl. assignment to works mgr. Willys Motors Inc., Toledo, 1952-54; mgr. assembly and mfg. services Willys Overland Export Corp., Toledo, 1955-59; asst. mng. dir. Willys Overseas S.A., Zug, Switzerland, 1959-61; adminstrv. dir. Kaiser Jeep Internat. Corp., Toledo, 1961-64, v.p., mng. dir., Oakland, Calif., 1964-66; group v.p. Eltra Corp., pres. Prestolite Internat. Co., N.Y.C., 1967-75; pres. Eltra Internat. Co., N.Y.C., 1973-75; corp. v.p. Xerox Corp., 1975—, pres. Xerox Latin Am. Group, 1975-78, group v.p. for Can.-Latin Am. and Middle East, 1978-80, group v.p. and pres. internat. ops., 1980-85, group v.p. ops. for U.S., Can., Europe, Middle East, Africa, Far East and Latin Am., 1982—; gen. ptnr., mng. dir. Kellner Di Leo & Co., 1986—; dir. Vulcan Materials Co., Engelhard Corp.; mng. dir. K.D. Equities, N.Y.Mem. U.S. Export Expansion Council, 1960, Commn. U.S.-Brazil Relations, 1980; chmn. bd. Codel Nat. Council, 1974. Bd. dirs. Friends of Philippines Found.; bd. dirs., mem. exec. com. Council of Ams.; vice-chmn. United Way campaign, New Canaan, New Canaan YMCA dr. Named Toledo's Outstanding Young Man, 1957, One of Ohio's Five Outstanding Young Men, 1957, One of America's Outstanding Young Men, 1966. Mem. Soc. Automotive Engrs., Woodward Engring. Soc. (pres.), U. Toledo Alumni Assn. (pres.), Blue Key, Kappa Sigma Kappa (pres.). Office: Kellner Di Leo & Co 40 Broad St New York NY 10004

ANTRIM, MINNIE FAYE, residential care facility administrator; b. Rochester, Tex., June 30, 1916; d. Charles C. Montandon and Myrtle Caldona (Brown) Montandon Taylor; m. Cecil C. Antrim, Jan. 1, 1938; children—Linda Faye Antrim Hathway, Cecil C. Student Central State Tchrs. Coll., Edmond, Okla., 1937. Asst. purchasing agt. Scenic Gen. Hosp., Modesto, Calif., 1955-68, Health Dept., Probation Dept., Stanislaus, Calif., 1955-68; owner, adminstr. Sierra Villa Retirement Home, Fresno, Calif., 1968-77, Mansion Home, Fresno, 1977—. Mem. Am. Coll. Health Care Adminstrs., Calif Bus. and Profl Club. Methodist. Club: Garden. Avocation: glee clubs. Home: 6070 E Townsend Fresno CA 93727

APATOFF, MICHAEL JOHN, finance executive; b. Harvey, Ill., June 12, 1955; s. William and Frances (Brown) A. BA, Reed Coll., 1980. Chief legis. asst. to U.S. Congressman Al Ullman Washington, 1978-80, spl. asst. to U.S. Congressman Tom Foley house majority whip, 1981-85; exec. v.p., chief oper. officer Chgo. Merc. Exch., 1986—. Bd. dirs. Mid-Am. chpt. ARC, 1987—, Chgo. Children's Choir, 1986—, Ill. Arts Alliance, Chgo., 1987—. Mem. Chgo. Coun. Fgn. Rels., Com. Fgn. Affairs, Mid-Am. Com., Chgo. Soc. Clubs, Met. Club, Execs. Club Chgo., Futures Industry Assn., Japan Am. Soc. Chgo. Democrat. Home: 405 N Wabash Apt #2911 Chicago IL 60611 Office: Chgo Merc Exch 30 S Wacker Dr Chicago IL 60606

APGAR, MAHLON, IV, real estate executive; b. Paterson, N.J., Jan. 14, 1941; s. Mahlon III and Dorothea (Tipper) A.; m. Anne Demarest Nelson, May 30, 1970; children: Frederick Clayton Demarest, Sarah Elisabeth Tipper, James Campbell Nelson. AB, Dartmouth Coll., 1962; postgrad., Oxford U., Eng., 1965; MBA, Harvard U., 1968. Assoc. McKinsey and Co., Inc., N.Y.C. and London, 1968-74; prin. London and Washington, 1974-80; pres. Heritage Devels., Ltd., Washington, 1980-85; pres., chief exec. officer Wellington Real Estate, Washington, 1985-87; mng. dir. Alex Brown Realty Services, Balt., 1987—; resch. assoc. Harvard Program on Tech. and Soc., 1968-69; vis. lectr. City and REgional Planning Harvard U., Cambridge, Mass., 1968-69; prin. advisor Sec. State Environment, London, 1972-74; urban advisor Minister Mcpl. and Rural Affairs, Saudi Arabia, 1974-78; devel. advisor Summa Corp. (Estate of Howard Hughes), Los Angeles, 1983-84; sr. v.p. Wellington Mgmt. Co./Thorndike, Doran, Paine & Lewis, Boston, 1985-87. Mem. F. St. Club. Author: Tackling Urban Problems, 1973; author and editor New Perspectives on Community Development, 1976; contbr. articles to profl. jours. Dir. World Affairs Council, Washington, 1982-87; mem. investment com. Magdalen Coll., Oxford, 1986—; mem. adv. council Am. Ditchley Found., N.Y.C., 1979—. Served to capt. U.S. Army, 1962-65, ETO. Recipient Arthur May award Am. Inst. Real Estate Appraisers, 1970. Fellow Royal Soc. Arts; mem. Am. Soc. Real Estate Counselors (cert.), Urban Land Inst. (vice chmn. comml. and retail council 1985—, chmn. internat. com. 1987—). Republican. Episcopalian. Clubs: Met. (Washington); Brooks's (London); Harvard (N.Y.C.); Pilgrims (N.Y.C.). Home: 7321 Brightside Rd Baltimore MD 21212

APOSTOLAKIS, JAMES JOHN, shipping company executive; b. N.Y.C., May 31, 1942; s. John George and Ann (Lampros) A. AB, U. Pa., 1962; LLB, Harvard U., 1965. Bar: N.Y. 1965. Atty. Dewey, Ballantine, Bushby, Palmer & Wood, N.Y.C., 1965-67; pres. Transoceanic Tank Ship Mgmt. Group, N.Y.C., 1968-72, Koplik Group Ltd., N.Y.C., 1983-84, A.G. Palmer & Co., Inc., N.Y.C., 1976—, Bradford Shipping, Inc., N.Y.C., 1973—, Bradmar Trading Corp., N.Y.C., 1975—; dir. Macmillan, Inc., Koplik Group, Ltd. Mem. Phi Beta Kappa. Clubs: Union, Metropolitan. Home: 150 E 69th St New York NY 10021 Office: Bradmar Trading Corp 505 Park Ave 3rd Fl New York NY 10022

APPEL, IRVING H(AROLD), optical manufacturing company executive; b. N.Y.C., Jan. 8, 1917; s. Ralph and Ada (Ader) A.; m. Gertrude Matlin, Jan. 16, 1938; children: Michaek E., Bonnie A., Kathy S. Grad. U.S. Army Air Force Aviation Cadet Sch., 1943. Inventory clk. Nat. Container Corp., Long Island City, N.Y., 1935-36; prodn. mgr. Kraft Corrugated Containers, Inc., Bayonne, N.J., 1936-42; gen. mgr. Republic Container Corp., Jersey City, 1945-49; gen. mgr. San Miguel Brewery Carton Plant, Manila, 1949-56; v.p. Cleghorn Folding Box Co., Lowell, Mass., 1957-64; pres. Lowell Corrugated Container Corp., 1959-64; exec. v.p. Prince Macaroni, Lowell, 1960-64, also bd. dirs.; pres., founder Welling Internat. Corp., Milford, Conn., 1964-79, chmn. bd. dirs., 1979-84, chmn. emeritus, 1984—; cons. Darier Asia Ltd. div. of Darier & Co, Geneva, 1988; bd. dirs. Conn. Bank & Trust Co., New Haven, Orange (Conn.) Nat. Bank. Trustee Conn. Visual Health Ctr. (chmn. 1984), Bridgeport; bd. dirs. Lake Copake Conservation Soc., Copake Lake, N.Y., pres. ARMDI, Golan. Served to 1st lt. USAAF, 1943-45, ETO, NATOUSA. Decorated D.F.C. Air medal with 5 oak leaf clusters; recipient cert. Appreciation Conn. Visual Health Ctr., Inc., 1975, Pres.'s award, 1977, Recognition award Flying Tigers, 1975, Recognition award Ambassador's Soc. Bd. Trustees, 1981, Recognition award State of Israel, 1980, Pub. Health award Conn. Visual Health Ctr., 1987, Mission of Mercy award Mogen David Adam, 1987; named Largest Individual Fund Raiser, Korea/Vietnam Meml., 1987. Mem. Aircraft Owners and Pilots Assn., 8th Air Force Hist. Soc., 2d Air Div. Assn., Air Force Assn. Home: 689 Royal Ln Orange CT 06477 Office: 65 Caswell St Milford CT 06460

APPEL, MICHAEL R(OBERT), corporation executive; b. N.Y.C., Aug. 13, 1938; s. Joseph and Frances (Soss) A.; m. Barbara Bleifer, Sept. 6, 1959; children: Alison, Jamie, Andrew. BS, Ohio State U., 1959, postgrad., 1959-60. CPA, N.Y. Sr. CPA Haskins and Sells, N.Y.C., 1960-65; controller Cartier Inc., N.Y.C., 1967-69; dir. money mgmt. Fischbach and Moore, Inc., N.Y.C., 1974-80; asst. treas. Fischbach Corp., N.Y.C., 1981-84, treas., 1984—, v.p., 1986—; cons. Mitsubishi Internat. Corp., N.Y.C., 1965-67. Mem. Nat. Assn. Corp. Treas., Fin. Execs. Inst., Soc. Internat. Treas., N.Y. State Soc. CPA's. Jewish. Office: Fischbach Corp 485 Lexington Ave New York NY 10017

APPLE, DAINA DRAVNIEKS, management analyst; b. Kuldiga, Latvia, USSR, July 6, 1944; came to U.S., 1951; d. Albins Dravnieks and Alina A. (Bergs) Zelmenis; divorced; 1 child, Almira Moronne; m. Martin A. Apple, Sept. 2, 1986. BS, U. Calif., Berkeley, 1977, MA, 1980. Economist U.S. Forest Service, Berkeley, 1976-84; mgmt. analyst officer U.S. Forest Service, San Francisco, 1984—. Author: Public Involvement In the Forest Service-Methodologies, 1977, Public Involvement-Selected Abstracts for Natural Resources, 1979, The Management of Policy and Direction in the Forest Service, 1982, An Analysis of the Forest Service Human Resource Management Program, 1984, Organization Design-Abstracts for Natural Resources Users, 1985; contbg. editor: Women in Natural Resources. Mem. Am. Forestry Assn., Assn. of Women in Sci., Sigma Xi, Phi Beta Kappa Assocs. (nat. sec. 1985—, pres. No. Calif. chpt. 1982-84, 1st v.p. 1981). Club: Commonwealth of Calif. (100 Leaders of Tomorrow). Home: PO Box 26155 San Francisco CA 94126 Office: US Forest Svc Engring Staff 630 Sansome St San Francisco CA 94111

APPLE, MARTIN ALLEN, high technology company executive; b. Duluth, Minn., Sept. 17, 1938; children: Deborah Dawn, Pamela Ruth, Nathan, Rebeccah Lynn. AB, ALA, U. Minn., 1959, MSci, 1962; PhD, U. Calif., 1968. Chmn. Multidisciplinary Drug Rsch. Group, U. Calif., San Francisco, 1974-78; pres., Internat. Plant Rsch. Inst., San Carlos, Calif., 1978-81; with EAN-Tech., Inc., Daly City, Calif., 1982-84, chmn. bd., 1983-84; with Adytum Internat., Mountain View, Calif., 1982—, chief exec. officer, 1983—; ptnr. ITR-France; adj. prof. computers in medicine U. Calif., San Francisco, 1982-84; bd. dirs. Holden-Day Pubs., 1987-88. Author: (with F. Myers) Review Medical Pharmacology, 1976; (with M. Fink) Immune RNA in Neoplasia, 1976; (with F. Becker et al) Cancer: A Comprehensive Treatise, 1977; (with M. Keenberg et al) Investing in Biotechnology, 1981; (with F. Ahmad et al) From Genes to Proteins: Horizons in Biotechnology, 1983; (with J. Kureczka) Status of Biotechnology, 1987; (with M. Baum) Business Advantage, 1987 (winner Excellence award Software Pubs. Assn. 1987); mem. editorial bd. Computers in Medicine. Recipient Citation East West Ctr. Bd. of Govs., 1988. Mem. Calif. Council Indsl. Innovation, 1982. Fellow Am. Coll. Clin. Pharmacology, Am. Inst. Chemists; mem. Assn. Venture Founders (bd. govs. 1982-83), East-West Center Assn. (bd. trustees 1982-88, vice chmn. 1983-85), Profl. Software Programmers Assn., Commonwealth Club of California, Leaders of Tomorrow (chmn. 1987-88), Phi Beta Kappa (mem. Phi Beta Kappa Assocs., Disting. Service award 1984, 85), Sigma Xi (bd. dirs., chmn. long-range strategic planning com. 1988—). Home: PO Box 391043 Mountain View CA 94039

APPLE, WILLIS WADE, banker; b. Winston-Salem, N.C., Nov. 24, 1951; s. James Woodard and Huldah F. (Booth) A.; m. Mary Florence Jones, Aug. 14, 1971; children: Mara Elizabeth, Lindsay Katharine. BS in Bus. Adminstrn., U. N.C., 1973, MBA, 1980, JD, 1980. Assoc. Holt & Watt, Reidsville, N.C., 1980-83; ptnr. Holt, Watt & Apple, Reidsville, N.C., 1983-85; solo practice 1985-87; v.p. corp. and strategic planning First Nat. Bank Reidsville, 1987—; dir. FNB Fin. Svcs. Corp. and Sub., First Nat. Bank Reidsville, 1985—. Pres. United Way of Reidsville, Inc., 1985; chmn. adminstrv. bd. Woodmont United Methodist Ch., 1983-85. 1st lt. USAF, 1973-76. Recipient Outstanding Young N. Carolinian award N.C. Jaycees, 1986, Disting. Svc. award Reidsville Jaycees, 1985. Mem. N.C. Bar Assn., ABA, N.C. Bankers Assn., Reidsville C. of C. (v.p. econ devel. 1987-88), Lions Club. Democrat. Methodist. Home: 614 Parkway Blvd Reidsville NC 27320 Office: First Nat Bank Reidsville 202 S Main St Reidsville NC 27320

APPLEBY, GEORGE ADDISON, aerospace company executive; b. Amarillo, Tex., Dec. 1, 1928; s. Harry Addison and Florence (Clemensen) A.; m. Mary Doreen Campbell, Sept. 3, 1955; children: Kerry Ann, John Addison, Thomas Scott. BA, Stanford U., 1951, MBA, 1956. Sales rep. Cowles Pub. Co., Spokane, Wash., 1956-60; v.p. sales Cougar Sawmills, Spokane, 1960-70; chmn. chief exec.officer Appleby Lumber Co., Spokane, 1970—, Precision Aerotech Inc., La Jolla, Calif., 1986—; dirs. Aero Tech., Wichita, Kans., Coast Aerotech Inc., Long Beach, Calif., chmn. bd. dirs. L&S Aerotech, Wichita, Micronics Internat., Brea, Calif. Lt. USN, 1951-54. Mem. Hayden Lake Country. Republican. Methodist. Home: 2470 Calle del Oro La Jolla CA 92037 Office: Precision Aerotech 7777 Fay Ave La Jolla CA 92037

APPLEMAN, BUFORD MARION, management consulting company executive; b. Fullerton, Calif., May 20, 1925; s. Milford Harold and Bessie Amelia (Olson) A.; A.A., Fullerton Jr. Coll., 1948; B.B.A., U. Tex., 1950; m. Virginia H. Maufrais, Apr. 28, 1946; children—Vicki, Susan. Indsl. engr., service mgr., dist. sales mgr. Tex. Foundries, Lufkin, 1950-62; mgr. asphalt sales Douglas Oil Co., Los Angeles, mgr. corp. planning, 1962-66; asst. to pres. Challenge-Cook Bros., Los Angeles, 1966-67; mgr. nat. account sales Taylor Machine Co., Louisville, Miss., 1967-68; v.p. leasing and maintenance contracts Crane Carrier Corp., Tulsa, 1968-74; prin. Appleman & Assos., Tulsa, 1974—; pres. Appleman Profit Systems, Inc., San Antonio, 1978—; cons. ready-mix concrete and concrete products industries; owner, ptnr. ready- mix truck and batch plants leasing cos. Served with USAAF, 1943-46; ETO. Mem. Nat. Ready Mixed Concrete Assn. (equipment maintenance com.), Tex. Aggregates and Concrete Assn. (chmn. allied div.). Republican. Methodist. Home and Office: 3427 Hunters Cir San Antonio TX 78230

APPLEWHITE, RALPH EUGENE, advertising executive; b. Detroit, Aug. 4, 1930; s. James Riley and Mary Aletha (Hall) A.; m. Dorothy Joan Wood, Dec. 28, 1957 (div. Dec. 1974); children: James Andrew, Erik Eugene. Student, Hanover Coll., 1948-49. Dir. circulation Courier Jour./Louisville Times, 1958-66; advt. sales rep. Advt. Specialties Co., Indpls., 1964-76; advt. sales mgr. Winters Assocs. Advt. Specialties Inc., Bloomington, Ind., 1976—. Rep. precinct committeeman, Jackson County, Ind., 1960-66; mem. alcohol beverage bd. Bartholomew County ABC Bd., 1982-85; res. dep. sheriff Jackson County Sheriff Dept., 1967-74, Bartholomew County Sheriff Dept., 1977-84. Lodge: Elks (officer). Office: Winters Assocs Advt Specialists 1589 Indianapolis Rd PO Box 864 Columbus IN 47202-0864

APSELOFF, DAVID A., finance executive; b. Hollywood, Fla., Nov. 26, 1958; s. Albert L. and Enid Sandra (Davis) A. BS in Acctg., U. Fla., 1980. CPA, Ga. Sr. acct. Arthur Andersen and Co., Atlanta, 1980-83; corp. contr. Flight Internat., Atlanta, 1983-86; v.p., chief fin. officer Cardiac Systems Inc., Atlanta, 1986—; with Senor Tech., Inc., 1988—; v.p., chief fin. officer Griffin (Ga.) Chrysler-Plymouth Dodge, 1987—, Fin. Con., Inc., 1987—. Loaned exec. Atlanta United Way, 1980, campaign asst., 1981-83. Mem. Am. Inst. CPA's, Ga. Soc. CPA's. Jewish. Home: 1602 Countryside Pl Smyrna GA 30080 Office: Cardiac Systems Inc 2009 Flightway Dr Atlanta GA 30341

ARAI, KIYOMARU, maritime and foreign commerce consultant; b. Toyko, June 2, 1918; s. Kiyoshi and Tokuko Arai; m. Sumiko Arai, Feb. 20, 1947 (dec. 1970); children: Chieko, Masao; m. Tomoko Arai, Feb. 2, 1972. BA, Tokyo U. Fgn. Affairs, 1941. Mgr., research commr. Nippon Yusen Kaisha, Ltd., Tokyo, 1941-74; dir., rep. Port San Diego, 1974-86; cons. in internat. transp. and commerce Yokohama, Japan, 1987—. Co-author: Containerization, 1973. Mem. World Trade Ctr. Club Japan. Home and Office: 971 Harajuku Totsuka, 245 Yokohama Japan

ARANGO, ANTHONY GLENN, chemical sales executive; b. Tampa, Fla., Nov. 14, 1945; s. Antonio Louis and Olga (Castro) A.; m. Loretta Dyer, Sept. 10, 1969 (div. 1975); 1 child, Anthony Glenn Jr.; m. Ruth Gordon, June 27, 1981. Student, Hillsboro Community Coll., 1970-74. Owner Diversified Maintenance Co., Tampa, 1970-77; mgr. sales Western-So. Life Ins. Co., Cin., 1978-80; pres. Ins. Planning Systems Inc., Tampa, 1980-84; chief exec. officer Dynex Industries Internat. Inc., Tampa, 1984—, also chmn.; cons. agt. Nat. Gen. Corp., Riyadh, Saudi Arabia, 1986—, Oriental Import Co. W.L.L., Safat, Kuwait, 1987—, Arab Domus Establishment Ministry, Riyadh, 1987—; cons. v.p. Inversiones Cusco corp., Lima, Peru, 1987—. Mem. Inter-Am. Security Orgn., Washington, 1987, Rep. Nat. Com., Washington, 1987. Served as petty officer 2d class USN, 1966-68. Mem. Am. Mgmt. Assn., Bldg. Owners Assn. Roman Catholic. Home: 4402 Beach Park Dr Tampa FL 33609 Office: Dynex Industries Internat PO Box 10858 Tampa FL 33679

ARASKOG, RAND VINCENT, telecommunications and electronics company executive; b. Fergus Falls, Minn., Oct. 30, 1931; s. Randolph Victor and Hilfred Mathilda A.; m. Jessie Marie Gustafson, July 29, 1956. B.S.M.E., U.S. Mil. Acad., 1953; postgrad., Harvard U., 1953-54. Spl. asst. to dir. Dept. Def., Washington, 1954-59; dir. mktg. aero. div. Honeywell, Inc., Mpls., 1960-66; former v.p. ITT Corp.; group exec. ITT Aerospace, Electronics, Components and Energy Group, Nutley, N.J., 1971-76; pres. ITT Corp., N.Y.C., 1979-85, chief exec. officer, 1979—, chmn. bd., chmn. exec. and policy coms., 1980—; dir. ITT Corp., Hartford Ins., Dayton-Hudson Corp., Shell Oil Corp., Dow Jones and Co.; chmn. Nat. Security Telecommunications Adv. Com., from 1983. Served with U.S. Army, 1954-56. Mem. Aerospace Industries Assn. (bd. govs.), Air Force Assn. (mem. exec. council). Episcopalian. Office: ITT Corp 320 Park Ave New York NY 10022

ARATANI, ROBERT, financial services executive; b. Scottsbluff, Nebr., Oct. 7, 1957; s. Andrew M. and Hedeiko (Uchida) A.; 1 child, Melanie M. BS, U. Wyo., 1979; MS, U. Nebr., 1981; postgrad., U. Minn., 1981-82. Assoc. Integrated Resources Mktg., Inc., Denver, 1983-84; sr. fin. analyst Empire Savs. and Loan Assn., Denver, 1984; v.p. Due Diligence, Inc., Littleton, Colo., 1985-86; dir. due diligence Multi-Fin. Corp., Englewood, Colo., 1987—; cons. Mgmt. Group, Inc., Denver, 1986—. Author newsletter, 1987; contbr. articles to profl. jours. Active Colo. chpt. Big Bros./Big Sisters, Denver, 1985—. Mem. Am. Econ. Assn., Am. Fin. Assn., Am. Agrl. Econ. Assn., Econometric Soc., Internat. Assn. Fin. Planners, Alpha Zeta, Gamma Sigma Delta. Home: 143 E Bluespruce Ct Highlands Ranch CO 80126 Office: Multi-Fin Corp 5350 S Roslyn St Ste 310 Englewood CO 80155

ARATO, PETER, marketing researcher; b. Budapest, Hungary, May 19, 1955; came to U.S., 1965; s. Steve and Friderika (Klein) A.; m. Harriet Su Tuchman, Mar. 5, 1983; 1 child, Lauren Melissa. BA, Queen's Coll., 1977; MBA, Baruch Coll., 1981. Mktg. research analyst J.B. Williams Co., N.Y.C., 1977-79; sr. mktg. research mgr. Lever Bros. Co., N.Y.C., 1981—. Mem. Am. Mktg. Assn. Home: 1781 Gregory Ave Merrick NY 11566 Office: Lever Bros Co 390 Park Ave New York NY 10022

ARBIB, JOHN A., construction company executive; b. Lawrence, N.Y., Sept. 18, 1924; s. Robert Simeon and Edna (Henry) A.; student Pa. State Coll., 1942-43, Ala. Poly. Inst., 1943, Columbia U., 1946-47; m. Leonore Grandlinger, June 5, 1949; children—John Paul, Peter Laurence, Diane Lynn. Partner, Robert S. Arbib & Co., N.Y.C., 1946-57; pres. Arbib Building Corp., Margate, Fla., 1958-62; pres. Custom Craft Homes of So. Fla., Inc., Boca Raton, 1962-65; v.p. VR Corp., Hallandale, Fla., 1965-68; v.p. Royal Palm Beach Colony Inc., Hallandale, 1968-72, St. Petersburg, Fla., 1971-72; v.p., gen. mgr. Pinebrook Bldg. Corp., Pembroke Pines, Fla., 1972-76; v.p. Pasadena Homes, Inc., gen. mgr. Pinebrook div., 1976-86; pres., chief exec. officer Multicon S.E., 1986—; gen. mgr. Pinebrook Bldg. Co., 1986—; pres. Home Owners Warranty Corp. of South Fla., 1974-76, v.p., 1977-81, dir., 1981—; dir. Home Owners Warranty Corp., Washington, 1974-80, mem. exec. com., 1979-80. Pres., Lakeville Estates, N.Y. Civic Assn., 1953-54; mem. Fla. Sec. Edn. Constrn. Industry Adv. Com., 1980-85; mem. Fla. Condominium Commn., 1972—; mem. Gov.'s Econ. Adv. Com., 1980-81. Bd. dirs. Govs. Philharmonic Orch. of Fla., Inc. (formerly Ft. Lauderdale Symphony) 1981—, v.p., mem. exec. com., 1983-86—; bd. dirs. Progress for Dade County, Fla., 1973—, Broward County Urban League, 1980-85; pres., bd. trustees Broward Philharmonic, 1988—; mem. Fla. Housing Fin. Agy., 1980—, vice chmn., 1980-82, chmn., 1983; mem. Broward County Bd. Rules and Appeals, 1975-81, mem. exec. com., 1979-81; trustee Fla. House, 1985—. Served with AUS, 1943-46, ETO. Named Builder of Month, Gen. Electric Corp., Oct. 1971. Mem. Builders Assn. S. Fla. (dir. 1966—, pres. 1973; Pres.'s award 1975, Builder of Year 1976), Fla. Home Builders Assn. (dir. 1969—, area v.p. 1973, sec. 1977, treas. 1978, pres. 1980, Fla. Builder of Yr. 1984), Nat. Assn. Home Builders (dir. 1970—, chmn. bus. mgmt. com. 1975-76, vice chmn. consumer affairs com. 1977, resolutions com. 1979-81, 85—, nat. v.p. 1981-82, planning com. 1982—, mortgage fin. com. 1982—, chmn. state and local housing fin. agys. com. 1983—, chmn. assn. planning com. 1985—, exec. com. 1985—, exec. com. Conf. Housing Agy. Chmn. and Commrs. 1983—, vice chmn. 1985), Nat. Inst. Bldg. Scis. (dir. tech. div.), Constrn. Council Fla. (pres. 1975, dir. 1974-82). Democrat. Unitarian (pres. Ft. Lauderdale ch. 1969, bd. dirs. 1965-70). Home: 2100 S Ocean Dr Unit 16BCD Fort Lauderdale FL 33316 Office: PO Box 8360 Pembroke Pines FL 33024

ARBON, GEORGENE KAY, banker; b. Denver, Apr. 27, 1949; d. Henry Peter and Mary Katherine (Begler) Hild; m. Ronald Erwin Derbin, June 10, 1967 (div. Sept. 1973); children: Rhonda Marie, Jeffrey Michael; m. James Reed Arbon, Mar. 10, 1974; 1 child, Jami Jean. Student, Met. State Coll., Denver, 1969-70. Sec. United Bank, Pueblo, Colo., 1972-73; asst. cashier 1st Nat. Bank Albuquerque, 1973-81; v.p. United N.Mex. Bank, Albuquerque, 1981—. Instr. ARC, Albuquerque, 1983—. Named Boss of Yr. Credit Women Internat., 1985. Mem. Albuquerque Fin. Instn. Security Officers Assn. (treas. 1984—), Internat. Assn. Credit Card Investigators (treas. 1985-86), Better Bus. Bur. (arbitrator Albuquerque br. 1984—). Democrat. Roman Catholic. Lodge: Civitan (lt. gov. Albuquerque 1985-86). Office: United New Mexico Bank 200 Lomas Blvd NW Albuquerque NM 87102

ARCHAMBAULT, JOHN KENEHAN, gas transmission company executive; b. Montreal, Que., Canada, Mar. 12, 1938; s. Bernard Archambault and Katherine (Kenehan) Archambault Choquette; m. Michele DuFour, Oct. 10, 1968; children—Patrick, Carolyn. BA, Princeton U., 1960; LLL, U. Montreal, 1966. Assoc. Pouliot, Mercure, LeBel, Montreal, 1966-73; gen. counsel TransCan. PipeLines, Toronto, Ont., 1973-75, v.p., gen. counsel, 1975-80, sr. v.p., 1983-88; exec. v.p. Trans Quebec & Maritimes, Montreal, 1980-83; pres., chief exec. officer Gt. Lakes Gas Transmission Co., Detroit, 1988—; bd. dirs. Internat. Pipeline Engring. Ltd., Toronto. Mem. Barreau de Quebec, U. Toronto Club, Grosse Pointe Hunt Club, Detroit Club, Renaissance Club, Detroit Athletic Club. Home: 204 Mainsail Ct Detroit MI 48207-5008 Office: Gt Lakes Gas Transmission Co 2100 Buhl Bldg Detroit MI 48226

ARCHAMBO, MICHAEL GERARD, advertising executive; b. Mpls., Nov. 21, 1957; s. John Francis and Carol Theresa (Wintheiser) A. Student, Goldenwest Coll. Draftsman with graphics dept. Borders and Assocs., Irvine, Calif., 1977-79; draftsman, engr. Rothert Engrs., Anaheim, Calif., 1979-82; account exec. Trader Mags., Irvine, 1984—. Mem. CAP, AFTRA. Republican. Office: Trader Mag 2621 Daimler Irvine CA 92700

ARCHER, ARTHUR ELLIOTT, chemicals, cleaning products company executive; b. Sisterville, W.Va., Nov. 16, 1943; m. Carol Arlene Bonar; children: Tera, Jennifer, Kara. BS in Chemistry, Marshall U., 1966. Analytical chemist Mobay Chems. Co., Pitts., 1966-70; gen. mgr. USS Chems., Pitts., 1970-80; mgr. strategic planning Mobil Chem. Co., Houston, 1980-83; v.p., gen. mgr. Church & Dwight Co. Inc., Princeton, N.J., 1983—; bd. dirs. Brotherton Chem. Co., Wakefield, Eng., Sales Y Oxidos, Monterrey, Mexico. Bd. dirs. Mercer Christian Acad., Trenton, N.J., 1983-86, Phila. Coll. of Bible, 1988—. Mem. Am. Mgmt. Assn., Chems. Mfrs. Assn. Republican. Baptist. Office: Church & Dwight Co Inc 469 N Harrison St Princeton NJ 08540-5297

ARCHER, CARL MARION, oil and gas company executive; b. Spearman, Tex., Dec. 16, 1920; s. Robert Barton and Gertrude Lucille (Sheets) A.; student U. Tex., Austin, 1937-39; m. Peggy Garrett, Aug. 22, 1939; children—Mary Frances, Carla Lee. Pres., Anchor Oil Co., Spearman, 1959—, Carl M. Archer Farms, Spearman, 1960—; gen. mgr. Speartex Grain Co., Spearman, 1967—, Speartex Oil & Gas Co., 1974—. Chmn. County Democratic Com., 1969—. Mem. Tex. Grain Dealers Assn., Tex. Grain and Feed Assn., Ind. Royalty Owners and Producers Assn., Nat. Grain Dealers Assn., Am. Petroleum Landmen Assn., Nat., Tex. Bankers Assns. Mem. Ch. of Christ. Clubs: Perryton, Borger Country, Amarillo. Home: PO Box 488 Spearman TX 79081 Office: 405 Collard St Spearman TX 79081

ARCHER, RICHARD EARL, product designer and alternative energy design consultant; b. Springfield, Ill., Aug. 24, 1945; s. Earl Wiley and Era Marie (Fentress) A.; m. Elizabeth Lou Lutz, Aug. 9, 1969; children—Jeremy Richard, William Earl. B.A. in Design, So. Ill. U., Carbondale, 1970; M.S., Gov.'s State U., 1979. Instr. design So. Ill. U., 1971-79, coordinator design program, 1979-80, asst. prof. comprehensive planning and design, 1980—; dir. Applied Alternatives. Mem. Nat. Alcohol Fuels Commn., 1980; chmn. Carbondale Energy Futures Task Force, 1980-81; mem. Ill. Legislature Alternative Energy Commn., 1981-83; mem. adv. panel U.S. Congl. Office Tech. Assessment, 1982; cons. creative problem solving U.S. Army War Coll. Editor: Ill. Solar Resource Adv. Council Grants Newsletter, 1979-81; contbr. articles to profl. jours.; originator Great Cardboard Boat Regatta. Recipient Outstanding Tchr. Year award Coll. Human Resources, So. Ill. U., 1979; U.S. Dept. Energy grantee, 1979-81; U.S. Dept. Labor grantee, 1978-79; Ill. Dept. Energy grantee, 1980-81; named Outstanding Tchr. of Yr., Sch. Art, 1985. Mem. Solar Lobby (dir. 1978-80). Home: RR 1 Box 667 DeSoto IL 62924 Office: So Ill U Design Program Bldg 0720 Carbondale IL 62901

ARCHIBALD, FRED JOHN, newspaper executive; b. Lincoln, Nebr., Sept. 10, 1922; s. Fred Irwin and Edna Esther (Olson) A. B.S., U.S. Mil. Acad., 1945. Commd. 2d lt. U.S. Army, 1945, advanced through grades to capt., 1951, served various assignments, U.S., Philippines, Japan, resigned, 1955; various exec. and managerial pub. relations positions in media and community relations Gen. Motors Corp., Detroit, Cleve., N.Y.C. and Washington, 1956-78; mng. editor Frederick News-Post, Md., 1978-85, assoc. pub., 1982-85; gen. mgr., editor News-Post News Service, Frederick, 1985-87, dir. industry relations, 1987—; lectr. journalism and pub. relations, various instns., 1947—; cattle breeder Armadale Farms, Frederick, 1964—. Gen. vice chmn., producer Frederick Arts Council Beaux Arts Ball, 1984-85. Decorated Army Commendation medal, Bronze Star medal. Mem. Airedale Terrier Club Am. (treas. 1959-61), Md. Polled Hereford Assn. (pres. 1979-81), Mil. Order Carabao, Am. Legion, Sigma Delta Chi, Sigma Alpha Epsilon. Clubs: Nat. Press, Army and Navy, Georgetown (Washington); Overseas Press (N.Y.C.). Democrat. Episcopalian. Avocations: theatrical producer, experimental gardening, art collecting, press and garden photography. Home: Armadale Farms PO Box 74 Frederick MD 21701 Office: Frederick News-Post PO Box 578 Frederick MD 21701

ARCHIBALD, NOLAN D., tools and household products company executive; b. Ogden, Utah, June 22, 1943; m. Margaret Hafen, June 8, 1967. AA, Dixie Coll.; BS, Weber State Coll.; MBA, Harvard U. Exec. v.p., gen. mgr. Sno Jet, Inc. div. Conroy, Inc., Burlington, Vt., 1970-77; sr. v.p., and pres. non-foods cos. Beatrice Foods, Chgo., 1977-85; chmn., pres., chief exec. officer The Black & Decker Corp., Towson, Md., 1985—; former All Am. basketball player. Named One of 10 Most Wanted Execs in U.S., Fortune Mag., Six Best Mgrs. in U.S., Bus. Week Mag. Office: Black & Decker Corp 701 E Joppa Rd Towson MD 21204

ARDIA, STEPHEN VINCENT, pump manufacturing company executive; b. Hackensack, N.J., Aug. 3, 1941; s. Vincent Henry and Anita Deborah A.; B.S., U.S. Merchant Marine Acad., 1963; M.B.A., Rutgers U., 1969; m. Virginia Ellis, July 11, 1964; children: David, Daniel, Deborah. Gen. mgr. Standard Pump Div., Worthington Pump Co., East Orange, N.J., 1976-79; v.p. internat. ops. Goulds Pumps Inc., Seneca Falls, N.Y., 1979-82, v.p. sales, 1982-84, pres., 1984-85, pres., chief exec. officer, 1985—; bd. dirs. Chase Lincoln Bank, Rochester, N.Y., Bus. Coun. N.Y. State. Bd. dirs. Women's Hall of Fame, Seneca Falls, N.Y., Pub. TV. Sta. WCNY, Cayuga Community Coll.; mem. adv. coun. Clarkson U. Sch. Mgmt.; pres. Hydraulic Inst. Mem. Skaneateles Country Club (bd. dirs.). Home: 3 W Lake St Skaneateles NY 13152 Office: Goulds Pumps Inc 240 Fall St Seneca Falls NY 13148

ARDINI, MARY-ANNE ELIZABETH, marketing executive; b. Boston, Feb. 24, 1955; d. Joseph Lawrence and Helen (McAnulty) A.; m. Steven J. Poleske. BA, Regis Coll., 1975, U. Mass., 1986. Field rsch. auditor Burke Mktg. Rsch., Cin., 1977-83; field dir. Abt Assocs., Inc., Cambridge, Mass., 1983—. Contbr. poetry pub. in various mags. counselor English as a second lang. program Washington Hill Community Assn., Roslindale, Mass., 1987-88. Mem. Mktg. Rsch. Assn. Democrat. Home: 818 Main St Melrose MA 02176 Office: 55 Wheeler St Cambridge MA 02130

AREHART, CATHERINE LEE, purchasing agent; b. Huntingburg, Ind., Dec. 31, 1954; d. Charles Henry and Dorothy Mae (Buechlein) Kelley; m. Daniel Lee Arehart, Mar. 27, 1982; 1 child, Christine Lee. Sec. Jasper (Ind.) Indsl. Supply Co., 1981-82; customer svc. rep. Touch of Class, Huntingburg, 1982-84; purchasing agt. Styline Industries, Huntington, 1984—. Coach softball N.E. Dubois, Ind., 1984. Democrat. Roman Catholic. Home: Rte 2 PO Box 3 Celestine IN 47521 Office: Styline Industries 431 4th St Huntingburg IN 47542

ARENA, PAUL RAYMOND, investment brokerage executive; b. Mpls., Apr. 26, 1958; s. Joseph James and Lorraine Irene (Gulden) A. Account exec. Alstead Strangis Dempsey Inc., Mpls., 1980-82, IRI Securities Corp., Mpls., 1982-83; v.p. Cralin Co., Palm Beach, Fla., 1983-85, Drexel Burnham Lambert Inc., Boca Raton, Fla., 1985-87; sr. v.p. Gulfstream Fin. Assn., Boca Raton, 1987—; pres. Arena Venture Group Inc., Boca Raton, 1986—. Bus. adviser North Palm Beach (Fla.) C. of C., 1984. Mem. Stockbrokers Soc., Gold Coast Investors Forum, Aircraft Owners and Pilots Assn. Republican. Roman Catholic. Home: 23120 L'ermitage Cir Boca Raton FL 33433 Office: GulfStream Fin Assn 2500 N Military Trail Ste 470 Boca Raton FL 33431

ARENTZ, ANDREW ALBERT, management consultant; b. Chgo., May 12, 1928; s. Andrew A. and Ruth J. (Gulbransen) A.; B.S.C.E., Ill. Inst. Tech., 1950; J.D., John Marshall Law Sch., 1960; m. Lillian Regina Ivanovsky, Sept. 1, 1950; children—Andrew Anton, Alethea Ruth, Paul David. Supr. ops. research AMF, Niles, Ill., 1959-62; assoc. dir. advanced transp. planning Gen. Am. Transp. Corp., Chgo., 1963-66, asst. to v.p. corp. planning, 1966-68; pres., chief exec. officer GARD, Inc., Niles, 1968-77; dir. planning and devel. GATX Corp., Chgo., 1977-83, spl. asst. to v.p. fin., 1983-84, dir. personnel research and benefits planning, 1984-86; pres. Arentz and Assocs., 1986—; Bd. dirs. Chgo. Bot. Garden, 1979-82, Luth. Sch. Theology, Chgo., 1972-78; mem. Synod Council, Met. Chgo. Synod, Evang. Luth. Ch. Am., 1987—; trustee Village of Riverwoods, 1969-73, 87—. Served with AUS, 1952-54. Home and Office: 333 Juneberry Rd Riverwoods IL 60015

ARGENTINE, PETER DOMINIC, financial analyst; b. Pitts., Feb. 22, 1948. BS in Math., U. Pitts., 1970; MBA, Duquesne U., 1972. Analyst Rockwell Internat., Pitts., 1972-76, mgr. exposure mgmt., 1976-78; mgr. banking H.J. Heinz Co., Pitts., 1978-80; treas. Carnation Internat., Los Angeles, 1980-85; v.p. fin., treas. Carnation Co., Los Angeles, 1985—. Avocations: golf, skiing. Office: Carnation Co 5054 Wilshire Blvd Los Angeles CA 90036

ARGIROPOULOS, JOHN GEORGE, construction company owner; b. Washington, Oct. 3, 1950; s. George Argiros and Mary Virginia (Tinsman) A.; m. Kathleen Susan O'Neill, July, 10, 1976. BA with distinction, U. Va., 1978. Project mgr. Peter Gordon Co., Capitol Heights, Md., 1978-82; owner Georgetown Roofing, Inc., Arlington, Va., 1982—. Served with U.S. Army, 1968-71, Vietnam. Club: Washington Golf and Country (Arlington).

ARGOBRIGHT, VICTOR WILLIAM, restaurant company executive; b. Blythe, Calif., July 2, 1948; s. Kenneth Earl and Doreen Elizabeth (Bird) A.; m. Kitty Irene Wood, Sept. 30, 1967; children: Victor William II, Derek, Jarrod, Rocky, Trenton. BS in Indsl. Mgmt., Ga. Inst. Tech., 1970; MBA, Ohio State U., 1986. Restaurant mgr. Bob Evans Farms Inc., Cin., 1971-72; dist. mgr. Bob Evans Farms Inc., Cin., Cleve., 1972-76; regional mgr. Bob Evans Farms Inc., Columbus, Ohio, 1976-80, v.p., dir. ops., 1980-88, sr. v.p., dir. ops., 1988—. Chmn. Canal Winchester (Ohio) Sch. Levy Com., 1980; pres. Canal Winchester Luth. Ch., 1985; vice chmn. Fairfield County Rep. Com.; advisor Va. Poly. Inst. Mem. Ohio Restaurant Assn. (vice chmn. polit. action com.). Home: 10620 Winchester St Canal Winchester OH 43110 Office: Bob Evans Farms Inc 3776 S High St Columbus OH 43207

ARICSON, LOUIS HOWARD, JR., investment analyst; b. N.Y.C., Jan. 20, 1951; s. Louis Howard Sr. and Clarice Gene (Peterson) A.; m. Deborah Sandy Schwartz, Jan. 10, 1982; children: Gillian, Jennifer, Brett. BS, Rensselaer Polytech. Inst., 1973; MBA, Wharton Coll., 1976. Budget analyst N.J. State Bur. Budget, Trenton, 1973-74; asst. adminstr. Med. Group, Memphis, 1974-75; cons. Ernst & Whinney, N.Y.C., 1977-79; mgr. AT&T, N.Y.C., 1979-81; sr. strategic planner Fed. Nat. Mortgage Assn., Washington, 1981-82; sr. fin. planner J.C. Penney, N.Y.C., 1982-83; pres. Aricson Enterprises, Roslyn, N.Y., 1983-87; investment analyst Fitch Investors Service, N.Y.C., 1987—; cons. Pechter-Fields, Bklyn., 1985-87. Fellow Fin. Analysts Fedn.; m. Inst. Chartered Fin. Analysts (cert. 1982), N.Y. Soc. Security Analysts, Omicron Delta Epsilon, Epsilon Delta Sigma. Office: Fitch Investors Svc 5 Hanover Sq New York NY 10004

ARIES, ROBERT S(ANCIER), chemical company executive, economist, consultant; b. Sofia, Bulgaria, July 21, 1919; came to U.S., 1939; s. Robert Emile and Sophie (Presente) A.; divorced; children: Vivian Aries Blount, Lynn O. BChemE, Poly. U., Bklyn., 1941, MChemE, 1943, PhD, 1947; MA in Econ., U. Minn., 1946; MSc, Yale U., 1948. Prin. Aries Internat., N.Y.C., 1945—, Aries, Paris, 1962-79; cons. Value Line, N.Y.C., 1953-56; adj. prof. U. Geneva, 1959-62; pres. DNA Econtech, N.Y.C., 1979—. Fellow AAAS; mem. Am. Econ. Assn., ASME, Metal Soc. of AIME, Inst. Food Technologists. Office: 49 E 41st St New York NY 10165

ARIKAWA, HIRO, industrial company executive; b. Tokyo, Nov. 27, 1926; s. Gorosaku and Ishi (Kawashima) A.; m. Mitsuko Kimura, Nov. 13, 1955; children: Kayoko, Kimiko. Grad., Japan Mil. Acad., 1945. Mgr. Tokiwa Trading Co., Tokyo, 1948-58; pres., chief exec. officer S.O.C. Corp. (formerly San-O Indsl. Co., Ltd.), Tokyo, 1958—, Nagano (Japan) S.O.C. Corp., 1967—, San-O Indsl. Corp., N.Y.C., 1970—, Brasan-O Eletronica Ltda., Sao Paulo, Brazil, 1973—; mem. indsl. adv. conf. Underwriters Labs, Inc., Chgo., 1973—; mem. Patent Commn.for Small to Medium Sized Enterprises, Japan Inst. Invention and Innovation, Tokyo, 1986—; dir. Japan Inst. Invention and Innovation, Tokyo, 1988—. Co-author: Electrical Fuses, 1987; patentee elec. fuse, other numerous patents in Japan and U.S. Trustee Den-En-Chofu Futaba Sch., Tokyo, 1986—. Served with Japanese Army, 1944-45. Recipient Dark Blue Ribbon Prime Minister's Office, 1982-87, Encouragement prize Chmn. Patent Attys. Assn., 1985, Dir. Gen. Japanese Patent Office, 1986. Mem. Rotary. Office: SOC Corp 43 Mori Bldg, 3-13-16 Mita, Minato-ku, Tokyo 108, Japan

ARIOLA, WAYNE PHILLIP, carpet company executive; b. Syracuse, N.Y., Oct. 17, 1934; s. Phillip F. and Lillian (Signor) A.; m. Mary J. Basile, Apr. 23, 1963; children: Wayne Jr., Chris, Nicole, Danielle. AB, Syracuse U., 1957. Gen. mgr. Callaway Mills, LaGrange, Ga., 1962-66; v.p. World Carpet Mill, L.A., 1966-76, Venture Industries, L.A., 1976-78, Columbus Mills, L.A., 1978-80; pres. E.T.C. Mills, Tustin, Calif., 1980-82, A&S Industries, Commerce, Calif., 1982—. Bd. dirs. Pacific Palisades Community Adv. Com., L.A., 1969, Pacific View Estates, Pacific Palisides, Calif., 1968-70, Rep. Roundtable. Lt. U.S. Army, 1958-60. Home: 350 Surfview Dr Pacific Palisades CA 90272

ARISON, MICKY, cruise line company executive; b. Tel Aviv, June 29, 1949. Student, U. Miami. Pres., chief exec. officer Carnival Cruise Lines Inc. Office: Carnival Cruise Lines Inc 5225 NW 87th Ave Miami FL 33178 *

ARISON, TED, cruise lines company executive, bank executive, real estate developer; b. Tel Aviv, Feb. 24, 1924; came to U.S., 1952; s. Meir and Vera (Avrutin) Arisohn; m. Mina Wassermam, Apr. 1948 (div.); children: Mickey Michael, Sharon Arison Sueiras; m. Marilyn B. Hersh Lin, Aug. 1968; 1 son, Michael A. Student, Am. U. Beirut, 1940-42. Mgr. M.Dizengoff & Co., Tel Aviv, 1946-48, 49-51; owner, chmn., pres. Tran-Air Co., N.Y.C., 1959-66, Arison Shipping Co., Miami, Fla., 1966-71, Hamilton Holding Co., Miami, Fla., 1979—, Carnival Cruise Lines, Miami, Fla., 1972—; trustee Nat. Found. Advancement in Arts, Miami, Fla., 1981—. Founder Soc. Univ. Founders U. Miami, Fla., 1981—; founder Albert Einstein Coll. Medicine, N.Y.C., 1983—, Mt. Sinai Med Ctr., Miami Beach, Fla., 1983, Tel Aviv U., 1983; mem. Republican Eagles, Washington, 1983—. Served to col. Israeli Army, 1948-49. Recipient Disting. Achievement award Albert Einstein Coll. Medicine, 1983. Republican. Jewish. Office: Carnival Cruise Lines Inc 5225 NW 87th Ave Miami FL 33178 *

ARKIN, ROBERT DAVID, lawyer; b. Washington, Feb. 15, 1954; s. William Howard and Zenda Lillian (Lieberman) A.; m. Rise Morgenstern, Dec. 29, 1974; children: Chelsea Morgenstern-Arkin, Nora Morgenstern-Arkin. BA, U. Pa., 1976, MA, 1976; JD, U. Va., 1979. Bar: Minn. 1980, Ga. 1987. Law clk. to chief justice Supreme Ct. Minn., St. Paul, 1979-80; assoc. Leonard, Street and Deinard, Mpls., 1980-84, ptnr., 1985-86; spl. asst. atty. gen. State of Minn., St. Paul, 1981; of counsel Trotter, Smith & Jacobs, Atlanta, 1986-89; ptnr. Minkin & Snyder, Atlanta, 1989—; mem. Tech. Rev. Com. Seed Money Venture Capital Product Loan Program, Minn. Office of Software Tech. Devel., St. Paul, 1985-86; vice chmn. Minn. Software Tech. Commn. (gubernatorial appointee), St. Paul, 1985-86. Exec. editor: Va. Jour. Internat. Law, Charlottesville, 1978-79; contbr. articles to profl. jours. Participant Leadership Mpls. of Greater Mpls. C. of C., 1984-85; mem. steering com. Young Leadership Devel., Mpls. Fedn. for Jewish Service, 1982-85; bd. dirs., mem. exec. com. Community Housing and Service Corp., Mpls., 1981-85. Mem. ABA (entertainment law, franchise law, computer law, bus. law and internat. sect.), Minn. Bar Assn. (chmn. internat. contracts com. 1985-86), Ga. Bar Assn. (computer, corp., internat., and entertainment law sects.) Atlanta Bar Assn., Computer Law Assn., Minn. Software Assn. (bd. dirs. 1986), Image Film and Video Assn. (bd. dirs. 1988—), Pi Gamma Mu. Democrat. Jewish. Home: 20 Battle Ridge Dr Atlanta GA 30342 Office: Minkin & Snyder One Buckhead Pla 3060 Peachtree Rd Ste 1100 Atlanta GA 30305

ARKLEY, ALFRED SAMUEL, management professor, management trainer and consultant; b. Spokane, Wash., Jan. 6, 1937; s. Stanley T. and Rose E. (Adatto) A.; m. Harriet Harvey, Nov. 10, 1965; children: Andy, Todd, Jed. AB, Harvard U., 1959; MA, Columbia U., N.Y.C., 1964, Mich. State U., 1968; PhD, Mich. State U., 1972. History tchr. U.S. Peace Corps, Sierra Leone, West Africa, 1961-63; social studies tchr. Lake Washinton Sch. Dist., Kirkland, Wash., 1964-66; asst. prof. polit. sci. Western Wash. U., Bellingham, 1970-75; pub. admin. fellow FAA, Washington, 1975-77; assoc. prof. mgmt. Sangamon St. U., Springfield, Ill., 1977-87; prof. mgmt. Sangamon St. U., 1987—; cons. Fed. Exec. Inst., Charlottesville, Va., 1985—. Recipient of Scholarship Harvard U., 1955-59, Pub. Adminstrn. Fellow Nat. Assn. Schs. of Pub. Adminstrn., Washington, 1975-77. Mem. Acad. Mgmt., Am. Soc. Pub. Adminstrn., Am. Polit. Sci. Assn. Home: 201 Wildrose Ln Rochester IL 62563 Office: Sangamon St U Mgmt Program Springfield IL 62794-9243

ARLEDGE, ROONE, television executive; b. Forest Hills, N.Y., July 8, 1931; s. Roone and Gertrude (Stritmater) A.; m. Joan Heise, Dec. 27, 1953 (div. 1971); children: Elizabeth Ann, Susan Lee, Patricia Lu, Roone Pinckney. BBA, Columbia Coll., 1952. With Dumont TV, 1952-53; producer-dir. children's and pub. affairs programming NBC, 1955-60; producer network sports ABC-TV, 1960-61, v.p. charge sports, 1963-68; pres. ABC News, 1968-85, ABC Sports, Inc., 1977-85; group pres. ABC News and Sports, 1985—; exec. producer all ABC sports programs, including 1964, 1968, 1972 Olympic games; created the Wide World of Sports program, 1961; producer entertainment spls. including Frank Sinatra, The Main Event at Madison Sq. Garden. (Recipient Emmy award 1958, 66, 67, 68, 69, 70, 71, 72, 73, 74, TV Guide award 1964, Cannes Film Festival Grand prize 1965, 66). Mem. Pres.'s Council on Phys. Fitness, also chmn. sports com. Served with AUS, 1953-54. George Foster Peabody awards internat. understanding (3); Nat. Headlines spl. citation, 1968; Saturday Rev. award; Distinguished Service award N.Y. chpt. Broadcast Pioneers, 1968; Kennedy Family award, 1972; award N.Y. chpt. Nat. Football Found. and; Hall of Fame, 1972; named Man of Yr. Nat. Assn. TV Program Execs.; named Man of Yr. Phila. Advt. and Sales Club; named Man of Yr. Football News; named Man of Yr. Ohio State U.; named Man of Yr. Gallagher Report. Office: ABC 1330 Ave of the Americas New York NY 10019 *

ARLEIN, DAVID L., investment banker; b. Newark, Nov. 13, 1938; s. Herman and Betty (Silverman) A.; m. Carol Phillipson, May 20, 1962 (div. 1985); m. Gail Haberman, Apr. 28, 1985; children: Wes J., Wendy J. BS, Bowling Green State U., 1960. Pres., chief fin. officer The Fin. Store, Denville, N.J., 1961—; bd. dirs. Am. Assurance Life, Deerfield Beach, Fla., 1987—. Author: Christmas Letters, 1985. Bd. mem. St. Barnabas Med. Ctr., Livingston, N.J., 1986. Mem. Internat. Assn. Fin. Planners (v.p. 1983), Registered Investment (pres. 1980). Republican. Office: The Fin Store 75 Bloomfield Ave Ste 12 Denville NJ 07834

ARLOW, ARNOLD JACK, advertising agency executive; b. Bklyn., Sept. 29, 1933; s. Louis and Sylvia (Spitzberg) A.; m. Phyllis Banschick, Apr. 20, 1958; children: Susan, Noah. B.F.A., 1978. Certificate in Art, Cooper Union, 1954. Art dir. N.Y. Times, 1958-61, Altman Stoller Advt., N.Y.C., 1961-65, Daniel & Charles Advt., N.Y.C., 1965, McCaffrey McCall Advt., N.Y.C., 1965-66; partner, creative dir. Martin Landey, Arlow Advt., N.Y.C., 1966-80; exec. v.p., creative dir. Geers Gross Advt., 1980-83; cons. communications industry 1983-84.; exec. v.p., creative dir. TBWA Advt., 1984—; tchr. design Wagner Coll., Staten Island, 1964-69. Alumni trustee Cooper Union, 1982-85. Served with USAF Res., 1961-66. Fulbright-Hays grantee Paris, 1954-55. Mem. N.Y. Art Dirs Club (bd. dirs., treas.), N.Y. One Club, Am. Inst. Graphic Arts. Democrat. Jewish. Home: 24 E 11th St New York NY 10003

ARMACOST, SAMUEL HENRY, bank executive; b. Newport News, Va., Mar. 29, 1939; s. George Henry and Verda Gae (Hayden) A.; m. Mary Jane Levan, June 16, 1962; children: Susan Lovell, Mary Elizabeth. BA, Denison U., 1961; MBA, Stanford U., 1964. With Bank of Am. NT & SA, San Francisco, 1961-81, v.p. mgr. London br., 1972-74, sr. v.p., mgr. San Francisco, 1975-77; exec. v.p. Europe, Middle East and Africa div. Bank of Am. NT & SA, London, 1977-79; exec. v.p., cashier Bank of Am. NT & SA, San Francisco, 1979-81; pres., chief exec. officer Bank of Am. and Bank Am. Corp., San Francisco, 1981-86; chmn., chief exec. officer Bank of Am., San Francisco, 1986-87; mng. ptnr. Merrill Lynch and Co., San Francisco, from 1987; now mng. dir. Merrill Lynch Capital Markets, San Francisco, 1988—; chmn. Bank Am. Internat. Ltd., London, Banco Comercial para America, Madrid; dir. Banco Intercontinental Espanol, Madrid, Bank Am. Internat. S.A., Luxembourg, Bank Am. N.Y., Fin. Group Kuwait, Banca d'America d'Italia, Milan, Societe Financiere puor le Pays d'Outre Mer, Geneva. Mem. Bankers Assn. for Fgn. Trade (dir.). Republican. Presbyterian. Clubs: Bohemian, Pacific Union, San Francisco Golf; Augusta (Ga.) Nat. Golf. Office: Merrill Lynch Capital Markets 101 California St Ste 1420 San Francisco CA 94111 *

ARMAGOST, ELSA GAFVERT, computer industry communications consultant; b. Duluth, Minn., Jan. 26, 1917; d. Axel Justus and Martina Emelia (Magnuson) Gafvert; m. Byron William Armagost, Dec. 8, 1945; children: David Byron, Laura Martina. Grad. with honors, Duluth Jr. Coll., 1936; BJ, U. Minn., 1938, postgrad. in pub. relations, bus. mgmt. and computer tech., 1965-81; PhD in Computer Communication Cons. Sci. (hon.), Internat. U. Found. Freelance editor, Duluth, 1939-42; procedure editor and analyst U.S. Steel, Duluth, 1942-45; fashion advt. staff Dayton Co., Mpls., 1945-48; systems applications and documentation mgr. Control Data Corp., Mpls., 1969-74, promotion specialist, mktg. editor, 1974-76, corp. staff coordinator info. on edn., 1976-78; instr. communications, publ. specialist, 1978-79, communication cons. peripheral products group, 1979-83; industry communications cons., 1983—; mem. steering com. U.S. Senatorial Bus. Adv. Bd., 1962-68; mem. U.S. Congrl. Adv. Bd., 1958-62; mem. adv. bd. North Cen. Deming Mgmt. Forum. V.p. Sewickley (Pa.) Valley Hosp. Aux., Sewickley Valley Mental Health Council; mem. Internat. Bible Study Fellowship; dir. publicity Sacred Arts Expo, World Affairs Council radio program, Pitts., 1962-68. Recipient Medal of Merit Rep. Presdl. Task Force. Mem. AAUW (1st v.p. Caracas, Venezuela), Women in Communication (dir. job mart), Am. Security Council (mem. adv. bd.), Internat. Platform Assn., Friends of Mpls. Inst. Art., Walker Art Inst., LWV (bd. dirs. Pitts. chpt.), Minn. Alumni Assn. (life), Am. Swedish Inst., Marsh Pk. Condominium Assn. (bd. mem.), Pi Epsilon (co-chmn. regional chpt., leadership award 1988), Toastmasters (Communications award 1984). Home and Office: 9500 Collegeview Rd Bloomington MN 55437

ARMBRUSTER, PAUL FREDERICK, credit union executive; b. Marion, Ohio, May 27, 1933; s. Harold E. Sr. and Pearl L. (Howman) A.; m. Barbara Seillman, May 10, 1952 (div. 1955); 1 child, Paula M.; m. Ruhann Ridge, May 26, 1967; children: Lynn Ann, Matthew, Mark Rogge. Cert., Internat. Acctg. Sch., Chgo., 1955, Phoenix Coll., 1983. Computer operator Cooper Tire and Rubber Co., Findley, Ohio, 1954-55; gen. mgr. Delaney Mobile Home Sales, Findley, Ohio, 1955-68, Christoff Estate Mobile Home Sales, Perrysburg, Ohio, 1969-70; mgr. Findlay Whirlpool Employee Fed. Credit Union, 1970-71; br. mgr. Clyde, 1971-76; owner, operator Mr. Big's Steak and Hoagie Shop, Mesa, Ariz., 1977-82; asst. mgr. SHS Employee Fed. Credit Union, Phoenix, 1980-82, pres., chief exec. officer, 1982—. Dir. pub. rels. Findlay Youth Baseball, 1967-76. Mem. Phoenix C. of C., Credit Union Execs. Soc., Ariz. Credit Union League, Credit Union Nat. Assn. Republican. Roman Catholic. Office: SHS Employee Fed Credit Union 1130 E McDowell Rd Phoenix AZ 85006

ARMOLD, JUDITH ANN, lawyer; b. Balt., Dec. 22, 1945; d. James Joseph and Mildred Louise (Swecker) A. BA, Western Md. Coll., 1967; JD, U. Md., 1971. Bar: Md. 1972, U.S. Dist. Ct. Md. 1972, U.S. Supreme Ct. 1980, U.S. Ct. Appeals (4th cir.) 1984. Tchr. French Balt. Pub. Schs., 1967-68; assoc. Venable, Baetjer and Howard, Balt., 1971-76, 89—; asst. atty. gen. Md. State Hwy. Adminstrn., Balt., 1976-77; asst. atty. gen., gen. counsel Md. Dept. State Planning, Balt., 1977-87; assoc. Cook Howard Downes & Tracy, Balt., 1987-89; trustee Md. Inst. for Continuing Profl. Edn. of Lawyers, Balt., 1979—, sec., 1986—; mem. inquiry com. Md. Atty. Grievance Commn., Annapolis, 1981-86, rev. bd., 1986-89; mem. steering com. Md. Land Use Round Table, 1986—; trustee Bar Assn. Ins. Trust, Balt., 1985-89, v.p., 1986-89—. Editor (notes and comments) Md. Law Rev., 1970-71. Mem. VISTA, 1967; bd. dirs. Doncaster Village Condominium Assn., Balt., 1977-79, Balt. Comml. Real Estate Women, 1989—. Mem. ABA, Am. Judicature Soc., Women's Bar Assn. of Md. (treas. 1974-78, sec. 1978-79), Md. Bar Assn. (state and local govt. law sect. council 1983—), Bar Assn. Baltimore County, Bar Assn. of Balt. City (exec. council 1979-80, young lawyers sect. council 1975-76, 78-80). Democrat. Presbyterian. Home: 1428 John St Baltimore MD 21217 Office: Venable Baetjer and Howard 210 Allegheny Ave PO Box 5517 Towson MD 21285-5517

ARMOUR, JAMES AUTHOR, military vehicle manufacturing company executive; b. Knoxville, Tenn., 1943. BS, Wayne U.; MBA, U. Detroit. Pres. AM Gen Corp., South Bend, Ind. Office: AM Gen Corp 701 W Chippewa Ave South Bend IN 46680-2600

ARMSTRONG, ALEXANDRA, financial advisor; b. Washington, Sept. 26, 1939; d. Rhoda Elizabeth (Forbes) Armstrong; m. Robert B. Phillips III, Aug. 1966 (div. Mar. 1971). BA in History, Newton (Mass.) Coll. Sacred Heart, 1960. Cert. fin. planner. Exec. sec. Ferris & Co., Washington, 1961-66, registered rep., 1966-77; sr. v.p. Julia Walsh & Sons, Washington, 1977-83; pres. Alexandra Armstrong Advisors Inc., Washington, 1983—. Contbr. articles to Ms. mag., profl. jours. Mem. Washington Jr. League, 1961—; vice chmn. Friends of Kennedy Ctr., Washington, 1987—; asst. treas. Nat. Capital coun. Boy Scouts Am., Washington, 1987, v.p., 1988—; mem. bd. visitors Georgetown U. Sch. Bus., 1988—; bd. dirs. Cultural Addliance Greater Washington. Named Bus. Woman of Yr., Washington Bus. and Profl. Women's Club, 1978; recipient award of excellence for commerce Boston Coll. Alumni Assn., 1985. Mem. Internat. Assn. for Fin. Planning (bd. dirs. 1980-87, chmn. emeritus, pres. 1986-87), Inst. Cert. Fin. Planners (bd. dirs. 1979-80), Nat. Assn. Securities Dealers (bus. conduct com. dist. 10 1986-89), Nat. Assn. Women Bus. Owners (pres. Capital area chpt. 1980-81), Nat. Women's Forum Bd., Tax Mgmt. and Fin. Planning Bd. (mem. adv. bd. 1987—). Republican. Roman Catholic. Home: 700 New Hampshire Ave NW Apt 1207 Washington DC 20037 Office: 1140 Connecticut Ave NW Ste 1100 Washington DC 20036

ARMSTRONG, ANNE LEGENDRE (MRS. TOBIN ARMSTRONG), former ambassador, corporate director, educator; b. New Orleans, Dec. 27, 1927; d. Armant and Olive (Martindale) Legendre; m. Tobin Armstrong, Apr. 12, 1950; children: John Barclay, Katharine A. Idsal, Sarita A. Hixon, Tobin and James L. (twins). Grad., Vassar Coll., 1949. Co-chmn. Rep. Nat. Com., 1971-73; del. Rep. Nat. Conv., 1964-84; counsellor to U.S. Pres., 1973-74; U.S. ambassador Gt. Britain, No. Ireland, 1976-77; chmn. adv. bd. Ctr. for Strategic and Internat. Studies (formerly affiliated with Georgetown U.), 1981-87, chmn. bd. trustees, 1987—; chmn. Pres.'s Fgn. Intelligence Adv. Bd., 1981—; commn. on Integrated Long Term Strategy, 1987; mem. Nat. Commn. Pub. Svc., 1988; pres. Nat. Thanksgiving Commn., 1986—; bd. dirs. Gen. Motors Corp., Halliburton Co., Boise Cascade Corp., Am. Express Co. Bd. regents Smithsonian Instn., 1978—; bd. overseers Hoover Instn., 1978—; co-chmn. Reagan-Bush Campaign, 1980; pres. Blair House Restoration Fund, 1985—. Recipient Rep. Woman of Yr. award, 1979, Texan of Yr. award, 1981, Presdl. Med. of Freedom award, 1987; named Tex. Women's Hall Fame, 1986. Mem. English-Speaking Union (chmn. 1978-80), Council Fgn. Relations, Tex. Womens Alliance (chmn. 1985—), Am. Assocs. of Royal Acad. Trust (trustee 1985—), Phi Beta Kappa. Clubs: Econ, N.Y; F St. (Washington).

ARMSTRONG, DAVID LYLE, finanical planner; b. Amarillo, Tex., May 26, 1958; s. Gail Arlen and Josephine Anne (Grissom) A.; m. Belinda Marie Powell, May 17, 1980; children: Tyler, Jon, Blaine,. BBA, U. Okla., 1982. CPA. Mem. Okla. Soc. CPA's (bd. dirs. personal fin. planning div.), Chartered Fin. Planners (bd. dirs. Okla chpt.). Home: 2809 Cynthia Cir Norman OK 73072 Office: Armstrong & Assocs 2420 Springer Dr Ste 110 Norman OK 73069

ARMSTRONG, GENE LEE, retired aerospace company executive; b. Clinton, Ill., Mar. 9, 1922; s. George Dewey and Ruby Imald (Dickerson) A.; B.S. with high honors, U. Ill., Urbana, 1948, M.S., 1951; m. Lael Jeanne Baker, Apr. 3, 1946; children—Susan Lael, Roberta Lynn, Gene Lee. With Boeing Aircraft, 1948-50, 51-52; chief engr. astronautics div., corp. dir. Gen. Dynamics, 1954-65; chief engr. Def. Systems GroupTRW, Redondo Beach, Calif., 1956-86, pvt. cons. systems engrng., 1986—. Mem. NASA Research Adv. Com. on Control, Guidance & Navigation, 1959-62. Served to 1st lt. USAAF, 1942-45. Decorated Air medal; recipient alumni awards U. Ill., 1965, 77; registered profl. engr., Calif. Mem. Am. Math. Soc., AIAA, Nat. Mgmt. Assn., Am. Def. Preparedness Assn. Club: Masons. Contbr. chpts. to books, articles to profl. publs. Home: 5242 Bryant Circle Westminster CA

92683 Office: Armstrong Systems Engring Co PO Box 86 Westminster CA 92684-0086

ARMSTRONG, JAMES HOUSTON, JR., accountant; b. Jacksonville, Fla., Aug. 27, 1947; s. James Houston and Agnes (Parramore) A.; m. Cathy Lee Cruse, Dec. 30, 1977; children: James III, William Michael. BA, Emory U., 1969; MBA, Ga. State U., 1975. CPA, Ga. Acct. Arthur Andersen & Co., Atlanta, 1975-78; gen. mgr. Augusta (Ga.) Nat., Inc., 1978—. Served with USN, 1969-72. Mem. Am. Inst. CPA's. Republican. Episcopalian. Club: Westlake Country (Augusta). Home: 3510 Preston Trail Augusta GA 30907

ARMSTRONG, JAMES RAYMOND, storage company executive, treasurer; b. Lowell, Mass., July 27, 1929; s. James Francis and Mary Elizabeth (Sexton) A.; m. Dorothy Elaine Dixon, Jan. 20, 1951; children: Deborah Ann, James Raymond Jr., Linda Ann. BA, Merrimack Coll., 1958. Accounts mgr. Burroughs Corp., Boston, 1953-64; regional sales mgr. Memorex Corp., Chgo., 1964-70; v.p. mktg. Computer Link Corp., Burlington, Mass., 1970-71; founder, pres., treas. Scopus Corp., Lowell, Mass., 1971—, Offsite Storage Inc., Lowell, Mass., 1971—; also bd. dirs. Offsite Storage Inc. Trustee St. John's Hosp., Lowell, 1978—; bd. incorporators Lowell 5Savs. Bank, 1982—. Sgt. U.S. Army, 1951-53. Mem. Lowell C. of C. and Industry (chmn. bd. dirs. 1983-84, Bus. Achievement award 1982), Vesper Country Club, KC. Democrat. Roman Catholic. Office: Scopus Corp 333 Aiken St Lowell MA 01853

ARMSTRONG, MICHAEL DAVID, investment banker; b. Bronxville, N.Y., May 7, 1955; s. Frank Alexander and Dorothy Ann (McEntegart) A.; m. Deborah Jane Lauderdale, Mar. 24, 1984; 1 child, David Coleman. BA, Washington and Lee U., 1977; MBA, Coll. William and Mary, 1982. Prodn. mgr., account exec. Austin Kelley Co., Atlanta, 1977-80; analyst 1st San Francisco Corp., Foster City, Calif., 1983-85, assoc., 1985-88; officer, sr. assoc. Bankers Trust Co., Atlanta, 1988—; fin. cons. AFP Ltd., Atlanta, 1983—. Mem. San Francisco Opera Assn., Mus. Soc. San Francisco, San Francisco Pub. T.V. Assn. Mem. Washington and Lee Alumni Club (Atlanta), Mu Beta Psi. Office: Bankers Trust Co 133 Peachtree St NE Ste 3600 Atlanta GA 30319

ARMSTRONG, OPAL MAE, insurance agent; b. Danville, Ky., Oct. 26, 1933; d. Robert Smith and Rosa Ellen (Benedict) Carrier; m. Cecil C. Clemons, Nov. 2, 1951 (div. 1970); children: Roger Michael, Cecile Joan; m. James E. Armstrong, May 13, 1971 (div. 1981). Student, Fla. Jr. Coll. With Taylor Drugs, Louisville, 1950-52, GE, Gainesville, Fla., 1961-63, Triangle Mobile Homes, Greensboro, N.C., 1963-65, Mobile Homes Brokers, Inc., Jacksonville, Fla., 1965-76, Amax Corp., Jacksonville, 1976-77, Dawson's Mobile Homes, Jacksonville, 1977-83; owner, mgr. Armstrong & Bosh Ins. Agy., Jacksonville, 1983—; ptnr., corp. mgr. Nobility Homes of Jacksonville, 1987—. Mail-out coord. Dem. Campaign Hdqrs., Louisville, 1955-56. Mem. Women Bus. Owners of North Fla. (bd. dirs., communication officer 1989—), Westside Businessmen's Club. Democrat. Home: 4305 Charleston Ln Jacksonville FL 32210 Office: Armstrong & Bosh Ins Agy 6114 Goodman Rd Jacksonville FL 32244

ARMSTRONG, ROBERT GEORGE, SR., financial planner; b. Peoria, Ill., Nov. 23, 1945; s. Robert Henry and Lura Elizabeth (Elgin) A.; m. Jill Lysbeth Robertson, July 1, 1976 (div. Aug. 1983); 1 child, Robert George II (dec.). BA, West Liberty State Coll., 1969. Cert. fin. planner. Chief exec. officer Panhandle Health Planning, Inc., Wheeling, W.Va., 1972-76; asst. dir. W.Va. Health Systems Agy., Charleston, W.Va., 1976-77; real estate agt. HomeFinders, Inc., Charleston, 1977-79; life underwriter Nat. Life Vt., Charleston, 1979-80; fin. planner Lanham, O'Dell & Constantino, Hurricane, W.Va., 1980—. Chmn. bd. Charleston Charity Horse Show, 1978-84. Recipient Outstanding Service award USPHS, 1975. Mem. Internat. Assn. Fin. Planners, Charleston C. of C., Oglebay Riding Club (Wheeling) (chmn. bd. 1972-76). Republican. Home: 1642 Virginia St E Charleston WV 25311 Office: Lanham O'Dell & Constantino 3981 Teays Valley Rd PO Box 537 Hurricane WV 25526

ARMSTRONG, ROBERT STEVENSON, JR., sales executive; b. Pitts., Aug. 14, 1954; s. Robert Stevenson and Mary Moreland (Coleman) A.; m. Alberta Louisa Scafuro, June 22, 1982; children: Kathryn Ballyreagh, Robert Stevenson III, Meredith Scafueo. AB, Wittenberg U., 1976. Asst. mgr. Minn. Fabrics, Inc., Washington, 1976-78; sales engr. K.J. Lesker, Inc., Pitts., 1979-82, sale regional mgr., 1982-83; pres. Telesis High Vacuum Equipment, Dallas, 1983—; bd. dirs. Potomac Scientific, Silver Spring, Md., United Mercantile Co., Pitts. Chmn., coord. John Anderson for Pres., Pitts., 1980. Mem. Am. Vacuum Soc., Pi Kappa Alpha. Republican. Presbyterian. Office: Telesis High Vacuum Inc 10705 Plano Rd Ste 100 Dallas TX 75238

ARMSTRONG, THEODORE MORELOCK, corporate executive; b. St. Louis, July 22, 1939; s. Theodore Roosevelt and Vassar Fambrough (Morelock) A.; m. Carol Mercer Robert, Sept. 7, 1963; children: Evelyn Anne, Robert Theodore. BA, Yale U., 1961; LLB, Duke U., 1964. Bar: Mo. 1964. With Miss. River Transmission Corp. and affiliated cos., 1964-85; corp. sec. Mo. Pacific Corp., 1971-75, River Cement Co., 1968-75; asst. v.p. Miss. River Transmission Corp., 1974-75, v.p. gas supply, 1975-79, exec. v.p., 1979-83, pres., chief exec. officer, 1983-85; exec. v.p. Natural Gas Pipeline of Am., 1985; sr. v.p. fin. and adminstrn. Angelica Corp., St. Louis, 1986—; bd. dirs. United Mo. Bank of St. Louis. Bd. dirs. Cen. Inst. for the Deaf, Tenn. Soc. of St. Louis, Boys Town Mo. Mem. ABA, Mo. Bar, Met. St. Louis Bar Assn., Phi Alpha Delta. Republican. Presbyterian. Clubs: Bellerive, St. Louis, Yale (St. Louis); Yale (N.Y.C.). Home: 43 Countryside Ln Saint Louis MO 63131 Office: Angelica Corp 10176 Corporate Sq Dr Saint Louis MO 63132

ARMSTRONG, THOMAS K., steel foundry executive; b. Ft. Polk, La., Feb. 27, 1954; s. Thomas K. and Patricia (Junkin) A.; m. Kathryn St. Germain, Oct. 2, 1972; children: Thomas K. III, Alexander D. BS in Indsl Engring., Ga. Inst. Tech., 1976. Area indsl. engr. E.I. DuPont de Nemours & Co., Seaford, Del., 1976-78; planning mgr. Tex. Steel Co., Ft. Worth, 1978-84, exec. v.p., 1985-87, pres., 1988—. Precinct chmn. Tarrant County Republican Com., 1979-87. Mem. Colonial Country Club. Episcopalian. Office: Tex Steel Co 3901 Hemphill St Fort Worth TX 76110

ARMSTRONG, WALTER PRESTON, JR., lawyer; b. Memphis, Oct. 4, 1916; s. Walter Preston and Irma Lewis (Waddell) A.; m. Alice Kavanaugh McKee, Nov. 3, 1949; children: Alice Kavanaugh, Walter Preston III. Grad., Choate Sch., Wallingford, Conn., 1934; A.B., Harvard U., 1938, J.D., 1941; D.C.L. (hon.), Southwestern at Memphis, 1961. Bar: Tenn. 1940. Practiced in Memphis, 1941—; assoc. firm Armstrong, Allen, Prewitt, Gentry, Johnston & Holmes (and predecessor firms), 1941-48, ptnr., 1948-86, of counsel, 1986—; Commr. for Promotion of Uniformity of Legislation in U.S. for Tenn., 1947-67. Author law rev. articles. Pres. bd. edn. Memphis City Schs., 1956-61; mem. Tenn. Higher Edn. Commn., 1967-84, chmn., 1974-75; mem. Tenn. Hist. Commn., 1969-80, hon. French consul, 1978-88. Pvt. to maj. AUS, 1941-46. Fellow Am. Bar Found. (sec. 1960-62), Tenn. Bar Found. (chmn. 1983-84), Am. Coll. Trial Lawyers; mem. ABA (ho. of dels. 1952-75), Tenn. Bar Assn. (pres. 1972-73), Memphis and Shelby County Bar Assn., Inter-Am. Bar Assn., Internat. Bar Assn., Fed. Bar Assn., Assn. Bar City N.Y., Am. Law Inst., Nat. Conf. Commrs. on Uniform State Laws (pres. 1961-63), Harvard Law School Assn. (sec. 1957-58), Order of Coif, Scribes (pres. 1960-61), Phi Delta Phi, Omicron Delta Kappa. Home: 1530 Carr Ave Memphis TN 38104 Office: Armstrong Allen Prewitt Gentry Johnston & Holmes 1900 One Commerce Sq Memphis TN 38103

ARMSTRONG, WILLIS COBURN, management consultant, former government official; b. N.Y.C., Apr. 2, 1912; s. James Claude and Hatte Amelia (Fairchild) A.; m. Martha Louise Schaffner, May 2, 1959; 1 child, Ian Coburn. BA, Swarthmore Coll., 1933; MA, Columbia U., 1934. Tchr. Horace Mann Sch., N.Y.C., 1934-39; mem. staff U.S. Embassy U.S. Dept. of State, Moscow, 1939-41; officer Lend Lease and Fgn. Econs. Adminstrn. U.S. Dept. of State, Washington, 1941-45, Officer War Shipping Adminstrn., 1945-46, officer Econ. Bur., 1946-58; counselor, minister U.S. Embassy U.S. Dept. of State, Ottawa, Can., 1958-62; dir. Brit. Commonwealth and No. Europe Affairs U.S. Dept. of State, Washington, 1962-64; econ. minister U.S. Embassy U.S. Dept. of State, London, 1964-67; asst. sec. state U.S. Dept. of State, Washington, 1972-74; assoc. dean Columbia U. Sch. Internat. Affairs, N.Y.C., 1967-69; pres. U.S. Council Internat. Bus., N.Y.C., 1969-72; Washington rep. U.S. Council Internat. Bus., 1974-82; mem. sr. rev. panel CIA, Washington, 1982-85; cons. British Petroleum, Washington, 1975-78, Burdeshaw Assocs., Washington, 1987—; bd. dirs. Flow Gen. Inc., McLean, Va., Atlantic Council U.S., Washington; prof., lectr. grad. courses Am. U., Columbia U., Johns Hopkins U., Georgetown U. Bd. dirs. English Speaking Union U.S., N.Y.C., 1978—. Mem. Cosmos Club, Nassau Club. Republican. Presbyterian. Home: 3226 Broad Br Terr Washington DC 20008

ARNALL, ELLIS GIBBS, lawyer, former governor of Georgia; b. Newnan, Ga., Mar. 20, 1907; s. Joe Gibbs and Bessie Lena (Ellis) A.; m. Mildred DeLaney Slemons, Apr. 6, 1935 (dec. June 29, 1980); children: Alvan Slemons, Alice Slemons Arnall Harty (dec. May 20, 1984); m. Ruby Hamilton McCord, July 15, 1981. Student, Mercer U., 1924; A.B., U. of South, 1928, D.C.L., 1947; LL.B., U. Ga., 1931; LL.D., Atlanta Law Sch., 1942, Piedmont Coll., 1943, Bryant Coll., 1948. Bar: Ga. 1931. Mem. Ga. Ho. of Reps., speaker pro tem, 1933-37; atty. gen. Ga., 1939-43, gov., 1943-47; pres. Columbus Nat. Life Ins. Co. (formerly Dixie Life Ins. Co.), Newnan, 1946-60, Soc. Ind. Motion Picture Producers, Beverly Hills, Calif., 1948-60, Ind. Film Producers Export Corp., Beverly Hills, 1953-60; sr. partner law firm Arnall, Golden & Gregory, Atlanta; chmn. bd. Coastal States Life Ins. Co., Atlanta, 1956-87, Atlanta Americana Motor Hotel Corp., 1949-86; vice chmn., dir. Sun Life Group, Inc.; dir. First Nat. Bank in, Newnan, 1949-85, Alterman Foods Inc., 1950-81, Midland Capital Corp., 1951-85, The Rushton Co., 1950-80, Simmons Plating Works, 1950-82, U.S. Office Price Stblzn., Feb.-Sept. 1952; mem. Nat. Commn. for UNESCO, 1947-51, 63-67; mem. U.S. del. Fifth Conf. UNESCO, Paris, 1949; mem. U.S. del. Anglo-Am. Film Conf., London, 1950, 53-56; nat. dir. U.S. Office Price 1953 Stabilization, Washington. Author: The Shore Dimly Seen, 1946, What the People Want, 1947. Mem. Franklin D. Roosevelt Warm Springs Meml. Commn., 1970—; trustee U. South, 1946-50, Mercer U., 1960-70. Named to Transp. Hall of Fame, 1977. Fellow Internat. Inst. Arts and Scis.; mem. Am. Judicature Soc., Nat. Assn. Life Ins. Co. (chmn. bd. 1955-81), Am., Fed., Ga. bar assns., Soc. Motion Picture Arts and Scis., Phi Beta Kappa, Phi Delta Phi, Kappa Alpha. Democrat. Club: Atlanta Lawyers. Home: 3 Muscogee Way NW Atlanta GA 30305 Office: Arnall Golden & Gregory 55 Park Pl Atlanta GA 30335

ARNBERG, ROBERT LEWIS, mathematician; b. San Francisco, Mar. 19, 1945; s. Wilbur H. and Elverne Evelyn (Lewis) A.; m. Judith Davis Urey, June 18, 1967 (div. 1977); 1 son, Christopher John. Student, U. Oreg., 1972-75, MA, 1969; AB, U. Calif.-Berkeley, 1967. Ops. rsch. systems analyst Hdqrs. Dept. of Army, Washington, 1969-72; sr. programmer Cons. & Designers, Beltsville, Md., 1975; cons., tchr., writer Cons. & Designers, Washington, 1976-78; programmer analyst Data Transformation Corp., Washington, 1978; mathematician, programmer, analyst Nat. Econ. Rsch. Assocs., Washington, 1978-80; rsch. fellow Logistics Mgmt. Inst., Washington, 1980-88; analyst ops. rsch. U.S. Geol. Survey, Reston, Va., 1988—; book reviewer Am. Assn. Advancement Sci., 1977—; instr. George Washington U., 1978; cons. Dept. Army, 1972; adj. asst. prof. U. Md., College Park, Md., 1988—. Author: AAM User's Guide, 1984, F16 FIMS User's Guide, 1982, Integrated Requirements and Inventory System User's Guide and Reference Manuals, 1988, Petroleum Quality Information System User's Guide and Performance Manual, 1988, Federal Energy Usage System User's Guide, 1988; others. Campaign worker Eugene McCarthy campaign 1976. Served to capt. U.S. Army, 1969-72. Mem. AAAS, Am. Math. Soc., Math. Assn. Am., Soc. for Indsl. and Applied Math., Internat. Congress of Mathematicians, N.Y. Acad. Scis., Washington Ethical Soc., Chi Psi. Home: 4107 W St NW Apt 202 Washington DC 20007 Office: US Geol Survey 206 National Ctr Reston VA 22902-5886

ARNDT, KENNETH EUGENE, banker; b. Milw., Mar. 19, 1933; s. Herbert E. and Anne B. (Kittel) A.; m. Lois Arndt; children: Victoria, Jeffrey. BS, Marquette U., 1955; MBA, NYU, 1961. Bank examiner Fed. Res. Bank of Chgo., 1955-57; account officer Pfizer Internat., N.Y.C., 1958-60; v.p. Chase Manhattan Bank, N.Y.C., 1960-80; v.p., area mgr. First Nat. Bank Chgo., 1981-87, fin. cons., 1987—. Author articles on trade with Japan and Far East. Mem. core com. N.J. Olympic Com., 1986. Served to 1st lt. U.S. Army, 1955-57. Mem. U.S. Korea Soc. (bd. dirs. 1984—), Asia Soc., Japan Soc. Home: 22 Sagamore Rd Bronxville NY 10708

ARNELL, ALVIN, management consultant, lecturer; b. Bklyn., Feb. 11, 1929; s. Aaron and Anna (Berr) A.; m. Helene, Feb. 17, 1952 (div. 1967); children: Susan, Peter, Eric; m. Elisse Jane, July 4, 1968; children: Andrew Frederick, Mathew Scott. Student, N.Y. State Inst. Applied Arts and Scis., 1946-47; BBA, Pace Inst., 1951; MBA (hon.), Osaka (Japan) U., 1964. Asst. advt. mgr. Doughnut Corp. Am., N.Y.C., 1946-48; advt. prodn. mgr. Ludwig Baumann, N.Y.C., 1948-51; direct mail mgr. Hecht Co., Washington, 1951-53; advt. mgr. Heat Timer Corp., Washington, 1953-56; pres. Miller Lauffer Printing Machinery, Washington, 1956-60; v.p. Halm Instrument Corp., Glen Head, N.Y., 1960-68; exec. v.p. Comml. Envelope Corp., Bronx, N.Y., 1968-76; pres. Vault Mgmt. Corp., Garden City, N.Y., 1976-83; cons., lectr. DIAlog Mgmt., Inc., Merrick, N.Y., 1979—, pres., 1983—; presenter seminars and workshops internat. disaster and recovery planning, corp. mgmt. Author: Standard Graphic Symbols, 1952, Effective Disaster/Recovery Planning, 1988; contbr. articles in bus. mgmt., mktg. and disaster/recovery planning. Recipient Greatests Contbn. to Community award Mayor's Office, N.Y.C., 1946; award UN Internat. Com. for Devel. Symbolic Lang., 1963. Home: 1945 Byron Rd Merrick NY 11566 Office: DIAlog Mgmt Inc 1945 Byron Rd Merrick NY 11566

ARNESON, GEORGE STEPHEN, manufacturing company executive, management consultant; b. St. Paul, Apr. 3, 1925; s. Oscar and Louvia Irene (Clare) A.; children: George Stephen Fernando, Deborah Clare Fernanda, Diane Elizabeth Fernanda, Frederick Oscar Fernando. BS in Marine Transp., U.S. Mcht. Marine Acad., 1945; BEE, U. Minn., 1949. Certified mgmt. cons. Sales engr. Hubbard & Co., Chgo., 1949-54; cons. Booz, Allen & Hamilton, Chgo., 1954-57; mgr. mktg. cons. services, dir. mktg., plant mgr. Borg-Warner Corp., Chgo., 1957-60; asst. gen. mgr., then v.p., gen. mgr. Delta-Star Electric div. H.K. Porter Co., Inc., Pitts., 1960-63; v.p., gen. mgr. elec. divs. Delta-Star Electric div. H.K. Porter Co., Inc., 1963-65; v.p. mktg. Wheeling Steel Corp., 1965-66; pres., chief exec. officer Vendo Co., Kansas City, Mo., 1966-72, also dir., chmn. exec. com.; pres., chmn. Dun-Lap Mfg. Co., Newton, Iowa, 1973-77; pres. Arneson & Co., Leawood, Kans., 1974—, Arneson, Compton & Hammond, Inc., Olathe, Kans., 1987—; bd. dirs. TelCon Assocs., Shawnee Mission, Kans. Contbr. articles on mgmt. cons., bus. valuation and appraisal of mgmt. to profl. jours. Chmn. adv. bd. Kans. Dept. Correctional, Topeka, 1980—. Served to lt. (j.g.) USNR, 1943-46. Recipient Outstanding Alumnus award U.S. Mcht. Marine Acad., 1968, Past Dir. award Automatic Merchandising Assn. Mem. Am. Soc. Appraisers (sr.), Inst. Mgmt. Cons. (cert. mgmt. cons.; chpt. pres., nat. bd. dirs.), Phi Gamma Delta (life), Alpha Phi Omega (life). Republican. Presbyterian. Clubs: Masons, KT, Shriners.

ARNETT, JAMES EDWARD, educator; b. Gullett, Ky., Oct. 3, 1912; s. Haden and Josephine (Risner) A.; A.B., San Jose State Coll., 1947, M.A., 1955; Ed.S., Stanford, 1959; m. Helen Mae Vallish, Mar. 23, 1943. Tchr., prin. pub. schs., Salyersville, Ky., 1930-41; tchr., adminstr. pub. schs., Salinas, Calif., 1947-52; owner-mgr. Arnett Apts., Salinas, 1950-53; tchr., Innes High Sch., Akron, Ohio, 1953-73; owner-mgr. Arnett Apts., Akron, 1953-72; dir. Educator & Exec. Co., 1962-73, Educator and Exec. Insurers, 1957-76, Educator and Exec. Life Ins. Co., 1962-76, Great Am. of Dallas Fire and Casualty Co., 1974-76, Great Am. of Dallas Ins. Co., 1974-76, J.C. Penney Casualty Ins. Co., 1976; cons., 1976-77. Mem. county, state central coms. Democratic party, 1952. Served with AUS, 1942-45. Mem. NEA (life mem.; del. conv. 1957-65), Ohio (del. convs. 1957-73), Akron (1st v.p. 1964-65, parliamentarian 1965-72), edn. assns., San Jose State Coll., Stanford alumni assns., Phi Delta Kappa. Home: 691 Payne Ave Akron OH 44302-1347 Office: 800 Brooksedge Blvd Westerville OH 43081

ARNETT, JAMES EDWARD, II, sales executive; b. Portsmouth, Ohio, Feb. 2, 1955; s. Baxter and Patricia (Pennington) A.; m. Mary Joan Mc Guire, Feb. 7, 1978. Student, Ashland Community Coll., 1975-84. Ins. broker Ashland, Ky., 1972-78; sales rep. E.R.A. Mktg. Research, St. Albans, W. Va., 1978-80, Clairol, Inc., N.Y.C., 1980-82; v.p. sales Arnett Bros. Coal Co. Inc., Ashland, 1982—, also bd. dirs.; pres., chief exec. officer So. Terminals, Inc. subs. Arnett Bros. Coal Co., Inc., 1988—, also bd. dirs. Named to Ho. Order Ky. Cols., 1977. Mem. Jaycees, Lamda Sigma Chi (treas. 1975-76). Clubs: Midlands Trade. Office: Arnett Bros Coal Co Inc PO Box 42155 Columbia SC 29206

ARNOFF, JUDITH UNGER, pharmaceutical company executive; b. Richmond, Va., May 14, 1946; d. Gary and Mary (Goldman) Unger; m. Lawrence Jay Arnoff, June 26, 1966. BS in Pharmacy, Temple U., 1968, MBA, 1982. Registered pharmacist, Pa. Staff pharmacist Del. County Meml. Hosp., Drexel Hill, Pa., 1968-69; sterile products pharmacist Albert Einstein Med. Ctr., Phila., 1969-74; mgr. tech. svcs. Elkins-Sinn, Inc., Cherry Hill, N.J., 1974-76, dir. tech. and mktg. svcs., 1976-78, dir. new bus. and market planning, 1978-81, v.p. adminstrn., 1981-85; v.p. Marsam Pharms., Inc., Cherry Hill, 1985—; chmn. pub. rels. com., bd. dirs. Phila. Drug Exchange, 1984-87, treas., 1988. Mem. Am. Soc. hosp. Pharmacists, Regulatory Affairs Profl. Soc., Rho Chi, Beta Gamma Sigma. Office: Marsam Pharms Inc Bldg 31 Olney Ave PO Box 1022 Cherry Hill NJ 08034

ARNOLD, DANIEL CALMES, financial executive; b. Houston, Mar. 14, 1930; m. Beverly Bintliff; children—Mrs. Randy Helms, Mrs. Tom Martin, Steven Arnold. B.B.A., U. Tex.-Austin, 1951, L.L.B., 1953. Ptnr. Vinson & Elkins, Houston, 1953-83; pres., dir. First City Bancorp. Tex., Inc., Houston, 1983-85, chmn. pres., dir., 1985-88; chmn., chief exec. officer Farm & Home Fin. Corp., 1989—; bd. dirs. Visa, U.S.A., Inc., 1985-87. Bd. dirs. Harris County Hosp. Dist., 1963-69, chmn. 1963-69; bd. dirs. Tex. Med. Ctr., Inc., Baylor Coll. Medicine; bd. dirs. Houston-Harris County chpt. ARC, chmn. 1970-72; chmn. bd. dirs. Met. Transit Authority Harris County, Tex., 1980-84. Mem. ABA, Tex. Bar Assn., Houston Bar Assn., Assn. Res. City Bankers. Methodist. Office: Farm & Home Fin Corp 400 1st City Tower 1001 Fannin St Houston TX 77002

ARNOLD, DOUGLAS RAY, bank executive; b. Pitts., Nov. 8, 1948; s. Harold Ramble and Grace Louise (Kauffman) A.; m. Janis Lee Schauerman, Aug. 3, 1974; children: Emily Jean, Bradley Scott. BS in Fin., Pa. State U., 1970. Owner Wheel Pump Inn, Phila., 1972-73; mgmt. trainee Continental Bank, Phila., 1973-75, ops. officer, 1976-77, adminstrv. v.p. ops., 1978-84, sr. v.p., 1984-88; group v.p. data processing Provident Nat. Bank, Phila., 1988—. Mem. Schuylkill Twp. Planning Commn., Phoenixville, Pa.; treas. Valley Forge Park Interpretion Assn., Pa. Served with U.S. Army, 1970-72. Republican. Presbyterian. Home: 165 Winterberry Ln Phoenixville PA 19460

ARNOLD, DOYLE LOUIS, banker; b. San Antonio, Sept. 19, 1948; s. Louis Carlisle and Elaine (Walker) A.; m. Anne Elizabeth Glarner, Apr. 6, 1985. BA, Rice U., 1970; MBA, Stanford U., 1976. Mgmt. cons. Touche Ross and Co., San Francisco, 1976-78, Edgar Dunn and Conover Inc., San Francisco, 1978-81; exec. asst. to dep. sec. Dept. Treasury, Washington, 1981-82; sr. dep. comptroller policy and planning Comptroller of the Currency, Washington, 1982-84; sr. v.p. strategic planning Wells Fargo and Co., San Francisco, 1984-86, sr. v.p., gen. auditor, 1986-87, sr. v.p. corp. strategy, 1987—. dir., treas. Satellite Sr. Homes Inc., Oakland, Ca., 1987—; mem. Private Industry Council, San Francisco, 1988. Lt. (j.g.) USN, 1970-73. Mem. World Affairs Council, Commonwealth Club. Republican. Presbyterian. Office: Wells Fargo & Co 420 Montgomery St San Francisco CA 94163

ARNOLD, G. DEWEY, JR., accountant; b. Montgomery, Ala., Jan. 30, 1925; s. G. Dewey and Janie Esther (Terry) A.; m. Dorothy Louise Wenger, Dec. 4, 1954; children: Susan O., G. Dewey III. B.A. in Econs, U. of South, 1949; postgrad. in acct., U. Tenn. C.P.A., Pa., D.C., Md. With Aladdin Industries, Inc., Nashville, 1949-50; with Price Waterhouse (C.P.A.s), 1950—; ptnr. Price Waterhouse & Co. (C.P.A.s), 1961—, ptn charge Washington office, 1965-76, mem. policy com., 1975-80, regional mng. ptnr., 1976-85; exec. dir. Nat. Commn. on Fin. Fraud, 1985-87; dir. Audit-Intelsat., 1987—; instr. acctg. Robert Morris Sch. Acctg., 1952-53; lectr., course dir. mgmt. acctg. Inst. Mexicano de Administracion de Negocias, A.C., 1958-64; bd. dirs. Washington Bd. Trade, 1973-75; mem. audit adv. com. Sec. Navy, 1972-75. Bd. dirs. Jr. C. of C., 1954-55; trustee Fed. City Council, 1966—; bd. dirs. Greater Washington Ednl. TV Assn., Inc., 1970-82, Minority Contractors Center, 1972-74, Redskins Found., 1973—, D.C. Mcpl. Research Bur., 1974-76, Wolf Trap Found., 1975—; chmn. bd. trustees Landon Sch., 1974-79; vice chmn. D.C. BiCentennial Commn., 1971-75. Served with USNR, 1943-45. Mem. Am. Inst. CPA's, D.C. Inst. CPA's, Nat. Assn. Accts., Md. Inst. CPA's, Am. Arbitration Assn. Episcopalian. Clubs: Chevy Chase, Burning Tree, Pine Valley Golf, Metropolitan (Washington); Rolling Rock. Office: Intelsat 3400 International Dr NW Washington DC 20008-3098

ARNOLD, JANE SUTTON, sales and marketing executive; b. Chgo.; d. John Carr and Florence Kathryn (Salter) Sutton; children: John Nolte, Kathryn Nolte, Alan Zachary. BS summa cum laude, U. Wis.-Milw., 1971, MS, 1976. Dir. Title III ESEA, Project Happe, Milw., 1974-76; dir. programs for gifted and talented Southeastern Wis. Gifted Consortium, Milw., 1976-82; dir. sales and tng. Marine Corp., Milw., 1982-84; v.p. sales and mktg. Bank One Wis. Trust Co. 1984—; mem. State Supt.'s Adv. Com. on Gifted and Talented, 1974-77; cons. Wis. Banking Assn., 1983—, ABA, AIB, BMA; pres. Wis. Council for Gifted and Talented, 1974-77, Wis. Assn. for Educators Gifted and Talented, 1975-77. Trustee Waukesha County Tech. Coll., 1985—, Girl Scouts Greater Milw., 1985-88; pres., bd. dirs. YWCA Greater Milw., 1985-88; mem. planning and allocation com. United Way Greater Milw., 1985-88, planned giving com. U. Wis.-Milw. Found., 1985-88. Author: Identifying the Gifted and Talented, 1976, Organizing Parent Discussion Groups, 1978. Recipient Ednl. Pacesetter award U.S. Office Edn., 1976. Mem. Am. Bankers Assn., Am. Inst. Banking, Bank Mktg. Assn., Mortar Board, Phi Delta Kappa. Office: Bank One Wis Trust Co 111 E Wisconsin Ave Milwaukee WI 53202

ARNOLD, JOHN H., bank executive; b. Plain Dealing, La., Oct. 7, 1931; s. Edward H. and Edna (Teutsch) A.; m. Wilda Kennon Arnold, Sept. 2, 1955; children: Steve Richard, J. Mark. BS, East Tex. Bapt. U., 1957; MS, New Orleans Bapt. Theol. Sem., 1959. Owner Church Supply Co., Houston, 1961-63; mgr. Ada Oil Co. Union, Houston, 1963-65, Monsanto Choc. Bayou Fed. Credit Union, Alvin, Tex., 1965-73; v.p. Tex. Credit Union League, Dallas, 1974-76; exec. v.p., chief operating officer S.W. Corp. Fed. Credit Union, Dallas, 1976—; chmn. credit com. U.S. Cen. Credit Union, Kansas City, 1985—; chmn. corp. forum Assn. Credit League Union Execs., Madison, Wis., 1980-82. Chmn. fin. com. East Tex. Bapt. U., Marshall, 1985—, also trustee. Home: 3811 Shady Hill Dallas TX 75229 Office: SW Corp Fed Credit Union PO Box 225147 Dallas TX 75265

ARNOLD, JOSHUA DAVID, asset manager; b. Camden, N.J., Jan. 9, 1951; s. Matthew Charles and Janet (Jaffe) A.; m. Janet Marcia Lubov, Oct. 25, 1975; children: Michael Benjamin, Judd Marcus, Marissa Beth. AB, Franklin and Marshall Coll., 1972; MA, U. Akron, 1975; cert., Coll. Fin. Planning, 1984. Registered fin. planner. Dir. Union Camp Inst., Zionsville, Ind., 1974-75; exec. dir. Herzel Camp Assn., St. Paul, 1975-77; rep. 1st Investors Corp., Edina, Minn., 1976-80; rep., pres. adv. council Pvt. Ledger Fin. Services, Edina, 1981—; owner Webb, Arnold, Markman & Co., Edina, 1981-87, Josh Arnold Investment Planning, Edina, 1987—; mem. fin. profl. advisors panel, Oakland, Calif., 1984—; talk show host and expert, Sta. KSTP, St. Paul, 1981-86, Sta. WCCO-TV, Josh's Jour. Sta. WCCO-TV, 1988-89, Money: The Inside Story, Sta. KLBB, 1989. Pub. Josh's Jour. of Investment Planning, 1988—. Bd. dirs., treas. Accessible Space, Inc., Mpls., 1983—; bd. dirs. Temple Israel, Mpls., 1985. Recipient Patriot award Pvt. Ledger Fin. Svcs., San Diego, 1985-88. Mem. Internat. Assn. Registered Fin. Planners, Inst. Cert. Fin. Planners, Assn. Registered Fin. Planners, Inc. Office: Josh Arnold Investment Planning 6800 France Ave S Ste 680 Edina MN 55435

ARNOLD, RICHARD WALKER, brokerage house executive; b. Melbourne, Victoria, Australia, Nov. 20, 1947; came to U.S., 1962; s. Ted Adamson and Helen Ruth (Down) A.; m. Vivian Lynn Giusto, Feb. 17, 1977; children: Carlie Lynn, Trevor Stephen. AB in Psychology, Stanford

U., 1968. With Raychem Corp., Menlo Park, Calif., 1966-71; v.p. Fin. Analysis, Inc., San Francisco, 1972-75; ind. fin. cons. San Francisco, 1976-77; asst. to pres. Charles Schwab Corp., San Francisco, 1977-79, chief fin. officer, 1980-84, exec. v.p. svc. delivery, 1984-85, exec. v.p. corp. devel., 1987—; dep. mng. dir. Bank of Am. Australia, Ltd., Melbourne, 1985-86; bd. dirs. Alabar Farms Property, Ltd., Victoria, Australia, Audio Lit., Inc., South San Francisco, Calif.; bd. advisors A-Mark Fin. Corp., Santa Monica, Calif., 1988, Am. Assn. Individual Investors, Chgo., 1981-85. Author: chpt. in Your Book of Financial Planning, 1984; contbr. articles to profl. jours. Bd. advisors Nat. Ctr. for Fin. Edn., San Francisco, 1983-85. Mem. N.Y. Stock Exch. (assoc.), Nat. Assn. Securities Dealers (prin. fin. and ops.), Mcpl. Securities Rulemaking Bd. (prin.).

ARNOLD, ROBERT DWAINE, stockbroker; b. Mpls., Jan. 13, 1935; s. Dwaine Berlwyn and Florence Eleanor (Copeland) A.; B.A. U. Iowa 1957; m. Linda Foster, July 8, 1960 (div. 1975); children—Angela Kay, Michele Rene, James Whitney. Registered rep. Quail & Co. Inc., Ottumwa, Iowa 1959-64, br. mgr. 1964-78; v.p. Dain Kalman & Quail, Cedar Rapids, Iowa 1972-78; resident v.p. Dain Bosworth Inc., Cedar Rapids 1978—. Pres., founder, dir. Robert F. Kennedy-Martin Luther King Meml. Scholarship Fund 1968-73; dir. Friends of Iowa Pub. Broadcasting Network 1968-78, pres. 1972; treas. Mid-Am. Council Boy Scouts Am. 1970; Iowa coord. Amnesty Internat. USA; bd. dirs. Iowa Civil Liberties Union. Served with U.S. Army 1957-59. Mem. Ottumwa C. of C. (v.p. 1970-73). Republican. Unitarian. Clubs: Rotary, Univ. Athletic. Home: 349 Parkland Dr SE Cedar Rapids IA 52403 Office: Dain Bosworth Inc PO Box 74330 Cedar Rapids IA 52407

ARNOLD, ROBERT LLOYD, investment broker; b. Seattle, June 18, 1952; s. Vern Lloyd and Ruth Francis (Bruty) A. Student, Bellevue Coll., Wash., 1971-71; BS magna cum laude, U. Wash., 1975; MS, Yale U., 1977. Lic. fed. securities agt. Group leader U.S. Govt., Miramonte, Calif., 1977-78; economist U.S. Govt., Walla Walla, Wash., 1978-79; gen. mgr. Full Value Roofing, Bellevue, 1979-81; transp. mgr. N.W. Hydra-Line, Inc., Seattle, 1981-83; owner Fairfields, Seattle, 1982—; investment broker Waddell & Reed, Inc., Seattle, 1983—; coord. Charles Givens Found., Seattle, 1984-85, 88—; lectr. Community Sch., Seattle, 1984—; guest speaker Kiwanis, Puyallup, Wash., 1985; seminar leader Chgo. Title Ins. Co, Seattle, 1985—. Fund raiser ARC, Seattle, 1984-85; vol. Seattle Capital Enlightenment, 1970—, Seattle Unity Ch., 1985—, apptd. fin. com., 1987—, chmn. fin. and adminstrn. com., 1988—. Grantee Bloedel Found., 1973-74, Bishop Soc. grantee, 1974-75; fellow Yale U., 1975-77. Mem. Yale Alumni Assn., Seattle Delta Group (lifetime) (chmn. 1985—), U. Wash. Alumni Assn., Xi Sigma Pi (treas. 1974-75). Republican. Office: Waddell & Reed Inc 200 W Thomas Ste 410 Seattle WA 98119

ARNOLD, WILLIAM EDWIN, manufacturing executive; b. Charleston, S.C., Aug. 13, 1938; s. Edwin Gustaf and Sara Louise (Hitchcock) A.; BA, Yale U., 1960. Pres., Dixon & Rippel, Inc., Saugerties, N.Y., 1965-70; v.p. Taj Enterprises Ltd., 1965-67, Bellern Research Corp., pres. Dixon & Rippel div., Saugerties, 1970-75; v.p. H & G Industries, Inc., pres. Indsl. Brush Div., Belleville, N.J., 1975-82; pres. World Brushworks, Inc., 1982-84; v.p., chief fin. officer Optimax III, Inc., N.Y.C., 1983-84; mng. dir. Brush Trading, Ltd., 1983-87; pres. Chestnut Holdings Ltd., 1985—; mng. dir. Cassi Properties, 1984—; pres. Swan Holding Ltd., 1985-88; bd. dirs. ARCS, 1986—. 1st lt. U.S. Army, 1961-63; with USAR, 1963-67. Mem. Internat. Platform Assn., Res. Officers Assn. Home: 19 Chestnut St Rhinebeck NY 12572 Office: PO Box 341 Rhinebeck NY 12572

ARNOLD, WILLIAM HOWARD, financial executive; b. N.Y.C., Feb. 6, 1934; s. William Tell and Edith Elizabeth (Tobin) A.; m. Nancy Jane Pennington, Dec. 28, 1963; children: William Howard Jr., Elizabeth Edith. BA, Colgate U., 1955. Cert. fin. planner. Billing mgr. R.H. Donnelley Co., N.Y.C., 1959-61; tax acct., fin. planner Phoenix, 1964—. Elder, trustee, pres. bd. trustees Morningside Presbyn. Ch., Phoenix. Mem. Nat. Soc. Pub. Accts., Ariz. Soc. Practicing Accts. (bd. dirs. 1976—, pres. Phoenix chpt. 1983-84), Nat. Assn. Enrolled Agts., Internat. Assn. Fin. Planning, Inst. Cert. Fin. Planners. Republican. Office: 1101 E Colter Phoenix AZ 85014

ARNOLD, WOOD, II, packaging company executive; b. Kansas City, Mo., Oct. 27, 1935; s. Charles and Eleanor (Beach) A.; m. Claire Ann Byrne, June 15, 1973; children: Ian H., Eliot C. BA, Northwestern U., 1957; MBA, Stanford U., 1959. Sales exec. Spencer Chem. Co., Kansas City, 1959-61; v.p. mktg. Redman Mfg. Co., Kansas City, 1961-72; pres. Package Devel. Corp., Kansas City, 1972—; speaker in field; bd. dirs. Kansas City Life Ins. Co. Exhibit mgr. Nelson Atkins Gallery, Kansas City, 1967. Mem. Soc. Plastics Engrs. Republican. Episcopalian. Office: Package Devel Corp 3100 Broadway Ste 1200 Kansas City MO 64111

ARNOLD, WYNN EDMUND, utilities executive, lawyer; b. Ludlow, Mass., Sept. 27, 1947; s. William Edmund and Barbara Eileen (Smith) A.; m. Helen Janice Falkson, Aug. 27, 1978; children: Sara Lesley, Merrin Falkson. Student, Glasgow U., Scotland, 1968-69; BA, U. N.H., 1970; JD, Suffolk U., 1981. Bar: N.H. 1981, Mass. 1982, U.S. Dist. Ct. N.H. 1981. Vol. U.S. Peace Corps, Ecuador, 1970-73; specialist office for civil rights HEW, Boston, 1974-78; specialist equal opportunity Office fed. Contract Compliance Programs, Boston, 1978-81; assoc. Tetler & Holmes, Hampton, N.H., 1981-83; exec. dir., sec. N.H. Pub. Utilities Commn., Concord, 1984—. Co-author, dir. (film) Despertad, 1972. Chmn. N.H. Episcopal Diosecan Stewardship Commn., Concord, 1986-88. Mem. Nat. Assn. Regulatory Utility Commrs. (exec. dirs. com.), N.H. Bar Assn. (long range planning com.), Mass. Bar Assn., Phi Delta Phi. Episcopalian. Office: NH Pub Utilities Commn 8 Old Suncook Rd Bldg 1 Concord NH 03301

ARNOTT, ROBERT DOUGLAS, investment company executive; b. Chgo., June 29, 1954; s. Robert James Arnott and Catherine (Bonnell) Cameron; m. Roberta Faith Baker, Oct. 28, 1979; 1 child, Robert Lindsay. BA, U. Calif., Santa Barbara, 1977. V.p. Boston Co., 1977-84; pres., chief exec. officer TSA Capital Mgmt., L.A., 1984-87; v.p., strategist Salomon Bros. Inc., N.Y.C., 1987-88; pres., chief investment officer First Quadrant Corp., Morristown, N.J. and Pasadena, Calif., 1988—. Editor: Asset Allocation, 1988; mem. editorial bd. Jour. Portfolio Mgmt., 1984—; contbr. articles to profl. jours. and chpts. to profl. books. Mem. Fin. Analysts Fedn., Inst. Internat. Rsch. (mem. adv. bd. 1988—). Democrat. Office: 1st Quadrant Corp 201 S Lake Ave Ste 607 Pasadena CA 91101

ARNSDORF, DENNIS A., printing company executive; b. Syracuse, N.Y., Jan. 5, 1953; s. Herbert Joseph and Vera Irene (Tishler) A.; m. Maxine Ellenberg, Apr. 11, 1976; children: Ilene, Laura. BS in Indsl. Labor Relations, Cornell U., 1975; MBA, U. Md., 1979. Sales rep. Procter and Gamble, Balt., 1975-77; br. mgr. Archer Systems Inc., Washington, 1978-80, dir. br. ops., 1980-84; regional mgr. Multicom Inc., Chevy Chase, Md., 1984-85; v.p., gen. mgr. Packard Press, Washington, 1986—. Mem. Anti-Defamation League, Nat. Trust Hist. Preservation. Mem. N. Va. Tech. Coun., Cornell U. Club. Office: Packard Press 1025 Connecticut Ave Washington DC 20036

ARNST, RANDALL RONALD, automotive executive; b. Cleve., Jan. 26, 1953; s. Victor J. and Alvina A. (Miller) A.; m. Cathy A. Arend, Nov. 7, 1981. B in Indsl. Engring., Gen. Motors Inst., 1976; MBA, John Carroll U., 1983. Coop. student Chevrolet Motor Div., Cleve., 1971-76, mech. engr., 1976-84; buyer New United Motor Mfg. Inc., Fremont, Calif., 1985-86; asst. mgr. direct purchasing New United Motor Mfg. Inc., Freemont, Calif., 1986-87, asst. mgr. prodn. control, 1987—. Mem. Am. Inst. Indsl. Engrs. Home: 1141 Derbyshire Dr Cupertino CA 95014 Office: New United Motor Mfg Inc 45500 Fremont Blvd Fremont CA 94538

ARNSTEIN, SHERRY PHYLLIS, health care executive; b. N.Y.C., Jan. 11, 1930; m. George E. Arnstein, June 26, 1951; BS, UCLA, 1951; MS in Communications, Am. U., 1963; postgrad. in systems dynamics MIT, summer 1976. Washington editor Current mag., 1961-63; staff cons. Pres. Com. on Juvenile Delinquency, 1963-65; spl. asst. to asst. sec. HEW, 1965-67; chief citizen participation advisor Model Cities Adminstrn., HUD, 1967-68; pub. policy cons., Washington, 1968-75; sr. research fellow HHS, Washington, 1975-78; v.p. govt. relations Nat. Health Council, Inc., Washington, 1978-85; exec. dir. Am. Assn. Colls. Osteo. Medicine, 1985—. Author: (with Alexander Christakis) Perspectives on Technology Assessment, 1975; editor: Government Relations Handbook Series, 1979-85, Washington Report Series, 1985. mem. editorial bd. Tech. Assessment Update, 1975-78, The Bureaucrat, 1975-83, Pub. Adminstrn. Rev., 1978-83, Health Mgmt. Quar., 1985. Contbr. articles to profl. jours. Bd. dirs. Youth Policy Inst. Office: Am Assn Colls Osteo Medicine 6110 Executive Blvd Ste 405 Rockville MD 20852

ARON, MARK G., corporate executive; b. Hartford, Conn., Jan. 27, 1943; s. Samuel H. and Florence A.; m. Cindy Sondik, June 1, 1966; 1 child, Samantha. B.A. summa cum laude, Trinity Coll., 1965; LL.B., Harvard U., 1968. Bar: Va., Mass., D.C. Asst. prof. law Osgood Hall Law Sch., York U., Toronto, 1968-70; assoc. Goulston & Storrs, Boston, 1970-71; atty., asst. gen. counsel then dep. gen. counsel U.S. Dept. Transp., Washington, 1971-81; asst. gen. counsel CSX, Richmond, Va., 1981-83, gen. counsel spl. projects, 1983-85; sr. v.p. corp. svcs. Chessie System R.R., Balt., 1985-86; sr. v.p. law and pub. affairs CSX Corp., Richmond, 1986—. Bd. trustees Va. Union U.; mem. Richmond Leadership Metro; bd. dris. Va. Literacy Found., Richmond Ballet; mem. Or Ami Cong. Mem. Va. Bar Assn., Mass. Bar Assn., D.C. Bar Assn., Bull and Bear Club, Willow Oaks Country Club. Home: 100 N Erlwood Ct Richmond VA 23229 Office: CSX Corp 1 James Ctr Richmond VA 23219

ARONSON, ARTHUR H., steel company executive; b. Troy, N.Y., July 9, 1935; s. George and Pauline (Lasdon) A.; m. Alice Ades, July 18, 1959; children—Terisa, Steven, Kristina, Betsy. B.S. in Metallurgy, MIT, 1958; M.S. in Metallurgy Engring., Rensselaer Poly. Inst., 1963, Ph.D. in Metallurgy, 1965. Mgr. ops. specialty steel Jones & Laughlin, Pitts., 1965-80; pres., chief exec. officer Cold Metal Products, Youngstown, Ohio, 1980-84; pres., chief operating officer Lukens Steel Co., Coatesville, Pa., 1984—; dir. Coatesville Fed. Savs. & Loan Assn., Pa. Contbr. articles to profl. jours.; patentee in field. Bd. dirs. Baldwin-Whitehall Sch. Dist., Pitts., 1969-73, Brandywine Hosp., Brandywine Valley Assn. Served to 1st lt. U.S. Army, 1959-61. Mem. Am. Iron and Steel Inst. Club: Racquet. Office: Lukens Steel Co 50 S 1st Ave Coatesville PA 19320

ARONSON, JASON, publisher; b. Minn., Jan. 25, 1928; s. Louis and Mollie (Weiner) A.; div.; 1 child, Jane; m. Joyce Kraus. BA, U. Minn., 1949, MD, 1953. Resident in psychiatry U. Minn. Hosps., 1954-57; asst. psychiatrist Harvard Med. Sch. and Mass. Gen. Hosp., 1959-64; editor-in-chief Internat. Jour. Psychiatry, 1962-70; pres. Jason Aronson Pubs., Inc., Northvale, N.J., 1964—. Served to capt. U.S. Army, 1957-79. Fellow Am. Psychiat. Assn. Office: Jason Aronson Pubs Inc 230 Livingston St Northvale NJ 07647

ARONSON, MARK BERNE, lawyer; b. Pitts., Aug. 24, 1941; s. Richard J. and Jean (DeRoy) A.; m. Ellen Jane Askin, July 20, 1970; children: Robert M., Andrew A., Michael D. BS in Econs., U. Pa., 1962; JD, U. Pitts., 1965. Bar: Pa. 1965, U.S. Dist. Ct. (we. dist.) Pa. 1965, U.S. Ct. Appeals (3d cir.) 1968, U.S. Ct. Claims 1978, U.S. Supreme Ct. 1966; lic. real estate broker, 1972. Sole practice, Pitts., 1965-66, 83—; sr. ptnr. Behrend & Aronson, Pitts., 1967-80, Behrend, Aronson & Morrow, Pitts., 1980-83. Past pres. Community Day Sch., Pitts., Rodef Shalom Jr. Congregation; past trustee Rodef Shalom Congregation, Pitts., 1979-87, trustee Pitts. Child Guidance Found., 1987—; mem., Pitts. Council on Edn., 1986—. Mem. Am. Trial Lawyers Assn. (sustaining mem., prior Pa. rep. to exchange com.), Pa. Trial Lawyers Assn. (Pres.'s Club), Allegheny County Bar Assn., N.Y. State Trial Lawyers Assn., Pa. Bar Assn., Am. Arbitration Assn. (mem. Nat. Panel Arbitrators). Republican. Jewish. Clubs: Concordia, Rivers. Lodge: Masons (master). Office: 429 4th Ave Ste 707 Pittsburgh PA 15219

ARROW, KENNETH JOSEPH, economist, educator; b. N.Y.C., Aug. 23, 1921; s. Harry I. and Lillian (Greenberg) A.; m. Selma Schweitzer, Aug. 31, 1947; children: David Michael, Andrew. B.S. in Social Sci., CCNY, 1940; M.A., Columbia U., 1941, Ph.D., 1951, D.Sc., 1973; LL.D. (hon.), U. Chgo., 1967, City U. N.Y., 1972, Hebrew U. Jerusalem, 1975, U. Pa., 1976; D.Social and Econ. Scis. (hon.), U. Vienna, Austria, 1971; D.Social Scis. (hon.), Yale, 1974; Doctor (hon.), Université René Descartes, Paris, 1974, U. Aix-Marseille III, 1985; Dr.Pol., U. Helsinki, 1976; M.A. (hon.), Harvard U., 1968; D.Litt., Cambridge U., 1985. Research assoc. Cowles Commn. for Research in Econs., 1947-49; asst. prof. econs. U. Chgo., 1948-49; acting asst. prof. econs. and stats. Stanford, 1949-50, assoc. prof., 1950-53, prof. econs., statistics and ops. research, 1953-68; prof. econs. Harvard, 1968-74, James Bryant Conant univ. prof., 1974-79; exec. head dept. econs. Stanford U., 1954-56, acting exec. head dept., 1962-63, Joan Kenney prof. econs. and prof. ops. research, 1979—; economist Council Econ. Advisers, U.S. Govt., 1962; cons. RAND Corp. Author: Social Choice and Individual Values, 1951, Essays in the Theory of Risk Bearing, 1971, The Limits of Organization, 1974, Collected Papers, Vols. I-VI, 1983-85; co-author: Mathematical Studies in Inventory and Production, 1958, Studies in Linear and Nonlinear Programming, 1958, Time Series Analysis of Inter-industry Demands, 1959, Public Investment, The Rate of Return and Optimal Fiscal Policy, 1971, General Competitive Analysis, 1971, Studies in Resource Allocation Processes, 1977, Social Choice and Multicriterion Decision Making, 1985. Served as capt. AUS, 1942-46. Social Sci. Research fellow, 1952; fellow Center for Advanced Study in the Behavioral Scis., 1956-57; fellow Churchill Coll., Cambridge, Eng., 1963-64, 70, 73, 86; Guggenheim fellow, 1972-73; Recipient John Bates Clark medal Am. Econ. Assn., 1957; Alfred Nobel Meml. prize in econ. scis., 1972, von Neumann prize, 1986. Fellow Am. Acad. Arts and Scis. (v.p. 1979-81), Econometric Soc. (v.p. 1955, pres. 1956), Am. Statis. Assn., Inst. Math. Stats., Am. Econ. Assn. (mem. exec. com. 1967-69, pres. 1973), AAAS (chmn. sect K 1983), Internat. Soc. for Inventory Research (pres. 1983—); mem. Internat. Econs. Assn. (pres. 1983-86), Nat. Acad. Scis., Am. Philos. Soc., Inst. Mgmt. Scis. (pres. 1963, chmn. council 1964), Finnish Acad. Scis. (fgn. hon.), Brit. Acad. (corr.), Western Econ. Assn. (pres. 1980-81). Office: Stanford U Dept Econs Stanford CA 94305

ARSCOTT, DAVID GIFFORD, investment company executive; b. Princeton, N.J., May 7, 1944; s. John Robert and Lois (Coffin) A.; m. Martha Porter Eskridge, Apr. 12, 1980; children: David Eskridge, William Tristram, Philip West, Devon Mathys Bunker. BA, Coll. Wooster, 1966; MBA, U. Mich., 1968. V.p., gen. mgr. Citicorp Venture Capital, San Francisco, 1967-78; mng. gen. ptnr. Arscott Norton & Assocs., Palo Alto, Calif., 1978-88; prin. Arscott Assocs., Atherton, Calif., 1988—; bd. dirs. Lam Rsch. Corp., Fremont, Calif. Deacon Calvary Presbyn. Ch., San Francisco, 1982; vestry clk. Trinity Parish, Menlo Park, Calif., 1987—. Mem. Nat. Venture Capital Assn., Western Assn. Venture Capitalists (pres. 1977), Am. Electronics Assn., Bohemian Club. Republican. Office: Arscott Assocs 3301 El Camino Real Atherton CA 94025

ARSHAM, GARY MARTIN, medical educator; b. Cleve., 1941; s. Sanford Ronald and Florence Gail A.; m. Diana Silver, 1971. AB cum laude, Harvard U., 1963; MD, Case-Western Res. U., 1967; PhD, U. Ill., 1971. Fellow in med. edn. U. Ill., Chgo., 1968-71; asst. then assoc. dean curriculum devel., asst. prof. medicine and health scis. communication SUNY, 1971-72; assoc. prof., prof. health professions edn. U. of Pacific, San Francisco, 1972-79; chmn. Council on Edn. Pacific Med. Ctr., San Francisco, 1976-81; v.p. Arsham Cons., Inc., San Francisco, 1981—; adminstr. Pacific Vision Found., 1977-84, dir. edn., 1983—; mem. nat. adv. bd. John Muir Hosp. Med. Film Festival, 1981—; mem. task force on interdisciplinary edn. Nat. Joint Practice Commn., 1973-74; bd. dirs. U.S.-China Ednl. Inst., 1980—, sec., 1986-88. Co-author: Diabetes: A Guide To Living Well, 1989; chief editor Family Medicine Reports, San Francisco, 1983. Fellow ACP; mem. Am. Ednl. Research Assocs., Assn. Am. Med. Colls., Assn. Study Med. Edn., Assn. Hosp. Med. Edn. (exec. com. 1980-84, sec.-treas. 1982-84), Am. Diabetes Assn. (bd. dirs. San Francisco chpt. 1984—, No. Calif. affiliate 1986-87, Calif. affiliate 1987—), Am. Assn. Diabetes Educators (assoc. editor 1985—), Calif. Med. Assn., San Francisco Med. Soc., Harvard Club San Francisco (bd. dirs. 1981-88, pres. 1984-86), Lane Med. Soc. (Sommelier 1985—), Am. Assn. Individual Investors (bd. dirs. San Francisco chpt. 1984-88), Tech. Security Analysts Assn. San Francisco. Office: Arsham Cons Inc PO Box 15608 San Francisco CA 94115

ARTHAREE, BARUTI LATEEF, paper company executive; b. Fresno, Calif., Nov. 6, 1952; s. Art and Georgia (Price) Hutchins; m. Bernadette Scott, Mar. 27, 1976; 1 child, Hasan Jahi. BA, Linfield Coll., 1974; postgrad., Calif. State U., Hayward, 1979-81, U. Calif., Berkeley, 1986. Sales rep. Boise Cascade Corp., Vancouver, Wash., 1974-77, San Francisco, 1977-81; product mgr. Boise Cascade Corp., Portland, Oreg., 1981-83; dist. mgr. Boise Cascade Corp., Cerritos, Calif., 1983-85; regional mgr. Boise Cascade Corp., Commerce, Calif., 1985—. Coach Am. Youth Soccer Orgn., Culver City, Calif., 1983-86, Culver City Little League, 1983-86. Named Outstanding Citizen, Portland Observer, 1976, Person on the Move, Black Enterprise, 1983, 88. Mem. Printing Industries Am., NAACP. Office: Boise Cascade Corp 5361 Alexander St Commerce CA 90049

ARTHUR, JOHN MORRISON, retired utility executive; b. Pitts., Aug. 17, 1922; s. Hugh Morrison and Ann Matilda (Crowe) A.; m. Sylvia Ann Martin, June 19, 1948; children: William Robert, John Martin, Andrew Scott. BEE, U. Pitts., 1944, MEE, 1947. With Duquesne Light Co., Pitts., 1944-87, asst. to chmn. bd. and pres., 1966-67, pres., 1967-68, chmn. bd., chief exec. officer, 1968-83, chmn. bd., pres., 1983-85, chmn. bd., 1986-87; ret. Duquesne Light Co., 1987; adv. bd. Mellon Bank N.A., Mellon Bank Corp.; bd. dirs. Mine Safety Appliances Co., Duquesne Light Co., Chambers Devel. Co. Trustee U. Pitts., Buhl Found. Served with AUS, 1942-43. Mem. IEEE, Engrs. Soc. Western Pa., Duquesne Club, Montour Heights Country Club, Rolling Rock Club. Office: Duquesne Light Co 1 Oxford Ctr 301 Grant St Pittsburgh PA 15279

ARTHUR, LLOYD, agricultural products company executive; b. 1930; married. Pres. Ind. Farm Bur. Coop., 1983—. Office: Ind Farm Bur Coop Assn Inc 120 E Market St Indianapolis IN 46204 *

ARTMANN, WILLIAM CHARLIE, financial executive; b. Jackson, Miss., May 13, 1957; s. Thomas Elton and Helen Bebe (Gilbert) A. BS, Miss. State U., 1979, MA, 1981; MBA, Delta State U., 1985. Instr. Miss. State U., 1980-81; researcher Ciba-Geigy Corp., Greenville, Miss., 1981-85; v.p. Profl. Planning Assocs., P.A., Jackson, 1985-87, ptnr., 1987—. Editor Narcissis Jour., 1975. Chmn. Bethel United Meth. Ch., Greenville, 1984-85. Named to Hall of Fame Miss. State U., 1981. Mem. Internat. Bd. Standards and Practices Cert. Fin. Planners (cert.), Internat. Assn. Fin. Planning, Nat. Assn. Life Underwriters, Internat. Sprock Assn. (pres. 1986-87, editor Sprock Ill. 1987). Office: Profl Planning Assocs PA 860 E River Pl Ste 107 Jackson MS 39202

ARTZ, FREDERICK JAMES, diversified manufacturing company executive; b. Pitts., Dec. 28, 1949; s. Ray Edison and Jean Elizabeth (McClurg) A.; m. Donna Marie Moschella, Dec. 16, 1977; children: James Randall, BrieAnn Elizabeth. BS in Adminstrn. and Mgmt. Sci., Carnegie Mellon U., 1972; MBA, U. Pitts., 1973. Indsl. engr. Spang and Co., Butler, Pa., 1973-74; retail buyer Sun Drug div. Spang Stores, Butler, 1974-79, internal auditor, 1979-82, acctg. mgr., 1982-88, treas., adminstr. pension plan, 1988—. Bd. dirs. Richland Youth Found., Gibsonia, Pa., 1988—. Mem. Beta Gamma Sigma. Office: Spang & Co PO Box 751 Butler PA 16003-0751

ARTZT, EDWIN LEWIS, consumer products company executive; b. N.Y.C., Apr. 15, 1930; s. William and Ida A.; m. Ruth Nadine Martin, May 12, 1950; children—Wendy Anne, Karen Susan, William M., Laura Grace, Elizabeth Louise. B.J., U. Oreg., 1951. Account exec. Glasser Gailey Advt. Agy., Los Angeles, 1952-53; with Procter & Gamble Co., Cin., 1953—; brand mgr. advt. dept. Procter & Gamble Co., 1956-58, asso. brand promotion mgr., 1958-60, brand promotion mgr., 1960, 62-65, copy mgr., 1960-62, advt. mgr. paper products div., 1965-68, mgr. products food div., 1968-69, v.p., 1969, v.p., acting mgr. coffee div., 1970, v.p., group exec., 1970-75, dir., 1972-75, 80—; group v.p. Procter & Gamble Co., Europe, Belgium, 1975-80; pres. Procter & Gamble Internat., 1980—; vice chmn. Procter & Gamble Co, 1980—. Past chmn. residential div. United Appeal; past chmn. Public Library Capital Funds campaign; past dist. chmn. Capital Fund Raising dr. Boy Scouts Am., past leadership tng. chmn.; past chmn. advt. com. Sch. Tax Levy, County Govt. Issue; past trustee Kansas City Philharmonic, Nutrition Found., Boys' Clubs Greater Cin.; past bd. dirs. Kansas City Lyric Theater; past bd. govs. Kansas City Art Inst. Mem. Am. C. of C. Belgium (v.p.), Conf. Bd. Europe (adv. council), Internat. C. of C. (exec. com. U.S. council), Nat. Fgn. Trade Council. Clubs: Queen City (Cin.), Cin. Country (Cin.), Comml. (Cin.). Home: 9005 Cunningham Rd Cincinnati OH 45243 Office: Procter & Gamble Co 1 Procter & Gamble Pla Cincinnati OH 45202 *

ARUNDEL, IAN BRESSON, art dealer; b. Mitchell, S.D., Feb. 22, 1914; s. Charles Henry and Mary Porter (Bresson) A.; student U. Mich., 1934-37; m. Millie Lewis Waugh, Nov. 8, 1952; children—Ann Waugh, Colin Waugh. Restorer paintings and art objects, Detroit, 1937-43; dealer antique art, conservator, Los Angeles, 1945-52; art dealer, appraiser, Los Angeles, 1952—; expert primitive tribal art, appraiser U.S. govt.; exhibited tribal art in group shows at Santa Barbara (Calif.) Mus. Art, Los Angeles County Mus. Art, Miami U., Pomona Coll., U. Calif. at Fullerton, Otis Art Inst. Served with AUS, 1943-45. Fellow Am. Inst. for Conservation Historic and Artistic Works; mem. Smithsonian Instn., Brit. Mus. Soc., Archives Am. Art, Mus. Alliance Los Angeles County Mus., Victorian Soc. Office: 7152 SE 13th Ave Portland OR 97202

ARVAY, NANCY JOAN, insurance company executive; b. Pitts., Aug. 27, 1952; d. William John and Cornelia (Prince) A. BA in History, Duke U., 1974; postgrad., Columbia U., 1974-75. Polit. and internat. communications specialist U.S. Senate Fgn. Relations Com., Washington, 1975-77; broadcast media relations rep. Am. Petroleum Inst., Washington, 1977-79; broadcast media relations rep. Chevron U.S.A., San Francisco, 1979-82, coordinator electronic news media relations, 1982-85; sr. media relations rep. Chevron Corp., San Francisco, 1985-87; dir. pub. relations Fireman's Fund Corp., Novato, Calif., 1987—; lectr. Dept. Interior-Park Service, Beckley, W.Va., 1983; chmn. pub. relations Internat. Oil Spill Conf., Washington, 1984-85. Author, coordinator: Research Studies in Business and the Media, 1980-83; contbg. author This Is Public Relations, 1985. Founding mem. San Francisco chpt. Overseas Edn. Group; mem. pub. relations com. World Affairs Council San Francisco. Mem. Pub. Relations Soc., Radio/TV News Dirs. Assn. (assoc.), San Francisco Women in Bus. Office: Firemen's Fund Corp 777 Marin Dr Novato CA 94998

ARZT, FRANK J., marketing executive; b. Budapest, Hungary, Apr. 7, 1937; came to U.S., 1957; s. Frank and Anna (Hadrevy) A.; m. Betty Ann Krieger, June 23, 1962; children: Frank G., Barbara, Pamela. BSME, Drexel U., 1962; MBA, Seton Hall U., 1966. Project mgr. Foster Wheeler Corp., Livingston, N.J., 1962-66, Sun Oil Co., Phila., 1966-69; dir. mktg. Sanda Inc., 1969-71; mktg. mgr. Scott Environ., Southampton, Pa., 1971-78; dir. mktg. IU Conversion Systems, Inc., Horsham, Pa., 1978-81; dir. internat. mktg. Exide Electronics Corp., Phila., 1981-84; dir. mktg. ADEC div. Wickes Mfg. Co., Swarthmore, Pa., 1984-88; v.p. mktg. and sales Nat. Drying Machinery Co., Phila., 1988—; lectr. in field. com. chmn. Dist. Export Council, Phila., 1978-85. Mem. ASME, Factory Automation Mfr.'s Assn. (officer), Internat. Trade Devel. Assn. (pres. 1973-74), Am. Def. Preparedness Assn., Rotary (officer 1977). Republican. Episcopalian. Home: 1021 Crozer Ln Springfield PA 19064

ASAHINA, ROBERT JAMES, editor, corporate executive; b. Toledo, June 25, 1950; s. Shoichi and Katherine (Kaneko) A. AM, NYU, 1974; B in Gen. Studies, U. Mich., Ann Arbor, 1972. Mng. editor The Pub. Interest, N.Y.C., 1975-78; adminstrv. editor GEO, N.Y.C., 1978-79; editor N.Y. Times, N.Y.C., 1979-82; arts editor Harper's Mag., N.Y.C., 1982-83; v.p., sr. editor Simon & Schuster, N.Y.C., 1983—; chmn. Tokunaga Dance Co., N.Y.C., 1985—. Contbr. numerous articles to jours. and mags. including The Wall Street Journal, Harper's, Art & Antiques. Office: Simon & Schuster 1230 Ave of the Americas New York NY 10020

ASAM, MICHAEL EVANS, credit union administrator; b. Honolulu, Mar. 27, 1948; s. Francis Peter and Annie Eulani (Copp) A.; m. Chu Cha Yang, Aug. 22, 1974. BBA in Mgmt., U. Hawaii, 1974. V.p. Hawaii Credit Union league, Honolulu, 1975-83; exec. v.p. AFL-CIO Hotel Workers Fed. Credit Union, 1983-85; v.p. Kona Community Fed. Credit Union, Kealakekua, Hawaii, 1985-87, pres., 1987—; chmn. bd. dirs. Pacific Corp. Fed. Credit

Union, Honolulu. Chief lobbyist Hawaii Credit Union League, Honolulu, 1981-83. Sgt. U.S. Army, 1968-71, Vietnam. Mem. Credit Union Exec. Soc., Hawaii Coun. Credit Union Exec. Soc., Big Island Credit Union Exec. Assn. (pres. 1985—), Lions (fin. chmn. Kona chpt. 1985-87, v.p. 1986-87). Democrat. Lutheran. Office: Kona Community Fed Credit Union PO Box 747 Kealakekua HI 96750

ASAM, ROBERT CHARLES, plastics process engineer; b. Phila., Dec. 9, 1942; s. Charles Arthur and Bette (Shisler) A.; m. Diane Karen Memmer, Apr. 30, 1966; children: Michael Robert, Barbara Eileen. BSChemE, Rensselaer Poly. Inst., 1964; MS in Polymer Chemistry, U. Akron, 1970. FDA coordinator Goodyear Tire & Rubber Co., Akron, Ohio, 1964-75; v.p. Asam Bros. Inc., Southampton, Pa., 1975-78, pres., 1978-81; process engr. Tenneco Chems., Burlington, N.J., 1979-81; sr. process engr. Hercules Inc., Burlington, 1981-83, RCA Videodisc Div., Indpls., 1983-84; sr. process engr., regulatory coordinator Sabin Corp., Bloomington, Ind., 1984-89, tech. dir., 1989—. Mem. Soc. Mfg. Engrs., Soc. Plastics Engrs. Republican. Jewish. Home: RR 2 Box 423 Poland IN 47868 Office: Sabin Corp PO Box 788 Bloomington IN 47401

ASBURY, LARRY WAYNE, real estate management company executive; b. Mexico City, Mo., Aug. 13, 1947; s. Donald Earl and Mary Juanita (Brower) A.; m. Debbie G. Widmer, Sept. 8, 1973. B.A. in Acctg., Southwest Mo. State U.-Springfield, 1973, postgrad., 1973-74. Cert. property mgr. Regional field rep. Vernon & James Smith Co., Dallas, 1973-76; v.p., regional mgr. Nat. Corp. Housing Partnerships, Nashville, 1976-79; v.p. Nat. Corp. Housing Partnerships, Washington, 1979-81, sr. v.p., 1981-86, exec. v.p., 1986—; v.p. NCHP Property Mgmt., Inc., Washington, 1979-81, sr. v.p., 1981-83, exec. v.p., 1983-84; pres. NCHP Property Mgmt., Inc., 1984—. Chmn. campaign United Way, Washington, 1981. Served with U.S. Army, 1967-70. Mem. Nat. Assn. Home Builders (ann. speaker 1983-89), Inst. Real Estate Mgmt., Nat. Leased Housing Assn. (speaker 1982, 85, 86), Nat. Apartment Assn. (pres. 1989—). Republican. Methodist. Home: 906 South Carolina Ave SE Washington DC 20003 Office: Nat Corp Housing Partnerships 1225 I St NW Washington DC 20005

ASCHAUER, CHARLES JOSEPH, JR., health products company executive; b. Decatur, Ill., July 23, 1928; s. Charles Joseph and Beulah Diehl (Kniple) A.; m. Elizabeth Claire Meagher, Apr. 28, 1962; children: Karen Claire, Thomas Arthur, Susan Jean, Karl Andrew. B.B.A., Northwestern U., 1950; certificate internat. bus. adminstr., Centre d'Etudes Industrielles, Geneva, Switzerland, 1951. Prin. McKinsey & Co., Chgo., 1955-62; v.p. mktg. Mead Johnson Labs. div. Mead Johnson & Co., Evansville, Ind., 1962-67; v.p., pres. automotive group Maremont Corp., Chgo., 1967-70; v.p., group exec. Whittaker Corp., Los Angeles, 1970-71; v.p., pres. hosp. products div. Abbott Labs., North Chicago, Ill., 1971-76; v.p., group exec. Abbott Labs., 1976-79, exec. v.p., dir., 1979—; bd. dirs. Benefit Trust Life Ins. Co., Chgo., Rust-Oleum Corp., Vernon Hills, Ill., Banc One Wis. Corp., Milw., Bank One, N.A., Milw. Lt. Supply Corps, USNR, 1951-55. Mem. Chgo. Pres.'s Orgn., Proprietary Assn. (bd. dirs.), Sigma Nu. Clubs: University (Chgo.), Economics (Chgo.); Sunset Ridge Country (Northbrook, Ill.); Fairbanks Ranch Country (Rancho Santa Fe, Calif.). Office: Abbott Labs Abbott Pk North Chicago IL 60064

ASCHER, JAMES JOHN, pharmaceutical executive; b. Kansas City, Mo., Oct. 2, 1928; s. Bordner Fredrick and Helen (Barron) A.; student Bergen Jr. Coll., 1947-48, U. Kans., 1946-47, 49-51; m. Mary Ellen Robitsch, Feb. 27, 1954; children—Jill Denise, James John, Christopher Bordner. Rep., B.F. Ascher & Co., Inc., Memphis, 1954-55, asst. to pres., Kansas City, Mo., 1956-57, v.p., 1958-64, pres., 1965—. Bd. dirs. Childrens Cardiac Center, 1964-70, pres., 1968-70; mem. central governing bd. Children's Mercy Hosp., 1968-80; bd. dirs. Jr. Achievement of Middle Am., 1970—, pres., 1973-76, chmn., 1979-81; edn. chmn. Young Pres.'s Orgn. 6th Internat. Univ. for Pres., Athens, 1975. Served to 1st. lt. inf., U.S. Army, 1951-53; Korea. Decorated Bronze Star, Combat Infantryman's Badge. Mem. Pharm. Mfrs. Assn., Drug, Chem. and Allied Trades Assn., World Bus. Council, Proprietary Assn., Chief Execs. Orgn., Midwest Pharm. Advt. Club, Sales and Advt. Execs. Club, Am. Mgmt. Assn. (pres.'s assn.), Kansas City C. of C., Am. Legion, VFW, Delta Chi. Clubs: Lotos, N.Y. Athletic; Kansas City; Mercury; Indian Hills Country (Prairie Village, Kans.); Rotary. Home: 6706 Glenwood Shawnee Mission KS 66204 Office: 15501 W 109th St Lenexa KS 66219

ASEER, GHULAM NABI, business executive; b. Sohawa, Punjab, Pakistan, Feb. 2, 1940; s. Dhanpat Rai and Kaniz Fatima A.; children from previous marriage: Tabassam, Shabana. MS, Punjab U., 1963; Shorthand degree, Danton Shorthand Sch., Delhi, India, 1959. Civilian clk. Army Sch. of Adminstrn., Kuldana-Murre Hills, 1958-59; stenographer Mangla Dam Project, Wapda, Mangla, 1960-62; asst. devel. officer Ideal Life Ins. Co., Karachi, 1963-64; prodn. officer Adamjee Ins. Co., Ltd., Lahore, 1965-66; proprietor Aseer Sohawy Corp., Lahore, Pakistan, 1968—. Muslim League. Clubs: Am. Library, Brit. Library. Avocation: reading. Office: Aseer Sohway Corp, GPO Box 1752, Lahore Punjab 54000, Pakistan

ASEN, SHEL F., publishing company executive; b. N.Y.C., May 30, 1937; s. Eli and Lillian (Handelson) A.; m. Dorothy Anne Waters, Apr. 28, 1963; children: Michael, Matthew. BBA in Acctg., CCNY, 1960. Auditor Apfel & Englander, CPAs, N.Y.C., 1960-64; dir. acctg. Metro Mail (Metromedia), Westbury, N.Y., 1964-66; successively info. analyst, mgr. prodn. cost, mgr. mfg. fin., mgr. mfg. fin. and paper, v.p. mfg. MCGraw-Hill, N.Y.C., 1966-85, sr. v.p. mfg., 1985-88, sr. v.p. mfg. and purchasing, 1988—; mem. faculty Folio Show; presenter convs., shows in field. Grade advisor, mgr. Kings Park (N.Y.) Youth Assn. Sgt. U.S. Army, 1960-65. Mem. Graphic Communications Assn. Office: McGraw-Hill Inc 1221 Ave of the Americas New York NY 10020

ASH, MARY KAY WAGNER, cosmetics company executive; b. Hot Wells, Tex., May 12; d. Edward Alexander and Lula Vember (Hastings) Wagner; m. Melville Jerome Ash, Jan. 6, 1966 (dec.); children: Marylyn Theard, Ben Rogers, Richard Rogers. Student, U. Houston, 1942-43. Mgr. Stanley Home Products, Houston, 1939-52; nat. tng. dir. World Gift Co., Dallas, 1952-63; founder, chmn. emeritus May Kay Cosmetics, Inc., Dallas, 1963—; speaker to various orgns. Bd. dirs. Wadley Inst. Molecular Medicine; chmn. bldg. fund. Prestonwood Bapt. Ch., Dallas; hon. chmn. Tex. Breast Screening Project, Am. Cancer Soc. Mem. Bus. and Profl. Women's Club. Office: Mary Kay Cosmetics Inc 8787 Stemmons Frwy Dallas TX 75247

ASHBY, DONALD WAYNE, JR., accountant; b. Camden, N.J., Feb. 17, 1926; s. Donald Wayne and Dorothy (Childers) A.; m. Jo Rutan, July 13, 1977; children—Pamela Anne, Donald Wayne III. B.S., Ohio State U., 1949. C.P.A., N.Y., Ohio. Partner Deloitte Haskins & Sells, C.P.A.s, 1961—; ptnr. in charge Columbus Office Deloitte Haskins & Sells, C.P.A.s, Ohio, 1961—; area mng. ptnr. Deloitte Haskins & Sells, C.P.A.s, 1986—, also bd. dirs. Served with USNR, 1944-46; with USAF, 1950-51. Mem. Am. Inst. C.P.A.s, Ohio Soc. C.P.A.s (pres. Columbus chpt. 1969), Ohio State U. Alumni Assn. (pres. 1981-83), Phi Gamma Delta. Episcopalian. Clubs: Scioto Country (treas. 1972-74), Columbus Athletic (pres. 1968), Execs. (pres. 1971), Columbus (pres. 1980-81), The Golf (treas. 1985—) (Columbus). Home: 4906 Riverside Dr Columbus OH 43220 Office: Deloitte Haskins & Sells 155 E Broad St Columbus OH 43215-3650

ASHBY, JOHN EDMUND, JR., marketing executive; b. Dallas, Mar. 5, 1936; s. John Edmund and Lillian Eloise (Cox) A.; B.B.A., U. Tex., 1957; m. Martha DeLarios; children—Vicki, Dana, Suzanne, Shelley, Elizabeth. Salesman, IBM, Corpus Christi, Tex., 1959-64, sales mgr., 1964-67; regional mgr. Recognition Equipment Inc., Dallas, 1967-69, v.p., 1969-81; v.p. Teknekron Fin. Systems, Dallas, 1981-83, exec. v.p. TRW Fin. Systems (formerly Teknekron Fin. Systems), 1983—. Served with USMC, 1957-59. Recipient Sales award Sales and Mktg. Execs. Assn., 1961, IBM, 1964. Mem. Sales and Mktg. Execs. Assn., Beta Theta Pi. Presbyterian. Home: 3429 Cornell Dallas TX 75205 Office: TRW Fin Systems 3100 Monticello Ste 612 Dallas TX 75205

ASHBY, ROGER ARTHUR, pulp and paper products company executive; b. Marieville, P.Q., Can., Nov. 2, 1940; s. Emmett Ashby and Aurore Ledoux; m. Marguerite Kelly, Feb. 12, 1966; children: Eric, Alexandre. BS in Commerce, U. Montreal, Can., 1963. Acct., then office mgr. Kimberly-Clark of Can., 1963-69; dir. adminstrv. svcs., then compt. Sopalin, S.A. subs. Kimberly-Clark Corp., Paris, 1969-71, dir. fin., 1971-72, v.p., mng. dir., bd. dirs., 1972-76; pres., chief exec. officer Spruce Falls Power & Paper Co. Ltd. subs. Kimberly-Clark Corp., Kapuskasing, Ont., Can., 1976-78; exec. v.p., chief operating officer, bd. dirs. Rolland Inc., 1978-80; exec. v.p. then pres. Domtar Pulp & Paper Products Group div Domtar, Inc., Montreal, 1980—; bd. dirs. Sintra Inc. Q.F.I.A., F.E.R.I.C. Mem. Soc. Mgmt. Accts. of Can., Soc. Cert. Gen. Accts. Can. (cert. gen. acct., Soc. Registered Gen. Accts. Can. (registered indsl. acct.), CPPA, Quebec Forest Industries Assn. (bd. dirs.). Clubs: St. James, Mont Bruno Country. Office: Domtar Pulp & Paper Products, 395 de Maisonneuve Blvd W, Montreal, PQ Canada H3A 1L6

ASHCOM, JOHN M., general management executive; b. Pitts., Apr. 7, 1945; s. John M. and Mary Grace (Herron) A. BSBA, Youngstown (Ohio) State U., 1969. Mgr. communications Rockwell Internat., Pitts., 1972-77; dir. communications Litton Industries, N.Y.C., 1977-78; dir. mktg. and communications Republic Steel-LTV, Canton, Ohio, 1979-86; gen. mgr. Hanel Storage Systems, Pitts., 1986—. Editor: Republic Profiler mag., 1979-84, Water Journal mag., 1972-78, Gas Line mag, 1972-78. Mem. Soc. Mfg. Engrs., Material Handling Inst., Am. Mgmt. Assn., Bus./Profl. Advertisers. Republican. Club: Clan Donald, Pitts. Office: Hanel Storage Systems 420 Rouser Rd Bldg 3 Pittsburgh PA 15108

ASHCRAFT, JOSEPHINE THOMPSON SAUNDERS, accountant; b. Greenwood, Miss., Sept. 5, 1961; d. John Dunklin Jr. and JoAnne (Gilliam) A. Honors exchange student, Westfield State U., 1983; BA in Religion, U. of South, 1984; BBA in Acctg., Delta State U., 1986; postgrad., Miss. Coll., 1986—. Gen. mgr., chief fin. officer Ashcraft Enterprises, Greenwood, 1984-85; project asst. Office of Auditor State of Miss., Jackson, 1985-86, internal auditor dept. health, 1988-89; contr. Univ. Press Miss., Jackson, 1986-88; fin. cons. Ashcraft Enterprises, 1985—. Mem. Nat. Assn. Coll. and Univ. Bus. Officers, Miss. Assn. Govtl. Purchasing Agts. Republican. Presbyterian. Home: 711 River Rd Greenwood MS 38930 Office: State Dept Health Underwood Bldg North State St Jackson MS 39206

ASHE, OLIVER RICHARD, government official; b. Washington, Nov. 25, 1933; s. Paul Joseph and Mary (Tomardy) A.; B.S., Georgetown U., 1955; M.B.A., Hofstra U., 1971; postgrad. Pace U., 1972—; m. Helen Marie Curtin, Feb. 15, 1958; children—Mary, Pauline, Margaret, Kathleen, Oliver, Cecilia, Caroline. Regional personnel rep. Marriott Corp., N.Y.C., 1965-68; personnel specialist Navy Resale System Office, N.Y.C., 1968-70, head, career mgmt., 1970-74, dep. dir., indsl. relations, 1974-76; dir. civilian personnel programs, spl. asst. to asst. sec. navy, manpower, res. affairs and logistics U.S. Dept. Def., Washington, 1976-81; asst. for adminstrn. Office Under Sec. of Navy, 1981—. Served to capt. U.S. Army, 1955-65. Recipient Sustained Superior Accomplishment award U.S. Govt., 1976, 78, 79, Outstanding Fed. Exec. award, 1983, 84, 85, Outstanding Sr. Exec. Svc. Performance awards, 1982, 83, 84, 85, 87, 86, Fed. Meritorious Mgmt. award, 1987, U.S. Presdl. Sr. Exec. Meritorious Svc. award, 1988, Disting. Exec. award U.S. Presdl. Rank, 1989. Author book chpt. Home: 10600 Vale Rd Oakton VA 22124

ASHER, GARLAND PARKER, international electronics retail company executive; b. Richmond, Va., Sept. 6, 1944; s. Harry Garland and Margie Gregory (Duke) A.; m. Elizabeth Tinkham Deszyck, June 29, 1968; children: Elaine Tinkham, Timothy Duke. BA in Polit. Sci., Randolph-Macon Coll., 1967; MBA in Internat. Fin., U. Pa., 1970. Fin. analyst Ford Motor Co., Dearborn, Mich., 1970-71; asst. v.p. research Kidder Peabody & Co., Inc., N.Y.C., 1971-77; dir. fin. planning Tandy Corp., Ft. Worth, 1977-86; v.p., treas. InterTAN, Inc., Ft. Worth, 1986—; bd. dirs. Craddock Allied Corp., Ft. Worth. Bd. dirs. Tarrant County Soc. Crippled Children and Adults, 1978—; mem. bd. assoc. Randolph-Macon Coll., 1986—. Mem. Inst. Chartered Fin. Analysts, Fin. Execs. Inst., Newcomen Soc. Republican. Presbyterian. Clubs: Ft. Worth, River Crest (Ft. Worth). Office: InterTAN Inc 2000 Two Tandy Ctr Fort Worth TX 76102

ASHER, JAMES LEONARD, mechanical engineer; b. Plainview, Tex., July 31, 1947; s. John Carr and Gertrude (Ely) A.; m. Rose Marie Fryman, June 7, 1969; 1 child, Joseph Lewis. BSME, Tex. Tech. U., 1971. Registered profl. engr., Tex., Colo. Jr. engr. Traves-Braun and Assocs. Inc., San Antonio, 1972-75; engr., office mgr. Traves-Braun and Assocs. Inc., Houston, 1975-78; engr. P & S Assocs. Inc., Houston, 1978-79, engr., corp. v.p., sec.-treas., 1979—. V.p. Spring Branch Oaks Civic Assn., Houston, 1977, pres., 1978-79; active Boy Scouts Am., 1986—. Mem. ASME, ASHRAE, Nat. Soc. Profl. Engrs. Republican. Office: P & S Assocs Inc PO Box 801701 Houston TX 77080-1701

ASHER, KAMLESH C., comptroller; b. Bombay, Dec. 22, 1953; came to U.S., 1982; s. Chhabildas D. and Manjula (Kapadia) A.; m. Surekha Kamlesh Kapadia, Jan. 5, 1983. B. Com., U. Bombay, 1975, LLB, 1977; MBA, U. Detroit, 1987. Cert. ship broker. Mgr. accounts Intermodal Transport, Bombay, 1978-83; traffic asst. Grancolombiana Inc., N.Y.C., 1983; auditor Norton Lilly & Co. Inc., N.Y.C., 1983-84; comptroller Multiface Inc., Garden City, Mich., 1984—. Mem. Am. Mgmt. Assn., Assn. Ship Brokers and Agts. (U.S.A.) Inc. Home: 6869 Plainfield Dearborn Heights MI 48127 Office: Multiface Inc 6721 Merriman Rd Garden City MI 48135

ASHFORD, JAMES KNOX, auto parts company executive; b. Starkville, Miss., Jan. 20, 1937; s. Charles Rabb and Nannie (Smith) A.; m. Jacqueline Martin, July 23, 1961; children: Diane Marie, James Knox, Catherine Nan. B.S. in Acctg., Miss. State U., 1958; grad., Advanced Mgmt. Program, Harvard U., 1976. Mgr. budgets Kern County Land Co., San Francisco, 1965-67; corp. controller Walker Mfg. Co., Racine, Wis., 1967-71, v.p. fin., 1971-73, exec. v.p., 1973-77; exec. v.p. fin. and adminstrn. Tenneco Automotive, Deerfield, Ill., 1977; pres. Monroe Auto Equipment Co. Mich. subs. Tenneco Automotive, 1978-81; v.p. corp. planning and devel. Tenneco Inc., Houston, 1981-82; pres., chief exec. officer Tenneco Automotive div. Tenneco Inc., 1982-87, J.I. Case Co., Racine, 1987—; bd. dirs. Automotive Info. Council, 1982-87. Served with USNR, 1954-62. Mem. Motor and Equipment Mfrs. Assn. (bd. dirs. 1982-85). Republican. Presbyterian. Home: 340 S Bluff's Edge Lake Forest IL 60045 Office: J I Case Co 700 State St Racine WI 53404 also: Monroe Auto Equipment Co International Dr Monroe MI 48161

ASHKIN, RONALD EVAN, financial planner; b. New Rochelle, N.Y., Apr. 5, 1957; s. Abraham and Arleen (Wollins) A.; m. Rajasperi Maliapen, Nov. 25, 1984. AB, Harvard U., 1977; MBA, U. Pa., 1982. V.p. Continental Chem. Corp., Terre Haute, Ind., 1978-83, pres., 1983-86; pres. New Concepts Inc., Terre Haute, 1987—; bd. dirs. A & C Distbg. Co., New Concepts, Inc., Terre Haute. Moderator TV show, Terre Haute, Ind., 1985-86. Mem. Terre Haute sch. adv. com., 1984-86; bd. dirs. Glenn Civic Ctr., Terre Haute, 1985-86. Recipient group study exchange grant Rotary Found., Sri Lanka and India, 1985-86; scholarship Harvard U., 1973-76. Mem. Leadership Terre Haute Alumni Assn. (chmn. 1986), Am. Prodn. and Inventory Control Soc. (local v.p. 1982-84, 86, local pres. 1985), Jr. Achievement (vol. cons.), Phi Beta Kappa. Jewish. Club: Country of Terre Haute. Lodge: Toastmasters (local v.p. 1981-82. Home: RR 23 PO Box 388 Terre Haute IN 47802 Office: New Concepts Inc 1330 Beech St Terre Haute IN 47804

ASHLEY, HOLT, aerospace scientist, educator; b. San Francisco, Jan. 10, 1923; s. Harold Harrison and Anne (Oates) A.; m. Frances M. Day, Feb. 1, 1947. Student, Calif. Inst. Tech., 1940-43; BS, U. Chgo., 1944; MS, MIT, 1948, ScD, 1951. Mem. faculty MIT, 1946-67, prof. aero., 1960-67; prof. aeros. and astronautics Stanford U., Palo Alto, Calif., 1967—; spl. research aeroelasticity, aerodynamics; cons. govt. agys., research orgns., indsl. corps.; dir. office of exploratory research and problem assessment and div. advanced tech. applications NSF, 1972-74; mem. sci. adv. bd. USAF, 1958-80; research adv. com. structural dynamics NASA, 1952-60, research adv. com. on aircraft structures, 1962-70, chmn. research adv. com. on materials and structures, 1974-77; mem. Kanpur Indo-American program Indian Inst. Tech., 1964-65; AIAA Wright Bros. lectr., 1981; bd. dirs. Hexcel Corp. Co-author: Aeroelasticity, 1955, Principles of Aeroelasticity, 1962, Aerodynamics of Wings and Bodies, 1969, Engineering Analysis of Flight Vehicles, 1974. Recipient Goodwin medal M.I.T., 1952; Exceptional Civilian Service award U.S. Air Force, 1972, 80; Public Service award NASA, 1981; named one of 10 outstanding young men of year Boston Jr. C. of C., 1956; recipient Ludwig-Prandtl Ring, West German DGLR, 1987. Fellow Am. Acad. Arts and Scis., AIAA (hon., assoc. editor jour., v.p. tech. 1971, pres. 1973, Structures, Structural Dynamics and Materials award 1969), Royal Aeronautical Soc. (hon.); mem. Am. Meterol. Soc. (profl., recipient 50th Anniversary medal 1971), AAAS, Nat. Acad. Engring. (aeros. and space engring. bd. 1977—, mem. council 1985—), Nat. Research Council (governing bd. 1987—),, Phi Beta Kappa, Sigma Xi, Tau Beta Pi. Home: 475 Woodside Dr Woodside CA 94062

ASHLEY, LAWRENCE ATWELL, JR., construction executive; b. Balt., Sept. 12, 1929; s. Lawrence Atwell Sr. and Theresa Lillian (Hartman) A.; m. Emma Faye Shepherd; children: Debra Lee, Lawrence Atwell III, Susan Lynn. BCE, U. Miss., 1956. Registered profl. engr., Tex., La. Engr. Brown & Root, Inc., 1957-64, project mgr., 1964-70; asst. constrn. mgr. Brown & Root, Inc., Raleigh, N.C., 1970-73; sr. constrn. mgr. Brown & Root, Inc., Houston, 1973-79, v.p., 1979-82, sr. v.p., 1982—; Advisor Sch. Engring. U. Miss., University, 1986-87; mem. Woods Order U. Miss., University, 1984-87. Served with USN, 1950-54. Mem. NSPE, Houston Engring. and Sci. Soc., Chi Epsilon. Republican. Home: 93 Auburn Ct Granbury TX 76048 Office: Brown & Root Inc 4100 Clinton Dr Houston TX 77001

ASHLIMAN, JOSEPH LYLE, JR., automotive leasing executive; b. Pitts., May 29, 1927; s. Joseph Lyle and Katherine L. (Voegler) A.; m. Audrey C. Baguet, July 28, 1948; children—Shirley Anne, Tracey Jo, Joseph Lyle III. Used car sales mgr. Mt. Lebanon Motors, Pitts., 1947-51; asst. to v.p. sales Lease Motor Vehicle Co., Pitts., 1951-60; exec. v.p. Foss Rental Co., Pitts., 1960-82; leasing mgr. Bob Smith Ford, Inc., Pitts., 1982-83; Pitts. br. mgr. Barrett Leasing Corp., 1983-85; leasing mgr. Bill Gray Leasing, Pitts., 1985—; profl. drummer, percussionist, 1948—. Mem. Bethel Park (Pa.) Sch. Bd., 1972-79, pres., 1977-78. Served with USN, 1945-47. Mem. Nat. Assn. Fleet Adminstrs., Am. Legion, VFW. Clubs: Elks, Kiwanis (past pres.) (Bethel Park). Home: 407 Broughton Rd Bethel Park PA 15102 Office: 2685 W Liberty Ave Pittsburgh PA 15216

ASHMORE, FRANK WILLIAM, real estate investment and development executive; b. Phila., Oct. 14, 1945; s. Francis William and Florence (Meehan) A.; m. Nancy M. Laskowski, Apr. 8, 1978; children: Peter F., Colin P. Bachelors, Villanove U., ME, 1967. Cert. Fin. Planner, 1987. Design engr. Ross Engring., New Brunswick, N.J., 1967-68; sales engr. Boston Filter Co., Charlestown, Mass., 1970-74; mortgage officer Latimer & Buck, Inc., Phila., 1974-76; dir. sales Colony Mortgage & Realty Corp., Bala Cynwyd, Pa., 1976-79; v.p. intamar Logistics, West Conshohocken, Pa., 1979-84, Triad Guaranty, Inc., Radnor, Pa., 1984—; v.p. Flanigan & Wycoff, Inc., Radnor, 1987—; bd. dirs. Kingsbury Condominium Assn., Malvern, Pa., 1987—. Pheresis donor ARC, Phila., 1978—. With U.S. Army, 1968-70, Vietnam. Mem. Inst. Cert. Fin. Planners, Inst. Cert. Fin. Planners (chair mem. com. Delaware Valley soc. 1987). Republican. Roman Catholic. Office: Triad Devel Co 200 Eagle Rd Ste 114 Wayne PA 19087

ASHRAF, KAMIAR, savings and loan executive; b. Tehran, Iran, July 2, 1960; came to U.S., 1982; s. Kazem and Pari Ashraf; m. Roxanne Jennet Perry, Oct. 27, 1984. BSC in Econs. with honors, U. London, 1982; MBA in Fin., U. Wash., 1983. Futures analyst Bardec Investment Corp., Santa Ana, Calif., 1984; 1st v.p. portfolio mgr. Hemet (Calif.) Fed. Savs. and Loan, 1984-88; mgr. risk mgmt. and investment rsch. Glendale (Calif.) Fed. Savs. and Loan, 1988—. Mem. Nat. Assn. Securities Dealers. Office: Glendale Fed Savs & Loan 201 W Lexington Dr Glendale CA 91202

ASHTON, THOMAS WALSH, investment banker; b. Rochester, N.Y., May 11, 1929; s. Charles Edward and Marie Margaret (Walsh) A.; B.S., U.S. Mil. Acad., 1952; M.B.A., Harvard U., 1957; m. Frances E. Hickey, May 16, 1953; children—Lucy M. Van Atta, Mary B. Ashton Anders, Monica H., William T; m. Mary K Joy, Dec. 20, 1978. Assoc. corp. fin. Eastman Dillon Union Securities, N.Y.C., 1957-61, gen. partner, 1967-69; asst. v.p. Harris Upham & Co., N.Y.C., 1961-67; v.p. duPont Glore Forgan, Inc., N.Y.C., 1971-73; sr. v.p. ABD Securities Corp., N.Y.C., 1973-75; fin. cons. Am. Cancer Soc. of N.Y.C., East West Group Inc.; chmn. Peninsular Investments, Treasure Island, Fla., 1977-87; cons. Dept. Commerce, 1971; chmn. Ashton Investments Inc., 1987—. Chmn. parents's council Smith Coll., 1974-76. Served with AUS, 1946-48, 52-55. Mem. Soc. Harvard Engrs. and Scientists (gov. 1974-75), West Point Soc. N.Y. (dir. 1971-75). Republican. Clubs: Army and Navy (Washington); Seminole Lake Country (Seminole, Fla.). Office: 153d Ave Madeira Beach FL 33708

ASHWORTH, BRENT FERRIN, lawyer; b. Albany, Calif., Jan. 8, 1949; s. Dell Shepherd and Bette Jean (Brailsford) A.; m. Charlene Mills, Dec. 16, 1970; children—Amy, John, Matthew, Samuel, Adam, David, Emily, Luke, Benjamin. B.A., Brigham Young U., 1972; J.D., U. Utah, 1975. Bar: Utah 1977. Asst. county atty. Carbon County, Price, Utah, 1975-76; assoc. atty. Frandsen & Keller, Price, 1976-77; v.p., sec., gen. counsel Nature's Sunshine Products, Spanish Fork, Utah, 1977—; bd. mem., gen. counsel Carbon County Nursing Home, Price, 1976-77. Chmn. Utah County Cancer Crusade Com., 1981-83; city councilman Payson City, Utah, 1980-82, mem. planning commn., 1980-82, mayor pro tem, 1982; bd. dirs. ARC, Utah County chpt., 1988—, Deseret Village Spanish Fork, Utah, 1988—. Mem. ABA, Assn. Trial Lawyers Am., Southeastern Utah Bar Assn. (sec. 1977), Utah State Bar, SAR, Phi Kappa Phi. Republican. Mormon. Lodge: Kiwanis. Home: 1965 N 1400 E Provo UT 84604 Office: Nature's Sunshine Products 1655 N Main St Spanish Fork UT 84660

ASHWORTH, ELINOR GENE, financial analyst; b. Phoenix, Dec. 12, 1942; d. Arvid Wick and Erma Gene (Grant) Cooper; m. Monroe Alfred Ashworth III, Aug. 1, 1964 (div. Aug. 1977); children: Leslie, Monroe. AA, Del Mar Coll., 1963; BA, U. Houston, 1978, MBA, 1980. Adminstrv. asst. audit dept. Houston Nat. Bank, 1976-78; analyst, portfolio mgr. Investment Advisors, Inc., Houston, 1978—, exec. v.p., 1980—, chief administrv. officer, 1985—, also bd. dirs. Trustee Sch. Woods., Houston, 1974-77; pres., bd. dirs. New Neighbors League, Houston, 1968-73; mem. Mus. Fine Arts, Houston, 1987—. Fellow Fin. Analyst Fedn. (chartered); mem. Houston Soc. Fin. Analysts (treas. 1986-87, v.p. 1987-88, pres. 1988-89, dir. 1989—), Investment Counsel Assn. Am., Phi Theta Kappa (pres.). Republican. Methodist. Office: Investment Advisors Inc 1100 Louisiana Ste 2600 Houston TX 77002

ASKEY, DONALD EDWIN, marketing executive; b. Washington, Dec. 16, 1946; s. Robert Francis and Ruth Janet (Kinney) A.; m. Phyllis Lynn Schwartz, May 25, 1969; children—Meredith, Thomas Elliott. B.A., U. Wis. Madison, 1968; A.M., Harvard U., 1973. Mgr., info. analyst U.S. Dept. Agr., Beltsville, Md., 1970-72, Lockheed Corp., Palo Alto, Calif., 1976-78; editor, publisher, mgr. Am.-Scandinavian Found., N.Y.C., 1972-76, Times-Mirror Corp., San Jose, Calif., 1978-79; v.p. Legasse Assocs., advt. agy., Walpole, N.H., 1979-81, Askey Assocs., advt. agy., Keene, N.H., 1981-87, Lynch, Ryan & Assocs., Westborough, Mass., 1987-88, Granite Bank, Keene, 1988—. Trustee Grand Monadnock Arts Council, Keene, 1982-85; bd. dirs. Keene YMCA; mem. Keene Zoning Bd. of Adjustment. Republican. Unitarian Universalist. Lodge: Rotary. Home: 19 Evergreen Ave Keene NH 03431 Office: Granite Bank 122 West St Keene NH 03431

ASKINS, ARTHUR JAMES, service executive, accountant; b. Phila., Dec. 12, 1944; s. William J. and Rita M. (O'Brian) A.; m. Nancy E. Paulsen, Apr. 28, 1979. BS, LaSalle U., 1967; MA, Rider Coll., 1971. CPA, Pa., N.J. Tchr. Cardinal Dougherty High Sch., Phila., 1967-70; pvt. practice acctg., 1967—; staff acct. Gross Master & Co., Jenkintown, Pa., 1970-74; asst. controller Hankin Trustee, Willow Grove, Pa., 1974-79; mgr. internal audit Resorts Internat. Hotel Casino, Atlantic City, N.J., 1979-87, dir. revenue acctg., 1987-89, dir. MIS, fin. spl. projects, 1988—. Recipient cert. of Commendation Twp. of Abington (Pa.), 1967, Disting. Service award Community Accts., Phila., 1982, Superstar award Resorts Internat. Casino-Hotel, 1982, Brotherhood award NCCJ, Atlantic City, 1983, Mgmt. award Resorts Internat. Casino Hotel, 1986, 1st Mgrs. award Resort Internat. Casino-Hotel, 1986, Outstanding Vol. Service award Big Bros./Big Sisters, 1987. Mem. Nat. Assn. Accts. (nat. bd. dirs. 1983-85), pres. South Jersey

Shore chpt. 1979-81, Community Affairs award Suburban Northeast Phila. 1978), Inst. Internal Auditors (bd. dirs. 1984—), Am. Inst. CPA's, N.J. Soc. CPA's, Pa. Inst. CPA's, Greater Mainland C. of C. (audit com. 1979—). Republican. Roman Catholic. Home: PO Box 398 Somers Point NJ 08244 Office: Resort Internat Hotel Casino North Carolina & Boardwalk Atlantic City NJ 08401

ASKINS, WALLACE BOYD, manufacturing company executive; b. Chgo., June 2, 1930; s. Wallace Fay and Evelyn Mae (Baker) A.; m. Trieste M. Olivieri, May 20, 1954; 1 child, Justin Wallace. B.A., Lake Forest (Ill.) Coll., 1952; J.D. with honors, John Marshall Law Sch., Chgo., 1961. Bar: Ill. 1961; C.P.A., Ill. Sr. accountant Ernst & Whinney (C.P.A.s), Chgo., 1952-55; controller, house counsel Nat. Lock Co., Rockford, Ill., 1955-65; asst. corp. controller Xerox Corp., Stamford, Conn., 1965-77; exec. v.p., chief fin. officer White Motor Corp., Cleve., 1977-81, chmn. bd., chief exec. officer, 1981-84; exec. v.p., chief fin. officer Armco Inc., Parsippany, N.J., 1984—, also bd. dirs.; bd. dirs. Neoax Corp., Corporate Property Services, Surety Title Agy., Inc. Mem. ABA, Am. Inst. CPA's, Fin. Execs. Inst., Ill. Soc. CPA's, N.Y. Soc. CPA's, Conn. Soc. CPA's, Ill. Bar Assn. Office: Armco Inc 300 Interpace Pkwy Parsippany NJ 07054

ASPATURIAN, SUZANNE DOHAN, public relations executive; b. Vienna, June 23, 1930; d. Emil and Gertrude (Schloesinger) Dohan; m. Vernon V. Aspaturian, Aug. 29, 1951; children: Heidi Jeanne, Nancy Lee. BA in Polit. Sci., UCLA, 1951. Mem. pub. relations staff Mutual Don Lee Broadcasting System, Hollywood, Calif., 1951-54; dir. publicity Bernie Kamins Pub. Relations, Hollywood, 1954-55; writer gen. extension program Pa. State U., University Park, 1955-56, conf. coordinator, 1964-65, writer, editor continuing edn., 1975-76; adminstrv. asst., research assoc. Neuropsychiat. Inst. UCLA, 1976-79; exec. asst. to pres. Western Los Angeles Regional C. of C., 1979-82; dir. communications, pub. affairs L.A. Bus. Coun., 1986—. Club: Publicity of Los Angeles, UCLA Alumni. Office: Los Angeles Bus Coun 10880 Wilshire Blvd 1103 Los Angeles CA 90024

ASPINALL, KEITH WILTON, management consultant; b. Southport, U.K., May 11, 1953; Came to U.S., 1978; MA in Philosophy, Politics, Econs., Christ Ch.-Oxford U., Eng., 1974; MBA with high distinction, Harvard U., 1980. Sr. auditor Touche Ross & Co., London, 1974-77; cons. Arthur Andersen & Co., London, 1977-78; v.p. Bain & Co., Boston, 1980—. Fellow Inst. Chartered Accts. in Eng. and Wales. Club: United Oxford and Cambridge. Home: 287 Marlboro St Boston MA 02116 Office: Bain & Co 2 Copley Pl Boston MA 02116

ASPIOTOU, KOULA, shipping company executive; b. Athens, Greece, July 19, 1946; d. John Aspiotis and Ana (Beni-Psalti) Seimenis; m. Nikitas Harhalakis, Mar. 1, 1981; children: Mando, Eriana. Diploma, Athens U., 1968. Jr. clk. Nat. Bank Greece, Athens, 1965-69; asst. to prof. constl. law Athens U., 1969; asst. v.p., sr. credit officer Bank of Am., Athens, 1969-85; mng. dir. Seastar Navigation Co. Ltd., Piraeus, Greece, 1985—; bd. dirs. Seastar Navigation Ltd., London, Seastar Chartering Ltd., Piraeus. Home: 1 Kithiron St, 145 62 Athens Greece Office: Seastar Group of Cos, 27/31 Hatzikiriakou St, 185 38 Piraeus Greece

ASQUINO, RICHARD ANTHONY, small business owner; b. New Bedford, Mass., July 16, 1943; s. Daniel and Alice (Martins) A.; m. Anne Marie Hallisey, Oct. 17, 1978; children: Rosemary, Peter Anthony, John Daniel. BSBA, Roger Williams Coll., 1988. Br. mgr. C.I.T., N.Y.C., 1969-74; workout specialist Durfee Attleboro Bank, Fall River, Mass., 1975-79, Shawmut Bank of Boston, 1980-81, Middleboro (Mass.) Trust co., 1981-83; gen. mgr. G.H.R. Engring. Assoc., Inc., New Bedford, 1984-86; pres. Robrik Assocs., Inc., Middleboro, 1986—, Re/Max Southeast Inc., Middleboro, 1986—, Quality Printers of New England, Middleboro, 1986—; owner Tech Leasing Co, Acushnet, Mass., 1985—. Office: Robrik Assocs Inc 438 W Grove St Middleboro MA 02346

ASSAEL, HENRY, marketing educator; b. Sofia, Bulgaria, Sept. 12, 1935; s. Stanley Isaac and Anna (Behar) A.; m. Alyce Friedman, Aug. 19, 1961; children: Shaun Eric, Brenda Erica. B.A. cum laude, Harvard U., 1957; M.B.A., U. Pa., 1959; Ph.D., Columbia, 1965. Asst. prof. mktg. Sch. Bus., St. John's U., Jamaica, N.Y., 1962-65, Hofstra U., Hempstead, N.Y., 1965-66; prof. mktg. Grad. Sch. Bus. Adminstrn., NYU, 1966—, chmn. mktg. dept., 1979—; cons. AT&T, N.Y. Stock Exchange, Nestle Co., Inc., GTE, CBS, Am. Can Co. Author: Educational Preparations for Positions in Advertising Management, 1966, The Politics of Distributive Trade Associations: A Study in Conflict Resolution, 1967, Consumer Behavior and Marketing Action, 1981, 3d edit., 1987, Marketing Management: Strategy and Action, 1985; also numerous articles; editor: A Century of Marketing, 33 vols, 1978, Early Development and Conceptualization of the Field of Marketing, 1978, History of Advertising, 40 vols., 1985. Mem. Am. Mktg. Assn., Assn. Consumer Research. Office: 100 Trinity Pl New York NY 10006

ASSAEL, MICHAEL, lawyer, accountant; b. N.Y.C., July 20, 1949; s. Albert and Helen (Hope) A.; m. Eiko Sato. B.A., George Washington U., 1971; M.B.A., Columbia U. Grad. Sch. Bus., 1973; J.D., St. John's Law Sch., 1977. Bar: N.Y. 1978, U.S. Dist. Ct. (so. and ea. dists.) N.Y. 1980, U.S. Supreme Ct. 1982; CPA, N.Y. Tax sr. Price Waterhouse & Co., N.Y.C. and Tokyo, 1977-78; pvt. practice law, N.Y.C., 1978—; pvt. practice acctg., N.Y.C., 1978—. Author: Money Smarts, 1982. Pres. bd. dirs. 200 Block East 74th Street Assn., 1982; bd. dirs. 200 E 74 Owners Corp., 1981—, treas., 1983-84, pres., 1984-85; mem. Yorkville Civic Council, tenant adv. com. Lenox Hill Neighborhood Assn., 1981-82. Recipient N.Y. Habitat/Citibank mgmt. achievement award, 1985. Mem. ABA, N.Y. State Bar Assn., N.Y. County Lawyers Assn., Am. Inst. CPA's, Am. Assn. Atty. CPA's, Inc., Nat. Assn. Accts., N.Y. State Soc. CPA's, Aircraft Owners and Pilots Assn. Clubs: N.Y. Road Runners, Columbia Bus. Sch. (N.Y.).

ASSAF, ALI YOUSSEF, investment executive; b. Maracaibo, Zulia, Venezuela, Sept. 22, 1947; came to U.S., 1973; s. Youssef Soleiman and Wadad Mohamed (Abdul-Baki) A.; m. Laurel Ann Green, Apr. 1, 1978; children: Zeina Nadine, Youssef Ali. BBA, Am. U. Beirut, 1973; MBA, Boston U., 1975. Internat. officer Mid. East, Africa div. Bank of Boston, 1975-80, asst. v.p., 1980-84; Mid. East rep. Bank of Boston, Cairo, 1981-82; branch mgr. Boston Bank Cameroon (affiliate of Bank of Boston), Yaounde, 1984-86, Universal Bakeries, Inc., Jacksonville, Fla., 1986-89; gen. mgr. O R Assaf Inc., Jacksonville; also bd. dirs. Assaf Inc., Jacksonville. Dist. commr. Lebaneese Boy Scouts Assn., Beirut, 1965-73; treas. Rabitat al Amal Al Ijtimaii, Beirut, 1969-73; mem. Am. Druze Soc., N.Y.C., 1977—. Mem. Am. Univ. of Beirut Alumni Assn., Optimist Internat., Riverside Club (chmn. membership com. 1987—). Republican. Moslem. Office: O R Assaf Inc 1605 Woodmere Dr Jacksonville FL 32210

ASTIGARRAGA, JOSE I(GNACIO), lawyer; b. Havana, Cuba, July 20, 1953; came to U.S., 1960, naturalized 1974; s. Jose Agustin and Carolina (Vila) A.; m. Nancy Louise Upchurch, Aug. 11, 1979; children: Carolina, Cristina. AA with honors, Miami Dade Community Coll., 1973; BBA summa cum laude, U. Miami, 1975; JD magna cum laude, 1978. Bar: Fla. 1978, U.S. Dist. Ct. (so. dist.) Fla. 1979, U.S. Dist. Ct. (mid. dist.) 1988, U.S. Ct. Appeals (5th and 11th cir.) 1981. Chief bailiff Dade County Juvenile and Family Ct., Miami, Fla., 1972-74; law clk.-bailiff 11th Jud. Cir., Miami, 1974-77; with firm Steel, Hector & Davis, Miami, 1978-84, ptnr., 1984—; adj. faculty U. Miami Sch. Law, Coral Gables, Fla., 1980-81; legal counsel Cuban Mus. Arts and Culture, 1985-88, Little Havana Activities and Nutrition Ctrs. of Dade County, Inc., 1987—. Contbr. article to Dade County Young Lawyers Manual, 1980. Mem. biomedical tech. sci. panel High Tech. and Industry Council, 1984-87, health care task force Beacon Council of Dade County, 1984-85; adminstrv. hearing officer Dade County Sch. Bd., Miami, 1982—; bd. dirs. Miami Children's Hosp., 1985-88, also chmn. quality assurance com., mem. fin. com.; bd. dirs. Miami Children's Hosp. Research Inst., Inc., 1986—, chmn. nominating com.; bd. dirs. Dade County Beacon Council Inc., 1985—; dir. Miami Coalition, Inc.; mem. exec. com., chmn. schs. task force; trustee Fla. Internat. Univ. Found., 1988—; dir. Miami Coalition, Inc.; mem. exec. com., chmn. Schs. Task Force; trustee Fla. Internat. U. Found., 1988—. Named Harvey T. Reid scholar U. Miami Sch. Law, 1975-78, Leonard T. Abess scholar, U. Miami, 1974-75; recipient Up and Comers Law award Price Water house and South Fla. Bus. Jour., 1988. Mem. ABA (com. on comml. fin. services, Uniform Comml. Code com., subcom. on comml. paper bank deposits and payment systems 1984), Fla. Bar Assn. (sec. civil procedure rules com. 1979-84), Dade County Bar Assn. (commr. jud. campaign practices commn. 1986-87), Cuban-Am. Bar Assn., U. Miami Sch. Law Alumni Assn. (bd. dirs. 1981-88), Greater Miami C. of C. (bd. govs. 1985-88, group chmn. econ. devel. sect. 1986-87, chmn. biotech task force 1984-86, hispanic affairs com. 1984—). Office: Steel Hector & Davis 200 S Biscayne Blvd Miami FL 33131

ASTON, JAMES WILLIAM, banker; b. Farmersville, Tex., Oct. 6, 1911; s. Joseph Alexander and Jimmie Gertrude (Jackson) A.; m. Sarah Camilla Orth, June 29, 1935 (dec. Mar. 25, 1989); 1 child, James William, Jr. BSCE, Tex. A&M U., 1933. Apprentice city mgr. City of Dallas, 1933-34, asst. city mgr., 1934-39, city mgr., 1939-41; city mgr. City of Bryan, Tex., 1939; v.p. Republic Nat. Bank, Dallas, 1945-55, exec. v.p., 1955-57, pres., 1957-61, pres., chief exec. officer, 1961-65, chief exec. officer, 1965-77, chmn. bd. dirs exec. com., 1977-87, cons., 1987—; Bd. dirs. Indsl. Properties Corp., Dallas; cons. NCNB Tex., 1988—. Bd. dirs. Hoblitzelle Found., Dallas, Southwestern Med. Found., Dallas, 1981—, Trinity Improvement Assn., Dallas; ex-official dir. Cotton Bowl Athletic Assn., Dallas; mem. Gov.'s Energy Adv. Counc., 1973; mem. adv. com. Dallas Citizens Counc. Recipient Disting. Am. award Nat. Football Found. and Hall of Fame, 1984, J. Erik Jonsson award for Voluntarism United Way, 1985. Mem. Dallas Clearing House Assn., Tex. Bankers Assn. (past pres.), Assn. Former Students Tex. A&M U. (pres. 1961), Tau Beta Phi, Beta Gamma Sigma. Home: 5000 Royal Ln Dallas TX 75229 Office: PO Box 660020 Dallas TX 75266-0020

ASTORGA, TONY M(ANUEL), accountant; b. Superior, Ariz., Dec. 14, 1945; s. Antonio Astorga and Esther L. (Luevano) Castro; divorced; children from previous marriage: Renee, Denise, Michelle; m. Milena Dora Cuellar, Apr. 29, 1984; children: Tabatha, Farah. BS in Acctg., Ariz. State U., 1970. CPA. Tax auditor II Ariz. Dept. Revenue, Phoenix, 1965-70; supervising sr. Peat, Marwick & Mitchell, Phoenix, 1970-75; ptnr. Astorga, Maurseth & Co., Phoenix, 1975-87; sr. v.p., treas. Blue Cross and Blue Shield Ariz., Phoenix, 1988—; bd. dirs. Blue Cross Blue Shield, Phoenix, Ariz. Acad., Phoenix, Ariz. Bd. dirs. Community Council, Phoenix, Friendly House, Phoenix, Info. and Referral Services, Phoenix, Valle del Sol, Phoenix, Ariz.-Mex. Commn., Phoenix; chmn., bd. dirs Ariz. Coliseum and Exposition Ctr., Phoenix, 1983—. Named one of Outstanding Young Men Am., U.S. Jaycees, Phoenix, 1980, to Ariz. State U. Bus. Alumni Hall of Fame, Tempe, 1985. Mem. Am. Inst. CPA's, Ariz. Soc. CPA's, Ariz. Hispanic C. of C. (Profl. of Yr. 1981-82), Ariz. State U. Acctg. Circle, Pi Kappa Alpha. Roman Catholic. Office: Blue Cross & Blue Shield Ariz. 2444 W Las Palmaritas Phoenix AZ 85021

ASUMADU, SAMPSON, pharmacist, financial consultant; b. Konogo, Ghana, July 19, 1952; came to U.S., 1974; s. Joseph and Mary (Akom) A.; m. Margaret Anochie, Nov. 13, 1985; children: Emmanuel, Rhoda, Rachel. BS in Pharm., Northeastern U., 1979, MS in Pharm., 1982; MBA, Arthur D. Little Coll., 1985. Registered pharmacist, D.C. Dir. ops. Ashanti Drug Stores, Ghana, West Africa, 1971-73; intern Boston Hosp. for Women, 1976-79; pharmacist Peter Bent, Brigham & Women's Hosp., Boston, 1979-81; supr. pharmacy U. Mass. Med. Ctr. U. Mass. Med. Ctr., Worcester, 1981-84; asst. Dir. pharmacy Greater S.E. Community Hosp., Washington, 1985—; pharmacist Peoples Drug Stores, Inc., Alexandria, Va., 1986-88; pres. Internat. Health and Devel. Corp.; cons. in field; inventor in field. Aronic Priesthood Ch. of Jesus Christ of Later Day Sts., Md., 1988. Mem. Soc. Hosp. Pharmacists, Fedn. Internat. Pharmacists (chartered), Am. Mgmt. Assn. Home and Office: 6602 Parkwood St Landover Hills MD 20784

ASWELL, DONALD LEE, utilities company executive; b. Downsville, La., July 19, 1926; s. Luther L. and Lucille C. (Aulds) A.; m. Virginia Loveless; children: Carol L., Marjorie J., Paul L. BS in Chemistry, La. State U., 1947. Registered mech. engr., La. Supt. sta. La. Power and Light Co., New Orleans, 1959-63, gen. supt. prodn., 1963-65, mgr. prodn., 1965-77, v.p. power prodn., 1977-83, sr. v.p. fossil ops., 1983-85, sr. v.p. energy supply, 1985—. Mem. ASME, Instrument Soc. Am. Democrat. Methodist. Home: 2641 Hudson Pl New Orleans LA 70131 Office: La Power & Light Co 1010 Common St PO Box 60340 New Orleans LA 70160

ATCHISON, MICHAEL DAVID, investor, investment bank executive; b. Gallup, N.Mex., Oct. 31, 1938; s. Thomas Wesely and Grace Dixon (Barber) A.; m. Margrit G. Koch, Feb. 18, 1961; children: Christina, Stephanie. MA in English, U. Tex., 1965, MBA in Fin., 1971. Mgr. bus. office Southwestern Bell, Dallas, 1965-70; v.p. 1st Nat. Bank Dallas, 1971-73; v.p., mgr. internat. div. Interfirst Bank-Houston, 1974-75; v.p. fin. and adminstrn. W.W. Young Interests Inc., Houston, 1975-82; founder, chief exec. officer M.D. Atchison Co., Houston, 1982—. Contbr. articles to profl. jours. With U.S. Army, 1958-60, ETO. Mem. Fin. Execs. Inst., Internat. Transp. Mgmt. Assn. (bd. dirs. 1976-79), Rotary. Republican. Lutheran. Home: 2219 Hickory Creek Kingwood TX 77339 Office: MD Atchison Co 15600 JFK Blvd Ste 500 Houston TX 77032

ATHERTON, JOHN W., JR., banker. Chmn., chief exec. officer CityFed. Fed. Savs. Bank, Palm Beach, Fla.

ATIEH, MICHAEL GERARD, accountant; b. Paterson, N.J., Aug. 8, 1953; s. Michael and Evelyn (Makoujy) A.; m Mary P. Higgins, May 9, 1976; children: Allison, Michael, Steven. BA in Acctg. and Econs., Upsala Coll., 1975. CPA, N.J. Auditor mgr. Arthur Young & Co., Newark, 1975-81; dir. acctg. standards Merck & Co., Rahway, N.J., 1981-82; dir. acctg. Merck & Co., Rahway, 1982-85, dir. investor relations, 1986-87, v.p. govt. relations, 1987—. Mem. com. Project Children, Pequannock, N.J., 1988. Mem. Am. Inst. CPAs, N.J. State Soc. CPAs, Nat. Investor Relations Inst. Republican. Roman Catholic. Office: Merck & Co 126 Lincoln Ave PO box 2000 Rahway NY 07065

ATKINS, RICHARD G., publishing company executive. Exec. v.p. telecommunications Macmillan Inc. Office: Macmillan Inc 866 3rd Ave New York NY 10022 *

ATKINS, SAMUEL JAMES, III, banker; b. Wichita Falls, Tex., Dec. 24, 1944; m. Catherine Lou Allen, Jan. 22, 1966; children: Lea Michele, Paige Elizabeth. B.S. in Petroleum Engring., U. Okla., 1968; M.B.A. in Fin., Harvard U., 1970. Petroleum engr. Shell Oil Co., Denver, 1967-68; with RepublicBank, Dallas, 1970-87, v.p., 1974-77, sr. v.p., div. mgr., 1977-80, sr. v.p., asst. dept. mgr., 1980-81, exec. v.p., 1981-87 ; exec. dir. Republic Bank Corp., 1982-87; exec. v.p. First RepublicBank, Dallas, 1987-88; exec. dir First RepublicBank Corp., 1987-88; group exec. v.p. NCNB, Tex. Nat. Bank, 1988—. Mem. Ind. Petroleum Assn. Am. (assoc., bd. dirs. 1984-86, 89), Am. Petroleum Inst. (assoc.), Am. Gas Assn. Republican. Methodist. Clubs: Dallas Petroleum, Royal Oaks Country (Dallas). Home: 9523 Robin Meadow Dallas TX 75243 Office: NCNB Tex PO Box 83104 Dallas TX 75283-3104

ATKINS, THOMAS JAY, lawyer; b. Detroit, Apr. 21, 1942; s. Robert Alfred and Dorothy Irene A.; m. Shirley Roberta Green, Dec. 21, 1968. BS in Engring., Wayne State U., 1965; MS in Engring., Rensselaer Poly. Inst., 1967; JD, San Joaquin Coll. Law, 1979; postgrad. Harvard Law Sch., 1979; MBA, UCLA, 1983. Bar: Calif. 1979. Cons. Ctr. for Advanced Studies, Gen. Electric Co., Santa Barbara, Calif., 1967-70; prin. Cen. Valley Distbrs., Visalia, Calif., 1970—, Thomas Jay Atkins, P.C., Visalia and Santa Barbara, 1979—, United Motor Supply, Inc., San Jose, Calif., 1986-88, O.E. Parts Supply, Inc., Fresno, 1988—; chmn. Calif. Merc. Inc., Tulare, 1980—. Recipient rsch. commendation NASA, 1969. Mem. ABA, Am. Mgmt. Assn., Engring. Soc. Detroit, Santa Barbara Yacht Club, Visalia Country Club, Regency Club, Visalia Racquet Club. Republican. Office: PO Box 3744 Visalia CA 93278 also: PO Box 524 Santa Barbara CA 93101

ATKINSON, ARLIS, construction executive; b. July 29, 1945; s. Homer H. and Emma A.; m. Linda K. Rhodes, Nov. 30, 1964; children: Mark A., Chanda K. Student, Manatee Community Coll., Bradenton, Fla., 1976-80. Area supt. Cather Industries, Sarasota, Fla., 1971-76; constrn. mgr. E & K of Fla., Sarasota, 1976-78, v.p., gen. mgr., 1978-82; owner, chief exec. officer Atkinson Plastering & Drywall, Inc., Bradenton, 1982—. Mem. Assn. Wall and Ceiling Ind. Internat. (bd. dirs. 1987-88), Assn. Bldg. Contractors, NAHB, Gulf Coast Builders Exchange, Fla. Wall and Ceilings Contractors Assn. (bd. dirs. 1983-86, pres. 1987-89). Club: Plaza (Bradenton). Lodges: Shriners, Masons (32 degree). Home: 1912 54th St E Bradenton FL 34208 Office: Atkinson Plastering & Drywall Inc 6003 28th St E Bradenton FL 34203

ATKINSON, EUGENE D., investment banker; b. Birmingham, Ala., Oct. 2, 1944; s. Thomas Eugene and Jewel Inez (Griffin) A.; m. Carol A. Deichman, Oct. 27, 1968; children—Shawn E., Trevor G. B.S., U.S. Mil. Acad., West Point, 1966; M.B.A., Harvard U., Boston, 1972. Assoc. Goldman Sachs & Co., N.Y.C., 1972-76; v.p. Goldman Sachs & Co., Tokyo, 1976-79, head Asian/Pacific region, 1979-84; ptnr. Goldman Sachs & Co., N.Y.C., 1984—; pres. Goldman Sachs (Japan) Corp., 1986-88; co-chmn. Goldman Sachs Internat., N.Y.C., 1988—. Contbr. articles to profl. jours. Served to capt. C.E., U.S. Army, 1966-70. Decorated Army Commendation medal with valor, Bronze Star.

ATKINSON, HAROLD WITHERSPOON, utilities consultant, real estate broker; b. Lake City, S.C., June 12, 1914; s. Leland G. and Kathleen (Dunlap) A.; B.S. in Elec. Engring., Duke, 1934; M.S. in Engring., Harvard U., 1935; m. Pickett Rancke, Oct. 6, 1946; children—Henry Leland, Harold Witherspoon. Various positions in sales, engring. Cambridge Electric Light Co. (Mass.), 1935-39, 46-73, asst. mgr. power sales dept., 1946-49, gen. mgr., 1957-73, dir., 1959-84, exec. v.p., 1972-73; mgr. Pee Dee Electric Membership Corp., Wadesboro, N.C., 1939-46; gen. mgr. Cambridge Steam Corp., 1951-73, v.p., 1959-73, dir. 1955-84. Chmn., Cambridge Traffic Bd., 1962-73; pres. Cambridge Center Adult Edn., 1962-64; v.p. Cambridge Mental Health Assn.; chmn. allocations com. Greater Boston United Community Services, 1971-72; chmn. Cambridge Commn. Services, 1955-56; adv. bd. Cambridge Council Boy Scouts Am.; mem. corp., chmn. camping com. Cambridge YMCA, 1964-71; chmn. Cambridge chpt. ARC, 1969-71; trustee of trust funds Town of Harrisville, N.H., 1976-83; treas. North Myrtle Beach Citizens Assn., 1982-84. Served from pvt. to capt. AUS, 1942-45. Registered profl. engr., Mass. Mem. IEEE (sr.), Mass. Soc. Profl. Engrs., Elec. Inst. (pres. 1971), Harvard Engring. Soc., Cambridge C. of C. (pres. 1957-58). Newcomen Soc. N.Am., Phi Beta Kappa, Tau Beta Pi, Pi Mu Epsilon. Clubs: Cambridge Boat (treas. 1962-65), Cambridge (pres. 1972-73); Carolina Golf; Bay Tree Golf; Plantation; Civitan (pres. Wadesboro 1940-41); Rotary (pres. Cambridge club 1959-60, v.p. North Myrtle Beach, S.C. club) Home: 705 Holloway Cir N North Myrtle Beach SC 29582 Office: PO Box 533 North Myrtle Beach SC 29597

ATKINSON, KENNETH ALLEN, oil company executive; b. Long Beach, Calif., Nov. 28, 1947; s. Milburn Tensley and Patricia June (Timberlake) A.; m. Jo Ann (Everett), Dec. 16, 1967. AA, Rio Hondo Coll., 1969; BSBA, Woodbury U., 1970. Corp. auditor Nat. Environment Corp., Orange, Calif., 1969-71; contr., sec., treas. Fuqua Homes, Inc., Arlington, Tex., 1971-77; administrv. asst. fin. Utah State U., Logan, 1977-79; asst. corp. contr. Flying J Inc., Brigham City, Utah, 1979-80; corp. contr. Flying J Exploration and Prodn., Billings, Mont., 1980—; cons. Billings, 1986—. Treas. Yellowstone County Rep. Com., Billings, 1987—, vice-chmn., 1986-87, precinct committeeman, Shepherd, Mont., 1984—; advisor, sponsor, Big Bros. and Big Sister, Billings, 1987. Fellow Coun. Petroleum Accts. Soc.; mem. Phi Gamma Kappa, YMCA Club. Republican. Home: 9242 Twelve Mile Rd Shepherd MT 59079 Office: Flying J Exploration & Prodn Inc 2906 1st Ave N North Billings MT 59101

ATKINSON, SHERIDAN EARLE, lawyer, financial and management consultant; b. Oakland, Calif., Feb. 14, 1945; s. Arthur Sheridan and Esther Louise (Johnson) A.; m. Margie Ann Lehtin, Aug. 13, 1966. 1 son, Ian Sheridan. B.S., U. Calif.-Berkeley, 1966, M.B.A., 1971; J.D., U. San Francisco, 1969. Bar: Calif. 1970. Prin. Atkinson & Assocs., fin. and mgmt. cons., corp. and bus. valuations, San Francisco, 1968—; assoc. Charles O. Morgan, Jr., San Francisco, 1972-76; pvt. practice, San Francisco Bay Area, 1976—. With USAR, 1970-76. Mem. ABA, Calif. Bar Assn. Republican. Office: 1327A Solano Ave Albany CA 94706

ATLAS, LIANE WIENER, publishing company executive; b. N.Y.C.; d. Louis and Frances (Ferne) Wiener; m. Martin Atlas, Mar. 5, 1944; children: Stephen Terry, Jeffrey L. AB, Vassar Coll., 1943; postgrad., Johns Hopkins U., 1953-55. Cert. fin. planner. Fgn. affairs officer Dept. State, Washington, 1962-68; sr. economist U.S. Commerce Dept., Washington, 1968-75, U.S. Treasury Dept., Washington, 1975-79, Riggs Nat. Bank, Washington, 1980-82; v.p. Fintapes Inc., Washington, 1984-87, pres., 1987—; mem. U.S. delegation UN Econ. Orgns., N.Y.C., Geneva, 1963, 64, 68, 79. Author: (book) Middle Eastern Financial Institutions, 1977; (audio cassettes) Financial Planning for Widowhood, 1986, Financial Planning for Divorce, 1987; freelance writer Changing Times and other mags., 1982-87. Treas. Entertaining People/Washington Home, 1986—. Fellow in econs. Johns Hopkins U., Balt., 1954-55; recipient Cert. of Appreciation U.S. Treasury Dept., Washington, 1977. Mem. Nat. Assn. Women Bus. Owners, Inst. Cert. Fin. Planners, Washington Ind. Writers, City Tavern Club, Vassar Club. Home: 2254 48th St NW Washington DC 20007 Office: Fintapes Inc PO Box 9754 Friendship Station Washington DC 20016

ATTARDO, LEWIS CHARLES, research administrator, consultant; b. Wilkes Barre, Pa., Dec. 3, 1950; s. Charles J. and Gertrude (Volpe) A.; children: Aimee, Jessica, Jill, L. Antonio. AS, Luzerne Community Coll., 1970; BA in Econs., Bloomsburg U., 1972. Appraiser SBA, Wilkes-Barre, Pa., 1972-73; comml. indsl. relocation specialist Redevel. Authority, City of Wilkes-Barre, 1973-75; dir. relocation Redevel. Authority, City of Lock Haven, Pa., 1975-78; coordinator community devel. Redevel. Authority, Dauphin County, Steelton, Pa., 1978-84; pres., chief exec. officer Attardo Enterprises, Harrisburg, Pa., 1976—; dir. Ben Franklin Tech. Ctr., Pa. State U. at Harrisburg, Middleton, Pa., 1984—; evaluator, panelist Commonwealth of Pa., 1987—, Role of Flexible Automation in Pa. Project, 1987-88; bd. dirs. Control Techtronics, Inc., Harrisburg, Pa., 1984—, Laser Communications, Inc., Lancaster, Pa., 1985-87, Pa. State U.-Harrisburg Small Bus. Devel. Ctr., WITF/TV Netsource; mem. tech. adv. council Pa. State U.-York, 1985—; v.p., bd. dirs., charter mem. Venture Investment Forum of Cen. Pa., Inc., 1986—; bd. dirs. Mfg. Tehc. Ctr. for South Cen. PA, York, 1988—; charter mem. The Wilson Ctr. Assocs., Washington, 1988—. Mem. Eastern Econ. Assn. (charter), Smithsonian (charter) Nat. Geog. Soc. (sec., bd. dirs.), Cen. Pa. Internat. Bus. Assn. (sec., bd. dirs. 1986—), AAAS (voting sec. K). Roman Catholic. Office: Pa State U Ben Franklin Tech Ctr Cen & No Pa Inc Middletown PA 17057 also: Attardo Enterprises PO Box 6186 Harrisburg PA 17112 also: Attardo Assocs 5508 Lily Pl Holiday FL 34691

ATTEBERRY, WILLIAM DUANE, diversified manufacturing company executive; b. Decatur, Ill., Mar. 24, 1920; s. William Herman and Lucile (Hunter) A.; m. Doris Jean Walker, Dec. 19, 1946; children: William Thomas, James Norman, Thomas Hunter. B.E., U. So. Calif., 1943. Engr. P.R. Mallory & Co., Indpls., 1946; v.p. Western Lead Products Co., Los Angeles, 1946-51; engr., prodn. mgr. chems. and metals div. Eagle-Picher Co., Cin., 1951-60; pres. chems. and metals div. Eagle-Picher Industries, Inc., Cin., 1960-65, exec. v.p. corp., 1965-67, pres., 1967-78, chmn. bd., 1978-85, chief exec. officer, 1968-82, also dir., chmn. exec. com.; dir. Fifth-Third Bank Cin., 1st Nat. Bank Joplin, Mo., Empire Dist. Electric Co., Xtek Inc., Kroger Inc., Vulcan Materials Co. Chmn. bd. dirs. Bethesda Hosp., bd. dirs. Joplin YMCA; trustee Ohio No. U., Boys Club Cin.; dir. Greater Cin. Found. Served to capt. USMCR, 1943-46, PTO. Recipient Engring. Alumnus award U. So. Calif., 1979, Great Living Cincinnatian award, 1988. Mem. AIME, Am. Zinc. Inst. (dir., v.p.), Queens City CLub (bd. govs. 1981—, v.p. 1988), Cin. Country Club, Tippecanoe Lake Country Club, Hole-in-the-Wall Golf Club (Fla.), Naples Yacht Club (Fla.), Bankers Club, Comml. Club (pres. 1987-88, Great Living Cincinatian 1988), Sigma Chi. Republican. Presbyterian (trustee). Clubs: Queen City, Cincinnati Country, Tippecanoe Lake Country (Ind.), Hole-in-the-Wall Golf (Fla.), Naples Yacht (Fla.), Bankers (Cin.), Commercial (Cin.)(pres. 1987-88). Office: Eagle-Picher Industries Inc 580 Walnut St Cincinnati OH 45202

ATTEBURY, WILLIAM HUGH, elevator company executive; b. Amarillo, Tex., Jan. 8, 1929; s. Arnold Gentry and Lula Vivian (Dunn) A.; student Iowa State Coll., 1947-49; B.A., Okla. U., 1951; m. Joyce B. Kallin, June 7,

1951; children—Julie Anne, William Arnold, Nancy Ellen, Elizabeth Grace, Edward Anton. Vice pres. Attebury Elevators, Inc., Amarillo, 1954—; pres. Bison Devel. Co., 1960—, A & S Steel Bldgs Inc., Amarillo, 1961—, El Poso Oil Co., Amarillo, 1969—, Bison Chem. Co., Port Neches, Tex., 1969—, ptnr. Tex. Beef Producers Group, 1978—; dir. Western Data, Inc., 1st Nat. Bank Amarillo, Master Films Co. Dir. Amarillo Bd. City Devel., 1969-73; adv. bd. Salvation Army, 1973-77; bd. mgrs. Amarillo Hosp. Dist., 1978-79; bd. dirs. Amarillo Children's Home, 1978-82; bd. dirs. Village of Hope, 1972-74; elder Westminster Presbyterian Ch., 1970—. Served with USNR, 1951-54; Korea. Mem. Panhandle Producers and Royalty Owners, Tex. Cattle Feeders Assn. (bd. dirs. 1981-83), Southwest Systems Builders Assn., Metal Bldg. Dealers Assn., Panhandle Grain Dealers Assn. Clubs: Amarillo, Amarillo Country. Home: 3202 Lipscomb St Amarillo TX 79109 Office: PO Box 7446 Amarillo TX 79109

ATWATER, FRANKLIN SIMPSON, business executive; b. New Britain, Conn., Aug. 24, 1916; s. George Franklin and Ida (Simpson) A.; m. Marion Jane Brian, May 9, 1947; children: Mary-Jane, Brian, Sally. B.S., MIT, 1938. Mem. staff MIT, 1938-39; with Fafnir Bearing Co. (div. Textron Inc.), New Britain, 1939-75, prodn. engr., indsl. engring. mgr., asst. gen. works mgr., gen. works mgr., 1956-59, v.p. mfg., 1959-63, v.p. ops., 1963-67, exec. v.p., 1967-69, pres., 1969-75; pres. Homelite, Charlotte, N.C., 1975-76, chmn., 1976-77; bus. advisor Internat. Exec. Service Corps, 1981-88; dir. Goss & DeLeeuw Machine Co., Fusion Systems Corp., Galileo Electro-Optics Corp., DBA Systems, Inc. Author: (with L.L. Bethel and others) Industrial Organization and Management, 1945, Essentials of Industrial Management, 1954, Production Control, 1942. Home: 91 Heritage Dr River Hills Plantation Clover SC 29710 Office: Homelite 14401 Carowinds Blvd Charlotte NC 28217

ATWATER, HORACE BREWSTER, JR., food company executive; b. Mpls., Apr. 19, 1931; s. Horace Brewster and Eleanor (Cook) A.; m. Martha Joan Clark, May 8, 1955; children—Elizabeth C., Mary M., John C., Joan P. A.B., Princeton U., 1952; M.B.A., Stanford U., 1954. Divisional v.p., dir. mktg. Gen. Mills. Inc., Mpls., 1958-65, mktg. v.p., 1965-70, exec. v.p., 1970-76, chief operating officer, 1976-81, pres., 1977-82, chief exec. officer, 1981—, chmn. bd., 1982—, also dir.; dir. Northwestern Nat. Life Ins. Co., Honeywell Inc., N.W. Bancorp. Trustee Princeton U., MacAlester Coll., Walker Art Ctr.; mem. adv. council Stanford U. Grad. Sch. Bus. Served to lt. USNR, 1955-58. Club: Woodhill Country (Wayzata, Minn.). Office: Gen Mills Inc 1 General Mills Blvd Minneapolis MN 55426 *

ATWATER, N. WILLIAM, engineering and construction executive; b. 1934. BS, Stevens Inst. Tech., Hoboken, N.J., 1956, MS, 1962. V.p. Foster-Wheeler Corp., Clinton, N.J., 1983-84, exec. v.p., 1984—; also pres., chief exec. officer Foster-Wheeler Internat. Corp. Office: Foster Wheeler Corp Perryville Corporate Pk Clinton NJ 08809

ATWELL, CHARLES MCHUGH, investment company executive; b. Washington, June 10, 1939; s. Charles Mervin and Monica Josephine (McHugh) A.; m. Pamela Ruth Durie, Jan. 8, 1966; children: Scott Patrick, Monica Rose. Cert. in investment banking, Georgetown U., 1966; MS, Am. Coll., 1983. CLU. V.p. Waddell & Reed Fin. Svcs., Kansas City, 1966—; presenter, counselor Trust for Insuring Educators, Reston, Va., 1983-87. Author: Accumulating Money, 1983. Cons. Boys and Girls Clubs Am., Kansas City, 1986—, ticket capt. 1988—; asst. dist. commr. Boy Scouts Am., Kansas City, 1988—; chmn. legacies Am. Cancer Soc., Johnson County, Kans., 1988—. Mem. Internat. Assn. Fin. Planners (pres. Kansas City chpt. 1977-79), bd. dirs. 1978-81, cons. 1986—), Am. Assn. for Continuing Edn., Coll. for Fin. Planning (Cons., advisor 1983—), Commerce Clearing House (adv. bd. 1987—). Republican. Roman Catholic. Office: Waddell & Reed Fin Svcs 2400 Pershing Rd PO Box 418343 Kansas City MO 64141-9343

ATWOOD, CLARK DENNIS, real estate developer; b. Denver, Feb. 2, 1953; s. George Clayton and Mildred Louise (Jose) A.; m. Sue Ann Teeters, Sept. 3, 1982; children: Tiffany, Holly, Jimmy, Trenton. BS in Indsl. Constrn. Mgmt., Colo. State U., 1975. Prodn. coordinator Wood Bros. Homes, Denver, 1972-76, constrn. mgr., 1976-78, spl. asst. to pres., 1978-79; v.p., div. mgr. Wood Bros. Homes, Albuquerque, 1979-82, San Antonio, 1982-84; div. pres. Nash Phillips Copus, Inc., Colo. Springs, Colo., 1984-87; sr. v.p., no. calif. div. mgr. SW Diversified, Inc., San Francisco, 1987—; v.p., bd. dirs. Albuquerque Homebuilders, 1980-82; bd. dirs. West Bay div. Bldg. Industry Assn.; co-chmn. Govt. Affairs Coun., 1988—. Chmn. builder group Pikes Peak United Way, 1985, chmn. real property div., 1986; tchr. Jr. Achievement Project Bus., 1986; com. person Rep. Com., Colo. Springs, 1985—; mem. growth policy coun. San Mateo Econ. Devel. Assn., 1987—. Recipient Mame award for Best Interior Design, 1984, 86. Mem. Econ. Devel. Council, Homebuilders Assn. of Colo. Springs (bd. dirs.), Home and Garden Show Home Builders Assn. (chmn. 1986), Young Builders Club (bd. dirs. San Antonio chpt. 1983-84), Sigma Lamda Qui. Methodist. Lodge: Demolay. Office: SW Diversified Inc 150 N Hill Dr Ste 35 Brisbane CA 94005

ATWOOD, DONALD JESSE, JR., federal official, former automobile manufacturing company executive; b. Haverhill, Mass., May 25, 1924; s. Donald Jesse and Doris Albertine (French) A.; m. Curina Harian, Sept. 8, 1946; children: Susan Albertine, Donald Jesse. BSEE, MIT, 1948, MSEE, 1950. With AC Electronics div. Gen. Motors. Corp., 1961-70, dir. Milw. ops., 1968-70, mgr. Indpls. ops. Detroit Diesel Allison div., 1970-73, 1st gen. mgr. Transp. Systems div., 1973-74, gen. mgr. Delco Electronics div., Kokomo, Ind., 1974-78, gen. mgr. Detroit, 1978-80, v.p., group exec., 1981-83, exec. v.p., 1984-87, vice-chmn., 1987-89, pres. GM Hughes Electronic Corp. div., 1985-89; Dep. Sec. of Def. designate Washington, 1989—; bd. dirs. Charles Stark Draper Lab. Corp. Bd. dirs. Automotive Hall of Fame Inc. Served with AUS, 1943-46. Mem. AIAA, Motor Vehicle Mfrs. Assn. (policy com.), Nat. Acad. Engring. (council), Soc. Automotive Engrs. Office: Dep Sec of Def Rm 3E 944 The Pentagon Washington DC 20301-1000 *

AU, ALICE MIU-HING, management consultant; b. Hong Kong, Feb. 12, 1958; d. Yuk Chong and Yuet Wah (Wong) A.; m. M. Anthony Wong, Jan. 3, 1982. BS in Engring. and Applied Sci., Yale U., 1981; MBA, Harvard U., 1986. Environ. engr. Digital Equipment Corp., Hudson, Mass., 1981-82, sr. process engr., 1982-84; mgmt. cons. McKinsey & Co., Inc., N.Y.C., 1986—; gen. ptnr. Advent Ptnrs., Dallas, 1986—, mng. ptnr. Advent Ptnrs. II, Dallas, 1987—; chmn. program com. Profl. Council, Boston, 1981-82. Club: Yale of N.Y. Home: 155 Cat Rock Rd Cos Cob CT 06807 Office: McKinsey & Co 55 E 52d St New York NY 10022

AU, EDWARD GUM HUNG, mechanical contractor; b. Honolulu, Feb. 28, 1924; s. Koon Ngon and Bow Jun (Ching) A.; m. Audrey Chew Hing, Jan. 18, 1944; children: Alvin, Baldwin, Carolyn, Derwin, Evelyn, Faye-Lynn. Apprentice Pearl Harbor (Hawaii) Naval Shipyard, 1940-44, pipefitter, shipfitter, 1947-51; foreman Kaimuki Plumbing, Honolulu, 1952-67; owner, pres., chmn. bd. dirs. Au's Plumbing & Metal Work, Inc., Honolulu, 1968—. Bd. dirs. Palolo Chinese Home, Honolulu, 1987—. Served with U.S. Army, 1944-45. Recipient Hawaii Bus. Top 250 award First Interstate Bank, Honolulu, 1985-87. Mem. Gen. Contractors Assn. Hawaii, Plumbing & Mech. Contractors Assn. Hawaii, Sheet Metal Contractors Assn., Chinese C. of C. Hawaii (pres., bd. dirs. 1987—), United Chinese Soc. (trustee 1987—), C. of C. of Hawaii (bd. dirs. 1987—), See Dai Doo Soc., Sheong Kar Heong Soc. Buddhist. Office: Aus Plumbing & Metal Work Inc 2265 Hoonee Pl Honolulu HI 96819

AUCELLO, JOSEPH G., investment company executive; b. Foggia, Italy, Mar. 20, 1960; came to U.S., 1969; s. Anthony and Angela (Ceddia) A.; m. Marie A. Cook, Oct. 25, 1985; 1 child, Angelina. BBA in Fin. and Investments, Bernard Baruch Coll., 1983. Trader, ins. and securities rep. Advest, Inc., Hartford, Conn., 1983—. Home: 13 Trinity Ln East Hartford CT 06118 Office: Advest Inc 280 Trumbull St Hartford CT 06118

AUCOTT, GEORGE W., rubber products and automotive services company executive; b. 1934; married. BS, Ursinus Coll., 1956. With Firestone Tire and Rubber Co., Akron, Ohio, 1956—, exec. v.p., 1980; corp. v.p., div. exec., v.p. ops. NA Tire, 1981; corp. exec. v.p., group pres. Firestone Internat., from 1982, World Tire; exec. v.p. World Tire group, 1986-88, pres., chief operating officer, 1988—, also bd. dirs. Office: Firestone Tire & Rubber Co 1200 Firestone Pkwy Akron OH 44317 other: Firestone Tire & Rubber Co 205 N Michigan Ave Ste 3800 Chicago IL 60601 *

AUER, MARILYN MILLS, banker; b. Port Huron, Mich., Apr. 30, 1936; d. James Carleton and Eunice Margaret (Foster) Mills; m. James Matthew Auer, Feb. 1, 1964; 1 child, Charles William. BS, Northwestern U., 1960; MS, U Wis., 1964. Tchr. Rockridge High Sch., Edgington, Ill., 1960-62; teaching asst. U. Wis., Madison, 1962-64; legal sec. Atty. Edmund P. Arpin, Neenah, Wis., 1964-66; lending asst. Republic Realty Mortgage Corp., Wauwatosa, Wis., 1972-79; editor Creative Homeowner Press, Milw., 1979-82; adminstrv. sec., asst. to govt. lending dept. 1st Bank, N.A., Milw., 1982-87, specialist, 1987—. Editor: The Baton of Phi Beta, 1964-70; freelance reviewer The Milw. Jour., 1972-84; contbr. to books by Creative Home Press. Mem. Milw. Symphony Chorus, 1975-86. Mem. Milw. Met. Assn. Profl. Mortgage Women (officer, editor newsletter, 1986—, sec. 1987-88, bd. dirs. 1987—), Phi Beta. Office: 1st Bank NA 201 W Wisconsin Ave Milwaukee WI 53259-1000

AUERBACH, ERNEST SIGMUND, lawyer, insurance company executive; b. Berlin, Dec. 22, 1936; s. Frank L. and Gertrude A.; 1 child, Hans Kevin. AB, George Washington U., 1958, JD, 1961. Bar: D.C. 1962, Pa. 1978, U.S. Dist. Ct. D.C. 1962, U.S. Ct. Appeals (D.C. cir.) 1962, U.S. Supreme Ct. 1971. Atty., So. Ry. Co., Washington, 1961-62; commd. 1st lt. U.S. Army, 1962, advanced through grades to maj., 1968; asst. staff judge adv. 1st Logistical Command, Saigon, Vietnam, 1966-67; internat. affairs div. Hdqrs. U.S. Army Europe, Heidelberg, Ger., 1967-70, chief, 1969-70; resigned, 1970; div. counsel Xerox Corp., Stamford, Conn., 1970-75; mng. atty. NL Industries, Inc., N.Y.C., 1975-77; asst. gen. counsel INA Corp., Phila., 1977-78, staff v.p. and assoc. gen. counsel, 1978-79, sr. v.p. INA Svc. Co., 1979-82, sr. v.p. CIGNA Worldwide Corp. div. CIGNA Corp., 1982-84, pres. internat. life and group ops., 1984—; mng. dir. Crusader Life Ins. PLC, Reigate, Eng., 1984-86, chmn. 1986-89. Mem. Am. Coun. on Fed. Republic Germany, computer systems tech. adv. com. Dept. Commerce, 1974-76. Col. USAR, 1970-85 . Decorated Legion of Merit with oak leaf cluster, Bronze Star. Contbr. articles to news and def. jours. Mem. ABA, Westchester-Fairfield Corp. Counsel Assn. (founding officer), Univ. Club, Nat. Arts Club. Avocation: running. Office: CIGNA Corp 1600 Arch St OL12 Philadelphia PA 19103

AUERBACH, JOSEPH, lawyer, educator; b. Franklin, N.H., Dec. 3, 1916; s. Jacob and Besse Mae (Reamer) A.; m. Judith Evans, Nov. 10, 1941; children: Jonathan L., Hope B. Pym. A.B., Harvard U., 1938, LL.B., 1941. Bar: N.H. 1941, Mass. 1952, U.S. Ct. Appeals (1st, 2d, 3d, 5th, 7th and D.C. cirs.), U.S. Supreme Ct. 1948. Atty. SEC, Washington and Phila., 1941-43, prin. atty., 1946-49; fgn. service staff officer U.S. Dept. State, Dusseldorf, W. Ger., 1950-52; ptnr. Sullivan & Worcester, Boston, 1952-82, counsel, 1982—; lectr. Boston U. Law Sch., 1975-76; lectr. Harvard Bus. Sch., Boston, 1980-82, prof., 1982-83, Class of 1957 prof., 1983-87, prof. emeritus, 1987—; bd. dirs. Nat. Benefit Life Ins. Co., N.Y.C., Valcom Inc., Omaha, J.L. Auerbach & Co., The Netherlands Antilles, Auerbach, Christenson, Taguiri, Inc., Boston. Author: (with S.L. Hayes, III) Investment Banking and Diligence, 1986, Underwriting Regulation and Shelf Registration Phenomenon in Wall Street and Regulation, 1987, also papers and articles in field. Mem. editorial bd., Harvard Bus. Rev. Bd. dirs. Friends of Boston U. Libraries; v.p., mem. exec. com. Shakespere Globe Ctr. (N.A.), N.Y.C., 1983—; trustee Mass. Eye and Ear Infirmary, Boston, 1981—, chmn. devel. com., 1985-88; trustee Old Colony Charitable Found., 1976—; mem. adv. bd., former chmn. devel. com. Am. Repertory Theatre, Cambridge, Mass., 1985—. Served with AUS, 1943-46. Decorated Army Commendation medal. Mem. ABA, Mass. Bar Assn., Harvard Class 1938 (class com.). Clubs: Federal, Harvard of N.Y.C. (mem. com. Class of 1938), Sky, Grolier, Shop, Harvard Mus. Assn., Sesquincentennial Harvard Musical Assn. (chmn.). Home: 23 Lime St Boston MA 02108 Office: Sullivan & Worcester One Post Office Sq Boston MA 02108 also: 1 Post Office Sq Boston MA 02109

AUERBACH, MARSHALL JAY, lawyer; b. Chgo., Sept. 5, 1932; s. Samuel M. and Sadie (Miller) A.; m. Carole Landsberg, July 3, 1960; children—Keith Alan, Michael Ward. Student, U. Ill.; J.D., John Marshall Law Sch., 1955. Bar: Ill. 1955. Sole practice Evanston, Ill., 1955-72; ptnr. in charge matrimonial law sect. Jenner & Block, Chgo., 1972-80; mem. firm Marshall J. Auerbach & Assocs., Ltd., Chgo., 1980—; mem. faculty Ill. Inst. Continuing Legal Edn. Author Illinois Marriage and Dissolution of Marriage Act, enacted into law, 1977; Historical and Practice Notes to Illinois Marriage and Dissolution of Marriage Act, 1980-88; contbr. chpts. to Family Law, Vol. 2. Fellow Am. Acad. Matrimonial Lawyers; mem. Ill. State Bar Assn. (chmn. family law sect. 1971-72), ABA (vice-chmn. family law sect. com. for liaison with tax sect. 1974-76). Home: 2314 Orrington Ave Evanston IL 60201 Office: 180 N LaSalle St Chicago IL 60601

AUGUSTINE, NORMAN RALPH, industrial executive; b. Denver, July 27, 1935; s. Ralph Harvey and Freda Irene (Immenga) A.; m. Margareta Engman, Jan. 20, 1962; children: Gregory Eugen, René Irene. B.S.E. magna cum laude, Princeton U., 1957, M.S.E., 1959; D English (hon.), Rennsselaer Poly. Inst., 1988. Research asst. Princeton U., 1957-58; program mgr., chief engr. Douglas Aircraft Co., Inc., Santa Monica, Calif., 1958-65; asst. dir. def. research and engring. U.S. Govt., Office of Sec. Def., Washington, 1965-70; v.p. advanced systems Missiles and Space Co., LTV Aerospace Corp., Dallas, 1970-73; asst. sec. army The Pentagon, Washington, 1973-75; undersec. army The Pentagon, 1975-77; v.p. ops. Martin Marietta Aerospace Corp., Bethesda, Md., 1977-82; pres. Martin Marietta Denver Aerospace Co., 1982-85, sr. v.p., info. systems, 1985, pres., chief operating officer, 1986-87, vice chmn., chief exec. officer, 1987-88, chmn., chief exec. officer, 1988—, also bd. dirs.; bd. dirs. Phillips Petroleum Co., Internat. Laser Systems, Inc., Orlando, Fla., Colo. Nat. Bank; mem. of corp. C.S. Draper Lab.; cons. Office of Sec. Def., 1971—, Exec. Office of Pres., 1971-73, Dept. Army, Dept. Air Force, Dept. Navy, Dept. Energy, Dept. Transp., mem. USAF Sci. Adv. Bd.; chmn. Def. Sci. Bd.; mem. NATO Group Experts on Air Def., 1966-70, NASA Research and Tech. Adv. Council, 1973-75; chmn. Space Systems and Tech. Adv. Bd., 1985—; chmn. adv. bd. dept. aeromech. engring. Princeton U., 1975-83; chmn. bd. visitors procurement and acquisition program Am. U., 1977-82; bd. advisors Center for Advancement of Procurement, Fla. State U.; chmn. adv. council, MIT Lincoln Lab. Author: Augustine's Laws; Mem. adv. bd.: Jour. of Def. Research, 1970—; asso. editor: Def. System Mgmt. Rev, 1977-82; editorial bd.: Astronautics & Aeros; contbr. articles to profl. jours. Trustee Johns Hopkins U.; fund raiser YMCA, Arlington, Tex., 1971-72; chmn. nat. program evaluation com., council v.p. Boy Scouts Am.; mem. Immanuel Presbyterian Ch., McLean, Va. Recipient Meritorious Service medal Dept. Def., 1970, Disting. Civilian Service medal Dept. Def., 1975, James Forrestal medal Nat. Security Indsl. Assn., 1988. Fellow Am. Astron. Soc., AIAA (hon., v.p. pub. policy 1978-82, dir. 1978-85 , pres. 1983-84, Goddard medal 1988), IEEE; mem. Am. Helicopter Soc. (dir. 1974-75), Nat. Acad. Engring., Internat. Acad. Astronautics, Assn. U.S. Army (pres. 1980-84), Nat. Security Indsl. Assn. (Forrestal medal 1988), Phi Beta Kappa, Sigma Xi, Tau Beta Pi. Office: Martin Marietta Corp 6801 Rockledge Dr Bethesda MD 20817

AULETTA, JOAN MIGLORISI, construction company executive, mortgage and insurance broker; b. N.Y.C., July 23, 1940; d. Angelo George and Ann (Passa) Miglorisi; A.B.S., Bklyn. Community Coll., 1957; m. E.V. Auletta, Oct. 5, 1958; children—Ann, Vincent, George, Jeanne. Owner-mgr. Auletta Realty, also owner-mgr. E&J Pancake House, L.I., N.Y., 1947-76; office and fin. mgr. Larchwood Constrn. Co., Farmingville, N.Y., 1976-77; prodn. mgr. Lawlor Industries, Holtsville, N.Y., 1977-79; real estate and fin. adv. Family Home Improvement Corp., Queens Village, N.Y., 1979-81; co-owner Total Home Constrn. Co., N.Y.C., 1981—; owner-mgr. Century 21, Echo Hills Realtors Inc., Miller Place, N.Y., 1987—, Tone-O-Matic, 1988—; owner-mgr. comml. property, 1970—. Roman Catholic. Home: 80 Smithtown Polk Blvd Centereach NY 11720 Home: 7107 N 70th Ave Fort Lauderdale FL 33319

AULETTA, LOUIS JOHN, SR., aerospace engineer; b. Torrington, Conn., Oct. 3, 1938; s. Louis Thomas and Elizabeth Ann (Torok) A.; m. Barbara Jean Scott, Feb. 27, 1960; children: Louis Jr., Lori, Tara, Mark. A in Elect. Tech., U. Hartford, 1961. Sr. test engr. Chandler Evans Div. Colt Industries, West Hartford, Conn., 1959-74; chief engr. Bauer Aerospace Inc., Farmington, Conn., 1974-77; v.p., gen. mgr. Bauer Aerospace Inc., Farmington, 1977-83, pres., chief exec. officer, 1983—; mem. adv. bd. U. Conn. Export Ctr., Storrs, 1986—, U. Hartford, 1987-88. Dir. Conn. World Trade Assn., Hartford, 1987-88, Farmington Park Assn., 1987-88; apptd. to Israel Exchange Commn. Recipient Exporter of Yr. award U.S. Small Bus. Adminstrn., 1988. Mem. Greater Hartford C. of C. (dir.). Republican. Roman Catholic. Lodge: Sons Italy. Home: 47 Edgewood Dr Torrington CT 06790 Office: Bauer Aerospace Inc Farmington Industrial Pk Farmington CT 06032

AULT, JOHN BRADY, insurance broker; b. Washington, July 18, 1951; s. John Miller and Beatrice Ann (Brady) A.; m. Alice Patricia Rowan, Apr. 14, 1973 (div. Jan. 1983); 1 child, Rebecca Marie; m. Susan Kay Jenkins, Apr. 30, 1988. AB in Econs., St. Louis U., 1973, MBA in Fin., 1976. Underwriter Reliance Ins. Co., St. Louis, 1973-76; v.p. Lawton, Byrne and Bruner, St. Louis, 1976-83; v.p. Marsh & McLennan Inc., St. Louis, 1983-87, Milw., 1987—. Mem. Ind. Ins. Agts., Mo. Athletic Club, Glen Echo Country Club. Home: 5506 N Kent Ave Whitefish Bay WI 53217 Office: Marsh & McLennan Inc 411 E Wisconsin Ave Milwaukee WI 53217

AULT, THOMAS JEFFERSON, III, manufacturing company executive, manufacturing consultant; b. Portland, Ind., June 23, 1911; s. Ross Earl and Olga (Sattler) A.; AS, Cumnock Coll., 1932; BA in Econs., UCLA, 1934; student Los Angeles Stock Exchange Inst., 1930-33; cert. Am. Mgmt. Assn. m. Mary C. Carr, June 30, 1938; 1 child, Brian Carr. With Borg-Warner Corp., Chgo., 1935-58, trainee Warner Gear div. Borg-Warner Corp., Muncie, Ind., 1935-37, buyer 1937-41; asst. purchasing agt., 1941-51, dir. purchasing, 1951-52, v.p. and asst. gen. mgr. Detroit Gear div., 1953-54, pres., 1954-57, pres., gen. mgr. Long mfg. div., Detroit, 1956-54; pres., chief exec. officer Saco-Lowell Shops, Boston, 1958-60, also dir.; pres., gen. mgr. The Budd Co., Detroit, 1960-64, dir. automotive div. Can., Mex., Argentina, 1960-64; v.p. McCord Corp., Detroit, 1965-68; pres., chief exec. officer Avis Indsl. Corp., Madison Heights, Mich., 1968-70, also dir.; pres., gen. mgr. Flyer Industries Ltd., Winnipeg, Man., Can., 1970-73, ; chmn. bd., chief exec. officer Saunders Aircraft Corp. Ltd., Gimi, Man., Can., 1972-73; chmn. bd., dir Austinite Corp., Southfield, Mich., 1970-74; chief exec. officer Superior Kendrick Bearings, Inc., Detroit, 1974-76, also dir.; chief exec. officer Washington (Ind.) Heat Transfer, Inc., 1976-79, also dir.; exec. v.p. Duffy Tool and Stamping Corp., Muncie, 1979-80 , also sr. exec. in residence lectr. and exec. in residence Ball State U. Coll. Bus., Muncie, Ind., 1979-84; pres. The T.J. Ault Co., 1987—; cons. to mgmt. Arthur D. Little Consulting, Inc., 1959—. Bd. dirs. United Found. of Southeastern Mich., 1961-64, ARC, Detroit, 1961-64, Jr. Achievement of Southeastern Mich., 1960-63, Employers Assn. of Detroit, 1955-58, Boston Mus. Sci., 1958-60, Mass. Meml. Hosp., 1958-60; chmn., Muncie Ind. Transit System, 1983-87 . Served to capt. U.S. Army, 1934-47. Recipient Purchasing Progress award Purchasing News, 1953, Outstanding Service award Jr. Achievement of Detroit, 1963, S.A.M. award, 1982; named to Automotive Hall of Fame, 1988, Coll. Bus. Prof. of Yr. Ball State Univ., 1983, All Univ. We-ness award Student Leadership Devel. Bd. Ball State Univ., 1984. Mem. President's Profl. Assn., Engring. Soc. Detroit, NAM, Mich. Mfrs. Assn., Soc. for Advancement Mgmt., Nat. Safety Council, Acad. of Mgmt., Am. Inst. Mgmt., Nat. Assn. Purchasing Mgmt., Am. Textile Machinery Assn., Automotive Parts Mfg. Assn., Farm Equipment Assn., Am. Ordinance Assn., Am. Soc. for Metals, Soc. Mfg. Engrs. (robotics internat.), Am. Prodn. and Inventory Control Soc., Am. Soc. Quality Control, U.S. C. of C., Air Conditioning and Refrigeration Inst., Econ. Club of Detroit (dir. 1961-64), Ind. Hist. Soc., Am. Security Council, Sigma Nu, Sigma Iota Epsilon, Delta Sigma Pi, Beta Gamma Sigma. Clubs: Elks, Masons, Shriners, Country of Detroit, University; La Coquille (Palm Beach); Delaware Country, Muncie (Muncie); Columbia (Indpls.), Rotary (Muncie). Contbr. articles on material control, long range planning and mgmt. to indsl. publs. Home: 4501 N Wheeling Ave Apt 3-102 Muncie IN 47304

AUMILLER, ROBERT JOHN, real estate developer; b. Balt., May 1, 1951; s. Joseph Robert and Frances Pearl (Beedle) A.; m. Susan Elizabeth Myers, June 26, 1971; children: Robert John Jr., Lacey E., Lauren C. BA, U. Md., 1970, JD, 1973. Bar: Md. 1973. Asst. state's atty State's Atty.'s Office, Baltimore City, Md., 1973-74; asst. atty gen. Atty. Gen.'s Office State of Md., Balt., 1974-76, spl. asst., 1976-78; assoc., ptnr. White, Mindel, Clarke & Hill, Towson, Md. and Balt., 1978-84; gen. counsel MacKenzie & Assocs., Inc., Towson, 1984-86, sr. v.p., 1987, exec. v.p. devel., 1988—; also bd. dirs. MacKenzie & Assocs., Inc.; bd. dirs. MacKenzie Properties, Inc., Towson, MacKenzie Services, Inc., Towson. Mem. gov.'s task force to study Md. tax ct., 1985-86; mem. Md. State Bd. Pub. Accountancy, 1980-86. Mem. ABA, Baltimore County Bar Assn., Md. State Bar Assn., Nat. Assn. Indsl. Office Parks (sec., treas. 1987-88), L'Hirondelle Club (bd. govs. 1984-88). Democrat. Roman Catholic. Home: 7604 Curving Ln Towson MD 21204 Office: MacKenzie & Assocs Inc 2328 W Joppa Rd Ste 200 Lutherville MD 21093

AURNER, ROBERT RAY, II, oil company and restaurant industry executive; b. Madison, Wis., Mar. 24, 1937; s. Robert Ray and Kathryn (Dayton) A.; m. Phyllis Barrett, 1957 (div. 1966); children: Sheryl, Roxanne, Kathryn, Suzanne, Robert III; m. Deborah Marion Lucas, Jan. 31, 1976; children: William Lucas, Christopher Ray. AA, Monterey Peninsula Coll.; BA, Calif. State U., Fresno; postgrad., U. Iowa, U. Calif.-Berkeley, Duquesne U. (formerly Duquesne Coll.). Lic. real estate broker; registered investment advisor. With mktg. dept. Shell Oil Co., San Francisco, 1957-62; mgr. real estate Gulf Oil corp., San Francisco and Oakland, Calif., 1962-67; real estate mgr., dir. Midwest ops. Sunray DX Oil Co., Tulsa, 1967-71, Milex, Inc., Plymouth Meeting, Pa., 1972-76; dir. Pitts. div. R1 Estate, A & P Supermarkets, Plymouth Meeting, Pa., 1976-78; real estate adminstr. Steak and Ale Restaurants div. Pillsbury Cos., Dallas, 1978-80; real estate mgr. Burger King Corp. div. Pillsbury Cos., N.Y. and Phila., 1980-86; real estate mgr. Pizza Hut div. Pepsi-Cola, Port Jefferson, N.Y., 1986-88; dir. real estate Pillsbury Cos., Port Jefferson, N.Y., 1988—; owner, pres. Auresco Corp. Ltd., Carson City, Nev., 1978, Energy Underwriters, Inc., Carson City, 1987—, Nathan's Famous, 1988—. With USNR, PTO. Named to Hon. Order Ky. Col., State of Ky., Commodore in Okla. Navy Gov. of Okla. Mem. Sigma Alpha Epsilon, USS Yellowstone Assn. (hon.), Buccaneer Club (pres.), Elks. Republican. Episcopalian. Home and Office: 28 Hewes St Port Jefferson NY 11776 also: PO Box 3434 Carmel CA 93921

AUSBERRY, MARSHAL LEE, financial executive; b. Winchester, Va., Mar. 27, 1957; d. Edgar Browning and Mary Magdeline (Mitchell) A.; m. Robyn Patrice Duke, Aug. 10, 1979; children: Marshal, Rian. BBA, James Madison U., 1979, MS in Acctg., 1982. CPA, Va. Gen. acct. I.C. Industries, Winchester, Va., 1979-80; plant acct. Richardson-Vicks Co., Winchester, 1980-84; asst. controller Busch Entertainment Corp. subs. Anheuser-Busch, Williamsburg, Va., 1984-88; mgr. gen. acctg. USA Today subs. Gannett, Arlington, Va., 1988—; adj. instr. Hampton (Va.) U., 1988; chmn. Life Line Ministeries, Inc., 1987—. Bd. dirs., treas. Tri-County Occupational Indsl. Ctr., Winchester, 1982-84; bd. dirs. Shenandoah Job Tng. Ptnrship Coun., Harrisonburg, Va., 1983-84. Mem. Nat. Assn. Accts. (dir. profl. devel., bd. dirs. 1987—). Baptist. Home: 6330 Shawndale Springfield VA 22152 Office: USA Today 1000 Wilson Blvd Arlington VA 22209

AUSERE, JOE MORRIS, food manufacturing company executive; b. Miami, Ariz., Sept. 29, 1929; s. Joe Perez and Josephine (Sanez) A.; B.S. in Indsl. Engring., Ariz. State U., 1952; m. Elizabeth Ann Oxford, Dec. 19, 1959; children—Melinda Jo., Leigh Ann, Michael Joseph. Sales and prodn. Rainbo Bread Co., Phoenix, 1942-52; prodn. cons. Campbell Taggart Inc., Dallas, 1952-60; v.p., gen. mgr. sales and prodn. Am. Foods Inc., Atlanta, 1960-66; exec. v.p. Merico, Inc., Carrolton, Tex., 1966-70, pres., 1970—, also dir. Served with Signal Corps, U.S. Army 1955-57. Republican. Baptist. Office: Merico Inc PO Box 5101 Carrollton TX 75011-5101

AUST, GERALD ALDRIC, finance holding company executive; b. Pulaski, Va., Jan. 20, 1950; s. Ernest Roy and Maxine (Gallimore) A.; m. Belinda Kay Akers, May 31, 1982. BS, Va. Poly. Inst. and State U., 1972; postgrad., U. Va., 1982. Br. officer Colonial Am. Nat. Bank, Roanoke, Va., 1973-76; v.p. Bank Shawsville, Va., 1976-79; asst. v.p. Crestar Bank, Roanoke, 1979-84, Cor East Savs. Bank, Roanoke, 1984; sr. v.p., chief adminstrv. officer, corp. sec. Heritage Fin. Corp., Richmond, Va., 1984—; bd. dirs. Am. Inst. Banking, Roanoke, Va. Campaign chmn. United Way, Roanoke, 1984.

Mem. Va. League Savs. Instns., Lions (bd. dirs. Salem, Va. chpt. 1983), Sigma Chi, Alpha Phi Omega. Office: Heritage Fin Corp 500 Forest Ave Richmond VA 23229

AUSTIN, EDWARD MARVIN, mechanical engineer, researcher; b. Rome, Ga., Nov. 15, 1933; s. Marvin Hart and Sarah Katherine (Youngblood) A.; m. Elizabeth Maria Geisz, Dec. 17, 1955; children: Jean, Diane, Judy. BS in Mech. Engring., Ga. Inst. Tech., 1955, MS in Mech. Engring., 1957. Registered profl. engr., N.C. Assoc. aircraft engr. Lockheed Aircraft Corp., Marietta, Ga., 1955; disting. mem. tech. staff Sandia Nat. Labs., Albuquerque, 1957—; sr. engr. Western Electric Co., Greensboro, N.C., 1968-71. Pres. Heights Br. YMCA, Albuquerque, 1974-75. Mem. ASME (treas. 1988—, N.Mex. sect.), Sigma Xi, Tau Beta Pi. Home: 3017 Matador Dr NE Albuquerque NM 87111 Office: Sandia Nat Labs PO Box 5800 Albuquerque NM 87185

AUSTIN, JOHN HOGG, JR., retired utilities executive; b. Bryn Mawr, Pa., Apr. 16, 1928; s. John Hogg and Helen Elizabeth (Miner) A.; m. Joan Dorothy Bickel, Oct. 14, 1950; children: Nancy, Thomas, Patricia, Katherine. B.S., Yale U., 1950. With Phila. Electric Co., 1950—, comptroller, 1967-71, v.p. finance and accounting, 1971-78, exec. v.p., dir., 1978-82, pres., dir., 1982-88, chief operating officer, 1980-88; bd. dirs. Meridian Bancorp, Inc., Phila. Suburban Water Co., Phila. Suburban Corp. Trustee United Way, So. Home Services; bd. dirs. YMCA of Met. Phila., Pa. Economy League. Mem. IEEE, Edison Electric Inst., Pa. Electric Assn. (exec. com.), Fin. Execs. Inst., Franklin Inst. Episcopalian. Clubs: Union League, Yale (Phila.). Home: 330 Bair Rd Berwyn PA 19312 Office: Phila Electric Co 2301 Market St Philadelphia PA 19101

AUSTIN, MARSHALL EDWARD, financial executive; b. Rochester, N.Y., Aug. 3, 1957; s. Delmer Edward and Betty Janet (Watt) A.; m. Janet Marie LaRosa, Feb. 16, 1980; children: Craig Thomas, Christine Mae Austin. BBA, Cleve. State U., 1979. Cert. fin. planner. Mgr. Toys R Us, Saginaw, Mich., 1980-84; cons. Creative Employee Benefits, Grand Blanc, Mich., 1984-87; fin. planner Eagle Equities, Glen Burnie, Md., 1987—. Mem. Inst. Fin. Planners, Internat. Assn. Fin. Planners. Republican. Baptist. Club: Exchange (Glen Burnie). Home: 8121 Turn Loop Rd Glen Burnie MD 21061 Office: Eagle Equities 400 Crain Hwy SW Glen Burnie MD 21061

AUSTIN, ROBERT EUGENE, JR., lawyer; b. Jacksonville, Fla., Oct. 10, 1937; s. Robert Eugene and Leta Fitch A.; div. Feb. 86; children: Robert Eugene, George Harry Talley. B.A., Davidson Coll., 1959; J.D., U. Fla., 1964. Bar: Fla. 1965, D.C. 1983, U.S. Supreme Ct. 1970; cert. in civil trial law Nat. Bd. Trial Advocacy, Fla. Bar. Legal asst. Fla. Ho. Reps., 1965; assoc. firm Jones & Sims, Pensacola, Fla., 1965-66; ptnr. firm Warren, Warren & Austin, Leesburg, Fla., 1966-68, McLin, Burnsed, Austin & Cyrus, Leesburg, 1968-77, Austin & Burleigh, Leesburg, 1977-81; sole practice Leesburg, 1981-83, Leesburg and Orlando, Fla., 1984-86; ptnr. firm Austin & Lockett P.A., 1983-84; ptnr. Austin, Lawrence & Landis, Leesburg and Orlando, 1986—; asst. state atty., 1972; mem. Jud. Nominating Commn. and Grievance Com. 5th Dist. Fla.; gov. Fla. Bar, 1983—. Chmn. Lake Dist. Boy Scouts Am.; asst. dean Leesburg Deanery, Diocese of Central Fla.; trustee Fla. House, Washington., U. Fla. Law Center, 1983—, chmn. 1988—. Capt. U.S. Army, 1959-62. Mem. Acad. Fla. Trial Lawyers, Am. Arbitration Assn., ABA, Am. Judicature Soc., Am. Law Inst., Assn. Trial Lawyers Am., Nat. Inst. Trial Advocacy, Def. Research Inst., Fed. Bar Assn., Lake County Bar Assn., Roscoe Pound Am. Trial Found., Kappa Alpha, Phi Delta Phi. Democrat. Episcopalian. Clubs: Timuquana Country (Jacksonville, Fla.); University (Orlando, Fla.). Home: 6300 N Silver Lake Dr Leesburg FL 32788 Office: Austin Lawrence & Landis 1321 W Citizens Blvd Leesburg FL 32748

AUSTIN, T. LOUIS, JR., construction company executive; b. 1919; married. BS, U. Ala., 1942. With Indsl. Generating Co., 1953-59; pres., chief exec. officer Tex. Power & Light Co., from 1967; various positions Tex. Utilities Co., 1953-72, pres., 1972-75, chmn., chief exec. officer, 1975-83; pres., chief exec. officer Brown & Root, Inc., Houston, 1983—, also bd. dirs.; bd. dirs. Halliburton Co. (parent), Dallas. Lt. USN, 1942-45. Office: Brown & Root Inc 4100 Clinton Dr Houston TX 77020

AUSTIN, TOM NOELL, tobacco company executive; b. Greeneville, Tenn., May 11, 1916; s. Clyde Bernard and Felice (Noell) A.; m. Emily Donaldson, Nov. 19, 1938; children: Tom Noell, Merrily (Mrs. Charles L. Teasley, Jr.), Jay Donaldson, Richard Lyon. Student, UCLA, 1936; B.A., U. Tenn., 1937. Shipping clk. Douglas Tobacco Co., 1937; with Austin Co., Greeneville, 1940—; v.p. Austin Co., 1944-48, pres., 1948-70; pres. Valley Realty Co., 1960—; chmn. bd. Austin Co., 1970—; dir. Sovran Fin. Corp./Cen. South; bd. dirs. Carolina and Northwestern Ry., Sovran Bank/Cen. South, First Nat. Bank, Greeneville, Sta. WETO-TV, Greeneville; v.p. Unaka Co., Greeneville, Austin Carolina Co., Kinston, N.C., Mullins Leaf Tobacco Co., S.C.; mem. Ky. and Tenn. Dist. Export Council; pres. Valley Realty Co., 1960—. Former trustee Tusculum Coll.; mem. devel. council U. Tenn.; dir. Tenn. Council on Econ. Edn. Mem. Japanese-Tenn. Soc., USA-Republic of China Trade Coun., USA-Bulgaria C. of C., USA-Egyptian C. of C., Exchange Club (Nashville, state pres. 1943-44), Omicron Delta Kappa. Republican. Methodist. Home: Rte 7 PO Box 127 Greeneville TN 37743 Office: Austin Co Hall & Cutler Sts Greeneville TN 37743

AUTERA, MICHAEL EDWARD, health care products company executive; b. Passaic, N.J., June 16, 1938; s. Michael and Laura (Vandervliet) A.; m. Martha Bolton Tilt, Jan. 31, 1959; children—Michael Edward, Katherine T., Stephen G. B.S., Lehigh U., 1960; M.B.A., Rutgers U., 1962. C.P.A., N.Y. Indsl. engr. Eastman Kodak Co., Rochester, N.Y., 1960-61; sr. accountant Haskins & Sells, C.P.A.s, N.Y.C., 1962-66; sr. v.p. adminstrn. , chief fin. officer Bristol-Myers Co., N.Y.C., 1966—. Mem. Puerto Rico USA Found. Bd. Mem. AICPA, N.Y. State Soc. CPAs, N.Y. Econ. Club, Beta Gamma Sigma. Presbyterian. Home: 300 Central Park West New York NY 10024 Office: Bristol-Myers Co 345 Park Ave New York NY 10154

AUTHIER, ROBERT NORMAN, real estate association executive; b. Holyoke, Mass., Aug. 26, 1949; s. Norman Phillip and Lillian Anne (Riopel) A.; m. Deborah Louise Howell, Oct. 6, 1979; children: Christopher John, Laura Annalise. BS in Pub. Relations, Boston U., 1971. Newswriter, reporter Daily Transcript-Telegram, Holyoke, 1968; dir. pub. relations Monadnock Music, Rindge, N.H., 1970; mem. pub. relations staff Publicity Inc., Boston, 1970-71; coordinator pub. relations and alumni Boston U., 1971-73; mgr. pub. relations Am. Lung Assn. Mass., Newton, 1974-76; dir. pub. relations Mass. Assn. Realtors, Boston, 1977-82, exec. v.p., 1988—. Mem. N.H. Assn. Realtors (v.p. 1982-88), Am. Soc. Assn. Execs. (cert.), New Eng. Soc. Assn. Execs. (bd. dirs. 1987-88, sec./treas. 1988—), Boston Computer Soc., Boston U. SPC Alumni Assn. (pres.), Scarlet Key, Mason. Office: Mass Assn Realtors 256 Second Ave Box 650 Waltham MA 02254

AUTRY, GENE (ORVON GENE AUTRY), actor, radio entertainer, broadcasting executive, baseball team executive; b. Tioga, Tex., Sept. 29, 1907; s. Delbert and Elnora (Ozmont) A.; m. Ina Mae Spivey, Apr. 1, 1932; m. Jacqueline Ellam, 1981. Grad., Tioga (Tex.) High Sch., 1925. R.R. telegraph operator Sapulpa, Okla., 1925; owner, chmn. bd. Calif. Angels; pres. Flying A Prodns.; owner Sta. KMPC AM & FM, Hollywood, Calif., Stas. KVI & KPLZ Radio, Seattle, Golden West Broadcasters; pres. several music and publ. cos. Made first phonograph record of cowboy songs, 1929; radio artist Sta. WLS, Chgo., 1930-34; motion picture actor, 1934-53, including In Old Santa Fe; starred in 88 musical Western feature pictures, 91 half-hour TV pictures 1950-55; has written or co-written over 200 songs including That Silver-Haired Daddy of Mine, 1931, You're the Only Star in My Blue Heaven, 1938, Dust, 1938, Tears On My Pillow, 1941, Be Honest With Me, 1941, Tweedle O'Twill, 1942, Here Comes Santa Claus, 1948; host Melody Ranch Theater Nashville Network, 1987, 88. Served with USAAF, 1942-45. Mem. Internat. Footprinters. Clubs: Masons (33 deg.), Shriners, Elks. Address: PO Box 710 Los Angeles CA 90078 Office: care Calif Angels PO Box 2000 Anaheim CA 92803

AVE, JOHN ROBERT, tobacco company executive; b. Lafayette, Ind., May 27, 1932; s. John and Zola Marie (Evans) A.; m. Aurora Gasparelli, Sept. 20, 1968; children: Christopher Evan, Dana Kathryn, Jonathan Eric. B.A., DePauw U., 1954; postgrad., Harvard U. Bus. Sch., 1956. With Lorillard Co., N.Y.C., 1973—; v.p. advt. and brand mgmt. Lorillard Co., 1973-77, sr. v.p. mktg., 1977-79, exec. v.p. mktg., 1979-84, pres., 1984—, chief exec. officer, 1985—. Served with USAF, 1956-60. Mem. Phi Beta Kappa. Methodist. Home: 1050 Park Ave New York NY 10128 Office: Lorillard Inc 1 Park Ave New York NY 10016

AVERITT, GEORGE RONALD, business owner; b. Birmingham, Ala., Aug. 28, 1949; s. George Garner and Sarah Luthinia (Allen) A.; m. Sallie Marie Dowling, Feb. 3, 1973; 1 child, Cory Thomas. BS, U. South Ala., 1972. Sales rep. Burroughs Corp., Columbus, Ga., 1972-77; sales rep. Gambro, Inc., 1978, mgr. regional sales, 1979-85; mfr.'s rep., owner MedTek Co., 1986—; cons. Mediq Mobile Svcs., Inc., Pennsauken, N.J, 1985—, Columbia Sci., Inc., Pennsauken, 1985—, Columbia Sci, Inc., 1987—, N-S Med. Products, Inc., Gainesville, Fla., 1987—. Mem. Radiology Soc. N.A., Orgn. Third Party Suppliers, Acad. Model Aeronautics. Methodist. Home and Office: 4501 Sears Rd Columbus GA 31907

AVERITT, RICHARD GARLAND, III, securities executive; b. Kearney, Nebr., Jan. 27, 1945; d. Richard Garland Jr. and Marguerite (Faubel) A.; m. Sandra Louise Smith, June 7, 1967; children: Dawn, Rick, Scott. BA, Duke U., 1967. Cert. fin. planner. Account exec. Merrill Lynch, Pierce, Fenner & Smith, Atlanta, 1976-78; v.p. mktg. Investment Mgmt. & Rsch., Inc., Atlanta, 1984-87, 1st v.p., 1987—. Officer, aviator USMC, 1967-76, lt. col. Res., 1976—. Mem. Internat. Assn. Fin. Planning (dir. Ga. chpt. 1978-79), Am. Arbitration Assn., Inst. Cert. Fin. Planners, Mensa, United Meth. Men Club (pres. 1987), Kiwanis. Republican. Office: Investment Mgmt & Rsch Inc 1647 Mt Vernon Rd Ste 250 Atlanta GA 30338

AVERY, WILLIAM JOSEPH, packaging manufacturing company executive; b. Chgo., June 20, 1940; s. Floyd Joseph and Margaret Mildred (Musard) A.; m. Sharon Bajorek, Sept. 5, 1959; children: Michelle, Martin, Sheryl. Grad. in indsl. mgmt., U. Chgo., 1968. With Crown Cork & Seal Co. Inc., 1959—; v.p. sales Crown Cork & Seal Co. Inc., Phila., 1974-79; sr. v.p. mfg. and sales Crown Cork & Seal Co. Inc., 1979-80, exec. v.p., 1980-81, pres., 1981—, also dir. Roman Catholic. Office: Crown Cork & Seal Co Inc 9300 Ashton Rd Philadelphia PA 19136 *

AVINA-RHODES, NINA ALVARADO, health facility director; b. Alamo, Tex., Nov. 29, 1944; d. Pedro Vasques Avina and Enriqueta Alvarado-Avina; m. James Lamar Rhodes Jr., Feb. 14, 1977; children: James Lamar III, Aaron Abraham, David Isaiah. BS in Bus. Adminstrn., Calif. State U., San Jose, 1973, postgrad., 1973-75; MA, La Salle U., 1988, postgrad., 1988—. Cert. tchr., Ariz.; cert. adult basic educator, Calif.; cert. ESL tchr., Calif. Instr. Ctr. for Employment Tng., Santa Clara, Calif., 1976-80; pres. Avina Bros. Trucking Co., Fresno, Calif., 1982-84; writer grants Quechan Nation Indian Tribe, Yuma, Ariz., 1984-86; exec. dir. Western Ariz. Health & Edn. Ctr., Yuma, Ariz., 1986—. Co-host program Sta. KTEH-TV, San Jose, 1983. Co-facilitator Vietnam Vets. Outreach Ctr., San Jose; bd. dirs. Ctr. for Employment Tng., Yuma, 1984—; mem. Milpitas Unified Sch. Bd., 1981-82. Recipient Humanitarian award VA, 1983, Humanitarian award Vietnamese Community of Santa Clara County, 1983, Citizen of Honor award Vietnam Combat Vets., Ltd., 1983; named Woman of Achievement Santa Clara County Bd. Suprs., 1983. Mem. NAFE, AMVETS (pres. aux. Yuma chpt. 1986—). Baha'i. Home: 1740 W 24th Ln Yuma AZ 85364 Office: Western Ariz Health & Edn Ctr 281 W 24th St Suite 136 Yuma AZ 85364

AVON, RANDY KALANI, investment banker; b. Honolulu, Sept. 25, 1940; s. Randolph Scott and Pualani (Mossman) A.; m. Joan Messmore, June 29, 1962; children: Eve, Emmy Lou, Jaimie, Bob, Randy. BS in Bus. Adminstrn., U. Fla., 1962. SE div. mgr. Rums of P.R., Miami, Fla., 1962-68; v.p. mktg. ContinentalInns Am., Memphis, 1968-70; pres. Corp. Pub. Relations and Mktg., Inc., Ft. Lauderdale, Fla., 1970—; pres., chief exec. officer Corp. and Fin. Cons., Inc., Ft. Lauderdale, Fla., 1976-82; pres. Security Investment Corp. Fla., 1967-75, Fla. Fixed Income Securities, Inc., 1975—. Author: The Future of the Tax Exempt Industry in Florida, 1980. Pres. United Cerebral Palsy, 1965; chmn. Ft. Lauderdale Community Relations Bd., 1966; apointee Pres.'s Council Econ. Advisors, 1988; trustee Ft. Lauderdale U., 1973-76; mem. Fla. Legislature, 1972-78. Recipient Outstanding Am. award Viva, 1974; Disting. Service award VFW, 1975, Legislator of Yr. award Condominium Owners Assn., 1976, Humanitarian award Broward County Rabbinical Assn., 1975, numerous others. Mem. Fla. Pub. Relations Assn. (v.p. 1971-72), West Broward C. of C. (v.p. 1978-79). Republican. Episcopalian. Lodge: Elks, Kiwanis. Office: 3051 N Federal Hwy Fort Lauderdale FL 33306

AWA, NGOZI MARY, investment and portfolio analyst; b. Calabar, Nigeria, Feb. 21, 1956; came to U.S., 1980; d. Edet Kalu Awa and Mary Nkese (Asuquo) A.; children: Collins, Elaine. BS, Cen. London Coll., 1980; diploma, Am. Inst. Banking, 1984; MBA, Marymount U., 1985. Rsch. asst. Marks & Spencer, London, 1979, Savon Drugs, Houston, 1980-81; fin. analyst Riggs Nat. Bank, Washington, 1981-85; mgr. budget and portfolio L'Enfant Pla. Properties Inc., Washington, 1985-86; fin. analyst Arnold and Porter, Washington, 1986-88; pres. Zee Fin. Svcs., Washington, 1987—; cons. fin. M. Dyson and Assoc., Washington, 1983—, Park Pl. Cafe, Washington, 1984-85, Akparanta and Assoc., Nigeria and Washington, 1981—, Mid-Atlantic Realty Group, Washington. Mem. com. United Way, Washington, 1982; pres. Internat. Student Union, London, 1980. Mem. Am. Mktg. Assn., Fin. Analyst Assn., Am. Mgmt. Assn., Inst. Mktg., Nigerian Inst. Mgmt., Brit. Inst. Mgmt. Roman Catholic. Clubs: Riggs Toastmasters (ednl. v.p. 1985) Advanced Toastmasters (adminstrv. v.p. 1986). Home: 2480 16th St NW #808 Washington DC 20009 Office: Zee Fin Svcs 2480 16th St NW Washington DC 20009

AWALT, ROBERT DONALD, computer executive, consultant; b. Balt., Aug. 19, 1954; s. Robert Francis and Rosalie Jayne (Kriete) A.; m. Katherine Joan Edgar, Apr. 4, 1981. BA in Math., BS in Computer Sci., Loyola Coll., 1976, MBA, 1978. Computer scientist Nat. Security Agy., Ft. Meade, Md., 1975-76; software mgr. Gen. Instrument Corp., Balt., 1976-83; v.p. devel. Muse Software, Balt., 1983-84; dir. mgmt. info. systems Tex. Instruments, Balt., 1984-88; pres. RDA Cons. Ltd., Balt., 1988—; mem. Ctr. Info. Systems Research, MIT, Boston, 1983—. Editor: (newsletter) Tech. Briefings, 1988—; contbr. articles to profl. jours. Pres. Hunt Valley (Md.) Community Assn., 1986-87, sec., 1983-86; vol. Md. State Senatorial Campaign, 1987. Mem. Assn. Computing Machinery, Digital Equipment Computer Users Soc. Office: RDA Cons Ltd 1133 Dulaney Gate Circle Hunt Valley MD 21030

AXEL, BERNARD, food service executive; b. Bklyn., May 23, 1946; s. Joseph and Irene (Rosen) A. BS, U. Ala., 1967; grad., Am. Inst. Banking, 1970. Asst. cashier, comptroller Nat. Bank of Commerce (formerly Am. Nat. Bank), Birmingham, Ala., 1967-72; supr. internat. travel Travel Anywhere, Birmingham, 1972; acctg. and purchasing agt. U.S. Dept. Justice, Texarkana, Tex., 1972-74; mgr. Styslinger Realty, Birmingham, 1974-75; pres. Christian's Inc., Birmingham, 1975—; gourmet chef WBRC-TV Morning show, Birmingham, 1983—. Contbr. recipes to mags. Judge March of Dimes Gourmet Gala, Birmingham, 1986; staff State of Ala., Montgomery, 1968-70; lt. govs. staff, 1980-84; bd. dirs. Temple Beth-El. Mem. Nat. Restaurant Assn. (mem. adv. bd. polit. action com. 1987—), Ala. Restaurant Assn. (bd. dirs. 1987—, pres. elect 1989), Jefferson County Restaurant Assn. (bd. dirs. 1981-83, 89—), Greater Birmingham Chefs Assn. (bd. dirs., Medal 1986), Birmingham Jaycees (treas. 1968-71), Chaine des Rotisseurs (maitre grillardin 1988—). Republican. Jewish. Club: Pine Tree Country (bd. dirs. 1968-71). Home: 2625 Highland Ave Birmingham AL 35205 Office: Christian's Inc 2300 Woodcrest Place Birmingham AL 35209-1304

AXEL, JOHN WERNER, office furniture manufacturing executive; b. Muscatine, Iowa, June 10, 1941; s. Chester Walter and Wilma Pauline (Marolf) A.; m. Joan Carol Urenn, June 6, 1964; children: Andrew, Brad. BS, Iowa State U., 1964; M in Govtl. Adminstrn., U. Pa., 1966. With Hon Industries, Muscatine, 1966—; internal auditor, asst. to pres. 1966, corp. planner, 1966-69, mgr. distbn. and customer service, 1996-72, v.p. adminstrn., 1972-78, v.p. fin., 1978—; bd. dirs. Mut. Selection Fund, Muscatine. Dir. Muscatine Community Sch. Bd., 1985—; chair Ea. Iowa Econ. Devel. Coun., 1987—. Joseph Wharton scholar, 1964-66; named Outstanding Young Alumnus Iowa State U., 1976. Mem. Nat. Office Products Assn., NAM, Nat. Investors Relations Inst. Episcopalian. Lodges: Rotary, Elks. Office: Hon Industries Inc 414 E 3rd St Muscatine IA 52761

AXELROD, NORMAN N(ATHAN), opticist, physicist; b. N.Y.C., Aug. 26, 1934; s. Louis E. and Sadie (Katz) A.; A.B., Cornell U., 1954; postgrad. U. Paris, France, 1958; Ph.D. in Optics and Physics, U. Rochester, 1959; m. Victoria Ann Grant, Mar. 21, 1975; children—Lauren Grant, Brian George. Aerospace scientist NASA, Goddard Space Flight Center, Washington, 1959-60; research fellow U. London, 1960-61; asst. prof. U. Del., 1961-65; mem. tech. staff Bell Labs., Murray Hill, N.J., 1965-72; prin. Axelrod Assocs., 1972—; dir. World Resources Devel. Co.; mem. adv. bd. Del. Dept. Edn., 1963-64; cons. Met. Mus. Art, N.Y.C., 1969-72; participant vis. scientist program Am. Inst. Physics, 1963-64; adviser to White House, 1969-70; cons. French Ministry Nat. Def. and War, 1971, C.R. Bard, Compuscan, CPC, Gen. Electric Co., IBM, ITT, Konishiroku, Johnson & Johnson, Perkin-Elmer, Sharp, Proctor & Gamble, RCA, Teradyne, Timken Co., Wall St. Jour. Fellow AAAS; mem. Am. Phys. Soc., Am. Optical Soc., IEEE, Soc. Mfg. Engrs., Machine Vision Assn. (cert. mfg. engr.), Del., N.Y. acads. sci., Electrochem. Soc., Sigma Xi, Sigma Pi Sigma, Pi Mu Epsilon. Editor: Optical Properties of Dielectric Films, 1968; book reviewer, cons. John Wiley & Sons, 1965-68, Rheinhold-Van Nostrand, 1968-70, Pergamon Press, 1969-70; contbr. articles to profl. jours. Patentee in field. Home: 445 E 86th St New York NY 10028 Office: Norman Axelrod Assocs 28 W 44th St New York NY 10036 also: 28 W 44th St New York NY 10036

AXFORD, ROY ARTHUR, nuclear engineering educator; b. Detroit, Aug. 26, 1928; s. Morgan and Charlotte (Donaldson) A.; m. Anne-Sofie Langfeldt Rasmussen, Apr. 1, 1954; children: Roy Arthur, Elizabeth Carole, Trevor Craig Charles. B.A., Williams Coll., 1952; B.S., Mass. Inst. Tech., 1952, M.S., 1955, Sc.D., 1958. Supr. theoretical physics group Atomics Internat., Canoga Park, Calif., 1958-60; asso. prof. nuclear engring. Tex. A&M, 1960-62, prof., 1962-63; asso. prof. nuclear engring. Northwestern U., 1963-66; asso. prof. U. Ill. at Urbana, 1966-68, prof., 1968—; cons. Los Alamos Nat. Lab., 1963—. Vice-chmn. Mass. Inst. Tech. Alumni Fund Drive, 1970-72, chmn., 1973-75; sustaining fellow MIT, 1984. Recipient cert. of recognition for excellence in undergrad. teaching U. Ill., 1979, 81; Everitt award for teaching excellence, 1985. Mem. Am. Nuclear Soc., ASME, AIAA, SAR (sec.-treas. Piankeshaw chpt. 1975-81, v.p. chpt. 1982-83, pres. chpt. 1984-86), Sigma Xi., Phi Kappa Phi, Tau Beta Pi. Home: 2017 S Cottage Grove Urbana IL 61801

AXILROD, STEPHEN HARVEY, investment banker, economist; b. N.Y.C., June 21, 1926; s. Jacob James and Pearl (Feltenstein) A.; m. Katherine Podolsky, July 1, 1950; children: Peter, Emily Axilrod Hildner, Richard. Student, So. Meth. U., 1943-44; AB magna cum laude, Harvard U., 1948; MA, U. Chgo., 1950, postgrad., 1951-52. Assoc. dir. div. research and statistics Fed. Res. Bd., Washington, 1970-73, advisor to bd. govs., 1973-76, staff dir. for monetary and fin. policy, 1976-86; economist domestic fin. Fed. Open Market Com., Washington, 1974-78, economist, 1978-81; staff dir., sec. Fed. Open Market Commn., Washington, 1981-86; vice chmn. Nikko Securities Internat., N.Y.C., 1986—; advisor Brookings Panel on Econ. Activity, Washington, 1986—, mem. investment com. Japan soc. Contbr. numerous articles on monetary policy, credit and securities markets and related matters to books, newspapers, mags. and profl. jours. Bd. overseers Lemburg program on internat. fin., Brandeis U. With USN, 1944-46. Mem. Phi Beta Kappa. Democrat. Office: Nikko Securities Co Internat Inc 200 Liberty St New York NY 10281

AYA, RODERICK HONEYMAN, tax consultant; b. Portland, Oreg., Sept. 17, 1916; s. Alfred Anthony and Grace Myrtle (Honeyman) A.; student U. Oreg., 1935-36, Internat. Accts. Soc., 1937-39, LaSalle Extension U., 1940-42, Walton Sch. Commerce, 1942, U. Calif. Extension, 1945; m. Helen Marjorie Riddle, June 16, 1945 (dec. Dec. 1983); children: Roderick Riddle, Deborah Germaine Aya Reynolds, Ronald Honeyman; m. Kathryn Rehnstrom Chatalas, June 22, 1986; stepchildren: John Todd, Paul Seth, Elizabeth Kate. Chief statistician Hotel Employers Assn., San Francisco, 1939-42; acct. Pacific Tel. & Tel. Co., San Francisco, 1942-52, spl. acct., 1952-63; tax acct., 1963-65; spl. acct. AT&T, N.Y.C., 1965-68, mgr. tax studies, 1968-73, div. mgr. tax research and planning, 1973-80; public acct., San Francisco, 1940—; music tchr., 1959—; v.p., treas., dir. Snell Research Assos., Inc., 1974-79; guest lectr. on taxes Westchester County Adult Edn. Program. Committeeman, Marin County council Boy Scouts Am., 1959-60, com. chmn., 1959-61; mem. Marin County Sheriffs' Reserve, 1963-65; law enforcement liaison com. on Juvenile Control; sec. Am. Nat. Standards Inst. Com. on Protective Headgear, 1967-80. Vice pres., treas., bd. dirs. Snell Meml. Found., 1957-80; trustee Snell Meml. Found. (U.K.), Ltd., 1972-88; mem. chmn.'s com. U.S. Senatorial Bus. Adv. Bd.; mem. Republican Presdl. Task Force; dir., past pres. Stuart Highlanders Pipe Band of San Francisco. Recipient Wisdom award of honor Wisdom Soc., 1970; Pres.'s Medal of Merit, 1981. Mem. ASTM, Nat. Soc. Pub. Accts., St. Andrews Soc., Telephone Pioneers Am., Soc. for Ethnomusicology (contbr. to jour.), U.S. Naval Inst., Phi Chi, Sigma Nu. Clubs: Corinthian Yacht (Tiburon, Calif.); Astoria Golf & Country; Sports Car of Am. (San Francisco region treas. 1957-58, dir. 1957-59); U.S. Yacht Racing Union. Author: The Legacy of Pete Snell, 1965; Determination of Corporate Earnings and Profits for Federal Income Tax Purposes, 2 vols., 1966. Home: PO Box 668 Seaside OR 97138

AYCOCK, HUGH DAVID, steel manufacturing company executive; b. Lilesville, N.C., 1930; married. With Nucor Corp., Charlotte, N.C., 1954—, div. shop supt., 1956-57, div. sales mgr., 1957-64, div. gen. mgr., 1964-65, pres., 1984—, also bd. dirs.; v.p. Nucor Steel SC div. Nucor Corp., 1965-84. Served with USN, 1950-54. Office: Nucor Corp 4425 Randolph Rd Charlotte NC 28211 *

AYERS, DONALD WALTER, tax preparation executive; b. Manhattan, Kans., Dec. 10, 1933; s. David Paul and and Marguerite Elizabeth (Stingley) A.; children: Donald Stephen, Karen Elizabeth. B.A., Kans. State Coll., 1955; postgrad., Kans. State U., 1961. C.P.A., Kans., Mo. Audit mgr. Peat, Marwick, Mitchell & Co. (C.P.A.s), Kansas City, Mo., 1961-73; v.p. fin., treas. H & R Block, Inc., Kansas City, 1973—. Served with USAF, 1955-60. Mem. Am. Inst. C.P.A.s, Mo. Soc. C.P.A.s, Fin. Execs. Inst., Nat. Assn. Accts. Republican. Episcopalian. Home: 1200 W 95th Ct Kansas City MO 64114 Office: H & R Block Inc 4410 Main St Kansas City MO 64111

AYERS, JAMES EDSON, corporate finance executive; b. Wood County, Ohio, June 14, 1932; s. Bert Melvern and Hazel Selma (Rudolph) A.; m. Shirley Ann Weber, June 4, 1966; children—Jonathan Albert, Julia Ann, Jeremy Alan. B.S., Bowling Green State U., Ohio, 1954; M.B.A., Washington U., St. Louis, 1958; grad. advanced mgmt. program, Harvard U., 1988. Various positions Dana Corp., Toledo, Ohio, 1964-74, dir. investor relations, 1975-80, asst. treas., 1980-83, corp. treas., 1983—, v.p., 1986—; v.p. fin., treas. Hayes-Dana Ltd., St. Catherine's, Ont., Can., 1974-75; dir. Diamond Savs. & Loan, Findlay, Ohio, 1983—. Dir., Toledo Area Govtl. Research Assn., 1983—. Served as sgt. U.S. Army, 1954-56. Mem. Fin. Execs. Inst., Nat. Assn. Corp. Treasurers. Home: 2391 Ayers Rd Millbury OH 43447 Office: Dana Corp 4500 Dorr St PO Box 1000 Toledo OH 43697

AYERS, RICHARD H., manufacturing company executive; b. Newton, Mass., Oct. 12, 1942; s. J. Robert and Virginia (Hixon) A.; m. Gay Boas, Aug. 12, 1964 (div. June 1973); children—Ashley C., Jennifer B., Bradford M.; m. Suzanne M. Lefebvre, Oct. 13, 1973; children—Kelly V., David R. B.S. in Indsl. Mgmt., MIT, 1965, M.S. in Indsl. Mgmt., 1965. Gen. foreman Wyman-Gordon Co., North Grafton, Mass., 1965-69; v.p. mfg. Britton Corp., Newington, Conn., 1969-72; line mfg. positions The Stanley Works, New Britain, Conn., 1972-85, pres., 1985—, chief operating officer, 1985-87, pres., chief exec. officer, 1987—, also dir.; dir. Conn. Mut. Funds, Hartford, Conn., So. New England Telecommunications Co.; assoc. dir. Perkin Elmer. Bd. dirs. New Britain Gen. Hosp., 1984—; trustee Hartford Grad. Ctr., 1986—. Am. Leadership Forum fellow, Hartford, 1985. Mem. Econ. Club N.Y., Hand Tools Inst. (bd. dirs. 1982-84), Nat. Assn. Mfrs. Republican. Club: Farmington Country (Conn.). Office: Stanley Works 1000 Stanley Dr New Britain CT 06053

AYLESWORTH, WILLIAM ANDREW, electronics company executive; b. Gary, Ind., Sept. 16, 1942; s. William Guy and Ann (Harnak) A.; children: Elisabeth, Sarah. BSEE, Cornell U., 1965; MS in Indsl. Adminstrn., Carnegie-Mellon U., 1967. Registered profl. engr., Tex. Various positions Texas Instruments, Inc., Attleboro, Mass. and Dallas, 1967-72; with treasury services dept. Texas Instruments, Inc., Dallas, 1972-80, asst. treas., 1980-82, treas., 1982-84, prin. fin. officer, 1984-85, chief fin. officer, 1985—; bd. dirs. Corp. Officers Dirs. Assurance Holding Ltd., Hamilton, Bermuda, Ark-wright-Boston Ins. Co., Atlanta, so. adv. bd., Children's Med. Ctr., Dallas. Bd. dirs. Children's Med. Ctr., Dallas, 1987—. Mem. Nat. Assn. Corp. Treas. (bd. dirs.), Fin. Execs. Inst., Tau Beta Pi. Office: Tex Instruments Inc 13500 N Central Expwy Dallas TX 75243

AYLOUSH, CYNTHIA MARIE, personnel director, corporate treasurer; b. Jackson, Mich., July 2, 1950; d. Leonard Edward and Violet Caroline (Kroeger) Ullrich; m. Abbott Selim Ayloush, June 21, 1980; children: Sasha Christine, Nadia Marie. AA, Fullerton Coll., 1970; diploma in fashion mdse., Brooks Coll., 1975; BS, Pepperdine U., 1980. Receptionist, Hydraflow, Commerce, Calif., 1968-74, personnel mgr., Cerritos, Calif., 1979—, treas., 1979—, corp. sec., 1985—; with sales dept. Robinson's, Cerritos, Calif., 1974-75, dept. mgr., 1975-79. Mem. Am. Soc. Personnel Adminstrs., Personnel Indsl. Relations Assn., Merchants and Mfrs. Assn., Cerritos C. of C. (dir. 1983—). Republican. Roman Catholic. Clubs: Soroptimist (sec. 1979—), Century, Pepperdine Univ. Office: Hydraflow 13259 E 166th St Cerritos CA 90701

AYLWARD, RONALD LEE, lawyer; b. St. Louis, May 30, 1930; s. John Thomas and Edna (Ketcherside) A.; m. Margaret Cecilia Hellweg, Aug. 10, 1963; children: Susan Marie, Stephen Ronald, Carolyn Ann. A.B., Washington U., St. Louis, 1952, J.D., 1954; student, U. Va., 1955. Bar: Mo. 1954, Ill. 1961, U.S. Supreme Ct. 1968. Assoc. Heneghan, Roberts & Cole, St. Louis, 1958-59; asst. counsel Olin Corp., East Alton, Ill., 1960-64; asst. gen. counsel INTERCO, Inc., St. Louis, 1964-66; asso. gen. counsel, mgr. law dept. INTERCO, Inc., 1966-69, asst. sec., 1966-74, gen. counsel, 1969-81, mem. operating bd., 1970—, v.p., 1971-81, mem. exec. com., dir., 1975—, exec. v.p., 1981-85, vice chmn. bd. dirs., 1985—; mem. dist. export council U.S. Dept. Commerce, 1974-77; dir., mem. exec. com. Boatmen's Nat. Bank St. Louis, 1982—, trust estates com., 1982-85, chmn. audit com., 1986—; bd. dirs. Boatmen's Bancshares, Inc., mem. audit com., 1984—, mem. compensation com., 1986—. Bd. dirs. St. Louis County chpt. Nat. Found. March of Dimes, 1974-84, sec., 1976-78, chmn., 1979-82; bd. dirs. Cardinal Ritter Inst., 1975—, St. Louis chpt. ARC, 1977-82, Linda Vista Montessori Sch., 1975-77; bd. dirs. Better Bus. Bur. Greater St. Louis, 1978-81; bd. dirs. YMCA Greater St. Louis, 1981—; bd. dirs., fin. com. United Way Greater St. Louis, 1986—; trustee St. Louis Council World Affairs, sec., 1977-84; chmn. lay bd. DePaul Health Center, 1979—, mem. exec. com. lay bd., 1981—; mem. lay adv. bd. Chaminade Coll. Prep. Sch., 1980—, chmn. bd. trustees, 1981-84; mem. lay bd. Acad. of the Visitation, 1981-85. Served with AUS, 1955-58. Mem. ABA, Mo. Bar Assn., St. Louis Bar Assn. (chmn. bus. law 1970-72, chmn. corp. law 1964-67, chmn. spl. projects 1964-65, moot ct. coms. 1966-67), Am. Judicature Soc., Am. Footwear Industries Assn. (nat. affairs, vice-chmn. 1970, chmn. 1971-75), Am. Apparel Mfrs. Assn. (dir. 1983-85), NAM (taxation com. 1970-76, pub. affairs com. 1973-76, govt. ops./expenditures com. 1973-78), St. Louis C. of C. (legis. and tax com. 1966-74, vice chmn. 1970-71), Asso. Industries Mo. (dir. 1973-80, exec. com. 1974-80, 2d v.p. 1974-76, pres. 1976-78), Am. Soc. Corp. Secs. (pres. St. Louis regional group 1972-73), Delta Theta Phi (dist. chancellor Mo. 70-79, pres. St. Louis alumni 1963). Clubs: Mo. Athletic (dir. 1976-78), Bellerive Country (dir. 1981-84), St. Louis. Home: 55 Muirfield Saint Louis MO 63141 Office: Interco Inc 101 S Hanley Rd Saint Louis MO 63105

AYRES, DAVID H., financial executive; b. Salem, Mass., Apr. 30, 1945; s. Samuel Loring and Mary (Davidson) A.; m. Jean Anderson, July 29, 1978; children: Jennifer, Geoffrey, Lauren. Bs, Cornell U., 1969, MBA, 1970. Trainee gobal credit Chase Manhattan Bank, N.Y.C., 1970-72, asst. treas., 1972-74; asst. to treas. Amax, Inc., Greenwich, Conn., 1974-78; sr. treasury adminstr. Amax, Inc., Greenwich, 1978-82, mgr. fin., 1982-86, dir. fin., 1986-88; dep. treas. Maritime Overseas Corp., N.Y.C., 1988-89, treas., 1989—. Mem. Soc. Colonial Wars, SAR. Republican. Congregationalist. Office: Maritime Overseas Corp 511 Fifth Ave New York NY 10017

AYRES, JUDITH ELIZABETH, environmental and business consultant; b. Akron, Ohio, Sept. 3, 1944; d. William Hanes and Mary Helen (Coventry) A.; m. John Woolfolk Burke, III, June 17, 1978; 1 child, Elizabeth Coventry Ayres. BA, Miami U., Oxford, Ohio, 1966; postgrad., Internat. Christian U., Mitaka, Japan, 1968; MPA, Harvard U., 1980. With U.S. Dept. Interior, 1972-78; communication-legis liaison person U.S. Dept. Interior, Ahchorage and Washington, 1974-78; cons. San Francisco, 1978-82; regional adminstr. EPA, San Francisco, 1983-87; prin. William D. Ruckelshaus Assocs., San Francisco, 1988—; lectr., speaker in field. Contbr. articles to numerous publs. Del. Republican. Nat. Conv., 1988; bd. dirs. Women's Leadership Fund, Kennedy Sch. Govt., Harvard U.; mem. bd. Conservationists for Bush; co-chmn. Bush for Pres., Marin County, Calif., 1988, Calif. Conservationists for Bush, 1988. Mem. Women's Forum West (bd. dirs.), Harvard Club, Lambda Alpha. Office: William D Ruckelshaus Assoc 100 Shoreline Hwy Mill Valley CA 94941

AYRES, RUSSELL WILLIAM, JR., retired construction and agricultural equipment company executive; b. Utica, N.Y., Mar. 8, 1926; s. Russell William and Helen A. (Gates) A.; m. Rebecca Thatcher, June 30, 1948; children—Russel William III, Carolyn, Stephen, Nancy. B.S.E.E., Yale U., 1948; M.E., U. Mich., 1946; postgrad. Harvard Bus. Sch., 1965. Mktg. mgr. Gen. Electric Co., 1948-61; corporate dir. strategic planning Westinghouse Air Brake Co., 1962-63; v.p., gen. mgr. Westinghouse Air Brake div. Am. Standard, 1963-70; pres., chief operating officer Mosler Safe Co., Hamilton, Ohio, 1971-78; sr. v.p. corp. ops. J.I. Case Co., Racine, Wis., 1978-82, sr. v.p., gen. mgr. service parts supply div., 1982-88. Chmn. bd. dirs. St. Lukes Hosp., Racine; v.p. fin. Racine Area United Way. Served with USN, 1943-46. Republican. Episcopalian. Club: Racine Country (Wis.).

AYRES, RUSSELL WILLIAM, III, lawyer; b. Schenectady, N.Y., Mar. 14, 1950; s. Russell William Jr. and Rebecca (Thatche) A.; m. Katherine E. Ayres; 1 child, Russell William IV. BA, Princeton U., 1972; MA, SUNY, Stony Brook, 1973; JD, Harvard U., 1976. Bar: Pa. 1976, U.S. Dist. Ct. (we. dist.) Pa. 1976. Assoc. Reed, Smith, Shaw & McClay, Pitts., 1976-83; assoc., gen. counsel The Hillman Co., Pitts., 1983—. Mem. ABA, Allegheny County Bar Assn., Am. Corp. Counsel Assn., Duquesne Club. Office: Hillman Co 1900 Grant Bldg Pittsburgh PA 15219

AZAR, RICHARD THOMAS, financial management consultant; b. Bklyn., June 3, 1954; s. Denis Anthony and Marie Elizabeth (Shakal) A. BA in Polit. Sci., U. S. Fla., 1976; MBA with honors, Pace U., 1979. CPA, N.Y. Sr. auditor, cons. Pannell Kerr Forster, N.Y.C., 1979-81; mgr. fin. systems and analysis, cons. svcs. group Ernst and Whinney, N.Y.C., 1982-85; mgr. fin. planning and controls, cons. svcs. group Price Waterhouse, N.Y.C., 1985-86; v.p., chief fin. officer N.Y. Real Estate Devel. Co., N.Y.C., 1986-87; prin. R.T. Azar and Assocs., N.Y.C., 1987-88; pres., founder CFO Resources Inc., N.Y.C., 1988—; cons. small bus. devel. ctr. Pace U., N.Y.C., 1987. Mem. AICPA (mgmt. adv. svcs. div.), N.Y. State Soc. CPA's (hotel, restaurant and club acctg. com. 1987), Nat. Assn. Accts. (N.Y. chpt.), Met. Club. Republican. Roman Catholic. Home: 335 E 51st St 4F New York NY 10022 Office: CFO Resources Inc 885 3d Ave Ste 2900 New York NY 10022

AZAROFF, LEONID VLADIMIROVITCH, physics educator; b. Moscow, June 19, 1926; came to U.S., 1939, naturalized, 1945; s. Vladimir Ivanovitch and Maria Yulievna (Odlen) A.; m. Carmen Wade, Mar. 9, 1946 (div. July 1968); m. Beth Sulzer, Mar. 4, 1972; children: David, Richard, Lenore. BS cum laude, Tufts Coll., 1948; PhD, MIT, 1954. Research physicist Armour Research Found., Chgo., 1953-54, sr. scientist, 1954-57; asso. prof. metall. engring. Ill. Inst. Tech., Chgo., 1957-61, prof., 1961-66; prof. physics, dir. Inst. Material Sci., U. Conn., Storrs, 1966—; guest physicist Brookhaven Nat. Lab., 1961, 62, 64; vis. prof. U. Mass., 1978-79, 85-86; cons. Owens-Ill., Philips Electronics, Hilger-Watts, Inc.; U.S. del. Internat. Union Crystallography, teaching commn., 1963-69; dir. Conn. Product Devel. Corp., Rogers Corp., Conn. Devel. Corp., 1977—; pres. Conn. Acad. Sci. and Engring., Hartford, Conn., 1976-82; translation editor Am. Inst. Physics, N.Y.C., 1958; bd. dirs. Conn. Product Devel. Corp., Hartford. Author: 7 books, including X-Ray Diffraction and X-Ray Spectroscopy, 1973; also articles. Served with AUS, 1944-46. Recipient Official Citation Conn. Gen. Assembly, Hartford, 1982. Fellow Am. Phys. Soc. (cons. editor), Mineral. Soc. Am.; mem. AAAS (dir.), IEEE (sr.), Am. Soc. Engring. Edn., Conn. Acad. Sci. and Engring. (pres. 1976-82), Am. Crystallographic Assn., Am. Inst. Mining Engrs., Am. Inst. Electronic Engrs., Internat. Union Physics, Internat. Union Crystal Growth, Sigma Xi (pres. Medford, Mass. chpt. 1947-48), Phi Kappa Phi, Sigma Pi Sigma. Democrat. Russian Orthodox. Home: PO Box 103 Storrs CT 06268 Office: U of Conn Inst of Materials Sci PO Box 136 Storrs CT 06268

AZAROFF, MARCELLA MARIE, engineering consulting company executive; b. Lincoln, Nebr., Nov. 5, 1938; d. John Joseph and Lillian Cecilia (Prochaska) Bohaty; m. Vladimir Azaroff, Feb. 1, 1958; children: Victor (dec.), Deena Ann, Andre Kurt, Tara Mae, Illya Lee. BBA, U. Nebr., 1984. Sec. Progressive Design, Inc., Omaha, 1968-72; sales coord. Cyclonaire div. HyMark Industries, Inc., Henderson, Nebr., 1973; adminstrv. asst. Cyclonaire Corp., Henderson, 1974-76, Upper Big Blue Natural Resource dist., State of Nebr., York, 1977-78; office mgr., bookkeeper Lincoln Indsl. Supply Co., 1978-82; staff acct. Jerome P. McCauley, CPA, Orlando, Fla., 1985, Spillane, Altman, McCauley & Leach, CPAs, Altamonte Springs, Fla., 1985; mgr. adminstrv. svcs., compt. Flex Automated Systems Inc., DeLeon Springs, Fla. and Silver Spring, Pa., 1986—, also bd. dirs.; bd. dirs. Wal-Mar Assocs., Lincoln. Active social, religious and speaking orgns. Mem. Nat. Assn. Accts., LWV. Democrat. Roman Catholic. Office: Flex Automated Systems Inc 3672 Marietta Ave Silver Spring PA 17575

AZAROW, CHARLES, retired sugar corporation executive; b. Jersey City, Dec. 12, 1918; s. Isaac and Ruth (Laurie) A.; m. Dolores Marie Willcockson. Student, Hudson Coll. With B.W. Dyer & Co., N.Y.C., 1937-52; v.p. sugar div. Pepsico, Purchase, N.Y., 1952-68; pres. sweetener div. Sucrest Corp., N.Y.C., 1968-77; pres. Revere Sugar Corp., N.Y.C., 1977-81; pres., chief exec. officer Nat. Sugar Refining, N.Y.C., 1981-82; vice chmn. Holly Sugar Corp., Colorado Springs, Colo., 1982-86; pres., chief exec. officer Holly Sugar Corp., Colorado Springs, 1986-88; cons. in sugar industry, 1988—. Counsilman Demarest, N.J., 1975-77. Served with U.S. Army, 1941-45. Mem. U.S. Beet Sugar Assn., Sugar Assn., Inc., Internat. Sugar Club (past pres.), Sugar Industry Technologists, N.Y. Coffee/Sugar Exchange (on spot com.). Office: Holly Sugar Corp 100 Chase Stone Ctr Colorado Springs CO 80903

AZCUENAGA, MARY LAURIE, government official. AB, Stanford U., 1967; JD, U. Chgo., 1973. Atty. FTC, Washington, 1973-75, asst. to gen. counsel, 1975-76, staff atty. San Francisco regional office, 1977-80, asst. regional dir., 1980-81, asst. to exec. dir., 1981-82, litigation atty. Office of Gen. Counsel, 1982, asst. gen. counsel for legal counsel, 1983-84, commr., Washington, 1984—. Office: FTC 6th & Pennsylvania Ave NW Rm 526 Washington DC 20580

AZZATO, LOUIS E., manufacturing company executive; b. N.Y.C., Oct. 8, 1930; s. John A. and Margaret (Ronca) A.; m. Margaret Jean McCarthy, June 25, 1955; children—Jean Bernadette and Patricia Bernadette Stephens (twins), John Kevin, Maureen Ann. BSChemE cum laude, CCNY, 1952. Process, project engr. Foster Wheeler Corp., Clinton, N.J., 1952-63; project mgr. Foster Wheeler Corp., 1963-67; v.p., mgr. progess plants and fired heater activities Foster Wheeler Italiana, Milan, 1967-74; sr. v.p., group exec. Foster Wheeler Corp., 1978-80, also bd. dirs., exec. v.p. equipment div. ops., 1980-81, pres., chief exec. officer, 1981-88; chmn., pres., chief exec. officer Foster Wheeler Corp., Clinton, N.J., 1988—; chmn. chief exec. officer Glitsch, Inc., Dallas, 1974-78; bd. dirs., chmn., pres. various subs. cos. of Foster Wheeler Corp, First Fidelity Bank, N.A., N.J., First Fidelity Bancorp. N.J.; bd. regents Seton Hall U., S. Orange, N.J., 1986. Patentee catalytic cracking. Mem. Am. Inst. Chem. Engrs., Industry Adv. Bd. ASME. Roman Catholic. Home: 22 Lord William Penn Dr Morristown NJ 07960

BAAR, JAMES A., public relations and corporate communications executive, author; b. N.Y.C., Feb. 9, 1929; s. A.W. and Marguerite R. B.; m. Beverly Hodge, Sept. 2, 1948; 1 son, Theodore Hall. A.B., Union Coll., Schenectady, 1949. Washington corr. UPI, also other wire service burs. and newspapers, 1949-59; sr. editor Missiles and Rockets mag., 1959-62; mgr. various news bur. ops. Gen. Electric Co., 1962-66; mgr. European Mktg. Communications Ops., 1966-70; pres. Gen. Electric subs. Internat. Mktg. Communications Cons., 1970-72; sr. v.p., dir. public relations Lewis & Gilman, Inc., Phila., 1972-74; exec. v.p. Creamer Dickson Basford, Inc., 1974-78; pres. Creamer Dickson Basford-New Eng., 1978-83; sr. v.p./mgr. Northeast region Hill & Knowlton, Inc., Boston, 1983-84; v.p. communications Computervision Corp., 1984-86; sr. v.p. Gray & Co. Pub. Communications and gen. mgr. Gray & Co., N.Y., 1986-87; exec. v.p., worldwide dep. dir. advanced tech. practice Hill & Knowlton, 1987—. Author: Polaris, 1960, Combat Missileman, 1961, Spacecraft and Missiles of the World, 1962; novel The Great Free Enterprise Gambit, 1980; also numerous articles. Bd. overseers New Eng. Conservatory Music. Mem. Nat. Investor Relations Inst., Pub. Relations Soc. Am., Counselors Acad., Internat. Pub. Relations Assn., Chi Psi, Nat. Press Club, Overseas Press Club, English Speaking Union (bd. dirs. Boston). Republican. Roman Catholic. Clubs: Hope (Providence); Union (Boston); Mohawk (Schenectady). Office: Hill & Knowlton Advanced Tech 800 South St Waltham MA 02154

BAAS, JAMES WILLIAM, real estate developer; b. Columbus, Ohio, May 14, 1945; s. Jacob Charles and Katherine (Schlecht) B.; m. Linda Hartlerode, Aug. 19, 1967; children: Daniel James, David William. BArch, Ohio State U., 1968; JD, Capital U., 1981. Bar: Ohio 1981, U.S. Dist. Ct. (so. dist.) Ohio 1981. Designer Smith, Hinchman & Grylls Assocs., Detroit, 1968-70; mgr. planning and design Multicon Properties Inc., Columbus, 1970-73; sr. v.p. Trott & Bean Architects Inc., Columbus, 1973-86; exec. v.p. Conquest Corp., Columbus, 1986-89, Pizzuti Devel. Inc., Columbus, 1989—. Vice cmn. Zoning and Planning Bd., Upper Arlington, Ohio, 1983-87; trustee St. Ann's Franciscan Found., St. Ann's Hosp., Westerville, Ohio, 1986—, Unverferth House, 1988—. Named to Pres.'s Club Cen. Ohio chpt. Am. Heart Assn., Columbus, 1986-87. Mem. ABA, AIA, Architects Soc. Ohio, Ohio State Bar Assn., Columbus Bar Assn., Nat. Assn. Indsl. and Office Parks (pres. cen. Ohio chpt. 1988-89), Athletic Club, Scioto Country Club. Republican. Lutheran. Home: 2120 Cheshire Rd Columbus OH 43221 Office: Pizzuti Devel Inc 250 E Broad St Ste 1900 Columbus OH 43215 also: 7380 Sand Lake Rd Orlando FL 32819

BABA, ISAMU, construction company executive; b. Oita, Japan, June 13, 1923; s. Gunroku and Kimiko Baba; m. Fumiko Takita, Nov. 3, 1948; children: Shiro, Kyoko Kojima. B in Engring., Osaka (Japan) U., 1945. Cert. architect, cons. engr., value specialist. Mgr. research and devel. Fujita Corp., Tokyo, 1965-75, dir., 1975-85, exec. v.p., 1985—. Author: The Method of Value Engineering in the Construction Industry, 1975, Basics of Construction Value Engineering, 1983, Application of Construction Value Engineering, 1983, Illustration of the Method of Keeping Costs Down in the Construction Industry, 1984. Recipient Presdl. citation Soc. Am. Value Engrs., 1981, Soc. award Associated Gen. Contractors of Japan, 1985. Mem. Internat. Council Bldg. Research, Studies and Documentation, Soc. Japanese Value Engrs. (councilor, Best Paper prize 1973, Promotional Achievment award 1984), Soc. Korean Value Engrs. (adviser), Archtl. Inst. Japan (trustee), Japan Soc. Civil Engrs., Japanese Cons. Engrs. Assn. Club: Tokyo Bridge. Lodge: Rotary. Home: 2-29-21 Irima-cho, Chofu-shi, Tokyo 182, Japan Office: Fujita Corp, 4-6-15 Sendagaya, Shibuya-ku, Tokyo 151, Japan

BABAR, RAZA ALI, industrial engineer, utility consultant, management educator; b. Shujabad, Punjab, Pakistan, May 29, 1947; came to U.S., 1972; s. Syed Mohammad Ali Shah and Syeda Hafeeza (Gilani) Bukhari; m. Sufia K. Durrett, July 23, 1974 (div. 1983); children: Azra Yasmeen, Imran Ali, Amenah Andaleep; m. Syeda Afshan Gilani, Aug. 23, 1983; children: Abdullah Ali, Hammad Ali, Omaima Ali. Pre engring. edn. Govt. Coll., Lahore, Pakistan, 1965; BS in Mining Engring., U. Engring. and Tech., Lahore, 1969; MS in Indsl. Engring., Wayne State U., 1978; postgrad Detroit Coll. Law, 1982, U. Mich., 1977-84. Engr., planner Bukhari Elec. Concern, Multan, Pakistan, 1969-70; mgr. mining ops. Felezzate Yazd Co., Iran, 1970-72; salesman Great Books, Inc., Chgo., 1972-73; field underwriter N.Y. Life Ins. Co., 1972-73; indsl. engr. Ellis/Naeyaert Assocs., Inc., Warren, Mich., 1973-74; grad. asst. dept. indsl. engring. and ops. rsch. Wayne State U., Detroit, 1974-75; prin. engr., work leader project svcs. div. Generation Constrn. Dept., Detroit Edison Co., 1975-79; tech. advisor Ministry of Prodn., Govt. Pakistan, Islamabad, 1979-80; chmn. dept. bus. adminstrn. Zakariya U., Multan, Pakistan, 1980-82; prin. engr. project controls Enrico Fermi 2 Detroit Edison Co., 1981-82, supr. Fermi 2 rate case task force, 1982-84, spl. projects engr. planning, 1984-88; mgr. econ. support svc. Syndeco, Inc., 1985-88; vis. prof. grad. Sch. Bus. Adminstrn., Wayne State U., 1987—; market planner Detroit Edison Co., 1988—. Author rsch. papers, presentations to Am. Assn. of Cost Engrs., Am. Power Conf., Internat. Assn. of Energy, Power and Environ. Systems. Founder Fedn. Engring. Assns. Pakistan, 1969; pres. acad. staff assn., mem. chancellor's com. Zakariya U., Pakistan, 1980-81; pres. Pakistan Cultural Group, Detroit, 1975-76; bd. dirs. Detroit Islamic Libr., 1976-77; mem. Econ. Outlook Conf., U. Mich., Ann Arbor, 1977-84, Rep. Presdl. Task Force Honor Roll, Rep. Nat. Com.; Recipient Pride of Performance medal Engring. U., Pakistan, 1967; Acad. Merit scholar Detroit Coll. Law, 1982. Mem. Am. Mgmt. Assn., Am. Mgmt. Assn. Internat., Econ. Club Detroit, Am. Inst. Indsl. Engrs., Am. Assn. Cost Engrs., Engring. Soc. Detroit, Am. Mktg. Assn., ESD Profl. Activities Coun., Pakistan Engring. Congress, Pakistan Inst. Mining Engrs., ABA (student chpt.), Am. Assn. of MBA Execs., Assn. Muslims Scientists and Engrs., Assn. Muslim Social Scientists, Internat. Platform Assn., Islamic Soc. N.Am., Am. Moslem Soc., Islamic Cultural Inst., Tanzeem-e-Islami Pakistan and N.Am., Pakistan Assn. of Am., Assn. of Pakistani Scientists and Engrs. in N.Am. Avocations: reading, writing, photography, sports, travel. Home: 15672 Golfview Dr Riverview MI 48192 Office: 2000 Second Ave Detroit MI 48226

BABAYANS, EMIL, financial planner; b. Tehran, Iran, Nov. 9, 1951; came to U.S., 1969; s. Hacob and Jenik (Khatchatourian) B.; m. Annie Ashjian. B.S., U. So. Calif., 1974, M.S., 1976; m. Annie Ashjian. Cert. fin. planner; chartered life underwriter, fin. cons. Pres. Babtech Internat., Inc., Sherman Oaks, Calif., 1975-85; sr. ptnr. Emil Babayans & Assocs., Woodland Hills, Calif., 1985—. Mem. Am. Mgmt. Assn., Nat. Assn. Life Underwriters, Inst. Cert. Fin. Planners, Internat. Assn. Fin. Planners, Am. Soc. CLU and Chartered Fin. Cons. Armenian Orthodox. Office: 21041 Burbank Blvd Suite 200 Woodland Hills CA 91367

BABCOCK, JANICE BEATRICE, health system specialist; b. Milw., June 2, 1942; d. Delbert Martin and Constance Josephine (Dworschack) B. BS in Med. Tech., Marquette U., 1964; MA in Healthcare Mgmt. and Supervision, Cen. Mich. U., 1975, postgrad. in Edn. in Health Care, 1975—. Registered med. technologist and microbiologist., clin. lab. scientist, Wis.; cert. bioanalytical lab. mgr. Intern St. Luke's Hosp., Milw., 1963-64; microbiologist St. Michael's Hosp., Milw., 1964-65; supr. clin. lab. svc. VA Regional Office, Milw., 1965-66; hosp. epidemiologist VA Ctr., Milw., 1966-74, supr. anaerobic microbiology and rsch. lab., 1974-78; adminstrv. officer, chief med. tech. VA Ctr., Wood, Wis., 1978-83, quality assurance coord., 1983-86, asst. to chief of staff profl. svcs., 1986—; rsch. assoc. dept. surgery Med. Coll. Wis.; tchr. in field Marquette U., U. Wis., Med. Coll. Wis. Contbr. numerous articles to profl. jours. Recipient Wood VA Fed. Woman's award, 1975, Profl. Achievement award Lab. World jour., 1981, Disting. Alumni award Cen. Mich. U., 1986. Fellow Royal Soc. Health, Am. Acad. Med. Adminstrs. (Wis. state dir. 1986—); mem. Internat. Acad. Healthcare Mgmt., Am. Soc. Microbiology, Am. Coll. Healthcare Execs., Am. Soc. Med. Tech. (Nat. Sci. Creativity award 1974, Nat. Microbiology Sci. (Achievement award 1978, Mem. of Yr. award 1979, Profl. Achievement Lectureship award 1981, French Lectureship award 1983), Assn. Practitioners in Infection Control, Fed. Execs. Assn., Wis. Hosp. Assn., AAUW, Nat. Geog. Soc., Marquette U. Alumni Assn. (Merit award 1979, Profl. Achievement award 1987), Assn. Marquette U. Women (bd. dirs. 1987-91, v.p. 1988-89), Holiday Camera Club, Alpha Mu Tau (pres. 1984-85), Alpha Delta Theta, Sigma Iota Epsilon, Alpha Delta Pi (Alumni Honor award 1979). Home: 6839 Blanchard St Wauwatosa WI 53213 Office: VA Med Center 5000 W National Ave Milwaukee WI 53295

BABCOCK, MICHAEL JOSEPH, retail company executive; b. Fort Riley, Kans., Sept. 10, 1941; s. David Edward and Dorothy Jayne (Viner) B.; m. Abigail Wilkins, Dec. 29, 1974: children: Michael Joseph, Elizabeth Anne, Catherine Nielsen, Rebecca Leigh. BA in Indsl. Psychology, U. Tulsa, 1965. Mem. corp. personnel staff 3M Co., St. Paul, 1965-67; mgr. wage and salary adminstrn. Famous-Barr Co., St. Louis, 1967-68; dir. exec. placement Famous-Barr Co., 1968-70; assoc. gen. mgr. Famous-Barr Co., Crestwood, Mo., 1970; v.p., personnel dir. Strouss' Co., Youngstown, Ohio, 1970-72; v.p. ops. and personnel Strouss' Co., 1972-73, May D & F, Denver, 1973-74; v.p. personnel May Co., L.A., 1974-75; sr. v.p. personnel May Co., 1976-80; sr. v.p. personnel and organizational devel. May Dept. Stores Co., St. Louis, 1976-80; chmn. bd. G. Fox & Co., Hartford, Conn., 1980-82; pres. Filene's, Boston, 1982-84; chmn. bd., chief exec. officer Filene's, 1984—; pres., chief exec. L.J. Hooker Retail Group, N.Y.C., 1987—; bd. dir. Liberty Mut. Ins. Cos. Bd. dirs., trustee Dana Farber Cancer Inst.; mem. Young Pres.'s Orgn. Mem. Nat. Retail Mcht. Assn. (bd. dirs.), Kappa Sigma. Republican. Episcopalian. Home: 274 Round Hill Rd Greenwich CT 06830 Office: L J Hooker Retail Group 361 Fifth Ave New York NY 10016

BABCOCK, THEODORE STODDARD, consultant; b. Bronxville, N.Y., July 14, 1950; s. Henry Nash and Mary Warner (King) B.; m. Lyn C. Ackerman, July 2, 1988. BA with distinction, U. Mich., 1973; MA, U. Va., 1974; MBA, Harvard U., 1982. Sales coordinator U.S. Grout Corp., Fairfield, Conn., 1974-76, dir. mktg., 1976-78, v.p. ops., 1978-80; product mgr. Internat. Paper, N.Y.C., 1982-84; program mgr. King-Casey, Inc., New Canaan, Conn., 1984-86; pres., chmn. Invasset Corp., New Canaan, Conn., 1986-88; pres., chmn., mng. dir. Dole Assoc., Katonah, N.Y., 1988—; pres., bd. dirs. Wesix Corp., Old Greenwich, Conn.; bd. dirs. Babcock Corp., Old Greenwich. Pres. alumni assn. Williston-Northampton Sch., Easthampton, Mass., 1977-78; trustee, 1979-84; trustee Mid-Fairfield Child Guidance Ctr., Norwalk, Conn., 1988—. Fellow English Speaking Union., Thomas Jefferson Meml. Found. Mem. Am. Mgmt. Assn. Democrat. Episcopalian. Club: Harvard (N.Y.C.). Home: 163 Bald Hill Rd N New Canaan CT 06840

BABCOCK, WARNER KING, entrepreneur, venture capitalist, investor; b. Bronxville, N.Y., Nov. 25, 1951; s. Henry Nash and Mary Warner (King) B.; m. Patricia Anne Joyner, Oct. 8, 1952; children: Elisabeth King, Mary Joyner, Stuart Warner. BA, U. N.C., 1974; MBA, Emory U., 1977. Regional mgr. U.S. Grout Corp., Greenwich, Conn., 1977-78, dir. corp. planning and service, 1978-79; pres. U.S. Waterproofing Inc., Fairfield, Conn., 1979-85, Babcock and King Inc., Fairfield, Conn., 1979-85, Babcock Group, New Canaan, Conn., 1985-88; founder, mng. dir. Advanced Materials Ptnrs. Inc., New Canaan, 1988—; bd. dirs. Robotic Retail Systems Corp., Koloramics Co., Gen. Colloid Corp. Patentee in field. Recipient Tech. award Constrn. Specification Inst., 1983. Fellow Am. Inst. Chemists; mem. ASTM, Am. Soc. Metals, Am. Chem. Soc., Materials Rsch. Soc., Comml. Devel. Assn., Am. Concrete Inst., Chemist Club, Rocky Point Club (pres. 1988—), Emory U. Club (pres. N.Y.C. 1980-81). Republican. Episcopalian. Office: Advanced Materials Ptnrs Inc PO Box 1022 49 Locust Ave New Canaan CT 06849-1022

BABER, WILBUR H., JR., lawyer; b. Shelby, N.C., Dec. 18, 1926; s. Wilbur H. and Martha Corinne (Allen) B.; B.A., Emory U., 1949; postgrad. U. N.C., 1949-50, U. Houston, 1951-52; J.D., Loyola U., New Orleans, 1965. Bar: La. 1965, Tex. 1966. Sole practice, Hallettsville, Tex., 1966—. Served with U.S. Army. Mem. ABA, La. Bar Assn., Tex. Bar Assn., La. Engring. Soc., Tex. Surveyors Assn. Methodist. Lodge: Rotary. Office: PO Box 294 Hallettsville TX 77964

BABICZ, LAURENCE WALTER, video executive; b. Chgo., Oct. 22, 1961; s. Walter Anthony and Betty Jean (Bruemmer) B. BS, DePaul U., 1984, postgrad., 1987. Analyst credit Marshall Field & Co., Chgo., 1984-86; treas. Imagewerks Inc., Chgo., 1986—. Canvasser, voter registration drive, Chgo., 1983-87.

BABISH, RICHARD CONSTANTINE, optical engineering consultant; b. Beverly, Mass., Sept. 17, 1918; s. Constantine Michael and Anna (Bennett)

B.; m. Josita Marie Dolan, May 20, 1945; children—James F., Joan M. B.S. in Physics, MIT, 1946. Lab. asst. Paramount News, N.Y.C., 1940-42; from engr. to v.p. Vitarama Corp., Huntington, N.Y., 1942-54; staff mem. Radiation Lab., MIT, Cambridge, 1944-45; engr. Perkin-Elmer Corp., Norwalk, Conn., 1949-1961, br. chief, 1961-1968, tech. dir., 1968-85; prin. cons., 1985—; tech. dir. Cinerama, Inc., Oyster Bay, N.Y., 1952-54, Cine Miracle Corp., N.Y.C. and Los Angeles, 1954-56; pvt. practice cons., 1985—; chmn. adv. bd. optics Norwalk State Tech. Coll., 1985—. Contbr. articles to profl. jours.; patentee in field. Fellow Optical Soc. Am.; mem. Soc. Photo-optical Instrumentation Engr., Internat. Commn. for Optics (U.S. com. 1985-87), Soc. Motion Picture and TV Engrs., AAAS. Avocation: photography. Home and Office: 74 Rivergate Dr Wilton CT 06897

BABSON, ARTHUR CLIFFORD, financial executive; b. Portland, July 19, 1909; s. Sydney Groham and Grace Bowditch (Campbell) B.; m. Margery Tindle Grey, Aug. 3, 1946; children—John Pell, Robert Grey. BS, U. Oreg., 1931. With Union Terminal Coldstorage Co., Jersey City, 1932-36, asst. supt., 1935-36; with Babson's Reports, Inc., Wellesley Hills, Mass., 1936-78, v.p., 1940-78; bd. dirs., mem. personnel coms. Home Group Inc., N.Y.C.; bd. dirs., mem. personnel coms. Home Ins. Co., N.Y.C. Chmn. Sherborn Bd. Selectmen, Mass., 1964-70; trustee Sawin Acad., 1975-85. U.S. Naval rep. lt. comdr., Sri Lanka and So. India, 1942-45. Mem. Pilgrims of U.S., Chi Psi. Episcopalian. Home: 8 Lookout Farm Rd South Natick MA 01760

BABSON, IRVING K., publishing company executive; b. Tel Aviv, Apr. 15, 1936; came to U.S., 1940; s. Matthew and Miriam B.; m. Laurie Babson; children—Stacey B., Mia L., Christopher. BBA, CCNY, 1957; postgrad. NATO seminars, Harvard U., 1965. Bd. dirs. Tribune/Swab-Fox Cos.; chmn. BMT Publs., Inc., Convenience Store News, U.S. Distbn. Jour., Gaming Bus. Mag., Smokeshop Mag., N.Y.C., Jour. Petroleum Mktg., N.Y.C.; ptr. Mag. Devel. Fund., Babson Family Investment. With AUS, 1956-57. Mem. Nat. Assn. Corp. Dirs. Club: Friars. Home: 10 E End Ave New York NY 10022 also: 19355 Turnberry Way North Miami Beach FL 33180 Office: 254 W 31st St New York NY 10001

BABYAK, MICHAEL, JR., financial planning executive; b. N.Y.C., Aug. 18, 1937; s. Michael and Mary (Prokop) B.; m. Ethel M. Babbitt, Apr. 29, 1961; children: Michel, Mary Alice, Marcia, Melissa, Michael II. Cert. life underwriting, Am. Coll., 1985; cert. fin. planning, Coll. Fin. Planning, 1988. Chartered fin. cons. Prin. Precision Fin. Services, Parsippany, N.J., 1970—; pres. Precision Pension Services, Inc., Randolph, N.J., 1975—; gen. agt. Am. United Life Ins. Co., Indpls., 1963—. Paul Harris fellow Rotary Internat. Found., 1976. Mem. N.J. Chartered Life Underwriters (bd. dirs. 1988—), Nat. Assn. Life Underwriters (pres. state chpt. 1978-79), Internat. Assn. Fin. Planners, Million Dollar Round Table (life, qualifying). Office: Precision Fin Svcs 1130 Rte 46 Parsippany NJ 07054

BACANI, NICANOR-GUGLIELMO VILA, civil structural engineer, consultant; b. Dagupan City, Pangasinan, Philippines, Jan. 10, 1947; s. Jose Montero and Felisa Lomibao (Vila) B.; m. Julieta San Antonio Carlos, June 24, 1972; children: Julinor, Jazmin, Joymita, Normina, Nicanor Jr. BCE, U. Philippines, 1968, MSE, 1973. Registered profl. engr., Philippines. Structural engr. FR Estuar, PhD. Assocs., Quezon City, Philippines, 1970-72; civil structural engr. BestPhil Cons., Dagupan City, 1972-73; engrng. mgr. Supreme Structural Products, Inc., Manila, 1974; chief engr. Tecphil Cons., Quezon City, 1974-76; v.p. Erectors, Inc., Makati, Philippines, 1977-81; pres. NGV Bacani & Assocs., various locations, 1981—; adviser, cons. Met. Manila Office of Commr. Planning, Manila, 1980—; profl. lectr. U. Manila Grad. Sch., Manila, 1982—; resource person Nat. Engrng. Ctr. U.P., Quezon City, 1983—; cons. Geo J Fosdyke Assocs., L.A., 1985—, Victor Constrn. & Devel., 1986—; pres. Mgmt. Design & Investment Co., 1987—, Stanley Assocs. Internat., 1988—. Author: A Reference for Engineers and Builders, 1983. Mem. Am. Mgmt. Assn., Internat. Assn. Bridge and Structural Engrs., Prestressed Concrete Inst., U. Philippines Alumni Engrs. Assn. (life), Assn. Structural Engrs. Philippines (bd. dirs. 4 terms).

BACCIGALUPPI, ROGER JOHN, agricultural company executive; b. N.Y.C., Mar. 17, 1934; s. Harry and Ethel (Hutcheon) B.; m. Patricia Marie Wier, Feb. 6, 1960 (div. 1978); children: John, Elisabeth, Andrea, Jason; m. Iris Christine Walfridson, Feb. 3, 1979. B.S., U. Calif., Berkeley, 1956; M.S., Columbia U., 1957. Asst. sales promotion mgr. Maco Mag. Corp., N.Y.C., 1956-57; mdsg. asst. Honig, Cooper & Harrington, San Francisco and L.A., 1957-58, 1958-60; asst. dir. merchandising Honig, Cooper & Harrington, 1960-61; sales rep. Blue Diamond Growers (formerly Calif. Almond Growers Exch.), Sacramento, 1961-64, mgr. advt. and sales promotion, 1964-70; v.p. mktg. Blue Diamond Growers (formerly Calif. Almond Growers Exch.), 1970-73, sr. v.p. mktg., 1973-74, exec. v.p., 1974-75, pres., 1975—; bd. dirs. Almond Bd. Calif., Nat. Coun. Farmer Coops., Grocery Mfrs. Am., Inc.; vice chmn., bd. dirs. Agrl. Coun. Calif., mem. consumer-producer com., adminstrn. com.; mem. U.S. adv. com. TRADE Negotiations, 1983—, U.S. adv. bd. Rabobank Nederlands. Vice chmn. Calif. State R.R. Mus. Fedn.; active Los Rios Community Coll. Dist.; bd. visitors U. Calif., Davis; vice chmn. Grad. Inst. of Cooperative Leadership, 1986—, chair, 1987—. With AUS, 1957. Mem. Calif. C. of C. (internat. trade com., bd. dirs. 1988—), Sacramento C. of C. (bd. dirs. host com. 1983), Calif. for Higher Edn., Grad. Inst. Coop. Leadership (chmn., trustee), Grocery Mfrs. Am., Inc. (mem., bd. dirs. 1988—), Sutter Club, Del Paso Country Club. Office: Calif Almond Growers Exch 1802 C St Sacramento CA 95814

BACH, PENELOPE CAROLINE, banker; b. Columbus, Ohio, Apr. 17, 1946; d. Clyde Aaron and Gayle)List(Palmer; m. Ronald Dean Bach, Sept. 14, 1968; children: Emily Robin, Allison Jeanne. BA, Ohio State U., 1968, MBA, 1982. Programmer, analyst The Huntington Nat. Bank, Columbus, 1968-75, asst. v.p., lead programmer, 1975-79, v.p., mgr. ops dept., 1979-85, sr. v.p., mgr. div, 1985—. Mem. Twing A Children's Hosp. Aux., Columbus, past pres.; treas. Child Care Resources, Zanesville, Ohio; chairperson Huntington Bankshares Polit. Action Com., Columbus. Mem. Nat. Corp. Cash Mgmt. Assn., Cen. Ohio Cash Mgmt. Assn. Republican. Episcopalian. Office: The Huntington Nat Bank 41 S High St Columbus OH 43287

BACHELOR, HERBERT JAMES, bank executive; b. San Diego, June 3, 1944; s. Herbert and Lorene (James) B.; m. Phyllis Kornblith, Aug. 21, 1965; children: Jeanne, Julia, Jonathan. BA, Harvard U., 1966, MBA, 1968. Sr. v.p. Shearson Am. Express, N.Y.C., 1968-78; vice chmn. Drexel Burnham Lambert, Inc., N.Y.C., 1978—, also bd. dirs.; bd. dirs. Days Inn Am., Atlanta. Office: Drexel Burnham Lambert Inc 60 Broad St New York NY 10004

BACHER, JUDITH ST. GEORGE, executive search consultant; b. New Rochelle, N.Y., July 14, 1946; d. Thomas A. and Rose-Marie (Martocci) Baiocchi; B.S., Georgetown U., 1968; M.L.S., Columbia U., 1971; m. Albert Bacher, Jan. 2, 1972; 1 son, Alexander Michael. Researcher, Time mag., N.Y.C., 1968-71; librarian Mus. Modern Art, N.Y.C., 1971-72; cons. Informaco Inc., N.Y.C., 1972-74, Booz-Allen & Hamilton, N.Y.C., 1974-79; prin. Nordeman Grimm/MBA Resources, N.Y.C., 1979—; mem. White House Adv. Com. on Personnel, Exec. Office of Pres., 1979-81; co-founder Research Roundtable, pres. 1981-83. Mem. Phi Beta Kappa. Office: Nordeman Grimm Inc 717 Fifth Ave New York NY 10022

BACHIK, MARK, finance company executive; b. Waco, Tex., Jan. 18, 1955; s. Joseph and Charlyne (Hannum) B.; m. Cathi Dawn Nelson, Oct. 1, 1977; children: Marcus Brandon, Christopher Ryan. BBA, Baylor U., 1977, MBA, 1978. Cert. fin. planner. Mgr. Shadows Investment Corp., Waco, 1974-76, statis. analyst, 1976; statis. analyst Rockwell Internat., Dallas, 1977; ops. analyst City of Waco, 1977-78; staff acct. Arthur Andersen & Co., Waco, 1978-79; mem. faculty Baylor U., Waco, 1979-81; pres., chmn. bd. Lake Shore Fin. Advisors, Inc., Waco, 1981—, The Vintage Group, Inc., Waco, 1986—; chmn. bd. Sterling Trust Co., Inc., Waco, 1986—; adv. dir. Cardinal Ind., Orlando, Fla., 1985-87, Commerce Clearing House, Inc., Chgo., 1986—; cons. Clifton Investment Co., Tucson, 1988—. Contbr. articles to profl. jours. Mem. Internat. Assn. Fin. Planners, Inst. Cert. Fin. Planners, Estate Planning Coun., Waco C. of C., Lions. Republican. Roman Catholic. Home: 3115 Woodlake Waco TX 76710 Office: Lake Shore Fin Advisors Inc 4547 Lake Shore Dr Waco TX 76710

BACHMAN, CAROL CHRISTINE, trust company executive; b. Buffalo, Jan. 20, 1959; d. Christian George and Joan Marie (Fincel) B. Student, Grad. Inst. Internat. Study, 1979-80; AB, Smith Coll., 1981; grad., New Eng. Sch. Banking, 1987. Trust asst. BayBank Middlesex, Burlington, Mass., 1984-85, sr. trust asst., 1985-87, trust adminstr., 1987, trust officer, 1987-88; estate settlement specialist Bank of Boston, 1988—. Mem. Nat. Assn. Female Execs. Roman Catholic. Home: 10 Marie Dr Wilmington MA 01887 Office: Bank of Boston 100 Federal St PO Box 1861 Boston MA 02105

BACHMAN, HENRY LEE, b. Bklyn., Apr. 29, 1930; s. Solomon and Frances (Cortese) B.; m. Doris Engelhardt, Dec. 8, 1951; children—Steven, Diane, Lorraine. BA in Elec. Engring., Poly. Inst. N.Y., 1951, MA in Elec. Engring., 1954; postgrad. Advanced Mgmt. Program, U., Harvard 1972. Engr., mgr. Wheeler Labs., Greenlawn, N.Y., 1951-55, exec. v.p., dir., Great Neck, N.Y., 1967-68, pres., dir., 1968-79; product line dir. Hazeltine Corp., Green Lawn, N.Y., 1970-72, v.p. quality assurance and logistics, 1973-75, v.p. quality assurance and customer svc., 1975-78, v.p. ops., 1978-84, v.p. engring., 1985—; chmn. L.I. Forum for Tech., 1985-86; mem. corp. bd. Poly. U., 1988—. Contbr. articles to profl. jours. Mem. Pres.'s Adv. Com. on Indsl. Innovation, 1979. Named Fellow and Disting. Alumnus Poly. Inst. N.Y., 1986; recipient Engring. Mgr. of Yr. award IEEE/Engring. Mgmt. Soc., 1985. Fellow IEEE (Centennial medal 1984, exec. v.p. 1984, treas. 1985, pres. 1987), Electronics Industries Assn.; mem. Nat. Indsl. Security Assn., Am. Soc. for Quality Control, Sigma Xi, Eta Kappa Nu, Tau Beta Pi. Avocation: sailing, opera, piano. Home: 5 Brandy Rd Huntington NY 11743 Office: Hazeltine Corp Mail Sta 1-5 Greenlawn NY 11740

BACHMAN, NATHAN DULANEY, IV, investment manager; b. Columbus, Ohio, Sept. 16, 1935; s. Nathan Dulaney III and Kathryn F. (Struble) B.; m. Lynda Mae Aughnay; children: Edward H., Nathan D., Keith F., Shannon Lee. BA cum laude, Princeton U., 1957; MBA, U. Va., 1961. Chartered fin. analyst Inst. Chartered Analysts, 1967. Investment analyst Fla. Capital Corp., Palm Beach, 1961-64; chief fin. officer and treas. Emery Industries, Inc., Cin., 1964-78; exec. v.p., chief fin. officer Burke Internat. Rsch. Corp., Cin., 1979-80; v.p. First Boston Corp., N.Y.C., 1980-82, Shearson Lehman Hutton, 1983—. Chmn. Corp. Fund Raising Cin. Ballet, 1984—. With USMCR, 1957-58. Recipient Community Service award Princeton U., 1987. Mem. Cin. Soc. Fin. Analysts (pres. 1975-76), Fin. Execs. Inst., Nat. Investor Rels. Assn., Inst. Chartered Fin. Analysts, Midwest Pension Conf., Terrace Pk. Club, Ohio Swim Club (pres. 1970-71, treas. 1967-70), Indoor Tennis Club, Cin. Tennis Club, Princeton Club Cin. Home: 9510 Cunningham Rd Cincinnati OH 45243 Office: Shearson Lehman Hutton 2300 Atrium II 221 E 4th St Cincinnati OH 45202

BACHMANN, DONALD M., accountant; b. N.Y.C.; s. Harry B. and Frances (Kestenbaum) B.; m. Harriet Harris, Dec. 11, 1960; children: Jill, Penny, Richard. BBA, CCNY, 1956. Ptnr. Blumberg, Block, Carter & Bachmann, C.P.A.'s, N.Y.C., 1960-69, Clarence Rainess & Co., C.P.A.'s, N.Y.C., 1970-72, Bachmann, Schwartz & Abramson, C.P.A.'s, N.Y.C., 1972—; chmn. N.Y. State Housing Fin. Agy., N.Y. State Med. Care Facilities Fin. Agy., N.Y. State Mcpl. Bond Bank, N.Y. State Project Fin. Agy.; chmn., chief exec. officer Applied DNA Systems Inc.; bd. dirs., treas. The Country Bank. Pres. Shield Inst. for Retarded Children, 1972—. With U.S. Army, 1962. Mem. N.Y. State Soc. C.P.A.'s (chmn. com. on cooperation with bankers), Am. Inst. C.P.A.'s, N.Y. Credit and Fin. Mgmt. Assn., Airline Owners and Pilots Assn., Capital Credit Club, Exchequer Credit Club, Checkmates Credit Club, 111 Credit Club, Masons, B'nai Brith. Office: Bachmann Schwartz Abramson 1450 Broadway New York NY 10018

BACHMANN, RICHARD ARTHUR, oil company executive; b. Green Bay, Wis., Dec. 6, 1944; s. Richard Arthur and Anita Sidonia (Dohmeyer) B.; m. Joanne Lois Klein, Aug. 24, 1968; children: Richard A., Joseph E., Christina J. BBA, Wis. State U., 1967; MBA, U. Wis., 1968. Mgr. fgn. fin. Exxon Corp., N.Y.C., 1968-78; v.p., treas. Itel Corp., San Francisco, 1978-81; exec. v.p. fin. and adminstrn. La. Land and Exploration Co., New Orleans, 1981—, also bd. dirs. Bd. dirs., mem. exec. com., sustaining membership com. chmn. New Orleans council Boy Scouts Am., 1984—, pres. 1988—; bd. dirs. Audubon Park and Zool. Garden. Home: 1404 Octavia St New Orleans LA 70115 Office: La Land & Exploration Co 909 Poydras St PO Box 60350 New Orleans LA 70160

BACHNER, DONALD JOSEPH, packaging manufacturing company executive; b. Chgo., Aug. 17, 1930; s. Louis Henry and Catherine Patricia (O'Connell) B.; m. Marie Kathleen Van Geertrvy, Mar. 16, 1974; children: Timothy, Patricia. BS cum laude, St. Mary's Coll., Winona, Minn., 1952. CPA, Ill. Asst. controller Chgo. Molded Products Corp., 1954-57; from chartered acct. to v.p., treas. Capitol Food Industries subs. Eversweet Foods, Inc., 1957-60; successively treas., v.p., pres. Capitol Food Industries subs. Bowey's Inc., 1960-67; v.p. internat. group Ill. Tool Works Inc., Chgo., 1967-80; pres. Am. Louver Co., Skokie, Ill., 1980-81; exec. v.p. Shred Pax Corp., Bensenville, Ill., 1982-83; gen. mgr. internat. div. Stewart Warner Corp., Chgo., 1983-88; pres., gen. mgr. Packaging Cos. subs. Axia, Inc., Oak Brook, Ill., 1988—, Dave Fischbein Co., Mpls., 1988—, Mid-Am. Machinery Co., Junction City, Kans., 1988—, Companie Fischbein S.A., Brussels, 1988—; bd. dirs. Contempory, Inc., Manitowoc, Wis. With U.S. Army, 1952-54. Fellow Internat. Operating Coun., Machinery and Allied Products Inst.; mem. Packaging Machinery Mfg. Inst., Rolling Green Country Club (Arlington Heights, Ill.), Delta Epsilon Sigma, Pi Kappa Delta. Office: D Fischbein Co 2700 30th Ave S Minneapolis MN 55406

BACHTELL, CLIFTON MERLE, investment banker; b. Greensboro, N.C., Sept. 8, 1937; s. Clifton Merle and Chrystal (Heeren) B.; m. June L. Minder, June 9, 1959 (div. 1974); m. Susan Redwood Lewis, June 28, 1975; 1 child, Christina Revercomb. BA, Duke U., 1959. With Crestar Bank, Richmond, Va., 1959-80; sr. v.p. Wheat First Securities, Richmond, Va., 1980—. Bd. dirs. Richmond Community Action Program, 1971-72; chmn. Church Hill Housing Corp., Richmond, 1971-73. Mem. Richmond Real Estate Group, Richmond Jaycees (pres. 1969-70, Outstanding Young Man 1968). Republican. Presbyterian. Clubs: Bull and Bear, Country of Va. (Richmond). Office: Wheat First Securities Inc 707 E Main St Richmond VA 23229

BACK, GEORGE LEONARD, television program syndicator; b. Bronx, N.Y., Nov. 20, 1939; s. Aaron and Anna (Herman) B.; m. Patricia Davis, Aug. 30, 1980; children: Alexandra Davis, Lauren Anne, Roxanne Eva. BBA, Hofstra Coll., 1962; M in Media Ecology, NYU., 1974, PhD in Media Ecology, 1979; HHD (hon.) Glassboro (N.J.) State Coll., 1983. Mgmt. trainee CBS/Columbia Group, N.Y.C., 1966, Chgo., 1967; div. mgr. ABC Films, Chgo., 1969, L.A., 1970; v.p., gen. mgr. mktg. Group W Prodns., N.Y.C., 1970-77; chief exec. Hughes TV Network, N.Y.C., 1977-79; exec. dir. Nat. Assn. TV Program Execs., 1979-82; prin. George Back & Assocs., N.Y.C., 1979—; pres. All Am. TV, 1982—, chmn. bd. dirs. 1985. Contbr. articles to TV jours. Mem. adv. bd. Babies Heart Fund, 1987. Capt. inf. U.S. Army Res., 1962-66. Mem. NATAS, World Future Soc. Jewish. Office: All Am TV 304 E 45th St 2nd Fl New York NY 10017

BACK, ROBERT WYATT, investment executive, consultant; b. Omaha, Dec. 22, 1936; s. Albert Edward Jr. and Edith (Elliott) B.; m. Linaya Gail Hahn, Aug. 30, 1964; children: Christopher Frederick, Gregory Franklin. BA, Trinity Coll., 1958; postgrad. London Sch. Econs. and Polit. Sci., 1959-60; MA, Yale U., 1960. CLU, chartered fin. analyst, fin. cons. Head trader, security analyst Lincoln Nat. Life Ins. Co., Fort Wayne, Ind., 1964-69; sr. investment analyst Allstate Ins. Co., Northbrook, Ill., 1969-72; investment adv. acct. mgr. Brown Bros. Harriman & Co., Chgo., 1972-74; asst. v.p., investment analyst Harris Trust & Savs. Bank, 1974-82; v.p. instl. research Prescott Ball & Turben, 1982-83, Blunt, Ellis & Loewi, Inc., 1983-84; v.p. instl. equity sales Rodman & Renshaw, Inc., 1984-87; v.p. instnl. research ins. Legg, Mason, Wood & Walker, Inc., 1987-89; mng. dir. instl. dept. Mongerson and Co. Security Corp., Chgo., 1989—; mng. dir. Backfocus Cons. & Referrals, Buffalo Grove, Ill., 1954—. Contbr. numerous articles to profl. jours. Mem. long-range planning com. Adlai Stevenson High Sch., Prairie View, Ill., 1980-82; chmn. investments Police Pension Fund Assn., Chgo., 1985-87; pres. Buffalo Grove Police Pension Fund, 1973—. Capt. USAFR, 1961-64. Woodrow Wilson fellow Yale U., 1958, English-Speaking Union fellow London Sch. Econs., 1959, Russian Research fellow Harvard U., 1960-61; subject of Superanalyst profile Crains Chgo. Bus., 1987. Fellow Fin. Analysts Fedn. (internat. del. 1974—); mem. Inst. Chartered Fin. Analysts (sec., bd. dirs. Chgo. chpt. 1980-84), Am. Coll. CLUs and Chartered Fin. Cons. (bd. dirs. 1986-87), Yale Club Chgo. (bd. dirs. alumni assn. del. 1972—), Yale Club Fort Wayne (pres. 1964-69), Yale Club N.Y.C., Trinity Club (mem. exec. com. Chgo. chpt. 1987—), Phi Beta Kappa, Pi Gamma Mu. Republican. Congregationalist. Avocations: skiing, international travel. Home: 942 Twisted Oak Ln Buffalo Grove IL 60090 Office: Mongerson & Co Securities Corp 135 S LaSalle St Chicago IL 60603

BACKENSTOSS, HENRY BRIGHTBILL, electrical engineer, consultant; b. Washington, Sept. 28, 1912; s. Ross Elwood and Susan Catherine (Brightbill) B.; m. Violet Pentleton, Jan. 23, 1942 (div. 1952); m. Bernadette Humbert, Sept. 24, 1954; 1 child, Martine Susan. BS, MEE, MIT, 1935. Registered profl. engr., Pa., Mass., Conn. Project mgr. Jackson & Moreland, Engrs., Boston, 1945-59; prof. power tech. Am. U. Beirut (Lebanon), 1959-61; spl. cons. Gen. Pub. Utilities Corp., N.Y.C., 1961-62; v.p. Jackson & Moreland Internat., Beirut, 1962-68; sr. cons. Gen. Pub. Utilities Svc. Corp., Reading, Pa., 1970-77; cons. Devel. Analysis Assocs., Cambridge, Mass., 1977-82; Govt. Saudi Arabia, 1962-69; panelist fuel crisis and power industry IEEE Tech. Conf., 1973. Contbr. articles to profl. publs. Bd. dirs. Reading Symphony Orch. (Pa.), 1975-86, Berks County Conservancy (Pa.), 1984—, Reading Mus. Found., 1986—, pres., 1988—. Mem. IEEE (life sr., power system engrng. com. 1952-87, Am Soc. Utility Investors, system econs. subcom. 1952-76), Nat. Soc. Profl. Engrs., Pa. Soc. Profl. Engrs., Sigma Xi (assoc.), Tau Beta Pi. Congregationalist. Home: 408 S Tulpehocken Rd Reading PA 19601

BACKER, WILLIAM MONTAGUE, advertising agency executive; b. N.Y.C., June 9, 1926; s. Bill and Ferdinanda (Legare) B.; m. Ann Allderdice Mudge, June 11, 1983. B.A., Yale U., 1950. Creative dir., vice chmn. McCann-Erickson, N.Y.C., 1954-79; pres. Backer & Spielvogel Inc., N.Y.C., 1979-87; vice chmn., exec. creative dir. Backer Spielvogel Bates Worldwide, N.Y.C., 1987—. Composer: (with others) Teach the World to Sing, 1975. Served with USNR, 1944-46. Mem. ASCAP. Episcopalian. Clubs: Orange County Hunt (Va.); Princeton. Office: Backer Spielvogel Bates Worldwide Inc 1515 Broadway New York NY 10036

BACON, GEORGE HUGHES, educational testing service analyst; b. Phila., Mar. 4, 1935; s. George Hughes and Alice Olive (Campbell) B.; div.; children: Christopher Scott, Melissa Ann Bacon White. BA in English Lit. and Music, Temple U., 1957; MS in Ednl. Adminstrn., U. Pa., 1968. Cert. tchr., Pa. Computer programmer 1st Pa. Bank, Phila., 1960-62, Phila. Nat. Bank, 1975-77; tchr. Davis Elem. Sch., Southampton, Pa., 1962-72; assoc. dir. Kranzley and Co., Cherry Hill, N.J., 1973-75; cons. facilities mgmt. Sci. and Computer Tech. Inc., Malvern, Pa., 1978-79; analyst lead systems Ednl. Testing Svc., Princeton, N.J., 1979-86, corp. analyst, 1987—; cons., lectr. computer software Abington (Pa.) Free Library, 1983-84, Jenkintown (Pa.) Music Sch., 1984, Fudan U., Shanghai, People's Republic China, 1985; invitational lectr., sr. tech. advisor UN Devel. Program Jao Tong U., Shanghai, 1988. Vol. aide Mercer County Geriatric Unit, Lawrenceville, N.J., 1986; music therapist Vital Age Community Ctr. for Elderly, Rockledge, Pa., 1986, Rydal (Pa.) Park Retirement Home, 1988; tutor Abington Free Library Literacy Project, 1988; mem. headmaster's coun. Am. Boy Choir, Princeton, 1987. With U.S. Army, 1958-60. Mem. Assn. Computing Machinery, Am. Assn. Adv. Sci., Assn. Systems Mgmt., Am. Ednl. Resch. Assn., Am. Evaluation Assn., Downtown Club, Temple U. Club, Faculty Club U. Pa., Manorlu Swim Club (Dresher, Pa.). Presbyterian. Home: 128 Blake Ave Philadelphia PA 19111

BACON, LEONARD ANTHONY, accounting educator; b. Santa Fe, June 10, 1931; s. Manuel R. and Maria (Chavez) Baca; m. Patricia Balzaretti; children—Bernadine M., Jerry A., Tiffany A. B.E., U. Nebr.-Omaha, 1965; M.B.A., U. of the Americas, Mexico City, 1969; Ph.D., U. Miss., 1971. CPA; cert. mgmt. acct., internal auditor. Commd. 2d lt. U.S. Army, 1951, advanced through grades to maj., 1964, served fin. and acctg. officer mainly Korea, Vietnam; ret., 1966; asst. prof. Delta State U., Cleveland, Miss., 1971-76; assoc. prof. West Tex. State U., Canyon, 1976-79; prof. acctg. Calif. State U., Bakersfield, 1979—; cons. Kershen Co. (now Atlantic Richfield Oil Co.), Canyon, 1979-80. Contbr. articles to profl. jours. U.S., Mex., Can., papers to profl. confs. Leader Delta area Boy Scouts Am., Cleveland, 1971-76; dir. United Campus Ministry, Canyon, 1976-79; minister Kern Youth Facility, Bakersfield, 1983—. Paratrooper Brazilian Army, 1955. Mem. Am. Acctg. Assn., Am. Inst. CPA's, Am. Assn. Spanish Speaking CPA's, Nat. Assn. Accts. (pres. Bakersfield chpt. 1981-82, Most Valuable Mem. award 1981), Am. Mgmt. Assn., Inst. Mgmt. Acctg., Calif. Faculty Assn., Acad. Internat. Bus., Inst. Internal Auditors, Inst. Cost Analysts, Alpha Kappa Psi (Dedicated Service award 1979). Clubs: Jockey (Rio de Janeiro). Lodges: Lions (v.p. Cleveland 1971-73), Kiwanis (v.p. 1974-79, A Whale of a Guy award, Cleveland 1975). Office: Calif State U 9001 Stockdale Hwy Bakersfield CA 93309

BACON, VICKY LEE, lighting services executive; b. Oregon City, Oreg., Mar. 25, 1950; d. Herbert Kenneth and Lorean Betty (Boltz) Rushford; student Portland Community Coll., 1974-75, Mt. Hood Community Coll., 1976, Portland State Coll., 1979; m. Dennis M. Bacon, Aug. 7, 1971; 1 dau., Randene Tess. With All Electric Constrn., Milwaukie, Oreg., 1968-70; with Lighting Maintenance Co., Portland, Oreg., 1970-78; service mgr. GTE Sylvania Lighting Services, Portland, 1978-80, br. mgr., 1980-83; div. mgr. Christenson Electric Co. Inc., Portland, 1983—. Mem. Nat. Secs. Assn., Illuminating Engring. Soc., Nat. Assn. Lighting Maintenance Contractors. Office: Christenson Electric Co Inc 111 SW Columbia Suite 480 Portland OR 97201

BACONRIND, PATRICIA LEE, educator; b. Sidney, Nebr., June 17, 1945; d. Wilber Lee and Leona H. (Juedes) Rhoades; m. Thomas S. Baconrind, July 28, 1979. BE, Midland Coll., 1967; MS, Kearney State Coll., 1970. Tchr. Nebraska City (Nebr.) High Sch., 1967-69; asst. prof. Wayne (Nebr.) State Coll., 1970-76; assoc. prof. Ft. Hays (Kans.) State U., 1976—; cons. Mktg. Small Bus. Devel. Ctr., Hays, 1986—, Iowa Beef Packers, South Sioux, 1974; coordinator Ft. Hays State U., 1987; pres. Hays Bd. Realtors, 1988—; instr. Small Bus. Devel. Ctr. Mem. Hays Library Com., 1984—, Nat. Humane Soc., Washington, 1986—; advisor Ft. Hays Mktg. Club, 1987, Mortar Bd., SCORE. Mem. Profl. Woman's Appraisal Assn., Am. Mktg. Assn., S.W. Mktg. Assn., Am. Real Estate Assn., Am. Inst. Real Estate Appraisers, Am. Real Estate Appraisers (bus. and industry Day Com.), Nat. Assn. Realtors, Kansas Assn. Realtors, Hays C. of C., Phi Kappa Phi, Tiger Club (Hays.). Office: Ft Hays State U 600 Park St Hays KS 67601

BACOT, JOHN CARTER, banker; b. Utica, N.Y., Feb. 7, 1933; s. John Vacher and Edna (Gunn) B.; m. Shirley Schou, Nov. 26, 1960; children: Elizabeth, Susan. A.B., Hamilton Coll., Clinton, N.Y., 1955; LL.B., Cornell U., 1958. Bar: N.Y. 1959. With firm Utica, 1959-60; with Bank of N.Y., N.Y.C., 1960—, pres., 1974-84, chief exec. officer, chmn., 1982—; also dir. Bank of N.Y.; bd. dirs. Home Life Ins. Co., Atlantic Reinsurance Co., Centennial Ins. Co., Bank of N.Y. Internat. Corp., Bank of N.Y. Co., Inc.; trustee Atlantic Mut. Ins. Co., Hamilton Coll. Mem. Econ. Club N.Y., Pilgrims of U.S., Assn. Res. City Bankers, N.Y. State Bar Assn., Council on Fgn. Relations. Episcopalian. Clubs: Montclair Golf, Links, Union. Home: 48 Porter Pl Montclair NJ 07042 Office: Bank NY Co Inc 48 Wall St New York NY 10286

BADALAMENTI, ANTHONY, accountant; b. St. Louis, Apr. 1, 1940; s. Sebastino and Grace (Orlando) B.; 1 child, Annette Marie. BS in Acctg., Washington U., 1970. CPA, Mo. Staff acct. Fischer & Fischer, CPA's, St. Louis, 1959-63; acct. McDonnell Aircraft Corp., St. Louis, 1963-65; asst. chief acct. Dempsey Tegler, Inc., St. Louis, 1965-66; contr. Cummins Mo. Diesel, Inc., St. Louis, 1966-67; sr. acct. Elmer Fox & Co., CPA's, St. Louis, 1967-71; pvt. practice acctg. St. Louis, 1972—; tchr. Meramec Community Coll., St. Louis, 1973-75. Mem. Am. Inst. CPA's, Mo. Soc. CPA's, Nat. Conf. CPA Practitioners, Crestwood-Sunset Hills C. of C. (pres. 1980-81, Bus. Profl. of Month award 1986), Rotary (pres. Crestwood-Sunset Hills Chpt. 1982-83). Republican. Roman Catholic. Home: 51 Heather Dr Saint Louis MO 63123 Office: 10805 Sunset Office Dr Saint Louis MO 63127-1095

BADDLEY, JAMES RICHARD, association administrator, educator; b. Water Valley, Miss., June 15, 1938; s. Richard Henry and Virginia Lee

(Vaughan) B.; m. Melvanna Lee Handley, Mar. 13, 1963; children: Melanie Ann, Scot Lee, Virginia Marie. BA, U. Miss., 1960, MS, 1963. Mem. faculty Biloxi (Miss.) Sch. Dist., 1961-62, Jackson (Miss.) Sch. Dist., 1962-65, Hinds Community Coll., Raymond, Miss., 1965-74; asst. dean U. Med. Ctr., Jackson, 1974-75; sr. v.p. Miss. Hosp. Assn., Jackson, 1975—. Mem. Am. Soc. Assn. Execs. Republican. Methodist. Office: Miss Hosp Assn PO Box 16444 Jackson MS 39056

BADER, GARY PAUL, human resource administrator; b. Ketchikan, Alaska, Dec. 9, 1940; s. Paul Peter and Irene Bessie (Jones) B.; m. Sheila Synnestvedt; 1 child, Benjamin; m. Dale Terry; children: Stephen, Moira, Cynda, Benjamin, Christopher. Mgr. human resources Alyeska Pipeline Service Co., Anchorage, 1979—. Pres. Anchorage Native Caucus, 1983; mem. Mcpl. Employees Relations Bd., Anchorage, 1982-87. Republican. Episcopalian. Home: 10701 Glazandf Dr Anchorage AK 99516 Office: Alyeska Pipeline Svc Co 1835 S Bragaw Anchorage AK 99512

BADER, STEPHEN LEIGH, communications executive; b. Louisville, May 28, 1942; s. Ralph Edward and Phyllis Del (Lucas) B.; m. Julie Ann Groot, Dec. 1960 (div. 1980); children: Barbara Ann, Natalie Lucas. Student, U. Louisville. Salesman Eve Printing Co., Louisville, 1964-66; v.p. R.L. White Co., Louisville, 1966-80; owner Lucas Investments, Louisville, 1975-83; territorial mgr. TMC of San Diego, 1983-85, pres., 1985—; bd. dirs. Clark-Bader, Inc., Louisville; vis. lectr. U. Calif., San Diego, 1985; chief exec. officer, pres. TMC Long Distance, Escondido Telephone. Mem. San Diego Employers Assn., Calif. Assn. Long Distance Tel. Cos., Alternative Carrier Telecommunication Assn., San Diego C. of C. Office: TMC San Diego 525 B St Ste 435 San Diego CA 92101

BADGER, ROBERT JOHN, JR., financial services company executive; b. Montezuma, Iowa, Oct. 10, 1940; s. Robert J.H. and Mildred J. (Trimble) B.; m. Cindia A. Clark, Apr. 19, 1975; children: Alec Guy, Jason Robert. BS in Social Scis., Iowa Wesleyan U., 1962; MS in History and Polit. Sci., Drake U., 1966. CLU; chartered fin. cons. Tchr. Pella (Iowa) Community Schs., 1962-64, Lincoln High Sch., Des Moines, 1964-69; salesman Prudential Ins. Co. Am., Des Moines, 1969; pres. John Badger & Assocs., Des Moines, 1972-80, Chartered Fin. Svcs., Ltd., Des Moines, 1982—, IA-SSURANCE Benefit Plans, Inc., Des Moines, 1980-87, Fin. Product Sales, Des Moines, 1987—. Contbr. articles to profl. jours. Trustee, mem. adminstrv. bd. Immanuel United Meth. Ch., Des Moines; cubmaster pack 81 Boy Scouts Am., 1980-84; scoutmaster troop 58, 1984-87; chmn. bd. dirs., chmn. exec. com., chmn. mental retardation/devel. disabled com. Polk County Health Svcs.; mem. ad hoc com. Broadlawns Hosp., Des Moines; mem. Polk County Long Range Health Care Planning Com.; bd. dirs. Iowa affiliate Am. Health Assn. Recipient Donald S. MacNaughton award Prudential Ins. Co. Am., 1980, God and Svc. award Boy Scouts Am. and Meth. Ch., 1987. Mem. Des Moines Assn. Life Underwriters (past pres.), Iowa Assn. Life Underwriters (past chmn. membership com.), CLU's Assn. (past program chmn.), Sales and Mktg. Execs. Cen. Iowa (past bd. dirs.), Des Moines Estate Planning Council, Sertoma (chmn. bd. dirs. 1986-88, Svc. to Mankind award). Republican. Office: Chartered Fin Svcs Ltd 936 8th St W Des Moines IA 50265

BADMAN, JOHN, III, architect, construction company executive; b. Kansas City, Mo., July 11, 1944; s. John II and Barbara (Smith) B.; m. Katherine Ballantine, May 12, 1984; children: Lindsay Cathryn, Barbara Smith, John IV. BA, Yale U., 1966, MArch, 1969, postgrad., 1969-70, M in Environmental Design, 1971. Registered architect, Conn. Gen. mgr. S.J. Willy, New Haven, Conn., 1971-73; v.p. Schumacher & Forelle, Great Neck, N.Y., 1973-77, exec. v.p., 1986-87; dir. planning and devel. Dravo Engrs., N.Y.C., 1977-81; sr. v.p. Parsons Brinckerhoff, N.Y.C., 1981-86, also bd. dirs.; prin. Ballantine and Badman Assocs., Architects and Land Planners, Greenwich, Conn., 1987—. Mem. Soc. Colonial Wars (steward 1986—, council 1987—, nominating com. 1988—, marshall 1988—), Nat. Council Archtl. Registration Bds. (cert.). Republican. Episcopalian. Clubs: Union League; Yale (N.Y.C.); Greenwich (Conn.) Country. Home: 77 John St Greenwich CT 06830 Office: Ballantine & Badman Assocs 108 Husted Ln Greenwich CT 06830

BADNER, BARRY, industrial engineer; b. Bklyn., Dec. 15, 1937; s. Hyman and Ray (Wachtelkoenig) B.; B. Indsl. Engring., N.Y. U., 1959, M.S. in Ops. Research, 1964; m. Heather Laurie, July 16, 1967; children—Ray Ann, Bruce Mitchell, David Alan. Engr., Burndy Corp., Norwalk, Conn., 1960-63, Estes Industries, Inc., N.Y.C., 1964-65, Drake, Sheahan/Stewart Dougall, N.Y.C., 1966-68; pres. Zelner and Badner, Inc., N.Y.C., 1969—; v.p., dir. Medinvent, Inc. Contbg. author: Hospital Special Care Facilities, 1981; co-inventor component mounting. Trustee Frisch Sch., Paramus, N.J.; v.p. United Jewish Community of Bergen County; trustee Jewish Braille Inst.; Congregation Ahavath Torah, Englewood. With U.S. Army, 1959-60. Mem.Inst. Mgmt. Consultants, Hosp. Mgmt. Systems Soc., Assn. Advancement Med. Instrumentation. Home: 261 Robin Rd Englewood NJ 07631 Office: 163 Engle St Englewood NJ 07631

BAEHREL, PETER WILLIAM, manufacturing company executive; b. Jamaica, N.Y., July 15, 1940; s. William Julius and Frances Elizabeth (Gingell) B.; student U. Fla., 1958-60; m. Judith Geuder, June 20, 1970; children—Michael Christian, Suzanne Michelle. Office mgr. Mehron Inc., N.Y.C., 1960-64; supr. facilities AMF Inc., White Plains, N.Y., 1965-73, mgr. facilities and equipment, purchasing agt., 1974-77, mgr. adminstrv. services and purchasing agt., 1978-81; dir. adminstrv. Services Carter-Wallace, Inc., N.Y.C., 1981—. Served with Army N.G., 1961-68. Mem. Soc. Food Service Mgmt., Purchasing Assn. Seven Counties, Nat. Fire Protection Assn., Employee Relocation Council, Adminstrv. Mgmt. Soc. Club: Rotary. Home: 21 Lark Ln Croton-on-Hudson NY 10520 Office: Carter Wallace Inc 767 Fifth Ave New York NY 10153

BAER, ALBERT MAX, metal products executive; b. N.Y.C., Feb. 6, 1905; s. Max and Bertha S. (Bodenheim) B.; m. Karla Bartels, May 2, 1976; 1 child, Margery Louise Baer Irish. Student CCNY, 1921-23, NYU, 1924-28, Columbia U., 1930-33; LL.D. (hon.), Hofstra U., 1967; D.C.S. (hon.), St. John's U., Jamaica, N.Y., 1971. Chmn. bd., chief exec. officer Imperial Schrade Corp. (formerly Imperial Knife Assoc. Cos. Inc.), N.Y.C., 1947—; chmn. bd. Cutlers Guild Ltd., Can.; bd. dirs. Durol S.A., Thiers, France, J.A. Henckels Imperial GmbH, Stag Cutlery Ltd., Listowel, Ireland, Sears, Roebuck & Co.; officer, dir. Acell Holdings Ltd., London, Acell Corp. of Am. Mem. adv. bd. Office Quartermaster Gen., U.S. Army, 1941-45; mem. council Sch. Gen. Studies, Columbia U., N.Y.C.; 1952—, chmn. council, 1952-63; mem. Rockefeller U. Council, N.Y.C.; mem. adv. council St. John's U.; dir. Christopher Columbus Quincentenary Found., Inc. Decorated Order of Merit (Poland); recipient Owl award Columbia U., 1963, Pirogov medal Acad. Med. Scis. USSR, 1965, Meml. medal J.E. Purkyne, Czechoslovak Soc. Cardiology, 1966, Illustrious Alumni award DeWitt Clinton High Sch., 1967, Internat. Gold Heart award Internat. Cardiology Found., 1968, Gold Heart award Am. Heart Assn., 1974, award of Merit, 1971, bronze medallion of City N.Y., 1968, Miguel Servet medal Spanish Heart Found., 1972; named Businessman of Yr., St. John's U., 1965; Hon. Water Commr., Ellenville, N.Y., 1987. Mem. Am. Fedn. Aging Research (dir.), All India Heart Found. (life), Nat. Hardware Alliance (Eng. hon. past pres.), Columbia Alumni Assn., Columbia Assocs. (life), NYU Albert Gallatin Assocs.; hon. mem. Spanish Heart Found. (assoc.), Federación Cardiológica (Argentina), Greek Cardiology Soc., Peruvian Caridology Found., Spanish Cardiology Soc., Instituto de Cardiologia Social (Lisboa, Portugal), Hofstra Mus. Fine Arts, South African Heart Assn., Singapore Nat. Heart Assn. Clubs: Am. (London); Am. Assembly of Columbia U., Ky. Cols., Century Country, Harmonie, Columbia U. Men's Faculty, Nippon. Clubs: Standard (Chgo.), Phyllis Court (Eng.). Lodges: Masons, St. George's Soc. Office: Imperial Schrade Corp 1776 Broadway New York NY 10019

BAER, RICHARD MYRON, college administrator; b. Chgo., May 26, 1928; s. Ernest Conroy and Elma Harriet (Billquist) B.; m. Carol Louise Moyer, Aug. 31, 1956; children: Dana. David, Caron, John. BS in Edn., No. Ill. State Teaching Coll., 1954; MS in Bus. Adminstrn., No. Ill. U., 1962, Cert. of Advanced Standing in Bus. Mgmt., 1967. Dist. field engr. Barber-Coleman Co., Rockford, Ill., 1957-62; coord., cen. stores No. Ill. U., DeKalb, 1962-67; dean, bus. svcs. Rock Valley Coll., Rockford, 1967-73; bus. mgr. Rockford Coll., 1973-81; v.p. fin., adminstrv. svcs. Met. Com. Coll., Omaha, 1981—. Sgt. U.S. Army, 1952-53, Korea. Mem. Nat. Assn. Coll. and Univ. Bus. Officers, Assn. Sch. Bus. Ofcls., Nebr. Community Coll. Bus. Officers (chmn. 1983-84), Sigma Iota Epsilon. Lodge: Rotary. Office: Met Community Coll PO Box 3777 Omaha NE 68118

BAER, ROBERT J., trucking company executive; b. Oct. 25, 1937, St. Louis; s. Charles M. and Angeline Baer; m. Jo Baer, Aug. 27, 1960; children: Bob Jr., Angie, Tim, Cathy, Kristen. BA, So. Ill. U., 1962, MS, 1964. Regional supr. div. recreation City of St. Louis, 1957-64; dep. dir. Human Devel. Corp., St. Louis, 1964-70; exec. asst. to co. exec. St. Louis County Govt, 1970-74; exec. dir. Bi-State Devel. Agy., St. Louis, 1974-77; v.p., gen. mgr. United Van Lines Inc. and subs., Fenton, Mo., 1977-80, exec. v.p., 1980-82, pres., chief operating officer, 1982—; pres. United Van Lines Inc. and UniGroup Inc., Fenton; bd. dirs. VanLiner Ins. Co., Fenton, adj. lectr. in bus. mgmt. Webster U., St. Louis, 1983—, Maryville Coll., St. Louis, 1984—. Pres. St. Louis Bd. Police Commn., 1984-89; bd. dirs. Thomas Dunn Meml. Adult Edn. Program (bd. dirs. program coordinator), St. Louis, 1957—. Mem. Am. Movers Conf. (bd. dirs., past chmn.), Household Goods Carriers' Bur. (chmn., bd. dirs. 1987—). Avocations: gardening, tennis, swimming, reading. Office: United Van Lines Inc 1 United Dr Fenton MO 63026

BAER, WILLIAM HAROLD, business executive; b. Eatontown, N.J., Dec. 6, 1947; s. Irving and Martha Ann (Ruddy) B.; BS in Bus. Adminstrn., Waynesburg Coll., 1971. Pres., Baldinos, Inc., Fayetteville, N.C., 1976—, Rondout Country Club, Ltd., Accord, N.Y., 1979-81, W.H.B. Cons., Accord, 1979-85, Baldinos Giant Jersey Subs, Inc., Hinesville, Ga., 1982-87, chmn., chief exec. officer, 1987; with Baldinos Mgmt. Group, Ltd., Augusta, Ga., 1987—; pres. Leisure Life Inc., Tinton Falls, N.J., 1980-87, Baldinos of Savannah, 1989— Pro Active Enterprises, Inc., Savannah, Ga., 1986-89, bd. dirs., 1989. Chmn. campaign March of Dimes, Liberty County, 1986-87; dir. Coastal Ga. March of Dimes, Savannah, 1986—. Served to 1st lt. USMC, 1971-75. Recipient Navy Achievement medal. Club: Coastal Racquet (Hinesville, Ga.) (pres. 1986-87, treas.-sec. 1987—). Office: PO Box 336 Accord NY 12404 also: 707 Marlboro Ct Hinesville GA 31313

BAERWALD, JOHN EDWARD, traffic engineer, educator; b. Milw., Nov. 2, 1925; s. Albert J. and Margaret M. (Brandt) B.; m. Elaine S. Eichstaedt, Apr. 3, 1948 (dec.); children: Thomas J., James K., Barbara Baerwald Bowman; m. Donna D. Granger, May 24, 1975. BS in Civil Engring., Purdue U., 1949, MS in Civil Engring., 1950, PhD in Civil Engring., 1956. Registered profl. engr., Calif., Ill., Ind. Research asst. Purdue U., 1949-50, research assoc., instr. hwy. engring., 1950-52, research engr., instr. hwy. engring., 1952-55; asst. prof. traffic engring. U. Ill., Urbana, Champaign, 1955-57; assoc. prof. traffic engring. U. Ill., Urbana, 1957-60, prof. traffic engring., 1960-69, prof. transp. and traffic engring., 1969-83, univ. traffic engr., 1957-63, dir. Hwy. Traffic Safety Ctr., 1961-83, prof. emeritus, 1983—; staff assoc. Police Tng. Inst., 1969—; cons. traffic engr., 1952—; pres. John E. Baerwald P.C., Santa Fe, 1983—; chmn. Champaign Parking and Traffic Commn., Ill., 1960-69; liaison mem. staff subcom. Ill. Gov.'s Ofcl. Traffic Safety Coordination Com., 1962-69, mem. subcom. hwy. safety program deficiencies, 1970-72; mem. Champaign-Urbana Urbanized Area Transp. Study, 1963-83, tech. adviser to policy com., 1963-75, chmn. policy com., 1977-83; mem. Ill. Sec. State Adv. Com. Vehicle Registration and Titling Matters, 1973-74; trustee Champaign-Urbana Mass Transit Dist., 1973-83, chmn., 1975-83; mem. tech. adv. com. Ill. Transp. Study Commn., 1977-81. Served with AUS, 1943-46. Recipient Pub. Service award Ill. Sec. State, 1976, past. pres. award Ill. Sec. Inst. of Transp. Engrs., 1983. Fellow ASCE, Inst. Transp. Engrs. (internat. pres. 1970, dir. 1964-65, 67-71, internat. council 1977-83, dir. Ill. sect. 1963-64, other offices and coms., exec. com. expert witness council 1986—, vice-chmn. 1988, chmn. 1989—, Past Pres.' award 1953, Theodore M. Matson Meml. award 1988); mem. Nat. Safety Council (dir. 1975-80, other offices and coms.), Am. Rd. and Transp. Builders Assn. (safety and environ. com. 1975-78, mem. transp. safety adv. council 1976-83, 89—, pres. edn. div. 1979, dir. 1979-83, mem. exec. com. 1979-80), Transp. Research Bd. (div. B council 1974-83, other offices and coms.), Pan Am. Hwy. Congress (best tech. paper award 1963, 67), Lions, Masons, Sigma Xi, Chi Epsilon. Lutheran. Home: RR 2 PO Box 927 Santa Fe NM 87505

BAETZ, W. TIMOTHY, lawyer; b. Cin., Aug. 5, 1944; s. William G. and Virginia (Fauntleroy) Baetz. BA, Harvard U., 1966; JD, U. Mich., 1969. Assoc. McDermott, Will & Emery, Chgo., 1969-74, income ptnr., 1975-78, capital ptnr., 1979—; mem. mgmt. com. McDermott, Will & Emery. Served with U.S. Army, 1969-75. Fellow Am. Coll. Probate Counsel; mem. ABA, Ill. State Bar Assn., Chgo. Bar Assn., Chgo. Counsel of Lawyers. Republican. Episcopalian. Club: Union League (Chgo.). Home: 500 Wisconsin Ave Chicago IL 60614 Office: McDermott Will & Emery 111 W Monroe St Chicago IL 60603

BAGDON, CHARLES ANTHONY, marketing executive; b. Waukegan, Ill., Aug. 5, 1946; s. Charles Anthony and Louise Bernice (Zelesnik) B.; m. Carolyn Mary Mack, June 9, 1973; children: Gregory, Brian, Mark. BBA, Northwestern U., 1968, MBA, 1969. Svc. rep. Ill. Bell, Waukegan and Skokie, 1971; bus. office supr. Ill. Bell, Libertyville, 1972-73; data engr. Ill. Bell, Chgo., 1974-75, account rep., 1976-77, acct. exec., 1978-80, account exec. industry cons., 1981-83; account exec., ind. cons. AT&T Communications, Rolling Meadows, Ill., 1984; primary account sales mgr. AT&T Communications, Rolling Meadows, 1985-86; sr. staff mktg. mgr. AT&T, Itasaca, Ill., 1987—; dir. Waukegan Savs. & Loan, 1973—. Author/editor: (pamphlets) Banking Opportunity Review, 1987, Insurance Opportunity Review, 1987, Health Care Opportunity Review, 1987. Pres. Lake Bluff (Ill.) Pk. Bd. Caucus, 1983-84; asst. cubmaster Boy Scouts Am., Lake Bluff, 1987-88; mem. parish pastoral coun. St. Mary's Ch., Lake Forest, Ill.; sec./treas. Lake Bluff Village Bd. Caucus, 1981-82. Served with U.S. Army, 1969-71. Recipient Evans Scholars Found. Alumni Assn Award, 1969. Mem. Telemktg. Assn., U.S. League Savs. and Loan Dirs. Roman Catholic. Home: 323 W Hawthorne Ct Lake Bluff IL 60044 Office: AT&T One Pierce Pl Fl 15 Itasca IL 60143

BAGLEY, COLLEEN, marketing executive; b. Mountain Home, Ark., Feb. 18, 1954; d. Roy Louis and Dorothy (Fry) B.; m. William A. Haskin, June 28, 1986. BA cum laude, U. South Fla., 1975. Lic. radio broadcaster, FCC 3d class. TV and radio producer Sta. WUSF-TV-FM, Tampa, Fla., 1974-76; TV announcer Sta. WFLA-TV, Tampa, 1974-76, news reporter, 1976-77, news producer, 1977-79; sr. producer Sta. KSTP-TV, Mpls., 1979-80; exec. producer Sta. WPVI-TV, Phila., 1980-82; dir. mktg. Grand Traverse Resort, Traverse City, Mich., 1982—; cons., bd. dirs. Enough Seminars, Phila., 1981-82. Contbg. author Strategic Hotel/Motel Marketing (Am. Hotel and Motel Assn. award), 1985. Mem. Traverse City Ski Council, 1983—, local host com. Nat. Govs.' Assn., 1986-87; chmn. N.Am. Vasa Cross Country Ski Race Mktg. Com., 1987-88. Mem. Traverse City Ad Club (awards for advt. excellence 1984-89), Traverse City C. of C. (air service transp. com. 1984-87), Grand Traverse Conv. and Visitors Bur. (mktg. com. 1984—), N.Am. Vasa Cross Country Ski Race Mktg. (chmn. 1987-88), No. Mich. Golf Council (exec. bd. 1986, 88, 89). Republican. Avocations: private pilot, aerobics, weightlifting, yoga, scuba diving. Home: 3471 Blackwood St Traverse City MI 49684 Office: Grand Traverse Resort 6300 US 31 N Grand Traverse Village MI 49610-0404

BAGNALL, GRAHAM EDWARD, financial executive; b. Birmingham, Eng., Jan. 20, 1948; came to Can., 1970; s. Herbert Edward and Marie Lily (Hall) B.; m. Christine Ryan Walker, Oct. 14, 1972; 1 child, Sarah. BA in Econs. with honors, U. Manchester, Eng., 1970; MBA, York U., Toronto, 1975. Chartered acct. V.p., treas. BCE Inc., Montreal, 1986—. Mem. Inst. Chartered Accts. Ont., Fin. Execs. Inst., University Club Montreal, MAAA Club. Home: 57 Thornhill Ave, Westmount, PQ Canada H3Y 2E3 Office: BCE, 2000 McGill College Ave, Montreal, PQ Canada H3A 3H7

BAHADUR, CHANCE, diversified food company executive; b. Agra, India, Nov. 22, 1942; came to U.S., 1959; s. Krishna and Rajeshwari (Mathur) B.; m. Donna Narolweski, Jan. 6, 1963; children—Mark, Miles. Sc.B., Agra U., India, 1959; S.B., Kans. State U., 1962; M.B.A., U. Chgo., 1969. C.P.A., Ill. Mktg. coordinator Ill. Inst. Tech. Research, Chgo., 1967-69; mgr. region Virtual Computer Services, Chgo., 1969-70; asst. to pres. Monsanto Environ. Chem. Systems, Chgo., 1970-73; corp. banking officer First Nat. Bank Chgo., 1973-76; dir. treasury ops. Esmark Inc., Chgo., 1976-77, asst. treas., 1977-82, treas., 1982-84; v.p., treas. Beatrice Cos., Inc., Chgo., 1984—, E-II Holdings, Inc., 1987-88; sr. v.p. fin., treas. Marriott Corp., Washington, 1988—. contbr. articles to profl. jours. Adv. Ill. Econ. Edn. Council, 1983. Mem. AICPA, Am. Inst. Chem. Engrs. (chmn. 1972-73), Ill. CPA Soc., Chgo. Council Fgn. Relations, Econ. Club Chgo. Clubs: Stonehenge Golf (Barrington), Biltmore; Monarch (Stuart, Fla.); Chicago; Meadow (Rolling Meadows); Wynstone (Barrington, Ill.). Office: Marriott Corp 10400 Fernwood Rd Washington DC 20058

BAHLINGER, RICHARD JOHN, beverage distributing company executive; b. Baton Rouge, La., Jan. 4, 1952; s. Peter Fabacher and Mary Claire (Bonnet) B.; m. André Marie Meyer, Dec. 28, 1973; 2 children: Mark Benjamin, Erin Elizabeth. BS in Indsl. Engring., La. State U., Baton Rouge, 1975; postgrad., Niagara U., 1982. Staff inds. engr. Chem. Group Olin Corp., Lake Charles, La., 1975-76; sr. inds. engr. Chem. Group Olin Corp., Cleveland, Tenn., 1976-79; maintenance supt. Chem. Group Olin Corp., Niagara Falls, N.Y., 1979-82; regional ops. mgr. Wholesale Ops. Div. Anheuser-Busch, St. Louis, 1982-85; pres., gen. mgr. Golden Eagle Distbg. Co., Tulsa, 1985—. Mem. exec. com. MDA; vol. Handi-Ham. Mem. Okla. Malt Beverage Assn. (bd. dirs. 1987—), Tulsa C. of C., Tulsa U. Hurricane Club, Tau Beta Pi. Republican. Roman Catholic. Office: Golden Eagle Distbg Co 2929 N Florence Tulsa OK 74110

BAHLS, GENE CHARLES, agricultural products company executive; b. Danville, Ill., June 9, 1929; s. Martin Joseph and Renetta Fredrica (Rook) B.; m. Marilyn Bernice Lane, June 9, 1951; children: Steven Charles (dec.), Sara Lynn Bahls Durre, David Lane. BMechE, Purdue U., 1951; postgrad., Miami (Ohio) U., 1958-59, Western Mich. U., 1965-66. Indsl. engr. Gardner Board & Carton Co., Middletown, Ohio, 1951-60; mgr. insdl. engring. Brown Paper Co., Kalamazoo, 1960-70; dir. engring. Armour Pharm. Co., Kankakee, Ill., 1970-76; dir. engring. Corn Processing div. Am. Maize Products Co., Hammond, Ind., 1976-80, v.p. ops., 1980-86, sr. v.p. mfg., 1986—; v.p. ops. sub. Am. Fructose Corp., Hammond, 1980—. Bd. dirs. Kankakee Symphony Assn., 1986—. Served with U.S. Army, 1954-56. Mem. Corn Refiners Assn. (bd. dirs.), Whiting, Ind. C. of C. Republican. Lutheran. Home: 2 Bristol Green Bourbonnais IL 60914 Office: Am Maize Products Co 1100 Indianapolis Blvd Hammond IN 46320

BAHR, MARK A., construction company executive; b. 1952; married. BSBA, Kans. State U., 1974. With Barton-Malow Co., Southfield, Mich., 1974—, asst. adminstr. acctg., 1974-77, asst. sec., 1977, treas., 1977-80, v.p., treas., 1980-81, exec. v.p., 1981—, also bd. dirs. Office: Barton-Malow Co PO Box 5200 Detroit MI 48235 Address: 27777 Franklin Rd Ste 800 Southfield MI 48034

BAIER, MARTIN, marketing consultant; b. Kansas City, Mo., Dec. 7, 1922; s. Harry and Yetta (Stein) B.; m. Dorothy Fay Rathbun, Mar. 7, 1948; 1 child, Donna Baier Stein. BBA, BS in Econs., U. Mo., Kansas City, 1943; MA in Econs., U. Mo., 1970. Circulation mgr. Box Office mag., Kansas City, Mo., 1937-42; advt. mgr. Tension Envelope Corp., Kansas City, 1946-54; gen. mgr. M.P. Brown, Inc., Burlington, Iowa, 1954-60; exec. v.p. Old Am. Ins. Co., Kansas City, 1960-87; mktg. cons., Kansas City, 1987—; adj. prof. mktg. U. Mo., Kansas City, 1969—; lectr. in field; bd. dirs. Path Mgmt. Industries, Inc., Leawood, Kans. Author: Elements of Direct Marketing; contbr. articles to profl. jours. Trustee Shepherd's Ctrs. Am., Kansas City, 1978—, adv. bd. for Direct Mktg. Ctrs., Kansas City and Washington, 1982—; bd. dirs. Mo. Repertory Theatre, Kansas City, 1968—. Recipient Faculty Service award Nat. Univ. Continuing Edn. Assn., 1984; named Mktg. Man of Yr., Sales and Mktg. Execs., Internat., 1979. Mem. Direct Mktg. Assn. (named Ins. Exec. of Yr., Edward N. Mayer award 1983), European Direct Mktg. Assn., Kansas City Direct Mktg. Assn. (Direct Marketer of Yr. 1984), Masons. Jewish. Home and Office: 121 W 48th St Suite 1102 Kansas City MO 64112

BAILEY, ANNETTE LEE, accountant; b. Suffolk, Va., June 30, 1958; d. Robert Lee and Anne Courtney (Reams) B. BSBA cum laude, Meredith Coll., 1979; postgrad., Va. Commonwealth U., 1980-85. Sales asst. Miller & Rhoads, Richmond, Va., 1975-79; pers. intern Graftek div. Exxon Co., Raleigh, N.C., 1979; sec. Fox-Huber Pers. Inc., Richmond, 1979-80, acctg. clk., 1980-81; bookkeeper Merrill Lynch Pierce Fenner & Smith, Richmond, 1980, lead bookkeeper, 1980; acctg. asst. Crestar Bank (formerly United Va.), Richmond, 1981-83; lease staff acct. Best Products Co. Inc., Richmond, 1983-87, supr. fixed asset acctg., 1987-89; mgr. gen. ledger acctg. Med. Coll. Va. Hosp., Richmond, 1989—. Mem. bell choir First Bapt. Ch., Richmond, 1979—; conv. del. Va. Rep. com., 1985. Shell Oil Co. scholar, 1976. Mem. NAFE, Nat. Assn. Accts., McCormack and Dodge Mid-Atlantic User Group (chmn. 1986-88, treas. 1988-89). Baptist. Home: 4901 Hillery Ct Richmond VA 23228 Office: Med Coll Va Hosp PO Box 152 MCV Sta Richmond VA 23298

BAILEY, BARRY DEE, oil, gas and mining company executive; b. Monahans, Tex., Apr. 20, 1954; s. Charles F. and Nadine Pearl (Schrader) B.; m. Linda Sue Edwards, July 16, 1977; children: Patrick Noble, Zachary Paul. BBA in Acctg., Tex. Tech. U., 1976. Tax acct. Griese & Kares CPA's, Houston, 1977-79; asst. controller Davis Walker Steel and Wire Co., Houston, 1979-81; controller, tax mgr. Houston Oil and Refining Co., 1981-83; fin. analyst O.I.L. Energy, Inc., Dallas, 1982-83; v.p., treas., sec. Exploration Co., San Antonio, 1984—, Luxello Properties Inc., San Antonio, 1986—. Mem. Assn. Corp. Secs. Republican. Lutheran. Office: Exploration Co 10101 Reunion Pl 10th Fl San Antonio TX 78216

BAILEY, ELIZABETH ELLERY, university dean; b. N.Y.C., Nov. 26, 1938; d. Irving Woodworth and Henrietta Dana (Skinner) Raymond; B.A. magna cum laude, Radcliffe Coll., 1960; M.S., Stevens Inst. Tech., 1966; Ph.D. (Bell Labs. grantee), Princeton U., 1972; children—James L., William E. Successively sr. tech. aid, assoc. mem. tech. staff, mem. tech. staff, supr. econ. analysis group, research head econs. research dept. Bell Labs., 1960-77; commr. CAB, 1977-83, v.p., 1981-83; dean Grad. Sch. Indsl. Adminstrn., Carnegie-Mellon U., 1983—; dir. Honeywell, Inc., Philip Morris, Coll. Retirement Equities Fund; adj. asst., then assoc. prof. econs. NYU, 1973-77; Founding mem., v.p. bd. trustees Harbor Sch. for Children with Learning Disabilities; trustee Princeton U., 1978-82, Presbyn. U. Hosp., 1984—, Brookings Inst., 1988—, Catalyst, 1988—; mem. exec. council Fedn. Orgns. for Profl. Women, 1980-82; chmn. Com. on Status of Women in Econs. Profession, 1979-82; mem. corp. vis. com. Sloan Sch. Mgmt., M.I.T., 1982-85; mem. adv. bd. Brookings Inst., 1987—, Center Econ. Policy Research, Stanford U., 1983—. Recipient Program Design Trainee award Bell Labs.; Mem. Am. Econ. Assn. (exec. com. 1981-83, v.p. 1985), Am. Assn. Collegiate Schs. Bus. (v.p. 1987-88). Author: Economic Theory of Regulatory Constraint, 1973; editor: Selected Economics Papers of William J. Baumol, 1976; Deregulating the Airlines, 1985; bd. editors Am. Econ. Rev., 1977-79, Jour. Indsl. Econs., 1977-84. Home: 220 Schenley Rd Pittsburgh PA 15217 Office: Carnegie-Mellon U 5000 Forbes Ave Pittsburgh PA 15213

BAILEY, EMILIE KATHRYN, sales and marketing executive; b. Bloomington, Ind., Oct. 12, 1946; d. Richard Charles and Marjorie (Kirkman) Koontz; m. Gerald Bailey, June 17, 1967 (div. Nov. 1985). Student, Lamar U., 1979, 87-89, Tex. Assn. Realtors Sch., 1985. Lic. real estate agt., Tex. Realtor, sales mgr. Dal Sasso Realty & Constrn., Nederland, Tex., 1979-81; realtor Am. Real Estate, Port Neches, Tex., 1981-82, Nordstrom & Assocs. Realtors, Port Neches, Tex., 1982-83; realtor, sales mgr. Mansard Builders, Inc., Beaumont, Tex., 1983-85; realtor Nash Phillips/Copus, Austin, Tex., 1985-86, Easter & Easter Realtors, Austin, 1986-87; nat. dir. sales, mktg. Oak Creek Mfg., Inc., Nederland, 1987-88; real estate agt. Don Moss & Assocs., Groves, Tex., 1987—; dir. sales, mktg. Heritage Oak Co., Crockett, Tex., 1989—. Mem. Bus. & Profl. Women's Club, Am. Bus. Women's Assn., Nederland C. of C., Port Neches-Nederland-Port Arthur Bd. Realtors (bd. dirs. 1983-85, chmn. hospitality com. 1982-83). Republican. Office: Heritage Oak Co PO Box 347 Crockett TX 75835 also: Don Moss & Assocs 3747 Charles Ave Groves TX 77619 Mailing: PO Box 7444 Beaumont TX 77706

BAILEY, FREDERICK EUGENE, JR., polymer scientist; b. Bklyn., Oct. 8, 1927; s. Frederick Eugene and Florence (Berkeley) B.; m. Mary Catherine Lowder, May 7, 1979. B.A., Amherst Coll., 1948; M.S., Yale U., 1950,

Ph.D., 1952. Sr. chemist Union Carbide Research Devel., 1952-59, group leader, 1959-62, asst. dir., 1962-69; mgr. mktg. research Union Carbide, N.Y.C., 1969-71; sr. research scientist Union Carbide Research Devel., South Charleston, W.Va., 1971—; adj. prof. chemistry Marshall U., Huntington, W.Va., 1975—; adj. prof. chem. engring. W.Va. Coll. Grad. Studies, 1981—; adj. prof. chemistry dept. U. Charleston, Morris Harvey Coll., 1962-63, 65; mem. grad. faculty W.Va. U., 1959-61; chmn. Gordon Research Conf. on Polymers, Calif. chmn., 1972, N.H. chmn., 1984; mem. Gordon Research Conf. Council; vice chmn. Gordon Research Conf. on Foams, 1990. Author: Poly(ethylene Oxide), 1976; editor: Initiation of Polymerization, 1983; (with K.N. Edwards) Urethane Chemistry and Applications, 1981; (with A. Eisenberg) Interactions in Macromolecules, 1986; patentee in field. Addison Brown scholar Amherst Coll., 1948; Forrest Jewett Moore fellow, 1949. Fellow AAAS, Am. Inst. Chemists (cert. chemist, Chem. Pioneer award 1987), N.Y. Acad. Scis.; mem. Am. Chem. Soc. (chmn. divisional officer caucus 1980-85, chmn. div. polymer chemistry 1976, councilor div. 1978—, com. sci. 1978, 82-83, gen. sec. Macromolecular secretariat 1978, divisional activities com. 1980-86, sec. divisional activities com. 1986, com. on coms. 1987—, Outstanding Sci. Achievement award Kanawha Valley sect. 1988). Republican. Episcopalian. Club: Tennis (Charleston, W.Va.). Home: 848 Beaumont Rd Charleston WV 25314 Office: Union Carbide Corp Tech Center South Charleston WV 25303

BAILEY, GLENN WALDEMAR, manufacturing company executive; b. Cleve., May 8, 1925; s. Harry W. and Elizabeth B.; m. Cornelia L. Tarrant, June 12, 1952. B.S., U. Wis., 1946; M.B.A., Harvard U., 1951. Project engr. Thompson Ramo Wooldridge, Cleve., 1946-49; fin. staff Ford Motor Co., Dearborn, Mich., 1951-54; mgr. fin. analysis Curtiss Wright Corp., 1954-57; asst. to v.p., gen. mgr. Overseas div. Chrysler Corp., Detroit, 1957-60; group gen. mgr. ITT Corp., N.Y.C., 1960-67; chmn. bd., pres. Keene Corp., N.Y.C., 1967-81, Bairnco Corp., N.Y.C., 1981—. Served to ensign USNR, 1943-46. Home: Ocean Reef Key Largo FL 33037 Office: Bairnco Corp 200 Park Ave New York NY 10166

BAILEY, IRVING WIDMER, II, insurance holding company executive; b. Cambridge, Mass., June 8, 1941; s. Harwood and Esther (Hill) B.; m. Nancy Lawrence, Sept. 21, 1963; children: Christopher L., Michele. Grad., Phillips-Exeter Acad., 1959; student, U. Paris, 1961-62; B.A. in French, U. Colo., 1963; M.B.A., NYU, 1968. Investment officer, asst. v.p. Mut. Life Ins. Co., N.Y.C., 1963-71; v.p. bond investment Phoenix Mut. Life Ins. Co., Hartford, Conn., 1971-76, sr. v.p. investments, 1976-81; exec. v.p., chief investment officer Capital Holding Corp., Louisville, 1981-87, pres., chief oper. officer, 1987-88, chmn., pres., chief. exec. officer, 1988—; also bd. dirs. 1988—; bd. dirs. Fed. Res. Bank St. Louis, Louisville br. Bd. dirs. Leadership Louisville Found., 1989—, U. Ky. Bus. Partnership Found., Lexington, 1981—; bd. govs. J.B. Speed Art Mus., 1988—; mem. exec. com. Ky. Econ. Devel. Corp., 1988—, Campaign for Greater Louisville, 1988—; mem. trust investment com. U. Louisville, 1982—. Mem. N.Y. Soc. Security Analysts, The Jefferson Club, River Valley Club. Republican. Presbyterian. Office: Capital Holding Corp 680 4th Ave PO Box 32830 Louisville KY 40232

BAILEY, JANET DEE, publishing company executive; b. Newark, Aug. 23, 1946; d. Richard and Mary Louise (Dee) Shapiro; m. John Frederick Bailey, May 9, 1971; 1 child, Jason David. BA, U. Del., 1968; MBA, Pace U., 1981. Prodn. editor Prentice-Hall, Inc., Englewood Cliffs, N.J., 1968-70; dir. publs. Spl. Libraries Assn., N.Y.C., 1970-76; dir. mktg. services Knowledge Industry Publs., White Plains, N.Y., 1978-81, v.p., 1984-85; dir. inventory and contracts Macmillan Book Clubs, N.Y.C., 1981-84; assoc. pub. dir. Elsevier Sci. Pub. Co., N.Y.C., 1985—. Mem. Assn. Am. Publishers (mem. jours. com.), Soc. for Scholarly Publishing. Office: Elsevier Pub Co 655 Ave of the Americas New York NY 10010

BAILEY, LAWRENCE RANDALL, SR., lawyer; b. Panama Canal Zone, Mar. 31, 1918; s. Charles W. and Clara Alma (Small) B.; m. Norma Thomas, May 20, 1961; children: Lawrence Jr., Bruce, Lamont, Susan. AB, Howard U., 1939, JD, 1942. Bar: N.Y. 1943, U.S. Dist Ct. (so. dist.) N.Y. 1950, U.S. Dist. Ct. (ea. dist.) N.Y. 1951, U.S. Ct. Appeals (4th cir.) 1960, U.S. Supreme Ct. 1953. Asst. counsel, pres. City Coun., N.Y.C., 1952-54; counsel, then vice chmn. Met. Transp. Authority, N.Y.C., 1970—, also bd. dirs.; chief counsel N.Y. State NAACP. Bd. dirs. Greater Jamaica (N.Y.) Devel. Corp. Chief warrant officer U.S. Army, 1943-48, PTO. Decorated Bronze Star. Mem. ABA, Nat. Lawyers Assn., Am. Trial Lawyers Assn., New York County Lawyers Assn., Met. Black Bar Assn., Howard U. Alumni Assn. Greater N.Y. (pres.). Democrat. Baptist. Home: 112-05 175th St Jamaica NY 11433 Office: 360 W 125th St New York NY 10027

BAILEY, LINDA DODSON, librarian; b. Freeport, Tex., Oct. 1, 1952; d. William Erroll and Helen Rose (McDowell) Dodson; m. John Randall Bailey, Aug. 31, 1985. BAin Teaching, Sam Houston State U., 1975; M Library and Info. Sci., U. Tex., 1986. Librarian Goose Creek Ind. Sch. Dist., Baytown, Tex., 1977-78, Channelview (Tex.) Ind. Sch. Dist., 1978-79; librarian Tenneco Inc., Houston, 1979-83, sr. librarian, 1983-88; core librarian Arthur Andersen and Co., Houston, 1988—. Mem. Spl. Librs. Assn., Houston Online User's Group, Houston Area Law Librs. Home: 13213 Bay Place Dr Baytown TX 77520

BAILEY, RAY VERNON, lawyer, patent atty., property mgr.; b. Royal, Iowa, Dec. 14, 1913; s. George Lewis and Marie (Albers) B.; B.A. cum laude, State U. Iowa, 1935, J.D. cum laude, 1937; m. Velda Maxine Sheldon, June 18, 1938; children—Theron Sheldon, George Bryan. Admitted to Iowa bar, 1937, Ill. bar, 1938; research patent counsel U.S. Gypsum Co., Chgo., 1937-39; asso. Home State Bank, Royal, 1940; partner Dick, Bailey & Fletcher, also Dick and Bailey, Des Moines, 1941-42; investigator U.S. Civil Service Commn., 1942-43; patent adviser Rock Island (Ill.) Arsenal, 1943-45; property mgmt., legal and patent work, Clarion, Iowa, 1945-74, Millers Bay, Milford, Iowa, 1974—; participant World Peace Through Law Ctr. Confs., Madrid 1979, Sao Paulo, Brazil 1981, Cairo 1983, Berlin 1985, Seoul, Korea, 1987 (mem. panel on real estate law), People to People's 6th Worldwide Conf., Aalborg, Denmark 1984. Dir., past pres. Okoboji Protective Assn.; owner Century Farm. Past mem. Iowa Ho. Reps., past mem. ethics com., departmental rules review com., banking laws revision com., fin. subcom. Iowa Higher Edn. Task Force; mem. Paxx World Found.-Peace Links Peace Mission to Jordan and Israel, 1989. Mem. exec. bd. Prairie Gold council Boy Scouts Am.; mem. Iowa Bd. Regents, 1969-81, past chmn. banking com.; mem. Iowa Coll. Aid Commn., 1971-81; past bd. dirs. Iowa Student Loan Liquidity Corp., also past chmn. bylaws com. past mem. alumni council U. Iowa; past chmn. public affairs com. Wright County Extension Council, past pres. Clarion Devel. Commn.; past mem. State of Iowa Com. on Mental Hygiene; mem. People to People Higher Edn. Adminstrs. Del. to People's Republic of China, 1978; mem. planning and goals com. World Peace Through Law Center, Nat. Com. Iowa Endowment 2000 campaign; past bd. dirs. Iowans for Tax Relief; past bd. dirs. U. Iowa Research Found.; Mem. Iowa Campaign Fin. Disclosure Commn.; sponsor U. Iowa Coll. of Law Faculty Library Lounge. Recipient Silver Beaver award Boy Scouts Am. Mem. ABA (patent legis, com.), Iowa (past mem. com. on patent, trademark and copyright law), Wright County, Dickinson County bar assns., State U. Iowa Alumni Assn. (past pres. Clarion chpt.), Iowa Patent Law Assn. (bd. dirs.), Dickinson County Taxpayers Assn. (bd. dirs.) , U. Iowa Parents Assn. (past pres.), Dickinson County Corn Growers Assn. (bd. dirs.), Northwest Iowa/Southwest Minn. U.S. Hwy. 71 Assn. (rep. City of Wahpeton), U. Iowa Pres.'s Club, Iowa State U. Order of the Knoll, Lions. Author papers in field. Address: Millers Bay RR 2 PO Box 190 Milford IA 51351

BAILEY, RICHARD BRIGGS, investment company executive; b. Weston, Mass., Sept. 14, 1926; s. George William and Alice Gertrude (Cooper) B.; m. Rebecca C. Bradford, June 20, 1950 (div. Dec. 1974); children—Ann, Elizabeth, Richard, Rebecca; m. Anne D. Prescott, Dec. 14, 1974 (div. 1980); m. Anita S. Lawrence, Sept. 12, 1980; 1 dau., Alexandra. B.A., Harvard, 1948, M.A., 1951; postgrad., Grad. Sch. Bus. Adminstrn., 1966. Prodn. engr. C. Brewer & Co., Honolulu, 1951-53; prodn. engr. Raytheon Co., Waltham, Mass., 1953-54; security analyst Keystone Custodian Funds, Boston, 1955-59; industry specialist Mass. Investors Trust, 1959-69; now mng. trustee; mng. partner Mass. Fin. Services, Co., Boston, 1969—; pres. Mass. Fin. Services, Co., 1978-82; chmn., dir. Mass. Fin. Services Co., 1982—; dir. Cambridge Trust Co., Lombard Odier Internat. Portfolio Mgmt. Ltd., London., Sun Life Assurance Co. Can. (U.S.); Chmn. Finance Com., Lincoln, Mass., 1966-68. Trustee Plimoth Plantation, Inc., Plymouth, Mass., Phillips Exeter Acad., Exeter, N.H., 1978-82; mem. adv. bd. Coll. Mental Health Center of Boston. Served to 2d lt., Signal Corps AUS, 1944-46. Decorated Letter of Commendation. Mem. Boston Security Analysts Soc. Republican. Episcopalian. Clubs: Knickerbocker (N.Y.C.), Harvard of N.Y. (N.Y.C.); Somerset (Boston); Eastern Yacht (Marblehead); Coral Beach and Tennis (Bermuda). Home: 63 Atlantic Ave Boston MA 02110 Office: 200 Berkeley St Boston MA 02116

BAILEY, ROBERT E., oil company executive; b. 1932. BBA, Ind. U., 1954; LLB, South Tex. Coll. Law, 1962. Ptnr. Arthur Andersen, Houston, 1958-72; chief fin. officer, exec. v.p. Damson Oil Corp., N.Y.C., 1972-82; exec. v.p. ENI, 1982-83; pres. Petro Corp., 1983-85; chief fin. officer, v.p. Gearhart Industries Inc., Ft. Worth, 1984—. Served with USAF, 1954-57. Office: Gearhart Industries Inc 1100 Everman Rd Fort Worth TX 76140

BAILEY, ROBERT LAURENCE, design firm executive; b. Coeur D'Alena, Aug. 8, 1938; s. Marshall Charles and Lillian Nora (Hanson) B.; m. Karin Elizabeth Wallace, June 1958 (div. 1965); children: Stuart Laurence, Diane Elizabeth; m. Martha Peters, Sept. 17, 1976. Student, Art Ctr. Coll. Design, 1958-61. Indsl. engr. Aeronutronics, Newport Beach, Calif., 1962-63; designer Skidmore Owings & Merrill, Portland, Oreg., 1963-72; pres. Robert Bailey Inc., Portland, 1972—. Mem. design rev. com. Portland City Planning Comm., 1980. Recipient Best of Environ. Graphics award Print Case Books, 1984, Silver medal Soc. Illustrators, 1985, Gold medal Soc. Art Dirs., 1986. Mem. AIA, Soc. Environ. Graphics Designers, Multnomah Club, Oreg. Yacht Club. Republican. Baptist. Office: Robert Bailey Inc 0121 SW Bancroft Portland OR 97201

BAILEY, RONALD WADE, energy systems executive; b. Dardanelle, Ark., Aug. 9, 1935; s. Darrell and Velma (Madden) B.; m. Betty Jo Ruffin, June 12, 1956; children: Rhonda, Ronald Wade Jr., Jil. BS, Ark. Tech. U., 1957; postgrad., U. Ark., 1957. Band instr. DeWitt (Ark.) High Sch., 1957-60; sales mgr. Smith Rice Mill, DeWitt, 1960-67; pres. Producers Rice Mill, Inc., Stuttgart, Ark., 1967-88, Stuttgart Etcetera Inc., 1974—, PRM Energy Systems, Inc., Stuttgart, Ark., 1983—; past. chmn. Fed. Reserve Bd., Little Rock, Ark. Leadership chmn. Boy Scouts Am., Stuttgart, 1980—; mem. Ark Adv. Council on Secondary Edn.; chmn. Grand Prairie Work Activity Ctr.; mem. Biomass Inst., Small Bus. Adv. Coun. Served to capt. Ark. Nat. Guard, 1953-67. Named to Hall of Distinction, Ark. Tech. Alumni Assn., Russellville, 1974. Mem. Assn. of Operative Millers., Assn. of Enerfy Engrs., Assn. Agrl. Engrs., Rice Millers Assn. (pres. 1972-73), Rice Council for Market Devel. (past. sec.), Stuttgart C. of C. (past pres.), Ark. Drier and Warehouseman Assn. Methodist. Home: 1821 Fairway Stuttgart AR 72160 Office: PRM Energy Systems Inc Bailey Bldg 1812 S Main St Stuttgart AR 72160

BAILEY, SCOTT ARTHUR, banker; b. Pottsville, Pa., Aug. 14, 1947; s. Roy E. and Eleanor C. (Thompson) B.; m. Melanie Kupiec, Aug. 25, 1969; children: Andrew, Todd. BS in Fin., Pa. State U., 1969; MBA, Drexel U., 1972. V.p., asst. to chmn. First Pa. Bank & Corp., Phila., 1969-81; v.p. corp. services S.E. Bank, N.Am., Miami, Fla., 1981-82, sr. v.p. corp. services, 1983-84, sr. v.p. nat. banking and fin. instns., 1984-85, sr. v.p. corp. planning and econs., 1985-88, sr. v.p. capital markets, merchant banking group, 1988—; bd. dirs. S.E. Internat. Trading Co., Miami. Pres., bd. dirs. Kappa Delta Rho Found., 1984. Mem. Am. Bankers Assn., Nat. Corp. Cash Mmgt. Assn. (cert. cash mgr.), Greater Miami C. of C. (biotech. com.), Greater Miami Opera Assn. (bd. dirs. 1986—), Internat. Wine & Food Soc. (bd. dirs. 1986—), Riviera Country Club, City Club of Miami, Twin Cedars Gun Club, Kappa Delta Rho (pres. local chpt. 1967-69). Republican. Episcopalian. Home: 6401 Maynada St Coral Gables FL 33146 Office: SE Bank NA 200 S Biscayne Blvd Miami FL 33131

BAILLIE, DEBORAH A., accountant; b. New Orleans, Mar. 8, 1956; d. Edgar M. and Frances A. (St. Romain) Giroir; m. John Baillie III, May 20, 1977; children: Jacob A., Rachel E. BBA, Loyola U., New Orleans, 1977. CPA, Alaska. Mem. staff Arthur Young & Co., New Orleans, 1977, Bateman Weatherspoon, Clarksville, Tenn., 1983-85; staff Arthur Young & Co., Anchorage, 1978-81, sr. staff mem., 1985-87; tax mgr. Ernst & Whitnet, Anchorage, 1987—. Home: 17707 Kiloana Ct Eagle River AK 99577 Office: 301 W Northern Lights Blvd #601 Anchorage AK 99503

BAILLIE, MARY HELEN, accounting executive; b. Clio, S.C., Aug. 18, 1926; d. Paul Clydus and Laurie (Easterling) Orr; grad. Carolina Bus. Coll., 1946; children—William Sinclair, Carol Anderson. Controller, George I. Clarke, Inc., Atlanta, 1953-57, DuBose Reed Constrn. Co./W. Carroll DuBose, Inc., Ft. Lauderdale, Fla., 1970-74; asst. controller H.B. Fuller Co., Ft. Lauderdale, 1975-76; owner M.H. Baillie & Assocs., Inc., Ft. Lauderdale, 1977—. Mem. Leadership Broward Alumni, 1985—, Ft. Lauderdale Sign Adv. Bd., 1983—, Broward County Commn. on Status of Women, 1985—; bd. dirs., treas. Women in Distress, 1984—. Mem. Nat. Accts. Assn. (dir. 1977-79, dir. spl. activities 1979—), Fla. Accts. Assn. (dir. 1977-79, sec. 1977-79), Ft. Lauderdale C. of C. (dir. 1979—), Internat. Assn. Fin. Planners. Republican. Clubs: Women's Execs. (dir. 1978-80, treas. 1978-80), Ft. Lauderdale Country. Home: 3471 NE 17th Terr Fort Lauderdale FL 33334 Office: MH Baillie & Assocs Inc 746 NE Third Ave Fort Lauderdale FL 33304

BAIMAN, GAIL, real estate broker; b. Bklyn., June 4, 1938; d. Joseph and Anita (Devon) Yalow; m. James F. Becker, Oct. 1970 (div. 1978); children—Steven, Susan, Barbara. Student Bklyn. Coll., 1955-57. Lic. real estate broker, N.Y., Pa., Fla. Personnel-pub. relations dir. I.M.C., Inc., N.Y.C., 1970-72; pres., broker Gayle Baiman Assocs., Inc., N.Y.C., 1972-74; v.p., broker Tuit Mktg. Corp., Mt. Pocono, Pa., 1974-83; pres., broker Ind. Timeshare Sales, Inc., St. Petersburg, Fla. and Mount Pocono, Pa., 1983—; mem. Nat. Timeshare Council. Arbitrator Better Bus. Bur. Mem. Am. Resort and Residential Developers Assn., Nat. Assn. Exec. Women. Avocations: reading, metaphysics, bowling. Office: Independent Timeshare Sales Inc 5680 66th St N Saint Petersburg FL 33709

BAIN, BRUCE ALAN, banker; b. Easton, Md., Jan. 9, 1957; s. Robert H. and Helen (O'Connor) B. AB in History, Duke U., 1979; MBA, Vanderbilt U., 1981. Fin. analyst Flagship Banks, Inc., Miami, Fla., 1981-84; mgr. asset and liability mgmt. Sun Bank/Miami, N.A., Miami, 1984—. Mem. Ft. Lauderdale Mus. of Art, 1986. Mem. Econ. Soc. South Fla., Alpha Tau Omega. Office: 1933 Players Pl North Lauderdale FL 33068

BAIN, LINDA VALERIE, executive development consultant; b. N.Y.C., Feb. 14, 1947; d. Carlton Louis and Helen V. (Boyd) B.; m. Samuel Green, Mar. 21, 1986. BA, CCNY, 1975. Exec. sec. N.Y.C. Dept. Social Services, 1966-70; program assoc. N.Y. State Dept. Mental Hygiene, N.Y.C., 1970-71, Nat. Council Negro Women, N.Y.C., 1973-79; sr. cons. Donchian Mgmt. Services, N.Y.C., 1980-85; pres., devel. cons. Bain Assocs., Inc., N.Y.C., 1985—; cons. Am. Express Co., Squibb Corp. Mem. Friends of Alvin Ailey, bd. dirs.; bd. dirs. The Friendly Place, Inc. Recipient Mary McLeod Bethune Recognition award Nat. Council Negro Women, 1974. Mem. Am. Soc. Tng. and Devel., Coalition of 100 Black Women, Council of Concerned Black Execs., Nat. Assn. Female Execs., Nat. and N.Y. Orgn. Devel. Network. Democrat. Office: Bain Assocs Inc PO Box 20789 New York NY 10025-9992

BAINBRIDGE, RUSSELL BENJAMIN, JR., oil and gas property management executive, consultant; b. Chgo., Feb. 24, 1945; s. Russell Benjamin, Sr. and Mary (Hudson) B.; m. Nancy H. Ferguson, Nov. 13, 1982. PhB, Duquesne U., 1968; MS in Geology, Iowa State U., 1976; MBA in Fin., DePaul U., 1980. Instr., Iowa State U., Ames, 1975-76; banking assoc. Continental Ill. Bank, Chgo., 1976-81; v.p. Penn Square Bank, Oklahoma City, 1981-82; sr. v.p. Union Bank and Trust, Oklahoma City, 1982-85; pres., chief exec. officer Magnolia Investors, Ltd., Oklahoma City, 1988—, also dir. Mem. governing bd. Okla. Mus. of Art Assocs., Oklahoma City, 1984—; pres. affiliate bd. Omniplex Assocs. Mem. AAAS, Am. Assn. Petroleum Geologists, Internat. Platform Assn., N.Y. Acad. Sci. Office: Magnolia Investors Ltd 123 NW 8th St Oklahoma City OK 73102

BAINS, HARRISON MACKELLAR, JR., financial executive; b. Pasadena, Calif., July 8, 1943; s. Harrison MacKellar and Celeste Adele (Callahan) B.; m. Leslie E. Tawney, Mar. 7, 1970; children: Harrison MacKellar, III, Tawney Elizabeth. B.A., U. Redlands, 1964; M.B.A., U. Calif., Berkeley, 1966. Asst. v.p. Citibank N.A., 1968-72; asst. treas. Richardson-Merrell Inc., 1972-76; asst. treas. Nabisco Inc., East Hanover, N.J., 1976-78, treas., 1978—, v.p., 1980-81; v.p., treas. Nabisco Brands, Inc., Parsippany, N.J., 1981-82, sr. v.p. fin., 1982-83, sr. v.p., treas., 1983-85; v.p., treas. RJR Nabisco Inc., Winston-Salem, N.J., 1985-86, sr. v.p., treas., 1987; sr. v.p., group exec. Chase Manhattan Bank, N.A., N.Y.C., 1987-88; v.p., treas. Bristol-Myers Co., N.Y.C., 1988—. Mem. Fin. Execs. Inst., Food Safety Council (treas. 1980—). Office: Bristol-Myers Co 345 Park Ave New York NY 10010

BAINTON, DONALD J., diversified manufacturing company executive; b. N.Y.C., May 3, 1931; s. William Lewis and Mildred J. (Dunne) B.; m. Aileen M. Demoulins, July 10, 1954; children—Kathryn C., Stephen L., Elizabeth A., William D. B.A., Columbia U., 1952; postgrad., Advanced Mgmt. Program, Rutgers U., 1960. With The Continental Group, Inc., 1954-83, gen. mgr. prodn. planning, 1967-68; gen. mgr. mfg. The Continental Group, Inc. (Eastern div.), 1968-73; gen. mgr. (Pacific div.), 1973-74, (Eastern div.), 1974-75; v.p., gen. mgr. ops. U.S. Metal, 1975-76; exec. v.p., gen. mgr. CCC-USA, 1976-78, corp. exec. v.p., pres. diversified ops., 1978-79; pres. Continental Can Co., 1979-81; pres. Continental Packaging, 1981-83, exec. v.p., operating officer parent co., 1979-83; chmn., chief exec. officer, dir. Viatech Inc., Syosset, N.Y., 1983—; dir. Cablec Inc., Appollo Industries, Dixie Metal Box Ltd. Gen. Pub. Utilities, Dixie Union. Bd. dirs. Columbia Coll. Served with USN, 1952-54, Korea. Mem. Nat. Center for Resource Recovery (dir.), Inst. Applied Econs. (dir.), Columbia U. Alumni Assn. Republican. Roman Catholic. Clubs: Milbrook Country (Greenwich, Conn.), Winged Foot (Mamaroneck, N.Y.), Chemical, Madison Sq. Garden (N.Y.C.), Union League (N.Y.C.). Office: Viatech Inc 1 Aerial Way Syosset NY 11791

BAINUM, STEWART WILLIAM, JR., health care and lodging company executive; b. Takoma Park, Md., Mar. 25, 1946; s. Stewart William Sr. and Jane Loretta (Goyne) B.; m. Sandra Ann Yarish, Sept. 26, 1987. BA, Pacific Union Coll., 1968; MBA, UCLA, 1970; postgrad. theology, Andrews U., 1971-72. V.p. Manor Care Inc., Silver Spring, Md., 1973-79, vice chmn., 1982-87, chmn., chief exec. officer, 1987—, also bd. dirs.; mem. Md. Ho. of Dels., Annapolis, 1979-83, Md. State Senate, Annapolis, 1983-87. Bd. dirs. Invest in Am., Washington, 1987; co-chmn. Dem. Forum, Montgomery County, Md., 1987; alt. del. Dem. Nat. Conv., San Francisco, 1984. Named Outstanding State Ofcl. of Yr., Young Democrats of Md., 1981; recipient Cert. of Merit, Common Cause of Md., Annapolis, 1982, 85, Torch of Liberty award Anti-Defamation League, Washington region, 1984. Office: Manor Care Inc 10750 Columbia Pike Silver Spring MD 20901

BAIRD, CHARLES FITZ, business executive; b. Southampton, N.Y., Sept. 4, 1922; s. George White and Julia (Fitz) B.; m. Norma Adele White, Sept. 13, 1947; children: Susan Fitz, Stephen White, Charles Fitz, Nancy Williams Harwood. A.B., Middlebury (Vt.) Coll., 1944; grad., Advanced Mgmt. Program, Harvard, 1960; LL.D. (hon.), Bucknell U., 1976. With Standard Oil Co., N.J., 1948-65; dep. European fin. rep. Standard Oil Co., London, 1955-58; asst. treas. Standard Oil Co., 1958-62; dir. Esso Standard SA Française, 1962-65; asst. sec. of navy (fin. mgmt.) 1966-67, undersec. of navy, 1967-69; v.p. fin. Inco Ltd., 1969-72, sr. v.p., 1972-76, vice-chmn., 1976-77, pres., 1977-80, chmn., chief exec. officer, 1980-87; bd. dirs. Inco Ltd., Bank of Montreal, Aetna Life and Casualty Co.; mem. President's Commn. Marine Sci., Engring. and Resources, 1967-69, Nat. Adv. Commns. on Ocean and Atmosphere, 1972-74; trustee Logistics Mgmt. Inst. Trustee Bucknell U., 1969—; chmn. bd. trustees, 1976-82; bd. advisers Naval War Coll., 1970-74. Served as capt. USMC, 1943-46, 51-52. Mem. Council Fgn. Relations, Chi Psi. Clubs: Chevy Chase (Md.); Short Hills (N.J.); Badminton and Racquet, Toronto, Maidstone (East Hampton, N.Y.); Bridgehampton (N.Y.). Home: 4423 Boxwood Rd Bethesda MD 20816 Office: Inco Ltd, 1 1st Canadian Pl, Toronto, ON Canada M5X 1C4

BAIRD, DUGALD EUAN, oilfield service company executive; b. Aberdeen, Scotland, Sept. 16, 1937; came to U.S., 1979; s. Dugald and Matilda Deans (Tennant) B.; m. Angelica Hartz, May 24, 1961; children—Camilla N., Maiken E. Student, Aberdeen U., Scotland, 1954-55; B.A. in Geophysics, U. Cambridge, 1960. Field engr. Schlumberger, Europe, Asia, Africa, 1960-69; asst. regional mgr. Schlumberger Overseas, Singapore, 1969-72; div. mgr. South Gulf div. Schlumberger Overseas, Dubai, 1972-74; personnel mgr. Schlumberger Tech. Services, Paris, 1975-79; exec. v.p. Schlumberger Ltd., N.Y.C., 1979-86, chmn., pres., chief exec. officer, 1986—. Office: Schlumberger Ltd 277 Park Ave New York NY 10017

BAIRD, MELLON CAMPBELL, JR., electronics industry executive; b. Corsicana, Tex., Feb. 24, 1931; s. Mellon Campbell and Katherine (Wasson) B.; m. Mary Beth Norman, Dec. 27, 1956. BBA, North Tex. State U., 1957, MBA, 1961. Adminstrv. asst. VARO Inc., Garland, Tex., 1957-59; western region mgr. VARO Inc., Los Angeles, 1959-61; dir. mktg. VARO Inc., Santa Barbara, Calif., 1961-63; exec. v.p., pres. F&M Systems Co., Dallas, 1963-74; pres. fed. systems group Sanders Assocs. Inc., Nashua, N.H., 1974-81; pres. def. & electronics group Eaton Corp., Cleve., 1981-86; pres., chief operating officer Tracor Inc., Austin, 1986-87, pres., chief exec. officer, 1988—. Served with USN, 1951-55. Mem. Nat. Security Indsl. Assn. (trustee 1974—), Navy League U.S. (life), Armed Forces Communications & Electronics Assn., Assn. Old Crows (life, tech. symposium chmn. 1987), Security Affairs Support Assn. (bd. dirs. 1988—), Tex. Assn. Taxpayers (bd. dirs. 1988—). Home: 4204 Green Cliffs Rd Austin TX 78746 Office: Tracor Inc 6500 Tracor Ln Austin TX 78725

BAISDEN, ELEANOR MARGUERITE, airline compensation executive, consultant; b. Bklyn., Nov. 7, 1935; d. Vernon McKee and Ethel Mildred (Cockle) Baisden. BA, Hofstra U., 1970. Clk., Trans World Airlines, N.Y.C., 1953-55, sec., 1955-64, compensation analyst, 1964-75, compensation mgr., 1975-85, dir. compensation and orgn. planning, 1985-88, dir. compensation and adminstrn., 1988—. Mem. Airline Personnel Dirs. Conf. (personnel com. 1984-85), Airline Tariff Pub. Co. (personnel com. 1978—), Nat. Fgn. Trade Council (compensation com. 1980-84), Internat. Personnel Assn. (co. rep. 1980-84), Mensa, Alpha Sigma Lambda (Scholar of Yr. 1965-66). Republican. Methodist. Club: Weatherby Lake Yacht (Mo.). Avocations: boating, swimming, piano, travel. Home: 7818 NW Scenic Dr Weatherby Lake MO 64152 Office: Trans World Airlines 11500 Ambassador Dr Kansas City MO 64153

BAKER, ALFRED STANLEY, II, data processing executive; b. Hopewell, Va., Oct. 27, 1947; s. Alfred Stanley and Koma Jo (Johnson) B.; BA in Math., Ill. Inst. Tech., 1970; m. Janet Marie Borowski, Feb. 15, 1969; children: Jennifer, Nathan. System software designer STAT-TAB, Chgo., 1968-71; supr. system software devel. Standard Oil Co. Ind., 1971-79; v.p., programming dir. Datamension Corp. (formerly Image Producers, Inc.), Northbrook, Ill., 1979-89; pres. Al Baker and Assoc., 1989—; speaker, cons. in field. Designer and author two popular spread sheet programs for IBM personal computers; author TRS-80 Programs and Applications for the Color Computer; also games for Apple, TRS-80, Atari and IBM PC. Home and Office: 3936 Sunset Ln Northbrook IL 60062 Office: 615 Academy Dr Northbrook IL 60062

BAKER, ANDREW HARTILL, clinical laboratory executive; b. London, Dec. 7, 1948; came to U.S., 1976; s. Charles David and Isobel Joyce (Taylor) B.; m. Susan Nancy Spector, Oct. 24, 1986; children: Laura, Sally, Thomas. Student, Framlingham Coll., Suffolk, Eng., 1961-66; diploma accountancy, City of London Polytechnique, 1968. Auditor Touche Ross, London, 1968-73; controller Corning Ltd., Essex, Eng., 1974-76; div. controller Corning Med., N.Y., 1977-79; asst. controller Corning Glass Works, N.Y., 1980-82; sr. v.p. Metpath Teterboro, N.J., 1982-85, pres., 1985—; chmn. MetWest, Inc., 1988; dir. Unilabs Corp., 1989; founder, dir. Med. Diagnostic Card, Inc., Hartill Ltd. Treas. United Way of Steuben County, Corning, N.Y., 1978-82; trustee Wayne Gen. Hosp., N.J., 1982-87. Fellow Inst. Chartered Accts. in Eng. and Wales. Mem. Ch. of Eng. Club: Honourable Arty. Co. (London). Home: 636 Winding Hollow Dr Franklin Lakes NJ 07417 Office: Metpath Inc 1 Malcolm Ave Teterboro NJ 07608

BAKER, ANN COLLINS, human resources consultant; b. Alton, Ill., Jan. 11, 1951; d. Jerre Churchill and Ruth Marie (Walder) Collins; m. Paul Allen Baker, Jan. 29, 1972 (div. 1987); 1 child, Andrew James. Student, U. Ill., 1969-71. Accounts receivable clk. Central Material Co., Champaign, Ill., 1971-72; with Carson Pirie Scott & Co., Chgo., 1972-84; regional trainer Carson Pirie Scott & Co., 1979-82, personnel adminstr., 1982-84; human resources cons. Chgo., 1984-85; human resources cons. Robertson Lowstuter, Deerfield, Ill., 1985-88, v.p., 1988—; guest lectr. bus. writing U. Wis., Milw., 1976; conductor seminars in field. Vol. fundraiser Misericordia-Heart of Mercy, 1984—. Mem. Am. Mgmt. Assn., Nat. Assn. Women in Careers. Roman Catholic. Home: 104 Brookwood Ct Vernon Hills IL 60061 Office: Robertson Lowstuter 104 Wilmot Rd Ste 110 Deerfield IL 60015

BAKER, BONNIE ANN, real estate broker; b. Rock Springs, Wyo., Apr. 5, 1946; d. Clarence Heber and Vivian Doan Sargent; m. Joel Cheney Baker, Feb. 7, 1969; children—Michelle Leigh, Joelle Doan. A.A., Western Wyo. Coll., 1971; B.F.A., U. Wyo., 1984. Lic. broker Wyo. Mem. public relations staff Janss Corp., Rock Spring, Wyo., 1980-81; salesman Sweetwater Realty, Green River, 1982-85; broker, owner Twin Pines Realty, Green River, 1985—; bd. dirs. Pioneer Nat. Title Co. Trustee, Western Wyo. Coll., 1977-84; mem. Democratic Precinct Com., Green River, 1977—; pres. Sweetwater County Dem. Women's Club, 1989; trustee Castle Rock Hosp. Spl. Dist., 1981-84; City of Green River Tourism Com., 1988—, Centennial Com., 1989—. Mem. Sweetwater County Bd. Realtors (chmn. com. 1983—), Green River C. of C. (bd. dirs. 1986—, pres. 1989), Rock Springs C. of C. Avocations: reading; painting; sculpture-lost wax, 1988—. Home: 392 Hillcrest Way Green River WY 82935 Office: Twin Pines Realty 489 W Flaming Gorge Way Green River WY 82935

BAKER, CALVIN D., financial services company executive; b. 1926; married. BS, Gwynedd-Mercy Coll. Pres. Community Fed. Savs., 1962-82; dir. Del. Valley Housing Council; pres. council Gwynedd-Mercy Coll.; with Atlantic Fin. Fed., Bala-Cynwyd, Pa., 1982—, now chmn., also bd. dirs. Office: Atlantic Fin Fed 50 Monument Rd Bala-Cynwyd PA 19004 *

BAKER, CAMERON, lawyer; b. Chgo., Dec. 24, 1937; s. David Cameron and Marion (Fitzpatrick) B.; m. Katharine Julia Solari, Sept. 2, 1961; children: Cameron III, Ann, John. Student, U. Notre Dame, 1954-57; AB, Stanford U., 1958; LLB, U. Calif., Berkeley, 1961. Bar: Calif. 1962, U.S. Dist. Ct. (so. dist.) Calif. 1962, U.S. Dist. Ct. (no. dist.) Calif. 1963, U.S. Ct. Appeals (9th) 1963. Assoc. Adams, Duque & Hazeltine, Los Angeles, 1961-62; mng. ptnr. Pettit & Martin, San Francisco,, 1972-81, 84-87; mem. exec. com Pettit & Martin, San Francisco, 1971-82, 84—; del. Union Internat. des Avocats, 1983—; mayor City of Belvedere, Calif., 1978-79. Mem. City Council, Belvedere, 1976-80, fin. com. San Francisco Lawyers Com. for Urban Affairs, 1986—, bd. dirs., 1975-83; bd. dirs. San Francisco Legal Aid Soc., 1971-72, Boalt Hall Alumni Assn., 1982-84. Mem. ABA (internat. bus. law com., law and acctg. com., small bus. com., law firms com.), Calif. Bar Assn. (corp. com., chmn. governing com. continuing edn. 1975), Bar Assn. of San Francisco (bd. dirs. 1966, 72-73, client relations com., chmn. pub. relations com.). Clubs: Bohemian (San Francisco), Tiburon Peninsula. Home: 38 Alcatraz Ave Belvedere CA 94920 Office: Pettit & Martin 101 California St 35th Fl San Francisco CA 94111

BAKER, CHARLES E., stockbroker; b. Carthage, Mo., June 17, 1946; s. Ernest Roy Baker and Doris Elaine (Law) Bradshaw. BS in Math., Ill. State U., Normal, 1975. Licensed stockbroker, 1976. Sales engr. Honeywell, Peoria, Ill., 1972-76; registered rep. Loewi & Co., Milw., 1976-79; v.p. Kidder Peabody & Co., White Plains, N.Y., 1979—; bd. dirs. TRISM, Inc. Bd. dirs. White Plains chpt. March of Dimes, 1986, mem. exec. com.; pres. White Plains Guild 1988—. Recipient March of Dimes Disting. Vol. Leadership award 1988. Mem. Profl. Photographers of Am., Kiwanis, Shriners, Masons. Lodge: Kiwanis (pres. White Plains chpt.), Masons. Home: 11 Lake St White Plains NY 10603 Office: Kidder Peabody & Co 123 Main St White Plains NY 10601

BAKER, CLARENCE ALBERT, SR., structural steel construction company executive; b. Kansas City, Kans., July 2, 1919; s. Earl Retting and Nancy Jefferson (Price) B.; student Kans. U., 1939-40, Finley Engring. Coll., 1937-39, Ohio State U., 1967, 69; m. Marjorie Ellen Yoakum, Mar. 19, 1959 (dec. Feb. 1981); children—Clarence Albert, Jorgeann Baker Hiebert; stepchildren—Robert Beale, Barbara Anne Stegner (Mrs. Robert T. Kenney II); m. 2d, Katherine V. Cochran, Nov. 6, 1982. With Kansas City (Kans.) Structural Steel Co., 1937-84, shop supt., 1959-68, v.p., plant mgr., 1968-73, v.p. plant ops., 1973-76, v.p. engring., 1976—, dir., 1969—. Curriculum adv. Kansas City (Mo.) Met. Jr. Coll., 1971-72, Kansas City Vocat. Tech. Sch., 1973—. Committeeman, Republican Party, 1970-72; chmn. City of Mission (Kans.) Rep. Party, 1970-72; councilman. City of Merriam (Kans.), 1957-59. Adv. bd. Wentworth Mil. Acad.; bd. dirs. Kansas City Jr. Achievement. Served with USNR, 1944-46. Mem. Am. Welding Soc. (pres. 1970-71, chmn. 1970, code com.), ASTM, Kans. Engring. Soc., Kans. City C. of C. Lodge: Masons. Home: 6635 Milhaven Dr Mission KS 66202 Office: 21st and Metropolitan Sts Kansas City KS 66106

BAKER, CLIFFORD HOWARD, marketing professional; b. Paoli, Ind., Oct. 14, 1932; s. James A. and Alice (Limeberry) B.; B.S., U.S. Mil. Acad., 1956; M.S., Purdue U., 1965; Ph.D., N.C. State U., 1972; m. Joan B. Meyer, Feb. 4, 1958; children—Steven Conrad, Bradford Nelson, Paul Milton, Jeffrey Todd, Douglas Ross, Matthew Kent. Indsl. mktg. exec. Tex. Instruments, Dallas, 1959-61; market research exec. Gen. Motors Corp., Kokomo, Ind., 1961-65; supr. market analysis Corning Glass Works, Raleigh, N.C., 1965-70; pres. Market Research and Statistics Co., 1970-71, Indsl. Edn. Inst., Mailmax, Raleigh and Columbia, S.C., Village Printer, Raleigh; v.p. Su Casa Mexican Restaurants, Raleigh, Quinn Mfg., Chapel Hill, N.C. Served with AUS, 1956-59. Recipient Nat. Def. Service medal West Point, 1956. Mem. IEEE, Assn. Grads. West Point, Alpha Kappa Psi (hon.), Delta Mu Delta (hon.). Mem. Ch. of Christ. Republican. Home: 4816 Deerwood Dr Raleigh NC 27612 Office: 4505 Creedmoor Rd Raleigh NC 27612

BAKER, DANIEL RICHARD, computer systems consultant; b. Rostock, Denmark, Mar. 19, 1932; came to U.S., 1936, naturalized, 1945; s. Arthur and Molly (Needman) B.; student Tufts Coll., 1949-51; B.A., Bklyn. Coll., 1957; postgrad. Fairleigh Dickinson U., 1961-64; postgrad. in math. Am. U., 1968; m. June Ellin Nebenzahl, Oct. 2, 1960; children—David Charles, Jill Alison. Tchr. math. N.Y.C. Public Schs., 1958-59; computer programmer Systems Devel. Corp., Paramus, N.J., 1959-61; programmer analyst ITT, Paramus, 1961-64; sr. mathematician Melpar Corp., Falls Church, Va., 1964-65; systems analyst Wolf Research & Devel. Corp., Badensburg, Md., 1965-66, Aries Corp., McLean, Va., 1966-68; sr. systems analyst N.Am. Rockwell Corp., Roslyn, Va., 1968-70; pres. Baker & Baker Data Assos., Fairfax Station, Va., 1970—; real estate broker; permanent group leader Dale Carnegie Sales Courses. Vol. ann. fund campaign Tufts Coll., 1976—. Served with AUS, 1954-55. Mem. No. Va. Assn. Realtors (multilist com., edn. com., pub. rels. com., 5-yr. Million Dollar Sales Club award), Va. Assn. Realtors (dir. 1977-80, 83—), Nat. Assn. Realtors, Am. Soc. Cybernetics, Silvanus Packard Soc. Club: Washington Tufts (v.p. 1975). Office: Baker & Baker Data Assocs 7310 Craftown Rd Fairfax Station VA 22039-2121

BAKER, DAVID E., company executive; b. Cin., Feb. 3, 1941; s. David E. and Marion I. (Robbins) B.; m. Judith L. Baker, Nov. 24, 1963; children: Glenn A., Eric. J. A in Engring., Lincoln Coll., Boston, 1976; BS, Northeastern U., 1976. Contract rep. Tech. Inc., Dayton, Ohio, 1964-66; dept. mgr. Areospace Rsch., Inc., Boston, 1966-72; reg. sales mgr. Advisor Security, Boston, 1972-73; sales mgr. Gamewell/Alarntronics, Boston, 1973-76, E.A.R. Corp., Indpls., 1976-81; product mgr. Esterline-Angus, Indpls., 1981-83; v.p., gen. mgr. U.S. Tap/Indiana Brass, Frankfort, 1983-85, Hansa Am., Inc., Michigan City, 1985—. Contbr. articles to profl. jours.; patentee in field. Mem. Nat. Fire Prevention Assn., Nat. Acoustical Assn., Nat. Kitchen and Bath Assn. Baptist. Office: Hansa Am Inc 1100 Boone Dr Michigan City IN 46360

BAKER, DAVID SCOTT, finance administrator, consultant; b. Fresno, Calif., Jan. 19, 1946; s. Elton Murray and Letha (Mitts) B.; m. Carol Elise Rosenfeld, July 26, 1970; children: Scott, Emily. BA, U. Puget Sound, 1968; MBA, Oreg. State U., 1970. Project dir. Ernst & Whinney, Tacoma, 1970-71; contr. Quali-cast, Chehalis, Wash., 1971-73; instr. Centralia (Wash.) Community Coll., 1972; adminstr. fin. Met. Hosps., Portland, Oreg., 1973-80; accounts mgr. Emanuel Hosp., Portland, Oreg., 1976-77; adminstr. fin. Kerr Ctrs., Portland, 1980—. Active Hospice House, Inc.; Cath. Youth Orgn.; treas. Portland Youth Philharm.; chmn. Opera Assn.; Country Classic Run. Recipient Service Commendation, Dept. Human Service, U. Oreg., 1988. Mem. Am. Soc. Pub. Adminstrs., Healthcare Fin. Mgmt. Assn., Alpha Kappa Psi. Club: 20/30 International (v.p. 1983-85). Office: Kerr Ctrs 424 NE 22d St Portland OR 97232

BAKER, DEXTER FARRINGTON, manufacturing company executive; b. Worcester, Mass., Apr. 16, 1927; s. Leland Dyer and Edith (Quimby) B.; m. Dorothy Ellen Hess, June 23, 1951; children: Ellen L., Susan A., Leslie A., Carolyn J. B.S., Lehigh U., 1950, M.B.A., 1957. Sales engr. Air Products & Chems., Inc., Allentown, Pa., 1952-56, gen. sales mgr., 1956-57, dir., 1964—, group v.p., 1967-68, exec. v.p., 1968-78, pres., 1978-88, chmn., chief exec. officer, 1986—; mng. dir. Air Products, Ltd., 1957-67, dir., 1964-80. Bd. assocs. Muhlenberg Coll.; trustee Lehigh U., Harry C. and Mary M. Trexler Found. Served with USNR, 1945-46; with U.S. Army, 1950-52. Mem. Am. Mgmt. Assn., Am. Inst. Chem. Engrs., Soc. Chem. Industry, Asa Packer Soc. Lehigh U., Theta Chi. Presbyterian (elder). Office: Air Products & Chems Inc Box 538 Allentown PA 18105

BAKER, DONALD, lawyer; b. Chgo., May 28, 1929; s. Russell and Elizabeth (Wallace) B.; m. Gisela S. Carli, Oct. 6, 1960; children: Caryna, Andrew, Russell. Student, Deep Springs Coll., Calif., 1947-49; J.D.S., U. Chgo., 1954. Bar: Ill. 1955, N.Y. 1964. Ptnr. Baker & McKenzie, Chgo., 1955—; bd. dirs. Trimedyne, Inc., Pharmatec, Inc. Bd. dirs. exec. com. Mid-Am. Com., Chgo., 1980—. Mem. ABA, Ill. Bar Assn., Chgo. Bar Assn., Internat. Trade Club Chgo. (bd. dirs. 1982-84). Club: Michigan Shores (Wilmette, Ill.). Office: Baker & McKenzie 130 E Randolph St Chicago IL 60601

BAKER, ERIC E., venture capitalist; b. Spencerville, Ont., Can., Aug. 27, 1933; s. Herman E. and Flora S. (Shannon) B.; m. Ann E. Relyea, Aug. 1, 1955; children: Rebecca, Charles, Melanie. BSc, Queen's U., Kingston, Ont., 1956; MS, MIT, 1958. Registered engr. Chem. engr. Cities Service Oil Co., Toronto, 1958; chem. sales profl. to ops. mgr. plastics and chems. Union Carbide Can., Toronto, 1959-71; v.p. Innocan Inc., Montreal, Que., Can., 1972-84; pres. Althamira Capital Inc., Montreal, 1984—; chmn. bd. Innopac, Inc., Toronto, Memotec Data Inc., Montreal, Biomira, Inc., Edmonton, Alta., Can.

BAKER, FRANCIS ELLSWORTH, electronics company executive; b. N.Y., Dec. 20, 1929; s. Francis Ellsworth and Cynthia (Gibbs) B.; m. Patricia Barry, May 27, 1975 (div.); children: Lucy, Cynthia, Francis, John; m. Karen Jean Dyson, Nov. 28, 2975; stepchildren: Kimberly, Kristen. A.B. cum laude, Harvard U., 1951, M.B.A., 1955. Bus. cons. Arthur D. Little, Cambridge, Mass., 1955-58; pres. Ven Cap Inc., Boston, 1959; pres. Andersen Group, Bloomfield, Conn., 1959—, also various subs.; dir. Conn. Nat. Bank. Chmn. Govs. Commn. on Tax Reform, Gov.'s Strike Force. Served to lt. USNR, 1951-53. Mem. Conn. Water Service Mfrs. Assn. (bd. dirs.). Clubs: N.Y. Yacht, Harvard (N.Y.C.). Home: 495 Deercliff Rd Avon CT 06001 Office: Andersen Group 1280 Blue Hills Ave Bloomfield CT 06002

BAKER, FREDERICK LLOYD, III, computer company executive; b. Chgo., May 11, 1941; s. Frederick Lloyd and Suzanne Berkeley (Budge) B.; B.S., 1963; M.B.A. (Roswell C. McCrea scholar), Columbia U., 1965; m. Mary York Reidy, June 8, 1968; children—Frederick Lloyd, IV, Marian York, Timothy Maurice Carr. Pricing analyst IBM World Trade Corp., N.Y.C., 1966-70, IBM World Trade Asia Corp., Tokyo, 1970-73; fin. analyst IBM World Trade AFE Corp., Westchester, N.Y., 1973-76, strategic planning mgr., 1976-78, mgr. functional planning, 1979-80, mgr. fin. ops.-Americas, 1980-82, mfg. fin. mgr., 1982-84; mgr. mfg. fin. evaluation IBM World Trade Asia Corp., Tokyo, 1984—. Rep., Greenwich (Conn.) Town Meeting, 1976-84. Served with USNR, 1965-66. Republican. Presbyterian. Clubs: Riverside Yacht, S.R., Tokyo Lawn Tennis. Office: IBM World Trade Asia Corp, Shuwa Kamiyacho Bldg, 3-13 Toranomon 4-chome, Minato-ku Tokyo 105, Japan

BAKER, GLORIA BETH, sales executive; b. Lancaster, S.C., Aug. 28, 1942; d. James Benjamin Baker and Belle (Hinson) Schafer; m. Larry D. Edgar, Feb. 26, 1960 (div. 1976); children: L. Dean, Dana Elizabeth, Damon Scott; m. James Edward Kleinschmidt, Aug. 27, 1988. Student, U. S.C., 1975-76, Columbia Mus. Art, 1966-67. Loan officer Columbia (S.C.) U.S. Employees Fed. Credit Union, 1975-79; mgr. SRCE Fed. Credit Union, Columbia, 1978-79, Lexco Fed. Credit Union, Cayce, S.C., 1979-80; mgr. customer svc. dept. Info. Resources (subs. Citicorp N.Y.), Columbia, 1980-81, sales exec., 1981—, sr. sales exec., 1986—. Mem. Southeastern Regional Credit Union Sch. Alumnia Assn. (treas. 1984-89). Home: 125 Milway Rd Irmo SC 29063 Office: Citicorp Info Resources PO Box 2844 Columbia SC 29202

BAKER, GUY EUGENE, insurance executive; b. San Bernardino, Calif., Apr. 16, 1945; s. Luther Thomas and Kathlyn (Dodds) B.; m. Colleen Dee Hubbard, July 15, 1967; children: Stacie, Todd, Andrew, Ellen. BA in Econs., Claremont Coll., 1967; MBA in Fin., U. So. Calif., 1968; MS in Fin. Svcs., 1984, MS in Mgmt., 1985. Cert. fin. planner; CLU; chartered fin. cons. Salesman Pacific Mut. Ins., Newport Beach, Calif., 1966—; pres., founder Assocs. in Ins. Concepts, Newport Beach, 1977—; mng. ptnr. Baker-Thomsen Assocs., Newport Beach, 1986—; chmn. Bayly Martin & Fay Compensation Strategies, Costa Mesa, Calif., 1984-86. Contbr. articles in field to profl. jours. Named Agt. of Yr. Gen. Agts. and Mgrs. Assn., 1978. Mem. Internat. Assn. Fin. Planners, Million Dollar Round Table (mgmt. council 1983, Top of the Table 1977—), CLU Soc., Assn. Life Underwriters (bd. dirs. 1986—), Orange County Life Underwriters (pres. 1977), Mission Viejo (Calif.) Country Club, Univ. Athletic Club Newport Beach. Republican. Home: 30172 Branding Iron Rd San Juan Capistrano CA 92675

BAKER, HAROLD CECIL, architect, consultant; b. Wheeling, W.Va., June 23, 1954; s. Harold Cecil Jr. and Virginia Ann (Gonot) B.; m. Amy Jean Taylor, Aug. 23, 1975; children: Nathan Taylor, Kyle Thomas. BS in Architecture, Ohio State U., 1978, MArch, 1980. Registered profl. architect, Fla., Ga., Ind., Md., Mich., Mo., N.C., Ohio, Okla., Penn., R.I., S.C., Tenn., Tex., Va. Project architect William Gilfillen Architects, Columbus, Ohio, 1977-79; v.p. Solar Design Group, Columbus, 1979-84; v.p. retail architecture Nexus Am., Columbus, 1984-86; prin. Harold C. Baker, AIA, Inc., Columbus, 1986—. Author: Town Franklin Design Guidelines, 1978. Solar Energy grantee Dept. Housing and Urban Devel., Dublin, Ohio, 1978, Silver award Inst. Bus. Designers, Nexus Corp. Hdqrs., 1985, Excellence award Columbus Inst. Bus. Designers, 1985. Mem. AIA (environ. awareness com. Columbus chpt. 1983-86, critic liaison high sch. design competition 1983-84, co-chmn. hon. award com. 1983-84, chmn. 1984-85), Architects Soc. Ohio. Republican. Roman Catholic. Office: Harold C Baker AIA Inc 673 High St Suite 204 Worthington OH 43085

BAKER, JACKSON ARNOLD, container shipping company executive; b. Saltville, Va., May 1, 1938; s. Joseph Arnold and Katherine Kimmons (Seale) B.; m. Carolyn Josephine Cantrell, Dec. 27, 1957; children—Allison Kimmons, Elizabeth Arnold. B.S. in Indsl. Mgmt, Ga. Inst. Tech., 1960. Dock foreman Roadway Express, Atlanta, 1960-63; asst. terminal mgr. Waterman of P.R., Mobile, Ala., 1963-65; with Sea-Land Service, Inc., 1965—; v.p. west coast SeaLand Service, Inc., Seattle, 1972-75, exec. v.p. Alaska div., 1975-84; group v.p. Atlantic div. Sea-Land Service, Inc., Iselin, N.J., 1984-86, vice chmn., chief operating officer, 1986-87, pres., chief operating officer, 1987—; also bd. dir. Sea-Land Corp., Iselin, N.J. Office: Sea-Land Corp 10 Parsonage Rd PO Box 800 Iselin NJ 08830

BAKER, JAMES ADDISON, III, secretary of state; b. Houston, Apr. 28, 1930; s. James A. and Bonner (Means) B.; m. Susan Garrett, Aug. 6, 1973; 8 children. B.A., Princeton U., 1952; LL.B., U. Tex., 1957. Bar: Tex. 1957. Mem. firm Andrews, Kurth, Campbell & Jones, Houston, 1957-81; undersec. Dept. Commerce, Washington, 1975-76; deputy chmn. del. ops. Pres. Ford Com., Washington, 1976; campaign chmn. George Bush, 1979-80; sr. adviser Reagan-Bush Com., 1980-81; mem. Reagan Transition Team, Washington, 1980-81; chief of staff White House, Washington, 1981-85; sec. Dept. Treasury, 1985-88.; campaign chmn. George Bush's Presidential campaign, 1988; sec. Dept. of State, 1989—. Trustee Woodrow Wilson Internat. Center for Scholars, Smithsonian Inst., 1977—. Served with USMC, 1952-54. Mem. ABA, State Bar Tex., Houston Bar Assn.; mem. Am. Judicature Soc.; Mem. Phi Delta Phi. Office: Dept State Office of the Sec 2201 C St NW Washington DC 20520

BAKER, JAMES EDWARD SPROUL, lawyer; b. Evanston, Ill., May 23, 1912; s. John Clark and Hester (Sproul) B.; m. Eleanor Lee Dodgson, Oct. 2, 1937 (dec. Sept. 1972); children: John Lee, Edward Graham (dec. Aug. 1988). A.B., Northwestern U., 1933, J.D., 1936. Bar: Ill. 1936, U.S. Supreme Ct. 1957. Practice in Chgo., 1936—; assoc. Sidley & Austin, and predecessors, 1936-48, ptnr., 1948-81; of counsel Sidley & Austin, 1981—; lectr. Northwestern U. Law Sch., 1951-52; Nat. chmn. Stanford U. Parents Com., 1970-75; mem. vis. com. Stanford Law Sch., 1976-79, 82-84, Northwestern U. Law Sch., 1980-89, DePaul U. Law Sch., 1982-87. Served to comdr. USNR, 1941-46. Fellow Am. Coll. Trial Lawyers (regent 1974-81, sec. 1977-79, pres. 1979-80); mem. ABA, Bar Assn. 7th Fed. Circuit, Ill. State Bar Assn., Chgo. Bar Assn., Soc. Trial Lawyers Ill., Northwestern U. Law Alumni Assn. (past pres.), Order of Coif, Phi Lambda Upsilon, Sigma Nu. Republican. Methodist. Clubs: John Evans (Northwestern U.) (chmn. 1982-85); University (Chgo.); John Henry Wigmore (past pres.); Midday (Chgo.), Legal (Chgo.), Law (Chgo.) (pres. 1983-85); Westmoreland Country (Wilmette, Ill.). Home: 1300 N Lake Shore Dr Chicago IL 60610 Office: Sidley & Austin 1 First Nat Pla Chicago IL 60603

BAKER, JAMES KENDRICK, specialty metals manufacturing company executive; b. Wabash, Ind., Dec. 21, 1931; s. Donald Dale and Edith (Swain) B.; m. Beverly Baker, Apr. 11, 1959; children—Betsy Ann, Dirk Emerson, Hugh Kendrick (dec.). A.B., DePauw U., 1953; M.B.A., Harvard U., 1958. Regional sales mgr. Arvinyl div. Arvin Industries, Inc., Columbus, Ind., 1958-60; gen. mgr. div. Arvinyl div. Arvin Industries, Inc., 1960-68, v.p., 1966-68, exec. v.p., 1968-81, pres., chief exec. officer, 1981—, also dir.; dir. Ind. Bell Telephone Co., Indpls., Ind. Nat. Corp., Pub. Service Ind., Plainfield. Bd. dirs. Associated Colls. Ind., De Pauw U.; pres. Columbus Found. for Youth, 1965, United Way of Bartholomew County, 1979; bd. dirs. Vinyl-Metal Laminators Inst. div. Soc. for Plastics Industry, 1960—, pres., 1963-64; vice chmn. Ind. Republican Conv., 1966. Served with AUS, 1953-55. Named Outstanding Boss C. of C., 1965; recipient Disting. Service award Ind. Jr. C. of C., 1966, Disting. Community Service award Columbus Area C. of C., 1983; named One of 5 Outstanding Young Men of Ind., 1966. Mem. Columbus C. of C. (bd. dirs.), Ind. C. of C. (bd. dirs.). Clubs: Rotary, DePauw University Alumni (pres. 1974), Harrison Lake Country. Home: 12044 W State Rd 46 Deer Crossing Columbus IN 47201 Office: Arvin Industries Inc 1531 E 13th St Columbus IN 47201

BAKER, JOHN RUSSELL, utilities executive; b. Lexington, Mo., July 21, 1926; s. William Frederick and Flora Anne (Dunford) B.; m. Elizabeth Jane Torrence, June 16, 1948; children—John Russell, Burton T. B.S., U. Mo., 1948, M.B.A., 1962. With Mo. Public Service Co., Kansas City, 1948—; treas. Mo. Public Service Co., 1966-68, v.p. fin., 1968-71, sr. v.p., 1971-73, exec. v.p., 1973—, also dir.; dir. Boatmen's Bank, Lee's Summit; lectr. fin. U. Mo.; pres., dir. Utilicorp B.C. Vice-pres. Mid-Continent council Girls Scouts, U.S., 1981; adv. council Sch. Acctg., U. Mo., Columbia. Recipient Outstanding alumnus award Sch. Adminstrn. U. Mo., Kansas City, 1965. Mem. Tax Execs. Inst. (pres. Kansas City 1968), U. Mo. Sch. Adminstrn. Alumni Assn. (pres. 1965), Edison Electric Inst. Republican. Methodist. Clubs: Kansas City, Blue Hills Country. Home: 205 Oxford Ln Lee's Summit MO 64063 Office: Utilicorp United Inc 911 Main Kansas City MO 64105

BAKER, JOHN STEWART, III, banker; b. Orange, N.J., Sept. 9, 1946; s. John Stewart Jr. and Roxanna Virginia (VanSant) Baker Betts; m. Pamela Virginia Colbert, July 29, 1972; children: Virginia, Cornelia, John Stewart IV. BS, Washington and Lee U., 1968; MBA, U. North Fla., 1981. V.p. Atlantic Nat. Bank, West Palm Beach, Fla., 1971-78; sr. v.p. Fla. Nat. Bank, Jacksonville, 1978—; chmn. bd. Fla. Payment Systems, Inc., Orlando, 1987—. Mem. fin. com. United Way, 1987; bd. dirs. Duval City chpt. Am. Cancer Soc., 19886—. 1st lt. inf. U.S. Army, 1968-71, Vietnam. Mem. Nat. Corp. Cash Mgmt. Assn., San Jose Country Club, Ponte Vedra Club. Methodist. Office: Fla Nat Bank 225 Water St Jacksonville FL 32201

BAKER, KERRY ALLEN, proprietary drug company executive; b. Selmer, Tenn., Sept. 21, 1949; s. Austin Clark and Betty Ann (Brooks) B.; m. Ellen Fleming. BIE, Ga. Inst. Tech., 1971; MBA, Ga. State U., 1973; JD, Memphis State U., 1987. With dept. law State of Ga., 1971-73; div. engr. N.W. Ga. div. Gold Kist Inc., Ellijay, Ga., 1977-80; sr. mfg. engr. Plough, Inc., Memphis, 1980-82, mgr. indsl. engring., 1983-86; supr. mfg. engring., 1986—. Served to capt. U.S. Army, 1973-77. Decorated Order of St. Barbara. Mem. Inst. Indsl. Engrs., Am. Mgmt. Assn., Soc. Advancement Mgmt., Am. Inst. Plant Engrs., Soc. Am. Mil. Engrs., Scabbard and Blade, Sigma Phi Epsilon, Pi Delta Epsilon, Alpha Phi Omega, Phi Delta Phi. Baptist. Lodge: Masons. Home: 3548 Evening Light Dr Bartlett TN 38135 Office: Plough Inc 3030 Jackson Ave Box 377 Memphis TN 38151

BAKER, LESLIE FRANCIS, construction company executive; b. Sabetha, Kans., Oct. 7, 1923; s. Perley Ross and Dora Ethel (Case) B.; m. Florence Pickerill, May 29, 1945; (dec. Jan. 1966); children: Debra, Michael; m. Charlotte Ann Phelps, Dec. 6, 1968; children: Deborah, Alison. Student, U. N.Mex., 1941-42, Colo. State U., 1942-43. Supt. Weeks Constrn. Co., Albuquerque, 1947-50; pres. Baker Wylie Constrn., Albuquerque, 1950-53, Baker Constrn. Co., Albuquerque, 1953—. Chmn. N.Mex. and West Tex. Health and Welfare Fund, 1984-87, N.Mex. Labor and Indsl. Commn., 1979—. Served as 1st lt. U.S. Army, 1943-46. Mem. Associated Gen. Contractors Am. (bd. dirs. 1980—, pres. N.Mex. bldg. br. 1980-81, chmn. legis. com. 1981-87, SIR award 1983). Sigma Nu. Republican. Clubs: Albuquerque Country. Lodge Elks. Home: 3021 San Pablo NE Albuquerque NM 87110 Office: Baker Constrn Co Inc 8360 Corona Loop NE Albuquerque NM 87113

BAKER, LESLIE MAYO, JR., banker; b. Brunswick, Md., May 22, 1942; s. Leslie Mayo Sr. and Betty Jane (Rinker) B.; m. Suzanne Baldwin Borum, Dec. 19, 1964; children: Leslie Roderic, Benjamin Spencer, Leslie Margaret Cecil. BA in English Lit., U. Richmond, 1964; MBA, U. Va., 1969. With Wachovia Bank and Trust Co., Winston-Salem, N.C., 1969—, asst. v.p., 1972-73, v.p. gen. loan adminstrn. office, then v.p. loan adminstrn. office, 1973-74, v.p., mgr. internat. dept., 1974-77, sr. v.p., mgr. internat. dept., 1977-80, exec. v.p. div. exec. adminstrn., 1980—. Trustee Southeastern Ctr. Contemporary Art, Winston-Salem, 1988; trustee Colgate Darden Grad. Sch., Charlottesville, 1982—; bd. visitors U. N.C. Grad. Sch., Chapel Hill, 1988; trustee Summit Sch., Winston-Salem, 1988. Capt. USMC, 1964-67, Vietnam. Mem. Robert Morris Assocs. (sr. assoc. Phila. 1980—). Episcopalian. Office: 1st Wachovia Corp PO Box 3099 Winston-Salem NC 27150

BAKER, ROBERT, manufacturing company executive; b. Bridgeport, Conn., Sept. 28, 1940; s. Irwin Henry and Ann (Keane) Baker; m. Patricia Ann Turoczi; children—Scott Allen, Christopher Keane. BA, U. Conn., Bridgeport, 1962. Asst. sales mgr., advt. mgr. Henry G. Thompson Co., subs. Vt. Am. Corp., Branford, Conn., 1971-74, nat. sales mgr., 1975-77; pres., gen. mgr. Magna div. Vt. Am. Corp., Elizabethtown, Ky., 1977-82, v.p., 1982-84, pres., chief exec. officer, 1984—, also bd. dirs.; dir. Vt. America; bd. dirs. Craftsman, 1987—. Bd. dirs. Jr. Achievement, Elizabethtown, 1978-82; instr. Project Bus., Elizabethtown, 1981-82. Served with USAR, 1963-64. Mem. Am. Supply Machine Mfrs. Assn. (bd. dirs.), Specialty Tool and Fastener Distbrs. Assn., Louisville C. of C. Club: Audubon Country (Louisville). Home: 310 Hidden Oak Way Louisville KY 40222 Office: Vt Am Corp 100 E Liberty St Louisville KY 40202

BAKER, ROBERT EDWARD, financial corporation executive, lawyer; b. Albion, Mich., May 6, 1930; s. Robert Charles and Loretto A. (Barrett) B.; m. Mary Anne Mulcahy, Feb. 20, 1965. B.B.A., U. Mich., 1952, LL.B., 1955. Bar: Mich. 1956. Atty. legal dept. Chrysler Corp., Detroit, 1955-64; with Chrysler Fin. Corp., 1964—; dir. Chrysler Fin. Corp., Troy, Mich., 1969—, v.p. corp. fin., 1970-80, v.p. fin., gen. counsel, 1980-85, vice chmn. bd., 1985—; dir. Mich. Nat. Bank, Southeastern Adv. Bd., Detroit, 1987; dir.

Am. Fin. Services Assn., 1972—, chmn. exec. com., 1983-84, pres. assn., 1978-79. Trustee Comprehensive Health Services of Detroit, 1972—, chmn. bd., 1977—. Served with CIC AUS, 1955-57. Recipient Disting. Service award Am. Fin. Services Assn., 1981. Mem. ABA, State Bar Mich., Fin. Execs. Inst., Am. Assn. Sovereign Mil. Order of Malta. Roman Catholic. Club: Orchard Lake Country (Mich.). Home: 4327 Stoneleigh Rd Bloomfield Hills MI 48013 Office: Chrysler Fin Corp 901 Wilshire Dr Troy MI 48084

BAKER, ROBERT WOODWARD, airline executive; b. Bronxville, N.Y., Sept. 3, 1944; s. Richard Woodward and Dorothy Marilyn (Garett) B.; m. Martha Jane Hauschild, June 11, 1966; children: Richard Woodward, Robert Woodward, William Garrett, Suzanne. B.A., Trinity Coll., 1966; M.B.A., U. Pa., 1968. Dir. ramp services Am. Airlines, Inc., N.Y.C., 1973-76; asst. v.p. mktg. adminstrn. Am. Airlines, Inc., 1976-77; v.p. so. div. Am. airlines, Inc., Dallas, 1977-79; v.p. freight mktg. Am. Airlines, Inc., Dallas-Ft. Worth Airport, 1979-80; v.p. sales and advt. Am. Airlines, Inc., 1980-82, v.p. mktg. automation systems, 1982-85, sr. v.p. info. systems, 1985, sr. v.p. ops., 1985—; sr. v.p. AMR Corp., 1987—. Office: Am Airlines Inc PO Box 619616 Dallas-Fort Worth Airport TX 75261-9616

BAKER, RONALD RAY, food products executive; b. Ft. Dodge, Iowa, Dec. 21, 1943; s. Harold E. and Ann Lavone (Hamen) B.; m. Ruth M. Hogan, Dec. 18, 1965; children: Bonnie, Sara, Jessica, Vanessa. BS, Marquette U., 1966. Salesman Parker Pen, Milw., 1965-66; programmer AC Electronics, Oak Creek, Wis., 1966-68; mgr. Marathon Electric, Wausau, Wis., 1968-75; dir. mfg. systems Am. Motors Corp., Southfield, Mich., 1975-77; mgr. bus. systems Reliance Electric, Euclid, Ohio, 1977-80; v.p. Stouffer Corp., Solon, Ohio, 1980-83, Nestle Enterprises, Solon, 1984; sr. v.p. Nestle Foods Corp., Purchase, N.Y., 1985—; bd. dirs. Beich, Inc., Bloomington, Ill., Cains Coffee Co., Oklahoma City, Fidco, White Plains, N.Y., Line Distbn. Services, Purchase, MJB Rice Co., Union City, Calif. Bd. dirs. March of Dimes, White Plains, 1986—. Mem. Waccabuc Club, Chagrin Valley Country Club. Roman Catholic. Home: 21 Silverbrook Ridgefield CT 06877 Office: Nestle Foods Corp 100 Manhattanville Rd Purchase NY 10577

BAKER, ROY E., accountant, educator; b. Kansas City, Mo., Dec. 6, 1927; s. Roy E. and Gladys (Cramer) B.; B.S., U. Kans., 1956, M.B.A., 1957; D.B.A., Harvard U., 1962; m. Doris Younger, May 16, 1976; 1 dau., Susan. Instr., U. Kans., 1957-59; asst. prof. Cornell U., 1962-67; program dir. acctg. U. Mo., Kansas City, 1967-71, chmn. dept., 1972-77, dir. research, 1971-72, prof. acctg., 1970—; cons. in health care; seminar leader in acctg. field. Served with USN, 1944-48, 50-52. C.P.A., Kans. Mem. Am. Acctg. Assn., Fin. Execs. Inst., Nat. Assn. Accts., Am. Inst. C.P.A.s, Mo. Soc. C.P.A.s, Mo. Assn. Acctg. Educators, Beta Gamma Sigma, Beta Alpha Psi. Mem. Ch. Nazarene. Club: Optimist (life). Author: Cases in Auditing, 1969; Budgeting for Hospitals, 1971; contbg. editor: Accountants Handbook; contbr. articles to profl. jours. Home: 11701 Wornall Rd Kansas City MO 64114 Office: Univ Mo Sch Bus Pub Adminstrn Kansas City MO 64110

BAKER, STEPHEN MICHAEL, logistics manager; b. Ardmore, Okla., Feb. 11, 1945; s. Charles Frederick and Mary Agnes (Breen) B.; m. Kathryn Marie Looker, July 9, 1966 (div. May 1980); m. Judith Reitz-Baker, Dec. 1, 1980. BA, Ohio State U., 1968; MBA, Tulane U., 1973; postgrad., U.S. Internat. U., San Diego, 1982—. Cert. profl. logistician. Enlisted U.S. Army, 1968, advanced through grades to maj., 1983, resigned, 1977, with res., 1970—; sr. research ptnr. Gen. Dynamics, Pomona, Calif., 1978-79; mem. technical staff Hughes Aircraft, Fullerton, Calif., 1979-81; supr. Rockwell Internat., Downey, Calif., 1981-88; mgr. Navcom Def. Electronics, Inc., El Monte, Calif., 1988—. Decorated Bronze Star; named Employee of Month, Rockwell Internat., 1983, 86. Mem. Orange County Soc. Logistics Engrs. (chpt. chmn. 1986-88, vice chmn. ops. 1985-86, tech. vice chmn. 1984-85), Logistics Edn. Found. (v.p. fin. 1987-88, 88—), Soc. Logistics Engrs. (cert.), Nat. Mgmt. Assn. Home: 18272 Roberta Cir Huntington Beach CA 92646 Office: Navcom Def Electronics Inc 4323 Arden Dr El Monte CA 91731-1997

BAKER, THOMAS EDGAR, oil company executive, lawyer; b. South Bend, Ind., Jan. 11, 1931; s. William Roger and Ruth (Stoll) B.; m. Mary Katherine Nunes, May 12, 1931; children: William R., Mary R., Thomas E. Jr., John J., Anne E. BS cum laude, U. Notre Dame, 1953; LLB, Georgetown U., 1960, LLM, 1962; LLM in Taxation, NYU, 1965. Bar: Va. 1961, N.Y. 1964, Tex. 1972; CPA, D.C. Mem. staff SEC, 1958-63; atty. Shell Oil Co., N.Y.C and Houston, 1963-75; gen. atty. Shell Oil Co., Houston, 1975-80, asst. gen. counsel, 1980-84, corp. sec., 1984—. Trustee Village Croton-on-Hudson, N.Y., 1969-71; bd. dirs. Soc. Performing Arts, 1988—. Served to lt. (j.g.) USN, 1953-56. Mem. ABA (budget officer, bus. law sect.), Am. Arbitration Assn., Am. Law Inst., AICPA, Tex. State Bar Assn. (chmn., sec. corp. counsel 1982-83), Houston City Bar Assn. (chmn. corp. counsel sec. 1987-88), Tex. Bus. Law Found.

BAKER, THOMPSON SIMKINS, mining company executive; b. Jacksonville, Fla.,, Aug. 25, 1905; s. John Daniel and Julia (Simkins) B.; m. Cynithia L'Engle, Nov. 23, 1931 (dec. Dec., 1967); children: Sarah Church, Edward L'Engle, John Daniel II; m. Sarah Burroughs, Apr. 12, 1970. B.S., Davidson Coll., 1926. With Fla. Rock Industries, Inc.(formerly Shands & Baker, Inc.), Jacksonville, Fla., 1929—; chmn. Fla. Rock Industries, Inc. (formerly Shands & Baker, Inc.), Jacksonville, Fla., 1973—. Home: 4167 Ortega Blvd Jacksonville FL 32210 Office: Fla Rock Industries Inc 155 E 21st St Jacksonville FL 32206

BAKER, WILLIAM GEORGE, publishing company financial executive; b. Bklyn., July 23, 1935; s. George Francis and Martha Mary (Klostermann) B.; m. Marilyn Rose Emmons, Oct. 10, 1959; children: Steven, Paul. BBA magna cum laude, St John's U., Bklyn., 1957; MBA, Pace U., 1967. C.P.A., N.Y. Mgr. Arthur Andersen & Co., N.Y.C., 1957-63; asst. treas. Harper & Row Pubs., Inc., N.Y.C., 1963-69, compt., 1969-71, v.p., compt., 1971-86, sr. v.p., compt., 1986-88, group v.p., 1988—. Served to cpl. USMC, 1958-59. Mem. Am. Inst. C.P.A.s, Fin. Execs. Inst. Club: University (N.Y.C.). Lodge: Masons. Home: 19 Lewis Ln Port Washington NY 11050 Office: Harper & Row Pubs Inc 10 E 53rd St New York NY 10022

BAKER, WILLIAM HERBERT, insurance company executive; b. Buffalo, Oct. 23, 1932; s. Guy Andrew and Ella Mae (Beeler) B.; BS in Econs., Purdue U., 1954; postgrad. Ball State U., 1956-58, Rider Coll., 1980-82; children: Scott Andrew, Karen Lynn. Prodn. supr., safety dir., labor relations supr. Gen. Motors Corp., Muncie, Ind., New Brunswick, N.J., Anderson, Ind., 1956-69; dir. personnel mgmt. N.J. Hosp. Assn., Princeton, 1969-75, v.p., 1975-81; sr. v.p. Middle Atlantic Shared Svcs. Corp., 1982-86; v.p. Ctr. for Health Affairs Ins. Svcs., Inc., 1986-88, corp. v.p., chief op. officer, 1989—; mem. faculty hosp. sems. . Former mem., v.p. Montgomery Twp. Bd. Edn., pres., 1977-80; past bd. dirs. Am. Heart Assn. N.J. affiliate; officer, former bd. dirs. Princeton Area United Fund; bd. dirs. Hightstown (N.J.) YMCA, 1988—. With CIC, AUS, 1954-56. Mem. Am. Mgmt. Assn., Am. Hosp. Assn., Am. Soc. Hosp. Personnel Adminstrn. Lutheran. Home: 95 Meadow Dr Hightstown NJ 08520 Office: 760 Alexander Rd CN-1 Princeton NJ 08540

BAKER-LIEVANOS, NINA GILLSON, jewelry store executive; b. Boston, Dec. 19, 1950; d. Rev. John Robert and Patricia (Gillson) Baker; m. Jorge Alberto Lievanos, June 6, 1981; children: Jeremy John Baker, Wendy Mara Baker, Raoul Salvador Baker-Lievanos. Student Mills Coll., 1969-70; grad. course in diamond grading Gemology Inst. Am., 1983; student in diamondtology designation Diamond Council Am., 1986—. Artist, tchr., Claremont, Calif., 1973-78; escrow officer Bank of Am., Claremont, 1978-81; retail salesman William Pitt Jewelers, Puente Hills, Montclair, Calif., 1981-83, asst. mgr., Montclair, 1983, mgr., Santa Maria, Calif., 1983—, corp. sales trainer, 1988—. Artist tapestry hanging Laguna Beach Mus. Art, 1974. Recipient Cert. Merit Art Bank Am., 1968. Mem. NAFE, Internat. Platform Assn., C. of C., Compassion Internat. Republican. Roman Catholic. Avocations: tapestry weaving, creative writing. Office: William Pitt Jewelers 158 Towne Ctr Santa Maria CA 93454

BAKHRU, ASHOK NARAINDAS, paper company executive; b. Jhansi, India, Mar. 23, 1942; s. Naraindas Jethanand and Saraswati Bakhru; m. Fay Thomas, Aug. 17, 1968; children—Romy, Jay. B.Tech., Indian Inst. Tech., Bombay, 1963; M.Indsl. Engring., Cornell U., 1965. Ops. research analyst Western Electric Co., Princeton, N.J., 1965-67; adminstr. ops. research Celanese Plastics Co., Newark, 1967-69; with Scott Paper Co., Phila, 1969—, sr. v.p., chief fin. officer, 1985—; bd. dirs. Arkwright Mut. Ins. Co., Waltham, Mass., Fidelcor Capital Inc., Phila., Pa.; trustee Internat. House of Phila. Mem. Phila. Treas. Club (pres. 1985-86), Fin. Exec. Inst., Delaware Valley Chief Fin. Officers. Home: 14 Dogwood Ln Glen Mills PA 19342 Office: Scott Paper Co Scott Pla Philadelphia PA 19113

BAKKE, M. RUSSELL, software engineer; b. LaCrosse, Wis., Apr. 1, 1945; s. Victor S. and H. Esther (Flugstad) B.; m. Leslie Ronica Garrison, Oct. 5, 1985. BA, St. Olaf Coll., 1967; BSEE, Air Force Inst. Tech., 1973; MBA, U. Utah, 1976; MSEE, U. Bridgeport, 1981. Cert. profl. engr. Asst. v.p., engr. Trans-Lux Corp., Norwalk, Conn., 1978-85; mgr. software Comml. Telecommunications, Inc., Santa Maria, Calif., 1985-86, Rockwell-Collins, Santa Ana, Calif., 1986; programmer, analyst Digital Fantasies Ltd., Huntington Beach, Calif., 1986—. Capt. USAF, 1968-78. Mem. IEEE, Mensa.

BAKKER, JONATHAN BUSHNELL, banker; b. Bogotá, Colombia, South America, Sept. 2, 1945; came to U.S. 1956; s. Arthur and Mary Louise (Bushnell) B. BA, U. Ill., 1969; MA, U. Conn., 1972, PhD., 1978. spl. lectr. U. R.I. and U. Hartford, 1978-84. Banking officer Mellon Bank, N.A., Pitts., 1985-87; asst. treas. UBAF Arab Am. Bank, N.Y.C., 1987-89; asst. v.p. Generale Bank, N.Y.C., 1989—. Contbr. articles to profl. jours. Bd. dirs. Pitts. New Music Ensemble, 1986-87, chmn. fin. com., 1986-87. Mem. U.S. C. of C. (rep. 1985). Office: Generale Bank 12 E 49th St New York NY 10017

BALADI, ANDRE, economic and business consultant; b. Heliopolis, Egypt, Mar. 11, 1934; Swiss citizen; s. Albert and Laura-Elena (Ventura) B.; m. Adrienne-Sylvia Barben, 1958; children: Viviane, Sibyl, Alex. Student English Sch., Jesuit Coll. and French Lycée, Cairo, Egypt, 1939-52; faculty of Scis., Beirut, Lebanon, 1952-53; grad. Inst. Internat. Studies, Geneva U., Switzerland, 1957; postgrad. Brit. Inst. Mgmt., London, 1959, IMEDE (Harvard U. Bus. Sch. European Program), IMI (Internat. Mgmt. Inst.), Switzerland, 1974-77. During studies UNO press corr. and econ. adviser to UNO Delegation, Geneva, 1955-57; internat. exec. Nestlé Co., Europe, Asia and U.S., also in charge joint ventures with Exxon, Mitsui, etc, 1958-72; corporate devel. dir. Lesieur, Paris, 1973-74; dir. Interfinexa, Compagnie Internationale pour le Dével., founded by Banque Nationale de Paris, Smith Barney Harris Upham, and Société Financière Européenne (Algemene Bank Nederland, Banca Nazionale del Lavoro, Bank of Am., Banque Bruxelles Lambert, Barclays Bank, BNP, Dresdner Bank, Sumitomo Bank, Union Bank of Switzerland), Geneva, 1974-77; dir. Soc. Gen. de Surveillance, Geneva, 1977-79; founder Baladi & Co., Internat. Devel. Group, Geneva, 1980—; chmn. Association pour l'Arbitrage Internat. en matière de Commerce et d'Industrie; expert Cour pour l'Arbitrage Internat. en matière de Commerce et d'Industrie, Geneva; lectr. Geneva U., various European academic and bus. orgns. Contbr. articles on econs. to profl. jours.; patentee in computer scis. Mem. Acad. Soc. Geneva, Ctr. Applied Studies in Internat. Negotiations, Mgmt. Ctr. Europe (Am. Mgmt. Assn.), Swiss Am. C. of C.; others. Clubs: Am. Internat., La Nautique Yacht (Geneva); Metropolitan (N.Y.C.). Address: Baladi & Co, 8 rue Toepffer, CH-1211 Geneva 12, Switzerland

BALAK, WILLIAM MARTIN, banker; b. Omaha, Apr. 21, 1937; s. William James and Martha (Lodl) B.; m. Vivian Ann Neasloney, July 1, 1980; children: Rebecca, Adam Z. BA, Creighton U., 1961. V.p. Dun and Bradstreet Inc., L.A., 1961-78, Norwest Banks, Omaha, 1978-85; exec. v.p., dir. Occidental Nebr. Fed. Savs. Bank, Omaha, 1985—; bd. dirs. Nebr. League Savs. Instns. Bd. dirs. Omaha Metro YMCA, 1979—, chmn., 1983-85, pres., 1983; bd. dirs. Omaha Summer Arts, 1987; mem. adv. council U. Nebr., 1984, bd. dirs., 1984—; admiral Navy of Nebr., Lincoln, 1978. Recipient Addy award Omaha Fedn. Advt., 1984, Internat. Creative Competition award, 1986. Mem. Omaha Club, Highland Country Club. Republican. Roman Catholic. Home: 6716 S 148 Circle Omaha NE 68137

BALANIS, GEORGE NICK, electrical engineer; b. Athens, Greece, Oct. 7, 1944; came to U.S., 1963, naturalized, 1977; s. Nicholas G. and Mary (Traganoudaki) B.; m. Toula Koutis, Nov. 15, 1971; children—Nikolas, Thalassa. BS with honors, Calif. Inst. Tech., 1967, MS, 1968, PhD, 1972; MBA, UCLA, 1987. Research asst. Calif. Inst. Tech., Pasadena, 1968-71; staff scientist Applied Theory, Inc., Los Angeles, 1971-77, Arete Assocs., 1977-80; sr. engr. Garrett Airesearch, Torrance, Calif., 1980-89; pres. Anotek, Santa Monica, Calif.. Contbr. articles to profl. jours. Mem. IEEE, ASME, Soc. Indsl. and Applied Math., Am. Math. Soc., Am. Acad. Mechanics, Tau Beta Pi, Sigma Chi. Greek Orthodox. Home: 2702 11th St Santa Monica CA 90405

BALAS, DEBORAH ANN, securities trader; b. Pitts., Feb. 24, 1957; d. William Julius and Rita Mae (McCann) B.; m. Roy Robert Lippin, Aug. 24, 1985. Student, Oxford U., Eng., 1977-78; BA in Philosophy, Chatham Coll., 1979. Officer Pitts. Nat. Bank, 1979-81; asst. treas. Discount Corp. N.Y., N.Y.C., 1981-83; asst. v.p. Donaldson, Lufkin & Jenrette, N.Y.C., 1983-84; v.p. CIC-Union Europeenne Internat., N.Y.C., 1985—. Mem. Phi Beta Kappa. Office: CIC Union Europeenne 520 Madison Ave New York NY 10022

BALBACH, STANLEY BYRON, lawyer; b. Normal, Ill., Dec. 26, 1919; s. Nyle Jacob and Gertrude (Cory) B.; m. Sarah Troutt Witherspoon, May 22, 1944; children: Stanley Byron, Nancy Ann Balbach Fehr, Barbara Balbach Lariviere, Edith. B.S., U. Ill., 1940, LL.D., 1942. Bar: Ill. 1942, Fla. 1980, U.S. Supreme Ct. 1950, U.S. Ct. Appeals (7th cir.) 1961. Ptnr. Couchman & Balbach, Hoopeston, Ill., 1945-48, Webber & Balbach, Urbana, 1948-81, Balbach, Fehr & Hodson, Urbana, 1981—; chmn. Nat. Title Assurance Fund, Inc.; nat. chmn. Jr. Bar Conf., 1955; pres., bd. dirs. Atty.'s Title Guaranty Fund, Champaign, Ill. Contbr. articles to profl. pubis. Chancellor Cen. Ill. Conf. United Meth. Ch., 1972-77. Capt. USAAF, 1942-45. Mem. ABA (ho. of dels. 1956, 65, chmn. spl. com. lawyers title guaranty funds 1962-70, standing mem. 1982—, past mem. council, econs. and real property, probate and trust law sects.), Ill. Bar Assn., Ill. Trial Lawyers Assn., Am. Coll. Probate Counsel (state chmn. 1975-77), Am. Agrl. Law Assn., Am. Judicature Soc., Am. Coll. Real Estate Lawyers, Masons, Rotary, Union Club, Urban League, Champ Country Club, Phi Delta Phi, Alpha Kappa Lambda. Home: 1009 S Douglas St Urbana IL 61801 Office: Balbach Fehr & Hodson 102 E Main St Ste 301 PO Box 217 Urbana IL 61801-0217

BALBIRER, ANDREW GORDON, food company executive; b. Phila., June 30, 1954; s. Gerald J. and Barbara (Tanenbaum) B.; m. Terri Marlene Engel, May 30, 1976; children: Staci Leigh, Kate Michelle. BBA, U. Mo., 1976. CPA, Ill. Sr. auditor Arthur Andersen & Co., Chgo., 1976-79; contr. Allied Van Lines, Broadview, Ill., 1980-81; supr. fin. reporting G.D. Searle & co., Skokie, Ill., 1981-83, mgr. profit analysis Nutrasweet div., 1983-85; asst. contr. NutraSweet Co. (subs. Monsanto Co.), Skokie, 1985-87, contr., 1987-88, v.p. fin., 1988—. Mem. AICPA, Ill. Soc. CPA's, Fin. Execs. Inst. Office: Nutrasweet Co Box 730 1751 Lake Cook Rd Deerfield IL 60015

BALCOM, GLORIA DARLEEN, computer administrative and marketing consultant; b. Porterville, Calif., July 23, 1939; d. Orel A. and Eunice E. Stadtmiller; A.A., El Camino Coll., 1959; student computer sci. Harbor Coll., 1976-77; m. Orville R. Balcom, July 23, 1971; stepchildren—Cynthia Lou, Steven Raymond. Personnel trainee AiResearch div. Garrett Corp., Los Angeles, 1959-60, sales promotion adminstr., 1960-64; sales rep. Volt Temporary Services, El Segundo, Calif., 1965-69, mgr., Tarzana, Calif., 1969-71; co-owner, co-operator Brown Dog Engring., Lomita, Calif., 1972-77; pres., owner, cons. MicroSly Mktg., Lomita, 1977—. Mem. Ind. Computer Cons. Assn., Am. Soc. Profl. and Exec. Women, Nat. Assn. Female Execs. Club: Torrance Athletic. Home and Office: 24521 Walnut St Lomita CA 90717

BALDASSARI, DENNIS, utilities executive; b. Pottstown, Pa., May 3, 1949; s. John Anthony and Rita Ida (Pietropalo) B.; m. Eileen Lourdes Moyer, Mar. 18, 1972; children: Michelle, Dennis John, Kathryn. BS in Commerce and Engring., Drexel U., 1972. Mgr. fin. planning Gen. Pub. Utilities Service Corp., Parsippany, N.J., 1977-78, asst. treas., 1978-79; treas., corp. sec. Jersey Cen. Power & Light, Co., Morristown, N.J., 1979-83, v.p., treas., 1983—, also bd. dirs. Mem. Nat. Assn. Corp. Treas. Roman Catholic. Office: Jersey Cen Power & Light Co Madison Ave at Punch Bowl Rd Morristown NJ 07960

BALDERSTON, THOMAS WILLIAM, banker, corporate administrator; b. Phila., Feb. 28, 1941; s. Hugh Eastburn and Pauline (Schaaf) B.; BS, Pa. State U., 1963; MBA, U. So. Calif., 1973; m. Louise Talmage, June 5, 1971; children: Kristin Clark, Thomas Talmage. Mktg. rep. Rohm & Haas Co., Phila., 1966-72; asst. v.p. Warburg Paribas Becker Inc., N.Y.C., 1973-77; sr. v.p. Blyth Eastman Paine Webber Health Care Funding Inc., N.Y.C., 1977-81, also dir.; chmn. bd., pres., founder Health Care Capital Alliance, Inc., 1981—; pres., founder Retirement Ctrs. Group, Inc., 1983—; gen. ptnr. Heather Hills Ltd. Partnership, 1984—; co-founder, vice chmn. bd. Genesis Health Ventures, Inc., 1985—; chief exec. officer Retirement Ctr. Network (joint venture ITD Group, Inc. and Retirement Ctr. Group, Inc.), 1985—; dir. Americare Corp., Columbus, Ohio, 1984-86. Served to 1st lt. C.E., U.S. Army, 1963-65. Mem. Am. Hosp. Assn., Fedn. Am. Hosps., Am. Health Care Assn., Am. Assn. Homes for the Aging, Nat. Assn. Ind. Living Ctrs., Nat. Assn. Sr. Living Ind., Pi Kappa Phi. Republican. Clubs: Round Hill (Greenwich, Conn.); Riverside Yacht (Conn.), Boca West. Office: 19500 Planters Point Way Boca West Boca Raton FL 33431-0970 also: RCG 986 Bedford St Stamford CT 06905 also: HCCA 34 Lake Dr S Riverside CT 06878

BALDONADO, ORLINO CASTRO, engineering and technical services company executive; b. Sta. Maria, Ilocos Sur, Jan. 16, 1942; came to U.S., 1968; s. Ambrocio Soliven and Venancia (Castro) B.; m. Estrella DeLuna Castillo, Dec. 26, 1968; children: Omar Castillo, Erika Castillo. Student, U. Philippines, 1958-60; BS, UCLA, 1962, MS, 1963, PhD, 1968; postgrad., Calif. Inst. Tech., 1963-65. Project scientist Holmes & Narver, Inc., Anaheim, Calif., 1962-74; mgr. Mechanics Rsch., Los Angeles, 1974-75, Systems Devel. Corp., Mclean, Va., 1976-79; pres., chief exec. officer EC Corp., Knoxville, Tenn., 1980—. Contbr. numerous articles to profl. jours. Named Regional Minority Entrepreneur of Yr. Minority Bus. Devel. Agy. U.S. Dept. Commerce, 1986, State and Regional Minority Small Bus. Person of Yr., SBA, 1986, Small Bus. Person of Yr. for Tenn., 1987; Southeastern Regional Entrepreneur of Yr., Venture Mag., 1987, Minority Contractor of Yr. Dept. Energy, 1987, Minority Contractor of Yr. Fed. Govt., 1987. Mem. Venture Exch. Forum, Nat. Contract Mgmt. Assn., Am. Def. Preparedness Assn., U.S.-Pan Asian Am. C. of C. Roman Catholic. Office: EC Corp 10511 Hardin Valley Rd Knoxville TN 37932

BALDWIN, EVERETT NEWTON, food company executive; b. Syracuse, N.Y., May 30, 1932; s. Stanley Everett and Velma Newton B.; m. Carol Fournier, Dec. 23, 1967; children: Gary Everett, Kristen Gay. A.B., Colgate U., 1954; grad., Advanced Mgmt. Program, Harvard U., 1975. With Procter and Gamble, 1957-62, unit sales mgr. New Eng., 1959-62; with Hunt-Wesson Foods, 1962-66, regional sales mgr. West Coast, 1964-66; with Wm. Underwood Co., 1966-75, exec. v.p., 1973-75; v.p. sales and mktg. Grocery Products div. The Pillsbury Co., 1975-77; with Land O'Lakes Foods, Land O'Lakes Inc., Mpls., 1977-82; group v.p. Land O'Lakes Foods, Land O'Lakes Inc., 1977-82; pres., chief exec. officer, dir. Welch Foods Inc., Concord, Mass., 1982—; dir. Nihon Welch, KK, Wausau Service Corp. Harvard Grad. Sch. fund agt. Advanced Mgmt. Program, 1970; incorporator Emerson Hosp., Concord, Mass. Served to capt. USAF, 1954-57. Mem. Grocery Mfrs. Am. (dir.), Nat. Food Processors Assn. (bd. dirs.), Nat. Food Brokers Assn. (prin. adv. group), Concord C. of C. (bd. dirs.). Home: 93 Charlis Farm Rd Carlisle MA 01741 Office: Welch Foods Inc 100 Main St Concord MA 01742

BALDWIN, GEORGE HEISLER, JR., food distribution executive; b. Phila., Feb. 11, 1946; s. George Heisler Sr. and Eleanor (Hughes) B.; m. Deedie Lewter, June 8, 1968; children: Denise Nicole, Geoffrey Heisler. BA, U. Kans., 1968; MBA, LaSalle U., 1982. Mgr. prodn. Balford Farms Dairy, Phila., 1972-76; mgr. sales Nelsons Ice Cream Co., Royersford, Pa., 1976-78; mgr. zone sales Harbisons Dairy, Phila., 1978-80; v.p. Milk Industry Mgmt. Corp., Bensalem, Pa., 1980—. Activist Rep. Party, Bucks County, Pa., 1986; acolyte coordinator God's Love Luth. Ch., Newton, Pa., 1988—; bd. dirs. Woodedge Farms Homeowners Assn., New Hope, Pa., 1988—. Lt. col. USMCR, 1968—. Mem. Union League Phila. (sec. armed services com. 1988—), Com. for Employers Support of Guard and Res. Republican. Lutheran. Home: 3 Chestnut Ln New Hope PA 18938

BALDWIN, HENRY FURLONG, banker; b. Balt., Jan. 15, 1932; s. Henry du Pont and Margaret (Taylor) B.; divorced; children: Mary Stevenson, Severn Eyre. AB, Princeton U., 1954. With Merc.-Safe Deposit & Trust Co., Balt., 1956; v.p. Merc.-Safe Deposit & Trust Co., 1963-65, sr. v.p., 1965, exec. v.p., 1965-70, pres., 1970-76, chmn. bd., 1976—; pres., dir. Merc. Bankshares Corp., 1970-84, chmn. bd., 1984—; bd. dirs. Balt. Gas and Electric Co., Merc. Safe Deposit & Trust Co., USF&G Corp., Flow Gen., Inc., Consol. Rail Corp., Wills Group, Inc., Constellation Holdings, Inc. Trustee Johns Hopkins U., Johns Hopkins Hosp. Served with USMCR, 1954-56. Office: Merc Bankshares Corp 2 Hopkins Pla PO Box 1477 Baltimore MD 21203

BALDWIN, LARELL HARDISON, insurance company executive; b. Hanford, Calif., May 12, 1940; s. Leo H. and Bernice (Gash) B.; m. Kathleen L. Hardison, June 23, 1979; children: Jennifer Lin, Leslie Kari, Richard Allen, Michael Maxwell. Student Pasadena Coll., 1958-61; grad. Alexander Hamilton Inst. Bus., 1967. V.p. mortgage lending div. Standard Life & Accident Ins. Co. of Okla., Phoenix, 1961-64; sales mgr. Peterson Baby Products Inc., Burbank, Calif., 1964-67; v.p. sales Rotorway Aircraft Corp., Tempe, Ariz., 1967-69; pres. Trans World Arts Inc., San Jose, Calif., 1969-75, Baldwin Assocs. Devel. Corp., Santa Cruz, Calif., 1975-80; ptnr., v.p. Assurance Distbg. Co. Ltd., Santa Ana, Calif., 1979-82; pres. Baldwin Assurance Mktg. Corp., 1982—; nat. cons. ins. cos., author, lectr.; bd. dirs. Am. Acrylic Industries. Author in field. Office: Baldwin Assurance Mktg Corp PO Box 66972 Scotts Valley CA 95066

BALES, WILLIAM BAXTER, transportation company executive; b. McAlpin, W.Va., Feb. 5, 1935; s. Charles Woodrow and Thelma (Hite) B.; m. Marga Larson, Jan. 9, 1960; children: Marna, William II, Charles. BS, Marshall U., 1957; student in law, U. Richmond, 1960-62. With Norfolk and Western Ry. Co., 1962-79; v.p. coal and ore traffic Norfolk So. Corp., Roanoke, Va., 1982—; v.p. Pocahontas Devel. Corp., Bluefield, W.Va., Pocahontas Land Corp.; bd. dirs., v.p. Norfolk So. Marine Services, Lamberts Point Barge Co., Inc., Bituminous Coal Research, Inc. Mem. Va. Dist. Export Council, Richmond, 1981—; bd. dirs. Roanoke Symphony Soc., 1986—, Roanoke County Sesquicentennial, 1988, United Way Roanoke Valley, 1988—. Served to capt. U.S. Army, 1957-59. Mem. Va. Mining and Reclamation Assn. (bd. dirs. 1988), Internat. Energy Agy. (assoc., Mem. coal industry adv. bd. 1986—), Vieging Coal and Energy Rsch and Devel. Com. (adv. bd. 1989—). Republican. Presbyterian. Clubs: The Sky (N.Y.); The Harbor (Norfolk); Hunting Hills Country (Roanoke), Waters Edge Country. Office: Norfolk So Corp 204 S Jefferson St Roanoke VA 24042-0070

BALICH, NICHOLAS SAMUEL, mining company executive; b. Bisbee, Ariz., Dec. 19, 1936; s. Samuel Steven and Noddie S. (Porobich) B.; m. Diana Houston Ragle, Sept. 11, 1969; children: Debra, Shannon, Barbara, Nicole, Sam, Stephanie. BSBA, U. Ariz., 1960. Underground mine and carpenter shop Copper Queen br. Phelps Dodge Corp., Bisbee, Ariz., 1955-56, chief acct., 1970-74; internal auditor Western Hdqrs. Phelps Dodge Corp., Douglas, Ariz., 1963-68; constrn. acct. Phelps Dodge Corp., Tyrone, N.Mex., 1968-70; asst. controller Phelps Dodge Corp., Douglas, 1974-79, controller Western ops, Western Hdqrs., 1979-87, v.p., 1987—; acct. Bisbee Daily Rev., 1961-63. Co-chairperson Ariz. Kidney Found., Phoenix, 1986-87, treas., 1985-86, bd. dirs., 1982—; mem. various coms. Sunkist Fiesta Bowl, Phoenix, 1985—; active, United Way; bd. dirs. Ariz. Theatre Co., Phoenix, 1987-88, mem. devel. com., 1988; mem. Phoenix Together, Valley Citizens League, Valley Contbns. Assn.; bd. dirs. Boys/Girls Clubs, 1989—. Mem. Ariz. Mining Assn. (chmn. tax com.), Ariz. Tax Rsch. Assn. (pres.

1988-89, 2nd v.p. 1987-88, fin. com. chmn. 1986-87), Wildcat U. Ariz., Ariz. C. of C. (tax com., 1989, bd. dirs. 1989—), Masons, Shriners, Elks, Sigma Alpha Epsilon. Republican. Mem. Serbian Orthodox Ch. Home: 5425 E Cholla St Scottsdale AZ 85254 Office: Phelps Dodge Corp 2600 N Central Ave Phoenix AZ 85004-3014

BALIKOV, HENRY R., lawyer; b. Bayshore, N.Y., May 23, 1946; s. Harold and Esther (Chernow) B.; m. Mary L. McMahon, 1976; children: Benjamin, Molly, Samuel. BA, Grinnell Coll., 1967; JD, U. Chgo., 1971. Bar: Ill. 1971, U.S. Supreme Ct. 1976. Adminstrv. asst. to chmn. Ill. Pollution Control Bd., 1972-73; enforcement atty. U.S. EPA, 1973-75, chief legal br., 1975-77; environ. counsel J.M. Huber Corp., 1977-79, govt. rels. counsel, Edison, N.J., 1979—; of counsel Synthetic Amorphous Silica and Silicates Industry Assn., 1985—; mem. Synthetic Amorphous Silica and Silicates Industry Assn., 1980—. Mem. Nat. Cooling Lake Policy Com., 1974-75, Nat. Noise Enforcement Adv. Com., 1975-76, Nat. Water Enforcement Policy Group, 1976-77, Hazardous Waste Treatment Coun., 1985-87. Recipient EPA Bronze medal, 1975; named one of Outstanding Young Men of Am. Nat. Jaycees, 1976; U.S. Congl. fellow, 1977. Mem. ABA, Ill. State Bar Assn., N.J. Assn. Corp. Counsel, AAAS, N.Y. Acad. Sci., Nat. Limestone Inst. (chmn. environ. com. 1983), Hazardous Material Control Rsch. Inst., Carbon Black Industry Com. for Environ. Health. Home: 304 Evergreen Dr Moorestown NJ 08057 Office: J M Huber Corp 333 Thornall St Edison NJ 08818

BALL, BEN CALHOUN, JR., management consultant, educator; b. Dallas, June 1, 1928; s. Ben C. Sr. and Kate (Mayers) B.; m. Helen Jean Moss, June 25, 1949; children: Jan, Mary, Barbara. BS, MIT, 1948, MS, 1949. V.p. Gulf Oil Corp., Pitts., 1949-78; faculty prin. MAC (Mgmt. Analysis Ctr.) Group Inc., Cambridge, Mass., 1978—; pres. Ball & Assocs., Cambridge, Mass., 1978—; vis. lectr., adj. prof. mgmt. and engring. MIT; vis. research fellow Ctr. for Policy Alternatives; vis. scientist engring., dir. integrated energy systems project MIT; chmn. energy modelling forum's working group Stanford U; mem. adv. com. U. Tex. Contbg. editor: Petroleum Management Mag.; author The Energy Aftermath: Blunders, Lessons & Prospects, 1989; contbr. numerous articles to profl. jours. Home: 1811 Trapelo Rd Waltham MA 02154 Office: Ball & Assocs PO Box 158 Cambridge MA 02142

BALL, BLAIR EVAN, mortgage company executive, consultant; b. Chgo., Sept. 7, 1954; s. John Roger and Dorothy Ruth (Boettcher) B.; m. Christi Ann O'Connor; 1 child, Blair Evan Jr. BBA in Mgmt., U. Okla., 1976. Mgr. Ken's Restaurant, Tulsa, 1976; production control staff R.R. Donnelley and Sons, Chgo., 1977-78; ptnr. Name Cons., Houston, 1978; adminstr., mktg. mgr. Xerox, Houston, 1978-83; loan officer Chase Manhattan Bank, Houston, 1983-84; v.p. Amerifirst Mortgage Corp., Houston, 1984-86, Meracor Mortgage, Houston, 1986—; chmn., chief exec. officer Flamingo Aviation, Inc., Houston, 1987—; pres. Quality Mortgage Service, Houston, 1986, Blair Ball & Assocs. Mem. Theatre Under the Stars. Mem. Mortgage Bankers Am. (polit. action com.), Greater Houston Assn. Mortgage Brokers (founder, pres., bd. dirs.), Dallas/Ft. Worth Mortgage Brokers Assn. (founder), Tex. Assn. Mortgage Brokers (founder), Nat. Assn. Mortgage Brokers (nominating com.), Nat. Sales and Mktg. Council, Tex. Mortgage Bankers (mortgage ins. com.), Houston Mortgage Bankers, Greater Houston Builders (golf champion 1985-86), Houston C. of C., Am. Biog. Inst., Positive Thinkers Club of Am. (founder Houston chpt.). Republican. Lutheran. Clubs: Toastmasters, Univ. (Houston), Westlake Fitness (fall fitness champion 1986, 87); Xerox Pres. Home: 15430 Rio Plaza Dr Houston TX 77083 Office: N Am Mortgage Co 900 Threadneedle #400 Houston TX 77079

BALL, CHARLES STEVEN, marketing professional; b. Columbus, Miss., June 10, 1960; s. Johnny Charles and Polly (Cannon) B.; m. Sharon Kaye Deadwyler, Aug. 6, 1983. BA, Samford U., 1982. Area sales rep. RJR/Nabisco Inc., Huntsville, Ala., 1982-84; asst. mktg. research Connections Inc., Birmingham, Ala., 1984-85; mktg. rsch. mgr. U. Ala. Hosps., 1985-86; dir. mktg. Univ. Credit Union, Birmingham, 1986—. Contbr. articles to profl. jours. Active Big Bros./Big Sisters, Birmingham, 1985-86. Mem. Am. Mktg. Assn., Pub. Relations Soc. Am., Pub. Relations Council Ala. Republican. Baptist. Home: 5208 Logan Dr Birmingham AL 35242 Office: Univ Credit Union 1117 14th St S Birmingham AL 35205

BALL, GEORGE L., securities company executive; b. Evanston, Ill.. B.A., Brown U. Pres. E. F. Hutton Group Inc. and E. F. Hutton & Co., N.Y.C., 1969-82; pres., chief exec. officer Prudential-Bache Securities, N.Y.C., 1983-86, chmn. and chief exec. officer, 1986—, also dir. Trustee Brown U.; mem. Presdl. adv. council Pvt. Sector Initiative; mem. bus. com. Met. Mus. Arts.; dir. Paper Mill Playhouse (the State Theatre of N.J.); bd. overseers Duke Comprehensive Cancer Ctr.; trustee Joint Council Econ. Edn.; chmn. Deafness Rsch. Found.; nat. trustee Nat. Symphony Orch.; trustee S. St. Seaport Mus. Mem. Securities Industry Assn., Bond Club N.Y. (v.p.). Office: Prudential-Bache Securities 199 Water St New York NY 10292

BALL, JAMES HERINGTON, lawyer; b. Kansas City, Mo., Sept. 20, 1942; s. James T. Jr. and Betty Sue (Herington) B.; m. Wendy Anne Wolfe, Dec. 28, 1964; children: James H., Steven Scott. AB, U. Mo., 1964; JD cum laude, St. Louis U., 1973. Bar: Mo. 1973, Ohio, 1976. Asst. gen. counsel Anheuser-Busch, Inc., St. Louis, 1973-76; v.p., gen. counsel, sec. Stouffer Corp., Solon, Ohio, 1976-83; sr. v.p., gen. counsel, sec. Nestle Enterprises, Inc., Solon, 1983—, Nestle Holdings, Inc., Wilmington, Del., 1984—. Editor-in-chief St. Louis U. Law Jour., 1972-73. Served to lt. comdr. USN, 1964-70, Vietnam. Mem. Ohio Bar Assn., Mo. Bar Assn. Office: Nestle Enterprises Inc 5757 Harper Rd Solon OH 44139

BALL, JAMES WILLIAM, check cashing company executive; b. Tacoma, June 23, 1942; s. Montgomery McKinley and Ann Marie Ball; m. Patricia Miller, July 29, 1977; children: Katherine Kendall, Molly Elizabeth. Student, St. Martin's Coll., Lacy, Wash., 1960-61, San Jose City Coll., 1966-68; BA, San Jose State U., 1970, MA, 1971; postgrad., U. Calif., Irvine, 1971-72. Store mgr. Food Villa Inc., San Jose, Calif., 1972-76; asst. mgr. Ralph's Inc., San Jose, 1976-78; pres., owner Ball Liquors Inc., San Jose, 1978-88; pres. Fast Cash Inc., San Jose, 1984—. Mem. Calif. Check Cashers Assn. (v.p. 1988—). Office: Fast Cash Inc 4110 Monterey Hwy San Jose CA 95111

BALL, ROY ORVILLE, engineer, educator; b. Washington, Oct. 24, 1945; s. Rura O. and Dorothy R. (Toynton) B.; m. Jacqueline Sue Childress, Apr. 4, 1970; children—Christian, David. B.S. in Civil Engring., U. Fla., 1967; M.S. in Environ. Engring., U. Tex., 1972; Ph.D., U. Del., 1976. Registered profl. engr., Del., Minn., Iowa, Ill. Facilities engr. U.S. Armor Ctr., Fort Knox, Ky., 1967-69; IBM, Fishkill, N.Y., 1970-71; environ. engr. DuPont, Newark, Del., 1972-77; asst. prof. engring. U. Tenn., Knoxville, 1978-80; mgr. process design Roy F. Weston, West Chester, Pa., 1980-81; prin. ERM, Chgo., 1981—; adj. faculty mem. Villanova U (Pa.), 1980, Drexel U., Phila., 1980. Co-author: Engineers Guide to Hazardous Waste Management, 1985. Contbr. articles to profl. publs. Holy Cross Sch. Bd., 1987—. Served to 1st lt. U.S. Army, 1968-69. Davis fellow, 1975-77. Mem. Holy Cross Sch. Bd., Deerfield, Ill., Am. Inst. Chem. Engrs., Air Pollution Control Assn., Water Pollution Control Fedn. Republican. Avocations: piano; chess. Home: 1130 Knollwood Deerfield IL 60015 Office: ERM-N Central Inc 102 Wilmot Rd Ste 300 Deerfield IL 60015

BALLA, (FERENC) BULCSU, hospital manager, clinical engineer; b. Budapest, Hungary, Feb. 23, 1934; came to U.S., 1977; naturalized, 1982; s. Jozsef and Maria (Balogh) B.; m. Gloria Male, Sept. 15, 1986. Diploma in Electronic Tech., MUM 13 Tech. Coll., Budapest, 1961; BSEE, KKMF Tech. Coll., Budapest, 1967. Electronic technician Orion TV-Radio Co., Budapest, 1959-63; dir. electronic instrument and customer service dept. HTSZ Co., Budapest, 1963-72; mgr. electronic instrument service dept. HIKI Co., Budapest, 1972-74; tech. mgr. GELKA Co., Budapest, 1974-76; clin. engr., mgr. clin. engring. Ill. Masonic Med. Ctr., Chgo., 1979—. With Hungarian Armed Forces, 1954-56. Mem. Assn. for the Advancement of Med. Instrumentation (cert. biomed. equipment technician 1982, cert. clin. engr. 1985). Republican. Buddhist. Home: PO Box 25500 Chicago IL 60625 Office: ILL Masonic Med Ctr 836 W Wellington Chicago IL 60657

BALLAM, SAMUEL HUMES, JR., retired corporate director; b. Phila., Apr. 12, 1919; s. Samuel Humes and Mary (McGarvey) B.; m. Dorothy Meadowcroft, May 1, 1943; children—Barbara J. Ballam Stephens, Samuel H., III. A.B., U. Pa., 1950; A.M.P., Harvard Bus. Sch., 1959. Fin. analyst Fidelity Bank, Phila., 1936-41, 46-48; investment officer Fidelity Bank, 1948-55, asst. to pres., 1955-56, v.p. br. system, 1956-60, sr. v.p. trust dept., 1960-66, exec. v.p. comml. dept., 1966-71; pres. Fidelcor, Inc., Phila., 1971-78; chief exec. officer Fidelcor, Inc., 1975-78; chmn. Am. Water Works Co., Inc., , 1985-88; dir. numerous corps. Life trustee U. Pa., Phila., 1970—; chmn. bd. dirs. Hosp. U. Pa., 1976-87; bd. dirs. Zool. Soc. Phila., 1978—, Balch Inst. for Ethnic Studies, Phila., 1964—, Geog. Soc. Phila., 1976—. Served to capt. USAF, 1951-52. Republican. Episcopalian. Clubs: Union League (v.p., dir.), Phila.; Merion Cricket. Home: 74 Middle Rd Bryn Mawr PA 19010 Office: Am Water Works Co Inc 1025 Laurel Oak Rd Voorhees NJ 08043

BALLANCE, ROBERT MICHAEL, manufacturing executive; b. Raleigh, N.C., Oct. 10, 1957; s. Robert Columbus and Elizabeth (Cyrus) B. AA, Louisburg Jr. Coll., 1977; BSME, N.C. State U., 1981; MBA, Duke U., 1988. Mfg. engr. Square D. Co., Knightdale, N.C., 1981-83; mech. process engr. Internat. Tel. & Tel., Raleigh, 1983-84, nat. acct. sales engr., 1984-85, sr. mgr. engr., 1985-86, mgr. contract assembly, 1986-87; chief adminstr. Holland Eye Clinic, Louisburg, N.C., 1987-88; purchasing engr. Raychem Corp, Fuquay-Varina, N.C., 1989—; pres. Gateway Labs., Louisburg, 1987-88; cons. Wake Forest (N.C.) Eye Clinic, 1987-88, East Wake Eye Clinic, Zebulon, N.C., 1987-88. Advisor Jr. Achievement, Knightdale, 1982; coach Capital Area Coccer League, Raleigh, 1986; v.p. Greencroft Nature Conservancy. Mem. N.C. Trail Assn. Republican. Home: 3628 Bond St Raleigh NC 27604

BALLANFANT, KATHLEEN GAMBER, newspaper executive, public relations company executive; b. Horton, Kans., July 11, 1945; d. Ralph Hayes and Audrey Lavon (Heryford) G.; m. Burt Ballanfant; children: Andrea, Benjamin. BA, Trinity U., 1967; postgrad. NYU, 1976, Am. Mgmt. Inst., 1977, Belhaven Coll., 1985. Pub. info. dir. Tex. Dept. Community Affairs, Austin, 1972-74; pub. affairs mgr. Cameron Iron Works, Houston, 1975-77, Assoc. Builders and Contractors, Houston, 1982-84; pres. Ballanfant & Assoc., Houston, 1977-82, 84—; pres. Village Life Inc., 1985—; pres., chief exec. officer Village Life Publs.; owner Village Life newspaper, Southwest Life newspaper, Houston Observer/Times newspaper, Village Life Printing & Typesetting; mem. adv. council on Construction Edn., Tex. So. U., Houston, 1984—; mem. task force on ednl. excellence Houston Ind. Sch. Dist., 1983—; mem. devel. bd. Inter First Fannin Bank, 1986-88. Author: Something Special-You, 1972, Prevailing Wage History in Houston, 1983; editor newspaper Bellaire Texan, 1981-82, Austin Times, 1971. Vice pres. West Univ. Republic Women's Club, Houston, 1984—; fgn. vis. chmn. Internat. Inst. Edn., Houston, 1980—; docent Houston Zoo, 1982. Named Tex. Woman of Achievement Tex. Womans Hosp., 1986; recipient Apollo IX Medal of Honor Gov. Preston Smith, 1970, Child Abuse Prevention award Gov. Dolph Briscoe, 1974, Tex. Community Newspaper Assn. (pres. 1988—, bd. dirs. 1987—). Mem. Bellaire C. of C. (bd. dirs. 1987—, sec., treas. 1988). Republican. Presbyterian. Lodge: Rotary. Avocations: traveling, racquetball, reading. Office: Ballanfant & Assoc 2514 Tangley Houston TX 77005

BALLANTINE, MORLEY COWLES (MRS. ARTHUR ATWOOD BALLANTINE), newspaper publisher; b. Des Moines, May 21, 1925; d. John and Elizabeth (Bates) Cowles; m. Arthur Atwood Ballantine, July 26, 1947 (dec. 1975); children—Richard, Elizabeth Ballantine Leavitt, William, Helen Ballantine Healy. A.B., Ft. Lewis Coll., 1975; L.H.D. (hon.), Simpson Coll., Indianola, Iowa, 1980. Pub. Durango (Colo.) Herald, 1952—, editor, pub., 1975-83, editor, chmn. bd., 1983—; dir. 1st Nat. Bank, Durango, 1976—, Des Moines Register & Tribune, 1977-85, Cowles Media Co., 1982-86. Mem. Colo. Land Use Commn., 1975-81, Supreme Ct. Nominating Commn., 1984—; mem. Colo. Forum, 1985—, Blueprint for Colo., 1985—; pres. S.W. Colo. Mental Health Ctr., 1964-65, Four Corners Opera Assn., 1983-86; mem. Colo. Forum, 1985—; bd. dirs. Colo. Nat. Hist. Preservation Act, 1968-78; trustee Choate/Rosemary Hall, Wallingford, Conn., 1973-81, Simpson Coll., Indianola, Iowa, 1981—, U. Denver, 1984—, Fountain Valley Sch., Colorado Springs, 1976—. Recipient 1st place award for editorial writing Nat. Fedn. Press Women, 1955, Outstanding Alumna award Rosemary Hall, Greenwich, Conn., 1969, Outstanding Journalism award U. Colo. Sch. Journalism, 1967, Distinguished Service award Ft. Lewis Coll., Durango, 1970; named to Colo. Community Journalism Hall of Fame, 1987. Mem. Nat. Soc. Colonial Dames, Colo. Press Assn. (bd. dirs. 1978-79), Colo. AP Assn. (chmn. 1966-67), Federated Women's Club Durango. Episcopalian. Club: Mill Reef (Antigua, W.I.) (bd. govs. 1985—). Address: care Herald PO Drawer A Durango CO 81302

BALLARD, LOWELL DOUGLAS, mechanical engineer; b. Seiling, Okla., June 27, 1933; s. Auty Wayne and Mabel (Henderson) Haynes; B.S., U. Md., 1962. Mech. engr. Rabinow Inc., Rockville, Md., 1962; mech. engr. Nat. Bur. Standards, 1962-82; export licensing officer Dept. Commerce, Washington, 1981-88; cons., 1989—; panel mem. Nat. Elec. Code, 1975 edit.; chmn. Joint Bd. on Sci. and Engring. Edn., 1981-82. Vice pres. South Townhouse Assn., 1974-77, pres., 1978. Served with USAF, 1954-58. Fellow Washington Acad. Sci.; sr. mem. IEEE; mem. Am. Def. Preparedness Assn., Philos. Soc. Washington, Optical Soc. Am. Presbyterian. Club: Toastmasters (area gov. 1981-82). Home: 7823 Mineral Springs Dr Gaithersburg MD 20877

BALLARD, ROGER K., treasurer; b. Bethesda, Ohio, Dec. 2, 1935; s. Glenn E. and Marie (Kirkpatrick) B.; m. Evelyn Eberts, Jan. 22, 1956; children: Cheryl Ballard James, David. BBA, Franklin U., 1967. Various positions Battelle Meml. Inst., Columbus, Ohio, 1953—, asst. treas. Mem. Fin. Execs. Inst. Republican. Home: 66 Berkeley Pl N Westerville OH 43081 Office: Battelle Meml Inst 505 King Ave Columbus OH 43201

BALLENGER, HURLEY RENÉ, electrical engineer; b. Jacksonville, Ill., Nov. 26, 1946; s. Leonard Hurley and Katherine Natalie (Daniel) B.; m. Sandra Ann Rubley, Dec. 9, 1986. Student, Ill. Coll., 1964-65, 75. Technician electronics div. Hughs Aircraft, Inc., Tucson, 1973; maintenance supr. Fiatallis N.Am., Springfield, Ill., 1973-75, project engr., 1975-83, plant engr., 1983-86; tech. advisor CNC/CAM Fiatallis Europe, Lecce, Italy, 1986-87; plant engr. Illini Tech., Inc., Springfield, Ill., 1988, mgr. mfg. engring., 1988—. Mem. career adv. bd. Lincoln Land Community Coll., Springfield, 1983-85. Served to staff sgt. USAF, 1965-72, Vietnam. Mem. Constrn. Industry Mfrs. Assn. (mem. energy com.). Lutheran. Office: Illini Tech Inc 615 E Kimble St Springfield IL 62703

BALLHAUS, WILLIAM FRANCIS, engineering executive; b. San Francisco, Aug. 15, 1918; s. William Frederick and Eva Rose Callero (O'Connor) B.; m. Edna Dooley, Feb. 13, 1944; children: William Francis, Katherine Louise, Martin Dennis, Mary Susan. AB, Stanford U., 1940, ME, 1942; PhD, Calif. Inst. Tech., 1947; LLD (hon.), Pepperdine U., 1980. Registered profl. engr. Aerodynamicist, structures engr. and preliminary design engr. Douglas Aircraft Inc., El Segundo, Calif., 1942-50; chief preliminary design engr. Convair, Ft. Worth, 1950-53; Mem. tech. adv. panel on aeros. Office Sec. Def., 1954-60; mem. NACA, 1954-57; chief engr. Northrop Aircraft, Hawthorne, Calif., 1953-57, v.p., gen. mgr. Nortronics div., 1957-61; exec. v.p., dir. Northrop Aircraft, Beverly Hills, Calif., 1961-65; pres. Beckman Instruments, Inc., Fullerton, Calif., 1965-83, chief exec. officer, 1983-84; bd. dirs. Northrop Corp., Union Oil Co. Calif., Republic Automotive Parts, Inc.; cons. Office of Critical Tables, Nat. Acad. Scis., 1958-65. Trustee Northrop U., Harvey Mudd Coll.; fellow Claremont U. Center; mem. adv. council Sch. Engring., Stanford U. William Switzer fellow Stanford U., 1940, Rosenberg fellow, 1941, Douglas Aircraft Co. fellow, 1947. Fellow AIAA; mem. Nat. Acad. Engring. (councillor 1982-88), Assn. U.S. Army (pres. Greater Los Angeles chpt. 1963-65, council of trustees 1965-69), Calif. Club, L.A. Country Club. Republican. Roman Catholic. Office: 1888 Century Park E Ste 2000 Los Angeles CA 90067

BALLIETT, JOHN WILLIAM, entrepreneur; b. Rochester, N.Y., Sept. 10, 1947; s. Charles Garrison and Burnetta Elizabeth (Purtell) B.; BS in Physics, Grove City Coll., 1969; postgrad. U. Rochester, 1969-71; m. Betsy Jane Van Patten, Jan. 25, 1969; 1 child, Noelle Elizabeth. Devel. engr. Eastman Kodak Co., 1969-70; scientist Tropel Inc., 1970, mgr. applied optics, 1971-72, mktg. mgr., 1972-73; exec. v.p., dir. Quality Measurement Systems Inc., Penfield, N.Y., 1973-77; pres. QMS Internat., Inc., Penfield, 1974-77, Balliett Assos., Sarasota, Fla., 1978—, Shore Lane Devel. Corp., 1981—; pres., pub. Suncoast TV Facts, Inc., Sarasota, 1979-81; pres. Charter One, Inc., Sarasota, 1981—; speaker at nat. and internat. timesharing confs. Founding dir. Internat. Found. for Timesharing. Mem. U.S. C. of C., Sarasota County C. of C., Am. Land Devel. Assn., Nat. Timeshare Council, Fla. Hotel-Motel Assn. Contbr. articles on timesharing to profl. publs. Patentee optical systems. Home: 1404 Westbrook Dr Sarasota FL 34231 Office: 4000 S Tamiami Trail Ste 210 Sarasota FL 34231

BALLMER, RAY WAYNE, minerals company executive; b. Santa Rita, N.Mex., May 6, 1926; s. Gerald Jacob and Martha Clara (Wilhelmsen) B.; m. Doris Jean Greer, July 8, 1945; children: Geraldine Lee, Ray James. B.S. N.Mex. Inst. Mining and Tech. in Mining Engring., 1949; M.S. in Indsl. Mgmt., MIT, 1960. Registered profl. engr., Ariz. Various exec. positions Kennecott Copper Corp., Salt Lake City, 1949-69; dir. ops., gen. mgr. Bougainville Copper Ltd., Panguna, Papua New Guinea, 1969-71; mng. dir. Bougainville Copper Ltd., Melbourne, Australia, 1971-75; exec. v.p. Amoco Minerals Co., Denver, 1975-82; vice chmn. Rio Algom Ltd., Toronto, Ont., Can., 1982—, also bd. dirs. Recipient Brown medal N.Mex. Inst. Mining and Tech., 1949; recipient Daniel C. Jackling award Soc. Mining Engrs., 1981; Sloan fellow, 1959. Mem. AIME, Mining and Metall. Soc. Am., Can. Inst. Mining (Toronto br.), Ontario Club. Club: Lambton Golf and Country (Toronto). Home: 228 Glen Rd, Toronto, ON Canada M4W 2X3 Office: Rio Algom Ltd, 120 Adelaide St W, Toronto, ON Canada M5H 1W5

BALOG, JAMES, investment banker; b. Vintondale, Pa., Sept. 9, 1928; s. Michael and Helen B.; m. Alvina Marie Bartos, Oct. 21, 1950; children: James Dennis, Stephen John, Michael George. B.S., Pa. State U., 1950; M.B.A., Rutgers U., 1958. Prodn. engr. Philco Corp., Lansdale, Pa., 1950; budget dir. Merck & Co., Rahway, N.J., 1951-61; v.p., assoc. fin. staff Electric Bond and Share Co., N.Y.C., 1962-63; v.p., dir. Auerbach Pollak & Richardson, N.Y.C., 1964-69; chmn. William D. Witter, Inc., N.Y.C., 1970-75; with Drexel Burnham Lambert, N.Y.C., 1976-87, vice chmn., 1985-87; chmn. Lambert Brussels Capital Corp., N.Y.C., 1988—, also bd. dirs.; chmn. 1838 Investment Advisors, Pa., 1988—; bd. dirs. Drexel Burnham Lambert Group, Pargesa Group, A.L. Labs., Coast U.S. Properties, Putnam Reins., Preinco Holdings, Inc. Mem. Watchung (N.J.) Bd. Edn., 1961-65; U.S. Bipartisan Commn. on Comprehensive Health Care. Mem. N.Y. Soc. Security Analysts, Econ. Club N.Y., The Sky Club, Spring Lake Bath and Tennis, Plainfield Country Club. Clubs: N.Y. Stock Exchange, Plainfield Country, Econ. of N.Y. Office: Lambert Brussels Capital Corp 405 Lexington Ave New York NY 10174

BALOG, RICHARD THOMAS, management consultant, educator; b. Balt., Sept. 15, 1951; s. Michael Anthony and Viola Ann (Wisniesky) B.; m. Laurie Sue Stone, Feb. 20, 1982. BA in Acctg., Loyola Coll., Balt., 1971. CPA, Md.; cert. internal auditor, fraud examiner. Sr. acct. Main LeFrantz, Balt., 1970-72; mgr. Blue Cross of Md., Inc., Balt., 1972-79, Inst. Internal Auditors Inc., Orlando, Fla., 1979-83; sr. mgr. Peat Marwick Main & Co., N.Y.C., 1983-88; chief exec. officer The Audit Resource Ctr., Inc., Jacksonville, Fla., 1988—; chmn. bd. dirs. Resource Ctrs. Inc., Jacksonville, 1989—; gov. Inst. Internal Auditors, Balt., 1974-79; mem. adj. faculty Fla. Community Coll., Jacksonville, 1988—. Editor: (periodical) Internal Auditing, 1984—; contbr. bus. articles to profl. jours. Scoutmaster Balt. council Boy Scouts Am., 1975-79, scoutmaster Wilton, Conn., council, 1984; asst. scoutmaster Passaic County Council, 1987—. Named Eagle Scout, Balt. council Boy Scouts Am., 1967. Mem. AICPA, Inst. Cert. Fraud Examiners, Inst. Internal Auditors (gov. 1974-79, outstanding profl. of yr., 1981), Md. Assn. CPA's, Nat. Assn. Accts., Inst Fin. Crime Prevention. Republican. Roman Catholic. Office: The Audit Resource Ctr 10991-55 San Jose Blvd Ste 106 Jacksonville FL 32223

BALOGH, LINDA JEAN, sales executive; b. Chgo., Sept. 24, 1950; d. Lurell and Laverne Carolyn (McFranklin) Powell; m. Steven Carl Gibbs, Jan. 29, 1969 (div. 1975); 1 child, Jennifer Carolyn; m. Randolph Curtiss Balogh, Dec. 7, 1987. Cert. in acctg., Knoxville Bus. Coll., 1972. With Sears Roebuck & Co., Knoxville, Tenn., 1967-68; dept. mgr. Loring AFB Exchange, Limestone, Maine, 1969-70; br. mgr. Republic Personnel Svc., Knoxville, 1971-73; sales counselor Vic Tanny Health & Racquet Club, Knoxville, 1973-75; ops. mgr. Wits Air Freight, Knoxville, 1975-77; dist. sales mgr. Burlington No. Air Freight, Nashville, 1977-81; field mgr. Cen. Air Freight, Nashville, 1982-84; account exec. Profit Freight Systems, Memphis, 1984-85, Flying Tigers, Memphis, 1985—; ptnr. Bay's Lawn & Landscape, Memphis, 1987—. Contbr. articles to profl. jours. Mem. Memphis Bus. and Profl. Women, NAFE, West Tenn. Traffic Club (bd. dirs. 1985-86). Democrat. Home: 3999 Friendly Way Memphis TN 38115 Office: Flying Tigers 3084 Connahbrook Dr Memphis TN 38116

BAMBERRY, CAROL ROSS, telemarketing manager; b. Elyria, Ohio; d. Edward Raymond and Caroline (Bozicevich) Ross; m. John Robert Bamberry, Feb. 16, 1975. BA, Notre Dame Coll. Ohio, Euclid, 1967; MEd, Boston State Coll., 1970; MBA, N.H. Coll., 1984. Tchr. Elyria (Ohio) Pub. Schs., 1963-65, Canton (Conn.) Pub. Schs., 1967-68; head tchr. Needham (Mass.) Pub. Schs., 1968-83; customer service supr. New Eng. Bus. Service, Groton, Mass., 1983-85; telemarketing mgr. New Eng. Bus. Service, Groton, 1985—; Coordinator Nat. Assn. Girls and Women in Sport, Reston, Va., 1981-83; cons. Mass. Interscholastics Athletics Assn., 1981-83. Editor handbook: Soccer Tips and Techniques, 1983. Named Coach of Yr., Boston Globe, 1977. Mem. Dir. Mktg. Assn., Am. Telemktg. Assn. Home: 12 Crestwood Ln Milford NH 03055 Office: New Eng Bus Svc 500 Main St Groton MA 01450

BANACH, ART JOHN, graphic artist.; b. Chgo., May 22, 1931; s. Vincent and Anna (Zajac) B.; grad. Art. Inst. of Chgo., 1955; pupil painting studies Mrs. Melin, Chgo.; m. Loretta A. Nolan, Oct. 15, 1966; children: Heather Anne, Lynnea Joan. Owner, dir. Art J. Banach Studios, 1949—, cartoon syndicate for newspapers, house organs and advt. functions, 1954—, owned and operated advt. agy., 1954-56, feature news and picture syndicate, distbn. U.S. and fgn. countries. Dir. Speculators S Fund. Recipient award 1st Easter Seal contest Ill. Assn. Crippled, Inc., 1949. Chgo. Pub. Sch. Art Soc. Scholar. Mem. Artist's Guild Chgo., Am Mgmt. Assn., Chgo. Assn. of Commerce and Industry, Chgo. Federated Advt. Club, Am. Mktg. Assn., Internat. Platform Assn., Chgo. Advt. Club, Chgo. Soc. Communicating Arts. Clubs: Columbia Yacht, Advt. Execs.; Art Directors (Chgo.). Home: 1076 Leahy Cir E Des Plaines IL 60016

BANAS, RICHARD FREDERICK, geographer; b. Hartford, Conn., June 8, 1948; s. Frank John and Sophie Wanda (Oliwka) B. AB, Assumption Coll., 1971; MS, Cen. Conn. State U., 1987. Market research analyst Advo-System, Inc., Hartford, 1971-72, Managed Mktg., Bolton, Conn., 1973; data technician Toner and Assocs., Inc., Seattle, 1974; research asst. Urban Data Ctr. U. Wash., Seattle, 1974-75, City of Seattle, 1975; fin. clk. State of Conn., Hartford, 1977-81, research analyst, 1981-82, accounts examiner, 1982—. Mem. AAAS, Assn. Am. Geographers, N.Am. Cartographic Info. Soc., Urban and Regional Info. Systems Assn., Gamma Theta Epsilon. Home: 8 Evans Ave East Hartford CT 06118

BANASIK, ROBERT CASMER, nursing home administrator, educator; b. Detroit, Dec. 8, 1942; s. Casmer John and Lucille Nathalie (Siperek) B.; BS in Mech. Engring., Wayne State U., 1965; MS in Indsl. Engring., Tex. Tech. Coll., 1967; MBA, Ohio State U., 1973, PhD, 1974; m. Jacqueline Mae Miller, Aug. 28, 1965; (div. 1985); children: Robert John, Marcus Alan, Jason Andrew; m. Barbara Jean Willows, Oct. 12, 1985. Mgmt. systems engr. Riverside Methodist Hosp., Columbus, Ohio, 1970, 71; owner, mgmt. systems cons. Banasik Assoc., Columbus, 1972—; dir. mgmt. systems engring. Grant Hosp., Columbus, 1973-78; owner, mgr. RMJ Investment Enterprises, Columbus, 1975-85; pres. Omnilife Systems, Inc., Columbus, 1979—, RMJ Mgmt., Inc., 1983-85. Bryant Health Ctr., Inc., Ironton, Ohio, 1983—, Equity Mgmt., 1985—; owner Omnivend, 1985—; adminstr. Patterson Health Ctr., Columbus, 1980—, Parkview Health Ctr., Inc., Volga, S.D, 1986—, Hamilton (Ohio) Health Ctr., Inc., 1986—, Shelby Manor Health Ctr., Inc., Shelbyville, Ky., 1986—, corp. sec. Clintonville Family Practice, Columbus, 1987—, Samaritan Care Ctr., Inc., Medina, Ohio, 1988—; asst.

prof. Capital U. Grad. Sch. Adminstrn., Columbus, 1973-79, assoc. prof., 1979—; pres. Banasik & Strayer Architects and Engrs., Columbus, 1988—; dir. Asset Data Systems, Columbus. Pres. bd. dirs. United Cerebral Palsy Franklin County, 1979-80; mem. founding bd. Support Resources, Inc., 1978-85; bd. dirs. Transp. Resources, Inc., 1979-80, Dennison Health Systems, 1988—, bd. dirs., 1988—; pres. indsl. adv. bd. Tex. Tech. U., 1987—; pres., bd. dirs. Ohio Acad. Nursing Homes, Columbus, 1986—. Registered profl. engr., Ohio; lic. nursing home adminstr., Ohio. Mem. Am. Hosp. Assn., NSPE (dir. Franklin County chpt. 1976-77), Ohio Soc. Profl. Engrs., Am. Inst. Decision Scis., Am. Coll. Health Care Adminstrs., Airplane Owner & Pilots Assn., Sigma Xi, Beta Gamma Sigma, Alpha Pi Mu, Phi Kappa Phi, Alpha Kappa Psi. Republican. Lutheran. Editor: Topics in Hospital Material Management, 1978-84; contbr. articles to profl. jours; participant expert witness testimony. Office: PO Box 8309 Columbus OH 43201

BANCROFT, ELIZABETH ABERCROMBIE, publisher, analytical chemist; b. Washington, Mar. 2, 1947; d. John Chandler and Ruth Abercrombie (Robinson) B.; A.B., Harvard U./Radcliffe Coll., 1979; postgrad. in forensic scis. John Jay Coll. Criminal Justice, 1982. Asst. dir. research Bagley Fordyce Research Labs., N.Y.C., 1979-83, dir. research and publs., Washington office, 1984-86; dir. Nat. Intelligence Book Ctr., 1986—; dir. Nat. Intelligence Study Ctr. Mem. Assn. Fgn. Intelligence Officers, Naval Intelligence Profls., Nat. Mil. Intelligence Assn., Nat. Intelligence Study Ctr., Assn. Ofcl. Analytical Chemists, Am. Chem. Soc., Am. Inst. Chemists, N.Y. Acad. Scis., Washington Book Pubs. Assn., Am. Bookseller Assn. Republican. Episcopalian. Clubs: Harvard of N.Y.C., Harvard/Radcliffe of Washington; Chemists of N.Y.; English Speaking Union of N.Y. and Washington. Home: 2737 Devonshire Pl NW Washington DC 20008 Office: Nat Intelligence Book Ctr 1700 K St NW Washington DC 20006

BANCROFT, PAUL, III, investment company executive; b. N.Y.C., Feb. 27, 1930; s. Paul and Rita (Manning) B.; B.A., Yale U., 1951; postgrad. Georgetown Fgn. Service Inst., 1952; m. Monica M. Devine, Jan. 2, 1977; children by previous marriage—Bradford, Kimberly, Stephen, Gregory. Account exec. Merrill Lynch Pierce Fenner & Smith, N.Y.C., 1956-57; asso. corporate finance dept. F. Eberstadt & Co., N.Y.C., 1957-62; partner Draper, Gaither & Anderson, Palo Alto, Calif., 1962-67; with Bessemer Securities Corp., 1967—; v.p. Venture Capital Investments, 1967-74, sr. v.p. securities investments, 1974-76, pres., chief exec. officer, dir., 1976-87; cons. Bessemer Securities Corp., 1988—; bd. dirs. Measurex Corp., Litton Industries, Inc., Albany Internat., Inc., Watts Industries, Inc., Scudder Devel. Fund, Scudder Capital Growth Fund, Scudder Internat. Fund, Scudder Internat. Bond Fund, Scudder Global Fund, Scudder Equity Income Fund, Scudder New Asia Fund, Maxim Integrated Products; ind. venture capitalist, 1988—; founder, past pres. and chmn. Nat. Venture Capital Assn.; trustee Carnegie Mellon U. Served to 1st lt. USAF, 1952-56. Clubs: River, Yale (N.Y.C.); Pacific Union, Bohemian (San Francisco). Home: Cheston Ln Rte 2 Box 314 E Queenstown MD 21658 Office: 1212 Ave of Americas Ste 1802 New York NY 10036

BANCROFT, RONALD MANN, manufacturing executive; b. Lewiston, Maine, Aug. 2, 1943; s. Ronald Percival and Maxine (Mann) B.; m. Sara Willis; children: Carrie Elizabeth, Emily Sara. BS, U.S. Naval Acad., 1965; MA, Oxford U., 1968. Commd. ensign USN, 1965, advanced through grades to lt. comdr., 1968-72, ret., 1972; ptnr. McKinsey & Co., Washington, 1972-83; sr. v.p. fin. and adminstrn. Bath (Maine) Iron Works Corp., 1983-87; chmn., chief exec. officer Paris Mfg. Corp., South Paris, Maine, 1987—; pres. Bancroft Enterprises, Portland, Maine, 1987—; chmn. chief exec. officer Paris Mfg. Corp., South Paris, Maine; bd. dirs. Biotherm, Inc. Bd. dirs. Maine Maritime Mus., Bath, 1985—. Rhodes scholar Oxford U., 1968. Mem. Fin. Execs. Inst. (chmn. so. Maine chpt. 1985-88). Republican. Congregationalist. Club: Leander (Henley, Eng.). Home: October Farm 224 Tuttle Rd Cumberland ME 04021 Office: Paris Mfg Corp 200 Western Ave Box 250 South Paris ME 04021

BAND, DAVID, investment banker; b. Edinburgh, Scotland, Dec. 14, 1942; s. David and Elisabeth (Aitken) B.; m. Olivia Rose Brind, June 1, 1973; children—David Robert Benjamin, Isabelle Olivia Eve. MA, Oxford U. Dir. J.P. Morgan & Co., Inc., London, 1981-86; mng. dir. Morgan Guaranty, Ltd., London, 1986-88; exec. v.p. Morgan Guaranty Trust Co.; chmn. J.P. Morgan Securities, Ltd., London; dir. Barclays PLC and Barclays Bank PLC; chief exec. officer Barclays de Zoete Wedd, London, 1988—; dep. chmn. The Securities Assn., 1986-88. Mem. The Hon. Co. Edinburgh Golfers. Office: Barclays de Zoete Wedd, Ebbgate House 2 Swan Ln, London EC4R 3TS, England

BANDER, NORMAN ROBERT, communications and information management consultant; A.B., Dartmouth Coll., 1954; postgrad. Harvard U., Columbia U., U. Pa., N.Y. U. Former sales research dir. Benton & Bowles, Inc., N.Y.C.; media program research dir. Lennen & Newell, Inc., N.Y.C.; dir. mktg., test analysis Gillette Co., Boston; dir. creative communication evaluation and advt. research J. Walter Thompson Co., N.Y.C.; pres. AdTracks and Bander & Assocs., Malvern, Pa., 1968-78, Sarasota, Fla., 1978—. Served as clin. psychologist, M.C., AUS, 1954-56. Mem. Am. Mktg. Assn. Clubs: Dartmouth, Yale (N.Y.C.). Author studies on mktg. and advt. effectivness, consumer behavior and public opinion. Office: AdTracks & Bander Assocs PO Box 190 Sarasota FL 34230

BANE, MARILYN ANNETTE, advertising executive; b. Ft. Worth, Aug. 26, 1943; d. Forest Nelson and Wilma Grace (Orr) B. BA, U. Tex., 1967. Copywriter Ted Bates and Co., Inc., N.Y.C., 1967-69, Grey Advt., Inc., N.Y.C., 1969-70; v.p., copy supr. Gary F. Halby Assocs., Inc., N.Y.C., 1970-73; exec. v.p., dir. account services Wells, Rich, Greene, Inc., N.Y.C., 1978-80, Wyse Advt., N.Y.C., 1983-87; v.p. advt. Maidenform, Inc., N.Y.C., 1987—. Mem. Fashion Group, Inc. Office: Maidenform Inc 90 Park Ave New York NY 10016

BANFER, FRANKLIN ARTHUR, II, financial planner; b. Johnstown, Pa., Sept. 22, 1959; s. Franklin Arthur and Marie Catherine (Frombach) B.; m. Ellen Lynn Smolleck, Oct. 23, 1981; 1 child, Franklin Arthur III. AA in Bus. Adminstrn., Pa. State U., 1979; diploma, Life Underwriters Tng. Coun., Washington, 1988. Chartered fin. cons.; chartered life underwriter. Asst. chef Ramada Inn, Clearfield, Pa., 1977-79; asst. mgr. Ramada Inn, Pitts., 1979-80; chef Brackenridge Heights Country Club, Natrona Heights, Pa., 1980-81; fin. planner Banfer Fin. Svcs., Johnstown, 1981—; moderator, tchr. Life Underwriters Tng. Coun., Johnstown, 1985-88. Mem. Cambria/Somerset Estate Planning Coun., Jaycees. Mem. Nat. Assn. Life Underwriters (Nat. Quality award 1986), Johnstown Assn. Life Underwriters (v.p. 1986-87, pres. 1988—, Mike Messina award 1985), Internat. Assn. Fin. Planning, Pa. Assn. Notaries, Johnstown Magic Guild (pres. 1982-84), Kiwanis. Republican. Lutheran. Home: 318 Robinson Ave Johnstown PA 15905 Office: Banfer Fin Svcs 211 Main St Johnstown PA 15901

BANG, CARMEN D., planning company executive; b. Clay County, Iowa, July 3; d. Willard C.J. and Norma (Hagedorn) Dethlefsen; divorced; children: Carole Dinkins, Marilyn Beman, Susan Curvel, Carla Clausen, H.W. (Bill). MS in Fin. Services, Am. Coll., Bryn Mawr, Pa., 1982, MS in Mgmt., 1985. CLU; chartered fin. cons. Asst. mgr. Spencer (Iowa) Sewing Machine Co., 1958-66; personnel supr. Wollard Aircraft Equipment, Miami, 1968-71; life ins. agt. Guardian Life Ins. Co., Miami, 1971—; exec. v.p. Pensions, Inc., Miami, 1978-82; pres. Plan Ahead, Inc., Miami, 1982—; mem. Dade County Mgmt. Bd, First Am. Bank and Trust, Miami, 1985—. Past sec., bd. dirs. Riverside Christian Ministries, Inc., Miami, 1981; past sec. mem. Miami Civic Music Assn., 1974—; chair person Riverside Christian Ministries Inc., 1987—. Mem. Miami Chpt. Am. Soc. CLU's (bd. dirs.), Estate Planning Coun. of Greater Miami, South Fla. Employee Benefits Coun. Republican. Lutheran. Lodges: Order Ea. Star, Daus. of Nile. Office: Plan Ahead Inc 1450 Madruga Ave Ste 204 Coral Gables FL 33146

BANIK, DOUGLAS HEIL, advertising executive; b. Camden, N.J., May 21, 1947; s. Wilmer Harry and Marie Grace (Heil) B.; m. Marcia Lynne Knotts, Jan. 31, 1981 (div. June 1986); children: Shannon Danae Vezina, Corey Jamison Vezina; m. Lauren Clark Abbe, Oct. 4, 1986; 1 child, Mark Mitchell Banik. AB, Harvard U., 1969; MA, U. Pa., 1970, PhD, 1973. Asst. prof. psychology Wellesley (Mass.) Coll., 1973-76; assoc. dir. rsch. Benton & Bowles, N.Y.C., 1976-79; v.p. rsch. Advt. Rsch. Found., N.Y.C., 1979-81; v.p., assoc. dir. rsch. Saatchi & Saatchi Compton, N.Y.C., 1981-83; v.p., dir. mktg. rsch. Ogilvy & Mather, L.A., 1983-86; sr. v.p., dir. rsch. and strategic planning D'Arcy Masius Benton & Bowles, Chgo., 1987—; cons. Med. Ctr., U. Calif., Davis, 1986, Columbia Pictures, Inc., Studio City, Calif., 1987. Editor: Jour. Advt. Rsch., 1979-80. Pres. Roosevelt Island Resident's Assn., N.Y.C., 1979-81; mem. com. infants, children, pregnant and lactating mothers White House Conf. on Nutrition Edn., 1979. Merit scholar Harvard U., 1965-69; Nat. Sci. Found. fellow U. Pa., 1969-73. Office: D'Arcy Masius Benton & Bowles 200 E Randolph Chicago IL 60601

BANIS, ROBERT JOSEPH, pharmaceutical company executive; b. N.Y.C., Oct. 26, 1943; s. Vincent Nicholas and Roberta Marie (Shwedo) B.; m. Lois Elaine Polson, Jan. 25, 1970; children: Andrea Berit, Lauren Nicole. BS, Cornell U., 1967; MS, Purdue U., 1969; PhD, N.C. State U., 1973; MBA, U. Chgo., 1982. Postdoctoral fellow Harvard U., Cambridge, Mass., 1973-75; sr. research scientist Armour Pharm. Co., Kankakee, Ill., 1975-79, tech. mgr. biochems. and parenterals, 1979-81, mgr. biochem. and pharm. devel., 1981-83; research group leader health care div. Monsanto, St. Louis, 1983-85; mgr. research ops. and fin. planning, health care div. Monsanto Co., St. Louis, 1985-86; mgr. research and fin. planning Searle, St. Louis, 1986-88, mgr. rsch. ops. and fin. planning, 1988—; adj. asst. bus. prof. U. Mo., St. Louis, 1987—. Contbr. articles to profl. jours. Postdoctoral fellow NIH, Harvard U., 1975. Mem. AAAS, Am. Chem. Soc., Phi Lambda Upsilon (chemistry hon.), Beta Gamma Sigma (bus. hon.). Office: Monsanto Co BB5A Saint Louis MO 63198

BANJOKO, ALIMI AJIMON, financial planner; b. Mona, St. Andrew, Jamaica, Nov. 11, 1954; came to U.S., 1980; s. Alton Alex and Martha Naomi (Needham) Harvey; m. Garnett Marlene St. Clair Clarke, Jan. 19, 1980; children: Che Lafianu, Pryha Krist-Loyé. BA (hons.), U. of the West Indies, Mona, 1978. Cert. fin. planner. Adminstrv. officer Ministry of Fgn. Affairs, Kingston, Jamaica, 1979; account exec., registered rep. John Hancock Cos., Boston, 1981-83; pres. PFS Group Inc., Bklyn., 1983—; sales rep. Morgan and Assocs., Bklyn., 1985—. Organizer 6th Congl. Dist. Rainbow Coalition, Far Rockaway, N.Y., 1984—; chmn. Capital Investment Plan, First Ch. of God, Far Rockaway, 1986—, trustee, 1985—. Mem. Inst. Cert. Fin. Planners, Internat. Assn. Fin. Planning, N.Y. Met. Ins. Brokers and Agts. Assn. (bd. dirs.). Office: PFS Group Inc 4919 Church Ave Brooklyn NY 11203

BANK, CHARLES NICKY, financial services company executive; b. Chgo., Sept. 29, 1943; s. Julius Charles and Sylvia (Kaplan) B.; m. Charlotte A. Hurt, Nov. 2, 1974; children—Bradley Tod, Martin Lee, Ryan Clayton, Darren Daniel. Student, Lincoln Jr. Coll., 1963-65. Clk. E.F. Hutton & Co., Inc., Chgo., 1966-69, account exec., 1969-73, br. mgr., 1973-85; nat. sales mgr. E.F. Hutton & Co., Inc., 1983—, sr. v.p. commodities, 1985—; dir. Hutton Internat. Ltd., E.F. Hutton Commodity Res. Fund. Ltd.; dir., v.p. E.F. Hutton Commodity Mgmt., Hutton Commodity Ptnrs., E.F. Hutton Futures Fund; mem. Mid Am. Commodity Exchange, Chgo., bd. dirs., 1981-83; mem. coms. Chgo. Bd. Trade; mem. Chgo. Bd. Trade Exchange, Chgo. Mercantile Exchange. Home: 1665 Duffy Ln Bannockburn IL 60015 Office: Prudential Bache Secutities 1900 E Golf Rd Schaumburg IL 60173

BANK, WILLIAM JULIUS, manufacturing company executive; b. N.Y.C., Dec. 17, 1913; s. Hyman and Mollie (Berg) B.; m. Esther Sawney Kaplan, Aug. 24, 1935; children: Barrie Alan, Michael Stephan, Marshall Peter. Student, U. Va., 1945, U. La., 1946, Purdue U., 1948. Foreman Simon Ackerman, 1929-36; mgr. Eagle Clothes, 1936-41; field insp. Phila. Q.M. Depot, 1941-42; plant mgr. Stuart Keith Mfg. Co., 1942-47; asst. v.p. Blue Ridge Mfrs., Inc., 1947-49, v.p. mfg., 1949-58, v.p. research and devel., 1958-59, asst. to pres., 1960, exec. v.p., 1961-68; exec. v.p. Imperial Shirt Co., 1961-68; ptnr. Jonbil Inc., 1966-67, exec. v.p., 1967-68, pres., 1968-70, owner, 1970—, chmn., chief exec. officer, 1984—; pres. Blue Jeans Mfg. Co., Inc., 1968—. Chmn. Employment Physically Handicapped, Lynchburg, Va., 1958; pres. Apparel Research Found. Mem. Am. Mgmt. Assn., Am. Soc. Personnel Mgmt., Soc. Advancement Mgmt., Am. Apparel Mfrs. Assn. (bd. dirs., mktg. com.), Nat. Acad. Scis. (adv. com. on textiles and apparel research), Inter Am. Commn. Textile Square Club (exec. com.). Lodges: Masons, Shriners. Home: 60 Ward Dr New Rochelle NY 10804 Office: Jonbil Inc 350 Fifth Ave New York NY 10001

BANKS, DAVID RUSSELL, health care executive; b. Arcadia, Wis., Feb. 15, 1937; s. J.R. and Cleone B.; married; children: Melissa, Michael. B.A., U. Ark., 1959. Vice pres. Dabbs, Sullivan, Trulock, Ark., 1963-74; chmn., chief exec. officer Leisure Lodges, Ft. Smith, Ark., 1974-77; registered rep. Stephens Inc., Little Rock, 1974-79; pres., chief operating officer Beverly Enterprises, Pasadena, Calif., 1979—; dir. Nat. Council Health Centers, Pulaski Bank, Little Rock. Served with U.S. Army. Office: Beverly Enterprises Inc 99 S Oakland Ave Pasadena CA 91101 *

BANKS, GORDON L., manufacturing representative; b. N.Y.C., Mar. 3, 1955; s. Russell and Janice (Reed) B. BS, Amherst Coll., 1978; JD, Boston U., 1981. Assoc. atty. Lord, Day, Lord, N.Y.C., 1981-83; asst. to pres. Enviro Spray Systems, Inc., Mont., Pa., 1984; mng. dir. Enviro Spray Systems, Inc., Hoboken, N.J., 1988—; bd. dirs. Grow Ventures Corp., N.Y.C., 1987—. Mem. Am. Horse Council. Club: Amherst. Office: Enviro Spray Systems Inc 5 Marine View Pla Hoboken NJ 07030

BANKS, HENRY STEPHEN, systems software company executive; b. Chgo., Nov. 13, 1920; s. Joseph S. and Mary V. (Sparrow) B.; m. Marjorie June Martin, Feb. 19, 1955; children: Pamela Kae, Kimberly Karen. BS, Loyola U., Chgo., 1944; MBA, Northwestern U., 1953. Commd 2d lt. USAF, 1941, advanced through grades to lt. col., 1955; with Res. 1955-80; sr. account mgr. Recordak Bus. Products div. Eastman Kodak, Cedar Rapids, Iowa, 1955-60; mgr. regional br. govt. Itek Bus. Products, Bethesda, Md., 1960-67; dir. mktg. DASA Corp., Andover, Mass., 1967-68; dir. product devel. Dymo Bus. Systems, Bethesda, 1968-81; v.p. mktg. Automation Horizons, Inc., Beltsville, Md., 1982-83; dir. govt. mktg. InterSystems Corp., Bethesda, 1984—; lectr. mktg. Coe Coll.; lectr. math. Loyola U.; cons. in field. Mem. MUMPS Users Group. Republican. Roman Catholic. Clubs: Bethesda Naval Officers, Ft. Myer Officers. Home: 7211 Radnor Rd Bethesda MD 20817 Office: InterSystems Corp 4520 East West Hwy S550 Bethesda MD 20814

BANKS, JAMES HOUSTON, trade association executive, public relations consultant; b. Waco, Tex., Nov. 3, 1925; s. Elijah Halbert and Eva Virginia (Haralson) B.; m. Mary Virginia Bussey, June 15, 1947; children: Virginia Anne, Janet Lynn Banks Tate. Student, U. Tex., 1943, 46-47, 58, 60. Various newspaper assignments Tex., 1941-53; pub. relations dir. Tex. State Tchrs. Assn., 1953-54; exec. asst. Gov. Allan Shivers, 1954-57, Gov. Price Daniel, 1957; Austin Correspondent Dallas Morning News, 1957-70; campaign publicity dir. U.S. Sen. Lloyd Bentsen, 1970; editor The Tex. Star, 1970-72; publicity dir. Sen. John G. Tower, 1972; exec. asst. Sen. John G. Tower, Austin, 1973-75; pub. rels. dir. Tex. R.R. Assn., Austin, 1975-89; pvt. practice pub. rels. cons. 1989—; editor Tex. Rys. mag.; free-lance writer and pub. relations cons., 1958—. Author: Money, Marbles & Chalk, 1971, Darrell Royal Story, 1973, Gavels, Grit & Glory, 1981, Corralling the Colorado, 1988; Austin correspondent Sports Illustrated mag. Mem. legis. com. State Bar of Tex., 1984-87; bd. dirs. Travis County Grand Jury Assn., Austin, 1986—. Served to 1st lt., USAF, 1943-45, 51-52. Recipient numerous writing awards, 1960—. Mem. R.R. Pub. Relations Assn. (pres. 1982), Assn. R.R. Communicators (v.p. 1981), Assn. R.R. Editors (disting. achievement awards 1976, 77, 78, 80, 81, 82), Football Writers Am., Tex. Sports Writers Assn., Sigma Delta Chi (pres. Austin chpt. 1962). Methodist. Clubs: Austin, Headliners (pres. 1976).

BANKS, ROBERT SHERWOOD, lawyer; b. Newark, Mar. 28, 1934; s. Howard Douglas and Amelia Violet (Del Bagno) B.; m. Judith Lee Henry; children—Teri, William; children by previous marriage—Robert, Paul, Stephen, Roger, Gregory, Catherine. A.B., Cornell U., 1956, LL.B., 1958. Bar: N.J. bar 1959, N.Y. State bar 1968. Practice law Newark, 1958-61; atty. E.I. duPont, Wilmington, Del., 1961-67; with Xerox Corp., Stamford, Conn., 1967-88; v.p., gen. counsel Xerox Corp., 1976-88; sr. counsel Latham & Watkins, N.Y.C., 1989—; bd. dirs. U. Conn. Rsch. and Devel. Corp., Fed. Judicial Ctr. Found., 1989—; mem. 2d cir. standing com on improvement of civil litigation. Mem. adv. council Cornell Law Sch.; trustee U.S. Supreme Ct. Hist. Soc.; bd. dirs. Ctr. for Pub. Resources. Mem. ABA, Am. Arbitration Assn. (panel arbitrators), Am. Judicature Soc. (mem. exec. com., bd. dirs.), Cornell Law Assn., Am. Corporate Counsel Assn. (bd. dirs., chmn. 1982-83), Conn. Bar Assn. Clubs: Aspetuck Valley Country, Jonathan's Landing. Office: Latham & Watkins 885 3rd Ave New York NY 10022

BANKS, RUSSELL, chemical company executive; b. N.Y.C., Aug. 2, 1919; s. Thomas and Fay (Cowen) B.; m. Janice Reed, July 19, 1949; 1 son, Gordon L. B.B.A., CCNY, 1936-40; J.D., N.Y. Law Sch., 1960. Bar: N.Y. 1961. Sr. acct. Selverne, Davis Co., N.Y.C., 1940-45; pvt. practice as C.P.A. N.Y.C., 1945-61; exec. v.p. Met. Telecommunications Corp., Plainview, N.Y., 1961-62; pres., chief exec. officer Grow Group, Inc. (formerly Grow Chem. Corp.), N.Y.C., 1962—; also dir. Grow Group, Inc. (formerly Grow Chem. Corp.); dir. Bainco Corp., Fenimore Fund. Editor: Managing the Small Company. Chmn. Liberty Cup Races; bd. dirs. N.Y.C. Harbor Festival Found. Recipient award of achievement Sch. of Bus. Alumni Soc. of CCNY, 1977; Winthrop-Sears medal Chem. Industry Assn., 1980. Mem. Nat. Paint and Coatings Assn. (past pres., bd. dirs., mem. exec. com.), Am. Mgmt. Assn. (gen. mgmt. planning council 1966—, also trustee), Solvent Abuse Found. for Edn. (bd. dirs.). Clubs: Metropolitan (N.Y.C.); Annabel's (London). Home: 1000 Park Ave New York NY 10028 Office: Grow Group Inc 200 Park Ave New York NY 10166

BANNES, LORENZ THEODORE, construction company executive; b. St. Louis, Oct. 24, 1935; s. Lawrence Anthony and Louise Clair (Vollet) B.; B.S. in Civil Engring., St. Louis U., 1957; m. Janet Ann Bruening, Aug. 10, 1957; children—Stephen W., Michael F., Timothy L. From project engr. to exec. v.p. Gamble Constrn. Co. Inc., St. Louis, 1960-69, pres., 1969-72; founder, pres. Bannes-Shaughnessy, Inc., St. Louis, 1972-77, chmn. bd., 1977-89 ; fornder, pres. Bannes Cons. Group Inc., 1989—; dir., v.p. St. Louis Constrn. Manpower Corp., 1977—. Tchr. civil engring. dept. St. Louis U., 1969—; tchr. contracting and constrn. methods U. Mo. Extension Center, 1970—; tchr. constrn. mgmt. Grad. Engring. Center, U. Mo., St. Louis, 1968—, tchr. constrn. mgmt. sch. Architecture, Washington U., St. Louis, 1974—; lectr. So. Ill. U., Edwardsville, 1982—; tchr. estimating concrete constrn.; tchr. Nat. Assn. Women in Constrn., 1973—; mem. seminar faculty World of Concrete, 1984—; Mem. adv. com. in civil engring. Florissant Valley Community Coll.; mem. adv. com. constrn. tech. Jefferson Coll. Chmn. trustees Aspenhof, 1973; adv. bd. Little Sisters of Poor, 1975—; nat. adv. bd. Sisters St. Joseph of Carondelet, 1985—, chmn. nat. devel., 1986—, chmn. nat. bd., 1987— (Distinguished Svc. award 1988); nat. bd. Living and Learning, Jesuit ednl. program for disadvantaged; mem. Human Rights Commn., Archdiocese of St. Louis, 1980—; chmn. bd. trustees Christian Bros. Coll. High Sch., St. Louis, 1980—, Sisters of St. Joe, v.p. Retirement Ctr., bd. dirs., 1988—. Served with USAF, 1957-60. Recipient Alumni Merit award St. Louis U., 1972, Appreciation award Sisters of St. Joe, 1988; named Man of Yr., Exec. Club of St. Louis U., 1978; named to Hall of Fame, Christian Bros. Coll. High Sch., 1981, St. Louis Small Bus. Entrepreneur of Yr., 1988. Mem. Nat. Soc. Profl. Engrs. (recipient Young Engr. of Year award 1971), Mo. Soc. Profl. Engrs. (chmn. Y.E. com., Constrn. Engr. of Yr. 1989), Concrete Council of St. Louis (pres. 1972-73, Distinguished Service award 1973), Assoc. Gen. Contractors Am. (Nat. Build/Am. award 1973), Assoc. Gen. Contractors St. Louis (Chmn. of Year 1973), ASCE (nat. com. constrn. research 1973-74), Am. Soc. Concrete Constructors (nat. bd. dirs. 1982—, nat. v.p. 1986—), Young Presidents Orgn., Sr. Execs. Org. Engrs. Club St. Louis (dir. 1975-76, 86—, hon. mem. 1986, award of merit 1987), Nat. Assn. Women in Constrn. (hon. mem., Disting. service award 1974), Mo. Soc. Profl. Engrs. (profl. engring. in constrn. award 1987, Entrepreneur of Yr. 1988), Xe Chi Epsilon (chpt. hon. mem. 1980). Home: 1345 Cragwold Rd Kirkwood MO 63122 Office: 6780 Southwest Ave Saint Louis MO 63143

BANNING, WILLIAM BENJAMIN, insurance executive; b. Florence, S.C., Mar. 9, 1953; s. Orville Fisher and Ruby (Bell) B.; m. Wanda Gore, Mar. 29, 1975; children: William Benjamin II, Angie. Student, Am. Coll., Bryn Mawr, Pa., 1984. CLU; Chartered Fin. Cons. Sales rep. Life Ins. Co. of Va., Florence, 1973-75; sales mgr. Life Ins. Co. of Va., Richmond, Va., 1975-79; tgn. cons. Life Ins. Co. of Va., Florence, 1979, agy. mgr., 1979-82, 1979-82; pres. Banning & Assocs. Inc., Florence, 1987—. Rep. committeman, Cloumbia, 1987—. Recipient Edwin F. Brooks award, Florence Assn. Life Underwrtiers, 1978-79. Mem. Cen. S.C. Gen. Agents and Mgrs. Assn., Cen. S.C. CLU Soc., S.C. Assn. LIfe Underwriters (bd. dirs. 1984—, pres. 1986-87). Baptist. Home: 126 Linnet Dr West Columbia SC 29169 Office: Banning and Assocs Inc 121 Executive Ct Dr Ste 103 Columbus SC 29210

BANNISTER, WILLIAM CHARLES, investor; b. Alexander, Kans., Mar. 25, 1937; s. Charles T. and Gladys B.; m. Marcia, Jan. 24, 1959; children: Mark, William T., Grant, Joel. BS, Ft. Hays State U., 1959, MS, 1962; postgrad., Okla. State U., 1967, Kans. U., 1970. Tchr. Radium (Kans.) Schs., 1959-60, prin., 1960-61; supt. Hanston (Kans.) Sch., 1962-64, Bazine (Kans) Schs., 1965-69; tchr. Ft. Hay State U., 1971-72; pvt. practice Hays, 1973—. Mem. Secondary Prins. Assn. Kans. (v.p.), Rooks County Tchr. Assn. (pres.), Kans. Farm Bur., Kans. Agr. Adv. Commn. (pres. 1975-76). Office: Bannister Trust Ltd 413 W 6th St Hays KS 67601

BANOVIC, ZLATKO JOSIP, electronic company executive; b. Virovitica, Slavonia, Yugoslavia, Mar. 10, 1951; s. Zvonko and Nada (Petraš) B.; m. Venuška Novoselnik, Apr. 30, 1977; children: Hrvoje, Ana. Diploma in electrotechnics engring., Electrotehnic Acad., Zagreb, 1974. Prof. Electrotechnic Medium Sch., Zagreb, 1974-76; maintenance engr. Televizia-Video Maintenance Dept., Zagreb, 1976-77, 78, sr. maintenance engr., 1978, sr. systems engr., 1979; head engr. Automatic Measurement Equipment, Zagreb, 1977-78; chief engr. Televizia-Video Maintenance Dept., Zagreb, 1980; owner Video Electronic Lab., Zagreb, 1986—; expert for electronics Republic Ct. of Croatia, Zagreb, 1986; video cons., projector various pvt. recording studios. Author: (sports competition videos) Central Video Masters, 1980-84. Recipient Achievement award AMPEX European Tng. Cen., 1980-85. Mem. United Engrs. Soc. Yugoslavia, United Republic Experts Ct. Croatia. Office: Video Electronic Lab Ltd, Vladimira Varicaka 2o, 41020 Zagreb Croatia, Yugoslavia

BANSAK, STEPHEN A., JR., investment banker; b. Bridgeport, Conn., Sept. 19, 1939; s. Stephen A. and Genevieve Bansak; m. Susan Jean Dizon, July 20, 1984; children: Cynthia A., Thomas S., Stephen A. III, Kirk C. BS, Yale U., 1961; MBA, U. Pa., 1968. With Kidder, Peabody & Co., Inc., N.Y.C., 1968—, v.p., 1971-75, co-mgr. dept. corp. fin., 1975-84; vice chmn. Kidder, Peabody Internat., 1984—; bd. dirs. Kidder Peabody P.R., KP Realty Advisers. Past trustee, v.p. Rumson (N.J.) Country Day Sch. Served to lt. USN, 1962-66, Vietnam. Mem. Securities Industry Assn. (chmn. corp. fin. com., rule 415 com.), Am. Stock Exchange (official). Clubs: Navesink Country, Yale of N.Y.C., Broad St. (bd. dirs., past pres.). Home: 33 Bellevue Ave Rumson NJ 07760 Office: Kidder Peabody & Co Inc 10 Hanover Sq New York NY 10005

BANTA, BERTON MERLE, manufacturing executive; b. Boston, June 3, 1960; s. Merle Henry Banta and June Mueller; m. Maude Darrell Chulay, Dec. 28, 1985. BA in Polit. Sci., Trinity Coll., 1983; MBA, Claremont Grad. Sch., 1985. Auditor Coopers & Lybrand, N.Y.C., 1983; customer and fin. services mgr. Telemktg. Communications of So. Calif., Pasadena, 1983-85; mgmt. cons. Arthur Anderson & Co., Los Angeles, 1986; asst. to v.p. Lawry's Restaurants, Inc./Van Frank Investments, Los Angeles, 1986-87; pres. Cee-Jay Research & Sales, Inc., Los Angeles, 1987—. Active San Marino Summer Baseball Camp, 1977-81; Lyndon Baines Johnson Congl. intern, Washington, 1982; pres. founder Pasadena Area Young Repubs., 1984—; founder Hunting for Art Gallery Jr. Fellows, San Marino, Calif. 1986—. Mem. Toastmasters (Jonathan Club), Pasadena Poly. High Sch. Alumni Exec. Com. Christian Scientist. Home: 267 S Roosevelt Pasadena CA 91107 Office: Cee-Jay Rsch & Sales Inc 13904 Maryton Ave Santa Fe Springs CA 90670

BANTA, MERLE HENRY, graphics equipment and service company executive; b. East St. Louis, Ill., Dec. 11, 1932; s. Albert Merle and Vivian Mae (Brown) B.; m. June M. Mueller, June 17, 1955; children—Brenda J. Williams, Berton M., Bradford C. B.S., Washington U., St. Louis, 1954; M.S., Iowa State U., 1955; M.B.A., Harvard U., 1961. Registered profl. engr.

Cons. McKinsey & Co., Los Angeles, 1961-64; chmn., pres., chief exec. officer Leisure Group, Los Angeles, 1964-84, Pacific Homes, Los Angeles, 1981-84; chmn., chief exec. officer AM Internat., Inc., Chgo., 1984—, pres., 1984-85, 88—; dir. Mark Controls Corp., Evanston, Ill., Leisure Group, Los Angeles, Pacific Homes, Los Angeles. Trustee Pasadena Poly. Sch., Calif., 1977—; bd. overseers Huntington Library, San Marino, Calif., 1972—. Served to lt. USN, 1955-59; North Africa. Recipient Daniel Mead award ASCE, 1955. Named Baker scholar Harvard U. Bus. Sch., Boston, 1961. Republican. Presbyterian. Clubs: California, Jonathon (Los Angeles); Economic, Chicago (Chgo.). Home: 180 E Pearson Apt 5006 Chicago IL 60611 Office: AM Internat Inc 333 W Wacker Dr Ste 900 Chicago IL 60606 *

BANTUVERIS, MIKE, consultant company executive; b. Racine, Wis., Dec. 25, 1935; s. Nickolas and Evangeline (Kallis) B.; children: Susan, Karen. BBA, U. Wis., 1963, MBA, 1964; postgrad., UCLA, 1978-82. Dir. mktg., devel. E&J Gallo Wine, Modesto, Calif., 1964-67; dir. strategic plan Gen. Mills, Mpls., 1967-70; dir. acquisitions, new bus. Internat. Multifoods, Mpls., 1970-73; v.p. dir. of ops. North Star Industries, L.A., 1973-75; pres., founder InterQuest Inc., Northridge, Calif., 1975—. Author: Strategic Boundaries Forming Industry Structure, 1981. With U.S. Army, 1954-59. Mem. Phi Beta Kappa, Phi Kappa Phi, Beta Gamma Sigma, Am. Soc. of Appraisers, Planning Execs. Inst., Am. Mgmt. Assn. Republican. Episcopalian. Office: InterQuest Inc 11145 Tampa Ave Ste 25 Northridge CA 91326

BANZHAF, CLAYTON HARRIS, retired merchandising company executive; b. Buffalo, Dec. 24, 1917; s. Joseph Maxmillian and Elizabeth (Harris) B.; m. Dolores J. Gavins, Dec. 30, 1962; children by previous marriage: Barbara Banzhaf Grimmett, Debra Banzhaf York, William Clay. M.B.A., U. Chgo., 1954. With Sears, Roebuck & Co., 1936-81, corp. asst. treas., 1958-60; sr. asst. treas. Sears, Roebuck & Co., Chgo., 1961-74; treas. Sears, Roebuck & Co., 1975-81, v.p., 1976-81, also dir.; pres., chief exec. officer Sears Roebuck Acceptance Corp., Wilmington, Del., 1963-72; dir. Sears Roebuck Acceptance Corp., 1972-81; former treas. Fleet Maintenance Inc., Lifetime Foam Products, Inc., Sears Finance Corp., Sears Internat. Finance Co., Sears Roebuck Internat. Inc., Sears Roebuck Overseas, Inc., Sears Roebuck de P.R. Inc., Terminal Freight Handling Co., Tower Ventures, Inc.; dir., chmn. audit com. Barclays Am. Corp.; former dir. Banco de Credito Internacional S.A., Homart Devel. Co., Lake Shore Land Assn., Inc., Sears Overseas Finance N.V., Western Forge Corp.; former officer other subs. Mem. com. banking, monetary and fiscal affairs U.S. C. of C., 1969-74; mem. exec. com. Chgo. Area council Boy Scouts Am., 1963-68, adv. bd., 1969-81; bd. dirs. Council Community Services, Chgo., 1975-77, United Way Met. Chgo., 1977-81; trustee Elmira (N.Y.) Coll., 1975-81; mem. com. on allied health evaluation and accreditation AMA, 1978-85; mem. bus. adv. council U. Ill., Chgo., 1978-81; mem. adv. bd. Coll. Health Related Professions, U. Fla., Gainesville, 1985—. Served to maj. AUS, 1941-46. Decorated Army Commendation medal. Mem. Fin. Execs. Inst. (pres. Chgo. 1972-73, nat. dir., exec. com. 1975-78, Midwest area v.p. 1977-78), Am. Assembly Collegiate Schs. Bus. (continuing accreditation com.), U. Chgo. Alumni Assn. (dir. 1966-67, v.p. 1968, pres. 1969, alumni council Grad. Sch. Bus. 1969, pres. 1972-75). Republican. Presbyterian. Clubs: Hound Ears, Long boat Key, Sarabay Country, Medinah Country. Home: 748 Dream Island Rd Longboat Key FL 34228 also: Hounds Ears Club Box 188 Blowing Rock NC 28605

BARAD, JILL ELIKANN, toy company executive; b. N.Y.C., May 23, 1951; d. Lawrence Stanley and Corinne (Schuman) Elikann; m. Thomas Kenneth Barad, Jan., 28, 1979; children: Alexander David, Justin Harris. BA English and Psychology, Queens Coll., 1973. Asst. prod. mgr. mktg. Coty Cosmetics, N.Y.C., 1976-77, prod. mgr. mktg., 1977; account exec. Wells Rich Greene Advt. Agy., Los Angeles, 1978-79; product mgr. mktg. Mattel Toys, Inc., Los Angeles, 1981-82, dir. mktg., 1982-83, v.p. mktg., 1983-85, sr. v.p. mktg., 1985-86, sr. v.p. product devel., from 1986, exec. v.p. product design and devel., exec. v.p. mktg. and product devel., 1988—. Charter mem. Rainbow Guild/Amie Karen Cancer Fund, Los Angeles, 1983, Los Angeles County Mus., 1985. Mem. Am. Film Inst. (charter). Office: Mattel Inc 5150 Rosecrans Ave Hawthorne CA 90250

BARAKET, EDMUND S., JR., general contractor, contracting consultant; b. N.Y.C., Oct. 10, 1947; s. Edmund S. and Agnes B.; student Pa. State U., 1967-69; A.A., Lehigh County Community Coll., 1971; m. Maryann; children—Christopher, Melissa, Joseph, Susan. Insp. metall. layout Bethlehem Steel Corp., 1967-69, mem. research and devel. staff, 1970-73; owner, mgr. Ed Baraket Gen. Contractors, Allentown, Pa., 1973—. Recipient award for restoration of early colonial family residences Keystone Publs., 1978. Mem. Gen. Contractors Assn. Lehigh Valley, Concrete Contractors Assn., Am. Soc. Concrete Constrn. Office: Ed Barket Gen Contractors 1322 Tweed Ave Allentown PA 18103

BARALT, CARLOS MANUEL, corporate executive, valuation and investment consultant; b. Havana, Cuba, Aug. 4, 1936; came to U.S., 1960; s. Luis A. and Lillian S. (Mederos) B.; m. Teresita Menendez Llanio, June 24, 1961; children: Sylvia, Cristina, Alicia, Anamaria. BS in Indsl. Engring., Lehigh U., 1962. Supr. systems dept. Whirlpool Corp., Evansville, Ind., 1963-67; sr. cons. corp. systems ITT Corp., N.Y.C., 1968-71; v.p. fin., adminstrn. Lyons Container Services Inc., Chgo., 1971-72; v.p. mktg. Am. Valuation Cons., Des Plaines, Ill., 1975-77; v.p. Marshall and Stevens Inc., N.Y.C., 1972-74, cons. internat. valuation, 1978-83; mgmt. cons. Arthur Andersen and Co., N.Y.C., 1983-85; chief exec. officer, chmn. bd. Homalite Inc., Wilmington, Del., 1985—; chief exec. officer, chmn. bd. Gen. Printing Corp., Wilminton, Del., 1987—; chmn., bd. dirs. Bacic Investment Counselors Inc., Cranbury, N.J., Cabris Corp., Wilmington. Contbr. articles to profl. jours. Mem. Nat. Assn. Accts., Assn. Corp. Growth, Alpha Pi Mu. Home: 24 Yeger Rd Cranbury NJ 08512 Office: Homalite Inc 11 Brookside Dr Wilmington DE 19806

BARBACHANO, FERNANDO G. R., banker; b. Merida, Yucatan, Mexico, Apr. 24, 1926; s. Fernando P. and Carmen (G.R.) B.; student Harvard U., U. Yucatan; m. Maruja G. Herrero, Dec. 21, 1947; children—Fernando, Maruja, Carmen, Cristina, Isabel, Juan. Founder, present chmn. constrn. co., food packing co., land-marine transp. co., airline co., also chain of hotels; founder 2 schs. tourism; developer Cozumel Island, Mexican Caribbean for tourists. chmn. bd. bank. Hon. consul of Guatemala in Merida, Mexico. Chmn. bd. dirs. Maya Found. Mem. Nat. Hotel Assn. (dir.), Nat. Travel Agts. Assn. (dir.), Merida C. of C. (dir.), Chamber Public Transport, Chamber Constrn., Chamber Tourism, Chamber Air Transport, Bankers Club, Internat. Assn. Travel Agts., Am. Soc. Travel Agts., Am. Hotel Mgmt. Assn., AMAV, AMH, COTAL, ICA. Club: Country. Home: 495 Montejo Ave, Merida Yucatan, Mexico Office: 472 60th St, Merida Yucatan, Mexico

BARBANELL, ROBERT LOUIS, financial executive; b. N.Y.C., June 30, 1930; s. Morris and Leah (Lorentz) B.; m. Carol Zeligson Feld, Nov. 26, 1960 (div.); 1 son, Edward M.; m. Betsy Shack, Feb. 1987. BS in Fin., NYU, 1952. With Loeb Rhoades & Co., N.Y.C., 1954-75; chmn., pres. Geon Industries, Inc., Woodbury, N.Y., 1975-77; v.p. fin. Azcon Corp., N.Y.C., 1977-79, Amcon Group, Inc., N.Y.C., 1979-80; pres. Amcon Group, Inc., 1981; sr. v.p. Bankers Trust Co., 1982-86, mng. dir., 1986—; Bd. dirs. Bond Investors Group, Inc. Bd. dirs. Lexington Sch. for Deaf, 1981—. Served with U.S. Army, 1952-54. Republican. Jewish. Clubs: University, Sky. Office: Bankers Trust Co 280 Park Ave New York NY 10017

BARBAROSH, MILTON HARVEY, investment baker; b. Montreal, Que., Can., Apr. 22, 1955; came to U.S., 1986; s. William and Ethel (Greenstone) B.; m. Ricki Tucker, June 1, 1980; children: Marli, Lori, Liana. B of Commerce and Acctg. with honors, Concordia U., Montreal, 1976; Can. Chartered Acct., McGill U., Montreal, 1977; MBA, York U., Toronto, Ont., Can., 1980. Sr. staff acct. Thorne, Ernst & Whinney, Montreal, 1976-79; mgr. merger and acquisitions Clarkson Gordon/Arthur Young, Toronto, 1980-84, Royal Bank of Can., Toronto, 1984-86; pres. JW Charles Group, Inc., Boca Raton, Fla., 1987-88, JW Charles Capital Corp., Boca Raton, 1986—. Author: (with others) The Acquisition Decision; editor M&A in Canada for Harris-Bentley Ltd. Fellow Can. Inst. Chartered Bankers; mem. The Can. Inst. of Chartered Bus. Valuators, Am. Soc. Appraisers (sr.), Securities Industry Assn. (membership com.), Inst. Chartered Accts. Ont., Quebec Order Chartered Accts., McGill U. Alumni, U. Toronto Alumni, Concordia U. Alumni, York U. Alumni, Boca Acad. (bd. dirs.), Pres.'s Club Fla. Atlantic U. (pres.), Boca Raton Hotel and Club. Office: JW Charles Capital Corp 980 N Federal Hwy Ste 310 Boca Raton FL 33432

BARBEE, WILLIAM HENRY, JR., business and government consultant, minister; b. Washington, Nov. 8, 1937; s. William Henry and Margaret Catherine (Coffman) B.; m. Elizabeth Ann Baumgardner, June 27, 1959; children: William Henry III, Marta Elizabeth, Erica Barbee Gardner, Christian Michael. BA, U. Md., 1970; MPA, U. So. Calif., 1976; PhD in Religion, Universal Life Ch., 1981, DD (hon.), 1981. Ordained to ministry Universal Life Ch., 1976. Reservations sales agt. Pan Am. World Airways, Washington, 1960; sales rep. Varig Airlines Brazil, Washington, 1961-63; sr. sales rep. Trans-World Airlines, Inc., Louisville, 1963-64; U.S. sales mgr., staff asst. to mng. dir. and chief exec. officer Civil Air Transport Co., Washington and Taipei, Republic of China, 1964-70; staff asst. Pacific Corp., Washington, 1964-70; mng. dir., chief exec. officer Barbee Cos., Washington, 1970—; chief exec. officer Nat. Conf. State Socs., Washington, 1986—, also bd. govs.; part-time lectr. bus. tech. Prince Georges Community Coll., Largo, Md., 1977-81; chief transp. br., spl. asst. to assoc. dir. adminstrn., expert cons. ACTION, Washington, 1970-72; mgmt. analyst VA, Washington, 1972-82, dep. dir. emergency mgmt. staff, 1982-84, mgr. nat. security and emergency preparedness programs Dept. Med. and Surgery, 1984—, past pres. VA Cen. Fed. Credit Union. Author: (with R. Pell, Jr.) A Program Evaluation--VA Chaplain Service, 1977; exec. editor Easy Money, 1976-80; editor: VFW Newsletter, 1979-80, GTS Newsletter, 1982-84; contbr. articles to profl. jours. Chmn. Mayor's Council on Sr. Citizens' Affairs City of New Carrollton (Md.), 1981-84; bd. dirs. Greater Washington Cherry Blossom Festival Com., 1986—; pres., chief exec. officer Vets. Adminstrn. Central Office Fed. Credit Union, Washington, 1976-80; bd. dirs. Asian Pacific Am. Heritage Council, Inc., Washington, 1982-83, Fed. Guamanian Assocs. Am., Inc., 1982-83; pres., chief. exec. officer Nat. Conf. State Socs., Washington, 1986-87. Served with USN, 1955-58. Mem. Am. Soc. Pub. Adminstrn., Met. Area Credit Union Mgmt. Assn., Nat. Aero. Assn., Assn. Mil. Surgeons U.S., Am. Soc. Psychical Research, Am. Soc. Assn. Execs., Calif. Soc. Psychical Study, Acad. Polit. Scis., Soc. for Philos. Study of the Paranormal, Nat. Emergency Mgmt. Assn., Nat. Emergency Mgmt. Coordinating Council, Aerobics Internat. Research Soc., Am. Legion, VFW (life), Guam Soc. Am., Nat. Aeronautic Assn., Armed Forces Communications and Electronics Assn., Nat. Assn. Uniformed Services Soc. Mil. Widows, Audubon Soc., Navy League, Guam Soc. Am. (bd. dirs., past pres.), Fedn. Guamanian Assns. Am. (bd. dirs.), Oceanic Soc., Nat. Geographic Soc., Am. Running and Fitness Assn., Smithsonian Assocs., Sigma Chi, others. Republican. Club: Advt. Met. Washington (edn. com.). Lodge: Rosicrucians. Home: Oakwood Knolls 6610 Adrian St New Carrollton MD 20784-3610 Office: VA Central Office Code 10B/EMS-1e NW 810 Vermont Ave NW Washington DC 20420-0001

BARBER, ANDREW BOLLONS, bank executive; b. Joliet, Ill., Apr. 8, 1909; s. Charles and Pauline Inez (Bollons) B.; student U. Ill., 1929-31; B.S., Northwestern U., 1939; m. Jo Ann McDonald, June 9, 1983; children—Suzanne (Mrs. Terrence J. Ryan), Nancy (Mrs. William Stone), Mary Jane (Mrs. Robert Holt); m. 2d, Jo Ann McDonald, June 9, 1983. Co-organizer, officer Union Nat. Bank, Joliet, Ill., 1940—, pres., 1972-73, chmn. bd., 1974—; vice chmn., dir. 1st Midwest Bancorp., Inc., 1946-82; dir. Citizens Nat. Bank, Waukegan, Ill., Nat. Bank North Chicago (Ill.), Streator (Ill.) Nat. Bank. Chmn. Will County Savings Bond Program, 1946-84; mem. Salem Village Bd. Trustees; chmn. Will County Land Clearance Commn., 1968-72; mem. Joliet Parking Commn., 1950-70; mem. Luth. Welfare Services Bd.; bd. dirs. Credit Bur. Will County; nat. assoc. bd. dirs. Boys Club Am., 1975—. Mem. C. of C. Kiwanian. Clubs: Country (Joliet, Ill.); Gt. Harbor Cay Flying; Three Rivers Yacht (Wilmington, Ill.); Chgo. Yacht; Tamboo (Bahamas). Home: 415 Western Ave Joliet IL 60435 Office: First Midwest Bancorp Inc 50 W Jefferson St Joliet IL 60431

BARBER, CHARLES EDWARD, journalist, newspaper executive; b. Miami, Fla., Oct. 30, 1939; s. James Plemon and Margaret Katherine (Grimes) B.; AA, Santa Fe Community Coll., 1971; m. Judith Margaret Tuck, May 28, 1960; children: Janet Lynn Wood, Christopher Edward. Prodn. mgr. dept. student publs. U. Fla., Gainesville, 1966-68, ops. mgr., 1968-70, asst. dir., 1970-72, dir., 1972-73, dir. div. publs., 1974; prodn. mgr. State Univ. System Press, Gainesville, 1975-76; pres., gen. mgr. Campus Communications, Inc., Gainesville, 1976—; assoc. pub., University News, 1987—; cons. in field. Mem. citizens adv. council Stephen Foster Elem. Sch., Gainesville, 1973-77; mem. Friends of Five, 1975-77, Friends of Library, 1975-77; chmn. book com. Fla. State Prison, 1973-85; bd. dirs. Gainesville High Sch. Band Boosters, 1978-79, 83-84, treas., 1984; key communicator Alachua County Sch. Bd., 1980—; spl. registered dep. sheriff Alachua County Sheriff's Dept., 1979—; mem. gifted students boosters Howard Bishop Middle Sch., 1980-82; dir. Howard Bishop Band Boosters, 1980-82; mem. pres.'s council U. Fla., 1978—; mem. Leadership Gainesville, 1979; pack com. chmn. Cub Scouts Am., 1977-78. With USCGR, 1957-65. Recipient Nat. 1st Place for Editorial Writing Hearst Found., 1965, Svc. award Santa Fe Community Coll., 1982; named nation's most disting. bus. adv. to coll. press, 1978; Cert. of Appreciation, Big Bros. and Big Sisters of Gainesville, 1984, Vols. for Internat. Student Affairs, 1986, 88, Fla. Track Club, 1988; Addy award Gainesville Advt. Fedn., 1986, 87. Mem. Am. Collegiate Network (adv. com.), Am. Advt. Fedn., Am. Newspaper Pubs. Assn., Associated Collegiate Press, Assn. for Edn. in Journalism and Mass Communications, Coll. Newspaper Bus. and Advt. Mgrs. (dir. 1981), Assn. Newspaper Classified Advt. Mgrs., Fla. Scholastic Press Assn. (newspaper judge 1981-85), Fla. Newspaper Advt. and Mktg. Execs. (chmn. edn. com.), Fla. Press Found., Fla. Press Assn., Fla. Press Club, Gainesville Advt. Fedn., (dir. 1979-80), Internat. Newspaper Fin. Execs., Internat. Newspaper Advt. and Mktg. Execs., Internat. Newspaper Mktg. Assn., Coll. Media Advisers, Soc. Newspaper Design, So. Univ. Newspapers (dir. 1980—), Printing Industries Fla., Gainesville Area C. of C. (com. of 100), Alligator Alumni Assn. (dir. 1980—, named Mr. Alligator 1986), Red Herring Club, Alchua Health Fitness Club, Sigma Delta Chi (treas. No. Fla. chpt. 1972-75, 86—), Alpha Phi Gamma. Democrat. Baptist (chmn. bd. deacons 1978, ch. moderator 1981-85). Adv. editor Fla. Quar., 1973-74; contbr. articles to profl. jours. Home: 4205 NW 21st Terr Gainesville FL 32605 Office: University News PO Box 14257 Gainesville FL 32604

BARBER, JIM ROBERT, financial planner; b. Huntington, W.Va., Feb. 9, 1952; s. James R. and N. June (Noble) B.; m. Cathy Lee Stevens, Mar. 10, 1973; children: Chad R., Cory S. Student, W.Va. U., 1970-72, Marshall U., 1972-73. Cert. fin. planner. Sales mgr. Lanier Bus. Products, Greensboro, N.C., 1976-81; fin. planner Edward D. Jones & Co., Greensboro, 1981—. Bd. dirs. Camp Carefree. Mem. Inst. Cert. Fin. Planners (cert.), Internat. Assn. Fin. Planners, Greensboro C. of C. (bd. dirs.), Kiwanis (chmn. bd.), Elks. Office: Edward D Jones & Co Forum VI Level 5 Greensboro NC 27408

BARBERA, FRANK ANTHONY, healthcare company executive; b. N.Y.C., Apr. 26, 1935; s. Antonio and Nicolena (Colella) B.; m. Joanna Maria Puccio, July 19, 1959; 1 child, Frank Jr. BBA, CUNY, 1956. CPA, N.Y. Sr. audit mgr. Ernst & Whinney, N.Y.C., 1956-72; v.p. fin. Polygram Corp., N.Y.C., 1972-75, Tosco Corp., Los Angeles, 1975-82; pres., chief exec. officer CompuMed Inc., Culver City, Calif., 1982—. Chmn. assessment bd. Town of Ossining, N.Y., 1970-74; pres. Young Reps., Ossining, 1973; mem. Rep. Town Com., Ossining, 1974. Mem. Am. Inst. CPAs, N.Y. State Soc. CPAs, Financal Execs. Inst. Roman Catholic. Home: 30208 Matisse Dr Rancho Palos Verdes CA 90274

BARBERA, MICHAEL ANTHONY, sales representative, consultant; b. Rochester, N.Y., Dec. 31, 1952; s. Anthony James and Ann Marie (DeYulio) B.; m. Amelia L. Tata, Sept. 13, 1975 (div. Apr. 1983); m. Sharon Nina Catanese, June 24, 1985. Cert. in leadership, No. Am. U., 1983. With data processing Xerox Corp., Rochester, 1970-74; pres. Barbera Painting Co., Rochester, 1974-77; corp. recruiter Mgmt. Recruiters, Rochester, 1977-80; sales rep. N.A. Van Lines, Rochester, 1980-83; v.p. sales Global Van Lines, Fairport, N.Y., 1983-86; sales rep. Marsellus Casket Co., Syracuse, N.Y., 1986—. Bd. dirs. YMCA, Greece, N.Y., 1983. Mem. N.Y. State Funeral Dirs. Assn., Rochester Realtors Assn., Rochester Profl. Sales Assn. Republican. Mem. Christian Ch. Home: 94 W Main St Honeoye Falls NY 14872 Office: Marsellus Casket Co 101 Richmond Ave Syracuse NY 13221

BARBIERI, ARTHUR ROBERT, chemicals company official; b. Paterson, N.J., June 10, 1926; s. Otto Arthur and Sadie (Maxwell) B.; student Rutgers U., 1957-58, Utah State U., 1962-69, Weber Coll., 1980—; m. Carole Jones, Dec. 26, 1979; children by previous marriage—Elaine, Debra, Donna. Asst. buyer Allen B. Dumont Labs., Clifton, N.Y., 1947-54; field supr. Housing Guild, Inc., Smithtown, N.Y., 1954-56; buyer Thiokol Co., Denville, N.J., 1956-60, sr. buyer, Brigham City, Utah, 1960-72, purchasing agt., 1972-85, sr. buyer, 1985-88. Bd. dirs. Brigham City Community Theatre, Thiokol Credit Union; precinct capt. Dem. party, 1973. Served with USN, 1944-46; PTO. Democrat. Clubs: Elks, Masons (past master, chmn. Grand Lodge Youth com. 1979), Shriners (pres. No. Utah club 1974-75), Jobs Daus. (asso. grand guardian 1978). Home: 3044 Jennie Ln Lake Havasu City AZ 86403

BARBIERI, ROCCO A., manufacturing company executive; b. 1936. BS, Villanova U., 1957. Controller Baker Industries Inc., Cedar Knolls, N.J., 1958-70; pres., chief exec. officer Gen. Felt Industries Inc., 1971—; exec. v.p. Knoll Internat. Holdings Inc., 1976; v.p. Knoll Internat. Inc., N.Y., 1978; pres., chief operating officer, chief exec. officer Knoll Internat. Inc., from 1981; pres., chief exec. officer Mich. Gen. Corp., from 1985; pres., chief exec. officer, dir. Mich. Gen. Investment Corp., Dallas, from 1985; now pres., chief operating officer, sr. mng. dir. Knoll Internat. Holdings Inc. Office: Gen Felt Industries Inc Park 80 Pla W-1 Saddle Brook NJ 07662 also: Knoll Internat Holdings Inc 153 E 53rd St New York NY 10022 *

BARBOUR, JAMES KEITH, chemical packaging and distribution company executive; b. N.Y.C., Jan. 30, 1948; s. James Morse and Rita Elizabeth (Edwards) B.; BA, Vanderbilt U., 1969; MBA with distinction, Adelphi U., 1973; m. Carole Barbour, June 25, 1982; children: Scott Ryan, Allison Cori, Daniel Adam. With N.Y. Telephone Co., N.Y.C., 1970-76; with AT&T, Morristown, N.J., 1977-78; v.p. mktg. and adminstrn., v.p. ops. Chas. Schaefer Sons, Inc. (name now Schaefer Salt & Chem.), Elizabeth, N.J., 1978-82, v.p., 1982-83, exec. v.p., 1983-87, chief op. officer, 1982-87, pres., prin., 1987—; prin., pres. Apocalypse Inc., 1983—; cons. in field communications, strategic planning, reorgn., tactical mktg., and negotiations. Mem. Rep. Congl. Com.; water safety instr. ARC. Mem. Am. Mktg. Assn., Nat. Assn. Chem. Distbrs., Sales Assocs. Chem. Industry, Nat. Pilots Assn., N.J. Chemists Club, Am. Mgmt. Assn., Aircraft Owners and Pilots Assn., U.S. Judo Assn., Scarsdale (N.Y.) Golf Club, Fairmount Country Club, Rainbow Springs Golf and Country Club, Beacon Hill Country Club (corp. mem.), Atlantic Highlands Yacht Club, Channel Club. Home: 933 W Front St Red Bank NJ 07701-5615 Office: Apocalypse Inc PO Box 236 Elizabeth NJ 07207

BARCA, GEORGE GINO, winery executive; b. Sacramento, Jan. 28, 1937; s. Joseph and Annie (Muschetto) B.; m. Maria Sclafani, Nov. 19, 1960; children—Anna, Joseph, Gina and Nina (twins). A.A., Grant Jr. Coll.; student LaSalle U., 1963. With AeroJet Gen. Corp., Sacramento, 1958-65, United Vintners, Inc., San Francisco, 1960-73; pres., gen. mgr. Barcamerica Corp., Sacramento, 1963—; pres., gen. mgr. Barca Wine Cellars, Calif. Wine Cellars, Inc., Calif. Grape Growers, Inc., Calif. Vintage Wines, Inc., Am. Vintners, Inc.; cons. in field. Named Best Producer of Sales, United Vintners, Inc. Mem. Calif. Farm Bur., Met. C. of C., Better Bus. Bur., Roman Catholic. Club: KC. Developer wine trademarks.

BARCA, KATHLEEN, marketing executive; b. Burbank, Calif., July 26, 1946; d. Frank Allan and Blanch Irene (Griffith) Barnes; m. Gerald Albino Barca, Dec. 8, 1967; children; Patrick Gerald, Stacia Kathleen. Student, Pierce Coll., 1964; B in Bus., Hancock Coll., 1984. Teller Security Pacific Bank, Pasadena, Calif., 1968-69, Bank Am., Santa Maria, Calif., 1972-74; operator Gen. Telephone Co., Santa Maria, Calif., 1974-83, supr. operator, 1983-84; account exec. Sta. KRQK/KLLB Radio, Lompoc, Calif., 1984-85; owner Advt. Unltd., Orcutt, Calif., 1986-88; regional mgr. A.L. Williams Mktg. Co., Los Alamos, Calif., 1988—; supr. Matol Botanical Internat., 1989—. Author: numerous local TV and radio commercials, print advt. Activist Citizens Against Dumps in Residential Environments, Polit. Action Com., Orcutt and Santa Maria; chmn. Community advt. Com., Santa Maria, Workshop EPA, Calif. Div., Dept. Health Svcs. State of Calif.; vice coord. Toughlove, Santa Maria; parent coord., mem. steering com. ASAP and Friends. Mem. Nat. Assn. Female Exec., Womens Network-Santa Maria, Cen. Coast Ad (recipient numerous awards), Santa Maria Valley C. of C. Democrat. Home and Office: 509 Shaw St PO Box 676 Los Alamos CA 93440

BARCLAY, DAVID KEATING, aquatic biologist, aquaculturist; b. Santa Monica, Calif., July 21, 1952; s. James Charles and Hildegarde (Roselle) B.; m. Christine Morgan, Jan. 21, 1979; children: Micah James Andrew, Benjamin David Christian. BS in Zoology, U. Hawaii, 1978. Asst. trainer Sea Life park, Waimanalo, Hawaii, 1971-72; rsch. asst. Naval Undersea Ctr., Kaneohe, Hawaii, 1974-75; marine mammal handler U. Hawaii, Honolulu, 1973-76; rsch. assoc. Rsch. Corp. U. Hawaii, Keahole Point, 1982-85; environ. technician Naval Ocean Systems Ctr., Kaneohe, 1975-77; asst. farm mgr. Aquatic Farms Ltd., Kaneohe, 1977-78; aquaculturist Trafalgar Housing Ltd., Hong Kong, 1981; cons. NSF, Kaneohe, 1982-83; owner, cons. Aquatic Culture and Design, Kapaau, Hawaii, 1986—; Pacific region sale mgr. Argent Chem. Labs., 1986—. Inventor aquaculture harvester; author tech. papers. Mem. North Kohala Bus. Assn., World Aquaculture Soc., Industry Adv. Council, Kona C. of C. Home and Office: PO Box 911 Kapaau HI 96755

BARCLAY, JAMES EDWARD, footwear company executive; b. Camden, N.Y., Mar. 12, 1941; s. John A. and Hazel I. (Leavenworth) B.; m. Jane Alice Chariton, Dec. 26, 1964; children: Sean, Kimberly, Adam. AAS, Morrisville Tech. Coll., 1961; BS, U. Ga., 1965. Sales rep. Gen. Foods, Atlanta, 1966-67; tech. sales rep. R.T. Vanderbilt Co., Inc., N.Y.C., 1967-69; dist. sales mgr. Beech Nut Foods, N.Y.C., 1969-70, div. sales mgr., 1970-72; nat. sales mgr. B.C. Recreational Industries, Braintree, Mass., 1972-79; v.p. sales and mktg. Reebok Internat., Ltd., Hingham, Mass., 1979-82; exec. v.p. Reebok Internat., Ltd., Avon, Mass., 1982-86; pres. footwear div. Reebok Internat., Ltd., Canton, Mass., 1986-87, exec. v.p., 1987—. Bd. dirs. Two/Ten Charity Trust, Watertown, Mass., 1986—. Office: Reebok Internat Ltd 150 Royal St Canton MA 02021

BARCLAY, RONALD DAVID, chemical company executive; b. Pitts., 1934; s. David Thompson and Olive Stewart (Bietel) B.; m. Gladys Anne Stoudt, July 11, 1959; children—Todd, Dana, Scott. B.B.A., U. Pitts., 1956; M.B.A., Lehigh U., 1965; Sr. Exec. Program, MIT, 1984. Market planning asst. Air Products & Chems., Inc., Allentown, Pa., 1956-57; treasury staff asst. Air Products & Chems., Inc., 1957-64, asst. treas., 1964-75, treas., 1975-82, v.p., treas., 1982—. Bd. dirs. Lehigh Econ. Advancement Project, Pa., 1979—, Health East Community Health Svcs. Orgn., Allentown, Pa., 1986—; with USCG, 1957-58. Republican. Presbyterian. Office: Air Products & Chems Inc PO Box 538 Allentown PA 18105

BARCUS, GILBERT MARTIN, medical products executive; b. N.Y.C., Sept. 20, 1937; s. Leon A. and Dorothy (Brownstein) B.; m. Sondra Ettin, May 6, 1961; children: David A., Ruth A. BS, NYU, 1959; MBA, L.I. U., 1969. Stock broker Ernst & Co., N.Y.C., 1962-65; sales mgr. McNeil Labs., Ft. Washington, Pa., 1965-75; mktg. mgr. USA Devices Ltd., New Brunswick, N.J., 1976-77; dir. product mgmt. TENS div. Stimtech, Inc., Mpls., 1977-78; products dir. Critikon, Inc., Raritan, N.J., 1979-80; v.p. mktg. Electro Biology, Inc., Fairfield, N.J., 1980-82; dir. sales, mktg. Medtronic/Med. Data Systems, Ann Arbor, Mich., 1982-85; v.p. corp. devel. Am. Biomaterials Corp., Princeton, N.J., 1985-86, sr. v.p., 1986-88; pres. Sandar Assocs., North Brunswick, N.J., 1980—; gen mgr. Creative Care Systems, Maplewood, N.J., 1986—; adj. prof. bus. CUNY, Middlesex Coll., Edison, N.J., 1986-88; lectr. dept. bus. Brookdale Community Coll., Bus. Week Mktg. Seminars, 1988. Contbr. articles to profl. jours. Chmn. Marlboro (N.J.) Fire Commn.; dir. Small Bus. Devel. Ctr. Middlesex County, 1988—. Fellow Assn. Advancement Med. Instrumentation, Internat. Assn. Study of Pain; mem. Ann Arbor C. of C. (legis. com.), NYU Alumni Assn. (dir. 1987—), Travis Pointe Country Club, NYU Club, Forsgate Country Club (v.p. 1986—), Pi Lambda Phi. Home and Office: 15 Wood Lake Ct North Brunswick NJ 08902

BARD, JOHN FRANKLIN, consumer products executive; b. Owatonna, Minn., Mar. 1, 1941; s. Franklin S. and Nina Carolyn (Geyer) B.; m. Barbara Ann Bowers, Aug. 1, 1964; children: Steven George, Kristin Elizabeth. BS in Bus., Northwestern U., 1963; MBA in Fin., U. Cin., 1972. With Procter & Gamble Co., Cin., 1963-78, internat. controller; group. v.p. Clorox Co., Oakland, Calif., 1978-84; pres. Physicians Formula Cosmetics, City of Industry, Calif., 1985—; exec. v.p., chief oper. officer Parent Co. Tambrands Inc., Lake Success, N.Y., 1985—; bd. dirs. Tambrands Inc. Bd. dirs. Alameda County YMCA, Oakland, 1979-87, Long Island United Way. Mem. Fin. Execs. Inst. Home: 25 Shore Dr Larchmont NY 10538 Office: Tambrands Inc 1 Marcus Ave Lake Success NY 11042

BARDFELD, LAWRENCE RICHARD, financial services executive, lawyer; b. N.Y.C., May 17, 1947; s. Max and Ann Helen (Rothbart) B.; m. Laura Ann Corsell, Sept. 20, 1986; 1 child, David Peter. BS, CCNY, 1970; MBA, Columbia U., 1971; JD, Fordham U., 1975. Bar: N.Y. 1976, D.C. 1978, Pa. 1988. Staff atty. SEC, Washington, 1975-77, spl. counsel, 1977-80, asst. dir., 1980-83; asst. gen. counsel Paine Webber, Inc., N.Y.C., 1983-85, v.p., assoc. gen. counsel, 1985-86; v.p., gen. counsel Pitcairn Fin. Mgmt. Group, Jenkintown, Pa., 1986-88, sr. v.p., gen. counsel, 1988—, also bd. dirs.; bd. dirs. Andrews/Nelson/Whitehead Corp., N.Y.C. Editor: Fordham Urban Law Jour., 1974-75. Office: Pitcairn Fin Mgmt Group 165 Township Line Rd Jenkintown PA 19046

BARDONER, JAMES LEO, retired manufacturing company executive; b. Lorain, Ohio, Aug. 17, 1918; s. James Ralph and Edith Margaret (Kutza) B.; m. Ruth Bradley Arndt, Nov. 3, 1944. Grad. high sch., Lorain. Foundry supr. Am. Crucible Co., Lorain, 1936-46, mgr. standards and methods, 1946-56, sales mgr., 1956-70, exec. v.p., 1970-74, pres., 1974-79; pres. Dorn Industries (formerly Am. Crucible Co.), Lorain, 1979-84, ret., 1984; bd. dirs. Lorrain Nat. Bank, LNB Bancorp., Lorain. Trustee Lorain Community Hosp., 1975—, chmn. bd. trustees, 1984—; trustee Lorain Pub. Library, 1977-88; pres. Greater Lorain County United Way, 1981; trustee Lorain County Community Coll. Found., 1981—, chmn. bd. trustees 1984-85. Mem. Elyria Country Club. Republican. Home: 3865 E Lake Rd Sheffield Lake OH 44054

BARDWIL, JOSEPH ANTHONY, investments consultant; b. Bklyn., Oct. 29, 1928; s. Najeb B. and Malvina (Galaini) B.; m. Valerie Pavilonis, Feb. 11, 1961; children—Anita, James, David, Joanna. B.S. in Econs, Wharton Sch., U. Pa., 1950; M.B.A., N.Y. U., 1956. Reporter, mgr. Dun & Bradstreet, Inc., N.Y.C., 1950-57; gen. investment mgr. Prudential Ins. Co., 1957-69; v.p. Hartz Mountain Corp., Harrison, N.J., 1969-88, Bardwil Assocs., Cranford, N.J., 1988—; Mem. adv. bd. First Jersey Nat. Bank. Mem. Fin. Analysts Fedn., N.Y. Soc. Security Analysts. Republican. Roman Catholic. Home and Office: 24 Shawnee Rd Cranford NJ 07016

BAREFOOT, BRIAN MILLER, financial service executive; b. Cin., Apr. 11, 1943; s. John Roy Jr. and Marjorie Isabel (Miller) B.; m. Pamela Howell Porter, Sept. 7, 1968; children: John, Katharine, Marjorie. BS, Babson Coll., 1966; MBA, Pace Coll., 1970. Trainee Merrill Lynch, N.Y.C., 1967-68, analyst, 1968-70; institutional salesman Merrill Lynch, Chgo., 1970-72; sales mgr. Merrill Lynch, Cleve., 1972-75; nat. sales mgr. Merrill Lynch, N.Y.C., 1975-76; mng. dir. Merrill Lynch, San Francisco and N.Y.C., 1976-84; sr. v.p., bd. dirs. Merrill Lynch, N.Y.C., 1984—. Trustee Babson Coll., Wellesley, Mass., 1986—, Kent Pl. Sch., Summit, N.J., 1988; bd. dirs. Summit (N.J.) YMCA, 1986—. Sgt. USAR, 1966-71. Mem. Econs. Club N.Y., Bond Club San Francisco, Bond Club N.Y., Beacon Hill Club (trustee 1988—), Baltusrol Golf Club, Bankers Club, Rockefeller Ctr. Club, Merchants Exchange Club of San Francisco. Republican. Episcopalian. Office: Merrill Lynch Pierce Fenner & Smith Inc World Financial Ctr New York NY 10280

BAREN, DAVID MORRIS, health care administrator; b. Chgo., Dec. 19, 1923; s. Elmon and Beckie (Bromberg) B.; m. Ann Welnak, Nov. 2, 1943; children: Terry Allen, Barbara Sue Cohen. Cert. Chem. Engring., Muskingum Coll., 1944; cer. pre-med., U. N.D., 1946; BS in Psychology, Roosevelt U., Chgo., 1947; MS in Psychology, U. Chgo., 1949, PhD, 1952. Psychologist, counselor City of Chgo., 1947-52, VA, Chgo., 1952-60; supr. of claims Ins. Co. of N.Am., Chgo., 1960-77; pres., chief exec. officer The Hosp. Annex Inc., Des Plaines, Ill., 1977—; exec. dir., chief exec. officer Cook DuPage Health Svcs., Des Plaines, Ill., 1977—; pres., chief exec. officer Preferred Providers of Met. Chgo., Maywood, Ill., 1984—, Profl. Recruitment Opportunities, Des Plaines, 1984—, Med. Network of Am., Des Plaines, 1987—. Author: Effects of Emotions on Memory, 1949. Bd. dirs. Family Svc., Village of Niles, Ill., 1978-87. With U.S. Army, 1942-46. Recipient scholarship U. Chgo. Mem. Am. Hosp. Assn., Continuity of Care, Health Profls. Jewish United Fund (bd. dirs.), Hispanic Health Alliance (bd. dirs.). Democrat. Jewish. Office: Cook DuPage Health Care 2700 River Rd #400 Des Plaines IL 60018

BARES, WILLIAM G., chemical company executive; b. 1941; married. B.S. in Chem. Engring., Purdue U., 1963; M.B.A., Case Western Res. U., 1969. Process devel. engr. Lubrizol Corp., Wickliffe, Ohio, 1963-67; group leader, pilot plant Lubrizol Corop., Wickliffe, Ohio, 1967-71; asst. dept. head Lubrizol Corp., Wickliffe, Ohio, 1971-72, dept. head., 1972-78, asst. to pres., 1978, v.p., 1978-80, exec. v.p., 1980-82, pres., dir., 1982—, chief operating officer, 1987—. Office: Lubrizol Corp 29400 Lakeland Blvd Wickliffe OH 44092 *

BARETZ, LLOYD JULE, holding company executive; b. N.Y.C., Oct. 2, 1945; s. Robert Elliott and Shirley (Schenendorf) B.; divorced; children: Elliott Joseph, Julie Lynn, Susanne Michele; m. Mia Young, May 4, 1984; 1 stepchild, Lizabeth. Grad., N.Y. Inst. Tech., 1967. Gen. mgr. Jeff Craig Assocs., Inc., Chgo., 1969-72; chief exec. officer Baretz and Assoc., Inc., Chgo., 1972-75, Fiscal Mgmt. Corp., Chgo., 1975-81; ptnr. B&B Fin. Cons., 1975-81, Cambridge Consol. Corp., Chgo., 1975—; pres. Lloydan, Inc., Gurnee, Ill., Skylark, Bristol, Ind., West Plains Furniture Cos., T.D. Holding Co, Markac, Oxford Capital Corp.; lectr. in field. With U.S. Army, 1967-69. Office: Cambridge Consol Corp 225 W Washington St Ste 1625 Chicago IL 60606

BARFIELD, BOURDON REA, investor; b. Amarillo, Tex., Oct. 28, 1926; s. Bourdon Ivy and Oliver Rea (Eakle) B.; BBA, U. Tex., 1951; m. Carolyn Grissom, Jan. 4, 1951; children: Deyanne, Amanda, Bourdon Ivy, John Callaway. Vice pres. Barfield Corp., Amarillo, 1951-57, pres. 1957—; pres. Guaranty Mortgage Corp., 1979—; dir. Mr. Burger Inc. Pres. Penbrooke Corp., Amarillo, 1969—. Mem. Durett Scholarship Com. Amarillo Pub. Schs., 1951—; area chmn. Crusade for Freedom, 1957; pres. Amarillo Symphony Orch., 1959-61; chmn. Citizens' Action Program, Amarillo, 1961-63; v.p. U. Tex. Dads' Assn., 1975—; mem. exec. com. Panhandle Plains Historical Soc., 1984, Llano Cemetery Bd, 1984; co-chmn. Amarillo Centennial Com., 1987. Mem. dist. Democratic Congl. Campaign Com., 1962-65, chmn., 1969; bd. dirs. Dallas Civic Opera, 1962, St. Andrew's Day Sch., Amarillo, 1962, Family Service Inc., Amarillo, 1969, Amarillo Art Ctr., 1972—; chmn. bd. dirs. Amarillo Pub. Library, 1963; exec. com. Panhandle Plains Mus., 1984—; co-chmn. Amarillo Centennial, 1987. Recipient Young Man of Yr. award Jr. C. of C., 1960, Man of Yr. award Amarillo Globe-News, 1988, award of Honor Downtown Amarillo Unltd. for Redevel. Work., 1966. Mem. Amarillo C. of C. (pres. 1961, named 1st Citizen of 2d. Century, 1987), U.S. C. of C. (dir. Civic Devel. Com. 1960), Jovian, 49ers, Vagabond Club, Masons (32 deg.), Rotary, Amarillo Country, Palo Duro, Beta Theta Pi. Episcopalian (lay reader, vestryman 1958-61). Home: 3201 Ong St Amarillo TX 79109 Office: 1620 Tyler St Amarillo TX 79105

BARGER, WILLIAM JAMES, savings company executive; b. Los Angeles, Nov. 1, 1944; s. James Ray and Aylene M. (Skinner) B.; m. Jane A. Cox, Jan. 30, 1988. BA, U. So. Calif., 1966; MA, Harvard U., 1970, PhD, 1972. Asst. prof econs. U. So. Calif., Los Angeles, 1971-76; v.p. Bank Am., Los Angeles, 1976-81; sr. v.p. Gibraltar Savs. Co., Beverly Hills, Calif., 1981-84, exec. v.p., 1984-88. Mem. Phi Beta Kappa.

BARGFREDE, JAMES ALLEN, lawyer; b. Seguin, Tex., Sept. 10, 1928; s. Herman Fred and Elsie (Vorpahl) B.; BS, Tex. A. and M. U., 1950; postgrad. Ohio State U., 1952-53; JD, St. Mary's U., 1957. Bar: Tex. 1957; m. Virginia Felts, Nov. 27, 1970; 1 child, Charles Allen. Registered profl. engr. Engr., Signal Corps, San Antonio, 1950-52; elec. engr. San Antonio Pub. Svc. Bd., 1953-58; patent counsel Hubbard & Co., Chgo., 1958-59; pvt. practiced law, Chgo., 1959-60, Houston, 1960—; assoc. Butler, Binion, Rice, Cook & Knapp, 1960-68; pvt. practive law, 1968-74, 75—; patent and legal counsel HydroTech Internat., Inc., 1977-81; ptnr. Bargfrede & Thompson, 1974-75. With USAF, 1952-53. Subcom. chmn. dist. com. on admissions Supreme Ct. Tex., 1988—. Mem. Houston Bar Assn. (chmn. automated equipment com. 1971-75, sub-com. chmn. bar admissions 1988—), State Bar Tex., Am. Intellectual Property Law Assn., Houston Intellectual Property Law Assn., Tex. State Bd. Law Examiners (sub-com. chmn. 1988—), Assn. Former Students Tex. A&M U., Houston Livestock Show and Rodeo (life), Delta Theta Phi. Baptist. Club: Briarcroft Civic (pres. 1979-82). Home: 5649 Piping Rock Ln Houston TX 77056 Office: 2323 S Voss Rd Houston TX 77057

BARHAM, CHARLES DEWEY, JR., electric utility executive, lawyer; b. Goldsboro, N.C., July 7, 1930; s. Charles Dewey and Helen Wilkinson (Douglass) Barham Hughes; m. Margaret Wright Crow, June 17, 1960; children: Margaret Douglass, Charles Dewey III. B.S., Wake Forest U., 1952, J.D., 1954. Bar: N.C. 1954. Asst. atty. gen. N.C. Dept. Justice, Raleigh, 1958-66; assoc. gen. counsel Carolina Power & Light Co., Raleigh, N.C., 1966-73; ptnr. Douglass & Barham, Raleigh, 1974-80; v.p., sr. counsel Carolina Power & Light Co., Raleigh, 1981-82, gen. counsel, 1982-87, sr. v.p., 1982—; chmn. bd., pres. Nuclear Mut., Ltd., Hamilton, Bermuda, 1981-86, dir.; gen. counsel World Nuclear Fuel Market, Atlanta, 1974-80; gen. counsel Meredith Coll., Raleigh, 1977-80, trustee, 1984-87; dir. regional bd. dirs. Wachovia Bank & Trust. Pres. Raleigh YMCA, 1982—. Capt. USNR, 1955-77. Mem. ABA, N.C. Bar Assn., Fed. Energy Bar Assn. Democrat. Baptist. Clubs: Raleigh Civitan (dir. 1974-77), Glen Forest (pres. 1977). Office: Carolina Power & Light Co PO Box 1551 Raleigh NC 27602 also: Carolina Power & Light Co 411 Fayetteville St Raleigh NC 27602

BARHYTE, DONALD JAMES, newspaper executive; b. Poughkeepsie, N.Y., May 16, 1937; m. Patricia E. Dressler, Dec. 27, 1958; children: Mark, Leslie. Student, U. Ky. Data processing mktg. rep. IBM, 1962-68; with Multimedia, Inc., Greenville, S.C., 1968—, asst. treas., then treas., 1971-73, v.p. fin., treas., 1973-77, v.p. fin. and adminstrn., treas., 1977-84, treas., chief fin. officer, 1985-87; pres. Multimedia Newspaper Co., 1987—; dir. S.C. Nat. Bank. Trustee, pres., St. Francis Community Hosp., 1979-80; bd. dirs., pres. United Way, 1985. Mem. Am. Mgmt. Assn., Am. Newspaper Pubs. Assn., So. Newspaper Pubs. Assn., Greenville C. of C. (v.p. community devel., dir.). Roman Catholic. Clubs: Poinsett, Biltmore Forest Country, Greenville Country. Home: 183 Chapman Rd Greenville SC 29605 Office: Multimedia Inc 305 S Main St PO Box 1688 Greenville SC 29602

BARILE, RONALD JOHN, electronics company executive; b. Cleve., Sept. 1, 1948; s. Anthony and Mary Frances (Verh) B.; m. Lynne Marie Tucker, Nov. 30, 1968; children: Anthony Lawrence, Cheryl Lynn, Ronald Christopher. AA in Data Processing, Riverside City Coll., 1972; BA in Mgmt., U. Redlands, 1982. Purchasing agt. Fleetwood Enterprises, Riverside, Calif., 1970—, computer ops. supr., 1970—, supply coordinator, 1979; real estate assoc. C.T. Smith, Riverside, 1979-81; dir. adminstrn. and fin. Synatek, Inc., San Bernardino, Calif., 1981-85, v.p., chief ops. officer, 1985-88, pres., 1988—; also bd. dirs. Dave Tucker & Assocs., Inc., San Bernardino, Calif. Served with USNR, 1969-70, Vietnam. Republican. Roman Catholic. Lodge: Rotary. Office: Synatek Inc PO Box 5249 San Bernardino CA 92412

BARIST, JEFFREY A., lawyer; b. Jersey City, Dec. 29, 1941; s. Irving and Lillian (Finkelstein) B.; m. Joan Elaine Travers, Feb. 19, 1967; children: Jessica, Alexis. AB, Rutgers U., 1963; JD, Harvard U., 1966. Bar: N.Y. 1967, U.S. Ct. Appeals (2d cir.) 1968, U.S. Dist. Ct. (so. dist.) N.Y. 1969, U.S. Supreme Ct. 1975. Law sec. U.S. Dist. Judge Irving Ben Cooper, N.Y.C., 1966-67; assoc. White & Case, N.Y.C., 1967-74, ptnr., 1974—. Contbr. articles to profl. jours. Fellow Am. Coll. Trial Lawyers; mem. Am. Law Inst. Office: White & Case 1155 Ave of Americas New York NY 10036

BARKER, CLAYTON ROBERT, III, lawyer; b. Statesville, N.C., Aug. 27, 1957; s. Clayton Robert Jr. and Alta Jo (Ellis) B. AB, Stanford U., 1979; postgrad., Tufts. U., 1982; JD, U. Va., 1983. Bar: N.Y. 1985. Assoc. Shearman & Sterling, N.Y.C., 1983-85, Skaddan, Arps, Slate, Meagher & Flom, N.Y.C., 1985—. Contbr. articles to profl. jours. Mem. ABA, Am. Soc. Internat. Law, N.Y. State Bar Assn. (internat. law and practice section, fgn. investment in U.S. bus. com.), Omicron Delta Kappa. Republican. Baptist. Office: Skadden Arps Slate Meagher & Flom 919 3d Ave New York NY 10022-9931

BARKER, CONSTANCE LEE MAY, insurance executive; b. Wilmington, Del., Nov. 13, 1957; d. John Rodney and Rebecca Lillian (Caleb) May; m. Rickie Robert Barker, Oct. 7, 1978; children: Nathan Dorry, Ashley Elizabeth. AA, Cecil Community Coll., 1977. Clk. J. Reese Short Agy., Cecilton, Md., 1977-80; agt. Sutton-Loder & Assocs., Newark, 1980-85; mgr. agy. Lassen, Marine & Webster, Elkton, Md., 1985—. Mem. Staff Young Dems., Elkton, 1987; active com. Cecil County Govt., Elkton, 1988—. Mem. Hartford-Cecil Ins. Women (se. 1988—), Cecil County C. of C. (bd. dirs. 1988—. Presbyterian. Home: 24 Elk Ranch Park Rd Elkton MD 21921 Office: Lassen Marine & Webster Inc 211 W Main St Elkton MD 21921

BARKER, FREDERICK HENRY, JR., elevator company executive; b. Syracuse, N.Y., Mar. 3, 1953; s. Frederick H. Sr. and Rose Anne (Zavidski) B. BS, Syracuse U., 1983. Field clk. Westinghouse Elevator Co., Syracuse, 1973-78, mktg. rep., 1980-83; application engr. Westinghouse Elevator Co., Millburn, N.J., 1978-80; br. and project mgr. Westinghouse Elevator Co., Buffalo, 1983-86; owner Barker Vertical Transp. Cons., Buffalo, 1986-88; dist. mgr. Delta Elevator Svc. Corp., Hartford, Conn., 1988—; cons. in field, Hartford 1988—. Author: (with others) Vertical Transp., 1986. Mem. Bldg. Owners and Mgrs. Assn. (bd. dirs. 1986-87), Buffalo C. of C. (participant community leadership seminars 1988), Alpha Sigma Lambda. Home: 140 Hawthorn St Hartford CT 06105 Office: Delta Elevator Svc Corp 83D Meadow St Hartford CT 06114

BARKER, HUGH ALTON, electric utility company executive; b. Stillwater, Minn., Nov. 26, 1925; s. George Clarence and Minerva (Register) B.; m. Janet M. Breitenbucher, Mar. 18, 1949; 1 child, Pamela J. BBA with distinction, U. Minn., 1949. C.P.A., Minn. Prin. Haskins & Sells, CPAs, Mpls., 1949-58; asst. to exec. v.p. Pub. Svc. Ind., Plainfield, Ind., 1958-60; fin. v.p. Pub. Svc. Ind., 1960-68, exec. v.p., 1968-74, pres., 1974-80, chief exec. officer, 1977—, chmn., 1980-88, dir., 1968—; bd. dirs. Bank One Indiana Corp, Bank One Indpls., NA, Bank One Plainfield, NA; mem. Ind. Commn. on Tax and Financing Policy, 1969-73, chmn., 1971-73. Bd. dirs. Assn. Colls. Ind.; mem. Ind. Acad., Ind. Local Govt. Property Tax Control Bd., 1973-74, Gov.'s Water Resources Study Commn., 1977-80; trustee Methodist Hosp., Indpls., 1975-81, Butler U.; bd. dirs. Edison Electric Inst., 1978-81, 83-86, 87-89, Ind. Legal Found., Inst. for Nuclear Power Operation, 1982-84. With AUS, 1944-45, ETO. Mem. Nat. Assn. Electric Cos. (bd. dir. 1974-78, chmn. 1978), Ind. Mfrs. Assn. (bd. dir. 1976-81), Ind. Electric Assn. (bd. dir., past pres.), Am. Inst. CPA's, Minn. Soc. CPA's, Ind. C. of C. (bd. dir. 1978—), Sigma Alpha Epsilon, Beta Gamma Sigma. Clubs: Columbia, Indpls. Skyline Athletic; Union League (Chgo.). Office: Pub Svc Co Ind Inc 1000 E Main St Plainfield IN 46168

BARKER, JIMMY LESTER, utility company executive; b. Robstown, Tex., Aug. 28, 1943; s. Lester Ray Barker and Billie Margaret (Younts) Owens; m. Shirley Agnes Marnick, Oct. 19, 1968 (div. 1979); children: Jimmy Lester Jr., Michelle Elizabeth; m. Mary Elizabeth Gaunt, Apr. 7, 1980; 1 child, Jessica Mae. BS in Engring. Sci., U. Tex., 1971. Registered profl. engr. Enlisted man U.S. Navy, 1964, advanced through grades to comdr., ret., 1975; sr. tng. engr. GE, Morris, Ill., 1975-76; sr. resident inspector U.S. Nuclear Regulatory Commn., Glen Ellyn, Ill., 1976-80, program mgr., 1984-86; mgr. area design Brown & Root, Inc., Bay City, Tex., 1980-81; site engring. and constrn. mgr. Houston Lighting & Power Co., Bay City, 1981-84; exec. asst. TU Electric Co., Dallas, 1986; mgr. engring. assurance TU Electric Co., Glen Rose, Tex., 1986—. Republican. Presbyterian. Office: TU Electric Co CPSES PO Box 1002 Glen Rose TX 76043

BARKER, KEITH RENE, investment banker; b. Elkhart, Ind., July 28, 1928; s. Clifford C. and Edith (Hausmna) B.; AB, Wabash Coll, 1950; MBA, Ind. U., 1952; children by previous marriage: Bruce C., Lynn K.; m. Elizabeth S. Arrington, Nov. 24, 1965; 1 child, Jennifer Scott. Sales rep. Fulton, Reid & Co., Inc., Ft. Wayne, Ind., 1951-55, office, 1955-59, asst. v.p., 1960, v.p., 1960, dir., 1961, asst. sales mgr., 1963, sales mgr., 1964, dir. Ind. ops.; sr. v.p. Fulton, Reid & Co., Inc., 1966-75; pres., chief exec. officer Fulton, Reid & Staples, Inc., 1975-77; ptnr. William C. Roney & Co., 1977-79; exec. com. Cascade Industries, Inc.; assoc. A.G. Edwards & Sons, Inc., 1984-89, v.p. investments, 1989—; dir. Fulton, Reid & Staples, Inc., Craft House Corp., Nobility Homes, Inc. Pres. Historic Ft. Wayne, Inc.; cons. to Mus. Historic Ft. Wayne; nominee, trustee Ohio Hist. Soc.; mem. Smithsonian Assocs.; bd. dirs. Ft. Wayne YMCA, 1963-64. Lt. USNR, 1952-55. Recipient Achievement certificate Inst. Investment Banking, U. Pa., 1959. Mem. Ft. Wayne Hist. Soc. (v.p.), Alliance Française, VFW (past comdr.), Co. Mil. Historians, Cleve. Grays, Am. Soc. Arms Collectors, 1st Cleve. Cavalry Assn., Nat. Assn. Securities Dealers (bus. conduct com.), Phi Beta Kappa. Episcopalian. Mason. Clubs: Beaver Creek Hunt, Cleve. Athletic, Rockwell Springs. Home: 351 Cranston Dr Berea OH 44017 Office: AG Edwards & Sons Inc 1965 E 6th St Cleveland OH 44114

BARKER, ORIN ROUNDY, software engineer; b. Salt Lake City, Dec. 2, 1939; s. Elvin Orin and Hertha Hildagard (Georgi) B.; m. LaVon Halse, Aug 4, 1965; children: Peter, Bel. BSEE, U. Utah, 1963, MA, 1965. Staff scientist GE, Syracuse, N.Y., 1965-87; research engr. Ill. Inst. Tech. Rsch. Inst., Rome, N.Y., 1987-89. Home: 312 Elm St Rome NY 13440-4146

BARKLEY, JOSEPH RICHARD, controller; b. Pa., Sept. 3, 1942; s. Joseph Harold and Rose Mary (Manger) B.; m. Diane Marie Bentivoglio, July 10, 1965; children: Christopher Michael, Patrick Joseph. BS Engring., U.S. Mil. Acad., 1965; MBA in Fin., Scranton U., 1975. Commd. 2d lt. U.S. Army, 1965, advanced through grades to maj., 1979, ret., 1979; fin. and analysis dir. Am. Express Corp., N.Y.C., 1978-82; asst. controller ops. div. Ins. Corp. N.Am., Phila., 1982-83; dir fin., adminstr. Cigna Corp., Phila., 1983-86; v.p., controller facilities div. Chase Manhattan Bank N.A., N.Y.C., 1986-88, v.p. controller Ins. Products Group, 1988—. Contbr. articles to profl. jours. Judge Newtown Election Bd., 1980—; mem. Council Rock Sch. Br., 1983-87; mem. Newtown Planning Commn., 1982. Decorated Combat Inf. Badge, Bronze Star. Mem. West Point Soc. Phila., Fin. Exec. Inst. Republican. Roman Catholic. Office: Chase Manhattan Bank Insurance Products Group 80 Pine St 10th Floor New York NY 10081

BARKLEY, PAUL C., airline holding company executive; b. 1929; married. BS, San Diego State Coll., 1958. With Arthur Young & Co., 1958-67, with Pacific Southwest Airlines, San Diego, 1967—, v.p. fin., 1968-73, sr. v.p. fin., chief operating officer, 1973-79, pres., chief operating officer, 1979-84, pres., chief exec. officer, 1984-89, now chmn. exec. com., also bd. dirs.; bd. dirs. Pancrete Inc. Served with USAF, 1951. Mem. Am. Inst. CPA's, Nat. Assn. Accts. Office: PS Group Inc PO Box 127405 San Diego CA 92112 *

BARKMAN, ANNETTE SHAULIS, real estate management executive; b. Somerset, Pa., Oct. 18, 1948; d. Norman Albert and Janice Lorraine (Robbins) S.; m. Jon A. Barkman, Dec. 1, 1983. B.A., Dickinson Coll., 1969; M.A., Indiana U. of Pa., 1975. Psychol. services asso. II Bedford/Somerset Mental Health Clinic, Somerset, 1972-78, Somerset State Hosp., 1978-79; pvt. practice hypnosis cons., Somerset, 1976—; pres. Habitability, Inc., real estate mgmt., Somerset, 1978—; exec. mgr. Gt. N.E. Land & Cattle Co., Somerset, 1980-82; owner, mgr. Somerset Credit and Collection Bur., 1981—; realtor James F. Custer Real Estate, 1980-87; Barkman Realty Inc., 1988—; cons. Somerset County Headstart Program, 1977, 78; mem., bd. dirs. Children's Aid Soc. Somerset, 1986—. Squadron comdr. CAP, Somerset, 1977-78, recipient Meritorious Service award, 1977. Mem. Somerset Welfare League, Chi Omega. Home: RD 8 Box 9 Somerset PA 15501 Office: 118 N Center Ave Somerset PA 15501

BARKSDALE, CLARENCE CAULFIELD, banker; b. St. Louis, June 4, 1932; s. Clarence M. and Elizabeth (Caulfield) B.; m. Emily Catlin Keyes, Apr. 4, 1959; children: John Keyes, Emily Shepley. A.B., Brown U., 1954; postgrad., Washington U. Law Sch., St. Louis, 1957-58, Stonier Grad. Sch. Banking, Rutgers U., 1964, Columbia U. Grad. Sch. Bus., 1968; LL.D. (hon.), Maryville Coll., St. Louis, 1976, Westminster Coll., Fulton, Mo., 1982. With Centerre Bank NA (formerly 1st Nat. Bank), St. Louis, 1958—, asst. cashier, 1960-62, asst. v.p., 1962-64, v.p., 1964, exec. v.p., 1968-70, pres., 1970-76, chief operating officer, 1974—, chmn. bd., chief exec. officer, 1976-88; also dir. Boatmen's Bancshores, Inc., St. Louis, vice chmn., 1988—; chmn., bd. dirs. Allied Bank Internat., Pet Inc., Wetterau Inc.; bd. dirs. Southwestern Bell Corp. Bd. dirs. Mo. Bot. Gardens, United Fund Greater St. Louis, Civic Progress Inc. Served with M.I. AUS, 1954-57. Mem. Am. Bankers Assn., Assn. Res. City Bankers, Alpha Delta Phi. Clubs: St. Louis, Mo. Athletic, St. Louis Country, Noonday, Brown University, Bogey (St. Louis); Links (N.Y.C.); Little Harbor (Harbor Springs, Mich.). Office: Boatmens Bancshares Inc 1 Centerre Pla Saint Louis MO 63101

BARKSDALE, PHILLIP DUNLAP, JR., banker; b. Jacksonville, Fla., Mar. 7, 1935; s. Phillip Dunlap and Helen Lee (Wilkens) B.; m. Marion Elizabeth Hathaway, Aug. 25, 1956; children—Karen, Kenneth, Judith. B.A. in Econs, U. Va., 1958; postgrad., N.Y. U. Grad. Sch. Bus., 1960-64. With Irving Trust Co., N.Y.C., 1960—; regional v.p. Irving Trust Co., 1970-72, sr. v.p., 1973, exec. v.p., 1974—. Trustee Citizens Budget Commn., 1977—. Served with U.S. Army, 1958-60. Mem. Assn. Res. City Bankers. Clubs: Wall St, Econ. N.Y. Office: Irving Trust Co 1 Wall St New York NY 10005

BARLETT, JAMES EDWARD, banker; b. Akron, Ohio, Jan. 1, 1944; s. Willard Paul and Pauline (Candlish) B.; m. Sue Patterson, June 20, 1964; 1 child, Jamie Catherine. B.A., U. Akron, 1967, M.B.A., 1971. Systems analyst B.F. Goodrich, Akron, Ohio, 1962-69; ptnr. Touche Ross & Co., Detroit, 1971-79; 1st. v.p., then sr. v.p. Nat. Bank Detroit, 1979-84; exec. v.p. NBD Bancorp and Nat. Bank Detroit, 1985—; bd. dirs. Computer Communications Am., Detroit, Cirrus System, Inc., also vice chmn. Trustee Sta. WTVS-TV, Detroit, 1984—, Detroit Country Day Sch., 1984—. Served to 1st lt. U.S. Army, 1967-69, Vietnam. Decorated Bronze Star, Army Commendation medal. Mem. Am. Bankers Assn., Mich. Bankers Assn., Detroit Athletic Club, Econ. Club, Bloomfield Hills Country Club, Red Run Golf Club. Republican. Episcopalian. Office: NBD Bancorp Inc 611 Woodward Ave Detroit MI 48226

BARLOW, WILLIAM PUSEY, JR., accountant; b. Oakland, Calif., Feb. 11, 1934; s. William P. and Muriel (Block) B.; student Calif. Inst. Tech., 1952-54. AB in Econs., U. Calif.-Berkeley, 1956. CPA, Calif. Acct. Barlow, Davis & Wood, San Francisco, 1960-72, ptnr., 1964-72; ptnr., J.K. Lasser & Co., 1972-77, Touche Ross & Co., San Francisco, 1977-78; self employed acct., 1978—. Co-author: Collectible Books: Some New Paths, 1979, The Grolier Club, 1884-1984, 1984; editor: Book Catalogues: Their Varieties and Uses, 2d edit., 1986; contbr. articles to profl. jours. Fellow Gleeson Libr. Assocs., 1969, pres., 1971-74; mem. Coun. Friends Bancroft Libr., 1971—, chmn., 1974-79; bd. dirs. Oakland Ballet, 1982—, pres. 1986—. Recipient Sir Thomas More medal Gleeson Libr. Assocs., 1989. Mem. Am. Water Ski Assn. (bd. dirs., regional chmn. 1959-63, pres. 1963-66, chmn. bd. 1966-69, 77-79, hon. v.p. 1969—), World Water Ski Union (exec. bd. 1961-71, 75-78), Grolier Club (N.Y.C.), Roxburghe Club (San Francisco), Book of Calif. Club (bd. dirs. 1963-76, pres. 1968-69, treas. 1971-83). Home: 1474 Hampel St Oakland CA 94602 Office: 449 15th St Oakland CA 94612

BARNARD, ROLLIN DWIGHT, financial executive, retired; b. Denver, Apr. 14, 1922; s. George Cooper and Emma (Riggs) B.; m. Patricia Reynolds Bierkamp, Sept. 15, 1943; children: Michael Dana, Rebecca Susan (Mrs. Paul C. Wulfestieg), Laurie Beth (Mrs. Kenneth J. Kostelecky). B.A., Pomona Coll., 1943. Clk. Morey Merc. Co., Denver, 1937-40; ptnr George C. Barnard & Co. (gen. real estate and ins.), Denver, 1946-47; v.p. Foster & Barnard, Inc., 1947-53; instr. Denver U., 1949-53; dir. real estate U.S. P.O. Dept., Washington, 1953-55; dep. asst. postmaster gen., bur. facilities U.S. P.O. Dept., 1955-59, asst. postmaster gen., 1959-61; pres., dir. Midland Fed. Savs. & Loan Assn., Denver, 1962-84; vice chmn. Bank Western Fed. Savs. Bank, 1984—; vice chmn. Western Capital Investment Corp., 1985—, pres.,

1985-87; dir. Verex Assurance Inc., 1983-86. Pres. Denver Area council Boy Scouts Am., 1970-71, mem. exec. bd., 1962-73; adv. bd. Denver Area council Boy Scouts Am, 1973—; chmn. Planning and Zoning Commn. Greenwood Village, Colo., 1969-73; mem. Greenwood Village City Council, 1975-77; mem. nat. council Pomona Coll., 1963—; bd. dirs. Downtown Denver Improvement Assn., pres., 1965; bd. dirs. Bethesda Found., Inc., 1973-82; bd. dirs. Children's Hosp., 1979-84, treas., 1983-84; bd. dirs., Rocky Mountain Child Health Services, Inc., 1982—; trustee Mile High United Fund, 1969-72, Denver Symphony Assn., 1973-74; mem. bd. Colo. Council Econ. Edn., 1971-80, chmn., 1971-76; trustee, v.p., treas. Morris Animal Found., 1969-81, pres., chmn., 1974-78, trustee emeritus, 1981—. Served to capt. AUS, World War II. Nominated One of Ten Outstanding Young Men in Am. U.S. Jaycees, 1955, 57; recipient Distinguished Service award Postmaster Gen. U.S., 1960; Silver Beaver award Boy Scouts Am., 1969; Outstanding Citizen of Year Sertoma, 1982; Colo. Citizen of Year Colo. Assn. Realtors, 1982. Mem. Denver C. of C. (pres. 1966-67), U.S. League Savs. Instns. (bd. dirs. 1972-77, vice chmn. 1979-80, chmn. 1980-81, mem. nat. legis. com., exec. com. 1974-77), Savs. League Colo. (exec. com. 1969-73, pres. 1971-72), Colo. Assn. Commerce and Industry (dir. 1971-76), Fellowship Christian Athletes (Denver area dir. 1963-76), Western Stock Show Assn. (dir. 1971—, exec. com. 1982—, 1st v.p. 1985—), Nu Alpha Phi. Republican. Presbyn. Clubs: 26 (Denver) (pres. 1970), Rotary (Denver) (dir. 1979-81, 2d v.p. 1980); Mountain and Plains Appaloosa Horse (pres. 1970-71), Roundup Riders of the Rockies (dir. 1979—, treas. 1980-87, v.p. 1987—). Home: 3151 East Long Rd Littleton CO 80121

BARNES, ANDREW EARL, newspaper editor; b. Torrington, Conn., May 15, 1939; s. Joseph and Elizabeth (Brown) B.; m. Marion Otis, Aug. 26, 1960; children: Christopher Joseph, Benjamin Brooks, Elizabeth Cheney. B.A., Harvard U., 1961. Reporter, bur. chief Providence Jour., 1961-63; from reporter to edn. editor Washington Post, 1965-73; met. editor, asst. mng. editor St. Petersburg Times, Fla., 1973-75, mng. editor, 1975-84; editor, pres. St. Petersburg (Fla.) Times, 1984—, chief exec. officer, 1988—; pres. Trend Mags., 1985—; pres., bd. dirs. Congl. Quar., 1985—; chmn. bd. dirs. Times Pub. Co., Poynter Inst., Modern Graphic Arts; bd. dirs. Newspaper Advt. Bur. Served with USAR, 1963-65. Alicia Patterson fellow, 1969-70. Mem. Fla. Soc. Newspaper Editors (pres. 1980-81), Am. Soc. Newspaper Editors. Home: 4819 Juanita Way S Saint Petersburg FL 33705 Office: St Petersburg Times 490 1st Ave S PO Box 1121 Saint Petersburg FL 33731

BARNES, CRAIG MARTIN, accountant; b. Oak Park, Ill., May 5, 1949; s. Raymond Herbert and Barbara Anne (Barlow) B.; m. Joyce Marie Brainard, Jan. 31, 1971; children: Annette Marie, Walter Martin. BS in Music Edn., U. Ill., 1971; BA in Acctg. and Fin., U. So. Fla., 1976. CPA, Tenn. Controller Fore Line Safe Co., Tampa, Fla., 1973-75, Fore Line Bldgs., Largo, Fla., 1973-75; EDP audit mgr. Comptroller of Treasury State of Tenn., Nashville, 1976-88; pvt. practice acctg. Gallatin, Tenn., 1986—. Mem., singer Nashville Symphony Chorus, 1982-86, coach Comptroller Sox Softball Team, Nashville, 1984-86. Ernst and Whinney scholar, 1976. Mem. Am. Inst. CPA's, Assn. Govt. Accts., Nat. Futures Assn., Gallatin C. of C., Phi Kappa Phi, Beta Alpha Psi. Seventh Day Adventist. Club: Chess (9th bd. 1966-67). Office: 425 S Water St Gallatin TN 37066

BARNES, DUDLEY MCBEE, financial planner; b. Clarksdale, Miss., Aug. 24, 1948; s. Harris H. and Jamye (Haskins) B.; m. Claire Ryan, Nov. 24, 1949; children: Ryan, Brook. BS, Miss. State U., 1970. Cert. fin. planner. Fin. planner Gainey & Assocs., Jackson, Miss., 1971-72; stockbroker Paine Webber, Jackson, 1972-73, Howard Weil, Clarksdale, Miss., 1973-76; fin. planner Barnes & Assocs., Inc., Clarksdale, 1976—; bd. dirs. VCR Enterprises, Inc., Clarksdale. Bd. dirs. Presbyn. Day Sch., Clarksdale, 1986—. Mem. Internat. Assn. Fin. Planning, Inst. Cert. Fin. Planners, Rotary. Presbyterian. Office: Barnes & Assocs Inc 252 Sunflower Ave Clarksdale MS 38614

BARNES, HELEN CROSS, banker; b. Portsmouth, Va., Mar. 26, 1945; d. Robert Lee and Frances Phyllis (Motley) Cross; m. L. Gary Barnes, Aug. 10, 1968. BA in Math., Westhampton Coll. of U. Richmond, 1967; spl. courses Am. Inst. Banking, Md. Bankers Sch. of U. Md. Tchr., York County Schs. (Va.), 1967-71; internal cons. Equitable Bank N.A., Balt., 1971-78, project mgr., 1978-82, v.p., dir. bank services, 1982—. Bd. dirs. exec. com., v.p. programs, corp. sec. Jr. Achievement Met. Balt., 1982—; mem. exec. bd., employment steering com., info. processing tng. ctr. steering com., asst. sec. Balt. Urban League, Inc., 1985—. Mem. Assn. Internal Mgmt. Cons., Assn. Info. Systems Profls., Office Tech. Mgmt. Assn., Am. Soc. Performance Improvement. Recipient Bronze Leadership award Nat. Bd. Dirs. Jr. Achievement, Inc. Republican. Methodist. Club: Argyle County (Silver Spring, Md.). Office: Equitable Bank NA 100 S Charles St Baltimore MD 21201

BARNES, JAMES E., energy company executive; b. Ponca City, Okla., 1934; married. Grad., Okla. State U.; grad. advanced mgmt. program, Harvard U. With Continental Pipe Line Co., 1956-62, Cherokee Pipe Line Co., 1962-64; with Conoco, Inc., Stamford, Conn., 1964-83, mgr. gas products div., 1964-65, gen. mgr. natural gas and gas products dept., 1965-70, v.p. purchasing, 1970-75, v.p. supply and trading, 1975-78, exec. v.p. supply and transp., 1978-83; sr. exec. v.p., chief operating officer Mapco, Inc., Tulsa, 1983-84, pres., chief exec. officer, bd. dirs., 1984—, chmn. bd., 1986—. Office: Mapco Inc 1800 S Baltimore Ave Tulsa OK 74119 •

BARNES, JOSEPH CURTIS, aircraft development executive; b. Ashland, Oreg., Jan. 1, 1913; s. Joseph Curtis and Flora Ellis (Bushong) B.; m. Janet A. Eames, Nov. 1, 1942; children: Joseph Curtis III, Robin Bushong Spiegel, Bonnie McClean Arndt. AB, Stanford U., 1935, MA, 1938; student V-7 program, USN Acad., 1940. Artist Walt Disney Studio, Burbank, Calif., 1938-40; with Barnes Bros., Medford, Orgn., 1940-80; chief exec. officer Tipsy Bee Research, Medford, 1980-86. Patentee vertical lift by flettner rotor; inventor silent lift vehicle, vehicle for vertical flight and ground transport. Served to lt. comdr. USNR, 1940-46, PTO. Mem. Am. Helicopter Soc. Republican. Home and Office: 4455 Fern Valley Rd Medford OR 97504

BARNES, KATHRYN WHITENER, banker; b. Arlington, Va., Nov. 21, 1957; d. Ralph Verlie and Alice Lee (Beard) Whitener; m. Harry Wallace Barnes, Jr., Oct. 3, 1987. BS in Mktg. Mgmt., Va. Tech. U., 1980. Comml. trainee First Union Nat. Bank, Charlotte, N.C., 1980; asst. credit mgr. First Union Nat. Bank, Greensboro, N.C., 1980-82, credit mgr., 1982-83; comml. loan officer Md. Nat. Bank, Rockville, 1983-86; asst. v.p. Md. Nat. Bank, Greenbelt, 1986-87, v.p., 1987-88; v.p., unit mgr. spl. corp. Signet Bank/Va., Vienna, 1988—. Democrat. Methodist. Home: 7200 Parsons Ct Alexandria VA 22306 Office: Signet Bank/Va 8330 Boone Blvd Ste 300 Vienna VA 22180

BARNES, LUTHER MATTHEW, III, manufacturing company executive; b. Rocky Mount, N.C., Oct. 6, 1936; s. Luther Matthew and Ruby Gold (Williams) B.; m. Margaret Ethel Daughtridge, Aug. 24, 1958; children: Margaret Ethel, Luther Matthew IV. AS, Campbell U., 1957; BS, U. N.C., 1959. V.p. Barnes Tin Shop, Rocky Mount, 1962-76, pres., 1976—; bd. dirs. Pioneer Savs. Bank, Rocky Mount. Bd. dirs. Edgecombe Community Coll. Found., Tarboro, N.C., 1987—, West Edgecombe Rescue Squad, Rocky Mount, 1983-87; mem. Rocky Mount Bd. Adjustment, 1983, Rocky Mount Planning Bd., 1984. Capt. USMC, 1959-62. Mem. U.S. Power Squadrons. Democrat. Presbyterian. Home: PO Box 1417 Rocky Mount NC 27802 Office: Barnes Tin Shop Inc 1741 Hardee Blvd Rocky Mount NC 27801

BARNES, RANDALL CURTIS, beverage company executive; b. Terre Haute, Ind., Aug. 23, 1951; s. Dean and Laverna B.; m. Brenda Czajka; 1 child, Jeffrey Ryan. BS with distinction, Stanford U., 1973, MBA with honors, 1978. Engagement mgr. McKinsey & Co., N.Y.C., 1978-81, sr. engagement mgr., 1981-84; fin. analyst (hqrs.) Gen. Mills, Mpls., 1973-74; fin. analyst Gen. Mills/ Red Lobster Inns, Orlando, Fla., 1974-75; supr. Gen. Mills/ Red Lobster Inns, Orlando, 1975-76, mgr. corp. fin. analysis, 1976; staff exec./ stategic planning Gen. Elec. Co., Fairfield, Conn., 1984-86; mgr. bus. devel. Gen. Elec. Co., Louisville, 1986; sr. v.p. stategic planning May Dept. Stores, St. Louis, 1986-87; sr. v.p. planning and new bus. devel. PepsiCo, Purchase, N.Y., 1987—. Office: Pepsico Inc Anderson Hill Rd Purchase NY 10577

BARNES, STEPHEN PAUL, sales executive; b. Corsicana, Tex., July 30, 1957; s. Paul Gordon and Barbara Jewell (Hawkins) B.; m. Tina Marie Dacus, Dec. 20, 1980 (div. May 1985); m. Kathie Jo Beck, Feb. 20, 1988. BS, Grand Canyon Coll., 1982. Cert. fin. planner. Sales rep. Phil Bramsen Distbrs., Mesa, Ariz., 1978-81, credit mgr., 1981-82; registered rep. John Hancock Fin. Svcs., Phoenix, 1983-86; mktg. mgmt. assoc. John Hancock Fin. Svcs., Boston, 1986-87; sales mgr. John Hancock Fin. Svcs., Phoenix, 1987—. Pub. address announcer Grand Canyon Coll. Home Basketball Games, Phoenix, 1977—; chmn. capital drive John C. Lincoln Day Care Ctr., Phoenix, 1987. Mem. Nat. Assn. Life Underwriters (nat. quality award 1985), Inst. Cert. Fin. Planners (sec., dir. Phoenix chpt.), Phoenix Life Underwriters Assn. (bd. dirs.), Phoenix City Club. Republican. Methodist. Home: 7516 N 22d St Phoenix AZ 85020 Office: John Hancock Fin Svcs 1430 E Missouri St Ste 250 Phoenix AZ 85014

BARNES, STEVEN J., food franchising company executive; b. 1919; married. With Odman Corp., 1938-52, Perlman Paper Co., 1952-61; with McDonald's Corp., Oak Brook, Ill., 1961—, exec. v.p., pres. internat. div., from 1968, now chmn. internat. div., ret., 1987. Office: McDonald Sales Corp 1 McDonald Pla Oak Brook IL 60521

BARNES, WALLACE, manufacturing executive; b. Bristol, Conn., Mar. 22, 1926; s. Harry Clarke and Lillian (Houbertz) B.; m. Audrey Kent, June 14, 1947 (div. Aug. 1962); children: Thomas Oliver, Jarre Ann; m. Mrs. Frederick B. Hollister, Jr. (div. Feb. 1973); 1 adopted son, Frederick Hollister; m. Joan C. Fierri, Mar. 3, 1973 (div. May 1985); m. Barbara Hackman Franklin, Nov. 29, 1986. BA, Williams Coll., 1949; LLB, Yale U., 1952; grad., Advanced Mgmt. Program, Harvard, 1973; LLB (hon.), U. Hartford, 1988. Bar: Conn. 1952. Assoc. firm Beach, Calder & Barnes (and predecessor), Bristol, 1952-55; partner Beach, Calder & Barnes (and predecessor), 1956-62; exec. v.p. Assoc. Spring Corp. (name changed to Barnes Group Inc.), 1962-64, pres., 1964-77, chmn., chief exec. officer, 1977—; pres. Nutmeg Air Transport, Inc., 1949-55; asst. to treas. Northeast Airlines, Inc., Boston, 1951; dir., mem. exec. com. Aetna Life & Casualty Co.; dir. Motalink Ltd., Wiltshire, Eng., Autoliaisons France S.A., Paris, Bank of New Eng. Corp.; pres. Bowman Products (Can.) Ltd.; pres. Wallace Barnes, Ltd.; dir., pres. Resortes Mecanicos S.A., Mexico City, Resortes Industriales del Norte S.A., Monterrey; pres. Assoc. Spring-Asia; chmn., dir. Barnes Group Found. Inc.; dir. Rogers Corp., Rohr Industries, Inc.; chmn., pres. Assoc. Spring Corp.; chmn. NHK-Assoc. Spring Suspension Components, Inc. Pres. Bristol Community Chest, 1956; bd. dirs., mem. exec. com. Bristol Boys Club, pres., 1965-68; mem. bd. regents, U. Hartford, 1981-87, chmn., 1988—; trustee Bristol Girls' Club Assn.; bd. dirs. New Eng. Legal Found., 1986—, New Eng. Council, 1980-83, Jr. Achievement N. Central Conn.; Nominee for Congress, 1st Congl. Dist. Conn., 1954; town chmn., Bristol, 1953-55; mem. Conn. Senate from 5th Dist., 1958-62, from 8th Dist., 1966-70, minority leader, 1969; Bd. dirs. Community Coun. of Capital Region, 1975-77, Hartford Symphony Soc., 1971-78, Coun. on Employment and Fair Taxation, 1978-80, Bus. Coalition on Health, 1983-88, Conn. Pub. Expenditure Coun., 1979-85; trustee Am. Clock and Watch Mus., Bristol Regional Environ. Ctr.; bd. trustees New Eng. Air Mus.; corporator Inst. of Living, Hartford; bd. dirs. Conn. Econ. Devel. Corp. Served as aviation cadet USAAF, 1944-45. Recipient distinguished service award Bristol Jaycees, Keystone award Boys Clubs of Am., 1967; Hon. Alumnus award U. Hartford, 1985. Mem. Am., Conn. bar assns., Am. Judicature Soc., Nat. Assn. Mfrs. (bd. dirs.), Am. Arbitration Assn., Bristol, Simsbury hist. socs., Newcomen Soc. N.Am., Conn. Bus. and Industry Assn., (past chmn., dir.), Bus.-Industry Polit. Action Com. , Am. Legion. Republican. Episcopalian. Clubs: Elk. (N.Y.C.), Economic (N.Y.C.), Yale (N.Y.C.), Williams (N.Y.C.); Hundred of Conn. Home: 1875 Perkins St Bristol CT 06010 Office: Barnes Group Inc 123 Main St Bristol CT 06010

BARNES, WALTER CARLYLE, JR., surgeon, medical director; b. Rutherford, N.C., May 25, 1922; s. Walter Carlyle and Mildred Elizabeth (Piehoff) B.; m. Pauline Ruth Lehman, May 25, 1948; children: Walter III, Abigail. BS, U. N.C., 1944; MD, Temple U., 1948. Diplomate Am. Bd. Surgery, Am. Coll. Surgery. Rotating intern Watts Hosp., U. N.C., Durham, 1948-49; resident in surgery Erlanger Regional Med. Ctr., Chattanooga, Tenn., 1949-54; fellow Horsley Svc., Richmond, Va., 1954-55; chief surgeon Southern Clinic, Texarkana, Ark., 1955-88; med. dir. St. Michael Hosp., Texarkana, Ark., 1988—. Contbr. articles to profl. jours. Pres. Tex. Regional Arts and Humanities Council, Texarkans, 1987-88, Caddo Council Boy Scouts Am., 1978; gov. bd. Texarkana Coll., 1984—. With U.S. Army, 1951-53, PTO. Fellow ACS, Southwestern Surgical Soc. (vice councilor 1970), Tex. Surgical Soc.; mem. AMA, Tex. Med. Assn. (bd. councilors 1960-70), Royal Acad. Medicine, Rotary. Methodist. Home: 3519 Olive St Texarkana TX 75503 Office: St Michael Hosp 6th and Hazel Texarkana TX 75502

BARNES, ZANE EDISON, communications company executive; b. Marietta, Ohio, Dec. 2, 1921; s. Emmett A. and Frances (Canfield) B.; children: Frances, Zane Edison, Shelley Barnes Donaho. BS, Marietta Coll., 1947. With Ohio Bell Tel. Co., 1941-60; asst. v.p. exec. ops. Ohio Bell Tel. Co., Cleve., 1961-63; gen. plant mgr. Ohio Bell Tel. Co., 1963-64, v.p. personnel, 1965-67; with engrng. dept. AT&T, N.Y.C., 1960-61; v.p., gen. mgr. Pacific N.W. Bell Tel. Co., Portland, 1964-65; v.p. ops. Pacific N.W. Bell Tel. Co., 1967-70; pres. Pacific N.W. Bell Tel. Co., Seattle, 1970-73, Southwestern Bell Tel. Co., 1973-74; pres., chief exec. officer, dir. Pacific N.W. Bell Tel. Co., St. Louis, 1974-86; chmn. bd., pres., chief exec. officer Southwestern Bell Corp., St. Louis, 1983-88, chmn. bd., chief exec. officer, 1988—; bd. dirs., chief exec. officer Southwestern Bell Corp.; dir. H & R Block, Inc., Gen. Am. Life Ins. Co., Reading & Bates Corp., INTERCO Inc. Pres., bd. dirs. St. Louis Variety Club; chmn. corp. adv. com. St. Louis Hugh O'Brian Youth Found.; bd. dirs. St. Louis Area Coun. Boy Scouts, Am. Productivity & Quality Ctr., Target; trustee Com. for Econ. Devel., Jefferson Nat. Expansion Meml. Assn.; life assoc. trustee Marietta Coll.; mem. Bus. Com. for Arts, Civic Progress, The United Negro Coll. Fund. Mem. Bus. Roundtable, Conf. Bd., Ctr. for Telecommunications Mgmt., Brookings Inst., Round Table, Backstoppers, Coalition of Chief Exec. Officers. Office: Southwestern Bell Corp 1 Bell Ctr Saint Louis MO 63101

BARNETT, DOUGLAS ELDON, agriculturist; b. Walnut Ridge, Ark., Feb. 11, 1944; s. Jewell Marvin and Emma Jean (Long) B.; m. Rosa Eileen Lacy, Mar. 17, 1973. BS in Edn., Ark. State U., 1967; MS, Northwestern State U., Natchitoches, La., 1970; PhD, U. Ky., 1974. Cert. tchr. Ark. Sci. instr. Maynard (Ark.) High Sch., 1968-69; biology instr. Paragould (Ark.) High Sch., 1969-70; grad. researcher U. Ky., Lexington, 1970, extension survey entomologist, 1971-76; survey coordinator U.S. Dept. Agriculture, Washington, 1976-77, nat. survey publ. mgr., 1978-81, agriculturist, 1981—. Contbr. articles to profl. jours. Mem. Entomol. Soc. Am. (sect. chmn. 1976—), Washington Emtomol. Soc., Sigma Xi.

BARNETT, ELIZABETH HALE, management consultant; b. Nashville, Mar. 17, 1940; d. Robert Baker and Dorothy (McCarthy) Hale; m. Crawford F. Barnett Jr., June 6, 1964; children: Crawford F. III, Robert H. BA, Vanderbilt U., 1962. Receptionist, sec. U.S. Atty. Gen. Robert F. Kennedy, Washington, 1962-64; free-lance cons. Atlanta, 1973-76; pres. E.H. Barnett & Assocs., Atlanta, 1976-83; trustee The Ga. Conservancy, Atlanta, 1978—, chmn. bd. trustees, 1986-88, also bd. dirs. Contbg. author: A New Agenda, 1982; contbr. articles to profl. jours. Bd. dirs. Jr. League of Atlanta, 1973-75; mem. Leadership Atlanta, 1976—; chmn., pres. bd. dirs. Vol. Coms. Art Mus. U.S. and Can., 1976-79; bd. dirs. The High Mus. Art, Atlanta, 1977—; chmn. bd. dirs. Met. Atlanta ARC, 1978-80, United Way of Met. Atlanta, 1981-84; mem. community adv. com. N.W. Ga. council Girl Scouts U.S., 1979-83; mem. council USO, Atlanta, 1981—; mem. bd. sponsor Atlanta Women's Network. Named one of Ten Outstanding Young Women of Am., 1977; honored by Ga. State Legis., Atlanta, 1978. Mem. LWV. Episcopalian. Office: The Ga Conservancy 8615 Barnwell Rd Alpharetta GA 30201

BARNETT, JOHN TERRANCE, marketing professional; b. Steubenville, Ohio, Sept. 20, 1949. Student, U. Steubenville, 1967-70; diploma, Pitts. Inst. Mortuary Sci., 1977-78. Tchr. Steubenville High Sch., 1970-71; br. mgr. C.I.T. Fin. Corp., N.Y.C., 1971-73; supr., credit analyst Ford Motor Credit, Dayton, Ohio, 1973-75; agt. Cen. States Agy., Jackson, Mich., 1975-76; mktg. prof. Ralph A. Hiller Co., Pitts., 1979—. Staff officer USCG Aux., Pitts., 1985-87. Mem. Nat. Fire Protection Assn., Am. Mktg. Assn., Profl. Personal Computer Users Group Pitts., Fluid Power Distbrs. Assn. Roman Catholic. Office: Ralph A Hiller Co 951 Killarney Dr Pittsburgh PA 15234

BARNETT, MARIE, real estate executive; b. LaGrange, Ga., May 19; d. George and D. (Moore) B.; m. James Stephens Dick, Dec. 5, 1960 (div.); children: Karen MarieDick Vidal, Sonya Stephens Dick Tafolla. Student, Fla. State U., 1955, U. Ga., 1956-58, Perry Coll., 1959; grad., Century 21 Internat. Mgmt. Acad., 1988. Lic. Calif. Dept. of Real Estate. Staff Mastrose Devel. Co., Palm Beach, Fla., 1962-65; pres., owner Century 21 Calif. Hills, Orange, Calif., 1973-79; real estate exec. F.M. Tarbell, Orange, Calif., 1979-85; pres., owner Century 21 Assocs., Newport Beach, Calif., 1985-88; real estate exec. Century 21 Inland Pacific, Newport Beach, Calif., 1988—. Pres. Jr. Auxiliary, Pass Christian, Miss., 1965; VIP panel Easter Seals, L.A., 1989; active 552 Club, Cancer Unit Hoag Hosp., Newport Beach, 1989, Cen Pac, Washington, 1989. Mem. Nat. Assn. of Realtors (Grad. Realtors Inst.), Calif. Assn. of Realtors (state dir. 1976, 78-79, realtor-assoc. rels. com., publicity com., co-chmn. Pvt. Property Week, 99 Club), East Orange Bd. of Realtors (chmn. spl. activities 1974-75, chmn. real estate fin. 1976, chmn. realtor-assoc. rels. com. 1977, chmn. Pvt. Property Week 1978, Pres.'s award 1978, chmn. Pvt. Property Week Luncheon 1980-81, communications com. 1980-81, 83, Pvt. Property Week com. 1981), Newport Harbor/Costa Mesa Bd. of Realtors (communications com. 1986—, CANTREE reception 1986, multiple listings com. 1987-88, chmn. Ann. Awards and Installation 1987, chmn. Equal Opportunity com. 1988), Corona Del Mar C. of C., Newport Harbor C. of C. Democrat. Office: Century 21 Inland Pacific 2 Corporate Plaza Newport Beach CA 92660

BARNETT, MARILYN, advertising agency executive; b. Detroit, June 10, 1934; d. Henry and Kate (Boesky) Schiff; B.A., Wayne State U., 1953; children: Rhona, Ken. Supr. broadcast prodn. Northgate Advt. Agy., Detroit, 1968-73; founder, part-owner, pres. Mars Advt. Co., Southfield, Mich., 1973—. Named Advt. Woman of Yr., Women's Club of Detroit, 1986, Outstanding Woman in Agy Mgmt., Am. Women in Radio and TV, Inc., 1987, Outstanding Woman in Broadcast, 1980. Mem. AFTRA (dir. 1959-67), Screen Actors Guild, Adcraft. Women's Adcraft. Creator, producer radio and TV programs, 1956-58; nat. spokesperson on TV, 1960-70. Club: Economic (Ad Woman of Yr. 1986). Office: 24209 Northwestern Hwy Southfield MI 48075 also: Mars Advt Co 5919 W 3d St Ste 1A Los Angeles CA 90036

BARNETT, NORMAN LAWRENCE, investment advisor; b. N.Y.C., Mar. 16, 1935; s. Herman Ben and Goldie Ann (Feiner) B.; B.S., N.Y. U., 1961; M.B.A., Harvard U., 1963, D.B.A., 1967; children—Jonathan David, Amy Elizabeth, Samuel Hamilton. Research fellow Harvard Bus. Sch., Boston, 1966-67; pres. Market Structure Studies, Inc., Cambridge, Mass., 1967-69, Venture Research & Capital Corp., Newton, Mass., 1969-71; v.p. White, Weld & Co., Boston, 1972-79; v.p., mgr. Cowen Investors Mgmt. Services, Boston, 1979-83; founder Norman L. Barnett & Co., Inc., Providence, 1983—. Mem. com. on resources Harvard Med. Sch., Boston, 1978-82; dir. Big Bros. of Boston, 1976-78, R.I. Philharm. Orch., 1985-88. Recipient Founders Day award N.Y. U., 1961. Mem. Harvard Bus. Sch. Assn. of R.I. (bd. dirs.). Club: Harvard. Contbr. articles to profl. jours.; developer portfolio mgmt. framework.

BARNETT, ROBERT STEVEN, data processing executive, consultant; b. Decatur, Ill., Feb. 1, 1950; s. Harry Dale Barnett and Mary Ellen (Fulk) Brown; m. Marcia Horner, June 16, 1971 (div. 1974); m. Catherine Jo Spence, Sept. 30, 1983. BA, So. Ill. U., 1973; MA, No. Ill. U., 1975. Owner Barney's Sampproﬁng, DeKalb, Ill., 1976; mgr. Protective Concrete Coatings, Cin., 1977; freelance writer Richmond, Va., 1978-82; founder, chief exec. officer Aesop Inc., Richmond, Va., 1983—. With USN, 1968-70. Mem. Better Bus. Bur. Offfice: Aesop Inc 301 E Franklin St Richmond VA 23219

BARNETT, THOMAS GLEN, manufacturing company executive; b. Olney, Ill., Aug. 15, 1946; s. Burl and Florence Ann (Gant) B.; m. Diana Kay O'Dell, Jan. 27, 1968; children—Kevin Thomas, Kelli Lyn. B.S. in Acctg., Millikin U., Decatur, Ill., 1968. C.P.A., Mo., Ill. Staff acct. Arthur Young & Co. (C.P.A.'s), Chgo., 1968-70; sr. acct. Arthur Young & Co. (C.P.A.'s), 1970-73, audit mgr., 1973-75; dir. internal audit Chromalloy Am. Corp., St. Louis, 1975-76; asst. controller Chromalloy Am. Corp., 1976-78, v.p., controller, 1978-80, exec. v.p. fin., 1979-87; chief fin. officer Marsh Co., Belleville, Ill., 1987—; dir. Protection Mutual Ins. Co. (So. region), Chgo., Landmark Bank Fairview Heights (Ill.). Mem. Fin. Execs. Inst., Am. Soc. C.P.A.'s, Mo. Soc. C.P.A.'s. Republican. Presbyterian. Clubs: St. Clair Country (Belleville) (pres. 1987—), Stadium (St. Louis). Office: Marsh Co 707 B St E Belleville IL 62221

BARNETTE, CURTIS HANDLEY, lawyer, steel company executive; b. St. Albans, W.Va., Jan. 9, 1935; s. Curtis Franklin and Garnett Drucella (Robinson) B.; m. Loris Joan Harner, Dec. 28, 1957; children: Curtis Kevin, James David. AB with High Honors, W.Va. U., 1956; postgrad. (Fulbright scholar), U. Manchester, 1956-57; J.D., Yale U., 1962; grad. advanced mgmt. program, Harvard U., 1974-75. Bar: Conn. 1962, Pa. 1968, U.S. Ct. Appeals (D.C. cir.) 1988. Mem. Wiggin & Dana, New Haven, Conn., 1962-67; atty. Bethlehem Steel Corp., Pa., 1967-70; gen. atty. Bethlehem Steel Corp., 1970-72, asst. sec., 1972-76, asst. gen. counsel, 1972-77, asst. to v.p., 1974-76, sec., 1976—, asst. v.p., 1976-77, v.p., gen. counsel, 1977-85, sr. v.p., 1985—, also bd. dirs.; lectr. U. Md., 1958-59; law tutor Yale U., 1962-67; dir. Sta. WLVT-TV. bd. dirs., vice chmn. Yale Law Sch. Fund; mem. Council Adminstrv. Conf. of the U.S., 1988—; mem. adv. bd. Minsi Trails council Boy Scouts Am.; bd. dirs. Pa. Bus. Roundtable, 1986—; bd. govs. Bethlehem Area Found; bd. dirs. W.Va. U. Found., 1987—. Served with U.S. Army Intelligence, 1956-57, USAR, 1958-67. Mem. ABA, Fed. Bar Assn., Pa. Bar Assn., Conn. Bar Assn., Northampton County Bar Assn., Am. Iron and Steel Inst., Assn. Gen. Counsel (pres. 1988—), Am. Soc. Corp. Secs. (chmn. 1986), Am. Law Inst., Stockholder Relations Soc. N.Y., Pa. Chamber Bus. & Industry (dir. 1985—), Pa. Bus. Roundtable (dir. 1986—), Nat. Council, Coll. of Law W.Va. U., Loblolly Bay Yacht Club, The Links, New Haven Lawn Club, Saucon Valley Club, Bethlehem Club, Blooming Grove Hunting and Fishing Club, Phi Beta Kappa, Beta Theta Pi, Phi Alpha Theta, Phi Delta Phi. Home: 1112 Prospect Ave Bethlehem PA 18018 Office: Bethlehem Steel Corp Martin Tower Rm 2018 701 E 3rd St Bethlehem PA 18016

BARNETTE, MARGE C., food service company executive; b. Honolulu, Dec. 15, 1944; d. William Leon B. BA in Acctg., Chaminade U., 1966. Supr. ARA/Slater Food Service, San Francisco, 1966-68; restaurant, catering mgr. Spencecliff Corp., Honolulu, 1968, gen. mgr., 1973-77; clubhouse mgr. Mid-Pacific Country Club, Lanikai, Hawaii, 1977; dir. dining services Tulane U., U. Houston ARA Services, New Orleans, 1978-79; ops. analyst ARA Services, Dallas, 1980; labor rels. mgr. Rockwell Internat. ARA Services, Los Angeles, 1981; dist. mgr. ARA Services, Phila., 1984-88; personnel dir. ARA Olympic Food Services, Los Angeles, 1983-84; dir. food svcs. Seattle organizing com. Seattle (Wash.) 1990 Goodwill Games, 1989—. Roman Catholic. Home: 10278 NE 129th Ln Kirkland WA 98034

BARNEVIK, PERCY NILS, electrical company executive; b. Simrishamn, Sweden, Feb. 13, 1941; s. Einar and Anna Barnevik; m. Aina Orvarsson, 1963; 3 children. MBA, Gothenburg Sch. Econs., Sweden, 1964; postgrad., Stanford U., 1965-66. With The Johnson Group, Sweden, 1966-69; with Sandvik AB, Sandviken, Sweden, 1969-80, group controller, 1969-75; pres. U.S. affiliate 1975-79, exec. v.p., 1979-80; pres., chief exec. officer ASEA, 1980-87; chmn. Sandvik AB, 1983—; pres., chief exec. officer Asea Brown Boveri Ltd., 1988—. Office: ABB Asea Brown Boveri Ltd, PO Box 8131, CH-8050 Zurich Switzerland other: Sandvik AB, S-81181 Sandviken Sweden

BARNEY, CHARLES LESTER, petroleum company executive; b. Shreveport, La., Nov. 4, 1925; s. Lester K. and Ruby Lee (Weeks) B.; B.S., Petroleum Engr., La. State U., 1949; m. Frances Jenkins, Oct. 13, 1944; children—Jerry, Charles, Merilyn. Ops. mgr. Mobil Can., 1964-66; gen. mgr., exploration and producing Mobil Germany, 1966-70; producing mgr. Mobil

Internat., 1970-71, planning mgr., 1971-72, mgr., acquisitions and concessions, 1972-74; corp. producing mgr. Mobil, 1974-75; v.p. drilling and prodn. Superior Oil Co., Houston, 1975-78, sr. v.p., prodn., sales, mfg. and planning, 1978-81, also dir.; chmn. bd., chief exec. officer McIntyre Mines Ltd., Can., 1979; chmn. bd., dir. Can. Superior Oil Ltd.; pres., chief exec. officer Mark Producing Inc., Houston, 1981-86; owner, chief exec. officer CLB & Assocs., Houston, 1986—. Served with USN, 1945-46. Mem. Soc. Petroleum Engrs., Mid-Continent Oil and Gas Assn. Episcopalian. Office: CLB & Assocs Tex Commerce Tower 600 Travis Houston TX 77002

BARNEY, JAMES SCOTT, mechanical engineer; b. Midwest City, Okla., Apr. 27, 1953; s. William Shores and Betty (Baldwin) B.; m. Susan Marie Haug, June 19, 1982; 1 child, William Michael. AA in Math and Sci., Montgomery Coll., Rockville, Md., 1977, AA in Engring., 1980; BS in Mech. Engring., U. Md., 1982. Pipe support engr. Bechtel Power Corp., San Clemente, Calif., 1982, instrument engr., 1982-84; contract coordinator Bechtel Constrn., Delta, Utah, 1984-85; mech. engr. Sperry Corp., Great Neck, N.Y., 1985; program mgt. engr. Sperry Corp., Waltham, Mass., 1985-86; sr. mem. engring. staff Unisys Corp., Waltham, 1986—. Served with U.S. Army, 1972-78. Recipient award Lincoln Arc Welding Found., 1982. Mem. Am. Soc. Mech. Engrs. (assoc.). Republican. Presbyterian. Home: 10 Reid Rd Chelmsford MA 01824 Office: Unisys Corp Def Systems 1601 Trapelo Rd Waltham MA 02154

BARNHARD, SHERWOOD ARTHUR, printing company executive; b. Newark, Mar. 14, 1921; s. Charles L. and Blanche (Tarnow) B.; m. Esther Lasky, Feb. 21, 1946; children—Ronald Harris, Paul Ira. BS, Franklin and Marshall Coll., 1942. With Lasky Co., Millburn, N.J., 1946—, exec. v.p., 1956-61, pres., 1961-86, chmn., 1986—; pres. N.J. Web and Sheetfed Color Lithographers; v.p. Daus. of Israel Geriatric Ctr., West Orange; N.J.; past trustee Temple Sharey Tefilo-Israel, South Orange, N.J.; bd. overseers N.Y.U. Ctr. Graphic Arts Mgmt. and Tech. Mem. Printing Industries N.J. (past pres.), Assn. Graphic Arts (past pres., past bd. dirs.), Met. Lithographers Assn. (past pres., mem. labor com.), Mktg. Communications Execs., Advt. Club N.Y., Zeta Beta Tau. Clubs: Crestmont Golf and Country (West Orange); Delair Country (Delray, Fla.).

BARNHILL, CHARLES WILLIAM, real estate broker and developer; b. Fairhope, Ala., Mar. 21, 1943; s. Charles Wilmer and Mary Virginia (Presley) B.; m. Paula Eve Stanley, June 7, 1969; children: Heather, Shelly, Shannon, Kristen. BS in Biology, U. Ala., University, 1965, MS in Chemistry, 1968; PhD in Biochemistry, U. Ala., Birmingham, 1974; postdoctoral fellow, U. South Ala., 1974-76. Pres., real estate broker Omega Properties Inc., Mobile, Ala., 1976—; pres. R&B Realty Inc., Mobile, 1984—; mem. adv. bd. First Ala. Bank, Spanish Ft., 1981—. Contbr. articles on biology to profl. jours. Active United Way, Mobile; v.p. Spanish Ft. PTA, 1986. Served to capt., U.S. Army, 1969-70. Mem. Real Estate Securities and Syndicati n Inst. (pres. Ala. chpt. 1982, sec.-treas. real estate securities inst.), Realtors Nat. Mktg. Inst. (comml. investment mem.), Ala. Realtors (bd. dirs. 1985-86). Republican. Methodist. Club: Toastmasters (Fairhope) (pres. 1978). Lodge: Kiwanis.

BARNUM, NAN MARTIN, advertising company executive; b. Lafayette, Ind., Sept. 3, 1951; d. Charles Walter Martin and Patricia Mae (Robertson) Kennedy; m. Mel B. Barnum, Jan. 1, 1982; children: Megan, Brenda. Student, Ray Vogue Sch. Comml. Design, Chgo., 1969-70, Purdue U., 1973-76. Graphic designer Loeb's Dept. Store, Lafayette, 1970-71; dir. promotion, talent Sta. WAZY-Radio, Lafayette, 1971-75; graphic designer Nat. Homes Corp., Lafayette, 1975-79, Hahn-Miskunas Advt., Lafayette, 1979-80; creative dir. Mktg. Resources, Lafayette, 1980-81; dir. mktg. Dan Pipkin Advt., Danville, Ill., 1981-82; pres. N.M. Barnum & Assocs., Belleville, Ill., 1982—; ptnr., dir. New Leaf, Inc., Belleville, 1982-86. Mem. coop. extension coun. bd. U. Ill., 1988—, steering com. Gateway United Worl of Difference Program, 1988—, steering com. 175th Anniversary of Belleville, 1987—; exec. bd. Downtown Belleville, 1986-87; bd. dirs. YWCA of St. Clair County, Belleville, 1986-87, pres. bd. 1987—. Lodge: Optimists. Office: NM Barnum & Assocs 117 S Charles Belleville IL 62220

BARNUM, WILLIAM DOUGLAS, communications company executive; b. Denton, Tex., July 28, 1946; s. Billie Douglas and Leticia Christina (Cox) B.; BSBA with distinction in Econs., Georgetown U., 1967; MBA, Fairleigh Dickinson U., 1985; m. Mary Ann Mook, Aug. 10, 1968. Acct., RCA Corp., Cherry Hill, N.J., 1967-68, Andros Island, Bahamas, 1968-70, budget and cost analyst, Cherry Hill, 1970, adminstr. telephone systems, 1970-73; mgr. project adminstrn. White Sands Radar Project, Holloman AFB, N.Mex., 1973-74; coordinator profit center acctg., N.Y.C , 1974-76, adminstr. globcom systems, N.Y.C., 1976-77, mgr. spl. project and accounts-payable, N.Y.C., 1978-79, mgr. fin., 1979-81, mgr. gateway ops., dir. field support services, 1982-88; sr. mgr. network services MCI Internat., 1988—; bd. dirs., chmn. fin. com. Morris/Sonerset County United Cerebral Palsy. Mem. Republican Presdl. Task Force. Mem. Am. Def. Preparedness Assn., Am. Security Council, NRA (life), Knifemakers Guild (hon.) Am. Knife Throwers Alliance (hon.), Mensa, Delta Phi Epsilon, Delta Mu Delta. Presbyterian. Author: Kroodley Made Knife Catalog, 1977. Home: PO Box 893 Far Hills NJ 07931 Office: MCI Internat 201 Centennial Ave Piscataway NJ 08854

BARON, RONALD HARVEY, manufacturing executive; b. Queens, N.Y., Oct. 28, 1950; s. George B. and Ruth (Strom) B.; m. Suzanne Lee Waxler, Aug. 20, 1972; children: Derek, Robyn. BS in Mgmt. Engring., Rensselaer Poly. Inst., 1972. Cost acct. Stecher-Traung-Schmidt, Rochester, N.Y., 1972-74; mgr. prodn. control Md. Paper Box, Balt., 1974-78; graphics mgr. Revlon, Ridgefield Park, N.J., 1978-79; engring. mgr. Winthrop-Atkins Co., Inc., Middleboro, Mass., 1979-81; ops. mgr. Winthrop-Atkins Co., Inc., Middleboro, 1981-85, v.p. mktg., 1985-86, pres., 1986—. Dir. RuPicola Prodns., Boston, 1985—; patentee in field. Pres. Scotts Level Community Assn., Balt., 1977; leader Boy Scouts Am., Stoughton, Mass., 1986-87. Mem. Assoc. Industries Mass., Printing Industries Am., Am. Assn. Indsl. Mfrs., Splty. Advt. Assn. Internat. (suppliers com.), Jaycees (Balt. chpt.). Republican. Jewish. Club: TEP (pres. 1970-72) (Troy, N.Y.). Office: Winthrop Atkins Co Inc Middleboro MA 02346

BAROUDY, BAHIGE MOURAD, biochemist, researcher; b. Beirut, Lebanon, July 1, 1950; came to U.S., 1973, naturalized, 1988; s. Mourad Bahige and Ludmila Adelheid (Obermuller-Haddad) B. B.S., Am. U. of Beirut, 1972; Ph.D., Georgetown U., 1978. Teaching asst. Wesleyan U., Middletown, Conn., 1973-74; research asst. Georgetown U., Washington, D.C., 1974-78, fellow, 1982, research assoc. prof., 1985—; vis. fellow scientist NIH, Bethesda, Md., 1979-81, vis. assoc. scientist, 1982-85. Contbr. articles to profl. jours., chpts. to books. Mem. Am. Soc. Biochemistry and Molecular Biology, Am. Soc. for Microbiology, Am. Soc. for Virology, Sigma Xi (award for outstanding publ. Georgetown U. chpt. 1977). Lutheran. Avocations: fencing; viola. Office: Georgetown U Dept Microbiology Div Virology & Immunology 5640 Fishers Ln Rockville MD 20852

BARR, ALBERT JOEL, public relations company executive; b. Phila., July 13, 1947; s. S. Stanley Barr and Elaine (Braslay) Buncher. BJ, George Washington U., 1969. Reporter, photographer Loudoun County-Times, Leesburg, Va., 1969-70; mgr. pub. relations and advt. ITT, Washington, 1970; asst. to sr. v.p. pub. relations Tobacco Inst., Washington, 1970-75; dir. pub. and congl. relations Nat. Assn. Regulatory Utility Commrs., Washington, 1975-76; dir. pub. relations Glass Packaging Inst., Washington, 1976-80; v.p. Henry J. Kaufman & Assocs., Inc., Washington, 1980-82; exec. v.p. S.K. O'Brien & Assocs., Inc., Washington, 1982-84; pres. A.J. Barr & Co., Washington, 1984—. Inventor computer program CARMA (computer-aided rsch. media analysis). Mem. Pub. Relations Soc. Am., Internat. Pub. Relations Assn., George Washington U. Alumni Assn. (com. on pub. relations), Nat. Press Club. Office: AJ Bar & Co 918 16th St NW Ste 603 Washington DC 20006

BARR, DAVID CHARLES, consulting firm executive; b. Camden, N.J., Apr. 10, 1950; s. John James and Margaret Ruth (Smith) B.; m. Susan Kae Moore; 1 child, David William. BBA, U. Miami, Coral Gables, Fla., 1972. Ptnr. Glazebrook Acctg. Agy., Miami, 1972-73; v.p. Fidelity Bank, Phila., 1973-81; chief fin. officer Pubco Corp., Tysons Corner, Va., 1981-83; v.p. Perpetual Am. Bank, Alexandria, Va., 1983-85; exec. v.p. Equibank, Pitts., 1985-86, Allegheny Beverage Corp., Cheverly, Md., 1986-87; mng. ptnr. Kane Maiwurm Barr Inc., Reston, Va., 1988—. Home: 1944 Upper Lake Dr Reston VA 22091 Office: Kane Maiwurm Barr 1850 Centennial Park Dr Reston VA 22091

BARR, KENNETH JOHN, mining company executive; b. Birmingham, Ala., Aug. 25, 1926; s. Archie and Mable Leona (Griffith) B.; m. Jeanne Bonner, Jan. 22, 1951; children: Marsha Jeanne, Kenneth John, Darren Clint. BS in Chem. Engring., Auburn U., 1947; grad., Advanced Mgmt. Inst. Northwestern U., 1964. Jr. petroleum engr. Stanolind Oil & Gas, Hobbs, N.Mex., 1948-49; chief engr. Amoco Prodn. Co., Tulsa, 1962-65; mgr. producing and v.p. producing dept. Amoco Can. Petroleum Co., Calgary, Alta, 1965-70; mgr. producing and v.p., div. mgr. Amoco Prodn. Co., New Orleans, 1970-73; mgr. supply dept. Standard Oil (Ind.), Chgo., 1973-75; exec. v.p. Amoco Internat., Chgo., 1975, Amoco Prodn. Co., Chgo., 1975-79; pres. Cyprus Mines (Std.), Los Angeles, 1979-80, Amoco Minerals Co., Denver, 1980-85; pres., chief exec. officer Cyprus Minerals Co., Denver, 1985—, also bd. dirs. Served with USAAF, 1945. Mem. Am. Mining Congress (bd. dirs. 1983—), AIME. Clubs: Snowmass (Aspen, Colo.); Longboat Key (Fla.). Office: Cyprus Minerals Co 9100 E Mineral Cir PO Box 3299 Englewood CO 80155

BARR, RONALD KENNETH, financial executive, controller; b. Miami Beach, Fla., Sept. 11, 1950; s. Burton Philip and Sybil Arlene (Freier) B.; m. Joy Frances Micale, Sept. 4, 1984. BBA, Iona Coll., 1974; MBA, Fordham U., 1987. CPA, N.Y. Acct. Deloitte, Haskins & Sells, Stamford, Conn., 1974-76; sr. acct. Thomas J. Lipton Inc., Englewood Cliffs, N.J., 1976-77; sr. fin. planning analyst Thomas J. Lipton Inc., Englewood Cliffs, N.J., 1977, supr. fin. planning, 1977-80, mgr. staff acctg., 1980-81, mgr. gen. acctg., 1981-82, mgr. fin. adminstrn.-tea buying, 1983; controller research and devel. ctr. Lever Bros. Co., Edgewater N.J., 1983—. N.Y. State Edn. Dept. regents scholar, 1967. Mem. Am. Inst. CPA's, N.Y. State Soc. CPA's. Office: Lever Rsch & Devel Ctr 45 River Rd Edgewater NJ 07020

BARRACK, WILLIAM SAMPLE, JR., petroleum company executive; b. Pitts., July 26, 1929; s. William Sample and Edna Mae (Henderson) B. B.S., U. Pitts., 1950; postgrad., Dartmouth Coll. With Texaco, Inc., N.Y., 1953-—; mktg. mgr. Northeast Texaco, Inc., 1953-62; dist. mgr. Texaco, Inc., Portland, Maine, 1962-63, Portland, 1963-65; asst. mgr. distbn. and devel. Texaco, Inc., N.Y., 1965-66, asst. mgr. mktg. research and project devel., 1966-67; asst. div. mgr. Texaco, Inc., Norfolk, Va., 1967-68; area dir. Texaco, Inc., Brussels, Belgium, 1968-70; gen. mgr. Texaco, Inc., N.Y., 1970; asst. to chmn. bd. Texaco, Inc., N.Y.C., 1971; v.p. internat. Europe Texaco, Inc., 1971-76, v.p. producing Eastern hemisphere, 1976-77; v.p. personnel and corp. services Texaco, Inc., White Plains, N.Y., 1977-80; chmn., chief exec. officer Texaco Ltd., London, Eng., 1980-83; sr. v.p. Texaco Inc., White Plains, N.Y., 1983—; pres. Texaco Oil Trading & Supply Co., White Plains, N.Y., 1983-84; dir. Caltex Petroleum Corp.; Mem. Naval War Coll. Found., Newport, R.I. Trustee Manhattanville Coll.; bd. dirs. Texaco Philanthropic Found., Mary Rose Soc. Served as comdr. USNR, 1951-53. Mem. Fgn. Policy Assn. N.Y. (gov.). Clubs: N.Y. Yacht; Ida Lewis Yacht; North Sea Yacht (Belgium); Woodway Country, Ox Ridge Hunt; Clambake (Newport, R.I.); Australian (Sidney, Australia). Office: Texaco Inc 2000 Westchester Ave White Plains NY 10650

BARRATT, ERIC GEORGE, accountant; b. Stokenchurch, England, Apr. 15, 1938; s. Frank Ronald and Winifred Mary (Hayward) B. Chartered acct. Ptnr. Tansley Witt & Co., London, 1966-79, Arthur Andersen & Co., London, 1979-82, MacIntyre Hudson, London, 1982—; dir. Automotive Products P.L.C., Leamington, 1977-86, Montague Boston Investment Trust P.L.C., London, 1982-85, Milton Keynes Devel. Corp., 1980-85. Chmn. Stokenchurch Parish Council, 1975-86; vice-chmn. Buckinghamshire County Council, Aylesbury, 1981-85; dir. Commn. for New Towns, 1986—; treas. Oriel Coll., Oxford, 1986. Fellow Inst. Chartered Accts. Conservative. Anglican. Clubs: Atheneaum, Carlton, City of London (London). Home: Stockfield, Stokenchurch HP14 3SX, England Office: MacIntyre Hudson, 28 Ely Pl, London EC1N 6RL, England

BARRE, LOREN D., manufacturing company executive; b. Benton City, Mo., Nov. 22, 1925; s. Thomas Horner and Ina (Baxter) B.; children—Lynn, Anne, Dana. B.S.E.E., U. Calif.-Berkeley, 1947; M.B.A., Stanford U., 1949. Registered profl. engr., Oreg. Sales rep. Allis Chalmers, Milw., 1949-56; sales staff RTE Corp., Waukesha, Wis., 1956-57, asst. to v.p., 1957-61, mktg. mgr., 1961-62, v.p. sales, 1962-65, v.p. mktg., 1965-68, sr. v.p. ops., 1968-70, pres., chief operating officer, 1970-76, pres., chief exec. officer, 1976-83, chmn. bd., chief exec. officer, 1983-88; dir. Stolper Industries, Menomonee Falls, Wis., Electronic Telecommunications, Inc., Waukesha, Wis. Bd dirs. Florentine Opera Co., Milw., Waukesha Meml. Hosp., 1974-83, vice chmn. 1976-80; regent Milw. Sch. Engring. Mem. IEEE. Clubs: Bluemound Golf and Country, University. Home: 929 N Astor St Apt 1902 Milwaukee WI 53202

BARREN, BRUCE WILLARD, merchant banker; b. Olean, N.Y., Jan. 28, 1942; s. James Lee and Marion Frances (Willard) B.; m. Roseanne Hundley, Apr. 17, 1976; children: James Lee, Christina Roseanne. BS, Babson Coll., 1962; MS, Bucknell U., 1963; grad. cert., Harvard U., 1967, Cambridge U., England, 1968. CPA, Pa., FCA, England. Sr. cons. Price Waterhouse, N.Y., 1963-67; v.p. Walston & Co., Inc., N.Y., 1967-70; sr. v.p. Delafield Childs, Inc., N.Y., 1970-71; chmn. The EMCO/Hanover Group, L.A., 1971—; vice-chmn. Four Winds Enterprises Inc., San Diego 1985-87; bd. dirs. various U.S. and internat. cos.; exec. mng. and gen. ptnr. Emco/Barren Fund 1988—. Recipient Disting. Svc. awards Calif. State Senate and State Assembly, Office of the Gov., Counties of L.A., Orange, Calif., San Diego, City of L.A.; U.S. Senate. Roman Catholic. Home: 1153 Chantilly Rd Los Angeles CA 90077 Office: EMCO Fin Ltd 1640 S Sepulveda Blvd Los Angeles CA 90025 also: 1932 Rittenhouse Sq Philadelphia PA 19103

BARRER, ROGER AARON, retail executive; b. N.Y.C., June 5, 1926; s. Aaron and Eva (Dranow) B.; children—Richard, Robert. B.S., NYU, 1948, M.S., 1950. Pres. Alexander's Inc., N.Y.C., 1948—; dir. Alexander's Inc., 1969—. Served with USAAF, 1944-46, ETO. Named Boy Scout of Yr., Boy Scouts Am., 1973. Office: Alexander's Inc 500 17th Ave New York NY 10018

BARRETT, CHARLES MARION, insurance company executive, physician; b. Cin., Mar. 10, 1913; s. Charles Francis and May (Ryan) B.; m. May Belle Finn, Apr. 27, 1942; children: Angela Barrett Eynon, Charles, John, Michael, Marian Barrett Leibold, William. AB, Xavier U., 1934, LLD (hon.), 1974; MD, U. Cin., 1938. Assoc. med. dir. Western & So. Life Ins. Co., Cin., 1942, med. dir., 1951-73, exec. v.p., 1965-73, pres., 1973-84, chmn. bd., chief exec. officer, 1984-88, chmn., 1988—; prof. depts. surgery and radiology U. Cin. Coll. Medicine, 1957-74, prof. emeritus, 1974—; chmn. Columbus Mut. Life Ins. Co., 1982—; bd. dirs. Procter & Gamble Co., Cin. Bell Inc. Bd. dirs. Our Lady of Mercy Hosp., Bethesda Hosp. and Deaconess Assn.; chmn. bd. trustees U. Cin., 1977, chmn. emeritus, 1987—; chmn. Cin. Bus. Com., 1986-87. Recipient Taft medal U. Cin., 1973, spl. award Ohio Radiol. Soc., 1974, Daniel Drake award, 1985; named Great Living Cincinnatian, 1987. Fellow Am. Coll. Radiology; mem. AMA, Life Ins. Assn. Am., Greater Cin. C. of C. (chmn. 1985-86), Knights of Malta, Alpha Omega Alpha. Office: Western & So Life Ins Co 400 Broadway Cincinnati OH 45202

BARRETT, FREDERICK CHARLES, engineering executive; b. Chgo., Apr. 1, 1949; s. Robert D. and Phyllis S. (Paul) B.; m. Wendy Lynn Freyer; 1 child, Richard. BSEE, Iowa State U., 1972; MBA with high honors, Lake Forest Coll., 1988. Registered profl. engr., Ill. Project. engr. Motorola, Inc., Schaumburg, Ill., 1972-76; sales rep. Computer Automation, Inc., Elk Grove Village, Ill., 1976-77; product engr. Entron Controls, Inc., Carol Stream, Ill., 1977-79; staff engr. AM Multigraphics, Mt. Prospect, Ill., 1979-81; sr. engr. Extel Corp., Northbrook, Ill., 1981-84; staff engr. Bell & Howell Co., Lincolnwood, Ill., 1984-88; dir. engr. Associated Rsch., Inc., Lake Bluff, Ill., 1988—; instr. Coll. Lake County, Grayslake, Ill., 1984. Patentee in field. Eugene Hotchkiss scholar Lake Forest Grad. Sch. Mgmt., 1988. Mem. IEEE. Office: Associated Rsch Inc 905 Carriage Park Ave Lake Bluff IL 60044

BARRETT, THOMAS JOSEPH, capital equipment company executive; b. Detroit, Oct. 26, 1934; s. Thomas Joseph and Thelma Louise (Johnson) B.; m. Charlene Elaine Ensslin, Feb. 22, 1963 (div. 1984); children: Kevin Patrick, Michael Dermot, Karen Marie, Kelly Susanne. BS, U. Detroit, 1960; MBA, U. Chgo., 1962. With B.F. Goodrich Co., 1962-82, gen. mgr., 1981-82; v.p. sales Siam Internat., Akron, Ohio, 1982-83; dir. braiding and winding products Rockwell Internat., Reading, Pa., 1984—. Mem. venture grant com. Berks County United Way, 1986, 87, 89, bd. dirs., 1987. With USN, 1954-56. Mem. Sales and Mktg. Execs. Assn. (v.p., bd. dirs.). Republican. Roman Catholic. Home: 4637 Sylvan Dr Reading PA 19606 Office: Rockwell Internat 200 N Park Rd Wyomissing PA 19610

BARRETT, THOMAS LEON FRANCIS, information technology software executive; b. Shenandoah, Pa., July 19, 1938; s. Thomas Francis and Leocadia Modesta (Pietkiewicz) B.; m. Helene Elizabeth Ryan, June 29, 1963; children: Kathleen Theresa, Maureen Patricia, Thomas Leon Francis, Jr. Student, Bloomsburg State Tchrs. Coll., 1956-57, Pa. State Inst. Tech., 1964-66; studetn, Villanova U., 1966-70; BS in Computer Scis., Pacific Western U., 1982. Profl. safe cracker Mosler Safe Co., Phila., 1958-66; programmer, mathematician Missile and Space div. Gen. Electric Co., Valley Forge, Pa., 1966-69, software engr., 1972-73; chief programmer SSD Gen. Electric Co., Phila., 1973-78; supr. software engring. Gen. Electric Co., Valley Forge, 1978-81, mgr. software engring. RSD, 1981-86, mgr. info. tech. software engring. RESD, 1986-88, sr. systems engr. Space Def. Initiative, 1988—; software cons. Programming Methods Inc., N.Y.C., 1969-70; programmer analyst GTE Data Svcs., Mt. Laurel, N.J., 1970-72. Treas. Intra County Swim League, Del. County, Pa., 1982-88; chmn. Cath. Charatics Dr. Sacred Heart Parish, 1980-81. Named Man of Yr. Sacred Heart Parish Clifton Hts., 1988. Mem. Holy Name Soc., Cath. Youth Orgn. (chief advisor 1972-85), Clifton Heights Swim Club (pres. 1987, 88, 89, swim team dir. 1976-81), Elks. Republican. Roman Catholic. Home: 18 Glenwood Cir Aldan PA 19018 Office: GE MD 4-010 Bldg 98 Blue Bell PA 19422

BARRETT, TOM HANS, rubber company executive; b. Topeka, Aug. 13, 1930; s. William V. and Myrtle B.; m. Marilyn Dunn, July 22, 1956; children: Susan and Sara (twins), Jennifer. Grad. Chem. Engr., Kans. State U., 1953; grad., Sloan Sch. Mgmt. MIT, 1969. With Goodyear Tire & Rubber Co., various locations, 1953—; pres. Goodyear Tire and Rubber Co., Akron, OH, 1982-89, chief oper. officer, 1982-89; chmn., pres., chief exec. officer Goodyear Tire & Rubber Co., Akron, Ohio, 1989—, also dir.; dir. A.O. Smith Corp., Rubbermaid Corp. Served with U.S. Army, 1953-55. Decorated officer with crown Order Merite Civil et Militaire, Luxembourg, 1976; recipient Sigma Phi Epsilon citation, 1979. Home: 2135 Stockbridge Rd Akron OH 44313 Office: Goodyear Tire & Rubber Co 1144 E Market St Akron OH 44316

BARRETT, WILLIAM JOEL, investment banker; b. Darien, Conn., Aug. 26, 1939; s. William J. and Virginia Barrett; BA, DePauw U., Greencastle, Ind., 1961; MBA, NYU, 1963; m. Sara Schrock, Sept. 1, 1962; children—William, Brian, Christopher, Peter. Investment analyst Met. Life Ins. Co., 1961-66; v.p. Gregory & Sons, investment bankers, 1966-69, G.A. Saxton, investment bankers, 1969-74; sr. v.p., Janney Montgomery Scott, Inc., N.Y.C., 1974—, also dir.; dir. ESI Industries, Inc., Heldor Industries, Inc., Shelter Components Corp., Fredericks Corp., TGC Industries, Inc.; bd. trustees Diocesan Investment Trust N.J. Republican. Episcopalian. Clubs: Navesink Country, Univ., India House, Bond of N.Y., Shrewsbury Sailing and Yacht, Sea Bright Lawn Tennis, Seabright Beach.

BARRIENTOS, ROBERT JOHN, art brokerage company executive; b. Lyons, Kans., Nov. 19, 1953; s. Frances Barrientos. Student, Hutchinson Jr. Coll., 1973; BA in History, Kans. Newman Coll., 1977; MA in Communications, Wichita State U., 1980. Mgr. El Mexico Cafe, Wichita, Kans., 1973-77; instr. Wichita State U., 1977-81; gen. mgr. Sta. KTEP-FM, El Paso, Tex., 1981-82; bd. dirs., cons. Fenix Inc., Wichita, 1982-84; owner, mgr. Robert Barrientos and Assocs., Wichita, 1983—; grant writer League United Latin Am. Citizens, Wichita, 1974-77; producer Sta. KAKE-TV, wichita, 1975-81; dir. pub. rels. Sta. KMUW-FM, Wichita, 1977-80, asst. gen. mgr., 1980-81; Corp. for Pub. Broadcasting tng. fellow Harvard U., 1979-81; dir. devel. Sta. KCUR-FM, Kansas City, Mo., 1989. Producer/writer TV documentaries, 1975—, radio dramas, 1980—; contbr. poetry to various publs. Mem. Wichita Employment/Tng. Council, 1978-81, Wichita Pvt. Industries Council, 1980-81, Greater Downtown Wichita, 1988, Wichita Econ. Devel. Commn. Home and Office: PO Box 36381 Kansas City MO 64111

BARRIGER, JOHN WALKER, IV, transportation executive; b. St. Louis, Aug. 3, 1927; s. John Walker and Elizabeth Chambers (Thatcher) B.; m. Evelyn Dobson, Dec. 29, 1955; children: John Walker V, Catherine Brundige. BS, MIT, 1949; CT, Yale U., 1950. With Santa Fe Ry., 1950-68, 70-83, supt. transp., 1965-68, mgr. staff studies and planning, Chgo., 1970-77, asst. v.p. fin., 1977-79, asst. to pres., 1979-83; dir. spl. services Santa Fe So. Pacific Corp., 1983-85, prin. John W. Barriger and Assocs., Chgo., 1985—; v.p. corp. devel. Venango River Corp., South Shore Ry., Chgo. Mo. and Western Ry., 1987-88; v.p. corp. devel., Chgo. Mo. and Western Ry., 1989— mgr. transp. controls div. Sylvania Info. Systems, Waltham, Mass., 1968-70; mem. vis. com. dept. civil engring. MIT, 1972-75; chmn. MIT Mgmt. Conf., Chgo., 1984. Trustee Village of Kenilworth (Ill.), 1978-85, North Suburban Mass Transit Dist., 1985—, chmn. railrod com., John W. Barriger III Nat. R.R. Library, St. Louis; bd. dirs. St. Louis Merc. Library. Served with USN, 1946. Recipient Bronze Beaver award MIT, 1975, Employee Campaign Chmn. of Yr. award United Way/Crusade of Mercy, 1979. Mem. Am. Assn. R.R. Supts. (bd. dirs. 1958-68), Am. Ry. Engring. Assn., Ry. Planning Officers Assn. (chmn. 1971-76), Transp. Research Bd., Transp. Research Forum, Western Ry. Club (pres. 1979-80), Newcomen Soc., MIT Alumni Assn. (bd. dirs. 1968-72), Delta Kappa Epsilon. Republican. Roman Catholic. Clubs: Econ. Chgo. Exec. Chgo., MIT Chgo. (pres. 1972-73), Kenilworth, Union League Chgo. Home: 155 Melrose Ave Kenilworth IL 60043 Office: 10 N Dearborn St Chicago IL 60602

BARRINGTON, BRUCE DAVID, corporate executive; b. Chgo., Apr. 9, 1942; s. Arthur Richard and Lorene Cora (Powell) B.; B.S. in Math., Bradley U., 1964; m. Gayle Marguerite Wilcoxen, June, 1970; children—Arthur Richard, II, Kenneth Alan, Paige Marguerite. Systems analyst Caterpillar Tractor Co., Peoria, Ill., 1965-67; mgr. hosp. systems devel. McDonnell Douglas Automation Co., Peoria, 1967-73; founder, dir. HBO & Co., Atlanta, 1973-83; mng. ptnr. Barrington Group; owner Hawk's Cay Resort; founder, chmn. Clarion Software Corp., Barrington Aviation, Inc. Bd. dirs., trustee Pine Crest Sch.; trustee Bradley U., First Presbyn. Ch., Pompano Beach, Fla., Dwight D. Eisenhower Soc. Named Centurian Disting. Alumnus Bradley U., 1985. Clubs: Country of Peoria; Lighthouse Point (Fla.) Yacht and Racquet, Adios Golf, Boca Raton Hotel and Club. Author: Clarion bus. computer language. Office: 150 E Sample Rd Ste 200 Pompano Beach FL 33064

BARRON, DORA JONES, quality engineering supervisor; b. Pinetops, N.C., Sept. 27, 1960; d. Willie James and Fannie (Jenkins) Jones; m. David Norris Barron, May 11, 1985. BS in Materials Engring., N.C. State U., 1982. Sr. mfg. engr. Black & Decker Corp., Tarboro, N.C., 1983—; instr. Edgecombe Tech. Coll., Tarboro, 1983—, computer programmer, 1984—, geometric tolerancing instr., 1985—. Active Wolfpack Club N.C. State U., Raleigh, 1987—. L.P. Doshi scholar N.C. State U. Sch. Engring., 1981, Scholastic Achievement award N.C. State Dept. Student Affairs, 1981-82. Mem. Soc. Mfg. Engrs., Am. Soc. Metals. Democrat. Baptist. Club: Youth Christian League (Crisp, N.C.) (advisor 1986—). Home: Rte 1 PO Box 421 Fountain NC 27829 Office: Black & Decker 3301 Main St Tarboro NC 27886

BARRON, INGE FALK, state official; b. Berlin, Oct. 26, 1927; came to U.S., 1941; d. Gustav Peter and Bettina (Schuller) Falk; widow; children: Diana, Alexander, Eleanor (dec.). BA, Barnard Coll., 1949; MA, Columbia U., 1951; cert., N.Y. Inst. Fin., 1953, Coll. Fin. Planning, Denver, 1987. Economist, researcher Nat. Bur. Econ. Rsch., Riverdale, N.Y., 1949-51; securities analyst A.G. Becker, A.M. Kidder, Smith Barney, N.Y.C., 1951-56; social worker Balt. Dept. Welfare, 1959-61; tchr. Balt. Sch. System, 1963-66; prof. econs. Morgan State U., Balt., 1966-67; chief rsch. Dept. Pub. Welfare State of Md., Balt., 1967-71, adminstr. dept. human resources, 1971-73, chief rsch. analyst for quality control, 1973-85, adminstr. Juvenile Svcs. Agy., 1985—; fin. cons. Barron Travel, Balt., 1985—. Fundraiser Assoc. Jewish Charities, Balt., Balt. United Way, Am. Israel Pub. Affairs Com., Washington. Mem. Am. Assn. Cert. Fin. Planners, N.Y. Soc. Securities Analysts, Balt. Fgn. Affairs Coun., Na'amat Hadassah, Zionist Orgn. Am. Home: 2100 W Rogers Ave Baltimore MD 21209 Office: State of Md Dept Juvenile Svcs 321 Fallsway Baltimore MD 21202

BARRON, JEFFERY ALLEN, project manager; b. Pitts., Mar. 30, 1958; s. Cecil Claire and Janet L. (Hittie) B. BSME, U. Pitts., Johnstown, 1980. Design checker Season-All Industries, Indiana, Pa., 1981, coord. mfg., 1982-83, mgr. tech. svcs., 1983-84; mgr. engring., quality control Reynolds Metals Products, Bourbon, Ind., 1984-85; project engr. Graham Arcthl. Products, York, Pa., 1985-87, project mgr., 1988—. Mem. Window to Riches Investment Club (asst. sec./treas. 1986, v.p. 1987, pres. 1988), Lions (sec. local club 1983, v.p. 1984), Moose. Republican. Lutheran. Home: 3400 Eastern Blvd Apt E-8 York PA 17402 Office: Graham Archtl Products 1551 Mt Rose Ave York PA 17405

BARRONE, GERALD DORAN, savings and loan association executive; b. Tujunga, Calif., 1931; married. BS, UCLA, 1955. Pres., chief exec. officer Fidelity Fed. Savs and Loan Assn., Glendale, Calif., from 1955, also bd. dirs.; now, pres., chief oper. officer Coast Savings and Loan Assn., L.A.; bd. dirs. Citadel Holding Corp., Glendale. Served with USN, 1951-53. Office: Coast Savings and Loan Assn 1000 Wilshire Blvd 22d Fl Los Angeles CA 90017 *

BARROW, THOMAS DAVIES, former oil and mining company executive; b. San Antonio, Dec. 27, 1924; s. Leonidas Theodore and Laura Editha (Thomson) B.; m. Janice Meredith Hood, Sept. 16, 1950; children—Theodore Hood, Kenneth Thomson, Barbara Loyd, Elizabeth Ann. B.S., U. Tex., 1945, M.A., 1948; Ph.D., Stanford U., 1953; grad. advanced mgmt. program, Harvard U., 1963. With Humble Oil & Refining Co., 1951-72; regional exploration mgr. Humble Oil & Refining Co., New Orleans, 1962-64, sr. v.p., 1967-70, pres., 1970-72, also dir.; exec. v.p. Esso Exploration, Inc., 1964-65; sr. v.p. Exxon Corp., N.Y.C., 1972-78, also dir.; chmn., chief exec. officer Kennecott Corp., Stamford, Conn., 1978-81; vice chmn. Standard Oil Co., 1981-85; investment cons. Houston, 1985—; mem. commn. on natural resources NRC, 1973-78, commn. on phys. sci., math. and natural resources, 1984-87, bd. on earth scis., 1982-84; dir. Tex. Commerce Bankshares, McDermott Internat. Inc., Am. Gen. Corp., GeoQuest Internat., Inc., Cameron Iron Works; trustee Woods Hole Oceanographic Instn., 20th Century Fund-Task Force on U.S. Energy Policy. Pres. Houston Grand Opera, 1985-87, chmn., 1987—; trustee Am. Mus. Natural History, Stanford U. 1980—, Baylor Coll. Medicine, Tex. Med. Ctr., 1983—, Geol. Soc. Am. Found., 1982-87. Served to ensign USNR, 1943-46. Recipient Disting. Achievement award Offshore Tech. Conf., 1973, Disting. Engring. Grad. award U. Tex., 1970, Disting. Alumnus, 1982, Disting. Geology Grad., 1985; named Chief Exec. of Yr. in Mining Industry, Fin. World, 1979. Fellow N.Y. Acad. Scis.; mem. Nat. Acad. Engring., Am. Mining Congress (bd. dirs. 1979-85, vice chmn. 1983-85), Am. Assn. Petroleum Geologists, Geol. Soc. Am., Internat. Copper Research Assn. (bd. dirs. 1979-85), Nat. Ocean Industry Assn. (bd. dirs. 1982-85), AAAS, Am. Soc. Oceanography (pres. 1970-71), Am. Geophys. Union, Am. Petroleum Inst., Am. Geog. Soc., Sigma Xi, Tau Beta Pi, Sigma Gamma Epsilon, Phi Eta Sigma, Alpha Tau Omega. Episcopalian. Clubs: Houston Country, Clove Valley, Petroleum, River Oaks Country, Ramada.

BARRY, ALLAN RONALD, ship pilot; b. Chgo., Jan. 28, 1945; s. Robert Edward and Stella Yvonne (Pellonari) B.; m. Ellen Conerly, May 1, 1971; 1 child, Elizabeth Anne. BS, U.S. Mcht. Marine Acad., 1967. Unltd. masters lic., Houston Ship Channel pilot's lic. USCG. Ship's officer Lykes Bros. S.S. Co., Inc., New Orleans, 1967-74; ship's pilot Houston Pilots, 1975—; pres., chief exec. officer Allan Barry, Inc., Houston, 1979—. Mem. Nat. Maritime Hist. Soc. Lt. USNR, 1967-82. Mem. U.S. Mcht. Marine Acad. Alumni Assn. (leadership contbr. 1978—), Nat. Audobon Soc., Houston Audubon Soc., Nat. Maritime Hist. Soc., Coun. Am. Master Mariners, Am. Pilots Assn., Am. Mcht. Marine Veterans, Propeller Club (bd. govs. Port of Houston 1986-88), Internat. Platform Assn. Republican.

BARRY, DONALD LEE, investment broker; b. Ft. Gordon, Ga., Sept. 1, 1953; s. C. Donald and Della (Newman) B.; m. Peggy Summerfield, Aug. 8, 1980 (div. June 1983). Student, Wichita State U., 1974-1981. Lic. stocks and commodity trader, life ins. agt. Instr. Cyr's Driving Sch., Wichita, Kans., 1974-78, v.p., 1978-81; investment broker A.G. Edwards & Sons, Wichita, 1981-85, v.p. investments, 1985—. Bd. dirs. Wichita Pub. Library, 1980, treas. 1981-83; bd. dirs. Interfaith Ministries Exec. Com., Wichita, 1983—; co-chmn. fin. com. to elect. Margalee Wright, Wichita, 1984. Served as cpl. USMC, 1972-74. Recipient Pres.'s Council award Oppenheimer Mgmt. Co., 1983, AG Edwards & Sons, 1986, 87, 88, 89. Mem. Am. Mensa Ltd., Internat. Assn. for Fin. Planners. Republican. Episcopalian. Club: Wichita. Home: 1303 Farmstead Wichita KS 67208 Office: AG Edwards & Sons 201 N Main Wichita KS 67202

BARRY, DONALD MARTIN, management consultant; b. Chgo., Jan. 27, 1944; m. Carol Braham, June 15, 1968; children: Patrick, Stephen, Michael. BS in Psychology, Loyola U., Chgo., 1967; MA in Psychology, So. Ill. U., 1971, PhD in Psychology, 1975; MBA in Fin., Rutgers U., 1985. Instr., research coordinator adminstrn. of justice So. Ill. U., Carbondale, 1972-75, asst. prof., 1975-77; assoc. prof. criminal justice Rutgers U., Newark, 1977-84; assoc. Dr. H. Tschudin Assocs Inc., River Vale, N.J., 1984—; cons. Dept. Justice, Washington, 1978-85, States of N.Y., 1983-84, N.J., 1982-84, Ill., 1974-75. Contbr. numerous articles to profl. jours. Research grantee Adminstrv. Office Cts. N.J., 1983, Law Enforcement Commn. Ill, 1975, 1st Jud. Cir. Ill., 1974. Mem. Inst. Mgmt. Cons. (cert.). Office: Dr H Tschudin Assocs 215 River Vale Rd River Vale NJ 07675

BARRY, DOUGLAS ALBERT, investment analyst; b. Manchester, Conn., Sept. 27, 1961; s. Philip Paul and Lena Sweet (Gray) B. BS in Fin., U. Conn., 1983, MBA, 1985. Analyst Mktg. Systems Devel. Corp., Rocky Hill, Conn., 1983-84; fin. analyst intern Lydall, Inc., Manchester, 1985-86; investment analyst Amherst Investment Mgmt. Co., Springfield, Mass., 1987—; cons. U.S. Small Bus. Adminstrn., Storrs, Conn., 1982. U. Conn. Alumni Assn. scholar, 1985. Mem. Hartford Soc. Fin. Analysts, Cen. Conn. Cash Mgmt. Assn. Home: 31 Belle Ave Enfield CT 06082 Office: Amherst Investment Mgmt Co 1414 Main St Springfield MA 01144

BARRY, FRANKLYN STANLEY, JR., holding company executive; b. Binghamton, N.Y., Oct. 26, 1939; s. Franklyn Stanley and Mildred Floy (Clewell) B.; m. Ann B. Searle, Mar. 9, 1962; children: Allison, Kevin, Kathleen. AB, Harvard U., 1961, MBA, 1967. With Fisher-Price Toys, Inc., East Aurora, N.Y., 1967-83; dir. mfg. Fisher-Price Toys, Inc., East Aurora, 1974-76, v.p. rsch., devel., 1976-78, exec. v.p., 1978-80, pres., 1980-83; chief exec. officer Software Distbn. Svcs., 1982-85; pres. Software Distbn. Services, 1985-87; chmn., chief exec. officer Sheridan Cos., Williamsville, N.Y., 1988—; regional dir. Marine Midland Bank, Buffalo; bd. dirs. Mcht.'s Mut. Ins. Co., Mcht.'s Group Inc. Bd. dirs. United Way of Buffalo and Erie County, 1980—, Sheehan Emergency Meml. Hosp., Buffalo, 1979—; chmn. Canisius Coll. Coun., 1979—. Served with USN, 1961-65. Mem. Buffalo Club, Harvard of Western N.Y. Club (pres. 1988—), Orchard Park Country Club, Youngstown Yacht Club. Office: 5166 Main St Williamsville NY 14221

BARRY, GREGORY STEVEN, electrical engineer; b. Winchester, Mass., July 18, 1959; s. Henry Francis Jr. and Jane Natalie (Coates) B.; m. Eleanor Ann Holbrook, May 11, 1985; children: Collin Henry, Nicole Marie. AAS, Berkshire Community Coll., 1982; B of Tech., Rochester (N.Y.) Inst. Tech., 1982. Assoc. engr. BTU Engring. Corp., North Billerica, Mass., 1982-83, controls engr., 1984, engring. section leader, 1984-86, engring. supr., 1986—. Mem. Nat. Fire Protection Assn. (cert.). Republican. Roman Catholic. Office: BTU Engring Corp 23 Esquire Rd North Billerica MA 01862

BARRY, JOHN EMMET, landscape architect; b. Oklahoma City, May 5, 1953; s. Jack Glasgow and Barbara (Bizzell) B.; children: Melissa Leigh, Christiann, John Emmet. BS in Environ. Design, U. Okla., 1975. Lic. landscape architect, Okla., Ga. Salesman Clifton Landscape Co., Tulsa, 1975-77; prin. John Barry Inc., Tulsa, 1977-85; mktg. dir. Kauffmann Group, Atlanta, 1985-86, D'Angelo Assocs., Atlanta, 1986-87; owner, mgr. Barry Design Group, Atlanta, 1987—; lobbyist Oklahomans for Landscape Architecture, 1977-79. Mem. Leadership Tulsa, 1979; bd. dirs. Downtown Tulsa Unltd., 1980-81; mem. Tulsa Parks and Recreation Study, 1981; mem. Tulsa Mayor's Braintrust Com., 1980; coord. John Zink for Senate, Broken Arrow, Okla., 1980. Mem. Am. Soc. Landscape Architects. Republican. Presbyterian. Office: 1335 Canton Rd Ste C Marietta GA 30066

BARRY, LEI, medical equipment manufacturing executive; b. Fitchburg, Mass., May 27, 1941; d. Leo Isaacson and Irene Helen (Melanson) Isaacson Godbout; m. Delbert M. Berry (div.); children: David M., Susan L.; m. Frank H. Mahan III, June 25, 1976; stepchildren: Jodi L., Sarah C., Amy S., Frank H. IV. Grad. high sch., Waltham, Mass. Advt. salesperson, broadcaster various radio and TV stas., N.C. and Tex., 1961-67; New Eng. sales rep. Hollister, Inc., Chgo., 1967-71, Northeastern sales mgr., 1971-76; v.p., ptnr. Mahan Assocs., Blue Bell, Pa., 1976—; pres. Blue Bell Bio-Med., Inc., 1982—. Mem. Whitpain Twp. Planning commn.; pres., bd. dirs. Interfaith of Ambler; dir. Elder, United Ch. of Christ, 1978— . Mem. Wissahickon Valley C. of C., Wissahickon Valley Hist. Soc. (past bd. dirs.), Wissahickon Valley Watershed Assn., Nat. Bus. and Profl. Women's Club, Health Industry Reps. Assn., Nat. Assn. Female Execs., Bus. Women's Network Phila., NOW. Republican. Avocations: tennis, skiing, gourmet cooking. Office: Blue Bell Bio-Med Inc PO Box 455 Blue Bell PA 19422

BARRY, RICHARD FRANCIS, III, newspaper publisher; b. Norfolk, Va., Jan. 18, 1943; s. Richard F. and Mary Margaret (Perry) B.; m. Carolyn Ann Kennett, Aug. 7, 1965; children: Carolyn Michelle, Christopher David. B.A., LaSalle Coll., 1964; J.D., U. Va., 1967. Bar: Va. 1967. Assoc. firm Kaufman, Oberndorfer & Spainhour (now Kaufman and Canoles), Norfolk, 1967-71; ptnr. 1972-73; corp. sec. Landmark Communications, Inc., Norfolk, 1973-74; pres., gen. mgr. Roanoke Times & World-News, Va., 1974-76; pres., gen. mgr. The Virginian-Pilot and The Ledger-Star, Norfolk, 1976-78, pub., 1983—; pres., chief operating officer, dir. Landmark Communications, Inc., Norfolk, 1978—, chief exec. officer, 1984—; dir. Greensboro News and Record, Inc., Times-World Corp., Telecable Corp., Newspaper Advt. Bur., Capital Gazette Newspapers Inc. Bd. dirs. Norfolk State U. Found., Chrysler Mus., Greater Norfolk Corp.; bd. dirs., pres., campaign chmn. United Way of South Hampton Rds.; bd. visitors, rector Old Dominion U.; trustee, v.p. U. Va. Colgate Darden Bus. Sch. Sponsors. Office: Landmark Communications Inc 150 W Brambleton Ave Norfolk VA 23510

BARRY, ROBERT MICHAEL, hospital executive; b. Boston, July 11, 1947; s. Walter Bradford and Glenda (Buckley) B.; m. Carolyn Cavicchi, Dec. 12, 1971 (div. 1979). BSBA, Stonehill Coll., 1969; MBA, Anna Maria Coll., 1978. Office mgr. Jordan Marsh Corp., Boston, 1969-72; chief acct. Worcester (Mass.) Hahnemann Hosp., 1973-75, asst. controller, 1975-78, controller, 1979-82, v.p. fin., treas., 1982-86, pres., chief exec. officer, 1986—; bd. dirs., trustee Gt. Brook Valley Health Ctr., Worcester, 1980—, Holden (Mass.) Hosp., 1986—. Mem. Healthcare Fin. Mgmt. Assn., Am. Coll. Healthcare Execs. (nominee). Republican. Roman Catholic. Lodge: K.C. Home: 4 Burncoat St Worcester MA 01605 Office: Worcester Hahnemann Hosp 281 Lincoln St Worcester MA 01605

BARRY, TIMOTHY FRANCIS, construction company executive; b. St. Louis, Aug. 1, 1951; s. Timothy Richard and Mary Margaret (Salmon) B.; m. Carol Sue Hill, Nov. 28, 1951; children: Michael, Elizabeth. BSCE, Northwestern U., 1972; BS Archtl. Engring., U. Kans., 1976. Registered profl. engr., Mo.; CPA, Md. Constrn. engr. Sverdrup & Parcel & Assocs., Washington, 1972-73; engring. and materials mgr. Butler Mfg. Co., Kansas City, Mo., 1976-80; project mgr. The George Hyman Constrn. Co., Washington, 1980-83; sr. v.p. McDevitt & Street Co., Richmond, Va., 1982-83. Home: 2109 Colesbury Dr Mechanicsville VA 23111 Office: McDevitt & Street Co 7200 Glen Forest Dr Ste 300 Richmond VA 23226

BARRY, WILLIAM EDWARD, computer executive; b. Torrington, Conn., Sept. 20, 1957; s. Robert James and Caroline (Kneisler) B. BA, U. Conn., 1979. Promotional sales asst. K-Mart Corp., Torrington, 1980-85; credit asst. Ingersoll Rand, Torrington, 1985-86; universal product code computer supr. IGA Supermarkets, Canton, Conn., 1986—. Contbr. articles to profl. jours. Active Easter Seal Drive, Watertown, Conn., 1985. Mem. Am. Mgmt. Assn., U. Conn. Alumni Assn. (mem. networking council 1979—), Spanish Club. Democrat. Roman Catholic. Home: 127 McGuiness St #2 Torrington CT 06790

BARSALONA, FRANK SAMUEL, theatrical agent; b. S.I., N.Y., Mar. 31, 1938; s. Peter and Mary (Rotunno) B.; m. June Harris, Sept. 1, 1966; 1 dau., Nicole. BA, Wagner Coll., S.I., 1958; postgrad., Herbert Berghof Sch., N.Y.C., 1959-60. Agt. Gen. Artists Corp., N.Y.C., 1960-64; founder, since pres. Premier Talent Agy., N.Y.C., 1964—; co-founder, pres. Phila. Fury, 1977-80; lectr., moderator music industry; co-owner WKSS Radio, Hartford, Conn., WMYF/WERZ-FM, Exeter, N.H. Bd. govs. T.J. Martell Leukemia Fund; bd. dirs. Rock & Roll Hall of Fame Mus. Recipient numerous awards Billboard Publs., cover subject spl. issue, 1984; named to Performance Mag. Hall of Fame, 1988. Mem. Internat. Adv. Coun., Mus. Am. Folk Art. Office: Premier Talent Agy 3 E 54th St New York NY 10022

BARSHOP, SAMUEL EDWIN, motel executive; b. Waco, Tex., Sept. 11, 1929; s. Joseph J. and Mary (Markusfeld) B.; m. Ann Kronish, Dec. 31, 1952; children: Bruce, Steven, Jamie. BBA in Internat. Trade, U. Tex., 1951; postgrad., Law Sch., St. Mary's U., 1952. Self-employed in real estate, office bldgs., shopping centers and land devel. Tex., 1951—; now pres., chmn., chief exec. officer, dir. La Quinta Motor Inns, San Antonio; established Sam Barshop Professorship in Mktg. Adminstrn. and 2 scholarships for minorities in Grad. Sch. Bus., U. Tex., also centennial professorships in nursing adminstrn. and bus., centennial lectureship in bus.; dir. S.W. Airlines Co., First Republic Bank Corp.; lectr. U. Tex.; mem. Motel Days Permanent Com., N.Y.C. Vice chmn. adv. council U. Tex. Coll. Bus., Adminstrn. Found., 1978-79, chmn., 1979-80, also chmn. devel./endowment com. and mem. exec. com. of adv. council; mem. Chancellor's Council and President's Assos., U. Tex.; former mem. coordinating bd. Tex. Coll. and Univ. System; former mem. Tex. Gov.'s Task Force Higher Edn.; bd. dirs. NCCJ, 1972—, San Antonio Econ. Devel. Found., San Antonio Festival; trustee S.W. Research Inst., San Antonio Med. Found.; chmn. parents com. Princeton U., 1972, 73; mem. San Antonio Com. for Arts; mem. devel. bd. U. Tex. Health Sci. Center, San Antonio; mem. adv. com. Tex. Lyceum; bd. regents U. Tex. System. Served to 2d lt. USAF, 1952-54. Named Man of Yr. Motel Brokers Assn. Am., 1978; recipient Disting. Alumnus award Coll. Bus. Adminstrn., U. Tex., 1979; bronze award for lodging industry Wall Street Transcript, 1980, 82. Club: Century (U. Tex. Coll. Bus. Adminstrn.) (dir.). Home: 212 La Rue Ann Ct San Antonio TX 78213 Office: La Quinta Motors Inns Inc 10010 San Pedro PO Box 32064 San Antonio TX 78216

BARSKE, BODO, holding company executive; b. Munich, July 30, 1938; came to U.S., 1982.; s. Kurt and Asta B.; m. Elizabeth Anne Voight, Feb. 14, 1985; 1 child, Anne Katherine; children from previous marriage: Holger, Florian. Law degree, U. Munich. cert. lawyer (assessor), Fed. Republic Germany. Fin. dir. Wacker Chemie GmbH, Munich, 1968-81; sr. v.p. Carl Zeiss, Inc., Thornwood, N.Y., 1982-88; v.p. Carl Zeiss, Inc. div. Am. Holding Co., Thornwood, N.Y., 1982-88; dep. mng. dir. U.G. Allgemeine Leasing, Munich, 1988—; sr. v.p. Zeiss Can. Ltd. div. Am. Holding Co., 1986-88. Mem. Am. Mgmt. Assn. Home: 36 Beechwood Way Scarborough-on-Hudson NY 10510

BARSY, IMRE JOSEPH, JR., marketing professional; b. Lancaster, Pa., Dec. 7, 1953; s. Imre Joseph and Helen Isabelle (Yeager) B.; m. Debra Ruth Mullennex, Mar. 12, 1979; 1 child, Imre Joseph III. BS in English, Davis and Elkins Coll., Elkins, W.Va., 1975. Editor-in-chief Tygart Valley Press, Elkins, 1976-81; assoc. editor Bicyling Mag., Emmans, Pa., 1981-84; industry editor Bicycle Guide Mag., Boston, 1984-86; communications dir. Specialized Bicycle Components, Morgan Hill, Calif., 1986—. Editor Buyers' Guide Edit., Bicycle Guide, 1984-86; contbr. articles to prof. mags. Mem. Sons of the Am. Legion. Democrat. Presbyterian. Office: Specialized Bicycle Components 15130 Concord Circle Morgan Hill CA 95037

BARTA, PAULA GENE, finance director; b. Rapid City, S.D., Jan. 30, 1952; d. Eugene Paul and Martha Louise (Langham) B.; m. William Lee Roberts, June 9, 1979; 1 child, Benjamin Lewis Roberts. BA, U. Colo., 1977; MBA, Harvard U., 1979. CPA, Calif. Program asst. Western States Arts Found., Denver, 1975-77; controller Jewish Family and Children's Services, San Francisco, 1979-83; acct. Deloitte Haskins & Sells, San Francisco, 1984-85, Touche Ross & Co., San Francisco, 1985-86; fin. dir. San Francisco Zool. Soc., 1987—. Mem. Am. Soc. Women Accts. (bd. dirs. 1988-89) Am. Woman's Soc. Cert. Pub. Accts., Nat. Assn. Accts., Phi Beta Kappa. Office: San Francisco Zool Soc Sloat Blvd at Pacific Ocean San Francisco CA 94132

BARTAK, GARY J., banker; b. Belleville, Kans., Sept. 11, 1953; s. Frank J. and Neva M. (Chopp) B.; m. Sara L. Schaefer, Oct. 15, 1983; children: Luke, Mark. Student, Kans. State U., 1975; BBA, Golden Gate U., 1983. CPA, Kans. Mgr. tax/audit Fox & Co. CPA's, Wichita, Kans., 1975-84; v.p. fin. SFM Venture Corp., Wichita, 1984-85; asst. controller Murfin Drilling Co., Wichita, 1985-87; v.p./cashier Citadel Bank of Wichita, 1987—; bd. dirs. State Bank of Colwich, Kans. Bd. dirs., treas. Wichita area Girl Scout council, 1981—. Mem. Am. Inst. CPA's, Kans. Soc. CPA's, Wichita C. of C. Lodge: KC. Home: 341 S Fountain Wichita KS 67218

BARTEAU, JOHN FRANK, restaurant executive; b. Springfield, Mass., Jan. 30, 1928; s. John Frank and Mary Elizabeth (Hunt) B.; m. Frances Melba Crockett; children: John F. III, Gilbert J., Suzanne, Peter H. Student, Norwich U., 1945-46; BA, Lehigh U., 1952, BSME, 1953. Engring. dir. AMF, York, Pa., 1953-72; v.p. devel. Church's Fried Chicken, San Antonio, Tex., 1972-79, sr. v.p. devel., mfg., 1984—; pres. Far West Products, San Antonio, 1979-80; v.p. devel. Ponderosa, Inc., Dayton, Ohio, 1980-84. Served with US Army, 1945-47. Mem. Phi Beta Kappa, Tau Beta Pi, Pi Tau Sigma. Home: Rte 2 PO Box 2045A Boerne TX 78006 Office: Church's Fried Chicken Inc 355A Spencer Ln PO Box BH001 San Antonio TX 78284

BARTEK, VICTORIA JEAN (VEE JAY), communications engineer; b. Pitts., Aug. 14, 1945; d. Elmer and Victoria (Mroz) B. Student, U. Pitts., nights 1974-77. With G.C. Murphy Co. Pitts., 1961-64; gen. clk. Bell Telephone, Pitts., 1964-67, staff aide, 1967-68, tech. asst., 1968-69, engring technician, 1969-70, engring. assoc., 1970-78; engr. Bell Telephone, Phila., 1978-79, Pitts., 1979—. Mem. Telephone Pioneers Am. Democrat. Roman Catholic.

BARTEL, RICHARD JOSEPH, real estate executive; b. Cedar Rapids, Iowa, Oct. 16, 1950; s. Donald William and Mary Annis (Crawford) B.; m. Sophie D. Piatkiewicz, Feb. 25, 1984; children: Michael Scott, Ashley Melanie, Sarah Catherine. BS in Acctg., U. Ill., 1973; MBA, Northwestern U., 1980. CPA; lic. real estate broker. Sr. acct. Price Waterhouse, Chgo., 1973-77; v.p., controller Marathon U.S. Realties, Inc., Chgo., 1977-84; v.p. project fin. Oxford Properties, Inc., Denver, 1984-85, Oxford Devel. Group Ltd., Toronto, 1985-86; sr. v.p. fin. ops. Cadillac Fairview Urban Devel., Dallas, 1986-87, Prentiss Properties Ltd., Inc., Dallas, 1987—. Mem. AICPA, Tex. Soc. CPAs. Republican. Roman Catholic. Home: 16207 Red Cedar Trail Dallas TX 75248 Office: Prentiss Properties Ltd Inc 1717 Main St Ste 5000 Dallas TX 75201

BARTELS, DONALD JAMES, freight company executive, consultant; b. Appleton, Wis., Apr. 17, 1956; s. Donald and Shirley Ann (Hanson) B.; m. Joann Catherine Zitske, Dec. 20, 1974; children: Stephanie, Andrew. Grad. high sch., Appleton. Owner D&J Custom Top, Appleton, 1977-81, D&J Freight Systems, Appleton, 1981-86; mgr. NM Transfer Co., Inc., Neenah, Wis., 1986-88; owner Bartels Enterprises, Menasha, Wis., 1986—; pres. Valley Bus. Users Group, Appleton, 1988. Home: N6983 Hwy 114 Menasha WI 54952 Office: Bartels Enterprises N6983 Hwy 114 Menasha WI 54952

BARTELS, GERALD LEE, association executive; b. Omaha, Dec. 28, 1931; s. Emil Frank and Mabel Anna (Denker) B.; children: Susan Bartels Reid, Jeri Bartels Blair, William Kimber, Robert Kimber, Michael Kimber. BA cum laude, Midland Coll., 1953. Cert. chamber exec. Dir. publicity Wittenberg U., Springfield, Ohio, 1955-56; Eastern projects mgr. Harry Krusz & Co., Lincoln, Nebr., 1956-59; gen. mgr. St. Paul Area C. of C., 1959-63; exec. v.p. Greater Macon (Ga.) C. of C., 1963-65; pres. Shrimp Boats, Inc., Macon, 1965-67; exec. v.p. Greater Greenville (S.C.) C. of C., 1967-76, Jacksonville (Fla.) C. of C., 1976-83, Atlanta C. of C. 1983—. Mem. Action Forum of Atlanta; bd. dirs. Atlanta Econ. Devel. Corp., Econ. Opportunity Atlanta. Served with U.S. Army, 1953-55; trustee Midland Coll. Recipient Gov. Nebr.'s award, 1982; named Man of Yr., Greenville Downtown Council, 1975, Man Of Yr., Elks Club, 1978. Mem. Am. C. of C. Execs. (chmn. 1982-83), So. Assn. Chamber Execs., Ga. C. of C. Execs. (bd. dirs. 1985-87, pres.-elect), S.C. C. of C. Execs. (pres. 1971), Atlanta C. of C. (pres. 1983—), Rotary. Episcopalian. Clubs: Commerce, Poinsett, Capital City.

BARTELS, JOACHIM CONRAD, marketing and publishing corporation executive; b. Ueberlingen, Germany, Dec. 3, 1938; came to U.S., 1966, naturalized, 1975; s. Conrad Heinrich and Charlotte (Simmendinger) B.; m. Beryl Garner, Mar. 6, 1965; children: Rachael M.J., Andreas H. Diploma in mech. engring., Coll. F. Trade and Industry, Giengen, Fed. Republic Germany; diploma in bus. adminstrn., Comml. Coll., Giengen, Fed. Republic Germany; grad. mgmt. program, Wharton Sch., U. Pa., 1973. Gen. mgr. No Nail Boxes Ltd., Ettelbruck, Luxemburg, 1963-66; sales mgr. N.Am. No Nail Boxes Ltd., Chester U.K. and Barrington N.J., 1967-68; v.p. Metal Edge Industries, Barrington, 1969-71; mgr. research and devel. Directory div. The Reuben H. Donnelley Corp., Phila., 1972-73; gen. mgr. Donnelley Mktg., Ettlingen, Fed. Republic Germany, 1974-76; v.p., regional mgr. Dun and Bradstreet Internat., Frankfurt, Fed. Republic Germany, 1977-79; v.p. Dun and Bradstreet Internat., N.Y.C., 1980-82, sr. v.p., 1983-85; sr. v.p. Bus. Mktg. div. The Dun and Bradstreet Corp., Wilton, Conn., 1986-87; sr. v.p. group planning and devel. The Dun and Bradstreet Corp. Bus. Info. Group, Murray Hill, N.Y., 1987—. Pub. Am. C. of C. in Germany, Frankfurt, 1978-80. Lodge: Rotary. Home: 239 Palmer Ct Ridgewood NJ 07450 Office: Dun & Bradstreet Corp Bus Info Group One Diamond Hill Rd Murray Hill NY 07974-0027

BARTELS, JUERGEN E., hotel company executive; b. Swinemuende, Ger., Sept. 14, 1940; s. Herbert and Lilli E. (Wendland) B.; m. Rachel M.P. Villemaire, Mar. 14, 1951. Final, Werner V. Siemens Sch., Hanover, W. Germany, 1956. Vice pres. Commonwealth Holiday Inns Can. Ltd., Can., 1971-76; exec. v.p. Ramada Internat., Brussels, Belgium, 1976-77; pres. Ramada Hotel Group, Phoenix, 1978-83; exec. v.p. Ramada Inns, Inc.; mem. Ramada Mgmt. Com.; pres., chief exec. officer Carlson Hospitality Group, Carlson Cos., Inc., Mpls., 1983—; dir. TGI Friday's Inc. Office: Carlson Cos Inc 12755 State Hwy 55 Minneapolis MN 55441

BARTELS, ROBERT RICHARD, securities analyst; b. Milw., Mar. 6, 1947; s. Eugene Ferdinand and Helen Ann (Van Beck) B.; m. Margarita Maria Casas, June 23, 1984; 1 child, William Robert. BS in Econs., Xavier U., 1969; MBA in Fin., Northwestern U., 1971. Chartered fin. analyst. Securities analyst Willaim Blair & Co., Chgo., 1973—, ptnr., 1981—. Mem. Inst. Chartered Fin. Analysts. Roman Catholic. Office: William Blair & Co 135 S LaSalle St Chicago IL 60603

BARTER, RUBY SUNSHINE, realtor; b. Omaha; d. Harry and Ruth (Gilman) Kolnick; m. Gerson Barter; children: Bruce, Mark, Sharon Sunshine Silverman, Peggy Sunshine Brooks, Jeffrey, Randi Sunshine Simon, JoAnne Sunshine Trombley, Ronald Sunshine. BS in Med. Tech., Creighton U.; postgrad., Clarkson Meml. Hosp. Sch. Med. Tech., U. Colo. Sch. Continuing Edn. Cert. Comml.-Investment Mems. Med. technologist Creighton Meml. St. Joseph Hosp.; realtor Nat. Real Estate and Mgmt. Co., Heller-Mark & Co., Walpin & Co., Denver; Mem. Mayors Adv. Com. on Denver's War on Poverty; project dir. Denver Citywide Headstart Vols.; mem. adv. com. Dialogue Regis Coll.; mem. exec. com. Anti-Defamation League, Hillel Councils; vol. Nat. Jewish Hosp., Jewish Community Ctr.; mem. exec. bd. Beth Joseph Congregation; active Adult Edn. Council Denver, Internat. House; Dolls for Democracy Lady Dever Pub. Schs. Mem. Nat. Real Estate Commn., Colo. Real Estate Commn., Denver Real Estate Commn. (liaison com.), Bd. Realtors, Real Estate Exchangers, Realtors Nat. Mktg. Inst., Real Estate Securities Syndication Inst. Home: 201 S Dexter St Denver CO 80222 Office: 1550 E 17th Ave Denver CO 80218

BARTH, ERNEST, chemical company executive; b. Vienna, Austria, Feb. 17, 1926; s. Jacob and Regina (Hecht) B.; m. Rita Spiegel, Dec. 30, 1951; 1 dau., Karen Nina. Pres., Continental Fertilizer Corp., N.Y.C., also v.p. Continental Ore Corp., 1953-72; pres. Agrico Internat., Inc., Tulsa and N.Y.C., 1972-73; pres. Beker Internat. Corp., Greenwich, Conn., also sr. v.p. Beker Industries, 1973-75; v.p. Philipp Bros./Engelhard Minerals & Chem. Corp., N.Y.C., 1975-77; sr. v.p. Beker Industries Corp., Greenwich, 1977-79; pres., dir. Superfos Am., Inc., Greenwich, 1979-85, chmn. bd., chief exec. officer, 1985-86; pres. Superfos Investments Ltd., Greenwich, 1985-86 ; dir. Mineral GMBH, Hamburg, Germany, Minex Corp. subs., Greenwich, 1978—; dir. affiliated cos.; cons. Chemie Linz AG of Austria, Balfour Maclaine Internat. Group—Wall St. Plaza. Mem. White House Food for Peace Council, 1962; co-chmn. U.S. Indsl. Mission to Korea, 1962. Clubs: Board Room (N.Y.C.); Burning Tree Country, Belle Haven (Greenwich, Conn.); Longboat Key (Sarasota, Fla.). Home: 25 Lindsay Dr Greenwich CT 06830 Office: 35 Mason St Greenwich CT 06830

BARTH, JOSEPH M., educator, financial planner; b. New York, Mar. 10, 1945; s. Stephen and Catherine (Connell) B.; m. Edith Louise Bamberger, Oct. 16, 1971; 1 child, Molly. BA, Iona Coll., 1962; MLS, St. John's U., 1969; MBA, Long Island U., 1983. Cert. fin. planner. Budget dir. U.S. Mil. Acad. Library, West Point, 1968—; pres. DATACO, Cornwall on Hudson, N.Y. Mem. Inst. Cert. Fin. Planners. Office: DATACO P O Box 364 Cornwall on Hudson NY 12520

BARTH, RICHARD, lawyer; b. N.Y.C., May 23, 1931; s. Alexander Haddon and Georgina (Grant) B.; m. Mary Elizabeth McAnaney, June 13, 1959; children: Leanore, Jennifer, Richard, Michele, Alexander. AB cum laude, Wesleyan U., 1952; LLB, Columbia U., 1955; postgrad., NYU, 1959-62. Bar: N.Y. 1958, N.J. 1966. Asso. firm Burke & Burke, 1957-65; gen. counsel, sec., mem. mgmt. com. CIBA, 1965-70; v.p., gen. counsel, mem. mng. com., dir. CIBA-GEIGY Corp., Ardsley, N.Y., from 1971, now pres., chief exec. officer, dir.; dir. Radio Shack Corp., 1964-65; bd. dirs. Bank of N.Y., 1989—, Irving Trust Co.; trustees Wesleyan U., Middletown, Conn., 1987—. Contbr articles to profl. jours. Mem. substandard housing bd., Summit, N.J., 1968-70. With AUS, 1955-57. Mem. Am., N.Y. Bar Assn., N.J. Bar Assn., Phi Delta Phi, Psi Upsilon. Home: 662 Guard Hill Rd Bedford NY 10506 Office: CIBA-GEIGY Corp 444 Saw Mill River Rd Ardsley NY 10502

BARTHELMAS, NED KELTON, investment banker; b. Circleville, Ohio, Oct. 22, 1927; s. Arthur and Mary Bernice (Riffel) B.; m. Marjorie Jane Livezey, May 23, 1953; children: Brooke Ann, Richard Thomas. B.S. in Bus. Adminstrn., Ohio State U., 1950. Stockbroker Ohio Co., Columbus, 1953-58; pres. First Columbus Corp., 1958—; pres., dir. Ohio Fin. Corp., Columbus, 1960—; trustee, chmn. Am. Guardian Fin., Republic Fin.; dir. Nat. Foods, Midwest Capital Corp., Capital Equity Corp., Midwest Nat. Corp., First Columbus Realty Corp., Court Realty Co., all Columbus. Served with Adj. Gen.'s Dept. AUS, 1945-47. Mem. Nat. Assn. Securities Dealers (past vice chmn. dist. bd. govs.), Investment Bankers Assn. Am. (exec. com. 1973), Investment Dealers Ohio (sec., treas. 1956-72, pres. 1973), Nat. Stock Traders Assn., Young Pres.'s Orgn. (pres. 1971), Nat. Investment Bankers (pres. 1973), Columbus Jr. C. of C. (pres. 1956), Ohio Jr. C. of C. (trustee 1957-58), Columbus Area C. of C. (dir. 1956, named an Outstanding Young Man of Columbus 1962), Newcomen Soc., Oxford Club, Executives Club, Stock and Bond Club, Columbus Club, Scioto Country Club (Columbus), Crystal Downs Country Club (Frankfort, Mich.), Kiwanis, Phi Delta Theta. Home: 1000 Urlin Ave Columbus OH 43212 Home (summer): 6498 Bixler Rd Beulah MI 49617

BARTHOLDSON, JOHN ROBERT, steel company executive; b. N.Y.C., Sept. 9, 1944; s. Nils and Judith (Kvist) B.; m. Carole Marie Duffy, Sept. 7, 1968; children: John Anders, Catherine Leigh, Kristen Elizabeth, Janet Louise. B.S., Pa. State U., 1966, M.B.A., 1970; student, Villanova U., 1967-68. Research and devel. engr. Gen. Electric Co., Valley Forge, Pa., 1966-69; treas. Norco Properties, Inc., Jacksonville, Fla., 1970-72, Warner Co., Phila., 1972-78, Lukens Steel Co., Coatesville, Pa., 1978—. Mem. Beta Gamma Sigma. Home: 1950 Standiford Dr Malvern PA 19355 Office: Lukens Steel Co 50 S 1st Ave Coatesville PA 19320

BARTHOLOMEW, ARTHUR PECK, JR., accountant; b. Rochester, N.Y., Nov. 20, 1918; s. Arthur Peck and Abbie West (Dawson) B.; m. Mary Elizabeth Meyer, Oct. 4, 1941; children: Susan B. Hall, Arthur Peck III, James M., Virginia L. A.B., U. Mich., 1939, M.B.A., 1940. With Ernst & Whinney, 1940-79, successively jr. accountant, partner charge Eastern dist., Detroit office, 1940-64, nat. office, Cleve., 1964-65, N.Y. office, 1965-79, also mem. mng. com.; instr. accounting U. Mich., 1940, George Washington U., 1945-46. Mem. Mich. Gov.'s Task Force for Expenditure Mgmt., 1963-64; mem. 2d Regional Plan Commn. N.Y.; Bd. dirs. Detroit League for Handicapped, 1952-64; treas. Grosse Pointe War Meml. Assn., 1961; bd. dirs., v.p. Greater N.Y. council Boy Scouts Am. Served from pvt. to capt. AUS, 1942-46. Mem. Nat. Assn. Accountants (pres. Detroit 1963-64, nat. pres. 1974-75), The Conf. Bd., Mich., N.Y. socs. C.P.A.s, Am. Inst. C.P.A.s, Phi Beta Kappa, Phi Kappa Phi, Beta Gamma Sigma, Phi Eta Sigma, Beta Alpha Psi, Phi Kappa Sigma. Republican. Presbyn. Clubs: Country (Detroit); Indian Harbor Yacht, Greenwich Country, Wall Street (pres. 1976-78); Gulf Stream Golf. Home: 6665 N Ocean Blvd Ocean Ridge FL 33435

BARTHOLOMEW, DONALD DELKE, inventor, business executive, engineer; b. Atlanta, Aug. 2, 1929; s. Rudolph A. and Rubye C. (Delke) B.; m. Paula Hagood; children: John Marshall, Barbara Ann, Deborah Paige, Sandra Dianne. Student in Physics, Ga. Inst. Tech., 1946-48, 55-58. Owner Happy Cottons and Jalopy Jungleland, Atlanta, 1946-48, Beach Hotel Supply, Miami Beach, Fla., 1949-50; engr. Sperry Microwave Electronics, Clearwater, Fla., 1958-61; v.p., owner Draft Pak, Inc., Tampa, Fla., 1961-65, Merit Plastics, Inc., East Canton, Ohio, 1966-79; pres., owner Modern Tech., Inc., Marine City, Mich., 1979—; owner, officer and dir. various internat. mfg. companies, 1981—. Patentee in field. Served as sgt. USAF, 1951-54. Mem. Soc. Automotive Engrs., Soc. Plastics Engrs. (dir. 1982), Soc. Mfg. Engrs., Holiday Isles Jr. C. of C. (founding dir.). Republican.

BARTINE, ALLEN R., mail order company executive; b. Marshalltown, Iowa, Apr. 2, 1945; s. Edwin Willard and Orpha L. (Froning) B.; m. Margot C. Friese, June 8, 1968; children: Todd A., Erin M. BS in Bus. and Econs., Iowa State U., 1967; MBA in Fin., Ind. U., 1969; Cert. in taxes, De Paul U., 1973. CPA, Ill. Sr. cons., auditor Touche Ross & Co., Chgo., 1969-74; exec. v.p. fin., dir. Am. Tara Corp., Chgo., 1974-84; chief fin. officer Dyson-Kissner-Moran Corp., Chgo., 1984-86; v.p. fin. and adminstrn. Aparacor, Inc., Evanston, Ill., 1986-89; chief fin. officer Popcorn Factory, Inc., Lake Bluff, Ill., 1989—. Dir. West Cen. Assn., Chgo., 1982-83; cubmaster Cub Scouts Am., Lake Forest, Ill., 1984; advancement chmn. Troop 46 Boy Scouts Am., Lake Forest, 1988; treas. Lake Forest Preservation Soc., Lake Forest, 1988. Mem. AICPA, Ill. Soc. CPAs, Am. Mgmt. Assn., Direct Mktg. Assn., Direct Selling Assn. Republican. Presbyterian. Office: Popcorn Factory Inc Lake Bluff IL 60044

BARTLETT, BRUCE REEVES, economist; b. Ann Arbor, Mich., Oct. 11, 1951; s. Frank and Marjorie (Stern) B. B.A., Rutgers U. 1973; M.A., Georgetown U., 1976. Spl. asst. to Congressman Jack F. Kemp, Washington, 1977-78; chief legis. asst. to U.S. Senator Roger Jepsen, Washington, 1979-80; dep. dir. Joint Econ. Com., U.S. Congress, Washington, 1981-83, exec. dir., 1983-84; v.p. Polyconomics, Inc., Morristown, N.J., 1984-85; sr. fellow Heritage Found., Washington, 1985-87; sr. policy analyst The White House, Washington, 1987-88; dep. asst. sec. for econ. policy Dept. Treasury, 1988—. Author: Coverup: The Politics of Pearl Harbor, 1941-46, 1978; Reaganomics: Supply Side Economics in Action, 1981; The Supply Side Solution, 1983. Contbr. articles to Washington Post, N.Y. Times, Wall Street Jour, numerous others. Served with USAF, 1973. Mem. Am. Econ. Assn. Republican. Home: 203 Yoakum Pkwy Apt 1822 Alexandria VA 22304 Office: Treasury Dept Rm 3445 Washington DC 20220

BARTLETT, CONNIE SUZANNE, account executive; b. San Angelo, Tex., Jan. 17, 1953; d. Maurice Vance and Joanna Ruth (Baker) B. BBA in Mktg., U. Tex., 1975. Mktg. rep. IBM, Detroit, 1975-76, Burroughs Corp., Austin, Tex., 1977; mktg. and tng. coordinator Systems Mktg. and Edn., Austin, 1978-79; nat. acct. exec. The Rsch. Inst. of Am., Austin, 1980—. Mem. Westwood Country Club (bd. dirs. 1986—, sec. 1987-88, chmn. tennis com. 1987—, mem. delinquent accts. com. 1987, food and beverage com. 1986-87). Democrat. Methodist. Office: The Research Inst of Am 90 5th Ave Austin TX 10011

BARTLETT, C(RAIG) SCOTT, JR., banker; b. Montclair, N.J., Apr. 24, 1933; s. Craig Scott Bartlett and Gertrude Louise (Selvage) Brown; m. Elizabeth Lewis, Nov. 7, 1959; children: Craig S. III, Laura Mason, Susan Ames. Student, Princeton U., 1951-53, 55-57; cert., Stonier Grad. Sch. Banking, 1966-68. Asst. sec. Chem. Bank, N.Y.C., 1957-64; v.p. Bank of N.Y., N.Y.C., 1964-68; assoc. corp. fin. Gregory and Sons, N.Y.C., 1968-69, G.A. Saxton and Co., N.Y.C., 1970-72, W.E. Burnet and Co., N.Y.C., 1972-73; exec. v.p. Nat. Westminster Bank U.S.A., N.Y.C., 1973—; arbitrator Nat. Assn. Security Dealers, N.Y.C., 1981—; bd. dirs. Nat. West U.S.A. Capital Corp, N.Y.C., Nat. West U.S.A. Credit Corp., N.Y.C., Fin. Services of N.Y., 1986—. Treas. Montclair (N.J.) Rehab. Orgn., 1985-86, Montclair Rep. County Com., 1978-83. Served with U.S. Army, 1953-55. Mem. Robert Morris Assocs. of N.Y. (pres. 1986-87). Episcopalian. Home: 64 Melrose Pl Montclair NJ 07042 Office: Nat Westminster Bank USA 175 Water St New York NY 10038

BARTLETT, DEDE THOMPSON, oil company executive; b. N.Y.C., Aug. 27, 1943; d. George Juul and Emilie Martha (Jones) Thompson; m. James Wesley Bartlett, Apr. 27, 1974; children: Katherine Morgan, John Eriksen. BA, Vassar Coll., 1965; MA, NYU, 1969. Corp. sec. Mobil Corp. and Mobil Oil Corp., N.Y.C., sec. of exec. coms., sec. bd. dirs.; bd. dirs. Mobil Found., N.Y.C., 1984-87, pres., dir. Mobil Found., N.Y.C., 1984-87. Trustee, vis. fellow Woodrow Wilson Nat. Fellowship Found., Princeton, N.J., 1983—. Mem. Am. Soc. Corp. Secs., Stockholder Relations Soc. N.Y., Vassar (Fairfield County, Conn.). Office: Mobil Corp 150 E 42nd St New York NY 10017

BARTLETT, DESMOND WILLIAM, engineering executive; b. Southampton, Eng., Feb. 11, 1931; came to U.S., 1971; s. Walter Hayward and Gladys (Akerman) B.; m. Joan Margaret Mitchell, July 19, 1952; children: Jennie Claire. Grad. Marine Engring., U. Coll., Southampton, 1951; diploma, Shippingport Nuclear, Pitts., 1961; exec. devel. diploma, Cornell U., 1978. chartered engr. U.K.; lic. chief engr., U.K. Ministry of Transport, nuclear power plant operator, U.K. Ministry of Def. Engr. officer Cunard Steamship Co., Liverpool, Eng., 1952-57; engr. Vickers Armstrong Ltd., Southampton, 1957-59; project mgr. Rolls Royce & Assocs., Derby, Eng., 1959-65; chief engr. Cammell Laird Shipbuilders & Engrs., Birkenhead, Eng., 1965-71; cons. Gibbs & Hill, Inc., N.Y.C., 1971-72; project dir. Westinghouse Electric Co., Pitts., 1972-79; pres. Dravo Engrs. Inc., Pitts., 1979-85, C.F. Braun, Inc., Alhambra, Calif., 1986—; bd. dirs. Dravotec spa, Milan, Italy, F.C. de Weger Bv, Rotterdam, Dravo-Still, Inc., Pitts., Worley Santa Fe Ltd., London, Santa Fe Braun (UK) Ltd, London. Decorated officer Order Brit. Empire (Eng.). Fellow Inst. Marine Engrs.; mem. ASME, Am. Nuclear Soc., Am. Mgmt. Assn., Project Mgmt. Inst., Am. Petroleum Inst., Coun. on Fgn. Rels. (L.A. com. on fgn. relations). Clubs: Duqesne.

BARTLETT, (HERBERT) HALL, motion picture producer, director; b. Kansas City, Mo., Nov. 27, 1929; s. Paul Dana and Alice (Hiestand) B.; m. Lupita Ferrer, Apr. 30, 1977 (div.); children: Cathy Bartlett Lynch, Laurie Bartlett Schrader. BA, Yale U., 1948. Owner, operator Hall Bartlett Prodn., Los Angeles, 1960—; pres. Jonathan Livingston Seagull Mcht. Co.; bd. dirs. James Doolittle Theatre, Hollywood, Calif., founder Music Ctr., Los Angeles. Producer, dir. (films) Navajo, 1953, Crazylegs, 1958, Unchained, 1957, All the Young Men, 1961, Durango, 1959, Zero Hour, 1961, The Caretakers, 1963, A Global Affair, 1968, Changes, 1968, Sandpit Generals, 1971, Jonathan Livingston Seagull, 1973, The Children of Sanchez, 1979, Catch Me If You Can, 1988, The Search of Zubin Mehta, 1975, The Cleo Laine Story, 1978, Comeback, 1983; author: The Rest of Our Lives, 1987. Mem. Friends of Library, Los Angeles, Cinema Circulus. Served to lt. USNR, 1949-51. Recipient 11 Acad. award nominations, Film Festival awards from Cannes 1961, 63, Venice 1959, 65, Edinburgh 1952, San Sebastian 1969, Moscow 1971, NCCJ 1955, Fgn. Press awards. Mem. Motion Picture Acad. Arts and Scis., Acad. TV Arts and Scis., Phi Beta Kappa. Republican. Presbyterian. Clubs: Bel-Air Country, Kansas City Country. Home: 861 Stone Canyon Rd Bel Air CA 90077 Office: 9200 Sunset Blvd Ste 908 Los Angeles CA 90069

BARTLETT, JOHN BRUEN, financial executive; b. Salt Lake City, Oct. 14, 1941; s. John B. and Helen Smith (Partridge) B.; children: Alison, Brian. B in Engring., U. Rochester, 1963; MBA, Rutgers U., 1968. CPA, Calif., Conn. Engr. Aerojet Gen., Sacramento, 1963-65, Hamilton Standard, Windsor Locks, Conn., 1965-67; acct., CPA Arthur Andersen & Co., San Francisco, 1968-76, Hartford, 1976-77; chief fin. officer UniFirst Corp., Wilmington, Mass., 1977—. Mem. Am. Inst. Profl. Cert. Accts., Fin. Exec. Inst., Treas. Club. Office: UniFirst Corp 68 Jonspin Rd Wilmington MA 01887

BARTLETT, LARRY LEE, drilling company executive; b. Lawton, Okla., Feb. 7, 1954; s. Jeri Lee and Vernace Ruth (Barker) B.; children by previous marriage: Leah Brooke, Jearl Lee. BS in Bus., Cameron U., 1976. V.p. Davis Jewel Box, Duncan, Okla., 1976-77; office mgr. Thomas Drilling Co., Duncan, 1977-81, v.p., 1981—. Mem. Internat. Assn. Drilling Contractors, Phi Kappa Phi. Home: 2016 Westbriar Rd Duncan OK 73533 Office: PO Box 400 Duncan OK 73534

BARTLETT, PAUL DANA, JR., agribusiness executive; b. Kansas City, Mo., Sept. 16, 1919; s. Paul D. and Alice May (Hiestand) B.; m. Joan Jenkins, May 14, 1949; children—J. Alison Bartlett Jager, Marilyn Bartlett Hebenstreit, Paul Dana III, Frederick Jenkins. BA, Yale U., 1941. Chmn. Bartlett and Co., Kansas City, Mo., 1961-77; pres., chmn. bd. Bartlett and Co. (formerly Bartlett Agri Enterprises, Inc.), Kansas City, 1977—; bd. dir. United Mo. Bank, United Mo. Bancshares. Lt. USN, 1942-46. Office: Bartlett & Co 4800 Main St Ste 600 Kansas City MO 64112

BARTLETT, THOMAS LEONARD, pet supply company executive; b. Cleve., May 25, 1950; s. Wesley James and Violet Virginia (Voigt) B.; m. Victoria Suzann Cowan, May 20, 1978; children: Welsey David, David Thomas. BS, Cornell U., 1972, MBA, 1974. Fin. analyst consumer electronics div. RCA, Indpls., 1974-75; fin. adminstr. black and white T.V. div. RCA, 1975-76, fin. adminstr. color T.V. div., 1976-77; mgr. processing group svcs. The Andersons, Maumee, Ohio, 1977-79; consumer group planning mgr. The Andersons, 1979-80, mktg. mgr. COB div., 1980-86, mgr. pet div., 1986—; bd. dirs. B & R Pet Supply, Inc., Grand Prairie, Tex., 1986—; mem. mgmt. com. L/M Animal Farms, Pleasant Plain, Ohio, 1986—. Loan exec. United Way N.W. Ohio, Toledo, 1983; mem. allocations com., 1985; chmn. allocations panel; mem. allocation and agy. rels. com., 1986—. Mem. Pet Industry Joint Adv. Coun. (bd. dirs. 1987, sec.-treas. 1988), Cornell Club (Toledo, secondary schs. com. 1982—). Home: 6123 Welsford Ct Maumee OH 43537 Office: The Andersons 1200 Dussel Dr Maumee OH 43537

BARTLETT, WALTER E., communications company executive; b. Marion, Ohio, Feb. 23, 1928; s. Clifford L. and Blanche (Paschall) B.; m. Marilyn L. Wright, Oct. 15, 1955; children: Suzanne Marie Bartlett Solimine, John Patrick, Robert Christopher. BBA, Bowling Green U., 1949; LittD, U.C., 1987. Nat. sales rep. Scripps Howard Newspapers, 1949-53; nat. sales rep. WLWC-TV (subs. Avco Broadcasting), Columbus, Ohio, 1953-55, v.p., gen. mgr., 1958-64; nat. sales mgr. Indpls. Times, 1955-58; v.p. Avco Broadcasting Corp., Avco Broadcasting-TV, Cin., 1964-76; v.p. Broadcasting-Multimedia Inc., Cin., 1976-77, pres., 1977-81; pres., chief operating officer Multimedia Inc., Cin. and Greenville, S.C., 1981-85, pres., chief exec. officer, 1985—, mem. exec. com., chmn. mgmt. com., also bd. dirs.; bd. dirs. Cen. Trust Co., Cin., Palmetto Bus. Forum, Columbia, S.C. Exec. producer (TV spl.) Donahue & Kids, 1980-81 (Emmy award). Chmn. Xavier U. Fund Drive, Cin., 1980; chmn. U. Cin. Fund Drive, 1982, chmn. bd. trustees, 1987, pres. exec. bd. dirs., 1989—; past mem. Ohio Ednl. TV Commn.; vice chmn. U. Cin. Found. Served to sgt. U.S. Army, 1950-52. Recipient Disting. Alumnus award Bowling Green U., 1980, Bd. Govs. award Nat. Acad. TV Arts and Scis., 1980, Am. Advt. Fedn. Silver medal award Cin. Advt. Club, 1981. Mem. Newspaper Advt. Bur. (bd. dirs. 1987—), Cin. C. of C. (past pres.), Ohio Assn. Broadcasters (past pres., Broadcaster of Yr. award 1974), TV Bur. Advt. (past chmn.), Nat. Assn. Broadcasters (past chmn. TV bd. dirs.). Clubs: Queen City, Coldstream Country, Bankers, Commonwealth, Recess (Cin.). Office: Multimedia Inc 305 S Main St Box 1688 Greenville SC 29602 also: Multimedia Inc 140 W 9th St Cincinnati OH 45202

BARTLEY, CHRISTOPHER JAYE, public information officer; b. Springfield, Ohio, July 20, 1953; s. Jack and Martha Arleen (Eastep) B.; m. Mary Ellen Flanagan, Sept. 27, 1986; 1 child, Meghan Elyse Bartley. AA, Sinclair Community Coll., 1977; BS, Bowling Green State U., 1980; MS, U. Dayton, 1983. Cert. tchr., Ohio . Tchr. Vandalia (Ohio)-Butler City Schs., 1980-84; pub. info. officer Ohio Atty. Gen.'s Office, Columbus, 1984—; cons. Springknoll Consultation Group.; mem. Montgomery County Career Edn. Adv. Bd., Dayton, 1984—. Treas. Ohio Assn. Coun. for Exceptional Children, Bowling Green, 1979-80, Miami Valley Coun. Exceptional Children, Dayton, 1980-84, Montgomery County Young Dems., 1983—, Ohio Young Dems. Am., Columbus, 1986-88. Mem. Pub. Rels. Soc. Am., Am. Assn. Polit. Cons., Optimists, KC. Roman Catholic. Home: 343 W Siebenthaler Ave Dayton OH 45405 Office: Atty Gen Dist 7 Office PO Box 6042 Dayton OH 45405

BARTOLACCI, GUIDO J., corporate executive; b. Phillipsburg, N.J., May 20, 1929; s. Augusto and Elvira Bartolacci; m. Margaret Lesko, June 21, 1952. Vice-chmn., chief oper. officer Laneco, Inc., Palmer, Pa. Office: Laneco Inc 3747 Hecktown Rd Palmer PA 18043

BARTOLI, DIANE S., social services administrator; b. Plains, Pa., Sept. 21, 1938; d. Anthony J. and Anice (Whiteley) Lupas; m. Bernard J. Bartoli, June 24, 1961; Judith Giovanelli, Eugene, Maria, Shelley. BS in Edn., East Stroudsburg U., 1960. Elem. sch. tchr. Levittown, Pa., 1960-61; owner, bookeeper A.J. Lupas Ins. Agy., Plains, 1977-83; owner, adminstr. Adult Services Unltd., Plains, 1983—; mem. task group Pa. State Com. on Elder Abuse, 1986; pres. NE Pa. Alzheimers Support Group, 1983—. Chair Dem. Com., Laflin, Pa., 1973, Laflin Borough Recreation Bd., 1972-80; gov.'s appointee Pa. Coun. on Aging, 1989. Recipient Chapel of the Four Chaplains award; named Woman of Yr. Penns Woods coun. Girl Scouts U.S., 1989. Mem. Nat. Adult Day Care Assn., Pa. Adult Day Care (bd. dirs. 1985—), Nat. Assn. Rehab. Facilities (coun. on aging), Am. Assn. Profl. Cons., Pa. Assn. Rehab. Facilities (chairperson subcom. comprehensive outpatient rehab.). Democrat. Roman Catholic. Club: Laflin Womens. Office: Adult Svcs Unltd Inc 220 S River St Plains PA 18705

BARTOLINI, BRUCE ANTHONY, trust company executive; b. Framingham, Mass., Mar. 4, 1950; s. Benjamin A. and Eleanor H. (Connery) B.; m. Pamela L. White, Apr. 4, 1974 (div. Apr. 1989). Student, Northeastern U., Boston, 1967-69, postgrad., 1986-88; BA in Biology, Framingham State Coll., 1971; postgrad., Keene State Coll., 1972. Sci. instr. Orford (N.H.) Acad., 1971-73; biology instr. J.P. Keefe Tech. Sch., Framingham, 1973—; pres. Bartolini Motor Sales, Inc., Medway, Mass., 1979—; trustee Milford Realty Devel., 1979—, Blackstone Realty, 1980; securities investor A.G. Edwards & Sons; mem. Concord Auto Auction, 1979—. Contbr. articles to profl. jours. With USAR, 1984—. Mem. NEA, Keefe Tech. Tchrs. Assn., Mass. Tchrs. Assn. Republican. Roman Catholic. Clubs: Southboro Rod and Gun (Mass.), Framingham Militia.

BARTON, BLAYNEY JONES, investment executive; b. Beaver City, Utah, Oct. 22, 1910; s. Ray Hunter and Emma Jay (Jones) B.; m. Hazel Lavina Whitaker, July 31, 1937; 1 son, John Whitaker. Student U. Utah, 1929-30, 33; LLB, George Washington U., 1938. Bar: Utah 1938, D.C. bar, 1938, U.S. Supreme Ct. bar, 1964; lawyer Reconstrn. Fin. Corp., Washington, 1938-40; spl. agt. FBI, N.Y., Va., Nebr., Calif., Utah, 1940-44; dir. indsl. and pub. relations Bayer Aspirin, Winthrop-Stearns Pharm. Co., Sterling-Winthrop Research Inst., Rensselaer, N.Y., 1945-51;dir. employee relations M & M Woodworking Co., Portland, Oreg., 1952-53; dir. labor relations Am. Stores Co. (name changed to Acme Markets, Inc.), Phila., 1954-56, v.p. labor relations, 1957-68; pres., chief negotiator, Food Indsutry Council, 1957-68, Meritorious Achievement award for stabilizing labor-mgmt. relations, Phila., 1965, acting dir. fed. labor-mgmt. relations Dept. Labor, Washington, 1968-70; pres. Barton Investment Co., 1971-84. Nat. committeeman Boy Scouts Am., 1950-51, commr. Ft. Orange council, Albany, N.Y., 1948-51; asst. dir. Albany Community Chest. 1949-51; missionary Ch. Jesus Christ Latter-Day Saints, Br. Isles, 1930-33; v.p. YMCA, 1950-51. Mem. Am. Arbitration Assn., Capitol Dist. Personnel Assn. (pres. 1946-51), Albany C. of C. (bd. dirs. 1949-51). Kiwanian (v.p. Albany, N.Y.), Rotarian. Clubs: Pa. Soc., Union League (Phila.). Office: PO Box 99 Berwyn PA 19312

BARTON, LEON SAMUEL CLAY, JR., architect; b. Orangeburg, S.C., Jan. 9, 1906; s. Leon Samuel Clay and Georgia (Hadley) B.; m. Alice Barbara Mosher, Dec. 2, 1941 (dec. Sept. 3, 1971); 1 child, Mary Jane (Mrs. Thomas C. Murray). B.S. in Architecture, Clemson U., 1928; postgrad., NYU, 1932-34, Atelier Morgan, N.Y.C., 1932-35, Inst. Effective Speaking & Human Relations, N.Y.C., 1952, N.Y. Med. Coll., 1966, Columbia U., 1970, Eastern Sch. Real Estate, N.Y.C., 1971; cert., U.S. Civil Def. Preparedness Agy., 1974, Summer Seismic Inst., U. Ill., 1978. Registered architect, Colo., Fla., Md., N.J., N.Y., S.C. certified Nat. Council Archtl. Registration Bds. Designer, draftsman engring. div. E.R. Squibb & Sons, 1928-35, dir. master planning, asst. to chief exec. engr., 1944-47; partner Barton & Pilafian, Architects & Engrs., Teheran, Iran; also cons. to Iranian Govt. Barton & Pilafian, Architects & Engrs., 1935-38; prin. Leon S. Barton, 1939-41; chief architect head archtl. dept. Robert & Co., Inc., Atlanta, 1941-44; naval architect shipbldg. div. Bethlehem Steel Co., 1944; with Vitro Corp. Am.(formerly The Kellex Corp. of Am.), N.Y.C.; chief architect nuclear energy projects U.S. AEC, 1948-54; sr. partner Barton and Pruitt and Assocs. (Architects, Engrs. and Planners), N.Y.C., 1954—; chmn. bd. pres. Walton Resiliant Floors, Inc., N.Y.C., 1968—. Project architect in charge: design Peter Cooper br. Chase Manhattan Bank, Shreve Lamb & Harmon Assocs., N.Y.C., 1947-48; Prin. works include Engring. and Maintenance Facilities Bldg, E.R. Squibb & Sons, New Brunswick, N.J., Vitro Research Lab. Facilities, Silver Spring, Md., Gen. Nuclear Research Lab. Facilities and Radiation Effects Research Lab. Facilities, Lockheed Aircraft Corp., Dawsonville, Ga., U.S. Food and Drug Adminstrn. Research Lab. and Office Facilities, Bklyn.; assoc. architect: (with Gen. Charles B. Ferris, Engrs.) Barnert Meml. Hosp. Center, Paterson, N.J. Recipient First Hon. mention Nat. WGN Broadcasting Theater Competition, 1934; Grand prize Internat. Teheran Stock Exchange (Bourse) Competition, 1935; First Hon. mention Prix de Rome archtl. Competition, 1935; Certificate of Merit for loyal and efficient services during World War II def. projects Robert & Co., Inc., 1944. Mem. AIA (corp. mem., mem. nat. task force for devel. health facilities research 1969-77, mem. publ. com. 1957-58, mem. pub. affairs com. 1967-68, mem. speakers bur. 1967-71, mem. hosp. and health com. 1967—, mem. sch. and coll. archtl. com. 1971-78, mem. urban planning com. 1972-78, mem. LeBrun Scholarship com. 1972-78, mem. criminal justice facilities com. 1974-75, mem. W. Side Hwy. subcom. 1973-75), N.Y. State Assn. Architects (corp. mem., mem. housing and urban devel. planning com. 1971-78, mem. sch. and coll. com. 1971-78, mem. honors and awards com. 1974-75, mem. environmental and community planning com. 1974-78), Am. Arbitration Assn. (nat. panel arbitrators 1970—), Greater N.Y. Hosp. Assn. (engring. adv. com. 1978—). Episcopalian. Home: PO Box 294 537 North Country Rd Saint James NY 11780 Office: Barton & Pruitt & Assocs 299 Madison Ave New York NY 10017

BARTON, LEWIS, food manufacturing company executive; b. N.Y.C., Mar. 9, 1940; s. Louis and Mary (Mosca) Bologna; m. Barbara Joan Hummell, Sept. 6, 1964; children—Glenn Scott, Gregory Jon. Student, Adelphi U., 1957-59. Sales rep. Olivetti Corp., N.Y.C., 1962-64, W. Ralston Co., Chgo., 1964-65, Milprint Co., N.Y.C., 1965-66; pres., founder Sigma Quality Foods (div. of Sugar Foods Corp.), Farmingdale, N.Y., 1966—. Patentee package design construction. Charter contbr. Statue of Liberty-Ellis Island Found., 1983; nat. mem. Smithsonian Assocs. Served with USAF, 1961-62. Named to Pres. Council for Ednl. Distinction, Adelphi U. Mem. Nat. Single Service Food Assn. (charter, chmn. 1977-79, Service award 1982), Internat. Food Service Mfrs. Assn., Am. Mgmt. Assn., Internat. Platform Assn., Italy-Am. C. of C., Dwight D. Eisenhower Soc. (founder). Republican. Clubs: Columbus Citizen's Found., Senator D'Amato's Senate (N.Y.C.), Carlton. Avocations: reading; woodworking; sailing; chess. Home: 45 Sutton Pl S New York NY 10022 Office: Sigma Quality Foods div of Sugar Foods Corp 21 W St New York NY 10006

BARTON, STANLEY, forest products company executive; b. Halesowen, Worcestershire, Eng., Dec. 30, 1927; came to U.S., 1957, naturalized, 1963; s. Lazarus and Alice (Faulkner) B.; m. Marion Brittain, Dec. 20, 1952; children—Carolyn Francesca, Andrea Elizabeth. B.Sc. (hons.), U. Birmingham, Eng., 1949; Ph.D., U. Birmingham, 1952. Group leader Naval Research Establishment, Halifax, N.S., Can., 1953-56; project coordinator Def. Research Chem. Labs., Ottawa, Ont., Can., 1956-57; devel. engr. Procter & Gamble, Cin., 1957-58; research and devel. group leader Procter & Gamble, 1958-59, research and devel. sect. head, 1959-69; tech. dir. food products-natural resources ITT, N.Y.C., 1969-76; sr. v.p. tech. and quality ITT Rayonier, Inc., Stamford, Conn., 1976—. Dist. chmn. United Appeal campaigns, Cin., 1964-65; sec. planning and zoning commn., Greenhills, Ohio, 1966-68. Mem. Am. Inst. Chem. Engrs., TAPPI, AAAS, Am. Theater Organ Soc., Cinema Organ Soc. Home: 10 White Woods Ln Westport CT 06880 Office: ITT Rayonier Inc 1177 Summer St Stamford CT 06904

BARWIG, MICHAEL EDWARD, oil company executive, consultant; b. Chicago Heights, Ill., May 4, 1951; s. Robert James and Bette Jean (Michael) B.; m. Joanne M. Yott, Sept. 4, 1971; children: Emily Jean, Michelle Marie, Jeffrey Michael, Nickolus Ryan. BS in Chem. Engring., Northwestern U., 1974. Registered profl. engr., Ill. Quality control foreman U.S. Steel, Gary, Ind., 1971-75; salesman Nalco Chem., Oakbrook, Ill., 1975-78; sr. buyer Inland Steel, East Chicago, Ind., 1978-83; v.p. sales Western Refining, Grand Junction, Colo., 1983-86; pvt. practice cons. Denver, 1986-87; mgr. Spruce Oil Corp., Denver, 1987—; lobbyist State of Colo. Inventor combustibles. Mem. AIME, Denver Oilmen's Assn., Renewable Fuels Assn., Colo. Petroleum Marketers. Republican. Roman Catholic. Office: Spruce Oil Corp 1801 Broadway Ste 1200 Denver CO 80202

BASEMAN, ROBERT LYNN, sales executive; b. Phila., May 19, 1932; s. Isadore and Esther (Troshinsky) B.; m. Renee Zinman, June 29, 1957 (div. Dec. 1986); children: Isadore Richard, Frank Mitchell, Jordan Mark, Russ Steven; m. Gwen Joy Roberts, Nov. 29, 1987. BS, Temple U., 1955. Sales mgr. Stevens Upholstery, Phila., 1955-61; br. mgr. Ency. Brit., Phila., 1961; dist. mgr. Ency. Brit., Phila. and Cin., 1962-65; div. mgr. Ency. Brit., Detroit, 1965-71; nat. sales mgr. Ency. Brit., Chgo., 1971-72; div. mgr. Ency. Brit., Phila., 1972-73; v.p. Ency. Brit., Chgo., 1973-82, exec. v.p., 1982-85, exec. v.p. worldwide sales mgmt. devel., 1985—; pres. Am. Learning Corp. (subs. of Ency. Brit.), Chgo., 1988—. Mem. Direct Selling Assn., Internat. Council Shopping Ctrs., Masons. Jewish. Home: 200 E Delaware Pl #20D Chicago IL 60611 Office: Am Learning Corp 200 S Michigan Ave Chicago IL 60604

BASFORD, JAMES ORLANDO, container manufacturing company executive; b. Akron, Ohio, Apr. 17, 1931; s. Napoleon Orlando and Hazel Martha (Fersner) B.; m. Mary Eleanor Hagmeyer, Mar. 16, 1957; children: Jeffrey James, Gregory Robert, Lisa Jean. Student, Kent State U., 1949-51, 55-58. Asst. sales mgr. San Hygene Mfg. Co., Akron, 1958-60; gen. sales mgr. Adjusta Post Mfg., Akron, 1960-64; area sales mgr. Gaylord Container, Columbus, Ohio, 1964-74; v.p. Buckeye Container Co., Wooster, Ohio, 1974-78, pres., 1978—, also bd. dirs.; bd. dirs. United Telephone of Ohio, Mansfield, Ohio. Dir. Boys Village, Smithville, Ohio, 1985—. Served with USAF, 1951-54, Korea. Mem. Wooster C. of C. (bd. dirs. 1977-80). Republican. Lutheran. Club: Wooster Country (pres. 1981-83). Lodge: Rotary (bd. dirs. Wooster club 1978-81). Home: 1097 Greens View Dr Wooster OH 44691 Office: Buckeye Corrugated Container 326 N Hillcrest Dr Wooster OH 44691

BASHFORD, ERIC RAINER, investment banker; b. Syracuse, N.Y., Sept. 30, 1959; s. Robert John and Audrey Ann (Kucinski) B. BA, Beloit Coll., 1981; MBA, U. Pa., 1988. Securities analyst Martin Simpson & Co., Inc., 1981-83, 1st Manhattan Co., N.Y.C., 1983-84; mng. ptnr. 1st Equity Mgmt., N.Y.C., 1984-85; v.p. R.C. Stamm & Co., Inc., N.Y.C., 1985-88; sr. v.p. J.T. Moran & co., Inc., N.Y.C., 1988—. Mem. N.Y. Soc. Security Analysts. Office: JT Moran & Co Inc 1 Whitehall St New York NY 10004

BASHKIN, LLOYD SCOTT, marketing and management consultant; b. Bridgeport, Conn., July 11, 1951; s. Jules Bernard and Luella (Kobre) B.; children: Marisa Elizabeth, Carly Michelle. BS in Fin., Syracuse U., 1973, MBA in Mktg. and Acctg., 1974; postgrad., Columbia U., 1975-78. Corp. staff mktg. cons. RCA, N.Y.C., 1974-77; mgr. entertainment, indsl. mktg. and nat. sales RCA, Cherry Hill, N.J., 1977-79; v.p. mktg. and sales CCA Electronics Corp. div. Singer Co., Cherry Hill, 1979-80; pres. Lloyd Scott & Co., Cherry Hill, 1980—, Sydex, Cherry Hill, 1987-88; adj. prof. grad. sch. Temple U., Phila., 1980-82, Drexel U., Phila., 1982—; speaker in field. Bd. trustee, chmn. mktg. com. Food Bank South Jersey, 1985—. Recipient Commendation award Gov. of N.J., 1981, SBA, 1983, Nat. Distbn. and Logistics Honorary award Delta Nu Alpha, 1973, Nat. Broadcasting Honorary award Alpha Epsilon Rho, 1979. Mem. Am. Mktg. Assn., So. Jersey C. of C. (chmn. small bus. action com. 1982-85, strategic planning and mktg. com. 1986—, bd. dirs. 1986—), Greater Cherry Hill C. of C. (chmn. small bus. coun. 1982-83), Rotary (bd. dris. Garden State club 1980-81). Lodge: Rotary (bd. dirs. Garden State club 1981-82). Office: Exec Mews Ste U-102 1930 E Marlton Pike Cherry Hill NJ 08003

BASILE, PAUL LOUIS, JR., lawyer; b. Oakland, Calif., Dec. 27, 1945; s. Paul Louis and Roma Florence (Paris) B.; m. Linda Lou Paige, June 20, 1970; m. 2d Diane Chierichetti, Sept. 2, 1977. BA, Occidental Coll., 1968; postgrad. U. Wash., 1969; JD, UCLA, 1971. Bar: Calif. Supreme Ct. 1972, U.S. Ct. Appeals (9th cir.) 1972, U.S. Dist. Ct. (cen. dist.) Calif. 1972, U.S. Dist. Ct. (no. dist.) Calif. 1985, U.S. Supreme Ct. 1977, U.S. Tax Ct. 1977, U.S. Ct. Clms. 1978, U.S. Customs Ct. 1979, U.S. Ct. Customs and Patent Appeals 1979, U.S. Ct. Internat. Trade 1981. Assoc., Parker, Milliken, Kohlmeier, Clark & O'Hara, Los Angeles, 1971-72; corporate counsel TFI Cos., Inc., Irvine, Calif., 1972-73; sole practice, Los Angeles, 1973-80; ptnr., Basile & Siener, Los Angeles, 1980-86; ptnr. Clark & Trevithick, Los Angeles, 1986—; gen. counsel J.W. Brown, Inc., Los Angeles, Calif., 1980—, asst. sec., 1984—; sec., gen. counsel Souriau, Inc., Valencia, Calif., 1981—; v.p., sec., dir., gen. counsel Pvt. Fin. Assocs., Los Angeles, 1983—. Trustee, sec. Nat. Repertory Theatre Found., 1975—, mem. exec. com. 1976—; mem. fin. com., bd. dirs. Calif. Music Theatre, 1988—; active Los Angeles Olympic Organizing Com.; dir. March Dimes Birth Defects Found., Los Angeles County, 1982-87, exec. com. 1983-86, sec. 1985-86; active Ketchum Downtown YMCA, Vols. Am. L.A.; bd. dirs. Canadian Soc. Los Angeles, 1980-83, sec., 1982-83; dist. fin. chmn. Los Angeles Area council Boy Scouts Am., 1982-83; active numerous other civic orgns. Mem. ABA, Can.-Am. Bar Assn., Los Angeles County Bar Assn., Italian-Am. Lawyers Assn., Asia Pacific Lawyers Assn., Fgn. Trade Assn. So. Calif., Can. Calif. C. of C. (dir. 1980-89, 2d v.p. 1983-84, 1st v.p. 1984-85, pres. 1985-87), French-Am. C. of C. (councilor 1979-84, v.p. 1980, 82-84), Los Angeles Area C. of C. (dir. 1980-81), Grand Peoples Co. (bd. dirs., 1985—, chmn. bd. 1986—), Japan-Am. Soc. So. Calif., L.A. World Affairs Council, Rotary, Jonathan Club. Democrat. Baptist. Home: 3937 Beverly Glen Blvd Sherman Oaks CA 91423 Office: Clark & Trevithick 800 Wilshire Blvd 13th Fl Los Angeles CA 90017

BASKA, JAMES LOUIS, wholesale grocery company executive; b. Kansas City, Kans., Apr. 3, 1927; s. John James and Stella Marie (Wilson) B.; m. Juanita Louise Carlson, Oct. 14, 1950; children: Steven James, Scott David. BSBA, U. Kans., 1949; JD, U. Mo., 1960. Bar: Kans. 1960. Pres., chief exec. officer Baska Laundry Co., Kansas City, 1951-62; ptnr. Rice & Baska, Kansas City, 1962-76; corporate sec., gen. counsel Assoc. Wholesale Grocers Inc., Kansas City, 1976-77, v.p., sec., gen. counsel, 1977-79, exec. v.p., chief fin. officer, sec., gen. counsel, 1979-84, pres., chief exec. officer, 1984—; pres., chief exec. officer Super Market Developers Inc., Super Market Investment Co. Inc., Grocers Dairy Co. Inc.; bd. dirs. United Mo. Bank of Kansas City, N.A. Served as staff sgt. U.S. Army, 1944-46. Mem. ABA, Kans. Bar Assn., Johnson County Bar Assn., Wyandotte County Bar Assn., Nat. Grocers Assn. (bd. dirs. 1980—, chmn. 1987-88), Food Mktg. Inst. (bd. dirs. 1988—). Republican. Roman Catholic. Office: Assoc Wholesale Grocers Inc 5000 Kansas Ave Kansas City KS 66100

BASKIN, C(HARLES) R(ICHARD), civil engineer, physical scientist; b. Houston, Mar. 6, 1926; s. Charles Todd and Bessie Emma (Heilig) B.; B.S. in Civil Engring., La. State U., 1953; m. Peggy June Holden, Dec. 31, 1952; children—Richard Karl, Sheila Frances. Design engr. City-Parish Dept. Pub. Works, Baton Rouge, 1953-57; city engr. City of Plaquemine (La.), 1957-58; sect. head, asst. chief engr. Tex. Bd. Water Engrs., Austin, 1958-62; asst. chief engr. Tex. Water Commn., Austin, 1962-65; asst. chief engr. and chief engr. Tex. Water Devel. Bd., Austin, 1965-77; dir. data and engring. services div. Tex. Dept. Water Resources, Austin, 1977-83; spl. asst. Office of Asst. Dir. Info. Systems, U.S. Geol. Survey, Reston, Va., 1983—. Chmn., Tex. Mapping Adv. Com., 1968-83, Water Oriented Data Programs sect. Tex. Interagy. Council on Natural Resources and the Environment, 1968-72, Tex. Natural Resources Info. System Task Force, 1972-83; mem. Non-Fed. Adv. Com. on Water Data for Public Use, 1970-83; chmn. Water Data Coordination Task Force, Interstate Conf. on Water Problems, 1975-83. Served with U.S. Army, 1944-47; p.o.w. Commd. Admiral Tex. Navy, 1961; recipient John Wesley Powell award U.S. Geol. Survey, 1972; registered profl. engr., La., Tex. Mem. Phi Kappa Phi, Tau Beta Pi (chpt. pres. 1950), Chi Epsilon, Phi Eta Sigma, Sigma Tau Sigma (pres. 1950). Adventist (elder). Avocations: photography, walking. Contbr. articles to profl. jours. Home: 1330 Quail Ridge Dr Reston VA 22094-1114 Office: US Geol Survey 801 National Ctr Reston VA 22092

BASLER, WAYNE GORDON, glass manufacturing executive; b. Cedar Rapids, Iowa, Aug. 16, 1930; children: Eric, Janelle, Peter. B.S. in Ceramic Engring., Iowa State U., 1953. With Ford Motor Co., 1960-72; dir. tech. devel. Guardian Industries, Detroit, 1972-77; pres. AFG Industries, Inc., Kingsport, Tenn., 1977—. Served to 1st lt. USAF, 1954-56. Republican. Presbyterian. Office: AFG Industries Inc 301 Commerce St Fort Worth TX 76102

BASS, CHARLES MORRIS, financial consultant; b. Miami, Fla., Sept. 21, 1949; s. Benjamin and Ellen Lucille (Williams) B; children—Cheryl Ellen, Benjamin Charles. B.A., U. Md., 1972; M.S., Am. Coll., 1982. C.L.U.; chartered fin. cons. Group rep. Monumental Life Ins. Co., 1972-73; agt. Equitable Life Ins. Co., N.Y., 1973-76; ptnr. Bass, Bridge and Assocs., Columbia, Md., 1976-81; pres. Multi-Fin Service, Inc., Balt., 1981-83; gen. mgr. Mfrs. Fin. Group, Denver, 1983-85; ptnr. Regency Econometrics Group, Denver, 1985—; speaker in field. Chmn. United Way Howard County, 1977-78; mem. Econ. Devel. Adv. Council Howard County, 1979-83. Served with USAF, 1968-71. Mem. Million Dollar Round Table, Nat. Assn. Life Underwriters, Am. Soc. C.L.U.s, Gen. Agts. and Mgrs. Assn., Columbia Life Underwriters Assn. (pres. 1982), Estate Planning Council, Howard County C. of C., Howard County Bus. Club, Columbia Bus. Exchange. Methodist. Home and Office: PO Box 621519 Littleton CO 80162

BASS, PERRY RICHARDSON, oil company executive; b. Wichita Falls, Tex., Nov. 11, 1914; s. E. Perry and Annie (Richardson) B.; m. Nancy Lee Muse, June 28, 1941; children: Sid R., Edward P., Robert M., Lee M. B.S. in Geology, Yale U., 1937; D. Humanitarian Service (hon.), Tex. Christian U., 1983. Chmn. Sid Richardson Carbon & Gas, Ft. Worth, 1959—; pres. Perry R. Bass, Inc., Ft. Worth, 1941—, also dir.; pres. Sid Richardson Found., Ft. Worth, 1960—, also dir.; dir. Bass Bros. Enterprises, Ft. Worth; mem. ad hoc com. Tex. Energy and Natural Resources Adv. Com.; mem. exec. com. Nat. Petroleum Council, Nat. Oil Policy Commn. on Possible Future Petroleum Problems; designer, builder fireboats for U.S. Navy. Active Longhorn council Boy Scouts Am.; chmn. Tex. Parks and Wildlife Commn., 1977-83; mem. adv. com. bd. visitors Univ. Cancer Found. of M.D. Andersen Hosp. and Tumor Inst.; bd. govs. Ochsner Found. Hosp. Recipient Silver Beaver award Boy Scouts Am., 1965, Silver Antelope award, 1969, Silver Buffalo award, 1976; Golden Deed award Ft. Worth Exchange Club, 1967; Disting. Civic Service award Dallas/Ft. Worth Hosp. Council, 1983. Mem. Am. Assn. Petroleum Geologists, Am. Petroleum Inst. (exec. com.), All Am. Wildcatters, Ind. Petroleum Assn. Am., Tex. Mid-Continent Oil and Gas Assn. (exec. com.). Clubs: Ft. Worth Boat, River Crest Country (Ft. Worth); Petroleum (Dallas and Ft. Worth); N.Y. Yacht; Royal Ocean Racing (London). Office: Perry R Bass Inc 201 Main St Fort Worth TX 76102 *

BASS, RAY HUDSON, credit union administrator; b. Watertown, Tenn., June 24, 1936; s. Aaron and Ellen Frances (Hudson) B.; m. Billie Loretta Willoughby, May 7, 1956; children: Amanda Rachelle, Kevin Ray. Mgr. Auto Glass Employee Fed. Credit Union, Nashville, 1959-80, pres., 1980—; chmn. Tenn. Credit Union League, Chattanooga, 1978-79. Pres. Dodson & Andrew Jackson PTA, Hermitage, Tenn., 1865-70. Home: 212 Ashawn Blvd Old Hickory TN 37138

BASS, ROBERT MUSE, entrepreneur; b. Ft. Worth, 1948; s. Perry Richardson and Nancy Lee (Muse) B.; m. Anne Bass, 1970; 3 children. BA, Yale U., 1970; MBA, Stanford U. V.p., bd. dirs. Bass Bros. Enterprises Inc., Ft. Worth, until 1985; prin. Robert M. Bass Group Inc., Ft. Worth, 1985—. Mem. Tex. State Hwy. and Pub. Transp. Commn., 1986-87; trustee Nat. Trust for Hist. Preservation; mem. collector's com. Nat. Gallery, Washington. Office: Robert M Bass Group Inc 201 Main St Fort Worth TX 76102 *

BASS, STEVEN MURRAY, public television executive; b. Atlantic City, N.J., Feb. 27, 1957; s. Walter and Catherine (Stump) B.; m. Sara Traut, May 12, 1984. BA, Bucknell U., 1979; MA in Bus., U. Wis., 1981. Mgr. spl. projects Sta. WHA-TV, Madison, Wis., 1981-82, asst. dir. membership devel., 1982; assoc. dir. devel. Pub. Broadcasting Svc., Washington, 1982-86, dir. devel., 1986-87, dir. nat. corp. support, 1987—; planning cons. Jewish Community Ctr. of Chgo., 1982; mktg. cons. State Hist. Soc. Madison, Wis., 1980; cons. Pa. House, Inc., 1979. Avocations: sailing, scuba diving. Home: 2107 Mason Hill Dr Alexandria VA 22306 Office: Pub Broadcasting Svc 1320 Braddock Pl Alexandria VA 22314

BASSETT, LAWRENCE C., management consultant; b. N.Y.C., Dec. 11, 1931; s. David Isaac and Genia Esther Bassett; m. Charlotte Corinne Margolis, Jan. 24, 1960; children: Wendy Jill, Craig Henrid, Heidi Jill, Evan Henrid. BA, NYU, 1953, MBA, 1958. Cert. mgmt. cons. Floor mgr. Franklin Simon & Co., N.Y.C., 1955-56; personnel mgr. Republic Carloading & Distbg. Co., N.Y.C., 1956-61; dir. personnel Clay Adams Inc., N.Y.C., 1961-63; asst. dir. personnel Montefiore Hosp. and Med. Ctr., N.Y.C., 1963-65; dir. personnel Hosp. for Joint Diseases and Med. Ctr., N.Y.C., 1965-67; sr. cons. Orgn. Resources Counselors Inc., N.Y.C., 1967-76; pres. Applied Leadership Tech. Inc., Bloomfield, N.J., 1976-86, The Bassett Cons. Group Inc., Thornwood, N.Y., 1986—; adj. prof. NYU, 1978—, Fairleigh Dickenson U., Teaneck, N.J., 1964-86; instr. Helene Fuld Sch. for Registered Nurses, N.Y.C., 1966-67. Author: Achieving Excellence, 1986; contbr. articles to profl. jours. Pres., v.p. Mt. Pleasant Bd. Edn., Thornwood, N.Y., 1973-76, 81-87. Served with U.S. Army, 1953-55. Mem. Soc. Profl. Mgmt. Cons. (bd. dirs., v.p.), Inst. Mgmt. Cons., Am. Soc. for Tng. and Devel., Am. Hosp. Assn., Am. Mgmt. Assn., Am. Arbitration Assn. Lodge: Masons. Home and Office: 1 Ilana Ln Thornwood NY 10594

BASSETT, MICHELLE SEGALL, corporate executive; b. Austin, Tex., July 23, 1955; d. Bernard E. and Muriel Lynnette (Lindstrom) Segall; m. Ronald Edward Bassett, June 17, 1988; 1 stepson, Robson Dismer. BBA in Mgmt., Tex. Christian U., 1977; postgrad., U. Houston, 1989—. Sales rep. NCR Corp., Dayton, Ohio, 1978-80, Hoffmann-LaRoche, Inc., Nutley, N.J., 1980-83; area sales mgr. Metromedia Long Distance, San Antonio, 1983-84, The Tigon Corp., Stamford, Conn., 1984-85; ptnr., pub. Bassett & Co., Galveston, 1986—. Vol. counselor juvenile probation dept. Harris County, Houston, 1988; crisis hotline counselor, Hotline, Austin, 1985; mem. Galveston Hist. Found., 1986—, pub. relations com. Grand 1894 Opera House, state bar grievance com. 4F, Harris County, Houston, 1988. Mem. Pi Beta Phi, Galveston Alumni Group. Episcopalian. Home: 1123 Sealy Galveston TX 77550 Office: Bassett & Co PO Box 3117 Galveston TX 77552

BASSETT, TINA, communication executive; b. Detroit; m. Leland Kinsey Bassett; children: Joshua, Robert. Student, U. Mich., 1974, 76-78, 81, Wayne State U., 1979-80. Advt. dir. Greenfield's Restaurant, Mich. and Ohio, 1972-73; dir. advt. and pub. relations Kresco, Inc., Detroit, 1973-74; pub's. rep. The Detroiter mag., 1974-75; pub. relations dir. Detroit Bicentennial Commn., 1975-77; prin. Leland K. Bassett & Assocs., Detroit, 1976-86; intermediate job devel. specialist Detroit Council of the Arts, 1977; project dir. Detroit image campaign Dept. Pub. Info., City of Detroit, 1975, spl. events dir., 1978; dep. dir. Dept. Pub. Info. City of Detroit, 1978-83, dir., 1983-86; pres., prin. Bassett & Bassett, Inc., Detroit, 1986—. Publicity chmn. Under the Stars IV, V, VI, VII, VIII, IX and X, Benefit Balls, Detroit Inst. of Arts Founders Soc., 1983-88, Detroit Inst. of Arts Centennial Ball, 1985, publicity chmn. Mich. Opera Theater, Opera Ball, 1987; program lectr. Wayne County Close-Up Program, 1984; mem. cen. planning com. Am. Assn. Mus.; mem. Founders Soc., Detroit Inst. Arts, North Rosedale Civic Assn.; mem. adv. bd. Detroit Jr. League., 1988—; mem. publicity choice Grand Prix Ball, 1989; co-chair producer Mus. Ball Ctr. for Performing Arts. Named Advt. Woman of Yr. Women's Advt. Club, 1989. Mem. Detroit Hist. Soc., Music Hall Assn. Club: Econ. Home: 18644 Gainsborough Rd Detroit MI 48223 Office: Bassett & Bassett Inc 672 Woodbridge St Detroit MI 48226-4302

BASTABLE, JOHN ANTHONY, airline executive; b. Dublin, Ireland, Dec. 27, 1944; came to U.S., 1982; s. Thomas Joseph and Eileen Monica (O'Connor) B.; m. Monica McCann, July 22, 1972; children: Conor, Eoin, Alan. BA with honors, U. Coll., Dublin, 1966. Grad. trainee Agr. Lingus-Irish Airlines, Dublin, 1967-68, indsl. engr., 1968-70, head pricing dept., 1970-73, head mktg. div., 1973-75, mktg. mgr., 1975-82; sr. v.p. N.A. Agr. Lingus-Irish Airlines, N.Y.C., 1982—; bd. dirs. Omni Hotel Corp., Hampton, N.Y. Mem. Internat. Air Transport Assn. (conf. chmn. 1978-82), European North Atlantic Carriers Assn. (chmn. 1987—), Airport Operators Coun. (dir. 1988—), Wings Club. Office: Aer Lingus 122 E 42d St New York NY 10168

BASTARDI, MARILYN PATRICIA, printing executive; b. Newark, Mar. 17, 1945; d. Anthony Frank and Janet Louise (Richliano) Petrozzino; m. Anthony Vincent Bastardi, June 24, 1967; children—Noelle, Anthony III, Matthew, Christian. B.A. in English, Caldwell Coll., 1966. Cert. elem. tchr., N.J. Tchr. Wayne Bd. Edn., N.J., 1966-68, supplemental tchr. learning disabilities, 1975-77; pres. Presto Printing Ctr., Parsippany, N.J., 1980—. Pres. GATEway No. N.J., 1978-80; mem. gifted edn. com. Hanover Twp. Bd. Edn., N.J., 1980; Named Rookie of Yr., Sir Speedy Franchises, 1981. Mem. Middle Atlantic Sir Speedy Owners Assn., AAUW (chmn. scholarship com. 1982), Caldwell Coll. Alumnae Assn. (exec. com. 1985—, sec. 1988-89, v.p. 1989-90), Delta Epsilon Sigma. Republican. Roman Catholic. Avocations: ice skating, gourmet cooking. Home: RD2 4 Southview Dr Boonton NJ 07005 Office: Sir Speedy Printing 1543 Route 46 Parsippany NJ 07054

BASTEDO, WAYNE WEBSTER, lawyer; b. Oceanside, N.Y., July 13, 1948; s. Walter Jr. and Barbara Catherine (Manning) B.; m. Bina Shantilal Mistry, Dec. 29, 1978. AB in Polit. Sci. cum laude, Princeton U., 1970; postgrad., NYU, 1977-78; JD, Hofstra U., 1978; LLM, NYU, 1988; postgrad., Fairleigh Dickinson U., 1988—. Bar: N.Y. 1980. Mgr. adminstrv. Law Jour. Seminars Press, N.Y.C., 1978-79; editor decisions and legal digests N.Y. Law Jour., N.Y.C., 1979-81; sole practice N.Y.C., 1981-82; atty. Western Union Corp., Upper Saddle River, N.J., 1983—; cons. litigation Exxon Corp., N.Y.C., 1982, Western Union Corp., Upper Saddle River, 1983; mem. corp. restructuring staff Western Union Corp., Upper Saddle River, 1986-89. Author: A Comparative Study of Soviet and American World Order Models, 1978, Who Has the Edge on Justice? Computer Services Alter Fair Play, 1979; assoc. editor Hofstra U. Law Rev. 1976-77; editor (directory series) Outside Counsel: Inside Director, 1976-81; contbr. articles to profl. jours. Mem. policy com. Roosevelt Island (N.Y.) Residents Assn., 1981-82. Served to lt. USN, 1970-75, Vietnam. N.Y. State Regents scholar, 1966-70, USN Officer Tng. scholar, 1967-70. Mem. ABA, N.Y. County Lawyers Assn. Democrat. Methodist. Home: 398 N Central Ave Ramsey NJ 07446 Office: Western Union Corp Office Gen Counsel 1 Lake St Upper Saddle River NJ 07458

BASTOKY, BRUCE MICHAEL, human resource executive; b. Cleve., June 15, 1953; s. Irving Benjamin and Esther (Naff) B.; m. Erin Kay Sebaugel, Jan. 21, 1989. Student, Cuyahoga Community Coll., 1971-73, U. Akron, 1984-85. Personnel/tng. adminstr. The May Co., Cleve., 1974-77; cons. Roth Young, Cleve., 1978-80; dir. human resources The Lawson Co., Cuyahoga Falls, Ohio, 1980-86, Cardinal Industries, Columbus, Ohio, 1986-89; pres. Mgmt. Group, Columbus, 1989—; mem. strategic planning bd. Profl. Secs. Internat., 1989. Author: Supervisor's Guide, 1985, Sixty Minute Mastery, 1987, Property Management First Aid Kit, 1988; producer (films/videos) The Visitor, 1984, Deli Heros, 1985. Mem. Youth Motivation Task Force, Akron, Ohio, 1983-86; officer Pvt. Industry Council, Akron, 1983-86. Recipient Silver Quill for Scriptwriting award Internat. Assn. Bus. Communicators, 1985, Best Film/Video Series award Nat. Assn. Convenience Stores, 1985, Exec. of Yr. award Profl. Secs. Internat., 1987. Mem. Am. Soc. Personnel Adminstrn. (bd. dirs. 1985-86), Am. Soc. Tng. and Devel., German Village Soc., Profl. Secs. Internat. (strategic planning bd. 1989—). Jewish. Home: 506 Lawrence Ave Columbus OH 43228 Office: Cardinal Industries Inc 4223 Donlyn Ct Columbus OH 43232

BATAYNEH, GHASSAN (JASON) RIZEK, investment advisor executive, portfolio manager; b. Amman, Jordan, Mar. 18, 1960; came to U.S., 1978; s. Rizk S. and Nasimeh R. (Adibe) B.; m. Karen Joan Bednar, Aug. 2, 1985. BBA, U. Wis., Milw., 1982; MBA in Fin. Investment and Banking, U. Wis., 1986. Investment analyst Nat. Projects and Investments Co., Ltd., Amman, 1982-83; teaching asst. U. Wis.-Milw., 1984-85; investment broker Geneva Securities, Inc., Schaumburg, Ill. and Milw., 1986-88; pres. Paragon Capital Mgmt., Inc., Milw., 1988—. Mem. Milw. Investment Analysts Soc., Fin. Analysts Fedn., Mensa, Beta Gamma Sigma. Home: PO Box 11833 Milwaukee WI 53211 Office: Paragon Capital Mgmt Inc 225 E Michigan St Ste 520 Milwaukee WI 53202

BATDORF, TERRIE LEE, banker; b. Toledo, June 7, 1949; d. Lawrence Edward and Alta F. (Segrist) B.; m. Harvey J. Osgood. BBA in Acctg., Ohio U., 1972; MS in Mgmt., Rensselaer Poly. Inst., 1975. Fin. trainee Pratt & Whitney Aircraft, 1972-74; acct. Medicare head office Aetna Life & Casualty Co., 1974-75; successively fin. analyst, ops. mgr., asst. v.p., project mgr., ops. head Citicorp processing treasury div., v.p. funds mgr. parent co. Citicorp, cash mgr. Citibank and Citicorp, fgn. exch. ops. channel head, 1975-88, mgr. exposure ops. Citibank, N.A. Mem. Nat. Assn. Accts. (past. bd. dirs), Ohio U. Alumni Assn. N.Y./N.J. (chpt. sec.), Phi Gamma Nu (regional dir., dir. edn. found.). Methodist. Club: Citibank Bridge. Home: 275-2OA W 96th St New York NY 10025

BATEMAN, DOTTYE JANE SPENCER, realtor; b. Athens, Tex.; d. Charles Augustus and Lillie (Freeman) Spencer; student Fed. Inst., 1941-42, So. Meth. U., Dallas Coll., 1956-58; m. George Truitt Bateman, 1947 (div. Apr. 1963); children—Kelly Spencer, Bethena; m. 2d, Joseph E. Lindsley, 1968. Sec. to state senator, Tyler, Tex., 1941-42; sec. to pres. Merc. Nat. Bank, Dallas, State Fair of Tex., Dallas, 1942-48; realtor, broker, Garland, Tex., 1956—; co-ptnr. Play-Shade Co.; appraiser Assoc. Soc. Real Estate Appraiser; auctioneer, 1963—; developer Stonewall Cave, 1964—, Guthrie East Estates. Pres., Central Elementary Sch. PTA, 1955-56, Bussey Jr. High PTA, 1956-57; former Rep. Precinct chairperson, Garland: mem. Rep. Senatorial Inner Circle, 1986—; den mother Cub Scouts Am., 1957-59; chmn. Decent Lit. Com., 1956-58; chmn. PTA's council, 1958; dir. Dallas Heart Assn., 1960, local chmn., 1955-57, county chmn., 1957-60; spl. dir. Henderson County Red Cross, 1945; local chmn. March of Dimes, 1961-63; mem. Dallas Civic Opera Com., 1963-64; mem. homemaker panel Dallas Times Herald, 1955-74, Nat. Rep. Womne and Regents, 1986—. Named Outstanding Tex. Jaycee-Ette Pres., 1953, hon. Garland Jay-Cee-Ette, 1956, hon. Sheriff, Dallas County, 1963; headliner Press Club Awards dinner, 1963-68. Mem. Garland, Dallas (chmn. reception com., past dir., mem. comml.-investment div., mem. make Am. better com. 1973-78, mem. beautify Tex. council 1977-78, by-laws com. 1977-78) bds. realtors, Auctioneers Assn., Internat. Real Estate Fedn., Soc. Prevention Cruelty to Animals, Dallas Women's (project chmn.). Garland (chmn. spl. services com. 1955-56) chambers commerce, Consejo Internacional De Buena Vecindad, Delphian Study Club, Eruditis Study Club, D.A.R. (Daniel McMahan chpt.). Christian Scientist. Clubs: Garland (past v.p., pres.), Tex. (past treas., ofcl. hostess) Jaycee-Ettes, Garland Fedn. Women's (past pres.), Garland Garden, Trinity Dist. Fedn. Women's (past pres.), Pub. Affairs Luncheon, Dallas Press (dir. 1973-74), chmn. house com. 1973-74, chmn. hdqrs. com. 1973-74). Home: 6313 Lyons Rd Garland TX 75043 Office: 5518 Dyer St #1 Dallas TX 75206

BATEMAN, JOHN ROGER, investment holding company executive; b. Medford, Oreg., Sept. 21, 1927; s. Joseph Nielson and Bessie Mable (Jackson) B.; children: David, Sally, Susan; m. Freddie Orlean Johnson, 1984. Student, U. Redlands, 1944-45, Mont. Sch. Mines, 1945, Colo. Coll., 1945-46, San Diego State Coll., 1948; B.S. with honors, U. Calif.-Berkeley, 1951, M.B.A., 1952. CPA, Tex., Calif. Acctg. trainee Standard Oil Co. Calif., San Francisco, 1952; sr. acct. Slavik & Ponder, CPAs, Corpus Christi, Tex., 1953-57; chief acct. Coastal States Corp., Corpus Christi, 1957-59, treas., 1959-66, v.p. fin., 1963-66; mng. ptnr. Bateman Investments, Corpus Christi, 1967—; with Bateman Alamo Group, Ltd., 1971-74, Bateman Meridian Group Ltd., 1972-75; mng. ptnr. Bateman Luxor Group Ltd., 1969-76; pres., chmn. bd. Bay Fabricators, Inc., 1973-78, dir., 1972-78; pres., chmn. bd. Bay Industries, Inc., 1975-78, Bateman Industries, Inc., 1976—, Bay Heat Transfer Corp., 1977-81; v.p., treas., dir. Integral Petroleum Corp., 1973-75; with Integral Energy Corp., 1975-79, Camden Drilling Co., 1974-79, Integral Drilling Co., 1974-79; dir. Guaranty Nat. Bank, 1972-75; ptnr. Jaro Leasing, 1980-85; dir. Summit Geophysical Internat., Inc., 1980-82; ptnr. Act I properties, 1981-84, First City Tower II, 1981—; chmn. bd. Bajon Signs Co., 1982; ptnr. Bajon Investments, 1980-87; chmn. bd. Bajon Corp., 1980-87, Bajon Devel. Corp., 1981-83. Bd. dirs., pres., treas. Little Theatre Corpus Cristi, 1964-68; ofcl. bd. 1st United Meth. Ch., 1964-67, 70-73, 78-80, 84-85; bd. govs. United Way Coastal Bend, 1964-67, 73-83, campaign chmn., 1977, pres., 1981; mem. exec. coun. USO, 1971-73; mem. YMCA Capital Devel. Camp Com., 1982, YWCA Capital Fund Adv. Com., 1982-85, co-chmn. YWCA Capital Fund Drive, 1985-87; chmn. So. Shore Christian Ch. Bldg. Renewal Camp, 1986; bd. dirs. Camp Fire Girls, 1967-69; Tex. Bd. Mental Health and Mental Retardation, 1981-88, vice chmn., 1985-87, chmn., 1987-88; mem. Tex. Health and Human Svcs. Planning Coun., 1987-88; del. Rep. Party of Tex. Convention, 1972, 76, 84; Tex. mem. Nat. Rep. Senatorial Com., 1978-81, Rep. Eagles, 1980-81; mem. Rep. Govs. Assn., 1980-81; co-chmn. Tex. Rep. Fin. Com., 1980-81.; bd. dirs. Crippled Children's Found. South Tex., 1985-86. Lt. (j.g.) UNSR, 1945-50. Mem. Tex. Soc. CPAs, Navy League U.S., Confederate Air Force, Pima Air. Mus., Corpus Christi Country Club, Town Club, Nueces Club, Rotary, Phi Beta Kappa, Beta Alpha Psi, Beta Gamma Sigma, Alpha Lambda Nu. Home: 401 Cape Cod Corpus Christi TX 78412 Office: 1668 S Staples Corpus Christi TX 78404

BATES, BARBARA J. NEUNER, municipal official; b. Mt. Vernon, N.Y., Apr. 8, 1927; d. John Joseph William and Elsie May (Flint) Neuner; B.A., Barnard Coll., 1947; m. Herman Martin Bates, Jr., Mar. 25, 1950; children—Roberta Jean Bates Jamin, Herman Martin III, Jon Neuner. Confidential clk. to supr. town Ossining (N.Y.), 1960-63; pres. BNB Assocs., Briarcliff Manor, N.Y., 1963-83, Upper Nyack Realty Co., Inc., Briarcliff Manor, 1966-71; receiver of taxes Town of Ossining (N.Y.), 1971—. Vice pres. Ossining (N.Y.) Young Republican Club, 1958; pres. Young Womens Rep. Club Westchester County (N.Y.), 1959-61; regional committeewoman N.Y. State Assn. Young Rep. Clubs, 1960-62; mem. Westchester County Rep. Com., 1963—; mem. Ossining Women's Rep. Club, 1960—, pres., 1984-85; mem. Westchester County Women's Rep. Club, 1957—. Mem. Jr. League Westchester-on-Hudson, DAR, N.Y. State Assn. Tax Receivers and Collectors, Receivers of Taxes Assn. of Westchester County, (legis. liaison, v.p., pres. 1984-85), Hackley Sch. Mothers Assn. (pres. 68), R.I. Hist. Soc., Ossining Hist. Soc., Ossining Bus. and Profl. Women's Club, Am. Soc. Notaries, Westchester County Hist. Soc., Briarcliff-Scarborough Hist. Soc. Congregationalist. Home: 78 Holbrook Ln Briarcliff Manor NY 10510 also: 663 Reynolds Rd Chepachet RI 02814

BATES, CHARLES WALTER, human resource executive; b. Detroit, June 28, 1953; s. E. Frederick and Virginia Marion (Nunneley) B. BA in Psychology and Econs. cum laude, Mich. State U., 1975, M in Labor and Indsl. Relations, 1977; postgrad. DePaul U., 1979-80; JD William Mitchell Coll. Law, 1984. Vista vol., paralegal, Legal Aid Assn. Ventura County, Calif., 1975-76; substitute tchr. social studies and history, Lansing, Holt and Okemos, Mich. pub. sch. systems, 1976-77; job analyst Gen. Mills, Inc., Mpls., 1977-78, plant personnel asst. II, Chgo., 1978-80, asst. plant personnel mgr. , Chgo., 1980-81, personnel mgr. consumer foods mktg., Mpls., 1981-82; personnel mgr. consumer foods mktg. divs., Saluto Pizza, Mpls., 1982-84; human resource mgr. Western div., Godfather's Pizza, Costa Mesa, Calif., 1984-85, Western region human resources mgr., Bellevue, Washington, 1985—. Candidate for lt. gov., 1982, Minn.; asst. scoutmaster Boy Scouts of Am., 1971—; candidate Sommanish Community Coun., Bellevue, 1989—. Named Eagle Scout, Boy Scouts Am., 1969; recipient God and Country award Boy Scouts Am., 1967, Scouter's Tng. award Boy Scouts Am., 1979. Mem. Nat. Eagle Scout Assn., Pacific NW Personnel Mgmt. Assn. (Lake Washington chpt.), Am. Soc. Personnel Adminstrn., Mich. State U. Alumni Assn., William Mitchell Coll. Law Alumni Assn. Libertarian. Unitarian-Universalist. Home: 232 168th Ave NE Bellevue WA 98008-4522 Office: Godfather's Pizza Inc 11400 SE Sixth St Ste 100 Bellevue WA 98004

BATES, CLARENCE EDWARD, JR., automotive executive; b. River-Rouge, Mich., Dec. 19, 1946; s. Clarence E. Sr. and Ethel M. (Covington) B.; divorced; 1 child, Jamil K. Student, Iowa State U., 1967; BA, Western Mich. U., 1969; MA, Eastern Mich. U., 1976. Tchr. Detroit Pub. Schs., 1969-70, Ecorse (Mich.) Pub. Schs., 1970-73; sales engr. Detroit Diesel Allison div. Gen. Motors, 1973-76; regional sales engr. Detroit Diesel Allison div. Gen. Motors, Edison, N.J., 1976-78, zone sales mgr., 1980-86; transmission acct. mgr. eastern regional sales Allison transmission div. General Motors, Clementon, N.J., 1987—. Pres. Trowbridge Condominium Assn., Clementon, N.J., 1985, sec. 1984-86. Republican. African Methodist. Office: GM Allison Transmission div PO Box 436 Clementon NJ 08021

BATES, JOHN WALTER, business educator; b. Bainbridge, Ga., Sept. 24, 1939; s. clarence F. and Lillian E. (Drake) B; m. Harriet Smith, July 1, 1961; children: Andrew, Robin. BCE, Ga. Inst. Tech., 1962; MBA in Econs., Ga. State U., 1967, PhD in Bus. Adminstrn., 1981. Registered profl. engr., Ga., Fla. Hwy. engr., chief urban planning, chief planning ops. researcher State of Ga., Atlanta, 1962-71; sr. planner transp., dir. planning, mgr. research and devel., mgr. mktg. and research Met. Atlanta Rapid Transit Authority, 1971-82; assoc. prof., dir. ctr. bus. for services Ga. Southwestern Coll., Americus, 1982—. Author: A Study of Demand for Transit Use, 1981; contbr. articles to profl. jours. Chmn. City of Americus Hist. Preservation Commn., 1986-89. Mem. Am. Mktg. Assn., Am. Planning Assn. (v.p. Ga. chpt. 1985, local mem. of yr. 1985), Nat. Assn. Bus. Economists, Rotary (sec. Americus club 1985-86), Masons, KT. Office: Ga Southwestern Coll Ctr Bus Svcs Americus CA 31709

BATES, LURA WHEELER, trade association executive; b. Inboden, Ark., Aug. 28, 1932; d. Carl Clifton and Hester Ray (Pace) Wheeler; B.S. in Bus. Adminstrn., U. Ark., 1954; m. Allen Carl Bates, Sept. 12, 1954; 1 dau., Carla Allene. Sec.-bookkeeper, then officer mgr. Assoc. Gen. Contractors Miss., Inc., Jackson, 1958-77, dir. adminstrv. services, 1977—, asst. exec. dir., 1980—; adminstr. Miss. Constrn. Found., 1977—; sec. AIA-Assoc. Gen. Contractors Liaisonship Coms., 1977—; sec. Carpenters Joint Apprenticeship Coms., Jackson and Vicksburg, 1977—. Sec., Marshall Elem. Sch. PTA, Jackson, 1962-64, v.p., 1965; sec.-treas. Inter-Club Council Jackson, 1963-64; tchr. adult Sunday sch. dept. Hillcrest Bapt. Ch., Jackson, 1975-82; Bapt. Women dir. WMU First Bapt. Ch., Crystal Springs, Miss., 1987—; mem. exec. com. Jackson Christian Bus. and Profl. Women's Council, 1976-80, sec., 1978-79, pres., 1979-80. Named Outstanding Woman in Constrn. Miss., 1962-63; Outstanding Mem. Nat. Assn. Women in Constrn., various times. Fellow Internat. Platform Assn.; mem. Nat. Assn. Women in Constrn. (chpt. pres. 1963-64, 76-77, nat. v.p. 1965-66, 77-78, nat. dir. Region 5, 1967-68, nat. sec. 1970-71, 71-72, pres. 1980-81, coordinator cert. constrn. assoc. program 1973-78, 83-84 guardian-controller Edn. Found. 1981-82, chmn. nat. bylaws com. 1982-83, 85-88, nat. parliamentarian 1983—), Nat. Assn. Parliamentarians, Delta Delta Delta. Editor NAWIC Image, 1968-69, Procedures Manual, 1965-66, Public Relations Handbook, 1967-68, Profl. Edn. Guide, 1972-73, Guidelines & Procedures Handbook, 1987-88; author digests in field. Home: 272 Lee Ave Crystal Springs MS 39059 Office: 2093 Lakeland Dr Jackson MS 39216

BATES, ROGER CHALON, communications executive; b. Highland Park, Ill., Nov. 4, 1935; s. Carl Everett and Cerretta Mae (Rogers) B.; m. Shelby Jeanne Reynolds, Aug. 26, 1956; children: Cerretta Kay Bates Kelly, James Walter. BA, Hendrix Coll., 1957. With Southwestern Bell Telephone Co., Oklahoma City, 1957—, asst. v.p. ops. staff, 1987—; mgr. acctg. AT&T Co., N.Y.C., 1968-69. Bd. dirs. Allied Arts Found., Oklahoma City, 1984—, Jr. Achievement, 1985—, United Way, 1987—, Mercy Hosp., 1986—. Mem. Telephone Pioneers Am. (pres. 1986-87), Fin. Execs. Inst. Republican. Presbyterian, Rotary. Home: 6002 Flaming Oaks Cir Norman OK 73071 Office: Southwestern Bell Telephone 800 N Harvey Rd Oklahoma City OK 73102

BATES, RUBY LEE, corporate administrator; b. Marion, La., July 14, 1940; d. Roy and Wordie B. (Boyette) Shelbon; m. Julius Green, Aug. 18, 1963 (div. 1968); 1 child, Dana; m. Charles Bates, June 30, 1976 (dec.). AA, Castlemont Coll., Oakland, 1957; SSA, Heald Coll., Oakland, 1958. Exec. sec. Golden State Ins., Oakland, 1958-66; adminstrv. office mgr. Simmons & Travis, Oakland, 1966-74; adminstrv. asst. Castle & Cooke, San Francisco, 1975-77, office coord., 1977-81, corp. bookkeeper, 1981-85; case adminstr. Kornblum, Kelly & Herlihy, San Francisco, 1986; case adminstr. Kornblum & McBride, San Francisco, 1986—. Editor: Handbook for Temporary Personnel, 1979, Basic Training Manual for Case Administrators, 1988. Vol., Gospel Voices, Oakland, 1971-85. Recipient Svc. award Bible Fellowship Ch., Oakland, 1976. Mem. NAFE, Gamma Phi Delta. Democrat. Baptist. Avocations: Gospel singing, walking, reading. Home: 3822 39th Ave Oakland CA 94619 Office: Kornblum & McBride 445 Bush St 6th Fl San Francisco CA 94108

BATEZA, JANE DENISE, manufacturing company executive; b. Flint, Mich., Oct. 27, 1955; d. Andrew Leroy and Betty Jean (Pruitt) Renfro; m. Philip Martin (div. 1986); children: Philip Martin II, Barbara Martin, Kharlos Martin. AS in Acctg., Marygrove Coll., 1986. Paralegal asst. Morgan and McClarty, Southfield, Mich., 1977; mgr. procurement div. Clipper Internat., Detroit, 1977-80, mgr. shipping and recieving, 1980-84, mgr. material control, 1984-86, controller, treas., 1986—, also bd. dirs., 1986—. Mem. Minority Bus. Devel. Council, Detroit C. of C., Bus. Club, Margrove Club. Republican. Office: Clipper Internat 8651 E Seven Mile Rd Detroit MI 48234

BATHON, THOMAS NEIL, financial services executive; b. Mt. Clemens, Mich., Apr. 18, 1961; s. Bernard Neil and Joan Catherine (Connell) B. BBA, Marquette U., 1983; MBA, DePaul U., 1984. Money fund analyst Kemper Fin. Services, Chgo., 1984-85, sr. market analyst, 1985-86, mgr. product devel., 1987; pres. Fin. Research Corp., Chgo., 1987—. Treas. Lawrence Hall Sch., Chgo., 1987-88; mem. Jr. Bd. Chgo. Easter Seal Soc., 1988—. Mem. Am. Mktg. Assn., Union League Club, Condors Rugby Club (Oak Park, Ill.). Republican. Roman Catholic.

BATISTE, ROBERT JOSEPH, military non-commissioned officer, educator; b. Pineville, La., Apr. 25, 1950; s. Leonard Joseph and Francis (Jacob) B.; m. Okee Hui Kong, July 2, 1982; children: Linden, Leonard, Chrysalis. AA, Los Angeles Coll., 1977; AS, Coll. Air Force, 1981; BS, U. Md., 1983; MA, Webster U., 1986. Enlisted USAF, 1968, advanced through grades to master sgt., 1983; aircraft maintenance engr. USAF, Castle AFB, Calif., 1969-70, Utapao, Thailand, 1970-71, 71-73, Wirthsmith AFB, Mich., 1971, Carswell AFB, Tex., 1974-76, Kadena AFB, Japan, 1976-78; mgmt. engr. USAF, Plattsburgh AFB, N.Y., 1978-80, Osan Air Base, Republic Korea, 1980-84, 87-88, Scott AFB, Ill., 1984-87; mgmt. engr. Utapao Air Base, Keesler AFB, Miss., 1988—; mgmt. engr. USAF, 1978—; instr. Cen. Tex. Coll., Osan Air Base, 1987-88, Gold Star Electronics, Osan City, Republic of Korea, 1987-88. Democrat. Roman Catholic. Home: 239 Coolidge Ave Biloxi MS 39531 Office: Utapao Air Base 3400 TCHTG/TTGUB Keesler AFB MS 39534

BATLA, RAYMOND JOHN, JR., lawyer; b. Cameron, Tex., Sept. 1, 1947; s. Raymond John and Della Alvina (Jezek) B.; m. Susan Marie Clark, Oct. 1, 1983; children: Sara, Charles, Michael, Traci. BS with highest honors, U. Tex., 1970, JD, with honors, 1973. Bar: Tex. 1973, D.C. 1973, U.S. Dist. Ct. D.C. 1974, U.S. Dist. Ct. (so. dist.) Tex. 1982, U.S. Ct. Appeals (D.C. cir.) 1974, U.S. Ct. Appeals (5th cir.) 1982, U.S. Ct. Appeals (10th cir.) 1978, U.S. Supreme Ct. 1977. Structural engr. Tex. Hwy. Dept., Austin, 1970; assoc. Hogan & Hartson, Washington, 1973-82, gen. ptnr., 1983—; dean's adv. bd. com. U. Tex. Law Sch., Austin, 1983—. Author: Petroleum Regulation Handbook, 1980; contbr. articles to profl. jours. Chmn. bd. deacons Meml. Bapt. Ch., Arlington, 1978-80; pres. bd. dirs., Randolph Square Condominium Assn., Arlington, 1986-87. Mem. ABA (mem. spl. com. for energy fin., vice chmn. energy com. 1981), Fed. Energy Bar Assn., Fed. Bar. Assn., D.C. Bar Assn., State Bar Tex., U. Tex. Law Sch. Assn. (bd. dirs.), Assn. Energy Engrs., Cogeneration Inst., City Club of Wash., Order of Coif, Phi Delta Phi, Chi Epsilon, Tau Beta Pi. Episcopalian. Home: 12406 Shari Hunt Grove Clifton VA 22024 Office: Hogan & Hartson 555 13th St NW Washington DC 20004

BATOR, CHRISTINE VICTORIA, lawyer; b. Linden, N.J., June 9, 1949; d. Walter Peter and Frances Mary (Padlo) B.; m. Norman Alfred Lehoullier, Jan. 19, 1975. BA, Seton Hall U., 1970, JD, 1975; LLM, NYU, 1982. Bar: N.J. 1975, U.S. Dist. Ct. 1975, N.Y. 1982. Law clk. to presiding justice Superior Ct. N.J., Flemington, 1975-76; dir. office legal affairs N.J. Dept. Health, Trenton, 1976—; ptnr. Carella, Byrne, Bain & Gilfillan, Roseland, N.J., 1982-88, Hannoch Weisman, Roseland, N.J., 1988—. Mem. ABA, N.J. Bar Assn. (chair edn. subcom. 1987-89, health and hosp. law sect.), Women's Polit. Caucus, Exec. Women N.J. (chmn. bd., appointments com.). Office: Hannoch Weisman 4 Becker Farm Rd Roseland NJ 07068

BATT, NICK, lawyer; b. Defiance, Ohio, May 6, 1952; s. Dan and Zenith (Dreher) B.; m. Jeannie Powers, May 8, 1987. BS, Purdue U., 1972; JD, U. Toledo, 1976. Bar: Ohio 1976. Asst. prosecutor Lucas County, Toledo, 1976-80, civil div. chief, 1980-83; village attorney, Village of Holland, Ohio, 1980—; law dir. City of Oregon, Ohio, 1984—; spl. counsel State of Ohio, 1983—. Mem. Maumee Valley Girl Scout Council, Toledo, 1977-80; bd. mem. Bd. Community Relations, Toledo, 1975-76; mem. Lucas County Democratic Exec. Com., 1981-83. Named One of Toledo's Outstanding Young Men, Toledo Jaycees, 1979. ABA, Ohio Bar Assn., Mem. Toledo Bar Assn., Ohio Council of Sch. Bd. Attorneys, Ohio Mcpl. Attorneys Assn., Toledo, K.C., Elks. Democrat. Roman Catholic. Office: 325 10th St Toledo OH 43624

BATTEN, FRANK, newspaper publisher, broadcaster; b. Norfolk, Va., Feb. 11, 1927; s. Frank and Dorothy (Martin) B.; m. Jane Neal Parke; children: Frank, Mary, Dorothy. A.B., U. Va., 1950; M.B.A., Harvard U., 1952. Reporter The Norfolk Ledger-Star; with advt. and circulation depts. The Virginian-Pilot and Norfolk Ledger-Star newspapers; v.p. The Norfolk Virginian-Pilot and Norfolk Ledger-Star newspapers, 1953, pub., 1954—; chmn. bd. Landmark Communications, Norfolk, 1967—; also chmn. Greensboro (N.C.) News & Record, Greensboro Record, Roanoke (Va.) Times & World-News, WTAR/WLTV Radio, Sta. KNTV, Sta. KLAS-TV and TeleCable Corp.; dir. Capital-Gazette Communications Inc., Annapolis, Md.; 2d vice chmn. AP, 1977-79, 1st vice chmn., 1979-81, chmn. bd., 1982-87; formerly chmn. AP Pension, Tech., Fgn. ops. coms.; past chmn. AP Nominating Com., Va. AP Members; former dir. So. Newspapers Pubs. Assn.; former chmn. bd. Newspaper Advt. Bur.; bd. dirs. Capital-Gazette Communications, Ind., Annapolis, Md., AP, also vice chmn., chmn. Trustee Culver Ednl. Found., U.S. Acad. Naval Found.; past chmn. bd. Old Dominion U.; past vice chmn. State Council Higher Edn. for Va.; past pres. and campaign chmn. Norfolk Area United Fund; chmn. com. for Internat. Naval Rev., 1957; trustee So. Newspaper Pubs. Found., Hollins Coll, U. Va. Grad. Bus. Sch. Sponsors. Served with U.S. Merchant Marine, World War II, also with USNR. Recipient Norfolk's First Citizen award, 1966. Mem. So. Newspaper Pubs. Assn. (past. bd. dirs. Am. Press Inst.), Norfolk C. of C. (pres. 1961), Am. Press Inst. (past bd. dirs.), Sigma Xi, Sigma Delta Chi, Delta Kappa Epsilon. Episcopalian. Clubs: Princess Anne Country, Norfolk Yacht (Norfolk). Office: Landmark Communications Inc 150 W Brambleton Ave Norfolk VA 23510

BATTEN, JAMES KNOX, newspaperman; b. Suffolk, Va., Jan. 11, 1936; s. Eugene Taylor and Josephine (Winslow) B.; m. Jean Elaine Trueworthy, Feb. 22, 1958; children: Mark Winslow, Laura Taylor, Taylor Edison. B.S., Davidson Coll., 1957; M. Pub. Affairs, Princeton, 1962. Reporter Charlotte (N.C.) Observer, 1957-58, 62-65; corr. Washington bur. Knight Newspapers, 1965-70; editorial staff Detroit Free Press, 1970-72; exec. editor Charlotte (N.C.) Observer, 1972-75; v.p. Knight-Ridder Newspapers, Inc., Miami, Fla., 1975-80, sr. v.p., 1980-82, pres., 1982-88, pres., chief exec. officer, 1988—; dir. AP. Trustee Davidson Coll. (N.C.), U. Miami. Served with AUS, 1958-60. Recipient George Polk Meml. award for regional reporting, 1968; Sidney Hillman Found. award, 1968. Mem. Greater Miami C. of. C. Methodist. Office: Knight-Ridder Inc 1 Herald Pla Miami FL 33101

BATTEN, MICHAEL ELLSWORTH, manufacturing company executive; b. Racine, Wis., Apr. 14, 1940; s. John Henry and Katherine (Vernet) B.; m. Gloria Strickland, July 6, 1963; children—John, Elizabeth, Louise, Timothy. B.A., Yale U., 1964; M.B.A., Harvard U., 1970. Account exec. Ted Bates & Co., N.Y.C., 1964-68; asst. sec. Twin Disc, Inc., Racine, Wis., 1970-71, sec. and asst. treas., 1971-75, v.p. and sec., 1975-76, exec. v.p., 1976-83, pres. and chief exec. officer, 1983—; bd. dirs. Briggs & Stratton Corp., Firstar Corp., Universal Foods Corp., Walker Forge, Inc., Racine. Trustee Prairie Sch., Racine, 1974—; bd. dirs. Jr. Achievement; exec. com. Pub. Expenditure Survey Wis. Mem. NAM (bd. dirs.), Machinery and Allied Products Inst., Soc. Automotive Engrs., Farm and Indsl. Equipment Inst., Racine Area Mfrs. and Commerce (dir.). Republican. Clubs: University, Milwaukee. Home: 3419 Michigan Blvd Racine WI 53402 Office: Twin Disc Inc 1328 Racine St Racine WI 53402

BATTLE, EDWARD GENE, energy resources executive; b. Mont Belvieu, Tex., June 19, 1923; s. Paul E. and Annie-Mae B. B.S., Tex. A&M U., 1954. Pres., chief exec. officer, dir. Norcen Energy Resources Ltd., Calgary, Alta., Can., 1975—; with Continental Oil Co., Tex., from 1954; evaluation engr. Medallion Petroleums, Ltd., 1957, v.p prodn., 1965, exec. v.p., 1966, pres., from 1973; pres., chief operating officer No. and Central Gas Corp., 1974—; bd. dirs. Argus Corp. Ltd., Labrador Mining & Exploration Co. Ltd., Liquid Carbonic Inc., M.A. Hanna Co. Mem. Assn. Profl. Engrs., Geologists and Geophysicists Alta., Assn. Profl. Engrs. Ont., Soc. Petroleum Engrs., AIME. Clubs: Calgary Golf and Country, Rosedale Golf. Office: Norcen Energy Resources Ltd, 715 5th Ave SW, Calgary, AB Canada T2P 2X7

BATTLE, WILLIAM CULLEN, lawyer; b. Charlottesville, Va., Oct. 9, 1920; s. John Stewart and Mary Jane (Lipscomb) B.; m. Barry Webb, Nov. 14, 1953; children: william Cullen Jr., Robert Webb, Jane Tavernor. BA, U. Va., 1941, LLB, 1947. Bar: Va., 1947, W.Va., 1947, U.S. Supreme Ct., 1950, U.S. Cir. Ct. (4th cir.), 1947. Atty. Columbia Gas System, Charleston, W.Va., 1947-50; ptnr. McGuire, Woods & Battle, Washington, 1950-61, 64-70; of counsel McGuire, Woods, Battle & Booth, Charlottesville, Va., 1988—; ambassador U.S. Govt., Canberra, Australia, 1962-64; chief exec. officer Fieldcrest Mills Inc., Eden, N.C., 1970-82, cons., 1982-87; bd. dirs. Black & Decker Inc., towson, Md., Mid. South Utilities, New Orleans; chmn. bd. W. Alton Jones Cell Sci. Ctr., Lake Placid, N.Y.; pres. Am. Textile Mfrs. Assn., 1980-81. Mem. State Council Higher Edn., Va., 1986—. Served to lt. comdr. USN, 1942-45. Decorated Silver Star; named Outstanding Textile Exec. Fin. News, 1977, Outstanding Textile Exec. Wall St. Transcript, 1977. Mem. Va. Bar Assn., U.S. Golf Assn. (pres. 1988—). Home: PO Box 1 Ivy VA 22945

BATTON, CALVERT VORWERK, appliance company executive; b. Cuyahoga Falls, Ohio, June 29, 1926; s. Ramsey T. and Mildred B. (Vorwerk) B.; student Bowling Green U., 1946; B.S. in Bus. Adminstrn., Kent State U., 1950, postgrad. Grad. Bus. Sch., 1960-63; m. Edith Sayre Jones, May 18, 1957; children—Susan, Sally, Pamela. With Hoover Co., Canton, Ohio, 1951—, auditor, 1951-53, mgr. br. office, 1953-56, mgr. field accounting, 1956-58, gen. office mgr., 1958-61, asst. budget mgr., 1961-62, mgr. adminstrv. services, 1962-64, asst. v.p., 1964-65, adminstrv. v.p., 1965-75, sr. v.p., 1986—. Bd. dirs. Canton Cultural Ctr.; bd. dirs., pres. Kent U. Found. Served with AUS, 1944-45. Mem. Adminstrv. Mgmt. Soc., Nat. Assn. Accountants, Am. Mgmt. Assn., Sigma Delta Epsilon. Republican. Presbyterian. Home: 30 Auburn Ave SE North Canton OH 44709 Office: Hoover Corp 101 E Maple North Canton OH 44720

BATTON, MONICA KIM, insurance company professional; b. Parkersburg, W.Va., July 3, 1956; d. William Ernest and Hope (Riddle) B.; 1 child, Jahda Hope. BA in Polit. Sci., W.Va. U., 1978; AA in Nursing, Wesley Coll., 1983; postgrad., Wilmington Coll., Georgetown, Del., 1988—. Res. librarian W.Va. U., Morgantown, 1978-79, tech. asst. II, 1979-80, tech. asst. I, 1980-81; nursing asst. Kent Gen. Hosp., Dover, Del., 1982-83, staff RN, 1983-86; rep. managed care Blue Cross and Blue Shield Del., Dover, 1986—. Chmn. pub. info. Am. Cancer Soc., Dover, 1985-86, chmn. pub. edn., 1986-87. Mem. Internat. Platform Assn., Peninsula Press Club. Office: Blue Cross & Blue Shield Del 901 S Governors Ave Dover DE 19901

BATTON, ROY EUGENE, golf course superintendent; b. Ft. Bragg, N.C., June 20, 1949; s. Joseph Henry Sr. and Lucille (Hobbs) B.; m. Norma Alease Best, Mar. 16, 1974 (div. Apr. 1985); m. Julia Hill Day, Aug. 15, 1987. BA in English, The Citadel, 1971. Rep. customer svc. Comml. Credit Corp., Wilmington, N.C., 1972-74; field rep. Wachovia Bank & Trust, Raleigh, N.C., 1974; asst. golf profl. Cape Fear Country Club, Raleigh, 1974-77; head golf profl. Boiling Springs Lakes Country Club, Southport, N.C., 1977-79; supt. golf course Fox Squirrel Country Club, Southport, 1979-81, Morehead City (N.C.) Country Club, 1981—. Mem. editorial quality rev. bd. Grounds Maintenance mag., 1987. 1st lt. USAR, 1971-86. Mem. Ea. N.C. Turf Assn. (pres. 1985-86), Carolinas Golf Course Supts. Assn., Turgrass Council N.C. (bd.dirs. 1985-86), Golf Course Supts. Assn. Am., Assn. of Citadel Men., Lions. Republican. Baptist. Home: 113 Taylor St Morehead City NC 28557 Office: Morehead City Country Club PO Box 604 Country Club Rd Morehead City NC 28557

BATTS, RICHARD BRYAN, chemical company executive; b. St. Louis, Oct. 17, 1933; s. Henry Thompson and Marie Katherine (Sutton) B.; m. Mary Kathleen Flowers, Jan 20, 1962; children: Bryan McCormick, Alyson Marie, Dory Ann. BA, Lafayette Coll., 1956. Trainee AT&T Corp., White Plains, N.Y., 1956; sales rep. Chase Brass & Copper Co., Waterbury, Conn., 1958-63; ter. mgr. Interstate Steel Co., Des Plaines, Ill., 1963-67; dist. mgr. Foseco, Inc., Cleve., 1967-72; sales dir. Resco, Chgo., 1973-75; gen. sales mgr. Brooks Tech. Co., Cleve., 1975-76, v.p., gen. mgr., 1976-78; v.p. Premier Indsl. Corp., Cleve., 1978-86; v.p. sales Stuart-Ironsides, Inc., Chgo., 1986-88, pres., 1988—. Bd. dirs. Chagrin Valley (Ohio) YMCA, 1976-80, Cath. Charities, 1987—. Capt. U.S. Army, 1956-58. Mem. Am. Mgmt. Assn., Am. Iron and Steel Engrs., Soc. Tribologists and Lube Engrs., Ind. Lubricant Mfrs. Assn. Republican. Roman Catholic. Office: Stuart-Ironsides Inc 7575 Plaza Ct Willowbrook IL 60521

BATTS, WARREN LEIGHTON, diversified industry executive; b. Norfolk, Va., Sept. 4, 1932; s. John Leighton and Allie Belle (Johnson) B.; m. Eloise Pitts, Dec. 24, 1957; 1 dau., Terri Allison. B.E.E., Ga. Inst. Tech., 1961; M.B.A., Harvard U., 1963. With Kendall Co., Charlotte, N.C., 1963-64; exec. v.p. Fashion Devel. Co., Santa Paula, Calif., 1964-66; dir. mfg. Olga Co., Van Nuys, Calif., 1964-66; v.p. Douglas Williams Assocs., N.Y.C., 1966-67; co-founder Triangle Corp., Orangeburg, S.C., 1967; pres., chief exec. officer Triangle Corp., 1967-71; v.p. Mead Corp., Dayton, Ohio, 1971-73; pres. Mead Corp., 1973-80, chief exec. officer, 1978-80; pres., chief operating officer Dart Industries, Inc., Los Angeles, 1980-81, Dart & Kraft, Inc., Northbrook, Ill., 1981-86; chmn., chief exec. officer Premark Internat. Inc., Deerfield, 1986—. Trustee Art Inst. Chgo., 1983—, Children's Meml. Hosp., Chgo., 1984—, Chgo. Symphony Orch., 1986—, The Menninger Found., 1988—. Office: Premark Internat Inc 1717 Deerfield Ave Deerfield IL 60015

BATZ, DALE LEE, dietician, medical facility administrator; b. Michigan City, Ind., Aug. 6, 1959; s. Norman and Shirley Ann (Jordan) B.; m. Cynthia Kruger, Nov. 3, 1984. BS, Valparaiso U., 1981. Asst. foodservice dir. Chgo. Osteopathic Hosp. ARA, 1982-84, food service dir. Battle Creek (Mich.) Adventist Hosp., 1984-87, asst. dir. cash ops. U. Chgo. Hosp., 1987—. Asst. youth dir. St. Peter's Luth. Ch., Battle Creek, 1987. Mem. Am. Dietitic Assn. Home: 4160 Oakmont Ct Crown Point IN 46307 Office: Univ Chgo Hosp 5841 S Maryland Chicago IL 60637

BAUCOM, SIDNEY GEORGE, lawyer; b. Salt Lake City, Oct. 21, 1930; s. Sidney and Nora (Palfreyman) B.; m. Mary B., Mar. 5, 1954; children—Sidney, George, John. BS, JD, U. Utah, 1953. Bar: Utah 1953. Pvt. practice Salt Lake City, 1953-55; asst. city atty. Salt Lake City Corp., 1955-56; asst. atty. Utah Power and Light Co., Salt Lake City, 1956-60, asst. atty., asst. sec., 1960-62, atty., asst. sec., 1962-68, v.p., gen. counsel, 1968-75, sr. v.p., gen. counsel, 1975-79, exec. v.p., gen. counsel, 1979-89, dir., 1988—; of counsel Jones, Waldo, Holbrook & McDonough, Salt Lake City, 1989—; bd. dirs. Utah Power and Light Co., Salt Lake City. Past chmn. Utah Coordinating Coun. Devel. Svcs., Utah Taxpayers Assn.; past mem. Mayor's Coun. Capitol Improvements, Utah Hoover Commn., Airport Bond Commn. Mem. Alta Club, Lions, Phi Delta Phi. Mormon. Home: 2248 Logan Ave Salt Lake City UT 84108 Office: Jones Waldo Holbrook & McDonough 1500 First Interstate Bank Bldg 170 S Main Salt Lake City UT 84101

BAUER, DALE ROBERT, publisher; b. Evanston, Ill., June 10, 1928; s. Valentine H. and Lutie (Jacobsen) B.; m. Sheila Gregory, Feb. 1955 (div. Aug. 1982); children: Richard Gregory, Courtney Anne; m. Peggy Kent, June 1986. BS in Econs., U. Pa., 1954. Pub. Med. World News, N.Y.C., 1966-72; group pub., v.p. McGraw-Hill, Inc., N.Y.C., 1972-76; pres. Billboard Pub., N.Y.C., 1976-78; pres. Standard Rate & Data Service, Inc., Wilmette, Ill., 1978-85, chmn. bd., 1985-88; group v.p. Macmillan, Inc., N.Y.C., 1981-88; pres. Edgewater Mgmt., Inc., Essex, Conn., 1989—; bd. dirs. Gallatin Div., NYU; past bd. dirs. Assn. Bus. Press, Am. Mag. Assn., Analytics Communications System, Inc., Reston, Va., Mag. Pubs. Am. Served to lt. (j.g.) USNR, 1946-52, Korea. Republican. Episcopalian. Club: University (N.Y.C.). Office: Edgewater Mgmt Inc Box 489 Essex CT 06426

BAUER, DANIEL GEORGE, financial executive; b. Halifax, Can., Sept. 10, 1960; came to U.S., 1964.; s. Joseph John and Catherine Ann (Pickett) B.; m. Tina Maria Chiusano, Aug. 27, 1988. BBA, U. Toledo, 1982; MBA, Fordham U., 1988. M.i.s. computer operator Champion Spark Plug. Co, Toledo, 1979-82; fin. systems supr. Macmillan, Inc., N.Y.C., 1982-84; mgr. fin. planning CBS, Inc., N.Y.C., 1984-85; mgr. treasury, current assets AT&T Corp., Murray Hill, N.J., 1985—; researcher Fin. Cons. Firm, Toledo, 1985—. Vol. United Way Bergen County, N.J., 1984-85; active Ohio Hist. Soc., N.J. Hist. Soc., SBA. Recipient Small Bus Achievement award Kersher Elevator Co., 1982. Mem. Nat. Assn. Credit Mgmt. (chmn. fin. com. N.J. chpt. 1987-88), Nat. Corp. Cash Mgmt. Assn., Fin. Execs. Inst., Strategic Planning Inst. Republican. Roman Catholic. Home: 81 Wentworth Rd Bedminster NJ 07921 Office: AT&T Corp 430 Mountain Ave Murray Hill NJ 07974

BAUER, EDWARD GREB, JR., lawyer, utilities executive; b. Jeannette, Pa., Aug. 10, 1928; s. Edward Greb and Virginia (Euwer) B.; m. Carolyn Large Isbell, May 8, 1954; children: Charlotte Large, Barbara Greb, Edward Greb III. B.A., Princeton U., 1951; LL.B., Harvard U., 1957. Bar: Pa. 1958. Atty. Ballard, Spahr, Andrews & Ingersoll, Phila., 1957-62; exec. asst. to Mayor James H.J. Tate, Phila., 1962-63; city solicitor Phila., 1963-70; v.p., gen. counsel Phila. Electric Co., 1970-88, sr. v.p., gen. counsel, 1988—; dir. Susquehanna Power Co., Susquehanna Electric Co., Adwin Realty Co., Adwin Equipment Co., Continental Bank, Eastern Pa. Devel. Co.; Bd. dirs. Phila. Crime Commn. Served with USAF, 1951-54. Mem. ABA, Pa., Phila. bar assns. Clubs: Union League (Phila.); Boca Raton Hotel and Club. Home: 652 Creighton Rd Villanova PA 19085 Office: Phila Electric Co 2301 Market St S-23-1 Philadelphia PA 19101

BAUER, NANCY MCNAMARA, television and radio network executive; b. Madison, Wis., Mar. 17, 1929; d. Richard Hughes and Lucy Jane (Whitaker) Marshall; B.A., U. Wis., 1950, M.S., 1963; m. J.B. McNamara, Dec. 29, 1952 (div. Mar. 1962); children—Margaret Ann, William Patrick; m. 2d, Helmut Robert Bauer, Mar. 4, 1974. Elem. tchr., Madison, 1963-66; specialist ednl. communications U. Wis., Madison, 1966-71, asst. prof., 1971-72; dir. educative services Ednl. Communications Bd., Wis. Ednl. TV and Radio Networks, Madison, 1972—; dir. Central Ednl. Network, 1973-80, 83—, exec. com., 1973-74, chmn. Instructional TV Council, 1977-79; adv. bd. Instructional TV Coop., 1972-75, exec. com., 1976-77; mem. instrnl. radio adv. com. Nat. Public Radio, 1979-82; mem. instructional TV adv. com. Public Broadcasting System, 1978-79, service com., 1980-83; mem ITV Study com. Corp. for Pub. Broadcasting, 1983-85. Ford Found. scholar, 1961-63; recipient Ohio State award, 1975, ABA Gavel award, 1975, Am. Legion Golden Mike award, 1976. Mem. Nat. Assn. Ednl. Broadcasters. Producer, writer numerous instructional series, as nationally distributed Patterns in Arithmetic and Looking Out Is In, TV, 1967, Inquiry: The Justice Thing, radio, 1973. Home: 127 Kensington Dr Madison WI 53704 Office: 3319 W Beltline Hwy Madison WI 53713

BAUER, PAUL DAVID, corporation executive; b. Buffalo, July 25, 1943; s. Norman Thomas and Rita Ann (Maloney) B.; m. Donna Marie Szlosek, May 6, 1967 (dec.); children: David, Lisa. B.S., Boston Coll., 1965. Supervising sr. Peat, Marwick, Mitchell & Co. (CPAs), Buffalo, 1965-70; with Tops Markets, Inc., Buffalo, 1970—, treas., 1972—, v.p., 1976-82, sr. v.p., 1982-89, exec. v.p., 1989—; pres. Niassociates, Inc., Buffalo, 1973—. Former treas. Studio Theatre Sch., Buffalo; sec. bd. dirs. Amherst Hockey Assn., 1977; mem. council on accountancy Canisius Coll., 1980; mem. pres.'s council, trustee D'Youville Coll.; past bd. dirs. Jr. Achievement., YMCA of Buffalo and Erie County; mem. Bishop's Lay Adv. Council; trustee Christ the King Sem. Mem. Nat. Assn. Accountants, Fin. Execs. Inst. Clubs: Park Country (Buffalo); Youngstown Yacht. Home: 49 Oakview Dr Williamsville NY 14221 Office: Tops Markets Inc 60 Dingens St Buffalo NY 14206

BAUER, RAYMOND GALE, manufacturers representative; b. Merchantville, N.J., June 19, 1934; s. Robert Irwin and Florence Winifred (Guyer) B.; A.A., Monmouth Coll., West Long Branch, N.J., 1955; B.B.A., U. Miami, 1958; m. Jayne Whitehead, Feb. 15, 1955; 1 dau., Linda Joan. Div. mgr. R.J. Reynolds Tobacco Co., Winston-Salem, N.C., 1959-68; Middle Atlantic mgr. U.S. Envelope Co., Springfield, Mass., 1968-74; div. sales mgr. Eastern Tablet Corp., Albany, N.Y., 1974-75; owner Ray Bauer Assos., mfrs. reps., Haddonfield, N.J., 1975—. Served with USAFR, 1959-64; officer Air Force Aux. Mem. Friends of Haddonfield (N.J.) Library, Haddonfield Civic Assn., Smithsonian Assos., Monmouth Coll., U. Miami alumni assns., Nat. Philatelic Soc., Am. Security Council, Air Force Assn., Am. Conservative Union, Am. Mgmt. Assn., Internat. Platform Assn., Lambda Sigma Tau, Lambda Chi Alpha. Clubs: Republican (Haddonfield), U.S. Senatorial, Arrowhead Racquet, Iron Rock Swim and Country. Home and Office: 132 Maple Ave Haddonfield NJ 08033

BAUER, THADDEUS, marketing executive; b. Worcester, Mass., Apr. 21, 1952; s. Roman and Krystyna (Sierak) B.; m. Jo Ann Mary, Aug. 3, 1974; children: Cristina, Andrew. AA, Worcester Jr. Coll., 1972; BSBA, Nichols Coll., 1974. Customer service coordinator Reed Roller Thread Die Co., Holden, Mass., 1976-79; customer service mgr. Presmet Corp., Worcester, 1979-80, sales engr., 1980-82, mgr. dist. sales, 1982-83, mgr. sales, 1983-86, dir. sales and mktg., 1986—. Treas. Henshaw Voters Assn., Leicester, Mass., 1986. Com. to Elect Ruth Kaminski, Leicester, 1988. Mem. Am. Powder Metallurgy Inst., Am. Soc. Metals. Club: Sales Execs. of Worcester. Home: 308 Henshaw St Leicester MA 01524

BAUERLE, TODD ALEX, financial planner; b. Auburn, N.Y., Mar. 27, 1960; s. Alexander and Barbara Ann (Wheeler) B.; m. Susan Taylor, Nov. 27, 1982; 1 child, Alexandria Sinclair Bauerle. BS in Aviation Mgmt., Embry-Riddle Aeronaut. U., 1982. Project adminstr. Embry-Riddle U., Daytona Beach, Fla., 1982-83; instructional designer Creativision, Inc., Holly Hill, Fla., 1983-84; fin. planner Bauerle Fin. Group, DeLand, Fla., 1984—. Mem. Nat. Assn. Life Underwriters, Internat. Assn. Fin. Planners, Rotary (bd. dirs. 1984). Home: 150 Shady Branch Trail De Land FL 32724 Office: Bauerle Fin Group 505 E New York Ave De Land FL 32724

BAUGE, CYNTHIA WISE, distributing company executive; b. Ottumwa, Iowa, Sept. 7, 1943; d. Donald Carlyle and Opal Dorthea (Douglas) W.; m. Harry Grant Bauge, May 1, 1965; 1 child, Melissa Anne. Student Iowa State U., 1962-64, Area XI Community Coll., Ankeny 1974-75. Legal sec. City of Ames, Iowa, 1965-69; acctg. mgr. Vivan Equipment Co., Ames, Iowa, 1969; asst. mgr. Bavarian Motor Lodge, Des Moines, 1969-71; bookkeeper TCP of Iowa, Des Moines, 1971-72, Moffitt Bldg Material co., Des Moines, 1972-73, CS Capital/Mid Am Growth Corp., West Des Moines, 1973-75; v.p. Grant Sales Inc., Plano, Tex., 1976—. Bd. dirs. Power, Allen, Tex., 1985-88, chmn. bd. dirs., 1986-88; bd. dirs. Cultural Arts Coun. of Plano, 1985-88, treas., 1986-87, v.p. classics, 1985-86; bd. dirs. North Tex. Rehab. Svcs., 1987—; adv. bd. Jr. League of Plano, 1988—; community bd. Physicians for Plano, 1988—. Mem. NAFE, Women's Div. C. of C. Plano (treas. 1981-82), Plano C. of C. (budget and fin. com., Athena/Bus. Woman of Yr. award 1986), Beta Sigma Phi. Republican. Lutheran. Avocations: home decorating, gaming. Office: Grant Sales Inc 1701 Capital Ave Plano TX 75074

BAUGH, COY FRANKLIN, corporate executive; b. Mt. Vernon, Ark., Feb. 7, 1946; s. Oather Lee Baugh and Eula Faye (Barnett) Baugh King; m. Cheryl Ann Linscott; 1 child, David F. AA, Glendale Coll., 1969; BS, Calif. State U., 1971; postgrad., Cornell U., 1978—. Sr. tax specialist Ernst & Winney, 1971-74; audit supr. Amfac, Inc., San Francisco, 1974-77, v.p., treas., 1984—; controller Fisher Cheese, Inc., Wapakoneta, Ohio, 1977-80, v.p. fin., 1980-84. Clubs: Treasurers (San Francisco) (sec., treas. 1987, v.p. 1988). Office: Amfac Inc PO Box 7813 San Francisco CA 94120

BAUGH, JOHN FRANK, wholesale company executive; b. Waco, Tex., Feb. 28, 1916; s. John Frank and Nell (Turner) B.; m. Eula Mae Tharp, Oct. 3, 1936; 1 child, Barbara (Mrs. Robert L. Morrison). Student, U. Houston, 1934-36. With A & P Food Stores, Houston, 1932-46; owner, operator Zero Foods Co., Houston, 1946-69; chmn. bd. Sysco Corp., Houston, 1969-85, sr. chmn. bd., 1986—; adv. dir. 1st City Nat. Bank of Houston; bd. dirs. Bank of Houston. Bd. dirs. Baptist Found. Tex.; founding trustee Houston Bapt. U.; chmn. deacons Bapt. Ch., Houston, 1954-55, chmn. bd. trustees, 1966-86; trustee Baylor U. Clubs: University, Petroleum, Lakeside Country (Houston); Quail Creek Country (San Marcos). Lodge: Rotary. Office: Sysco Corp 1390 Enclave Pkwy Houston TX 77077

BAUGH, LYNDA LOUISE, real estate company executive; b. Riverside, Calif., Apr. 15, 1962; d. Perry Dean and Sandra Louise (Macek) B. Student, Belmont Coll., 1980, Phillips Bus. Coll., 1981-82. Owner, pres. Reel Time Recording Co., Houston and Nashville, 1982-84; pvt. practice acctg. Nashville, 1985; real estate agt. About Town, Inc., Nashville, 1986-87, Faxon Homes, Nashville, 1987-89; real estate sales & mktg. Phillips Builders Inc, Nashville, 1989—. Fund raiser Bullshooters, Nashville, 1986—; pres. beautification Percy Priest Woods Homeowners, Nashville, 1987—. Mem. NAFE, Nashville Bd. Realtors (chmn. community svcs. 1988). Roman Catholic. Home: PO Box 201 Brentwood TN 37024-0201

BAUKNIGHT, CLARENCE BROCK, wholesale and retail company executive; b. Anderson, S.C., May 14, 1936; s. John Edward and Theodosia (Brock) B.; m. Harriet League, June 29, 1959; children: Harriet League, Clarence Brock. B.S., Ga. Inst. Tech., 1958. Dist. mgr. Wickes Corp., and predecessor, Atlanta, 1960-65; exec. v.p. Builder Marts Am., Inc., Greenville, S.C., 1965-70, pres., chief exec. officer, 1970-87; chmn. bd. dirs., pres. Builder Marts Am., Inc., 1987-88; chmn. bd. dirs., chief econ. officer Builderway, Inc., Enterprise Computer Systems, Inc. Mem. policy adv. bd. Joint Ctr. Urban Studies Harvard U., 1984-88; trustee Greenville Hosp. System, Bumcombe St. United Meth. Ch., 1985— (chmn. 1989). Mem. Chief Exec. Orgn., World Bus. Council, Phi Delta Theta. Methodist. Clubs: Greenville Country; Poinsett (Greenville); Wildcat Cliffs, Highlands Country (Highlands, N.C.), Cullasaja. Lodges: Masons, Shriners. Home: 111 Rockingham Rd Greenville SC 29607 Office: Builder Marts Am PO Box 47 Greenville SC 29602

BAUM, ALLYN ZELTON, magazine editor, writer; b. Chgo., Oct. 22, 1924; s. Moses and Effie Florence (Kaufman) B. BJ, Northwestern U., 1948. Gen. mgr., bur. chief Internat. News Photo Service, Berlin and Paris, 1948-50; gen. mgr. United Press Photos, Berlin and Frankfürt, Fed. Republic Germany, 1950-52; photo editor The Am. Daily, London, 1953-54; assoc. editor Coronet mag., N.Y.C., 1955-57; staff photographer The New York Times, N.Y.C., 1957-67; sr. editor Med. Econs. mag., Oradell, N.J., 1967—. Author: The Worst Place in the World, 1965, Glove Compartment Guide to Car Care, 1973; photography represented in permanent collections Mus. Modern Art, Met. Mus. Art, Eastman House. Sgt. USAAF, 1943-46. Recipient 21 N.Y. Times Pub.'s Awards, Jesse Neal award Am. Book Pubs. Assn., 1972, other awards for photography. Mem. Internat. Motor Press Assn., Players Club (N.Y.C.), Silurians. Unitarian. Home: 425 E 51st St Apt 2-E New York NY 10022 Office: Med Econs 680 Kinderkamack Rd Oradell NJ 07649

BAUM, HERBERT MERRILL, food company executive; b. Chgo., Dec. 6, 1936; s. Jack William and Ruth Frances (Ginsburg) B.; m. Diane Jean Kale, Nov. 1, 1975 (div. Sept. 1977); m. Karen Rochelle Oberman, Dec. 22, 1983. BSBA, Drake U., 1958. Account exec. Stern, Walters & Simmons, Chgo., 1962-66, Doyle, Dane, Bernbach, Chgo., 1966-69; v.p., account dir. Needham, Harper & Steers, Chgo., 1969-78; assoc. dir., dir. new products Campbell Soup Co., Camden, N.J., 1978, v.p. mktg., 1978-84, exec. v.p. U.S. Div., 1984-85; pres. Campbell USA, Camden, 1985—, sr. v.p., 1986—; bd. dirs. Chem. Bank N.J.; trustee Cooper Hosp., Camden, 1981—, Rider Coll., Lawrenceville, N.J., 1986—. Bd. dirs. Nat. Hispanic U., Oakland, Calif., 1987—, Advt. Coun. Inc., N.Y., Advt. Edn. Found., Coun. Better Bus. Burs., Washington; chmn. Media/Advt. Partnership Drug Free Am., N.Y.C., 1986—. With U.S. Army, 1958-59. Mem. Assn. Nat. Advertisers (bd. dir. 1982—, chmn. 1985-86), Am. Mgmt. Assn., Union League. Home: 910 Chanticleer Cherry Hill NJ 08003 Office: Campbell Soup Co Campbell Pl Camden NJ 08101

BAUM, JOHN ROBERT, architectural woodwork manufacturing company executive; b. Harrisburg, Pa., Aug. 11, 1942; s. John Harry and Virginia Hale B.; B.S., Lehigh U., 1964; M.B.A., Northwestern U., 1966; m. Jo Ann Snyder; children—Robin Hale, Edward Erich. Pres., owner J.R. Baum, Inc., Hanover, Pa., 1967-77; bus. broker Gaugher-Letham, Camp Hill, Pa., 1978-79; pres. Ivan C. Dutterer, Inc., Hanover, 1979—; dir. First Fed. Savs. & Loan, Hanover, Blue Shield of Pa., Camp Hill, Pa., Commonwealth Communications Services, Inc., Harrisburg. Bd. dirs. Hanover Pub. Sch. Dist. Mem. Archtl. Woodwork Inst. Home: 404 Dart Dr Hanover PA 17331 Office: Ivan C Dutterer Inc 115 Ann St Hanover PA 17331

BAUM, RICHARD THEODORE, engineering company executive; b. N.Y.C., Oct. 3, 1919. BA, Columbia U., 1940, BS, 1941, MS, 1948. Registered profl. engr. Nat. Bur. Engring. Registration, N.Y., D.C., 20 other states. Engr. Electric Boat Co., Groton, Conn., 1941-43; with Jaros, Baum & Bolles, N.Y.C., 1946—, ptnr., 1958-86, ptnr. emeritus, cons. to firm, 1986—; mem. adv. council, faculty of engring. and applied sci. Columbia U., N.Y.C., 1972—. Served to 1st lt. USAAF, 1943-46. Egleston medalist Columbia U., 1985. Fellow Am. Cons. Engrs. Council, ASME, ASHRAE; mem. Nat. Acad. Engring., NSPE, Nat. Soc. Energy Engrs., Nat. Research Council (chmn. bd. bldg. research bd.), Am. Arbitration Assn. (panel of arbitrators 1973—), Council on Tall Bldgs. and Urban Habitat (vice chmn. N.Am. chpt., mem. steering group). Club: Univ. (N.Y.C.). Office: Jaros Baum & Bolles 345 Park Ave New York NY 10154

BAUMAN, EARL WILLIAM, accountant, government official; b. Arcadia, Nebr., Jan. 30, 1916; s. William A. and Gracia M. (Jones) B.; B.S. with honors, U. Wyo., 1938; postgrad. Northwestern U., 1938-39; m. Margaret E. Blackman, Oct. 21, 1940 (dec. 1984); children—Carol Ann Bauman Ammerman. Earl William Jr. Acct., Haselmire, Cordle & Co., Casper, Wyo., 1939-42; asst. dir. fin. VA, Chgo., 1946-49, chief acctg. group VA, Washington, 1949-52, supr. systems acctg. GAO, Washington, 1952-55; supervising auditor GAO, Washington, 1955-58; dir. finance, asst. dir. Directorate Acctg. and Fin. Policy, Office Asst. Sec. Def., Washington, 1958-63; tech. asst. to comdr. AF Acctg. and Fin. Ctr., Denver, 1963-73; mem. investigations staff Ho. of Reps. Appropriations Com., 1953-54; prof. acctg. Benjamin Franklin U., 1960-63; mem. exec. council Army Finance, 1963-64; dir. Real Estate Investment Corp., 1962-64; sr. ptnr. EMB Enterprises, 1973—; chmn. Acctg. Careers Council Colo., 1969-71. Chmn. Aurora Citizens Adv. Budget Com., 1975-76; chmn. fin. and taxation com. Denver Met. Study, 1976-78. Served with AUS, 1942-46; col. Res., now ret. C.P.A. Mem. AICPA, Wyo. Assn. C.P.A.s, Fed. Govt. Accts. Assn. (nat. v.p. 1972-73, pres. Denver 1973-74), Army Finance Assn., Am. Soc. Mil. Comptrollers, Denver Am. Soc. Mil. Comptrollers (pres. 1968-69), Citizens Band Radio Assn. (pres. 1963), Nat. Assn. Ret. Fed. Employees (Aurora 1072 pres. 1986-87), Alpha Kappa Psi, Beta Alpha Psi, Phi Kappa Phi. Club: Columbine Sertoma (pres. 1975-76). Avocations: photography, tennis, collector cars. Home: 536 Newark Ct Aurora CO 80010

BAUMAN, JACK C., manufacturing executive; b. Dobbsferry, N.Y., Feb. 22, 1926; s. Charles A. and Martha (Suter) B.; m. Constance Morman, Mar. 1955 (div. Oct. 1973); children: Lynn, Jennifer, Sara; m. Carol Jean Dufour, Aug. 2, 1974; children: Lisa, Tracey. BA in English, Colgate U., 1950; AMP, Harvard U., 1972. Mktg. mgr. Union Camp Corp., Wayne, N.J., 1962-63, asst. to exec. v.p., 1963-66, gen. mgr. Honeycomb div., 1966-70, gen. mgr. bag div., 1970-78; pres. PCL Packaging Inc., Remington, Va., 1978-82; cons. Charlottesville, Va., 1982-84; gen. mgr. Bigelow Packaging Inc., Greenville, S.C., 1984—. Bd. dirs. United Way Ridgewood N.J., 1968, Boy Scouts Am., Chgo, 1960; regional dir. Civil Def. Adminstrn. LaGrange Park, Ill., 1960-61. Served as sgt. USMC, 1944-46, PTO. Republican. Presbyterian. Home: 10 Parkins Pl Greenville SC 29607 Office: Bigelow Packaging Inc PO Box 2740 Greenville SC 29602

BAUMANN, FRED WILLIAM, paper company executive; b. Lexington, Ky., May 27, 1945; s. Frederick William and Elizabeth P. (Goetz) B.; m. Mitchell Ann Ward, Jan. 25, 1974; children: Hilary Mitchell, Margaret Elizabeth, Ryan Frederick. BBA, Western Ky. U., 1968. pres. Regency Group, Lexington, 1985—; bd. dirs. United Group, Monroe, La. Salesman Baumann Paper Co., Inc., Lexington, 1971-79, v.p., 1974, pres., 1979, chmn. Bd., 1982—. Sgt. U.S. Army, 1969-70, Vietnam. Decorated Bronze Star. Mem. Ky. Hotel and Motel Assn. (Disting. Svc. award). Democrat. Home: 198 Juniper Dr Versailles KY 40383 Office: Baumann Paper Co Inc 1601 Baumann Dr Lexington KY 40512

BAUMANN, KURT DAVID, software company executive; b. Pittsfield, Ill., June 15, 1959; s. William R. and Beverly A. (Ionson) B.; m. Michaela M. Barry, Oct. 31, 1985. Student, U. Ill., 1978-81. Programmer U. Ill., Champaign, 1979-82; microprogrammer Duosoft Inc., Champaign, Ill., 1981-83; software mgr. Continuous Learning Corp., Cambridge, Mass., 1983-84; pres., chief exec. officer Learning Tree Software Inc, Reston, Va., 1984-89; pres. InterCon Corp., Reston, 1988—; cons. AT&T Info. Systems, Freehold, N.J., 1984-86, MAC Assist, Reston, 1988—. Author ESL software programs for Spanish speakers, physics software games. Mem. EDUCOM, AFNORD (bd. dirs.), Assn. for Computing Machinery, IEEE, Soc. Mfg. Engrs. Home: 4 Pheasant Run Sterling VA 22170 Office: InterCon Systems Corp 64950 Community Pla Sterling VA 22170

BAUMANN, RONALD EDWIN, real estate executive, chemical company executive; b. Oak Park, Ill., Aug. 31, 1933; s. Edwin Walter and Sylvia J. (Zak) B. Student, Va. Mil. Inst., 1951-52; BS, Northwestern U., 1955. Mgmt. trainee Marshall Field and Co., Chgo., 1955-56; pres. C&B Devel. Corp., West Milford, N.J., 1960-75; with land acquisition dept. Union Carbide Corp., N.Y.C., 1963-69, mgr. spl. projects, 1970-75, nat. mgr. bldgs. and site svcs., 1975-83; dir. corp. real estate Union Carbide Corp., Danbury, Conn., 1984—; bd. dirs. Personal Computer Techs. Group Inc., Danbury. Mem. Somers (N.Y.) Archtl. Bd., 1985—. Commd. USAF, 1956-59. Mem. Nat. Assn. Corp. Real Estate Execs. (pres. Fairfield, Conn.-Westchester, N.Y. chpt. 1987-89), Indsl. Devel. Rsch. Council, Urban Land Inst. Republican. Presbyterian. Home: 198 Heritage Hills Dr Somers NY 10589

BAUMGARTNER, ALLAN RODNEY, computer company executive; b. N.Y.C., May 27, 1938; s. John Herbert and Claire Regina (Strobele) B.; B.S., Carnegie Inst. Tech., 1960; m. Dolores Zalewski, Dec. 4, 1975; children—Yvette Selena, Brendon Allan Hans. Product mgr. Westinghouse Electric Corp., Sunnyvale, Calif., 1966-67, data processing devel. mgr., 1967-71; data communications designer Pacific Telephone Co., San Francisco, 1971-74, internal cons., 1974-78; cons. to advanced communications system AT&T, Morristown, N.J., 1976-77; dir. tech. strategy Nat. Semicondr. Corp., San Diego, 1979-80, dir. software mktg. subs. Nat. Advanced Systems, Inc., Mountain View, Calif., 1980-83, pres. Gyrus Systems Corp., San Diego, 1983-84; v.p. sales and mktg. System Specialists and Cons., 1984-86; pres. Internat. Computer Contracting Corp., San Jose, Calif., 1986—; IBM analyst Dataquest, San Jose, 1987—; cons. mgmt. data processing, Data Quest Inc., 1987—. Capt. C.E., U.S. Army, 1960-65. Mem. Data Processing Mgmt. Assn., IEEE, Assn. Data Processing Service Orgns. Republican. Home: 4221 Quimby Rd San Jose CA 95148 Office: Internat Computer Contracting Corp 1758 G Junction Ave San Jose CA 95112

BAUMHART, RAYMOND CHARLES, university president; b. Chgo., Dec. 22, 1923; s. Emil and Florence (Weidner) B. BS, Northwestern U., 1945; PhL, Loyola U., 1952, STL, 1958; MBA, Harvard U., 1953; DBA, Harvard, 1963; LLD (hon.), Ill. Coll.; DHL (hon.), Scholl Coll. Podiatric Medicine, Rush U., Chgo. Joined Jesuit Order, 1946; ordained priest Roman Cath. Ch., 1957. Asst. prof. mgmt. Loyola U., Chgo., 1962-64, dean Sch. Bus. Adminstrn., 1964-66, exec. v.p., acting v.p. Med. Ctr., 1968-70, pres. of univ., 1970—; dir. Jewel Cos., Inc., Continental Ill. Corp. Author: An Honest Profit, 1968, (with Thomas Garrett) Cases in Business Ethics, 1968, (with Thomas McMahon) The Brewer-Wholesaler Relationship, 1969; corr. editor: America, 1965-70. Trustee Boston Coll., 1968-71, St. Louis U., 1967-72; bd. dirs. Coun. Better Bus. Burs., 1971-77, Cath. Health Alliance Met. Chgo., from 1986; mem. U.S. Bishops and Pres.'s Com. on Higher Edn., 1980-84, Jobs for Met. Chgo., 1984-85. Lt. (j.g.) USNR, 1944-46. Decorated Order of Cavalier Italy; recipient Râle medallion Boston Coll.; John W. Hill fellow Harvard U., 1961-62, Cambridge Ctr. for Social Studies rsch. fellow, 1966-68. Mem. Assn. Jesuit Colls. and Univs. (bd. dirs.), Fedn. Ind. Ill. Colls. and Univs. (bd. dirs.), Comml. Club, Econ. Club, Mid-Am. Club. Home: 6525 N Sheridan Rd Chicago IL 60626

BAUMWOLL, JOEL PHILIP, advertising and public relations executive; b. Bronx, N.Y., May 22, 1940; s. Harold and Marie (Vascovitz) B.; m. Ellen May Wolberg, June 20, 1963; children: Lisa Quincy, Michael Wolberg. BA, Fairleigh Dickinson U., 1962; postgrad. in clin. and social psychology U. Mich., 1963; postgrad. in social psychology NYU, 1964. V.p., dir. ops. Queen Applied Research Co., N.Y.C., 1962-66; v.p., assoc. dir. research Grey Advt. Inc., N.Y.C., 1966-72; sr. v.p. in charge research, planning J. Walter Thompson Co., N.Y.C., 1972-76, sr. v.p., group account dir., 1978-80, exec. v.p. mktg., 1980; pres. N.Y. div. Needham, Harper & Steers, Inc., 1980-84; vice chmn. Needham, Harper & Steers USA, 1982-85; pres. Joel Baumwoll Assocs., Inc., 1985—; mng. ptnr. Baumwoll & Tannen Assocs. Inc., 1985—; trustee Market Sci. Inst., 1972-75. Trustee Walden Sch., 1977-83, Post Grad. Ctr. Mental Health, 1977—. Mem. Market Research Council, Copy Research Council, Advt. Research Found., Am. Mktg. Assn. (bd. dirs. N.Y. chapter), Pub. Info. Council, Am. Cancer Soc. (dir.). Home: 144 W 86th St New York NY 10024 Office: 540 Madison Ave New York NY 10022

BAUSHER, VERNE C(HARLES), banker; b. Reading, Pa.; s. La Verne H. and Helen M. (Dornes) B.; m. Sandra Stamm Bausher, May 20, 1965; children: Christopher S., Gretchen S., Samantha A., Andrew P. BS, Drexel U., 1961; MBA, Northwestern U., 1962. Asst. v.p. Cen. Nat. Bank of Cleve., 1962-69; v.p. Meridian Bank (formerly American Bank and Trust Co. of Pa.), Reading, 1969-83; exec. v.p. Penn Savs. Bank, Wyomissing, 1983-87; exec. v.p., chief lending officer Germantown Savs. Bank, Bala Cynwyd, Pa., 1987—. Trustee, v.p. Pub. Edn. Found. for Berks County, 1986—; trustee, treas. Burn Found. of NE and East Pa., 1987—; bd. dirs. Wilson Sch. Dist., West Lawn, Pa., 1977—, Berks County Intermediate Unit, Reading, 1977—, YMCA of Reading, 1987—. Republican. Lutheran. Home: 1502 Whitfield Blvd Reading PA 19609 Office: Germantown Savs Bank City Line and Belmont Aves Bala-Cynwyd PA 19004

BAVOSO, WILLIAM DAVID, lawyer; b. Passaic, N.J., Nov. 3, 1946; s. William Joseph and Katherine (Patrisso) B.; m. Sharon Ann Hillman, Aug. 30, 1969; children: Amy R., Katherine E., David W., John C. BS, U. Fla., 1968; JD, St. John's U., 1971. Ptnr. Bavoso, Fox & Coffill, Port Jervis, N.Y., 1971—; atty. City of Port Jervis, Port Jervis City Sch. Dist., Port Jervis Indsl. Devel. Agy., Norstar Bank, Middletown Savs. Bank, Arcs Mortgage Inc., Bank of N.Y., Key Bank, Mchts. Bank, Hawley, Pa., Port Jervis Community Devl. Agy., Port Jervis Devel. Corp., Town of Greenville, N.Y., Town of Deerpark (N.Y.) Planning Bd., Town of Lumberland (N.Y.) Planning and Zoning Bd.; mem. adv. bd. Mercy Community Hosp., United Penn Bank. Elder 1st Presbyn. Ch. Port Jervis; mem. Port Jervis Zoning Commn. Served to capt. U.S. Army, 1968. Mem. N.Y. State Bar Assn., Fla. Bar Assn., Pa. Bar Assn., Orange County (N.J.) Bar Assn., Minisink Valley Hist. Soc. (bd. dirs.). Democrat. Office: Bavoso Fox & Coffill 19 E Main St Port Jervis NY 12771

BAXENDELL, SIR PETER (BRIAN), transportation and trading executive; b. Runcorn, Eng., Feb. 28, 1925; s. Leslie Wilfred Edward and Evelyn Mary (Gaskin) B.; m. Rosemary Lacey, 1949; children: Anne, Gillian, Peter, John. BSc, ARSM, Royal Sch. Mines, London; DSc (hon.), Heriot-Watt U., Queen's U. Belfast, U. London, U. Tech. Loughborough. With Royal Dutch/Shell Group, 1946—, mng. dir. Shell-BP Nigeria, 1969-72, mng. dir. Royal Dutch/Shell Group, London, 1973-85, chmn. Shell U.K., 1974-79; chmn. Shell Transport & Trading Co. PLC, 1979-85, also bd. dirs.; chmn. Shell Can. Ltd., 1980-85; dir. Shell Oil Co., U.S.A., 1982-85, Shell Transport & Trading Co. PLC, 1973—, Hawker Siddeley Group PLC, 1984—, chmn. 1986—, Inchcape PLC, 1986—; bd. dirs. Sun Life Assurance Co. Can. Decorated comdr. Order Brit. Empire, 1972, Knight bachelor, 1981, Comdr. Order Orange-Nassau, 1985; fellow Imperial Coll. Sci. and Tech. Fellow Inst. Petroleum, Fellowship Engring., Inst. Mining and Metallurgy. Address: Shell Ctr, London SE1 7NA, England Office: Hawker Siddeley Group Pub, Ltd, 18 St James's Sq, London SW1Y 6DG, England

BAXTER, DONALD EUGENE, financial planner; b. Lamar, Mo., Aug. 6, 1951; s. Helen (Schwalje) B.; m. Diane Kay Dickey, Jan. 2, 1970; children: Michelle, Justin. Student, Rockhurst Coll., Kansas City, Mo., 1970-71; AA, Longview Community Coll., Lee's Summit, Mo., 1973; BA, U. Mo., 1976. CLU; cert. fin. planner. Agt. New Eng. Life Ins. Co., St. Louis, 1976-79, 81-82, Home Life N.Y., Clayton, Mo., 1979-81; pres. Donald E. Baxter, Inc., Wichita, Kans., 1982—, Profl. Svc. Corp., Wichita, 1982-85, Westlake Securities Inc., Agoura Hills, Calif., 1983-84, Tital Capital Corp., Tustin, Calif., 1984-85, Primeline Fin. Group, Wichita, 1985—. County dir. Election Com. for Emerson for Congress, Rolla, Mo., 1982; trustee Christ in Youth, Joplin, Mo., 1985—. Mem. Wichita Cert. Fin. Planners (sec. 1986-87, program chmn. 1987-88), Ozark Life Underwriters (treas. 1980-81, program chmn. 1981-82), Adminstrv. Mgmt. Soc. (mktg. com. 1986-87). Republican. Office: Primeline Fin Group 224 E Douglas St Ste 100 Wichita KS 67202

BAXTER, FRED EDWIN, JR., lawyer; b. Pitts., Sept. 13, 1943; s. Fred Edwin and Jeanne Lynn (Galbreth) B.; m. Carolyn Wilson, June 17, 1967; children: Fred Edwin III, Nicole Marie. BA, Muskingum Coll., 1965; JD, Ohio No. U., 1968. Bar: Pa. Supreme Ct 1969, U.S. Ct. Appeals (3rd cir.) Pa. 1976, Fed. Dist. Ct. 1972, U.S. Supreme Ct. 1982. Atty. Allegheny County Pub. Defender, Pitts., 1969-72; assoc. Gondelman & Baxter, Pitts., 1972-88, Grogan, Graffam, McGinley & Lucchino, Pitts., 1988—; bd. dirs. Astrotech Internat., Inc., Pitts. Mem. Ross Twp. Planning Commn., Pitts., 1972-75, Ross Twp. Zoning Bd., 1975-78. 1st lt. U.S. Army, 1968-74. Mem. ABA, Pa. Bar Assn., Assn. Trial Lawyers Am., Pa. Borough Solicitors Assn., Pa. Mcpl. Authorities Assn., Highland Country Club. Office: Grogan Graffam McGinley and Lucchino 3 Gateway Ctr 22d Fl Pittsburgh PA 15222

BAXTER, RALPH FELIX, chemical company executive; b. Hamburg, Germany, Aug. 31, 1925; came to U.S., 1941, naturalized, 1944; s. Felix and Irmy (Münden) B.; m. Janice Phillips, 1960; children: David P., Eric F., Robert. Student, Rensselaer Poly. Inst., 1943-44, UCLA, 1946-48; B.S. in Mech. Engring, U. Calif.-Berkeley, 1949. Asso. Gen. Air Conditioning Corp., 1949-50; group project mgr. Rheem Mfg. Co., 1950-56; asst. to pres., dir. mfg. Revell, Inc., 1956-59; with Hunt Foods & Industries, Inc., 1959-67, dir. corp. planning. gen. mgr. ops. v.p. ops., 1959-64, v.p. corp. planning and analysis, 1964-67; sr. v.p. Avery Internat. Inc., Marino, Calif., 1967—; instr. div. extension UCLA, 1959-60; pres. So. Calif. Industry Edn. Council, 1971-73; v.p. Industry Edn. Council of Calif., 1973-81. Mem. White House Fellowship Commn., 1979-81. Served with AUS, 1943-46. Mem. Inst. Mgmt. Scis. (nat. chmn. coll. on planning 1966-68), Am. Arbitration Assn., Nat. Panel Arbitrators, Am. Ordnance Assn. (Walsh Meml. award 1953), Calif. Mfrs. Assn. (dir. 1981-88, vice chmn. 1988—). Home: 1263 N Citrus Dr La Habra CA 90631 Office: Avery Internat Corp 150 N Orange Grove Blvd Pasadena CA 91103

BAXTER, ROBERT HENRY, software executive; b. Jersey City, June 1, 1940; s. Robert H. and Dorothy M. (Garrison) B.; m. Doris E. Rush, Oct. 4, 1977 (div. 1986); children: Christine, Kelly, Sean. BS, USAF Acad., 1962; MA, Oxford U., Eng., 1964; grad., Royal Coll. Def. Studies, Eng., 1979. Commd. 2d lt. USAF, 1962, advanced through grades to brig. gen., 1984; served as aide to chief of staff USAF hdqrs., Pentagon, Washington, 1974-77; dep. comdr. ops. 52d Tactical Fighter W5 USAF, Spangdahlem, Fed. Republic Germany, 1978; dir. fighter ops. hqrs. Europe USAF, Ramsteon, Fed. Republic Germany, 1979-80; comdr. 31st Tactical Fighter Wing, Langley AFB, Va., 1981-82; dir. programs USAF hqrs., Pentagon, 1984-85; ret. USAF, 1985; sr. v.p. Nat. Guardian Corp., Greenwich, Conn., 1985-87; pres., chief exec. officer Ins. Software Systems Inc., Tarrytown, N.Y., 1987—, also bd. dirs. Contbr. articles to profl. jours. Rhodes scholar, 1962; White House fellow, 1972. Mem. White House Fellows Assn., Assn. Am. Rhodes Scholars, USAF Assn. Office: Ins Software Systems Inc 120 White Plains Rd Tarrytown NY 19591

BAXTER, TURNER BUTLER, independent oil operator; b. Dermott, Ark., Mar. 13, 1922; s. Robert Wiley and Sallie Hollis (Murphy) B.; BBA, U. Tex., 1947; MBA, Pepperdine U., L.A., 1976; m. Pauline Taylor Bond, June 7, 1947; children—David Bond, Paula Taylor. With Rio Grande Nat. Life Ins. Co., Dallas, 1947-67, sr. v.p., 1963-67; engaged in investments, 1967-75, 79—; ind. oil operator, 1979—; pres. Shelby Office Supply Inc., Dallas, 1975-79. Pres. Dallas Health and Sci. Mus., 1953-56; adv. bd. Dallas Community Chest Trust Fund, 1976—; v.p. Circle Ten council Boy Scouts Am., 1970-74. With USAAF, 1943-46. Recipient Silver Beaver award Boy Scouts Am., 1968. Mem. Salesmanship Club Dallas. Methodist. Clubs: Kiwanis (pres. 1966), Dallas Country, Petroleum (Dallas). Home: Rte 4 Box 304 Kaufman TX 75142 Office: PO Box 620 Kaufman TX 75142-0620

BAYARDI, ELIZABETH AUDREY, health care administrator; b. Valley Stream, N.Y., Sept. 7, 1948; d. James Robert and Audrey (Pierce) Boerckel; m. Armand Bayardi, Oct. 30, 1971; children: Adrian, Julia. BA cum laude, Middlebury Coll., 1970; MBA, Boston U., 1982. Service advisor N.Y. Telephone Co., N.Y.C., 1971-74; mgr. patient access systems Harvard Community Health Plan, Boston, 1974-76; asst. adminstr. Harvard Community Health Plan, Cambridge, Mass., 1976-80; regional health ctr. adminstr. Harvard Community Health Plan, Wellesley, Mass., 1980-84; exec. v.p. Meml. Health Plan, Worcester, Mass., 1984-86; pres., chief exec. officer Health Ins. Plan of N.J., Medford, 1986—. Singer Chorus pro Musica, Boston, 1974-86, Princeton, N.J., 1986—; trustee Germaine Lawrence Sch., Arlington, Mass., 1984-86, chair devel. com., 1986. Mem. Phi Beta Kappa. Democrat. Quaker. Home: 544 Pineville Rd Upper Makefield PA 18940 Office: Health Ins Plan NJ 100 Horizon Blvd Robbinsville NJ 08691

BAYAT, ARSALAN, health science facility administrator; b. Tehran, Iran, Jan. 10, 1960; came to U.S., 1976; s. Ardashir Bayat and Badri Merat; m. Gerry Dawn Towle, May 24, 1980. BS, Ft. Hays State U., 1981. Acct. Schatz, Fletcher & Assocs., Augusta, Maine, 1981-83; auditor exec. dept. State of Maine, Augusta, 1983-84; chief fin. officer Coastal Econ. Devel., Bath, Maine, 1984-85; account mgr. Sebasticook Valley Hosp., Pittsfield, Maine, 1985-87; asst. adminstr. Down East Community Hosp., Machias, Maine, 1987—; cons. Pittsfield, 1985-87. Mem. Healthcare Fin. Mgmt. Assn., Jaycees (internal v.p. Augusta chpt. 1982, v.p. fin. 1983). Moslem. Home: PO Box 472 Machias ME 04654 Office: Down East Community Hosp RR PO Box 11 Machias ME 04654

BAYBAYAN, RONALD ALAN, lawyer; b. Paia, Hawaii, July 4, 1946; s. Celedonio Ladresa and Carlina (Domingo) B.; m. Dianne Lea, June 14, 1969 (div. June 1985); children: Alycia Kay, Amber Lea; m. Sharyn Dee Huckins, Dec. 31, 1985. BA, Coe Coll., 1968; JD, Drake U., 1974. Bar: Iowa 1977, U.S. Dist. Ct. (so. dist.) Iowa 1977, U.S. Tax Ct. 1978, U.S. Dist. Ct. (no. dist.) Iowa 1980, U.S. Ct. Appeals (8th cir.) 1985, U.S. Supreme Ct. 1985, U.S. Dist. Ct. Hawaii 1986. Asst. law librarian Drake U., Des Moines, 1974-77; assoc. Law Office Mike Wilson, Des Moines, 1977-78; sole practice Des Moines, 1978—; bd. dirs. Berkley & Co. Amb. Bd. dirs. Wakonda Christian Ch., 1989—. Served with USAF, 1969-73. Mem. ABA, Iowa Bar Assn., Polk County Bar Assn., Am.-Filipino Assn. Iowa (bd. dirs. 1986), Bass Anglers Sportsman Soc. (Iowa chpt. pres. 1979-82). Republican. Mem. Wakonda Christian Ch. Club: Mid-Iowa Bassmasters (past pres., past v.p., past sec.) (Des Moines). Home: 1520 Birch Norwalk IA 50211 Office: 5609 Douglas Des Moines IA 50310

BAYER, WILLIAM EMIL, JR., healthcare executive; b. Phila., Oct. 1, 1958; s. William Emil Sr. and Mary Elizabeth (Germsheid) B.; m. Judi Mae Batchelor, Sept. 12, 1987. AS, Hahnemann U., 1980; BS, Phila. Coll. Textiles & Sci., 1987. Staff respiratory therapist Albert Einstein Med. Ctr., Phila., 1980-81, clin. coordinator ICU, 1981-82, supr. respiratory therapy dept., 1982-84; dir. respiratory therapy div. Quality Care Med. Equipment, Conshohocken, Pa., 1984-86; ptnr. Med. Express Inc., Bensalem, Pa., 1986—. Mem. Am. Assn. Respiratory Care. Club: Exchange (Levittown, Pa.). Home: 434 N Mt Vernon Cir Bensalem PA 19020 Office: Med Express Inc 4802 Neshaminy Blvd Bensalem PA 19020

BAYERLEIN, RICHARD EDWARD, manufacturing executive; b. Milw., Dec. 30, 1928; s. Roland W. and Ruth N. (Vanderjagt) B.; m. Carol Cathryn Moss, Oct. 18, 1952; children: Steven R., Douglas G., Beth E. BSME, U. Wis., 1950. Registered profl. engr. Pres. Bay-San Co. Inc., Waukesha, Wis., 1950—; pres. Filtration Systems Inc., Waukesha, 1980—, also bd. dirs.; bd. dirs. Mixer Systems Inc., Pewaukee, Wis., Fluid Power Energy Inc., Waukesha. Mem. Soc. Automotive Engrs. (chmn. Milw. sect. 1972). Republican. Methodist. Clubs: Wis. (Milw.)(pres. 1984-86), Bluemound Golf and Country, Western Racquet. Lodge: Masons (master 1960). Office: Filtration Systems W229 N591 Foster Ct Waukesha WI 53186

BAYLE, GENERES DUFOUR, financial planner; b. New Orleans, Aug. 14, 1933; s. Joseph Dufour and Alice (Waggaman) B.; m. Emily Friend, Oct. 24, 1964; children: Lizette, Valerie, Stephanie, Aimee. BBA, Tulane U., 1955. Field underwriter Mut. N.Y., New Orleans, 1958-59; benefits cons. Marsh & McLennan, New Orleans, 1969-76, Demmas & Bayle, New Orleans, 1976-84; fin. planner Fin. Cons. Group, New Orleans, 1984—; v.p., bd. dirs. Nezpique Corp., Wilmington, Del., 1980-88; pres. Valencia, Inc., New Orleans, 1984-86. Chmn. bd. trustees Youth Alternatives, Inc., New Orleans, 1984—. Capt. USAF, 1955-57. Mem. Am. Soc. CLU's (pres. New Orleans chpt. 1976-77), Inst. Cert. Fin. Planners (cert., v.p. Gulf Coast Soc. 1988—), Essex Club (pres. 1985-86), Stratford Club. Office: Fin Cons Group Inc 3900 Causeway Blvd Ste 725 Metairie LA 70002

BAYLEY, MARK TOWNSEND, sales executive; b. Atlanta, Apr. 26, 1950; s. Harold Raymond and Winifred (Boyce) B.; m. Susan Werner, Dec. 3, 1983 (div.); m. Danna Kendall, Sept. 21, 1988. BS, Pa. State U., 1972. With Certainteed Corp., Valley Forge, Pa., 1975—, account mdse. mgr., 1986-87, regional sales mgr., 1987—. Home: 421 Gateway Blvd Huron OH 44839 Office: Certainteed Corp 11519 US Rt 250 North Milan OH 44846

BAYLIS, ROBERT MONTAGUE, investment banker; b. N.Y.C., Aug. 20, 1938; s. Chester, Jr. and Dorothy Montague (Smith) B.; m. Lois Margaret Wells, Apr. 6, 1963; children: Robert Wells, David Martin, John Chester. A.B., Princeton U., 1960; M.B.A., Harvard U., 1962. Chartered financial analyst. Mng. dir. First Boston Corp., N.Y.C., 1963—. Served with M.C. U.S. Army, 1962-63. Mem. Securities Industry Assn., N.Y. Soc. Security Analysts, Nat. Assn. Bus. Economists, New York Stock Exchange. Clubs: Weeburn Country; Wall Street (N.Y.C.), University (N.Y.C.); Nassau, Cap and Gown. Home: 116 Delafield Island Rd Darien CT 06820 Office: 1st Boston Corp Park Avenue Pla New York NY 10055

BAYLISS, LARRY DALE, advertising executive; b. St. Louis, Aug. 19, 1940; s. Arthur Lamoine and Helen Ruth (Balling) B.; m. Mariann Stuckenschneider, June 24, 1961; 1 child, Kathleen Ann Bayliss. AA in Mktg., Washington U., St. Louis, 1968, AA in Bus. Adminstrn., 1979, BBA, 1979. With sales promotion Wagner Electric Corp., St. Louis, 1958-67; mgr. Skinner & Kennedy Co., St. Louis, 1967-68; adminstrv. asst. The Boatmen's Nat. Bank, St. Louis, 1968-69, systems analyst, 1969-71, asst. cashier, 1971-72, prin. asst. cashier, 1972-73, asst. v.p., 1973-75, v.p., 1975-83, 1983-84, sr. v.p., 1984—; pres. B&B Advt. Agy., St. Louis, 1983—. Creater, dir. (film) Katie, 1982 (Nat. Kidney Found. Pub. Svc. award 1982). Bd. dirs. Mental Health Assn., St. Louis, Wishing Well Found., St. Louis; vice chmn. The Salvation Army, St. Louis. Recipient Cert. of Excellence First Advt. Agy. Network, 1974, Flair award St. Louis Soc. Communicating Arts, 1975, Clio award, 1977, Fin. World Mag. award, 1979, 80, 81, 82, 83; named Ad Man of Year St. Louis, 1989, Ad Man of Yr. 9th Dist. Am. Advt. Fedn., 1989. Mem. Advt. Club Greater St. Louis (pres. 1987-88, chmn. bd. dirs. 1989), Bank Mktg. Assn., Ill. and Mo. Bank Mktg. Assn. (chmn. bd. 1978-79), Regional Commerce and Growth Assn., Mo. Athletic Club, Press Club. Roman Catholic. Office: Boatmen's Bancshares Inc 100 N Broadway Saint Louis MO 63102

BAYNARD, MILDRED MOYER (MRS. ROBERT S. BAYNARD), civic worker, corporate executive; b. Lincoln, Nebr., May 10, 1902; d. Charles Calvin and Flora (Harter) Moyer; m. Robert S. Baynard, May 24, 1927; 1 child, Lester B. Student, Sullins Coll., 1921, U. So. Calif., 1922; BA, U. Nebr., 1925. Tchr. pub. schs., Lincoln, 1926-27, Crescent City, Fla., 1925-26; sec. Venice Land Co., Inc., 1949-69; sec. Fla. Bridge Co., 1960-68; ptnr. Ind. Parking, 1965-72; v.p. Venice-Nokomis Bank, Venice, Fla., 1947-62, bd. dirs., 1947-62; pres. Venice Land Co., 1969-72. Mem. editorial adv. bd. Florida Lives. Mem. Fla. State Dist. Welfare Bd., 1948-52; pres. bd. dirs. YWCA, 1953-56; Fla. chmn. Nat. Soc. Prevention Blindness, 1957-60, bd. dirs., 1960-67, v.p., 1963-66; nat. v.p., pres. Fla. affiliate Nat. Soc. to Prevent Blindness, 1958-64, v.p., 1967-68, also mem. Fla. exec. com., hon. life mem., hon. bd. dirs., exec. com. Fla. affiliate, 1983-85; bd. dir. Ctr. for Blind, 1956; pres. Suncoast div. Arthritis Found. Inc., 1966-67; mem. nat. voter adv. bd. Nat. Security Coun.; pres. North Ward PTA, 1938; mem. The Nat. Conservative Found., Heritage Found., Rep. Nat. Com., The Conservative Caucus, Inc., Nat. Rep. Senatorial Com., sec. St. Petersburg (Fla.) Woman's Club, 1945-46; mem. St. Margaret's Guild, St. Thomas Episcopal Ch., St. Petersburg; trustee St. Petersburg Jr. Coll. Devel. Found., Inc., 1984—; Dem. precinct committeewoman, 1936. Recipient Outstanding Citizen's award Pinellas County Commn., 1964, Cable award, 1964, Shield award, 1973, Sarah Schwab Deutsch award, 1978. Mem. U.S. Coun. for World Freedom, Stuart Soc., St. Petersburg Hist. Soc., Mus. Fine Arts, All Childrens Hosp. Guild, U. Neb. Alumni Assn., Mus. of Fine Arts, Nat. Taxpayers Union, DAR., St. Petersburg Bar Aux., Delta Gamma (province officer 1950-56, conv. chmn. 1964, Cable award 1964, Shield award 1973, house corp. 1969—, hon. fellow found. 1974—), Sorosis Club, Yacht Club of St. Petersburg, Panhellenic, Women's Club, Interlock (sec. 1942-44), Venice Nokomis Woman's (life). Lodges: Women of Rotary (pres. Venice chpt. 1962), Women of Rotary (St. Petersburg). Home: 627 Brightwaters Blvd NE Saint Petersburg FL 33704

BAYOL, IRENE SLEDGE, information services specialist; b. Franklin County, N.C., Oct. 11, 1933; d. Walter Ernest and Nonie (Parrish) Sledge; m. Charlie Morton Hamlet, Aug. 23, 1950 (div. Mar. 1956, dec. 1981); 1 child, Marcia Jean; m. Jerome Stollenwerch Bayol, Aug. 9, 1958 (div. May 1972, dec. 1980); children: Jerome Jr., Susan Carol, Keenan Jules. Student, Louisburg (N.C.) Jr. Coll., 1952-53, U. Va., 1970, No. Va. Community Coll., 1984, Am. U., 1986—. Computer equipment analyst USAF, Washington, 1970-73; supr. GSA, Washington, 1973-84; computer equipment specialist GSA Inst. for Info. Tech., Washington, 1984-85; policy officer GSA, Washington, 1985-87, agy. liaison mgr., 1987—; ind. real estate agt., 1973—. Mem. Porlf. Women's Coub, Toastmistress Club, Travel Club, Investments Club. Episcopalian.

BAYS, KARL DEAN, business executive; b. Loyall, Ky., Dec. 23, 1933; s. James K. and Myrtle (Criscillis) B.; m. Billie Joan White, June 4, 1955; children: Robert D., Karla. BS, Eastern Ky. U., 1955, LLD (hon.), 1977; MBA, Ind. U., 1958; DCS (hon.), Union Coll., Ky., 1971. With Am. Hosp. Supply Corp., Evanston, Ill., 1958-85, pres., bd. dirs., 1970, chief exec. officer, 1971-85, chmn. bd., 1974-85; chmn. bd. Baxter Internat., Deerfield, Ill., 1985-87; chmn., chief exec. officer Whitman Corp., Chgo., 1987—; also bd. dirs. IC Industries, Inc., Chgo.; bd. dirs. Amoco Corp. Delta Air Lines, Inc., No. Trust Corp. Trustee emeritus Duke U., Northwestern U.; life mem. bd. dirs. Lake Forest Hosp. Served with USMCR, 1955-57. Recipient Trojan MBA Achievement award U. So. Calif., 1972, Horatio Alger award, 1979, Disting. Alumni Service award Ind. U., 1977; named Outstanding Alumnus Eastern Ky. U., 1973, Mktg. Man of Year Sales and Mktg. Execs. Assn. Chgo., 1977, Outstanding Chief Exec. Officer in hosp. and health-care supplies industry, Fin. World, 1981-82, 85, Outstanding Chief Exec. Officer in hosp. supply industry, Wall St. Transcript, 1980, 84. Clubs: Econ., Comml., Mid-Am. (Chgo.); Glen View; Old Elm, Onwentsia. Office: Whitman Corp 111 E Wacker Dr Chicago IL 60601

BEACH, ARTHUR O'NEAL, lawyer; b. Albuquerque, Feb. 8, 1945; s. William Pearce and Vivian Lucille (Kronig) B.; B.B.A., U. N.Mex., 1967, J.D., 1970; m. Alex Clark Doyle, Sept. 12, 1970; 1 son, Eric Kronig. Admitted to N.Mex. bar, 1970; assoc. firm Smith & Ransom, Albuquerque, 1970-74; assoc. firm Keleher & McLeod, Albuquerque, 1974-75, ptnr., 1976-78, shareholder firm Keleher & McLeod, P.A., Albuquerque, 1978—; teaching asst. U. N. Mex., 1970. Bd. editors Natural Resources Jour., 1968-70. Mem. State Bar N.Mex. (unauthorized practice of law com., adv. opinions com., med.-legal panel, legal-dental-osteo.-podiatry com., jud. selection com.), Am., Albuquerque (dir. 1978-82) bar assns., State Bar Specialization Bd. Democrat. Mem. Christian Sci. Ch. Home: 2015 Dietz Pl NW Albuquerque NM 87107 Office: Keleher & McLeod PA PO Drawer AA Albuquerque NM 87103

BEACH, ROBERT PRESTON, accountant, fraternal organization executive; b. Portland, Oreg., Jan. 29, 1916; s. Henry Edward and Olga Ruth (Lindblad) B.; m. Barbara Frances Harvey, July 12, 1941; 1 dau., Barbara Anne Beach Meek. B.S., U. Calif.-Berkeley, 1938; M.B.A., Harvard U., 1940. C.P.A., Mass. Acct., Coopers & Lybrand, Boston, 1940-42, 46-53; sec. corp. Brown & Sharpe Mfg. Co., Providence, 1953-55; bus. mgr. Metcalf & Eddy, Boston, 1956-60; practice acctg., Boston, 1961—; corporator First Am. Bank for Savs., Boston, 1974-86; guest lectr. Boston U., 1966-67. Treas., Republican Town Com., Natick, Mass., 1948-53; clk. First Congregational Ch. in Wellesley Hills (Mass.), 1967-72; mem. corp. New Eng. Bapt. Hosp. Health Care Corp. and New Eng. Bapt. Hosp. Corp., Boston, 1964—; trustee Leonard Morse Hosp., Natick, 1950-53. Served as lt. comdr. USN, 1942-46; PTO. Fellow Am. Inst. C.P.A.s, Mass. Soc. C.P.A.s (various coms.); mem. SAR (treas. Mass. chpt. 1975-77), Conf. Grand Secs. in N.Am. (sec.-treas. 1976-85, pres. 1985-86), Beta Alpha Psi. Club: Harvard (Boston). Lodge: Masons (editor publs. 1966—, grand sec. 1968—. 33d degree, D.S.M. and Henry Price medals 1963, 66, Philip C. Tucker medal 1983, past presiding officer many orgns., trustee Masonic Edn. and Charity Trust 1982—). Home: 250 Beacon St Boston MA 02116 Office: Grand Lodge of Masons 186 Tremont St Boston MA 02111

BEADLE, JOHN GRANT, manufacturing company executive; b. Chgo., Dec. 16, 1932; s. John G. and Katharine (Brady) B.; m. Lee Oliver, Apr. 11, 1955; children: Katharine, John. B.A., Yale U., 1954. Salesman Pure Oil Co., Jacksonville and Tampa, Fla., 1957-59, Kordite Co., Tampa, New Orleans, 1959-61; with Union Spl. Corp., Chgo., 1961—; exec. v.p. Union Spl. Corp., 1972-75, pres., chief operating officer, 1975-76, pres., chief exec. officer, 1976-84, chmn., chief exec. officer, 1984—; bd. dirs. Woodward Governor Co., Rospatch Corp., Grand Rapids, Mich., Portec Corp.; past pres., bd. dirs. Juvenile Protection Assn.; past chmn., bd. dirs. Midwest Indsl. Mgmt. Assn.; past chmn. Internat. Council Machinery and Allied Products Inst. Trustee Allendale Sch. for Boys; bd. dirs. Greater N. Michigan Ave. Assn.; trustee, past pres. Castle Park Assn. Served with USAF, 1954-57. Mem. Northwestern U. Assocs., Chgo. Com., Am. Apparel Machinery Mfrs. Assn. Republican. Episcopalian. Clubs: Skokie Country (Glencoe, Ill.); Mchts. and Mfrs, Commonwealth, Comml. Office: Union Special Corp 222 N LaSalle St Ste 900 Chicago IL 60601

BEAL, ILENE, bank executive. BA, Wellesley Coll., 1967. Mgmt. trainee Nat. Shawmut Bank, Boston, 1967-71; from asst. sec. to exec. v.p. BayBanks, Inc., Boston, 1972—; successively asst. v.p., v.p., sr. v.p. BayBanks, Inc., now exec. v.p., asst sec. Office: BayBanks Inc 175 Federal St Boston MA 02110

BEAL, ROBERT LAWRENCE, real estate executive; b. Boston, Sept. 10, 1941; s. Alexander Simpson and Leona M. (Rothstein) B. B.S. cum laude, Harvard U., 1963, M.B.A., 1965. Vice pres., ptnr. Beacon Cos., Boston, 1965-76; ptnr. The Beal Cos.; exec. v.p. Beal and Co., Inc., Boston, 1976—; dir., mem. exec. com., mem. lending com. Provident Instn. Savs., 1983-86; dir., mem. exec. com. U.K.-Am. Properties; chmn., dir. Mass. Indsl. Fin. Agy., 1976—; instr. real estate Northeastern U., 1969-75. Bd. dirs. Boston Zool. Soc., 1972-86, pres., 1980, chmn. 1981-84, hon. chmn., 1985; mem. vis. com. Sch. Mus. Fine Arts, Boston, 1974-76; overseer Boys Club Boston, 1975—; mem. corp. Belmont Hill Sch.; trustee Beth Israel Hosp., 1981—, mem. bldg. and grounds com., 1976-82, 86; dir. Harvard Coll. Fund Council, 1972-73, capital fund dr. Class '63, 1979-85, co-chmn. 25th reunion; exec. bd. Boston chpt. Am. Jewish Com., 1987—; bd. dirs. Boston Mcpl. Research Bur., 1978—; trustee The Partnership, Inc., 1981—, New Eng. Aquarium, 1987—; bd. dirs. Boston Housing Partnership, Inc., 1983—; mem. adv. task force John F. Kennedy Library, 1982—; bd. overseers Mus. Fine Arts, Boston, 1988—. Mem. Nat. Realty Com. (dir., past sec., mem. exec. com. 1974—, v.p., vice chmn.), Mass. Assn. Realtors (dir. 1979-81), Greater Boston Real Estate Bd. (dir. 1970-72, 76—, pres. 1978-79), Am. Soc. Real Estate Counselors, Bldg. Owners-Mgrs. Assn. Boston (dir. 1970-72), Ripon Soc. (co-founder, nat. treas. 1968-73, nat. governing bd. 1979—), Nat. Assn. Real Estate Appraiser (cert.), Mass. Taxpayers Found. (dir. 1980-86), Inst. Property Taxation (affiate), Internat. Assn. Assessing Officers (primary subscribing mem. 1982—), Beacon Hill Civic Assn. (dir. 1975-79), Bostonian Soc. (life), Greater Boston C. of C. (execs. club). Republican. Jewish. Home: 21 Brimmer St Boston MA 02108 Office: Beal and Co Inc 15 Broad St Ste 800 Boston MA 02109

BEALE, GEORGIA ROBISON, historian; b. Chgo., Mar. 14, 1905; d. Henry Barton and Dora Belle (Sledd) Robison; m. Howard Kennedy Beale, Jan. 2, 1942; children: Howard Kennedy, Henry Barton Robison, Thomas Wight. AB, U. Chgo., 1926, AM, 1928; PhD, Columbia U., 1938; student Sorbonne and Coll. de France, 1930-34. Reader in history U. Chgo., 1927-29; lectr. Barnard Coll., 1937-38; instr. Bklyn. Coll., 1937-39; asst. prof. Hollins (Va.) Coll., 1939-41, Wellesley Coll., 1941-42, Castleton (Vt.) State Coll., 1968-70; vis. asso. prof. U. Ky., Lexington, 1970-72; professorial lectr. George Washington U., 1983-84. Author: Revelliere-lépeaux, Citizen Director, 1938, 72, Academies to Institut, 1973, Bosc and the Exequatur, 1978; contbg. author Historical Dictionary of the French Revolution, 1985; also articles. Mem. Madison (Wis.) Civic Music Assn. and Madison Symphony Orch. League, 1958—; hon. trustee Culver-Stockton Coll., 1974—. Univ. fellow Columbia U., 1929-30. Mem. AAUW (European fellow 1930-31), Am., So. hist. assns., Soc. French Hist. Studies, Western Soc. French History (hon. mem. exec. council), Am., Brit. socs. 18th century studies, Phi Beta Kappa, Pi Lambda Theta, Phi Alpha Theta, Pi Kappa Delta. Clubs: Reid Hall (Paris); Brit. Univ. Women's (London). Address: The Ridge Orford NH 03777 also: 2816 Columbia Rd Madison WI 53705 also: 110 D St SE Washington DC 20003

BEALE, WALTER MICHAEL, shoe retail executive; b. Suffolk, Va., May 23, 1955; s. Walter III and Rebecca Ann (DeJarnette) B. BSBA, Old Dominion U., 1977. CPA, Va. With Peak, Drescher and Whitfield, Franklin, Va., 1977-83, mgr. acctg. and auditing svcs., 1981-83; controller Russell and Holmes Corp., Suffolk, 1983-86, v.p. fin., 1986—. Asst. treas. Sycamore Bapt. Ch., Franklin, 1984—, chmn. bldg. fin. com., 1983—. Fellow AICPA, Va. Soc. CPAs; mem. Forks of the River Ruritan Club (pres. 1983), Lions (treas. Franklin chpt. 1985—). Home: 144 River Point Dr Suffolk VA 23434 Office: Russell & Holmes Corp 139 N Main St Suffolk VA 23434

BEALL, DONALD RAY, manufacturing company executive; b. Beaumont, Calif., Nov. 29, 1938; s. Ray C. and Margaret (Murray) B. B.S., San Jose State Coll., 1960; M.B.A., U. Pitts., 1961; postgrad., UCLA. With Ford Motor Co., 1961-68; fin. mgmt. positions Newport Beach, Calif., 1961-66; mgr. corp. fin. planning and contracts Phila., 1966-67; controller Palo Alto, Calif., 1967-68; exec. dir. corp. fin. planning N.Am. Rockwell, El Segundo, Calif., 1968-69, exec. v.p. electronics group, 1969-71; exec. v.p. Collins Radio Co., Dallas, 1971-74; pres. Collins Radio Group, Rockwell Internat. Corp., Dallas, 1974-76, Electronic Ops., Dallas, 1976-77; exec. v.p. Rockwell Internat. Corp., Dallas, 1977-79; pres., chief operating officer Rockwell Internat. Corp., Pitts., 1979-88; chmn. bd., chief exec. officer Rockwell Internat. Corp., El Segundo, Calif., 1988—; bd. dirs. Interfirst Corp.; mem. Pres.'s Export Council, 1981-85; bd. overseers U. Calif., Irvine, 1988—. Past Dallas met. chmn. Nat. Alliance Bus.; mem. Dallas Citizens Council; past bd. dirs. United Way of Met. Dallas, So. Methodist U. Found. Sci. and

Engring.; bd. dirs. Dallas Council World Affairs; trustee U. Pitts.; gen. campaign chmn. Western Pa. affiliate Am. Diabetes Assn.; vice chmn. region IV Los Angeles County United Way, 1984-85; mem. Brit.-N.Am. com. Bus.-Higher Edn. Forum. Recipient award of distinction San Jose State U. Sch. Engring., 1980. Mem. Armed Forces Communications and Electronics Assn. (nat. dir.), Electronic Industries Assn., Aerospace Industries Assn. (chmn. bd. govs. 1987), Soc. Automotive Engrs., Soc. Mfg. Engrs. (hon.), Def. Preparedness Assn., Young Pres.'s Orgn., Navy League of U.S., Sigma Alpha Epsilon, Beta Gamma Sigma. Office: Rockwell Internat Corp 2230 E Imperial Hwy El Segundo CA 90245

BEALMEAR, MICHAEL WILLIAM, accounting company executive, consultant; b. Corpus Christi, Tex., Aug. 30, 1947; s. William Gus and Helen (Lentz) B.; m. Carolyn Mary Mall, May 26, 1985; 1 child, William Todd. BS in Engring., U. Tex., 1970; BS in Math., Rice U., 1973. Regional mng. ptnr. Peat Marwick, Mitchell & Co., Miami (Fla.), San Francisco, N.Y.C., 1973-84; ptnr., nat. dir. info. tech. cons. Coopers & Lybrand, N.Y.C., 1984—. Contbr. over 50 articles to technical computing jours. Mem. Chancellor's Council U. Tex., Austin, 1986-88; bd. dirs. N.Y. Zool. Soc., 1987-88. Mem. IEEE, Assn. Data Processing Software and Services Orgn. (bd. dirs., 1987-88), Assn. Computing Machinery (chpt. pres., 1980), Nat. Assn. Corp. Dirs., Rockefeller Ctr. Club (N.Y.C.), N.Y. Racquet and Tennis Club. Avocations: motor racing, photography. Home: 13 Hen Hawk Ln Westport CT 06880 Office: Coopers & Lybrand 1251 Ave of the Americas New York NY 10020

BEALS, VAUGHN LEROY, JR., vehicle manufacturing company executive; b. Cambridge, Mass., Jan. 2, 1928; s. Vaughn LeRoy and Pearl Uela (Wilmarth) B.; m. Eleanore May Woods, July 15, 1951; children: Susan Lynn, Laurie Jean. B.S., M.I.T., 1948, M.S., 1954. Research engr. Cornell Aero. Lab., Buffalo, 1948-52, MIT Aero Elastic and Structures Research Lab., 1952-55; dir. research and tech. N.Am. Aviation, Inc., Columbus, Ohio, 1955-65; exec. v.p. Cummins Engine Co., Columbus, Ind., 1965-70, also dir.; chmn. bd., chief exec. officer Formac Internat., Inc., Seattle, 1970-75; dep. group exec. Motorcycle Products Group, AMF Inc., Milw., 1975-77; v.p. and group exec. Motorcycle Products Group, AMF Inc., Stamford, Conn., 1977-81; chief exec. officer Harley-Davidson, Inc., Milw., 1981-89, chmn., 1981—; mem. adv. bd., chmn. exec. com. Traffic Inst. Northwestern U.; bd. dirs. Simplicity Mfg., Inc., R.F. Richard Corp., First Wis. Nat. Bank, Milw., First Wis. Corp. Bd. dirs. Greater Milw. Com., Bus. Against Drunk Drivers, Inc. Mem. Met. Milw. Assn. Commerce, Nat. Assn. Mfrs. Clubs: University, Milw. Country (Milw.). Home: 1707 E Fox Ln Milwaukee WI 53217 Office: Harley-Davidson Inc 3700 W Juneau Ave Milwaukee WI 53201

BEAM, FRANCIS H., JR., account, consultant; b. Cleve., Nov. 12, 1935; s. Francis H. and Helen Elizabeth (Race) B.; m. Virginia Mae Judd, July 24, 1954; children: Jennifer Carroll, Francis H. III, Judd Andrew. BA, Yale U., 1957; MBA, Harvard Bus. Sch., 1959. CPA, Ohio. Staff Ernst and Whinney, Cleve., 1959, ptnr., 1967-78; vice-chmn., regional mng. ptnr. Ernst and Whinney, Chgo., 1978-81; vice-chmn. planning Ernst and Whinney, Cleve., 1981-84, vice-chmn., regional mng. ptnr., 1984-88; mng. dir. TBN Holdings, Cleve., 1988—. Mem. AICPA, Union Club, Pepper Pike Club, Country Club, Tavern Club. Republican. Presbyterian. Home: 2755 Lander Rd Pepper Pike OH 44124 Office: TBN Holdings Lander Ctr 3550 Lander Rd Pepper Pike OH 44124

BEAM, FRANK LETTS, communications corporation executive; b. Mount Vernon, Ohio, Apr. 10, 1942; s. James Alfred and Margaret Adele (Rudin) B. B.S.B.A., Northwestern U., Evanston, 1964. With advt. dept. ITT Bell and Gossett, Morton Grove, Ill., 1961-62; exec. trainee Leo Burnett Co., Chgo., 1964-65; acct. exec. Young and Rubicam, Chgo., 1965-67; prin., founder Frank L. Beam Co., Chgo., 1967-80; founder, pres. Beam Communications, Key Biscayne, Fla., 1981—; co-founder Beam Laser Systems, Inc., 1986, Allbev, Inc., Charlotte, N.C., 1986; with Lloyd's of London, 1989—. Author: Effects of the Inner Six Outer Seven on Damlier-Benz ATG, 1961. Co-founder Key Biscayners for Responsive Govt., 1985; mem. steering com. Rep., 1972. Mem. Broadcast Pioneers, Nat. Assn. Broadcasters, Internat. Radio and T.V. Soc., Mayflower Desendents, SAR. Presbyterian. Clubs: Chig. Yacht; Key Biscayne Yacht, Surf (Miami). Avocations: boating, music, photography. Home: 201 Crandon Blvd Key Biscayne FL 33149 Office: Beam Communications Corp 50 W Mashta Dr Key Biscayne FL 33149

BEAM, WALTER WILLIS, retired oil and gas company executive; b. Denison, Tex., July 25, 1921; s. Orville Wray and Lucy Carey (Fischer) B.; m. Margeretta Wood, Sept. 11, 1943; children: Walter W., Chester W. B.S.M.E., Tex. A&M U., 1946; M.S.M.E., Okla. State U., 1952. Design engr. Dow Chem. Co., Freeport, Tex., 1946-47, Freeport Sulphur Co., 1947-48; design engr. Conoco, Inc., Ponca City, Okla., 1948-86, ret. v.p. engring.; bd. dirs. Pioneer Bank and Trust Co., Ponca City. Patentee liquified natural gas. Bd. dirs. Westminster Village, Ponca City Opportunity Ctr.; adv. bd. Okla. Christian Coll. Sch. Engring. Served with USAF, 1943-45, CBI. Decorated D.F.C. with two oak leaf clusters; decorated Air medal with seven oak leaf clusters, others. Mem. Ponca City C. of C. (chmn. bd. 1986), Okla. Soc. Profl. Engrs. (past pres. chpt.). Democrat. Mem. Ch. of Christ (elder). Lodge: Rotary. Home: 1400 Reveille Dr Ponca City OK 74604

BEAMER, JO ANN JEAN, forging company executive; b. Dedham, Iowa, June 15, 1939; d. William Columbus and Neva Belle (Randolph) Dennis Delzell; m. Michael R. Beamer, July 10, 1973; children—Steven Dean Pease, Donald Lee Newman, Karey Lee (Newman) Davidofsky; stepchildren: Christopher Michael, Shelli. Student Chaffey Jr. College, U. Nev. Exec. sec. Aerojet Gen. Corp., Azusa, Calif., Nuclear Rocket Devel. Sta., Jackass Flats, Nev., 1959-62, 64-68; exec. sec. safety and test ops. Pan Am. World Airways, Nuclear Rocket Devel. Stat., 1962-64; personnel and safety asst. safety and personnel Survival Systems Co., Ontario, Calif., 1968-71; personnel mgr. Hooker Industries, Ontario, 1971-74; asst. terminal mgr. CMD Transp. Co., Vernon, Calif., 1977-80; personnel mgr. Schlosser Forge Co., Cucamonga, Calif., 1980—; guest speaker Ontario Community Hosp. Active Chino (Calif.) High Sch. Band Boosters. Mem. Nat. Assn. Female Execs., Mchts. and Mfrs. Assn., Personnel Indsl. Relations Assn. Home: 5729 Portsmouth St Chino CA 91710 Office: Schlosser Forge Co 11711 Arrow Route St Cucamonga CA 91730

BEAN, BRUCE WINFIELD, lawyer; b. Albany, N.Y., Dec. 19, 1941; s. William Joseph and Ruth Elizabeth (Lafferty) B.; m. Barbara Bryant Hunting; children: Austin Bryant, Ashley Elizabeth. AB, Brown U., 1964; JD, Columbia U., 1972. Bar: N.Y. 1973, Calif. 1981. Law clk. to judge U.S. Ct. Appeals (2d cir.), 1972-73; assoc. Simpson Thacher & Bartlett, N.Y.C., 1973-76, Patterson, Belknap, Webb & Tyler, N.Y.C., 1976-80; counsel fin. and planning Atlantic Richfield, Los Angeles, 1980-85; sr. v.p., gen. counsel The Home Group Inc., N.Y.C., 1985—; bd. dirs. Home Capital Services, Inc., Gruntal Fin. Corp., Imperial Premium Fin., Inc., Cole Haan Holdings Inc. Served to col. USAFR, 1964-86, Vietnam. Mem. N.Y. State Bar Assn. (chmn. spl. com. on mil. and veterans affairs). Office: The Home Group Inc 59 Maiden Ln 28th Fl New York NY 10038-4548

BEAN, FRANK WILSON, soft drink marketing executive, lawyer, advertising and public relations executive; b. Bloomington, Ill., Jan. 14, 1940; s. Wilson Rosemond and Beatrice (Mill) B.; m. Joyce Travis Whitsel, June 11, 1960; children—Brenton Sewell, Kimberly Whitsel. B.S., U. Fla., 1962, M.A. in Journalism and Communication, 1963; J.D., Woodrow Wilson Coll. Law, 1983. Bar: Ga. 1984, Ga. Supreme Ct., Ga. Appeals Ct., U.S. Dist. Ct. (no. dist.) Ga. 1984. Staff rep. pub. relations Coca-Cola Co., Atlanta, 1968-72, services mgr. pub. relations, 1972-76; mgr. corp. sport sponsorships Coca-Cola Export Corp., Atlanta, 1976-79, mgr. internat. sports, 1980—; instr. DeKalb Community Coll. (Ga.), 1975-78. Adv. com. U. Fla., 1978-81. Bd. dirs. mgmt. Northside YMCA, Atlanta, 1984—. Served to capt. USAF, 1963-68. Recipient Golden Eagle award CINE, 1980. Mem. Pub. Relations Soc. Am. (accredited), Atlanta Jaycees (v.p. 1968-74), Alpha Delta Sigma, Pi Kappa Alpha. Republican. Episcopalian. Club: Capital City (Atlanta). Avocations: writing, fishing, water skiing. Home: 275 Forrest Lake Dr NW Atlanta GA 30327 Office: Coca-Cola Co Coca-Cola Pla Atlanta GA 30313

BEAR, LARRY ALAN, lawyer; b. Melrose, Mass., Feb. 28, 1928; s. Joseph E. and Pearl Florence B.; B.A., Duke U., 1949; J.D., Harvard U., 1953; LL.M. (James Kent fellow), Columbia U., 1966; m. 2d, Rita Maldonado, Mar. 29, 1975; children: Peter, Jonathan, Steven. Admitted to Mass. bar, 1953, N.Y. bar, 1967; trial lawyer firm Bear & Bear, Boston, 1953-60; cons. legal medicine P.R. Dept. Justice, also prof. law U. P.R. Law Sch., 1960-65; legal counsel, then commr. addiction services City N.Y., 1967-70; dir. Nat. Action Com. Drug Edn., U. Rochester (N.Y.), 1970-77; individual practice, N.Y.C., also public affairs radio broadcaster Sta. WABC, 1970-82; U.S. legal counsel Master Enterprises of P.R., 1982—; adj. prof. fin. Grad. Sch. Bus. Adminstrn. NYU, 1986—; spl. cons. to the Ctr. for New Era Philanthropy and Human Service Systems, Inc., 1987—; vis. prof. legal medicine Rutgers U. Law Sch., 1969; mem. alcohol and drug com. Nat. Safety Council, 1972-82; cons. in field. Mem. public policy com. Advt. Council, 1972—; mem.-at-large Nat. council Boy Scouts Am., 1972-85. Mem. Am. Bar Assn., N.Y. State Bar Assn., Forensic Sci. Soc. Gt. Britain, Acad. Colombiana de Ciencias Medico-Forenses. Club: Harvard (N.Y.C.). Author: Law, Medicine, Science and Justice, 1964; also articles. Home: 95 Tam O'Shanter Dr Mahwah NJ 07430 also: Ctr for New Era Philanthropy 7 Wynnewood Rd Wynnewood PA 19096

BEARD, PETER LYNDON, lawyer; b. Albuquerque, Oct. 24, 1959; s. Donald Sinclair and Nancy Caroline (Foscue) B. AB in Econ., Davidson Coll., 1983; JD, Syracuse U., 1986. Bar: Md. 1986, D.C. 1989. Econ. analyst U.S. Senate Com. on the Budget, Washington, 1981-82; assoc. Semmes, Bowen & Semmes, Balt., 1986-88; atty. Habitat for Humanity Internat. Inc., Americus, Ga., 1988—. Youth advisor Damascus (Md.) United Meth. Ch., 1987-88; adult leader Boy Scouts Am., Damascus, 1984-88. Mem. ABA, Md. Bar. Assn. Republican. Office: Habitat for Humanity Habitat and Church Sts Americus GA 31709

BEARDSLEE, DANIEL BAIN, venture capitalist, educator; b. Flint, Mich., Mar. 25, 1960; s. Kelly Bain and Joyce Ann (Adamson) B.; m. Susan Helen Mousseau, Mar. 12, 1983. BSME, GM Inst., 1983; MS in Mgmt., MIT, 1986. Computer systems engr. AC Spark Plug div. GM, Flint, 1983-84; cons. Arthur D. Little, Inc., Cambridge, Mass., 1985-86; v.p. fin. and adminstrn. Data to Info., Troy, Mich., 1986-87; asst. to pres. Demery Mgmt. Group, Birmingham, Mich., 1987—; lectr. Oakland U., Rochester, Mich., 1987—; adj. faculty Macomb Community Coll., Warren, Mich., 1988. Mem. Inventor's Council of Mich., Southeastern Mich. Venture Group, Mich. Tech. Council. Home: 7483 Deep Run Apt 1022 Birmingham MI 48010 Office: Demery Seed Cap Fund 3707 W Maple Rd Birmingham MI 48010

BEARDWOOD, BRUCE ALLAN, chemical company executive; b. Pawtucket, R.I., Apr. 3, 1936; s. Houghton and Barbara (Wright) B.; m. Marjorie Swan Jackson, July 26, 1958 (div. Mar. 1966); children: Bruce Allan, Lisa; m. Judith Kay Fredricks, Oct. 15, 1966; children: Susan, Matthew, Jenny. BChemE, Yale U., 1958. With E.I. DuPont de Nemours & Co., Wilmington, Del., 1958—; salesman Chgo., 1963-66; sales developer Wilmington, 1966-70; dist. sales mgr. Cleve., 1970-73; mktg. mgmt. Wilmington, 1973-78, dir. planning, 1978-79, dir. indsl. films, 1979-81, gen. mgr. fabrics and finishes, 1981-83, v.p. fabricated products, 1983—. V.p. Boy Scouts Am., 1982—; trustee Tatnall Sch., 1983—; bd. dirs. Del. Symphony, 1986—. Mem. Sigma Xi, Tau Beta Pi. Clubs: Greenville Country; Rodney Sq.; DuPont Country. Lodge: Rotary. Office: E I Du Pont de Nemours & Co 1007 Market St-FPD Wilmington DE 19898

BEATTY, JOHN TOWNSEND, JR., investment banker; b. Evanston, Ill., Feb. 18, 1936; s. John Townsend and Jane (Confer) B.; m. Marila M. Miller, Sept. 8, 1962; children—John Townsend III, William Oeric, Emily Frances. B.A., Yale U., 1958; M.B.A., U. Chgo., 1966. Regional mgr. Allis-Chalmers Mfg. Co., Bangkok, Thailand, 1966-69; v.p. Halsey Stuart & Co., Chgo., 1969-72; 1st v.p. Smith Barney, Harris Upham & Co., Chgo., 1972-86; dir. Miss. Valley Airlines, 1981-85, dir. Green Tree Acceptance Corp., 1982-85. Sr. Warden St. James the Less Ch., Northfield, Ill., 1987; mem. sch. bd. Sunset Ridge Sch., 1976-83; dir. United Way, 1975-80. Served with U.S. Army, 1958-61. Clubs: Chgo., Econs. (membership com. 1987); Sunset Ridge Country.

BEATY, JOHN THURSTON, JR., investment company executive; b. N.Y.C., Apr. 7, 1944; s. John Thurston and Julia (Corscaden) B.; m. Anne L. Mehringer, Feb. 8, 1986. Grad., Choate Sch., 1962; BA magna cum laude, Princeton U., 1966; MBA with high distinction, Harvard U., 1968. Spl. asst. Office Sec. Def., Washington, 1968-70; v.p. Davidge & Co., Washington, 1970-84, pres., chief exec. officer, 1984—; bd. dirs. Newfound Corp., Washington, Venture Capital Fund New Eng., Boston. Trustee United Way, Washington, 1969—, Cathedral Choral Soc., Washington, 1981—, St. John's Child Devel. Ctr., Washington, 1980-84, Washington Hosp. Ctr., 1989—; vol. Montgomery County Hist. Soc., Bethesda, Md., 1984—. Named Vol. of Yr., United Way, 1987. Mem. Investment Counsel Assn., Met. Club, North Lake George Yacht Club (Hague, N.Y.), Cap and Gown (Princeton), Phi Beta Kappa. Episcopalian. Home: 5312 Allandale Rd Bethesda MD 20816 Office: Davidge & Co 1747 Pennsylvania Ave NW Washington DC 20006

BEAUBIEN, DAVID JAMES, electronics company executive, consultant; b. Montague, Mass., Sept. 20, 1934; s. Arthur and Helen Agnes (Moreau) B.; m. Mary Ann Robert, Sept. 21, 1957; children: Arthur F., Patricia M., Mark C. BSEE, U. Mass., 1957. Registered profl. engr., Mass. Pres., founder Cambridge Systems, Inc., Newton, Mass., 1959-67; asst. to pres. EG&G, Inc., Bedford, Mass., 1967-77; v.p. EG&G, Inc., Wellesley, Mass., 1977-82, sr. v.p., 1982—; bd. dirs. Kidder Peabody Family Mut. Funds, N.Y.C., MetraByte Corp., Taunton. Vice chmn. then chmn. Bd. Regents Pub. Higher Edn., Boston, 1980-88; trustee U. Mass., 1979-80. Recipient Disting. Alumnus award U. Mass., 1983. Mem. Am. Meteorol. Soc., Sigma Xi. Roman Catholic. Home: 12 N Taylor Hill Montague MA 01351 Office: EG & G Inc 45 William St Wellesley MA 02181

BEAUDOIN, LAURENT, industrial, recreational and transportation company executive; b. Laurier Station, Que., Can., May 13, 1938; s. P.A. and Yvonne (Rodrigue) B.; m. Claire Bombardier, Aug. 29, 1959; children—Nicole, Pierre, Elaine, Denise. B.A., Ste. Anne U., N.S., Can., 1957; M. Commerce, Sherbrooke U., 1960, D. Bus. Adminstrn. (hon.), 1971. Partner firm Beaudoin, Morin, Dufresne & Assos., Quebec, Que., 1961-63; comptroller Bombardier Ltd., Valcourt, Que., 1963-64; gen. mgr. Bombardier Ltd., Montreal, Que., 1964-66; pres. Bombardier, Inc., Montreal, Que., 1966-86, chmn., chief exec. officer, 1979—; bd. dirs. Bombardier-Rotax GmbH, Gunskirchen, Austria, Entreprises de J.-Armand Bombardier, Montreal, Bombardier Corp. Inc., Malone, N.Y., Bell Can. Enterprises, Alcan Aluminum Ltd. Hon. v.p. Que. Provincial council Boy Scouts Can.; Bd. govs. Faculté d'Adminstrn., U. Sherbrooke, Que. Decorated officer Order Can. Fellow Inst. Chartered Accountants; mem. C. of C. Que. (gov.). Office: Bombardier Inc Ste 1700, 800 Rene Levesque Blvd W, Montreal, PQ Canada H3B 1Y8

BEAUDOIN, ROBERT LAWRENCE, small business owner; b. Newberry, Mich., Nov. 22, 1933; s. Leo Joseph and Edith Wilhelmina (Graunstadt) B.; m. Margaret Cecelia Linck, June 20, 1953; children: Eugene Robert, Kathleen Therese, Annette Marie, Suzanne Margaret. Student, Marquette U., 1952-53. With Fisher plant Gen. Motors, 1953; dock hand State of Mich., St. Ignace, 1953; sch. bus driver Engadine (Mich.) Consol. Schs., 1957; owner, operator Beaudoin's Texaco, Beaudoin's Cafe, Naubinway, Mich., 1956-82, Beaudoin's Cafe and Marathon, Naubinway, 1982-83, Beaudoin's Cafe, Naubinway, 1956—; bd. dirs. Naubinway Mchts. Inc., 1985—. Mem. Naubinway July 4th Com., 1954—; past mem. Naubinway Port commn., Garfield Twp. Planning, zoning commn.; vol. fireman Garfield Twp. Fire Dept., Naubinway, 1980—; mem. recreation com. Garfield Twp. Bd., Engadine, 1983; support fellow N.G. and Res., support mem. U.S. Army Recruiting Main Sta., Detroit; mem. U.S. Air Force Ground Observer Corp. Recipient Cert. of Appreciation, U.S. Army Recruiting Main Sta., Detroit, 1971, Statement of Support, N.G. and Res., 1976. Mem. West Mackinac C. of C., Nat. Fedn. Ind. Bus. (mem. adv. bd. 1971—, 20 yr. award 1985), KC (dist. dep. 1988—). Roman Catholic. Club: Hiawatha Sportsmans (mem. bd. govs. Engadine 1965-67), Engadine Trap Shooting. Lodges: KC (grand knight 1979-83, Mich. State Council membership and program dir. East Marquette diocese 1984-88), Lions (3d v.p. Engadine club 1970-71), Kofe (grand knight Mich. state coun. 1979-83, program dir. east Marquette diocese Mich state coun. 1984-88, supreme coun. dist. deputy 1988—). Home: PO Box 143 E Main St Naubinway MI 49762 Office: Beaudoins Cafe PO Box 143 US Hwy 2 Naubinway MI 49762

BEAUDREAULT, EDGAR JOSEPH, JR., investment company executive; b. Putnam, Conn., May 19, 1948; s. Edgar Joseph and Wilhelmina (Huber) B.; 1 child, Brooke Elise. BS, Fairfield U., 1970; JD, New England Sch. Law, 1974; LLM, Boston U. Sch. Law, 1977. Regional sales mgr. Am. Gen., Boston, 1979-81; nat. sales mgr. Am. Gen., Houston, 1981-83; v.p. Am. Capital, Atlanta, 1983-86; sr. v.p. Johnson Lane, Atlanta, 1986-88, Interact Mgmt., Atlanta, 1988—. Mem. Ga. Pub. TV. Mem. ABA, Investment Co. Inst., Retail Security Brokers Ga. (bd. dirs.), Foresters Am. Democrat. Roman Catholic. Home: 12315 Charlotte Dr Alpharetta GA 30328 Office: Interact Mgmt 35 Glenlake Pkwy Ste 245 Atlanta GA 30328

BEAUGRAND, KENNETH LOUIS, lawyer, business executive; b. N.Y.C., Oct. 19, 1938; BA, Brown U., 1960; LLB, Columbia U., 1963; LLM, U. London, 1964; m. Augusta Newell Wood Barnard, Nov. 22, 1969; 3 children. Bar: N.Y. 1964, Ont. 1977. Assoc. Willkie, Farr & Gallagher, N.Y.C., 1964-68; solicitor I.O.S. Ltd. Fin. Services, Geneva, 1968-69, sec., 1969-71, v.p., dir., gen. counsel, 1972-73; v.p., dir., gen. counsel Value Capital Services, Amsterdam, 1971-72; assoc. Aird, Zimmerman & Berlis, 1973-77; v.p., sec., gen. counsel Eaton Bay Fin. Services Ltd., Toronto, 1977-79, sr. v.p., gen. counsel, 1979-82, sr. v.p. ins. and fund. divs., 1982-83, sr. v.p. ops., 1983-85; exec. v.p. 1985-86, sr. v.p. investments The Imperial Life Assurance Co. of Can., Toronto, 1986-87, exec. v.p., chief operating officer, 1987—. Bd. dirs. Laurentian Mut. Funds, Viking Mut. Funds, Eaton Funds Mgmt., Ltd., Laurier Life, chmn., chief exec. officer, bd. dirs. Imbrook Properties, Ltd. Avocations: tennis, skiing, sailing. Clubs: University, Toronto Lawn Tennis. Office: The Imperial Life Assurance Co of Can, 95 St Clair Ave W, Toronto, ON Canada M4V 1N7

BEAUPRE, MICHAEL CARL, financial executive; b. Kalamazoo, Jan. 30, 1944; s. Herbert and Doris Irene (Bruni) B.; m. Barbara Joyce Stern, Feb. 27, 1965; children: Michael D., David J., Bonnie L., Steven J., Lindsey M. BA, U. Wis., Milw., 1965, postgrad., 1973; postgrad., U. Wash., Seattle, 1972. V.p. St. Francis Savs. & Loan, Milw., 1965-72; exec. v.p. Wis. Fin. Services, Milw., 1972-74; v.p. Rep. Savs. & Loan, Milw., 1974-78; regional mgr. PMI Mortgage Ins. Co., Los Angeles, 1978-81; sr. v.p. Nat. Home Equity Corp., Los Angeles, 1981-83; pres. BSC Mortgage Corp., Torrance, Calif., 1983—; v.p. Sterling Bancorp., Los Angeles; bd. dirs. Sterling Bank, Los Angeles. Mem. Mortgage Bankers Am. Republican. Lutheran. Clubs: Pensiula Racquet (Rancho Palos Verdes, Calif.); Rolling Hills Racquet (Torrance). Home: 41 Santa Catalina Dr Rancho Palos Verdes CA 90274 Office: BSC Mortgage Corp 2377 Crenshaw Blvd #350 Torrance CA 90501

BEAVEN, DOUGLAS FREDERICK, management consultant; b. Cambridge, Eng., May 17, 1939; came to U.S., 1939; s. Robert H. and Carolyn (Michel) B.; m. Janet Wood, July 2, 1966; children: Kirsten, Anne. BA, Denison U., 1961; postgrad., U. Pitts., 1964-65. V.p. Booz, Allen & Hamilton, N.Y.C., 1966-77; pres. D.F. Beaven Assocs., Inc., Rye, N.Y., 1977-80; ptnr. Coopers & Lybrand, Boston, 1980—, head strategic planning and productivity practice. Mem. Nat. Assn. Bus. Officers, Coll. and Univ. Systems, Wellesley (Mass.) Country Club. Republican. Mem. United Ch. of Christ. Office: Coopers & Lybrand 1 Post Office Sq Boston MA 02109

BECHERER, HANS WALTER, agricultural equipment manufacturing executive; b. Detroit, Apr. 19, 1935; s. Max and Mariele (Specht) B.; m. Michele Beigbeder, Nov. 28, 1959; children: Maxime, Vanessa. B.A., Trinity Coll., Hartford, Conn., 1957; student, Munich U., Germany, 1958; M.B.A., Harvard U., 1962. Exec. asst. office of chmn. Deere & Co., Moline, Ill., 1966-69; gen. mgr. John Deere Export, Mannheim, Germany, 1969-73; dir. export mktg. Deere & Co., Moline, Ill., 1973-77, v.p., 1977-83, sr. v.p., 1983-86, exec. v.p., 1986-87, pres., chief operating officer, 1987—, also bd. dirs.; dir. U.S.-Yugoslav Econ. Council, Deere & Co.; mem. industry sector adv. com. U.S. Dept. Commerce, 1975-81. Vice pres., trustee St. Katharine's-St. Mark's Sch., Bettendorf, Iowa, 1983. Served to 1st lt. USAF, 1958-60. Mem. Farm and Indsl. Equipment Inst. (bd. dirs. 1987—). Republican. Roman Catholic. Clubs: Rock Island Arsenal Golf (Ill.); Davenport (Iowa). Home: 788 25th Ave Ct Moline IL 61265 Office: Deere & Co John Deere Rd Moline IL 61265

BECHTEL, STEPHEN DAVISON, JR., engineering company executive; b. Oakland, Calif., May 10, 1925; s. Stephen Davison and Laura (Peart) B.; m. Elizabeth Mead Hogan, June 5, 1946; 5 children. Student, U. Colo., 1943-44; BS, Purdue U., 1946, D. in Engring. (hon.), 1972; MBA, Stanford U., 1948; DSc (hon.), U. Colo., 1981. Registered profl. engr., N.Y., Mich., Alaska, Calif., Md., Hawaii, Ohio, D.C., Va., Ill. Engring. and mgmt. positions Bechtel Corp., San Francisco, 1941-60; pres. Bechtel Corp., 1960-73, chmn. of cos. in Bechtel group, 1973-80; chmn. Bechtel Group, Inc., 1980—; bd. dirs. IBM; former chmn. Bus. Council; life councillor, past chmn. Conf. Bd.; mem. policy com. Bus. Roundtable; mem. Labor-Mgmt. Group, Nat. Action Council on Minorities in Engring., from 1974. Trustee, mem., past chmn. bldg. and grounds com. Calif. Inst. Tech.; mem. pres.'s council Purdue U.; mem. adv. council Stanford U. Grad. Sch. Bus. Served with USMC, 1943-46. Decorated officer French Legion of Honor; recipient Disting. Alumnus award Purdue U., 1964, Disting. Alumnus award U. Colo., 1978; Ernest C. Arbuckle Disting. Alumnus award Stanford U. Grad. Sch. Bus., 1974; Man of Yr. Engring. News-Record, 1974; Outstanding Achievement in Constrn. award Moles, 1977; Disting. Engring. Alumnus award U. Colo., 1979; Herbert Hoover medal, 1980; Washington award Western Soc. Engrs., 1985, Chmn.'s award Am. Assn. Engring. Socs., 1982. Fellow ASCE (Engring. Mgmt. award 1979, Pres. award 1985), Instn. Chem. Engrs. (U.K., hon.); mem. AIME, Nat. Acad. Engring. (past chmn., chmn. industry adv. bd.), Calif. Acad. Scis. (hon. trustee), Am. Soc. French Legion of Honor (bd. dirs.), Fellowship of Engring (U.K., fgn. mem.), Chi Epsilon, Tau Beta Pi. Clubs: Pacific Union, Bohemian, San Francisco Golf (San Francisco); Claremont Country (Berkeley, Calif.); Cypress Point (Monterey Peninsula, Calif.); Thunderbird Country (Palm Springs, Calif.); Vancouver (B.C.); Ramada (Houston); Links, Blind Brook (N.Y.C.); Met. (Washington); Augusta (Ga.) National Golf; York (Toronto); Mount Royal (Montreal). Office: Bechtel Group Inc 50 Beale St PO Box 3965 San Francisco CA 94119

BECK, ALBERT, manufacturing company executive; b. N.Y.C., Jan. 14, 1928; s. Albert Christian and Mabel Agnes (Dunn) B.; m. Jean Norma Russ, June 16, 1951; children—Nancy, Richard, Douglas. B.S., Fairleigh Dickinson U., 1950; M.S., Rutgers U., 1956. Product line mgr. Tung Sol Electric Inc. div. Wagner Electric, Bloomfield, N.J., 1951-66; dir. quality control IT&T, Brussels, Belgium, 1966-69; asst. dir. product ops. IT&T, N.Y.C., 1969-72, dir. N.Am. staff, 1972-73; v.p. ops. Grinnell Fire Protection Co., Providence, 1973-79 exec. v.p., 1979; exec. v.p. Grinnell Corp., 1986—. Mem. bd. edn. Wayne, N.J., 1964. Served with A.C., USN, 1945-47. Mem. Am. Soc. Quality Control (sr.), Nat. Fire Sprinkler Assn. (treas., bd. dirs. 1987), Sigma Xi. Republican. Office: Grinnel Corp 3 Tyco Pk Exeter NH 03833

BECK, ANDREW JAMES, lawyer; b. Washington, Feb. 19, 1948; s. Leonard Norman and Frances (Greif) B.; m. Gretchen Ann Schroeder, Feb. 14, 1971; children: Carter, Lowell, Justin. BA, Carleton Coll., 1969; JD, Stanford U., 1972; MBA, Long Island U., 1975. Bar; Va. 1972, N.Y. 1973. Assoc. Casey, Lane & Mittendorf, N.Y.C., 1972-80, ptnr., 1980-82; managing ptnr. Haythe & Curley, N.Y.C., 1982—. Trustee Bklyn. Heights Synagogue, 1980-81, Bklyn. Heights Montessori Sch., 1988—. Mem. ABA, Va. State Bar Assn., New York State Bar Assn., Assn. of Bar of City of N.Y. Home: 71 Willow St Apt 1 Brooklyn NY 11201 Office: Haythe & Curley 437 Madison Ave New York NY 10022

BECK, BRENDA FAYE, communications company executive; b. Grenada, Miss., June 1, 1952; d. Thomas Watson, Jr. and Dorothy Eloise (Clemons) McCaulla; m. Lee Roy Tubbs, Oct. 10, 1971 (div. 1977); m. Charlie Eugene Beck, Apr. 14, 1980; children: Lee Gabriel, Thomas Hugh, Brenda Georgianna, (stepchild) Alethea Dawn. Student, U. Miss., 1978, George Meany Ctr. Labor Studies, 1984, Homes Jr. Coll., 1988—. Long distance operator South Central Bell Telephone, Grenada, 1969-83; computer operator South Central Bell Telephone, Houston, 1975-76; asst. chief operator South Central

Bell Telephone, Grenada, 1977; TSPS operator AT&T Communications, Grenada, 1980, chmn. quality of worklife, 1987—; directory editor Telephone Pioneers Am., Grenada, 1980-81; editor Union First Class, Communications Workers Am., Grenada, 1984—, job steward, 1985—. Editor: Telephone Pioneers Am. Cookbook, 1981. Asst. coach Grenada Soccer League, 1985—; fund raiser Am. Cancer Soc., Grenada, 1986, St. Jude Children's Hosp., Memphis, 1987. Named Operator of the Year, 1973; recipient first place award Hobby Directory for Telephone Pioneers Am., 1980, first place editorial writing award Communications Workers Am./AFL-CIO, 1984. Mem. Future Pioneers Am. Republican. Baptist. Home: 815 Mary Ave Grenada MS 38901-4907 Office: AT&T Communications 404 1st St Grenada MS 38901

BECK, ROBERT RANDALL, investment management executive; b. San Francisco, July 2, 1940; s. Lester L. and Eunice (Hague) B. AB with cert. in pub. affairs, Woodrow Wilson Sch. Princeton U., 1982; MBA, Harvard U., 1967. Producer, dir. Les Films Numero Uno, Paris, 1963-65; with State St. Rsch. and Mgmt. Co., Boston, 1967—, ptnr., 1973-85; mng. ptnr. Marble Arch Ptnrs., 1985—; bd. dir. Mastery Edn. Corp., Petrogen, Inc., Exovir, Inc.; United Artists Communications, Inc.; chmn. Coline Disto SA/Pais; chmn. bd. Am. Mobile Systems, Inc. Bd. trustee, treas. Huntington Theatre, Boston; mem. corp. New Eng. Deaconess Hosp., mem. investment com. Lt. USN, 1962-64. Mem. Boston Soc. Security Analysts. Home: Forest Rd HC 63 Box 76 East Alstead NH 03602 Office: Marble Arch Ptnrs 75 State St Boston MA 02109

BECK, WILLIAM HAROLD, JR., lawyer; b. Clarksdale, Miss., Aug. 18, 1928; s. William Harold and Mary (McGaha) B.; m. Nancy Cassity House, Jan. 30, 1954; children—Mary, Nancy, Katherine. B.A., Vanderbilt U., 1950; J.D., U. Miss., 1954. Bar: Miss. 1954, La. 1960. Atty., Clarksdale, Miss., 1954-57; asst. prof. Tulane U., 1957-59; ptnr. Foley & Judell, New Orleans, 1959-88; of counsel, 1988—. Served to capt., AUS, 1951-53. Mem. ABA, La. Bar Assn., Miss. Bar Assn., SAR, Soc. Colonial Wars, S.R. Office: Foley & Judell 535 Gravier St New Orleans LA 70130

BECKER, CRAIG STEVENS, institute of technology official; b. N.Y.C., Aug. 2, 1952; s. Morris and Adele (Naftel) B. BA in History, SUNY, Oneonta, 1974; MPA, SUNY, Albany, 1976; MS in Acctg., Northeastern U., 1979. CPA, N.Y. Budget analyst Ohio Legis. Budget Office, Columbus, 1976-77; mgmt. analyst Ga. Dept. Audits, Atlanta, 1977-78; from asst. to staff to sr. acct. Peat Marwick Main & Co., Albany, Ga., 1979-82; mgmt. cons. Peat Marwick Main & Co., N.Y.C., 1982-84, sr. cons., 1984-86, mgr., 1987-89; chief fin. officer Stevens Inst. Tech., Hoboken, N.J., 1989—. Mem. Am. Soc. for Pub. Adminstrn., N.Am. Conf. on Ethiopian Jeery (treas., bd. dirs. N.Y.C. chpt. 1986—). Office: Stevens Inst Tech Castle Point on Hudson Hoboken NJ 07003

BECKER, DAVID ALAN, venture capitalist; b. N.Y.C., Oct. 15, 1964; s. Robert Edward and Geraldine (Lerner) B. BS in Econs., U. Pa., 1986. Staff acct. KMG Main Hurdman, N.Y.C., 1985; portfolio mgr. The Revere Fund, Inc., N.Y.C., 1988—; assoc. BV Capital Mgmt., Inc., N.Y.C., 1986—; bd. dirs. United Color Press, Monroe, Ohio, Foster Med. Supply, Inc., Dedham, Mass. Interviewer U. Pa., 1987—. Republican. Office: BV Capital Mgmt Inc 575 Fifth Ave Ste 1700 New York NY 10017

BECKER, EDWARD A., accounting educator, consultant; b. Phila., Jan. 9, 1938; s. Henry L. and Anne M. (Miller) B.; m. Esther Lipson, Aug. 23, 1959 (div. Oct. 1970); children: Felisa R., Jacki M. BS in Acctg., Temple U., 1959; MBA, Drexel U., 1967; PhD, Pa. State U., 1984. CPA, Washington, Pa., N.C. Sr. staff acct. Jack H. Felzer & Co., CPA, Bala Cynwyd, Pa., 1960-67; sr. corp. staff auditor Radio Corp. of Am., N.Y.C., 1967-68; regional controller Laventhol & Horwath, CPA, Phila., 1968-70; treas., controller Scanforms, Inc., Bristol, Pa., 1970-72; controller Empire Assocs., Inc., Phila., 1972-76; sr. staff acct. Friedlander Dunn & Co., CPA, Jenkintown, 1976-77; asst. prof. Bucknell U., Lewisburg, Pa., 1977-83, Va. Commonwealth U., Richmond, 1983-84; assoc. prof. U. N.C., Wilmington, 1984-86; prof., dir. master acctg. program Nova U., Ft. Lauderdale, Fla., 1986—; cons. Lauderhill, Fla., 1986—; mem. New Hanover (N.C.) County Commrs.' Performance Adv. Task Force, 1985-86; frequent speaker for profl. orgns. Reviewer Acad. Accounting Historians Working Paper series, 1982—; editorial bd. Pa. CPA Spokesman/Pa. CPA Jour., 1980-82, 84-85; contbr. articles to profl. jours. Recipient Legion of Honor Chapel of the Four Chaplains, Temple U., 1982. Mem. Beta Gamma Sigma. Home: 7166 NW 49th Ct Lauderhill FL 33319 Office: Nova U Dept Acctg 3301 College Ave Fort Lauderdale FL 33314

BECKER, FRANK JOE, banker; b. Olpe, Kans., Jan. 23, 1936; s. Frank Xavier and Hattie Florentene Becker; m. Barbara Ann Brinkman, June 4, 1960; children: Paula, Connie, Ann, Frank. BSCE, Kans. U., 1958. Chief exec. officer 1st Nat. Bank and Trust Co., El Dorado, Kans., 1979—; past pres. Kans. Motor Carriers, Topeka; bd. dirs. Kans. Gas and Electric Co., Wichita, Great West Life and Annuity Ins. Co., Lawrence, Kans. Comdg. gen. Kans. Cavalry, Topeka, 1983-86; co-chmn., bd. dirs. Kans. Inc., Topeka, 1986—; bd. dirs. Susan B. Allen Meml. Hosp., El Dorado, 1977—, Kans. Bd. Regents, Topeka, 1985-87. Named Vol. of Yr., State of Kans., 1986. Mem. Kans. U. Alumni Assn. (bd. dirs. endowment assn. greater univ. fund, engring. adv. com.). Lodge: KC (grand knight, dist. dep. El Dorado chpt. 1965-67). Office: 1st Nat Bank & Trust Co PO Box 945 El Dorado KS 67042

BECKER, JAMES WILLIAM, natural resource and transportation holding company executive; b. Mpls., Sept. 19, 1942; s. John W. and Beatrice M. (Crowe) B.; m. Jane Claassen Furber, Feb. 24, 1968; children: Stephen William, Thomas Lawrence. BA in Polit. Sci., U. Minn., 1964, JD, 1967. Bar: Minn. 1967, Wash. 1982. Atty. Burlington No. R.R. Co., St. Paul, 1972-78, asst. gen. solicitor, 1978-81, asst. gen. counsel, 1981-84; asst. v.p. law Burlington No. Inc., Seattle, 1984-85, v.p. law, 1985-86, v.p., gen. counsel, 1986-87, sr. v.p. law, 1987—. Trustee endowment fund Bellevue Philharmonic Orch., Seattle, 1987. Mem. ABA, Wash. State Assn., Minn. Bar Assn. Club: Overlake Country (Bellevue, Wash.). Home: 4231 90th Ave SE Mercer Island WA 98040 Office: Burlington No Inc 999 3rd Ave Seattle WA 98104-4097

BECKER, JEFFREY SCOTT, administrator, marketing director; b. Massapequa, N.Y., Dec. 7, 1960; s. Theodore and Barbara B. BA in Pub. Relations, U. Miami, Fla., 1982; cert. mgmt. studies, U. Miami, 1982, MBA in Fin., 1984. Exec. dir., controller The Ea. Sun Adult Congregate Living Facility, Miami Beach, Fla., 1984-86; adminstr. Plaza at James Adult Congregate Living Facility, Miami Beach, 1986—; mng. dir. The Renaissance Hotel, Miami Beach, 1986—, adminstr., 1988—; ops. officer The Pointe Adult Communities, 1989—; cons. to adult living facilities with Becker and Becker, various cities, 1986—. Dep. supr. of nat. elections, Miami, 1986. Mem. Jaycees (Miami Beach), Gerontol. Soc. Am., Am. Biog. Inst. Rsch. (bd. advisors). Republican. Jewish. Lodge: B'nai B'rith (vol. 1984—). Home: 7375 NW 34th ST Lauderhill FL 33149 Office: 1800 E Oakland Park Blvd Fort Lauderdale FL 33306

BECKER, KARL MARTIN, holding company executive; b. Glenridge, N.J., May 30, 1943; s. Alfred Martin and Helen K. (Gramse) B.; m. Barbara A. Benton, Feb. 19, 1966; children—Glenn M., Mark W. A.B., Yale U., 1965; J.D., U. Chgo., 1968. Bar: Ill. Assoc. Vedder Price Kaufman Kammholz, Chgo., 1968-75, ptnr., 1975-78; asst. gen. counsel Esmark, Inc., Chgo., 1978-83, assoc. gen. counsel, 1983-84; v.p., gen. counsel, sec. Swift Ind. Corp., Chgo., 1985-86, sr. v.p., gen. counsel, sec., 1986; sr. v.p., gen. counsel Beatrice Cos., Inc. and BCI Holdings Corp., Chgo., 1986-87, E-II Holdings, Inc., Beatrice Co., Chgo., 1987-88, Beatrice Co., Chgo., 1988—. Mem. Chgo. Bar Assn., ABA. Club: Monroe. Home: 924 Forest Ave Wilmette IL 60091 Office: Beatrice Co 2 N LaSalle St Chicago IL 60602

BECKER, KATHLEEN LENT, nurse, educator, healthcare administrator; b. San Diego, Nov. 16, 1954; d. John William and Elinore (Lepird) Lent; m. Peter J. Becker, Sept. 29, 1979; 1 child, Graham Wiley. BS in Nursing, U. Md., 1977, MS, 1983. Primary nurse intensive care Washington Hosp. Assn., 1978-80; primary nurse discharge planner Vis. Nurse Assn., Balt., 1979-80; nurse Johns Hopkins Hosp., Balt., 1983-84, nurse adminstr., 1985-87; v.p. Cons. for Health and Allied Professions Inc., Balt., 1983—; instr. Johns Hopkins U., Balt., 1984—; cons. Health Care for Homeless, Balt., 1986, 88, Williams and Wilkens Pub. Co., Balt., 1987, Johns Hopkins Health Plan, Balt., 1985. Contbr. articles to profl. jours. Staff Health Task Force on Nursing Home Regulations, Balt., 1983, East Balt. Task Force on Hypertension, 1985-86, Sperks-Glencoe (Md.) Community Assn., 1986—. Mem. Am. Nurses Assn., Md. Nurses Assn. (chmn. nominating com. 1988—, mem. legis. com., 1987—), Council Nurse Practitioners, Kappa Kappa Gamma. Democrat. Lutheran. Office: Johns Hopkins U 600 N Wolfe St Baltimore MD 21205

BECKER, MICHAEL LEWIS, advertising executive; b. Toledo, Oct. 30, 1940; s. Nathan M. and Carolyn (Strasburger) B.; m. Katherine Riesdorph, Mar. 25, 1966; children: Danielle, Adam, Rachel. BS, Syracuse U., 1962. Helicopter traffic reporter Radio Sta. WJRZ, Newark, 1962-64; copywriter Papert, Koenig, Lois, N.Y.C., 1965-68; copywriter, copy chief, sr. v.p., group creative dir. Young & Rubicam, N.Y.C., 1968-83; vice-chmn., chief creative officer Ted Bates Worldwide, N.Y.C., 1983-86; exec. v.p. Ted Bates Worldwide, 1986; exec. v.p., sr. creative dir. Batten, Barton, Durstine & Osborn, N.Y.C., 1986-87; chief creative officer Wunderman Worldwide, N.Y.C., 1987—; asso. vis. prof. Pratt U., Bklyn., 1973-79. With N.J. N.G. Recipient Venice Film Festival Gold and Silver Lions, Internat. Broadcasting awards, CLIO awards, N.Y. Art Dirs. Club awards, N.J. Art Dirs. Club award. Mem. Copy Club of N.Y. Jewish. Office: Wunderman Worldwide 675 Ave of the Americas New York NY 10010

BECKER, RAY EVERETT, data processing executive; b. Grand Rapids, Mich., Jan. 14, 1937; s. Lawson Everett and Virginia Jane (Shellman) B.; m. Mary Rita Warren, Aug. 18, 1960 (div. 1972); children: Elizabeth Anne, Catherine Virginia; m. Arlyss Ellen Roeber, Aug. 12, 1974. AB in Engring., Dartmouth Coll., 1959, MS in Engring and Bus. Adminstrn., 1960; MS in Mgmt., MIT, 1974. Project adminstr. Astro Electronics div. RCA, Hightstown, N.J., 1961-65; bus. mgr.radar lab. Missile Systems div. Raytheon Corp., Bedford, Mass., 1965-68; mgr. mgmt. systems Missile Systems div. Raytheon Corp., Bedford, 1968-70, mgr. adminstrn. and data processing, 1970-73; program mgr. Missile Systems div. Raytheon Corp., Lowell, Mass., 1981-85; mgr. comml. svcs. Raytheon Svc. Co., Burlington, Mass., 1974-75; dir. mktg. Raytheon Svc. Co., Burlington, 1975-80; v.p., mgr. Mideast area Raytheon Overseas Ltd., Riyadh, Saudi Arabia, 1980-81; v.p., gen. mgr. Info. Svcs. div. Keane Inc., Boston, 1985—. Home: 132 Stow Rd Harvard MA 01451 Office: Keane Inc 10 City sq Boston MA 02129

BECKER, ROBERT CHARLES, electrical engineer; b. Madison, Wis., June 15, 1954; s. James Oscar and Eunice Carol (Ziemke) B. BSEE, U. Wis., 1976, MSEE, 1980, PhD in Elec. Engring., 1985. Engr./scientist Collins Arionics Group Rockwell Internat., Cedar Rapids, Iowa, 1977-79; prin. research engr. Gallium Arsenide Components Group Unisys, Eagan, Minn., 1984-88; prin. rsch. scientist systems and rsch. ctr. Honeywell Corp., Mpls., 1988—; cons. J.P. Langan and Assocs., St. Louis Park, Minn., 1984-86. Mem. IEEE. Office: Honeywell Corp 3660 Technology Dr Minneapolis MN 55418

BECKER, ROBERT LEE, industrial automation specialist; b. Adrian, Minn., June 15, 1950; s. Alfred H. and Esther H. (Slater) B.; m. Mary Olson, Nov. 24, 1971; children: Heather, Chad. BME, N.D. State U., 1972; MBA, Oakland U., 1980. With Allen-Bradley Co. div. Rockwell Internat., 1972—; sales engr. Rockwell Internat., Boston and Detroit, 1973-83; dist. mgr. Rockwell Internat., Davenport, Iowa, 1983-86, Denver, 1986—. Mem. Instrument Soc. Am., Soc. Mfg. Engrs., Rocky Mountain Elec. League, Tae Kwon Do Assn. (1st degree black belt), Elks. Home: 7536 Parkview Mountain St Littleton CO 80127 Office: Allen Bradley Co 14828 W 6th Ave Golden CO 80401

BECKER, WILLIAM ADOLPH, insurance association executive; b. Kenosha, Wis., July 2, 1933; s. Adolph Gustav and Helen Marie (Rasmussen) B.; BA, William and Mary Coll., 1957; diploma Cornell U., 1958; m. Mildred Lois Behr, Dec. 13, 1952; children: Verne W., Bradford S., Gregory T. CLU; registered health underwriter. Mgr., Commodore Maury Hotel, Norfolk, Va., 1957-59; field underwriter Home Life Ins. Co. of N.Y., Norfolk, 1959-61; asst. to gen. agt. Union Mutual Life Ins. Co., Richmond, Va., 1961-65; supr. Aetna Life & Casualty, Richmond, 1965-70, mktg. dept. field dir., 1970-71, gen. agt., Utica, N.Y., 1971-74, Syracuse, N.Y., 1974-77; v.p. Life Underwriter Tng. Council, Washington, 1977-82, field exec., mgr. confs. and meetings, 1982—. instr. C.L.U. diploma program, 1973-74, Life Underwriter Tng. Council, Richmond, 1964-68. Mem. Va. Health Ins. Council Hosp. Relations Com. Served with USN, 1950-54. Recipient Louis I. Dublin award for pub. service, 1976, 77. C.L.U. Mem. Am. Soc. C.L.U.'s (pres. Mohawk Valley chpt. 1973-74, pres. No. Va. chpt. 1987-88), Utica Assn. Life Underwriters (pres. 1972-73), N.Y. Assn. Life Underwriters (regional v.p. 1977-78), Am. Soc. Tng. and Devel., Greater Washington Soc. Assn. Execs., Ins. Conf. Planners, Gen. Agts. and Mgrs. Assn., Richmond Assn. Life Underwriters, Nat. Assn. Health Underwriters, Richmond Assn. Health Underwriters, Va. Assn. Health Underwriters, No. Piedmont Assn. Life Underwriters. Republican. Contbg. editor LIMRA Mgrs. Mag., Dow Jones Irwin Pub. Co., Bests Convention Guide, 1988. Office: Life Underwriter Tng Coun 1922 F St NW Washington DC 20006

BECKETT, GRACE, economics educator emerita; b. Smithfield, Ohio, Oct. 7, 1912; d. Roy Martin and Mary (Hammond) Beckett. AB, Oberlin Coll., 1934, AM, 1935; PhD, Ohio State U., 1939. Music supr. Pub. Schs., Kelleys Island, Ohio, 1935-36; grad asst. econs. Ohio State U., 1936-39; assoc. prof. econs. and music Ind. Central Coll., 1939-41: with U. Ill., Champaign-Urbana, 1941—, asst. prof. econs., 1945-51, assoc. prof. econs., 1951-73, assoc. prof. emerita Coll. Commerce and Bus. Adminstrn., 1973—. Author: Reciprocal Trade Agreements Program, 1941, 72; contbr. profl. pubs. Mem. Am. Econ. Assn., Music Educators Nat. Conf., Ill. Music Educators Assn., Econ. History Assn., Am. Finance Assn., Am. Hist. Assn., AAAS, N.Y. Acad. Scis., Ohio Acad. History, Ohio Hist. Soc., Winchester-Frederick County (Va.) Hist. Soc., Ill. Music Tchrs. Assn., Music Tchrs. Nat Assn., Interlochen Alumni Assn. (life), Nat. Band Assn., U. Ill. Alumni Assn. (assoc.), Friends of Art of the Allen Meml. Art Mus. at Oberlin Coll., Nat. Sch. Orch. Assn., Krannert Art Mus. Assos. (U. Ill.), Ohio State U. Alumni Assn., Nat. Honor Soc., Mary Ball Washington Mus. and Library, Met. Mus. Art (N.Y.C.) (nat. asso.), Oberlin Coll. Alumni Assn., Alpha Lambda Delta (hon.), Phi Beta Kappa, Pi Lambda Theta, Phi Chi Theta (hon.). Methodist. Club: Women's at the University of Ill., Oberlin Coll. Half-Century. Address: PO Box 386 Urbana IL 61801

BECKETT, JOHN R., business executive; b. San Francisco, Feb. 26, 1918; s. Ernest J. and Hilda (Hansen) B.; m. Dian Calkin, Nov. 27, 1947 (dec. June 1968); children: Brenda Jean, Belinda Dian; m. Marjorie Abenheim, July 1969. AB, Stanford U., 1939, MA, 1940. Valuator Pacific Gas & Electric Co., 1941-42; utility fin. analyst Duff and Phelps, 1942-43; utility fin. expert SEC, 1943-44; asst. to pres. Seattle Gas Co., 1944-45; investment banker Blyth and Co., 1945-60, v.p., 1955-60; pres. Transam. Corp., 1960-79, chmn. bd. dirs., 1968-82, chief exec. officer, 1965-80, chmn. exec. com., 1982—, also bd. dirs.; bd. dirs. Kaiser Aluminum and Chem. Co., Tex. Eastern Corp., Bank Am., BankAm. Corp., Clorox Co. Clubs: San Francisco Golf, Pacific Union, Bohemian (San Francisco); Cypress Point (Pebble Beach, Calif.). Office: Transamerica Corp 600 Montgomery St San Francisco CA 94111

BECKETT, THEODORE CORNWALL, lawyer; b. Heidelberg, Fed. Republic of Germany, Nov. 21, 1952 (parents Am. Citizens); s. Theodore Charles and Daysie Margaret (Cornwall) B.; m. Patricia Anne McKelvy, June 18, 1983; 1 child: Anna Kathleen. BA, U. Mo., 1975, JD, 1978. Bar: Mo. 1978, U.S. Dist. Ct. (we. dist.) Mo. 1978. Ptnr. Beckett & Steinkamp, Kansas City, Mo., 1978—. Bd. dirs. Kans. Spl. Olympics, 1979-84, legal advisor, 1984—. Mem. ABA, Mo. Bar Assn., Kansas City Bar Assn., Mo. Assn. Trial Attys., Assn. Trial Lawyers Am., Kansas City Club, Carriage Club, Beta Theta Pi. Democrat. Presbyterian. Office: Beckett & Steinkamp 1400 Commerce Bank Bldg PO Box 13425 Kansas City MO 64199

BECKMAN, ARNOLD ORVILLE, chemist, instrument manufacturing company executive; b. Cullom, Ill., Apr. 10, 1900; s. George W. and Elizabeth E. (Jewkes) B.; m. Mabel S. Meinzer, June 10, 1925; children: Gloria Patricia, Arnold Stone. BS, U. Ill., 1922, MS, 1923; PhD, Calif. Inst. Tech., 1928; DSci (hon.), Chapman Coll., 1965; LLD (hon.), U. Calif., Riverside, 1966, Loyola U., L.A., 1969, Whittier Coll., 1971, U. Ill., 1982, Pepperdine U., 1977; DHL (hon.), Calif. State U., 1984. Rsch. assoc. Bell Tel. Labs., N.Y.C., 1924-26; chem. staff Calif. Inst. Tech., 1926-39; v.p. Nat. Tech. Lab., Pasadena, Calif., 1935-39; pres. Nat. Tech. Lab., 1939-40, Helipot Corp., 1944-58, Arnold O. Beckman, Inc., South Pasadena, Calif., 1946-58, Beckman Instruments, Inc., Fullerton, Calif., 1940-65; chmn. bd. Beckman Instruments, Inc. (sub. SmithKline Beckman Corp.), from 1965; vice chmn. SmithKline Beckman Corp., 1984-86; bd.dir. Security Pacific Nat. Bank, 1956-72, adv. dir., 1972-75; bd. dir. Continental Airlines, 1956-71, adv. dir., 1971-73. Author articles in field; inventor. Mem. Pres.'s Air Quality Bd., 1970-74; chmn. System Devel. Found., 1970-88; chmn. bd. trustees emeritus Calif. Inst. Tech.; hon. trustee Calif. Mus. Found.; bd. overseers House Ear Inst., 1981—; trustee Scripps Clinic and Rsch. Found., 1971-83, hon. trustee, 1983—; bd. dirs. Hoag Meml. Hosp. With USMC, 1918-19. Benjamin Franklin fellow Royal Soc. Arts.; named to Nat. Inventors Hall of Fame, 1987. Fellow Assn. Clin. Scientists; mem. Am. Acad. Arts and Scis., L.A. C. of C. (bd. dir. 1954-58, pres. 1956), Calif. C. of C. (dir., pres. 1967-68), Nat. Acad. Engring. (Founders Award, 1987), N.A.M., Am. Inst. Chemists, Instrument Soc. Am. (pres. 1952), Am. Chem. Soc., AAAS, Social Sci. Rsch. Coun., Am. Assn. Clin. Chemistry (hon.), Newcomen Soc., Sigma Xi, Delta Upsilon, Alpha Chi Sigma, Phi Lambda Upsilon. Clubs: Newport Harbor Yacht, Pacific. Home: 107 Shorecliff Rd Corona del Mar CA 92625 Office: 100 Academy Dr Irvine CA 92715

BECKMAN, JAMES WALLACE BIM, economist, business executive; b. Mpls., May 2, 1936; s. Wallace Gerald and Mary Louise (Frissell) B. B.A., Princeton U., 1958; Ph.D., U. Calif., 1973. Pvt. practice econ. cons., Berkeley, Calif. 1962-67; cons. Calif. State Assembly, Sacramento, 1967-68; pvt. practice market research and econs. consulting, Laguna Beach, Calif., 1969-77; cons. Calif. State Gov.'s Office, Sacramento 1977-80; pvt. practice real estate cons., Los Angeles 1980-83; v.p. mktg. Gold-Well Investments, Inc., Los Angeles 1982-83; pres. Beckman Analytics Internat., econ. cons. to bus. and govt., Los Angeles and Lake Arrowhead, Calif., 1983—. Served to maj. USMC 1958-67. NIMH fellow 1971-72. Fellow Soc. Applied Anthropology; mem. Am. Econs. Assn., Am. Statis. Assn., Am. Mktg. Assn. (officer), Nat. Assn. Bus. Economists (officer). Democrat. Presbyterian. Contbr. articles to profl. jours. Home: Drawer 2350 Crestline CA 92325

BECKMAN, JUDITH KALB, financial counselor and planner, lecturer, writer; b. Bklyn., June 27, 1940; d. Harry and Frances (Cohen) Kalb; m. Richard Martin Beckman, Dec. 16, 1961; children: Barry Andrew, David Mark. BA, Hofstra U., 1962; MA, Adelphi U., 1973, cert. fin. planning, 1984. Promotion coordination pub. rels. Mandel Sch. for Med. Assts., Hempstead, N.Y., 1973-74; exec. dir. Nassau Easter Seals, Albertson, N.Y., 1974-76; dir. pub. info. Long Beach Meml. Hosp., N.Y., 1976-77; account rep. First Investors, Hicksville, N.Y., N.Y.C., 1977-78; sales asst., then account exec. Josephthal & Co. Inc., Great Neck, N.Y., 1978-81; v.p., cert. fin. planner Arthur Gould Inc., Great Neck, 1981-88; pres. Fin. Solutions (affiliated with Seco West Ltd., Goldner Siegfried Assocs. Inc.), Westbury, N.Y., 1988—; adj. instr. Adelphi U., Garden City N.Y., 1981-83, Molloy Coll., Rockville Ctr., N.Y., 1982-84; lectr. SUNY-Farmingdale, 1984-85; creater, presenter seminars, workshops on fin., investing, 1981—. Fin. columnist The Women's Record, 1985—; writer quar. newspaper The Reporter, 1987. Recipient citation for leadership Town of Hempstead, N.Y., 1986, L.I. Press Club award Bus. Column, 1987. Coord. meat boycott, L.I., 1973; co-founder, chairperson L.I. del. High Profile Men and Women, Colonie Hill, Hauppauque, N.Y., 1985; sec., treas. L.I. Alzheimer's Found., 1989—. Recipient Bus. Writer award Press Club, 1987, Mentor award SBA, 1989. Mem. Nat. Assn. Women Bus. Owners L.I. (bd. dirs. 1987—), Women's Econ. Developers of L.I. (bd. dirs. 1985—), Internat. Assn. Fin. Planners (L.I. chpt.), Inst. Cert. Fin. Planners, L.I. Ctr. Bus. and Profl. Women (pres. 1984—), C.W. Post Tax Inst., Am. Soc. Women Accts. Republican. Jewish. Avocations: theater, classical music, opera, reading. Home: 2084 Beverly Way Merrick NY 11566 Office: Fin Solutions care Goldner Siegfried Assocs Inc 51 Locust Ave Ste 304 New Canaan CT 06840

BECKNELL, PATRICIA ANN, design company manager; b. Spartanburg, S.C., May 6, 1950; d. Joseph Lloyd and Annie (Wofford) B. Student, U.S.C., 1969-70; BS in Bus. Mgmt., Limestone Coll., 1978-81. Market research asst. Spartan Mill Sales, Spartanburg, 1970-73; bookkeeper, auditor Realtec Inc., Sapphire, N.C., 1973-76; computer coordinator Internat. Minerals and Chemical, Spartanburg, 1976-84; mgr. Tropical Design Inc., Lyman, S.C., 1984-88, pres., 1988—; also bd. dirs. Tropical Design Inc., Lyman; pres. Tropical Design USA, Lyman, 1988—, also bd. dirs.; pres. Tropical Design BHM, Birmingham, Ala., 1988—; also bd. dirs. Tropical Design BHM, Birmingham. Mem. Am. Bus. Women's Assn. (pres. 1983-84, v.p. 1982-83, rec. sec. 1981-82, Woman of the Yr. 1983), Inst. Bus. Designers, Upper State Apt. Assn. Episcopalian. Office: Tropical Design Inc 190 Murphy Rd Lyman SC 29365

BECKSTEDT, JOHN EDGAR, investment banker; b. Milw., May 12, 1947; s. Carl A. and Ada (Kelley) B.; BA, Wis. State U., 1971; postgrad. John Marshall Law Sch., 1971-73; m. Linda Nienow, June 12, 1971; children—John Edgar, Robert Christopher. Law clk. firm Walsh, Case and Coale Assos., Chgo., 1971-73; mgr. sales and leasing Royal Truck & Trailer Co., Chgo., 1974-80; v.p. Seng Truck Leasing Co., Bensenville, Ill., 1980-84; Lyons Leasing and Equipment Co., 1984-86; pres. The Chgo. Corp., 1986—; mgr. ptnr. FIBS, 1985—; dir. H.P. Transfer Co., Seng Warehouse & Distbn. Co. Sec. Wilmette (Ill.) Coun. for Comml. Renewal, 1976-77; co-chmn. Wilmette Fourth of July Commn., 1976, 77, 78; precinct capt. Rep. Com., Wilmette, 1975—; plan commr. for Wilmette, 1980—; bd. dirs. Wilmette United Way, 1979-84. Named Outstanding Young Man Am., Jaycees, 1978. Mem. Chgo. C. of C., Ill. Trucking Assn., Traffic Club Chgo., Truck Rental and Leasing Assn. Am., Wilmette Jaycees (external v.p. 1976-77, 78-79), U.S. Yacht Racing Union, Nat. Handball Assn. Am., Whitewater Alumni Assn., Phi Alpha Delta, Phi Sigma Epsilon (chpt. v.p. 1968-69), Phi Sigma Kappa. Roman Catholic. Home: 2501 Thornwood Rd Wilmette IL 60091 Office: Heart Truck & Trailer Sales 600 N Thomas Dr Bensenville IL 60106

BECKWITH, RODNEY FISK, management consultant; b. Passaic, N.J., Oct. 24, 1935; s. Raymond Fisk and Nancy Angel (Oberdorf) B.; B.M.E. with distinction, Cornell U., 1958; M.B.A. with distinction, Harvard U., 1963; m. Elizabeth Ann Wedemann, July 23, 1960; children:Allison Beckwith Melson, Kimberly Hall. Plant engr. Western Electric Co., Kearny, N.J., 1960-61; sr. asso. Cresap, McCormick and Paget, Inc., N.Y.C., 1963-68, prin., N.Y.C., 1968-72, v.p., Melbourne, Australia, 1972-77, v.p., dir., exec. com., N.Y.C., 1977-83; v.p., dir. Fin. Instns. Services, 1983-84, v.p., dir. internat. 1984—. Bd. dirs. Am. C. of C., Australia, 1975-77. Served with USN, 1958-60, to lt. USNR, 1960-65. Mem. Inst. Mgmt. Cons.'s (founding), Delta Upsilon. Presbyterian. Clubs: Harvard, Board Room (N.Y.C.); Australian (Melbourne); Wee Burn Country (Darien, Conn.). Home: 8 Nolen Ln Darien CT 06820 Office: Fin Instns Svcs 245 Park Ave New York NY 10017

BECRAFT, FRANK JOSEPH, natural gas company executive; b. Sioux Falls, S.D., Nov. 29, 1943; s. John Richard and Esther Irene (Moore) B. ; m. Sandra Sue Alm, Dec. 20, 1969; children: Malinda, John. BS, Drake U., 1965; grad. Program for Mgmt. Devel., Harvard U., 1979. Sr. rep. No. Natural Gas Co., Houston and Midland, Tex., 1965-74; v.p. Northwest Pipeline Co., Salt Lake City, 1974-84; exec. v.p. Valero Transmission Co., San Antonio, 1984-86; sr. v.p. natural gas div. Valero Energy Corp., San Antonio, 1984—; pres., chief operating officer Valero Transmission Co., San Antonio, 1986—. Chmn. commerce and industry div. United Way, San Antonio, 1985; exec. chmn. Explorer Scouts Boy Scouts Am., San Antonio, 1987. Mem. So. Gas Assn. (bd. dirs. 1985—), Natural Gas Men of Houston, Assn. of Tex. Intrastate Natural Gas Pipelines, Interstate Natural Gas Assn. Am. Methodist. Clubs: Dominion Country, Giraud (San Antonio).

BEDESEM, MICHAEL PETER, electronics executive; b. N.Y.C., Apr. 1, 1942; s. Peter and Mildred M. Bedesem; m. Joan Keenan (div. 1974); children: Peter, Kristin, Scott, Erik; m. Elizabeth Bickelhaupt, Feb. 14, 1974; children: Adrianne, Barbara. BS in Physics, Bucknell U., 1964; MS in Physics, Western Res. U., 1966. Mktg. mgr. LeCroy Corp., Spring Valley, N.Y., 1966-74, exec. v.p., 1974-86, pres., 1986—, also bd. dirs. Office: LeCroy Corp 700 S Chestnut Ridge Rd Chestnut Ridge NY 10977

BEDFORD, ROBERT GEORGE, furniture company executive; b. Cleve., July 24, 1943; s. Edward A. and Mary Ane (Stupar) B.; m. Barbare Ane (Samodell) B., Apr. 1, 1967; children: Robert C., Amy K., Patience A., Deanne A. BBA, John Carroll U., 1965; MBA, Ball State U., 1967. With sales and mgmt. Litton Industries Inc./P.T.N., Beverly Hills, Calif., 1967-74; industry sales mgr. Rexnord, Milw., 1974-79; sr. product mgr., gen. mgr. Sunarhauserman Inc., Cleve., 1980—; owner, cons. Bartel Assocs., Cleve., 1984—. Author pamphlet Plan for Planning for Vols., 1984 (hon. mention AMA Pub.). Planning coordinator Cleve. Roman Catholic Archdiocese, 1981—; instr., dir. Contract Mag.'s Workshops, Chgo., 1987—. Recipient 35 Yrs. Recognition award Jr. Achievement, 1983. Mem. Product Mgrs. Assn. (regional officer 1981-87). Republican. Home: 17843 Fox Hollow Dr Strongsville OH 44136 Office: Sunarhauserman Inc 5711 Grant Ave Cleveland OH 44129

BEDI, RAHUL, general management professional; b. Patiala, Punjab, India, Sept. 27, 1941; came to U.S., 1979; s. Satya Vrat and Laj Bedi; m. Susham Dhameja, Dec. 11, 1969; children: Varun, Purva. MSc, J&K U., Jammu, India, 1962; cert bus. adminstrn., Imede Mgmt Devel. Inst., Lausanne, Switzerland, 1971; MBA, NYU, 1982. Asst. mgr. Singlo Tea Co., Calcutta, India, 1964-72; estate mgr. Dooars Tea Co., Calcutta, 1972-74; dep. dir. Tea Bd. India, Brussels, 1974-79; chief exec. officer Tea Bd. of India, N.Y.C., 1979—. State rep. Experiment in Internat. Living, 1967-74. Recipient Best Asst. Mgr. award Bd. Dirs., Calcutta, 1971. Mem. Tea Council U.S.A. Inc. (bd. dirs. 1979—), Tea Council Can. (bd. dirs. 1979—), Internat. Platform Assn., India C. of C. of Am. (v.p. 1981—), Internat. Platform Assn., Imede Alumni Assn., Beta Gamma Sigma. Club: Chief Exec. Officers (N.Y.C.). Office: Tea Bd India 445 Park Ave New York NY 10022

BEDIKIAN, RHONDA COLETTE, accountant, financial consultant; b. Jersey City, Jan. 20, 1950; d. Hyman and Marie-Jose Gabrielle (Gerard) Rodetsky; m. Bruce Melvin Miller, Aug. 16, 1969 (div. Aug. 1976); 1 child, Brent Joseph; m. Johnny Nobar Bedikian, Dec. 29, 1985; 1 child, Denise Sarah. AA, Bergen Community Coll., 1976; BS in Acctg. and Fin., U. So. Calif., 1978. Bookkeeper JMRH Inc., Tarzana, Calif., 1977-79; jr. acct. Motown Records Inc., Hollywood, Calif., 1979-80; chief acct. Chrysalis Records Inc., Los Angeles, 1980-83; acctg. mgr. Platt Music Corp., Torrance, Calif., 1983; asst. controller Contempo Casuals Inc. Div. Neiman-Marcus, Los Angeles, 1984-88; dir. acctg. Capitol Records, Inc. Div. Thorn-EMI, Hollywood, Calif., 1988—; cons. in field. Active City of Hope, Am. Ballet Theatre, The Ahmanson Theatre. Office: Capitol Records Inc 1750 N Vine St HV8 Hollywood CA 90028

BEDNARIK-HANSEN, JULIA MARIE, accountant, auditor; b. Oconto Falls, Wis., May 30, 1959; d. Edward Michael and Utibela Ludmila (Bobik) B.; m. Lee Edmund Hansen, Sept. 3, 1983. BBA, U. Wis., Oshkosh, 1983; postgrad., Columbus (Ga.) Coll., 1984, Chaminade U., 1984; M. in Acctg., U. Hawaii, 1987. CPA, Hawaii. Teller 1st Wis. Nat. Bank, Oshkosh, 1983-84; sr. auditor Terry Wong, CPA, Inc., Honolulu, 1986—; acctg. researcher, 1986—. vol. Ft. Shafter Chapel, 1986-88. Mem. Am. Prodn. and Inventory Control Soc. (cert.), Mil. Wives' Club, Beta Gamma Sigma. Republican. Home: 2520-D Village Ln Oshkosh WI 54904

BEDROSIAN, EDWARD ROBERT, investment management company executive; b. Chgo., June 30, 1932; s. Kesrow and Rebecca (Babian) B.; m. Diane Yvonne Morse, Aug. 25, 1956; children: Dawn Eve, Cynthia Sarah, Edward Robert. B.S.C.E., Ill. Inst. Tech., 1954; M.S.C.E., M.I.T., 1955; M.B.A., Harvard U., 1964. Registered profl. engr., Mass. Treas. Ea. Shokcrate Corp., Bound Brook, N.J., 1964-65; v.p., treas. Polaroid Corp., Cambridge, Mass., 1965-87; chmn. Merganser Capital Mgmt. Corp., Combridge, Mass., 1987—; bd. dirs. Nat. Micronetics, Inc. Served with USNR, 1955-60. Mem. Fin. Execs. Inst., Treasurers Club of Boston. Conglist. Home: 43 Wingate Rd Wellesley MA 02181 Office: Merganser Capital Mgmt Corp 1 Cambridge Ctr Cambridge MA 02142

BEDROSSIAN, PETER STEPHEN, lawyer, business executive; b. Hoboken, N.J., Sept. 15, 1926; s. Nishan and Helen (Jamagotchian) B.; m. Jean M. Reynolds, Jan. 1951 (div. Oct. 1962); children: Peter, Alice Marie; m. JoAnn H. Thorpson, Nov. 16, 1962 (div. July 1986); children: Stephanie Ann, Jennifer Ann. B.B.A., St. Johns U., 1949, J.D., 1954. Bar: N.Y. 1954, Calif. 1973. Chief acct. Stauffer Chem. Co., N.Y.C., 1948-58; dir. taxes Stauffer Chem. Co., 1958-76, asst. treas., 1961-76; mem. firm Dobbs, Berger & Molinari, San Francisco, 1976-80; pres. Parrot Ranch Co., San Francisco, 1982—; v.p., dir. Stauffer Chem. Internat., Geneva, Switzerland, 1959-62; Vice chmn. Nitron Inc., Cupertino, Calif.; dir. Kali-Chemie Stauffer, Hannover, Germany, Stauffer Chem. Co. Internat. Served with AUS, 1944-46. Mem. Am., N.Y., Calif. bar assns., Tax Execs. Inst. (pres. N.Y. chpt.), Internat. Assn. Assessing Officers, Am. Electronics Assn., Am. Legion, Phi Delta Phi, Alpha Kappa Psi. Club: N.Y. Athletic (N.Y.C.); Beach and Tennis (Pebble Beach, Fla.). Address: PO Box 122 Pebble Beach CA 93953-0122

BEDSWORTH, JAMES HOWARD, investment company executive, accountant, financial planner; b. Kansas City, Kans., Jan. 21, 1936; s. Charles R. and Lottie I. (Wheatley) B.. m. Mary Sue Card, Sept. 7, 1958; children: John B., Bryan T., Jennifer K., J. Andrew, Jason T. BS, Olivet Nazarene Coll., 1958; MBA, U. Okla., 1960; cert., Coll. for Fin. Planning, Denver, 1981. CPA, Mich., Kans. Jr. acct. Touche, Ross and Co., Kansas City, Mo., 1960-62; acct., sr. acct. Sinderson Henning and Mueller, Kansas City, Kans., 1962-64; v.p. fin., sec.-treas., bd. dirs. Marantette and Co., Detroit, 1964-67; comptroller 1st of Mich. Corp., Detroit, 1968-70; pres., chief exec. officer, bd. dirs. Alexander Hamilton Fin. Inc., Farmington Hills, Mich., 1970-73; regional sales mgr. Monex Internat. Ltd., Troy, Mich., 1974-75; exec. v.p., owner Internat. Trading Group Ltd., Southfield, Mich., 1976-78; v.p. mktg. U.S. Mut. Real Estate Investment Trust, Detroit, 1978-80; pres., owner Bedford Internat. Corp., Grosse Pointe, Mich., 1981—. Author: How to Choose a Financial Planner and Why You Should, 1984; contbr. articles to profl. jours. Bd. dirs., fund raiser Grosse Pointe Little League Baseball, 1978-84. Mem. AICPA, Inst. Cert. Fin. Planners (cert.), Mich. Assn. CPAs, Registry Fin. Planning Practitioners, Internat. Assn. for Fin. Planning (v.p., exec. v.p., pres., chmn. southeast Mich. 1978-84), Midwest Assn. for Fin. Planning (pres., chmn. bd. 1984-86), Optimist (bd. dirs. Grosse Pointe 1986-88). Office: Bedford Internat Corp PO Box 36430 Grosse Pointe MI 48236

BEEBE, LEO CLAIR, industrial equipment executive, former educator; b. Williamsburg, Mich., July 20, 1917; s. Fred Grant and Rena (Allton) B.; m. Jan Wyss, Mar. 11, 1966; children—Leo Peter, Anne Lorraine. BS in Edn., U. Mich., 1939; postgrad., Wayne U., 1942-43; MA, Glassboro State Coll., 1985. With Ford Motor Co. (various locations), 1945-72; gen. mgr. consumers products div. Philco-Ford, Phila.; also exec. v.p. Philco-Ford, until 1972; prof. mgmt. Glassboro State Coll., 1972-85, dean bus. adminstrn., 1977-85; chmn. bd. John Hancock Health Plan of Pa., 1982—; dir. K-Tron Internat., 1976—, chmn., chief exec. officer, 1985—; mgr. winning Ford Motor racing team culminating in 1st U.S. 1-2-3 victory in 24 hour endurance race, LeMans, France, 1966; cons. Nat. Council Better Bus. Burs., 1972-74, sec. HEW, 1978-81. Author numerous manuals, articles speeches on refugee and hardcore disadvantaged employment. Vice chmn. Pres. Eisenhower's Com. for Hungarian Refugees; dir. program to resettle 36,000 refugees; dir. Cuban Refugee Center, Miami, 1960; chief exec. Pres. Johnson's Program for Hardcore Employment, 1968; mem. Pres. Johnson's Commn. for Exec. Exchange; chmn. Civic Com. on Sch. Needs, Dearborn, Mich., 1958; pres. Dearborn Boys' Club, 1955-60; chmn. numerous campaigns YMCA, United Fund; bd. dirs. Reading is Fundamental; trustee Va. Union U.; Trustee Misericordia Coll., 1983—; chmn. bd. dirs. United Way Gloucester County. Served with USNR, 1942-45. Recipient Gold plate award for achievement Nat. Acad. Achievement, 1969. Mem. Nat. Alliance Businessmen (founding pres.), Indsl. Audio Visual Assn. (past pres.), C. of C. So. N.J. (bd. dirs., vice chmn.). Episcopalian. Club: Rotary (past dist. gov.). Home: 108 Glenn Rd Ardmore PA 19003 Office: K-Tron Internat Pitman NJ 08071

BEEBY, KENNETH JACK, lawyer, food company executive; b. Peoria, Ill., May 21, 1936; s. Harold J. and L. and Elizabeth (Otten) B.; m. Shelley Jean Seip, June 14, 1959; children—Kathryn Jean, Sara Jane, Christine Vivian. B.A., Beloit (Wis.) Coll., 1958, J.D., Northwestern U., 1961. Bar: Ind. 1961, Ill. 1961, Mo. 1962, Mass. 1974. Staff atty. Seven-Up Co., St. Louis, 1961-73; house counsel, then chief legal officer Ocean Spray Cranberries, Inc., Hanson, Mass., 1973-77; v.p., gen. counsel Ocean Spray Cranberries, Inc., Plymouth, Mass., 1977—, sec., 1982—. Mem. ABA, Mass. Bar Assn., Am. Corp. Counsel Assn., Am. Soc. of Corp. Secs., Ancient and Illustrious Order of Colfax. Office: Ocean Spray Cranberries Inc 225 Water St Plymouth MA 02360

BEECH, CHARLES WILLIAM, JR., manufacturing company official; b. Mobile, Ala., Oct. 27, 1961; s. Charles William and Esther Faye (Patrick) B. BS, U. Ala., 1985. Mfg. control supr. MacMillan Bloedel Inc., Pine Hill, Ala., 1985—. Vol. tutor Tuscaloosa (Ala.) Pub. Schs., 1981; vol. ARC, 1978-80. Baptist. Home: 12 Bridgeport Camden AL 36726 Office: MacMillan Bloedel Inc Pine Hill AL 36769

BEECHER, EARL WILLIAM, marketing professional; b. Chgo., June 18, 1942; s. Adolph Bernard and Dorothy M. (McEwen) B.; m. Dec. 1, 1962; children: Katherine, Ann. BS in Bus., St. MatthewsU., 1964; A in Fin., Loyola U., 1967; LHD (hon.), Mt. Sinai Theol. Sem., 1971. Sales rep. Burroughs Corp., Detroit, 1964-67; br. mgr. Friden Co., Chgo., 1967-71; dir. mktg. Friden Co., San Leandro, Calif., 1971-75; pres. Standard Bus. Machine Co., Los Angeles, 1975-81; nat. sales mgr. Xerox Corp., Dallas, 1981-83; pres. EBS Data, Denver, 1983-86; v.p. Hedman Co., Chgo., 1986—; pres. Comml. Resources, Denver, 1981—, also bd. dirs.; bd. dirs. Roma Corp., 1984-86. Rep. precint cpt., Shaumburg, Ill., 1969; rep. fund raiser, Dallas, 1982. Mem. Machine Dealers Assn., Alpha Psi Omega (bd. dirs. 1971), Duke of Manchester Hunt Club, Cape Cod Yacht Club. Office: Comml Resources Inc 3 Golf Ctr Ste 267 Hoffman Estates IL 60195

BEECHER, ROBERT WILLIAM, accounting company executive; b. Boston, Aug. 13, 1931; s. Leslie Dade and Ellen Frances (Duggan) B.; m. Myrna Joy MacClary, Mar. 19, 1955 (div. Dec. 1983); children—Joy A. Beecher Emerson, Gregory R., Joel T., Jennifer E., Pamela M.; m Georgina Marie Canty, July 11, 1984. B.S. summa cum laude, Boston U., 1957. C.P.A., N.Y., Mass. Acct. Peat, Marwick, Mitchell & Co., Boston and N.Y.C., 1957-65; ptnr., mng. ptnr. Peat, Marwick, Mitchell & Co., White Plains, N.Y. and Boston, 1965-81; vice chmn. Peat, Marwick, Mitchell & Co., Boston, 1981-84; dep. chmn. Peat Marwick Main & Co. (formerly Peat, Marwick, Mitchell & Co.), N.Y.C., 1984—. Past corporator Mus. of Sci., Boston; past mem. bd. visitors Boston U.; past mem. Mass. Gen. Hosp., Boston, Mass. Fgn. Bus. Council; past treas. Newton-Wellesley Hosp., Wellesley, Mass.; past mem. bd. dirs. Boston Mcpl. Research Bur., Greater Boston C. of C. Served with U.S. Army, 1952-54 Korea. Mem. Am. Inst. C.P.A.s, N.Y. State C.P.A.s, Mass. Soc. C.P.A.s, Nat. Assn. Accts., Beta Gama Sigma. Republican. Clubs: Board Room, Economic (N.Y.C.). Office: Peat Marwick Main & Co 767 Fifth Ave New York NY 10153

BEED, DAVID JAMES, insurance company executive; b. Hampton, Iowa, Jan. 7, 1945; s. David and Marjorie (Baker) B.; m. Cheryl McDaniel,, June 21, 1969 (div. 1979); 1 child, Jennifer C.; m. Allison Barringer, Jan. 16, 1981; 1 child, Ian. BA, U. Iowa, 1968. Regional group mgr. Prudential, L.A., 1971-76; asst. mgr. Fidelity Mut., Beverly Hills, Calif., 1976-78; v.p. CIMA, Washington, 1978-83; sr. v.p. group mktg. Transam., Los Angeles, 1983-87, exec. v.p., chief mktg. officer, 1987—. Mem. benefits com. D.C. Spl. Olympics, Family Crisis Ctr. 1st lt. U.S. Army, 1968-71. Mem. Kiwanis. Office: Transam Life Cos 1150 S Olive St Los Angeles CA 90015

BEEMSTER, JOSEPH ROBERT, manufacturing executive; b. Chgo., Nov. 11, 1941; s. Joseph Z. and Emily (Dehaus) B.; BA, DePaul U., 1962; postgrad. Ill. Inst. Tech., 1976, 77, U. Minn., 1979, 80; m. Judith L. Schefers, Sept. 7, 1963; children—David, Susan. Mfg. mgr. Johnson & Johnson, Chgo., 1967-71, mgr. safety and security, 1971-78; corporate dir. safety and health Pacific Dunlop GNB Inc., St. Paul, 1978-88; dir. loss control svcs. Richard Oliver Risk Mgrs., 1988—. Author: Safe Work Practices for Workers Exposed to Lead; producer videotapes on health and safety tng. Chmn., Bolingbrook (Ill.) Human Relations Commn., 1971-77. Mem. Am. Soc. Safety Engrs., Am. Indsl. Hygiene Assn. Home: 1606 Hadley Ct Wheeling IL 60090 Office: 3227 Wilke Rd Ste 2701 Arlington Heights IL 60004

BEERMAN, ALBERT LOWELL, accountant; b. Atlanta, Nov. 21, 1934; s. Mannie Robert and Celia (Bergman) B.; m. Bonnie Zuber (div. Mar. 1986); children: Cindy, Carol; m. Glenda Ilene Novak, May 26, 1986. BA, Rice U., 1956. Staff acct. Arthur Young & Co., Houston, 1956-57; staff acct. Farb Miller & Co., Houston, 1957-58, pntr., 1958-68; pntr. Alexander Grant & Co., Houston, 1969-70, Chgo., 1970-79; pntr. Touche Ross & Co., Atlanta, 1979—; mem. U. Tex. Acctg. Adv. Council, Austin, 1978—. Contbr. articles to mags. Pres. Jewish Vocat. Service, Atlanta; mem. Rice U. Fund Council, 1977-80. Mem. Am. Inst. CPA's, Ga. Soc. CPA's, Belgian-Am. C. of C. (bd. dirs., exec. com.), Rice Alumni Orgn. (chmn.). Clubs: Standard, Commerce (Atlanta). Home: 2 Misty Ridge Manor Atlanta GA 30327 Office: Touche Ross & Co 225 Peachtree St Atlanta GA 30043-6901

BEERMANN KAPPALADONNA, JUDITH COUNTESA ANA, investment and real estate company executive; b. Falls City, Nebr., May 19, 1945; d. August and Minnie Sophie (Ohlensehlen) Biermann; m. William August Beermann, Feb. 13, 1977 (dec. Dec. 1979); children—Kristine Kay, Angeline Ann; m. Otto Von Bismarchi, June 24, 1984. M.A., Kans. State U., 1966; postgrad. Moana Coll., 1971. Saleslady, Rudy's, Falls City, 1960-61, with Kappala Donna Enterprises Systems Inc., Honolulu, 1967—, pres., exec. owner, 1984—; mem. Charles Schwab & Co., Inc., 1985. Del., Republican Conv., Honolulu, 1983-84; trustee Honolulu Bay Hosp. Assn., Hawaiian Bankers Assn. (bd. dirs.). Mem. Am. Mgmt. Assn., Am. Entrepreneurs Assn., Hawaiian Real Estate Assn. (bd. dirs.), Nat. Assn. Female Execs. Lutheran. Clubs: Kamabemaha, Rose of Hawaii, Club House Hawaii, Sorority Club Hawaii. Avocations: golf, water skiing. Home: 7316 Maple St Omaha NE 68134

BEERNINK, DARRELL WAYNE, actuary, life insurance company executive; b. Maurice, Iowa, Oct. 28, 1937; s. Harold William and Henrietta (Vermeer) B.; m. Alyce E. Poelman, Aug. 28, 1965; children: Bryan Scott, Kristen Joy, Sara Lynne. AA, Northwestern Coll., Orange City, Iowa, 1957; BA, Hope Coll., 1959; MS, U. Iowa, 1961. CLU; CPCU. Actuary, v.p. State Farm Life Ins. Co., Bloomington, Ill., 1961—, State Farm Life & Accident Ins. Co., Bloomington, 1961—, State Farm Annuity Co., Bloomington, 1961—. Bd. dirs. Home Sweet Home Mission, Bloomington. Fellow Soc. Actuaries, Life Office Mgmt. Assn.; mem. Am. Acad. Actuaries, Am. Coll. Life Underwriters, Am. Inst. Property and Liability Underwriters. Republican. Baptist. Office: State Farm Life Ins Co One State Farm Pla Bloomington IL 61710

BEESLEY, THOMAS EDWARD, chemical executive; b. Somerville, N.J., June 28, 1937; s. Edward and Mary (Koval) B.; m. Mary Anne Engel, Dec. 26, 1959; children: Thomas David, Mark Vincent, Margaret Ann. BS, Mt. St. Mary's Coll., 1959; MS, St. John's U., Jamaica, N.Y., 1961. Biochemist researcher Bristol-Meyers Co., Hillside, N.J., 1961-62; researcher Merck, Sharpe & Dohme, Rahway, N.J., 1962-67; founder, dir. research and devel. Quantum Industries, Fairfield, N.J., 1967-70, pres., 1970-72; v.p. tech. Whatman Chem. Separation, Clifton, N.J., 1972-83; founder, pres. Advanced Separation Techs. Inc., Whippany, N.J., 1983—. Contbr. research articles to tech. jours.; patentee extraction apparatus, bonded phase materials for chromatographic separations. Mem. Am. Chem. Soc. Republican. Roman Catholic. Office: ASTEC 37 Leslie Ct Whippany NJ 07981

BEETHAM, STANLEY WILLIAMS, consumer products executive; b. Montpelier, Idaho, Nov. 2, 1933; s. Harry Stanley and Mary (Williams) B.; 1 child, Lara Mary; m. Barbara Burnham Barnard, June 20, 1987. BA, Wesleyan U., 1956; MA, U. Amsterdam (Netherlands), 1957; postgrad. Harvard U., 1958-59, U. Wash., 1959-60. Internat. market mgr. U.S. Rubber/Uniroyal, N.Y.C., 1960-63; corp. mktg. cons. Gen. Electric Co., N.Y.C., 1963-65; assoc. dir. Benton & Bowles, Inc., N.Y.C., 1965-67; dir. corp. planning Esmark, Chgo., 1967-72; dir. corp. planning Consol. Packaging Co., Chgo., 1972-74; sr. cons. Booz Allen Hamilton/Hay Assocs., N.Y.C. and Phila., 1975-80; sr. v.p. U.S. Tobacco Co., Greenwich, Conn., 1981-87; pres. S.W. Beetham & Assocs., Ridgefield, Conn., 1987—. Contbr. articles in field. Candidate for U.S. Congress from 13th Ill. Dist., 1972, 74; chmn. roundtable Westchester (Conn) Planning Forum. Fulbright scholar, 1956, Marshall scholar, 1957; Woodrow Wilson fellow, 1958. Mem. N.Am. Soc. Corp. Planning, Nat. Assn. Bus. Economists, Council for Urban Econ. Devel., Internat. Soc. for Planning and Strategic Mgmt., Phi Beta Kappa. Home and Office: 62 Old Branchville Rd Ridgefield CT 06877

BEETLE, GEORGE ROBERT, engineer, consultant; b. Camden, N.J., Feb. 17, 1940; s. George Bradley and Vivian May (Stock) B.; m. Susan Grant, Jan. 15, 1963; children: Christopher, Gregory Alan, Stephanie. BA in Govt., BCE, Lafayette Coll., 1962; MPA in Econs., Princeton U., 1966. Registered profl. engr., Pa., Conn., Del., Fla., Ind., Md., Mass., N.J., N.Y., Ohio, Oreg., Tenn., Va., Wis. Spl. asst. to gen. mgr. Southeastern Pa. Transp. Authority, Phila., 1966-68; social research coordinator City Planning Commn., Phila., 1968; cons. engr. Louis T. Klauber & Assocs., Phila., 1969-72, ptnr., 1972-76; pres. George Beetle Co., Phila., 1976—. Bd. dirs. Southeastern Pa. Transp. Authority, Phila., 1980-81; vol. Peace Corps, Sialkot, Pakistan, 1962-64. Mem. Am. Econ. Assn., Am. Soc. Civil Engrs., Am. Ry. Engring. Assn. Democrat. Presbyterian. Clubs: Princeton (Phila.) (treas., pres. 1976-78); Princeton (N.Y.). Home and Office: 533 Arbutus St Philadelphia PA 19119

BEFOURE, JEANNINE MARIE, writer, accounting and business consultant; b. N.Y.C., Aug. 6, 1923; d. Thomas James and Frances Marie (Thompson) Nicholson; m. Willard Rockne, Oct., 1940 (div. 1946); children—Rodger Lloyd, Lenore Irene; m. Jean Maure Befoure, Aug. 3, 1974. BS in Communications magna cum laude, Woodbury U., 1979, MBA, 1981. Audit clk. Sears Roebuck, Seattle, 1946-50; supr. materials USN, Guam, 1951-52; pvt. practice accounting, Nev., Calif., Ariz., 1953-68; chief oper. officer, chief exec. officer Yearound Bus. Svcs., Las Vegas, Nev., 1969-73; writer, cons. The JM People, San Gabriel, Calif., 1982—; TV producer Channel 20, El Monte, Calif., TV access producer Channel 3, El Monte, 1987—, researcher mgmt. tng. methods, 1988—; instr. bus. and indsl. mgmt. Calif. Community Colls., 1979-82; mem. IRS/Tax Practioner Bd., Las Vegas, 1972-73; tutor Lauback Lit. Action, L.A., 1981—; researcher asult edn. methods for bus., 1988—. Author children's stories and poetry, bus. articles. Trainer Kellogg Found.-United Way, L.A.; founding sec. Homeowners of Golden Valley, Ariz., 1961. Mem. World Future Soc., Assn. MBA Execs., Greater L.A. Press Club, Phi Gamma Kappa. Republican. Religious Scientist. Avocations: photography, poetry.

BEGEL, THOMAS M., manufacturing company executive; b. 1942; married. Student, U. Mo. With E.I. Du Pont de Nemours and Co., 1964-66, Boise Cascade Corp., 1966-72; sr. v.p. Wheelabrator-Frye Inc., 1972-81; chmn., chief exec. officer Pullman Co., 1981—, now chmn., pres., chief exec. officer, also bd. dirs. Office: Pullman Co 182 Nassau St Princeton NJ 08540 *

BEGG, PETER ROBERT, banker; b. Pitts., July 8, 1951; s. Peter and Elizabeth (Jadlocki) B.; m. Deborah Ann Bawden, Oct. 16, 1971. BA, Rutgers U., 1973. Asst. mgr. F.W. Woolworth Co., Pitts., 1973; supr. D.L. Clark Co., Pitts., 1974; work mgmt. analyst Pitts. Nat. Bank, 1974-77, mgr. availability planning, 1977-78, asst. v.p., 1979, budget coord. ops., 1979-81, v.p., mgr. corp. svcs., 1982—; bd. dirs. Tri-State Automated Clearing House Assocs. Mgr. Swissvale Boys Baseball Assn., Pitts., 1979-85; bd. dirs. West Penn Football Ofcls. Assn., 1981—, Woodland Hills Drug and Alcohol Abuse Council, Pitts., 1982-85; pres. Newmy Sch. PTA, Pitts., 1981-82. Mem. Bank Adminstrn. Inst. (pres. Pitts. chpt. 1987). Republican. Methodist. Club: Edgewood Country. Home: 200 Lynn Ann Dr New Kensington PA 15068 Office: Pitts Nat Bank 960 Fort Duquesne Blvd Pittsburgh PA 15222

BEGHINI, VICTOR GENE, oil company executive; b. Greensboro, Pa., Oct. 24, 1934; s. Peter Victor and Beatrice Katherine (Minor) B.; m. Anna Mae Wancheck, July 7, 1956. B.S. in Petroleum Engring., Pa. State U., 1956; postgrad. in mgmt. devel., Harvard Bus. Sch., 1974; LLD (hon.), Marietta Coll., 1988. Registered profl. engr., La. With Marathon Oil Co., various locations, 1956-73; mgr. corp. risk Marathon Oil Co., Findlay, Ohio, 1973-75; mgr. prodn. ops. Marathon Oil Co., Cody, Wyo., 1975-77; coordinating mgr. prodn. ops. Marathon Oil Co., Findlay, 1977-78, v.p. supply and transp., 1978-82; v.p. supply and transp. Marathon Petroleum Co., Findlay, 1982-83, pres., 1984-85, dir., 1982-85; pres. Marathon Oil Co., Findlay, 1987—, also bd. dirs.; bd. dirs. Tex. Oil and Gas Corp.; mem. corp. policy com. USX Corp., 1987—. Trustee Ohio No. U., Ada, 1981-84. Recipient Chauncey Rose award Rose Poly. Inst., Terre Haute, Ind., 1981; named Disting. Alumnus Pa. State U., 1985. Mem. Soc. Petroleum Engrs., Am. Petroleum Inst. (bd. dirs.), Natural Gas Supply Assn. (chmn. 1987-88). Republican. Roman Catholic. Club: Elks. Office: Marathon Oil Co 539 S Main St Findlay OH 45840

BEHLMER, CURT RANDOLPH, recording engineer, consultant; b. Encino, Calif., Aug. 5, 1960; s. Rudolph Herman and Sandra Lee (Wightman) B.; m. Anna Gabellieri, July 22, 1984. Sound engr. Lion's Gate Films, Inc., Los Angeles, 1977-79; chief engr. Ryder Sound Services, Inc., Hollywood, Calif., 1979—; pres. Studio Systems, Inc., Studio City, Calif., 1988—; pres. Studio Systems, Inc., Studio City, Calif., 1988—. Mem. Acad. TV Arts and Scis. (gov. 1987—, Emmy awards 1981, 85, 87, 88), Acad. Motion Picture Arts and Scis., Soc. Motion Picture TV Engrs., Audio Engring. Soc., Internat. Alliance Theatrical Stage Employees. Home: 11500 Canton Dr Studio City CA 91604 Office: Ryder Sound Svcs Inc 1161 N Vine St Hollywood CA 90038

BEHM, FORREST EDWIN, glass manufacturing company executive; b. Lincoln, Nebr., July 31, 1919; s. Forrest E. and Lisle (Jacobson) B.; m. Ethel E. Groth, Aug. 11, 1943; children—Courtney Ann, Douglas, Brian, Gregory. B.S., U. Nebr., 1941, LL.D., 1965. With Corning (N.Y.) Glass Works and affiliates, 1946-86; pres. Corning Internat., 1965-75, sr. v.p. staff, 1975-80, dir. Corning Glass Works, 1975-86, sr. v.p., gen. mgr. Elec. and Electronics Group, 1980-82, sr. v.p. ops., 1982-83; dir. quality for mgmt. com. Corning Glass Works, 1983-86, advisor, cons., 1986—; bd. dirs. Goulds Pumps Inc.; former mem. bd. govs. Electronic Industries Assn.; bd. advisers Malcolm Baldrige Nat. Quality award, sr. examiner, 1989. Served to maj. AUS, 1942-46. Mem. Nebr. Football Hall of Fame; elected to Nat. Coll. Football Hall of Fame, 1988. Mem. Electronic Industries Assn. (bd. govs.), Beta Gamma Sigma. Republican. Presbyterian. Clubs: Corning Country; Baltusrol Golf. Home: 3 Briarcliff Dr Corning NY 14830 Office: Corning Glass Works 80 E Market St Ste 303 Corning NY 14830

BEHNKE, WALLACE BLANCHARD, JR., utility executive; b. Evanston, Ill., Feb. 5, 1926; s. Wallace Blanchard and Dorothea (Bull) B.; m. Joan F. Murphy, Sept. 24, 1949; children: Susan F., Ann B., Thomas W. B.S., Northwestern U., 1945, B.E.E., 1947. With Commonwealth Edison Co., Chgo., 1947—; dist. supt. Commonwealth Edison Co., Crystal Lake, Ill., 1956-58; div. engr. Commonwealth Edison Co., Joliet, Ill., 1958-60; area mgr. Commonwealth Edison Co., Mount Prospect, Ill., 1960-62; div. v.p. Commonwealth Edison Co., Chgo., 1962-66; asst. to pres. Commonwealth Edison Co., 1966-69, v.p., 1969-72, exec. v.p., 1972-80, vice chmn., 1980—, also bd. dirs.; dir. LaSalle Bank Lakeview, Chgo., Tuthill Pump Co., Duff & Phelps Selected Utilities, Inc., Calumet Industries Inc. Bd. govs. Argonne Nat. Lab.; bd. dirs. United Way Chgo., Ill. Inst. Tech., Ill. Inst. Tech. Research; trustee, pres. Protestant Found. Chgo.; Served to lt. USNR, 1943-46, 50-52. Fellow IEEE; mem. Nat. Acad. Engring., Am. Nuclear Soc., Western Soc. Engrs., Nat. Planning Assn. (trustee), Power Engring. Soc. (pres.), Phi Delta Theta. Clubs: Econ, Chgo, Comml., Hinsdale Golf (Ill.). Home: 411 S Elm St Hinsdale IL 60521 Office: Commonwealth Edison Co One 1st National Pla Box 767 Chicago IL 60690

BEHRENDT, BILL LEE, infosystems specialist; b. Kirksville, Mo., Oct. 21, 1958; s. Carl and Dora Lee (Kirkham) B.; m. Kathrine Louise Rowland, Oct. 21, 1987. Student, NE Mo. State U., 1981. Computer programmer Hannibal, Mo., 1981-85; actor various, Hollywood, Calif., 1985-86; freelance software designer Unionville, Mo., 1986; data entry, computer cons. City of Unionville, 1986-87; tech. writer, software designer Hollister, Inc., Kirksville, Mo., 1987—; owner Show-Me Ware, Novinger, Mo., 1988—; owner Lincoln St. Computing, Unionville, 1986—. Author: 30 Games for the Timex/Sinclair, 1983, Music and Sound for the Commodore 64, 1983, Conquering the Commodore 64 Kingdom, 1984; (with HanK Librach) Using the Commodore 64 in the Home, 1983. Lutheran. Home and Office: Rte 1 PO Box 173-E Novinger MO 63559

BEHRENDT, RICHARD PAUL, securities trader; b. Green Bay, Wis., Mar. 17, 1944; s. Walter and Rose Annette (Papa) B. BS, Marquette U., 1987. Cert. fin. planner. Co-owner, pres. Behrendt's Inc. Groceries, Milw., 1970-79; realtor Merrill, Lynch Realty Inc., Milw., 1982; investment broker Stifel, Nicolaus & Co., Milw., 1983—. Mem. parish council St. Augustine Ch., Milw., 1987-88, pres., 1986. Mem. Inst. Cert. Fin. Planners. Republican. Roman Catholic. Home: 2636 S 124th St West Allis WI 53227 Office: Stifel Nicolaus & Co Inc 615 E Michigan St Suite 400 Milwaukee WI 53202

BEHRENS, DAVID ALAN, financial service executive; b. Fremont, Nebr., Feb. 3, 1963; s. Arthur L. and Margaret J. (Rath) B. CLU; LUTCF; registered investment advisor. Prin. David A. Behrens & Assocs., Omaha, Nebr., 1988—. Mem. Nat. Assn. CLUs, Skyline Country Club (com. pres.). Home: 9022 Gary Cir Omaha NE 68138 Office: David A Behrens & Assocs 11516 Nicholas St Omaha NE 68154

BEIAN, ROBERT EDWARD, manufacturing company executive; b. Estherville, Iowa, Aug. 22, 1937; s. Trygve Edward and Clara Sofie (Handeland) B.; m. Norma Maude Breon, May 27, 1960; children: Robert Edward Jr. (dec.), Kristine Ann. Student, Iowa Weslyan Coll., 1959-62. Asst. bus. mgr. Iowa Weslyan Coll., Mt. Pleasant, 1959-62; asst. personnel dir. Goldwaters Dept. Stores, Phoenix, 1962-65; contract adminstr. Goodyear Aerospace Corp., Litchfield Park, Ariz., 1965-67; mgr. field office Goodyear Aerospace Corp., St. Louis, 1967-70; mgr. internat. mktg. Goodyear Aerospace Corp., Litchfield Park, 1970-74, mgr. internat. contracts, 1974-83, mgr. contract mgmt., 1983-87; dir. contracts and bus. planning Loral Def. Systems Ariz., Litchfield Park, 1987—. Served with U.S. Navy, 1956-69. Mem. Nat. Contract Mgmt. Assn., Ariz. State Bar (internat. sect.), Ariz. World Trade Assn. Republican. Lutheran. Home: 1402 W Frier Dr Phoenix AZ 85021 Office: Loral Def Systems PO Box 85 Litchfield Park AZ 85340

BEIGHEY, LAWRENCE JEROME, metal and plastic containers company executive; b. Akron, Ohio, June 24, 1938; s. Jac Laverne and Martha Rose (Vestal) B.; m. Carole Anne LaFlamme, Dec. 11, 1970; children: Basil, Susan, Thomas, Timothy, Elizabeth, Anne. BS in Indsl. Engring., Pa. State U., 1960. Registered profl. engr., Pa.; cert. data processor. Mgr. internat. div. Brockway (Pa.), Inc., 1968-76, mgr. energy div., 1976-78, project mgr., 1978-79, plant mgr., 1979-81, mgr. mfg. staff and services, 1981-83; exec. v.p. Brockway Standard, Atlanta, 1983-86, pres., 1986—; v.p. Brockway, Inc., Jacksonville, Fla., 1986—. Bd. dirs. Boy Scouts Am., DuBois, Pa., 1978-80, YMCA, DuBois, 1981-83; mem. sch. bd. Brockway Area Sch. Dist., 1981-83; pres. Jaycees, DuBois, 1964. Mem. Steel Shipping Container Inst. (bd. dirs. 1986), Data Processing Mgmt. Assn. (bd. dirs. 1966-68). Republican. Lutheran. Club: Dunwoody (Ga.) Country. Lodge: Masons.

BEIGHLE, DOUGLAS PAUL, lawyer; b. Deer Lodge, Mont., June 18, 1932; s. Douglas Paul Beighle and Clarice Janice (Driver) Kiefer; m. Gwendolen Anne Dickson, Oct. 30, 1954; children: Cheryl, Randall, Katherine, Douglas J. B.S. in Bus. Adminstrn., U. Mont., 1954; J.D., U. Mont, 1958; LL.M., Harvard U., 1960. Bar: Mont. 1958, Wash. 1959, U.S. Supreme Ct. 1970. Assoc. Perkins & Coie, Seattle, 1960-67, ptnr., 1967-80; v.p. contracts Boeing Co., Seattle, 1980-81, v.p. contracts, gen. counsel, sec., 1981-86; sr. v.p., sec. Boeing Co., 1986—; chief legal counsel Puget Sound Power & Light Co., Bellevue, Wash., 1970-80, dir., 1981—; bd. dirs. Peabody Holding Co., St. Louis, Washington Mut. Savs. Bank, Seattle. Nat. dir. Jr. Achievement, Colorado Springs, 1981—; trustee Mcpl. League Seattle, 1983-88, U. Mont. Found., Missoula, 1983—; dir. Wash. Gives, 1988—, Maritime Ctr., 1988—. lst. lt. USAF, 1954-56. Harvard U. Law Sch. fellow, 1959. Mem. ABA, Mont. Bar Assn., Wash. State Bar Assn. (chmn. advt. law sect. 1959-60), Seattle-King County Bar Assn., Nat. Assn. Mfrs. (bd. dirs., regional vice-chmn. 1988—), Rainier Club, Yacht Club. Republican. Presbyterian. Office: Boeing Co 7755 E Marginal Way S Seattle WA 98108

BEIM, DAVID ODELL, investment banker; b. Mpls., June 2, 1940; s. Raymond Nelson and Moana (Odell) B.; m. Elizabeth Lucile Artz, Aug. 29, 1964; children—Amy Marie, Nicholas Frederick. B.A. with honors, Stanford U., 1963; B.Phil. (Rhodes scholar), Oxford (Eng.) U., 1965. With First Boston Corp., N.Y.C., 1966-75; v.p. First Boston Corp., 1971-75, head project finance, 1973-75; exec. v.p. Export-Import Bank U.S., Washington, 1975-77; head corp. fin. Bankers Trust Co., N.Y.C., 1978-86, sr. v.p., 1978-79, exec. v.p., 1979-86, mem. mgmt. com., 1986-87; mng. dir. Dillon Read & Co., 1987—. Pres. Wave Hill, Inc.; trustee Markle Found., Outward Bound, Inc. Mem. Council Fgn. Relations. Home: Dodgewood Rd Riverdale NY 10471 Office: Dillon Read & Co 535 Madison Ave New York NY 10022

BEIMERS, GEORGE JACOB, financial executive; b. Grand Rapids, Mich., Dec. 30, 1930; s. Jacob Beimers and Betty Marie (Ashby) Gerold; m. Susannah Shrack, June 5, 1952 (div. 1972); m. Gertrude Hii, Apr. 5, 1986; children: Linda Sue Barrie, Mark George, Pamela Ann. BS in Edn., Western Mich. U., 1952; MEd in Adminstrn., U. Ariz., 1960, MEd in Psychology, 1976; degree in internat. rels., Johns Hopkins U., Bologna, Italy, 1970. Instr. polit. sci. Tucson Pub. Schs., 1957-87; instr. psychology and sociology U. Ariz., Tucson, 1972-87; v.p. New Era Corp., Tucson, 1970-71; pres. Beimers Properties and Investment Co., Tucson, 1972—. Author: Luck, the Human Factor, 1983; editor Blackboard mag., 1960. With U.S. Army, 1953-55. Recipient Golden Poet award World of Poetry, 1987, award of merit, 1987. Mem. U.S. Boat Owners Assn., Sierra Club. Republican. Office: PO Box 30541 Tucson AZ 85751

BEINHOCKER, GILBERT DAVID, investment banker; b. Phila., July 7, 1932; s. Joseph A. and Florence (Shlifer) B.; B.A., Pa. State U., 1954; M.S., U. Pa., 1958; D.Eng., U. Detroit, 1968; m. Barbara Broadley, Dec. 17, 1960; children—Eric David, Elizabeth Broadley, Robert Marc. Engring. dir. Epsco, Inc., 1958-61; pres. Syber Corp., Natick, Mass., 1961-64; div. mgr. Tech. Measurement Corp., 1964-65; dir. advanced planning Am. Optical Co., 1965-66; chmn. bd. Microdyne Instruments, Inc., Waltham, Mass., 1967-69; pres., chief exec. officer, dir. Mgmt. Scis., Inc., Cambridge, Mass., 1968—; dir. Nat. Info. Services Inc., Cambridge; chief exec. officer, dir. Eurocom Inc., Cambridge, 1975—; dir. corp. finance Moors and Cabot, Boston, 1976-82; v.p., treas., dir. First New Eng. Corp. Fin., Inc., 1982—; pres. Excalibur Ventures, Inc.; chmn. bd. Paragon Plastics Inc.; bd. chmn., chief exec. officer Regal Internat., bd. dirs. Waterman Industries Corp.; sr. lectr. U. Detroit, 1967-68. Recipient Nat. Fight for Sight citation Nat. Council to Combat Blindness, 1963. Mem. AAAS, IEEE, Assn. Computing Machinery, Internat. Fedn. Med. Electronics and Biol. Engring., Internat. Soc. Clin. Electroretinography, Assn. Research Ophthalmology, Am. Def. Preparedness Assn., Am. Mgmt. Assn., Instrument Soc. Am., Am. Assn. Med. Instrumentation, Pi Lambda Phi. Democrat. Author: Theory and Operation of Stardac Computers, 1960, also articles. Patentee in field. Home: 36 Beatrice Cir Belmont MA 02178 Office: Excalibur Ventures Inc 1 Boston Pl Ste 3400 Boston MA 02108

BEISER, GERALD J., paper products company executive; b. Hamilton, Ohio, Nov. 11, 1930; s. Ralph M. and Eunice (Platt) B.; m. Delores Joy Reynolds, Oct. 8, 1960; children: Jeffrey Gerald, Jennifer Joy. A.B., Earlham Coll., 1952; M.B.A., U. Mich., 1956. Mgmt. trainee Champion Papers, Hamilton, 1956-60; asst. to v.p. finance Champion Papers, 1960-67; dir. budgets and forecasts U. S. Plywood-Champion Papers Inc. (name later changed to Champion Internat.), 1967-69, spl. asst. to chmn., 1968, dir. fin. planning, 1969-70, treas., 1970-72, v.p., treas., 1972-75, sr. v.p. fin., 1975—; mem. nat. adv. bd. Chem. Bank, N.Y.C., Fairfield County adv. bd. Conn. Nat. Bank; mem. N.Y. adv. bd. Allendale Ins.; bd. dirs. Weldwood Can., Ltd. Served with AUS, 1952-54. Mem. Am. Paper Inst. (chmn. fin. mgmt. com. 1978-80), The Conf. Bd.'s Coun. Fin. Execs., Alpha Kappa Psi. Club: Economic (N.Y.C.). Home: 7 Fraser Rd Westport CT 06880 Office: Champion Internat Corp 1 Champion Pla Stamford CT 06921

BEIT, HUGO HERBERT, private investor, trustee; b. Frankfurt am Main, Fed. Republic Germany, Oct. 9, 1930; s. Herbert James Beit von Speyer and Elisabeth (de Neufville) Lehmann; m. Louise Christine de Angelis, May 31, 1980; 1 child, Lili Sophie. B in Engring., Yale U., 1953; MBA, Columbia U., 1961. Field service engr. Babcock & Wilcox Co., N.Y.C., 1953-59; ind. trustee 1961—; bd. dirs. Cerbini Research Corp., Port Chester, N.Y. Mem. ASME (assoc.), Yale Sci. and Engring. Assn., Inc. (bd. dirs., sec. 1964—). Republican. Clubs: Yale, Club at the World Trade Ctr. (N.Y.C.); The Grad. Assn. (New Haven). Home: 19 E 72d St New York NY 10021-4145 Office: 19 E 72d St New York NY 10021-4145

BEKKUM, OWEN D., retired gas company executive; b. Westby, Wis., Mar. 2, 1924; s. Alfred T. and Huldah (Storbakken) B.; m. Dorothy A. Jobs, Aug. 26, 1950. B.B.A., U. Wis., 1950; postgrad., Northwestern U. C.P.A. With Arthur Andersen & Co., 1951-57, Hertz Corp., 1957-62; with No. Ill. Gas Co., Aurora, 1963-88, asst. comptroller, 1966-68, comptroller, 1968-70, adminstrv. v.p., 1970-73, exec. v.p., 1973-76, pres., 1976-87, chief exec. officer, 1981-87, vice chmn., 1988. Bd. dirs. Jr. Achievement, Chgo., 1975-79, vice chmn., 1976-79; bd. dirs. Protestant Found. Greater Chgo., 1975-89, pres., 1985-87; bd. dirs. Pace Inst., 1977-83, Andrew Corp., 1980-89; bd. dirs. Am. Scandinavian Council, 1987—, chmn., 1988—. Served with AUS, 1943-46. Mem. Am. Mgmt. Assn., Am. Gas Assn. (dir. 1978-82, 83-87), Inst. Gas Tech. (dir. 1978-82), Gas Research Inst. (dir. 1982-88). Clubs: Economic, Comml., Mid-Day (Chgo.). Home: 805 St Stephens Green Oak Brook IL 60521

BELAU, JANE CAROL GULLICKSON, computer products and services company executive; b. Fertile, Minn., Oct. 21, 1934; d. Solon Hubert and Orpha (Love) Gullickson; m. Paul G. Belau, June 22, 1957; children: Steven, Matthew, Nancy Belau Collins. Student, Concordia Coll., Moorhead, Minn., 1952-53; grad., RN, Fairview Hosp. Sch. Nursing, 1956; postgrad., U. Minn. Spl. events dir. Retail Merchants Assn., 1966-71; cons. U.S. HEW, Washington, 1971-77; commr. Minn. State Corrections Authority, Mpls., 1974-75; cons. McKnight Found., Mpls., 1974-78; commr. Minn. State Cable Communications Bd., 1975-78; v.p. state mktg. and govt. affairs Control Data Corp., Mpls., 1978—; cons. in field. Illustrator: Fashiongrams; producer-host cable TV program Community Affairs; contbr. articles to profl. jours. Bd. advisors U. Minn. Grad Sch., 1985—; chmn. nat. adv. council St. John's U., Minn., 1986—; bd. dirs. Minn. Meeting, 1986—, Minn. High Tech Council, 1986—, Minn. Alliance for Sci., 1986—, Minn. Acad. Sci., 1985—; pres. Rochester (Minn.) Area Econ. Devel. Co., 1986—; v.p., bd. dirs. Nat. Luth. Acad., 1985—; founding dir. Vinland Nat. Ctr.; founder Nat. Conf. Developmental Disabilities; chmn. Nat. Developmental Disabilities Adv. Council. Named Bus. and Profl. Woman of Yr., 1974; recipient Outstanding Leadership award Internat. Assn. Women Execs., 1981. Mem. Am. Electronics Assn. (Minn. govtl. chmn.), Women's Econ. Roundtable Minn. (founder, bd. dirs.), U.S. C. of C. (nat. health care com.). Club: Mpls. Decathlon. Home: 433 9th Ave SW Rochester MN 55901 Office: Control Data Corp 8100 34th Ave S Minneapolis MN 55440

BELCHER, FORREST RENFROW, management consultant; b. Tulsa, Mar. 5, 1922; s. John Cheslow and Sarah Blanche (Renfrow) B.; student Okla. State U., 1939-42, Okla. U., 1944; B.A. in Psychology, U. Tulsa, 1947, M.A. in Psychology, 1949; postgrad. in psychology U. Houston, 1950-52; m. Betty Dings, June 2, 1943; children—Forrest Ray, Gail, Michael, Lynne. With Amoco Prodn. Co., 1948-69, employee relations supr., Houston, 1955-57, tng. and devel. cons., Tulsa, 1957-69; mgr. tng. and devel. Amoco Corp., Chgo., 1970-78; pvt. practice mgmt. cons., Tulsa, 1978—; pres. Mega Cons., Inc., Tulsa, 1981—; adj. prof. Okla. State U.; gen. chmn. First Internat. Tng. and Devel. Conf., Geneva, 1972; chmn. First Inter Am. Tng. Conf., Caracas, Venezuela, 1971; cons., speaker First S.E. Asia Tng. Conf., Manila, 1974; speaker in field; founder, chmn. Woodlands Group, a tng. and devel. think tank; cons. to mgmt. groups, Europe, S.Am., Can., U.S. Served with inf. U.S. Army, 1942-45; ETO. Decorated Purple Heart. Mem. Am. Soc. Tng. and Devel. (life; pres. 1970, Gordon M. Bliss Meml. award 1979), Am. Assn. Humanistic Psychology, U. Tulsa Alumni Assn. Democrat. Unitarian. Author booklet: How to Form a National Training Society, 1971; contbr. articles to profl. jours. Office: 10 Lookout Ln Diamond Head Sand Springs OK 74063

BELCHER, LARRY RAY, electronics executive; b. St. Joseph, Mo., Feb. 16, 1946; s. Orville E. and E. Pauline (Andrew) B.; m. Dianne M. Kuntz, July 22, 1967; children: Dawn Denise, Kristina Rhea. BS in Mktg., U. Tex., Dallas, 1978, BS in Fin., 1979. Mgr. Family Fin., Kansas City, Mo., 1967-73; regional v.p. Kensington Mortgage, Dallas, 1973-78; fin. adm. Tex. Instruments, Dallas, 1978—; prin. LDL Enterprises, Dallas, 1986—. Served as sgt. USAF, 1964-67. Republican. Methodist. Home: 1904 Cornmwall Ln Sachse TX 75040 Office: Tex Instruments 8505 Forest Ln Dallas TX 75234

BELDEN, THOMAS MACKAY, securities company executive; b. Camden, N.J., Jan. 4, 1954; s. Duane MacKay and Gloria Marie (Paladino) B.; m. Margaret Rose Petito, Apr. 30, 1983; 1 child, Meredith MacKay. BA, Williams Coll., 1976; MS, NYU, 1977. Fin. cons. Coopers & Lybrand, N.Y.C., 1976-79; fin. analyst, asst. treas. J.P. Morgan & Co. Inc., N.Y.C., 1980-82; treasury analyst, asst. v.p. Morgan Guaranty Trust Co N.Y., N.Y.C., 1982-85; instl. sales, v.p. J.P. Morgan Securities, Inc., N.Y.C., 1985—. Presbyterian. Clubs: University (N.Y.C.); Taconic Golf (Williamstown, Mass.); Pelham Country (Pelham, N.Y.); Williams (N.Y.C.). Home: 372 Central Park W New York NY 10025 Office: J P Morgan Securities Inc 23 Wall St New York NY 10015

BELDOCK, DONALD TRAVIS, corporation financial executive; b. N.Y.C., May 29, 1934; s. George and Rosa (Tribus) B.; m. Lucy Geringer, Apr. 23, 1971; children: John Anthony, Gwen Ann, James Geringer Christopher. B.A., Yale U., 1955. Mdse., fin. exec. R. H. Macy & Co., N.Y.C., 1955-60; mng. ptnr., fin. cons. D. T. Beldock & Co., N.Y.C., 1961-66; pres., chief exec. officer, chmn. fin. com. BASIX Corp. (formerly Basic Resources Corp.), N.Y.C., 1966-69, chmn. bd., pres., chief exec. officer, 1970-88; chmn., dir. White Shield Greece Oil Corp., N.Y.C., 1969-88; chmn., chief exec. officer, dir. Fundamental Properties, Inc., N.Y.C., 1989—; bd. dirs. Winko-Matic Signal Co., Norcross, Ga., Phoenix; bd. dirs. Packard Press Corp., Phila., chmn., chief exec. officer, 1987—; founding ptnr. Transp. Infrastructure Adv. Group; chmn., dir. White Shield Greece Oil Corp., N.Y.C.;chmn., pres., chief exec. officer, bd. dirs. Primavera Products, Inc., 1989—. Chmn. bd. trustees Strang Clinic-Preventive Medicine Inst., 1968—; mem. bd. advisors Chem. Bank, 1985-88; bd. dirs. Renewable Energy Inst., 1981-86; trustee Am. Symphony Orch., 1979—; chmn. bd. dirs. Teamwork Found., 1980—; mem. com. Nat. UN Day, 1978-87; mem. N.Y. Gov's. commn. Voluntary Enterprise, 1985-88; chmn. N.Y. Gov's. commn. subcom. Foster Care Ind. Living, 1986—; bd. advisers U. Hawaii Free Fellowship Program, 1982-86; mem. pvt. sector adv. panel on infrastructure financing Senate Budget Com., 1984-88; mem. exec. com. Yale U. Devel. Bd., 1983—, , bd. govs. Honoree testimonial dinner United Jewish Appeal, 1960. Mem. Am. Mgmt. Assn., Fgn. Policy Assn., Assn. of Yale U. Alumni (nat. class rep. 1983-86, gov. 1986—). Clubs: Lotos, Yale, Westchester Country. Office: Fundamental Properties Inc 880 Third Ave New York NY 10022

BELFIGLIO, GERALD LOUIS, steel company executive; b. Pitts., Nov. 6, 1948; s. Louis E. and Ann K. Belfiglio; m. Katheleen A. Di Cecco, Apr. 11, 1970; children: Christopher,P., Susanne M. BS, Pa. State U., 1970; MBA, U. Pitts., 1985. CPCU. Casualty underwriter Aetna C & S, Pitts., 1970-73; office mgr. ins. agy. Aetna C & S, Cannonsburg, Pa., 1973-75; asst. v.p. Johnson & Higgins, Pitts., 1975-78; risk mgr. Allegheny Internat., Pitts., 1978-81; dir. risk mgmt. Allegheny Ludlum Corp., Pitts., 1981—. Mem. Risk Ins. Mgmt. Soc. (assoc., pres. Pitts. chpt. 1981, bd. dirs. 1987—, sec., editor newsletter 1982—; nat. chmn. govtl. affairs 1987—, nat. exec. com. 1989—), Pitts. C. of C. (risk mgmt. specialist task force on port authority transit 1986, chmn. com. tort reform task force 1986—, chmn. govt. affairs 1987-89). Office: Allegheny Ludlum Corp 1000 Six PPG Pl Pittsburgh PA 15222

BELIN, DAVID WILLIAM, lawyer; b. Washington, June 20, 1928; s. Louis I. and Esther (Klass) B.; m. Constance Newman, Sept. 14, 1952 (dec. June 1980); children—Jonathan L., James M., Joy E., Thomas R., Laura R. B.A., U. Mich., 1951, M.B.A., 1953, J.D., 1954. Bar: Iowa 1954. Ptnr. Herrick & Langdon, 1955-62, Herrick, Langdon, Sandblom & Belin, 1962-66; sr. ptnr. Herrick, Langdon, Belin, Harris, Langdon & Helmick, 1966-78, Belin, Harris, Helmick, Tesdell, Lamson & McCormick, Des Moines, 1978—; dir. Kemper Mut. Funds., Midwest Newspapers, Inc.; counsel President's Commn. on Assassination of President Kennedy (Warren Commn.), 1964; exec. dir. Commn. on CIA Activities within the U.S. (Rockefeller Commn.), 1975; mem. Pres.'s Com. on Arts & Humanities, 1984—. Author: November 22, 1963: You Are the Jury, 1973, Final Disclosure, 1988. Bd. dirs. Des Moines Civic Music Assn., 1959-61, Des Moines Community Drama Assn., 1961-64, Des Moines Symphony, 1968-70, U. Mich. Alumni Assn., 1963-66. Served with AUS, 1946-47. Recipient Henry M. Bates Meml. award U. Mich. Law Sch., Brotherhood award NCCJ, 1978; hon. orator U. Mich., 1950. Mem. Soc. Barristers, Order of Coif, Phi Beta Kappa, Phi Kappa Phi, Delta Sigma Rho, Beta Alpha Psi. Club: Michigamua. Office: 2000 Financial Ctr Des Moines IA 50309

BELIN, JACOB CHAPMAN, paper company executive; b. DeFuniak Springs, Fla., Oct. 28, 1914; s. William Jacob and Addie (Leonard) B.; m. Myrle Fillingim, Nov. 28, 1940; children—Jacob Chapman, Stephen Andrew. Student, George Washington U., 1935-38. Dir. sales St. St. Joe Paper Co., Fla., 1949-56; v.p. St. Joe Paper Co., 1956-68, pres., dir., 1968—, chmn. bd., chief exec. officer, 1982—; pres., dir. St. Joseph Land & Devel. Co., Jacksonville Properties, Inc.; chmn., chief exec. officer St. Joe Container Co.; chmn. bd., dir. New Eng. Container Co.; chmn. Florala Telephone Co., Gulf Telephone Co.,; chmn., pres. St. Joseph Telephone & Telegraph Co.; dir. St. Joseph Tel. & Tel. Co., Talisman Sugar Corp. Bd. dirs. Nemours Found., Alfred I. duPont Found.; trustee Estate of Alfred I. DuPont. Mem. Elks, Rotary, Kappa Alpha. Baptist. Office: St Joe Paper Co 1650 Prudential Dr Jacksonville FL 32207

BELIVEAU, MARTHA OATES, business education educator; b. Gastonia, N.C., Sept. 25, 1944; d. Grady and Helen (White) Oates; m. Paul Roland Beliveau, May 27, 1977. B.S., We. Carolina U., 1967; M.A., 1969; Ed.S., Ga. State U., 1981. Cert. tchr., Ga. Sec. to Congressman B. Whitener, Washington, 1965; instr. Haywood Tech. Inst., Clyde, N.C., 1967-68; instr. Gaston Coll., 1968-73; adminstrv. asst. Pilot Internat. Hdqrs., Macon, Ga., 1973; instr. Macon Jr. Coll., 1973-75; asst. prof., coordinator bus. edn. Clayton State Coll., 1975-82, assoc. prof., 1982—; communications cons. Mem., Mid-Ga. Symphony Guild. Mem. AAUW, Assn. Info. Systems Profls., Am. Vocat. Assn., Ga. Vocat. Assn., Nat. Bus. Edn. Assn., Adminstrv. Mgmt. Soc., So. Bus. Edn. Assn., Ga. Bus. Edn. Assn., Pilot Internat. (dir.), Delta Pi Epsilon. Lutheran (mem. Southeastern Synod ch. ext. com., mem. ch. council, fin. chmn., treas.), Delta Pi Epsilon. Club: Pilot International. Contbg. author: Business Writing: Concepts and Applications, 1983. Club: Pilot of Macon (Ga.). Home: 890 River North Blvd Macon GA 31211 Office: Clayton State Coll Office Adminstrn & Tech Morrow GA 30260

BELK, IRWIN, retail executive; b. Charlotte, N.C., Apr. 4, 1922; s. William Henry and Mary Leonora (Irwin) B.; m. Carol Grotnes, Sept. 11, 1948; children: William Irwin, Irene Belk Miltimore, Marilyn Belk Wallis, Carl Grotnes. BS in Commerce, U. N.C., 1946; LLD (hon.), Mo. Valley Coll., 1977. Dir. Belk Fin. Co.; officer and dir. Belk Group Stores, Charlotte; chmn., dir. PMC, Inc., Raleigh, N.C.; chmn. bd. Monroe Hardware Co.; dir. Fidelity Bankers Life Ins. Co., Richmond, Va., First Union Nat. Bank of N.C., Charlotte, Lumbermen's Mut. Casualty, Co., Chgo., Stonecutter Mills, Spindale, N.C.; Past pres. men's council N.C. Synod, Presbyn. Ch.; mem. exec. com. Hist. Found. Presbyn and Reformed Chs. (Montreat), N.C. Past pres. N.C. div. Am. Cancer Soc.; trustee N.C. Symphony Soc.; chmn. U.S. Olympic Com. for N.C.; past mem. City of Charlotte Urban Redevel. Com.; mem. N.C. Ho. of Reps., 1959-60, 61-62, N.C. Senate, 1963-66, N.C. Legis. Council, 1963-64, Legis. Research Commn., 1965-66, Democratic nat. committeeman for, N.C., 1969-72; del. Dem. Nat. Convs., 1956, 60, 64, 68, 72; bd. dirs. Med. Found. N.C., N.C. State Bus. Found. N.C., Chapel Hill, Ednl. Found., Found. of U. N.C., Charlotte, Sch. of Design, N.C. State U.; bd. dirs., mem. exec. com. N.C. Assn. for Blind; bd. dirs., past pres. N.C. chpt. Nat. Soc. Prevention Blindness; ho. dels. Am. Cancer Soc.; bd. dirs. Charlotte Opera Assn.; bd. govs. U. N.C.; trustee Queens Coll., Charlotte, Presbyn. Coll., Clinton, S.C.; bd. advisors Belk Found.; mem. adv. council Wingate (N.C.) Coll.; bd. visitors Babcock Grad. Sch. Mgmt., Wake Forest U.; former bd. assos. Meredith Coll., Raleigh; bd. counselors Erskine Coll., Due West, S.C.; bd. advisers Western Carolina U., Cullowhee, N.C.; former bd. advisers Campbell Coll., Buies Creek, N.C. Served with USAAF, World War II. Recipient Outstanding Young Man award Charlotte, 1954-57. Mem. Charlotte Mchts. Assn., Charlotte C. of C. (exec. com., dir.), N.C. Presbyn. Hist. Soc. (past pres.), Charlotte Country Club, Myers Park Country Club, Charlotte City Club, Sky Club, Masons, Shriners, Lions (past pres., past dist. gov.), Kappa Alpha, Delta Sigma Pi. Democrat. Presbyterian (elder, past deacon). Clubs: Masons (Charlotte, dist. gov.), Shriners (Charlotte, dist. gov.), Lions (Charlotte, dist. gov.) (past pres.); Charlotte City (Charlotte), Charlotte Country (Charlotte), Charlotte Execs. (Charlotte) (past pres.), Charlotte Carrousel (Charlotte) (past pres.), Myers Park Country (Charlotte); Sky (N.Y.C.). Home: 9200 Winged Bourne Rd Charlotte NC 28210 Office: Belk Group Stores 6100 Fairview Rd Ste 640 Charlotte NC 28210

BELK, THOMAS MILBURN, corporate executive; b. Charlotte, N.C., Feb. 6, 1925; s. William Henry and Mary Leonora (Irwin) B.; m. Katherine McKay, May 19, 1953; children: Katherine Belk Morris, Thomas Milburn, Jr., Hamilton McKay, John Robert. BS in Mktg., U. N.C., 1948. With Belk Stores Services, Inc., 1948—, pres., 1980—; bd. dirs. NCNB Corp., Mut. Savs. & Loan Assn., Bus. Devel. Corp. of N.C. Bd. dirs. Mecklenburg County council Boy Scouts Am., Presbyn. Home at Charlotte, U. N.C. at Chapel Hill Found., Inc.; bd. dirs. YMCA, pres., 1978-79; gen. chmn. Shrine Bowl of Carolinas, 1963-64, United Appeal, 1959; past pres. United Community Service; trustee Charlotte Community Coll. System, 1958-65, Montreat-Anderson Coll., 1964-68, St. Andrews Presbyn. Coll., Laurinburg, N.C., 1967-71, Crossnore (N.C.) Sch., Inc., Davidson (N.C.) Coll., 1974—, Endowment Fund, 1975-78, Presbyn. Hosp., Charlotte; trustee U. N.C., Charlotte, 1975—, chmn. 1982—; mem. bd. visitors Wake Forest U. Served to lt. (j.g.), USN, 1943-46. Named Young Man of Yr., Jr. C. of C., 1960, Man of Yr., Charlotte News, 1962, Tarheel of Week, Raleigh News & Observer, 1964, Man of Yr., Delta Sigma Pi, 1962. Mem. Charlotte C. of C. (chmn. 1977), N.C. Citizens for Bus. and Industry (past pres.), Cen. Charlotte Assn. (pres. 1965-66), Mountain Retreat Assn. (past chmn. bd. trustees). Democrat. Clubs: Charlotte Country, Quail Hollow Country, Country of N.C., Biltmore Forest, Grandfather Golf and Country (Linville, N.C.). Lodges: Rotary, Masons, Shriners (Charlotte bd. dirs.). Home: 2441 Lemon Tree Ln Charlotte NC 28211 Office: Belk Stores Svcs 308 E 5th St Charlotte NC 28202 other: PO Box 31788 Charlotte NC 28231

BELKIN, HERBERT ALLEN, music company executive; b. N.Y.C., May 4, 1939; s. Max William and Estelle (Hopfenbloom) B.; m. Roberta Deanna Steele; children: Gregory Allen, Matthew William. BA, U. Nebr., 1962, MA (hon.), 1977; JD, Rutgers U., 1965. Bar: N.Y. 1965. Conciliator, sr. atty. Equal Employment Opportunity Commn., Washington, 1965-68; dir. NBC, N.Y.C., 1968-70; counsel, gen. mgr. Capitol Records, Inc., Hollywood, Calif., 1970-72; v.p. mktg. Atlantic Rec. Corp., N.Y.C., 1972-75; sr. v.p. ABC Records, Inc., Los Angeles, 1975-78; pres. Mobile Fidelity Sound Lab., Petaluma, Calif., 1978—; cons. Theater Now, Inc., N.Y.C., 1978-80, Pickwick Internat., Inc., Mpls., 1978-80, By the Numbers, San Jose, Calif., 1985—; vis. prof. Sonoma State U., Cotati, Calif., 1981-85. Fundraiser Carter for Pres. campaign, Los Angeles, 1976, 80, Douglas Bosco for Ho. Reps. campaign, Occidental, Calif., 1984, 86; entertainment chmn. Jackson for Pres. campaign, Los Angeles, 1976; sponsor Redwood Arts Council, Occidental, 1980, 87. Fellow Ford Found., 1965. Mem. ABA. Democrat. Unitarian. Office: Mobile Fidelity Sound Lab 1260 Holm Rd Petaluma CA 94952

BELKNAP, JOHN C., financial executive; b. Colombo, Sri Lanka, Aug. 29, 1946; s. Robert Jackson B. and Elsie (Green) Pearson; m. Ann D. Underhill, Aug. 24, 1974. BA, Cornell U., 1968, MBA, 1970. CPA, N.Y. Sr. acct. Arthur Young & Co., N.Y.C., 1970-73; asst. contr. Kay Corp., N.Y.C., 1973-74; v.p., chief fin. officer Kay Corp., 1979-85; chief fin. officer Kay Jewelers, Inc., Alexandria, Va., 1974-79; exec. v.p., chief fin. officer Seligman & Latz, Inc., N.Y.C., 1986-88, also bd. dirs.; vice chmn., chief exec. officer Tru-Rem Corp., N.Y.C., 1988—; bd. dirs. Am. Vision Ctrs., Inc., Adrien Arpel, Inc. Mem. Am. Inst. CPA's, N.Y. Soc. CPA's. Republican. Episcopalian. Club: Belle Haven (Greenwich, Conn.), Univ. (N.Y.C.). Home: 286 Round Hill Rd Greenwich CT 06831 Office: Tru-Rem Corp 521 Fifth Ave New York NY 10005

BELKNAP, MICHAEL H. P., real estate developer; b. South Bend, Ind., Oct. 27, 1940; s. Paul E. and Mary Elizabeth (Gibb) B.; B.A., Harvard U., 1963, J.D., 1967; LL.B., Cambridge (Eng.) U., 1965; m. Dorothy Callaway, Aug. 12, 1967; children—Michael, Jenny Warner, Matthew Gibb. Admitted to N.Y. bar, 1969; asso. Sullivan & Cromwell, N.Y.C., 1967-70; dir. Council on Environment, Office of Mayor City of N.Y., 1970-72; v.p., gen. counsel Corporate Property Investors, N.Y.C., 1972-75; v.p. Levitt & Sons Inc., Greenwich, Conn., 1975-78; pres. Belknap Co. Ltd., Canaan, N.Y., 1978—. English Speaking Union fellow, 1963-64. Mem. Urban Land Inst. Democrat. Episcopalian. Home: PO Box 94 Canaan NY 12029 Office: Warner Crossing Rd Canaan NY 12029

BELL, BRYAN, real estate, oil investment executive, educator; b. New Orleans, Dec. 15, 1918; s. Bryan and Sarah (Perry) B.; B.A., Woodrow Wilson Sch. Pub. and Internat. Affairs, Princeton, 1941; M.A., Tulane U., 1962; m. Rubie S. Crosby, July 15, 1950; children—Rubie Perry Gosnell, Helen Elizabeth, Bryan, Beverly Saunders, Barbara Crosby. Pres., Tasso Plantation Foods, Inc., New Orleans, 1945-66; partner Bell Oil Cos., New Orleans, 1962—; gen. ptnr. 26 ltd. partnerships in oil, real estate and venture capital, 1962—; instr. econs. of real estate devel. Sch. Architecture, Tulane U., New Orleans, 1967—; instr. entrepreneurship, Univ. Coll. Mem. Garden Dist. Assn., 1964—. Bd. dirs. United Fund for Greater New Orleans Area, 1964-71, pres., 1968-69; chmn. Human Talent Bank Com., New Orleans, 1969—; mem. City Planning Commn., New Orleans, 1956-58; mem. bd. Met. Area Com., 1968—, pres., 1971—; bd. dirs. Bur. Govtl. Research, 1966—, pres., 1971—; chmn. com. Met. Leadership Forum, 1969—; mem. bd. New Orleans Area Health Council, 1966-70; bd. dirs. Tulane-Lyceum, 1947-51, Family Service Soc., 1951-58, pres., 1956-58; bd. dirs. St. Martin's Protestant Episcopal Sch., 1964-68, Metairie Park Country Day Sch., 1967-71; bd. dirs. Trinity Episcopal Sch., chmn., 1958-68; chmn. Trinity Christian Community, 1975—; bd. dirs. Christ Spirit of 76 Com., Fedn. Chs., 1975—, pres., 1984; bd. dirs. aux. Lighthouse for Blind; bd. dirs. Alton Ochsner Med. Found., 1983—. Served to 1st lt. AUS, World War II. Recipient Benemerenti Papal honor from Pope John Paul II, Weiss Brotherhood award NCCJ, 1983, Times Picayune Loving Cup City of New Orleans, 1985. Mem. New Orleans C. of C., Princeton Alumni Assn. La. (pres. 1962-63), Fgn. Realtions Assn. Democrat. Episcopalian (vestry 1960—, jr. warden 1968-70, sr. warden 1970-72). Clubs: Internat. House, Boston, New Orleans Lawn Tennis, Wyvern, Lakeshore, Pickwick, New Orleans Country. Address: 1331 3d St New Orleans LA 70130

BELL, CHARLES EUGENE, JR., industrial engineer; b. N.Y.C., Dec. 13, 1932; s. Charles Edward and Constance Elizabeth (Verbelia) B.; B. Engring., Johns Hopkins U., 1954, M.S. in Engring., 1959; m. Doris R. Clifton, Jan. 14, 1967; 1 son, Scott Charles Bell. Indsl. engr. Signode Corp., Balt., 1957-61, asst. to plant mgr., 1961-63, plant engr., 1963-64, div. indsl. engr., Glenview, Ill., 1964-69, asst. to div. mgr., 1969-76, engring. mgr., 1976—; host committeeman Internat. Indsl. Engring. Conf., Chgo., 1984. Served with U.S. Army, 1955-57. Registered profl. engr., Calif. Mem. Am. Inst. Indsl. Engrs. (pres. 1981), Indsl. Mgmt. Club Central Md. (pres. 1964), Nat. Soc. Profl. Engrs., Ill. Soc. Profl. Engrs., Soc. Plastics Engrs. Republican. Roman Catholic. Home: 1021 W Old Mill Rd Lake Forest IL 60045 Office: Signode Corp 3610 W Lake Ave Glenview IL 60025

BELL, DAVID ARTHUR, advertising agency executive; b. Mpls., May 29, 1943; s. Arthur E. and Frances (Tripp) B.; m. Gail G. Galvani; children: Jenny L., Jennifer L., Jeffrey D., Ashley Tripp, Andrew Joseph. B.A. in Polit. Sci., Macalester Coll., 1965. Account exec. Leo Burnett, Chgo., 1965-67; pres. Knox Reeves, Mpls., 1967-74; pres. Atlantic div. Bozell & Jacobs, 1974-85; vice chmn. Bozell, Jacobs, Kenyon & Eckhardt (name now Bozell Inc.), 1986—, also mem. exec. com.; bd. dirs. Bus. Publs. Audit. Nat. com. coordinator United Way Am., Minn., 1975—; trustee Macalester Coll., 1970-78. Recipient centennial medallion Macalester Coll., 1974; named disting. alumnus Macalester Coll., 1978; recipient Minn. Airman of Yr. award, 1967. Mem. Am. Advt. Fedn. (vice-chmn. nat. bd. dirs.), Bus. Publs. Audit (bd. dirs.). Republican. Presbyterian. Club: Minikahda (Mpls.). Home: 47 E 88th St New York NY 10128 Office: Bozell Inc 40 W 23rd St New York NY 10010

BELL, EDWARD FRANCIS, telecommunications company executive; b. Evanston, Ill., 1930. BSEE, U. Ill., 1951; MBA, Northwestern U., 1960. With Ill. Bell Telephone Co., 1952-62, 64-75, former asst. v.p. corp. planning; engr. AT&T, 1962-64; v.p. engring. & corp. planning Ohio Bell Telephone Co., Cleve., 1976-78, exec. v.p., 1978-83, chief operating officer from 1978, pres., 1983—, now chief exec. officer, also bd. dirs.; bd. dirs. Ameritrust Co., Ohio Bell. Served with U.S. Army, 1951-53. Office: Ohio Bell Telephone Co 45 Erieview Pla Cleveland OH 44114

BELL, GEORGE DE BENNEVILLE, investment banker; b. Phila., Feb. 6, 1924; s. John Cromwell and Sarah (Baker) B.; m. Roberta Howard McVey, May 2, 1953; children: Sophie Bell Ayres, George de Benneville Jr., James T. B.A., Yale U., 1948; postgrad., U. Pa. Law Sch., 1948-49. With Drexel & Co., Phila., 1949-66, ptnr., 1956-66; sr. v.p., dir. Drexel Harriman Ripley, Phila., 1967-70; v.p. Dillon Read & Co., N.Y.C., 1971-73; sr. v.p., dir. Janney Montgomery Scott Inc., Phila., 1974-78, exec. v.p., dir., 1978-82, co-chmn., dir., 1982—; vice chmn. JMS Resources, Phila.; v.p., bd. dirs. GS Ventures, Inc.; v.p., treas. K.B. Equities, Inc.; mem. regional firms adv. com. N.Y. Stock Exch., 1983-86; bd. govs. Am. Stock Exch., Inc. Bd. dirs. The Lankenau Hosp., Phila., 1966—, Inst. for Cancer Research, Phila., 1968—, Fox Chase Cancer Ctr., Phila., 1974—; trustee So. Home for Children, 1956-66, Lankenau Med. Rsch. Ctr., Main Line Health, Inc. Served as 2d lt. USAF, 1943-45. Mem. Bond Club Phila. (past gov.), Bond Club N.Y. (past gov), Investment Bankers Assn. (past. v.p., bd. dirs.), Phila. Stock Exchange (past vice chmn., bd. dirs.), Assn. Stock Exchange Firms. (past gov.). Republican. Episcopalian. Clubs: Racquet (pres. 1976-79) (Phila); Pine Valley Golf (N.J.); Links (N.Y.C.); Augusta Nat. Golf, Gulph Mills Golf, Merion Cricket, The Cts. Home: 1226 Rock Creek Rd Gladwyne PA 19035 Office: Janney Montgomery Scott Inc 5 Pennsylvania Center Pla Philadelphia PA 19103

BELL, GEORGE EDWIN, retired physician, insurance company executive; b. Canton, Ohio, Dec. 6, 1923; s. George Edwin and Florence Lea (Clark) B.; m. Evelyn Maxine Adams, Apr. 20, 1946; children: Richard, John, Jeffrey, David. Student, Wooster Coll., 1941-42, Yale U., 1943; M.D., Ohio State U., 1947; postgrad., U. Pa., 1954-55. Am. Bd. Life Ins. Medicine. Intern Del. Hosp., Wilmington, 1947-48, resident in medicine, 1948-49; resident in pathology Aultman Hosp., Canton, Ohio, 1949-50; resident in medicine Ohio State U. Hosp., Columbus, 1955-56, asst. clin. prof. medicine, 1970-89; ltd. practice medicine Central Ohio Med. Group, Columbus, 1971-89; dir. med. service Columbus State Hosp., 1958-66, dir. research lab., 1966-69, med. dir., 1968-89; v.p. Nationwide Ins. Co., Columbus, 1980-89; chmn. dept. medicine Grant Hosp., Columbus, 1975-77. Contbr. articles to profl. jours.; programmer computer programs for use in lab. office, 1967—; contbr. abstracts to med. jours. Advisor Columbus Pub. Health Nursing Dept., 1967-79; vol. physician Ecco Family Practice Clinic, 1970-74; bd. dirs. Columbus Council on Alcoholism, 1973-77, League Against Child Abuse, 1979-83, Recreation Unltd., 1985—; ad hoc data processing com. chmn. Columbus Acad. Medicine, 1980-81. Served as med. officer USAF, 1951-53. Fed., state, pvt. research grantee, 1958-59; recipient Vol. Services cert. Ohio Dept. Mental Health, 1981, Service plaques J.C. Penney Co., 1981, Service plaques Columbus Health and Life Claim Assn., 1983. Fellow ACP, Am. Life Ins. Med. Dirs. Assn.; mem. AMA, Am. Council Life Ins. (chmn. human resources com.), Acad. Medicine Columbus and Franklin County (history and archives com. 1982—), Midwestern Med. Dirs. Assn. (pres. 1985-86), Pres.'s Club, Kappa Mu Epsilon. Home: 66 Campusview Blvd Worthington OH 43235

BELL, JOHN LEWIS, manufacturing executive; b. Marion, Ind., June 5, 1942; s. John Lewis and Lauvonnia C. (Kinder) B.; children by previous marriage; children: John Lewis, Robert; m. Toni Grant, June 5, 1988. Student, Ind. U., 1960-62; B.B.A., U. Miami, 1965; M.B.A., Ball State U., 1971; M.A., in Psychology, 1977; Ph.D., Purdue U., 1980. Treas. Bell Fibre Products Corp., Marion, 1966-68; pres., treas. Bell Fibre Products Corp., 1968-71, pres., chief exec. officer, 1971-81, chmn. bd., chief exec. officer, 1981—; pres. Bell Gallery Photog. Art; chmn. bd. Am. Bank and Trust Co., Marion. Bd. dirs. Lakeview Wesleyan Ch. Mem. Am. Inst. Mgmt., Am. Mgmt. Assn., Soc. Advancement Mgmt., Young Pres.'s Orgn., Alpha Kappa Psi. Clubs: Kiwanis (Marion), Meshingomesia Country (Marion). Office: Bell Packaging Corp 3102 S Boots St Marion IN 46953

BELL, MARY E. BENITEAU, accountant; b. San Antonio, Dec. 20, 1937; d. Thomas Alfred and Mary Elizabeth (McMurrain) Beniteau; BBA, Baylor U., 1959; MBA, U. Tex., 1960; m. William Woodward Bell, May 31, 1969; children: Susan Elizabeth, Carol Ann. Teaching asst. U. Tex., Austin, 1959-60; prin. Deloitte, Haskins & Sells, C.P.A.s, Dallas, 1960-69; county auditor Brown County, Tex., 1972-78; pvt. practice acctg., Brownwood, Tex., 1969—; acct. Brownwood Regional Hosp. Women's Aux., 1969—. Mem. bus. and audit com. Bapt. Gen. Conv. Tex., 1985—, vice chmn., 1987-88, chmn., 1988-89. Named Outstanding Woman Over 35, Brownwood Jaycees, 1986, Outstanding Com. Chmn., Dallas chpt. CPA's, 1968-69; CPA, Tex. Mem. Brownwood C. of C. (dir. 1979-82, sec.-treas. 1981-82), Tex. Soc. CPA's (dir. 1979-82, chair relations with AICPA com. 1988-89, trustee found. 1981—, sec.-treas. 1982-84, pres. 1984-86), AICPA's, Am. Soc. Women Accts., Am. Woman's Soc. CPA's, Abilene Chpt. CPA's (dir. 1984-85, 87-88, CPA of Yr. 1984-85), Brownwood Com. CPA's (pres. 1987-88), AAUW, Pi Beta Phi, Baylor U. Alumni Assn. (dir. 1979-82). Baptist. Clubs: Brownwood Woman's (pres. 1980-81), Rotary Ann of Brownwood (pres. 1983-84. Home: PO Box 1564 Brownwood TX 76804 Office: 109 N Fisk St Brownwood TX 76801

BELL, MICHAEL BRUCE, executive benefits planner; b. Los Angeles, Dec. 27, 1943; s. Walter Edwin Marion and Julia Evelyn (Pyle) B.; m. Rosalie Jean Paneno, June 30, 1964 (div. 1981); children: Darren Scott, Michael Bradley, Bryen Anthony; m. Malea Kathleen Wong, Feb. 4, 1984. AA, El Camino Coll., 1964; BS, Pepperdine U., 1965; MBA, U. So. Calif., 1967. Prin. Wheat-Bell & Assocs., Los Angeles, 1967-70; asst. gen. agt. Mass. Mut. Life, Los Angeles, 1970-79; v.p. Century Fin. Corp., Los Angeles, 1979-80; prin. Michael B. Bell & Assocs., Los Angeles, 1980-86; pres. Exec. Benefits Group, Inc., Los Angeles, 1986—; bd. dirs. K & K Labs., Inc., Carlsbad, Calif. Mem. Million Dollar Round Table (Top of Table 1986-87), Am. Soc. CLUs, Am. Soc. Chartered Fin. Analysts (bd. dirs. 1973—), Life Underwriters Assn Los Angeles, U. So. Calif. MBA Alumni Assn. (pres. 1973), Commerce Assocs. U. So. Calif. (bd. dirs. 1974), Sertoma (v.p. 1974-78), Jonathan Club (com. chmn. 1976—). Republican. Roman Catholic. Office: Exec Benefits Group Inc 417 S Hill St Suite 1070 Los Angeles CA 90013

BELL, MILDRED BAILEY, law educator; b. Sanford, Fla., June 28, 1928; d. William F. and Frances E. (Williford) Bailey; m. J. Thomas Bell, Jr., Sept. 18, 1948 (div.); children—Tom, Elizabeth, Ansley. AB, U. Ga., 1950, JD cum laude, 1969; LLM in Taxation, N.Y. U., 1977. Bar: Ga. 1969. Law clk. U.S. Dist. Ct. No. Dist. Ga., 1969-70; prof. law Mercer U., Macon, Ga., 1970—; mem. Ga. Com. Constl. Revision, 1978-79; v.p., bd. dirs. Arrowhead Travel Inc. Mem. ABA, Ga. Bar Assn., Phi Beta Kappa, Phi Kappa Phi. Republican. Episcopalian. Bd. editors Ga. State Bar Jour., 1974-76; contbr. articles to profl. jours., chpts. in books. Home: 516 High Point North Rd Macon GA 31210 Office: Mercer U Law Sch Georgia Ave Macon GA 31207

BELL, P. JACKSON, railroad executive; b. Portsmouth, Va., Dec. 31, 1941; s. John Henry and Lois Belle (Hendrix) B.; m. Virginia Phillips Inman, Apr. 11, 1981; children by previous marriage: Scarlett Lee, Christopher J. B.S.B.A., Northwestern U., 1963; M.A., U. S.C., 1964. Mgmt. cons. McKinsey & Co., Washington, 1967-73; dir. corp. planning Washington Post Co., 1973-77; asst. to pres. Allegheny Airlines, Washington, 1977-78; v.p.-long range planning USAir Inc, Washington, 1978-83, sr. v.p.-fin., 1983-86, exec. v.p.-fin., 1986-89; v.p.-fin., chief fin. officer USAir Group, 1984-89; exec. v.p., chief fin. officer Burlington Northern Inc., Ft. Worth, 1989—; mem. bd. cons. Riggs Nat. Bank, Washington, 1986-88. Served to capt. USMC, 1964-67, Vietnam. Mem. Air Transport Assn. Am. (chmn. econs. and fin. council 1986, chmn. audit and fin. com. 1987—). Office: Burlington No Inc 777 Main St Fort Worth TX 76102

BELL, RICHARD EUGENE, grain company executive; b. Clinton, Ill., Jan. 7, 1934; s. Lloyd Richard and Ina (Oglesby) B.; m. Maria Christina Mendoza, Oct. 22, 1960; children—David Lloyd, Stephen Richard. B.S. with honors, U. Ill., 1957, M.S., 1958. Internat. economist Dept. Agr., Washington, 1959-60; dir. grain div. Dept. Agr., 1969-72; agrl. attache Am. embassies in Ottawa, Can., Brussels, and Dublin, Ireland, 1961-68; asst. sec. agr. internat. affairs and commodity programs 1973-77; pres. Riceland Foods Inc., Stuttgart, Ark., 1977—; now also chief exec. officer Riceland Foods Inc.; pres., dir. Commodity Credit Corp., also Fed. Crop Ins. Corp., 1975-77; exec. sec. President's Agrl. Policy Com., 1976-77; rep. Internat. Wheat Council, London, 1970-77; adv. World Food Conf., Rome, 1974. Recipient Disting. Service award Dept. Agr., 1975. Mem. Alpha Gamma Rho, Alpha Zeta. Republican. Mem. Christian Ch. (Disciples of Christ). Office: Riceland Foods Inc 2120 Park Ave PO Box 927 Stuttgart AR 72160

BELL, RICHARD G., corporate lawyer; b. Billings, Mont., Sept. 16, 1947; s. George A.W. and Mary Helen (Sharp) B.; m. Linda Carol Riggs, June 21, 1969; children: Stephen, Geoffrey. AB, Stanford U., 1969; JD, U. Calif., San Francisco, 1972. Bar: Calif. Assoc. Finch, Sauers, Player & King, Palo Alto, Calif., 1972-76; ptnr. Finch, Sauers, Player & Bell, Palo Alto, 1976-83; gen. counsel Watkins-Johnson Co., Palo Alto, 1983—. Bd. dirs. Family Service Assn., Palo Alto, 1981-87. Mem. ABA, Calif. Bar Assn., Santa Clara County Bar Assn., Peninsula Assn. Gen. Counsel. Republican. Episcopalian. Office: Watkins-Johnson Co 3333 Hillview Ave Palo Alto CA 94302

BELL, RICHARD HARDING, II, venture capitalist; b. Columbus, Ohio, Dec. 26, 1946; s. Richard Harding and Cynthia May (Kyper) B.; m. Paulise G. Rossetti, Nov. 17, 1973; children: Christina, Carleigh, Richard III, Michael Jonathan. Student, Ohio Wesleyan U., Ohio Wesleyan U. and Franklin Coll., Lugano, Switzerland. Registered corp. agt., Del. Circulation dir. Rolling Stone mag., San Francisco, 1970-71; mgmt. cons. various nat. mags., 1972-79; bus. mgr. Enterprise Pub. Co., Wilmington, Del., 1980-81; pres., founder Harvard Bus. Services, Wilmington, 1981—, also bd. dirs.; bd. dirs. Highlights for Children mag., Columbus, Tripledge Wiper Corp., Bensalem, Pa.; founder, bd. dirs. Corp. Law Ctr. Del., Wilmington, 1985; mem. Del. Valley Venture Group. Chmn. venture capital task force Del. State C. of C., Wilmington, 1984-85; chmn. capital com. Del. Gov.'s High Tech. Task Force, Wilmington, 1986-87; mem. bidco rev. com. devel. office State of Del., gov.'s small bus. com., bus. and econ. devel. com.; fund raising chmn. Franklin Coll. Mem. Venture Capital Stock Market Assn. (bd. dirs. 1982-84, founding com.), Lyon's Eye Found. (life), Del. State C. of C., Del. Valley Venture Group, Personal Computer Users Groups. Republican. Episcopalian. Club: Brandywine Country (Wilmington). Lodge: Lions.

BELL, ROBERT ARNOLD, sales and promotions executive; b. Springfield, Mass., Oct. 12, 1950; s. Irwin and Vivian (Rulnick) B.; m. Brandi Merryl Kane; 1 child, Jolie Eve. Student, Babson Coll., 1968-72. V.p. Standard Svcs., Springfield, 1972-74; exec. v.p. Marden-Kane, Inc., N.Y.C., 1974-87, pres., 1987—. Treas. new leadership div. North Shore U. Hosp., Manhasset, N.Y., 1985—, assoc. trustee. Mem. Promotion Mktg. Assn. Am. (chmn. membership N.Y.C. chpt. 1984—, sec. 1986—, vice chmn., outstanding chmn. award 1985). Club: Fresh Meadow Country (Great Neck, N.Y.) Lodge: Friars. Office: Marden-Kane Inc 410 Lakeville Rd Lake Success NY 11042

BELL, ROBERT COLLINS, lawyer; b. St. Joseph, Mo., Sept. 19, 1912; s. Robert Cook and Mamie Burke (Collins) B.; m. Mary-Katherine Morris, Mar. 22, 1941; children—Robert III, Marianne. Student Carleton Coll., 1929-32; A.B., U. Minn., 1933; J.D., Harvard U., 1936. Bar: Minn. 1936, Conn. 1942, D.C. 1949, N.Y. 1953. Assoc. Fowler, Youngquist, Furber, Taney and Johnson, Mpls., 1936-37; atty. U.S. Wage and Hour Div.-Minn., N.D., S.D., Mont., 1939-40; chief tax amortization sect. War Prodn. Bd., 1940-42; assoc. Cummings and Lockwood, Stamford, Conn., 1942-52; ptnr. Smith Mathews, Bell and Solomon, N.Y.C., 1952-62; practice, New Canaan, Conn., 1962—; pros. atty., New Canaan, 1948-50. Mem. War Dept. Bd. Contract Appeals, Office of Under Sec. of War, 1944-45. Mem. ABA, Conn. Bar Assn., Internat. Bar Assn. Democrat. Congregationalist. Clubs: Harvard (N.Y.C.); Tokeneke (Darien, Conn.); Masons. Obtained judgments totalling over 25 million dollars on behalf of the Pottawatomi, Miami and Chippewa Indian Tribes in U.S. Ct. Claims and U.S. Indian Claims Commn. Home and Office: 528 Main St New Canaan CT 06840

BELL, ROBERT KINSLOE, JR., real estate appraiser; b. Somers Point, N.J., Nov. 1, 1934; s. Robert Kinsloe and Elizabeth (Kress) B.; m. Jean Miller Bell, Nov. 11, 1959 (div. Jan. 1972); 1 child, Robert Kinsloe III; m. Barbara Barracliff Maul, Sept. 15, 1984. BA in Econs., Rollins Coll., 1957. Real estate salesman Morrison Real Estate, Ocean City, N.J., 1960-62; owner Bell Realty, Ocean City, 1962-72; real estete appraiser Rex-McGill Realty, Orlando, Fla., 1972-82; pres., owner Bell & Irwin, Inc., Orlando, 1982—; owner, instr. Cape May County Real Estate Sch., Ocean City, 1968-73. Mem. Presl. Task Force, Washington, 1982-88; trustee Ocean City Tabernacle Assn., 1988—; bd. dirs. Ocean City C. of C., 1969-72. Served with USN, 1957-59. Mem. Am. Inst. Real Estate Appraisers (regional profl. standards panel 1985-89, nat. com. on MAI experience rating 1989—, admissions com. 1975-89), N.J. Assn. Realtors (v.p. 1972), Ocean City Bd. Realtors (pres. 1970), Penn. Soc. S.R. Republican. Methodist. Clubs: Orlando Tennis and Racquet. Office: Bell & Irwin Inc 509 W Colonial Dr Orlando FL 32804

BELL, SHARON KAYE, accountant; b. Lincoln, Nebr., Sept. 14, 1943; d. Edwin B. and Evelyn F. (Young) Czachurski; m. James P. Kittrell (div. Sept. 1974); children: Nathan James, Nona Kaye; m. Joseph S. Bell, June 5, 1976; stepchildren: Patricia, Bobbie, Linda. Various positions mgmt., bookkeeping 1961-71; bookkeeper Internat. Harvester, Chesapeake, Va., 1971-73, Cheat'AH Engring., Santa Ana, Calif., 1973-74, Fre Del Engring., Santa Ana, Calif., 1974-75; bookkeeper/mgr. Tek Sheet Metal Co., Santa Ana, Calif., 1975-79; owner, bookkeeper Bell's Bookkeeping, Huntington Beach, Calif., 1979-86, Fountain Valley, Calif., 1986-88, Laguna Hills, Calif., 1988—. Mem. Nat. Assn. Accts. (dir. 1985-86, sec. 1986-87, v.p. 1987—), Nat. Notary Assn., NAFE, Wives of Submarine Vets. World War II (v.p. Los Angeles chpt. 1986-87), Nat. Soc. Pub. Accts. Republican. Office: Bell's Bookkeeping PO Box 2713 Laguna Hills CA 92654-2713

BELL, THOMAS DEVEREAUX, JR., manufacturing company executive; b. Niagara Falls, Nov. 2, 1949; s. Thomas Devereaux and Lenore (Chisholm) B.; m. Margaret McDaniel, Jan. 17, 1975 (div.); 1 child, Thomas Devereaux, III; m. Jennifer Holtzman, Dec. 27, 1987. Student, U. Tenn., 1967-70, George Washington U., 1973, NYU, 1984-88. Exec. dir. Presdl. Inaugural Ball Com., Washington, 1972; dep. div. dir. Com. to Reelect the Pres., Washington, 1971-72; adminstrv. asst. U.S. Senator William Brock, Washington, 1973-75; pres., chief exec. officer Bell and McDaniel, Washington, 1975-76, Holder, Kennedy, Dye & Bell, Nashville, 1976-79; chmn., chief exec. officer Creative Communications Corp., Washington, 1979-82; pres., chief exec. officer Hudson Inst., Indpls., 1982-87; exec. v.p. Ball Corp., Muncie, Ind., 1987—; bd dirs. Operation Enterprise, Am. Mgmt. Assn., N.Y.C., Merchants Nat. Bank & Trust Co., Indpls., Merchants Nat. Corp., Indpls., Ball Corp., Muncie, Ind., Clark Equipment Co., South Bend, Ind., Cin. Milicron, Cin., Am. States Ins. Cos., Indpls., Lincoln Nat. Corp., Ft. Wayne, Ind., Hudson Inst., Indpls., Nat. Alliance of Bus., Washington; chmn. bd. dirs. Ctr. for Naval Analyses, Alexandria. Mem. Transition Team for Pres. Ronald Reagan, Washington, 1981; bd. dirs. Indpls. Mus. Art; trustee Butler U., Indpls. Mem. Indpls. C. of C. (bd. dirs. 1985-87). Republican. Clubs: Skyline, University (Indpls.); Delaware Country, Muncie, Ind. Office: Ball Corp 345 S High St PO Box 2407 Muncie IN 47307-0407

BELL, THOMAS ROWE, natural gas transmission company executive; b. Chattanooga, Feb. 26, 1928; s. Joseph Sumner and Hattie Bush (Rowe) B.; m. Agnes Louise Slaughter, Dec. 29, 1956; children: Bush A., Thomas Rowe, Mary E., David L. B.S. in Bus., U. Tenn., 1950. With E. Tenn. Natural Gas Co., 1950—, dir. sales devel., asst. treas., 1959-64, v.p., 1964-72; pres. E. Tenn. Natural Gas Co., Knoxville, 1973—; also dir. E. Tenn. Natural Gas Co.; past chmn. mgmt. com. Knoxville Internat. Energy Expn., 1979—. Trustee Ft. Sanders Reginal Med. Ctr.; bd. dirs. Webb Sch.; past pres. Met. Knoxville YMCA. Served with AUS, 1950-52. Mem. Am. Gas Assn., Ind. Natural Gas Assn., So. Gas Assn. (dir.), Tenn. Gas Assn. (past pres.), Sigma Phi Epsilon. Presbyterian. Office: E Tenn Natural Gas Co 8200 Kingston Pike PO Box 10245 Knoxville TN 37919

BELL, WILLIAM JOSEPH, cable television company executive; b. Jersey City, Dec. 10, 1939; s. William Joseph and Mary Jane (Egan) B.; m. Ellen Jules McInerney; children: Michael, Sally, Thomas, Timothy, Jennifer. BA in Econs., St. Peter's Coll., 1961. With Dun & Bradstreet, Union Carbide, Riegel Paper Corp., 1962-71; asst. treas. Gen. Instrument Corp., 1971-79; exec. v.p., then pres. Cablevision Systems Corp., Woodbury, N.Y., from 1979, now vice chmn., 1979—; bd. dirs. Continental Bank, Garden City, N.Y. Office: Cablevision Systems Corp 1 Media Crossways Woodbury NY 11797

BELL, WILLIAM NEAL, automobile dealership executive; b. Plymouth, Mass., Dec. 11, 1959; s. William Farmer and Claudette Fay (Wallace) B. Student, Fla. State U., 1978-79, U. Md., Munich, Fed. Republic Germany, 1980-81. Writer, vocalist Pentagram, Blacksburg, Va., 1980-83; meat cutter Cooks Supermkt., Alexandria, Va., 1984-85; waiter Clyde's, Tysons, Va., 1984-85; salesman Rosenthal Nissan, Tysons Corner, 1985-87; sales mgr. Rosenthal Dodge, Arlington, Va., 1987-88; mem. Nissan Profl. Sales Guild, Arlington, 1986—; fin. mgr. Rosenthal Mazda, Arlington, 1988—. Composer songs; lyricist, composer Complete Works, 1983-84. Mem. Nissan Profl. Sales Guild. Republican. Baptist. Clubs: Independence (Arlington); Porsch Am. (Fairfax, Va.). Home: 6067 Netherton St Centreville VA 22020 Office: Rosenthal Automotive 1550 Wilson Blvd Ste 700 Arlington VA 22209

BELLANGER, SERGE RENÉ, banker; b. Vimoutiers, France, Apr. 30, 1933; s. René Albert and Raymonde Maria (Renard) B.; MBA, Paris Bus. Sch., 1957. With Citibank, 1966-73, Paris br., 1966-69, world corp. relations officer for Europe, N.Y.C., 1969-73, asst. v.p., 1969-71, v.p., 1972-73; sr. v.p., gen. mgr. N.Y. br. Crédit Industriel et Comml., 1973-79, exec. v.p., gen. mgr., 1979-84, exec. v.p., gen. mgr. CIC-Union Européenne Internat. et Cie, 1984—, also U.S. gen. rep. CIC Group, 1973-88; prof. banking French Banking Inst., 1961-64; mem. adv. com. French House, Columbia U., 1976—, mem. U.S. Com. Fgn. Trade Advisors for France, 1979-83, v.p. U.S. com., 1984-85, exec. v.p. 1985—. Chmn. internat. banking course New Sch. Social Research, N.Y.C., 1981-83. Served with French Air Force, 1958-60. Decorated Algeria Commemorative medal, chevalier Legion of Honor. Mem. French-Am. C. of C. (councillor 1973-74, exec. com. 1974-80, v.p. 1980-82, exec. v.p. 1982-83, nat. pres. 1983—, pres. N.Y. chpt. 1983—), French Overseas Assn., Inst. Fgn. Bankers (trustee 1975-77, v.p. 1977-79, chmn. legis. and regulatory com. 1977-79, chmn. 1979-80), Société Lyonnaise de Banque (bd. dirs. 1986—), Assn. for the Promotion of French Sci., Industry and Tech., 1986—, pres. 1986—), N.Y. Futures Exchange (dir. 1980-87, chmn. fgn. exchange steering com. 1981-82), N.Y. Cotton Exchange (bd. dirs. fin. instrument exchange div. 1985—), Bank Adminstrn. Inst. (editorial bd. World of Banking Mag. 1981—, columnist 1986—). Clubs: Board Room, River (N.Y.C.); Automobile de France (Paris). Home: 860 UN Pla Apt 23/24C New York NY 10017 Office: 520 Madison Ave New York NY 10022

BELLAS, ALBERT CONSTANTINE, investment banker; b. Steubenville, Ohio, Sept. 15, 1942; s. Constantine Michael and Kiki (Michalopoulos) B.; m. Kay Mazzo, Dec. 21, 1978; children—Andrew James, Kathryn Kiki. B.A., Yale U., 1964; J.D., U. Chgo., 1967; M.B.A., Columbia U., 1968. Assoc. Dillon, Read & Co., Inc., N.Y.C., 1968-72; v.p. Goldman Sachs & Co., N.Y.C., 1973-76; gen. ptnr. Loeb Rhoades & Co., N.Y.C., 1976-78; exec. v.p., dir. Loeb Rhoades Hornblower, Inc., N.Y.C., 1978-79; sr. exec. v.p., dir. Shearson Am. Express, Inc., N.Y.C., 1979-83; sr. exec. v.p. Shearson Lehman Hutton Inc., N.Y.C., 1983—; allied mem. N.Y. Stock Exchange. Bd. dirs. Lincoln Ctr. for Performing Arts, N.Y.C., 1987—, Sch. Am. Ballet, N.Y.C., 1975-85, vice chmn., 1986-87, chmn., 1987—; mem. investment com. Mercersburg Acad., Pa., 1987—; mem. day sch. com. Brick Ch., N.Y.C., 1985-88. Mem. ABA, Ohio Bar Assn., Maidstone Club, Yale Club, City Midday Club. Home: 1130 Park Ave New York NY 10128 Office: Shearson Lehman Hutton 2 World Trade Ctr 100th Fl New York NY 10048

BELLEGO, HERVE MELAINE, chemical company executive; b. Plumelin, France, Nov. 9, 1947; came to U.S., 1974; M. Chem. E., Ecole Nat. Superieure des Industries Chimiques, Nancy, France, 1970; MS in Mgmt., Boston U., 1983. Tech. sales rep. Rohm & Haas, Paris, France, 1972-74; mktg. specialist Rohm & Haas, Phila., 1974-76; mgr. European extrusion market Gen. Electric Corp., Bergen OpZoom, Holland, 1976-79; gen. mgr. Thiokol-Ventron Europe, Brussels, 1979-82; v.p. mktg. Ventron div. Morton Thiokol, Inc., Danvers, Mass., 1982-85, v.p., gen. mgr. Ventron div., 1985—. Office: Ventron div Morton Thiokol 150 Andover St Danvers MA 01923

BELLER, GARY A., financial services company executive; b. N.Y.C., Oct. 16, 1938; s. Charles W. and Jeanne A. B.; m. Carole P. Wrubel, Nov. 22, 1967; 1 child, Jessie Melissa. BA, Cornell U., 1960; LLB, NYU, 1963, LLM, 1971. Bar: N.Y. 1963. Various positions gen. counsel's office Am. Express Co., N.Y.C., 1968-82, exec. v.p. and gen. counsel, 1983—. Editorial bd. Ctr. Pub. Resources (Alternatives), N.Y.C. Bd. dirs. Lenox Hill Neighborhood Assn.; bd. dirs., vice chmn. Citizens' Crime Commn. of N.Y.; mem. lawyers com. Nat. Ctr. for State Cts. Mem. ABA, Bar Assn. City N.Y., N.Y. County Bar Assn. (com. corp. law depts.), Harvard Bus. Sch. Club, Doubles Club. Office: Am Express Co Am Express Tower World Fin Ctr New York NY 10285-5130

BELLER, GERALD STEPHEN, former insurance company executive; b. Phila., Aug. 6, 1935; s. Nathan and Adelaide B. (Goldfarb) B.; C.L.U., Am. Coll., Bryn Mawr, Pa., 1972; m. Nancy R. Nelson, June 8, 1968; children—Fay A., Mark S., Royce W., Merrilee A., Marie A., Frank A. Spl. agt. Prudential Ins. Co., San Bernardino, Calif., 1959-62, div. mgr., 1962-66; agy. supr. Aetna Life & Casualty Co., Los Angeles, 1966-69, gen. agt., 1969-77. Magician Magic Castle, Hollywood, Calif. Mem. adult correctional adv. coun. San Bernardino County, Calif. Served with USAF, 1953-57. Recipient Man of Year award, 1961; Manpower Builders award, 1966-69; Agy. Builders award, 1970-72; Pres.'s Trophy award, 1973-74; Nat. Mgmt. award, 1973-76. Mem. Los Angeles Life Underwriters Assn., Am. Soc. C.L.U.s, Golden Key Soc. of Am. Coll., Internat. Exec. Svc. Corps. (vol.), Calif. Assn. Life Underwriters, Los Angeles County C.L.U.s. Home: 20625 Tonawanda Rd Apple Valley CA 92307

BELLES, ANITA LOUISE, management engineer, educator; b. San Angelo, Tex., Aug. 30, 1948; d. Curtis Lee and Margaret Louise (Perry) B.; m. John Arvel Willey, July 13, 1969 (div. Aug. 1978); children: Suzan Heather, Kenneth Alan. BA, U. Tex., 1972; MS in Health Care Adminstrn., Trinity U., 1984. Registered emergency med. technician; cert. CPR instr., emergency med. technician tchr., La. Regional emergency med. service tng. coordinator Bur. Emergency Med. Service, Lake Charles, La., 1978-79; exec. dir. Southwest La. Emergency Med. Service Council, Lake Charles, 1979-83; project coordinator Tulane U. Med. Sch., New Orleans, 1982-83; dir. La. Bur. of Emergency Med. Service, Baton Rouge, 1982; pres. Computype, Inc., San Antonio, 1983-86, Emergency Med. and Safety Assocs., La. and Tex., 1982—; dir. family planning Bexar County Hosp. Dist., Tex., 1987; mgmt. engr. Inpatient Support Applications, 1987-88; instr. grad. sch. health care adminstrn. S.W. Tex. State U. Editor A.L.E.R.T., 1980-83, San Antonio Executive News, 1987—, Family Living, 1987-88; feature writer Bright Scrawl, 1985-86; contbr. numerous articles on emergency med. services to profl. jours. Bd. dirs. Thousand Oaks Homeowner's Assn., sec., treas., 1985; active Trinity U. Health Care Alumni Assn., Jr. League San Antonio, The Parenting Ctr., Baton Rouge, 1982-83, Jr. League Lake Charles, 1982, Campfire Council Pub. Relations Com., Lake Charles, 1982; newsletter editor Community Food Co-Op, Newsletter Editor, 1979; vol. Lake Charles Mental Health Ctr., 1974. Recipient Outstanding Service award La. Assn Registered Emergency Med. Technicians, 1983, Southwest La. Assn. Emergency Med. Technicians, 1983; named Community Leader KPLC TV, Lake Charles, 1981, regional winner Assn U. Programs in Health Adminstrn., HHS Sec's. Competitions for Innovations in Health, 1982. Mem. Nat. Assn. Emergency Med. Technicians., Tex. Assn. Emergency Med. Technicians, Am. Coll. Health Care Execs., Am. Assn. Automotive Medicine, Southwest La. Assn. Emergency Med. Technicians (founding mem., v.p. 1979-80, CPR com. chmn. 1980-81, pub. relations com. chmn. 1981-82, bd. dirs. 1980-82), Am. Mgmt. Assn., Nat. Soc. Emergency Med. Service Adminstrs., Nat. Coalition Emergency Med. Services, Am. Composition Assn. Methodist. Office: Bexar County Hosp Dist 4502 Medical Dr San Antonio TX 78284

BELLESSA, JAMES LLOYD, JR., equity research analyst; b. Seattle, Nov. 22, 1946; s. James Lloyd and Jeanne Ann (Bingham) B.; m. LuAnn Woodward, Jan. 28. 1971; children: Michelle, Nicole, Gina, Jull, Karen, Alicia, Melanie. BA, Brigham Young U., 1971; MBA, 1973. Analyst, portfolio mgr. Western Asset Mgmt. Co., L.A., 1973-77; asst. trust investment officer Idaho First Nat. Bank, Boise, 1977-83; v.p., dir. research D.A. Davidson and Co., Gt. Falls, Mont., 1983—. Mem. Salt Lake City Soc. Fin. Analysts, Fin. Analysts Fedn., Inst. Chartered Fin. Analysts (cert. CFA). Republican. Mormon. Home: 3409 6th Ave S Great Falls MT 59405 Office: 8 3rd St N Great Falls MT 59403

BELLINGER, JOHN DOOLEY, banker; b. Honolulu, May 13, 1923; s. Eustace L. and Lei (Williams) B.; m. Joan Simms, Apr. 7, 1945; children: Dona, Jan, Neil. Student, U. Hawaii, 1941-42, LL.D. (hon.), 1982; LHD (hon.), Hawaii Loa Coll., 1986. With First Hawaiian Bank (and predecessor), Honolulu, 1942—; pres., chief exec. officer First Hawaiian Bank (and predecessor), 1969—, chmn. bd., 1979—, also bd. dirs.; chief exec. officer, chmn. bd. First Hawaiian, Inc., also bd. dirs.; chmn., chief exec. officer First Hawaiian Credit Corp.; chmn., chief exec. officer, dir. 1st Hawaiian Leasing, Inc.; dir. Alexander & Baldwin, Honolulu, Matson Nav. Co., Hawaiian Telephone Co., Pacific Resources Inc., Restaurant Suntory, U.S.A., Halekulani Corp.; mem. Gov.'s adv. bd. Underwater Cable Transmission Project. Chmn. Japan-Hawaii Econ. Council; chmn., bd. dirs. Pacific Internat. Ctr. for High Tech.; bd. dirs. North Hawaii Community Hosp., Inc.; civilian aide to sec. Army for Hawaii; chmn. U.S. Army Civilian Adv. Steering Com.; trustee Francis H.I. Brown Found., Punahou Sch., Japan-Am. Inst. Mgmt. Sci. Fund; hon. trustee Bishop Mus.; bd. dirs. East-West Ctr. Found. Served with AUS, 1946-47; bd. govs. Japanese Cultural Ctr. Hawaii. Decorated Disting. Civilian Service Medal Sec. of Army, 1980; recipient Disting. Citizen award Congl. Medal of Honor Soc., 1981; decorated ProPatria award, 1984, Torch of Liberty award Anti-Defamation League of B'nai B'rith, 1984, Businessman of Yr. award Hawaiian Bus./Profl. Assn., 1984; Gen. Creighton W. Abrams medal, David Malo award Rotary Club Honolulu, 1986, Community Relations award of excellence Dept. Army, 1987; 3d Class Order Rising Sun, 1985; named Hawaii Disting. Citizen, Boy Scouts Am. Aloha council, 1987; numerous others. Mem. Hawaii C. of C. (bd. dirs.), Assn. U.S. Army, Navy League, Hawaii bankers assns. Clubs: Hawaiian Civic, Oahu Country, Waialae Country (Honolulu) (bd. dirs., past pres.); The 200 (treas., past pres.). Office: First Hawaiian Bank 165 S King St Honolulu HI 96813

BELLIS, ARTHUR ALBERT, financial executive, government official; b. Worcester, Mass., June 16, 1928; s. Frank Clayton and Ruth Porter (Gordon) B.; m. Barbara Swift, Feb. 22, 1952 (div. 1969); children—Bradford, Susan; m. E. Deborah Shea, May 28, 1972; children—Cynthia, Michael. B.S. in B.A., Boston U., 1952. Asst. credit mgr. Procter & Gamble, N.Y.C., 1955-56; asst. supr. capital budget Western Union, N.Y.C., 1956-58; corp. budget analyst CBS, N.Y.C., 1958-64; account exec. Edwards & Hanley, N.Y.C., 1964-66, Spencer Trask, Worcester, 1966-70; sr. securities compliance examiner SEC, Boston, 1970—. Advisor Explorer program Mohegan council Boy Scouts Am., 1966-70; mem. Worcester Rep. Com., 1952-53, Rep. Presdl. Task Force, 1984-85; mem. fin. com. Town of Yarmouth, 1982-86. Recipient Superior Performance award SEC, 1976, 1986; Medal of Merit, Pres. of U.S., 1985. Mem. Aircraft Owners and Pilots Assn., Internat. Platform Assn. Methodist. Lodge: Masons. Avocation: flying. Home: 14 Ice House Rd South Yarmouth MA 02664 Office: John McCormack Courthouse and Post Office Bldg 7th Fl Boston MA 02109

BELLISTON, TRACY BLAINE, financial executive; b. Nephi, Utah, May 19, 1956; s. Blaine F. and Rosalie (Harmon) B.; m. Jill Barney, May 9, 1980; children: T. David, Stephen B., Michael B. A in Mktg., Dixie Coll., 1977; BBA, So. Utah State U., 1983; postgrad., Am. Coll., 1985. CLU; chartered fin. cons. Gen. agt. Investors Life, Provo, Utah, 1981-83; assoc. Intermountain Fin. Group, Salt Lake City, 1983-85, Brock & Assocs., Salt Lake City, 1983-86; assoc. Mass. Mut. Cos., Salt Lake City, 1986-88, unit supr., 1986-88, dist. mgr., 1989—; dir. fin. planning Integrated Fin. Designs, Inc., Salt Lake City, 1986-87, Strategic Planners Group, Inc., Salt Lake City, 1987—; speaker in field. Bd. dirs. Arsenal Alliance Youth Soccer Assn., Salt Lake City, 1987—. Mem. Internat. Assn. Fin. Planning, Am. Soc. Chartered Life Underwriters and Chartered Fin. Cons. (bd. dirs. Utah chpt.), Nat. Assn. Life Underwriters. Republican. Mormon. Home: 9948 Yorkshire Dr Salt Lake City UT 84065 Office: Mass Mut Cos 4 Triad Ctr Ste 600 Salt Lake City UT 84180

BELLMORE, LAWRENCE ROBERT, JR., financial planner; b. Flint, Mich., May 1, 1947; s. Lawrence R. and Vaneta O. (Wortz) B.; m. Patricia Antonopolos, Dec. 27, 1969; 1 son, Lawrence Robert III; m. 2d, Susan Marie Thompson, Aug. 1979; 1 son, Samuel Ryan; 1 stepdau., Stacy Marie Thompson. B.S. in Mech. Engring., Gen. Motors Inst., 1970; MBA, U. Pitts., 1987. Cert. fin. planner. Engr. in tng. Gen. Motors Inst., Flint, Mich., 1969-70; dist. service and parts mgr. Detroit zone Buick Motor Div., Flint, Mich., 1970-72; mgr. fleet maintenance N.Am. Van Lines, Ft. Wayne, Ind., 1972-74, Eazor Express, Pitts., 1974-75; br. mgr. Pullman Trailmobile, Inc., Lancaster, Pa., 1975-79, Jersey City, N.J., 1976-77, Balt., 1977-79; pres. Lyco Truck Sales & Service, Inc. and Lyco Leasing, Inc., Montoursville, Pa., 1979-81, L.R. Bellmore & Assocs., Montoursville, Pa., 1981—; registered rep. Waddell & Reed, Inc., 1982-83; nat. sales mgr. R. Dummont & Co., GMBH W.Ger. in U.S., 1982; founder LRBA Assocs., Inc., Bus. Brokers & Investment Banking, 1987—; mng. exec. Integrated Resources Equity Corp., Montoursville, 1987—; mktg. dir. Muncy Homes, Inc. Bd. dirs. Black Hawk Home Owners Assn., 1972-74. Mem. Internat. Assn. Fin. Planners, Internat. Assn. Cert. Fin. Planners, Full Gospel Bus. Men's Fellowship, Internat. Republican. Lodges: Rotary, Sertoma. Home: RD 5 Box 576 Muncy PA 17756 Office: L R Bellmore & Assocs 113 S Main St Muncy PA 17756

BELLRINGER, STEPHEN TERRENCE, gas company executive; b. Birmingham, Eng., July 5, 1946; married. B of Commerce, U. Windsor, 1968, MBA, 1969. Pres. Union Gas Ltd., 1968—; vice chmn. Can. Gas Assn., past chmn. Ont. Gas Assn. Trustee Pub. Gen. Hosp., Chatham, Ont.; vice chmn. bd. govs. U. Windsor. Office: Union Gas, 50 Keil Dr N, Chatham, ON Canada N7M 5M1

BELLUOMINI, FRANK STEPHEN, accountant; b. Healdsburg, Calif., May 19, 1934; s. Francesco and Rose (Giorgi) B.; m. Alta Anita Gifford, Sept. 16, 1967; 1 child, Wendy Ann. AA, Santa Rosa Jr. Coll., 1954; BA with honors, San Jose State U., 1956. CPA, Calif. Staff acct. Hood, Gire & Co., CPA's, San Jose, Calif., 1956-60, ptnr., 1960-66; ptnr. Touche Ross & Co., CPA's, San Jose, 1967—, ptnr.-in-charge San Jose office, 1971-85, sr. ptnr. San Jose office, 1985—. Mem. adv. bd. Salvation Army, San Jose, 1979-85, San Jose Children's Council, 1982—; trustee Santa Clara County (Calif.) United Way, 1979-83, v.p. planning and allocations, 1981-83, vice chmn., 1985-87, chmn. 1987-89; bd. dirs. San Jose Mus. Art, 1984-86. Named Disting. Alumnus, San Jose State U. Sch. Bus., 1978. Mem. Santa Clara County Estate Planning Council (pres. 1979-80), Calif. Soc. C.P.A.'s (pres. chpt. 1968-69, state v.p. 1976-77), Am. Inst. C.P.A.'s (chmn. state and local govt. com. 1976-79), San Jose State Alumni Assn. (treas. 1960-61, dir. 1961-62, exec. com. 1961-62), San Jose State Acctg. Round Table (bd. dirs., treas. 1982-87), Beta Alpha Psi (San Jose State U. Outstanding Alumnus award 1986). Roman Catholic. Club: San Jose Rotary (dir. 1979-81, trustee and treas. San Jose Rotary Endowment 1976-83).

BELLVILLE, RALPH EARL, banker; b. Lynn, Mass., June 15, 1925; s. Harold Eugene and Edith Floy (Simpson) B.; m. Crescentia Ranftl, Oct. 16, 1954. AB, Harvard U., 1950. Asst. mgr. No. Trust Co., Chgo., 1955-60; v.p. United Calif. Bank, L.A., 1960-69; exec. v.p. Security Pacific Nat. Bank, L.A., 1969-85; pres. REB Cons., Santa Monica, Calif., 1985—; bd. dirs. Security Pacific Overseas Corp., Security Pacific Overseas Investment Corp., Security Pacific Asian Bank, Hong Kong, Security Pacific Ltd., Sydney, Australia. Active L.A. Com. on Fgn. Rels. With inf. U.S. Army, 1943-46. Decorated Bronze Star with oak leaf cluster. Mem. Global Econ. Action Inst., Asia Soc., Jonathan Club, Internat. Club, Harvard Club So. Calif. Home: 211 24th St Santa Monica CA 90402 Office: REB Cons 211 24th St Santa Monica CA 90402

BELNIAK, ROBERT KAROL, editor, concert promoter; b. Springfield, Mass., Feb. 14, 1945; s. Adam and Lena (Rodgers) B.; m. Deborah Ann Fydenkevez, Aug. 7, 1987; children: Carolyn, Alan. AA, Grahm Jr. Coll., 1970. Merchandiser Schenley Industries Inc., Springfield, Mass., 1971—. Editor Echoes of the Past mag., 1987—; producer, on air personality sta. WTCC-FM, Springfield, 1977-88. Recipient Best Oldie Program award Valley Advocate Newspaper, 1986. Roman Catholic.

BELSKY, IRA M., apparel industry executive; b. N.Y.C., July 7, 1952; s. Irving and Sylvia (Liquerman) B.; m. Dorothy P. Lullen, Feb. 11, 1979; 1 child, Brian. BA summa cum laude, U. Pa., 1973; JD, Stanford U., 1979. Bar: Calif. 1979. Asst. to gov. State of Ill., Chgo., 1973-76; assoc. O'Melveny & Myers, Los Angeles, 1979-83; exec. v.p., founder Spear Fin. Services Inc., Los Angeles, 1983-86, also bd. dirs.; chief exec. officer Banff Ltd., N.Y.C., 1986—; bd. dirs. Investors Retirement and Mgmt. Corp., Santa Barbara, Calif., Micro Electronics Tech., Boston. Mem. Phi Beta Kappa. Democrat. Office: Banff Ltd 1410 Broadway New York NY 10018

BELSKY, MARTIN A., defense company executive. Exec. v.p. Unisys Corp., Detroit. Office: Unisys Corp Unisys Pl PO Box 418 Detroit MI 48232 *

BELTEAU, KENNETH RAYMOND, electrical engineer; b. N.Y.C., Jan. 16, 1946; s. Raymond Lawrence and Virginia (Chamberlin) B.; m. Sharon Ann Lalumandier, Dec. 26, 1970; children: Chad Kenneth, Kevin Raymond, Jocelyn Carol. BSEE, La. State U., 1968; MBA, U. Houston, 1974. Registered profl. engr., Tex. Engr. Gulf Refining Co., Houston and New Orleans, 1968-74; sr. pipeline engr. Gulf Refining Co., Houston, 1974-75; dir. pipeline regulations Oil Corp., Houston, 1978-81; supt. ops. and maintenance Gulf Oil Corp., Houston, 1976-78; dir. pipeline regulations and tariffs Gulf Pipeline Co., Houston, 1981-83, dir. planning and econs., 1983-85; sr. engr. ARCO Pipe Line Co., Independence, Kans., 1985-88; sr. planning analyst ARCO Pipe Line Co., Independence, 1988—; alt. owner rep. South Pass Block 49 Pipeline System, 1979-85, Sabine Pass Block 13 Pipeline System, 1979-85, Clovelly-Alliance-Meraux Pipeline System, 1979-85, West Delta Pipeline System, 1979-85; bd. dirs. Dixie Pipe Line co. Contbr. papers to profl. publs. Chmn. memberships ARCO Civic Action Program, 1989—; adviser Jr. Achievement, 1975; active Boy Scouts Am., presently dist. rep.; water safety instr. ARC; dir., v.p., treas. Tex. Excavation Safety System Inc., Dallas, 1983-86; bd. dirs. Independence Day Care Ctr.; coach Glenshire Soccer Club, 1981-85, Independence Soccer Club, 1985-86, Braeburn Little League, 1983-85, asst. coach Babe Ruth Baseball, 1988. With U.S. Army, 1970-71. Mem. IEEE, Tex. Soc. Profl. Engrs., Nat. Soc. Profl. Engrs., Assn. Energy Engrs., Tex. Mid-Continent Oil & Gas Assn. (chmn. pipeline com. 1982-84), Soc. Am. Mil. Engrs., Independence Country Club, ARCO Employees Club (v.p. 1987-88), KC, Am. Legion, Sigma Iota Epsilon. Republican. Roman Catholic. Home: 3001 Crown Dr Independence KS 67301 Office: ARCO Pipe Line Co ARCO Bldg Independence KS 67301

BELZBERG, BRENT STANLEY, financial executive; b. Calgary, Alta., Can., Jan. 1, 1951; s. Hyman and Jenny Belzberg; m. Lynn Rosen, Jan. 6, 1979; children: Bram David, Kate Sonja, Zachary William. B in Commerce, Queen's U., Kingston, Ont., 1972; LLB, U. Toronto, 1975. Solicitor Tory, Tory, Deslauriers and Binnington, Toronto, Ont., 1975-79; v.p., dir. First City Trust Co., Vancouver, B.C., 1979—; sr. v.p. First City Fin. Corp., Vancouver, 1979—; chmn., chief exec. officer First City Devel. Corp., Toronto, 1979—; pres., chief operating officer 1st City Trustco Inc., Toronto, 1988—, also bd. dirs.; bd. dirs. Cantel Inc., Pioneer Lifeco Inc. Bd. dirs. United Synagogue Day Sch., Toronto, 1987, Olympic Trust of Can., Toronto, Gallatea Art Internat., Toronto, 1987, Weizman Inst., Mt. Sinai Hosp., Israel Bonds Can.; assoc. chmn. major gifts United Jewish Appeal of Met. Toronto, 1987—; mem. Can. Coun. Christians & Jews; mem. pres.'s com. U. Toronto. Jewish. Club: Cambridge (Toronto), Oakdale Golf & Country. Office: First City Trustco Inc, 200 King St W Ste 1600, Toronto, ON Canada M5H 3T4

BELZBERG, SAMUEL, finance and trust companies executive; b. Calgary, Alta., Can., June 26, 1928; s. Abraham and Hinda (Fishman) B.; m. Frances Cooper; children: Cheryl Rae, Marc David, Wendy Jay, Lisa. B.Comm., U. Alta., Edmonton, 1948. Chmn., chief exec. officer First City Fin. Corp. Ltd.; chmn. First City Trust Co.; bd. dirs. Enserv Corp., Am. Eagle Petroleums Ltd., First City Industries, Inc., Scovill, Inc., Pioneer Life Assurance Co.; hon. dir. Cantel Inc. Home: 3489 Osler St, Vancouver, BC Canada V6H 2W4 Office: First City Fin Corp Ltd, 777 Hornby St, Vancouver, BC Canada V6Z 1S4

BELZBERG, WILLIAM, financial company executive; b. 1932; married. Vice pres., dir. First City Fin. Corp. Ltd. Can.; pres., chief exec. officer Far West Fin. Corp., Newport Beach, Calif., 1976-80, chmn. bd., 1978—, dir.; chmn. bd., pres., chief exec. officer Far West Sav. and Loan Assn., Newport Beach. Office: Far W Fin Corp 4001 MacArthur Blvd Newport Beach CA 92660 *

BELZER, ALAN, diversified manufacturing company executive; b. Bklyn., Nov. 27, 1932; s. Morris and Vera B.; children: Debra, Frances. B.S., NYU, 1953. With Allied Corp., N.Y.C., 1955—; gen. mgr. plastic film bus. Allied Corp., 1970-71; pres. Allied Corp. (Fabricated Products div.), 1971-72; v.p. ops. Allied Corp. (Fibers div.), 1972-73, exec. v.p., pres., 1973-75; group v.p. Corp. Office, 1975-79; group v.p., pres. Fibers and Plastics Co., 1979-83, corp. exec. v.p., pres. engineered materials sector, 1983-88, corp. pres., chief operating officer, 1988—; bd. trustees Manhattan Bowery Corp., N.Y., 1987—. Served with USCGR, 1953-55. Mem. N.Am. Soc. for Corp. Planning (bd. dirs. 1968), Opportunity Resources for the Arts (bd. dirs. 1981), Chem. Mfrs. Assn. (bd. dirs. 1983—). Office: Allied-Signal Inc Columbia Rd & Park Ave Morristown NJ 07960 *

BEMBERIS, IVARS, marketing professional; b. Riga, Latvia, Sept. 25, 1941; came to U.S., 1950; s. Arvids Bemberis and Lina (Baumanis) Caune; m. Jeannette Arnold, June 14, 1964; children: Scott Ivars, Kimberly Ann. AB in Engring. Sci., Dartmouth Coll., 1964, BCE, 1965, M in Engring., 1966. Registered profl. engr., Conn., Iowa. Engr. Dorr Oliver, Inc. now Amicon div. of W.R. Grace and Co., Stamford, Conn., 1968—; then market devel. mgr. membrane venture unit Dorr Oliver, Inc. now Amicon div. of W.R. Grace and Co., Stamford, now mgr. indsl. mkgt., 1988—. Contbr. articles on membrane processing to profl. jours. Chmn. Nat. Phonathon Dartmouth Dean's Fund, 1983-86; coach, supr. Soccer Club Ridgefield, Conn., 1975-80. With U.S. Army, 1966-68, Vietnam. Decorated Bronze Star. Mem. Am. Inst. Chem. Engrs., Inst. Food Technologists, Water Pollution Control Fedn., N.Am. Membrane Soc., Dartmouth Soc. Engrs. (pres. 1976-78, exec. com. 1972-82). Democrat. Lutheran. Clubs: Dartmouth (New Canaan, Ridgefield and Wilton)(treas. Dartmouth chpt. 1978-88. Office: W R Grace and Co Amicon Div 24 Cherry Hill Dr Danvers MA 01923

BEMIS, HAL LAWALL, engineering and business executive; b. Palm Beach, Fla., Jan. 30, 1912; s. Henry E. and Elise (Lawall) B.; m. Isabel Mead, June 27, 1942 (div.); children—Elise, Carolyn, Claudia; m. Jeanne Chatham, June 5, 1982. B.S., M.I.T., 1935. With Campbell Soup Co., 1935-53; mgr., asst. to pres., v.p., dir. Campbell Soup Co., Ltd., 1946-53; organizer, pres. Mariner Corp., 1954—; v.p. Hosp. Food Mgmt., Inc., 1954-57; sec., treas. Bell Key Corp., 1955—; v.p. Coral Motel Corp., 1963—; pres. Jennings Machine Corp., 1957—; cons. Coopers & Lybrand, 1973—; dir., mem. exec. and audit coms. Publicker Industries; chmn., dir. Phila. Reins. Corp.; dir. Ott, Hertner, Ott & Assos., Colonial Savs. Bank. Past pres. Commn. Twp. Lower Merion, Pa.; bd. dirs., vice chmn. Spring Garden Coll.; exec. bd. Com. of 70; chmn. bd. Am. Cancer Soc.; bd. dirs. Delaware Valley area Nat. Council on Alcoholism; adv. bd. Salvation Army; past trustee Haverford Sch.; dir. Phila. Port Corp., West Phila. Corp., Phila. Indsl. Devel. Corp.; trustee United Fund, Young Men's Inst.; pres., trustee Greater Phila. Found.; bd. dirs. Am. Diabetes Assn., M.I.T. Devel. Found., Broad St. So. Com.; mem. corp. bd. Goodwill Industries, Garrett-Williamson Found. Served 1st lt. to lt. col. AUS, 1942-45. Decorated Legion of Merit with oak leaf cluster, Bronze Star medal; Croix de Guerre (France). Mem. Greater Phila. C. of C. (past chmn. bd., past pres.), SAR, S.R., Pa. Soc., Newcomen Soc., Mil. Order World Wars, Mil. Order Fgn. Wars, Am. Legion (past comdr.), Tau Beta Pi, Delta Psi. Clubs: Union League (pres.), Racquet, Rittenhouse, Penn, Philadelphia; St. Anthony (N.Y.C.), Merion Golf (Ardmore, Pa.); Merion Cricket (dir.) (Haverford, Pa.); Bachelor's Barge, IV Street, Pine Valley Golf, Sunday Breakfast, Right Angle, Toronto Golf, Royal Canadian Yacht, Brit. Officers. Home: 101 Cheswold Ln Haverford PA 19041 Office: 410 Lancaster Ave Haverford PA 19041

BEMIS, JAMES RAYFIELD, international banking executive; b. El Paso, Tex., Mar. 1, 1953; s. Robert Eugene and Jennie Marie (Navas) B.; m. Lynn Luanne Thurman, July 28, 1979; children: Marisa Lynne, Meghan Elizabeth. AA with honors, Ventura Coll., 1974; BA with honors, U. Calif., 1977; MBA, UCLA, 1987. Data analyst City of Santa Barbara, Calif., 1978-79; staff asst. City of Oxnard, Calif., 1979-80, mgmt. analyst, 1980-83, budget dir., 1983-85, econ. devel. mgr., 1985-87; v.p. Sumitomo Trust and Banking Co., Ltd., Los Angeles, 1987—; mem. Oxnard Capital Improvement Program Com., 1983—, Oxnard Debt Fin. Task Force, 1985—, Oxnard EDP Task Force, 1984—. Contbr. articles on research and mgmt. devel. to profl. jours. Mem. Friends of the Library, Oxnard, 1983—, Santa Clara Parish, Oxnard, 1980—. Mem. Govt. Fin. Officers Assn. (Disting. Budget Presentation 1985), Am. Soc. Pub. Adminstrs., Mfrs. and Processors Assn. (sec. 1986), Mcpl. Mgmt. Assts. of So. Calif., Calif. Mcpl. Utilities Assn. (legis. com. 1982-85), Calif. Econ. Devel. Assn. (govt. liaison com. 1986). Republican. Roman Catholic. Home: 234 Goldenwood Circle Simi Valley CA 93065 Office: Sumitomo Trust & Banking Co Ltd 333 S Grand Ave Ste 5300 Los Angeles CA 90071

BEN, JOAN, paralegal; b. Rockland, Maine, Aug. 1, 1967; d. Emilio Jaime and Maria Angela (Cardenas) B. Grad. with honors, Casco Bay Coll., 1987. Paralegal Hiscock & Barclay, Augusta, Maine, 1987-88, P.J. Perrino, Jr., Augusta, 1988—. Mem. Maine Assn. Paralegals. Roman Catholic. Office: PJ Perrino Jr 124 State St Augusta ME 04330

BENAPFL, WILLIAM JOSEPH, accountant; b. Pasadena, Calif., Aug. 26, 1956; s. John Roscoe and Janice Jean (Murphy) B.; m. Lea Sunseri, Aug. 25, 1984; children: Brendan, Christine. BSBA, Calif. State U., Hayward, 1979. Fin. acct. Pacific Coast Producers, Santa Clara, Calif., 1980-87; corp. controller Pacific Coast Producers, Santa Clara, 1987—. Mem. Nat. Assn. Accts. (bd. dirs. local chpt. 1982-84, 85-86, v.p.1984-85, 86-87), Nat. Soc. Accts. Coops., San Jose Athletic Club. Republican. Roman Catholic. Office: Pacific Coast Producer PO Box 4240 Santa Clara CA 95054

BENAVIDES, LUIS JORDAN, bonding and insurance executive; b. San Antonio, June 5, 1949; s. Julius Winn Benavides and Irma (Cordova) McIntyre; m. Mary Esther Fernandez, June 13, 1971; children: Luis Xavier, Joshua Adam, Angela Alyssa. BBA, St. Mary's U., San Antonio, 1971; postgrad. comml. lending, U. Okla., 1983. Cert. nat. bank examiner, master residential appraiser. Salesman Richardson-Merrell Corp., Wilton, Conn., 1972-75; nat. bank examiner Conptroller of Currency, Fargo, N.D., 1975-81; v.p. loan rev. First State Bank, Abilene, Tex., 1981; sr. v.p. investments First West Fin. Corp., Lubbock, Tex., 1982; sr. v.p. loan adminstrn. Security Nat. Bank, Lubbock, 1983; head comml. lending Exchange Nat. Bank, San Antonio, 1984; sr. ptnr. Banker Econ. Services of Tex., Lubbock, 1984-86; regional mgr. Fin. Services Network, San Antonio, 1986-87; pres. Benavides Agy., San Antonio, 1987—; cons. USDA-FHA, State of Ala., 1985; speaker in field. Contbr. articles to profl. jours. Bd. dirs. I.I.S.A. Tex., 1989, Arroyo Ltd.-R.E. Developer, Abilene, 1981-84; Hhispanic membership chmn. Boy Scouts Am., West Tex. Panhandle; coordinator West Tex. Econ. Devel. and Small Bus. Seminar, 1986; area chmn. West Tex. Diocesan Campaign for Advance Gifts; mem. fin com. Diocese of Lubbock, steering com. NISD Bond '88; pres. parish council Our Lady of Guadalupe Ch. Mem. Nat. Assn. Master Appraisers, Abilene Mexican Am. C. of C. (pres. 1980-81), Am. Subcontractor Assn., Ind. Ins. Agts. Tex. Republican. Roman Catholic. Office: Benavides Agy 1603 Babcock Ste 151 San Antonio TX 78229

BENCHLEY, ROBERT STAFFORD, publishing executive; b. Newton, Mass., July 27, 1950; s. Edwin Allen Jr. and Barbara Carol (Donegan) B.; m. Rosemary Power, June 17, 1972 (div. May 1983); m. Andrea T. Gabriel,

Sept. 20, 1987. BA, Syracuse U., 1974. Asst. editor Food and Drug Packaging Mag., N.Y.C., 1972-74, assoc. editor, 1974-75, mng. editor, 1975-83; editor and pub. Benchmark Mag., N.Y.C., 1983-86; pub., editorial dir. Franchise Mag., N.Y.C., 1986-87; cons. N.Y.C., 1987-88; publ. dir. Custom Mags. Inc., N.Y.C., 1988—; screener nat. mag. awards, 1981-87; treas. Am. Mus. of Pub., 1985-87. Author numerous free lance articles; editor various pubs. Recipient 1st prize for cover design, Am. Soc. Bus. Press Editors,1979, Jesse H. Neal award Am. Bus. Press, 1980. Mem. Am. Soc. Mag. Editors, Soc. Profl. Journalists. Home: 51 Fuller Brook Rd Wellesley MA 02181

BENCKE, RONALD LEE, financial executive; b. Maynard, Iowa, Feb. 9, 1940; s. Floyd B. and Emilie W. (Reinhardt) B.; m. Mary Kay Scott, Dec. 19, 1961; children: Stephen, Patrick, Desiree, Matthew, Joshuah. BA, Wartburg Coll., 1962; PMD, Harvard U., 1981. Fin. analyst Gen. Electric, Danville, Ill., 1962-65; controller Ansul Co., Marinette, Wis., 1965-66; systems mgr. Chamberlain Corp., Elmhurst, Ill., 1966-69; cons. Westinghouse Electric, Pitts., 1969-74; v.p., controller Westinghouse Credit Corp., Pitts., 1974-83; v.p., chief fin. officer Westinghouse CreditCorp., Pitts., 1983-88, pres., 1988—, also bd. dirs. Scoutmaster Boy Scouts Am., Chgo., 1967; chmn. United Way, 1985; elder Presbyn. Ch. Mem. Fin. Execs. Inst., Planning Exec. Inst., Harvard U. Bus. Sch. Assn. (pres.), Nat. Rev. Appraisers, Mortgage Underwriters Assn. Republican. Club: Harvard-Yale-Princeton (Pitts.). Office: Westinghouse Credit Corp 1 Oxford Centre Pittsburgh PA 15219

BENDER, ANTHONY JOSEPH, management consultant; b. Cumberland, Md., Mar. 4, 1958; s. John Andrew and Filomena Ann (Dearcangelis) B.; m. Hilda Mae Thein, Oct. 31, 1981 (div. Jan. 1985). BS in Econs., Frostburg (Md.) State U., 1981; MBA, Shippensburg U. Pa., 1985. Systems analyst Corning Glass Works, Greencastle, Pa., 1981-85; programmer, analyst Ingersoll-Rand, Charlotte, N.C., 1985; mgr. mgmt. cons. sect. Price Waterhouse, Charlotte, 1985—; instr. Tech. Coll. Alamance, N.C., 1987. Mem. Am. Prodn. and Inventory Control Soc. (cert., instr. local chpt. 1986, 87). Democrat. Roman Catholic. Club: Charlotte Textile. Home: 1426 Lilac Rd Charlotte NC 28209 Office: Price Waterhouse One NCNB Pla Ste 3200 Charlotte NC 28280

BENDER, CHARLES CHRISTIAN, retail home center executive; b. Bklyn., July 4, 1936; s. Charles C. and Virginia R. (Rahlfs) B.; m. Jean Ann Couper; children: Lori Ann, Hallie Couper. BA, Hillsdale Coll., 1959; MBA, U. Mich., 1960. Buyer Dayton Hudson, Detroit, 1962-69; v.p., gen. mdse. mgr. Wickes Lumber, Saginaw, Mich., 1969-81; gen. mgr. Wickes B.V., Utrecht, Netherlands, 1981-84; pres., chief exec. officer, owner Busy Beaver Bldg. Ctrs., Pitts., 1984—. Served with U.S. Army, 1960-61. Mem. Home Ctr. Industry Pres. Coun. (bd. dirs. 1986—), Home Ctr. Inst. (adv. coun. 1984—), St. Margaret's Meml. Hosp. Found. (mem. corp. leadership coun.). Republican. Presbyterian. Clubs: Fox Chapel Yacht, Pitts. Field. Home: 310 Buckingham Rd Pittsburgh PA 15215 Office: Busy Beaver Bldg Ctrs Inc 701 Alpha Dr Pittsburgh PA 15238

BENDETSEN, KARL ROBIN, business executive, lawyer; b. Aberdeen, Wash., Oct. 11, 1907; s. Albert M. and Anna (Benton) B.; m. Billie McIntosh, 1938; 1 son, Brookes McIntosh; m. Maxine Bosworth, 1947; 1 dau., Anna Martha; m. Gladys Ponton de Arce Heurtematte Johnston, 1972. A.B., Stanford U., 1929, J.S.D., 1932. Bar: Calif., Oreg., Ohio, N.Y., Wash., D.C., U.S. Supreme Ct. Practiced law Aberdeen, Wash., 1932-40; mgmt. counsel 1946-47; cons. spl. asst. to sec. U.S. Dept. Def., 1948; asst. sec. Dept. Army, 1948-50, under sec., 1950-52; dir. gen. U.S. R.R.s, 1950-52; chmn. bd. Panama Canal Co., 1950-54; counsel Champion Papers, 1952-53, v.p. Tex. div., 1953-55, v.p. ops., 1955-60, chmn. bd., pres., chief exec. officer, 1960-67; dir. Westinghouse Electric, 1961-80; chmn., pres., chief exec. officer Champion Internat., 1967-72; dir. N.Y. Stock Exchange, 1972-82; chmn. exec. com. Champion Internat., 1973-75; spl. U.S. rep. with rank of ambassador to W.Ger., 1956, spl. U.S. ambassador to Philippines, 1956; chmn. adv. com. to sec. Dept. Def., 1962; vice chmn. Def. Manpower Commn., 1974-76; bd. overseers Hoover Instn.; chmn. panel on Strategic Def. Initiative for Pres. Reagan, 1980-84. Directed evacuation of Japanese from West Coast, 1942. Served to col. U.S. Army, 1940-46; spl. rep. sec. of war to Gen. MacArthur 1941. Decorated D.S.M. with oak leaf cluster, Silver Star, Legion of Merit with 2 oak leaf clusters, Bronze Star with 3 oak leaf clusters and Combat V, Army Commendation medal with 3 oak leaf clusters, medal of Freedom; Croix de Guerre with Palm; officer Legion of Honor (France); Croix de Guerre with palm (Belgium); mem. Order Brit. Empire; recipient Disting. Civilian Service medal. Mem. Theta Delta Chi. Episcopalian. Clubs: Links (N.Y.C.), Metropolitan (N.Y.C.), Brook (N.Y.C.); Chicago; Washington Athletic (Seattle); Bohemian (San Francisco), Pacific Union (San Francisco); F Street (D.C.), Georgetown (D.C.); Everglades (Palm Beach, Fla.), Bath and Tennis (Palm Beach, Fla.). Home: 2918 Garfield Terr NW Washington DC 20008 Office: Champion Internat 1850 K St Ste 1185 Washington DC 20006

BENDIX, WILLIAM EMANUEL, equipment manufacturing company executive; b. Los Angeles, Feb. 24, 1935; s. Emanuel S. and Katharine (Rinkle) B.; m. Joyce McCune, June 7, 1957; children—Bruce, Louise, Linda. B.S. in Engring, UCLA, 1957; M.B.A. with distinction, Harvard U., 1962. With mfg. and engring. mgmt. dept. Litton Industries, Calif., 1962-65; prin. Theodore Barry and Assos., Los Angeles, 1965-70; v.p. ops., div. pres., group v.p., dir., pres., chief exec. officer Mark Controls Corp., Evanston, Ill., 1970—. Served to lt. (j.g.) USNR, 1957-60. Mem. Valve Mfrs. Assn. Am. (chmn. 1989—), Tau Beta Pi. Home: 611 Longwood Glencoe IL 60022 Office: Mark Controls Corp 5202 Old Orchard Rd Skokie IL 60077

BENEDICT, LINDA SHERK, insurance company executive; b. Hartford, Conn., Jan. 25, 1945; d. Robert William and Marjorie Joan (Drysdale) Sherk; m. Geoffrey Clinton Benedict, Sept. 13, 1969 (div. 1981). AB in Social Psychology, Harvard U., 1967; MBA in Fin., U. Conn., 1980. CLU. Analyst market rsch. Polaroid Corp., Cambridge, Mass., 1967-70, Transaction Tech., Cambridge, 1970-72; mgr. market rsch. Ocean Spray Cranberries, Hanson, Mass., 1972-76; with Conn. Gen. Life, Bloomfield, 1976-86, regional v.p. claims, 1983-86; v.p. claims and svcs. Blue Cross & Blue Shield, Balt., 1986—; v.p. , gen. mgr. individual market div. Blue Cross & Blue Shield of Md., Balt., 1986—; pres. Sterling Health Svcs., Inc. Blue Cross & Blue Shield of Md., Balt., 1988—. Chmn. Blue Cross United Way campaign, Balt., 1987; mem. fin. com., bd. dirs. Meals on Wheels, Balt., 1987—; bd. dirs. Columbia/Freestate Health System, Balt., 1987—; chmn. fin. com. Lit. Vols., Hartford, 1985-86, bd. dirs. 1984-86. NSF grantee, 1966-67. Mem. Am. Mgmt. Assn., C. of C. Bloomfield (pres. 1977-79). Office: Blue Cross & Blue Shield Md 700 E Joppa Rd Baltimore MD 21204

BENEDICT, ROBERT EDWARD, automotive safety device manufacturing executive; b. Newark, Mar. 11, 1923; s. Michael Douglas and Evelyn (Spangenberger) B.; m. Dorothy Burdick, June 9, 1945; children: Christine, Mark Burdick, Hubbard Stewart. BS in Marine Transp., MIT, 1944. Analyst, supr. Moore McCormack Lines, Inc., N.Y.C., 1944-51, P.R. Econ. Devel. Adminstrn., San Juan, 1951-53; asst. dir. purchases Celanese Corp. Am., Charlotte, N.C., 1953-55; budget dir. Am. Export Lines, Inc., N.Y.C., 1955-58; mgr. mktg. and adminstrn. Phelps Dodge Internat. Corp., N.Y.C., 1958-70, gen. mgr., 1960-62, v.p., 1962-65, exec. v.p., 1965-68, pres., chief exec. officer, 1968-70; pres. Am. Mail Line, Ltd., Seattle, 1970-73; v.p. Everett Steamship Corp., San Mateo, Calif., 1973-75; pres. Tucor Services, Inc., San Francisco, 1975-77; freelance mgmt. cons. San Mateo, 1978-81; mgmt. cons. Gilbert C. Jones Inc., N.Y.C., 1981-85; pres. AP Industries, Inc., Toledo, 1985-87, also bd. dirs.; chmn., chief exec. officer, bd. dirs. automotive ignition interlock blood-alcohol breath analysis device mfg. co. Autosense Corp., Hayward, Calif., 1988—; mem. Pacific Basin Econ. Devel. Council, San Francisco, 1971-73; mem. Com. of 100, Toledo, 1987—; bd. dirs. SeaGate Venture Mgmt., Inc., Toledo. With U.S. Army, 1943. Mem. Inverness Club, Toledo Club, PGA West Club, Tau Beta Pi. Democrat. Office: Autosense Corp 3501 Breakwater Ave Hayward CA 94545

BENHAM, ROBERT S., utility executive; b. Newark, 1938. Grad., Vanderbilt U., 1961, LLB, 1963. Ptnr. Williams, Benham and McDaniel, Memphis; former commr. Memphis Gas and Water div., chmn. Office: Memphis Light Gas & Water Div 220 S Main St Memphis TN 38101

BENIGNO, THOMAS DANIEL, real estate developer, lawyer; b. Queens, N.Y., July 29, 1954; s. John Baptiste and Ernesta Mary (Yannaco) B.; m. Maria Angelica Vasquez, Jan. 26, 1980; children: Diana Maria, Laura Michelle. BA with honors, Hofstra U., 1976; JD, Yeshiva U., 1979. Bar: N.Y. 1981. Atty. Legal Aid Soc., Bronx, N.Y., 1976-84; ptnr. Benigno, Cassisi & Cassisi, Floral Park, 1984-87; pvt. practice Floral Park, 1987—; pres. Gurben Properties, Inc., Floral Park, 1987—. Mem. N.Y. State Bar Assn., Nassau County Bar Assn., N.Y. State Trial Lawyers Assn., N.Y. State Defenders Assn. Democrat. Roman Catholic. Office: PO Box 789 Valley Stream NY 11582

BENJAMIN, BURTON IRVING, farm supply cooperative executive; b. Hastings, Minn., Oct. 14, 1938; s. Harry Mertes and Florence Elizabeth (Severson) B.; m. Carol Fenner, Oct. 10, 1964; children: Dean, Nancy, Russell. Constrn. foreman Northwestern Bell Telephone Co., St. Paul, 1964-69; chief exec. officer Tomorrow Valley Coop., Amherst, Wis., 1971-80, Cloverbelt Coop., Wausau, Wis., 1982—. Served with U.S. Army, 1962-64, Korea. Republican. Lutheran. Home: 9672 River Rd Amherst WI 54406 Office: Cloverbelt Coop Svcs 1202 N 1st St PO Box 1327 Wausau WI 54402

BENJAMIN, JAMES COVER, controller, manufacturing company executive; b. Peoria, Ill., Oct. 25, 1952; s. Kenneth Edward and Jane (Cover) B.; m. Catherine Louise Guthrie, June 8, 1974; children: Jennifer, Sara, Eric. BS, U. Ill., 1974. CPA, Wis., Ill. Sr. audit mgr. Price Waterhouse, Peoria, Ill., Milw. and London, 1974-86; controller, v.p. Harnischfeger Industries, Brookfield, Wis., 1986—. Mem. Am. Inst. CPA's, Wis. Inst. CPA's, Ill. Inst. CPA's, Fin. Exec. Inst. Office: Harnischfeger Industries Inc PO Box 554 Milwaukee WI 53201

BENJAMIN, JEFFREY ROYCE, media executive; b. Lansing, Mich., Mar. 15, 1954; s. Royce M. and Ann E. (Wettlaufer) B. BA, U. Mich., 1978, MBA, 1980. Auditor Arthur Andersen & Co., Detroit, 1979; sr. auditor Arthur Young & Co., Los Angeles, 1980-83; controller, mgr. Los Angeles Olympic Organizing Com., 1983-85; treas., chief fin. officer Global Media, Ltd., Washington, 1986-88; dir. fin. and adminstrn. CBS/Sony Imagesoft Inc., L.A., 1988—. Bd. dirs., treas. Live Aid Found., Los Angeles, 1985—; chmn. bd. Rock Against Drugs Found., 1986—. Mem. Beta Alpha Psi. Home: 839 N Hayworth Ave Los Angeles CA 90069 Office: CBS/Sony Imagesoft Inc 9200 Sunset Blvd Ste 820 Los Angeles CA 90069

BENKE, NORMAN R., trucking company executive; b. Portland, Oreg., Sept. 12, 1931; s. Reinhold and Johanna (Baumann) B.; m. Marion Larson, Sept. 5, 1953; children: Martin E., Christopher R., Gregory R., Linda S. BBA, U. Oreg., 1955; student, Columbia U., 1972, Harvard U., 1978. From div. acct. to sr. v.p. fin. Consol. Freightways, Inc., Palo Alto, Calif. 1st lt. U.S. Army, 1955-57. Mem. Nat. Acctg. and Fin. Coun. of Am. Trucking Assn. (pres. 1980, chmn. 1981), Bankers Club, Portland Yacht Club.

BENKE, ROBIN PAUL, librarian; b. Trinidad, W.I., Jan. 30, 1953; came to U.S., 1967; s. Albert Theodore and Rita A. (Riva) B. BA, Hampden-Sydney Coll., 1975; MLS, Peabody Coll., 1978. Librarian Clinch Valley Coll. U. Va., Wise, 1978—. Compiler reference and bibliography workbook, 1987. Pres. Appalachian Traditions Inc., 1987; bd. dirs. Pro-Art Assn., Wise, 1983. Mem. Am. Library Assn., Assn. Coll. Rsch. Librs. (mem. bibliographic instrn. sect. policy com.), Southeastern Library Assn., Va. Library Assn. (editor region I newsletter), Va. Edn./Media Assn., Am. Assn. U. Profs., Beta Phi Mu, Kappa Delta Pi. Republican. Episcopalian. Home: PO Box 1519 Wise VA 24293 Office: Clinch Valley Coll College Ave Wise VA 24293

BENN, DOUGLAS FRANK, computer and telecommunications consulting and services company executive; b. Detroit, May 8, 1936; s. Frank E. and Madeline (Pond) B.; m. Shirley M. Flanery, July 16, 1955; children—Christopher, Susan, Kathy. A.A., Jackson Jr. Coll., 1956; student, U. Mich., 1957-58; BS in Math., Mich. State U., 1960, MA, 1962; cert. data processing (NSF scholar), Milw. Inst. Tech., 1965; postgrad., U. Wis., 1965-66; Ed.Adminstrn., Washington U., 1972; MS in Computer Sci., So. Meth. U., 1982, postgrad., 1989—. Diecaster Diecast Corp., Jackson, Mich., 1955-60; tchr. math. and sci. Lansing (Mich.) Public Schs., 1960-64; chmn. computer sci. dept. Kenosha (Wis.) Area Tech. Inst., 1964-67, registrar, 1966-67, mgr. data processing, 1965-67; sr. systems analyst Abbott Labs., North Chicago, Ill., 1967-68, sr. project leader, 1968-69; dir. data processing div. St. Louis Public Schs., 1969-74; dir. div. info. systems dept. mental health State of Ill., Springfield, 1974-78; dir. data processing div. Med. Computer Systems, Inc., Dallas, 1978; dir. bus. adminstrn. Dallas County Mental Health Center, 1979-80; prof. computer sci. So. Meth. U., Dallas, 1979-82; sr. dir. corp. research and devel. Blue Cross & Blue Shield of Tex., Dallas, 1980-83; v.p. mgmt. info. services Western States Adminstrs., Fresno, Calif., 1984-88; chmn. bd., pres. The Benn Group, Inc., Merced, Calif., 1987—; lectr. and adv. Council of Great Cities Public Sch. Systems, 1969-74; cons. Ill. Med. Soc., 1976-78, Wis. Bd. Vocat., Tech. and Adult Edn., 1964-67; co-dir. mgmt. adv. group Ill. Dept. Mental Health, 1974-78; adv. Tex. Gov.'s Task on Mental Health, 1980. Contbr. articles on data processing systems to profl. publs. Dist. supt. Kenosha council Boy Scouts Am., 1965-66. Mem. Data Processing Mgmt. Assn., Assn. for System Mgmt. (Disting. Service award 1980, Merit award 1976, Achievement award 1978, chpt. pres. 1976-77), Am. Arbitration Assn. Presbyterian. Club: So. Meth. U. Faculty. Home and Office: 3244 Stanford Dallas TX 75205

BENNER, HENRY, JR., publishing company executive; b. Phila., May 21, 1942; s. Henry J. and Marian (Dowling) B.; m. Beverley McNeil Grow, June 15, 1966; children: Henry McNeil, John Patterson, Julia Dowling. BS, Georgetown U., 1964; MBA, U. Va., 1966. Comml. lending officer Md. Nat. Bank, Balt., 1969-72; v.p. comml. lending First Va. Bank, Falls Church, 1972-73; v.p. holding co. First Va. Banks, Inc., Falls Church, 1974; pres. First Va. Bank (Cen.), Charlottesville, 1974-81; gen. exec. fin. Worrell Newspapers, Inc., Charlottesville, 1981-83; pres. Brown Pub. Co., Cin., 1983—; bd. dirs. Va. Banker's Assn., Richmond, 1980. Trustee St. Ann's Belfield Sch., Charlottesville, 1977-84; sec., treas., Colgate-Darden Sch., Charlottesville, 1978-81. Served to capt. U.S. Army, 1966-69, ETO. Mem. Ohio Newspaper Assn., Inland Daily Press Assn. (group newspaper com.). Republican. Episcopalian. Clubs: Cin. Country; Farmington Country (Charlottesville); Washington Golf and Country (Arlington, Va.). Lodge: Rotary. Home: 3498 Arnold St Cincinnati OH 45226 Office: Brown Pub Co 3152 Linwood Ave PO Box 9239 Cincinnati OH 45209

BENNERT, ARTHUR JAMES, insurance company executive; b. Maplewood, N.J., June 3, 1926; s. William James and Lillian Catherine (Cordes) B.; m. Ethna Christine Wilkinson, Oct. 9, 1954; children: Ethna Marlie, Arthur Jr., Keith. BS in Bus. Adminstrn., Seton Hall U., 1950. Adjustor INA Ins. Co., Newark, 1953-55, claim supr., 1955-57; claim supr. North British Ins. Co., N.Y.C., 1957-58; adjustor Ohio Casualty Ins. Co., Newark, 1958-59; claim supr. Ohio Casualty Ins. Co., Hamilton, 1959-74, asst. sec., 1974-76, v.p., 1976-84, sr. v.p., 1984—. Sgt. U.S. Army, 1944-46, ETO. Republican. Roman Catholic. Home: 5659 Kingsbury Rd Fairfield OH 45014 Office: Ohio Casualty Ins Co 136 N 3rd St Hamilton OH 45025

BENNET, DOUGLAS JOSEPH, JR., public radio executive; b. Orange, N.J., June 23, 1938; s. Douglas Joseph and Phoebe (Benedict) B.; m. Susanne Klejman, June 27, 1959; children: Michael, James, Holly. B.A., Wesleyan U., Middletown, Conn., 1959; M.A., U. Calif., Berkeley, 1960; Ph.D., Harvard, 1968. Asst. to econ. adv. AID, New Delhi, India, 1963-64; spl. asst. to Am. ambassador to India, 1964-66; asst. to Vice Pres. Hubert H. Humphrey, 1967-69; adminstrv. asst. to U.S. Senator Thomas Eagleton, 1969-73, to U.S. Senator Abraham Ribicoff, 1973-74; staff dir. com. budget U.S. Senate, 1974-77; asst. sec. state congressional relations 1977-79; adminstr. AID, Washington, 1979-81; pres. Roosevelt Ctr. for Am. Policy Studies, 1981-83; pres., chief exec. officer Nat. Pub. Radio, Washington, 1983—. Bd. visitors Inst. Policy Scis. and Pub. Affairs Duke U. Mem. Council Fgn. Relations, Nat. Acad. Pub. Adminstrn., Inst. for East West Security Studies (bd. dirs.). Democrat. Home: 3206 Klingle Rd NW Washington DC 20008 Office: Nat Pub Radio 2025 M St NW Washington DC 20036

BENNETT, ALAN JEROME, electronics executive, physicist; b. Phila., June 13, 1941; s. Leon Martin and Reba (Perry) B.; m. Frances Kitey, June 16, 1963; children: Sarah, Rachel, Daniel. BA, U. Pa, 1962; MS, U. Chgo., 1963, PhD, 1965. Physicist rsch. and devel. ctr. GE, Schenectady, N.Y., 1966-74, br. mgr. rsch. and devel. ctr., 1975-79; dir. electronics lab. Gould Inc., Rolling Meadows, Ill., 1979-84; v.p. rsch. Varian Assocs., Palo Alto, Calif., 1984—. Contbr. articles to profl. jours. Fellow NSF, 1963-65, 66. Mem. AAAS, IEEE (sr.), Am. Phys. Soc., Phi Beta Kappa, Sigma Xi. Home: 233 Tennyson Ave Palo Alto CA 94301 Office: Varian Assoc 611 Hansen Way Palo Alto CA 94303

BENNETT, BARBARA ESTHER, controller; b. Norfolk, Nebr., Nov. 24, 1953. AA, Northeastern Nebr. Community Coll., Norfolk, Nebr., 1973; student, U. Nebr., 1980, U. Colo., Denver, 1985, Harvard U., 1985. Bookkeeper McIntosh, Inc., Norfolk, 1971-77; credit, office mgr. Goodyear Service Stores Inc., Norfolk, 1977-81; pvt. practice acct. Norfolk, 1971-81; base adminstr. Evergreen Helicoptors Inc., Greeley, Colo., 1981-82; pvt. practice acctg. and tax service Denver, 1984—; acctg. supr, asst. controller Saltzgitter Machinery, Inc., Louviers, Colo., Saltzgitter, Fed. Republic Germany., 1982-85; corp. controller Satter, Inc., Denver, 1985—. Phi Theta Kappa, Phi Beta Lambda. Republican. Lutheran. Club: 4H. Home: 963 S Patton Ct PO Box 19070 Denver CO 80219 Office: Satter Distbg Co Inc 4100 Dahlia Denver CO 80207

BENNETT, EDWARD JAMES, lawyer; b. Newton, Iowa, Dec. 27, 1941; s. Erskine Francis and Malvina Esther (Goodhue) B.; m. Virginia Lee Cook, Jan. 30, 1965; children: Elizabeth, Edward James. BA, U. Iowa, 1964, JD, 1966. Bar: Iowa 1966, U.S. Dist. Ct. (so. dist.) Iowa 1967. Atty. Diehl, Clayton & Cleverley, Newton, 1966-70; atty. The Maytag Co., Newton, 1970-74, sr. atty., 1974-80, assoc. counsel, 1980-85, asst. sec., asst. gen. counsel, 1985—. Chmn. Civil Svc. Commn., Newton, 1980-86; mem. Newton Zoning Bd. Adjustment, 1978—, chmn. 1978-85; sec., trustee Newton Community Ctr., Inc., 1976—. Mem. ABA, Iowa State Bar Assn. (chmn. Trade Regulation Com. 1981—), Iowa Assn. Bus. and Industry (Unemployment Compensation Com. 1973—), Newton Country Club. Republican. Presbyterian. Home: RR 2 PO Box 616 Newton IA 50208 Office: Maytag Corp 403 W 4th St N Newton IA 50208

BENNETT, GARY PAUL, technical services company executive; b. Newport, R.I., June 26, 1941; s. Paul Buchanan and Alzada Eugenia (Trapp) B.; m. Frances Lawrence Bunting, June 2, 1963; children: Christine F., Gary Paul Jr. BS in Math., U. S.C., 1963; M in Engring. Adminstrn., George Washington U., 1972. Ops. research analyst U.S. Govt., Carderock, Md., 1969-72; with Analysis & Tech. Inc., North Stonington, Conn., 1972—, now exec. v.p., 1978—, chief oper. officer, 1984—; pres., chief exec. officer A&T Tech. Services Inc., New London, Conn., 1977-80; bd. dirs. Analysis & Tech. Inc., Structured Tech. Corp., Waterford, Conn., Automation Software Inc., Kingstown, R.I. Author tech. manuals. Trustee Westerly Community Hosp., R.I., 1987—. Served to lt. comdr. USN, 1963-69, USNR, 1969-72. Scholarship NROTC, 1960-63, U. S.C., 1960-61. Mem. Navy League, Submarine League, Am. Mgmt. Assn. Democrat. Clubs: Wadawanuck Yacht (Stonington, Conn.). Home: RFD 3 PO Box 69F Montauk Ave Stonington CT 06378

BENNETT, JACK FRANKLIN, oil company executive; b. Macon, Ga., Jan. 17, 1924; s. Andrew Jackson and Mary Eloise (Franklin) B.; m. Shirley Elizabeth Goodwin, Sept. 17, 1949; children: Jackson Goodwin, Philip Davies, Hugh Franklin, Elizabeth Fraser. BA, Yale U., 1944; MA, Harvard U., 1949, PhD, 1951. Negotiator Joint U.S.-U.K. Export Import Agy., Berlin, Germany, 1946-47; teaching fellow finance Harvard, 1949-51; spl. asst. to adminstr. Tech. Assistance Program, U.S. Dept. State, Washington, 1951-52; economist U.S. Mut. Security Agy., Washington, 1952-53; sr. economist Presdl. Commn. on Fgn. Econ. Policy, 1954; sr. fgn. exch. analyst Exxon Corp., N.Y.C., 1955-58; dep. European fin. rep. Exxon Corp., London, 1958-60; treas. Esso. Petroleum Co., Ltd., London, 1960-61; asst. treas. Exxon Corp., N.Y.C., 1961-65; mgr. gen. econs. dept. Exxon Corp., 1965-66, mgr. coordination and planning dept., 1966-67; gen. mgr. supply dept. Exxon Co., U.S.A., Houston, 1967-69; v.p., dir. Exxon Internat., N.Y.C., 1969-71; sr. v.p. Exxon Corp., N.Y.C., 1975-88, also bd. dirs., ret., 1989; dep. undersec. for monetary affairs U.S. Dept. Treasury, Washington, 1971-74, undersec. for monetary affairs, 1974-75; bd. dir. Discount Corp. N.Y., Tandem Computer Co., Mass. Mut. Ins. Co., Dean Witter Mut. Funds. Contbr. articles to profl. jours. Trustee Com. Econ. Devel. With USNR, 1943-46. Mem. Coun. Fgn. Rels., University Club (N.Y.C.), Stanwich Club (Greenwich, Conn.), York (Maine) Club. Republican. Office: 1 Rockfeller Pla Rm 1250 New York NY 10020

BENNETT, JAMES LOUIS, management consultant, radar specialist; b. Elmira, N.Y., Jan. 31, 1938; s. Albert Jr. and Vera Lena (Wheat) B.; m. Edith Mildred Wagnon, Oct. 12, 1974; children: James Louis, Christy Lou, Harry A., Vera L., Dorothy. BBA, U. Alaska, Fairbanks, 1969; MBA, U. Alaska, Anchorage, 1973. Housing mgmt. officer FAA, Anchorage, 1969-75; assoc. prof. bus. adminstrn. Chapman Coll., Cold Bay, Alaska, 1975-78, Ea. Wyo. Coll., Lusk, 1981—; mgmt. cons. Alaska, Wyo. and Md., 1973—; chief sector field office FAA, Cold Bay, 1975-78; radar technician Balt.-Washington Internat. Airport, Md., 1978-80; chief sector field office Lusk, Wyo., 1980-83; mgr. sector field office Casper, Wyo., 1983, mgr. sector field office II, 1986—; real estate appraiser, 1981—; constrn. insp., 1981—; bd. dirs. J&J Enterprises, Willard Fisheries Co. Author: History of Air Traffic Control, 1968, Development in Alaska, 1968; bus. columnist Lusk Herald, 1982-84. Bd. dirs. Casper Fed. Exec. Council, 1985. Served with USN, 1956-60. Recipient Spl. Achievement award FAA, 1971, 81, Meritorious Service award, 1969, 85, 87, Outstanding Achievement award, 1979, 80. Mem. Am. Soc. Public Adminstrn., Internat. Conf. Sports Car Clubs (regional chmn. 1967-69), Fairbanks Sports Car Club (pres. 1966-68), Alaska Sports Car Club, Am. Assn. Arbitrators (comml. arbitrator 1986, panel and autoline arbitrator), Better Bus. Bur. Republican. Jewish. Lodges: Shriners, Masons (past master local lodge), Order Eastern Star (past patron 1984), Harmony (past master 1985), Internat. Order Job's Daus. (assoc. guardian 1982). Home: 7220 W Riverside Dr Casper WY 82604 Office: Natrona County Internat Airport 8411 Fuller St Casper WY 82604

BENNETT, JEROME, cement company executive; b. Greenwood, Miss., Oct. 20, 1922; s. Harry and Jennie (Arenzon) B.; m. Julie M. Boyd, Sept. 6, 1947; children: Jerome, Jack, Henry. B.S., La. State U., 1943; postgrad., Wharton Sch., U. Pa., 1946. With Ford Motor Co., Dearborn, Mich., 1950-65; dep. comptroller ITT, 1965-66; dep. dir. Latin ops. Ford Motor Co., 1966-69; v.p. Office of the pres. Xerox Corp., Stamford, Conn., 1969-75; exec. v.p., chief fin. officer White Motor Corp., Eastlake, Ohio, 1975-76; pres., chief operating officer White Motor Corp., 1976-79; sr. v.p., chief fin. officer Lonestar Inc., Greenwich, Conn., 1979—. Served with U.S. Army, 1943-46. Mem. Pa. Inst. C.P.A.s. Clubs: Metropolitan (N.Y.C.); Union (Cleve.), Kirtland Country (Cleve.); Greate Bay (Somers Point, N.J.), Atlantic City Country (Northfield, N.J.); John's Island (Fla.); Greenwich Country (Conn.). Home: Pheasant Lane Greenwich CT 06830 Office: Lone Star Industries Inc 1 Greenwich Pla PO Box 5050 Greenwich CT 06836

BENNETT, JESSIE F., lawyer; b. Bridgeport, Conn., Mar. 2, 1958; d. Cornelius T. and Jessie F. (Sutcliffe) B. BS in Fin. with honors, Fairfield U., 1980; JD magna cum laude, U. Bridgeport, 1986. Bar: Conn., U.S. Dist. Ct. Conn., U.S. Dist. Ct. (so. dist.) N.Y.,D.C. Jud. clk. U.S. Dist. Ct., New Haven, 1986; atty. Chapman & Moran, Stamford, Conn., 1986, Cohen & Wolf, Danbury, Conn., 1987, Davidson, Driscoll & Naylor, Norwalk, Conn., 1988—. Mem. ABA, ACLU, Conn. Bar Assn., Danbury Bar Assn., Greater Bridgeport Bar Assn., Assn. Trial Lawyers Am., Conn. Trial Lawyers Assn., Westport Bar Assn., D.C. Bar Assn., Conn. Civil Liberties Union, Phi Delta Phi, Phi Alpha Delta (Am. Jurisprudence award in Remedies and Family Law, Kristin Ann Carveth Meml. Scholastic award). Roman Catholic. Home: 280 Hooker Rd Bridgeport CT 06610

BENNETT, JOHN RICHARD, medical equipment manufacturing company executive; b. N.Y.C., June 18, 1952; s. Herbert Edward and Mary (Macario) B.; m. Robin Ann Laffer, Oct. 15, 1977; children: Adam, Lindsay, Matthew. BS, SUNY-Albany, 1977; MBA, Dowling Coll., 1988. CPA, N.Y. Staff acct. Joseph Zak and Co., Patchogue, N.Y., 1977-81, ptnr., 1981-83; controller Atomic Products Corp., Shirley, N.Y., 1983-86, v.p., chief fin.

officer, 1986—; mem. adj. faculty Suffolk County Community Coll., Selden, N.Y., 1982—. Mem. AICPA, N.Y. State Soc. CPAs, Kiwanis (treas. Patchogue 1987, v.p. 1988). Office: Atomic Products Corp 49 Natcon Dr Shirley NY 11967

BENNETT, J(OHNNY) MARVIN, academic administrator, controller; b. Columbia, Mo., Apr. 9, 1933; s. Alvy and Maggie L. (Lewis) B.; m. Norma Sapp, June 21, 1952; children: Jane, Keith, Joy, Lorna. Student, U. Mo. Dir. bus. systems U. Mo., Columbia, 1955-75, Clemson (S.C.) U., 1975-80; controller Cen. Mo. State U., Warrenburg, 1980—, treas., 1982—, asssoc. v.p. for fin., 1986—. Pres. Lenoir, Inc. Retirement Community, Columbia, 1985-87, bd. dirs. 1987—. Mem. Nat. Assn. Coll. and Univ. Bus. Officers, Rotary. Republican. Home: Rte 5 PO Box 905 Warrenburg MO 64093 Office: Cen Mo State U 213 Adminstrn Bldg Warrensburg MO 64093

BENNETT, MICHAEL JOHN, management consultant; b. Nottingham, U.K., May 31, 1934; s. John and Elsie (Parkin) B.; m. Diana Rose Hardy, Sept. 19, 1959: children: Sarah Elizabeth, Fiona Lesley, James Michael. BA, Cambridge (Eng.) U., 1959. Plant mgr. ICI, Wilton, Eng., 1959-63; devel. engr. Humphreys & Glasgow Ltd., London, 1963-65, devel. mgr., 1965-67; v.p. Humphreys & Glasgow Ltd., N.Y.C., 1967-69; tech. dir. Chem. Systems Internat. Ltd., N.Y.C., London, 1969-73; mgr. dir. Chem. Systems Internat. Ltd., London, 1973-86; pres., chief exec. officer Charles H. Kline & Co. Inc., Fairfield, N.J., 1986. Patentee in field. Served with RAF, 1952-55. Fellow Inst. Chem. Engrs., Royal Soc. Arts, Mfrs. Commerce; mem. Am. Inst. Chem. Engrs. Episcopalian. Club: Royal Automobile (London). Office: Kline & Co Inc 165 Passaic Ave Fairfield NJ 07006

BENNETT, ROYAL FREDERICK, infosystems specialist, consultant; b. Birmingham, Ala., Nov. 13, 1957; s. Robert Nelson and Jean (Monroe) B.; m. Julia D. Evesque, Dec. 11, 1982. Systems technician South Cen. Bell Telephone, Sylacauga, Ala., 1978-82; sales rep. South Cen. Bell Advanced Systems, Birmingham, 1982-84; mem. staff computer systems support Bell South Advanced Systems, Birmingham, 1984—. Reader Nat. Pub. Radio, 1987—. Republican. Methodist. Home: 816 Saulter Rd Homewood AL 35309 Office: Bell South Advanced Systems 3000 Riverchase Galleria Suite 1500 Birmingham AL 35244

BENNETT, SAUL, public relations agency executive; b. N.Y.C., Oct. 21, 1936; s. Philip and Ruth (Weinstein) Ostrove; m. Joan Marian Abrahams, Aug. 15, 1965; children—Sara, Charles, Elizabeth. B.S. in Journalism, Ohio U., Athens, 1957. Engaged in public relations 1963—; account supr., then v.p. Rowland Co. (public relations), N.Y.C., 1965-74; v.p., then sr. v.p. Robert Marston and Assocs., N.Y.C., 1974-78; exec. v.p. Robert Marston and Assocs., 1978-86, partner, 1979—, sr. exec. v.p., 1986—; pres. Robert Marston Mktg. Communications Inc., 1988. Served with USAR, 1958-59, 61-62. Office: Robert Marston & Assocs Inc 485 Madison Ave New York NY 10022

BENNEY, DOUGLAS MABLEY, marketing executive, consultant; b. Cold Spring Harbor, N.Y., Aug. 7, 1922; s. William Mabley and Wilhelmina (Walters) B.; m. Eugenia Sammis, Sept. 30, 1944 (div. Jan. 1980); children: William Douglas, Barbara Gates, Robert Scott; m. Barbara Mueller, July 8, 1983; stepchildren: Gregory Carmichael, Andrew Carmichael. Navy air cadet U. N.C.-Chapel Hill, 1943, Cornell U., 1943; student in engring. Purdue U., 1939-41; A.B., Colgate U., 1946-49; postgrad. Columbia U., 1951-52; With Curtis Publs., Phila., 1950-63, editor, assoc. pub. Jack & Jill, 1960-63; mktg. mgr. edn. div. Doubleday & Co., N.Y.C., 1963-67; advt. and sales mgr. Hearst Book div. N.Y.C., 1967-68; v.p. creative services Nat. Liberty Corp., Valley Forge, Pa., 1968-72; v.p. mktg. Gerber Life Ins. Co., N.Y.C., 1972-75; sr. mktg. officer Internat. Group Plans, Washington, 1975-78; v.p. mktg. Maxon Adminstrs., Inc., Washington, 1978-88; exec. v.p. A&B Advt., Inc., Temple Hills, Md., 1988—. Patentee newspaper inserts, self-mailers. Served as ensign AC, USN, 1943-46; PTO. Recipient award Artists Guild Del. Valley, 1969, Direct Mail Mktg. Assn., 1965, Myasthenia Gravis Found., 1985. Mem. Direct Mktg. Assn., Direct Mktg. Assn. Washington, Direct Mktg. Creative Guild, Greater Washington Soc. Assn. Execs. Club: Woodlawn Country (Alexandria, Va.). Avocations: woodworking; sailing; photography; scuba diving.

BENNINGTON, KENNETH BRADFORD, operations professional; b. Phila., Mar. 29, 1950; s. Kenneth Bradford Jr. and Lillian Madelyn Bennington; m. Mary Elizabeth Melody, Apr. 8, 1972; children: Michael P., Daniel E., Ryan J. BA, LaSalle U., 1971; MA, Villanova U., 1975; MBA, Drexel U., 1982. Sr. planner Merck & Co. Inc., West Point, Pa., 1977—. Coach, umpire Deep run Valley Sports Assn., Hilltown Township, Pa., 1980—; chmn. Hilltown Twp. Planning Commn., 1983—; mem. Hilltown Twp. Civic Assn., 1987, Neshaminy watershed adv. com., 1987—; mem. MADD, Hilltown Hist. Soc., 1988—. Capt. U.S. Army, 1973-77, Korea. Mem. Am. Legion. Republican. Roman Catholic.

BENNITT, MICHAEL PAUL, savings and loan executive; b. El Dorado, Kans., Sept. 21, 1955; s. Paul A. and Colleen I. (Wartick) B.; m. Deborah Jane Johnson, Jan. 11, 1980; children: Breanna Michelle, Benjamin Michael. Student, Ozark Bible Coll., Joplin, Mo., 1973-74, NE Mo. State U., 1974-76; BS in BA and Acctg., Mo. So. State U., 1979. Lic. life, health ins. State of Mo. Store mgr. Zales Jewelers, Joplin, Mo., 1979-81; dir. mktg. Doss Office Systems, Springfield, Mo., 1981-87; dir. sales Mid-Am. Banking Services, Springfield, 1987; investment services mgr. Great So. Savs. & Loan, Springfield, 1987—; pres. Great So. Capital Mgmt., 1987—. Mem. Nat. Assn. Securities Dealers (cert. gen. registered rep. & prin.), Springfield C. of C. (bus. and industry com., masters com., ambassadors com.), Rotary, Phi Theta Kappa, Omicron Delta Epsilon. Republican. Home: 1431 S Fairwood Springfield MO 65804 Office: Great So Savs & Loan 430 South Ave Springfield MO 65806

BENO, CANDICE LYNN, chemical company executive; b. New Brunswick, N.J., Mar. 25, 1951; d. Andrew Jule and Claire May (Blanchard) B. BA magna cum laude, U. Conn., 1973, MS in Biochemistry, 1974. Grad. asst. U. Conn., 1973-75; lab. technician Linde div. Union Carbide Corp., Keasbey, N.J., 1976-78, sr. lab. technician, 1978-79; regional tech. supr. Linde div. Union Carbide Corp., South Plainfield, N.J., 1979; asst. staff engr. Linde div. Union Carbide Corp., Springfield, N.J., 1979-82, staff engr., 1982-84; tech. bus. cons. Linde div. Union Carbide Corp., Danbury, Conn., 1984-85; staff engr. Linde div. Union Carbide Corp., Somerset, N.J., 1985-87; mgr. Linde div. Union Carbide Corp., Springfield, 1987—; supr. Werner Erhard & Assocs., Edison, N.J., 1984-87; guest seminar leader, 1985—, course mgr., 1984-86. Mem. Compressed Gas Assn. (chmn. 1984—, vice chmn. 1982-88), Am. Soc. Quality Control, Semiconductor Equipment and Material Inst. (co-chmn. 1987—, editor jour. Homstic Health 1982-88, Outstanding Svc. award 1984-88, Leadership award, 1988), Mortar Bd., Phi Beta Kappa, Phi Kappa Phi. Democrat. Home: 1000 W 8th St Plainfield NJ 07063 Office: Union Carbide Corp Linde Div 150 Morris Ave PO Box 699 Springfield NJ 07081

BENSCHIP, GARY JOHN, manufacturing company executive; b. Chgo., Aug. 27, 1947; s. Melville John and Eleanor (Melin) B.; m. Susan Diane Mattson, Sept. 19, 1970; 1 child, Jaclyn. BS in Fin., U. Ill., Chgo., 1969; MBA, DePaul U., 1971. Budget analyst R.R. Donnelly & Sons, Chgo., 1969-73; rep. DuPont Walston, Chgo., 1973-74; mgr. fin. ops. Sun Electric Corp., Crystal Lake, Ill., 1974-78; dir. fin. analysis Cenco, Inc., Oak Brook, Ill., 1979-83; treas. Amerace Corp., Hackettstown, N.J., 1983—. Mem. Beta Gamma Sigma, Delta Mu Delta. Office: Amerace Corp 8 Campus Dr Arbor Cir S Parsippany NJ 07054-0254

BENSCHNEIDER, DONALD, agricultural products company executive; married. With Landmark Inc., Columbus, Ohio, pres., 1975; chmn. bd. dirs. Countrymark Inc. Office: Countrymark Inc 4565 Columbus Pike PO Box 1206 Delaware OH 43015 *

BENSCOTER, THOMAS DONALD, communications company executive; b. Lansing, Mich., Dec. 6, 1950; s. Donald Leon and Ruth (Stoffel) B.; m. Christine Lee Galt, July 27, 1974; children: Jill, Ryan. BS, U. So. Calif., 1973, MBA, 1974. V.p. fin. Span Internat., Inc., Scottsdale, Ariz. and Riyadh, Saudi Arabia, 1976-85; chief fin. officer, treas. Comven, Inc., Phoenix, 1986-88; exec. v.p. Communications Ventures, Inc., Scottsdale, 1988—. Mem. Assn. for Corp. Growth. Republican. Roman Catholic. Club: U. So. Calif. Alumni (Ariz.) (bd. dirs. 1977-88, treas. 1985-88). Office: Communications Ventures Inc 7492 E Timberlane Ct Scottsdale AZ 85258

BENSEN, ANNETTE WOLF, graphic art company executive; b. Bklyn., Aug. 7, 1938; d. Isidor and Sylvia Wolf; m. Gene Bensen, Oct. 14, 1979. A.A.S., N.Y.C. Community Coll., 1958; postgrad., Pratt Inst., 1974-75. With Wagner-Ellsberg, Inc., N.Y.C., 1958-62; art dir. Island Pen Mfg. Inc., Stacie Pen, Curtis Rand Industries, Inc., N.Y.C., 1962-68; with G.S. Lithographers, Inc., N.Y.C., 1968-70; partner, pres. Rembrandt's Mother, Inc., N.Y.C., 1970-72; co-owner, pres. Film Comp., Inc., N.Y.C., 1972-75; mgr. Expertype, Inc., N.Y.C., 1975—; adj. lectr. N.Y.C. Community Coll., 1971-75. Mem. Advt. Women N.Y., Assn. Graphic Arts , Club Printing Women N.Y. (pres.), Sales Assn. Graphic Arts (exec. bd.), Typographers Assn. N.Y., Women in Prodn. Inc., Aircraft Owners and Pilots Assn. Office: Expertype Inc 44 W 28th St New York NY 10001

BENSON, BRUCE DAVEY, oil and gas company executive; b. Chgo., July 4, 1938; s. P. Bruce and Harriet (Fentress) B.; m. Nancy Lake, 1963; children: James, David, Ann. BA in Geology, U. Colo., 1964; postgrad., Cornell U., 1957-61, Colo. Sch. Mines, 1964-65. Field geologist Exxon, 1964; pres. Benson Mineral Group, Inc., Golden, Colo., 1965—. Fin. chmn. Colo. Rep. Com., Denver, 1984-87, chmn., 1987—; bd. dirs. Boy Scouts Am., Denver, 1987—; pres. bd. trustees Berkshire Sch., Sheffield, Mass., 1986—. Mem. Geol. Soc. Am., Soc. Econ. Paleontologists and Mineralogists, Rocky Mountain Assn., Kans Ind. Oil and Gas Assn., Petroleum Club, Denver Athletic Club. Republican. Office: Benson Mineral Group Inc 1536 Cole Blvd Ste 220 Golden CO 80401

BENSON, CHARLES EDWARD, aircraft company executive; b. Dubuque, Iowa, Dec. 13, 1912; s. John Alexander and Katie Martha (Butcher) B.; m. Dorothy Mae Seibert, Sept. 20, 1941 (div. Aug. 1951); m. Maxine Luella Welch, Feb. 10, 1952; children: Linda Jeanne, Thomas Charles, Carol Ann. Cert. aircraft and engine meahanic, mechanic examiner; lic. marine navigator. Ind. mechanic on heavy equipment and marine engines 1926-37; machinist Miami (Fla.) Ship Bldg. Co., 1937-38; mechanic Eastern Airlines, Miami, 1938-41; mechanic, instr. San Antonio, 1941-46; owner, mgr. Benson Aero-Motive Co., San Antonio, 1946-48, Benson Aero-Motive Inc., San Antonio, 1948—. Designer, developer shipboard fire fighting trainer simulating on-deck aircraft crash landing, numerous others. Home: 8810 Post Oak San Antonio TX 78217 Office: Benson Aero-Motive Inc 1442 Parkridge San Antonio TX 78216

BENSON, DAVID ALAN, pension fund administrator; b. Newark, June 8, 1953; s. Robert William and Esther Louise (Porazzo) B.; m. Shari Loe, May 12, 1979; children: Adrienne Lee, Christopher Hardy. BA, Yale U., 1975; MBA, U. Pa., 1977. Fin. analyst Exxon Corp., N.Y.C., 1977-79, 83-85; sr. fin. analyst Exxon Chem Co., Darien, Conn., 1979-82; mgr. acctg. Esso Pappas, Athens, Greece, 1982; mgr. investments and analysis Elf Aquitaine, Inc., Stamford, Conn., 1986—. Mem. Nat. Investment Sponsor Fedn., Pension Group E., Yale Club of Montclair. Office: Elf Aquitaine Inc PO Box 10037 Stamford CT 06904

BENSON, DONALD ERICK, holding company executive; b. Mpls., June 1, 1930; s. Fritz and Annie (Nordstrom) B.; m. Ann M. Braaten, Jan. 20, 1951; children: Linda K., Nancy A., Stephen D. BBA in Acctg., U. Minn., 1955. CPA, Minn. From staff to ptnrship. Arthur Andersen & Co., Mpls., 1955-68; pres. MEI Corp., Mpls., 1968-86; now exec. v.p. Bank Shares Inc., Mpls., also bd. dirs.; pres. MEI Diversified Inc., Mpls., 1986—, also bd. dirs.; bd. dirs. Marquette Bank Mpls., Minn. Twins Baseball Club, Mass Mut. Corp. Investors. Bd. dirs. Meth. Health Care Minn., Mpls.; chmn. Bethel Coll. Found., St. Paul; bd. dirs., past pres. Boys and Girls Clubs Mpls. Served with U.S. Army, 1951-53. Mem. Am. Inst. CPA's, Minn. CPA Soc. Clubs: Mpls., Interlachen Country (bd. dirs., treas., fin. com.). Office: MEI Diversified Inc 90 S Sixth St Minneapolis MN 55402

BENSON, E. STEPHEN, investment banker; b. Greenwich, Conn., June 13, 1947; s. Edgar Slifer Benson and Gloria Diana (Diaz) Searles; m. Joan Maria Chiappetta, Aug. 3, 1969; children: Edgar Stephen, Belding Barnes, Hartman Slifer. AB in Econs., Lafayette Coll., 1969; MBA, Columbia U., 1971. V.p. Dean Witter and Co., N.Y.C., 1971-77; mng. dir. Salomon Bros. Inc., N.Y.C., 1977-88; gen. ptnr. Gibbons Green van Amerongen, N.Y.C., 1988—; bd. dirs. Grad. Sch. Bus. Columbia U., Sheller-Globe Corp., Am. Bank Stationery Co. Office: Gibbons Green van Amerogen 600 Madison Ave New York NY 10022

BENSON, KATHERINE ALICE, psychology educator; b. Mpls., June 12, 1949; d. Gerald Philip and Gladys Irene (Berg) B.; m. James Lyman Staebler, Aug. 8, 1981 (div. Sept. 1986); 1 child, David James. B.A. summa cum laude, U. Minn., 1972; M.S., U. Mass.-Amherst, 1976, Ph.D., 1979. Instr. psychology U. Mass., Amherst, 1977-78; asst. prof. U. Minn., Morris, 1978—. Precinct chmn. Ward 1 Stevens County Democratic-Farmer-Labor Party, 1982-85, dir., 1986—. Grantee Council on Liberal Edn., 1980, U. Minn. Grad. Sch., 1981-83; U. Minn. Grad. Sch. fellow, 1983; Bush Found. sabbatical fellow, 1985-86. Mem. Minn. Commn. on Martin Luther King, Jr., Holiday. Mem. Minn. Women Psychologists, AAAS, Am. Psychol. Assn., Soc. Research in Child Devel., Nat. Women's Studies Assn., NOW (Minn. chpt. adv. bd. 1983-84), Bus. & Profl. Women. Unitarian-Universalist. Contbr. articles to profl. jours. Office: U Minn Div Social Sci Morris MN 56267

BENSON, KENNETH SAMUEL, corporate executive; b. Vancouver, B.C., Can., Aug. 12, 1937; s. Samuel and Ruby Gertrude (Poole) B.; m. Inara Blums, Aug. 8, 1964. B.Com., U. B.C., 1961, LL.B, 1962. Bar: called to B.C. bar 1963. Articled student-at-law Ellis, Dryer and Co., Vancouver, 1962-63; petroleum landman Atlantic Refining Co., Alta., Can., 1963-65, Corpus Christi and Dallas, Tex., 1963-65; barrister, solicitor Guild, Yule and Co., Vancouver, 1965-68; barrister, solicitor, corp. sec. Bulkley Valley Forest Industries Ltd., Vancouver, 1968-72; barrister, solicitor, asst. corp. sec. Cominco Ltd., Vancouver, 1972-80, corp. sec., 1980-84; v.p., corp. sec. Cominco Ltd., 1984-85; v.p. adminstrn., sec. Can. Pacific Enterprises Ltd., Calgary, Alta., Can., 1985; v.p. adminstrn. Can. Pacific Ltd., Calgary, 1985-86, v.p. personnel and adminstrn., 1986—; bd. dirs. Reserve de la Petite Nation, Inc., 1985—, Syracuse China of Can. Ltd., Can. Pacific Enterprises Ltd. Mem. Can. Bar Assn., Law Soc. B.C. (conf. bd. U.S.), Sporting Club du Sanctuaire Montreal, Conf. Bd. Can. Home: 6150 Ave du Boise Apt 10 F-G, Montreal, PQ Canada H3S 2V2 Office: Can Pacific Ltd, Ste 800 Pl du Canada, PO Box 6042 Sta A, Montreal, PQ Canada H3C 3E4

BENT, MICHAEL WILLIAM, realty company executive, consultant; b. Oakland, Calif., Mar. 7, 1951; s. William Camp and Lorene (Howson) B.; children: John D., Chelsea L.; m. Laurie Sue Nelson, Dec. 15, 1984. Student Rutgers U., 1969-72. Lic. real estate broker. V.p. Century 21 Kato & Co., Denver, 1979-80; broker, mgr. Century 21 Hasz & Assocs., Denver, 1980-81; sec. Metro Brokers, Inc., Denver, 1982-83, v.p., 1983-84; sec., dir. Metro Brokers Fin. Svcs., Inc., 1984-85, dir., 1984-86, Metro Brokers, Inc., 1982-85 ; broker, owner Metro Broker M. Bent Realty & Mgmt. Co., Aurora, Colo., 1981-88; pres., broker Piney Creek Realty, Inc., 1988—; bd. dir. Metro Brokers, Inc.; past pres. Country Club Real Estate, Inc. Com. chmn., Boy Scouts Am., 1987—. Mem. Denver Bd. Realtors, Aurora Bd. Realtors, Realtors Nat. Mktg. Inst., Internat. Assn. Fin. Planners (cert. comml. investment mem., cert. residential specialist, grad. realtors inst.). Republican. Roman Catholic. Club: Optimist (pres. 1982-84, Heather Ridge chpt.). Home: 17096 E Dorado Cir Aurora CO 80015 Office: Piney Creek Realty Inc 15434 E Orchard Rd Aurora CO 80015

BENT, ROBERT OLIVER, II, oil company executive; b. Mineola, N.Y., May 17, 1941; s. Robert McKinley and Edith Charlotta (Tastrom) B.; m. Karen Sevening, May 28, 1970; 1 child, Robert Oliver III. BA, BS, Brown U., 1963; MBA, U. Chgo., 1966. Various positions Amoco Corp., Chgo., 1966—, dir. ins., 1988—; bd. dirs. Highland Community Bank, Chgo. Bd. dirs. Marianjoy Rehab. Ctr., Wheaton, Ill., 1976—, chmn., 1988—,. Mem. Naperville Country Club. Office: Amoco Corp 200 E Randolph St Chicago IL 60680

BENTCOVER, BRUCE JAY, financial executive; b. Chgo., Dec. 25, 1954; s. Irving T. and Carolyn (Cohen) B.; m. Debra Lynn Shlifka, Aug. 19, 1979; children: Erin, Jeffrey. BA, Ea. Ill. U., 1975; MBA, U. Chgo., 1979. Fin. analyst Evang. Hosp. Assn., Oak Brook, Ill., 1977-79; bus. analyst, project leader Xerox Corp., Chgo., 1979-80; European treas. G.D. Searle & Co., Skokie, Ill., 1980-85; asst. treas. Ecolab, Inc., St. Paul, 1985-86, v.p., treas., 1986—. Mem. Fin. Execs. Inst., Nat. Assn. Corp. Treas., St. Paul Athletic Club. Home: 661 Cheyenne Ln Mendota Heights MN 55120 Office: Ecolab Inc Ecolab Ctr 370 Wabasha St Saint Paul MN 55102

BENTLEY, ALFRED YOUNG, JR., telecommunications manufacturing company executive; b. Boston, Dec. 22, 1943; s. Alfred Young Bentley and Virgina (Ellis) Rhone; m. Geraldine Giaccone, Apr. 21, 1968; children: Alfred Young III, Suzanne Kathleen. BE, Stevens Inst., 1965. Systems engr. data processing div. IBM Corp., Newark, 1965-73; cons. systems and programming corp. hdqrs. IBM Corp., Armonk, N.Y., 1973-76; mgr. market requirements office products div. IBM Corp., Franklin Lakes, N.J., 1976-81; dir. product mgmt. Exxon Office Systems Co., Stamford, Conn., 1981-83, v.p. product mgmt., 1983-85; exec. dir. AT&T Info. Systems, Morristown, N.J., 1985-88, AT&T Systems Integration Div., Bridgewater, N.J., 1988—. Roman Catholic. Home: 243 Central Ave West Caldwell NJ 07006 Office: AT&T 55 Corporate Dr Bridgewater NJ 08807-6991

BENTLEY, DAVID MICHAEL, real estate broker; b. Franklin, Ind., June 19, 1959; s. James Lewis and Mary Lucille (Addison) B.; m. Maggie Robles, Nov. 22, 1980. Student, U. Ariz., 1977-80. Sales agt. Roy H. Long Realty Co., Tucson, 1980-82, asst. sales mgr., 1982-83, comml. sales agt., 1983-84; pres. Benteq Corp., Tucson, 1984-88, Calif. Land Devel., San Diego, 1988—. Mem. Ad Hoc Com. Pima County Planning & Zoning Commn.; adv. mem. Comml. Brokers Econ. Task Force, Tucson. Mem. Nat. Assn. of Realtors, Ariz. Assn. Realtors, Tucson Bd. Realtors, Southern Ariz. Homebuilders Assn. (exec. land devel. coms., pub. relations chmn.), Comml. Investment Council (designate, cert. comml. investment mem. 1987), Southern Ariz. Cert. Comml. Investment Mem. (exec. officer). Republican. Episcopalian. Office: 4660 La Jolla Village Dr Ste 750 San Diego CA 92122

BENTLEY, FRED DOUGLAS, SR., lawyer; b. Marietta, Ga., Oct. 15, 1926; s. Oscar Andrew and Ima Irene (Prather) B.; m. Sara Tom Moss, Dec. 26, 1953; children: Fred Douglas, Robert Randall. BA, Presbyn. Coll., 1949; JD, Emory U., 1948. Bar: Ga. 1948. Sr. mem. Bentley & Dew, Marietta, 1948-51; ptnr. Bentley, Awtrey & Bartlett, Marietta, 1951-56, Edwards, Bentley, Awtrey & Parker, Marietta, 1956-75, Bentley & Schindelar, Marietta, 1975-80, Bentley, Bentley, Bentley & Bentley, Marietta, 1980—; pres. Beneficial Investment Co., Adirondack, Inc., Newmarket, Inc., Happy Valley, Inc., Bentley & Sons, Inc.; chmn. bd. Charter Bank and Trust Co.; trustees Kennesaw Coll. Mem. Ga. Ho. of Reps., 1951-57, Ga. Senate, 1958; past pres. Cobb County (Ga.) C. of C.; hon. curator Bentley Rare-Book Gallery, Kennesaw Coll. Served with USN. Named Citizen of Yr., C. of C., 1951, Leader of Tomorrow, Time mag., 1953, Vol. Citizen of Yr., Atlanta Jour./Constn., 1981. Mem. Nat. Trial Lawyers Assn., Assn. Trial Lawyers Am., Ga. Trial Lawyers Assn., ABA, Ga. Bar Assn., Am. Jurisprudence Soc., Hon. Blue Key Frat. Democrat. Methodist. Clubs: Rotary (Marietta); Georgian (bd. dirs.) (Atlanta). Home: 1441 Beaumont Dr Kennesaw GA 30144 Office: 260 Washington Ave Marietta GA 30060

BENTLEY, FRED DOUGLAS, JR., lawyer; b. Marietta, Ga., Aug. 27, 1955; s. Fred Douglas and Sara Tom (Moss) B.; m. Patricia Ann Foster, Dec. 17, 1983; children: Thomas Rhett, John Matthew. BBA in Acctg., U. Ga., 1977; JD, Emory U., 1980. Bar: Ga. 1980, La. 1983, Tex. 1986, U.S. Ct. Appeals (11th cir.) 1982, U.S. Dist. Ct. (no. dist.) Ga. 1982, U.S. Dist. Ct. (so. dist.) Tex., U.S. Ct. Appeals (5th cir.) 1983, U.S. Dist. Ct. (ea. and mid. dists.) La. 1983. Ptnr. Bentley & Bentley, Marietta, 1980-83; assoc. Phelps, Dunbar, Marks, Claverie & Sims, New Orleans, 1983-86; the Permian Corp., Houston, 1986-87; ptnr. Bentley, Bentley & Bentley, 1987—; faculty Phillips Jr. Coll., Metaire, La., 1983. Dist. rep. Republican Party Big Shanty Dist., Kennesaw, Ga., 1982-83; trustee The Cove at Walden; bd. dirs. The Tommy Nobis Ctr. Am. Cancer Soc. Recipient Jour. Cup award Atlanta Constn. Newspaper, 1973; Outstanding Young Men of Am. award Jaycees, 1981. Mem. ABA, Fed. Bar Assn., Ga. State Bar Assn., La. State Bar Assn., Tex. State Bar Assn., Houston Bar Assn., Cobb County C. of C. (trustee 1982-83), Am. Corp. Counsel Assn., Phi Delta Phi. Republican. Roman Catholic. Lodge: Rotary (Marietta), KC. Home: 171 Mountain Brook Dr Marietta GA 30064 Office: Bentley Bentley & Bentley 260 Washington Ave Marietta GA 30060

BENTLEY, JOHN GREGORY, entrepreneur; b. Rome, Ga., Oct. 27, 1961; s. Bobby John and Peggy Delores (Green) B. BS in Bus. Mgmt., U. Tenn., Chattanooga, 1984. Vice pres. ops. Bentley Fabrics, Rossville, Ga., 1977-82; ptnr. Bentley's, Ft. Oglethorpe, Ga., 1982-85, owner, chief exec. officer, 1985—. County coord. Hamilton Jordan for U.S. Senate Campaign, 1986; treas. Catoosa County Commn. on Bicentennial U.S. Constn., 1987—; mem. Catoosa County Democratic Com., 1988—; mem. Ft. Oglethorpe City Coun., 1988—; city clk. Town of Ft. Oglethorpe. Mem. Catoosa County C. of C., Lakeview-Ft. Oglethorpe Jaycees (pres. 1982-83, treas. 1984-86, Jaycee of Yr. award 1982). Methodist. Home: 304 Park Lake Dr Fort Oglethorpe GA 30742 Office: 304 Lafayette Rd Fort Oglethorpe GA 30742

BENTLEY, LISA JANE, retail executive; b. Lansdale, Pa., Mar. 20, 1936; d. Fred Olin and Beulah Sailor (Flagler) Ricker; m. Ronald F. Pepka, May 20, 1956 (div. 1969); 1 child, Ronald Glenn; m. John Lee Bentley, July 30, 1972. Student, Fresno (Calif.) State U., 1949-51; ordained, Living Bible Ctr., Phoenix, 1987. Mgr., owner Arthur Murray, N.Y.C., Phila. and Key West, Fla., 1956-65; interior designer Lisa's Interiors, Phila., 1965-75; exec. cons. Snelling & Snelling, Phila., 1975-78; pres., treas. Bentley Glass and Mirror, Inc., Las Vegas, Nev., 1979—; also chmn. bd. dirs. Bentley Glass and Mirror, Inc., Las Vegas; pres., treas. Bentley Enterprises, Inc., Las Vegas, 1980—, also chmn. bd. dirs.; pres., treas. Bentley Interiors Worldwide, Las Vegas, 1982—; tchr. Higher New Thought Ctr., Las Vegas, 1987—. Pastor, minister, pres., sec. Worldwide Outreach Awareness Ctr., 1987—; founder, chmn. bd. dirs., pres., sec. metaphysical tchr., healer, counselor Nev. Inst. Applied Metaphysics Inc., 1987—; v.p. Mt. Charleston (Nev.) Home Owners Assn., 1987. Mem. Associated Gen. Contractors, Internat. New Thought Alliance, Glazing Contractors Assn. (legis. chmn. 1985, fin. chmn. 1985, membership chmn. 1985). Office: Bentley Glass & Mirror 3230 Polaris #20 Las Vegas NV 89102

BENTLEY, ROBERT CLYDE, architect; b. Livermore, Calif., July 5, 1926; s. Clyde Edward and Doris Katherin (Taylor) B.; m. Patricia Ann Grant, Sept. 10, 1948 (div. 1974); children: Grant Patrick, Linda Dori, William Clyde; m. Elizabeth Aldrin Hench, June 7, 1974; stepchildren: Anders Hench, Colleen Hench, Carolyn Hench. BA, U. Calif.-Berkeley, 1950; grad. Anthony Sch. Real Estate, 1982. Registered architect, Calif. Pvt. practice architecture, Los Altos, Calif., 1959— ; Architect of University of Nations Scheme on Alcatraz Island on San Francisco Bay for AIA, 1988—. mng. employee Advanced Interiors, San Jose, 1982-83; interior contractor Red Lion Inn, San Jose, 1982-83, Marriott Hotel, San Jose, 1982-83; architect's rep. San Jose Airport, 1980-81; realtor El Monte Properties, Los Altos, 1980-85 ; asst. city planner Yakima Wash., 1958-59; dir. Bentley Engrs., 1950-75; elec. takeoff estimator of tube Bay Area Rapid Transit, San Francisco, 1967-68. Mem. housing code commn. Yakima City Planning Dept., 1959. Served to lt. (j.g.) USNR, 1944-45. Recipient Spark Plug award, Oakland Jaycees, 1965. Mem. Phi Delta Theta. Democrat. Unitarian. Home: 595 Jay St Los Altos CA 94022 Office: 745 Distel Dr Los Altos CA 94022

BENTLY, DONALD EMERY, electrical engineer; b. Cleve., Oct. 18, 1924; s. Oliver E. Bently and Mary Evelyn (Conway) B.; m. Susan Lorraine Pumphrey, Sept. 1961 (div. Sept. 1982); 1 child, Christopher Paul. BSEE with distinction, Iowa State U., 1949, MSEE, 1950; DS (hon.), U. Nev., 1987. Registered profl. engr., Calif., Nev. Pres. Bently Nev. Corp., Minden, 1961-85, chief exec. officer, 1985—; chief exec. officer Bently Rotor Dynamics and Research Corp., Minden, 1985—; also chmn. bd. dirs. Bently Nev. Corp., Minden; chmn. bd. dirs. Gibson Tool Co., Carson City, Nev., 1978—. Contbr. articles to profl. jours.; inventor in field. Served with USN, 1943-46, PTO. Named Inventor or Yr., State of Nev. Invention and Tech. Council, 1987. Mem. IEEE, Am. Petroleum Inst., Soc. Tribologists and Lubrication Engr., ASME, Sigma Xi, Tau Beta Pi, Eta Kappa Nu. Episcopalian. Home:

Bently Buckeye Ranch Minden NV 89423 Office: Bently Nev Corp 1617 Water St Minden NV 89423

BENTON, JACK MITCHELL, bank executive, human resources executive; b. Bakersfield, Calif., July 15, 1941; s. James Edwin and Alice Kathryn (Hawthorne) B.; m. Suzanne Wilken, June 14, 1964; children: Mitchell Brian, Andrea Katherine. BS in Acctg., Calif. State U., Chico, 1964. CPA, Calif., N.Y. Acct. Arthur Young & Co., Los Angeles, 1964-68; chief fin. officer Newport Nat. Bank, Newport Beach, Calif., 1968-70; mng. dir. human resources Chase Manhattan Bank & Chase Manhattn Capital Markets Corp., N.Y.C., 1970-87; sr. v.p., mgr. human resources Bank Tokyo, Ltd.-N.Y. Agy. Bank Tokyo Trust Co., N.Y.C., 1987—. Served with USCG, 1960-61, USCGR, 1961-68. Mem. AICPA, Am. Soc. Pers. Adminstrn., Calif. Soc. CPAs, N.Y. State CPAs, Shek-O Country (Hong Kong). Republican. Club: Snek-O Country (Hong Kong). Home: 30 Maple Ave Madison NJ 07940 Office: Bank Tokyo Ltd 100 Broadway New York NY 10005

BENTON, PHILIP EGLIN, JR., automobile company executive; b. Charlottesville, Va., Dec. 31, 1928; s. Philip Eglin and Orient (Nichols) B.; m. Mary Ann Zadosko, May 23, 1974; children: Katherine Benton Harris, Deborah A., Cynthia Benton Nelson, Philip Eglin, III, Paula R. AB in Econs. and Math. magna cum laude, Dartmouth Coll., 1952; MBA in Fin. with highest distinction, Amos Tuck Sch., 1953. With Ford Motor Co., 1953—; v.p. truck ops. Ford of Europe 1977-79; v.p. Ford Div., Detroit, 1979-81; v.p. sales ops. N.Am. Auto Ops., Detroit, 1981-85; exec. v.p. diversified products Dearborn, Mich., 1985-86; exec. v.p. Ford Internat. Automotive Ops. Ford Motor Co., Dearborn, Mich., 1986-87; pres. Ford Automotive Group, Dearborn, 1987—. Exec. com. Highway Users Fedn. for Safety and Mobility; trustee Mich. Opera Theatre; bd. dirs. United Found.; mem. Pres.'s Soc., The Edison Inst., Founders Soc., Detroit Inst. Arts; bd. overseers Amos Tuck Sch. Bus. Adminstrn.; exec. com. Meadow Brook. Served with USMCR, 1946-48. Mem. Am. Inst. for Contemporary German Studies (bd. dirs.), Detroit Hist. Soc. (trustee), Detroit Zool. Soc., The Old Club, Bloomfield Hills Country Club, Grosse Pointe Club, Dartmouth Club Detroit. Office: Ford Motor Co The American Rd Dearborn MI 48121

BENWAY, JOSEPH CALISE, finance executive; b. Providence, Nov. 11, 1949; s. Joseph and Connie (Grimaldi) B.; m. Susan Duffy, Aug. 18, 1984. AS, R.I. Jr. Coll., 1969; BA, Boston U., 1971; MBA, Washington U., 1975. Sr. fin. analyst AMOCO, Chgo., 1975-78; asst. controller Marsteller Inc., Chgo., 1978-81, controller, 1981-83; chief fin. officer, exec. v.p. fin. Burson-Marsteller, N.Y.C., 1983—, also bd. dirs.; bd. dirs. Rogers Merchandising, Lombard, Ill.; mem. Young & Rubicam Fin. Operating Com., N.Y.C., 1985—. Home: 202 Highbrook Ave Pelham NY 10803 Office: Burson Marsteller 230 Park Ave S New York NY 10003

BENZ, BRADLEY, portfolio manager; b. Neenah, Wis., Mar. 24, 1964; s. Evans C. and Geraldine S. (Robinson) B. BBA, U. Wis., Whitewater, 1986. Investment mgr. Associated Bank, Neenah, 1986—. Republican. Home: 3532 N Gillett Appleton WI 54915 office: Associated Bank 100 W Wisconsin Ave Neenah WI 54956

BENZAK, LOUIS RICHARD, investment counselor; b. Allentown, Pa., Aug. 27, 1939; s. Louis Anton and Emma Ann (Yany) B.; B.S., Pa. State U., 1961; m. Virginia Ann Scully, Nov. 17, 1973; children—Christopher Louis, Jeffrey John, Caroline Ann. Second v.p. Chase Manhattan Bank, N.Y.C., 1962-68; sr. v.p. Loeb Rhoades & Co., N.Y.C., 1969-77; pres. Spears Benzak & Co. (now Spears, Benzak, Salomon & Farrell, Inc.), N.Y.C., 1978—; chmn., dir. SBSF Fund, Inc. Bd. dirs., treas. Muscular Dystrophy Assn. Am., 1977—, Benedict Found. for Ind. Schs., Am. Farmland Trust, Washington; trustee Rye Hist. Soc., Rye Country Day Sch.; Served with U.S. Army, 1962. Mem. N.Y. Soc. Security Analysts. Clubs: Knickerbocker (N.Y.C.); Apawamis, Am. Yacht (Rye, N.Y.). Home: 225 Highland Rd Rye NY 10580-1833 Office: Spears Benzak Salomon & Farrell 45 Rockefeller Plaza New York NY 10100

BENZIGER, PETER HAMILTON, utility executive; b. N.Y.C., Nov. 28, 1926; s. Alfred Felix and Nannie Merrick (Hamilton) B.; m. Joan Patricia Kelly, June 22, 1971; children—John Mitchell, Elizabeth Roberts. B.S. in Engring., Princeton U., 1949. Registered profl. engr., D.C., Md. With Potomac Electric Power Co., 1949—; sr. v.p. generation Potomac Electric Power Co., Washington, 1973-89; vice chmn., chief operating officer Potomac Capital Investments subs. Potomac Electric Power Co., Washington, 1989—. With USNR, 1944-46. Mem. ASME, Assn. Edison Illuminating Cos., Met. Washington Bd. Trade. Republican. Roman Catholic. Clubs: Chevy Chase Country, Metropolitan. Home: 5207 Westbard Ave Bethesda MD 20816 Office: Potomac Capital Investments Corp 900 19th St NW Washington DC 20006

BEN-ZVI, PHILLIP NORMAN, insurance company executive, actuary; b. Bklyn., June 3, 1942; s. Samuel and Anna (Yaffe) Ben-Zvi; m. Susan Grossberg, Feb. 17, 1968; children: Michael, Sharyn, Jonathan. BS, CCNY, 1963. V.p., actuary Royal Ins. Co., N.Y.C., 1963-80; v.p., sr. actuary Continental Corp., Piscataway, N.J., 1980-81, sr. v.p., 1981—; vice chmn. bd. Nat. Coun. on Compensation Ins., N.Y.C., 1987—; bd. dirs. Ins. Inst. for Highway Safety, Washington, 1985—. Fellow Casualty Actuarial Soc. (pres. 1985-86), Can. Inst. Actuaries; mem. Am. Acad. Actuaries (v.p. 1987—), Casualty Actuaries N.Y. (past pres.), Internat. Actuarial Assn. Jewish. Home: 14 Guy Dr East Brunswick NJ 08816 Office: Continental Corp One Continental Dr Cranbury NJ 08570

BERARDESCO, MICHAEL RICHARD, teacher; b. Irvington, N.J., May 15, 1951; s. Harry N. and Adeline M. (DeRick) B.; m. Carolyn Anne Tobey, June 23, 1973; 1 child, Mark David. BFA cum laude, Md. Inst. Coll. of Art, 1973. Apprentice F. Schonbach, Washington, 1972; tchr. Md. Inst. Coll. of Art, Balt., 1973-74; freelance artist archtl. renderings Balt., 1971-73, New Providence, N.J., 1973-80, Chatham, N.J., 1980-84; prin., owner Michael Berardesco Assoc., Chatham, 1984—; tchr. N.J. Ctr. for Visual Arts, 1988—. Freelance artist archtl. renderings, Balt., 1971-73, New Providence, N.J., 1973-80, Chatham, 1980-84. Home: 12 Pine St Chatham NJ 07928 Office: 2 N Passaic Ave Chatham NJ 07928

BERARDI, JOHN FRANCIS, publishing company executive; b. Waterbury, Conn., Mar. 9, 1943; s. John August and Coletta (Gannon) B.; m. Karen Anne Fahey, Sept. 4, 1967; children: Maura, John, Meghan. BBA, Cleve. State U., 1970. CPA, Ohio. Audit sr. Ernst & Whinney, Cleve., 1970-76; controller staff AM Internat., Shaker Heights, Ohio, 1976-78; v.p. controller Harvest Cos. (subs. Harcourt Brace Jovanovich), Cleve., 1978-82, exec. v.p., 1982-84; controller Harcourt Brace Jovanovich Inc., Orlando, Fla., 1984-85, v.p., controller, 1985-86, sr. v.p., treas., 1986—; also bd. dirs. Harcourt Brace Jovanovich Inc., 1988—. Advisor Jr. Achievement, Cleve., 1972-76; group leader Cath. Charities, Cleve., 1979-84; council mem. St. Brendan Ch., North Olmsted, Ohio, 1982; bd. dirs. Bishop Moore High Sch., Orlando, 1986. Served with USN, 1961-66. Mem. Fin. Execs. Inst. Republican. Club: Sabal Point Country (Longwood, Fla.). Office: Harcourt Brace Jovanovich Inc 6277 Sea Harbor Dr Orlando FL 32887

BERCK, CINDY JO, service executive; b. Indpls., June 13, 1963; d. Stephen Raymond and Marjorie Kay (Steinmetz) Rasmussen; m. John Henri Berck, May 18, 1985. BS, Butler U., 1987. With cardiology dept. Sch. Medicine, Ind. U., Indpls., 1977-82, adminstrv. asst., 1983-85; adminstr. Inst. Health Enhancement div. Personnel Devel. Group, Indpls., 1985—, coordinator EAP program, 1987—; corp. sec. Personnel Devel. Group, Indpls., 1987—, asst. dir., 1987. Co-editor: (newspaper) Wellness Watch, 1986—. Vol. collector Am. Cancer Soc., Indpls., 1985—; vol. donations com. Am. Council for the Blind, Indpls., 1986—, Indpls. Humane Soc., 1986—. Mem. Indpls. Alliance for Health Assn., Kappa Kappa Gamma Alumni Group. Presbyterian. Club: Columbia. Office: Personnel Devel Group 222 E Ohio St Ste 800 Indianapolis IN 46204

BERDICK, LEONARD STANLEY, insurance broker; b. New Rochelle, N.Y., Aug. 13, 1938; s. Julius and Fay (Jaffe) B.; m. Arlene Jean Kaufman, Oct. 31, 1968. B.A., Colgate U., 1960; M.A., Columbia U., 1963; student, U. N.C. Law Sch., 1960-61. Broker, dir., agt. Leonard S. Berdick Agy., S.I., N.Y., 1975—. Committeeman, Liberal Party, 1974—. Mem. Nat. Assn. Life Underwriters, N.Y. Ins. Brokers Assn., Life Suprs. Assn., Acad. Polit. Sci., Colgate U., Columbia U., U. N.C. alumni assns. Jewish. Club: Colgate Univ. Home: 2 Elmwood Park Dr Staten Island NY 10314 Office: Leonard S Berdick Agy 280 Madison Ave Ste 905 New York NY 10016

BERDROW, STANTON K., power company executive; b. Long Beach, Calif., Oct. 4, 1928; s. Earl Lester and Martha Ann B.; m. Rosa R. Rottger, Feb. 22, 1951; children—Nancy, John, Matthew. B.S., Armstrong Coll., Berkeley, Calif., 1950; postgrad. Sch. Bus. Syracuse U., 1951-52. Dist. advt. and sales promotion mgr. The Pennzoil Co., Los Angeles, 1953-59; v.p., mgmt. supr. Batten, Barton, Durstine & Osborn, Inc., San Francisco, 1960-77; v.p., dir. acctg. services Commart Communications, Santa Clara, Calif., 1978-80; v.p. communications and pub. affairs Sierra Pacific Power Co., Reno, 1980—. Adminstr. Sierra Pacific Charitable Found., 1987—; bd. dirs. PBS-TV, Reno. Served with U.S. Army, 1946-48. Mem. Am. Advt. Fedn. (Best in the West award 1985), Pub. Utility Communicators Assn. (1st award complete campaign 1986, 88, 1st award employee communications 1984), Am Mktg. Assn. (recipient Silver Effie award N.Y. chpt., 1987, 88), Pub. Relations Soc. Am. (past pres. Sierra Nev. chpt.), Reno Advt. Club, Newcomen Soc. Republican. Clubs: Innisfree Beach (Lake Tahoe, Calif.); Rotary. Contbr. articles to profl. jours. Home: 3925 Skyline Blvd Reno NV 89509 Office: Sierra Pacific Power Co PO Box 10100 Reno NV 89520

BERDUX, WILLIAM JAMES, JR., optical instruments manufacturing company executive; b. San Diego, Mar. 13, 1947; s. William James and Beatrice Naomi (Martin) B.; m. Barbara Love, Feb. 14, 1976; children: Sabrina M., Chelsie L. B.S. in Bus. Mgmt., San Diego State U., 1973. Mgmt. trainee Union Bank, San Diego, 1973-73, Los Angeles, 1973, comml. loan officer, San Francisco, 1974-76; dir. B.H.R. Fin. Services, Inc. div. Argo Industries, Inc., Los Angeles, 1976-78; v.p. gen. mgr. Argo Trading Co., Inc. div. Argo Industries, inc., Laguna Hills, Calif., 1978-81; v.p., mng. dir. Argo Industries, Inc., Laguna Hills, 1978-81; internat. sales and mktg. mgr., Bausch & Lomb, Inc., Pasadena, Calif., 1981—. Served with USAF, 1965-69. Home: 27382 Celanova Mission Viejo CA 92692-3345

BERE, JAMES FREDERICK, diversified manufacturing company executive; b. Chgo., July 25, 1922; s. Lambert Sr. and Madeline (Van Tatenhove) B.; m. Barbara Van Dellen, June 27, 1947; children—Robert Paul, James Frederick, David Lambert, Lynn Barbara, Becky Ann. Student, Calvin Coll., 1940-42; B.S., Northwestern U., 1946, M.B.A., 1950. With Clearing Machine Corp. div. U.S. Industries, Inc., 1946-53, gen. mgr., 1953-56; gen. mgr. Axelson Mfg. Co. div., 1956, pres., 1957-61; pres., gen. mgr. Borg & Beck div. Borg-Warner Corp., Chgo., 1961-64; group v.p. Borg-Warner Corp., 1964-66, exec. v.p. automotive, 1966-68, corp. pres., 1968-84, chief exec. officer, 1972-86, chmn. bd., from 1975; Dir. Abbott Labs., North Chicago, Time, Inc., Hughes Tool Co., Ameritech, Tribune Co., Temple-Inland Inc., Kmart Corp.;. Trustee U. Chgo. Served as lt. AUS, 1943-45. Mem. Am. Mgmt. Assn., Bus. Roundtable, Bus. Council, Alpha Tau Omega.

BERENSON, RICHARD WILLIAM, computer software company executive; b. Boston, Nov. 13, 1958; s. Richard Arthur and Judith Cynthia (Woodbury) B.; m. Barbara Sue Fischbein, June 12, 1983. BA, Harvard U., 1980, MBA, 1984; JD, Harvrd U., 1984. Bar: Mass. 1984, N.Y. 1984. Mem. tech. staff AT&T Bell Labs., Whippam, N.J., 1984-85; product mgr. Palladian Software, Inc., Cambridge, Mass., 1985-87, dir. product devel., 1987-88; pres. Foresight Systems, Inc., Newton, Mass., 1988—; treas. Found. for Space Bus. Research, Boston, 1984. Mem. Brookline (Mass.) fin. com. Mem. Mass. Bar Assn., N.Y. Bar Assn., Am. Assn. Artificial Intelligence.

BERENSON, ROBERT LEONARD, advertising agency executive; b. Chgo., Nov. 14, 1939; s. James Morton and Harriet Ruth (Fisher) B.; m. Elizabeth Segal, Sept. 9, 1962; 1 dau., Cindy Elizabeth. B.A., Syracuse U., 1961; M.S.J., Northwestern U., 1962. Mgmt. trainee Grey Advt., Inc., N.Y.C., 1964-67; v.p., account supr. Grey Advt., Inc., 1967-70, v.p., mgmt. supr., 1970-71, sr. v.p., mgmt. rep., 1971-77, exec. v.p., 1977-82, exec. v.p. adminstrn. and account mgmt., 1982—; guest lectr. mktg. U. Conn., Syracuse U., Northwestern U., St. John's U., 1974-88. vice chmn. bd. dirs. Better Business Bur.; bd. dirs. P.O.P. Radio Inc. 1st lt. U.S. Army, 1962-64. Jewish. Home: 7 Farmers Rd Kings Point NY 11024 Office: Grey Advt Inc 777 3rd Ave New York NY 10017

BERES, MARY ELIZABETH, management educator, organizational consultant; b. Birmingham, Mich., Jan. 19, 1942; d. John Charles and Ethel (Belenyesi) B. B.S., Siena Heights Coll., Adrian, Mich., 1969; Ph.D, Northwestern U., 1976. Joined Dominican Sisters, 1960; tchr., St. Francis Xavier Sch., Medina, Ohio, 1962-64, St. Edward Sch., Detroit, 1964-67; tchr. Our Lady of Mt. Carmel Sch., Temperance, Mich., 1967-69, asst. prin., 1968-69; tchr. math. St. Ambrose High Sch., Detroit, 1969-70; vis. instr. Cornell U., 1973-74; assoc. prof. orgn. behavior Temple U., Phila., 1974-84; assoc. prof. mgmt. Mercer U. Atlanta, 1984—; cons. in field. Contbr. chpts. to books; organizer of symposia in areas of corp. leadership and cross-cultural communication. Bd. trustees Adrian Dominican Ind. Sch. System (Mich.), 1971-79; bd. dirs. Ctr. for Ethics and Social Policy, Phila., 1980-84; Bd. trustees Adrian Dominican Ind. Sch. System, Adrian, Mich., 1971-79; mem. Atlanta Clergy and Laity Concerned, 1986—; mem. Econ. Pastoral Implementation Com. of Archdiocese of Atlanta, 1988—. Recipient Legion of Honor membership Chapel of the Four Chaplains, Phila., 1982; Disting. Teaching award Lindback Found., 1982, Cert. for Humanity, Mercer U., 1985; mem. program planning com. of interdepartmental group in bus. adminstrn. U. Ctr. in Ga., 1987—, chair, 1988—. Mem. Acad. Mgmt., Indsl. Relations Research Assn., Acad. Internat. Bus. (program com. southeast U.S. region 1987, chairperson mgmt. track 1988), The So. Mgmt. Assn., Assn. Social Econs (interdepartmental group in bus. adminstrn., U. Ctr. in Ga., program planning com. 1987—, chairperson 1988—), So. Ctr. Internat. Studies, Nat. Assn. Female Execs. Democrat. Roman Catholic. Office: Mercer U Sch Bus and Econs 3001 Mercer University Dr Atlanta GA 30341

BERETZ, PAUL BASIL, management/business consultant; b. Washington, Oct. 15, 1938; s. O. Paul and Marthe (Szabo) B.; m. Jane M. Beretz; children: Charles, Melissa, John, Michele, Claudine. BBA, U. Notre Dame, 1960; MBA, Golden Gate U., 1974. Mgr. cen. credit Union Carbide Corp., Atlanta, San Francisco, N.Y.C., 1961-81; gen. mgr. Bayox/Almac Co., Oakland, Calif., 1981-83; asst. treas. Crown Zellerbach Corp., San Francisco, 1983-86; prin. P.B. Beretz and Co., Bus. Cons., San Francisco, 1986—. Author: Managing Commercial Credit, 1981; contbr. articles to profl. jours. Mem. Credit Rsch. Found. (bd. trustees 1983-86), U. Notre Dame Nat. Alumni Assn. (bd. dirs. 1983-86). Democrat. Roman Catholic.

BERFAS, JAY JOSEPH, advertising executive; b. N.Y.C., Nov. 8, 1947; s. Bernard Benjamin and Hilda Devorah (Raifaisen) B.; m. Carolyn Joan Zeizel, June 20, 1970; children: Carly, Scott. BA, Queens Coll., 1969; MA, NYU, 1973. Tchr., guidance counselor N.Y.C. Bd. Edn., 1969-76; account exec. Instl. Investor, N.Y.C., 1977-78; mgr. Midwest advt. Instl. Investor, Chgo., 1978-80; from dir. U.S. advt. to v.p., dir. advt. Instl. Investor, N.Y.C., 1981—. Mem. Nat. Investor Rels. Inst., Fin. Communications Soc. Office: Instl Investor 488 Madison Ave New York NY 10022

BERG, GORDON HERCHER, banker; b. New Haven, May 14, 1937; s. J. Edward and Dazma (Hercher) B.; m. Ruth Gardner, Aug. 26, 1961; (div. 1985); children: Elizabeth, Deborah, Mary, Beatrice, Gordon; m. Patricia Pridham, Apr. 27, 1985. AA, Mitchell Coll.; BA, Ohio Wesleyan U., 1959; MBA, NYU, 1963; grad., Stonier Grad. Sch. Banking, 1967; MTS, Harvard U., 1988. Asst. sec. Irving Trust Co., N.Y.C., 1959-64; v.p. New England Merchants Bank, Boston, 1964-68; ptnr. The Sprague Co., Boston, 1968-70; pres., chief exec. officer Berg & Co. Inc., BMFC, Inc., Boston, 1971—; pres. Gordon Berg Co., Boston, 1984—. Contbr. articles to prfl. jours. Trustee New England Meml. Hosp., Stoneham Mass., Jordan Hosp., Plymouth Mass., Derby Acad., Hingham, Mass. 1972-83. Mem. Mortgage Bankers Assn. Am. (cert. mortgage banker 1983), Duxbury Yacht Club, Masons. Episcopalian. Office: Gordon Berg Co Exchange Pl Fl 36 Boston MA 02109

BERG, JAMES ALLEN, association executive; b. Buffalo, Mar. 22, 1940; s. Carl William and Marion (Shutt) B.; m. Carol Betty Pearl, June 20, 1963; children: Jonathan, Ryan. BS in Edn., SUNY, Buffalo, 1963, MS in Adminstrn., 1967. Cert. tchr., adminstr., N.Y. Tchr. Tonawanda (N.Y.) Schs., 1963-66; tchr., prin. Ellicottville (N.Y.) Schs., 1966-67; prin. West Seneca (N.Y.) Schs., 1967-70, Lancaster (N.Y.) Schs., 1970-77; pres. Applied Imagination, East Aurora, N.Y., 1970—; exec. dir. Greater East Aurora C. of C., 1980—; cons. East Aurora Devel. Corp., 1985—, Erie Community Coll., Orchard Park, N.Y., 1985—; bd. dirs. (founding dir.) Toytown U.S.A., Inc. Fellow N.Y. State C. of C.; mem. Am. C. of C. Execs., Suburban C. of C. Execs. Republican. Office: East Aurora C of C 666 Main St East Aurora NY 14052

BERG, LEE MICHAEL, jewelry retail executive; b. Dallas, Nov. 22, 1948; s. Lee Henry and Rose Marion (Levine) B.; m. Brenda Gartner, June 27, 1971; children: Ryan, Scott, Chad. AA, Kemper Mil. Jr. Coll., Boonville, Mo., 1969; BA, So. Meth. U., 1971. With Corrigan's Fine Jewelry, Dallas, 1971-73; supr. Bailey, Banks and Biddle Jewelers, Phila., 1973; sr. v.p. Fine Jewelers Guild of Zales Corp., N.Y.C., 1974-76; owner Lee Michaels Fine Jewelry, Baton Rouge, 1978—; owner, mgr. Shreveport, La., 1981—, Lafayette, La., 1985—, Hammond, La., 1987—. Bd. dirs. Baton Rouge Symphony, 1986—, Congregation B'Nai Israel, Baton Rouge, 1984-86, The Jewish Fedn., Baton Rouge, 1981-84, 1988—; mem. Young Pres. Orgn. Mem. Am. Gem Soc., The Diamond High Council of Antwerp (Belgium), Jewelers of Am. (bd. dirs. 1986—), Cortana Mall Merchants Assn. (pres. 1983-86), Baton Rouge C. of C. (bd. dirs. 1988—), La. Retailers Assn. (bd. dirs. 1988—), Jewelers of Am. (treas., bd. dirs. 1988—). Jewish. Office: 9337 Cortana Pl Baton Rouge LA 70815

BERG, PAUL EDWARD, investment consultant; b. New Haven, June 12, 1941; s. John Edward and Dazma Charlotte (Hercher) B.; m. Cynthia Wattenberg, June 6, 1970; children: Christina Elizabeth, John Spencer. BS in Bus. Econs., Lehigh U., 1963. Pension trust officer Chase Manhattan Bank, N.Y.C., 1964-68; v.p. Reynolds Securities Inc., N.Y.C., 1968-75; dir. investment svcs. A.S. Hansen, Inc., Chgo., 1975-82; pres. Berg Fiduciary Cons., Inc., Port Chester, N.Y., 1982—; chmn. Plan Sponsor Network, Port Chester, N.Y., 1984—; bd. dirs. A.S. Hansen, Inc., Chgo. Mem. Zoning Bd. Appeals, Scarsdale, N.Y., 1984-87, bd. dirs. 1978-79; mem. Ad Hoc Transp. Com., Scarsdale, 1981-84, chmn. Ad Hoc Indoor Pool Coms.,1988-89; elder Hitchcock Presbyn. Ch., Scarsdale, 1988—. Sgt. USAR, 1963-69. Mem. Larchmont (N.Y.) Yacht Club, Fox Meadow (Scarsdale) Tennis Club. Office: 363 Westchester Ave Portchester NY 10573

BERG, RICHARD T., meat and food products company executive; b. 1925. BS, U. Md., 1950. Pres., chief exec. officer Hygrade Food Products Corp., 1950-60, 70-75; v.p. ops. John Morell and Co., 1960-69; exec. v.p. ops. Wilson Foods Corp., Oklahoma City, 1975-81, pres., 1981—, also chief operating officer, dir. Office: Wilson Foods Corp 4545 N Lincoln Blvd Oklahoma City OK 73105 *

BERG, STANTON ONEAL, firearms and ballistics cons.; b. Barron, Wis., June 14, 1928; s. Thomas C. and Ellen Florence (Nedland) Silbaugh; student U. Wis., 1949-50; LL.B., LaSalle Extension U., 1951; postgrad. U. Minn., 1960-69; qualified as ct. expert witness in ballistics various cts.; m. June K. Rolstad, Aug. 16, 1952; children—David M., Daniel L., Susan E., Julie L. Claim rep. State Farm Ins. Co., Mpls., Hibbing and Duluth, Minn., 1952-57, claim supt., 1957-66, divisional claim supt., 1966-70; firearms cons., Mpls., 1961—; regional mgr. State Farm Fire and Casualty Co., St. Paul, 1970-84; bd. dirs. Am. Bd. Forensic Firearm and Tool Mark Examiners, 1980—; instr. home firearms safety, Mpls.; cons. to Sporting Arms and Ammunition Mfrs. Inst.; internat. lectr. on forensic ballistics. Adv. bd. Milton Helpern Internat. Center for Forensic Scis., 1975—; mem. bd. cons. Inst. Applied Sci., Chgo.; cons. for re-exam. of ballistics evidence in Sirhan case Superior Ct. Los Angeles, 1975; mem. Nat. Forensic Ctr., 1979—, internat. study group in forensic scis., 1985—; chmn. internat. symposiums on forensic ballistics, Edinburgh, Scotland, 1972, Zurich, 1975, Bergen, Norway, 1981. Served with CIC, AUS, 1948-52. Fellow Am. Acad. Forensic Sci.; mem. Assn. of Firearm and Tool Mark Examiners (exec. council 1970-71, Distinguished Mem. and Key Man award 1972, exam. and standards com., spl. honors award 1976, nat. peer group on cert. of firearms examiners 1978—), Forensic Sci. Soc., Internat. Assn. Forensic Scis., Internat. Assn. for Identification (mem. firearms subcom. of sci. and practice com. 1961-74, 86-89, chmn. firearm subcom. 1964-66, 69-70, lab. research and techniques subcom. 1980-81, life and disting. mem. 1947—), Firearms Western Conf. Criminal and Civil Problems (sci. adv. com.), Am. Legion, Army Counter-Intelligence Corp. Vets. Assn., Interactive Assn. Forensic Scis., Internat. Assn. Identification (disting. mem. 1988), Browning Arms Collectors Assn. (life), Am. Ordnance Assn., Nat. Rifle Assn. (life mem.), Minn. Weapons, Internat. Cartridge Collectors Assns., Internat. Reference Orgn. Forensic Medicine and Scis, Internat. Assn. Bloodstain Pattern Analysts, Internat. Study Group in Forensic Scis. Contbg. editor Am. Rifleman mag., 1973-84; mem. editorial bd. Internat. Microform Jour. Legal Medicine and Forensic Sciences, 1979—, Am. Jour. Forensic Medicine and Pathology, 1979—; contbr. articles on firearms and forensic ballistics to profl. publs. Address: 6025 Gardena Ln NE Minneapolis MN 55432

BERG, STEPHEN WARREN, government official; b. Washington, Jan. 21, 1948; s. Isidore and Dorothy (Faust) B.; BA, Tulane U., 1970; MS, Shippensburg State Coll., 1976; m. Linda Ann Burns, Nov. 7, 1975; children: Ashley Michelle, Marcus Alan. Program analyst Dept. Army, New Cumberland, Pa., Ft. Monmouth, N.J., Chambersburg, Pa., 1972-75; program mgr. Army Office Environ. Program, Washington, 1975-76; chief, directorate support br. Army Corps of Engrs., Washington, 1976-78; chief coordination and support br. Public Bldgs. Service, Washington, 1978-79, chief mgmt. control and analysis br., 1979-82, sr. planner policy and planning office, 1982-86; operational dir. Office Assoc. Adminstr. for Ops., GSA, Washington, 1986—; exec. officer Coop. Adminstrv. Support Program, 1987—, Pres.'s Council on Mgmt. Improvement, 1987—. Mem. Acad. Polit. Sci., Am. Soc. Public Adminstrn. Home: 12453 Galesville Dr Gaithersburg MD 20878 Office: 18th and F Sts NW Washington DC 20405

BERGAU, FRANK CONRAD, real estate, commercial and investment properties executive; b. N.Y.C., Sept. 17, 1926; s. Frank Conrad and Mary Elizabeth (Davie) B.; BA in English, St. Francis Coll., Loretto, Pa., 1950; MS in Edn. and English, Potsdam (N.Y.) State U., 1969; m. Rita I. Korotkin; children: Mary, Rita, Francis, Theresa, Veronica. Tchr. English Gouverneur (N.Y.) Schs., 1962-81, dir. continuing edn., 1968-81, summer prin., 1974-80; project dir. St. Lawrence County (N.Y.) Bd. Co-op. Ednl. Services, Canton, 1974; pres. Irenicon Assos. Bd. dirs. St. Lawrence County Assn. Retarded Children, 1965—; pres. bd. dirs. Gouverneur Library. Mem. Gouverneur C. of C. (dir. 1963-66), Lake County Bd. Realtors, NEA, N.Y. Assn. Continuing Edn. (dir.). Certified as tchr., supr., adminstr., N.Y. Club: Gouverneur Luncheon. Lodge: Kiwanis (charter mem. Clermont).

BERGEN, D. THOMAS, business executive; b. Albert Lea, Minn., June 16, 1930; s. Dr. Francis J. and Grace Frances (Donovan) B.; m. Sarah E. Lampert, Aug. 12, 1961 (div. 1980); children: Peter Lampert, Katherine O'Shaughnessy, Margaret Donovan. AB, Harvard U., 1952, MBA, 1954. Regional transp. mgr. DEWline Project, Fed. Electric div. ITT, Can., Arctic and No. Alaska, 1956-58; various positions in internat. ops. Honeywell Inc., Mpls., Fed. Republic Germany, India, France, U.K., 1958-69; pres. Am. Hoist and Derrick (Europe) Corp., London and Zurich, Switzerland, 1969-72, Bergen-Billings Inc., predecessor cos., N.Y.C., Washington, London, 1973—; bd. dirs. numerous corps. Author: German Expressionist Drawings in the Collection of D. Thomas Bergen, 1978; contbr. articles on visual arts to mags., newspapers; lectr. on visual arts. Vice pres. Jr. Achievement, Mpls., 1962-65; asst. sec. Am. Chapel in London, 1975-78; exec. com. Busch-Reisinger Mus., Harvard U., 1975—; trustee New Eng. Electric Ry. Hist. Soc., 1951-56. Served to 1st lt. USAF, 1954-56. Mem. Coll. Art Assn. Republican. Roman Catholic. Clubs: Harvard (N.Y.C. art and architecture com. 1978-83); Bucks, Naval and Military, Harvard, Inst. of Dirs. (London), Edgewater Country (Albert Lea, Minn.). Home: 23B Holland Rd, London W14 8HJ, England Office: Bergen-Billings Inc PO Box AB 1666 FDR Sta New York NY 10150

BERGER, ANDREW L., investment banker, lawyer; b. N.Y.C., Dec. 10, 1946; s. Harry and Jennie (Kronenberg) B.; m. Brook Jaye Horowitz, June 16, 1968; children—Adam Linley, Douglas Bradley. BS, Lehigh U., 1968; JD, Columbia U., 1971. Bar: N.Y. 1972. Assoc. Cravath, Swaine & Moore, N.Y.C., 1971-78; ptnr. Rivkin, Sherman & Levy, N.Y.C., 1979-81; mem.

exec. com., adminstrv. mng. dir. L.F. Rothschild & Co. Inc., N.Y.C., 1981-88, pres., 1987-88; mem. exec. com. L.F. Rothschild Holdings Inc., 1986-88; chmn. bd., trustee L.F. Rothschild Managed Trust, 1986-88; chmn. bd. L.F. Rothschild Fund Mgmt. Inc., 1986-88, also bd. dirs., 1986-88; mng. dir. Wertheim Schroder & Co. Inc., N.Y.C., 1988—; chmn. bd., trustee Hampton Utilities Trust, 1988. Mem. ABA, N.Y. Bar Assn., Assn. of Bar of City of N.Y. Office: Wertheim Schroder & Co Inc 787 7th Ave New York NY 10019-6016

BERGER, FRANK S., consumer products company executive; b. N.Y.C., Nov. 6, 1936; s. Ernest A. and Anna (Weiss) B.; m. Judith Kugel, Jan. 15, 1966; children: Evan, Stacey. B.A., Queens Coll., 1958; M.B.A., N.Y. U., 1960; postgrad., Law Sch., 1961, IBM Edn. Center, 1960. Supr. dept. mktg. and fin. analysis Lever Bros., 1959-61; v.p. fin. and adminstrn. Pacific Enterprises, 1961-62; mem. corp. mktg. staff Joseph E. Seagram & Sons, Inc., 1962-63; mktg. asst. to mgr. cen. div. Calvert Distillers, 1964, asst. mgr. Fla. region, 1965, mgr. N.J. region, 1966-67, asst. mgr. Ea. div., 1967-68, mgr. So. div., 1969-70; v.p., gen. sales mgr. Frankfort Distillers, 1970-71, exec. v.p. mktg. and fin., 1972-73; pres. Gen. Wine & Spirits Co., N.Y.C., 1973-76, Seagram Distillers Co., 1976-77, House of Seagram, 1978-79; dir. Joseph E. Seagram & Sons, Inc., 1974-79; chmn. bd. Quadrillon Investments Inc., 1980-86, Viceroy Imports, Inc., 1981-86; chmn. Hazel Bishop Cosmetics, Paramus, N.J., 1981-87; exec. dir. Majestic PLC, 1987-88; exec. dir. Falchi Enterprises, L.I., N.Y., 1987-89, pres., chief exec. officer, 1989—. Trustee N.Y. Hall of Sci.; Chmn. N.Y. Lunch-o-Ree Boy Scouts Am., United Jewish Appeal, Gaucho Basketball Assn., Cystic Fibrosis Soc.; exec. com. wine and spirits div. Anti-Defamation League, Pro-Am. tennis sponsor Cerebral Palsy; bd. dirs. Bronfman Found. Served with AUS, 1958. Mem. Am. Mgmt. Assn., Am. Mktg. Assn, N.Y. C. of C., Young Pres.' Orgn., A.I.M. Clubs: Advt. of N.Y, N.Y. Sales Execs.

BERGER, HAROLD, lawyer, engineer; b. Archbald, Pa., June 10, 1925; s. Jonas and Anna (Raker) B.; m. Renee Margareten, Aug. 26, 1951; children: Jill Ellen, Jonathan David. B.S. in Elec. Engring, U. Pa., 1948, J.D., 1951. Bar: Pa. 1951. Since practiced in Phila.; judge Ct. of Common Pleas, Phila. County, 1971-72; Chmn., moderator Internat. Aerospace Meetings Princeton U., N.J., 1965-66; chmn. Western Hemisphere Internat. Law Conf., San Jose, Costa Rica, 1967; chmn. internat. Confs. on Aerospace and Internat. Law, Coll. William and Mary; permanent mem. Jud. Conf. 3d Circuit Ct. of Appeals; mem. County Bd. Law Examiners, Phila. County, 1961-71; chmn. World Conf. Internat. Law and Aerospace, Caracas, Venezuela, Internat. Conf. on Environ. and Internat. Law, U. Pa., 1974, Internat. Confs. on Global Interdependence, Princeton U., 1975, 79; mem. Pa. State Conf. Trial Judges, 1972-80, Nat. Conf. State Trial Judges, 1972—; chmn. Pa. Com. for Independent Judiciary, 1973—. Mem. editorial advisory bd.: Jour. of Space Law, U. Miss. Sch. of Law, 1973—; Contbr. articles to profl. jours. Mem. Bar Assn.We the People 200 Com. for Constn. Bicentennial. Served with Signal Corps AUS, 1946-48. Recipient Alumnus of Year award Thomas McKean Law Club, U. Pa. Law Sch., 1965, Gen. Electric Co. Space award, 1966, Nat. Disting. Achievement award Tau Epsilon Rho, 1972, Spl. Pa. Jud. Conf. award, 1981. Mem. Inter-Am. Bar Assn. (past chmn. aerospace law com.), Fed. Bar Assn. (chmn. class action and complex litigation com. Phila. chpt. 1986—, past nat. chmn. com. on aerospace law, pres. Phila. chpt. 1983-84, nat. exec. council, nat. chmn. fed. jud. com., Presdl. award 1970, Nat. Distinguished Service award 1978, nat. com. 1987 bi-centennial of U.S. Constn.), ABA (Spl. Presdl. Program medal 1975, past chmn. aerospace law com., mem. state and fed. ct. com., nat. conf. of state trial judges), Phila. Bar Assn. (chmn. jud. liaison com. 1975, past chmn. internat. law com. 1977), Assn. U.S. Mems. Internat. Inst. Space Law Internat. Astronautical Fedn. (dir.), Internat. Acad. Astronautics Paris (past v.p.). Office: 1622 Locust St Philadelphia PA 19103

BERGER, JAMES CHARLES, research and information center administrator; b. Wilmington, Del., Nov. 9, 1941; s. Theodore and Grace (First) B.; m. Linda Simon, Oct. 24, 1975. BA, U. Del., 1965; MA, U. Mass., 1968; PhD, U. Conn., 1973; Diploma, Chubb Inst., 1988. Asst. prof. Newton (Mass.) Coll., 1972-75; research assoc. Fairleigh Dickinson U., Teaneck, N.J., 1975-76; research dir. John Jay Coll. Criminal Justice, N.Y.C., 1976-88; pvt. practice in computer cons. Morristown, N.J., 1988—; cons. Nat. Orgn. Black Law Enforcement Execs., Washington, 1977, Nat. Assn. Legal Assts., Tulsa, 1981, Ctr. Applied Research and Analysis in the Social Scis., Bklyn., 1981—. Author: Criminal Justice Education, 1980; also articles. Cons. Jewish Family Service of Del., Wilmington, 1974-75. Grantee NSF, 1974, Conn. Research Found., 1971-72; hon. mem. research bd. advisors Am. Biographical Inst., 1988. Mem. Am. Assn. Pub. Opinion Research, Am. Polit. Sci. Assn., Am. Soc. Pub. Adminstrn., Pi Sigma Alpha, Pi Alpha Alpha. Jewish. Home: 7 Olyphant Pl Morristown NJ 07960

BERGER, JUDITH ELLEN, physician recruitment and health care consulting firm executive; b. Bklyn., Mar. 17, 1948; d. Eugene and Lillian (Rosensweig) Frankel; m. Stephen G. Schoen, Feb. 15, 1982; 1 child by previous marriage: Scott Berger. Student Franklin Pierce Coll., 1966-67, New Coll. Social Research, 1971, 73-74. Recruiter, Fanning Personnel, N.Y.C., 1967-71; sales mgr. Roth Young, N.Y.C., 1974-77; v.p., sr. sales cons. Corson Group, N.Y.C., 1977-79; pres. MD Resources, Inc., Miami, Fla., 1979—. Contbr. articles and papers to profl. lit. Vol. worker Miami unit Am. Cancer Soc., 1984—. Named to Inc Mag. 500, 1984, Outstanding Young Working Woman, Glamour Mag., 1985, Disting. Entrepreneur Shearson Lehman Bros., 1987-88, Successful Woman Entrepreneur, 1987. Mem. Nat. Assn. Physician Recruiters (bd. dirs., sec. 1985—), Am. Mktg. Assn. (chpt. bd. dirs. 1984—), Am. Group Practice Assn. (assoc.), Med. Group Mgmt. Assn. (assoc.). Avocations: skiing, scuba diving, aviation, biking, hiking. Office: MD Resources Inc 7835 Galloway Rd Ste 200 Miami FL 33173

BERGER, KAY, public relations executive; b. Pitts., Feb. 18, 1939; d. Alex and Eve (Lando) Singer; m. Ted Stern, Mar. 24, 1984. B.S., UCLA, 1961; M.B.A., Pepperdine U., 1981. Demonstrator Carl Byoir Pub. Relations, Los Angeles, 1960-66; mgr. home econs. Calavo Co., Los Angeles, 1966-69; asst. dir. consumer relations Thermador-Waste King Corp., Los Angeles, 1961-66; exec. v.p. western div. Harshe-Rotman & Druck, Inc. (now Ruder Finn & Rotman), Los Angeles, 1969-80; pres. western region Manning, Selvage & Lee, Inc., Los Angeles, 1980-84; exec. v.p. U.S. regional ops. Manning, Selvage & Lee, Inc., Chgo., 1985-88, exec. v.p. European ops., 1988—, also dir., chmn. long range planning and fin. coms. Mem. com. 1986 Chgo. Internat. Theatre Festival; pub. relations adv. com. grad. sch. U. Chgo.; bd. dirs. New City YMCA. Recipient 1st place award Nat. Council Farm Coops., 1967, Los Angeles Advt. Women, 1967, cert. creative excellence U.S. Indsl. Film Fair, 1974. Mem. Home Economists in Bus. (group chmn. Los Angeles chpt. 1968-69), Internat. Assn. Bus. Communicators, Nat. Investor Relations Inst., Pub. Relations Soc. Am. Home: 875 N Dearborn St Apt 18E Chicago IL 60610 also: 26 Montpelier Pl, London SW7 1HW, England

BERGER, LANCE ALLEN, publishing and information executive; b. Bklyn., July 12, 1943; s. Henry and Ruth (Hirschhorn) B.; m. Dorothy Roberta Turk, June 13, 1965; children—Adam, Craig, Cheryl, Nancy. B.A., Bklyn. Coll., 1965, M.A., 1967. Mgr. mgmt. resources CPC Internat., Englewood Cliffs, N.J., 1976-77, dir. human resources, 1977-79; dir. orgn. devel. Continental Can, Stamford, Conn., 1979-80; prin. Hay Group, N.Y.C., 1980-81, sr. prin., 1981-83, ptnr. gen. mgr., Phila., 1983-84, exec. v.p., 1984-87, v.p., mng. dir. 1987-88; mng. dir. MLR Publishing, 1988—; ; vice chmn. Pequonnock Valley Mental Health, N.J., 1974-78; mem. Council of Bus. Advisors, Teaneck, N.J., 1975-78, Community Leadership Program, Phila., 1983—. Contbr. to profl. jours. Mem. Am. Soc. Personnel Adminstrn., Am. Soc Tng. Devel., Planning Forum, Manalapan Jaycees (sec. 1971-74), Am. Mgmt. Assn., Am. Compensation Assn., Am. Soc. Tng. & Devel. Home: 17 Courtney Circle Bryn Mawr PA 19010 Office: Hay Group 229 S 18th St Philadelphia PA 19103

BERGER, RICHARD STEIL, synthetic fiber company executive; b. N.Y.C., Apr. 28, 1929; s. Elmer S. and Elsie (Feinberg) B.; m. Freeda Schatzberg, Aug. 15, 1954; children: Eugene, Steven (dec.). BS, Stanford U., 1950; MS, PhD in Organic Chemistry, U. Wis., 1954. Chemist Shell Devel. Co., Emeryville, Calif., 1956-65; mgr. fiber chemistry br. Phillips Petroleum Co., Barlesville, Okla., 1965-70; dir. research projects Phillips Fibers Corp., Greenville, S.C., 1970-73; dir. strategic planning Phillips Fibers Corp., Greenville, 1973-86, dir. planning and budgeting, 1986—. Contbr. articles to tech. jours.; patentee in polymer and fiber field. Chmn. Salute to Edn., Greenville County, S.C., 1973. Served with U.S. Army, 1954-56. Mem. Planning Forum, Sigma Xi, Alpha Chi Sigma, Tau Beta Pi, Phi Lambda Upsilon. Lodge: Elks. Office: Phillips Fibers Corp PO Box 66 Greenville SC 29602

BERGER, STEPHEN, public agency executive; b. N.Y.C., July 11, 1939; s. Saul and Paula (Rosenzweig) B.; B.A., Brandeis U., 1959; m. Cynthia C. Wainwright, Sept. 24, 1977. Editor, Crowell-Collier Publs., N.Y.C., 1961-62; exec. asst. to Rep. Jonathan Bingham, N.Y.C., 1964-68; pres. PCM Corp., N.Y.C., 1969-73; exec. dir. N.Y. Study Commn. on N.Y.C., 1972-73; dir. Studies Commn. on Critical Choices for Ams., N.Y.C., 1973-74; commr. N.Y. Dept. Social Services, Albany, 1975-76; dir. N.Y. Office Planning Services, Albany, 1975; exec. dir. N.Y. Emergency Fin. Control Bd., N.Y.C., 1976; mem. N.Y. Bd. Social Welfare, 1977; dir. corp. devel. Oppenheimer & Co., Inc., N.Y.C., 1981-82; investment banker Odyssey Ptnrs., N.Y.C., 1983-85; chmn. U.S. Ry. Assn., Washington, 1980-87; prof. public adminstrn. N.Y.U., 1977-85; Bd. dirs., chmn. fin. com. N.Y. Met. Transp. Authority, 1979-85; exec. dir. Port Authority N.Y. and N.J., 1985—, Intergovtl. Policy Adv. Com. (office U.S. trade rep. 1988—). Served with U.S. Army, 1962-63. Democrat. Jewish. Office: Port Authority NY & NJ 1 World Trade Ctr New York NY 10048

BERGER, WILLIAM ERNEST, newspaper publisher; b. Ferris, Ill., June 6, 1918; s. William George and Ethel (Nelson) B.; student Carthage Coll., 1935-38; m. Jerry June Barnes, Feb. 26, 1943; children—William Edward, Barbara, John Jeffrey. Newspaper editor and pub., Hondo, Tex., 1946-65, 81—; commr. Tex. Water Rights Commn., Austin, 1965-69; pres. Assoc. Tex. Newspapers, Inc., 1957—; pres. South Tex. Press, Inc., Hondo, 1979—; owner Sta. KRME Hondo, 1969—. Treas., Medina Meml. Hosp., Hondo, 1962-64. Del., Tex. Democratic Conv., 1962, 64, 66, 68, Nat. Dem. Conv., 1968. Served with AUS, 1942-46. Mem. Tex. Press Assn. (pres. 1963), South Tex. Press Assn. (pres. 1954), Sigma Delta Chi (chpt. treas. 1967-69). Methodist. Clubs: Headliners, Lions (Hondo past pres.).

BERGERSON, DAVID RAYMOND, lawyer, manufacturing company executive; b. Mpls., Nov. 23, 1939; s. Raymond Kenneth and Katherine Cecille (Langworthy) B.; m. Nancy Anne Heeter, Dec. 22, 1962; children—W. Thomas C., Kirsten Finch, David Raymond. B.A., Yale U., 1961; J.D., U. Minn., 1964. Bar: Minn. 1964. Assoc. Fredrikson Law Firm, Mpls., 1964-67; atty. Honeywell Inc., Mpls., 1967-74, asst. gen. counsel, 1974-82, v.p., asst. gen. counsel, 1983-84, v.p., gen. counsel, 1984—; bd. dirs. Honeywell Fin. Inc., Mpls. Bd. dirs. Pillsbury United Neighborhood Services, Inc., Mpls., 1983—, officer, 1984—. Mem. ABA, Minn. State Bar Assn., Hennepin County Bar Assn., Am. Corp. Counsel Assn. (officer Minn. chpt. 1986, bd. dirs. Minn. chpt. 1987). Republican. Club: Minneapolis. Home: 2303 Huntington Point Rd E Wayzata MN 55391 Office: Honeywell Inc Honeywell Pla Minneapolis MN 55408

BERGESON, SCOTT, retail executive; b. Logan, Utah, Feb. 7, 1938; s. Harold E. and Reba M. (Butler) B.; m. Elaine Ann Johnson, Sept. 7, 1962; children: Eric S., Todd K., Paula A., Jill E., Amy K., Sean M. B.S., Brigham Young U., Provo, Utah, 1962, M.B.A., 1965. With Skaggs Cos., Inc., 1972-79, corp. sec., 1977-79; v.p., sec. Am. Stores Co., Salt Lake City, 1979-81; pres., chief exec. officer subs. co. Am. Stores Mgmt. Systems Co., 1981-83; exec. v.p. Am. Stores Co., 1983-86; chmn. bd., chief exec. officer Osco Drug , Inc., Oak Brook, Ill., 1987-88; sr. v.p. Am. Stores Co., Salt Lake City, 1989—. Democrat. Mormon. Office: Am Stores Co 5201 Amelia Earhart Dr Salt Lake City UT 84130-0658

BERGETHON, KAARE ROALD, educational consultant, former college president; b. Tromso, Norway, June 8, 1918; came to U.S., 1926, naturalized, 1930; s. Maximilian and Petra Rudd (Olsen) B.; m. Katherine Lind, Apr. 4, 1942; children: Bruce L., Peter R. A.B., DePauw U., 1938; M.A., Cornell U., Ithaca, N.Y., 1940, Ph.D., 1945; Litt.D., Brown U., 1959, Franklin and Marshall Coll., 1959; LL.D., Rutgers U., 1959, Muhlenberg Coll., 1959, Lehigh U., 1959, Waynesburg Coll., 1960, DePauw U., 1961, Gannon Coll., 1978, Lafayette Coll., 1978, Temple U., 1978, Allegheny Coll., 1979, Bloomfield Coll., 1980. With Walter Kidde Constructors Inc., N.Y.C., 1938-39, 41-44; instr. German Syracuse (N.Y.) U., 1945-46; instr. German Brown U., 1946-47, asst. prof. German, asst. to chmn. div. modern langs., 1947-52, assoc. dean, 1952-55, assoc. prof. German, 1953-58, dean, 1955-58, prof. German, 1958; pres. Lafayette Coll., Easton, Pa., 1958-78; pres. emeritus Lafayette Coll., 1978—; interim chief exec. and cons. Bloomfield (N.J.) Coll., 1979-80, interim pres., cons., 1986-87; vice chmn. Econ. Devel. Council of N.Y.C., Inc. and; exec. dir. Nat. Alliance of Bus. of N.Y.C., 1980-81; interim pres. New Eng. Coll., Henniker, N.H., 1981-82, pres., 1982-85; ednl. cons. Easton, 1985—; interim pres., cons. Wells Coll., Aurora, N.Y., 1987-88; bd. dirs. Am. Home Products Corp. Author: Grammar for Reading German, 1950, alt. edit., 1963, rev. edit., 1979, also articles in profl. publs. Past pres. Presbyn. Coll. Union; past pres. Middle States Assn. Colls. and Secondary Schs.; trustee Charlotte W. Newcombe Found., Princeton, N.J. Mem. Phi Beta Kappa, Phi Eta Sigma, Phi Kappa Phi, Beta Theta Pi, Sigma Delta Chi, Alpha Phi Omega. Presbyterian. Clubs: University (N.Y.C.), Northampton Country (Easton). Home: 303 Brynwood Dr Easton PA 18042

BERGEVIN, YVON JOSEPH, construction company executive; b. Shoreham, Vt., Aug. 30, 1942; s. Louis and Jeanne (DeForge) B.; m. Karen Gibson, June 13, 1970; children—Kristen, Christopher. B.A., U. Vt., 1964; M.B.A., U. Chgo., 1977. V.p. ops. F.A. Tucker, Inc., Rutland, Vt., 1968-72; v.p. Myers-Oak Comml. Constrn., Chgo., 1973; corp. estimator L. E. Myers Co., Chgo., 1974-77, equipment mgr., 1977-79; v.p. equipment Flintkote Stone Products, Hunt Valley, Md., 1979-82; exec. v.p. Genstar Stone Products Co., Hunt Valley, 1982-87; pres., chief operating officer The Driggs Corp., Capitol Heights, Md., 1987—. Bd. dirs. Md. Safety Council, Balt., 1984-87; mem. Greater Balt. Com., 1984—; div. chmn. United Way of Central Md., 1985-87, team chmn., 1987; mem. Montgomery County Civil War Roundtable, 1988—. Served to 1st lt. U.S. Army, 1964-66. Mem. Nat. Sand and Gravel Assn. (bd. dirs. 1985-87). Home: 10900 Edison Rd Potomac MD 20854 Office: The Driggs Corp 8700 Ashwood Dr Capitol Heights MD 20743

BERGFELD, C. DANIEL, management consultant; b. Bronxville, N.Y., Dec. 27, 1942; s. Albert Joseph and Elizabeth (Palmer) B. BA, Yale U., 1965; MMS, Stevens Inst. Technology, 1967. Cert. Mgmt. Cons. Program mgr. Office of the Mayor, City of N.Y., 1967-70; pres. Bergfeld & Assocs., 1971-73; sr. assoc. Cresap, McCormick & Paget, 1973-75; ptnr. Case and Co., 1976-82; mktg. dir. Coopers & Lybrand, N.Y.C., 1983-86, mgmt. cons. fin. services group, 1987—. Author: Strategic Pricing, 1981; contbg. author The Architect's Guide to Facility Programming, 1979. Trustee Westminster Choir Coll., Princeton, N.J. Mem. Inst. Mgmt. Cons., Am. Mktg. Assn., Swedish-Am. C. of C. Quaker. Clubs: Yale Club of N.Y.C., Blue Hill Troupe Ltd., Saugatuck Shores. Home: 300 Central Park W Apt 29H New York NY 10024 Office: Coopers & Lybrand 1251 Avenue of the Americas New York NY 10020

BERGHOLD, JOSEPH PHILIP, business executive; b. Allentown, Pa., Mar. 5, 1938; s. Joseph Norton and Cecilia (Boandl) B.; m. Kay Rose Binder, June 11, 1960; children: Karin A., J. Hans, Miles P. BA, Muhlenberg Coll., 1960; MBA, NYU, 1963; postgrad., Stanford U., 1973. Asst. treas. Polymer Corp., Reading, Pa., 1967-69; fin. v.p. Automated Health Systems, Burlingame, Calif., 1969-71, Six Flags, Inc., Los Angeles, 1972; v.p., treas., group v.p. internat. operations Koracorp Industries, San Francisco, 1973-80; v.p., treas. Levi Strauss & Co., San Francisco, 1980-82; sr. v.p., chief fin. officer Ryan Homes, Inc., Pitts., 1983-86; exec. v.p., chief fin. officer parent co. NVRyan, McLean, Va., 1987—; pres., chief exec. officer NVR Fin. Services Group, McLean, 1987—. Trustee Muhlenberg Coll.; mem. adv. bd. Sloan program Stanford U. Grad. Sch. Bus Adminstrn.; bd. dirs. Atlantic Coun. U.S. Sloan fellow, 1973. Mem. Nat. Investor Inst. Republican. Home: 340 Chesapeake Dr Great Falls VA 22066 also: Ryan Homes Inc 100 Ryan Ct Pittsburgh PA 15205

BERGLEITNER, GEORGE CHARLES, JR., investment banker; b. Bklyn., July 16, 1935; s. George Charles and Marie (Preitz) B.; m. Betty Van Buren, Oct. 29, 1966; children—George Charles III, Michael John, Stephen William. B.B.A., St. Francis Coll., Bklyn., 1959; M.B.A., Coll. City N.Y., 1961; Ph.D. in Bus. Adminstrn. (hon.), Colo. State Christian Coll. Dir. instl. sales A.T. Brod & Co., N.Y.C., 1965-66; dir. instl. sales Weis, Voisin & Cannon, Inc., N.Y.C., 1966-67, C.B. Richard, Ellis & Co., N.Y.C., 1967-68; pres. Stamford (N.Y.) Fin. Co., also bd. dirs.; pres. M.J. Manchester & Co., Fashion & Time, Inc., B.J.B. Graphics, Inc., First Coinvestors, Inc., Smart Fit Foundations, Inc., Jay Co., Computer Holdings Corp., Ltd., Delhi Mfg. Corp.; pres. Delhi Chems., Inc., Walton; chmn. bd. dirs. Delhi Industries, Delhi Mfg. Inc., Delhi Internat., Inc., Luxembourg, Bio-Life, Inc., Bio-Vite, Inc.; bd. dirs. Alpha Capital Corp., Am. Energy Mgmt. Corp., Stamford Fin., Electronic Tax Ctrs., Inc., Leonia Enterprises, L.I. Venture Capital Group, L.I. Venture Group, N.Y. Venture Capital Group, N.Y. Venture Group, Maritime Transp. & Tech., Inc., Vital Signs Inc., Delaware County Real Estate Corp., InterPharm Inc.; exec. v.p. Cove Abstract Corp., also bd. dirs.; mem. Nat. Stock Exchange, N.Y. Merc. Exchange, Phila.-Balt.-Washington Stock Exchange. Chmn. Franciscan Fathers Devel. Program, 1967-71; mem. President's Council, Franciscan Spirit award, 1959—; pres. South Kortright Central Sch.; chmn. No. Catskills Econ. Devel. Council.; Regent St Francis Coll.; bd. dirs. Econ. Devel. Council Delaware County, Printing Trade Sch., Community Hosp., Stamford, N.Y., Western Catskills Community Revitalization Council, Inc. Served with U.S. Army, 1952-55. Recipient St. Francis Coll. Alumni Fund award, 1965; John F. Kennedy Meml. award, 1972; Internat. award for service to investment comm., 1972; Paul Harris fellow Rotary Internat. Mem. Security Traders Assn. N.Y., Nat. Security Traders Assn., AIM, Cath. War Vets., Assn. Investment Bankers, Honor Legion N.Y.C. Police Dept., Coll. City N.Y. alumni assns. Republican. Club: Stamford Country. Lodges: KC, Moose, Rotary (pres. Stamford 1980-81, Paul Harris fellow). Home: Red Rock Rd Stamford NY 12167 Office: Stamford Fin Bldg Stamford NY 12167

BERGMAN, BRUCE JEFFREY, lawyer; b. N.Y.C., May 15, 1944; s. Lawrence A. and Myrna (Coe) B.; m. Linda A. Cantor, May 30, 1971; children: Jennifer Dana, Jason Cole. BS, Cornell U., 1966; JD, Fordham U., 1969. Bar: N.Y. 1970, D.C. 1987, U.S. Dist. Ct. (so. dist.) N.Y. 1971, U.S. Supreme Ct. 1973, U.S. Dist. Ct. (ea. dist.) N.Y. 1973, U.S. Ct. Appeals (2d cir.) 1973. Assoc. law firm Jarvis, Pilz, Buckley & Treacy, N.Y.C., 1970-76; ptnr. law firm Pedowitz & Bergman, Garden City, N.Y., 1976-80; dep. county atty. Nassau County, Mineola, N.Y., 1980-84; counsel Jonas Libert & Weinstein, Garden City, 1981-84; ptnr. Roach & Bergman, 1984—; adj. assoc. prof. NYU Real Estate Inst., N.Y.C., 1981—. Author: New York Mortgage Foreclosures, 1983; contbr. numerous articles to legal jours.; contbg. editor: Mortgages and Mortgage Foreclosure in New York, 1982. Councilman, City of Long Beach, N.Y., 1980-88. Mem. ABA, N.Y. State Bar Assn., Nassau County Bar Assn. (dir., chmn. real property law com.), Am. Coll. Real Estate Lawyers, Cornell Club (past pres.). Republican. Home: 12 Hawthorne Ln Lawrence NY 11559 Office: Roach & Bergman 600 Old Country Rd Garden City NY 11530

BERGMAN, BRUCE JOHN, electronics executive; b. Virginia, Minn., June 16, 1941; s. Elmer William and Mary Ann (Elias) B.; m. Janet Lee Phillips, Jan. 13, 1962; children: Rebecca, Bret. BEE, U. Minn., 1964; MBA, U. So. Calif., 1971. Devel. engr. Gen. Dynamics/Convair, San Diego, 1964-65; devel. engr. mgr. Honeywell, Inc., Mpls., 1965-71; gen. mgr. Control Data Corp., Mpls., 1971-83; chmn., chief exec. officer Xylogics, Inc., Burlington, Mass., 1983—. Author of various articles. Mem. Am. Electronics Assn. Republican. Lutheran. Club: Nashawtuc Country (Concord, Mass.). Office: Xylogics Inc 53 Third Ave Burlington MA 01803

BERGMAN, CHARLES EMMETT, marketing executive; b. Bklyn., Dec. 29, 1924; s. Charles Waldemar and Harriet Frances (McCoy) B.; m. Donna Marie Riedinger, Oct. 8, 1955; children: Therese Anne, Lise Marie. BEE, Clarkson U., 1950; MBA, Case Western Res. U., 1959. Mgr. mktg. Bailey Controls Co., Wickliffe, Ohio, 1950-86; cons. tech. mktg., Cleve., 1986—; SCORE cons. SBA; lectr. mktg. Case Western Res. U., 1960-65. Editor: KASH Directory, 1988. Advisor Jr. Achievement Program, Cleve., 1973. Served with U.S. Navy, 1943-46, PTO. Mem. Instrument Soc. Am., U. Club. Republican. Roman Catholic. Home: 2424 N Taylor Rd Cleveland Heights OH 44118-1336

BERGMAN, DANN WAYNE, training company executive; b. Cleve., May 26, 1953; s. Sanford Alvin and Carol Ileen (Sonkin) B.; m. Beverly Lynn May, June 23, 1974; 1 child, Erinn Nicole. BA, Toledo U., 1975, MEd, 1977; postgrad., Ohio U., 1971-74. Instructional tech. Courseware, Inc., San Diego, 1977-80, project dir., 1981-84; project dir. Solar Turbines, San Diego, 1980-81; dir. custom devel. McGraw-Hill Tng. Systems, Elmar, Calif., 1984-87; editorial dir. McGraw-Hill Tng. Systems, Del Mar, Calif., 1987-89; mktg. dir. Vital Learning Corp., Del Mar, 1989—; instr. Nat. U., San Diego, 1981—. Contbr. articles to profl. jours. Mem. Am. Soc. Tng. and Devel., Am. Telemktg. Assn., Nat. Soc. for Performance and Instrn. Office: Vital Learning Corp PO Box 641 Del Mar CA 92014

BERGMAN, JUDSON TAFT, banker; b. Crookston, Minn., Feb. 1, 1957; s. Clinton Benjamin and Juanita Jeanette (Moritz) B.; m. Susan Claire Heche, Nov. 3, 1979; children: Elliot, Elisabeth, Natalie. BA, Wheaton (Ill.) Coll., 1979; MBA, Columbia U., 1983. Assoc. John Nuveen & Co., N.Y.C., 1982-83; assoc. John Nuveen & Co., Chgo., 1983-85, asst. v.p., 1986, v.p., 1987, v.p. and dir. mergers and acquisitions, 1987—. Author: Merging Health Care Orgns., 1987. Del. Brit.-Am. Conf. for Successor Generation, St. Louis, 1988. Mem. Chgo. Coun. Fng. Rels., Lake Forest (Ill.) Club. Office: John Nuveen & Co Inc 333 W Wacker Dr Chicago IL 60606

BERGMAN, KLAUS, utility executive, lawyer; b. Nurnberg, Fed. Republic Germany, May 24, 1931; came to U.S., 1936; s. Ludwig and Else (Wertheimer) B.; m. Barbara E. Redman, Jan. 30, 1954; children: Nicole V.F., Cathryn L. AB, Columbia U., 1953, LLB, 1955. Bar: N.Y. Assoc. Mudge Rose Guthrie & Alexander, N.Y.C., 1959-65; asst. gen. counsel Am. Electric Power Service Corp., N.Y.C., 1965-71; v.p. Allegheny Power System, Inc., N.Y.C., 1971-82, exec. v.p., 1982-85, pres., chief exec. officer, dir., 1985—, chief exec. officer and dir. various subs.; now also chmn., chief exec. officer Monongahela Power Co., Fairmont, W.Va.; dir. Ohio Valley Electric Co., Piketon Ohio. Served to lt. (j.g.) USCGR, 1956-59.

BERGMANN, CARL KENZIG, corporate professional; b. Washington, Nov. 9, 1929; s. Everett A. Sr. and Anna Mae (Meany) B.; m. Lucy Allensworth Beremann, Nov. 5, 1955; children: Allison, Jeffrey, Cynthia, Diane, Catherine. Student, Georgetown U., 1948; BCS, Ben Franklin U., 1951, MCS, 1954. Various positions from exec. v.p., sec. to treas. Bergmann Ins., Arlington, Va., 1949—; pres. G & G Liquore Co.; exec. v.p., treas. Bergmann's Cleaning, Inc., Arlington; pres. Tri-State Laundry, 1987—. Served with U.S. Army, Korea. Mem. Internat. Fabric Inst. Republican. Roman Catholic. Lodge: KC. Office: Bergmann's Inc 2147 Lee Hwy Arlington VA 22201

BERGONZI, FRANK MICHAEL, retail drug store chain executive; b. Lebanon, Pa., Aug. 2, 1945; s. Michael D. and Dorothy M. (Burkholder) B.; m. Polly Ann Mayhoffer, June 24, 1967 (div. Apr. 1985); children: Megan Ann, Peter Michael; m. Gail Elizabeth Forbes, Nov. 25, 1986. BSBA, Susquehanna U., 1967. CPA, Pa. Staff acct. Main Hurdman, Harrisburg, Pa., 1967-69; asst. v.p., asst. controller Rite Aid Corp., Harrisburg, 1969-77, v.p., 1977-85, sr. v.p. fin., 1985—. Office: Rite Aid Corp PO Box 3165 Harrisburg PA 17011

BERGSLAND, THOMAS GRANT, manufacturing company executive; b. LaCrosse, Wis., Sept. 6, 1933; s. Grant Christian and Myrtle Helene (Staff) B.; m. Katherine Jeanne Smith, Sept. 7, 1957; children: Kristin, Erica, Emily, Peter. BSME, Northwestern U., 1956, MBA, 1957. Indsl. engr. Trane Co., LaCrosse, 1958-66, plant mgr., 1966-75, works mgr., 1975-81; gen. mgr. Crenlo, Inc., Rochester, Minn., 1981-83; pres. Elektro Assemblies, Inc., Rochester, 1983—; bd. dirs. Norwest Bank Rochester. Bd. dirs. Minn. Pub. Radio, Rochester. 1st lt. USAR, 1958-63. Mem. C. of C. (bd. dirs.), Lake City YachtClub, Rochester Golf and Country Club (bd. dirs.), Rotary Club (bd. dirs.). Republican. Episcopalian. Office: Elektro Assemblies Inc 522 NW 6th Ave Rochester MN 55901

BERGSTRESSER, PATRICIA ANN, media/promotion strategist; b. Ishpeming, Mich., Nov. 17, 1944; d. Valmore Paul and Irma Barbara (Parlato) Johnson; children: Christopher John, Scott Kenneth. Student, U. Grenoble, France, 1964. Various positions ABC (KGO-TV), 1973-74; pub. relations specialist Levinson and Assocs., Hollywood, Calif., 1975-76; freelance writer CBS, Hollywood, 1975-76; with Nat. Iranian Radio/TV, Tehran, 1978-79, CBS News, Tehran, Iran, 1979; freelance promotion San Francisco, 1980-85; founder Columbia Promotional Systems, 1985—. Media strategist campaign for Bd. Suprs., San Francisco; former mem. exec. bd. Sch. of the Arts; pub. relations com. World Affairs Council. Office: Press Club San Francisco 555 Post St San Francisco CA 94102

BERGSTROM, JOHN JACOB, manufacturing and research executive; b. Waterloo, Iowa, Nov. 29, 1925; s. Daniel Everett and Johanna Elizebeth (Hansen) B.; m. Jo Ann Straight, July 21, 1946; children: Becky Ann Forsberg, Lori Jo Ruhlman. BA, U. No. Iowa, 1949; postgrad., State U. Iowa, 1951-52. Mathematician Chamberlain Mfg. Corp., Waterloo, Iowa, 1954-55, project leader, 1955-58, engring. supr., 1958-66, asst. gen. mgr., 1966-70, gen. mgr., 1970-73; group v.p. Chamberlain Mfg. Corp., Elmhurst, Ill., 1973-79, exec. v.p., 1979-85, pres., 1985—, also bd. dirs.; bd. dirs. Mason Chamberlain Inc., Picayune, Miss., Mfg. Scis. Corp., Oakridge, Tenn., Saco (Maine) Def. Inc. Patentee in field; contbr. articles to profl. jours. Served with USN, 1943-46, PTO. Mem. Am. Def. Preparedness Assn. (bd. dirs. 1987—, Tech. Leadership award 1973, Firepower award 1986). Unitarian. Home: 1124 Perry Dr Palatine IL 60067 Office: Chamberlain Mfg Corp 845 Larch Ave Elmhurst IL 60126

BERK, ALAN S., accounting company executive; b. N.Y.C., May 11, 1934; s. Phil and Mae (Buchberg) B.; m. Barbara Binder, Dec. 18, 1960; children—Charles M., Peter M., Nancy M. BS in Econs., U. Pa., 1955; MS in Bus., Columbia U., 1956. Staff acct. Arthur Young & Co., N.Y.C., 1956-57; mgr., prin. Arthur Young & Co., 1957-67, dir., 1975—, ptnr., 1976—, chief fin. officer, 1984; sr. v.p. Avco Corp., Greenwich, Conn., 1967-75. With U.S. Army, 1957. Mem. Am. Inst. CPA's, N.Y. State Soc. CPA's, Fin. Execs. Inst. Clubs: Board Room (N.Y.C.); Burning Tree Country (Greenwich), Landmark. Home: 14 Cornelia Dr Greenwich CT 06830 Office: Arthur Young & Co Nat Office 277 Park Ave New York NY 10172

BERK, ALEXANDER, beverage company executive. Formerly v.p. Schenley Industries Inc., Dallas, to 1988, now pres., chief exec. officer, 1988—. Office: Schenley Industries Inc 12270 Merit Dr Ste 600 Dallas TX 75251 *

BERK, JAMES EDWARD, sales executive; b. N.Y.C., Sept. 26, 1945; s. Francis A. and Florence (Jacques) B.; m. Laureen L. Maroney, June 30, 1979; children: Kimberly Ann, Deborah Ann, James Joseph. BBA, CCNY, 1969, MBA, 1972. Product mgr. Garland Ranges, Maspeth, N.Y., 1965-72; v.p. sales White Consol. Industries, Greenville, Mich., 1972-78; v.p. mktg. Kelvinator Appliances div. White Consol. Industries, Grand Rapids, Mich., 1978-79; exec. v.p. Midland Electronics, Kansas City, Mo., 1979-80; sr. v.p. Western Auto, Kansas City, 1980-82; exec. v.p. Otasco div. Rapid Am., Tulsa, 1982-85; sr. v.p. Caldor, Norwalk, Conn., 1985-86; pres. Wholesale Club, Indpls., 1986—, also bd. dirs. Dir. West Mich. Health Systems, Grand Rapids, 1977-79; trustee Indpls. Civic Theatre, 1987—. Republican. Home: 11045 Queens Way Carmel IN 46032 Office: The Wholesale Club 7260 Shadeland St Indianapolis IN 46250

BERK, JAMES LAWRENCE, II, entertainment executive, television and motion picture producer, author, composer; b. Akron, Ohio, Aug. 2, 1960; s. James L. and Cheryl Berk. BA, Yale U., 1982; MBA, Duke U., 1984. Asst. to Pres. Multimedia Entertainment, N.Y.C., 1984-86, asst. to v.p. program mktg., 1986; pres. Platinum Entertainment, Inc., 1986—. Author: (screenplays) Digging Up Scotland, Blind Justice, Cellarfull of Dreams, Open Season; (musical compositions) Where Did I Go Wrong?, Tides Are Turning, In My Life, Living Without Your Love, Love Like Red Wine; (novels) The Making of Michael Helms, Open Season; (play) That's Life!; (television programs) Perfect Match, A Girl in a Million, Whereabouts, You Name It, Indecent Interval. Home: 1850 Indian Hills Trail Akron OH 44313 Office: Platinum Entertainment Inc 255 E 49th St PO Box 4C New York NY 10017

BERK, PEGGY FAITH, public relations/financial consultant; b. N.Y.C., Feb. 3, 1951; d. Stanley and Naomi Elaine (Herskowitz) B.; divorced; 1 child, Mason Ben-Yair. Student, NYU, 1968-71, New Sch. for Social Rsch., 1971-73. News editor Herald Newspapers, N.Y.C., 1972-73; mktg. liaison U.S. Dept. Commerce, Tel Aviv, Israel, 1973; mgr. fgn. currency dept. Bank Le'umi BM, Arad, Israel, 1974-75; exec. v.p. Peter Small & Assocs., N.Y.C., 1978-81; prin., pres. Strategic Communications, N.Y.C., 1981—; cons. sr. v.p. The Rowland Co., N.Y.C., 1984-85; prin., pres. BFP Internat. Inc., N.Y.C., 1987—; cons. Coun. on Fin. Aid to Edn., N.Y., 1979-81, Global Link, Tokyo, 1986—; bd. dirs. New Networking Aquisition Corp., Hartford, Conn., 1988. Contbr. numerous news articles. Bd. dirs. Child Net, Inc., Mass., 1987—. Mem. Citiwomen, Women's Am. ORT. Office: Strategic Communications 276 Fifth Ave New York NY 10001

BERKE, MICHAEL, marketing executive; b. N.Y.C., Apr. 28, 1939; s. Robert and Hanna B.; m. Monica Karen Mishkin, June 23, 1962; children: Alison Ruth, Adam Robert. BA in Mktg., NYU, 1967. Regional mgr. Continental Leasing Corp., Edison, N.J., 1968-70, Cavanaugh Leasing-Bank Va., Ft. Lee, N.J., 1971-72, Leasco Capital Equipment Corp., Great Neck, N.Y., 1972-75; v.p. mktg. Industralease Corp., Lake Success, N.Y., 1975-78; sr. v.p. mktg. Sussex Leasing Corp., Great Neck, 1978-85; sr. v.p. Eaton Fin. Corp., Framingham, Mass., 1985—. Contr. articles to profl. jours. Mem. Assn. Equipment Lessors (bd.dirs. 1986-88), Am. Assn. Equipment Lessors. Office: Eaton Fin Corp 27 Hollis St PO Box 9104 Framingham MA 01701

BERKLEY, ROGER LAWRENCE, textile manufacturing executive; b. Paterson, N.J., July 1, 1946; s. Robert Howard and Barbara Ina (Glasgall) B.; m. Elaine Deborah Gleich, Dec. 23, 1979; children: Daniel Harris, Sarah Rose. BA, Columbia U., 1968; cert. in mgmt., Am. Mgmt. Assn., 1987. Tchr. Fieldston Sch., Bronx, N.Y., 1970-72; asst. v.p. Weave Corp., Hackensack, N.J., 1973-78, v.p., 1978-83, exec. v.p., 1983-86, pres., 1986—. Candidate for mayor Borough of Woodcliff Lake, N.J., 1983; county committeeman Bergen County Dem. Orgn., Hackensack, 1982-83; mem., v.p. Bd. of Edn. Woodcliff Lake, 1984—. Mem. Am. Textile Mfrs. Inst. (upholstery fabrics com. 1979—, mktg. com. 1987—), Am. Mgmt. Assn., Men's Club Temple Emanuel, Wombats Softball. Democrat. Jewish. Office: Weave Corp 401 Hackensack Ave Hackensack NJ 07601

BERKMAN, JACK NEVILLE, lawyer, corporate executive; b. London, Eng., Feb. 12, 1905; came to U.S., 1908, naturalized, 1922; s. Hyman L. and Sarah (Hellman) B.; m. Sybiel B. Altman, Aug. 27, 1933 (dec. May 1964); children: Myles P., Monroe E., Stephen L.; m. Lillian Duban Rojtman, Jan. 26, 1970. AB, U. Mich., 1926; JD, Harvard U., 1929. Bar: Ohio 1930. Practiced in Steubenville, until 1968; chmn. bd., pres. Rust Craft Broadcasting Co.; operating Sta. WSTV-AM-FM-TV, Steubenville, Sta. WJKS-TV, Jacksonville, Fla., Sta. WRDW-TV, Augusta, Ga., Sta. WTYM, Tampa, Fla., Sta. WEYI-TV, Saginaw, Mich., Sta. WROC-AM-FM-TV, Rochester, N.Y., Sta. WRCP-AM-FM, Phila., Sta. WPIT-AM-FM, Pitts., Sta. WRCB-TV, Chattanooga, Sta. WWOL-AM-FM, Buffalo, N.Y., also Rust Craft Cable; vice chmn. bd., chmn. exec. com. Rust Craft Greeting Cards Boston, N.Y.C. and Pitts., (which also operated Rust Craft Ltd., Eng., Can., France), 1958-79; chmn., chief exec. officer, dir. Associated Communications Corp., N.Y.C., Pitts., 1979—. Subs. of ACC, Associated American Artists, N.Y.C., Celcom Commun. Corps. (Cellular operations, Pitts., Albany, Rochester, Buffalo, N.Y.), WSTV, Inc. Steubenville, (RAdio AM-FM), Past dir. Union Savs. Bank and Trust Co., Sinclair Bldg., Steubenville; past chmn. Tri-State Indsl. Commn. Author: (play) Playing God, 1931, also short stories, articles. Pres., trustee Sybiel B. Berkman Found., Steubenville; dir. emeritus Retina Found. Devel. Bd.; founding mem. Soc. of Friends, Japan House, N.Y.C.; Fellow Aspen Inst. Humanistic Studies; mem. Nat. Council of the Rockefeller U., adv. bd. Skin Cancer Found.; Nat. Council of Met. Opera; ABA, FCC Bar Assn.; Ohio Bar Assn. (past pres. jr. bar); Am. Soc. for Tehnion (life trustee); Harvard Law Sch. Assn., N.Y.; Internat. Radio & TV Soc. N.Y.C.; Special Rep. to 350th Anniversary Celebration of Harvard U.; mem. Dean's Adv. Council of Harvard Law Sch., Cambridge, Mass., mem. Bd. Overseers' Com. on Univ. Resources of Harvard Coll., Cambridge, Mass. Clubs: Harvard-Yale-Princeton, Variety (Pitts.); Friars, Harvard, Harmonie (N.Y.C.). Office: Associated Communications 680 Fifth Ave 11th Fl New York NY 10019

BERKMAN, MARSHALL L., manufacturing company executive; b. Steubenville, Ohio, 1936; (married). A.B., Harvard U., 1958, M.B.A., 1960, J.D., 1963. Pres. Rust Craft Greeting Cards, Inc., 1967-79; with Ampco-Pitts. Corp., 1979—, chmn., chief exec. officer, 1979—, also dir.; bd. dirs. Louis Berkman Co., Value Line, Inc., U.S. Biochem. Corp. Office: Ampco-Pitts Corp 600 Grant St Ste 4600 Pittsburgh PA 15219

BERKNESS, BRAD JOHN, systems analyst; b. St. Paul, Feb. 14, 1961; s. Richard Harvey and Nancy Jean (Alexander) B. BA in Econs., U. Wash., 1983. Systems analyst Boeing-Computing Mgmt. Orgn., Kent, Wash., 1984—; ptnr. Systems Design Cons., Seattle, 1988. Mem. Omicron Delta Epsilon. Home: 10912 SE 254th Pl Apt B101 Kent WA 98031 Office: Boeing Computing Mgmt Orgn PO Box 3707 Seattle WA 98124

BERKOFF, CHARLES EDWARD, pharmaceutical executive; b. London, Sept. 29, 1932; came to U.S., 1963; s. Maurice and Dora (Landy) B.; m. Frances Elaine Price, Aug. 17, 1961; children: Timothy, David, Kevin. BS in Chemistry, U. London, 1956, DIC, 1958; PhD, Imperial Coll., U. London, 1959. Chartered chemist. Dir. SmithKline Beckman Group, Phila., 1964-83; exec. v.p. ImuTech, Inc., Huntingdon Valley, Pa., 1983-84; pres., chief exec. officer Antigenics, Inc., Horsham, Pa., 1984—, Creative Licensing Internat., Inc., Horsham, 1987—; research assoc. Johns Hopkins U., Balt., 1959-60; sr. research fellow Southampton U., Eng., 1960-61; mem. Adv. Council Smithsonian Sci. Info. Exchange, Washington, 1976-82. Contbr. articles to profl. jours.; patentee numerous U.S. and fgn. patents. Monsanto Research fellow Imperial Coll. Sci. and Tech., 1956-59; Fulbright scholar, 1959-60; recipient Statue of Victory World Culture prize Centro Studi e Ricerche Delle Nazioni, 1985. Fellow Am. Chem. Soc., Royal Soc. Chemistry; mem. Entomol. Soc., Am. Inst. Chem. Engrs., Licensing Execs. Soc. Republican. Unitarian. Club: Engrs. Club of Phila. Home: 59 Twin Brooks Dr Willow Grove PA 19090 Office: Antigenics Inc 700 Business Center Dr Horsham PA 19044

BERKOVITCH, BORIS S., bank executive, lawyer; b. Odessa, Russia, Feb. 24, 1921; s. Samuel and Pauline B.; m. Barbara E. Sinclair, children—Joanne, Ellen. B.S., N.Y. U., 1947; LL.B., Columbia U., 1949. First dep. supt. banks State of N.Y., 1963-64; ptnr. Root Barrett Cohen Knapp & Smith, 1964-66; sr. v.p., gen. counsel J. P. Morgan & Co. Inc. and Morgan Guaranty Trust Co. of N.Y., N.Y.C., 1966-83, vice chmn. bd., 1983-86. Served with USMC, 1942-46, 51-52. Mem. Am. Law Inst., Assn. Bar City N.Y. Clubs: India House, County Limerick Hunt. Home: 55 Lincoln Ave Purchase NY 10577 Office: 23 Wall St New York NY 10015

BERKOWITZ, STANLEY BEHR, surgeon, medical consultant, business executive; b. Bklyn., Aug. 1, 1926; s. Arthur and Eva Berkowitz; m. Karen Dianne Daigger, 1964; children: Anthony Brett, Bruce Jordan. BA, Columbia U., 1947; MD, SUNY, N.Y.C., 1951. Diplomate Am. Bd. Surgery. Rotating intern Mt. Zion Hosp., San Francisco, 1951-52, resident in surgery, 1952-53, 54-56, chief resident surgeon, 1956-57; resident in neurosurgery U. Calif., San Francisco, 1953-54; pvt. practice surgery San Francisco, 1957-77; assoc. clin. prof. surgery U. Calif., San Francisco, 1969-78; med. cons. Calif. Dept. Health, Oakland, 1977—; hematology instr. SUNY, Bklyn., 1951; pres. Bask Industries, Burlingame, Calif., 1964—; med. dir. Zenith/Monarch Nat. Ins., Los Angeles, 1961-65; negotiator Calif. Physicians Union, Sacramento, 1983-85; ins. cons. No. Calif. Portuguese Fraternal Assn., Oakland, 1987—. Author: Differential Diagnosis: A Memory Tickler, 1967; creator med. software; contbr. articles to profl. jours. With U.S. Army, 1945-46. Recipient F.I. Harris award Mt. Zion Med. Ctr., 1952. Fellow ACS, Am. Coll. Quality Assurance and Utilization Rev. Physicians; mem. Internat. Soc. for Technology Assessment in Health Care, Union Am. Physicians (treas., bd. dirs. 1971-76). Democrat. Jewish. Home: 400 Dwight Rd Burlingame CA 94010 Office: Calif Dept Health Svcs 1433 Webster St Ste 100 Oakland CA 94612

BERKOWITZ, STEVE, publishing company executive. V.p. fin. and adminstrn. Macmillan Pub., N.Y.C. Office: Macmillan Pub 866 3rd Ave New York NY 10022 *

BERKSHIRE, GERALD LYNN, accountant; b. Wooster, Ohio, Feb. 6, 1951; s. Eugene Emerson and Bernice Leona (Korns) B.; m. Kathryn Jayne Mueller, July 30, 1977; children: Geoffrey Eugene, Jessica Lynne. BA in Acctg., U. Akron, 1973; MBA, Case Western Res. U., 1980. Tax auditor State of Ohio, Akron, 1973-75; tax acct. Standard Oil Co., Cleve., 1975-79; sr. tax acct. Warner & Swasey Co., Cleve., 1979-80; sr. tax analyst Sherwin-Williams Co., Cleve., 1980-81, mgr. state and local taxes, 1981-83, dir. money and banking, 1984—. Mem. Treas. Club of Cleve., Am. Mgmt. Assn., Nat. Assn. Corp. Treas. Home: 1165 Chatham Pl Rocky River OH 44116 Office: Sherwin Williams Co 101 Prospect Ave Cleveland OH 44115

BERKSON, ROBERT GARY, stockbroker; b. Bklyn., Feb. 14, 1939; s. Martin and Jeanne (Wolin) B.; B.S. in Econs., Hofstra U., 1960; m. Deanna Feinberg, Mar. 26, 1972. Sec./treas. Packer, Wilbur & Co., Inc., N.Y.C., 1961-70; pres. A.J. Carno Co., Inc., N.Y.C., 1971—; pres. Berkson's Bldg. Corp., N.Y.C., 1961—, with First Jersey Securities Inc., N.Y.C., 1975-80; chmn. The Triad Corp. Planning and Communications, Inc.; bd. dirs. Am. Friends of Haifa U.; v.p. Rob-Len Amusement Corp. Trustee Children's Med. Fund. of N.Y.; assoc. trustee L.I. Jewish Hosp. Mem. N.Y. Merc. Exchange. Clubs: Pine Hollow Country, Whitehall. Home: 50 Broadway New York NY 10004 Office: First Jersey Securities Inc 50 Broadway New York NY 10004

BERLIN, ALAN DANIEL, lawyer, oil company executive; b. Bklyn., Oct. 20, 1939; s. Joseph Jacob and Rose (Smith) B.; m. Renee Wellinger, Dec. 22, 1962; children—Nicole Suzanne, Allison Leigh. B.B.A., CCNY, 1960; LL.B., NYU, 1963, LL.M., 1968. Bar: N.Y. 1963. Assoc. Aranow, Brodsky, Bohlinger, Einhorn & Dann, N.Y.C., 1965-68; asst. counsel Gen. Electric Co., N.Y.C., 1968-70; tax counsel Norton Simon Inc., N.Y.C., 1970-77; pres. Belco Petroleum Corp., N.Y.C., 1977—; asst. prof. Pace U. Grad. Sch. Bus., 1977-85. Author monographs on fed. income tax. Bd. dirs. Mental Health Assn., Westchester; vice chmn. Briarcliff Manor (N.Y.) Peoples Caucus. Served with U.S. Army, 1963-65. Mem. Am. Bar Assn., N.Y. State Bar Assn., Assn. Bar City N.Y., Inter-Am. Bar Assn. Lodge: Masons. Office: 1 Dag Hammarskjold Pla New York NY 10017

BERLIN, BARRY NEIL, investment executive; b. Martinsville, Va., Dec. 6, 1954; s. Theodore and Zelda (Berlin). BS, U. Va., 1977; MBA, Northwestern U., 1978. Chartered fin. analyst. Econ. analyst, v.p. First Nat. Bank Tulsa, 1978-82; sr. counselor Wachovia Bank, Winston-Salem, N.C., 1983-87; v.p., mgr. First Wachovia Capital Mgmt., Atlanta, 1988—; mem. coun. examiners Inst. Chartered Fin. Analysts, Charlottesville, Va., 1984—. Participant Leadership Tulsa, 1982; trustee Temple Israel, Tulsa, 1981-82; com. co-chmn. Leadership Winston-Salem, 1984-85—; founder, chmn. Jewish Young Adults Tulsa, 1980-81; v.p. Temple Emanuel, 1985-87. Fellow Atlanta Soc. Fin. Analysts (bd. dirs.). Republican. Avocations: triathletics, bridge.

BERLIN, JEROME CLIFFORD, lawyer, accountant, real estate developer; b. N.Y.C., Aug. 23, 1942; s. Benjamin R. and Muriel (Weintraub) B.; BSBA, U. Fla., 1964, JD, 1968; m. Gwen Tischler, July 30, 1977; children: Bret Jason, Sharon Nicole, Ashley Lauren. Acct., Peat, Marwick, Mitchell & Co., Houston, 1968-69; mem. law firm Jerome C. Berlin, Miami, Fla., 1969-71; pres. Sterling Capital Investments, Inc., Miami, 1971-80; pres., chief operating officer Robino-Ladd Co., Del., also Inprojet Corp., Miami, 1974-80; individual practice law, Miami, 1980—. Chmn., Dade County Zoning Appeals Bd., 1971-73; chmn. bd. Signature Gardens, 1984—; chmn. bd. Duex Michel, Inc. 1984—; vice chmn. bd. dirs. Anti-Defamation League, 1979-83, chmn. Fla. regional bd., 1984-87, nat. commn. of Anti-Defamation League, 1981—; chmn. Fla. Com. of 100; mem. long-range planning com. Miami Children's Hosp., 1980— mem. citizens bd. Fla. Crime Prevention Commn., 1982; mem. world bd. dirs. Am. Israele Pub. Affairs Com., 1984-86, mem. exec. bd. dirs., 1987—; bd. dirs. Democratic Nat. Com., 1985—; bd. dirs., treas. Alexander Muss High Sch., Israel; nat. fin. chmn. Dem. Senatorial Campaign Com., 1987—; mem. exec. com. Dem. Nat. Fin. Council, 1985—; bd. dirs. Temple Beth Am., Miami; mem. exec. bd. Juvenile Diabetes Found., U. Miami Project Newborn; bd. overseers Hebrew Union Coll., 1983—. C.P.A., Fla., Tex. Mem. Am. Inst. C.P.A.s, Fla. Inst. C.P.A.s, Tex. Soc. C.P.A.s, Fla. Bar Assn., Am. Assn. Attys. and C.P.A.s, Fla. Thousand (chmn.), Fla. Soc. of Fellows (chmn.). Jewish. Home: 5425 SW 92d St Miami FL 33156

BERLIN, MARTIN H., electronics company executive; b. N.Y.C., Feb. 15, 1934; s. Jesse J. and Martha (Malawista) B.; m. Rosalyn Klein, Nov. 3, 1963; children: Allison Mara, Jonathan Evan. BS, NYU, 1954, MBA, 1960. Supr. Prod. Planning Budd Electronics Inc., L.I., N.Y., 1956-63; supr. inventory and material control ACF Electronics Inc., Paramus, N.J., 1963-65; mgr. materials Airtron div. Litton Industries, Morris Plains, N.J., 1965-66; mgr. materials planning Narda Microwave Inc., Plainview, N.J., 1966-68; dir. materials, v.p. Hazeltine Corp. div. Emerson Elec., Greenlawn, N.Y., 1968—. Loaned exec. Urban League, L.I., 1987. With U.S. Army, 1954-56. Mem. Elec. Industries Assn. (steering com. 1980—; past chmn., mem. materials procurement com.), L.I. Forum for Tech. (bd. dirs. 1985-86), Purchasing Mgmt. Assn. of N.Y., Am. Prodn. and Inventory Control Soc. Office: Hazeltine Corp Greenlawn NY 11740

BERLIN, STEVEN RITT, oil company financial official; b. Pitts., July 1, 1944; s. Sidney D. and Pauline (Ritt) B.; student Carnegie Mellon U., 1964-67; B.S. in Bus. Adminstrn., Duquesne U., 1967; M.B.A., U. Wis., 1969; m. Vera Y. Leffman, June 9, 1968; children—Leslie, Jessica, Loren. Prof., U. Houston, 1970-72; various fin. positions Cities Service Co., Tulsa, 1973-83; v.p. fin. Citgo Petroleum, Tulsa, 1983-85, gen. mgr., 1985-86, chief fin. officer, 1986—; speaker various industry, profl. seminars; instr. U. Tulsa. Bd. dirs. Tulsa Ind. Living Ctr.; sec., treas. Green T Club of Tulsa. Various univ. and govt. research grants; C.P.A. Mem. Am. Inst. C.P.A.s, Am. Acctg. Assn., Am. Inst. for Decision Scis., World Future Soc., Okla. Soc. C.P.A.s, Am. Assembly Collegiate Schs. Bus., Stanford U. Alumni Assn., Beta Gamma Sigma Alumni Club. Jewish. Avocations: jogging, reading. Home: 230 E 19th St Tulsa OK 74119 Office: Citgo Petroleum Corp PO Box 3758 Tulsa OK 74102

BERLINER, HENRY ADLER, JR., banker, lawyer; b. Washington, Feb. 9, 1934; s. Henry Adler and Josephine (Mitchell) B.; m. Bodil Iversen, Sept. 16, 1961 (div. Aug. 1984); children: Marie Christine, John Mitchell, George Iversen; m. Margaret Rouse, Sept. 22, 1985; 1 child, Meghan Mitchell. BA, U. Mich., 1956; JD, George Washington U., 1964. Bar: D.C. 1965, U.S. Supreme Ct. 1968. Assoc. Graighill, Aiello, Gasch & Craighill, Washington, 1964-66; asst. U.S. atty. Dept. Justice, Washington, 1966-67; ptnr. Berliner & Maloney, Washington, 1969-84; pres., chief exec. officer 2d Nat. Fed. Savs. Bank, Salisbury, Md., 1972—; chmn. Pennsylvania Avenue Devel. Corp., Washington, 1984-89. Contbr. articles to profl. jours. Chmn. D.C. del. Nat. Republican Conv., 1972, 76; mem., chmn. D.C. Commn. on Jud. Disabilities and Tenure, 1973-78; chmn. corp. adv. bd. Second Genesis, Inc., Bethesda, Md., 1985—. Lt USNR, 1956-59. Mem. Met. Club, Chevy Chase Club (Md.), Annapolis Yacht Club (Md.), Phi Delta Phi (internat. pres.), Sigma Chi. Episcopalian. Office: 2d Nat Fed Savs Bank 2045 West St Annapolis MD 21401

BERLINER, WILLIAM MICHAEL, business educator; b. Aug. 24, 1923; s. Samuel L. and Anna (Josephine) B.; m. Bertha A. Hagedorn, Apr. 27, 1946. B.S., N.Y. U., 1949, M.B.A., 1953, Ph.D., 1956. With Continental Casualty Co., 1941-42 45-46; retail div. mgr. B.F. Goodrich Co., 1949-50; asst. purchasing agt. Cutler-Hammer, Inc., 1950-51; mem. faculty N.Y. U., N.Y.C., 1951—; prof. mgmt. and orgnl. behavior, chmn. dept. mgmt. N.Y. U., 1965-74; dir., cons. OTI Services, Inc., 1958—; cons. Mfrs. Hanover Trust Co., 1956—; edn. adviser Am. Inst. Banking sect. Am. Bankers Assn., 1962—; Ford Found. cons. exec. program, N.Y.C. and Met. Area, 1961-65; mem. policy com. Regents Coll. Univ. of State of N.Y. Kellogg Found.; cons. exec. program Boys Clubs Am., 1962-67; faculty Stonier Grad. Sch. Banking, 1970—, Bank Personnel Grad. Sch., Am. Bankers Assn., 1980—; ednl. cons. Bank Adminstrn. Inst., 1976-81, Grad. Sch. Banking, U. Wis., 1982—, N.Y. State Bankers Assn., 1977—; policy and adv. com. Non-collegiate sponsored instrn. program, Univ. State of N.Y., 1983—, policy com. mem. Regents Coll. degrees, 1970—. Author: (with F.A. DePhillips and J.J. Cribbin) Management of Training Programs, 1960, (with W.J. McLarney (dec.) Management Practice and Training, Cases and Principles, 1974, Managerial and Supervisory Practice, 1979. Served to 1st lt. USAAF, 1942-45. Decorated D.F.C., Air medal with 6 oak leaf clusters, Purple Heart; Ford Found. grantee, 1960. Mem. Acad. Mgmt., Am. Soc. Personnel Adminstrn. (accredited personnel diplomate), Am. Mgmt. Assn., Am. Mktg. Assn., Beta Gamma Sigma, Alpha Kappa Psi. Home: 27 Perkins Rd Greenwich CT 06830 Office: NYU Grad Sch Bus Adminstrn 100 Trinity Pl New York NY 10006

BERLIOZ, GEORGES LOUIS, lawyer; b. Izieux, France, July 14, 1943; s. Louis Marie and Julie Marthe (Mollard) B.; B.A. with honors in Physics, U. Calif., Berkeley, 1963, B.A., LL.B., 1966; Lic. en Droit, U. Paris, 1969, D.E.S. Dr. Public, 1969, D.E.S. Dr. Prive, 1970, Dr. Droit with highest honors, 1971; m. Brigitte Anne Houin, July 4, 1974; 1 son, Pierre Roger Louis. Reader in physics U. Calif., Berkeley, 1961-63, research asst. law Boalt Hall, 1965-66; asst. U. Paris Law Sch., 1970-71; admitted to bar, 1969; prof. U. Lille Law Sch., 1971-75; lectr. U. Paris Law Sch., 1979—; avocat à la Cour de Paris, 1969—; sr. partner firm Berlioz, Ferry, David, Lutz, Rochefort, Paris, 1978—; sr. ptnr. firm Berlioz & Co., Paris, Brussels, London, N.Y.C.; mem. com. experts Codification Internat. Contracts, 1979; vis. lectr. internat. seminars. Sec.-gen., then pres. Union des Etudiants pour le Progrès, Paris, 1966-69. Maj. Walter Dinkelspiel scholar, 1964; John Woodman Ayer fellow, 1965. Mem. Internat. Bar Assn., Union Internat. des Avocats, Assn. des Docteurs en Droit, Assn. Droit et Commerce, Am. Tax Inst., Boalt Hall Alumni Assn. Author: Le Contrat d'Adhésion, 2d edit., 1976; co-author: L'Information et le Droit Privé , 1978; Les Eurocrédits, 1981; La loi française et l'activité internationale des entreprises; editor, Internat. Contract Law and Fin. Rev., 1980—; editorial advisor, corr. Jour. Bus. Law; contbr. articles to profl. jours. Home: 94 rue du Bac, Paris 75007 France Office: 68 Blvd de Courcelles, 75017 Paris France

BERLOW, ROBERT ALAN, lawyer; b. Detroit, Feb. 11, 1947; s. Henry and Shirley (Solovich) B.; m. Elizabeth Ann Goldin, Sept. 20, 1972; children: Stuart, Lisa. BA, U. Mich., 1968; JD, Wayne State U., 1971. Bar: Mich. 1971. Asst. to dean Wayne State U., Detroit, 1971-72; mem. Radner, Radner, Shefman, Bayer and Berlow, P.C., Southfield, Mich., 1972-78; gen. counsel Perry Drug Stores, Inc., Pontiac, Mich., 1978-80, gen. counsel, sec., 1980-82, v.p., gen. counsel, sec., 1982-88, sr. v.p., gen. counsel, sec., 1988—. V.p. United Hebrew Schs. Detroit, Southfield, Mich., 1987—. Mem. Mich. Bar Assn. (panelist real property sect. 1986, Homeward Bound series), Inst. Continuing Legal Edn. (panelist 1985, 87), Internat. Council Shopping Ctrs. (round table leader nat. law conf. 1986, 88). Office: Perry Drug Stores Inc 5400 Perry Dr PO Box 1957 Pontiac MI 48056

BERMAN, GEORGE RICHARD, planning consulting company executive; b. N.Y.C., Aug. 11, 1935; s. Arthur Harold and Claire Cecile (Blumenthal) B.; B.Chem. Engring., Yale U., 1956, M.Eng., 1960; M.B.A., Columbia U., 1963; m. Rochel Udovitch, Sept. 10, 1961; children—Joshua Asher, Jonathan Eli. Mktg. tech. rep. Monsanto Chem. Co., Springfield, Mass., 1960-62; process/project engr. Shell Chem. Co., Woodbury, N.J., 1963-65; dir. bus. planning Philip Morris U.S.A., N.Y.C., 1965-77; pres. Devon Mgmt. Resources, Inc., Yonkers, N.Y., 1977—; bd. dirs. Recall, Inc., Nat. Computer Ctr. for Indsl. Applications, Inc.; lectr. stats. and ops. research Richmond (Va.) Coll., 1967, NYU Grad. Sch. Bus., 1969; assoc. prof. ops. research Pace U., 1985—. Served to lt. USNR, 1956-59. Mem. Inst. Mgmt. Scis., N.Am. Soc. Corp. Planning, Am. Prodn. and Inventory Control Soc., Am. Inst. Chem. Engrs. Republican. Jewish. Clubs: Yale (N.Y.C.); Mory's. Contbr. articles to profl. jours. Office: 84 Franklin Ave Yonkers NY 10705

BERMAN, RICHARD JAY, investment banker; b. Mamaroneck, N.Y., June 25, 1942; s. Henry and Augusta (Taninbaum) B. BS, NYU, 1964, MBA, 1972; JD, Boston Coll., 1969; postgrad. Hague Acad. Internat. Law, 1969. Dir. mergers and acquisitions Norton Simon, Inc., N.Y.C., 1970-75; v.p. Bankers Trust Co., N.Y.C., 1975-80, sr. v.p., 1981-82; pres. Am. Acquisition Co., N.Y.C., 1982—, Henber Bldg. Corp., N.Y.C., since 1978—; founder Lindy Petroleum Corp., 1980; chmn. bd. dirs. Prestolite Battery Co.

Can.; bd. dirs. H. Brammer Corp., Bank Lease Cons., Inc., Profiles Internat., Inc. Contbg. author: (handbook) Mergers, Acquistions and Buyouts, 1981. Mem. bd. overseers NYU Bus. Sch.; mem. Republican Nat. Com., Mus. Modern Art. Mem. Boston Coll. Law Sch. Alumni Assn., NYU Alumni Assn., Sandwich Mus. Home and Office: 16 E 53d St 7th Fl New York NY 10022

BERMAN, RICHARD MILES, lawyer; b. N.Y.C., Sept. 11, 1943; s. Samuel and Sophie (Berman) B.; m. Emily Krasna, May 29, 1979 (div. Nov. 1983). BS, Cornell U., 1964; JD, NYU, 1967; diploma of comparative law U. Stockholm, 1968, internat. law, 1970. Bar: N.Y. 1971. Assoc., Davis Polk & Wardwell, N.Y.C., 1970-74; exec. asst. Sen. Jacob K. Javits, N.Y.C., 1974-78; gen. counsel, exec. v.p., dir. Warner Amex Cable Communications Inc., N.Y.C., 1978-86; gen. counsel, sec. MTV Networks Inc., N.Y.C., 1983-86; ptnr. LeBoeuf, Lamb, Leiby & MacRae, N.Y.C., 1986—; exec. dir. N.Y. State Alliance to Save Energy Inc., N.Y.C., 1977-78. Mem. fellowships and grants com. Am.-Scandinavian Found, N.Y.C., 1977-78; bd. dirs. Citizens Com. for N.Y.C. Inc., 1977—. Recipient 3 Am. Jurisprudence awards; Thord-Gray fellow Am.-Scandinavian Found, 1967-68; Donald Frank Sussman Meml. scholar Cornell U., Judge Valente, Clarence Palitz and Jacob Levy Found. scholar NYU Sch. Law, 1964-67. Mem. U.S. Jr. Davis Cup Squad (met. N.Y.C.), Assn. Bar City N.Y. Republican. Jewish. Avocations: tennis horseback riding, house restoration. Home: 230 E 73d St Apt 6E New York NY 10021 Office: LeBoeuf Lamb Leiby & MacRae 520 Madison Ave New York NY 10022

BERMAN, RICHARD PHILIP, retail executive, lawyer, accountant; b. Bklyn., Jan. 15, 1943; s. Louis and Anne Jean (Guskin) B. MA in Sci., Rutgers U., 1967; JD, NYU, 1969. Pres. World-Wide Assocs., N.Y.C., 1959, U. Colo., 1960-63, Badge-King Internat. Corp., 1963-65, World-Wide Assocs. Corp., 1965, Berman Assocs., 1965-68, Berman's Realty & Constrn. Corp., 1968-69, R. Philip Berman Esq. & Assocs., 1969-75, Berman's Empire Diamond Jewelry & Antiques, Forest Hills, N.Y., 1975—. Mem. Assn. Trial Lawyers Am., Internat. Assn. CPAs, N.Y. State Soc. CPAs, Pub. Rels. Am. Home and Office: 98-15 Horace Harding Expy Forest Hills NY 11368

BERMAN, STANLEY, retail executive; b. Quincy, Mass., Jan. 25, 1934; s. Benjamin and Sophie (Katz) B.; m. Sandra Wolff, June 1, 1955; children: David, Terri Duff. BA, U. Mass., 1956; postgrad. Program for Mgmt. Devel., Harvard U., 1969. Various acctg. positions leading to div. controller Grossman's Inc., Braintree, Mass., 1953-69; v.p., controller Evans Retail Group, Braintree, 1970-78; exec. v.p. adminstrn. Grossman's Inc., Braintree, 1978—; pres. Grossman Employee Fed. Credit Union, Braintree, 1960. Mem. Home Ctr. Leadership Council, 1985—; pres. Temple B'Nai Shalom, Braintree, 1971. Office: Grossman's Inc 200 Union St Braintree MA 02184

BERMAN, STEWART, data processing executive; b. N.Y.C., Oct. 13, 1944; s. Jack Joseph and Julia (Segal) b.; m. Sarah Vida Isaacoff; children: Alisa Gwen, Franklin Seth, Shari Aviva. BEE, CCNY, 1966, MEE, 1969; MBA in Acctg., Fordham U., 1978. Engr. Edo Corp., Queens, N.Y., 1966-69, GT&E Rsch. Lab., Queens, 1969-72; systems programmer MTA, N.Y.C., 1972-75; ptnr. Coopers and Lybrand, N.Y.C., 1975—; bd. dirs. Riverbay Corp., Bronx, N.Y., 1979-86. Pres. Coop City Dem. Club, Bronx, N.Y., 1988—; dist. leader 81st Assembly Dist. Bronx County, N.Y., 1988—. Mem. IEEE, Assn. for Computing Machinery, Knights of Pythias. Democrat. Jewish. Home: 34 B Adler Pl Bronx NY 10475 Office: Coopers & Lybrand 1251 Ave of the Americas New York NY 10020

BERMAS, STEPHEN, lawyer; b. N.Y.C., Apr. 27, 1925. BS, Cornell U., 1949, D in Juridical Sci., 1950; LLM, NYU, 1957. Bar: N.Y. 1950. Assoc. Wagner, Quillinan, Wagner & Tennant, N.Y.C., 1950-51; law sec. to chief justice U.S. Dist. Ct. (so. dist.) N.Y., N.Y.C., 1951-55; assoc. Gordon, Brady, Caffrey & Keller, N.Y.C., 1955-59; ptnr. Medine & Bermas, N.Y.C., 1959-63, Feltman & Bermas, N.Y.C., 1964-66; sr. atty. Columbia Gas System Corp., N.Y.C., 1966-69; asst. gen. counsel Continental Group Inc., N.Y.C., 1970-77, assoc. gen. counsel, 1978-82; v.p., gen. counsel Continental Can Co. Inc., Norwalk, Conn., 1982-86, exec. v.p., gen. counsel, 1987—; instr. law Queen's Coll, N.Y.C., 1964-68. Mem. ABA, N.Y. State Bar Assn., Nassau County Bar Assn. Office: Continental Can Co Inc 800 Connecticut Ave Norwalk CT 06856

BERN, RONALD LAWRENCE, construction company executive; b. Anderson, S.C., Aug. 23, 1936; s. Samuel Harris and Minnie (Siegel) B.; m. Elaine Kay Lefkowitz, Dec. 25, 1960; children: Brett Alan, Melissa Lynn. BA in Journalism, U. S.C., 1958, MA in Journalism, 1961. Writer William Barton Marsh Co., N.Y.C., 1958-59; editor, writer Univac div. Sperry Rand, N.Y.C., 1959-60; editor, mgr. Bell Telephone Labs., N.Y.C., 1961-63; pres. Ronald Bern Co., N.Y.C., 1964-85; corp. sr. v.p. The LVI Group, Inc., N.Y.C., 1985—; cons. AT&T Co., N.Y., N.J., 1966-85; bd. dirs. NICO Constrn. Co., N.Y., Space Design Group, N.Y., Talon Corp. Author" An American in the Making, 1960, The Successful Salesman, 1972, The Legacy, 1975; contbr. articles to profl. publs. Bd. dirs. North Brunswick Little League, N.J., 1975-79; mem. North Brunswick Planning Commn., 1984. Served with U.S. Army, 1958-59, 61-62. Fellow S.C. Press Assn., 1960. Mem. South Caroliniana Soc. Democrat. Jewish. Home: 37 Hidden Lake Dr North Brunswick NJ 08902 Office: The LVI Group Inc 345 Hudson St New York NY 10014

BERNARD, DAVID A., investment advisor; b. Toronto, Ont., Can., Dec. 19, 1945; s. Seymour and Evelyn (Gensior) B.; m. Francine Claire Gouvin, Oct. 24, 1981; children: Claire Rose, Maximilian David. Student, Columbia U. Pres. D.A. Bernard & Co., N.Y.C., 1967-74, Tower Funding, Inc., N.Y.C., 1974-79; v.p. MCANY, Inc., N.Y.C., 1979-81; bd. dirs. Concord Assets Group, Inc., N.Y.C., 1981—. Dir. Com. for a Rep. Assembly, Albany, N.Y., 1983—. Clubs: The Sky , N.Y. Croquet (N.Y.C.). Home: 234 Park Ave Palm Beach FL 33480

BERNARD, FORSYTHE, oil company executive; b. N.Y.C., Jan. 3, 1928; s. Elimelich Max and Frances Fannie (Waxman) N.; m. Jane Louise England, Aug. 5, 1983 (div. Dec. 1987). Student, Midwestern State U., 1945-49. Expeditor Chance Vought Aircraft Co., Grand Prairie, Tex., 1952-54; photographer Color Lab . Cleve., 1955-57; chief exec. officer N. Ohio Photography, Loraine, 1957-58; traveling salesman Pitts. Gartor Co., Columbus, Ohio, 1958-61, Pa-Je Jewelry, Columbus, 1961-62; chief exec. officer A-1 Driver Tng. Sch., Dallas, 1962-70; cantor Niesenson's Jewish Broadcasting Svc., Cleve., 1970-77; social svc. worker III Cuyahoga County, Cleve., 1978-84; adminstr. Brit. Petroleum Co., Cleve., 1988—. Candidate for U.S. Senate from Tex., 1966. With USN, 1949-50. Mem. Jewish War Vets. (sr. vice comdr. Dallas 1965-69). Home: 1710 Prospect Ave Cleveland OH 44115 Office: Brit Petroleum Co 200 Public Sq Cleveland OH 44114

BERNARD, JACQUELYN LEE, brokerage house executive; b. New Orleans, June 5, 1958; d. Louis Joseph and Shirley Ann (Barnes) B.; m. Danny Ray Hurst, July 11, 1981 (div. 1984). BS, U. Tenn., 1982. CPA, Tenn. Affiliate broker Southland Realty Co., Dyersburg, Tenn., 1977-78; auditor Newbill and Henry, Dyersburg, Tenn., 1980-82, Peat Marwick Mitchell and Co., Memphis, 1982-83; controller Mike Rose Oil Co., Trenton, Tenn., 1983-84; investor acctg. mgr. Union Planters Nat. Bank, Memphis, 1984; computer conversion cons. First Nationwide Mortgage Strategies, Memphis, 1985-86; fin. cons. Vining-Sparks Securities Inc., Memphis, 1986-88, securities broker, 1988—; instr. in acctg. Mid-South Voct. Sch., W. Memphis, Ark., 1983. mem. TWIGS Together We Initiate Growth support group for LeBon Heur Children's Hosp., Memphis, 1987—. Mem. AICPA, Tenn. Soc. CPAs., Phi Kappa Phi. Republican. Methodist. Home: 6564 Whitetail Ln Memphis TN 38115 Office: Vining-Sparks Securities Inc 889 Ridgelake Blvd Memphis TN 38119

BERNARD, JACQUES NIELS, venture capitalist; b. Lyons, Rhone, France, Sept. 27, 1938; s. Rene G. and Eliette S. (Granyi) B.; m. Sophie M. Blanc, Dec. 21, 1960; children: Jean-François, Laurence, Nicolas. M.Sc., Ecole Polytechnique, Paris, 1960; B.A., Faculté de Droit et Scis. Economiques, Paris, 1964. Mktg. mgr. Schlumberger, Mpls., Paris, 1965-69; planner, planning mgr. IBM Systems Devel. Div., Nice, France, Harrison, N.Y., 1969-74; product line mgr. IBM-Europe, Paris, 1974-78; dir. Consultronique, Paris, 1979-82, mng. dir., 1982-88; geschaeftsfuhrer Consultronik, Frankfurt, W.Ger., 1983-88; dir. Leisystem S.A., Lyons, France, 1981-87; gen. ptnr. Tech. Investment Ptnrs., Paris, San Francisco, 1988—; mem. conf. bd. Served to lt. French Army, 1960-62. Recipient Medaille Commemorative Algerie, 1962. Mem. Institut de l'Enterprise (conf. bd.), Am. C. of C. (Frankfurt, Paris). Roman Catholic. Home: 8 Rue de Jarente, 75004 Paris France

BERNARD, JAMES WILLIAM, industry executive; b. Brainerd, Minn., June 25, 1937; s. Paul Raymond and Maybelle Gertrude (Fynskov) B.; m. Maureen Day, Sept. 6, 1958; children: David, Kenneth, Kathleen. BS, U. Oreg., 1960. Trainee Univar Corp., San Francisco, 1960-61; resident mgr. Univar Corp., Honolulu, 1961-65; sales mgr. Univar Corp., San Francisco, 1965-67; v.p. Univar Corp., Phoenix, 1967-71; v.p. Univar Corp., San Francisco, 1971-74, corp. v.p., 1974-82; sr. v.p. Univar Corp., Seattle, 1982-83, exec. v.p., 1983-86, pres., chief exec. officer, 1986—, also bd. dirs.; bd. dirs. U. Wash. Exec. MBA Program, Seattle, 1984—, VMR Corp., Bellevue, Wash. Mem. Am. Chem. Soc., Seattle C. of C., Columbia Tower Club, Rainier (Seattle) Club. Republican. Office: Univar Corp 801 Second Ave Ste 1600 Seattle WA 98104

BERNARD, KENNETH JOHN, manufacturing executive; b. Bridgeport, Conn., Jan. 8, 1958; s. Frank A. and Elizabeth (Hirsh) B.; m. Bonnie E. Slama, June 15, 1985; 1 child, Katherine. BA, Tufts U., 1980; MBA, U. Balt., 1986. Service rep. Otis Elevator/United Tech., Balt., 1981-83, sales rep., 1983-86; br. mgr. Otis Elevator/United Tech., Stamford, Conn., 1987—. Republican.

BERNARD, PHILIP JOSEPH, investment company representative; b. Alexandria, La., Mar. 17, 1959; s. Philip J. and Carol A. (Boudreaux) B.; m. Mary D. Schaff, May 4, 1985. BS in Bus. Adminstrn., U. New Orleans, 1984. Registered rep. Pioneer Western Investment Group, Metairie, La., 1984—. Recipient Trail Blazer award, 1985, Pioneer Club award, 1987. Mem. Nat. Assn. Securities Dealers. Republican. Office: Pioneer Western Investment Group 3330 W Esplanade Ave Ste 310 Metairie LA 70002

BERNBACH, JOHN LINCOLN, advertising executive; b. 1944; s. William Bernbach. Grad. polit. sci., Georgetown U. Trainee account mgmt., then v.p. account services Gilbert Advt., 1966-72; with DDB Needham Worldwide, Inc. (formerly Doyle Dane Bernbach), Paris, 1972-79, London, 1979-84; pres., chief exec. officer internat. div. DDB Needham Worldwide, Inc. (formerly Doyle Dane Bernbach), N.Y.C., 1984-86, pres., 1986—. Office: DDB Needham Worldwide Inc 437 Madison Ave New York NY 10022

BERNDT, JOHN EDWARD, telecommunications company executive; b. Hartford, Wis., May 22, 1940; s. Alvin John and Myra Rosalie (Scherger) B.; m. Donna Jean Harker, June 15, 1963; children: Susan, Andrew, Carolyn, Mary. BSEE, U. Wis., 1963. Various technical and mgmt. positions Wis. Telephone Co., 1961-79; asst. v.p. bus. svcs. AT&T, Basking Ridge, N.J., 1979-83; v.p. market planning AT&T Internat., Basking Ridge, 1983-85, pres., chief exec. officer, 1985-87; sr. v.p. internat. svcs. AT&T Bus. Markets, Morristown, N.J., 1987-89; pres. AT&T Internat. Comml. Svcs., Morristown, 1989—. Mem. policy adv. com. U.S. Trade Rep. Svcs., Washington, 1987—, Nat. Adv. Coun. Bus. Edn., N.Y.C., 1987—, bd. visitors Fuqua Sch. Bus. Duke U., Durham, N.C., 1987—, bd. advisors Ctr. Internat. and Strategic Studies, Washington, 1986—; trustee Am. Grad. Sch. Internat. Mgmt., Phoenix, 1986—, Internat. Inst. Communication, London, 1989—; bd. dirs. Bus. Coun. Internat. Understanding, N.Y.C., 1986-87, U. Wis. Found., Madison, 1987—. Recipient disting. svc. award Coll. Engring. U. Wis., Madison, 1988; named Officer de l'Order de la Couronne Govt. Belgium, Brussels, 1989. Mem. IEEE, Coun. Fgn. Rels., Fairmount Country Club (Chatham, N.J.), Chatham Squash and Racquet Club. Republican. Presbyterian. Office: AT&T 412 Mt Kemble Ave Rm N503 Morristown NJ 07960

BERNER, ARTHUR SAMUEL, finacial institution executive; b. N.Y.C., Nov. 12, 1943; s. Hyman and Sylvia Berner; BA, CCNY, 1964; JD, NYU, 1967; children: Jocelyn, Evan. Bar: N.Y. 1967, Tex. 1980. Assoc. firm Cahill & Gordon, N.Y.C., 1967-70; with Inexco Oil Co., Houston, 1970-85, v.p. legal, sec., 1972-85; exec. v.p., gen. counsel, corp. sec. United Fin. Group Inc., Houston, 1985—. Bd. dirs. Soc. Performing Arts, Houston Grand Opera, Houston Symphony, Tex. Opera Theatre, Delia Stuart Dance Co., Jewish Fedn., Jewish Community Ctr., Jewish Family Service, Anti-Defamation League; pres. Am. Jewish Com.; bd. dirs. Ctr. Internat. Affairs. Mem. ABA, Houston Bar Assn., City Bar Assn., Tex. Bar Assn., N.Y. State Bar Assn. Jewish. Office: United Fin Group Inc 5718 Westheimer Ste 2200 Houston TX 77057

BERNER, LAWRENCE MICHAEL, holding company executive; b. New Orleans, Sept. 26, 1942; s. Paul Louis and Mary Louise Berner; m. Diane Rita Muhs, May 22, 1965 (div. 1968); m. Doris Marie Chancey, July 29, 1972; children: Dana Marie, Lauren Theresa. BS in Acctg., U. New Orleans. CPA, La. Audit mgr. Peat, Marwick & Mitchell, New Orleans and Balt., 1964-70; treas. Mech. Equipment Co., New Orleans, 1971; acctg. mgr. Stewart Enterprises, Inc., New Orleans, 1971-72, v.p. fin., 1972-80, exec. v.p., 1980-84, pres., 1984—. Served with USNG, 1965-71. Mem. Am. Inst. CPA's, La. Soc. CPA's, Fin. Execs. Inst. Republican. Roman Catholic. Clubs: Colonial Golf and Country (Harahan, La.) (pres. 1981-85); Metairie (La.) Country. Office: Stewart Enterprises Inc 110 Veterans Memorial Blvd Metairie LA 70005

BERNETT, THEODORE BYRON, educator, management consultant; b. Chgo., Aug. 30, 1924; s. Joseph and Julia (Gorski) B.; B.S. in M.E., U. Ill., 1950; student bus. adminstrn., U. Wis., Milw., 1953-54; m. Helen Brower, Apr. 23, 1949; children—Richard, Michael, James. Julie, Amy. founder T.B. Bernett & Assos., Kenosha, Wis., 1980—. Served with USNR, 1943-46. Home: 6622 59th Ave Kenosha WI 53142-2931

BERNEY, JOSEPH HENRY, appliance manufacturing company executive; b. Balt., May 7, 1932; s. Eugene Philip and Blanche (Ney) B.; m. Phyllis Pearlove, Jan. 18, 1956; children: Richard, Philip, Julia, David. BS, U. Pa., 1953; MS, Columbia U., 1954. C.P.A., Va., Wis. Staff acct. Touche, Niven, Bailey & Smart, C.P.A.s, N.Y.C., 1954, A.M. Pullen & Co., C.P.A.s, Richmond, Va., 1954-56; vice chmn. Nat. Presto Industries, Inc., Eau Claire, Wis., 1956—, also bd. dirs.; officer, bd. dirs. Nat. Holding Investment Co., Canton Mfg. Corp., Jackson Sale & Storage, Presto Mfg. Co., Nat. Pipeline Co. Bd. dirs. Outward Bound, Inc., United Fund Eau Claire, U. Wis.-Eau Claire Found., Eau Claire YMCA, Minn. Outward Bound Sch.; past pres. Chippewa Valley council Boy Scouts Am. Mem. Am. Inst. C.P.A.s, Va., Wis. socs. accountants, Beta Gamma Sigma, Delta Sigma Rho. Home: PO Box 1331 Eau Claire WI 54702 Office: care Nat Presto Industries Inc 3925 N Hastings Way Eau Claire WI 54703

BERNHARDT, ARTHUR DIETER, housing consultant; b. Dresden, Germany, Nov. 19, 1937; came to U.S., 1966; s. Rudolf B. and Charlotte (Bernhardt). Dipl. Ing., U. Tech., Munich, W. Ger., 1965; postgrad., U. So. Calif., 1966-67; M. City Planning, MIT, 1969. In various postions with bldg. projects 1965-68; dir. Program in Industrialization of Housing Sector, MIT, Cambridge, 1969-76, pres., 1977—; chief exec. officer, dir. Program in Industrialization of Housing Sector, MIT, Cambridge and N.Y.C., 1989—; internat. housing industry cons., Cambridge, Mass. & N.Y.C., 1973—; asst. prof. MIT, 1970-76. Author book; contbr. articles to profl. jours. Mem. exec. com. Mass. Gov.'s Adv. Com. on Manufactured Housing, 1974-75; NRC del. 8th Gen. Assembly Internat. Council Bldg. Research, 1974. Fed. Republic Germany fellow, 1965, 66, 67, 68; MIT fellow, 1968, 69; MIT grantee, 1970; Fed. Republic Germany grantee, 1965; Alfred P. Sloan Found. grantee, 1970; Dept. Commerce grantee, 1972; HUD grantee, 1972, 74. Mem. Internat. Council Bldg. Research, Am. Acad. Polit. and Social Sci., Am. Planning Assn., Deutscher Hochschulverband, Am. Judicature Soc. (assoc.). Home: New York NY Office: PO Box 2288 New York NY 10185

BERNHARDT, LEWIS JULES, retired brokerage executive, novelist; b. N.Y.C., Sept. 22, 1937; s. Henry and Jean Bernhardt; m. Rochelle Solomon, Aug. 7, 1960; children: Marc Stuart, Jay Michael. BA, U. Md., 1964, MA, 1965; MA, Princeton U., 1967, PhD, 1970. Asst. prof. Rutgers U., New Brunswick, N.J., 1970-76; from sales trainer, account exec. and analyst to v.p. Halpert Oberst & Co., Millburn, N.J., 1976-83; 2d v.p., fin. cons. Shearson, Lehman Bros., East Brunswick, N.J., 1983-87; v.p., dir. mktg., sales trainer Baird, Patrick Capital Group, Inc., West Orange, N.J., 1987—; Bulgarian exchangee Internat. Research & Exchange Bd. in affiliation with Kliment Ohhrid Univ., 1971, Soviet exchangee Internat. Research & Exchange Bd. in affiliation with Moscow State Univ., 1973. Editor: Poems and Idylls of Saul Chernikhovsky, 1974; author computer tutorials, RUSSJAZ, 1974. Served with U.S. Army, 1960-63. Ford Found. Regional Studies fellow, 1968. Jewish. Club: Princeton (N.Y.C.). Lodge: B'nai Brith (v.p. local chpt. 1979-83). Home: 5 Norton Rd East Brunswick NJ 08816 Office: 5 Norton Rd East Brunswick NJ 08816-1703

BERNICK, HOWARD BARRY, manufacturing company executive; b. Midland, Ont., Can., Apr. 10, 1952; came to U.S., 1974, naturalized, 1976; s. Henry and Esther (Starkman) B.; m. Carol Lavin, May 30, 1976; children: Craig, Peter, Elizabeth. B.A., U. Toronto, Ont., 1973. Investment banker Wood Gundy Ltd., Toronto, 1973-74, First Boston Corp., Chgo., 1974-77; dir. of profit planning Alberto Culver Co., Melrose Park, Ill., 1977-79, v.p. corp. devel., 1979-81, group v.p., chief fin. officer, 1981-85, exec. v.p., 1985-88, pres., chief operating officer, 1988—, also bd. dirs. Office: Alberto-Culver Co 2525 Armitage Ave Melrose Park IL 60160

BERNINGER, RONALD WILLIAM, biochemist; b. Bloomsburg, Pa., Apr. 3, 1945; William Jackson and Bethena (Peckne) B.; m. Virginia Wise, Aug. 3, 1968. BS in Chemistry, Drexel U., 1968; PhD, U. Pitts., 1972. Fellow in immunology Johns Hopkins U. Sch. Medicine, Balt., 1975-77, instr., 1977-79, asst. prof., 1979-80; asst. prof. Tufts U. Sch. Medicine, Boston, 1980-86; sr. scientist NeoRx Corp., Seattle, 1986—; mem. Biomedical Research Grant Support Com., Boston, 1982-86; site visit mem. Nat. Inst. Health, Washington, 1980, mem. spl. rev., 1985-86; reviewer profl. jours., 1977-86. Author: Alpha-1-Andtrypsin Laboratory Manual, 1978; contbr. articles to profl. jours. Served as capt. U.S. Army, 1972-75. Mem. AAAS, Am. Chem. Soc., N.Y. Acad. Sci. Lutheran. Home: 10018 64th Pl W Everett WA 98204 Office: NeoRx Corp 410 W Harrison Ave Seattle WA 98119

BERNOSKY, HERMAN GEORGE, retail gasoline dealer; b. Minersville, Pa., Aug. 16, 1921; s. Peter and Mary Bernosky; student Rider Coll., Trenton, N.J., 1947-48. With Bernosky's Exxon Sta., Llewellyn, Pa., 1940-42, 46—, owner, operator, 1949—. Treas. Minersville Area Bicentennial, 1976. Served with AUS, 1942-46; ETO. Decorated Bronze Star (3). Mem. Internat. Platform Assn., Am. Legion. Democrat. Roman Catholic. Club: Minersville Lions (past pres., dir. 1957—). Home: 622 Lytle St Minersville PA 17954 Office: PO Box 170 Llewellyn PA 17944

BERNSTEIN, AARON, retail apparel executive; b. Minsk, Russia, Oct. 30, 1904; came to U.S., 1908, naturalized, 1940; s. George and Anna B.; student public schs., N.Y.C.; m. Ida Lebowitz, June 3, 1928; children: Charlotte Strauss, Gloria Sir. Gen. mgr. Gordon Dept. Store, West Point, Miss., until 1940; pres. Ruth Shops, Inc., Columbus, Miss., 1940—. Jewish. Office: Ruth Shops Inc 101 104 109 S 5th Main St Columbus MS 39701

BERNSTEIN, ALLEN RICHARD, publishing executive; b. Chgo., Feb. 14, 1941; s. Harry and Esther (Sider) B.; m. Barbara Elaine Rottenberg, May 7, 1972; children: Howard, David, Michael. BS, Calif. Inst. Tech., 1962; MA, UCLA, 1964, PhD, 1965. Pres. Acad. Info. Service Inc., Bowie, Md., 1974—. Author: Tax Guide for College Teachers, 1989, Tax Guide for Engineers, 1989; also papers in mathematical logic. Home and Office: Acad Info Svc Inc 7809 Chestnut Ave Bowie MD 20715

BERNSTEIN, ARTHUR HAROLD, venture capital executive; b. N.Y.C., June 8, 1925; s. Charles and Eva (Aronson) B.; m. Barbara R. Ettinger, June 24, 1951; children: Jeffrey R., Diane. B of Chem. Engring., Cornell U., 1947, LLB, 1950. Bar: N.Y. 1950, Fla. 1956, Calif. 1972, U.S. Supreme Ct. 1962, U.S. Dist. Ct. (so. dist.) N.Y. 1951, U.S. Dist. Ct. (ea. dist.) N.Y. 1952, U.S. Ct. Appeals (2d cir.) 1952. Staff atty. N.Y. Cen. R.R. Co., N.Y.C., 1950-55; gen. counsel Ryder System, Inc., Miami, 1955-58, v.p., treas., 1958-65; sr. assoc. Lazard Freres & Co., N.Y.C., 1966-68; v.p. Norton Simon, Inc., Los Angeles, 1968-70; sr. v.p. Max Factor & Co., Los Angeles, 1970-77; pres. Bancorp Capital Group Inc., Bancorp Venture Capital Inc., L.A., 1988—, also bd. dirs.; bd. dirs. Ryder System, Inc., Miami, Redken Labs., Inc., Canoga Park, Calif.; mng. ptnr. Calif. Capital Investors, Los Angeles, 1980—. Served with USN, 1943-46, PTO. Mem. ABA. Jewish. Office: Bancorp Venture Capital Inc 11812 San Vicente Blvd Los Angeles CA 90049

BERNSTEIN, BERNARD, lawyer, corporate executive; b. Bklyn., Feb. 9, 1929; s. Irving and Esther (Schriro) B.; m. Carmel Roth, June 24, 1973. AB, Syracuse U., 1950; JD, Harvard U., 1953. Bar: N.Y. With Philipp Bros., Inc. subs. Salomon Inc. (formerly Minerals and Chems. Philipp, Englehard Minerals & Chems. Corp., Phibro-Salomon, Inc.), N.Y.C., 1965—; now gen. counsel, sec. Philipp Bros., Inc. subs. Salomon Inc. (formerly Phibro-Salomon, Inc.), N.Y.C., also bd. dirs. Served with AUS, 1953-55. Mem. ABA, Am. Arbitration Assn. (bd. dirs., mem. exec. com.). Home: 25 E 86th St New York NY 10028 Office: Philipp Bros Inc 1221 Ave of the Americas New York NY 10020

BERNSTEIN, CARYL SALOMON, lawyer; b. N.Y.C., Dec. 22, 1933; d. Gustav and Rosalind (Aron) Salomon; m. William D. Terry, June 12, 1955 (div. 1967); children: Ellen Deborah, Mark David; m. Robert L. Cole, Jr., Oct. 25, 1970 (div. 1975); m. George K. Bernstein, June 17, 1979. B.A. with honors, Cornell U., 1955; J.D., Georgetown U., 1967. Bar: D.C. 1968, U.S. Dist. Ct. D.C. 1968, U.S. Ct. Appeals (D.C. cir.) 1968, U.S. Supreme Ct. 1971. Atty. Covington & Burling, Washington, 1967-73; staff atty. Overseas Pvt. Investment Corp., Washington, 1973-74, asst. gen. counsel, 1974-77, v.p. for ins., 1977-81; sr. v.p., gen. counsel, sec. Fed. Nat. Mortgage Assn., Washington, 1981-82, exec. v.p., gen. counsel, sec., 1982—; bd. dirs. Citizens Bank of Md., Nat. Housing Conf., Citizens Bank Md. Contbr. articles to profl. jours., chpt. to book; mem. bd. editors Georgetown Law Jour., 1966; mem. editorial adv. bd. Housing and Devel. Reporter, 1986-87. Mem. bd. regents Georgetown U., 1986—; bd. dirs. Council for Ct. Excellence, Washington, 1986—. N.Y. Regents scholar, 1951-55. Mem. ABA, Fed. Bar Assn., D.C. Bar Assn., Phi Beta Kappa, Phi Kappa Phi. Office: Fed Nat Mortgage Assn 3900 Wisconsin Ave NW Washington DC 20016

BERNSTEIN, HOWARD NATHANIEL, equipment distributor executive; b. Chgo., Feb. 21, 1923; s. Sol and Eleanor (Kaplan) B.; m. Barbara Paula Ruby, June 21, 1953 (div. Nov. 1968); children: Lisa Lynn Millspaugh, Leslie Ellen Sandler; m. Harriet Kopel, Sept. 7, 1973. Student, Wilson Jr. Coll., 1941-43, Northwestern U., 1946-51. Mgr. sales Sterling Lumber and Supply Co., Chgo., 1946-53; owner, pres. Atlas Lift Truck Rentals and Sales, Chgo., 1951—. Served to lt. USN, 1943-46. Mem. Material Handling Equipment Distbrs. Assn. (pres. 1965-66). Office: Atlas Lift Truck Rental & Sales 5050 N River Rd Chicago IL 60176

BERNSTEIN, IRWIN FREDERICK, apparel company executive; b. Bklyn., Mar. 11, 1933; s. Bernard and Edna (Levy) B.; m. Liela Soberman, Oct. 11, 1956; children: Barbara, Ruth, Brian. BA, Columbia U., 1954, MS, 1955. With Maidenform, Inc., Bayonne, N.J., 1958—, mgr. info. systems, 1967-75; exec. v.p. Maidenform Sportswear div. Maidenform, Inc., N.Y.C., 1971, materials mgr., 1973-75; distbn. dir. Maidenform Sportswear div. Maidenform, Inc., Bayonne, 1975, asst. v.p. planning and adminstrn., 1976-81, v.p. planning and adminstrn., 1982—. Chmn. data coord. com. U.S. Olympic Com., Colorado Springs, Colo., 1985-89; pres. Garden State Games, Trenton, 1986—. Recipient Alumni Athletic award Columbia Varsity C Club, 1973. Mem. Am. Apparel Mfrs. Assn. (chmn. mgmt. systems com. 1975-77), Am. Arbitration Assn., U.S. Fencing Assn. (pres. 1976-80), Westfield (N.J.) Tennis Assn. (pres. 1983-85); Shore Athletic Club, Rotary. Office: Maidenform Inc 154 Ave E Bayonne NJ 07002

BERNSTEIN, JOSEPH, lawyer; b. New Orleans, Feb. 12, 1930; s. Eugene Julian and Lola (Schlemoff) B.; B.S., U. Ala., 1952; LL.B., Tulane U., 1957; m. Phyllis Maxine Askanase, Sept. 4, 1955; children: Jill, Barbara, Elizabeth R, Jonathan Joseph. Clk. to Justice E. Howard McCaleb of La. Supreme Ct., 1957; admitted to La. bar, 1957; assn. firm Jones, Walker, Waechter, Poitevent, Carrere & Denegre, 1957-60, partner, 1960-65; gen. practice New

Orleans, 1965—; gen. counsel Alliance for Affordable Energy. Past pres. New Orleans Jewish Community Ctr., Met. New Orleans chpt. March of Dimes. Trustee New Orleans Symphony Soc.; past mem. adv. council New Orleans Mus. Art; past nat. exec. com. Am. Jewish Com. Served to 2d lt. AUS, 1952-54. Mem. Am., La., New Orleans bar assns., Phi Delta Phi, Zeta Beta Tau. Democrat. Jewish. Home: 3119 Prytania Ave New Orleans LA 70115

BERNSTEIN, RICHARD A., publishing company executive; b. N.Y.C., June 28, 1946; s. Sidney and Ethel Helen (Shankman) B.; m. Amelia Fishman, Nov. 21, 1944; children: Bradley Ross, Jennifer Anne. BA in Econs., NYU, 1968. V.p. Pease & Ellman Inc., N.Y.C., 1968-73; pres. P&E Properties Inc., N.Y.C., 1973—; chmn. Western Pub. Co. Inc., N.Y.C., 1984—; chmn., pres., chief exec. officer Western Pub. Group Inc., N.Y.C., 1984—; chmn. Gen. Med. Corp., Richmond, Va., 1987—, Harris Wholesale Co., Cleve., 1988—; chmn., pres., chief exec. officer Penn Corp., 1986—; bd. dirs. Hosp. for Joint Diseases, N.Y.C., N.Y. State Employee Retirement System, N.Y.C.; mem. bd. overseers NYU Schs. Bus. and Pub. Adminstrn.; trustee NYU; mem. Chem. Bank Adv. Bd., 1985—. Trustee Police Athletic League, N.Y.C., 1982—; chmn. N.Y. State Commn. on Regulation of Lobbying, Albany, 1982-86; candidate for comptroller City of N.Y., 1981. Served with U.S. Army, 1969. Fellow Yeshiva U., N.Y.C., 1986. Mem. Econ. Club N.Y. Republican. Jewish. Office: Western Pub Group Inc 444 Madison Ave New York NY 10022

BERNSTEIN, SIDNEY, lawyer; b. Bronx, N.Y., May 3, 1938; s. Meyer and Ethel (Sloop) B.; m. Joyce Elaine Blum, July 7, 1963 (div. 1979); children: Michael Louis, Sheryl Lyn; m. Andra Jane Schutz, June 6, 1982 (div. 1987). B.A., Columbia U., 1960; J.D., Cornell U., 1964. Bar: N.Y. 1966, U.S. Dist. Ct. (we. dist.) N.Y. 1966, U.S. Dist. Ct. (so. dist.) N.Y. 1978, U.S. Ct. Appeals (D.C. cir.) 1980, U.S. Supreme Ct. 1971. Jr. editor Lawyer's Coop. Pub. Co., Rochester, N.Y., 1964-65, asst. mng. editor, 1966-71, editor Case and Comment Mag., 1966-71; sr. mng. editor Matthew Bender & Co., N.Y.C., 1971-75, asst. to pres., 1976-83; chief exec. officer, pres. Kluwer Law Book Pubs., Inc., N.Y.C., 1984-89; counsel Tolmage, Peskin, Harris & Falick, N.Y.C., 1988—; faculty Nat. Coll. Advocacy, 1977—; adj. faculty Sch. Continuing Edn., NYU, 1980-81. Mem. editorial bd. Trial Mag., 1982-83; mem. editorial adv. bd. Am. Criminal Law Rev., 1972-74; exec. editor: Nat. Law Rev. Reporter, 1981-83; editor-in-chief: Belli Soc. Internat. Law Jour.; editor: Criminal Defense Techniques, 6 vols., 1977-83; Columnist Supreme Ct. Rev., Trial Mag. contbr. articles to profl. jours. Mem. Roscoe Pound. Found.; pres. Belli Soc., 1985-86. Mem. ABA, Am. Law Inst., Am. Soc. Writers on Legal Subjects (past pres.), Assn. Trial Lawyers Am., N.Y. Trial Lawyers Assn., Nat. Assn. Criminal Def. Lawyers, Am. Judicature Soc., Trial Lawyers for Pub. Justice, Golda Meir Assn., Vols. for Israel, Masons. Republican. Jewish. Home: W Shore Towers 101 Gedney St Nyack NY 10960 Office: 20 Vesey St New York NY 10007

BERNSTEIN, STEPHEN LOUIS, lawyer; b. N.Y.C., Nov. 22, 1933; s. Jack and Gertrude (Kalz) B.; m. Phyllis Goldberg, Jan. 16, 1960; children: Kenneth, Gail, Jeffrey. BA, Columbia Coll., 1955; LLB, Harvard U., 1958. Sole practice N.Y.C., 1958-67; gen. counsel Am. Midland Corp., Englewood Cliffs, N.J., 1967—. Home: 565 Clubhouse Rd Woodmere NY 11598 Office: Am Midland Corp 270 Sylvan Ave Englewood Cliffs NJ 07632

BERNT, BENNO ANTHONY, financial executive; b. Bielitz, Austria, Mar. 14, 1931; came to U.S., 1953, naturalized, 1961; s. Victor and Grete (Meissner) B.; m. Constance Smigel, June 22, 1957; children: Karin, Eric, Steve. BS in Engring. cum laude, Fed. Inst. Tech., Vienna, Austria, 1952; DCS in Internat. Econs. cum laude, U. Commerce, Vienna, 1953; MBA, Carnegie Mellon U., 1954. Fin. and mfg. exec. Chrysler Corp., 1954-59; mfg. and bus. planning exec., subs. gen. mgr. Whirlpool Corp., 1959-68; pres. Cissell Mfg. Co., Louisville, 1968-70; gen. mgr. Simonds Abrasive Co., Phila., 1970-73; v.p. fin. ESB Ray-O-Vac Corp., Phila., 1973-76, exec. v.p., dir., 1977-78; pres. Ray-O-Vac Co., Madison, Wis., 1979-82; sr. v.p. fin. and planning, chief fin. officer Nat. Intergroup Inc., Pitts., 1983-87; chmn. The Griffin Group, Pitts., 1988—; bd. dirs. Manpower Inc. Treas., bd. dirs., Pitts. Symphony; trustee Carnegie Mellon U.; vice chmn. Pitts. Pub. Broadcasting Co.; bd. dirs. Pitts. Ctr. for Arts. Mem. Duquesne Club, Pitts. Golf Club, Fox Chapel Golf Club, Union League. Home: 308 Schenley Rd Pittsburgh PA 15217 Office: Griffin Group 308 Schenley Rd Pittsburgh PA 15217

BERNTHAL, HAROLD GEORGE, health care company executive; b. Frankenmuth, Mich., June 11, 1928; s. Wilfred Michael and Olga Bertha (Stern) B.; m. Margaret Hrebek, Jan. 25, 1958; children—Barbara Anne, Karen Elizabeth, James Willard. B.S. in Chemistry, Mich. State U., 1950. Chmn. CreBern Inc., Wilmette, Ill., 1986—; bd. dirs. Becor Western, Inc., First Nat. Bank, Lake Forest, Ill., Nat. Standard Corp., Nalco Chem. Co., Butler Mfg. Co. Trustee Northwestern Meml. Hosp., Chgo., Valparaiso (Ind.) U., Wheat Ridge Found. Served with AUS, 1950-52. Clubs: Chicago, Economic, Commercial (Chgo.); Knollwood; Old Elm. Office: 1144 Wilmette Ave Wilmette IL 60091

BERQUIST, KENNETH GIFFORD, electronics executive; b. Worcester, Mass., Dec. 26, 1950; s. Robert C. and Priscilla (Gifford) B.; m. Gail C. Jackson, Mar. 18, 1983; children: Rebecca, Jenna, Heather. Grad. exec. devel. program, Cornell U., 1979; BBA, Calif. Coast U., 1980. Project engr. BASF, Bedford, Mass., 1968-79; gen. sales mgr. Gould, Inc., Cleve., 1974-81; mktg. dir. Analogic Corp., Danvers, Mass., 1981-82; exec. v.p., chief ops. officer Wayne Kerr, Inc., Woburn, Mass., 1982-86; pres., chief exec. officer Assemtest, Haverhill, Mass., 1987—, also chmn. bd. dirs.; bd. dirs. MJT Assocs., Nashua, N.H., DSI, Woburn, Mass. Author: Current Fad in Matrix Organizations, 1980. Mem. IEEE, Am. Mgmt. Assn. Home: 7 Wabanaki Way Andover MA 01810 Office: Assmetest 88 Essex St Haverhill MA 01830

BERRA, JOHN MICHAEL, measurement and control instrumentation company executive; b. St. Louis, Aug. 24, 1947; s. Joseph Mario and Geraldine (Brunelli) B.; m. Charlotte Lynne King, Oct. 4, 1969; children: James Mathew, Daniel John, Jennifer Anne. BS in Systems and Automatic Control Engring., Washington U., St. Louis, 1969. Instrument engr. Monsanto Co., St. Louis, 1969-72; sr. instrument engr. J.F. Pritchard & Co., Kansas City, Mo., 1972-74; control system specialist Beckman Instruments, Houston, 1974-76; successively CPI mktg. mgr., industry mktg. mgr., dir. sales and mktg., v.p. sales and mktg., sr. v.p./gen. mgr. Rosemount Inc., Eden Prairie, Minn., 1976-86, pres., 1986—, also bd. dirs. With U.S. Army Res., 1970-74. Mem. Instrument Soc. Am., Sci. Apparatus Makers Assn. (bd. dirs. 1986—), Hazeltine Nat. Golf Club (Chaska, Minn.). Roman Catholic. Home: 11207 Radisson Dr Burnsville MN 55337 Office: Rosemount Inc 12001 Technology Dr Eden Prairie MN 55344

BERREY, ROBERT FORREST, lawyer; b. Oak Park, Ill., Dec. 7, 1939; s. Rhodes Clay and Regina (Kasprovich) B.; m. Betsy Kate Meyer, Sept. 8, 1968; children—Adam Forrist, Ellen Catherine, Kevin Joseph. AB, Harvard U., 1962; JD, U. Chgo., 1968. Bar: Ill. 1969, Ohio 1986. With firm Torshen, Fortes & Eiger, Chgo., 1970-75; atty. Jewel Companies, Inc., Chgo., 1975-76; sec. Jewel Companies, Inc., 1976-80, v.p., sec., gen. counsel, 1980-85; v.p., gen. counsel Philips Industries Inc., 1986—. With AUS, 1962-65. Mem. ABA. Clubs: Sunset Ridge Country, NCR Country. Home: 20 Walnut Ln Oakwood OH 45419 Office: Philips Industries Inc 4801 Springfield St Dayton OH 45431

BERRIE, RUSSELL, sales executive, business owner; b. N.Y.C., Mar. 18, 1933; s. Nathan and Naomi (Edleman) B.; m. Kathy Bohbot (div. Dec. 1983); children: Brett, Richard, Leslie, Scott; m. Uni Juliana Yang, Dec. 29, 1983; children: Nicole Alanna, David Benjamin. Student, NYU, U. Fla. Toy salesman Modern Toy Co., Chgo., 1956; pvt. practice mfrs. rep. Ft. Lee, N.J., 1957-66; mfrs. rep., pres., chmn. bd. dirs. Russ Berrie & Co. Inc., Palisades Park, Oakland, N.J., 1963—; lectr. in field; owner N.Y. Knights Arena Football Team. Holds numerous copyrights in field. Bd. overseers NYU Grad. Sch. Bus., 1986—; founding mem., bd. dirs. Boys Town Jerusalem Found. Am., N.Y.C., Jewish Hosp. and Rehab. Ctr., Jersey City; trustee United Jewish Community Bergen County, River Edge, N.J., Jewish Community Ctr. on Palisades, Tenafly; founder Yeshiva U. Sch. Bus., N.Y.C.; chmn. Israeli Bus. Conf. Hebrew U., Jerusalem, 1986. Recipient Ayuda award Ayuda Toy Dr., 1984-85, Rizzuto award UNICO Nat. Italian-Am. Service Orgn., 1987, Gate of Jerusalem award Boys Town Jerusalem, 1987, Humanitarian award Cath. Community Services, 1986, Entrepreneur of Yr. award Venture Mag. and Arthur Young, 1988; named Man of Yr., Cath. Community Services, 1986. Mem. Toy Mfrs. Am., Am. Bus. Conf. Jewish. Office: Russ Berrie & Co Inc 111 Bauer Dr Oakland NJ 07436

BERRY, BOB RAY, nursery executive; b. Sanger, Calif., Sept. 29, 1938; s. Fred and Molly (McClaine) B.; m. Shireldean Wilcox, Sept. 3, 1960; children: Burl Robert, Brian Rodney, Holley, Cher Reneé. BS, NE State U., 1961; postgrad., Harvard U., 1981. Salesman Ozark Nurseries, Tahlequah, Okla., 1961-68; chmn., pres. Am. Nursery Products, Inc., Tahlequah, 1968-86, chmn., chief exec. officer, 1986—; v.p., bd. dirs. Mid-Western Transit, Inc., Mid-Western of Tenn., Inc., McMinnville, Beauty Grow Barks, Inc., Great Lakes Evergreens, Inc., Northland Evergreens, Inc.; pres. bd. dirs. Am. Foliage, Inc.; bd. dirs. Phyton Technoligies, Inc. Chmn. Okla. State Dept. Transp. Commn., 1987—. Republican. Methodist. Office: Am Nursery Products Inc 5 Miles West Hwy 51 Tahlequah OK 74464

BERRY, DAVID PAUL, electronics company executive; b. Stoneham, Mass., Dec. 4, 1940; s. Paul Andrew and Margaret (Meuse) B.; m. Margaret Berry; children: Michael, Mark, Kathryn; m. Alice Daborn, children: Suzanne, Lisa, James. BEE, Tufts U., 1962; postgrad., Northeastern U., European Inst. Bus. Adminstrn., 1981. Salesman, sales mgr. Hewlett Packard Co., Waltham (Mass.) and Washington, 1962-65; salesman, with mktg. dept. DPD, GEM region IBM, Cambridge, Mass., 1965-68; sales mgr. Info. Dynamics, Reading, Mass., 1968-69, Graphic Systems Div. RCA, Boston, 1969-71; salesman, sales mgr. Digital Equipment Corp., Waltham, 1971-74; mgr. mktg. Digital Equipment Corp., Maynard, Mass., 1974-76; mgr. edn. products group European product line Digital Equipment Corp., Geneva, 1976-82; mgr. med. systems Digital Equipment Corp., Hudson, Mass., 1982-83; mgr. U.S. sales tng. Digital Equipment Corp., Stow, Mass., 1983-84; mgr. mid-Am. dist. sales Digital Equipment Corp., St. Louis, 1984—. Chmn. auction event Sta. KETC-TV, St. Louis, 1985-88; dist. chmn. activities com. St. Louis Council Boy Scouts Am., 1988—. Mem. Regional Commerce and Growth Assn., Stadium Club. Office: Digital Equipment Corp 721 Emerson Rd Saint Louis MO 63141

BERRY, ELSA LOUISE, investment banker; b. N.Y.C., July 31, 1956; d. Robert Meyers and Erna Louise (Mueller) B.; m. Alain D. Bankier, May 18, 1985. BA in Econs., Nanterre U., Paris, 1978; MBA, Hautes Etudes Commls., Paris, 1980. Assoc. cons. Faulhaber & Co., Boston, 1980-82; v.p. Cheverny Assocs., N.Y.C., 1982-84; founding ptnr., mng. dir. Vendome and Co., Inc., N.Y.C., 1984-89; exec. v.p. Banexi Internat. Svcs. (N.Am.) Corp., N.Y.C., 1989—. Mem. French-Am. C. of C., Assn. Corp. Growth, French-Am. Bus. Execs. Club: 600 (N.Y.C.). Home: 322 W 57th St Apt 36S New York NY 10019 Office: Banexi IFS 499 Park Ave New York NY 10022

BERRY, EVE MARIE, executive; b. Austin, Tex., July 21, 1950; d. Jim Smither and Helen (Kirby) B.; m. Anthony Joseph Smokovich, Sept. 16, 1979; children: Erin, Sean. BA, Ind. U., 1972, MA, 1977. Program dir. human resources City Bloomington, Ind., 1973-75, dep. controller, 1975-77; sr. cons., trainer The Grantsmanship Ctr., Los Angeles, 1977-79; pres. Mgmt. Dimensions, Inc., Nashville, 1978—; v.p. EQUICOR-Equitable HCA Corp., N.Y.C., Nashville, 1986-88; cons. Equitable, N.Y.C., 1978-86, 88, Chase Manhattan Bank, N.Y.C., 1983-85, 88, Mfrs. Hanover, N.Y.C., 1985-86, Reuters, N.Y.C., 1988—, Citicorp, N.Y.C., 1988—. Mem. Planning Forum, Am. Soc. Tng. Devel., Fin. Women's Assn. N.Y.C. Home: 1206 Chickering Rd Nashville TN 37215 Office: Mgmt Dimensions Inc 1801 West End Ave Nashville TN 37203

BERRY, JOHN DOUGLAS, financial executive; b. San Francisco, May 17, 1944; s. Roy Milam and Mary Elizabeth (Mackin) B.; m. Pamela Lynn Patrich, Nov. 6, 1971; 1 child, Kierstin. AA in Bus. Adminstrn., Foothill Coll., 1966; BS in Acctg., San Jose State U., 1968. CPA, Tex. Sr. auditor Price Waterhouse, San Francisco, 1968-72; internal audit dir. Natomas Co., San Francisco, 1972-76; contr. Natomas Internat., Houston, 1976-78; V.p. finance Natomas N.Am., Houston, 1978-84, Elf Aquitane, Houston, 1984-85; fin. cons. Hallador Inc., Sacramento, Calif., 1987, Lone Star Technologies, Dallas, 1987—. Fund raiser United Way, Houston, 1984. With U.S. Army, 1968-70, Vietnam. Decorated Bronze star U.S. Army, 1969; Acctg. Honor Soc. scholar San Jose State U., 1966. Mem. AICPA, Tex. Soc. CPA's, Petroleum Accts. Soc., San Jose State Bus. Alumni, Wimbledon Racquet (Spring, Tex.) Club. Republican. Roman Catholic. Home: 6903 Farnaby Ct Spring TX 77379 Office: Lone Star Technologies Inc 2200 W Mockingbird Ln Dallas TX 75235

BERRY, NORMAN CHARLES, advertising agency executive; b. London, June 15, 1931; came to U.S., 1979; s. Charles William and Marjorie B.; (divorced); children: Lucy Elizabeth. Student Brit. schs. With Young & Rubicam Ltd., London, 1952-64; copy chief Young & Rubicam Ltd., 1958-64; founder, pres. Davidson, Pearce, Berry & Spottiswoode, London, 1964-79; exec. v.p., dir., head creative dept. Ogilvy & Mather Inc., N.Y.C., 1979-83, pres., 1985—; creative head Ogilvy & Mather Worldwide, N.Y.C., 1983—; chmn., chief exec. officer, creative head Ogilvy & Mather Inc., N.Y.C., 1987—; pres. Internat. Creative, 1987—. Served as officer Brit. Army, 1949-51, Korea. Fellow Inst. Practitioners in Advt. Office: Ogilvy Group Inc 2 E 48th St New York NY 10017

BERRY, RICHARD ROWLAND, manufacturing company executive; b. Chgo., Feb. 17, 1932; s. Richard Benson and Leta Lodema (Rowl) B.; m. Joan Widicus Harrison, Aug. 8, 1954; children—Richard H., Karen L., Scott R. B.S. in Metall. Engring, U. Ill. Engring. trainee brass group Olin Corp., 1954, v.p. mfg. from, 1970; group pres. Olin Corp., East Alton, Ill., 1980-83; exec. v.p., dir. Olin Corp., Stamford, Conn., 1983—; bd. dirs. Ill. Power Co., 1988—. Bd. dirs. Atlanta U., Ill. Power Co. Served with U.S. Army, 1955-57. Mem. United Ch. of Christ. Office: Olin Corp 120 Long Ridge Rd PO Box 1355 Stamford CT 06904

BERRY, ROBERT BASS, construction executive; b. Tulsa, Jan. 29, 1948; s. Guy Leonard and Barbara (Bass) B.; m. Catherine Cowles, Jan. 16, 1971; children: Matthew Knipe, Eli Banjamin. BA in Fin., Okla. U., 1970. Ops. mgr. D.C. Bass & Sons Constrn., Inc., Enid, Okla., 1971-73; chief exec. officer, exec. v.p. D.C. Bass & Sons Constrn., Inc., Enid, 1973-75, pres., 1975—; chief exec. officer, pres. Mosher Devel. Co., Enid, 1975—; pres. Bobsfarm, Inc., Enid, 1975—. Mem. Okla. Acad. for State Goals, Oklahoma City, 1985—, Gov.'s Internat. Trade Team, 1986-88; nat. dir. Am. Friends of the Game Conservancy, Washington; founding advisor Leadership Okla., Oklahoma City, 1986, Habitat for Humanity, Enid, 1984; chmn. State Alcohol Beverage Law Enforcement Commn., Oklahoma City, 1984-88; chmn. State Tort and Liability Task Force, 1986-87, State Right to Work Task Force, 1986-88; bd. dirs. Enid Wellness Ctr., 1985-87, Enid Joint Indsl. Found., 1984—. Capt. C.E., U.S. Army, 1971. Named Exec. of Yr. Profl. Secs. Internat., 1981; recipient Pres.' Coun. award Phillips U., 1984, Developer's award Heritage League of Enid, 1985. Mem. Okla. State C. of C. (bd. dirs. 1986—, chmn.), Enid C. of C. (bd. dirs. 1975-78, 81-84), Associated Gen. Contractors (Legis. team 1985-87), Young Pres.' Orgn., Okla. Futures. Republican. Presbyterian. Club: Grand Nat. Quail Hunt (Enid). Office: DC Bass & Sons Constrn Co 205 E Maine Enid OK 73702

BERRY, ROBERT VAUGHAN, electrical, electronic manufacturing company executive; b. Newark, Mar. 24, 1933; s. Harold Silver and Elizabeth Lippincott (Vaughan) B.; m. Victoria Shaw, Mar. 8, 1958; children—Patricia E., Michael V. B.A., Dartmouth Coll., 1954. With Thomas & Betts Corp., Bridgewater, N.J., 1957—; dir. Thomas & Betts Corp., 1972-85, v.p. fin., 1975-83, sr. v.p., 1983—; pres. Thomas & Betts Internat., Inc., 1975; bd. dirs. Ames Rubber Corp., Hamburg, N.J. Trustee Carrier Found. Psychiat. Hosp., Belle Mead, N.J., 1984—. Served to 1st lt. Airborne Corps U.S. Army, 1954-57. Republican. Clubs: Baltusrol Golf (Springfield, N.J.); Rock Spring (West Orange, N.J.); Summerlea Golf and Country (Montreal, Que., Can.); Wentworth (Surrey, Eng.); Mid Ocean (Bermuda); Royal and Ancient Golf of St. Andrews (Scotland). Office: Thomas & Betts Corp 1001 Frontier Rd Bridgewater NJ 08807-0993

BERRY, ROBERT WORTH, lawyer, educator, retired army officer; b. Ryderwood, Wash., Mar. 2, 1926; s. John Franklin and Anita Louise (Worth) B. B.A. in Polit. Sci., Wash. State U., 1950; J.D., Harvard U., 1955; M.A., John Jay Coll. Criminal Justice, 1981. Bar: D.C. 1956, Pa. 1961, Calif. 1967, U.S. Supreme Ct. 1961. Research assoc. Harvard U., 1955-56; atty. Office Gen. Counsel U.S. Dept. Def., Washington, 1956-60; staff counsel Philco Ford Co., Phila., 1960-63; dir. Washington office Litton Industries, 1967-71; gen. counsel U.S. Dept. Army, Washington, 1971-74, civilian aide to sec. army, 1975-77; col. U.S. Army, 1978-87; prof., head dept. law U.S. Mil. Acad., West Point, N.Y., 1978-86; retired brigadier gen. U.S. Mil. Acad., 1987; mil. asst. to asst. sec. of army, Manpower and Res. Affairs Dept. of Army, 1986-87; asst. gen. counsel pub. affairs Litton Industries, Beverly Hills, Calif., 1963-67; resident ptnr. Quarles and Brady, Washington, 1974-78; dir., corp. sec., treas., counsel G.A. Wright, Inc., Denver, 1987—. Served with U.S. Army, 1944-46, 51-53, Korea. Decorated Bronze Star, Legion of Merit, Disting. Service Medal; recipient Disting. Civilian Service medal U.S. Dept. Army, 1973, 74, Outstanding Civilian Service medal, 1977. Mem. Fed. Bar Assn., Phi Beta Kappa, Phi Kappa Phi, Sigma Delta Chi. Methodist. Clubs: Army Navy, Army Navy Country, Nat. Lawyers.

BERRY, SUSAN PATRICIA, director of business resource center; b. Marietta, Ohio, July 7, 1956; d. Daniel Timothy and Constance C. (Gagnon) Reese; divorced; 1 child, Jan Elizabeth. BA magna cum laude, Marietta Coll., 1983; MBA cum laude, Ohio U., 1984. Mktg. coordinator Kardex Systems Inc., Marietta, 1985-86; assoc. dir. Bus. Resource Ctr. Marietta Coll., 1986-87, dir. Bus. Resource Ctr., 1987—; bd. dirs. Marietta Small Bus. Enterprise Ctr., Small Bus. Inst., Ohio Indsl. Tng. Program. Mem. Am. Soc. Tng. and Devel. (treas. Ohio Valley chpt.), Am. Mktg. Assn. (bd. dirs.), Econ. Roundtable of Ohio Valley, Ohio Assn. for Adult and Continuing Edn., Nat. Assn. Female Execs., Small Bus. Inst. Dirs. Assn. Republican. Roman Catholic. Office: Marietta Coll 105 Thomas Hall Marietta OH 45750

BERRY, THOMAS CLAYTON, securities broker, brokerage owner, energy company owner; b. Roswell, N.Mex., May 23, 1948; s. Homer C. and Betty J. (Cronic) B.; m. Bonnie L. Shamas, May 30, 1969; children: Lisa C., Joshua E. AA, N.Mex. Mil. Inst., 1969; Assoc. course in real estate, 1984, NASD DPP rep. and prin. courses, 1983. Farmer Berry Farms, Dexter, N.Mex., 1969-72; sec., dir. Victor & Assoc., Phoenix, 1972-74; dir., foreman Berry Land & Cattle, Dexter, 1974-82; v.p., dir. Trinity Investment Corp., Roswell, 1982-83; pres., dir. Jordache Investments, Roswell, 1982-83; v.p., dir. Diamond Braich Realtors, Roswell, 1982-83; v.p., dir. Tierra Fin. Group, Roswell, 1985-86, pres., dir., 1986—; v.p., dir. Tierra Capital Corp., Roswell, 1984-86, pres., dir., 1986—; pres., dir. Tierra Energy Corp., Roswell, 1987—. Deacon North Phoenix Bapt. Ch., Phoenix, 1973-74; bd. dirs. First Assembly of God Ch., Roswell, youth group sponsor, 1978—; coach Roswell Youth Soccer, 1978—. Named one of Outstanding Men of Am., 1982. Mem. Nat. Assn. Securities Dealers, Roswell Realtor Assn., N.Mex. Realtor Assn.,. Republican. Mem. Nazarene Ch. Home: 2010 Brazos Roswell NM 88201 Office: Tierra Fin Group Inc 400 N Pennsylvania Roswell NM 88201

BERRY, VIRGIL JENNINGS, JR., management consultant; b. Pine Bluff, Ark., Dec. 20, 1928; s. Virgil J. and Harriett F. (Gannaway) B.; m. Alice Ann Adams, Dec. 22, 1948; children: Carol, Scott, Janet, Wade. BE, Vanderbilt U., Nashville, 1948; MS in Chem. Engring., Calif. Inst. Tech., Pasadena, 1949; PhD in Chem. Engring. and Physics, Calif. Inst. Tech., 1951. Dir. planning and coordination Sinclair Oil Corp., N.Y.C., 1966-69; sec. corp. mgmt. com. Sinclair Oil Corp., 1968-69; mgr. internat. fin. control and coordination Atlantic Richfield Co., N.Y.C., 1969-70; sr. v.p.-corp. R&D Jos. Schlitz Brewing Co., Milw., 1970-75; sr. v.p. ops. Jos. Schlitz Brewing Co., 1975-78; pres. Chgo. Extruded Metals Co., 1979-82, Berry & Co., Chgo., 1982-84; v.p. A.T. Kearney Inc., Chgo., 1984—. Contbr. numerous articles to profl. jours. Home: 800 N Washington Hinsdale IL 60521 Office: A T Kearney Inc 222 S Riverside Pla Chicago IL 60606

BERRY, WILLIAM MARTIN, financial consultant; b. Chgo., June 21, 1920; s. William John and Mary Frances (Martin) B.; m. Julia McIntire Vail, Dec. 19, 1972; children: William E., Mary P., Peter D. BS, St. Mary's Coll., 1941; MA, DePaul U., 1949. Div. controller Hughes Aircraft Co., Culver City, Calif., 1950-55, TRW, Redondo Beach, Calif., 1955-58; mgr. mgmt. cons. dept. Peat, Marwick, Mitchell and Co., Los Angeles, 1958-61; v.p. Litton Industries Inc., Beverly Hills, Calif., 1961-74; chmn., chief exec. officer Northwestern Nat. Ins. Co., Milw., 1974-84; sole practice cons. Milw., 1984—; bd. dirs. Marine Corp., Milw., Astronautics Corp. Am., Milw., Graphic Strategies, Inc., Sunnyvale, Calif., Am. Med. Bldgs. Inc., Milw. Bd. dirs. Columbia Hosp., Milw., 1976—, Milw. Assn. Commerce, 1976-81, Milw. Symphony Orch., 1974-81, United Performing Arts Fund., Milw., 1977-81. With U.S. Army, 1941-46. Mem. Fin. Execs. Inst., Milw. Club, Milw. Country Club, Univ. Club. Republican. Home and Office: 13800 N Birchwood Ln Mequon WI 53092

BERRY, WILLIAM WILLIS, utility executive; b. Norfolk, Va., May 18, 1932; s. Joel Halbert and Julia Lee (Godwin) B.; m. Elizabeth Mangum, Aug. 23, 1958; children: E. Preston, John Willis, William Godwin. BSEE, Va. Mil. Inst., 1954; MS in Commerce, U. Richmond, 1964. Registered profl. engr., Va. Engr. Gen. Electric Co., 1954-55; with Va. Power, Richmond, 1957—, v.p. div. ops., then sr. v.p. comml. ops., 1976-78, exec. v.p., 1978-80, pres., chief operating officer, 1980-83, pres. chief exec. officer, 1983-85, chmn., chief exec. officer, 1985-86; chmn., chief exec. officer Dominion Resources, Richmond, 1986—; bd. dirs. Sovran Fin. Corp., Norfolk, Ethyl Corp., Richmond, Universal Corp., Richmond. Trustee Union Theol. Sem., Richmond. 1st lt. AUS, 1955-57. Republican. Clubs: Richmond Kiwanis (past pres.), Commonwealth, Country of Va, Downtown, Norfolk Yacht and Country. Office: Dominion Resources Inc 701 E Byrd St Richmond VA 23219

BERSON, BERTRAND LEVINE, electronics executive; b. Bklyn., Jan. 20, 1938; s. Irving A. Levine and Charlotte (Yawnick) Berson; 1 stepchild, Lawrence; m. Joyce Ellen Peterson; children: Ilene, Jennifer; 1 stepchild, Teri Romero. BEE, CCNY, 1960; MSEE, U. Rochester, 1963. Head microwave device rsch. RCA David Sarnoff Rsch. Ctr., Princeton, N.J., 1966-73; mgr. rsch. and devel. Hewlett-Packard Microwave, San Jose, Calif., 1973-80; v.p., gen. mgr. semiconductor div. Avantek Microwave, Santa Clara, Calif., 1980-81; pres. Cons. in Tech., Mountain View, Calif., 1981-83, Interdevices, Mountain View, Calif., 1983-86; v.p. sales and mktg. Acrian, Mountain View, 1986-87; pres. Berson and Assocs., Mountain View, 1986—. Contbr. articles to profl. jours.; patentee in field. Mem. West Windsor (N.J.) Bd. of Health, 1970-73, N.J. Conservation Commn., 1970-73. With USAR, 1960-66. Recipient Cert. of Appreciation, U.S. Dept. of Def. Mem. Microwave Theory and Techniques Soc. (Recognition award), USAF Communications and Electronics Assn., Old Crows. Office: Berson & Assocs 655 Castro St Ste 3 Mountain View CA 94041

BERSTEIN, IRVING AARON, technology executive; b. Providence, Oct. 11, 1926; s. Robert Louis and Laura (Sperber) B.; m. Susan D'Amico, Apr. 16, 1972; children: Johnathan Louis, Robert Laurance. ScB in Chemistry, Brown U., 1946; PhD in Chemistry, Cornell U., 1950. Pres. Controls for Radiation Inc., Cambridge, Mass., 1960-71; dir. med. div. AGA Corp., Secaucus, N.J., 1971-72; asst. dir. rsch. programs Harvard-MIT div. Health Scis. and Tech., Cambridge, 1972-85; pres. Berstein Tech. Corp., Lexington, Mass., 1979—; chmn. bd. Hygeia Scis. Inc., Newton, 1980-87, pres. 1985-87, sr. sci. advisor 1987—, also dir.; spl. ltd. ptnr. Oasis Ptnrs., Boston, 1988—; bd. dirs. Cellular Transplantation Scis. Inc., Collaborative Rsch. Inc., Bedford. Contbr. articles to profl. jours. Frances Wayland scholar Brown U., 1945. Mem. 49ers Inc. (chmn. N.E. chpt. 1983-84), Harvard Club, Cornell Club, Brown Club, Sigma Xi. Jewish. Office: Berstein Tech Corp 42 Buckman Dr Lexington MA 02173

BERSTICKER, ALBERT CHARLES, chemical company executive; b. Toledo, Mar. 22, 1934; s. Albert Charles and Lillian (Schorling) B.; m. Frances Ploeger, Sept. 15, 1956; children: Steven, Susan, Karen, Cristina. M.S. in Geo-Chemistry, Miami U., Oxford, Ohio, 1957. Chemist Interlake Iron Corp., Toledo, 1956; engr. Mobile Producing Corp., Billings, Mont., 1957-58; with Ferro Corp., Cleve., 1958—; asst. to group v.p. internat. Ferro Corp., 1973-74, group v.p. internat., 1974-76, exec. v.p. ops., chief operating officer, 1976—. pres., chief operating officer, 1988—, also dir.; dir. Ferro Enamel Espanola, S.A., Castellon, Spain, Ferro Holland B.V., Rotterdam, Metal Portuguesa, S.A.R.L., Lisbon, Duramax, Inc., Nissan Ferro Organic Chem. Co. Ltd., Tokyo, Ferro Far East, Ltd., Hong Kong, Ferro Indsl. Products, Ltd., Oakville, Ont., Can., Queen City Distbrs., Ltd., Downsview, Ont., Ferro South East Asia Pte., Ltd., Singapore, Replas Inc., Evansville, Ind., Cleve. Electric Illuminating Co., Employers Resource Council, Cleve., Soc. Bank, Cleve. State U. Devel. Found. Editor: Symposium on Salt, 1963. Chmn. Cleve. Area Devel. Council; trustee Cleve. Roundtable. Mem. Am. Ceramics Soc., Spanish Ceramics Soc., Chem. Mfg. Assn., Leadership Cleve. Episcopalian. Office: Ferro Corp 1 Erieview Pla Cleveland OH 44114

BERTGES, RICHARD PAUL, mortgage broker, real estate investor; b. Erie, Pa., Feb. 12, 1952; s. Robert Paul and Mary Catherine (Sullivan) B.; m. Deborah Mae Gilmour Bertges, June 1982; 1 child, Ryan. BS in Fin., Penn State U., 1974. Expediter Zimmerman Electric, Erie, 1974-75; real estate salesman Price Real Estate, Erie, 1975-77; real estate broker Springhurst Realty, Erie, 1977-82; letter carrier U.S. Postal Service, Erie, 1982-87; comptroller Liberty Mortgage Corp., Erie, 1987—, acct., 1982—. Mem. Erie Maennerchor Club, East Erie Turners Club, Zukor Club. Democrat. Roman Catholic. Office: Liberty Mortgage Corp 3818 Liberty St Erie PA 16509

BERTHELSEN, JOHN ROBERT, printing company executive; b. Albert Lea, Minn., July 23, 1954; s. Robert Eugene and Erna Catherine (Petersen) B.; m. Debra Denise Peterson, June 29, 1974; children: Angela Marie, Derek John. Student public schs. Albert Lea, Minn. Prodn. worker Arrow Printing Co., Albert Lea, 1972-73; journeyman Munson Printing Co., Red Wing, Minn., 1973-75; prep. foreman O'Connor Printing Co., Sioux Falls, S.D., 1975-76; preparation supr. Modern Press Inc., Sioux Falls, 1976-79; gen. mgr. Suttle Press, Inc., Waunakee, Wis., 1979-82, pres., 1982—. Recipient 1st place Nat. Skill Olympics (printing), Vocat. Indsl. Clubs Am., 1972, Gold award best managed printing co. Nat. Assn. Printers and Lithographers, 1983, 87, 88, Silver award Mgmt. Plus Program Nat. Assn. Printers and Lithographers, 1986. Mem. Madison Craftsmen (pres. 1983-85, named Craftsman of the Yr. 1987), Internat. Assn. Printing House Craftsmen (gov. 6th dist. 1985-87, internat. treas. 1987—), Wis. State Council on Printing (dir. 1988—). Office: Suttle Press Inc 806 S Division St PO Box 370 Waunakee WI 53597

BERTOVIC, PATRICIA A., real estate executive; b. Bronx, N.Y., Mar. 19, 1947; d. George Edward and Elizabeth Louise (Cullen) Scheuerman; m. Thomas Robert Bertovic, Dec. 28, 1974; 1 child, Kevin Thomas. With Blue Cross and Blue Shield, Garden City, N.Y., 1967-70; acctg. clk. Reliance Ins. Co., Garden City, 1970-72, personal lines rating supr., 1972-73; personal lines underwriter Reliance Ins. Co., Mechanicsburg, Pa., 1973-74, adminstrv. mgr., 1974-84; ins. recruiter Ins. Svcs., Camp Hill, Pa., 1984-86; relocation dir. Thompson Wood Real Estate, Camp Hill, 1986—. Asst. coach Upper Allen Soccer, 1987; parent rep. Children's Family Ctr., Messiah Village, Mechanicsburg, 1988—; mem. concession com. Mechanicsburg Little League, 1988—. Mem. Adminstrv. Mgmt. Soc. (dir. bd. dirs. 1988, sec. bd. dirs. 1989), NAFE, Trade Winds Club. Democrat. Roman Catholic. Home: 602 Somerset Dr Mechanicsburg PA 17055 Office: Thompson Wood Real Estate Inc 3813 Market St Camp Hill PA 17011

BERTRAND, FREDERIC HOWARD, insurance company executive; b. Montpelier, Vt., Aug. 5, 1936; s. George Joseph and Delores Gertrude (Mallory) B.; m. Elinor Maude Pierce, June 11, 1960; children: Kimberly Sue, Michael Scott, John Frederic (dec.). B.S. in Civil Enging. magna cum laude, Norwich U., 1958; postgrad., Georgetown U. Law Sch., 1961-63, Carnegie-Mellon U. Sch. Indsl. Adminstrn., 1967-68; J.D., Coll. William and Mary, 1967. Bar: Vt., Va.; registered profl. engr., Vt. Engr.-adminstr. CIA, Washington, 1960-70; dir. Chittenden Trust Co., Montpelier, 1989—; mem. exec. bd. Chittenden Trust Co., Montpelier, 1975-86, dir. Mountain Region, 1986—; bd. dirs. Union Mut. Fire Ins. Co., New Eng. Guaranty Ins. Co., Montpelier, Cen. Vt. Pub. Svcs. Co., Rutland; civilian aide to sec. of army, Washington, 1981—. Chmn. Montpelier Bd. Appeals, 1972-76; chmn. charter revision com. City of Montpelier, 1973, alderman, 1974-76, pres. city council, 1975-76, mayor, 1976-78; vice chmn. Montpelier Republican Com., 1973-74; Bd. dirs. Central Vt. Econ. Devel. Corp., 1985—; mem. Vt. State Rep. Com., 1974-76, Vt. Bus. Roundtable (bd. dirs., treas. 1987—); trustee Kellogg-Hubbard Library, Montpelier, 1978-82, Norwich U., Northfield, Vt., 1979-85. Recipient Outstanding Alumnus award Norwich U., 1980. Mem. ABA, Vt. Bar Assn., Va. Bar Assn., Washington County Bar Assn., Theta Chi, Epsilon Tau Sigma. Republican. Roman Catholic. Office: Nat Life Ins Co National Life Dr Montpelier VT 05604

BERTY, J(OHN) JEFFRY, fire protection company executive; b. Belfonte, Pa., June 26, 1953; s. John J. and Ruth K. (Hart) B.; m. Judith Ann Young, Sept. 5, 1987; m. Susan M. Klingerman, Sept. 2, 1972 (div. Jan. 1986); children: Jennifer Rene, Larissa Raye, Jason Ryan, David Armand, Angela Ruth, Jaclyn Grace. BS, Ind. U., 1975; postgrad., Ind. U., Indpls., 1988—. CPA, Ind. Staff acct. to audit mgr. Cooper & Lybrand, Indpls., 1975-83; controller Crime Control, Inc., Indpls., 1983-84; ptnr. J. Berty Cons., Indpls., 1984-85; v.p. fin. Culligan Fireprotection, Inc., Indpls., 1985—. Pres. St. Gabriel Parish Council, Indpls., 1981-83; active United Way of Greater Indpls., 1983-84. Mem. Am. Inst. CPA's, Ind. CPA Soc., Nat. Assn. Accts., Ind. U. Alumni Assn. Republican. Roman Catholic. Clubs: Indpls. Country, Indpls. Athletic.

BERUBE, JACQUES B., communications company executive; b. St. Léon-le-Grand, Que., Can., Sept. 11, 1941; s. Paul and Rose-Anne (Lefrançois) B.; m. Nicole Berube, Sept. 9, 1967; children: Manon, Lyne Julie. BS, Laval U., 1965. With Bell Can., 1966—, v.p., 1983-87; exec. v.p. Que., 1987—; bd. dirs. Télébec, Bell-Northern Rsch. Ltd. Mem. Montreal (Que.) C. of C. Ltd. Office: Bell Can, 1050 Beaver Hall Hill, Montreal, PQ Canada H2Z 1S4 also: Bell Can, 2800 700 de La Gauchetière St, Montreal, PQ Canada H3B 4LI *

BESABE, RENATO C., comptroller; b. Manila, Jan. 9, 1945; came to U.S., 1972; s. Vicente and Felisa (Candido) B.; m. Edna Magdangal, July 22, 1978; children: Eileen, Renato Jr., Elissa. BBA, U. of the East, The Philippines, 1966; MBA, St. John's U., 1985. CPA, The Philippines. Audit clk. ABS-CBN Broadcasting Corp., Quezon City, The Philippines, 1969-70; audit staff asst. Amon Trading Corp., Makati Rizal, The Philippines, 1971-72; internat. ops. officer Security Pacific Internat. Bank, N.Y.C., 1973-81; sr. examiner Soc. Gen., N.Y.C., 1981-85; comptroller Banco Indsl. de Venezuela, N.Y.C., 1985—; chmn. bd. dtrustees pension plan, mem. Exec. com. Banco Indsl. de Venezuela. Mem. Fin. Exec. Inst., Am. Mgmt. Assn. Inst. Internat. Bankers, Bankers Adminstrn. Inst. Home: 34 Denton Pl Staten Island NY 10314 Office: Banco Indsl de Venezuela 400 Park Ave New York NY 10022

BESCH, HENRY ROLAND, JR., pharmacologist, educator; b. San Antonio, Sept. 12, 1942; s. Henry Rol and Monette Helen (Kasten) B.; m. Frankie R. Drejer; 1 child, Kurt Theodore. B.Sc. in Physiology, Ohio State U., 1964, Ph.D. in Pharmacology (USPHS predoctoral trainee 1964-67), 1967; USPHS postdoctoral trainee, Baylor U. Coll. Medicine, Houston, 1968-70. Instr. ob-gyn. Ohio State U. Med. Sch., Columbus, 1967-68; asst. prof. Ind. U. Sch. Medicine, Indpls., 1971-73, assoc. prof., 1973-77, prof., 1977, Showalter prof. and chmn. pharmacology and toxicology, 1977—; Can. Med. Research Council vis. prof., 1979, investigator fed. grants, mem. nat. panels and coms., cons. in field. Contbr. numerous articles pharm. and med. jours.; mem. editorial bds. profl. jours. Fellow Brit. Med. Research Council, 1970-71; Grantee Showalter Trust, 1975—. Fellow Am. Coll. Cardiology; Mem. AAAS, Am. Assn. Clin. Chemistry, Am. Fed. Clin. Research, Am. Heart Assn., Am. Physiol. Soc., Am. Soc. Molecular Biol. Chemists, Am. Soc. Pharmacology and Exptl. Therapeutics, Assn. Med. Sch. Pharmacologists, Biochem. Soc., Cardiac Muscle Soc., Internat. Soc. Heart Research (exec. com. Am. sect.), Nat. Acad. Clin. Biochemistry, N.Y. Acad. Scis., Sigma Xi. Office: Ind Univ Sch Medicine 635 Barnhill Dr Indianapolis IN 46202

BESCHERER, EDWIN A., JR., business information services company executive; b. Bklyn., Nov. 19, 1933; s. Edwin A. and Dorothy (Herbert) B.; m. Jane Madsen, June 11, 1955; children: John, Timothy, Karen, Katherine. B.S., Purdue U., 1955. With fin. depts. Gen. Electric Co., Fairfield, Conn., 1955-74, mgr. corp. fin. analysis, 1974-78; v.p., controller Dun & Bradstreet Corp., N.Y.C., 1978-82, sr. v.p. fin., chief fin. officer, 1982-87, exec. v.p. fin., chief fin. officer, 1987—. Mem. Fin. Execs. Inst. Home: 38 English Dr Wilton CT 06897 Office: Dun & Bradstreet Corp 299 Park Ave New York NY 10171

BESER, JACQUES, aeronautical engineer; b. Wilrijk, Belgium, Apr. 20, 1950; s. Huna and Odette B.; m. Lauraine Chammas, Oct. 12, 1980; 1 child, David. Student, U. Libre de Bruxelles, 1970; BS in Engring., Calif. Inst. Tech., 1973, MS in Aero., 1973; PhD in Aero., Stanford U., 1978. Mgr. systems analysis dept. Intermetrics, Inc., Huntington Beach, Calif., 1977-84; program mgr. systems analysis dept. TAU Corp., Long Beach, Calif., 1984-88; pres., founder JB Systems, Santa Ana, Calif., 1988—. Contbr. articles to profl. jours. Mem. Inst. Navigation, AIAA, IEEE. Office: JB Systems 3 Hutton Ctr Dr Ste 920 Santa Ana CA 92707

BESS, JEROME, advertising and public relations executive; b. Bayonne, N.J., Nov. 8, 1922; s. Herman M. and Molly C. Galanter B.; m. Jean Abelson, June 1, 1948; children: John H., Andrea. B.S. in Bus., Ind. U., 1946. Broadcast advt. mgr. Robert Hall Clothes Inc., N.Y.C., 1950-62; exec. v.p. RKO Gen. Broadcasting, N.Y.C., 1962-67; v.p., gen. mgr. WOR-TV, Channel 9, N.Y.C., 1967-69; pres. Sawdon & Bess Inc., advt., N.Y.C., 1969-79, chmn., 1975-79; pres., chmn. Sawdon & Bess subs. Ted Bates WorldWide, N.Y.C., 1979-83; now chmn. AC&R/DHB & Bess Advt., Inc. subs. Saatchi Saatchi Worldwide, N.Y.C. Served to 1st lt. USAAF, 1943-46. Mem. Am. Assn. Advt. Agys., Internat. Radio-TV Soc., Friars Club, Mountain Ridge Country, Troon Country Club (Scottsdale, Ariz.). also: 3800 E Lincoln Dr Phoenix AZ 85018 Office: AC&R/DHB & Bess Advt Inc 16th E 32nd St New York NY 10016

BESSER, JOHN EDWARD, lawyer; b. Iowa City, May 15, 1942; s. Edward L. and Martha E. (Taylor) B.; m. Suzanne Taylor, June 18, 1965; children: Sharon, Brian, Lorraine, Warren. AB, U. Rochester, 1964; JD, Northwestern U., 1967. Bar: Mo. 1967. Assoc. Morrison & Hecker, Kansas City, Mo., 1967-71; with Xerox Corp., Stamford, Conn. and Rochester, N.Y., 1971-81, counsel internat.; v.p. adminstrn., gen. counsel, sec. Barnes Group, Inc., Bristol, N.Y., 1981—. V.p., bd. dirs. Conn. Soc. to Prevent Blindness, Madison, Conn., 1983—; participant Am. Leadership Forum, Hartford, Conn., 1987—. Mem. ABA, Mo. Bar Assn. Office: Barnes Group Inc 123 Main St Bristol CT 06010

BESSIE, SIMON MICHAEL, publisher; b. N.Y.C., Jan. 23, 1916; s. Abraham and Ella (Brainin) B.; m. Constance Ernst, Sept. 12, 1945; children: Nicholas, Katherine; m. Cornelia Schaeffer, Dec. 21, 1968. B.A. magna cum laude, Harvard U., 1936. Reporter Newark Star Eagle, 1936; research dept. RKO-Radio Pictures, 1936-38; editor Market Research Monthly, 1938; free-lance writer Europe, Africa, 1938-39; assoc. editor, war editor, war corr. Look mag., 1940-42; editor Harper & Bros., 1946-52, gen. editor, 1952-59; co-founder Atheneum Pubs., 1959, pres., 1963-75; sr. v.p. Harper & Row, N.Y.C., 1975-81, v.p., 1988—, also bd. dirs., 1975-87; pres. Joshuatown Pub. Assocs., N.Y.C., 1981—; co-pub. Cornelia and Michael Bessie Books, 1981—; lectr. English Columbia U., 1953-59; dir. Novel Workshop, New School, 1959-63, Franklin Book programs, 1963-72; chmn. vis. com. Harvard U. Press, 1972-78, bd. dirs., 1980—; bd. dirs. Am. Book Pubs.' Council, 1964-69, Ctr. for Communication, 1981—; chmn. trade book div. Assn. Am. Publishers, 1970-72, bd. dirs., 1972-76, chmn., 1974-75, chmn. freedom to read com., 1975-78, internat. freedom to publish com., 1975—; mem. exec. com. Ctr. for the Book, Library of Congress, 1979—, chmn., 1983—. Author: Jazz Journalism, 1938; Contbr. numerous articles to mags. Bd. overseers vis. com. dept. history Harvard U., 1964-77; chmn. lit. panel Nat. Arts Council, 1971-74, chmn. spl. projects panel, 1974-81; chmn. bd. advisors Sta. WNET, 1979-83, trustee, 1983—; chmn. book com. Alfred P. Sloan Found., 1986—. Served as chief news bur. psychol. warfare br., 1943-44, Algiers, Sicily, Italy; chief psychol. warfare combat team 1944, So. France; dep. dir. USIS, 1944-46, France. Recipient Medal of Freedom, 1946, Curtis Benjamin award Assn. Am. Pubs., 1986. Mem. Council Fgn. Relations, Assn. Harvard Alumni (dir. 1974-77), Phi Beta Kappa. Clubs: Century Assn. (N.Y.C.), Harvard (N.Y.C.); Federal City (Washington). Home: Joshuatown Rd Lyme CT 06371 Office: 10 E 53d St New York NY 10022

BESSON, MICHEL LOUIS, manufacturing company executive; b. Nancy, France, Mar. 14, 1934; came to U.S., 1980; s. Marcel Louis and Germaine (Savignac) B.; m. Marie Jose Ellie, May 19, 1967; children: Frederique, Pascal, Thomas. Diploma in Engring., Ecole Centrale des Arts et Mfrs., Paris, 1959; M.S. in Chem. Engring., M.I.T., 1960. From engr. to chmn. bd. and chief exec. officer Cellulose du Pin, 1962-80; pres., chief exec. officer CertainTeed Corp., Valley Forge, Pa., 1980—, also bd. dirs.; bd. dirs. Sq. D, First Fidelity Bancorp, St. Gobain, Inc.; bus. ptnr. Pa. Acad. Fine Arts, 1984—. Bd. dirs. Greater Phila. C. of C., 1981—; bd. dirs. Greater Phila. Internat. Network, 1981—; trustee Inst. Internat. Edn., 1982—; trustee Acad. Natural Scis., 1981-85, Lycée Francais de New York, 1986—; corp. ptnr. Phila. Mus. Art, 1981—; French fgn. trade advisor Comite Nat. des Conseillers du Commerce Exterieur, 1982—; mem. Phila. Com. Fgn. Relations, 1982—; bd. dirs. St. Joseph's U., 1983-85; bd. dirs. Urban Affairs Partnership, 1982—; active World Affairs Coun., 1982—. With French Air Force, 1960-62. Recipient Leadership award M.I.T., 1980. Mem. French-Am. C. of C. (councillor 1981—). Club: Union League, Sunday Breakfast. Office: Certainteed Corp 750 E Swedesford Rd PO Box 860 Valley Forge PA 19482

BEST, CRAIG DOUGLAS, controller; b. Rockford, Ill., July 21, 1947; s. Raymond and Ethel (Jensen) B.; m. Rhonda L. Chaney, Feb. 21, 1975; 1 child, Elizabeth. BS, Rockford Coll., 1973; MBA, No. Ill. U., 1976. Asst. v.p. Home Fed. Savs. & Loan, Rockford, 1976-77; treas. Robert Trigg & Sons, Rockford, 1977-80, Rock Valley Internat., Rockford, 1980-82; contr. Geraghty Industrial and Equipment, Rockford, 1982-85, Mott Bros., Rockford, 1985—; cons. acct., Rockford, 1982—. With USAF, 1974-75. Mem. Nat. Assn. Accts. Republican. Office: Mott Bros 9075 Main St Rockford IL 61101

BEST, JONATHAN ERIC, controller, accountant; b. Newark, Oct. 4, 1955; s. Seymour and Cecelia Norma (Mallow) B. BS in Bus. and Econs., Lehigh U., 1977. CPA, N.J. Sr. acct. Coopers & Lybrand, N.Y.C., 1977-80; sr. corp. auditor Times Mirror Co., Inc., L.A., 1980-85; asst. controller Morning Call, Inc., Allentown, Pa., 1985-87, controller, 1987—. Mem. Am. Inst. CPAs, N.J. State Soc. CPAs, Internat. Newspaper Fin. Execs. Office: Morning Call Inc 101 N 6th St Allentown PA 18105

BEST, RICHARD ALLEN, JR., architect; b. Somers Point, N.J., Apr. 26, 1957; s. Richard Allen Sr. and E. Jeanne (Cunningham).B. BA, U. N.C., 1979, BArch, 1980; MArch, UCLA, 1982. Registered architect, Calif. Intern architect Urban Innovations Group, Los Angeles, 1981; designer, draftsman Charles Moore, Inc., Los Angeles, 1982-84; sr. draftsman WZMH Group, Inc., Los Angeles, 1984-85, project cpt., designer, 1985-87; with Elbasani & Logan Architects, Berkeley, Calif., 1987; owner Richard A. Best, Jr. Architect, Beverly Hills, Calif., 1988—; teaching asst. UCLA Sch. Archtecture, 1981-82. Co-author: Un Storico Aldente, 1981; co-designer Mercatale e Albergo, 1981; designer Beverly Hills Civic Ctr., 1982 (1st place 1982); capt., designer Mission Inn, Riverside, Calif., 1986. Fellow UCLA, 1980; scholar UCLA, 1981, Bell Telephone Co., N.J., 1977; named one of Outstanding Young Men Am., Nat. Jaycees, 1982. Mem. AIA. Democrat. Methodist. Home: 9364 Beverlycrest Dr Beverly Hills CA 90210 Office: 9364 Beverlycrest Dr Beverly Hills CA 90210

BEST, ROBERT WAYNE, gas transmission company executive, lawyer; b. Nappanee, Ind., Oct. 8, 1946; s. Wayne and Helen F. (Kendall) B.; m. Mary Beth Hoffman, Apr. 7, 1967; children—Stephanie, Sean, Ashley. B.S., Ind. State U., 1968; J.D., Ind. U., 1974. Bar: Ky., Ind. Atty. Tex. Gas Transmission Corp., Owensboro, Ky., 1974-79, sr. atty., 1979-81, gen. counsel, 1981-82, v.p., gen. counsel, 1982-85, pres., chief exec. officer, 1985—; dir. Cardinal Fed. Savs. Bank. Bd. dirs. Leadership Owensboro, Brescia Coll., Mercy Hosp., Ky. Ind. Coll. Fund., United Way Owensboro-Daviess County; mem. exec. com. Strategies for Tomorrow; mem. Ky. Econ. Devel. Corp. Mem. ABA, Ky. Bar Assn., Ind. Bar Assn., Fed. Energy Bar Assn. Democrat. Roman Catholic. Home: 1212 Woodbridge Trail Owensboro KY 42301 Office: Tex Gas Transmission Corp 3800 Frederica St Owensboro KY 42301

BESTERVELT, PEGGY LEE, franchise organization executive; b. St. Joseph, Mich., Dec. 21, 1961; d. Theodore Robert and Margaret Anne (Troost) B. BA, U. Mich., 1984. Research asst. U. Mich., Ann Arbor, 1984-86; ops. coordinator Molly Maid, Inc., Ann Arbor, 1986—; pres. B & D Acctg. Inc., Ann Arbor, 1986-88. Co-editor-in-chief Mich. Jour. Polit. Sci., 1980-84. Mem. congl. casework Congressman Mark D. Siljander, 4th Dist. office, 1982. Mem. Nat. Assn. Female Execs. Republican. Baptist. Office: Molly Maid Inc 3001 S State St #707 Ann Arbor MI 48108

BESTGEN, WILLIAM HENRY, JR., financial planner; b. Quincy, Mass., June 23, 1947; s. William Henry and Ebba Violet (Fristam) B.; m. Ann Marie Mahoney, Apr. 12, 1975; children: Brad William, Lauren Ann. BA, Northeastern U., 1970. CLU; chartered fin. cons. Fin. planner Bay Fin., Waltham, Mass., 1970—; pres. Yankee Planners, Inc., Middleboro, Mass. Mem. exec. bd. Boston Estate and Bus. Planning Coun. Mem. Am. Soc. CLU's, Nat. Assn. Life Underwriters, Internat. Assn. Fin. Planners, Million Dollar Round Table (life). Republican. Lutheran. Home: 100 Holland Ave Stoughton MA 02072

BESTWICK, ROBERT DAVID, investment banker; b. Grove City, Pa., Sept. 11, 1956; s. David Moore and Rosemary Elizabeth (Walker) B. BA, Colgate U., 1978; MBA, Syracuse U., 1981. Ops. fin. analyst Johnson & Johnson Corp., New Brunswick, N.J., 1981-83, mktg. fin. dir., 1983-85; investment banker William Sword & Co. Inc., Princeton, N.J., 1985—; bd. dirs. S.L. Schlegel Co. Inc., Reading, Pa.; cons. Tray-Pak Corp., Reading, 1982—, BRD Real Estate, Reading, 1982—. Mem. Beta Gamma Sigma. Republican. Lutheran. Clubs: Yale, Deke (N.Y.C.). Home: 19-13 Aspen Dr Plainsboro NJ 08536 Office: William Sword & Co Inc 22 Chambers St Princeton NJ 08542

BESTWICK, WARREN WILLIAM, construction company executive; b. Missoula, Mont., June 27, 1922; s. William Andrews and Beatrice Anna (Eddy) B.; student Glendale Coll., 1941, U. Mont., 1942; BA, U. Wash., 1949; m. Glenette Haas, Sept. 11, 1949; children: Sharon Kaye, Carol Eddy, Jan Marie. Sr. acct. Frederick & Nelson, Seattle, 1950; controller, bus. mgr. Virginia Mason Hosp., Seattle, 1958-64; controller Bumstead Woolford Co., Seattle, 1964-68; controller, treas. Wash. Asphalt Co., Seattle, 1968-72; exec. v.p., sec. treas. Wilder Constrn. Co., Inc., Bellingham, Wash., 1972-77, pres., 1977—, also dir.; bd. dirs. TRC Thermal Reduction, Ltd., Cost Cutter Foods, Bellingham; treas., dir. Vincent Contracting, Inc., Vincent Corp.; past chmn. Area IV advisory bd. Wash. Dept. Commerce and Econ. Devel.; mem. adv. bd. to U.S. Bank of Washington. Mem. adv. council Mt. Baker Boy Scouts Am.; past pres., bd. dirs. Shuckson Found. Whatcom County. Served to col., pilot USMCR, 1942-74. Decorated DFC (3), Air medal (7). Mem. Assn. Wash. Bus. (past. dir.), Whatcom County Devel. Council (past dir. and pres.), Bellingham C. of C. (past dir.), Marine Res. Officers Assn. (past dir. Seattle), Res. Officers Assn., Marine Corps League, Associated Gen. Contractors Am., The Beavers Constrn. (hon.), United For Wash., U. Wash. Alumni Assn., Ret. Officers Assn., Marine Aviation Assn. Clubs: Wash. Athletic (Seattle); Bellingham Golf and Country, Bellingham Yacht; Rotary (past pres.). Home: 233 N State St Bellingham WA 98225 Office: Wilder Constrn Co Inc 2006 State St N Bellingham WA 98225 also: 11301 Lang St Anchorage AK 99515

BESZTERCZEY, LESLEY MARGARET, bank holding company executive; b. Otley, Eng., Mar. 14, 1945; came to U.S., 1979; d. John Geoffrey Jim and Kathleen Mary (Clapham) Scott; m. Akos Csaba Beszterczey, Aug. 17, 1968; children: Sara, Stephen. BE, McGill U., 1966; MS in Acctg., Northeastern U., 1982. CPA, Mass. Tchr. math. pub. schs., Montreal, Que., Can., 1966-67, 69-73, Hull, Que., 1967-69; mem. audit staff Arthur Young & Co., Boston, 1982, mem. tax staff, 1983-85; corp. tax dir., v.p. Multibank Fin. Corp., Dedham, Mass., 1985—. Mem. AICPA, Mass. Soc. CPAs, Tax Execs. Inst., Delta Kappa Gamma, Beta Gamma Sigma. Home: 47 Pioneer Rd Hingham MA 02043

BETANCOURT, ELISA, financial executive; b. N.Y.C., June 14, 1962; d. Godofredo and Mirtha (Tolosa) B. AAS, La Guardia Coll., 1986; student, St. John's Coll., 1987—. Financial coordinator La Guardia Med. Group, Forest Hills, N.Y., 1986—; pres. MBS, Woodhaven, N.Y., 1987—. Mem. Am. Assn. Med Assts. Home: 87-26 95th St Woodhaven NY 11421

BETANZOS, LOUIS, banker; b. Dearborn, Mich., Oct. 30, 1936; m. Nancy Ann Dorr, May 1, 1965; children: Deborah, Ramon, Sandra. BS, U. Detroit, 1958; postgrad., Wayne State U., 1965, Williams Coll., 1977. Trader Chrysler Corp., Highland Park, Mich., 1963-64; export fin. specialist Chrysler Corp., Detroit, 1964-65; sr. trader Nat. Bank Detroit, 1965-67, mgr. bond dept., 1967-79, 1st v.p., 1979-81, sr. v.p., 1981-84; exec. v.p., treas. NBD Bancorp, Detroit, 1984—; bd. dirs. NBD Mortgage Co., Troy, Mich., 1986—. Trustee U. Detroit, 1985—; bd. dirs. Mcpl. Adv. Coun., 1979—, Citizens Rsch. Coun., 1986—. With U.S. Army, 1961-63. Mem. Pub. Securities Assn. (bd. dirs. 1987—), Detroit Club, Pine Lake Country Club (Orchard Lake, Mich.). Republican. Roman Catholic. Home: 2890 Lakewoods Ct Orchard Lake MI 48033 Office: NBD Bancorp Inc 611 Woodward Ave Detroit MI 48226

BETHEA, BARRON, lawyer, electrical hardware manufacturing, former state legislator; b. Birmingham, Ala., May 20, 1929; s. Malcolm and Wilma (Edwards) B.; student U. of South, 1948-50; B.S., U. Ala., 1952, LL.B., 1953; m. Phyllis Parker, Sept. 8, 1967; children—Barron Augustus, Elizabeth Ann. Admitted to Ala. bar, 1953; practiced in Birmingham, 1953-54; founder Barron Bethea Co., Inc., elec. hardware mfrs., Birmingham, 1957, chmn., pres., sec., treas., 1957—. Mem. Ala. Democratic Exec. Com., 1958-62; mem. Ala. Ho. of Reps., 1962-66. Mem. mgmt. bd. Five Points YMCA, 1962. Served as 1st lt. USAF, 1954-56. Mem. Ala. State Bar, Birmingham Bar Assn., Asso. Industries Ala., Birmingham C. of C., Am. Judicature Soc., Scabbard and Blade, Phi Gamma Delta, Phi Alpha Delta. Methodist. Elk. Club: Downtown. Patentee in field. Home: 4963 Spring Rock Rd Birmingham AL 35223 Office: Barron Bethea Co Inc PO Box 2202 Birmingham AL 35201

BETHEA, CHARLES, real estate analyst, consultant; b. Phila., July 14, 1933; s. Sampson Benjamin Washington and Mary Elizabeth (Melvin) B.; m. Carmen Romero, Oct. 31, 1971; 1 child, Angela Regan. BBA, U. Pa., 1975; student, Temple U., 1977-79. Engring. aide I City of Phila., 1953-56, engring aide II, 1956-65, real estate asst. I, 1965-70, real estate asst. II, 1970-81; real estate rep. McDonald's Corp., Cherry Hill, N.J., 1981-83; asst. mgr. real estate Consol Rail Corp., Phila., 1983-86; corp. analyst-real estate Shared Med. Systems Corp., Malvern, Pa., 1986-88; pvt. practice cons. Phila., 1981—. Author booklet How to Avoid Foreclosure, 1984. Mem. adv. bd. Lee Cultural Ctr., Phila., 1969; real estate advisor Adv. Community Devel. Corp., 1973; real estate sites and selection com. Sch. Dist. Phila., 1970-81; exec. com. New Path Montessori Sch., Phila., 1983; real estate cons. Phila. Bd. Dirs. of City Trusts, 1965-81; spl. counsel to Phila. city solicitor for negotiating econ. terms of City-Pa. Railroad agreements, 1972-76; mem. Morris Arboretum. Recipient Commonwealth of Pa. scholarship, 1973-75. Mem. Wharton Club of Phila., Faculty Club of U. Pa., U. Pa. Real Estate Soc. Democrat. Baptist. Home: 1041 E Sydney St Philadelphia PA 19150

BETHUNE, JOHN JOHNSON, economics educator; b. Clinton, N.C., Aug. 8, 1956; s. John Lauchlin Bethune and Lee (Daughtry) Bethune Peak; m. Kathryn Ferrari, Aug. 3, 1985; 1 child, Kathryn Thelma. BA, Campbell U., 1979; MA, U. N.C., Greensboro, 1981; PhD, Fla. State U., 1987. Research asst. U. N.C., Greensboro, 1979-80; research assoc. USDA, Greensboro, 1980-81; instr. Fla. State U., Tallahassee, 1981-84; statistician Econ. Research Services, Tallahassee, 1984; prof. econs. Bellarmine Coll., Louisville, 1984—; cons. Bank Louisville, 1988—. Articles editor Ky. Jour. Econs. and Bus. Mem. Am. Econ. Assn., So. Econ. Assn., Ky. Econ. Assn. (exec. bd. 1987—), History of Econs. Soc., Internat. Schumpeter Soc. (co-founder). Presbyterian. Home: 2527 Broadmeade Louisville KY 40205 Office: Bellarmine Coll Newburg Rd Louisville KY 40205

BETON, JOHN ALLEN, communications company executive; b. Chgo., Aug. 25, 1950; s. John Henry and Anne Marilyn (Joseph) B.; BS, U. Ill., 1972; MBA, DePaul U., 1975. Market analyst ITT Telecommunications, Des Plaines, Ill., 1972-73, mgr. mktg. svcs., 1973-75, mgr. market planning, Hartford, Conn., 1975-77, area mgr., Detroit, 1977-80, mgr. mktg. ops., Des Plaines, Ill., 1980-81; v.p. mktg. NEC Tele., Inc., Melville, N.Y., 1981-82; v.p. mktg. Summa Four, Inc., Manchester, N.H., 1982-85; pres. Alston div. Conrac Corp., 1985—. Mem. Am. Mktg. Assn., Am. Philatelic Soc., Pitcairn Islands Study Group, Phi Eta Sigma, Phi Kappa Phi, Beta Gamma Sigma. Presbyterian (deacon). Home: 97 E Highland Ave Unit D Sierra Madre CA 91024 Office: Conrac Corp 1600 S Mountain Ave Duarte CA 91010

BETSALEL, HARVEY, business executive; b. Montreal, Jan. 31, 1947; s. Louis and Mary (Fagan) B.; m. Lynne Hops, Dec. 25, 1971; children: Richard, Michael. B in Commerce, Sir George Williams U., Montreal, Que., Can., 1968; MBA, York U., Toronto, Ont., Can., 1972. Ops. research analyst Bank of Montreal, 1969-70, investment analyst, 1972-77; mgr., treasury Standard Brands Ltd., Toronto, 1977-79; internat. fin. officer Bank of Nova Scotia, Toronto, 1979-80; treas. Motorola Can. Ltd., Toronto, 1980-84; v.p., treas. Motorola Can. Ltd., Ottawa, Ont., 1985—, Mitel Corp., Ottawa, Ont., 1984—. Mem. Soc. Fin. Analysts, Ottawa Cash Mgmt. Soc., Ottawa Carleton Bd. Trade. Office: Mitel Corp, 350 Legget Dr, Kanata, ON Canada K2K 1X3

BETTI, JOHN A., automobile manufacturing company executive; b. Ottawa, Ill., Jan. 6, 1931; s. Louis and Ida (Dallari) B.; m. Joan Doyle, Aug. 22, 1953; children: Diane , Denise, Donna, Joan. B.S. in Mech. Engring, Ill. Inst. Tech., 1952; M.S. in Engring, Chrysler Inst. Engring., 1954; postgrad., U. Detroit, 1963. Registered profl. engr., Mich. Student engr. to asst. chief engr. Chrysler Corp., 1952-62; with Ford Motor Co., 1962—, chief light truck engr., chief engine engr., chief car planning mgr., chief car engr., then v.p., gen. mgr. truck ops., 1975-76; v.p. product devel. Ford of Europe, Inc., Warley, Essex, Eng., 1976-79, also dir.; v.p. powertrain and chassis ops. Ford N.A., Mich., 1979-83; v.p. mfg. and bus. devel. Ford N.A. Automotive Ops., Dearborn, Mich., 1983-84; exec. v.p. tech. affairs and operating staffs Ford Motor Co., Mich., 1985-88; dir. Ford Motor Co., Dearborn, Mich., 1985—, exec. v.p. diversified products ops., 1988—; chmn. bd. Ford Motor Co. Caribbean Inc., 1979-84, Ensite Ltd., Can., 1979-84; dir. Ford of Germany, 1978, Ford of Mex., 1984-85; past instr. Lawrence Inst. Engring., Wayne State U., Detroit; bd. dirs. Truck Hist. Mus., 1975-76; mem. exec. com. Western Hwy. Inst.; chmn., bd. trustees GMI Engring. and Mgmt. Inst., 1985—; chmn. Ford Aerospace Corp., 1988—; dir. Ford New Holland, Inc., 1988—; chmn. Ford Electronics and Refrigeration Corp., 1988—; dir. Park Ridge Corp., 1988. Bd. dirs. Mich. Opera Theatre, 1984-87; trustee Detroit Inst. for Children, 1985—; mem. nat. adv. com. U. Mich. Engring. Sch., 1985—. Recipient Alumni Profl. Achievement award Ill. Inst. Tech., 1980; John Morse Meml. scholar. Mem. Soc. Automotive Engrs., Nat. Acad. Engring., Tournament Players Club of Mich., Tau Beta Pi, Pi Tau Sigma, Alpha Sigma Phi, Beta Omega Nu. Clubs: Bloomfield Hills (Mich.) Country; Tournament Players Club Mich. Office: Ford Motor Co The American Rd Dearborn MI 48121

BETTMAN, GARY BRUCE, lawyer; b. N.Y.C., June 2, 1952; s. Howard G. and Gretel J. (Pollack) B.; m. Michelle Weiner, Aug. 24, 1975; children: Lauren, Jordan, Brittany. BS, Cornell U., 1974; JD, NYU, 1977. Bar: N.Y. 1978, N.J. 1978, U.S. Dist. Ct. (so. and ea. dists.) N.Y. 1979. Assoc. Proskauer Rose, N.Y.C., 1977-80, Gutkin, Miller et al, Milburn, N.J., 1980-81; asst. gen. counsel NBA, N.Y.C., 1981-84, v.p., gen. counsel, 1984-89, sr. v.p., gen. counsel, 1989—. Mem. N.Y. State Bar Assn., Assn. of Bar of City of N.Y., N.J. Bar Assn., Sports Lawyers Assn. (bd. dirs. 1985—), Phi Kappa Phi. Office: Nat Basketball Assn Olympic Tower 645 Fifth Ave New York NY 10022

BETTS, ANN BRANTLY, sales executive; b. Nashville, Apr. 22, 1947; d. Samuel David and Isabel Annie (Livingstone) Brantly; m. Hugh Martin Brown, Apr. 29, 1972 (div. 1977); m. James Michael Betts, Aug. 11, 1984. BS in Edn., Austin Peay State U., 1969. Teller First Tenn. Nat. Bank, Memphis, 1969-70; with Xerox Corp., Memphis, 1970-82; sales exec. Raytheon Data Systems, Dallas, 1982; maj. account sales trainer Panasonic Office Products, Dallas, 1982-84; dealer rep. Ricoh Corp., Austin, 1985-86; sales exec. OCE, Austin, 1986-87; dir. sales tng. and devel. The Hartford, Conn., 1987—. Republican. Presbyterian. Home: 6830 Constitution Ln Charlotte NC 28210 Office: The Hartford Hartford Pla Hartford CT 06115

BETTS, JAMES WILLIAM, JR., financial analyst, consultant; b. Montclair, N.J., Oct. 11, 1923; s. James William and Cora Anna (Banta) B.; m. Barbara Stoke, July 28, 1951; 1 dau., Barbara Susan (dec.). B.A., Rutgers U., 1946; M.A., U. Hawaii, 1957. With Dun & Bradstreet, Inc., 1946-86, service cons., 1963-64, reporting and service mgr., 1964-65, sr. fin. analyst, Honolulu, 1965—; owner, operator Portfolio Cons. of Hawaii, 1979—. Served with AUS, 1942-43. Mem. Am. Econ. Assn., Western Econ. Assn., Atlantic Econ. Soc. Republican. Episcopalian.

BETZ, EDWARD BERGAN, paper company executive; b. Seattle, Aug. 17, 1934; s. Edward Ferndinand and Clara Matilda (Bergan) B.; m. Marlene Phyllis Braun, June 20, 1959; 1 son, Edward Bergan. B.A., U. Wash., 1956. Prodn. and cost acct. Scott Paper Co., Everett, Wash., 1960-65, plant acct., Sandusky, Ohio, 1965-67, mfg. acct., Phila., 1967-70; controller Scott Graphics, Inc., Holyoke, Mass., 1970-74; asst. corp. controller Scott Paper Co., Phila., 1974-79, v.p., controller, 1979—. Bd. dirs. Taylor Hosp. Found., Ridley Park, Pa., 1985; adv. coun. Coll. Bus. and Econs. U. Del., Newark, 1987. Served to lt. USNR, 1956-60. Mem. Am. Paper Inst., Fin. Execs. Inst. Presbyterian. Club: Waynesborough Country. Office: Scott Paper Co Scott Plaza I Philadelphia PA 19113

BEUTNER, ROGER EARL, manufacturing executive; b. Essen, Fed. Republic Germany, June 15, 1930; came to U.S., 1930; s. Emil Henry and Melitta (Wolleman) B.; m. Marcia Susan Gailband, Aug. 10, 1957; children: Sheryl, Austin, Brian. BS in Mech. Engring., Stevens Inst. Tech., Hoboken, N.J., 1952; BS in Indsl. Engring., NYU, 1961; MBA, Ga. State U., 1965. Registered profl. engr., Mo. Staff engr. Chase Bag Co., N.Y.C., 1960-62; prodn. engr. Boyle Midway div. AHPC, N.Y.C. and Atlanta, 1962-67; plant mgr. Bristol-Myers corp., St. Louis, 1967-70; sr. v.p. ops. Amway Corp., Ada, Mich., 1970—; pres. Mich. Chem. Council, Lansing, 1988—. Mich. Rep. Precinct del., Grand Rapids, 1984—; engring. bd. visitors Grand Valley U., Grand Rapids, 1987—, Western Mich. U., Kalamazoo, 1983—. Capt. USAF, 1952-56. Mem. Am. Inst. Indsl. Engr., Nat. Soc. Profl. Engrs., Mich. Chem. Council (pres. 1988—), Chem. Spec. Mfrs. Assn. (chmn. bd. dirs. 1979-87), Tau Beta Pi, Alpha Pi Mu. Republican. Jewish. Home: 155 Hidden Lake Ct SE Grand Rapids MI 49506 Office: Amway Corp 7575 E Fulton Rd SE Ada MI 49355

BEVACQUA, RONALD ANTHONY, food products executive; b. Jersey City, Dec. 14, 1945; s. Guido Ferrar and Anna (Lostumbo) B.; m. Joan Marie Stanley, May 25, 1968; children: Dawn Nicole, Stefanie Michele. BS, NYU, 1967. CPA, N.J. Plant mgr. Pepperidge Farm Inc. Campbell Soup Co., Downingtown, Pa., 1980-82; v.p., controller Mrs. Paul's Kitchens Campbell Soup Co., Phila., 1982-84, Campbell Soup U.S.A., Camden, N.J., 1984-85; exec. v.p., chief fin. officer Interstate Bakeries, Kansas City, Mo., 1985—. Mem. Am. Inst. CPA's, N.J. Soc. CPA's, Nat. Assn. Accts. Home: 3612 W 122 Terrace Leawood KS 66209 Office: Interstate Bakeries Corp 12 E Armour Blvd Kansas City MO 64141

BEVAN, ROBERT LEWIS, lawyer; b. Springfield, Mo., Mar. 23, 1928; s. Gene Walter and Blanche Omega (Woods) B.; m. Ronice Diane Gartin, Jan 25, 1977; children: Matthew Gene, Lisa Ann. AB, U. Mo., 1950; LLB, U. Kansas City, 1957. Bar: Mo. 1957, D.C. 1969. Adminstrv. asst. U.S. Senator T. Hennings Jr., Washington, 1957-60; legis. asst. U.S. Senator E.V. Long, Washington, 1960-69; sr. govt. relations counsel Am. Bankers Assn., Washington, 1970-84; ptnr. Hopkins & Sutter, Washington, 1984—. Ghost author: The Intruders, 1967; contbg. editor U.S. Banker, 1985-88. Fieldman Dem. Nat. Com., 1968. Served with U.S. Army, 1946-47, 1951-53. Mem. ABA (adminstrv. law sect., bus. law sect., chmn. banking law com.). Democrat. Methodist. Club: Exchequer (Washington). Home: 310 N Pitt St Alexandria VA 22314 Office: Hopkins Sutter Hamel & Park 888 16th St NW Washington DC 20006

BEVERETT, ANDREW JACKSON, merchandising executive; b. Midland City, Ala., Feb. 21, 1917; s. Andrew J. and Ella Levonie (Adams) B.; B.S., Samford U., 1940; M.B.A., Harvard U., 1942; m. Martha Sophia Landgrabe, May 26, 1951; children—Andrew Jackson III, James Edmund, Faye A. Various exec. positions in corporate planning and mgmt. United Air Lines, Chgo., 1946-66; dir. aviation econs., sr. mktg. and econ. cons. Mgmt. and Econs. Research, Inc., Palo Alto, Calif., 1966-71; sr. economist Stanford Research Inst., Menlo Park, 1971-72; pres. Edy's on the Peninsula stores, 1973-78; real estate broker, fin. and tax cons., Saratoga, Calif., 1979—. Served from ensign to lt. USNR, 1942-46. Mem. Nat. Assn. Enrolled Agts., Nat. Assn. Realtors, Pi Gamma Mu, Phi Kappa Phi. Home: 19597 Via Monte Dr Saratoga CA 95070 Office: 12175 Saratoga Sunnyvale Rd Suite A Saratoga CA 95070

BEVILLE, R. HARWOOD, shopping center development executive; b. Phila., Aug. 30, 1940; s. Ross Harwood and Edna Mae (LaFon) B.; m. Judith Ann Miles; children—Ross H., Melissa Ann. B.S. in Mech. Engring., U. Md., 1962; M.B.A., Harvard U., 1964. Various positions FMC Corp., 1964-66, asst. to pres. Bolens div., 1966-67, gen. mgr. recreational vehicle mfg. and sales, 1967-68; sr. analyst U.S. Bur. Budget, Washington, 1968-70; dir. corp. planning Rouse Co., Columbia, Md., 1970-73, v.p., 1973-75, sr. v.p., chief fin. officer, 1975-78, exec. v.p., 1978—; trustee Internat. Council Shopping Ctrs. Chmn. campaign for excellence, mem. bus. adv. council U. Md.; mem. bus. adv. council Anne Arundel County, Md.; bd. dirs. Traditional Acupuncture Inst. Home: 1300 Eva Gude Dr Crownsville MD Office: Rouse Co 10275 Little Patuxent Pkwy Columbia MD 21044

BEVINGTON, VIRGINIA APPLEGARTH, financial planning and investment advisor; b. Atlanta, Feb. 24, 1953; d. William Francis and Alice Lenore (Vollmer) Applegarth; m. E. Milton Bevington Jr., Jan. 4, 1974 (div. 1987); children: Alden Keene, Elizabeth Rickey. BA cum laude, Vanderbilt U., Nashville, 1974. CLU; cert. fin. planner; chartered fin. cons. Pension analyst Sun Life Can., Atlanta, 1974-77; trust adminstr. Trust Co. Bank, Atlanta, 1977-78; fin. planning cons. Roe, Martin and Nieman, Atlanta, 1978-79; pres. GRAM Group, Winchester, Mass., 1984-87; sr. fin. planner APEX Adv. Services, Cambridge, Mass., 1987-88, v.p., 1988-89; ptnr. TFC Fin. Mgmt., Boston, 1989—; mem. adv. bd. fin. planning Boston U. Contbg. editor Fin. Planning mag., 1986—; author Protecting Your Family with Insurance, 1989. Mem. Boston Bus. Assn. (pres. 1988—), Internat. Assn. for Fin. Planning (bd. dirs. Boston chpt. 1987-88, sec. 1988—), Am. Soc. CLUs and chartered fin. cons., Inst. Cert. Fin. Planners. Democrat. Office: TFC Fin Mgmt 176 Federal St Boston MA 02110

BEVIS, JAMES WAYNE, manufacturing company executive; b. Quincy, Fla., Sept. 29, 1934; s. Harold Wayne and Maude (Kelly) B.; m. Bettye Jane Johns, Aug. 29, 1954; children—Harold, Graydon, Tina. B.S. in Indsl. Engring., U. Fla., 1959. With Gen. Electric, 1959-69; v.p. Rupp Industries, Mansfield, Ohio, 1969-73; v.p. ops. Rolscreen Co., Pella, Iowa, 1973-80, pres., chief exec. officer, 1980—. Republican. Home: Rt 3 Pella IA 50219 Office: Rolscreen Co 102 Main St Pella IA 50219

BEYER, WILLIAM EDWARD, financial executive; b. Portland, Oreg., Oct. 10, 1950; s. Peter William and Doris May (Ulin) B.; m. Jeannetta Louise Jensen, June 29, 1974 (div. Jan. 1988); children: Erik William, Jessica Louise. BS in Acctg., Portland State U., 1978. Ops. officer U.S. Nat. Bank Oreg., Portland, 1974-76; contract auditor U.S. Army CE, Portland, 1977; fin. analyst Portland GE, 1978-82, cash mgr., 1982-85; treasury mgr. Portland Gen. Corp., 1986—. Contbr. to various mags. Mem. contbns. com. United Way Columbia-Willamette (Oreg.), Portland, 1979; mem. allocations com. United Way, 1980-82. With USAF, 1970-73. Mem. Nat. Corp. Cash Mgmt. Assn. (bd. dirs. 1987—, chmn. publs. com. 1988), Portland Cash Mgrs. Assn. (cert.). Democrat. Lutheran. Home: 3455 NE 34th St Portland OR 97212 Office: Portland Gen Corp 121 SW Salmon St Portland OR 97204

BEYERLEIN, FRITZ WERNER, manufacturing company executive; b. Berlin, Mar. 13, 1936; came to U.S., 1967; s. Fritz and Gertrud (Jaeger) B.; 1 child, Dagmar Bettina. BS in Chemistry, Tech. U. Karlsruhe, 1958; MS in Phys. Chemistry, U. Munich, 1960; PhD, Tech. U. Aachen, 1966. Sect. mgr. semicondr. tech. devel. Siemens Corp., Munich, 1958-66; sect. mgr. assembly tech. devel. Fairchild Rsch. & Devel., Palo Alto, Calif., 1967-68; engring. mgr. Nat. Semicondr., Santa Clara, Calif., 1968-69; dept. mgr. worldwide assembly and packaging ops. Signetics Corp., Sunnyvale, Calif., 1964-76; pres., owner tech. cons. svc., Sunnyvale, 1976-83; v.p. mfg. Cypress Semicondr. Corp., San Jose, Calif., 1983—; cons. in field. Patentee in field. Mem. German Chem. Soc., French Engring. Soc. Home: 941 Olympus Ct Sunnyvale CA 94087

BEYMER, CLYDE EASTON, bank executive; b. Huchinson, Kans., Aug. 12, 1920; s. Clyde Elmer and Ethel M. (Jones); m. Barbara J., June 17, 1942; children: E. Easton, Gary C., Robert K. BA in Econs., Ft. Hays State U., 1942. Pres. Beymer & Beymer Inc., Lakin, Kans., 1946—; pres., chmn. bd. dirs. Kearny County Bank, Lakin, 1975—; dir. Plains Petroleum Co., Lakewood, Colo., 1985—. Lt. U.S. Army, 1942-46. Republican. Methodist. Home: Country Heights Lakin KS 67860 Office: Kearny County Bank 221 N Main Lakin KS 67860

BHATIA, NAVIN CHANDRA, structural engineer; b. Gujranwala, Punjab, India, Mar. 18, 1942; came to U.S., 1970; s. Kundan Lal and Shanti Devi Bhatia; m. Uma Haryal, Feb. 11, 1979; children: Ramona, Shaun. MSCE, Ill. Inst. tech., 1973, postgrad., 1973-76, 80-82. Registered profl., structural engr., Ill. Constrn. engr. M/S Bharat Constrn. Co., Bombay, 1962-65; field engr. M/S Bertlin & Ptnrs., Bombay, 1965-70; structural engr. Sargent & Lundy, Chgo., 1973-76, sr. structural engr., 1976-79, sr. engring. analyst, 1979—. Yoga and meditation practitioner Himalayan Inst., Glenview, Ill., 1985—. Mem. ASCE, Am. Soc. Egrs. from India (pres. Chgo. chpt. 1985-87). Home: 932 Kentucky Ln Elk Grove Village IL 60007 Office: Sargent & Lundy 55 E Monroe Chicago IL 60603

BIAGO, ANTHONY JOSEPH, real estate corporation executive, accountant; b. Exeter, Pa., Feb. 24, 1938; s. Albert and Rose (Bianco) B.; m. Barbara Ellen Killiri, Oct. 8, 1960; children: Denise Ann, Anthony Joseph Jr. AS in Mgmt., Middlesex Coll., 1971; BS in Acctg., Rutgers U., 1974; MBA in Fin., La Salle U., 1980. Controller Tujax Industries, N.Y.C., 1969-72; pres. Porter Foods, Inc., Linden, N.J., 1973-79; v.p. fin. Elizabeth Iron Works, Union, N.J., 1980-83; pres. Ace Brokers, Union, N.J., 1983—, ABBCO Devel. Corp., Kenilworth, N.J., 1983—; appraiser-cons. N.J. Cts., State of N.J., 1983—. Chmn. Boy Scouts Am., Cranford, N.J., 1979-80; com. mem. Rep. Party, Union, 1977-81; treas. Cranford Rep. Com., 1980-81; mem. Cranford Zoning Bd. Adjustments, 1980-82. Served with U.S. Army, 1956-59. Mem. Rutgers Alumni Assn., Delta Sigma Pi (pres. 1972-73). Roman Catholic. Lodge: KC (pres. 1960). Office: Ace Bus Brokers & ABBCO Devel Corp 1527A Stuyvesant Ave Union NJ 07083

BIALOCK, MARION GALE, professor in economics; b. Paragould, Ark., July 12, 1948; s. Rupert Leonard and Vera Mae (StevensonO B.; m. Marlys Ann Storck, Aug. 2, 1969; children: Bart, Jacob. BSBA, U. Ark., 1970, MA, 1972; PhDin Econs., Okla. State U., 1980. Instr. of econs. Ga. So. Coll., Statesboro, 1971-73; grad. asst. Okla. State U., Stillwater, 1973-75, instr. of econs., 1975-76, rsch. assoc., 1976-77; asst. prof. of econs. U. Evansville(Ind.), 1977-83; assoc. prof. of econs. Harlaxton Coll., Gratham, Eng., 1983—; econ. cons. law firms in Ind., Ky., Ill., 1980—. Author numerous papers in field. Mem. So. Regional Sci. Assn., So. Econs. Assn., Duck Lodge. Office: U Evansville 1800 Lincoln Ave Evansville IN 47722

BIANCA, ANDREW MICHAEL, computer software executive; b. Mineola, N.Y., May 22, 1956; s. Victor Anthony and Rita Mary (Lusardi) B. BA in Managerial Econs. and Engring. Sci., SUNY, Stony Brook, 1980; MS, Ariz. State U., 1988. Research asst. HEW project, SUNY, Stony Brook, 1977, research asst. Nat. Hwy. Traffic Safety Adminstrn., 1978; account rep. Micro Computer Brokers, Phoenix, 1981-83; research asst. Ariz. State U., Tempe, 1984; pres. Amber Info. Systems, Phoenix, 1983—. Mem. Digital Equipment User Group, VAX User Group Ariz., Mensa, Alpha Zeta. Office: Microtech 3039 W Kristal Phoenix AZ 85027

BIANCHI, CHARLES PAUL, financial executive, consultant; b. Texarkana, Tex., Sept. 3, 1945; s. Angelo Paul and Jewel Evelyn (LaFayette) B.; m. Stephanie Ellquist, Aug. 11, 1973; children: Charles Brandon LaFayette, Canaan Desiree Ellquist. BA, Dickinson Coll., 1967; M in Bus. Mgmt., Cen. Mich. U., 1976. Cert. fin. planner, registered investment adviser. Employment orientation instr. Pa. Bur. Employment Security, Scranton, 1971-72; mgmt. analyst Defense Logistics Agy., Phila., 1972-75; program, sr. budget analyst Defense Logistics Agy., Alexandria, Va., 1975-78; fed. budget specialist Exec. Office Pres. OMB, Washington, 1978-83; owner, prin. Charles P. Bianchi Fin. Planning and Investment Adv. Services, Arlington, Va., 1985—; internal cons. Inter-Am. Devel. Bank, Washington, 1983-89; pres. Wealth Conservancy Internat., 1989—; OMB rep. Am. Assn. Budget and Program Analysts, Washington, 1976-77; registered rep. affiliate Tucker Anthony, R.L. Day, 1987-89. Mem. World Affairs Coun. Washington. Served with Peace Corps, 1969-71. Mem. Inst. Cert. Fin. Planners, Internat. Assn. Fin. Planning, Fin. Analysts Fedn., Washington Soc. Investment Analysts, Assn. Returned Peace Corps Vols., Theta Chi. Home: 224 N Fillmore St Arlington VA 22201

BIANCHI, PHILIP WILCKES, stockbroker; b. N.Y.C., Apr. 12, 1931; s. Albert William and Helen Gladys (Wilckes) B.; B.S. in Indsl. Mgmt., M.I.T., 1953; m. Marion Ayer Bigelow, Mar. 6, 1976; children by previous marriage—Felicia Anne, Elizabeth Alexandra. With USM Corp., Boston, 1957-77, mgr. balance payments, 1971-74, adminstr. policies, procedures, 1974-77; with Drexel Burnham Lambert Inc., Boston, 1977-89, Smith Barney, Boston, 1989—. Served with USAF, 1953-55. Episcopalian. Clubs: Country (Brookline); Union Boat (Boston). Office: Smith Barney One Federal St Boston MA 02110

BICANICH, THOMAS PAUL, business educator; b. Simpson, Pa., Dec. 12, 1931; s. Thomas and Rose Marie (Vranich) B. BE, Ind. U. Pa., 1957, MEd, 1965; EdD, U. Pitts., 1970. Cert. tchr. Instr. Monessen (Pa.) High Sch., 1957-65; assoc. prof. U. Pitts., 1965—; evaluator project Dept. Edn. Harrisburg, Pa., 1965—. Contbr. articles to profl. jours. Served in U.S. Navy, 1949-53. Mem. Pa. Bus. Edn. Assn. (pres. 1975-76, recipient Outstanding Post-Secondary award 1981), Tri-State Bus. Edn. Assn. (pres. 1970, life), Ea. Bus. Edn. Assn. (v.p. 1969-70, Nat. Assn. Bus. Tchr. Edn. (dir. research 1977-78), Delta Pi Epsilon (pres. 1973-75, sponsor 1975—). Office: U Pitts 4M21 Forbes Quadrangle Pittsburgh PA 15260

BICK, DAVID GREER, health care marketing executive; b. Toledo, June 29, 1953; s. James D. and Carol Jean (Hermann) B.; children: Jennifer Kelly, Jesse Quinn, Matthew Adam, Wylie Christine. BE, U. Toledo, 1975; cert. health cons. Purdue U., 1981. Dist. mgr. Blue Cross Northwest Ohio, Tiffin, 1977-79, regional mgr., Sandusky, 1979-81, dir. sales, Toledo, 1981-82; v.p. mktg. Blue Cross/Blue Shield Central N.Y., Syracuse, 1983; exec. dir. Preview-Health Benefits Mgmt. of Ohio, Toledo, 1984-87, chief mktg. exec. Medchoice/Dentachoice HMO Blue Cross and Blue Shield of Ohio, 1984-87, v.p. sales and support sevices, mut. health services, 1988; v.p. slaes and mktg. Family Health Plan HMO, 1989—. Author: Paupers and Profiteers (poetry). Mem. Toledo Found. for Life, PTA, People's Med. Soc., The Park Ridge Ctr. Inst. for the Study of Health, Faith & Ethics, Toledo Zoological Soc., Toledo Mus. Art. Mem. Am. Coll. Utilization Rev. Physicians, Hastings Ctr./Inst. & Soc. of Ethics and Life, Am. Hosp. Assn., U.S. Tennis Assn., U. Toledo Alumni Assn., Toledo C. of C., Boilermaker Club (Purdue), Rotary. Avocations: photography, golf, basketball, skiing, tennis. Roman Catholic. Home: 4000 Sylvania Ave #58 Toledo OH 43623 Office: Family Health Plan HMO 333 Fourteenth St Toledo OH 43624

BICKEL, BERTRAM WATKINS, retired comptroller; b. Mt. Carmel, Pa., Jan. 26, 1925; s. George Isaac and Edith (Watkins) B.; m. Charis Irene Henry, June 8, 1946; 1 son, Keith David. Grad. high sch. Head teller Union Nat. Bank, Mt. Carmel, 1946-50; nat. bank examiner 1951-61; sr. v.p., comptroller Merchants Nat. Bank, Allentown, Pa., 1961-76; comptroller Norton Oil Co., Phillipsburg, N.J., 1977-87, ret., 1987; Accounting adviser Lehigh County Community Coll. Bd. dirs. treas. Allentown YMCA. Served with USNR, 1943-46. Mem. Bank Adminstrn. Inst. (dir.), Am. Legion. Republican. Presbyn. Clubs: Masons; Brookside Country (Macungie, Pa.) (dir.); Livingston (Allentown), Lehigh Valley (Allentown); Willow Brook Golf (Catasauqua, Pa.). Home: 509 Longacre Dr PO Box 714 Cherryville PA 18035

BICKEL, FLOYD GILBERT, III, investment counselor; b. St. Louis, Jan. 10, 1944; s. Floyd Gilbert II and Mary Mildred (Welch) B.; B.S. in Bus. Adminstrn., Washington U., St. Louis, 1966; M.S. in Commerce, St. Louis U., 1968; m. Martha Wohler, June 11, 1966; children—Christine Carleton, Susan Marie, Katherine Anne, Jennifer Anne, Laura Elizabeth, Andrew Barrett (dec.). With research dept. Yates, Woods & Co., St. Louis, 1966-67; asst. br. mgr. E.F. Hutton & Co., Inc., St. Louis, 1967-70; asst. v.p., resident mgr. Bache & Co., Inc., St. Louis, 1970-72; pres. Donelan-Phelps Investment Advisors, Inc., St. Louis, 1972-80; first v.p., dir. consulting services E.F. Hutton & Co., Inc., St. Louis, 1980-88, v.p. Merrill Lynch and Co., 1988—; pres., dir. Drew Petroleum, Inc. Biclan, Inc.; pres. Bicmel, Inc.; chmn., dir. Data Research Assos., Inc., St. John's Bancshares, Inc. Mem. City of Des Peres (Mo.) Planning and Zoning Commn., 1975-76; chmn. St. Louis County Bd. Equalization, 1976-79; pub. safety commr. City of Des Peres, 1977-80, mem. audit and fin. com., 1980-86; mem. Gov.'s Crime Commn., 1981—; bd. dirs. Villa Duchesne Sch. Mem. Internat. Soc. Cert. Employee Benefit Specialists, Internat. Found. Employee Benefit Plan, St. Louis Soc. Fin. Analysts, Bellerive Country Club (bd. dirs., treas.), Beaver Creek Club, St. Louis Club, John's Island Club, Commanderie de Bordeaux Club. Republican. Presbyterian. Contbr. bus. articles to mags. Home: 30 Huntleigh Woods Saint Louis MO 63131 Office: Merrill lynch & Co 607 S Lindbergh Blvd Saint Louis MO 63131

BICKERTON, JOHN THORBURN, pharmaceutical executive; b. Windsor, Ont., Can., Apr. 6, 1930; came to U.S., 1972; s. Edward Levi and Catherine (Thorburn) B.; m. Natalie Katherine Kasurak, Aug. 20, 1955; children: Katherine, John, Paul. B in Commerce, Queen's U., Kingston, Ont., 1953. Auditor Price Waterhouse & Co., Windsor, 1953-57; asst. controller Parke Davis subs. Warner Lambert Co., Detroit, 1957-72; controller Warner Lambert Internat., Morris Plains, N.J., 1972-80, v.p. fin. Europe, 1980-82; v.p. fin. Parke Davis subs. Warner Lambert Co., Morris Plains, N.J., 1982—. Episcopalian. Home: 16 Summit Rd Morristown NJ 07960

BICKETT, THOMAS J., petrochemical company executive, accountant; b. 1939. BS, Pa. State U., 1962. CPA. With S.D. Leidesdorf & Co., 1962-73; with Witco Corp., N.Y.C., 1973—, controller, 1977-81, v.p., 1980-81, v.p. fin. adminstrn., 1981-84, exec. v.p. fin. adminstrn., from 1984, now pres., chief op. officer, also bd. dirs. Mem. Am. Inst. CPAs. Office: Witco Corp 520 Madison Ave New York NY 10022 *

BICKFORD, GEORGE PERCIVAL, lawyer; b. Berlin, N.H., Nov. 28, 1901; s. Gershon Percival and Lula Adine (Buck) B.; m. Clara L. Gehring, Apr. 6, 1933 (dec. Dec. 1985); 1 dau., Louise G. Boyd; m. Jessie B. McGaw, May, 1986 (div. Nov. 1988). A.B. cum laude, Harvard, 1922, LL.B., 1926. Bar: Ohio 1926. Since practiced in Cleve.; asso. firm Arter & Hadden, partner, 1940—; instr. Hauchung U., Wuchang, China, 1922-23; instr. taxation Western Res. Law Sch., 1940-47; lectr. Indian history and culture Cleve. Coll., 1948-50; gen. counsel FHA, Washington, 1958-59; hon. consul of India 1964—; Mem. Cleve. Moral Claims Commn., 1935-37. Mem. Cuyahoga County Rep. Exec. Com., 1948-58, 60—; Trustee Am. U. in Cairo; vis. com. fine arts dept. Harvard, 1962-68, 72-78; trustee, former v.p. Cleve. Mus. Art; trustee Cleve. Inst. Art.; mem. Nat. Com. for Festival of India in U.S., 1985; mem. adv. com. Asia Soc. Houston, 1986. Served with Ohio N.G., 1926-29; from capt. to lt. col. JAG dept. AUS, 1942-46. Decorated Legion of Merit. Mem. Am., Ohio, Cleve. bar assns., Cleve. Council World Affairs (trustee). Episcopalian (standing com. Diocese Ohio 1951-63, chancellor 1962-77). Clubs: Union (Cleve.), Rowfant (Cleve.); Army and Navy (Washington); Harvard (N.Y.C.). Home: 13415 Shaker Blvd #12K3 Cleveland OH 44120

BICKFORD, JEWELLE W., investment banker; b. Evanston, Ill., Dec. 12, 1941; d. James A. Wooten and Phyllis (Taber) Kades; m. Nathaniel J. Bickford, Feb. 1, 1962; children: Laura C., Emily A. BA, Sarah Lawrence Coll., 1974. Trustee, chair com. on gen. programs and issues Community Svc. Soc., N.Y.C., 1973-77; dir. community bd. assistance unit Office of the

Mayor, N.Y.C., 1977-80; v.p. Citibank, N.A., N.Y.C., 1980-84; v.p. Dillon, Read & Co., Inc., N.Y.C., 1984-85, sr. v.p., 1985-88; pres. Trepp Fin. Svcs., Inc., N.Y.C., 1988—; mem. adv. bd. First Womens Bank, 1975-78. Trustee South Street Seaport Theater, chmn. bd. 1978-83; trustee Coro Found., Citizens Com. for Children; bd. dirs. Phoenix House Found.; trustee, sec. bd. trustees Fountain House; mem. exec. com. of fin. coun. Dem. Nat. Com. Mem. Fin. Womens Assn. (bd. dirs.). Democrat. Episcopalian. Club: River (N.Y.C.). Home: 969 Fifth Avenue New York NY 10021 Office: Trepp Fin Svcs Inc 275 Madison Ave New York NY 10016

BICKFORD, JOHN VAN BUREN, coal company executive; b. Roanoke, Va., 1934. Grad., Va. Poly Inst., 1955. Pres., dir. Westmoreland Coal Sales Co., Phila.; dir. Eastern Coal & Coke Co. Office: Westmoreland Coal Co 700 The Bellevue 200 S Broad St Philadelphia PA 19102

BICKMORE, DANFORD MARK, finance company executive; b. Santa Maria, Calif., Jan. 19, 1948; s. David Keith and Norma (Bird) B.; m. Christine Smith, June 28, 1973 (div. Dec. 1982); children: Mark, Scott, Tara; m. Myrna Corine Johnson, Mar. 6, 1985; children: Corinne, Connie, Kevin, Karen. BS, Calif. State U. Acct. Sunworld, Inc., Bakersfield, Calif., 1980-81, Tosco Corp., Bakersfield, Calif., 1981-82; spl. asst. to pres. Adam, Midvale, Utah, 1982-85; pres., founder Fin. Extensions Corp., Mesa, Ariz., 1985—; bd. dirs. Phase III Market, Mesa; bd. dirs., participant Nat. Leadership Inst., N.Y.C. Sustaining mem. Rep. Nat. Com., Washington, 1986; pres. Students in Free Enterprise, Bakersfield, 1981. Served with U.S. Army, 1969-71, Vietnam. Recipient Cert. of Appreciation Pres. U.S. Richard M. Nixon, 1971. Mem. Nat. C. of C. Republican. Mormon. Office: Fin Extensions Corp PO Box 2153 Mesa AZ 85204

BICKNER, BRUCE PIERCE, agriculture and natural resources executive; b. Chgo., Sept. 21, 1943; s. Arno A. and Dorothy P. (Pierce) B.; m. Joan Alice Johnson, July 29, 1967; children: Brian, Kevin, Julie. B.A., DePauw U., 1965; J.D., U. Mich., 1968. Bar: Ill. 1968, Wis. 1968. Law clk. U.S. Dist. Ct., Milw., 1969; ptnr. Sidley & Austin, Chgo., 1970-75; chmn., chief exec. officer Dekalb (Ill.) Corp., 1976—; bd. dirs. Depco, Inc., Denver, DeKalb Energy Can. Ltd., Calgary, Alta., Pride Petroleum Svcs. Inc., Houston, Lindsay Mfg. Co., Nebr. Mem. ABA. Republican. Mem. Evangelical Covenant Ch. Am. Office: DeKalb Corp 3100 Sycamore Rd De Kalb IL 60115

BIDDLE, ANTHONY JOSEPH DREXEL, III, investment banker; b. Washington, Nov. 30, 1948; s. Anthony Joseph Drexel Biddle Jr. and Margaret (Atkinson) Biddle Robbins; m. Karen M. Erskine, Dec. 23, 1970; children: Anthony Joseph Drexel IV, Cordelia Erskine Drexel. BS in Econs., Cornell U., 1970; MBA in Fin., U. Pa., 1975. 2d v.p. Chase Manhattan Bank, N.Y.C., 1975-77; mgr. Chase Manhattan Ltd., London, 1977-79; v.p. Flint Hills Drilling Co., Winfield, Kans., 1979-81; ptnr. Hale and Assocs., Washington and Winfield, 1979-81; pres. Drexel Biddle and Co. Inc., Phila., 1982—; ptnr. L.T. Funston and Co. Inc., Phila., 1987-88; mng. dir. The Hanseatic Group Inc., Phila., 1988—; owner, dir. Constn. Cruise Lines Inc., Phila., 1988—. Contbg. author: Legal Aspects of the Management Process, 1976. Bd. advisors Boys Harbor Inc., N.Y.C., 1972—; bd. dirs. Charity Ball Inc., Phila., 1981—, Phila. Ship Preservation Guild, 1982—, Independence Hall Assn., Phila., 1984—, Drexel U. Friends, Phila., 1987—; founding co-chmn. Arthur Ross Gallery, U. Pa., 1982—; assoc. trustee U. Pa., 1983-87; trustee Nat. Inst. for Music Theater, Kennedy Ctr., Washington, 1985-87. With USN, 1970-73. Mem. Wharton Olympus Inc. (chmn. Europe-Mid East and Asia 1978-79), Soc. of Cin., Phila. Club, Athenaeum Club, Army-Navy Club, U. Club, Royal Automobile Club, Travellers Club. Home: 638 Panama St Philadelphia PA 19106

BIDDLE, DONALD RAY, aerospace company executive; b. Alton, Mo., June 30, 1936; s. Ernest Everet and Dortha Marie (McGuire) B.; student El Dorado (Kans.) Jr. Coll., 1953-55, Pratt (Kans.) Jr. Coll., 1955-56; B.S. in Mech. Engring., Washington U., St. Louis, 1961; postgrad. computer sci. Pa. State U. Extension, 1963; certificate bus. mgmt. Alexander Hamilton Inst., 1958; m. Nancy Ann Dunham, Mar. 13, 1955; children—Jeanne Kay Biddle Bednash, Mitchell Lee, Charles Alan. Design group engr. Emerson Elec. Mfg., St. Louis, 1957-61; design specialist Boeing Vertol, Springfield, Pa., 1962; cons. engr. Ewing Tech. Design, Phila., 1962-66; chief engr. rotary wing Gates Learjet, Wichita, Kans., 1967-70; dir. engring. Parsons of Calif. div. HITCO, Stockton, Calif., 1971—. Cons. engr. Scoutmaster, counselor, instl. rep. Boy Scouts Am., St. Ann, Mo., 1958-61; mem. Springfield Sch. Bd., 1964. Mem. Am. Helicopter Soc. (sec.-treas. Wichita chpt. 1969), ASME, Am. Mgmt. Assn., ASTM, Am. Inst. Aeros. and Astronautics, Exptl. Pilots Assn. Republican. Methodist (trustee, chmn. 1974-76, 84-86, staff parish 1987-88). Patentee landing gear designs, inflatable rescue system, glass retention systems, adjustable jack system, cold weather start fluorescent lamp, paper honeycomb core post-process systems. Home: 1140 Stanton Way Stockton CA 95207 Office: HITCO 3437 Airport Way Stockton CA 95206

BIDDLE, GARY JAMES, manufacturing company executive; b. Tiffin, Ohio, Nov. 9, 1938; s. Harold J. and Virginia (Lang) B.; m. Jeanne Castelluccio, May 9, 1981; children: Amanda J., Gregg G. AA, Rider Coll., 1971, BS in Commerce, 1975. Various staff positions Am. Standard, Inc., Tiffin, 1957-66; mfg. cons. Am. Standard, Inc., N.Y.C., 1966-69; mgr. product control Am. Standard, Inc., Trenton, N.J., 1969-73; dir. mgmt. info. systems Am. Standard, Inc., Piscataway, N.J., 1973-83; staff v.p. mgmt. info. systems Am. Standard, Inc., N.Y.C., 1983-86, v.p. info. systems, 1986—. Club: Union League (N.Y.C.). Home: 32 Riverview Terr Belle Mead NJ 08502 Office: Am Standard Inc 40 W 40th St New York NY 10018

BIDERMAN, CHARLES ISRAEL, real estate investor; b. N.Y.C., Oct. 24, 1946; m. Brenda Carol Nicholson (div.); 1 child, John Patrick; m. Cheryl Marie Johnson, Sept. 8, 1985; 1 child, Christopher Isaac. BA, Bklyn. Coll., 1967; MBA, Harvard U., 1971. Assoc. editor Barron's Fin. Weekly, 1971-73; pres. Charles Biderman & Co., N.Y.C. and Nashville, 1973-77, 80—, Market St. Devel. Corp. (formerly Nashville Mgmt. Corp.), 1976-80; fin. editor Wall St. Final, N.Y.C. Constructed over 200 homes including Gaslite Condominiums and Lafayette Townhouses, Seaside Park, N.J., Three Pence Brooke Townhomes, Jackson, N.J., Quail Farms, Jackson. Bd. dirs. Tenn. Dance Theater, 1977-80. Served with USAF, 1966-67. Home: 36 Linda Dr Jackson NJ 08527 Office: The Charles Biderman Co PO Box 1325 Jackson NJ 08527

BIDLACK, JERALD DEAN, manufacturing company executive; b. Oakwood, Ohio, Nov. 18, 1935; s. Ansel Carol and Vivian Irene (Huff) B.; m. Ruth Heidenescher, Dec. 24, 1953; children: Jeffrey, Cynthia, Timothy, Bethann, Deborah. B.S.M.E., Tri-State U., 1956; postgrad., Wayne State U., 1959. Registered profl. engr., N.Y. Sr. engr. Cadillac Gage Co., Warren, Mich., 1956-63; engring. mgr. indsl. Moog Inc., East Aurora, N.Y., 1963-67; mng. dir. Moog Inc., Boeblingen, Republic of Germany, 1967-69; pres. internat. ops. Moog Inc., East Aurora, 1969—; adj. lectr. SUNY-Buffalo, 1979—; dir. Moog Inc., Moog Gmbh, Moog Controls Ltd., Moog Sarl, Moog Japan. Patentee in field. Mem. com. Boy Scouts Am., East Aurora, 1973-76. Mem. Young Pres.'s Orgn. (chpt. chmn. 1981-82), Fluid Power Soc., Nat. Soc. Profl. Engrs., Buffalo and Erie County C. of C. Club: Country of Buffalo. Home: 323 Windsor Ln East Aurora NY 14052 Office: Moog Inc East Aurora NY 14052

BIDWELL, JAMES TRUMAN, JR., lawyer; b. N.Y.C., Jan. 2, 1934; s. James Truman and Mary (Kane) B.; m. Gail S. Bidwell, Mar. 6, 1965 (div.); children: Hillary Day, Kimberly Wade, Courtney E.; m. Katharine T. O'Neil, July 15, 1988. B.A., Yale U., 1956; LL.B., Harvard U., 1959. Bar: N.Y. 1959. Atty. U.S. Air Force, Austin, Tex., 1959-62; assoc. firm Donovan, Leisure, Newton & Irvine, N.Y.C., 1962-68, ptnr., 1968-84; ptnr. White & Case, N.Y.C., 1984—. Pres. Youth Consultation Service, 1973-78. Mem. ABA, Fed. Bar Assn., N.Y. State Bar Assn., N.Y. County Lawyers Assn. Episcopalian. Club: Ch. N.Y.C. (pres. 1983-87). Lodge: Am. Friends of St. George's (pres. 1987—). Office: White & Case 1155 Ave of the Americas New York NY 10036

BIEBER, OWEN F., labor union official; b. North Dorr, Mich., Dec. 28, 1929; s. Albert F. and Minnie (Schwartz) B.; m. Shirley M. Van Woerkom, Nov. 25, 1950; children: Kenneth, Linda, Michael, Ronald, Joan. H.H.D., Grand Valley Coll., 1983; hon., Ferris State Coll., 1986. Rep. Internat. Union UAW, Grand Rapids, Mich., 1961-72, asst. regional dir. Region ID, 1972-74, regional dir Region ID, 1974-80; v.p. Internat. Union UAW, Detroit, 1980-83, pres., 1983—. Chmn. Kent County Dem. Com., Wyoming, Mich., 1964-66, mem. exec. bd., 1966-80; del. Nat. Dem. Convs., 1968, 76, 80. Named Labor Man of Yr., Kent County AFL-CIO, 1965. Mem. NAACP (life), Grand Rapids Urban League. Roman Catholic. Club: Economic of Detroit. Office: Internat Union United Automobile Aerospace & Agrl Implements Workers Am 8000 E Jefferson Ave Detroit MI 48214

BIEDERMANN, BROOKE, business owner; b. Chgo., June 2, 1950; d. Melvin Taylor and Barbara (Brent) B. BA, Skidmore Coll., 1972. Flight attendant Am. Airlines, Jamaica, N.Y., 1972-89; owner, pres. Switch Internat., Lyndhurst, N.J., 1986—. Mem. Assoc. Profl. Republican. Episcopalian. Home: Twin Ponds Ln Wilton CT 06897 Office: Switch Internat 291 Pine St Lyndhurst NJ 07071

BIEGELSEN, ELAINE LANDER, accountant; b. St. Louis, Feb. 8, 1939; d. Louis and Edna (Schramm) Lander; m. Paul Simeon Biegelsen, June 29, 1961; children: Elizabeth, Rebecca, Annie. BS, Washington U., St. Louis, 1961; MS, Purdue U., 1964; MBA, Xavier U., 1984. CPA, Ohio. Tchr. phys. edn. Fairborn (Ohio) City Schs., 1961-62; with payroll, personnel depts., coord. Glen Manor Home, Cin., 1980-81; acct., supr. Clayton Scroggins & Assocs., Cin., 1981-86; acct. William H. Lammert & Co., CPAs, Cin., 1986—. Mem. AICPA, Ohio Soc. CPAs, Am. Soc. Women Accts. (bd. dirs. 1988—), Cin. Women's Forum. Office: ...

BIEGLER, DAVID W., gas company executive; b. 1946; married. BS, St. Mary's U., 1968; postgrad., Harvard U., 1980. With Enserch Exploration Inc., 1966-78, petroleum engr., 1968-70, dist. petroleum engr., 1970-72, staff petroleum engr., then mgr. revenue control, 1972-74, chief engr., 1974-75, dir. engring. mktg. planning, then v.p. processing engring. mktg., 1975-77, v.p. land and mktg., 1977-78; exec. v.p. Pool Arabia, 1978-79; exec. v.p. eastern hemisphere Pool Intairdril, 1979-80; pres. Pool Well Servicing Co., 1980-84; pres. U.S. ops. Pool Co., 1984-85; pres., chief operating officer Lone Star Gas Co. div. Enserch Corp., Dallas, 1985—. Office: Lone Star Gas Co 301 S Harwood St Dallas TX 75201

BIEL, FREDRICK WILLIAM, savings and loan executive; b. Seattle, Apr. 13, 1938; s. William Harry and Leonora (LaForte) B.; m. Carolyn Jean Glaser, Aug. 19, 1942; children: Jean Marie, Margaret Ann. BA, U. Washington, 1961. Salesman McPherson Realty, Seattle, 1967; asst. mgr. Seattle First Nat. Bank, 1967-69; loan analyst IDS Mortgage Corp., Seattle, San Francisco, 1969-71; asst. v.p. Golden West Fin. Corp., Oakland, Calif., 1971-76; div. mgr. secondary market Mortgage Guaranty Ins. Corp., Los Angeles, 1976-78; v.p. Lloyds Bank Calif., Los Angeles, 1978-82; exec. v.p. Home Owners Savings & Loan Assoc., Boston, 1982—; bd. dirs. Home Fed. Mortgage Corp., Boston. Served to capt. with USAF, 1962-67. Mem. Mortgage Bankers Assn. Republican. Episcopalian. Office: Home Owners Fed Savs & Loan 3 Burlington Woods Burlington MA 01803

BIEL, GEORGE EVERETT, human resource executive; b. Frankfurt-am-Main, Germany, Mar. 9, 1949; came to U.S., 1953; s. Fred W. and Ingeborg E. (Weber) B.; m. Wendy D. Biel, Oct. 27, 1973; children: Scott, Brad. BSBA in Indsl. Psychology, CUNY, 1972; MA in Indsl. Psychology, Springfield Coll., 1973. Personnel rels. rep. Chase Manhattan Bank, N.Y.C., 1973-75; sr. employee rels. rep. Travlers Cheques div. Am. Express Co., N.Y.C., 1975-77, compensation mgr. internat. banking div., 1977-78; employee rels. advisor Celanese Fibers Mktg. Co., N.Y.C., 1978-79; employee rels. supr Celanese Fiber Industries, Inc., Shelby, N.C., 1979-81; domestic and expatriate supr. Esso Inter-Am., Inc. div. EXXON, Coral Gables, Fla., 1981-85; expatriate adminstrn. div. mgr. Internat. Colombia Resources Corp. subs. Exxon, Barranquilla, Colombia, 1985-88; cons. Drake Beam Morin, Inc., 1988-89; v.p. Manchester Inc., Parsippany, N.J., 1989—; founding mem., bd. dirs. Internat. Com. Employee Relocation Coun., Washington, 1982-85; founding mem. S. Fla. Relocation Network, Miami, 1981-85. Co-author: Guide to Employee Relocation and Relocation Policy Development, 1983. Bd. dirs. Colombo Americano Community Com., Barranquilla, 1985-88. Office: Manchester Inc 4 Gatehall Dr Parsippany NJ 07054

BIELECKI, PAUL MICHAEL, manufacturing executive; b. Boston, Nov. 22, 1947; s. Michael J. and Rosemary C. (Shannon) B.; m. Phyllis Ann Amoroso, Apr. 29, 1983; children: Kristine, Bryan, Kimberly. AA in Bus., Newbury Jr. Coll., Boston, 1979; BS in Bus., N.H. Coll., Manchester, 1981, MBA, 1982; MBL, Boston U., 1983. Planner RCA, Burlington, Mass., 1967-71; buyer Microwave Assn., Burlington, 1971-73, sr. buyer, 1973-74, sub. contracts mgr., 1974-75, purchasing mgr., 1975-76, materials mgr., 1976-78, acquisitions mgr., 1978-80; dir. materials Data Precision/Analogic, Danvers, Mass., 1981-84; ops./materials mgr. Ferro-Fluidics, Inc., Nashua, N.H., 1984—; v.p. cons. service Adv. Systems Concepts, Danville, N.H., 1978-84; bd. dirs. Hilton Electric Profl. Constrn., Hampstead, N.H.. Mem. Planning Bd., Danville, 1985-86, chmn. planning bd.; mem. Zoning Bd., 1986-88, mem. Cable Commn., 1985-88. With U.S. Army, 1967-71, Vietnam. Mem. Am. Prodn. Inventory Control, Profl. Purchasing Mgmt. Assn. Republican. Roman Catholic. Home: 14 Hampstead Rd S Danville NH 03881 Office: Ferro-Fluidics Inc 40 Simon St Nashua NH 03061

BIELORY, LEONARD, allergist, immunologist, medical school administrator; b. Neptune, N.J., Nov. 17, 1954; s. Max and Bessie (Spielberg) B.; m. Marilyn Miriam Gilan, July 5, 1981; children: Brett Phillip, Barry Mark. BS, Lehigh U., 1976, MS, 1976; MD, N.J. Med. Sch., 1980. Intern, resident U. Md. Hosp., Balt., 1980-82; clin. assoc. NIH, Bethesda, Md., 1982-85; dir. div. allergy and immunology N.J. Med. Sch., Newark, 1985—. Contbr. rsch. papers to profl. jours., chpt. to books. Bd. dirs. Congregation Israel, Springfield, N.J., 1988. Recipient Young Investigator award Am. Acad. Allergy and Immunology, 1985; Schering Corp. Travel grantee, 1985. Fellow ACP, Am. Acad. Allergy and Immunology; mem. Med. Soc. N.J. Jewish. Office: NJ Med Sch 185 S Orange Ave I-512 Newark NJ 07103-2757

BIELUCH, PHILIP JAMES, actuary; b. Hartford, Conn., Mar. 1, 1955; s. William Charles and Nellie (Sidor) B.; m. Gayle Denise Ashley, Feb. 16, 1985. BS in computer, Trinity Coll., 1976. Chartered life underwriter; chartered fin. cons. Actuarial assoc. Covenant Life Ins., Hartford, 1973-77; asst. v.p. Huggins & Co., Hartford, 1977-79; v.p. Sorensen & Assocs., Hartford, 1979-80; assoc. actuary Security-Conn., Avon, 1980-81; pres. Delta Actuaries, Inc., Hartford, 1982-85; cons. Tillinghast, A Towers Perrin Co., Hartford, 1985—, prin., 1986—. Fellow Soc. Actuaries; mem. Am. Acad. Actuaries, Am. Soc. CLU's, Conference of Actuaries in Pub. Practice. Republican. Roman Catholic. Clubs: University (Hartford) (bd. dirs. 1985-88). Home: 152 Woodruff Rd Farmington CT 06032 Office: Tillinghast One Commercial Pla Hartford CT 06103

BIERNACKI-PORAY, WLAD OTTON, architect; b. Lwow, Poland, June 9, 1924, came to U.S., 1950, naturalized, 1955; s. Roman Alexander and Ewa Valeria (Biernacki) P.; m. Zofia Maria Balicki, Aug. 15, 1947; children—Krystyna Cora, Teresa Nora, Marek Victor. BA, U. Rome, 1948; MA, Univ Coll., London, 1950. Registered architect, U.S., U.K., Can., Poland. Assoc. architect A. Alvarez Assocs., Montclair, N.J., 1951-54; chief designer, ptnr. Howard T. Fisher Assoc., N.Y.C., 1954-55; prin. Biernacki-Poray & Assocs., N.Y.C. and Montclair, N.J., 1955—; pres. Mike Poray & Assocs. Engring. Ltd., Nigeria; chmn. Poray, Peter & Assocs. Ltd., London; pres. Am. Biotech. Corp., Montclair, 1975—. Prin. works include: U.S. Fed. Office Bldg., Newark, 1968, Pediatric Inst. and Med. Acad., Krakow, Poland. Bd. dirs. Albert Schweitzer Fellowship, N.Y.C., 1975—, pres. Am. Rsch. Hosp., N.Y.C., 1960—. Lt. Arty., 1939-45, ETO, NATOUSA. Mem. Interplan Assn. Engrs. (pres. 1966-80), Am. Tower Assn. (pres. 1970—), AIA, Knights of Souvereign Order of St. John, Jerusalem Order of Malta. Roman Catholic. Office: Biernacki-Poray & Assocs 45 Park St Montclair NJ 07042

BIERSTEDT, PETER RICHARD, lawyer, consultant; b. Rhinebeck, N.Y., Jan. 2, 1943; s. Robert Henry and Betty (MacIver) B.; m. Carol Lynn Akiyama, Aug. 23, 1980. AB, Columbia U., 1965, JD cum laude, 1969; cert., U. Sorbonne, Paris, 1966. Bar: N.Y. 1969, U.S. Supreme Ct. 1973, Calif. 1977. Atty. with firms in N.Y.C., 1969-74; sole practice 1971, 75-76; with Avco Embassy Pictures Corp., Los Angeles, 1977-83; v.p., gen. counsel Avco Embassy Pictures Corp., 1978-80, sr. v.p., 1980-83, dir., 1981-83; gen. counsel New World Entertainment (formerly New World Pictures), L.A., 1984-87, exec. v.p., 1985-87; sr. exec. v.p. Office of Chmn. New World Entertainment (formerly New World Pictures), Los Angeles, 1987—, also bd. dirs.; pres. subs. New World Prodns. and New World Advt. New World Pictures, 1985—; guest lectr. U. Calif., Riverside, 1976-77, U. So. Calif., 1986, UCLA, 1987; bd. dirs. New World Pictures (Australia), Ltd., FilmDallas Pictures, Inc., Cinedco, Inc., Motion Picture Assn. Am., 1980-83. Mem. Motion Picture Assn. Am. (dir. 1980-83), Acad. Motion Picture Arts and Scis. (exec. br.), Am. Film Inst., N.Y. State Bar Assn., L.S. County Bar Assn., ACLU., AAAS. Democrat.

BIESENDORFER, WILLIAM JOE, management company executive, entrepreneur; b. Council Bluffs, Iowa, Aug. 7, 1943; s. Arthur William and Mildred Eileen (Witter) B.; m. Diane Louise Gartner, July 24, 1964; children: John David, Jennifer Marie. BArch, U. Nebr., 1967. Appraiser, constrn. analyst VA, Denver, 1971-76, asst. chief appraiser, 1976-79, chief appraiser, 1979-81, asst. loan officer, 1981-84; pres., owner Mgmt. Specialists Inc., Westminster, Colo., 1982—. Mem. com. appeals Arvada (Colo.) Urban Renewal Authority, 1985-88. Served to lt. USN, 1967-71. Mem. Community Assn. Inst., Denver Homebuilders Assn. Republican. Lutheran. Office: Mgmt Specialists Inc 8670 Wolff Ct Ste 150 Westminster CO 80030

BIGBIE, CHARLES ROY, III, underwriter; b. Tulsa, Oct. 9, 1959; s. Charles Roy Mr. and Virginia Elizabeth (Hittson) B.; m. Betty L. Brown, June 21, 1980; children: Angela L., Cheryl E. BS in Chem. Engring., U. Tulsa, 1981; cert., Am. U., Bryn Mawr, Pa., 1987. CLU, chartered fin. cons. Mgr. data processing Spectron Corp., Tulsa, 1977-80; sales mgr. Smithco Engring., Tulsa, 1980-83; underwriter The New Eng., Tulsa, 1983—. Pres. Tulsa Fire Buff Assn., 1980; hon. mem. Tulsa Fire Dept., 1977. Mem. Am. Inst. Chem. Engrs. (sec. 1985), Nat. Assn. Life Underwriters, Tulsa Assn. Life Underwriters, Million Dollar Roundtable (life). Episcopalian. Club: Astronomy (Tulsa) (observing chmn. 1985-86). Lodge: Kiwanis. Home: 3144 S Atlanta Ave Tulsa OK 74105 Office: The New Eng 8023 E 63d Pl #750 Tulsa OK 74133

BIGGAR, JAMES MCCREA, food company executive; b. Cleve., Dec. 5, 1928; s. Hamilton Fisk and Ruth Carolyn (McCrea) B.; m. Margery Dean Stouffer, Dec. 29, 1950; children: Elizabeth, James, William, David. B.S. in Mech. Engring. and Engring. Adminstrn., Case Inst. Tech., 1950. With Reliance Electric Co., Cleve., 1950-60, mgr. alternating current products, 1955-60; with frozen foods div. Stouffer Corp., Cleve., 1960-70, mktg. v.p., 1960-66, v.p., gen. mgr., 1966-68, pres., 1968-70; v.p. food service group Litton Industries, Solon, Ohio, 1970-72; pres., chmn. bd., dir. Stouffer Corp., Solon, Ohio, from 1972; chmn., chief exec. officer Nestle Enterprises, Inc., Solon, Ohio, 1983—, also dir.; pres., chief exec. officer, dir. Nestle Holdings Inc., Wilmington, Del., 1985—; bd. dirs. Nat. City Corp. of Cleve., Sherwin-Williams Co., Cleve. Pres. Orange Local Sch. Bd., Pepper Pike, Ohio, 1967-68; v.p. Vocat. Guidances Svcs., Cleve., 1970-76; trustee Cleve. Clinic, Cleve. Tomorrow, Greater Cleve. Growth Assn., Playhouse Square Found., Univ. Sch., 1981-83; exec. v.p. Cleve. Devel. Advisors, Inc.; bd. govs. Women's Econ. Alliance; bd. overseers Exec. Coun. Fgn. Diplomats. Mem. Am. Frozen Food Inst. (past chmn., dir.), Grocery Mfrs. Am. (dir.), Phi Kappa Psi, Theta Tau, Beta Gamma Sigma. Presbyterian. Clubs: Cleve. Country, Clevelander, Pepper Pike Country, Rolling Rock.

BIGGART, JAMES H., JR., corporate finance executive; b. N.Y.C., Sept. 22, 1952; s. James H. and Charlotte M. (Britton) B.; m. Joy C. Johnson, June 26, 1982; children: Matthew James, Trevor Dickinson. BS in Fin., U. Va., 1974; MBA, U. Conn., 1975; cert. advanced study in fin., Fairfield (Conn) U., 1988. CPA, Conn. Tax staff Arthur Andersen & Co., N.Y.C., 1975-78, tax. sr., 1978-80, tax mgr., 1980-84; dir. taxes Hubbell, Inc., Orange, Conn., 1984-86, asst. treas., 1986-87, treas., 1987—, acct., cert. cash mgr., 1987—. Mem. Tax Execs. Inst., Fin. Execs. Inst., Nat. Corp. Cash Mgmt. Assn. Republican. Roman Catholic. Office: Hubbell Inc 584 Derby Milford Rd Orange CT 06477-4024

BIGGERS, RALPH LEE, structural engineer; b. Charlotte, N.C., Dec. 23, 1941; s. Ralph Lee and Sara Wilma (Kidd) B.; m. Sally Anne Miller, June 21, 1969; children: Lee Anne, Sara Katherine, Katie Grace. BS, N.C. State U., 1964; MS, San Diego State U., 1973. Registered profl. engr., N.C., Calif., Ala.; registered structural engr., Calif. Constrn. foreman Roanoke Constrn. Co., Roanoke Rapids, N.C., 1964-65; design engr. Whitman-Atkinson, San Diego, 1969-70; project mgr. Scott Meml., San Diego, 1970-71; sr. engr. Inter-City Engrs., Inc., San Diego, 1971-73, Atkinson, Johnson & Spurrier, Inc., San Diego, 1974—, corp. sec., 1977—, also bd. dirs., 1980—, exec. v.p., 1986—; lectr. civil engring. San Diego State U., 1976-77, 82. Pres. Christian Heritage Retirement Ctr., San Diego, 1980-82; v.p. Christian Unified Schs. San Diego, 1983-84; trustee Scott Meml. Bapt. Ch., El Cajon, Calif., 1986—. Served to lt. USN, 1965-69, capt. USNR. Mem. ASCE, Soc. Am. Mil. Engrs., Structural Engrs. Assn. Calif., Am. Concrete Inst., Cons. Engrs. Assn. Calif., Naval Res. Assn. Republican. Home: 2409 Cerro Sereno El Cajon CA 92019 Office: Atkinson Johnson & Spurrier Inc 4121 Napier St San Diego CA 92110

BIGGERS, STAN WALLACE, retail executive; b. Charlotte, N.C., July 13, 1943; s. Wallace Hemby and Margaret (Donkel) B.; m. Joanne Broyles, Nov. 27, 1969; children: Julie, Kimberly. AB in Econs., Pfeiffer Coll., 1969. Adminstrv. asst. Ivey's Dept. Store, Greenville, S.C., 1969-70, store mgr., 1971-72, buyer, 1972-75, corp. buyer, 1975; mgr. div. mdse. Belk Dept. Stores, Myrtle Beach, S.C., 1975-88; pres. Standard Office Equipment Co., Albemarle, N.C., 1976—. Scoutmaster Boy Scouts Am., Albemarle, 1977—; pres. Community Concert Assn., Albemarle, 1983-85; v.p. Downtown Devel., Albemarle, 1986-89; bd. dirs. adv. bd. Small Bus., Albemarle, 1984-86. Served with U.S. Army, 1962-65. Recipient Silver Beaver award Boy Scouts Am., 1988; named Dist. Leader Boy Scouts Am., 1987. Mem Nat. Fedn. Ind. Bus. (guardian), Nat. Office Products Assn., Carolina Office Products Assn., Albemarle C. of C. (bd. dirs. 1987-89, Retailer of Yr. 1982), Rotary (pres. Albermarle club 1982-83 , Paul Harris fellow 1983). Democrat. Methodist. Office: Standard Office Equipment Co 175 N 2d St Albemarle NC 28001

BIGGERS, WILLIAM JOSEPH, corporation executive; b. Great Bend, Kans., Mar. 16, 1928; s. William Henry and Frances (Jack) B.; m. Eathil Bonner, Nov. 17, 1956 (div. July 1981); children: Frances, Patricia; m. Diane McLaughlin, Feb. 14, 1983. B.A., Duke U., 1949. C.P.A., Ga. Pub. acct. 1949-55; sec.-treas. Parker, Helms & Langston, Inc., Brunswick, Ga., 1955-59, Stuckey's, Inc., Eastman, Ga., 1959-60; sec.-treas., v.p. finance Curtis 1000 Inc., 1961-69; v.p. Am. Bus. Products, Inc., Atlanta, 1969-73, chief exec. officer, 1973-88, chmn. bd., 1983—; also dir.; trustee ABP Profit Sharing Trust; Trustee Ga. Council Econ. Edn.; mem. mgmt. conf. bd. Emory U. Grad. Sch. Bus.; bd. dirs. Com. Publicly Owned Cos., Carriage Industries, Inc., Vt. Am. Corp., Joint Council on Econ. Edn.; mem. listed co. adv. com. N.Y. Stock Exchange. Bd. visitors Berry Coll.; bd. dirs. Atlanta Area council Boy Scouts Am. Served with USNR, 1946; Served with AUS, 1950-52. Mem. Am. Inst. C.P.A.s, Ga. Soc. C.P.A.s, Fin. Execs. Inst., Am. Mgmt. Assn., Phoenix Soc. Atlanta, Conf. Bd., NAM, Phi Kappa Psi. Clubs: Capital City, Georgian, Ashford, Marietta County. Lodge: Rotary. Office: Am Bus Products Inc 2100 Riveredge Pkwy Ste 1200 Atlanta GA 30328

BIGLEY, WILLIAM JOSEPH, JR., control engineer; b. Union City, N.J., May 8, 1924; s. William Joseph and Mary May (Quigley) B.; B.M.E., Rensselaer Polytech. Inst., 1950; M.S. in Elec. Engring., N.J. Inst. Tech., 1962, M.S. in Computer Sci., 1973; Ed.D., Fairleigh Dickinson U., 1984; m. Hannelore Hicks, June 24, 1950; children—Laura C., William Joseph IV, Susan J. Project engr. Tube Reducing Corp., Wallington, N.J., 1953-58, Flight Support, Inc., Metuchen, N.J., 1958-59, Airborne Accessories, Inc., Hillside, N.J., 1959-61; prin. staff engr. in control engring. Lockheed Electronics Co. div. Lockheed Aircraft, Inc., Plainfield, N.J., 1961—. Prof. engring. electronics Newark Coll. Engring., 1961-62; prof. cons. engr. Automatic Control Systems, 1958—. Mem. council Boy Scouts of Am., Scotch Plains, N.J., 1960-63. Served with AUS, 1943-44; served with USNR, 1944-46. Named Engr.-Scientist of Yr., Lockheed Electronics Co., Inc., 1980, recipient Robert

E. Gross award for tech. excellence, 1980; Achievement Honor Roll award N.J. Inst. Tech. Alumni Assn., 1982; registered profl. engr., N.Y., N.J., Calif. Mem. Nat. Soc. Profl. Engrs., IEEE, ASME, NRA, Instrument Soc. Am., Am. Mgmt. Assn., Tau Beta Pi (eminent engr. 1986). Contbr. articles to profl. jours. Home: 1641 Terrill Rd Scotch Plains NJ 07076 Office: Lockheed Corp Hwy 22 Plainfield NJ 07060

BIJUR, PETER I., petroleum company executive; b. N.Y.C., Oct. 14, 1942. BA in Polit. Sci., U. Pitts., 1964; MBA Columbia U., 1966; m. Anne Bijur. Various dist. and regional sales positions Texaco, Inc., 1966-71, mgr. Buffalo (N.Y.) sales dist., 1971-73, asst. mgr. to v.p. for pub. affairs, 1973-75, staff coordinator dept. strategic planning, 1975-77, asst. to exec. v.p., 1977-80, mgr., Rocky Mountain Refining & Mktg. 1980-81, asst. to chmn. bd., 1981-83; pres. Texaco Oil Trading and Supply Co., 1984, v.p. spl. projects, 1984-86; pres., chief exec. officer Texaco Can. Inc., Don Mills, Ont., 1987, also bd. dirs; chmn., pres., chief exec. officer Texaco Can. Resources, Calgary, Alta., 1988; chmn., chief exec. officer Texaco Ltd., London, 1989—. Office: Texaco Ltd, #1 Knightsbridge Green, London, ON Canada SW1X 7QJ

BILECKI, RONALD ALLAN, financial planner; b. Cin., July 15, 1942; s. Allan Frederick and Ruth Hilda (Parker) B.; m. Judy A. Newberry, Jan. 25, 1964; children: Sherry D. Longo, Sean P. BA in Chemistry, Calif. State U., 1968. Cert. fin. planner; registered investment adviser. Ins. agt. N.Y. Life Ins., Covina, Calif., 1973-75; asst. mgr. N.Y. Life Ins., Los Angeles, 1975-79; pvt. practice Rosemead, Calif., 1979-81; pres. Fin. Designs Corp., San Gabriel, Calif., 1981—; fin. planning cons. So. Calif. Edison, Rosemead, 1986—, Los Angeles Dept. of Water and Power, 1986—. Mem. Gideons, Covina, 1987. Mem. Internat. Assn. Fin. Planning, Registry Fin. Planning Practitioners. Republican. Office: Fin Designs Corp 7220 Rosemead Blvd #206 San Gabriel CA 91775

BILLER, ALAN DAVID, management and pension consultant; b. N.Y.C., Sept. 4, 1944; s. Newman M. and Dorothy (Jacobs) B.; m. J. Elizabeth Burack, Sept. 11, 1966; children: Katherine N., Margaret L. BA, Yale U., 1965; MPhil, U. of London, 1967; PhD, Columbia U., 1970; MBA, Harvard U., 1975. Asst. prof. philosophy Pomona Coll., Claremont, Calif., 1970-72; loan officer Wells Fargo, San Francisco, 1975-78; sr. cons. A.D. Little Inc., San Francisco, 1979; dir. investment industries SRI Internat., Menlo Park, Calif., 1979-82; pres. Alan D. Biller & Assocs., Palo Alto, Calif., 1982—. Contbr. articles to profl. jours. Pres. Childrens Ctr. of Stanford, Calif., 1978-79; bd. dirs., treas., chmn., Peninsula French-Am. Sch., Palo Alto, Calif., 1982—. Fellow NEH 1972, Woodrow Wilson, Eldridge, Yale-Carnegie 1965; Baker scholar, Harvard U. Bus. Sch., 1975. Clubs: Berzelius (New Haven), Century (Cambridge, Mass.), Ladera Oaks (Portola Valley, Calif.). Home: 121 Fulton St Palo Alto CA 94301 Office: Alan D Biller & Assocs Inc PO Box 30 Palo Alto CA 94302

BILLER, JOEL WILSON, lawyer, former foreign service officer; b. Milw., Jan. 17, 1929; s. Saul Earl and Mildred (Wilson) B.; m. Geraldine Pollack, May 1, 1955; children—Sydney, Andrew, Charles. B.A., U. Wis., 1950; J.D., U. Mich., 1953; M.A., Northwestern U., 1959. Bar: Wis. 1953. Atty. Milw., 1953-55; vice consul Am. consulate, Le Havre, France, 1956-58; econ. officer Am. Embassy, The Hague, Netherlands, 1959-62; internat. relations officer State Dept., Washington, 1962-66; econ. officer, asst. dir. AID mission, Quito, Ecuador, 1966-69; econ. counselor Am. embassy, Buenos Aires, Argentina, 1969-71; dir. AID mission, Santiago, Chile, 1971-73; spl. asst. to undersec. state for econ. affairs Washington, 1973-74; spl. asst. to dep. sec. state 1974, dep. asst. sec. state for comml. and spl. bilateral affairs, 1974-76, dep. asst. sec. state for transp., telecommunications and comml. affairs, after, 1976; practice of law Milw., 1980—; v.p. Manpower Inc., Milw., 1979—. Mem. Am. Fgn. Service Assn., Wis. Bar Assn. Office: Manpower Inc 5301 N Ironwood Rd PO Box 2053 Milwaukee WI 53202

BILLER, LESLIE STUART, banker; b. N.Y.C., Mar. 16, 1948; s. Max David and Sylvia (Gottesman) B.; m. Sheri Jean Wolfson, Aug. 7, 1969; 1 child, Kimberly. BS in Chem. Engring., CCNY, 1969; MBA in Mgmt., Xavier U., 1973. Engr. Proctor & Gamble, Cin., 1969-73; prodn. analyst Citicorp., N.Y.C., 1973-76; bus. mgr. Citicorp., Italy, 1976-82; regional bus. mgr. Citicorp., Eng., 1982-85; exec. v.p. consumer markets Bank Am., San Francisco, 1985-87; exec. v.p. strategic planning and acquisitions Norwest Corp., Mpls., 1987—. Office: Norwest Corp 6th & Marquette Minneapolis MN 55479

BILLER, MORRIS (MOE BILLER), union executive; b. N.Y.C., Nov. 5, 1915; m. Anne Fiefer, Aug. 24, 1940 (dec.); children: Michael, Steven; m. Colee Farris, Jan. 1987. Student, Bklyn. Coll., 1936-38, CCNY, 1946. With U.S. Postal Service, 1937—; active Am. Postal Workers Union, Washington, 1937—, now pres.; active Manhattan-Bronx Postal Union (N.Y. Metro Area Postal Union), 1959-60, N.E. regional coordinator, 1972-80, gen. pres., from 1980; bd. dirs. Union Labor Life Ins., Co.; exec. v.p. pub. employee dept. AFL-CIO; pub. mem. fed. adv. council occupational safety and health Dept. Labor. Bd. dirs. Assn. Children with Retarded Mental Devel., United Way Internat.; adv. bd. Cornell U. Trade Union Women Studies Program; adv. council Empire State Coll.; nat. bd. dirs., fed. thrift adv. council A. Philip Randolph Inst.; nat. labor chairperson March of Dimes Telethon, 1948; bd. dirs. Fund for Assuring an Ind. Retirement; v.p., Muscular Dystrophy Assn. Served with AUS, 1943-45, ETO. Recipient Disting. Service award N.Y.C. Central Labor Council, 1977; recipient Community Service award N.Y.C. Central Labor Council, 1979, Spirit of Life award City of Hope, 1982, Walter P. Reuther Meml. award Ams. for Democratic Action, 1982. Mem. Combined Fed. Campaign (exec. com.), N.Y.C. Central Labor Council (exec. bd dirs.), Central Labor Council (bd. dirs. central rehab.), Coalition Labor Union Women, Postal, Telegraph and Telephone Internat. (mem. exec. com.), NAACP, A. Philip Randolph Inst. Office: Am Postal Workers Union 1300 L St NW Washington DC 20005

BILLICK, L. LARKIN, financial and marketing executive; b. Des Moines, Sept. 15, 1948; s. Lyle Larkin and Florence Carlson B.; BS, U. Kans., Lawrence, 1970; grad. Inst. Bank Mktg., U. So. Calif., La. State U., 1978; m. Kathryn Rose Gildner, Aug. 14, 1971; children: Kelly Lynne, Brett Larkin. Group ins. trainee Bankers Life Co., Des Moines, 1970-71; nat. advt. rep. Stoner Broadcasting Co., Des Moines, 1971-74; advt. account supr. Mid-Am. Broadcasting, Des Moines, 1974-75; dir. pub. realtions and mktg. Iowa Bankers Assn., Des Moines, 1975-77; asst. v.p., advt. mgr. corp. staff Marine Banks, Milw., 1977-79, v.p. advt., 1979-81; pres. Billick Fin. Mktg. Group, 1981-82; 1979-81; sr. v.p. mktg. Univ. Savs. Assn., Houston, 1982-84; mgmt. supr. W.B. Doner Advt./S.W., Houston, 1984-86; pres. The Strategists, Inc., Houston, 1986—. Bd. dirs. Grad. Inst. Bank Mktg., La. State U., 1978-79; chmn. communications Milwaukee County Performing Arts Center, 1978-79; advt., promotion cons. to polit. candidates; chmn. communications council United Performing Arts Fund Milw., 1978-79; dist. coordinator State Del. for Jimmy Carter, 1972-80; chmn. communications com. Milwaukee County council Boy Scouts Am., 1979-80; bd. dirs. Katy (Tex.) Nat. Little League, 1984-89, Katy Youth Football, 1984-86, Katy Taylor High Sch. Booster Club, 1988—. Mem. Bank Mktg. Assn. (chmn. advt. council 1980-81, mem. nat. conv. com. 1980-82), Am. Bankers Assn. (mem. nat. mktg. conf. com. 1980), Am. Advt. Fedn. (public service com. 1980-81), Am. Mktg. Assn., U. Kans. Alumni Assn. (life), Milw. Advt. Club (v.p., bd. dirs. 1978-81). Democrat. Roman Catholic. Home: 910 Caswell Ct Katy TX 77450 Office: The Strategists Inc 1360 Post Oak Blvd Ste 2400 Houston TX 77056

BILLIG, ERWIN H., manufacturing company executive; b. 1927. Student, Loughborough U. With Wilmot Breeden Tru flo Ltd., 1960-72; v.p., group exec. Chgo. Pneumatic Tool Co., 1972-76; group v.p. Masco Corp., 1976-84, exec. v.p., 1984-87; pres., chief operating officer Taylor, Mich., 1987—. Office: Masco Industries Inc 21001 Van Born Rd Taylor MI 48180 *

BILLIMORIA, FAROKH (BILL), financial planning executive; b. Bombay, Aug. 13, 1943; came to U.S., 1966; s. Manchershaw N. and Meher Billimoria; m. Huty F. Kelawala, Dec. 22, 1974; children: Jimmy, Eric. BSME, Victoria Jubilee Tech. Inst., Bombay, 1965; BS in Indsl. Engring., Ill. Inst. Tech., 1967, MS in Indsl. Engring., 1970, MBA in Fin., U. Chgo., 1973. CPA, Ill.; cert. fin. planner. Systems analyst/programmer J. T. Ryerson & Son Inc., Chgo., 1967-71; sr. systems analyst Washington Nat. Ins. Co., Evanston, Ill., 1971-74; mgmt. cons. Ernst & Whinney, Chgo., 1974-78; sr. mgmt. cons. A.T. Kearney, Inc., Chgo., 1978-82; pres. Integrated Fin., Inc., Arlington Heights, Ill., 1982—. Mem. Internat. Assn. for Fin. Planning Inc. (treas. greater O'Hare chpt. 1983-84, exec. v.p. 1984-85, pres. 1985-87), Inst. for Cert. Fin. Planners. Republican. Zoroastrian. Lodge: Rotary Internat. (program chmn. Arlington Heights 1986-87). Home: 1081 King Charles Ct Palatine IL 60067 Office: Integrated Fin Inc 605 E Algonquin Rd Suite 160 Arlington Heights IL 60005

BILLINGS, PATRICIA ANNE, human resources manager; b. N.Y.C., Feb. 21, 1943; d. George James and Anne Marie (Murray) B. BS in Edn. cum laude, Seton Hall U., 1971; MA in Am. Studies, Fairfield U., 1976. Cert. elem. and secondary tchr., N.Y., N.J., Conn. Various teaching positions Conn., N.Y., 1962-78; tng. specialist Morgan Guaranty Trust Co., N.Y.C., 1979-81; asst. treas. Bankers Trust Co., N.Y.C., 1981-83, asst. v.p., 1983-84; mgr. tng. Emery & Purolator Worldwide, Wilton, Conn., 1984—; bd. dirs. Long Ridge Sch., Stamford, Conn., 1986—; cons. in field. Active Personnel Commn. City of Stamford, 1986. Mem. Am. Soc. Tng. and Devel. Democrat. Roman Catholic. Office: Emery & Purolator Worldwide Old Danbury Rd Wilton CT 06897

BILLINGS, THOMAS NEAL, computer and publishing executive, consultant; b. Milw., Mar. 2, 1931; s. Neal and Gladys Victoria (Lockard) B.; A.B. with honors, Harvard U., 1952, M.B.A., 1954; m. Barta Hope Chipman, June 12, 1954 (div. 1967); children—Bridget Ann, Bruce Neal; m. Marie Louise Farrell, Mar. 27, 1982. Vice pres. fin. and adminstrn. Copley Newspapers Inc., La Jolla, Calif., 1957-70; group v.p. Harte-Hanks Communications Inc., San Antonio, 1970-73; exec. v.p. United Media, Inc., Phoenix, 1973-75; asst. to pres. Ramada Inns, Inc., Phoenix, 1975-76; exec. dir. Nat. Rifle Assn., Washington, 1976-77; pres. Ideation Inc., Washington, 1977-81; chmn. Bergen-Billings Inc., N.Y.C., 1977-80, Franchise Mgmt. Corp., Reno, 1988—; pres. The Assn. Service Corp., San Francisco, 1978-88, Accuprint Inc., Carlsbad, Calif., 1989—; pres. Recorder Printing and Pub. Co. Inc., San Francisco, 1980-82; v.p. adminstrn. Victor Techs. Inc., Scotts Valley, Calif., 1982-84; mng. dir. Saga-Wilcox Computers Ltd., Wrexham, Wales, 1984-85; chmn. Thomas Billings & Assocs., Inc., Reno, 1978—, Intercontinental Travel Svc. Inc., Reno, 1983—, Oberon Internat. Ltd., 1985-86; dir., chief exec. officer Insignia Solutions group, High Wycombe, England, Cupertino, Calif., 1986-89; bd. dirs. Lenny's Restaurants Inc., Wichita, Kans., Tymyndr Corp., Dover Del., Zzyzzyx Corp., Reno; guest lectr. in field. Bd. dirs. Nat. Allergy Found., 1973—, The Wilderness Fund, 1978—, San Diego Civic Light Opera Assn., 1965-69; chief exec. San Diego 200th Anniversary Expn., 1969. Served with U.S. Army, 1955-57. Recipient Walter F. Carley Meml. award, 1966, 69. Fellow U.K. Inst. Dirs.; mem. Am. Newspaper Pubs. Assn., Inst. Execs. Inc. (dir.), Inst. Newspaper Controllers, Am. Assn. V.P.s (dir.), Sigma Delta Chi. Republican. Clubs: West Side Tennis, LaJolla Country; Washington Athletic; San Francisco Press; Harvard (N.Y.C.); Elks. Author: Creative Controllership, 1978; editor The Vice Presidents' Letter, 1978—, Intercontinental News Service, London, England, 1985—; pub. The Microcomputer Letter, 1982—, Synthetic Hardware Update, 1987—. Office: 100 W Grove St Ste 360 Reno NV 89509 also: 1255 Post St Ste 625 San Francisco CA 94109

BILLINGSLEY, JAMES RAY, telephone company executive; b. Rome, Ga., Jan. 22, 1927; s. Charles White and Loral Tabitha (Barker) B.; m. Helen Lee Brown, May 7, 1960; children: James Ray, Jr., Walter Brown, Ann Barker, John Charles. Student, NOrth Ga. Coll., 1944-45, NYU, 1945; J.D., U. Miss., 1950. Bar: Miss. bar 1950, N.Y. bar 1958. Atty. U.S. Dept. Labor, Birmingham, Ala., 1950-55, Washington, 1955-56; atty. Western Electric Co., N.Y.C., 1956-60; v.p. regulatory matters Western Electric Co., 1973-74; atty. N.Y. Telephone Co., N.Y.C., 1960-67; gen. atty. N.Y. Telephone Co., 1967-70, v.p. revenues, 1970-73; v.p. fed. regulation AT&T, N.Y.C., 1974-83, sr. v.p. fed. regulation, 1984—; mng. gen. ptnr. Tolten Ltd. Partnership; mem. bd. advisors U. Miss. Ctr. for Telecommunications:. Trustee, treas. Henry L. and Grace Doherty Charitable Found. Served with U.S. Army, 1944-47. Mem. ABA, N.Y. Bar Assn. (public utilities com. 1967—), Fed. Communications Bar Assn., N.Y. Ole Miss Alumni Club (bd. dirs.). Presbyterian. Clubs: Manursing Island (Rye); Internat., Congressional Country (Washington). Office: AT&T 295 N Maple Ave 17-4342K2 Basking Ridge NJ 07920

BILLINGTON, BRIAN JOHN, executive recruiter, consultant; b. Chgo., Dec. 12, 1931; s. William Howard and Gladys (Waterton) B.; m. Marlene Ann Sherry; children: Brian J. Jr., Williams Howard III. BBA, Roosevelt U., 1957. Asst. personnel mgr. Allstate Ins. Co., Northbrook, Ill., 1959-64; v.p. Far West Fin., Los Angeles, 1964-67; mgr. Price Waterhouse, Los Angeles, 1967-73; pres. Billington & Assocs., Inc., Los Angeles, 1973—. Patron Los Angeles County Mus. of Art, 1980—; founder Los Angeles Music Ctr., 1985—. Served with U.S. Army, 1952-54. Mem. Calif. Exec. Recruiters Assn., Brit. Am. C. of C. Republican. Episcopalian. Club: Dana Strand (Dana Point, Calif.), Beverly Hills Country (Calif.). Home: 1150 Chantilly Rd Los Angeles CA 90077 Office: Billington & Assocs Inc 3250 Wilshire Blvd Los Angeles CA 90010

BILSING, DAVID CHARLES, controller, corporate executive; b. Upper Sandusky, Ohio, Mar. 15, 1933; s. John Reuben and Mary Victoria (Neate) B.; m. Dorothy L. Emerson, Sept. 17, 1955; children—Karen, Michael, Linda. B.S., Ohio U., 1955. C.P.A., Ill. Acct. trainee AMSTED Industries, Chgo., 1955-59; asst. plant controller AMSTED Industries, 1959-61, div. controller, 1962, mgr. cost acctg., 1963-65, asst. controller, 1965-69; corp. controller Beloit Corp., Wis., 1969-73, Baxter Labs., Deerfield, Ill., 1973-79; corp. controller Reynolds Metals Co., Richmond, Va., 1979-88, v.p. controller, 1988—. Served with AUS, 1956-58. Mem. Ill. Soc. C.P.A.'s, Am. Inst. C.P.A.'s, Nat. Assn. Accts., Fin. Execs. Inst. Home: 1 Broad Run Rd Manakin-Sabot VA 23103 Office: Reynolds Metal Co 6601 Broad Street Rd Richmond VA 23261

BILTZ, STUART JAMES, health care administrator; b. Cin., Apr. 29, 1946. BA, Hanover Coll., 1968; MS in Health Care Adminstrn., Trinity U., San Antonio, 1972. Adminstr. Inst. Phys. Medicine and Rehab. Inc., Louisville, 1972-74, Travis Clinc Found., Jacksonville, Tex., 1974-75; asst. adminstr. HCA Med. Plaza Hosp., Ft. Worth, Tex., 1975-78; adminstr. HCA Woman's Hosp. Tex., Houston, 1978-83, HCA Spring Br. Meml. Hosp., Houston, 1983-86; v.p. HCA Houston Div., Kingwood, Tex., 1986-87; pres., chief operating officer HCA Wesley Med. Ctr., Wichita, Kans., 1987—. Mem. bd. govs. Fedn. Am. Hosps., Little Rock, Ark., 1988—; trustee Inst. Logopedics, Wichita, Kans., 1988—; treas., bd. dirs. Greater Houston Hosp. Council, 1984-87. Served with U.S. Army, 1968-70. Mem. Am. Coll. Hosp. Adminstrs., Kans. Hosp. Assn., Wichita Area C. of C. Republican. Roman Catholic. Office: HCA Wesley Med Ctr 550 N Hillside Wichita KS 67214

BILZERIAN, PAUL ALEC, real estate executive; b. Miami, Fla., June 18, 1950; s. Oscar A. and Joan I. (Barrie) B.; B.A., Stanford U., 1975; M.B.A., Harvard U., 1977; m. Terri L. Steffen, Sept. 17, 1978; children: Dan, Adam. Asst. dir. World Data Analysis Ctr., Stanford, Calif., 1974-75; treasury assoc. Crown Zellerbach Corp., San Francisco, 1977-78; chmn. bd. Internat. Broadcasters, Inc., Seminole, Fla., 1978-79; exec. v.p. Nat. Bus. Enterprises, Inc., Sacramento, 1979-82; pres. So. Bus. Enterprises, Inc., St. Petersburg, Fla., 1982—, also dir.; pres. Bicoastal Oil & Gas Corp., Sacramento, Calif., 1984—; pres. Bicoastal Fin. Corp., 1986—; chmn., chief exec. officer Singer Co.; dir. Southbay Hardware Co., Inc., Sarasota, Fla. Served to 1st lt. U.S. Army, 1968-71. Decorated Bronze Star. Club: Harvard Bus. Sch. Home: 1914 Carolina Ave NE Saint Petersburg FL 33703 Office: 501 E Kennedy Blvd Ste 1900 Tampa FL 33602-4933 also: The Singer Co 15438 N Florida Ave Ste 205 Tampa FL 33602 also: 1264 S Tamiami Trail Ospre FL 33559 *

BINCH, JAMES GARDNER, merchant banker; b. Toronto, Ont., Can., July 11, 1947; came to U.S., 1972; s. Wilfred Reese and Elizabeth Bowie (Gardner) B.; m. Susan Badgerow May, Aug. 20, 1970; children: Winston, Devon. BS in Econs., BS in Engring., Princeton U., 1970; MBA, U. Pa., 1972. Assoc. Cresap, McCormick & Paget, Inc., N.Y.C., 1972-77, prin., 1977-78; dir. bus. devel. bldg. products div. Champion Internat., Stamford, Conn., 1978-79, v.p. bus. planning, 1979-80; v.p. strategic planning Combustion Engring. Co., Stamford, 1980-85; exec. v.p. C-E Lummus Crest, Inc., Bloomfield, N.J., 1985, pres., 1985-87; pres., bd. dirs. Trinity Capital Corp., Stamford, 1987—; bd. dirs. Gulfstar Petroleum Corp., Houston, APL Group, Wilton, Conn., ATCO, Inc., Greenwich, Conn. Chmn. New Canaan (Conn.) chpt. ARC, 1982-84; bd. dirs. Partnership for N.J., 1985-87. Mem. N.J. C. of C. (bd. dirs. 1985-87), N.Y. Yacht Club, Country Club New Canaan. Episcopalian. Office: Trinity Capital Corp One Station Pl Stamford CT 06902

BINDER, AMY FINN, public relations company executive; b. N.Y.C., June 13, 1955; d. David and Laura (Zeisler) Finn; m. Ralph Edward Binder, Aug. 15, 1976; children: Ethan Max, Adam Finn, Rebecca Eve. BA with honors, Brown U., 1977. Freelance photographer N.Y.C., 1977-78; account exec. Newton & Nicolazza, Boston, 1978-79, Agnew, Carter, McCarthy, Boston, 1979-80; dir. pub. relations City of New Rochelle, N.Y., 1980-82; dir. urban communications Ruder-Finn, N.Y.C., 1982-85, v.p., 1985-86, exec. v.p., 1986-87, pres., 1987—; bd. dirs. Castle Art Gallery, New Rochelle. Photographer: Museum without Walls, 1975, The Spirit of Man: Sculpture of Kaare Nygaard, 1975, Knife Life and Bronzes, 1977, St. Louis: Sculpture City, 1988. Mem. Madrid com. Sister City program, N.Y.C.; bd. dirs. New Rochelle Community Fund. Democrat. Jewish. Office: Ruder Finn Inc 301 E 57th St New York NY 10022

BINDER, DAVID FRANKLIN, lawyer, author; b. Beaver Falls, Pa., Aug. 1, 1935; s. Walter Carl and Jessie Maivis (Bliss) B.; m. Deana Jacqueline Pines, Dec. 25, 1971; children—April, Bret. B.A., Geneva Coll., 1956; J.D., Harvard U., 1959. Bar: Pa. 1960, U.S. Ct. Appeals (3d cir.) 1963, U.S. Supreme Ct. 1967. Law clk. to chief justice Pa. Supreme Ct., 1959-61; counsel Fidelity Mut. Life Ins. Co., Phila., 1964-66; ptnr. Bennett, Bricklin & Saltzburg, Phila., 1967-68; mem. Richter, Syken, Ross, and Binder, Phila., 1969-72, Raynes, McCarty, Binder, Ross and Mundy, Phila., 1972—; mem. faculty Pa. Coll. Judiciary; lectr., course planner Pa. Bar Inst. Recipient Disting. Alumnus award Geneva Coll., 1981. Mem. ABA, Pa. Bar Assn., Phila. Bar Assn., Assn. Trial Lawyers Am. (lectr.), Pa. Trial Lawyers Assn. (lectr.), Phila. Trial Lawyers Assn., Harvard Law Sch. Assn. Clubs: Peale, Union League. Author: Hearsay Handbook, 1975, ann. supplements, 2d edit., 1983. Office: Raynes McCarty Binder Ross & Mundy 1845 Walnut St Ste 2000 Philadelphia PA 19103

BINDER, GARY, marketing professional; b. Brookline, Mass., June 14, 1944; s. Jack and Rose (Tatelman) B.; m. Joan Golub, Oct. 1, 1967; children: Alan Jay, David Michael. BS in Fin., Boston U., 1966; MBA in Econs., NYU, 1968. Economist GM, N.Y.C., 1968-72; sr. fin. analyst McCall Pub. Co., N.Y.C., 1972-73; mgr., dir. mktg. and planning Foote & Davies, Inc., Atlanta, 1973-79, v.p. mktg. and planning, 1979-85; v.p. market planning and rsch. Treasure Chest Advt. Co., Inc., Glendora, Calif., 1985—. Office: Treasure Chest Advt Co Inc 511 W Citrus Edge Glendora CA 91740

BINDER, MITCHELL BARRY, electronics executive; b. N.Y.C., June 1, 1955; s. Al and Anne (Kraman) B.; m. June Linda Harris, Sept. 3, 1978; children: Jessica, Evan. BS in Econs., U. Pa., 1977. CPA, N.Y. Staff acct. Saul L. Klaw & Co., N.Y.C., 1977-79; with Richard A. Eisner & Co., N.Y.C., 1979-83; v.p. fin. Orbit Instrument Corp., Hauppauge, N.Y., 1983—. Mem. AICPA, N.Y. State Soc. CPAs. Republican. Jewish. Office: Orbit Instrument Corp 80 Cabot Ct Hauppauge NY 11788

BINDER, WILLIAM HARRY, food products executive; b. Boston, Aug. 16, 1922; s. Edward and Anna (Snyder) B.; m. Alice Buscelle, Apr. 10, 1953. Grad., Boston Latin Sch., 1939; BA, Harvard U., 1947; postgrad., NYU, 1949-52. Dist. sales mgr. Hudson Pulp & Paper Corp., N.Y.C., 1952-65; v.p. Romar Tissue Mills, Woodside, N.Y., 1965-72; pres. Bennington (Vt.) Tissue Mills, 1972-77, William H. Binder Enterprises, N.Y.C., 1977—; v.p. Trans-Cullinaire Publ., N.Y.C., 1977-81; cons. David's Cookies, N.Y.C., 1985—; instr. N.Y. Tech. Coll. Contbr. articles to trade publs. Mem. fund-raising com. Vietnam Meml. Commn., N.Y.C., 1985-86. Col. USAR, 1950-67. Mem. Food and Beverage Assn. Am. (chmn. exec. com. 1986—, named Man of Yr. 1985), Grocery Mfrs. N.Y. (pres. 1965-67), N.Y. Soc. Mil. and Naval Officers (pres. 1985-87), 7th Inf. Regt. Club, Yale Club, B'nai B'rith (pres. Harvest lodge 1961-63). Democrat. Jewish. Home and Office: 35 Sutton Pl Apt 3C New York NY 10022

BINDLEY, WILLIAM EDWARD, pharmaceutical executive; b. Terre Haute, Ind., Oct. 6, 1940; s. William F. and Gertrude (Lynch) B.; m. Martha Leinenbach, June 10, 1961; children: William Franklin, Blair Scott, Sally Ann. BS, Purdue U., 1961; grad. wholesale mgmt. program, Stanford U., 1966. Asst. treas. Controls Co. Am., Melrose Park, Ill., 1962-65; vice-chmn. E.H. Bindley & Co., Terre Haute, 1965-68; chmn. bd., chief exec. officer Bindley Western Industries, Inc., Indpls., 1968—; Scholl Scholarship guest lectr. Loyola U., Chgo., 1982; guest lectr. Young Pres. Orgn., Palm Springs, Calif. and Dallas, 1981, 82, 84; guest instr. Ctr. for Entrepreneurs, Indpls., 1983; bd. dirs. AmeriTrust Ind. Corp.; disting. lectr., mem. adv. bd. Georgetown U., 1989—. State dir. Bus. for Reagan-Bush, Washington and Indpls., 1980; trustee Indpls. Civic Theatre, St. Vincent Hosp., Indpls., U.S. Ski Team; bd. dirs. Nat. Entrepreneurship Found.; mem. pres.'s coun. Purdue U., West Lafayette, Ind.; hon. sec. of state State of Ind.; trustee Marian coll., Indpls. Named hon. Ky. Col., 1980, "Sagamore of the Wabash" Gov. Orr., State of Ind. Mem. Young Pres. Orgn. (area dir., chmn. 1982, award 1983), Nat. Wholesale Druggists Assn. (dir. 1981-84, Svc. award 1984), Purdue U. Alumni Assn. (life), Woodstock Club, Meridian Hills Countryn Club. Republican. Roman Catholic. Office: Bindley Western Industries Inc 4212 W 71st St Indianapolis IN 46268

BINGHAM, CHARLES W., wood products company executive; b. Myrtle Point, Oreg., 1933. Grad., Harvard U., 1955, JD, 1960. Now exec. v.p. Weyerhaeuser Co.; bd. dirs. Puget Sound Power & Light Co. Mem. Nat. Forest Products Assn. (bd. govs.). Office: Weyerhaeuser Co Weyerhauser Way Federal Way WA 98003

BINGHAM, JULES, ship broker; b. Amsterdam, The Netherlands, Sept. 21, 1921; came to U.S., 1945; naturalized, 1951; s. David and Therese B.; m. Helen Jarro, Sept. 27, 1956; 1 stepson, Lawrence Christian. BA, Haverford Coll., 1947; MA, Sch. of Advanced Internat. Studies, Johns Hopkins U., 1948. With W. Rountree Ship Brokers, N.Y.C., 1949-50; ship broker Shipping Enterprises Corp., N.Y.C., 1950-55, Ocean Freighting and Brokerage Corp., N.Y.C., 1955-60; pres. Bingham Bigotte Shipping Co., Inc. and affiliated cos., N.Y.C., 1960-76, sr. ptnr., 1976—. Mem. Assn. Shipbrokers and Agts. Club: Plandome (N.Y.) Country Club. Home: 180 Sands Point Rd Sands Point NY 11050 Office: Bingham Bigotte & Co 90 Broad St New York NY 10004

BINGLE, KIMBERLY ANN, securities analyst; b. Rochester, Pa., Sept. 17, 1963; d. Donald Edward and Lois JoAnn (Harrison) B. Student, Inst. U. de Tech., Nice, France, 1985; BA in Fin., Pa. State U., 1986. Sr. securities analyst Nationwide Ins. Co., Columbus, Ohio, 1986—; investment advisor J.A. Allan Inc., Beaver Falls, Pa., 1988. Mem. Phi Eta Sigma, Golden Key, Columbus Jaycees. Office: Nationwide Ins Co 1 Nationwide Pla Columbus OH 43216

BINGO-DUGGINS, KAREN LEIKO, personnel specialist; b. Honolulu, Dec. 15, 1942; d. Warren Tsutomu and Shizue (Shiroma) Bingo; m. Michael Oniel Bingo-Duggins, Aug. 18, 1976. Student, Chaminade Coll., 1963-64; BA, U. Hawaii, 1965. Classification trainee Pacific region U.S. Army, Okinawa, Japan, 1967-71, personnel staffing specialist Pacific region, 1971-72; position classification specialist U.S. Army, San Francisco, 1972-74; personnel mgmt. specialist material comand U.S. Army, Washington, 1974, mgmt. employee specialist material command, 1974-76, personnel evaluation specialist material command, 1976-78, classification specialist, 1978-80; personnel mgmt. specialist USAF, Washington, 1980-84, chief sr. exec. service mgmt., 1984—. Mem. Internat. Personnel Adminstrn., Minority Women in Govt., Fed. Exec. Inst. alumni Assn. Home: 4327 Stream Bed Way Alexandria VA 22306 Office: Hdqrs USAF/DPCZ Pentagon Rm 4E232 Washington DC 20330-5060

BINKLEY, NICHOLAS BURNS, banking executive; b. Pasadena, Calif., Oct. 31, 1945; s. John Thomas and Marijane (Tucker) B.; m. Diana Padelford Binkley, Aug. 3, 1974; children: Pepper Alexandra, Byron Jack. Student, Univrsite-d'Aix/Marseille, Aix-en-Privence, France, 1966-67; BS in Polit. Sci., Colo. Coll., 1968; MA in Internat. Studies, Johns Hopkins

U., 1971. From London sr. credit analyst to middle-East asst. treas. of Petroleum div. Chase Manhattan Bank, N.Y.C., 1973-75; pvt. practice investments N.Y.C., 1975-77; from asst. v.p. to v.p., regional mgr. Security Pacific Nat. Bank, Los Angeles, 1977-83; 1st v.p. to sr. v.p. to exec. v.p., vice chmn., chief oper. officer Fin. Svcs. System Security Pacific Corp., San Diego, 1983—. Vol. Peace Corp., Tunisia, 1968-70; campaign mgr. U.S. COngl. Campaign, Pasadena, 1972—. Office: Security Pacific Corp 10124 Old Grove Rd San Diego CA 92131

BINNS, JAMES W., watch manufacturing company executive; b. Los Angeles, July 16, 1946; s. John H. and Elizabeth R. (Sturtevant) B.; m. Lynn L. Binns, Nov. 2, 1979; children: Jeffrey, Gregory, Russell. BS, UCLA, 1967, MS, 1969; MBA, U. So. Calif., 1973. Engring. sr. Lockheed Aircraft, Los Angeles, 1968-73; dir. fin. planning Rockwell Internat., Pitts., 1973-78; treas. Timex Group Ltd., Middlebury, Conn., 1978-80, chief fin. officer, 1980-83, pres., chief operating officer, 1983-85, chief exec. officer, 1985—; prof. bus. Orange Coast U., Santa Ana, Calif., 1975-76. Chmn. corp. campaigns United Way Greater Waterbury, Conn., 1979-80; bd. dirs. Conn. Bus. and Industry Assn. Mem. Beta Gamma Sigma. Republican. Methodist. Office: Timex Group Ltd Park Rd Middlebury CT 06762

BINNS, WALTER GORDON, JR., automobile manufacturing company executive; b. Richmond, Va., June 8, 1929; s. Walter Gordon and Virginia Belle (Matheny) B.; A.B., Coll. William and Mary, 1949; A.M., Harvard U., 1951; M.B.A., N.Y. U., 1959; m. Alberta Louise Fry, Apr. 1, 1972; 1 dau., Amanda; 1 stepdau., Clarissa. Trainee, Chase Nat. Bank, N.Y.C., 1953-54; with Gen. Motors Corp., N.Y.C., 1954—, asst. treas., 1974-82, chief investment funds officer, 1982—, v.p. 1986—; bd. dirs. Gen. Motors Acceptance Corp., Motors Ins. Corp., Futures Industry Assn.; investment adv. com. N.Y. State Common Retirement Fund; mem. pension mgrs. adv. com. N.Y. Stock Exchange; fin. instruments adv. com. Chgo. Mercentile Exchange. Trustee ARC Retirement System, Citizens Budget Commn., N.Y.C., Endowment Assn. Coll. William and Mary, Joint Council Econ. Edn., Fin. Execs. Research Found.; bd. dirs. Alcoholism Council Greater N.Y., Community Fund of Bronxville, Eastchester Tuckahoe, Inc. Served with U.S. Army, 1951-53. Mem. Fin. Execs. Inst. (chmn. com. on employee benefits 1977-80, com. on investment of employee benefit assets, 1985-88), Am. Pension Conf., Economic Club of N.Y., Phi Beta Kappa, Beta Gamma Sigma. Clubs: Bronxville (N.Y.) Field; Harvard (N.Y.C.), Grolier; Recess (Detroit). Home: 21 Crows Nest Rd Bronxville NY 10708 Office: GM 767 Fifth Ave New York NY 10153 also: GM Gen Motors Bldg Detroit MI 48202

BINTZ, CHARLES THOMAS, stockbroker; b. Salt Lake City, Dec. 9, 1923; s. Charles Carroll and Denise (Karrick) B.; m. Dorothy Cornish, Apr. 28, 1945; children: Dorothy, Martha, Charles, Brian. BA, Cornell U., 1947. Vice pres. sales W. H. Bintz Co., Salt Lake City, 1958-67, chmn. bd., 1970-84; acct. exec. Merrill Lynch, Salt Lake City, 1967-77, v.p., 1977—; chmn. Diversified Investment Corp., Salt Lake City, 1970-84. Bd. dirs. YMCA, Westminster Coll. Found., Am. Protectors Ins. Corp. Served with USNR, 1943-45. Methodist. Clubs: Alta, Salt Lake Tennis, Salt Lake Country. Home: 2550 Elizabeth St Salt Lake City UT 84106 Office: Merrill Lynch Pierce Fenner & Smith 60 East South Temple Salt Lake City UT 84111

BIONDI, FRANK J., JR., entertainment company executive; b. N.Y.C., Jan. 9, 1945; s. Frank J. and Virginia (Willis) B.; m. Carol Oughton, Mar. 16, 1974; children: Anne, Jane. BA, Princeton U., 1966; MBA, Harvard U., 1968. Assoc.-corp. fin. Shearson Lehman Hutton Bros. Inc., N.Y.C., 1970-71, Prudential Bache Securities, N.Y.C., 1969; prin. Frank J. Biondi Jr. & Assocs., N.Y.C., 1972; dir. bus. analysis Teleprompter Corp., N.Y.C., 1972-73; asst. treas., assoc. dir. bus. affairs Children's TV Workshop, N.Y.C., 1974-78; dir. entertainment program planning HBO, N.Y.C., 1978, v.p. programming ops., 1979-82, exec. v.p. planning and adminstrn., 1982-83, pres., chief exec. officer, 1983, chmn., chief exec. officer, 1984; exec. v.p. entertainment bus. sector The Coca-Cola Co., 1985; chmn., chief exec. officer Coca-Cola TV, 1986; pres., chief exec. officer Viacom Internat. Inc., N.Y.C., 1987—, also bd. dirs.; bd. dirs. Viacom Inc., N.Y.C. Trustee Citizens Budget Commn., N.Y.C.; bd. dirs. Leake-Watts Child Care Agy., Yonkers, N.Y., 1975, Morningside Nursing Home, Bronx, N.Y., 1977, Mus. Broadcasting, N.Y.C., Am. Mus. of Moving Image, N.Y.C. Recipient Best of a New Generation award Esquire mag., 1984. Mem. Internat. Radio and TV Soc. (former treas. and v.p.), Ctr. for Communications, Am. Mus. of Moving Image, Mus. of Broadcasting, Am. Film Inst., Riverdale Yacht Club, Princeton of N.Y. Club. Office: Viacom Internat Inc 1211 Ave of the Americas New York NY 10036

BIPPUS, DAVID PAUL, manufacturing company executive; b. Evansville, Ind., Nov. 25, 1949; s. James Paul and Mary Louise (Elder) B.; m. Kohnne Susann Heikens, Aug. 28, 1971; 1 child, Laura. BS, Iowa State U., 1971; MBA with honors, Boston U., 1975. Tech. mgr. Ill. Dept. Transp., Springfield, 1976; asst. dir. planning Horace Mann Ins. Co., Springfield, 1976-79; mgr. fin. planning Hydro-Transmission div. Sundstrand Corp., Ames, Iowa, 1979-82; controller Hydraulics div. Sundstrand Corp., Rockford, Ill., 1982-84; v.p. fin., sec., treas. Suntec Industries, Inc., Rockford, 1984—; bd. dirs. Cotta Trans. Co., Rockford, 1976—; instr. Lincoln Land Community Coll., Springfield, 1976-78. Dir. Rockford Civic New Comers, 1982-85; mem. Story County Planning & Zoning Commn. Served to 1st lt. U.S. Army, 1972-76. Mem. Fin. Exec. Inst., Soc. of CPCU's, Nat. Assn. Accts., Am. Legion. Republican. Lutheran. Club: Forest Hills Country. Home: 2627 Norwood Dr Rockford IL 61107 Office: Suntec Industries Inc PO Box 7010 2210 Harrison Ave Rockford IL 61125

BIRCHBY, KENNETH LEE, banker; b. Columbus, Ind., Feb. 1, 1915; s. Ernest Lee and Constance Douglas (Pinsent) B.; m. Julia C. Barsch, Apr. 12, 1941; children—Kenneth Lee, John D. LL.B., St. Johns U., 1949; postgrad., Grad. Sch. Banking, Rutgers, 1956. With Brevoort Savs. Bank, Bklyn., 1936-42; comptroller Brevoort Savs. Bank, 1945-48; spl. agt. FBI, 1942-45; auditor, v.p. Jamaica (N.Y.) Savs. Bank, 1948-66; exec. v.p. Hudson City Savs. Bank, Jersey City, 1966-68; pres. Hudson City Savs. Bank, 1968—, chmn., chief exec. officer, 1981—; also dir., instr. Grad. Sch. Savs. Banks, Brown U.; adv. counsel Conf. State Bank Suprs.; mem. N.J. Banking Adv. Bd. Mem. Mayor's Adv. Com., 1971—; v.p., bd. dirs. Hudson County chpt. ARC., Bergen council Boy Scouts Am.; past bd. dirs. N.J. Coll. Fund Assn.; past regent St. Peter's Coll. Mem. Savs. Banks Assn. N.J. (pres. 1970-72), New York Assn., Jersey City C. of C. (pres., dir.), Assn. Former FBI Agts., Savs. Banks Auditors and Comptrollers Assn. N.Y. (past pres.), Nat. Assn. Mut. Savs. Banks (com. chmn., pres. 1974-75), C. of C. and Industry No. N.J. (dir.). Clubs: Northampton Colony Yacht (Southampton, L.I.) (dir.); Ridgewood Country, Essex, Bergen Carteret. Home: 12 Pine Tree Dr Saddle River NJ 07458 Office: Hudson City Savs Bank 80 Century Rd W Paramus NJ 07652

BIRCHENOUGH, KAREN BROWN, management consultant; b. Santa Ana, Calif., July 7, 1942; d. Wendell Maurice Brown and Jacqueline Ann (Morgan) Voris; m. Robert Anderson, Feb. 24, 1960 (div. Nov. 1962); children: T. Eileen Boeckholt, Tory Annette Cramer; m. Robert J. Birchenough Jr., Feb. 12, 1972 (dec. Nov. 1982); children: Robert J. III, James R. III. Grad. high sch., Red Bluff, Calif. Credit supr. Gensler-Lee Diamonds, Oakland, Calif., 1962-68; acct. U.S. Army, Munich, Fed. Republic Germany, 1968-71, Omni Mobile Homes, Athens, Tenn., 1972-73; farm mgr. B-K Ranch, Pulaski, Tenn., 1972-75; school bus driver Giles County Schs., Pulaski, 1973-75; agt. Patterson Real Estate, Houma, La., 1979-82; owner K&V Investments, Inc., Houston, 1983—, The Brief-Case Success Motivation Inst., Houston, 1987—; instr. San Jacinto Jr. Coll. Cen. Campus, Houston, 1988—; conductor seminars Houston YWCA, 1988. Journalist, news writer Brooks (Tex.) Citizen, 1988—; illustrator books The Garden, 1986, Single Man's Survival Kit, 1988. Mem. Texans for Civil Justice, Houston, 1987-88; chair Spring Forest/Dunmoor versus Friendswood, 1988. Mem. Clear Lake City (Tex.) C. of C. Republican. Club: Toastmasters. Lodge: Rotary. Office: The Brief-Case 17223 Mercury Dr Houston TX 77058

BIRCHER, EDGAR ALLEN, lawyer, placement company executive; b. Springfield, Ohio, Apr. 28, 1934; s. John Clark and Ethel Ann (Speakman) B.; m. Lavinia Brock, Sept. 30, 1978; children: Douglas, Stephen, Todd, Karen. B.A., Ohio Wesleyan U., 1956; J.D., Ohio State U., 1961; postgrad., Columbia U., 1974, Stanford U., 1975. Bar: Ohio 1962, Tex. 1973. Assoc. Fuller, Seney, Henry & Hodge, Toledo, 1962-64; with Cooper Industries, Inc., Houston, 1964—, v.p., 1977-88, gen. counsel, 1977-88; pres. Flex Law, Inc., Houston, 1988—. With USAF, 1956-59. Mem. ABA, Tex. Bar Assn., Phi Delta Theta, Phi Delta Phi, Houston Club, Bob Smith Club, Knights of Momus. Home: 1501 Harborview Circle Galveston TX 77550

BIRD, L. RAYMOND, investor; b. Plainfield, N.J., Jan. 22, 1914; s. Lewis Raymond and Bessie (MacCallum) B.; student N.Y. U., 1946-47; m. May Ethel Siercks, June 5, 1949. With shipping dept. Horn & Hardart Co., 1936-46, control auditor, 1946-49, gen. supt. in commissary, 1949-51; asst. to treas. fin. and legal Lockheed Electronics Co. (formerly Stavid Engring., Inc.), 1951-55, treas., 1955-60; pres., dir. State Bank of Plainfield (N.J.), 1960-62; investor, 1962—; treas. Route Twenty Two Corp. Plainfield area committeeman Young Life Campaign, Inc.; pres. Plainfield Camp of Gideons, 1956—; mem. exec. com., treas. Christian Bus. Men's Com. of Central Jersey, 1956—bd. dirs. Child Evangelism Fellowship N.J.; bd. dirs. Sudan Interior Mission; chmn. bd. trustees, chmn. exec. com., chmn. fin. and investments com. Barrington Coll.; trustee Evangelistic Com. Newark and Vicinity. Served from pvt. to 1st lt. 6th Armored Div., AUS, 1941-45. Mem. Am. Mgmt. Assn., Plainfield Area C. of C. Baptist (deacon). Home and office: 18 Maplewood Dr Whiting NJ 08759

BIRD, RALPH GORDON, utilities company executive; b. Highland Park, Mich., Sept. 9, 1933; s. Thurman Elmer and Gladys May (Stephenson) B. BS, U.S. Naval Acad., 1956; MS, USN Postgrad. Sch., 1969. Commd. ensign USN, 1956, advanced through grades to rear adm., 1979, various sea assignments primarily in nuclear powered submarines, 1956-67, comdg. officer USS Archerfish (SSN 678), 1970-74, sr. mem. U.S. Pacific fleet nuclear propulsion examining bd., 1974-76; sr. instr., chief of naval ops. sr. officers ship material readiness course USN, Idaho Falls, Idaho, 1976-77; chief of staff, submarine force U.S. Pacific fleet USN, Pearl Harbor, Hawaii, 1977-79; dir. logistics and security assistance Pacific Command USN, 1979-81; dep. chief naval material for logistics Naval Material Command USN, Washington, 1981-84; ret. USN; pvt. practice cons. to nuclear utility industry 1984-86; sr. v.p. nuclear Boston Edison Co., 1987—. Decorated Def. Superior Service medal, 4 Legion of Merit awards. Mem. Am. Nuclear Soc. Office: Boston Edison Co 800 Boylston St Boston MA 02199

BIRD, ROBERT CARL, state agency adminstrator; b. West Allis, Wis., Sept. 1, 1931; s. Rowland Greenwood and Clara Marie (Lindenborn) B.; m. Mary Emma Ireland, June 4, 1954; children: Steven Carl, Timothy Curtis, Sandra Leigh, Carol Marie. BS, U. Fla., 1953, MEd, 1958; postgrad., Duke U., 1962, U. Tex., 1964-65; PhD, Fla. State U., 1970. Cert. tchr. Tchr. Hendey County Schs., LaBelle, Fla., 1953-55, Palm Beach County Schs., West Palm Beach, Fla., 1955-64; instr. Lake-Sumter Jr. Coll., Leesburg, Fla., 1965-67, Polk Community Coll., Winter Haven, Fla., 1970-71; prof. U. Cen. Fla., Orlando, 1971-87; planner Fla. Dept. Community Affairs, Tallahassee, 1987—; cons. Electron Macine Corp., Umatilla, Fla., 1965-67, Addison Wesley Pub. Co., Reading, Mass., 1978-79, Harcourt Brace Jovanovich Pub. Co., Orlando, 1983-85, Lake Dist. Schs., Tavares, Fla., 1983-85. Author: Elementary Drug Education, 1979; editor Fast Jour., 1982-85; co-author lab manual; contbr. numerous articles to various jours. Bd. dirs. citizens com.East Orange County Community Ctr., Union Park, Fla., 1984-86. Grantee NSF, 1962 64-65. Mem. Fla. Assn. Sci. Tchrs. (bd. dirs. 1974-84, outstanding educator, 1983), Sigma Phi Epsilon. Democrat. Methodist. Home: 1850 Folkstone Rd Tallahassee FL 32312 Office: Dept Community Affairs 2740 Centerview Dr Tallahassee FL 32399

BIRGER, JORDAN, business executive; b. Winthrop, Mass., Nov. 10, 1922; s. Louis John and Ruth (Berman) B.; B.S., Tufts U., 1943; m. Barbara Ann Featherman, Aug. 7, 1955; children—Chet Bradley, Jon Sanford. Founder, treas. Orkney Assos., Waltham, Mass., 1950-70; founder Bee Plastics, Inc., Waltham, 1960, pres., 1960-68; treas. 214 Assos., Inc., Waltham, 1966-68; partner Ridge Assos., Cambridge, Mass., 1968-69; mgr. consumer products div. Amoco Chem. Corp., Waltham, 1968—; founder, pres., chmn. Family Products, Inc., Tyngsborough, Mass., 1972-88. Mem. alumni council Tufts U., 1974—, mem. bd. overseers Coll. Engring., 1988—, chmn. Capital fund dr. Coll. Engring., 1981-84, mem. vis. com., 1982—. Served with AUS, 1944-46. Recipient Disting. Service awards Tufts U. Coll. Engring., 1973, Tufts Alumni Assn., 1982; pres., chmn., Family Products, Inc., 1986; mem. new campaign steering com., Coll. Engring Tufts U., 1987, mem. bd. of overseers, 1988—. Fellow Soc. Tufts; mem. Am. Chem. Soc., Soc. Plastic Engrs., Phi Epsilon Pi. Republican. Jewish. Mason. Home: 145 Sargent Rd Brookline MA 02124 Office: Family Products Inc Tyngsborough MA 01879

BIRK, ROGER EMIL, federal mortgage association executive; b. St. Cloud, Minn., July 14, 1930; s. Emil S. and Barbara E. (Zimmer) B.; m. Mary Lou Schrank, June 25, 1955; children: Kathleen, Steven, Mary Beth, Barbara. BA, St. John's U., 1952. Mgr. Merrill Lynch, Pierce, Fenner and Smith, Inc., Ft. Wayne, Ind., 1964-66, Kansas City, Mo., 1966-68; asst. div. dir. Merrill Lynch, Pierce, Fenner and Smith, Inc., N.Y.C., 1968-70, div. dir., 1971-74, pres., 1974-76, chmn., 1980-85; pres. Merrill Lynch & Co., N.Y.C., 1976-81, chmn., chief exec. officer, 1981-85, chmn. emeritus, 1985—; chmn. bd. Internat. Securities Clearing Corp., N.Y.C., 1986-87; pres., chief operating officer Fed. Nat. Mortgage Assn., Washington, 1987—; dir. N.Y. Stock Exchange, 1981-85, vice chmn., 1983-85; mem. Bus. Roundtable, 1981-85, Pres.'s Commn. on Exec. Exchange, 1981-85, Pres.'s Pvt. Sector Survey on Cost Control, 1982-85. Chmn. nat. adv. council St. John's U., 1975-76, bd. regents, 1975-78; trustee U. Notre Dame, 1981—. Served with AUS, 1952-54. Mem. Nat. Assn. Securities Dealers (mem. long-range planning com. 1975-78), Council on Fgn. Relations. Club: Navesink Country (Middletown, N.J.). Office: Fed Nat Mortgage Assn 3900 Wisconsin Ave NW Washington DC 20016 *

BIRKELUND, JOHN PETER, investment company banking executive; b. Chgo., June 23, 1930; s. George R. and Ruth (Olsen) B.; m. Constance I. Smiles, Oct. 25, 1958; children: Gwynne, Elizabeth Oberbeck, Constance Olivia, Diana. AB, Princeton U., 1952. Cons. Booz Allen & Hamilton, Chgo., 1956; v.p. Amsterdam Overseas Corp., N.Y.C., 1956-67; co-founder, chmn., dir. New Court Securities Corp., N.Y.C., 1967-81; pres. Dillon, Read & Co., Inc., N.Y.C., 1981-87, chmn., 1988—; bd. dirs. NAC Re Corp., Greenwich, Conn., Fifth 956 Corp., N.Y.C. Trustee Brown U., Providence, R.I., 1984— . Served to lt. USNR, 1953-55. Mem. Council Fgn. Relations, Phi Beta Kappa. Clubs: Princeton Cap & Gown, Downtown Assn., The Links (N.Y.C.), Univ. (N.Y.C.). Home: 956 Fifth Ave New York NY 10021 Office: Dillon Read & Co Inc 535 Madison Ave New York NY 10022

BIRKHEAD, EVAN, publishing executive; b. Syracuse, N.Y., June 22, 1960; s. Guthrie Sweeney and Louise (Gartner) B. BA, Tufts U., 1982; MS, Syracuse U., 1983. Asst. editor Hardcopy mag. Seldin Pub. Co., Placentia, Calif., 1983-84, assoc. editor, 1984-85; east coast editor Seldin Pub. Co., Boston, 1986-87; sr. editor Tech. Horizons in Edn. Jour., Santa Ana, Calif., 1985-86; east coast editor DEC Profl. Press, Lexington, Mass., 1988—. Democrat. Home: 89th St #411 Medford MA 02155 Office: Profl Press 238 Bedford St Ste 3 Lexington MA 02173

BIRKHOLZ, GABRIELLA SONJA, communications executive; b. Chgo., Apr. 11, 1938; d. Ladislav E. and Sonja (Kosner) Becvar. BA in Communications and Bus. Mgmt., Alverno Coll., 1983. Editor, owner Fox Lake (Wis.) Rep., 1962-65, McFarland (Wis.) Community Life and Monona Community Herald, 1966-69; bur. reporter Waukesha (Wis.) Daily Freeman, 1969-71; community relations staff Waukesha County Tech. Inst., Pewaukee, Wis., 1971-73; pub. relations specialist JI Case Co., Racine, Wis., 1973-75, corp. publs. editor, 1975-80; v.p., bd. dirs. publs. Image Mgmt., Valley View Ctr., Milw., 1980-82; pres. Communication Concepts, Unltd., Racine, 1983—; guest lectr. Alverno Coll., U. Wis.; adj. faculty U. Wis.-Parkside. Contbr. articles to profl. jours. Bd. dirs. Big Bros./Big Sisters Racine County, Girl Scouts Racine County; mem. Downtown Racine Devel. Corp., Downtown Racine Assn.; mem. community adv. bd. Sta. WGTD-FM. Recipient awards Wis. Press Assn., Nat. Fedn. Press Women; named Wis. Woman Entrepreneur of Yr., 1985. Mem. Internat. Assn. Bus. Communicators (accredited mem.; bd. dirs. 1982-85, various awards), Wis. Women Entrepreneurs (Entrepreneurial Spirit award 1985), Alverno Alumnae Assn., Sigma Delta Chi. Home: 3045 Chatham St Racine WI 53402 Office: 927 Main St Racine WI 53403

BIRKHOLZ, RAYMOND JAMES, metal products manufacturing company executive; b. Chgo., Nov. 11, 1936; s. Raymond I. and Mary (Padian) B.; m. Judy Ann Richards, Apr. 23, 1966; children: Raymond J. Jr., Scott C., Matthew R. BSME, Purdue U., 1958; MBA, U. Chgo., 1963. Registered prof. engr., Ill. V.p. apparatus div. Gen. Cable Corp., Westminster, Colo., 1973-77; v.p. ops. metals div. Ogden Corp., Cleve., 1977-80; v.p. mfg. and engring. Ogden Corp., N.Y.C., 1980-81, pres. indsl. products, 1981-84, v.p., 1984-86; pres., chief oper. officer Amcast Indsl. Corp., Dayton, Ohio, 1986—. Home: 1070 Beryl Trail Centerville OH 45459 Office: Amcast Indsl Corp PO Box 98 Dayton OH 45401

BIRKS, G(EORGE) DRUMMOND, retail executive; b. Montreal, Que., Can., Feb. 18, 1919; s. Henry Gifford and Lilian Cockshutt (Drummond) B.; m. Muriel Scobie (dec. 1979); m. Anne Loheac, Feb. 1984. B. Commerce, McGill U., Montreal, 1940. With Henry Birks & Sons Ltd, Montreal; dir. numerous cos. Served with Can. Army, 1940-46. Office: Henry Birks & Sons Ltd, 1240 Phillips Sq, Montreal, PQ Canada H3B 3H4

BIRKY, JOHN EDWARD, banker, consultant; b. Minier, Ill., July 16, 1934; s. John G. and Gertrude K. (Nafziger) B.; m. Susan Becker, Dec. 13, 1937; children: John Brian, Kathleen Debera. BS in Indsl. Adminstrn., U. Ill., 1957; postgrad., Ohio State U., 1957; MBA, Case Western Res. U., 1975. Cert. data processor. Asst. to mgr. Caterpillar Tractor Co., Peoria, Ill., 1957-61; cons. Sutherland Co., Peoria, 1961-63; mgr. United Research Services, San Mateo, Calif., 1963-69; dir. Case Western Res. U., Cleve., 1969-72; v.p. Fed. Res. Bank, Cleve., 1972-79; exec. v.p. Banc Systems Assn., West Lake, Ohio, 1979-83; exec. v.p. Citizens Banking Corp., Flint, Mich., 1983—, also chmn. auto com., mem. corp. exec. com., 1986-88; bd. dirs. Citizens Banking Corp.; speaker various profl. confs.; bd. dirs. Citizens Bank, Flint, Comml. Nat. BAnk, Berwyn, Ill., Citizens Leasing Corp., Grand Rapids, Mich., Citizens Bank, Mich., Comml. Nat. Bank, Berwyn, Ill., Citizens Leasing Corp., Grand Rapids, Mich. Contbr. articles to banking jours. Mem. Rep. precinct com., Sierra Vista, Ariz., 1964-65; life mem. Pres.'s Task Force, Washington, 1980-88; advisor automation commn. ARC, Flint, 1987; mem. exec. bd., treas. Flint Inst. Music, 1986-88, vice-chmn.; elder, lay pastor First Presbyn. Ch., Flint, 1988-91. Capt. USAF, 1957-60. Mem. Am. Bankers Assn., U. Ill. Alumni Assn. (life), Am. Legion, Univ. Club Flint, City Club Flint, Warwick Hills County Club (Grand Blanc, Mich.), Walden Country Club (Aurora, Ohio), Masons, Shriners, Acacia (life, vice-chmn. local chpt. 1988-90). Republican. Clubs: Warwick Hills Country (Grand Blanc, Mich.); Walden Country (Aurora, Ohio), University (Flint). Lodges: Masons, Shriners. Home: 6099 Rolling Green Grand Blanc MI 48439 Office: Citizens Banking Corp 1 Citizens Banking Ctr Flint MI 48502

BIRLE, JAMES ROBB, investment banker; b. Phila., Jan. 25, 1936; s. John George and Mildred C. (Donnelly) B.; m. Mary Margaret McDaniels, Jan. 28, 1961; children—James Robb, Jr., Anne Margaret, Alexandra Lea, John George II. B.S.M.E., Villanova U., 1958. Design engr., sales specialist atomic power equipment Gen. Electric Co., San Jose, Calif., 1958-72; gen. mgr. nuclear energy mktg. Gen. Electric Co., San Jose, 1972-77; v.p., gen mgr. far east area div. Gen. Electric Co., N.Y.C., 1977-81; v.p., gen mgr. air condition div. Gen. Electric Co., Louisville, 1981-82; sr. v.p., group exec. constrn. and engring. services group Gen. Electric Co., Westport, Conn, 1982-85; sr. v.p. corp. trading ops. Gen. Electric Co., N.Y.C., 1985-88; ptnr. The Blackstone Group, N.Y.C., 1988—. Bd. dirs. Nat. Foreign Trade Council, 1985—, Bus. Council Internat. Understanding, 1985—. Republican. Roman Catholic.

BIRMINGHAM, MARTIN F., banker; b. Rochester, N.Y., Oct. 30, 1921; s. Edward M. and Mary Elizabeth (Egleton) B.; m. Ann Louise Bayer, Sept. 30, 1950; children: Katherine J., Mary L., Mark R., Martin K. V.p. Abstract & Title Ins. Co. (now div. Title Guarantee Co.), Rochester, 1940-54; with Marine Midland Bank, Rochester, 1954—, 1968-73, pres., 1973—, regional chmn., 1987—; also dir., exec. v.p. Marine Midland Bank, N.Y.C. Bd. dirs. United Way Rochester, St. John Fishers Coll., Gannet Found., Inc., St. Ann's Home and Heritage, Strong Mus., Genessee Country Mus.; bd. dirs., chmn. Exec. Svc. Corps, Rochester. With USAAF, 1943-45. Mem. Greater Rochester C. of C. (bd. dirs.),. Clubs: Automobile of Rochester, Country of Rochester, Oak Hill Country, Genessee Valley. Office: Marine Midland Bank 1 Marine Pla Rochester NY 14639

BIRNBAUM, ROBERT JACK, lawyer; b. N.Y.C., Sept. 3, 1927; s. Joseph M. and Beatrice (Herman) B.; m. Joy E. Mumford, June 2, 1957; children—Gregg Gordon, Julie Beth. B.S., NYU, 1957; LL.B., Georgetown U., 1962. Bar: D.C. 1963. Atty. SEC, Washington, 1961-66; with Am. Stock Exchange, N.Y.C., 1967-85, pres., 1977-85; pres. N.Y. Stock Exchange, N.Y.C., 1985-88; spl. counsel Dechert Price & Rhoads, N.Y.C., 1988—. Served with USCGR, 1945-46. Office: Dechert Price & Rhoads 477 Madison Ave New York NY 10022

BISAGA-CHATTINGER, APRIL DARLENE, marketing executive, health facility administrator; b. Wisconsin Rapids, Wis., Apr. 8, 1950; d. Lawrence C. and Arlene Ella (Hause) Lee; m. Emil Mark Bisaga, July 1, 1972 (dec. 1984); children: Richard L. Bisaga, April L. Bisaga; m. Paul Francis Chattinger, June 29, 1985. RN, Deaconess Hosp., Milw., 1971; BS in Nursing, Govs. State U., University Park, Ill., 1981; postgrad., Keller Grad. Sch. Mgmt., Chgo., 1985—. Charge nurse Milw. Children's Hosp., 1972-73; charge nurse critical care St. James Hosp. Med. Ctr., Chicago Heights, Ill., 1972-75, trauma coordinator, 1975-78, dir. emergency health edn., 1978-84, dir. ednl. services, 1984-86, dir. mktg. and emergency health edn., 1986—; cons. Zabo Industries, Oak Brook, Ill., 1984, Ford Motor Co., Chicago Heights, 1986. Bd. dirs. Am. Cancer Soc., Cook County, Ill., 1986—. Recipient Award of Excellence Nat. Registry Emergency Med. Technicians, 1981. Mem. Am. Mktg. Assn., Am. Bus. Women Club, Altrusa Women's Club (sec. 1986—). Roman Catholic. Office: St James Hosp Med Ctr Rte 30 & Chicago Rd Chicago Heights IL 60411

BISBEE, GERALD ELFTMAN, JR., investment company executive; b. Waterloo, Iowa, July 12, 1942; s. Gerald Elftman Bisbee and Maxine Cole Prather; m. Linda Elaine Ude, Aug. 22, 1970; children: Gerald Elftman III, Katherine Elizabeth. BA, North Cen. Coll., Naperville, Ill., 1967; MBA, U. Pa., 1972; PhD, Yale U., 1975. Adminstr. Northwestern U. Med. Ctr., Chgo., 1967-70; asst. prof. Yale U., New Haven, 1974-78, assoc. dir. health services, 1975-78; pres. Hosp. Research and Ednl. Trust, Chgo., 1978-84; v.p., shareholder Kidder, Peabody & Co., N.Y.C., 1984-87; chmn., chief exec. officer Sequel Corp., New Canaan, Conn., 1987—; adj. prof. Northwestern U., Kellogg Sch. of Mgmt., Evanston, Ill., 1979-83; mem. visiting com. Harvard U. Health Services, Boston, 1986—, exec. adv. com. Weatherhead Sch. of Mgmt. Health Systems Program, Case Western Res. U., Cleve., 1984-86; bd. dirs. Cerner Corp., Yamaichi Funds, Inc., Geriatrics and Med. Ctrs., Inc. Author: (book) Multihospital Systems: Policy Issues for the Future, 1981, co-author: Managing the Finances of Health Institutions, 1980, Financing of Health Care, 1979, Musculo-skeletal Disorders: Their Frequency of Occurrence and Their Impact on the Population of the United States, 1978. Mem. adv. com. Waveney Care Ctr., New Canaan, 1987. Grantee USPHS, Washington, 1972-75. Mem. Yale Club (N.Y.). Office: Sequel Corp 73 Grove St New Canaan CT 06840

BISHOP, DAVID NOLAN, electrical engineer; b. Memphis, Jan. 14, 1940; s. Robert Allen Bishop and Sara Frances (Gammon) Marett; m. Lois Margaret Baudouin, Nov. 16, 1963; children: Julie Frances, Anne Marie. BSEE, Miss. State U., 1962, MSEE, 1965. Registered profl. engr., La., Miss., Tex., Fla. Constrn. engr. Chevron Oil Co., New Orleans, 1964-70, lead constrn. engr., 1970-72, sr. constrn. engr., 1972-78; staff elec. engr. Chevron U.S.A., Inc., New Orleans, 1978-82, sr. staff elec. engr., 1982-85, elec. engring. cons., 1985—; offshore safety and anti-pollution equipment rep. Am. Petroleum Inst., 1982-86. Contbr. articles to profl. jours. Asst. scoutmaster Boy Scouts Am., Metairie, La., 1964-69; mem. adminstrv. bd. St. Matthew's United Meth. Ch., Metairie, 1974-76; mem. adv. com. U. Tex., Austin, Petroleum Extension Tex., 1980—; mem. engring. adv. com. Miss. State U., 1982—, chmn. curriculum and rsch. subcom., 1986—. Mem. Instrument Soc. Am. (sr., sect. pres. 1977-78, dist. v.p. 1983-85, chmn. coun. v.p.'s 1984-85, v.p. standards of practice 1988—), Tau Beta Pi, Phi Eta Sigma, Eta Kappa Nu, Omicron Delta Kappa. Republican. Home: 8704 Darby Ln

River Ridge LA 70123 Office: Chevron USA Inc 935 Gravier St New Orleans LA 70112

BISHOP, DONALD CURTIS, printing company executive; b. Fort Collins, Colo., Mar. 30, 1939; s. Donald Charles and Dorothy Katherine (Horney) B.; m. Jo Glen Taylor, June 27, 1959; children: Lori Lee, Donald Charles. BA, Whittier Coll., 1961. Prodn. worker Penn Lithographics Inc., Cerritos, Calif., 1955-63, v.p., 1963-67, pres., 1967—; dir. alumni rels. Whittier (Calif.) Coll., 1965-66. Chmn. bd. Whittier Area Baptist Fellowship, 1983; trustee Biola U., La. Mirada, Calif., 1984-85, Bethel Coll. Devel. Found., St. Paul, Minn., 1983. Mem. Graphic Arts Tech. Found., Printing Industries of Am. (chmn. bd. 1986-87, Graphic Arts/Lewis Meml. Exec. of the Yr. 1988), Printing Industries of So. Calif. (pres. 1976-77, Man of the Yr. 1979), Nat. Assn. of Printers and Lithographers, Friendly Hills Country Club. Republican. Baptist. Home: 15916 La Lindura Dr Whittier CA 90603 Office: Penn Lithographics Inc 16221 Arthur St Cerritos CA 90701

BISHOP, DORI SUZANNE, accountant; b. Balt., Aug. 17, 1957; d. Daniel Henry and Dorothy Denton (Bliss) Honeman; m. James Edward Bishop, Jr., Apr. 18, 1982; children: James Edward II, Rachel Kelly. BS in Acctg., Towson State U., 1979. CPA, Md. Staff acct. Lacy and Hedberg, Honolulu, 1980; mgr. Ernst and Whinney, Balt., 1980-86; dir. taxes Jiffy Lube Internat. Inc., Balt., 1986—. Chmn. com. for on-site day care, Jiffy Lube Internat. Inc., 1988. Mem. AICPA, Md. Assn. CPAs, Am. Women's Soc. CPAs. Democrat. Presbyterian. Office: Jiffy Lube Internat Inc 7008 Security Blvd Ste 300 Baltimore MD 21207

BISHOP, GENE HERBERT, banker; b. Forest, Miss., May 3, 1930; s. Herbert Eugene and Lavonne (Little) B.; m. Kathy S. Bishop, May 27, 1983. B.B.A., U. Miss., Oxford, 1952. With First Nat. Bank, Dallas, 1954-69; sr. v.p., chmn. sr. loan com. First Nat. Bank, 1963-68, exec. v.p., 1968-69; pres., dir. SBIC subs. First Dallas Capital Corp.; pres. Lomas & Nettleton Fin. Corp., Dallas, 1969-75, Lomas & Nettleton Mortgage Investors, Dallas, 1969-75; chmn., chief exec. officer Merc. Nat. Bank, Dallas, 1975-81, MCorp., Dallas, 1975—; dir. Lomas & Nettleton Fin. Corp., Lomas & Nettleton Mortgage Investors, Southwest Airlines Co., Republic Fin. Services, Inc. Bd. dirs. Southwestern Med. Found., State Fair Tex.; trustee, Children's Med. Center; mem. Dallas Citizens Council, Dallas Council World Affairs. Served to 1st lt. USAF, 1952-54. Mem. Assn. Res. City Bankers. Methodist. Clubs: Dallas Petroleum, Terpsichorean, Idlewild, Brook Hollow Golf. Office: MCorp PO Box 655415 Dallas TX 75265-5415

BISHOP, GEORGE WILLIAMS, III, supply company executive; b. Williamson, W.Va., May 11, 1936; s. George W. and Dorothy Ann (Scott) B.; BEE, Va. Mil. Inst., 1958; postgrad. U. Va., 1959; m. Nancy Lee Long, Dec. 4, 1976; 1 child, Rebecca Lee; children by previous marriage: George Williams IV, Angela, Brett, Dale Scott. Mgr. elec. div. Buchanan Williamson Supply Co., Grundy, Va., 1962-64, exec. v.p., 1964-77, pres., chmn., 1977-85, dir., 1964-85 ; v.p., gen. mgr. Wingfield & Hundley, Inc., Richmond, Va., 1966-69, pres., 1969-72; chmn. Grundy Coal and Dock Co., 1977-85 , Royal Mgmt. Cons., 1983-86. Served to capt. USAF, 1959-62. Mem. Rotary (local pres. 1965-66). Republican. Presbyterian. Home: 710 Sharon Dr Johnson City TN 37601 Winter Home: 1020 Ponce de Leon Dr Fort Lauderdale FL 33316

BISHOP, GORDON BRUCE, journalist; b. Paterson, N.J., Jan. 1, 1938; s. Charles E. and Freda Mary (Romyns) B.; m. Jeanne Ann Reed, June 30, 1962; children: Jennifer, Elizabeth. Student, Am. Acad. Dramatic Arts, 1957; B.A., Rutgers U., 1967. Reporter, columnist Herald-News, Passaic, N.J., 1959-67; investigative reporter, columnist Star-Ledger, Newark, N.J., 1969—; lectr. Rutgers U., Princeton U. Author: (with Frank Papps) The Purple Canary, 1963, Holding Onto Nothing, 1969, Gems of New Jersey, 1985, Greater Newark: A Microcosm of America, 1989; producer: Public Broadcasting System documentary TV film It's My Home, 1980; producer-collaborator (musical) Crispus, 1986. Environ. commr. Eatontown, N.J., 1973-76. Recipient Disting. Pub. Service award N.J. Profl. Soc. Engrs., Nat. Environ. awards Scripps-Howard Found., 1971-75; Nat. Conservation awards Washington Journalism Ctr., 1971-72; Conservation award N.J. Audubon Soc., 1973; named Man of Yr. AABC Congregation, Irvington, N.J.; N.J. Press Assn. awards, 1971-88; N.J. Pub. Health Assn. award, 1987; Mid-Atlantic States Air Pollution Control Assn. Disting. Service award, 1987; named N.J. Journalist of Yr., 1986, N.J. Literary Hall of Fame, 1987.; Pub. Service award N.J. Profl. Journalism Soc., 1972, 73, 74, 76, 78, N.J. Conf. Mayors award, 1974; Nat. Recycling award Nat. Recycling Assn., 1973; Gold medal N.J. Garden Club, 1980; award Ballew/McFarland Found., 1981, N.J. Agrl. Soc., 1981; Nat. Wildlife Fedn.'s Nat. Conservation Achievement award, 1987; Inst. Internat. Edn. scholar, U. Manchester, Eng., 1972. Mem. Rutgers U. Alumni Assn. Office: The Star-Ledger Star-Ledger Pla Newark NJ 07101

BISHOP, JAMES FRANCIS, executive search consulting company executive; b. Chgo., Mar. 14, 1937; s. Francis Joseph and Margaret Rose (Nagle) B.; m. Shirley Ann McNulty, Oct. 13, 1962; children: Michael Francis, Noreen Maura, James Francis Jr. BA, Marquette U., 1961, MA, 1965. Spl. agt. Office of Naval Intelligence, Chgo., 1962-65; sr. assoc. Burke & O'Brien Assoc., Inc., N.Y.C., 1965-67, v.p., 1967-74, sr. v.p., 1974-78, pres., 1978-83; pres. Burke, O'Brien & Bishop Assoc., Inc., Princeton, N.J., 1983—; pres. Frog Family, Inc., Princeton, 1986—. Bd. trustees George St. Playhouse, 1988—, St. Francis Med. Ctr., Trenton, N.J.; councilman Piscataway (N.J.) Reps., 1967-80; City of Piscataway, 1968-71. With USMC, 1954-57. Mem. Marquette U. Alumni Assn. (v.p. 1985-87, pres. 87-88). Republican. Roman Catholic. Clubs: Union League (Chgo.); Marquette (N.Y.C.), Forsgate Country. Home: 33 Richard Ct Princeton NJ 08540 Office: Burke O'Brien & Bishop Assocs 100 Thanet Cir Ste 108 Princeton NJ 08540

BISHOP, RONALD E., insurance company executive. BS, U. Maine, 1953, Husson Coll., 1960. Sr. v.p. Nat. Life Ins. Co., 1976-83, exec. v.p., 1983-85, vice chmn. bd., 1985—, also bd. dirs. Office: Nat Life Ins Co National Life Dr Montpelier VT 05604

BISHOP, SID GLENWOOD, union official; b. Gladehill, Va., Nov. 11, 1923; s. Clarence Glenwood and Lillian Helen (Onks) B.; grad. U.S. Naval Trade Sch., 1942; certificate in coll. labor relations Concord Coll., Athens, W.Va., 1961; m. Margaret Lucille Linkous, June 6, 1947. Telegraph operator Virginian R.R., 1946-47, C & O R.R., 1947-62; local chmn. Order R.R. Telegraphers, 1960-62, gen. chmn. C & O-Virginian R.R.'s, 1962-68; 2d v.p. Transp-Communication Employees Union, St. Louis, 1968-69; v.p. transp.-communication div. Brotherhood Ry. and Airline Clks., Rockville, Md., 1969-73, asst. internat. v.p., 1973—; mem. subcom. Labor Research Adv. Council, Dept. Labor, 1975, mem. com. on productivity, tech., growth Bur. Labor Statistics, 1975-77. Served with USN, 1941-46. Mem. AFL-CIO, Canadian Labor Congress, Hunting Hills Home Owners Assn., VFW, Chantilly Nat. Golf and Country Club, Elks, Masons, K.T., Shriners. Democrat. Home and Office: 5211 Chukar Dr SW Roanoke VA 24014

BISHOP, WARNER BADER, business executive; b. Lakewood, Ohio, Dec. 13, 1918; s. Warner Brown and Gladys (Bader) B.; m. Katherine Sue White, Dec. 15, 1944; children: Susan, Judith, Katharine, Jennifer; m. Barrie Osborn, Feb. 4, 1967 (div. Dec. 1980); children: Wilder, Brooks.; m. Susan Bragg Howard, June 3, 1982. A.B., Dartmouth, 1941; M.B.A., Amos Tuck Grad. Sch., 1942; grad. Advanced Mgmt. Program, Harvard U., 1955. With Archer-Daniels-Midland Co., Cleve., 1946-59; successively sales rep., export mgr., sales mgr., divisional gen. mgr., asst. v.p. Archer-Daniels-Midland Co., 1946-56, v.p., 1956-59; pres. Fed. Foundry Supply Co., 1957-59, Wyodak Clay & Chem. Co., 1957-59, Basic, Inc., until 1963, Union Fin. Corp., Cleve., 1963-74; pres. Union Savs. Assn., 1963-74, chmn., 1970—; chmn., pres. Transohio Financial Corp., Cleve., 1974-85; dir. Blue Cross-Blue Shield Ohio, Med. Cons. Imaging Co.; trustee Med. Cleve. Mut.; dir. Med. Life Ins. Co.; sec. Foundry Ednl. Found., 1956-60. Contbr. articles to trade jours. Gen. campaign mgr. Cleve. Area Heart Soc., bd. chmn., 1960-61; mem. corp. Fenn Coll.; Bd. dirs. Ohio Heart Soc.; chmn. Highland Redevel. Corp., 1963-68; pres. Council High Blood Pressure; dir. Am. Heart Soc., 1963-68; 1964-69. Served to lt. USNR, 1942-45; comdg. officer escort vessels. Clubs: Union (N.Y.C.); Meadow (Southampton, N.Y.); Chagrin Valley Hunt, Union, Kirtland Country, Tavern (Cleve.); Bath and Tennis, Everglades (Palm Beach, Fla.). Home: 300 S Ocean Blvd Penthouse B Palm Beach FL 33480 also: Two Bratenahl Pl Apt 14D Bratenahl OH 44108

BISHOP, WILLIAM WADE, advertising executive; b. Mt. Vernon, N.Y., Apr. 17, 1939; s. Kenneth Farrington and Dorothea (Renz) B.; m. Jacqueline Kenton, May 21, 1966; children: William Jr., Christopher. BA, Ohio Wesleyan U., 1961. Account exec. Ogilvy & Mather, Grey, BBDO, N.Y.C., 1964-72; v.p. Ted Bates, N.Y.C., 1972-74; category mgr. Gen. Foods Corp., White Plains, N.Y., 1974-79; mng. dir. Mktg. Corp. Am., Westport, Conn., 1979-80; exec. v.p. MCA Advt., N.Y.C., 1980-84, pres., chief exec. officer, 1984-86; pres. MCA Communications Group, 1987—, Ally & Gargano, N.Y.C., 1986-89; bd. dirs. Consumer Healthcare Communications Inc. Served with USMC, 1962-68. Mem. Am. Assn. Advt. Agys., Melrose Club (Hilton Head, S.C.). Republican. Congregationalist. Office: Ally & Gargano Inc 805 Third Ave New York NY 10022

BISIEWICZ, ALAN WALTER, insurance executive, social work consultant; b. Springfield, Mass., Jan. 27, 1951; s. Fred and Eleanor Ann (Innarelli) B.; m. Susan Patricia Duffy; 1 child, Zachary. BA, Amherst Coll., 1973; MSW, Smith Coll., 1978. Sch. adjustment counselor Northampton (Mass.) Pub. Schs., 1978-81; psychiatric social worker Community Care Mental Health Ctr., Springfield, 1981-82; asst. prof. psychiatry U. Mass. Med. Sch., Northampton, 1982-83; dir. employee assistance program Mass. Mut. Life Ins. Co., Springfield, 1983—; bd. dirs. Pioneer Valley Consumer Counseling Service, Springfield; cons. Osborn (Mass.) Clinic, 1983—. Mem. Nat. Assn. Social Workers, Am. Assn. Profl. Hypnotherapists, Assn. Labor/Mgmt., Adminstrs. and Cons. on Alcoholism. Roman Catholic. Office: Mass Mutual Life Ins Co State St Springfield MA 01111

BISNO, ALISON PECK, investment banker; b. Little Rock, Apr. 3, 1955; d. Robert A. and Sue (Redyard) Peck; m. Edward Jay Bisno, June 15, 1980; 1 child, Adam, Amy. BBA in Fin., Memphis State U., 1977; student, U. Tex., Austin, 1979. Chartered fin. analyst. Mgmt. training program First Tenn. Bank, Memphis, 1977-80; customer service, comml. lending rep., asst. mgr., fin. analyst Fed. Express, Memphis, 1980-81; fin. analyst Coastal Corp., Houston, 1981-82; underwriter Stephens, Inc., Little Rock, 1982—, analyst-securities, 1983-84, dir. of research, 1984-88, v.p., 1988—. Mem. Inst. of Chartered Fin. Analysts, N.Y. Soc. of Security Analysts, Nat. Assn. of Securities Dealers. Office: Stephens Inc 114 E Capitol Ave Little Rock AR 77201

BISPHAM, THOMAS PEDDER, investment banker; b. N.Y.C., Aug. 30, 1945; s. Robert Gedney and Barbara (Woodward) B.; m. Barbara Shea, Dec. 27, 1975; children: Thomas Pedder Jr., Barbara Harlin. BA, Lafayette Coll., 1972; postgrad., NYU, 1975-78. Asst. v.p. energy and minerals worldwide Chem. Bank, N.Y.C., 1972-78; v.p. energy and minerals Irving Trust Co., N.Y.C., 1978-81; dir. fin. cons. Dames & Moore, N.Y.C., 1981-82; v.p. pvt. equity group Bankers Trust Co., N.Y.C., 1982—. Contbr. articles to profl. jours. Lay reader, chalice bearer and usher Church of the Heavenly Rest, N.Y.C.; bd. dirs. Lincoln Hall, N.Y.C., 1975-82; treas. The Blue Hill Troupe, Ltd., N.Y.C., 1985-87; sec. West 93d Block Assn., N.Y.C., 1981—; vol. UN We Believe, N.Y.C., 1974-88—; trustee Union Chapel, Siasconset, Mass., 1987—; bd. dirs. Children's Heart Fund, N.Y.C., 1986—, Mus. City N.Y.; spl. vol. Children's Christmas Part, 1988; coach West Side Soccer League, 1987—. Served with USN, 1965-69. Mem. AIME (N.Y. section treas. 1982-83, bd. dirs. econ. and fin. subsection), Soc. Mining Engrs of AIME, Can. Inst. Mining and Metall. Engrs., Cogeneration Inst. of Assn. Energy Engrs., Vet. Corps Arty. N. Y. (Distinguished Service award 1980), Nat. Assn. Energy Service Cos. (bd. dirs. 1987—), Am. Mining Congress (fin. adv. council exec. com. 1982-84), Psi Upsilon. Republican. Episcopalian. Clubs: Siasconset Casino Assn. (Ma.); Sankaty Head Golf and Beach (Siasconset, Mass.). Lodge: Masons (steward 1981-82). Home: 210 Riverside Dr New York NY 10025 Office: Bankers Trust Co 280 Park Ave New York NY 10015

BISSELL, JOHN HOWARD, marketing executive; b. Bklyn., July 8, 1935; s. Donald Henry and Lillian (Eckberg) B.; m. Joan Becker, Sept. 7, 1963; children: John Edward, Mary Katherine. BA in Polit. Sci., Yale U., 1956. Brand mgr. Procter and Gamble, Inc., Cin., 1960-71; v.p., new products mktg. Frito-Lay, Inc., Dallas, 1971-80; v.p. mktg. The Stroh Brewing Co., Detroit, 1980-85; sr. v.p., spl. products div. The Stroh Brewery Co., Detroit, 1985—; pres. Pacific Health Beverage Co. subs. The Stroh Brewery Co., Detroit, 1985—. Chmn. corp. funds campaign Sta. WTVS, Detroit, 1986; exec. bd. dirs. Detroit council Boy Scouts Am., 1983-86. Served as 1st lt. USAF, 1957-59. Mem. Assn. Nat. Advts. Republican. Presbyterian. Clubs: Birmingham Athletic, Renaissance; Yale (N.Y.). Home: 3310 Morningview Terr Birmingham MI 48010

BISSON, ANDRE, transportation executive; b. Trois-Rivieres, Que., Can., Oct. 7, 1929; s. Roger and Marcelle (Morin) B.; m. Reine Levesque, June 13, 1953; children: Helene, Isabelle. BA, Laval U., Que., 1950, M.Commerce, 1953; MBA, Harvard U., 1955, LHD (hon.), U. Du Quebec, 1985. Asst. prof. bus. adminstrn. Laval U., 1955-63, assoc. prof., 1963-66; dir. Inst. Can. Bankers, Montreal, Que., 1966-71; gen. mgr. Bank of N.S., Montreal, 1971-77, v.p., gen. mgr., 1977-83, sr. v.p., gen. mgr., 1983-87; pres. Logistec Corp., 1987—, Donohue Inc., Donohue Watance Inc., Columbia Computing Services Inc.; bd. dirs. Power Fin. Corp., L'Union Can. Cie d'Assurance, Que. Chmn. bd. Notre Dame Hosp., Montreal, 1977—, Fondation canadienne de perfectionnement en affaires; bd. dirs. U. Montreal, 1979—, Fondation de l'Universitié du Québec à Montréal, Montreal Bd. Trade, Théâtre du Noveau Monde, European Inst. Bus. Adminstrs., Fontainebleau, France, 1977—. Named Man of Month, Revue Commerce, Montreal, 1979; mem. Order of Can., Gov. Gen., Ottawa, 1982; recipient medal Gloire de l'Escolle, Laval U. Alumni Assn., Que., 1982, Hermes trophy Laval U., 1988. Fellow Inst. Can. Bankers (hon.), mem. French C. of C. in Can. (pres. 1983-85), International Fin. Ctrs. Orgn. Montreal, Société d'Investissement Jeunesse, Province of Que. C. of C. (exec. com. 1976-80). Roman Catholic. Clubs: Mount Royal (com. 1987), St. James (com. 1975-78), Canadian of Montreal, Harvard Bus. Montreal (pres. 1971), St.-Denis (bd. 1984) (Montreal).

BITTEN, ROBERT DENZER, chemical company executive; b. Jersey City, Mar. 26, 1933; s. Robert Mooney and Florence Amelia (Denzer) B.; B.S. in Chemistry, W.Va. Wesleyan Coll., 1957; m. Betty Bertine Elkin, Sept. 4, 1959; children—Vicky, James, Robert. Sales rep. Allied Chem. Corp., N.Y.C., 1957-59, Ja-Ro Chem., Inc., Dallas, 1959-61, Lucidol (div. Pennwalt Corp.) Buffalo, 1961-64, Southwest dist. mgr., 1964-66, mgr. field sales, 1966-78, v.p. mktg., 1978—. Mem. adv. administrv. bd. Christ United Meth. Ch. (Buffalo); active Little League Football (Buffalo). Served in USN, 1953-55. Recipient Clare E. Bacon Exec. award Soc. Plastics Industry, 1983. Mem. Chem. Week Adv. Bd. Mem. Chemists Club, Soc. Plastics Industry (bd. dirs. 1987—, exec. com., policy com.; vice chmn. nat. meeting 1977, chmn. 33d Ann. Tech. Conf. and Exhibit of Reinforced Plastic/Composites Inst. 1978, Man of Yr. 1983), Am. Chem. Soc., Benzene Ring Soc., Vinyl Inst. Am. (exec. bd. dirs.), Alpha Sigma Phi. Methodist. Clubs: Audubon Golf, Ionosphere, Red Carpet, Masons, Shawnee Country, Grand Island Rod and Gun. Selected to represent plastics industry in U.S. govt. sponsored tour of Europe, 1976; contbr. articles to profl. jours. Office: Lucidol Penwalt Corp Div 1740 Military Rd Buffalo NY 14240

BITTER, JOHN LEONARD, JR., investment banker; b. Johnson City, Tenn., Dec. 14, 1932; s. John Leonard and Millicent (Ffolliott) B.; m. Carol Manneschmidt, Apr. 7, 1961; 1 child, John III. BS in Geology, U. Ariz., 1958. Analyst Met. Life, N.Y.C., 1960-62; assoc. N.Y. Securities, N.Y.C., 1962-67, ptnr., 1968-70; v.p. E.F. Hutton, Charlotte, N.C., 1972-84; 1st v.p. Interstate/Johnson Lane, Atlanta, 1984—; bd. dirs. Communication Cable Inc., Siler City, N.C. Served with USN, 1951-55, Korea. Mem. Assn. Corp. Growth. Republican. Episcopalian. Clubs: Ravinia (Atlanta); Biltmore Forest (Asheville, N.C.). Home: 46 Olde Ivy Sq Atlanta GA 30342 Office: Interstate/Johnson Lane 975 Johnson Ferry Rd Atlanta GA 30342

BITTEROLF, WOLFGANG, marketing consultant; b. Vienna, Austria, June 15, 1941; came to U.S., 1978; s. Karl Eugen B. and Hilda Anna (Weiner) Roesler; m. Faith Anne Timlin, Dec. 20, 1969; children: Paul Anthony, Stephen Karl. Degreee in Advt. and Sales, Hochschule fuer Welthandel, Vienna, Austria, 1966. Mg.. mktg. Lever S.A., Caracas, Venezuela, 1968-76, Beecham-Venezuela, Caracas, 1975; mktg. dir. Bristol-Myers Venezuela, Caracas, 1976-78, Vesuvius Crucible Co., Pitts., 1979-83; prin. Bitterolf Mktg., Pitts., 1984—. Mem. Rotary. Office: Bitterolf Mktg 1378 Freeport Rd Pittsburgh PA 15238

BITTLE, D. DENISE, residential construction and sales executive; b. Anniston, Ala., Apr. 15, 1957; d. Alvin Lester and Eunice (Roberts) B.; 1 child, Jennifer. Student, U. Montevallo, 1975-76. V.p. Don Sills Enterprises, Anniston, 1976—. Pianist Woodland Park Bapt. Ch., Anniston, 1980-87; dir. Girls in Action, Anniston, 1984—; mem. Anniston Bd. Realtors, Anniston, 1984-86. Republican. Office: Don Sill Enterprises PO Box 3342 Oxford AL 36203

BIXBY, SUSAN K., marketing executive; b. Mason City, Iowa, Mar. 3, 1952; d. Kenneth R. and Marilyn (Greenlee) Church; m. Steven Bixby, May 31, 1971; children: Patrick, Ashleigh. BS in Mktg., George Mason U., 1981. Founder, owner Orion Mktg., Manassas, Va., 1983—. dir. Patchwork Proverbs, Winston-Salem, N.C. Mem. Beta Epsilon Phi, Jr. Women's Club of Manassas. Office: Orion Mktg PO Box 2149 Manassas VA 22110

BIXLER, ALICE LORRAINE HILL, security lock company official; b. Moore, Okla., Jan. 15, 1935; d. Robert Edward and Alma Alice (Fraysher) Hill; m. Kenneth A. Bixler; children: Debra Hrboka, Pamela Spangler, Eric Shiver, Lorraine Smith. Grad., Patricia Stevens Modeling Sch., Orlando, Fla., 1963; student, Draughton Sch. Bus., Oklahoma City, 1968-69, Troy State U., 1970-71, Ventura Coll., 1974; AA in Gen. Edn., Rose Coll., Midwest City, Okla.; BS in Bus. and Acctg., Central State U., 1977; student, U. Okla., 1977-78. Former mode; rep. Gravity Drop and Dead Bolt Lock Inc., Oxnard, Calif., 1977—. Home: 3699 Lemon Ave Oxnard CA 93033 Office: Gravity Drop & Dead Bolt Lock Inc PO Box 2242 Oxnard CA 93034

BJERCKE, ALF RICHARD, business executive; b. Oslo, May 30, 1921; s. Richard and Birgit (Brambani) B.; student Mass. Inst. Tech., 1939-41; m. Berit Blikstad, Mar. 15, 1946; children—Leif Richard, Haakon Richard, Ingerid, Berit. With Alf Bjercke A/S, Oslo, 1945—, partner, 1950—, vice chmn., 1966-69, chmn., 1969—; dir. A/S. Jotungruppen, 1972-83, chmn. corp. council, 1983—; chmn. bd. Nydalens Compagnie, 1982-88; with Addis Ababa, Nat. Chem. Ind. Ltd., 1966-75; chmn. Norwater (Norske Vannkilder A/S.), ABC Produkter A/S, Scanpump A/S, 1972-78, Vallenova, Inc., Oslo, 1984-88; chmn., dir. Oplandske Dampskibsselskab, 1981—; dir. Norwegian Shipping & Trade Jour., 1962-81, Atheneum Forlag, Vallenova Inc.; chmn. Jotungruppen A/S, Kolding, Denmark, 1966-88; vice chmn. Akershus Broiler Co., chmn. Chilinvest A/S., Pan Art Gallery, Vinland Film A/S & Co.; dir. Atheneum Pub. Co., Mosvold Overseas Trading Co., Atheneum Communications, Inc., Alamo Co. Hon. consul gen. Tunisia in Norway; vice chmn. Norwegian Spring Water Assn.; chmn. council Kofoed Sch., 1962-80; mem. Norway's Olympic Com., 1971-74; mem. exec. com. Norwegian UNIDO Council, del. conf.; Norway del. Econ. Commn. for Africa; mem. Norwegian Arbitration Bd. for Competitive Questions; chmn. Soc. for Protection Ancient Towns, Soc. for Reconstrn. of Old Christiania, 1968—; mem. council Norsk Sjofartsmuseum; chmn. bd. Norway's Bus. Mus., 1980-88; Norwegian mem. adv. com. Sail Tng. Assn., London; past chmn. Nordic Adv. Council for Industry; mem. Commn. 3 CIOR, Norwegian chmn. Rotary Internat. Campaign Polio Plus (eradicating polio). Mem. campaign com. Norwegian Conservative party, 1974, council mem. Oslo'dagere '86, '88; bd. dirs. Artists Gallery of Oslo, 1957-69; vice chmn. East Norway Sailing Sch. Ship Assn., 1961-78; chmn. Norwegian-Ethiopian Soc., 1954-70; chmn. council Norway-Am. Assn.; chmn. fin. com. Norwegian World Wild Life Fund Bd. Reps.; Norwegian rep. Operation Sail 76; bd. dirs. A Smoke-free Generation, 1980; chmn. Norwegian Ch. Council, 1984; bd. dirs. Care (Norway), 1984, Norwegian Orgn. Asylum Seekers, 1984. Major Royal Norwegian Air Force, 1941-45; maj. Res. Mem. Norwegian Assn. Industries (past dir.), Color Council Norway (chmn. 1958-69, 72-81), Norwegian Paint Mfrs. Assn. (past chmn.), Norway Athletic Assn. (chmn. 1968-72), Wine and Food Soc., World Wildlife Fund 1001 Club, Phi Delta Gamma. Clubs: Rotary (dist. gov. 1980-81, vice chmn. world community service); Oslo Bus. Men's (dir. 1968-70). Pub.; From the Diplomatic World, 1983, Dragonene, 1988. Contbr. articles in several fields to profl. jours.; columnist jour. Farmand. Home: 14 President Harbitzgate 0259, Oslo 2 Norway Office: Solleveien 2a, 1324 Lysaker Norway

BJONTEGARD, ARTHUR MARTIN, JR., banker; b. Lynn, Mass., Mar. 23, 1938; s. Arthur M. and Irma W. (Cook) B.; m. Wilma Joy Golding, Oct. 15, 1966; children—Arthur M., Karla Kristin. B.A., Duke U., 1959; J.D., U. Va., 1962; postgrad., Stonier Grad. Sch. Banking, Rutgers U., 1966; grad. advanced mgmt. program, Harvard U. Sch. Bus., 1974. Bar: N.J. 1962, S.C. 1967. Bank examiner U.S. Treasury Dept., Richmond, Va., 1962-66; trust officer S.C. Nat. Bank, Columbia, 1966-74; sr. v.p. S.C. Nat. Bank, 1974-81; pres. S.C. Nat. Corp., Columbia, 1981-84; vice-chmn. S.C. Nat. Corp., 1984—, dir., 1982—; bd. dirs. S.C. Nat. Bank, 1986. Pres. United Way of the Midlands, Columbia, 1984-85, S.C., 1986-87, Univ. Assocs., Columbia, 1984-85, Friday Luncheon Club, Columbia, 1984, Spring Valley Ednl. Found., 1986—; chmn. Columbia Community Relations Council, 1984. Named Vol. of Yr., Urban League, Columbia, 1984. Mem. S.C. Bar Assn., Palmetto Soc., S.C. Bankers Assn. (Outstanding Young Banker 1973), Thomas Jefferson Soc., S.C. C. of C. (v.p. 1986—). Episcopalian. Clubs: Forest Lake Country, Palmetto (Columbia); Spring Valley Country. Office: SC Nat Corp 1426 Main St Columbia SC 29226-0001

BJONTEHGARD, ARTHUR MARTIN, JR., bank executive; b. Lynn, Mass., Mar. 23, 1938; s. Arthur Martin Sr. and Erma Winifred (Cooke) B.; m. Wilma G. Bjontegard, Oct. 15, 1966; children: Arthur Martin III, Karla K. BA, Duke U., 1959; JD, U. Va., 1962; postgrad., Stonier Grad. Sch. Banking, 1966, Harvard U., 1976. Bar: N.J. 1962. Sr. v.p. S.C. Nat. Bank, Columbia, 1969-75, exec. v.p., 1975-81; pres. S.C. Nat. Corp., Columbia, 1981-84, vice-chmn., 1984—. Past pres. United Way Midlands; bd. dirs. Cen. Carolina Found.; pres. Spring Valley Edn. Found., S.C. Council Econ. Edn. Named Young Banker Yr., S.C. Bankers Assn., 1973, Man Yr., Columbia Urban League, 1986. Mem. N.J. Bar Assn., S.C. Bar Assn., S.C. C. of C., Forest Lake Club, Spring Valley Club. Home: 33 Sunturf Cir Columbia SC 29223 Office: SC Nat Corp 1426 Main St Columbia SC 29226-0001

BJORKHOLM, PAUL JAMES, engineering company executive, physicist; b. Milw., May 27, 1942; s. Jack Warren and Marion Beatrice (Anderson) B.; m. Pauline L. Pasko, Aug. 12, 1967; children: Jonathan Olof, Jill Katherine. BA, Princeton U., 1964; MA, U. Wis., 1965, PhD, 1969. Sr. scientist Am. Sci. and Engring., Inc., Cambridge, Mass., 1969-73, staff scientist, 1973, sr. staff scientist, 1973-83, v.p. rsch., 1983-85, sr. v.p. med. and security sci., 1985-87, sr. v.p. rsch., 1987—. Contbr. articles to profl. jours.; patentee in field. Nat. Cancer Inst. grantee. Mem. Am. Assn. for Physicists in Medicine, Am. Phys. Soc., Am. Soc. for Nondestructive Testing. Home: 4 Beach Rd Sharon MA 02067 Office: Am Sci & Engring Inc Ft Washington Cambridge MA 02139

BJORNBAK, MARK PHILIP, printing company executive; b. Detroit, May 19, 1958; s. Russell G. and Helen (Knapp) B.; m. Lucy Lane, June 27, 1981; children: James, Samantha, Lydia. Student, Sch. Craft Coll., Livonia, Mich., 1978; BA in Human Rels., Judson Coll., 1981. Cert. firefighter, emergency med. technician, Ill. Buyer, salesman Bed 'n' Stead, Plymouth, Mich., 1972-79; alcohol treatment asst. share program Lyden Family Svc., Franklin Park, Ill., 1981-84; mgr. sales Dundee Press Inc., West Dundee, Ill., 1984—; firefighter, emergency med. technician Village of West Dundee, 1986—; graphics coordinator, cons. Health Quest, Dundee, Ill., 1986—. Mem. Mus. Sci. and Industry, Chgo.; indsl. chmn. Fox Valley Postal Customers Coun., 1987-88. State of Mich. scholar, 1977. Mem. West Dundee Firefighters Assn., Dundee C. of C. (chmn. mktg. com. 1986-87, bd. dirs. 1987—), Cardunal C. of C. Baptist. Office: Dundee Press Inc 109 N Second St Dundee IL 60118

BJORNSON, CARROLL NORMAN, small business owner; b. Bklyn., Sept. 6, 1929; s. Karl Olaf and Bertha Jacobine (Olsen) B.; m. Edith McBride Cameron, Jan. 11, 1963; children: Lisa Carol, Karl Cameron (dec.). BS, U.S. Mcht. Marine Acad., 1950; MBA, Harvard U., 1956. Owners rep. Shipowner Hilmar Reksten, Bergen, Norway, 1957-63; service mgr. Stolt-Nielsen, Inc., Greenwich, Conn., 1963-68, v.p., 1964-69; pres. Stolt-Nielsen, Inc., Japan, 1969-71; pres. Stolt-Nielsen, Inc., Greenwich, Conn., 1971-77, exec. v.p., 1977-85; owner, pres. Md. Marine Inc., Houston, Tex., 1985—; dir. Stolt Tankers & Terminals (Holdings) S.A., Greenwich, 1977—. Dir. Norwegian-Am. C. of C., N.Y.C., 1979-85; trustee Am. Mcht. Marine Mus., 1985—. Served to lt. USNR, 1953-55. Mem. N.Y. Yacht Club, Harvard Bus. Sch. Club Greater N.Y., Inc. Republican. Home: 45 Nutmeg Dr Greenwich CT 06831 Office: Md Marine Inc 8 Sound Shore Dr Greenwich CT 06836

BJORNSTAD, THOMAS SHELDON, financial planner; b. Eau Claire, Wis., Oct. 26, 1955; s. Robert Ogden and Leah Jean (Sheldon) B.; m. Lorrie Susan Auman, Aug. 21, 1976; children: Joel, Jodi, Aimee-Christine. BA, St. Olaf Coll., 1977. Cert. fin. planner, 1989. Sales rep. IDS, South Bend, Ind., 1980-81; office adminstr. P.E.B.S.C.O., South Bend, Ind., 1981-83; v.p. adminstrn. Combined Capital Securities, South Bend, Ind., 1983-85; dir. fin. planning Everett Reasoner Adv. Corp. (named changed to Miller Reasoner Adv. Corp.), Elkhart, Ind., 1985—. Mem. Internat. Assn. Fin. Planners (bd. dirs. Michiana chpt. 1987-88).

BLACHLY, JACK LEE, oil company executive, lawyer; b. Dallas, Mar. 8, 1942; s. Emery Lee and Thelma Jo (Budd) B.; m. Lucy Largent Rain, Jan. 15, 1972; 1 son, Michael Talbot. B.B.A., So. Meth. U., 1965, J.D., 1968. Bar: Tex. 1968, U.S. Ct. Appeals (5th cir.) 1969, U.S. Supreme Ct. 1975, U.S. Tax Ct. 1977. Trust officer InterFirst Bank Dallas, N.A., 1968-70; ptnr. firm Reese & Blachly, Dallas, 1970-71; assoc. firm Rain Harrell Emery Young & Doke, Dallas, 1971-76; staff atty. Sabine Corp., Dallas, 1976-77, mgr. legal dept., 1977-80, v.p., gen. counsel, 1980—. Mem. ABA, Tex. Bar Assn., Dallas Bar Assn., Am. Soc. Corp. Secs. Baptist. Clubs: Chaparral, Dallas Gun, Northwood, Dallas Petroleum (Dallas). Office: Rain Harrell Emery Young & Doke 2001 Ross Ave Ste 1000 Dallas TX 75201

BLACK, ALEXANDER, lawyer; b. Pitts., Nov. 19, 1914; s. Alexander and Ruth (Hay) B.; m. Jane Mevay McIntosh, Apr. 23, 1955; children: F. Kristin Hoeveler, Kenneth M., Elizabeth H. Black Watson. AB, Princeton U., 1936; LLB, Harvard U., 1939. Bar: Pa. 1940, U.S. Supreme Ct. 1955, U.S. Ct. Appeals (3d cir.) 1957, U.S. Ct. Claims 1959, U.S. Ct. Appeals (Fed. cir.) 1982. Law clk. Buchanan, Ingersoll P.C. and predecessors, Pitts., summers 1936-39, assoc., 1939-51, ptnr., 1951-85, shareholder, 1980-85, of counsel, 1985—. Served to lt. USNR, 1942-46, PTO. Mem. ABA, Pa. Bar Assn., Allegheny County Bar Assn., Am. Law Inst., Am. Coll. Trial Lawyers, Am. Coll. Real Estate Lawyers, Am. Bar Found., Pa. Bar Found., Am. Judicature Soc., Panel of Arbitrators, Am. Arbitration Assn., Assn.Panel of Arbitrators. Republican. Presbyterian. Clubs: Harvard/Yale/Princeton, Duquesne (Pitts.); Princeton (N.Y.C.); Edgeworth (Sewickley, Pa.). Home: 1309 Beaver Rd Sewickley PA 15143 Office: Buchanan Ingersoll PC 600 Grant St 57th Fl Pittsburgh PA 15219

BLACK, CHARLES ALDEN, economist, aquatic engineer; b. Oakland, Calif., Mar. 6, 1919; s. James Byers and Katharine (McElrath) B.; m. Shirley Temple; children: Linda Susan, Charles A. Jr., Lori Alden. BA, Stanford U., 1940, MBA, 1946; postgrad., Harvard U., 1941. Purchasing asst. Castle & Cooke Ltd., San Francisco, 1946-48; asst. to pres. Hawaiian Pineapple, Honolulu, 1948-50; mgr. bus. ops. SRI Internat., Menlo Pk., Calif., 1953-58; mgr. fin. relations Ampex Corp., Redwood City, Calif., 1958-64; v.p., co-founder Pacific Mariculture, Pescadero, Calif., 1964-68; pres., chmn. Mardela Corp., Woodside, Calif., 1969—; co-founder, chmn. bd. Marquest Group, Inc., Pocasset, Mass., 1985—, Marine Imaging Systems Inc., Marine Telepresence, Inc. Comdr. USN, 1941-45. Mem. Marine Tech. Soc., World Mariculture Assn., Woods Hole Oceanographic Inst. (mem. corp. bd.), Oceanic Inst., Bohemian Club, Pacific Union Club, Beta Sigma (hon.). Republican. Home and Office: 115 Lakeview Dr Woodside CA 94062

BLACK, CHARLES ROBERT, oil company executive; b. Abilene, Tex., Aug. 29, 1935; s. Taylor Flow and Mildred Opal (Griffin) B.; m. Billie Katherine Huckabay, June 2, 1956; children—Kevin Robert, Susan Kay Black Handley. B.S. in Petroleum Engring., Tex. Tech. U., 1958. Field engr. Texaco Inc., Monument, N.Mex., 1958-59; area engr. Texaco Inc., Andrews, Tex., 1959-60; reservoir engr. Texaco Inc., Midland, Tex., 1960-61, div. proration engr., 1961-64, div. secondary recovery engr., 1965-66; dist. engr. Texaco Inc., Wichita Falls, Tex., 1966-67; sr. petroleum engr. Texaco Inc., Houston, 1967-68; asst. to div. gas supt. Texaco Inc., New Orleans, 1968-69; asst. to gen. mgr. Texaco Inc., N.Y.C., 1969-70, crude oil coordinator, 1970-74, asst. to v.p. producing, 1974-75, mgr. Middle East ops., 1976; pres., gen. mgr. Texaco Iran, London, 1977-79; gen. mgr. Texaco Oil Trading, London, 1979-80; v.p. trading Texaco Oil Trading & Supply, White Plains, N.Y., 1980-83; pres. Texaco Internat. Trader Inc., White Plains, 1980-83; v.p. Texaco Inc., White Plains, 1983—; sr. v.p. Texaco Middle East-Far East, White Plains, 1983, pres., 1984-87; pres. Texaco Latin Am./West Africa, Coral Gables, Fla., 1987—; dir. numerous Texaco subs.; mem. adv. council Am.-Saudi Bus. Roundtable, N.Y.C., 1984-87; dir. Caribbean/Cen. Am. Action Commn., Washington, 1987—. Trustee Tex. Tech. Alumni Endowment Fund, Lubbock, 1984—; dir. New World Symphony, 1988—, Miami Opera, 1988—, Fla. Internat. Scholarship Found., 1988—; mem. nat. steering com. Tex. Tech. Enterprise Campaign, Lubbock; elder Presbyn. Ch. of U.S., Midland, Tex.; mem. Deacon Noroton Presbyn. Ch., Darien, Conn.; mem. adv. council Georgetown U. Ctr. for Arab Studies, Washington, 1984-87; mem. citizen com. U. Miami, 1987—; mem. com. 21 Coral Gables C. of C., 1987—. Served to radarman 2d class USNR, 1953-61. Recipient Disting. Alumni award Tex. Tech. U., 1979, Disting. Engr. award, 1980. Mem. Am. Arab Assn. for Commerce and Industry, Soc. Petroleum Engrs., Tex. Tech. Ex-Students Assn., Coral Gables C. of C. (trustee 1987—), Greater Miami C. of C. (trustee 1988—), Phi Gamma Delta, Pi Epsilon Tau, Phi Eta Sigma. Republican. Office: Texaco Inc 150 Alhambra Cir Coral Gables FL 33134

BLACK, CONRAD MOFFAT, corporate executive; b. Montreal, Que., Can., Aug. 25, 1944; s. George Montegu and Jean Elizabeth (Riley) B.; m. Shirley Gail Hishon. B.A., Carleton U., 1965; LL.L., Laval U., 1970; M.A. in History, McGill U., 1973; LL.D. (hon.), St. Francis Xavier U., 1979, McMaster U., 1979; Litt.D. (hon.), U. Windsor, 1979. Chmn., co-owner Eastern Twps. Pub. Co., Ltd., La Soc. de Publication de l'Avenir de Brome Missisquoi Inc., Farnham, Que., 1967—; chmn. Sterling Newspapers Ltd., Vancouver, 1971—, Dominion Malting Ltd., Winnipeg, 1976—; chmn. bd., chmn. exec. com. Argus Corp. Ltd., Toronto, 1979—, chief exec. officer, 1986—; chmn., chief exec. officer The Ravelston Corp. Ltd., 1986—, Hollinger Inc., 1986—; chmn. The Daily Telegraph, 1987, Saturday Night Mag., Inc., 1987, Unimédia Inc., 1988; dep. chmn. Am. Pub. Co., 1987; vice chmn. Norcen Energy Resources Ltd., 1986—; mem. exec. com., dir. Can. Imperial Bank Commerce, 1983—; dir. Algoma Central R.R., Brascan Ltd., Can. Marconi Co., Carling O'Keefe Breweries of Can. Ltd., Confederation Life Ins. Co., Domgroup Ltd., Eaton's of Can. Ltd., T. Eaton Acceptance Co. Ltd., The Fin. Post Co. Ltd., M.A. Hanna Co., Cleve., Hees Internat. Bancorp Inc., Tridel Enterprises, Inc. Author: Duplessis, 1977. Bd. dirs Clarke Inst. Psychiatry Found., 1989—; patron Malcolm Muggeridge Found.; mem. adv. bd. St. Mary's Hosp., West Palm Beach, Fla. Mem. Trilateral Commn., Americas Soc. (chmn.'s council), Internat. Inst. for Strategic Studies, Bilderberg Meetings (adv. group, steering com.). Clubs: Toronto, York, Toronto Golf, The Granite (Toronto); University (Montreal), Mount Royal (Montreal); The Everglades (Palm Beach). Office: 10 Toronto St, Toronto, ON Canada M5C 2B7

BLACK, DAVID SCOTT, accountant; b. Canandaigua, N.Y., Aug. 28, 1961; s. John Robert and Carol Laverne (Malcho) B.; m. Laurie Jean Price, July 26, 1986. BS in Acctg., Liberty Bapt. Coll., 1983; MS in Acctg., Rochester Inst. Tech., 1984. CPA. Asst. prof. Liberty U., Lynchburg, Va., 1984-87, dir. acctg., 1987—. Mem. Nat. Assn. Accts., Am. Inst. CPA's, Va. Soc. CPA's. Baptist. Home: 303 Willow Oak Terr Forest VA 24551 Office: Liberty U Box 20000 Lynchburg VA 24506

BLACK, DAVID STATLER, lawyer; b. Everett, Wash., July 14, 1928; s. Lloyd Llewelyn and Gladys (Statler) B.; m. Nancy Haskell, July 26, 1952; children: David Lloyd, Andrew Haskell, Kathleen Louise. B.A., Stanford U., 1950; LL.B., U. Wash., 1954. Bar: Wash. 1954, D.C. 1969, Kans. 1979. Assoc. firm Preston, Thorgrimson & Horowitz, Seattle, 1954-57; asst. atty. gen. Wash. State; also counsel Wash. Pub. Service Commn., 1957-61; gen counsel Bur. Pub. Roads, Dept. Commerce, 1961-63; vice chmn. Fed. Power Commn., 1963-66; adminstr. Bonneville Power Adminstrn., 1966-67; under-sec. Dept. Interior, 1967-69; v.p. Dreyfus Corp., 1969-70; mem. firm Pierson, Ball & Dowd, Washington, 1970-79; v.p., gen. counsel The Kans. Power & Light Co., Topeka, 1979-82, sr. v.p. law, 1982-87, pres., chmn. bd., chief exec. officer, 1987—. Mem. Wash. State, D.C., Kans., Am. bar assns., Phi Delta Phi, Delta Kappa Epsilon. Office: Kans Power & Light Co PO Box 889 Topeka KS 66601

BLACK, ERROLL VIC, insurance company executive; b. Phila., Apr. 15, 1945; s. Erroll Victor and Mabell (Pallanch) B.; m. Nancy Carol Hertsch, Mar. 17, 1983; children: Erroll, Eric, Maura, Carey. BSME, Pa. State U., 1967; MS in Fin. Services, Am. Coll., 1979. CLU. Dist. sales mgr. Met. Life Ins. Co., N.Y.C., 1968-78; asst. v.p. mktg. Sun Life Ins. Co., Balt., 1978-82; agy. dir. Charlotte (N.C.) Liberty Mut. Co., 1982-86; field mgmt. cons. Western-So. Life Ins. Co., Cin., 1986—; bd. dirs. Decisions Inc., Balt. Co-author: Improving Performance, 1981, Persistency Pays, 1981; editor: Career Path to Success, 1980; author tng. materials. Mem. Am. Coll. CLU's, Am. Coll. Chartered Fin. Cons., Internat. Assn. Fin. Planners, Charlotte Sales and Mktg. Execs., Am. Soc. CLU and Charterd Fin. Cons., Am. Soc. Tng. and Devel., Charlotte Assn. Life Underwriters, Life Ins. Mktg. and Research Assn., U.S. Power Squadron, Gen. Agts. and Mgrs. Assn. Home: Box 30304 Charlotte NC 28230 Office: Western So Life Ins Co 400 Broadway Cincinnati OH 45202

BLACK, FREDERICK HARRISON, electrical manufacturing company executive; b. Des Moines, Nov. 11, 1921; s. Frederick H. and Aurora (Brooks) B.; B.S. in Engring. Physics, Fisk U., 1949; M.B.A., Pepperdine U., 1972; D.Ed., U. Mass., 1975; m. Kay Browne; children—Joan, Lorna, Jai, Crystal. Field engring. mgr. Burroughs Co., 1955-59; sr. engr. Convair Astronautics, 1959-60; project engr. N.Am. Aviation, 1960-61, Gen. Electric Co., Phila., 1961-63, Aerospace Corp., 1963-66; mgr. minority relations Gen. Electric Co., Fairfield, Conn., 1966-73, mgr. equal opportunity, minority relations, safety and security, 1973-75, mgr. compliance spl. interest group programs corp. pub. relations, 1975-86. Past pres. Bethune Mus. Archives; exec. dir. Watts orgn.; bd. dirs. Interracial Council Bus. Opportunities and Nat. Minority Bus. Campaign. Served to 2d lt. AUS, 1941-44. Mem. AIAA, IEEE, Am. Soc. Personnel Adminstrn. Home: 13643 Prince William Dr Midlothian VA 23113 Office: Nat Press Bldg 529 14th St Ste 1063 Washington DC 20045

BLACK, JAMES GARY, utility company executive; b. Conway, S.C., Mar. 31, 1938; s. Richard Eugene and Annie Rebecca (Tedder) B.; m. Harriet Kay Hook, June 1, 1963; children: Harriet Rebecca, Jonathan McCrae. BS, Newberry Coll., 1961. Epidemiologist U.S. Health Dept., Columbia, S.C., 1961-62; indsl. engr. Shakespheare Co., Columbia, 1962-63; credit clk. S.C. Electric & Gas Co., Columbia, 1963-66, supr. cash records, 1966-78, asst. treas., 1978—. Served as staff sgt. USNG, 1961-67. Mem. Nat. Corp. Cash Mgmt. Assn., Cash Mgmt. Assn. S.C. (v.p. 1980, pres. 1981), West Columbia C. of C. Lutheran. Club: Country of Lexington (S.C.). Lodge: Lions. Office: SC Electric & Gas Co 1426 Main St Columbia SC 29201

BLACK, JEREMY JOSEPH, financial analyst; b. Cleve., Feb. 9, 1952; s. Joseph Montgomery and Eloise (Goodwin) B.; m. Nancy Pryce, July 8, 1978; children: Jennifer Nicole, Jonathan Joseph, Julie Elizabeth. BS, No. Ariz. U., 1976; MDiv, Conservative Bapt. Theol. Sem., 1980. Cert. fin. planner. Prof. philosophy Colo. Christian Coll., Morrison, 1980-82; div. mgr. D.W. Hannech and Assocs., Lakewood, Colo., 1980-81; gen. ptnr., commodity trading advisor Advanced Futures Systems Ltd., Lakewood, 1983-87; fin. planner Mountain States Investments and Fin. Services, Lakewood, 1981-85; v.p., treas. Interfin. Corp., Lakewood, 1984-86; pres. Advanced Investment Software, Lakewood, 1987—, Interfin. Corp., Lakewood, 1986—; co-gen. ptnr. Navigator Fund Ltd., Denver, 1987—; gen. ptnr. Futures Growth Fund Ltd., Lakewood, Colo., 1984—. Mem. Internat. Assn. Fin. Planners, Inst. Cert. Fin. Planners, Lakewood C. of C. Republican. Baptist. Home: 8009 W Fremont Ave Littleton CO 80228 Office: Interfin Corp 8101 E Prentice Ave Ste 805 Englewood CO 80111

BLACK, JOE ED, business executive; b. Snyder, Tex., Aug. 8, 1933; s. Joel Alex and Bonnie Ruth (Davis) B.; m. Susan Faye Webb, Oct. 17, 1958; children: Cynthia Jeanne, Randall Harvey; m. Carole Linda Kingery, Sept. 15, 1986 (div. Dec. 1988). Student, Hardin-Simmons U., 1951-55. Asst. golf profl. Abilene (Tex.) Country Club, 1953-56; tournament player PGA Tour, 1955-57, asst. tournament dir., 1958-61, tournament dir., 1961-64; golf profl. Brookhaven Country Club, Dallas, 1964-84; v.p. golf ops. Club Corp. of Am., Dallas, 1964-84; pres. Western Golf Properties, Inc., Scottsdale, Ariz., 1985—; mem. rules com. Masters Golf Tournament, Augusta, Ga., 1960—; mem. policy bd. PGA Tour, Sawgrass, Fla., 1977-82; chmn. 1983 PGA Ryder Cup Matches, 1983; chmn. Pga Championship, 1979, 80. Contbr. articles to profl. jours. Mem. Tex. Golf Hall of Fame, 1981. Mem. Profl. Golfers Assn. Am. (pres. 1981-82). Republican. Methodist. Clubs: Desert Highlands Golf Club, Desert Mountain Golf Club (Scottsdale, Ariz.), Brookhaven Country Club (Dallas). Home: 5634 N Scottsdale Rd Scottsdale AZ 85253 Office: Western Golf Properties Inc 711 E Greenway Rd Scottsdale AZ 85260

BLACK, KENT MARCH, electronics company executive; b. Carrollton, Ill., Oct. 25, 1939; s. Kenneth Wilbur and Alta Jane (March) B.; m. Karen Anne Jones, Aug. 5, 1960; children: Elizabeth Anne, Nancy Jane. B.S.E.E., U. Ill., 1962. With Rockwell Internat., 1962—; various engring. mgmt. positions Rockwell Internat., Cedar Rapids, Iowa, 1962-72, program dir. satellite communications systems Govt. Telecommunications div., 1972-76; v.p., gen. mgr. Collins Telecom Systems div. Rockwell Internat., Dallas, 1976-78; pres. Electronic Systems Group Rockwell Internat., Anaheim, Calif., 1978-80, exec. v.p. def. electronic ops., 1980-81; corp. v.p., pres. comml. electronics ops. Rockwell Internat., Dallas, 1981-86, corp. v.p., pres. electronics ops., 1986—. Bd. dirs. United Way of Met. Dallas, 1982-88, Dallas County Community Coll. Dist. Found., Inc., Assn. for Higher Edn. N. Tex. ; mem. adv. bd. Coll. Engring. U. Ill.; mem. exec. bd. Circle Ten council Boy Scouts Am.; mem. devel. bd. U. Tex.-Dallas; chmn. U.S. Savs. Bond Campaign, Dallas, 1982-84, 87; chmn. U.S. Savs. Bonds Nat. Seminar, 1985-86. Mem. Nat. Mgmt. Assn. (Silver Knight of Mgmt. award 1980, Gold Knight of Mgmt. award 1989). Office: Rockwell Internat Corp Electronics Ops 1200 N Alma Rd Richardson TX 75081

BLACK, ROBERT PERRY, banker; b. Hickman, Ky., Dec. 21, 1927; s. Burwell Perry and Veola (Moore) B.; m. Mary Rives Ogilvie, Oct. 27, 1951; children: Patty Rives, Robert Perry. B.A., U. Va., 1950, M.A., 1951, Ph.D., 1955. Part-time instr. U. Va., 1953-54; research assoc. Fed. Res. Bank, Richmond, Va., 1954-55, assoc. economist, 1956-58, economist, 1958-60, asst. v.p., 1960-62, v.p., 1962-68, 1st v.p., 1968-73, pres., 1973—; asst. prof. U. Tenn., 1955-56; lectr. U. Va., 1956-57; mem. Gov.'s Adv. Bd. Revenue Estimates, 1976—; mem. adv. bd. Health Corp. Va., 1981—; advisor to bd. trustees Edn. Found of State Bank Suprs., 1986-88. Contbr. articles to profl. jours. Past mem. adv. bd. Central Richmond Assn.; former trustee Collegiate Schs., past chmn.; mem. Assn. for Preservation of Va. Antiquities, 1971—; adv. council Robert E. Lee council Boy Scouts Am., 1977-78; bd. dirs. Richmond Eye and Ear Hosp.; past pres. United Way Greater Richmond, active Corp. Div., 1986; bd. dirs., mem. exec. com., treas., chmn. fin. com. Downtown Devel. Unltd., 1975-86; chmn. adv. com. Ctr. Banking Edn., Va. Union U., 1977-79; trustee E. Angus Powell Endowment for Am. Enterprise, 1980-88; mem. adv. bd. Ctr. for Advanced Studies, U. Va., 1986—, Va. Union U. Sch. Bus., 1986-88; Retreat Leader Leadership Met. Richmond, 1986; mem. Gov.'s Adv. Bd. on Budget, 1974—; bd. dirs. Richmond Eye and Ear Hosp. Authority, 1988—; mem. com. Richmond Renaissance Riverfront, 1988—; mem. Forum Club, 1987—. With AUS, 1946-47. Recipient George Washington Honor medal award Freedoms Found. Valley Forge, 1978. Mem. Am. Econ. Assn., So. Econ. Assn., Am. Fin. Assn., Richmond Soc. Fin. Analysts, Am. Inst. Banking, Raven Soc., Mgmt. Discussion Group (chmn. 1980-81), Va. Inter-Govt. Inst. (bd. dirs. 1986—), Va. State Golf Assn., Va. Seniors Golf Assn., Country of Va. Club (bd. dirs. 1980-85, 88, v.p. 1981-83, pres. 1983-85), Phi Beta Kappa (past pres. Richmond chpt.), Beta Gamma Sigma, Alpha Kappa Psi, Kappa Alpha. Methodist. Home: 10 Dahlgren Rd Richmond VA 23233 Office: Fed Res Bank 701 E Byrd St Richmond VA 23219

BLACK, THEODORE HALSEY, manufacturing company executive; b. Jersey City, Oct. 22, 1928; s. Theodore Charles and Mary (Carroll) Bl; m. Marilyn Rigsby, 1979; children: Deborah, Theodore Jr., Susan, Zelda, Carol, Brian, Marilyn. BSEE, U.S. Naval Acad., Annapolis, 1953; Advanced Mgt. Program, Harvard U., 1974. Salesman, sales mgr. Ingersoll-Rand Co., N.Y.C., 1957-67, gen. mgr. turbo products div., 1967-72, v.p., 1972-87; pres., chief oper. officer Ingersoll-Rand Co., Woodcliff Lake, N.J., 1988, chmn., pres., chief exec. officer, 1988—; pres., chief exec. officer Dresser-Rand Co., Corning, N.Y., 1987-88; bd. dirs. Gen. Pub. Utilities, Parsippany, N.J., 1988—, Zeigler Coal Holdings Co., St. Louis, 1985—. Trustee Bus. Coun. for UN, Boy Scouts Am. Capt. USMC, 1946-49, 53-59. Recipient Naval Aviator award USN, Corpus Christi, Tex., 1955. Mem. Machinery and Allied Products Insustry Assn. (exec. com.). Roman Catholic. Office: Ingersoll-Rand Co 200 Chestnut Ridge Rd Woodcliff Lake NJ 07675

BLACK, THOMAS JOHN, hospital executive; b. Orange, N.J., July 29, 1943; s. Frank M. and Edith A. (Flanagan) B.; m. Gaetana M. Thomas, June 5, 1966; children: Ashley Ann, Tracy Ann, Thomas John. BS in Acctg., St. Peter's Coll., 1967. CPA, N.J. Staff asst. Main Hurdman, CPA's, N.Y.C., 1967-71; mgr. Fox & Co., CPA's, Paterson, N.J., 1971-74; dir. fin. St. Joseph's Hosp. and Med. Ctr., Paterson, 1974-75, asst. adminstr., 1975-80, v.p. fin. affairs, 1980-89, mem. pension plan com., 1984—, sr. v.p. fin. affair, 1989—; trustee V.H.S. Mgmt., Inc., 1987—, H.H.S.V. MRI Corp., 1985—. With budget rev. and fin. com. Diocese of Paterson, 1982-86. Mem. Healthcare Fin. Mgmt. Assn. (reinbursement com., chief fin. officer com.), AICPA, N.J. Soc. CPA's, Denville (N.J.) Jaycees, Coun. Fin. N.H. Hosp. Assn. Republican. Office: St Josephs Hosp and Med Ctr 703 Main St Paterson NJ 07503

BLACK, WILLIAM GORDON, transportation executive; b. Winnipeg, Man., Can., Aug. 9, 1927; s. William Fotheringham and Mary Teresa (Douglas) B.; children: Sandra, Perelandra, Andra-Lee, Gordon. Grad. in acctg., U. Man., 1949. Chartered acct. Sr. acct. William Gray & Co., Winnipeg, 1944-50, Peat, Marwick, Mitchell, Winnipeg and Montreal, 1951-54; treas. Kingsway Transports, Montreal, Que., Can., 1955-60; with Can. Steamship Lines, Montreal, 1961-81, successively sec.-treas., comptroller, v.p. fin., sr. v.p.; sr. v.p., dep. chmn. The CSL Group Inc., Montreal, 1981-88, also bd. dirs., dep. chmn., 1989—; bd. dirs. Argyll Energy Inc., Toronto, Can. Steamship Lines Inc., Can. Shipbuilding and Engring. Inc., St. Catherine's, Voyageur Enterprises Inc., Montreal, Atlantic Container Express, Montreal, Atlantic Searoute Ltd., Halifax, Oceanic Fin. Corp., Bermuda, Newterm Ltd., St. John's. Mem. Inst. Chartered Accts. Man., Inst. Chartered Accts. Que., Fin. Execs. Inst., Assn. for Can. Pension Fund Mgmt., Standard Protective and Indemnity Assn. (bd. dirs. 1979—), Can. Shipowner's Mut. Assn. (chmn., bd. dirs. 1976—), Standard Compensation Actual Liability Assn. (chmn., bd. dirs. 1977—). Clubs: St. James, Beaconsfield (Montreal). Home: 566 Victoria, Westmount Can H3Y 2R6 Office: CSL Group Inc, 759 Victoria Sq, Montreal, PQ Canada H2Y 2K3

BLACKBURN, CHARLES LEE, oil company executive; b. Cushing, Okla., Jan. 9, 1928; s. Samuel and Lillian (Beall) B.; m. Mary Ann Bullock Colburn, July 14, 1984; children: Kern A., Alan J., Charles L., Derek R. BS in Engring. Physics, U. Okla., 1952. With Shell Oil Co., 1952-86, exec. v.p. exploration and prodn., 1976-86; pres., chief exec. officer Diamond Shamrock Corp. (name changed to Maxus Energy Corp., 1987), Dallas, 1987—; chmn., pres., chief exec. officer Maxus Energy Corp., 1987—. Served with U.S. Army, 1946-48. Mem. Am. Petroleum Inst. (dir.), Soc. Petroleum Engrs., Mid-Continent Oil and Gas Assn., Tau Beta Pi, Sigma Tau. Methodist. Clubs: Houston Country, Coronado; Dallas Country, Dallas Petroleum. Office: Maxus Energy Corp 717 N Harwood St Dallas TX 75201 *

BLACKBURN, MARSH HANLY, food brokerage executive, consultant; b. Ft. Thomas, Ky., Nov. 13, 1929; s. Hanly R. and Lois (Marsh) B.; m. Margret Pettit, Feb. 2, 1952, (div. 1970); children: Steven, Kevin, Marsha; m. Mary Klimek, June 19, 1976. BS in Mktg., Ind. U., 1952. Pres. Sales Force Cos., Inc., Chgo., 1973-79; chmn., chief exec. officer Sales Force Cos., Inc., 1979—; chmn. adv. com. Uniform Code Coun., Dayton, Ohio, 1984—; mem. exec. com., 1985—. Mem. Ind. U. Sch. Bus. Coun., Bloomington, 1975-78; trustee Food Industry Crusade Against Hunger, St. Louis, 1986—. With U.S. Army, Korea. Decorated Bronze Star. Mem. Chief Execs. Orgn., Nat. Food Brokers Assn., Chgo. Pres.'s Assn. (chmn. 1976-78), Merchandising Execs. Club, Am. Mgmt. Assn. (mem. gen. mgmt. coun. 1973—), Am. Inst. Food Distbn. (trustee N.Y.C., 1985—), Met. Club, Chgo. Yacht Club, Econs. Club (Chgo.). Office: Sales Force Cos Inc 4333 Transworld Rd Schiller Park IL 60176

BLACKBURN, ROBERT EUGENE, internal auditor, retired; b. Brookville, Ohio, June 28, 1923; s. Harry William and Mary Esther (Wolfe) B.; m. Dorothy Viola Bloom, Aug. 21, 1949; children: Kevin, Kyle. BA, Defiance (Ohio) Coll., 1947, BS, 1947; MA, Miami U., Oxford, Ohio, 1951. CPCU. With Motorists Mut. Ins. Co., Columbus, Ohio, 1952—, casualty and property sales mgr., 1968-74, underwriting mgr., 1974-82, internal auditor, 1982-88. Coun. pres. Clinton Heights Luth. Ch., Columbus, 1976; pres. music assn. Centennial High Sch., Columbus, 1978, 79; loaned exec., Franklin County United Way, 1985, 86, 87, 88. With USN, 1943-46, PTO. Mem. Nat. Assn. CPCU (bd. dirs. Columbus chpt. 1981-84), Defiance Coll. Alumni Assn. (bd. dirs. 1982-85). Republican. Home: 6041 Winstead Rd Columbus OH 43235

BLACKBURN, WYATT DOUGLAS, insurance executive; b. Amarillo, Tex., July 6, 1954; s. Wyatt W. and Marjorie C. (Wyre) B.; m. Deborah L. Garland, Feb. 28, 1987. BBA, W. Tex. State U., 1976. Staff acct. Harvey, Messenger & Co. CPA's, Amarillo, 1974-77; audit mgr. Martin W. Cohen & Co. CPA's, Dallas, 1977-78; sr. v.p. adminstrv. ops., 1978-88, sr. v.p., chief fin. officer, Bankers Assurance Group, Arlington, Tex., 1988—. bd. dirs. State & County Mut. Fire Ins. Co., State Nat. Ins. Co., State Nat. Life Ins. Co., Tex. Mem. Am. Inst. CPA's, Tex. Soc. CPA's, Omicron Delta Epsilon. Home: 2510 Lake Ridge Red Oak TX 75154

BLACKBURN-FIELDS, DENISE, financial executive; b. Williamson, W.Va., Dec. 7, 1955; d. Tracy Rupert and Newana Yvonne (Stevens) Blackburn; m. Stephen J. Fields, Apr. 2, 1983. AA, So. W.Va. Community Coll., 1976; BA, Marshall U., 1979, MA, 1982; grad. with honors Sch. Bank Mktg., 1986, diploma, Am. Inst. Banking, 1988. Accounts adjustor Ashland Fin. Co., South Williamson, Ky., 1973-74; dir. payroll Mingo County Bd. Edn., Williamson, 1974-77; sec. spl. projects coordinator Marshall U., Huntington, W.Va., 1978-79; market researcher First Huntington Nat. Bank, 1980-81; mktg. dir. First Bank Ceredo (W.Va.), 1981-83; mktg. officer Flat Top Nat. Bank, Bluefield, W.Va., 1983—; instr. Marshall U., 1980-83, Concord Coll., 1986—, Bluefield State Coll., 1987—. Contbr. articles to profl. jours. Vol. Am. Heart Assn., Bluefield, United Way, Am. Cancer Soc. W.Va. Bd. Regents ednl. scholar, 1974-82. Fellow Communicator's Roundtable of Va's. (1st v.p.), Am. Soc. Advt. and Promotion, Am. Mktg. Assn., Bank Mktg. Assn., Am. Inst. Banking (pub. relations office 1982-83), W.Va. Bankers Assn., Pub. Relations Soc. Am., Charleston Advt. Club, Quota Club of South Bluefield (bd. dirs.), Kappa Delta Pi, Pi Omega Pi. Home: 11 Rolling Hills Princeton WV 24740 Office: Flat Top Nat Bank 211 Federal St PO Box 950 Bluefield WV 24701

BLACKERBY, JAMES WILLIAM, financial planner; b. Denver, Mar. 6, 1950; s. Robert Ernest and Beverly Lois (Stonebraker) B.; m. Susan Louise Clark, May 29, 1971; children: Christopher, Karen, Brian. BA, U. Colo., 1972; MPA, U. R.I., 1975. Asst. treas. Old Stone Bank, Providence, 1976-78; supervising cons. Ernst & Whinney, Providence, 1978-80; supr. mgmt. Auditor Gen. Office, Providence, 1980-84; planner IDS Fin. Svcs., Wakefield, R.I., 1984—; dist. mgr. IDS Fin. Svcs., Providence, 1985-87, corp. liason, 1987—; bd. dirs. Am. Mussel Inc., Galilee, R.I.; mem. Faculty Bus. Sch. U. R. I., Kingston, 1988—. Treas. Peace Dale Congl. Ch., 1985—; coach Little League Baseball, Soccer, Narragansett, R.I., 1982—. Mem. Am. Soc. Pub. Adminstrs. (pres. R.I. chpt. 1982-83), Inst. Cert. Fin. Planners (cert.), Internat. Assn. Fin. Planners, Wakefield C. of C., Rotary. Home: 12 Perkins Ave Narragansett RI 02882 Office: IDS/Am Express 336 Main St Wakefield RI 02879

BLACKHAM, ANN ROSEMARY (MRS. J. W. BLACKHAM), realtor; b. N.Y.C., June 16, 1927; d. Frederick Alfred and Letitia L. (Stolfe) DeCain; m. James W. Blackham Jr., Aug. 18, 1951; children: Ann C., James W. III. AB, Ohio Dominican Coll., 1949; postgrad., Ohio State U., 1950. Mgr. br. store

Filene & Sons, Winchester, 1950-52; broker Porter Co. Real Estate, Winchester, 1961-66; sales mgr. James T. Trefrey, Inc., Winchester, 1966-68; pres., founder Ann Blackham & Co. Inc., Realtors, Winchester, Mass., 1969—. Mem. bd. econ. advisors to Gov., 1969-74; participant White House Conf. on Internat. Cooperation, 1965; mem. Presdl. Task Force on Women's Rights and Responsibilities, 1969; mem. exec. council Mass. Civil Def., 1965-69; chmn. Gov.'s Commn. on Status of Women, 1971-75; regional dir. Interstate Assn. Commn. on Status of Women, 1971-74; mem. Gov. Task Force on Mass. Economy, 1972; mem. Gov.'s Judicial Selection Com., 1972, Mass. Emergency Fin. Bd., 1974-75; corporator, trustee Charlestown Savs. Bank, 1974-84; corporator Winchester Hosp., 1983—; mem. Winchester 350th Anniversary Commn.; mem. design rev. commn. Town of Winchester; bd. dirs. Phoenix Found., Bay State Health Care, Mass. Taxpayers Found., Speech and Hearing Found.; mem. regional selection panel White House Fellows, 1973-74; mem. com. on women in service U.S. Dept. Def., 1977-80; 2d v.p. Doric Dames, 1971-74, bd. dirs., 1974—; ; dep. chmn. Mass. Rep. State Com., 1965-66; sec. Mass. Rep. State Conv., 1970, del., 1960, 62, 64, 66, 70, 72, 74, 78; state vice chmn. Mass. Rep. Fin. Com., 1970; alt. del.-at-large Rep. Nat. Conv., 1968, 72, del., 1984; pres. Scholarship Found., 1976-78, Mass. Fedn. Women's Clubs; mem. Winchester 350th Aniversary Commn. Recipient Pub. Service award Commonwealth of Mass., 1978, Merit award Rep. Party, 1969, Pub. Affairs award Mass. Fedn. Women's Clubs, 1975; named Civic Leader of Yr., Mass. Broadcasters, 1962. Mem. Greater Boston Real Estate Bd. (bd. dirs.), Mass. Assn. Real Estate Bds. (bd. dirs.), Nat. Assn. Real Estate Bd. (women's council). Brokers Inst., Council Realtors (pres. 1983-84), Winchester C. of C. (bd. dirs.), Greater Boston C. of C., Nat. Assn. Women Bus. Owners, ENKA Soc., Capitol Hill Club, Ponte Vedra Club, Winchester Boat Club, Winchester Country Club, Wychemere Harbor Club, Womens City Boston Club, Winton Club (sec., bd. dir.). Home: 60 Swan Rd Winchester MA 01890 Office: Ann Blackham & Co Inc 11 Thompson St Winchester MA 01890

BLACKMAN, CLARK MONROE, II, accounting executive, consultant; b. Kansas City, Mo., Mar. 9, 1956; s. Richard Clark and Mary Jo (Martin) B.; m. Julia Maria Claus, Aug. 3, 1980; children: Clark Monroe III, Jennifer Marie. BBA, U. Iowa, 1979, MA, 1980; cert., Coll. Fin. Planning, Denver, 1986. CPA, Colo. Acct. Arthur Andersen & Co., Denver, 1980-83; v.p. Money Mgmt. Group, Ltd., Denver, 1983-85; fin. cons. Friedman, Eisenstein, Raemer & Schwartz, Chgo., 1986-87, head personal cons. group, 1987—. Contbr. articles to profl. jours. Mem. Am. Inst. CPAs, Internat. Assn. Fin. Planners, Inst. Cert. Fin. Planners. Home: 1710 Biesterfield St Elk Grove Village IL 60007 Office: Friedman Eisenstein Raemer & Schwartz 401 N Michigan Ave Chicago IL 60611

BLACKMAN, JAMES RAY, tax director; b. Allegan, Mich., Mar. 21, 1942; s. Dale Elmer and Delloricia (Reed) B.; m. Gloria Ann Petersen, Dec. 30, 1961; children: James Jr., Ruth, Jonathan, Jeffrey. BBA, Ariz. State U., 1974. Acct. U-Haul Co., Portland, Oreg., 1962-64; tax mgr. U-Haul Co., Phoenix, 1964-76; tax dir. Firstar Corp., Milw., 1976—. Mem. Tax Execs. Inst. (treas. 1984-85, sec. 1985-86, regional v.p. 1986-87, v.p. 1986-87, pres. Milw. chpt. 1987-88). Home: 503 W Dean Rd Fox Point WI 53217 Office: Firstar Corp 777 E Wisconsin Ave Milwaukee WI 53201

BLACKMAN, JAMES TIMOTHY, automobile dealer; b. Lakeland, Fla., Dec. 10, 1951; s. James Ogden and Bernice (Green) B.; m. Martile Rebecca Sudduth, Feb. 5, 1983; children: Brittany Rebecca, Brooke Lansing. Student, U. Fla., 1969-71. Pres. Jim Blackman Ford, Sebring, Fla., 1972—, Sebring Leasing & Rent-A-Car, Inc., 1976—, Bros. Two Developers, Inc., Sebring, 1979—; pres. Capt. D's Seafood of Highlands and Okeechobee Counties. Crusade chmn. Am. Cancer Soc., Highland County, Fla., 1986—, pres. 1988—; chmn. Com. of 100, Sebring, 1977-78; co-chmn. Sebring C. of C., 1975-78; bd. dirs. Sebring Airport Authority, 1986—, chmn., 1988; bd. deacons 1st Presbyn. Ch., 1976—, past chmn. Mem. Fla. Automobile Dealers Assn. (bd. dirs. 1984-88). Democrat. Presbyterian. Lodge: Kiwanis (local pres. 1977-78). Home: 2808 Sunrise Dr Sebring FL 33870 Office: Jim Blackman Ford Inc 3201 Hwy 27 South PO Box 433 Sebring FL 33870

BLACKWELL, RICHARD MANNING, lawyer; b. Plainfield, N.J., Mar. 21, 1940; s. Howard M. and Anna (Sutton) B.; m. Louise Blackwell, 1965; children: Craig M., David M. AB, Brown U., 1962; LLB, Yale U., 1965. Bar: N.Y. 1966. Atty. Met. Life Ins. Co., N.Y.C., 1965-73, asst. gen. counsel, 1973-76, assoc. gen. counsel, 1976-79, v.p. and ins. counsel, 1979-85, v.p. and sec., 1985—; dir., officer various subsidiaries of Met. Life Ins. Co. Contbr. articles to profl. jours. Mem. ABA, Am. Soc. Corp. Secs. Home: 267 Holly Hill Mountainside NJ 07092 Office: Met Life Ins Co 1 Madison Ave New York NY 10010

BLADES, HERBERT WILLIAM, pharmaceutical company executive; b. Dubuque, Iowa, Apr. 27, 1908; s. Walter and Nellie (Quilliam) B.; m. Jane Larison Marshall, June 1, 1933; children—John William, William Stoddard. B.S., Northwestern U., 1931. Gen. mgr. John Wyeth and Bro., Can., Ltd., 1935-38; v.p., gen. mgr. Kolynos Co., 1938-43; asst. to pres. Am. Home Products Corp., 1943-46, exec. v.p., 1960—, also dir.; exec. v.p. Wyeth Labs. div., 1946-56, pres., 1956-71, chmn. bd., 1971-73; dir. Carlo Erba, S.p.A., Milan, Italy, Provident Mutual Life Ins. Co. Phila., Phila. Nat. Bank, Phila.; Cons. White House Conf. on Aging, 1961; dir. Pa. Plan to Develop Scientists Med. Research.; Bd. dirs. Bryn Mawr (Pa.) Hosp., Pharm. Mfrs. Assn. Found., Inc.; bd. mgrs. Wistar Inst. Recipient Order of Honneur et Merite Republic Haiti, 1959. Mem. Pharm. Mfrs. Assn. (dir.), Delta Upsilon. Presbyn. (elder, trustee). Clubs: Racquet (Phila.); St. Davids (Wayne). Home: Villa 37 1400 Waverly Rd Gladwyne PA 19035 Office: Am Home Products Corp PO Box 8299 Philadelphia PA 19101

BLAHA, JAMES JOSEPH, merger and acquisition intermediary; b. Berwyn, Ill., June 8, 1937; s. James Joseph and Libby (Baxa) B.; m. Barbara Lynn Clark, June 17, 1960; children: James Clark, Bradley, Robert. BS, Northwestern U., 1959; MBA, SUNY, Buffalo, 1964. With Westinghouse Electric Corp., 1959-84; controller Westinghouse Electric Corp., Bridgeport, Conn., 1969-72; contr. Westinghouse Electric Corp., Chgo., 1974-84, mgr. strategic products, 1972-74; pres. Bus. Holding Co., Oak Brook, Ill., 1985—; prin. Bus. Appraisal Co., Oak Brook, 1984—. Mem. adminstrv. bd. Northwestern U., Evanston, Ill., 1976-81; bd. dirs. Coll. DuPage, Glen Ellyn, Ill., 1976-83, chmn., 1979-83. Recipient cert. of appreciation Ill. Assn. Sch. Bds., 1983. Mem. Am. Mktg. Assn., Am. Mgmt. Assn., Am. Soc. Appraisers, Assn. Corp. Growth, Ill. Community Coll. Trustee Assn. (exec. officer 1978-79, Cert. of Merit 1984). Club: Cress Creek (Naperville). Home: 1040 Summit Hills Naperville IL 60540 Office: Bus Appraisal Co One Lincoln Ctr Ste 1090 Oakbrook Terrace IL 60181

BLAHA, JOSEPH WADE, newspaper publisher; b. Omaha, Sept. 17, 1938; s. Joseph Mathew Blaha and Margaret Dora (Taney) Butler; m. Karen B. Carlson, Sept. 17, 1982; children: Mark, Roberta, Steven, Jennifer, Margaret. BA, St. Mary's Coll., 1961; postgrad., San Francisco State Coll., 1963. Advt. salesman San Francisco Examiner, 1963-65; advt. dir. Polk County Itemizer-Observer, Dallas, Oreg., 1965-68; gen. mgr. Ukiah (Calif.) Daily Jour., 1969-70; publisher Polk County Itemizer-Observer, Dallas, 1971-78; pub. Lake Oswego (Oreg.) Rev., 1978-84; v.p. Times Newspapers Inc., Tigard, Oreg., 1985-87; v.p., chief oper. officer Community Newspapers Inc., Beaverton, Oreg., 1988; pres., chief exec. officer Robinson Pub. Corp., Seattle, 1989—, also bd. dirs.; pres., bd. dirs. Am. Community Pub. Inc. Mem. Nat. Newspapers Am., Suburban Newspapers Am., Oreg. Newspaper Pubs. Assn. (pres. 1987-88), Wash. Newspapers Pubs. Assn. Roman Catholic. Office: Robinson Pub Corp 207 SW 150th Seattle WA 98166

BLAICH, LARRY MASON, real estate developer, entrepreneur; b. Buffalo, N.Y., Oct. 13, 1949; s. Mason Carl and Roberta (Copeland) B.; m. Janice Rosamund Stephenson, July 1, 1972; children: Jonathan David, Kristin Dawn. BA, Rutgers U., 1971; MBA, Cornell U., 1974. CPA, N.Mex., N.Y. Sr. acct. Arthur Andersen & Co., N.Y.C., 1973-75; asst. v.p. McGraw Hill, Inc., N.Y.C., 1975-77; v.p. fin. H.A. Simpson & Assoc. Devel. Co., Denver, 1977-79; ptnr., pres. LMB & Assocs., Inc., Denver, 1979-82; ptnr., v.p. Cauwels & Davis Assoc., Inc., Albuquerque, 1982-88; v.p. Tres Santos Trading Co., Albuquerque, 1988—. Author: Real Estate Transactions, Tax Planning, 1980; inventor red phosphorescent TV screen, 1973. Real estate cons. Boy Scouts Am., Albuquerque, 1984; coach Am. Youth Soccer Orgn., Albuquerque, 1986—; deacon Hoffmantown Bapt. Ch., Albuquerque, 1986—; bd. dirs. Fellowship of Christian Athletes, Albuquerque, 1987—. Mem. Am. Inst. CPAs, N.Mex. Soc. CPAs, CPAs in Pvt. Practice (bd. dirs.), Nat. Assn. Home Builders, Toastmasters Internat. (aacomplished toast master). Republican. Baptist. Office: Tres Santos Trading Co Inc 1100 Second St NW Albuquerque NM 87102

BLAINE, DEVON, public relations executive; b. Lynwood, Calif., Sept. 16, 1947; d. Harold W. and Ruth Mae (Decho) Schulz; m. Robert Beau Baur, Feb. 1970 (div.). Student UCLA, 1965-66. Owner, founder Blaine Group, Los Angeles, 1975—. Mem. exec. com. White House Conf. on Small Bus., 1980, 82, So. Calif. chmn., 1986; mem. exec. com. Calif. State Conf. Small Bus., 1980, 82, 84; mem. blue ribbon planning com. Calif. State Conf. Small Bus., 1984; mem. Gov. Brown's Small Bus. Adv. Council; co-chmn. Calif. Delegation White House Conf. on Small Bus., 1986. Mem. Nat. Small Bus. Assn., Women in Bus., Nat. Assn. Women Bus. Owners (past chpt. pres. Woman Entrepreneur of Yr. award 1987), Pub. Rels. Soc. Am., Book Publicists So. Calif., Women in Show Bus., Women's Nat. Book Assn., Nat. Small Bus. United (pres. Calif. chpt. 1989), Calif. Small Bus. United (pres.), L.A. Venture Assn. (pres. 1989), Variety Club, Publicity Club N.Y. Democrat. Lutheran. Office: The Blaine Group 7465 Beverly Blvd Los Angeles CA 90036

BLAIR, BOBBY CHARLES, chemical engineer; b. Arcadia, Kans., Sept. 21, 1941; s. Charles Warren and Hazel Louise (Wyckoff) B.; B.S. in Chem. Engrng., Okla. State U., 1964; M.B.A., U. Tulsa, 1969. With Phillips Petroleum Co., 1964—, mktg. research engr., Bartlesville, Okla., 1974-77, mktg. and tech. analyst, 1977-80, mining chems. project dir., Bartlesville, 1980-85; gas sales specialist, 1985-86; gas sales coord., Naperville, Ill., 1986—. Wentz Found. Service scholar. Mem. Phi Theta Kappa, Sigma Tau. Republican. Mem. Christian Ch. (Disciples of Christ). Co-inventor, patentee high speed fibrillation process.

BLAIR, DENNIS EARL, financial planner; b. Crothersville, Ind., Feb. 8, 1947; s. Earl Otis and Mary Viola (Meeks) B.; m. Nancy Lynn Kollock, Aug. 20, 1968 (div. Oct. 1980); children: Ryan J., Megan E., Hanna J. BS in Bus. Edn., Ball State U., 1969. CLU, ChFC. Tchr. Monroe Community Sch. Corp., Cowan, Ind., 1969-72; real estate assoc. Blair Real Estate & McKibben Realtors, Muncie, Ind., 1972-75; ins. agt. Prudential Ins. Co., Muncie, 1975-78, Ins. and Risk Mtm., Muncie, 1979-82; with ins. and fin. planning div. David B. Stocker & Assocs., Muncie, 1982-86; fin. planner IDS Fin. Svcs., Inc., Muncie, 1986—. Fundraiser United Way, Muncie, 1986—, YMCA, Muncie, 1986—, Ball State U., Muncie, 1986—. Mem. East Cen. Assn. Life Underwriters (pres. 1980-81), East Cen. Ind. Estate Planning Council (sec. 1987), Nat. Assn. Life Underwriters, Am. Soc. CLUs and ChFCs, Internat. Assn. for Fin. Planning, Sertoma (pres. Muncie chpt. 1980-81). Republican. Office: IDS Fin Svcs Inc 2020 W McGalliard PO Box 950 Muncie IN 47308

BLAIR, EDWARD MCCORMICK, JR., investment banker; b. Balt., June 20, 1942; s. Edward McCormick and Elizabeth (Iglehart) B.; m. Frances de Bretteville, Aug. 3, 1969; children: Helen, Edward, Jane. BA, Stanford U., 1965; MBA, Harvard U., 1971. With Morgan Guaranty Trust Co., N.Y.C., 1971-74; trader William Blair & Co., Chgo., 1974-79, ptnr. corporate fin., 1979—; bd. dirs. Research Industries, Salt Lake City, Chgo. Dock and Canal Trust. Vice chmn. Brookfield Zoo, Chgo., 1985; trustee Latin Sch., Chgo., 1986-88, Pullman Found., Chgo., 1986—. Lt. USNR, 1966-69. Office: William Blair & Co 135 S LaSalle St Chicago IL 60603

BLAIR, J. KENT, JR., securities analyst; b. Binghamton, N.Y., Dec. 11, 1938; s. J. Kent Sr. and Bertha M. (Schippers) B.; children by previous marriage: J. Kent III, Katharine W., Peter M., Amanda H.; m. Prudence Ellen Lewis, Jan. 26, 1986. AB, Colgate U., 1961; MS in Indsl. Adminstrn., Carnegie-Mellon U., 1963. Bus. analyst Merck & Co., Inc., Rahway, N.J., 1963-68; v.p. Auerbach, Pollack & Richardson, N.Y.C., 1968-75, Donaldson, Lufkin & Jenrette, N.Y.C., 1975—. Trustee Cen. Presbyn. Ch., Summit, N.J.; bd. dirs. Alliance Internat. Health Care Fund, N.Y.C., 1983—. Recipient Maroon citation Colgate U., 1981. Mem. Fin. Analyst Fedn., N.Y. Soc. Security Analysts, Glen Rock (N.J.) Athletic Club, Beacon Hill Club (N.J.). Office: Donaldson Lufkin & Jenrette 140 Broadway New York NY 10005

BLAIR, JAMES BURTON, lawyer; b. Elkins, Ark., Oct. 27, 1935; s. William Joe and Mildred (Woosley) B.; m. Margaret Gibson, Aug. 17, 1957 (div. 1974); children: Heather Elaine, Arden Sue, James Rufus; m. Diane D. Divers, Sept. 1, 1979. BA, U. Ark., 1955, JD, LLB, 1957. Bar: Ark. 1975, U.S. Dist. Ct. (we. dist.) Ark. 1957, U.S. Ct. Appeals (8th cir.) 1958, U.S. Supreme Ct. 1968. Assoc. Crouch & Jones, Springdale, Ark., 1957-58; jr. ptnr. Crouch, Jones & Blair, Springdale, 1958-63; ptnr. Crouch, Blair & Cypert, Springdale, 1963-64, Crouch, Blair, Cypert & Waters, Springdale, 1968-75; sr. ptnr. Blair, Cypert, Waters & Roy, Springdale, 1975-80; gen. counsel Tyson Foods, Inc., Springdale, 1980—; dir. Tyson Export Sales, St. Thomas, V.I., 1985—. Vice-chmn. U. Ark. Bd. Trustees, Fayetteville, 1988—; chmn. State Bd. Higher Edn., Ark., 1985; nat. committeeman, Dem. Nat. Com., Washington, 1980-84. Fellow Am. Coll. Trial Lawyers, Ark. Bar Found.; mem. ABA, Ark. Bar Assn. Home: 1011 Tanglebriar Fayetteville AR 72701 Office: Tyson Foods Inc 2210 Oaklawn Dr Springdale AR 72764

BLAIR, ROBERT EDWARD, retail executive, marketing professional; b. Balt., Feb. 14, 1946; s. John Thomas and Anna Louise (Golibart) B.; m. Anita Louise Zimmerman (div. Nov. 1983). BS, Mt. St. Mary's Coll., 1968. Sales rep. Pfizer, Inc., Salisbury, Md., 1971-74; hosp. rep. Pfizer, Inc., Balt., 1974-76; sales rep. Telemed, Inc., Columbia, Md., 1976-78; regional sales mgr. Cardiac Datacorp., Inc., Columbia, 1978-79; nat. sales mgr. Cardiac Datacorp., Inc., Bloomfield, Conn., 1979-81, dir. mktg. and sales, 1981-84, v.p. mktg. and sales, 1984—. 1st lt. with USMC, 1968-71, Vietnam. Democrat. Roman Catholic. Office: CDI Med Svcs 1280 Blue Hills Ave Bloomfield CT 06002

BLAIR, SAMUEL DAVIDSON, food company executive, consultant; b. Greenville, Pa., Aug. 10, 1927; s. Melvin Austin and Mildred (Billig) B.; m. Eleanor Reichert (div. 1978); children: David, Mark, Nancy; m. 2d, Emily-Jean Gurreri. BS, Allegheny Coll., 1950. Purchasing agt. Westinghouse Electric Corp., Meadville, Pa., 1950-52, The Bryant Electric Co., Bridgeport, Conn., 1952-55; dir. purchasing J.B. Williams Co., Glastonbury, Conn., 1956-58; mgr. gen. purchasing Beech-Nut Lifesavers Corp., Canajoharie, N.Y., 1958-64, asst. v.p. ops., 1964-70; dir. distbn. and planning Beech-Nut Lifesavers Corp., N.Y.C., 1970-74; v.p. distbn. The Nestle Co. Inc., White Plains, N.Y., 1974-84; sr. v.p. materials mgmt. Nestle Foods Corp., Purchase, N.Y., 1984—; pres. Nestle Properties Inc., N.Y., 1982—, Line Distbn. Services Inc., Purchase, 1980—. Mem. devel. com. Internat. Multiple Sclerosis Soc., London, 1986-88. Served with USN, 1945-47. Mem. Grocer Mfrs. Assn., Nat. Assn. Purchasing Mgmt., Nat. Counsel Phys. Distbn. Republican. Clubs: Canajoharie Country (pres. 1958-60), Ft. Rensselaer (pres. 1960-63). Home: 6 Florian Ct Westport CT 06880

BLAIR, THOMAS MICHAEL, accountant, auditor; b. Knoxville, Tenn., Mar. 15, 1957; s. John Thomas and Helen (McCants) B.; m. Mary Linda Sparry, Mar. 13, 1982; children: Lauren Elizabeth, Michele Leigh. BS in Bus. Adminstrn. and Acctg., U. Tenn., 1979. CPA, Tenn. Fin. auditor TVA, Knoxville, 1980-83, field supr. fin. audit, 1983-85, project mgr. contract audit, 1985—. Mem. AICPA, Tenn. Soc. CPA's, Assn. Govt. Accts. Republican. Presbyterian. Home: 236 Mohawk Cir Seymour TN 37865 Office: TVA Knoxville TN 37901

BLAKE, CHRISTIAN, financial executive; b. Bellows Falls, Vt., Oct. 16, 1933; s. Carl Wesley and Marian (Fair) B.; divorced; children: Melanie, Mark, Staci. BS, Ariz. State U., 1959. Pres., chief exec. officer Tri-I Cos., Westminster Station, Vt. Candidate for selectman Town of Bellows Falls, 1988. Lt. USAF, 1951-55. Republican. Office: Tri-I Cos PO Box 177 Westminster Station VT 05159

BLAKE, GARY BOMAN, advertising executive; b. San Diego, Apr. 1, 1947; s. Ross Clifford and Cecily Anne (Boman) B.; m. Susanne Rosling (div. Sept. 1985); 1 child:, Ashley Lauren; m. Lynette Gaye Holland, Sept. 7, 1985; 1 child, Ryan Winslow. BA in Polit. Sci. and Psychology, Whittier (Calif.) Coll., 1969; postgrad., U. Copenhagen, 1970-71. Mktg., mdse. cons. J. Walter Thompson, Copenhagen, 1969-72, Warner/Electra/Atlantic, San Francisco, 1972-74, Warner Bros. Records, Burbank, Calif., 1976-79; creative dir. Lambert & Blake, Inc., San Francisco, 1979-81; pres. The Blake Agy., Inc., San Francisco, 1981—; bd. dirs. Transam. Trading Corp., Salinas, Kans. Fund raiser Mt. Diablo coun. Boy Scouts Am., 1985-86; mem. adv. coun. Berkeley Pub. Edn. Found., 1987-88. Recipient Clio award for radio comml. Meaningful Details, 1981, Award of Excellence Mead Ann. Report Show, 1986, Merit award San Francisco Art Dirs. Show, 1986, Cert. of Merit Bus. Profl. Advt. Assn. West-Zitel Ann. Report, 1987. Mem. San Francisco Art Dirs. Club (v.p. 1982-83, pres. 1983-84), San Francisco Advt. Club (civic affairs com., Cable Car award 1986), Western States Advt. Club, Rotary. Republican. Methodist. Home: 32 The Plaza Dr Berkeley CA 94705 Office: The Ice House 151 Union St Ste 451 San Francisco CA 94111

BLAKE, GILBERT EASTON, air conditioning company executive; b. Glendale, Calif., June 7, 1953; s. Easton and Barbara Lee (Hunt) B.; m. Joye Trottier, June 5, 1975; children: Kristopher, Xela, Kamaron, Joseph, Alexander, Andrew. Student, Brigham Young U., 1974-75. Owner, pres. Blake Roofing, Salt Lake City, 1976-77; pres. Conjoy Inc., Salt Lake City, 1977-85, Conjoy Enterprises, Inc., Salt Lake City, 1985—; v.p., bd. dirs. Associated Funding Inc., Salt Lake City, Classy Sandwich, Murray, B&T Classic Enterprises, Inc. Scoutmaster Salt Lake City Council Boy Scouts Am., 1982-84; judge concourse d'Elegance Car Show, U. Utah, 1983—, Auto Expo Car Show, 1985—. Republican. Mormon. Office: Conjoy Enterprises Inc 5218 S Pinemont Murray UT 84123

BLAKE, JANE SALLEY, publishing company executive, small business owner; b. Tallahassee, Fla., Sept. 3, 1937; d. George Lawrence Salley and Eleanor (King) Hookham; m. Arthur Copeland Blake Jr., Sept. 5, 1959; children: A. Copeland III, Tarrant Salley. BA, Fla. State U., 1958. Exec. sec. Hist. Homes Found., Louisville, 1975-76; chair Ky. Heritage Bicentennial, Louisville, 1976; founder, pres., chmn. Arts Forum, Inc., Louisville, 1978-84; pres. Blake Publs., Inc., Louisville, 1983-86; pres., prin. The Center mag., Inc., Louisville, 1986—, J.S. Blake Pub. Group, Louisville, 1986—. V.p. Art Ctr. Assn., Louisville, 1967-72; bd. dirs., publicity chair Children's Theatre, 1968; v.p., bd. dirs. Crusade vs. Crime, 1972-74; bd. dirs. Farmington Hist. Home, 1973-75, 77-80, actor/singer Lunchtime Theatre, 1974; mem. Theatre A La Carte troupe, 1976-77; founder, chmn. Potpourri of the Arts, 1979-83; mem. pub. rels. com. Jefferson County Police, 1987-88; mem. YWCA, 1988. Mem. Pub. Rels. Soc. Am. (Landmark of Excellence award 1988), Advt. Club Louisville (13 Louie awards for publs. 1981-84), Women in Communications, The Entrepreneur Soc. (bd. dirs.), Bus. Advocates, Louisville C. of C., Soc. Profl. Journalists, Women's Club Louisville, Women's Alliance, Sigma Delta Chi. Republican. Episcopalian. Home: 2006 Round Ridge Rd Louisville KY 40207 Office: The Center Mag Inc 118 Bauer Ave Louisville KY 40207

BLAKE, JOHN FREEMAN, financial lawyer; b. Santa Clara, Calif., June 29, 1950; s. Freeman Dawes and Teresa (Seneker) B.; m. Linda Humphlett, Aug. 27, 1977; children: William, Braden. AB cum laude, U. Calif., Berkeley, 1972; postgrad., Tufts U., 1972-73; JD, U. San Francisco, 1979. Bar: Calif., D.C. Asst. v.p., fin. counselor Bank Am., San Francisco, 1974-79; assoc. McCutchen, Doyle, Brown & Enersen, San Francisco, 1979-80, Trembath, McCabe, Schwartz, Evans & Levy, Concord, Calif., 1980-83, Silverstein & Mullens, Washington, 1983-87; sole practice Washington, 1987—; mem. Joint Adv. Com. Calif. Continuing Edn. of Bar, 1981-83; adj. prof. estate planning Golden Gate U., San Francisco, 1982-83, George Washington U., Washington, 1984—; numerous seminars, lectures, forums. Author: Tax Management Financial Planning (4 vols.), 1985, also exec. editor; author and editor: Financial Planning After the Tax Reform Act of 1986; prepared numerous manuals, pamphlets on Calif. probate laws, estate planning; contbr. articles to Money mag., profl. jours. Active Washington Estate Planning Council. Mem. ABA, Calif. State Bar Assn., Internat. Assn. Fin. Planning (nat. bd. dirs. 1985—), Registry Fin. Planning Practitioners, Phi Beta Kappa. Office: 1101 Connecticut Ave NW Ste 1201 Washington DC 20036

BLAKE, KEVIN E., marketing executive; b. Mpls., Dec. 23, 1958; s. Ewald E. and Majorie I. (Van Dusen) B.; 1 child, Stepen. Student, Normandale Community Coll., Bloomington, Minn., 1976-77, U. Minn., 1977-79. Customer service rep. Ozark Air Lines, Sioux City, Iowa, 1979-80; sales rep. Ozark Air Lines, Peoria, Ill., 1980-82; dist. mktg. mgr. Ozark Air Lines, San Diego, 1982-86; mgr. mktg. automation systems Ozark Air Lines, St. Louis, 1986-87; account mgr. Trans World Airlines, St. Louis, 1987; mgr. passenger sales Trans World Airlines, Mpls., 1987—. Mem. St. Paul Conv. and Visitors Bur. Mem. San Diego SKAL Club (bd. dirs. 1983-86), San Diego SABRE Club, Sales Mktg. Execs., Mpls. C. of C., St. Paul C. of C. Club: San Diego Skal (bd. dirs. 1983-86). Office: TWA Inc 2 Appletree Sq Ste 426 Bloomington MN 55425

BLAKE, LEROY CARL, marketing executive; b. Hot Springs, Ark., June 19, 1935; s. Carlton LeRoy and Elfie Mae (Bacon) B.; m. Irene Elvin, Feb. 14, 1982. BS, Tex. Christina U., 1957; B of Fgn. Trade, Am. Grad. Sch. Internat. Mgmt., 1967; MBA, Fairleigh Dickinson U., 1982. Mgr. Plasta-Flex div. C.L. Blake & Assocs., Ft. Worth, 1958-66; mktg. mgr. Philip Morris Internat., Caracas, Venezuela and Buenos Aires, 1967-71; dir. internat. mktg. Joseph Dixon Crucible Co., Jersey City, 1973-83; mgr. worldwide mktg. Capital Controls Co., Colmar, Pa., 1986—; adj. prof. internat. mktg. Montclair (N.J.) State Coll., 1983; cons. in field. Contbr. articles on mktg. to various publs. Organizer, Tarrant County Rep. Party, Ft. Worth, 1960-62, precinct chmn., 1961-62, asst. County chmn., 1962. Mem. Assn. Polit. Risk Analysts, TAPPI, Instrument Soc. Am., Am. Mgmt. Assn. Home: 150 W Shoen Rd Exton PA 19341 Office: Capital Controls Co Inc 3000 Advance Ln Colmar PA 18915

BLALOCK, RAYMOND BUSH, ophthalmologist, business executive; b. Huntsville, Tex., Oct. 19, 1927; s. William Ben and Minnie Sue Blalock; m. Winona M. Blalock, Aug. 15, 1948; children Raynona, Renee, Ray. MD, U. Tex., Galveston, 1950. Diplomate Am. Bd. Ophthalmology. Gen. practice medicine 1951-62; practice medicine specializing in ophthalmology Huntsville, Tex., 1965—; clin. instr. dept. ophthalmology U. Tex. Med. Br., Galveston, 1965-75, clin. asst. prof., 1975-85, clin. assoc. prof., 1986—; bd. dirs. 1st Nat. Bank, vice chmn. bd., 1982-86, chmn. bd., 1987—; bd. dirs. 1st Huntsville Corp. Served with USN, 1956-57. Mem. AMA, Tex. Med. Assn., Tri-County Med. Assn., Am. Acad. Opthalmology, Houston Opthal. Assn., Scotch Highlands Breeders Assn. (pres. 1984-87, chmn. bd. 1988—), Am. Internat. Charolais Assn. Presbyterian. Home: 510 Riverside Dr Huntsville TX 77340 Office: 1400 13th St Huntsville TX 77340

BLANCHARD, TOWNSEND EUGENE, diversified technical services company executive; b. Du Quoin, Ill., Jan. 30, 1931; s. Townsend and Anna Belle (Jackson) B.; m. Norma Louise Barr, Dec. 18, 1960; children: John Barr, Susan Melody, Jayne Ann Blanchard Reishus, Stephen Eugene. BS, U. Ill., 1952; MBA, Harvard U., 1957. Cons. Ill. Sch. Bond Svc., Monticello, 1958-62; co-founder, treas., chief fin. officer Americana Nursing Ctrs., Monticello, 1962-75; v.p. fin., treas., chief fin. officer, chief of staff Cenco, Inc., Chgo., 1975-79; sr. v.p., chief fin. officer, dir. DynCorp., McLean, Va., 1979—. Elder Presbyn. Ch.; bd. dirs. Combined Health Appeal, 1986—. Lt. USNR, 1952-55. Decorated Spl. Commendation letter. Mem. Fin. Execs. Inst. (pres. 1988-89), Fin. Mgmt. Assn., Delta Sigma Phi (trustee nat. found. bd. 1982—, pres. 1988—, Harvey H. Hebert award 1975). Clubs: U. Ill. Alumni (Washington), Harvard U. (Washington); Econ. (Chgo.). Home: 1222 Aldebaran Dr McLean VA 22101 Office: DynCorp 2000 Edmund Halley Dr Reston VA 22091

BLAND, PETER GEORGE, bank executive; b. Essex, Eng., Mar. 19, 1937; came to U.S., 1983; s. George Henry Roberts and Margaret (Clarkson) B.; m. Ann Elizabeth Johnson, June 6, 1959; children: Nicola Anne, Susan Elizabeth. Grad. Peter Symonds Churchers Coll., Winchester, Eng., 1953; diploma Inst. Bankers, 1961. With Barclays Bank, Eng. and Wales, 1953-79, local dir., Bristol, Eng., 1979-83, chmn. exec. com., dir. Barclays Am. Corp., 1983-87, Charlotte, N.C., dir. Barclays Am. Comm. Services, Inc. and pres. Barclays Am. Bus. Credit, Inc., Hartford, Conn., 1983-89; chief oper. officer Barclays Bank of N.Y., N.Y.C., 1989—. Mem. Inst. Bankers (U.K.), Manchester Bus. Sch. Assn., Gwent C. of C. (treas. 1974-79). Conservative.

Mem. Ch. of Eng. Club: Hartford. Home: 72 Hampshire Dr Glastonbury CT 06033 Office: Barclays Bank NY 75 Wall St New York NY 10265

BLANEY, MICHAEL, lawyer; b. Jersey City, June 21, 1953; s. George R. and Anne M. (Ryan) B.; m. Mary Jane Reddington, Nov. 1, 1985; 1 child, Patrick M. BA, Holy Cross Coll., Worcester, Mass., 1975; JD, Seton Hall U., 1980. Bar: N.J. 1980; U.S. Dist. Ct. (fed. dist.) N.J. 1980. Investigator Hudson County Pros. Office, Jersey City, 1977-79; legal asst. Bell Labs., Whippany, N.J., 1979-81; atty. Combustion Engring., Bloomfield, N.J., 1981-84; sr. atty. Combustion Engring., Stamford, Conn., 1984—. Mem. N.J. Bar Assn., Westchester-Fairfield County Corp. Counsel Assn. Office: Combustion Engring Inc 900 Long Ridge Rd Stamford CT 06904

BLANFORD, IRVING IVEY, banker; b. Portsmouth, Va., Jan. 8, 1899; s. George Thomas and Claude Meredith (Sessoms) B.; student Va. Mil. Inst., 1918; m. Gladys Simmons Johnson, Sept. 7, 1935 (dec. 1966); children—Virginia Caroline Blanford Nicewander, Gladys Sessoms Blanford Godwin, Claudia Maria Blanford Hubbard. Radio operator Panama R.R., 1920; sec. Comml. Hardware Co., Norfolk, Va., 1922-25; salesman Chas. Syer & Co., Norfolk, 1926-28; food broker, New Bern, N.C., 1928-29; mfrs. rep. Nat. Sugar Refining Co., N.J., N.Y.C., 1930-41; exec. dir. pub. housing City of New Bern, 1945-69; chmn. exec. com. Bank of New Bern, 1959-63, pres., 1962-72, dir., 1957-72; dir. New Bern Morris Plan Co., 1943-57; chmn. local bd. NCNB, New Bern, 1972—; mem. Centenary United Meth. Ch. Clubs: New Bern Golf & Country, Elks (exalted ruler 1938), Masons, Shriners, Rotary (pres. 1928-29), Eastern Carolina Yacht (treas. 1956-57), Dunes. Home: 1604 Tryon Rd New Bern NC 28560 Office: 2119 Neuse Blvd New Bern NC 28560

BLANK, CHARLES EUGENE, accounting company executive; b. Jacksonville, Ill., May 26, 1929; s. John Lavern and Lucile Mary (Jokisch) B.; m. Dolores May Mahn, May 14, 1955; children: David Eugene, James Michael. BS in Commerce, St. Louis U., 1952. CPA, Tex. Ptnr. Ernst & Whinney, 1952—. With USMC, 1947-49. Mem. Am. Inst. CPAs, Bent Tree Country Club (Dallas), Bellerive Country Club (St. Louis). Republican. Roman Catholic. Home: 10411 Strait Ln Dallas TX 75229 Office: Ernst & Whinney 2001 Ross Ave Ste 2800 Dallas TX 75201

BLANK, DAVID, advertising agency executive; b. N.Y.C., Dec. 30, 1923; s. Jacob and Rose (Schwartz) B.; m. Ann Zable, Feb. 13, 1944; children—Jenise Blanc, Jacqueline France, Richard Blank. B.S. in Bus., NYU, 1949. Supr. adminstrn. div. VA, 1946-48; buyer Darling Carriage Co., 1948-50; mdse. mgr., 1950-54; v.p. merchandising, 1954-57; v.p. sales Joy Toy Corp. and mdse. mgr. Wholesale City, v.p. merchandising Darling Stores, 1956-57; pres. Crestwood Advt., Inc., N.Y.C, 1957-74; chmn., pres. Burroughs Research and Devel. Corp., Marketing Alliance Ltd., U.S. Consumer Products; pres., chmn. bd. Blank & Kempner Advt., Inc./Mutual Media, Inc.; v.p. Hobar Group; v.p., dir. L.D.M. Mktg., Inc.; pres. Lester David Mktg. Corp.; rep. MCA Corp.; dir., mem. exec. com. China Trade Corp. Cons., 1974—; pres. B&J Mktg. Ltd., St. Augustine, Fla.; chmn. bd. Daric Media Inc. Contbr. articles to profl. jours. Adviser Amvets Com. of Concern for Release Am. Prisoners of War Vietnam; hon. fire chief N.Y. State Fire Fighters Assn., 1970; campaign chmn. senator Nick Spano, mayor Angelo Martinelli, congressman Toricelli, councilman O'Rourke and County Legislator Lee, Rep. Party, 1981, county exec. Andrew O'Rourke; chmn. bd., pres. Midchester Jewish Ctr., Zionist Orgn. of Am.; v.p. bd. govs. Yonkers Fedn.; v.p., bd. dirs. United Synagogue Jewish Community Ctr. Served to 1st lt. USAAF, 1942-46. Mem. Jewish War Vets (vice comdr.), DAV, Odd Fellows (dist. dep., grand master). Home: 35 Ardell Rd Bronxville NY 10708 Office: Mutual Media Inc 675 Third Ave New York NY 10017

BLANK, GEORGE WILLIAM, III, entrepreneur, consultant; b. Phila., June 1, 1945; s. George W. and Betty Marion (Drinnan) B.; m. Linda Kay Cotten, Aug. 19, 1967; children: George W. IV, Robert Alan. AB, Eastern Coll., St. Davids, Pa., 1971; MDiv, Princeton Theol. Sem., 1974. Ordained to ministry Presbyn. Ch., 1975. Pastor Calvary Presbyn. Ch., Leechburg, Pa., 1975-79; editor-in-chief Softside Pubs., Milford, N.H., 1979-81; editorial dir. Creative Computing, Morris Plains, N.J., 1981-82; pres. NuClas Corp., Denville, N.J., 1982—; cons. Office Tech. Assessment, U.S. Congress, Washington, 1981; founder, bd. dirs. Computer Action Learning, Summit, N.J., 1983—; speaker Nat. Computer Conf., Houston, 1981. Author: The Creative Atari, 1981, (computer program) Wordscope, 1985; editor: Pathways Through the ROM. Pres. Leechburg Ministerium, 1977-79; v.p. Meals on Wheels, Leechburg, 1976-79; asst. scoutmaster, Boy Scouts Am., Coatesville, Pa., 1969-71, Morris Plains, 1985-86, dist. commr. Morris County, 1986—. Served with U.S. Army, 1965-68. Mem. IEEE. Office: NuClas Corp 239 Fox Hill Rd Denville NJ 07834

BLANK, LAWRENCE FRANCIS, computer consultant; b. Detroit, Oct. 4, 1932; s. Frank A. and Marcella A. (Pieper) B.; m. Carol Louise Mann, Oct. 12, 1963; children: Ann, Steven, Susan, Lori. BS, Xavier U., 1954. Asst. engr. Gen. Electric Co., Evendale, Ohio, 1956-60; research engr. Gen. Dynamics Corp., San Diego, 1960-62; mem. tech. staff Computer Scis. Corp., El Segundo, Calif., 1962-64; programming mgr. IBM, Los Angeles, 1964-69, Xerox Corp., El Segundo, 1969-74; ind. computer cons., 1974—. Mem. Assn. Computing Machinery, Ind. Computer Cons. Assn. Home and Office: 212 Via Eboli Newport Beach CA 92663

BLANK, PETER JOSEPH, investment banker; b. N.Y.C., Aug. 18, 1933; s. Joseph Peter and Catherine (Kupera) B.; m. Charlene Margaret Kogler, Feb. 27, 1960; children: Kathleen Blank Ensley, Barbara, Peter Jr. Student, St. Petersburg (Fla.) Jr. Coll.; BS in Advt., U. Fla., 1959; diploma, Am. Savs. and Loan Inst., Chgo., 1969. Advt. dir. Home Fed. Savs. & Loan Assn., St. Petersburg, 1959-65, v.p., 1965-80; sr. v.p. Home Fed. Bank Fla., St. Petersburg, 1980-85; sr. v.p. mktg. Barnett Bank Pinellas County, St. Petersburg, 1986-88; exec. v.p. Atlantic Securities, Inc., Tampa, 1988—; pres., chmn. bd. dirs. Pinellas Service Corp. Pres., chmn. St. Petersburg Cert. Devel. Corp., 1988—; commr. Pinellas County Employees Rels. Com., Clearwater, Fla., 1988—; chmn. Com. of 100 of Pinellas County. Sgt. USAF, 1952-56. Mem. Bank Mktg. Assn., Fin. Insts. Mktg. Assn. (pres. 1960-61), St. Petersburg C. of C. (treas. 1965), Lions (pres. St. Petersburg chpt. 1964-65). Democrat. Roman Catholic. Office: Atlantic Coast Securities Inc 4830 W Kennedy Blvd Suite 350 Tampa FL 33609

BLANKEMEYER, BRUCE JAMES, marketing professional; b. Lebanon, Pa., May 31, 1952; s. Eugene A. and Ruth J. (Hickman) B. BBA in Mktg., U. Cin., 1984. Gen mgr. McDonald's of Cin., 1976-78; sales broker G.A. Newman & Assocs., Akron, Ohio, 1978-79; account rep. Lubriquip Houdaille, Cleve., 1979-84, account mgr., 1984-85; product mgr. ALT Controls, Inc., Richmond, Va., 1985—. Republican. Roman Catholic. Office: Alt Controls Inc 705 Air Park Rd Ashland VA 23005

BLANKENSHIP, BARBARA STEWART, heating and air company executive; b. Wilmington, Del., Dec. 20, 1949; d. William Robert and Beatrice Mae (Pierson) Stewart; m. Stephen Nathaniel Blankenship, May 26, 1984; stepchildren: Stephen, Shelley, Nathan. BS, U. Del., 1972. Tchr. Carroll County Schs., Mt. Airy, Md., 1976-78; sec., treas. Cundiff Heating and Air Inc., Roanoke, Va., 1979—; also bd. dirs. Cundiff Heating and Air Inc., Roanoke; bd. dirs., sec., treas., ptnr. Cundiff Duct Cleaning Svcs., Inc.; controller, ptnr. Barjer Properties, Roanoke, 1986—. Bd. dirs., sec. Beechwood West Homeowners Assn., 1988—. Mem. Roanoke Network Managerial and Profl. Women (bd. dirs. 1986—), Nat. Assn. Accts., Nat. Assn. Plumbing, Heating and Cooling Contractors. Office: Cundiff Heating and A/C Inc 4426 Palmer Ave NE Roanoke VA 24019

BLANKENSHIP, DAVID LYNN, insurance company executive; b. Manchester, Iowa, Mar. 24, 1951; s. Earle Robert and Marvel Lucille (McFarland) B.; m. Lois Annabelle Carter, June 19, 1972; children: Carrie Lynn, Troy David. BBA, U. Iowa, 1973; MBA, Marquette U., 1977. Pres. Aegon USA Realty Advisors, Inc., Cedar Rapids, Iowa, 1983—, Cedar Income Fund 1, Ltd., Cedar Rapids, 1984—, USP Real Estate Investment Trust, Cedar Rapids, 1985—, Cedar Income Fund 2, Ltd., Cedar Rapids, 1986—; v.p. Life Investors Ins. Co., Cedar Rapids, 1984—, Pacific Fidelity Life Ins. Co., Cedar Rapids, 1985—, Bankers United Life Ins. Corp., —, 1984—, Fin. Investors Life Ins. Corp., —, 1984—, NN Investors Life Ins. Co., Inc., —; sr. v.p. MidAm. Mgmt. Corp., —, 1985—. Office: Aegon USA Realty Advisors 4333 Edgewood Rd NE Cedar Rapids IA 52499

BLANKENSHIP, DWIGHT DAVID, business owner; b. Ashland, Ky., Mar. 18, 1944; S. David Earl and Dorthy Irene (King) B.; m. Joyce Eddy, Mar. 1, 1969 (div. Oct. 1984); children: Dwight W., Cheryl L. Grad. high sch., Ashland, Ky. Owner, mgr. Royal Pool, Sarasota, Fla., 1970-72, Am. Indian Jewelry, Sarasota, Fla., 1972-78, Daves Enterprises, Big Pine Key, Fla., 1978-86, D & D Enterprises, Ocala, Fla., 1986—, Master Mktg. Prodn. Co., Bradenton, Fla., 1987—, Gold Designs, Bradenton, Fla., 1987—. Home: 6716 26th St W Bradenton FL 34207 also: Gold Designs Cortez Pla E 661 44 Ave W Bradenton FL also: Master Mktg Cortez Pla E 661 44th Ave W Bradenton FL

BLANKENSHIP, HARRIS BRADLEY, construction executive; b. Alamogordo, N. Mex., Aug. 10, 1951; s. Robert G. Blankenship and Eula Pearl (Linson) Altoff; m. Velta June Ross, May 23, 1975 (div. Aug. 1985); children: Jason Bradley, Karrie Ann. Student in arch. tech., Anoka Tech. Inst., 1971-72. Draftsman Miles Homes, Inc., Mpls., 1972-74; draftsman, estimator H.T. Coker Constrn. Co., Alamogordo, 1974-75; estimator, project mgr. Sanford Constrn., Alamogordo, 1975-79; mgr. Chaparral Builders, Inc., Hobbs, N.Mex., 1979—. Democrat. Baptist. Lodges: Elks (Alamogordo club esquier, 1978-79), Lions (sec. treas. Hobbs Downtown club 1982, 85-86), Moose. Home: 718 Luna Hobbs NM 88240 Office: Chaparral Builders Inc 315 S Leech Hobbs NM 88240

BLANKENSHIP, RANDALL AUSTON, distribution manager; b. Miami, Okla., Mar. 11, 1960; s. Ernest Auston and Carolyn Sue (Phillips) B.; m. Melanie Ann Klaus, Mar. 8, 1980; children: Matthew Adam, Ryan Auston. Grad. high sch., Fairland, Okla. Territory mgr. Rasor-West Distbn., Miami, Okla., 1981—. Home: 6 F NW Miami OK 74354 Office: Rasor-West Distbn Co 1500 Newman Rd Box 440 North Miami OK 74358

BLANKFORT, LOWELL ARNOLD, newspaper publisher; b. N.Y.C., Apr. 29, 1926; s. Herbert and Gertrude (Butler) B.; m. April Pemberton; 1 child, Jonathan. BA in History and Polit. Sci., Rutgers U., 1946. Reporter, copy editor L.I. (N.Y.) Star-Jour., 1947-49; columnist London Daily Mail, Paris, 1949-50; copy editor The Stars & Stripes, Darmstadt, Germany, 1950-51, Wall St. Jour., N.Y.C., 1951; bus., labor editor Cowles Mags., N.Y.C., 1951-53; pub. Pacifica (Calif.) Tribune, 1954-59; free-lance writer, Europe, Asia, 1959-61; co-pub., editor Chula Vista (Calif.) Star-News, 1961-78; co-owner Paradise (Calif.) Post, 1977—, Monte Vista (Colo.) Jour., Ctr. (Colo.) Post-Dispatch, Del Norte (Colo.) Prospector, 1978—, Plainview (Minn.) News, St. Charles (Minn.) Press, Lewiston (Minn.) Jour., 1980—, Summit (Colo.) Sentinel, New Richmond (Wis.) News, 1981-87, Yuba City Valley Herald, Calif., 1982-85, TV Views, Monterey, Calif., 1982-87, Summit County Jour., Colo., 1982-87, Alpine (Calif.) Sun, 1987—. Contbr. articles on fgn. affairs to newspapers. Mem. Calif. Dem. Cen. Com., 1963. Named Outstanding Layman of Yr. Sweetwater Edn. Assn., 1966, Citizen of Yr. City of Chula Vista, 1976, Headliner of Yr. San Diego Press Club, 1980. Mem. ACLU (pres. San Diego chpt. 1970-71), Calif. Newspaper Pubs. Assn., World Affairs Council San Diego (1st v.p. 1988—, exec. bd. mem.), Internat. Ctr. Devel. Policy (nat. bd. 1985—), World Federalist Assn. (nat. exec. bd., pres. San Diego chpt. 1984-86), Soc. Profl. Journalists Home: Old Orchard Ln Bonita CA 92002 Office: 315 4th Ave Ste S Chula Vista CA 92010

BLANKINSHIP, HENRY MASSIE, data processing executive; b. Providence, Sept. 27, 1942; s. Ernest Randolph and Henrietta (Massie) B.; m. Linda Ferber, Jan. 17, 1981; children: John Byron, Kevin Mark, Sara Jane. Student, Rollins Coll., 1962-63, U. Va., 1963-66. Mgmt. analyst First Va. Bankshares Corp., Falls Church, 1967-72; head systems planning br. Navy Recruiting Command, Arlington, Va., 1972-80; head computer network devel. Navy Mil. Personnel Command, Arlington, Va., 1980-83, head software engring., 1983-84; head Navy Personnel Data Systems, Arlington, Va., 1984-88, Navy Personnel and Manpower Data Systems Mgmt., Arlington, Va., 1988—. Nat. corr. Karate Illustrated Mag., 1976-79. Head Karate instr. YMCA, Fairfax County, Va.; police spl. teams cons., Fairfax County. Recipient Outstanding Navy Civilian Service award, 1975, 76, 77, 78, 79, 81, 82, 84, Gold Wreath U.S. Navy, 1977, Navy Spl. Acts award, 1983; named Ea. Region Nat. Karate champ, black belt (5th degree), 1968-73. Mem. Am. Mgmt. Assn., Nat. Assn. Combative Arts, Am. Tae Kwon Do Assn., U.S. Karate Assn., Internat. Martial Arts Assn. (pres.), U.S. Kickboxing Assn., Tai-Fung Martial Arts Assn. Republican. Office: Navy Personnel & Manpower Data Systems Mgmt PO Box 1610 Arlington VA 22210

BLANKLEY, WALTER ELWOOD, manufacturing company executive; b. Phila., Sept. 23, 1935; s. George William and Martha Emily (McCord) B.; m. Rosemary Deniken, Aug. 16, 1958; children: Stephen Michael, Laura Ann. B.S.M.E., Princeton U., 1957. Mgr. planning Ametek Hunter Spring, Hatfield, Pa., 1965-66, gen. mgr., 1966-69; asst. to pres. Ametek, Inc., San Francisco, 1969-71; v.p. Ametek, Inc., Watsonville, Calif., 1971-78, group v.p., 1978-82, sr. v.p., 1982—; dir. Kinark Corp., Tulsa, 1988—; bd. dirs. Kinark Corp., Tulsa, Okla., Am. Stock Exchange. Mem. Aluminum Extruders Council (pres. 1974-76, dir. 1971-78). Office: Ametek Inc PO Box 351 Watsonville CA 95076

BLANTON, JACK SAWTELLE, oil company executive; b. Shreveport, La., Dec. 7, 1927; s. William Neal and Louise (Wynn) B.; m. Laura Lee Scurlock, Aug. 20, 1949; children: Elizabeth Louise Blanton Wareing, Jack Sawtelle Jr., Eddy Scurlock. BA, U. Tex., 1947, LLB, 1950. Bar: Tex. 1950. With Scurlock Oil Co., Houston, 1950-88, v.p., 1956-58, pres., 1958-83, chmn. bd., 1983-88; pres. Eddy Refining Co.; bd. dirs. Southwestern Bell Corp., Tex. Commerce Bank N.A., Gordon Jewelry Corp., Ashland Oil Inc., Baker Hughes Inc., Burlington No. Past chmn. bd. trustees St. Luke's United Meth. Ch., Houston; chmn. bd. regents U. Tex. System, 1985-89; past vice chmn., former bd. dirs. Meth. Hosp., Houston. Mem. Mid-Continent Oil and Gas Assn. (past pres.), Houston C. of C. (life), Sons Rep. of Tex. (past pres. San Jacinto chpt.), Sam Houston Meml. Assn., Nat. Tennis Assn., U.S. Lawn Tennis Assn., Tex. Ind. Oil Producers and Refiners, Ex-Students Assn. U. Tex. (past pres.), Houston C. of C. (chmn. 1985-86), Delta Kappa Epsilon, Phi Delta Phi, Phi Alpha Delta. Clubs: Houston (Houston) (past pres.), River Oaks Country (Houston); El Dorado Country (Palm Springs, Calif.). Office: RepublicBank Ctr 700 Louisiana St Ste 3920 Houston TX 77002

BLANTON, JOHN ARTHUR, architect; b. Houston, Jan. 1, 1928; s. Arthur Alva and Caroline (Jeter) B.; BA, Rice U., 1948, BS in Architecture, 1949; m. Marietta Louise Newton, Apr. 10, 1953 (dec. 1976); children: Jill Blanton Lewis, Lynette Blanton Rowe, Elena Diane. With Richard J. Neutra, Los Angeles, 1950-64; pvt. practice architecture, Manhattan Beach, Calif., 1964—; lectr. UCLA Extension, 1967-76, 85, Harbor Coll., Los Angeles, 1970-72. Mem. Capital Improvements Com., Manhattan Beach, 1966, city commr. Bd. of Bldg. Code Appeals; mem. Bd. Zoning Adjustment. Served with Signal Corps, U.S. Army, 1951-53. Recipient Best House of Year award C. of C., 1969, 70, 71, 83, Preservation of Natural Site award, 1974, design award, 1975, 84. Mem. AIA (contbr. book revs. to jour. 1972—, recipient Red Cedar Shingle/nat. merit award 1979), Soc. Archtl. Historians. Club: Rotary. Six bldgs. included in A Guide to the Architecture of Los Angeles and Southern California; works featured in L'architettura mag., 1988. Office: 2100 Sepulveda Blvd Ste 14 Manhattan Beach CA 90266

BLASIUS, DONALD CHARLES, appliance company executive; b. Oak Park, Ill., June 10, 1929; s. Ervin A. and Frances C. (Critchfield) B.; m. Carle Ann Forslew, Oct. 11, 1952; children: Douglas Charles, Ann Louise. BSBA, Northwestern U., 1951. Various exec. positions McCulloch Corp., 1953-68; various exec. positions J.I. Case Co., 1968-74, v.p., gen. mgr. div., 1970-72, sr. v.p., gen. mgr. div., 1972-74; exec. v.p., chief operating officer Tappan Co., Mansfield, Ohio, 1974-76, pres., chief exec. officer, 1976-84, chmn. bd., chief exec. officer, 1984-86; chmn., chief. exec. officer home products group White Consol. Industries, Inc., Columbus, Ohio, 1986-88, pres., 1989—; bd. dirs. Ohio Edison Co., Akron, several AB Electrolux N. Am. cos.; dep. mem. group exec. mgmt. com. AB Electrolux, Stockholm, Sweden, 1988—. Served with Spl. Services, AUS. Home: 2370 Pebblebrook Westlake OH 44145 Office: White Consol Industries Inc 11770 Berea Rd Cleveland OH 44111

BLASS, GERHARD ALOIS, educator; b. Chemnitz, Germany, Mar. 12, 1916; came to U.S., 1949, naturalized, 1955; s. Gustav Alois and Anna (Mehnert) B.; m. Barbara Siegert, July 16, 1945; children—Andrew, Marcus, Evamaria, Annamaria, Peter. Abitur, Oberrealschule Chemnitz, 1935; Dr. rer. nat., Universität Leipzig, 1943. Asst. Institut für Theoretische Physik, Leipzig, 1939-43; research cons. Siemens & Halske, Berlin, 1943-46; dozent math. and physics Oberrealschule, Nuremberg, 1946-47, Ohm Polytechnikum, Nuremberg, 1947-49; prof. physics Coll. St. Thomas, St. Paul, 1949-51; prof. physics U. Detroit, 1951-81, chmn. dept., 1962-71; guest prof. U. Baroda, India, spring, 1967. Author: Theoretical Physics, 1962, Weil Hiersein viel ist Poems in German, 1987. Fellow AAAS; mem. Soc. Asian and Comparative Philosophy, Esperanto League N.Am., Sigma Pi Sigma. Roman Catholic. Home: 4441 Stewart Rd Metamora MI 48455

BLASS, WALTER PAUL, consultant, management educator; b. Dinslaken, Germany, Mar. 31, 1930; came to U.S., 1941, naturalized, 1947; s. Richard B. and Malvi (Rosenblatt) B.; B.A., Swarthmore Coll., 1951; postgrad. Princeton U., 1951-52; M.A., Columbia U., 1953; m. Janice L. Minott, Apr. 2, 1954; children—Kathryn, Christopher, Gregory. Asst. Laos and Cambodia desk officer ICA, Washington, 1957-58; gen. mgr. R.B. Blass Co., Deal, N.J., 1958-61; economist AT&T, N.Y.C., 1961-66; country dir. Peace Corps, Afghanistan, 1966-68; asst. v.p. revenue requirement studies N.Y. Telephone Co., N.Y.C., 1968-70, dir. corp. planning, 1970-82; dir. strategic planning AT&T, N.Y.C., 1982-85 (ret.); pres., Strategic Plans, Unltd., Warren, N.J., 1985—. Exec. Fellow-in-Residence, Martino Grad. Sch. Bus. Adminstrn., Fordham U., N.Y.C., 1986—; cons. McKinsey & Co., Telecommunications Authority Ireland, McDonnell Douglas, Heller Fin., Inc.; lectr. in field; vis. prof. U. Grenoble, France, 1988. Trustee Guilford Coll., 1975—. Served to lt., j.g., USNR, 1953-56. Woodrow Wilson Found. sr. fellow, 1974—. Mem. N.Y. Acad. Scis., Soc. Values in Higher Edn. (dir. 1983-86), Am. Econ. Assn., Nat. Assn. Bus. Economists, N.Am. Soc. Corp. Planning (dir. 1972), Royal Econ. Soc., Princeton Club. Co-author: The Strategic Planning Handbook, 1982. Home and Office: 6 Casale Dr Warren NJ 07060

BLATHERWICK, GERALD D., telecommunications executive; b. Kansas City, Mo., July 5, 1936; s. E.L. and Nell Blatherwick; m. Anne Taylor, June 11, 1960; children: Kate, Nell. BS in Journalism, U. Kans., 1958. With Southwestern Bell Telephone Co., Kans., Mo., and Tex., 1963-78, 82-86, pub. relations mgr., San Antonio, 1975, pub. relations dir., 1975-78, v.p. pub. relations, St. Louis, 1982-86; v.p. pub. relations Southwestern Bell Corp., St. Louis, 1984-86, vice chmn., dir. human resources and corp. communications, 1986-88, vice chmn., dir. human resources, corp. communications and govt. relations, 1988—; asst. v.p. Pacific Telephone and Telegraph Co., San Francisco, 1978-79, v.p. pub. relations, 1979-82; pres. Southwestern Bell Found.; bd. dirs. Southwestern Bell Corp., Southwestern Bell Telephone, Southwestern Bell Publs., Southwestern Bell Mobile Systems, Metromedia Paging Svcs., Inc., U.S. Telephone Assn., Boatmen's Trust Co.; chmn. Southwestern Bell Corp., Washington; mem. conf. bd., adv. coun. on human resource mgmt; chmn. communications 1992 PGA Tournament. Chmn. bd. Dance St. Louis; bd. dirs. St. Louis Symphony, Mary Inst. of St. Louis, Nat. Action Council for Minorities in Engring.; pres. Arthur W. Page Soc.; past bd. dirs. ARC, San Francisco, United Way, San Francisco Ballet, YMCA Greater St. Louis, Arts and Edn. Council; past bd. govs. Econ. Literacy Coun. Calif.; trustee Mo. Botanical Gardens. Lt. (j.g.) USN, 1959-62. Clubs: Bellerive Country, Missouri Athletic, St. Louis, Stadium, Town and Country Racquet, Racquet Club of Ladue, Mo., Golf Club of Okla. Home: 26 Fordyce Ln Saint Louis MO 63124 Office: SW Bell Corp One Bell Ctr Saint Louis MO 63101

BLATTNER, MEERA MCCUAIG, educator; b. Chgo., Aug. 14, 1930; d. William D. McCuaig and Nina (Spertus) Klevs; m. Minao Kamegai, June 22 1985; children: Douglas, Robert, William. B.A., U. Chgo., 1952; M.S., U. So. Calif., 1966; Ph.D., UCLA, 1973 . Research fellow in computer sci. Harvard U., 1973-74; asst. prof. Rice U., 1974-80; asso. prof. applied sci. U. Calif. at Davis, Livermore, 1980—; adj. prof. U. Tex., Houston, 1977—; vis. prof. U. Paris, 1980; program dir. theoretical computer sci. NSF, Washington, 1979-80. NSF grantee, 1977-81. Mem. Soc. Women Engrs., Assn. Computing Machinery, IEEE Computer Soc. Contbr. articles to profl. jours. Office: U Calif Davis/Livermore Dept Applied Sci Livermore CA 94550

BLAU, HARVEY RONALD, lawyer; b. N.Y.C., Nov. 14, 1935; s. David and Rose (Kuchinsky) B.; m. Arlene Joan Garrett, Mar. 21, 1964; children: Stephanie Elizabeth, Melissa Karen, Victoria Gayle. A.B., N.Y.U., 1957, LL.M., 1965; LL.B., Columbia U., 1961. Bar: N.Y. 1961. Practiced in N.Y.C., after 1961; sr. partner firm Blau, Kramer, Wactlar & Lieberman, P.C., Jericho, N.Y., 1975—; law sec. to U.S. Dist. Judge Cooper So. Dist. N.Y., 1962-63; asst. U.S. atty. So. Dist. N.Y., 1963-66; chmn. Instrument Systems Corp., Oneita Industries Inc., Universal Holding Corp., John Adams Life Ins.; bd. dirs. ARX, Inc., Nu Horizons Electronics Corp., VTX Electronics Inc., L.I. div. of The Bank of N.Y. Trustee Village of Old Westbury. Served to capt. JAGC, AUS, 1958-66. Mem. Fed. bar assns., Assn. Bar City N.Y., Bar Assn. Nassau County. Home: 125 Wheatley Rd Old Westbury NY 11568 Office: Instrument Systems Corp 100 Jericho Quadrangle Jericho NY 11753 also: Oneita Industries Inc Dogwood Ave Andrews SC 29510

BLAU, JOEL MICHAEL, financial consultant; b. Chgo., Apr. 15, 1959; s. Sam Joseph and Laurel Helene (Witz) B.; m. Susan Lynn Kaufman, Apr. 17, 1982; children: Jason, Jamie. BBA, Drake U., 1981. Cert. Fin. Planner. Commodity and stockbroker Frazier Parrott div. Heinold Commodities, Chgo., 1981-83; investment rep. Great Am. Fed. Savs., Oak Park, Ill., 1983-84, Mid-Am. Fed. Savs., Naperville, Ill., 1984-85; fin. planner 1985-86; cons. Fin. Integrity Group, Chgo., 1986—. Columnist "Investment Exchange", Cicero-Berwyn (Ill.) Life, 1983. Mem. Inst. Cert. Fin. Planners, Alpha Epsilon Pi. Jewish. Home: 1255 Elmwood Deerfield IL 60015 Office: Fin Integrity Group 8755 W Higgins Ste 1170 Chicago IL 60631

BLAUCH, BRENT WILLIAM, coal company executive; b. Harrisburg, Pa., Oct. 29, 1951; s. Richard M. Blauch and Mary A. (Machamer) Warren; m. Cathy Ann Dobbs, June 16, 1973; children: Laura Nicole, Tammie Lynne. BSCE, U. Pitts., 1973. Registered profl. engr., Pa. Project mgr. Skelly & Loy, Harrisburg, 1973-78; co-owner Robins & Assocs., Mechanisburg, Pa., 1978-81; pvt. practice cons. engr. Mechanisburg, Pa., 1981-82; assoc. dep. sec.dept. environment resources State of Pa., Harrisburg, 1982-84; dep. dir. Office Surface Mining, U.S. Dept. Interior, Washington, 1985; spl. project officer U.S. Dept. Interior, Harrisburg, 1986; v.p. Environ. Power Corp., Camp Hill, Pa., 1986—; cons. Mining Cos., U.S. Dept. Interior, Pa. and Washington, 1985—. Coach Cumberland Valley All Girls Softball Assn., Mechanisburg, 1987—. Mem. Pa. Mining Profls. (pres. 1979-82), Nat. Coal Coun. Republican. Methodist. Home: 1109 Orrs Bridge Rd Mechanisburg PA 17055 Office: Environ Power Corp 4 Lemoyne Dr Lemoyne PA 17043

BLAYDES, DAVID LEE, financial consultant; b. Mendota, Ill., Feb. 21, 1955; s. Raymond and Ruby (Glidewell) B.; m. Susan Marie McLennan, Sept. 15, 1985; children: Bridgette Nicole, Lauren Marie. BS, Olivet U., 1977; postgrad., Coll. for Fin. Planning, 1988—. Owner, pres. Integrated Fin. Resources, Ltd., Oak Brook, Ill., 1981—; lectr. corp. retirement planning seminars. Contbr. articles to profl. jours. Mem. Internat. Assn. Registered Fin. Planners (registered fin. planner), Inst. Cert. Fin. Planners (cert. fin. planner), Internat. Assn. for Fin. Planners (registry), Nat. Assn. of Estate Planners. Home: 940 Cherry Hills Ln Naperville IL 60540 Office: Integrated Fin Resources Ltd 2001 Midwest Rd Oak Brook IL 60521

BLAZIEK, WILLIAM LOUIS, casino and hotel executive; b. Oakland, Calif., Apr. 21, 1944; s. Herman Louis B. V.p. sales and mktg. Del Webb Hotels, Las Vegas, Nev., 1969-81; sr. v.p. sales and mktg. Resorts Internat. Casino Hotel, Atlantic City, 1982—; mem. U.S. Mktg. Council on Internat. Tourism, Washington, 1984—. Served to 1st lt. U.S. Army, 1966-69. Mem. Am. Soc. Assn. Execs., Hotel Sales and Mktg. Assn. Internat. Roman Catholic. Office: Resorts Internat Casino Hotel Boardwalk & N Carolina Ave Atlantic City NJ 08404

BLECKER, NAOMI PERLE, credit manager; b. N.Y.C., Mar. 3, 1956; d. Sidney and Zelda (Pologe) B. Student, CUNY, 1973-77. Credit mgr. new accounts Gimbel's Dept. Store, N.Y.C., 1975-78; credit mgr. Eue/Screen Gems div. Columbia Pictures Corp., N.Y.C., 1977-82, JSL Video Services, Inc. subs. AME, Inc., N.Y.C., 1982—. Mem. Nat. Assn. Credit Mgmt. (chmn. motion picture and t.v. group 1982—), Nat. Assn. Female Execs., Am. Jewish Congress. Democrat. Home: 141-30 Pershing Crescent Briarwood New York NY 11435

BLEEKE, JOEL ALLEN, management consultant; b. Port Washington, Wis., Feb. 19, 1953; s. Milton Henry and Corliss Marie (Sachse) B. BA, Carthage Coll., 1975; JD, Northwestern U., 1979, MS in Fin., 1979. Prin. McKinsey & Co., Inc., Chgo., 1979—. Contbr. articles on fin. and corp. strategy to U.S. and internat. bus. publs. Clubs: University, Economic. Office: McKinsey & Co Inc 20 S Clark St Ste 2700 Chicago IL 60603

BLEIBERG, ROBERT MARVIN, financial editor; b. Bklyn., June 21, 1924; s. Edward and Frances (DuBroff) B.; m. Harriet Evans, May 1948 (div. Mar. 1953); 1 dau., Ellen; m. Sally Diane Beverly, Oct. 25, 1956; 1 son, Richard Beverly. B.A., Columbia, 1943; M.B.A., N.Y. U., 1950; D.C.Sc., Hillsdale Coll., 1977. v.p. Dow Jones & Co., Inc. Asso. editor: Prudden's Digest of Investment and Banking Opinions, N.Y.C., 1946; asso. editor: Barron's Nat. Bus. and Financial Weekly, N.Y.C., 1946-54; editor, 1955-81, pub., 1980-88, editorial dir., 1981—. Served with inf. AUS, 1943-45, PTO. Decorated Purple Heart; recipient GBA Alumni Achievement award, NYU, 1981. Mem. N.Y. Soc. Security Analysts., N.Y. Fin. Writers Assn. (Elliott V. Bell award), Mont Pelerin Soc., Econ. Club N.Y., Phi Beta Kappa, Phi Beta Kappa Assos. Home: 25 Central Park W New York NY 10023 Office: Barron's Nat Bus & Fin Weekly Dow Jones & Co Inc 200 Liberty St New York NY 10281

BLEIDT, BRADFORD CHESTER, financial planner; b. South Charleston, W.Va., Mar. 12, 1954; s. Robert A. and Mary F. (Gush) B.; m. Denise S. Bleidt; children: Christian, Taylor, Travis. BGS, U. Ky., 1976. Pres. Park Ave. Assocs., Lexington, Ky., 1977-79; agt., rep. Phoenix Mut., Boston, 1980-85; pres. Fin. Perspectives Planning Svcs. Inc., Boston, 1985—. Mem. Internat. Assn. Fin. Planners, Soc. CLUs and Chartered Fin. Cons. Democrat. Methodist. Office: Fin Perspectives Planning Svcs One Exeter Pla Boston MA 02116

BLENKO, WALTER JOHN, JR., lawyer; b. Pitts., June 15, 1926; s. Walter J. and Ardis Leah (Jones) B.; m. Joy Kinneman, Apr. 9, 1949; children—John W., Andrew W. BS, Carnegie-Mellon U., 1950; JD, U. Pitts., 1953. Bar: Pa. 1954. Practice law, Pitts., 1954—; ptnr. Eckert, Seamans, Cherin & Mellott. Active Churchill Vol. Fire Co., 1970-82; charter and hon. mem. Wilkinsburg Emergency Med. Service. Served with U.S. Army, 1944-46, ETO. Decorated Bronze Star. Fellow Am. Coll. Trial Lawyers; mem. ABA, ASME, Pa. Bar Assn., Allegheny County Bar Assn., Am. Patent Law Assn., Patent Law Assn. Pitts. (pres. 1977-78), Assn. Bar City of N.Y., Engrs. Soc. Western Pa., Internat. Patent and Trademark Assn. Clubs: Duquesne, Univ., Rolls-Royce Owners (bd. dirs. 1982-84, v.p. publs. 1984-87, treas. 1987—). Avocation: old cars. Home: 4073 Middle Rd Allison Park PA 15101 Office: Eckert Seamans Cherin & Mellott 600 Grant St Pittsburgh PA 15219

BLESSING, WILLIAM R., telecommunications executive; b. Ft. Belvoir, Va., Aug. 12, 1955; s. Roger F. and Jeanne (Shafer) B.; m. Anne Harlenske, June 16, 1979; 1 child, John R. BS, U. Kans., 1977; MBA, Stanford U., 1981. CPA, Kans. Fin. analyst United Telecom, Shawnee Mission, Kans., 1981-82; mgr. planning U.S. Sprint, Shawnee Mission, 1982-83, dir. fin., 1983-85, v.p. network adminstrn., 1985-86, v.p. strategic mktg., 1986—. Mem. Fin. Execs. Inst., Sigma Chi. Home: 2100 W 61st Terr Shawnee Mission KS 66208 Office: US Sprint PO Box 8417 Shawnee Mission KS 64114

BLEVINS, CHARLES RUSSELL, publishing executive; b. Kittaning, Pa., Apr. 6, 1942; s. Clarence Ray and Elizabeth Sarah (Warren) B.; m. Gale Watkins Crittenden, Dec. 16, 1967; children: Charles Jr., Rush. BS, Ind. U., 1964. Asst. prodn. exec. Wall St. Jour., Cleve., D.C. and Princeton, 1964-71, Gannett Co. Inc., El Paso Agy., El Paso, Tex., 1971-76; prodn. exec. Rockford Newspapers, Rockland, Ill., 1976-77; corp. prodn. dir. Gannett Corp. Hdqrs., Rochester, N.Y., 1977-79; v.p., prodn. Gannett Corp. Hdqrs., Arlington, Va., 1979-89; pres. Chuck Blevins & Assocs., Co., Tysons Corner, Va., 1989—; speaker European Printing Conf., Newspaper Quality Meeting Conf.; chmn. Conf. Quality-Newspaper Assn., chmn. Conf. Research & Engring. Council, Chgo. creator quality standards, operating procedures USA Today, 1981-86. Mem. Am. Newspaper Pub. Assn. (tech. com. 1985—), Research and Engring. Council fo Graphic Arts (v.p., 1985—), Rochester Inst. Tech. Council, W. Va. Inst. Tech. Adv. Council, Inca Fiej Research Assn. (press com.), Sigma Chi. Club: Westwood Country (Vienna). Office: Chuck Blevins Assocs Co 8321 Old Court House Rd Tysons Corner VA 22182

BLEVINS, DONNA LYNNE, real estate executive; b. Oak Ridge, Tenn., Apr. 21, 1949; d. Carl David and Peggy (Reasor) B. BFA in Advt. cum laude, North Tex. State U., 1977. Ind. mktg. cons. 1972—; with Blevins Investment Real Estate, Bonita Springs, Fla., 1983—. Author: (book) Trade Secrets of Buying and Selling Real Estate, 1985, (home study courses) Buy and Sell Real Estate, 1985, 86; creator audio tapes; contbr. articles to profl. jours. Mem. Nat. Assn. Realtors (cert. comml. investment mem.), Fla. Assn. Realtors, Nat. Speakers Assn., Realtors Nat. Mktg. Inst. Office: Blevins Investment Real Estate 27761 New US 41 Bonita Springs FL 33923

BLEVINS, GARY LYNN, architect, real estate broker; b. St. Charles, Ark., Feb. 17, 1941; s. Franklin Monroe and Frances Pauline (Breland) B. BS in Architecture, U. Tex., 1964, BArch, 1969; MBA, So. Meth. U., 1974; postgrad. U. Tex., Dallas, 1975-76. Registered architect, Tex., Fla.; lic. real estate broker, Tex.; cert. Nat. Council Archtl. Registration Bds., Constrn. Specifications Inst. Draftsman, Omniplan Architects, Dallas, 1969-70; project mgr. STB Architects, Dallas, 1970-71; designer Architectonics, Inc., Dallas, 1971-72; architect Envirodynamics, Inc., Dallas, 1972-75; architect/real estate broker Gary L. Blevins Co., Dallas, 1975-77, Trammell Crow Co., Dallas, 1977-83; architect, owner Gary L. Blevins, AIA; real estate broker, owner Gable Cos.; v.p., mgr. Farr Constrn. Co., Dallas, 1983-85; owner Dallas Tennis and Sports Club, 1987—; instr. El Centro Coll., 1981-85. Served with USN, 1964-67, Vietnam. Mem. AIA (coms. design, urban planning), Tex. Soc. Architects, Am. Planning Assn., Nat. Assn. Realtors, Tex. Assn. Realtors, Greater Dallas Bd. Realtors. Constrn. Specifications Inst., The 500, Inc., Dallas Classic Guitar Soc. Dallas Mus. Fine Arts, Dallas Symphony Assn. So. Meth. U. M.B.A. Assn., U.S. Tennis Assn., Tex. Tennis Assn., Dallas Tennis Assn. Republican. Methodist. Home: 1026 Tranquilla Dallas TX 75218 Office: 9400 N Central Expwy Ste 1312 Dallas TX 75214

BLEVINS, WILLIAM EDWARD, banker; b. Pocahontas, Va., Oct. 18, 1927; s. Howard Muncey and Elsie Jane (Wire) B.; m. Mary Hester Jenkins, Aug. 25, 1951; children—Jeffrey Alexander, Jennifer Lynn McEldowney, Bradley Edward. A.B., Marshall Coll., 1951; M.P.A., CCNY, 1960. Personnel mgr. Equitable Life, N.Y.C., 1951-66; asst. v.p., dir. mgmt. devel. Nat. Bank Detroit, 1966-69, v.p., dir. personnel, 1969-74, sr. v.p., dir. personnel, 1974—; sr. v.p., dir. personnel NBD Bancorp, Detroit, 1980—; dir. Blue Cross & Blue Shield Mich., Detroit, Human Resources Council AMA, 1979-84, 87—. Trustee Bon Secour Hosp., Grosse Pointe, Mich., 1975-84; bd. dirs. Oxford Inst., 1987—. Served with USAF, 1946-47. Recipient Outstanding Alumnus award Marshall U., 1976. Mem. Alpha Bank Personnel Group (founder, chmn. 1972-74, 86), Mich. Personnel Indsl. Relations Group (chmn. 1980—), Am. Inst. Banking (bd. dirs., bd. regents, chmn. 1983—), Am. Soc. Employers (bd. dirs. 1970—, treas. 1970—), Bank Adminstrn. Inst. (mem. human resources commn. 1983—), Am. Bankers Assn. (bd. dirs. 1974-75). Republican. Congregationalist. Clubs: Detroit Athletic, Country Club; Grosse Pointe Yacht. Office: NBD Bancorp Inc 611 Woodward Ave Detroit MI 48226

BLICHER, BERT, finance company executive; b. N.Y.C., Dec. 23, 1943; s. Barney and Adele (Zaitz) B.; m. Marci Ann Friedman, Nov. 28, 1979; children: Nicole Robyn, Ryan David. B.B.A., U. Pa., 1972. Prin. P&B Personnel Inc., Phila., 1972-75; pres., chief operating officer Oxford First Corp. and subs., Phila., 1975—; chmn. fin. com. Nat. Timesharing Council; pres. Internat. Found. Time Sharing, Washington. Author (manual) Timeshare Financing, 1984. Bd. dirs. Gatehouse Phila., 1973-79. Named Man of Month, Phila. Jaycees, 1974. Mem. Am. Resort and Residential Devel. Assn. (formerly Am. Land Devel. Assn.) (treas. bd. dirs.), Nat. Second Mortgage Assn., Pa. Employment Assn. (pres. 1974), Phi Sigma Kappa. Office: Oxford First Corp 7300 Old York Rd Philadelphia PA 19126

BLIER, BERNARD BENEDICT, management consultant; b. Scranton, Pa., Sept. 22, 1917; s. Bernard Carl and Margaret Genevieve (McDonough) B.; m. Dorothy Ruth Hayes, July 7, 1956. Student, U. Scranton, 1935-37. Pub. affairs dir. Pa. Dept. Labor and Industry, 1938-42, War Manpower Commn., 1942-43, Office of Price Adminstrn., 1943, VA, Phila., 1945-48; dir. City Planning Commn., Scranton, 1946-67; pub. affairs dir. Scranton C. of C., 1950-54; dir. Scranton Redevel. Authority, 1954-68, Northeastern Pa. Indsl. Devel. Commn., 1950-80; mgmt. cons. Bernard B. Blier & Assocs., Scranton, 1950—; cons. Pa. Coal Research Bd., 1955-62; legis. cons. Pa. Indsl. Devel. Authority, 1955-61; cons. Pa. R.R. Task Force, 1973-74; v.p. govt. affairs Heckethorn Mfg. Co., 1986-87; pres. Heckethorn Techs., 1986—. Dir. Spl. Pa. Senate Com. on Waste Disposal, Recycling and Energy Resources, 1976; cons. U.S. Dept. Commerce energy panel, 1974-75, Fed. Anthracite Task Force, 1978-79, 1984—; exec. v.p. U.S. Anthracite Council, 1985—; devel. cons. U. of Scranton, 1985-87; pres. Mulberry Devel. Corp. Served with AUS, World War II. Mem. Am. Econ. Devel. Council, Nat. Press Club, Am. Commn. on East-West Accord, Am. Mgmt. Assn., Pub. Relations Soc. of Am., Am. Mktg. Assn. Democrat. Roman Catholic. Club: Scranton. Home: 1774 E Mountain Rd Scranton PA 18505 Office: Chamber of Commerce Bldg Scranton PA 18503

BLINDER, MARTIN S., publishing company executive; b. Bklyn., Nov. 18, 1946; s. Meyer and Lillian (Stein) B.; m. Janet Weiss, Dec. 10, 1983. BBA, Adelphi U., 1968. Account exec. Bruns, Nordeman & Co., N.Y.C., 1968-69; v.p. Blinder, Robinson & Co., Westbury, N.Y., 1969-73; treas. BHB Prodns., Los Angeles, 1973-76; pres. Martin Lawrence Ltd. Edits., Van Nuys, Calif., 1976—, also chmn. bd. dirs.; pres., dir. Corp. Art Inc., Visual Artists Mgmt. Corp., Art Consultants Inc.; lectr. bus. symposia. Contbr. articles to mags. and newspapers; appeared on TV and radio. Mem. Dem. Nat. Com.; mem. benefit com. AIDS project, L.A., 1988; bd. dirs. Very Spl. Arts, 1989, chmn. visual arts Internat. Very Spl. Arts Festival, 1989; patron Guggenheim Mus., N.Y.C., Mus. Modern Art, N.Y.C., L.A. County Mus. Art, L.A. Mus. Contemporary Art (hon. founder), Whitney Mus. Am. Art, Palm Springs Mus. Art, Hirschhorn Mus., Washington, Skirball Mus., L.A., Diabetes Found. of City of Hope, B'nai B'rith Anti-Defamation League, Very Spl. Arts; mem. Citizens for Common Sense; bd. dirs., pres. Rsch. Found. for Crohns Disease. Read into Congl. Record, 1981, 83, 86, 88; recipient resolution of commendation L.A. City Coun., 1983, State of Calif. resolution for contbn. to arts in Calif., 1983, Merit award Republic Haiti for contbn. to arts, 1985, U.S. Senate commendation, 1983, County of Los Angeles Bd. Suprs. resolution for Contbn. to arts in So. Calif., 1983, Gov. of R.I. resolution for contbns. to arts, 1985. Nov. 18, 1985 declared Martin S. Blinder Day in Los Angeles in his honor by Mayor Tom Bradley. Office: Martin Lawrence Ltd Edits 16250 Stagg St Van Nuys CA 91406

BLISS, JERRY EVAN, safety engineer; b. Battle Creek, Iowa, Apr. 8, 1949; s. Ernest Dale and Evelyn (Colleran) B.; m. Ann M. Zenk, June 7, 1980. BA, U. No. Iowa, 1979. Electrician Heetland Electric Co., Laurens, Iowa, 1971-75; tchr. driver's edn. Thomas Jefferson High Sch., Council Bluffs, Iowa, 1979-80; safety engr. Aetna Life and Casualty Ins. Co., Omaha, 1980-82, sr. safety engr., 1983-87; supt. safety engring. dept. Aetna Life and Casualty Ins. Co., Des Moines, 1987—. Served with USN, 1967-70, Vietnam. Mem. VFW, Am. Soc. Safety Engrs. Democrat. Roman Catholic. Lodge: KC (trustee, faithful navigator Council Bluffs club). Home: 1549 S 12th Ave W Newton IA 50208 Office: Aetna Life & Casualty 500 E Court Des Moines IA 50309

BLISS, STANLEY MICHAEL, leasing executive; b. Cleve., Oct. 13, 1939; s. George Judson and Rose (Robbins) B.; m. Sheila Bernice Novel, Oct. 26, 1972; children: Gregg, Steven, Marc. BS, Ohio State U., 1961. Analytical reporter Dun & Bradstreet, Cleve., 1962-67; asst. credit mgr. Stouffer Foods Corp., Cleve., 1967-69; credit mgr. Allstate Ins., Cleve., 1969; credit officer Ford Motor Credit Co., Cleve., 1969-79; nat. credit mgr. TransUnion Leasing Corp., Chgo., 1979-82; dir. credit Deutsche Credit Corp., Deerfield, Ill., 1982-84; v.p. credit Heller Fin., Inc., Chgo., 1984-86, Circle Bus. Credit, Indpls., 1986—. Mem. Am. Mgmt. Assn. (assoc.), Am. Assn. Equipment Lessors. Avocations: golf, boating. Home: 1399 Carey Ct Carmel IN 46032 Office: Circle Bus Credit Inc 8720 Castle Creek Pkwy Indianapolis IN 46250

BLITZ, DANIEL, electronics engineer; b. N.Y.C., Feb. 8, 1920; s. Samuel and Amelia (Hirsch) B.; m. Peggy Schulder, Aug. 5, 1963. BS, MIT, 1940. Research engr. Radio Corp. of Am., Camden and Princeton, N.J., 1940-47, Raytheon Mfg. Corp., Waltham, Mass., 1947-51; co-founder Sanders Assocs., Inc., Waltham, 1951; research engr. Sanders Assocs., Inc., Waltham and Nashua, 1951-87; corp. engr. Sanders Assocs., Inc., Nashua, N.H., 1974-80; engring. fellow Sanders Assocs., Inc., 1980-87, cons., 1987—; cons. in field. Patentee in field (50). Chmn. Spl. Com. on Radar Altimeters, Radio Tech. Commn. for Aeronautics, 1979-82; mem. Spl. Com. on Loran-C Receivers, Radio Tech. Commn. for Marine Services., 1978-79. Mem. IEEE (life), Soc. Photographic Scientists and Engrs., Soc. Motion Pictures and TV Engrs., AAAS. Home and Office: 242 Beacon St Boston MA 02116

BLITZSTEIN, DAVID S., benefit consultant; b. Phila., May 5, 1954; s. William and Anna (Golub) B.; m. Edie Ruth Sonnenmark, May 28, 1978; children: Jesse S., Gina Rose. BA, U. Pa., 1976; MS in Labor Studies, U. Mass., 1978. Rsch. assoc. United Food and Comml. Workers, Washington, 1978-84; rsch. economist United Mine Workers Am., Washington, 1984-87; union trustee 1978 Retired Constrn. Benefit Trust, Washington, 1984—, United Mine Workers Am. 1985 Constrn. Workers Pension Plan, Washington, 1985—; adminstr. corp. campaign office United Mine Workers Am., Washington, 1987-89; sr. benefit cons. Poulin Assocs., Inc., Washington, 1989—; rep. Coun. Instl. Investors, Washington, 1988—; mem. labor com. U.S. Bur. Labor Stats., Washington, 1980—. Mem. Internat. Found. Employee Benefits, Indsl. Rels. Rsch. Assn. Democrat. Jewish. Home: 2701 Beechmont Ln Silver Spring MD 20906 Office: Poulin Assocs Inc 1250 24th St NW Ste 600 Washington DC 20037

BLIWAS, JAMES CHARLES, financial planning company executive; b. Milw., Nov. 3, 1946; s. Philip R. and Joyce Shirley (Strauss) B. BA, U. Minn., 1968; postgrad., U. Chgo., Purdue U., 1976, 85. With Sta. WCCO-TV, Mpls., 1966-68; bus. correspondent Sta. KTVU-TV, San Francisco, 1968-71; asst. editor Bus. Week Mag., Chgo., 1971-76; dir. planning and bus. devel. Mid Am. Commodity Exchange, Chgo., 1976-80; sr. cons. N.Y Stock Exchange, 1980-82; staff aide, pres. com. productivity The White House, Washington, 1981; exec. v.p. Von Hertzen Fin. Services, Inc., Hopkins, Minn., 1982-89; dir. mktg. Oppenheimer, Wolff & Donnelly, St. Paul, 1989—. Author: The Bellini Letter, 1985; writer, producer: (TV program) Daytime, 1982; writer: (TV movies) Throwaway Kids, 1982, Fox-Hunt, 1983; producer, host radio program "A Matter of Money", 1989—. Bd. dirs. Hopkins Area Little League, 1985—, coach, 1984—. Mem. Entrepreneur's Resource Group, Nat. Assn. Law Firm Mktg. Profls., Inner Circle Forum, Nat. Assn. Life Underwriters, Minn. Assn. Life Underwriters, Million Dollar Round Table. Office: Oppenheimer Wolff & Donnelly 1700 First Bank Bldg Saint Paul MN 55101

BLIWAS, PHILIP R., insurance executive, tax and financial planner; b. Milw., June 28, 1920; s. Rubin and Caroline B.; student U. Wis., 1937-40, U. Ind., 1946-47; LLB, Marquette U., 1947; postgrad. Columbia U., 1942, Ind. U. Law Sch., 1946-47, Purdue U. Ins. Inst., 1980-81. Cert. farm estate planning U. Minn., 1977; cert. Keypact Inst. Advanced Studies, 1979; m. Joyce Shirley Strauss; children: James Charles, Janice M. Sec., Charles Strauss Shoes, Milw., 1947-51; pres., gen. mgr., chief exec. officer Korbe Shoe, Inc., Mpls., 1951-74; field underwriter N.Y. Life Ins. Co., 1975-79; gen. agt., owner Philip Bliwas Agy., Chaska, Minn., 1978—; founder, chief exec. officer Janus Fin. Mktg. Corp., 1980-84, Von Hertzen Fin. Services, Inc., 1978-86; speaker fin. seminars, 1987-88. Del. to county and state convs. Minn. Dem. Farm Labor Party, 1972, 76, 80; vol. work Carver County Family Services, sr. citizens tax preparation. Served to lt. USN, 1941-46; PTO. Recipient Life Ins. Nat. Sales Achievement ann. award Nat. Assn. Life Underwriters, 1978-82, Nat. Quality award, 1977, 78, 81; named Top Life Ins. Producer of 1981, Nat. Travelers Life Co. Mem. Nat. Assn. Life Underwriters, Million Dollar Round Table (life, qualifying, Top of Table 1982). Home: 110922 Von Hertzen Cir Chaska MN 55318 Office: Philip Bliwas Agy Hopkins MN 55343

BLOCH, BARRY STEVEN, retail executive; b. St. Louis, Mar. 23, 1948; s. Gustav and Mildred Bloch; m. Denise Helene Zabrack; children: Robert Lawrence, Margaret Sarah. BS in Bus. Adminstrn., Drake U., 1970; JD, Northwestern U., 1974. Bars: Ill., Nebr. Staff v.p. Kimberly-Clark Corp., Neenah, Wis., 1976-84; v.p. Jaffe Lighting & Supply, Inc., St. Louis, 1984—. Mem. Beta Gamma Sigma.

BLOCH, HENRY WOLLMAN, tax preparation company executive; b. Kansas City, Mo., July 30, 1922; s. Leon Edwin and Hortense Bienenstok; m. Marion Ruth Helzberg, June 16, 1951; children: Robert, Thomas M., Mary Jo, Elizabeth Ann. BS, U. Mich., 1943; DBA (hon.), Avila Coll., Kansas City, Mo., 1977; LLD (hon.), N.H. Coll., 1983. Ptnr. United Bus. Co., 1946-55; pres., chief exec. officer H & R Block, Inc., Kansas City, 1955—, also dir.; dir. Commerce Bankshares, Inc., Kansas City, Southwestern Bell Corp., CompuServe, Inc., Graphic Tech. Past trustee Clearinghouse for Midcontinent Founds.; past bd. dirs. Menorah Med. Ctr.; bd. dirs., past pres. Menorah Med. Ctr. Found.; former mem. pres.'s adv. coun. Kansas City Philharmonic Assn.; chmn., dir. H & R Block Found.; pres. of trustees U. Kansas City, Nelson-Atkins Mus. Art; former trustee Am. Mus. Assn.; bd. dirs. Jewish Fedn. and Coun. Greater Kansas City; dir., past pres. Civic Coun. Greater Kansas City; gen. chmn. United Negro Colls. Fund, 1986; bd. dirs. St. Luke's Hosp.; former mem. bd. dirs. Coun. of Fellows of Nelson Gallery Found., Am. Jewish Com.; former mem. bd. govs. Kansas City Mus. History and Sci.; bd. dirs. Midwest Rsch. Inst., Kansas City Symphony, Greater Kansas City Community Found.; gen. chmn. Heart of Am. United Way Exec. Com., 1978; past met. chmn. Nat. Alliance Businessmen; former mem. bd. regents Rockhurst Coll.; former mem. bd. chancellor's assocs. U. Kans. at Lawrence; former mem. bd. dirs. Harry S. Truman Good Neighbor Award Found.; bd. dirs. Internat. Rels. Coun.; bd. dirs., v.p. Kansas City Area Health Planning Coun.; past pres. Found. for a Greater Kansas City; dir. Mid-Am. Coalition on Health Care, St; Luke's Found.; trustee Jr. Achievement of Mid-Am.; vice chmn. corp. fund Kennedy Ctr.; 1st lt. USAAF, 1943-45. Decorated Air medal with 3 oak leaf clusters; named Mktg. Man of Yr. Sales and Mktg. Execs. Club, 1971, Chief Exec. Officer of Yr. for svc. industry Fin. World, 1976, Mainstreeter of Decade, 1988, Entrepreneur of Yr., 1986; recipient Disting. Exec. award Boy Scouts Am., 1977, Salesman of Yr. Kansas City Advt. Club, 1978, Civic Svc. award Hyman Brand Hebrew Acad., 1980, Golden Plate award Am. Acad. Achievement, 1980, Chancellor's medal U. Mo.-Kansas City, 1980, Pres.'s trophy Kansas City Jaycees, 1980, W.F. Yates medal for disting. svc. in civic affairs William Jewell Coll., 1981, bronze award for svc. industry Wall Street Transcript, 1981, Disting. Missourian award NCCJ, 1982, Lester A. Milgram Humanitarian award, 1983, Hall of Fame award Internat. Franchise Assn., 1983; named to Bus. Leader Hall of Fame Jr. Achievement, 1980. Mem. Greater Kansas City C. of C. (past pres.), C. of C. Greater Kansas City (Mr. Kansas City award 1978), Oakwood Country Club, River Club, Carriage Club, Kansas City Racquet Club. Jewish. Office: H&R Block Inc 4410 Main St Kansas City MO 64111

BLOCH, PAUL, public relations executive; b. Bklyn., July 17, 1939; s. Edwin Lionel and Antoinette (Greenberg) B. B.B. Polit. Sci., UCLA, 1962. Publicist Rogers & Cowan, Beverly Hills, Calif., 1962-70, v.p., 1970-75, sr. v.p., ptnr., 1975-83, exec. v.p., sr. ptnr., 1983—. Advisor Pres.'s Council on Phys. Fitness and Sports, Washington, 1982—; asst. Am. Cancer Soc., United Way, Am. Diabetes Assn., UNICEF, 1975—; adv. council Orange County Sheriff's Dept., 1980—. Served with U.S. Army, 1957. Mem. Publicists Guild of Am. (award for publicity campaign for Brian's Song 1972), Country Music Assn. Clubs: Pips. Office: Rogers & Cowan 10000 Santa Monica 4th Fl Los Angeles CA 90067

BLOCK, DOUGLAS CARL, wholesale company executive; b. Lancaster, Wis., Sept. 8, 1953; s. LeRoy Carl and Marjorie Eleanor (Hickin) B.; m. Shirley Ann Dimmer, May 26, 1979; children: Daniel LeRoy, Kristin Marie, Bryan Douglas. BS, U. Wis., 1974, MBA, 1976. CPA, Wis. Acct. Peat, Marwick, Mitchell & Co., Rock Island, Ill., 1975; sr. acct. Great-Thornton, Madison, Wis., 1976-80; controller Rowley-Schlimgen, Inc., Madison, Wis., 1980-81; v.p. Bryant Industries, Inc., Madison, Wis., 1981-86; sec.-treas. Automatic Temperature Supplies, Inc., Madison, Wis., 1986—. Mem. Am. Inst. CPA's, Wis. Soc. CPA's. Office: Automatic Temperature Supplies Inc 1023 E Main St Madison WI 53703

BLOCK, LEONARD NATHAN, drug company executive; b. Bklyn., Dec. 21, 1911; s. Alexander and Tillie (Goetz) B.; m. Adele Goldberg, Oct. 8, 1936; children: Peggy Davis (Mrs. Richard M. Danziger), Thomas Roger. B.S., U. Pa., 1933; L.H.D. (hon.), Mt. Sinai Sch. Medicine, 1985. Sr. chmn. Block Drug Co., Inc., Jersey City, 1933—. Mem. N.Y.C. Com. of Foster Care of Children, 1966-69; mem. Bd. Social Welfare, 1969-77, vice chmn., 1974-77; treas. Child Welfare Info. Services, 1972-84; bd. dirs. Welfare Research, Inc., 1980; Bd. dirs. Fedn. Jewish Philanthropies, 1953—, asso. chmn. bd., chmn. distbn. com., 1958-63, chmn. communal planning com., 1964-68; bd. dirs., treas. Lincoln Ctr. for the Performing Arts, 1977-84. Recipient award N.Y. State Welfare Conf., 1972, Naomi and Howard Lehman award, 1974, Disting. Service award Fedn. Jewish Philanthropies, 1984. Clubs: Harmonie, Hollywood Golf, Ocean Beach. Home: 535 Park Ave New York NY 10021 Office: Block Drug Co Inc 257 Cornelison Ave Jersey City NJ 07302

BLOCK, PAMELA JO, vocational administrator; b. Freeport, Ill., May 25, 1947; d. Carl and Leona Mae (Stukenberg) B. BS, Iowa State U., 1969; MEd, U. Ill., 1973. Tchr. Palatine (Ill.) High Sch., 1969-85, dept. chairperson, 1973-85; mgr. N.W. Suburban Career Coop., Palatine, 1985—; cons. Household Internat., Prospect Heights, Ill., 1982-83; evaluator Ill. State Bd. Edn., 1976—. Contbr. articles to profl. jours. Bd. dirs. Ill. Women's Agenda, Chgo., 1986-87; mem. Suburban Adv. Council United Way, 1984-87. Named one of Outstanding Young Women of Ill., 1982, Charlotte Danforth Woman of Achievement, N.W. suburban chpt. Women in Mgmt., 1989. Mem. AAUW (pres. Wheeling-Buffalo Grove, Ill. br. 1982-84, chair Ill. div. found. 1985-87, program com., cons. nat. found. 1987—, mem. rsch. adv. panel 1989—), Am. Vocat. Assn. Lutheran. Lodge: Rotary (vocat. service com. chair Buffalo Grove club 1987-88). Home: 190 Woodstone Dr Buffalo Grove IL 60089 Office: NW Suburban Career Coop 1750 S Roselle Rd Palatine IL 60067

BLOCK, RUTH, retired insurance company executive; b. N.Y.C., Nov. 7, 1930; d. Albert and Celia (Shapiro) Smolensky; BA, Adelphi U., 1952; m. Norman Block, April 5, 1952. With Equitable Life Assurance Soc. of U.S., 1952-87, v.p., planning officer, 1973-77, sr. v.p. in charge individual life ins. bus., 1977-80, exec. v.p. individual ins. bus.'s, 1980-87, duties expanded to include all individual and small group lines of bus., group life and health bus.'s, chief ins. officer, 1984-87; bd. dirs. Amoco Corp., Avon, Ecolab Inc., Tandem Fin. Group, 12 ACM Mut. Funds; trustee Life Underwriter Tng. Coun., 1983-85; chmn., chief exec. officer Equitable Variable Life Ins. Co., 1981-84; vis. exec. Mobil Co. U. Iowa, 1978. Bd. dirs. Stamford (Conn.) YWCA, 1977-80; nat. chmn. Equitable United Way, 1978. Recipient Disting. Alumni award Adelphi U. Sch. of Bus., 1979, Catalyst award 1983, WEAL award, 1983, N.Y.C. YMCA award. Mem. Nat. Assn. Securities Dealers (gov. at large 1982-84), Data Processing Mgmt. Assn., Com. of 200. Office: PO Box 4653 Stamford CT 06906

BLODGETT, ELSIE GRACE, association executive; b. Eldorado Springs, Mo., Aug. 2, 1921; d. Charles Ishmal and Naoma Florence (Worthington) Robison; m. Charles Davis Blodgett, Nov. 8, 1940; children: Carolyn Doyel, Charleen Bier, Lyndon Blodgett. Student Warrensburg (Mo.) State Tchrs. Coll., 1939-40; BA, Fresno (Calif.) State Coll., 1953. Tchr. schs. in Mo. and Calif., 1940-42, 47-72; owner, mgr. rental units, 1965—; exec. dir. San Joaquin County (Calif.) Rental Property Assn., Stockton, 1970-81; prin. Delta Rental Property Owners and Assocs., 1981-82; propr. Crystal Springs Health World, Inc., Stockton, 1980-86; bd. dirs. Stockton Better Bus. Bur. Active local PTA, Girl Scouts U.S., Boy Scouts Am.; bd. dirs. Stockton

Goodwill Industries. Named (with husband) Mr. and Mrs. Apt. Owner of San Joaquin County, 1977. Mem. Nat. Apt. Assn. (state treas. women's div. 1977-79), Calif. Ret. Tchrs. Assn. Republican. Methodist. Lodge: Stockton Zonta. Home and Office: 2285 W Mendocino Ave Stockton CA 95204

BLODGETT, FORREST CLINTON, economics educator; b. Oregon City, Oreg., Oct. 6, 1927; s. Clinton Alexander and Mabel (Wells) B.; B.S., U. Omaha, 1961; M.A., U. Mo., 1969; Ph.D., Portland State U., 1979; m. Beverley Janice Buchholz, Dec. 21, 1946; children—Cherine (Mrs. Jon R. Klein), Candis Melis, Clinton George. Joined C.E., U.S. Army, 1946, commd. 2d lt., 1946, advanced through grades to lt. col., 1965; ret. 1968; engring. assignments Japan, 1947-49, U.K., 1950-53, Korea, 1955-56, Alaska, 1958-60, Vietnam, 1963; staff engr. 2d Army Air Def. Region, Richards-Gebaur AFB, Mo., 1964-66; base engr. Def. Atomic Support Agy., Sandia Base, N.Mex., 1966-68; bus. mgr., trustee, asst. prof. econs. Linfield Coll., McMinnville, Oreg., 1968-73, assoc. prof., 1973-83, prof., 1983—; pres. Blodgett Enterprises, Inc., 1983-85; founder, dir. Valley Community Bank, 1980-86, vice chmn. bd. dirs., 1985-86. Commr., Housing Authority of Yamhill County (Oreg.), chmn., 1980-83; mem. Yamhill County Econ. Devel. Com., 1978-83; bd. dirs. Yamhill County Found., 1983—. Decorated Army Commendation medal with oak leaf cluster; recipient Joint Service Commendation medal Dept. of Def. Mem. Soc. Am. Mil. Engrs. (pres. Albuquerque post 1968), Am. Econ. Assn., Western Econ. Assn. Internat., Nat. Retired Officers Assn., Res. Officers Assn. (pres. Marion chpt. 1976), SAR (pres. Oreg. soc. 1985-86), Urban Affairs Assn., Pi Sigma Epsilon, Pi Gamma Mu, Omicron Delta Epsilon (Pacific NW regional dir. 1978—). Republican. Episcopalian. Lodge: Rotary (pres. McMinnville club 1983-84). Office: Linfield Coll McMinnville OR 97128

BLODGETT, FRANK CALEB, food company executive; b. Janesville, Wis., Apr. 22, 1927; s. Frank Caleb Pickard and Dorothy (Korst) B.; m. Jean Ellen Fountain, June 23, 1951; children: Caleb J., Barbara F., David K. Grad., Beloit Coll., 1950; postgrad., Advanced Mgmt. Program, Harvard U., 1969. First v.p., dir. Frank H. Blodgett Inc., Janesville, 1947-61, pres., dir., 1961-62; with Gen. Mills Inc., Mpls., 1961—, v.p., dir. mktg., 1967-69, gen. mgr., v.p., 1969-73, group v.p., 1973-76, exec. v.p., 1976-80, vice chmn., 1981—, chief fin. and adminstrv. officer, 1985—; dir. Gen. Mills Inc., 1980—; dir. Medtronic, Inc., Northwestern Nat. Life Ins. Co., Diversified Energies, Inc.; bd. dirs. Cereal Inst., 1970-76, chmn., 1973-74: trustee Nutrition Found., 1980-84, Gen. Mills Found., 1980—. Trustee Washburn Child Guidance Center, 1972-75, Beloit Coll., 1976—. Served with U.S. Navy, 1944-46, PTO. Mem. Millers Nat. Fedn., Young Millers Orgn. (past pres.), U.S. C. of C. (bd. dirs. 1982-88), Greater Mpls. C. of C. (bd. dirs. 1975-76), Phi Kappa Psi (trustee alumni bd. Beloit 1961-62), Phi Eta Sigma. Home: 688 Hillside Dr Wayzata MN 55391 Office: Gen Mills Inc 1 General Mills Blvd PO Box 1113 Minneapolis MN 55426-1348

BLOEMSMA, MARCO PAUL, investor; b. Heemstede, Netherlands, July 20, 1924; s. Philippus and Wilhelmina Geertruida (Bonebakker) B.; LLM, Leyden U., 1948; m. Mieke Harten, Sept. 23, 1955; children: Marco Reinier, Barbara Patricia, Michiel Alexander. Lawyer firm van der Feltz, Voûte & Riechelmann, 1948-49; assoc., then ptnr. Blackstone, Rueb & van Boeschoten, 1951-72; pres. C. Harten Holding B.V., The Hague, 1972-85; pres. Bloemsma Holding B.V.; hon. chmn. KTI-group; chmn. Ten Doesschate-group; dir. Volvo Bedryfswages B.V., Mauritshuis Found.; positions held include: dir., pres. chmn. Patino-group; chmn. Lips United-group, ICL Nederland B.V., Auto-Palace-group; dir. Mobil Chemie B.V., Ambac B.V., Ned. Mij. Mijnbouwkundige Werken N.V., Polak & Schwarz N.V., Lockheed Europe N.V., Vulcaansoord N.V., Merck Sharp en Dohme Nederland N.V., Svenska Metallverken/Granges Nederland B.V., Author nat. reports on fiscal and corp. subjects. Served with Dutch Naval Reserve, 1949-51. Hon. Ky. col. since 1962. Clubs: Cercle Interalliée (Paris); Amstel (Amsterdam); Wittenburg (Wassenaar); Royal Bachelors (Gothenborg); Cercle Litteraire (Lausanne). Home: 5 Ave de Crousaz, 1010 Lausanne Switzerland

BLOM, NICOLE JAN, advertising sales executive; b. Seattle, Oct. 3, 1958; d. Daniel Charles and Ellen Lavon (Stewart) B. Student Am. Conservatory Theatre, 1978; BA in Theatre, U. Wash., 1981. Profl. dancer, actress, Seattle, 1976-80; assoc. dir. devel. pub. rels. officer The Bush Sch., Seattle, 1981-83; acctg. rep., advt. dir. Pacific Northwest mag., Seattle, 1983-86; assoc. advt. mgr. Esquire mag., N.Y.C., 1986-88; mgr. eastern advt. Esquire mag., 1988—. Fund raising co-chmn. Bob Ellis for Wash. State Legislature, 1982. Mem. Advt. Women of N.Y., U. Wash. Alumni Assn., Gamma Phi Beta Alumni Assn. Clubs: Women's Univ., Junior League of N.Y. Avocations: sailing, reading, travel, skiing.

BLOMBERG, ROBERT N., underwriter; b. New Britain, Conn., July 14, 1956; s. Norman and Ingrid (Young) B.; m. Lori J. Fanning, May 9, 1987. BS, Barrington Coll., 1978; MBA, U. Conn., 1985. Mgr. D.M. Reed, Inc. div. Allied Stores, Trumbull, Conn., 1978-80; underwriter, asst. sec. Travelers Ins. Co., Hartford, Conn., 1980—. Active Wintonbury Ch., Bloomfield, Conn., 1976—, Big Bros./Big Sisters Conn., Hartford, 1987—; violinist Farmington (Conn.) Symphony, 1982—. Home: 75 Hilltop Dr Simsbury CT 06070 Office: The Travelers One Tower Sq Hartford CT 06183

BLOMQUIST, ROBERT OSCAR, banker; b. Passaic, N.J., Aug. 19, 1930; s. Oscar and Adeline Louise (Hotaling) B.; m. Audrey M. Korn, Apr. 4, 1954; children: Dana C., Carin E. BA, Allegheny Coll., Meadville, Pa., 1952; MS, Columbia, 1953. With Chase Manhattan Bank, N.Y.C., 1957-76; gen. mgr. Chase Manhattan Bank, U.K., 1970; regional exec. Chase Manhattan Bank, U.K., Scandinavia, Africa, 1971; sr. v.p., group exec. Chase Manhattan Bank, Europe and Africa, 1971-74, Nat. Banking Group, 1975-76; pres., dir. Chase Manhattan Leasing Corp., Chase Nat. Svcs. Corp., Chase Manhattan Realty Leasing Corp., 1974-76; chmn. Chase Banks-Internat., Chgo., L.A. and Houston, 1974-76; pres., dir. Franklin State Bank, Somerset, N.J., 1976-80; vice chmn., dir. Mercantile Bank, N.A., St.Louis, 1980-87; chief credit officer Integra Fin. Corp., Pitts., 1988—; bd. dirs. Luth. Brotherhood Life Ins. Co., Mpls.; dir. Robert Morris Assocs., 1987-88. Contbr. articles to profl. jours. Bd. dirs. Luther N.W. Sem., St. Paul, 1982-85; trustee Thiel Coll., Greenville, Pa., 1988—. Lt. USNR, 1954-59. Mem. Bellerive Country Club (St. Lousi), Univ. Club (St. Louis), Duquesne Club (Pa.). Home: 2044 Lake Marshall Dr Gibsonia PA 15044 Office: Integra Fin Corp 4th & Wood Sts Pittsburgh PA 15222

BLOOD, EDWARD LINFORD, consumer products company executive; b. Logan, Utah, Sept. 17, 1945; s. Howard L. and Marcelle (Linford) B.; m. Martha Louise Hughes, Dec. 18, 1969; children: Laurie Jean, Amy Louise, Timothy Edward, Kristen Elizabeth. Security analyst Smith Barney & Co., N.Y.C., 1971-75; sr. industry analyst Baker, Weeks & Co., N.Y.C., 1975-77; v.p. research Dain Bosworth & Co., Mpls., 1977-81; dir. strategic analysis Gen. Mills Inc., Mpls., 1981-85, dir. strategic analysis and investor communications, 1985-86, v.p. strategic planning and analysis, 1986—. Bd. dirs. Bus. Econ. Edn. Found., Mpls., 1988—. SP4 USNG, 1968-74. Fellow Chartered Fin. Analysts (chartered 1977); mem. The Planning Forum (pres. 1985-86), Twin Cities Security Analysts. Office: General Mills Inc 1 General Mills Blvd Minneapolis MN 55426

BLOOM, ARNOLD SANFORD, lawyer; b. Syracuse, N.Y., Sept. 3, 1942; s. Benjamin and Sarah (Kushner) B.; m. Cirelle Dvorin, July 20, 1967; children: Brooke, Jessica, Evan. B.S., Syracuse U., 1964, M.B.A., 1967, J.D., 1967; LL.M., NYU, 1968. Bar: N.Y. 1967, U.S. Dist. Ct. (so. dist.) N.Y. 1972, U.S. Supreme Ct. 1986. Assoc. Marshall, Bratter, Greene, Allison & Tucker, N.Y.C., 1968-74; sr. atty. Kane-Miller Corp., Tarrytown, N.Y., 1974-78, gen. counsel, 1978-87, v.p., 1980-87; v.p., gen. counsel Russ Berrie and Co., Inc., Oakland, N.J., 1988—. Mem. ABA, N.Y. State Bar Assn., Order of Coif, Justinian Soc., Beta Alpha Psi, Alpha Kappa Psi. Home: 8 Suzanne Ln Chappaqua NY 10514 Office: Russ Berrie & Co Inc 111 Bauer Dr Oakland NJ 07436

BLOOM, DAVID RONALD, retail drugs company executive; b. Toronto, Can., Apr. 20, 1943; s. Samuel and Tillie Bloom; m. Molly Rosenbloom, May 8, 1966; children: Corinne, Michael. BSc in Pharmacy, U. Toronto, 1967. Pharmacist Plaza Drugs, Toronto; assoc. Shoppers Drug Mart Ltd., Toronto, dir. ops., v.p. ops., exec. v.p. ops., pres. cen. Ont. and Man. regions, pres., chief exec. officer, 1983—, also chmn. bd. dirs.; pres. Top Drug Mart, Toronto; chief exec. officer, chmn. Imasco Drug Retailing Group, Toronto, 1987—, Peoples Drugs, Alexandria, 1987—. Co-chmn. Juvenile Diabetes Found., Toronto, 1987; bd. dirs. Mi. Sinai Hosp., Toronto. Mem. Young Pres. Orgn., Imasco Ltd. (bd. dirs.), Can. Trust (bd. dirs.), Retail Council Can. (bd. dirs.), Koffler Inst. for Pharmacy Mgmt. (bd. dirs.). Office: Shoppers Drug Mart, 225 Yorkland Blvd, Willowdale, ON Canada M2J 4Y7 other: Peoples Drug Stores Inc 6315 Bren Mar Dr Alexandria VA 22312

BLOOM, HAROLD EDWARD, marketing executive; b. N.Y.C., May 4, 1946; s. Sidney and Rose B.; BBA, U. Miami, 1968; MBA, City U. N.Y., 1971; m. Ellen T. Friedman, July 14, 1973; children: Allison, Robert. Project dir. Monar Market Planning, N.Y.C., 1968-71; asst. tech. dir. Grey Advt., N.Y.C., 1971-73; market research mgr. ITT Continental Baking, Rye, N.Y., 1973-74; mgr. consumer research Coca-Cola, Atlanta, 1973-78; dir. market research Pillsbury Co., Mpls., 1978-79; dir. market research STP Corp., Ft. Lauderdale, Fla., 1979-82; pres. Cons. in Mktg. Research, Coral Springs, Fla., 1982-84; v.p. mktg. research Tupperware Worldwide, Orlando, Fla., 1984—. Mem. Am. Mktg. Assn., Advt. Fedn. Greater South Fla., Am. Mgmt. Assn. Home: 400 Beech Tree Ln Longwood FL 32779 Office: Tupperware Worldwide PO Box 2353 Orlando FL 32802

BLOOM, JAMES EDWARD, financial company executive; b. Milw., Aug. 24, 1941; s. Edward Harry and Clarina Louise (Hoppe) B. Cert. in radiology tech., Columbia Hosp., 1963; AA in Edn. with honors, Milw. Area Tech. Coll., 1964; BBA in Sales and Mktg. Bus. Mgmt. with honors, Concordia Coll., 1968; postgrad. in mgmt. scis., Marquette U., 1969-72. Radiologic technologist Columbia Hosp., Milw., 1963-69; asst. adminstr. Bel Air Convalescent Ctr., Inc., Milw., 1969-70; asst. mktg. mgr. Champion Internat. Inc., Milw., 1970-72, human resources mgr., safety and tng. dir., 1972-75; corp. dir. indsl. rels. Weyenburg Shoe Mfg. Co., Milw., 1975; gen. mgr. Aqua Spray, Inc., Milw., 1976; mgmt. cons. Bloom & Assocs., Milw., 1976—; pres. Mortgage Fin. Co., Milw., 1985—; guest lectr. mgmt. Milw. Area Tech. Coll., 1974-75, Marquette U., Milw., 1975, U. Wis., Milw., 1975; advisor on bus. devel. State of Wis., 1978—. Mem. Am. Mgmt. Assn., Am. Soc. for Tng. and Devel., Indsl. Rels. Rsch. Assn., Am. Soc. for Personnel Adminstrn., Am. Soc. Safety Engrs., Assn. for Corp. Growth, Am. Soc. Radiologic Technologists. Home: 8060 N Navaho Rd Fox Point WI 53217 Office: Mortgage Fin Corp 1 Park Pla 11270 W Park Pla Milwaukee WI 53224

BLOOM, MICHAEL EUGENE, communications executive; b. Pittsburg, Calif., Jan. 16, 1947; s. Benjamin Bernard and Mildred (Haims) B.; m. Deborah Ann Bresler, Aug. 6, 1977; children: Benjamin Solomon Bresler, Miriam Hannah Bresler. BA in Sociology, U. Calif.-Santa Barbara, 1969, postgrad. elec. engring., 1969-71; MBA, Stanford U., 1979. Broadcaster, Sta. KCSB-FM, Santa Barbara, 1964-68, gen. mgr., 1968-69; broadcaster KKIS-AM, Pittsburg, Calif., 1965, KMUZ-FM, Santa Barbara, 1965-67, KTMS-AM-FM, Santa Barbara, 1967-69; mem. tech. staff Gen. Rsch. Corp., Santa Barbara, 1970-72; mgmt. scientist, cons. Sci. Applications, Inc., LaJolla, Calif., 1973-74, Planning and Mgmt. Cons. Corp., Cleve., 1974, Bloom Enterprises, Santa Monica, Calif., 1975-77; project team leader, sr. programmer Bendix Field Engring. Corp., Sunnyvale, Calif., 1977; retail product planner Crocker Nat. Bank, San Francisco, 1978; dir. corp. devel. Am. TV & Communications Corp., Englewood, Colo., 1979-82, dir. new bus. devel., 1983-84, dir. bus. and tech. devel., 1984-85; dir. video svcs. devel. Pacific Bell, San Francisco, 1985-86, dir. product strategy and devel., San Ramon, Calif., 1986-87, dir. market strategy group, 1987-88, dir. customer premises Broadband Mktg. div., 1988—, Japan task force, 1988—; chmn. communications bd. U. Calif.-Santa Barbara; v.p., bd. dir. Intercollegiate Broadcasting System, Inc., 1967-70; founder, dir. U. Calif. Radio Network, 1967-69; chmn. systems standards task force on teletext Nat. Cable TV Assn., 1980-81. Adv. coun. Coll. Info. Studies, U. Denver, 1982-85. Recipient Pres.'s Merit award U. Calif., 1965. Mem. IEEE, Am. Mktg. Assn. (exec.), Soc. Cable TV Engrs., Nat. Cable TV Assn., U. Calif.-Santa Barbara Alumni Assn. (life), Stanford U. Bus. Sch. Alumni Assn. (program chmn. Rocky Mountain chpt. 1982-85), Stanford U. Alumni Assn. (life). Author: (with L.A. Sibley) Carrier Current System Design, 1967. Office: Pacific Bell 2600 Camino Ramon 1 S 953 San Ramon CA 94583

BLOOM, RODNEY MERLIN, chemical company executive; b. Davenport, Iowa, Aug. 25, 1933; s. Frederick Merlin and Zelma Irene (Gilbert) B.; m. Mary Lou Jones, Oct. 3, 1952; children: Robert, Dean, Lynne, Jeffrey, Cathleen. BS in Acctg., U. Iowa, 1959; postgrad., Harvard U., 1978, Stanford U., 1979. CPA, Ill. Audit supr. Ernst and Whinney, Chgo., 1959-66; mgr. fin. ops. Nalco Chem. Co., Naperville, Ill., 1966-68, asst. treas., 1968-69, treas., 1969-75, controller, 1969-75, v.p., 1975-81, sr. v.p., chief fin. officer, 1981—; bd. dirs. Nalcomex, Mex., Nalfloc Ltd., Eng., Nalco Chem. Ltd., Hong Kong. Served with U.S. Army, 1953-55. Mem. Am. Inst. CPAs, Ill. Soc. CPAs, Fin. Execs. Inst., Econ. Club. Republican. Lutheran. Club: Glen Oak Country (Glen Ellyn, Ill.). Home: 21W745 Dorchester Ct Glen Ellyn IL 60137 Office: Nalco Chem Co 1 Nalco Ctr Naperville IL 60566

BLOOM, STUART PERCY, management consultant; b. Port Elizabeth, Republic of South Africa, Dec. 2, 1952; s. Barnet and Miriam (Kolnick) B. B Comml. Sci., Rhodes U., S. Africa, 1975; cert. theory accountancy, U. Cape Town, S.Africa, 1977; MBA, NYU, 1980. CPA, Tex.; chartered acct., Republic of South Africa. Acct., mgmt. cons. Bass Gordon Willis, Cape Town, 1975-78; sr. mgr. mgmt. adv. services Deloitte Haskins & Sells, N.Y.C., 1980—. Contbr. gen. mgmt. articles to profl. jours. Mem. Inst. Mgmt. Cons., Am. Inst. CPA's, South African Inst. Chartered Accts., The Plannning Forum, Assn. For Corp. Growth.

BLOOMFIELD, KEITH MARTIN, management consultant; b. Bronx, N.Y., Sept. 11, 1951; s. Monroe Louis and Shirley B. (Mason) B.; B.A., Windham Coll., 1973; M.S., Syracuse U., 1974; m. Adrienne Donna Young, Sept. 2, 1979. Personnel/cons. Automatic Data Processing Inc., Clifton, N.J., 1975-78; cons. European Am. Bank, N.Y.C., 1978-79; cons. Consol. Edison N.Y., 1979-81; div. mgr. Pepsi-Cola Mgmt. Inst., Purchase, 1981-87 ; cons. Pepsi-Cola Co., Purchase, 1981-87; sr. program mgr. Learning Internat., Stamford, Conn., 1987—; pres. Katbird Communications, White Plains, N.Y., 1977—. Mem. public info. com. Westchester div. Am. Cancer Soc.; mem.-at-large Am. Cancer Soc.; mem. White Plains Bd. Edn. Adv. Com. on Cable TV; trustee Temple Israel Ctr. Mem. Nat. Acad. TV Arts and Scis., Syracuse U. Alumni. Club: Men's (pres.). Contbr. short stories to various publs.; writer stage and screen plays. Home: 260 Garth Rd Scarsdale NY 10583

BLOOMGARDEN, KATHLEEN FINN, public relations executive; b. N.Y.C., June 9, 1949; d. David and Laura (Zeisler) Finn; m. Zachary Bloomgarden; children: Rachel, Keith, Matthew. BA, Brown U., 1970; MA, Columbia U., PhD. Pres. Rsch. & Forecasts, N.Y.C., Ruder, Finn & Rotman, N.Y.C., 1988—. Bd. dirs. N.Y. Arthritis Found. Mem. Pub. Relations Soc. Am., Nat. Investor Relations Inst., Pharm. Advt. Coun., Swedish-Am. C. of C, CARE (bd. dirs.). Jewish. Home: 1084 North Ave New Rochelle NY 10804 Office: Ruder Finn & Rotman Inc 301 E 57th St New York NY 10022

BLOSKAS, JOHN D., financial executive; b. Waco, Tex., July 13, 1928; s. George and Alvina (Schrader) B.; m. Anna Louise Nelson, Feb. 7, 1955; children: Suzzanne (dec.), John D., Kenneth Douglas. Exec. sec. Waco Jr. C. of C., 1953-55; assoc. editor Mexia (Tex.) Daily News, 1955-56; dir. publicity Valley C. of C., Weslaco, Tex., 1956-57; religion editor Houston Chronicle, 1957-58; v.p. pub. relations annuity bd. Southern Bapt. Conv., Dallas, 1958-81, v.p., endowment officer annuity bd., 1984—; v.p. Lady Love Cosmetics, Dallas, 1981-84. Author: Staying in the Black, Financially, Living Within Your Means; editor: THe Years Ahead. Served with USNR, 1945-49, 50-51. Mem. Southern Baptist (past pres.), Tex. Bapt. (past pres.) pub. relations assns., Pub. Relations Soc. Am. (accredited), Religious Pub. Relations Council, Sales and Mktg. Execs., Baptist Devel. Officers Assn., Assn. Baptist Found. Execs., Fellowship Chritians in Arts, Media and Entertainment. Home: 5816 Clendenin Dallas TX 75228 Office: 511 N Akard Bldg PO Box 2190 Dallas TX 75201

BLOUCH, TIMOTHY CRAIG, food company executive; b. Lebanon, Pa., June 26, 1954; s. Charles and Elaine (Krick) B.; m. Donna Joyce Walmer, June 18, 1977. AA, Harrisburg Area Community Coll., 1974; BBA, Pa. State U., 1977. Prodn. supr. Kraft, Inc., Allentown, Pa., 1977-78; prodn. supr. Hershey (Pa.) Chocolate USA, 1978-82, mgr. inbound and fleet ops., 1982-83, mgr. inbound ops., 1983-84, mgr. transp. rates, 1984-86, mgr. traffic services, 1986—. Republican. Office: Hershey Chocolate USA 19 E Chocolate Ave Hershey PA 17033

BLOUNT, WINTON MALCOLM, construction and manufacturing company executive; b. Union Springs, Ala., Feb. 1, 1921; s. Winton Malcolm and Clara B. (Chalker) B.; m. Carolyn Self Blount, Dec. 22, 1981; children: Winton Malcolm III, Thomas A., S. Roberts, Katherine Blount Miles, Joseph W. Student, U. Ala., 1939-41; LHD, Judson Coll., 1967; D. in Humanities, Huntingdon Coll., 1969; LLD, Birmingham-So. Coll., 1969; DCL, U. Ala., 1969, DSci., 1971; D. in Pub. Service, Seattle-Pacific Coll., 1971. Pres., chmn. bd. Blount Bros. Corp., Montgomery, Ala., 1946-68; postmaster gen. U.S. Washington, 1969-71; chmn. exec. com. Blount, Inc., Montgomery, Ala., from 1973, chmn. bd., chief exec. officer, 1974—; dir. Union Camp Corp., Munford Inc., World Mail Ctr., Inc. Chmn. Ala. Citizens for Eisenhower, 1952; Southeastern dir. Nixon-Lodge, 1959-60; Bd. dirs. United Appeal Montgomery; bd. dirs. Montgomery YMCA, also life mem.; former trustee So. Research Inst.; trustee Rhodes Coll.; trustee, pres. pro tempore. U. Ala.; bd. visitors Air U., Maxwell AFB, 1971-73; mem. adv. council U.S. Army Aviation Mus., Ft. Rucker, Ala. Served with USAAF, 1942-45. Named one of four Outstanding Young Men Ala., 1956; named Man of the Year Montgomery, 1961, Citizen of the Year Montgomery Advertiser, 1987; recipient citation for distinguished service to City of Montgomery, 1966; Ct. Honor award Montgomery Exchange Club, 1969; Nat. Brotherhood award NCCJ, 1970; Silver Quill award Am. Bus. Press, 1971; Golden Plate award Am. Acad. Achievement, 1980; non-mem. award Outstanding Achievement in Constrn. The Moles, 1980. Mem. Am. Mgmt. Assns. (trustee), Bus. Council, Conf. Bd., NAM (Golden Knight Mgmt. award Ala. Council 1962), U.S. C. of C. (nat. pres. 1968), Ala. C. of C. (pres. 1962-65), Newcomen Soc. N.Am. Presbyn. (deacon). Club: Rotarian. Home: 5801 Vaughn Rd Montgomery AL 36116 Office: Blount Inc 4520 Executive Park Dr Box 949 Montgomery AL 36116

BLOUNT, WINTON MALCOLM, III, investment executive; b. Albany, Ga., Dec. 14, 1943; s. Winton Malcolm Jr. and Mary Katherine (Archibald) B.; m. Lucy Durr Dunn, June 6, 1970; children: Winton Malcolm IV, K. Stuart, William, Judkins. Student, U. Ala., 1962-63; B.A., U. South, 1966; M.B.A., U. Pa., 1968. With Blount Bros. Corp., Montgomery, Ala., 1968-73, project mgr., 1972-73; with Mercury Constrn. Corp., Montgomery, 1973-77; pres. Mercury Constrn. Corp., 1975-77; chief exec. officer, chmn. bd. Benjamin F. Shaw Co., Wilmington, Del., 1977-88; pres., chief operating officer Blount Internat., Ltd., Montgomery, 1980-83, pres., chief exec. officer, 1983-85; chmn., chief exec. officer Blount Internat., Ltd., 1985-87; sr. v.p. Blount Inc., 1985-87, vice chmn., 1987-89; bd. dirs. Dunn Constrn. Co. Birmingham, Ala., 1st Ala. Bank of Montgomery, N.A., Ala. Power Co. Mem. fin. com. Ala. Republican party, 1980-82; bd. dirs. Montgomery YMCA, Episcopal High Sch., Montgomery Acad., Ala. Pub. Affairs Research Council, 1979-81; active Tukabatchee area council Boy Scouts Am., 1980-83; bd. visitors Coll. Commerce and Bus. Adminstrn., U. Ala., 1983-88; mem. bd. control Com. of 100; bd. dirs. Bus. Council Ala. Mem. Young Pres.'s Orgn., Ala. C. of C. (dir.), Montgomery C. of C. (dir.), Del. C. of C. (dir. 1979-80), NAM (dir. 1982-85). Episcopalian. Clubs: Beavers, Moles. Office: PO Box 5060 Montgomery AL 36195

BLUE, ROBERT LINSON, retired insurance company executive; b. Jackson Center, Ohio, Sept. 6, 1912; s. Clyde Leroy and Alta Margaret (Linson) B.; m. Ann Greiner, Feb. 20, 1937; children: Virginia Ann Blue Thabes, Sarah Blue Prior. BS in Fin. and Law, Ohio State U., 1934. Agt., field asst., asst. mgr. Travelers Ins. Co., Columbus, Ohio, 1942; founder, gen. mgr. R.L. Blue & Co., Miami, Fla., 1946-83; founder Savs. Ins. Group, Miami, 1968-83, retired, 1983; counsel on USA savs. and loans Lloyds-London, Miami, 1985—. Author ins. manuals For U.S. Savings and Loan League, 1964, 67. Served to lt. comdr., USN, 1942-46. Mem. Million Dollar Roundtable (life), NALU, Am. Assn. Mng. Gen. Agts. (hon. life). Republican. Presbyterian. Clubs: Bath (Miami); Grandfather Golf and Country (Linville, N.C.). Lodges: Masons, Royal Order of Scotland. Home: 1700 NE 105 St #303-4 Miami Shores FL 33138 Office: Law Office Ste 520 10800 Biscayne Blvd Miami FL 33161

BLUESTEIN, PAUL HAROLD, management engineer; b. Cin., June 14, 1923; s. Norman and Eunice D. (Schullman) B.; m. Joan Ruth Straus, May 17, 1943; children: Alice Sue Bluestein Greenbaum, Judith Ann. B.S., Carnegie Inst. Tech., 1946, B.Engring. in Mgmt. Engring., 1946; M.B.A., Xavier U., 1973. Registered profl. engr., Ohio. Time study engr. Lodge & Shipley Co., 1946-47; adminstrv. engr. Randall Co., 1947-52; partner Paul H. Bluestein & Co. (mgmt. cons.), 1952—, Seinsheimer-Bluestein Mgmt. Services, 1964-70; gen. mgr. Baker Refrigeration Co., 1953-56; pres., dir. Tabor Mfg. Co., 1953-54, Bluejay Corp., 1954—, Blatt & Ludwig Corp., 1954-57, Jason Industries, Inc., 1954-57, Hamilton-York Corp., 1954-57, Earle Hardware Mfg. Co., 1955-57, Hermas Machine Co., 1956—, Panel Machine Co., Ermet Products Corp., 1957-86, Tyco Labs., Inc., 1968-69, All-Tech Industries, 1968; gen. mgr. Hafleigh & Co., 1959-60; sr. v.p., gen. mgr. McCauley Ind. Corp., 1959-60; gen. mgr. Am. Art Works div. Rapid-Am. Corp., 1960-63; sec.-treas., dir. Liberty Baking Co., 1964-65; pres. Duquesne Baking Co., 1964-65, Goddard Bakers, Inc., 1964-65; pub. Merger and Acquisition Digest, 1962-69; partner Companhia Engenheiros Indsl. Bluestein Do Brasil, 1970-84; v.p., gen. mgr. Famco Machine div. Worden-Allen Co., 1974-75; exec. v.p., gen. mgr. Peck, Stow & Wilcox Co., Inc., 1976-77; mem. Joint Engring. Mgmt. Conf. Com., 1971-78. Com. mem. Cin. Art Mus. With AUS, 1943-46. Mem. ASME, Internat. Inst. Indsl. Engrs., Am. Soc. Engring. Mgmt., C.I.O.S.-World Council Mgmt. (dir., 1982-87). Home and Office: 3420 Section Rd Amberley Village Cincinnati OH 45237

BLUHM, NEIL G., real estate company executive; b. 1938; married. B.S., U. Ill.; J.D., Northwestern U. Bar: Ill. Ptnr. firm Mayer, Brown & Platt, Chgo., 1962-70; pres. JMB Realty Corp., Chgo., from 1970; pres., trustee JMB Realty Trust, Chgo., 1972—. Office: JMB Realty Corp 900 N Michigan Ave Chicago IL 60611

BLUM, EDWARD HOWARD, investment banker; b. Washington, Jan. 1, 1940; s. Irwin Ellis and Esther (Wolff) B.; m. Marlene H. Witman, June 8, 1965; children: Daniel Joseph, Matthew Alan. BS, Carnegie-Mellon U., 1961; MS, Princeton U., 1963, PhD, 1965. Asst. prof. Princeton (N.J.) U., 1965-67; sr. scientist, project leader, dir. rsch., v.p. Rand Corp., N.Y.C. and Santa Monica, Calif., 1967-76; dir. advanced tech. U.S. Dept. Energy, Washington, 1976-80; v.p., exec. dir. Merrill Lynch Capital Markets, Washington and N.Y.C., 1980-86; pres., vice chmn. bd. Md. Nat. Investment Banking Co., Greenbelt, 1986-89; pres., chief exec. officer Blum & Co., Inc., Reston, Va., 1989—; mem. adv. bd. Solar Energy Rsch. Inst., Denver, 1983—; mem. Fed. Pvt. Sector Ptnrship Bd., Denver. Editor Jour. Urban Analysis, 1970-77; contbr. articles to profl. jours. Trustee U. Detroit, 1970-79; chmn. subcom. Gen. Adv. Com. to Create Regional Sci. and Tech. High Sch., Fairfax County, Va., 1984-85. Recipient award Inst. Mgmt. Sci., 1974, Ops. Rsch. award NATO, 1976. Home: 2417 Luckett Ave Vienna VA 22180 Office: Blun & Co Inc 11800 Sunrise Valley Dr Ste 322 Reston VA 22091

BLUM, JACK ARTHUR, lawyer, trade association executive; b. N.Y.C., Aug. 5, 1941; s. Isador and Ruth (Klar) B.; m. Nancy Dee Gordon, June 15, 1967 (div. 1975); 1 son, Justin; m. Carole Kathleen Kauffman, Dec. 22, 1984. B.A., Bard Coll., 1962; J.D., Columbia U., 1965. Bar: D.C. 1968. Asst. counsel Senate Antitrust Subcom., Washington, 1966-72; assoc. counsel Senate Fgn. Relations Com., 1972-76; pres. Ind. Gasoline Marketers Council, Washington, 1976-87; ptnr. Blum, Nash & Railsback, Washington, 1977-87; appointed Spl. Counsel U.S. Senate Fgn. Relations Com., Washington, 1987—; cons. UN Centre on Transnational Enterprises, N.Y.C., 1977. Trustee Bard Coll., 1972-78, Center for Devel. Policy, 1980-86; bd. dirs., pres. Nat. Consumers League, Washington, 1967—. Mem. ABA, Fed. Bar Assn., D.C. Bar Assn. Democrat. Home: 1676 Homewood Landing Rd Annapolis MD 21401 Office: Com on Fgn Rels US Senate Washington DC 20510

BLUM, PETER, management consultant; b. Ried, Austria, Oct. 8, 1950; came to U.S., 1951; s. Nikolaus and Maria (Gross) B.; m. Cynthia Esteves, Feb. 14, 1976; children: Kristen, Eric. BS in Metallurgy and Materials Sci., Lehigh U., 1972, MS in Metallurgy and Materials Sci., 1973; MBA, U. Pa.,

1981. Mgr. Airco Rsch. Labs., Murray Hill, N.J., 1974-79; researcher Wharton Applied Rsch. Ctr., Phila., 1980-81; cons. Cresap, McCormick and Paget, N.Y.C., 1981—, prin., 1986—. Contbr. articles to profl. jours.; patentee in field. NSF fellow, 1972-73. Mem. Beta Gamma Sigma. Office: Cresap McCormick & Paget 245 Park Ave New York NY 10167 also: Telesis 127 Dorrance St Providence RI 02903

BLUMBERG, PHILIP FLAYDERMAN, real estate developer; b. Miami, Fla., Nov. 10, 1957; s. David and Lee (Dickens) B.; m. Lina Esther Waingortin, Apr. 13, 1986; 1 child, David. BBA, U. N.C., 1979; MBA, Harvard U., 1983. Pres. Am. Ventures Corp., Miami, Fla., 1979—; mng. ptnr. Banyan Reach ltd., Cutler Ridge, Fla., 1979; pres. Real Data Systems, Inc., Miami, 1984, Fort Dallas Assocs., Miami, 1985; chmn. exam. com. Profl. Savs. Bank, Coral Gables, Fla., 1985—; bd. dirs. Brickell Area Assn. Trustee Colony Performing Arts Theater, Miami Beach, 1985; bd. advs. New World Sch. Arts, Miami, 1985; mem. U. Miami Venture Council, Coral Gables, 1984; co-chmn. Japan-Miami Bus. Council, 1987—; trustee Beacon Council, 1988—; bd. dirs. City of Miami Downtown Devel. Authority, 1988—, Brickell Area Assn., 1988—. Mem. Japan-Am. Soc. of S. Fla. (bd. dirs. 1988—). Clubs: City (founding mem.), Bankers, Harvard (Miami). Home: 2430 Brickell Ave Apt 306-A Miami FL 33129 Office: Am Ventures Corp 1443 S Miami Ave Miami FL 33130

BLUME, MARSHALL EDWARD, finance educator; b. Chgo., Mar. 31, 1941; s. Marshall Edward Blume and Helen Corliss (Frank) Gilbert; m. Loretta Ryan, June 25, 1966; children—Christopher, Caroline, Catherine. S.B., Trinity Coll., Hartford, Conn., 1963; M.B.A., U. Chgo., 1965, Ph.D., 1968; M.A. (hon.), U. Pa., 1970. Lectr. applied math. Grad. Sch. Bus., U. Chgo., 1966, instr. bus. fin. and applied math., 1967; lectr. fin. U. Pa., Phila., 1967, asst. prof., 1968-70, assoc. prof., 1970-74, prof., 1974-78, Howard Butcher prof., 1978—, chmn. dept., 1982-86, assoc. dir. Rodney White Ctr., 1978-86; dir. Rodney White Ctr., 1986—; mem. U.S. Compt. Gen. adv. bd. on Oct. 1987 stock market crash, 1987-88; prof. fin. European Inst., Brussels, 1975-76, New U. Lisbon, Portugal, 1982; vis. prof. Stockholm Sch., spring 1976, U. Brussels, 1975. Author: Mutual Funds and Other Institutional Investors, 1970; The Changing Role of the Individual Investor, 1978; The Structure and Reform of the U.S. Tax System, 1985; editor: Encyclopedia of Investments, 1982; The Complete Guide to Investment Opportunities, 1984; assoc. editor Jour. Fin. and Quantitative Analysis, 1967-76, Jour. Fin. Econs., 1976-81, Jour. of Portfolio Mgmt., 1985—; mng. editor Jour. Fin., 1977-80, assoc. editor, 1985-88 . Contbr. articles to profl. publs. Trustee Trinity Coll., Hartford, Conn., 1980-86. Mem. Am. Fin. Assn. (officer 1977-80), Am. Econs. Assn. Home: 204 Woodstock Rd Villanova PA 19085 Office: U Pa White Ctr Fin Rsch 3250 Steinberg Hall Philadelphia PA 19104

BLUMENTHAL, W. MICHAEL, manufacturing company executive, former secretary Treasury; b. 1926. BS, U. Calif., Berkeley, 1951; MA, MPA, Princeton U., 1953, PhD, 1956. Rsch. assoc. Princeton U., 1954-57; v.p., bd. dirs. Crown Cork Internat. Corp., 1957-61; dep. asst. sec. for econ. affairs State Dept., 1961; apptd. Pres.'s dep. spl. rep. for trade negotiations with rank of amb. 1963-67; pres. Bendix Internat., 1967-70; also bd. dirs. Bendix Corp., 1967-77, vice-chmn., 1970-71, pres., chief operating officer, 1971-72, chmn., pres., chief exec. officer, 1972-77; sec. of Treasury Washington, 1977-79; also bd. dirs. UNISYS Corp. (formerly Burroughs Corp.), Detroit, 1979—; vice-chmn., chief exec. officer Unisys Corp. (formerly Burroughs Corp.), Detroit, 1980-81, chmn., chief exec. officer, 1981—; bd. dirs. N.Y. Stock Exchange, Tenneco, Inc., N.Y. Stock Exch., Chem. N.Y. Corp. and subs. Chem. Bank. Bd. dirs. Greater Phila. First Corp., The Phila. Orch., Detroit Renaissance, New Detroit, Detroit Symphony Orch.; v.p., bd. dirs., mem. exec. com. United Found. Detroit. Mem. Bus. Council, Bus. Roundtable, Am. Econ. Assn. Club: Economic of Detroit (bd. dirs.). Office: Unisys Corp PO Box 500 Blue Bell PA 19424

BLUMSTEIN, MICHAEL WES, securities analyst; b. Bklyn., Sept. 13, 1956; s. Stanley Blumstein and Gloria May (Rosenkrantz) Spitalnik; m. Eve Caligor, Sept. 8, 1985; 1 child, Jonah Andrew. AB, Brown U., 1978; MBA with distinction, Harvard U., 1983. Chartered fin. analyst. Reporter UPI, Providence, 1977-79, Miami Herald, Ft. Lauderdale, Fla., 1979-81; reporter bus. and fin. N.Y. Times, 1983-85; securities analyst First Boston Corp., N.Y.C., 1985—. Mem. N.Y. Soc. Security Analysts. Jewish. Office: First Boston Corp Park Ave Pla New York NY 10055

BLUMSTEIN, WILLIAM A., insurance company executive; b. N.Y.C., Mar. 21, 1948; s. Norman L. and Susan (Shapiro) B.; m. Ellen Goldsmith, Sept. 12, 1970; children: Amy Beth, Sara Lynn, Rachel Hope. BBA, Pace U., 1970; postgrad. Coll. of Ins., 1977-79. CPCU. From trainee to casualty underwriter Hartford Ins. Group (Conn.), 1970-72; broker, agt. account exec. Barco Assos., Inc., N.Y.C., 1972-74; broker, agt. account exec. Blume & Blumberg Inc., N.Y.C., 1974-75, v.p., treas., 1975-80; pres. Blume & Blumstein, Inc., N.Y.C., 1980-85, Blumstein & Levine Inc., 1985—; chmn. bd. dirs. Aetna N.Y.C. Gemini User Group, 1985-86; bd. dirs. Joint Purchasing Corp., adv. coun. mem. Aetna, 1988—. Trustee Westchester Reform Temple, 1976—, sec., 1981-83, 87—, v.p., 1983-87, 89—, pres. Men's Club, 1976-80, trustee Men's Club, 1980—; trustee Jewish Home and Hosp. for Aged, 1980—, asst. sec., 1983-85, treas., 1985—; adv. coun. Aetna Casualty Ins. Co., 1988—, chmn., 1989—; mem. West Quaker Ridge Assn.; elected to Scarsdale Citizen's Com., 1987—. Mem. Coun. Ins. Brokers Greater N.Y., Profl. Ins. Agts. Assn., Ind. Ins. Agts. Assn., Town Club, Century Country Club, B'nai B'rith, Sigma Zeta Chi Alumni Assn. (past. pres., sec.). Home: 70 Penn Blvd Scarsdale NY 10583 Office: 15 E 41st St New York NY 10017

BLUNDELL, WILLIAM RICHARD C., electric company executive; b. Montreal, Apr. 13, 1927; s. Richard C. and Did Aileen (Payne) B.; m. Monique Audet, Mar. 20, 1959; children: Richard, Emily, Michelle, Louise. B.A.Sc., U. Toronto, 1949. Registered profl. engr., Ont. Sales engr. Can. Gen. Electric Co., Toronto, 1949-51, travelling auditor, 1951, various fin. positions, 1951-66, treas., 1966-68, v.p.-fin., 1968-70, v.p., exec. consumer div., 1970-72; v.p., exec. apparatus div. Can. Gen. Electric Co., Lachine, Que., 1972-79; pres., chief exec. officer Camco Inc., Weston, Ont., 1979-83; pres., chief operating officer Can. Gen. Electric Co. Ltd., Toronto, 1983-84; chmn., chief exec. officer Gen. Electric Can. Inc., 1985—; bd. dirs. Alcan Aluminium Ltd., AmocoCan., Inc. Home: 45 Stratheden Rd, Toronto, ON Canada M4N 1E5 Office: GE Can Inc, 2300 Meadowvale Ave, Mississauga, ON Canada L5J 3Y2

BLUNT, ROGER RECKLING, construction and engineering company executive; b. East Providence, R.I., Oct. 12, 1930; s. Harry Weeden and Bertha Mildred (Reckling) B.; m. DeRosette Yvonne Hendricks, June 9, 1956; children: Roger Reckling, Jennifer Mari, Amy Elizabeth, Jonathan Hendricks. BS, U.S. Mil. Acad., 1956; MS in Civil Engring., MS in Nuclear Engring., MIT, 1962. Registered profl. engr., D.C., N.Y. Commd. 2d lt. U.S. Army, 1956, advanced through grades to lt. col., served with CE, 1956-69; sr. assoc. Harbridge Ho., Inc., Washington, 1969-71; chief exec. officer, chmn. Blunt Enterprises, Inc., Essex Constrn. Corp., Washington, 1971—; dir. Potomac Electric Power Co. Trustee Greater Washington Research Ctr.; bd. dirs., dir. Greater Washington Bd. Trade; bd. dirs. U. Md. Found., Md. Water Resources Adv. Commn.; bd. regents U. Md.; v.p. fin. and dir. Northeastern regional bd. Boy Scouts Am. Maj. gen. USAR (ret.). Registered profl. engr., D.C., N.Y. State; cert. nuclear plant engr., C.E. Mem. Nat. Soc. Profl. Engrs., D.C. Soc. Profl. Engrs., D.C. C. of C., West Point Soc. D.C., Res. Officers Assn., Assn. of U.S. Army, Sr. Army Res. Commanders Assn., Alpha Phi Alpha, Sigma Pi Phi. Presbyterian (elder). Club: Kiwanis of Washington. Office: 2018 5th St NE Washington DC 20002

BLUTT, MITCHELL JONATHAN, physician; b. Windsor, Conn., Mar. 4, 1957; s. Herbert and Rose (Deckel) B. BA, U. Pa., 1978, MD, 1982, MBA, 1987. Diplomate Am. Bd. Internal Medicine. Intern, then resident N.Y. Hosp., Cornell Med. Ctr., N.Y.C., 1982-85; fellow clin. scholars program Robert Wood Johnson Program U. Pa., Phila., 1985-87; assoc., then v.p., then gen. ptnr. Chem. Venture Ptnrs., N.Y.C., 1987—; adj. asst. prof. medicine N.Y. Hosp. Cornell Med. Ctr., 1987—. Contbr. articles to profl. jours. Recipient Kaiser Health Care award Kaiser Found., U. Pa., 1987, George Kirkham award Cornell Med. Coll., 1985. Mem. AMA, ACP, Am. Acad. of Med. Dirs., Soc. of Gen. Internal Medicine, Sphinx Soc., Phi Beta Kappa, Beta Gamma Sigma.

BLYTH, MICHAEL LESLIE, food company executive; b. Cleethorpes, Lincolnshire, Eng., Aug. 20, 1950; came to U.S., 1976; s. Cyrill Leslie and Doris Rene (Cullum) B.; m. Macon Williamson, Sept. 10, 1977; children: Matthew Leslie, Mallory Macon. MSc, Reading U., 1973; MBA, Northwestern U., 1978. Mgr. mktg. Prestold No. Ltd., Manchester, U.K., 1973-76; mgmt. cons. MAC Group, Chgo., 1978-83; sector dir. planning and bus. devel. Am. Hosp. Supply, Evanston, Ill., 1983-84; exec. v.p. Alcar Group, Skokie, Ill., 1984-85; v.p. corp. strategy Kraft Inc., Glenview, Ill., 1985-86, v.p. and dir. mktg., 1986—; bd. dirs. Council on Health Promotion, Chgo. Fulbright scholar, 1976-78. Mem. Assn. for Corp. Growth, Chgo. Planning Forum (bd. dirs. 1986—), English Speaking Union, Chgo. Advt. Club, Chgo. Council on Fgn. Relations. Office: Kraft Inc Kraft Ct Glenview IL 60025

BOAND, CHARLES WILBUR, lawyer; b. Bates County, Mo., Aug. 19, 1908; s. Albert and Edith Nadine (Pipes) B.; m. Phoebe Bard, Aug. 2, 1980; children: Bard, Barbara. AA, Jr. Coll. Kansas City; JD summa cum laude, U. Mo., Kansas City; MBA, LLB cum laude, U. Chgo. Bar: Mo. 1931, D.C. 1936, Ill. 1937, U.S. Supreme Ct. 1935, U.S. Ct. Appeals (1st, 2d, 5th, 6th, 7th, 9th, 10th, 11th and D.C. cirs.), trial bar of U.S. Dist. Ct. (no. dist.) Ill. Assoc. Moore & Fitch, St. Louis, 1933; atty. Gen. Counsel's Office, U.S. Treasury Dept., 1933-36; assoc. Wilson & McIlvaine, 1937-42, ptnr., 1945-88, chmn. exec. com., 1974-86, sr. ptnr., 1982-88; spl. counsel Burke, Wilson & McIlvaine, Chgo., 1988—; mem. Nat. Conf. Lawyers and CPA's, 1976-82. Mem. grad. sch. bus. council U. Chgo., 1961-68, citizens bd., vis. com. to libraries, 1985—; trustee Muskingum Coll., 1965-79; stated clk. Presbyn. Ch. Barrington, 1962-65. Served as officer USNR, 1942-45, lt. comdr. Res. (ret.). Mem. ABA, Ill. Bar Assn. (chmn. exec. com. corp. securities law sect. 1954-56), Chgo. Bar Assn. (chmn. com. corp. law 1963-64), Fed. Bar Assn., 7th Circuit Bar Assn., U. Chgo. Alumni Assn. (pres. 1975-80, alumni cabinet 1964-70, 72-80, v.p. 1973-74, 1st Alumni Disting. Service award 1981), U. Chgo. Law Sch. Alumni Assn. (pres. 1968-70, bd. dirs. 1950-72), Order of Coif, Chgo. Soc. Law Clubs, Beta Gamma Sigma, Sigma Chi, Phi Alpha Delta. Clubs: Chgo., Mid-Am., Met., Law, Legal (Chgo.); Barrington Hills (Ill.) Country (bd. dirs. 1947-55); Los Caballeros Golf (Ariz.). Home: 250 W County Line Rd PO Box 567 Barrington Hills IL 60011 Office: Burke Wilson & McIlvaine 500 W Madison St Ste 3700 Chicago IL 60606

BOARDMAN, BRUCE E., manufacturing company executive; b. Kansas City, Mo., Aug. 26, 1942; s. George Riley and Elizabeth May Boardman; m. Marilyn L. Moehring, Nov. 29, 1969; children: Adam, Molly, Elizabeth. BS in Metallurgy, Purdue U., 1965. Metall. engr. Republic Steel Co., Chgo., 1965-68; metall. engr. Deere & Co., Moline, Ill., 1968-85, mgr. metals rsch., 1985—. Mem. Am. Soc. for Metals (chpt. chmn. 1973, Outstanding Young Mem. award 1974), Soc. Automotive Engrs., U.S. Advanced Ceramics Assn. (bd. dirs.). Home: 13 Westwood Dr Genesco IL 61254 Office: Deere & Co 3300 River Dr Moline IL 61265

BOARDMAN, MICHAEL NEIL, lawyer; b. N.Y.C., Jan. 7, 1942; s. Martin Vincent and Hannah (Greisman) B.; m. Constance Hallie Kramer, Aug. 28, 1966; children—Adam Lawrence, Amy Suzanne. AB, Syracuse U., 1964; JD, Seton Hall U., 1967. Bar: N.J. 1968, U.S. Dist. Ct. N.J. 1968, U.S. Supreme Ct. 1971. Assoc., Liebowitz, Krafte & Liebowitz, Englewood, N.J., 1968-69; ptnr. Boardman & Epstein, Saddle Brook, N.J., 1969-75; sole practice, Saddle Brook and Ridgewood, N.J., 1975—; designated counsel State of N.J. Office of Pub. Defender, 1970-77; mem. skills tng. course faculty Inst. Continuing Legal Edn., Newark, 1976—; vice-chmn. Bergen County dist. fee arbitration com. Supreme Ct. N.J., 1987-88 , chmn. 1988-89; lectr. Inst. Continuing Legal Edn., Newark, 1979—. Democratic committeeman County of Bergen, N.J., 1974-76; mem. Citizens Com. to Study Declining Enrollment, Glen Rock, N.J., 1975-77; panelist Matrimonial Early Settlement Program, Bergen County, 1978—; mem. Glen Rock Jewish Ctr.; mem. profl. adv. bd. Nat. Hypoglycemia Assn., Inc., 1985—. Mem. ABA, N.J. State Bar Assn., Bergen County Bar Assn., Am. Judicature Soc., NOW, Adoptive Parents Orgn. Bergen County Club. Home: 48 Glen Blvd Glen Rock NJ 07452 Office: 4 Franklin Ave Ridgewood NJ 07451

BOARMAN, GERALD JUDE, distribution executive, religious organization administrator; b. Indpls., July 12, 1940; s. John Eldon and Agnes (Dugan) B.; m. Susan Marie Schmalz; children: Gerald II, Jeffrey, Michael, Daniel. Student, Purdue U., 1959; student, Butler U., 1960, W. Va. State U., 1964. Br. mgr. Dynamic Distbrs., Indpls., 1959-62; paper sales rep. Proctor & Gamble, St. Albans, W.Va., 1963-65; instr. soap salesman Proctor & Gamble, Camp Hill, Pa., 1965-66; equipment salesman Breuer Electric Mfg. Co., Camp Hill, 1967-69; v.p. Janitor Supply House, Inc., Harrisburg, Pa., 1969-80; sec. Servo Systems, Inc., Harrisburg, 1977-80; chmn. bd. dirs., founder Bortek Industries, Inc., Mechanicsburg, Pa., 1980—; chmn. bd., founder Multi-Media Ministries, Inc., Mechanicsburg, 1980—; pres., founder World Christian Monetary Fund, Mechanicsburg, 1987—; chmn. bd. Task Masters, Inc., Mechanicsburg, 1981-87; mem. pres.'s adv. council CBN Univ., Va. Beach, 1987. Speaker Nat. Edn. Ctr. Thompson Inst., Harrisburg, 1984; city fin. mgr. Americans for Robertson, Washington, 1987. Mem. Internat. Sanitary Supply Assn., Bldg. Service Contractors Assn. Internat. Republican. Home: 478 Woodcrest Dr Mechanicsburg PA 17055 Office: Bortek Industries Inc 4713 Old Gettysburg Rd Mechanicsburg PA 17055

BOBBE, RICHARD A., management consultant; b. N.Y.C, June 4, 1920; s. Arthur Louis and Mina (Praeger) B.; m. Carol Norwalk, Jan. 27, 1945; children: Leland George, Judith Helene. BS in Indsl. Engring., Lehigh U., 1941; MBA, Harvard U., 1947. Mgr. material plan and control Am. Houses, Inc., N.Y.C., 1947-49; salary adminstr., dir. employee relations Emerson Radio Corp., N.Y.C., 1949-55; plant mgr. Gen. Interiors, Inc., Bklyn., 1955-57; dir. acquisitions and comml. devel. Continental Copper and Steel, N.Y.C.; sr. ptnr. Robert H. Schaffer & Assocs., Stamford, Conn.; adj. prof. Hofstra U., Hempstead, N.Y., 1984—. Contbr. articles to profl. jours. Served to lt. comdr. USNR, 1945-47. Mem. Inst. Mgmt. Cons. (founding). Democrat. Jewish. Home: 678 Morton Ave Franklin Square NY 11010 Office: Robert H Schaffer & Assoc 401 Rockrimmon Rd Stamford CT 06903

BOBERG, LARON CAPBARAT, importer, retailer; b. San Rafael, Calif., May 2, 1947; d. Joseph Lauren and Anna Marion (Schlosser) Capbarat; m. Robert Arthur Boberg, Oct. 2, 1976; 1 child, Lauren Lynn. Student, No. Ariz. U., 1965-68, U. Hawaii, 1972, Hong Kong U., 1984. Realtor Frank Howard Adams Co., Novato, Calif., 1972-75; property mgr. R&B Devel. Co., Los Angeles, 1975-76; realtor Willoughby & Assocs., Portland, Oreg., 1980-82; owner Far East Shoppers, Hong Kong, 1983-85, Oriental Merc. Co., Raleigh, N.C., 1985—. Del. Wake County Dem. Com., Raleigh, 1988; facilities chmn. N.C. Women's Resource Ctr., Raleigh, 1988; active in Women's Forum N.C., 1988. Mem. Triangle Chpt. N.C. World Trade Assn., N.C. Nat. Assn. Women Bus. Owners (pres. 1987-88). Roman Catholic. Office: Oriental Mdse Co 4205 Pleasant Valley Rd Ste 254 Raleigh NC 27612

BOCCHICCHIO, LUCILLE M., information technology executive. BS in Math. with honors, U. R.I., 1961. Engr., computer analyst Sikorsky div. United Tech., Stratford, Conn., 1961-64; systems programmer, analyst Sperry Corp., N.Y.C., 1964-65; sr. cons. Advanced Computer Techniques, N.Y.C., 1965-69; dir. tng. Levin-Townsend Service Corp., N.Y.C., 1969-70; pres., mgmt. cons. L.M. Bocchicchio, Ltd., N.Y.C., 1970—. Author: Our Child's Medical History, 1982; contbr. articles to profl. jours.

BOCCHINO, LINDA ELIZABETH, jewelry store executive, registered nurse; b. Lynn, Mass., Sept. 28, 1948; d. Anthony Hamilton and Ruth J. (Moran) Dyczus; m. Anthony Bocchino. Student, Fitchburg (Mass.) State Coll., 1967; RN Diploma, Burbank Hosp., 1969. RN, Mass. Surgical nurse Beverly (Mass.) Hosp., 1970-71; charge nurse Louise Caroline Nursing Home, Saugus, Mass., 1971-72; supr. nursing Saugus Hosp., 1972-78; with sales dept. Germain Monteil Cosmetics, Peabody, Mass., 1978.; pres. Martoni Jewelers, Peabody and Medford, Mass., 1978—. Author poem published in 1989 New American Anthology (Golden Poet award 1988). Named Top 100 Women in Bus. Boston Woman Mag., 1988. Mem. Gemological Inst. Am. (v.p. New Eng. Alumni Assn.), Eastern Star, Royal Chpt., Mass.-R.I. Jewelers Assn. (bd. dirs. 1988—). Office: Martoni Jewelers Inc 215 Newbury St Peabody MA 01960 also: 340 Middlesex Ave Medford MA 02155

BOCCITTO, ELIO, publishing company executive. With Berlitz Internat. Inc., N.Y.C., 1961—, former tchr., then various positions including v.p. for East Asia, v.p. for U.S. and Can., sr. v.p. Europe, pres., 1982—; v.p. Macmillan, Inc., N.Y.C., 1988—. Office: Macmillan Inc 866 3rd Ave New York NY 10022

BOCK, JEFFREY WILLIAM, lawyer; b. Mpls., Mar. 26, 1950; s. Frederick Garland Bock and Vera (Lewer) Randall; m. Elaine Drinkwater, Dec. 5, 1976 (div. 1981). BA, Dartmouth Coll., 1972; JD, U. Chgo., 1975. Bar: Oreg. 1975. Assoc. Tonkon, Torp & Galen, Portland, Oreg., 1975-78, McEwen, Hanna & Gisvold, Portland, 1978-81; corp. counsel Thermo Electron, Waltham, Mass., 1981-83; assoc. Perkins Coie, Portland, 1983—. Mem. Univ. Club, Founders Club. Office: Perkins Coie 111 SW 5th Ave Ste 2500 Portland OR 97204

BOCKELMAN, JOHN RICHARD, lawyer; b. Chgo., Aug. 8, 1925; s. Carl August and Mary (Ritchie) B. Student, U. Wis., 1943-44, Northwestern U., 1944-45, Harvard U., 1945, U. Hawaii, 1946; B.S. in Bus. Adminstrn, Northwestern U., 1946; M.A. in Econs, U. Chgo., 1949, J.D., 1951. Bar: Ill. 1951. Atty.-advisor Chgo. ops. office AEC, 1951-52; asso. firm Schradzke, Gould & Ratner, Chgo., 1952-57, Brown, Dashow & Langeluttig, Chgo., 1957-59, Antonow & Weissbourd, Chgo., 1959-61; partner firm Burton, Isaacs, Bockelman & Miller, Chgo., 1961-69; individual practice law Chgo., 1970—; prof. bus. law Ill. Inst. Tech., Chgo., 1950-82; lectr. econs. DePaul U., Chgo., 1952-53; dir. Beale Travel Service, Inc; dir., sec. Arlington Engring. Co.; dir., v.p. Universal Distbrs., Inc. Pres. 1212 Lake Shore Dr. Condo Assn. Served with USNR, 1943-46. Mem. Am. Bar Assn., Ill. Bar Assn., Chgo. Bar Assn., Cath. Lawyers Guild Chgo., Phi Delta Theta. Clubs: Lake Point Tower (Chgo.), Barclay Ltd. (Chgo.), Whitehall (Chgo.), Internat. (Chgo.); Anvil (East Dundee, Ill.). Home: 1212 Lake Shore Dr Chicago IL 60610 Office: 104 S Michigan Ave Ste 808 Chicago IL 60603

BOCKERSTETTE, JOSEPH A., management consultant; b. Lexington, Ky., Nov. 19, 1957; s. Paul Edward and Sue Carolyn (Richardson) B.; m. Jennifer Lee Trauth, June 27, 1981; 1 child, Lindsey Anne. BS in Indsl. Engring., U. Cin., 1981. Cert. in prodn. and inventory mgmt. Cons. Main Hurdman, Cin., 1982-83; cons. Coopers-Lybrand, Cin., 1984, mgr. mfg. cons., 1986—, dir. mfg. cons., 1988—; v.p. ops. Texstyle, Inc., Cin., 1985. Mem. Inst. Indsl. Engring. (mgmt. div. dir. 1988, pres Cin. chpt. 1987), Am. Prodn. Inventory Control Soc. Home: 5911 Red Oak Dr Fairfield OH 45014 Office: Coopers & Lybrand 201 E 4th St Cincinnati OH 45202

BOCKHAUS, JAMES HOWARD, manufacturing company executive; b. Keokuk, Iowa, Feb. 25, 1939; s. Howard Burton and Mary Irene (Zimmerman) B.; A.B. cum laude, Harvard Coll., 1960; M.S., Syracuse U., 1968; m. Nancy Jean Beattie, July 7, 1965; children—Kimberly Kristen, Jay Bradford. With Gen. Electric Co., Fairfield, Conn., 1960-75, mgr. European mfg. automation ops., 1970-72, mgr. strategic planning cons., 1973-75; dir. corp. strategy devel. Internat. Paper Co., N.Y.C., 1975-77; v.p. corp. planning LTV Corp., Dallas, 1977-81; chmn., bd., pres. ATEC Internat. Inc., Arlington, Tex., 1981-86; sr. cons. The Directorate, Carollton, Tex., 1986-87; sr. v.p., gen. mgr. Ambac Internat. Corp., Columbia, S.C., 1987—. Trustee, Dallas Ballet Assn., 1978-86; bd. dirs. Citizens Found. Syracuse, 1967-68. White House fellow, 1968-69. Mem. N. Am. Soc. Corp. Planning (past pres. Dallas-Ft. Worth chpt.), Planning Execs. Inst. (past pres. Dallas-Fort Worth), Assn. Corp. Growth (past chmn. membership Dallas-Fort Worth), White House Fellows Assn., Columbia C. of C. (chmn. Indsl. Chief Execs. group 1988—), Faculty House of Carolina, Wildewood Country Club (Columbia). Republican. Presbyterian. Home: 104 Cowdray Park Dr Columbia SC 29223-8126 Office: Ambac Internat Corp I-77 and Killian Rd Columbia SC 29202

BOCKIAN, DONNA MARIE, data processing executive; b. N.Y.C., June 4, 1946; d. Forrest Mager and Mary C. (Lovelace) Hastings; m. James Bernard Bockian, Sept. 16, 1984; children: Vivian Shifra, Adrian Adena, Lillian Tova. BA in Psychology, Vassar Coll., 1968; diploma in systems analysis NYU, 1978. Computer programmer RCA, N.Y.C., 1968-71; systems analyst United Artists Corp., N.Y.C., 1971-78; project leader Bradford Nat. Corp., N.Y.C., 1978-81; project mgr. Mfrs. Hanover Trust, N.Y.C., 1981-83; project mgr. Chem. Bank, N.Y.C., 1983-86; mgr. fin. systems Salomon Bros., N.Y.C., 1986-87, v.p. James B. Bochian and Assocs., 1987—. Mem. Assn. Women in Computing (exec. com. 1982-83), Vassar Club. Avocation: photography. Home: 26 Farmhouse Ln Morristown NJ 07960

BOCKIAN, JAMES BERNARD, computer systems executive; b. Jersey City, Sept. 16, 1936; s. Abraham and Evelyn (Skner) B.; m. Donna M. Hastings; children: Vivian Shifra, Adrian Adena, Lillian Tova. B.A., Columbia U., 1953; M.Pub. Adminstrn., U. Mich., 1955; M.A., Yale U., 1957. Vice-consul, 3d sec. Embassy, Dept. State, Washington and abroad, 1957-61; sr. systems analyst J.C. Penney Co., N.Y.C., 1961-67; mgr. systems services, head dept. systems projects adminstrn. McDonnell Douglas Automation Co., East Orange, N.J., 1967-76; prin. James B. Bockian & Assocs., Inc., Morristown, N.J., 1976—; dir. info. systems Comml. Computer Systems, Inc., Norwalk, Conn., 1976-79; v.p. mgmt. info. systems Thomas Cook, Inc., 1980-83, exec. cons. to Thomas Cook Group; lectr. in field. Grad. fellow Yale U., 1957. Mem. Internat. Assn. Cybernetics, Assn. Computing Machinery, Data Processing Mgmt. Assn., Am. Mgmt. Assn., Systems and Procedures Assn. Jewish. Clubs: Yale (N.Y.); Royal Danish Yacht (Copenhagen). Author: Management Manual for Systems Development Projects, 1979; Project Management for Systems Development, 1981; AT&T User Guide to Information Systems Development, 1980. Contbr. treatises and articles to profl. publs. Home: 26 Farmhouse Ln Morristown NJ 07960 Office: Olde Forge E Ste 26-5B Morristown NJ 07960

BOCKMANN, BRUCE RICHARD, investment banker; b. Boston, Nov. 17, 1938; s. Finn O. and Charlotte (Cox) B.; m. Maria Kathryn Bentivoglio, Mar. 6, 1982; children: Mary Stewart, Jill, Nathaniel. BA cum laude, Bowdoin Coll., 1960; MBA, Harvard U., 1967. Mng. dir. Morgan Stanley, N.Y.C., 1967—. Mem. spl. events com. Am. Ballet Theatre, N.Y.C., 1984-85; patron The Australian Opera, Sydney, 1986—; chmn. Harvard Bus. Sch. Class of 67 Alumni Fund, 1980-82; trustee Com. for Econ. Devel. of Australia, 1986—. Served to lt. USN, 1960-65. Mem. Australia Am. Soc. N.Y. Club: Doubles (N.Y.). Home: 84/86 Wolseley Rd, Point Piper, Sydney New South Wales, Australia 2027 Office: Morgan Stanley Internat Inc, MLC Centre Martin Place, Sydney New South Wales 2000, Australia

BODDEN, JAMES MANOAH, II, investment consultant; b. Port Arthur, Tex., Nov. 15, 1951; s. James Manoah and Dorothy Mae (Foreman) B.; m. Lana Arline Jackson, May 1, 1981; children—James Manoah, III, Natasha Arline. A.A.S. in Banking, Internat. Coll. Cayman Islands, 1976, B.A. in Bus. and Econs., 1976. Sr. cert. valuer; registered property mgr. Mgr. Bodden Motors, Ltd., Grand Cayman, 1969-73; asst. mgr. J.M. Bodden & Co. Ltd., Grand Cayman, 1973-77; v.p. J.M. Bodden & Son Internat. Ltd., Grand Cayman, 1977-81; pres., chmn. bd. Internat. Fin. Cons., Ltd., Grand Cayman, 1981-83; pres., mng. dir. Select Internat. Properties, Ltd., 1983—. Founding mem. Jr. C. of C. Cayman Islands, 1971; mem. Cayman Islands Tourism Adv. Bd., 1979. Mem. Ind. Cons. Am., Cayman Islands Real Estate Assn. (founding mem., v.p. 1987—) Internat. Middle East Assn., Internat. Orgn. Real Estate Appraisers, Internat. Inst. (internat. mem.). Office: Cayman Airways Ltd, Airport Rd Breezy Castle, Grand Cayman Cayman Islands

BODINE, ARTHUR WILLIAM, finance company executive; b. Chico, Calif., Aug. 19, 1943; s. Angus Olsen and Amber Louise (Ohlin) B.; m. Elana Jan McBurney, Aug. 14, 1965; children: Bradford Sterling, Brynley, Barrett Alexander. BA in Polit. Sci. and Econs., UCLA, 1967; MBA, Harvard U., 1969. Sr. analyst The Bank of N.Y., N.Y.C., 1970-72; v.p. research Scudder, Stevens & Clark, N.Y.C., 1972-79; investment officer Tchrs. Ins. Annuity Assn./Coll. Retirement Fund, N.Y.C., 1979-81; dir. investment research Citicorp, N.Y.C., 1981-86; sr. ptnr. J.P. Morgan Equities, Inc., N.Y.C., 1987—; chmn., chief exec. officer Crimson Realty Advisors, N.Y.C., 1979; mem. adv. bd. Spinnaker Investor Ptnrs., N.Y.C., 1987—, Univ. Enterprises; vis. lectr. London Sch. Econs., 1986, Oxford U. Author: Finding Tomorrow's Investments Today, 1982. bishop, presiding trustee Latter Day Saints Ch., N.Y.C., 1973-78, mem. high council, 1978-79; pres. West End Apts. Co-op, N.Y.C., 1978. Fellow Fin. Analysts Fedn. (bd.

dirs.), Investment Tech. Assn.; mem. Internat. Soc. Fin. Analysts (founding dir. 1985—), N.Y. Soc. Security Analysts (pres., bd. dirs. 1981—, Vol. of Yr. 1986), Research Dirs. Forum (founding dir. 1982—), Sigma Alpha Epsilon. Republican. Office: JP Morgan Equities Inc 23 Wall St New York NY 10015

BODINE, MARY C., healthcare facility executive; b. Topeka, Oct. 17, 1942; d. Louis M. and Margaret E. (Carr) B. AS in Respiratory Therapy, Community Coll. Denver, 1970; BA in Community Health Edn., Washburn U., 1978; MPA, U. Kans., 1982, cert. in health care services adminstrn., 1984. Tech. dept. head respiratory therapy and cardiology St. Mary's Hosp., Grand Junction, Colo., 1970-71; supr. St. Francis Hosp. and Med. Ctr., Topeka, 1971-73, adminstrv. dir. cardio-respiratory sect., 1973-82; intern in hosp. adminstrn. U. Kans., Topeka, 1985; exec. v.p. DePaul Hosp., Cheyenne, Wyo., 1986—. Mem. Zonta. Democrat. Roman Catholic. Office: DePaul Hosp 2600 E 18th St Cheyenne WY 82001

BODINE, RALPH E., food products company executive; b. 1942. AB, Princeton U., 1966. With Sunkist Growers Inc., Calif., 1977—; chmn. Sunkist Growers Inc., 1986—, also bd. dirs. With USNR, 1961-63. Office: Sunkist Growers Inc PO Box 7888 Van Nuys CA 91409-7888 *

BODKIN, FRANCIS FISHER, JR., stockbroker; b. N.Y.C., June 8, 1944; s. Francis Fisher and Elizabeth Alice (Burtenshaw) B.; B.S.B.A., Georgetown U., 1967; m. Irene Fox, Aug. 15, 1970; children—Madeleine, Elizabeth. Mgr. instl. services Edwards and Hanly, N.Y.C., 1970-76, Colin Hochstin & Co., N.Y.C., 1976-78; mng. ptnr. Bodkin Satloff & Co., N.Y.C., 1978-82; pres. Bodkin Securities Co., Inc., 1982—. Mem. Security Traders N.Y., N.Y. Stock Exchange. Republican. Episcopalian. Clubs: Heights Casino (past gov.); St. Andrews Soc. N.Y. (past chmn.); Bklyn.; Point O'Woods Assn.; Masons. Home: 2 Grace Ct Brooklyn Heights NY 11201 Office: Bodkin Securities Co Inc 26 Broadway 26th Fl New York NY 10004

BODKIN, LAWRENCE EDWARD, inventor, research development company executive, gemologist; b. Sapulpa, Okla., May 17, 1927; s. Clarence Elsworth and Lillie (Moore) B.; m. Ruby Emma Pate, Jan. 15, 1949; children: Karen Bodkin Snead, Cinda, Lawrence Jr. Student, Fla. State U., 1947-50; grad., Gemological Inst., 1969. Chief announcer, program dir., mgr. various radio stations, Winter Haven, Fla., Tallahassee and Jacksonville, Fla., 1947-60; ind. jewelry salesman and appraiser Underwood Jewelers, 1961-87; pres. Bodkin Jewelers and Appraisers, Jacksonville, 1984—, Telanon, Jacksonville, 1981—, Bodkin Co., Jacksonville, 1974—; chmn., chief exec. officer Bodkin Corp., Jacksonville, 1975—; dir. product safety and R & D Innovative Designer Products, Kendall Park, N.J., 1989—; cons. gem and mineral groups, Jacksonville, 1960—, numerous corps. and industries (on inventions); lectr. in field. Author: Dual Imagery of Ultra Speed Bodies, 1971, Miniatures, 1976; contbr. articles to sci. publs.; inventor Universal-Fault Circuit-Interrupter, 1973; holder of over 15 U.S. and fgn. patents. Mem. Jacksonville Mus. Sci. and Hist., 1981—, Jacksonville Symphony Assn., 1985—, Cummer Gallery Art, Jacksonville, 1985—. Served with U.S. Army, 1945-47, ETO. Mem. Am. Gem Soc. (cert.), Fla. State U. Alumni Assn, Mensa Internat. Clubs: San Jose Country (Jacksonville); Ponte Vedra Country (Fla.). Home: 1149 Molokai Rd Jacksonville FL 32216 Office: 5991 Chester Ave Ste 111 Jacksonville FL 32217

BODKIN, RUBY PATE, corporate executive, real estate broker, educator; b. Frostproof, Fla., Mar. 11, 1926; d. James Henry and Lucy Beatrice (Latham) P.; m. Lawrence Edward Bodkin Sr., Jan. 15, 1949; children: Karen Bodkin Snead, Cinda, Lawrence Jr. BA, Fla. State U., 1948; MA, U. Fla., 1972. Lic. real estate broker. Banker Lewis State Bank, Tallahassee, 1944-49; ins. underwriter Hunt Ins. Agy., Tallahassee, 1949-51; tchr. Duval County Sch. Bd., Jacksonville, Fla., 1952-76; pvt. practice realty Jacksonville, 1976—; tchr. Nassau County Sch. Bd., Jacksonville, 1978-83; sec., treas., v.p. Bodkin Corp., R&D/Inventions, Jacksonville, 1983—; pvt. practice tutoring, Jacksonville; substitute tchr. Duval County Sch. Bd., 1980—. Mem. Jacksonville Symphony Guild, 1985—, Mus. Sci. And History Guild, Jacksonville, 1959—, Southside Woman's Club, Jacksonville, 1957—, Garden Club Jacksonville, 1976—. Recipient 25 Yr. Service award Duval County Sch. Bd., 1976, Tchr. of Yr. award Bryceville Sch., 1981. Democrat. Baptist. Clubs: San Jose Country; Ponte Vedra Oceanfront Resort. Home: 1149 Molokai Rd Jacksonville FL 32216 Office: Bodkin Jewelers & Appraisers PO Box 16482 Jacksonville FL 32216

BODMAN, SAMUEL W., III, chemical company executive; b. Chgo., Nov. 26, 1938; s. Samuel W. Jr. and Lina (Hervel) B.; children: Elizabeth L., Andrew M., Sarah H. B.S. in Chem. Engring., Cornell U., 1960; Sc.D., MIT, 1964. Tech. dir. Am. Research and Devel., Boston, 1965-70; Prof. and lectr. MIT, Cambridge, Mass., 1964—; v.p. Fidelity Venture Assn., Boston, 1970—; pres. Fidelity Venture Assn., 1974-77, chmn., 1977; pres. Fidelity Mgmt. and Research Corp., Boston, 1977-86, FMR Corp., until 1986; pres., chief operating officer Cabot Corp., Waltham, Mass., until 1988, now chmn., chief exec. officer, 1988—; dir. SKOK Inc., Cambridge, Mass., Addressograph Farrington, Boston, Modar, Natick, Mass., Continental Cablevision, Boston. Trustee Multiple Sclerosis Soc., Mass. chpt., 1982; corp. mem. Babson coll., Wellesley, Mass., 1982. Mem. Boston C. of C. (dir. 1983—). Episcopalian. Home: 29 Chestnut St Boston MA 02108 Office: Cabot Corp 950 Winter St Waltham MA 02254-9073 *

BODNAR, JOHN, III, financial planner; b. Rahway, N.J., Aug. 8, 1958; s. John Jr. and Barbara Joan (Bogus) B.; m. Karen Fielding, Nov. 25, 1984; children: John Winthrop, Jacqueline Fielding. BA, Hobart Coll, 1981. Sr. v.p. Ford Fin. Group, East Hanover, N.J., 1981-87; pres. Bodnar Fin. Services, Florham Park, N.J., 1987—; cons. Pioneer Mortgage and Fin. Services, Florham Park, 1982—. Councilman Mus. Council, Clark, N.J., 1982-84; cochmn. Rahway State Prison Lifer's Adv. Bd., 1982—; pres. Rep. Club, Clark, 1983—. Named Qualifying Mem. Million Dollar Roundtable, 1986. Mem. Nat. Assn. Life Underwriters (chmn. pub. service com. Newark chpt. 1982—, Nat. Sales award 1985-88, Nat. Quality award 1987), Internat. Assn. Fin. Planners, Inst. Cert. Fin. Planners, Trust for Hist. Preservation. Roman Catholic. Office: Bodnar Fin Svcs 256 Columbia Turnpike Ste 108A Florham Park NJ 07932 •

BODNER, EMANUEL, industrial scrap metals recycling company executive; b. Houston, July 25, 1947; s. Eugene and Eve (Pryzant) B.; BBA, U. Tex., Austin, 1969; m. Jennifer L. Holt, Sept. 13, 1981; children: Jessica Elyse, Jeremiah. Vice pres. Bodner Metal & Iron Corp., Houston, 1969—. Bd. dirs. Cy-Champ Utility Dist., 1978-79, Tex. Rehab., 1985—, Tex. Council on Disabilities; mem. Tex. Legis. Council, Citizens Adv. Commn. Study of Vocat. Rehab., 1970-72; mem. removal of archtl. barriers com. Tex. Rehab. Assn., 1971; mem. handicapped access program task force Tex. Dept. Human Resources, 1978-79; mem. bd. Tex. Rehab. Commn., 1985—, Tex. Council on Disabilities ; mem. Tex. Gov.'s Com. on Employment of Handicapped, vice chmn. employment devel. sub-com. 1981-82; mem. new leadership exec. com. State of Israel Bonds, 1984. Mem. Inst. Scrap Recycling Industries (nat. public relations com., nat. fgn. trade com.; dir. Gulf Coast chpt. 1977-84, chmn. chpt. public relations com. 1978-83, editor Gulf Coast Reporter 1978-85, sec. Gulf Coast chpt. 1984-85, treas. 1985, 2d v.p. 1986-87, chmn. membership com. 1986-87, 1st v.p. and chair conv. com. 1987—, Outstanding award 1985), Ex-Students Assn. U. Tex., Alpha Epsilon Pi (life). Jewish. Clubs: Shriners, Masons (32 deg.). Office: Bordner Metal & Iron Corp 3660 Schalker Dr Houston TX 77026

BODNEY, JAY VICTOR, brokerage house executive; b. Kansas City, Mo., Nov. 25, 1943; s. Daniel Fred and Retha (Silby) Bodney; m. Arleen Boschele, Nov. 12, 1966 (div. 1981); 1 child, Jay Max. AS, Kansas City Jr. Coll., 1963; BS in Edn., U. Mo., 1965. Tchr. Shawnee Mission (Kans.) High Sch. Dist., 1965-69; stockbroker Francis I. Dupont & Co., Kansas City, 1969-70, Paine Webber, Kansas City, 1970-71; nat. sales tng. mgr. Paine Webber, N.Y.C., 1971-72, N.Y. instnl. sales, 1972-73; v.p. instnl. sales Paine Webber, Kansas City, 1974-76; v.p., mgr. Paine Webber Real Estate Securities, Kansas City, 1977-85; v.p., mgr. mortgage banker Paine Webber Mortgage Fin., Kansas City, 1985-87; v.p. instnl. sales Dean Witter Reynolds Inc., Kansas City, 1988—. Mem. Kans. Adv. Coun. on Arts with Handicapped, 1986—. Republican. Jewish. Home: 12424 Cambridge Circle Leawood KS 66209 Office: Dean Witter Reynolds Inc 4435 Main St Ste 700 Kansas City MO 64111

BODONY, STEPHEN GERALD, publishing company executive; b. Balt., Dec. 11, 1947; s. Stephen George and Martha Faye (Sharp) B.; m. Mary Margaret Bowman, Aug. 3, 1974; children: Daniel, Adam. BSBA, Wright State U., 1970. Office mgr. controller F.D. Borkholder & Co., Nappanee, Ind., 1970-73; controller, chief fin. officer Franklin Coach Co., Nappanee, 1973-74, Newmar Industries, Inc., Nappanee, 1974-77; v.p. Newmar Industries, Inc., 1977-78; ops. auditor Leisure Time Products, Nappanee, 1978-79; pvt. practice cons. Nappanee, 1979-80; chief fin. officer Hanson Silo Co., Lake Lillian, Minn., 1980-86; v.p. gen. mgr. Hanson Silo Co., Lake Lillian, 1986-88, chief fin. officer, 1988; chief fin. officer Internat. Computer Programs Inc., Indpls., 1988—. Dir. Crisis Pregnancy Ctr., Willmar, Minn., 1987—; trustee First Baptist Ch., 1985-86. Served to lance cpl. USMC, 1979. Baptist. Home: 750 Sunblest Blvd Fishers IN 46038

BOE, MYRON TIMOTHY, lawyer; b. New Orleans, Oct. 30, 1948; s. Myron Roger and Elaine (Tracy) B. BA, U. Ark., 1970, JD, 1973; LLM in Labor, So. Methodist U., 1976. Bar: Ark. 1974, Tenn. 1977, U.S. Ct. Appeals (4th, 5th, 6th, 7th, 8th, 9th, 10th, 11th cirs.) 1978, U.S. Supreme Ct. 1978. City atty. City of Pine Bluff, Ark., 1974-75; sec.-treas. Ark. City Atty. Assn., 1975; labor atty. Weintraub-Dehart, Memphis, 1976-78; sr. ptnr. Rose Law Firm, Little Rock, 1980—. Author: Handling the Title VII Case Practical Tips for the Employer, 1980; contbr. book supplement: Employment Discrimination Law, 2d edit., 1983. Served to 2d lt. USAR, 1972-73. Recipient Florentino-Ramirez Internat. Law award, 1975. Mem. ABA (labor sect. 1974—, employment law com. 1974—), Ark. Bar Assn. (sec., chmn. labor sect. 1978-81, ho. of dels. 1979-82, Golden Gavel award 1983), Def. Research Inst. (employment law com. 1982—), Am. Trial Lawyers Assn., Ark. Trial Lawyers Assn., Ark. Assn. of Def. Counsel, Ark. Bd. of Legal Specialization (sec. 1982-85, chmn. 1985—, labor, employment discrimination, civil rights). Office: Rose Law Firm 120 E Fourth St Little Rock AR 72201

BOEHM, GEORGE EDGAR, manufacturing and distributing executive; b. Dayton, Ohio, Aug. 18, 1931; s. Irwin Geroge Boehm and Martha B. (Mynes) Baldridge; m. Margaret Ann Chervenka, Oct. 15, 1959; children: Lynn Marie Boehm Jordan, Julie Ann Boehm Bonner. BBA in Acctg., Ohio State U., 1959. Sr. auditor Deloitte, Haskins & Sells, Milw., 1959-66; v.p. Aetna Bus. Credit Co., High Point, N.C., 1966-70; pres. Water Bonnet Inc., Coburn Industries Inc. and Advance Finishing Inc. all subs. Equity Nat. Industries Inc., Atlanta, 1970-74; exec. v.p. Cunningham Art Products Inc., Stone Mountain, Ga., 1974-75; cons. Stone Mountain, 1975; exec. v.p. Plaid Enterprises Inc., Norcross, Ga., 1975—. Mem. AICPA, Nat. Assn. Accts., Wis. Inst. CPA's, Atlanta Athletic Club, Masons, Pi Kappa Alpha Alumni Assn. Home: 1755 Tamworth Ct Dunwoody GA 30338 Office: Plaid Enterprises Inc PO Box 7600 Norcross GA 30091

BOEKE, NORBERT HENRY, heating, ventilating and air conditioning company executive; b. Anna, Ohio, Aug. 31, 1940; s. Sylverius and Loretta (Henke) B.; m. Carol Ann Gramza, Nov. 3, 1962; children: Kevin Michael, Mark Anthony. Student, U. Toledo, 1959-61. Design engr. Buehrer & Stough Architects and Engrs., Toledo, 1961-67; sales engr. Fry Bros. Heating and Air Conditioning, Toledo, 1967-77; dir. plant ops. Parkview Hosp., Toledo, 1977-81; chief exec. officer Noron, Inc., Toledo, 1981—; mem. com. Ohio Environ. Svcs., 1979, Ohio Dept. Devel., 1987; cert. auditor Ohio Dept. Energy, 1979; mem. tech. adv. com. Ohio Hosp. Assn., 1980, Hosp. Coun. NW Ohio, 1980, heating, ventilating & air conditioning adv. com. Tera Tech. Coll. Contbr. articles to profl. publs. Coach, bd. dirs. Youth Travel Ice Hockey, N.W. Ohio Amateur Hockey Assn., Greater Toledo Area Hockey Assn., 1978-85; tournament marshall Ohio State Hockey Championships, Sylvania, 1984. Mem. Toledo Heating and Air Conditioning Contractors Assn. (trustee), Bass Anglers Sportsmans Soc., Nat. Rifle Assn., So. Mich. Sportsmans Club. Roman Catholic. Home: 2255 Angel Ave Toledo OH 43611 Office: Noron Inc 3025 E Manhattan Blvd Toledo OH 43611

BOEKENHEIDE, RUSSELL WILLIAM, forest products company executive; b. St. Louis, Dec. 6, 1930; s. William George and Mildred (Hann) B.; m. Frances Jeanne Deguire, 1958 (div. 1964); children: Mark, Louise, Susan; m. Barbro Helena Martinson, June 18, 1966. B.A. in Econs., Blackburn Coll., 1952. Personnel mgr. Vickers Inc., Joplin, Mo., 1959-64; dir. personnel Kendall Co., Boston, 1964-73; v.p. personnel Nestle Co., White Plains, N.Y., 1973-76; v.p. indsl. relations Union Camp Corp., Wayne, N.J., 1976-84, sr. v.p., 1984—; U.S. mgmt. del. Textile div. ILO, Geneva, Switzerland, 1971. Trustee Blackburn Coll., Carlinville, Ill., N.J. Ind. Coll. Fund; adv. bd. Riegel and Emory Human Resource Research Ctr., U. S.C. Served with U.S. Army, 1952-54. Mem. Am. Paper Inst. (chmn. employee relations com. 1978-80, chmn. labor relations com. 1980-82). Republican. Club: Indian Trail (Franklin Lakes, N.J.). Home: 352 Algonquin Rd Franklin Lakes NJ 07417 Office: Union Camp Corp 1600 Valley Rd Wayne NJ 07470

BOELTER, ROBERT, advertising agency executive; b. Eau Claire, Wis., Nov. 21, 1940; s. Robert H. and La Vyne M. (Sherman) B.; B.S., U. Wis., Madison, 1965; m. Maureen Kennedy; children: Christopher, Bridget, Robert. Art dir. Waldbilling & Besteman, Inc., Madison, 1966-67; creative dir. Stephan & Brady, Inc., Madison, 1967-70; art dir. Hoffman, York, Baker & Johnson, Chgo., 1970-71, Milw., 1971-73; pres. Advt., Boelter & Lincoln, Madison and Milw., 1973—; tchr. Madison Area Tech. Coll., 1966-67, mem. comml. art adv. bd., 1976-88; bd. dirs. Homestar Video, Inc.; sec., bd. dirs. Zins, Boelter & Lincoln, Inc. Recipient numerous awards for advt. creative work, including: Madison Advt. Club, 1967-70, 74—, Milw. Advt. Club, 1977, Milw. Art Dirs. Club, 1966-71, Milw. Soc. Communicating Arts, 1972-76, Am. Advt. Fedn., 1975-81, Am. Bus. Press Assn., 1972, CLIO, 1979, N.Y. One Show, 1981, Bank Mktg. Assn., 1979-81, Rockford Advt. Club, 1980. Mem. Dane County Humane Soc., 1986—. Mem. Am. Mktg. Assn. (chpt. pres. 1981), Madison Advt. Club, Madison Art Center, Downtown Madison Inc. (dir. 1979-84), Greater Madison C. of C., North Central Briarders (founding pres. 1976-77), Briard Club Am. (pres. 1983-84), Nat. Dog Breed Club, Nat. Model Railroaders Assn., Chgo. and Northwestern Hist. Soc., Milw. Road Hist. Soc., Mid-Continent Ry. Mus., Pro-Com. Home: 1706 Camelot Dr Madison WI 53705 Office: PO Box 1665 123 E Doty St Madison WI 53701

BOEMI, A. ANDREW, banker; b. N.Y.C., Mar. 3, 1915; s. S. and Marietta (Boemi) B.; B.C.E., Coll. City N.Y., 1936, M.C.E., 1938; m. Flora Dorothy DeMuro, Apr. 26, 1941; children—Andrew A., Marcia Rosamond Buchanan. Engr., Gibb & Hill, Cons. Engrs., N.Y.C., 1937; city planner N.Y. Planning Comm., 1938-41; cons. U.S. Bur. Budget, Exec. Office of President, Washington, 1942; asst. loan officer, planning cons., asst. v.p., v.p. First Fed. Savs. & Loan, Chgo., 1946-57; pres., chief exec. officer Madison Bank & Trust Co., Chgo., 1957-84, chmn. bd., 1974—; pres., chmn. bd. Madison Fin. Corp., Chgo., 1974-84, chmn. bd., chief exec. officer, 1985-87, chmn. bd., 1987— ; chmn., bd. dirs. Madison Nat. Bank of Niles (Ill.), 1st Nat. Bank of Wheeling (Ill.), MFC Mortgage Co.; chmn. Century Savings Bancorp, 1988—. Mem. exec. com. Archdiocesan Commn. Human Relations and Ecumenism, 1969-72; mem. Mayor's Commn. Landmarks Preservation Council, 1972-75. Bd. dirs. Met. Housing and Planning Council, 1950—, pres., 1975-76; mem. Elem. Sch. Bd., Park Ridge, Ill., 1953-59, pres., 1956-59; citizens bd. Loyola U., Chgo.; chmn. Joint Action Com. Civic Assns. for location Chgo. campus U. Ill., 1960-61; chmn. Gateway Com., Chgo., 1958-63; bd. dirs. Duncan YMCA, 1964-77; mem. Exec. Svc. Corp., 1988—; mem. adv. bd. Cath. Charities, 1986—. Served to lt. comdr. USNR, 1942-46. Recipient commendation ribbon from sec. navy, World War II; decorated Knight Order Holy Sepulchre of Jerusalem. Mem. Am. Bankers Assn., Ill. Bankers Assn. (fed. legis. and regulation com.), ASCE, Am. Inst. Planners, Navy League U.S., Newcomen Soc. N.Am., Am. Legion, Knights of Malta (decorated), Lambda Alpha, Alpha Beta Gamma. Republican. Clubs: Economic, Bankers, University (Chgo.); Park Ridge Country. Home: 1110 N Lake Shore Dr Apt 7-S Chicago IL 60611 Office: 400 W Madison St Chicago IL 60606

BOESCHENSTEIN, WILLIAM WADE, glass products manufacturing executive; b. Chgo., Sept. 7, 1925; s. Harold and Elizabeth (Wade) B.; m. Josephine H. Moll, Nov. 28, 1953; children: William Wade, Michael M., Peter H., Stephen S. Student, Phillips Acad., 1944; B.S., Yale, 1950. With Owens-Corning Fiberglas Corp., 1950—, br. mgr., Detroit, 1955-59, v.p. central region, 1959-61, v.p. sales br. operations, Toledo, 1961-63, v.p. marketing, 1963-67, exec. v.p., 1967-71, pres., 1971-88, chief exec. officer, 1972—, chmn., 1981—, dir., 1967—; dir. Prudential Ins. Co. Am., FMC Corp., Chgo., M. A. Hanna Co., Cleve. Trustee Toledo Mus. Art, Phillips Acad., Andover, Mass., Edison Inst.; mem. nat. bd. Smithsonian Assocs. Mem. The Bus. Council, The Conf. Bd. Clubs: Links (N.Y.C.), Toledo (Toledo), Inverness (Toledo), Belmont Country (Perrysburg, Ohio), Augusta (Ga.), Nat. Home: 3 Locust St Perrysburg OH 43659 Office: Owens-Corning Fiberglas Corp Fiberglas Tower Toledo OH 43659

BOESEL, MILTON CHARLES, JR., lawyer, business executive; b. Toledo, July 12, 1928; s. Milton Charles and Florence (Fitzgerald) B.; m. Lucy Laughlin Mather, Mar. 25, 1961; children—Elizabeth Parks, Charles Mather, Andrew Fitzgerald. B.A., Yale, 1950; LL.B., Harvard, 1953. Bar: Ohio bar 1953, Mich. bar 1953. Of counsel firm Ritter, Boesel & Robinson, Toledo, 1956—; pres., dir. Michabo, Inc.; dir. 1st Nat. Bank of Toledo. Served to lt. USNR, 1953-56. Episcopalian. Clubs: Toledo, Toledo Country; Leland Country (Mich.). Home: 2268 Innisbrook Rd Toledo OH 43606 Office: Ritter Boesel & Robinson 810 First Fed Pla Toledo OH 43604

BOETTCHER, ARMIN SCHLICK, lawyer, banker; b. East Bernard, Tex., Apr. 12, 1941; s. Clem C. and Frances Helene (Schlick) B.; B.B.A., U. Tex., Austin, 1963, J.D., 1967; m. Virginia Nan Barkley, Apr. 13, 1963; children—Lynn Frances, Laura Anne. Various positions personal trust dept. Republic Bank Houston 1967-75, sr. v.p., trust officer, head trust dept., 1975-82; dir. Union State Bank, East Bernard, Union Motor Co., Inc., East Bernard, Bess Mgmt. Corp., Houston. Bd. dirs. Whispering Oaks Civic Club, 1980-85, pres., 1981. Mem. Houston Bus. and Estate Planning Council, Houston Estate and Fin. Forum, Tex., Houston Bar Assns., Sigma Chi, U. Tex. Ex-Students Assn. (life). Methodist. Club: Meml. Forest (dir. 1981-83). Office: 2500 Tanglewilde Ste 277 Houston TX 77063

BOETTCHER, BRYAN CLAIR, advertising executive; b. Marinette, Wis., Feb. 3, 1956; s. Lloyd Clarence and Audrey Eloise (Knudson) B.; m. Mary Beth Waeghe, May 28, 1979; children: Brooke, Brent, Brennan. BS, U. Wis., Green Bay, 1978. Relocation specialist City of Green Bay Planning, 1978-81; v.p. Orde Advt. Co., Green Bay, 1981—. Mem. adv. council Green Bay Visitor and Conv. Bur., 1981—; mem. St. John's Bd. Edn., 1988—. Mem. Tips Club of Green Bay (sec./treas. 1981—), Ashwauben Bus. Assn., Howard-Soamico Bus. Assn. Clubs: Nat. Phoenix (sec./ treas. 1982—), Univest (sec. 1986—). Home: 978 Southern Cross Rd Green Bay WI 54303 Office: Orde Advt Co 300 S Taylor St Green Bay WI 54303

BOGAARD, WILLIAM JOSEPH, lawyer; b. Sioux City, Iowa, Jan. 18, 1938; s. Joseph and Irene Mary (Hensing) B.; B.S., Loyola Marymount U., Los Angeles, 1959; J.D. with honors, U. Mich., 1965; m. Claire Marie Whalen, Jan. 28, 1961; children—Michele, Jeannine, Joseph, Matthew. Bar: Calif. 1966. Ptnr. firm Hufstedler, Miller, Kaus & Beardsley, Los Angeles, 1971-82; exec. v.p., gen. counsel First Interstate Bancorp, Los Angeles, 1982—. Mem. Pasadena (Calif.) City Council, 1978-86; mayor City of Pasadena, 1984-86. Served to capt. USAF, 1959-62. Mem. Am. Bar Assn., Los Angeles County Bar Assn. (Outstanding Corp. Counsel award 1987). Office: 1st Interstate Bancorp 707 Wilshire Blvd Los Angeles CA 90017

BOGAN, MARY FLAIR, stockbroker, former actress; b. Providence, July 9, 1948; d. Ralph A.L. and Mary (Dyer) B.; B.A., Vassar Coll., 1969. Actress, Trinity Sq. Repertory Co., R.I., Gretna Playhouse, Pa., Skylight Comic Opera, Milw., Cin. Playhouse, Playmakers' Repertory, Va.; mem. nat. co. No Sex, Please, We're British; also TV commls., 1970-77; account exec. E.F. Hutton & Co., Inc., Providence, 1977-86; account v.p. Paine Webber, 1986—; econ. reporter Sta. WPRI-TV, 1982-85, Sta. WJAR-TV, 1987—. Treas. Red Bridge Council Rep. Women; chmn. new mems. com. R.I. Fedn. Rep. Women. Recipient Century Club award, 1980, 81, 82, 83, 85; Blue Chip Sales award, 1983, 85, Pacesetter Sales Award, 1986, 87. Mem. Internat. Platform Assn., Newport Preservation Soc., Providence Preservation Soc. Clubs: Providence Art, Turks Head, Brown Faculty. Home: 18 Cooke St Providence RI 02906 Office: Sta WJAR-TV 1520 Hospital Trust Tower Providence RI 02903

BOGAN, NEIL EARNEST, lawyer; b. Des Moines, Oct. 21, 1945; s. William Eldirage and Cynthia Marie (Faulkner) B.; m. Carolyn Sue Martin, Aug. 9, 1968; children: Tiffany Lynn, Tyler Douglas, Tadd Justin Pace. BA, U. Okla., 1967; JD, U. Tulsa, 1970. Bar: Okla. 1970, U.S. Dist. Ct. (no. dist.) Okla. 1970, U.S. Ct. Appeals (10th cir.) 1975, U.S. Supreme Ct. 1980. Legal intern Jones, Givens, Brett, Gotcher & Doyle, Tulsa, 1970, assoc., 1970-75; v.p. Jones, Givens, Gotcher, Bogan & Hilborne, Tulsa, 1975—, mng. atty., 1987; bd. dirs. Douglas-Gordon Ltd., Petroleum Mktg. Co., Tulsa Nat. Bank, mem. loan com., 1984—; lectr. in field. Captain Indian Nations council Boy Scouts Am., 1987; patron N.E. Okla. chpt. Am. Heart Assn., 1987, Tulsa Opera Inc., 1988; com. mem. annual fund drive Philbrook Art Ctr., 1985, 86; mem. adminstrv. bd. Asbury Meth. Ch. 1988—, fin. com., 1988—; office coordinator annual fund drive United Way, 1986, 87, 88; coordinator fund raising com. U. Tulsa Coll. of Law, 1986; trustee U. Tulsa, 1989—. Named Alumnus of Month, U. Tulsa, 1988. Fellow Okla. Bar Found. (trustee 1989—), Am. Bar Found.; mem. ABA (del. 1989—), Am. Judicature Soc., Okla. Bar Assn. (pres.-elect 1989, v.p. 1984, bd. govs. 1984-87, 89—, chmn. budget com. 1989), Tulsa County Bar Assn. (bd. dirs. 1983—, pres. 1987-88, chmn. med.-legal com. 1989, Pres. award 1984, Disting. Svc. award 1986), Tulsa Bus. Builders Assn. (pres. 1985, Silver Star cert. 1988), Okla. Fellowship Christian Athletes (bd. reps. 1987—), Nat. Conf. Bar Pres., Southern Conf. Bar Pres. Republican. Methodist. Office: Jones Givens Gotcher Bogan & Hilborne 3800 1st National Tower Tulsa OK 74103

BOGART, HOMER GORDON, paper and pulp company executive; b. New Rochelle, N.Y., July 28, 1922; s. Harold Garfield and Mildred Helen (Moses) B.; B.A. in History, Dartmouth Coll., 1945; m. Skaidrite Ozols, Feb. 22, 1962; children—Bonnie, Gary, David, Imants. Tchr., coach Vt. Acad., Saxtons River, 1945-48; owner, mgr. H.G. Bogart Distbg. Co., Kalamazoo, 1949-51; sales mgr. Food Processing Equipment Co., 1951-58; asst. sales engr. Sutherland Paper Co., Kalamazoo, 1958-61, sales mgr., Kalamazoo and N.Y.C., 1961-68; nat. sales mgr. Brown Co., N.Y.C., 1964-68; sales mgr. Perkins-Goodwin Co., Inc., Chgo., 1968-77, v.p. sales, 1975-77, pres., chief exec. officer, 1977-85., pres. paper mktg. group, 1986—; const. to pres. Andrews/Nelson/Whitehead. Trustee, Paper Tech. Found., Inc., Western Mich. U., Kalamazoo; bd. dirs. Chgo. Health Mgmt. Orgn. Served with U.S. Army, 1942-43. Mem. TAPPI. Republican. Episcopalian. Clubs: Sae, Marco Polo. Contbr. articles to profl. jours. Home: 3305 Robincrest Northbrook IL 60062 Office: Perkins-Goodwin Co Inc 540 Frontage Northfield IL 60093

BOGATER, RAYMON L., trucking company executive; b. Cleve., Nov. 25, 1939; s. Theodore Frank and Estelle Margaret (Nadwodny) B.; m. Jeanette Jaksic, May 5, 1973. BBA, Bowling Green U., 1965. Self-employed in trucking industry Cleve., 1965-67; mgr. traffic and softgoods Fabri-Ctrs. of Am., Beachwood, Ohio, 1967-69; mgr. distbn. and warehouse Gaylords Nat. Corp., Cleve., 1969-72; mgr. fleet ops., delivery, transfer Higbee Co., Cleve., 1972-79; gen. mgr. food distbn. Lawson Co., Akron, Ohio, 1979-80; v.p. ops. A-Gar Trucking & Painting, Inc., Cleve., 1980-83; v.p., gen. mgr. Accurate Moving Co., Inc., Cleve., 1983-87; pres. First Choice Gen. Contractors, Inc., Cleve., 1988—; pres. Servpro of Lake County, Willoughby, Ohio. Mem. Assn. Specialists in Cleaning & Restoration, Am. Trucking Assn., Cleve. Area Bd. Realtors, Beta Theta Pi. Republican. Russian Orthodox. Club: Elks, Westlake Yacht, Lorain Country. Home: 2192 West Blvd Cleveland OH 44102 Office: First Choice Gen Contractors 3400 St Rocco Ct Cleveland OH 44102

BOGDAN, JAMES E., chief financial officer; b. Milw., Mar. 3, 1948; s. Edward John and Audrey (Westphal) B.; m. Patricia Ann Noohan, June 18, 1973; children: Steven, Matthew, Gregory. BBA magna cum laude, U. Notre Dame, 1970. CPA, Wis. Sr. auditor Price-Waterhouse & Co., Milw., 1970-74; v.p., owner Peterson Chem., Sheboygan, Wis., 1974-76; corp. controller Albert Trostel & Sons, Milw., 1976-80; v.p. McQuay, Inc., Milw., Mpls., 1980-84; fin. exec. Parker Pen Co., Janesville, Wis., 1984-85; v.p. fin. Sordoni Enterprises, Forty Ft., Pa., 1986-87; v.p., chief fin. officer C-TEC Corp., Wilkes-Barre, Pa., 1987—. Chmn. Vols. of Am. of N.E. and Pa., Wilkes Barre, 1987—; pres. Franklin Nat. Little Leauge, Franklin, Wis., 1983; active Vols. Am. League. Mem. Fin. Exec. Inst. Roman Catholic.

Home: RD 1 Box 519-1 Dallas PA 18612 Office: C-TEC Corp 46 Public Sq Wilkes-Barre PA 18703-3000

BOGDAN, LIVIUS SILVIU, real estate developer; b. Bucharest, Romania, Nov. 28, 1932; s. Silviu and Margaret (Laurentzy) B.; m. Florina Tanasescu, Feb. 22, 1955 (div. 1957); m. Margareta Batsu, July 2, 1962. MA, Archtl. Inst., Romania, 1955; BArch, Met. Collegiate, London, 1966. Am. Reg. Architect; lic. personal property broker, Calif.; cert. registered appraiser, Ariz. Dir. architecture and engring. Govt. Agy., Romania, 1957-66; v.p., sr. project dir. Welton/Becket, N.Y.C., 1967-78; pres. 1st Regency Devel. Corp., N.Y., Fla., London, 1978-84; v.p. E&E Devel. Corp., L.A., 1985-87; pres. Regal Regency Devel. Corp, North Hollywood, Calif., 1988—; mortgage underwriter, Ariz., 1983. Mem. Condo Developers Council of Am., Am. Land Devel. Assn., Am. Hotel and Motel Assn., Merchants-Brokers Exchange, Audobon, Masons. Republican.

BOGDANOVICH, JOSEPH JAMES, food company executive; b. San Pedro, Calif., May 9, 1912; s. Martin Joseph and Antoinette (Simich) B.; m. Nancynell Swaffield, Apr. 3, 1937; children—Martin, Robert, Joseph James. Student, Sch. Commerce, U. So. Calif., 1934. With Star-Kist Foods, Inc., Terminal Island, Calif., 1926—, adminstrv. asst., 1937-44, pres., from 1944; sr. v.p., dir. H.J. Heinz Co., Pitts., now vice-chmn., dir.; Mem. Calif. Marine Research Com., 1960-66; ofcl. adviser joint U.S.-Japanese Tuna Conf., 1959, 62. Bd. dirs. Marymount Coll., South Palos Verdes Estates, Calif. Club: Virginia Country (Long Beach, Calif.). Office: H J Heinz Co 600 Grant St Pittsburgh PA 15219

BOGDANOWICZ-BINDERT, CHRISTINE ANNE, investment banker; b. Leuven, Belgium, Sept. 5, 1951; came to U.S., 1976; d. Jerzy and Anne (Leskiewicz) Bogdanowicz; m. Detlef Bindert, July 29, 1974; children: Yannick Alexander. M in Econs., Cath. U. Louvain, 1974; M in Advanced Govt. Studies, Coll. Europe Studies, Bruges, Belgium, 1975. Credit officer Mitteleuropaische Handelsbank, Frankfurt, Fed. Republic of Germany, 1975-76; economist Internat. Monetary Fund, Washington, 1976-80; sr. v.p. internat. govt. adv. svcs. Shearson Lehman Hutton Inc., N.Y.C., 1980-85, sr. v.p. corp. fin., 1985-89; sr. v.p. corp. fin. Shearson Lehman Hutton Inc., Frankfurt, Federal Rep. Germany, 1989—; chmn. trends analysis com. Council of Americas, N.Y.C., 1984-86; cons. Fgn. Policy Assn., N.Y.C., 1984-86; adj. prof. Fordham U., N.Y.C., 1984-86, Columbia U., N.Y.C., 1985—. Editor: The Supranationals, 1986, Solving the Global Debt Crisis: Strategies and Controversies from Key Stakeholders, 1989; mem. editorial adv. bd. The Internat. Economy, 1988—; mem. editorial rev. bd. Columbia Jour. World Bus., 1987—; contbr. articles to profl. jours. Bd. dirs. Hudson Guild, N.Y.C., 1986-89; bd. dirs., mem. fin. com. Women's World Banking, N.Y.C., 1986—; mem. council Overseas Devel. Council, Washington, 1987—. Mem. North South Roundtable. Roman Catholic. Office: Shearson Lehman Hutton AG, Wilhelm-Leuschner Str 41, D 6000 Frankfurt/Main Federal Republic Germany

BOGER, DAN CALVIN, economics educator, statistical and economic consultant; b. Salisbury, N.C., July 9, 1946; s. Brady Cashwell and Gertrude Virginia (Hamilton) B.; m. Gail Lorraine Zivna, June 23, 1973; children—Gretchen Zivna, Gregory Zivna. B.S. in Mgmt. Sci., U. Rochester, 1968; M.S. in Mgmt. Sci., Naval Postgrad. Sch., Monterey, Calif., 1969; M.A. in Stats., U. Calif.-Berkeley, 1977, Ph.D. in Econs., 1979. Cert. cost analyst; cert. profl. estimator. Research asst. U. Calif.-Berkeley, 1975-79; asst. prof. econs. Naval Postgrad. Sch., Monterey, Calif., 1979-85, assoc. prof., 1985—; cons. econs. and statis. legal matters CSX Corp, others, 1977—. Assoc. editor The Logistics and Transportation Rev., 1981-85; mem. editorial rev. bd. Jour. Tranp. Research Forum, 1987—; contbr. articles to profl. jours. Served to lt. USN, 1968-75. Flood fellow Dept. Econs., U. Calif.-Berkeley, 1975-76; dissertation research grantee A.P. Sloan Found., 1978-79. Mem. Am. Econ. Assn., Am. Statis. Assn., Econometric Soc., Math. Assn. Am., Inst. Mgmt. Sci., Ops. Research Soc. Am. (sec., treas. mil. applications sect. 1987—), Sigma Xi. Home: 61 Ave Maria Rd Monterey CA 93940 Office: Naval Postgrad Sch Code 54Bo Monterey CA 93943

BOGGS, KEVIN SCOTT, accountant; b. L.A., Oct. 31, 1964; s. Richard and Lola (May) B. BA, Pacific Union Coll., 1987. Staff acct. Loma Linda (Calif.) Community Hosp., 1987—. Home: 871 W Walnut Ave Monrovia CA 91016 Office: Loma Linda Community Hosp 25333 Barton Rd Loma Linda CA 92354

BOGGS, WILLIAM BRADY, quality engineering consultant; b. Atlanta, Nov. 15, 1943; s. William Brady and Callie Kathleen (Jordan) B.; m. Rebecca Lynn Taunton, Feb. 26, 1966; children—Jason Alan, Brian Daniel. BS in Physics, Ga. Inst. Tech., 1965; MS, Fla. State U., 1970, MBA, 1971; postgrad N.C. State U., 1979-80; diploma in Bible and Doctrine, Berean Sch. of Bible, 1985. Cert. quality engr. Am. Soc. Quality Control. Radar systems analyst Calspan Corp., Buffalo, 1972-74; sect. head research systems engring. BASF Corp. (formerly Am. Enka Co.), Enka, N.C., 1974-78, mgr. research systems engring., 1978-82, research staff statistician, 1982-83, engring. staff statistician, 1983-87, head fibers div. statis. services, 1988—; pres. Alpha Quality Services, Inc., Candler, N.C., 1985—. Contbr. papers to profl. conf. Sr. comr. Royal Rangers outpost 46 Christian ministry for boys, Asheville, 1984-85, sect. comdr. Gt. Smoky Mountain sect. N.C. dist., 1986—. Served to capt. U.S. Army, 1965-68. Mulliken fellow, 1968-70, Fla. State U. fellow, 1970-71. Mem. Am. Soc. Quality Control, Am. Statis. Assn., Tau Beta Pi, Phi Kappa Phi, Sigma Pi Sigma, Pi Eta Sigma, Sigma Iota Epsilon, Beta Gamma Sigma. Mem. Assembly of God. Clubs: Full Gospel Businessmens Fellowship (treas. 1980, sec. 1981-82); Frontiersman Camping Fraternity N.C. Avocations: photography, camping. Home: Rte 2 PO Box 391-A Candler NC 28715 Office: BASF Corp Fibers Div Enka NC 28728

BOGLE, JOHN CLIFTON, investment company executive; b. Montclair, N.J., May 8, 1929; s. William Yates, Jr. and Josephine (Hipkins) B.; m. Eve Sherrerd, Sept. 22, 1956; children: Barbara, Jean, John Clifton, Nancy, Sandra, Andrew. A.B., Princeton U., 1951. With Wellington Mgmt. Co., Phila., 1951-74; asst. to pres. Wellington Mgmt. Co., 1954-62, sec., adminstrv. v.p., 1962-66, exec. v.p., 1966-67, pres., chief exec. officer, 1967-74; chmn., chief exec. officer Vanguard Group Investment Cos. (Wellington Fund, Windsor Fund, others), Valley Forge, Pa., 1974—; dir. Meritor Fin. Group, 1969—; dir., mem. exec. com. Gen. Accident Ins. Group, dir., chmn. fin. com. Mead Corp. Contbr. numerous articles to profl. jours., chpts. to books. Chmn. bd. trustees Blair Acad.; bd. dirs. Nat. Constitution Ctr.; adv. council econs. dept. Princeton U.; adv. council Center for Fin. Insts., U. Pa.; chmn. fin. com. Bryn Mawr (Pa.) Hosp. Mem. Nat. Assn. Securities Dealers (investment cos. com. 1967-74, long-range planning com. 1973-74), Investment Co. Inst. (gov. 1969-81, chmn. 1969-70). Clubs: Merion Cricket (Haverford), Merion Golf (Ardmore); Union League (Phila.). Home: 418 N Rose Ln Haverford PA 19041 Office: Vanguard Group 1300 Morris Dr PO Box 876 Valley Forge PA 19482

BOGOMOLNY, RICHARD JOSEPH, retail food chain executive; b. 1935, Cleve.; married. BS, Case Western U., 1957, JD, Cleve. State U., 1961. With Eagle Ice Cream Co., 1955-68, Fisher Foods Inc., 1968-72, Pick-N-Pay Supermarkets Inc., 1972-78; with First Nat. Supermarkets, Cleve., 1978—, pres., chief exec. officer, now chmn., chief exec. officer, 1983—. Office: First Nat Supermarkets Inc 17000 Rockside Rd Cleveland OH 44137 *

BOGUE, BRUCE, insurance agent; b. Los Angeles, Sept. 24, 1924; s. Charles Luther and Viola (Adam) B.; m. Tays Myrl Tarvin, Dec. 18, 1945; children: Tays Elizabeth, Charles Luther II. BA, U. Calif. at Los Angeles, 1947; grad. Inf. Staff and Command Sch. U.S. Army, 1948. Agt. Mut. Benefit Life Ins. Co., Los Angeles, 1948-55, prodn. mgr., 1955-62; gen. agt. Guardian Life Ins. Co., Los Angeles, 1962-85, agt., 1985—; tchr. ins. UCLA. Contbr. articles to profl. jours. Precinct capt., poll watcher, hdqrs. chmn., fund raising chmn., campaign chmn. for Rep. party. Served to capt. inf. AUS, 1942-46, ETO. Recipient Man of Affairs award Los Angeles Wilshire Press, Los Angeles Mirror News, 1958, Nat. Mgmt. award 1980-85. Mem. Million Dollar Round Table (life), Am. Soc. CLUs, Assn. Advanced Life Underwriters, Nat. Assn. Life Underwriters, U. Calif. at Los Angeles Alumni Assn. (life). Congregationalist. Clubs: California; Monrovia Tennis; Los Angeles. Home: 2200 Homet Rd San Marino CA 91108 Office: Guardian Life Ins Co 617 S Olive St #1000 Los Angeles CA 90014

BOHAN, THOMAS E., advertising company executive. Exec. v.p., mgmt. dir. Saatchi and Saatchi DFS Inc., N.Y.C. Office: Saatchi & Saatchi DFS Inc 375 Hudson St New York NY 10014-3220 *

BOHANAN, DAVID JOHN, management consultant; b. Utica, N.Y., Dec. 13, 1946; s. Clifton Ralph and Florence Susan (Dunham) B.; m. Judith Ann Petrocci, July 31, 1977; children: Luke, Jacob. BFA in Ceramics and Painting, Alfred U., 1968; BS in Commerce, U. Md., 1979; MBA in Mgmt., Boston U., 1981. Pub. R&R in the Med Mediterranean Pubs. Srl., Vicenza, Italy, 1974-81; pvt. practice fin. cons. Jersey City, 1981-86; agt. S&B Practice Mgmt. Assocs., Jersey City, 1983—, bus. cons., 1986—; fin. planner Fin. Found., Inc., Jersey City, 1986—, investment advisor, 1987—; rep. Nathan & Lewis Securities, Inc., N.Y.C., 1982—. Capt. field arty., U.S. Army, 1968-74, Vietnam. Decorated Bronze Star with oak leaf cluster. Mem. Inst. Cert. Fin. Planners (cert.). Republican. Home: 369 Woodlawn Ave Jersey City NJ 07305 Office: Fin Found Inc 314 Rte 22W Ste G Greenbrook NJ 08812

BOHANNON-KAPLAN, MARGARET ANNE, publisher, lawyer; b. Oakland, Calif., July 6, 1937; d. Thomas Morris and Ruth Frances (Davenport) Bohannon; m. Melvin Jordan Kaplan, Feb. 2, 1961; children—Mark Geoffrey, Craig Andrew, Stephen Joseph, David Benjamin, Jonathan Michael. Student Smith Coll., 1955-56, U. Cin., 1956; B.A. in Philosophy, U. Calif.-Berkeley, 1960; LL.B., LaSalle Extension U., 1982. Bar: Calif. 1982. Engaged in property mgmt., real estate investment Kaplan Real Estate, Berkeley and San Francisco, 1961-77; investment exec. Wellington Fin. Group, San Francisco, 1977—; cons. fin. planning and law, San Francisco and Carmel, Calif., 1982—; pres. Wellington Publs., Carmel, 1983—, Exec. Advt., Carmel, 1983—. Author: (pseudonym Helen P. Rogers), Everyone's Guide to Financial Planning, 1984, Social Security: An Idea Whose Time Has Passed, 1985, The American Deficit: Fulfillment of a Prophecy?, 1988, The Election Process, 1988, The Deficit: 12 Steps to Ease the Crisis, 1988. Mem. ABA, Calif. Bar Assn., Calif. Real Estate Assn., Inst. Cert. Fin. Planners, Estate Planning Council, The Federalist Soc., Internat. Platform Assn. Club: Commonwealth (San Francisco). Avocations: figure skating, violin, hiking. Office: PO Box 223159 Carmel CA 93922

BOHLEN, RICHARD W., manufacturing company executive; b. N.Y.C., Dec. 27, 1935; s. Richard and Mathilda Katherine (Buck) B.; m. Gwendolyn Ann Beran, July 9, 1960; children: Jeannette Louise, Christine Anne. BS, MIT, 1957; postgrad. Darmstadt (W.Ger.) Tech. Inst., 1960-61; MS, Poly. Inst. N.Y., 1962; MBA, Calif. State U.-Fullerton, 1968. Engr., project engr. aircraft, missile design Grumman Aerospace Corp., 1957-62; with Rockwell Internat., Pitts., 1962—, Apollo engring. mgr., space shuttle program mgr., 1962-72, dir. engring. indsl. products group, 1972-73, dir. bus. strategy, corp. staff, 1973-76, v.p. bus. devel., gen. indsl. ops., 1976-77, v.p., gen. mgr. utility and indsl. ops., 1977-80, pres. Mcpl. and Utility Div., 1980-86; pres. Mcpl. and Utility Div., 1980-86, pres. Measurement and Flow Control Div., 1986-87, sr. v.p. ops., 1988—; dir. GF Corp., Two-Six Inc. Mem. City L.A. Mayor's Fin. Task Force Projected Expenditures Subcom., 1988. Mem. Gas Appliance Mfrs. Assn., Am. Water Works Assn., AIAA, Am. Mgmt. Assn., Am. Gas Assn., Nat. Assn. Corp. Dirs., Nat. Assn. Bus. Economists, Pacific Coast Gas Assn. (bd. dirs., chmn. 1986-87), Beta Gamma Sigma, Sigma Phi Epsilon. Clubs: Pitts. Field, Pitts. Athletic Assn.

BOHLKEN, DEBORAH KAY, data processing executive; b. Anchorage, Nov. 16, 1952; d. Darrell Richard and Gertrude Ann (Merkel) B. BA, U. Ark., 1975, MSW, 1977. Specialist community devel. State of Ark., Little Rock, 1976-77, supr. community area, 1977-78, mgr. evaluation and data processing, 1978-80; corp. analyst Systematics, Inc., Little Rock, 1980-83, mgr. corp. planning and rsch., 1983-85, group mgr., planning, rsch. Washington Congl. liasion, 1985—. Contbr. articles and papers to profl. publs. Bd. dirs. Cen. Ark. Radiation Therapy Inst. Hotline, Little Rock, 1980-82, Cancer Soc., Little Rock, 1986—; state chair Cansurmount, Little Rock, 1985—. Nat. Juvenile Justice Law Enforcement Adminstrn. explimary data processing grantee, 1976-78. Mem. NAFE, Nat. Assn. Bank Svcs., Cash Mgrs. Assn., Fin. Mgrs. Assn., Mortgage Bankers Assn., U.S. Savs. and Loan Assn., Am. Mgmt. Assn. Democrat. Methodist. Office: Systematics Inc 4001 Rodney Parham Rd Little Rock AR 72212

BOHN, JOHN AUGUSTUS, JR., banker, lawyer; b. Oakland, Calif., Oct. 31, 1937; s. John Augustus and Virginia G. Bohn; m. Barbara Neukom, 1962; children—Linnea, John N., Maya, Cameron. A.B. cum laude, Stanford U., 1959, postgrad. Sch. Credit and Fin. Mgmt., 1979; postgrad., London Sch. Econs., 1960; LL.B., Harvard U., 1963. Bar: Calif. 1963, Guam 1965, Trust Ter. Pacific 1965, U.S. Supreme Ct. 1986. Pvt practice San Francisco, Guam, Trust Ter. Pacific, 1964-67; v.p. Wells Fargo Bank, San Francisco, 1967-68, 74-81, Tokyo, 1968-72, Los Angeles, 1972-74; spl. asst. to Sec. Treasury Dept. Treasury, 1981; U.S. ambassador to Asian Devel. Bank, Manila, 1981-84; vice-chmn. Export-Import Bank of U.S., Washington, 1984-86; pres., chmn. Export-Import Bank of U.S., 1986—. Mem. Calif. Commn. on Ednl. Fin., 1977-78; founding ptnr. Washington Pacific Group, 1980; bd. dirs. Alliance for Am. Innovation, 1980; chmn. Mgmt. and Evaluation Commn., Calif. Bd. Edn., 1981. Fulbright fellow, 1960. Mem. State Bar Calif., Bar of Guam, Bar Trust Ter. of Pacific. Office: Export-Import Bank US 811 Vermont Ave NW Washington DC 20571

BOHON, ELLIS G(RAY), accountant, management and tax consultant; b. LaBelle, Mo., Sept. 1, 1902; s. Frank W. and Lee (Ellis) B.; m. Joyce L. Finlayson, Apr. 15, 1939; children: Walter Duncan, Ellis Gray II (dec.). Student Westminster Coll., Fulton, Mo., 1920-21; BS cum laude, Knox Coll., Galesburg, Ill., 1924; postgrad. Walton Sch. Commerce, 1927-29, Northwestern U., 1930-33, 1935, 1965-66, YMCA Community Coll., 1963-71, Chgo. Bd. Trade Grain Inst., 1955-56 (all Chgo.); CPA, U. Ill., 1935. Enrolled as atty. Tax Ct. U.S.A.; CPA, Ill., Ky., Iowa, Mo. Staff accountant Ernst & Ernst, CPA's, Chgo., 1927-30; partner R. L. Pearce & Co., CPAs', 1930-36; propr. E. G. Bohon & Co., CPA's, 1936—; former lectr. Am. Inst. Banking, Walton Sch. Commerce, Ill. Inst. Tech., Chgo., Lake Forest (Ill.) Coll. Author papers. Former advisor, treas. Lakes chpt. Order DeMolay, bus. men's adv. council Jones Comml. High Sch. (Chgo.). Member Am. Inst. CPA's, Am. Accounting Assn., Ill. (past chmn. tech. com.), Ia. socs. CPA's, Nat. Assn. Accountants, Am. Arbitration Assn., Accounting Research Assn., Am. Inst. Laundering, Ky. Hist. Soc., Midwest Bus. Adminstrn. Assn., Phi Delta Theta. Presbyterian. Clubs: Masons, Shriners (treas. club 1978), Union League, Univ. of Evanston. Home: 523 E North Ave Lake Bluff IL 60044 Office: PO Box 431 Lake Bluff IL 60044

BOICE, CRAIG KENDALL, management consultant; b. Portland, Oreg., June 25, 1952; s. Charles A. and Audrey (Larson) B.; m. Jacinta E. Remedios, Nov. 21, 1979. BA summa cum laude, Beloit Coll., 1973; MA, Yale U., 1974, M.Phil., 1976, M in Pub. and Pvt. Mgmt., 1979. Instr. fellow philosophy Yale U., New Haven, 1978-79; economist Overseas Pvt. Investment Corp., Washington, 1978; sr. cons. Coopers and Lybrand, Washington and London, 1979-81; v.p. ops. Internat. Licensing Network, N.Y.C., 1981-82; pres., chmn., chief exec. officer Boice Dunham Group, N.Y.C., 1983—; adj. asst. prof. NYU, 1984—. Cons. Lake Placid Olympic Organizing Com., (N.Y.), 1979, New Haven Homesteading Program, 1979. Mem. Computer and Automated Systems Assn., Soc. Mfg. Engrs., Corp. Growth Assn., Soc. Photog. Scientists and Engrs., Planning Forum., World Future Soc., Internat. Platform Assn. Democrat. Office: Boice Dunham Group 437 Madison Ave New York NY 10022

BOISSEAU, JERRY PHILIP, financial services company executive; b. Plattsburgh, N.J., June 5, 1939; s. Augustine Arthur and Genevieve Francis (Poland) B.; m. Linda Gael Cummings Aug. 18, 1961; children: Gregory Philip, Lisa Michele. B of Gen. Studies, U. Nebr., 1970; MEd in Adminstrn., Fitchburg State Coll., 1978; MBA, Western New Eng. Coll., 1981. Cert. fin. planner; registered investment advisor. Commd. 2d lt. field artillery U.S. Army, 1963, advanced through grades to lt. col., 1979, ret., 1981; account exec. Prudential-Bache Securities, Springfield, Mass., 1981-87; pres. Arlington Beach Co., Seaside Park, N.J., 1987—; propr., mgr. Amherst Fin. Services, Seaside Park, 1987—; instr./lectr. U. Mass., Amherst, 1982-87, Greenfield (Mass.) Community Coll., 1983-86. Mem. Inst. Cert. Fin. Planners, Internat. Assn. Fin. Planning, Toms River C. of C., Rotary (pres. Amherst chpt. 1986-87), KC (4th degree). Roman Catholic. Home and Office: 500 N Bayview Ave PO Box 591 Seaside Park NJ 08752

BOK, JOAN TOLAND, utility executive; b. Grand Rapids, Mich., Dec. 31, 1929; d. Don Prentiss Weaver and Mary Emily (Anderson) T.; m. John Fairfield Bok, July 15, 1955; children: Alexander Toland, Geoffrey Robbins. A.B., Radcliffe Coll., 1951; J.D., Harvard U., 1955. Bar: Mass. 1955. Assoc. Ropes & Gray, Boston, 1955-61; pvt. practice Boston, 1961-68; atty. New Eng. Electric System, Westborough, Mass., 1968-73; asst. to pres. New Eng. Electric System, 1973-77, v.p., sec., 1977-79, vice chmn., dir., 1979-84, chmn., 1984—; vice chmn.,bd. dirs. NEES Energy Inc.; bd. dirs., chmn., New Eng. Power Co.; bd. dirs. Mass. Electric Co., Narragansett Electric Co., Bank of New Eng. N.A., Bank of New Eng. Corp., Dennison Mfg., Monsanto Co., Norton Co. Bd. dirs. Com. for Econ. Devel.; trustee Library of Boston Athenaeum; former pres. Harvard Bd. Overseers; councillor Am. Antiquarian Soc.; mem. of the corp. Mass. Gen. Hosp., MIT. Fellow Am. Bar Found.; mem. ABA, Boston Bar Assn., Woods Hole Oceanographic Instn., Phi Beta Kappa. Unitarian. Home: 53 Pinckney St Boston MA 02114 Office: New Eng Electric System 25 Research Dr Westborough MA 01581

BOLAJI, ROTIMI MICHAEL, accountant, operational research consultant; b. Okemesi-Ekiti, Nigeria, Mar. 3, 1952; s. Ibiloye Ezekiel and Ojuolape Abigael (Ojo-Odide) B.; m. Aduke Janet Adeoti, Mar. 11, 1981; children: Oluwatola Peter, Oluwafunmilola Deborah, Paul Oluwatuyi. Ordinary Nat. Diploma in Acctg., Poly. Ibadan, Nigeria, 1975, Higher Nat. Diploma in Acctg., 1978. Acctg. supr. Nigerian Nat. Petroleum Co., Lagos, 1979-82; acct., co. sec. Tixo Ltd., Ibadan, 1982-83, Abdulai & Amimolo Co. Ltd., Ibadan, 1983-84; internal auditor Ekiti-Akoko Agrl. Devel. Projects, Ikole-Ekiti, Nigeria, 1984-85; fin. mgr. Nigerian Telecommunications Ltd., Lagos, 1985-86; mng. dir. Mgmt. & Profl. Services Ltd, Ibadan, 1986—; audit mgr./cons. Opeabayomi & Co., Ibadan, 1986; bd. dirs. Profl. Edn. Ctr., Jos., Nigeria; prin. ptnr. Rotimi Bolaji & Co. Mem. Brit. Inst. Mgmt., Inst. Chartered Accts. Nigeria (assoc., chartered), Am. Mgmt. Assn. Clubs: Christian Pen Witness (Ibadan) (pres. 1977-86, editor newsletter 1977). Home: Obala Compound, PO Box 18, Okemesi-Ekiti Nigeria Office: Mgmt & Profl Services Ltd, N6/390B Polytechnic Rd, PO Box 15304, Ibadan Nigeria

BOLAK, HALIL DOGAN, petroleum company executive; b. Istanbul, Turkey, Oct. 14, 1961; s. Ahmet Aydin and Ayse Selma (Gürsan) B.; m. Ümit Nazli Alpay, Aug 10, 1984; 1 child, M. Sinan. BS in Engring., U. Rochester, 1983, MBA, 1985. With, bd. dirs. Türkpetrol T.A.S., Istanbul, Marmara Petrol A.S., Istanbul, Turtel A.S., Istanbul, Tüdas A.S., Istanbul; cons. in field; bd. dirs. Merkez Ins. A.S. Mem. Beta Gamma Sigma, Turkish Touring Club. Office: Turkpetrol TAS, Muallim Naci Cad 100, Istanbul Turkey

BOLAND, GERALD LEE, financial executive; b. Harrisburg, Pa., Apr. 2, 1946; s. Vincent Harry and Alice Jane (Geiste) B.; m. Elaine Frances Glenn, Oct. 25, 1980; 1 child, Peter Alexander. BS, Lebanon Valley Coll., 1968. Acctg. trainee Armstrong Cork Co., Millville, N.J., 1968; payroll supr., plant ops. accountant, 1969-70; sr. fin. acct. Lancaster (Pa.) Gen. Hosp., 1970-71, mgr. gen. acctg., 1972; corp. acctg. mgr. HMW Industries, Inc., Lancaster, 1972; corp. controller Fleck-Marshall Co. subs. Gable Industries, Lancaster, 1973-74, sec.-treas., 1974-75; controller Dominion Psychiat. Treatment Center, Falls Church, Va., 1975-76; controller, dir. fin. Miller & Byrne, Inc., Rockville, Md., 1976-79; v.p. internal auditing Medlantic Healthcare Group, 1979-88; v.p. ops. Kapner, Wolfberg & Assocs., Van Nuys, Calif., 1988—. Mem. Am. Acctg. Assn., Nat. Assn. Accts., Hosp. Fin. Mgmt. Assn., Eastern Fin. Assn., Am. Hosp. Assn., Am. Mgmt. Assn., Fin. Mgmt. Assn., Inst. Internal Auditors. Methodist. Home: 6309 Gallery St Bowie MD 20715

BOLAND, THOMAS EDWIN, banker; b. Columbus, Ga., July 8, 1934; s. Clifford Edwin and Helen Marjorie (Robinson) B.; m. Beth Ann Campbell, May 23, 1959; children—Susan Ann, Thomas Edwin. Student, Emory U., 1952-54, grad. Advanced Mgmt. Program, 1972; B.B.A., Ga. State U., 1957; postgrad., Stonier Grad. Sch. Banking, Rutgers U., 1964-66. With First Nat. Bank of Atlanta, 1954—, v.p., 1968-71, group v.p., 1972-73, sr. v.p., 1974-78, exec. v.p., in charge in credit policy, 1979-86; exec. v.p., chief adminstrv. officer First Nat. Bank of Atlanta and First Atlanta Corp., 1981-86, vice chmn., chief adminstrv. officer, 1987—; v.p. First Atlanta Internat. Corp., 1979—; exec. v.p. First Wachovia Corp., 1985—; chmn. bd. dirs. 1st Atlanta Bank, Wilmington, Del., 1987—; bd. dirs. First Nat. Bank Atlanta, First Atlanta Corp., First Atlanta Leasing, Minbanc Capital Corp., Washington, 1988, mem. investment com., 1978-86. Trustee Atlanta Bapt. Coll., 1970-72; trustee, mem. endowment com., mem. investment com. Ga. Bapt. Found., Atlanta, 1980-86, treas., 1980—; mem. Christian Life Commn., So. Bapt. Conv., Nashville, 1985—; mem. pres.'s council Mercer U., Macon, Ga., 1980-86, 88, trustee, 1986-88; bd. visitors Emory U., 1982-86; mem. exec. bd. Atlanta area council Boy Scouts Am., 1982, v.p. fin., 1986-87, pres., 1988—. Served with AUS, 1957. Recipient Disting. Salesman award Sales and Mktg. Execs., 1968; named Disting. Alumnus Coll. Bus. Adminstrn., Ga. State U., 1986. Mem. Am. Bankers Assn. (cert. comml. lender, bank card com. 1964-66), Robert Morris Assocs. (security dealers relations com. 1974-75, chmn. Met. Atlanta Area 1979-81, chmn. and dir. Eastern Group, Southeastern chpt. 1981, pres. and dir., So. chpt. 1982, chmn. policy div. council 1984-86, 2d v.p. 1986-87, 1st v.p. 1987-88, pres. 1988-89, nat. bd. dirs. 1984—), Ga. State U. Alumni Assn. (exec. com. and bd. dirs. 1979—, pres. 1985-86), Ga. State U. Found. (chmn. bd. trustees, 1988—). Clubs: Cherokee Town and Country, Capital City, Rotary (Atlanta). Home: 4986 Buckline Crossing Dunwoody GA 30338 Office: 1st Nat Bank 2 Peachtree St NE Atlanta GA 30383

BOLANDER, GLEN S., JR., food manufacturing company executive; b. N.Y.C., Sept. 24, 1946; s. Glen S. and Lucille B. (Amols) B.; m. Diana L. Smith, Feb. 1, 1969; 1 child, Lori D. AA, Southwestern Jr. Coll., Chula Vista, Calif., 1967; BA, San Diego State U., 1969; MBA, Calif. State U., 1978. Fireman Montgomery Fire Dept., Chula Vista, 1967-69; tech. sales rep. chems. div. Pfizer, Inc., N.Y.C., 1972-78; sales broker Bradford Co., Palos Verdes, Calif., 1978-80; pres., owner Contract Mfg. Services, Livermore, Calif., 1980-82; v.p. indsl. Grist Mill Co., Lakeville, Minn., 1982-85, v.p. sales, 1985-86, exec. v.p., 1986-87, pres., 1987—, also bd. dirs. Lt. USNR, 1969-72. Mem. Inst. Food Technologists (treas. no. Calif. chpt. 1972—), Am. Assn. Cereal Chemists, Am. Mgmt. Assn. Methodist. Office: Grist Mill Co PO Box 430 Lakeville MN 55044

BOLAS, EDWARD S., controller; b. Ft. Lee, Va., May 26, 1952; s. Kenneth H. and Lois E. (Stokes) B.; m. Mary P. Doll, July 7, 1973; 2 children. Student, U. Nebr., 1970-71; AA, Met. Tech. Community Coll., Omaha, 1980. Bookkeeper Vernon Dolleck, CPA, Omaha, 1980; regional acctg. mgr. Continental Care Ctrs., Omaha, 1980-83; regional acct. Beverly Enterprises, Inc., Omaha, 1983-85; chief fin. officer Mobridge Regional Hosp., S.D., 1985-88; controller Am. Bus. Forms, Glenwood, Minn., 1988—; Pres. elect Benson Community Council, Omaha, 1975-78; coach Cath. Youth Soccer Assn., Omaha, 1983-84; cubmaster Boy Scouts Am., Mobridge, 1985-88. Mem. Healthcare Fin. Mgrs. Assn. Republican. Methodist. Lodge: Masons. Office: Am Bus Forms Inc 31 E Minnesota Ave Glenwood MN 56334-0218

BOLCH, CARL EDWARD, JR., lawyer, corporation executive; b. St. Louis, Feb. 28, 1943; s. Carl Edward and Juanita (Newton) B.; m. Susan Bass; children: Carl, Allison, Natalie, Melanie, Jordan. B.S. in Econs, U. Pa., 1964; J.D., Duke U., 1967. Bar: Fla. 1967. Chmn. bd., chief exec. officer Racetrac Petroleum, Inc., Atlanta, 1967—. Edition editor: Close Corporations, 1967. Mem. ABA, Fla. Bar Assn., Soc. Ind. Gasoline Marketers (pres. 1987-89). Office: Racetrac Petroleum Inc PO Box 105035 Atlanta GA 30348

BOLDING, DAVID CHRISTIAN, controller, oil and gas consultant; b. Shreveport, La., Aug. 2, 1953; s. Grady Palmer and Charlotte Grace (Matson) B.; m. Paula Lynn Peters, June 9, 1972 (div. 1984); children: Brian Michael, Katharine Lyn; m. Ursula Skuta, Oct. 7, 1986. BS in Bus. Mgmt., Notre Dame U., 1975. CPA, Tenn., Kans., Nev., Okla. Staff acct. Price Waterhouse & Co., Memphis, 1975-77; mgr. acctg. dept. Jones, Sanborn, McDaneld & Jantz, Hutchinson, Kans., 1977-78; v.p. Nev. First Corp., Winnemucca, 1978-82; controller oil and gas explorationdiv. Drillers, Inc., Oklahoma City, 1982-85; controller Goldman Investments, Oklahoma City, 1985—; bd. dirs. Polo Prodn. Co., Oklahoma City, Camelot Sq., Inc.,

Oklahoma City, M&L Petroleum Co., Oklahoma City, Pima Enterprises, Inc., Tucson, Preston Capitol, Inc., Houston. Coach City of Edmond (Okla.) Park and Recreation, 1985—, YMCA Sports Program, Edmond, 1985—. Recipient John C. Pangborn scholarship Notre Dame U., 1974-75. Mem. AICPAs, Kans. Soc. CPAs. Methodist. Home: 2022 Three Stars Edmond OK 73034 Office: Goldman Investments 1140 NW 63d St 300 PO Box 1748 Oklahoma City OK 73107

BOLDOSSER, NANCY SHILAY, telecommunications company executive; b. N.Y.C., June 5, 1957; d. Nicholas and Olga (Chanevich) S.; m. Randy Richard Boldosser, June 13, 1981. BS in Acctg., Lehigh U., 1979, MBA, 1979. CPA, N.J., Pa.; cert. internal auditor. Staff auditor Price Waterhouse, N.Y.C., 1979-80, sr. tax acct., 1981; sr. tax acct. Deloitte Haskins & Sells, Allentown, Pa., 1981-82; mfg. acct. AT&T, Allentown, 1982-83; resident audit head AT&T, Reading, Pa., 1984-86; staff mgr. results and reporting Data Sytems Group AT&T, Morristown, N.J., 1986-87; controller svcs. product line Data Systems Group AT&T, Morristown, 1987-88, products mgr. data networking products and network systems, 1988—. Mem. AICPA, Inst. Internal Auditors. Republican. Episcopalian. Office: AT&T 184 Liberty Corner Rd Rm 2NQ04 Warren NJ 07060-0908

BOLDRY, J(OSEPH) STUART, JR., bank executive; b. Pitts., July 15, 1956; s. Joseph Stuart and Miriam Brown (Anderson) B.; m. Jennifer Paula Zittnan, Apr. 26, 1986. BA in Econs., Boston Coll., 1978; MBA, U. Chgo., 1982. Supr. bankcard ops. Harris Trust & Savs. Bank, Chgo., 1979-80, human resource coord., 1980-82, remittance processing mgr., 1982-84, systems project mgr., 1984-85, check processing mgr., 1985-87, retail products mgr., 1988—; cons. jobsearch workshop North Park Coll., Chgo., 1981-86; pres., organizer ABLE Unisys User Group, 1985-86. Co-author: Current Trends in Wholesale Remittance Pocessing, 1986. Recipient Order of Cross and Crown award, 1978. Mem. Boston Coll. Alumni Assn., U. Chgo. Alumni Assn., Univ. Club. Republican. Roman Catholic.

BOLEN, SHARRON LEE, state agency administrator; b. Chgo., Sept. 2, 1943; d. Oscar L. and Louise Bolen; divorced; 1 child, Sean M. Student, Loyola U., Chgo. and Rome, 1963-64; BA, Marquette U., 1965. Case worker Dept. Pub. Aid Cook County, Chgo., 1966-67; job developer Ill. Dept. Labor, Chgo., 1967-70; research asst. Mathmatica, Princeton, N.J., 1976-77; family counselor Family Counseling Service, Princeton, 1976-77; program coordinator N.J. Dept. Labor, Trenton, N.J., 1978-84; mgmt. trainer N.J. Dept. Transp., Trenton, 1984-88, supr. mgmt. tng., 1988—. Author: Employer Relations, 1981, Back Problems Preservation, 1985, Situatoral Leadership, 1986. Co-chmn. Four Season Ballet, Princeton, 1986. Mem. Cert. Pub. Mgr. Soc. (cert.). Home: 27 Witherspoon Princeton NJ 08540 Office: NJ Dept Transp 1035 Parkway Ave Trenton NJ 08625

BOLEY, DENNIS LYNN, construction company executive; b. Lima, Ohio, Aug. 27, 1951; s. James Cloyral and Joan Marie (Bevington) B.; m. Marjorie Ann Ribic, Dec. 13, 1975; children: Lisa Marie, Amanda Michelle. BSCE, Tri State Coll., 1974; MSCE, Ga. Inst. Tech., 1977. Registered profl. engr., Pa., Ohio; registered profl. land surveyor, Pa. Staff engr. D'Appolonia Cons. Engrs., Inc., Pitts., 1974-77, asst. project engr., 1977-78, project engr., 1978-82, mgr. civil group, 1982-83; dir. engring. research and devel. Nicholson Constrn. Co., Pitts., 1983-87, v.p., 1987—. Contbr. more than 25 articles to profl. jours. Lay speaker, councilman Alpha Luth. Ch., Turtle Creek, Pa., 1986-87. Mem. ASCE (sec. Pitts. sect. 1980-83, bd. dirs. 1984-85, v.p. 1985-86, pres. 1986-87, past pres. 1987—, Outstanding Young Civil Engr. of Yr. 1987), Engrs. Soc. West Pa. Republican. Office: Nicholson Constrn Co PO Box 98 Bridgeville PA 15017

BOLGER, ROBERT JOSEPH, retired trade association executive; b. Phila., Aug. 9, 1922; s. Harold Stephen and Edna (Adams) B.; m. Helen Siegfried, May 22, 1954; children: Robert, Mary T., Cynthia A., Ann M., Catherine B., David A. BS, Villanova U., 1943; postgrad., Northwestern U., 1945-46, U. Pa., 1946-47, U. Geneva, 1948-49; Dr. Pharmacy (hon.), Mass. Coll. Pharmacy, 1983. Salesman Container Corp., Phila., 1947; supr. sales Kraft Food Co., Phila., 1949-52; overseas mgr., dir. retail relations Smith, Kline Beckman Corp., Phila., 1952-62; asst. to exec. v.p. Nat. Assn. Chain Drug Stores, Inc., Arlington, Va., 1962-67, pres., 1967-87, ret., 1987; founder, developer Robert J. Bolger Assocs., 1988—; bd. dirs. Barr Labs., Pomona, N.Y., 1988—, Am. Pharm. Inst., Washington, 1988—, Am. Found. Pharm. Edn.; bd. dirs. Nat. Drug Trade Conf., pres., 1974-82. Bd. dirs. Alexandria (Va.) Hosp., Nat. Council on Patient Info. and Edn. Served to lt. comdr. USNR, 1943-45, PTO. Decorated Air medal; named Man of Yr. Cosmetic and Toiletry sect. United Jewish Appeal, 1972, Chain Exec. of Yr., Chain Drug Rev., 1979; recipient Torch of Learning award Am. Friends of Hebrew U., 1987, Chain Drug Rev. Bd. Lifetime Achievement award, 1988, Robert B. Begley award for contbns. to chain drug industry, 1988. Mem. Am. Pharm. Assn., Com. of 100, U. S. C. of C., Cen. Council Nat. Retail Assns. (chmn.), Am. Retail Fedn. (bd. dirs.), Nat. Assn. Retail Druggists, Phamracists Against Drug Abuse (bd. dirs. 1986—), Am. Soc. Assn. Execs., Nat. Assn. Execs. Club (bd. dirs.), Key Exec. Industry Council. Clubs: Belle Haven Country (Alexandria); Met. (N.Y.C.); Seaview Country (Absecon, N.J.). Home: 7705 Maid Marian Ct Alexandria VA 22306 Office: Robert J Bolger Assocs 413 N Lee St Alexandria VA 22314

BOLGER, THOMAS EDWARD, telecommunications company executive; b. Norfolk, Nebr., Sept. 4, 1927; m. Mae Nelson, Nov. 26, 1949; children: Patrick, Thomas, Nancy, Mollie, Ann. BSEE, S.D. Sch. Mines and Tech., 1949, D in Bus. Sci. (hon.), 1987. Engr. Northwestern Bell Telephone Co., 1948-54; dist. plant supt. Northwestern Bell Telephone Co., Minn., 1957-59; chief engr. Northwestern Bell Telephone Co., Des Moines, 1959-61; engr. AT&T, N.Y.C., 1955-57; v.p., gen. mgr. Pacific Northwest Bell Telephone Co., Portland, Oreg., 1961-64; v.p. ops. Pacific Northwest Bell Telephone Co., Seattle, 1964-67, pres., 1967-70; pres. Chesapeake and Potomac Telephone Cos., Washington, 1970-74; exec. v.p. AT&T, Basking Ridge, N.J., 1974-83; chmn. Bell Atlantic Corp., Phila., 1984—, chief exec. officer, 1984-89; chmn. Bell Atlantic Network Services, Inc., 1984-87; mem. bd. trustees Nat. Geographic Soc.; dir. Govt. Employees Ins. Corp., PNC Fin. Corp., Ashland Oil, Inc.; adv. dir. Pitts. Nat. Bank. Bd. dirs. Jr. Achievement Met. Washington, 1970-72, Met. Washington Urban Coalition, trustee Nat. Action Council for Minorities in Engring., 1975-82, Joint Council on Econ. Edn., 1975—, Pacific Sci. Ctr. Found., 1964-70, Providence Hosp., Seattle, 1964-70, Consortium of Univs., Com. for Econ. Devel., 1984-86, Washington Ctr. for Met. Studies; trustee, v.p. project planning Fed. City Council, also mem. exec. com.; trustee Cen. Assn. Seattle, 1967-70, also v.p.; v.p. Met. Washington Bd. Trade; gen. campaign chmn. United Givers Fund Nat. Capital Area, Washington; mem. Washington Citizens Council Nat. Council on Crime and Deliquency, 1967-70, Seattle Found., 1967-70; mem. adv. council Grad. Sch. Bus. Adminstrn. U. Washington, 1967-70, mem. vis. com. Grad. Sch. Pub. Affairs, 1967-70; mem. adv. com. Salvation Army Greater N.Y., 1975-78. Served with USN, 1945-46. Mem. Bus. Roundtable, Brookings Council, IEEE, Northwest-Midwest Membership Council, Union League, Eta Kappa Nu. Clubs: City (Washington); Burning Tree, Alfalfa, Royal Poinciana Golf, George Town, Quail Creek Country, Congl. Country. Office: Bell Atlantic Corp 1600 Market St Philadelphia PA 19103 *

BOLGER, TIMOTHY JOSEPH, savings and loan association executive; b. Jacksonville, Fla., Sept. 11, 1955; s. Joseph Frances and Catherine (Shea) B. BS in Fin. and Bus. Econs., The Am. U., 1977, MBA in Fin., 1980. Asst. cashier Kennedy Bank & Trust, Bethesda, Md., 1976-78; mktg. devel. specialist Fed. Home Loan Mortgage Corp., Washington, 1980-82; v.p. Dominion Fed. Savs. & Loan, McLean, Va., 1982-84, sr. v.p., 1984-86, exec. v.p., 1986—; bd. dirs. Gramling Engring., Bethesda, Dominion Mortgage Funding Corp., Dominion Funding Corp.; sr. v.p. Dominion Mortgage Ctrs., Inc. Contbr. (with others) articles to various profl. jours. Mem. Am. Inst. Banking, Montgomery County Young Bankers, Washington Soc. Investment Analysts, Inc.

BOLICK, ERNEST BERNARD, JR., housing administrator; b. Boone, N.C., May 7, 1933; s. Ernest Bernard and Mary Virginia (Moretz) B.; A.B., Lenoir-Rhyne Coll., 1955; M.Div., Luth. So. Sem., 1958; M.A., U. N.C., 1968, Ed.D., 1978; m. Rose J'neane Edwards, Aug. 10, 1973; 1 child, Maria Theresa. Cert. housing mgr., 1984. Mission organizer Luth. Ch. Am., Fla. 1958-63; instr. history U. N.C., 1965-66; dean men Louisburg Coll. 1968-69; library rep. McGraw-Hill Book Co., N.Y.C. 1969-70; real estate broker, Greensboro, N.C. 1970—; dean instrn. Winsalm Coll., 1977-79; housing coordinator Western Piedmont Council of Govts, Hickory, N.C., 1979-84; chmn. profl. devel. group N.C. Housing Assn., 1986—; asst. exec. dir. Graham Housing Authority, N.C., 1984— , systems adminstr., 1986-87. Pres. Mental Health Assn., Sanford, Fla., 1959-62; mem. St. John Luth. Church Council, Hudson, N.C., 1984. Research grantee U. N.C. 1975-76. Cert. housing mgr. Mem. AAUP, Sect. 8 Housing Assn. (sec., program com. chmn. 1985-86, chmn. profl. devel. com. 1986—), So. Bus. Coll. Assn., Southeastern Coll. Personnel Assn., Alamance County Credit Union (bd. dirs., treas. 1986—). Democrat. Home: 248 Brookberry Cir Chapel Hill NC 27514

BOLIN, WILLIAM, data processing executive; b. Phoenix, Jan. 9, 1945; s. Harvey Wesley and Julia (Hentz) B.; m. Paula Bolin, Apr. 1, 1972; children: Tracy, Autum. BS in Edn., No. Ariz. U., 1978. Systems analyst State Health Dept., Phoenix, 1969-74, Samaritan Health Service, Phoenix, 1974-79; mgr. info. systems Med Tronics, Inc., Tempe, Ariz., 1979-84, Talley Industries, Inc., Phoenix, 1984—. Bd. dirs. Community Coll., Phoenix, 1984-86. Mem. APICS, Data Processing Mgmt. Assn., Am. Prodn. and Inventory Control Soc. Office: Talley Industries Inc 2800 N 44th St Phoenix AZ 85008

BOLING, JOHN CARL, computer software company executive, statistical and computer software educator; b. Parkersburg, W. Va., Mar. 2, 1949; s. John Lafayette and Anna Mildred (Brown) B.; m. Kathleen Marie Haaser, Aug. 24, 1974; children: Jonathan, Todd, Michelle. BS, Va. Tech. 1971, MA, 1973; PhD U. Tenn., 1979. Faculty Va. Tech., Blacksburg, 1973-74; mgr. statis. cons. U. Tenn. Computing Ctr., Knoxville, 1976-78; statistician TVA, Knoxville, 1978-80; adj. faculty U. Tenn., Knoxville, 1978-80; dir. SAS Inst., Cary, N.C., 1980—; dir. Va. Tech. Alumni Assn., Blacksburg, 1978—; stat. cons. Knoxville Orthopedic Clinic, 1978-80. Contbr. articles on video, computer based and instructional computer software tng. Served to staff sgt. USAR, 1974-80. Named Outstanding Young Men in Am., Jaycees, 1978. Mem. Am. Statis. Assn. (chair program statis. computing sect. 1988), Internat. TV Assn., Phi Beta Kappa, Phi Kappa Phi, Phi Eta Sigma, Omicron Delta Kappa, Phi Delta Kappa. Republican. Methodist. Avocations: running, racquetball, tennis, golfing, music. Home: 103 Deer Park Ln Cary NC 27511 Office: SAS Inst PO Box 8000 Cary NC 27511

BOLLENBACH, STEPHEN FRASIER, hotel executive; b. Los Angeles, July 14, 1942; s. Walter and Betty (Mason) B.; m. Suzanne Weimer, Apr. 13, 1963 (div. Dec. 1969); m. Barbara May Christeson, Dec. 31, 1970; children: Christopher, Keat. BS in Fin., UCLA, 1965; MBA, Calif. State U., 1968. Chief fin. officer D.K. Ludwig Group, N.Y.C., 1977-80; sr. v.p. fin., treas. Marriott Corp., Washington, 1982-86; sr. v.p., chief fin. officer Holiday Corp., Memphis, 1986—, also bd. dirs.; chmn., chief exec. officer S.W. Savs. and Loan, Phoenix, 1980-82. Trustee Christian Bros. Coll., Memphis, 1988—. Mem. Urban Land Inst., Industry Real Estate Financing Adv. Council. Home: 393 Sweetbriar Rd Memphis TN 38119 Office: Holiday Corp 1023 Cherry Rd Memphis TN 38117

BOLLER, RONALD CECIL, financial executive; b. Cleve., Mar. 12, 1939; s. Ernest Russell and Rose B.; m. Marilyn L. Emery, Oct. 14, 1967 (div. 1982); children: Lori J., Lisa L. BS, Purdue U., 1962; MBA, U. Chgo., 1970. Engr. system sales and application Leeds & Northrup Co., North Wales, Pa., 1965-68; with Owens-Ill., Inc., Toledo, 1970—, dir. planning, rsch. and analysis, 1977-78, mgr. corp. real estate, 1978-80, mgr. portfolio mgmt. and benefit funds, treasury, 1980-81, dir. benefit fin., treasury, 1981-87, v.p., dir. benefit fin., 1988-89, 1989—. Pres. Great Lakes Credit Union, Toledo, 1976-77. Served to 1st lt. USAF, 1962-65. Office: Owens-Ill Inc One SeaGate Toledo OH 43666

BOLLINGER, BOB JAMES, financial planner; b. Stillwater, Okla., Nov. 22, 1953; s. Bob James Bollinger and Juanita Louise (Belknap) Sipe; m. Julie Carol Belden, Sept. 6, 1975 (div. May 1979), m. Julia Lynn Reid, June 3, 1989. BA in Zoology, Okla. State U., 1976; cert., Coll. Fin. Planning, 1987, postgrad., 1986—. Owner Bollinger Constrn., Stillwater, 1980-83; salesperson Fin. Planning Corp., Am., Inc., Stillwater, 1983-84; fin. planner Fin. Planning Ctr., Inc., Oklahoma City, 1984—; securities rep. FSC Securities Corp., Oklahoma City, 1984-88, registered prin., 1988—; pres. BJB Adv., Inc., Stillwater, 1987—; owner Golden Eagle Enterprises, Stillwater, 1980-84, Bollinger Property Mgmt., Stillwater, 1985-87, Okla. Biol. Supply, Stillwater, 1988—. Chmn. estate planning coun. First United Meth. Ch., Stillwater, 1986—. Named one of Outstanding Young Men Am., U.S. Jaycees, 1984. Mem. Inst. Cert. Fin. Planners, Internat. Assn. for Fin. Planning. Republican. Office: BJB Adv Inc 205 W 7th Ste 203A Stillwater OK 74074

BOLLINGER, JOHN, architect, planner, consultant; b. London, Apr. 12, 1943; came to U.S., 1948, naturalized 1953.; s. Luzar and Sarah Rosalie (Mayer) B.; m. Paula Jean Carter, Jan. 29, 1947; 1 child, Lara Renee. BArch, U. So. Calif., 1966, MArch, 1968, D in Bldg. Sci., 1971; cert. in pub. adminstrn., Calif. State U., Long Beach,, 1978. Registered architect, Calif.; lic. gen. contractor, Calif. Project coordinator Bank of Am., Los Angeles, 1972-75; sr. planner City of Long Beach, Calif., 1975-84; project mgr. World Trade Ctr., Port of Long Beach, 1979-84; prin. John Bollinger Architect, Fullerton, Calif., 1976—; prin. contractor Bldg. Resources Interface, Fullerton, 1982—; pres. The Mentor Group, Los Angeles, 1984—; v.p. Trans-Pacific Mortgage, Vancouver, Can., 1987—; lectr. U. So. Calif., Idylwild, Calif., 1970—; teaching asst. architecture U. S. Calif., Los Angeles, 1968-71; cons. for World Trade Ctrs. in Oxnard, Pomona, Santa Ana, San Diego, Fresno, Calif. Co-author: (master plan report) Polb Master Plan, 1979 (E-Star award 1979), feasibility study for World Trade Ctr., (Willy award 1982). Bd. dirs. Forum for Cultural and Ednl. Exchange, Beverly Hills, Calif., 1975; chmn. Jewish Bus. and Profl. Network of Orange Co., 1987; sec. gen. So. Calif. World Trade Ctrs. Council, 1985; mem. Town Hall, Los Angeles, 1978—. Weyerhauser Found. grantee, 1969, AIA fellow, Los Angeles, 1965, U. So. Calif. Archtl. Guild fellow, 1968. Mem. AIA, Am. Inst. of Planners, World Trade Ctrs. Assn., Internat. Bus. Assn., Long Beach C. of C., U. So. Calif. Alumni Assn. Democrat. Jewish. Lodge: Lions. Home: 717 N Carhart Ave Ste 64 Fullerton CA 92633 Office: The Mentor Group 9200 Sunset Blvd Los Angeles CA 90069

BOLLMEIER, EMIL WAYNE, manufacturing company executive; b. Hurst, Ill., Jan. 16, 1925; s. Emil Philip and Flossie Louise (Swain) B.; m. Nancy Lee Mercier, Feb. 9, 1972; children—David Wayne, Ann Louise, Paul Wesley. B.S. in Chem. Engring, U. Nebr., 1947; postgrad., U. Minn., 1949-51. With 3M Co., St. Paul, 1947-82; div. v.p. electro products div. 3M Co., 1965-72, group v.p. elec. products group, 1973-83, mem. 3M ops. com.; chief exec. officer, gen. ptnr. C-TEK Ltd. Partnership, 1983—; pres. Dynex Research, Inc., 1983—; chmn. bd., pres. Global Thermoelectric Power Systems Ltd., 1985-86. Patentee in field. Mem. Planning Commn., Mendota Heights, Minn., 1960-65; chmn. Republican Party, Dakota County, Minn., 1965-68. Served with USNR, 1945-46. Fellow IEEE; mem. Nat. Elec. Mfrs. Assn. (bd. govs.), Sigma Xi, Sigma Tau. Presbyterian. Home: 265 Burlington Rd Saint Paul MN 55119

BOLNER, CLIFTON JOSEPH, food company executive; b. San Antonio, Tex., July 30, 1928; s. Joe and Josephine (Grandjean) B.; B.S. (Disting. Mil. Grad.), Tex. A&M U., 1949; m. Rosalie Richter, Jan. 20, 1949; children—Tim, Mike, Deb, Cindy, Bev, Chris, Mary. Partner, Bolner's Grocery & Meat Market, San Antonio, 1949-55; pres. Bolner's Fiesta Products, Inc., San Antonio, 1955—, chief exec. officer, 1980—; a founder, dir. Exchange Nat. Bank, San Antonio, 1980-85 ; dir. Kelly Field Nat. Bank, Kelly Field Nat. Bancshares. Pres., Cath. Family and Children Services, San Antonio, 1968-69; chmn. fin. com. San Antonio Archdiocese, 1978-79;chmn. ann. awards dinner NCCJ, 1974; chmn. fin. com. Our Lady of Grace Parish, 1970-74, pres. parish council, 1970; mem. adv. bd. St. Peter's Children's Home; celebrity waiter Leukemia Soc., 1985-88; trustee, bd. dirs. San Antonio Area Found., 1988—; bd. dirs. San Antonio Symphony Soc., 1973—, San Antonio Mus. Assn., 1973—, chmn. trustee mgmt. com., 1986— , Opera Superman, 1975—, San Antonio Muscular Dystrophy Assn., 1975-85; mem. devel. bd. Incarnate Word Coll., 1974—; mem. adv. bd. St. Mary's U., 1983—; San Antonio Cath. rep. NCCJ, 1978-83. 1st lt. USAF, 1950-52. Recipient Disting. Alumni award Cen. Cath. High Sch., 1979; Gocery Supplier of Yr. citation Federated Foods, U.S.A.; Archbishop Furey Outstanding award medal, 1969; honoree NCCJ, 1982. Mem. Produce Mktg. Assn. (dir. retail div. 1980—), Am. Spice Trade Assn. (membership com. 1977-79), Oblate Asso., Assn. of Holy Family Guilds. Roman Catholic. Clubs: KC, San Antonio Serra Vocation, Italo Am. Young Men's, St. Paul's Men's, Soc. of Mary Assos. Home: 110 W Lynwood St San Antonio TX 78212 Office: Bolner's Fiesta Products Inc 426 Menchaca St San Antonio TX 78207

BOLNICK, HOWARD JEFFREY, insurance company executive; b. Detroit, Oct. 27, 1945; s. Arnold J. and Rebecca (Schuff) B.; m. Kay Zimring, Nov. 29, 1970; children: Lori Ann, Lee Scott. BA with honors, U. Mich., 1966; MBA, U. Chgo., 1970. Actuary CNA Ins. Cos., Chgo., 1967-76; prin. Coopers & Lybrand, Chgo., 1976-80; pres. Celtic Life Ins. Co., Chgo., 1980—. Contbr. articles to profl. and trade publs. Bd. dirs. Schwab Rehab Ctr., Chgo., 1982-85, Mt. Sinai Med. Ctr., Chgo., 1985-87, Ill. Comprehensive Health Ins. Plan, Chgo., 1987—. Fellow Soc. Actuaries; mem. Am. Acad. Actuaries, Health Ins. Assn. Am. (bd. dirs. 1988—), Standard Club. Jewish. Office: Celtic Life Ins Co 208 S LaSalle St Ste 1950 Chicago IL 60604

BOLOGNA, CALOGERO ANTONIO, controller, corporate executive; b. Trappeto, Italy, Feb. 25, 1957; came to U.S., 1966; s. Giovanni and Nunzia (Marchese) B. BBA in Fin. Mgmt., Calif. State U., Long Beach, 1980. Asst. storekeeper, acctg. clk. Downey (Calif.) Community Hosp., 1976-80; chief fin. officer, controller Stout Roofing Inc., Downey, 1980—. Democrat. Roman Catholic. Office: Stout Roofing Inc 9705 Washburn Rd Downey CA 90241

BOLOTSKY, DAVID ALEXANDER, securities analyst; b. N.Y.C., Jan. 26, 1963; s. Marvin and Laura Lipton (Lipschitz) B. BA, SUNY, Binghamton, 1985. Gen. mgr. Slipped Disc Records, Binghamton, 1984-85; securities analyst First Boston Corp., N.Y.C., 1985-87, Goldman, Sachs & Co., N.Y.C., 1987—. Mem. Merchandising Analysts Group, Phi Beta Kappa. Jewish. Office: Goldman Sachs & Co 85 Broad St New York NY 10004

BOLT, ROBERT LOUIS, business owner, minister; b. Buffalo, Sept. 23, 1953; s. Robert Ellsworth and Katherine Theresa (Sampson) B.; m. Shirely A. Trulin, (div. Feb. 1982); m. Marie Elizabeth Lambrix, Sept. 4, 1982; 1 child, Annette Marie. Student, Ch. Scientology, 1974; cert., Internat. Tng. Sch., 1981. Mgr. Arby's Roast Beef, Tonawanda, N.Y., 1974-79; comml. real estate assoc. Reeves Real Estate, Buffalo, 1979-81; pres. Mike's giant Submarines, Inc., Buffalo, 1981—; counselor, minister Ch. Scientology, Buffalo, 1973-74, counselor, personnel and communications exec., 1978-83. Sec. Kenmore (N.Y.) Mchts. Assn., 1987, v.p., 1988, pres. 1989. Republican. Office: Mike's Giant Submarines 289 W Ferry Buffalo NY 14213

BOLTON, JOANN R., financial executive; b. Libertyville, Ill., Apr. 25, 1946; d. Robert Keith and Marvene Ruth (Smith) B.; 1 child, Janis Clytee. BA, Carthage Coll., 1969; MBA, Roosevelt U., 1977. Mem. credit staff Am. Hosp. Corp., Evanston, Ill., 1969-71; credit analyst Outboard Marine Co., Waukegan, Ill., 1972-80; credit mgr. Abbott Labs., North Chicago, Ill., 1980—. Mem. Chgp. Midwest Credit Assn. Lutheran. Office: Abbott Labs 1400 Sheridan Rd North Chicago IL 60064

BOLTON, KENNETH ALBERT, corporate professional. s. Albert and Myrtle (Nelting) B.; m. Maryanne Lavelle, Oct. 27, 1940; children: Katharine, Ann. BS in Indsl. Engring., Pa. State U., 1978; MBA, Kennedy Western U., Agoura Hills, Calif., 1988. With Western Electric, Allentown, Pa., 1961-63; system mgr. Western Electric, Phila., 1963-72; mgr. MCS Mgmt. Internat., Washington, 1972-80, Coopers & Lybrand, Phila., 1980-82; dir. cons. Worden & Risberg, Phila., 1982-83; v.p. mktg. Laminated, Inc., Hatfield, Pa., 1983-86; pres. Mgmt. Internat., Phila., 1986—; bd. dirs. Ent., Internat., Phila., 1978—. Contbr. articles to profl. jours. Advisor Jr. Achievement, Media, Pa., 1970. Mem. NSPE, Phila. C. of C. (bd. dirs. 1975, lobbyist small bus. coun. 1978), Engrs. Club. Republican. Home: 2979 W School House Ln Philadelphia PA 19144 Office: Mgmt Internat The Kenilworth Ste 706 Philadelphia PA 19144-9969

BOLTON-SMITH, CARLILE, JR., telecommunications company executive, lawyer; b. Washington, Sept. 3, 1937; s. Carlile and Anne Cavendish (Boyle) B.-S. BA, Amherst Coll., 1959; JD, Columbia U., 1966. Bar: N.Y. 1966, D.C. 1966. Assoc. Cravath, Swaine & Moore, N.Y.C., 1966-73; asst. sec., asst. gen. counsel MCI Telecommunications Corp., N.Y.C., 1973-76; v.p., asst. sec., asst. gen. counsel MCI Telecommunications Corp., Washington, 1976—, v.p., sec., asst. gen. counsel, 1982—. Served with USN, 1960-63. Office: MCI Communications Corp 1133 19th St N W Washington DC 20036

BOMBARDIER, ANDRÉ J. R., manufacturing company executive; b. Valcourt, Que., Can., Dec. 31, 1942; divorced; children: Jean-Francois, Isabelle, Charles, Louis. BA, U. Sherbrooke, Que., 1969. Pres. Les Entrepriess de J.-Armand Bombardier Ltd.; vice chmn. Bombardier Inc., Montreal, Que. Roman Catholic. Home: 761 St Joseph St, Valcourt, PQ Canada J0J 1EO Office: Bombardier Inc Ste 1700, 800 Rene-Levesque Blvd W, Montreal, PQ Canada H3B 1Y8

BOMZER, DAVID J., human resources professional; b. N.Y.C., Dec. 5, 1961; s. Herbert Wallace and Estie Ann Bomzer. BS, Mich. State U., 1983; MA, U. Ill., 1985. Sr. human resources rep. Data Gen. Corp., Westboro, Mass., 1985—; guest lectr. various ednl. inst., 1986-87. Mem. Am. Soc. Personnel Adminstrs., Am. Compensation Assn. Office: Data Gen Corp 4400 Computer Dr Westborough MA 01580

BONACCI, DONALD NICHOLAS, petroleum corporation executive; b. N.Y.C., Oct. 2, 1929; s. Daniel John and Fay A. (Giamondi) B.; m. Frances Milanowycz, Sept. 13, 1952; children: Daniel, Michele, Donald, Jr. B.A., N.Y. U., 1951. Personnel mgr. Combusion Engring., Inc., Windsor, Conn., 1955-60; dir. personnel United Nuclear Corp., Elmsford, N.Y., 1961-69; v.p. Orgn. Resources, Inc., Boston, 1969-73; sr. v.p. adminstrn. Commonwealth Oil, Inc., Ponce, P.R., 1973-78; sr. v.p. adminstrn. and human resources Tesoro Petroleum Corp., San Antonio, 1978—. Served as 1st lt. U.S. Army, 1951-53. Mem. Am. Soc. Personnel Adminstrs., Am. Petroleum Inst. Club: Oak Hills Country, Dominican Country. Office: Tedoro Petroleum Corp 8700 Tesoro Dr San Antonio TX 78286

BONAIUTO, PAUL MARIO, manufacturing company executive, financial officer; b. Boston, Dec. 8, 1950; s. Paul and Lucy S. (Cianci) B.; m. Wendy Sinnott, Aug. 4, 1973; children: Jennifer, Laura, Marianne. BBA, U. Mass., 1972. Internal auditor L. Grossman & Sons, Braintree, Mass., 1972-74; with Ludlow Corp., 1974-82; internal auditor Ludlow Corp., Needham, Mass., 1974-76; acctg. mgr. Ludlow Corp., Temple City, Calif., 1976-78; plant controller Ludlow Corp., Chgo., 1978-80, Paoli, Pa., 1980-82; v.p., chief fin. officer Graphic Packaging Corp., Paoli, 1982—; dir. Colorpac, Inc., Franklin, Ohio, 1986. Mem. Nat. Assn Accts., Flexible Packaging Assn. Republican. Roman Catholic. Home: 420 Berkley Rd Exton PA 19341 Office: Graphic Packaging Corp PO Box 500 Paoli PA 19301

BONAR, JOHN ALEXANDER, marketing professional; b. Chgo., Sept. 12, 1941; s. Alexander and Josephine Anne (Chmura) B; m. Nancy Carol Safarcyk; children: Michael John, Douglas John. BS, U. Ill., 1964, MS, 1965. Tooling engr. Boeing Airplane Co., Seattle, 1965-68; ceramic engr. Howmet Corp., Dover, N.J., 1968-69; sr. engr. Exxon Research and Engring., Florham Park, N.J., 1969-72; corrosion engr. Esso Standard Libya, Marsa El Grega, 1972-74; mktg. mgr. Carborundum Co., Niagara Falls, N.Y., 1974-77; regional sales mgr. Carbrundum Co., Niagara Falls, N.Y., 1977-82, mktg. mgr., 1982-85; mktg. dir. AO Smith, Florence, Ky., 1985—. Author: Corr and Chem Resis. Masonry, 1986. Contbr. articles to profl. jours. Mem. Am. Car Soc., Am. Soc. for Metals, Am. Iron and Steel Inst. Home: 11959 Timerberlake Dr Cincinnati OH 45249

BONAR, LUCIAN GEORGE, business executive; b. Lodz, Poland, June 1, 1934; emigrated to Can., 1941; s. Henry and Janina (Wierska) B.; m. Stephanie Leonard, June 1, 1963; children—Justin Gray, Daphne Leonard. B.A.Sc. in Metall. Engring., U. Toronto, 1958; M.S. in Metallurgy, U. Calif., Berkeley, 1959; Ph.D., Cambridge (Eng.) U., 1962. Mgr. product planning Falconbridge Ltd., Toronto, Ont., 1962-70; pres. Bonar Assocs. Ltd., Toronto, 1970-72; sr. v.p. comml., nickel div. Amax Inc., Greenwich,

Conn., 1972-80; pres. mineral resources div. Cabot Corp., N.Y.C., 1980-81; v.p. mktg. and sales Falconbridge Ltd., Toronto, 1981-86; chmn., chief exec. officer Eldorado Nuclear Ltd., Ottawa, Ont., Can., 1987-88; pres., dir. Bonar Assocs. Ltd., Toronto. Author: The Nickel Industry, 1971. Athlone fellow, 1959; Nat. Research Council Can. spl. scholar, 1961. Mem. AIME, Am. Soc. Metals, Metals Soc., Assn. Profl. Engrs. Ont. Clubs: Royal Can. Yacht, Toronto, National, Badminton and Racquet (Toronto); Oxford and Cambridge (London). Home: 96 Glen Rd, Toronto, ON Canada M4W 2V6 Office: 120 Adelaide St W, Ste 409, Toronto, ON Canada M5H 1T1

BOND, NELSON LEIGHTON, JR., health care executive; b. Glen Ridge, N.J., Apr. 17, 1935; s. Nelson Leighton and Dorothy Louise (Minsch) Hudson B.; m. Susan Priscilla McDonald, June 7, 1958 (div. May 1981); children: Sally Louise, Nelson Leighton III, Trevor Paul, Elizabeth Prescott, Susan Bond Kearney; m. Gwendolen Nash Gorman, July 24, 1982. BA, Lehigh U., 1957; MBA, Harvard U., 1966. Dist. mgr. McGraw Hill, Inc., N.Y.C., 1957-64; assoc. McKinsey and Co., Inc., N.Y.C., 1966-68; fin. analyst Drexel Harriman Ripley, Inc., N.Y.C., 1968-69; instl. salesman Faulkner Dawkins and Sullivan, N.Y.C., 1969-70; v.p. Alex Brown and Sons, Balt., 1970-77; pres., dir. Blood Pressure Testing, Inc., Reisterstown, Md., 1977—; pres. Consumer Micrographics, Inc., Balt., 1980-83; pres. Medscreen, Inc., Balt., 1987—, also bd. dirs.; bd. dirs. Clark Pendelton Realty, N.Y.C.; dir. Offutt Securities, Inc., 1987—, Nat. Health Systems, Inc., 1987—, Med. Test Systems, Inc., 1988-89, Lifescreen, Inc., 1989—. Pres. Parents' Club St. Paul's Sch., Brooklandville, Md., 1978-79. 1st lt. USAR, 1958-60. Foote, Cone and Belding fellow Harvard U., 1965. Republican. Episcopalian. Office: Medscreen Inc PO Box 1053 Reisterstown MD 21136-1053

BOND, RICHARD MILTON, utility company executive; b. Spokane, Wash., Apr. 23, 1924; s. Joseph McKinley and Ethel (Campbell) B.; m. Pat Hendrickson, June 30, 1946; children: David Preston, Marc Douglas, Andrew Joseph. Student, Calif. Inst. Tech., 1942-43; BA, BS, U. Calif., Berkeley, 1946; student, U. So. Calif., 1945-46. Lic. comml. pilot. Sales engr. Ingersoll Rand Corp., N.Y.C. and Phila., 1947-48; adminstrv. asst. Bendix Aviation, North Hollywood, Calif., 1949-50; v.p. sales Calor Gas Co., San Francisco, 1950-57; v.p., mng. dir. Vancouver Island Gas Co., Nanaimo, B.C., Can., 1957-65; pres. Solar Gas Co., Spokane, 1955-87, Solar Gas Ltd., Nanaimo, 1958—; mem. Wash. Ho. Reps., Olympia, 1974-86. Rep. Wash. Sate Legis., Olympia, 1975-87; del. Rep. Nat. Convs., Phila., 1948, Kansas City, Mo., 1976, Dallas, 1984. Named Legislator Yr., Young Ams. for Freedom, 1977, Legislator Yr., Wash., Legislator Yr. Conservative Union and Wash. Taxpayers Assn., 1977, Eagle Scout Boy Scouts Am., South Pasadena, Calif., 1938. Mem. Nat. Propane Gas Assn. (bd. dirs. 1966—), Am. Legis. Exchange Council (bd. dirs. 1985-87, named Outstanding Legislator 1984), Assoc. Engrs. Spokane (pres. 1973-74), Air Force Assn. (v.p. 1970-76). Lodge: Rotary (bd. dirs. Nanaimo club 1964-65). Office: Solar Gas Ltd, PO Box 12, Nanaimo, BC Canada V9R EK4

BOND, ROGER, metal parts manufactring executive; b. Paterson, N.J., Jan. 21, 1937; s. Claude Guilbert and Gladys (Freden) B.; m. Ruth Ann Donovan, Aug. 30, 1958; children: Robert, Siri, Craig. MEd, Stevens Inst. Tech., 1958, M in Mgmt. Sci., 1964. Prodn. scheduling mgr. Scovill Mfg. Co., Caldwell, N.J., 1965-68; systems engrs. Scovill Mfg. Co., Waterbury, Conn., 1968-70; maintenance control mgr. Scovill Mfg. Co., Waterbury, 1970-72, mgr. mfg. engring., 1972-75; mgr. engring. William Prym, Inc., Dayville, Conn., 1975-77; mgr. div. Milford Rivet & Machince Co., Elyria, Ohio, 1977-83; mgr. mfg. ops. Hoover Universal, Cumming, Ga., 1983-85; exec. v.p. Abbott Ball Co., West Hartford, Conn., 1985-88; pres. Abbott Ball Co., West Hartford, 1988—; chmn. Lorain County Mfr's coun., Ohio, 1982. Inventor in field. Cubmaster Cheshire (Conn.) Coun. Boy Scouts Am., 1974. Mem. Commerce and Industry Assn. (pres. 1983). Republican. Lutheran. Office: Abbott Ball Co R R Pl West Hartford CT 06110

BONES, JOSEPH RICHARD, accountant; b. Edmonton, Alta., Can., Sept. 13, 1936; s. Thomas Joseph and Margaret Monica (Lambertus) B.; chartered acct. Inst. of Chartered Accts. of Ont. (Can.); m. Deanna M. Pollard, May 30, 1959; children—Jo-Anne, Michael, Maureen. Ops. and methods officer Govt. of Can. Comptroller of Treas., Ottawa, Ont., 1961-62; partner Ward Mallette C.A.s (internationally BDO/Binder), Ottawa, 1962—, exec. partner 48 offices in Ont., also nat. chmn. Fellow Chartered Accts. Inst. of Ont. (pres.); mem. Can. Inst. Chartered Accts. (life), Assn. of Kinsmen Clubs (life), Ottawa Chartered Accts. Assn. Roman Catholic. Clubs: Laurentian, K.C. (Ottawa). Home: 26 Leaver, Ottawa, ON Canada K2E 5P6 Office: Ward Mallette, 120 Adelaide St W #1020, Toronto, ON Canada M5H 1T1

BONFIELD, GORDON BRADLEY, JR., oil and gas company executive; b. Grand Rapids, Mich., May 23, 1926; s. Gordon Bradley and Helen Louise (Gutekunst) B.; m. Ardella Mae Cowan, Aug. 27, 1949; children: Gordon Bradley III, Kenneth S. B.A., Colgate U., 1950; student, Advanced Mgmt. Program, Harvard, 1967. Pres., dir. Packaging Corp. Am. (and predecessor cos.), Evanston, Ill., 1974-81; chmn. bd., chief exec. officer Packaging Corp. Am. (and predecessor cos.), 1981-82; sr. v.p. Tenneco, Inc., Houston, 1982—, also group exec. Sr. fellow Am. Leadership Forum; mem. chmn. Tex. Research League, Houston Symphony, Vols. Am.; chmn. Houston Job Training Partnership Council; bd. dirs. ARC, Tex. Inst. Arts in Edn., Tex. Assn. Taxpayers, Business Arts Fund, Initiatives for Children; mem. State Adv. Council Community in Schs.; vice chmn. Bus. Art Fund; trustee Found. for Bus., Politics and Econs. Served with U.S. Army, 1944-46. Office: Tenneco Inc Tenneco Bldg Houston TX 77002

BONGIORNO, JOHN JACQUES, financial corporation executive; b. Uniontown, Pa., Jan. 12, 1938; m. Judith Ann Miles; children: Stephen, Vanessa. BBA in Acctg., Duquesne U., 1962. CPA, Ill. Sr. auditor Touche Ross & Co., Chgo., 1962-66; audit supr. Alexander Bratt & Co., Caracas, Venezuela, 1966-67; controller Chrysler Fin. Corp., Troy, Mich., 1967-80; asst. controller Chrysler Corp., Highland Park, Mich., 1980-81; v.p., ops. Internat. Harvester Credit Corp., Schaumburg, Ill., 1981-84; v.p. fin. Navistar Internat. Corp., Chgo., 1984—; pres. Navistar Fin. Corp., Schaumburg, 1984—. Served with U.S. Army, 1956-58. Home: 1323 Glenmore Ct Barrington IL 60010 Office: Navistar Fin Corp 600 Woodfield Schaumburg IL 60196

BONHAG, THOMAS EDWARD, insurance executive, financial consultant; b. Bronxville, N.Y., Jan. 19, 1952; s. Herman Arthur and Anne Elizabeth (Sage) B.; m. Noreen Patricia Early, Apr. 24, 1976 (div. Dec. 1981); m. Cornelia Hackett Lyons, Oct. 8, 1983. BS, Fordham U., 1973; MBA, St. John's U., 1979; postgrad., Am. Coll., 1979-84. CLU; cert. fin. planner, chartered fin. cons. Field sales rep. Colgate-Palmolive Co., N.Y.C., 1973-74; employee relations officer The Chase Manhattan Bank, N.Y.C., 1974-78; agt., dist. mgr. The Equitable Life Assurance Soc., N.Y.C., 1979-83; dir. mktg. ops. northeastern region The Equitable Life Assurance Soc., Edison, N.J., 1984—; fin. cons. Am. Geriatrics Soc., N.Y.C., 1983—. Mem. Hoboken (N.J.) Environ. Com., 1983—. Am. Soc. CLU's, Nat. Assn. Life Underwriters, Internat. Assn. Fin. Planning, Assn. for MBA Execs. Republican. Roman Catholic. Home: 706 Orange Ave Cranford NJ 07016

BONHAM, PHILLIP ERIC, real estate executive; b. Pasadena, Calif., June 7, 1942; s. Lyle Leonard and Isobel Muriel (McAughey) B.; m. Sandra Diane, Apr. 26, 1969; children: Lara Michelle, Ashley Marin. BA, San Jose (Calif.) State U., 1968, MA, 1970; JD, Calif. Western U., 1977. Prin. Phil Bonham & Co., San Diego, 1979-83; with investments dept. Marcus & Millichap, San Diego, 1983-85, John Burnham & Co., San Diego, 1985-86; dir. corp. accounts New Am. Network, San Diego, 1986-87; v.p. Kenneth S. Hayashi Corp., San Diego, 1987-88, pres., 1988—; chmn. Mgmt. Alert, San Diego, 1988—; pres., chmn. bd. dirs. Internat. Capital Asset Group Ltd., La Jolla, Calif. Mem. Sigma Chi. Republican. Presbyterian. Home: 1368 Clove St San Diego CA 92106

BONI, ROBERT EUGENE, industrial company executive; b. Canton, Ohio, Feb. 18, 1928; s. Frank and Sara Boni; m. Janet Virginia Klotz, Aug. 16, 1952; children: Susan, Leslie. B.S. in Metall. Engring, U. Cin., 1951; M.S., Carnegie Inst. Tech., 1954, Ph.D., 1954. Research engr. Armco Inc., Middletown, Ohio, 1956-61, sr. research engr., 1961-68, mgr. applied sci., 1968-70, dir. metall. research, 1970-75, asst. v.p. research and tech., 1976, v.p. research and tech., 1976-78, group v.p. material resources and strata energy, 1978-80, group v.p. steel group, 1980-82, exec. v.p., chief operating officer, 1982-83, pres., chief exec. officer, 1985-86; chmn., chief exec. officer Armco Inc., Parsippany, N.J., 1986—. Patentee in field. Bd. dirs. N.C. Cen. U., Alexander and Alexander Services, Inc., GMI Engring. & Mgmt. Inst. Served with U.S. Army, 1954-56. Recipient Disting. Engring. Alumnus award U. Cin., 1970. Mem. AIME (Fairless award Iron & Steel Soc. of AIME 1987), Indsl. Research Inst., Am. Iron and Steel Inst., Am. Iron and Steel Engrs., ASTM, Welding Research Council. Office: Armco Inc 300 Interpace Pkwy Parsippany NJ 07054

BONIOL, EDDIE EUGENE, investments executive; b. Port Arthur, Tex., Sept. 14, 1931; s. Willie Bernice and Leila Evelina (Chase) B.; diploma in acctg. Tyler Comml. Coll., 1949; student Baylor U., 1955-56, La. Coll., 1956, SUNY, 1981—; m. Margaret Faye Aguillard, Feb. 5, 1966; children: Joe Ed, Mark Eugene, Liesl Michelle. Various positions Comml. Credit Co., Bus. Services Group, Balt., 1959-73, area dir., 1970-73; freelance mgmt. cons. Dallas, 1973; v.p. Tex. Western Fin. Corp., Dallas, 1974-76; asst. v.p. Citicorp Bus. Credit Inc., Dallas, 1976-78; v.p. fin. and adminstrn., also chief fin. officer Superior Iron Works & Supply Co. Inc., Shreveport, La., 1978-80; sr. v.p., chief fin. officer Latham Resources Corp., Shreveport, 1980-81; pres. Decca Leasing Corp., Shreveport, 1981—; chmn., chief exec. officer Red River & Gulf Resources, Inc., Shreveport, 1982—; pres. Med. Bus. Services, Inc., Shreveport, 1982-86; cons. in field. Trustee La. Coll., 1984—, vice-chmn., 1987-89. Served with USN, 1950-53. Cert. credit analyst, credit and fin. analyst. Republican. Baptist. Lodge: Lions (pres. LeCompte, La. club, 1959, pres. North Shreveport club 1988—, founder, 1st pres. South Shreveport club). Home: 8606 Rampart Pl Shreveport LA 71106 Office: 1953 E 70th St Ste 2 Shreveport LA 71105

BONMARTINI, FRANCESCO, chemical company executive; b. Rome, Oct. 21, 1926; came to U.S., 1954; s. Giovanni and Giacinta Tracagni B.; m. Charlotte Doelger, Apr. 23,1960; children: Giovanni, Gioia. D in Chemistry, State U. Rome, 1952. Rsch. chemist St. Oil N.J. (name changed to Exxon), Linden, 1952-59; area sales mgr. St. Oil N.J. (name changed to Exxon), N.Y.C., 1960-62; dirigente Montecatini (name changed to Montedison), Milan, 1962-66; pres., Tecpac J.V. div. Hercules/Riegel Paper, Brussels, 1967-69; with Hercules, Inc., 1969—; corp. v.p. market devel. Hercules, Inc., Wilmington, Del., 1985—. Patentee in field. Served to 2d lt. Italian Army, 1944-45. Clubs: Circolo Caccia (Rome); VicMead Hunt (Greenville). Home: 900 DuPont Rd Wilmington DE 19807 Office: Hercules Inc Hercules Pla Wilmington DE 19894

BONNES, CHARLES ANDREW, lawyer; b. Bklyn., Jan. 23, 1941; s. Charles Andrew and Beverly (Bade) B.; m. Cynthia Crane Rich, Aug. 7, 1965; children—Jocelyn Winthrop, Andrew Rich. BA, Dartmouth Coll., 1962; LLB, Yale U., 1965. Bar: N.Y. 1965. Assoc. Olwine, Chase, O'Donnel & Weyher, N.Y.C., 1965-76; corp. sec. Airco, Inc., Montvale, N.J., 1977-84; v.p., gen. counsel The BOC Group, Inc., Montvale, 1984—. Mem. ABA. Home: 154 Carlisle Terr Ridgewood NJ 07450 Office: BOC Group Inc 575 Mountain Ave Murray Hill NJ 07974

BONNEY, JOHN DENNIS, oil company executive; b. Blackpool, Eng., Dec. 22, 1930; s. John P. and Isabel (Evans) B.; 4 children from previous marriage; m. Elizabeth Shore-Wilson, Aug. 1986; 1 child. B.A., Hertford Coll., Oxford U., Eng., 1954, M.A., 1959; LL.M., U. Calif., Berkeley, 1955. Oil adviser Middle East, 1959-60; fgn. ops. adviser, asst. mgr., then mgr. Chevron Corp. (formerly Standard Oil Co. of Calif.), San Francisco, 1960-72, v.p., from 1972, vice chmn., 1987—, also dir. Clubs: Commonwealth; World Trade (San Francisco); Univ. (N.Y.C.); Oxford and Cambridge (London). Office: Chevron Corp 225 Bush St San Francisco CA 94104

BONNINGTON, VICKI VAN VELSON, lawyer; b. Rochester, N.Y., June 17, 1950; d. James Maurice and Virginia Oatlean (Clark) Van V. BS in Nursing magna cum laude, SUNY, Brockport, 1975, BS in Sociology summa cum laude, 1975, BS in Biology summa cum laude, 1975; JD summa cum laude, Syracuse U., 1983. Bar: N.Y. 1984, Mass. 1985; registered nurse, N.Y. Instr. anatomy and physiology lab. State U. Coll., Brockport, N.Y., 1973-75; instr. human biology Rochester Mus. and Sci. Ctr., 1973-75; nurse Strong Meml. Hosp., Rochester, 1975-79; clin. intern Seifert, Sedley & Co., London, 1981; summer assoc. Nixon, Hargrave, Devans & Doyle, Rochester, 1982; fed. law clk. U.S. Dist. Judge, Syracuse, N.Y., 1983-85; assoc. Bingham, Dana & Gould, Boston, 1985—. Bd. visitors Syracuse U., 1987—. Mem. ABA, Mass. Bar Assn., Boston Bar Assn. Methodist. Office: Bingham Dana & Gould 150 Federal St Boston MA 02110

BONO, ANTHONY SALVATORE EMANUEL, II, data processing executive; b. N.Y.C., Nov. 24, 1946; s. Anthony S.E. and Lola M. (Riddle) B. BA in Polit. Sci., Hartwick Coll., 1969; cert. in info. systems analysis, UCLA, 1985. Mgmt. trainee Mfrs. Hanover Trust Co., N.Y.C., 1973-74; supr. client services Johnson & Higgins of Calif., Los Angeles, 1974-77, account exec. comml. accounts, 1977-80, coordinator internal systems, 1981-83, mgr. systems devel., 1983-89, v.p., mgr. systems devel., 1989—. Deacon Westwood Presbyn. Ch., 1982-85. Served with USAF, 1969-73. Named Airman of Yr., San Bernadino C. of C., 1970. Mem. Assn. Systems Mgmt. (dir. publicity and awards 1982-84, corr. sec. 1984-85), Channel Island Mensa, Alpha Sigma Phi. Republican. Home: 15010 E Reedley St Moorpark CA 93021 Office: Johnson & Higgins 2029 Century Park E Los Angeles CA 90067

BONO, JACK ALEX, research laboratory executive; b. Cokeburg Junction, Pa., May 10, 1925; s. Dominick and Maria (Tosi) B.; m. Bette Jackson, Feb. 28, 1946; children: Meri Bono McCarthy, Bette, Steve, John. BS, Northwestern U., 1946. With Underwriters Labs. Inc., Northbrook, Ill., 1946—, now pres. Served with USNR, 1943-46. Fellow Soc. Fire Protection Engrs., ASTM; mem. Nat. Soc. Profl. Engrs. Episcopalian. Club: Union League (Chgo.). Office: Underwriters Labs Inc 333 Pfingsten Rd Northbrook IL 60062

BONOMO, JOSEPH RALPH, military officer; b. N.Y.C., Mar. 20, 1951; s. Ralph J. Anita R. (Curiale) B. BBA, Iona Coll., 1973; MPA, SUNY, Albany, 1975; student, USN Officer Candicate Sch., Newport, R.I., 1976, Navy Supply Corps Sch., Athens, Ga., 1976, USN Submarine Sch., Groton, Conn., 1977; MS, Naval Postgrad. Sch., 1985. Data adminstr. Welfare Research Inc., Albany, N.Y., 1975-76; advanced through grades to lt. comdr. USN; supply officer USS Henry Clay Blue Crew, Charleston, S.C., 1977-79, Fighter Squadron 101, Oceana, Va., 1979-81; aviation support officer USS Constellation, San Diego, 1981-83; info. systems officer Comdr. Naval Air Foce, U.S. Atlantic Fleet, Norfolk, Va., 1985-88, USS Saratoga, 1988—. Vol. WHRO Pub. TV, Norfolk, 1987-88; mem. Smithsonian Assocs., Washington, 1984-88; mem. Planetary Soc., Pasadena, Calif., 1983-88, Nat. Geog. Soc., Washington, 1986-88. Mem. Supply Corps Sch. Alumni Assn., Hampton Roads Supply Corps Assn., Iona Coll. Alumni Assn., U.S. Naval Inst., Delta Lambda Kappa. Roman Catholic. Office: USS Saratoga Supply Dept FPO NY NY 09543-2740

BONSAL, RICHARD IRVING, textile mills executive; b. Palmyra, N.J., June 19, 1920; s. Alonzo Felten and Jennie (Weart) B.; m. Jean Caven, Oct. 18, 1947; children: Julia Lynn, Sarah Bonsal Miller, Martha Bonsal Day. BE in Mech. Engring., Yale U., 1942. Lic. profl. engr., N.Y., N.J. Rsch. engr. E.I. DuPont de Nemours & Co., Inc., Wilmington, Del., 1942-47; with Joshua L. Baily & Co., Inc., Hoboken, N.J., 1947—; pres. Joshua L. Baily & Co., Inc., Hoboken, 1967—; bd. dirs. Mayfair Mills, Arcadia, S.C. Commn. Town of Montclair (N.J.), 1972-80, dep. mayor, 1972-76; trustee The Mountainside Hosp. Recipient Community Svc. award Montclair Jaycees, 1982, Citizenship award Svc. Clubs Council Montclair, 1985. Mem. ASME (life), Am. Textile Mfg. Inst. (past chmn. textile mkt. com.), Am. Arbitration Assn. (arbitrator), Merchants Club (pres. 1969-74, 84-89), Montclair Golf Club, Union League Club, Princeton (N.Y.C.), Bradford Bath and Tennis, Upper Montclair County Club (Clifton, N.J.)(pres. 1969-71), Sigma Xi (assoc.), Tau Beta Pi. Home: 264 Upper Mountain Ave Upper Montclair NJ 07043 Office: Joshua L Baily & Co Inc 2 Hudson Pl Hoboken NJ 07030

BONSIGNORE, MICHAEL ROBERT, electronics company executive; b. Plattsburg, N.Y., Apr. 3, 1941; s. Marco Romulo and Alice Marie (Enders) B.; m. Sheila Ani Gorman, June 7, 1963; children—Michelle, Michael Robert, Christopher. BS, U.S. Naval Acad., 1963; postgrad. Tex. A&M U. With Honeywell, Inc., 1969-71, 73—, v.p. mktg., 1977-80, v.p. ops. Honeywell Marine Systems, Seattle, 1981-83, pres. Honeywell Europe, Brussels, 1983-86, exec. v.p. internat., 1987, pres. internat., 1987— ; bd. dirs. Donaldson Co. Mem. adminstrv. staff Tex. A&M U., 1972; cons. Bd. dirs. United Way King County, 1981-83, Jr. Achievement Seattle, 1981-83; mem. adv. coun. U.S. Trade Rep. (Investment Policy Adv. Com.), Office Tech. Assessment; mem. devel. bd. Global Leadership U. Mich.; bd. dirs. Minn. Orch., Met. Econ. Devel. Assn.; mem. adv. bd. Minn. Trade Office. Lt. USN, 1963-69. Mem. Sea-Space Symposium (pres. 1981), Am. C. of C. Brussels (v.p.), Nat. Assn. Underwater Instrs., U.S. Naval Acad. Alumni Assn. (past pres.), Met. Econ. Devel. Assn., U.S. Power Squadron Club. Republican. Roman Catholic. Office: Honeywell Inc Honeywell Pla Minneapolis MN 55408

BONSKY, JACK ALAN, chemical company executive, lawyer; b. Canton, Ohio, Mar. 12, 1938; s. Jack H. and Pearl E. Bonsky; A.B., Ohio U., 1960; J.D., Ohio State U., 1964; m. Carol Ann Portmann, Sept. 2, 1960; children—Jack Raymond, Cynthia Lynn. Bar: Ohio 1964, U.S. Dist. Ct. (so. dist.) Ohio 1969. With Metcalf, Thomas & Bonsky, Marietta, Ohio, 1964-69, Addison, Fisher & Bonsky, Marietta, 1969-70; asst. counsel GenCorp., Inc. (formerly Gen. Tire & Rubber Co.), Akron, Ohio, 1970-75, assoc. gen. counsel, 1975-86, asst. sec., 1977-86, v.p. and sec., 1986; v.p., sec., gen. counsel DiversiTech Gen., Inc., 1986-87; v.p., gen. counsel GenCorp Polymer Products, 1988—; solicitor City of Marietta, Ohio, 1966-67; legal advisor City of Marietta Bd. of Edn., 1966-67; police prosecutor, Belpre, Ohio, 1969-70; comml. law instr. Am. Inst. Banking, 1969; dir. Frontier Holdings, Inc., Denver, Frontier Airlines, Denver, 1985 (merged with People Express Airlines, 1985). Mem. Marietta Income Tax Bd. of Rev., 1966-67; mem. Traffic Commn., 1966-69, chmn., 1967; mem. Civil Service Commn., 1969; trustee Urban League, 1978-81, pres., 1980-81; trustee Akron Community Service Ctr., 1978-81, United Way of Summit County, 1982—; bd. dirs. Washington County Soc. for Crippled Children, 1964-70; bd. dirs. S.E. Ohio unit Arthritis Found., 1967-70, chmn., 1968-70; mem. Washington County Health Planning Com., 1968-70; mem. ho. of dels. Ohio Easter Seal Soc., 1968-70. Recipient Akron Community Service Ctr. and Urban League Leadership award, 1981. Mem. Ohio Bar Assn. Home: 4234 Idlebrook Dr Akron OH 44313 Office: GenCorp Polymer Products 350 Springside Dr PO Box 3545 Akron OH 44309-3545

BONWICK, ROY EDWIN, merger and acquisition executive; b. Ottawa, Ont., Can., May 27, 1929; came to U.S., 1962; s. Edwin Thomas and Rose (Farris) B. BA in Commerce, Carleton U., Ottawa, 1950. CPA. Auditor, fin. mgr., analyst GE, Can. and U.S., 1950-63; fin. mgr. Litton Industries, Orange, N.J., 1963-70; dir. treasury svcs. Olin Corp., New Haven, 1970-76; assoc. mergers and acquisitions Sowers, Lewis, Wood & Assocs., Old Greenwich, Conn., 1976-78; pres. Roy Bonwick Assocs., Inc., Branford, Conn., 1979—. Mem. Internat. Assn. Merger and Acquisition Cons., Assn. Corp. Growth, Inst. Chartered Accts. of Ont. Office: Roy bonwick Assocs Inc 5 S Main St Ste 522 Branford CT 06405

BOOE, JAMES MARVIN, chemical engineer; b. Austin, Ind., Nov. 12, 1906; s. James Ross and Grace (Hesler) B.; B.S., Butler U., 1928; m. Dortha Maud Weaver, July 30, 1938; children—James Marvin, Ann Marie, John Weaver. Chemist, Indpls. Plating Co., 1929; chief chemist P. R. Mallory & Co., 1929-45, dir. electrochem. research, 1945-51, exec. chem. engr., 1951-53, dir. chem. and metall. research corp. labs., 1953-63; dir. chem. labs. Mallory Capacitor Co., Indpls., 1963-72, cons., 1972—. Advisory bd. Am. Security Council; charter mem. Rep. Presdl. Task Force; bd. dirs. Irvington Benton House Assn.; pres., bd. dirs. Irvington Hist. Landmarks Found. Accredited profl. chemist Am. Inst. Chemists. Recipient Army-Navy E civilian award, Naval Ordnance Devel. award. Fellow Am. Inst. Chemists; mem. Am. Chem. Soc., Electrochem. Soc., Irvington Hist. Soc., Am. Def. Preparedness Assn., Indpls. Scientech Soc. (bd. dirs.), Smithsonian Instn. (asso.), Indpls. Mus. Art, Goodwill Industries, Ransburg YMCA, Presbyterian (elder, trustee). Lodge: Kiwanis. Patentee in field (38). Research on electrolytic capacitors, batteries, resistors, semiconductors. Home: 548 N Audubon Rd Indianapolis IN 46219 Office: Mallory Capacitor Co 3029 E Washington St Indianapolis IN 46201

BOOGAERTS, JOHN JOSEPH, JR., architect, map publisher, urban planner; b. Alexandria, La., Mar. 30, 1934; s. John Joseph and Eunice Loenie (Muse) B.; m. Florence May Macdonald, June 1, 1961; children: Charrette, Whitmore, Pieter, Wijngaert. BArch, Tulane U., 1962; MS in Urban Planning, Columbia U., 1965. Project planner Milan Engring. Ltd., Belize, Brit. Honduras, 1960-62; planner, mem. staff New Orleans City Planning Commn., 1962-63; architect Skidmore Owings & Merrill, 1966-68; prin., urban designer N.Y.C. Housing and Devel. Adminstrn., 1968-74; pres. Boogaerts & Assocs. PC, N.Y.C. and Riyadh, Saudi Arabia, 1975—, Middle East Info. Co., Stamford, Conn. and Al Kohbar, Saudi Arabia, 1978—; cons. UN, 1975, 77, Cen. Planning Orgn., Yemen Arab Republic, 1975, Ministry of Mcpl. and Rural Affairs and Ministry of Info., Kingdom of Saudi Arabia, 1977-78; guest lectr. Columbia U., 1969, NYU, 1975-76, Princeton (N.J.) U., 1975-76. Producer pub. series of guide maps of cities and countries of Middle East. Mem. Manhattan Community Bd. 8, 1968-75, chmn. E. 86th St. corridor com., 1968-75; Republican candidate Ho. of Reps. 18th Congl. Dist., 1974; mem. steering com. Carnegie Hill Neighbors, Inc., 1968-75, N.Y. Mcpl. Art Soc., 1968—; speakers bur. N.Y.C. Charter Revision Commn., 1975; pres. Columbia Archtl. and Planning Alumni, 1974-76; active Rep. Town Com., Greenwich, Conn., 1988—. William Kinne Fellows travel grantee, 1964. Mem. AIA, Am. Inst. Cert. Planners, Greenwich (Conn.) Rep. Town Com. Republican. Roman Catholic. Clubs: University (N.Y.C.), N.Y. Road Runners, Riyadh Scuba Divers; Symposium (Greenwich). Home: 315 Valley Rd Cos Cob Greenwich CT 06807-1814

BOOK, JOHN KENNETH (KENNY), retail store owner; b. Hillsboro, Ill., June 26, 1950; s. Vern Ray Book and Pearl Iva (Foster) Book Alford; m. Betty L. Christy, Dec. 23, 1981; children: Elizabeth Marie Dunn, Leslie Michelle Dunn. Asso. in Acctg., Ky. Bus. Coll., 1974. Laborer, Lexington (Ky.) Army Depot, 1968-70; machine operator A.O. Smith, Mt. Sterling, Ky., 1971-72; laborer Irvin Industries, Lexington, 1973-75; owner Kenny's Signs & Bus. Services, Winchester, Ky., 1977—; research bd. advisors ABI. Active Winchester Sch. Bd., 1976, 78; city commnr. 1977, 79, 81, 83, 87; mayor Winchester, 1985. Named to Hon. Order Ky. Cols., 1973. Mem. Ky. Sheriff's Assn. (hon.). Democrat. Office: Kenny's Signs & Bus. Svcs 25 E Broadway PO Box 840 Winchester KY 40391-0840

BOOKER, BRIAN RAYMOND, wholesale company executive; b. L.I., N.Y., Sept. 17, 1959; s. Howard and Shiela (Carter) B.; m. Judy Kay Mead, May 31, 1986; 1 child, Adam Howard. AA, Sierra Coll., 1981; student, Calif. State U., Chico, 1982-84. Clk. Raley's, Sacramento, 1980-82; v.p., sales mgr. B&H Wholesale, Inc., Sacramento, 1982—. Office: B&H Wholesale Inc PO Box 41157 Sacramento CA 95838

BOOKER, LARRY FRANK, accountant; b. Mobile, Ala., May 22, 1950; s. Frank and Helen Louise Booker; m. Prudence E. Porter, Sept. 1, 1972; children: Jennifer Erin, Meggan Leah. BA, U. S.Ala., 1972; student, U. N.C., 1976-77. CPA, Pa., Ala. Research economist Research Triangle Inst., Durham, N.C., 1974-76; with Providence Hosp., Mobile, 1978-80; pvt. practice acctg. Mobile, 1981—; enrolled IRS. Vol. Jr. Achievement. Mem. Nat. Assn. Accts., Nat. Soc. Pub. Accts., Ala. Assn. Pub. Accts. (past dist. pres., bd. dirs.). Lodge: Kiwanis. Home: 2121 LucknerCt Mobile AL 36618 Office: 2100 Airport Blvd Suite 201 Mobile AL 36606

BOOKOUT, JOHN FRANK, JR., oil company executive; b. Shreveport, La., Dec. 31, 1922; s. John Frank and Lena (Hagen) B.; m. Mary Carolyn Cook, Dec. 21, 1946; children: Beverly Carolyn, Mary Adair and John Frank III (twins). Student, Iowa Wesleyan Coll., 1943, Centenary Coll., 1946-47; LLD (hon.), Centenary Coll., 1987; BSc, U. Tex., 1949, MA, 1950; DSc (hon.), Tulane U., 1978. Geologist Shell Oil Co., Tulsa, 1950-59, div. exploration mgr., 1959-61; area exploration mgr. Shell Oil Co., Denver, 1961-63, The Hague, Netherlands, 1963-64; mgr. exploration and prodn. econs. dept. Shell Oil Co., N.Y.C., 1965, v.p. Denver exploration and prodn. area, 1966; v.p. Southeastern exploration and prodn. region Shell Oil Co., New Orleans, 1967-70; pres., chief exec. officer, dir. Shell Can. Ltd., Toronto,

Ont., 1970-74; exec. v.p., dir. Shell Oil Co., Houston, 1974-76, pres., chief exec. officer, dir., 1976-88; dir., mem. exec. com. Shell Petroleum Inc., 1988—; dir. Royal Dutch Petroleum Co., 1988—; bd. dirs. Irving Trust Co., Royal Dutch Shell, Shell Petroleum, Inc.; chmn. adv. bd. Inst. Bioscis. and Tech. Tex. A&M U. Active chancellors council U. Tex.; bd. dirs. Meth. Hosp., Houston; mem. regional adv. bd. Inst. Internat. Edn.; mem. U.S. Fish and Wildlife Found. Served with USAAF, 1942-46. Decorated Air medal with 3 oak leaf clusters; comdr. Order of Orange-Nassau (The Netherlands), 1988; recipient Disting. Service award Nat. Assn. Secondary Sch. Prins., John Rogers award Southwestern Legal Fedn., 1986; named Outstanding Chief Exec. Domestic Integrated Oil Co. Wall St. Transcript, 1982-84, Disting. Alumnus U. Tex., 1981. Mem. Am. Assn. Petroleum Geologists, Nat. Petroleum Council (former chmn.), Houston C. of C., The Conf. Bd. (bd. dirs.), Am. Petroleum Inst. (bd. dirs., past chmn. bd., mgmt. com.), 25 Year Club Petroleum Industry (bd. govs. SW dist.), Internat. C. of C. (U.S. Council; trustee), Council on Fgn. Relations Inc., All-Am. Wildcatters Assn., Bus. Roundtable (mem. policy com.), Am. Council on Edn. (bus.-higher edn. forum), Nat. Fish and Wildlife Found. (bd. dirs.). Home: PO Box 2463 Houston TX 77252 Office: 1 Shell Pla Houston TX 77001

BOOKSHESTER, DENNIS STEVEN, retail company executive, b. Chgo., Nov. 26, 1938; s. Jack and Dorothy (Goldblatt) B.; m. Karen Schwartz, July 2, 1967; children: Allison, Jacklyn. BS, U. Ala., 1960. Salesman to sr. v.p. merchandise Burdines, Miami, 1961-77; pres. Sibley, Lindsey & Curr div. Assoc. Dry Goods, N.Y.C., 1977-78, chmn. and chief exec. officer, 1978-82; pres. Caldor div. Assoc. Dry Goods, N.Y.C., 1982-83; chmn. and chief exec. officer dept. stores Carson Pirie Scott & Co., Chgo., 1983-84, vice chmn., chief exec. officer retail group, 1984—, also bd. dirs.; bd. dirs. Midway Airlines, Chgo., Northwestern Corp. Trustee The latin Sch. Chgo. Served as cpl. U.S. Army, 1960-66. Mem. Young Pres.' Orgn. Office: Carson Pirie Scott & Co 1 S State St Chicago IL 60603 also: Carson Pirie Scott & Co 36 S Wabash Ave Chicago IL 60603

BOONE, DAVID EARLE, banker, educator; b. Oakland, N.J., Mar. 13, 1933; s. Barret E. and Sophia A. (Earle) B.; BBA, Adelphi U., 1970, cert. in Fin., 1970, MBA, 1973; cert. Am. Inst. Banking, 1968; m. Joan Diane Rochelle Rosenhouse, Mar. 23, 1959; children: Barry Michael Earle, Nancy Ellen Wolf, Douglas Mark Bartlett. Dep. dept. head small bus. loan Mfrs. Hanover Trust Co., N.Y.C., 1968-69, regional credit asst., 1970-71, asst. sec., 1971, loan officer, 1971-75, regional loan officer, 1976, asst. v.p., 1977, officer in charge spl. tng. sect., 1977-81, dep. mgr. Fifth Ave. br., 1981-82; corporate loan officer Queens-Bronx Corporate Banking Center, 1982-85; v.p. corp. banking div. Norstar Bank, 1985; mem. cash mgmt. com. Norstar Bankcorp., 1986-87; adj. lectr. bus. adminstrn. Adelphi U., Garden City, N.Y., 1973, adj. lectr. fin. off campus grad. bus. program, 1973-77, adj. instr. fin., 1978, adj. asst. prof. banking and fin., 1979-85, adj. assoc. prof. banking and fin., 1986—, mem. devel. com. Grad. Bank Mgmt. Inst., Sch. Banking, 1980-87; instr. banking Am. Inst. Banking, N.Y.C., 1978, Hunter Coll., N.Y.C., 1977; Bd. dirs. East End Civic Assn., 1965-68, v.p., 1966-68. Served with USAF, 1951-55. Mem. Nat. Assn. of Accts., Bank Credit Assocs. of N.Y., Robert Morris Assocs. (chmn. com. for coop. with public accts. 1980-81, bd. govs. 1981-82, chmn. domestic lending div. 1981-84, regent Loan Mgmt. Seminar 1982-83, 1st v.p. chpt. 1984-85, pres. N.Y. chpt. 1985-86, bd. of govs. N.Y. chpt. 1986—, forward planning com. 1986—), Nat. Domestic Loan Coun., Adelphi U. Bus. Schs. Alumni Assn. (exec. bd. 1983—, chmn. ways & means com. 1983-87, Wayndach Sch. & Bus. Alliance (devel. coun. 1986—), Long Island Forum Tech. Home: 60 Bedell Ave Hempstead NY 11550 Office: Norstar Bank 1660 Walt Whitman Rd Melville NY 11747

BOONE, LOUIS EUGENE, business and management educator, author; b. Robertsdale, Ala., May 5, 1941; s. Louis Warren and Helen H. (Hadley) B.; m. Patsy Gayle Jones, May 28, 1964; children—Barry, Christopher. B.S., Delta State U., 1963; M.S., So. Miss. U., 1964; Ph.D., U. Ark., 1969. Chmn. div. mgmt. and mktg. U. Tulsa, 1969-79; prof. bus. adminstrn. U. Central Fla., 1979-82; Ernest G. Cleverdon chair bus. and mgmt. U. South Ala., 1982—; Sir Ian Potter disting. prof. Caulfield Inst., Melbourne, Australia, 1976. Adv. editor in mgmt. and mktg. PennWell Books, Tulsa; assoc. editor So. Bus. Rev.; mem. editorial rev. bd. Jour. Exptl. Learning and Simulation, Jour. of Acad. Mktg. Sci.; author: Management Perspectives in Marketing, 1972, Classics in Consumer Behavior, 1977; (with Edwin Hackleman) Marketing Strategy, 1975; (with Harold Segal and David L. Kurtz) Le Marketing: Realite Canadienne, 1975; (with James C. Johnson) Marketing Channels, 1977; (with David L. Kurtz) Foundations in Marketing, 1977, Marketing Mastery Guide, 1981, L'Enterprise D'Aujourd'Hui: Structure et Dynamique, 1984; Management, 3d edit., 1987, Contemporary Marketing, 6th edit., 1989, Personal Financial Management, 1989, (with David L. Kurtz and Joseph A. Braden) The Sales Management Game, 2d edit., 1979; (with M. Dale Beckmen and David L. Kurtz) Le Marketing: Realite Contemporaine, 1980, Foundations of Marketing, 4th edit., 1988, Foundations of Marketing Essentials Edition, 1986; (with Donald A. Bowen) The Great Writings in Management and Organizational 1987; (with Kurtz, Applebaum and Beckman Contemporary Canadian Business, 1987; (with C. Patrick Fleenor and David L. Kurtz) CEO: Who Makes It to the Top in America, 1989; contbr. articles to profl. jours. Mem. Southwestern Mktg. Assn. (founding pres. 1973), So. Mktg. Assn. (v.p. 1976, 77), Am. Mktg. Assn. (pres. Tulsa chpt. 1979, disting. svc. award 1979), Acad. Mgmt., Bienville Clib, Isle Dauphine Club. Home: 11555 Jeff Hamilton Rd Mobile AL 36695 Office: U South Ala Mobile AL 36688

BOONSTRA, CORNELIS, food products company executive; b. 1938; married. With Unilever NV, 1955-62; with Zwivel Handelmij NV, 1962-74, v.p., 1965-66, pres. SRV ops., 1966-74; pres. Intradal NV, 1974-83; vice chmn. bd. Date Douwe Egberts NV, 1983-84, chmn., 1984—; sr. v.p. Sara Lee Corp., 1986-88, exec. v.p., 1988—. Office: Sara Lee Corp 3 First National Pla Chicago IL 60602 also: Douwe Egberts NV, Keulsekade 143, 3532AA Utrecht Netherlands *

BOORE, LEWIS ALEXANDER, VI, investment executive; b. Somerville, N.J., July 6, 1959; s. Lewis Alexander V and Shirley Mae (Schmitt) B.; m. Sandra Shelley, Mar. 16, 1983 (div. May 1985); 1 child, Lewis; m. Danna Lee Shansby Demetre, June 28, 1985; children: Jamie Lee, Jillann, Michael, Lewis Alexander VII. BS in Engring., U.S. Mil. Acad., 1981; postgrad., San Jose (Calif.) State U., 1987. Registered profl. engr., Calif. Engr. sales div. Avantek, Inc., Santa Clara, Calif., 1986-88; account exec. Drexel Burnham Lambert, Palo Alto, Calif., 1988—. Capt. U.S. Army, 1981-86. Named Revolution Man of Yr., DAR, 1977, Man of Yr., Jaycees, 1984. Mem. U.S. Mil. Acad. Alumni Assn., Assn. Old Crows, Palo Alto Rugby Club. Republican. Episcopalian. Home: 921 Jungfrau Ct Milpitas CA 95035 Office: Drexel Burnham Lambert 5 Palo Alto Sq Palo Alto CA 94306

BOOSEY, JOHN ARTHUR, management consultant, engineer; b. Little Rock, Ark., Aug. 19, 1929; m. Artie McConnell, Nov. 16, 1953; children: John A. Jr., Debra Gary. BSEE, U. Tex., 1951, MBA, 1955, JD, 1957; MBA, La. State U. Sr. v.p. EBASCO Svcs., N.Y.C., 1978-88; pres. Enseroh Internat. Devel. Corp., N.Y.C., 1978-88. Office: Ebasco Svcs Inc 2 World Trade Ctr New York NY 10048

BOOTE, ALFRED SHEPARD, marketing researcher, educator; b. N.Y.C., May 21, 1929; s. Alfred Denton and Katharine (Kerrison) B.; m. Joan Peterson, July 9, 1960 (div. Sept. 1963); m. Heath Drury, June 1, 1973. BA, Colgate U., 1951; MBA, Columbia U., 1953, M in Philosophy, 1974, PhD, 1975; MA, Stanford U., 1957. Research mgr. design and market research labs., Container Corp. of Am., 1961-63; assoc. dir. mktg. research Pepsi-Cola Co., 1963-65; dir. mktg. research Far East area, PepsiCo Internat., 1965-67, dir. mktg. research Worldwide,, 1967-70; pvt. practice mktg. research cons. clients include Singer Co., McDonald's Corp., GTE, Gen. Elec. Co., Magic Chef Corp., and others. N.Y.C., 1970-75; cons. Arthur D. Little, Inc., Cambridge, Mass., 1975-76; gen. mgr., dir. research Decision Research Corp., Lexington, Mass., 1976-78; dir. mktg. research Singer Co., Stamford, Conn., 1978-81; mng. dir., founder Psychographics Research Corp., Inc., Bedford, N.Y., 1981-86; v.p. research Smith Stanley & Co., Inc., Darien, Conn., 1983-87; adj. assoc. prof. sociology Hunter Coll., 1983; adj. lectr. mktg. research Nichols Coll., 1985; vis. prof. mktg. Clark U., 1985—. Mem. editorial rev. bd. Jour. of Advt., 1982-87; mem. editorial bd. Psychology and Mktg., 1983-85; contbr. articles in field to profl. jours. Mem. Planning Commn., Woodstock, Conn.; mem. Regional Planning Commn. Northeast Conn., 1987—. Served to lt. (j.g.) U.S. Navy, 1953-56. Mem. Am. Assn. Pub. Opinion Research, Am. Sociol. Assn., Am. Mktg. Assn., Mkt. Research Soc. Hong Kong (founder, 1st chmn.), Alpha Kappa Delta, Alpha Kappa Psi. Home: Bull Hill Woodstock CT 06281 Office: Clark U Grad Sch Mgmt Worcester MA 01610

BOOTH, CHARLES LOOMIS, JR., banker; b. Des Moines, Aug. 6, 1933; s. Charles L. and Nancy Washington (Miller) B.; Baccalaureat, French Inst., Athens, Greece, 1952; B.A., Harvard U., 1956, LL.B., 1960. Vice pres., sr. investment officer Am. Security and Trust, Washington, 1965-72; sr. v.p. Alliance Capital, N.Y.C., 1972-74; exec. v.p., chief investment officer Bank of N.Y., N.Y.C., 1974—. Mem. N.Y. Soc. Security Analysts. Clubs: Metropolitan (Washington); University (N.Y.C.). Office: Bank NY 48 Wall St New York NY 10286

BOOTH, DOUGLAS WADE, utility company executive; b. Atlanta, 1924. Student, Washington & Lee U., 1942; B.S.E.E., U. Ala., 1947. With Duke Power Co., Charlotte, N.C., 1952—, v.p. mktg., 1965-71, dir., 1968, sr. v.p. retail ops., 1971-76, exec. v.p., 1976-82, pres., chief operating officer, 1982—; bd. dirs. Barclays Am. Corp. Trustee U. N.C. at Charlotte, Brevard (N.C.) Coll. Office: Duke Power Co 422 S Church St Box 33189 Charlotte NC 28242

BOOTH, ELIZABETH MARIE, banker; b. N.Y.C., Oct. 29, 1944; d. James Charles Hudson Booth and Elsa-Marie (Opp) Koehler; m. Edward J. Michel, Aug. 10, 1963 (div. 1987); children: Bartlett, Barrett, Edward, David. BA, Barnard Coll., 1965; MS, CCNY, 1966; MBA, Western Conn. State U., 1986. Dir. devel. Wyckham Rise, Washington, Conn., 1982; tchr. Norwalk (Conn.) Pub. Schs., 1985-87; exec. community banker Conn. Bank & Trust, Greenwich, 1987-88; asst. mgr. Union Trust Co., Stamford, Conn., 1988—. Cons., bd. dirs. Alton Bay (N.H.) Bible Conf., 1983—. NSF scholar, 1960. Mem. Am. Mus. Natural History, New Canaan Nature Ctr., Smithsonian Assocs., Barnard Coll. Club (v.p. Fairfield, Conn. chpt. 1980—), NAFE, Fairfield Network Female Execs. Republican.

BOOTH, I(SRAEL) MACALLISTER, photographic products company executive; b. Atlanta, Dec. 7, 1931; s. Charles Victor and Charlotte Ann (Beattie) B.; m. Frances Marie Henry, Sept. 22, 1956; children—David M., Thomas H., Mary E., Charlotte M. B.M.E., Cornell U., 1955, M.B.A., 1958. With Polaroid Corp., Cambridge, Mass., 1958—, v.p., 1976-78, exec. v.p., 1980-84, chief operating officer, 1982-86, pres., 1984—, chief exec. officer, 1986—. Served to capt. USAF, 1955-57. Episcopalian. Office: Polaroid Corp 549 Technology Sq Cambridge MA 02139

BOOTH, JOHN LOUIS, service executive; b. Danville, Va., May 15, 1933; s. William Irvine and Melba (Harvey) B.; m. Ann Fennell, May 23, 1959; children: Mark, Robin. BA, U. Richmond, 1958; ThM, Dallas Theol. Sem., 1962, ThD, 1965; postgrad., Ariz. State U., 1972, 79. Pastor Skyway Bible Ch., Seattle, 1964-66, Mount Prospect (Ill.) Bible Ch., 1966-71, Camelback Bible Ch., Paradise Valley, Ariz., 1971-78; counselor Camelback Counseling Ctr., Phoenix, 1978-79; dir. Paradise Valley Counseling, Inc., Phoenix, 1980—; chmn. bd. Paradise Valley Counseling, Inc., 1980—; chmn. bd. Paradise Valley Counseling Found., Inc., Phoenix, 1982—; adj. prof. Grand Canyon U., 1981—, Southwestern Coll., Phoenix, 1979—, Talbott Theol. Sem. Phoenix Ext., 1983-85; seminar speaker frequent engagements, 1965—. Author: Understanding Today's Problems, 1980, Marriage by the Master Plan, 1980, Equipping for Effective Marriage, 1983, (tape series) Starting Over, 1982, Enjoying All God Intended, 1988. Precinct committeeman Rep. Party, Phoenix, 1983-84, 87-88; chaplain Arizona State Senate, Phoenix, 1973. Mem. Christian Assn. for Psychol. Studies, Internat. Assn. Biblical Counselors. Baptist. Club: Pinewood Country (Munds Park, Ariz.). Office: Paradise Valley Counseling Inc 10210 N 32d St Ste 211 Phoenix AZ 85028

BOOTH, WALLACE WRAY, retired electronics and aerospace executive; b. Nashville, Sept. 30, 1922; s. Wallace Wray Booth and Josephine England; m. Donna Cameron Voss, Mar. 22, 1947; children: Ann Conley (Mrs. F. Brian Cox), John England. BA, U. Chgo., 1948, MBA, 1948. Various positions Ford Motor Co., Dearborn, Mich., 1948-59; v.p. fin., treas. dir. Ford Motor Co., Toronto, Ont., 1959-63; mng. dir., chief exec. officer Ford Motor Co. Australia, Melbourne, 1963-67; v.p. corp. staffs, indsl. products Philco-Ford Corp., Phila., 1967-68; sr. v.p. corp. staffs, mem. exec. com. Rockwell Internat. Corp., El Segundo, Calif., 1968-75; pres., chief exec. officer United Brands Co., Boston, 1975-77, also dir.; chmn. Ducommon, Inc., L.A., 1977-88, pres., chief exec. officer, 1978-88; bd. dirs. Rohr Industries, Litton Industries, Inc., Navistar Internat. Corp., Chgo., 1st Interstate Bank, L.A., Arrow Electronics, Inc., N.Y. Past chmn. United Way, L.A.; pres. Children's Bur. Los Angeles. Served to 1st lt. USAAF, 1943-46.

BOOTHROYD, HERBERT J., insurance company executive; b. Mason City, Iowa, Dec. 23, 1928; s. Herbert L. and Clara (Schmitt) B.; m. Barbara Elizabeth Dunne, Feb. 9, 1961; children: Diane Lea, John Herbert. A.B., U. Mich., 1952, A.M., 1953. Enrolled actuary, 1976. With Mass. Mut. Life Ins. Co., 1953-57; with New Eng. Mut. Life Ins. Co., Boston, 1957-87; v.p. New Eng. Mut. Life Ins. Co., 1967-77, sr. v.p. pension ops., 1977-82, exec. v.p. group ops., 1983-87; dir. New Eng. Pension and Annuity Co., 1980-87, pres., 1981-87; pres., dir. New Eng. Gen. Life, 1983-85; dir. New Eng. Gen. Life, New Eng. Variable Life Ins. Co. Contbg. author: Life and Health Insurance Handbook, 1973. Bd. dirs. New Eng. chpt. Am. Diabetes Assn., 1979-84; bd. govs. Handel and Haydn Soc., 1984—, sec., 1986—; mem. nat. Campaign Com. U. Mich., 1983—. Served with AUS, 1946-47. Fellow Soc. Actuaries; mem. Better Bus. Bur. Eastern Mass (dir. 1980-88, vice chmn. and mem. exec. com. 1985-88), Am. Council Life Ins., Am. Acad. Actuaries, Internat. Congress Actuaries, Phi Beta Kappa, Theta Delta Chi. Home and Office: 51 Indian Hill Rd Weston MA 02193

BORDA, RICHARD JOSEPH, insurance executive; b. San Francisco, Aug. 16, 1931; s. Joseph Clement and Ethel Cathleen (Donovan) B.; m. Judith Maxwell, Aug. 30, 1953; children: Michelle, Stephen Joseph. AB, Stanford U., 1953, MBA, 1957. With Wells Fargo Bank, San Francisco, 1957-70; mgr. Wells Fargo Bank, 1963-66, asst. v.p., 1966-67, v.p., 1967-70; exec. v.p. adminstrn. Wells Fargo Bank, San Francisco, 1973-85; asst. sec. Air Force Manpower Res. Affairs, Washington, 1970-73; vice chmn. Nat. Life Ins. Co., Montpelier, Vt., 1985—, also bd. dirs. Pres. Air Force Aid Soc., Washington; trustee Scholarships for Children of Am. Mil. Personnel. Served to lt. col. USMCR, 1953-55. Recipient Exceptional Civilian Service, 1973. Mem. Marine Corps Res. Officers Assn., Air Force Assn., Phi Gamma Delta. Republican. Episcopalian. Clubs: Army-Navy (Washington); Calif. (Los Angeles); Burlington (Vt.) Country; Pulgrims (N.Y.C.). Lodge: Masons. Office: Nat Life Ins Co National Life Dr Montpelier VT 05604

BORDELON, SCOTT EDWARD, certified financial planner; b. New Orleans, July 6, 1955; s. Eugene Joseph Bordelon and Gwendolyn (Deimel) Martino; m. Charlotte Anne Aucoin, Feb. 14, 1986; 1 child, Carly Kristin. Student, U. New Orleans; cert. fin. planner, Coll. Fin. Planning, 1984, postgrad. Ins. exec. Guardian Life Ins. Co., New Orleans, 1978-82; fin. planner Hebert Simon Co., New Orleans, 1982-86; cert. fin. planner Northlake Fin. Advisors, Covington, La., 1986—. Mem. Internat. Assn. Fin. Planners, Inst. Cert. Fin. Planners, Gulf Coast Soc. Inst. Cert. Fin. Planners (bd. dirs. 1987—). Republican. Roman Catholic. Home: 70200 7th St Covington LA 70433 Office: North Lake Fin Advisors Rte 8 PO Box 211-D Covington LA 70433

BORDERS, CHARLES EDWARD, electric utility company executive; b. Bloomfield, Ind., Dec. 30, 1925; s. Roy A. and Roberta E. (Yount) B.; m. Margie Lou O'Hearn, Apr. 13, 1947; children: Kathleen Montgomery, Kristine Fresch, Brian C. B.S. in E.E., U. Notre Dame, 1947. Jr. geophysicist Carter Oil Co., Rolling Fork, Miss., 1947; with Indpls. Power & Light Co., 1947—, sr. v.p., 1976—. Chmn. Better Bus. Bur., Indpls., 1981-82; pres. Indpls. Opera Co., 1982-83; chmn. NCCJ, Indpls., 1982-83. Mem. Ind. Electric Assn. (chmn. 1981). Clubs: Indpls. Athletic, Columbia, Highland Golf & Country (dir. 1981-83). Home: 6140 Sunset Ln Indianapolis IN 46208 Office: Indpls Power & Light Co 25 Monument Cir Indianapolis IN 46206

BORDERS, ROBERT SHIVELY, sales executive; b. Louisville, May 11, 1943; s. Robert and Martha (Mann) B.; m. Sharron Lee Wilham, Apr. 16, 1966; children: Karen, Scott, Laura, Bethany. BA in Physics, U. Louisville, 1973, postgrad., 1973-75. Engring. technician Am. Standard, Louisville, 1965-66; sr. sales rep. Xerox, Louisville, 1971-75; nat. sales mgr. DCE Vokes Inc., Louisville, 1975-86; nat. sales mgr. Amox div. VBM, Louisville, 1986—. Contbr. articles to profl. jours. With USN, 1967-71. Mem. Am. Welding Soc., Am. Foundryman's Soc. Republican. Baptist. Office: VBM-Amox Div 1402 W Main St Louisville KY 40201

BOREL, RICHARD WILSON, radio station executive, communications consultant; b. Columbus, Ohio, June 10, 1943; s. Richard Alfred and Margaret (Wilson) B.; m. Kathy Teaford, July 17, 1965; 1 child, Meredith Lynn. BS in Mktg., Ohio State U., 1964; MBA in Fin., U. Pa., 1966. Mgr. sales and svcs. budgets TWA, N.Y.C., 1966-69; mgr. planning and devel. John Blair & Co., N.Y.C., 1969-76; v.p., sta. mgr. Sta. WHOH Corp., Boston, 1976-84; sr. v.p., chief oper. officer Ea. Exclusives, Inc., Boston, 1984-85; pres., chief oper. officer Borel & Co., Dover, Mass., 1985-86, Metro Net, Inc., Boston and Vt., 1986-89; v.p. sales and mktg., chief adminstrv. officer Target Prodns., Inc., Boston, 1989—. Author: (with others) Broadcast and Cable Management, 1986. Mem. New Eng. Broadcasting Assn. (pres. 1977-78), Wharton Club (bd. dirs. 1988—), Beta Gamma Sigma. Republican. Episcopalian. Home: 6 Circle Dr Dover MA 02030

BORELLI, FRANCIS J(OSEPH) (FRANK), insurance brokerage and consulting firm financial executive; b. Bklyn., Sept. 2, 1935; s. Anthony and Ida Borelli; m. Madlyn Quadrino, June 25, 1960; children: Frank, Richard. BBA, Baruch Coll. CUNY, 1956. C.P.A., N.Y. With Deloitte Haskins & Sells, 1956-79, ptnr., 1968-79, mng. ptnr. in charge Bergen County, N.J. office, 1976-79; sr. v.p. fin. and adminstr., dir. Airco, Inc., Montvale, N.J., 1980-84; sr. v.p., chief fin. officer, dir. Marsh & McLennan Cos., Inc., N.Y.C., 1984—; bd. dirs. United Water Resources, Nanuet Nat. Bank, N.Y. Bd. dirs. Nat. Multiple Sclerosis Soc.; active numerous pub. service orgns. Mem. Fin. Execs. Inst. (bd. dirs.), Am. Inst. C.P.A.s, N.Y. State Soc. C.P.A.s. Clubs: Ridgewood Country; Broad St. Office: Marsh & McLennan Cos Inc 1221 Ave of Americas New York NY 10020

BOREN, HUGO, corporation executive; b. Buenos Aires, Apr. 17, 1943; came to U.S., 1952, naturalized, 1961; s. Samuel and Clara Angela (Lorenzi) B.; m. Camille Christensen, Feb. 15, 1974; children: Craig, Mark, Michael, Christine, Paul. B in Engring. Sci., Brigham Young U., 1969, MBA, 1971. Auditor IML Freight, Salt Lake City, 1972-73; controller Nature's Way Products, Provo, Utah, 1971-72; staff planner Bechtel Group, San Francisco, 1973-74; pres. Visher Systems, Inc., 1974—; v.p. Murdock Internat., Provo, 1975—, also bd. dirs.; v.p. Murdock Tech., Provo, 1984—, also bd. dirs. Explorer scout leader Boy Scouts Am., Provo, 1981-84; coach Youth Soccer, Basketball, Softball clubs, Provo, 1981—; Ecclesiastical leader Ch. of Jesus Christ of Latter Day Saints, Provo, 1975—. Republican. Home: 1097 E 2570 N Provo UT 84604 Office: Murdock Internat Corp 10 Mountain Springs Pkwy Springville UT 84663

BOREN, WILLIAM MEREDITH, business executive; b. San Antonio, Oct. 23, 1924; s. Thomas Loyd and Verda (Locke) B.; m. Molly Brasfield Sarver, Dec. 3, 1976; children: Susan, Patricia, Janet, Jenny, Burton, Cliff. Student, Tex. A&M U., 1942-43, Rice U., 1943-44; B.S. in Mech. Engring., Tex. U., 1949. Vice pres., gen. mgr. Rolo Mfg. Co., Houston, 1949-54; mgr. sales engring. Black, Sivalls & Bryson, Houston, Oklahoma City, 1955-64; pres., dir., mem. exec. com. Big Three Industries, Inc., Houston, 1965—; dir. Bowen Tool Co., Houston. Inventor Classic Bridge game. Trustee SW Research Inst., San Antonio; bd. dirs. Houston Econ. Devel. Coun. Served to lt. (j.g.) USN, 1943-46. Mem. French/Am. C. of C. (bd. dirs. Houston chpt.), Internat. Oxygen Mfrs. Assn., Tau Beta Pi, Pi Tau Sigma. Republican. Home: 11214 Montebello Ct Houston TX 77024 Office: Big Three Industries Inc PO Box 3047 Houston TX 77253

BORENSTEIN, MILTON CONRAD, lawyer, manufacturing company executive; b. Boston, Oct. 21, 1914; s. Isadore Sidney and Eva Beatrice B.; m. Anne Shapiro, June 20, 1937; children: Roberta, Jeffrey. AB cum laude, Boston Coll., 1935; JD, Harvard U., 1938. Bar: Mass. 1938, U.S. Dist. Ct. 1939, U.S. Ct. Appeals 1944, U.S. Supreme Ct. 1944. Pvt. practice law Boston, 1938—; officer, dir. Sweetheart Paper Products Co., Inc., Chelsea, Mass., 1944-61; pres. Sweetheart Paper Products Co., Inc., Chelsea, 1961-83, chmn. bd., 1984; with Sweetheart Plastics, Inc., Wilmington, Mass., 1958—; v.p. Sweetheart Plastics, Inc., Wilmington, 1958-84, also dir.; v.p. Md. Cup Corp., Owings Mills, 1960-77, exec. v.p., treas., 1977-84, also dir.; Bd. dirs. Am. Assocs. Hebrew U., 1968—. Trustee Boston Coll., 1979-87, assoc. trustee, 1987—, chmn. estate planning coun., 1981-83, mem. council exec. com., 1984—; trustee Combined Jewish Philanthropies, Boston, 1969—, N.E. Sinai Hosp., Stoughton, Mass., 1974—, Ben-Gurion U., 1975-85, 87—; bd. overseers Jewish Theol. Sem. Am., 1971—; mem. pres.'s coun. Sarah Lawrence Coll., 1970-79; pres. Congregation Kehillath Israel, Brookline, Mass., 1977-79, hon. pres., 1979—; mem. pres.'s coun. Brandeis U., 1979-81, fellow, 1981—; v.p. Assoc. Synagogues of Mass., 1980-81; bd. dirs. nat. governing coun. Am. Jewish Congress, 1984—. Recipient Community Svc. award Jewish Theol. Sem. Am., 1970. Mem. ABA, Boston Bar Assn. (bicentennial com. 1986-87), Mass. Bar Assn., Chelsea C. of C. (dir.). Clubs: Harvard (Boston and N.Y.C.), Harvard Faculty, 100. Lodges: Masons, Shriners. Home: 273 Eliot St Chestnut Hill MA 02167 Office: Concorde Assocs & the of Office Milton C Borenstein 1 Devonshire Pl Ste 2912 Boston MA 02109

BORENSTINE, ALVIN JEROME, search company executive; b. Kansas City, Mo., Dec. 14, 1933; s. Samuel and Ella C. (Berman) B.; m. Roula Alakiotou, Dec. 31, 1976; Ella Marie and Sami (twins). B.S. in Econs., U. Kans., 1956; M.B.A., U. Pa., 1960. Analyst, Johnson & Johnson, New Brunswick, N.J., 1961-62; systems mgr. Levitt & Sons, Levittown, N.J., 1962-66; dir. mgmt. info. svcs. Warner Brothers Co., Cambridge, Mass., 1966-71; mgr. fin. and adminstrv. systems Esmark, Inc., Chgo., 1971-72; pres. Synergistics Assocs. Ltd., Chgo., 1972—; mem. bus. adv. coun., Program Able Hellenic Dimensions. Mem. bus. adv. coun. St. Xavier U., Program Able, Hellenic Dimensions. Mem. Assn. for Systems Mgmt. (pres. Boston chpt. 1969, Disting. Svc. award 1970), Soc. Info. Mgmt. Systems and Procedures Assn. rsch. fellow, 1959-60; Eddie Jacobson Found. scholar, 1958-60. Club: Carlton. Lodge: B'nai B'rith. Home: 6033 N Sheridan Chicago IL 60660 Office: Synergistics Assocs Ltd 320 N Michigan Ave Ste 1803 Chicago IL 60601

BORER, EDWARD TURNER, investment banker; b. Phila., Nov. 30, 1938; s. Robert Chamberlin and Helen Elizabeth (Clawges) B.; B.S., U. Pa., 1960; m. Amy Hamilton Ryerson, Aug. 8, 1959; children—Edward Turner, Catherine Hamilton, Elizabeth Taft. Rep., Hopper Soliday & Co., Inc., Phila., 1960-67, v.p. research, 1967-73, sec., 1971-85, sr. v.p., 1973-82, exec. v.p., 1982-84, pres., 1984-88, also bd. dirs.; dir. Manchester Gas Co. (N.H.), 1965-88, pres., 1970, chmn. bd., chmn. exec. com., 1970-82; chmn. bd. EnergyNorth, Inc., 1982—; dir., sec. Disaster Control, Inc., 1981-83, Omni Oil & Gas Mgmt. Co., 1981-84; dir. Hopper Soliday Corp., 1988-89; founder, treas., sec., dir. Creative Information Systems, Inc., Chadds Ford, Pa., 1967-77; v.p. Sovereign Investors, 1980-86 ; dir. Energy North Natural Gas, Inc., Energy North Propane, Inc. (formerly Rent-A-Space of New Eng., Inc.). Chmn. West Met. Area-Wide Com., Regional Med. Program, 1969-70; pres, bd. dirs. Phila. Corp. for Fin. Investment, Phila. Corp. for Investment Svcs., Phila. Corp. for Investment Mgmt., 1989—. Pres. Swarthmore Home and Sch. Assn., 1973; bd. dirs. Freedom Valley council Girl Scouts U.S.A., 1974-75, also chmn. finance com.; bd. dirs., chmn. fin. com. Planned Parenthood Southeastern Pa., 1980-85, dir. 1988; treas., 1986-87 trustee George W. South Meml. Ch. of the Adv., Phila., 1978-88. Served to 1st lt., Q.M.C., AUS, 1961-62. Chartered fin. analyst. Mem. Fin. Analysts Fedn., Phila. Securities Assn. (dir. 1979-83, v.p. 1980-81, pres. 1981-82), Nat. Assn. Securities Dealers (arbitrator 1982—, chmn. dist. 11 and bus. conduct com. 1986), Fin. Analysts Phila. (treas. 1976-77), N.Y. Soc. Security Analysts, Am. Arbitration Assn. (arbitrator 1988—), Delta Upsilon. Episcopalian (vestryman 1970-73, 74-77, 85-88). Club: Union League (Phila.). Home: 125 Guernsey Rd Swarthmore PA 19081 also: Box 643 Saint John VI 00831 Office: 2103 Fidelity Bldg Philadelphia PA 19109

BORG, MALCOLM AUSTIN, communications company executive; b. N.Y.C., Jan. 28, 1938; s. Donald Gowen and Flora (Austin) B.; m. Sandra Jean Agemian, Sept. 9, 1961; children—John Austin, Jennifer Ann, Stephen Agemian. B.S. in English Lit, Columbia, 1965; postgrad., Harvard U., 1970; LHD (hon.), Ramapo (N.J.) Coll., 1985. Editorial trainee Bergen Evening Record (named changed to Bergen Record, 1984), Hackensack, N.J., 1959—; gen. assignment reporter Bergen Evening Record (named changed to Bergen Record, 1984), 1960-62, adminstrv. asst. to pub., 1963-64, asst. pub., 1965-66, v.p., 1967-68, exec. v.p., 1968-70, pres., 1971-78, chief exec. officer, 1971—, chmn. bd., 1975—; chmn. bd. Gateway Communications, Inc. subs. Macromedia Inc., Cherry Hill, N.J., 1978—; chmn. bd., chief exec. officer Macromedia, Inc. Holding Co., Hackensack, 1983—; chmn. bd., dir. Gremac, Inc.; bd. dirs. Ferag, Inc., Bristol, Pa. Active numerous civic orgn. , 1965—; bd. dirs. Wolfeboro (N.H.) Camp Sch., 1970—; mem. Palisades Interstate Park Commn., 1974—; chmn. Submarine Meml. Assn., Hackensack, 1974—; trustee Aviation Hall of Fame, N.J., 1979—; mem. Bergen County adv. bd. Nat. Council on Alcoholism, 1978—; mem. adv. council Sch. Gen. Studies, Columbia U., 1981—, mem. nat. campaign com. Fund for Columbia, 1983-87. With U.S. Army, 1956-58. Recipient 1st William H. Spurgeon III award Bergen council Boy Scouts Am., 1972, Whitney M. Young award, 1986; Torch of Liberty award Anti-Defamation League, B'nai B'rith, 1973, ann. communications and leadership award Greater N.Y. dist. 46 Toastmasters Internat., 1976, Service to Others award N.J. div. Salvation Army, 1977, ann. community leadership award NO. N.J. Interprofl. Council, 1977, Man of Yr. award Holy Name Hosp., 1977, Editor of Yr. award Nat. Press Photographers Assn., 1985, Owl award Columbia U., 1986, Citizen's award Acad. Medicine N.J., 1986. Mem. Am. Newspaper Publs. Assn., Am. Soc. Newspaper Editors, N.J. Press Assn., Soc. Profl. Journalists-Sigma Delta Chi, Bergen County C. of C. (bd. dirs. 1967-74), Hill Sch Alumni Assn. (pres. 1973-76), N.J. C. of C. (bd. dirs. 1977-79), Advt. Council (bd. dirs. 1978-85). Clubs: Arcola Country (Paramus, N.J.); Englewood Field (N.J.); Mid Ocean (Tucker's Town, Bermuda); Harvard (N.Y.C.), Club at World Trade Ctr. (N.Y.C.); Bath and Tennis (Spring Lake, N.J.); Knickerbocker Country (Tenafly, N.J.); Manasquan River Golf (Brielle, N.J.); Tournament Players (Ponte Verda, Fla.), Moselem Springs Golf Club (Fleetwood, Pa.). Office: Macromedia Inc 150 River St Hackensack NJ 07601-7172

BORGHESE, LIVIO M., investment bank executive; b. 1938. MBA, U. Pa., 1961. With Bear Stearns Cos. Inc., N.Y.C., 1968-88, exec. v.p.; chmn. internat. investment banking Prudential-Bache Capital Funding, N.Y.C., 1988—. Office: Prudential-Bache Capital Funding 1 Seaport Pla New York NY 10292

BORGIA, ANDREA GEORGE, insurance broker; b. Glendale, Calif., Oct. 12, 1950; s. John and Margaret (Cabodi) B.; m. Catherine Marie Lutz, July. 26, 1980; children: Jenna Catherine, Alexander John. BA in Bus., U.S. Internat. U., 1973. CLU. Pvt. practice insurance broker San Diego, 1974-84; ptnr. BYCO, San Diego, 1984—. Mem. 44th Congl. Dist. Adv. Com., San Diego; mem. bd. dirs. Community Congress of San Diego. Mem. San Diego Assn. Life Underwriters, Nat. Assn. Life Underwriters (Health Ins. Quality award, 1976, 80, Nat. Sales Achievement award 1979), Am. Soc. CLU'S, Million Dollar Round Table, Ariz. State Alumni Assn., U.S. Internat. U. Alumni Assn., San Diego State Alumni Assn. (pres. circle mem.). Republican. Roman Catholic. Club: San Diego Track. Home: 1112 Solana Dr Del Mar CA 92014 Office: BYCO 409 Camino del Rio S Suite 300 San Diego CA 92108

BORHI, CAROL, data processing executive; b. N.Y.C., Oct. 23, 1949; d. Carl and Elsie Elizabeth (Varady) Chaky; m. Nicholas Anthony Borhi, Sept. 23, 1972; children: Christy Nicole, Nicholas James. Assoc. in Applied Sci., Manhattan Community Coll., 1970; student, Hunter Coll., 1967-68, 70-71. Programmer asst. N.Y. Telephone, N.Y.C., 1970-73, programmer, 1974-76, programmer analyst, 1976-83; staff analyst Nynex Service Co., N.Y.C., 1984-87; systems analyst Nynex Corp., N.Y.C., 1987; assoc. dir. Nynex Corp., White Plains, N.Y., 1987—; pres. Personal Touch Computing, N.Y.C., 1981-86. Mem. Telephone Pioneers Am. (charter), Creative Investors Am. Republican. Roman Catholic. Club: Sacred Heart. Office: Nynex Corp 1111 Westchester Ave White Plains NY 10604

BORIS, WILLIAM O., advertising agency executive; b. Gary, Ind., Jan. 7, 1939; s. Oscar and Betty Boris; divorced; children: Darcy, Tara. BS, Ind. U., 1965, MBA, 1966. With Caterpillar Tractor Co., 1965; exec. v.p. Leo Burnett Co., Chgo., 1966—, chmn. investment com., chmn. adminstrn. com., mem. fin. com., also bd. dirs.; instr. Ind. U., Bloomington, 1967-69, guest lectr., 1982-84, mem. adv. bd. coun.; guest lectr. U. Minn., 1985. Contbg. author: Principles of Marketing, 1983. Sgt. U.S. Army, 1958-60. Mem. Chgo. Assn. Commerce and Industry (bd. dirs. 1983). Republican. Presbyterian. Home: 275-B Island View Ln Barrington IL 60010 Office: Leo Burnett Co Inc 1 Prudential Pla Chicago IL 60601

BORK, WALTER ALBERT, oil company executive; b. Chgo., Apr. 21, 1927; s. Walter Albert and Frances (Raczka) B.; m. Claire Elizabeth Connolly, Dec. 6, 1958; 1 son, Richard. B.S. in Petroleum Engring, U. Okla., 1951. Gen. mgr. corp. supply and distbn. Mobil Oil Corp., N.Y.C., 1972-77, v.p., 1977, v.p. sales and supply div., 1984, now bd. dirs. Served with U.S. Army, 1951-53. Republican. Roman Catholic. Office: Mobil Oil Corp 150 E 42nd St New York NY 10017

BORKAN, WILLIAM NOAH, biomedical electronics company executive; b. Miami Beach, Fla., Apr. 29, 1956; s. Martin Solomon and Annabelle (Hoffman) B.; B.S.E.E., Carnegie Mellon U., 1977; Ph.D., Sussex Coll. Tech., 1979; married. Tech., Dominicks' Radio & TV Co., Miami Beach, 1971-74; computer programmer Mt. Sinai Hosp., Miami Beach, 1973-74; chief studio engr. WGMA, Hollywood, Fla., 1973-74; disc. jockey WBUS-FM, Miami Beach, 1974; chief rec. engr. Dukoff Recording Studios', Miami, 1974-75; rec. studio design and constrn. TSI, Hollywood, Fla., 1975-77; chief design engr. Lumonics Co., Miami, 1974; service mgr. 21st Century Electronics Co., Miami, 1975; lab. tech. Carnegie-Mellon U.; mgr. Tech. Electronics Co., Pitts., 1976; pres. Borktronics Co. Miami, 1974-84; cons. specialist in neurobiometrics St. Barnabas Hosp., N.Y.C., 1978-83; rec. studio designer FXL Studios, Sunrise, Fla., 1978; pres., chief exec. officer Electronic Diagnostics, Inc., 1978-83, pres., chief exec. officer NeuroMed, Inc., 1980—; mem. coll. curricular coms. E.E. Dept. Grantee Carnegie Corp. and Carnegie Mellon U. Mem. Am. Soc. Heating, Refrigeration and Air Conditioning Engrs., Assn. Energy Engrs., Soc. Automotive Engrs., Assn. for Advancement Med. Instrumentation, AAAS, N.Y. Acad. Scis., Audio Engring. Soc. Author publs. in field; patentee in field. Home: 3364 NE 167th St North Miami FL 33160 Office: NeuroMed Inc 5000 Oakes Rd Fort Lauderdale FL 33314

BORKOVITZ, HENRY SAMUEL, engineering company executive; b. Chgo., Dec. 4, 1935; s. Leon and Goldye (Anoff) B.; m. Suzan Flanzbaum, June 1961 (div. 1972); children: Debra, Benjamin, Leah; m. Gaye Gayler, July 31, 1983; 1 stepchild, Suzanne Benson. Student, U. Ill., 1954-56; BS in Elec. Engring., Ill. Inst. Tech., 1958, MS in Elec. Engring., 1962; MBA, U. Chgo., 1970. Registered profl. engr., Ill. Design. Devel. engr. Lindberg Engring. Co., Chgo., 1953-62; chief devel. engr. ElectroSeal Corp., Des Plaines, Ill., 1962-64; dir. engring. Sola Electric div. Gen. Signal Corp., Elk Grove Village, Ill., 1964-81; v.p. engring. Realist, Inc., Menomonee Falls, Wis., 1981—. Patentee in field. Pres. Rogers Park Montessori Sch., Chgo., 1965. With U.S. Army, 1959. Mem. IEEE. Office: Realist Inc N93 W16288 Megal Dr Menomonee Falls WI 53051

BORLAND, VIRGINIA ANN, fashion specialist, fiber company executive; b. N.Y.C., Mar. 8, 1929; d. Charles Peter and Margaret Elise (Swane) S.; m. J. Nelson Borland, Nov. 13, 1969 (separated 1987). BA, Wells Coll., 1951. Publicist J. Walter Thompson Advt. Agy., 1952-55, Grey Advt., 1960; fashion dir. Cunningham & Walsh, N.Y.C., 1961-85, Avtex Fibers, Inc., N.Y.C., 1986—; cons., fashion editor Fashion Galleria mag., KTA, MMI, BASF Fibers. Vol. pediatric ward Meml. Hosp., 1953-84. Mem. Fashion Group (gov. 1975-77, found. dir. 1983-84), Inner Circle, Color Assn. U.S.A. (chmn. women's apparel color selection com.), Round Table Fashion Execs., Fashion News Workshop, N.Y. Jr. League. Republican. Episcopalian. Home: 110 East End Ave New York NY 10028 Office: The Fashion Galleria 110 West 40th St New York NY 10018

BORMAN, FRANK, airlines company executive, former astronaut; b. Gary, Ind., Mar. 14, 1928; s. Edwin Borman; m. Susan Bugbee; children: Fredrick, Edwin. B.S., U.S. Mil. Acad., 1950; M. Aero. Engring, Calif. Inst. Tech., 1957; grad., USAF Aerospace Research Pilots Sch., 1960, Advanced Mgmt. Program, Harvard Bus. Sch., 1970. Commd. 2d lt. USAF, advanced through grades to col., 1965, ret., 1970; assigned various fighter squadrons U.S. and Philippines, 1951-56; instr. thermodynamics and fluid mechanics U.S. Mil. Acad., 1957-60; instr. USAF Aerospace Research Pilots Sch., 1960-62; astronaut With Manned Spacecraft Ctr., NASA, until 1970; command pilot on 14 day orbital Gemini 7 flight Dec. 1965, including rendezvous with Gemini 6; command pilot Apollo 8, 1st lunar orbital mission, Dec. 1968; sr. v.p. for ops. Eastern Air Lines, Inc., Miami, Fla., 1970-74, exec. v.p., gen. operations mgr., 1974-75, pres., chief exec. officer, 1975-85, chief exec. officer, 1975-86, chmn. bd., 1976-86; vice chmn., dir. Tex. Air Corp., Houston, from 1986. Recipient Distinguished Service award NASA, 1965; Collier Trophy. Nat. Aeros. Assn., 1968. Office: Patlex Corp 205 W Boutz Rd Bldg 4 Ste 4 Las Cruces NM 88005 also: Patlex Corp 20415 Nordhoff St Chatsworth CA 91324 *

BORN, ALLEN, mineral and energy development company executive; b. Durango, Colo., July 4, 1933; s. C. S. and Bertha G. (Tausch) B.; m. Patricia Beaubien, Mar. 23, 1953; children—Michael, Scott, Brett. B.S. in Metallurgy and Geology, U. Tex.-El Paso, 1958. Exploration geologist El Paso Natural Gas, Tex., 1958-60; metallurgist Vanadium Corp. Am., 1960-62; gen. foreman Pima Mining, 1962-64; asst. supt. MolyCorp, 1964-67; chief metallurgist and supt., mgr. AMAX Inc., Greenwich, Conn., 1967-76, pres., chief operating officer, 1985—; chief exec. officer AMAX Inc., 1986-88, chmn., chief exec. officer, pres., 1988—; pres., chief exec. officer Can. Tungsten Mining Corp. Ltd., 1976-81; pres. AMAX of Can. Ltd., 1977-81; pres., chmn., chief exec. officer Placer Devel. Ltd., Vancouver, B.C., Can., 1981-85; chmn, chief exec. officer, pres. Amax Inc., Greenwich, Conn., 1988—; chmn. bd. Alumax, Inc., Amax Gold, Inc.; bd. dirs. Can. Tungsten Mining Corp., Aztec Mining Co. Ltd., Australia, Aztec Resources. Contbr. numerous articles to mining jours. Served with U.S. Army, 1952-55. Mem. AIME, Am. Mining Congress (bd. dirs.). Republican. Clubs: Sky (N.Y.C.); Indian Harbor Yacht (Greenwich, Conn.); Vancouver. Office: Amax Inc Amax Ctr PO Box 1700 Greenwich CT 06836

BORNS, ROBERT AARON, real estate developer; b. Gary, Ind., Oct. 24, 1935; s. Irving Jonah and Sylvia (Mackoff) B.; m. Sandra Solotkin Mar. 30, 1958; children: Stephanie, Elizabeth, Emily. BS, Ind. U., 1957. Account exec. Reynolds & Co., Chgo., 1957-59, Francis I. duPont Co., Indpls., 1960; owner, operator Borns & Co., Indpls., 1960-63; chmn. Borns Mgmt. Corp., Indpls., 1963—; bd. dirs. Heritage Venture Ptnrs., Indpls. Power and Light Co., IPALCO Enterprises. Bd. dirs. Indpls. Mus. of Art-Life, Corp. Community Council; bd. dirs.; mem. bd. vis. Jewish Studies Program, Ind. U. Recipient Enterprise award Indpls. Bus. Jour., 1982. Jewish. Mem. Econ. Club (bd. dirs.), Univ. Club. Office: Borns Mgmt Corp 200 S Meridian St Indianapolis IN 46225

BOROCHOFF, CHARLES ZACHARY, manufacturing company owner; b. Atlanta, Apr. 11, 1921; s. Isadore and Pauline (Reisman) B.; m. Ida Dorothy Sloan, Jan. 11, 1942; children—Lynn Borochoff Gould, Toby Ann Borochoff Bernstein, Jean Sue Borochoff Shapiro, Lance Mark. LLB, Atlanta Law Sch., 1941. Exec v.p. So. Wire & Iron Works, Atlanta, 1936-63; pres. Borochoff Properties, Inc., real estate, Atlanta, 1954—, Designs Unlimited, Inc., Atlanta, 1964—, Scottdale Enterprises, Atlanta, 1972—; chmn. Borochoff Realty; exec. v.p. Imperial SE; pres. CDR Mfg. Co. Mem. High Museum of Art (patron 1955—), Corcoran Gallery (patron); Nat. Conf. Christians and Jews, 1967—, Planned Parenthood, 1970—. Trustee Atlanta Playhouse, 1971—; bd. dirs. Little Miss Ga. Pageant, Little Mr. Dogwood Festival Pageant; mem. program com. Nat. UN Day, 1977, 78; mem. nat. adv. bd. Am. Security Council. Mem. DeKalb C. of C. (econ. devel. com. 1975), Nat. Retail Wholesale Furniture Assn., Internat. Home and Furniture Reps. Assn., Am. Mgmt. Assn. (Presdl. Club), String & Splinter Club Inc., Nu Beta Epsilon. Jewish. Lodges: Masons, Shriner (32 deg.), B'nai B'rith. Clubs: Atlanta Music, Progressive, Jockey. Home: 3450 Old Plantation Rd NW Atlanta GA 30327 Office: 733 Glendale Rd NE Scottdale GA 30079

BOROD, DONALD LEE, lawyer; b. Cleve., June 22, 1947; s. Jules Arthur and Hortense Edith (Cowan) B.; m. Jane Duclos Hudson, Nov. 11, 1978; children: James Hudson, Catherine Duclos. B.A., U. Mich., 1969; J.D., Columbia U., 1972. Bar: N.Y. 1973, Conn. 1984. Assoc. firm Dewey, Ballantine, Bushby, Palmer & Wood, N.Y.C., 1972-81; assoc. gen. counsel Kollmorgen Corp., Hartford, Conn., 1981-83, gen. counsel, 1983-86, v.p., gen. counsel, 1986—. Harlan Fiske Stone scholar Columbia U., 1971. Mem. ABA, Conn. Bar Assn., Am. Corp. Counsel Assn., Assn. Bar City N.Y. Club: Hartford Golf. Office: Kollmorgen Corp 10 Mill Pond Ln Simsbury CT 06070

BORON, FRANK THOMAS, plastics company executive; b. New Castle, Pa., Oct. 17, 1941; s. Joseph Michael and Helen (Billyk) B.; m. Janet Julia Smyczek, Jan. 9, 1965; children: David, Stacey, Kathryn, Aaron, Claire, Ethan. BSME, Cleve. State U., 1964. Registered profl. engr., Ohio. With B.F. Goodrich Chem. Co., 1964-84; product mgr. B.F. Goodrich Chem. Co., Cleve., 1972-78, new products mgr., 1978-82, market mgr., 1982-84; pres. Falcon Mktg. Services, Lakewood, Ohio, 1979—; exec. v.p. BioPlastics Co., Inc., North Ridgeville, Ohio, 1984—, North Coast Compounders, Inc., North Ridgeville, 1989—; tchr. Lake Erie Coll., Painesville, Ohio, 1983; bd. dirs. Comml. Devel. Assn., Washington. Gen. chmn. Derby A Golf Classic, Juvenile Diabetes Found., Elyria, Ohio, 1987, 88. Mem. Sales and Mktg. Execs. Lorain County, U.S. Equine Mktg. Assn., Comml. Devel. Assn. Republican. Roman Catholic. Office: BioPlastics Co Inc 4935 Mills Indsl Pkwy North Ridgeville OH 44039

BOROWSKI, JENNIFER LUCILE, corporate administrator; b. Jersey City, Oct. 23, 1934; d. Peter Anthony and Lucy (Zapolska) B. BS, St. Peter's Coll., 1968; postgrad., Pace Coll., 1976-77. Mgr. benefits Amerada Petroleum Corp., N.Y.C., 1951-66, Mt. Sinai Hosp., N.Y.C., 1966-67; mgr. payroll Haskins & Sells, N.Y.C., 1967-74; mgr. payroll and payroll tax Cushman & Wakefield, Inc., N.Y.C., 1975—. Mem. Am. Payroll Assn. (bd. dirs. 1979-81, cert.), Am. Mgmt. Assn., Am. Soc. Payroll Mgrs. Republican. Roman Catholic. Home: 36 Front St North Arlington NJ 07032 Office: Cushman & Wakefield Inc 1180 Ave of the Americas New York NY 10036

BORRECA, JOHN PETER, building materials manufacturing executive; b. N.Y.C., May 1, 1953; s. John Benedict and Ellen Loretta (McElroy) B.; m. Francine Kathleen Manetz, Apr. 24, 1976; children: Jason John, Michael Christopher. Student, CUNY, 1971-73; BA, U. South Fla., 1975. CPA, N.J. Sr. acct. The Celotex Corp., Tampa, Fla., 1975-77; plant controller The Celotex Corp., Texarkana, Ark., 1978-80; mgr. ops. adminstrn. The Celotex Corp., Tampa, 1982-83, dir. fin. acctg., 1983-85, v.p. fin., 1985-88; controller Insul-Coustic Div., Sayreville, N.J., 1980-82; v.p., chief fin. officer, treas. Jim Walter Corp., Tampa, 1988—. Fellow N.J. Soc. CPA's, Nat. Assn. Accts. Democrat. Roman Catholic. Office: Jim Walter Corp 1500 N Dale Mabry Hwy Tampa FL 33607

BORRELL, JERRY, magazine editor; b. El Paso, Tex., May 23, 1952; s. Gerald Joseph and Harriet (Green) B.; divorced; children: Sean, Allistair. BA, U. Miami, 1975; MS, Cath. U., 1981. Researcher U.S. Congress, Washington, 1976-79; sr. editor Computer Graphics, San Francisco, 1979-81; editor in chief Digital Design, Boston, 1981-83; sr. editor MiniMicro Systems, Boston and San Jose, Calif., 1983-85; editor-in-chief Macworld, San Francisco, 1985—. Contbr. numerous articles to profl. publs. Mem. Assn. Computing Machinery, Soc. Info. Display, Sigma Delta Chi. Home: 2000 Broadway #712 San Francisco CA 94115 Office: Macworld Inc 501 2d St 5th fl San Francisco CA 94107

BORST, MICHAEL J., financial systems analyst; b. Chgo., Mar. 8, 1955; s. James J. and Stephanie L. (Searle) B.; m. Janet Sue Israel, June 25, 1983; 1 child, Brian. BS in Fin., No. Ill. U., 1977; MBA in Systems, DePaul U., 1983. Gen. ledger specialist Playboy Enterprise, Chgo., 1978-80; info. systems analyst Old Ben Coal Co., Chgo., 1980-84; fin. systems analyst Handy Dan Home Improvement, Inc., San Antonio, 1984-86; acctg. systems officer MBank Alamo, San Antonio, 1986—; pres. Software Insights Cons., San Antonio, 1986—. Author: (software program) Wheel of Wealth, 1986. Vol. March of Dimes, San Antonio, 1985—; mem. St. Francis of Assissi, San Antonio, 1985—. Republican. Roman Catholic. Home: 4506 Honey Locust Woods San Antonio TX 78249 Office: MBank Alamo PO Box 900 San Antonio TX 78293

BORSUM, JAMES CARL, food company executive; b. Ann Arbor, Mich., Apr. 7, 1958; s. Jerry Carl and Helen Gertrude (Draminski) B.; m. Deborah Dee Troxel, Sept. 8, 1979. Student, U.S. Naval Acad., 1976-78; BS with high honors, Mich. State U., 1980, MS, 1981; MBA, U. Chgo., 1986. Engr. in tng. Kellogg Co., Battle Creek, Mich., 1978-79; engring. asst. USDA, East Lansing, Mich., 1979-80; grad. asst. Mich. State U., East Lansing, 1980-81; process/computer engr. CPC Internat., Winston-Salem, N.C., 1981-83; ops. mgr. CPC Internat., Summit-Argo, Ill., 1983-86; plant mgr. New Tech Snacks, Inc., Joliet, Ill., 1986-87, sales mgr., 1987-88, v.p., 1988-89, v.p., gen. mgr., 1989—. With USN, 1976-78. Mem. Am. Soc. Agrl. Engrs. Home: 4085 Garden Ave Western Springs IL 60558 Office: New Tech Snacks Inc 2409 McDonough St Joliet IL 60436

BORTEN, WILLIAM H., research company executive; b. N.Y.C., Mar. 1, 1935; s. David and Susan B.; m. Judith Sue Becker, Feb. 13, 1957; children: Jeffry, Daniel, Matthew. B.B.A., Adelphi U., Garden City, N.Y., 1957. Controller Avien, Inc., Woodside, N.Y., 1959-63; asst. gen. mgr. Fairchild Industries, Germantown, Md., 1963-71; exec. v.p., treas. Atlantic Research Corp., Alexandria, Va., 1971-80; pres. Atlantic Research Corp., 1980—, chief exec. officer, 1986—, also dir. Advisor for bus. and industry State Bd. for Community Colls., Richmond, Va., 1983—; trustee Adelphi U., Garden City, N.Y., 1982—, The Treatment Ctrs. for Montgomery County; founder Montgomery Village Day Care Ctr., Gaithersburg, Md., 1972; bd. dirs. Fairfax County Pub. Schs. Found., 1986—, Venture Clinic, 1986. Mem. Nat. Assn. Accountants. Office: Atlantic Rsch Corp 5390 Cherokee Ave Alexandria VA 22312

BORUM, RODNEY LEE, financial executive; b. nr. High Point, N.C., Sept. 30, 1929; s. Carl Macy and Etta (Sullivan) B.; m. Helen Marie Rigby, June 27, 1953; children: Richard Harlan, Sarah Elizabeth. Student, U. N.C., 1947-49; BS, U.S. Naval Acad., 1953. Design-devel. engr. GE, Syracuse, N.Y., 1956-58; design-devel. engr. GE, Cape Kennedy, Fla., 1956-58, missile test condr., 1958-60, mgr. ground equipment engr., 1960-61, mgr. ea. test range engring., 1961-65; adminstr. Bus. and Def. Svcs. Adminstrn.-Dept. Commerce, 1966-69; pres. Printing Industries Am., Arlington, Va., 1969-85, staff cons., 1985-86, mem. exec. com., 1969-85, dir.; pres. W.H. Rigby Cons., 1985-86; exec. v.p. Amasek Inc., Cocoa, Fla., 1986-87; assoc. Fin. Svcs. Orgn., Cocoa, Fla., 1987—; sec. Graphic Arts Show Corp.; dir. Inter-Comprint Ltd., Strangers Cay, Ltd.; mem. governing bd. Comprints Internat. Mem. exec. coun. Cub Scouts Am., 1965; bd. dirs. Brevard County United Fund (Fla.), 1964-65, v.p., 1964-65; bd. dirs. Brevard Beaches Concert Assn., 1965; mem. edn. coun. bd. dirs. Graphic Arts Tech. Found., Pitts., 1970-86; trustee, founder Graphic Arts Edn. and Rsch. Trust Fund, Arlington, Va., 1978-85; candidate for Congress from 11th dist. Fla. 1st lt. USAF, 1953-56. Named Boss of Yr., C. of C., 1965; recipient Bausch and Lomb Sci. award, 1947, Am. Legion award, 1952. Mem. U.S. Naval Inst., U.S. Naval Acad. Alumni Assn., Graphic Arts Coun. N.Am. (bd. dirs. 1977—), Phi Eta Sigma. Methodist.

BOSKIN, MICHAEL JAY, economist, educator; b. N.Y.C., Sept. 23, 1945; s. Irving and Jean (Kimmel) B.; m. Chris Dornin, Oct. 20, 1981. AB with highest honors, U. Calif., Berkeley, 1967, MA in Econs., 1968, PhD in Econs., 1971. Asst. prof. Stanford (Calif.) U., 1970-75, assoc. prof., 1976-78, prof., 1978—, dir. Ctr. for Econ. Policy Research, 1986—, Wohlford prof. econs., 1987—; chief economic adviser Office of the Pres., Washington, D. C., 1989—; vis. prof. Harvard U., Cambridge, Mass., 1977-78; cons. in field; bd. dirs. Equitec-Siebel Mut. Fund Group, Oakland, Calif. Author: Too Many Promises: The Uncertain Future of Social Secruity, 1986, Reagan and the Economy: Successes, Failures Unfinished Agenda, 1987; contbr. articles to profl. jours. Faculty Research fellow Mellon Found., 1973. Mem. Am. Council on Capital Formation (bd. dirs. 1986—), Nat. Chamber Found. (bd. dirs. 1987—). Office: Stanford U Dept Econs Stanford CA 94305 *

BOSMAN, ROBERT ALLAN, oil company executive; b. Jacksonville, Fla., Feb. 17, 1957; s. Archie Robert and Frances (Hurst) B.; m. Cynthia Denise Petty, Apr. 12, 1980; children: Lisa Michelle, Brian Allan. Assoc., St. Johns River Community Coll., Palatka, Fla., 1977; B in Acctg., U. No. Fla., 1979. Acct. Eastern Seaboard Petroleum, Jacksonville, 1979-81, credit mgr., 1981-83, acctg. mgr., 1983-85, sales exec., 1987—; internat. bus. developer First Union Nat. Bank, Jacksonville, 1985-87. Mem. Jacksonville C. of C. Internat. (bd. dirs. 1985-87). Republican. Congregationalist. Club: Propeller (bd. dirs. 1980-83) (Jacksonville). Home: 822 Ibis Rd Jacksonville FL 32216 Office: Ea Seaboard Petroleum 6531 Evergreen Ave Jacksonville FL 32206

BOSNER, KEVIN CHARLES, finance company executive; b. Rochester, N.Y., Oct. 23, 1951; s. John A. and Sabina (Lyons) B.; m. Mary Catherine Cleary, Oct. 27, 1973; children: Richard, Alanna. BA in English and Edn., Le Moyne Coll., 1973; MBA in Fin. and Acctg., Rochester Inst. Tech., 1977. Mgr. and owner Allied Indsl. Laundry, Rochester, 1973-77, Temstad, Inc., Rochester, 1977-81; with Case Hoyt Corp., Rochester, 1981-88; corp. contr. Case Hoyt Corp., 1986-88; v.p. fin. IMPCO, Inc., Rochester, 1988—. Mem. Nat. Assn. Accts. Home: 796 Blue Creek Dr Webster NY 14580 Office: IMPCO Inc 100 Rockwood St Rochester NY 14610

BOSSEN, WENDELL JOHN, insurance company executive; b. Vienna, S.D., Nov. 11, 1933; s. Hans Simonsen and Clara Patrina (Yorseth) B.; m. Jean Davidson, Jan. 6, 1956; children: Mark, Monica. Student, S.D. Sch. Mines, 1952. CLU. Agt. Northwestern Nat. Life Ins. Co., Mpls., 1957-61, dist. mgr., staff mgr., 1961-68, br. mgr., 1968-72, div. v.p., 1972-77; exec. v.p., chief operating officer Inter-Ocean Ins. Co., Cin., 1977-84; sr. v.p. corp. mktg. Mut. Benefit Life Ins. Co., Newark, 1984—; cons. Newark Performing Arts Corp., 1986. Author: Businessmens Guide to Insurance, 1981; contbr. articles to profl. jours. Chmn. ARC, Waterstown, S.D., 1962, Northeast S.D. chpt. United Way, Watertown, 1963, Waterstown County Reps., 1963-64; mem. exec. com. S.D. Reps., Pierre, 1964; bd. dirs. Am. Luth. Ch., Cin., 1979. Recipient Danforth Found. award, 1952. Mem. Nat. Assn. Life Underwriters (pres. Watertown chpt. 1960-61, v.p. state chpt. 1961-62), Chartered Life Underwriters, Life Ins. Mktg. Research Assn. (com. chmn. 1975). Club: Golden Valley Country (Mpls). Lodges: Elks (pres. 1962-63), Lions (pres. 1961, 73), Kiwanis. Home: 149 Wexford Way Basking Ridge NJ 07920 Office: Mut Benefit Life Ins Co 520 Broad St Newark NJ 07101

BOSSERT, PHILIP JOSEPH, information systems executive; b. Indpls., Feb. 23, 1944; s. Alfred Joseph and Phyllis Jean (Cashen) B.; m. Jane Elisabeth Shade, June 29, 1968. BA in Econs., Rockhurst coll., 1968; cert. in Philosophy, U. Freiburg, Fed. Republic Ger., 1970; MA in Philosophy, Washington U., St. Louis, 1972, PhD in Philosophy, 1973. Asst. prof. philosophy Hawaii Loa Coll., Honolulu, 1973-76, pres., 1978-86; dir. Hawaii com. for the humanities Nat. Endowment for the Humanities, Honolulu, 1976-77; dir. long range planning Chaminade U., Honolulu, 1977-78; pres. Strategic Info. Solutions, Honolulu, 1986—; mgr. strategic info. systems GTE Hawaiian Telephone, Honolulu, 1987—; cons. Ssangyong Bus. Group, Seoul, Korea, 1987—, Nat. Assn. Colls. Univs. and Bus. Officers, Washington, 1980—. Author: Strategic Planning and Budgeting, 1989; author, editor numerous books on philosophy; contbr. articles to profl. jours. Sgt. U.S. Army, 1962-65. Fulbright-Hays fellow, 1968-70, Woodrow Wilson fellow, 1972-73, Nat. Endowment for Humanities fellow, 1976. Mem. Data Processing Mgmt. Assn., Soc. Corp. Planners, Rotary Club. Office: Strategic Info Solutions Inc PO Box 37849 Honolulu HI 96837

BOSSIDY, LAWRENCE ARTHUR, utility company executive; b. Pittsfield, Mass., Mar. 5, 1935; B.A. in Econs., Colgate U., m. 1956; children: Lynn, Larry, Paul, Pam, Nancy, Mary Jane, Lucy, Michael, Kathleen. With Gen. Electric Co., 1957—, former exec. v.p., sector exec. services and materials Gen. Elec. Co., Fairfield, Conn., vice chmn., dir.; now chmn., dir. Gen. Electric Credit Corp. (now Gen. Electric Capital Corp.), N.Y.C. Mem. Elfun. Roman Catholic. Office: GE Capital Corp 570 Lexington Ave New York NY 10022 *

BOSSIER, ALBERT LOUIS, JR., shipbuilding company executive; b. Gramercy, La., Nov. 29, 1932; s. Albert Louis and Alba Marie (Dufrense) B.; m. Jo Ann Decedue, Jan. 11, 1958; children—Albert Louis III, Brian, Donna, Steven. BS, La. State U., 1954, BSEE, 1956; J.D., Loyola U., New Orleans, 1971. Registered profl. engr., La. With Avondale Shipyards, Inc., New Orleans, 1957—, elec. supt., 1961-67, gen. plant supt., 1967-69, v.p. prodn. ops., 1969-72, exec. v.p., 1972-78, pres., from 1978, now chmn., chief exec. officer. Bd. dirs. Better Bus. Bur. of New Orleans, C. of C. of New Orleans and River Regions. Served as 1st lt. Signal Corps AUS, 1956. Mem. ABA, La. Bar Assn., Am. Welding Soc., Navy League of U.S. (pres. Greater New Orleans council 1981—). Club: Propeller (New Orleans). Office: Avondale Industries Inc PO Box 50280 New Orleans LA 70150

BOSSOLA, ANTOINETTE, financial executive; b. St. Louis, Sept. 18, 1956; d. Raymond L. and Sylvia L. (Woods) B.; m. James R. Disano, Oct. 3, 1987. BS in Communications, U. Mo., 1979. Cert. fin. planner. Exec. organizer C.J. Thomas Co., St. Louis, 1979-84; fin. planner Integrated Resources Equity Corp., St. Louis, 1985-87, Pension and Retirement Resources, St. Louis, 1987—. Contbr. articles to profl. publs. Chmn. St. Louis Civil Service Commn.; coordinator 13th Ward, St. Louis. Mem. Inst. Cert. Fin. Planners, Internat. Assn. Fin. Planning. Club: Carlysle Sailing Assn. (sec. 1987—). Home: 1816 Lafayette Saint Louis MO 63104 Office: Pension & Retirement Resources 1715 Deer Tracks Trail Ste 120 Town and Country MO 63131

BOST, PATRICIA JAMES, financial executive; b. St. Louis, Feb. 9, 1943; d. Lewis Edmond and Lena (Vance) James; m. Larry Edward Bost. Student, Drury Coll., 1961; BS with honors, Washington U., 1969; MBA with honors, So. Ill. U., 1982; postgrad., George Washington U., 1988—. With Monsanto Co., St. Louis, 1962-75, acctg. mgr., 1975-1982; vis. asst. prof. U. N.Mex., Albuquerque, 1983-86; vis. asst. prof. George Washington U., Washington, 1986, doctoral fellow, 1989—; instr. acctg. George Mason U., Fairfax, Va., 1986-87; contr. Clean Sites, Inc., Alexandria, Va., 1988-89; trainer Roy Walters & Assoc., N.J., 1976-82; instr. acctg. George Washington U., 1986. Contbr. articles and book rev. to profl. publs. Mem. scholarship com. Air Force Wives Club, N.Mex., 1985; leader St. Louis area Girl Scouts U.S., 1978. Mem. Nat. Assn. Accts., Inst. Mgmt. Accts. (cert.), Am. Acctg. Assn., Acad. Internat. Bus., Tex. Soc. Club, Porsche of Am. Club. Methodist. Home: 1587 C Eglin Way Bolling AFB Washington DC 20336

BOSTIAN, DAVID BOONE, JR., financial company executive; b. Charlotte, N.C., Feb. 12, 1943; s. David Boone and Clara Edna (Kanoy) B.; A.B. (Disting. Mil. grad.), Davidson Coll., 1964; M.B.A. (Bus. Found. scholar), U. N.C., 1965; m. Mary Rodgers Hunter, Sept. 11, 1965; 1 son, Robert Boone. Dir. market services Hayden, Stone Inc., N.Y.C., 1967-72; v.p., dir. market research Loeb, Rhoades & Co., N.Y.C., 1972-76; pres. Bostian Research Assocs., Inc., N.Y.C., 1977—; lectr. Wharton Bus. Sch., Columbia U., N.Y. Inst. Fin., New Sch., Conf. Bd.; expert witness U.S. Senate Fin. Com., U.S. Gold Commn., Joint Econ. Com.; econ. advisor to Exec. Office of the Pres., U.S. Treasury Dept., Fed. Reserve. Mem. Rep. Nat. Com.; mem. U.S. Senate Bus. Adv. Bd., Pres.' Econ. Policy Advisory Bd. Served to lt. U.S. Army, 1965-67. Named one of Outstanding Young Men Am., 1978. Mem. Am. Fin. Assn., N.Y. Soc. Security Analysts (govt. relations com.), Inst. Chartered Fin. Analysts, Fin. Analysts Research Found., Blue Chip Economists, Nat. Assn. Bus. Economists, N.Y. Assn. Bus. Economists, Nat. Bur. Econ. Research, Ne Ultra Soc. of Davidson Coll., Ballet Theater Found., Internat. Platform Assn., Internat. Assn. Bus. Economists, Pres.'s Assn. Am. Mgmt. Assn., World Future Soc., U. N.C. Alumni Assn. (trustee), N.C. Society of N.Y. (trustee), Alpha Phi Omega. Republican. Presbyterian. Clubs: U.S. Senatorial; Economic (N.Y.C.). Author: (with others) Methods and Techniques of Business Forecasting, Encyclopedia of Stock Market Techniques, A Question of National Economic Security, Toward a Synthesis of Random Walk and Market Analysis, Market Analysis and Portfolio Strategy, The New American Boom. Home: Suffolk Ln Tenafly NJ 07670 Office: Bostian Rsch Assocs Inc 360 Madison Ave New York NY 10017

BOSTON, WALLACE ELLSWORTH, JR., healthcare executive, financial consultant; b. Salisbury, Md., May 28, 1954; s. Wallace Ellsworth Sr. and Barbara Ellen (Widdowson) B. AB, Duke U., 1975; MBA, Tulane U., 1978. CPA, Md. Mktg. trainee John Deere Indsl. Equipment Co., Moline, Ill., 1978; acct. Price Waterhouse, Balt., 1978-80, sr. cons., 1980-83, mgr. cons., 1983; v.p. fin., chief fin. officer Nat. Realty Services, Inc., Vienna, Va., 1984-85, sr. v.p syndications, 1985-86; v.p. fin. Meridian Healthcare, Towson, Md., 1986—; also bd. dirs. Meridian Healthcare; bd. visitors Montebello Rehab. Hosp., Balt. Contbr. articles to profl. jours. Mem. Md. Assn. CPA's (mem. mgmt. adv. services com. 1980-84, mem. industry com. 1988—), Am. Inst. CPA's, Inst. Mgmt. Acctg., Am. Mgmt. Assn., Internat. Assn. Fin. Planners, McDonogh Sch. Alumni Assn. (pres. 1986), Duke Univ. Alumni Assn. (pres. Balt. chpt. 1983-84). Republican. Methodist. Clubs: Balt. Country, Ctr. (Balt.). Home: 7 Louis Edward Ct Hunt Valley MD 21030 Office: Meridian Healthcare 515 Fairmount Ave Towson MD 21204

BOSWELL, GARY TAGGART, electronics company executive; b. Ft. Worth, Dec. 24, 1937; s. David W. and Marjory (Taggart) B.; B.A., Tex. Christian U., 1958, M.S., 1965; postgrad. San Diego State Coll., 1960-61; m. Margaret Ruth Yelvington, Sept. 8, 1957; children—Michael David, Margaret McQuiston, Susannah Ruth. Scientist U.S. Govt., White Sands (N.M.) Missile Range, 1958-59; research engr. Gen. Dynamics, San Diego, 1959-60; programmer Bell Helicopter, Hurst, Tex., 1960-63; sect. head Collins Radio Co., Dallas, 1963-68; mgr. software devel. Tex. Instruments, Inc., Austin, 1968-72; mgr. ASC (Advanced Sci. Computer) Mktg., 1973-75, mgr. ASC div., 1975-76, mgr. computer systems, 1976-80, mgr. global positioning systems, 1980-81, mgr. TI engring. systems, 1981-83, v.p. equipment group, mgr. intelligent systems div., 1983-86, pres. Aydin Monitor Systems, Ft. Washington, Pa., 1987-88, Aydin Computer and Monitor, Horsham, Pa., 1988—. Mem. Am. Nat. Fortran Standards Com., 1970-74. Mem. Assn. Computing Machinery, Snipe Class Internat. Racing Assn. Club: White Rock Sailing. Designer several Fortran Compliers. Winner Western Hemisphere Snipe championship, 1970, also other maj. regattas. Home: 1130 Welsh Rd Ambler PA 19002 Office: Aydin Computer & Monitor 700 Dresher Rd Horsham PA 19004

BOSWELL, GEORGE MARION, JR., orthopedist, health care facility administrator; b. Dallas, May 12, 1920; s. George Marion and Viola (Scarbrough) B.; m. Veta M. Fuller, Oct. 30, 1958; children: Brianna Boswell Brown, Kama, Maia. BS, Tex. Tech U., 1940; MD, U. Tex., Southwestern Dallas, 1950. Diplomate Am. Acad. Orthopaedic Surgery. Intern Parkland Hosp., Dallas, 1950-51; resident gen. surgeryand orthopedic surgery Parkland, Baylor and Scottish Rite Hosps., Dallas, 1951-55; practice medicine specializing in orthopedics Dallas, 1955—; v.p. med. affairs Baylor Health Care System, Dallas, 1982—; pres., owner Bee Aviation Inc., Dallas, 1968—, Boswell Realty Inc., Dallas, 1971—; lectr., cons. on health care delivery. Contbr. articles to profl. jours. Fellow ACS; mem. AMA, Am. Acad. Orthopaedic Surgery (Key Man U.S. Congress 1980—), Am. Hosp. Assn., Tex. Hosp. Assn. (Key Man Tex. Legislature 1980—, council on hosp. staffs), Flying Physicians (pres. Tex. 1960-64). Republican. Methodist. Club: Cresent (Dallas). Home: 4849 W Lawther Dr Dallas TX 75214 Office: Baylor Health Care System 3201 Worth St Dallas TX 75226

BOSWELL, HENRY OLIVER, retired oil company executive; b. Corsicana, Tex., June 13, 1929; s. Henry Oliver and Opal B.; m. Jean Sylvia Wirtz, Sept. 4, 1954; children: Henry Oliver, Laura Jean Schulze, Diane Elizabeth McGowen, Mary Gail Smith. B.S. in Petroleum Engring., U. Houston, 1954; grad. advanced mgmt. program, U. Western Ont. Sch. Bus., Can., 1969. Engr. Stanolind Oil & Gas Co., Houston and Lake Charles, La., 1953-57; engring. supr. Pan Am. Petroleum Corp., New Orleans, Tulsa, Houston and Beaumont,, Tex., 1957-70; v.p.-prodn. Amoco Can., Calgary, Alta., 1970-73, pres., 1973-75; v.p.-prodn. Amoco Internat. Oil Co., Chgo., 1975-78; v.p.-Africa and Middle East Amoco Internat. Oil Co., Houston, 1978-79, exec. v.p., 1979-81; pres.-internat. Amoco Prodn. Co., Chgo., 1981-83, pres., 1983-87; dir. Amoco Corp., 1983-87; bd. dirs. Rowan Cos., Cameron Iron Works, ServiceMaster Industries, Inc. Trustee Am. U. in Cairo, 1985—. Served as 2d lt. U.S. Army, 1946-48. Mem. Am. Petroleum Inst., Soc. Petroleum Engrs., Nat. Ocean Industries Assn. (dir. 1984—), 25-Yr. Club Petroleum Industry, Petroleum Club (Houston). Republican. Baptist. Home: 34 S Bay Dr Bullard TX 75737

BOTELHO, RICHARD PAUL, manufacturing company executive; b. Fall River, Mass., Oct. 31, 1949; s. William Couto and Alice Sylvia Botelho; m. Diane Marie Luz, Sept. 27, 1969; children: Tracy Lynn, Julie Ann. AS in Acctg., Bristol Community Coll., 1969; BS in Acctg., Johnson and Wales Coll., Providence, 1973. Acct. Flint Bus. Service, Fall River, 1968-69; cost acct. Mt. Hope Machinery Co., Taunton, Mass., 1969-73; asst. comptroller Cliftex Corp., New Bedford, Mass., 1973; cost acctg. mgr. St. Regis Paper, Attleboro, Mass., 1974-77; matls. mgr. St. Regis Paper, Attleboro, 1977-78; comptroller Colonial Industries, Framingham, Mass., 1978-81; fin. and matls. mgr. Victor Electronics, Southboro, Mass., 1981-82; founder, treas., v.p. The Alternative Group, Inc., Worcester, Mass., 1982-84; v.p. fin. Standard Fin-Pipe Radiator Corp., Clinton, Mass., 1984-87; owner Controller's Office, Software Devel. Firm, Attleboro, 1987—. Trustee Darlington Congl. Ch., 1977-79; exec. v.p. Bristol County Young Reps., 1968, 69. Mem. Bus. Adminstrn. Soc. (pres. 1969). Clubs: Attleboro Power Squadron, Greenwich Yacht. Lodges: Eastern Star, Masons (master). Home: 168 Bishop St Attleboro MA 02703 Office: Software Devel Co Contr's. Office 168 Bishop St Attleboro MA 02703

BOTHE, DAVIS ROSS, consulting firm executive, educator; b. Bonduel, Wis., Dec. 16, 1950; s. Oscar Theodore and Berdine Grace (Ross) B. BS in Applied Math., U. Wis., Milw., 1973, MBA, 1976. Sr. statis. analyst Gen. Motors Co., Detroit, 1976-85; pres. Internat. Quality Inst., Inc., Northville, Mich., 1985—; also bd. dirs. Internat. Quality Inst., Inc. Author: Break Through to Quality Excellence, 1984, Industrial Problem Solving, 1986; producer (video tape) Let Your Process Do the Talking, 1983; also articles. Mem. Am. Soc. for Quality Control (cert. reliability, quality engr.), Am. Soc. for Metals, Am. Statis. Assn., Soc. Automotive Engrs., Math. Assn. Am. Lutheran. Home: 19525 Dartmouth Pl Northville MI 48167 Office: Internat Quality Inst Inc 19525 Dartmouth Place Northville MI 48167

BOTHFELD, EDWARD ELMS, manufacturing executive; b. Boston, July 25, 1924; s. Henry S. and Anna (Elms) B.; m. Nancy Clausen, Jan. 26, 1964; children: Dorothy, Sandra, Edward, Henry, Tracy. AB, Harvard U., 1946; MBA, Northwestern U., Evanston, 1963. Engr. Philco, Phila., 1947-51; prodn. control mgr. Motorola, Chgo., 1952-62; dir. mfg. Knowles Electronics, Chgo., 1962-68; pres. Synchro-Start Products, Inc., Skokie, Ill., 1968—. Pres. Skokie Valley United Way, 1986; bd. dirs. Coll. Ednl. Found., 1988—. Lt. USN, 1942-46, 1951-53. Mem. Engine Generator Set Assn. Republican. Clubs: Skokie Country (Glencoe, Ill.); Ridge and Valley Tennis (Glenview, Ill.). Lodge: Rotary (pres. 1986-87). Home: 530 Hoyt Ln Winnetka IL 60093 Office: Synchro Start Products Inc 625 W Howard St Niles IL 60648

BOTHWELL, JOSEPH CONRAD, JR., electronics company executive; b. Palmer, Mass., Aug. 2, 1923; s. Joseph Conrad and Katherine Louise (Utley) B.; m. Maureen Rhona Gilbride, Sept. 24, 1949; children: Brian J., Bruce A., Douglas J. AB, Harvard U., 1944, MBA cum laude, 1949. Sr. v.p. M/A Com., Inc., Burlington, Mass., 1952—; industry advisor ICC, 1989; bd. dirs. Spectran Corp., New Eng. Household Moving and Storage. Bd. dirs. Boston Heart found., New Eng. Deaconess Hosp. 1st lt. U.S. Army, 1942-46, PTO. Mem. Internat. Communications Conf. (chmn. fin. com. 1978, industry advisor 1988). Clubs: Harvard (Boston), Univ. (Boston). Home: 11 Cornell Rd Wellesley MA 02181 Office: M/A-COM Inc 7 New England Executive Pk Burlington MA 01803

BOTKIN, MONTY LANE, manufacturing manager; b. Lubbock, Tex., Mar. 26, 1951; s. Louis A. and Geneva O. (Marlin) B.; m. Barbara J. Searls, July 24, 1971; 1 child, Nicholas L. BA, Tex. Tech U., 1975. Supr. Tex. Instruments, Inc., Lubbock, 1976-77, Abilene, Tex., 1977-78; electronic ctr. mgr. Tex. Instruments Supply Co., Palo Alto, Calif., 1978-81; mfg. mgr. home computers Tex. Instruments, Inc., Lubbock, 1981-83, mfg. mgr. calculator, 1983-87, mfg. mgr. ednl. products, 1987—. Coordinator Lubbock chpt. United Way, 1981—, loaned exec., 1981—, Lubbock chpt. United Blood Services, 1985—; vol. Lubbock chpt. March of Dimes, 1986—. Mem. Am. Mfg. for Excellence Westexins (treas. 1987—), Toastmasters. Home: 4207 88th St Lubbock TX 79423 Office: Texas Instruments, 2301 N University, Lubbock United States

BOTRUFF, BARRY ALAN, credit reporting executive; b. Hammond, Ind., Apr. 18, 1952; s. Richard E. and Leona (Mates) B.; m. Penelope D. Stevens, Nov. 1975; children: Christopher A., Renee N. BBA, Ferris State U., 1975. Field adjuster Gen. Electric Credit Corp., Highland, Ind., 1975; mgr. credit/collection Gen. Electric Credit Corp., Highland, 1975-76; dsu mgr. Gen. Electric Credit Corp., Indpls., 1976; br. mgr. Gen. Electric Credit Corp., Merrillville, Ind., 1976-78; adminstrv. asst. Trans Union Credit Info., Chgo., 1978-81; ops. mgr. Trans Union Credit Info., St. Louis, 1981-83; v.p., gen. mgr. Trans Union Credit Info., Dayton, Ohio, 1983-87; reg. v.p. Trans Union Credit Info., Dayton, 1987—. Office: Trans Union Credit Info Co 115 E Third St Dayton OH 45402

BOTTANI, ALDO ARTHUR, JR., communications company executive, electrical engineer; b. Union City, N.J., May 1, 1926; s. Aldo A. and Zilda (Bartolemei) B.; m. Jean Bottani, Sept. 3, 1949 (dec. Aug. 1971); m. Lee Defina, Oct. 27, 1973; children: Brian Kelly, Steven. BEE, NYU, 1950. Various engring. positions Long Lines Dept. AT&T Co., N.Y.C., 1950-52, various engring. supervisory positions, 1954-60, various engring. mgmt. positions, 1961-63; radio engr. AT&T, Chgo., 1963-68; mktg. mgr. AT&T, N.Y.C., 1968-84; dir. cellular planning Metro Mobile CTS, Inc., N.Y.C., 1984-86, v.p. engring., 1986-88. Mem. Nat. Def. Exec. Res., 1984—. col. U.S. Army, 1952-54, Korea. Mem. IEEE (sr. chpt. chmn. 1985-88), Radio Club Am. Roman Catholic. Club: Unico (Paramus, N.J.). Office: Metro Mobile CTS Inc 110 E 59th St 36th fl New York NY 10022

BOTTNER, IRVING JOSEPH, cosmetic company executive; b. Bronx, N.Y., Jan. 15, 1916; s. Sigmund and Rose (Habercorn) B.; m. Elaine Schiff, Sept. 8, 1940 (div. Aug. 1958); children—Barbara, Jeffrey; m. Roslyn Ilene Miller, Feb. 14, 1961. B.S., NYU Sch. Commerce, 1937; M.S., NYU Grad. Sch. Bus., 1939. C.P.A., N.Y. C.P.A. Seidman & Seidman, N.Y.C., 1938-41; v.p., treas. Lewyt Corp., N.Y.C., 1941-56, Revlon, Inc., N.Y.C., 1956; pres. Kno-Mark Esquire Shoe Polish (subsidiary Revlon), 1959; group v.p. in charge of subsidiaries Revlon, Inc., N.Y.C., 1965-68; pres. Revlon Profl. Products Group, 1968—; sr. v.p. Revlon, Inc., N.Y.C., 1980—; pres. Revlon-Realistic; chmn. Roux Labs., Gen. Wig (subsidiaries); dir. Henry Colomer Co. Barcelona, Spain, Revlon Profl. Products Inc. Canada (all subs. Revlon). Inventor "through-the-wall" air conditioner, vacuum cleaner; Revlon Sensor Perm and MP-200 Hair Conditioner. Named Man of Yr. City of Hope, N.Y. State Chpts., 1965. Republican. Jewish. Clubs: Friars (N.Y.C.); Hampshire Country (Mamaraneck, N.Y.); Del-Aire Country (Delray Beach, Fla.). Home: 4780 Cherry Laurel Ln Delray Beach FL 33445 Office: Revlon Profl Products Group 555 57th St New York NY 10019

BOTTORFF, DENNIS C., banker; b. Clarksville, Ind., Sept. 19, 1944; s. Irvin H. and Lucille H. B.; m. Jean Brewington, Aug. 21, 1964; children: Todd, Chad. BE, Vanderbilt U., 1966; MBA, Northwestern U., Evanston, Ill., 1968. Pres. Commerce Union Bank, Nashville; also exec. v.p. Commerce Union Corp., Nashville; chmn., chief exec. officer Commerce Union Bank and Commerce Union Corp., Nashville, 1984-87; vice chmn., chief oper. officer, dir. Sovran Fin. Corp., Norfolk, Va., 1987—; bd. advisors The Jack C. Massey Grad. Sch. of Bus. (Belmont Coll., Nashville); trustee Com. for Econ. Devel.; mem. Assn. of Res. City Bankers, Young Presidents' Orgn.; bd. dirs. Shoney's Inc. Bd. dirs. Va. Symphony. Mem. Hampton Rds. C. of C., Farmington Country Club (Charlottesville, Va.), The Harbor Club, Town Point Club (Norfolk), Princess Anne Country Club (Virginia Beach, Va.). Presbyterian. Clubs: Belle Meade Country, Cumberland. Home: 600 55th St Virginia Beach VA 23451 Office: Sovran Fin Corp Sovran Ctr 1 Commercial Pl Norfolk VA 23501

BOTTS, KENNETH EDWARD, accountant; b. Phenix City, Ala., Jan. 28, 1949; s. Casper Orin Botts and Audrey Alene (Dykes) Botts Baker; m. Linda Diane Eskridge, Sept. 22, 1979 (div. 1984); m. Rebecca Braswell, June 6, 1987. BSBA, Auburn U., 1971; MBA, Ga. State U., 1975, M in Taxation, 1986. CPA, Ga. Supr. acct. May, Zima & Co. CPAs, Atlanta, 1973-77; sr. auditor Royal Crown Cos., Inc., Atlanta, 1978-81; fin. analyst Rollins, Inc., Atlanta, 1982; owner, pres. Kenneth E. Botts, P.C. CPA, Norcross, Ga., 1982—. With U.S. Army, 1971-73. Mem. AICPA, Ga. Soc. CPAs. Republican. Presbyterian. Home: 3775 Laurel Brook Way Lithonia GA 30058 Office: 1770 Indian Trail Rd Ste 190 Norcross GA 30093 also: PO Box 97 Lilburn GA 30226

BOTZ, WAYNE RAY, auditor; b. Berlin, July 4, 1957; s. Raymond Edward and Dorothea Marie (Brosewski) B.; m. Judith Ann Botz, Nov. 19, 1982. BSBA, St. Louis U., 1979. CPA, Mo. Auditor Laventhol & Horwath Co., St. Louis, 1979-81; sr. auditor Fox & Co., St. Louis, 1982-84; asst. controller Taylor, Morley, Simon Co., St. Louis, 1984-85; dir. internal auditing, v.p. Community Fed. Savs. and Loan Assn., St. Louis, 1985—. Mem. St. Louis Ambs's. Mem. Am. Inst. CPA's, Mo. Soc. CPA's, Fin. Mgrs. Soc.(sec. St. Louis chpt. 1989—). Republican. Roman Catholic. Home: 3150 Allen Saint Louis MO 63104 Office: Community Fed Savs and Loan Assn 1 Community Federal Ctr Saint Louis MO 63131

BOUCHER, JOSEPH WILLIAM, lawyer, accountant, business owner, teacher, writer; b. Menominee, Mich., Oct. 28, 1951; s. Joseph W. and Patricia (Coon) B.; m. Susan M. De Groot, June 4, 1977; children: Elizabeth, Bridget, Joseph William III. BA, St. Norbert Coll., 1973; JD, U. Wis., 1977, MBA in Fin., 1978. Bar: Wis. 1978, U.S. Dist. Ct. (we. dist.) Wis. 1978; CPA, Wis. Adminstrv. aide to Senator Wis. Senate, Madison, 1977; ptnr. Murphy, Stolper et al., Madison, 1978-84, Stolper et al., Madison, 1985—; lectr. bus. U. Wis., Madison, 1980—. Contbr. articles to Wis. Bar Assn. Bd. dirs. United Way, Dane County, Wis., 1986-89; bd. advisors St. Mary's Med. Ctr., Madison, 1989—. Named one of Outstanding Young Men Am., 1978, Wis. Lawyer Adv. Yr., SBA, 1983. Mem. ABA, Wis. Bar Assn., Dane County Bar Assn., Am. Inst. CPA's, Wis. Inst. CPA's, U. Wis. Bus. Alumni Assn. (bd. dirs. 1980-87), Am. Inst. CPA's (bd. examiners, bus. law subcom.). Roman Catholic. Home: 5925 S Hill Dr Madison WI 53705 Office: Stolper et al 7617 Mineral Point Rd Madison WI 53717

BOUCHIE, MICHAEL CHARLES, sales executive; b. St. Louis, Apr. 16, 1955; s. Charles Rudolph and Mary Ann (Porzenski) B.; m. Brenda Sue Kojis, Jan. 6, 1979; children: Timothy Michael, Tara Jeanne, Anne Elizabeth, Benjamin Thomas. BA, La. State U., 1985. Program and music dir. Sta. KRRV, Alexandria, La., 1979-82; air talent promotions, dir. sales Sta. WSLG, Gonzales, La., 1982-85; regional sales mgr. J.B. Cable Ads, Inc., Shreveport, La., 1986-87, gen. sales mgr., 1987—. Team mgr. Alexandria Little League Baseball, 1979, 80. Served with USAF, 1973-77. Mem. Am. Advt. Assn. Club: Cenla Advt. Republican. Roman Catholic. Home: 135 Carroll St Shreveport LA 71105 Office: JB Cable Ads Inc 635 Stoner Ave Shreveport LA 71101

BOUDREAU, EDWARD JOSEPH, JR., financial company executive; b. Cambridge, Mass., Oct. 16, 1944; s. Edward Joseph and Anella (Sakowich) B.; B.S., Boston U., 1966; postgrad. Am. U., 1966-67; M.B.A., Suffolk U., 1971; Sr. Exec. Program Stanford U., 1984; m. Janet Forsberg, May 26, 1968; children—Nancy, Mark. With John Hancock Mut. Life Ins. Co., Boston, 1967-88 , trainee, 1967-68, adminstrv. asst., 1968, treasury officer, 1968-70, treasury officer, asst. dir. banking relations, 1970-75, corp. banking service officer, 1975-78, gen. dir. banking and short-term investment, asst. treas., 1979, 2d v.p., 1980—, v.p., treas., 1981—, sr. v.p., treas., 1986-87, sr. v.p. spl. corp. assignments, 1987-88; pres., chief exec. officer John Hancock Advisers Inc., 1989—; chmn. bd. John Hancock Adviser Internat. Ltd., 1989—; chmn. bd. First Signature Bank and Trust, 1982—, JH Distributors Inc.; Mem. Nat. Assn. Corp. Treas. (assoc.), Boston Treasurer's Club, Winchester Country Club, N.E./Can. Bus. Council (bd. dirs. 1986—). Contbr. articles to profl. jours. Office: John Hancock Advisers Inc 101 Huntington Ave Boston MA 02199

BOUDREAU, NANCY ANNA, banker; b. Portola, Calif., Oct. 29, 1947; d. William Ellis and Hazel Harriett (Sanders) Bennett; m. James Louis Boudreau, Apr. 2, 1966; children: Rene' Christine, Jamie Danielle. Student, U. Wis., River Falls, 1965, U. Wis., Stevens Point, 1965-67; BA, Winona State U., 1975. Instr. evening sch. Western Wis. Tech. Inst., La Crosse, 1972-75; youth placement specialist Job Service Wis., La Crosse, 1975-82; human resource officer First Bank La Crosse, 1982-83, asst. v.p. ops. and human resources, 1983-84, asst. v.p., 1984-86; v.p. ops. First Bank of Platteville (Wis.), 1986-87, exec. v.p., 1987-89, pres. banking and adminstrn., 1989—, also bd. dirs.; instr. Am. Inst. Bankers, Madison, Wis., 1985—; corp. sec. First Nat. Bank of Platteville, 1988—; bd. dirs. Platteville Area Indsl. Devel. Corp.; v.p. First Shares Inc. Contbr. articles to profl. jours. Pres. YMCA, La Crosse, 1985; co-chmn. YM-YW Joint Exec. Com., La Crosse, 1985; div. chmn. United Way, La Crosse, 1980-86; bd. dirs. Luth. Hosp. Corp., La Crosse, 1986. Grantee Coop. Ednl. Services Agy., 1974-75. Mem. Am. Soc. Personnel Adminstrs., Wis. Bankers Assn. (bd. dirs., treas. bank mktg. sect. 1988, vice-chmn. 1989), La Crosse Area Personnel Assn. (pres. elect 1986), Greater L Crosse C. of C., Platteville C. of C. (bd. dirs., pres.), Bank Mktg. Assn. (adv. coun.). Republican. Methodist. Club: AVANT Women in Bus. Leadership (La Crosse). Lodges: Rotary (Platteville), Rotary Internat. Office: First Nat Bank of Platteville 170 W Main St Platteville WI 53818

BOUDREAUX, THOMAS LEE, energy company executive; b. Port Neches, Tex., July 18, 1947; s. Lee Robert and Vivian Rose (Manuel) B.; m. George Ann Jones, Sept. 5, 1970; children—Carrie, Lori. B.B.A. in Acctg., Lamar U., 1970. C.P.A. Staff acct. Arthur Andersen & Co., Houston, 1970-74, mgr., 1974-75, 77-79, ptnr., 1979-83; exec. dir., dir. acctg. Pub. Utility Commn. Tex., Austin, 1976-77; vice chmn. bd. dirs. Entex, Houston, 1984—; bd. dirs. SLT Communications, Inc., Houston, Tex. Rsch. League. Bd. dirs. Tex. Assn. Taxpayers, Inc., Tex. Rsch. League, Jr. Achievement S.E. Tex., Inc. Mem. Am. Inst. C.P.A.s, Tex. Soc. C.P.A.s, Am. Gas Assn., So. Gas Assn. Roman Catholic. Clubs: Petroleum, Houston, Lakeside Country. Office: Entex PO Box 2628 Houston TX 77252-2628

BOUGHTON, MAUREEN ELLA, marketing executive; b. Sydney, Australia, Feb. 11, 1944; came to U.S., 1965, naturalized, 1973; d. Patrick Yelverton and Joan Patricia (Heath) Williams; divorced; children: Edward, III, Tracy Yelverton. Ed. pvt. schs., Australia. Account exec. Sta. KKOP-FM, Redondo Beach, Calif., 1976-77; pres. MAV Enterprises, Ventura, Calif., 1977-83, Boughton Enterprises Inc., Ventura, 1980—; mng. dir., chief fin. officer Henrob Corp., Torrance, Calif., U.S. subs. Henrob S.A., Geneva, 1984—; pres. Design Innovators, 1987—. Fashion and beauty editor South Bay mag., Calif. Good Life mag., Big Valley mag., also Skin Care mag., 1977-80. Mem. Am. Mgmt. Assn., NAFE, Am. Soc. Profl. and Exec. Women. Republican. Christian Scientist. Lodge: Soroptimists Internat. Home: 2611 Ruhland Ave #4 Redondo Beach CA 90278 Office: Henrob Corp Exec Hdqtrs 3551 Voyager St #106 Torrance CA 90503

BOUILLIANT-LINET, FRANCIS JACQUES, management consultant; b. Garches, France, Aug. 20, 1932; came to U.S., 1977; s. Jacques Achille and Virginia Sutton (McKee) B.-L.; m. Elga Wood, Oct. 14, 1960 (div. 1978); m. Carolyn Jeanine Taylor, Nov. 17, 1978. Diploma in sci., Admiral Farragut Acad., 1948; post., Hautes Etudes Commerciales, Paris, 1949, Duke U., 1949-50. Mgmt. trainee Harry Ferguson Cos., Europe, 1951-57; sales promotion mgr. Massey-Harris-Ferguson, Paris, 1957-59; gen. programs mgr. Massey Ferguson Ltd., Coventry, Eng., 1959-63; coord. office of pres. Massey Ferguson Ltd., Toronto, Ont., Can., 1963-65; group product mgr. Massey Ferguson Ltd., Toronto, 1966-68; dir. internat. logistics Allis Chalmers Corp., Milw., 1968-71; joint mng. dir. LePiol, s.a.r.l., Cannes, France, 1971-77; chmn. bd., chief exec. officer FBL, Inc., Hurtsboro, Ala., 1977—, also bd. dirs.; exec. dir. H.J. Crawley, Ltd., Leamington, Eng., 1961-66; cons. pres. White Motor Corp. Europe, Milan, Italy, 1974-75; bd. dirs. F.J.B., Inc., Thermal, Calif. Author (manual) The New Product Process, 1963. Mem. Columbus Mus. Art and Sci., 1982; assoc. mem. Nat. Trust Hist. Preservation, Washington, 1982; charter founder Ronald Reagan Rep. Ctr., Washington, 1987. Sgt. French Armed Forces, 1953-57, Algerian War. Mem. Am. Soc. Agrl. Engrs. (affiliate), Brit. Inst. Mgmt., Calif. Farm Bur. Fedn., Ala. Farm Bur. Fedn., Ala. Sheriff's Assn. (hon.), Capital City Club, La Quinta Country Club. Office: FBL Inc PO Box 298 Hurtsboro AL 36860-0298

BOULANGER, ROBERT N., insurance company executive; b. Springfield, Mass., Apr. 4, 1933; s. Henry Joseph and Jeannette Mary (Guerette) B.; m. Joyce Pauline DeFontes, Sept. 13, 1955; children: Debra Ann, David Robert, Jennifer Ann, Julie Elizabeth. BS in Acctg. and Fin., Bryant Coll., 1953; postgrad., Syracuse U., 1969. Sr. auditor Comery, Davison & Co., Providence, R.I., 1956-61; controller Berkshire Hathaway, Inc., New Bedford, Mass., 1961-67; dir. corp. acct. SCM Corp., N.Y.C., 1967-72; sr. v.p. fin. Diners Club, Inc., N.Y.C., 1972-81; v.p., corp. controller Continental Corp., Cranbury, N.J., 1981—. Sgt. U.S. Army, 1953-56. Mem. Am. Inst. CPA's, Fin. Execs. Inst. Office: Continental Corp One Continental Dr Cranbury NJ 08570-0001

BOULINE, STEPHEN ERIC, controller; b. Porcell, Okla., Nov. 21, 1957; s. George Dean and Patricia Jean (Richards) B. BBA, Tex. Tech U. Sec. treas. The Processing Ctr., Houston, 1980-82; controller Security Assocs. Internat., Houston, 1982-88; controller, chief fin. officer Siege Industries, Houston, 1988—; gen. ptnr. Bouline and Sons; cons. Tax Bookkeeping Services, Houston. Fin. adv. Meml. Hosp. Systems, Houston, 1983—; state fin. chmn. Young Reps. Tex., 1986; mem. Harris County Young Reps. (v.p. 1983-84); shift capt. Reagan-Bush Campaign, Houston, 1984; state chmn. Tex. Young Reps. Fedn., 1987-88; area chmn. Kent Hance for Tex. R.R. commr., 1988; alt. del. State Rep. Conv., 1988. Named an Outstanding Young Man Am., Jaycees, Houston, 1984, Yr. Man of Yr., Tex. Young Reps., 1984. Republican. Methodist. Home: 203 Blue Willow Houston TX 77042 Office: Siege Industries 1024 W Loop North Houston TX 77055

BOUNDS, LAURENCE HAROLD, gas company executive; b. Newcastle, Wyo., Feb. 15, 1922; s. James Henry and Blanche Agnes (McKay) B.; B.S., Simpson Coll., 1943; postgrad. Columbia, 1943; m. Dorothy May Bostrom, Nov. 20, 1965; 1 stepson, Allen J. McDowell. With comptroller dept. Kemper Ins., Chgo., 1947-51; sec.-treas. W&J Constrn. Co., 1951-64; auditor, Roosevelt Hotel, Jacksonville, Fla., 1964-66; v.p. Western Natural Gas Co., Jacksonville, 1966—, also sec., dir. Served to lt. USNR, 1942-46. Mem. Navy League, U. Fla. Pres.' Council, Jacksonville Symphony Assn., Alpha Tau Omega, Episcopalian. Clubs: Island (St. Simon's, Ga.); Tournament Players (Ponte Vedra, Fla.). Home: 6926 Bakersfield Dr Jacksonville FL 32210 Office: Western Natural Gas Co 2960 Strickland St Jacksonville FL 32205

BOUNDS, WILLIAM G., accountant; b. Memphis, Aug. 25, 1950; s. James Othell and Doris Berniece (Wilson) B.; m. Rebecca Lynn Schell, Feb. 17, 1973; children: Megan, Erin, Micah. BSBA, U. Mo., St. Louis, 1972. CPA, Mo.; cert. fin. planner. Ptnr. Lester Witte & Co., CPAs, St. Louis, 1973-8l, Bounds, Poger & O'Donnell, CPAs, St. Louis, 1981—. Mem. AICPA, Mo. Soc. CPA's, Internat. Assn. for Fin. Planning, Inst. Cert. Fin. Planners, Clayton Club (Mo.). Office: Bounds Poger & O'Donnell 120 S Central Ave Saint Louis MO 63105

BOURGUIGNON, PHILIPPE ETIENNE, service executive; b. Salins, Jura, France, Jan. 11, 1948; came to U.S., 1981; s. Jacques Yves and Paule (Clement) B.; m. Martine Monique LeMardeley, June 25, 1977; children: Emilie, Sebastien. Maitrise Scis. Econ., Aix (France) U., 1971; MBA, Paris U., 1974. Project mgr. Synthese Documentaire, Paris, 1971-72, Systembau, Munich, 1973; v.p. devel. Novotel Asia, Middle East, Paris, 1974-78; exec. v.p. Accor North Am., N.Y.C., 1978-84; pres., chief exec. officer Accor Asia Pacific, Los Angeles, 1984—; also bd. dirs. Accor Internat., N.Y.C., 1987—; bd. dirs. Island in the Sun, Costa Mesa, Calif., Compagnie Hoteliere du Pacific, Paris. Active Rassemblement Pour Republique, Valence, 1969. Mem. Young Pres. Orgn. Roman Catholic. Home: 2632 Westridge Rd Los Angeles CA 90049

BOURKE, WILLIAM OLIVER, metals company executive; b. Chgo., Apr. 12, 1927; s. Robert Emmett and Mable Elizabeth (D'Arcy) B.; m. Elizabeth Philbey, Sept. 4, 1970; children: William Oliver, Judith A., Andrew E., Edward A. Student, U. Ill., 1944-45; B.S. in Commerce, DePaul U., 1951. With Ford Motor Co., Dearborn, Mich., 1956-60, nat. distbn. mgr., 1960-64; gen. sales mgr. Ford Can., Toronto, Ontario, 1964-67; asst. mng. dir. Ford Australia, Melbourne, 1967-70, mgr. dir., 1970-71; pres. Ford Asia-Pacific and South Africa, Inc., Melbourne, 1971-72, Ford Asia-Pacific, Inc., Melbourne, 1972-73; pres. Europe, Inc., 1973-75, chmn. bd., 1975-80; exec. v.p. Ford N.Am. Automotive Ops., Dearborn, 1980-81, also bd. dirs.; exec. v.p. Reynolds Metals Co., Richmond, Va., 1981-83, pres., chief oper. officer, 1983-86, pres., chief exec. officer, 1986-88, chief exec. officer, 1988—, also chmn. bd. dirs., also bd. dirs.; bd. dirs. Premark Internat., Inc., Merrill Lynch. 1st lt. M.I. U.S. Army, 1944-48. Mem. U.S. C. of C. (bd. dirs.). Office: Reynolds Metals Co 6601 Broad Street Rd Richmond VA 23261 also: Can Reynolds Metals Co Ltd, 420 Sherbrooke St W, Montreal, PQ Canada H3G 1K9

BOURN, HARRY JOSEPH, investment advisor; b. Jacksonville, Ill., Sept. 17, 1940; s. Harry Haxton and Mary Dell (Barber) B.; m. Marilyn Mae Armstrong, June 17, 1962; children: Jeffrey Joseph, Rebecca. BS in Agr., U. Ill., 1962, MS in Agr. Econs., 1963. Fieldman East Cen. Farm Bus., Farm Mgmt., Monticello, Ill., 1965-69; farm mgr. The Northern Trust Co., Chgo., 1969-72, regional mgr., 1972-76, gen. mgr., 1976-80; pres. Am. Agr. Investment Mgmt. Co., Inc., Lombard, Ill., 1980—. Elder Christian Ch. Clarendon Hills, Ill., 1970—; pres. Lisle Ill. Sch. Dist., 1979-84. Served to 1st lt. U.S. Artillery, 1963-65. Mem. Am. Soc. Farm Mgrs. and Rural Appraisers (accredited farm mgr., bd. dirs.), Chgo. Farmers Club, Am. Assn. Agr. Econs., Ill. Soc. Farm Mgrs. and Rural Appraisers (past pres.), Lions (pres. local club 1968). Republican. Home: 5605 Westview Ln Lisle IL 60532 Office: Am Agr Investment Mgmt Inc 631 E Butterfield Rd Ste 302 Lombard IL 60148

BOURNE, BILLY WAYNE, account executive; b. Hannibal, Mo., Sept. 6, 1950; s. Billy Harold and Dorothy Ellen (Rutherford) B.; m. Janet Carroll, Apr. 9, 1979; children: Kristin, Matthew. BA in Econs., U. Mo., Rolla, 1972; MBA in Mktg., U. Mo., Columbia, 1977. Sales trainee Honeywell, Inc., St. Louis, 1977-78, sales engr., 1978-81, sales engr. II, 1981-83, sr. sales rep., 1983-88, account exec., 1988—. With U.S. Army, 1972-74. Mem. ASHRAE. Office: Honeywell Inc 11842 Borman Dr Saint Louis MO 63146

BOURNE, JOHN DAVID, city finance executive; b. Barbados, West Indies, July 6, 1937; s. Daniel E. and Clarissa M. (Foster) B.; B.B.A., Baruch Coll., City U. N.Y., 1972; M.B.A., L.I. U., 1974. Mgr., Household Fin. Corp., N.Y.C., 1963-72, N.Y.C. Off-Track Betting Corp., 1972—; notary pub., 1964—; prof. bus. adminstrn. St. Joseph's Coll., Bklyn., 1982—, Coll. of Adelphi U., 1986—. Served with USAF, 1959-63. Mem. Baruch Coll., L.I. U. alumni assns. Democrat. Home: 144-36 182d St Springfield Gardens NY 11413

BOURNE, MARK HOWARD, investor advisor; b. Cambridge, Mass., May 12, 1946; s. Nathan and Irene Bourne; m. Ina Bourne; children: Daniel, Andrew. BA in Econs., U. Mass., 1968. V.p. mktg. and strategy Fidelity Mgmt. & Rsch., Boston, 1980-82; dir. rsch. Marathon Investment Mgmt., Chestnut Hill, Mass., 1982—; cons. in field; weekly TV and radio appearances. Office: Marathon Investment Mgmt 220 Boylston St Chestnut Hill MA 02167

BOUSQUETTE, WILLIAM C., financial executive; b. Detroit, Oct. 11, 1936; s. William Harvey and Darleen Elizabeth (Keller) B.; m. Diane Claudia Bickle, Dec. 1, 1956; children—Kevin, Matthew, Janine, Gregory, William, Jr. B.B.A., U. Detroit, 1958, M.B.A., 1962. Asst. corp. controller Ford Motor Co., Dearborn, Mich., 1961-81; v.p. fin. controls Rockwell Internat., Pitts., 1981-84; chief fin. officer Emerson Electric, St. Louis, 1984—. Office: Emerson Electric Co 8000 W Florissant Saint Louis MO 63136

BOUSTANY, FREM FREM, JR., physician, wholesale bakery executive; b. Lafayette, La., May 7, 1928; s. Frem Frem and Beatrice (Joseph) B.; B.S., Tulane U., 1948, M.D., 1950; m. Angell Fakouri, Jan. 6, 1957; children—Deborah, Jennifer, Stephanie. Intern, Charity Hosp., New Orleans, 1950-51, resident, 1951-54; practice medicine specializing in ob-gyn, Crowley, La., 1958-69; v.p. Huval Baking Co., Lafayette, 1950-70, pres., 1970-76, chief exec. officer, 1976—; dir. Flowers Industries, Inc., Thomasville, Ga., La. Bank & Trust Co., Crowley, City Savs. Bank & Trust Co., DeRidder, La. Mem. flowers pension and audit com., bd. dirs. Woman's Hosp., Lafayette; bd. dirs. Lafayette Boys Club, 1972-75, Jr. Achievement, 1972-76; v.p. United Giver's Fund, Lafayette, 1974-78, bd. dirs., 1970-78. Served with M.C., USAF, 1954-56. Mem. AMA, La. Med. Soc., Am. Bakers Coop. (past chmn., pres.), Am. Bakers Assn., So. Bakers Assn. (gov.), Am. Inst. Baking, Rotary (pres. Lafayette chpt., sec. local dist.). Democrat. Roman Catholic. Clubs: Bayou Bend Country, Crowley Town ; Lafayette Town, City, Krewe of Gabriel, Krewe of Zeus, Order of Troubadours (Lafayette); Camelot (Baton Rouge); K.C. Home: 200 Oakwater Dr Lafayette LA 70503 Office: Huval Baking Co Box 2339 Lafayette LA 70502

BOUTILLIER, ROBERT JOHN, accountant; b. Newark, Jan. 1, 1924; s. William and Millicent (Davies) B.; m. Marie C. Humphries, June 24, 1945; children: Robert Allan, Suzanne Marie. B.S., Rutgers U., 1948. C.P.A., N.J. With Peat, Marwick, Mitchell & Co., 1943-82, ptnr., 1955-82, ptnr. charge Newark office, 1960-70, mem. adv. com. and Eastern area, ptnr., 1965-70, ptnr. in charge U.S. ops., 1970-77, vice-chmn., 1977, ret., 1982; lectr. Rutgers U.; dir. Prudential Ins. Co. Am., Howard Savs. Bank. Bd. dirs. Newark YM-YWCA.; trustee Rutgers, The State U. Mem. Am. Inst. C.P.A.s, N.J. Soc. C.P.A.s, Newark Jaycees (pres. 1956-57, Outstanding Young Man of Yr. 1957), Newark Assn. Commerce and Industry, Delta Sigma Pi, Beta Gamma Sigma. Republican. Presbyterian. Clubs: Rotary of N.Y, Baltusrol Golf (past pres., gov.), Echo Lake Country, Seaview Country, Ocean Reef. Home and Office: 920 Minisink Way Westfield NJ 07090

BOUTIN, DAVID JOSEPH, printing company owner; b. Sanford, Maine, May 4, 1947; s. Amedee George Boutin and Eleita Leona (Beaudoin) Carrier; m. Faye Rogers, Jan. 19, 1974; 1 child, Christopher Joseph. BA, St. Bonaventure U., 1970. Lic. realtor, Md. Sales supr. K&M Jewelry, N.Y.C., 1974-80; salesman Kelly Press, Cheverly, Md., 1980-85, Sara Lee Foods Corp., Chgo., 1975-87; realtor Real Estate Counselors, Glen Burnie, Md., 1985-87; pres. Am. Internat. Printing, Arnold, Md., 1985-87; realtor Long and Foster Realtors, Severna Park, Md., 1987—. Mem. Anne Arundel County Bd. Realtors, Severna Park, 1985-86. Served to 1st lt. U.S. Army, 1971-74. Mem. D.C. Friends of Ireland. Roman Catholic. Lodge: Kiwanis (Central Anne Arundel, Md.) (pres., 1986—). Home: 1A St Ives Dr Chartwell Severna Park MD 21146 Office: Am Internat Printing PO Box 9733 Arnold MD 21012

BOUTTE, DAVID GRAY, lawyer; b. Kingman, Ariz., Sept. 6, 1944; s. Riley Joseph and Audray Echo (Bowden) B.; m. Caroline Ruth Regitko, June 27, 1981; children: Ryan Gray, Gray Douglas, Banks David Gray. BA in History, Calif. State U., Long Beach, 1966; JD, U. So. Calif., 1972. Bar: Calif. 1973, U.S. Ct. Appeals (9th cir.) 1973, D.C. 1976, U.S. Supreme Ct. 1976, U.S. Ct. Appeals (D.C. cir.) 1976. Asst. to chief engr. Norris Industries, Inc., L.A., 1964-66; law clk. to presiding justice U.S. Ct. Appeals (9th cir.), L.A., 1972-73; law clk. to chief justice Warren Burger U.S. Supreme Ct., Washington, 1973-74; assoc. O'Melveny & Myers, L.A., 1974-78; dir. staff task force U.S. Dept. Def., Washington, 1978-80; gen. counsel alt. energy div. Mobil Oil Corp., N.Y.C., 1980-83; mgr. planning coordination Mobil Chem. Co., Stamford, Conn., 1983-86; gen. counsel internat. div. Mobil Oil Corp., 1986—. Editor-in-chief So. Calif. Law Rev., 1971-72. Commr. L.A. Pub. Commn. on County Govt., 1974-75. Capt. USMC, 1966-69, Vietnam. Decorated Purple Heart. Mem. ABA (chmn. young lawyers div., internat. law commn., 1975-76), Order of Coif, Sleepy Hollow Country Club (Scarborough, N.Y.). Republican. Episcopalian. Office: Mobil Oil Corp 150 E 42nd St New York NY 10017

BOUVIER, CHRISTIAN RENÉ, audit manager, administration educator; b. Paris, Nov. 13, 1940; s. Raymond and Charlotte (Mirault) B.; m. Jacqueline Boulard, Nov. 4, 1968; children: Romuald, Aldric, Thibault, Astrid. Capitaine au long Cňurs, 1967; CPA, France. Mate and fist mate Mcht. Navy, 1960-68, with mktg. dept., then fin. dept. IBM, Paris, 1969-84; audit dir. Hutchinson then Nouvelles-Galeries, 1984-88. Author: Audit and Computer, 1983. Served with French Navy, 1961-62. Mem. Inst. Internal Auditors. Roman Catholic. Home: 68 Rue de l'Ermitage, 95320 Saint-Leu-la-Forêt France Office: 66 Rue des Archives, 75003 Paris France

BOUVIER, JOHN ANDRE, JR., lawyer, corporate executive, legal and financial consultant; b. nr. Ocala, Fla., May 16, 1903; s. John Andre and Ella (Richardson) B.; m. Helen A. Schaefer, June 6, 1928 (dec. 1983); children: Helen Elizabeth (Mrs. William Spencer), John Andre III, Thomas Richardson; m. Barbara Carney; children: Mark B. Carney, Kevin P. Carney. Student, Davidson Coll., 1922-24; AB, U. Fla., 1926, LLB, 1929, JD, 1969; MBA, Northwestern U., Evanston, Ill., 1930; LHD (hon.), Windham Coll., 1977; D of Commerce (hon.), Ft. Lauderdale Coll., 1985. Bar: Fla. bar 1929. Practiced in Gainesville, 1929, Miami, 1930—; specialist corp., real estate and probate law, cons. atty.; gen. counsel Patterson & Maloney, Ft. Lauderdale; chmn. exec. com. Permutit Co., 1964-73; chmn. bd. Prosperity Co.; vice chmn. bd. Ward Indsl. Corp.; chmn. bd., pres. Pantex Mfg. Corp., Nat. Leasing Inc., Miami; pres. Knaust Bros., Inc., K-B Products Corp., Iron Mountain Atomic Storage Vaults, Inc., West Kingsway, Inc., East Kingsway, Inc., South Kingsway, Inc.; pres., dir. Ace Solar Constrn. Co., Southport Apts., BMB Devel. Co., Hendricks Devel. Corp.; sec. 50th St. Heights, Inc., Knight Manor, Inc., Dade Constrn. Co. (all Miami), Karen Club Apt. Hotel, Ft. Lauderdale, C&S Banking Corp., Landmark Banking Corp. Fla., Farquhar Machinery Co., BMB Devel. Corp., Hendricks Isle Devel. Corp. Author monographs, newspaper articles in field. Bd. dirs. Syracuse Govtl. Research Bur.; dir., sec. Wilson Garden Apts. Inc. Commr., Dade County council Boy Scouts Am.; chmn. Malecon Com. Dade County; mem. Planning Council Zoning Bd. Miami; chmn. Coxsackie-Athens Area Redevel. Com.; vice chmn. Nat. Parkinson Found.; bd. dirs., trustee Miami Boys Clubs; trustee Windham Coll., Westminster Manor, Gateway Terrace. Mem. Internat. Platform Assn., Am. Judicature Soc., ABA, Fla. Bar Assn., Dade County Bar Assn., Broward County Bar Assn., Miami C. of C., Sigma Chi (Order of Constantine). Presbyterian. Clubs: Miami Beach Rod and Reel, Riviera Country, Ft. Lauderdale Yacht, Skaneateles (N.Y.) Country, Ponte Vedra Country, Tower, Capitol Hill. Lodge: Masons, Shriners, Elks, Rotary. Home: 608 Intracoastal Dr Fort Lauderdale FL 33304 Office: 6888 NW 7th Ave Miami FL 33150 also: Bienvenue Blowing Rock NC 28605 also: PO Box 14 Climax NY 12042 Mailing Address: Box 7254 Fort Lauderdale FL 33338

BOVA, ALBERT JOSEPH, JR., controller, accountant; b. Allentown, Pa., June 4, 1954; s. Albert Joseph Sr. and Doris Alice (Ehrhardt) B.; m. Ann Marie Eckenrode, June 5, 1982; children: Emily, Maria, Theresa. BBA, Lehigh U., 1976. CPA, Pa. Jr. staff acct. Palmer & Co., CPAs, Easton, Pa., 1976-79; sr. staff acct. Abraham & Co., CPAs, 1979-83; div. contr. Creative Displays and Adams Outdoor Advt., Bethlehem, Pa., 1983—. Mem. Am. Inst. CPA's, Pa. Inst. CPA's, Nat. Assn. Accountants, (bd. dirs. communications com. 1984-86). Republican. Office: Adams Outdoor Advt 2176 Ave C LVIP Bethlehem PA 18017

BOVEY, TERRY ROBINSON, insurance executive; b. Oregon, Ill., May 13, 1948; s. John Franklin and Frances (Robinson) B.; m. Diana Carmen Rodriguez, Aug. 29, 1970 (div. July 1980); 1 child, Joshua; m. Kathy Jo Johnston, Sept. 14, 1985: stepchildren: Lara, Mickey, Keri; 1 child, Courtney. Student, Ariz. Western Coll., 1966-68, Grand Canyon Coll., 1968-69; BBA, U. Ariz., 1972. Salesman All-Am. Dist. Co., Yuma, Ariz., 1972-76; dist. asst. mgr. Equitable Life Ins., Yuma, 1976-81; gen. sales mgr. Ins. Counselors, Yuma, 1981-83; mng. gen. agt. First Capital Life Ins. Co., Ariz., N.Mex., So. Calif. and N.C., 1983—; regional commnr. Ariz. Interscholastic Assn., Yuma, 1972-88. mem. Century Club, Boy's Club of Yuma. Mem. Nat. Assn. Life Underwriters (nat. sales achievement award 1979, 82, 84, 86, 87, Nat. Quality award 1984-88), Life Underwriters Polit. Action Com., Tucson City Assn. Republican. Presbyterian.

BOWDEN, ELBERT VICTOR, economics educator; b. Wrightsville, N.C., Nov. 25, 1924; s. James Owen and Dovie Ellen (Phelps) B.; m. Doris Adele Fales (div.); children: Elbert V. Jr., Richard Ashley, Doris Ellen, Jack Bryson, William Austin, Joyce Leigh; m. Judith Louise Holbert; children: Kristen R., Amy L. BA in Econs. and Polit. Sci. with high distinction, U. Conn., 1950; MA in Econs., Duke U., 1952, PhD in Econs., 1957. Grad. asst. dept. econs. Duke U., Durham, N.C., 1950-53, instr. dept. econs., 1953-54, 55-56; rsch. assoc. Bur. Bus. Rsch. U. Ky., Lexington, 1954-55; assoc. prof. Norfolk (Va.) Coll. of William and Mary (name now Old Donimion U.), 1956-59, prof., chmn. dept. econs., 1959-63; prof. econs. Elmira (N.Y.) Coll., 1963-64, SUNY, Fredonia, 1970-75; exec. dir. Upper Peninsula Com. for Area Progress, Escanaba, Mich., 1964-65; chief economist, chief of mission Robert R. Nathan Assocs. Trust Terr. Econ. Devel. Team, Saipan, Mariana Islands, 1965-67; assoc. prof., rsch. economist Tex. A&M U., 1967-70; chief econ. adviser, project mgr. Fiji Regional Planning Project UN, Suva, 1975-77; prof. econs., chair banking Appalachian State U., Boone, N.C., 1977—; dir. Houston-Galveston (Tex.) Area Project Fed. Water Pollution Control Adminstrn. and Tex. Water Quality Bd., 1967-69; testifier Interstate Commerce Commn., U.S. Senate Pub. Works Com., U.S. Senate Com. on Interior and Insular Affairs, 1964-66; asst. Blue Ridge Electric Membership Corp.; speaker Olean (N.Y.) Bus. Inst., 1979; cons., presenter seminars, workshops in field. Author: Revolution in Banking: Regulatory Changes, the New Competitive Environment and the New World for the Financial Services Industry in the 1980s, 1984, Economic Evolution: Principles, Issues, Ideas--Through the Looking Glass of Time, 2d rev. edit, 1985, Principles of Economics: Theory, Problems, Policies, 5 rev. edit., 1986, 6th edit., 1989, numerous others; contbr. articles, papers and book reviews to profl. publs. and orgns. Mem. fin. com. City of Seven Devils, N.C.; asst. N.C. Dept. Marine Fisheries; mem. adv. bd. Stadewide Taxpayers Ednl. Coalition. With U.S. Mcht. Marine, 1943-46, PTO. Ford Found. fellow, 1960. Mem. AAAS, AAUP, Am. Bus. Communication Assn., Am. Econ. Assn., Am. Fin. Assn. (committeman 1960-61), Atlantic Econ. Soc., Community Colls. Social Scis. Assn., Ea. Fin. Assn., Fin. Mgmt. Assn., Regional Sci. Assn., So. Econ. Assn., So. Fin. Assn., So. Regional Sci. Assn., Southwestern Social Sci. Assn. (chmn. interdisciplinary symposium on urban and regional problem solving 1970), Western Econ. Assn., Western Regional Sci. Assn. (mem. program planning com. 1978-69), Gamma Chi Epsilon, Omicron Delta Epsilon. Home: PO Box 1461 Boone NC 28607 Office: Appalachian State U Chair Banking Office Boone NC 28608

BOWDEN, HUGH KENT, oil company executive; b. Chanute, Kans., Oct. 17, 1933; s. John Ona and Iva Nanette (McEver) B.; m. Constance Rae Kiser, June 13, 1958; children: Barry J., Cynthia Bowden Danyla. BS in Chem. Engring., U. Kans., 1954; MS in Mgmt., MIT, 1968. Engr. Conoco Inc., U.S. and London, 1954-70; v.p., gen. mgr. Conoco Italy, Milan, Italy, 1968-70; asst. mgr., product supply and distbn. Conoco Inc., N.Y.C., 1970-71, mgr. logistics, 1971-75, gen. mgr. logistics, 1975-78, v.p. logistics & downstream planning, 1978-81; v.p. refining & mktg., Europe Conoco Inc., London, Eng., 1985-87; chmn., mng. dir. Conoco Ltd., London, 1981-87; v.p. refining and mktg. N.Am. Conoco Inc., Houston, 1987—; v.p. E. I. du Pont de Nemours & Co., Wilmington, Del., 1987—; bd. dirs., exec. com. Cit-Con Oil Corp., Lake Charles, La. Bd. dirs., mem. exec. com. Theatre Under the Stars, Houston, 1988—; nat. assoc. Boys Clubs of Am., N.Y.C., 1988—; adv. bd. U. Kans. Sch. Engring., 1988—. Served with U.S. Army, 1955-57. Recipient Sloan fellowship, MIT, 1967-68. Mem. Am. Petroleum Inst. (mktg. exec. com., gen. com. mktg.), Nat. Petroleum Refiners Assn. & Hwy. Users Fed., Washington (bd. dirs.). Republican. Methodist. Clubs: Petroleum, Pine Forest Country (Houston). Office: Conoco Inc MC-3084 PO Box 2197 Houston TX 77252

BOWDEN, JAMES ALVIN, construction company financial executive; b. Vernal, Utah, Mar. 19, 1948; s. Alvin George and Erva (Kirk) B.; m. Jane Ruth Taylor, May 31, 1973; children—Scott James, Julie, Jeffrey Taylor, Camille, Timothy Kirk. B.S. in Civil Engring., Brigham Young U., 1972, M.B.A., 1974. Planning analyst Morrison Knudsen Corp., Boise, 1974, asst. mgr. corp. planning, 1974-75, mgr. fin. analysis, 1975-78, asst. treas., 1978-83, v.p. fin. real estate subs., 1983-84, treas., 1984-86; v.p. and treas., 1986—; spl. instr. Boise State U., 1977-78. Bd. dirs. Boise chapter ARC, 1982—, treas., 1984-86, vice chmn. 1986-87, chmn. 1987-88, nat. nominating com. 1989—; mem. United Way, Boise, 1980-85; bd. dirs. Fundsy, 1985—. Mem. Beta Gamma Sigma. Republican. Mormon. Home: 10058 W Ironclad Ct Boise ID 83704 Office: Morrison Knudsen Corp Morrison Knudsen Pla Boise ID 83729

BOWDEN, OTIS HEARNE, II, management consulting firm executive; b. Stuttgart, Ark., Jan. 2, 1928; s. Otis Hearne and Donna (Trice) B.; B.S. in Bus. Adminstrn., Washington U., 1950, M.B.A., 1953; m. Helen Carol Lamar, June 25, 1949. Financial analyst St. Louis Union Trust Co., St. Louis, 1950-53; dist. mgr. TRW, Inc., Cleve., 1953-63; dir. Mass Transit Center, B.F. Goodrich Co., Akron, Ohio, 1963-67; v.p. E.A. Butler Assocs., Inc., Cleve., 1967-71; pres. Bowden & Co., Inc., Cleve., 1972—; guest lectr. Akron U., 1972—. Nat. promotion dir. Laymen's Hour Radio Broadcast, 1959-63; chmn. commerce and industry div. United Fund of Greater Cleve., 1962; pres. Am. Baptist Men of Ohio, 1962-63; trustee Alderson-Broaddus Coll., Philippi, W.Va., 1965-76; vice chmn. bd. dirs. Eastern Coll., Phila.; alumni bd. govs. Washington U., St. Louis; bd. dirs. Am. Bapt. Fgn. Mission Soc., 1962-71; regional dir. Project Winsome Internationale; vice chmn. adv. bd. Salvation Army of Greater Cleve., 1979—, also chmn. program com. Served with USMCR, 1951. Mem. Am. Mgmt. Assn., Ohio Cons. Assn. (pres. 1982), Am. Mktg. Assn., Red Apple Country Club, Rotary (trustee 1975-77, Paul Harris fellow 1978), Union Club, Assn. Exec. Search Cons. (bd. dirs.) Office: Bowden & Co Inc 5000 Rockside Rd Cleveland OH 44131

BOWEN, BRETT HEALD, financial services executive; b. Chgo., May 24, 1941; s. Fredrick Raymond and Holly (Laws) B.; m. Sandra Lee Ervin, Aug. 21, 1965 (div. Aug. 1988); children: Brandon, Brady, Bryan. BSBA, U. Ill., 1964. Staff auditor Washington Nat. Ins. Co., Evanston, Ill., 1964-68, supr. internal auditing, 1968-70, asst. mgr., then mgr. internal auditing, 1970-76; dir. internal audits Washington Nat. Corp., Evanston, 1976-81; compliance officer Washington Nat. Equity Co., Evanston, 1985; dept. head., dir. internal audits Washington Nat. Corp., Evanston, 1982-85, v.p. auditing, 1986—, v.p. compliance officer, 1988—, also bd. dirs.; auditor Park Ridge (Ill.) 20th Century Jrs. Club, 1978-88. Author: Control Guidelines for the Processing of Data, 1980. Treas., bd. dirs. Park Ridge Jaycees, 1965-77; ballot collector Chgo. Rep. Orgn., 1970; advisor Park Ridge Parks Bd., 1982-88. With USMC, 1959-60. Mem. Am. Soc. CLU's, Life Office Mgmt. Assn., EDP Auditors Assn., Ins. Affiliated Broker/Dealers, Inst. Internal Auditors, Park Ridge Golf League (pres. 1978, 82, treas. 1984), Washington Nat. Ins. Bowling League (pres. 1973-76), Nat. Assn. Cert. Fraud Examiners. Home: 4831 W Conrad St Apt 213 Skokie IL 60077 Office: Washington Nat Corp 1630 Chicago Ave Evanston IL 60201

BOWEN, JOHN RICHARD, chemical company executive; b. Passaic, N.J., May 5, 1934; s. Nathan S. and Florence R. (Schubarth) B.; m. Patricia Joanne Meinke, Feb. 4, 1956; children: Kenneth Alan, Teresa Lynn. B.B.A., U. Mich., 1956, M.B.A., 1957. C.P.A. With Price Waterhouse & Co., Detroit, 1958-66; v.p. Corning Internat. Corp., 1966-72; controller U.S. Postal Service, 1972-74; v.p. fin. Morton Thiokol, Inc., Chgo., 1974—. Home: 42 Little Marryat St Cary IL 60013 Office: Morton Thiokol Inc 110 N Wacker Dr Chicago IL 60606

BOWEN, J(OHN) WILLIAM, management consultant; b. Newton, Mass., Nov. 20, 1944; s. John S. and Ruth C. (Zoller) B.; m. Carlyn D. Lundin, Sept. 1, 1966 (div. Feb. 1978); children: Carl J., Jeffrey S.; m. Christina M. Edwards, Oct. 12, 1985. BS, Worcester Poly. Inst., 1966; MBA, Harvard U., 1970. With City of N.Y., 1970-74; v.p. Chase Manhattan Bank, N.Y.C., 1974-77; sr. assoc. Booz, Allen & Hamilton, N.Y.C., 1977-80; dir. of planning Gen. Electric Credit Corp., Stamford, Conn., 1980-81; mng. v.p. First Manhattan Cons. Group, N.Y.C., 1981—. Named George F. Baker scholar at Harvard U., 1969.

BOWEN, PATRICK HARVEY, retail store executive; b. Cin., July 7, 1939; s. Albert Vernon and Elsie Matilda (Harvey) B.; 1 child, Harvey Shaw. BA, Marietta Coll., 1961; JD, Duke U., 1964; MBA, Columbia U., 1975. Bar: N.Y. 1965. Assoc. Mudge, Rose, Guthrie, Alexander & Ferdon, N.Y.C., 1964-66; atty. Kennecott Copper Corp., N.Y.C., 1966-71, asst. counsel, 1971-79, asst. gen. counsel, 1979-83, asst. sec., 1980-83; sr. assoc. atty. Allied Stores Corp., N.Y.C., 1983-87, v.p., gen. counsel, sec., 1987-88, v.p., 1988—; Mem. ABA, Conn. Bar Assn., N.Y. State Bar Assn., Assn. of Bar of City of N.Y., Am. Soc. Corp. Secs., Westchester-Fairfield Corp. Counsel Assn. Office: Allied Stores Corp 2001 W Main St Ste 140 Stamford CT 06902

BOWEN, ROBERT C., publishing company executive; b. Rossville, Ga., Sept. 15, 1941; s. William O. and Sarah (Williams) B.; m. Wanda L. Clark, July 2, 1965; 1 child, Natalie Michele. B.S., U. Chattanooga, 1967, M.Ed.,

1969. Tchr., counselor, coach Catoosa County Bd. Edn., Rossville, Ga., 1967-69; dir. research and evaluator Bibb County Bd. of Edn., Macon, Ga., 1969-71; evaluation cons. CTB-McGraw Hill Co., Winter Park, Fla., 1972-74; dist. mgr. so. states CTB-McGraw Hill Co., 1974-75, regional mgr. midwestern states, 1976-77; nat. sales mgr., dir. mktg. Gregg-McGraw Hill, N.Y.C, 1977-78, v.p., gen. mgr., 1982-84; gen.mgr. EDL-McGraw Hill, N.Y.C, 1978-79; group v.p. for sch. pub. McGraw-Hill Book Co., N.Y.C, 1979-81, v.p. mktg., 1981-82; gen. mgr., v.p. Gregg-McGraw Hill, N.Y.C., 1983; v.p., gen. mgr. Coll.-McGraw-Hill, N.Y.C., 1984; exec. v.p. edn. and tng. McGraw-Hill Book Co., N.Y.C., from 1985; now pres. SRA, Chgo. Mem. Nat. Task Force on Edn., 1984—. Mem. Assn. Am. Pubs. (chmn. sch. div. 1981-82), Literacy Vols. Am. (bd. dirs. 1979—). Baptist. Home: 3 Hereford Dr Princeton Junction NJ 08550 Office: SRA 155 N Wacker Dr Chicago IL 60606 *

BOWEN, ROBERT STEVENSON, diversified company executive; b. Chgo., Dec. 4, 1937; s. Earl McDonald and Helen T. (Stevenson) B.; m. Jane Carlson, Oct. 13, 1973; children: Thomas, Anne. A.B., North Park Coll., Chgo., 1955; B.S., Northwestern U., 1958; M.B.A., Harvard U., 1961; postgrad., U. Stockholm, (Sweden), 1963-64. Sr. planning mgr. Ford Motor Co., Dearborn, Mich., 1961-72; v.p. mktg. and internat. Zenith Radio Corp., Chgo., 1972-80; pres. sales and mktg. group Firestone Tire and Rubber Co., Brook Park, Ohio, 1980-84; pres., chief exec. officer Comnet Corp., Greenbelt, Md., 1984—; chmn., chief exec. officer Group I Software Inc., Greenbelt, 1987—; chmn. bd. Zenith Time S.A., LeLocle, Switzerland, 1974-78; bd. dirs. Ford Labs., Moonachie, N.J. Trustee Nat. 4-H Council, Chevy Chase, Md., 1980-84, Chesapeake Acad., Arnold, Md., 1987—. George F. Baker scholar Harvard Bus. Sch., 1960; Fulbright scholar, 1963-64. Office: Comnet Corp 6404 Ivy Ln Ste 500 Greenbelt MD 20770

BOWEN, W. J., gas company executive; b. Sweetwater, Tex., Mar. 31, 1922; s. Berry and Annah (Robey) B.; m. Annis K. Hilty, June 6, 1945; children: Shelley Ann, Barbara Kay, Berry Dunbar, William Jackson. B.S., U.S. Mil. Acad., 1945. Registered profl. engr., Tex. Petroleum engr. Delhi Oil Corp., Dallas, 1949-57; v.p. Fla. Gas Co., Houston, 1957-60; pres. Fla. Gas Co., Winter Park, Fla., 1960-74; pres., chief exec. officer Transco Cos., Inc., Houston, 1974-81; chmn. Transco Cos., Inc. (name changed to Transco Energy Co.), Houston, 1976—; chief exec. officer Transco Energy Co., Houston, 1981-87, also bd. dirs.; bd. dirs. James River MCorp. chmn. bd. dirs. YMCA, Houston, United Way of Tex. Gulf Coast; nat. bd. Smithsonian Assn.; trustee bd. Baylor Coll. Medicine, Jesse H. James Sch. of Bus., Rice U . Served with AUS, 1945-49. Mem. U.S. Energy Assn. (1st vice-chmn., com. of U.S. world energy conf.). Episcopalian. Office: Transco Energy Co 2800 Post Oak Blvd Houston TX 77056

BOWEN, WILLIAM JOSEPH, management consultant; b. N.Y.C., May 13, 1934; s. Edward F. and Mary Alice (Drooney) B.; divorced; children: William J., Timothy M., Priscilla A., Robert B.; m. Betsy Bass, Oct. 31, 1983. BS, Fordham U., 1956; MBA, NYU, 1963. Trainee Smith, Barney, N.Y.C., 1959-61; asst. v.p. Citicorp, N.Y.C., 1961-67; v.p. Hayden, Stone, N.Y.C., 1967-69; 1st v.p. Shearson Hammill, N.Y.C., 1969-73; assoc. Heidrick & Struggles, 1973-77, ptnr., 1977—; mgr. Heidrick & Struggles, Chgo., 1978-81, pres., chief exec. officer, 1981-83; vice chmn. Heidrick & Struggles, N.Y.C., Chgo., 1983—. Served to capt. USAF, 1956-59. Republican. Clubs: Chgo.; Onwentsia (Lake Forest, Ill.); N.Y., Marco Polo, Union League (N.Y.C.). Office: Heidrick & Struggles Inc 125 S Wacker Dr 2800 Chicago IL 60606

BOWER, BRUCE EDWARD, financial planner; b. Romeo, Mich., Apr. 6, 1950; s. Allan M. and Eleanor F. (Schoof) B.; m. Joy M. Kaufman, July 21, 1979; 1 child, Steven Michael. BS in Engring. summa cum laude, Mich. State U., 1972, MS summa cum laude, 1973. Lead design engr. Black & Veatch Cons. Engrs., Dallas, 1973-76; internat. project dir. Black & Veatch Cons. Engrs., Kansas City, Mo., 1976-80; tax incentive mgr. Kidder, Peabody & Co., Kansas City, Mo., 1980-84; exec. v.p., owner Fin. Advisory Service Inc., Overland Park, Kans., 1984—; adv. dir. Research Hosp., Kansas City, 1982—. Mem. Chmn.'s Club Heart of Am. United Way, Kansas City, 1986—. Mem. Inst. Cert. Fin. Planners, Internat. Assn. Fin. Planners. Republican. Episcopalian. Home: 9714 Overbrook Rd Leawood KS 66206 Office: Fin Advisory Svc Inc 10955 Lowell Ste 420 Overland Park KS 66210

BOWER, JEAN RAMSAY, court administrator, lawyer; b. N.Y.C., Nov. 25, 1935; d. Claude Barnett and Myrtle Marie (Scott) Ramsay; m. Ward Swift Just, Jan. 31, 1957 (div. 1966); children: Jennifer Ramsay, Julia Barnett; m. Robert Turrell Bower, June 12, 1971. A.B., Vassar Coll., 1957; J.D., Georgetown U., 1970. Bar: D.C. 1970. Exec. dir. D.C. Dem. Central Com., Washington, 1969-71; sole practice, Washington, 1971-78; dir. Counsel for Child Abuse and Neglect Office, D.C. Superior Ct., 1978—. Mem. Mayor's Com. on Child Abuse and Neglect, 1973—, vice chmn., 1975-79; mem. Family Div. Rules Adv. Com., 1977—; pres., bd. dirs. C.B. Ramsay Found., 1984—. Mem. mgmt. bd. Child Advocacy Ctr., 1980— . Mem. Women's Bar Assn. (found. 1986—), D.C. Bar Assn., Women's Bar Assn. Found (bd. dirs. 1986). Named Washingtonian of the Yr., Washingtonian Mag., 1979, Woman Lawyer of the Yr., Women's Bar Assn., D.C., 1985. Office: DC Superior Ct Room 4235 500 Indiana Ave NW Washington DC 20007

BOWER, MARVIN D., insurance company executive; b. Stanford, Ill., July 20, 1924; s. Charles Howard and Marjorie Dale (Garst) B.; m. Mari Morrissey, June 1, 1946 (dec. 1981); children: Stacie (Mrs. John Killian), Jim, Pete, Molly (Mrs. Christopher Miller), Tom, John.; m. Carolyn Paine Newland, Apr. 24, 1983; stepchildren: Linda (Mrs. Bradford Gleason), Lori (Mrs. Paul Lorenz), Leslie, William, David. Ph.B., Ill. Wesleyan U., 1948. C.L.U. Agt. Northwestern Mut. Life, Bloomington, Ill., 1949-52; with State Farm Life Ins. Co., 1952—; sec. for Can. State Farm Life Ins. Co., Toronto, 1955-58; exec. v.p., sec. State Farm Life and Accident Assurance Co., 1961—, also bd. dirs.; v.p. health State Farm Mut. Auto Ins. Co., 1968—; exec. v.p. State Farm Life Ins. Co., Bloomington, Ill., 1973—, chmn. bd., 1985—, also dir. Served to capt. AUS, 1943-46. Fellow Life Office Mgmt. Inst.; mem. Phi Gamma Delta. Home: 49 Country Club Pl Bloomington IL 61701 Office: State Farm Life Ins Co 1 State Farm Pla Bloomington IL 61710

BOWERMAN, CHARLES LEO, oil company executive; b. Crawfordsville, Ind., Dec. 16, 1939; s. Thomas Edward and Hazel (Melvin) B.; m. Coralea Weir, June 12, 1960; children—Cynthia, Cristina, Candace. A.B., Wabash Coll., 1961. Jr. job analyst Phillips Petroleum, Bartlesville, Okla., 1961-62, sales trainee, 1962-64, various mktg. dept. positions, 1964-84, v.p. mktg., 1984-88; sr. v.p. petroleum products Phillips Petroleum, Bartlesville, 1988—. Mem. exec. bd. Cherokee Area council Boy Scouts Am.; trustee Boys Club of Bartlesville. Mem. Am. Petroleum Inst. (former chmn. gen. com. mktg.), Okla.-Kans. Oil and Gas Assn. (bd. dirs. 1985—), Hillcrest Country Club, Masons, Royal Order Jesters. Republican. Office: Phillips Petroleum Co Phillips Bldg Bartlesville OK 74004

BOWERS, BARBARA LEE, marketing consultant; b. St. Louis, Mar. 13, 1948; d. Grover William Bowers and Mary (Brewer) Ehlen. BA, St. Louis U., 1972; MA, Webster U., 1976. Art tchr. Webster Groves Sch. Dist., St. Louis, 1971-78; adminstrv. asst. to pres. BHN Advt., St. Louis, 1979-80; dir. advt. Medicine Shoppe Internat., St. Louis, 1980-83; dir. pub. rels. Sta. KSDK-TV, St. Louis, 1983-84; account exec. Tretter-Gorman, Inc., St. Louis, 1984-85; v.p. regional mktg. Community Psychiat. Ctrs., Santa Anna, Calif., 1985-86; owner, mktg. cons. In-House Mktg. Consulting, Santa Anna, 1986—. Contbr. numerous articles to profl. jours. Promotions chairwoman St. Louis chpt. March of Dimes, 1984, event chairwoman, 1988. Mem. Am. Mktg. Assn., Pub. Rels. Soc. Am. Republican. Roman Catholic. Office: In-House Mktg Cons 604 County Hill Dr Saint Louis MO 63119

BOWERS, DANIEL KENT, electric power industry executive; b. Ft. Wayne, Ind., Sept. 15, 1947; s. Arnold F. and Thelma D. (Merriman) B.; m. Nancy C. Burns, July 24, 1970 (div. May 1980); children: Stephanie, Stacy. BSBA, Ind. U., Ft. Wayne, 1970; MBA, U. Ariz., 1972, MS in Fin., 1973. Staff acct. Sanford, Myers & Dewald, CPAs, Ft. Wayne, 1969; adj. prof. bus. U. Ariz., Tucson, 1972-73; prof. bus. Ariz. Western. Coll., Yuma, 1973-75; ar. analyst advance planning Idaho Power Co., Boise, 1975-76, mgr. corp. modeling, 1976-77, asst. to v.p. fin., 1977-78, asst. treas., 1978-80, treas., 1980—, v.p., 1987—. Mem. exec. com. Jr. Achievement Idaho, Inc., Boise, 1986—; mem. bus. com. Boise Neighborhood Housing Svcs., 1987—; vol. YMCA, Boise, 1985—. Mem. Edison Electric Inst., N.W. Electric Light and Power Assn., Am. Fin. Assn., Nat. Assn. Corp. Treas., Risk Ins. Mgmt. Soc., Nat. Assn. Rate of Return Analysts. Office: Idaho Power Co PO Box 70 Boise ID 83707

BOWERS, DOUGLAS EDWARD, insurance executive; b. Royston, Ga., Dec. 18, 1947; s. Waco and Betty Frances (Thompson) B.; m. Sabra Elaine Slater, May 1, 1969; 1 child, Dana Lorraine. Student, Ga. State U., 1973-74; AA, DeKalb Community Coll., Clarkston, Ga., 1973. Credit rep. Gulf Oil Corp., Atlanta, 1968-70; credit mgr. Ga.-Pacific, Inc., Atlanta, 1970-72; credit rep. Moore Handley, Inc., Pelham, Ala., 1972-73, ctr. store mgr., 1973-75; ins. agt. Equitable Life, Atlanta, 1975-78, 82-85, dist. mgr., 1978-82; bus. cons., owner Bowers & Assocs., Duluth, Ga., 1983—; pres., owner, founder BAF Systems, Inc., 1988—. Named Rookie of Yr. Gen. Agts. and Mgrs. Assn., 1976, Equitable Life, 1976-78. Mem. Am. Soc. CLU's, Atlanta Assn. Life Underwriters, Million Dollar Round Table, Gwinnett County C. of C., Atlanta Jaycees (sec. 1978). Lodge: Optimists (pres. Duluth chpt. 1988-89). Home: 3514 Debbie Ct Duluth GA 30136 Office: PO Box 760 Duluth GA 30136

BOWERS, GRAYSON HUNTER, building parts manufacturing company executive; b. Frederick, Md., Nov. 18, 1897; s. Grayson Eichelberger and Chrisse Byrd Dell (Firestone) B.; ed. Gettysburg Coll., 1919; m. Isabel Houck, June 6, 1921 (dec. Dec. 1961); children: Grayson Hunter, Charles R., Alice Josephine Bowers Butler; m. 2d, Frances L. Crilly, June 20, 1964. Vice pres. William D. Bowers Lumber Co. and pres. allied corps., Frederick, 1919—; pres. Fidelity Bldg. & Loan Assn., 1961-80; Mt. Olivet Cemetery Co.; sr. v.p., dir. Fredericktown Bank & Trust Co., 1931-79; dir., officer Lumbermens Merchandising Corp., Wayne, Pa., 1945-70. Alderman, City of Frederick, 1928-34; pres. Bd. Election Suprs., 1934-38, Frederick City Planning Commn., 1943-70; trustee Hood Coll., 1950-74; mem. adv. council Md. Hosp. Constrn., 1968-71. Served to 1st lt. U.S. Army, 1919. Club: Masons. Mem. Frederick County Hist. Soc. (pres. 1965-67, 70-72). Home: 101 Council St 1st Fl Frederick MD 21701 Office: William D Bowers Lumber Co 10620 Woodsboro Pike Woodsboro MD 21798

BOWERS, MARJORIE ERIKA, school director; b. Landshut, Fed. Republic Germany, Dec. 22, 1948; (parents Am. citizens); d. Robert Theodore and Erika Auguste (Ertl) B. BA, U. Ky., 1971, MA, 1972. Elem. tchr. Bellevue (Ky.) Bd. Edn., 1971-75, Ft. Thomas (Ky.) Bd. Edn., 1975-82; prin. Boone Co. Bd. Edn., Florence, Ky., 1982-85, exec. dir. to supt., 1985—; mem. State Adv. Com. on Inservice Tng., Frankfort, Ky., No. Ky. U. Adminstrs. Preparation Study Group, Highland Heights, 1986-87, No. Ky. U. Steering Com. No. Ky. Collaborative, Highland Heights; chairperson Ky. Assn. Sch. Execs. Study Group on Support for Prins., Frankfort. Bd. dirs. Boone County Ednl. Found., Florence, 1986-88; mem. Boone County Adv. Com. for At Risk Studies, Florence, 1987-88. Named to Ky. PTA Prin.'s Honor Roll, 1985; Nat. Assn. Elem. Prins. fellow, 1985; Boone County Writing Inst. grantee, 1986, Boone County Writing to Read grantee, 1986. Mem. Ky. Assn. Sch. Adminstrs., Ky. Ednl. Leadership Inst. (bd. dirs. 1983-88), Ky. Inst. for Women, Ky. Arabian Horse Assn., Internat. Horse Assn., Delta Kappa Gamma, Phi Delta Kappa (pres. 1977-88). Democrat. Roman Catholic.

BOWERS, PATRICIA ELEANOR FRITZ, economist; b. N.Y.C., Mar. 21, 1928; d. Eduard and Eleanor (Ring) Fritz. Student scholar, Goucher Coll., 1946-48; B.A., Cornell U., 1950; M.A., NYU, 1953, Ph.D., 1965. Statis. asst. Fed. Res. Bank N.Y., N.Y.C., 1950-53; lectr. Upsala Coll., East Orange, N.J., 1953-59; researcher Fortune mag., N.Y.C., 1959-60; teaching fellow NYU, N.Y.C., 1960-62, instr., 1962-64; mem. faculty Bklyn. Coll., CUNY, 1964—, prof. econs., 1974—. Author: Private Choice and Public Welfare, 1974. Sec. Friends of the Johnson Mus., Cornell U., 1989—. Mem. Am. Econ. Assn., Econometric Soc., N.Y. Acad. Scis., Fgn. Policy Assn., Women's Econ. Round Table, Met. Econ. Assn. (sec. 1963-68, pres. 1974-75), Am. Statis. Assn. (univs. chmn. ann. forecasting confs. 1970-71, 71-72), City Island Yacht Club, NYU Club, Kappa Alpha Theta. Home: 145 E 16th St New York NY 10003 Office: CUNY Bklyn Coll Dept Econs Brooklyn NY 11210

BOWERS, RICHARD STEWART, JR., lawyer; b. Boston, Jan. 9, 1946; s. Richard Stewart and Doris Elizabeth (Rich) B.; m. Ellen Kathleen Rice, June 12, 1971; children: Richard Stewart III, Raymond Clark, Dwight Rice. BA cum laude, Harvard U., 1967; JD, Boston Coll., 1970. Bar: Mass. 1971, U.S. Dist. Ct. Mass. 1972, U.S. Ct. Appeals (1st cir.) 1972. Assoc. Harnish, Mansfield, Marsh & Macdonald, Waltham, Mass., 1970-71, Robert S. Marsh Law Office, Waltham, 1972-73; ptnr. Bowers & Bowers, Boston, 1973-78; corp. atty. Coachmen Industries, Inc., Elkhart, Ind., 1979-84, asst. v.p.-legal, 1985-87, v.p.-legal, 1988—. Pres. Nat. Ry. Hist. Soc. Boston Chpt., Newton, Mass., 1970-72; v.p. Nat. N.Y. Cen. R.R. Mus., Elkhart, Ind., 1987—; trustee Protestant Guild for Blind, Belmont, Mass., 1975-78. Republican. Methodist. Lodge: Rotary (sec. Boston chpt. 1978). Home: 17552 County Rd 10 Bristol IN 46507 Office: Coachmen Industries Inc 222 Middlebury St Elkhart IN 46516

BOWERS, ROBERT EARL, financial executive software firm; b. Elberton, Ga., Sept. 3, 1956; s. William Marvin Jr. and Francis Blanche (Salmond) B.; m. Cynthia Ann Lawrence, May 3, 1980; children: Robert Lawrence, William Ryan, Matthew Brett. BS in Acctg. summa cum laude, Auburn U., 1978. CPA, Ga. Audit mgr. Arthur Andersen & Co., Atlanta, 1978-84; v.p. fin., treas. Stockholder Systems, Inc., Norcross, Ga., 1984-87, exec. v.p., 1987—. Campaign treas. Newt Gingrich for Congress, Riverdale, Ga., 1984; mem. pub. affairs com. Atlanta C. of C., 1983-84; deacon, past treas. Christian Ch. Fellow Ga. Soc. CPAs, Auburn U. Acctg. Alumni (bd. dirs. 1985-87), Woodward Acad. Alumni, (treas., bd. dirs. 1980-87). Republican. Home: 3450 Aubusson Terr Alpharetta GA 30201 Office: Stockholder Systems Inc 4411 E Jones Bridge Rd Norcross GA 30092

BOWERS, RUSSEL TODD, banker; b. Orlando, Fla., Mar. 31, 1956; s. Leo Elzian and Alice Juanita (Spinks) B.; m. Kim Elaine Ackley, June 23, 1979; children: Christopher Garrett, Jonathan Thomas. BSBA, U. Cen. Fla., 1977; grad., Stonier Grad. Sch., 1988. Tax asst. Sun Banks, Inc., Orlando, 1977-78, asst. gen. accct., 1978-80, fin. analysis mgr., 1980-81, fin. reporting mgr., 1981-82; v.p., contr. SunBank, N.A., Orlando, 1982-83, sr. v.p., chief fin. officer, 1983—. Treas. Host Com. Cen. Fla., Orlando, 1986-88; participant Leadership Orlando, 1988; trustee Orlando Sci. Ctr.; bd. dirs. Leukemia Found. Cen. Fla. Mem. Fin. Execs. Inst., Nat. Assn. Accts., U. Cen. Fla. Alumni Assn. (pres. 1986), Citrus Club, Beta Gamma Sigma (hon.), Sigma Chi Alumni (pres. 1988). Democrat. Roman Catholic. Home: 9249 Sonia St Orlando FL 32825 Office: SunBank NA 200 S Orange Ave Orlando FL 32802

BOWHERS, VINCENT CARROLL, insurance underwriter; b. West Seneca, N.Y., Jan. 24, 1928; s. William Henry and Ethel Katherine (Carroll) B.; m. Helen Marie Statz; children: James V., William J., Robert T., Vincent C. Jr. BBA, Canisius Coll., 1950, DHL (hon.), 1984; postgrad., Purdue U., 1950-51. CLU, N.Y., Pa., Mass. Agt. John Hancock Co., Buffalo, 1950-51, tng. supr., 1952, mgr. sales, 1953-55, asst. gen. agt., 1956-60, gen. agt., 1961-67; gen. agt. John Hancock Co., Phila., 1967-71, Boston, 1972—; pres. Gen. Agts. & Mgrs. Conf., Washington, 1982-83. Chmn. County div. Buffalo United Way, 1964-65, Comml. div. Phila. United Way, 1971. Served with USN, 1945-46. Recipient John W. Yates Meml. award Los Angeles Gen. Agts. & Mgrs. Assn., 1983; named to Gen. Agts. and Mngrs. Hall of Fame, 1988. Mem. Mass. Life Underwriters Assn. (pres. 1980-81, Meeham award 1984), Boston CLU's (Albert E. Richardson award 1987, dir. 1987), Boston Estate Planning Council (pres. 1981-82), Boston Gen. Agts. & Mgrs. Assn. (pres. 1975-76), Boston Mgmt. Round Table (chmn. 1983-84), Research Agys. Group (chmn. 1984-85), Agy. Mgmt. Tng. Council (chmn. 1986-87), John Hancock Gen. Agts. Assn. (pres. 1981-82), Life Underwriters Tng. Council (trustee). Republican. Roman Catholic. Clubs: Down Town (Boston), Weston, Mass. Golf, The Buffalo. Home: 31 Sylvan Lane Weston MA 02193 Office: John Hancock Co 1 Winthrop Sq Boston MA 02110

BOWIE, KAREN LORRAINE, banker; b. Washington, Aug. 30, 1961; d. James Henry and Ramona C. (Harris) Johnson. BBA, Xavier U., 1983. Mgr. trainee 1st Nat. Bank Cin., 1983, portfolio mgr., 1983-87, trust officer, 1987-88; asst. v.p. Cen. Trust Co., Cin., 1988—. Vol. fin. devel. ctr. YWCA, Cin., 1987—. Fellow Inst. Chartered Fin. Analysts; mem. Cin. Urban Bankers (treas. 1985-86), Internat. Assn. Fin. Planning, Cin. Soc. Fin. Analysts, Am. Inst. Banking (bd. vos., v.p. fin., acctg. instr. 1986—), Xavier U. Alumni Assn. Office: Cen Trust Co 201 E 5th St Cincinnati OH 45202

BOWLBY, RICHARD ERIC, computer systems analyst; b. Detroit, Aug. 17, 1939; s. Garner Milton and Florence Marie (Russell) B.; m. Gwendoline Joyce Coldwell, Apr. 29, 1967. B.A., Wayne State U., 1962. With Ford Motor Co., Detroit, 1962-65, 66—, now computer systems analyst; pres. 1300 Lafayette East-Coop., Inc., 1981-82. Mem. Antiquaries, Friends Detroit Pub. Library, Friends Orch. Hall. Club: Founders Soc. (Detroit). Office: Ford Motor Co 300 Renaissance Ctr Ste 3000 PO Box 43314 Detroit MI 48243

BOWLES, BARBARA LANDERS, food company executive; b. Nashville, Sept. 17, 1947; d. Corris Raemone Landers and Rebecca Aima (Bonham) Jennings; m. Earl Stanley Bowles, Nov. 27, 1971; 1 son, Terrence Earl. B.A., Fisk U., 1968; M.B.A., U. Chgo., 1971. Chartered fin. analyst, 1977. Banker to v.p. First Nat. Bank of Chgo., 1968-81; asst. v.p. Beatrice Cos., Chgo., 1981-84; v.p. investor relations Kraft Inc., Chgo., 1984—. Recipient Salute to Am.'s Top 100 Black Bus. and Profl. Women award Delta Sigma Theta and Dollars & Sense Mag., 1985. Mem. Fin. Analysts Fedn., Nat. Assn. Investment Clubs, Nat. Investor Relations Inst., Chicago Fisk Alumni Assn. (pres. 1983-85). Mem. United Ch. of Christ. Club: University (Chgo.). Avocations: tennis, bridge. Office: Kraft Inc Kraft Ct Glenview IL 60025

BOWLES, EDNA MATHILDA, government relations consultant; b. Callao, Peru, Mar. 7, 1928 (parents Am. citizens); d. James Martin and Eloise Matilde B.; B.S., Universidad Nacional de San Marcos, Lima, Peru, 1946; postgrad. Bryce Coll., 1947. Mem. staff, office of econ. counselors Argentine embassy, Washington, 1947-50; researcher, statistician Nat. Labor-Mgmt. Council on Fgn. Trade Policy, Washington, 1950-51; mgr. Washington office L.M. MacDonnell, 1951-53; asst. sec.-treas. Tech. Resources Corp., Washington, 1953-54; Washington editor, asst. to pub. Americas Daily/Diario Las Americas, Miami, Fla., 1954-66; govt. relations cons., 1966—; acting treas. Ten Eyck Assos., Washington, 1962-64; acting exec. dir. Inst. Socio-Econ. Studies, Ltd., Washington, 1973-74; asst. to pres. Lead-Zinc Producers Com., Washington, 1975; asso. govt. relations rep. Martin-Marietta Aluminum Co., Washington, 1975; dir. communications Am. Assn. Port Authorities, Washington, 1977; assoc. cons. Cons. Capacities Group, Inc., 1984—. Dir. publicity D.C. Young Republicans, 1952-54; nat. dir. publicity Nat. Citizens Com. for Columbus Day, 1955-60; staff aide service D.C. chpt. ARC; vol. counselor Barney Neighborhood House, Washington. Mem. Am. Soc. Tng. and Devel., Nat. Planning Assn., World Future Soc., Nat. Assn. Female Execs. Republican. Methodist. Office: 3636 16th St NW Ste B-1105 Washington DC 20010

BOWLES, MICHELE JOYCE, administrative assistant; b. Lansing, Mich., Jan. 3, 1961; d. Robert Nelson and Joyce Olive (Allday) B. BA, Gemological Inst. Am., San Francisco, 1980. Dancer Happendance, Lansing, 1982-86; office mgr. Shaw's Jewelers, Lansing, 1979-81; adminstr. asst. Meijer, Inc., Lansing, 1981—. Mem. Internat. Assn. Quality Circles. Republican. Mem. Christian Sci. Ch. Home: 600 Cherry St Lansing MI 48933 Office: Meijer Perishables Inc 3301 S Creyts Rd Lansing MI 48917

BOWLING, JAMES CHANDLER, consultant; b. Covington, Ky., Mar. 29, 1928; s. Van Dorn and Belinda (Johnson) B.; m. Ann Jones, Oct. 20, 1951; children: Belinda, Nancy, James Jr., Stephanie. B.S., U. Louisville, 1951; LL.D. (hon.), Murray U., 1976, U. Ky., 1981. Various positions from campus rep. to v.p. sales and corp. relations Philip Morris, Inc., N.Y.C.; then exec. v.p., group v.p., dir. marketing, asst. to chmn. bd., sr. v.p., dir., now cons.; dir. Miller Brewing Co., Seven Up Co.; bd. dirs., mem. exec. com. Tobacco Inst., Washington.; sr. adv. bd. Burson-Marsteller; advisor USIA; bd. dirs. Cherokee Farms, Union Trust, Darien, Conn., Centurion, Inc., Centurion Stables, Inc.; chmn. bd. Prnews.; chmn. Bowling Investments, Inc. Author: How To Improve Your Personal Relations, 1959. Mem. nat. council Boy Scouts Am., 1961—; trustee Boy Scout Mus.; justice of peace, Rowayton, Conn., 1960-68; vice-chmn. Clean World Internat.; chmn. Pub. Affairs Council, Washington; bd. overseers U. Louisville; bd. dirs., former pres., former chmn., Keep Am. Beautiful; bd. dirs. Nat. Automatic Merchandising Assn.; trustee Berea Coll., Midway Jr. Coll.; bd. dirs. Ky. Ind. Coll. Found., Nat. Tennis Found. and Hall of Fame, U. Ky. Devel. Council., Lambda Chi Alpha Found. Served with AUS, World War II, PTO. Recipient Kolodny award as outstanding young exec. in tobacco industry, 1963; named U.S. Young Businessman of Year St. John's U., 1967, Outstanding Alumnus U. Louisville, 1970, 86, Kentuckian of Year, 1977; elected to Tobacco Industry Hall of Fame, 1976. Mem. Nat. Assn. Tobacco Distbg. (dir. exec. mgmt. div.), Pub. Relations Soc. Am., Sales Execs. Club N.Y., The Kentuckians (past pres.), Laymen's Nat. Bible Assn. (v.p., dir.), World Press Inst. Episcopalian. Clubs: Wee Burn Country; Union League (N.Y.C.). Home: 13 Tokeneke Trail Darien CT 06820 Office: 230 Park Ave S New York NY 10003

BOWMAN, BARBARA SHERYL, banker; b. Cleve., Sept. 2, 1953; d. Bert and Shirley Marie (Regan) B. BS magna cum laude, Calif. State U., Fresno, 1976; postgrad., Am. Grad. Sch. Internat. Mgmt., 1976; MBA magna cum laude, Loyola-Marymount U., 1980. Asst. to pres. Aerol Co., Los Angeles, 1976-77; mgmt. trainee First Interstate Bank of Calif., Los Angeles, 1977-78; mgr. consumer credit Brentwood, Calif., 1978-79; asst. v.p. Beverly Hills, Calif., 1979-82, v.p., 1982-84, v.p., sales mgr., 1985-89; v.p. Mercantile Nat. Bank, Los Angeles, 1982; sr. v.p. Fimsa subs. First Interstate Bancorp, Los Angeles, 1988, Houston, 1989—; v.p., asst. mgr. Real Estate div. Fical, San Diego, 1986-87; speaker San Diego Mortgage Bankers Assn., 1986. Mem. Nat. Assn. Female Execs., Am. Bus. Women's Assn., Nat. Assn. Bank Women (v.p. Los Angeles chpt. 1984-86), Loyola-Marymount Alumni Assn., Bldg. Industry Assn., St. Mary's Acad. Alumni Assn., Phi Kappa Phi. Republican. Roman Catholic. Office: Fimsa 650 N Sam Houston Pkwy Houston TX 77060

BOWMAN, DAVID WESLEY, lawyer; b. Mpls., Dec. 14, 1940; s. Burton F. and Eldred (Frudenfeld) B.; m. Patricia L. Schlimme, Nov. 26, 1975; children—Christopher B., Sarah K., David W., Tully B., Ashley B. B.A., U. Iowa, 1964, J.D., 1967. Bar: Iowa 1967. Asst. counsel Dept. Navy, Washington, 1968-72, Firestone Corp., Akron, Ohio, 1972-77; counsel Harris Corp., Melbourne, Fla., 1977-80, v.p., sec., gen. counsel documation, 1980-81, sector counsel, 1981-83; v.p., sec., gen. counsel Harris Graphics Corp., 1983-87; sr. v.p., gen. counsel MAPCO Inc., Tulsa, 1987—. Mem. ABA, Fed. Bar Assn., Iowa Bar Assn., Nat. Contract Mgmt. Assn., Nat. Security Indsl. Assn. Episcopalian. Home: 3104 S Columbia Cir Tulsa OK 74105 Office: MAPCO Inc PO Box 645 Tulsa OK 74101-0645

BOWMAN, LARRY ALAN, association executive; b. Lebanon, Pa., Mar. 18, 1948; s. Herbert Merle and Lucille Helen (Blouch) B.; m. Kathleen C. Wall, July 9, 1977; children: Alexis Wall, Samuel Meyer. BA in Polit. Sci., Lebanon Valley Coll., 1970; MPA, SUNY, Albany, 1977; postgrad., U. Del., 1985, U. Md., 1985. Caseworker Pa. Dept. Pub. Welfare, Phila., 1970-75; dir. govt. affairs Schenectady County C. of C., N.Y., 1977-83; pres. Chemung County C. of C., Elmira, N.Y., 1983—. Author: Everything You Always Wanted to Know About Forming a Local Political Action Committee, 1979. Co-chmn. promotional com. Corning Classic LPGA, 1986—; mem. adv. coun. Elmira Pioneers/Red Sox Baseball Club, 1989—; vol. United Way Cheming County, Elmira, 1985, United Way of Schenectady County, 1981-83; bd. dirs. Regional Energy Devel. Corp., Corning, N.Y., 1988—, So. Tier Econ. Growth Corp., Elmira, 1985—, Mark Twain Arts Coun., Elmira, 1987—. Mem. Am. C. of C. Execs., N.Y. State C. of C. Execs. (pres. elect 1988), Elmira Country Club. Democrat. Methodist. Home: 322 Larchmont Rd Elmira NY 14905 Office: Chemung County C of C 215 E Church St Elmira NY 14901

BOWMAN, MONROE BENGT, architect; b. Chgo., Aug. 28, 1901; s. Henry William and Ellen Mercedes (Bjork) B.; m. Louise Kohnmann, Nov.

1944; 1 son, Kenneth Monroe; B.Arch., Ill. Inst. Tech., 1924. Registered architect, Ill., Wis., Ind., Ohio, Colo. Asso., Benjamin H. Marshall, Chgo., 1926; exhibited models and photographs of Bowman Bros. comtemporary designs at Mus. Modern Art, N.Y.C., 1931; pvt. practice architecture, Chgo., 1941-44; asso. Monroe Bowman Assos., Chgo., 1945—; cons. Chgo. Dept. City Planning, City of Sparta (Wis.), Alfred Shaw, Architect. Mem. Navy League U.S. Important works include Boeing Aircraft bldgs., Wichita, Kans., Emerson Electric bldgs., St. Louis, Maytag Co., Newton, Iowa, Douglas Aircraft bldgs., Park Ridge, Ill., Shwayder Bros. bldgs., Denver, Clark Equipment Co., Buchannon, Mich., Radio-TV Sta. WHO, Des Moines, Foote, Cone & Belding offices, Chgo., Burridge Devel., Hinsdale, Ill., Yacht Club and recreational facilities, Lake Bemiji, Minn., United Airlines offices downtown Chgo., Automatic Sprinkler Corp., Chgo., King Machine Tool div. Am. Steel Foundries, Cin., Marine Terr. Apts., Chgo., Dorchester Park Apts., Chgo., Manteno (Ill.) State Hosp., No. Ill. Gas Co. bldgs., LaGrange, Joliet, Streator and Morris, 1340 Astor St. Apt. Bldg., Burnham Center, Chgo., NSF, Green Bank, W.Va., Naval Radio Research Sta., Sugar Grove, W.Va., Columbus Boy Choir Sch., Princeton, N.J., office bldg. and hotel, Charleston, W.Va. Home: 730 Ridge Ave Evanston IL 60201

BOWMAN, NED DAVID, medical administrator; b. Chattanooga, July 15, 1948; s. Ned Turner and Ernie (White) B.; stepmother Charlotte (Bramlett) B.; m. Linda Carol Eggers, Sept. 18, 1970; children: Bob, Jean, Beth, Scott, Ben. BS, U. Tenn., 1971, MBA, Vanderbilt U., 1982. Adminstr. Oak Ridge Orthopedic Clinic, 1971—; cons. med. adminstrn. Mem. Oak Ridge Human Resources Bd., 1975; past pres. Anderson County Health Council, 1980-81; adv. com. vocat. edn. Oak Ridge city schs., 1977; treas. UN Com. Oak Ridge, 1977, 81. Bd. dirs. Oak Ridge Boys Club; mem. wood badge patrol, advisor to explorer post Boy Scouts Am. Recipient certs. of appreciation City of Oak Ridge, Oak Ridge City Schs. Mem. AAAS, UN Assn. U.S., Soc. Advancement Mgmt. (cert. appreciation 1975, v.p. 1975), Nat. Audubon Soc., Oak Ridge C. of C. (past bd. dirs.), N.Y. Acad. Sci., Med. Group Mgmt. Assn. (past pres. Tenn. chpt.), Am. Coll. Med. Group Adminstrs., Nat. Assn. Orthopedic Clinic Adminstrs., Tenn. Secondary Schs. Athletic Assn., Tenn. Med. Group Mgmt. Assn. Nat. Fedn. Interscholastic Ofcls. Assn., Tenn. Conservation League, Orthopedics Overseas. Mormon. Lodge: Rotary. Avocation: basketball ofcl. Home: 502 Delaware Ave Oak Ridge TN 37830 Office: 145 E Vance Rd Oak Ridge TN 37830

BOWSHER, CHARLES ARTHUR, government official; b. Elkhart, Ind., May 30, 1931; s. Matthew A. and Ella M. (West) B.; m. Mary C. Mahoney, Dec. 14, 1963; children: Kathryn M., Stephen C. BS, U. Ill., 1953; MBA, U. Chgo., 1956; DSc in Bus. Adminstrn. (hon.), Bryant Coll., 1984. C.P.A., Ill. Ptnr. Arthur Andersen & Co., Chgo., 1956-67, Washington, 1971-81; asst. sec. of Navy for fin. mgmt. Dept. Def., Washington, 1967-71; comptroller gen. U.S., 1981—; mem. nominating com. Acctg. Hall Fame, adv. com. Fin. Acctg. Standards Bd., structural review com. Govt. Acctg. Standards Bd. Mem. adv. council dept. sociology Princeton U., bd. advisors Wharton Govt. and Bus. Program, Wharton's Fishman-Davidson Ctr. for Study Service Sector, vis. com. Miami U., Conf. Bd.; bd. dirs. Am. Productivity Ctr.; hon. bd. Ctr. Excellence Govt.; adv. com. office for govtl. acctg. research and edn. U. Ill., bus. adv. council; pub. sector com. Internat. Fedn. of Accts.; adv. council Office of Tech. Assessment; bd. of overseers Wharton Sch., U. Pa.; mem. nat. comm. to prevent infant mortality; mem. vis. com. Sch. Bus., U. So. Calif.; chmn. Nat. Adv. Commn. on Law Enforcement. Served with AUS, 1953-55. Recipient Distinguished Pub. Service award U.S. Navy, 1969, Distinguished Pub. Service award Dept. Def., 1971. Mem. Am. Inst. CPAs, Nat. Assn. Govt. Accts., Nat. Acad. Pub. Adminstrn., Am. Mgmt. Assn. (gen. mgmt. council), Alumni Assn. Grad. Sch. Bus. U. Chgo. (v.p. 1965-67), Pi Kappa Alpha, Beta Alpha Psi (adv. forum). Clubs: Burning Tree (Washington). Home: 4503 Boxwood Rd Bethesda MD 20816 Office: GAO 441 G St NW Rm 7000 Washington DC 20548

BOWYER, GARY NEAL, financial executive consultant; b. Joliet, Ill., Feb. 15, 1947; s. Dee and Martha (Sullivan) B. BA in Internat. Rels., Purdue U., 1969; MBA in Fin., Boston U., 1974. Acct. supr. Comml. Credit Bus. Loans, Chgo., 1974-77; credit, ops. mgr. ITT Comml. Fin., Chgo., 1977-87; v.p. Mellon Fin. Svc., Oak Brook, Ill., 1982-87; pres. Gary N. Bowyer and Assocs., Chgo., 1987—. With U.S. Army, 1970-72, Vietnam. Mem. Internat. Assn. Fin. Planners, Inst. Cert. Fin. Planners (v.p. communications 1987—, bd. dirs. Chgo. Chpt., 1987—), Nat. Assn. Personal Fin. Advisors, Park Ridge C. of C. (small bus. chmn. 1988). Home: 747 W Brompton Chicago IL 60657 Office: Gary N. Bowyer & Assocs Inc 6405 N Avondale Chicago IL 60631

BOX, BARRY GLENN, aerospace engineer, military officer; b. Hillsboro, Tex., Oct. 13, 1958; s. Jimmy and Virginia (Morgan) B. BS in Engring., U.S. Mil. Acad., 1981; MBA, So. Meth. U., 1987—. Commd. 2d lt. U.S. Army, 1981, advanced through grades to capt., 1984, resigned, 1986; program mgr. E-Systems, Garland, Tex., 1986-88; sr. aerospace engr. Boeing Aerospace Corp., Corinth, Tex., 1986—. Jr. bd. dirs. Park Cities Bapt. Ch., Dallas, 1986—. Decorated Meritorious Service medal. Mem. West Point Soc. North Tex. (bd. dirs. 1986—), Raffles Club (founding mem.). Avocations: running, scuba, racquetball, chess. Home: 3440 Tiberglen Rd #183 Dallas TX 75287-3420 Office: Boeing Aerospace Corp 7801 S Stemmons Frwy Corinth TX 75065-9119

BOXER, ROBERT L., lawyer; b. N.Y.C., Apr. 26, 1953; s. Jack and Elaine (Krinsky) B.; m. Susan S. Rodio, Oct. 23, 1982; children: Eric, Laura. BA in Econs., SUNY, Stony Brook, 1974; JD, U. Mich., 1977. Bar: N.Y. 1977, U.S. Dist. Ct. N.Y. 1978. Assoc. Middleton and Wilson, Rochester, N.Y., 1977-81; corp. counsel Sykes Datatronics Inc., Rochester, N.Y., 1981-83; corp. gen. counsel, sec. Moscom Corp., East Rochester, N.Y., 1983—. Mem. Phi Beta Kappa. Office: Moscom Corp 300 Main St East Rochester NY 14445

BOXLEY, LINDY CALVIN, corporate professional; b. Richmond, Va., Aug. 2, 1931; s. Lindsay Stevens and Beatrice (Courtney) B.; m. Adeline Conley, Sept. 12, 1970; m. Margaret Loretta Heilig, Oct. 13, 1950 (div. 1967); children: William Alan, Steven Lee. Grad. high sch., Orange, Va. Salesman Martin Furniture Co., Inc., Culpeper, Va., 1950-51, Tappahannock, Va., 1951-52; asst. Martin Furniture Co., Inc., Tappahannock, 1952-57; sec.-treas. Tidewater Furniture Co., Inc., Mathews, Va., 1957-65; treas. Martin Furniture Co., Inc., Culpeper, 1965-86, pres., 1986—. Methodist. Clubs: Tappahannock (pres. 1957). Lodge: Mathews Lions Club (tail twister 1961, lion tamer 1963). Home: 1116 Meander Dr Culpeper VA 22701 Office: Martin Furniture Co 125 E Davis St Culpeper VA 22701

BOYARSKY, VAL DAVID, manufacturing executive, information systems specialist, management consultant; b. Kiev, USSR, July 15, 1960; came to U.S., 1978; parents David and Belle (Vishnevski) B. AS in Computer Tech., Spring Garden Coll., 1981; BS in Computers and Mgmt., Temple U., 1984, MBA in Mgmt. Ops., 1988. Lead programmer Schaevitz Engring., Pennsauken, N.J., 1980-82, sr. systems analyst, 1982-85, mgr. systems and programming, 1985-87; dir. mgmt. info. systems Rotor Clip Co., Somerset, N.J., 1987-89; dir. MIS Telenex Corp. (div. Gen. Signal), Mt. Laurel, N.J., 1989—; cons. in field. Mem. Am. Prodn. Inventory Control Soc., Northeastern HP Users Group, Am. Mgmt. Soc., Assn. Computer Machinery, Am. Math. Soc., N.J. Chess Assn., Karate Club. Republican. Jewish. Home: 56 Knollwood Dr Cherry Hill NJ 08002

BOYCE, ALLAN R., business executive; b. Chgo., Aug. 27, 1943; s. John Allan and Ruth (Palmer) B.; m. Sally Ely, June 28, 1969; children—Laura, Jennifer. B.A., Dartmouth Coll., 1965; M.B.A., Stanford U., 1969. With Burlington No. R.R., St. Paul, 1969-81; asst. v.p. exec. dept. Burlington No. R.R., 1976-81; v.p. pub. affairs Burlington No., Inc., Seattle, 1981-84; sr. v.p. human resources Burlington No., Inc., 1984-88; sr. v.p. human resources, adminstrn. Burlington Resources, 1989—. Bd. dirs. Mcpl. League, Seattle, 1981—. Served to lt. USNR, 1965-67.

BOYCE, DANIEL HOBBS, financial planning company executive; b. Flint, Mich., Oct. 19, 1953; s. James Edward and Alice Marilyn (Hobbs) B.; m. Suzanne Kay Williams; children: Kenneth C., Geoffrey A., Stephen J. BA, U. Mich., 1974, MA, 1978. Rep. Mut. Svc. Corp., Detroit, 1982-87; prin. Investment Mgmt. & Rsch. Inc., Atlanta, 1987—; treas., chief fin. officer Ctr. Fin. Planning Inc., Birmingham, Mich., 1988—; v.p. Southworth, Boyce & McFawn Planning Corp., Troy, Mich., 1982-85; owner, fin. planner Daniel H. Boyce Fin. Adv. Svcs., Birmingham, 1985-88; mem. adj. faculty Coll. Fin. Planning, Denver, 1985—; mem. adv. council cert. program in personel fin. planning Oakland U., Rochester, Mich., 1987—; edn. cons. Nat. Ctr. for Fin. Edn., Denver, 1985—. Bi-weekly columnist Money Matters, Legal News newsletter, 1984-86; monthly columnist Personel Fin. for suburban Detroit newspaper chain, 1987—. Mem. Detroit Soc. of Inst. of Cert. Fin. Planners (pres. 1986-87, chmn. 1987-88), Internat. Assn. Fin. Planning (bd. dirs. SE Mich. chpt. 1984-87), Internat. Soc. Cert. Employee Benefit Specialists. Office: Ctr Fin Planning Inc 877 S Adams Ste 202 Birmingham MI 48009

BOYCE, DONALD NELSON, diversified industry executive; b. Buffalo, May 4, 1938; s. Nelson W. and Mary A. (Gillis) B.; m. Jeris Jane Smith, Sept. 22, 1956; children: Mark D., Tammy J., Timothy R., Daniel E. BS, Rochester Inst. Tech., 1967, postgrad., 1969-71. Acct. Sylvania Electric Products Co., Buffalo and Batavia, N.Y., 1956-59; acct., systems mgr., controller Constrn. Equipment div. Eaton Corp., Batavia, 1959-69; controller Strippit div. Houdaille Industries, Inc., Akron, N.Y., 1969-72; treas. Houdaille Industries, Inc., Northbrook, Ill., 1972-79, v.p. fin. and adminstrn., 1979-84, exec. v.p., dir., 1984-86, pres., dir., 1986-87, pres., chief exec. officer, dir., 1987-88; chmn., pres. IDEX Corp., Northbrook, 1988—, also bd. dirs.; mem. adv. bd. Marine Bank-Western, Batavia, 1967-69; dir. S.E. Banking Corp., Miami, Fla., S.E. Bank, N.A., Miami, Band-It Inc., Denver, Lubriquip Inc., Cleve., Vibratech Inc., Buffalo, N.Y., Strippit Inc., Akron, N.Y., Viking Pump, Cedar Falls, Iowa, Warren Rupp Inc., Mansfield, Ohio, Morgan Products, Oshkosh, Wis., Morgan Products Ltd., Oshkosh, Wis. Mem. bd. edn. Oakfield-Ala. Central Sch., 1970-77. Mem. Machinery and Allied Products Inst. (exec. com.), Coun. for Advanced Tech., Am. Mgmt. Assn., Monroe Club. Republican. Methodist. Home: 1251 N Sheridan Rd Lake Forest IL 60045 Office: IDEX Corp 630 Dundee Rd Northbrook IL 60065

BOYCE, DOREEN ELIZABETH, educational foundation executive; b. Antofagasta, Chile, Apr. 20, 1934; d. George Edgar and Elsie Winifred Vaughan; B.A. with honors, Oxford (Eng.) U., 1956, M.A. with honors, 1960; Ph.D., U. Pitts., 1983, D. in Hum. Lit., Westminster Coll., 1986; m. Alfred Warne Boyce, Aug. 11, 1956; children—Caroline Elizabeth, John Trevor Warne. Lectr. and tutor in econs. U. Witwatersrand, South Africa, 1960-62; provost and dean of faculty, prof. econs. Chatham Coll., Pitts., 1963-79; prof. econs., chmn. dept. econs. and mgmt. Hood Coll., Frederick, Md., 1979-82; exec. dir. Buhl Found., Pitts., 1982—; dir. Duquesne Light Co., Dollar Bank, FSB, Microbac Labs., Inc. Del. White House Conf. on Small Bus., 1980; mem. Gov.'s Conf. Small Bus., 1979-82; trustee Franklin and Marshall Coll., 1982—, Frick Edn. Commn., 1980—, Buhl Sci. Ctr., 1982—; mem. citizens sponsoring com. Allegheny Conf. Community Devel., 1982—; mem. Fed. Jud. Nominating Commn., 1977-79, Pa. Gov.'s Commn. on Financing of Higher Edn., 1983-85 bd. dirs. World Affairs Council, 1984—. Mem. Am. Econs. Assn., Exec. Women's Council, Am. Assn. Higher Edn. (mem. com. prof. devel. Council Founds.), Grantmakers of Western Pa. (pres.). Office: The Buhl Found 4 Gateway Ctr Rm 1522 Pittsburgh PA 15222

BOYCE, TIMOTHY JOHN, real estate executive; b. New Haven, Oct. 19, 1954; s. Thomas William and Rose F. (Eagan) B.; m. Tara McGowan, Aug. 19, 1978; children: Owen, Patrick. BS, Georgetown U., 1975; JD, MBA, U. Pa., 1979. Bar: Conn. 1979. Assco. Cummings & Lockwood, Stamford, Conn., 1979-81; asst. gen. counsel Daseke Group, Inc., Stamford, 1981-84; v.p., gen. counsel Hawthorne Group, Inc., Stamford, 1984-86, pres., 1986—; cons. Southampton Tree Farm, N.Y., 1987, Island Devel., Inc., N.Y.C., 1987-88. Author: The Duty of Fair Representation, 1979. Mem. Conn. Bar Assn., Phi Beta Kappa. Office: Hawthorne Group Inc 60 Guernsey Ave Stamford CT 06901

BOYD, DAVID PRESTON, business educator; b. Amsterdam, N.Y., Oct. 19, 1943; s. David Preston and Mignon (Finch) B. BA in English Lit., Harvard U., 1965; DPhil in Behavioral Scis., Oxford U., 1973. Asst. headmaster Dedham Country Day Sch., Mass., 1965-69; co-owner The Old Cambridge Co., Mass., 1973-77; instr. Coll. Bus. Adminstrn., Northeastern U., Boston, 1977-78, asst. prof., 1978-82, assoc. prof., 1982-87, prof., 1987—, acting dean, 1987, dean, 1987—; Patrick F. and Helen C. Walsh research prof., 1985-86, chmn. human resources mgmt. dept., 1986-87, mem. univ. editorial bd., 1984-89. Author: Elites and Their Education, National Foundation for Educational Research, 1973, also numerous articles. Recipient Excellence in Teaching award Northeastern U., 1980; Northeastern U. grantee, 1982-84, Control Data Corp., 1983, NYU, 1985. Home: 65 Grove St Wellesley MA 02181 Office: Northeastern U 101 Hayden Hall Boston MA 02115

BOYD, JOE DAN, farm journal editor; b. Winnsboro, Tex., Jan. 9, 1934; s. James Daniel and Dolly Fay (Tinney) B.; m. Barbara Ann Evers, Dec. 19, 1955; children: Tara, Colin, Logan. BS, Tex. A&M Coll., 1957; MA, U. Pa., 1969. Writer farm news Star-Telegram, Ft. Worth, 1957; assoc. editor Nat. Future Farmer, Alexandria, Va., 1958-60; field editor Farm Jour., Montgomery, Ala., 1960-62; assoc. mng. editor Farm Jour., Phila., 1963-67, regional editor, 1968; regional editor Farm Jour., Memphis, 1969-72, Dallas, 1973—; editor Cotton Today, Dallas, 1978—. Contbr. articles to farm and folklore jours. 2d lt. F.A., U.S. Army, 1957-58. Mem. Am. Agrl. Editors Assn. (bd. dirs. 1985—), Soc. Profl. Journalists, Sigma Delta Chi, Dallas Agrl. Club (bd. dirs.). Methodist. Home: 2701 Raintree Dr Plano TX 75074 Office: Farm Jour Inc 811 S Central Expwy Ste 525 Richardson TX 75080

BOYD, JOHN KENT, advertising executive; b. Portsmouth, Ohio, Oct. 17, 1910; s. Lambert Thomas and Faery Ann (Ritter) B.; student Tulane U., New Orleans, 1927-29; m. Jeanne Marie Dunlap, Dec. 26, 1935; children: John Kent, Barbara Ann. Mem. staff advt. dept. Am. Rolling Mill Co., Middletown, Ohio, 1929-31; advt. mgr. Pitts. and Midway Coal Mining Co., Kansas City, Mo., 1932-35; v.p. Ferry-Hanly Co., 1935-44; ptnr. Bruce B. Brewer & Co., Kansas City and Mpls., 1944-66; pres., chief exec. officer Bruce B. Brewer Co., Inc., 1967-72, chmn. bd., chief exec. officer, 1972-75; dir. Marco Mfg. Co.; past pres., dir. Quivira, Inc.; pres. Kaybee, Inc. Cochmn. United Funds publicity com., 1953; dir. United Cerebral Palsy Assn. of Kansas City; active Boy Scouts Am.; bd. govs. Starlight Theatre Assn., YMCA, Quiet Birdmen; bd. dirs. Kansas City Crime Commn. Adv. com. FAA Kanas City Air Traffic Control. Named Man of Yr. in Gen. Aviation, 1969; recipient silver medal Am. Advt. Fedn., 1972. Mem. AIM, Nat. Aero. Assn., Am. Legion, Kansas City Sr. Golf Assn., Kansas City Promotion Com., Airplane Owners and Pilots Assn. (nat.). Am. Mktg. Assn. (dir. Kansas City chpt.), Am. Royal Assn. (gov.), C. of C., Snipe Class Internat. Racing Assn., Nat. Pilots Assn. (dir.) Am. Bonanza Soc., Air Force Assn., Silver Wings, Kansas City Advt. Club, Sales Execs. Club, Quivira Country Club, Mission Hills Country Club, Aero of Kansas City Club, OX5 of Am. Club, Capital Hill Club (Washington), Quivira Sailing Club (past commodore), Diamondhead Yacht and Country Club, Bay-Waveland Yacht Club. Author: Jerry Dalrymple, 1931, Crowded Skies, 1969. Home: 3400 Yacht Club Cir Bay Saint Louis MS 39520 Office: 6512 Maple Dr Mission KS 66202

BOYD, MORTON, banker; b. Louisville, June 7, 1936; s. Morton and Pauline Boyd; m. Anne Theobald; children—Anne Chambers, Robert Morton. B.A., U. Va., grad. Stonier Grad. Sch. Banking, 1964. With First Nat. Bank of Louisville, 1959—, pres., chief adminstrv. officer, 1981—, also bd. dirs.; exec. v.p. First Ky. Nat. Corp., pres., 1987—, chief exec. officer, 1988—, also bd. dirs. holding co.; bd. dirs. First Ky. Nat. Corp. Holding Co., First Ky. Trust Co., Nat. Processing Co., Louisville Bd. Fed. Res. Bank of St. Louis, Broadway Project Corp. Mem. Louisville fund for the Arts, 1984—; bd. overseers U. Louisville; trustee Bellarmine Coll. Served to 2d lt. U.S. Army, 1958-59. Mem. Assn. Res. City Bankers. Episcopalian. Office: 1st Ky Nat Corp PO Box 36000 Louisville KY 40233

BOYD, ROBERT GIDDINGS, JR., mental health facility administrator; b. San Juan, Mar. 16, 1940; s. Robert Giddings and Laura Jean (Stephenson) B.; m. Amanda Gail Rasmussen, July 28, 1967 (div. 1977); 1 dau., Stephanie Gail; m. Denise Ann Ryll, Dec. 10, 1978; 1 son, Robert Giddings III. B.A. in Sociology, Coll. William and Mary, 1962; postgrad. in bus. mgmt., George Washington U., 1965-67. Lic. in real estate, Ariz. Supr. staff services Bellcomm, Inc., Washington, 1964-67; budget mgr. Goodbody & Co., N.Y.C., 1968-70; bus. mgr. Westminster Sch., Simsbury, Conn., 1970-76; pres., gen. mgr. F & R Enterprises, Inc., Scottsdale, Ariz., 1976-78; mng. dir. San Diego Symphony Assn., 1981-84; v.p. fin. mental health facility San Diego Ctr. for Children, 1985—; pub. speaker San Diego Symphony, 1982—. Served to 1st lt. U.S. Army, 1962-64. Mem. Am. Symphony Orch. League, Am. Mgmt. Assn, Am. Arts Alliance, Combined Arts and Ednl. Council, San Diego Employers Assn. Republican. Office: San Diego Ctr Children 3002 Armstrong St San Diego CA 92111

BOYD, WILLIAM B., former manufacturing company executive; b. Palestine, Tex., Jan. 30, 1924. B.S., Tex. A&M U., 1948. Gen. mgr. household refrigeration Gen. Electric Co., to 1975; pres. Carrier Air Conditioning Co., N.Y.C., group environ. and energy systems group, successively v.p., gen. mgr. plumbing products div. corp. v.p. group exec., western hemisphere bldg. products group, sr. v.p. bldg. products group; chief operating officer Am. Standard Inc., N.Y.C., to 1985, vice chmn., 1985-86, chief exec. officer, 1985-89, chmn., 1986-89, pres., 1987-89, also dir.; dir. Stanley Interiors Corp. Office: Am Standard Inc 40 W 40th St New York NY 10018 *

BOYER, DAVID SCOTT, manufacturing company executive; b. Detroit, Nov. 15, 1942; s. Francis P. and Margaret (Mitchell) B.; m. Patricia Tews, Oct. 15, 1966; children: Aimee, Joe, Julie. BS, St. Joseph's Coll., 1964; postgrad., U. Detroit, 1965, Harvard Bus. Sch., 1976. Account mgr. Texaco, 1966-68; account mgr. Teleflex Auto div. Teleflex, Inc., Troy, Mich., 1968-72, sales mgr., 1972-75; mgr. industry comml. group Teleflex Inc., Troy, Mich., 1975-78, v.p. auto group, 1978-85, pres. comml. group, 1985-86; pres., chief operating officer Teleflex Inc., Limerick, Pa., 1986—. Served with USCGR. Mem. Soc. Automobile Engrs., Engring. Soc. Detroit, Soc. Mfg. Engrs., Soc. Plastics Engrs., Engring. Soc. for Advancing Mobility Land Sea Air and Space. Office: Teleflex Inc 155 S Limerick Rd Limerick PA 19468

BOYER, GEOFFREY FREDERICK, financial executive; b. Plainfield, N.J., Apr. 13, 1945; s. Daniel B. Boyer Jr. and Margaret Bette (Masie) Moeller; m. Janet Louise Stout, June 24, 1972; children: Geoffrey F. Jr., Jennifer L. BA in History, Bates Coll., Lewiston, Maine, 1967; cert., Coll. Fin. Planning, 1986. V.p. Pro Services, Inc., Flourtown, Pa., 1976-77; prin. McBryde & Co., Allentown, Pa., 1977-83; ins. broker Alden-Levine Assocs., Allentown, Pa., 1978-83; pres., investment advisor Boyer Fin. Group, Inc., Allentown, Pa., 1983—; asst. treas., dir. PennBerks Investors, Inc., Boyertown, Pa., 1972—; asst. sec., dir. Boyertown Properties, Inc., 1972—. Patentee computer investment tool, 1987. Deacon, Faith Evang. Free Ch., 1983-85, chmn. fin. com., 1983—. Mem. Internat. Assn. Fin. Planning (pres. Lehigh Valley chpt. 1984-87, chmn., 1987—), Inst. Cert. Fin. Planners, Allentown C. of C. (mem. small bus. coun. 1984—, dir. small bus. coun. 1988—). Republican. Office: Boyer Fin Group 1259 S Cedar Crest Blvd #336 Allentown PA 18103

BOYER, GEORGE EDWARD, JR., financial planner; b. Newark, Nov. 12, 1955; s. George Edward Sr. and Myra (Tersigni) B. AAS in Bus. Adminstrn., County Coll. of Morris, Randolph, N.J., 1977. Br. acctg. clk. Keuffel and Esser, Morristown, N.J., 1977-79; audit clk. II First Nat. Bank Allentown, Pa., 1979-80; prodn. analyst Country Miss, Easton, Pa., 1980-85; registered rep. Waddell and Reed, Allentown, 1986—. Mem. Nat. Assn. Securities Dealers. African Meth. Episcopal. Home: 901 Apt E George St Easton PA 18042

BOYER, ROBERT ALLAN, business executive; b. Detroit, Mar. 2, 1934; s. Robert Allan and Elizabeth (Szabo) B.; divorced; children: Jennifer, Stephen, Lorna. MBA, Cornell U., 1959. Exec. asst. to pres. Merck & Co., Inc., Rahway, N.J., 1962-68; dir. fin. TWA Corp., N.Y.C., 1972-69; nat. dir. fin. Coopers & Lybrand, N.Y.C., 1972-79; dir. adminstrn. Sullivan & Cromwell, N.Y.C., 1979-; chmn., founder Legal Execs. Group, Law Firm Tech. Group, 1979. Mem. congl. support com. Rep. Party, N.Y., 1980—. Mem. ABA, Assn. Legal Adminstrs. (exec. com. 1986-87), Aircraft Owners and Pilots Assn. Republican. Presbyterian. Club: Echo Lake Country (Westfield, N.J.). Office: Sullivan & Cromwell 125 Broad St New York NY 10004

BOYHAN, EDWARD RALPH, investment executive; b. Teaneck, N.J., Nov. 8, 1945; s. George Edward and Olive Constance (Thomas) B. BA in Psychology, Occidental Coll., 1964; MS in Computer Sci., NYU, 1970, MBA in Econ., 1979-88. Systems programmer NYU, N.Y.C., 1967-72; sr. staff Securities Industry Automation Corp., N.Y.C., 1972-82; v.p. Salomon Bros. Inc., N.Y.C., 1982—; cons. Parsons & Whittemore, N.Y.C., 1977-81. Mem. IEEE, Am. Mgmt. Assn., Assn. Computing Machinery. Office: Salomon Bros Inc 1 New York Pla New York NY 10004

BOYLAN, JOHN LESTER, financial executive, accountant; b. Columbus, Ohio, Aug. 23, 1955; s. James Robert and Ruth Isabella (Capes) B.; m. Susan Marie Stakes, May 21, 1983; 1 child, David. BBA, Ohio State U., 1977. CPA, Ohio. Staff acct. Deloitte, Haskins & Sells, Columbus, 1977-79, sr. acct., 1979-83, mgr., 1983-86; dir. fin. planning Lancaster Colony Corp., Columbus, 1986—, asst. treas., 1987—. Office: Lancaster Colony Corp 37 W Broad St Columbus OH 43215

BOYLAN, MARK THOMAS JAY, real estate corporation officer; b. Kansas City, Mo., June 8, 1961; s. Stephan Mickich and Carroll (Jay) B. BBA, So. Meth. U., 1984. Analyst First Bank System Mortgage Corp., Kansas City, 1984-86; v.p. Pearce, Urstadt, Mayer & Greer Realty Corp., Leawood, Kans., 1986—. Republican. Presbyterian. Home: 2505 W 84th St Leawood KS 66206 Office: Pearce Urstadt Mayer Greer Realty Corp 11100 Ash Ste 100 Leawood KS 66206

BOYLAN, WILLIAM ALVIN, lawyer; b. Marshalltown, Iowa, Sept. 18, 1924; s. Glen D. and Dorothy I. (Gibson) B.; m. Nancy Dickson, Aug. 5, 1950; children: Ross, Laura. Student, U. Iowa, 1943-44; B.A., Drake U., 1947; LL.B., Harvard U., 1950. Bar: Ill. 1950, N.Y. bar 1952. Practiced in N.Y.C., 1952—; mem. firm Gould & Wilkie, N.Y.C., 1987—; bd. dirs. Tribune Oil Corp. Contbr. articles to profl. jours. Served with USAAF, 1943-46. Mem. ABA, N.Y. State Bar Assn., Assn. Bar City N.Y., Fed. Bar Council, Phi Beta Kappa, Sigma Alpha Epsilon. Episcopalian. Clubs: Harvard, The Down Town Assn. Home: 108 E 82d St New York NY 10028 Office: Gould & Wilkie 1 Wall St 34th Fl New York NY 10005

BOYLE, BRYAN DOUGLAS, senior computer systems engineer; b. Fall River, Mass., June 11, 1956; s. Edwin Clayton and Lucille Annemarie (Gouin) B.; m. Paula DeAngelis, Jan. 19, 1980 (div. Mar. 1983). BA in Communications, Fordham U., 1978. Computer designer ABC, N.Y.C., 1978-85; system engr. IMR Systems, Leavenworth, Kans., 1985-86; sr. engr. Data Gen. Corp, 1986—; editor Globecom Pub., Prairie Village, Kans., 1981-85 ; pres. Beta Processing, Bronx, 1981-87; computer cons. Soc. Broadcast Engrs., Indpls., 1983-86, Roncom Broadcast Design, Fairfield, N.J., 1984-87. Software author Bi-Tech Enterprises, Bohemia, N.Y., 1980-83; computer editor Broadcast Communication, 1981-84; contbg. editor Broadcast Mgmt./Engring. Mag., 1984-86; editor Broadcast Communications mag., 1981-83. Decorated Order Knight of St. George the Martyr, Sovereign Mil. Mem. Soc. Broadcast Engrs. (sec. 1977-80, 85—, award 1983), Sovereign Mil. and Hosp. Order of St. John of Jerusalem, Knights of Malta knight of honor and merit). Republican. Roman Catholic. Lodge: Knights of Malta (knight of honor and merit), Order of St. John of Jerusalem (hospitaler). Avocations: automobile restoration, racing, pvt. pilot.

BOYLE, FRANCIS JOSEPH, transportation and energy company executive; b. Manchester, N.H., Oct. 23, 1945; s. Hugh A. and Victoria (Gabashian) B.; m. Barbara Ann Genest, June 7, 1969; children—Blair, Paige. B.S., St. Joseph's U., 1967; M.B.A., Temple U., 1971. C.P.A. Auditor Arthur Young & Co., Phila., 1967-69; mgr. IU Internat., Phila., 1971-77; v.p., treas. U.S. Filter Corp., N.Y.C., 1977-82, treas., 1982-83, v.p., treas., 1983-85; sr. v.p., chief fin. officer El Paso Natural Gas Co., El Paso, 1985—. Served with USAR, 1967-73. Mem. Fin. Execs. Inst., Am. Inst. C.P.A.s. Office: El Paso Natural Gas Co PO Box 1492 El Paso TX 79978

BOYLE, JOAN F., actuary; b. Rahway, N.J., Sept. 13, 1947; d. Edward V. and Florence M. (Assell) Hojecki; m. John P. Boyle, Apr. 26, 1970 (div. Aug. 1985). BA in Econs., Douglass Coll., 1969. Various positions Blue

Cross/Blue Shield of N.J., Newark, 1969-80, dir. actuarial dept., 1980-82, asst. v.p., actuary, 1982-84, v.p., actuary, 1984-86, exec. v.p., 1986-89, chief fin. officer, 1989—. Mem. Am. Acad. Actuaries. Republican. Roman Catholic. Home: 1881 North Gate Rd Scotch Plains NJ 07076 Office: Blue Cross/Blue Shield NJ 33 Washington St Newark NJ 07101

BOYLE, JOHN WILLIAM, retail executive; b. Darlington, Wis., Feb. 20, 1929; s. John Joseph and Nora Catherine (Whalen) B.; m. Helen Ann Martin, Aug. 11, 1951; children: John, Ann, Ellen, James, Susan, Robert. BBA in Acctg., U. Wis., 1950. CPA, Ill. Staff acct. Arthur Andersen & Co., Chgo., 1953-57, mgr., 1957-63, ptnr., 1963-72; exec. v.p. May Dept. Stores Co., St. Louis, 1972-78, vice-chmn., 1978-80, chmn. bd. dirs., 1980-83; sr. v.p. fin. and adminstrn. Jack Eckerd Corp., Clearwater, Fla., 1983—, also bd. dirs. Treas. Senator Jack Danforth Campaigns, St. Louis, 1974-83; bd. dirs. Boys Hope, St. Louis, 1978—, Abilities Rehab. Ctr., Inc., Clearwater, 1986—. Sgt. U.S. Army, 1951-53. Mem. AICPA. Republican. Roman Catholic. Office: Jack Eckerd Corp 8333 Bryan Dairy Rd Largo FL 34647 Mailing: PO Box 4689 Clearwater FL 34618

BOYLE, RICHARD GUY, electronics company executive; b. Preston, Conn., June 10, 1938; s. Charles and Ruth (Porter) B.; m. Muriel F. Maslak, Nov. 4, 1961; children: Kerry Jeanne, Kimberly Ann, Kyle Guy. B.B.A., Western New Eng. Coll., Springfield, Mass., 1965, M.B.A., 1968; A.M.P., Harvard U., 1982. Fin. planning mgr. Hamilton Standard div. UTC, Windsor Locks, Conn., 1961-70; contr. Dunham-Bush subs. Signal Corp., West Hartford, Conn., 1970-76; fin. v.p. Brand-Rex Co. (now BRIntec Corp.), Willimantic, Conn., 1976-79, sr. v.p., 1979-82, exec. v.p., 1982-88, pres., chief exec. officer, 1988—. Served with U.S. Army, 1957-60, Korea. Mem. Fin. Execs. Inst. Club: Harvard Bus. Sch. Home: 127 Grandview Dr Glastonbury CT 06033 Office: Brintec Corp 1600 W Main St Willimantic CT 06226

BOYLE, WALTER OTT, brokerage house executive; b. Louisville, Feb. 8, 1921; s. Lee R. and Rose B. (Burton) B.; m. Margaret E. Turner, Dec. 26, 1942 (dec. July 1969); children: Gerald, Margaret, Patricia; m. Jeannine Louise Fisher, Feb. 4, 1970 (dec. Feb. 1986); children: Lawrence, Nancy, Janice, Scott; m. Bonnie L. Kramer, June 25, 1986; 1 child, Donald. AB, U. Louisville, 1942. Various exec. positions A&P Tea Co., Louisville, Detroit, N.Y.C., 1945-67; v.p. fin. Benner Tea Co., Burlington, Iowa, 1968; sr. v.p. and chief fin. officer Allied Supermarkets, Detroit, 1968-73; sr. v.p., chief fin. officer Penn Fruit Co., Phila., 1974-75; owner Boyle Assoc., Louisville, 1975—. Served to lt. comdr. USN, 1942-45, 1950-52, Korea. Republican. Roman Catholic. Home and Office: 503 Cheskirk Pl Louisville KY 40243

BOYLE, WILLIAM PICKARD, JR., food company executive; b. N.Y.C., Mar. 21, 1933; s. William Pickard and Jane (McKennan) B.; m. Patricia Ann Schrock, July 14, 1962; children: William Pickard III, Katharine McKennan. BS, Cornell U., 1955, MBA, 1956. Sales supr. Pillsbury Co., Mpls., 1958-60; sales rep. Flint Ink Corp., Detroit, 1960-63; with J.M. Smucker Co., Orrville, Ohio, 1963—, v.p. mktg., 1972-81, sr. v.p., pres. internat. div., 1981—. 1st lt. U.S. Army, 1956-58. Mem. N.Am. Soc. Corp. Planning, Am. Mktg. Assn., Communicators Club. Republican. Home: 12 Public Sq Medina OH 44256 Office: J M Smucker Co Strawberry Ln Orrville OH 44667

BOYLES, WILLIAM RAY, JR., shipbuilding company executive; b. Detroit, May 20, 1948; s. William Ray and Pauline (Potter) B.; m. Phyllis Diane Fowler, Jan. 16, 1971; children: William, Steven, Robyn, Bryant. Student, Ga. State U., 1968; BBA in Acctg., Ga., 1975. CPA, Ga. Audit sr. Arthur Young & Co., Atlanta, 1975-78; internal auditor Fuqua Industries, Atlanta, 1978-79; contr. Mitchell Steel Co., Nashville, 1979-80; internal audit mgr. Am. Ship Bldg. Co., Tampa, Fla., 1980-83, contr., 1984—. 1st lt. U.S. Army, 1968-73. Mem. AICPA. Republican. Baptist. Home: 4206 Briarberry Ln Tampa FL 33624 Office: Am Ship Bldg Co 2502 Rocky Pointe Rd Tampa FL 33607

BOYNTON, WILLIAM LEWIS, electronic manufacturing company official; b. Kalamazoo, May 31, 1928; s. James Woodbury and Cyretta (Gunther) B.; ed. pub. schs.; m. Kei Ouchi, Oct. 8, 1953. Asst. mgr. Speigel J & R, Kalamazoo, 1947-48; served with U.S. Army, 1948-74, ret., 1974; with Rockwell/Collins div., Newport Beach, Calif., 1974-78, supr. material, 1978-81, coord., 1981-88; supr. coord. Rockwell/CDC, Santa Ana, Calif., 1981—, coord. investment recovery, 1982-86, shipping and material coordinator, 1987-88, material coordinator, 1988, environ. coordinator Rockwell/SPD, Newport Beach, 1988—; mem. faculty Western Mich. U., 1955-58. Trustee Orange County Vector Control Dist., 1980—; mem. adv. panel for bus./econ. devel. Calif. State Legislature, 1979-86. Decorated Bronze Star. Mem. Assn. U.S. Army, Assn. U.S. Army, Non-Commd. Officers Assn., Nat. Mgmt. Assn., Nat. Geog. Soc. Republican. Roman Catholic. Home: 5314 Lucky Way Santa Ana CA 92704 Office: 4311 Jamboree Rd Newport Beach CA 92660

BOYNTON, WYMAN PENDER, retired lawyer; b. Portsmouth, N.H., Oct. 8, 1908; s. Harry Edwin and Helen Catherine (Pender) B.; m. Mildred Elizabeth Ballard, Feb. 1, 1935; children: Elizabeth Ballard Boynton Larsen. BS, MIT, 1931; LLB, U. Mich. 1936. Bar: N.H. 1936, U.S. Dist. Ct. 1946; registered profl. engr. With C.E. Walker & Co., 1931-33; jr. acct. J. Ben Hart, 1934; mem. Jeremy R. Waldron, 1936-39, Waldron & Boynton and successors Boynton, Waldron, Doleac, Woodman & Scott, P.A., Portsmouth, N.H., 1940-86; trustee Portsmouth Coop. Bank, 1946-81, chmn. bd. 1976-81. Asst. scoutmaster, then scoutmaster Boy Scouts Am., 1931-33, mem. troop com. and dist. com. 1936-40, mem. coun. exec. bd. 1951-60, coun. commr., 1953-54, coun. pres. 1957-58; mem. Portsmouth Athenaeum, N.H. Hist. Soc., Soc. for Preservation of New Eng. Antiquities; trustee Portsmouth Hist. Soc., 1940-86, v.p., 1946-85, 87—, pres., 1985-87; trustee Mark H. Wentworth Home for Chronic Invalids, 1948-81, pres. 1950-81; pres. Chase Home for Children, 1950-77, trustee 1946—; trustee Portsmouth YWCA, 1949-70; pres. Portsmouth Athenaeum, 1977-80; trustee Portsmouth Pub. Libr., 1955-70; trustee N.H. Indsl. Sch., Manchester, 1955-66, chmn. 1958-66; mem. Portsmouth Spl. Water Com., 1958-62; mem. Portsmouth City Mgr. Charter Com., 1947-49; mem. N.H. Hos. of Reps., 1933-34; mem. Portsmouth City Coun., 1937-38; county atty. Rockingham County, 1947-50; mem. Portsmouth Sch. Bd., 1954-58, 62-70; del. Rep. Nat. Conv., Chgo., 1952; mem. N.H. Constl. Conv., 1974. Commd. 2d lt. USAR, 1931 C.E., U.S. Army, 1940-45, ETO; col. res., 1945-61. Decorated Bronze Star; recipient Silver Beaver award Daniel Webster Council Boy Scouts Am., 1958, Portsmouth C. of C. Community Svc. award, 1978. Mem. ABA, N.H. Soc. Profl. Engrs., NSPE, N.H. Land Surveyors Assn., Soc. Am. Mil. Engrs. Republican. Congregationalist. Clubs: Rotary (Paul Harris award 1985), Wentworth Fairways, Pease AFB Golf. Home: 668 Middle St Portsmouth NH 03801

BOYS, GEORGE WARING, investment counselor; b. Charlotte, N.C., June 12, 1938; s. George W. and Muriel (Dole) B.; m. Elizabeth Carpenter; child: Elizabeth. BS, N.C. State U., Raleigh, 1960; postgrad., NYU, 1962. Account. exec. Smith Barney, N.Y.C. and Charlotte, 1962-70; v.p. Loomis-Sayles and Co., Boston, 1970-77; pres. G. Waring Boys Co. Inc. (now Boys, Arnold & Co. Inc.), Asheville, N.C., 1977—. Mem. Fin. Analysts Fedn., N.C. Soc. Fin. Analysts, Investment Co. Inst. Republican. Episcopal. Office: Boys Arnold & Co Inc PO Drawer 5255 Asheville NC 28813

BOYSEN, LARS, bank executive; b. Vejle, Denmark, Aug. 23, 1948; came to U.S., 1975; s. Svenn and Erna (Thomsen) B.; m. Mary E. Arnold, June 7, 1986. BS in Bus. Adminstrn., The Aarhus Sch. Bus., Denmark, 1973, MS in Econs., 1975; postgrad., U. Wash., 1981-82. Mktg. research analyst Santa Fe Fed., San Bernardino, Calif., 1975-77, mktg. research mgr., 1977-79, v.p., mktg. dir., 1979-81; v.p., office adminstrn. mgr. Pacific Fed. Savs. & Loan Assn., Costa Mesa, Calif., 1981-82; v.p., human resources and corp. research dir. Pacific Savs. Bank, Costa Mesa, 1982-86, sr. v.p. corp. services, 1986—. Recipient First award The Advt. Club, Los Angeles, 1979, Andy award of merit The Advt. Club, N.Y.C., 1980. Mem. Calif. League Savs. and Loan Assns. (human resources). Office: Pacific Savs Bank 1901 Newport Blvd Costa Mesa CA 92927

BOYSEN, MELICENT PEARL, finance company executive; b. Houston, Dec. 1, 1943; d. William Thomas and Mildred Pearl (Walker) Richardson; m. Stephen M. Boysen, Sept. 10, 1961 (dec. 1973); children: Marshella, Stephanie, Stephen. Student, Cen. Mo. State, 1973-75. Owner, pres. Boysen Enterprises, Kansas City, Mo., 1973—, Boysen Agri-Services, Kansas City, 1984—; fin. cons., underwriter New Eng. Life Ins. Co., Kansas City, 1978-81; cons. San Luis Rey (Calif.) Tribal Water Authority, Wind River (Wyo.) Reservation, Cheyenne River (S.D.) Sioux, Iroquois Nations (N.Y.) 1983—; bd. dirs. Visible Horizons 1987—. Founding bd. dirs. Rose Brooks Ctr. battered women, Kansas City, 1979—, treas., 1979-81. Mem. Internat. Fin. Planners Assn., Internat. Agri-Bus. Assn., DAR, Kans. C. of C. and Industry, Kansas City C. of C. Republican. Methodist. Office: Boysen Enterprises PO Box 9104 Shawnee Mission KS 66201

BOZE, FRED ADWELL, pharmaceutical company executive; b. Suffolk, Va., Feb. 28, 1946; s. Fred Adwell Jr. and Isabell (Mathews) B.; m. Linda Jones (div. Aug. 1982); m. Susan Seagle, May 4, 1984; 1 child: Carolyn Elizabeth. AS in Engring., Chowan Coll., 1964-66; BS in Math. Edn., Old Dominion U., 1970. Tchr. Norfolk (Va.) City Schs., 1970-71, Deep Creek High Sch., Chesapeake, Va. 1971-72; mgmt. trainee Peoples Drug Store, Norfolk, 1972-74, asst. mgr., 1974-75, mngr. technician, 1975-88; sales mgr. Metro Restaurant Equipment Co., Norfolk, 1988-89; exec. Freddy's RX, Hampton, Va., 1989—. Mem. Kiwanis (bd. dirs., sec. local chpt. 1979-80, bd. dirs. 1983-86, v.p. 1983-84, pres. Norfolk chpt. 1984-85). Republican. Episcopalian. Home: 482 Cranston Ln Virginia Beach VA 23452

BOZZONE, ROBERT P., steel company executive; b. 1933; married; 3 children. BS, Rensselaer Poly Tech. Inst., 1955. With Allegheny Ludlum Steel Corp., Pitts., 1955—, former v.p., gen. mgr., former exec. v.p., gen. mgr., now pres., chief operating officer, from 1985, also bd. dirs. Office: Allegheny Ludlum Steel Corp 1000 6th PPG Pl Pittsburgh PA 15222 *

BRACEWELL, ROBERT EDWARD LEE, telecommunication satellite company executive; b. Citronelle, Ala., June 4, 1930; s. Robert Edward Lee and Opal (Hinton) B.; m. Sue Ann Alldredge, Apr. 1960 (div. Aug. 1974); m. Margaret Susan Griggs, Apr. 9, 1977; children: Robert Edward Lee III, Victoria Teresa, Jenifer Diana, Steven Bradley. Student U. Ala., 1953-54, Springhill Coll., 1954-55, Tulane U., 1955-56. Dir. comml. systems Brown Engring. (Teledyne), Huntsville, Ala., 1963-67; computer application engr. Gen. Electric Co., Huntsville, 1965-67; program mgr. Sperry Univac, Blue Bell, Pa., 1967-73; dir., sr. v.p. Internat. Computers Plc, London, 1973-79; exec. v.p. Internat. Computers, Falls Church, Va., 1979-81; asst. v.p. Am. Satellite Co., Rockville, Md., 1981-84; program mgr. IBM Corp., McLean, Va., 1985—; vis. lectr. U. Mo., 1970-71, U. Edinburgh, 1976; cons. Govt. of N.Z., 1976-77, Province of Alta., Can., 1980. Author: Project Management, 1975; designer on-line prodn. and inventory control for paper industry, 1962, optical computer input, 1966. With U.S. Army, 1949-52, Korea. Decorated Bronze Star, Purple Heart (4). Mem. Brit. Computer Soc. (assoc.), Masons. Republican. Methodist.

BRACKEN, GARY K., controller; b. Worland, Wyo., July 29, 1939; s. Carl A. and Betty G. (Groven) B.; m. Dorothy V., Dec. 30, 1961; children: Carlee, Kevin. BS, Mont. State U., 1961. CPA, Colo. Acct. Peat, Marwick, Main, Billings, Mont., 1964-69; v.p., controller Tele-Communications Inc., Denver, 1969—. Office: Tele-Communications Inc 22595 Wellshire Sta Denver CO 80222

BRACKENRIDGE, ELOISE WILSON, industrial communications consultant; b. Taylor, Tex., Oct. 22, 1939; d. John Adams III and Eloise (Wilson) B. BFA in Communications, U. Tex., 1961, MA in Communications, 1969. Fgn. service staff officer U.S. Dept. State, Washington, 1961-66; campaign aide Rep. George Bush, Houston, 1970; communications cons. Austin (Tex.), Houston, and Washington, 1970-73; pub. relations mgr. Tex. Internat. Airlines, Houston, 1973-75; communications mgr. Dresser Industries Inc., Houston, 1975-83; v.p. corp. communications CRS Sirrine Inc., Houston, 1983-86; indsl. communications cons. Houston, 1986—; mng. ptnr. Brackenridge and Eilert, Houston and Austin, 1972—; bd. dirs. Hobby Community Bank, Houston. Author: Mota Bonita, 1979; editor: Anthology of Communication Theory, 1967; prod. and dir. ednl. and indsl. film series, 1970-73; contbr. articles to profl. jours. Mem. selection bd. USIA, Washington, 1971; active Houston Council Performing Arts, Houston Econ. Devel. Forum; patron Houston Jr. League, 1974—. Recipient Meritorious Honor award U.S. Dept. State, 1964, Best Nat. Trade Show Exhibit award U.S. Trade Show Assn., 1982, Nat. Excellence award Soc. Mktg. Profl. Services, 1985, numerous awards for advt. and speaking. Mem. Internat. Platform Assn., Phi Kappa Phi, Alpha Epsilon Rho. Republican. Episcopalian. Club: Houston Forum. Home: 3524 Greystone Dr #199 Austin TX 78731

BRACKETT, RONALD E., lawyer; b. Rockford, Ill., May 10, 1942; s. F. Earl Brackett and Anne (Christenberry) Townsend; m. Susan Carol Tucker, June 11, 1966 (div. June 1972); m. Susan Catherine Stichnoth, May 31, 1975; 1 child, Charles William. BA, Trinity Coll., 1964; JD, U. Mich., 1967. Bar: N.Y. 1968. Assoc. Rogers & Wells, N.Y.C., 1968-74, ptnr., 1974—; bd. dirs. King Kullen Grocery Co. Inc., Westbury, N.Y. Mem. ABA, N.Y. State Bar Assn., Phi Beta Kappa. Republican. Presbyterian. Office: Rogers & Wells 200 Park Ave Pan Am Bldg New York NY 10166

BRACY, MICHAEL BLAKESLEE, energy company executive; b. St. Louis, Dec. 13, 1941; s. Webb B. and Jane (Blakeslee) B.; m. Ella Bingham Cox, June 13, 1970. B.S. in Engring. Physics, U.S. Naval Acad., 1963. With Chase Manhattan Bank, N.A., N.Y.C., 1969-77, v.p. public utilities div., 1973-77; with El Paso Co., Houston, 1977-84, v.p., 1979-84, sr. v.p., 1979-84, chief fin. officer, 1979-84; exec. v.p. fin. and adminstrn. Arkla Inc., 1984-88; pres. Arkla Pipeline Group, 1988—. Served as officer USN, 1963-69. Mem. Fin. Execs. Inst. Clubs: N.Y. Athletic; City Midday (N.Y.C.); Shreveport Country, Southern Trace Country, University, Cambridge (Shreveport, La.). Office: Arkla Inc PO Box 21734 Shreveport LA 71151

BRADBURY, JOHN DANIELS, b. N.Y.C., Apr. 9, 1941; s. Warren Ball and Mary Elizabeth (Brennemann) B.; AB, Harvard U., 1963; m. Judith Barrett Horowitz, July 17, 1969; children—Douglas, Mitchell, Kristin, Andrew. Ptnr. W.B. Bradbury Co., N.Y.C., 1963-74; pres., owner Mil. Media Inc., N.Y.C., 1974—. Pres., Bentley Sch. PTA, 1972-73; sec. 257 Cen. Park W. Inc., 1980-82; vice chmn. Phillips Exeter Fund Raising Campaign for Manhattan, 1980. Mem. Am. Logistics Assn., Nat. Assn. Pubs. Reps., The Chief Execs. Officers Club. Club: Harvard of N.Y.C. Office: Mil Media Inc 2109 Broadway New York NY 10023

BRADDOCK, RICHARD S., banker; b. Oklahoma City, Nov. 30, 1941; s. Robert L. and Mary Alice (Krueger) B.; m. Susan Schulte, Feb. 14, 1978; 1 child, Christina; children by previous marriage: Jennifer, Richard, Derek. B.A., Dartmouth Coll., 1963; M.B.A., Harvard Bus. Sch., 1965. Mktg. staff General Foods, White-Plains, N.Y., 1965-73; staff Citicorp, N.Y.C., from 1973, now sector exec. in charge of worldwide consumer fin. services, info. bus., investor relations, corp. pub. affairs, customer affairs, corp. advt., also bd. dirs.; bd. dirs. Visa Internat., Visa USA, San Francisco; bd. dirs. Eastman Kodak. Bd. dirs. Cancer Research Inst., N.Y.C.; mem. Council on Foreign Rels. Office: Citicorp 399 Park Ave New York NY 10043

BRADEN, WILLIAM EDWARD, trading company executive, consultant; b. Milw., Dec. 29, 1919; s. Armond Edward and Eve Ninette (Fuller) B.; AB, Harvard U., 1941; m. Sonoyo Matsuda, Jan. 23, 1950 (dec.); children: Amy, Wythe Edward, Robert Fuller, William Samuel; m. Margaret Peterson Bowen, Oct. 16, 1987. Foreman, Procter & Gamble Mfg. Co., Quincy, Mass., 1941-42; civilian employee War Dept., Changchun, Manchuria, 1946-47; pres. Pacific Projects Ltd., Tokyo, 1948—; pres. Taihei Boeki Co., Ltd., Tokyo, 1955-80, chmn. bd., 1980-86; dir. Ferro Far East Ltd., Hong Kong, Ferro Enamels (Japan) Ltd., Osaka, Nissan Ferro Organic Chem. Co., Ltd., Tokyo, Palace Housing Co., Ltd., Tokyo, Taiwan Longson Co. Ltd., Taipei. Served with AF, USNR, 1943-45. Mem. Am. Japan Soc., Am. C. of C. in Japan, Japan Am. Soc. Honolulu, Pacific and Asian Affairs Council Honolulu (gov. 1984—), Chamber Music Soc. Hawaii (dir. 1984—), Asia Soc. N.Y.C. Clubs: Harvard (N.Y.C., Tokyo, Honolulu); Tokyo Am.; Fgn. Correspondents (Japan) (asso. mem.).

BRADER, JAMES BERNARD, telephone company executive; b. Omaha, Dec. 15, 1933; s. Harry Bernard and Agnes Ellen (Dimmnick) B.; m. Mary Ann Dulacki, Sept. 9, 1961; children: Elizabeth, James II, Anne, Laura, Kristina. Student in Bus. Adminstrn., U. Nebr., Omaha, 1958-62. Craftsman Northwestern Bell Telephone Co., Omaha, 1951-60, engr., 1960-62, traffic chief, 1962-64, supr. facilities, 1966-67, mgr. planning, 1967-77, mgr. tng., 1977-80, mgr. fin., 1980-85, mgr. media relations, 1985—; v.p. ops. Flex-i-pak, Schreveport, La., 1964-66. Sgt. U.S. Army, 1956-60. Mem. Nebr. Press Assn., Omaha Press Club, Nebr. Broadcasters Assn., German/Am. Club. Republican. Roman Catholic. Home: 3617 S 114th St Omaha NE 68144 Office: Northwestern Bell Telephone Co 100 S 19th St Room 1270 Dodge Omaha NE 68102

BRADFORD, BARBARA REED, lawyer; b. Cleve., June 13, 1948; d. William Cochran and Martha Lucile (Horn) B.; m. Warren Neil Davis, Oct. 9, 1976 (separated 1986). BA, Pitzer Coll., 1970; JD, Georgetown U., 1975, MBA, 1985. Bar: N.Y. 1976, D.C. 1976. Staff asst. Sen. Edward M. Kennedy, Washington, 1970-71; assoc. Breed, Abbott & Morgan, N.Y.C., 1975-76, Verner, Liipfert Law Firm, Washington, 1976-78; atty. AID Dept. of State, Washington, 1978-83, atty. trade and devel. program staff, 1986—; pres. Georgetown Export Trading, Inc., Washington, 1984-86. Bd. dirs. Jr. League, Washington, 1977-78. Mem. D.C. Bar Assn., Fed. Bar Assn., Bar of State of N.Y., Potomac Hunt Club. Democrat.

BRADFORD, CHARLES LOBDELL, management consultant; b. Chgo., Apr. 29, 1936; s. Charles Lobdell and Margaret Ann (Gorman) B.; m. Sally Ann Amundson, June 20, 1959; children: Barbara Bruhn, Robert Wesley, Cynthia Amundson. AB, Dartmouth Coll., 1958; MBA, Amos Tuck Sch. Bus. Adminstrn., 1959. Various positions upto sr. v.p. Bradford Paper Co., Holland, Mich., 1959-80; pres., chmn. and chief exec. officer Ctr. for Simplified Strategic Planning, Glen Arbor, Mich., 1981—; seminar instr. at various univs. Author: Simplified Strategic Planning Manual, 1981. Pres. Holland Bd. of Edn., 1968-80, Ottawa Intermediate Sch. Dis., 1970-80. Mem. Planning Forum. Episcopalian. Office: Ctr for Simplified Strategic Planning PO Box 348 Glen Arbor MI 49636

BRADFORD, DENNIS DOYLE, hotel company executive, real estate broker; b. Tulsa, Sept. 5, 1945; s. Doyle Earl and Elta (Price) B.; m. Richie Deloris Dawson. BSBA in Econs., U. Tulsa, 1969. Sales and mktg. rep. Xerox Corp., Oklahoma City, 1969-72; comml. loan officer Mager Mortgage Co., Oklahoma City, 1973-74; pvt. practice real estate Oklahoma City, 1973—; pres., owner Bradford Oil Co., Oklahoma City, 1977-80; pres. Blazer Oil Co., Oklahoma City, 1980—; v.p. Petro So., Inc., Tampa Fla., 1983-84; ptnr. Coachman Inns, Oklahoma City, 1981-86; chmn., pres., chief exec. officer Coachman Inc., Oklahoma City, 1985—; vice chmn. nat. adv. council to SBA, Washington, 1984—; del. White House Conf. on Small Bus., Washington, 1986; bd. dirs. CraftWorld Internat., Inc., Tampa, Okla. Med. Ctr. Found. Mem. Nat. Cowboy Hall of Fame, Okla. Heritage Assn., Okla. County Hist. Soc.,Air Force Assn., Young Pres.'s Organ. Oklahoma City C. of C. Republican. Methodist. Clubs: Oklahoma City Golf and Country; Beacon. Home: 6711 Avondale Dr Oklahoma City OK 73116 Office: Coachman Inc 301 NW 63d St Suite 500 Oklahoma City OK 73116

BRADFORD, MILTON DOUGLAS, insurance company executive; b. Wright, Minn., Sept. 1, 1930; s. Milton T. and Irene J. (Wainer); m. Arlene J. Ryberg, Aug. 31, 1950 (div. 1974) children: Milton A., Douglas D.; m. Eunice H. Nelson, May 10, 1974. AS, Bismarck Coll., 1950. Auditor Provident Life Ins. Co., Bismarck, N.D., 1950-64, controller, 1964-70, v.p., controller, 1970-80, v.p., treas., controller, 1980-87, sr. v.p., treas., 1987—. Republican. Lodges: Masons, Shriners. Home: 1915 Catherine Dr Bismarck ND 58501 Office: Provident Life Ins Co 316 N 5th Bismarck ND 58501

BRADFORD, ROBERT EDWARD, supermarket executive; b. Roanoke, Va., June 27, 1931; s. Miller Hughes and Helen (Gardner) B.; m. Margaret Strader, Dec. 27, 1956 (div. June 1970); children: Joseph Charles, Stephen Frederick; m. Nancy Rourke, Nov. 12, 1970; 1 child, Laura Ann. Grad., Washington and Lee U., 1954. New dir. WMAL Radio and TV, Washington, 1957-58; adminstrv. asst. rep. Richard Poff (Rep.-Va.), Washington, 1958-68; exec. dir. Ill. Rep. Com., Springfield, 1968-71; adminstrv. asst. Senator Bill Brook (Tenn.), Washington, 1971-73; dir. govt. affairs Firestone Tire and Rubber Co., Washington, 1973-77; exec. v.p. Food Mktg. Inst., Washington, 1977-80; pres., chief exec. officer Nat. Restaurant Assn., Washington, 1980-81; sr. v.p. Great A&P Tea Co., Washington, 1981-83, Safeway Stores, Oakland, Calif., 1983—. Bd. dirs. Pub. Affairs Council, Washington, 1983-86, Keep Am. Beautiful, N.Y.C., 1984—, Friends of Arts, San Francisco, 1984—, 2d Harvest, Chgo., 1985—, Nat. Easter Seals Soc., Chgo., 1986—. Served to capt. U.S. Army, 1954-57. Recipient 17 Radio Journalism awards AP, 1954-57; Harvard U. fellow (hon.), 1970-71. Republican. Methodist. Clubs: F St. (Washington); Capitol Hill (Washington); River Bend (Great Falls, Va.).

BRADFORD, ROBERT ERNEST, motion picture producer; b. Berlin; came to U.S., 1946, naturalized, 1953; s. Siegfried and Doris (Herzberg) B.; m. Barbara Taylor, Dec. 24, 1963. Student, Marie Curie Coll., Paris, 1937; A.B., U. Geneva, 1945. Prodn. cons. Distbn. Corp. Am., N.Y.C., 1946-53; exec. v.p. Jesse L. Lasky Prodns., Beverly Hills, Calif., 1953—; exec. v.p., dir. Samuel Bronston Prodns., N.Y.C., 1955—; exec. v.p. Franco London Films Internat., Ltd., Montreal; pres. Franco London Film S.A., Paris, Franco London Music, Ltd., London; head feature prodn., exec. producer Hal Roach Studios, Hollywood, Calif., 1959—; dir. Hy-Ford Prodns., Inc., Hy-Ford Europea, Rome, Jack London Prodns.; lectr. internat. affairs and interracial problems, 1950—; cons., dir. Nat. Found. for Good Govt., 1952; cons. Internat. Study Tour Alliance, 1951—. Producer: John Paul Jones, Walter Bros., 1958, The Scavengers, Hal Roach Studios, 1959, If You Remember Me, 1959-60, The Golden Touch, 1959-60, Simon Bolivar, 1965, To Die of Love, 1971, Sweet Deception, 1972, Impossible Object, 1973, Hold the Dream, 1986, Voice of the Heart, 1988, Act of Will, 1988, To Be The Best, 1989. Pub. relations dir one-world award com. Am. Nobel Anniversary Com. Served with French Intelligence, 1940-45. Recipient citation for outstanding work and civic achievements Greater N.Y. Citizens Forum, 1952. Office: 450 Park Ave New York NY 10022

BRADFORD, WILLIAM EDWARD, JR., publishing company executive; b. Denver, May 11, 1948; s. William Edward and Jean Geddes (Simson) B. BA, Trinity Coll., Hartford, Conn., 1971; MA, New Sch., 1974; MBA, U. Denver, 1976. With Braford-Robinson Printing Co., Denver, 1976-78, v.p., 1978-80; v.p. Bradford Pub. Co., Denver, 1980-84, pres., 1984—. Mem. Nat. Composition Assn., Printing Industries Am., Mountain State Printing Industries, Mountain State Employees Council, Denver C. of C. Club: DAC (Denver). Office: Bradford Pub Co 1743 Wazee St Denver CO 80202

BRADLEY, BETH ANN, printing company representative; b. Ft. Rucker, Ala., Mar. 24, 1963; d. David Bernard and Pamela Jane (Steele) B. BA in English, U. N.H., 1985. Sales rep. Dartmouth Printing Co., Hanover, N.H., 1986—; speaker at pub. seminars. Contbr. articles to profl. publs.; inventor printing implement. Mem. Nat. Abortion Rights Action League; fundraiser Westmonte Recreation Ctr., Altamonte Springs, Fla., 1987—. Mem. Am. Mgmt. Assn., NOW, Fla. Mag. Assn. (com. chair), Toastmasters. Democrat.

BRADLEY, E. MICHAEL, lawyer; b. N.Y.C., Apr. 13, 1939; s. Otis Treat Bradley and Marian Booth (Alling) Ward; m. Judith Allen Thompson, June 29, 1962; children: Jennifer Treat, Michael Thompson, Thomas Alcott, Samuel Allen. BA, Yale U., 1961; LLB, U. Va., 1964. Bar: N.Y., 1965. Assoc. Davis, Polk & Wardwell, N.Y.C., 1964-72; assoc. Brown & Wood, N.Y.C., 1972-73, ptnr., 1974—; lectr. Practicing Law Inst., N.Y.C., 1970-79; 86, Am. Law Inst.-ABA, Phila., 1977-78; arbitrator Am. Arbitration Assn., N.Y.C., 1975—. Contbg. editor: The Use of Experts in Corporate Litigation, 1978, Securites Law Techniques, 1985. Bd. dirs. Bennett Coll. Found., N.Y.C., 1984—; trustee Salisbury (Conn.) Sch., 1987—. Mem. ABA, N.Y. State Bar Assn., Fed. Bar Assn., Assn. Bar City N.Y. Republican. Presbyterian. Clubs: River, Union, Coral Beach, The Downtown Assn., Hillsboro, Quogue Field, Shinnecock Yacht. Home: 888 Park Ave New York NY 10021 Office: Brown & Wood 1 World Trade Ctr New York NY 10048

BRADLEY, JOHN ANDREW, hospital management company executive; b. Hammond, Ind., Aug. 3, 1930; s. Andrew C. and Florence (Wolfe) B.; m. Judith E. Salmi, June 1, 1955; children: John Michael, Kerry Kathleen, Kelly Ann. BS, Loras Coll., 1952; MHA, St. Louis U., 1955, PhD, 1962. Asst. adminstr. Incarnate Word Hosp., St. Louis, 1958-61; with Santa Rosa Med. Ctr., San Antonio, 1961-69; from v.p. to sr. v.p. Am. Medicorp, Inc., San Antonio, 1969-78; with Am. Healthcare Mgmt., Dallas, 1978—, pres., 1978-84, chmn., chief exec. officer, 1985—. Served to capt. AUS, 1953-56. Home: 5611 Harbor Town Dr Dallas TX 75287 Office: Am Healthcare Mgmt 14160 Dallas Pkwy Ste 900 Dallas TX 75240

BRADLEY, KIRK JACKSON, oil company executive; b. Atlanta, Nov. 27, 1962; s. Roger Junie and Patricia Vaughn (Proctor) B. BBA, U. Ga., 1984; MBA, Duke U., 1986. Asst. to pres. Lee-Moore Oil Co., Sanford, N.C., 1985-87, pres., 1987—; pres. Govs. Club Devel. Corp., Chapel Hill, N.C., 1988—; sec./treas. Carolina Trace Properties, Inc., Sanford, 1986-87, chmn. bd. dirs., 1987—; asst. to chmn. The Pantry, Inc., Sanford, 1988—; vice chmn. bd. dirs. First Carolina Bank, Sanford. Named one of Outsanding Young Men Am., 1986. Mem. Country Club of N.C., Carolina Trace Country Club, Ashford Club, Georgian Club, Elks, Moose. Office: Lee-Moore Oil Co Drawer 9 Sanford NC 27330

BRADLEY, LAWRENCE JOHN, trade association executive; b. Phila., Mar. 20, 1957; s. James Daniel and Katherine May (Lambert) B.; m. Nancy Theresa Smargiassi, May 2, 1981; children: Katherine, Nicholas, Larry, Michael. Student, Charles Morris Price Sch., 1978, Rutgers U., 1978-81. Office coordinator Penn-Del-Jersey chpt. Nat. Elec. Contrs. Assn., Phila., 1975-77; dir. edn. Penn-Del-Jersey chpt. Nat. Elec. Contrs. Assn., 1977-80, labor relations rep., 1980-82, asst. dir., 1982-85, exec. dir., 1985—. Chmn. Phila. Crusade campaign Am. Cancer Soc., 1977-78; registered lobbyist, Pa., 1981-88; mem. Elec. Contractors Polit. Action Com. 1st recipient Angelo P. Morella award Poor Richard's Club Phila., 1978. Mem. Internat. Assn. Elec. Inspectors (bd. dirs., exec. bd. ea. sect. 1987-88), Am. Soc. Assn. Execs., Pa.-Jersey-Del.-Md. Elec. Alliance (v.p. govtl. affairs, bd. dirs. 1985-88), Delaware Valley Soc. Assn. Execs., Del. C. of C., Pa. C. of D., Phila. C. of C. Roman Catholic. Club: Congressional (Washington). Home: 47 Appletree Ln Sewell NJ 08080 Office: Penn-Del-Jersey Chpt NECA 336 Suburban Sta Bldg Philadelphia PA 19103

BRADLEY, THOMAS L., sales and marketing executive; b. Clinton, Iowa, Apr. 20, 1946; s. Max J. and Dolores Bradley. BBA, Western Ill. U., 1969. Owner, mgr. Bradco Investments, Belleville, Ill., 1968-74; gen. mgr. Internat. Funding, Denver, 1974-80, Suncatcher, Sacramento, 1980-83; owner, mgr. Colortec Images, San Diego, 1985—, Bradley Internat., Sacramento and San Diego, 1980—; v.p. Realty Group Investments, San Diego, 1986—; owner Bradco Investment Co., 1988—; cons. Artisianes Titicaca, La Paz, Bolivia, 1976-85, Dept. Energy and Land, Sacramento, 1980-82; U.S. liaison Robert Lehrer Exports, Lima, Peru, 1975-84; bd. dirs. Satori Enterprises, San Diego, 1982—, Aries, Denver, 1977-79. Author: Iowa Poems, 1978, Iowa poetry Assn. award, 1978, Starting Business--A Primer, 1985; contbr. articles and photographs to jours. and newsletters. Vol. fund raising Heart Assn., Belleville, Ill., 1970; asst. chmn. Democratic presdl. election, 1972, chmn. voter registration, 1968; chmn. fund raising Photo Products Assn., 1986. Mem. Am. Internat. Mktg. Assn., Northwest Apparel Assn., Calif. Apparel Assn., Midwest Apparel Assn., San Diego Bd. Realtors, San Diego Life Underwriters, Photo Products Assn. (founder 1986). Democrat. Clubs: American Golf, San Diego Golf, Torrey Pines Golf. Lodge: Toastmasters. Home: 3558 6th Ave San Diego CA 92103 Office: Bradley Internat 3558 6th Ave San Diego CA 92103

BRADLEY, WALTER D., real estate broker, owner; b. Clovis, N.M., Oct. 30, 1946; s. Ralph W. and M. Jo (Black) B.; m. Debbie Shelly; children: Tige, Lance, Nicole. Student Eastern N.M. U., 1964-1967. Supr. Tex. Instruments, Dallas; mgr., salesman Nat. Chemsearch, Irving, Tex., Colonial Real Estate, Clovis, 1976; mem. N.Mex. Senate, 1989—. V.p., bd. dirs. Clovis Indsl. Commn., 1983-86, pres. econ. devel., 1987; bd. dirs. United Way, Clovis, 1984-86, Curry County Blood Adv. Bd., Clovis, 1980-85; chmn. Curry County Reps., Clovis, 1984-88; Cosmos Soccer, Clovis, 1984. Mem. Realtors Assn. N.Mex. (v.p., bd. dirs. 1982-85, v.p. 1987-88), Clovis Bd. Realtors (pres. 1982), Clovis C. of C., Curry County Jaycees, N.M. Jaycees. Baptist. Lodge: Lions. Home: 2020 Fairway Terr Clovis NM 88101 Office: Colonial Real Estate PO Box 1154 910 Colonial Parkway Clovis NM 88101

BRADLEY, WILLIAM SUTTON, chemical company executive; b. Buffalo, Feb. 22, 1935; s. Donald Devere and Helen Elizabeth (Sutton) B.; m. Nelly Antonia Johanna van Leeuwen, Sept. 17, 1959; children: Peter, David, Timothy, Michelle. BA, Hamilton Coll., 1956; postgrad., U. Pa., 1956-57. Salesman Comml. Chems. Inc., Buffalo, 1957-58, asst. treas., 1961-68, treas., 1968-72, pres., 1972—; dir. K.N. Aronson Inc., corp. sec. Trustee Medaille Coll., Buffalo, 1981-88; bd. dirs., trustee SUNY Adv. Council, Buffalo, 1987—; pres., bd. dirs. Salvation Army, Buffalo, Evening News Crippled Children's Camp, Buffalo. Lt. U.S. Navy, 1958-61. Mem. Hamilton Coll Alumni Assn. (nat. pres. 1986-88). Republican. Episcopalian. Home: PO Box 53 Getzville NY 14068 Office: Comml Chems Inc 211 Hertel Ave Buffalo NY 14207

BRADSHAW, CHARLES JACKSON, food service company executive; b. 1936. Student, Wofford Coll., 1959. Salesman Pierce Motor Co., 1959-61; pres. Spartan Food Systems Inc., Spartanburg, S.C., 1961-69, chmn. bd., 1969-86; pres., chief operating officer Transworld Corp., 1984-86. Served to lt. AUS. Office: Bradshaw Investments Inc 812 E Main St Spartanburg SC 29302

BRADSHAW, DELMA LEE, accountant, educator; b. Greenville, S.C., Apr. 17, 1950; s. Joseph Napoleon and Mary Ann (Webb) B.; m. Julia Paulette Sellers, Dec. 17, 1970 (div. 1972); m. Patricia Ann Ormand, Aug. 29, 1980; children: Ashley Morgan, Joseph Buckley. BA magna cum laude, Piedmont Coll., 1974. CPA, S.C. Staff acct. Rogers, Brigman & Leach, CPA's, Greenville, 1970-73, Elliot, Davis & Co., CPA's, Greenville, 1974-76; tax specialist Dobson & Dobson, Attys. at Law, Greenville, 1976-78; acctg. mgr. William W. Brown, CPA's, Greenville, 1978-80; pvt. practice in acctg. Greenville, 1980-82; mng. ptnr. Bradshaw, Gordon & Clinkscales, P.A., CPA's, Greenville, 1984—; adj. instr. Greenville Tech. Coll., 1974—; speaker in field. Fellow AICPA, S.C. CPA's (pub. rels. com.), N.C. CPA's. Baptist. Home: 522 Golf Course Rd Piedmont SC 29673 Office: Bradshaw Gordon Clinkscales & Shaw PA CPA's 630 E Washington St Greenville SC 29602

BRADSHAW, HOWARD HOLT, management consulting company executive; b. Phila., Feb. 28, 1937; s. Howard Holt and Imojean (Campbell) B.; m. Loretta Warren Sites, Aug. 13, 1982; children by previous marriage—Elaine Allen, Howard Holt. B.A., Yale U., 1958; postgrad., Duke U., 1958-60. Cert. mgmt. cons. Western Electric Co., various locations, 1960-67; personnel mgr., head behavioral scis. cons. Celanese Fibers Co., Charlotte, N.C., 1967-72; pres. Orgn. Cons., Inc., Charlotte, 1972—; cons. in field. Author: Personal Power, Self Esteem and Performance, 1983; The Management of Self Esteem, 1981; mem. editorial rev. bd. Jour. Mgmt. Issues; contbr. articles to profl. jours. Regional chmn. Constl. Party of Pa., Harrisburg, 1964-66; pres. Coordinated Planning League, Inc., Charlotte, 1972-74; exec. com. Citizens for Effective Govt., Inc., Charlotte, 1987—. Recipient cert. of appreciation Charlotte Police Dept., 1969, Mecklenburg County Com., 1970. Mem. Inst. Mgmt. Cons., Am. Psychol. Assn., Soc. Indsl. and Organizational Psychology, Am. Soc. Tng. and Devel., Orgnl. Devel. Network. Republican. Presbyterian. Home: 3031 Arundel Dr Charlotte NC 28209 Office: Orgn Cons 1913 Charlotte Dr Charlotte NC 28203

BRADSHAW, NANCI MARIE, business executive; b. Schenectady, Aug. 21, 1940; d. Leo Arthur and Angela Bertha (Bonk) Bradshaw; m. William Clayton Hoehn, Oct. 12, 1963 (div. 1979); children: Sharon Ann, Theresa Lynn. BS, Skidmore Coll., 1977. Asst. to pres. Schenectady Indsl. Drafting, 1978-79; bus. exec. math dept. SUNY, Albany, 1979-86, sec. council on acad. freedom and ethics, 1983-85; Evangelist Newspaper, Albany, 1986-89; cons., lectr. trustee, v.p., sec. Help Ctr., Inc., Troy, N.Y., 1982—; lectr., cons. Organizational Mgmt., Albany, Schenectady and Troy, 1984—. Coordinator, originator Pre-Kindergarten PTO, Schenectady, 1976-78, Sunday sch. program Immaculate Conception Ch., Schenectady, 1970-79; mem. Pruyn Cultural Ctr., N.Y. Mem. Nat. Assn. Female Execs., N.Y. Acad. Scis., Math. Assn. Am., Am. Mgmt. Assn. Republican. Roman Catholic. Lodge: Soroptimist Internat. Avocations: refinishing antiques, reading, music, fitness. Home: 157 Maple Ave Troy NY 12180 Office: Albany Cath Press Inc 39 Philip St Albany NY 12207

BRADT, GEORGE EUGENE, leather wholesale company executive; b. Rockwood, N.Y., July 29, 1935; s. Melvin and Edith (Sterling) B. Student, Fulton Montgomery Community Coll., 1980. Leather grader Fowes Bros. & Co., Inc., Gloversville, N.Y., 1962-67; supr. Warden Leathers, Inc., Gloversville, 1967-83; corp. pres. G. Levor & Co., inc., Gloversville, 1983—; bd. dirs. Neal & Morey Leather Co., Gloversville. Mem. exec. com. Fulton County Rep. Com., Gloversville, 1984—; bd. advisor Salvation Army, Gloversville, 1985—; pres. Rockwood Rural Cemetery Assn., Johnstown, Y.Y., 1978—; chmn. Town of Ephratah Rep. Com., Johnstown, 1984—; mem. coun. Boys Scouts Am., Gloversville, 1987—; active Fulton County Rep. Club. With N.Y. N.G., 1953-62. Mem. Fulton County Pilots Assn. (treas. 1989). Home: RD 2 Rt 10 Johnstown NY 12095 Office: G Levor & Co Inc PO Box 866 Gloversville NY 12078

BRADY, DAVID GENE, electronics executive; b. Mpls., May 29, 1942; s. Gene W. and Joan C. (Burke) B.; m. Joan F. Goodoien, Sept. 14, 1962; children: Cathrine, Mark, Jennifer. Student, U. Minn., 1961-63, Rockford Coll., 1971-72. Indsl. engr. Donaldson Co., Mpls., 1962-66, Univac Inc., Mpls., 1966-67, Honeywell Inc., Mpls., 1967-69; engring. mgr. Arnold Engring. Inc., Marengo, Ill., 1969-73; dir. mfg. Magnetic Controls Inc., Mpls., 1973-84; v.p. ops. Moniterm Inc., Mpls., 1984—. Served to cpl. USMC, 1960-67. Mem. Paradigm. Republican. Baptist. Office: Moniterm Inc 5740 Green Circle Dr Minnetonka MN 55343

BRADY, GEORGE MOORE, JR., real estate executive, mortgage banker; b. Balt., Aug. 6, 1922; s. George Moore and Ellen Latimer (Atkinson) B.; BA, Johns Hopkins U., 1947; JD, U. Md., 1949; m. Maria Nomita von Barby, Dec. 3, 1971; children by previous marriage: Elizabeth Grant Brady Andrews, Frances Relyea Brady Siegler, Ellen Atkinson Brady Glaessner, George Moore, Madeleine Vaughn, Richard Grant. Sr. v.p. The Rouse Co., Columbia, Md., 1950-70; chmn. bd. Rouse-Wates, Columbia, 1970-72; pres., chief exec. officer Nat. Corp. for Housing Partnerships, Washington, 1972-87; ret. 1988, bd. dirs. The Rouse Co., First Am. Bank, NA, washington, Enterprise Social Investment Corp., Pre Nat. Corp. for Housing Partnerships. Mem. Md. State Planning Commn., 1980—; chmn. Ptnrs. for Livable Places; bd. dirs. Nat. Housing Conf. With U.S. Army. Decorated Purple Heart. Mem. Sovereign Mil. Order of Malta So. Assn. Clubs: Metropolitan (Washington); Chevy Chase (Md.).

BRADY, GUY, JR., agricultural export sales executive; b. Miller, Ark., Sept. 23, 1946; s. Guy Sr. and Lucy Elma (Fox) B.; m. Rochelle Christi Ford, Apr. 15, 1971 (div. Sept. 1982); 1 child, Rebecca Lynn. BS, U. Ark., 1970, MS in Econs., 1972. Grain mcht. Goodpasture, Inc., Houston, 1972-79; export grain mcht. Interstate Grain Corp., Houston, 1979-86, exec. v.p., 1986—. Home: 2122 Park York Dr #7 Katy TX 77450

BRADY, JAMES JOSEPH, publisher; b. Bronx, N.Y., Feb. 14, 1949; s. Francis Thomas and Catherine Veronica (Quinn) B.; m. Mary Jane Miceli, May 2, 1971. BBA, CCNY, 1971. Salesman, mktg. rep. Sun Oil Co., 1971-83, Noxell Corp., 1971-83, Honeywell Corp., 1971-83; licensee Burroughs Corp., 1983—; publisher Community Pride Publs., 1986—; local newspaper columnist, 1985—; commentator weekly radio program Brady On Business, 1985—; cons. in field. Trustee Our Lady of Sorrows Roman Catholic Ch., Mercerville, N.J., 1987—. Princeton C. of C. (small bus. council 1987). Office: Community Pride Publs CN 5245 Princeton NJ 08543

BRADY, JAMES THOMAS, accounting company executive; b. N.Y.C., July 11, 1940; s. James Joseph and Beatrice (Condon) B.; m. Francine Palermo, Nov. 5, 1966; children: James Mark, Linda Elizabeth. BBA, Iona Coll., 1962. CPA, N.Y. Staff auditor Arthur Andersen & Co., N.Y.C., 1962-63, 65-69, audit mgr., 1969-75, audit ptnr., 1975-76; audit ptnr. Arthur Andersen & Co., Melville, N.Y., 1976-78; mng. ptnr. L.I. Arthur Andersen & Co., Melville, 1978-85; mng. ptnr. Balt. Arthur Andersen & Co., 1985—. Trustee Iona Coll., New Rochelle, N.Y., 1983—; pres. pub. policy Greater Balt. Com., 1988, Huntington (N.Y.) Arts Council, 1981-83; chair Inroads of Balt., 1985—, L.I. Coalition for Fair Broadcasting, 1983-85; sr. co-chair NCCJ Md. Region, Balt., 1988—. With U.S. Army, 1963-65. Mem. Am. Inst. CPA's, Md. Assn. CPA's, N.Y. State Soc. CPA's, Iona Coll. Alumni Assn. (Doyle Award 1983), Hillendale Country Club (Phoenix, Md.). Democrat. Roman Catholic. Home: 10631 Pot Spring Rd Cockeysville MD 21030 Office: Arthur Andersen & Co 201 N Charles St Baltimore MD 21201

BRADY, NICHOLAS FREDERICK, secretary of the treasury; b. N.Y.C., Apr. 11, 1930; s. James C. and Eliot (Chace) B.; m. Katherine Douglas, Sept. 5, 1952; children: Nicholas Frederick, Christopher D., Anthony N., Katherine C. B.A., Yale U., 1952; M.B.A., Harvard U., 1954. With Dillon, Read & Co., Inc., N.Y.C., 1954-82, chmn., chief exec. officer, 1982—; dir., chmn. exec. com. Purolator Courier Corp., Inc., Basking Ridge, N.J., 1983—; appointee to U.S. Senate from N.J. to fill unexpired term of Harrison Williams 1982, resigned, Dec. 1982; secretary Dept. of the Treasury, Washington, 1988—; dir. Bessemer Securities Corp., Doubleday & Co., Ga. Internat. Corp., Wolverne World Wide Inc., ASA Ltd., Media Gen. Inc., NCR Corp. Trustee assoc. Boys' Club Newark.; Reagan appointee MX missile devel. options panel, Central Am. Study Commn., 1983. Clubs: Bond (N.Y.C.), Lunch (N.Y.C.) (bd. govs.), Links (N.Y.C.). Office: Treasury Dept 15th & Pennsylvania Aves NW Washington DC 20220 *

BRADY, PEGGY JOE, oil company executive, consultant; b. Grimsley, Tenn., May 24, 1941; d. Paul Earl and Daisy Elease (Demonbreun) Stults; m. Robert Collins Whited, Oct. 9, 1959 (dec. July 1975); children—Paula Diane, Robert Wayne, Wesley Dale (dec.); m. James Dexter Brady, Mar. 10, 1984. A.B., U. Tenn., 1972-73. Insp. Colonial Mfr., Jamestown, Tenn., 1957-60; clk. Frisch's, Inc., Dayton, Ohio, 1960-64, Tenn. Dept. Pub. Health, Nashville, 1967-69; acct. Tenn. Dept. Safety, Nashville, 1969-73; service rep. IRS, Nashville, 1973-74; pvt. practice acctg., Crossville, Tenn., 1977-79; exec. asst. Vol. Energy, Inc., Crossville, 1979-82; owner Brady Enterprises; corp. officer H. Stonewell Service, Inc., Crossville, 1982—; cons. to oil and gas industries. Com mem. Young Democrats, Nashville, 1967-69; officer/del. PTA, Nashville, 1966-68; counselor Wautauga council Boy Scouts Am., 1968-69; bd. dirs. Community Action Services, Cumberland, 1985-86, 86-87, 87-88; advisor Am. Inst. for Cancer Research, 1984. Mem. Tenn. Oil and Gas Assn., Nat. Assn. Female Execs. Club: Order Eastern Star. Office: Harold Stonewell Svc Inc PO Box 2768 Hwy 127 Crossville TN 38557 also: Brady Enterprises Hwy 127 PO Box 2646 Crossville TN 38557

BRADY, ROBERT LINDSAY, publisher; b. Titusville, Pa., July 3, 1946; s. Francis J. and Dorothy (Lindsay) B.; m. Margaret Schmidt, July 30, 1977; 1 child, Lindsay Louise. BA, U. Notre Dame, 1971; JD, U. Conn., 1978. Bar: Conn. 1980. Mng. editor Official Assoc. Press Almanac, Essex, Conn., 1971-74; v.p. editorial Inst. for Mgmt., Old Saybrook, Conn., 1974-78; pres., pubs. Bus. and Legal Reports Inc., Madison, Conn., 1978—. Author: Law for Personnel Managers, 1981, Employment at Will, 1986, Before You Say: You'll Have to Go, 1986; editor in chief Personnel Mgrs. Legal Reporter, 1978—, What to Do About Personnel Problems, 1985—. Served with U.S. Army, 1968-70. Mem. Conn. Bar Assn., Am. Soc. Personnel Adminstrs. Office: Bus & Legal Reports 64 Wall St Madison CT 06443

BRADY, THOMAS DENIS, controller; b. Prescott, Ariz., June 2, 1955; s. Ormond Denis and Mary (Mei) B.; m. Kimberley Jo Huber, Apr. 21, 1978. BSBA, Ariz. State U., 1977, BS in Fin., 1983. Lic. real estate agt., Ariz., ins. agt. Ariz. Controller Twin Knolls Market, Inc., Mesa, Ariz., 1977-81; ins. agt. William Kirkendale & Assocs., Phoenix, Ariz., 1981; supr. accounts receivable dept. Associated Grocers Ariz., Phoenix, 1981-84; asst. controller SW Restaurant Systems, Inc., Tempe, Ariz., 1984-86; controller, treas. SW Restaurant Systems, Inc., Tempe, 1986—; bd. dirs., treas. Dobbins Enterprises, Durable Products Inc., United Comml. Realty, Inc.; controller, treas., Canyon Provisions, Inc., Tempe, 1986—, also bd. dirs. Active Dennis DeConcini for U.S. Senate campaign, 1976. Mem. Nat. Restaurant Assn., Ariz. Restaurant Assn., Mesa-Tempe-Chandler Bd. Realtors, Scottsdale Bd. Realtors. Democrat. Roman Catholic. Home: 3440 E Edgewood Ave Mesa AZ 85204 Office: SW Restaurant Systems 1979 E Broadway Rd Suite 3 Tempe AZ 85282

BRAFF, HOWARD, brokerage house executive, financial analyst; b. Bklyn., July 18, 1952; s. Emanuel and Rose (Schlamberg) B.; m. Cindi Louise Sansone, Mar. 25, 1975; 1 child, Shana. BA in Math. and Psychology summa cum laude, Hofstra U., 1974, MBA in Fin., 1984. Fin. mgr. Save On Oil, Inc., Merrick, N.Y., 1974-83; acct. exec., portfolio mgr., high-tech. and health care ind. analyst Laidlaw, Adams & Peck, Inc., Westbury, N.Y., 1983-86; ind. investment adv. Merrick, 1977-83; account exec., portfolio mgr. high tech and health care industry analyst Investors Ctr. Inc., Farmingdale, N.Y., 1986-87; health care industry analyst, portfolio mgr. Strasbourger Pearson Tulcin Wolff Inc., N.Y.C., 1987-88; br. mgr. Olde Discount Corp., Hicksville, N.Y., 1988—. Mem. Phi Beta Kappa. Home: 1790 Meadowbrook Rd Merrick NY 11566 Office: Olde Discount Corp 267 Old Country Rd Hicksville NY 11801

BRAFFORD, WILLIAM CHARLES, chemical company executive; b. Pike County, Ky., Aug. 7, 1932; s. William Charles and Minnie (Tacket) B.; m. Katherine Jane Prather, Nov. 13, 1954; children—William Charles III, David A. JD, U. Ky., 1957; LLM (fellow), U. Ill., 1958. Bar: Ky. 1957, Ga. 1965, Tax Ct. U.S 1965, Ct. Claims 1965, Ohio 1966, U.S. Ct. Appeals 1966, U.S. Supreme Ct. 1970, Pa. 1973. Trial atty. NLRB, Washington and Cin., 1958-60; atty. Louisville & Nashville R.R. Co., Louisville, 1960-63, So. Bell Telephone Co., Atlanta, 1963-65; asst. gen. counsel NCR Corp., Dayton, Ohio, 1965-72; v.p., sec., gen. counsel Betz Labs., Inc., Trevose, Pa., 1972—; dir. Betz Process Chems., Inc., Betz, Ltd. U.K., Betz Paper Chem. Inc., Betz Energy Chems., Inc., Betz S.A. France, B.L. Chems., Inc., Betz GmbH, Germany, Betz Entec, Inc., Betz Ges. GmbH, Austria, Betz NV Belgium, Betz Sud S.p.A., Italy, Betz Internat. Inc., Betz Europe Inc., Primex Ltd., Barbados. Served as 1st lt. C.I.C. AUS, 1954-56. Mem. Am. Soc. Corp. Secs., Nat. Assn. Corp. Dirs., Atlantic Legal Found. Republican. Presbyterian. Office: Betz Labs Inc 4636 Somerton Rd Trevose PA 19047

BRAGA, DANIEL, management consultant; b. Oporto, Portugal, Feb. 14, 1946; s. Daniel Sr. and Teresa (de Meireles) B.; m. Monika Bäuerle; 1 child, Diana. Grad., Inst. Superieur des Scis. Econs. et Commerciales, Paris, 1979, Ctr. de Perfectionnement aux Affaires, Paris, 1982. Inventory mgr. D.A.F. France, Survilliers, 1970-73; asst. to v.p. ops. Manpower France, Paris, 1973-79; personnel dir. Erom France, Paris, 1980-84; dir. ops. Ordinter, Paris, 1984-85; pvt. practice in mgmt. cons. Paris, 1985—; v.p. Assn. pour la Promotion des Entreprises, La Celle Saint-Cloud, 1985—; bd. dirs. Syndicat des Profls. du Marche du Travail Temporaire Work Services Fedn., Paris, 1985-86. Editor: (newspaper) Permedias; developer fin. software. V.p. Centro de Pesquisas Espaciais, Porto, Portugal, 1966—. Home and Office: 100 Blvd Massena, 75013 Paris France

BRAGER, WALTER S., retired food products corporation executive; b. Kewaunee, Wis., Oct. 20, 1925; s. Walter and Rose (Dorner) B.; m. Lois Jean Park, May 31, 1952; children: Kimberly Ann Brager Erickson, James C., Todd J. BSMechE, U. Wis., 1950, MBA, 1951; cert. exec. devel., Cornell U., 1960. Indsl. engring. mgmt. Oscar Mayer & Co., Madison, Wis., 1951-66, corp. ops. mgr., 1966-71, v.p. East Cen. region, 1971-74, v.p. East Cen. and Southwest regions, 1974-77, v.p. regional mgmt., 1977-78, group v.p. regional mgmt. and ops., 1978, group v.p. regional mgmt., ops. and engring., 1978-80, group v.p. ops. and engring., 1980-85; exec. v.p. Oscar Mayer Foods Corp., Madison, 1985-88, also bd. dirs.; Bd. dirs. Subzero Freezers Co., 1973—. Chmn. Edgewood High Sch. Adv. Bd., Madison, 1968-71; pres., bd. dirs. Wis. AgriBus. Council, Madison, 1971-75; mem. United Way Dane County, div. chmn., 1972-74; mem. United Madison Community Found., chmn., 1981, bd. dirs., 1974-81; mem. indsl. liaison council U. Wis. Coll. Engring., 1980-87. Served with USAF, 1943-46. Recipient Disting. Service award U. Wis. Coll. Engring., 1979. Mem. Wis. Mfrs. and Commerce Assn. (bd. dirs., exec. com. 1977-79), Madison C. of C. (bd. dirs., v.p. 1971-74), Bascom Hill Soc. Republican. Roman Catholic. Clubs: Madison, Nakoma Country (bd. dirs. 1969-72) (Madison); Maple Bluff Country, Lakeway Yacht and Country. Home and Office: 821 Sunfish St Austin TX 78734

BRAGG, GEORGE LEE, computer company executive; b. Ada, Okla., Aug. 24, 1932; s. George Lee and Delza E. (Thompson) B.; m. Mary Ann Elizabeth Underwood, Jan. 30, 1958; children: Daniel L., David E., James S., Julie A. B.S. in Bus. Adminstrn., Pepperdine U., 1954; postgrad., Free U. Berlin, W. Ger., 1957-58, U. So. Calif., 1965, UCLA, 1968. Exec. dir. corp. devel. N.Am Aviation, Rockwell, El Segundo, Calif., 1959-71; founder, pres. Dawson & Bragg, Inc., Los Angeles, 1971-73; dir. bus. devel. Collins Radio Co., Dallas, 1973-74; v.p. corp. devel. Memorex Corp., Santa Clara, Calif., 1974-81; pres., chief exec. officer Telex Computer Products, Inc. (subs. The Telex Corp.), Tulsa, 1981-88; chmn. Telex Computer Products, Inc., Tulsa, 1984-88; pres., chief operating officer The Telex Corp., Tulsa, 1986-88; pres. Memorex Telex N.V., Tulsa, 1988—, also bd. dirs., adv. bd. Bd. advisors Literacy and Evangelism Internat., Tulsa, 1983—; mem. So. Growth Policies Bd., Raleigh, N.C., 1986—, Tulsa C. of C., 1983—; bd. dirs. Okla. Sci. and Tech. Council, 1985—, Philbrook Art Mus., Tulsa, 1986—, Arts and Humanities Council, Tulsa, 1985—; chmn. Univ. Ctr., Tulsa, 1987—; bd. govs. Okla. Christian Coll.; mem. commn. on the Future of the South, 1986. Served with U.S. Army, 1955-56. Mem. Gov's Corp. Execs. Okla., Tulsa Econ. Devel. Found., Computer and Communications Industry Assn. (exec com.). Republican. Presbyterian. Office: Memorex Telex 6422 E 41st St Tulsa OK 74135

BRAGG, MICHAEL ELLIS, lawyer; b. Holdrege, Nebr., Oct. 6, 1947; s. Lionel C. and Frances E. (Klinginsmith) B.; m. Nancy Jo Aabel, Jan. 19, 1980; children: Brian Michael, Kyle Christopher. BA, U. Nebr., 1971, JD, 1975. Bar: Alaska 1976, U.S. Dist. Ct. Alaska 1976, Nebr. 1976, U.S. Dist. Ct. Nebr. 1976. Assoc. White & Jones, Anchorage, 1976-77; field rep. State Farm Ins., Anchorage, 1977-79, atty. corp. law dept., Bloomington, Ill., 1979-81, sr. atty., 1981-84, asst. counsel, 1984-86, counsel dept. corp. law, 1986-88; asst. v.p., counsel gen. claims dept. State Farm Fire and Casualty Co., 1988—; lectr., contbr. legal seminars. Contbr. articles to legal and ins. jours., also regional editor various publs. Bd. dirs. Friends of Arts, Bloomington, 1984-85, McLean County Crime Prevention Com., 1988—; pres. McLean County Crime Detection Network, 1988—. Served with USNG, 1970-76. Mem. ABA (vice chmn. property ins. com. 1986—, corp. counsel and antitrust coms., various offices tort and ins. practices sect. 1986—), Am. Corp. Counsel Assn., Internat. Platform Assn., Def. Rsch. Inst. Republican. Unitarian. Club: Crestwicke Country. Office: State Farm Ins Cos 112 E Washington Ste 12N Bloomington IL 61701

BRAGINTON-SMITH, BRIAN S., marketing professional; b. Hyannis, Mass., May 23, 1953; s. John Desmond and Dorothy Rose (Intraversato) B.; m. Beth-Ellen Braginton-Smith (div. Apr. 86); 1 child, Bret Alexander. Student, Capecod Community Coll., 1972-73, Suffolk U., 1975-76, Bryant Coll., 1976-77. Sales rep. Dalton Assoc. Inc., Cumberland, R.I., 1976-77, M. Brown Inc., Boston, 1977-79; pres. Braginton-Smith Assoc., Ashland, Mass., 1979-86; ea. regional mktg. mgr. Hag Inc., Greensboro, N.C., 1986-87; pres. Utilitech Inc., Yarmouth Port, Mass., 1987—; cons. Hag USA, Greensboro, N.C., 1986-88, Wolff Wire Corp., Luddington, Mich., 1988—. Author: Computer Child, 1988; contbr. articles to profl. jours. Inventor Programate, 1984. Active Parade com., Cumberland, R.I., 1986; active Yarmouth Port (Mass.) Hist. Soc., 1987. Fellow Rotary Internat. Home: 112 Freeboard Ln Yarmouthport MA 02675

BRAHA, THOMAS I., business executive; b. Austin, Tex., Sept. 3, 1947; s. Jacob and Valentine (Capone) B.; m. Nancy Elizabeth Rowe, Mar. 31, 1973; children—Nancy Elizabeth, Jeanne Valentine, Travis Ian. B.S.M.E., U. Tex., 1969; M.B.A., Temple U., 1971; postgrad., N.Y. U., 1971-73. Engr. Davis Electronics, Inc., Austin, 1967, Whirlpool Corp., Evansville, Ind., 1968; project engr. ITE Imperial Corp., Phila., 1969-71; sr. supply analyst Mobil Oil Corp., N.Y.C., 1971-74; pres. Western Hemisphere Bulk Oil (U.S.A.), Inc., N.Y.C., 1974-75; pres., chief exec. officer Braha Oil Inc., Braha Oil Ltd., Braha Oil B.V., Braha Estates, Inc., Braha Farms, Braha Profit and Pension Trusts. Mem. Am. Mgmt. Assn., ASME, Inst. Petroleum (U.K.), Nat. Petroleum Refining Assn., Am. Petroleum Inst. Office: Braha Holding Co PO Box 787 Bryn Mawr PA 19010

BRAITHWAITE, RALPH RHEY, executive search consultant; b. Manchester, Conn., Nov. 30, 1946; s. Harold Rhey and Constance Marie (Kelly) B.; divorced, 1972; children: Aimee Elizabeth, Richard Rhey; m. Elizabeth P. Taylor, Dec. 7, 1985. BA in Psychology, Cen. Conn. State Coll., 1973, MS in Counseling, 1974; MBA in Organizational Behavior, U. Hartford, Conn., 1981. Dir. vet. affairs Manchester (Conn.) Community Coll., 1973-78, mem. adj. faculty psychology, 1974-79; devel. cons. U. Hartford, 1979-82, mem. adj. faculty, 1979—; devel. cons. Cigna Corp., Bloomfield, Conn., 1982-85; prin. Deane, Howard & Simon Inc., Hartford, 1985—. With U.S. Army, 1966-70. Mem. Am. Mktg. Assn., Am. Soc. Tng. and Devel., Instrument Soc. Am., Organzational Devel. Network. Office: Deane Howard & Simon 81 Wethersfield Ave Hartford CT 06114

BRALICH, RICHARD ALLEN, industrial company executive; b. Sharon, Pa., Dec. 27, 1957; s. Joseph Thomas and Mary Dorothy (Mason) B. BA cum laude, Westminster Coll., New Wilmington, Pa., 1979; postgrad. bus. adminstrn., U. Pitts., 1987—. CPA, Ohio, Pa. Sr. acct. Hill, Barth & King, CPA's, Youngstown, Ohio, 1979-82; contr. PBI Investments, West Middlesex, Pa., 1982-83; sr. internal auditor Ampco-Pitts. Corp., 1983-85; contr., adminstrv. mgr. New Castle (Pa.) Industries, Inc., 1986—. Active United Way, Sharon, 1981-82. Mem. AICPA, Pa. Inst. CPA's. Republican. Roman Catholic. Office: New Castle Industries Inc 1399 Countyline Rd New Castle PA 16101

BRALY, TERRELL ALFRED, diversified investments executive; b. San Antonio, Dec. 1, 1953; S. James Willard and Joyce (Judkins) B.; m. Patricia Empain, June 27, 1977; children: Vanessa, Jennifer, Edward. BSBA, Babson Coll., 1977. Asst. to dir. Empain/Schneider Group, Paris, 1977-78; gen. ptnr. Empain/Braly Investments, Paris, N.Y.C. and Dallas, 1978-82; pres. Concerts Unltd., Inc., N.Y.C., 1978—, Elite Concerts Internat., Dallas, 1983—, T.A. Braly & co., Denver, 1983—; guest lectr. Babson Coll., Wellesley, Mass., 1977—; trustee J. J. Booth Trusts, Denver, 1987—. Co-author: Days of Pleasure, Years of Pain, 1988. Named Disting. Entrepreneurs, Babson Coll., 1976. Mem. ASCAP, Am. Mgmt. Assn. (Pres.'s assn.), Bentwood Country Club. Republican. Episcopalian. Home: 6120 S Harvard Tulsa OK 74136 Office: 8177 S Harvard Ste 221 Tulsa OK 74137

BRAMBLE, RONALD LEE, business and legal consultant; b. Pauls Valley, Okla., Sept. 9, 1937; s. Homer Lee and Ethyle Juanita (Stephens) B.; m. Kathryn Louise Seiler, July 2, 1960; children: Julia Dawn, Kristin Lee. AA, San Antonio Coll., 1957; BS, Trinity U., 1959, MS, 1964; JD, St. Mary's U., 1975; DBA, Ind. No. U., 1973. Mgr., buyer Fed-Mart, Inc., San Antonio, 1959-61; tchr. bus. San Antonio Ind. Sch. Dist., 1961-65, edn. coordinator, bus. tng. specialist, 1965-67; assoc. prof., chmn. dept. mgmt. San Antonio Coll., 1967-73; prin. Ron Bramble Assocs., San Antonio, 1967-77; pres. Adminstrv. Research Assocs., Inc., 1977-82; v.p. PIA, Inc., 1982-83; v.p. fin. Solar 21 Corp., 1983-84, sr. staff Ausburn, Astoria & Seale (formerly Ausburn, O'Neill & Assocs.), San Antonio, 1984—; lectr. bus., edn. and ch. groups, 1965—. Cons. editor: Prentice-Hall, Inc., Englewood Cliffs, N.J., 1969-71; contbr. articles to profl. jours. Cert. lay speaker Meth. Ch. Served with AUS, 1959. Recipient Wall Street Jour. award Trinity U., 1959, U.S. Law Week award, 1975. Mem. ABA, San Antonio C. of C., Adminstrv. Mgmt. Soc. (pres. 1966-68, Merit award 1968), Bus. Edn. Tchrs. Assn. (pres. 1964), Sales and Mktg. Execs. San Antonio (bd. dirs. 1967-68, Disting. Salesman award 1967), Internat. Platform Assn., Internat. Assn. Cons. to Bus., Nat. Assn. Bus. Economists, Acad. Mgmt., Christian Legal Soc., Comml. Law League Am., Phi Delta Phi, Lions. Republican. Home: 127 Palo Duro San Antonio TX 78232 Office: Ausburn Astoria & Seale 100 NE Loop 410 Suite 1070 San Antonio TX 78216

BRAMHALL, ROBERT RICHARD, management consultant; b. Ft. Smith, Ark., Oct. 30, 1927; s. Richard Marion and Ima Lucille (Stovall) B.: AB in Social Rels., Harvard U., 1951, MBA, 1960; m. Mary Margaret Bundy, Aug. 10, 1957; children—Robert Richard Jr., Laura Louise. With Gen. Electric Co., Fairfield, Conn., 1954-66, Philco-Ford subs. Ford Motor Co., Phila., 1966-68, Warwick Electronics subs. Whirlpool Corp., Niles, Ill., 1968-70; prin. Bramhall Assocs., Lake Forest, Ill., 1970—; cons. to Rockwell Internat., Bunker-Ramo Corp., Dan River Inc., Molex, Spartan Mills, Rollins, Inc., Lubrizol Corp., Sears (Can.) Ltd., Northrop Corp. Pres. Chgo. Tennis Patrons, Inc., 1974-75. Served with U.S. Army, 1946-48. Winner Singles and Doubles Vt. State Tennis Championship, 1956; runner-up U.S. Clay Ct. Doubles' Championships (with Bobby Riggs). Republican. Presbyterian. Club: Harvard of Chgo. Home: 855 Buena Rd Lake Forest IL 60045 Office: Bramhall Assocs 222 Wisconsin Bldg PO Box 783 Lake Forest IL 60045

BRAMSON, FRANK HARRIS, stock brokerage company executive; b. Wausau, Wis., Aug. 27, 1946; s. Ronald Abert and Selma Jane (Greenwald) B.; B.A. in Fin., U. Ill., 1968; m. MaryLiz Stone. With Freehling & Co., Chgo., 1968-87, account exec., 1969-78, partner, 1978-85, mng. ptnr., 1985-86; spl. ltd. ptnr. Cowen & Co., 1986—; allied mem. N.Y. Stock Exchange, 1978-86, Am. Stock Exchange, 1978-86. Pres. jr. bd. dirs. Thresholds Mental Health Rehab. Center, Chgo., 1976-78; mem. fund-raising bd. Goodman Theatre. Mem. Nat. Assn. Securities Dealers (prin.), Chgo. Fgn. Relations Council, Bond Club Chgo., Lake Shore Country. Home: 969 Sheridan Rd Glencoe IL 60022 Office: Cowen & Co Freehling Div 190 S La Salle St Chicago IL 60603

BRANCA, RALPH MICHAEL, corporation executive; b. Mt. Vernon, N.Y., July 1, 1935; s. Frank E. and Emma (Ruggerio) B.; m. Ida M. Bernabei, Oct. 24, 1953; children: Anthony, Ralph, Emma, Christopher, Jeffery. PhD, Harvard U., 1970. Dir. mgmt. info. systems GE, Bridgeport, Conn., 1966; dir. fin. and adminstrn. USM Corp., Shelton, Conn., 1966-70, gen. mgr. spl. fasteners, 1971-78, v.p. ops fastener group, 1978-79; pres. Bailey, N.H., 1979-81; v.p. corp. devel. Emhart Corp., Farmington, Conn., 1981-88, v.p. indsl. sect., 1988—. Bd. dirs. West Lordship Beach Corp., Stratford, Conn., 1974-78, bd. dirs., 1976-86. Mem. Mergers and Acquisition Round Table, Assn. Corp. Growth. Roman Catholic. Home: 8 Old Green Rd Trumbull CT 06611 Office: Emhart Corp PO Box 2730 Hartford CT 06101

BRANCH, BARRINGTON HEATH, real estate executive; b. Atlanta, May 9, 1940; s. William Harllee and Katherine Quintard (Hunter) B.; m. Mary Ellen Busbee, Aug. 24, 1963 (div. Dec. 1986); children: Barrington Heath Jr., Ellen Elizabeth. BA, Davidson Coll., 1962; JD, Duke U., 1966. Assoc. Hansell, Post, Brandon and Dorsey, Atlanta, 1966-71; exec. v.p. Portman Properties, Atlanta, 1971-84; exec. v.p., ptnr. Vantage Properties, Inc., Atlanta, 1984-87; exec. v.p. Algernon Blair Group, Inc., Montgomery, Ala., 1987-89, Corporex Cos., Inc., Cin., 1989—. Bd. dirs. Sheltering Arms Day Care Ctrs., Atlanta, 1969-75, Atlanta YWCA, 1980-84, Urban Property Devel. Council Duke U., Durham, N.C., 1985—; mem. bd. vis. Davidson (N.C.) Coll., 1983—, Grady Meml. Hosp., Atlanta, 1985—; vol. counsel Atlanta Commn. on Crime and Juvenile Delinquency, 1967-68. Served with U.S. Army, 1962-65. Mem. ABA, Ga. Bar Assn., Urban Land Inst. (assoc.), Soc. Internat. Bus. Fellows (bd. dirs. nat. adv. bd. 1986—, pres. 1981-83), Davidson Coll. Atlanta Alumni Assn. (pres. 1975), Nat. Alumni Assn. Davidson Coll. (v.p., bd. dirs. 1986), Westminster Alumni Assn. (pres. 1969-70). Presbyterian. Clubs: Piedmont Driving, Capital City (Atlanta); Montgomery Country. Office: Corporex Cos Inc PO Box 75020 Cincinnati OH 45275

BRANCHFLOWER, LYLE, business executive; b. Seattle, Sept. 25, 1940; s. Norman H. and Edith R. (Williams) B.; m. Nancy Wildermuth; children: Hillary, Christine. BA, U. Pa., 1962, MBA, 1968. Cost analyst Kimberly-Clark Corp., Anderson, Calif., 1969-70; mergers and acquisitions analyst Pacific Lighting Corp., Los Angeles, 1970-73; pres. RG Mfg. Co., San Pedro, Calif., 1973-75, dir., 1973-77; project mgr. TRW, Redondo Beach, Calif., 1976-77; instr. Fed. Correctional Inst., Terminal Island, 1975; cons. Spl. Offender Ctr. Wash. State Reformatory; spl. cons. TCA Films, Palos Verdes Estates, Calif., 1976-85; ptnr. Conley-Branchflower Stables, 1980-81, Branchflower-Carr Prodns., 1982-85, B.F. Leasing, 1982-85; pres. Branchflower Investment Co., 1980—; v.p. H.E.S., Inc., 1981; pres. LWBCo., 1985—; mem. exec. com. Corp. Interviewing Network, 1985—. Contbr. articles to profl. jours.; patentee in field of mechs. Assoc. vestryman St. Peter's Episcopal Ch., San Pedro, 1975-76; adv. bd. Salvation Army, San Pedro, 1975-78; active fund raising YMCA, San Pedro, 1976-78; vestryman St. Aidan's Episcopal Ch., Camano Island, Wash., 1980; mem. adv. com. Marysville (Wash.) Pub. Schs., 1987—. Served to lt. USN, 1961-65. Mem. U. Pa. Alumni Club of Wash. (bd. govs. 1985—), Mensa. Republican. Clubs: Seattle Tennis, Wharton MBA. Lodge: Kiwanis. Home: 13614 56th Ave NE Marysville WA 98270

BRAND, FRANK A., electronics company executive; b. Bklyn., June 26, 1924; s. Charles A. and Louise S.; m. Elaine M. Donohue, June 29, 1946; children: Kathleen Ann, Nancy Jeanne, Frank A. Jr., Robert Edward, Jeannette Marie, Thomas Patrick. BS, Poly. Inst. Bklyn., 1950, MS, 1958; PhD, UCLA, 1970. Dir. R&D programs in microwave semiconductor and quantum electronic devices U.S. Army Electronics Command, 1950-67, chief Integrated Electronics div., 1967-71; exec. v.p., chief operating officer M/A-Com, Inc., Burlington, Mass., 1982-86, acting chief exec. officer, 1986-87, sr. v.p., chief tech. officer, 1987—; adj. prof. Monmouth Coll., 1958-70. Fellow IEEE, Bd. Fellows of Poly. U.; mem. Deans Coun. UCLA. Home: 249 Alexander Palm Rd Boca Raton FL 33452 Office: M/A-Com Inc 7 New England Executive Pk Burlington MA 01803

BRAND, JOSEPH LYON, lawyer; b. Urbana, Ohio, Aug. 11, 1936; s. Vance and Katherine (Lyon) B.; children: Elizabeth Brand Schell, Stephanie Lyon, Joseph Howard (dec. 1983). AB, U. Mich., 1958; MA, Ohio State U., 1959; JD with honors, George Washington U., 1963. Bar: Ohio and D.C. 1963. Ptnr. Patton, Boggs & Blow (and predecessor), 1967—; professorial lectr. comparative law George Washington U. Nat. Law Ctr., 1983—. Trustee Urbana U., 1981-83. Mem. ABA (chmn. com. banking and fin. sect. internat. law 1971-72), Washington Inst. Fgn. Affairs, Washington Fgn. Law Soc., Internat. Bar Assn., D.C. Bar Assn., Am. Soc. Internat. Law, George Washington Law Alumni Assn. (pres. 1988-89), Order of Coif (chpt. pres. 1970-71). Home: PO Box 540 Great Falls VA 22066 Office: Patton Boggs & Blow 2550 M St NW Washington DC 20037

BRANDEIS, BARRY, management consultant; b. Phila., May 3, 1946; s. Norman and Jennie (Yousin) B.; B.S. in Psychology, Pa. State U., 1968, M.B.A. in Mgmt., 1970; M.B.A. in Fin., Baruch Coll., CUNY, 1974, post-grad. in bus., 1975; m. Renee Riesenberg, Apr. 4, 1971; children—Adam, Marisa. Account exec. Meridian Securities Co., Bala Cynwyd, Pa., 1968-70; instr. Pace U. Grad. Sch., also Baruch Coll., 1968-75; asst. to chmn. Wasko Gold Products Corp., N.Y.C., 1975-77, v.p. fin., 1977-80, exec. v.p., 1980-83; group exec. Holding Capital Group, 1984-85; chief exec. officer Budoff, Inc., 1985—; with Craftex Creations Inc., 1989—; adj. assoc. prof. Pace U. Grad. Sch. Bus. Mem. U.S. Senate Bus. Adv. Bd. Mem. AAUP, Internat. Precious Metals Inst. (charter), Assn. M.B.A. Execs., P.R. C. of C. in U.S. (bd. dirs.), Internat. Platform Assn., N.Y. Acad. Scis., Omicron Delta Kappa, Psi Chi. Home: 15 Cooper Dr Great Neck NY 11023 Office: 685 Fifth Ave New York NY 10022

BRANDI, JAY THOMAS, finance educator; b. Bennington, Vt., Feb. 9, 1947; s. Joseph Andrew and Lillian Ruth (Docherty) B. BS, Kans. State U., 1975; MBA, Tex. Christian U., 1976; PhD, U. Ariz., 1985. Supr. fin. investigations Fla. Div. of Securities, Tallahassee, 1976-77, asst. dir., 1977-79; asst. prof. fin. U. Louisville, 1982-88, assoc. prof. fin., 1988—; cons. Ky. Revenue Cabinet, Frankfort, 1984-85; pres. and cons. Finplan Assocs., Louisville, 1982—; acad. coordinator Equine Industry Program, U. Louisville, 1987-88; adj. faculty U. Denver Coll. for Fin. Planning. Contbr. numerous articles to profl. jours. Curriculum coordinator, mem. steering com. Project Build, Louisville, 1985—; lobbyist Office of Controller, Fla., 1977-79. Served with U.S. Army, 1967-69, 1971-74. Mem. Internat. Assn. Fin. Planning (v.p., bd. dirs. Ky. chpt. 1986—), Fin. Mgmt. Assn., Acad. Fin. Socs., Am. Fin. Assn., Eastern Fin. Assn., So. Fin. Assn., Southwestern Fin. Assn., Louisville C. of C. (devel. fin. steering com., venture capital/capital gains preference task force), Am. Legion, VFW, Phi Kappa Phi, Beta Gamma Sigma, Delta Sigma Pi, Alpha Phi Omega. Democrat. Roman Catholic. Home: 1030 Stivers Rd Louisville KY 40207 Office: U Louisville Sch Bus Louisville KY 40292

BRANDIMORE, STANLEY ALBERT, holding company executive, lawyer; b. Highland Park, Mich., Aug. 20, 1927; s. Albert James B. and Genevieve (McCormick) Weideman; m. E. Kennedy Greene, Dec. 27, 1952; children: Vanessa Brandimore Lund, Darrell Stanley. B.B.A. in Acctg., U. Miami, Fla., 1954; J.D., U. Miami, 1957. Bar: Fla. 1957, U.S. Supreme Ct. 1968. Instr., lectr. acctg. U. Miami, 1954-57; atty. Fla. Pub. Service Com., Tallahassee, 1957-59; atty. Fla. Power Corp., St. Petersburg, 1959-63, asst. gen. counsel, 1963-68, v.p., gen. counsel, 1968-75, sr. v.p., gen. counsel, 1975-83; exec. v.p., gen. counsel Fla. Progress Corp., St. Petersburg, 1983—. Served with USN, 1945-48, 50-52. Mem. St. Petersburg Bar Assn. (treas. 1964-65), Fla. Bar Assn., ABA, St. Petersburg C. of C. (bd. govs.), St. Petersburg Jr. Coll. Alumni Assn. (bd. dirs.). Republican. Clubs: Suncoasters, Tiger Bay, Presidents; Treasure Island Tennis and Yacht (Fla.) (bd. govs., rear commodore). Home: 8573 42d Ave N Saint Petersburg FL 33709 Office: Fla Progress Corp 240 1st Ave S Ste 300 PO Box 33042 Saint Petersburg FL 33701

BRANDIN, DONALD NELSON, bank holding company executive; b. N.Y.C., Dec. 28, 1921; s. Nils F. and Dorothy May (Mead) B.; m. Mary Elliott Keyes, Jan. 1, 1982; children: Robert N., Patricia Brandin Barnes, Douglas M.; 1 stepdau., Elizabeth E. White. A.B., Princeton U., 1944. With Bankers Trust Co., N.Y.C., 1946-56; with Boatmen's Nat. Bank, St. Louis, 1956-89; chmn. exec. com. Boatmen's Nat. Bank, 1968-70, pres., chief operating officer, 1971-72, chmn. bd., pres., chief exec. officer, 1973-78, chmn. bd., chief exec. officer, 1978-84, chmn. bd., 1984-85, also dir.; exec. v.p. Boatmen's Bancshares, Inc., St. Louis, 1969-72; chmn. bd., chief exec. officer Boatmen's Bancshares, Inc., 1973-88, chmn. bd., 1988-89; dir. EAC Corp., St. Louis, Sigma-Aldrich Corp., Laclede Gas Co., all St. Louis. Bd. dirs. Arts and Edn. Council Greater St. Louis, St. Louis Symphony Soc., Washington U. Served to capt. AUS, 1943-46. Mem. Assn. Bank Holding Cos., Assn. Res. City Bankers, Am. Banking Assn., Mo. Bankers Assn., Bank Adminstrn. Inst., Robert Morris Assocs., Fed. Adv. Council 8th Dist. (bd. dirs., pres.). Clubs: Blind Brook (Purchase, N.Y.); St. Louis, Old Warson Country, Bogey, (St. Louis); Garden of Gods (Colorado Springs, Colo.). Office: Boatmen's Bancshares Inc PO Box 236 Saint Louis MO 63166

BRANDNER, J. WILLIAM, publishing company executive, insurance company executive; b. S.I., N.Y., Apr. 1, 1937; s. J. Kenneth and Mary D. (Monaghan) B.; children: John William, Robert, Kathleen, Peggy Ann, Jill; m. Karen J. Pohnan, Apr. 13, 1987. B.B.A., Manhattan Coll., 1958. C.P.A., N.Y., N.J. Audit mgr. Arthur Andersen & Co., N.Y.C. and Newark, 1958-71; asst. controller Harcourt Brace Jovanovich, Inc., N.Y.C., 1971-73, controller, 1973-78; v.p. Harcourt Brace Jovanovich, Inc., N.Y.C., Orlando, 1976-86; treas., chief fin. officer Harcourt Brace Jovanovich, Inc., Orlando, Fla., 1978-86, sr. v.p., chief fin. officer, 1980-86; chmn., chief exec. officer HBJ Ins., Orlando, Fla., 1982—; exec. v.p., bd. dirs. Harcourt Brace Jovanovich, Orlando, Fla., 1985—. bd. visitors U. Central Fla. Coll. Bus., 1979—. Mem. Am. Inst. C.P.A.s, N.Y. State Soc. C.P.A.s. Republican. Roman Catholic. Club: Milbrook Country (Greenwich, Conn.); Bay Hill Country (Orlando, Fla.). Home: 6216 Indian Meadow Dr Orlando FL 32819 Office: Harcourt Brace Jovanovich Inc 6277 Sea Harbor Dr Orlando FL 32887 also: HBJ Bldg Orlando FL 32887

BRANDON, EDWARD BERMETZ, banker; b. Davenport, Iowa, Sept. 15, 1931; s. William McKinley and Mary Elizabeth (Bermetz) B.; m. Phyllis Anne Probeck, Aug. 7, 1954; children: William M., Robert P., Beverly A., Beth A., E. Matthew. B.S., Northwestern U., 1953; M.B.A., Wharton Sch. Banking & Fin., 1956. Mgmt. trainee Nat. City Bank, Cleve., 1956-61, sr. v.p., corp. banking head, 1978-79, exec. v.p. corp. banking group, 1979-82, vice chmn., 1982-83, pres., 1984-87, chief exec. officer, 1985—; exec. v.p. Nat. City Corp., 1982-83, pres., dir., 1986-88, chmn., chief exec. officer, 1987—, dir., 1986—; bd. dirs. Standard Products Co. Trustee, exec. com. Greater Cleve. Growth Assn.; trustee John Carroll U.; chmn. bd. trustees Cleve. Orch., St. Vincent Charity Hosp., NCCJ, Leadership Cleve., United Way Svcs.; exec. com. Greater Cleve. YMCA; bd. advisors, exec. com. Notre Dame Coll. of Ohio; Playhouse Sq. Found. Lt. USN, 1953-55. Mem. Am. Bankers Assn., Ohio Bankers Assn. (bd. dirs.), Assn. Res. City Bankers, Assn. Bank Holding Cos., Internat. Monetary Conf., Union Club, Shaker Heights Country Club, Firestone Country Club, Pepper Pike Club, 50 Club, Tavern Club, Kirtland Country Club. Republican. Methodist. Office: Nat City Corp 1900 E 9th St Cleveland OH 44114-3484

BRANDS, JAMES EDWIN, medical products executive; b. Lebanon, Ind., July 5, 1937; s. Edwin Herman and Pearl Irene (Brown) B.; m. Gail Marian Knight, Sept. 12, 1959; children: Jeffrey, Scot, Alan, Susan. AB, Wesleyan U., Middletown, Conn., 1959; MBA, U. Chgo., 1961. CPA, Mo. Staff acct., mgr. Arthur Andersen & Co., Chgo., 1961-71; ptnr. Arthur Andersen & Co., St. Louis, 1971-82; sr. v.p. Scherer-Storz, Inc., Atlanta, 1982-86; exec. v.p. Scherer Scientific Ltd., Atlanta, 1986—, also bd. dirs.; bd. dirs. Scherer Healthcare Inc., Atlanta, Biofor, Inc., Waverly, Pa.; bd. dirs., v.p. Nat. Travel Mgmt. Inc., Atlanta; owner-mgr. Brands & Co., St. Louis, 1981-86, Atlanta, 1987—. Mem. Am. Inst. CPA's, Mo. Soc. CPA's, Ga. Soc. CPA's. Republican. Presbyterian. Clubs: Bellerive Country (St. Louis) (chmn., trustee club grounds 1984-86); Country of the South (Atlanta), Vinings (Atlanta); Profl. Golfers Assn. Nat. Golf (Palm Beach Gardens, Fla.). Home: 4330 Bancroft Valley Country Club of the South Alpharetta GA 30201 Office: Scherer Scientific Ltd 2895 Paces Ferry Rd Atlanta GA 30339

BRANDSTETTER, BRUCE GEORGE, architect, engineer; b. Cin., Jan. 18, 1956; s. Lawrence Francis and Elaine (Dwertman) B.; m. Betsy Anne Beard, June 14, 1980; children: Timothy George, Paul Gordon. BCE, Ohio State U., 1978; postgrad., Northwestern La. State U., 1979, Xavier U., 1980. Registered profl. engr., Ohio, Ky. Field engr. Turner Constrn., Houston, 1978-79; civil engr. KZF, Inc., Cin., 1979-82; prin. Brandstetter/Carroll, Cin., 1982—. Coordinator baptismal preparation, Guardian Angels Ch., Cin., 1983-86, bldg. com.; facilitator of chief exec. officers, Cin. C. of C., 1982—; United Appeal Fund Drive Account mgr. Greater Cin. Ctr. Econ. Edn. Entrepreneurship Day, 1986; co-chmn. bldg. com. Mayor's Commn. on Infra Structure; mem. Leadership Cin., 1987-88. Mem. ASCE, Ohio Airport Mgrs. Assn., Am. Pub. Works Assn., Cin. C. of C. (Cin. Inst. Small Enterprise communications com.), Ohio State Alumni Assn., Cin. Rotary Club (chmn. various coms., bd. dirs. 1989—). Roman Catholic. Home: 2371 Bretton Dr Cincinnati OH 45244 Office: Brandstetter/Carroll Inc 424 E Fourth St Cincinnati OH 45202

BRANDT, DONALD EDWARD, utilities company executive; b. St. Louis, July 22, 1954; s. Edward H. and Margaret E. (Hertling) b.; m. Jeanine M. Pulay, Nov. 1, 1986; 1 child, Matthew. BSBA, St. Louis U., 1975. CPA, Mo. Audit mgr. Price Waterhouse, St. Louis, 1975-83; sr. v.p. fin. and acctg. Union Electric Co., St. Louis, 1983—. Mem. Fin. Execs. Inst., Am. Inst. CPA's, Mo. Soc. CPA's. Roman Catholic. Club: Mo. Athletic (St. Louis). Office: Union Electric Co PO Box 149 Saint Louis MO 63166

BRANDT, RICHARD PAUL, communications and entertainment company executive; b. N.Y.C., Dec. 6, 1927; s. Harry and Helen (Satenstein) B.; m. Helen H. Kogel, May 31, 1975; children: Claudia, David, Matthew, Thomas; 1 stepdau., Jennifer. B.S. with high honors, Yale U., 1948. With Trans-Lux Theatres Corp., 1950-54, v.p., 1952-54; with Trans-Lux Corp., 1954—, v.p., 1959-62, pres., 1962-80, chmn. bd., 1974—; also chief exec. officer, dir.; dir. Am. Book-Stratford Press, Inc., 1962-87, mem. exec. com., 1969-87; dir. Brandt Theatres, Presdl. Realty Corp.; founding gov. Ind. Film Importers & Distbrs. Am., 1959-63, bd. dirs., 1959-69; v.p., mem. exec. com. Theatre Owners Am., 1962-65; mem. bill of rights com. Council Motion Picture Orgns., 1963-65; bd. dirs. Film Soc. Lincoln Ctr., 1968-71; mem. N.Y. State Bus. Adv. Com. on Mgmt. Improvement, 1966-70; chmn. bd. Univ. Settlement Soc., 1964-66, hon. pres., bd. dirs., 1966-77; dir. Am. Theatre Wing, 1970—, United Neighborhood Houses, 1968-73; bd. dirs., treas. Settlement House Employment Devel., 1969-72; trustee, mem. exec. com. Am. Film Inst., 1971—, vice chmn., 1980-83, chmn. bd., 1983-86, chmn. emeritus 1986—; trustee Mus. Holography, 1979-82; mem. Tony awards mgmt. com., 1986—. Mem. adv. bd. Communications Art Program, Coll. Santa Fe, 1987—. Named Exhibitor of Yr., ShoWest, 1984. Mem. Nat. Assn. Theatre Owners (dir. 1957-78, exec. com. 1965-78, Sherrill Corwin award 1983), Phi Beta Kappa, Sigma Xi. Clubs: Yale, Landmark. Office: Trans-Lux Corp 110 Richards Ave Norwalk CT 06854

BRANDT, RICHARD PAUL, sales executive; b. Providence, Oct. 5, 1961; s. David and Shirley Marion (Wilk) B. BBA cum laude, Boston U., 1983. Exec. trainee May Dept. Stores-Hechts, Washington, 1983-84, asst. buyer, 1984-85, buyer, 1986-87; nat. sales mgr. Jasmin Footwear, Pennsauken, N.J., 1988—. Active B'nai B'rith Youth Orgn., Brookline, Mass., 1979—. Mem. Am. Mktg. Assn., Am. Mgmt. Assn., Two-Ten Found., Western Shoe Assn., Mid-Atlantic Shoe Travelers Assn., Boston U. Alumni Assn. Republican. Jewish. Home: 11 N 2d St Philadelphia PA 19106

BRANDZEL, JACOB REUBEN, accountant; b. Chgo., June 23, 1939; s. Harold and Rose B.; m. Janice Rae Jackson, Jan. 13, 1962; children: Barbara, Robert. BS, DePaul U., 1961; JD with honors, John Marshall Law Sch., 1968. CPA, Ill., Pa. Revenue agt., conferee IRS, Chgo., 1961-68; ptnr. Laventhol & Horwath, Chgo., 1968—. Contbr. articles to profl. jours. Mem. profl. adv. com. Jewish United Fund, Chgo., 1968—; dir., com. chmn. Anti-Defamation League, Chgo., 1980-84. Served to staff sgt. USAF, 1962-68. Mem. ABA, AICPA, Ill. CPA Soc., Met. Club (Chgo.), Locust Club (Phila.). Home: 133 Woods Lane Radnor PA 19087 Office: Laventhol & Horwath 1845 Walnut St 19th Fl Philadelphia PA 19103

BRANN, EDWARD R(OMMEL), editor; b. Rostock, Mecklenburg, Germany, May 20, 1920; s. Guenther O.R. and Lilli (Appel) B.; came to U.S., 1938, naturalized, 1966; BA, Berea Coll., 1945; MA, U. Chgo., 1946; postgrad. U. Wis., 1948-56; m. Helen Louise Sweet, Dec. 9, 1948; children: Johannes Weidler, Paul George. Asst. membership sec. central YMCA, Chgo., 1946-48; asst. editor Credit Union Mag., Madison, Wis., 1955-65; dir. hist. projects, asst. dir. publs. CUNA Internat., Inc., Madison, 1965-70, staff historian, 1958-65; asst. dir. publs. Credit Union Nat. Assn., Inc., Madison, 1970-72, 83-84, asst. dir. communications, 1973-83, sr. editor Credit Union mag., 1973-84, coordinator Innovative Ideas Center, 1980-84; contbg. editor Credit Union Exec. mag., 1982-84; dir. hist. projects World Council of Credit Unions, Inc., 1970-79, dir. European relations, 1972-83. Active ARC, various coms. Dane County chpt., vol. cons., 1984—. Recipient Christo et Ecclesiae award Concordia Coll., Milw., 1968, Distinguished Alumnus award Berea Coll., 1977, Risser award Dane County chpt. ARC, 1983; named Ky. col. Mem. Am. Hist. Assn., NEA, Assn. Higher Edn., Luth. Laymen's League, Wis. Hist. Soc., Delta Phi Alpha, Pi Gamma Mu. Lutheran. Contbr. articles to profl. jours. Home: PO Box 383 Madison WI 53701 Office: PO Box 5905 Madison WI 53705

BRANNAN, WILLIAM C., financial executive; b. McKeesport, Pa., Feb. 22, 1949; s. Charles W. and Amy (Campbell) B.; m. Suzanne Brannan, Aug. 8, 1970; children: William J., Laura. BA in Bus., Adelphi U., 1970. Chartered fin. analyst. Fin. advisor Fin. Cons. Group Ltd, Edinboro, Pa., 1971-81, First Fin Group, Ann Arbor, Mich., 1981-83; chief fin. officer TSM, Inc., Ann Arbor, 1983—; bd. dirs. LSSM, Detroit. Mem. Inst. for Econometric Rsch., Am. Bus. Assn., Am. Mgmt. Assn., Fin. Mgrs. Soc., Nat. Wildlife Fedn., Nat. Assn. Fin. Cons., Detroit Econ. Club, Rotary. Republican. Lutheran.

BRANSCOMB, LEWIS MCADORY, physicist; b. Asheville, N.C., Aug. 17, 1926; s. Bennett Harvie and Margaret (Vaughan) B.; m. Margaret Anne Wells, Oct. 13, 1951; children—Harvie Hammond, Katharine Capers. A.B. summa cum laude, Duke U., 1945, D.Sc. (hon.); M.S., Harvard U., 1947, Ph.D., 1949; D.Sc. (hon.), Poly. Inst. N.Y., Clarkson Coll., Rochester U., U. Colo., Western Mich. U., Lycoming Coll., U. Ala., Pratt Inst.; Rutgers U., Lehigh U., U. Notre Dame; L.H.D. (hon.), Pace U. Instr. physics Harvard U., 1950-51; lectr. physics U. Md., 1952-54; vis. staff mem. Univ. Coll., London, 1957-58; chief atomic physics sect. Nat. Bur. Standards, Washington, 1954-60; chief atomic physics div. Nat. Bur. Standards, 1960-62; chmn. Joint Inst. Lab. Astrophysics, U. Colo., 1962-65, 68-69; chief lab. astrophysics div. Nat. Bur. Standards, Boulder, Colo., 1962-69; prof. physics U. Colo., 1962-69; dir. Nat. Bur. Standards, 1969-72; chief scientist, v.p. IBM, Armonk, N.Y., 1972-86; mem. corporate mgmt. bd. IBM, Armonk,

1983-86; dir. pub. policy program Kennedy Sch. Govt., Harvard U., Cambridge, Mass., 1986—, Albert Pratt pub. service prof., 1988—; mem.-at-large Def. Sci. Bd., 1969-72; mem. high level policy group sci. and tech. info. Orgn. Econ. Coop. and Devel., 1968-70; mem. Pres.'s Sci. Adv. Com., 1965-68, chmn. panel space sci. and tech., 1967-68; mem. Nat. Sci. Bd., 1978-84, chmn., 1980-84; mem. Pres.'s Nat. Productivity Adv. Com., 1981-82; mem. standing com. controlled thermonuclear research AEC, 1966-68; mem. adv. com. on sci. and fgn. affairs Dept. State, 1973-74; mem. U.S.-USSR Joint Commn. on Sci. and Tech., 1977-80; chmn. Com. on Scholarly Communications with the People's Republic of China, 1977-80; chmn. Carnegie Forum Task Force on Teaching as a Profession, 1985-86; dir. Mobil Corp., Lord Corp., Mitre Corp., Draper Labs., Inc.; mem. pres.'s bd. visitors U. Okla., 1968-70; mem. astronomy and applied physics vis. coms. Harvard U. 1969-83, bd. overseers, 1984-86 ; mem. physics vis. com. M.I.T., 1974-79; mem. Pres.'s Com. Nat. Medal Scis., 1970-72; bd. dirs. Am. Nat. Standards Inst., 1969-72; trustee Carnegie Instn., 1973—, Poly. Inst. N.Y., 1974-78, Vanderbilt U., 1980—, Nat. Geog. Soc., 1984—, Woods Hole Oceanographic Instn., 1985—. Editor: Rev. Modern Physics, 1968-73. Served to lt. (j.g.) USNR, 1945-46. USPHS fellow, 1948-49; Jr. fellow Harvard Soc. Fellows, 1949-51; recipient Rockefeller Pub. Service award, 1957-58, Gold medal exceptional service Dept. Commerce, 1961, Arthur Flemming award D.C. Jr. C. of C., 1962, Samuel Wesley Stratton award Dept. Commerce, 1966, Career Service award Nat. Civil Service League, 1968, Proctor prize Research Soc. Am., 1972. Fellow Am. Phys. Soc. (chmn. div. electron physics 1961-68, pres. 1979), AAAS (dir. 1969-73), Am. Acad. Arts and Scis.; mem. Nat. Acad. Scis. (council 1972-75), Nat. Acad. Engring. (Arthur Bueche award), Washington Acad. Scis. (Outstanding Sci. Achievement award 1959), Nat. Acad. Public Adminstrn., Am. Philos. Soc., Phi Beta Kappa, Sigma Xi (pres. 1985-86). Club: Am. Yacht (Rye, N.Y.). Office: Harvard U Kennedy Sch Govt 79 J F Kennedy St Cambridge MA 02138

BRANSON, HARLEY KENNETH, lawyer; b. Ukiah, Calif., June 10, 1942; s. Harley Edward and Clara Lucile (Slocum) B.; 1 child, Erik Jordan. AA, San Francisco City Coll., 1963; BS in Acctg. and Fin., San Jose State U., 1965; JD, Santa Clara U., 1968. Bar: Calif. 1969, U.S. Dist. Ct. (so. dist.) Calif. 1969, U.S. Ct. Appeals (9th cir.) 1969, U.S. Tax Ct. 1969, U.S. Ct. Customs and Patent Appeals 1970, U.S. Supreme Ct. 1973. Law clk. to judge U.S. Ct. Appeals (9th cir.), San Diego, 1968-69; ptnr. Klitgaard & Branson, Inc., San Diego, 1969-72; assoc. Jennings, Engstrand & Henrikson, San Diego, 1972-76, ptnr., 1976-78; div. counsel Ralston Purina Co., San Diego, 1978-83; group gen. counsel Castle & Cooke, Inc., San Diego, 1983-85; gen. counsel, corp. sec. Bumble Bee Seafoods, Inc., San Diego, 1985—, also bd. dirs., exec. v.p. Editor Santa Clara Law Rev., 1967-68. Mem. Mission Valley Unified Planning Com., 1978; bd. dirs. Mission Valley Coun., San Diego, 1977-78; coach Peninsula YMCA Soccer, San Diego, 1978-79. James B. Emery scholar and Farmers Ins. Group scholar Santa Clara U., 1966-68. Mem. ABA (corp., banking and bus. law, and internat. law sects.), Calif. Bar Assn., Am. Soc. Corp. Secs., Nat. Food Processors Assn. (lawyer com., claims com.), Am. Corp. Coun. Assn. (pres. San Diego County 1987-88). Republican. Club: San Diego Tennis and Racquet. Office: Bumble Bee Seafoods Inc 5775 Roscoe Ct San Diego CA 92123

BRANSON, JAY WALLACE, financial planner; b. Lapeer, Mich., Sept. 29, 1956; s. Jacob Wallace and Nina Jean (Henderson) B. Student, U. Mich, 1974-76, Coll. for Fin. Planning, 1986-87. Gen. mgr. Tex. Wholesale Distbrs., Houston, 1977-82; mgr. ops. Saks 5th Ave, Houston, 1982-84; fin. planner Cigna Individual Fin. Svcs., Houston, 1984=86; prin. Childs, Branson, Fowlkes, CFP, Houston, 1986—. Mem. mus. collectors group Mus. Fine Arts, Houston, 1985—; bd. dirs. Chocolate Bayou Theater Co., Houston, 1987—; mem. Mus. Guild, Houston, 1987—. Mem. Houston Soc. Inst. Cert. Fin. Planners, Inst. Cert. Fin. Planners, Internat. Assn. Fin. Planners. Republican. Office: Childs Branson Fowlkes 4544 Post Oak Pl #100 Houston TX 77027

BRASE, INGRID ELISABETH, chemist; b. Port Jefferson, N.Y., May 9, 1955; d. Ottokar Anton and Elisabeth Josephine (Becker) Woerner; m. John D. Brase, Nov. 12, 1983; children: Christopher, Joseph. BS, SUNY, Oneonta, 1977; MBA, Rider Coll., 1983. Research chemist Nat. Starch and Chem. Corp., Bridgewater, N.J., 1977-78, devel. chemist, 1979-81, supr. tech. mktg. devel., 1981-86, supr. market devel., 1986-87, mgr. product devel., sr. project supr., 1988—. Patentee drilling mud dispersants. Mem. Am. Chem. Soc., Nat. Assn. Corrosion Engrs., Cooling Tower Inst. Office: Nat Starch & Chem Corp Finderne Ave Bridgewater NJ 08807

BRASHEAR, DAVID MARK, venture capitalist; b. Pitts., Apr. 18, 1961; s. James Edward and Judith Elaine (Brugh) B. BS in Econ., U. Pa., 1983; MBA, Havard U., 1987. Rsch. analyst Strategic Planning Assocs., Inc., Washington, 1983-85, assoc., 1987-88; venture analyst Hillman Ventures, Inc., Pitts., 1986; assoc. Hillman Ventures East, Inc., Vienna, Va., 1988—; bd. dirs. Phoenix Telecom, Inc. Chmn. mktg. com. Alexandria chpt. ARC, 1984. Home: 811 Wolfe St Alexandria VA 22314 Office: Hillman Ventures East 8000 Towers Crescent Dr Vienna VA 22180

BRASWELL, STEPHEN R., insurance company executive; b. Manila, Philippines, Feb. 24, 1940; s. L. Render and Elizabeth W. B.; m. Ernestine Dunlap; children: Elisabeth Dunlap, Wylly Willingham, Catherine Spalding, Stephen Render Jr., Grayson Sides. B.S., Duke U., 1962. With Prudential Ins. Co. Am., 1963—; pres. Southwestern ops. Prudential Ins. Co. Am., Houston, 1980-84; sr. v.p. Prudential Ins. Co. Am., Newark, 1984-87, sr. v.p. individual ins. services dept., 1987-88; pres. Prudential Property Casualty Ins. Co., Holmdel, N.J., 1988—, chmn., 1988—, also bd. dirs.; chmn. Prudential Comml. Ins. Co., Prudential Gen. Ins. Co., Pru-LMI Comml. Ins. Co., 1988—; bd. dirs. Prudential Reinsurance Co., Prudential Ins. Brokerage, Inc. Trustee Monmouth Coll.; past trustee Children's Psychiat. Ctr., N.J.; mem. adv. bd. Amigos de las Americas; mem. Gov.'s Commn. on Future Ind. Higher Edn., N.J. Mem. Rumson Country Club, Florida Yacht Club. Republican. Episcopalian. Home: Riverfields Rumson NJ 07760

BRATTON, WILLIAM EDWARD, electronics executive, management consultant; b. Dallas, Oct. 25, 1919; s. William E. and Edna (Walker) B.; m. Betty Thume, May 30, 1942; children: Dale, Janet, Donna. AB in Econs., Stanford U., 1940; MBA, Harvard U., 1945. From v.p. to pres. Librascope, Glendale, Calif., 1947-63; v.p., gen. mgr. Ampex, Culver City, Calif., 1963-66; pres. Guidance Tech., Santa Monica, Calif., 1967-68; v.p. electronics div. Gen. Dynamics, San Diego, 1969-72; pres. Theta Cable T.V., Santa Monica, 1974-82; pres., chief exec. officer Stagecoach Properties, Salado, Tex., 1959—; bd. dirs. PDA Engring. Served to lt. (j.g.) USNR, 1944-46. Republican. Episcopalian. Club: El Niguel Country (Laguna, Calif.) (pres. 1978-79). Office: PDA Engring 2975 Red Hill Costa Mesa CA 92626

BRAUDE, MICHAEL, board of trade executive; b. Chgo., Mar. 6, 1936; s. Sheldon and Nan B.; m. Linda Rae Miller, Aug. 20, 1961; children—Peter, Adam. B.S., U. Mo., 1957; M.S., Columbia U., 1958. Vice pres. Commerce Bank, Kansas City, Mo., 1960-73; vice pres. Mercantile Bank, Kansas City, Mo., 1966-73; exec. v.p. Am. Bank, Kansas City, Mo., 1973-84; pres., chief exec. officer Kansas City Bd. Trade, Mo., 1984—; bd. dirs. Overland Park Savs. & Loan, Kans., Cell Tech. Inc., Boulder, Colo. Author: Managing Your Money, 1975, also 12 childrens books. Pres. Metr. Community Coll. Found., Kansas City, Mo., 1982-84; mayor City of Mission Woods, Kans., 1982-84. Mem. Futures Industry Assn., Nat. Futures Assn. (bd. dirs.), Nat. Grain Trade Council (bd. dirs.), U. Mo. Alumni Assn (bd. dirs. 1985—). Jewish. Club: Homestead Country (Prairie Village, Kans.). Home: 5319 Mission Woods Terr Shawnee Mission KS 66205 Office: Kans City Bd Trade 4800 Main St Ste 303 Kansas City MO 64112

BRAUER, HARROL ANDREW, JR., broadcasting executive; b. Richmond, Va., Oct. 17, 1920; s. Harrol Andrew and Bertie (Gregory) B.; m. Elizabeth Anne Hill, May 18, 1946; children: Harrol Andrew III, William Lanier, Gregory Hill. BA, U. Richmond, 1942; LLD, Christopher Newport Coll. Chief announcer, program dir., account exec. various radio stas. in Va., 1939-42, 45-49; assoc. WVEC radio, Hampton, Va., 1949-80; v.p., dir. sales Sta. WVEC-TV, Hampton, 1953-82; v.p. Peninsula Cable Corp., 1966-82; chmn. Wyatt Bros., 1983—; bd. dirs. Peninsula Broadcasting Corp. Pres. Hampton Community Chest, 1951-52; crusade chmn. Peninsula unit Am. Cancer Soc., 1960—. Mem. Hampton Sch. Bd., 1963—, vice chmn., 1964-68, chmn., 1968-70; pres. Hampton Parking Authority, chmn. 1988—; bd. dirs. YMCA, Va. USO; bd. dirs., vice chmn. Va. Pub. Telecommunications Bd., chmn. 1985—; Soc. Founders of Mace Christopher Newport Coll., 1988—; chmn. bd. trustees Hampton Roads Ednl. TV Assn., 1965-70; rector Christopher Newport Coll., 1976-82; co-chmn. for 375th Anniversary Celebration City of Hampton, 1985; v.p., founder Chesapeake Acad., 1988—. Served as lt. USNR, 1942-45. Recipient Disting. Service medallion Christopher Newport Coll., NCCJ award, Disting. Citizen award City of Hampton. Mem. Hampton Retail Mchts. Assn. (past pres., bd. dirs.), Chesapeake Acad. Found. (vice-chmn. 1988—), Jamestowne Soc., Peninsula C. of C. (past bd. dirs.), Broadcast Pioneers, Sigma Alpha Epsilon. Clubs: Commonwealth, Indian Creek Yacht and Country, James River Country, Hampton Yacht, Peninsula Exec.'s (past pres., bd. dirs.); Town Point. Lodge: Kiwanis (past bd. dirs., pres., lt. gov.). Home: 35 N Boxwood St Hampton VA 23669

BRAUKUS, ROBERT MICHAEL, utilities executive; b. Wallace, Idaho, May 8, 1941; s. Joseph John and Anna Francis (Matusavage) B.; m. H. Jane Kennaugh, June 8, 1968; children: Susan, Greg. BSEE, Seattle U., 1965. Registered profl. engr., Calif., Wash., Idaho, Mont., Oreg., Alaska. Asst. engr. Puget Sound, Power & Light Co., Bellevue, Wash., 1968-71, communication engr., 1971-72, relay engr., 1972-75, asst. supt. substas., 1975-77, supt. T&D, 1977-80, dir. communication and system protection, 1982—; mgr. operation div. Chugach Electric, Anchorage, 1980-82. Co. co-chmn. United Way Fund, King County, Wash., 1986; mem. Engring. Advancement Council Seattle U., 1987-88; committeeman Mcpl. Leage, Bellevue, 1987; coord. capital campaign Salvation Army, Seattle, 1987; fund raiser Am. Cancer Soc., Bellevue, 1988; co. rep. 1990 Goodwill Games, Wash., 1988; bd. dirs. Bellevue Arts Assn. Lt. USNR, 1965-68, Vietnam. Recipient Citizen Community award Bellevue Downtown Park Com., 1987, Engr. Yr. award Puget Sound Engring. Council, 1989. Mem. IEEE (Seattle sect.), NSPE, Am. Soc. Quality Control, Electric Power Rsch. Inst. (adv. bd. integrated utility communication systems), Rotary. Republican. Roman Catholic. Office: Puget Sound & Light Co 13635 NE 80th St Redmond WA 98052

BRAUN, HELEN MARIE, financial services executive; b. Chgo.; d. Hubert Jacob Jr. and Evelyn Marta B. BA, Fordham U., 1979. Exec. asst. Goldman, Sachs & Co., N.Y.C., 1970-79; asst. to officer Morgan Guaranty Trust Co. of N.Y., N.Y.C., 1979-82, mgmt. trainee, 1982-83, asst. sec., 1983-86; asst. v.p. J.P. Morgan Investment Mgmt., Inc., N.Y.C., 1986—. Mem. editorial bd. Convent of Sacred Heart, N.Y.C., 1980-86, mem. alumnae bd., 1981-86. Mem. benefit com. Am. Harvest Benefit, N.Y.C., 1985—.

BRAUN, MICHAEL ALAN, data processing executive; b. Albany, N.Y., Oct. 25, 1949; s. Murry and Marjorie (Leopold) B.; m. Leslie Hope, July 4, 1971; children: Michelle, Amy. BA, U. Rochester, 1971, MBA, 1972. Mktg. rep. IBM Corp., N.Y.C., 1972-77; program adminstr. IBM Corp., Raleigh, N.C., 1978-79; mgr. mktg. IBM Corp., Charlotte, N.C., 1979-80; mgr. product mktg. IBM Corp., White Plains, N.Y., 1981-83; adminstr. asst. to div. pres. IBM Corp., White Plains, 1984; mgr. product typewriter devel. IBM Corp., Lexington, Ky., 1985-86; dir. planning IBM Corp., White Plains, 1986; dir. channel mgmt. IBM Corp., Montvale, N.J., 1987-88; mgr. northeastern area IBM Corp., N.Y.C., 1988—. Office: IBM Corp 590 Madison Ave New York NY 10022

BRAUN, ROBERT CLARE, retired association and advertising executive; b. Indpls., July 18, 1928; s. Ewald Elsworth and Lila (Inman) B.; B.S. in Journalism-Advt., Butler U., 1950; postgrad. Ind. U., 1957, 66. Reporter, Northside Topics Newspaper, Indpls., 1949, advt. mgr., 1950; asst. mgr. Clarence E. Crippen Printing Co., Indpls., 1951; corp. sec. Auto-Imports, Ltd., Indpls., 1952-53; pres. O. R. Brown Paper Co., Indpls., 1953-69; pres., chief exec. officer Robert C. Braun Advt. Agy., 1959-70, Zimmer Engraving Inc., Indpls., 1964-69; former chmn. bd. O. R. Brown Paper Co., Zimmer Engraving, Inc.; advt. cons. Rolls-Royce Motor Cars, 1957-59; exec. dir., chief exec. officer Historic Landmarks Found., Ind., 1969-73; exec. v.p., Purchasing Mgmt. Assn. Indpls., 1974-85; cen. dist. coordinator Ind. Regional Minority Supplier Devel. Council, 1985-88; pres. A.P.S. Industries, Inc., 1979—; nat. pres. Associated Purchasing Publs., 1981-85; gen. mgr. Midwest Indsl. Show, 1974-85, Midwest Office Systems and Equipment Show, 1974-85, Grand Valley Indsl. Show, 1974-85, Evansville Indsl. Show, 1982-85, Ind. Bus. Opportunity Fair, 1985-88. Chmn., Citizens' Adv. Com. to Marion County Met. Planning Dept., 1963; pres. museum com. Indpls. Fire Dept., 1966-76; mem. adv. com. Historic Preservation Commn. Marion County, 1967-73; Midwestern artifacts cons. to curator of White House, Washington, 1971-73; mem., chmn. Mayor's Contract Compliance Adv. Bd., 1977—; mem. Mayor's Subcom. for Indpls. Stadium, 1981-83; adv. bd., exec. com. Inpls. Office Equal Opportunity 1982—; mem. Ind. Minority Bus. Opportunity Council, 1985-88; mem. Met. Mus. Art, Indpls. Mus. Art. Bd. dirs. Historic Landmarks Found. Ind., 1960-69; dir., sec. Ind. Arthritis and Rheumatism Found., 1960-67, pres., 1969, dir., 1970—, dir. Asso. Patient Services, 1976—; pres. Amanda Wasson Meml. Found., 1961-72, Huggler-Ault Meml. Trust, 1961-72. Recipient Meritorious Service award St. Jude's Police League, 1961; citation for meritorious service Am. Legion Police Post 56, 1962; Tafflinger-Holiday Park appreciation award, 1973; Nat. Vol. Service Citation, Arthritis Found., 1979; Margaret Egan Meml. award Ind. Arthritis Found., 1980; Indpls. Profl. Fire Fighters meritorious service award, 1982. Mem. Marion County Hist. Soc. (dir. 1964—, pres. 1965-69, 74-76, 1st v.p. 1979), Am. Guild Organists (mem. Indpls. chpt., charter mem. Franklin Coll. br.), Indpls. Humane Soc., Ind. Museum Soc. (treas., dir. 1967-74), Internat. Fire Buff Assos., Indpls. Second Alarm Fire Buffs (sec.-treas. 1967, pres. 1969), Ind. Hist. Soc., Nat. Hist. Soc., Nat. Trust Historic Preservation, Smithsonian Assn., Friends of Cast Iron Architecture, Soc. Archtl. Historians, Am. Heritage Soc., N.A.P.M. Editors Group (nat. sec. 1979-81, nat. chmn./pres. 1981-84), Am. Assn. State and Local History, Decorative Arts Soc. Indpls., Ind. Soc. Assn. Execs., Nat. Assn. Purchasing Mgmt. (W.L. Beckham internat. pub. relations award 1983), Purchasing Mgmt. Assn. Indpls. (dir. 1974—), Victorian Soc. Am. (nat. sec. 1971-74), Lambda Chi Alpha, Alpha Delta Sigma, Sigma Delta Chi, Tau Kappa Alpha. Club: Indpls. Press, Rolls-Royce Owners. Author: The Mr. Eli Lilly that I Knew, 1977. Editor: Historic Landmarks News, 1969-74; Hoosier Purchasor mag., 1974-85, I.R.M.S.D.C. News, 1985-88. Contbr. articles to profl. jours. Home: 1415 W 52d St Indianapolis IN 46208

BRAUN, WARREN LLOYD, radio engineer; b. Postville, Iowa, Aug. 11, 1922; s. Karl William and Cornelia (Mueller) B.; BSEE, Valparaiso Tech. Inst., 1940-41, Capitol Engring. Inst., 1953, Alexander Hamilton Inst., 1953, DSc (hon.) Shenandoah Coll. Registered profl. engr., Va., S.C.; m. Lillian Cooke Stone, May 24, 1942; children: Warren L. (dec.), Dikki Carol. Chief engr. Sta. WKEY, 1941, Sta. WSVA, 1941, later gen. mgr. Sta. WSVA-AM-FM-TV; v.p. EWSP Corp.; E.S.M.W.T.P. sect. head, 1942-45; charge installation stas. WSIR, WTON, WSVA-FM, WJMA, TV stas. WAAM-TV and WSVA-TV, Blue Ridge TV cable facilities, 1945-60; asst. gen. mgr., dir. engring. WSVA-AM-FM-TV, 1959-63; v.p. Market Dimensions, Inc.; chief exec. officer, chmn. bd. ComSonics, Inc., 1972—, Shenandoah Valley Devel. Corp., 1972—.Panel 4 mem. TV Allocations Study Orgn.; chmn. Harrisonburg-Rockingham County Recreational Study Commn.; chmn. Upper Valley Regional Park Authority; mem. Va. Citizens Coun. for Recreation; mem. Va. Air Pollution Control Bd., 1966-73, Va. State Water Control Bd., 1974-82, vice-chmn., 1976-77, chmn., 1977-78, Harrisonburg-Rockingham County Regional Sewer Authority; commr. Ohio River San. Commn., 1974-82, chmn., 1978-80; v.p. Harrisonburg-Rockingham County Community Concert Assn.; mem. SE USA and Japan Bd. Trade Assn. Va., 1972—; bd. dirs. Richmond Regional Export Coun. , Va. Cultural Laureate Found.; bd. dirs. Employee Stock Ownership Coun. Am., 1977—, vice-chmn., 1984-85, pres. 1985-86, chmn. 1987—. Recipient Jefferson Davis medal, 1961, A.S.E. Internat. award, 1969. Fellow Audio Engring. Soc., Internat. Consular Acad. (Reitzke award 1972); mem. Nat. Assn. Broadcasters (nat. chmn. tape standards com., engring. adv. com. 1966), IEEE, Va. Assn. Professions (v.p 1972-73, pres. 1974-75), Va. Soc. Profl. Engrs. (bd. dir., pres. Skyline chpt., named Engr. of Yr. 1965, Disting. Svc. award 1974), Nat. Soc. Profl. Engrs. (mem. air pollution control task force), Acoustical Soc. Am., Soc. Motion Picture and T.V. Engrs., Am. Soc. Heating Refrigerating and Air Conditioning Engrs., Nat. Soc. Profl. Engrs. (mem. air pollution control task force), Electronics Industry Assn. (mem. broadband communications standards com.), Harrisonburg-Rock County C. of C. (pres. 1965, Harrisonburg-Rockingham Man of Yr. 1965, Exec. of Yr. 1983, Businessman of Yr. 1985), Am. Soc. Testing and Materials, Va. Acad. Scis. (dir., exec. com.), Va. C. of C. (chmn. world trade com. 1969-71, bd. dirs. 1973-77, v.p. 1975-77), Elks (Richmond). Office: ComSonics Inc 1350 Port Republic Rd Harrisonburg VA 22801

BRAUSA, G. STEVEN, insurance company executive; b. Mattoon, Ill., Apr. 18, 1951; s. Ralph Jerome and Margaret May (Stevenson) B.; m. Vida Minoo, Dec. 20, 1975; children: Heather Renee, Robyn Nichol, Andrew Michael. BS, U. Kans., 1973; MBA, U. Tex., 1977. Analyst Arthur Anderson Co., Kansas City, Mo., 1977-78; securities analyst Tchrs. Inc. and Annuity, N.Y.C., 1978-79, sr. securities analyst, 1979-80, sr. portfolio analyst, 1980-82, asst. investment officer, 1982-84, investment officer, 1984-85, asst. v.p., 1985-87, 2nd v.p., 1987-88, v.p. securities, 1988—. Served to 1st lt. USAF, 1973-75. Republican. Office: Tchrs Ins & Annuity Assn 730 Third Ave New York NY 10017

BRAVERMAN, LOUISE M., architect; b. N.Y.C., Nov. 23, 1948; d. Don S. and Madlyn (Barotz) B.; m. Steven Z. Glickel, July 1, 1984; 1 child, Jennifer Liberty. BA, U. Mich., 1970; MArch, Yale U., 1977. Registered architect, N.Y. Ptnr., architect Austin Braverman Patterson, Architects, N.Y.C. and Southport, Conn., 1982—; guest design critic Yale U., Columbia U., U. Pa., Cooper Union U., Syracuse U., Bryn Mawr Coll., Ohio State U. Mem. Am. Inst. Architects, Archtl. League, Assn. Real Estate Women, Nat. Women's Mus. (charter). Club: Yale (N.Y.C.). Office: Austin Braverman Patterson Architects 39 E 31 St New York NY 10016

BRAVMANN, LUDWIG, investment banker; b. Würzburg, Fed. Republic Germany, Apr. 15, 1925; came to U.S, 1941; s. Samuel and Flora (Lehmann) B.; m. Lotte Simon, March 20, 1949; children: Judith Kaufthal, Carol. Student, CCNY, 1952-53. Silversmith Durham Silver, N.Y.C., 1941-43, 46-52; with Oppenheimer & Co., N.Y.C., 1952-62, ptnr., 1962—. Trustee United Jewish Appeal Fedn., Yeshiva U. Served with U.S. Army, 1943-46. Decorated Bronze Star. Jewish. Office: Oppenheimer & Co Inc World Financial Ctr New York NY 10281

BRAVO, CARLOS EDUARDO, finance executive; b. Santurce, P.R., Jan. 20, 1959; s. Carlos E. and Dolores (Almenar) B; m. Rose Pazos, Dec. 23, 1983; children: Otto, Sheena. BS in Aerospace Engring., U. Fla., 1981, MS in Engring. and Applied Maths., 1983; MBA, Northwestern U., 1988. Registered profl. engr., Fla. Salesman MacGregor Auto Sales, Gainesville, Fla., 1979-80; project dir., cons. CEB Engring., Gainesville, 1980-85; computer techniques specialist GE, Gainesville, 1983-85; sr. test engr. Snap-on-Tools, Kenosha, Wis., 1985; project mgr. Snap-on-Tools, Kenosha, 1985-86, mgr., bus. devel., 1987—; pres. Bravo Internat., Kenosha, 1988—. Capt. United Way, Gainesville, 1983-85. Mem. Soc. for Indsl. and Applied Math., Soc. Automotive Engrs., Exptl. Aircraft Assn. Republican.

BRAWLEY, BILLY FRANK, oil company executive; b. Erick, Okla., Oct. 24, 1929; s. Samuel Franklin and Ida Mae (Moore) B.; m. Maxine M. Ellis, Nov. 25, 1949; children: Phyllis Lea Tidwell, William Wade. BS in Petroleum Engring., U. Okla., 1956. Sr. engr. Sunray DX Oil Co., Wichita, Kans., 1960-62; div. methods engr. Sunray DX Oil Co., Houston, 1962-64; dist. engr. Sunray DX Oil Co., Roswell, N.Mex., 1964-69; regional mgr. engring. Sun Exploration & Prodn. Co., Ventura, Calif., 1969-73; mgr. Calif. offshore Sun Exploration & Prodn. Co., Ventura, 1973-76; ops. mgr. Sun Exploration & Prodn. Co., Houston, 1976-80; dist. mgr. Sun Exploration & Prodn. Co., Valencia, Calif., 1980-84; gen. dist. mgr. Sun Exploration & Prodn. Co., Denver, 1984-88; exec. v.p. H&W Drilling Fluids Inc., Denver, 1988—. Chmn. Santa Clarita Valley United Way, Valencia, 1982; exec. com. Los Angeles United Way, Region 1, 1982, bd. dirs., 1982; bd. dirs. Boys & Girls Club Am., Valencia, 1983. Served as sgt. U.S. Army, 1950-52. Named Vol. of Yr., United Way, Valencia, 1984. Mem. Rocky Mountain Oil and Gas Assn. (bd. dirs. 1987—), Soc. Petroleum Engrs. (chpt. chmn. 1968-69), Am. Petroleum Inst., Internat. Assn. Drilling Contractors. Republican. Mem. Disciples of Christ Ch. Home: 3008 E Nichols Cir Littleton CO 80122 Office: H&W Drilling Fluids Inc 5524 S Prince St Littleton CO 80120

BRAY, ARTHUR PHILIP, management science corporation executive; b. San Francisco, Sept. 23, 1933; s. Arthur T. and Anna F. (Nevin) B.; m. Grace McCarthy, June 16, 1956; children: Bernard, Peter, Erin, Eileen, Mary, Florence. AA, San Francisco City Coll., 1953; BSME with highest honors, U. Calif., Berkeley, 1955. Registered profl. engr., N.Y., Calif. With nuclear power systems div. GE, San Jose, Calif., 1955-84; v.p., gen. mgr. nuclear power systems div. GE, San Jose, 1978-84; exec. v.p. Mgmt. Analysis Co., San Diego, 1984-86; pres., chief exec. officer Mgmt. Analysis Co. Internat., San Diego, 1986—; pres., chief exec. officer Renewable Resources Systems, Inc., Menlo Park, Calif., 1986-88, vice chmn., mng. dir., 1988—; bd. dirs. CommBank of San Francisco, 1978-82, Sequoia Nat. Bank, 1986—, Superstill Tech., Redwood City, Calif., Thermal Energy Storage., Inc., San Diego, SAI Geothermal Co., Santa Clara, Calif.; bd. chmn. Goose Lake Lumber Co., Lakeview, Oreg., 1987—, Teal-Tech, Inc., Santa Clara, 1987—. Co-author: Nuclear Power and the Public, 1970; author: Key Computer Programs in Heat Transfer and Reactor Analysis, 1956, rev. edit., 1964; patentee in field. Bd. fellows, regent Bellarmine Coll. Prep., San Jose., U. Santa Clara, Calif., mem. dean's adv. council Sch. Engring., San Jose State U.; founding. mem. San Jose Reperatory Co., 1980-84. Recipient Ernest O. Laurence Meml. award U.S. Dept. Energy, 1977. Mem. Nat. Acad. Engring., Am. Nuclear Soc., ASME, Atomic Industrial Forum, Olympic Club, Phi Beta Kappa, Tau Beta Pi, Pi Tau Sigma. Republican. Roman Catholic. Office: Renewable Resources Systems Inc Bldg 4 Ste 160 3000 Sand Hill Rd Menlo Park CA 94025

BRAY, WILLIAM ALBERT, communications executive; b. Bethany, Mo., Dec. 4, 1924; s. Chester Sharp and Goldie Mae (Meyer) B.; m. Jo Anne Pace, Feb. 8, 1953; children: David Pace, Brenda Anne. BJ, U. Mo., 1948. Editor, pub. The Odessan, Odessa, Mo., 1948-56; assoc. prof. journalism U. Mo., Columbia, 1953-84; exec. dir. Mo. Press Assn., Columbia, 1953—. Editor: (continuing series) Publisher's Handbook; Mo. Press News, 1953-85. Apointee by gov. adv. bd. Mo. State Hist. Archives, Jefferson City, Mo., 1982—; mem. Columbia Futures Com., 1987. Served as sgt. with inf. U.S. Army, 1943-46, ETO. Recipient Mo. Honor medal U. Mo., 1985, Disting. Service award Nat. Assn. Secs. State, 1985. Mem. Nat. Newspaper Found. (trustee, 1982-87), Newspaper Assn. Mgrs. (pres. 1958-59, Am. Newspaper Reps. (sec. 1960-65), Nat. Newspaper Assn. (bd. dirs. 1959-60, com. long-range planning, Disting. Service award 1966, Amos award 1985), Mo. Associated Dailies (sec., treas. 1960—), Mo. Press Found. (sec. 1984—), Sigma Delta Chi. Democrat. Mem. Christian Ch. (Disciples of Christ). Office: Mo Press Assn 802 Locust Columbia MO 65201

BRAYMER, MARGUERITE ANNETTA, optical company executive; b. Camden, N.J., Mar. 25, 1911; d. Arthur Thomas and Annetta May (Sherman) Adams; m. Raymond A. Dodd, Sept. 12, 1931; 1 child, Peter R.; m. Lawrence Braymer, Mar. 25, 1950 (dec.). Student, South Jersey Law Sch., 1929-30. Freelance writer various mags., 1950-54; decorating editor Woman's Day mag., N.Y.C., 1944-53; sec. Questar Corp., New Hope, Pa., 1950-65, pres., advt. dir., 1965-76, chmn., advt. dir., 1976—; pres., founder Questar Libr. Sci. and Art, New Hope, 1980—. Author America's Homemaking Book, 1957, America's Cookbook, 1963. Active Small Bus. Task Force, Washington, 1982-84; trustee New Sch. of Music, Phila., 1973-83. Recipient Bus. Achievement award, Cen. Bucks C. of C., Bucks County, Pa., 1985. Democrat. Episcopalian. Home: PO Box 157 New Hope PA 18938 Office: Questar Corp PO Box 59 New Hope PA 18938

BRAYSON, ALBERT ALOYSIUS, II, educational association administrator; b. Port Jefferson, N.Y., June 28, 1953; s. Albert Aloysius and Julie Elizabeth (Krantz) B.; m. Barbara Norris Skretch, June 18, 1977; children: Albert III, Caroline Elizabeth. BA, Elmira (N.Y.) Coll., 1975; MS in Edn., Adelphi U., 1979. Tchr. Lake Grove (N.Y.) Sch., 1975-77, asst. headmaster, 1977-79, exec. dir., 1979—; pres. Lake Grove Sch. and Treatment Ctrs., Durham, Conn., 1985—; cons. Valleyhead Sch., Lenox, Mass., 1985—; grant reviewer U.S. Govt., 1985-87. Treas. Lake Grove Village Ind. Party, 1980. Mem. Nat. Assn. Pvt. Schs. for Exceptional Children, Council for Exceptional Children, Council for Assn. Services to Exceptional Services, Orgn. to Assure Services to Exceptional Students. Republican. Lodge: Lions (pres. 1986). Club: Stony Brook Yacht. Office: Lake Grove Sch Moriches Rd Lake Grove NY 11755

BRAZ, EVANDRO FREITAS, management consultant; b. Rio de Janeiro, Apr. 20, 1943; came to U.S., 1966; s. Jose Nunes and Edir (Freitas) B.; B.S. in Mech. Engring., Rio de Janeiro U., 1965; M.S. in Indsl. Engring., Columbia U., 1967, M.B.A. (OAS fellow), 1968; m. Darline Kristina Ryther, Dec. 28, 1968; children—Erica Denise, Daniel William, Max Elliot. Assoc. engr., Mass Transit Authority, Rio de Janeiro, 1964; prodn. engr. Gen. Electric Corp., Rio de Janeiro, 1965-66; cons. mgmt. cons. services Coopers & Lybrand, N.Y.C., 1968-72, mgr. mgmt. cons. services, 1972-76, prin., partner mgmt. cons. services, 1976-81, prin. partner nat. office, 1981-85, N.Y. Office, 1986—. Registered profl. engr., Brazil. Mem. Inst. Mgmt. Cons. (cert.), Inst. Mgmt. Scis., Nat. Assn. Accts., Am. Prodn. and Inventory Control Soc., Am. Arbitration Assn., Am. Constrn. Owners Assn. Roman Catholic. Club: Mt. Kisco (N.Y.) Country. Home: 14 Whitlaw Close Chappaqua NY 10514 Office: Coopers & Lybrand 1251 Ave of the Americas New York NY 10020

BREATHITT, EDWARD THOMPSON, JR., lawyer, railroad executive; b. Hopkinsville, Ky., Nov. 26, 1924; s. Edward Thompson Sr. and Mary Josephine (Wallace) B.; m. Lucy Alexander Breathitt; children: Mary Frances, Linda Key, Susan Holleman, Edward Thompson III. BS in Commerce, U. Ky., 1947, LL.B., 1950, JD, 1970, LL.D. (hon.), 1965; LL.D. (hon.), U. Marshall, 1966, Ky. Wesleyan, 1967. Bar: Ky. 1950, U.S. Supreme Ct. 1974. Assoc. Trimble, Soyars & Breathitt, Hopkinsville, 1960-62; gov. State of Ky., Frankfort, 1963-67; assoc. Trimble, Soyars & Breathitt, Hopkinsville, 1968-72; v.p. Southern Railway Co., Washington, 1972-82; v.p. Norfolk Southern Corp., Washington, 1982-86, sr. v.p., 1986—; bd. dirs. Castleton Farm Inc., Lexington, Ky., 1982—; mem. adv. bd. Am. Security Bank, Washington, 1987; bd. dirs. Morehead State U., 1986—; mem. Ky. Econ. Devel. Corp., 1979—. Mem. legis. State of Ky., Frankfort, 1952-56; chmn. and pres. Commn. on Rural Property, Washington, 1965-67; pres. Commn. to Fulfill These Rights, Washington, 1965-67. Served with USAAF, 1942-45. Named Conservationist of Yr. Nat. Wildlife Fedn. and Outdoor Life Mag., 1966; recipient Conservationist award U.S. Dept. of Interior, 1967, Lincoln Key award for Civil Rights, 1966. Fellow U. Ky.; mem. Ky. Bar Assn., D.C. Bar Assn. Democrat. Methodist. Club: Metropolitan, Chevy Chase, Burning Tree (Washington); Pendenis (Louisville, Ky.). Home: 892 Canton Heights #1 Cadiz KY 42211 Office: Norfolk So Corp 1050 Connecticut Ave NW #740 Washington DC 20036

BREBACH, GRESHAM T., JR., accounting company executive; b. Mpls., Nov. 14, 1940; m. Judith Stephenson; children: Gregory, Elizabeth, Amanda, Mark. BS in Engring., U. Ill., 1962, MBA, 1964. With cons. div. Arthur Andersen & Co., Chgo., 1964-74, cons. ptnr., 1974-84; ptnr.-in-charge cons. div. Arthur Andersen & Co., N.Y.C., 1984-87, mng. ptnr. U.S. cons., 1987—. Mem. U. Ill. Commerce Assn., 1978—, pres., 1983-84. Mem. University Club Chgo.

BRECHT, SALLY ANN, corporate quality assurance executive; b. Trenton, N.J., Aug. 5, 1951; d. Charles L. and Helen (Orfeo) B. BBA, Coll. William & Mary in Va., 1973; MBA, Rider Coll., 1981. Electronic data processing auditor McGraw Hill, Inc., Hightstown, N.J., 1976-79, State of N.J., Mercerville, 1979-80, NL Industries, Hightstown, 1980-84; systems tech. planning specialist Ednl. Testing Service, Princeton, N.J., 1984-85, acting div. dir. application devel., 1985-87, mgr. computer standards and security, 1987-88, asst. dir. office corp. quality assurance, 1988—. Office: Ednl Testing Svc Rosedale Rd Princeton NJ 08520

BREDESEN, PHILIP NORMAN, chemical company executive; b. Oceanport, N.J., Nov. 21, 1943; s. Philip Norman and Norma (Walborn) B.; m. Andrea Conte, Nov. 22, 1974; 1 child, Benjamin. AB in Physics, Harvard U., 1967. Dir. systems devel. Searle Medidata, Lexington, Mass., 1970-73; div. mgr. Searle Medidata, London, 1973-75; dir. spl. project Hosp. Affiliates Internat., Nashville, 1975-78; v.p. internat. div. INA Health Care Group, Nashville, 1978-80; chmn. HealthAm. Inc., Nashville, 1980-86, Clin. Pharms., Nashville, 1986—; bd. dirs. Coventry Corp, Ft. Worth, 1st Commonwealth, Chgo., Convenient Home Services, Ft. Lauderdale, Fla. Bd. dirs. United Way of Middle Tenn., Nashville, 1985, Nashville Bus. Incubation Ctr., 1985, Nashville Symphony, 1985; candidate for mayor, Nashville, 1987—; candidate for U.S. Ho. of Reps. (5th dist.) Tenn. Democrat. Presbyterian. Home: 1724 Chickering Rd Nashville TN 37215 Office: Clin Pharms Inc 3310 W End Ave Nashville TN 37203

BREDIN, J(OHN) BRUCE, real estate executive; b. Wilmington, Del., June 1, 1914; s. Robert and Margaret (Starrett) B.; student Coll. William and Mary, 1932-34, U. Pa., 1938-40, LLD (hon.) Coll. William and Mary; m. Octavia M. duPont, Aug. 4, 1945; children—Stephanie S. du P. B. Speakman, Margaretta Starrett Bredin Brokaw, Jonathan Bruce, Alletta Bredin-Bell, Laura L. Bredin Hussey, Antonia duPont Massie. Civilian employee U.S. Govt., 1934-38; with E.I. du Pont de Nemours & Co., 1939-45, 49-52, Texaco, 1945-46; pres. Bredin Realty Co., 1950-81; Participant in Smithsonian expdns. to Africa and West Indies; mem. spl. fine arts com. Dept. State; chmn. Fund for the Diplomatic Reception Rms. Found., Dept. State; mem. trustee adv. com. Longwood Gardens Inc.; mem. devel. com. Woods Hole Oceanographic Inst.; pres. Bredin Found.; founding chmn. Henry Francis Du Pont Collectors Circle; emeritus bd. dirs. Med. Center of Del.; trustee Unidel Found.; trustee, vice chmn. Henry Francis du Pont Winterthur Mus.; trustee Endowment Assn. Coll. William and Mary; hon. trustee Foxcroft Sch. (life), U. Del.; bd. dirs. U. Del. Library Assocs.; pres. Bartol Research Inst. U. Del.; mem. fin. com. Christ Ch., Christiana Hundred; lifetime trustee & dir. Med. Ctr. Del. Hosp. Found.; corp. mem. Nantucket Cottage Hosp.; Hon. fellow Smithsonian Instn.; mem. Del. Acad. Medicine (dir.), Hist. Soc. Del. (trustee), Am. Competitive Enterprise System (hon. life dir.) Confrerie des Chevaliers du Tastevin. Clubs: Vicmead Hunt, Greenville Country, Wilmington, Wilmington Country; Corinthian Yacht (Phila.); Everglades, Soc. of Four Arts (Palm Beach, Fla.); Gulf Stream Bath and Tennis, Gulf Stream Golf (Delray Beach, Fla.); Nantucket Yacht, Sankaty Head Golf (Nantucket); Met. (Washington). Home: PO Box 3598 Wilmington DE 19807 Office: 5724 Montchanin Bldg PO Box 87 Wilmington DE 19899

BREEN, JOHN GERALD, manufacturing company executive; b. Cleve., July 21, 1934; s. Hugh Gerald and Margaret Cecelia (Bonner) B.; m. Mary Jane Brubach, Apr. 12, 1958; children: Kathleen Anne, John Patrick, James Phillip, David Hugh, Anne Margaret. B.S., John Carroll U., 1956; M.B.A., Case Western Res. U., 1961. With Clevite Corp., Cleve., 1957-73, gen. mgr. foil div., 1969-73, gen. mgr. engine parts div., 1973-74; group v.p. indsl. group Gould Inc., Rolling Meadows, Ill., 1974-77, exec. v.p., 1977-79; pres. Sherwin Williams Co., Cleve., 1979-86, chief exec. officer, 1979—, chmn., 1980—, also dir.; dir. Parker Hannifin Corp., Cleve., Nat. City Bank, Cleve., Mead Corp., Dayton, Ohio. Served with U.S. Army, 1956-57. Clubs: Pepper Pike, Union, Cleve. Skating. Home: 2727 Cranlyn Rd Shaker Heights OH 44122 Office: Sherwin-Williams Co 101 Prospect Ave NW Cleveland OH 44115

BREEN, PATRICIA HELEN HALL, financial consultant; b. Detroit, Sept. 15, 1926; d. John William and Ethel Viola (Mardian) Hall. BBA, U. Mich., 1949; postgrad. U. Mich.-Detroit, 1953-54. Policy and procedure sec. Gen. Motors Central, Detroit, 1949-50; trust investment analyst Nat. Bank of Detroit, 1950-51; investment analyst Baxter & Co., Cleve., 1952; sr. fin. cons. Merrill Lynch, Farmington Hills, Mich., 1957—; founder, chmn., pres., chief exec. officer Good Food Co., Livonia, Mich.; radio and TV lectr. Mem. Nat. Assn. Female Execs. (pres. Oakland County 1985-87), U. Mich. Alumnae Assn. (bd. dirs. 1973-74). Republican. Roman Catholic. Club: Detroit Boat (Belle Isle, Mich.), 300, Oakland County Reps. Avocations: silversmithing, oil painting, writing, water- and snow-skiing, golf. Home: 17959 University Park Dr Livonia MI 48152 Office: Merrill Lynch Pierce Fenner & Smith Inc Triatria Bldg Ste 260 32255 Northwestern Hwy Farmington Hills MI 48018

BREEN, SEAN PATRICK, publisher; b. Teaneck, N.J., Oct. 15, 1954; s. John Patrick and Catherine Elizabeth (Giblin) B. BA, U. Dayton, 1976; MBA, Emory U., 1981. Reporter, editor Jour. Herald, Dayton, Ohio, 1976-81; mktg. intern Milliken and Co., Spartanburg, S.C., 1981-82; freelance editor Atlanta, 1982-83; staff writer Atlanta Bus. Chronicle, 1983-84; mng. editor S. Fla. Bus. Jour., Miami, 1984-85, editor, 1985-86, pub., 1986—, pres., 1987—. Area rep. Emory U. Sch. bus., 1987—; mem. S. Fla. Coordinating Council, 1987—. Mem. Advt. Fedn. Greater Miami. Home: 2715 Tigertail Ave PH 1 Coconut Grove FL 33133 Office: S Fla Bus Jour 7950 NE 53rd St Ste 210 Miami FL 33166

BREEN, THOMAS ALBERT, financial services executive; b. Ft. Benning, Ga., Apr. 18, 1956; s. Thomas Alden and Anne Marie (Brun) B.; m. Linda Whitney, June 16, 1979; children: Matthew, Andrew. BSBA in Acctg., Colo. State U., 1979. CPA, Colo. With audit staff Coopers & Lybrand, Denver, 1979-81; audit supr. Hein & Assocs., Denver, 1981-84; v.p. fin. Orion Broadcast Group, Inc., Denver, 1984-89, Englewood, Colo., 1989—; bd. dirs. FN Realty Svcs., Inc., Pasedena, Calif., Vehicle Resource Corp., FNRS Fin. Corp. Mem. AICPA, Colo. Soc. CPA's. Office: Orion Broadcast Group Inc 6061 S Willow Dr Ste 117 Englewood CO 80111

BREEN, THOMAS JOHN, form publishing company executive; b. Chgo., May 29, 1948. BS in Mech. Engring., U. Ill., 1971; MBA, Northwestern U., 1975. With Am. Can Co., Chgo., 1971-72, Northwest Ind., Chgo., 1972-74, Rockwell Internat., various locations, 1974-79; group pres. Rand McNally, Skokie, Ill., 1979—. Patentee in field. Office: Rand McNally & Co 8255 N Central Park Ave Skokie IL 60076

BREEZE, FRANK V., manufacturing company executive; b. Centralia, Ill., July 28, 1924; s. Clint F. and Fredia I. (Beadle) B.; divorced; children: Mark Furmon, Clint R., Chris Francis, Kurt Douglas, Lynn Breeze Schultz. BSME, U. Mo., Rolla, 1949, hon. degree, 1967; postgrad., Harvard U. Engr. trainee PPG Industries, Inc., Crystal City, Mo., 1949-52, project engr., 1952-54, asst. to plant engr., 1954-55, asst. plant engr., 1955-57, fabrication engr., 1957-58, supt. fabrication, 1958-59, asst. plant mgr., 1959-60, plant mgr., 1960-69, gen. mgr. window glass plants, glass div., 1969-71, mgr. primary glass, flat glass div., 1971-72, dir. planning and devel., glass div., 1972-73, v.p., asst. gen. mgr. glass div., 1973, v.p., gen. mgr. glass div., 1973-77, group v.p. glass, 1977-80, sr. v.p., 1980-84; vice chmn. bd. dirs., chief adminstrv. officer PPG Industries, Inc., Pitts., 1984—, also bd. dirs.; bd. dirs. Armstrong World Industries, Lancaster, Pa. Served to staff sgt. U.S. Army, 1943-45, ETO. Decorated Bronze Star, Purple Heart. Mem. Nat. Assn. Mfrs. (bd. dirs. 1981—). Republican. Clubs: Duquesne (Pitts.); Rolling Rock (Ligonier), Laurel Valley Golf. Office: PPG Industries Inc 1 PPG Pl Pittsburgh PA 15272

BREEZLEY, ROGER L., banker; b. Williston, N.D.; married. B.B.A., U. N.D. C.P.A., Oreg. Acct. Haskins & Sells, 1960-68; v.p. Moduline Internat. Inc., 1968-77; with U.S. Bancorp, Portland, Oreg., 1977—, with corp. devel. and fin. analysis depts., 1977-79, sr. v.p. fin. analysis planning, 1979-80, exec. v.p., 1980-82, treas., 1980—, vice chmn., 1982-87, chief operating officer, 1983-87, dir., chmn., chief exec. officer, 1987—; exec. v.p. U.S. Nat. Bank of Oreg. (subs.), Portland, 1980-82, vice chmn., chief operating officer, 1982—; also dir. U.S. Nat. Bank of Oreg. (subs.). Office: US Bancorp US Bancorp Tower 111 SW 5th Ave PO Box 8837 Portland OR 97208

BREHM, FREDERICK CARL, management consultant; b. N.Y.C., June 3, 1930; s. Frederick Karl and Jeanette Eleanor (Reuthe) B.; m. Barbara Louise Hebb, Aug. 2, 1952; children: Susan Ellen, Barbara Ann, Mary Jo, Frederick Carl III, Caroline Louise. BA cum laude, U. Conn., 1953; postgrad. in bus., NYU, 1958-65. With Hazeltine Corp., Greenlawn, N.Y., 1956-88, sr. v.p. govt. products, 1984-86, sr. v.p., govt. systems, 1986-88; pres. Def. Resources Internat., Inc., Huntington, N.Y., 1988—. Pres. East Gate Assn., Inc., Lloyd Harbor, N.Y., 1986-88. Served with USAF, 1953-56. Recipient Meritorious Pub. Service medal USN, 1982. Mem. Nat. Security Indsl. Assn. (chmn. ASW com. 1980-82, mem. exec. com. 1982—, Charles B. Weakley award 1983), Armed Forces Communications and Electronics Assn., Air Force Assn., Assn. U.S. Army, Navy League U.S. Republican. Presbyterian. Home: 1 East Gate Rd Lloyd Harbor NY 11743

BREITBARTH, LARRY ALLEN, business valuation analyst; b. Harvey, Ill., Nov. 16, 1963; s. Donald Marnell and Suzanne (Wakeham) B.; m. Jessica Heath, Aug. 2, 1986. BA in Fin. cum laude, U. Ill., 1985; MBA, U. Chgo., 1988. Bus. valuation analyst Arthur Andersen & Co., Chgo., 1985—. Mem. Phi Beta Kappa. Lutheran. Office: Arthur Andersen & Co 10 S La Salle 32d Fl Chicago IL 60603

BREITBARTH, S. ROBERT, manufacturing company executive; b. Newark, N.J., July 15, 1925; s. Jacob and Rose (Brandman) B.; m. Laurel Patricia Stroh, Oct. 30, 1949; children: Meredith Jane, Jill Gretchen. B.E.E., Cornell U., 1949. Vice pres. Gen. Cable Corp., Greenwich, Conn., 1966-77; exec. v.p. Gen. Cable Corp., 1976-78; pres. Gen. Cable Internat., Inc., 1978-85, also dir.; v.p. GK Technologies, Inc., 1979-82; pres. Waterbury (Conn.) Wire Inc., 1987—, also bd. dirs.; bd. dirs. Bankest Capital Corp., Miami. Treas. Stony Point Assn., Westport, Conn., 1973-75, pres., 1975-76, 87-88. Served with USAAF, 1944-46. Decorated Venezuela-Orden al Merito en el Trabajo Primera Clase. Mem. U.S. Investment in Spain Com. (chmn. 1977-80), Spain-U.S. C. of C. (bd. dirs.), Wire Assn., IEEE, Cornell Soc. Engrs. Home: 2 Stony Point Westport CT 06880

BREITKREUZ, GEORGE WILLIAM, publishing company executive; b. West New York, N.J., Feb. 22, 1928; s. Henry B.; m. Viola Kinkel, 1950; children: Thomas, Linda, Steven, Kenneth. B.B.A., Pace U., 1950. Auditor Ernst & Ernst (C.P.A.s), N.Y.C., 1951-54; v.p., treas. Am. Heritage Pub. Co., N.Y.C., 1955-70; v.p. fin. Daniel Starch & Staff, Mamaroneck, N.Y., 1970; v.p. fin., treas. Elba Systems Corp., Denver, 1970-73; exec. v.p. fin. and corp. services Houghton Mifflin Co., Boston, 1973—; also dir. Houghton Mifflin Co. Served with AUS, 1946-47. Mem. Fin. Execs. Inst. Baptist. Home: 52 Fairoaks Ln Cohasset MA 02025 Office: Houghton Mifflin Co 1 Beacon St Boston MA 02107

BREITWEISER, WILLIAM DAN, investment executive; b. Pitts., Oct. 19, 1948; s. John Frederick Nicholas and Jeanne Eleanor (Jones) B.; m. Lyn Varney, Dec. 12, 1967 (div. Mar. 1970); 1 child, Karen Elaine; m. Brenda Lee Beener, Apr. 4, 1971 (div. Oct. 1978); m. Carole Lee Moore, July 14, 1979. Grad. high sch., Bethel Park, Pa., 1966. Lic. commodities broker, ins. agt., Pa. Adjuster Singer Co., Pitts., 1966-67, salesman, asst. mgr., 1968-70; owner Southland Sewing Ctr., Pitts., 1970-78; mgr., salesman Pool City, Pitts., 1978-85; investment advisor Paine Webber, Pitts., 1985—. Mem. Beallsville Boro Council, 1988. Served with USAF, 1967-68. Methodist. Lodge: Masons. Home: PO Box 264 Beallsville PA 15313 Office: Paine Webber 525 William Penn Pl 35th Fl Pittsburgh PA 15219

BREMER, JOHN PAUL, management consultant; b. St. Louis, Apr. 11, 1926; s. Jesse Currier and Eunice Sibylla (Schaus) B.; student U. Ill., 1946-47, U. Lausanne, 1947-48, Sorbonne, Paris, 1948; M.B.A., U. Chgo., 1955. Sales, tech. rep. IBM Corp., Washington, 1955-58; sr. data processing cons. Vaule & Co., Providence, 1958-63; co-founder, pres. Systemation, Inc., Boston, 1963-71; sr. cons., mgr. Mgmt. Cons. Group, Keane Assocs., Wellesley, Mass., 1971-74; pres. Bremer Assocs., Inc., Boston, 1974—. Served with AUS, 1944-46. Lutheran. Club:University (Boston), Algonquin. Home: 191 Commonwealth Ave Boston MA 02116 Office: 8 Newbury St Boston MA 02116

BRENDLE, DOUGLAS DAVID, retail executive; b. Elkin, N.C., July 4, 1928; s. James David and Edna (Arnold) B.; m. Lydia Jane Underwood, Aug. 21, 1954; 1 child, Adelia Jane. Student, Wake Forest U., 1947; BS in Acctg., Bowling Green U., 1950. Buyer/salesman Brendle's Cash Wholesale, Inc., Elkin, N.C., 1952-55, buyer/salesman, sec.-treas., 1956-66, sec., treas., 1956-84, pres., chief exec. officer, 1984—, also chmn. bd. dirs. Trustee Bapt. Childrens' Homes, Thomasville, N.C., Wake Forest U., advisor bus. sch.; advisor Campbell U., Appalachian State U., Boone, N.C. Sgt. U.S. Army, 1950-52. Democrat. Baptist. Office: Brendles Inc 1919 N Bridge St Elkin NC 28621 Home: 2000 Georgia Ave Winston-Salem NC 27104

BRENDLEY, DONALD JOSEPH, financial executive; b. East St. Louis, Ill., Oct. 4, 1935; s. Fred W. and Agnes M. (Clancy) B.; m. Dolores A. Cummings, June 30, 1956; children: Donald, Keith, David, Craig. BS in Bus. Adminstrn., So. Ill. U., 1966; EDP, Cornell U., 1981. Budget analyst McDonnell-Douglas Co., St. Louis, 1964-66; plant controller Arvin Industries, Oneida, Tenn., 1966-68; asst. controller Hobbs div. Stewart Warner, Inc., Springfield, Ill., 1968-73; v.p., controller Revere Copper & Brass Co., Clinton, Ill., 1973-85; v.p. fin. The Knapheide Mfg. Co., Quincy, Ill., 1985—, also bd. dirs.; instr. acctg. Richland Community Coll., Decatur, Ill. 1981-85. Bd. dirs. YMCA, Clinton, 1982-85. Served with USAF, 1957-60. Mem. Nat. Assn. Accts. (bd. dirs. 1978-81), Clinton C. of C. Lodges: Elks, KC. Office: The Knapheide Mfg Co 436 S 6th St Quincy IL 62306

BRENDSEL, LELAND C., federal mortgage company executive. married. D. in Fin., Northwestern U.; prof., U. Utah. Prof. U. Utah; economist Farm Credit Banks, Fed. Home Loan Bank, Des Moines; exec. v.p., chief fin. officer Fed. Home Loan Mortgage Corp., Washington, 1982, pres., chief exec. officer. Office: Fed Home Loan Mortgage Corp 1759 Business Center Dr PO Box 4115 Reston VA 22090 *

BRENGEL, FRED L., manufacturing company executive; b. Hicksville, N.Y., 1923; married. B.S. in Mech. Engring., Stevens Inst. Tech., 1944. With Johnson Controls Inc. (formerly Johnson Service Co.), Milw., 1948—, v.p. sales, 1965-67, pres., 1967-86, chief exec. officer, 1967-88, chmn., 1985—, also dir.; bd. dirs. First Wis. Corp., Heil Co., Wis. Bell, Harley-Davidson. Served to lt. USN, 1943-46. Office: Johnson Controls Inc 5757 N Green Bay Ave Box 591 Milwaukee WI 53201 *

BRENNAN, BERNARD FRANCIS, retail chain store executive; b. Chgo., 1938; married. B.A., Coll. St. Thomas, 1964. With Sears, Roebuck & Co., Chgo., 1964-76; with Sav-A-Stop, Inc., 1976-82, group v.p.-service mdse. group, 1976-78, pres., chief operating officer, 1978-79, pres., chief exec. officer, 1979-82, chmn., 1982; exec. v.p. Montgomery Ward & Co., Inc., Chgo., 1982-83, pres., chief exec. officer, 1985—; pres. Household Merchandising Inc., Des Plaines, Ill., 1983-85. Served with U.S. Army, 1958-60, 62. Office: Montgomery Ward & Co Inc 1 Montgomery Ward Pla Chicago IL 60671 *

BRENNAN, CHARLES MARTIN, III, construction company executive; b. New Haven, Jan. 30, 1942; s. Charles Martin Jr. and Margaret Mary (Gleeson) B.; m. Mary Day Ely, June 22, 1966; children: Elizabeth Martin, Cynthia Herrick. BA, Yale U., 1964; MBA, Columbia U., 1969. Gen. mgr. New Haven Malleable Iron co., 1966-68; fin. analyst Scovill Mfg. co., 1969-71; treas. Cerro Corp., N.Y.C., 1971-74, Gould Inc., Chgo., 1974-76; mng. dir. Imperial Trans Europe N.V. (46 percent subs. of Gould Inc.), London, 1976-79; v.p. Latin Am. Gould, Inc., Sao Paulo, Brazil, 1979-80; sr. v.p., chief. fin. officer Gould, Inc., Chgo., 1980-88, sr. v.p., asst. to chmn. bd., 1988—, also bd. dirs.; chmn., chief exec. officer L.E. Myers Group, Inc., Oak Brook, Ill., 1988, The L.E. Myers Co. Group, Oak Brook, 1988—; bd. dirs. Northwest Meml. Hosp., Better Govt. Assn. Mem. Chgo. Club, Econ. Club. Republican. Episcopalian. Office: L E Myers Co Group 1010 Jorie Blvd Oak Brook IL 60521

BRENNAN, CIARAN BRENDAN, accountant, independent oil producer, real estate developer; b. Dublin, Ireland, Jan. 28, 1944; s. Sean and Mary (Stone) B. BA with honors, Univ. Coll., Dublin, 1966; MBA, Harvard U., 1973; MS in Acctg., U. Houston, 1976. Lic. real estate broker, Calif. Auditor Coopers & Lybrand, London, 1967-70; sr. auditor Price Waterhouse & Co., Toronto, Ont., Can., 1970-71; project acctg. specialist Kerr-McGee Corp., Oklahoma City, 1976-80; contr. Cummings Oil Co., Oklahoma City, 1980-82; chief fin. officer Red Stone Energies, Ltd., 1982, Hibernia Oil Inc., 1980—; treas., chief fin. officer Leonoco, Inc., 1982-87, JKJ Supply Co., 1983-87, Saturn Investments Inc., 1983-87, JFL Co., 1984-87, Little Chief Drilling & Energy Inc., 1984-85; chief fin. officer St. Regis Resources Corp., Culver City, Calif., 1988; pres. Ciaran Brennan Corp., 1980, Rathgar Securities, Inc., 1989—; bd. dirs., cons. small oil cos.; adj. faculty Okla. City U., 1977-86; vis. faculty Cen. State U., 1977-86. Contbr. articles to profl. jours. Mem. Inst. Chartered Accts. England and Wales, Inst. Chartered Accts. Can., Inst. Chartered Accts. in Ireland, AICPA, Tex. Soc. CPAs, Okla. Soc. CPAs, Calif. Soc. CPAs. Republican. Roman Catholic.

BRENNAN, DAVID LEO, lawyer, steel and transportation company executive; b. Akron, Ohio, July 5, 1931; s. Daniel Clark and Josephine (Winum) B.; m. Ann Amer, July 6, 1957; children: Elizabeth Ann, John Bernard, Kathleen Louise, Nancy Jane. BS, Ohio State U., 1953; LLB, Case Western Res. U., 1957; LLD (hon.), U. Akron, 1985. Bar: Ohio, 1957. Ptnr. Amer Cunningham Brennan Co. LPA, Akron, 1958—; chmn. bd. The Brenlin Group, Akron, 1975—. Mem. exec. com. Akron Regional Devel. Bd., 1988—. Mem. ABA, Ohio Bar Assn., Akron Bar Assn., Soc. Benchers. Republican. Roman Catholic. Home: 1200 Sunset View Dr Akron OH 44313 Office: The Brenlin Group 670 W Market St Akron OH 44303 also: Amer Cunningham Brennan Co 159 S Main St Akron OH 44308

BRENNAN, EDWARD A., retail and financial services executive; b. Chgo., Jan. 16, 1934; s. Edward and Margaret (Bourget) B.; m. Lois Lyon, June 11, 1955; children: Edward J., Cynthia Walls, Sharon Lisnow, Donald A., John L., Linda. BA, Marquette U., Milw., 1955. With Sears, Roebuck and Co., 1956—; exec. v.p. So. terr. Sears, Roebuck and Co., Atlanta, 1978-80; pres., chief operating officer for merchandising Sears, Roebuck and Co., Chgo., 1980-81, chmn. bd., chief exec. officer mdse. group, 1981-84, pres., chief operating officer, 1984-86, chmn., pres., chief exec. officer, 1986—, also bd. dirs.; bd. dirs. Minn. Mining & Mfg. Co., Chgo. Council Fgn. Relations; mem. bd. trustees Savs. and Profit Sharing Fund of Sears Employees. Trustee, Marquette U., De Paul U.; mem. Chgo. Urban League, 1980—, Chgo. Mus. Sci. and Industry, The Sears Roebuck Found.; chmn. bd. govs. United Way Am. Mem. Pres.' Export Council, Bus. Roundtable, Conf. Bd. Office: Sears Roebuck & Co Sears Tower Chicago IL 60684

BRENNAN, EMMET JAMES, III, personnel consultant; b. St. Louis, Oct. 4, 1945; s. Emmet James Jr. and Rita Katherine (Perkinson) B.; student St. Louis U., 1963-65, Washington U., St. Louis, 1965-70, U. Mo., St. Louis, 1975; B.A. with honors in Mgmt., Webster U., 1978; m. Elizabeth Jane Webb, Mar. 7, 1970. Pers. specialist Otto Faerber & Assos., St. Louis, 1965-70; indsl. rels. pers. mgr. Rexall Drug Co., St. Louis, 1970-71; compensation analyst Dart Industries, Los Angeles, 1971-74; corp. wage and salary adminstr., pers. devel. assoc. Mallinckrodt, Inc., St. Louis, 1974-78; dir. St. Louis office Sullivan, Eisemann & Thomsen, St. Louis, 1978-80; pres. Brennan, Thomsen Assocs., Inc., Chesterfield, Mo., 1980—; asst. dir. Compensation Inst., 1981-82; guest lectr. various univs. and profl. socs. Lector, Incarnate Word Roman Cath. Parish. Served with U.S. Army, 1966-68. Mem. Am. Compensation Assn., Am. Soc. for Pers. Adminstrn., Adminstrv. Mgmt. Soc. (bd. dirs.), Nat. Com. on Pay Equity (job evaluation task force), Compensation and Benefits Network; Chesterfield C. of C., St. Louis Writers Guild, Phi Kappa Theta. Author: Geographic Salary and Cost of Living Differentials, 1980; The Compensation Audit, 1981; Payout, 1987, Performance Mgmt., 1988; contbg. editor, founding mem. bd. editorial advisors Personnel Jour., 1984—; St. Louis mgr. Today's Mgr., 1985—; contbr. articles to mag. Office: Brennan Thomsen Assocs Inc 106 Four Seasons Ctr Chesterfield MO 63017

BRENNAN, JOHN JOSEPH, mutual fund company executive; b. Boston, July 29, 1954; s. Francis Patrick and Mary Josephine (Gilhooley) B.; m. Catharine Barbara Joyce Brennan, May 17, 1980; children: William Thomas, Kara Boggs. AB, Dartmouth U., 1976; MBA, Harvard U., 1980. Planner N.Y. Bank for Savs., 1976-78; fin. mgr. S.C. Johnson & Son, Inc., Racine, Wis., 1980-82; asst. to the chmn. The Vanguard Group, Inc., Valley Forge, Pa., 1982-85; sr. v.p., chief fin. officer The Vanguard Group, Inc., 1985-86, exec. v.p., 1986—, also dir., 1987—; dir. ICI Mut. Ins. Co., 1988—. Mem. Fin. Exec. Inst., No-Load Mut. Fund Assn. (gov. 1985—, exec. v.p. 1986—). Roman Catholic. Office: Vanguard Group Investment Cos 1300 Morris Dr Wayne PA 19087

BRENNAN, PATRICK FRANCIS, printing paper manufacturing executive; b. N.Y.C., Aug. 1, 1931; s. Patrick F. and Mary Ellen (Costello) B.; m. Barbara Fleischman; children: Sean, Peter, Gerald. Grad., Fordham U., 1957; Advanced Mgmt. Cert., Harvard U., 1983. Dist. mgr. Consol. Papers, Inc., N.Y.C., 1963-67; regional mgr. Consol. Papers, Inc., Chgo., 1967-71, nat. sales mgr., 1971-76, v.p. sales, 1976-84; exec. v.p. Consol. Papers, Inc., Wisconsin Rapids, Wis., 1984-88, pres., 1988—; bd. dirs. Consol. Water Power Co., Wisconsin Rapids, Mead Realty, Wisconsin Rapids, Northland Cranberries, Inc.; bd. dirs. paper sci. and engring. U. Minn. Coll. Natural Resources. Mem. Am. Paper Inst., Rotary, Bulls Eye Country Club (Wisconsin Rapids) (bd. dirs. 1988—). Office: Consol Papers Inc 231 1st Ave N PO Box 8050 Wisconsin Rapids WI 54494

BRENNAN, SHELIQUE DENEE, advertising executive; b. Sandusky, Ohio, Nov. 5, 1957; d. Charlton Lee I and Jessie Bernadine (Mischler) Seville; m. Scott Edward Brennan, May 25, 1986; children: Charlton Lee Seville II, Sheena Jean Seville. AA, Alaska U., 1978; student, Terra Tech., 1980-82. Data entry computer operator USA Today, Mansfield, Ohio, 1984-85; dist. mgr. USA Today, Sandusky, 1984, Sanduskly Register, 1985, Toledo Blade, Sandusky, 1985; advt. dir. Willard (Ohio) Junction, 1986-88; advt. sales rep. Willard Times Junction newspaper, 1988—; tax cons. Federated Tax, Willard, 1986—; notary pub., Willard, 1980—. Republican. Lutheran. Office: Willard Times Junction 211 Myrtle Ave Willard OH 44890

BRENNEN, WILLIAM ELBERT, management consultant; b. Mo., Sept. 30, 1930; s. William E. and Frances (Andrew) B.; m. Natalia Summers, Nov. 14, 1958 (div. 1979); children: William, Natalia Jane, Elizabeth; m. Sharon Russell, Aug. 8, 1987. BS, U.S. Mcht. Marine Acad., 1952; MBA, U. Chgo., 1964. Ship's officer, traffic and ops. mgr. States Marine Lines Inc., Korea and Japan, 1952-61; with Case & Co./Stevenson Jordan & Harrison, Inc. Mgmt. Cons., Chgo. and N.Y.C., 1961-68; dir. internat. materials mgmt. Internat. Minerals & Chems., Skokie, Ill., 1968-71, Abbott Labs., North Chicago, Ill., 1971-73; pres. W.E. Brennen Cons., Inc. (name changed to Brennen Cons. Inc. 1987), 1987-88—; mgmt. cons., Evanston, Ill., 1973-88, South Bend, Ind., 1988—; v.p., mng. prin. Fry Cons., 1982-88. Lt. (j.g.) USNR, 1953-55. Mem. Am. Mktg. Assn. (pres. Chgo. chpt. 1982-83, bus. mktg. coun., 1987-89, Mktg. News editorial rev. bd., editorial adv. bd.), Inst. Mgmt. Cons. (dir. Chgo. chpt. 1987—), Turnaround Mgmt. Assn., South Bend/Mishawaka C. of C., Elkhart C. of C. Episcopalian. Office: 300 N Michigan South Bend IN 46601-1239

BRENNER, DONALD ROBERT, fuel oil company executive; b. Jersey City, July 29, 1936; s. Jerome Lewis and Muriel M. (Ehlen) B.; m. Ginette Adam, June 10, 1977; children: Michael, Jerome II, Robert. BA, Dartmouth Coll., 1958. V.p. Air Pilot Oil Co., Secaucus, N.J., 1958-63; sales mgr. Amerada Hess, Woodbridge, N.J., 1963-68; pres. Metro Fuel Co., Inc., Ridgefield, N.J., 1968—, Metro Oil & Chem. Corp., Ridgefield, 1968-85; vice-chmn. bd. dirs. The Trust Co. N.J.; bd. dirs. Truco Bancorp. V.p. Jerome L. and Muriel Brenner Charitable Found.; trustee Dwight Englewood (N.J.) Sch., Englewoood Hosp., Felician Coll., Lodi, N.J. Mem. Ridgefield Mfrs. Assn. Clubs: Ridgefield Exchange. Lodge: Elks. Home: PO Box 721 Alpine NJ 07620 Office: Metro Fuel Co Inc 1011 Hudson Ave PO Box 335 Ridgefield NJ 07657

BRENNER, MARSHALL LEIB, lawyer; b. N.Y.C., Aug. 8, 1933; s. Samuel and Ruth (Novak) B.; m. Gwen A. Krakower, Aug. 9, 1959; children: Scott David, Louri Ann, Robin Lynn. BA, St Lawrence U., Canton, N.Y., 1955; JD, Bklyn. Law Sch., 1959. Bar: N.Y. 1960, U.S. Dist. Ct. (no. and ea. dists.) N.Y. 1960, U.S. Ct. Claims 1964, U.S. Supreme Ct. 1964, U.S. Dist. Ct. (so. dist.) N.Y. 1969. Assoc. Spitz & Levine, Poughkeepsie, N.Y., 1960-62; sr. ptnr. Brenner, Gordon & Lane, Poughkeepsie, 1977—; chief appeals sect. Dutchess County Pub. Defenders Office, Poughkeepsie, 1966-78; tchr. law Marks Realtors/Appraisors, Poughkeepsie and Fishkill, N.Y., 1968-72, Robert-Mark Realtors, Hopewell Junction, N.Y., 1979—; lectr. Dutchess County Realty Bd. for Sales/Broker Lic. Applicants, 1985—. Contbr. articles to profl. jours. Pres., bd. dirs. Sloper-Willen Community Ambulance, Wappingers Falls, N.Y., 1966-79; bd. dirs. Poughkeepsie Jewish Community Ctr., 1980-82, Dutchess County Assn. for Sr. Citizens, Dutchess County Youth Bd. Served to capt. U.S. Army, 1956-63. Mem. N.Y. State Bar Assn., Dutchess County Bar Assn., N.Y. State Trial Lawyers Assn. Republican. Jewish. Clubs: Harding (Poughkeepsie) (pres. 1968-69); County Players (Wappingers Falls) (bd. dirs. 1963-74). Lodges: Masons, Rotary (pres. 1973-74, 78-79, Govs. Trophy 1978). Home: 30 Robin Rd Poughkeepsie NY 12601 Office: Brenner Gordon & Lane 35 Market St Poughkeepsie NY 12601

BRENNER, RONALD JOHN, pharmaceutical industry executive; b. Bethlehem, Pa., June 9, 1933; s. Sam Ralph and Frieda V. E. (Buck) B.; m. Sally Gaskill, Oct. 24, 1964; children: Carol L., Nancy G., Katherine E., Richard J. BS in Pharmacy, U. Cin., 1955; MS in Pharm. Chemistry, U. Fla., 1957, PhD in Pharm. Chemistry, 1959. Research scientist McNeil Labs., Ft. Washington, Pa., 1958-66, dir. devel. research, 1966-67, exec. dirs. new products, 1967-70, exec. v.p., 1974-78; v.p. Johnson & Johnson Internat., New Brunswick, N.J., 1970-74; pres. McNeil Pharm. Co., Ft. Washington, 1978; co. group chmn. Johnson & Johnson Co., New Brunswick, 1978-82, v.p., 1982-84; pres., chief exec. officer CYTOGEN Corp., Princeton, N.J., 1984—; Trustee Phila. Coll. Pharmacy and Sci., 1976—; mem. N.J. Gov.'s Commn. on Sci. and Tech., Task Force on Acad.-Indsl. Innovation; mem. adv. bd. Scripps Clinic and Research Found. Trustee Phila. Coll. Pharmacy and Sci., 1976—; bd. dirs. Am. Found. Pharm. Edn., 1983—. Mem. Am. Pharm. Assn., AAAS, Acad. Pharm. Scis., Soc. Chem. Industry, Pharmacists Against Drug Abuse Found. (v.p., trustee). Office: CYTOGEN Corp 600 College Rd E Princeton NJ 08540

BRENT, WILLIAM H., hospital financial executive; b. Youngstown, Ohio, Dec. 15, 1943; s. Howard and Nora (Parchment) B.; m. Adrianne Faye Mann, Aug. 20, 1982; children: David C., Dyanna L. BS in Health Care Adminstrn., George Washington U., 1975, MBA in Fin., 1979; postgrad., Nova U. Enlisted USN, 1963, advanced through grades to lt. comdr., 1981, ret., 1985; comptroller Naval Hosp. USN, Quantico, Va.; from head fin. systems to dir. resource execution Bur. Medicine and Surgery USN, Washington; comptroller Naval Hosp. USN, Bethesda, Md.; fin. systems coord. Georgetown U. Hosp., Washington, 1985—. Decorated Silver Star, Purple Heart, Cross of Gallantry, others. Mem. Health Care Fin. Mgmt. Assn., Am. Coll. Health Care Adminstrs., Assn. Mil. Comptrollers, Assn. MBA Execs., Am. Assn. Individual Investors. Democrat. Roman Catholic. Home: 906 Cox Ave Hyattsville MD 20783 Office: Georgetown U Hosp 3800 Reservoir Rd NW Washington DC 20007

BRENTLINGER, PAUL SMITH, venture capital executive; b. Dayton, Ohio, Apr. 3, 1927; s. Arthur and Welthy Otello (Smith) B.; m. Marilyn E. Hunt, June 23, 1951; children: Paula, David, Sara. BA, U. Mich., 1950, MBA, 1951. With Harris Corp., Melbourne, Fla., 1951-84, v.p. corp. devel., 1969-75, v.p. fin., 1975-82, sr. v.p. fin., 1982-84; gen. ptnr. Morgenthaler Ventures, Cleve., 1984—; bd. dirs. Ferro Corp., Cleve., Hypres, Inc., Elmsford, N.Y., Allegheny Ludlum Corp., Pitts. Mem. Fin. Execs. Inst., Phi Beta Kappa. Clubs: Union (Cleve.). Home: 2755 Eaton Rd Shaker Heights OH 44122 Office: Mortgenhaler Ventures 700 National City Bank Bldg Cleveland OH 44114

BRENTNALL, R. MICHAEL, medical clinic executive; b. Creston, Iowa, Jan. 21, 1943; s. Ivan Randal and Alice Irene (Yount) B.; B.S., Calif. State U., 1966; m. Connie J. Hower, June 3, 1967; children—John Michael, Terry David. Sr. acct. Cooper & Lybrand, San Francisco and Palo Alto, Calif., 1966-71; div. controller Arcata Graphics, San Jose, Calif., 1971-73; adminstr. Creston Med. Clinic (Iowa), 1973—. Elder, Presbyterian Ch., 1979-82. C.P.A., Iowa. Mem. Am. Inst. C.P.A.s, Iowa Soc. C.P.A.s, Med. Group Mgrs. Assn., Creston C. of C. (dir. 1979-82), Beta Alpha Psi. Republican. Clubs: Crestmoor Golf, Elks. Home: 309 S Stone St Creston IA 50801 Office: Creston Med Clinic 526 New York Ave Creston IA 50801

BRESANI, FEDERICO FERNANDO, international corporate business executive; b. Lima, Peru, Apr. 27, 1945; came to U.S., 1964; s. Federico L. and Beatriz (Ferrer) B.; m. Patricia Anne Grannis, Aug. 26, 1972; children: Christina Anne, Vianna Clarissa. BS in Elect. Engring., Milw. Sch. of Engring., 1970; MBA, Fairleigh Dickinson U., 1980. Engr. Cerro Corp., Lima, Peru, 1973-76; supr. Cerro Corp./CMP, N.Y.C., 1976-77, mgr., 1978, purchasing mgr., 1979-80; product mgr. Schumag, Inc., Norwood, N.J., 1980-82, v.p., 1982; sales, mktg. mgr. EVG, N.Y.C., 1983-85, v.p., 1986—. Mem. The Wire Assn. Internat., Wire Reinforcement Inst., Concrete Reinforcement Steel Inst., Mining Club, Chemists Club (N.Y.C.), Omicron Delta Epsilon. Home: 77 Chuckanutt Dr Oakland NJ 07436 Office: EVG 60 E 42d St New York NY 10165

BRESLIN, MICHAEL EDWARD, advertising agency executive, lawyer; b. N.Y.C., Apr. 27, 1937; s. John and Catherine (Malley) B.; m. Catherine Regina Cleary, May 30, 1959; children: Catherine Mary, John Joseph, Patricia Mary, Mary Kay. B.B.A., Pace U., 1960; J.D., Fordham U., 1964. Communications cons. N.Y. Telephone Co., N.Y.C., 1955-60; atty., coordinator labor relations and adminstrn. NBC, N.Y.C. and Chgo., 1960-67; exec. v.p., gen. counsel, sec. Leo Burnett Co. Inc., Chgo., 1979—; past chmn. legal affairs com. Am. Advt. Assn. Am.; mem. govt. relations com. Am. Assn. Advt. Agys. Mem. Am. Assn. Advt. Agys. Republican. Roman Catholic. Clubs: Chgo. Athletic Assn, Executive of Chgo. (dir.), Plaza. Home: 395 Westwood Dr Barrington IL 60010 Office: Leo Burnett Co Inc Prudential Pla Chicago IL 60601

BRESLIN, THOMAS RAYMOND, manufacturing executive; b. St. Paul, May 13, 1944; s. Raymond Edward and Marion Evelyn (Thomas) B.; m. Frances Lee Preiner, June 6, 1964; children: Sean Edward, Heather Maire. BA, Coll. St. Thomas, 1968. Asst. to pres. Richard Mfg. Co., Mpls., 1959-69; sales engr. Mid Continental Engring., Mpls., 1969-72; v.p. K.Y., Inc., Mpls., 1972-74; cons., gen. mgr. Metals Engring., St. Paul, 1974-76; v.p. Richard Mfg. Co., Eden Prairie, Minn., 1976—; bd. dirs. Gallery Photo, New Brighton, Minn.; pres. 120 Creative Corner, Mpls., 1971-77. Pres. Pike Lake PTA, New Brighton, 1974; chmn. Pike Lake Library Com., New Brighton, 1975. Mem. Photo Mktg. Assn. Republican. Roman Catholic. Home: 1246 North Court New Brighton MN 55112

BRESSLER, DIANE SUSAN, investment company executive; b. Toledo, June 9, 1956; d. Robert and Ruth B. BBA, Tri-State U., Ind., 1978; MBA, U. Chgo., 1980. Assoc. Hayes/Hill Inc., Chgo., 1980-81, sr. assoc., 1981-83, prin., project mgr., 1983-84; project mgr. MAC Group, Chgo., 1984-86; v.p. Alliance Capital, N.Y.C., 1986-88; v.p. mktg., sales CIC Asset Mgmt., 1988—. Cons., Bus. Vols. for the Arts, Chgo., 1984-86; bd. dirs., treas. 18 E. Owners Assn., N.Y.C., 1986—; bd. dirs. Women's Nat. Rep. Com. Chgo., 1984-86, David Puszh Dance Co., 1986—. Mem. Fin. Analysts Fedn., Am. Statistical Assn., Am. Mktg. Assn., U. Chgo. Sch. Bus. Alumni Assn. (bd. dirs. 1986—), Delta Mu Delta. Club: Chgo. Bus. Sch. (bd. adv. 1986—). Home: 18 E 63rd St New York NY 10021 Office: CIC Asset Mgmt 180 Maiden Ln New York NY 10038

BRESSLER, FERN WILLIAM, banker, controller; b. Lewistown, Pa., Aug. 29, 1953; s. Marvin Milton and Margaret Cathrine (Wagner) B.; m. Sherry Malaine Anderson, Oct. 16, 1976; children: Jannon Marie, Eric William. BS in Acctg., York Coll., 1975. CPA, Pa. Jr. acct. Richard H. Flowers II, CPA, Harrisburg, Pa., 1975-77; staff acct. Stambaugh, Dorgan & Co., Inc., York, Pa., 1977-78, sr. acct., 1978-79, supr. audit div., 1979-81; audit mgr. Drovers & Mechs. Bank, York, 1981-83, contr., 1984-85, v.p., contr., 1985—. Mem. adv. bd. West York Sch. Dist., 1986—. Mem. AICPA, Pa. Inst. CPAs, Nat. Assn. Accts. (bd. dirs. 1986—, v.p. 1987—, Most Valuable Mem. York chpt. 1987-88). Lutheran. Home: 2406 Opal Rd York PA 17404

BRESSLER, RICHARD MAIN, railroad executive; b. Wayne, Nebr., Oct. 8, 1930; s. John T. and Helen (Main) B.; m. Dianne G. Pearson, Apr. 17, 1981; children: Kristin M., Alan L. B.A., Dartmouth Coll., 1952. With Gen. Electric Co., 1952-68; v.p., treas. Am. Airlines Inc., 1968-72, sr. v.p., 1972-73; v.p. finance Atlantic Richfield Co., Los Angeles, 1973-75, sr. v.p. fin., 1975-77; pres. Arco Chem. Co., 1977-78, exec. v.p., 1978-80; pres., dir. Burlington No., Inc., St. Paul, 1980—, chief exec. officer, 1980-88; chmn. Burlington No., Inc., Seattle, 1982—; dir. Baker Internat., El Paso Co., Seafirst Corp., Honeywell Inc., Gen. Mills, Inc.; trustee Penn Mut. Life Ins. Co. Office: Burlington No Inc 999 3rd Ave Seattle WA 98104 *

BRESTICKER, ROBERT BARUCH, manufacturing company executive; b. Pitts., Jan. 15, 1955; s. Samuel and Claire (Bossack) B. BA, Dartmouth Coll., 1975, MBA, 1982; postgrad., Northwestern U. CPA, Ill. Mfg. asst. Gen. Mills, West Chicago, Ill., 1982-83, coordinator new info. systems devel., 1983; auditor, cons. Arthur Young & Co., Chgo., 1983-86; sr. mfg. planning analyst Motorola, Inc., Schaumburg, Ill., 1986-87, mgr. prodn. control sect., 1987—. Served to lt. (j.g.) USN, 1974-80. Mem. Am. Prodn. and Inventory Control Soc., Soc. Mfg. Engrs. Republican. Jewish. Home: 21 Kristin Pl Apt 1202 Schaumburg IL 60195 Office: Motorola Inc 1301 E Algonquin Rd Schaumburg IL 60196

BRESTOFF, NELSON ELLIOTT, lawyer; b. Detroit, Oct. 20, 1948; s. Philip F. and Dee (Parker) B.; m. Lois Ellen Montague, Aug. 30, 1975; children: Daniel Richard, Jonathan Robert. BS, UCLA, 1971; MS, Calif. Inst. Tech., 1972; JD, U. So. Calif., 1975. Practice law Woodland Hills, Calif. Bd. dirs. Planning and Conservation League, 1974-78; mem. specific plan citizens adv. com. Ventura/Cahuenga Corridor, 1987—, co-chmn. 101 Corridor Transp. com., 1987—; founding chmn. Valley Sci. Found., 1988—. Author: How to Borrow Money Below Prime, 1985, How to Write Off Your Downpayment, 1986. Mem. West Los Angeles Regional C. of C. (bd. dirs. 1979-83), Los Angeles City Atty. Small Bus. Adv. Council, Valley Industry and Commerce Assn. (bd. dirs. 1987—). Home: 5735 Rolling Rd Woodland Hills CA 91367 Office: Brestoff Law Corp 5959 Topanga Canyon Blvd Woodland Hills CA 91367

BRETHEN, ROBERT HERSCHELL, building components manufacturing company executive; b. Rochester, N.Y., June 29, 1926; s. Milton R. and Ethyl H. (Herschell) B.; m. Alma Hommel; children: Karen E., David M. B.S., Syracuse U., 1949. Regional sales mgr. Delco Appliance div. Gen. Motors Corp., Rochester, 1949-62; v.p., gen. mgr. Kitchen Machine div. Toledo Scale Corp., Rochester, 1963-68; group v.p. Fuqua Industries, Atlanta, 1968-71, Nat. Service Industries, Atlanta, 1971-73; pres. Philips Industries, Inc., Dayton, Ohio, 1973—, chief exec. officer, 1986—, also bd. dirs.; bd. dirs. Hobart Bros. Mfg. Co., 1st Nat. Bank. Trustee Miami Valley Hosp., Syracuse U.; bd. dirs. Jr. Achievement of Dayton, Miami Valley, Inc. Mem. Dayton C. of C. (solicitations rev. com.), Sigma Phi Epsilon. Republican. Home: 2445 Ridgeway Rd Dayton OH 45419 Office: Philips Industries Inc 4801 Springfield St PO Box 943 Dayton OH 45401

BRETT, ARTHUR CUSHMAN, JR., banker; b. Bronxville, N.Y., Mar. 23, 1928; s. Arthur Cushman and Mary Kathryn (Clark) B.; m. Mary Elizabeth Cunliffe, Aug. 21, 1954; children: Margaret Brett Uzarski, Catherine Brett Main, John, Patricia, Matthew. B.S., Fordham U., 1953; M.B.A., NYU, 1959. Asst. v.p. Bowery Savs. Bank, N.Y.C., 1950-68; instl. registered rep. Salomon Bros., N.Y.C., 1968-71, 73-75, Blyth Eastman Dillon, Boston, 1971-73; v.p. Mut. Am. Life Ins. Co., N.Y.C., 1975-78; v.p. investments, sec. East River Savs. Bank, N.Y.C., 1978-80; sr. v.p. investments, treas. Apple Bank for Savs., N.Y.C., 1980—. Mem. investment com. Social Sci. Research Council, 1976-86, NYU Fed. Credit Union, 1983—. Mem. N.Y. Soc. Security Analysts, Nat. Assn. Bus. Economists, Nat. Assn. Corp. Treas., Money Marketeers NYU, Fin. Club/Bus. Forum NYU (bd. dirs. 1983-87). Roman Catholic. Club: World Trade Ctr. Home: 2514 Redding Rd Fairfield CT 06430 also: 441 Ocean Ave Stratford CT 06497 Office: Apple Bank Savs 205 E 42d St New York NY 10017

BREUM, ROBERT PAUL, software developer; b. Spokane, Wash., Oct. 15, 1952; s. Ralph Franklin and Eleanor (Merriam) B.; m. Linda Sue Garver, May 28, 1977; children: Erik Franklin, Roger Alan. Student, Vanderbilt U., 1971-76. Systems engr. Electronic Data Systems, Dallas, 1977-79; sr. systems engr. MSI Data Corp., Altamonte Springs, Fla., 1979-82; sales engr. John Fluke Mfg. Co., Orlando, Fla., 1982-84, Teradyne, Inc., Winter Park, Fla., 1984-86; owner, mgr. Computer Fenestrations, Lake Monroe, Fla., 1986—.

BREWER, DAVID MADISON, lawyer; b. Bordeaux, Gironde, France, July 8, 1953; s. Herbert L. and Paulyne B. (Ver Benec) B.; m. Andrea M. Bordiga, May 20, 1978; children: James David Madison, Caroline Elizabeth, Geoffrey Andrew. AB summa cum laude, Yale U., 1975, JD, 1978. Bar: N.Y. 1979. Assoc. atty. Cravath Swaine & Moore, N.Y.C., 1978-84; assoc. gen. tax counsel Union Pacific Corp., Bethlehem, Pa., 1984—. Editor Yale Law Jour., 1977-78. Policy Asst. Office of the Campaign Mgr., Bush-Quayle Campaign, 1988; bd. dirs. Yale Law Sch. Fund, 1989—; spl. gifts chmn. Yale Coll. Class of 1975 and Law Sch. Class 1978, 1985—. Mem. N.Y. Bar Assn., Phi Beta Kappa. Republican. Episcopalian. Clubs: Yale (N.Y.C.); Mory's (New Haven, Conn.). Office: Martin Tower Eighth & Eaton Ave Bethlehem PA 18018

BREWER, EDWARD EUGENE, tire and rubber company executive; b. Findlay, Ohio, July 19, 1925; s. William B. and Edna (Hurrel) B.; m. Joyce K. Josephsen, Feb. 7, 1948; children: Stephen, Rebecca, Mary, Sara, Debra. B.S. in Mech. Engring., Purdue U., 1949. With Cooper Tire & Rubber Co., Findlay, 1949-56, v.p., 1956-70, exec. v.p., 1970-77, pres., chmn. bd., 1977-82, chmn. bd., chief exec. officer, 1982—. Home: 857 S Main St Findlay OH 45840 Office: Cooper Tire & Rubber Co Lima & Western Aves Findlay OH 45840

BREWER, MARK, accountant; b. Waynesboro, Tenn., Dec. 19, 1955; s. Carmack and Lorene (Baker) B.; m. Terri Brewer, May 20, 1977; children: Philip, Ashley. BA, Freed-Hardeman Coll., 1977. Internal auditor HCA Corp., Nashville, 1977-78; asst. controller Redmond Park Hosp., Rome, Ga., 1978-79; controller Smith County Meml. Hosp., Carthage, Tenn., 1979-81, Redmond Park Hosp., Rome, 1981-84; chief fin. officer Coliseum Pk. Hosp., Macon, Ga., 1984—; bd. dirs. Coliseum Assocs., Macon, Middle Ga. Christian Sch., Macon. Dir. youth Southside Ch. of Christ, Macon, 1988—. Mem. Hosp. Fin. Mgmt. Assn., Lions. Republican. Office: HCA Coliseum Med Ctr 350 Hospital Dr Macon GA 31213 Home: 1391 Beaver Oaks Dr Macon GA 31210

BREWER, OLIVER GORDON, JR., corporate executive; b. Winston-Salem, N.C., Dec. 8, 1936; s. Oliver Gordon and Lula Irene (Masencup) B.; m. Gail Olt, Aug. 29, 1959; children: Nancy Lynne, Oliver Gordon III. B.A., Guilford Coll., 1960; postgrad., Dartmouth Coll.; A.M.P., Harvard Bus. Sch., 1983. With Phila. Nat. Bank, 1963-70, regional v.p., 1969-70; treas. Alco Standard Corp., Valley Forge, Pa., 1970—; v.p. Alco Standard Corp., 1973-86, v.p. fin., treas., 1986—; dir. Corp. Ins. and Reins Ltd., Bermuda, Sun Distbrs. Inc., Phila. Chmn. J. Wood Platt Caddie Scholarship Trust. Mem. Pa. Golf Assn. (pres. 1975-76, past exec. com., sectional affairs com.). Clubs: Huntingdon Valley (Pa.) Country, Pine Valley (N.J.) Golf. Home: 3645 Holt Ln Huntingdon Valley PA 19006 Office: Alco Standard Corp PO Box 834 Valley Forge PA 19482

BREWER, WILLIAM DIXON, utilities executive; b. Muskogee, Okla., Sept. 8, 1936; s. Earl C. and Ethyl A. (Collins) B.; m. Barbara Amy Zola, Oct. 12, 1968; children: Christopher Colston, Boyd Dixon. BS in Petroleum Engring., BSME, U. Okla., 1959, MME, 1960. Mem. staff mfg. mgmt. program GE, various, 1962-65; advt. materials specialist GE, Warren, Mich., 1965-67, mgr. advt. materials, 1967-70; mgr. materials GE, Mexico City, 1970-72, gen. mgr. controls, 1972-74; mgr. components GE, Erie, Pa., 1974-76; mgr. mfg. lighting div. Crouse Hinds, Syracuse, N.Y., 1976-82; v.p., gen. mgr. dist. equipment Crouse Hinds, Charlottesville, Va., 1982-86; pres. McGraw-Edison Power Systems, Pitts., 1982—. V.p. Oakland County (Calif.) Young Reps., 1968; chmn. major firms fund drive, bd. dirs. United Way, Albemarle County, Va., 1984-85. Lt. (j.g.) USN, 1960-62. Home: 1014 Tall Trees Dr Pittsburgh PA 15241 Office: Cooper Power Systems PO Box 2850 Pittsburgh PA 15230

BREYER, JAMES WILLIAM, venture capitalist; b. New Haven, July 26, 1961; s. John Paul and Eva (Karman) B.; m. Susan Zaroff, June 20, 1987. BS, Stanford U., 1983; MBA, Harvard U., 1987. Sr. bus. analyst McKinsey & Co., N.Y.C., 1983-85; assoc. Accel Ptnrs., San Francisco, 1987—. Baker scholar Harvard U., 1987. Mem. Nat. Venture Capital Assn., Western Assn. Venture Capitalists, Harvard Club(N.Y.C.), Harvard Bus. Sch. Club of No. Calif. Office: Accel Ptnrs 1 Embarcadero Ctr San Francisco CA 94111

BRIAR, GEORGE MATHEW, architectural hardware supply company executive; b. Bristol, Pa., Aug. 1, 1950; s. George M. and Joan C. (Elmer) B.; m. Judith Ann Talarico, Apr. 15, 1974; children: Dominique, Daniel, Jesse. BA cum laude, Lycoming Coll., 1972. CPA, N.Y. Sr. acct. Deloite, Haskins & Sells, N.Y.C., 1972-76; mgr. cost and fin. analyses Cartier-Wallace, Inc., N.Y.C., 1976-79; plant controller Revlon, Inc., N.Y.C., 1979-82; controller Bobby McGee's U.S.A., Inc., Phoenix, 1982-85; v.p. fin. and treas. Atlantic Hardware Supply Corp., N.Y.C., 1985—. Mem. Am. Inst. CPA's, Constrn. Fin. Assn. (N.Y.C. chtp.) Lycoming Coll. Alumni Assn., Tau Kappa Epsilon (pres. 1973). Home: 15 High St Allentown NJ 08501 Office: Atlantic Hardware Supply Corp 601 W 26th St New York NY 10001

BRICHTA, PAUL, toy parts and raw materials company executive; b. Ostrava, Czechoslovakia, Sept. 27, 1931; s. Fred and Else B.; B.S. in Econs., Wharton Sch., U. Pa., 1954; m. Hannah Glassman, Jan. 21, 1967; children—Elaine, Lisa. Sales rep. Foods div. Lever Bros. Co., 1956-58; v.p. mktg. sales Jolly Toys Inc., N.Y.C., 1958-69; exec. v.p. Assoc. Indsl. Designers Ltd., N.Y.C., 1969-73; pres. Dicker Internat. Inc., N.Y.C., 1973—, also subs. Ozen Sound Devices Inc., N.Y.C., Tokyo. Pres., N.Y. Times Youth Forums Alumni. Served to 1st lt. Mil. Intelligence, U.S. Army, 1954-56. Mem. Met. Opera Guild (sponsor). Clubs: U. Pa. of L.I., Wharton Bus. Sch. of N.Y. Home: 71 Meadow Woods Rd Great Neck NY 11020 Office: Dicker Internat Inc 225 Broadway New York NY 10007

BRICKER, GARY ROBERT, insurance broker; b. Colver, Pa., Aug. 11, 1940; s. Robert Fay and Aletha (Curry) B.; children: Deborah, Donna. Ins. broker Bricker Ins. Agy., Landover, Md., 1962—; realtor Bricker Real Estate & Investment Co., Landover; semi-precious metal buyer Gold Brick, Landover. Served with U.S. Army, 1958-61. Republican. Baptist. Lodges: Masons, Shriners, Elks, Moose.

BRICKER, WILLIAM HAROLD, oil and gas producing and refining company executive, private investor; b. Detroit, Jan. 29, 1932; B.S. in Agr., Mich. State U., 1953, M. Hort., 1954; m. Doris Arlene Bricker, Apr. 30, 1955. With Diamond Shamrock Chem. Co., Dallas, 1969—, v.p. biochems., 1969-72, pres., 1973-74; v.p. Diamond Shamrock Corp. (name changed to Maxus Energy Corp., 1987), Dallas, 1973-74, chief operating officer, 1974-75, pres., 1975-76, 86—, chief exec. officer, 1976-79, 86-87, chmn. bd., 1979-87; chmn., chief exec. officer Skyline Investments, Inc., 1987—, D.S. Energy Svcs.; bd. dirs. Lloyd West Corp., Am. Ball Mfg. Corp., LTV Corp., Blue Coral, Inc., Trammell Crow Real Estate Investors. Bd. govs.; bd. dirs. Kent Waldrep Nat. Paralysis Found.; past mem. communications com. Dallas Citizens Coun., Dallas Mus. Fine Arts, Dallas Symphony Mus.; mem. ARC, bus. adminstrn. and devel. coun. Tex. A&M U. Mem. Dallas Petroleum Club. Clubs: Preston Trail Golf, Brook Hollow, Tower (bd. govs.). Office: Skyline Investments Inc 1 Bent Tree Ste 520 16475 Dallas Pkwy Dallas TX 75248

BRICKHILL, CHRISTOPHER JOHN, software company executive; b. Perth, Australia, Oct. 30, 1946; s. Lloyd Westley Brickhill and Harriet Mary (Jude) Sorrell. BA, U. Melbourne, Australia, 1967, BSc, 1969; MSc, U. Essex, Eng., 1972; postgrad., Oxford (Eng.) U., 1972-75. Systems engr. Cable and Wireless Co., Eng., 1975, Chase Manhattan Bank, N.Y.C., 1976; mgr. Bankers Trust Co., N.Y.C., 1977-80, Citibank Corp., N.Y.C., 1980-82; pres. Intelcom Data Systems, Inc., N.Y.C., 1982—. Author: What is Mathematical Logic?, 1972.

BRICKLEY, STEPHEN CRAIG, manufacturing executive; b. Boston, Mar. 7, 1951; s. Stephen Fran and Margaret Mary (Gallagher) B.; m. Betty Ann White, May 17, 1986. BSME, Northeastern U., 1974; MSE, Boston U., 1987. Sales engr. Abcor Inc., Cambridge, Mass., 1974-75; design engr. Gen. Electric Co., Portland, Maine, 1975-77; product engring. mgr. Cargocaire Engring., Amesbury, Mass., 1977-82, v.p. devel., 1982-86, gen. mgr., 1986—. Mem. IEEE, Am. Soc. Mech. Engrs., Am. Soc. Heating Refrigeration and Air Conditions Engrs. (tech. advisor, absorption com. 1988). Office: Cargocaire Engring Co 79 Monroe St Amesbury MA 01913

BRICKMAN, JOSEPH MARK, funeral director; b. Cleve., May 1, 1953; s. Frank George and Marian Veronica (Frohnapple) B.; m. Kathleen Mary Delis, Oct. 3, 1980; children: Patrick, Julie, Jonathan. Diploma in mechanics, L/S Denver Automotive, 1973; student, Lakeland Community Coll., 1973-76; diploma in mortuary sci., Pitts. Inst. Mortuary Sci., 1978. Lic. funeral dir. Funeral dir., embalmer Brickman & Sons Funeral Home, Euclid, Ohio, 1978—. Mem. Ohio Embalmers Assn., Cleve. Embalmers Assn., Cuyahoga County Funeral Dir. Assn. (2d v.p. 1986). Roman Catholic. Office: Brickman & Sons Funeral Home 21900 Euclid Ave Euclid OH 44117

BRIDENDALL, JOHN PHILIP, financial executive; b. Lake Charles, La., June 7, 1950; s. Philip and Caroline (Ford) B.; m. Toby Beerman; children: Melissa, Carolyn, Ashley. BS, U. Tenn., 1972; MBA, U. Pa., 1974. CPA, Ga., Ky., Tenn. Asst. v.p. Brown-Forman Corp., Louisville, 1981-83; sr. v.p., pres., dir. corp. devel. Brown-Forman Distiller Corp., Louisville, 1986—; bd. dirs. polit. action com. Brown-Forman Distiller Corp.; sr. v.p., chief fin. officer Jack Daniel Distillery, Nashville, 1983-86, also bd. dirs.; bd. dirs. Lenox, Inc., Lawrenceville, N.J. Bd. dirs. Ky. Opera Assn., Louisville, 1987—. Mem. Am. Inst. CPA's. Office: Brown-Forman Corp PO Box 1080 Dixie Hwy Louisville KY 40210

BRIDGE, ALAN R., personnel director; b. Salt Lake City, Feb. 9, 1948; s. Joseph K. and Mari E. (Dietz) B.; m. Eileen Walton, June 2, 1977; children: Melanie, Kevin, Robert, Jeffrey. BS, U. Utah, 1973; MA, Brigham Young U., 1977. Personnel analyst Salt Lake City Corp., 1977-78, personnel analyst II, 1978-, sr. personnel analyst, 1979, adminstr. pub. safety program, 1979-80, employee rels. mgr., 1980-81, personnel dir., 1981—; cons. Utah League of Cities and Towns, Salt Lake City, 1978-84, St. George City, Utah, 1986-87; adj. prof. Salt Lake Community Coll., 1987—; prof. mgmt. U. Phoenix, 1987—. Com. mem. Employers Com. for Support of the N.G. and Res., Salt Lkae City, 1987. Mem. Western Region Internat. Personnel Mgmt. Assn. (pres. 1987-88), Beta Gamma Sigma Soc., Utah Chpt. Internat. Personnel Mgmt. Assn. (pres. 1985). Republican. Mormon. Home: 5959 S 2700 W Salt Lake City UT 84118 Office: Salt Lake City Corp 324 South St Rm 530 Salt Lake City UT 84111

BRIDGEFORD, GARY JAMES, electronics company executive; b. Waukegan, Ill., Dec. 12, 1947; s. Kermit M. and Marion (Neuens) B. BS, Milw. Sch. Engring., 1970; MBA, U. Iowa, 1974. Indsl. engr. Amana (Iowa) Refrigeration, Inc., 1970-72, treasury analyst, 1972-77; ops. analyst Joseph Schlitz Brewing Co., Milw., 1977-78; fin. analyst Johnson Controls, Inc., Milw., 1978-79, mgr. risk and fleet services, 1979-84, controller internat. ops., 1984-85, mgr. corp. risk mgmt., 1985—. Mem. Machinery and Allied Products Inst. Risk Mgmt. Counsel, Risk and Ins. Mgmt. Soc. (bd. dirs., treas.). Roman Catholic. Office: Johnson Controls Inc PO Box 591 Milwaukee WI 53201

BRIDGES, JOSEPH HENRY, financial services company executive; b. Greensboro, N.C., Jan. 23, 1943; s. Henry Lee and Clarice (Hines) B.; m. Susie Ligon, Dec. 29, 1978; children: Kelley, Jenaffer. BA, Wake Forest U., 1965; MBA, U. N.C., 1971. V.p., sec. Bank N.C., N.A., Raleigh, 1971-80; v.p., treas. Guardian Fed. Savs. & Loan, Washington, 1980-82; contr. Tower Fed. Credit Union, Annapolis Junction, Md., 1982-86, v.p. fin., 1986-88; pres., chief exec. officer Treas. Dept. Fed. Credit Union, Washington, 1988—. Served to capt. U.S. Army, 1966-69. Mem. Fin. Execs. Inst. Episcopalian. Lodge: Rotary (sgt. at arms 1987). Home: 12304 Triple Crown Rd Gaithersburg MD 20878 Office: Treas Dept Fed Credit Union Treas Annex Rm 126 Washington DC 20220

BRIDGEWATER, BERNARD ADOLPHUS, JR., footwear and specialty retailing company executive; b. Tulsa, Mar. 13, 1934; s. Bernard Adolphus and Mary Alethea (Burton) B.; m. Barbara Paton, July 2, 1960; children: Barrie, Elizabeth, Bonnie. A.B., Westminster Coll., Fulton, Mo., 1955; LL.B., U. Okla., 1958; M.B.A., Harvard, 1964. Bar: Okla. 1958, U.S. Supreme Ct. 1958, U.S. Ct. of Claims 1958. Asst. county atty. Tulsa, 1962; assoc. McKinsey & Co.; mgmt. cons. McKinsey & Co., Chgo., 1964-68, prin., 1968-72, dir., 1972-73, 75; assoc. dir. nat. security and internat. affairs Office Mgmt. and Budget, Exec. Office Pres., Washington, 1973-74; exec. v.p. Baxter Travenol Labs., Inc., Chgo. and Deerfield, Ill., 1975-79, dir., 1975-85; pres. Brown Group, Inc., Clayton, Mo., 1979—, chief exec. officer, 1982—, chmn., 1985—, also dir.; bd. dirs. FMC Corp., Chgo., Boatmen's Bancshares, Inc., St. Louis, Centerre Nat. Bank, St. Louis, McDonnell Douglas Corp., St. Louis, ENSERCH Corp., Dallas; cons. Office Mgmt. and Budget, 1973, 75. Author: (with others) Better Management of Business Giving, 1965. Trustee Rush-Presbyn.-St. Luke's Med. Center, 1974-84, Washington U., St. Louis, 1983—, Barnes Hosp., St. Louis, 1987—; bd. visitors Harvard U. Bus. Sch., 1987—. Served to lt. USNR, 1958-62. Recipient Rayonier Found. award Harvard U., 1963; George F. Baker scholar, 1964. Mem. Beta Theta Pi, Omicron Delta Kappa, Phi Alpha Delta. Clubs: Chgo.; River (N.Y.C.); St. Louis Country, Log Cabin (St. Louis); Indian Hill Country (Winnetka, Ill.). Office: Brown Group Inc 8400 Maryland Ave Clayton MO 63105

BRIDGFORTH, ROBERT MOORE, JR., aerospace engineer; b. Lexington, Miss., Oct. 21, 1918; s. Robert Moore and Theresa (Holder) B.; student Miss. State Coll., 1935-37; B.S., Iowa State Coll., 1940; M.S., M.I.T., 1948; postgrad. Harvard U., 1949; m. Florence Jarnberg, November 7, 1943; children—Robert Moore, Alice Theresa. Asst. engr. Standard Oil Co., of Ohio, 1940; teaching fellow M.I.T., 1940-41, instr. chemistry, 1941-43, research asst., 1943-44, mem. staff div. indsl. cooperation, 1944-47; asso. prof. physics and chemistry Emory and Henry Coll., 1949-51; research engr. Boeing Airplane Co., Seattle, 1951-54, research specialist 1954-55, sr. group engr., 1955-58, chief propulsion systems sect. Systems Mgmt. Office, 1958-59, chief propulsion research unit, 1959-60; chmn. bd. Rocket Research Corp. (name now Rockcor, Inc.), 1960-69, Explosives Corp. Am., 1966-69. Fellow Brit. Interplanetary Soc., AIAA (asso.), Am. Inst. Chemists; mem. Am. Astronautical Soc. (dir.), AAAS, Am. Chem. Soc., Am. Rocket Soc. (pres. Pacific NW 1955), Am. Ordnance Assn., Am. Inst. Physics, Am. Assn. Physics Tchrs., Tissue Culture Assn., Soc. for Leukocyte Biology, N.Y. Acad. Scis., Combustion Inst., Sigma Xi. Home: 4325 87th Ave SE Mercer Island WA 98040

BRIDSTON, PAUL JOSEPH, financial executive; b. Grand Forks, N.D., May 28, 1928; s. Joseph and Anna (Pederson) B.; m. Peggy C. Cullen, Aug. 26, 1955; children—Peter, Rebecca, Sarah. BA magna cum laude, Yale U., 1950; MBA, Stanford U., 1952. Sec.-treas. First Fed. Savs. & Loan Assn., Grand Forks, N.D., 1955-61, pres., 1962-81, chmn. bd., 1961-82; pres. J.B. Bridston Ins. Co., 1963-75; chief Housing Guaranties Program for Latin Am., AID, Washington, 1964-65; cons. U.S. Dept. State, 1968-70; asst. insp. gen. fgn. assistance, 1970; mem. N.D. Ho. of Reps., 1972-74; chmn. Pioneer Mountain Mortgage Bank, 1980-84; con. Paul J. Bridston & Assocs., 1984-88; vis. prof. mgmt. U. Okla. 1988—. Pres. Grand Forks YMCA, 1959-60, GrandForks United Fund, 1961-62; bd. dirs. Tyrone Guthrie Theatre, Mpls., 1963-69, Boys Club Am., 1963-69; chmn. Martin County Atlantic-Pacific Housing, Inc., Fla., 1984-86. With USNR, 1952-55. Mem. Nat. Savs. and Loan League (bd. dirs. 1961), U.S. Savs. League (chmn. internat. devel. com. 1968-69), Yale U. Alumni Assn., Stanford Alumni Assn. Lutheran. Clubs: Augusta Nat., Fed. City, Tulsa Country. Lodge: Elks. Home: 6843 Tall Pines Rd Bemidji MN 56601 Office: 300 S 5th St Grand Forks ND 58201

BRIDWELL, CHARMAINE CLAUDETTE, financial officer; b. Chula Vista, Calif., June 25, 1953; d. Charles Mike and Louise Julia (Flegal) Erreca; m. Dennis Wayne Bridwell, July 7, 1971 (div. 1976); 1 child, Joshua Wayne. Student, Southwestern Coll., Chula Vista, 1971. Bookkeeper Erreca's, Inc., Spring Valley, Calif., 1973-81, chief fin. officer, 1981—. Home: 1507 Sunrise Shadow Ct El Cajon CA 92019 Office: Erreca's Inc 8555 Paradise Valley Rd Spring Valley CA 92077

BRIED, HENRY WILLIAM, manufacturing company official mechanical engineer; b. Teaneck, N.J., June 17, 1933; s. Henry F. and Rose M. Bried; married; children by previous marriage: Kathleen, James, Henry William, Stephen. ME, Stevens Inst. Tech., 1965. Tech. planning engr. Gen. Electric Co., Phila., 1958-60; product design engr. Gen. Electric Co., Valley Forge, Pa., 1961-63; mgr. mil. aerospace systems Washington, 1965-68; mgr. WWMCCS Program Honeywell Info. Systems, Phoenix, 1968-71, mgr. prodn. programs, 1968-74; mgr. info. systems Motorola, Inc., Phoenix, 1974-76, mgr. participative mgmt. program, 1976-80, corp. dir. participative mgmt. program, 1980-82; pres., chief exec. officer Economy Plumbing Supply, Scottsdale, Ariz., 1982—. Pres. Kiva-Kaibab Little League, 1972-74, coach, 1969-76; coach Wheaton Boys Club, 1961-68; pres. Layhill Rd. Citizens Assn., 1965-68; bd. dirs. Ariz. Boys Community, 1976-79, Phoenix Urban League, 1988—; vice-chmn. bd. dirs. Found. Sr. Adult Living, 1982-86; mem. rate rev. com. Cen. Ariz. Health Systems Agy., 1981—; mem. Rep. Nat. Com.; bd. dirs. P.S.D.A. Served to 1st lt., Ordinance Corps, U.S. Army, 1955-58. Mem. ASME, Air Force Assn., U.S. Navy League. Roman Catholic. Home: 8501 E Cholla St Scottsdale AZ 85260 Office: Economy Plumbing Supply 3922 W Indian School Rd Scottsdale AZ 85019

BRIEN, ROBERT L., management consultant; b. Pitts., Dec. 10, 1937; s. Donald G. and Louise (Lerch) B.; m. Yvonne Brien, Jan. 31, 1964 (div. 1986); children: Garen, Andrea, Alison; m. Maxie Slack, Aug. 22, 1986. BS, Cornell U., 1963; MA, Temple U., 1970, PhD, 1974. Cert. psychologist, Pa. Psychologist Mgmt. Scientists, Phila., 1971-73; prin., cons. Miller, Ginsburg & Brien, Phila., 1973-86, The Haverford Group, Bristol, Va., 1986—; bd. dirs. Atelier Internat., Inc., N.Y.C., Office Improvements, Inc., Manchester, Pa., Manchester Industries. Author: (with others) Omega Management, 1982. With U.S. Army, 1964-66. Mem. Merion Cricket Club, Country Club of Bristol, Bermuda Anglers Club. Republican. Episcopalian. Office: The Haverford Group 211 Winsor Ln Haverford PA 19041

BRIGGS, DANIEL L., county official; b. Washington, June 22, 1952; s. Gerald L. and Corinne (Merkt) B.; m. Elise Mears, Apr. 17, 1982; children: Ryan, Christopher, Kaitlyn. BA, St. Lawrence U., 1974; JD, U. Bridgeport, 1980. Councilman Town of Thompson, Monticello, N.Y.; acting judge Village of Monticello; treas. Sullivan County, Monticello, 1983—; mem. adj. faculty Sullivan County Community Coll., Loch Sheldrake, N.Y. Mem. exec. com. Sullivan County Rep., N.Y.; mem. exec. com., Sullivan County chpt. ARC; vol. Loch Sheldrake Fire Dept., Monticello Vol. Ambulance Corps. Mem. Govtl. Fin. Officers Assn., N.Y. State Treas. Assn. Lodges: Lions, Elks. Office: Sullivan County 100 North St Monticello NY 12701

BRIGGS, GEORGE MADISON, civil engineer; b. Albany, N.Y., May 4, 1927; s. Franklin H. and Emma E. (Briggs) B.; B.S. in C.E., Purdue U., 1952; M.P.A., SUNY, Albany, 1968; m. Jean M. Cully, Oct. 31, 1954; children—George Madison, Barbara Jean. Engr., N.Y. State Dept. Public Works, Albany, 1952-56, asst. planning and location engr. dist. 1, 1956-60, resident engr. Saratoga County, 1961-64; asso. civil engr. N.Y. State Dept. Transp., Albany, 1965-67, dir. hwy. maintenance, 1968-72, dir. maintenance, 1972-80, asst. commr. ops., 1980-83; pres. Briggs Engring., P.C., Greenwich, N.Y., 1983—; exec. dir. N.Y. Bituminous Distbrs. Assn.; mem. coms. Transp. Research Bd., Nat. Acad. Scis.; instr. Fed. Hwy. Adminstrn.'s Course in bridge maintenance for state DOT bridge maintenance technicians and suprs. Co-author Am. pub. works assn. Roads and Streets Manual. Chmn. transp. com. 1980 Olympic Winter Games; cons. FHWA, Saudi Arabia, 1983, OAS, Caracas, Venezuela, 1984. Mem. Planning Bd. Town of Easton. Served with AUS, 1945-47. Registered profl. engr., N.Y. Mem. Nat. Soc. Profl. Engrs., N.Y. State Soc. Profl. Engrs. (pres. Tri-County chpt.), Am. Public Works Assn., Nat. Inst. Transp. (exec. council), Nat. Assn. State Hwy. and Transp. Ofcls. (vice chmn. maintenance com., task force leader bridge maintenance), SAR (v.p. chpt.), Soc. Mayflower Descs. Mem. Soc. Friends. Clubs: Masons, Shriners, Elks. Contbr. articles to profl. publs. Home and Office: Burton Rd #1 Box 401M Greenwich NY 12834

BRIGGS, GRAHAM RUFUS, financial executive; b. Grimsby, Lincolnshire, Eng., Apr. 20, 1939; came to U.S., 1966; s. Arthur George and Ruth Lillian (Whipps) B.; m. Jane Therese Corcoran, April 26, 1969; children: Graham Seton, Sarah Jane. MA, Cambridge U., Eng., 1962; MS, Cranfield Inst. Tech., Eng., 1965; MBA with distinction, Harvard U., 1967. Asst. to pres. ABEX Corp., N.Y.C., 1967-69; v.p. fin. Edn. for Mgmt. Inc., Boston, 1969-71; mgr. strategic planning AIRCO Inc., Montvale, N.J., 1971-74; v.p. fin. Computer Identics Corp., Westwood, Mass., 1974-80; pres. Fin. Mgrs. Inc., Needham, Mass., 1980-83; v.p. fin. Charles River Data Systems Inc., Framingham, Mass., 1983-89, The Anderson Cos., Marshfield, Mass., 1989—. Author: The Theory and Practice of Management Control, 1970; contbr. articles to profl. jours. Mem. Fin. Exec. Inst., Cambridge U. Metall. Soc. (founder). Republican. Episcopalian. Home: 45 Hoover Rd Needham MA 02194 Office: The Anderson Cos 1025 Plain St Marshfield MA 02050

BRIGGS, JOHN PORTER, financial executive; b. Orange, Calif., Feb. 26, 1953; s. Lowell Porter and Henrietta (Spence) B.; m. Donna Josephine Frederic, May 18, 1979; children: John Nathan Arron, Daniel Avry, Jeremy Ryan, Nolan Frederic. BA, Calif. State U., Fullerton, 1976; JD, Tulsa U., 1979. Bar: Okla. 1979. Assoc. Warren F. Young & Assocs., Tulsa, 1979-81; pres. Baytide Securities, Tulsa, 1981, WhitMar Securities Co., Tulsa, 1983-84; v.p., gen counsel WhitMar Exploration Co., Tulsa, 1981-84; sr. v.p. Polaris Energy Devel. Co. (formerly Petromark Resources Co.), Tulsa, 1984-88, pres., chief fin. officer, 1988—; also bd. dirs. Petromark Resources Co., Tulsa; bd. dirs. Golden Sitka Resources, Vancouver. Mem. ABA, Okla. Bar Assn., Okla. Ind. Petroleum Assn., Cedar Ridge Country Club. Democrat. Methodist. Office: Polaris Energy Devel Co 7030 S Yale #800 Tulsa OK 74136

BRIGGS, MALCOLM NORTHRUP, financial consultant; b. Fountain Hill, Pa., July 30, 1947; s. John Danforth and Agatha Crane (Robb) B.; m. Rebecca Rogan Newell, July 30, 1977; children: Evan, Connor, Aynsley, Malcolm Jr., John II. BA cum laude, Harvard U., 1969. With Bethlehem (Pa.) Steel Co., 1969-72; v.p. Covert & Assocs., Allentown, Pa., 1972-81; sr. v.p. Andesa Cos., Allentown, 1981—; pres. Andesa Investments Corp., Allentown, 1985—, Andesa Realty Corp., Allentown, 1985—. Mem. adult com. Young Life, Lehigh Valley, Pa., 1977-82; chmn. Scripture Union U.S.A., Upper Darby, Pa., 1988—. With USAR, 1969-76. Mem. Cert. Fin. Planners, Saucon Valley Country Club (Bethlehem), Spee Club (Cambridge, Mass.). Office: Andesa Cos 1621 N Cedar Crest Blvd Allentown PA 18104

BRIGGS, PAUL W(ELLINGTON), former utility company executive; b. Fairport, N.Y., Nov. 9, 1922; s. C. LeRoy and Erma B.; m. Beatrice Schroeder, Oct. 14, 1950; children: David, Peter, Thomas. A.S. in Acctg. and Fin, Bentley Coll., 1942. With Rochester Gas and Electric Corp., N.Y., 1945-88; sr. v.p. fin. and gen. services Rochester Gas and Electric Corp., 1973-74, pres., 1974-80, chmn. bd., chief exec. officer, 1980-88, also dir., chmn., exec. & fin. com.; dir. Norstar Bank, Norstar Trust Co., Norstar Investment Adv. Services, Inc. Bd. dirs. United Way of N.Y. State, N.E. Midwest Inst.; trustee Eastman Dental Center, Rochester, Rochester Inst. Tech.; bd. dirs. Rochester Philharm. Orch., Inc. Served in AC U.S. Army, 1943-45. Lutheran. Clubs: Country (Rochester), Genesee Valley (Rochester). Office: Rochester Gas & Electric Corp 89 East Ave Rochester NY 14649

BRIGGS, PHILIP, insurance company executive; b. Paris, Feb. 28, 1928; s. Robert E. and Madeleine (Boell) B. (parents Am. citizens); m. Jean M. Sloan, July 9, 1949; children—Karen, Heather, Peter. A.B., Middlebury Coll., 1948. With Met. Life Ins. Co., N.Y.C., 1948—; v.p., gen. mgr. Met. Life Ins. Co., 1971-73, sr. v.p., 1973-77, exec. v.p., 1977-86, vice chmn. bd. dirs., 1986—. Vice chmn. bd. trustees Coll. Ins. Served with AUS, 1946-48, 50-51. Fellow Soc. Actuaries, Am. Acad. Actuaries; mem. Nat. Planning Assn., Health Ins. Assn. Clubs: Stanwich Golf (Greenwich, Conn.); Sky (N.Y.C.). Home: 520 Stanwich Rd Greenwich CT 06830 Office: Met Life Ins Co 1 Madison Ave New York NY 10010

BRIGHAM, HENRY DAY, JR., lawyer; b. Pittsfield, Mass., Dec. 12, 1926; s. Henry Day and Gladys M. (Allen) B.; m. Catherine T. Van't Hul, Dec. 16, 1961; children—Henry Day, Johan Van't Hul, Alexander Frederick. B.A., Yale U., 1947, J.D., 1950. Bar: N.Y. 1951, Mass. 1966. Assoc., Milbank Tweed Hope & Hadley, N.Y.C., 1951-52, 54-56, Simpson Thacher & Bartlett, N.Y.C., 1956-66; v.p., gen. counsel, dir. Eaton & Howard, Inc., Boston, 1966-73, pres., 1973-79, v.p., chmn. exec. com. Eaton & Howard, Vance Sanders Inc., 1979-81, v.p., chmn. exec. com. Eaton Vance Corp., 1981—; pres., trustee Eaton Vance Cash Mgmt. Fund, Boston, 1974—; v.p., dir. Eaton Vance Spl. Equities Fund, Inc., Boston, 1969—; v.p., trustee Eaton Vance Tax Free Reserves, Boston, 1982—, Money Market Trust, Boston, 1981—, The Wright Managed Equity Trust, Boston, 1982—, Bond Trust, Boston, 1983—, Stovall/21st Consistent Return Trust, N.Y.C., 1986—; dir. Investors Bank & Trust Co., Boston. Pres., Trustees of Donations of Episcopal Diocese of Mass., 1984—; sec. Chestnut Hill Assn. (Mass.), 1969—. Served to lt. USNR, 1952-54, MTO. Mem. Investment Co. Inst. (bd. govs.), Investment Counsel Assn. Am. (bd. govs.), Phi Beta Kappa, Phi Delta Phi. Republican. Episcopalian. Clubs: Country (Brookline, Mass.); Tennis & Racquet, Downtown, Harvard, Longwood Cricket (Boston); Tarratine Yacht (Islesboro, Maine). Office: Eaton Vance Corp 24 Federal St Boston MA 02110

BRIGHAM, SAMUEL TOWNSEND JACK, III, lawyer; b. Honolulu, Oct. 8, 1939; s. Samuel Townsend Jack, Jr. and Betty Elizabeth (McNeil) B.; m. Judith Catherine Johnson, Sept. 3, 1960; children: Robert Jack, Bradley Lund, Lori Ann, Lisa Katherine. B.S. in Bus. magna cum laude, Menlo Coll., 1963; J.D., U. Utah, 1966. Bar: Calif. 1967. Asso. firm Petty, Andrews, Olsen & Tufts, San Francisco, 1966-67; accounting mgr. Western sales region Hewlett-Packard Co., North Hollywood, Calif., 1967-68; atty. Hewlett-Packard Co., Palo Alto, Calif., 1968-70; asst. gen. counsel Hewlett-Packard Co., 1971-73, gen. atty., asst. sec., 1974-75, sec., gen. counsel, 1975-82, v.p., gen. counsel, 1982-85, v.p. adminstrn., gen. counsel, 1985—; lectr. law Menlo Coll.; speaker profl. assn. seminars. Bd. dirs. Palo Alto Area YMCA, 1974-81, pres., 1978; bd. govs. Santa Clara County region NCCJ; bd. trustees Menlo Sch. and Coll. Served with USMC, 1957-59. Mem. Am. Bar Assn., Calif. Bar Assn., Peninsula Assn. Gen. Counsel, MAPI Law Council, Am. Corp. Counsel Assn. (chmn. 1985, bd. dirs. 1983—), Am. Soc. Corp. Secs. (pres. No. Calif. Chpt. 1983—). Home: 920 Oxford Dr Los Altos CA 94022 Office: Hewlett-Packard Co 3000 Hanover St Palo Alto CA 94304

BRIGHT, H. DAVID, financial executive; b. Columbus, Ohio, Aug. 9, 1934; m. Carol Ann Polivka, July 30, 1960 (dec. July 1981); children: David, Christopher, William (dec.), Kathleen; m. Cynthia Page Subby, 1987. BBA, Marquette U., 1960. CPA, Calif. Sr. acct. Price Waterhouse & Co., Chgo., 1960-64; controller Dart Industries, Los Angeles, 1964-70; group controller Whittaker Corp., L.A., 1970-72; sr. v.p. fin. Nat. Edn. Corp., Irvine, Calif., 1972-78, pres., chief exec. officer, 1978-88; chmn., chief exec. officer Nat. Edn. Corp., Irvine, 1988, chmn., chief exec. officer, pres., 1989—; bd. dirs. Fluorocarbon Corp., Laguna Niguel, Calif., Brinderson Corp., Newport Beach, Calif., MPRI, Alexandria, Va. Trustee Falcon Found., Colorado Springs, Colo., Marquette U., Milw., Laguna Art Mus., Costa Mesa, Orange County Performing Arts Ctr., Costa Mesa; speaker Rep. Nat. Conv., New Orleans, 1988. Served with U.S. Army, 1952-56. Named Chief Exec. Officer of Yr. Fin. World Mag. Mem. Fin. Execs. Inst., Newport Beach Country Club, Big Canyon Country Club, Rotary (Paul Harris fellow). Roman Catholic. Office: Nat Edn Corp 18400 Von Karman Dr #1100 Irvine CA 92715

BRIGHT, HARVEY R., petroleum corporation executive; b. Muskogee, Okla., Oct. 6, 1920; s. Christopher R. and Rebecca E. (Van Ness) B.; m. Mary Frances Smith, May 27, 1943 (dec. Apr. 1971); children—Carol (Mrs. James B. Reeder), Margaret (Mrs. Jerry R. Petty), Christopher R., Clay Van Ness; m. Peggy Braselton, Dec. 15, 1972. B.S., Tex. A&M U., 1943. Ptnr. Bright & Co. (oil producers), Dallas; bd. dirs. State Fair of Tex., Dallas, Reynolds Penland Co., Bright Mortgage Co., Dallas; chmn. bd. dirs. Bright Truck Leasing Corp., Dallas; chmn. bd. dirs., chief exec. officer Bright Banc Savs. Assn., Dallas. Dir. State Fair of Tex., Dallas; chmn. bd. Children's Health Services of Tex., Dallas. Served with AUS, World War II. Home: 4500 Lakeside Dr Dallas TX 75205 Office: 2355 Stemmons Bldg Dallas TX 75207

BRIGHT, MARILYN AGNES, retail executive; b. Beacon, N.Y., Apr. 25, 1946; d. Alfred Joseph Meurant and Agnes Mary (Ketcham) Kusmaul; m. Edward Albert DiTullo, Dec. 13, 1969 (div. Feb. 1985); children: Donna Lynn DiTullo Weller, Donald Thomas; m. Gregory Lawrence Bright, May 2, 1987. Student, Catonsville (Md.) Community Coll., 1984—. Sec. IBM Corp., East Fishkill, N.Y., 1967-71; credit clk. Sears Roebuck & Co., Balt., 1973-74; wxec. sec. Calvert Gen. Contaractors, Ellicott City, Md., 1974-76; adminstr. Dictaphone Corp., Balt., 1976—. Recipient One Standard Excellence award F.T. Allen, Pitney Bowes, 1987. Republican. Roman Catholic. Home: 520-103 Pinehurst Circle Westminster MD 21157 Office: 11438 Cronridge Dr Ste W Owings Mills MD 21117

BRIGNOLO, JOSEPH BARTHOLEMEW, photographer; b. Bridgeport, Conn., Oct. 1, 1920; s. Bartolomeo and May (Smith) B.; m. Claudette Dean, Jan. 26, 1951 (dec. 1973); m. Karen Anne Conley, Dec. 20, 1973; children: Joseph B., Antoinette C. A of Fine Arts, Sch. Modern Photography, N.Y., 1942; student, U. Miami (Fla.), 1948-53. Asst. photographer Brignolo Studio, Bridgeport, 1938-41; pres. Brignolo Studio, Coral Gables, Fla., 1946-65, N.Y.C., 1965-77; owner Joseph B. Brignolo Photography, Chester, N.Y., 1977—; lectr. Profl. Photographers Soc. of N.Y., Newburg, 1980, Brooks Inst., Santa Barbara, Calif., 1982; cons. The Image Bank, 1983. Numerous exhibitions as a photographer; (books) The Image Bank, 1983, Thailand, 1987; Manhattan, N.Y., 1986. Founder, bd. dirs. Glenbrook (Conn.) Civil Assn., 1968-72; scout master Boy Scouts Am., Coral Gables, 1963-65; lectr.. adviser Monroe (N.Y.)-Woodbury Sch. System, 1985-88. Sgt. ULS Army, 1942-45, ETO. Named Best in Show Brit. Assn. Indsl. Editors, London, 1985. Mem. Am. Soc. Mag. Photographers, Conn. Profl. Photographers Assn., DeMolay, Masons. Home: Oxford Springs Rd Chester NY 10918

BRILES, STEPHEN LEROY, civil engineer; b. Kansas City, Kans., Apr. 2, 1953; s. Victor Leroy and Bernice (Potter) B.; m. Cynthia Lee Byers, June 2, 1973; children: Jared M., Janelle M., Aubry N. BSCE, U. Kans., 1976; MBA, Webster U., Kansas City, Mo., 1984. Registered profl. engr., Ill., Ohio, Iowa, Mo., Kans. Project engr. Marley Cooling Tower Co., Mission, Kans., 1975-79, Black & Veatch Engr., Overland Park, Kans., 1979-83; project mgr. Payless Cashways, Inc., Kansas City, Mo., 1983—. Sr. advisor Mid-Am. Jr. Achievement, Overland Park, Kans., 1978; deacon Kansas City Bapt. Temple, 1985. Mem. Mo. Soc. Profl. Engrs. (chmn. indsl. div. 1982), ASCE, Chi Epsilon, Tau Beta Pi. Baptist. Home and Office: Payless Cashways Inc 10428 Oakmont Overland Park KS 66215

BRILEY, MARTHA CLARK, insurance company executive; b. Glen Ridge, N.J., May 31, 1949; d. David Ormiston and Marion Jane (Drury) Clark; m. Richard Keith Dentel, Dec. 29, 1972 (dec. Feb. 1974); m. Joseph Coyle Briley, Mar. 25, 1978; children: Christopher, Alexis. AB, Brown U., 1971; MBA, Harvard U., 1978. CLU, 1986, chartered fin. cons., 1987. Asst. treas., trainee Chase Manhattan Bank, N.Y.C., 1971-74, 2d v.p. corp. fin., 1974-76, v.p., team leader corp. lending, 1978-81; v.p. corp. fin. Prudential Ins. Co., Newark, 1981-83, v.p., treas., 1983-89; pres., chief exec. officer Prudential Power Funding Assocs., Newark, 1989—. Trustee Brown U., 1987—, Ind. Coll. Fund of N.J., 1988—. Recipient Alumni Svc. award Brown U., Providence, R.I., 1984. Mem. Fin. Womens Assn. (bd. dirs.), Treas.'s Group N.Y., Assn. Alumni Brown U. (bd. dirs., mem. exec. com. 1982-87, treas. 1982-84). Republican. Presbyterian. Office: Prudential Power Funding Assocs 4 Gateway Ctr 100 Mulberry St Newark NJ 07102

BRILL, ALAN RICHARD, financial executive; b. Evansville, Ind., July 5, 1942; s. Gregory and Bernice Lucille (Froman) B.; A.B., DePauw U., 1964; M.B.A., Harvard U., 1968; m. Bonnie Faye Phillips, May 26, 1973; children—Jennifer Leigh, Katherine Anne, Alison Elizabeth. Mgmt. cons. Peace Corps, Ecuador, 1964-66; sr. acct., cons. Arthur Young & Co., N.Y.C., 1968-71; v.p. ops. Charter Med. Mgmt. Co., Inc. and v.p.-controller Hosp. Investors, Atlanta, 1972-73; v.p., treas., dir. Worrell Newspapers, Inc., and Worrell Broadcasting Inc., Charlottesville, Va., 1973-79; pres. Brill Assos., Evansville, Ind., 1979—, Brill Media Co., Inc., Evansville, 1980—. Mem. AICPA, N.Y. State Soc. C.P.A.s, Inst. Newspaper Controllers and Fin. Officers. Republican. Methodist. Clubs: Farmington Country (Charlottesville); Safari Internat. Home: 211 E Jennings Newburgh IN 47630 Office: PO Box 3353 Evansville IN 47732

BRILL, RONALD MITCHEL, retail executive; b. N.Y.C., Sept. 12, 1943; s. Morris William and Esther (Gelman) B.; m. Lisa Sue Feldman, Dec. 31, 1969; children—Matthew, Jonathan. B.S., Fairleigh Dickinson U., 1966. C.P.A., Calif. Mem. audit staff Arthur Andersen & Co., Los Angeles, 1966-69, audit sr., 1969-71, audit mgr., 1971-76; dir. audit services Handy Dan Home Improvement Ctrs., Inc., City of Commerce, Calif., 1976-78; controller Home Depot, Inc., Atlanta, 1978-80, v.p. fin., treas., 1981-84, sr. v.p., chief fin. officer, 1984—. Contbr. monthly columns to mag. Fin. sec. Temple Emanu-el, Atlanta, 1984. Mem. Nat. Retail Mchts. Assn., Am. Inst. C.P.A.s, Calif. Soc. C.P.A.s, Inst. Internal Auditors. Office: The Home Depot Inc 2727 Paces Ferry Rd Atlanta GA 30339

BRILL, STEVEN, magazine editor; b. Queens, N.Y., Aug. 22, 1950; m. Cynthia Margolin; children: Emily Jane, Sophia. BA summa cum laude, Yale U., 1972, JD, 1975. Asst. to the Mayor City of N.Y.C., 1972-74; contbg. editor, columnist New York mag., 1974-76; law columnist and writer

Esquire mag., N.Y.C., 1977-79; founder, editor-in-chief American Lawyer mag., N.Y.C., 1978-82; exec. v.p. AM-LAW Pub. Corp., N.Y.C., 1978-82; pres., chief exec. officer, editor-in-chief AM-LAW Pub. Corp., 1982—. Author: Firearms Control--A Research and Policy Report, 1976, The Teamsters, 1978; freelance writer Harper's mag., 1974-76. Recipient John Hancock award for Bus. Journalism, 1976, Nat. Mag. Award for Essays and Criticism, 1983. Mem. Phi Beta Kappa. Office: AM-LAW Newspaper Pubs 600 Third Ave New York NY 10016

BRILLHART, DAVID WINTHROP, banker; b. Bethlehem, Pa., Jan. 9, 1925; s. David H. and Elizabeth L. (Lehr) B.; B.S., U.S. Mil. Acad., 1946; M.B.A., N.Y. U., 1960; m. Joan Jeffris, Mar. 5, 1948; children—Jeff, Sally, Jon. Vice pres. Morgan Guaranty Trust Co., N.Y.C., 1954-72; exec. v.p. S.E. First Nat. Bank of Miami (Fla.), 1972-76; pres., chief exec. officer 1st Bancshares of Fla., Inc., Boca Raton, 1977-79; chmn. David Brillhart and Assos., Miami, 1979—; dir. Lehigh Valley Bank, Bethlehem, Pa., Constrn. Specialties, Inc., Cranford, N.J., Independence Bancorp, Perkasie, Pa. Served to capt. AUS, 1946-54. Mem. N.Y. Soc. Security Analysts, AIM, Am. Mgmt. Assn. Clubs: Standard, Coral Reef Yacht, Miami (Miami). Home: 5401 SW 98th Terr Miami FL 33156 Office: David Brillhart & Assocs 5900 SW 73d St Miami FL 33143

BRILLIANDE, ROBERT, insurance executive; b. Paris, France, Sept. 14, 1909; s. Isiah and Sophia (Gerine) B.; B.A., U. Hawaii, 1935; m. Irvine Tewksbury Baptiste, June 25, 1938; children—Robert Irving II, Gary Shawn, Timothy Wayne, Michael Bruce, Karen Joy. Editor, pub. Waikiki Pictorial News, 1935-37; engaged in ins. bus., 1937—; pres., treas. Brilliande Ins. Agy., Ltd., 1944-79, emeritus, 1979—; founder Financial Security Life Ins. Co., Ltd., Honolulu, 1950, pres., from 1950, chmn., from 1950, now emeritus chmn. and pres.; pres., treas. Reliable Investment Corp., Ltd., 1953—, Hawaii Underwriting Co., Ltd., 1953-79. Founder-patron Chamber Music Soc. Honolulu, Hawaiin Opera Theatre; patron Royal Circle of Honolulu Symphony Soc., Commedia, Inc., repertory theatre. Bd. dirs. Inst. Orch. and Ensemble Hawaii, Honolulu Community Theatre. Served with U.S. Army, 1930-36. Mem. Nat. Assn. Life Underwriters (life mem. Million Dollar Round Table), Ins. Accounting and Statis. Assn., Life Office Mgmt. Assn., Nat. Assn. Life Cos., Am. Mgmt. Assn., Gen. Agts. and Mgrs. Assn. Hawaii, Assn. Life Underwriters Hawaii, Hawaii Claims Assn., Am. Risk and Ins. Assn., Internat. Monetary and Fin. Soc. Hawaii (founder, 1st pres.), First Hawaii Shakespearean Soc. (pres. 1974), Nat. Skeet Shooting Assn., U.S. Tennis Assn. (past exec. com.), Hawaii Tennis Assn. (founder, 1st pres.) Lawn Tennis Assn., AAU (bd. mgrs. for weightlifting, organizer, 1st pres. weightlifting assn. Hawaii), Honolulu Acad. Arts, U. Hawaii Theater Guild, Honolulu Community Theater (dir. 1979—), U. Hawaii Alumni Assn., Hist. Soc. Bishop Mus. Assn., N.Y. Shavians, African Soc. Denmark (hon. life), Game Conservation Internat., East African Profl. Hunters Assn. (hon. life), Internat. Platform Assn., Internat. Shakespeare Assn., African Soc. Denmark (life), Bernard Shaw Soc. N.Y., Alliance Francaise, Phi Delta Phi. Clubs: Masons (K.T., 32d deg.), Safari Internat. (founder, 1st pres. Hawaii chpt., mem. internat. bd.), Aloha Skeet and Trap Hawaii (hon. life), Club de Regatas Corona Fishing (Tampico, Mexico), Hickam Rod and Gun (hon. life), Sailfish and Tarpon Mexico, Haura Marlin de Tahiti (founder), Hawaii, Kona Big Game Fishing, Honolulu Automobile, Honolulu Press (life). Home: 3671 Diamond Head Rd Honolulu HI 96816

BRIMMEKAMP, CARL GERD, foreign trade company executive; b. Hamburg, Germany, Aug. 7, 1928; s. Carl and Charlotte Eugenie (Steinwachs) B.; student U. Hamburg; B.A. in Econs., Bklyn. Coll., 1955; postgrad. N.Y. U., 1955-56; M.B.A., U. Calif., Berkeley, 1961; m. Ruth M. Lingg, Sept. 5, 1953; children—Thomas L., Susanne L., Kristina S. Sales engr. Ferrostaal Overseas Corp., N.Y.C., 1952-56; gen. mgr., sec.-treas. Ferrostaal Pacific Corp., San Francisco, 1957-62; pres. Carl G. Brimmekamp Co., San Francisco, N.Y.C., 1962-73; pres., chief exec. officer Krupp Internat., Inc., Harrison, N.Y., 1970-79, Carl G. Brimmekamp & Co., Inc., Stamford, Conn., 1979—; chmn. Brimmekamp Corp., San Rafael, Calif., 1980—. Co-founder, German-Am. Round Table, San Francisco, 1958; founder German-Am. Trade Adv. Bd., 1962-66; bd. dirs. Gulf Atlantic Machine and Tool Co., Inc., Mobile, Ala., Koch Material Handling Systems, Inc., Stamford, Conn. Served with U.S. Army, 1953-55. Mem. TAPPI, Wire Industry Assn., German-Am. C. of C. (dir. 1971-74, 76-79, exec. com. 1976-79). Republican. Presbyterian. Clubs: Landmark (Stamford); World Trade, Univ. (San Francisco); Greenwich (Conn.) Country; Met. Opera, Met. (N.Y.C.); Fripp Island (S.C.); Duquesne (Pitts.); Deutscher Verein. Office: Carl G Brimmekamp & Co Inc 102 Hamilton Ave Stamford CT 06901

BRINCKMAN, DONALD WESLEY, industrial company executive; b. Chgo., Mar. 17, 1931; m. Beverly Washo; children: Scott, Bonny, Barbara, Donna, Dawn. BS, Northwestern U., 1954, MBA, 1959; D Bus. Mgmt. (hon.), Judson Coll., 1987. Mktg. researcher Elgin (Ill.) Watch Co., 1954; market research mgr. Crane Corp., Evanston, Ill., 1955-59, Johnson Motors, Waukegan, Ill., 1959-60; v.p., gen. mgr. replacement C/R Industries, Elgin, 1960-74; pres., chief exec. officer Safety-Kleen Corp., Elgin, 1968—; bd. dirs. Johnson Worldwide Assocs. Chmn. indsl. div. Elgin United Way, 1985; mem. adv. Elgin Community Coll., 1987-88; trustee Coe Coll., Cedar Rapids, Iowa, 1987—; bd. mgrs. Sherman Hosp., Elgin, 1982—. Named fellow Ill. Bus. Hall of Fame, 1986. Mem. Am. Bus. Conf. (founding), Ill. C. of C., Motor Equipment Mfrs. Assn. Republican. Roman Catholic. Office: Safety-Kleen Corp 777 Big Timber Rd Elgin IL 60123

BRINEGAR, BILL WAYNE, telecommunications executive; b. Haskell, Tex., Sept. 2, 1941; s. William T. and Opal M. (Howard) B.; m. Shelva J. Waugh, Feb. 27, 1965 (div. Feb. 1986); children: Billy Gene, Tod Von. Student, Richland Coll., 1976-79. Engring. mgr. Rockwell Collins, Richardson, Tex., 1966-79; dir. engrs. Sci. Atlanta, Norcross, Ga., 1979-84; chief exec. officer Digital Transmission Systems, Inc., Norcross, 1984-88, ANBC, Inc., Norcross, 1989—; advisor CEO Round Table, Atlanta, 1985—; bd. dirs. Advance Tech. Devel. Inst. Patentee threshold extension switch, video clamp, variable amplitude delay equalizer. Served with USN, 1960-64. Mem. IEEE (sr.), Am. Electronics Assn. (chmn. membership com. 1986—). Baptist. Office: ANBC Inc 3000 Northwood Pkwy Ste 235 Norcross GA 30071

BRINEGAR, CLAUDE STOUT, oil company executive; b. Rockport, Calif., Dec. 16, 1926; s. Claude Leroy Stout and Lyle (Rawles) B.; m. Elva Jackson, July 1, 1950 (div. 1983); children: Claudia, Meredith, Thomas; m. Katharine (Schellenger) Potter, May 14, 1983. BA, Stanford U., 1950, MS, 1951, PhD, 1954. V.p. econs. and planning Union Oil (now Unocal), L.A., 1965; pres. pure oil div. Union Oil (now Unocal), Palatine, Ill., 1965-69; sr. v.p., pres. refining and mktg. Union Oil (now Unocal), L.A., 1969-73; U.S. sec. of transp. Washington, 1973-75; sr. v.p. adminstr. Unocal Corp., L.A., 1975-85, exec. v.p., chief fin. officer, 1985—; bd. dirs. AmTrack, Washington; founding dir. Consol. Rail Corp., Washington, 1974-75. Author: monograph on econs. and price behavior, 1970; contbr. articles to profl. jours. on statistics and econs. Sgt. U.S. Air Corp, 1945-47, Korea. Mem. Am. Petroleum Inst. (bd. dirs. 1976-85), Calif. Club, Georgetown Club, Internat. Club, Phi Beta Kappa. Republican. Office: Unocal Corp Unocal Ctr 1201 W 5th St Los Angeles CA 90017

BRINK, JOHN WILLIAM, finance corporation executive; b. Chgo., July 14, 1945; s. M.W. and Alice L. (Nelson) B.; m. Cynthia Hollowell, Jan. 2, 1982; children: Bethany, Peter, Gwendolyn, Courtney. BBA, U. Wis., 1967; MBA, West Tex. State U., 1970. Comml. lending officer Huntington Nat. Bank of Columbus, Ohio, 1970-72; asst. treas. Peabody Internat., Galion, Ohio, 1972-75; v.p., treas. Avis, Inc., Garden City, N.Y., 1975-82, Savin Corp., Valhalla, N.Y., 1983; A.G. Becker Paribas, N.Y.C., 1983-84, U.S. Surg. Corp., Norwalk, Conn., 1984; pres. Treasury Adv. Corp., Pound Ridge, N.Y., 1985-86; sr. v.p., treas., chief fin. officer, Green Tree Acceptance, Inc., St. Paul, 1986—; mem. faculty Franklin U. Gen. Evening Coll., Columbus, 1971-75. Served with AUS, 1968-70. Mem. Am. Mgmt. Assn. (fin. div. steering com. 1978-82), Hazeltine Nat. Golf Club. Office: Green Tree Acceptance Inc 345 Saint Peter St Saint Paul MN 55102-1639

BRINKER, THOMAS MICHAEL, finance executive; b. Phila., Sept. 8, 1933; s. William Joseph and Elizabeth C. (Feeley) B.; m. Doris Marie Carlin, Oct. 11, 1958; children—Thomas Michael, James E., Joseph F., Diane M. Student, St. Joseph's U., U. Pa.; M.S. in Fin. Services, Am. Coll., 1980. Registered investment advisor. With Ice Capades, 1951-52, 56; with Casa Carioca, Garmisch, Fed. Rep. Germany, 1954-56; profl. ice skating tchr. and mfrs. rep. Ridley Park, Pa., 1956-60; agt., div. mgr. Prudential Ins. Co., Phila., 1960-65; gen. agt. Mut. Trust Life Ins. Co., 1965-70; pres., founder Fringe Benefits Inc., Havertown, Pa., 1970—, Fin. Foresight Ltd., Havertown, Pa., 1983—; adj. prof. Pa. State U., 1984—, St. Joseph's U., 1985—. Host. weekly radio show: Financial Forum, WWDB-FM, 1982—; author: Hi, I'm Tom Brinker, You're on WWDB, 1987; columnist: Financially Yours, 1983—; ghostwriter: Nat. Assn. Life Underwriters' Fin. Fitness campaign, 1985; contbr., author, conductor of seminars on fin. planning; contbr. articles to profl. jours. Pres., Delaware County Estate Planning Council, 1979-80, Pipeline Inc., Springfield, Pa., 1970-71; dir. nat. council Invest-in-Am., 1986. Served with US Army, 1954-56. Recipient Nat. Quality awards Nat. Assn. Life Underwriters, 1966—, Nat. Sales Achievement awards, 1970—. Mem. C.L.U. (chartered fin. cons.), Delaware County Life Underwriters (pres. 1975-76, 82-83), Am. Coll. Life Underwriters, Nat. Assn. Life Underwriters, Million Dollar Round Table (life and qualifying mem., court of table 1988), Internat. Platform Assn., Internat. Assn. Fin. Planners (admitted registry fin. planning practitioners 1984, Del. Valley chpt. 1986-88, v.p. 1986-88, pres. Del. Valley chpt. 1989—). Roman Catholic. Clubs: Lake Naomi (v.p. bd. govs. 1982, pres. 1986), The Manor, Knights of Columbus. Home: 115 Locust Ave Springfield PA 19064 Office: 1 N Ormond Ave Township Line Rd Havertown PA 19083 also: Rte 940 PO Box 219 Pocono Summit PA 18346

BRINKLEY, JAMES WELLONS, investment company executive; b. Suffolk, Va., Jan. 30, 1937; s. Lee and Gertrude Rachel (Wright) B.; m. Dana Lynn Brenner, June 12, 1959; children: Robert, Douglas, Susan. Student, U. Richmond, 1955-56; BA in Econs., Coll. William & Mary, 1959. Exec. v.p. Mason & Co., Investment Bankers & Brokers, Newport News, Va., 1962-70; exec. v.p. Legg, Mason, Wood & Walker, Inc., Balt., 1970-84, pres., 1984—, also bd. dirs.; sr. exec. v.p., bd. dirs. Legg Mason, Inc., Balt., 1982—. Dir. The Leadership Greater Balt. Com.; chmn. investment com. Coll. William and Mary, Williamsburg, Va., trustee endowment com., bd. vis.; mem. investment com. Episcopal Ministries, Balt. Capt. U.S. Army, 1960-62. Mem. Balt. Soc. Security Analysts, Nat. Fedn. Fin. Analysts, Securities Industry Assn. (dir.), Legal Mutual Liability Soc. Balt. (dir.), Md. Acad. Scis. (dir., vice chmn.), Bond Club Balt., Rotary. Office: Legg Mason Wood Walker Inc Legg Mason Tower 111 S Calvert St Baltimore MD 21202

BRINKMAN, LINDA, manufacturing company executive; dietitian; b. Medford, Wis., Jan. 15, 1952; d. Clarence and Elizabeth (Scheuer) W.; m. David P. Brinkman, Apr. 25, 1981; children: Sarah, Matthew. BS, in Edn., No. Ill. U., 1973, MS in Nutrition, 1976. Registered dietitian. Extension adviser U. Ill., Champaign, 1973-74; home economist Jewel Foods, Melrose Park, Ill., 1976-78; technologist Quaker Oats, Barrington, Ill., 1978-82; owner A.C.E., Elburn, Ill., 1981—; instr. Waubonsee Community Coll., Sugar Grove, Ill., 1984—. Author mag. column, 1983. Avocations: gourmet cooking, needle crafts, spinning. Home: N4628 Felland Rd Mauston WI 53948 Office: Am Cat Emporium Rte 1 Box 292A Camp Douglas WI 54618

BRINKMAN, RICHARD GENE, oil company executive; b. LaPorte, Ind., Aug. 4, 1927; s. Wilbert Carl and Ruth (Reeder) M.; m. Audrey A. Benson, Aug. 13, 1955 (dec.); 1 child, Lisa B. Brinkman. Student, Valparaiso U., 1947; B.S., Ind. U., 1951, postgrad., 1953; postgrad., U. N.Mex., 1951. With Texaco Inc., N.Y.C., 1956—, asst. comptroller financial reporting, 1963-67, asst. comptroller internat., 1967, asst. comptroller adminstrn., 1968-69, staff coordinator strategic planning, 1969-70, treas., 1971-77, v.p. fin. and econs., 1977-84, v.p. chmn.'s office, 1984-86, sr. v.p., chief fin. officer, 1986—; mem. adv. bd. Mfrs. Hanover Trust Co.; dir. Heddington Ins. Ltd., Heddington Brokers Ltd. Past dir. parents council St. Mary's Coll., Notre Dame, Ind.; bd. dirs. White Plains (N.Y.) Hosp. Med. Ctr. Served with AUS, 1945-47; mem. Dean's Adv. Council Ind. U. Grad. Sch. Bus. Served with USAF, 1951-53. Mem. Acad. Grad. Fellows Ind. U. Sch. Bus. Am. Petroleum Inst. Club: Woodway Country (Darien, Conn.). Office: Texaco Inc 2000 Westchester Ave White Plains NY 10650

BRINKMANN, KARL DWANE, sales executive; b. Bryan, Tex., Oct. 10, 1957; s. Hubert Eldie and Bobbye Louise (Poehl) B.; m. Rhonda Lynn Wilson, June 9, 1984. BS, Tex. A&M U., 1978. Electronics technician O.I. Corp., College Station, Tex., 1978-82, service technician, 1982-85, sales coord., 1985, inside sales mgr., 1985-88, gen. sales mgr., 1988—. Mem. bldg. and grounds com. First United Meth. Ch., Bryan, 1986—. Mem. Water and Waste Water Analysts Assn. Home: 724 Edgewood Dr Bryan TX 77802

BRINKS, KENNETH JOHN HENRY, milling company executive; b. Quincy, Ill., May 18, 1935; s. William Michael and Grace Marie (Bergman) B.; m. Sharon Lee DeWitt, Dec. 27, 1957 (div. 1972); m. Darlene Mary Ann Ghelfi, Apr. 7, 1973; children—Vonnie, Danney, Sheri, Bradley. Student U. Ill., 1953-55; B.A., Quincy Coll., 1958. Purchasing agt. Electric Wheel div. Firestone Tire, Quincy, 1959-60; credit corr. Moorman Mfg. Co., Quincy, 1959-63; office mgr. Bell Grain & Milling Inc. Subs. Moorman Mfg. Co., Perris, Calif., 1963-64, sec., 1964-65, dir., 1965—; treas., sec., 1965-73, v.p. and treas., 1973-83, exec. v.p. and treas., 1983-87, chief fin. officer, gen. mgr., 1987—; sec. Bellmilling Corp. (subs.), Escondido, Calif., 1964-65, treas., sec., 1965-73, pres., chief exec. officer, 1973—; div., chmn. Marshall's Pullets Inc.. Bd. dirs., former treas. Nehi-Kai Villas Homeowners Assn., pres. 1986—. Served to sgt. 1st class U.S. Army. Mem. Toastmasters (treas., v.p., pres.). Lodge: Lions (treas., div.). Office: Bell Grain & Milling 17971 Highway 215 Perris CA 92370

BRINSON, RANDY EUGENE, business consultant; b. Lafayette, Ind., Mar. 13, 1948; s. Charles William and Edna M. (Denney) B.; student SUNY, 1966-71, 75, 77, De Vry Inst. Tech., Chgo., 1972-73. Field engr. Sorbus Inc., Albany, N.Y., 1973-74; purchasing mgr. Artcraft Concepts, Ballston Lake, N.Y., 1974-78; rep. Dow Hickam Pharms., Houston, 1979; owner Rebco, Clifton Park, N.Y., 1977-82; cons. Lela Computer Suitors, Inc., Albany, 1982—; co-organizer Am. Discovery, Inc., Buffalo, 1972. Co-chmn. Wayne Wagner for Congress Camp, 1974; mem. Volunteers in Tech. Assistance, Mt. Ranier, Md., 1975—; mentor for gifted children Guilderland (N.Y.) Sch. Dist.; mem. Nat. Republican Com. Mem. Mensa. Mem. Reformed Ch. Am. Office: Lela Computer Suitor Inc PO Box 357 Clifton Park NY 12065

BRINZA-MANKA, TAMERA ANN, audiologist; b. Muskegon, Mich., Aug. 24, 1961; d. Milton Andrew and Elizebeth Ann (Warmus) B.; m. Steve R. Manka, June 28, 1986. BS in Speech and Hearing, Ind. State U., 1983; MA in Audiology, Ball State U., 1985. Audiologist Northside Rehab. Assn., Indpls., 1985, Witham Meml. Hosp., Lebanon, Ind., 1985; audiologist, owner Beltone Hearing Aid Ctr., Terre Haute, Ind., 1985—. Mem. Am. Speech, Lang. and Hearing Assn., Ind. Speech and Hearing Assn., Nat. Hearing Aid Soc., Am. Acad. Audiology, Gamma Phi Beta. Club: Country of Terre Haute. Office: Beltone Hearing Aid Ctr 809 Merchants Bank Bldg Terre Haute IN 47807

BRISCOE, JOHN H., accountant; b. Corpus Christi, Tex., Oct. 22, 1957; s. William H. and Doris (Gautier) B.; m. Tanya L. Jones, Sept. 9, 1983; 1 child, Adam. BBA in Acctg., U. Tex., 1981. CPA, Tex.; chartered bank auditor. Sr. supr. Peat Marwick Mitchell & Co., Corpus Christi, 1981-85; mgr. Ernst & Whinney, Corpus Christi, 1985-87; v.p., chief fin. officer Gen. Gas Resources Inc., Corpus Christi, 1987-88; v.p., chief fin. officer, co-founder AMMEX Energy Corp., Corpus Christi, 1988—. Mem. AICPA, Tex. Soc. CPA's, Petroleum Accts. Soc. (mem. council), South Tex. Savs. and Loan League (programs com. 1986), Corpus Christi C. of C. Republican. Presbyterian. Office: AMMEX Energy Corp 710 N Mesquite Corpus Christi TX 78401

BRISKIN, BERNARD, finance executive; b. N.Y.C., May 21, 1924; s. Samuel Jacob and Sara (Myers) B.; m. Judith Esther Friedman, Apr. 30, 1972; children—Jeffrey, Deborah, Julie, stepchildren—Rex Wilder, Cam Wilder. B.A., UCLA, 1949. Staff asst. Norton Simon, Inc., 1950-60; self-employed 1960-63; pres. Telautograph Corp., 1963-78; pres., chief exec. officer Arden Group, Inc., Compton, Calif., 1978—. Served with USMC, 1943-45. Office: Arden Group 2020 S Central Ave Compton CA 90220

BRITT, GEORGE GITTION, JR., association executive; b. Bklyn., May 19, 1949; s. George Gittion and Mary Jane (Pattillo) B.; m. Yvonne Oles, Nov. 24, 1974. BA in Polit. Sci., Cheyney State Coll., 1972; postgrad. U. Mich., 1974. Communications asst. U. Pa. Hosp., 1968-70; chmn. Phila. Community Devel. Program, 1970-72; chmn. Pa. Dept. Commerce, Phila., 1972-74; chmn. Nat. Assn. Puerto Rican Youth, Phila., 1974—; chief exec. officer, chmn. Britt, Morales, Patterson, McGhee Corp., 1976—; pub. relations counsellor United Minority Enterprise Assocs; chief operating officer Ricky Espinoza and Assocs. Mem. Phila. Democratic Exec. Com., 1970-76; candidate for Pa. Legislature, 1970, 72, for mayor of Phila., 1975, 79, for City controller, 1981, for U.S. Ho. of Reps., 1978; mem. Council for Equal Job Opportunity, 1970—, pres. 1981. Named Hon. Citizen, Tex., 1972, Mpls., 1972, Ark., 1978, Ala., 1978, Minn., 1978, W.Va., 1978. Mem. Am. Soc. Pub. Adminstrn., Internat. City Mgmt. Assn., Assn. Govt. Accts., Nat. Service League, Nat. League Cities, Nat. Mcpl. League. Baptist. Clubs: N.Y.C., Faculty of U. Pa., Hilltop. Home: 906 S 60th St Philadelphia PA 19143

BRITT, GERALD F., food products company executive; b. 1932; married. BA, U. Chgo., 1951. Exec. v.p., gen. mgr. W. W. Moyer, from 1976; with Gerber Products Co., Fremont, Mich., 1957—, budget dir., 1964-69, asst. to pres., 1969-72, dir. corp. personnel, 1972-80, corp. v.p., 1980-82, v.p. human resources, 1982-86, exec. v.p., 1986—. With U.S. Army, 1954-56. Office: Gerber Products Co 445 State St Fremont MI 49412 *

BRITT, GLENN ALAN, publishing company executive; b. Hackensack, N.J., Mar. 6, 1949; s. Walter E. Britt and Helen (Bell) Crupi; m. Barbara Jane Little, Oct. 25, 1975. AB, Dartmouth Coll., 1971, MBA, 1972. Controller's asst. Time, Inc., N.Y.C., 1972-74; fin. dir. Iran project, Time-Life Books Time, Inc., Alexandria, Va., 1976-78; dir. video group new bus. devel. Time, Inc., N.Y.C., 1980-81, sr. v.p. fin. video group, 1984, v.p., treas., 1986-88, v.p., chief fin. officer, 1988—; v.p., treas. Manhattan Cable TV, N.Y.C., 1974-76; v.p. network and studio ops. Home Box Office, Inc., N.Y.C., 1978-80, sr. v.p., chief fin. officer, 1984-86; sr. v.p. fin. Am. TV and Communications Corp., Stamford, Conn., 1981-84. Mem. Fin. Exec. Inst. Club: N.Y. Athletic. Office: Time Inc Time & Life Bldg New York NY 10020

BRITT, RUSSELL WILLIAM, utility executive; b. Mar. 28, 1926. B.S. in Elec. Engring., U. Wis., 1946, B.B.A., 1948. With Wis. Electric Power Co., Milw., 1948—, asst. controller, 1960-62, controller, 1962-77, treas., 1969-73, v.p. fin., controller, 1973-75, exec. v.p., controller, 1975-77, exec. v.p., 1977-82, pres., chief operating officer, 1982—. Office: Wis Energy Corp 231 W Michigan St PO Box 2046 Milwaukee WI 53201 *

BRITT, TERESA MARIE, banker; b. Elmhurst, Ill., Dec. 29, 1961; d. Thomas P. Britt. BS in Fin. and Econs., Elmhurst Coll., 1984; MBA in Fin. and Mktg., Ill. Benedictine Coll., 1988. Adminstrv. asst. Fin. Resource Network, Evanston, Ill., 1979-81, credit analyst, 1981-83, officer comml. loans, 1983-84; officer comml. loans Marine Midland Bank, Chgo., 1984—. Mem. Chgo. Council Fgn. Relations, 1984—. Democrat. Roman Catholic. Office: Marine Midland Bank 250 S Wacker Dr Ste 900 Chicago IL 60606

BRITTAIN, BEVERLY ANNE, accountant; b. Denville, N.J., July 6, 1959; d. Ellsworth Donald and Ruth Stephanie (Gammelin) Allis; m. David Ross Brittain, May 15, 1982. BA in Acctg., U. Fla., 1981. CPA, Fla. Sr. acct. Baker & Campbell, CPA's, Tampa, Fla., 1982—; asst. pres. Christian Homebuilders, Tampa, 1987—. Mem. AICPA, Aux. Bar Assn., Fla. Inst. CPA's. Republican. Methodist. Home: 469 W Davis Blvd Tampa FL 33606 Office: Baker & Campbell CPA's 200 S MacDill Ave Tampa FL 33609

BRITTING, ROBERT JOSEPH, advertising executive, marketing professional; b. Newark, Aug. 3, 1948; s. George August and Stephanie Ethel (Novak) B.; m. Nancy Jane Hennig, June 25, 1972; 1 child, Robert Joseph II. Student, Fairleigh Dickinson U., 1976, MBA in Mktg., 1979. Account supr. Rolf W. Rosenthal div. Olgivy and Mathers, N.Y.C., 1976-79; v.p., account supr. Klemptner Advt. div. Saatchi & Saatchi, 1979-80; dir. mktg. Clark O'Neill, Fairview, N.J., 1980-82; v.p., account supr. Vicom Assocs. div. Foote Cone Belding, N.Y.C., 1982-85, M.E.D. Communications, Woodbridge, N.J., 1985-87; v.p. mktg. WX Word Tronics, Prospect Park, N.J., 1987—, also bd. dirs. Mem. Pharm. Advt. Council. Republican. Roman Catholic. Home: 25 Rosewood Ct West Windsor NJ 08550 Office: Word Tronics Corp 316 North Sixth St Prospect Park NJ 07506

BRITZ, DIANE EDWARD, investment company executive, chemical trader; b. York, Pa., June 15, 1952; d. Everett Frank and Billie Jacqueline (Sherrill) B.; m. Marcello Lotti, Sept. 9, 1978; children: Ariane Elizabeth, Samantha Alexis. BA, Duke U., 1974; MBA, Columbia U., 1982. Asst. mgr. Columbia Artists, N.Y.C., 1974-76; gen. mgr. Eastern Music Festival, Greensboro, N.C., 1977-78; v.p. Britz Cobin, N.Y.C., 1979-82; pres. Pan Oceanic Mgmt., N.Y.C., 1983—, also bd. dirs.; pres. Pan Oceanic Advisors, Ltd., 1988—, also bd. dirs; bd. trustees Turtle Bay Music Sch. Mem. Bus. Vols. For Arts; class chmn. Duke U. Ann. Fund Drive. Mem. Fin. Women's Assn., Nat. Assn. of Female Execs., Columbia Bus. Sch. Quaker. Clubs: Doubles, Wings (N.Y.C.). Office: Pan Oceanic Mgmt Ltd 122 E 42d St Suite 205 New York NY 10168

BRO, KENNETH ARTHUR, plastic manufacturing company executive; b. Tsingdao, Shandung, China, Aug. 28, 1921 (parents Am. citizens); s. Albin Carl and Marguerite (Harmon) B.; m. Patricia Welch, May 6, 1944; children—William, Peter, Kenneth M., Patricia, Elizabeth, A. Charles. B.S., Northwestern U., 1949. Purchasing agent Welch Mfg. Co., Chgo., 1950-56; v.p. Welch Sci. Co., Chgo., 1957-64; v.p., co-owner Webb Plastic Co., Northbrook, Ill., 1965-87, ret. 1987. Chmn. bd. trustees Northland Coll., Ashland, Wis., 1957, 70-74; pres. bd. dirs. Chgo. Commons Assn., 1962, 70-74; dist. chmn. bd. dirs. Jr. Achievement, Chgo., 1970, 72-74; pres. Found. for Sci. Relaxation, 1965—. Served to pvt. 1st class U.S. Army, 1944-46, ETO. Decorated Bronze Star, Purple Heart. Mem. Am. Vaccum Soc., Am. Assn. Physics Tchrs. Republican. Congregationalist. Clubs: Indian Hill (Winnetka, Ill.); University, Chgo. Yacht, Economic, Executive (Chgo.). Avocations: sailing; flying; travel. Home: 375 Sheridan Rd Winnetka IL 60093 Office: 629 Green Bay Rd Ste 9 PO Box 583 Wilmette IL 60091

BROAD, ELI, financial services and home construction company executive; b. N.Y.C., June 6, 1933; s. Leon and Rebecca (Jacobson) B.; m. Edythe Lois Lawson, Dec. 19, 1954; children: Jeffrey Alan, Gary Steven. B.A. cum laude in Bus. Adminstrn, Mich. State U., 1954. Acct. 1954-56; asst. prof. Detroit Inst. Tech., 1956-57; co-founder Kaufman & Broad, Inc., Los Angeles, 1957; pres., chmn. Kaufman & Broad, Inc., 1957-72, part-time chmn., 1973-75, chmn., chief exec. officer, 1976—; chmn., chief exec. officer Sun Life Ins. Co. Am., Balt., 1976-79; dir. Sun Life Ins. Co. Am., 1979—; chmn., chief exec. officer Sun Life U.S.A., 1986—; chmn. Sun Life Group Am., Atlanta, 1978—; dir. Fed. Nat. Mortgage Assn., 1984—, Anchor Nat. Life Ins. Co., 1986—; past dir. Verex Corp.; real estate adv. bd. Citibank, N.Y.C. Dir. devel. bd. Mich. State U., 1969-72; mem. Nat. Indsl. Pollution Control Council, 1970-73; co-founder Council Housing Producers; chmn. Los Angeles Mayor's Housing Policy Com., 1974-75; del. Democratic Nat. Conv., 1968; pres. Calif. Non-Partisan Voter Registration Found., 1971; bd. dirs. Nat. Energy Found., 1979—, NCCJ, YMCA, Los Angeles United Way, Haifa U.; bd. dirs., trustee Windward Sch.; mem. acquisition com. Los Angeles County Mus. Art, 1979-81; exec. com. Internat. Forum for Los Angeles World Affairs Council; exec. com., bd. fellows Claremont Colls.; adv. bd. Inst. Internat. Edn.; chmn. founding bd. trustees Mus. Contemporary Art, Los Angeles, 1980—; vis. com. U. Calif. at Los Angeles Grad. Sch. Mgmt.; trustee City of Hope, Calif. State Univs. and Colls.; trustee Pitzer Coll., 1979—, chmn. bd. trustees, 1972-79. Recipient Man of Year award City of Hope, 1965; Golden Plate award Am. Acad. Achievement, 1971; Humanitarian award NCCJ, 1977; Housing Man of Yr. Nat. Housing Conf., 1979; Am. Heritage award Anti-Defamation League, 1984. Mem. Beta Alpha Psi. Clubs: Regency, Hillcrest Country (Los Angeles). Home: 1 Oakmont Dr Los Angeles CA 90049 Office: Kaufman & Broad Inc 11601 Wilshire Blvd Los Angeles CA 90025

BROAD, KENNETH CHARLES, computer company executive; b. Traverse City, Mich., Aug. 30, 1944; s. Delbert M. and Louise D. (Getchell) B.; m.

Debra S. Wheeler, June 5, 1982; 1 child, Jeremy M. BS, Cen. Mich. U., 1967, MA, 1969. Instr. psychology U. No. Iowa, Cedar Falls, 1968-73; real estate broker K.C. Bee Realty, Cedar Falls, 1973-78; sales rep. Digital Equipment Corp., Farmington Hills, Mich., 1978-81; sr. sales rep. Perkson-Elmer, Southfield, Mich., 1982-84; regional sales mgr. Human Designed Systems, Livonia, Mich., 1984—. Office: Human Designed Systems 2768 Foster Ave Ste 100 Ann Arbor MI 48108

BROADBENT, AMALIA SAYO CASTILLO, advertising executive, graphic arts designer; b. Manila, May 28, 1956; came to U.S., 1980, naturalized, 1986; d. Conrado Camilo and Eugenia de Guzman (Sayo) Castillo; m. Barrie Noel Broadbent, Mar. 14, 1981; children: Charles Noel Castillo, Chandra Noel Castillo. BFA, U. Santo Tomas, 1978; postgrad. Acad. Art Coll., San Francisco, Alliance Francaise, Manila, Karilagan Finishing Sch., Manila, Manila Computer Ctr.; BA, Maryknoll Coll., 1972. Designer market research Unicorp Export Inc., Makati, Manila, 1975-77; asst. advt. mgr. Dale Trading Corp., Makati, 1977-78; artist, designer, pub. relations Resort Hotels Corp., Makati, 1978-81; prodn. artist CYB/Young & Rubicam, San Francisco, 1981-82; freelance art dir. Ogilvy & Mather Direct, San Francisco, 1986; artist, designer, owner A.C. Broadbent Graphics, San Francisco, 1982—. Works include: Daing na Isda, 1975, (Christmas coloring) Pepsi-Cola, 1964 (Distinctive Merit cert.), (children's books) UNESCO, 1973 (cert.). Pres. Pax Romana, Coll. of Architecture and Fine Arts, U. Santo Tomas, 1976-78, chmn. cultural sect., 1975; v.p. Atelier Cultural Soc., U. Santo Tomas, 1975-76; mem. Makati Dance Troupe, 1973-74. Recipient Merit cert., Inst. Religion, 1977. Mem. Alliance Francaise de San Francisco, Nat. Assn. Female Execs. Roman Catholic. Office: A C Broadbent Graphics 407 Jackson St Ste 302 San Francisco CA 94111

BROADBENT, ROBERT R., retail company executive; b. Lisbon, Ohio, May 25, 1921; s. Raymond and Ruth Edna (Schoonover) B.; m. Mary; 1 son, William Stuart. B.S., U. Akron, Ohio, 1946. Personal asst. to Cyrus S. Eaton, Cleve., 1946-49; various positions in retailing 1949-58; exec. v.p., dir. Higbee Co., Cleve., 1958-73; pres., vice chmn. bd. Higbee Co., 1979-84, chmn. bd., 1984-89; also dir.; chmn. bd., chief exec. officer Gimbel's, N.Y.C., 1973-76; pres., chief exec. officer Liberty House-Mainland, San Francisco, 1976-79; dir. Huntington Bank N.E. Ohio, D.H. Homes Co. Ltd., New Orleans, LISC, N.Y.C. Bd. dirs., exec. com. Greater Cleve. Growth Assn.; bd. dirs. Kent State Found., Cleve. Tomorrow, Cleve. 500 Found.; trustee Kent State U. Served with USAAF, 1943-45, ETO. Decorated D.F.C., Air medal with 4 oak leaf clusters. Mem. Am. Retail Fedn. (bd. dirs.). Clubs: Cleve. Racquet (Cleve.), Cleve. Country (Cleve.), Union (Cleve.); Union League (N.Y.C.). Office: Higbee Co 100 Public Sq Cleveland OH 44113

BROADDUS, CHARLES DAVID, manufacturing company executive; b. Irvine, Ky., Oct. 17, 1930; s. Beverley S. and Lula M. (Congleton) B.; m. Ruth Banister, June 22, 1957; children—Michael, Daniel, Elizabeth. A.B., Centre Coll., Danville, Ky., 1952; M.S., Auburn U., 1954; Ph.D., U. Fla., 1960. Chemist U. Ky., Lexington, 1955-56; instr. Centre Coll., 1956-57; chemist research Procter & Gamble Co., Cin., 1960—, v.p. research, 1984—. Contbr. articles to profl. jours.; patentee in field. Home: 867 Carini Ln Cincinnati OH 45218 Office: Procter & Gamble Co Miami Valley Labs PO Box 398707 Cincinnati OH 45239-8707

BROADHEAD, JAMES LOWELL, business executive; b. New Rochelle, N.Y., Nov. 28, 1935; s. Clarence James and Mabel Roseader (Bowser) B.; m. Sharon Ann Rulon, May 6, 1967; children: Jeffrey Thorton, Kristen Ann, Carolyn Mary, Catherine Lee. B.M.E., Cornell U., 1958; LL.B., Columbia U., 1963. Bar: N.Y. 1963. Mech. engr. sales dept. Ingersoll-Rand Co., 1958-59; asso. Debevoise, Plimpton, Lyons & Gates, N.Y.C., 1963-68; asst. sec. St. Joe Minerals Corp., N.Y.C., 1968-70, sec., 1970-77, gen. counsel, 1973-74, v.p. devel., 1976-77, exec. v.p., 1980-81, pres., 1981-82, also dir.; sr. vp. GTE Corp., Stamford, Conn., 1984-88; also pres. GTE Corp. telephone ops., Stamford, Conn., 1984-88; chmn., chief exec. officer Energy Research Corp., Danbury, Conn., 1973-74; v.p. St. Joe Petroleum Co., N.Y.C., 1974-76; pres. St. Joe Zinc Co., Pitts., 1977-80; exec. v.p., dir. U.S. Industries, 1983; sr. v.p. GTE Corp., N.Y.C., 1984-88; pres., chief exec. officer FPL Group Inc.; bd. dirs. Barnett Banks Inc. Editor: Columbia Law Rev., 1963. Served with U.S. Army, 1960-61. Club:; Union League, Middlesex. Home: PO Box 088801 North Palm Beach FL 33408 Office: FPL Group Inc PO Box 08801 North Palm Beach FL 33408

BROADHURST, AUSTIN, JR., executive recruiter; b. Boston, Aug. 9, 1947; s. Austin and Deborah (Lowell) B.; BA, Williams Coll., 1969; MBA, Harvard U., 1972; m. Janine Boyajian, June 15, 1974; children: Robert James, Lauren Cox. With sec.'s office HEW, Washington, 1972-76; asst. to corp. exec. v.p. Travenol Labs., Deerfield, Ill., 1976-78, group product mgr., 1978-79; dir. corp. planning Nat. Med. Care, Boston, 1979-80, corp. v.p., 1980-83; sr. v.p. UHA Enterprises, N.Y.C., 1983-84; pres., chief exec. officer, dir. OcuSystems, Inc., 1985-86; exec. dir. Russell Reynolds Assn. 1986-88, mng. dir., 1988—. Corporator New Eng. Bapt. Hosp., 1982-83; active Squam Lakes Assn., N.H. Episcopalian. Clubs: Harvard of N.Y., Milbrook. Home: 45 Patterson Ave Greenwich CT 06830 Office: Russell Reynolds Assn 3 Landmark Sq Stamford CT 06901

BROADHURST, NORMAN NEIL, foods company executive; b. Chico, Calif., Dec. 17, 1946; s. Frank Spencer and Dorothy Mae (Conrad) B.; BS, Calif. State U., 1969; MBA, Golden Gate U., 1975; m. Victoria Rose Thomson, Aug. 7, 1976; 1 son, Scott Andrew. With Del Monte Corp., San Francisco, 1969-76, product mgr., 1973-76; product mgr. Riviana Foods, Inc., div. Colgate Palmolive, Houston, 1976-78; new products brand devel. mgr. foods div. Coca Cola Co., Houston, 1978-79, brand mgr., 1979-82, mktg. dir., 1982-83; v.p. mktg. Beatrice Foods Co., Chgo., 1983-86; pres., chief operating officer Famous Amos Chocolate Chip Cookie Co., Torrance, Calif., 1986-88; corp. sr. v.p., gen. mgr. Kerr Glass Mfg., L.A., 1988—. Chmn. youth soccer program Cystic Fibrosis; pres., chmn. South Coast Symphony, 1985-88. Recipient Cystic Fibrosis Community Svcs. award, 1982; bd. dirs. Literacy Vols. Am., Inc., 1987—. Mem. Am. Mgmt. Assn., Am. Mktg. Assn., Toastmasters Internat. (past chpt. pres.). Home: 5009 Queen Victoria Woodland Hills CA 91364 Office: Kerr Glass Mfg 1840 Century Park E Los Angeles CA 90067

BROCK, CHARLES MARQUIS, lawyer; b. Watseka, Ill., Oct. 8, 1941; s. Glen Westgate and Muriel Lucile (Bubeck) B.; m. Elizabeth Bonilla, Dec. 17, 1966; children: Henry Christopher, Anna Melissa. AB cum laude, Princeton U., 1963; JD, Georgetown U., 1968; MBA, U. Chgo., 1974. Bar: Ill. 1969, U.S. Dist. Ct. (no. dist.) Ill. 1969. Asst. trust counsel Continental Ill. Nat. Bank, Chgo., 1968-74; regional counsel Latin Am., Can. Abbott Labs., Abbott Park, Ill., 1974-77, regional counsel, Europe, Africa and Middle East, 1977-81, div. counsel, 1981—; sec. mgmt. com. TAP Pharms., 1985—; bd. dirs. Ningbo Abbott Biotech., Ltd. Served with Inter-Am. Def. Coll., U.S. Army, 1964-66. Mem. ABA, Chgo. Bar Assn., Phi Beta Kappa. Republican. Clubs: Princeton (Chgo.); Princeton (N.Y.C.), Mich. Shores (Wilmette, Ill.). Home: 1473 Asbury Ave Winnetka IL 60093 Office: Abbott Labs Abbott Park IL 60064

BROCK, GERALD WAYNE, federal agency administrator; b. Hanford, Calif., Mar. 31, 1948; s. Aston A. and Leila L. (McAtee) B.; m. Ruth Carol Reisner, June 27, 1971; children: Jane, Sara, David, James. BA, Harvard U., 1970, PhD, 1973. Asst. prof. U. Ariz., Tucson, 1973-78; assoc. prof. Bethel Coll., St. Paul, 1978-79; econ. cons. Brock Econ. Rsch., St. Paul, 1979-83; economist FCC, Washington, 1983-86, chief acctg. and audits div., 1986-87, chief common carrier bur., 1987—. Author: The U.S. Computer Industry, 1975, The Telecommunications Industry, 1981. Office: FCC Common Carrier Bur 1919 M St NW Washington DC 20554

BROCKHAUS, ROBERT HEROLD, SR., business educator, consultant; b. St. Louis, Apr. 18, 1940; s. Herold August and Leona M (Stutzke) B.; m. Joyce Patricia Dees, June 13, 1970; children—Cheryl Lynn, Robert Herold. B.S. in Mech. Engring., U. Mo.-Rolla, 1962; M.S.I.A., Purdue U., 1966; Ph.D., Washington U., St. Louis, 1976. Mgr. Ralston-Purina, St. Louis, 1962-69; pres. Progressive Mgmt. Enterprises, Ltd., St. Louis, 1969—; asst. prof. mgmt. sci. St. Louis U., 1972-78, assoc. prof., 1978-84, prof., 1984—; dir. Small Bus. Inst., St. Louis U., 1976-86; dir. Inst. Entrpreneurial Studies, 1987—, Coro Found., 1987—, Mo. Inventores Assn., 1988—; state adminstr. Mo. Small Bus. Devel. Ctrs., St. Louis, 1982-86, state dir., 1987—; Schoen prof. entrepreneurship Baylor U., 1981; McAninch prof. entrepreneurship Kans. State U., 1985-87 . Co-author: Encyclopedia of Entrepreneurship, 1982; Building A Better You, 1982; Nursing Concepts for Health Promotion, 1979, Art and Science of Enterpreneurship, 1985; editor Journal of Consulting, 1988—; also contbr. articles to profl. jours. Bd. dirs. City Venture, St. Louis, 1982-86, CORO Found., 1987—, Mo. Inventors Assn., 1988—; del White House Conf.on Small Bus., 1986. Recipient Disting. Service award Pi Kappa Alpha, 1972; Fulbright fellow, U. Waikato, N.Z., 1985. Fellow Internat. Council for Small Bus. (sr. v.p. 1981-83, internat. pres. 1983-84, bd. dirs. 1983, v.p. 1986, exec. dir. 1987—), Nat. Small Bus. Inst. Dirs. Assn. (nat. v.p. 1980-82, nat. pres. 1982-83); mem. Acad. Mgmt. (nat. program chmn. 1977-78), Fenton Jaycees (treas.). Mem. United Ch. of Christ. Club: Executive (St. Louis) (moderator 1973-86). Avocations: swimming; sailing; camping. Home: 10000 Hilltop Dr Saint Louis MO 63128

BROCKSBANK, ROBERT WAYNE, retired oil company executive; b. Hudson, N.Y., June 2, 1924; s. Harold Ten Eyck and Helen (Beeler) B.; m. Grace Mary Wright, June 24, 1944 (div. 1976); children—Leslie B. Lucas, Stephanie B. Rodgers, Sydney B. Kirchner; m. Karin Paulson, Oct. 6, 1979. B.S. in Commerce, Drexel U., 1947. Varsity athletic coach Friends Central Prep. Sch., Phila., 1946; with Socony Vacuum Oil (now Mobil), Paulsboro, N.J., 1947-55; staff asst., mfg. employee relations Socony Mobil Oil (now Mobil), N.Y.C., 1955-57; asst. employee relations mgr. Mobil Oil, N.Y.C., 1957-59, mgr. coll. relations, 1959-85. Contbr. articles to profl. jours. Cons., Council on Career Devel. for Minorities, Dallas, 1964—, bd., 1968—, chmn., 1981—, chmn. emeritus, 1988—. Nat. Urban League Summer Fellowship and Career Awareness Program, 1966-81; dir. Southeastern Econ. Devel. Found., Atlanta, 1976-85; trustee Tougaloo (Miss.) Coll., 1977—, bd. dirs. 1977—; exec. adv. council Soc. Hispanic Profl. Engrs., Los Angeles, 1977-84; chmn. bus. adv. com. Hampton (Va.) Inst., 1978-81, mem., 1978-86; mem. minority engring. corp. adv. bd. U. Md., 1979-85, chmn., 1979-81; mem. bd. visitors Drexel U. Sch. Bus., Phila., 1980—; dir. Nat. Consortium for Grad. Degrees for Minorities in Engring., South Bend, Ind., 1981-84. Served to maj. USMC 1942-46, 50-52. Named Friend of the Univ., Va. State U., 1981; Mem. Emeritus, N.C. Central U. Bus. Adv. Council, 1983; Trustee of Edn., League of Latin Am. Citizens, 1983; Robert W. Brocksbank endowed scholarship fund established in his honor, 1985; recipient Pericles award Nat. Employment Mgrs. Assn., 1986, Martin Luther King Dream award Nat. Assn. Negro Profl. and Bus. Women's Clubs, Inc., 1988. Mem. Am. Assembly Coll. Schs. of Bus. (dir. 1980-82, com. Upward Mobility for Minorities in Bus.), Coop. Edn. Assn., Am. Soc. Engring. Edn., Mexican-Am. Engring. Soc., Western Coll. Placement Assn., Southern Coll. Placement Assn., S.W. Coll. Placement Assn., Tex. Assn. Chicanos in Higher Edn., Internat. Platform Assn., Am. Indian Sci. and Engring. Soc. (adv. bd. 1982—, chmn. 1985-88), Midwest Coll. Placement Assn., Middle Atlantic Placement Assn. (hon.), Eastern Coll. Personnel Officers (hon. 1984, dir. 1961-63). Republican. Presbyterian. Clubs: Marine Meml. Club (San Francisco); Marine Officers Assn. (Quantico, Va.). First Person to be featured 3 times on page 1 of Wall Street Journal.

BROCKWAY, PETER CRAIG, investment comapny executive; b. N.Y.C., Aug. 5, 1956; s. Robert Ezra and Hope (Morehouse) B.; m. Susan Perry, Apr. 30, 1983; 1 child, Vanessa. BBA, Stetson U., 1978; MBA, Harvard U., 1980. Dir. planning Photo Electronics Corp., West Palm Beach, Fla., 1980-82; v.p. SE Bank, Miami, Fla., 1982-85; chief fin. officer Wood Gundy Properties, Inc., Baton Raton, Fla., 1985-86; v.p. Trivest, Inc., Miami; v.p. Atlantis Group, Inc., Miami, Biscayne Holdings, Inc., Miami, 1986—. Presdl. scholar Stetson U., 1977. Republican. Presbyterian. Office: Trivest Inc 2665 S Bayshore Dr Miami FL 33133

BRODECKI, JOSEPH MICHAEL, financial executive; b. Landsberg, Fed. Republic Germany, Dec. 12, 1946; came to U.S., 1949; naturalized, 1956.; s. Boleslaw Henry and Sonia (Piekarska) B.; m. Shelley G. Spivack, Sept. 16, 1979; children: Talia, Ariella. BS in Psychology, Va. Commonwealth U., 1970, MS in Indsl. Psychology, 1976; MS in Social Services Adminstrn., Case Western Res. U., 1978; Cert. Fin. Planner, Coll. Fin. Planning, 1985. Indsl. services specialist State of Va., Richmond, 1972-74; exec. dir. campus programs Jewish Community Fedn. Richmond, 1974-76, B'nai B'rith Internat., Washington, 1974-76; campaign mgr. Jewish Community Fedn. Cleve., 1976-83; fin. planner, registered rep. Pvt. Ledger, San Diego, 1986—; investment advisor Planners Fin. Svcs., Mpls., 1988—; assoc. exec. dir. Mpls. Fedn. Jewish Service, 1983—; bd. dirs., v.p. Colony TV Inc., Richmond; bd. dirs. Handforms, Inc., Cleve., Talia Inc., Oneida, N.Y.; fundraising cons.; nat. dir. fin. resource devel. U.S. Holocaust Meml. Mus., Washington. Mem. com. Fedn. Community Planning Com., Cleve., 1979-81; campaign div. chmn. United way, Cleve., 1981; nat. campaign chmn. Case Western Res. Mandel Sch. Applied Social Scis., Cleve., 1982-83. Recipient Fedn. Exec. Recruitment and Edn. Program award Council Jewish Fedns., 1976-78, Jaycees Outstanding Young Man of Am., 1977, Vivian Rabineau Meml. award Council Jewish Fedns., 1985, Pinchas Sapir award United Jewish Appeal, 1983, 85, 86. Mem. Internat. Assn. Cert. Fin. Planners, Twin Cities Assn. Cert. Fin. Planners (founding mem.), Met. Washington D.C., Md. and Va. Consortium of Cert. Fin. Planners, Psi Chi, Alpha Epsilon Pi. Club: Cleve. City. Home: 9004 Wandering Trail Dr Potomac MD 20854 Office: US Holocaust Meml Council 2000 L St NW Washington DC 20036

BRODERICK, ANTHONY JAMES, federal government administrator; b. N.Y.C., Feb. 23, 1943; s. Anthony James and Geraldine (Cummings) B.; m. Sylvia Fantasia, May 30, 1967; children: Sean, Pia. BS in Physics, St. Bonaventure U., 1964. Project mgr. pvt. industry, various locations, 1964-71; physicist U.S. Dept. Transp., Cambridge, Mass., 1971-76; staff chief environment and energy FAA, Washington, 1976-79, tech. advisor aviation standards dept., 1979-82, dep. assoc. adminstr. aviation standards dept., 1982-85, assoc. adminstr. aviation standards dept., 1985-88, assoc. adminstr. reg. and cert., 1988—. Author numerous sci. and tech. articles; patentee in field. Recipient Arthur S. Fleming award, Jaycees, 1979, Presdl. Meritorious Exec. Rank award, 1982, Sr. Exec. Service awards, U.S. Govt., 1983-87. Mem. Air Traffic Control Assn. Roman Catholic. Home: PO Box 3423 Warrenton VA 22186 Office: FAA Dept Regulation and Cert 800 Independence Ave SW Washington DC 20591

BRODERICK, RICHARD JAMES, fiberglass company executive; b. Beverly, Mass., Sept. 7, 1921; s. David and Winifred A. (Mc Donough) B.; m. Mildred R. Carter; children—Judith A. Lane, Philip M., Kenneth R., Kathleen R. Broderick Colbert. B.B.A., Boston U., 1947. Contracting officer Sylvania Electric Products, Salem, Mass., 1945-47; treas. Bomac Labs., Inc., Beverly Mass., 1947-59; chmn., pres. Metcom, Inc., Salem, 1959-72; chmn. Digilab, Inc., Cambridge, 1972-79; gen. mgr. Indikon Co., Cambridge, 1979-80; v.p. gen. mgr. Highline Industries, Inc., Lawrence, Mass., 1980—; v.p., dir. Light Schoppe Inc., Watertown, Mass., dir. Bay Bank & Trust Co., Beverly, Viable Systems Inc., Sherborn, Mass., Fryco, Inc., Phoenix; mgmt. cons. R.J. Broderick & Assocs., Beverly. Inventor microwave switch, 1965. Chmn. Beverly unit ARC, 1960; pres. Beverly Parish Council, 1980. Served with USCG, 1942-45. Mem. Electronic Industries Assn. (v.p. 1962-65), Solar Energy Industries Assn. Roman Catholic. Office: Highline Industries Inc 225 Essex St Lawrence MA 01840

BRODEUR, RICHARD DENNIS, advertising agencyexecutive; b. Concord, N.H., Mar. 31, 1953; s. Richard Delvanie and Patricia Elizabeth (Noonan) B.; m. Judy Karen Hecht, Oct. 23, 1976; children: Nicholas Lyle, Patrick Addison, Rachel Ann. BA, U. N.H., 1975. Art dir. Agrafiotis Assocs., Inc., Manchester, N.H., 1978-83; art dir. Eagle Advt., Inc., Manchester, 1983, creative dir., 1983—, v.p., 1987—, ptnr., 1988—; instr. illustration Notre Dame Coll., Manchester, 1988—; freelance designer, illustrator. Exhibitor area art shows. Active N.H. Percent for Art Program. Mem. N.H. Advt. Club (numerous awards), N.H. Creative Club, Assn. Canado-Am. Republican. Roman Catholic. Home: 189 Arah St Manchester NH 03104 Office: Eagle Advt Inc 1361 Elm St Suite 408 Manchester NH 03101

BRODNIK, CARL JOSEPH, JR., accountant; b. Indpls., Dec. 31, 1949; s. Carl Joseph, Sr. and Ruth Ada (Stephenson) B.; m. Patrice Marie Wilcox, May 18, 1974; children: Christopher Michael, Joel Martin. BA, Marian Coll., 1975. CPA, Ind. Supr. FMC Corp., Indpls., 1968-78; mem. staff Howard R. Nixon CPA, Indpls., 1978-80; sr. internal auditor City of Indpls., 1980-87; acct. Nixon Brodnik & Co., P.C., Indpls., 1987-88; contr. Showalter, Pee & Skripsky, Inc., Indpls., 1989—. Rep. vice precinct committeeman, Indpls., 1986—. Mem. Am. Inst. CPA's, Ind. CPA Soc. (mem. nonprofit orgns. com. 1985—), Inst. Internal Auditors (chmn. continuing edn. com. 1987—). Roman Catholic. Office: Showalter Pee & Skripsky Inc 8440 Woodfield Crossing Blvd Ste 460 Indianapolis IN 46240

BRODO, DONNA MARIE, accountant; b. Atlantic City, Mar. 13, 1957; d. Howard H. and Dorothy (Merkord) Berchtold; m. Thomas Joseph Brodo, Aug. 22, 1987. BA in Econs., Rutgers U., 1979. CPA, N.J. Asst. staff mgr. N.J. Bell, Newark, 1979-80, assoc. staff mgr., 1981-83, staff mgr., 1985-87; staff mgr. AT&T Communications, Rockville, Md., 1983-84; sr. fin. analyst GPU Svc. Corp., Parsippany, N.J., 1987—. Mem. AICPA, N.J. Soc. CPA's. Roman Catholic. Home: 19 Mount Vernon Sq Verona NJ 07044 Office: 100 Interpace Pkwy Parsippany NJ 07054

BRODSKY, LLOYD, management educator; b. Phila., Dec. 18, 1955; s. William and Audrey (Lesse) B. BA, Vassar Coll., 1976; MS, U. Calif., San Francisco, 1979; MBA, U. Calif., Berkeley, 1979; PhD, MIT, 1988. Cons. Index Systems, Cambridge, Mass., 1980-81; software engr. Hewlett-Packard, Waltham, Mass., 1981-83; asst. prof. Sch. Mgmt. Boston U., 1987—. Mem. Amnesty Internat. Mem. Am. Assn. Artificial Intelligence. Democrat. Jewish. Club: Appalachian Mountain (Boston) (trip leader 1983-87). Office: Boston U Sch Mgmt 704 Commonwealth Ave Boston MA 02215

BRODSKY, ROBERT JAY, wholesale executive; b. Chgo., June 1, 1939; s. Victor Robert and Anille (Evans) B.; m. Anna-Marie H. Miller, June 21, 1969; children: Paul, David. AB, U. Chgo., 1961, MBA, 1962. With J.J. Brodsky & Sons, Inc., Chgo., 1962—, pres., 1986—. Served to 1st lt. C.E., Mil. Police, Ill. Army Reserve N.G., 1962-68. Mem. Nat. Candy Wholesalers Assn., Ill. Assn. Tobacco and Candy Distbrs. (bd. dirs. 1987—). Republican. Jewish. Office: J J Brodsky & Sons Inc PO Box 19700 7300 S Kimbark Ave Chicago IL 60619

BRODSKY, WILLIAM J., mercantile exchange executive. Pres. Chgo. Mercantile Exchange. Office: Chgo Merc Exch 30 S Wacker Chicago IL 60606 *

BRODY, ALAN JEFFREY, commodity exchange executive; b. Newark, Apr. 19, 1952; s. Robert and Marcia (Ostroff) B.; m. Miriam Kahan, May 22, 1977. B.A., Northwestern U., 1974; J.D., Rutgers U., 1977. Bar: N.Y. 1978, N.J. 1978. Assoc. Baer Marks & Upham, N.Y.C., 1977-80; v.p. counsel Commodity Exchange Inc., N.Y.C., 1980-81, pres., chief exec. officer, 1981-89, chmn., 1987-88; v.p. Commodities Exchange Ctr. Inc., 1981-84, alternate dir., 1984—; mem. commodity panel policy adv. com. to U.S. trade rep.; mem. council Found. Internat. Futures and Commodities Inst., Geneva. Mem. ABA, N.J. Bar Assn., Assn. of Bar of City of N.Y. (commodities regulation com.), New York County Lawyers Assn., Nat. Futures Assn. (bd. dirs., exec. com.), Futures Industry Assn. (past mem. exec. com. law and compliance div.), Am. Copper Council (bd. dirs.), Copper Club (bd. dirs.), Swiss Commodities & Futures Assn. (bd. dirs.). Office: Commodity Exch Inc NY Commodities Exch Ctr 4 World Trade Ctr New York NY 10048

BRODY, KENNETH DAVID, investment banker; b. Phila., June 30, 1943; s. Herbert Brody and Esther (Forman) Brody Shimberg; m. Judy E. Donahue, Feb. 5, 1964 (div. Feb. 1974); m. Helen M. Tandler, Apr. 6, 1974 (div. Oct. 1978); m. Carolyn J. Schwenker, June 26, 1987. B.S.E.E. with high honors, U. Md., 1964; M.B.A. with high distinction, Harvard U., 1971. Foreman and staff asst. Chesapeake & Potomac Telephone Co., Washington, 1964-66; with Goldman, Sachs & Co., N.Y.C., 1971—, ptnr., 1978—. Bd. dirs. Alvin Ailey Am. Dance Theater, N.Y.C., 1981—, Inst. for Art and Urban Resources, 1987—, Urban Research Found., 1987—. Served to capt. U.S. Army, 1966-69. Baker scholar, 1970; Loeb Rhoades fellow, 1971. Mem. Urban Land Inst. (comml. and retail devel. council 1987), Tau Beta Pi, Eta Kappa Nu, Omicron Delta Kappa, Alpha Tau Omega. Democrat. Unitarian. Club: Harvard (bd. mgrs. N.Y.C.). Office: Goldman Sachs & Co 85 Broad St New York NY 10004

BRODY, NANCY LOUISE, lawyer; b. Chgo., Nov. 17, 1954; d. Mitchell and Grace Yaden (Williams) Block; m. Daniel Matthew Brody, Oct. 28, 1979. BA, U. Mich., 1975; JD, Loyola U., Chgo., 1979. Bar: Ill. 1979, Pa. 1980, Ariz. 1981. Sec., gen. counsel Block & Co., Inc., 1981—, also bd. dirs. Bd. dirs. Ind. YMCA, 1986-87, Charlottesville YMCA, 1989—. Named one of Outstanding Young Women Am., 1983. Life fellow Am. Bar Found., Pa. Bar Found. (bd. dirs. 1984-88); mem. ABA (ho. dels. 1986-88, state membership chmn. Pa. 1986-88), Ill. State Bar Assn., Pa. Bar Assn. (bd. govs. 1984-87, chairperson 1985-86 treas. young lawyers div. 1983-84), Internat. Platform Assn., Zonta (parliamentarian Ind. chpt. 1985-86, 87-88), Pi Beta Phi. Republican. Office: Block & Co Inc 108 Second St NE Charlottesville VA 22901

BROEKEMA, DIRK, JR., mortgage banker; b. Chgo., Feb. 5, 1936; s. Dirk and Sophie Broekema; m. Doris Deal; children: Detje, Dirk III. B.S. in Fin., U. Ariz., 1960. Exec. v.p. Union Bank, Tucson, 1963-68, regional v.p., Los Angeles, 1968-73; exec. v.p. U.S. Fin., Inc., San Diego, 1973-75; pres. St. Paul Title, San Diego, 1976-77; chief exec. officer, chmn. bd. Bowest Corp., La Jolla, Calif., 1978—. Bd. dirs. Scripps Clinic and Research Found., La Jolla. Served to capt. U.S. Army, 1960-63. Republican. Episcopalian. Club: La Jolla Country (bd. dirs.).

BROER, EILEEN DENNERY, management consultant; b. Phila., Sept. 7, 1946; d. Vincent Paul and Jane Dorothy (Knight) Dennery; m. Paul Alan Broer, Nov. 26, 1970 (div. 1980); m. Charles Kenneth ReCorr, Sept. 10, 1981; 1 child, Matthew Vincent; stepchildren: Kenneth, Christopher. BA, Coll. Mt. St. Vincent, 1969. Media dir., control mgr. Merrill Anderson Co., N.Y.C., 1970-72; adminstrv. asst. fin. McCall Pattern Co., N.Y.C., 1972-74, personnel specialist, 1974-77, mgr. employee rels., 1978; dir. personnel Notions Mktg. Inc., N.Y.C., 1978-79; 2nd v.p. personnel Manhattan Life Ins. Co., N.Y.C., 1979, v.p. human resources, 1980-82; v.p. human resources McM Corp., Raleigh, N.C., 1982-85; pres. The Human Dimension, 1985—; bd. dirs. Ctr. For Health Edn. Inc.; adj. faculty writing NYU, 1975-78. Mem. Human Resource Planning Soc., Orgn. Devel. Network, Nat. Assn. Women Bus. Owners (pres. N.C. chpt. 1988-89), Am. Soc. for Tng. and Devel., Raleigh C. of C., Gestalt Inst. Cleve. Office: The Human Dimension 975 Walnut St Ste 354 Cary NC 27511

BROGGI, MICHAEL, marketing executive; b. Los Angeles, June 19, 1942; s. Roger Edward and Thelma Cecile (Marchal) B.; m. Sharon Boyd; children: Michael Jr., Stephen. AA in Journalism, Los Angeles Valley Coll., 1961; grad., USAF Sch. Medicine, Montgomery, Ala., 1962; BA in Mktg. and Communications, Calif. State U., Northridge, 1967; cert. bus. and real estate, San Bernardino Coll., 1975; MBA, Calif. Pacific U., 1988, PhD in Bus. Adminstrn., 1989. Ops. staff Disneyland, Anaheim, Calif., 1960-63; newswriter, reporter Sta. KGIL, San Fernando, Calif., 1963-67; mem. corp. mktg. staff Walt Disney Prodns., Burbank, Calif., 1967-70; mgr. pub. relations Magic Mountain Amusement Park, Valencia, Calif., 1970-72; exec. v.p., gen. mgr. Lake Arrowhead, Calif., 1972-75; dir. adminstrv. svcs. Marriott Corp. Gt. Am. Theme Park, Santa Clara, Calif., 1975-78; v.p., dir. mktg. Mktg. and Fin. Mgmt. Enterprises, Inc., Woodland Hills, Calif., 1978-87; pres. Michael Broggi & Co., Farmington Hills, Mich., 1987—; lectr. Calif. Poly. State U., Pomona, Calif. State U., Northridge, Moorpark (Calif.) Community Coll., Los Angeles Valley Coll., U. So. Calif., Acad. Ambulatory Surgery, Scottsdale, Ariz., Los Angeles Publicity Club, San Francisco Advt. Club, Orange County Advt. Club. Mem. Fire Commn., Spl. Dep. Commn., San Bernardino County. Mem. Am. Mktg. Assn., Cultural Found., Internat. Platform Assn., Am. Soc. Profl. Cons., Nat. Ry. Hist. Soc., Journalism Alumni Assn. Office: Michael Broggi & Co 33533 W 12 Mile Rd #330 Farmington Hills MI 48331

BROGLIATTI, BARBARA SPENCER, television and motion picture executive; b. Los Angeles, Jan. 8, 1946; d. Robert and Lottie (Goldstein) Spencer; m. Raymond Haley Brogliatti, Sept. 19, 1970. B.A. in Social Scis. and English, UCLA, 1968. Asst. press. info. dept. CBS TV, Los Angeles, 1968-69, sr. publicist, 1969-74; dir. publicity Tandem Prodns. and T.A.T. Communications (Embassy Communications), Los Angeles, 1974-77, corp. v.p., 1977-82, sr. v.p. worldwide publicity, promotion and advt. Embassy

Communications, Los Angeles, 1982-85; sr. v.p. worldwide corp. communications Lorimar Telepictures Corp., Culver City, Calif., 1985-89; chmn. Brogliatti Co., Burbank, Calif., 1989—; bd. govs. TV Acad., Los Angeles, 1984-86. Bd. dirs. KIDSNET, Washington, 1987—. Recipient Gold medallion Broadcast Promotion and Mktg. Execs., 1984. Mem. Dirs. Guild Am., Publicists Guild, Acad. TV Arts and Scis. Office: Brogliatti Co 3601 W Olive Ave Ste 430 Burbank CA 91505

BROIDIS, GARY MICHAEL, accountant; b. Queens, N.Y., Nov. 3, 1964; s. David and Shirley (Lipke) B. BS, SUNY, Oneonta, 1986; MBA, SUNY, Binghamton, 1987. Programmer Automatic Data Processing, N.Y.C., 1986; mgr. Hilltop Cafe, Binghamton, 1986-87; mgmt. trainee fin. reporting Oppenheimer & Co. Inc., N.Y.C., 1987-88; cost analyst Avon Products, Inc., 1988—.

BROKENBAUGH, DEBORAH, computer systems analyst; b. Williamstown, N.J., May 27, 1954; d. Arthur and Dolores (Johnson) Jackson; m. James Edward Brokenbaugh Jr., Sept. 2, 1972; children: Nicholas Keshawn, James Edward III. Grad. high sch., Williamstown, N.J. Policy claims clk. Penn Mutual Life Ins. Co., Phila., 1975-78, programmer, 1978-82; sr. programmer Assistance Retainer Management Systems Inc., Wilmington, Del., 1983-85; programmer analyst Assistance Retainer Management Systems Inc., Wilmington, 1985-86, sr. programmer analyst, 1986, mng. programmer analyst, 1986—. Supt. Allen AME Ch. Sunday Sch., Williamstown, 1983-85; sec. Gloucester Twp. Midget Football Assn., 1986-87. Mem. Delaware Valley DB2/SQL-DS Users' Group. Methodist. Home: 132 W North St Clayton NJ 08312 Office: Foulkwood Profl Bldg 2036 Foulk Rd Suite 202 Wilmington DE 19803

BROMELKAMP, DAVID JOHN, accountant; b. Poughkeepsie, N.Y., Aug. 2, 1960; s. Henry James and Elaine Teresa (Kuhl) B. BS, St. John's U., 1982; postgrad., Coll. St. Thomas, 1988—. CPA, Minn. Mgr. Durafin Radiator Corp., St. Paul, 1984-85; acct. Mork, Harvey and Co., St. Paul, 1985-86, Stirtz, Bernards and Co., Mpls., 1986-88; investment exec. Dain Bosworth Inc., Mpls., 1988—. Mem. AICPA, Am. Mgmt. Assn., Minn. World Trade Assn., Minn. Soc. CPAs. Republican. Roman Catholic. Home: 2628 Harriet Ave S Minneapolis MN 55408

BROMFIELD, WILLIAM MARKHAM, management information company executive; b. Albany, N.Y., Sept. 11, 1946; s. Clair Jr. and Mary Kate (Patton) B.; m. Susanne Courtney Wilson, Oct. 3, 1970; children: Arianne Diana, Markham Graves. Student, Suffield Acad., 1964, U. Va., 1968. Cons. mgmt. N.Y.C., 1968-69, Boston, 1970-77, Arlington, Va., 1977-82; pres. Market Response, Inc., Miami, Fla., 1982-84; v.p. mktg. Corp. Solutions Am., Chantilly, Va., 1986-87, pres., 1987—. Office: Corp Solutions Am 14310 Sullyfield Cir Chantilly VA 22021

BROMLEY, DAVID ALLAN, physicist, educator; b. Westmeath, Ont., Can., May 4, 1926; s. Milton Escort and Susan Anne (Anderson) B.; m. Patricia Jane Brassor, Aug. 30, 1949; children—David John, Karen Lynn. BS in Engring. Physics, Queen's U., Kingston, Ont., 1948, MS in Physics, 1950; PhD in Nuclear Physics, U. Rochester, 1952; MA (hon.), Yale U., 1961; Dr. Nat. Phil. (hon.), U. Frankfurt, 1978; Docteur (Physique) (hon.), U. Strasbourg, 1980; DSc (hon.), Queen's U., 1981, U. Notre Dame, 1982, U. Witwatersrand, 1982, Trinity Coll., 1988; LittD (hon.), U. Bridgeport, 1981; Dott. (hon.), U. Padua, 1983; LHD (hon.), U. New Haven, 1987. Operating engr. Hydro Electric Power Commn. Ont., 1947-48; research officer Nat. Research Council Can., 1948; instr., then asst. prof. physics U. Rochester, 1952-55; sr. research officer, sect. head Atomic Energy Can. Ltd., 1955-60; asso. prof. physics, asso. dir. heavy ion accelerator lab. Yale, 1960-61; prof. physics, dir. Yale (A.W. Wright Nuclear Structure lab.), 1961—, chmn. physics dept., 1970-77, Henry Ford II prof., 1972—; bd. dirs. UNC Resources Inc., Barnes Engring. Co., NE Bancorp Inc., Union Trust Co., United Illuminating Corp., Chronar, Inc.; cons. Brookhaven, Argonne, Berkley and Oak Ridge Nat. Labs., Bell Telephone Labs., IBM, GTE; mem. panel nuclear physics Nat. Acad. Scis., 1964, chmn. com. on nuclear sci., 1966-74, chmn. physics survey, 1969-74; mem.-at-large, mem. exec. com. div. phys. scis. NRC, 1970-74, mem. exec. com., assembly phys. and math. scis., 1974-78, mem. naval sci. bd., 1974-78; mem. high energy physics adv. panel ERDA, 1974-78; mem. nuclear sci. adv. panel NSF and Dept. Energy, 1980—; mem. White House Sci. Council, 1981—, U.S./USSR Joint Coordinating Com. for Rsch. on Fundamental Properties Matter, 1972—, Nat. Sci. Bd., 1988—; chmn. Office Phys. Scis., 1975-78, Dept. of Energy INSF Panel on Electron Accelerator Facilities, 1983, Gandhi-Reagan Presdl. Com. on Indo-U.S. Cooperation in Sci. and Tech., 1983—, Sarney-Reagan Presdl. Com. on Brazil-U.S. Cooperation in Sci. and Tech., 1987—, Jr. Faculty Fellowship Com. David and Lucile Packard Found., 1988; vice chmn. White House Panel on Health of U.S. Univs., 1985-86; adv. bd. Inst. Nuclear Power Ops., 1983-85, Electric Power Rsch. Inst., 1984—. Editor: Physics in Perspective, 5 vols, 1972, Large Electrostatic Accelerators, 1974, Nuclear Detectors, 1978, Heavy Ion Science, 8 vols, 1981-84; co-editor: Procs. Kingston Internat. Conf. on Nuclear Structure, 1960, Facets of Physics, 1970, Nuclear Science in China, 1979; assoc. editor: Annals of Physics, 1968—, Am. Scientist, 1969-81, Il Nuovo Cimento, 1970—, Nuclear Instruments and Methods, 1974—, Science, Technology and the Humanities, 1978—, Jour. Physics, 1978—, Nuclear Science Applications, 1978—, Technology in Soc, 1981—; cons. editor: McGraw Hill Series in Fundamentals of Physics, 1967—, McGraw Hill Ency. Sci. and Tech. Bd. dirs. Oak Ridge Assoc. Univs., 1977-80, U. Bridgeport, 1981—. Recipient medal Gov. Gen. Can., 1948, U.S. Nat. medal of sci., 1988, Disting. Alumnus award U. Rochester, 1986; NRC fellow, 1952; fellow Branford Coll., 1961—; Guggenheim fellow, 1977-78; Humboldt fellow, 1978, 85; Benjamin Franklin fellow Royal Soc. Arts, London, 1979—. Fellow Am. Phys. Soc. (mem. council 1967-71), Am. Acad. Arts and Scis., AAAS (chmn. physics sect. 1977-78, pres.-elect 1980, pres. 1981—, chmn. bd. 1982—); mem. Can. Assn. Physicists, European Phys. Soc., Conn. Acad. Arts and Scis., Conn. Acad. Sci. and Engring. (council 1976-78), Internat. Union Pure and Applied Physics (U.S. nat. com. 1969—, chmn. 1975-76, v.p. 1975-81, pres. 1984-87), Southeastern Univ. Research Assn. (bd. dirs. 1984—), Council on Fgn. Relations, Sigma Xi (pres. Yale 1962-63). Home: 35 Tokeneke Dr North Haven CT 06473 Office: Yale Univ/Wright Nuclear Structure Lab 272 Whitney Ave New Haven CT 06511

BROMS, CHARLES HOWARD, oil executive; b. McKeesport, Pa., Aug. 6, 1942; s. Charles Howard and Dorothy (Cairns) B.; m. Karen Elaine Tracy, July 27, 1968; children: Kirsten, J.B. BA in Econs., Crove City Coll., 1964. Mgr. mktg. ARCO, Los Angeles, 1964-78, mgr. planning, 1978-80, mgr. govt. relations, 1980-85, mgr. pub. issues, 1985—; adivsor John F. Kennedy Sch. Govt. and Energy & Environ. Policy Ctr. Harvard U., 1985—. Commr. La Mirada (Calif.) Planning Commn., 1981-84. Mem. Am. Petroleum Inst., The Cousteau Soc., Los Angeles C. of C., U. Los Angeles Club, Alta Vista Country Club. Home: 936 Rashford Dr Placentia CA 92670 Office: ARCO 515 S Flower St Los Angeles CA 90071

BRONER, HERBERT JORDAN, home furnishings company executive; b. Chelsea, Mass., Jan. 10, 1928; s. Irving and Rose L. (Pliner) B.; m. Janice I. Broner, Sept. 9, 1951; children: Lisa F., Karen R., Frank A. A.B., Middlebury Coll., 1949; postgrad., George Washington U. Furniture buyer Hecht Co., Washington, 1948-53; exec. v.p. Rowe Furniture Co., Salem, Va., 1954-67; also dir.; dir. mktg. Mohasco Corp., Amsterdam, N.Y., 1968-71; pres. Unagusta Corp., Waynesville, N.C., 1971-72; also dir.; pres. Cort Furniture Rental Corp.; group v.p. rental ops. Mohasco, 1972-80, exec. v.p., 1980, pres., chief operating officer, 1980-83, pres., chief exec. officer, 1983-85, chmn. bd., pres., chief exec. officer, 1985—, dir., 1980—; bd dirs. Welbilt Corp., N.Y.C., 1971-72, Hechinger Co., Landover, Md., 1988—; adv. bd. dirs. Mfrs. Hanover Trust Co., N.Y.C., 1988—; bd. govs. Dallas Furniture Market Ctr., 1985—. Mem. Niskayuna (N.Y.) Conservation Adv. Council. Served with USNR, 1948-56. Recipient Brotherhood award Furniture div. NCCJ, 1982, Torch of Liberty award Anti-Defamation League, 1986. Mem. Furniture Rental Assn. Am. (former dir.), Am. Furniture Mfrs. Assn. (dir. 1983—), Am. Mgmt. Assn., Delta Upsilon. Office: Mohasco Corp 4401 Fair Lakes Ct Fairfax VA 22033

BRONES, LYNN A., financial executive; b. Albert Lea, Minn., Dec. 16, 1954; s. Max B. and Marge (Thrond) B.; m. Laura L. Schaal, May 26, 1984; 1 child, Brock A. BSS, Cornell Coll., Mt. Vernon, Iowa, 1977; JD, U. Iowa, 1980, MBA, 1985. Cert. fin. planner. Fin. cons. Farm Credit Banks, Omaha, 1980-84; trust dept. head Boone (Iowa) State Bank, 1984-85; mgr. fin. services Century Cos., Waverly, Iowa, 1985—. Mem. adv. sales com. LIMRA, Hartford, Conn., 1986—, liason mem. 1986—. Mem. Inst. Cert. Fin. Planners, Internat. Assn. Fin. Planning, Registry Fin. Planning Practitioners (Cert. of Appreciation 1986), Nat. Ctr. for Fin. Edn., Life Ins. Mktg. Rsch. Assn. Home: 1504 Circle Dr Waverly IA 50677 Office: Century Co Heritage Way Waverly IA 50677

BRONFMAN, CHARLES ROSNER, distillery executive; b. Montreal, Que., Can., June 27, 1931; s. Samuel and Saidye (Rosner) B.; m. Andrea Morrison, 1982; children: Stephen Rosner, Ellen Jane. Student, McGill U., 1948-51. With The Seagram Co., Ltd., 1951—, v.p., dir., 1958-71, exec. v.p., 1971-75, pres., 1975-79; dept. chmn. Seagram Co. Ltd., 1979-86, chmn. exec. com., 1975—, co-chmn., 1986—; chmn. bd. Montreal Baseball Club Ltd., CRB Found.; hon. chmn., dir. Super-Sol Ltd., Israel; dir. E.I. duPont de Nemours & Co., Power Corp. Can. past pres. Allied Jewish Community Services, Montreal; life gov. Jewish Gen. Hosp.; 23 for hon. chmn. Can.-Israel Securities Ltd. (State of Israel Bonds Can.); bd. dirs. Can. Council Christians and Jews. Clubs: Montefiore (Montreal), Mt. Royal (Montreal), Saint-Denis (Montreal), Elm Ridge Golf and Country (Montreal); Palm Beach Country. Office: Seagram Co Ltd, 1430 Peel St, Montreal, PQ Canada H3A 1S9

BRONFMAN, EDGAR MILES, distillery executive; b. Montreal, Que., Can., June 20, 1929; s. Samuel and Saidye (Rosner) B. Student, Williams Coll., 1946-49; B.A., McGill U., 1951; LHD (hon.), Pace U., 1982; LLD (hon.), Williams Coll., 1986. Chmn. adminstrv. com. Joseph E. Seagram & Sons, Inc., 1955-57, pres., 1957-71; chmn., chief exec. officer, pres. Distillers Corp.-Seagram Ltd., Montreal, 1971-75; now chmn., chief exec. officer Seagram Co. Ltd. and Joseph E. Seagram & Sons Inc.; bd. dirs. Am. Technion Soc., Internat. Exec. Service Corps, E.I. duPont de Nemours & Co. Citizens Com. for N.Y.C., U.S.-USSR Trade and Econ. Council; pres. Samuel Bronfman Found., World Jewish Congress; mem. exec. com. Am. Jewish Congress, Am. Jewish Com.; chmn. Anti-Defamation League N.Y. Appeal; bd. dirs. Am. com. Weizmann Inst. Sci., Israel; chmn. planning com., mem. adv. council Sch. of Internat. and Pub. Affairs, Columbia U. Named Chevalier de la Légion d'Honneur French Govt. Mem. Ctr. for Inter-Am. Relations, Council Fgn. Relations, Hundred Year Assn. N.Y., United Jewish Appeal, Fedn. Jewish Philanthropies (hon. chmn.), Com. for Econ. Devel., Fgn. Policy Assn., Bus. Com. for Arts, Inc., Union Am. Hebrew Congregations (bd. dels.), B'nai B'rith Internat. (bd. overseers). Office: Joseph E Seagram & Sons Inc 375 Park Ave New York NY 10152

BRONFMAN, PETER FREDERICK, investment banker; b. Montreal, Que., Can., Oct. 2, 1929; s. Allan and Lucy (Bilsky) B.; m. Diane Feldman Theodora Reitsma (div.); children—Linda, Bruce, Brenda; m. Lynda Hamilton. Student, Lawrenceville Sch., 1948; B.A., Yale U., 1952. Chmn. Eoper Enterprises Ltd., Toronto. Office: Brascan Ltd Box 48, Commerce St Postal Sta, Toronto, ON Canada M5L 1B7

BRONOCCO, TERRI LYNN, telecommunications company executive; b. San Antonio, Jan. 7, 1953; d. Lawrence and Jimmie Doris (Mears) B.; m. Martin L. Lowy, July 5, 1975 (div. Jan. 1979). Student in communications U. Tex.-Austin, 1970-73. Pub. relations mgr. Assocs. Corp., Dallas, 1976-79; editor-in-chief Nat. Tax Shelter Digest, Dallas, 1979; fin. editor Dallas/Ft. Worth Bus., Dallas, 1979-80; pub. affairs dir. Gen. Telephone Co., Lewisville, Tex., 1980-82; pub. info. mgr. GTE Corp., Stamford, Conn., 1982-83, media communications mgr., 1983-84, media relations and communications mgr., 1984-86; v.p. external affairs U.S. Sprint Communications Co., Dallas, 1986-88; v.p. external affairs U.S. Sprint, Washington, 1988—. Fundraiser, pub. relations counsel Am. Shakespeare Theatre, Stratford, Conn., 1984-86; bd. dirs. Music Found. for the Handicapped, Bridgeport, Conn., 1984-86; precinct chmn. Dallas County Dem. Party, 1982; bd. dirs. Far Mill River Assn., Stratford, 1983-86; mem. adv. commn. State Tex. Emergency Communications, 1987—. Recipient award for Newspaper Series Dept. Transp., 1980. Mem. Internat. Assn. Bus. Communicators (Best Photograph award 1977), Women in Communications (Matrix award 1985), Women in Mgmt., Am. Mgmt. Assn., Dallas C. of C. (telecommunications com. 1987, Spl. Recognition award 1978). Roman Catholic. Home: 1600 N Oak St Arlington VA 22201 Office: US Sprint Communications Co 2002 Edmund Halley Dr Reston VA 22091

BRONSARD, JOSEPH ALFRED, pulp and paper company executive; b. Waterbury, Conn., May 30, 1933; m. Marlene R. Cook, Sept. 9, 1961. BME, N.J. Inst. Tech., 1968; MA in Sci., Trenton State Coll., 1970. Registered profl. engr., N.J. Dir. engring. Triangle Industries, New Brunswick, N.J., 1963-68; v.p., plant mgr. Homasote Corp., Trenton, N.J., 1968—. Contbr. articles to profl. pubs. Mem. ASME, TAPPI, Soc. Plastics Engrs., Fluid Power Soc. (chpt. pres. 1974), Engring. Club. Home: 7 Verona Ave Trenton NJ 08619 Office: Homasote Corp Lower Ferry Rd West Trenton NJ 08628

BRONSON, KENNETH CALDEAN, communications company executive; b. Kensington, Kans., Apr. 15, 1933; s. Lloyd and Lottie Belle (Bierman) B.; m. Edith Jeanette MacArthur, Feb. 1, 1959; children: Brian, Laura, Linda. Student, Kans. U., 1951-55; AB, Washburn U., 1959. Sports writer Topeka Daily Capital, 1952-59; state editor Topeka Capital-Jour., 1959-61; editor, pub. Pierce City (Mo.) Leader-Jour., 1961-62; news editor Topeka State Jour., 1962; mng. editor Independence (Mo.) Examiner, 1962-64, editor, 1964-66; editor, pub. Morning Sun, Pittsburg, Kans., 1966-77; v.p. Stauffer Communications, Topeka, 1976—. Author: 1000 News Story Ideas, 1986. Mem. Kans. Commn. on Judicial Qualifications, Topeka, 1974—; pres. Pittsburg C. of C., 1970; bd. dirs. William Allen White Found., 1968—. Served with USN, 1955-57. Mem. Am. Newspapers Pubs. Assn. (com. chmn. 1983-84), Inland Daily Press Assn. (found. dir. 1986—), Kans. Press Assn. (bd. dirs. 1970-76, pres. 1975-76). Mem. Christian Ch. (Disciples of Christ). Home: 3850 SW Chelmsford Topeka KS 66610 Office: Stauffer Communications Inc 616 SE Jefferson St Topeka KS 66607

BROOK, GARY FRED, accountant; b. Chicago, Nov. 9, 1961; s. Marvin A. and Jeanne A. (Suhring) B.; m. Jeanette Marie Heniff, Oct. 12, 1985; children: Sarah, Austin. CPA, Ill. Mem. staff Touche Ross & Co., Chgo., 1985-87; supr. accounts receivable Highland Superstores, Inc., Lansing, Ill., 1987-88; fin. analyst McDonald's Corp., Oak Brook, Ill., 1988—. Mem. Am. Inst. CPA's, Ill. CPA Soc. Office: McDonald Corp McDonald Pla Oak Brook IL 60521

BROOKE, EDNA MAE, business educator; b. Las Vegas, Nev., Feb. 10, 1923; d. Alma Lyman and Leah Mae (Ketcham) Shurtliff; m. Bill T. Brooke, Dec. 22, 1949; 1 child, John C. BS in Acctg., Ariz. State U., 1965, MA in Edn., 1967, EdD, 1975. Grad. teaching asst. Ariz. State U., Tempe, 1968-69; prof. bus. Maricopa Tech. Coll., Phoenix, 1967-72, assoc. dean instl. services, 1972-74; prof. bus. and acctg. Scottsdale (Ariz.) Community Coll., 1974—; cons. in field. Author: The Effectiveness of Three Techniques Used in Teaching First Semester Accounting Principles to Tech. Jr. College Students, 1974. Mem. Nat. Bus. Edn. Assn., Western Bus. Edn. Assn., Ariz. Bus. Edn. Assn., Am. Acctg. Assn., Delta Pi Epsilon. Home: 2139 E Solano Dr Phoenix AZ 85016 Office: Scottsdale Community Coll 9000 E Chaparral Scottsdale AZ 85252

BROOKER, THOMAS KIMBALL, investment banker; b. Los Angeles, Oct. 1, 1939; s.Robert Elton and Sally Burton Harrison (Smith) B.; m. Nancy Belle Neumann, 1966; children: Thomas Kimball Jr., Isobel, Vanessa. BA in French Lit., Yale U., 1961; MBA, Harvard U., 1968; MA in Art History, U. Chgo., 1989. Assoc. in corp. fin. Morgan Stanley & Co., Inc., N.Y.C., 1968-73, v.p., 1973-75, mng. dir., 1976-88; head Chgo. office Morgan Stanley & Co., Inc., 1978-88; pres. Barbara Oil Co., Chgo., 1989—, also bd. dirs.; bd. dirs. Zenith Electronics Corp.; gov. Midwest Stock Exchange, 1980-88, vice chmn., 1986-88; mem. Lloyd's of London. Mem. vis. com. Library at U. Chgo., Yale U. Pres. Council, 1980-84; assoc. fellow Saybrook Coll. Yale U.; bd. dirs. Lyric Opera Chgo., Ctr. for Am. Archeology, 1980-84, Alliance Francaise-Maison Francaise de Chgo., Chgo. Council Fgn. Relations; vice chmn., trustee Newberry Library; chmn. Yale U. Com. on Library, 1980-84; trustee Yale Library Assocs., chmn. 1976-79; trustee Piermont Morgan Library. Served as lt. USN, 1962-66. Mem. Securities Industry Assn. (exec. com. cen. states dist.), Conseil d' Administrn. Assn. Internationale de Bibliophilie. Clubs: Chgo., Comml., River (N.Y.C.), Knickerbocker (N.Y.C.), Grolier (N.Y.C.), The Casino, Saddle & Cycle, Edgartown Yacht (Mass.), Quadrangle, Racquet Chgo., Rockaway Hunt. Home: 1500 N Lake Shore Drive Chicago IL 60610 Office: Barbara Oil Co One First Nat Pla Ste 2656 Chicago IL 60609

BROOKMAN, ANTHONY RAYMOND, lawyer; b. Chgo., Mar. 23, 1922; s. Raymond Charles and Marie Clara (Alberg) B.; m. Marilyn Joyce Brookman, June 5, 1982; children: Meribeth Brookman Farmer, Anthony Raymond, Lindsay Logan Christienson. Student Ripon Coll., 1940-41; BS, Northwestern U., 1947; JD, U. Calif.-San Francisco, 1953. Bar: Calif. 1954. Law clk. to presiding justice Calif. Supreme Ct., 1953-54; ptnr. Nichols, Williams, Morgan, Digardi & Brookman, 1954-68; sr. ptnr. Brookman & Hoffman, Inc., Walnut Creek, Calif., 1968—. Pres., Young Republicans Calif., San Mateo County, 1953-54. Served to 1st lt. USAF. Mem. ABA, Alameda County Bar Assn., State Bar Calif., Lawyers Club Alameda County, Alameda-Contra Costa County Trial Lawyers Assn., Assn. Trial Lawyers Am., Calif. Trial Lawyers Assn. Republican. Clubs: Masons, Athenian Nile, Crow Canyon Country, Shriners. Pub. Contra Costa New Register. Office: Brookman and Hoffman 901 H St Ste 200 Sacramento CA 95814 also: 1990 N California Blvd Walnut Creek CA 94596 also: 2119 W March Ln Ste A Stockton CA 95207

BROOKS, ANNMARIE MANZI, electrical contracting executive; b. Methuen, Mass., Sept. 13, 1953; d. Albert Peter and Anna Louise (Mikolajczyk) Manzi; m. Wayne Clinton Brooks. AA, Bradford (Mass.) Coll., 1973; BA, U. N.H., 1975; MS, Georgetown U., 1977. Cert. fluency in Italian Lang. Sr. researcher, translator Nat. Geographic Soc., Washington, 1977-84; asst. treas. Manzi Elec. Corp., Lawrence, Mass., 1984—; v.p., treas. Windjammer Constrn. Co. and Windjammer Properties, Seabrook, N.H., 1984—; media cons., Washington, 1980-84. Photographer for book: Mills, Mansions, Mergers, 1982. Democrat. Roman Catholic. Home: 123 Atlantic Ave Seabrook NH 03874 Office: Manzi Elec Corp PO Box 69 Lawrence MA 01842

BROOKS, ANTOINETTE MARIE, real estate executive; b. Worcester, Mass., Dec. 3, 1940; d. Philip F. and Madeline (Rondinone) Inangelo; m. Richard E. Brooks, Dec. 27, 1958; children: Richard E. Jr., Marlo L., Jeffrey Paul. A in Bus., Cen. NE Coll., 1958; student, Thomas Edison Sch., 1959, Am. Inst. Banking, 1973, Lee Inst. Real Estate, 1965. Credit clk. Pub. Finance Co., Worcester, Mass., 1958-61; asst. treas. Trans Ea. Corp., Worcester, Mass., 1961-65; pres. Antoinette M. Brooks Real Estate Assocs., Worcester, 1965-79; sales rep. Dennison's Mfg. Co., Framingham, Mass., 1979-81; mgr. N.E. Indsl. Park, Holliston, Mass., 1982-83, Coldwell Banker, Resdl., Northborough, Mass., 1983—. Justice of the Peace, Mass., 1983—. Mem. Women's Council Realtors, Greater Worcester Bd. Realtors (coms. 1977—), Nat. Assn. Female Execs. (bd. dirs. local chpt. 1987), Nat. Assn. Realtors, Mass. Assn. Realtors, Worcester Bd. Realtors (profl. standards com. 1987—, speaker 1987), Worcester Order Son's of Italy. Democrat. Roman Catholic. Home: 293 Davis St Northborough MA 01532 Office: Re-Max Real Estate Assocs Pendalton Sq Main St Northborough MA 01532

BROOKS, CLAUDIA A., software executive, consultant; b. Atlanta, Jan. 18, 1957; d. John William and Annette (Thompson) B.; m. Robert A. Davis, Mar. 22, 1974 (div. Aug. 1978); 1 child, Robert. Student, Coastal Carolina Community Coll., Jacksonville, N.C., 1977-78; AA in Computer Sci., Clayton Jr. Coll., Morrow, Ga., 1980; BBA in Info. Systems, Ga. State U., 1984. Cert. in Info. Systems, Bus. Adminstrn. Data processing, fin. coordinator UFCW Union and Employers Trust Fund, Atlanta, 1981; programmer, analyst, asst. data ctr. mgr. Davidson Mineral Properties, Inc., Atlanta, 1981-82; product specialist, programmer Info. Systems Am., Inc., Atlanta, 1982-83; programmer, analyst Software Shop Systems, Inc., Atlanta, Farmingdale, N.J., 1983-85; mgr. product devel. Software Shop Systems, Inc., Farmingdale, 1985-88. Vol. op. new life USN, Guam, 1975, vol. asst. Indochina refugee effort ARC, Guam, 1975. Mem. NAFE, Mensa, Cousteau Soc. Presbyterian.

BROOKS, GARY, management consultant; b. Bklyn., Feb. 28, 1934; s. Nathan R. and Rose (Stern) B.; S.B., MIT, 1955; M.S., U. Rochester, 1959; m. Felice Ruth Dobbin, May 23, 1956; children—Andrew, Leslie Ellen. Project engr. Gen. Electric Co., Pittsfield, Mass., 1955-56; engr., new product supr. Eastman Kodak Co., Rochester, N.Y., 1956-64; v.p. ops. Peerless Photo Products, Inc., Shoreham, N.Y., 1964-68; cons., project mgr. Technomic Consultants, N.Y.C., 1969-71; v.p., div. gen. mgr. Scott Graphics, Inc., Holyoke, Mass., 1971-76; v.p., mng. prin. Pace Cons. Group, Hartford, Conn., 1976-86; founder, mng. ptnr. Allomer Ptnrs., N.Y.C. and Ashburnham, Mass., 1987—; adj. prof. U. Rochester, 1958-59, C.W. Post Coll., 1968-70, U. Mass., Amherst, 1978-85. Pres. Temple Isaiah, Stony Brook, N.Y., 1970-71; trustee, v.p. Sinai Temple, Springfield, Mass., 1973-80. Served with U.S. Army, 1956. Mem. Inst. Mgmt. Consultants, Turnaround Mgmt. Assn., MIT Alumni of N.Y. , N.Am. Soc. Corp. Planning, Sales and Mktg. Execs. Western Mass. (pres. 1980-81), 100 Club. Republican. Home: 325 E 77th St New York NY 10021

BROOKS, GEORGE ANDREW, lawyer, educator; b. N.Y.C., May 11, 1900; s. George H. and Mary Agnes (Winifred (O'Hara) B. A.B. with sr. class hons., Fordham U., 1924, J.D. (LL.B.) cum laude, 1927, LL.D. (hon.), 1952; LL.M., NYU, 1951; LL.D. (hon.), Scranton U., 1953. Bar: N.Y. 1928, U.S. Dist. Ct. (so. and no. dists.) N.Y. 1938, U.S. Dist. Ct. (no. dist.) Ind. 1939, U.S. Ct. Appeals (2d cir.) 1941, U.S. Dist. Ct. (ea. dist.) N.Y. 1946, U.S. Tax Ct. 1947, U.S. Ct. Appeals (3d cir.) 1949, U.S. Supreme Ct. 1958. Tchr. Regis High Sch., N.Y.C., 1924-27; Seton Hall High Sch., South Orange, N.J., 1924-30; practice, N.Y.C. and Tuckahoe, N.Y., 1928-34; with Gen. Motors Corp., N.Y.C., 1934-65, dir. N.Y. legal staff, 1941-65, corp. sec., 1947-65, sec. fin. policy com., 1947-58, sec. fin. com., 1958-65; lectr. law Fordham U., N.Y.C., 1929-35, adj. asst. prof., 1965-70, adj. assoc. prof., 1970-72, adj. prof. law, 1972—; prof. Seton Hall Coll., South Orange, N.J., 1924-34; atty. Union Free Sch. Dist. 1, Town of Eastchester, Westchester County, N.Y., 1930-56; legal cons., prodn. div. Nat. Def. Adv. Commn., Washington, 1940; arbitrator Nat. Assn. Securities Dealers, Inc. Bd. dirs. Legal Aid Soc. Westchester County, 1964-75, sec., 1965-72, pres., 1972-74; bd. dirs. Lavelle Sch. for Blind, N.Y.C., 1956—, v.p. 1971-78, pres., 1978-80, pres. emeritus; trustee emeritus Fordham U.; bd. dirs. Westchester Legal Services, Inc., 1967-85, N.Y. County Lawyers Assn., 1965-71, Rose Hill Housing Devel. Fund Corp.; trustee St. Agnes Hosp., White Plains, N.Y., 1982-87. Served with U.S. Army, 1918. Created knight of Malta; recipient Alumni Achievement award Fordham Coll., 1959, Encaenia award Fordham Coll., 1959, medal of Achievement Fordham Law Alumni Assn., 1968, Bene Merenti medal Fordham U., 1979, Law Sch. award Fordham U., 1984. Fellow N.Y. Bar Found.; mem. U.S. Cath. Hist. Soc. (bd. dirs. 1958-84, v.p. 1964-66, pres. 1966-68), ABA, Fed. Bar Assn., Comml. Law League of Am., Westchester County Bar Assn., Cath. Lawyers Guild (bd. dirs. 1958-61), N.Y. State Bar Assn. (ho. of dels. 1972-77), Fordham U. Alumni Fedn. (bd. dirs. 1955-64), Fordham Law Alumni Assn. (bd. dirs. 1960-75), Assn. Bar City N.Y., Fordham Coll. Alumni Assn. (pres. 1948-52). Republican. Clubs: University, N.Y. Athletic (N.Y.C.). Home: Eton Hall 127 Garth Rd Apt 5A Scarsdale NY 10583

BROOKS, HAROLD LEE, administrative services executive; b. Cattaraugus, N.Y., July 7, 1917; s. Paul Ambrose and Erma Mae Brooks; m. Virginia Elizabeth Albee, June 24, 1939; children: Donna Jean, Murray Lee, Paul Allen, Hugh Albee, Marlene Yvonne, Jon Harold, Marianne Rae. Assoc. in Arts and Scis., Richland Coll., 1978. Propr. grocery store, Elmira, 1946-47; acctg. supr. Holiday Inn, Dallas, 1972-75; buyer Control and Computing Devices, Garland, Tex., 1975-80; pres. Ad-Serv, Inc., Garland, 1982-88; chief instr. Navy Sea Cadets, 1980-84. Mem. task force to recommend curriculum for purchase mgrs. Dallas Community Colls., 1978. Served with U.S. Army, 1947-72. Mem. Purchasing Mgrs. Assn. Dallas, Am. Legion (post comdr. 1958-59). Club: Flying (pres. 1953-55, 56-57). Lodges: Masons, Lions (pres. Diamonhead chpt., chmn. archtl. control com., chmn. media and pub. rels. com.). Home: 3269 Holly Hill Rd Hot Springs AR 71913-7032

BROOKS, JERRY CLAUDE, textile company executive; b. College Park, Ga., Apr. 23, 1936; s. John Bennett and Mattie Mae (Timms) B.; B.S., Ga.

Inst. Tech., 1958; m. Peggy Sue Thornton, Feb. 26, 1961; children: Apryll Denise, Jerry Claude, Susan Vereen. Safety engr. Cotton Producers Assn., Atlanta, 1959-64, dir. safety and loss control, 1964-70; dir. corporate protection Gold Kist, Inc., Atlanta, 1970-81; dir. corporate safety J.P. Stevens, 1981-84, dir. Safety and Security, 1984-86, dir. health and safety, 1986-88, dir. loss control Am. Yarn Spinners assn., 1988—; instr., Ga. Safety Inst., Athens, Ga., 1971—. Bd. dirs. Greater Lithonia (Ga.) Homeowners Assn., Ga. Soc. Prevention of Blindness, Ga. Safety Council. Served with AUS, 1958-59. Mem. Am. Soc. Safety Engrs. (chpt. pres. 1968-69, regional v.p. 1974-76), Nat. Safety Council (gen. chmn. fertilizer sect. 1969-70, gen. chmn. textile sec. 1985-87), So. Safety Conf. (v.p. bus. and industry 1968-74, pres. 1974), Am. Soc. Indsl. Security, Ga. Bus. and Industry Assn. (dir.; named outstanding mem. 1981), Internat. Assn. Hazard Control Mgrs. (chpt. pres. 1979—). Clubs: Masons, Rosicrucians; Exchange (pres. 1969-70; Book of Golden Deeds award 1981) (Lithonia). Home: Rte 5 PO Box 100 Kings Mountain NC 28086 Office: Am Yarn Spinners Assn PO Box 99 Gastonia NC 28053

BROOKS, JERRY REX, paper company executive; b. New Castle, Ind., Sept. 29, 1944; s. Rex E. and Mildred P. (Beam) B.; m. Marilyn Fletcher (div.); children: Teresa, Richard; m. Elizabeth A. Bell, Dec. 29, 1984; children: Brian, Amy. MS, Purdue U., 1974. Comd. 2nd lt. U.S. Army, 1967; advanced through grades to maj. U.S. Army, Vietnam, 1978; personnel mgr. Burrough's Corp., Dallas, 1978-79; mgr. mgmt. devel. Internat. Paper Co., Shreveport, La., 1979-82, Mobile, Ala., 1982-85; div. tng. mgr. Mead Paper Co., Chillicothe, Ohio, 1985—. Author: Teroman, 1988. Mem. Am. Soc. Tng. and Devel., Lions, Optimists. Home: 6228 Beaver Lake Dr Grove City OH 43123 Office: Mead Paper Co PO Box 2500 Chillicothe OH 45601

BROOKS, JOHN LAWRENCE, III, high technology company finance executive; b. Boston, Feb. 16, 1951; s. John Lawrence and Nancy Ann (Foley) B.; m. Susan Anne Sakalinski, Oct. 27, 1974. BBA, U. Mass., 1972, MS in Bus. Adminstrn., 1973. CPA, Mass, cert. fin. planner. Sr. mgr. Arthur Andersen & Co., Boston, 1973-82; chief fin. officer Contrex Inc., Billerica, Mass., 1982-83; pvt. practice acctg. and fin. planning, Chelmsford, Mass., 1982—; ptnr. Alexander, Aronson, Finning & Co. P.C., Westboro, Mass., 1983-85; v.p. fin. and ops. Encore Computer Corp., Marlboro, Mass., 1985, Advanced Systems Design Corp., Newton, Mass., 1986, Strato Med. Corp., Beverly, Mass., 1986—. Sec. Chelmsford Jaycees, 1981-82. Fellow Am. Inst. CPA's; mem. Mass. Soc. CPA's, Nat. Assn. Accts., Beta Gamma Sigma. Roman Catholic. Home: 42 Spaulding Rd PO Box 208 Chelmsford MA 01824-0208

BROOKS, PHILIP BARRON, retired public accountant, b. N.Y.C., Apr. 20, 1914; AB cum laude, Rider Coll., 1935; m. Betty R. Ralston; children: Richard L., Michael B., Philip J., Jeffrey R. Pvt. practice pub. acctg., Montclair, N.J., 1937-67; founder, chmn. bd., chief exec. officer Bank of Bloomfield (N.J.), 1972-74; past pres. Surf Club Apts., Inc., Surfside, Fla.; past treas., dir. Computer Spltys. Corp., Palisades Park, N.J.; founder, ret. dir. Garden State Title Ins. Co., Montclair; founder, ret. pres., chief exec. officer TransJersey Bancorp.; founder, ret. dir. Garden State Mortgage Agy., Inc., Montclair, N.J.; dir. Nortek, Inc., Providence, R.I.; formerly lectr. tax subjects; panel mem. Am. Arbitration Assn. Former trustee, treas. Youth Employment Service, Montclair Urban Coalition, 1968-71; trustee emeritus Rider Coll.; former trustee Montclair Community Hosp. Recipient Disting. Alumnus award Rider Coll., 1974. CPA, N.J., N.Y. Mem. Fla., N.J., socs. CPA's. Am. Inst. CPA's, Rider Coll. Alumni Assn. (nat. pres. 1965-67, past trustee), Grand Jury Assn. Essex County, N.J. Hosp. Assn., Montclair C. of C. (dir., pres. 1966-69, past trustee), N.J. Hist. Soc., U.S. Croquet Assn., U.S. Navy League, Zeta Beta Tau. Clubs: Spring Lake Bath and Tennis, Spring Lake Golf, Green Gables Croquet, La Gorce Country, Fairway Mews Golf and Raquet, Com. of One Hundred (dir.) (Miami, Fla.); Surf (treas., bd. govs., past sec.) (Surfside, Fla.); One Hundred (former trustee, treas.) (Montclair); N.Y. Athletic; Montclair Elks (past exalted ruler). Home: Surf Club Apts Surfside FL 33154

BROOKS, RICHARD MALLON, money management executive; b. Akron, Ohio, May 3, 1928; s. Bryant John and Sophia Beadle (Mallon) B.; B.S., Yale U., 1950; M.B.A., U. Calif.-Berkeley, 1960; m. Sidney Hedin, Dec. 2, 1961; children—David, Scott, Susan. With Calif. and Hawaiian Sugar Co., San Francisco, 1957-78, fin. analyst mgr. raw sugar dept., 1957-67, sr. v.p. fin. and adminstrn., 1968-78; v.p. fin. Amfac, Inc., San Francisco, 1979-80, sr. v.p., chief fin. officer, 1980-84; v.p. fin., treas. Lucky Stores, Inc., Dublin, Calif., 1984-87; pres.., chief exec. officer SFA Mgmt. Corp., San Francisco, 1987—; mem. western adv. bd. Arkwright Boston Ins. Co., 1977-82; bd. dirs. Longs Drug Stores, 1988—, BEI Electronics Inc., 1987—. Pres. Piedmont council Boy Scouts Am., 1980-81; 1st v.p. Oakland Mus. Assn., 1978-79, 85-87, dir., 1974-80, 85—; trustee Coll. Prep. Sch., 1982—; trustee Golden Gate Scouting, 1980-84. Served to 1st lt. Air N.G., 1951-56. Mem. Fin. Officers of No. Calif. (pres. 1974-75), Pensions West (pres. 1975-79), Fin. Execs. Inst. Republican. Episcopalian. Clubs: Pacific-Union, Berkeley Tennis, Olympic. Home: 20 Sierra Ave Piedmont CA 94611

BROOKS, ROBERT ALEXANDER, oil company executive; b. Ft. Knox, Ky., Sept. 12, 1944; s. Robert and Meredith (Boller) B.; m. Carol Mateer, Aug. 13, 1966; children—Alison, Joy, Robert, Deborah. B.S., U. Ill., 1966; M.S., La. State U., 1969, Ph.D., 1970. Assoc. La. Water Resources Research Inst., Baton Rouge, 1966-70; scientist Conoco, Ponca City, Okla., 1970-74; team leader uranium exploration U.S. Geol. Survey, Denver, 1974-77; v.p. minerals Energy Res. Group, Wichita, Kans., 1977-82, BHP Petroleum (Americas), v.p. oil exploration, 1982-86; pres. Resource Masters Assocs., Wichita, 1986-88, Team Resources Corp., 1988—; chief exec. officer Rio Gold Mining Ltd., 1987—; rep. uranium resource com. UN, Rome, 1976. Contbr. articles to profl. jours. Mem. Am. Assn. Petroleum Geologists, Soc. Econ. Geologists, Denver Regional Exploration Geologists (pres. 1977-80), Kans. Geol. Soc. Republican. Presbyterian. Clubs: Wichita Country, Wichita; Hiwan (Evergreen, Colo.). Avocations: skiing, tennis, swimming, scuba. Home: 646 Edgewater St Wichita KS 67230 Office: Resource Masters Assocs 646 Edgewater Suite 100 Wichita KS 67230

BROOKS, SAM ALLEN, health care company executive; b. Waco, Tex., Jan. 29, 1939; s. Sam Allen and Macil Clare (Reynolds) B.; m. Linda Daniel, Apr. 27, 1968; children—Wendy, Dan, Ashley. Grad., Baylor U., 1962. Mgr. Ernst & Whinney, Dallas, 1961-69; treas., controller Hosp. Corp. Am., Nashville, 1969-81, exec. v.p. fin., 1969-85, v.p., treas., 1972-74, fin. v.p., treas., 1974-78, sr. v.p. fin., treas., 1978-81, sr. v.p. fin., 1981-84; chmn. Beverly Investment Properties, Inc., Pasadena, Calif., 1985—; bd. dirs. Sovran Bank/Cen. South, Nashville Kinetic Concepts, Inc., San Antonio, Hunter-Melnor, Inc., Memphis, MicroBilt, Inc., Atlanta, Phy Cor, Nashville, Rebound, Inc., Nashville, Beverly Investment Properties, Pasadena. Bd. dirs. Comprehensive Devel. Evaluation Ctr. Vanderbilt U., Nashville, St. Bernard's Sch. for Exceptional Children, Nashville. Served to 1st lt. USAR, 1960-67. Mem. Tenn. Soc. C.P.A.s, Tex. Soc. C.P.A.s. Office: Beverly Investment Properties Inc 3401 W End Ave PO Box 13 Nashville TN 37203

BROOKS, WILLIAM SIDNEY, construction executive; b. Florence, Ala., Jan. 11, 1935; s. Roland Mozel and Margaret Marie (Cromwell) B.; m. Nancy Ann Walker, July 20, 1957; children: Barbara Ann Umenhoffer, Kathryn Elizabeth Kendall. BSME, U. Ala., 1957. Main engr. Union Carbide, Oak Ridge, Tenn., 1957-1960; field supr. Rust Engr. Co., 1960-65; constrn. mgr. Rust Engr. Co., Pitts., 1965-70; staff engr. W.Va. Pulp and Paper, Covington, Va., 1963-65; dir. constrn. Procon, Des Plaines, Ill., 1970-71; constrn. mgr. Dilavo, Pitts., 1971-78; sr. v.p. Blount Constrn. Group, Montgomery, Ala., 1978—. Named Disting. Engr. fellow U. Ala., 1988. Mem. ASME, Am. Council Constrn. Edn., Constrn. Industry Inst., Assoc. Gen. Contractor, Capital City Club, Willow Point Country Club.

BROOKSTONE, ARNOLD F., paper packaging company executive; b. Chgo., Apr. 8, 1930; s. Reuben F. and Florence (Kabiller) B.; m. Adrienne Lee Haft, June 12, 1954; 1 dau., Susan Gail. BS, U. Ill., 1950; postgrad., Northwestern U., 1950-51; JD, DePaul U., 1952. Bar: Ill. 1953; C.P.A., Ill. Ptnr. Golman, Brookstone & Co. (C.P.A.s), Chgo., 1952-65; with Stone Container Corp., Chgo., 1965—; v.p., controller Stone Container Corp., 1969-72, v.p., treas., 1972-73, v.p. fin., treas., 1973-77, sr. v.p. fin., treas., 1977-81, sr. v.p., chief fin. and planning officer; v.p., bd. dirs. various subsidiaries Stone Container Corp.; bd. dirs. Continental Glass & Plastic, Inc., Forest Ins. Ltd., Prairie Packaging Corp.; bd. dirs., chmn. fin. com. Donnelly Corp., chmn., bd. dirs. World Horizons, Inc.; bd. dirs., v.p. Seminole Kraft Corp.; bd. dirs. Stone Forest Industries; lectr. Fin. Execs. Inst., 1966, Nat. Audio-Visual Inst., 1955-56, Northwestern U. Grad. Sch. Mgmt., 1977; bd. dirs. Stone Savannah River Pulp and Paper Corp. Bd. dirs. Young Men's Jewish Council, Chgo., 1954-58; pres., dir. Child, Inc., 1958-65; former dir. Council Jewish Elderly. Mem. Am. Paper Inst. (fin. mgmt. steering com.), Am. Inst. CPAs, Fin. Execs. Inst., Ill. Soc. CPAs, Green Acres Country Club (treas., bd. dirs.), Standard Club, Internat. Club, Tau Epsilon Phi. Jewish. Office: Stone Container Corp 150 N Michigan Ave Chicago IL 60601

BROOME, BARRY DEAN, estate and financial planning consultant; b. Gaffney, S.C., Jan. 24, 1942; s. Walter Dean and Virginia Mae (Moss) B.; BA, U. Cen. Fla., 1973, J.D., Atlanta Law Sch., 1987; m. Janis M. Black, Feb. 14, 1969; children—Gina Michelle, Tina Marie, Jana Malia, Barry Dean II. Pres., Barry Broome Co., estate and fin. planning, Jacksonville, Fla., 1963-78; dir. tng. and sales devel. Gulf Life Ins. Co., Jacksonville, 1978-81; adj. instr. fin. planning Ga. State U. cons. to ins. cos. in so. states, Dunwoody, Ga., 1981—; advisor to securities industry in S.E. Mem. fin. com. North Fla. council Boy Scouts Am., 1978-81; fin. chmn. various Republican candidates on state and local level; mem. bishopric Ch. of Jesus Christ of Latter-day Saints, 1974-75, stake pres., 1976-80, mem. high council, 1975-76. Recipient spl. commendation Health Ins. Assn. Am., 1981; C.L.U.; chartered fin. cons. Mem. Am. Soc. C.L.U.s, Internat. Assn. Fin. Planning, Nat. Assn. Life Underwriters, Am. Arbitration Assn., Internat. Platform Assn. Contbr. articles on advanced underwriting to profl. publs. Home: 3497 Dunwoody Club Dr Dunwoody GA 30350 Office: Ga State U PO Box 888831 Atlanta GA 30356

BROPHY, JOSEPH THOMAS, insurance company executive; b. N.Y.C., Oct. 25, 1933; s. Joseph R. and Mary (Mitchell) B.; m. Carole A. Johnson, June 8, 1957; children—Thomas J., David W., Patricia J., Maureen A., Kathleen M. BS cum laude, Fordham U., 1957; grad. sr. exec. program, Sloan Sch., MIT, 1987. Mathematician Vitro Labs., West Orange, N.J., 1957; dir. mgmt. info. systems Prudential Ins. Co., Newark, 1957-67; v.p. Huggins & Co. (cons. actuaries and mgmt. cons.), Phila., 1967-68; v.p., chief actuary Bankers Nat. Life Ins. Co., 1968-72; sr. v.p. Travelers Corp., Hartford, Conn., 1972—; bd. dirs. Engineered Bus. Systems, Security Settlement Corp., Travelers Diebold Tech. Co., Execucom, Inc., Travtech, Inc., Travelers TPA, Inc., Applied Expert Systems; cons. in field, 1967—; enrolled actuary Employee Retirement Income Security Act (ERISA). Author: A User's Guide to Project Management. Tech. editor: Actuarial Digest. Pres. St. Patrick's Pipe Band, Inc.; bd. dirs. Catholic Family Services; corporator St. Francis Hosp.; chmn. adv. bd. info. scis. Grad. Bus. Sch., Fordham U., Bronx, N.Y. Served with USMCR, 1949-50; with AUS, 1952-54. Recipient Disting. Info. Sci. award Data Processing Mgmt. Assn., 1986. Fellow Soc. Actuaries; mem. Am. Acad. Actuaries, Acoustical Soc. Am., Hartford Actuaries Club, N.Y. Actuaries Club, Am. Arbitration Soc. (arbitrator), Greater Hartford C. of C. (bd. dirs.). Club: Hartford. Home: 33 Rushleigh Rd West Hartford CT 06117 Office: Travelers Corp 1 Tower Sq Hartford CT 06183

BROPHY, THEODORE F., telephone company executive; b. N.Y.C., Apr. 4, 1923; s. Frederick H. and Muriel W. (Osborne) B.; m. Sallie M. Showalter, Sept. 16, 1950; children: Stephen F., Anne R. A.B., Yale U., 1944; LL.B., Harvard U., 1949. Bar: N.Y. Assoc. Root, Ballantine, Harlan, Bushby & Palmer, N.Y.C., 1949-55; gen. counsel Lummus Co., 1955-58; counsel Gen. Telephone Co., N.Y.C., 1958-59; v.p., gen. counsel Gen. Telephone & Electronics Corp. (now GTE Corp.), 1959-68, exec. v.p., gen. counsel, 1968-72, pres., 1972-76, chmn. bd., 1976-88, chief exec. officer, 1976-88; bd. dirs. Reader's Digest Assn., Inc., Procter & Gamble Co.; past chmn. U.S. del. to Word Adminstrv. Radio Conf. on Space Svcs.; mem. regulatory adv. com. N.Y. Stock Exchange Bd. Mem. Greenwich Hosp. Assn.; trustee Smith Coll., Kent Sch. Lt. (s.g.) USNR, 1944-46. Mem. Bus. Council. Office: 60 Arch St Greenwich CT 06830

BROSIUS, ARTHUR JAMES, energy company consultant; b. Summerville, Pa., Nov. 11, 1913; s. Edwin Franklin and Dorothy Viola (Wolfgang) B. BS, U. Pitts., 1935, ML, 1940. Cert. transp. practictioner. Acct. Dravo Corp., Pitts., 1935-39; asst. auditor Union Barge Line Corp. and subs., Pitts., 1939-44; ops. asst. Union Barge Line Corp. and subs., 1945-48, asst. v.p., 1949-54, adminstrv. asst. to pres., 1954-59, asst. to pres., 1959-62; v.p., bd. dirs. Union Barge Line Corp., 1962-73, Union Mechling Corp. and subs., Pitts., 1973-79; v.p. Derby Coal Co. div. Derby & Co., Inc., Pitts., 1980-82; cons. Derby Coal Co. div. Derby & Co., Inc., 1982-85, Philbro Energy, Inc., Greenwich, Conn., 1985—; bd. dirs. Water Resources Congress, Washington, 1986—, Nat. Waterways Conf., Washington, 1987—. Trustee U. Pitts., 1969-71. Recipient Disting. Alumnus award U. Pitts., 1972. Mem. Am. Soc. Transp. and Logistics (founder), Nat. Def. Transp. Assn. (life), Traffic Club Pitts. (life), Waterways Assn. Pitts (past pres.), Greater Pitts. C. of C. (bd. dirs. 1964-73), U. Pitts. Alumni Assn. (bd. dirs. 1975—), Propeller Club U.S.A. (bd. govs. Port Pitts. 1987—), Duquesne Club (Pitts.), Beta Gamma Sigma. Republican. Presbyterian. Home: 154 N Bellefield Ave Pittsburgh PA 15213 Office: Phibro Energy Inc PO Box 2800 Pittsburgh PA 15230

BROSS, JOHN JOSEPH, automobile dealership executive; b. Troy, N.Y., Sept. 16, 1939; s. John Joseph and Dorothy Rose (Rodgers) B.; m. Barbara Ann Kramer (div. 1982); children: John J. III, Kevin M., Michael W. Grad. high sch., Albany, N.Y. Owner, operator Bross Texaco Service, Albany, 1965-70; technician Metroland Motors, Albany, 1979-73; dir. service Back Bay Motors, Boston, 1973-78; dir. fixed ops. Colony Motors, Edgartown, Mass., 1978-79; mgr. service Braymans, Attleboro, Mass., 1979-80, Midway Auto Ctr., Framingham, Mass., 1980-81; pres. Jack Bross Assocs., Groveland, Mass., 1981-83; gen. mgr. Merrimack Valley Datsun, Haverill, Mass., 1982-83; sr. cons. Dealer Mgmt. Assn., Exeter, N.H., 1983-88; founder Achiever Group, Bradford, Mass., 1989—. Served with USMC, 1961-64. Mem. Soc. Automotive Engrs., Haverhill C. of C., Neuro Linguistic Programing Practitioners. Home: 3C Manor Dr PO Box 98 Groveland MA 01834 Office: Achiever Group 394 S Main St Bradford MA 01835

BROSSEAU, LUCIEN, insurance company executive; b. Montreal, Que., Can., Jan. 28, 1920; s. Rosario and Zelia (Dufour) B.; m. Gilberte Brosseau, July 14, 1940; children: Michel (Mrs. Myren Puchuluteguy), Micheline (Mrs. James W. Gilbert), Lesley (Mrs. Andre Wery). Diploma Gen. Math., U. Laval, Can., 1946, Acturial Diploma, U. Edinburgh, Scotland, 1951. Actuary, La Solidarite Ins. Co., Quebec City, Que., 1951-59; lectr. faculty of commerce U. Laval, Quebec, 1954-55; mng. dir. La Survivance Ins. Co., St. Hyacinthe, Que., 1959—, v.p., 1968-76, pres., 1976—, also dir.; pres. Hotel-Dieu de St-Hyacinthe, 1972—. Gov. Fedn. Socs. d'Histoire du Que., 1987; pres. Centraide Richelieu-Yamaska, 1988—. Recipient Canadian Silver Jubilee medal, 1978. Mem. Corp. of Charted Adminstrs. Que. (pres. 1973-75), Can. C. of C. (pres. 1963-65), Montreal Inst. Investment Analysis, Am. Inst. Mgmt. (fellow pres.'s council), Actuarial Club Montreal, Can. Health Life Ins. Assn. (bd. dirs. 1981-83, pub. relations com. 1978). K.C. Home: 2580 St Pierre St W, Saint Hyacinthe, PQ Canada J2T 4R9 Office: 1555 Girouard W, Saint Hyacinthe, PQ Canada J2S 2Z6

BROTBECK, GEORGE NATHAN, software company executive; b. Chattanooga, July 30, 1946; s. Charles Bourbon and Eva Mae (Watkins) B.; m. Mary Emeline Wise, Feb. 1, 1969 (div. Sept. 1974); m. Mary Jane Adams, Feb. 27, 1978; children: Rebekah Kelly, Sarah Elizabeth. BA in Math., U. Chattanooga, 1969; MA in Math., U. N.Mex., 1973, postgrad., 1975. Staff mem. Los Alamos (N.Mex.) Nat. Lab, 1969-76; sr. programmer analyst Edison Community Coll., Ft. Myers, Fla., 1976-78; supr. engring. software Gen. Dynamics, Pomona, Calif., 1978-80; mgr. mktg. and customer support Harris Computer Systems div., Ft. Lauderdale, Fla., 1980-81; group software mgr. Digital Equipment Corp., Atlanta, Ga., 1981-85; v.p. info. systems Colwell Systems Inc., Champaign, Ill., 1985-87; dir. systems and ops. Addamax Corp., Champaign, 1987-88; v.p. ops. Profl. Mgmt. Inst., Tulsa, 1988—; instr. Calif. Poly. Inst., Pomona, 1979. Mem. Unit 4 Sch. Dist. Computer Curriculum Adv. Com. Mem. Am. Mgmt. Assn., Assn. for Systems Mgmt., Data Processing Mgmt. Assn. (pres. East Cen. Ill. chpt.), Soc. for Info. Mgmt. Democrat. Methodist. Lodge: Rosicrucians. Home: 7818 E 77th St Tulsa OK 74133 Office: Profl Mgmt Inst 7169 S Braden Tulsa OK 74136

BROTHERS, JOHN ALFRED, chemical company executive; b. Huntington, W.Va., Nov. 10, 1940; s. John Luther and Genevieve (Monti) B.; m. Paula Sprague Benson, June 21, 1975. B.S., Va. Poly. Inst., 1962, M.S., 1965, Ph.D., 1966; postgrad advanced mgmt. program, Harvard U., 1981. With Internat. Nickel Co., 1962-64; with Ashland Oil, Inc., Ky., 1966—; sr. v.p. Ashland Oil, Inc., 1983-87; sr. v.p., group operating officer Ashland Oil Inc., 1987—; with Ashland Chem. Co., Columbus, Ohio, 1974—; pres. Ashland Chem. Co., Columbus, 1983—; bd. dirs. Ameritrust Corp., Cleve., Drew Chem. Co.; adj. prof. engring. Ohio State U., 1978—, pres. bus. adv. council, 1981—. Bd. dirs. Columbus Mus. Art, Mt. Carmel Hosp., Ohio Dominican Coll., 1984—. NSF fellow, 1965-66; named Outstanding Young Man U.S. C. of C., 1972. Mem. Am. Petroleum Inst., Mfg. Chemists Assn., Columbus C. of C. (bd. dirs.), Tau Beta Pi, Phi Kappa Phi. Republican. Clubs: Scioto Country, Rolling Rock, Muirfield Country, Mill Reef, Scioto Valley (treas.). Office: Ashland Chem Co PO Box 2219 Columbus OH 43216

BROTHERS, JOHN WAYNE, accountant; b. Norfolk, Va., Oct. 14, 1950; s. John Meredith and Nina (Hayman) B.; m. Evelyn Ruth Brown, June 14, 1974; children: John Meredith, Carie Lynn, Fritz Meredith. BS, Old Dominion U., 1974; postgrad. bank adminstrn., U. Wis., 1983. CPA, Va. Cost acct. Va. Nat. Bank, Norfolk, 1975-77, asst. acctg. officer, 1977-79; acctg. officer Sovran Bank, Norfolk, 1979-84, v.p., 1984-86, 1st v.p., 1986—; ptnr. Brothers & Palmer, Norfolk, 1983, Brothers Ventures, Norfolk, 1981; acctg. tchr. Am. Inst. Banking, Norfolk. Mem. Ocean View Bapt. Ch.; dir. budget Ocean View Bapt. Ch., Norfolk, deacon, 1982; chmn. Ocean View Endowment Fund, Norfolk; treas. Sch. for Bank Adminstrn. Class of 1983; pres. Meadowbrooke/Hunt Club Point Civic League. Mem. Am. Inst. CPA's, Am. Inst. Banking, Bank Adminstrn. Inst. (treas. 1988-89). Home: 6810 Woodridge Dr Norfolk VA 23518 Office: Sovran Fin Corp World Trade Ctr 101 E Main St Ste 200 Norfolk VA 23510

BROTHERS, THOMAS JOHN, financial consultant, lawyer; b. Tokyo, Nov. 13, 1949; (parents Am. citizens); s. Jerome Ray and Sue Brothers; m. Sherril Mae Feely, Apr. 4, 1970; children: Jessica C., Maggie E., John Thomas. BA, U. Wash., 1971; JD, U. Pacific, 1979. Bar: Washington 1979. Analyst State Of Calif., Sacramento, 1975-80; resettlement coord. Archdiocese of Seattle, Sacramento, 1980-81; exec. dir. Cuban Refugee Resettlement of Washington, Inc., Seattle, 1981-87; fin. cons. Merrill Lynch, Everett, Wash., 1987—. Vice chmn. Refugee Forum Puget Sound, Seattle, 1981-82; pres. Leadership Tomorrow Alumni Assn., Seattle, 1985-86; del. Snohomish County Rep. Com., 1988. With U.S. Army, 1971-74. Mem. Washington State Bar Assn., Travel Com., Inter-profl. Com. Home: 1232 S Lake Stickney Dr Lynnwood WA 98037 Office: Merrill Lynch 2930 Wetmore Ave Everett WA 98201

BROTT, JAMES DONALD, tire company executive; b. Akron, Ohio, Jan. 24, 1964; s. Donald Alton and June Christine (Hoover) B. A in Criminal Justice, U. Akron, 1985. Computer operator Brott, Kusmotz, Magliore and Mardir, Akron, 1980-85; pres., founder Dynamic Tire Co., Akron, 1985—. Mem. Nat. Tire Dealers Assn., Ohio Tire Dealers Assn., Ohio Young Tire Dealers Assn. (pres. 1986-87), Nat. Young Tire Dealers Assn. (exec. bd. dirs. 1986-87), Am. Mgmt. Assn. Republican. Home: 790 Portage Lake Dr Akron OH 44319 Office: Dynamic Tire Co 1615 S Arlington St Akron OH 44306

BROUCEK, WILLIAM SAMUEL, printing plant manager; b. Statesboro, Ga., July 27, 1950; s. Jack Wolf and Emily Louise (Kupferschmid) B.; m. Sara Carolyn Bennett, May 10, 1975; children—Samuel Josiah, William Bennett. B.B.A., Ga. So. Coll., 1972. Adminstr. Willingway Hosp., Statesboro, Ga., 1972-73; dept. mgr. Deluxe Check Printers, Inc., Jacksonville, Fla., 1975-78, asst. prodn. mgr., 1978-82, asst. plant mgr., 1982-83, mgr. Atlanta plant, 1984—. Bd. dirs. Ga. So. Coll. Alumni Assn., Statesboro, 1980-81; vol. Am. Cancer Soc., Jacksonville, 1981-83; elder Eastminster Presbyn. Ch. Mem. Stone Mountain Indsl. Park Assn., DeKalb County C. of C., Republican. Clubs: Smokerise Swim (Stone Mountain, Ga.), YMCA, Aircraft Owners and Pilots Assn. Avocations: aviation, old cars. Mailing Address: PO Box 1337 Tucker GA 30085

BROUGHTON, RAY MONROE, economic consultant; b. Seattle, Mar. 2, 1922; s. Arthur Charles and Elizabeth C. (Young) B.; BA, U. Wash., 1947, MBA, 1960; m. Margret Ellen Ryno, July 10, 1944 (dec.); children: Linda Rae Broughton Hellenthal, Mary Catherine Broughton Boutin; m. 2d, Carole Jean Packer, 1980. Mgr. communications and managerial devel. Gen. Electric Co., Hanford Atomic Products Ops., Richland, Wash., 1948-59; mktg. mgr., asst. to pres. Smyth Enterprises, Seattle, 1960-62; dir. research Seattle Area Indsl. Council, 1962-65; v.p., economist (mgr. econ. research dept.) First Interstate Bank of Oreg., N.A., Portland, 1965-87; ind. economic cons., 1987—; mem. econ. adv. com. to Am. Bankers Assn., 1980-83; mem. Gov.'s Econ. Adv. Council, 1981-88; dir. Oregonians for Cost Effective Govt., 1989—; instr. bus. communications U. Wash., Richland, 1956-57. Treas., dir. Oreg. affiliate Am. Heart Assn., 1972-78, chmn., 1980-81, dir., 1980-84. Served to 1st lt. U.S. Army, 1943-46; ETO. Mem. Western Econ. Assn., Pacific N.W. Regional Econ. Conf. (dir. 1967—), Nat. Assn. Bus. Economists (co-founder chpt. 1971), Am. Mktg. Assn. (pres. chpt. 1971-72), Alpha Delta Sigma. Episcopalian. Author: Trends and Forces of Change in the Payments System and the Impact on Commercial Banking, 1972; contbg. editor Pacific Banker and Bus. mag., 1974-80.

BROUILLARD, JOHN CHARLES, retail company executive; b. Brockton, Mass., Apr. 7, 1948; s. Francis Arthur Brouillard and Marie Virginia Carroll; m. Elaine Ferguson, Oct. 12, 1974; children: John Jr., Carolyn, Michael, Diane, Jeffrey. BMechE, U. Mass., 1970; MBA, U. Pa., 1974. CPA, Mass. Sr. cons. Arthur Andersen & Co., Boston, 1974-77; sr. v.p. Hill Dept. Stores, Canton, Mass., 1977—. Served with U.S. Army, 1971-73. Office: Hills Dept Stores 15 Dan Rd Canton MA 02021

BROUILLETTE, WILLIAM GREGORY, publishing executive; b. Bethesda, Md., Apr. 23, 1954; s. Robert Tate and Catherine (Clark) B.; m. Nancy Elizabeth Plummer, Apr. 25, 1981; children: Molly Ann, Gregory Thomas. BA, Georgetown U., 1976, MA, 1977. Sales rep. Equipro Corp., Rockville, Md., 1979-81; mem. staff sales and mgmt. Donnelly Directory Dun & Bradstreet, Washington, 1980-83; mem. dept. human resources and tng. Thomson Directories, Manchester, England, 1984-86; mgr. sales Thomson Directories, Glasgow, Scotland, 1984-86; mgr. area sales Donnelly Directory, Richmond, Va., 1986, Rockville, 1987—. Mem. Ad Club Washington, Germantown (Md.) C. of C. Roman Catholic. Office: Donnelley Directory 6011 Executive Blvd Rockville MD 20852

BROUSSARD, JAMES MICHAEL, wholesale distribution executive; b. St. Martinville, La., Sept. 7, 1946; s. Dizier Joseph and Eunice Marie (Berard) B.; m. Susan Rose Kirk, Sept. 1, 1972; 1 child, Kirk. BA in Econs., UCLA, 1973; MS in Mgmt. and Adminstrn., U. Tex., Dallas, 1981. Cost adminstr. Rockwell Internat., Newport Beach, Calif., 1973-76; supr. cost control Rockwell Internat., Dallas, 1976-78; contr. Mermaq, Inc., Dallas, 1978-80; regional mgr. fin. svcs. GTE Svc. Corp., Dallas, 1980-82; dir. mgmt. svcs. Anderson Clayton Foods, Dallas, 1982-84, contr., 1984-86; v.p., corp. contr. Fox Meyer Corp., Dallas, 1987—. Sgt. USAF, 1966-69. Mem. Fin. Execs. Inst., Nat. Assn. Accts., Indian Creek Golf Club (Carrollton, Tex.). Republican. Episcopalian. Office: Fox Meyer Corp 1220 Senlac Dr Carrollton TX 75006

BROWER, MYRON RIGGS, architect, interior designer, educator; b. Muscatine, Iowa, Dec. 8, 1949; s. Myron Orson and Marcene P. (Shafnett) B. BArch, Ariz. State U., 1973, BA in Edn., 1977. Registered architect, Ariz., Calif. Architect in tng. Fenlason Assocs., Architects, Tempe, Ariz., 1975-77; pres. Myron Riggs Brower, Architect, Inc., Scottsdale, Ariz., 1977—; prof. Scottsdale Community Coll., 1982—. Mem. AIA, Am. Soc. Interior Designers. Republican.

BROWN, ALLYN STEPHENS, retired newspaper publisher and consultant; b. New Castle, Ind., Feb. 7, 1916; s. Leroy Nicholas and Alice (Stephens) B.; A.B., Amherst Coll., 1938; m. Ellen Louise Kellogg, June 20, 1942; children—Allyn Stephens Jr., Dianne Kellogg (Mrs. Daniel R. Cherry). With Evening Times, Sayre, Pa., 1939-50, co-pub. 1946-50; pres. Owego

(N.Y.) Gazette, Inc., 1948-50; bus. mgr. Goldsboro (N.C.) News-Argus, 1950-52; with Graphic Equipment div. Fairchild Camera, Plainview, N.Y., 1953-56, 60-65; pres. pub. Brown-Thompson Newspapers, Inc., Union City, Pa., 1956-82; cons., 1982—. Served with USAAF, 1943-46. Mem. Sigma Delta Chi. Home: 3319 Heritage Dr Hendersonville NC 28739

BROWN, ANDREW JOSEPH, opinion research company executive; b. Allentown, Pa., Feb. 10, 1945; s. John Michael and Verna Estelle (Peters) B.; m. Martha Jane Moyer, Jan. 22, 1972; children: Nathan Andrew, Melanie Jane. BS, Iowa State U., 1968; MBA, Temple U., 1971. Asst. claims mgr. Blue Cross of Lehigh Valley, Allentown, 1968-69; rsch. assoc. Chilton Rsch. Svcs., Radnor, Pa., 1972-78, v.p., 1978, assoc. dir., 1979-82; exec. v.p. Opinion Rsch. Corp., Princton, N.J., 1982-85, pres., 1985-86, chief exec. officer, 1986—; bd. Pub. Relations News, N.Y.C. Bd. dirs. Thomas Edison State Coll., Trenton, N.J., 1986—; trustee Princeton United Way, 1987—. Served with USAF, 1963-64. Mem. Am. Mktg. Assn., Nassau Club. Home: Pennington NJ 08534 Office: Opinion Rsch Corp PO Box 183 Princeton NJ 08542

BROWN, ANNE, insurance broker; b. Boston, Aug. 4, 1941; b. Leon R. and Adrienne (LaPointe) Bouchard; m. Erik R. Brown, June, 10, 1961 (div. 1977); children: Allison , Lindsey. Sales asst. Northwestern Mut. Life Ins. Co., Boston, 1963-77; dir. mktg. Bradley Ins. Planning, Chestnut Hill, Mass., 1978-84; pvt. practice ins. brokerage Marstons Mills, Mass., 1984—; promotional cons., 1977-84; cons. to ins. agts. and brokers on mktg. techniques, 1980—. Mem. Nat. Assn. Life Underwriters, Inst. Contemporary Art, Boston Life Underwriters Assn., Boston Visual Artists Union, Mid Cape Racquet Club (Yarmouth, Mass.), Corinthian Yacht Club (Marblehead). Home and Office: 1026 River Rd Marstons Mills MA 02648

BROWN, ANTHONY WYNN, information systems company executive; b. Bay City, Mich., Apr. 6, 1961; s. Erwin Junior and Lorraine Mildred (Duquette) B.; m. Dawn Marie Loomis, Aug. 28, 1982. A of Data Processing, Delta Coll., 1982. Asst. computer programmer Ford Forestry Ctr., Houghton, Mich., 1979-80; computer operator Frankenmuth (Mich.) Mut. Ins. Co., 1980-82, ops. programmer, 1982-84; sr. tech. operator Genesse Mchts. Bank, Flint, Mich., 1984-85; mgr. computer systems Bobier Tool Supply Inc., Flint, 1985-88, v.p. info. systems, 1988—; pres. D.M.I.S. Users Group, 1988—; chmn. New Port Richey, Fla., 1987—. Dir. Sch. Millage Campaign, Bay City, Mich., 1978; instr. religious edn. St. John Vianney Parish, Saginaw, Mich., 1987—. Mem. Engring. Soc. Detroit, Soc. for Machine Intelligence, Interex, Data Processing Mgmt. Assn., Saginaw C. of C. (mem. com. 1987). Roman Catholic. Club: Pioneer (Saginaw). Home: 411 S Porter Saginaw MI 48602 Office: Bobier Tool Supply Inc G-4163 Corunna Rd Flint MI 48532

BROWN, B. R., coal company executive; b. 1932; married. B.S., U. Ark., 1958. Sr. v.p. Conoco, 1975-77; with Consolidation Coal Co. (subs. Du-Pont), Pitts., 1977—; exec. v.p., then pres. and chief operating officer, chief exec. officer Consolidation Coal Co., Pitts., 1987—, also bd. dirs.; dir. Ky. Found. for Energy Tech. Devel., Inc., Am. Mining Congressmem. Dept. Energy's Innovation Control Tech. Adv. Panel, Jefferson Energy Found. Nat. Steering Com.; dir. Orgn. Resource Counselors, Inc., Indsl. Rels. Counselors, Inc. Mem. excellence program adv. coun. Lamar U.; trustee Carnegie Mellon U., mem. fin. com., student affairs com.; v.p. Allegheny Trails coun. Boy Scouts Am.; mem. Vietnam Vets. Leadership Adv. Bd. Mem. Am. Coal Found., Assn. for the Devel. Inland Navigation in Am.'s Ohio Valley, Living Lakes, Inc., Bituminous Coal Ops. Assn. (dir.), Internat. Energy Agy. (coal industry adv. bd.), Nat. Coal Coun. (coal policy com., exec. com.), Nat. Coal Assn. (past. chmn.), Nat. Coal Coun. (past vice chmn.), Greater Pitts. C. of C., Regional Indsl. Devel. Corp. Pa., Nat. Safety Coun. (gov.), Duquesne Club. Office: Consolidation Coal Co 1800 Washington Rd Pittsburgh PA 15241

BROWN, BARTON, automotive company executive; b. Glen Cove, N.Y., Sept. 21, 1924; s. Andrew Malcolm and Julia Marie (terKuile) B.; m. Priscilla Thomason, May 9, 1953; children—Barbara Kerr Brown Swafford, Suzanne Goree Brown Irwin. S.B., S.M., MIT, 1950. Various positions parent co. and subs. Gen. Motors Corp., 1950-65; mng. dir. Continental div. Gen. Motors Corp., Antwerp, Belgium, 1965-68; dir. staff ops. overseas div. Gen. Motors Corp., N.Y.C., 1968-78; dep. dir. Latin Am. div. Gen. Motors Corp., Detroit, 1978-80, exec. dir. Asia div., 1980-83, v.p., 1983—. Served as sgt. USAF, 1943-46. Republican. Office: GM 3044 W Grand Blvd Detroit MI 48202

BROWN, BENJAMIN A., financial executive; b. N.Y.C., Feb. 13, 1943; s. Horace A. and Lillian A. (Hurwitz) B.; m. Elinore Carole Abravanel, Aug. 8, 1968; children—Adam Howard, Dina Lauren. B.B.A. in Acctg., Adelphi U., 1964; M.B.A. in Fin. and Investments, Baruch Coll. CUNY, 1971. Acct. Samuel Greiff C.P.A., Atty., Forest Hills, N.Y., 1963-66; v.p. research dept. Walston & Co., N.Y.C., 1967-73; treas. ENSERCH Corp., Dallas, 1974-78, v.p. fin., 1978-82, v.p. fin. relations, 1982—. Mem. Fin. Execs. Inst., N.Y. Soc. Security Analysts, Am. Gas Assn. (chmn. fin. com. 1983-85), Am. Petroleum Inst., Petroleum Investors Relations Assn. Clubs: Dallas Athletic, 2001. Home: 7342 Blythdale Dallas TX 75248 Office: ENSERCH Corp 300 S St Paul Dallas TX 75201

BROWN, BERNARD BEAU, chemical executive; b. Phila., Apr. 15, 1925; s. Solomon and Pearl (Gaz) B.; m. Shirley C. Mark, Sept. 1, 1947; children: Eric, Aimee. BS in Chemistry, Temple U., 1945; MS in Chemistry, U. Mich., 1947, PhD in Organic Chemistry, 1949. Lectr. in chemistry U. Mich., Ann Arbor, 1947-49, sr. chemist research inst., 1949-51; mgr. research Olin Mathieson, New Haven, 1951-59; v.p. research and devel. Penick Div. CPC Internat., Lyndhurst, N.J., 1959-80, A.L. Lab Inc., Ft. Lee, N.J., 1980—. Home: 146 Tudor Oval Westfield NJ 07090 Office: AL Labs Inc One Executive Dr Fort Lee NJ 07024

BROWN, BRITT MURDOCK, banker; b. Wichita, Kans., Aug. 1, 1952; s. Harry Britton Jr. and Ann Louise (McCarthy) B.; m. Sally Melissa Andrews, Nov. 26, 1982; children: Aaron Britton, Jacqueline Lea, Ruse Murdock. B of Bus. Adminstrn. and Econs., Wichita State U., 1974. Investment officer Fourth Nat. Bank, Wichita, 1974-80; investment broker A.G. Edwards & Sons, Wichita, 1980; v.p., trust officer Kans. State Bank and Trust Co., Wichita, 1980-83, sr. v.p, trust officer, 1983-86, exec. v.p., trust officer, 1986-87, exec. v.p., sr. trust officer, 1987—; exec. v.p. Kans. State Fin. Corp., Wichita, 1987—; sec., treas. Sun Eagle Enterprises, Wichita, Britt Brown Ptnrship., Wichita, M. M. Murdock, Wichita. Advisor Senator Robert Dole, Washington, 1983—; chmn. bd. dirs. Holy Family Ctr., Wichita, 1974—, Sedgewick County Civil Service Bd., 1985—; bd. govs. Wichita State U., 1980—; bd. dirs. Police and Fire Retirement Bd., Wichita, 1985—; mem. Kans. State Political Action com., 1987—, Wichita Crime commn., pres., 1988. Named one of Outstanding Young Men Am., 1981. Mem. Am. Inst. Banking, Kans. Ind. Oil and Gas Assn., Wichita Estate Planning Council (v.p. 1984-86), Wichita C. of C., Nat. Conf. Christians and Jews (bd. dirs. 1986—), Paul Revere Found. Republican. Roman Catholic. Clubs: Wichita (bd. dirs. 1985—), Wichita Country. Office: Kans State Bank & Trust Co 123 N Market Wichita KS 67202

BROWN, BRUCE, insurance company executive; b. Stamford, Conn., July 25, 1931; m. Mary Thorpe, Aug. 31, 1954; children—Richard B., David T., Katherine R. B.S., U. Conn., Storrs, 1953. C.L.U. V.p. Am. Republic Ins. Co., Des Moines, 1970-77; sr. v.p. Provident Life & Accident Co., Chattanooga, Tenn., 1977-83; pres., chief exec. officer Monarch Life Ins. Co., Springfield, Mass., 1983—. Served to 1st lt. U.S. Army, 1953-55. Home: AC Boyden Rd Conway MA 01341 Office: Monarch Life Ins Co 1 Monarch Pl Springfield MA 01133

BROWN, CHARLES DANIEL, chemical corporation executive; b. Mineral Springs, Ark., Oct. 31, 1927; s. Leonidas Carlton and Willie Pearl (Graves) B.; m. Marjorie Ann Fischer, June 1, 1951; children: Brant Carlton, Karyn Danette, Christopher Daniel. B.S. in Civil Engring., U. Ark, 1951. With E.I. DuPont de Nemours & Co., Inc., Wilmington, Del., 1951—, v.p. engring. dept., 1982—. Task force chmn. constrn. industry cost effectiveness project: books Report on Problems of United States Construction Industry, 1978-81 (Engring. News Record-Constrn. Industry Man of Year award 1982). Served with AUS, 1946-47, PTO. Mem. Bus. Roundtable (chmn. constrn. com. N.Y.C. 1981-83), Theta Tau. Methodist. Clubs: Kennett Square Country (Pa.); Wilmington Country; DuPont Country (Wilmington). Home: 8 Hickory Ln Chadds Ford PA 19317 Office: E I Du Pont de Nemours & Co Engring Dept Louviers Bldg PO Box 6090 Newark DE 19714

BROWN, CLAYTON WARREN, construction executive; b. Buffalo, June 6, 1930; s. Raymond Frank and Elizabeth Melvina (Mager) B.; m. Jeannine Laurel Roper, Oct. 9, 1948; children: Cynthia, Eric, Rebecca, Adam. Student, Ill. Inst. Tech., 1948-50. V.p. Chgo. Ornamental Iron Co., Melrose Park, Ill., 1957-68, M.W. Iron Works Co., Chgo., 1968-77; pres. Brand Indsl. Services, Inc., Park Ridge, Ill., 1977—; chmn. Brand/Site Services, Inc., St. Paul, 1987—; bd. dirs. Barrier Systems Co., Cleve. Trustee Village of Palatine, Ill., 1967-74, Village of Kildeer, Ill., 1977-81. Episcopalian. Office: Brand Indsl Svcs 1420 Renaissance Dr Park Ridge IL 60068

BROWN, COLIN W(EGAND), diversified company executive, lawyer; b. Port Jefferson, N.Y., Mar. 26, 1949; s. Keirn C. and Jane (Schuhl) B.; m. Cynthia Porter, Aug. 21, 1971; children—Courtney, Alec, Seth. BA, Williams Coll., 1971; JD, Duke U., 1974. Bar: N.Y. 1975, N.C. 1983. Assoc. Simpson Thacher & Bartlett, N.Y.C., 1974-81; sr. v.p.-gen. counsel Cannon Mills Co., Kannapolis, N.C., 1981-82; v.p., gen. counsel Fuqua Industries, Inc., Atlanta, 1982—. Mem. Leadership Atlanta, 1987-88, adv. bd. Atlanta Legal Aid Soc.; bd. dirs. Fulton County (Ga.) Heart Assn., Spl. Audiences, Inc.; exec. Egleston Hosp. Mem. ABA, Am. Corp. Counsel Assn. (pres. Ga. chpt.). Home: 400 King Rd NW Atlanta GA 30342 Office: Fuqua Industries Inc 4900 Gaeorgia Pacific Ctr Atlanta GA 30303

BROWN, CONNIE YATES, small business owner; b. Carthage, Mo., Apr. 29, 1947; d. Charles Lee and Eunice Jane (Farmer) Yates; m. Larry Edward Brown, June 19, 1982; 1 step-dau., Tammy Lynn Brown. B.S., Pittsburg State U., 1969. Cert. home economist. With White Shield Oil and Gas/Petro-Lewis, Tulsa, 1969-74, dept. supt., 1971-74; with Southwestern Bell Telephone Co., 1975-79; owner, mgr. Abbyco, Inc., rental, sales carpet cleaning equipment, Tulsa, 1978—; sec.-treas. R.D.R. Assn. Inc.; lectr. in field. Active Okla. Rep. Party. Named Rookie of Yr., Tulsa div. Southwestern Bell Yellow Pages, 1976; sales award winner Rug Doctor Licensee of Yr., 1981, 85. Mem. Home Economists in Bus., Am. Home Econs. Assn., Met. Tulsa C. of C., Equipment Rental Dealers Assn. Eastern Okla., Tulsa Alumnae Panhellenic (bd. dirs. com. collegiate rels.), Pitts. State U. Alumni Assn. (past pres. Tulsa chpt.), Tulsa Area Women Bus. Owners, Tulsa Women's Found., Resonance, Order of Rainbow for Girls, Phi Upsilon Omicron, Alpha Gamma Delta (nat. dir. alumnae devel. 1984-86). Home: 7806 S Evanston Ave Tulsa OK 74136 Office: Abbyco Inc 8600 S Lewis Ave Tulsa OK 74137

BROWN, CONNY RAY, mechanical engineer; b. Bryan, Tex., Oct. 21, 1947; s. Charlie Ray Brown and Helen Victoria (Kosh) Bean; m. Nancy Faith Wiedeman, Jan. 6, 1978. BSME, Tex. A&M U., 1970. Registered profl. engr. Tex., Ill., Ky., Ariz. Design engr. CRSS, Houston, 1970-83, egring. programmer, v.p., 1983—. Served to capt. U.S. Army, 1970-78. Mem. ASME, ASHRAE (pres. local chpt. 1972-73, mem. soc. com. 1972—). Republican. Roman Catholic. Office: CRSS PO Box 22427 Houston TX 77227

BROWN, DANIEL, independent art consultant, critic, small business owner; b. Cin., Nov. 4, 1946; s. Sidney H. and Genevieve Florence (Elbaum) B.; m. Ellen Neveloff, May 24, 1970; m. 2d, Jane Felson, Sept. 14, 1980; stepchildren—Christopher Minton, Scott Minton. A.B. cum laude, Middlebury Coll., 1968; A.M., U. Mich., 1970; postgrad. Princeton U., 1971-72. Dir. cultural events U. Cin., 1972, spl. asst. to pres., 1973; v.p., corp. sec. Brockton Shoe Trimming Co., Cin., 1974—; instr. Art Acad. Cin., 1980—; prin. Daniel Brown, Inc.; curator KZF Gallery, Cin., 1987—; art critic Cin. Mag., 1980-83, Cin. Art Acad. Newsletter, Provincetown Arts, 1988—; art commentator Sta. WKRC-TV, Cin., art and movie critic Sta. WCPO-TV, Cin., 1986; art critic USA Arts; frequent guest lectr. on arts; guest curator New Art from Academe: An Overview The Cen. Exchange, Kansas City, Mo., 1988, Figure It Out! inaugural exhibition Katz and Dawgs Gallery, Columbus, Ohio, 1988, Lyrical Abstractions, 1989, Design of the Future, 1989, Contemporary Landscape Kencabco Co., Cin., 1988, A Critic's Choice: Art of the '90's, Northern Ky. U., 1989; guest co-curator Cincinnati Yesterday and Today Tangeman Fine Arts Gallery U. Cin., 1987, guest curator, 1988; frequent guest lectr. on arts; permanent curator The KZF Art Gallery, Cin., 1987—; corr. editor: Dialogue Mag., 1986, art reviewer 1983—; author: David Brumbeck: The Romantic Classicist, 1989, Tom Bacher: High Tech American Impressionist, 1989 . Recipient The Critic's Purse award, Dialogue mag., 1985. Mem. exhbns. com. Contemporary Arts Ctr.; mem. membership com. Cin. Art Mus.; sec., bd. dirs. Mercantile Library, 1985—, treas. 1986, chmn. programs com., 1987—, Young Wing; trustee Contemporary Arts Ctr. 1984—, co-chmn. artists adv. bd., 1987, Vocal Arts Ensemble, 1984, Enjoy the Arts, 1985-88, v.p. 1986; mem. bd. advisors Cin. Artists Group Effort, 1986-88; guest curator Carnegie Arts Ctr., Covington, Ky., 1986—; juror art competitions Cin. and Columbus, Ohio, 1986-87. Mem. Shoe and Leather Club, Two-Ten Nat. Found., Internat. Platform Assn. Club: University (Cin.). Home: 3900 Rose Hill Ave Apt 401B Cincinnati OH 45229 Office: Brockton Shoe Trimming Co 212 E 8th St Cincinnati OH 45202

BROWN, DANIEL HERBERT, lawyer, manufacturing company executive; b. N.Y.C., Feb. 22, 1933; s. Harry and Celia (Weiner) B.; m. Myrna Serotick, June 15, 1958; children: Ian, Jennifer, Eric. A.B., CCNY, 1955; J.D., Fordham U., 1960. Bar: N.Y. 1961. Assoc. Brumbaugh, Free Graves & Donohue, N.Y.C., 1960-68; with Rheem Mfg. Co., N.Y.C., 1968—, v.p., sec., gen. counsel, 1973—, also bd. dirs.; bd. dirs. Rheem U.S. Holdings, Inc., Rheem Export Sales Corp, Rheem Textile Systems, Inc; legal adv. com. Mid-Atlantic Legal Found., 1983—. Served to 1st lt. AUS, 1955-57. Mem. N.Y. Patent Law Assn. (gov. 1971-74, com. profl. ethics 1979-82), Assn. Bar City N.Y. (mem. legal assistance com. 1967-71, profl. responsibility com. 1969-73), Gas Appliance Mfrs. Assn. (chmn. task force on consumer legislation 1975—, mem. legis. com. 1974—), Am. Bar Assn. (sect. antitrust law, chmn. corp. law depts. 1988—), Assn. Bar City N.Y. (com. corp. law depts. 1978-86), Am. Corp. Counsel Assn. (pres. Greater N.Y. chpt. 1986—). Home: 21 The Fenway Roslyn Estates NY 11576 Office: Rheem Mfg Co 350 Park Ave New York NY 10022

BROWN, DAVID, motion picture producer, writer; b. N.Y.C., July 28, 1916; s. Edward Fisher and Lillian (Baren) B.; m. Liberty LeGacy, Apr. 15, 1940 (div. 1951); 1 son, Bruce LeGacy; m. Wayne Clark, May 25, 1951 (div. 1957); m. Helen Gurley, Sept. 25, 1959. AB, Stanford U., 1936; MS, Columbia U., 1937. Apprentice San Francisco News and Wall St. Jour., 1936; night editor, asst. drama critic Fairchild Publs., 1937-39; editorial dir. Milk Research Council, 1939-40; assoc. editor Street & Smith Publs., 1940-43; assoc. editor, exec. editor, editor-in-chief Liberty mag., 1943-49; editorial dir. Nat. Edn. Campaign, A.M.A., 1949; assoc. editor, mng. editor Cosmopolitan mag., 1949-52; mng. editor, story editor, head scenario dept. 20th Century-Fox Film Corp. Studios, Beverly Hills, Calif., 1952-56, mem. studio exec. com., 1956-60, producer, 1960-62; v.p., dir. story operation 20th Century Fox Film Corp., Beverly Hills, Calif., 1964-69, exec. v.p. creative operations, 1969-70, dir., 1968-70; exec. v.p. creative operations, dir. Warner Bros., 1971-72; ptnr. Zanuck/Brown Co., N.Y.C., 1972—; exec. story editor, head scenario dept., editorial v.p. New Am. Library World Lit., Inc., 1963-64; final judge for best short story pub. in mags. Benjamin Franklin Mag. ann. awards, 1955-58. Author: Brown's Guide to Growing Gray, 1987; contbr. articles to Am. mag., Collier's, Harpers, Sat. Evening Post, others; editor: I Can Tell It Now, 1964, How I Got That Story, 1967; contbr.: Journalists in Action, 1963; producer: (films) The Sting, 1973, The Sugarland Express, 1974, The Eiger Sanction, 1975, Jaws, 1977, MacArthur, 1977, Jaws II, 1978, The Island, 1980, Neighbors, 1981, The Verdict, 1982, Target, 1985, Cocoon, 1985. Trustee com. on film Mus. Modern Art, N.Y.C. Served as 1st lt., M.I. AUS, World War II. Mem. Acad. Motion Picture Arts and Scis., Producers Guild Am., Am. Film Inst. (vice-chmn., trustee, mem. exec. com.). Clubs: Players (N.Y.C.), Dutch Treat (N.Y.C.), Century Assn. (N.Y.C.), Overseas Press (N.Y.C.); Nat. Press (Washington); Coffee House (N.Y.C.). Office: The Manhattan Project Ltd 711 Fifth Ave New York NY 10022

BROWN, DAVID FAIN, financial executive; b. N.Y.C., Feb. 19, 1941; s. William Heren and Fain (Goodson) B.; m. Sheila Duckworth, June 20, 1970 (div. Dec. 1975); m. Nancy Ann Verity, Oct. 24, 1982; children: Fain Kelley, Kathryn Verity. B.A. in Econs., Rutgers U., 1964, LL.B., 1966. Assoc. Cravath, Swaine & Moore, N.Y.C., 1966-72; v.p., gen. counsel City Investing Co., N.Y.C., 1972-85; chmn. bd. Gen. Devel. Corp., Miami, Fla., 1985—; bd. dirs. Motel 6 G.P. Inc., Dallas, Work Wear Corp. Inc., Cleve. Mem. vis. com. Rosenstiel Sch. Marine and Atmospheric Sci., U. Miami, 1988—. Served as pvt. USMCR, 1958-64. Mem. N.Y. Bar Assn. Republican. Clubs: Knickerbocker, The Links, N.Y. Athletic (N.Y.C.); Coral Reef Yacht (Miami). Home: 158 S Prospect Dr Coral Gables FL 33133 Office: Gen Devel Corp 1111 S Bayshore Dr Miami FL 33131

BROWN, DONALD GRADY, banker; b. Lynchburg, Va., Nov. 4, 1949; s. Robert Wilmot and Wanda (Spencer) B.; m. Jeannette Corell, June 18, 1977; children: Donald Grady Jr., Jennifer Ann, Christina Elain. BBA, Va. Poly. Inst. and State U., 1972. Communication rep. Chesapeake and Potomac Telephone Co., Lynchburg, 1972-73; br. mgr. N.C. Nat. Bank, Greensboro, 1973-77; mktg. dir. N.C. Nat. Bank, Charlotte, 1977-80; sr. loan and credit officer N.C. Nat. Bank, Greenville, 1980-86; city exec. N.C. Nat. Bank, Thomasville, 1986—. Bd. dirs. Thomasville YMCA, 1988—, Salvation Army, Thomasville, 1987—, H.P.T. Family Services; mem. Davidson County Community Coll. found., 1988—. Mem. Thomasville C. of C. (v.p. econ. devel. 1988). Republican. Methodist. Club: Colonial Country (Thomasville). Lodge: Rotary. Home: 200 Lake Dr E Thomasville NC 27360

BROWN, DOREEN LEAH HURWITZ, development company executive; b. Marseille, France, June 11, 1927; came to U.S., 1939, naturalized, 1941; d. Nathan and Anne (Silverstone) Hurwitz; m. Donald L. Brown, Dec. 30, 1951 (dec.); children: Claudia Geraldine, Nicole Deborah. BA cum laude, Bryn Mawr Coll., 1947. Adminstrv. asst., interpreter, translator FAO, Washington, 1949-51; with Aldon Constrn. & Mgmt. Corp., Washington, 1951—, v.p., exec. officer, 1977—; consumer liaison Nat. Acad. Scis., 1973. Author: Window on Washington: the Trade Deficit. Nat. chmn. nat. affairs Nat. Council Jewish Women, N.Y.C., 1971-75; pres. Consumer Edn. Council on World Trade, 1973-78, Consumers for World Trade, Washington, 1977—; mem. Women's Nat. Dem. Club, 1960—; mem. Internat. Trade Importers and Retailers Textile Adv. Com., Dept. Commerce. Mem. Bryn Mawr Coll. Alumnae Assn., World Trade Forum. Club: Woodmont Country. Office: Aldon Constrn& Mgmt Corp 1001 Connecticut Ave NW Ste 800 Washington DC 20036

BROWN, DUNCAN FRASER, insurance company executive; b. Boston, May 8, 1921; s. William Eustis and Estelle Marguerite (Wolff) B.; m. Olivia Ramsey, May 2, 1945; children: Olivia, Duncan II, Peter, Melissa, Anne. AB, Harvard Coll., 1942. CLU. Agy. mgr., agt. Union Cen. Life, Cin., 1946-54; gen. agt. State Mut. Life Assurance Co., Burlington, Vt., 1954-57; supr. of agys. Worcester, Mass., 1957-62; pres., chmn. Brown Bridgman & Co., Burlington, 1962-83; pres. Simson, Brown, Pastore & Zais, South Burlington, 1987—, Simson, Brown & Co., South Burlington, 1983—; bd. dirs. Vt. Fin. Services, Brattleboro, Vt. Chmn. Vt. Hosp. Data Coun., Waterbury, Vt., 1982-84, Vt. Water Resources Bd., Montpelier, Vt., 1980-82, Dist. Environ. Com., Essex Junction, Vt., 1971-80. Lt. comdr. USNR, 1942-46, ATO, ETO. Mem. Am. Soc. CLU, Leash Club, Harvard Club. Republican. Episcopalian. Home: 75 Old Farm Rd South Burlington VT 05403

BROWN, EDWARD SHERMAN, computer sales representative; b. Lansing, Mich., May 6, 1940; s. Raymond Edward and Jennie W. (Maki) B.; A.A., Compton (Calif.) Coll., 1970; A.A. in Bus. Adminstrn., Santa Ana Coll., 1975; BA in Mktg., Fullerton State U., 1976, MS in Mgmt., Cardinal Stritch Coll., 1985; m. Edith Volk; 1 dau., Angela Renee. Sr. technician Rockwell Internat., Anaheim, Calif., 1962-69; sr. digital system technician Hughes Aircraft, Fullerton, Calif., 1969-70; engr. spl. systems Gen. Automation, Anaheim, 1970-76, engring. mgr., 1976-77, sales mgr., 1977-78, sales mgr. computer systems, Milw., 1978-80; sales engr. computer systems div. Perkin-Elmer, Brookfield, Wis., 1980-82, sales mgr. data systems div., Overland Park, Kans., 1982-83; sr. sales rep. tech. computer systems Digital Equipment Corp., Brookfield, Wis., 1983—; cons. in field. Served with U.S. Army, 1959-62. Mem. Central Mich. Rocket Soc. (past v.p.), Sales Mktg. Execs. Kansas City, Mid-Am. Masters Track and Field Assn. (race dir.), Pi Sigma Epsilon, Alpha Gamma Sigma. Club: Variety of Wis. (dir.). Home: 2200 S Layton Blvd Milwaukee WI 53215 Office: Digital Equipment Corp 150 N Patrick Blvd Brookfield WI 53005

BROWN, ELBERT LEON, manufacturing company executive; b. Meridian, Miss., Nov. 10, 1938; s. Elbert L. Brown and Josephine (McLaurin) Cutler; m. Patricia A. Tashlin, Apr. 15, 1966 (div. June 1976); children: Shirley, Sonya; m. Dale J. Dunkel, Jan. 15, 1977; children: Laurie Quermann, Amy Quermann, Jennifer Quermann. BS in Chem. Engring., U. Miss., 1960; MBA, Stanford U., 1968. Fin. analyst Raychem. Corp., Menlo Park, Calif., 1968-69, mgr. planning, 1969-70, chief fin. officer, 1970-72, dir. R&D, 1973-77, gen. mgr. conductive polymer div., 1977-81, dir. strategic planning, ops., 1982-88, group gen. mgr. display techs., 1988—; dir. Taliq Corp., Sunnyvale, Calif., 1983—, Andus Corp., Los Angeles, 1983—, Menlo Care, Inc., Palo Alto, Calif., 1986—, Landec Labs., Inc., Redwood City, Calif., 1987—. Campaign worker for senate and congl. seat, 1982, 84. Served as a lt. in USN, 1960-66. Mem. Fremont Hills Country Club, Los Altos Tennis Club. Republican. Congregationalist. Office: Raychem Corp 300 Constitution Menlo Park CA 94025

BROWN, FAYETTE, III, electronics executive; b. Cleve., June 2, 1943; s. Fayette Jr. and Louisiana (Draper) B.; m. Laurie Wheeler, Aug. 27, 1966; children: L. Melissa, Alexander H. BA, Yale U., 1965; MBA, U. Va., 1967. With Harris Corp., Melbourne, Fla., 1967-79, v.p. corp. devel., 1985—; liaison dir. Matra-Harris Semicondrs., Melbourne, Fla., 1979-83; dir. mktg. Digital Products div. Harris Semicondr. Co., Melbourne, 1983-85. Office: Harris Corp 1025 W NASA Blvd Melbourne FL 32919

BROWN, FREDERICK HAROLD, insurance company executive; b. Troy, N.Y., Apr. 21, 1927; s. Harold Lamphere and Maida Adelaide (Wooden) B.; m. Mary Lee Lamar, Aug. 12, 1950; children: Deborah Elaine Wright, Frederick Harold. BS in Mech. Engring., Bucknell U., 1949. Registered profl. engr., Wis., Pa., Tenn. With CIGNA and Subs., Phila., 1949-73, asst. v.p., 1970-71, v.p., 1971-73; founder, pres., chief exec. officer Jersey/Internat. Group, Cherry Hill, N.J., 1973-84 ; pres., chief exec. officer Admiral Ins. Co. subs. W.R. Berkeley Corp., Greenwich, Conn., 1979-84; sr. v.p. W.R. Berkley Corp., Greenwich, 1984-87; chmn. bd. Investors Ins. Holding Corp. and all subs., 1987—. Contbr. articles to profl. jours. Mem. Phila. Fire Prevention Com., 1958-68; exec. treas. Camden County (N.J.) Rep. Orgn., 1968-73; clk. bd. chosen freeholders of Camden County, 1969-73; active United Fund, Boy Scouts Am. Served with USNR, 1944-46. Named Citizen of Yr., INA, 1970. Mem. Soc. Fire Protection Engrs., Nat. Fire Protection Assn., Conf. Spl. Risk Underwriters, U.S. Jaycees (hon. life, Outstanding State V.P. 1961, Outstanding Nat. Dir. 1962). Episcopalian. Clubs: Tavistock (N.J.) Country; St. James's; Atrium (N.Y.), Channel (N.J.).Lodge: Kiwanis (Haddonfield). Home: 45 Ocean Ave Apt 4-B Monmouth Beach NJ 07750 Office: Investors Ins Holding Corp 100 Metro Park S CN-007 Laurence Harbor NJ 08878

BROWN, MRS. GARDNER RUSSELL See GILLICE, SONDRA JUPIN

BROWN, GLENDA CAROL, insurance executive, small business owner; b. Jackson, Miss., June 30, 1949; d. Troy Snow and Bonnie Glenn (Gill) Brown Jr., A.A. in Radio and TV, Marjorie Webster Jr. Coll., 1969; B.A. in Radio and TV, U. Md., 1974; M.A. in Bus. Mgmt. and Supervision, Central Mich. U., 1975. Adminstrv. asst. Dept. Navy (NTDA), Washington, 1970-78; tech. writer, editor VSE Engring., Alexandria, Va., 1979; agt. Aetna Life Ins. Co., McLean, Va., 1979-84; gen. agt. Western Fidelity Ins. Co., Washington, 1985—; real estate agt. ERA House of Burgesses, Vienna, Va. Mem. NAFE, D.C. Assn. Life Underwriters, Profl. Ins. Agts., Arlington C. of C., No. Va. Bd. Realtors. Avocations: reading, piano, tennis, ice skating, phys. fitness. Home and Office: 7561 Vogels Way Springfield VA 22153

BROWN, G(LENN) WILLIAM, JR., lawyer; b. Waynesville, N.C., June 9, 1955; s. Glenn William Sr. and Evelyn Myralyn (Davis) B.; m. Amy Margaret Moss, Apr. 14, 1984. BS in Biology and Polit. Sci., MIT, 1977; JD, Duke U., 1980. Bar: N.Y. 1981. Assoc. Donovan Leisure Newton & Irvine, N.Y.C., 1980-84; assoc. Sidley & Austin, N.Y.C., 1984-87, ptnr., 1988—. Editorial bd. Duke Law Jour. Mem. ABA (sect. internat. law com., internat. fin. and comml. transactions, and pvt. internat. law. 1988—), Assn. of Bar of City of N.Y. (uniform state laws com. 1984-87). Democrat. Mem. Dutch Reform Ch. Home: 171 State St Brooklyn Heights NY 11201 Office: Sidley & Austin 875 Third Ave New York NY 10022

BROWN, H. W(ILLIAM), railroad company executive; b. Bryn Mawr, Pa., July 29, 1938; s. Howard W. and Viola (Vercoe) B.; m. Constance Forster, Mar. 7, 1964; children: Bradley J., Diana. B.S. in B.A., Bucknell U., 1960. C.P.A., Pa. Audit mgr. Price Waterhouse & Co., Phila., 1962-68; controller, ops. mgr. Bioren & Co., Phila., 1968-70; controller Ins. Co. N. Am., Phila., 1970-72; sr. v.p., chief fin. officer Investment Annuity, Inc., Valley Forge, Pa., 1972-78; v.p., treas. Consol. Rail Corp., Phila., 1978-86, sr. v.p. fin., chief fin. officer, 1986—; bd. dirs. Phila. Nat. Bank, Trailer Train Co. Served with U.S. Army, 1960-62. Mem. Fin. Execs. Inst., Am. Inst. C.P.A.s, Pa. Soc. C.P.A.s. Home: 4137 Jackson Dr Lafayette Hill PA 19444 Office: Consol Rail Corp 6 Penn Center Pla Rm 1806 Philadelphia PA 19103

BROWN, HARLAN JAMES, acquisition and industrial studies executive; b. Altoona, Pa., Dec. 16, 1933; s. Lindsey A. and E. Grace (Ackerman) B.; m. Christina L. Chapman, July 17, 1987; 1 child, Harlan James II. M in Engring., Colo. Sch. Mines, 1957; MBA, George Washington U., 1967. Field engr. Beckman Instruments, Arlington, Va., 1957-59; ptnr. Shaheen, Brown & Day, Denver, 1959-60; v.p. Nat. Engring. Service subs. NES, Inc., Washington, 1960-63; pres. NSC Internat., Washington, 1963-67; chmn. bd., chief exec. officer Harlan Brown & Co., Inc., McLean, Va., 1967—; seminar and video lectr. various corps. Mem. IEEE, Am. Soc. Metall. Engrs., Am. Chem. Soc., Am. Mgmt. Assn., Blue Key, Theta Tau, Sigma Delta Psi, Alpha Tau Omega. Methodist. Clubs: Regency Sport. Author: (with Mock and Shuckett) Financing for Growth, 1971, Discovring the Growth Niche, Chief Executives, 1982, Planning Review, 1985. Home: 1800 Old Meadow Rd McLean VA 22102 Office: Harlan Brown & Co Inc 6861 Elm St McLean VA 22101

BROWN, HAROLD, scientist, educator, corporate director, consultant, former secretary of defense; b. N.Y.C., Sept. 19, 1927; s. A.H. and Gertrude (Cohen) B.; m. Colene Dunning McDowell, Oct. 29, 1953; children: Deborah Ruth, Ellen Dunning. A.B., Columbia U., 1945, A.M., 1946, Ph.D. in Physics (Lydig fellow 1948-49), 1949. Research scientist Columbia U., 1945-50, lectr. physics, 1947-48; lectr. physics Stevens Inst. Tech., 1949-50; research scientist U. Calif., Berkeley, 1951-52, staff mem., group leader E.O. Lawrence Radiation Lab., 1952-60; dir. Lawrence Livermore (Calif.) Lab., 1960-61; dir. def. research and engring. Dept. Def., Washington, 1961-65; sec. Dept. Air Force, Washington, 1965-69; pres. Calif. Inst. Tech., Pasadena, 1969-77; disting. vis. prof. Sch. Advanced Internat. Studies Johns Hopkins U., Washington, 1981-84, chmn. Fgn. Policy Inst., 1984—; dir. AMAX, CBS, IBM, Philip Morris Inc., Cummins Engine Co., Synergen Inc.; mem. Polaris Steering Com., 1956-58; cons., mem. Air Force Sci. Adv. Bd., 1956-61, Pres.'s Sci. Adv. Com., 1958-61; sr. sci. adviser Conf. Discontinuance Nuclear Tests, 1958-59; U.S. del. SALT, Helsinki, Vienna and; Geneva, 1969-77; chmn. Tech. Assessment Adv. Council to U.S. Congress, 1974-77; mem. exec. com. Trilateral Commn., 1973-76. Author: Thinking About National Security: Defense and Foreign Policy in a Dangerous World, 1983. Decorated Medal of Freedom; named One of 10 Outstanding Young Men U.S. Jaycees, 1961; recipient Medal of Excellence Columbia U., 1963; Joseph C. Wilson award in internat. affairs, 1976; award for disting. contbns. to higher edn. Stony Brook Found., 1979. Mem. Nat. Acad. Engring., Am. Phys. Soc., Am. Acad. Arts and Scis., Nat. Acad. Scis., Council on Fgn. Relations, N.Y.C. (dir. 1983—), Phi Beta Kappa, Sigma Xi. Clubs: Bohemian (San Francisco); California (Los Angeles); Athenaeum (London). Office: Johns Hopkins U Fgn Policy Inst 1619 Massachusetts Ave NW Washington DC 20036

BROWN, HENRY BEDINGER RUST, financial management company executive; b. Pitts., Feb. 13, 1926; s. Stanley Noel and Elizabeth Fitzhugh (Rust) B.; m. Betsey Jean Smith, Mar. 27, 1954; children—Peter, Alexander, Elizabeth, Harriet. A.B., Harvard U., 1948. Asst. v.p. Citibank, N.Y.C., 1954-63; 2d v.p. Tchrs. Ins. & Annuity Assn., N.Y.C., 1963-68; chmn. Res. Fund, N.Y.C., 1970-83; pres. Depositors 1st Nat. Bank, N.Y.C., 1984—, Res. Mgmt. Co., Inc., Leesburg, Va., 1984—. Councilman Town of Westfield, N.J., 1982-84. Served with USNR, 1944-46.

BROWN, IRA BERNARD, data processing executive; b. N.Y.C., July 18, 1927; s. David and Ruth (Ehrlich) B.; m. Myra Dipkin, Oct. 31, 1954; children: Rene, Lori. BS, U.S. Mcht. Marine Acad., 1949; MS, Drexel U., 1959. Data processing mgr. Sperry Rand, Syosset, N.Y., 1962-66; corp. systems mgr. Loral Corp., Scarsdale, N.Y., 1966-68; chmn. bd., pres., chief exec. officer Brandon Systems Corp., Secaucus, N.J., 1968—. Mem. Assn. for Computing Machinery, Assn. for Systems Mgmt., C. of C. Clubs: Lake Mohawk Country; Sales Exec. of N.Y. Lodges: Compass 1019 F&AM. Home: 2000 Linwood Ave Apt 8V Fort Lee NJ 07024 also: 7 Oakwood Trail Lake Mohawk Sparta NJ 07871 Office: Brandon Systems Corp 1 Harmon Pla Secaucus NJ 07094

BROWN, JACK H., supermarkets company executive; b. San Bernardino, Calif., June 14, 1939 . Student, San Jose State U., UCLA. Vice pres. Sages Complete Markets, San Bernardino, 1960-71, Marsh Supermarkets, Yorktown, Ind., 1971-77; pres. Pantry Supermarkets, Pasadena, Calif., 1977-79; pres. mid-west div. Cullum Cos., Dallas, 1979-81; pres., chief exec. officer Stater Bros. Markets, Colton, Calif., 1981—; chmn. bd. dirs. Stater Bros. Inc., 1986—; dir. Life Savs. & Loan Assn., San Bernardino. Trustee, U. Redlands, Calif.; bd. dirs. Goodwill Industries of Inland Empire, San Bernardino; bd. councillors Calif. State U., San Bernardino. Served with USNR, 1958-60. Named Sagamore of the Wabash, Gov. Ind., 1978. Mem. Western Assn. Food Chains (v.p., bd. dirs., pres. 1987-88), Calif. Retailers Assn. (bd. dirs.), Food Mktg. Inst., So. Calif. Grocers Assn., Food Employers Council (bd. govs.). Republican. Presbyterian. Lodge: Elks. Office: Stater Bros Markets 21700 Barton Rd Colton CA 92324

BROWN, JAMES ALLEN, JR., chemist, microbiologist; b. Akron, Ohio, May 23, 1926; s. James Allen and Bessie Louise (Smart) B.; m. Lillie Mae Rice, Sept. 9, 1951. BS, U. Akron, 1949; postgrad., Ohio State U., 1951-52; MS, Kent State U., 1952; PhD, Howard U., 1968. Pub. health microbiologist Cleve. Pub. Health Dept., 1953-54; clin. microbiologist VA Hosp., Wilmington, Del., 1954-56; div. chief lab. VA Hosp., Indpls., 1956-63; research microbiologist Walter Reed Army Med. Ctr., Washington, 1963-67; supr. tech. info. specialist EPA Nat. Air Pollution Control Adminstrn., Washington, 1967-70; research scientist UniRoyal Chem, Inc., Naugatuck, Conn., 1970-77, Ford Motor Co, Dearborn, Mich., 1977—. Contbr. articles to sci. jours. Served with U.S. Army, 1944-46. Fellow Am. Acad. Microbiologists, Am. Pub. Health Assn., Am. Inst. Chemists; mem. Am. Chem. Soc., Nat. Orgn. Black Chemists and Chem. Engrs., N.Y. Acad. Scis. Democrat. Home: 29830 W 12 Mile Rd #301 Farmington Hills MI 48018 Office: Ford Motor Co 20000 Rotunda Dr Rm S-3198 PO Box 2053 Dearborn MI 48121

BROWN, JAMES CHANNING, engineering company executive; b. Spartanburg, S.C., Mar. 29, 1944; s. James Earl and Edna Lillian (Lavender) B.; m. Sharon Ann Huxhold, June 13, 1964; children: Jason Channing, Todd Christopher, Michelle Lynn. Grad., Fall's Coll., 1963. Supr. engring. services Memcor Co., Huntington, Ind., 1973-76; div. mgr. RDS, Grand Rapids, Mich., 1976-79; corp. pres. MidAm. Design Services, Ft. Wayne, Ind., 1979—; pres. Master Circuits, Inc., Kokomo, Ind., 1984—; pres. Inc. 500, 1987; adv. com. Ind. Vocat. Tech. Coll. Patentee in field. Served as sgt. U.S. Army, 1964-67, Vietnam. Mem. Soc. Mfg. Engrs., Inc. 500. Republican. Lodge: Shriners. Home: 9923 Neil Armstrong Ct Fort Wayne IN 46804 Office: MidAm Design Svcs Inc 10206 Lima Rd Fort Wayne IN 46818

BROWN, JAMES CREIGHTON, transportation executive; b. Evanston, Ill., Sept. 9, 1952; s. Walter Creighton and Jeanette (Snyder) B.; m. Anne Elizabeth Wicher, Nov. 26, 1976; children: Elizabeth, Christopher, Kimberly. BA in Psychobiology, U. Calif., Santa Cruz, 1974; postgrad., Menlo Sch. Bus. Adminstrn., Menlo Park, Calif., 1975-76. CPA, Calif., Oreg. Staff auditor Arthur Andersen & Co., San Francisco, 1976-79; internal control mgr. Georgia-Pacific Corp., Portland, Oreg., 1979-82; controller BRAE Corp., San Francisco, 1982-85, Am. President Spl. Commodities, Salinas, Calif., 1985—. Mem. Am. Inst. CPA's, Calif. Soc. CPA's. Republican. Episcopalian. Office: Am President Spl Commodities 955 Blanco Cir Ste #D Salinas CA 93901

BROWN, JAMES EARLE, tax manager, accountant; b. Marlin, Tex., Aug. 10, 1950; s. James Mitchell and Thelma Mae (Rhamy) B.; m. Cheri Lee Propp, Sept. 17, 1983. BBA, Tex. Tech. U., 1973. CPA, Tex. Tax acct. Placid Oil Co., Dallas, 1973-74, Frito-Lay, Inc., Dallas, 1974-76; tax acct. Dresser Industries, Inc., Dallas, 1976, internat. tax acct., 1976-79; sr. tax acct. The Western Co. of N. Am., Ft. Worth, 1979-80, mgr. state tax, 1980-81, mgr. fed. tax, 1981-82, asst. dir. taxes, 1982-83; tax mgr. Color Tile, Inc., Ft. Worth, 1983—. Mem. Tax Execs. Inst., Am. Inst. CPA's, Tex. Soc. CPA's, Sigma Nu. Republican. Methodist. Home: 4540 Saldana Dr Fort Worth TX 76133 Office: Color Tile Inc 515 Houston St Fort Worth TX 76102

BROWN, JAMES FREDERICK, food service executive; b. St. Louis, Apr. 20, 1941; s. Lester Belden and Cecilia (Best) B.; m. Sue Anne Blessing, June 29, 1963; children: Stephanie, Kristen, Justin. BS, Miami U., Oxford, Ohio, 1963; MBA, UCLA, 1964. Security analyst Ohio Co., Columbus, 1964-66; exec. v.p. Sybra, Inc., Grand Blanc, Mich., 1966-70; v.p. fin. G L Enterprises, Inc., Milw., 1970-74; chmn., chief exec. officer Bankers Mortgage Corp., St. Paul, 1974-81, Hart Ski Mfg. Co., Inc., St. Paul, 1977-81; sr. v.p., treas. Economy Co., Oklahoma City, 1981-84; pres., chmn., chief exec. officer Bankers Inter-Funding Co., Inc., St. Paul, 1985—; chmn., chief exec. officer 1 Potato 2, Inc., Mpls., 1986—; cons. Am. Edn. Computer, Inc., Palo Alto; cons. Goldeneye Products, Inc., Mpls., 1985—, also bd. dirs.; bd. dirs. Bankers Restaurants, Inc., Mpls. Mem. dean's coun. UCLA Grad. Sch. Mgmt., Sci. Mus. Minn. Mem. St. Paul Athletic Club. Republican. Presbyterian. Home: 11 Lost Rock Ln North Oaks MN 55127 Office: 1 Potato 2 Inc 5640 International Pkwy Minneapolis MN 55428

BROWN, JAMES THOMPSON, JR., computer information scientist; b. Orange, N.J., Jan. 3, 1935; s. James Thompson and Marjorie (Hale) B.; m. Alice Beasley, Oct. 3, 1959; children—Kathryn, James. B.M.E., Cornell U., 1957; M.S., Stanford U., 1964. Applied sci. rep. IBM Corp., Schenectady, N.Y., 1957-59, corp. staff mem., White Plains, N.Y., 1960-68; cons. Case & Co., Stamford, Conn., 1969-74, dir., 1975-83, pres., 1983-84; pres. Tom Brown & Co., Wilton, Conn., 1985—. Mem. Internat. Assn. Chain Stores (adviser, speaker 1971—), Nat. Grocers Assn. (adviser 1983—), Am. Inst. Indsl. Engrs. (sr. mem.), Inst. of Mgmt. Scis. Republican. Home: 119 Middlebrook Farm Rd Wilton CT 06897 Office: Tom Brown & Co PO Box 431 Wilton CT 06897

BROWN, JAMES TYLER, retired investment consultant; b. Rockville, Ind., Nov. 8, 1904; s. Charles John and Grace Mae (LeFevre) B.; m. Faith Saxton Grant, Nov. 25, 1967. A.B., De Pauw U., 1926; M.B.A., Harvard U., 1928; grad. Rutgers U. Sch. Banking, 1949. Asst. prof. U. Oreg., Eugene, 1928-29; mem. investment research dept. Wood Struthers & Co., N.Y.C., 1930-36; mgr. research dept. Shields & Co., N.Y.C., 1936-37; mem. investment dept. Mellon Securities Corp., Pitts., 1938-42; v.p. Mellon Nat. Bank, Pitts., 1946-69. Trustee DePauw U., Greencastle, Ind., 1955-74; trustee, treas. St. Barnabas, Inc., Gibsonia, Pa., 1974—. Served to col. U.S. Army, 1942-45. Republican. Presbyterian. Clubs: Univ. (Pitts.), Harvard Yale Princeton; Univ. (Winter Park, Fla.), Harvard.

BROWN, JERRY GLENN, manufacturing company executive; b. Birch Tree, Mo., Aug. 19, 1933; s. Glenn Oliver and Alma Pearl (Brown) B.; m. Shirleen Wolfe, Oct. 16, 1953; 1 dau., Theresa Ann. B.S., S.W. Mo. State U., Springfield, 1953; postgrad., St. Louis U., 1956-58. With McDonnell Douglas Corp., St. Louis, 1956—; v.p. McDonnell Douglas Corp., 1972—, treas., 1975—, chief fin. officer, 1984—; dir. McDonnell Douglas Fin. Corp. Pres. Delmar Baptist Ch. Endowment Fund; trustee Mo. Baptist Hosp.; bd. dirs. United Way. Served with AUS, 1954-56. Home: 13325 Crossland Saint Louis MO 63131 Office: McDonnell Douglas Corp PO Box 516 Saint Louis MO 63166

BROWN, JOHN ARTHUR, financial planner; b. Atmore, Ala., Mar. 20, 1941; s. James David and Mary Frances (Vickery) B. BS, Fla. State U., 1965. Cert. fin. planner. Area sales mgr. CIBA/Geigy, Summit, N.J., 1967-84; fin. planner IDS/Am. Express, Mpls., 1984-86; owner, mgr. John Brown Fin. Planning, Fairhope, Ala., 1986—. Bd. dirs. Contact Mobile, Ala., 1984, 85, others. Mem. Internat. Assn. Fin. Planning (v.p. 1987-88, pres. 1988—), Nat. Ctr. for Fin. Edn., Sertoma (bd. dirs.). Republican. Methodist. Office: John Brown Fin Planning 305 N Section St Fairhope AL 36532

BROWN, JOHN FRED, steel company executive; b. Floydada, Tex., May 20, 1941; s. Rex. R. Brown and Martha L. (McCleskey) Mayfield; m. Karolyn Kay Robertson, July 31, 1960; children: John Robert, Jonathan David, William Charles. BSME, U. Wis., 1968; MBA, Tex. Tech U., 1978. Staff engr. Continental Oil Co., Houston, 1971-73; sr. buyer Continental Oil Co., Lake Charles, La., 1973-74; v.p. WedgeCor, Inc., Billings, Mont., 1974-76; chmn., chief exec. officer Tri-Steel Structures, Inc., Denton, Tex., 1976-87, Dallas, 1987—; chmn., chief exec. officer Hawk Industries, Inc., Denton, 1978—. Contbg. author: Steel Homes, 1985. Served with U.S. Army, 1968-69, Vietnam. Decorated Bronze Star. Mem. Ctr. for Entrepreneurial Mgmt. (CEO Club). Mem. Ch. of Christ. Club: Denton Country. Home: Rte 1 PO Box 362E Denton TX 76201 Office: Tri-Steel Structures Inc 5800 Campus Circle in Las Colinas Irving TX 75063

BROWN, JOHN LOTT, educator; b. Phila., Dec. 3, 1924; s. John Lott and Carolyn Emma (Francis) B.; m. Catharine Hertfelder, June 11, 1948; children: Patricia Carolyn, Judith Elliott, Anderson Graham, Barbara Smith. B.S. in Elec. Engring, Worcester (Mass.) Poly. Inst., 1945, D.Sc. (hon.), 1984; M.A., Temple U., 1949; Ph.D., Columbia U., 1952. Personnel tng. and personnel mgr. Olney foundry Link-Belt Co., Phila., 1948-50; tech. dir. air force contract, dept. psychology Columbia U., 1952-54; head psychology div., aviation med. lab. Naval Air Devel. Center, Johnsville, Pa., 1954-59; dir. grad. tng. program physiology 1962-65; asst., then asso. prof. physiology U. Pa. Med. Sch., 1955-65; prof. physiology and psychology Kans. State U., 1965-69; dean Grad. Sch., 1965-66, v.p. acad. affairs, 1966-69; prof. optics and psychology, dir. center visual sci. U. Rochester, N.Y., 1969-78; pres., prof. psychology, physiology and opthalmology U. South Fla., Tampa, 1978-88, Regents prof., 1988—, pres. emeritus, 1988—; chmn. com. vision NRC-Nat. Acad. Scis., 1965-70; chmn. vision research program com. Nat. Eye Inst., 1975-78; trustee Worcester Poly. Inst., 1970-83, mem. alumni council, 1975-76; trustee Illuminating Engring. Research Inst., 1974-79; mem. U.S. nat. com. Internat. Commn. Optics, 1977; bd. dirs. Pioneer Bank, Fla., Am. Ship Bldg. Co. Author chpts. in books, also monographs, articles, 1953—; cons. editor: Perception and Psychophysics, 1972—; editorial adv. bd.: Vision Research, 1971-77. Bd. dirs. Pub. Broadcasting Service, 1980-83, Mid-Am. Inst. Profl. Devel., 1980-82, Fla. Gulf Symphony, 1979-81, Tampa Gen. Hosp. Found., 1980-81; mem. Fla. Council 100, 1978-88; mem. corp. bd. Tampa Performing Arts Hall, 1980-88; chmn. Tampa Bay Area Research and Devel. Authority, 1979-86, Tampa Bay Area Fgn. Affairs Com., 1979—; chmn. bd. dirs. H. Lee Moffitt Cancer Ctr. and Research Inst., 1984-88. Served with USNR, 1943-46. Recipient Research Career Devel. award NIH, 1961-62, Robert Goddard award Worcester Poly. Inst., 1969; sr. research fellow USPHS, 1959-61; grantee NIH; grantee NSF; grantee Office Naval Research; grantee Nat. Eye Inst.; grantee NIMH; grantee NASA. Fellow Optical Soc. Am. (exec. council Rochester chpt. 1975-76, asso. editor jour. 1972-77), Am. Psychol. Assn., AAAS; mem. Assn Research Vision and Ophthalmology (pres. 1978), Soc. Neurosci., Psychonomic Soc., Fla. Assn. Colls. and Univs. (pres. 1988—), Sigma Xi, Tau Beta Pi, Psi Chi, Phi Eta Sigma, Phi Kappa Phi, Omicron Delta Kappa, Phi Gamma Delta. Quaker. Home: 1405 Julie Lagoon Lutz FL 33549 Office: Univ South Fla 4202 Fowler Ave Tampa FL 33620-6150

BROWN, JOHN M., gas company executive; b. Sproul, Pa., Nov. 25, 1924; s. John Brown; m. Wanda D. Brown, June 4, 1949; children: Linda JoAnn Brown Anderson, Patricia Ann. BSME, W.Va. U., 1949. Mgmt. trainee Pa. Gas Co., Erie, 1949-53; foreman, dist. engr. Warren, Pa., 1953-55; asst. supt. 1955-64, chief engr., 1964-66, v.p., 1966-67, sr. v.p., 1967-72, pres., 1972-74; exec. v.p. Nat. Fuel Gas Distbn., Buffalo, N.Y., 1974; pres. Nat. Fuel Gas Distbn., Buffalo, 1978, pres., chief exec. officer, 1979—; sr. v.p. Nat. Fuel Gas Co., Buffalo, 1974-76, exec. v.p., 1976; v.p. Seneca Resources Corp., Buffalo, 1976-77; sr. v.p. Nat. Fuel Gas Supply Corp., Buffalo, 1977-78, exec. v.p., 1978; v.p. Penn-York Energy Corp., Buffalo, 1978-79; bd. dirs. N.Y. State Com. for Jobs and Energy Independence, N.Y.C., 1st Nat. Bank Pa., Erie, Erie County Indsl. Devel. Corp., Buffalo. C0-chmn. Buffalo-Erie County Labor-Mgmt. Council, 1984—; bd. dirs. Blue Cross We. N.Y., Buffalo, 1982—. Served with USN, 1943-46, PTO. Mem. Am. Gas Assn., Pa. Gas Assn. (bd. dirs.), NAM (energy com.), N.Y. Gas Group (exec. com.), Onsite Fuel Cell Users Group (bd. dirs.). Republican. Lutheran. Clubs: Buffalo; Orchard Park Country (N.Y.). Office: Nat Fuel Gas Distbn Corp 10 Lafayette Sq Buffalo NY 14203 also: Nat Fuel Gas Co 30 Rockefeller Pla New York NY 10112

BROWN, JOHN ROBERT, manufacturing company executive; b. Duncombe, Iowa, Mar. 20, 1935; s. John William and Helen Sue (Hoyt) B.; m. Rosemary Louise Ohnemus, Sept. 3, 1955; children: Julie, Kathryn, John, Margaret, Timothy, Maureen, Sheila, Bridget. BSME, U. Notre Dame, 1956. Plant mgr. Dodge div. Reliance Electric Co., Rogersville, Ind., 1970-74; v.p. mfg. Campbell-Hausfeld div. Scott Fetzer Co., Harrison, Ohio, 1974-76; asst. v.p. prodn. Robroy Industries, Inc., Verona, Pa., 1976-84, v.p. prodn., 1984-85, v.p. ops., 1985—; mfg. cons., adv. dir. Morristown (Tenn.) Coll. Contbr. articles to profl. jours. Bd. dirs. PTA, So. Bend, Ind., 1968-69; 73-74; chmn. Hawkins County United Fund, Rogersville, Tenn.; pres. St. Catherine's Parish Council, Wildwood, Pa., 1986. Republican. Roman Catholic. Club: Notre Dame (Pitts.). Lodge: Elks. Home: 1009 Arborwood Dr Gibsonia PA 15044 Office: Robroy Inds Inc River Rd Verona PA 15147

BROWN, JOSEPH DAVID, business educator, marketing executive; b. Columbus, Ohio, Dec. 19, 1937; s. William Elvin and Jessie Mae (Wrightsel) B.; m. Marcia Lee Hahn, June 10, 1964; children—Rhonda, Jeffrey, Scott, Douglas. BS, Ohio State U., 1959, MS, 1960, PhD, 1964. Asst. prof. mktg. U. Ga., 1963-68; assoc. prof. dept. mktg. Ball State U., Muncie, Ind., 1963-70, dir., Bur. Bus. Research, 1970-85, prof. mktg., 1973—; pres. Brown & Assocs., Inc., Muncie, 1980—; research dir. Bonsib, Inc., Ft. Wayne, Ind., 1980—; dir. City Machine Tool & Die Co., Muncie. Author: Strategic Marketing for Music Educators, 1985; contbr. articles to profl. jours. Elder Presbyterian Ch.; pres. bd. dirs. Jr. Achievement-Ind., Muncie, 1977-78; pres. Ind. Redevel. Commn., Muncie, 1970-78. Recipient Outstanding Research award Sears and Roebuck Found. U. Ga. Mem. Assn. for Univ. Bus. and Econ. Research, Am. Mktg. Assn., Ind. Econ. Forum, Eastern Ind. Econs. Club. Avocations: reading golf, travel. Home: 2208 Pineview Dr Muncie IN 47300 Office: Ball State U Muncie IN 47306

BROWN, JOSEPH LEONARD, manufacturing executive; b. Americus, Ga., Jan. 21, 1906; s. Lucian and Minnie (Horton) B.; m. Eleanor Ruth Gallagher, Feb. 22, 1936; children: Neil Norbert, Wayne Lucian. BS in Gen. Engring., Ga. Inst. Tech., 1928, ME, 1935. Student engr. Stone & Webster Inc., Boston, 1928-29; gas engr. Stone & Webster Inc., N.Y.C., 1935-36; plant engr. Haverhill (Mass.) Gas Light Co., 1929-35; pres. Brown Equipment & Mfg. Co., Charlotte, N.C., 1936-43; project engr. Liberty Aircraft Products, Farmingdale, N.Y., 1943-46; pres., chmn. bd. Brown Truck & Trailer Mfg. Co., Charlotte, 1946-87, Brown Equipment Mfg. Co., Charlotte, 1987—. Patentee truck clearance lamp, truck axle aligning tool, floor truck engagement mechanism. Mem. Charlotte Engrs. (v.p. 1947-50). Republican. Methodist. Home: 1530 Lilac Rd Charlotte NC 28209 Office: Brown Equipment Mfg Co PO Box 32214 Charlotte NC 28232

BROWN, JOSEPH SIMON, JR., food company executive; b. Jeanerette, La., June 1, 1907; s. Joseph Simon and Septima Alexandrine (Fortier) B.; m. Mary Sylvia Sandoz, June 18, 1930; children: Gordon Sandoz, Norman Sandoz, Joseph Simon III, Sylvia Sandoz Brown Putnam. Grad., St. Peter's Coll., New Iberia, La., 1924. Ptnr., founder J.S. Brown & Son, New Iberia, La., 1926-56; founding ptnr., chmn. bd. Bruce Foods Corp., New Iberia, La., 1956—; founder, dir., v.p. City Bank Trust Co., New Iberia, La., 1958—. Recipient award of Appreciation, City Bank and Trust Co. of New Iberia, 1983. Mem. New Iberia C. of C., Nat. Food Processors Assn., La. Yam Council, Internat. Trade Mart., World Trad Ctrs. Assn. Democrat. Roman Catholic. Clubs: The Plimsoll div. Internat. Trade Mart (New Orleans), World Trade Ctr., Internat. House of New Orleans. Home: 924 E Main St New Iberia LA 70560 Office: PO Box 1030 New Iberia LA 70561-1030

BROWN, J(OSEPH) THEODORE, software company consultant; b. Cleve., July 10, 1924; s. Joseph Parker and Lulu Jean (Raney) B.; m. Garnett Marie Stout, Sept. 15, 1945; children: Judith M. Yeager, Theresa J. Norwark, Victoria E. Rush, Anne Catherine Brown. BChemE, U. Dayton, 1945; postgrad., U. Cin., 1945-47. Chemist NCR Corp., Dayton, Ohio, 1947-49, lab. mgr., 1949-73; rsch. chemist bus. forms div. NCR Corp., Miamisburg, Ohio, 1973-80, lab. mgr., 1980-87; cons. NCR Corp., Dayton, 1987—; instr. U. Dayton, 1952-67. Mem. Am. Chem. Soc. (sec. Dayton sect. 1953, 71-72, chmn. 1973), ASTM, Math. Assn. Am., Cobrentz Soc. Home and Office: 815 Princewood Ave Dayton OH 45429

BROWN, KAREN CHRISTINE, healthcare company executive, accountant; b. Galesburg, Ill., Mar. 7, 1951; d. Ernest Vail and Inez Ruth (Schollerman) Stevenson; children: Collin Weston Summers, Christopher Winfield Summers. BS in Acctg. summa cum laude, Ill. State U., 1981. CPA, Ill.; cert. mgmt. acct. Staff acct. I, Henning, Strouse, Jordan, CPA's, Bloomington, Ill., 1982-83, staff acct. II, 1983-84; asst. v.p. fin. Heritage Enterprises, Inc., Bloomington, 1985-86, v.p. fin., 1986—. Deacon Univ. Christian Ch., Normal, Ill., 1983-85; bd. dirs. McLean County Ctr. for Human Svcs., Bloomington, 1986—, treas., 1987—. Mem. AICPA, Ill. CPA Soc. (long term care com. 1985—), Ill. Health Care Assn. (com. mem. 1987—). Home: 1305 Chadwick Dr Normal IL 61761 Office: Heritage Enterprises Inc 115 W Jefferson St Bloomington IL 61701

BROWN, KENNETH CHARLES, business executive; b. Ft. Collins, Colo., July 9, 1952; s. Charles Calvin and Barbara Ann (Brookhart) B.; m. Victoria Marie Martin, July 27, 1984; children: Bryson John Kenneth, Charles Brookhart, Theodore McFarlane. BSME, Cornell U., 1974; MA in Engring. Sci. and Econs., Oxford U., Eng., 1977. Registered profl. engr., Colo. Assoc. engr. Stone & Webster Engring. Corp., Boston, 1974-75; with Solar Energy Rsch. Inst., Golden, Colo., 1977-80, sr. engr., 1979-80, mgr., 1980; mgr. Sci. Applications Internat., Golden, 1980-82; mgr. Price Waterhouse, Denver, 1982-84, sr. mgr., 1984; v.p. Inspiration Resources Corp., N.Y.C., 1985—. Contbr. chpts. to books. Mem. Cornell U. Council, 1979-83, Rhodes Scholarship Selection Com., Topka, Mpls., 1978-84. Recipient World Rowing Championship Gold medal, Fedn. Internat. Soc. d'Aviron, 1974; Rhodes scholar, 1975. Mem. Internat. Assn. Energy Economists, The Planning Forum, Cornell Soc. Engrs., Cornell Club. Republican. Episcopalian. Home: 215 Old Kings Hwy N Darien CT 06820 Office: Inspiration Resources Corp 250 Park Ave New York NY 10177

BROWN, KENNETH GEORGE, banker; b. London, Aug. 14, 1936; came to U.S., 1983; s. George Henry and Amelia (French) B.; m. Rosemary Tozler, May 7, 1960 (div. 1981); children: Matthew Stuart, Simon James; m. Elisabeth May Borchardt, Apr. 10, 1983. From various positions to gen. mgr. Midland Bank & co., London, 1952-83; pres., chief exec. officer Midland Internat. Trade Services, N.Y.C., 1983-88; mng. dir. Midland Montagu, N.Y.C., 1988—. Mem. Chartered Inst. of Bankers, Inst. of Petroleum, Brit. Am. C. of C. (bd. dirs. 1987—), Scarsdale Golf Club, Boardroom Club. Office: Midland Montagu 560 Lexington Ave New York NY 10022

BROWN, KEVIN MICHAEL, treasurer; b. Morristown, N.J., June 15, 1948; s. Michael Xavier and Jean Margaret (McCormack) B.; m. Patricia Lynn Macce, Nov. 16, 1975; children: Meredith Lynn, Michael Kevin. BS in Bus. Mgmt., Monmouth Coll., 1971. Sales mgr. ISD, Inc., Union, N.J., 1971-76; dir. profit share plan, trustee Brown Dist. Corp., Fairfield, N.J., 1981—; mng. ptnr. Brown Gypsum Co., Fairfield, 1985—, 55 Laura Equities, Morristown, 1987—; sec, treas. Brown Distbg. Corp., Fairfield, 1976—, bd. dirs. Active in Peck Sch. PTA, Morristown, Assumption Sch. PTA, Morristown, Blackberry Hills Property Owners Assn., Morristown. Mem. Ceiling and Interior Systems Contractor Assn., Drywall and Interior Systems Contractor Assn., Bldg. Contractors Assn. of N.J., Porsche Club, Spring Brook Country Club, Basking Ridge Golf Club. Roman Catholic. Home:

Laura Ln Morristown NJ 07960 Office: Brown Distbg Corp 18 Commerce Rd Fairfield NJ 07006

BROWN, LARITA EARLY DAWN, publisher, computer and educational products manufacturing executive; b. Santa Monica, Calif., Dec. 21, 1937; d. Robert Walter and Lela Shirley (Sims) B. AA, Santa Monica City Coll., 1956; BA, Los Angeles State U., 1973; D (hon.), Boston U., 1977; Masters, LaSalle U., postgrad. Tchr. parochial sch. Gardena, Calif., 1968-70; supr. Early Childhood programs/tchr. Los Angeles City Schs.-Headstart Program, 1970-72; project asst. Mayor's Office Employment and Job Devel., Los Angeles, 1972-76; community services specialist U.S. Dept. Commerce, Washington, 1976-81; owner, founder N and Out Publishing Co., Richardson, Tex., 1984—; dir. tutorial programs resource ctrs.; cons. human resources, Dallas area, 1985—; contractor Reading Is Fundamental assn., 1984; robot programmer; computer scis. specialist, cons.; founder, dir. Skooter Sam Ednl. Software Co., Dallas; founder Electronics Tech. Consortium; founder (pvt. sch.) Skooter Sam New Age Space Sch. Author: Ginalyn's Surprise, 1984, Skooter Sam in Texas, 1985, Skooter Sam Series, Queens/Kings of African Heritage, African American Inventors, Skooter Sam: Key to the Future, others; patentee numerous childrens' computer products. Active Dallas PTA Council; supr. various polit. campaigns, Calif. and Tex., 1970—; advisor youth and coll. student div. NAACP, 1981-82; media cons. Nat. Womens Polit. Caucus, Hollywood, Calif., 1976. Recipient trophy from Los Angeles County Community Colls., 1980, Service award U. So. Calif., 1970, Dallas Kiwanis Clubs, 1984, Silver Poet award, 1986, Sesquicentennial Tex. Logo award, 1986, Gold Seal award; named hon. citizen. Mem. Anthropol. Assn. Am., Phi Beta Alpha Gamma. Methodist. Office: N & Out Pub-Mfg PO Box 2712 Richardson TX 75083

BROWN, LISA ANN, portfolio manager; b. Reading, Pa., Aug. 30, 1956; d. Franklin George And Phyllis Mary (Fox) B.; m. John Michael Millet, Aug. 8, 1981 (div. Feb. 1984). BS in Econs., U. Pa., 1978; MBA with honors, N.Y.U., 1981. Mktg. rep. NCR Corp., Ft. Washington, Pa., 1978-79; dealer sales rep. and analyst Exxon Co. USA, Linden, N.J., 1981-84; coord. bank relations Pennzoil Co., Houston, 1984-86; mgr. portfolio First Union Corp., Charlotte, N.C., 1986—; ptnr. Options Trading Co., Houston, 1984-86. Fundraiser Am. Heart Assn., Houston, 1985. Recipient Exxon Excellence award, 1982. Mem. N.C. Bond Club, Wharton Alumni Assn. (sec. 1985-86), Wharton Women's Assn., Beta Gamma Sigma, Alpha Mu Alpha. Home: 3825 Selwyn Ave Charlotte NC 28209 Office: First Union Corp One First Union Ctr FNDS DC-8-0600 Charlotte NC 28288-0600

BROWN, LLOYD GEORGE, oil company executive; b. Falmouth, Trelawny, Jamaica, Feb. 25, 1944; s. Benjamin Louis and Rosa Maud (McCook) B.; m. Joanna Agatha Nyack, July 4, 1970; children: Donovan George, Keena Monique. Diploma in agr., Jamaica Sch. Agr., Spanish Town, 1965; BS, Tuskegee (Ala.) Inst., 1969; MBA, Columbia U., 1971. Citrus officer Citrus Growers Assn. Ltd., Kingston, Jamaica, 1965-67; budget officer CUNY, 1971-72; mkt. planning mgr. Massey-Ferguson, Inc., Des Moines, 1972-73; indsl. sales rep. Esso Standard Oil SA Ltd., Kingston, 1973-74, asst. to sales mgr., 1974-76; sales coordinator Esso West Indies Ltd., Kingston, 1976-77, refinery coordinator, 1977-78, econ. planning adv., 1978-82; econ. planning adv. Petrojam Ltd., Kingston, 1982-88; mgr. Petroleum Co. of Jamaica Ltd., Kingston, 1989—; cons. Dimpex Assocs., Inc., N.Y.C., 1971, MBA Mgmt. Cons., Inc., N.Y.C., 1970-71. Mem. Kay Kourt Assn. (pres. 1983—). Anglican. Lodges: Rotary (com. chmn.), Masons. Office: Petroleum Co Jamaica, 96 Marcus Garvey Dr, PO Box 241, Kingston Jamaica

BROWN, LOIS HEFFINGTON, health facility administrator; b. Little Rock, Mar. 28, 1940; d. Carl Otis and Opal (Shock) Heffington; M. Ivy Roy Brown, June 21, 1984; children: Carletta Jo Rice, Roby Lynn Rice, Pherby Allison Graham, Phelan Missy Graham. Student, Guilford Tech. Community Coll., Jamestown, N.C., 1974-75, 77, 80. Cert. hearing aid audiologist, specialist. Sec. Berger Enterprises, West Memphis, Ark., 1962-65; office mgr. Beltone Hearing Care Ctr., Greensboro, N.C., 1975-81; owner Hearing Care Ctr., Cullman, Ala. 1982-85, Miracle-Ear Ctr., Cullman, Decatur, Fultondale, Jasper and Birmingham, Ala., 1985-87; pres. L&I Corp., Cullman, Decatur, Fultondale, Jasper and Birmingham, 1987—. Gov.-appointed Ala. Bd. Hearing. Mem. Nat. Hearing Aid Soc., Ala. Hearing Aid Dealers Assn. (sec. 1984-86, v.p. 1986-88, bd. dirs. 1988—), Women of the Moose. Republican. Baptist. Home: Rte 1 PO Box 113A Danville AL 35619 Office: L&I Corp 2109 A Danville Rd SW Decatur AL 35601

BROWN, MARK TERRILL, hotel executive, electronics executive; b. Dodge City, Kans., June 21, 1953; s. Maynard Virgil and Evelyn Christina (Lietzan) B.; m. Donna Rae Seibel, June 11, 1977; children: Amanda Marie, Jennifer Lee. Student, St. Mary of the Plains Coll., 1971-72, Colo. U., 1988—. Owner War Eagle Jewelers, Liberal, Kans. and Estes Park, Colo., 1967—; gen. mgr. Moreno Tewahay Inc., Estes Park, 1979-88, treas., 1988—; pres. Hobit Industries, Estes Park, 1985—; v.p. The Estes Park Trolley Corp., 1987—; gov. Best Western Internat., 1985—; bd. dirs. Colo. Connections, Boulder. Inventor automatic telephone quotation system, Hobit 2000, 1985. Planning commr. Town of Estes Park, 1988—, trustee 1984-88; bd. dirs. Estes Park C. of C., 1983-84; commr. econ. devel. Larimer County, 1988—; bd. dirs. Internat. Aspenfest, pres. 1981-83. Mem. Am. Hotel & Motel Assn., Colo. Wyo. Hotel & Motel Assn., Estes Park Accomodations Assn. (pres. 1983-84). Republican. Roman Catholic. Lodge: Elks. Office: Hobit Industries PO Box 282 Estes Park CO 80517

BROWN, MELVIN F., corporate executive; b. Carlinville, Ill., June 4, 1935; s. Ben and Selma (Frommel) B.; m. Jacqueline Sue Hirsch, Sept. 2, 1962 (dec.); children: Benjamin Andrew, Mark Steven. A.B., Washington U., 1957, J.D., 1961. Bar: Mo. bar 1961. Pvt. practice St. Louis, 1961-62; asst. to gen. counsel Union Elec. Co., St. Louis, 1962-65; sec., atty. ITT Aetna Corp., St. Louis, 1965-72; v.p., gen. counsel ITT Aetna Corp., 1972; also dir.; corp. sec., gen. counsel ITT Financial Corp., 1974-77, exec. v.p., 1977—; now also pres. ITT Comml. Fin. Corp., also dir.; Dir. Civic Employment Corp., 1970—, Medicine Shoppe Internat.; mem. Interracial Conf. Bus. Opportunities, 1969—. Mem. Mo. Commn. Democratic Party Constn. By-laws and Party Structure, 1969-70, Mo. Dem. Platform Com., 1966, 68; mem. Bd. Adjustment City of Clayton, Mo., 1974—; Chmn. St. Louis chpt. Am. Jewish Com., 1968—; mem. funding council Suzuki Automotive Found. for Life. Served to capt. AUS, 1957-64; mem. Res. Hon. col. Mo. Gov.'s staff. Mem. Bar Assn. Met. St. Louis (pres. young lawyers sect. 1965-66), Mo. Bar Assn. Office: ITT Comml Fin Corp 8251 Maryland Ave Clayton MO 63105

BROWN, MERRILL MARK, publishing executive, corporate planner; b. Phila., Aug. 2, 1952; s. Fred R. and Gertrude (Katz) B.; m. Barbara S. Kappalman, May 25, 1980; children: Jessica, Rachel. BA in Polit. Sci., Washington U., St. Louis, 1974. Reporter Media Gen. News, Winston-Salem, N.C., 1974-75; Washington corr. Media Gen. News, 1975-78; fin. writer Washington Star, 1978-79; fin. writer Washington Post, 1979-82, N.Y. corr., 1982-84; dir. bus. devel. Washington Post Co., 1984-85; exec. editor Channels Mag., N.Y.C., 1985-87, editor, 1987—. Contbr. World Book Year Book, 1982-86; free-lance writer. Office: Channels Mag 19 W 44th New York NY 10036

BROWN, MICHAEL STEVEN, healthcare communications consultant; b. Columbus, Ohio, Oct. 20, 1950; s. David Bernard and Sally (Smigelsky) B.; m. Jane Ellen Klein, Sept. 11, 1983; children: Elizabeth S., Zachary A., Emily F., Abigail I. BS in Microbiology, Ohil State U., 1972; MA in Edn. Communications, Ohio State U., 1973. Writer, dir. film prodn. unit Iowa State U., Ames, 1973-75; media coord. Iowa State Ctr., 1975-77; dir. Ednl. Med. Ctr. Tufts-New Eng. Media Ctr., Boston, 1977-83; v.p. programming The Am. Network, Milw., 1983; pres. Telehealth Assocs., Needham, Mass., 1983-89; dir. edn. & tng. svcs. Granada Hosp. Group, Inc., Burlington, Mass., 1989—; instr. dept. community medicine Tufts U., Boston, 1981; pres. Boston Healthcare Cable Consortium, 1981-83. Editor, pub. profl. directories and market rsch. reports. Bd. overseers Boston Community Access and Programming Found., 1981-83. Mem. Assn. Biomed. Communications Dirs. (treas. 1981-83), Health Scis. Communications Assn. (bd. dirs. 1980-81), Pharm. Advt. Coun. Home: 11 Willow St Needham MA 02192 Office: Granada Hosp Group Inc 21 B St Burlington MA 01803

BROWN, NORMAN AMES, academic adminisrator; b. Seattle, Dec. 2, 1944; s. Gordon Eldridge and Barbara (Fleming) B.; m. Doris E. Fillingame, Sept. 4, 1964 (div.); children: Jefferson Alec, Nicole Leslie; m. Judy Kathleen Gokel, July 13, 1980. BA, Wash. State U., 1966; MA, George Washington U., D.C., 1967; DBA, George Washington U., 1969; JD, Georgetown U., 1969. Bar: Calif., 1985. Asst. to v.p. Gen. Mills, Inc., Mpls., 1969-72; mktg. mgr. Bethlehem Steel COrp., Nashville, 1972-76; dir. mktg. Miles Labs., Berkeley, Calif., 1976-83; licensing assoc. U. Calif., Berkeley, 1984-86; dir. tech. tranfer U. Utah, Salt Lake City, 1986—; pres. Innovation Dynamics, Oakland, 1976-86; cons. in field; bd. dirs. Portable Med. Labs. Inc., San Diego. Mem. Calif. Bar Assn., Licening Execs. Soc., Soc. U Patent Adminstr. (edn. com.), Mountain West Venture Capital Assn. Office: U Utah Tech Tranfer Office Salt Lake City UT 84108

BROWN, NORMAN JAMES, financial manager; b. Concord, N.H., May 12, 1942; s. Gilman D. and Katherine (Tucker) B.; m. Catherine Murphy, Sept. 17, 1983. BBS cum laude, N.H. Coll., 1968. CPA, Tenn. Acct. Peat Marwick Mitchell & Co., Portland, Me., 1968-69; audit mgr. Internal Audit Service div. VA, Washington, 1969-77; fin. mgr. regional office VA, Nashville, 1980—; supr. auditor Office Inspector Gen., Austin, Tex., 1977-80. With USAF, 1960-64. Mem. Assn. Govtl. Accts., Mid. Tenn. Fed. Exec. Assn., Moose. Republican. Reorganized Ch. of Jesus Christ of Latter-day Saints. Home: PO Box 22604 Nashville TN 37202 Office: VA Regional Office 110 9th Ave S Nashville TN 37203

BROWN, NORMAN WESLEY, advertising agency executive; b. Columbus, Ohio, Jan. 27, 1931; s. Leonard and Alvena (Folker) B.; m. Blanche; children—Pamela, Kendall; m. Lynn Godfrey, Jan. 3, 1980; children—Justin Godfrey, Brendan Godfrey. B.A., Ohio State U., 1953; M.B.A., Harvard U., 1958. Account exec. Foote, Cone & Belding, Los Angeles, 1959-63, account supt., 1963-73, gen. mgr., 1973-79; gen. mgr. Foote, Cone & Belding, Chgo., 1979-81, pres., from 1981, chief exec. officer, 1982—, chmn.; chmn. bd., chief exec. officer, dir. Foote, Cone & Belding Communications Inc., Chgo. Mem. bus. adv. council Chgo. Urban League, 1983—; bd. govs. Sch. Art Inst. Chgo., 1983—; dir. Chgo. Council on Fgn. Relations. Served to 1st lt. USAF, 1954-56. Mem. Am. Assn. Advt. Agys. (gov. at large 1983—). Republican. Clubs: Tavern, East Bank (Chgo.), Saddle and Cycle. Home: 209 E Lake Shore Dr Chicago IL 60611 Office: Foote Cone & Belding Communications Inc 101 E Erie St Chicago IL 60611 *

BROWN, OWSLEY, II, diversified consumer products company executive; b. Louisville, Sept. 10, 1942; s. William Lee Lyons and Sara (Shallenberger) B.; m. Christina Lee, Oct. 26, 1968; children—Owsley, Brooke Lee, Augusta Wilson. BA, Yale U., 1964; MBA, Stanford U., 1966. With Brown Forman Corp., Louisville, 1961-83, pres., 1983—; chmn., chief exec. officer Brown-Forman Beverage Co. Div. Brown-Forman Corp., Louisville, 1986—. Pres. Actors Theatre, 1985; bd. dirs. Greater Louisville Fund for Arts. Served to 1st lt. U.S. Army, 1966-68. Republican. Episcopalian. Clubs: Pendennis, Louisville Country, Wynn Stay, Filson. Office: Brown Forman Corp 850 Dixie Hwy Louisville KY 40210 *

BROWN, PHILLIP STEPHEN, biological products company executive, lawyer; b. Kansas City, Mo., Apr. 6, 1936; s. Louis and Evelyn (Strauss) B.; m. Peedee Roseroot, July 19, 1959; children: David L., Melissa Brown Rooker, Michael E. BS, U. Wis., 1958; JD, U. Mich., 1961; postgrad., Harvard U., 1974. Bar: Mo. 1962, U.S. Dist. Ct. (ea. and we. dists.) Mo. 1962, U.S. Ct. Appeals (8th cir.) 1962, U.S. Supreme Ct. 1969, U.S. Ct. Appeals (5th cir.) 1972. Assoc. Tucker, Murphy, Wilson, Lane & Kelly, Kansas City, Mo., 1961-66, Achtenberg, Sandler & Balkin, Kansas City, 1966-67; asst. pros. atty. Jackson County, Kansas City, 1967-68; asst. gen. counsel Kansas City So. Industries, Inc., 1968-70, gen. counsel, 1970-80, v.p. govt. affairs, 1980—; pres. Midcon Labs Inc. subs. Kansas City So. Industries, Kansas City, 1985-88. Pres. Grassland Heritage Found., Shawnee Mission, Kans., 1985—; bd. dirs., past chmn. Swope Pkwy. Health Ctr., Kansas City, 1982—; bd. dirs. Nat. Found. for Soil & Water Conservation, Washington, 1982—. Served with U.S. Army, 1958-59. Fellow Soc. of Fellows, Nelson-Atkins Mus. Art; mem. Mo. Bar Assn., Kansas City Bar Assn. Club: Kansas City. Home: 4232 Brookridge Dr Fairway KS 66205 Office: Kansas City So Industries Inc 114 W 11th St Kansas City MO 64105

BROWN, RAY LEE, business educator; b. Columbus, Ohio, Nov. 25, 1930; s. John Lee and Audrey Louise (Cott) B.; B.S., Ohio State U., 1953, Ph.D., 1972; M.B.A., Harvard U., 1963; m. June Edna Gibbs; children—Ellen, Sheryl, Linda, Victor, Gregory, Carol. Tax acct. Gen. Electric Co., Schenectady, 1953; commd. 2d lt. USAF, 1954, advanced through grades to col., 1974; assigned Office Comptroller USAF, also Office Sec. Def.; ret., 1975; asst. prof. acctg. U. Denver, 1975-79; v.p., chief fin. officer Congressional Info. Service, Inc., 1980; prof. Loyola Coll., Balt., 1981-84; Calif. State U.-Sacramento, 1985—; cons., lectr. for several orgns. Decorated Legion of Merit; C.P.A.; cert. managerial acct. Mem. Am. Acctg. Assn., Nat. Assn. Accts., Assn. Govt. Accts. (research award 1978), Beta Gamma Sigma, Beta Alpha Psi. Contbr. articles to profl. jours. including Harvard Bus. Rev. and Jour. of Accountancy. Address: Dept Accountancy 6000 J St Sacramento CA 95819

BROWN, RICHARD HARRIS, telecommunications executive; b. New Brunswick, N.J., June 3, 1947; s. Harris Ransford and Winifred Veronica (Clelland) B.; m. Christine C. Demler, Sept. 27, 1969; children—Ryan, Allison. B.S. cum laude, Ohio U., 1969. Mgr., Ohio Bell Tel. Co., Columbus and Toledo, 1969-74, dist. mgr., Toledo, 1974-79, div. mgr., Cleve., 1979-81; v.p. engring. United Telephone System, Inc., Westwood, Kans., 1981-82; v.p. ops. United Telephone Co. of Midwest, Overland Park, Kans., 1982-83; v.p. ops., chief operating officer United Telephone Co. of Fla., Altamonte Springs, Fla., 1983-87, also dir.; sr. v.p. human resources, adminstrn., United Telecommunications Inc., Westwood, 1987-88; pres. Sprint Svcs. div. United Telecommunications, 1988—; bd. mgrs. Vista-United Inc., Kissimmee, Fla., 1983-86; bd. dirs. North Supply Co., United Telephone Co. of N.J., United Telephone Co. of Pa., United Telephone S.E. Group, United Telephone, Midwest Group. Bd. dirs. Northwest Ohio Cystic Fibrosis Found., Toledo, 1976-78; East Cleveland YMCA, 1978-80. Served with Army N.G., 1969-74. Mem. Orlando C. of C., Fla. State C. of C. (chmn. utilities communications com.), Hallbrook Country Club. Republican. Home: 12605 Juniper Circle Leawood KS 66209 Office: United Telecommunications Inc PO Box 11315 Kansas City MO 64112

BROWN, ROBERT, manufacturing executive; b. N.Y.C., Jan. 16, 1931; s. Samuel and Dorothy (Keppler) B.; m. Barbara Schwartz, Oct. 8, 1953 (div. 1984); m. Angelika Jansen, Oct. 18, 1986. BBA, CCNY, 1957. CPA, N.Y. Sr. acct. M.R. Feinod & Co., N.Y.C., 1957-61; v.p. ops. Ehrenratch Photo-Optic, Roosevelt Field, N.Y., 1961-65; exec. v.p. BFL Communications, Plainview, N.Y., 1965-74, Seatrain Lines Inc., N.Y.C., 1974-81, Chromalloy Gas Turbine Corp., San Antonio, 1982—. With U.S. Army, 1950-51, Korea. Republican. Office: Chromalloy Gas Turbine Corp 4430 Director Dr San Antonio TX 78219

BROWN, ROBERT CORNING, II, savings and loan executive; b. Cin., June 13, 1950; s. Robert Corning and Shirley Ann (Bossenberger) B.; m. Lois Dorothy Betsch, Apr. 17, 1977 (div. June 1987); children: Stephanie, Jennifer; m. Barabara Ann Franke, Sept. 25, 1987; children: Stacy, Brad. Student, Cornell U., 1969-71. Assoc. auditor First Nat. Bank, Cin., 1971-77; asst. v.p. Eagle Savs. Assn., Cin., 1977-83; sr. v.p. Ky. Mortgage Co., Lexington, 1983-84; exec. v.p. First Investment Mortgage Co., Cin., 1984-87; v.p. Merit Savs. Assn., Cin., 1987—; instr. Sundrex Inst. Cin., Great Oaks Vocat. Schs., Cin; bd. dirs. Empire Mortgage Co., Columbus, Ohio. Contbr. articles to newspapers, profl. jours. Mem. SW Ohio Savs and Loan League (lending and pub. relations coms.). Republican. Roman Catholic. Home: 794 Shoreham Circle Cincinnati OH 45255 Office: Merit Savs Assn 4318 Montgomery Rd Cincinnati OH 45212

BROWN, ROBERT JOHN, accountant; b. Belfast, Northern Ireland, Jan. 7, 1944; s. George and Matilda (Girvan) B.; m. Nelda Mae Wade, Nov. 5, 1966; 1 child, Erin Roberta. BBA, Wayne State U., 1967. CPA, Calif. Staff Ernst & Whinney, Detroit, 1966-82, ptnr.-in-charge cons., 1982-85; mng. ptnr. Ernst & Whinney, San Diego, 1985—; chmn. Corp. Fin. Coun., San Diego, 1987-88. Mem. exec. com. San Diego State U. Pres.'s Coun., 1988. Sgt. USAFR, 1969-75. Mem. Mich. Assn. CPA's (bd. dirs. 1983-85), Fairbank Ranch Country Club (membership and fin. com. 1987-88), Pine Lake Country Club, Detroit Athletic Club. Republican. Presbyterian. Office: Ernst & Whinney 110 West A St Ste 1000 San Diego CA 92101

BROWN, RONALD, stock broker; b. Chgo., Aug. 30, 1930; s. Arthur S. and Eleanor (Smith) B.; B.S., Purdue U., 1953; M.B.A., N.Y. U., 1957; m. Patricia Joan Miner, Aug. 2, 1952; children—Mitchell Ronald, Valerie Patricia. Security analyst E.W. Axe & Co., Tarrytown, N.Y., 1955-56, Stillman, Maynard, N.Y.C., 1956-61; instl. salesman Clark Dodge & Co., N.Y.C., 1961-67; gen. partner Buttonwood Assocs., Jersey City, 1967-71; pres. Personal Investment Mgmt. Co., Mahwah, N.J., 1971-72; asst. v.p., account exec. E.F. Hutton N.Y.C., 1972-77; v.p. Dean Witter Reynolds, Inc., 1979—. Rockland County Republican committeeman, 1958-60. Served with U.S. Army, 1953-55. Mem. N.Y. Soc. Security Analysts, Inst. Chartered Fin. Analysts, Fin. Analysts Fedn., Kappa Sigma. Clubs: Madison Square Garden (N.Y.C.); Landmark (Stamford, Conn.); Scarsdale Golf. Contbr. articles to profl. jours. Home: 400 E 54th St New York NY 10022 Office: 2 World Trade Ctr New York NY 10048

BROWN, RONALD OSBORNE, telecommunications and office information systems consultant; b. Winchester, Mass., Apr. 9, 1941; s. Herbert Walcott and Madeleine Louise (Osborne) B.; m. Annette M. Brown; children—Melinda E., Jeffrey J. B.Sc. with distinction, U. Maine, 1963; M.Sc., Tufts U., 1965; Ph.D., Queens U., Kingston, Ont., 1972. Mem. tech. staff RCA Corp., Burlington, Mass., 1965-66; research assoc. Queen's U., Kingston, Ont., 1966-71; mem. sci. staff BNR, Ottawa, Ont., 1971-72; sr. systems engr. GTE Corp., Needham, Mass., 1973-83; mgr. Coopers & Lybrand, Boston, 1983-87, nat. dir, 1987-88; ind. cons., 1988—; program coordinator Northeastern U., Boston, 1976—; cons. Bell Can., 1968-71; tech. adv. TP & T Mag., Littleton, Mass., 1984-89, contbg. editor, 1989—; faculty adv. council Nat. Communications Forum, 1986—. Contbr. articles to profl. jours. Mem. IEEE, Assn. Profl. Engrs. Ont., Tau Beta Pi, Phi Kappa Phi, Eta Kappa Nu. Home: Quaker Ridge Rd PO Box 470 South Casco ME 04077 Office: 28 Tappan St Melrose MA 02176

BROWN, SANDRA JANE, pharmaceutical research company executive; b. N.Y.C., July 7, 1945; d. Walter Joseph and Ina Buckley (McClurg) B. A.S., Dean Jr. Coll., 1965. Med. sec. Bergen Pines County Hosp., Paramus, N.J., 1965-66; adminstrv. asst. Info. Handling Services, Englewood Cliffs, N.J., 1966-70; clin. research assoc. Biometric Testing, Inc., Englewood Cliffs, 1970-79; corp. sec., dir. Pharma Control Corp., Englewood Cliffs, 1979—; sec./treas. TDI Pharm. Systems, Englewood Cliffs, 1980-83; v.p. Chateau Condo Assn., Cliffside Park, N.J., 1982—. Office: Pharma Control Corp 661 Palisade Ave Englewood Cliffs NJ 07632

BROWN, SANDRA MARIE, dog breeder, consultant; b. LaFollette, Tenn., July 10, 1958; d. Gene and Beaulah M. (Letner) Hale; m. Thomas Garrett Brown, Dec. 12, 1981. Student, Lincoln Meml. U., 1973-76. Asst. restaurant and catering mgr. Holiday Inns. Inc., Knoxville, 1975-80; singer and TV personality Knoxville, 1976-80; dog breeder and designer of pet clothes Paw Pals Inc., Knoxville, 1987—; cons. Humane Soc., Knoxville, 1986, K-9 Acad., Knoxville, 1986, Little Bits Creations, LaFollette, 1985—. Author: Life in Applachia, 1973. Mem. Nat. Republican Com., 1987; spokesperson Crestwood Mills Orgn., 1982-87, Knox County Homeowners Assn. , 1986—. Mem. Knox County Humane Soc. (top breeder poodles 1984), Northshore Animal League. Baptist. Clubs: Deane Hill Country, Young Women's Auxiliary (pres. 1970-73), Sweet Adelines. Home: 308 Bridgewater Rd Knoxville TN 37923

BROWN, SANDRA WILLIAMS, data processing executive; b. N.Y.C., May 14, 1945; d. Edward Barnwell and Miriam Virginia (Anderson) Williams; BS in Edn., Northwestern U., 1967. With IBM, 1967—, regional equal opportunity program mgr., N.Y.C., 1973-75, Gen. Bus. Group/Internat. personnel programs adv., White Plains, N.Y., 1975-77, Gen. Bus. Group/Internat. mgr. exec. compensation, 1977-78, adminstrv. asst. to IBM corp. dir. personnel programs, Armonk, N.Y., 1979, mgr. personnel resources Systems Product div., White Plains, 1979-80, hdqrs. personnel mgr., 1980-81, mgr. hdqrs. personnel, info. systems and communications group, 1982-83, mgr. corp. retirement and capital accumulation, 1983-84, dir. mgmt. and exec. devel. Ams. Far East Corp. div., 1984-88, dir. personnel programs Latin div., 1988, dir. personnel corp. hdqrs., 1988; dir. U.S./ Tri-State Hdqtrs. Personnel, 1988 . Episcopalian.

BROWN, SHARON GAIL, company executive, consultant; b. Chgo., Dec. 25, 1941; d. Otto and Pauline (Lauer) Schumacher; B in Gen. Studies, Roosevelt U.; m. Robert B. Ringo, Aug. 2, 1984; 1 dau. by previous marriage, Susan Ann. Info. analyst Internat. Minerals & Chems., Northbrook, Ill., 1966-71, programmer analyst, 1971-74; programmer analyst Procon Internat. Inc. subs. UOP Inc., Des Plaines, Ill., 1974-76, systems analyst, 1976-77, project leader, 1977-78; mgr. adminstrv. services, 1978-82; spl. cons. to pres. IPS Internat., Ltd., 1982-83; spl. cons. to pres. CEI Supply Co. div. Sigma-Chapman, Inc., 1984-87, ptnr. and co-founder Brown, Ringo & Assocs., 1987—; data processing cons. Mem. Buffalo Grove (Ill.) Youth Commn., 1978-82; mem. adv. com. UOP Polit. Action Com., 1979-82; Mem. Rep. Senatorial Com. Inner Circle. Mem. Am. Mgmt. Assn., Chgo. Council on Fgn. Rels., Lake Forest-Lake Bluff Hist. Soc. Home: 550 E Deerpath Lake Forest IL 60045

BROWN, SHIRLEY MAE, hospital administrator; b. Sioux City, Iowa, Dec. 5, 1930; d. Joseph Earl and Amy Louise (West) Peiffer; widowed; children: Dennis Leroy, Tommy Lee, Gary Eugene. Grad. high sch., Huntington, Ind. Dietary aide Huntington Meml. Hosp., 1960-65, nurses' aide, 1965-71, dir. purchasing, 1971-88. Mem. Am. Bus. Women's Assn. (pres. Huntington chpt. 1977, 81, 88, Woman of Yr. 1977, 88). Home: 536 Joe St Huntington IN 46750 Office: Huntington Meml Hosp 1215 Etna Ave Huntington IN 46750

BROWN, STEPHANIE SMITH, accountant; b. New Orleans, Aug. 9, 1952; d. Manuel John and Audrey (Coustat) S.; m. Terence C. Brown, Aug. 25, 1973. Student, La. State U.; BS in Acctg., U. Md., 1974. CPA, Md. Jr. acct. Carday Assocs., Washington, 1974-78, acctg. mgr., 1978; sr. acct. Essex Corp., Alexandria, Va., 1978-87, controller, 1987—. Home: 8404 Autumn Way Clinton MD 20735 Office: Essex Corp 333 N Fairfax St Alexandria VA 22314

BROWN, STEPHEN LANDESMAN, investment company executive; b. N.Y.C., July 13, 1938; s. Paul Landesman and Sadie (Collins) Brown; m. Barbara Jane Spitz, Aug. 22, 1964; children: Spencer, Andrew, Christina. AB, Brown U., 1961; LLB, NYU, 1965. V.p. Goodkind and Co., N.Y.C., 1966-72; gen. ptnr. Monness Williams and Co., N.Y.C., 1975-78; v.p. Rosenkranz and Co., N.Y.C., 1979-82; chmn. S.L. Brown and Co., N.Y.C., 1983—, The Franklin Holding Corp., N.Y.C., 1986—; bd. dirs. Andal Corp., Copley Fin. Services Corp.; advisor Copley Fund; trustee Wilbraham and Monson Acad., Wilbraham, Mass. Mem. Assn. Corp. Growth. Club: City Athletic (N.Y.C.), Doubles (N.Y.C.), Metropolis Country (White Plains, N.Y.). Office: S L Brown & Co 767 Fifth Ave New York NY 10153

BROWN, STEPHEN LEE, insurance company executive; b. Providence, July 6, 1937; s. Eugene R. and Florence M. (Zetlin) B.; m. Arleen Claire Elliott, June 12, 1960; children: Beverly, William. AB, Middlebury Coll., 1958. With John Hancock Mut. Life Ins. Co., Boston, 1958—, asst. actuary, 1963-67, assoc. actuary, 1967-70, 2d v.p., 1970-73, v.p., actuary, 1973-77, sr. v.p., treas., 1977-81, exec. v.p., 1981-87, pres., chief ops. officer, vice chmn. bd., 1987—, also bd. dirs.; trustee Alfred P. Sloan Found., N.Y.C., 1986—; bd. dirs. John Hancock Subs. Inc., Boston, John Hancock Freedom Securities Corp., N.Y.C. Bd. dirs. Boston Housing Partnership, Inc., Boston, 1984—; bd. dirs. Boston Police Athletic League, 1987—; trustee Mus. of Sci., Boston. Served as 1st lt. U.S. Army, 1958-59. Fellow Soc. Actuaries; mem. Am. Acad. Acad. Actuaries, Actuaries Club Boston. Clubs: Algonquin, Commercial, Economic (Boston). Office: John Hancock Mut Life Ins PO Box 111 Boston MA 02117

BROWN, STEPHEN ROBERT, manufacturing executive; b. London, England, Apr. 22, 1939; arrived in U.S., 1980; s. Henry Robert and Anne (Platten) B.; m. Lesley Maunsell, Apr. 16, 1966; children: Hilary, Christopher, Michael, Rebecca. MA, Oxford U., England, 1962; MBA, U. Western Ont., 1970. Acct. Shell Internat. Petroleum Co. Ltd., Genoa, Italy, Oman, 1963-68; fin. mgr. Alcan Can. Products Ltd., Toronto, 1970-72; mfg. mgr. Alcan Extrusions, Kingston, Ont., 1972-74, Alcan Rolled Products, Kingston, Ont., 1975-78; gen. mgr. cen. region Alcan Bldg. Products, Toronto, 1978-80; v.p. planning Alcan Aluminum Corp., Cleve., 1980-82; pres. Alcan Bldg. Products Co., Warren, Ohio, 1982-85, Alcan Rolled Products Co., Cleve., Toronto, 1985—; exec. v.p. Alcan Aluminum Corp., Cleve., 1985—, also bd. dirs.; bd. dirs. Logan Aluminum Inc., Russellville, Ky., Alcan Smelters and Chems. Ltd., Montreal. Active United Way, Cleve., 1987. Mem. The Aluminum Assn. Anglican. Clubs: Country, Cleve. Racquet (Pepper Pike, Ohio); York, Toronto Lawn Tennis. Office: Alcan Aluminum Corp 100 Erieview Pla Cleveland OH 44114

BROWN, VICTOR HATFIELD, financial executive; b. Phila., Sept. 17, 1929; s. Geary and Blanche B. (Hatfield) B.; B.S. in Econs., U. Pa., 1951, M.B.A., 1954; Ph.D., U. Buffalo, 1957; m. Joan A. Hewitt, Jan. 22, 1955; children: Cynthia Joan, Douglas Victor, Paul Arthur. Acct., Charles S. Rockey & Co., Phila., 1951-53; instr. acctg. U. Pa., Phila., 1953-54; internal auditor Bur. Audits, City of Phila., 1954; chmn. acctg. dept. U. Buffalo, 1954-58; partner Touche Ross & Co., N.Y.C., 1958-71; controller Standard Oil Co. (Ind.), Chgo., 1971-76, v.p. and controller, 1976-81; exec. v.p., chief fin. officer and dir. Firestone Tire & Rubber Co., Akron, Ohio, 1981-82; mem. Fin. Acctg. Standards Bd., Norwalk, Conn., 1983—. Mem. Nat. Assn. Accts., Am. Inst. C.P.A.s, Am. Acctg. Assn., Fin. Execs. Inst. Club: Econ. Contbr. articles to profl. jours. Office: Fin Acctg Standards Bd 401 Merritt 7 PO Box 5116 Norwalk CT 06856-5116

BROWN, VICTOR MCCLEAVE, accounting executive, controller, financial analyst, consultant; b. Atlanta, Nov. 14, 1958; s. Joseph Hedrick and Wilma Loree (McCleave) B.; m. Kim LeVette, June 6, 1987. Student, Ga. State U., 1982. Tax processor Coopers & Lybrand, CPA's, Atlanta, 1979-80; corp. intern trainee fin. Lockleed Ga. Co., Marietta, 1981-82, adminstrv. assoc. fin., 1982-83, acct., 1983-85, sr. acct., 1985-87; fin. analyst Dobbs Houses, Inc., College Park, Ga., 1987—; owner Brown's Bookkeeping & Tax Svc., Atlanta, 1983—; acctg. mgr. C&S Ins. Svcs., Inc., Atlanta, 1988—; v.p. fin. Lockleed Mgmt. Assn., Marietta, 1987. Fundraiser Butter St. YMCA. Mem. Nat. Assn. Accts., Ga. Assn. Pub. Accts., Socius Strata Club (v.p. 1982-87), Alpha Phi Alpha (exec. sec. 1979-82). Home: 468 Waterford Rd NW Atlanta GA 30318 Office: Atlantic Assocs Inc 2973 Baker Ridge Dr NW Atlanta GA 30318

BROWN, WENDELL HOWARD, investor, financial planner; b. New Albany, Ind., Nov. 13, 1947; s. Howard Stanley and Estol Mae (Rhodes) B.; m. Linda Ellen Wright, Feb. 16, 1969 (div. Jan. 1983); m. Rebecca Kathleen Zimmerman, Sept. 10, 1983. BS, Oakland City (Ind.) Coll., 1969; MS, Ind. State U., 1972; Cert. in banking, Am. Inst. Banking, 1979; Cert. in counseling, Purdue U., 1984, MBA in Fin., 1988. Cert. Fin. Planner, Ind. Instr. acctg. Benton Community Sch. Corp., Fowler, Ind., 1969-72; sr. auditor Sears, Roebuck & Co., Chgo., 1972-75; sr. v.p., trust officer Fowler State Bank, 1975-86; fin. advisor The New Eng., Boston, 1988—; bd. dirs. Am. Inst. Banking, Lafayette, Ind. Pres. United Fund, Fowler, 1979, 80; bd. dirs. Fowler Park Assn., 1981, Benton Pub. Library, Fowler, 1982-86, sec. 1982-86; investment counselor Council for Aging, Fowler, 1985. Mem. Internat. Assn. Fin. Planning, Assn. for MBA Execs., Krannert Grad. Student Assn. for MBAs, Benton Country Club (pres. 1983-85), Rotary. Democrat. Methodist. Home: 7949 Rockridge Ct Indianapolis IN 46268 Office: The New Eng 11711 N Meridian Ste 400 Carmel IN 46032

BROWN, WILLIAM L., banker; b. Hendersonville, N.C., Feb. 1, 1922; s. William W. and Sarah (Maxwell) B.; m. Helen Presbrey, June 1947; children: Kathryn H., Richard P., Steven J., Melissa M. Student, Mars Hill Coll., Newberry Coll.; M.B.A., Harvard, 1947. With First Nat. Bank Boston, 1949—, asst. v.p., 1949-59, v.p., 1959-66, sr. v.p., 1966-69, exec. v.p., 1969-71, pres., chief operating officer, 1971-83, chmn., chief exec. officer, 1983-87; chmn. Bank of Boston Corp., 1983-89; ret; dir. Stone & Webster, Inc., N.Y.C., Standex Internat. Corp., Salem, N.H., Gen. Cinema Corp., Boston, Liberty Mut. Ins. Co., Boston, Liberty Mut. Fire Ins. Co., Boston., Liberty Life Assurance Co. of Boston. Bd. overseers Children's Hosp. Med. Ctr., Boston; trustee Boston Coll., Boston Plan Excellence in Pub. Schs. trustee, mem. corp. Mus. of Sci.; bd. dirs. Jobs for Mass., Inc., JFK Library Found.; mem. corp. Northeastern U. Served to lt. USNR, World War II. Office: 1st Nat BankBoston 100 Federal St Boston MA 02110

BROWN, WILLIAM LEE LYONS, JR., consumer products company executive; b. Louisville, Aug. 22, 1936; s. William Lee Lyons and Sara (Shallenberger) B.; m. Alice Cary Farmer, June 13, 1959; children—William Lee Lyons III, Alice Cary, Stuart Randolph. B.A., U. Va., 1958; B.S., Am. Grad. Sch. Internat. Mgmt., 1960. Sales rep. Brown-Forman Corp., Phoenix, 1960-61; v.p. Louisville, 1965-68; sr. v.p. Ariz., 1968-72, exec. v.p., 1972-76, pres., chief exec. officer, 1976-83, chmn., chief exec. officer, 1983—; asst. v.p. Jos. Garneau Co. import div. Brown-Forman, N.Y.C., 1961-62, dir., Paris, France, 1962-65; bd. dir. Brown-Forman Corp., First Ky. Nat. Corp. Louisville, Nat. City Corp., Cleve.; mem. Pres's. Adv. Com. for Trade Negotiations. Mem. Nat. Rep. Senatorial Trust Com.; dir. Am. Bus. Conf., Washington; bd. visitors U. Va. 1st lt. U.S. Army, 1958-59. Decorated chevalier de L'Ordre du Merite Agricole France; hon. consul France. Mem. Soc. Sons Colonial Wars, U. Va. Alumni Assn. (past pres.), Travellers Club, Fishers Island Club, River Valley Club, Pendennis Club, Louisville Country Club, University Club. Episcopalian. Home: Fincastle Prospect KY 40059 also: Fishers Island NY 06390 Office: Brown Forman Corp 850 Dixie Hwy Louisville KY 40210

BROWN, WILLIAM PATRICK, manufacturing company executive; b. Denver, Mar. 25, 1945; s. William Emmett and Marie (Sullivan) B.; m. Karin Sue Anderson, Feb. 10, 1973; children: Matthew Todd, Jennifer Nicole. BBA, U. Ariz., 1967. Asst. mgr. Kmart, Inc., 1967-71, ops. mgr., 1971-74; mfg. mgr. Tertronix, Inc., Beaverton, Oreg., 1974-83, materials mgr., 1983-84, ops. mgr., 1984-85, dir. mktg. and sales, 1985-88; bus. devel. mgr. Nelco Tech. Inc., Tempe, Ariz., 1988—. Mem. Am. Mktg Assn., Am. Mgmt. Assn., Soc. Mfg. Engrs., Am. Prodn. Inventory Control Soc. Republican. Home: Rte 4 PO Box 707 Hillsboro OR 97123

BROWNE, BROOKS HALSEY, venture capitalist; b. New Haven, Aug. 12, 1949; s. Elmer Teare and Joyce (Thompson) B.; m. Anne Tooke, Feb. 16, 1980. BA, Williams Coll., 1972; MBA, Harvard U., 1976. Account officer Citibank N.A., N.Y.C., 1972-74; mng. dir. Overseas Pvt. Investment Corp., Washington, 1976-84; sr. v.p. Allied Capital Corp., Washington, 1984—. Mem. Nat. Venture Capital Assn., Nat. Assn. Small Bus. Investment Cos. Office: Allied Capital Corp 1666 K St NW Ste 901 Washington DC 20006

BROWNE, CLIFFORD LOREN, JR., hospital and nursing home administrator; b. Omaha, Sept. 21, 1928; s. Clifford Loren and Adena Ivern (Fry) B.; m. Phyllis Jean Blair, June 6, 1953; children: Ronald, Rockwell, Sandra, Gina. BSBA, S.W. Mo. State U., 1956; MPA in Hosp. Adminstrn., U. Mo., Kansas City, 1970; cert. in health execs. devel., Cornell U., 1979. Asst. airport dir. City of Springfield (Mo.), 1953-58; budget examiner State of Mo., Jefferson City, 1958-66; assoc. adminstr. Kansas City Gen. Hosp., 1966-73; adminstr. Truman Med. Ctr. East, Kansas City, 1973—; vice chmn. bd. dirs. John Knox Village Retirement Ctr., Lee's Summit, Mo., 1983—. Com. mem. Mo. Title XIX Disbursement, 1984—; counselor-bishop Sante Fe stake Reorganized Ch. of Jesus Christ Latter-day Saints, Independence, Mo., 1985—; bd. dirs. Hope House, Independence, 1986—, Herald House, Independence, 1988; bd. govs. Community Mental Health Ctr.-South, Grandview, Mo., 1985—. Served as warrant officer U.S. Army, 1948-52, Korea. Recipient award of merit Kansas City council Boy Scouts Am., 1986. Fellow Am. Coll. Health Care Execs., Am. Coll. Health Care Adminstrs.; mem. Mo. League Nursing Home Adminstrs., Am. Hosp. Assn. (governing council on aging, 1987—, region 6 policy bd. 1987—), Mo. Hosp. Assn. (chmn. com. on long term care 1985—). Democrat. Lodges: Masons, Rotary. Office: Truman Med Ctr East 7900 Lees Summit Rd Kansas City MO 64139

BROWNE, EDMUND JOHN PHILLIP, oil company executive; b. Hamburg, Fed. Republic Germany, Feb. 20, 1948; came to U.S., 1986; s. Edmund and Paula Browne. MA in Physics, Cambridge U., Eng., 1969; MS in Bus., Stanford (Calif.) U., 1981. Registered profl. engr., United Kingdom. Petroleum engr. Brit. Petroleum Co., N.Y., Calif. and Alaska, 1969-79; regional petroleum engr. Brit. Petroleum Co., London, 1979-80, group treas., 1981-83; mgr. forties Brit. Petroleum Co., Aberdeen, Scotland, 1983-84; comml. mgr.. Brit. Petroleum Co., London, 1984-86; exec. v.p., chief fin. officer Standard Oil Co. of Ohio, Cleve., 1986-87, chief exec. officer, 1987—; chief fin. officer BP America, Inc., Cleve., 1987—; adv. bd. mem. Weatherhead Sch. Mgmt., Cleve., 1986—; bus. adv. council Carnegie-Mellon U., Pitts., 1986—; bd. dirs. BP Exploration Co. Bd. dirs. Cleve. Ballet, Cleve. Clinic. Trevelyan open scholar. Fellow Inst. Mining and Metallurgy. Clubs: Athenaeum (London); Union (Cleve.).

BROWNE, SUSAN ELIZABETH, construction executive; b. Gastonia, N.C., Sept. 22, 1961; d. Thomas Banks and Jane Senter (Hiltzheimer) B. BSCE, N.C. State U., 1983; MBA, U. N.C., Charlotte, 1989. Assoc. engr. Carolina Power & Light Co., Raleigh, 1983-85; estimator, project mgr. Beam Constrn. Co., Inc., Cherryville, N.C., 1985-88, v.p., 1988—. Mem. Cherryville C. of C. (bd. dirs.), Beta Gamma Sigma. Democrat. Presbyterian. Home: 305 S Jacob St Cherryville NC 28021 Office: Beam Constrn Co Inc 601 E Main St Cherryville NC 28021

BROWNELL, BARRY CLAYTON, restaurant executive; b. Portland, Oreg., Jan. 11, 1922; s. Ambrose and Helen Alison (Phillips) B.; m. Gloria Maxine Bertha Mierow, June 24, 1944 (div.); children: Michael, Timothy, Barbara, Charles, Janice, Ardythe, Marilyn, Roger, Curtis, Marcia; m. Laura Marion Kennelly, Apr. 26, 1980. BA, Reed Coll., 1943. Owner, mgr. Oreg. Kimberchicks' Inc., Gladstone, 1944-60; owner Brownell Sound & Hi Fi, Inc., Oregon City, 1960—, also chmn. bd.; owner, chief exec. officer A.P. Corral Inc., Portland, 1984—, Red Steer Restaurant & Lounge, Portland, 1984—. Mem. Greater Portland Conv. and Visitors Assn. Mem. Oreg. Farm Bur. Fedn. (v.p. 1946-60), Oreg. Restaurant and Hospitality Assn., Masons, Rotary (pres. North Portland 1987-88). Republican. Methodist. Office: Red Steer Restaurant & Lounge 2514 N Marine Dr Portland OR 97217

BROWNELL, EDWIN ROWLAND, banker; b. Tampa, Fla., Sept. 19, 1924; s. Clarence DeWolf and Helen Lucy (Hill) B.; m. Helen Marie Kegel, Jan. 22, 1948 (dec. Apr. 1967); 1 child, Nancy; m. Blanche Rosina Parisi, Dec. 26, 1967; children: Elizabeth, Elaine, Evelyn. BCE, U. Fla., 1947. Registered profl. surveyor, Fla., Ark., Ga., Miss., Nev., N.D., S.D., S.C., Tenn., W.Va. Cadastral engr. City of Miami, Fla., 1948-53; pres., real estate salesman E.R. Brownell & Assocs., Inc., Miami, 1953—; pres., chief exec. officer, chmn. Brickellbanc Savs. Assn., Miami, 1985—, also bd. dirs.; chmn. surveying adv. com. U. Fla., Gainesville, 1974—; mem. degree accrediation team Nat. Council Engring. Examiners, S.C., 1985—, 60 person team that evaluated engring. readiness of U.S. Armed Forces; chmn. engring. adv. com. Fla. State Bd. Regents, Tallahassee, 1982-85. Elected county surveyor State of Fla., Dade County, 1956-60; chmn. Zoning Bd. Adjustment, Coral Gables, Fla., 1978-87; vice chmn. Coral Gables Planning and Zoning Bd., 1987—; bd. dirs. Boys Club of Miami, 1980-83; mem. Com. of 100, Miami, Fla. Fellow Am. Congress Surveying and Mapping (pres. 1980-81, Surveying Excellence award 1977), NSPE (pres. 1978-79), Fla. Soc. Profl. Surveyors (hon., Fla. Land Surveyor of Yr. 1973, pres. 1978-79), Dade County Chpt. Fla. Soc. Profl. Surveyors (pres. 1965-69); mem. NSF, Am. Soc. Photogrammetry and Remote Sensing (Presdl. citation 1982), Am. Soc. Photogrammetry Found. (vice chmn. 1985—), Am. Mil. Engrs., Am. Planning Assn., Internat. Geog. Info. Found. (vice-chmn.), Miami Bd. Realtors, Fla. Planning and Zoning Assn. (S. Fla. chpt.), Fla. Assn. Cadastral Mappers, Bus. Inc., Sierra Club (pres. 1977), NSF, Com. of 100, Bus. Inc., Lambda Alpha Internat., Kappa Alpha. Republican. Roman Catholic. Clubs: Coral Gables Country, Riviera Country (Coral Gables); Holly Hills Country (Sapphire, N.C.). Lodges: KC, Kiwanis. Home: 1207 Sorolla Ave Coral Gables FL 33134 Office: E R Brownell & Assocs Inc 3152 Coral Way Miami FL 33145

BROWNING, DAVID STUART, lawyer; b. Amarillo, Tex., June 6, 1939; s. Stuart W. and Pauline (Rogers) B.; m. Judith Helen Jackson, July 31, 1958; 1 son, Mark. B.A., U. Tex., 1960, J.D., 1962; M.A., Johns Hopkins U., 1964. Bar: D.C. bar 1963, Tex. bar 1964, N.Y. bar 1970. Atty. firm Fulbright & Jaworski, Houston, 1964-70; asst. counsel Schlumberger Ltd., N.Y.C., 1970-75; sec., gen. counsel Schlumberger Ltd., 1976—. Contbr. articles to legal jours. Mem. Am., N.Y. State, Tex., Houston bar assns., Assn. Bar City N.Y., Am. Soc. Internat. Law, Southwestern Legal Found. (adv. bd.), Am. Soc. Corporate Secs. Office: Schlumberger Ltd 277 Park Ave New York NY 10172

BROWNING, PETER CRANE, packaging company executive; b. Boston, Sept. 2, 1941; s. Ralph Leslie and Nancy (Crane) B.; m. Carole Ann Shegog, Dec. 14, 1963 (div. 1974); children: Christina, Jennifer; m. Kathryn Ann Klucharich, July 27, 1974; children: Kimberly, Peter. AB in History, Colgate U., 1963; MBA, U. Chgo., 1976. Salesman, mktg. rep. White Cap div. Continental Can, Northbrook, Ill., 1964-75; mgr. mktg. Conally Venture div. Continental Can, 1975-79; gen. mktg. and sales mgr. Bondware div. Continental Can, 1979-81, v.p., gen. mgr., 1981-84; v.p. gen. mgr. White Cap. div. Continental Can, 1984-86, exec. v.p., operating officer, 1986—; bd. dirs. Conn. Chem. Ltd., Toronto, Can. Bd. dirs. Keep Am. Beautiful. Mem. Am. Mktg. Assn., Norwalk C. of C. Republican. Episcopalian. Clubs: Meadow (Rolling Meadows, Ill.), Carlton (Chgo.), Field (New Canaan, Conn.). Home: 11 Silver Ridge Rd New Canaan CT 06840 Office: Continental Can Co Inc 800 Connecticut Ave Norwalk CT 06856

BROWNING, REBA SMITH, bus contractor; b. Jacksonville, Fla., Dec. 5, 1926; d. Reuben F. and Emmie Ruth (Hopkins) Smith; m. Richard McGuire, July 26, 1945 (div. July 1949); children—Michael Vernon, Patricia Gail; m. Elwood Likens Browning, Aug. 17, 1957; 1 child, Bruce Morgan. Ed. pub. schs., Jacksonville. Bus owner, contractor Duval County Schs., Jacksonville, 1969-75; owner, pres. Browning Transp., Inc., Jacksonville, 1975—; driver tng. instr. Mem., sec. Fla. Vol. Chaplain Cert. Com., Jacksonville, 1984-85. Recipient Outstanding Christian of Yr. award Hogan Baptist Brotherhood, Jacksonville, 1971; Nat. Safety Slogan of Yr. award Gateway Transp., 1972. Mem. Nat. Fedn. Ind. Bus., U.S. C. of C., Duval County Sch. Bus Contractor's Assn. (pres. 1970-73, 81-83, bd. dirs.), Nat. Save-the-Children Club, Jacksonville Be-a-Friend Club. Republican. Baptist. Avocations: public speaking; poetry; furniture refinishing. Office: Browning Transp Inc 8655 Phillips Hwy Jacksonville FL 32216

BROWNING, ROY WILSON, JR., educational administrator; b. Oketo, Kans., Oct. 2, 1928; s. Roy Wilson and Elva B. (Ward) B.; m. Geraldine L. Green, Dec. 27, 1950; children: Roy Wilson III, Christine S., Julie A. BA with honors, Ottawa U., 1950; MDiv, Phillips U., 1955; MS, Emporia State U., 1960; EdD, U. Kans., 1968. Cert. tchr. and adminstr., Kans. Real estate salesman Hayden Turner Realty, Ottawa, 1948-50; fund raiser assoc. Spencer Mitchell Assocs., Kansas City, Mo., 1952-54; dir. secondary edn. Topeka United Sch. Dist. 501, 1962-68; asst. dep. supt. Topeka Unified Sch. Dist. 501, 1968-71, asst. supt., 1974—; adj. prof. Kans. State U., Manhattan, 1987—; bd. dirs. Swedish Am. State Bank, Courtland, Kans. Trustee Phillips U., Enid, Okla., 1968-80, Ottawa U., 1981—; vice chmn. Topeka/Shawnee County Health Bd., 1975; mem. com. on orgns. Nat. ARC; v.p. Capital Area ARC, 1988. Chaplain USAF, 1956-59, ret. col. Res., 1988. Recipient Outstanding Community Svc. award Modern Woodman Am., Topeka, 1986, Meritorious Svc. citation Rotary Internat. Found., 1985; U.S. Office Edn. travel/study grantee, India, 1967; Paul Harris fellow Rotary Internat., 1986. Mem. Nat. Assn. Pupil Personnel Adminstrn. (trustee 1984-87), Kans. Assn. Supervision and Curriculum Devel. (pres.), United Sch. Adminstrs. (bd. dirs.), Nat. Assn. Supervision and Curriculum Devel. (bd. dirs.), Mil. Chaplains Assn. (life, sec. treas. 1971—), Capital Area Res. Officers Assn. (pres. 1982), Rotary (pres. Topeka club 1970). Republican. Mem. Christian Ch. (Disciples of Christ). Office: Topeka Unified Sch Dist 501 624 W 24th St Topeka KS 66611

BROWNLEY, JOHN FORREST, fast food executive; b. Buffalo, July 24, 1942; s. John William and Gertrude Elizabeth B.; B. Mgmt. Engring., Rensselaer Poly. Inst., 1965; MBA in Mktg., U. Pa., 1967; m. Dorothy Robohm, Sept. 26, 1971; children—Christopher, David. Cons., 1970-71; with Scott Paper Co., 1971-80; treas. Wendy's Internat., Inc., Dublin, Ohio, 1981-88, sr. v.p. fin., treas., 1988—. Bd. dirs. United Cerebral Palsey, Columbus and Franklin Counties. With USNR, 1967-69. Mem. Fin. Execs. Inst., Columbus Treasurers Club, Nat. Assn. Corp. Treas. (bd. dir.). Home: 2459 Wenbury Rd Upper Arlington OH 43220 Office: Wendy's Internat Inc 4288 W Dublin Granville Rd Dublin OH 43017

BROWNSTEIN, HARRIS ALLEN, automotive company executive; b. N.Y.C., Feb. 8, 1958; s. Bernard Morris and Annette (Hirsch) B.; m. Debra Rose Casale, Sept. 14, 1959. BS in Biochemistry, SUNY, 1980. Sales rep. Habberstad BMW Dealer, N.Y.C., 1980-83, Legend Porsche-Audi-Saab Ltd., Amityville, N.Y., 1984—; research cons. automotive sales. Editor, actor TV shows, 1986, 87, video pubs., 1986, 87. Named Top Salesman in U.S., Audi, Porsche, 1985, 86, 87, 88, one of Top Five Salesman in USA for Saab Automobiles, 1987, 88. Jewish. Office: Legend Porsche Audi Saab Ltd 158 Merrick Rd Amityville NY 11701

BROXSON, EVELYN LIPSCOMB, data processing executive; b. Corsicana, Tex., Aug. 30, 1948; d. Elwin David and Mildred Bonner Lipscomb; m. Marion Donald Broxson, May 13, 1967; children: Marion Donald Jr., Matthew Dane, Melinda Denise. AS, Navarro Coll., 1968. Mgr. data processing E.W. Hable & Sons Inc., Corsicana, 1969-73, Parrott Oil Corp., Dallas, 1973-75; pvt. practice contract programmer Dallas, 1975-76; mgr. data processing Five Stars Distbrs. Inc., Dallas, 1976-82, Designers Collection Inc., Dallas, 1982—. Mem. council City of Eureka, Tex., 1982-88; vol. 4-H Clubs Navarro County, Corsicana. Recipient Alumni award Navarro County 4-H Clubs. Mem. Dallas-Ft. Worth System 34/36 User Group. Presbyterian. Club: Corsicana Classic Car (sec., treas. 1984-85). Home: Rte 6 PO Box 134 Eureka TX 75110 Office: Designers Collection Inc 1207 Round Table Dr Dallas TX 75247

BROZA, LYNNE, accountant; b. Neptune, N.J., Aug. 17, 1955; d. Allan Benjamin and Arline (Lichtenstein) B. BS in Polit. Sci., Franklin & Marshall Coll., 1977; postgrad., Pace U., 1986—. CPA, N.J. Claims adjuster Liberty Mut. Ins. Co., Cherry Hill, N.J., 1978-79; mgr. tax dept. Broza, Block & Rubino, CPA, P.A., Asbury Park, N.J., 1980—. Active Amnesty Internat. Fellow Am. Inst. CPAs, N.J. Soc. CPAs; mem. Am. Bus. Appraisers, Greater Twp. of Ocean C. of C (treas.). Democrat. Jewish. Office: Broza Block & Rubino 601 Grand Ave Asbury Park NJ 07712

BROZEN, YALE, economist, educator; b. Kansas City, Mo., July 6, 1917; s. Oscar and Sarah (Sholtz) B.; m. Lee Parsons, Apr. 26, 1962; children—Yale II, Reed. AA, Kansas City Jr. Coll., 1936; MA, U. Chgo., 1940, PhD, 1941. Asst. prof. social sci. U. Fla., 1940-41; asst. prof. econs. Ill. Inst. Tech., 1941-44, assoc. prof., 1944-46; asso. prof. econs. U. Minn., 1946-47, vis. prof. econs., 1948; prof. econs. Northwestern U., Evanston, Ill., 1947-57; dir. Research Transp. Center, 1957-59; prof. econs. U. Chgo., 1957—; dir. research mgmt. program U. Chgo. (Grad. Sch. Bus.), 1959-67, dir. applied econ. program, 1960—; adj. scholar Am. Ent. Inst., 1972—; Cons. State Dept., 1956-63; vis. prof. econs São Paulo, Brazil, 1954, Rikkyo U., Tokyo, 1964, U. Va., 1965, Grad. Inst. Internat. Studies, 1969; research assoc. Social Sci. Research Council, 1949; cons. pub. utility econs. Cook County State's Atty's Office, 1950; dir. econ. tng. Am. Tel. & Tel. Co., 1951; cons. President's Materials Policy Commn., 1951, Anti-Trust Div., Dept. Justice, 1952, NSF, 1954-55, N.A.M., 1954-55, Loewi & Co., 1969; Dir. Univ. Nat. Bank, West Burton Place Corp., Carus Corp. Author: Workbook for Economics, 1946, Textbook for Economics, Vol. I, 1948, Advertising and Society, 1974, The Competitive Economy, 1975, Concentration, Mergers, and Public Policy, 1982, Mergers in Perspectives, 1982. Civilian tng. adminstr. Signal Corps U.S. Army, 1942-43. Mem. Am. Econ. Assn., Mont Pelerin Soc., Phi Beta Kappa, Delta Sigma Pi. Clubs: Quadrangle (Chgo.), Technology (Chgo.). Home: 1380 Dartmouth Rd Flossmoor IL 60422 Office: U Chgo 1101 E 58th St Chicago IL 60637

BRUBAKER, JAMES EDWARD, engineer; b. Chgo., Feb. 24, 1935; s. Samuel James and Mary Louise (Alward) B.; m. Phyllis Ann Evans, Aug. 18, 1956; children: David, Richard, Lisa, Mark. BS in Gen. Engring., U. Ill., 1956, MSME, 1957. Instr. English U. Ill., 1956-57; with Westinghouse Electric Corp., Pitts., 1959—, prin. engr. Clinch River Breeder Reactor, 1975-83, prin. engr. MX missile, 1984-85; prin. engr. West Valley Nuclear Demonstration Westinghouse Electric Corp., Boff, N.Y., 1985-87; prin. engr. machinery tech. div. Westinghouse Electric Corp., Pitts., 1987—; chmn. Mechanism Design Com., Pitts., 1965; cons. USN, USAF and DOE. Patentee in field; editor Mechanism Design Manual and Mil. Spl. Mem. Pleasant Hills Athletic Assn. (pres. 1976-77). Republican. Lodge: Lions (pres. 1984-85). Home: 372 Cavan Dr Pittsburgh PA 15236 Office: Westinghouse MTD Pittsburgh PA 15236

BRUBAKER, KAREN SUE, tire manufacturing company executive; b. Ashland, Ohio, Feb. 5, 1953; d. Robert Eugene and Dora Louise (Camp) B. BSBA, Ashland Coll., 1975; MBA, Bowling Green State U., 1976. Supr. tire ctr. ops. BF Goodrich Co., Akron, Ohio, 1976-77, supr. tire ctr. acctg., 1977-79, asst. product mgr. radial passenger tires, 1979-80, product mgr. broadline passenger tires, 1980-81, group product mgr. broadline passenger and light truck tires, 1981-83, mktg. mgr. T/A high tech radials, 1983-86; product mgr. B.F. Goodrich T/A radials, The Uniroyal Goodrich Tire Co., Akron, 1986—. Sect. chmn. indsl. div. United Way, Akron, 1983-86. Recipient Alumni Disting. Service award Ashland Coll., 1986; Alpha Phi Clara Bradley Burdette scholar, 1975. Mem. Am. Mktg. Assn. (pres. Akron/Canton chpt. 1982-83, Highest Honors award 1983, v.p. bus. mktg., elected to nat. bd. dirs. 1984-86, v.p. profl. chpts., 1987—), Susan B. Anthony Soc. of Akron Women's Network, Nat. Assn. Female Execs., Zonta, Beta Gamma Sigma, Omicron Delta Epsilon. Home: 1862 Indian Hills Trail Akron OH 44313 Office: The Uniroyal Goodrich Tire Co 600 S Main St Akron OH 44397-0001

BRUBAKER, PETER P., communications executive; b. Lancaster, Pa., Nov. 13, 1946; s. Henry C. and Margaret (Posey) B.; m. Margaret Wolfe Donnelly, June 29, 1968; children: Patrick D., Joshua P. BA, Wesleyan U., 1972; MBA, Harvard U., 1974. Lending officer Mellon Bank, Pitts., 1974-77; mgr. corp. services Susquehanna Broadcasting Co., York, Pa., 1977-78, dir. fin., 1978-80, v.p. fin., 1980—, v.p. cable div., 1979-86; pres. Susquehanna Cable Co. subs. Susquehanna Broadcasting Co., York, Pa., 1986—; Mem. copyright com. Nat. Cable TV Assn., Washington, 1987—. Mem. Kidney Found. of York (treas. 1980-88), York Polit. Action Com. (treas. 1984—), Hist. York Inc. (pres. 1987—). Served with USAF, 1967-71, Vietnam. Mem. Cable TV Adminstrn. and Mktg., 1986. Moravian. Clubs: Downtown of York (bd. dirs. 1983-84), Harvard (N.Y.C.). Lodge: Rotary. Office: Broadcasting Co Susquehanna Cable Co 140 E Market St York PA 17401

BRUCE, HARRY JAMES, transportation company executive; b. Newark, July 2, 1931; s. John William and Anna Margaret (Ackerman) B.; m. Vivienne Ruth Jennings, Sept. 10, 1955; children: Robert, Stacy, Bethann. B.S., Kent State U., 1957; M.S., U. Tenn., 1959; cert. Advanced Mgmt. Program, Harvard U., 1979. Diplomate: cert. Am. Soc. Transp. and Logistics; 1960. Transp. research asst. U.S. Steel Co., Pitts., 1959-64; dir. market devel. Spector Freight Co., Chgo., 1964-67, v.p. mktg., 1967-69; dir. distbn. Joseph Schlitz Brewing Co., Milw., 1969-71, asst. v.p. plant ops., 1971-72; v.p. mktg. Western Pacific R.R., San Francisco, 1972-75; sr. v.p. mktg. Ill. Central R.R., Chgo., 1975-83, chmn., chief exec. officer, 1983—; also dir. Ill. Central Gulf R.R., Chgo.; bd. dirs. LaSalle Bank Lake View, Chgo., A.P. Green Industries Inc., Mexico, Mo. Author: How to Apply Statistics to Physical Distribution, 1967, Distribution and Transportation Handbook, 1971; inventor vari-deck, 1970. Bd. dirs. Glenwood Sch. for Boys, Ill.; mem. adv. bd. U. Tenn.; bus. adv. com. Northwestern U. Served to 1st lt. U.S. Army, 952-55, ETO. Mem. Newcomen Soc., Nat. Council Phys. Distbn., Nat. Freight Transp. Assn., Nat. Def. Transp. Assn., Northwestern U. Assocs. Republican. Presbyterian. Clubs: Glenview (Ill.); Chicago, Mid-Am. (dir.) (Chgo.); Metropolitan (N.Y.C.). Home: 88 Woodley Rd Winnetka IL 60093 Office: Ill Cen RR Co 233 N Michigan Ave Chicago IL 60601

BRUCE, MARVIN E., corporate executive; b. Sylvester, Ga., July 29, 1928; s. Thomas Peter and Bobbie (Cobb) B.; m. Carolyn Couch, June 19, 1949; children: Carol Lynn Smith, Janet C. Bruce. LLB, John Marshall U., 1948. V.p. Uniroyal Tire Co., N.Y.C., 1950-72; pres., chief exec. officer TBC Corp., Memphis, 1972—, also bd. dirs.; bd. dirs. Krug Internat. Dayton, Ohio,

Union Planters Corp., Memphis; chmn. bd. Memphis Internat. Motorsports, 1987—. Chmn. campaign com. Boy Scouts Am., Memphis, 1986-87. Mem. Nat. Tire Dealers, Automotive Parts and Accessories, Memphis Country Club (Memphis), Univ. Club. Democrat. Baptist. Office: TBC Corp 4770 Hickory Rd Memphis TN 38115

BRUCK-MUNRO, BETH ANNE, company executive; b. Richmond, Ind., Sept. 23, 1958; d. Edward Walter and Jayne Elizabeth (Dickerson) Bruck; m. Gregory D. Campbell, Sept. 20, 1980 (div. Feb. 1983); m. Arthur Duane Munro, May 25, 1986. AA in Bus. Adminstrn., St. Petersburg Jr. Coll., 1978; BA in Acctg., U. South Fla., 1980. CPA, Fla. Staff acct. Main Hurdman CPAs (now Peat Marwick & Co.), St. Petersburg, Fla., 1980-82; chief acct. Innova, Inc., Clearwater, Fla., 1982-83, controller, 1983-86; controller Med. High Tech. Internat., Inc., Clearwater, 1986—. Mem. Fla. Inst. CPA's, Phi Kappa Phi. Republican. Presbyterian. Office: Med High Tech Internat Inc 14155 58th St N Clearwater FL 34620

BRUECKNER, ROBERT DAVIS, data processing executive; b. Loudon, Tenn., Apr. 14, 1935; s. Mynhart Oswald and Eva Helen (Davis) B.; m. Mary Lucile Sully, June 1 1956; children: Susan Alice, William James. BA, U. Chattanooga, 1960. Data processing mgr. Chattem Drug & Chem., Chattanooga, 1961-65; plant acct. Container Corp. Am., Chattanooga, 1965-67; data processing mgr. Chattanooga Glass Co., 1967-74; mgr. info. systems Dorsey Trailers, Inc., Elba, Ala., 1974—; cons. Sewell Plastics, Inc., Atlanta, Ga., 1978, 82; instr. evening div. Chattanooga, State Tech. Coll., 1970, Cleve. (Tenn.) State Community Coll., 1972, Enterprise (Ala.) State Jr. Coll., 1980. V.p. Lutheran PTA, Chattanooga, 1973; pres. Elba High Band Boosters, 1977, Elba PTA, 1978. Served to capt. USAR, 1961-71. Mem. Cert. Systems Profl., Data Processing Mgmt. Assn., COMMON. Republican. Methodist. Home: 1481 Cherokee Ln Elba AL 36323 Office: Dorsey Trailers Inc 701 Hickman Ave Elba AL 36323

BRUEN, WALTER PATRICK, JR., pharmaceutical executive; b. Evergreen Park, Ill., Sept. 20, 1936; s. Walter Patrick and Marian Rose (Larney) B.; m. Anna Marie Gregory, Apr. 23, 1960; children: Walter Patrick III, Maura Ann, Michael Gregory, Bridget Marie. BS in Civil Engring., Ill. Inst. Tech., 1958; MBA, Ind. U., 1963. Registered profl. engr., Ill., Ind. Sr. indsl. engr. Eli Lilly and Co., Indpls., 1965-67, sr. compensation analyst, 1967-69, corp. trainee, 1969-70, mgr. compensation, 1970-72, mgr. compensation and benefits, 1972-77, exec. dir. compensation, 1978—; dir. mfg. and adminstrn. Eli Lilly France, Paris, 1977-78; mem. steering com. Project 777, 1985—. Bd. dirs. Children's Bur. Indpls., 1979—, pres., 1985-87; mem. personnel com. Indpls. Mus. Art, 1982—. Served to lt. Civil Engr. Corps, USN, 1958-65, capt. Res. Mem. ASCE, Soc. Am. Mil. Engrs., Am. Compensation Assn., Council on Employee Benefits (trustee 1988—), Naval Res. Assn. (life), Navy League U.S. Republican. Roman Catholic. Home: 10624 Winterwood Carmel IN 46032 Office: Eli Lilly & Co Lilly Corp Ctr Indianapolis IN 46285

BRUETT, WILLIAM HUBER, JR., bank executive; b. N.Y.C., Jan. 11, 1944; s. William H. Bruett; B.A. in Econs., St. Lawrence U., 1966; M.B.A., St. John's U., 1971; m. Karen Diesl; 1 child, Lindsey. With Mfrs. Hanover Trust Co., N.Y.C., 1966-83, asst. sec., 1969-70, asst. v.p., 1971-73, v.p., 1973-76, officer in charge Fifth Avenue Corp. Banking Ctr. 1976-78, corp. cash mgmt. officer in charge, 1978-82, sr. v.p., 1980, fin. services group sr. v.p., officer in charge, 1982-83; pres., chief exec. officer Chittenden Corp. and Chittenden Bank (subs.), Burlington, Vt., 1984—, also bd. dirs.; bd. dirs. Green Mountain Power Corp., Health Ins. of Vt., Shelburne Farms, New Eng. Council, Greater Burlington Indsl. Corp., Cynosure, Inc.; com. of founders Vt. Venture Capital Fund; steering com. Vt. Bus. Roundtable. Mem. Vt. Bankers Assn. (pres. 1989-90). Office: Chittenden Corp 2 Burlington Sq PO Box 820 Burlington VT 05402

BRUGGER, HUBERT ANTON, financial holding company executive; b. Lindau, Germany, Feb. 26, 1933; came to U.S., 1961, naturalized, 1965; Betriebswirt, U. Munich, 1958; grad. internat. mktg. Northwestern U., 1961; B.A. in Bus. Adminstrn., M.B.A. in Econs., Ph.D. in Internat. Econs., all Columbia Pacific U.; m. Gisela Schruut, May 21, 1961; children—Joern-Eric Walter, Beatrice Caroline. Founder, Autohaus Brugger, Inc., Redwood City, Calif., 1966—, Brugger Corp., fin. holding and investment co., Redwood City, 1968—, also chmn. bd.; bd. dirs. Pacific Bank of San Francisco; chmn. Western AG Systems, Inc., chmn. BayCity Land Co., Inc.; chmn. Brokway Corp., Nev. Bd. regents Columbia Pacific U. Mem. Internat. Economists Assn., Internat. Assn. Pvt. Investment Bankers, Internat. Soc. Financiers (cert. internat. financier), U.S. Senatorial Bus. Adv. Bd. Home: 25 Haciendas Dr Woodside CA 94062 Office: Brugger Plaza Ctr Convention Way Redwood City CA 94063

BRUGGER, JOERN-ERIC WALTER, real estate company executive, lawyer; b. Nuremburg, Fed. Republic Germany, July 11, 1962; came to U.S., 1962; s. Hubert Anton and Gisela Eva (Schruut) B. BS in Biology, UCLA, 1985; JD, Santa Clara U., 1989. Adminstrv. asst. Autohaus Brugger, Redwood City, Calif., 1985-86; v.p. automobile div. Brugger Corp., Redwood City, 1986-87; v.p. BayCity Land Co., Redwood City, 1987-88, pres., 1989—; corp. sec. Western AG Systems, Inc., Redwood City, Bankers Indemnity Corp., Redwood City, Brockway Corp., Reno. Republican. Roman Catholic. Office: BayCity Land Co Inc 370 Convention Way Ste 300 Redwood City CA 94063

BRUHN, HANS-JUERGEN, auditor, consultant; b. Hamburg, Federal Republic Germany, Jan. 13, 1940; s. Hans Friedrich and Herta Catherina (Iden) B.; m. Ursula Leu, May 12, 1967; children: Urte. Anke, Silke. Inspector Fed. Post-Telephone-Telecommunication Adminstrn., Hamburg, 1960-68; group leader EDP Post-Telephone-Telecommunications Research Plant, Darmstadt, Fed. Republic Germany, 1968-71; audit officer EDP Fed. Audit Office, Frankfurt, Fed. Republic Germany, 1971-81; sr. audit officer Fed. Audit Office, Frankfurt, Fed. Republic Germany, 1986-89; auditor Internat. Bd. Auditors for NATO, 1989—; project mgr. Ministry of Fin., Ankara, Turkey, 1981-85; chief cons. Hendrikson Associated Cons., Eschborn, Fed. Republic Germany, 1981-85. Author: Engagement of Computer Capacity in Terms of Commercial Efficiency, 1973, Audit Aspects in the Utilization of EDP, 1974, Manual of EDP Audit, 1975. Pres. German Folk Music Soc., Wehrheim, 1976. Grantee Minister Posts and Telecommunications, Bonn, 1969. Mem. Verband der Beamten der Obersten Bundesbehörden EV im Deutschen Beamtenbund. Lutheran. Home: Steinweg 8, D-6393 Wehrheim 3 Federal Republic of Germany Office: Internat Bd Auditors for NATO, NATO Hdqrs, B-1110 Brussels Belgium

BRULL, PIERRE SIGMUND, banker; b. Neuilly, France, July 25, 1934; came to U.S., 1957; s. Charles K. and Rita (Markwald) B.; m. Susan K. Fogarty, June 8, 1961 (div. 1964); 1 child, Jennifer L. BA, Cambridge U., 1955; MBA, Columbia U., 1957; MA, Cambridge U., 1960. Fin. analyst Exxon Corp., N.Y.C., 1957-61; v.p. rsch. Dominick & Dominick, N.Y.C., 1961-71; dir. rsch. Hanseatic Corp., N.Y.C., 1971-73; fin. analyst 1st Manhattan Co., N.Y.C., 1973-77; v.p., dep. mng. dir. U.S. Trust Co., London, 1977-80; v.p., dir. investor relations Bank of N.Y., 1980—. Mem. Bank Investor Relations Assn. (bd. dirs. 1983—), Fin. Analyst Fedn., N.Y. Soc. Security Analysts (chmn. corp. relations com. 1987—), Nat. Investors Relations Assn. (v.p. 1987—), Fin. Symposium of N.Y. Home: 1060 Park Ave New York NY 10128 Office: Bank of NY 52 William St New York NY 10286

BRUMBACK, CHARLES TIEDTKE, communications executive; b. Toledo, Sept. 27, 1928; s. John Sanford and Frances Hannah (Tiedtke) B.; m. Mary Louise Howe, July 7, 1951; children: Charles Tiedtke Jr., Anne V., Wesley W., Ellen P. BA in Econs., Princeton U., 1950; postgrad., U. Toledo, 1953-54. CPA, Ohio, Fla. With Arthur Young & Co., CPAs, 1950-57; bus. mgr., v.p., treas., pres., chief exec. officer, dir. Sentinel Star Co. subs. Tribune Co., Orlando, Fla., 1957-81; pres., chief exec. officer Chgo. Tribune subs. Tribune Co., 1981-88, pres., chief oper. officer, 1988—; also bd. dirs. Tribune Co., Chgo. Trustee Robert R. McCormick Charitable Trust, Northwestern U., Culver Ednl. Found., Chgo. Symphony Orch. Northwestern Meml. Hosp., chmn, 1987—. Served to 1st lt. U.S. Army, 1951-53. Decorated Bronze star. Mem. AICPA, Ohio, Fla. Socs., CPAs, Fla. Press Assn. (treas. 1969-76, pres. 1980, bd. dirs.), Am. Newspaper Pubs. Assn. (bd. dirs.), Comml. Club of Chgo., Chgo. Club, Tavern Club. Home: 1500 N Lake Shore Dr Chicago IL 60610 Office: Chgo Tribune Co 435 N Michigan Ave Chicago IL 60611

BRUMBAUGH, JOHN A., JR., electrical engineer; b. Pittsburg, Kans., Aug. 23, 1927; s. John A. and Leona G. (Finley) B.; m. Shirley Jean Ellis, July 8, 1950; children: Mark Alan, Steven Thomas, Scott Andrew. Design engr. McNally Pitts. Mfg. Co., Pittsburg, 1949-55; plant engr. Morton Salt Co., Hutchinson, Kans., 1955-59; asst. plant mgr. Morton Salt Co., Port Huron, Mich., 1959-65; plant mgr. Morton Salt Co., Grand Salne, Tex., 1965-70; facility mgr. Morton Salt Co., Hutchinson, Kans., 1970-84, Morton Salt div. Morton Thiokol, Inc., Rittman, Ohio, 1984—. Lt. USNR, 1945-46. Recipient Boss of Yr. award Bus. and Profl. Women, 1979. Mem. Assn. Commerce and Industry (dir. 1974-84), Tex. Mfs. Assn., (dir. Dallas chpt. 1966-70), East Tex. C. of C. (dir. 1968-70), Am. Legion, Lions (pres. local club 1964-65). Home: 431 Allen Dr Wadsworth OH 44281 Office: Morton Salt div Morton Thiokol Inc 151 S Industrial Rittman OH 44270

BRUML, ROBERT WOLF, investment banker; b. Cleve., May 12, 1954; s. Edgar and Marjorie (Wolf) B.; m. Cynthia Gardner, Aug. 30, 1981; 2 children: Andrew Gardner, Madeliene Gardner. BA in Econs., U. Rochester, 1976; MBA, U. Pa., 1978. Auditor Peat, Marwick & Main, Cleve., 1978-79; sr. v.p. Golenberg & Co., Cleve., 1979-86; v.p. Intercapco, Inc., Cleve., 1979-86; pres. Bruml Capital Corp., Cleve., 1986—. Mem. Assn. Corp. Growth (v.p. membership 1986-88). Office: Bruml Capital Corp 1717 E 9th St Ste 914 Cleveland OH 44114-2803

BRUMM, PAUL MICHAEL, banking executive; b. Cin., Oct. 18, 1947; s. Paul Frederick and Jeane (Faine) B.; m. Linda Ann Phillips, Dec. 28, 1968 (div. Dec. 1982); children: Anna Ulrika, Nicholas David. Jaqualine Dorothy Speier, June 25, 1983. BA in Econs., U. Cin., 1969, MBA in Fin., 1976. Various positions The Fifth Third Bank, Cin., 1966-77, v.p., 1981-85, v.p., treas., trust officer, 1985-89; treas. Fifth Third Bancorp, Cin., 1985-87, sr. v.p., treas., 1987—; v.p., gen. mgr. Med. Funding Svcs., Inc., Cin., 1977-81; bd. dirs., mem. fin. com. BHC Securities Inc., Phila., 1985-89. Chmn. The Salvation Army Bus. Adv. Bd., Cin., Disabilities Svcs. Allocations Com. Community Chest, Cin.; trustee Med. Found. Cin. Mem. Fin. Execs. Inst., Delta Mu Delta. Republican. Roman Catholic. Club: Bankers (Cin.), Univ., Cin. Athletic, Coldstream Country. Home: 1891 Berkshire Ln Cincinnati OH 45230 Office: Fifth Third Bank 38 Fountain Sq Pla Cincinnati OH 45263

BRUMMER, DONALD E., grain merchandising executive; b. Albert Lea, Minn., May 23, 1944; s. Philip J. and Loretta (Schultz) B.; m. Pamela Brummer, Nov. 13, 1987. Merchandiser then regional mgr.then v.p. Pillsbury Co., Mpls., 1966—. Dir. Mpls. Grain Exchange, Nat. Grain Trade Council. Sgt. USMCR, 1965-71. Mem. Nat. Grain and Feed Assn., Mpls. Athletic Club, Minn. Valley C. of C. Republican. Roman Catholic. Office: Mpls Grain Exch 150 Grain Exchange Bldg Minneapolis MN 55415

BRUNETTI, WAYNE HENRY, utilities executive; b. Cleve., Oct. 13, 1942; s. Henry Joseph and Lillian (Lupo) B.; m. Mary Kelly, Aug. 17, 1963; children: Kelly Christine, Andrew Wayne. BSBA in Acctg., U. Fla., 1964; student program for mgmt. devel., Harvard U., 1974. Acct. Fla. Power and Light Co., Miami, Fla., 1964-68, systems analyst, 1968-69, project coordinator, 1969-72, mgr. property acctg., 1972-73, mgr. corp. acctg., asst. comptroller, 1973-77, asst. to v.p. pub. affairs, 1977-80, dir. energy mgmt., 1980, v.p. energy mgmt., 1980-83, v.p. divs., 1983-84, group v.p., 1984-87, exec. v.p., 1987—; bd. dirs. Sun Bank Miami. Bd. dirs. South Miami Hosp. Found., 1986—, Haven Ctr., Inc., Miami, 1986—, United Way of Dade County, Miami, 1986—. Mem. Associated Industries Fla. (bd. dirs. 1986—). Democrat. Roman Catholic. Office: Fla Power & Light Co PO Box 029100 Miami FL 33102-9100

BRUNGOT, GEORGE OLIVER ROBERT, insurance company executive; b. Berlin, N.H., Aug. 26, 1923; s. Sivert Matias and Hilda C.F. (Johnson) B.; m. Dolores Jean Ferree, July 6, 1949; children: George Robert, Karl Douglas, Susan Christine. Student, U. N.H., 1941-43; BS in Naval Sci., U.S. Naval Acad., 1946. CLU; chartered fin. cons., Md. Commd. ensign USN, 1946, advanced through grades to lt., 1952, resigned, 1954; spl. agt. Prudential Ins. Co., Boston, 1949-51; dist. mgr. Jefferson Standard, Annapolis, Md., 1954-68; ind. agt. George Brungot and Assocs., Annapolis, 1968—. Treas. Evang. Presbyn. Ch., Annapolis, 1985—. Recipient Pres. Cabinet award Shenandoah Life Ins. Co., Roanoke, Va., 1985-88, Pres.'s Council award 1986, Qualified Nat. Quality award Nat. Assn. Life Underwriters, 1955-89. Mem. Anne Arundel Life Underwriters (pres. 1960), Chesapeake Personal Computer Users Group (pres., founder 1984), Am. Soc. CLU's and Chartered Fin. Cons. (Balt. chpt.), Million Dollar Round Table (Honor Roll award 1957—). Democrat. Club: Annapolis Yacht. Lodges: Civitan (pres. Annapolis chpt. 1960-61), Elks. Home and Office: PO Box 747 Annapolis MD 21404

BRUNI, JEROME V., brokerage house executive; b. Portland, Maine, Sept. 26, 1948; s. James P. and Hilla B.; m. Pamela Sue Ingram; children: Kristopher, Alan. BS, USAF Acad., 1970; MA, UCLA, 1971. Ops. research officer Rome Air Devel. Ctr., N.Y., 1971-74; chief data analysis Pacific Air Forces, 1974-76; systems/econ. analyst U.S. Dept. Def., Albuquerque, 1976-79; asst. prof. econs. USAF Acad., Colorado Springs, Colo., 1979-84; v.p. Smith Barney, Colorado Springs, 1984—. Author: Cadel Financial Planning Guide, 1982; author newsletter Counterpoint, 1981-84. Named Outstanding Instr., USAF Acad., 1981, 82, Outstanding Stockbroker, Money mag., 1987, Outstanding Writer, Econs. dept. Air Force Acad., 1983. Mem. Internat. Assn. Fin. Planners.

BRUNING, ANTHONY STEVEN, lawyer; b. St. Louis, Oct. 24, 1955; s. Frederick Charles Jr. and Pauline (Shrum) B.; m. Cynthia Louise Leonard, Nov. 2, 1979; children: Anthony Steven Jr., Ryan Leonard, Michele louise. BA, U. Mo., 1977; JD, St. Louis U., 1980. Atty. Leritz, Reinert & Duree PC, St. Louis, 1980—. Mem. Mo. Bar Assn. (rep. exec. com., young lawyers sect. coun. 1983-87), St. Louis Met. Bar Assn., ABA, Ill. Bar Assn., Mo. Assn. Trail Attys., Assn. Trail Lawyers Am., Mo. Athletic Club. Office: Leritz Reinert & Duree PC 812 N Collins Lacledes Landing Saint Louis MO 63102

BRUNK, JAMES FREDERICK, sales executive; b. Balt., Apr. 22, 1951; s. John William and Shirley Anne (Moran) B.; m. Jean Elizabeth Crowley; children: Alexander, Christopher. BSCE and Environ. Engring., Cornell U., 1973. Sales engr. MCC Powers, San Leandro, Calif., 1980-82; regional sales mgr. MCC Powers, San Francisco, 1983-85; nat. sales mgr. MCC Powers, North Brook, Ill., 1985-86; dir. sales Landis & Gyr Powers, Buffalo Grove, Ill., 1987—. Served to lt. USN, 1973-79. Mem. ASHRAE, Nat. Fire Protection Assn., Am. Mktg. Assn., Assn. Energy Engrs. (sr.). Republican. Roman Catholic. Office: Landis & Gyr Powers 1000 Deerfield Pkwy Buffalo Grove IL 60015

BRUNNER, GORDON F(RANCIS), household products company executive; b. Des Plaines, Ill., Nov. 6, 1938; s. Frank Anthony and Alfreida Elizabeth (Eslinger) B. ; m. Nadine Marie Slosar, Aug. 10, 1963; children: Christine Marie, Pamela Ann, Meggan Therese. BChemE, U. Wis., 1961; MBA, Xavier U., Cin., 1965. With Procter & Gamble Co., 1961—; mgr. product coordination European Ops. Procter & Gamble Co., Brussels, 1977-81, mgr. research and devel. European Ops., 1981-83; mgr. research and devel. U.S. Procter & Gamble Co., Cin., 1983-85, v.p. research & devel. U.S., 1985-87, sr. v.p. research & devel. U.S., 1987—. patentee in field. Adv. bd. St. Ursula Villa, Cin., 1987; group chmn. United Way, Cin., 1987. Evans scholar alumni. Mem. Engring. Soc. Cin. Republican. Roman Catholic. Clubs: Queen City, Hyde Pk. Country (Cin.). Home: 7300 Sanderson Pl Cincinnati OH 45243 Office: Procter & Gamble Co Ivorydale Tech Ctr 5299 Spring Grove Ave Cincinnati OH 45217

BRUNNER, KEELY SHERMAN, aerospace company executive; b. Reading, Pa., Jan. 1, 1939; s. Keely S. and Alice M. (Geissler) B.; m. Loraine Bardowski (div. 1974); children: Megan, Mark; m. Nancy J. Eaton, Aug. 16, 1976; children: Jessica, Douglas. BS in Mech. Engring., Drexel U., 1962; MS in Bus. Adminstrn., Colo. State U., 1974. Bus. mgr. Ball Aerospace Systems, Boulder, Colo., 1976-82, 84-86, mgr. strategic planning, 1982-84; bus. mgr. Ball Corp., Westminster, Colo., 1986-88; dir. mgmt. systems Ball Corp., Broomfield, Colo., 1988—. Mem. Project Mgmt. Inst. Home: 222 Forrest Ln Boulder CO 80302 Office: Ball Aerospace Systems Group 10 Long's Peak Dr Broomfield CO 80020-2510

BRUNNER, RICHARD FRANCIS, shipyard executive; b. New Orleans, Sept. 9, 1926; s. Raymond Francis and Eunice (Laux) B.; m. Vivian Elizabeth Mayer, July 25, 1948; children: Dale Ann, Richard G., Scott T. B.S. in Mech. Engring., Tulane U., 1951. With Avondale Industries Inc., New Orleans, 1945—, now exec. v.p., chief operating officer, bd. dirs. Served with USNR, 1944-46. Mem. Soc. Naval Architects and Marine Engrs., Navy League, Tau Beta Pi. Roman Catholic. Office: Avondale Industries Inc PO Box 50280 New Orleans LA 70150

BRUNNER, VERNON ANTHONY, marketing executive; b. Chgo., Aug. 9, 1940; s. Frank Anthony and Alfrieda (Eslinger) B.; divorced; children: Jack Daniel, Amanda Josephine; m. Sharon Ann Walschon, July 1, 1972; 1 child, Suzanne Marie. BS in Pharmacy, U. Wis., 1963. Registered pharmacist. Mgr. store Walgreen Co., Chgo., 1963-71; dist. mgr. Walgreen Co., Deerfield, Ill., 1971-75, dir. merchandising, 1975-77, dir. mktg., 1977-78, v.p. mktg., 1978-82, sr. v.p. mktg., 1982—. Mem. Evans Scholar Alumni Assn. Roman Catholic. Office: Walgreen Co 200 Wilmot Rd Deerfield IL 60015

BRUNNER, WILLIAM FRANCIS, biochemist; b. Bronx, N.Y., Dec. 18, 1948; s. William Francis and Anne Luceile (Fitzpatrick) B.; m. Bernadette Elizabeth MacDougall, May 6, 1978; children: Alison Anne, William Lawrence. BS in Chemistry, Manhattan Coll., 1971; MS in Biochemistry, N.Y. Med. Coll., 1984. Research asst. Manhattan Coll., Bronx, 1973-74; research scientist N.Y. State Psychiat. Inst., N.Y.C., 1974-86; sr. pharmacologist ICI Ams. Inc., Wilmington, Del., 1986—. Mem. AAAS, Am. Chem. Soc., N.Y. Acad. Sci., Am. Inst. Chemists, Am. Soc. for Pharmaceutics and Experimental Therapeutics, Sigma Xi. Roman Catholic. Avocations: stamp collecting, hiking, canoeing, skiing. Office: ICI Ams Inc Molecular & Neurochem Pharmacology Wilmington DE 19897

BRUNO, GRACE ANGELIA, accountant, educator; b. St. Louis, Oct. 11, 1935; d. John E. and Rose (Goodwin) B. BA, Notre Dame Coll., 1966; MEd, So. Ill. U., 1972; MAS, Johns Hopkins U., 1983; PhD, Walden U., 1985. CPA, Mo., Md., N.J. Tchr. Sisters of Notre Dame, St. Louis, 1962-80; pres. Bruno-Potter, Inc., Avon-By-The-Sea, N.J., 1981—; asst. treas., instr. acctg. Coll. of Notre Dame of Md., Balt., 1978-79, treas., 1979-80; asst. prof. acctg. Georgian Ct. Coll., Lakewood, N.J., 1985—; fin. advisor James Harry Potter Gold Medal Award, N.Y.C., 1980—. Elected to Internat. Platform Assn., 1987. Mem. Am. Inst. CPA's (tax div.), N.J. Soc. CPA's, N.J. Bus. Educators, St. Louis Bus. Educators (treas. 1972-73). Democrat. Roman Catholic. Home and Office: 419 Third Ave Avon By The Sea NJ 07717

BRUNO, LOUIS LEONARD, JR., wine wholesaler; b. Youngstown, Ohio, Sept. 21, 1947; s. Louis Leonard and Rose Marie (Hoffman) B.; m. Marcia Ann Hoover, June 7, 1969; children: Louis III, Matthew. BS in Math., Marquette U., 1973. Wine mgr. Met. Liquor Co., Inc., Milw., 1973-78; pres., chief exec. officer Bruno Wines & Spirits Inc., Milw., 1978—; pres. Lou Bruno Sch. Wine, Ltd., Milw., 1983—; instr. Met. Arts Program U. Wis., Milw., 1985—. Wine writer Milw. Jour., 1985-86. Com. chmn. Milw. Symphony, 1981; pres. St. Mary's Parish Council, Pewaukee, Wis., 1986. Mem. Confrerie de la Chaine des Rostisseurs. Republican. Roman Catholic. Home: 1335 Barrington Woods Dr Brookfield WI 53005 Office: Bruno Wines & Spirits Inc 21100 W Capitol Dr Pewaukee WI 53072

BRUNO, NICHOLASJOSEPH, marketing professional; b. Jersey City, Mar. 13, 1938; s. Dominick Joseph and Catherine (Costantino) B.; m. Donna Albanese, Sept. 17, 1966; children: Nicholas Albanese, Brookes Anthony, Dean Joseph. Student, Farleigh Dickinson U., 1959-61. Govt. account rep. AM Internat., N.Y.C., 1962-66; nat., govt. account mgr. sales programming mgr. Xerox Corp., N.Y.C., 1966-76; nat. account br. mgr. Savin Corp., N.Y.C., 1976-78; dir. govt. mktg. GSBM, Mountainside, NJ, 1978-83; nat. major account mktg. mgr. Minolta Corp., Ramsey, N.J., 1983—. Mgr. Little League, Manalapan, N.J., 1975-82; scout master Boy Scouts Am., Manalapan, 1975-85, chmn. com., Colts Neck, N.J., 1987-88. Served with U.S. Army, 1957-59. Republican. Roman Catholic. Office: Minolta Corp 101 Williams Dr Ramsey NJ 07446

BRUNO, RONALD G., retail food company executive. married. BS, U. Ala., 1974. With Bruno's Inc., Birmingham, Ala., v.p. sales, now pres., chief operating officer. Office: Bruno's Inc 300 Research Pkwy Birmingham AL 35211

BRUNS, DANNY LEE, healthcare association executive; b. Wayne, Nebr., Oct. 16, 1949; s. Wilbur Lee and Betty L. (Wacker) B.; m. Barbara Kay Temple, Sept. 1, 1970; children: Kristin Suzanne, Joshua Lee, Amanda Marie. Student, S.D. State U., 1967-69, S.W. Minn. State Coll., 1970-71. Mgmt. cons., project coordinator, then asst. v.p. South Cobb Med. Ctr., Austell, Ga., 1974-77; asst. to pres., v.p. devel., then project devel. officer Med. Investment Corp., Montezuma, Ga., 1977-82; dir. acquisitions and devel., then exec. v.p. Beverly Enterprises, Inc., Rockville, Md., 1982-86; chief exec. officer Trinity Living Ctrs., Inc., Williamsburg, Va., 1986—. Mem. Ga. Gov.'s Council on Aging, Atlanta, 1976-77; bd. dirs. St. Luke's Luth. Ch., Montezuma, 1976-78. Mem. Ga. Health Care Assn. (bd. dirs., mem. reimbursement com. 1975-76). Republican. Office: Trinity Living Ctrs Inc 161C John Jefferson Sq Williamsburg VA 23185

BRUNSON, JOHN SOLES, lawyer; b. Houston, Jan. 8, 1934; s. Nathan Bryant and Jonnie E. (McMillan) B.; BBA, Baylor U., 1956, LLB, 1958, JD, 1965; m. Joan Erwin, Dec. 26, 1953: children—W. Mark, Dana Ruth. Bar: Tex., 1958, U.S. Supreme Ct., 1961; assoc. Dillingham, Schleider & Lewis, Houston, 1958-64; ptnr. Brunson & Brill, Houston, 1964-70, Baker, Heard & Brunson, Houston, 1970-72, Brunson & Erwin, Houston, 1972-84; pres. Gold Acorn Capital Corp., Clavis Investment Corp.; chmn. Carat Refining Co. Mem. Harris County (Tex.) Dem. Exec. Com., 1959-65; mem. Tex. Dem. Exec. Com., 1968-74. Mem. State Bar Tex., Houston Bar Assn., Am. Bar Assn. Baptist. Clubs: Houston, Houstonian. Office: 11 Briar Hill Houston TX 77042

BRUNSON-THUROW, SUSAN MARIE, insurance company executive; b. Dallas, July 23, 1956; d. Albert Wayne and Vera Elizabeth (Sullins-Dean) Brunson; m. Harold A. Thurow, May 17, 1986; 1 child, Frances Elizabeth. BMus in Edn, Tex. Wesleyan Coll., Ft. Worth, 1978. Music tchr. Aledo (Tex.) Ind. Sch. Dist., 1978-80; ins. agt. Ky. Cen. Life, Arlington, Tex., 1980-82; gen. ptnr. Thurow Ins. Agy., Arlington, 1982—. Mem. Great S.W. Assn. Life Underwriters (pres. 1987-88), Ind. Agts. Assn. Presbyn., C. of C. (edn. com.), Arlington Amateur Radio Club. Office: Thurow Ins Co 1503 A Nora Dr Arlington TX 76013

BRUSCA, ROBERT ANDREW, economist; b. Detroit, Mar. 14, 1950; s. Andrew Adam and Doris Rita (Lozon) B.; m. Candice Steinman, Sept. 2, 1973. BA, U. Mich., 1973; MA, Mich. State U., 1976, PhD, 1977. Chief economist Fed. Res. Bank of N.Y., N.Y.C., 1977-82; economist, fedwatcher Irving Trust Co., N.Y.C., 1982-85; chief economist The Nikko Securities Co Internat., Inc., N.Y.C., 1986—; adj. prof. Columbia U., 1978—; appeared frequently on TV, radio as fin. specialist, 1983—. Author (column) Money Current, Fin. World mag., 1987-88, Econ. Currents, 1988—; contbr. articles in field. Mem. Money Marketeers NYU (bd. dirs. 1988—), Paupack Hills Golf Club (Greentown, Pa.). Office: Nikko Securities Co Internat 200 Liberty St Tower A 28th Fl New York NY 10081

BRUSH, DAVID ELDEN, broadcast executive; b. Albany, Oreg., Oct. 24, 1950; s. Leonard Gilmore and Helen Elizabeth (Kirkpatrick) B.; m. Donella J. Urban, Aug. 24, 1974 (div. 1987). Student, Oreg. State U., 1968-69, Chemeketa Community Coll., 1976; AS, Linn-Benton Community Coll., 1980. Lic. FCC 1st class radiotelephone operator. Electronics technician Toad Hall Hi-Fi, Corvallis, Oreg., 1974-76, Corvallis Audio-Video Systems, 1976-78, Albany TV, Oreg., 1978; programmer Forrest Industries Ins. Exchange, Albany, 1980-81; owner/operator Tangent TV Cable Co., Oreg., 1984—; programmer analyst Summit Info. Systems, Inc., Corvallis, 1981-85, tech. support rep., 1985-87, sr. tech. document writer, 1987—. Author: Tangent City Charter, 1981. Photographer Tangent Rural Fire Protection Dist., 1979-85 (named Rookie of Yr. 1980) councilman, City of Tangent, 1980-81, 1st elected mayor City of Tangent, 1981-85; instrumental in obtaining City of Tangent's 1st state-approved land-use plan, 1985, city's 1st sewer system, 1981-85. Served with USCG, 1970-74. Mem. Electronics Technicians Assn. 1979—, Internat. Soc. Cert. Electronics Technicians. Republican. Methodist. Lodge: Fairmount Grange #252. Office: Tangent TV Cable Co PO Box 201 Tangent OR 97389

BRUST, SUSAN MELINDA, telecommunications executive; b. N.Y.C., Sept. 27, 1951; d. Stanley Milton and Preva Joan (Simons) B.; m. William S. Boorstein; 1 child, Jon Bradley. BA in Geology, Hunter Coll., 1973; postgrad., Bernard Baruch Coll., 1988—, Tel Aviv U., 1971, U. Colo., 1973. Sales rep. Burroughs Corp., N.Y.C., 1976-81; pvt. network specialist Tymnet, Inc., N.Y.C., 1981-85; regional sales mgr. Dama Telecommunications, N.Y.C., 1985-87; account exec. Network Equipment Technologies, N.Y.C., 1987—; ind. telecommunications cons. Brust & Associates, N.Y.C., 1983—. Mem. NOW, N.Y.C., 1979—; exec. bd. mem. Jewish Guild for the Blind, N.Y.C., 1975; assoc. Spl. Olympics, N.Y.C., 1984—. Mem. Nat. Assn. Female Execs., Assn. Women in Computing, Empire Women in Telecommunications. Democrat. Home: 101 W 79 St New York NY 10024 Office: Network Equipment Techs 33 Whitehall St New York NY 10017

BRUYNES, CEES, manufacturing company executive; b. The Netherlands, Aug. 3, 1932; s. Arie and Petronella (Borst) B.; m. Elly Nagel, Feb. 1, 1963; children: Irene W., Jan Paul. Grad., Chr. Lyceum, Arnhem, Netherlands, 1951. With N.V. Philips' Gloeilampenfabrieken, Netherlands, 1953-71; pres., chief exec. officer Philips Can., 1971-74; exec. v.p. N. Am. Philips Corp., N.Y.C., 1975-78, pres., chief operating officer, 1978—, chief exec. officer, 1981—, chmn., 1985-88; chmn., pres., chief exec. officer Consol. Electronics Industries Corp., Stamford, Conn., 1988—. Served with Dutch Air Force, 1951-53. Clubs: Landmark (Stamford), Sky (N.Y.C.), Netherlands (N.Y.C.), Greenwich (Conn.) Country, Lyford Cay, Round Hill. Home: Khakum Wood Greenwich CT 06830 Office: 1 Landmark Sq Stamford CT 06901

BRYAN, DAVID TENNANT, media company executive; b. Richmond, Va., Aug. 3, 1906; s. John Stewart and Anne Eliza (Tennant) B.; m. Mary Harkness Davidson, May 11, 1932 (dec. Feb. 1987); children: Mary Tennant, John Stewart, Florence. Student, U. Va., 1925-28; LL.D., U. Richmond, 1973. Chmn., dir. Media Gen., Inc.; former publisher Richmond Times-Dispatch and Richmond News Leader, to 1978. Hon. trustee Va. Union U.; overseer Hoover Instn. Mem. Am. Newspaper Pubs. Assn. (pres. 1958-60), Soc. of Cin., Va. Hist. Soc. (pres. 1978-81), Sigma Delta Chi. Clubs: Commonwealth (Richmond), Country of Va. (Richmond); Farmington Country (Charlottesville); St. Anthony (N.Y.C.), Union (N.Y.C.); Nat. Press (Washington), Alfalfa (Washington); Bohemian (San Francisco). Home: Ampthill Rd Richmond VA 23226 Office: Media Gen Inc 333 E Grace St Richmond VA 23219

BRYAN, JERRY LYNN, advertising and public relations executive; b. Poplar Bluff, Mo., Oct. 17, 1939; s. Chester Lee and Bernita Louise (Henson) B.; m. Melva Pauline Tate, June 28, 1959; children: Jeffrey Lynn, Bernita Ruth, Jay Matthew. B in Journalism, U. Mo., 1961. News dir. Sta. KLIK, Jefferson City, Mo., 1962-67; pres. sec. Gov. Mo., Jefferson City, 1967-73; v.p. Wright & Manning, Inc., St. Louis, 1973-77; dir. communications Consol. Aluminum, St. Louis, 1977-78; mgr. bus. devel. Sverdrup Corp., St. Louis, 1978-81, dir. corp. communications, 1981—. Mem. nat. adv. bd. U. Mo. Sch. Journalism, 1984—, world trade council Regional Commerce and Growth Assn., St. Louis, 1985—; bd. dirs. Press Club Met. St. Louis, 1985—, St. Louis Journalism Found., 1987; mem. exec. com., bd. dirs. Confluence St. Louis, 1987—, St. Louis Mental Health Assn., 1987—. Mem. Pub. Relations Soc. Am. (exec. com. corp. sect. 1986—, chmn.-elect 1988, chmn. 1989, bd. dirs. St. Louis chpt. 1987—), Internat. Assn. Bus. Communicators (pres. St. Louis chpt. 1987, chmn. internat. awareness 1986, dist. IV Communicator of Yr. 1985), Bus. Profl. Advt. Assn. (pres. St. Louis chpt. 1985-86, internat. v.p. 1986-87, treas. 1987-88, vice-chmn. 1988-89, Chpt. of Yr. Leadership award 1986, St. Louis Profl. of Yr. award 1988). Democrat. Baptist. Club: Mo. Athletic. Home: 1411 Silverleaf Ln Saint Louis MO 63146 Office: Sverdrup Corp 801 N 11th Saint Louis MO 63101

BRYAN, JOHN HENRY, JR., food and consumer products company executive; b. West Point, Miss., 1936. B.A. in Econs. and Bus. Adminstrn, Rhodes Coll., Memphis, 1958. Joined Bryan Foods, 1960; with Sara Lee Corp. (formerly known as Consol Food Corp.), Chgo., 1960—, exec. v.p. ops., 1974-75, pres., chief exec. officer, 1975-76, chmn. bd., chief exec. officer, 1976—; also dir. Sara Lee Corp. (formerly known as Consol Food Corp.); dir. Amoco Corp., First Chgo. Office: Sara Lee Corp 3 First National Pla Chicago IL 60602-4260

BRYAN, JOHN STEWART, III, newspaper publisher; b. Richmond, Va., May 4, 1938; s. David Tennant and Mary Harkness (Davidson) B.; m. Alice Pyle Zimmer, June 15, 1963 (div. 1985); children—Elizabeth Talbott, Anna Saulsbury. B.A., U. Va., 1960. Advt. salesman Burlington Free Press, Vt., 1963-65; reporter The Tampa Times, Fla., 1965-67, v.p., 1968-76; pub. The Tampa Tribune and Times, Fla., 1976-77; pres., pub. Richmond Times-Dispatch, Richmond News Leader, Va., 1978—; bd. dirs. Media Gen., Inc., Richmond, 1974—, vice chmn., exec. v.p., 1985—; bd. dirs. AP, 1984—, Newspaper Advt. Bur., 1977—, Mut. Ins. Cos., Bermuda. Pres. Tampa Bay Art Ctr., 1970, Tampa Citizens Safety Council, 1971, Tampa United Way, 1974, Fla. Gulf Coast Symphony, 1977, Jr. Achievement of Richmond, 1981, Goodwill Industries of Richmond, 1982; trustee U. Tampa, 1972-78, St. Catherine's Sch., 1979-82, Va. Council Econ. Edn., 1980—, Episcopal High Sch., Alexandria, Va., 1980-86, Va. Found. Ind. Colls., 1984—; mem. council advisers U. South Fla., 1975-77. Served with USMC, 1960-62. Recipient medal of Honor, DAR, 1983. Mem. Fla. Soc. Newspaper Editors (life), So. Newspapers Pubs. Assn. (bd. dirs. 1973-75, found. chmn. 1978-79, pres. 1981-82), Fla. Press Assn. (life, pres. 1971-72, Disting. Service award 1976), Va. Press Assn. (bd. dirs. 1980-86), Am. Newspaper Pubs. Assn. (premium fund com. 1977—), World Bus. Coun., Fla. Council of 100, Sigma Delta Chi. Clubs: Bohemian (San Francisco), Alfalfa, Country of Va., Commonwealth, Tampa Yacht and Country; University (Tampa). Home: 4608 Sulgrave Rd Richmond VA 23221 Office: Media Gen Inc 333 E Grace St Richmond VA 23219

BRYAN, RICHARD RAY, real estate development executive, construction executive; b. Centerville, Iowa, Apr. 15, 1932; s. Ashley Chester and Celia Mildred (Wright) B.; m. Shirley Erline Wilson, Dec. 17, 1955; children: Scott Douglas, Shari Kay. BS, Tex. A&M U., 1956; MS, Stanford U., 1957; student advanced mgmt. program Harvard U., 1986. Lic. real estate broker, Tex.; registered profl. engr., Tex. Project mgr. H.B. Zachry Co., San Antonio, 1957-63, 69-70, v.p., 1985-87, sr. v.p., 1987—, also bd. dirs.; project mgr. Zachry Internat., Lima, Peru, 1964-68; gen. mgr. Trans-Pecos Materials Co., Odessa, Tex., 1968-69; project mgr., v.p. Gerald D. Hines Interests, Houston, 1970-75, sr. v.p., 1979-80; bd. dirs., gen. mgr. Hines Overseas Ltd., Athens, Greece, 1976-78; sr. v.p. Cadillac Fairview, Urban Devel. Inc., Houston, 1981-85; bd. dirs. Met. Resources. Mem. Greater Austin/San Antonio Corridor Council, profl. devel. com. Ctr. for Constrn. Edn. Tex. A&M U., visual arts com. Tex. A&M U.; bd. dirs. San Antonio Econ. Devel. Found.; mem. adminstrv. bd. United Meth. Ch. Served with USAF, 1950-52, Korea. Fellow ASCE; mem. Newcomen Soc. N.Am, Nat. Geog. Soc., Urban Land Inst. (mem. devel. infrastructure and services council), Constrn. Industry Inst. (adv. bd.), Tex. Assn. Taxpayers (bd. dirs.), Smithsonian Assocs., Earthwatch. Clubs: Giraud, Dominion Country, Circumnavigators. Home: 7618 Woodhaven San Antonio TX 78209

BRYAN, ROBERT FESSLER, former investment analyst; b. New Castle, Pa., Jan. 19, 1913; s. Harry A. and Nell (Fessler) B.; m. Elaine A. Norwood, Sept. 7, 1940; children: Diane Elaine (Mrs. James M. Lyon), Barbara Norwood (Mrs. Michael C. Bowen); m. Dorothy Darr MacKenzie, Aug. 11, 1961; m. Gertrude B. Bruneau, Feb. 10, 1978. A.B. summa cum laude, Oberlin Coll., 1934; Ph.D., Yale, 1939. Instr. econs. Yale U., 1935-36, 37-39, Princeton U., 1936-37; economist Lionel D. Edie & Co., Inc., N.Y.C., 1939-40; asst. v.p. Lionel D. Edie & Co., Inc., 1943-45, v.p., 1946-48; price exec., rubber br. OPA, 1941-42; economist Goodyear Aircraft Corp., Akron, Ohio, 1943; with J.H. Whitney & Co., N.Y.C., 1948-50; partner J.H. Whitney & Co., 1951-59; financial v.p., treas., dir. Whitney Communications Corp., 1959-69; dir. M.L. Ready Assets Trust, Merrill Lynch Capital Fund, M.L. Basic Value Fund; partner Whitcom Investment Co., 1967-69. Mem. exec. com. Yale Grad. Sch. Council, 1969-73; trustee Oberlin Coll., 1960-70. Mem. Am. Mgmt. Assn (finance council 1952-55), Phi Beta Kappa. Clubs: Ocean (Delray Beach, Fla.), Gulfstream Golf, Gulfstream Bath & Tennis (Delray Beach, Fla.), Apawamis (Rye, N.Y.); Mt. Bruno Country (Montreal, Que). Home: 200 N Ocean Blvd Delray Beach FL 33444 also: 52 Water's Edge Rye NY 10580

BRYAN, WILLIAM DAVID, investment officer; b. Laurel, Miss., May 11, 1947; s. Charles Clark and Marion (White) B.; m. Nancy White, Oct. 17, 1970; children: Shawn, Jonathan, Timothy. BS in Bus., Miss. State U., 1973; Diploma, Stock Market Inst., Phoenix, 1979; postgrad., Troy State U., 1981-83. Account exec. Merrill, Lynch, Pierce, Fenner & Smith, Pensacola, Fla., 1973-84; chief investment officer BB&T, Wilson, N.C., 1984—. chmn. Pensacola Seafood Festival, 1977-80; troop leader Boy Scouts Am., Wilson, 1986-88. 1st lt. U.S. Army, 1979-73. Mem. Sertoma Club. Democrat. Wesleyan. Home: 3310 Teal Dr Wilson NC 27893 Office: BB&T 223 W Nash St Wilson NC 27893

BRYANT, JAMES ARTHUR, restaurant executive; b. Chester, Pa., Apr. 13, 1949; s. James A. and Doris C. (Johnson) B.; m. Yvonne Olivia Hose, July 18, 1970; 1 child, Jason Chase. BS, Ky. State U., 1971. Master claims adjuster Nationwide Ins. Co., Columbus, Ohio, 1972-78; captive ins. agt. Nationwide Ins. Co., Louisville, 1978-83; risk mgr. Chi-Chi's Inc., Louisville, 1983-85, dir. risk mgmt., 1985%. Mem. Risk Ins. Mgmt. Soc. Democrat. Baptist. Office: Chi-Chi's Inc 10200 Linn Station Rd Louisville KY 40232

BRYANT, KAREN WORSTELL, financial consultant; b. Cadillac, Mich., Sept. 7, 1942; d. Harley Orville and Rose Edith (Bell) Worstell; children: Lynda Jean, Tracey Jo, Cynthia Jill, Troy Thomas; m. Robert Melvin Bryant, Nov. 29, 1968. Student, Cen. Mich. U., 1963-67, Mich. State U., 1966, Johns Hopkins U., 1982-83. Sales rep. Xerox Corp., Southfield, Mich., 1972-74; cons. employment contracts Policy Study Group, Johnson & Johnson, IBM World Trade Asia and others, Tokyo, 1974-79; area sales mgr. Universal Plastics, McLean, Va., 1979-81; exec. product mgr. The Western Union Telegraph Co., Upper Saddle River, N.J., 1981-86; dir. mktg. and sales support The Nat. Guardian Corp., Greenwich, Conn., 1986-88; fin. cons. Shearson Lehman Hutton, Pearl River, N.Y., 1988—. Mem. NAFE, Internat. Platform Assn. Republican. Home: 19 Sky Meadow Rd Suffern NY 10901 Office: Shearson Lehman Hutton One Blue Hill Pla Pearl River NJ 10965

BRYANT, ROBERT PARKER, retired food service and lodging executive; b. Staten Island, N.Y., May 13, 1922; s. Thomas V. and Rosanna (McRoberts) B.; m. Barbara Carlson; children—Elizabeth Bryant Wright, Robert, Christine Bryant Ablutz, Catherine Bryant Swanson, Martha McMahon. B.S., Cornell U., 1947. Exec. v.p. restaurant ops. Marriott Corp., Washington, 1966-74; corp. v.p. ops. Marc's Big Boy, Milw., 1974-75; group v.p. Burger King Corp., Miami, Fla., 1975-76; pres., chief exec. officer Dobbs Houses, Inc., Memphis, 1976-88, also bd. dirs.; vice chmn., chief exec. officer food service and lodging group Carson Pirie Scott & Co., Chgo., from 1981, also dir.; dir. Commerce Union Bank, Memphis, West Electric Co., Toronto. Bd. dirs. Bus. Vols. for the Arts, Chgo., Chgo. area council Boy Scouts Am. Served as officer U.S. Army, 1942-46. Democrat. Presbyterian. Club: University (Chgo.), Union League (Chgo.); N.Y. Athletic (N.Y.C.) Lodge: Rotary. Home: PO Box 4010 Glen Arm MD 21057

BRYANT, SANDRA RENEE, municipal administrative executive; b. Norfolk, Va., July 29, 1959; d. James Thomas and Wincie (Jackson) B. BA in Polit. Sci, Old Dominion U., 1981, MA in Urban Studies, 1988. Credit leader Gen. Electric Co., Chesapeake, Va., 1981-84; adminstrv. analyst City of Suffolk, Va., 1984-86, sr. adminstrv. analyst, 1986; asst. city mgr. City of Emporia, Va., 1986-89; pub. affairs officer Henrico County, Richmond, Va., 1989—. Treas. Emporia-Greensville affiliate Am. Heart Assn., 1987-88, program chmn., 1988—; vice chmn. Prince George-Hopewell Emporia Community Diversion Program, 1986, 88-89; fiscal agt. Emporia Greensville Recreation Adv. Commn.; grants adminstr. Emporia-Greensville Airport Commn.; coordinator Community Improvement Council; adv. bd. Southampton Community; bd. dirs. Southeastern Tidewater Opportunity Project, Inc., 1984-86, South Cen. Pvt. Industry Council, 1986-89, Community Diversion Incentive Program, 1986-89; coordinator Emporia-Greensville-Jarratt Community Improvement Council, 1986-89; mem. region bd. Conf. of Minority Pub. Adminstrs., 1989—. Old Dominion U. grantee, 1984-85. Mem. Nat. Recreation and Parks Soc., Am. Parks and Recreation Soc., Nat. Assn. Female Execs. (bd. dirs. 1986, Am. Soc. Pub. Adminstrs. (affiliate, planning com.), Internat. City Mgmt. Assn. (profl. devel. com. 1987—, assoc., award 1985), Va. Local Govt. Mgrs. Assn., Va. Analyst Network, Va. Parks and Recreation Soc., Emporia-Greensville C. of C. Roman Catholic. Home: 8636 Eversham Rd Richmond VA 23229 Office: Henrico County Office Pub Affairs PO Box 27032 Richmond VA 23273

BRYANT, TANYA (MRS. GLENDELL W. DOBBS), real estate executive; b. Sliema, Island of Malta, May 15, 1920; d. Jose Louis and Vera (Jarmonkine) Mifsud; student pvt. schs.; m. Arthur J. W. Pitt, Nov. 17, 1937 (div. Feb. 1952); children—Natasha, Valerie Pitt Deeds, F. David, Micheline Pitt Magdaleno; m. 2d, William Cullen Bryant, Dec. 29, 1959 (div. June 1960); m. 3d, Jack F. Cutler, May 4, 1963 (div. Oct. 1968); m. 4th, Glendell W. Dobbs, Mar. 1969. Came to U.S., 1949, naturalized, 1957. Imported model Jacques Heim, Paris, France, 1949-50; Conover model all major fashion shows and TV shows U.S., 1950-52; sportswear buyer, exec. trainee Neiman Marcus, Dallas, 1952-54; mgr. ladies wear Broadway Dept. Store, Panorama City, Calif., 1954-56; owner, buyer Brides and Besides shops, Los Angeles, Bakersfield, Westwood, Calif., 1956-60; owner Tanya Bryant, Realtor, Lodi, Calif., 1957—; pres. San Joaquin Software Systems, Inc. Originator, dir. Pamper House, Rockefeller Center, 1952. Staff asst. ARC, London, 1942-45; gray lady, Los Angeles, 1957-60. Bd. dirs. Better Bus. Bur., 1976—; mem. San Jose City Tenant/Landlord Com., 1975-79. Mem. Women's Council Nat. Assn. Real Estate Bds. (chpt. pres. 1966, 69), San Fernando Valley Bd. Realtors (dir. 1966), Stockton Bd. Realtors (chmn. investment div. Dist. 7), Lodi Bd. Realtors (bd. dirs. 1983—), Calif. Real Estate Assn. (dir. 1966-72, chmn. public relations 1969, 70, polit. affairs com. 1972-74, legis. com. 1973), San Jose Real Estate Bd. (dir. 1970, sec. 1970), Internat. Inst. Valuers (sr. cert. valuer), Internat. Platform Assn., C. of C. (dir. 1966), Internat. Traders Club. Contbr. articles to profl. jours. Home: 11421 Fortyniner Cir Gold River CA 95670 Office: 107 W Lockeford St Lodi CA 95240

BRYANT, TARBY CHALMER, real estate merchant banker; b. Dunham, N.C., Dec. 5, 1942; s. T. Chalmer and Edna (Sockwell) B.; m. Leslie Johnsen, Oct. 22, 1969. BA, Davidson Coll., 1964; MBA, Ga. State U., 1969. Pres. Nat. Auto Assn., Atlanta, 1969-84, vice-chmn., 1984—; gen. ptnr. Braemar Group Ltd., Atlanta, 1971—; hotel developer and cons. Braemar Group Ltd., Atlanta, 1975. Pres. Atlanta Jaycees, 1971-72, Atlanta Econ. Devel. Corp., 1985-86; chmn. Community Rels. Commn., Atlanta, 1975; fin. chmn. Atlantans for Maynard Jackson, 1973; mem. policy com. Coun. of Urban Econ. Devel., 1985-86. 1st lt. U.S. Army, 1965-67, Vietnam. Named one of Five Outstanding Young Man, Atlanta Jaycees, 1975. Mem. Am. Auto Touring Alliance (pres. 1983-85), AITourisme (mgmt. com. 1983-85). Republican. Presbyterian. Clubs: World Trade (Atlanta). Lodge: Rotary. Home: 4030 Paper Mill Rd Marietta GA 30067 Office: Braemer Group Ltd 225 Peachtree St Ste 1650 Atlanta GA 30303

BRYDON, HAROLD WESLEY, entomologist, writer; b. Hayward, Calif., Dec. 6, 1923; s. Thomas Wesley and Hermione (McHenry) B.; m. Ruth Bacon Vickery, Mar. 28, 1951 (div.); children: Carol Ruth, Marilyn Jeanette, Kenneth Wesley. AB, San Jose State Coll., 1948; MA, Stanford U., 1950. Insecticide sales Calif. Spray Chem. Corp., San Jose, 1951-52; entomologist, fieldman, buyer Beech-Nut Packing Co., 1952-53; mgr., entomologist Lake County Mosquito Abatement Dist., Lakeport, Calif., 1954-58; entomologist, adviser Malaria Eradication Programs ICA (name changed to AID), Kathmandu, Nepal, 1958-61, Washington, 1961-62, Port-au-Prince, Haiti, 1962-63; dir. fly control research Orange County Health Dept. Santa Ana, Calif., 1963-66; free-lance writer in field, 1966—; research entomologist U. N.D. Sch. Medicine, 1968; developer, owner Casierra Resort, Lake Almanor, Calif., 1975-79; owner Westwood (Calif.) Sport Shop, 1979-84; instr. Lassen Community Coll., Susanville, Calif., 1975—; mem. entomology and plant pathology del. People to People Citizen Ambassador Program, China, 1986. Research and publs. on insecticides, mech. methods for dispersing insecticides, biol. control parasites of houseflies. Served with USNR, 1943-46. Recipient Meritorious Honor award for work in Nepal, AID, U.S. Dept. State, 1972. Mem. Entomol. Soc. Am., Am. Mosquito Control Assn., Pacific Coast Entomol. Soc., Am. Legion. Republican. Methodist. Club: Commonwealth of California. Lodges: Masons, Rotary. Home: PO Box 312 Westwood CA 96137

BRYE, FREDERICK LOEL, JR., insurance executive, accountant, consultant; b. Hobart, Ind., Dec. 30, 1953; s. Frederick Loel Sr. and Betty Jane (Perrin) B.; m. Carlie Ruth DeLorme; children: Lindsay Brooke, Matthew Ross. BBA, No. Mich. U., 1976. CPA, Mich., Wis., Fla. Acct. Anderson, Tackman & Co. CPAs, Marquette, Mich., 1976-81; controller Red Lobster Seafood Processing, St. Petersburg, Fla., 1981-85; treas. Nat. Ins. Services, Inc., Tampa, Fla., 1985—; bd. dirs., East Bay Fin. Services, Inc., Nat. Benefit Adminstrs., Inc., officer 1987—; pres. East Bay Benefit Systems, Inc., 1987—; cons. in field. Mem. Am. Inst. CPAs, Mich. Assn. CPAs, Fla. Inst. CPAs, Profl. Inst. Mass Marketers, Tampa C. of C. Republican. Home: 503 Penn National Rd Seffner FL 33584 Office: Nat Ins Svcs Inc 3629 Queen Palm Dr Tampa FL 33619

BRYSON, GARY SPATH, cable television and telephone company executive; b. Longview, Wash., Nov. 8, 1943; s. Roy Griffin and Marguerite Elizabeth (Spath) B.; m. Suzanne D. Groteluesschen, Oct. 18, 1969; children: Kelly Suzanne, Lisa Christine. A.B., Dartmouth Coll., 1966; M.B.A., Tuck Sch., 1967. With Bell & Howell Co., Chgo., 1967-79; pres. consumer group, also consumer and audio-visual group Bell & Howell Co., 1977-79; chmn. bd., chief exec. officer Bell & Howell Mamiya Co., Chgo., 1979-81; exec. v.p. Am. TV & Communications Corp., subs. Time, Inc., Englewood, Colo., 1981-88; v.p. diversified group US West, Englewood, 1988-89, pres. cable communications div., 1989—. Mem. Phi Beta Kappa, Sigma Alpha Epsilon. Republican. Lutheran. Home: 5246 S Jamaica Way Englewood CO 80111 Office: US West 9785 Maroon Cir Ste 210 Englewood CO 80112

BRYSON, JOHN E., utilities company executive; b. N.Y.C., July 24, 1943; m. Louise Henry. B.A. with great distinction, Stanford U., 1965; student, Freie U. Berlin, Federal Republic Germany, 1965-66; J.D., Yale U., 1969. Bar: Calif., Oreg., D.C. Asst. in instrn. Law Sch., Yale U., New Haven, Conn., 1968-69; law clk. U.S. Dist. Ct., San Francisco, 1969-70; co-founder, atty. Natural Resources Def. Council, 1970-74; vice chmn. Oreg. Energy Facility Siting Council, 1975-76; assoc. Davies, Biggs, Strayer, Stoel & Boley, Portland, Oreg., 1975-76; chmn. Calif. State Water Resources Control Bd., 1976-79; vis. faculty Stanford U. Law Sch., Calif., 1977-79; pres. Calif. Pub. Utilities Commn., 1979-82; ptnr. Morrison & Foerster, San Francisco, 1983-84; sr. v.p. law and fin. Calif. Edison Co., Rosemead, 1984; exec. v.p., chief fin. officer SCEcorp. and So. Calif. Edison Co., 1985—; lectr. on pub. utility, energy, communications law.; former mem. exec. com. Nat. Assn. Regulatory Utility Commrs., Calif. Water Rights Law Rev. Commn., Calif. Pollution Control Financing Authority; former mem. adv. bd. Solar Energy Research Inst., Electric Power Research Inst., Stanford Law Sch.; bd. dirs. Pacific Am. Income Shares Inc. Mem. bd. editors, assoc. editor: Yale U. Law Jour. dir. or trustee World Resources Inst., Washington, Calif. Environ. Trust, Claremont U. Ctr., Grad. Sch., Stanford U. Alumni Assn. Woodrow Wilson fellow. Mem. Calif. Bar Assn., Oreg. Bar Assn., D.C. Bar Assn., Nat. Assn. Regulatory Utility Commrs. (exec. com. 1980-82), Stanford U. Alumni Assn. (bd. dirs. 1983-86), Phi Beta Kappa. Office: So Calif Edison Co 2244 Walnut Grove Rosemead CA 91770

BUBB, HARRY GEIPLE, insurance company executive; b. Trinidad, Colo., Dec. 16, 1924; s. Harry H. and Grace Alleine (Geiple) B.; June 9, 1951; children—Melinda, Howard, Susan, John, Mary. BA in Econs, Stanford U., 1946, MBA, 1949; grad., Advanced Mgmt. Program, Harvard U., 1973. With Pacific Mut. Life Ins. Co., 1949—, asst. v.p., 1966-68, then v.p., 1968-72, sr. v.p. group ins., 1972-75, pres., 1975—, chief exec. officer, 1986—, chmn. bd., 1987—. Bd. dirs. Orange County Bus. Com. for Arts, United Way of Orange County, Calif. Econ. Devel. Corp., Com. Econ. Devel.; trustee U.S. Acad. Decathlon, Newport Harbor Art Mus. Served as pilot USNR, World War II. Mem. Calif. C. of C. (bd. dirs.), Los Angeles C. of C. (bd. dirs.). Clubs: Lincoln of Orange County, Balboa Yacht, California, Center. Home: 27 Beacon Bay Newport Beach CA 92660 Office: Pacific Mut Life Ins Co 700 Newport Center Dr Newport Beach CA 92663

BUBECK, NANCY E., human resources executive; b. Trenton, N.J., Mar. 16, 1954; d. Frederick S. Bubeck Jr. and Phyllis E. (Henderson) Bodine. BA, Stockton State Coll., 1978. Lic. cert. social worker, Mass. Social worker various pvt. orgns., Boston, 1979-83; ins. adminstr. Boston Properties, 1982-84; personnel adminstr. Biotechnica Internat. Inc., Cambridge, Mass., 1984-87; mgr. human resources Genzyme Corp., Boston, 1987—. Mem. Indsl. Biotechnology Assn., Mass. Biotechnology Assn., Internat. Assn. Personnel Women, Am. Mgmt. Assn., Zeta Tau Alpha. Democrat. Presbyterian. Office: Genzyme Corp 75 Kneeland St Boston MA 02111

BUCCELLA, WILLIAM VICTOR, lawyer; b. Seattle, Oct. 23, 1943; s. Fred J. and Adeline J. (Carriero) B.; m. Mary A. O'Shea, Aug. 26, 1967; children—Mark Brendon, Jennifer Ball, Peter James. B.S., Canisius Coll., 1965; J.D., Cornell U., 1968. Bar: N.Y. 1968, U.S. Dist. Ct. (we. dist.) N.Y. 1972. Law clk. U.S. Dist. Ct. (we. dist.) N.Y., 1972-74; assoc. Diebold & Millonzi, Buffalo, 1974-77; assoc. gen. counsel Wheelabrator-Frye Inc., Hampton, N.H., 1977-81, gen. counsel, 1981-83; v.p., asst. gen. counsel The Signal Cos. Inc., La Jolla, Calif., 1983-86; mng. dir., gen. counsel The Henley Group Inc., La Jolla, 1986—; dir. New Eng. Legal Found., Boston. Served to lt. JAGC, USN, 1969-72. Mem. ABA, N.Y. State Bar Assn. Office: Henley Group Inc 11255 N Torrey Pines Rd La Jolla CA 92073

BUCCHIERI, PETER CHARLES, countant; b. Bristol, Conn., Nov. 2, 1955; s. Carmelo Charles and Josephine Maria (Winzereth) B.; B.S., Central Conn. State U., 1978; m. Karen O'Connell, Oct. 11, 1975 (div. 1987); 1 child, Sara; m. Lorinda Carol Smart, July 8, 1988. Pres. Bucchieri & Lochet, Inc., Orleans, Mass., 1978; pres. Investment Timing and Research Inc., 1982—, pres. Eastham Travel, 1986—. Mem. Orleans Bd. Trade, 1978—. Cert. fin. planner. Mem. Internat. Assn. Fin. Planners, Inst. Cert. Fin. Planners, Nat. Assn. Security Dealers, Investment Cos. Inst. and Securities Industry Assn. Republican. Roman Catholic. Contbr. articles to various newspapers. Avocations: skiing, reading. Home: 8 Prides Path Orleans MA 02653 Office: Bucchieri & Lochet Inc 12 Main St Orleans MA 02653

BUCHALTER, STUART DAVID, retail paint company executive; b. Los Angeles, Aug. 13, 1937; s. Irwin R. and Ethel M. B.; children: Stephanie, Michael, Douglas. B.A., U. Calif., Berkeley, 1959; LL.B., Harvard U., 1962. Bar: Calif. 1963, D.C. 1975. Partner firm Buchalter, Nemer, Fields & Younger, Los Angeles, 1964-80; spl. counsel SEC, 1975; chmn. bd. Standard Brands Paint Co., Torrance, Calif., 1980—; dir. City Nat. Bank, Beverly Hills, Calif., Lorimar Telepictures, Culver City, Calif. Author articles in field. Vice pres. Am. Jewish Com., 1979, 86; trustee Jewish Community Found. of Greater Los Angeles; bd. dirs. Constl. Rights Found. Served with USCG, 1962-63. Mem. State Bar Calif., D.C. Bar Assn., Los Angeles Area C. of C. (bd. dirs.). Office: Standard Brands Paint Co 4300 W 190th St Torrance CA 90509

BUCHANAN, BRENDA J., computer manufacturing executive; b. San Diego; d. Fred and Annie M. (Winston) B. BS in Math., Physics and Chemistry, U. Denver; MA in Math., Washington U., 1973; postgrad. McGill U., 1973-75, U. Cologne, Fed. Republic Germany. Math. instr. Washington U., St. Louis, 1969-71; programmer/analyst United Aircraft of Can., Longueil, Que., 1971-73; ops. research analyst Consol. Bathurst Ltd., Montreal, Que., 1973-76; corp. new product planning mgr. Digital Equipment Corp., Maynard, Mass., 1976-80, new product program mgr., Springfield, Mass., 1980-84, tapes bus. mgr., 1984-88, corp. purchasing program office mgr., Northboro, Mass., 1986-88, dist. mfg. mgr., Marlboro, Mass., 1988—; mem. Digital Equipment Women's Adv. Com., 1986—. Leader, Can. Girl Guides, Montreal, 1972-74; mem. mayor's blue ribbon com. Dept. Pub. Works, Springfield, 1983. Fulbright fellow, Fed. Republic

Germany; recipient Experiment in Internat. Living award Fed. Republic Germany, 19. Mem. Can. Ops. Research Soc., LWV (bd. dirs.), Strathmore Shire Assn. (trustee 1987—). The Profl. Council, Alpha Kappa Alpha (Basileus, Ivy of Yr., Denver chpt.). Democrat. Baptist. Club: Links, Inc. (Springfield) (treas. 1984-86). Home: 4E Strathmore Shire PO Box 49 North Uxbridge MA 01538 Office: Digital Equipment Corp 3 Results Way (MR03-2/J20) Marlborough MA 01752-9103

BUCHANAN, JAMES MCGILL, economist, educator; b. Murfreesboro, Tenn., Oct. 2, 1919; s. James McGill and Lila (Scott) B.; m. Anne Bakke, Oct. 5, 1945. BS, Middle Tenn. State Coll., 1940; MA, U. Tenn., 1941; PhD, U. Chgo., 1948; D honoris causa, U. Giessen, 1982, U. Zurich, 1984, George Mason U., U. Valencia, New U. Lisbon, 1987, Ball State U., City U. London, 1988. Prof. econs. U. Tenn., 1950-51; prof. econs. Fla. State U., 1951-56; prof. econs. U. Va., 1956-62, Paul G. McIntyre prof. econs., 1962-68, chmn. dept., 1956-62; prof. econs. U. Calif., Los Angeles, 1968-69; univ. disting. prof. econs. Va. Poly. Inst., 1969-83, George Mason U., 1983—; dir. Ctr. for Pub. Choice, 1969—; Fulbright research scholar, Italy, 1955-56, Ford Faculty research fellow, 1959-60; Fulbright vis. prof. Cambridge U., 1961-62. Author: (with C.L. Allen and M.R. Colberg) Prices, Income and Public Policy, 954, Public Principles of Public Debt, 1958, The Public Finances, 1960, Fiscal Theory and Political Economy, 1960, (with G. Tullock) The Calculus of Consent, 1962, Public Finance in Democratic Process, 1966, The Demand and Supply of Public Goods, 1968, Cost and Choice, 1969, (with N. Devletoglu) Academia in Anarchy, 1970; Editor: (with R. Tollison) Theory of Public Choice, 1972, (with G.F. Thirlby) LSE Essays on Cost, 1973, The Limits of Liberty, 1975, (with R. Wagner) Democracy in Deficit, 1977, Freedom in Constitutional Contract, 1978, What Should Economists Do?, 1979, (with G. Brennan) The Power to Tax, 1980; (with G. Brennan) The Reason of Rules, 1985; Liberty Market and State, 1985, Economics: Between Predictive Science and Moral Philosophy, 1987, Economics: Between Predictive Science and Moral Philosophy, 1987, Explorations in Constitutional Economics, 1989; contbr. articles to profl. jours. Served as lt. USNR, 1941-46. Decorated Bronze Star medal. Recipient Nobel Prize in Economics, 1986. Fellow Am. Acad. Arts and Scis.; mem. Am. Econ. Assn. (exec. com. 1966-69, v.p. 1971, dist. fellow 1983—, Seidman award 1984), So. Econ. Assn. (pres. 1963), Western Econ. Assn. (pres. 1983), Mt. Pelerin Soc. (pres. 1984-86). Home: PO Box G Blacksburg VA 24063 Office: George Mason U Dept Econs 4400 University Dr Fairfax VA 22030

BUCHANAN, LEE ANN, communications company executive; b. Albuquerque, July 6, 1955; d. William Henry Buchanan and Juanita Irene (Pilgrim) Wood; m. Charles Stanton Wood, Jan. 17, 1987. BA, U. Calif., Irvine, 1977. Exec. asst. Congressman William Thomas, Washington, 1979-83; dep. chief staff Gov. George Deukmejian, Sacramento, Calif., 1983-84; v.p. client services Nelson-Ralston-Robb Communications, Costa Mesa, Calif., 1985—. Bd. govs. Rep. Assocs. of Orange County, 1985—; founding sec. Orange County Young Reps., 1985. Mem. Internat. Assn. Bus. Communicators, Am. Assn. Polit. Cons., Pub. Relations Soc. Am., U. Calif.-Irvine Alumni Assn. Office: Nelson-Ralston-Robb Communications 125 E Baker St 180 Costa Mesa CA 92626

BUCHANAN, PETER TOWNLEY, investment banker; b. Orange, N.J., Sept. 12, 1934; s. Percy H. and Ruth C. (Townley) B.; m. Lane Eichhorn, Oct. 20, 1956; children: Richard T., Linda V. AB with honors, Princeton U., 1956. With CS First Boston Inc. and predecessor co., N.Y.C., 1956-57, 60—; v.p. First Boston Corp., N.Y.C., 1967-73, mgr. equity securities dept., 1972-74, exec. v.p., dir. charge trading, sales, ops. and administrn., 1974-78, pres., 1978—, chief exec. officer, 1983—, also dir., pres., chief operating officer, 1978-83; pres., chief exec. officer First Boston Inc. (parent), N.Y.C., 1983—, also dir.; bd. dir. N.Y. Stock Exch.; mem. adv. com. Grad. Sch. of Indsl. Adminstrn. at Carnegie Mellon U.; mem. adv. coun. grad. sch. bus. Stanford Univ.'s ; mem. fin. com. Joint Coun. on Econ. Edn.; bd. dirs. Ethics Resource Ctr., Inc., N.Y.C. Ptnrship, Inc. Bd. dirs. Alzheimer's Disease and Related Disorders Assn.; trustee Greater N.Y. Couns. Boy Scouts Am. Capt. USAF, 1957-60. Mem. Security Traders Assn. N.Y., Securities Industry Assn. (governing council), bd. dirs., exec. com., vice chmn. 1981—). Clubs: Bond (N.Y.C.), Princeton (N.Y.C.); links, Morris County Golf, Baltusrol Golf, Castle Pines Golf Club. Home: 32 Crescent Rd Madison NJ 07940 Office: 1st Boston Corp Park Avenue Pla New York NY 10055

BUCHANAN, ROBERT CAMPBELL, corporate professional; b. Appleton, Wis., May 13, 1940; s. William Eugene and Josephine (Breneman) B.; m. Bonnie Glidden, Aug. 5, 1961; children: Scott Gustavus, Phillip Edward, Emily Virginia. BA, Lawrence Coll., 1962; MBA, Dartmouth Coll., 1967. With Fox River Paper Co. div. Fox Valley Corp., Appleton, 1967-74, exec. v.p., 1973-74, pres., 1974-79; pres., chief operating officer Fox Valley Corp., Appleton, 1979-80, pres., chief exec. officer, 1980—; bd. dirs. Am. Paper Inst., Banc One, Milw. and Appleton, W.H. Brady Co., Milw., Ariens Co., Brillion, Wis., Charter Mfg. Co., Wis. Assoc. Mfrs. & Commerce, Madison, Wis. Dir. Appleton Devel. Coun., 1982, United Health Svcs., 1980-81; trustee Lawrence U., 1979—, Inst. Paper Chemistry, 1986-88. Mem. Wis. Paper Group (dir. 1976-83), The Young Pres. Orgn. (chmn. Wis. 1983-84), Exec. Com., North Shore Club, Menasha Club, Fla. Country Club, Boynton Beach Club. Republican. Congregationalist. Home: W6309 Firelane 9 Menasha WI 54952 Office: Fox Valley Corp 600 S Vulcan St Appleton WI 54915

BUCHANAN, TERI BAILEY, public relations executive, marketing agency owner; b. Long Beach, Calif., Feb. 24, 1946; d. Alton Hervey and Ruth Estelle (Thompson) Bailey; m. Robert Wayne Buchanan, Aug. 14, 1964 (div. May 1979). BA in English with highest honors, Ark. Poly. Coll., 1968. With employee communications AT&T, Kansas City, Mo., 1968-71; freelance writer Ottawa, Kans., 1971-73; publs. dir. Ottawa U., 1973-74; regional info. officer U.S. Dept. Labor, Kansas City, 1974-75; owner, operator PBT Communications, Kansas City, 1975-79; sr. pub. affairs rep., sr. editor, exhibit supr., communications specialist Standard Oil/Chevron, San Francisco, 1979-84; owner The Resource Group/Mktg. Pub. Relations, San Francisco, 1984—; bd. Golden Gate U. Hosp. Mgmt. Dept., San Francisco, 1984—; mem faculty Golden Gate U. Pub. Relation Masters Program, San Francisco, 1987. Pub. relations trainer Bus. Vols. for Arts, San Francisco, 1985—; pro-bono cons. Black Tie Soc.-Mayor's Fund-Homeless, San Francisco, 1987. Recipient Internat. Assn. Bus. Communicators Bay Area Gold and Silver awards, 1984. Mem. Publicity Club, Pub. Relations Round Table, San Francisco Conv. and Visitors Bur., San Francisco C. of C., Concord C. of C., Commonwealth Club Calif. (vice chmn. pub. relations com. 1984—). Democrat. Congregationalist. Office: The Resource Group 555 De Haro St #340 San Francisco CA 94107

BUCHHOLZ, DAVID LOUIS, accountant; b. Wisconsin Rapids, Wis., Aug. 13, 1936; s. Lawrence Frank and Edna Ella (Benz) B.; m. Arlene Jean Benke, June 6, 1959 (div. 1982); children: Lisa Lynn Shuttleworth, Shawn Leslie Skidmore, Dana Gaye; m. Vera Rose Wombwell, June 2, 1984. Student, Wis. State Coll., 1953-54; BBA, U. Wis., 1958. CPA, Ill., Iowa, La., Mich. Head Chgo. tax div. Arthur Andersen & Co., Chgo., 1975-79, tax practice dir., 1978-79, mng. dir. tax practice, 1979-80, mng. dir. tax policies & procedures, 1980-81, mng. ptnr. tax practice, 1981—. Campaign chmn. Am. Cancer Soc., Chgo. area, 1973, Cook county area, 1974, State of Ill., 1975; regional co-chmn. NCCJ, Chgo., 1979—; com. mem. U. Chgo. Fed. Tax Planning Com., Chgo., 1979—; bd. visitors U. Wis. Sch. Bus., Madison. Mem. Am. Inst. CPA's (various tax coms.), Ill. Soc. CPA's, Econ. Club Chgo., Internat. Fiscal Assn., Ill. Inst. Continuing Legal Edn., Bascom Hill Soc. of U. Wis. Clubs: Univ., Mid-Am. Office: Arthur Andersen & Co 69 W Washington St Ste 3500 Chicago IL 60602

BUCHHOLZ, KRISTI MICHELLE ATCHLEY, health and beauty aids executive; b. Knoxville, Tenn., May 6, 1962; d. Oliver Wendell and Montie Jane (Rogers) Atchley; m. James William Buchholz Jr., May 9, 1987. BS in Advt., U. Tenn., 1985. Sales rep. Internat. Playtex, Dover, Del., 1985-87; mgr. key account ter. Shulton U.S.A., Collierville, Tenn., 1987-89, area mgr., 1989—; speaker in field. Singer Friendship Ambassador Club, 1978-79; active local polit. campaigns. Mem. Women in Advt., Univ. Tenn. Advt. Club. Republican. Baptist.

BUCHHOLZ, WILLIAM JAMES, communications specialist, educator; b. Ladysmith, Wis., July 17, 1945; s. James Fossegard and Hazel Winnefred (Crandell) B.; m. Dorothy Ann Kostka, June 17, 1967; children: Christopher, Jeffrey. BA, U. Wis., Eau Claire, 1967; MA, Ohio U., 1968; PhD, U. Ill., 1976. Grad. asst. U. Ill., Urbana, 1972-76; asst. prof. English, bus. communication Bentley Coll., Waltham, Mass., 1976-83, assoc. prof., 1983—, dir. undergrad./grad. bus. communication program, 1988—; cons. 1978—; mgr. pubs. Scholastech Inc., Cambridge, Mass., 1983—. Editor/author: Communication Training and Consulting in Business, Industry and Government, 1983; contbg. editor The Challenge of Change: Managing Communications and Building Corporate Image in the 1990's, 1989; contbr. articles to profl. jours. NDEA-IV fellow, 1967-68; FIPSE grantee, 1986, 87. Mem. Assn. for Bus. Communication, Soc. Tech. Communication, Assn. for Profl. Writing Cons., Internat. Platform Assn. Roman Catholic. Home: 69 School St Lexington MA 02173 Office: Bentley Coll Grad Ctr 175 Forest St Waltham MA 02154-4705

BUCHIN, STANLEY IRA, management consultant; b. N.Y.C., Sept. 7, 1931; s. K. and Bertha (Handman) B.; S.B., M.I.T., 1952; M.B.A, Harvard U., 1956, D.B.A., 1962; m. Jacqueline Thurber Chase, Sept. 14, 1957; children—Linda C., David L., Gordon T. Asst. to treas. Bay State Abrasives, 1956-58; research asst. Harvard Bus. Sch., 1958-59, research assoc., 1959-60, instr., 1960-61, lectr., 1961-62, asst. prof., 1962-66, assoc. prof., 1966-69; pres. Applied Decision Systems, Wellesley, Mass., 1969-78; v.p. Temple, Barker & Sloane, Inc., Lexington, Mass., 1975-80, sr. v.p., 1980—, also dir.; dir. Wellesley Volkswagen, Capital Formations Corp., Diamond Machining Tech. Multicomp. Trustee, treas. Human Relations Service, 1973-82; trustee Gould Farm; mem. adv. com. Brandeis U. Dept. Mental Health. Served in Chem. Corps, U.S. Army, 1952-54. IBM fellow, 1962-63; George F. Baker scholar, 1956. Mem. Am. Mktg. Assn., Inst. Mgmt. Sci., Fin. Mgmt. Assn., Tau Beta Pi. Republican. Congregationalist. Clubs: Stage Harbor Yacht, Harvard (Boston), Cambridge Boat. Home: 65 E India Row Boston MA 02110 Office: Temple Barker & Sloane 33 Hayden Ave Lexington MA 02173

BUCHMANN, GARY JOHN, accountant, consultant; b. Paterson, N.J., Nov. 22, 1957; s. William A. and Gertrude (Pelhak) B. BBA, Bucknell U., 1979. CPA, N.J., N.Y. Mgr. Null N. Fish & Co., CPA's, Englewood Cliffs, N.J., 1979-87; pvt. practice acctg. Hawthorne, N.J., 1987—. Fellow N.J. Soc. CPA's; mem. Am. Inst. CPA's, N.Y. Soc. CPA's. Republican. Methodist. Home and Office: 9 Third Ave Hawthorne NJ 07506

BUCHNER, JAMES, real estate and economic development executive; b. Middletown, Conn., Aug. 9, 1932; s. Frank D. and Anna R. (Augeri) B.; A.A., Compton Coll., 1956; B.A., Whittier Coll., 1958; B.S. in Mech. Engring., West Coast U., 1969, M.S. in Mgmt. Fin., 1972; m. Dora Guerrero, Dec. 26, 1964; 1 son, Donald. Sales rep. Los Angeles Dept. Water and Power, 1960-61, comml. lighting specialist, 1961-62, govtl. sales cons., 1962-64, power sales cons., 1964-68, promotional planner, 1968, power sales engring. assoc., 1968-69, supr. market research, 1969-72; citrus grower, 1969—; devel. dir. City of Placentia, Calif., 1972-77; founder, pres. Real Estate Cons. & Assocs., Whittier, Calif., 1977—; pres., chief exec. officer Econ. Devel. Corp. Orange County, Orange, Calif., 1977-83; bd. dirs. Unisen Corp. Mem. Calif. Statewide Econ. Stblzn. Com., 1972-80; mem. exec. com. So. Calif. Econ. and Job Devel. Council, 1977-81; mem. So. Calif. Residential Research Com., 1969-73; bd. dirs. Los Angeles Dept. Water and Power Employees Credit Union, 1970-72, asst. treas., 1971, treas., 1972; bd. dirs. Orange County Family Service Assn., 1976-81, v.p. 1981; community chmn. March of Dimes, 1976-77; chmn. Orange County Task Force on Pvt. Sector Employment Incentives. Served with USN, 1953-55. Cert. econ./indsl. developer, lic. real estate broker. Mem. Illuminating Engring. Soc. Home: 5536 Adele Ave Whittier CA 90601

BUCHSBAUM, SOLOMON JAN, physicist; b. Stryj, Poland, Dec. 4, 1929; came to U.S., 1953, naturalized, 1957; s. Jacob and Berta (Wassertheil) B.; m. Phyllis N. Isenman, July 3, 1955; children: Rachel Joy, David Joel, Adam Louis. B.S., McGill U., 1952, M.S., 1953; Ph.D., Mass. Inst. Tech., 1957. Mem. tech. staff Bell Labs., Murray Hill, N.J., 1958-61; dept. head Bell Labs., 1961-65, dir., 1965-68; v.p. Sandia Labs., Albuquerque, 1968-71; exec. dir. Bell Labs., 1971-76, v.p., 1976-79, exec. v.p., 1979—; research in gaseous and solid state plasmas, communications; sr. cons. Def. Sci. Bd., chmn., 1972-77, 81—; mem. AEC Controlled Thermonuclear Fusion Com., 1965-72, Pres.'s Sci. Adv. Com., 1970-73, Pres.'s Com. on Sci. and Tech., 1975-76; mem. fusion power coordinating com. ERDA, 1972-76, adv. group sci. and tech. NSF, 1976-77; chmn. Energy Research Adv. Bd., 1978-81; mem. Naval Research Adv. Com., 1978-81; mem. vis. com. M.I.T., 1977—, mem. corp. devel. com., 1980—; cons. Office Sci. and Tech., 1976-82; chmn. White House Sci. Council, 1982—; trustee Rand Corp., 1982—; mem. Draper Lab. Corp., 1983—; bd. dirs.; bd. Govs. Argonne Nat. Lab., 1985—. Assoc. editor: Revs. Modern Physics, 1968-72, Jour. Applied Physics, 1968-70, Physics of Fluids, 1963-64; co-author: Waves in Plasmas, 1963; contbr. numerous articles to profl. jours. Trustee Argonne Univs. Assn., 1979-82. Moyse traveling fellow, 1953-54; IBM fellow, 1954-56; recipient Anna Molson Gold medal, Sec. of Def. medal for Outstanding Pub. Service, 1977; Sec. of Energy award for Exceptional Pub. Service, 1981; Nat. Medal of Sci., 1986. Fellow Am. Phys. Soc. (chmn. div. plasma physics 1968, mem. council 1973-76), IEEE (Frederk Philips award 1987), Am. Acad. Arts and Scis., AAAS; mem. Nat. Acad. Engring. (exec. com. 1975-76), Nat. Acad. Scis., Cosmos Club. Office: AT&T Bell Labs Crawfords Corner Rd Holmdel NJ 07733

BUCHWALD, ELIAS, public relations executive; b. N.Y.C., Feb. 5, 1924; s. Louis and Sara (Gottfried) B.; m. Oct. 25, 1952; children: Monita, Lee Ezer, Gena Golda. B. Chem Engring. Sch. Tech. CCNY, 1944. Process engr. Union Carbide, Oak Ridge, 1946-48; acct. exec. Sheldon, Morse, Hutchins & Easton, N.Y.C., 1948-50; sr. assoc. Harold Burson, Pub. Relations, N.Y.C., 1950-52; v.p. Burson-Marsteller, N.Y.C., 1952-75, vice chmn., 1975—; pres. Marsteller Found., N.Y.C., 1980—; vice chmn. Cohn & Wolfe, 1988—. Contbr. articles to profl. jours. Served with U.S. Army, 1944-46. Mem. Pub. Relations Soc. Am. (pres. N.Y. chpt. 1987-88, chmn. bd. ethics and profl. standards 1988-89, Presdl. Citation 1980-82, 1987, 88), Am. Inst. Chem. Engrs. Republican. Jewish. Home: 1020 Park Ave New York NY 10028 Office: Burson Marsteller 230 Park Ave S New York NY 10003

BUCHWALD, LEE E., investment banker; b. N.Y.C., Jan. 2, 1958; s. Elias and Gloria F. (Mayer) B. BA, Columbia U., 1978, MBA, 1982. Mgmt. cons. McKinsey & Co., N.Y.C., 1977-78, William E. Hill & Co., N.Y.C., 1978-79; investment banker Smith Barney, Harris Upham & Co., N.Y.C., 1979-81, Rothschild Inc., N.Y.C., 1982—. Home: 115 4th Ave Apt 5C New York NY 10003 Office: Rothschild Inc One Rockefeller Pla New York NY 10020

BUCK, CHRISTIAN BREVOORT ZABRISKIE, independent oil operator; b. San Francisco, Oct. 18, 1914; s. Frank D. and Zayda Justine (Zabriskie) B.; student U. Calif., Berkeley, 1931-33; m. Natalie Leontine Smith, Sept. 12, 1948; children—Warren Zabriskie, Barbara Anne. Mem. engring. dept. U.S. Potash Co., Carlsbad, N.Mex., 1933-39; indl. oil operator, producer, Calif., 1939-79, N.Mex., 1929—, owner, operator farm, ranch, Eddy County, N.Mex., 1951-79; dir. Belridge Oil Co. until 1979; dir. Buck Ranch Co. (Calif.) Served with RAF, 1942-45. Democrat. Episcopalian. Club: Riverside Country (Carlsbad). Home: 108 W Alicante Rd Santa Fe NM 87501 Office: PO Box 2183 Santa Fe NM 87504

BUCK, DANIEL KARL, insurance executive; b. Wichita, Kans., Sept. 4, 1953; s. Benjamin Harrison and kathryn Rose Buck; m. Gloria Ann Norris, Sept. 10, 1977 (div. Apr. 1986); children: Brett Daniel, Bryan Benjamin. Student, Pratt (Kans.) Jr. Coll., 1973; cert. in exec. fringe benefits, Purdue U., 1987. CLU. Career agt. Security Mut. Life, Wichita, 1974-85; owner, pres. Ins. Strategies, Inc., 1985—. Chmn. Diabetes Bike-a-thon, Wichita, 1982. Mem. Nat. Assn. Life Underwriters, Million Dollar Rountable, Cosmopolitan Club (pres. Wichita chpt. 1984-85), Masons., Shriners. Republican. Roman Catholic. Office: Ins Strategies Inc 807 N Waco Ste 11 Wichita KS 67203

BUCK, WILLIAM MAJOR, JR., coal company executive; b. Phila., June 4, 1931; s. William Major and Mabel Irene (Mattis) B.; m. Jacquelin Rae Machin, June 26, 1959; children—Allyson Paige, Jennifer Leigh. B.A. in

Liberal Arts, Wesleyan U., Middletown, Conn., 1953; M.B.A., U. Chgo., 1960. Mgmt. trainee, supr. ring, asst. to labor relations mgr. The Budd Co., Phila. and Gary, Ind., 1953-62; labor relations mgr. Miles Labs., Elkhart, Ind., 1962-64; employee relations mgr. Internat. Minerals & Chem. Co., Bartow, Fla., 1964-66; v.p. employee relations Consumer Products Group, The Singer Co., N.Y.C., 1966-75; v.p. employee relations, officer Berwind Corp., Phila., 1975-78; sr. v.p. adminstrn. Peabody Holding Co., Inc., St. Louis, 1978—. Trustee Sta. KETC Pub. Broadcasting St. dir. Jr. Achievement Greater Miss. Valley, 1981, ARC, St. Louis Bi-State chpt., 1986. Served with M.I. Corps, AUS, 1953-55. Presbyterian. Club: Mo. Athletic. Office: Peabody Holding Co Inc 301 N Memorial Dr Saint Louis MO 63102

BUCKINGHAM, RICHARD L(EROY), computer company executive; b. Huntington, Ind., Sept. 27, 1945; s. Ralph L. and Luella (Sell) B.; m. Cheryl A. Robins, June 10, 1967; children: Blake, Amber. BA, Wabash Coll., 1967; MBA, Harvard U., 1973. Mgr. fin. Gen. Mills Inc., Mpls., 1973-78; asst. treas. Wheelabrator-Frye Inc., Hampton, N.H., 1978-81; treas. Computervision Corp., Bedford, Mass., 1981-87, v.p., treas., 1987-88; v.p., treas. Prime Computer Inc., Natick, Mass., 1988—. Served to lt. (j.g.) USNR. Mem. Nat. Assn. Corp. Treas. Home: 2 Prescott Ln Hampton Falls NH 03844 Office: Prime Computer Inc Prime Pk Natick MA 01760

BUCKINGHAM, RICHARD SHERWOOD, soft drink company executive; b. Bridgeport, Conn., July 20, 1932; s. Clyde Sherwood and Melicent Camp (Wilcox) B.; m. Martha Virginia Hedeman, Dec. 17, 1955; children: Linda Buckingham Thomson, Stephen Sherwood. BA, Middlebury Coll., 1954. Div. mgr. Continental Can Co., St. Louis, 1958-68, gen. mgr., 1969-72; mgr. new bus. devel. Continental Can Co., N.Y.C., 1972-74; mgr. nat. sales Luxo-Lamp Corp., Port Chester, Conn., 1974-77; v.p. Cadbury Schweppes, Inc., Stamford, Conn., 1977—. Pres., bd. dirs. Vol. Ctr. S.W. Conn., Stamford, 1987—; v.p Stamford United Way, 1984—. Lt. USNR, 1953-57. Republican. Home: 67 Old Kings Hwy Wilton CT 06897 Office: Cadbury Schweppes Inc High Ridge Park Stamford CT 06905

BUCKLER, SHELDON A., photographic company executive; b. N.Y.C., May 18, 1931; s. Morris H. and Mollie M. (Smith) B.; m. Dorothea J. Chandler, June 30, 1978; children—Julie, Eve, Sarah. B.A., NYU, 1951; Ph.D., Columbia U., 1954. Research assoc. U. Md., 1954-56; research group leader Am. Cyanamid Co., Stamford, Conn., 1956-62; mgr. organic unit AMF, Springdale, Conn., 1962-64; with Polaroid Corp., Cambridge, Mass., 1964—; exec. v.p. Polaroid Corp., 1980—; dir. Lord Corp. Contbr. articles to profl. jours.; patentee in field. Trustee U. Union U. 1973-75; bd. mgrs. Mass. Eye and Ear Infirmary, 1985—; mem. adv. bd. Am. Repertory Thetre, 1988—. Served with U.S. Army, 1954-56. Mem. Am. Chem. Soc., Phi Beta Kappa. Office: Polaroid Corp 549 Technology Sq Cambridge MA 02139

BUCKLEY, CONK, JR., sales director, financial consultant; b. Springfield, Ill., Apr. 21, 1941; s. Conk Sr. and Veronica (Hoffmann) B.; m. Paula Buckley, Sept. 1, 1962; children: Conk III, Shannon. BA in Econs., U. Iowa, 1965. CLU, Chartered Fin. Cons. Systems analyst Franklin Life Ins., Springfield, 1965-67, supr., 1967-71, dept. mgr., 1971-75, dist. agt., 1975-76, gen. agt., 1976-77, supt. of agys., 1975-77, agy. v.p., 1977-79; regional sales dir. Franklin Life Ins., Leawood, Kans., 1979—. Fellow Life Mgmt. Inst.; mem. Kansas City Gen. Agts. and Mgrs. (bd. dirs. 1982-83, treas., sec., v.p. 1984-85, 86, pres. 1987, regional membership chmn. 1988—). Republican. Roman Catholic. Office: Franklin Life Ins 4701 College Blvd Ste 110 Leawood KS 66211

BUCKLEY, ELLIOT ROSS, government official, lawyer; b. N.Y.C., June 18, 1921; s. Edmund Langford and Beryl (Meeks) B.; m. Mary Smallpage, May 1, 1948; children—Elliot Ross, Margaret Buckley Doll, John Smallpage, Brian Langford, Michael Stewart. B.A., U. Tex., Austin, 1943; J.D., Tulane U., New Orleans, 1949. Bar: La. 1949. Atty. Gulf Oil Corp., Shreveport, La., 1950-52; sole practice law New Orleans, 1953-56, 59-64; atty. Gulf Oil Corp., New Orleans, 1956-59; tchr., asst. prin. Sam Barthe Sch., Metairie, La., 1964-69; atty. advisor U.S. Dept. Justice, Washington, 1969-82; gen. counsel Occupational Safety and Health Rev. Commn., Washington, 1982-84, commr., 1984, chmn., 1984—. Mem. Westbriar Civic Assn., Vienna, Va., 1972—; mem. Town Council, Vienna, 1976-86; mem. Fairfax County Republican Commn., Va., 1984-86, Orleans Parish (La.) Rep. Commn., 1954-56, 60-62, La. State Rep. Cen. Commn., 1954-56. Served with USAAF, 1943-46; candidate for Mayor of New Orleans, 1962. Mem. La. State Bar Assn., ABA, Phi Delta Phi, Delta Kappa Epsilon. Republican. Roman Catholic. Home: 108 St Andrews Dr Vienna VA 22180 Office: Occupational Safety & Health Rev Commn 1825 K St NW Washington DC 20006

BUCKLEY, JOHN WILLIAM, financial company executive; b. Parkersburg, W.Va., Feb. 28, 1932; s. George Brady and Clara Ellen (Humphrey) B.; m. Rena Mae Gaudreau, Aug. 9, 1958; children—Karen Lynn, Jeffrey Scott. Student, Dartmouth Coll., 1950-52; BS, Boston U., 1957; MBA, NYU, 1963. Chartered fin. analyst. Securities analyst Mut. Benefit Life Ins. Co., Newark, 1957-64; securities analyst IDS Fin. Svcs., Mpls., 1964-71, treas., v.p., 1971—. Treas. Mpls. Soc. for Blind, 1981. Served with U.S. Army, 1952-55. Mem. Twin Cities Soc. Securities Analysts, Lions. Republican. Episcopalian. Home: 4801 Aspasia Ln Edina MN 55435 Office: IDS Fin Corp IDS Tower Minneapolis MN 55474

BUCKLEY, KEVIN TIMOTHY, information and sales processing executive; b. N.Y.C., July 30, 1949; s. Terrence Dennis and Anna (Dietz) B.; m. Lidna Heberer (div. June 1983); 1 child, Kerry. BA, Pace U., 1972. Customer svcs. mgr. Lewco Securities, N.Y.C., 1972-73; regional v.p. Kalvar Corp., Mpls., 1973-88, also former mem. bd. dirs.; pres. The Protector Corp., Boulder, Colo., 1988—. N.Y. Edn. Assn. Regents scholar, 1967. Mem. Assn. for Info. and Image Mgmt., Data Processing Mgmt. Assn., U.S. Power Squadron. Roman Catholic. Home: 336 Parkway Ct Minneapolis MN 55419 Office: The Protector Corp 6681 Arapahoe Boulder CO 80301

BUCKLEY, RICHARD BENNETT, asset management company executive; b. Providence, Nov. 7, 1942; s. Alfred and Helen (Searles) B.; m. Karen Owen, May, 1982; 1 child, Owen Searles. BA, Denison U., 1965; JD, Syracuse U., 1968; EMBA, U. New Haven, 1982. Successively asst. dean, dir. placement, dean admissions, lectr. ins. law, assoc. dean, dir. placement, dir. admissions, asst. prof. law Syracuse (N.Y.) U., 1968-74, assoc. prof. law, 1974-77; pres. Schiavone Tire & Rubber Reclamation Corp., New Haven, Conn., 1978-80, Schiavone Sports, New Haven, 1978-80; v.p. Cowen Asset Mgmt., N.Y.C., 1980-87, spl. ltd. ptnr., 1986—, sr. v.p., 1987—; chmn. bd. Founders Bank, New Haven, 1985—; prin. Maple Valley Ski Area, West Dummerston, Vt., 1985—; mentor Yale U. Sch. Orgn. and Mgmt., New Haven, 1987—. Author: Handbook on Profl. Ethics and Responsibility, 1973; mng. editor Ins. Counsel Jour., 1971-87; contbr. legal articles to profl. jours. Mem. ABA, N.Y. Bar Assn., Order of Coif, Phi Sigma Alpha, Phi Delta Phi, Quinnipiack Club (bd. govs.), Rotary (pres. 1987-88, Spl. Pres. award 1982-83, Rotarian of Yr. 1985-86). Home: 34 Grove Hill Rd Sachem's Head CT 06437 Office: Cowen Asset Mgmt 205 Whitney Ave Ste 317 New Haven CT 06511

BUCKLEY, STEPHEN, JR., auditor; b. Boston, May 28, 1949; s. Stephen and Catherine (Long) B.; m. Susan Palmer Bliss, Sept. 16, 1972; children: Sarah, Daniel, Timothy. AB in Econs., Bowdoin Coll., 1971; MS in Acctg., Northeastern U., 1973. CPA, Mass. Audit ptnr. Arthur Young & Co., Boston, 1973—. Treas. Boston Latin Sch. Found., 1988—; chmn. Medfield (Mass.) Indsl. Fin. Authority, 1986—. Mem. Am. Inst. CPAs, Mass. Soc. CPAs, New Eng. Brit. Bus. Assn. (bd. dirs., treas.). Clubs: Charles River Country (Newton, Mass.), Bay (Boston). Home: 60 Millbrook Rd Medfield MA 02052 Office: Arthur Young One Boston Pl Boston MA 02102

BUCKMAN, HARLEY ROYAL, insurance company executive; b. Mpls., Apr. 7, 1907; s. Royal George Buckman and Menna (Sievers) Schwarz; married, Oct. 24, 1934; children: Ned, Todd. BBA, U. Minn., 1943. Pres. H. R. Buckman CLU & Assocs., Inc., Milw., 1940—; pres. Pension Mgmt. Inc., Milw., 1955—; chmn. bd. dirs. Polyval Inc., San Gabriel, Calif. 1980—. Contbr. articles to profl. jours. Recipient Nat. Quality award Nat. Assn. Life Underwriters, Wis. Assn. Mental Health (past state chmn.).

Mem. Milw. Assn. Chartered Life Underwriters, Wis. Assn. Mental Health (past state chmn.). Republican. Club: Milw. Country. Office: HR Buckman CLU & Assocs 5225 N Ironwood Rd Ste 118 Milwaukee WI 53217

BUCKMAN, ROBERT HENRY, chemical company executive; b. Louisville, Dec. 1, 1937; s. Stanley Joseph and Mertie (Willigar) B. BSChemE, Purdue U., 1959; MBA in Stats., U. Chgo., 1961. Asst. to pres. Buckman Labs., Memphis, 1961-63, sec.-treas., 1963-71, vice chmn. bd. dirs., sec-treas., 1971-80, pres., chmn. bd., 1980-84, chmn. of bd., pres., chmn. of bd., 1984—. Mem. Tenn. Dist. Export Council, Patron Arts Appreciation Found., Memphis, Rhodes Coll. Exec. Com., Memphis, 1981—, Met. Inter-Faith Assn. Devel. Bd., Memphis, 1985—; chmn. devel. com. Rhodes Coll. Bd. Trustees, Memphis, 1981—; exec. com. Future Memphis, 1986—. Mem. Am. Mgmt. Assns., Econ. Club of Memphis (bd. dirs. 1986—), Mid-South Exporters Roundtable (Exporter of the Year, 1987), Pickwick Yacht Club, Memphis Power Squadron (Past commdr.), Memphis Racquet Club, Phi Circle Omicron Delta Kappa. Republican. Presbyterian. Office: Buckman Labs Inc 1256 N McLean Blvd Memphis TN 38108

BUCKNER, FRED LYNN, chemical company executive; b. Salt Lake City, Feb. 29, 1932; s. Faye Wanita (MacDaniel) B.; m. Faye Robinson; children: Cole, Dallas, Troy. BSME, U. Utah, 1958. Devel. engr. Bacchus works Hercules Inc., Salt Lake City, 1961-63, sr. devel. engr., 1963-64; tech. sales rep. polymers dept. Hercules Inc., Wilmington, Del., 1964-66, market supr. polymers dept., 1966-69, sales mgr. film, 1969-73, dir. sales film packaging div., 1973-78, dir. film worldwide bus. ctr., 1978-81, dir. organics bus. group, 1981-83, group v.p. organics, 1983-84; pres. Hercules Engineered Polymers Co., Wilmington, 1984-86; pres. Hercules Specialty Chems. Co., Wilmington, 1986-87, also bd. dirs., pres., chief operating officer, 1987—. Trustee Med. Ctr. Del.; Served with USAR, 1951-54. Office: Hercules Inc 1313 N Market St Wilmington DE 19894

BUCKNER, LINDA IVERSON, insurance, software, and marketing consultant, writer; b. Lincoln, Nebr., July 14, 1950; d. Joseph Thomas and Henrietta Mae (McClure) Fisher; m. David Lynn Iverson, Dec. 29, 1967 (div. May 1980); children: Rachelle, Meggan, Elyssa; m. John David Buckner, Apr. 17, 1981. BS in Bus., U. S.D., 1974; student in Direct Mktg., Northwestern U., 1986-87. Lic. life, accident and health ins. agt., 1980, property and casualty agt., 1985. Mktg. rep. ESCO, Northfield, Ill., 1975-76; sales mgr. Safecom, Inc., Schaumburg, Ill., 1976-79; account exec. CNA, Inc., Chgo., 1979-81; mktg. mgr. Computer Sci. Corp., Chgo., 1981-83; ptnr., v.p. mktg. Buckner & Assocs., Wheaton, Ill., 1981—; account exec., mgr. nat. accounts devel. Marsh-McLennan Group, 1984-86; pres. Buckner & Assocs., 1986—; cons. Ins. Agy. Automation, 1979-81, CARA Corp., Lombard, Ill., 1983-84. Dem. election judge, DuPage County, Ill., 1977—; mem. DuPage County Citizens Adv. Com., 1978-80; mem. Hoffman Hallmark Choir, 1978-80, fundraiser Acad. Performing Arts, Chgo., 1981—. Mem. NAFE, Nat. Assn. Ins. Women, Soc. Mgmt. Info. Systems (assoc.), Data Processing Mgmt. Assn., Am. Mgmt. Assn., Am. Soc. Assn. Execs., Chgo. Soc. Assn. Execs., Direct Mktg. Assn. Home and Office: Buckner & Assocs 505 W Union St Wheaton IL 60187

BUCKSBAUM, MARTIN, real estate developer; b. Marshalltown, Iowa, July 31, 1920; s. Louis and Ida Bucksbaum; married, 1967; 1 child, Mary. Student, Marshall Coll., 1939. Pres. Cashway Super Markets, Marshalltown, 1950-60; pres. Gen. Mgmt. Corp., Des Moines, 1960—, chmn., 1975—; chmn. Gen. Mgmt. Corp., Los Angeles, 1985—. Office: Gen Growth Cos 215 Keo St Des Moines IA 50306

BUCKSTEIN, MARK AARON, lawyer; b. N.Y.C., July 1, 1939; s. Henry Al and Minnie Sarah (Russ) B.; m. Rochelle Joan Buchman, Sept. 11, 1960; children: Robin Beth, Michael Alan. BS in Math., CCNY, 1960; JD, NYU, 1963. Bar: N.Y. 1963, U.S. Dist. Ct. (so. and ea. dists.) N.Y. 1965, U.S. Supreme Ct. 1981. Assoc., Russ & Weyl, Massapequa, N.Y., 1963-64; assoc. counsel Mut. Life Ins. Co. N.Y., N.Y.C., 1964-65; assoc. Moses & Singer, N.Y.C., 1965-67, Leinwand, Maron & Hendler, N.Y.C., 1967-68; sr. ptnr. Baer Marks & Upham, N.Y.C., 1968-86, sr. v.p. external affairs, gen. counsel Trans World Airlines, Inc. N.Y.C., 1986—, also bd. dirs.; spl. prof. law Hofstra U. Law Sch., Hempstead, N.Y., 1981—; bd. dirs. Bayswater Realty & Capital Corp., N.Y.C., Travel Channel Inc., N.Y.C.; mem. exec. com. Herzfeld & Stern, N.Y.C., 1981-84. Trustee, Bronx High Sch. Sci. Found., 1984—. Mem. ABA, N.Y. Bar Assn., Am. Arbitration Assn. (arbitrator), Internat. Bar Assn. Democrat. Jewish. Lodge: KP (past dep. grand chancellor 1978). Avocations: tennis, music, theater, puzzles. Office: TWA Inc 100 S Bedford Rd Mount Kisco NY 10549

BUCKWALTER, ALAN ROLAND, III, bank executive; b. N.Y.C., Feb. 21, 1947; s. Alan Roland Jr. and Mary (Ackerman) B.; m. Linda Marie Castellano (div. 1979); 1 child, Lisa Jeanine; m. Helen Aline Kraft, Aug. 29, 1981; children: Robert Alan, Katherine Anne. Diploma, Valley Forge Mil. Acad., 1966; BA, Fairleigh Dickinson Coll., 1970; postgrad., Stanford U., 1985. Mng. dir. Chemical Bank, N.Y.C., 1970—. Mem. Union League Club (admission com., house com.). Home: 139 E 63rd St New York NY 10021 Office: Chem Bank 277 Park Ave New York NY 10172

BUCUZZO, ESTELLE LEMIRE, machine and tool company executive; b. Manchester, N.H., Apr. 3, 1927; d. William Joseph and Eva Marie (Racette) Lemire; m. James Michael Bucuzzo; children: William, Andrea, Lisa, Laura. BS, Simmons Coll., Boston, 1947. Sec. Sta. WEEI Radio, Boston, 1947, Sta. WLAW Radio, Lawrence, Mass., 1947-52; buyer's clk. Western Electric Co., North Andover, Mass., 1953-59; v.p. J.M.B. Machine Tool Co., Haverhill, Mass., 1962—. Republican. Roman Catholic. Home: 41 Eudora St Haverhill MA 01830 Office: JMB Machine & Tool Co Inc 15 Hale St Haverhill MA 01830

BUDD, EDWARD HEY, insurance executive; b. Zanesville, Ohio, Apr. 30, 1933; s. Curtis Eugene and Mary (Hey) B.; m. Mary Goodrich, Aug. 24, 1957; children: Elizabeth, David, Susan. B.S. in Physics, Tufts U., 1955. With The Travelers Cos., Hartford, Conn., 1955—; v.p., then sr. v.p. The Travelers Cos., 1967-76, pres., chief operating officer, 1976-82, chief exec. officer, 1982—, chmn. bd., 1982—, also dir., pres., 1985—; bd. dirs. Delta Air Lines, GTE Corp., The Inst. of Living. Fellow Casualty Actuarial Soc.; mem. Bus. Roundtable, Am. Acad. Actuaries, Am. Ins. Assn. (immediate past chmn., dir., exec. com.), Bd. Overseers Inst. for Civil Justice. Episcopalian. Office: Travelers Indemnity Co 1 Tower Sq Hartford CT 06183

BUDD, GENE F., finance executive; b. Cleve., Sept. 4, 1938; s. Frank J. and Helen Budd; m. Regina M. Golenski, Sept. 4, 1958; children: Darlene, Jaye. BS, Kent State U., 1960, MBA, 1965; postgrad., Case Western Res. U., 1978-79. Various fin. positions Glidden Co., Cleve., 1960-67; asst. mgr. investments Chessie Systems Inc., Cleve., 1967-69; asst. to treas. AM International., Cleve., 1969-72; asst. treas. Cin. Milacron Inc., 1972-77; treas. Samuel Moore Co. div. Eaton Corp., Cleve., 1977-79; asst. treas. Lamson and Sessions Co., Cleve., 1979-80, treas., 1980-82, v.p., treas., 1982-83, v.p. fin., treas., 1983-87, sr. v.p. fin. and adminstrn., 1987—; mem. adv. bd. Allendale Ins. Co., 1988—. Served to 1st lt. U.S. Army, 1961-62. Mem. Fin. Execs. Inst., Cleve. Treas. Club., Cleve. Security Analysts, Fin. Analysts Fedn. Home: 2412 Victoria Pkwy Hudson OH 44236 Office: Lamson & Sessions Co 25701 Science Park Dr Cleveland OH 44122

BUDKEVICS, GIRTS JANIS, financial planner; b. Bklyn., July 10, 1952; s. Boriss and Ilga (Prods) B. BA in Communications, Hofstra U., 1975. Sales rep. Martin L. Stroll, Inc., Hartsdale, N.Y., 1976-79; asst. mgr. Nassau Splty. Steel, Garden City, N.Y., 1979-82; sales rep. Smith Corona, Anaheim, Calif., 1982-83, Royal Consumer Bus. Products, L.A., 1983-87; fin. planner IDS/Am. Express, Long Beach, Calif., 1987—. Mem. Internat. Assn. Fin. Planners, Internat. Soc. Preretirement Planners, 1987—, Latvian Assn. So. Calif. (bd. dirs. 1987—), West Coast Latvian Athletic Assn. (pres. 1986—), Latvian Folk Dance Ensemble Club (bd. dirs. 1986-87), Sports Club Riga So. Calif. (pres. 1986—), Riga Volleyball Club (pres. 1985-86), Lettonia frat. (pres. So. Calif. chpt. 1987—). Republican. Lutheran. Home: 812 5th St Manhattan Beach CA 90266 Office: IDS Fin Svcs 900 E Wardlow Rd Suite C Long Beach CA 90807

BUDNICK, ERNEST JOSEPH, television broadcast executive; b. N.Y.C., July 3, 1948; s. Louis and Caroline (Probert) B.; m. Susan Swingle, Sept. 8, 1984. Cert. Data Processing, Comml. Programming Unltd., N.Y.C., 1968; grad., Dale Carnegie Inst., 1988. Owner Underground Records, N.Y.C., 1970; systems analyst Ins. Services, N.Y.C., 1973-77; pres., owner Bernard Friedman Video Prodns., N.Y.C., 1973-85; systems analyst Mfrs. Hanover, N.Y.C., 1977-80; mgr. TV and satellite prodn. Salomon Bros., Inc., N.Y.C., 1980—. Composer, singer, engr. (single) Keep on Playing, 1980. Mem. Am. Film Inst. (council mem. 1984—). Democrat. Home: 10 W 15th St New York NY 10011 Office: Salomon Bros Inc 2 New York Plaza New York NY 10004

BUDNITZ, ARRON EDWARD, lawyer, consultant, educator; b. Hanover, N.H., Feb. 27, 1949; s. Harry and Frieda Sara (Altscitz) B. AB, Dartmouth Coll., 1971; MBA, Boston U., 1973, LLM in Taxation, 1981; JD, Suffolk U., 1979; Cert., Coll. Fin. Planning, 1984. Bar: Fla. 1979, Mass. 1979, N.H. 1980, U.S. Dist. Ct. Mass. 1979, U.S. Dist. Ct. N.H. 1980, U.S. Tax Ct. 1979, U.S. Ct. Appeals (1st cir.) 1979, Maine 1987, U.S. Dist. Ct. Maine 1987. Sole practice Newport, N.H. and Winthrop, Mass., 1979—; adj. faculty N.H. Coll., Manchester and Salem, 1984-86. Mem. ABA, Fla. Bar Assn., Mass. Bar Assn., N.H. Bar Assn., Maine Bar Assn., Dartmouth Lawyers Assn., Inst. Cert. Fin. Planners, Internat. Assn. Fin. Planning, N.H. Estate Planning Council, Intertel, Phi Delta Phi. Democrat. Jewish. Home: 1 Pond St #1-F Winthrop MA 02152-1023 Office: PO Box #508 Newport NH 03773-0508

BUECHE, WENDELL FRANCIS, manufacturing company executive; b. Flushing, Mich., Nov. 7, 1930; s. Paul D. and Catherine (McGraw) B.; m. Virginia M. Smith, June 14, 1952; children: Denise, Barbara, Daniel, Brian. B.S.M.E., U. Notre Dame, 1952. With Allis-Chalmers Corp., 1952—; dist. mgr. Detroit, 1961-64, sales and mktg. mgr., 1964-69; group exec. v.p. West Allis, Wis., 1973-76, exec. v.p. elec. groups, 1976-77, exec. v.p., chief adminstrv. and fin. officer, 1977-80, chief adminstrv. officer, 1977-80, exec. v.p., head solids process equipment sector and fluids processing group, chief fin. officer, 1980-81, pres., chief operating officer, dir., 1981-83, pres., chief exec. officer, dir., 1984—, chmn., 1986-88; ret. chief exec. officer and chmn. Allis-Chalmers Corp., West Allis, Wis., 1988; dir. M&I Marshall Illsley Bank., M&I Corp., Wis. Gas Corp., WICOR, Inc. Mem. The Chgo. Com., 1981—, Greater Milw. Com., 1981—; mem. council Med. Coll. Wis., 1983—, engrng. adv. coun. U. Notre Dame. Mem. IEEE, ASME, AIME, Machinery and Allied Products Inst., Nat. Sand and Gravel Assn. (dir.), Nat. Elec. Mfrs. Assn. (gov.). Clubs: Milwaukee Country, Westmoor Country. Office: Allis-Chalmers Corp PO Box 512 Milwaukee WI 53201

BUEHRIG, JAMES OTTO, JR., real estate company executive; b. St. Louis, Mar. 30, 1954; s. James O. and Shirley M. (Peters) B.; m. Nancy A. Striebel, Aug. 16, 1974; children—Matthew, Gregory, Amanda. B.S., Northeast Mo. State U., 1976. CPA, Mo. Sr. acct. Peat, Marwick & Mitchell, St. Louis, 1975-79; controller Mason-Cassilly Inc., 1979-81; sr. v.p., chief fin. officer J.L. Mason Group, Inc., St. Louis, 1981—, also dir.; dir. Germania Bank, Ill., EMCI, Corp. & Continental Security Life Ins. Co., Jefferson City, Mo., J.L. Mason Realty and Investments, Inc., St. Louis, The J.L. Mason Group S.W. Fla., Inc., Orlando, J.L. Mason Group Tampa Bay (Fla.), Inc. Mem. devel. bd. Cardinal Glennon Children's Hosp., St. Louis, 1984—. Mem. Am. Inst. CPAs, Mo. Soc. CPAs, Nat. Assn. Accts., Am. Mgmt. Assn., Eagle Scout Assn. Roman Catholic. Office: J L Mason Group Inc 5020 Tamiami Trail N Naples FL 33940

BUEHRLE, MAUREEN ANNE, trade association executive, small business manager, manufacturer; b. Sandusky, Ohio, Mar. 17, 1952; d. John Anthony and Patricia Ann (Wolverton) Rogers; m. Richard Aquinas Knuff, March 16, 1974 (div. 1977); m. David Lawrence Buehrle, Sept. 30, 1977. Student, St. Mary's Coll., Notre Dame, Ind., 1970-72; BA, Ohio State U., 1974; postgrad., Wright State U., 1975-76. CPA, Ohio, Pa.; cert. mgmt. acct. Acct. Nat. Bd. Boiler/Pressure Vessel Inspectors, Columbus, Ohio, 1973-75; fin. aid officer Urbana (Ohio) Coll., 1975-76; office mgr. Mellman-Peterka & Co., Dayton, Ohio, 1976-79; pvt. practice acctg. Dayton, 1979-80, 82-86; fin. mgr. Montgomery Co. Community Action Agy., Dayton, 1980-82; mfr. The Herbal Connection, Marietta, Pa., 1985—; bus. mgr. Cramers' Posie Patch, Columbia, Pa., 1987—; treas. Internat. Herb Growers and Marketers' Assn., Silver Spring, Pa., 1986-87; exec. dir. Internat. Herb Growers and Marketers' Assn., Silver Spring, 1987—. Mem. Soc. for the Improvement of Conditions for Stray Animals, Dayton, 1977; exec. bd. Friends of Carriage Hill Farm, 1981-85. Mem. NAFE, NOW, Am. Assn. Women CPA's, Nat. Assn. Accts., Ohio Soc. CPA's. Republican. Home: 21 N Gay St Marietta PA 17547 Office: IHGMA PO Box 281 Silver Spring PA 17575

BUELL, GLENN DEXTER, JR., computer systems and engineering services company executive; b. Dallas, Aug. 31, 1934; s. Glenn Dexter and Jo Mae (Burlison) B.; m. Romula Geraldine Barrios, Feb. 15, 1962; children—Gregory Glenn, Jeffrey Glenn. B.S., Tex. A&M U., 1956; M.S., U. So. Calif., 1965; Ph.D., UCLA, 1969. Engr. McDonnel-Douglas, Long Beach, Calif., 1965-69; dir. Rockwell Internat., Anaheim, Calif., 1969-79; mgr. Hughes Helicopters, Culver City, Calif., 1979-80; v.p., div. gen. mgr. Comarco, Inc., Anaheim, Calif., 1980-82, pres., 1982-87, chief operating officer, 1982-84, chief exec. officer, 1984-87, chmn. bd. dirs., 1986-87; pres. Titan Engrng. Services, Inc, San Diego, 1988—. Served to capt. USAF, 1957-62. Republican. Lutheran.

BUENGER, CLEMENT LAWRENCE, banker; b. Cin., Apr. 27, 1926; s. Clement Lawrence and Estelle (Pelzer) B.; m. Ann McCabe, Apr. 22, 1950. Student, U. Wis., 1943-44; B.S.B.A., Xavier U., Cin., 1950. Acct. Kroger Co., Cin., 1950; exec. v.p. Selective Ins. Co., Cin., 1952-67, Life Ins. Co. Ky., Louisville, 1967-69; chmn., chief exec. officer Fifth Third Bank, Cin., 1969—; also dir. Fifth Third Bank; dir., pres. Fifth Third Bancorp., parent co. Fifth Third Bank; bd. dirs. Cin. Gas and Electric Co. Pres. Fund for Ind. Schs. Cin.; trustee Xavier U.; bd. dirs. Greater Cin. Airport, INROADS; mem. Cin. Bus. Com.; mem. adv. bd. Cin. Council World Affairs. With USN, 1943-45. Mem. Assn. Res. City Bankers, Greater Cin. C. of C. (trustee). Republican. Roman Catholic. Clubs: Cin. Country, Bankers, Comml, Queen City. Office: Fifth Third Bancorp 38 Fountain Square Pla Cincinnati OH 45263

BUFFETT, WARREN EDWARD, corporate executive; b. Omaha, Aug. 30, 1930; s. Howard Homan and Leila (Stahl) B.; m. Susan Thompson, Apr. 19, 1952; children: Susan, Howard, Peter. Student, U. Pa., 1947-49; B.S., U. Nebr., 1950; M.S., Columbia, 1951. Investment salesman Buffett-Falk & Co., Omaha, 1951-54; security analyst Graham-Newman Corp., N.Y.C., 1954-56; gen. partner Buffett Partnership, Ltd., Omaha, 1956-69; chmn. bd. Berkshire Hathaway, Inc., Nat. Indemnity Co., Nat. Fire & Marine Ins. Co., See's Candy Shops, Inc., Columbia Ins. Co., Buffalo Evening News; bd. dirs. Capital Cities/ABC, Solomon, Inc. Bd. govs. Boys Clubs Omaha, 1962—; life trustee Grinnell Coll., 1968—; trustee Urban Inst. Office: Berkshire Hathaway Inc 1440 Kiewit Pla Omaha NE 68131 also: Buffalo News 1 News Pla Buffalo NY 14240

BUFKIN, ISAAC DAVID, energy diversified company executive; b. Haynesville, La., May 16, 1922; s. Floran E. and Pauline E. B.; m. Lee Elmo Renfrow, Apr. 23, 1944; children: Peggy Bufkin Gerst, David Michael. BS, La. Tech. U., 1948. Mech. engr. NACA, Langley Field, Va., 1948-49; with Tex. Eastern Transmission Corp., Houston, 1949-79, v.p. gas mktg. and rates, 1968-71, v.p. gas ops., 1971-79; exec. v.p. Tex. Eastern Corp., Houston, 1979, pres., chief operating officer, 1979-80, pres., chief exec. officer, 1980-86, chmn. bd., chief exec. officer, 1980-87, chmn. bd. dirs., 1987—; bd. dirs. Conf. Bd.; mem. Interstate Oil Compact Commn. Bd. dirs. Stehlin Found. for Cancer Research; life bd. dirs. La. Tech. Engring Found. Served with USAAF, 1943-46. Mem. La. Engring. Soc., Nat. Soc. Profl. Engrs., Soc. Gas Lighting, Gas Men's Roundtable Washington, Newcomen Soc. N. Am. Baptist. Office: Tex Ea Corp 1221 McKinney PO Box 2521 Houston TX 77010

BUFORD, BRENDA L., mortgage company executive; b. Kansas City, Mo., July 18, 1951; d. Wayne O'Brien and Mary A. Anderson; m. Christopher A. Becker, April 7, 1981 (div. Dec. 31, 1985); m. James D. Buford, April 11, 1987. Loan officer Mid-Cen. Mortgage, Kansas City, 1971-73; office mgr. Comfort Trane Heating & Cooling, Overland Park, Kans., 1973-75; treas. Anchor Fin. Corp., Leawood, Kans., 1975—; bd. dirs. Anchor Ins. Services, Inc.; asst. treas. Anchor Life Assurance Co. Leawood, 1984—. Mem. Friends of Art; Fin. Insts. Mktg. Assn. Lutheran. Office: Anchor Fin Corp 9400 Mission Rd Box 6826 Leawood KS 66216

BUFORD, JACK WILLIAM, consultant; b. Topeka, July 22, 1912; s. Charles Homer and Bess (Thomas) B.; m. Helen Malott, Dec. 27, 1934; children: Anne Ludwin, Thomas. BSCE, U. Wash., 1933; MS in Engring., Harvard U., 1934. Various positions Pa. RR, 1934-50; sr. v.p. internat. ops. Hanna Mining Co., Cleve., 1950-77; cons., 1977—. Served to lt. col. U.S. Army, 1941-46. Mem. Am. Iron and Steel Inst., AIME. Republican. Clubs: Union (Cleve.); Rolling Rock (Ligonier, Pa.); Paradise Valley Country (Ariz.); Westwood Country (Rocky River, Ohio). Lodges: Masons, Shriners. Home and Office: 7337 E Echo Ln Scottsdale AZ 85258

BUGATCH, BERYL, brokerage research administrator; b. Balt., Apr. 27, 1945; s. Samuel I. and Edith (Leaderman) B.; m. Nanette Sauber, June 29, 1969; 1 child, Samantha. BS in Econs., U. Pa., 1966; MBA, Harvard U., 1968. Dir. advanced computer techniques Office of U.S. Sec. Def., Washington, 1968-69; pres. B. Bugatch Stores, Inc., Balt., 1969-83; dir. instl. research Baker, Watts & Co., Inc., Balt., 1983—. Democrat. Jewish. Home: 3410 Wood Valley Dr Baltimore MD 21208 Office: Baker Watts & Co 100 Light St Baltimore MD 21202

BUGGIE, FREDERICK DENMAN, management consultant; b. Toledo, Mar. 27, 1929; s. Horace and Loraine (Denman) B.; B.A., Yale U., 1956; M.B.A., George Washington U., 1961; m. Betty Jo Chilcote, Sept. 7, 1951; children—Martha Louise Buggie Kenney, John Chilcote. Sales engr. Alcoa, Balt. and Phila., 1956-66; pres. Gt. Lakes Research Inst., Erie, Pa., 1967-69; mktg. mgr. Technicon Instruments, Tarrytown, N.Y., 1969-71; program mgr. Innotech, Norwalk, Conn., 1971-76; pres. Strategic Innovations Internat., Lake Wylie, S.C., 1976—, SII Strategic Innovations A.G., Zurich, Switzerland; founder, chmn. Strategic Innovations Internat. Ltd., Bedford, England, Strategic Innovations B.V., Amsterdam, The Netherlands; conf. leader, lectr.; adj. prof. various univs. Served with USAF, 1950-54. Mem. Assn. Corp. Growth, The Planning Forum, C.D.A., EVAF, Inst. of Dirs. Clubs: Weston Field; Yale N.Y.C.; Yale London. Author: New Product Development Strategies, 1981. Home: 8 Sunrise Point Lake Wylie SC 29710 Office: Strategic Innovations Internat 12 Executive Ct Lake Wylie SC 29710

BUHLER, ROBERT ANDREW, banker; b. Racine, Wis., Nov. 9, 1956; s. Robert Walter and Eunice Jean (Berg) B.; m. Violetta Kapsalis, June 24, 1984. BA in Acctg. and Fin., U. Wis., 1978, MBA, 1979. Banking officer Continental Ill. Nat. Bank, Chgo., 1980-83, 2d v.p., capital markets, 1983-84; mgr. Can. Imperial Bank Commerce, Chgo., 1984-85, sr. mgr., 1985, asst. gen. mgr., 1985-86, v.p. capital markets, 1987—. Clubs: University, East Bank (Chgo.), Exec. Club Chgo. Office: Can Imperial Bank Commerce 30 N LaSalle St Suite 4100 Chicago IL 60602

BUIST, RICHARDSON, banker; b. Bklyn., Aug. 8, 1921; s. George Lamb and Adelaide (Richardson) B.; student Yale U.; m. Jean Mackerley, Oct. 2, 1948; children—Peter Richardson, Jean Morford Buist, Mary Elizabeth Buist Flores. Advt. copy writer Ecloss Co., Sparta, N.J., 1946-48; advt. mgr. Sussex County Ind., 1948-50, Dover Advance, 1950-53; bus. mgr. N.J. Herald, Newton, 1953-70; dir., v.p. The N.J. Herald, Inc., 1958-70, pub., 1967-70; dir. N.J. Press Assn., 1966-70; asst. sec., asst. treas. Morford Co., 1965-72, pres., 1986— ; trust officer Midlantic Nat. Bank/Sussex & Mchts., Newton, 1971-88, Midlantic Nat. Bank, Edison, N.J., 1972-86, cons., 86—; bd. dirs. North Jersey Health Care Corp. Pres. Sussex County chpt. Am. Cancer Soc., 1956-58, Sussex County Music Found., 1959-61; mem. Morris-Sussex Area Health Facilities Planning Council, 1965-68, bd. govs., 1962-88; v.p. Sussex County Council Arts, 1971-73. Chmn. pub. relations Morris-Sussex Area Council Boy Scouts Am., 1986-88; trustee Sussex County Music Found., 1955-75; v.p., chmn. fin. devel. com. Newton Meml. Hosp., 1966-68, bd. govs. 1962-88, pres. bd. govs., 1968-71, chmn., 1971-73, bd. govs. 1962-88; founding incorporator, trustee NW Jersey Health Care, 1971-76; trustee, mem. exec. com. regional health planning council Health Systems Agy., 1976-82, 1984-87, v.p., 1978-79; trustee United Way of Sussex County, 1984—, spl. gifts chmn., 1984-88; dir. North Jersey Health Care Corp., 1988—; chmn. bd. trustees Prime Care Inc., 1989—. Mem. N.J. Vet. Med. Soc. Aux. (del. 1979-82, 88), Am. Vet. Med. Soc. Aux. (nat. chmn. legis. com., 1986-88). Clubs: Morristown (N.J.). Lodge: Rotary (pres. 1967-68, Paul Harris Fellow award 1988). Home: Sand Pond Rd RR 2 Box 668-A Hamburg NJ 07419 Office: 93 Spring St Newton NJ 07860

BULL, BRIAN STANLEY, physician, educator, medical consultant and business executive; b. Watford, Hertfordshire, Eng., Sept. 14, 1937; came to U.S., 1954, naturalized, 1960; s. Stanley and Agnes Mary (Murdoch) B.; m. Maureen Hannah Huse, June 3, 1963; children: Beverly Velda, Beryl Heather. B.S. in Zoology, Walla Walla Coll., 1957; M.D., Loma Linda (Calif.) U., 1961. Diplomate: Am. Bd. Pathology. Intern Yale U., 1961-62, resident in anat. pathology, 1962-63; resident in clin. pathology NIH, Bethesda, Md., 1963-65; fellow in hematology and electron microscopy NIH, 1965-66, staff hematologist, 1966-67; research asst. dept. anatomy Loma Linda U., 1958, dept. microbiology, 1959, asst. prof. pathology, 1968-71, assoc. prof., 1971-73, prof., 1973—, chmn. dept. pathology, 1973—; cons. to mfrs. of med. testing devices; pres. Med. Devices Co., San Bernadino, Calif. Bd. editors Jour. Clin. and Lab. Haematology, U.K.; editor-in-chief Blood Cells N.Y.-Heidelberg; contbr. chpts. to books and numerous articles to med. jours.; patentee in field. Served with USPHS, 1963-67. Nat. Inst. Arthritis and Metabolic Diseases fellow, 1967-68; recipient Daniel D. Comstock Meml. award Loma Linda U., 1961, Merck Manual award, 1961, Mosby Scholarship Book award, 1961; Ernest B. Cotlove Meml. lectr. Acad. Clin. Lab. Physicians and Scientists, 1972. Fellow Am. Soc. Clin. Pathologists, Am. Soc. Hematology, Coll. Am. Pathologists, Fed. Drug Adminstrn. panel on hematology, Nat. Com. on Clin. Lab. Standards, Internat. Com. on Hematology Standards, N.Y. Acad. Scis.; mem. AMA, Assn. Pathology Chmn., Calif. Soc. Pathologists, San Bernardino County Med. Soc., Acad. Clin. Lab. Physicians and Scientists, Am. Assn. Pathologists, Sigma Xi, Alpha Omega Alpha. Seventh-day Adventist. Office: Loma Linda U Sch Medicine 11234 Anderson Loma Linda CA 92350

BULL, JAMES WILLIAM, financial executive; b. Lockport, N.Y., Dec. 5, 1952; s. William Howard and Mary Elizabeth (Murphy) B. BS, U. Buffalo, 1978. Materials mgmt. Harrison Radiator div. GMC, Lockport, N.Y., 1978-84; fin. planning cons. Upstated Profl. Planning, Buffalo, 1984-87; mgr. fin. div. The Baker Fin. Group, Lockport, 1987—. Dir. Charitable Giving com. Eastern/Niagara United Way, 1987—, div. mgr., 1986, 87. Mem. Internat. Assn. Fin. Planners, Alpha Omega Alpha, Tuscalora Club. Republican. Roman Catholic. Home: 3 Longcroft Dr Lockport NY 14094 Office: The Baker Fin Group 111 Main St Lockport NY 14094

BULL, RICHARD SUTTON, JR., paper company executive, lawyer; b. Chgo., Jan. 21, 1926; s. Richard Sutton and Sara Rozet (Smith) B.; m. Lois Karna Werme, July 19, 1950; children: Lois Karna Bull Bouton, Sara Annette Bull Swiatlowski, Richard Sutton, Harry Calvin, Mary Ellen Frantz. Student, Ill. State U., 1944, 46, Columbia U., 1944-45; B.A., Yale U., 1948, J.D., 1951; LL.M. (Food Law Inst. fellow), NYU, 1952. Bar: Ill. 1953, U.S. Supreme Ct. 1963. Instr. econs. Stone Coll., New Haven, 1950-51; atty. Swift & Co., 1952-57, Bradner Cen. Co., Chgo., 1957—; pres. Bradner Cen. Co., 1965-66, pres., chmn. bd., 1966—; sec., treas., bd. dirs. Clearview Farms; bd. dirs. Security Chgo. Corp., First Security Bank, Chgo. Past bd. dirs. Duncan Med. Ctr., YMCA, 1968-75, Evan. Health Found., Oak Brook, Ill., 1984-87; mem. USS Abraham Lincoln Commissioning Com.; trustee, bd. dirs. Goodwill Industries, 1975-80, vice chmn., 1977-79; mng. dir. Civic and Arts Found., vice chmn., 1978-89; Chgo. Crime Commn., 1983—, bd. dirs., treas.; assoc. Northwestern U., Met. Chgo. Air Force Community Council, 1983—; asst. treas. Chgo. Crime Commn.; mem. Coll. DuPage Adv. Council. Served with USNR, 1944-46. John Robins fellow Food and Drug Inst. NYU, 1951. Mem. Chgo. Bar Assn., Chgo. Assn. Commerce and Industry (dir. 1973-87, gen. sec. 1980-81), Am. Arbitration Assn. (nat. panel arbitrators 1968—), Pres.' Assn, Graphic Arts and Paper Assn. (pres. 1968-69), Edward Moss Martin Soc. (past pres.), Paper Club (dir., past pres.), Yale Club, Union League Chgo. (bd. dirs. 1980-83, sec. 1985-87), Chgo. Econ. Club, Yale Club N.Y.C., Ruth Lake Country Club, Khyble Bay Yacht Club (past commodore 1972-73, bd. govs. 1970—).

Presbyterian. Home: 4 Countryside Ct Hinsdale IL 60521 Office: Bradner Cen Co 333 S Des Plaines St Chicago IL 60606

BULLARD, ROBERT MARVIN, sales and distribution company executive; b. Atlanta, Dec. 12, 1931; s. Harold Bryant and Sarah Edna (Johnston) B.; m. Ann Wilkins, Apr. 4, 1959; children—Suzanne Bullard Houser, Robin Bullard Segarro, Robert Johnston. B.S., Ga. Inst. Tech., 1953. Sales engr. process control div. Honeywell, Atlanta, 1957-60, br. mgr., Charlotte, N.C., 1960-65, industry mgr., Ft. Washington, Pa., 1965-67, mgr. market sales, 1967-69, mgr. new bus. devel., 1969-70, mgr. mktg., 1970-71; dir. mktg. Electronics Corp. Am., Cambridge, Mass., 1971-72; v.p. mktg. process control div. LFE Corp., Waltham, Mass., 1972-75; mktg. mgr. indsl. controls div. Harvey Hubbell Co., Madison, Ohio, 1975-77; corp. v.p., div. pres. Pacific Sci. Co., Santa Ana, Calif., 1977-84; pres., chmn. bd. TechSci. Internat., Santa Ana, 1984—; v.p. Go Controls, Inc., Whittier, Calif., 1984-87, also bd. dirs. Served to capt. USAF, 1954-57; Eng. Mem. Instrument Soc. Am. (sr.), Mem. Les Amis du Vin, Orange County Wine Soc., Am. Inst. Wine and Food, Mensa. Republican. Presbyterian. Home: 24316 Cataluna Circle Mission Viejo CA 92691 Office: TechScience Internat Inc 3020 N Hesperian Santa Ana CA 92706

BULLIS, EUGENE MARTIN, computer company executive, financial executive; b. Watertown, N.Y., May 10, 1945; s. Homer M. and Eleanor L. (Loucks) B.; m. Linda J., Oct. 22, 1966; children: Anthony, Jeffrey, Joellen. BBA, Colby Coll., 1967. CPA, Mass. With Ernst and Whinney, Boston, 1967-79, ptnr., 1978-79; v.p., internat. controller Wang Labs., Inc., Lowell, Mass., 1979-81, sr. v.p., corp. controller, 1981-83, sr. v.p., corp. controller, treas., 1983—, chief fin. officer, 1988—. Trustee St. John's Hosp., Middlesex Community Coll. Office: Wang Labs Inc 1 Industrial Ave Lowell MA 01851

BULLOCK, DAVID FRASER, airline executive; b. Taber, Alta., Can., Apr. 6, 1955; s. Evan James and Mary Grace (Kirkvold) B.; m. Jennifer Lee Smith, Apr. 22, 1977; children: Tiffany, Sabrina, Michael, Angela, David. BS in Econs., Brigham Young U., 1978, MBA, 1980. Cons. Bain and Co., Boston, 1980-82; mgr. Bain and Co., Menlo Park, Calif., 1983-84; ptnr. Bain Capital, Menlo Park, Calif., 1984-86; v.p. Medivision, Menlo Park, Calif., 1984-86; exec. v.p., chief fin. officer World Airways/WorldCorp, Oakland, Calif. and Herndon, Va., 1986—; also bd. dirs. World Airways/WorldCorp. Mormon. Office: World Corp 13873 Park Ctr Rd Herndon VA 22071

BULLOCK, DAVID JOHN, financial planning company executive; b. Boise, Idaho, Apr. 25, 1956; s. Harry Cliffe and LaVaughn (Hunter) B.; m. Kathleen Amelia Packer, Sept. 12, 1979; children: Steven, James, Jeffrey. BS, Brigham Young U., 1980. Pvt. practice fin. planning Provo, Utah, 1978-80; pvt. practice investment banking Denver, 1980-84; v.p. JMB Realty Corp., Denver, 1984-87; div. mgr. IDS/Am. Express, Inc., Denver, 1987—; bd. dirs. Interfin. Securities, Inc. Mem. Rep. Presdl. Task Force, 1980—. Mem. Internat. Assn. Fin. Planners. Mormon. Clubs: Cherry Hills Country (Englewood, Colo.), Tucson Country. Office: IDS/Am Express Inc 1141 W El Dorado Pl Suite C200 Tucson AZ 85715

BULLOCK, PETER BRADLEY, tool company executive; b. Tipton, Eng., June 9, 1934; s. William Horace Bradley and Catherine (Garner) B.; B.Sc., U. London; m. Joyce Rea, Nov. 1, 1958; children—Claire Elizabeth Bradley, Penelope Jane Bradley. With Nat. Coal Bd., 1959-65, Thomas Potterton Ltd., 1966-67, Fibreglass Ltd., 1965-66, 67-69; pres., mng. dir., Flymo Ltd.; dir. Electrolux Ltd.; joint mng. dir. Electrolux Group UK; group chief exec. James Neill Holdings PLC, 1983—, Spear & Jackson Internat. PLC, 1986—; chmn. Neill Tools Ltd., 1983—; ; pres., dir. gen. AMV (France), 1986—; bd. dirs. 600 Group Plastic Ltd. Co. Served with Brit. Army, 1956-58. Chartered engr., U.K. Mem. Inst. Energy, Inst. Mktg., Inst. Dirs. Conservative. Mem. Ch. of Eng. Clubs: Arts of London, Leander, Phyllis Court. Home: The Cottage, Queenwood, Watlington, Oxford OX9 5HW, England other: The Mill Cottage, Edale, via Sheffield, Derbyshire S30 2ZE, England Office: Handsworth Rd, Sheffield S13 9BR, England

BULLOCK, WILLIAM CLAPP, JR., banker; b. Bronxville, N.Y., June 28, 1936; s. William and Elizabeth (Van Wagnen) B.; m. Edith Swain, June 21, 1958; children: Wendy, Martha, Sarah, Bill. B.A., Yale U., 1958; postgrad., NYU, 1958-60. Asst. treas., asst. v.p. nat. div. Morgan Guaranty Trust Co., N.Y.C., 1958-69; v.p., sr. loan officer Merrill Trust Co., Bangor, Maine, 1969-71, exec. v.p., 1971-73, pres., 1973-80, pres., chief exec. officer, 1980-82, chmn. bd., pres., 1982—; pres. Merrill Bankshares Co., 1973-80, pres., chief exec. officer, 1980-82, chmn. bd., pres., 1982—; chmn. Merrill, Norstar Bank, Bangor, 1988-89; pvt. practice as fin. cons. 1989—; bd. dirs. Courier Gazette, Pepsi-Cola Bottling Co., Maine Capital Corp., Fleet Fin. Group, Providence, R.I., Bangor Hydro-Electric Co., Eastern Maine Health Care, Fed. Res. Bank Boston. Bd. dirs. Gov. Longley's Task Force on Indian Land Claims, 1979-80; bd. dirs. Associated Industries of Maine, 1978-81; bd. dirs. New Eng. Council, 1981—, former pres. Mem. Maine Bankers Assn. (dir., former pres.), Am. Bankers Assn., Maine C. of C. (former dir.). Clubs: Yale, N.Y. Anglers. Home and Office: RFD 2 PO Box 121 Orrington ME 04474

BULLOUGH-LAZAR, LYNN DIANE, sales executive; b. N.Y.C., Jan. 16, 1958; d. John Frank and Dorothy (Baines) Bullough; m. Henry David Lazar, Nov. 1, 1986. BA in Communications, Speech and Theater, Fairleigh Dickinson U., 1981. Mktg. rep. On-Line Software Internat., Ft. Lee, N.J., 1984-87; program dir. Med. Weight Mgmt., Teaneck, N.J., 1987—. Actress/singer: (plays) South Pacific, Chicago, Kiss Me Kate, Company, A Loss of Roses, Scrambled Feet, Jerry's Girls, I'm Getting My Act Together; soloist telethon Muscular Dystrophy Assn. Active benefits "AIDS: Our Fears, Our Hopes", Bergen County Health Conf. Mem. Theta Alpha Phi. Democrat. Episcopalian.

BULMAN, WILLIAM PATRICK, data processing executive; b. Corona, N.Y., Jan. 11, 1925; s. William T. and Bridget A. (Gibbons) B.; ABS, U. Upper N.Y., 1947; BBA, Syracuse (N.Y.) U., 1949, MBA, 1978; m. Jane G. Jones, June 30, 1952. In systems/programming Mohawk Airlines, Utica, N.Y., 1951-55; data processing mgr. Gold Medal Packing, Utica, 1956-59, West End Brewing, Utica, 1960-73; coordinator on-line data processing systems Sperry-Univac, Utica, 1973-76, data processing mgr., 1976-77; programmer/analyst MDS, Herkimer, N.Y., 1977-86; sr. programmer, analyst, Momentum Techs., Herkimer, N.Y., 1986-89; ret., 1989; pvt. cons., 1989—. Served with USN, 1941-46. Mem. Data Processing Mgmt. Assn. (v.p., treas.), Assn. Systems Mgmt. Address: 35 Ashwood Ave Whitesboro NY 13492

BULOVIC, DANICA, banker; b. Civljane, Yugoslavia, Feb. 20, 1937; came to U.S., 1984; d. Jovan and Manda (Knezevic) Zrilic; m. Ljubomir Bulovic, July 5, 1964; children: Aleksandar, Vladimir. BS in Law, Belgrade U., 1962. Officer Jugobanka, Belgrade, Yugoslavia, 1956-60, chief exec. officer, 1961-83; sr. ops. officer Jugobanka N.Y. Agy., N.Y.C., 1984—. Home: 163 Coligni Ave New Rochelle NY 10801 Office: Jugobanka NY Agy 500 Fifth Ave New York NY 10110

BULZA, ARLENE, retail buyer; b. Gary, Ind., Jan. 11, 1940; d. Henry J. and Henrietta K. (Weber) B. AA, Stephens Coll., Columbia, Mo., 1960. Buyer H. Gordon & Sons, Gary, 1960-64; buyer, merchandiser 5-7-9 Shops, Chgo., 1964-69, Flair of Boston, 1969-76, Young Insiders, N.Y.C., 1976-78; pres., owner Competitive Purchasing, N.Y.C., 1978-86; buyer, merchandiser M.D. Assocs., N.Y.C., 1987-88; owner A&M Off-Price Brokers, N.Y.C., 1989—. Home: 300 E 40th St Apt 3T New York NY 10016

BUMPERS, W. CARROLL, finance corporation executive. Chmn. Greyhound Fin. Corp., Phoenix. Office: Greyhound Fin Corp Mail Sta 1931 Phoenix AZ 85077 *

BUNCE, JOHN WILLIAM, electronics executive; b. Milw., Aug. 16, 1949; s. John Peter and Dorothy Flora (Guertz) B.; m. Nancy Lucille Montano, July 3, 1977; children: Emily, Abigail. BSEE, MIT, 1971; MBA, Harvard U., 1977. Cons. McKinsey & Co., Chgo., 1977-78; nat. svc. mgr. MCC Powers div. Mark Controls, Northbrook, Ill., 1978-82; v.p. mktg. sales MCC Clayton Mark div. Mark Controls, Lake Zurich, Ill., 1982-83; pres. Intellitech, Inc., Northbrook, 1983—. Lt. (j.g.) USNR, 1971-75.

BUNCHER, JAMES EDWARD, business executive; b. Moline, Ill., Sept. 19, 1936; s. Ralph Frank and Mae Loretta (Eis) B.; m. Mary Alice Dodge, Sept. 3, 1961; 1 son, Douglas James. BS in Acctg., U. Ill., 1961, M of Acctg. Sci., 1962. CPA, Ill. Staff auditor Peat, Marwick, Mitchell & Co., St. Louis, 1962-63; controller, asst. v.p. Durkee Consumer Foods div. SCM Corp., Cleve., 1963-72; controller Hosp. Products div. Abbott Labs., North Chicago, Ill., 1972-74; pres., chief operating officer Hosp. Affiliates Internat., Inc., Nashville, 1974-79, 80-81, INA Healthplan, Dallas, 1979-80, 81-82; pres., chief exec. officer Republic Health Corp., Dallas, 1982-87; prin. Horizon Cos., Dallas, 1987—. Served with USN, 1956-58. Methodist. Clubs: Gleneagles Country. Office: Horizon Cos 11220 Harry Hines Dallas TX 75229-0667

BUNDSCHUH, GEORGE AUGUST WILLIAM, insurance company executive; b. Yonkers, N.Y., Sept. 24, 1933; s. George and Anna B.; m. Joanne Detjen; children: Russell, Erica. B.B.A., Pace U., 1955; M.S., Columbia U. Grad. Sch. Bus., 1959. Chartered fin. analyst. With N.Y. Life Ins. Co., N.Y.C., 1959—; sr. v.p. N.Y. Life Ins. Co., 1979-80, exec. v.p., 1980-84, vice chmn., 1984—. Trustee Pace U. Served with AUS, 1956-58. Mem. Inst. Chartered Fin. Analysts. Office: NY Life Ins Co 51 Madison Ave New York NY 10010

BUNKER, RODNEY BRUCE, financial executive; b. Saranac Lake, N.Y., Mar. 7, 1943; s. Lionel Arthur and Cora Mae (Morgan) B.; m. Patricia Ann Somers, Apr. 5, 1963; children: Patti, Tracy, Michael. BBA in Acctg., U. Nebr.-Omaha, 1970; MBA, U. Dayton, 1974. Commd. 2d lt. USAF, 1970, advanced through grades to capt., ret., 1981; cost analyst Aero. Systems Div. USAF, Wright-Patterson AFB, Ohio, 1970-74, budget dir. materials lab., 1974-76; mgmt. effectiveness insp. Systems Command Insp. Gen. USAF, Andrews AFB, Md., 1976-78, budget dir. test and evaluation systems command, 1978-80; controller, asst. gen. mgr. Tex. Peripherals, Odessa, 1980-84; exec. dir. fin. Lubbock (Tex.) Ind. Sch. Dist., 1984—; bd. dirs. Direct Reimbursement Service Inc., Lubbock, Bunker Christmas Country, Inc., Lubbock, Profl. Benefits Ins. Co., Houston. Mem. Govt. Fin. Officers Assn. (del. Cert. Achievement 1984-85, 86-87), Tex. Assn. Sch. Bus. Officials (vice chmn. 1988-89, chmn. 1989—, Cert. Achievement 1984-85, 86-87). Republican. Baptist. Home: Box 351 Smyer TX 79367 Office: Lubbock Ind Sch Dist 1628 19th St Lubbock TX 79401

BUNN, CHARLES NIXON, strategic business planning consultant; b. Springfield, Ill., Feb. 8, 1926; s. Joseph Forman and Helen Anna Frieda (Link) B.; student U. Ill., 1943-44; BS in Engring., U.S. Mil. Acad., 1949; MBA, Xavier U., Cin., 1958; m. Cecine Cole, Dec. 26, 1951 (div. 1987); children: Sisene, Charles; m. Marjorie Fitzmaurice, Apr. 5, 1988. Flight test engr. Gen. Electric Co., Cin., also Edwards AFB, Calif., 1953-59; sr. missile test engr., space systems div. Lockheed Aircraft Corp., USAF Satellite Test Center, Sunnyvale, Calif., 1959-60, 63-70, economist, advanced planning dept., 1961-63; economic and long-range planning cons., Los Altos, Calif., 1970-73; head systems planning, economist, strategic bus. planning, Western Regional hdqrs. U.S. Postal Service, San Bruno, Calif., 1973-78; strategic bus. planning cons., investment analysis cons., 1978-79; strategic bus. planning Advanced Reactor Systems dept. Gen. Electric Co., Sunnyvale, Calif., 1979-84; strategic planning cons., 1984—. Served with inf. paratroops U.S. Army, 1944-45, with inf. and rangers, 1949-53; Korea. Decorated Battle Star (5). Mem. Nat. Assn. Bus. Economists, World Future Soc., Sigma Nu. Episcopalian. Home and Office: 222 Incline Way San Jose CA 95139

BUNN, DONALD WALTER, II, construction company executive; b. Laramie, Wyo., Sept. 2, 1951; s. Donald Walter and Doris Lenora (Lathrop) B. Student, U. Wyo., 1970-73; BS, Ariz. State U., 1986. Pres. Don Bunn II Contrn., Laramie, 1977-80, Bio-Phase, Laramie, 1980-82; with market research Chanen Constrn., Phoenix, 1983-84; dir. client services Walpole Contracting Corp., Mesa, Ariz., 1985; v.p., dir. client services Butterfield Magnum Inc., Scottsdale, Ariz., 1985-86; dir. mktg. Skidmore Contracting, Mesa, 1986-87; dir. mktg. and bus. devel. Ninteman Constrn. Co., San Diego, Calif., 1987-88; mgr. sales T.B. Penick and Sons, Inc., San Diego, 1988—; cons. real estate Scottsdale Marine, 1984-85, cons. mktg., 1986—. Mem. Soc. Mktg. Profl. Services, Central City Assn., World Affairs Council. Home: 1051 Archer St San Diego CA 92109 Office: TB Penick & Sons Inc 864 34th St San Diego CA 92109

BUNT, JAMES RICHARD, electric company executive; b. St. Cloud, Minn., Sept. 24, 1941; s. Eberhard Joseph and Christine Frances (Bromberg) B.; m. Arlene Anita Weisberg, Aug. 12, 1965; children: Gregory, Ashlee. B.A., U. S.D., Vermillion, 1967; M.A., Claremont Grad. Sch., Calif., 1968. Mgmt. trainee Gen. Electric Co., Schenectady, N.Y., 1968-70, corp. auditor, 1970-73; mgr. fin. ops. Nuclear Energy div. Gen. Electric Co., San Jose, Calif., 1973-77; cons. fin. planning Gen. Electric Co., Fairfield, Conn., 1977-79; mgr. fin. planning and analysis MABG, Louisville, 1979-81; v.p., comptroller Gen. Electric Fin. Services Inc. and Gen. Electric Credit Corp., Stamford, Conn., 1981-87; v.p. corp. exec. office Gen. Electric Co., Fairfield, Conn., 1987—; bd. dirs. Coherent Gen., Inc., Powerex, Inc. Fellow NDEA, 1967. Mem. Fin. Execs. Inst., Elfun Soc., Phi Beta Kappa. Republican. Roman Catholic. Club: Redding Country. Home: 447 Thayer Pond Rd Wilton CT 06897 Office: GE 3135 Easton Turnpike Fairfield CT 06431

BUNTEN, JOHN RICHARD, banker; b. Topeka, Kans., July 3, 1932; m. Anne Wootten Blalock, June 30, 1956; children—John Richard Jr., Anne W., Betty B., Richard B. B.S. in Bus., U. Kans., 1954; M.B.A., U. Tex., 1959. With Republic Bank Dallas, 1959-86 , v.p., 1965-71, sr. v.p., 1971-74, exec. v.p., 1974-77, sr. credit officer, vice chmn., 1977-82, vice chmn., mng. dir. Corp. Banking, 1982-86, mng. dir. Secura Group, 1986-88; pres. First City Bank Dallas, 1988—. bd. dirs. Southwestern Sch. Banking So. Meth. U., Am. Healthcare Mgmt., Inc. Trustee Dallas Hist. Soc., Baylor Coll. Dentistry, Sr. Citizens Coun. st lt. USAF. Mem. Phi Gamma Delta, Dallas Country Club, Dallas Club. Office: 1st City Bank 1700 Pacific Dallas TX 75266-1700

BUNTING, ROBERT L., engineer; b. Balt., Feb. 18, 1946; s. Robert B. and Helen M. (Osborne) B.; m. Mary Jo Woods, Sept. 4, 1987. BS in Bus. Adminstrn., U. Balt., 1976. Tech. writer Bendix Field Engring., Balt., 1967-72; prodn. coordinator Port City Press, Balt., 1972-74; tech. writer Ward Machinery Co., Balt., 1974-79; sr. engr. Westinghouse Def. Industry, Balt., 1979—. Mem. Soc. for Tech. Communications, Soc. for Logistics Engrs., Printing Industries of Md. Home: 2908 Crystal Palace Ln Baltimore MD 21122 Office: Westinghouse Def Industry 7312 Parkway Dr Bldg 105 MS6320 Hanover MD 21076-1199

BUNTROCK, DEAN LEWIS, waste management company executive. With Waste Mgmt., Inc., Oak Brook, Ill. 1968—, chmn., chief exec. officer, dir.; mem. bd. trustees Chgo. Symphony Orch. Office: Waste Mgmt Inc 3003 Butterfield Rd Oak Brook IL 60521 *

BUNZEL, MARK JOHN, digital imagery executive, educator; b. Milw., May 13, 1954; m. Deena Hostick. BA in Bus., Rutgers U., 1976. Dir. prodn., cons. Jack Morton Prodns., N.Y.C., 1976-81; pres., chief exec. officer Avion Communications Inc., N.Y.C., 1981-84; chmn., chief exec. officer CompuVision, Santa Clara, Calif., 1982-85, Avtex Research Corp., San Jose, Calif., 1985—; instr. U. Calif., Santa Cruz, 1987—. Recipient gold and bronze awards N.Y. Internat. Film Festival, 1979, 80. Office: Avtex Rsch Corp 5979 Starwood Dr San Jose CA 95120

BUONANNI, BRIAN FRANCIS, health care facility administrator, consultant; b. Pawtucket, R.I., Sept. 2, 1945; s. James and Roselle B.; m. Lynne Buonanni (div. 1982); children: Donna, Karen, Jamie; m. Diane Pilar Buonanni, Feb. 23, 1985. BA, Providence Coll., 1967; EdM, Boston Coll., 1968; M in Health Adminstrn., St. Louis U., 1973. Lic. nursing home adminstr., N.J. Rehab. counselor, tchr. R.I. Assn. for Blind, Providence, 1968-71; adminstrv. resident Carney Hosp., Boston, 1972; asst. adminstr. Alton (Ill.) Meml. Hosp., 1973-77, Gnaden Huetten Meml. Hosp., Lehighton, Pa., 1977-80; v.p. ops. Burdette Tomlin Hosp., Cape May Ct. House, N.J., 1980-85; chief oper. officer St. Elizabeth's Hosp., Elizabeth, N.J., 1985—; pres. Health Care Practice Mgmt., Jenkinstown, Pa., 1984—; chmn., mem. adv. bd. Shifa, McFaul & Lyons, Morristown, N.J., 1987—; mem. rev. com. N.J. Health Council, Trenton, 1987—. Fellow Am. Coll. Healthcare Execs.; mem. NAACP, Nat. Assn. Purchasing Agts., Rotary. Home: 12 Coldevin Rd Clark NJ 07066 Office: St Elizabeth Hosp 225 Williamson St Elizabeth NJ 07207

BUONGIORNO, JOSEPH PETER, engineer; b. Hoboken, N.J., Apr. 5, 1947; s. Daniel James and Victoria (Bruno) B.; m. Ellen Joan Ruvere, Sept. 27, 1969; children: Rachel, Gina. BSCE, Newark Coll. Engring., 1969, MSCE, 1972. Registered profl. engr., N.J. Assoc. engr. Goodkind & O'Dea, Inc., Clifton, N.J., 1969-78; sr. engr. Davy McKee Corp., Berkeley Heights, N.J., 1978-79, Lockwood Greene, N.Y.C., 1979-80, Lurgi Corp., Inc., River Edge, N.J., 1980-81, C.F. Braun Inc., Murray Hill, N.J., 1981-83; supervising engr. Nabisco Brands, Inc., Parsippany, N.J., 1983—. Chmn. Hopatcong (N.J.) Zoning Bd., N.J., 1978-88, mem. Planning Bd., 1984-86; vice chmn. United Meth. Ch. bldg. com., 1987—. Mem. ASCE. Republican. Clubs: Elba Beach (pres. 1980, 86-87), Hopatcong Rifle & Pistol (pres. 1979). Office: Nabisco Brands Inc 200 Deforest Ave East Hanover NJ 07936

BUONICONTI, NICHOLAS A., tobacco company executive; b. Springfield, Mass., 1940. Grad., U. Notre Dame, 1962; JD, Suffolk U., 1968. Pres., chief oper. officer UST, Inc., Greenwich, Conn. Office: UST Inc 100 W Putnam Ave Greenwich CT 06830

BUONO, ANTOINETTE THERESA, accountant; b. Bklyn., July 17, 1965; d. Rudolf James and Angelina Theresa (Genovese) B. BBA in Pub. Acctg. magna cum laude, Pace U., 1987. CPA, N.Y. With Peat Marwick Main & Co., N.Y.C., 1986—, acct., 1987, sr. acct., 1988—. Mem. N.Y. State Soc. CPAs, Alpha Chi. Roman Catholic. Home: 1130 59th St Brooklyn NY 11219 Office: Peat Marwick Main & Co 345 Park Ave New York NY 10154

BURCH, CHARLES WILLIAM, SR., security service executive; b. Long Beach, Calif., July 30, 1959; s. Lawrence Leiland Burch and Carolyn Hattie (Kestner) Belon; m. Jenny m. Sterna, May 27, 1980 (div. June 1981); m. Jean Elaine Duncan, July 14, 1986; 1 child, Charles William Jr. Student, Big Ben Community Coll., 1978. Security guard, personell mgr. Tahoe Mountain Security, South Lake Tahoe, Calif., 1987, gen. mgr., 1987-88; prin. Burch Security Svc., South Lake Tahoe, 1989—. With U.S. Army, 1976-79. Mem. Calif. State Nusmatic Assn. Democrat. Morman. Office: Burch Security Svc PO Box 15150 South Lake Tahoe CA 95702

BURCH, CRAIG ALAN, electronics executive; b. Geneva, Nebr., May 13, 1954; s. J.J. and R. Eleanor (Bean) B. BS in Elec. Engring., BS in Biology, MIT, 1977. Product specialist Siemens Med., Iselin, N.J., 1977-79, product mgr., 1979-80, nat. sales mgr. computer tomography, 1986-88; sr. sales specialist Siemens Med., Phila., 1981-85; pres. Micro Devices Corp., Princeton, N.J., 1985—; v.p. Intelligent Prodn. Systems Inc., Deerfield Beach, Fla., 1988—. Methodist. Home: 3 Hawthorne Ln East Windsor NJ 08520 Office: Micro Devices Corp 301 N Harrison St Bldg B Princeton NJ 08540

BURCH, JOHN CHRISTOPHER, JR., investment banker; b. Nashville, Jan. 18, 1940; s. John Christopher and Frances Vivian (Harris) B.; m. Susan Marie Klein, Sept. 13, 1969; children—Frances Marie, Christina Polk, John Christopher III. B.A., Vanderbilt U., 1966. Credit analyst Bank N.Y., N.Y.C., 1966-70; v.p. instl. sales Loeb Rhoades & Co., N.Y.C., 1970-75, J.C. Bradford & Co., Nashville, 1976-82; mng. dir. Equitable Securities Corp., Nashville, 1982—. Active Com. Fgn. Relations, Nashville, 1976, N.C. Soc. Cin., Raleigh, 1979. Served with U.S. Army, 1962-65. Mem. Nashville Security Dealers Assn., Fedn. Fin. Analysts. Episcopalian. Clubs: Belle Meade Country, Cumberland (Nashville). Home: 705 Hillwood Blvd Nashville TN 37205 Office: Equitable Securities Corp First American Ctr Nashville TN 37238

BURCH, JOHN WALTER, mining equipment company executive; b. Balt., July 14, 1925; s. Louis Claude and Constance (Boucher) B.; B.S. in Commerce, U. Va., 1951; postgrad. U.S. Coast Guard Acad., 1951; m. Robin Neely Sinkler, Apr. 19, 1952; children—John C., Robert L., Charles C., Anne N. With Procter & Gamble Co., Phila., 1953-65, sales mgr., 1960-65; v.p. Warner Co., Phila., 1965-73; chmn. bd., chief exec. officer S.S. Keely Co., Phila., 1973-75; pres., chmn. bd., chief exec. officer Burch Materials Co., Inc., Wayne, Pa., 1975—; dir. Eagle's Eye, Inc., Wayne. Bd. dirs. Nat. Multiple Sclerosis Soc., 1970-81, v.p., mem. exec. com., 1974-77; bd. dirs. Pa. Sports Hall of Fame, 1974—, v.p., mem. exec. com., 1974-79; chmn. Am. Legion Tennis Tournaments for State of Pa., 1975-82; mem. U.S. Congl. Adv. Bd., 1982—; bd. dirs. Eagle's Eye Lacrosse Club, 1982—. Served with USN, 1943-46, USCG, 1951-53. Mem. Am. Mgmt. Assn., Soc. Advancement of Mgmt., Internat. Platform Assn. Republican. Roman Catholic. Clubs: Merion Cricket, Merion Golf. All-Am. in lacrosse, 1949. Home: 412 Conestoga Rd Wayne PA 19087 Office: Burch Materials Co Inc 685 Kromer Ave Berwyn PA 19312

BURCH, PHILIP J., utilities executive, auditor, consultant; b. Paducah, Ky., Mar. 6, 1937; m. Judith Ann Reaves, May 14, 1960; children: Michael, Tracy, Jeff, Amy, Christopher. BBA, Merrimack Coll., 1972; MBA, Murray (Ky.) State U., 1977. Product mgr. Gen. Electric Corp., Milw., Boston, 1960-72; systems mgr. Diano Corp., Boston, 1972-76; sr. ops. analyst Arkla, Inc., Shreveport, La., 1977-85; mgr. mktg. services Arkla, Inc., Little Rock, 1985—; mem. faculty La. State U., Shreveport, 1979-80; adv. Red River Desk & Derrick, Shreveport, 1983-85. Pres. Ark. Cystic Fibrosis, Little Rock, 1988—. Mem. Am. Gas Assn. (chmn. com. rsch. seminars), Nat. Assn. Accts. (dir. publicity com. 1979), Data Processing Mgmt. Assocs., South County Jaycees (pres. 1967). Home: 11 Tucker Creek Rd Conway AR 72032 Office: Ark La Gas Co 400 E Capitol Little Rock AR 72203

BURCHAM, STEPHEN DALE, treasurer; b. Huntington, W.Va., Nov. 17, 1956; s. Dale and Margery Elizabeth (Thomas) B.; m. Deborah Lee Lowe, June 12, 1977; children: Jodi, Jessica. BBA, Ohio State U., 1981. CPA, Ohio. Auditor Auditor of State of Ohio, Columbus, 1981; sr. acct. Hayflich & Steinberg CPA's, Huntington, 1981-86; treas. Fairland Local Sch. Dist., Proctorville, Ohio, 1986—. Named Outstanding Young Man Am., 1987. Mem. Am. Inst. CPA'a, Ohio Soc. CPA's, Ohio Assn. Sch. Bus. Ofcls. (v.p. Southern Hills chpt. 1987-88), Ohio State U. Alumni Assn., Lions (treas. 1987—). Democrat. Methodist. Home: RR 4 Box 147 Proctorville OH 45669 Office: Fairland Local Sch Dist RR 4 Box 201 Proctorville OH 45669

BURCHARD, ELLEN WILLIAMS, actress, producer, artist, writer; b. Newport, R.I., June 13, 1913; d. Clarence Raymond and Mary Christine (Stewart) Williams; m. John Church Burchard, Feb. 6, 1943; 1 child, John Church. Studied painting with William Van Dresser, 1943, Stephen Olszewski, 1975-85; studied acting U. Wis., 1944, Stella Adler Studio, 1954-56, Herbert Berghof Studio, 1957-65, Harold Clurman's Profl. Acting Classes, N.Y.C., 1960-62. Actress on Broadway, films and TV, also in Rome and London; founder Carriage House Theatre, Little Compton, R.I., 1958, producer, artistic dir., actress Pro Summer Repertory Co., 1958-76; off-Broadway producer, N.Y.C., 1958-76; producer, artistic dir. Actors Repertory Co., Little Compton, 1976-85; actress R.I. Playwrights Theatre Summer Festival, Providence, 1985; lyricist Morning Song, 1979; playwright Marguerite, 1978, Scenes from the Past, 1979; off-Broadway roles include Journey to Endor, 1987-88; editor (poetry) To Diana, 1985. Founder, pres. Young Women's Rep. Club, Newport, 1935-37, 46-54, Little Compton Rep. Club, 1946-57, Newport Players Guild, 1936-42, 46-52; founder, 1st v.p. New Eng. Council Young Reps., 1932-37; Young Nat. Committeewoman Rep. Nat. Com., 1932-43. Mem. Actors Equity Assn., Screen Actors Guild, AFTRA, R.I. Short Story Club (pres. 1982-85), R.I. Water Color Soc., Newport Art Mus., Westport Art Club, Bus. Womens Club (charter, Newport). Congregationalist. Club: Mosaic (founder) (Newport).

BURCHMAN, HOWARD BARRY, consultant; b. N.Y.C., Feb. 19, 1951; s. Paul and Bernice (Rosenblum) B. BA, Middlebury Coll., 1973; student, U. London, 1973-74. Rsch. analyst U.S. Dept. Housing and Urban Devel., Washington, 1974-76; dir. program devel. Urban Homesteading Assistance

Bd., N.Y.C., 1976-78; owner Howard Burchman and Assocs., N.Y.C., 1978-87; ptnr. Burchman Terrio Cons., N.Y.C., 1987—. Author: Profit-Non Profit Partnerships, 1983, Office Space for Non Profits, 1986. Cons. Fund for the City of N.Y., 1984-86, Trinity Ch., Wall St., N.Y.C., 1985-88, N.Y. State Div. of Substance Abuse; vice chmn. Community Bd. 7, Manhattan, N.Y.C., chmn. Housing Com., 1984-88; bd. dirs. Ardor Found., N.Y.C., 1988—. Democrat. Jewish. Home: 79th St Boat Basin New York NY 10024 Office: Burchman Terrio Cons 180 Varick St 17th Fl New York NY 10014

BURCK, NEIL ARTHUR, marketing professional; b. Portland, Oreg., Dec. 23, 1957; s. Wayne Arthur Burck and Rose Marie (Dooley) Tracy; m. Susan Marie Mansker, Sept. 4, 1982; children: Conner John, Maren Inga. BS, Oreg. State U., 1982. Prodn. supr. Alaska Packers Assn., Newport, Oreg., 1979-80; sales trainee Advanced Bus. Computers, Tigard, Oreg., 1982; mgr. mktg. Verticon Computer Ctr., Bend, Oreg., 1983; mktg. coord. Xytec Corp., Bend, 1983-85; product specialist Floating Point Systems, Inc., Beaverton, Oreg., 1985-86; mgr. mktg. communications Key Tech., Inc., Walla Walla, Wash., 1987—. Bd. dirs. Walla Walla Coun. on Child Abuse and Neglect; mem. civic adv., bd. Walla Walla Gen. Hosp.; active Luth. Family Svcs., Bend, 1985. Avocations: outdoor activities, running, cycling, basketball, hiking. Home: 1826 Hilbrooke Dr Walla Walla WA 99362-0030 Office: Key Tech Inc PO box 1617 Walla Walla WA 99362-0030

BURDEN, JAMES EWERS, lawyer; b. Sacramento, Oct. 24, 1939; s. Herbert Spencer and Ida Elizabeth (Brosemer) B.; m. Kathryn Lee Gardner, Aug. 21, 1965; children—Kara Elizabeth, Justin Gardner. BS, U. Calif.-Berkeley, 1961; JD, U. Calif.-Hastings Coll. Law, 1964; postgrad. U. So. Calif., 1964-65. Bar: Calif. 1965, Tax Ct. U.S. 1969, U.S. Supreme Ct. 1970. Assoc. Elliott and Aune, Santa Ana, Calif., 1965, White, Harbor, Fort & Schei, Sacramento, 1965-67; assoc. Miller, Starr & Regalia, Oakland, Calif., 1967-69, ptnr., 1969-73; ptnr. Burden, Aiken, Mansuy & Stein, San Francisco, 1973-82; ptnr. James E. Burden, Inc., San Francisco, 1982—; ptnr. Austex Oil & Gas Co., Luling, Tex., Judgment Oil and Gas Co., Lockhart, Tex., Northpoint Investment Co., San Francisco; underwriting mem. Lloyds of London, 1986—; corp. sec. Doric Devel., Inc., Alameda, Calif.; sec. Harbor Bay Isle Assocs., Alameda; instr. U. Calif.-Berkeley, 1968-74, also Merritt Coll. Mem. ABA, Claremont Country Club, San Francisco Grid Club, San Francisco Comml. Club, Commonwealth of Calif., The American Club Ltd. (London). Contbr. articles to profl. jours. Office: 200 California St 5th Fl San Francisco CA 94111

BURDEN, JOHN W., III, retail company executive; b. 1937; married. BS, Lehigh U., 1959. With Bambergers, Newark, 1959-71; with Federated Dept. Stores, 1971—, v.p. gen. mgr. Burdines subs., 1973-76, exec. v.p. Burdines subs., 1976-78, pres. Burdines subs., 1978-81, chmn. bd. Abraham & Strauss subs., 1981-85, vice chmn. bd. dirs., 1985-88; chmn., chief exec. officer Campeau Corp. (Allied Federated Dept. Stores unit), 1988—. Office: Federated Mdse Svcs 1440 Broadway 13th Fl New York NY 10018 also: Allied Stores Corp 1114 Ave of the Americas New York NY 10036 *

BURDITT, GEORGE MILLER, JR., lawyer; b. Chgo., Sept. 21, 1922; s. George Miller and Flora Winifred (Hardie) B.; m. Barbara Helen Stenger, Feb. 17, 1945; children: Betsey Burditt Blessing, George M., Deborah Burditt Norton, Barbara Burditt Perry. BA, Harvard U., 1944, LLB, 1948. Bar: Ill. 1949, U.S. Dist. Ct. (no. dist.) Ill. 1952, U.S. Ct. Appeals (7th cir.) 1961, U.S. Ct. Appeals D.C. 1962, U.S. Ct. Appeals (4th cir.) 1974, U.S. Supreme Ct. 1974, U.S. Ct. Appeals (2d cir.) 1978, U.S. Ct. Appeals (9th cir.) 1987. With law dept. Swift & Co., Chgo., 1948-54; assoc. Chadwell & Kayser and predecessors, Chgo., 1955-69; ptnr. Burditt, Bowles and Radzius, chartered, Chgo., 1969—; dir. Gerber Products Co.; adj. prof. Northwestern U. Sch. Law; gen. counsel Food and Drug Law Inst.; mem. Ill. State Ho. of Reps., 1965-72, asst. majority leader, 1971-72; Rep. candidate U.S. Senate, 1974. 2d lt. USAAF, 1943-45. Named Outstanding Legislator, Better Govt. Assn., 1969, 71; recipient Presdl. award Cook County Bar Assn., 1981. Mem. ABA, Ill. State Bar Assn., D.C. Bar Assn., Chgo. Bar Assn. (pres. 1980-81), N.Y. Bar Assn., Fed. Bar Assn., Met. Bar Leaders Caucus (pres. 1981-82), Harvard Law Sch. Assn. (pres. 1988—), Harvard Law Soc. of Ill. (pres. 1980-81), Union League Club, Econ. Club, Mid-Day Club, Crystal Downs Country Club, Law of Chgo. Club (pres. 1980-81). Contbr. articles on food and drug laws to profl. jours. Office: Burditt Bowles & Radzius 333 W Wacker Dr Chicago IL 60606

BURDON, WILLIAM FONTAINE, advertising executive; b. Ware, Mass., Dec. 21, 1926; s. Paul P. and Dorothy S. (Schaninger) B.; Assoc. B.A., Curry Coll., Boston, 1951; m. Leonora Foronda, Sept. 10, 1954; children—Susan Lee, Linda Marie. With NBC, 1952-54; exec. v.p., creative dir. Marvin Hult & Assocs., advt., Peoria, Ill., 1955-61; pres. Burdon Advt., Inc., Peoria, 1962-82; pres. Burdon & Oakley, Inc., Peoria, 1982—. Mem. adv. bd. YWCA. Landmarks Found. Served with U.S. Army, 1945-47. Author published poetry. Home: 1827 W Sunnyview Dr Peoria IL 61614 Office: Burdon & Oakley Inc 2523 W Reservoir Blvd Peoria IL 61615

BURENGA, KENNETH L., publishing executive; b. Somerville, N.J., May 30, 1944; s. Nicholas Burena Jr. and Louanna (Chamberlin) B.; m. Jean, Oct. 29, 1964; children: Kean L., Diene M. BS, Rider Coll., 1970. Budget acct. Dow Jones & Co. Inc., South Brunswick, N.J., 1966-67, asst. mgr. data processing control, 1968-69, staff asst. for systems devel., 1970-71, mgr. systems devel. and control, 1972-76, circulation mktg. mgr., 1977-78, circulation sales dir., 1979-80, v.p. circulation, circulation dir., 1980-86; chief fin. officer and adminstrv. officer Dow Jones & Co. Inc., N.Y.C., 1986-88; gen. mgr. Dow Jones & Co. Inc., 1989—, Wall Street Journal, 1989—; bd. dirs. Telerate Inc., N.Y., Dow Jones Courier. Bd. dirs. Better Bus. Bur., N.Y., 1987. Served to staff sgt. USAR. Mem. Fin. Execs. Inst. Office: Dow Jones & Co Inc 200 Liberty St New York NY 10281

BURESH, THOMAS GORDON, financial services executive; b. Green Bay, Wis., Oct. 7, 1951; s. Norbert E. and Dorothy M. (Kreilkamp) B.; m. Suzan Lee Rickbeil, Mar. 21, 1980. BBA, U. Wis., 1973. CPA, Wis.; cert. fin. planner; registered investment advisor. Staff acct. Ernst & Whinney, Milw., 1973-75; sr. acct. Ernst & Whinney, Chgo., 1975-77; ptnr., v.p. Suby, Von Haden & Assocs., Madison, 1977—; pres. SVA Planners, Inc., 1987—. Gen. mem. United Way Dane County, Madison, 1984-87; bd. dirs. Arthritis Found., Milw., 1986—, So. Dist. chmn., 1986-88. Mem. Am. Inst. CPA's, Wis. Inst. CPA's, Internat. Assn. Fin. Planning, Inst. Cert. Fin. Planners. Roman Catholic. Home: 7865 E Oakbrook Circle Madison WI 53717 Office: Suby Von Haden & Assocs SC 901 Whitney Way Madison WI 53711

BURGENER, ROBERT HOWARD, corporate professional, consultant; b. Los Angeles, Apr. 20, 1936; s. Arnold and Jane (Howard) B.; m. Diane Burgener, July 10, 1961 (div. 1985); children: Robert H., Douglas S.; m. Carolyn Richards, Aug. 23, 1987. BS, U. Utah, 1958. Pres. Utah Assn. Music Dealers, Salt Lake City, 1958-65, EMI Energy Corp, Salt Lake City, 1969-83, EMI of Pacific, Hawaii, 1981-83; sec. Real Estate West, Salt Lake City, 1972-76; exec. sec. Am. Inter-Med. Supply, Salt Lake City, 1983—, Universal Leasing Corp., Salt Lake City, 1986—; cons. Cinemaware Corp., Westlake village, Calif., 1983—; bd. dirs. Software Rsch. & Devel. Corp.; pres. CCC Corp. dba Unshippers Assn., 3d party billing Co. Airborne Express, Calif., Fla. and Mass., 1988—. Sgt. U.S. Army, 1955-62. Home: 2844 Millcreek Rd Salt Lake City UT 84109 Office: 4190 Highland Dr Salt Lake City UT 84124

BURGER, LEWIS STEPHEN, legal services company executive; b. Bklyn., Aug. 6, 1941; s. Julius Sidney Burger and Eve (Gordon) Tucker; m. Pamela Enid Burger, Dec. 23, 1964 (div.); children: Michael, Allison; m. Judith Friedberg, July 31, 1983; 1 child, Amy Rachel. BA, L.I. U., 1963; JD, Bklyn. Law Sch., 1968. Bar: N.Y. 1968, U.S. Supreme Ct. 1974, D.C. 1983. Asst. dist. atty. Nassau County, 1969-70; sr. ptnr. Burger & LaVallee, Freeport, N.Y., 1970-80; sole practice Hauppauge, N.Y., 1980-81; sr. ptnr. Burger, Kramer, Feldman & Kirschner, Hauppauge, 1981-83; chmn., chief exec. officer group and prepaid legal svc. plans Nationwide Legal Svcs. Inc., Hartsdale, N.Y., 1983-87; chmn., chief exec. officer Premier Legal Access Systems (Mialamy Mktg. Corp.), 1987-88, Premier Affinity Resources, N.Y.C., 1987—; vice-chmn. Spend Today and Retire Tomorrow, Inc., 1988—; bd. dirs. Nat. Resource Ctr. for Consumers of Legal Svcs.; moderator conv. panel on entrepreneurial legal plans Am. Prepaid Legal Svcs. Inst., 1983, mem. pub. edn. com.; spl. advisor U.S. Congl. Adv. Bd. Appearances on radio and tv programs including Sta. WCBS-TV, Take Two Sta. WQXR-FM, Long Island Spotlight, Dialogue 101 Sta. WCBS Radio, Barry Gray Show Sta. WMCA Radio, Good Morning San Antonio, Sta. WNBC Radio, CNN; editor Long Beach (N.Y.) Rep. Paper; contbr. articles to profl. jours. Mem. U.S. Congl. Adv. Bd. Mem. Former Asst. Dist. Atty.'s Assn. Nassau County, Nat. Dist. Atty.'s Assn., Nat. Assn. Criminal Def. Lawyers. Jewish. Home and Office: Premier Legal Access Systems 139 Boulder Ridge Rd Scarsdale NY 10583 also: Nationwide Legal Svcs Inc 475 Park Ave S New York NY 10016

BURGESS, ARTHUR HARRY, accountant; b. Sharon, S.C., Oct. 25, 1903; s. Arthur Calhoun and Mary (Love) B.; m. Sara Elizabeth Doll, Nov. 30, 1933; children: Sara Elizabeth Burgess Frazer, Arthur Harry. Student Furman U., 1921-23. Pub. acct., Hickory, N.C., 1928—; chmn. bd. Arthur H. Burgess & Co. Mem. adv. bd. trustees Queens Coll.; elder Presbyn. Ch. Mem. Am. Inst. CPA's, N.C. Assn. CPA's, Sharon Found. CPA's (pres.). Paul Harris fellow. Clubs: Lake Hickory Country (Hickory); Charlotte (N.C.) City. Home: 322 3d Ave NE Hickory NC 28601 Office: Arthur H Burgess Co 1st Union Fin Ctr Ste 610 200 1st Ave NW PO Box 2587 Hickory NC 28603

BURGESS, BRUCE HOWLAND, real estate executive; b. Rutherford, N.J., Dec. 26, 1950; s. Edward Sisson and Shirley (Westervelt) B.; m. Martha Jane Tweedy, Nov. 3, 1979; children: Andrew David, Geoffrey Edward, Stephanie Ann. BA in Bus. and Fin., Montclair State Coll., 1972; student, Real Estate Inst. NYU, 1974-76. Lic. real estate broker, N.Y., Tex., Okla. Office leasing broker Cross & Brown Co., N.Y.C., 1972-74; project mgr. Draper & Kramer, Inc., Phila., 1974-76; second v.p. real estate Chase Manhattan Bank, N.Y.C., 1976-79; gen. mgr. Joshua Muss & Assoc., Dallas, 1979-83; pres., chmn. Burgess Mgmt. Corp., Dallas, 1983—; trustee Fed. Bankruptcy Ct., Dallas, 1983—; advisor Retirement Housing Corp., Dallas, 1985—; specialist in problem real estate analysis and disposition; guest lectr. Richland Coll., Dallas, 1984-85; assoc. dir. Griffin Capital Corp., N.Y.C. and Dallas, 1987—; bd. dirs. Signworks Devel., Inc., Dallas, B/D Contractors, Inc., Dallas. Republican. Presbyterian. Office: Burgess Mgmt Corp 5501 LBJ Fwy Suite 311 Dallas TX 75240

BURGESS, BRYAN ELIJAH, communication executive; b. Sparta, Tenn., Oct. 27, 1937; s. Elijah B. and Pauline (Pennington) B.; m. Leslie Hindman, Sept. 12, 1979; children: Belinda, Susan Urquhart, Paula Cook, Wendy Murdzak. BSEE, Tenn. Tech. U., 1960; MSEE, U. Ala., 1965; PhD summa cum laude, U. Tenn., 1976. Registered profl. engr. Ala. V.p. Nashville Speedways Inc., 1968-70; cons. Intergraft, Huntsville, Ala., 1976-78; dir. research Motlow St. Community Coll., Tullahoma, Tenn., 1970-76; mgr. utility services Sci. Applications Inc., Huntsville, 1978-83; mgr. nat. sales Avco Electronics, Huntsville, 1983-85; mgr. ops. Bell S. Services Inc., Birmingham, Ala., 1985—. Mem. Phi Kappa Phi. Office: Bell South Svcs 3535 Colonnade Pkwy South S2E1 Birmingham AL 35243

BURGESS, DAVID, lawyer, government official; b. Detroit, Nov. 30, 1948; s. Roger Edward and Claire Theresa (Sullivan) B.; m. Rebecca Culbertson Stuart, 1985 (dec. 1988). BS in Fgn. Service, Georgetown U., 1970, MS in Fgn. Service, 1978, JD, 1978. Research asst. Gerogetown U. Sch. Bus. Adminstrn., Washington, 1975, asst. to dean, 1975-76; research asso., prof. Acad. in the Public Service, Washington, 1976-79; asst. editor Securities Regulation Law Report; legal editor Internat. Trade Reporter, Bur. Nat. Affairs, 1978-79; atty. Cadwalader, Wickersham & Taft, Washington, 1979-81; mng. editor Bur. Nat. Affairs, Washington, 1981-82; dir. U.S. Peace Corps, Niamey, Niger, 1982-84, Rabat, Morocco, 1984-85; dir. policy planning, mgmt. Peace Corps, Washington, 1985-87; dir. Bur. Human rights and Humanitarian Affairs U.S. Dept. of State, Washington, 1987—; speaker workshops Minority Legis. Edn. Program, Ind. Assn. Cities and Towns, Georgetown U. Continuing Edn. Program, Communications Workers Am., Colo. State U., U. Wis. Alumni rep. Internat. Sch. Bangkok, 1972-74. Author: Financing Local Government, 1977, 2d edit., 1978, Preparation of the Local Budget, 2 vols., 1976, 2d edit., 1978, Local Government Accounting Fundamentals, 2d edit., 1977, Understanding Federal Assistance Programs, 2d edit., 1978, The POW/MIA Issue: Perspectives on the National League of Families, 1978; contbr. articles to publs. Served with USAF, 1970-74. Mem. ABA, D.C. Bar Assn., Wash. Internat. Trade Assn., Am. Soc. Internat. Law, Am. Acad. Arts and Scis., Acad. Polit. Sci., Washington Fgn. Law Soc., Federalist Soc., Ripon Soc., Amnesty Internat., U.S. Assn. Internat. Commn. Jurists, Internat. Platform Assn., Republican Nat. Lawyers Assn., World Affairs Council, Georgetown U. Alumni Assn. (bd. govs. 1975—, class rep. 1971—). Roman Catholic. Clubs: Nat. Press, Pres.'s. Home: 3115 N 1st Pl Arlington VA 22201 Office: US Dept State Bur Human Rights & Humanitarian Affairs 2201 C St NW Washington DC 20520

BURGESS, JANET HELEN, interior designer; b. Moline, Ill., Jan. 22, 1933; d. John Joseph and Helen Elizabeth (Johnson) B.; student Augustana Coll., Rock Island, Ill., 1950-51, U. Utah, Logan, 1951-52, Marycrest Coll., 1959-60; m. Richard Everett Guth, Aug. 25, 1951; children: John Joseph, Marshall Claude, Linnea Ann Guth Layman Sinclair; m. Milan Andrew Vodick, Feb. 16, 1980. One-person shows: El Pao, Bolivar, Venezuela, 1952-62; represented in pvt. collections, U.S., Europe, S.Am.; producer, designer Playcrafters Barn Theatre, Moline, Ill., 1963-65; designer, gen. mgr. Grilk Interiors, Davenport, Iowa, 1963-87; dir. Fine Arts Gallery, Davenport, 1978-84; chmn. bd. Product Handling, Inc., Davenport, 1981-88; owner mail order bus. Amazon Vinegar & Pickling Works Drygoods, Davenport. Contbr. articles to profl. jours.; design work featured in Gift & Decorative Accessories mag., 1969, 80, Decor mag., 1979. Bd. dirs. Rock Island Art Guild, 1974—, Quad Cities Arts Council, 1980-84 ; bd. dirs. Village of East Davenport (Iowa) Assn., 1973-84 , pres., 1981; bd. dirs. Neighborhood Housing Services, Davenport, Davenport Area Conv. and Tourism Bur., 1981; mem. adv. bd. interior design dept. Scott Community Coll., 1975-80; mem. Mayor's Com. Historic Preservation, Davenport, Iowa, 1976-77, 85—; bd. dirs. retail com. Operation Clean Davenport, 1981; mem. 16th Iowa Civil War Re-enactment Union. Mem. Gift and Decorative Accessories Assn. (nat. merit award 1969), Am. Soc. Interior Designers (assoc.), Nat. Trust Hist. Preservation, Preservation Group, State Iowa Hist. Soc. Home: 2801 34th Ave Ct Rock Island IL 61201 Office: 2218 E 11th St Davenport IA 52803

BURGESS, JEANNE LLEWELLYN, international consumer products corporation executive, research foundation executive; b. New Albany, Ind., Aug. 6, 1923; d. Jesse Joel and Lydia Ann (Young) Llewellyn; m. Quentin F. Burgess, Dec. 24, 1941 (dec. Nov. 1984). Student, Ind. U., 1948-49, Ind. U. SE, New Albany, 1979. Supr. policy dept. Wabash Life Ins. Co., Indpls., 1952-53; claim examiner Acacia Mut. Life Ins. Co., Washington, 1954-61; exec. sec. System Devel. Corp., Falls Church, Va., 1962-64; mgr. stockholder relations Brown-Forman Corp., Louisville, 1965-88; sec., treas. Airline Mushroom Producers, New Albany, 1977-84; exec. dir. Sylvan Forest Inst., Louisville, 1984—. Co-editor Corporate Fact Book, 1987; mgr. Brown-Forman Ann. Report, 1970-88; contbr. numerous poems and articles for mags. and newspapers. Active arts council, Floyd and Orange Counties, Ind. and met. Louisville 1977—; mem. adv. bd. Gov.'s Task Force on Forest Mgmt., Indpls., 1980; cons. Jr. Achievement, Floyd County, 1981-82, judge nat. essay contest, 1983; bd. dirs. Flyd City Histl. Soc., Fairview Historic Cemetery, New Albany; mem. Dodrasquicentennial Celebration Com. New Albany, 1988; del. citizens ambassador program People to People Internat., 1988. Recipient Clarion Merit award Women In Communications, 1982, Cert. of Accomplishment Four Seasons Wine Symposium, N.Y.C., 1970. Mem. Nat. Investor Relations Ins., Corp. Transfer Agts. Assn., Am. Forestry Assn., Nat. Assn. Investors (corp. adv. bd. 1981-83), So. Ind. Poets and Writers Assn. Republican. Methodist. Home: 4000 Persimmon Ln New Albany IN 47150

BURGESS, JOSEPH EDWARD, human resources executive; b. Kingstree, S.C., May 18, 1935; s. Joseph Ting and Earline Burgess; m. Clara M. Skipwith, May 14, 1966 (div. Sept. 1968). BA, W.Va. State Coll., 1958; MA, New Sch. of Social Research, 1983. Mktg. rep. Mobil Oil Corp., N.Y.C., 1964-69; asst. dir. Nat. Urban League, N.Y.C., 1969-71; dir. minority relations Babcock & Wilcox, N.Y.C., 1971-78; dir. EEO adminstrn. Anheuser-Busch, St. Louis, 1978-79; dir. EEO GAF Corp., N.Y.C., 1979-82; asst. v.p. Met. Life, N.Y.C., 1982-87; dir. human resources Skidmore, Owings & Merrill, N.Y.C., 1987; dep. dir. EEO NYC Health and Hosp. Corp., N.Y.C., 1987—; cons. Fayetteville (N.C.) State U., 1984—; chmn. N.Y/N.J. Liaison Group, N.Y.C., 1985-87; dep. dir. EEO N.Y.C. Health and Hosp. Corp., 1987—. Councilman Yonkers (N.Y.) City Council, 1986; mem. NAACP, Black Democrats of Westchester County, Westchester, N.Y., 1985. Recipient Presdl. citation The White House, 1981, commendation Nat. Urban League, 1980, Bronco plaque Fayetteville State U., 1985. Mem. NAACP (Yonkers br.), Nat. Urban Affairs Council. Methodist. Home: 300 Palisade Ave #3N Yonkers NY 10703 Office: NYC Health & Hosp Corp 125 Worth St New York NY 10013

BURGESS, ROBERT K., construction company executive; b. 1944. BS, Mich. State U., 1966. With Pulte Home Corp., West Bloomfield, Mich., 1983—, v.p. corp. devel., 1983-84, sr. v.p., 1984-85, chief operating officer, exec. v.p., 1985-86, pres., chief operating officer, 1987—, also bd. dirs. Office: Pulte Home Corp 33 Bloomfield Hills Pkwy Ste 300 Bloomfield Hills MI 48013 *

BURGESS, T. PETER, management consultant; b. Preston, Eng., Jan. 8, 1940; married; 2 children. BA, Cambridge U., 1961, MA, 1966; cert. chartered acctg., Coopers & Lybrand, London, 1965, FCA, 1975. Engr. Davy Ashmore Group, 1961-62; planner, field acct. H.A. Simons Ltd., 1966-67; subs., div. contr. Aerosol Techniques, Inc., 1967-70; corp. budget mgr., fin. contr., v.p. mfg. Gulton Industries, Inc., 1970-74; chief fin. officer Continental Seafoods, Inc., Africa, Middle East, Latin Am.,U.S., Europe & Japan, 1974-78; prin., cons. Burgess Mgmt. Assocs., 1978—; mem. fisheries planning Cote d'Ivoire, 1978, Nigeria, 1978, U.S.A., 1980, Burma, 1981, French Guinee, 1982, Madagascar, 1982, Thailand, 1983, North Yemen, 1983, South Yemen, 1983, Liberia, 1983, West Africa, 1984, Senegal, 1985, Kuwait, 1985, Guinee Conakry, 1986, Guinee Bissau, 1986, Mozambique, 1987, fisheries devel., Nigeria, 1988; agricultural planning, India, 1978, U.S.A., 1981, 85; mgmt. consultancy, Madagascar, 1980, 81, 85, 87, Nigeria, 1986,Saudi Arabia, 1988; devel. planning, Ethiopia, 1987, Lesotho, 1987, Malawi, 1987, So. Africa, 1988; project supervision, Benin, 1986. Home: 221 E 66th St Apt 4C New York NY 10021 Office: Burgess Mgmt Assocs 1173A 2d Ave Ste 221 New York NY 10021

BURGHARDT, KURT JOSEF, marketing professional, infosystems specialist; b. Mainz, Fed. Republic of Germany, June 8, 1935; came to U.S., 1957; s. Karl Franz and Aenne Elizabeth (Lohr) B.; m. Alison Gertrude Koch, Dec. 9, 1980; children: Lars, Kristina. Student, U. Frankfurt, Fed. Republic of Germany, 1956-57; BBA, U. Wis., 1957, MBA, 1960. Mgmt. trainee A.C. Nielsen, Chgo., 1960-62, asst. to pres., 1962-66; nat. sales mgr., v.p. Neodata Services, Boulder, Colo., 1966-76, exec. v.p., div. mgr., 1976-77; pres. Neodata Services, Louisville, 1977—, also chmn. bd. dirs., exec. v.p.; bd. dirs. 1st Nat. Bank, Boulder. Contbr. articles to profl. jours. Former pres. and tenure mem. Philharm. Soc., Boulder; mem. endowment bd. dirs. Arts and Humanities Assembly of Boulder; active Boulder Econ. Council. Served with U.S. Army, 1960. Mem. Audit Bur. Circulation, Direct Mail Mktg. Assn., City and Regional Mag. Assn., Mag. Pubs. Assn., Boulder C. of C., U. Colo. Relations Assn. (bd. dirs.), Accord Assn. (bd. dirs.), XYZ Club, Boulder Country Club, Phi Beta Kappa. Office: Neodata Svcs PO Box 4586 Boulder CO 80306

BURGHART, WILLIAM ROBERT, banker; b. Chanute, Kans., Aug. 3, 1949; s. Ralph William and Betty Irene (Wilson) B.; m. Joyce Ellen Griffith, Aug. 20, 1970; children: Valinda Michelle, Vince McClain. AA, Neosho County Community Coll., 1969; BA, Emporia (Kans.) State U., 1971. Asst. v.p. Emporia State Bank and Trust Co., 1970-77; sr. v.p. Prairie State Bank, Augusta, Kans., 1977-83; pres. Citadel Bank Augusta, 1983—, also bd. dirs. Mem. sch. bd. Unified Sch. Dist. 402, Augusta, 1981-85; fin. sec. Christ Luth. Ch., Augusta, 1983-84, 86-87. Mem. Augusta C. of C. (pres. 1985-86). Republican. Clubs: Optimists (pres. 1980-81, 82-83)(Augusta). Office: Citadel Bank Augusta 645 State Augusta KS 67010

BURGMAN, DIERDRE ANN, lawyer; b. Logansport, Ind., Mar. 25, 1948; d. Ferdinand William Jr. and Doreen Yvonne (Walsh) B. BA, Valparaiso U., 1970, JD, 1979; LLM, Yale U., 1985. Bar: Ind. 1979, U.S. Dist. Ct. (so. dist.) Ind. 1979, N.Y. 1982, U.S. Dist. Ct. (so. dist.) N.Y. 1982, U.S. Ct. Appeals (7th cir.) 1982, U.S. Ct. Appeals (D.C. cir.) 1984, U.S. Ct. Appeals (2d cir.) 1984, U.S. Supreme Ct. 1985. Law clk. to chief judge Ind. Ct. Appeals, Indpls., 1979-80; prof. law Valparaiso (Ind.) U., 1980-81; assoc. Dewey, Ballantine, Bushby, Palmer & Wood, N.Y.C., 1981-84, Cahill Gordon & Reindel, N.Y.C., 1985—. Note editor Valparaiso U. law rev., 1978-79; contbr. articles to law jours. Mem. bd. visitors Valparaiso U. Sch. Law, 1986—, chmn., 1989—. Ind. Bar Found. scholar, 1978. Mem. ABA (trial evidence com., profl. liability com.), Assn. of Bar of City of N.Y. (com. profl. responsibility), N.Y. County Lawyers Assn. (asst. chmn. com. Supreme Ct. 1987-88, Outstanding Svc. award 1988). Home: 164 E 61st St New York NY 10021 Office: Cahill Gordon & Reindel 80 Pine St 17th Fl New York NY 10005

BURGMEIER, CHARLES RICHARD, accountant; b. Dubuque, Iowa, Jan. 15, 1954; s. James Alphonse and Joanne Justin (Keffeler) B.; m. Paula Elizabeth Zerull, Sept. 17, 1977; children: Nicholas James, Joseph Paul, Elizabeth Ann. BBA, U. Iowa, 1976. CPA, Iowa; cert. fin. planner. Staff McGladrey & Pullen, Clinton, Iowa, 1976-81, mgr., 1981-84, ptnr., 1984—. Mem. fin. com. Mercy Hosp., Clinton; chief auditor United Way, Clinton, 1980-83, chmn. budget and allocation, 1987, bd. dirs., 1987—. Recipient Disting. Service award Clinton Jaycees, 1987. Mem. AICPA, Iowa Soc. CPA's, Rotary Club. Home: 3607 Valley Ln Clinton IA 52732 Office: McGladrey & Pullen 223 Wilson Bldg Clinton IA 52732

BURGOYNE, JAMES FREDERICK, greeting card company executive; b. Phila., Feb. 1, 1936; s. Harry and Esther (O'Neil) B.; m. Mary Louise McDevitt, Apr. 18, 1959; children: James F., William J., Mary E., Kristen A. BS in Acctg., St. Joseph's U., Phila., 1958. Pres. Burgoyne Inc., Phila., 1976—. Chmn. WCAU-TV Neighborhood Fund., Phila., 1987. Capt. USMC, 1958-62. Mem. Cedarbrook C. of C., Vesper Club. Republican. Roman Catholic. Office: Burgoyne Inc 2030 Byberry Rd Philadelphia PA 19116

BURGSTRESSER, RICHARD ALBERT, JR., sales executive; b. Phila., Sept. 2, 1954. BA, Marietta Coll., 1976. Mgr. audio mktg. Panasonic Co., Secaucus, N.J., 1981-85, mgr. nat. sales div. radio cassettes, 1985-88, mgr. nat. sales adminstrn., 1988—. Office: Panasonic Co 1 Panasonic Way Secaucus NJ 07094

BURGUIERES, PHILIP JOSEPH, metal products company executive; b. Franklin, La., Sept. 3, 1943; s. Denis P.J. and Emma L. (LeBlanc) B.; m. Cheryl A. Courrege, Aug. 21, 1965; children: Emily Louise, Philip Martial. BS in Mech. Engring, U. Southwestern La., 1965; MBA, U. Pa., 1970. Adminstrv. asst. Cameron Iron Works, Inc., Houston, 1971, fin. mgr. European ops., 1972-75, v.p. corp. svcs., 1975-77, v.p. and gen. mgr. forged products div., 1977-79, exec. v.p. ops., 1979-81, pres., chief operating officer, 1981-85, pres., chief exec. officer, 1986—, chmn. bd., 1987—; chmn. bd. dirs. J.M. Burguieres Co., Ltd., Franklin; bd. dirs. Panhandle Ea., Houston, Tex. Commerce Bancshares. Chmn. Duchesne Acad. Sacred Heart, Houston, 1987. Served with USN, 1966-69. Mem. Am. Petroleum Inst. (bd. dirs.), Petroleum Equipment Suppliers Assn. (pres. 1986-87), Nat. Petroleum Coun., Greater Houston C. of C. (bd. dirs.), Nat. Ocean Industries Assn., Petroleum Club of Houston (pres. 1988—), Tau Beta Pi, Pi Tau Sigma. Roman Catholic. Office: Cameron Iron Works Inc PO Box 1212 Houston TX 77251

BURICK, MARY FRANCES, banker, former government official; b. Youngstown, Ohio, Dec. 22, 1952; d. Joseph and Carol Marie (Vlasic) B.; B.A. in Econs., Youngstown State U., 1975; M.A. in Econs., U. Okla., 1981. Fin. analyst examiner Ohio Div. Bank Supervision, Columbus, 1975; liquidator div. liquidation FDIC, Washington, 1975-83, liquidator-in-charge Cleve. office, 1979-83; credit officer Nat. City Bank, Cleve., 1983-84; asst. v.p. credit and loan adminstrn., bus. banking exec. Society Nat. Bank, Cleve., 1984—; instr. Cleve. State U. Mem. Nat. Assn. Bus. Economists, Am. Mgmt. Assn., Am. Soc. Profl. and Exec. Women, NAFE, Nat. Assn. Bank Women (state pub. affairs chmn. 1988—), Internat. Platform Assn. Roman

Catholic. Clubs: Cleve. Bus. Economist, Women's City of Cleve. Home: 26523 Normandy Bay Village OH 44140

BURK, DANA PRAG, industrial engineer; b. Portland, Oreg., Apr. 13, 1960; d. John Allen Prag and Anne Elizabeth (Marshall) Jay; m. Alan E. Burk, Apr. 16, 1983. BS in Indsl. Engring., U. Portland, 1983. Scheduler Neltech Devel., Portland, 1981-82, mng. engr., 1982-83; dry storage supr. Gourmet Brands, Boardman, Oreg., 1983-86, quality assurance supr., 1986-87; indsl. engr. Lamb-Weston, Boardman, 1987—.

BURK, JACK ANDREW, investment co. exec.; b. Springfield, Tenn., Mar. 19, 1935; s. Andrew Jackson and Elizabeth Ethelyne (Revels) B.; student Central Bible Inst., Springfield, Mo., 1953-54, So. Calif. Coll., Costa Mesa, 1955; student San Fernando Valley Coll., 1956; m. Alice Jean Jackson, Apr. 24, 1965; children—Teresa Lynn, Cheryl Ninette, Loren Dwayne. With Rocketdyne div. N. Am. Aviation Santa Susana Rocket Test sect., 1959-65; with Equity Funding Corp., 1965-73, area. v.p. So. Calif., Century City, 1970-71, v.p., resident mgr., Tarzana, Calif., 1972-73; founder, pres. Preferred Exec. Programs Inc., Woodland Hills, Calif., 1973-76; mem. adv. com. Am. Pacific Life Ins. Co., San Rafael, Calif., 1973-77; dir. bus. affairs Peoples Found., Fresno, Calif., 1977-84; gen. mgr. PF Communications Inc., Fresno, 1979-84; mgmt. cons. TV stas. and prodn. facilities, 1984-85; dist. sales mgr., Omega Video, Inc., Lawndale, Calif., 1985-86; major account rep. U.S. Sprint, 1987—. Mem. Nat. Assn. Securities Dealers, Nat. Assn. Life Underwriters, Internat. Assn. Fin. Planners. Republican. Home: 9391 E Ellery Clovis CA 93612

BURKART, ROBERT E., research foundation administrator. PhD, Purdue U. Various mgmt. positions personnel, sales tng. Hoechst-Celanese; mgr. Mgmt. Devel. Svcs. Indsl. Rsch. Inst., N.Y.C. Office: Indsl Rsch Inst 1550 M Street NW Washington DC 20005

BURKE, DANIEL BARNETT, communications corporation executive; b. Albany, N.Y., Feb. 4, 1929; s. J. Frank and Mary (Barnett) B.; m. Harriet Shore, Aug. 31, 1957; children: Stephen, J.Frank, James, Sarah, William. A.B., U. Vt., 1950; M.B.A., Harvard, 1955. Various positions product mgmt. and devel. Jell-O div. Gen. Foods Corp., 1955-61; gen. mgr. WTEN-TV, Albany, 1961-64; corporate v.p. WTEN-TV, 1962; gen. mgr. WJR AM/FM, Detroit, 1964-69; corporate exec. v.p., dir. WJR AM/FM, 1967; pres. pub. div. Capital Cities Broadcasting Corp., N.Y.C., 1969-72; pres., chief operating officer Capital Cities Broadcasting Corp., 1972-85, Capital Cities ABC Inc., 1986—; bd. dirs. Rohm & Haas Co., Avon Products, Inc., Conrail. Bd dirs. Cities in Schs. Inc., Nat. Urban League, Am. women's Econ. Devel. Corp., Am. Film Inst.; past chmn. bd. trustees U. Vt.; past chmn. bd. trustees Med. Mission Sisters, Phila. Served to 1st lt., inf. AUS, 1951-53, Korea. Mem. Phi Delta Theta. Office: Capital Cities/ABC Inc 24 E 51st St New York NY 10022

BURKE, JACQUELINE YVONNE, telecommunications executive; b. Newark, Apr. 10, 1949; d. Trim and Viola (Smith) Russell; m. Harry Clifford Burke Jr., Aug. 20, 1968 (div. 1977); 1 child, Terence Christopher. Student, Howard U., Washington, 1966-67. Teaching asst. Barringer High Sch., Newark, 1967; course developer Prudential Property and Casualty Ins., Newark, 1968-74; exec. Ad-A-System, Avenel, N.J., 1974-77; staff mgr. AT&T, Basking Ridge, N.J., 1977-83; quality assurance mgr. ops. and engring. Bell Communications Research, Morristown, N.J., 1984-86, dir. traffic routing adminstr., mem. tech. staff, 1986—; instr. Summer Tech. Edn. Program, Morristown, 1987. Instr. Youth for Christ, Fanwood, N.J., 1984-86; cons., instr. Black Achievers/YMCA, Newark, 1985; pres. Archway Pregnancy Ctr., Elizabeth, N.J., 1985—; counselor, Restoration House Youth Ctr., 1988—, Teen Crisis Hot-Line, 1988—. Recipient Tribute to Woman in Industry award, 1985, Black Achiever award, 1985, Sojourner Truth award, 1989, Bellcore Synergy III cert., 1989; named Outstanding Young Woman Am., 1985. Mem. Nat. Assn. Negro Bus. and Profl. Women's Club, Inc., Career Options/YWCA, Am. Mgmt. Assn., Tribute to Women and Industry (speaker, mem. mgmt. forum 1985—). Democrat. Home: 229 West Ave South Plainfield NJ 07080 Office: Bell Communications Rsch 435 South St Rm 1J325 Morristown NJ 07960

BURKE, JAMES EDWARD, manufacturing company executive; b. Rutland, Vt., Feb. 28, 1925; s. James Francis and Mary (Barnett) B.; B.S. in Econs., Holy Cross Coll., 1947; M.B.A., Harvard U., 1949; m. Alice Eubank, Apr. 27, 1957 (dec.); children: Mary Clotilde, James Charles; m. 2d, Diane W. Burke, Nov. 7, 1981. Sales rep., then asst. brand mgr., brand mgr. Procter & Gamble, 1949-52; product dir. Johnson & Johnson, 1953-54, dir. new products, 1954-57, dir. advt. and merchandising, 1957-58, v.p. advt. and merchandising, 1958-62, gen. mgr. Baby Products Co. div., 1962-64, exec. v.p. mktg., 1964-65, gen. mgr. Johnson & Johnson Products Co. div., 1965-66, pres. 1966-70, chmn. bd., 1970-71, corp. dir., mem. exec. com., 1973-76, dir., mem. exec. com. parent co., 1965—, vice-chmn. exec. com., from 1971, chief exec. officer, chmn. bd. parent co., 1976—; dir. IBM, Prudential Ins. Co. Mem. vis. com. bd. overseers Harvard Coll. Med. Sch. and Sch. Dental Medicine; bd. dirs. United Negro Coll. Fund; vice-chmn. Corp. Fund Kennedy Ctr.;mem. policy and planning commn. Bus. Roundtable; mem. Pres.'s Commn. Exec. Exchange, Pres.'s Pvt. Sector Survey on Cost Control in Fed. Govt.; mem. Trilateral and Nat. Commns. on Pub. Service; vice chmn. bus. council bd. dirs. Council on Fgn. Relations. Served as ensign USN, World War II; PTO. Mem. Conf. Bd. (vice chmn.). Office: Johnson & Johnson 1 Johnson & Johnson Pla New Brunswick NJ 08933 also: Johnson & Johnson 501 George St New Brunswick NJ 08903 *

BURKE, JOHN JAMES, utility executive; b. Butte, Mont., July 25, 1928; m. Nancy M. Calvert, July 12, 1952; children: Cheryl Burke Harris, Mary Burke Orizotti, Kathleen, John James, III, Elisabeth. BS in Bus., BA in Law, U. Mont., 1950, J.D., 1952. Bar: Mont. 1952, U.S. Supreme Ct. 1957. Ptnr. Weir, Gough, Booth and Burke, Helena, 1954-59; atty. Mont. Power Co., Butte, 1959-67, v.p., 1967-78, exec. v.p., 1979-84, vice chmn. bd. dirs., 1984—; bd. dirs. Blue Cross/Blue Shield Mont. Trustee U. Mont. Found., Carroll Coll. Mont., Mont. Hist. Soc., 1988—; pres. City-County Planning Bd., 1966-78; past dir. Vigilante council Boy Scouts Am., Shining Mountains council Girl Scouts U.S. Served to capt. JAGC, USAF, 1952-54, with Res. 1954-61. Mem. ABA (mem. council pub. utility law sect.), Silver Bow County Bar Assn., Mountain States Legal Found. (bd. dirs), Lazard Freres Spl. Equity Fund (bd. dirs.), Nat. Assn. Mfrs. (bd. dirs.), Edison Electric Inst. (exec. adv. com. on planning), Butte C. of C. (v.p. 1965-72), U. Mont. Alumni Assn. (past bd. dirs.), Phi Delta Phi. Roman Catholic. Clubs: Montana, Butte Country, Elks, Rotary (sec. Helena 1955-58); 116 (Washington). Home: 50 Burning Tree Ln Butte MT 59701 Office: Mont Power Co 40 E Broadway Butte MT 59701

BURKE, MARGARET ANN, computer and communications company specialist; b. N.Y.C., Feb. 25, 1961; d. David Joseph and Eileen Theresa (Falvey) B. BS in Computer Sci., St. John's U., Jamaica, N.Y., 1982. Software specialist C&P Telephone Co., Washington, 1983—. Commr. C&P Telephone Softball League, 1986—; mem. Corcoran Gallery of Art, 1989—. Mem. Nat. Assn. Female Execs., Alliance Francaise, Nat. Fedn. Rep. Women, League Rep. Women D.C., Smithsonian (resident assoc. 1988—), Am. Film Inst. Roman Catholic. Home: 4422 42d St NW Washington DC 20016 Office: C&P Telephone Co 13101 Columbia Pike Silver Spring MD 20904

BURKE, MICHAEL DONALD, oil and gas company executive; b. Salem, Oreg., Feb. 27, 1944; s. James Michael Burke and Mary Jane (Farrington) Gage; m. Louise Mennow, June 3, 1972; children—Kendra Anne, Michael John. B.S. in Chem. Engring., Tex. A&M U., 1966; M.B.A. in Fin. and Mktg., U. Tex., Austin, 1970. Mktg., product mgr. PPG Industries, Pitts., 1966-76; cons. PACE Cons., Houston, 1976-78; mktg. mgr. ICI Americas (CCPC), Houston, 1978-80; dir. Tri-State Synfuels Tex. Eastern Corp., Houston, 1980-82; v.p. mfg. La Gloria Oil & Gas Co. subs. Tex. Eastern Corp., Houston, 1982-84, pres., 1984—; pres. Tex. Eastern Products Pipeline Co. subs. Tex. Eastern Corp., Houston, 1986—; group v.p. Tex. Eastern Corp., 1986—; pres. Personal Devel. Forum, Houston, 1982—. Chmn. Tex. Eastern Polit. Action Com., Houston, 1985-86, United Way Campaign Effectiveness Council, Houston, 1986, Houston chpt. Am. Leadership Forum, 1987—; bd. dirs. Houston Mental Health Assocs., 1987—, ARC, 1987—, Sam Houston council Boy Scouts Am. Mem. Nat. Petroleum Refiners Assn. (bd. dirs. 1984—), Am. Petroleum Inst. (gen. refining com. 1982-84), Tex. Eastern Toastmasters (pres. 1984), Houston C. of C. (chmn. Houston Bus. Group 1986-88), Corpus Christi Jaycees (past dir.), Southbriar Community Assn. (past pres.). Republican. Roman Catholic. Clubs: Petroleum of Houston, Forum of Houston. Office: Tex Ea Corp 1221 McKinney PO Box 2521 Houston TX 77252

BURKE, STEVEN CHARLES, healthcare administration executive; b. Atlanta, May 23, 1951; s. Charles Hulett and Carole Ruth (Mason) B.; m. Margaret Hudgins, Aug. 9, 1975; 1 child, David. BA, U. So. Sewanee, 1973; MHA, Duke U., 1975. Planning analyst Greenville Hosp., S.C., 1975-78, asst. dir. facility devel. and constrn., 1978-79, asst. v.p. planning, 1979-83; dir. planning and mktg. Youngstown Hosp. Assn., Ohio, 1983-84, v.p. planning and mktg. Western Res. Care System, Youngstown, 1984-86; v.p. mktg. Richland Meml. Hosp., Columbia, S.C., 1986—; bd. dirs. Palmetto Sr. Care, Columbia. Mem. Am. Coll. Healthcare Adminstrs., Am. Soc. Hosp. Planning and Mktg., Am. Mgmt. Assn., Carolinas Soc. Hosp. Planning and Mktg., S. C. Hosp. Assn. (planning com.), Greater Columbia C. of C. (prospect identification com. 1978, 88), Soc. Strategic Healthcare Mgmt. of Hosp. Assn. Pa. Episcopalian. Avocations: choral singing, racquetball, woodworking, bicycling. Home: 6720 Sandy Shore Rd Columbia SC 29206 Office: Richland Meml Hosp 5 Richland Med Park Columbia SC 29203

BURKER, HARRY SNYVELY, JR., electrical equipment manufacturing executive; b. June 25, 1928; married;. Student, Fenn Coll. With Cleve. Graphite Bronze Co., 1944-52; with Clevite Corp., 1952-69, Gould, Inc., 1969-83; with Siemens Energy & Automation Inc., Atlanta, 1983—, v.p., gen. mgr. ITE Elec. Products div., 1983-84, sr. v.p., 1984-85, pres., chief exec. officer, 1985—, also bd. dirs. Bd. dirs. Nat. Assn. Elec. Distbrs. Edn. Found. Mem. Nat. Elec. Mfrs. Assn. Home: 41 Vernon Glen Ct Dunwoody GA 30338 Office: Siemens Energy & Automation Inc 223 Perimeter Center Pkwy Atlanta GA 30346

BURKET, RICHARD EDWARD, agriprocessing executive; b. Sandusky, Ohio, Apr. 25, 1928; s. Firm C. and Marie (Bock) B.; m. Carolyn Anne McMillen, Feb. 22, 1951 (div. 1979); children: Leslie, Buffie, Lynn Murphy Burket. B.A., Oberlin Coll., 1950. Tech. sales mgr. Rhoades Equipment Co., Ft. Wayne, Ind., 1954-55; with Chemurgy div. Central Soya Co., Ft. Wayne, Ind., 1955-69; dir. mktg. Chemurgy div. Central Soya Co., Chgo., 1966-69; v.p. protein specialties Archer Daniel Midland Co., Decatur, Ill., 1969-74, v.p., asst. to pres., 1974-80; v.p., asst. to chmn. Archer Daniel Midland Co., Decatur, 1980—; mem. Gov.'s Task Force on Future Rural Agriculture. Bd. dirs. Decatur Area Arts Council, 1972-84; bd. dirs. Macon County United Way, 1974-77, Boys Club, Decatur, 1979-86, Decatur Metro C. of C., 1982-87; mem. Millikin U. Assocs., Macon County Econ. Devel. Found., St. Mary's Hosp. Adv. Bd., Ill. Agriculture Export Adv. Com. Served to 1st lt. U.S. Army, 1974-77. Mem. Inst. Food Technologists, Am. Mgmt. Assn., Soy Protein Council (chmn. 1974-76), Gov.'s Rural Affairs Council, U.S. Sweetener Producers Group, Ill. Agrl. Export Adv. Com., Ill. 4-H Found. Bd. Clubs: Decatur, Decatur Country. Home: Rte 1 PO Box 84A Blue Mound IL 62513 Office: Archer Daniels Midland Co 4666 Faries Pkwy Decatur IL 62525

BURKETT, MARGIE EILENE, corporation executive; b. Somerset, Pa., Oct. 15, 1951; d. Theodore Roosevelt and Arretta Mae (Hetrick) Stoner; m. Harris G. Custer, July 4, 1969 (div. 1977); m. Richard Earl Burkett, Mar. 20, 1982; children: Tracy Sue, Richard Shane. AA, Cambria Rowe Bus. Coll., 1971. Sec. Stoner Enterprises, Inc., Friedens, Pa., 1969-77, computer operator, 1977-82, v.p., 1982—, also bd. dirs. Republican. Home and Office: Stoner Enterprises Inc RR #1 Friedens PA 15541

BURKHARDT, CHARLES HENRY, author, association executive, lecturer, consultant; b. Bklyn., June 17, 1915; s. Adolph Michael and Mildred (Herman) B.; m. Lillian Sanders, Jan. 31, 1942; children: Gregory Charles, Christopher Michael. BS, St. John's U., 1938; postgrad. Pratt Inst., 1947-48. .Service mgr., asst. sales mgr. Concord Oil Corp., N.Y.C., 1939-43; instr. heat engring. Walter Hervey Jr. Coll., N.Y.C., 1947-49; dir. edn. Perfex Corp., Milw., 1949-51; gen. mgr. Paragon Maintenance Co., Mineola, N.Y., 1951-55; mng. dir., sec.-treas. Oil Heat Inst. Am., N.Y.C., 1955-60; v.p. Nat. Oil Fuel Inst., N.Y.C., 1960-62; exec. v.p. New Eng. Fuel Inst. Boston, 1962-81, pres., 1981-86; cons. Standard Oil Co. N.J., 1957-58, Bacharach Instrument Co., 1947, Richfield Mfg. Co., 1948, Arthur D. Little Inc., 1987, Global Petroleum Inc., 1986-87, Centennial and Atlantic Mutual Ins. Cos., 1987—, Scully Signal Co., 1986—, Nutter, McClennan & Fish, Boston, 1987—, Rich, May, Bilodeau & Flaherty, Boston, 1988—, Hinshaw, Culbertson, Moelmann, Hoban & Fuller, Chgo., 1988—, CNA Ins. Co., 1988—, New London (Conn.) Mutual Ins. Co., 1989, Robins Kaplan Miller and Ciresi, Minn., 1989; mem. fuel oil mktg. adv. com. Dept. Energy, 1974-1980, residential conservation task force; del. New Eng. Energy Congress, 1978, White House Conf. on Small Bus.; chmn. fuel oil marketeers' fin. viability task force SBA; mem. Mass. state residential conservation adv. com.; trustee St. Elizabeth's Hosp., Brighton, Mass., 1985—; nat. coordinator 1985 Oil Heat Centennial Celebration. Pres. New Eng. Fuel Inst. Edn. Found., 1983-86, cons. 1987, 88, 89. Served to capt. AUS, 1943-46. Granted Knighthood Equestrian Order of the Holy Sepulchre, Jerusalem, 1986; recipient Disting. Achievement award New Eng. Oil Heat Industry, 1972; certs. of commendation Conn. Petroleum Assn., 1974, 80; Oil Man of New Eng. award Better Home Heat Council N.H., 1975; Certificate of Appreciation, Soc. Mfg. Engrs., 1976; 15th Anniversary commendation New Eng. Fuel Inst., 1977; Man of Yr. award Met. Energy Council, 1984. Mem. Am. Soc. Heating, Refrigeration and Air Conditioning Engrs. (life), Am. Soc. Assn. Execs., Nat. Soc. Bus. Economists, ASTM. Republican. Roman Catholic. Author: Residential and Commercial Air Conditioning, 1959, Baseboard Heating, 1952, Domestic and Commercial Oil Burners, 1969. The Oil Heating Technician, 1957. Home: 770 Boylston St Boston MA 02199

BURKHART, CARL HENRY, engineer; b. Phila., Dec. 28, 1940; s. George Henry and Dorothy (Lessing) B.; m. Barbara Hope Smolen, June 13, 1962; 1 child, Susan Lynn Burkhart Regan. BS in Engring., U.S. Coast Guard Acad., 1962; BS in Civil Engring., U. Ill., 1966; MS in Engring. Mgmt., Northeastern U., 1969. Registered profl. engr., Pa., S.C. Joined USCG, 1958, commd. ensign, 1962, advanced through grades to comdr., 1977; engring. watch officer USCG, Boston, 1962-65, civil engr., 1966-69; civil engr. USCG, Washington, 1979-72, London, 1972-75; chief engring. sect. USCG, Washington, 1975-79, energy mgmt. officer, 1979-82; ret. USCG, 1982; gen. services adminstr. City of Greenville, S.C., 1982-84; project mgr. O'Neal Engring., Inc., Greenville, 1984-86, bus. mgr., 1986—. Author, editor: USCG Tower Manual, 1978. Vol. Am. Cancer Soc., Bowie, Md., Greenville, 1979-84; Sister Cities Internat., Greenville, 1986—; Symphony Guild, 1987—. Mem. Soc. Am. Mil. Engrs., Nat. Soc. Profl. Engrs., Nat. Asbestos Council, Am. Soc. Civil Engrs. Home: 13 Hiawatha Dr Greenville SC 29615 Office: O'Neal Engring Inc 850 S Pleasantburg Dr Greenville SC 29607

BURKITT, BRUCE WARREN, oil company executive; b. Bozeman, Mont., Apr. 11, 1949; s. William Hollis and Anne Arliene (Ronning) B.; m. Cynthia Ann Mossman, June 22, 1974. BS in Bus., Mont. State U., 1972; MBA, Okla. U., 1978. With Conoco Inc., Houston, 1978-85, coordinator gas supply, 1985-86, adminstrv. mgr., 1986-87, dir. mktg., 1987—. Served to capt. U.S. Army, 1972-77. Office: Conoco Inc PO Box 2197 Houston TX 77252

BURLESON, KAREN TRIPP, lawyer; b. Rocky Mount, N.C., Sept. 2, 1955; d. Bryant and Katherine Rebecca (Watkins) Tripp; m. Robert Mark Burleson, June 25, 1977. BA, U. N.C., 1976; JD, U. Ala., 1981. Bar: Tex. 1981, U.S. Dist. Ct. (so. dist.) Tex. 1982, U.S. Ct. Appeals (fed. cir.) 1983. Law clerk Tucker, Gray & Espy, Tuscaloosa, Ala., 1978-81, to presiding justice Ala. Supreme Ct., Montgomery, summer 1980; atty. Exxon Prodn. Research Co., Houston, 1981-86, coordinator tech. transfer, 1986-87; assoc. Arnold, White and Durkee, Attys. at Law, Houston, 1988—. Contbr. articles to profl. jours. Recipient Am. Jurisprudence award U. Ala., 1980, Dean's award, 1981. Mem. Houston Bar Assn. (internat. transfer tech. com. 1983-84), Houston Intellectual Property Lawyers Assn. (outstanding inventor com. 1982-84, chmn. student edn. com. 1986, sec. 1987-88, bd. govs. 1987-88, chmn. awards com. 1988-89), Tex. Bar Assn. (antitrust law com. 1984-85, chmn. Internat. Law com. of Intellectual Property Law Sect. 1987-88), ABA, Am. Intellectual Property Lawyers Assn. , Phi Alpha Delta (clk. 1980). Republican. Methodist. Office: Arnold White & Durkee PO Box 4433 Houston TX 77210

BURLEY, JACK LYNN, food products executive; b. Pitts., Apr. 26, 1942; s. Andrew C. and Lynda B. (Jackson) B.; m. Jo Anne Elaine Cobb, May 29, 1965; children: Diana Lynne, Jack Lynn. BS, Pa. State U., 1965; MBA, U. Pitts., 1974. Acct. Fed. Power Commn., Washington, 1965-68; assoc. mgr. fin. Gen. Foods Corp., White Plains, N.Y., 1968-70; sr. cost analyst Heinz U.S.A. div. H.J. Heinz Co., Pitts., 1970-71, mgr. fin. planning, 1971-74, gen. mgr. fin. planning, 1974-83, controller, 1983-85, v.p. fin., 1985-87, v.p. fin. and adminstrn., 1987—. Bd. dirs. Urban League Pitts., 1986—; bd. dirs. Neighborhood Ctrs. Assn., Pitts., 1985-88, bus. sch. alumni soc. bd. Pa. State U., 1985-88, Cen. Blood Bank, 1988—. Served with U.S. Army, 1966-68. Recipient Black Achievers award Tzik mag., 1980, Black Arts Festival Alumni award Pa. State U., 1984. Mem. NAACP (Pitts. br.), Pa. C. of C. (bd. dirs. 1988—), Omega Psi Phi. Democrat. Presbyterian. Home: 104 Windsor Ct Monroeville PA 15146 Office: H J Heinz USA Div 1062 Progress St Pittsburgh PA 15212

BURLINGAME, JOHN HUNTER, lawyer; b. Milw., Apr. 27, 1933; s. Leroy James and Mary Janet (Burchard) B.; m. Carolyn Elizabeth Beachley, Aug. 27, 1960 (div. Feb. 1981); children: Carolyn, Janet, Amy, Alexander; m. Dorcas Hodges, June 5, 1982. BS, U. Wis., 1960, LLB, 1963. Bar: Ohio 1964. From assoc. to ptnr. Baker & Hostetler, Cleve., 1963—. Lt. USN, 1955-59. Mem. ABA, Cleve. Bar Assn., Pepper Pike Club, Union Club, Metropolitan Club. Republican. Presbyterian. Office: Baker & Hostetler 3200 National City Ctr Cleveland OH 44114

BURM, FORREST HENRY, transportation executive; b. Chgo., Mar. 14, 1930; s. Joseph F. and Helen (Kobler) B.; m. Darlene Benson, Mar. 12, 1949; children: Daniel, Diane. Student, U. Ill., Chgo., 1947-49. Supr. first line Watson Bros. Transp., Chgo., 1948-52; with Yellow Freight System, Inc., Overland Park, Kans., 1952—; sr. v.p. Yellow Freight System, Inc., Overland Park, 1981—. Office: Yellow Freight System 10990 Roe Ave Overland Park KS 66211

BURMAN, MARSHA LINKWALD, lighting manufacturing executive, marketing professional; b. Balt., Jan. 9, 1949; d. William and Lena (Ronin) Linkwald; m. Robert Schlosser, July 2, 1972 (div. 1980); m. John R. Burman, June, 1986; children—Melanie, David, Heather, Richard. B.S. cum laude in Edn., Kent State U., 1970, M.A. summa cum laude in Sociology, 1971. Cert. secondary edn., Ohio. Spl. project dir. Tng. and Research Ctr., Planned Parenthood, Chgo., 1978; with mgmt. edn. ctr. Gould, Inc., Chgo., 1979, program adminstr., 1979-80; systems trainer Lithonia Lighting, 1981, mgr. tng. and edn., 1981-86, dir. mktg., tng. and devel., 1986—. Author: (booklet) Putting Your Best Foot Forward (award Am Soc. Tng. and Devel.), 1982; author, editor Dictionary of Lighting Industry Terminology, 1988 . Facilitator single parenting interaction group, Atlanta, 1984-85. U.S. Office Edn. grantee, 1971. Mem. Lithonia Lighting Mgmt. Club (v.p. 1982-83), Am. Soc. of Tng. and Devel. (bd. dirs. 1982, spl. projects. dir. Atlanta chpt. 1982, Vol. of Yr., Community Leader Am. 1987, 89), Toastmasters. Avocation: reading. Office: Lithonia Lighting Div Nat Svc Industries 1400 Lester Rd Conyers GA 30207

BURNES, RICHARD MELLIER, JR., venture capitalist; b. Boston, Mar. 13, 1941; s. Richard Mellier and Ruth (Carney) B.; m. Nonnie Steer, June 22, 1963; children: Gordon M., Sarah S., Ethan M. BA, Harvard U., 1963; MBA, Boston U., 1970. Credit analyst Nat. Shawmut Bank, Boston, 1963-65; analyst Fed. St. Capital Corp., Boston, 1965-68, v.p., 1968-70; gen. ptnr. Charles River Ventures, Boston, 1970—; dir. Bytex Corp., Southborough, Mass., ChipCom Corp., Waltham, Mass., Epoch Systems, Inc., Marlborough, Mass., Seragen, Inc., Hopkinton, Mass., Summa Four, Inc., Manchester, N.H. Pres. Middlesex Sch. Bd. Trustees, Concord, Mass., 1985—; bd. dirs. Boston Ctr. Adult Edn., 1972-77; trustee Cantata Singers, Boston, 1970—, treas., 1977-81. Mem. Nat. Venture Capital Assn. (bd. dirs. 1985—). Office: Charles River Ventures 67 Batterymarch St Boston MA 02110

BURNET, THORNTON WEST, marketing executive; b. Cin., Aug. 27, 1917; s. David and Agnes McClung (West) B.; B.S. in Commerce, U. Va., 1940; m. Mary Elizabeth Charlton, Aug. 14, 1948; 1 son, Thornton West. Asst. treas. Lincoln Service Corp., Washington, 1941-50, v.p., sec., 1950-59; v.p. mktg. Am. Fin. Mgmt. Corp., Silver Spring, Md., 1959-76; v.p., treas., dir. Monet Constrn. Co., Fairfax, Va., 1962-84; v.p. mktg. Am. Directory Service Agy., Silver Spring, 1976-83; sec., treas., dir. Worldwide Yellow Pages, 1979-87. Committeeman, Boy Scouts Am., 1945—; trustee W. C. Westlake Found., 1960—, Children's Mission, Pitts., 1980-83; pres. bd. trustees Fletcher Meml. Library, 1962-86. Served with U.S. Army, 1940-43. Mem. Alpha Kappa Psi. Republican. Episcopalian (vestryman, past sr. warden). Home: 10800 Hunters Valley Rd Vienna VA 22180 Office: 1398 Lamberton Dr Silver Spring MD 20902

BURNETT, JAMES ROBERT, aerospace company executive; b. Eldorado, Ill., Nov. 27, 1925; s. James Lawrence and Edith Lillian (Bramlett) B.; m. Betty Anne Knox, Aug. 18, 1949; children—James William, Karen Jean, Susan Anne, Janice Leigh. B.S. in Elec. Engring., Purdue U., 1946, M.S. in Elec. Engring., 1947, Ph.D., 1949, D.Engring. (hon.), 1969. Assoc. prof. elec. engring. Purdue U., Lafayette, Ind., 1946-56; dir. electromech. lab. TRW Systems Group, Redondo Beach, Calif., 1956-61; minuteman program mgr. TRW Systems Group, San Bernardino, Calif., 1961-66, mgr. ops., 1966-69; v.p., asst. gen. mgr. TRW Systems Group, Redondo Beach, 1969-70, v.p., gen. mgr. systems engring. and integration div., 1970-74, sr. v.p., 1974-77, asst. gen. mgr., 1977-82, v.p., gen. mgr. Def. Systems group, 1982-86; ex-ec.v.p., dep. gen. mgr. S&D sector TRW Inc. Group, 1986—; dir. OEA, Inc., Denver. Served to 1st lt. USMC, 1943-50. Recipient Air Force Systems Command award; Charles A. Coffin fellow. Fellow AIAA; mem. IEEE, Nat. Acad. Engring. Republican. Office: TRW S&D Sector 1 Space Park Redondo Beach CA 92078

BURNETT, ROBERT A., publisher; b. Joplin, Mo., June 4, 1927; s. Lee Worth and Gladys (Plummer) B.; m. Gloria M. Cowden, Dec. 25, 1948; children: Robert A., Stephen, Gregory, Douglas, David, Penelope. AB, U. Mo., 1948. Salesman Cowden Motor Co., Guthrie Center, Iowa; then Equitable Life Assurance Soc., Joplin, Mo.; now chmn., chief exec. officer Meredith Corp.; bd. dirs. Whirlpool Corp., Norwest Bank Des Moines, ITT, Iowa Resources, Dayton Hudson Corp. Past chmn. Travel Industry of Am.; bd. dirs. Grinnell Coll. Served with AUS, 1945-46. Mem. NAM (bd. dirs.), Phi Delta Theta. Congregationalist. Home: 2942 Sioux Ct Des Moines IA 50321 Office: Meredith Corp 1716 Locust St Des Moines IA 50336

BURNHAM, J. V., sales executive; b. Pascagoula, Miss., May 23, 1923; s. George Luther and Eli Vashti (Hough) B.; m. Patti Lauri Latham, May 18, 1946; children: James Steven, Jon Douglas, Richard Scott, Bruce Edward, Vernon Alan. AA, Jones County (Miss.) Jr. Coll., 1946; AS, Rochester Inst. Tech., 1948; BS, U. Houston, 1951, MEd, 1953. Mgr. The Progress-Item, Ellisville, Miss., 1948-51; asst. prof., asst. mgr. U. Houston Journalism and Printing Plant, 1950-57; estimator, product supt. purchasing Chas. P. Young Co., 1965-67, asst. sec.-treas., 1967-69, v.p. sales, 1969—. Assoc. editor Am. Oceanography, 1968-71; southwest corr. Inland Printer and Nat. Lithographer, 1952-60. Pres. Printing Industries of Gulf Coast, Houston, 1971-73; chmn., bd. dirs. Tex. Printing Edn. Found., Houston; bd. dirs. Mus. of Printing History, Houston. Served to lt. (j.g.) USNR, 1943-46. Recipient Scouters award Boy Scouts Am., 1960, Scouters Key award Boy Scouts Am., 1965, Wood Badge award Boy Scouts Am., 1964; named Man of Yr., Houston Graphics Soc., 1968, Printing Industry of Gulf Coast, 1970. Mem. Houston Advt. Club, Bus. and Profl. Advt. Assn., Pres's. Club of Charles P. Young Co. (charter, Outstanding Sales Achievement award), Houston Lithographic Club, U.S. Hist. Soc., Nat. Eagle Scout Assn., Nat. Rifle Assn., Houston Craftsmens Club (hon. life., past pres., Ben Franklin award 1971). Republican. Methodist. Clubs: Braeburn Country, Newport Country, Goebel Collectors (Houston); The Landing at Seven Coves (Conroe, Tex.); Westwood Country (Trinity, Tex.).

BURNHAM, SHEILA KAY, accountant; b. Alliance, Ohio, May 7, 1955; d. Donald Everald and Marilyn Arlene (Datz) B. AS, Cen. Ohio Tech. Coll., 1977. CPA, Ohio. Staff acct. E.A. Guelde & Assocs., Newark, Ohio, 1973; staff acct., sr. acct. Wells & Snyder, Newark, 1973-78; mgr. Wells, Snyder, Digman & Co., Newark, 1978-83; acctg. instr. Cen. Ohio Tech. Coll., Newark, 1982-83; prin. Digman, Burnham & Co., Newark, 1983-84, Sheila K. Burnham, CPA, Newark, 1984—; panelist Tax Facts Radio and TV program, Columbus, Ohio, 1983—. Bd. dirs., treas. The Easter Seal Soc. of Licking County, Newark, 1983—, pres. 1987—; treas. Ohio Easter Seal Soc. 1988—; pres. The Ctr. for Alternative Resources, Newark, 1987—; bd. dirs. YWCA, 1988—, treas., 1988—; Big Sister, Newark, 1984—; mem. adv. com. for acctg. tech. Cen. Ohio Tech. Coll., Newark, 1984—; instr. Vol. Income Tax Assistance Program, Newark, 1985—; trustee, mem. adminstrv. bd., chairperson fin., choir mem., Sunday Sch. tchr. Christ United Meth. Ch., Newark, 1969—; mem. Leadership Tomorrow, 1988-89. Recipient Outstanding Alumni award Cen. Ohio Tech. Coll., 1983. Mem. Ohio Soc. CPA's, Am. Womens Soc. CPA's, Am. Soc. Women Accts., Newark Area C. of C., Mental Health Assn., Leadership Tomorrow, Zonta Internat. Republican. Methodist. Home: 345 Central Ave Newark OH 43055 Office: 85 N Third St Newark OH 43055

BURNISON, BOYD EDWARD, lawyer; b. Arnolds Park, Iowa, Dec. 12, 1934; s. Boyd William and Lucile (Harnden) B.; m. Mari Amaral; children: Erica Lafore, Alison Katherine. BS, Iowa State U., 1957; JD, U. Calif., Berkeley, 1961. Bar: Calif. 1962, U.S. Supreme Ct. 1971, U.S. Dist. Ct. (no. dist.) Calif. 1962, U.S. Ct. Appeals (9th cir.) 1962, U.S. Dist. Ct. (ea. dist.) Calif. 1970. Dep. counsel Yolo County, Calif., 1962-65; of counsel Davis and Woodland (Calif.) Unified Sch. Dists., 1962-65; assoc. Steel & Arostegui, Marysville, Calif., 1965-66, St. Sure, Moore & Hoyt, Oakland, 1966-70; ptnr. St. Sure, Moore, Hoyt & Sizoo, Oakland and San Francisco, 1970-75; v.p. Crosby, Heafey, Roach & May, P.C., Oakland, 1975—, also bd. dirs. Adviser Berkeley YMCA, 1971—; adviser Yolo County YMCA, 1962-65, bd. dirs. 1965; bd. dirs. Easter Seal Soc. Crippled Children and Adults of Alameda County, Calif., 1972-75, Moot Ct. Bd., U. Calif., 1960-61; trustee, sec., legal counsel Easter Seal Found., Alameda County, 1974-79, hon. trustee, 1979—. Paul Harris fellow. Fellow ABA Found.; mem. ABA (labor rels. and employment law sect., equal employment law com. 1972—), Nat. Conf. Bar Pres.'s, State Bar Calif. (spl. labor counsel 1981-84, labor and employment law sect. 1982—), Alameda County Bar Assn. (chmn. memberships and directory com. 1973-74, 80, chmn. law office econs. com. 1975-77, assn. dir. 1981-85, pres., 1984, vice chmn. bench bar liaison com. 1983, chmn. 1984, Disting. Svc. award 1987), Yolo County Bar Assn. (sec. 1965), Yuba Sutter Bar Assn., Bar Assn. San Francisco (labor law sect.), Indsl. Rels. Rsch. Assn., Sproul Assoc. Boalt Hall Law Sch. U. Calif. Berkeley, Iowa State Alumni Assn., Order Knoll, Round Hill Country Club, Rotary, Pi Kappa Alpha, Phi Delta Phi. Democrat. Home: 2500 Caballo Ranchero Dr PO Box 743 Diablo CA 94528 Office: Crosby Heafey Roach & May 2300 Lake Merritt Pla Bldg 1999 Harrison St Oakland CA 94612

BURNLEY, JAMES H., IV, lawyer; b. High Point, N.C., July 30, 1948; s. James Horace and Dorothy Mary (Rockwell) B.; m. Jane Nady. B.A. magna cum laude, Yale U., 1970; J.D., Harvard U., 1973. Assoc. Brooks, Pierce, McLendon, Humphrey & Leonard, 1973-75; ptnr. Turner, Enochs, Foster, Sparrow & Burnley, P.A., 1975-81; dir. VISTA, 1981-82; assoc. dep. atty. gen. Dept. Justice, Washington, 1982-83; gen. counsel Dept. Transp., Washington, 1983, dep. sec., 1983-87, sec., 1987-89; assoc. Shaw, Pittman, Potts & Trowbridge, Washington, 1989—. Office: Shaw Pittman Potts & Trowbridge 2300 N St NW Washington DC 20037

BURNS, DAN W., manufacturing company executive; b. Auburn, Calif., Sept. 10, 1925; s. William and Edith Lynn (Johnston) B.; 1 child, Dan Jr. Dir. materials Menasco Mfg. Co., 1951-56; v.p., gen. mgr. Hufford Corp., 1956-58; pres. Hufford div. Siegler Corp., 1958-61; v.p. Siegler Corp., 1961-62, Lear Siegler, Inc., 1962-64; pres., dir. Electrada Corp., Culver City, Calif., 1964-85; chief exec. officer Sargent Industries, Inc., L.A., 1985-88, now chmn. bd. dirs.; chmn. bd. dirs., chief exec. officer Arlington Industries, Inc.; dir. Gen. Automotive Corp., Dover Tech. Internat., Inc. Bd. dirs. San Diego Aerospace Mus., Smithsonian Inst. Served to capt. U.S. Army, 1941-47; prisoner of war Japan; asst. mil. attache 1946, China; a.d.c. to Gen. George C. Marshall 1946-47. Mem. Orgn. Am. States Sports Com. (dir.). Clubs: Los Angeles Country, St. Francis Yacht, Calif., Conquistadores del Cielo, Garden of the Gods. Home: 10851 Chalon Rd Bel Air Los Angeles CA 90077 Office: 833 Moraga Dr Ste 4 Bel Air Los Angeles CA 90049

BURNS, DANIEL HOBART, management consultant; b. Atlanta, Jan. 26, 1928; s. Hobart H. and Florence (Kuhn) B.; B.A., U. Ala., 1949; grad. Armed Forces Staff Coll., 1966, Air Command and Staff Coll., 1969, Air War Coll., 1972; postgrad. U. S.C., 1975, Regent Coll., U. B.C., 1978-79, Trinity Episcopal Sch. for Ministry, 1979-80; m. Barbara Ann Grimsley, Jan. 15, 1949 (div. July 1974); children—Eric Grimsley, Daniel Hobart, Barbara Bennett, Arlene Chester; m. 2d, Ann Lyn Horrell, Sept. 28, 1979; children: Jessica Florence, Stephen John. Account exec. Sta. WCOS, Columbia, S.C., 1949-51; sales mgr. sta. WIS, Columbia, 1951-57; ins. agt. Aetna Life Ins. Co., Columbia, 1957-60; propr. Daniel H. Burns Co., mgmt. cons., broker, Columbia, 1960—; pres., dir. Nat. Search, Inc., 1966—, Indsl. Surveys, Inc., 1968—; Alliance Bldg. Industries, 1971-84; cons., Ednl. TV Network, govts. of Israel, Greece, W. Ger., Fed. Grants Projects, S.C. Ednl. TV Network; guest lectr. U. S.C.; cons. sales mgmt. and market analysis, analytical and conceptual problem solving; owner Western Rare Books-Fine Art Assocs., 1983—. Pres., Schneider Sch. PTA, 1963-66; supr. registration City of Columbia, 1962-69; asst. project dir., statewide law enforcement edn. through TV, 1966-69; cons. Pitts. Leadership Found., 1980-81; dist. commr. Boy Scouts Am.; pres., chmn. ward 15 Republican Party; pres., bd. dirs. Internat. Communications Resources Found.; bd. dirs. Travelers Aid Assn. Am., Nat. Council USO; Columbia Sch. Theology for Laity; bd. dirs., exec. com. Consol. Agys. of United Funds; Richland County chpt. Nat. Found. Served with USAAF, 1943-46; lt. col. USAF Res. ret. Mem. S.C. Football Ofcls. Assn., Columbia Real Estate Bd., Air Force Assn., Am. Y-Flyer Yacht Racing Assn., AAUP, Am. Mgmt. Assn., Nat. Assn. Ednl. Broadcasters, Soc. for Advancement Mgmt., Am. Soc. Real Estate Appraisers, Interprofl. Cons. Council, Nat. Assn. Security Dealers, Soc. Am. Archivists, Nat. Hist. Soc., Internat. Platform Assn., Hist. Columbia Found., S.C. Press Assn., Columbia C. of C., Am. Soc. Personal Adminstrn., Sierra Club, Columbia Lyric Opera, Internat. Christian Leaders, Fellowship Christian Athletes, English Speaking Union, N. Am. Yacht Racing Union, Sigma Phi Epsilon. Episcopalian/Anglican. Clubs: Charleston (S.C.) Yacht; Yachting of Am., Workshop Theatre, First Nighters, Columbia Squash Racquets, Town Theatre, Masons (Shriner), Lions. Author publs. in field. Home: 2130 11th St Boulder CO 80302 Office: PO Box 1725 Boulder CO 80306 Other: 46 Punga Grove, Whangarei New Zealand

BURNS, DAVID CRAIG, lawyer; b. Waterloo, Iowa, Apr. 19, 1949; s. Cecil Joseph and Eileen Elizabeth (Schuster) B.; m. Sarah Ann Sizemore, June 1, 1974 (div. 1978); m. Barbara Lynn Stauth, Mar. 8, 1980; children: Justin, David. BA in Polit. Sci., U. Iowa, 1971; JD, U. Kans., 1974. Bar: Kans. 1974, U.S. Dist. Ct. Kans. 1974. Assoc., then ptnr. Speir, Stroberg, Sizemore, Burns and Gillmore, P.A. (formerly called Speir, Stroberg & Sizemore), Newton, Kans., 1974—; bd. dirs. Midland Nat. Bank, Newton, Walton (Kans.) State Bank, Hertzler Rsch. Found., Halstead, Kans. Served to 1st lt. USAR, 1974-75. Mem. ABA, Kans. Bar Assn., Am. Sch. Attys. Assn., Am. Hosp. Attys. Assn., Newton Country Club (bd. dirs. 1979-83). Republican. Roman Catholic. Home: Rt 1 Box 197AA Moorlands West Newton KS 67114 Office: Speir Stroberg Sizemore Burns and Gillmore PA 809 Main St Box 546 Newton KS 67114

BURNS, DEBORAH DENISE, financial planner, broker; b. Houston, Mar. 15, 1953; d. Allie (Burns) Sneed; divorced; 1 child, James E. Beard. BS in Psychology, U. Houston, 1983. Collection clk. Foley's Dept. Store, Houston, 1973-76; clk. U.S. P.O., Houston, 1976-81; office mgr. LFA, Inc., Houston, 1981-83; ind. sales agt. First Continental Ins. Co., Houston, 1983-86; unit mgr. Summit Mktg. Group, Houston, 1985—, broker, 1985—. counselor Julia C. Hester House United Way Agy., Houston, 1984. Roman Catholic. Office: First Continental Ins Co 2303 Smith Houston TX 77006

BURNS, EDWARD EARL, JR., controller, accountant. s. Edward Earl Sr. and Leona Eugene (Andrews) B.; m. Ann Michele Lawson, Dec. 25, 1976; children: Edward E. III, Jonathan, Marie. BBA, Ga. State U., 1975. CPA, Ga. Auditor State of Ga., Atlanta, 1975-76; sr. staff acct. Harris, Kerr, Forster, CPAs, 1976-80; internal auditor Cox Enterprises, Inc., 1980-83; asst. contr. Cox Ariz. Publ., Inc., Mesa, 1983-88, contr., 1988—. Asst. scoutmaster Boy Scouts Am., Mesa, 1987-88; cons. Jr. Achievement, Mesa and Phoenix, 1986-87; bd. dirs., treas., coach Little League Baseball, Mesa, 1987-88. Mem. Am. Inst. CPAs, Ga. Soc. CPAs, Ariz. Soc. CPAs. Republican. Luthern. Home: 1527 E McClellan Mesa AZ 85203 Office: Cox Ariz Publ Inc 120 W First Ave Mesa AZ 85210

BURNS, ELIZABETH MURPHY, media executive; b. Superior, Wis., Dec. 4, 1945; d. Morgan and Elizabeth (Beck) Murphy; m. Richard Ramsey Burns, June 24, 1984. Student U. Ariz., 1963-67. Promotion and programming sec. Sta. KGUN-TV, Tucson, 1967-68; programming and traffic sec. Sta. KFMB-TV, San Diego, 1968-69; owner, operator Sta. KKAR, Pomona, Calif., 1970-73; co-owner Evening Telegram Co. (parent co. Murphy Stas.); pres. Morgan Murphy Stas., Madison, Wis., 1976—; dir. Nat. Guardian Life Ins. Co., various media stas. and corps. Mem. adv. bd. Wis. Chamber Orch., Madison, 1983—; bd. dirs. Duluth/Superior Symphony, Minn., 1985, TV Bur. of Advt.; bd. dirs. N.E. Midwest Inst., 1984—, now chmn. bd. dirs. Mem. Nat. Assn. Broadcasters, Wis. Broadcasters Assn. Republican. Roman Catholic. Clubs: Madison, Nakoma Country; Northland Country (Duluth), Boulders Country (Carefree, Ariz.). Avocations: golf, tennis, travel. Home: 180 Paine Farm Rd Duluth MN 55804 Office: Sta WISC-TV 7025 Raymond Rd Madison WI 53711

BURNS, GROVER PRESTON, retired physicist; b. nr. Hurricane, W.Va., Apr. 25, 1918; s. Joshua Alexander and Virgie (Meadows) B.; m. Julia Belle Foster, Nov. 4, 1941; children: Julia Corinne Burns Jefferson, Grover Preston. AB, Marshall U., 1937; postgrad., Duke U., 1939-40; MS, W.Va. U., 1941; postgrad., U. Md., 1946; DSc (hon.), Colo. State Christian Coll., 1973. Tchr. high sch., W.Va., 1937-40; fellow W.Va. U., 1940-41; instr. physics U. Conn., 1941-42; asst. prof. Miss. State Coll., 1942-44, acting head physics dept., 1944-45; asst. prof. physics Tex. Tech. Coll., 1946; assoc. prof. math. Marshall U., 1946-47; research physicist Naval Research Lab., Washington, 1947-48; asst. prof., chmn. physics dept. Mary Washington Coll., 1948-68; assoc. prof., chmn., 1968-69; supr. statis. analysis sect. Am. Viscose div. FMC Corp., 1950-67; pres. Burns Enterprises Inc., Fredericksburg, Va., 1958—; mathematician Naval Surface Weapons Ctr., 1967-81; staff mathematician Unisys Corp., 1982-87; cons. FMC Corp., 1984-86. Author: A Story of My Life, 1988reviewer Am. Jour. Pysics; contbr. articles to profl. jours.; patentee in thermometers, conductivity testers and star finders. Served with AUS, 1945-46. Mem. Phys. Soc., AAUP, Am. Assn. Physics Tchrs. Home: 600 Virginia Ave Fredericksburg VA 22401

BURNS, HENRY KNOX, III, corporate executive; b. Macon, Ga., Apr. 2, 1941; s. Henry Knox Jr. and Anne (Holmes) B.; m. Katharine Stark Miller, Aug. 24, 1962; children: Henry IV, Stuart, Hubert. Student, Ga. Tech. Inst., 1959-64. Plant mgr. Burns Brick Co., Macon, 1964-75, sec., treas., 1972-75; prin. Burns Automation, Macon, 1973-75, Newton, Ala., 1975-80; prin. Burns Clay Products, Newton, Ala., 1975-80; plant mgr. Elgin (Tex.) Butler Brick, 1981-83; prin. Burns Machinery, Inc., Dothan, Ala., 1983—. Patentee in field. Mem. Am. Ceramic Soc., Dothan Houston County C. of C. Presbyterian. Home: 400 S Park Dothan AL 36301 Office: Rt 1 Box 69-C Dothan AL 36301

BURNS, IVAN ALFRED, grocery products and industrial company executive; b. Leamington Spa, England, Jan. 18, 1935; s. Cecil Ivan and Dorothy Constance (Mote) B.; m. Angela Loeffel, May 16, 1959; children: Pauline Cecile, Charla Cheyney, Claudine. BS, Coventry Coll., 1958. Various positions Deere & Co., Moline, Ill., 1960-64; dir. internat. ACF Industries Inc., N.Y.C., 1972-75, v.p., 1975-81, pres., chief operating officer, 1981-83, chmn., chief exec. officer, 1983-84; pres. corn refining div. CPC Internat. Inc., Englewood Cliffs, N.J., 1985-87, exec. v.p. adminstrn., 1987—, also bd. dirs.; bd. dirs. Continental Corp., N.Y.C. Patentee valve, 1980. Bd. dirs. United Way, New York, 1984-85; mem. bus. adv. bd. Northwestern U., 1983—. Mem. Conf. Bd. Republican. Mem. Ch. of England. Clubs: Sky, Pres.'s, Econ. (N.Y.C.). Home: Deer Park Rd New Canaan CT 06840 Office: CPC Internat Inc International Pla Englewood Cliffs NJ 07632

BURNS, JAMES FRANCIS, JR., bank executive; b. N.Y.C., July 9, 1937; s. James Francis and Sarah (Mulligan) B.; children: Kimberly, Karen, Karla. B.B.A., Loyola U., Los Angeles, 1959. Audit mgr. Arthur Andersen & Co., Los Angeles, 1959-66; controller St. Joseph Hosp., Burbank, Calif., 1966-68; with First Interstate Bank, Los Angeles, 1970-82, v.p., chief fin. officer, 1972-75, sr. v.p., chief fin. officer, 1975-78, exec. v.p., chief fin. officer, 1978-82; exec. v.p. fin. First Interstate Bancorp, Los Angeles, 1982—; mem. bus. adv. coun. Loyola U., L.A., 1981—. Mem. Am. Inst. CPAs. Republican. Roman Catholic. Office: 1st Interstate Bancorp 707 Wilshire Blvd Los Angeles CA 90017

BURNS, JOHN DUDLEY, chemical company executive; b. Houston, May 18, 1933; s. John Heard Burns and Annie (Lee) Peeples B.; m. Margaret Alice Garrett, May 19, 1962; children—John Arthur, Dan Garrett, Kevin Norman, William Dudley. B.A. in Chem. Engring., Rice U., 1955, B.S. in Chem. Engring., 1956; grad. Program for Mgmt. Devel., Harvard U., 1973. Asst. gen. mgr. Conoco Chems. div., Saddle Brook, N.J., 1973-75; v.p. comml. Conoco Chems. div., Houston, 1975-78; v.p., gen. mgr. ops. Conoco Chems. div., 1978-79, sr. v.p., 1979-80; exec. v.p. chems. Conoco, Inc., 1980-84; pres., chief exec. officer Vista Chem. Co., 1984—, also chmn. Mem. adv. coun. Zool. Soc. Houston, 1983—, Rice U. Fund Coun. Mem. Soap and Detergent Assn. (dir.), Soc. Chem. Industry. Clubs: River Oaks, Westlake (bd. govs. 1982—). Home: 10 Stillforest Houston TX 77024 Office: Vista Chem Co 15990 N Barkers Landing Rd Houston TX 77079

BURNS, JOHN JOSEPH, JR., business executive; b. Cambridge, Mass., June 27, 1931; s. John Joseph and Alice (Blake) B.; m. Barbara Ann Miller, Oct. 18, 1958; children: John J. III, Christine, Gregory, Timothy, Jennifer. B.S. in Fin, Boston Coll., 1953; M.B.A., Harvard U., 1955. Asso. buying dept. and arbitrage dept. Goldman Sachs & Co., N.Y.C., 1957-63; assoc. N.Y. Securities, N.Y.C., 1963-67, gen. ptnr., 1968; v.p. fin., dir. Alleghany Corp., N.Y.C., 1968-77, pres., dir., 1977—, mem. exec. com., 1977—; bd. dirs. Chgo. Title & Trust Co.; bd. dirs. Shelby (Ohio) Ins. Co., Cyclops Industries Inc., Pitts. Served with USN, 1955-57. Roman Catholic. Club: Oyster Harbors. Office: Alleghany Corp 55 E 52d St New York NY 10055

BURNS, KENNETH JONES, JR., lawyer, natural resources company executive; b. Cleve., Oct. 3, 1926; s. Kenneth Jones and Isabel (Nanson) B.; m. Edith Louise Mitten, June 23, 1949; children: Deborah, Kenneth Jones III, Sarah, Elizabeth, Nancy, Andrew. B.S., Northwestern U., 1948, J.D., 1951. Bar: Ill. 1951, Ohio 1972. Asso. Jenner & Block, Chgo., 1951-60; partner Jenner & Block, 1961-72; sr. v.p., gen. counsel, sec. Anchor Hocking Corp., Lancaster, Ohio, 1972-79; v.p., gen. counsel Internat. Minerals & Chem. Corp., Northbrook, Ill., 1979—; legal counsel Chgo. Jr. Assn. Commerce and Industry, 1955-58; lectr. Northwestern U. Sch. Law, 1955. Pres. Wilmette Civic Improvement Assn., 1958-62; v.p., dir. Citizens of Greater Chgo., 1961-64; mem. Chgo. Crime Comm.; bd. dirs. Am. Bar Endowment, 1975—, v.p., 1981-83, pres., 1983-85. Served with USNR, 1945-46, 51-52. Recipient Key award Chgo. Jr. Assn. Commerce, 1956. Fellow Am. Bar Found. (dir. 1983-85); mem. ABA (chmn. jr. bar conf. 1961-62, ho. of dels. 1962-64, 71—, asst. sec. 1967-71, sec., gov. 1971-75), Ill. Bar Assn., Chgo. Bar Assn. (bd. mgrs. 1961-63), Am. Bar Retirement Assn. (bd. dirs. 1982-86), Assn. Gen. Counsel, Chgo. Barrister Inn (pres. 1966-67), Legal Club Chgo. (exec. com. 1981-82), Law Club Chgo., Order of Coif, Sigma Chi, Phi Delta Phi. Club: Skokie (Ill.) Country. Home: 15 Warrington Dr Lake Bluff IL 60044 Office: Internat Minerals & Chem Corp 2315 Sanders Rd Northbrook IL 60062

BURNS, LAWRENCE ALOYSIUS, JR., data processing executive, accountant; b. Cin., Aug. 5, 1949; s. Lawrence Aloysius and Marjorie Mary (Wiegele) Burns; m. Peggy Louise Watkins , June 16, 1979; 1 child, Eric; stepchildren: Amy Steers, Mikal Steers. BS, U. Cin., 1971, M in Bus., 1977, postgrad., 1978-79. Staff acct. Arthur Andersen & Co., Cin., 1979-81; programmer, analyst Applied Solutions, Inc., Cin., 1981-84, dir. of proprietary software, 1984—; vis. lectr. U. Cin., 1978-79; ind. tax cons., Cin., 1977—. Asst. coach Coll. Hill Knothole, Cin., 1980-84; mem. Cin. Updowntowners, 1977-79. Served with U.S. Army, 1971-73. Mem. Am. Inst. CPA's, Mensa, Phi Beta Kappa, Beta Gamma Sigma. Roman Catholic. Home: 6661 Plantation Way Cincinnati OH 45224 Office: Applied Solutions Inc 1228 Walnut St Ste 5210 Cincinnati OH 45215

BURNS, LEO RICHARD, financial planner; b. Quincy, Mass., Sept. 30, 1939; s. Leo Henry and Mary Elizabeth (Conroy) B.; m. Arlene Frances Goodrow, Sept. 2, 1961 (div. Feb. 1969); children: Leo R., Maureen Ann, Kim Darlene; m. Rosemary Frances Ciccarelli, Aug. 23, 1969; children: Patrick Michael, Eric Christopher. Cert. fin. planner. Gold team fin. planner IDS Fin. Services, Fitchburg, Mass., 1975—; owner, clk. Leominster (Mass.) Automotive Warehouse, Inc., A-1 Auto Parts, Inc., Leominster; owner, treas. Med. Access Interant., Inc., Fitchburg, Mass.; cons. various orgns., Mass., 1975—; lectr. Northeastern U., Boston, 1987—. Co-author: The Experts Guide to Managing and Marketing a Successful Financial Planning Practice, 1988. Pres. North Cen. Alcoholism Commn., Leominster, 1984-89. With USN, 1958-62. Mem. Internat. Assn. Fin. Planning (bd. dirs. Boston 1987-88), Inst. Cert. Fin. Planners (treas. Boston 1986—), Rotary (pres. 1985-86). Republican. Roman Catholic. Office: IDS Fin Svcs Inc 348 Lunenburg St Fitchburg MA 01420

BURNS, MICHAEL EDWIN, accountant; b. Chgo., Aug. 15, 1963; s. Edwin F. and Jean H. B. BS in Acctg. with honors, U. Ill., Champaign, 1985. CPA, Ill. Acct. Arthur Andersen & Co., Chgo., 1985—. Mem. Am. Inst. CPA's, CPA Soc., U. Ill. Alumni Assn. (life). Office: Arthur Andersen & Co 33 W Monroe St Chicago IL 60603

BURNS, MICHAEL JOSEPH, manufacturing executive; b. Passaic, N.J., Feb. 18, 1943; s. Michael Joseph and Ellen Kathryn (Warman) B.; m. Emma Anne, Dec. 19, 1964; children: Michael, Jeffrey, Tricia, Stephen. B.A. in English, William Paterson Coll., Wayne, N.J., 1964; J.D., Seton Hall U., Newark, 1975. Bar: N.J. 1975. Purchasing analyst Am. Brands Co., 1972-75; div. purchasing mgr. Dutch Boy Paints, NL Industries, 1975-76; v.p. purchasing Dutch Boy, Inc., 1977-78; pres., gen. mgr. Dutch Boy, Inc. (Dutch Boy coatings div.), 1978-80; pres., chief exec. officer Kroehler Mfg. Co., Naperville, Ill., 1980-83; pres., chief operating officer Rymer Co., Rolling Meadows, Ill., 1983-88; pres. Emerald Group, Lake Forest, Ill., 1988—. Served to capt. USMCR, 1964-67, Vietnam. N.J. State scholar; recipient Disting. Alumni award Wm. Paterson Coll. Mem. ABA, Am. Arbitration Assn. Presbyterian. Office: 113 Surrey Ln Lake Forest IL 60045

BURNS, MITCHEL ANTHONY, transportation services company executive; b. Las Vegas, Nev., Nov. 1, 1942; s. Mitchel and Zella (Pulsipher) B.; m. Joyce Jordan, Nov. 14, 1962; children: Jill, Mike, Shauna. BS in Bus. Mgmt, Brigham Young U., 1964; MBA in Fin., U. Calif., Berkeley, 1965; postgrad., Fla. Internat. U., 1989. With Mobil Oil Corp., N.Y.C., 1965-74, controller, 1970-72, cost-of-living coordinator, 1973, fin. analysis mgr., 1973-74; with Ryder System, Inc., Miami, Fla., 1974—, exec. v.p., chief fin. officer, 1978-79, pres., chief ops. officer, 1979-83, pres., chief exec. officer, 1983-85, chmn., pres., chief exec. officer, 1985—, also bd. dirs.; exec. v.p., chief fin. officer, pres. Ryder Truck Rental, Inc., 1980-81; bd. dirs. J.C. Penney Co., Inc., Pfizer, Inc., S.E. Banking Corp., S.E. Bank, N.A.; trustee U. Miami, 1984—; mem. nat. adv. coun. sch. mgmt. Brigham Young U., 1981—. Mem. bd. visitors Grad. Sch. Bus. Administrn. U. N.C., Chapel Hill, 1988—; bd. dirs., trustee United Way Dade County, Fla.,1981—, chmn. Dade County Campaign, 1988. Named Marketer of Yr. Acad. Mktg. Sci., 1983, Americanism award Anti-Defamation League, 1984, Bus. Leader of Yr. The Miami News, 1985, Ricks Coll. Bus. Leader of the Century, 1989, Fin. World Chief Exec. Officer of Yr. in Transp.: Freight & Leasing, 1984, 85, 87; recipient Boneh Yisroel Builder award Greater Miami Jewish Fedn., 1989, Silver medallion award Nat. Conf. Christians & Jews, 1988, Community Svc. award Advt. Fedn. Gt. Miami, 1987. Mem. U.S. C. of C. (bd. dirs. 1985—), U.S. Chamber Svcs. Industries Coun. (chmn. 1987-88). Office: Ryder System Inc 3600 NW 82nd Ave Miami FL 33166

BURNS, RICHARD RAMSEY, lawyer; b. Duluth, Minn., May 3, 1946; s. Herbert Morgan and Janet (Strobel) B.; divorced; children: Jenny, Brian; m. Elizabeth Murphy, June 14, 1984. BA with distinction, U. Mich., 1968, JD magna cum laude, 1971. Bar: Calif. 1972, U.S. Dist. Ct. (no. dist.) Calif. 1972, U.S. Ct. Appeals (9th cir.) 1972, Minn. 1976, U.S. Dist. Ct. Minn. 1976, Wis. 1983, U.S. Tax. Ct. 1983. Assoc. Orrick, Herrington, Rowley & Sutcliffe, San Francisco, 1971-76; ptnr. Hanft, Fride, O'Brien, Harries, Swelbar & Burns P.A., Duluth, 1976—; gen. counsel Evening Telegram Co., Superior, Wis., 1982—, Murphy TV Stas., Madison, Wis., 1982—. Chmn. Duluth-Superior Area Community Found., 1983—; chmn. Quetico Lifecare Corp., Duluth, 1987—. Named Outstanding Young Man of Am., 1987, 89, Duluth Jr. C. of C., 1980. Fellow Am. Coll. Probate Counsel; mem. Calif. Bar Assn., Wis. Bar Assn., Minn. Bar Assn., 11th Dist. Bar Assn. (chmn. ethics com.), Arrowhead Estate Planning Council (pres. 1980), Northland Country Club (pres. local chpt. 1982-84), The Boulders Club, Kitchi Gammi Club, Athletic Club. Republican. Home: 180 Paine Farm Rd Duluth MN 55804 Office: Hanft Fride O'Brien Harries Swelbar & Burns PA 1000 First Bank Pl Duluth MN 55802

BURNS, ROBERT FRANCIS, convenience store corporation executive; b. Oak Park, Ill., Nov. 26, 1928; s. Robert F. and Amiee C. (Regis) B.; m. Annabelle Flitcraft, June 17, 1950; children: Gayle, Constance, Nancy, Tricia. AB, Oberlin Coll., 1950. Various positions Union Oil Co. of Calif., L.A., St. Louis, Kansas City, Mo. and New Orleans, 1950-57, Wilshire Oil Co. of Calif., L.A., 1957-59, Gulf Oil Co., L.A. and Houston, 1959-78; v.p., gen. mgr. Lucky Stores-Checker Auto div., Phoenix, 1978-82; sr. v.p. Circle K Corp., Phoenix, 1982—. Office: Circle K Corp 1601 N 7th St Phoenix AZ 85006

BURNS, ROBERT MICHAEL, marketing executive; b. Monmouth, Ill., Dec. 8, 1938; s. Robert McNamera and Kathryn (Lutrell) B.; m. Shirley Ann Meyer, May 21, 1963; children: Robin, Robert, Tammy, Amy, Julie, Mark. Student, Knox Coll., 1956, U. Ark., 1957-58; BA, Mo. State U., 1965; postgrad., U. Md., 1973. Pvt. practice gen. agt. 1968-72; v.p. Swift & Co. Ins. Group, Chgo., 1972-77; regional dir. Realty World Corp., Washington, 1977-78; exec. v.p. Ptnrs. Internat., Washington, 1978-80; pres. Breakthru Mktg., Inc., Milw., 1980—; cons. Red Carpet/Guild, San Diego, 1986—; co-founder Strategic Mgmt. Inst., Milw., 1988; bd. dirs. Ptnrs. Internat., Cedar Rapids, Iowa, 1979-81. Author: The Sales Process, 1986; co-author The Psychology of Winning, 1983; inventor computer closed-loop mgmt. system. Served with U.S. Army, 1963-65. Recipient numerous awards for Outstanding Sales, Mktg. and Mgmt. ins., real estate and franchising. Republican. Methodist. Home: 16560 W Nancy Ln Brookfield WI 53005 Office: Breakthru Mktg Svcs Inc 21675 Doral Rd Waukesha WI 53186

BURNS, RONALD JAMES, manufacturing equipment company executive; b. Michigan City, Ind., Apr. 18, 1937; s. Melvin B. and Alice K. (Shindler) B.; m. Sandra Kay Bratton, June 19, 1960; children—Dwight, Rhonda. B.S. in Bus, Ind. U., 1959. Methods analyst Ryerson Steel Co., Chgo., 1960; dir. ops. analysis Asso. Corp., South Bend, Ind., 1960-70; v.p., gen. mgr. Allis-Chalmers Corp., Milw., 1970-80, sector exec., v.p., 1980-84, sr. v.p., chief fin. officer, 1984—. Served with U.S. Army N.G., 1959-65. Office: Allis-Chalmers Corp 1205 S 70th St Milwaukee WI 53201

BURNS, SANDRA K., lawyer, educator; b. Bryan, Tex., Aug. 9, 1949; d. Clyde W. and Bert (Rychlik) B.; 1 son, Scott. BS, U. Houston, 1970; MA, U. Tex.-Austin, 1972, PhD, 1975; JD, St. Mary's U., 1978. Bar: Tex. 1978; cert. tchr., adminstr., supr. instrn., Tex. Tchr. Austin (Tex.) Ind. Sch. Dist., 1970-71; prof. child devel./family life and home econs. edn. Coll. Nutrition, Textiles and Human Devel. Tex. Woman's U., Denton, 1974-75; instrnl. devel. asst. Office of Ednl. Resources div. instrnl. devel. U. Tex. Health Sci. San Antonio, 1976-77; legis. aide William T. Moore, Tex. Senate, Austin, fall, 1978, com. clk.-counsel, spring, 1979; legal cons. Colombotti & Assocs., Aberdeen, Scotland, 1980; corp. counsel 1st Internat. Oil and Gas, Inc., 1983; contracted atty. Humble Exploration Co., Inc., Dallas, 1984; assoc. Smith, Underwood, Dallas, 1986-88; pvt. practice, Dallas, 1988—; atty. contracted to Republic Energy Inc., Bryan, Tex., 1981-82, ARCO, Dallas, 1985; vis. lectr. Tex. A&M U., fall 1981, summer, 1981; lectr. home econ. Our Lady of the Lake Coll., San Antonio, fall, 1975. Mem. ABA, State Bar of

Tex., Phi Delta Kappa. Contbr. articles on law and edn. to profl. jours. Office: 8300 Douglas Ave Ste 800 Dallas TX 75225

BURNS, WARD, textile company executive; b. New Bedford, Mass., May 31, 1928; s. Frederick Lloyd and Pauline (Ward) B.; m. Cynthia A. Butterworth, Dec. 19, 1964; children: Helen Abby, David Ward, Walton Lloyd. B.A., Amherst Coll., 1950; M.B.A., Harvard U., 1952; spl. student, NYU, 1955-57. C.P.A., N.Y. Mgr. Price Waterhouse & Co. (C.P.A.s), N.Y.C., 1954-62; assoc. Laurence S. and David Rockefeller, Brussels, Belgium, 1962-65; with J.P. Stevens & Co., Inc., N.Y.C., 1965-88, controller, 1969-78, group v.p., 1978-80, pres., 1980-86, vice chmn., 1987-88; also dir., mem. exec. com.; bd. dirs. Stevens Graphics, Inc., Atlanta; cons. ARS, Milan, Italy, HVL, Brussels, ARCO, Florence and Milan, 1963-65. Mem. editorial adv. bd.: Jour. Accountancy, 1969-72. Treas., dir. Internat. Sch. Brussels, 1963-65; pres. bd. dirs. Internat. Sch. Brussels Found., N.Y.C., 1965—; pres., bd. dirs. Friends New Cavell Hosp. Inc., 1972-78. Served as capt. USAF, 1952-53. Mem. Am. Inst. C.P.A.'s, N.Y. State Soc. C.P.A.'s, Financial Execs. Inst., St. Andrews Soc., Phi Alpha Psi, Phi Kappa Psi. Clubs: University, Links, Economics (N.Y.C.); Pilgrims, Sky; Edgartown Yacht. Office: 1133 Ave of the Americas 45th Fl New York NY 10036

BURNSIDE, FRANK BOYLE, marketing professional; b. Wilkes-Barre, Pa., Feb. 14, 1950; s. Frank Boyle and Peggy (Davis) B.; m. Candace Mohr, Aug. 26, 1972; children: Holly, Michael. BS, Kings Coll., 1974; MBA, U. Pa., 1977. Mgr. merchandise productivity John Wanamaker Inc., Phila., 1976-77, mgr. sales, econ. fin. analysis, 1978-79; mgr. market research and analysis C-TEC Corp., Wilkes-Barre, Pa., 1979-85, mgr. corp. devel. and planning, 1986—; v.p. Northeast Pa. Personal Computer Users Group, Pittston, 1987—. Columnist Op/ Wilkes-Barre Times Leader. Grad. Leadership Wilkes-Barre, 1984; bd. dirs. Wyoming Hist. and Geolog. Soc., Wilkes-Barre, 1979—; trustee Georgetown Settlement Assn., 1980—; columnist Wilkes-Barre Times Leader, 1988—; deacon First Presby. Ch., Wilkes-Barre. Mem. The Planning Forum, Westmoreland Club. Home: PO Box 142 RD #1 Noxen PA 18636 Office: C-TEC Corp PO Box 3000 46 Public Sq Wilkes-Barre PA 18703-3000

BURNSIDE, WALDO HOWARD, department store executive; b. Washington, Nov. 5, 1928; s. Waldo and Eleanor B.; m. Jean Mae Culbert, June 24, 1950; children: Diane Louise, Leslie Ann, Arlene Kay, William Howard. B.S., U. Md., 1949. With Woodward & Lothrop, Washington, 1949-80; divisional mdse. mgr. Woodward & Lothrop, 1957-65, v.p., gen. mdse. mgr., 1965-74, exec. v.p., 1974-78, pres., 1978-80; also dir.; vice chmn., chief operating officer Carter Hawley Hale Stores, Inc., Los Angeles, 1980-83, pres., chief operating officer, 1983—; dir. Security Pacific Corp. Trustee Md. Ednl. Found.; trustee St. John's Hosp. and Health Ctr. Found.; trustee, past chmn. U. Md. Alumni Internat. Mem. Ind. Colls. So. Calif. (bd. dirs.), Los Angeles Area C. of C. (bd. dirs.), Automobile Club So. Calif. (bd. dirs.), Phi Kappa Phi, Sigma Chi. Episcopalian. Clubs: California, Los Angeles Country, N.Y. Athletic. Office: Carter Hawley Hale Stores Inc 550 S Flower St Los Angeles CA 90071

BURNSTEIN, FRANCES, commercial association executive; b. N.Y.C., Oct. 13, 1935; d. Benny and Yetta Kirshenbaum; m. Barry Burnstein, Oct. 16, 1955; children: Steven, Barbara, Lori. Student, CCNY, 1953-55; grad., Insts. Orgn. Mgmt., 1983. Dep. mayor Twp. of Cherry Hill, N.J., 1975-77; exec. dir. Cherry Hill C. of C., 1977-88, pres., 1988—; commr. Camden County Parks, 1986-88. Trustee Cooper Found. Med. Ctr., Camden, N.J., 1980-89, Police Athletic League, 1976—; bd. dirs. ARC, Camden County, 1981—, Guidance Ctr., 1982-84, Cherry Hill unit Am. Heart Assn., 1986—; trustee Ronald McDonald House of Kids, Camden County United Way, 1981—, v.p., 1981-84, pres.'s cabinet, 1982-84; co-chair Del. River Region Tourism Council, 1983; exec. adv. coun. Rutgers U. Sch.Bus., 1985—. Named Newsmaker of Yr., Cherry Hill C. of C., 1984; Frances Burnstein Little League Softball Field dedicated to her, 1980; selected for cover of N.J. Woman Mag., 1986; named one of seven Women to Watch in 1986, State of N.J., Bus. Watch 1989 Bus. Jour. N.J. Mem. N.J. Assn. C. of C. (v.p.), N.J. Assn. C. of C. Execs. (v.p. 1987—), Am. Assn. C. of C., Am. Assn. C. of C. Communications Council, Nat. Assn. Membership Dirs., Nat. Assn. Female Execs., Am. Mgmt. Assn., Am. Heart Assn. (bd. dirs. Camden County chpt. 1987—). Republican. Jewish. Lodge: Garden State Rotary (Person of Yr. 1980). Office: Cherry Hill C of C 1060 Kings Hwy N Cherry Hill NJ 08034

BURR, JAMES HUGH, securities analyst; b. Washington, Oct. 31, 1948; s. James Joseph Burr and Anne Bowman Carter; divorced; married 2d. Diana Louise Roswick, Aug. 10, 1985. AB, Bowdoin Coll., 1970; MA, Duke U., 1972; JD, Fordham Sch. Law, 1979; MBA, NYU, 1986. Bar: N.Y. 1980. Legis. analyst bur. of budget City of N.Y., 1972-76; sr. analyst N.Y.C. Fin. Control Bd., 1976-82; v.p., mgr. staff devel. Moody's Investors Svc., N.Y.C., 1982—. Contbr. articles to profl. jours. Capt. U.S. Army, 1972-78. Mem. ACLU, Nat. Assn. Bond Lawyers. Democrat. Episcopalian. Home: 312 Carroll Close Tarrytown NY 10591 Office: Moody's Investors Svc 99 Church St New York NY 10007

BURR, RICHARD ALLEN, marketing professional; b. Claremont, N.H., Sept. 23, 1938; s. William McKinley and Lena (Prud'Homme) B.; m. Valerie Fitz, Nov. 12, 1964 (dec. 1984); children: Jennifer Lynn, Allison Anne, Katherine Ewing; m. Cynthia Carlson, Aug. 17, 1985; stepchildren: Erik Carlson, Freya Lee, Toren Marshall. BS in Pharmacy, Mass. Coll. Pharmacy, Boston, 1960; MBA, Boston Coll., 1971. Registered pharmacist, Mass. V.p. R.A. Gosselin and Co. Inc., Dedham, Mass., 1956-72; mgr. mktg. rsch. Dow Pharm., Indpls., 1972-74; mgr. comml. rsch. Dow-Lepetit, Indpls., 1974-75; mgr. mktg. rsch. and devel. Dow Chem. USA, Indpls., 1975-81; dir. mktg. rsch. and devel. Merrell Dow Pharm., Cin., 1981-87; pres. R.A. Burr and Co. Inc., Cin., 1987—; mem. adv. bd. Walker Rsch. Inc., Indpls., 1984—. Treas. Fall Creek PTA, 1979-80. Mem. Assn. Nat. Advertisers, Advt. Rsch. Found., Midwest Pharm. Advt. Council, Pharm. Mktg. Rsch. Group., Biomed. Mktg. Assn., World Future Soc., Am. Mktg. Assn., Am. Mgmt. Assn., Am. Pharm. Assn., Am. Soc. Hosp. Pharmacy. Home and Office: 8783 Arcturus Dr Cincinnati OH 45249

BURROW, TERRY BRUCE, real estate developer; b. Long Beach, Calif., Jan. 11, 1943; s. James M. and Willa Dean (Mull) B.; m. Sharon Gayle Young; children: Terri, Shelley, Ross, Debbie. Student, Harbor Jr. Coll., Wilmington, Calif. Ops. officer Wilmington (Calif.) Mut. Savs. and Loan, 1961-66; real estate mgr. Taco Bell, Torrence, Calif., 1966-68; pres. Realty Assocs. Brokerage, Inc., Jonesboro, Ark., 1983—, Realty Assocs. Cos., Inc., Jonesboro, Ark., 1983—. Named to Million Dollar Club Ark. Realtors Assn., 1981; Top Volume Sales Producer Jonesboro Bd. Realtors, 1983, Salesman of Yr., 1979, Realtor of Yr., 1983. Mem. Internat. Council Shopping Ctrs. (state dir. govtl. affairs com. 1986-89), Nat. Assn. Corp. Real Estate Execs. (founding), Nat. Assn. Realtors, Am. Coll. Real Estate Cons., Jonesboro Realtors Assn. (life mem. Million Dollar Club 1983), Jonesboro Bd. Realtors (pres. 1982-84, Realtor of Yr. 1983), Ark. Arts Council, Jonesboro Fine Arts Council. Republican. Baptist. Office: Realty Assocs Cos Inc 2005 Highland Dr Jonesboro AR 72401

BURROWS, BRIAN WILLIAM, research and development manufacturing executive; b. Burnie, Tasmania, Australia, Nov. 15, 1939; came to U.S., 1966; s. William Henry and Jean Elizabeth (Ling) B.; m. Inger Elisabeth Forsmark; 1 child, Karin. ScB, U. Tasmania, 1960, ScB with honors, 1962; PhD, Southampton U., 1966. Staff scientist Tyco Labs., Inc., Waltham, Mass., 1966-68; lectr. Macquarie U., Sydney, Australia, 1969-71; chief sect. Battelle-Geneva, Switzerland, 1971-75; group leader Inco, Ltd., Mississauga, Ont., Can., 1976-77; lab. dir. Gould, Inc., Rolling Meadows, Ill., 1977-86; v.p. rsch. USG Corp., Chgo., 1986—; bd. dirs. U.S. Gypsum Co., Chgo. Contbr. articles to tech. jours.; patentee in field. Mem. Am. Chem. Soc., Materials Rsch. Soc., IEEE, AAAS, Indsl. Rsch. Inst. (co. rep.), Meadow Club (Rolling Meadows, Ill.). Home: 835 Fairfax Ct Barrington IL 60010 Office: USG Corp 101 S Wacker Dr Chicago IL 60606

BURROWS, JOHN EDWARD, communications company executive; b. Englewood, N.J., Aug. 6, 1950; s. Laurence McCallum and Pauline Hannah (McClave) B. BA in Journalism, Rutgers U., 1972. From staff asst. to account exec. Ogilvy & Mather Inc., N.Y.C., 1977-80; mgr. sales devel. CBS Radio Spot Sales, N.Y.C., 1980-81; dist. dir. affiliate relations CBS Radio Network, N.Y.C., 1981-84, dir. affiliate relations, 1984-86, v.p. affiliate relations, 1986-87; v.p. news and sports affiliate relations CBS Radio Networks, N.Y.C., 1987—. Author: A Country Heart, 1983. Episcopalian. Home: 130 Overlook Ave Hackensack NJ 07601 Office: CBS Radio Networks 51 W 52d St New York NY 10019

BURRUS, DANIEL ALLEN, research company executive, consultant; b. Portland, Oreg., Aug. 22, 1947; s. Joe Howard and Mary Kathleen (Boelk) B. BS, U. Wis., Oshkosh, postgrad; postgrad., U. Wis., Milw. Lifetime teaching cert., Wis. Founder, pres. Burrus Media Prodns., Brookfield, Wis., 1978-80, Burrus Powered Gliders, Waukesha, Wis., 1980-82, Midwest Skynasaurs, Waukesha, 1982-84, Ultrasports Inc., Waukesha, 1982-84, Burrus Research Assocs., Inc., Waukesha, 1983—; cons. various fed. and state credit unions, ins. cos., U.S. banks, univs. and corps.; speaker in field. Editor: Applied Science Rev., 1985, 88; author, editor: Tech. Futures Newsletter, 1985—; author: (audio tape learning systems) The Future of Education, 1985, Beyond Megatrends, 1985, Teaching Creativity, 1986, Futureview: A Look Ahead, 1986, Maximizing Your Creativity, 1989; author: Futureview: How to Shape the Future and Become a Master of Change, 1989, Beyond Competition: Winning Now and in the Future, 1989; writer, dir., producer: (films) Deja Vu, 1972, Phantasmagoria, 1972, The New Adventures of Superman, 1972; contbr. articles to profl. publs. Recipient 2 First Place awards Milw. Film Festival, 1973-74, First Place award Carroll Coll. Film Festival, 1979. Mem. Internat. Platform Assn., Internat. Personal Robot Assn. (founding), Nat. Speakers Assn., Wis. Profl. Speakers Assn. (bd. dirs. 1985-87, pres. 1988, Speaking Star award 1988), Exptl. Aircraft Assn. Home: 2761 S 149th New Berlin WI 53151 Office: Burrus Rsch Assocs PO Box 1354 Waukesha WI 53187

BURSHTAN, ALVIN, wholesale company executive; b. Preston, Iowa, Feb. 15, 1935; s. Sam and Esther (Jacobson) B.; m. Ann Carol Lichtenstein, Dec. 8, 1960; children—Sharon, John, Lauri. B.A., U. Iowa, 1956. Promotion dir. KCRG-AM and TV, Cedar Rapids, Iowa, 1956-57; account exec. Ettinger Advt. Agy., Cedar Rapids, 1957-59; asst. advt. dir. Eagle Food Ctr., Rock Island, Ill., 1959-63; v.p. advt. Super Food Services, Chgo., 1963-68, sr. v.p. mktg., Dayton, Ohio, 1968-85, exec. v.p. mktg., 1986—. Served with U.S. Army, 1957. Mem. Dayton Sales and Mktg. Execs. Club, Alpha Delta Sigma. Jewish. Home: 4808 Laurelann Dr Kettering OH 45429 Office: Super Food Svcs Inc 3233 Newmark Dr Dayton OH 45342

BURSON, HAROLD, public relations executive; b. Memphis, Feb. 15, 1921; s. Maurice and Esther (Bach) B.; m. Bette Ann Foster, Oct. 30, 1947; children: Scott, Mark. BA, U. Miss., 1940; DHL (hon.), Boston U., 1988. Corr., reporter Memphis Comml. Appeal, 1938-40; dir. Ole Miss News Bur., Oxford, Miss., 1939-40; dir. pub. relations H.K. Ferguson Co., N.Y.C., 1941-43; chmn. Burson-Marsteller, N.Y.C., 1953—; dir., mem. exec. com. Young & Rubicam, N.Y.C.; officer, dir. Burson-Marsteller subs. in Can., Latin Am., Europe, Australia, Asia; mem. adv. council Emory U. Bus. Sch. Chmn. bd., mem. exec. com., Joint Council on Econ. Edn.; mem. exec. com. Young Astronauts Council, 1984-88; bd. dirs., exec. com., v.p. public info. Nat. Safety Council, 1968-76; bd. dirs. Kennedy Center Prodns., Washington, Catalyst Inc.; former trustee World Wildlife Fund, 1979-81, Found. for Public Relations Research and Edn.; trustee Hackley Sch., Tarrytown, N.Y., 1968-76; mem. Fine Arts Commn., 1981-85. Served with AUS, World War II. Named Public Relations Profl. of Year Public Relations News, 1977, 89; recipient Gold Anvil award Public Relations Soc. Am., 1980; Horatio Alger award, 1986; Arthur Page award U. Tex., 1986; named to U. Miss. Hall of Fame, 1980. Mem. Am., Internat. public relations assns., N.Y. Soc. Security Analysts, Am. Philatelic Soc., N.Y. Acad. Medicine (assoc.), Blue Key, Overseas Press, Marco Polo Club, Mid-Am. Club, Internat. Club, Scarsdale Golf Club, Econ. Club of N.Y. (dir., trustee), Horatio Alger Assn. (dir.), Omicron Delta Kappa. Home: 260 Beverly Rd Scarsdale NY 10583 Office: Burson-Marsteller 230 Park Ave S New York NY 10003

BURSTEIN, JACK DAVID, banking executive; b. Poland, Sept. 27, 1945; came to U.S., 1949; s. Charles and Gene (Kohn) B.; m. Gilda Adler, June 11, 1966; children: Melanie, Lisa, Jason, Jonathan. BA, CUNY, 1966. CPA, N.Y., Fla. CPA Seidman & Seidman, N.Y.C., 1968-70; ptnr. Schechter, Beame, Burstein, Price & Co., Miami, Fla., 1970-86; pres., chief exec. officer Am. Capital Corp., Miami, Fla., 1984—; chmn., chief exec. officer Transcapital Fin. Corp., Miami, Fla., 1988—; chmn. bd. Transohio Savs. Bank, 1988. Contbr. articles to profl. jours. Bd. dirs. Greater Miami Jewish Fedn., Miami; bd. dirs. Beth Israel Congregations, Miami Beach, Fla.; chmn. Hebrew Acad., Miami Beach; founder Mt. Sinai Hosp., Miami Beach. Mem. Am. Inst. CPA's, Dade County Chpt. CPA's, Fla. Inst. CPA's, N.Y. State Inst. CPA's. Republican. Office: Transcapital Fin Corp 1221 Brickell Ave Miami FL 33131

BURSTON, RICHARD MERVIN, business executive; b. Brookline, Mass., Oct. 31, 1924; s. Mark and Anita (Andrews) B.; m. Phoebe Harvey Hopkins, Aug. 29, 1958; children—Abby Lyn, Seth Hopkins, Joshua Craig, Mark Andrews, Amanda Lee. B.A., Bowdoin Coll., 1949; M.B.A., Harvard U., 1952. Mgr. beauty dept. Kendall Co., Boston, 1953-58; regional sales mgr. M. Pier Co., Ft. Lauderdale, Fla., 1958-59; nat. sales mgr. Ozon Products, Inc., Bklyn., 1959-63; v.p., co-founder Burston/Larkin Assocs., Stamford, Conn., 1964—; pres., chief exec. officer Excalibur, Inc., Stamford, 1981—; founder, pres. Burston Inc., Stamford, 1987—; dir. Nat. Beauty and Barber Reps. Assn., N.Y.C., 1973-74, Louv Yacht Yard, Norwalk, Conn., 1969-73; cons. Ruckel Mfg., Inc., N.Y.C., 1969-87. Dir. Roxbury Babe Ruth, Stamford, 1969-85; pres., dir. Roxbury-Riverbank Little League, Stamford, 1971-82; trustee Miramichi Rod & Gun Club, Lyttleton, New Brunswick, Can., 1980—; fund raiser Bowdoin Coll., Brunswick, Maine, 1984—. Served to lt. USNR, 1943-46, PTO. Recipient Man of Yr. award United Beauty Supply Corp., Bridgeport, Conn., 1983. Mem. Beauty and Barber Supply Inst., Am. Beauty Assn. Republican. Jewish. Clubs: Landmark, North Stamford Exchange (dir. 1984-86), Miramichi Rod & Gun, Bowdoin (Southwest Conn.); Spartan. Lodge: Masons. Avocations: fly fishing; sailing, commemorative plates, oriental rugs. Home: 156 Riverbank Dr Stamford CT 06903 Office: Burston Inc 300 Broad St #804 Stamford CT 06901

BURT, DAVID A., grocery and drugstore company executive; b. 1920; married. Announcer, producer Sta. KMOX, St. Louis, 1946-48; sta. mgr. St. Joseph Valley Broadcasting Co., 1948-49; sales rep. Chgo. Tribune, 1949-53; advt. mgr. Kroger Co., 1956-60, mktg. mgr., 1960-62, div. v.p., 1962-71, regional v.p., 1971-75, v.p., 1975-86, sr. v.p., 1986—. Office: Kroger Co 1014 Vine St Cincinnati OH 45202 *

BURT, JAMES MELVIN, sugar manufacturing company executive; b. Los Angeles, June 20, 1933; s. Earl Jefferson and Sara Frances (Cook) B.; m. Lynne A. Johnson, June 18, 1954; children: Kathleen, Karen, Peggy, Laurie. B.A., Occidental Coll., Los Angeles, 1955. With Lever Bros. Co., N.Y.C., 1959-65, Heinz Co., Pitts., 1965-69; v.p., dir. consumer products Facelle Co., Oxnard, Calif., 1969-73; v.p., dir. brokerage ops. Bromar Inc., Newport Beach, Calif., 1973-80; sr. v.p. sales and mktg. C & H Sugar Co., San Francisco, 1980—. Served as capt. USMC, 1955-58. Mem. Am. Mgmt. Assn. (mktg. council 1981-82). Republican. Presbyterian. Clubs: Sharon Heights (Menlo Park, Calif.); World Trade (San Francisco). Office: C&H Sugar Co 1390 Willow Pass Rd Concord CA 94520

BURT, MARVIN ROGER, financial advisor, investment manger; b. L.A., Mar. 5, 1937; s. Henry Howard Burt and Iris Faith (Green) Welton; m. Joy Lee Rougk, July 20, 1958; children: Sandra Marie, Scott Marvin. BA, UCLA, 1958; MPA, George Washington U., 1965, D in Pub. Adminstrn., 1969. Cert. fin. planner; registered fin. planning practitioners. Mgmt. trainee Bank Am., L.A., 1961-62; program analyst Dept. Def., Washington, 1962-65, Exec. Office Pres., Washington, 1965-66; mem. sr. research staff Resource Corp., Bethesda, Md., 1966-67; sr. cons. Peat Marwick Mitchell, Washington, 1967-68; cons. Potomac, Md., 1968-69; mem. sr. staff Urban Inst., Washington, 1969-72; pres. Burt Assocs., Inc., Bethesda, 1972—, Inst. Human Resources Research, Bethesda, 1973-82; asst. v.p. Sci. Applications Internat., McLean, Va., 1982-85; cons. govt. agys., Washington, 1965-82. Author: (books) Options for Improving the Care of Neglected and Dependent Children, 1971, Policy Analysis, 1974, A Comprehensive Emergency Services System for Neglected and Abused Children, 1977, Drug Abuse, 1979, Children of Heroin Addicts, 1980 ; contbr. articles to profl. jours. Chmn. coun. on ministries North Bethesda United Meth. Ch., 1975-76, 81-82, chmn. bd. dirs., 1977-78; mem. Community Coordinated Child Care, Bethesda, 1976-77. USPHS grantee, 1977-82. Fellow AAAS; mem. Ops. Rsch. Soc. Am. (chmn. tech. sect. 1979-80), Internat. Assn. Fin. Planning (v.p. nat. capital chpt. 1987—), Inst. Cert. Fin. Planners. Lodge: Rotary (bd. dirs. 1987—). Home: 5 Willowgate Ct Bethesda MD 20817 Office: Burt Assocs Inc 7200 Wisconsin Ave Ste 1008 Bethesda MD 20814

BURT, RICHARD MAX, lawyer; b. Phila., Dec. 8, 1944; s. Joseph Frank and Louise Esther (Kevitch) B.; m. Katherine Anne Hedrick, Apr. 25, 1965 (div.); children: Corinne, Julie. BA, Gettysburg (Pa.) Coll., 1965; JD, Dickinson Sch. of Law, 1969. Bar: N.Y. 1970, U.S. Dist. Ct. (so. dist.) N.Y. 1972, U.S. Ct. Appeals (2d cir.) 1972. Assoc. Donovan, Leisure, Newton & Irvine, N.Y.C., 1969-73; asst. counsel Sandoz, Inc., East Hanover, N.J., 1974-78; v.p., sec. Sandoz Corp., N.Y.C., 1978-88; sec. Sandoz Nutrition Corp., Mpls., 1983-88, Master Builders Inc., 1985-88; v.p. fin. and devel., chief fin. officer Sandoz Pharm. Corp., E. Hanover, N.J., 1989—. Mem. ABA, Westchester-Fairfield Corp. Counsel Assn., Internat. Bar Assn., Am. Corp. Counsel Assn. Office: Sandoz Corp 608 Fifth Ave New York NY 10020

BURT, WALLACE JOSEPH, JR., insurance company executive; b. Burlington, Iowa, Apr. 1, 1924; s. Wallace Joseph and Lela (Catlow) B.; student Iowa State Coll., 1942, U. Wis., 1945; m. Alice Olmsted, June 22, 1946; children—Lockwood, David, Virginia. Vice pres., dir. 1st Ins. Fin. Co., Des Moines, 1946-50, Northeastern Ins. Co., Hartford, Conn., 1950-59; pres., owner Hail Reinsurance Mgmt., Inc., Ormond Beach, Fla., 1960—; chmn. Burt & Scheld, Inc., Ormond Beach, 1961—; chmn. U.S. br. Hamburg Internat. Reins. Co., 1976—; chmn. First N.Y. Syndicate Corp., 1979—, W.J. Burt Mgmt., Inc., N.Y.C., 1979—; pres. Ormond Reins. Co.; dir., v.p. Barnett Bank, Ormond Beach; underwriting mem. Lloyd's of London; mem. N.Y. Ins. Exchange, 1983—. Trustee, pres. Ormond Beach Meml. Hosp. Served to 1st lt. USAAF, World War II. Decorated D.F.C., Purple Heart, Air medal with 5 oak leaf clusters. Home: 222 Riverside Dr Ormond Beach FL 32074 Office: 146 S Atlantic St Ormond Beach FL 32074

BURTIS, EDWARD DAVID, banker; b. Buffalo, Dec. 4, 1941; s. E. Robert and Ruth (Curtiss) B.; m. Mary Margaret Chiles, Apr. 20, 1968; children: David Monfort, Stephen Chiles. BS in Econs., U. Pa., 1963, MBA in Mktg., 1965. Analyst, mgr. Bd. Govs. Fed. Res., Washington, 1971-76; v.p. ops., v.p. cash mgmt. Am. Security Bank, Washington, 1977-81; v.p. product mgmt. Phila. Nat. Bank, 1981-82; v.p. corp. services Dominion Bankshares Corp., Roanoke, Va., 1982—. Devel. chmn. Am. Heart Assn., Roanoke, 1985-86, bd. dirs., 1986—, v.p. 1987—. Mem. Nat. Automatic Clearing House Assn. (bd. dirs. 1986—), Va. Automated Clearing House Assn. (bd. dirs., mem. exec. com. 1983—, pres. 1986-88). Club: Hidden Valley Country (Salem, Va.). Home: 2631 Southwood Dr Roanoke VA 24018 Office: Dominion Bankshares Corp Box 13327 Roanoke VA 24040

BURTNER, ROGER LEE, research geologist, oil company administrator; b. Hershey, Pa., Mar. 31, 1936; s. Bruce Lemmuel and Bernetta Viola (Quigle) B.; m. Carol Ann Spitzer, Aug. 1, 1965; 1 child, Pamela Sue. BS cum laude, Franklin and Marshall Coll., 1958; MS, Stanford U., 1959; PhD, Harvard U., 1965. Assoc. research geologist Calif. Research Corp. div. Standard Oil Co. of Calif., La Habra, 1963-64, research geologist, 1964-68; exploration geologist Tex. div. Standard Oil Co. of Calif., Corpus Christi and Houston, 1968-69; research geologist Chevron Oil Field Research Co. div. Chevron Corp., La Habra, 1969-74, sr. research geologist, 1974-77, sr. research assoc., 1977—, petrology group project leader, 1975-80, supr. electron microscopy lab., 1977-82. Contbr. articles to sci. jours. Founder Christ Coll. Irvine, 1976, Orange County Permorming Arts Ctr., Costa Mesa, Calif., 1979; trustee Christ Coll. Irvine Found., 1989—; mem. Friends of Christ Coll. Irvine, Fullerton (Calif.) Arboretum, 1983—, Orange County Master Chorale, 1978-81, Christ Coll. Community Chorale, 1983—; bd. dirs. Luth. High Sch. Assn. Orange County, Orange, Calif., 1975-81, 88—, pres., 1977-79, v.p. 1979-81; v.p. Prince of Peace Luth. Ch., Anaheim, Calif., 1980-86, 89—, pres. 1986—. NSF fellow, 1958-60. Fellow Geol. Soc. Am.; mem. Am. Assn. Petroleum Geologists, Soc. Econ. Paleontologists and Mineralogists, Clay Minerals Soc. (councilor 1981-84), Geochem. Soc., Los Angeles Basin Geol. Soc., Audubon Soc., Orange County Wheelman, Sierra Club, Internat. Assn. Geochemistry and Cosmochemistry, Sigma Xi, Phi Beta Kappa. Republican. Home: 721 E Harmony Ln Fullerton CA 92631 Office: Chevron Oil Field Rsch Co PO Box 446 La Habra CA 90631

BURTON, DELMAR LEE, insurance company executive; b. Kansas City, Kans., Dec. 25, 1929; s. Delmar Leroy and Helen Elmina (Wood) B.; m. Glenna L. Branstetter, July 22, 1951; children: Deborah, Dan. B.S., U. Mo., 1951. Underwriter Nat. Surety Corp., Kansas City, Mo., 1951, Ohio Casualty Co., Hamilton, 1953-55; Underwriter Employers Reins. Corp., San Francisco, 1956-71, v.p., 1971-78, sr. v.p., 1978-83; exec. v.p. Employers Reins. Corp., Overland Park, Kans., 1983—; bd. dirs. Emplòyers Reinsurance Corp., Bates Turner Inc., 1st Fidelity Equity Corp. With U.S. Army, 1951-53, Korea. Republican. Mem. United Ch. of Christ. Clubs: Merchants Exchange, Kansas City. Office: Employers Reins Corp 5200 Metcalf St PO Box 2991 Overland Park KS 66201

BURTON, DOROTHY JO, management consultant; b. Mexico, Mo.; d. Joe Wheeler and Gladys Leah (Robison) Hanson; B.S., Washington U., St. Louis, 1961; M.B.A., So. Ill. U., 1982; m. W. Wesley Burton, Jr.; children—Carole, Barbara, John, Wesley W. Engr., McDonnell Aircraft, St. Louis, 1952-64; sr. engr. McDonnell Douglas Astron., St. Louis, 1964-70; sr. cons. McDonnell Douglas Automation Co., St. Louis, 1970-80, sect. mgr., 1980; now prin. Mgmt. Systems Assocs., Lake St. Louis, Mo.; cons. in field. Mem. Am. Assn. Cost Engrs., Project Mgmt. Inst. Republican. Presbyterian. Home: 16 Rue Grand Lake Saint Louis MO 63367 Office: 1000 Lake Saint Louis Blvd Ste 219 Saint Louis MO 63367

BURTON, EARL GILLESPIE, III, lawyer; b. St. Louis, Sept. 20, 1952; s. Earl Gillespie Jr. and Patricia Joan B.; m. Carol Joy Edwards, May 31, 1980; 1 child, Sara Frances. BBA in Fin., U. Mo., 1976, JD, 1980. Bar: Mo. 1980. Legal intern Mo. Atty. Gen., Jefferson City, 1978-80; assoc. gen. counsel Clayton (Mo.) Brokerage Co., 1980-86; pvt. practice Clayton, 1987—; bd. dirs. Ins. Mgmt. Group, St. Louis. Trustee Gateway chpt. Leukemia Soc. Am., St. Louis, 1988—. Mem. ABA, Mo. Bar Assn., Order of Barristers. Methodist. Home: 1124 Foxworth Ct Ballwin MO 63011 Office: Earl Gillespie III 14 S Central Ste 210 Clayton MO 63105

BURTON, JOHN CAMPBELL, university dean, educator, consultant; b. N.Y.C., Sept. 17, 1932; s. James Campbell and Barbara (French) B.; m. Jane Garnjost, Apr. 6, 1957; children: Eve Bradley, Bruce Campbell. B.A., Haverford Coll., 1954; M.B.A., Columbia U., 1956, Ph.D., 1962. C.P.A., N.Y. Staff acct. Arthur Young & Co., N.Y.C., 1956-60; prof. acctg. and fin. Grad. Sch. Bus. Columbia U., N.Y.C., 1962-72, Arthur Young prof. acctg. and fin., 1978—, dean Grad. Sch. Bus., 1982-88; chief acct. SEC, Washington, 1972-76; dep. mayor fin. City of N.Y., 1976-77; dir. Scolastic Inc., Bowery Savs. Bank; dir., chmn. audit com. Commerce Clearing House Inc., 1979—, First Pa. Corp.-First Pa. Bank, 1982-85; mem. U.S. Comptroller Gen. Cons. Panel, 1978—; bd. dirs. Accts. for Pub. Interest, 1978-85. Editor: Corporate Financial Reporting: Conflicts and Challenges, 1969, Corporate Financial Reporting: Ethical and Other Problems, 1972, (with Russell Palmer and Robert Kay) Handbook of Accounting and Auditing, 1981, The International World of Accounting: Challenges and Opportunities, 1981; author: Accounting for Business Combinations, 1970, (with W.T. Porter) Auditing: A Conceptual Approach, 1971, (with H. Goodman, A. Phillips and M. Vasarhelyi) Illustrations and Analysis of Disclosures of Inflation Accounting Information, 1981; contbr. articles to profl. jours. Pres., trustee Millbrook Sch. (N.Y.), 1958—; trustee ex officio Am. Assembly, 1982-88. Recipient Disting. Scholar award Hofstra U., 1975; Ford Found. fellow, 1961-62. Mem. Am. Inst. C.P.A.s (council 1980-83), Am. Acctg. Assn. (acad. v.p. 1980-82), Am. Fin. Assn., Am. Econ. Assn., Fin. Execs. Inst., Assn. Govtl. Accts. Pres., trustee. Clubs: Metropolitan (N.Y.C.); Lake Sunapee Yacht (N.H.). Home: 130 E End Ave Apt 12A New York NY 10028 Office: Columbia U 625 Uris Hall New York NY 10027

BURTON, RAYMOND CHARLES, JR., trailer train company executive; b. Phila., Aug. 29, 1938; s. Raymond Charles and Phyllis (Clifford) B. BA,

Cornell U., 1960; MBA, U. Pa., 1963. Various operating positions Santa Fe Ry. Co., 1963-68, asst. controller, 1968-69; asst. treas. Santa Fe Industries, Chgo., 1969-74; asst. v.p. planning, treas. Burlington No., Inc., 1974-79; v.p. and treas. Burlington No., Inc., St. Paul and Seattle, 1979-82; v.p. planning Internat. Harvester Co., Chgo., 1982; pres., chief exec. officer Trailer Train Co., Chgo., 1982—, Railbox Co., Railgon Co., Chgo., 1982—. 1st lt. U.S. Army, 1960-61. Mem. Met. Club, Chgo. Club, Tower Club, Sea Island Club. Republican. Presbyterian. Office: Trailer Train Co 101 N Wacker Dr Chicago IL 60606

BURTON, RICHARD GREENE, paper company marketing executive; b. Pawtucket, R.I., Jan. 4, 1936; s. Fred Marsden and Winifred Congdon (Greene) B.; m. Nancy Jane Fairgrieve, June 27, 1959; children: Jeffrey Greene, Janet Lynn, Steven Richard. BA, Duke U., 1958. Salesman Riegel Paper Corp., Chgo., 1958-66; sales mgr. publ. papers Mead Corp., Chgo., 1966-75, regional sales mgr., N.Y.C., 1976-79, v.p. sales, Dayton, Ohio, 1979-82; v.p. mktg. Paper Corp. Am., Valley Forge, Pa., 1982—. Mem. mktg. com. Phila. div. Am. Cancer Soc. Mem. Sales Assn. Paper Industry (program chmn. 1964-65, v.p. Chgo. region 1965-66, Man of Yr. award 1966). Republican. Clubs: Naperville (Ill.) Country; Waynesborough Country (Paoli, Pa.). Home: 1533 Sugartown Rd Paoli PA 19301 Office: Paper Corp Am 1325 Morris Dr Wayne PA 19087

BURTON, RICHARD MAX, management educator; b. Rushville, Ill., Aug. 12, 1939; s. Arlie H. and Mabel E. (Hoyt) B.; m. Nadine Ferdman; 1 child, Aziel. BS, U. Ill., 1961, MBA, 1963, D in Bus. Adminstrn., 1967. Asst. prof. Naval Postgrad. Sch., Monterey, Calif., 1967-70; prof. Duke U., Durham, N.C., 1970—; chmn. bd. trustees Durham County Hosp. Corp., 1987—. Co-author: Designing Efficient Organizations, 1984, Innovation and Entrepreneurship in Organizations, 1986; contbr. articles to profl. jours.; departmental editor: Mgmt. Sci., Providence, 1986—. Exec. dir. LEAD Adv. Council, Durham, 1985—. Office: Duke U Fuqua Sch Bus Durham NC 27706

BURWELL, DUDLEY SALE, retired food distribution executive; b. Ebenezer, Miss., Nov. 21, 1931; s. Clement Lucas B. and Winfree Henry (Burwell); m. Joan Fay Berman, July 26, 1952; children: Lana, Dudley S., Joel B., Gregory Todd, Troy E. Student, Holmes Jr. Coll., 1950, Draughons Bus. Coll., 1951; grad., LaSalle Extension U., 1965. With Lewis Grocer Co., Indianola, Miss., 1954—, v.p., sec., 1972-79, pres., chief exec. officer, 1979-87; pres., chief exec. officer Sunflower Stores, Inc., Indianola, Miss., 1979-87; pres. So. Bus. Specialists Inc. doing bus. as Corp. Investment Internat., Jackson, Miss., 1988—. Bd. dirs. Miss. Econ. Council. Served with USMC, 1952-54. Mem. Am. Inst. C.P.A.s, Miss. Soc. C.P.A.s, Indianola C. of C. (pres. 1976-77). Methodist. Lodge: Rotary. Home: 11 Highland Meadows Jackson MS 39211 Office: Corp Investment Internat 188 E Capitol St 1 Jackson Pl Ste 1250 Jackson MS 39201

BUSBY, JAMES MERWIN, business machines company executive; b. Williamsburg, W.Va., May 18, 1931; s. Calvin and Rose (Ray) B.; B.S., Empire State Coll., 1978; m. Emilie Saundra DeBernardis, Dec. 28, 1968; children—Nancy Ann Marler, Karl Ray, Gary Wayne, Christopher Lud, Allison Brooke. Enlisted U.S. Army, 1952, advanced through grades to maj., 1969; ret., 1973; mgr. devel. assurance Xerox Corp., Rochester, N.Y., 1973—. Committeeman, Monroe County Republican Com., 1975—; mem. Zoning Bd. Appeals Town of Perinton, N.Y., 1979-85, chmn., 1984-85; pres. Roundtree Homeowners Assn., 1975-82. Decorated Bronze Star medal. Cert. data processor. Mem. Xerox Mgmt. Assn., IEEE, Aircraft Owners and Pilots Assn., Data Processing Mgmt. Assn. (founding pres. No. Va. chpt.), Ret. Officers Assn. (pres. 1975-76), Alpha Mu Sigma. Republican. Roman Catholic. Home: 14 Shagbark Way Fairport NY 14450 Office: Xerox Corp Xerox Sq Rochester NY 14644

BUSCH, AUGUST ADOLPHUS, III, brewery executive; b. St. Louis, June 16, 1937; s. August Adolphus and Elizabeth (Overton) B.; m. Susan Marie Hornibrook, Aug. 17, 1963 (div. 1969); children: August Adolphus IV, Susan Marie II; m. Virginia L. Wiley, Dec. 28, 1974; children: Steven August, Virginia Marie. Student, U. Ariz., 1957-58, Siebel Inst. Tech., 1960-61. With Anheuser-Busch, Inc., St. Louis, 1957—, sales mgr., 1962-64, v.p. mktg. ops., 1964-65, v.p., gen. mgr., 1965-74, pres., 1975-79, chief exec. officer, 1975—, chmn. bd., 1977—; chmn., pres. Anheuser Busch Cos., Inc., St. Louis, 1979—, also bd. dirs.; v.p. Busch Properties, Inc., St. Louis; bd. dirs. St. Louis Nat. Baseball Club, Mfrs. Railway Co., Southwestern Bell Corp., Gen. Am. Life Ins. Co., Emerson Electric Co.; trustee St. Louis Refrigerator Car Co. Mem. adv. bd. St. John Mercy Med. Ctr.; bd. dirs. United Way Greater St. Louis, St. Louis Symphony Soc.; bd. overseers Wharton Sch. U. Pa.; pres. exec. bd. Boy Scouts Am. Clubs: St. Louis, Frontenac Racquet, St. Louis Country, Racquet (St. Louis); Noonday, Log Cabin, Stadium. Office: Anheuser-Busch Cos Inc 1 Busch Pl Saint Louis MO 63118

BUSCH, NOEL HENRY, banker; b. Jordan, Minn., Dec. 9, 1940; s. Albert Meinrad and Hildegarde Sophie (Bauer) B.; m. Bertina Nancy Lee Helgeson, July 9, 1966; children: Maria Renee, Lavinia Christine, Owen Martin, Mark Allen, Amineh Adrienne. BA, U. Minn., 1965. Legis. and bus. devel. counsel various trade assns., 1966-71; chief exec. officer Ind. Bankers Minn., Mpls., 1972-75; prin. organizer, founding dir., chief exec. officer Ind. State Bank Minn., Mpls., 1975-81; chmn. bd. Ind. Bankers Credit Corp., Mpls., 1980-82; pres. Ind. Bancservices Exch., Mpls., 1981-82; founding dir., pres., chief exec. officer, chmn. exec. com. Ind. Bankers Bank Fla., Orlando, 1982—; chmn. Bankers Bank Council; founding dir., pres. Bankers' Bankcorp. of Fla., 1989—; prin. organizer, founding exec. officer bankers bank movement. Named Banker Advocate of Yr. Orlando C. of C., 1985, Fin. Services Advocate of Yr. U.S. Small Bus. Adminstrn., Jacksonville, Fla., 1985. Mem. Ind. Bankers Assn. Am., Fla. Bankers Assn., Community Bankers Fla. Republican.

BUSCHMANN, SIEGFRIED, business executive; b. Essen, Germany, July 12, 1937; s. Walter and Frieda Maria (von Stamm) B.; m. Rita Renate Moch, May 7, 1965; children—Verena, Mark. Diploma, Wilhelms U. Various exec. positions Thyssen AG, Duesseldorf, Fed Republic of Germany, 1964-82; pres. Thyssen Holding Corp., Troy, Mich., 1982—; sr. v.p. Budd Co., Troy, Mich., 1982-83, sr. v.p., chief fin. officer, 1983-86, vice chmn., chief fin. officer, 1986—. Office: Budd Co 3155 W Big Beaver Rd PO Box 2601 Troy MI 48084

BUSFIELD, ROGER MELVIL, JR., trade association executive; b. Ft. Worth, Feb. 4, 1926; s. Roger Melvil and Julia Mabel (Clark) B.; student U. Tex., spring 1943, summer 1946; B.A., Southwestern U., 1947, M.A., 1948; Ph.D., Fla. State U., 1954; m. Jean Wilson, Mar. 26, 1948 (div. Oct. 1960); children—Terry Jean, Roger Melvil III, Timothy Clark; m. Virginia Bailey, Dec. 1, 1962; 1 dau., Julia Lucille. Asst. prof. Southwestern U., 1947-49; instr. U. Ala., 1949-50, Fla. State U., 1950-54; asst. prof. speech Mich. State U., 1954-60; editorial services specialist Oldsmobile div. Gen. Motors Corp., Lansing, Mich., 1960; gen. publs. supr. Consumers Power Co., Jackson, Mich., 1960-61; asso. dir. Mich. Hosp. Assn., Lansing, 1961-73; exec. dir. Ark. Hosp. Assn., Little Rock, 1973-81, pres., 1981—. Trustee, Central Mich. U., 1967-73, chmn., 1970; mem. Mich. Gov.'s Commn. on Higher Edn., 1972-74; mem. Ark. Gov.'s Emergency Med. Services Adv. Council, 1975—, chmn., 1978-84; mem. Ark. Gov.'s Task Force on Rural Hosps., 1988-89, Ark. Dept. of Health Long Range Planning Com., 1988-89. Served with USMC, 1943-46. Named Tex. Outstanding Author, Theta Sigma Phi, 1958; recipient Disting. Alumnus award Southwestern U., 1971; Senate-House Concurrent Resolution of Tribute, Mich. Legis., 1973. Mem. Am. Soc. Assn. Execs., Ark. Soc. Assn. Execs. (pres. 1981-82), Public Relations Assn. Mich. (pres. 1966), Speech Communications Assn., Am. Coll. Health Care Execs., State Hosp. Assn. Exec. Forum (sec., treas. 1989), Am. Hosp. Assn. (council legis. 1975-77, council allied and govtl. relations 1983-86). Methodist. Club: Rotary (Little Rock). Author: The Playwright's Art, 1958, Arabic transl., 1964; (with others) The Children's Theatre, 1960; editor Theatre Arts Bibliography, 1964; contbr. articles to profl. jours.; author profl. motion picture scenarios. Home: 48 Tally Ho Ln Little Rock AR 72207 Office: Ark Hosp Assn 1501 N University Ste 400 Little Rock AR 72207

BUSH, EDWARD CHURCH, stock broker, rancher; b. Beeville, Tex., May 25, 1953; s. Edward Milton and Mary Kathryn (Church) B. BA, Tulane U., 1977. Acct. exec. Legg, Mason, Howard, Weil, New Orleans, 1979—; rancher Atascosa County, Tex., 1957—. Advisor Jr. Achievement, New Orleans, 1980-86, Friends of the Audubon Zoo, New Orleans. Mem. SAR (state treas. 1986—), Soc. Colonial Wars, Soc. War of 1812, Sons of Republic of Tex., Sons of the Revolution, San Antonio Club, New Orleans Country Club, Round Table, New Orleans Essex Club, Washington Army and Navy Club, Blue Key Phi Alpha Theta, Kappa Alpha Order. Republican. Presbyterian. Home: 2801 St Charles Ave Apt #K New Orleans LA 70115 Office: Howard Weil LaBouisse Friedrichs 1100 Poydras St Ste 900 New Orleans LA 70163

BUSH, EDWIN FRANKLIN, JR., lawyer; b. Hartford City, Ind., July 30, 1944; s. Edwin Franklin and Estella Marie (Burklo) B.; children: Edwin F. III, Susan Marie. BS, Ball State U., 1966; JD, Ind. U., Indpls., 1972. Bar: Wis. 1973, Ind. 1973, U.S. Dist. Ct. (so. dist.) Ind. 1973, U.S. Dist. Ct. (ea. and we. dist.) Wis. 1973. Law clk. to presiding justice Ind. Supreme Ct., Indpls., 1972-73; assoc. Gibbs, Roper, Loots & Williams, Milw., 1973-78; legal counsel Johnson Controls Inc., Milw., 1978-80; sr. legal counsel Appleton (Wis.) Papers Inc., 1980-86, asst. gen. counsel, asst. sec., 1986—. Chmn. Parking Transit Commn., Appleton, 1982-87; bd. dirs. Friends Mosquito Hill Nature Ctr., Appleton, 1980-84. Mem. ABA, Wis. Bar Assn., Outagamie County BAr Assn., Am. Corp. Counsel Assn. Home: 1504 N Nicholas Appleton WI 54914 Office: Appleton Papers Inc PO Box 359 Appleton WI 54912

BUSH, HOWARD JAMES, marketing professional; b. Clifton Springs, N.Y., Apr. 3, 1953; s. Sanford Clark and Marie (Brockhuizen) B.; m. Paula Lorraine Packard, , June 7, 1975; children: James, Jeffrey. BS, U.S. Mil. Acad., 1975; MBA, Harvard U., 1982. Ops. mgr. AT&T Long Lines, Boston, 1981; strategic planning analyst Seaboard Systems Railroad, Jacksonville, Fla., 1982-83; dir. mktg. Seaboard Systems Railroad, Jacksonville, 1983-86; asst. v.p. mktg. CSX Transp., Balt., 1986-88; asst. v.p. network devel. CSX Transp., Jacksonville, Fla., 1988—; Superintendant Cliftondale Meth. Ch., Saugus, Mass., 1981; coach, Jacksonville Youth Soccer, Jacksonville, 1984-85, Lutherville, Timonium (Md.) Recreation, 1987. Served to capt. U.S. Army, 1975-80. Recipient Outstanding Man of the Year award Jaycees, 1981. Mem. Transp. Club. Republican. Home: 8429 Papelon Way Jacksonville FL 32217 Office: CSX Transp 500 Water St Jacksonville FL 32202

BUSH, JACK EUGENE, retail executive; b. Skidmore, Mo., Oct. 10, 1934; s. Harold Travis Bush and Aletha Virginia (Case) Quinn; m. Mary June Birbeck, June 28, 1953; children: Paula Annette, Tracy Lynn. Student, Air Force Inst., 1953-58; BS, U. Mo., 1958. Owner Bush Seed Co., King City, Mo., 1953-56; various mgmt. and exec. positions J.C. Penney Co., N.Y.C., 1958-80; v.p. Zayre Corp., Framingham, Mass., 1980-85; v.p. Roses Stores, Henderson, N.C., 1985-86, sr. v.p., 1986, pres., chief operating officer, 1986—, also bd. dirs. Bd. dirs. YMCA, Henderson, 1986-88. Served to capt. USAF, 1953-58. Named Hon. Citizen, City of Memphis, 1982, State of Tenn., 1980, Hon. State Trooper, State of Ga., 1980, Lt. Col., Gov.'s Staff State of Ga., 1981; named to Hon. Order Ky. Cols. Mem. Internat. Mass Retailers Assn., Am. Mgmt. Assn., Nat. Retail Mgmt. Inst., Pres.'s. Assn., Beta Gamma Sigma. Republican. Club: Henderson Country, Ky. Cols. Home: 3101 Cameron Dr Henderson NC 27536 Office: Rose's Stores Inc PO Box 947 Henderson NC 27536

BUSH, PAUL STANLEY, furniture company executive; b. Olean, N.Y., May 5, 1936; s. Stanley and Sophia Bush; m. Debbie Bush, July 29, 1972. BME, Rensselaer Poly. Inst., 1957. Applications engr. Clark Bros. div. Dresser Clark, Olean, 1957-58; sales mgr. Bush Bros. Products, Inc., Little Valley, N.Y., 1959-61; v.p., treas. Bush Bros. Products, Inc., Little Valley, 1961-71; pres., chief exec. officer Bush Industries, Inc., Little Valley, 1971-86, Jamestown, N.Y., 1986—. Patentee shelf position holding device, also containers. Bd. dirs. Chautauqua County chpt. ARC. Recipient Bus. Citizenship award Western N.Y. Assn. Youth Burs. and Bds., 1987; named Outstanding Exec. of Yr., Secs. Assn. Jamestown, 1987. Mem. Mfrs. Assn. Jamestown Area, Indsl. Mgmt. Club (award of excellence 1987), Young Pres. Orgn., Am. Mgmt. Assn., World Bus. Council, Pres. Assn., Elkdale Country Club (pres.), Moonbrook Country Club. Home: 35 W Lake St Lakewood NY 14750 Office: Bush Industries Inc 1 Mason Dr Jamestown NY 14701

BUSHRE, PETER ALVIN, financial executive; b. Ketchikan, Alaska, Dec. 14, 1943; s. Robert Almon and Violet Orene (Neal) B. BS, U. Ariz., 1967, MA in Acctg., 1971. Staff auditor Peat Marwick Mitchell & Co., Honolulu, 1971-72; sr. auditor Touche Ross & Co., Anchorage, 1972-73; sr. legis. auditor State of Alaska, Juneau, 1973-76, comptroller, 1976-78, treas., 1978-83; comptroller Alaska Permanent Fund Corp., Juneau, 1983—; pres. Bushre Trading and Investment Co., Douglas, Alaska, 1980—. Republican. Baptist. Home: PO Box 28 Douglas AK 99824

BUSKIRK, PHYLLIS RICHARDSON, economist; b. Queens, N.Y., July 19, 1930; d. William Edward and Amy A. Richardson; m. Allen V. Buskirk, Sept. 13, 1950; children: Leslie Ann, William Allen, Carol Amy, Janet Helen. AB cum laude, William Smith Coll., 1951. Rsch. asst. W.E. Upjohn Inst. for Employment Rsch., Kalamazoo, 1970-75, rsch. assoc., 1976-83, sr. staff economist, 1983-87. Co-editor Bus. Conditions in the Kalamazoo Area, Quar. Rev., 1979-84, asst. editor Bus. Outlook for West Mich., 1984-87. Mem. Civil Svc. Bd. City of Kalamazoo, 1977—, chmn., 1981—; trustee First Presbyn. Ch., Kalamazoo, 1984-87, chmn., 1985, 86, mgr. adminstrn. and fin., 1987—; trustee Sr. Citizens Fund, Kalamazoo, 1984—, corp. restructuring com. 1985-86. exec. bd. 1986-88; bd. dirs. Heritage Community Kalamazoo, 1988—; pres., bd. dirs. Westland Meadows, 1988—. Mem. Indsl. Rels. Rsch. Assn., Nat. Assn. Ch. Bus. Adminstrn., Presbyn. Ch. Bus. Adminstrn. Assn. Clubs: P.E.O., Kalamazoo Network. Office: 321 W South St Kalamazoo MI 49007

BUSKUHL, CARL THOMAS, financial analyst; b. Brisbane, Australia, July 27, 1952; s. Paul E. and Joyce Marie (Clarke) B.; m. Gayle Hoxie, May 24, 1980; children: Travis Lloyd, Curtis Paul. BA in Fin., U. Puget Sound, 1977. Fin cons., account exec. Merrill Lynch, La Jolla, Calif., 1977-82; v.p. Detwiler, Ryan and Co., San Diego, Calif., 1982-84; investment assoc. Jensen Securities, Portland, Ore., 1984-85; fin. analyst U.S. Dept. Energy BPA, Portland, 1985-88, Sacramento (Calif.) Mcpl. Utility Dist., 1988—. With USMC, 1970-72. Mem. Assn. Gov. Accts., Masons, Sigma Nu. Republican. Methodist. Office: 6201 S St PO Box 15830 Sacramento CA 95852-1830

BUSSE, LEONARD WAYNE, banker; b. Chgo., June 29, 1938; s. Edwald William and Elsie Helen (Weidner) B.; m. Gretchen Gnuam Beal, Sept. 7, 1963; children—Whitney Lee, Carter Douglas. B.S., Purdue U., 1960; postgrad., Northwestern U., 1964-67. C.P.A. With Continental Ill. Corp., Chgo., 1963—, v.p., 1973-81, sr. v.p., 1981—, controller, 1984—, head internat. banking dept., 1985; exec. v.p. Continental Bank, Chgo., 1985-89; assoc. Alfred Checchi Assocs., L.A., 1989—. Bd. dirs., treas. McGraw Wildlife Found., Elgin, Ill., 1982—. Mem. Robert Morris Assn., Am. Inst. C.P.A.s. Republican. Lutheran. Club: Chicago.

BUSSELL, GLENDA FOWLER, mental health director; b. Louisville, Jan. 4, 1934; d. James Boxley and Clara Theresa (Ryan) Fowler; m. Harold Dean Bussell, Aug. 16, 1963 (div. 1973); 1 child, Scott Fowler. BA, Western Ky. U., 1955; MSW, U. Louisville, 1965. Asst. prof. social work Ohio State U., Columbus, 1970-74, adj. lectr., 1978-79; exec. dir. N. Cen. Mental Health Svcs., Columbus, 1974—; bd. dirs. Mental Health Corps. Am. Enterprises Inc., Tallahassee, Fla. Bd. dirs. Cen. Ohio Adolescent Ctr., Columbus, 1979, YWCA, 1979-81, Columbus Area Internat. Program, 1983-85. Mem. Nat. Assn. Social Workers (sec. 1980-81), Assn. Mental Health Adminstrs., Acad. Cert. Social Workers, Met. Columbus Club, Phi Kappa Phi. Democrat. Office: N Cen Mental Health Svcs 1301 N High St Columbus OH 43201

BUSTEED, BEATRICE, financial planner; b. L.A., Jan. 8, 1938; d. Ignacio and Clemencia (Armijo) Val Verde; m. Donald J. Busteed, Jan. 23, 1982. AA, Trade Tech. Jr. Coll., 1975; BA, Calif. State U., L.A., 1974; MBA, Pepperdine U., 1983. Pvt. sec., bookkeeper E.S. Dulin, L.A., 1962-72, Neil Petree, 1968-73; sec., paralegal O'Melveny & Myers, 1973-86, personal fin. mgr., 1980—; rep. Fin. Network Investment Corp., 1984—. Rockwell Internat. fellow Pepperdine U., 1982. Mem. Internat. Assn. for Fin. Planning, Inst. Cert. Fin. Planners, Nat. Notary Assn., Mensa (bd. dirs. greater L.A. area 1975-78), Phi Kappa Phi. Republican. Roman Catholic. Home: 5530 Thornburn St #204 Los Angeles CA 90045 Office: 3250 Wilshire Blvd Ste 900 Los Angeles CA 90010

BUSTER, WILLIAM FRANK, business equipment manufacturing company executive; b. Oak Creek, Colo., Nov. 20, 1927; s. Frank Lafayette and Francis (Lamb) B.; m. Evelyn Marie Johnson, Sept. 15, 1951; children—Barbara Anne, Patricia Johanna. B.S.E.E., Milw. Sch. Engring., 1953. With NCR Corp., 1971—, gen. mgr., San Diego, 1974-76, v.p., 1976-77, v.p., Dayton, Ohio, 1977-80, sr. v.p., 1980-83, exec. v.p., 1983—; Served with USAF, 1946-49. Office: NCR Corp 1700 S Patterson Blvd Dayton OH 45479

BUTCHER, HOWARD, III, investment banker; b. Ardmore, Pa., Jan. 28, 1902; s. Howard Jr. and Margaret (Keen) B.; m. Elizabeth Crosswell McBee Jan.8, 1936 (dec. Oct. 1972); children: Howard IV, McBee, Jonathan; m. Elizabeth Shryock, June 1973. BA, U. Pa., 1923, LLD (hon.), 1967; PhD in Civil Law (hon.), St. Joseph's Coll., 1968; LLD (hon.), PMC Colls., 1969. Cert. investment banker. Sr. ptnr. Butcher and Sherrerd, Phila., 1948-68; chmn. emeritus Butcher and Singer Inc., Phila., 1968—. Office: Butcher and Singer Inc 1500 Walnut St Philadelphia PA 19102

BUTCHKO, ROBERT EDWARD, manufacturing company executive; b. Jan. 7, 1946; s. Edward John and Irene (Waskiewicz) B.; m. Janice Fetchko, June 14, 1969 (div. Nov. 1984); children: Robert Andrew, Jennifer Ann. BSME, N.J. Inst. Tech., Newark, 1979. Mgr., plant and mfg. engr. Pyralarm, Inc., Dublin, Ga., 1975-78; mgr. facilities planning Pyrotronics Div. Baker Industries, Cedar Knolls, N.J., 1978-79; mgmt., energy cons. Engrs., Inc., Newark, 1980-81; mgr. automation implementation ADT, Inc., N.Y.C., 1981-84, mgr. spl. service programs, 1984-85; mgr. direct and retail mktg. ADT, Inc., Parsippany, N.J., 1986-87; mgr. mfg. engring. ADT, Inc., Clifton, N.J., 1987—. Adv. bd. Factory mag., Chgo., 1974-75; bd. dirs. Dublin Civic Theater, Dublin, Ga., 1977; troop bd. mem. Stanhope chpt. Boy Scouts Am., Stanhope, N.J., 1983-84; bd. mem., v.p. Lenape Valley High Sch. Band, Stanhope, 1985-86. 2d class petty officer USN, 1967-69, Vietnam. Mem. SME/EM, SMTA. Democrat. Roman Catholic. Lodge: KC. Home: 58 Lynne Dr Andover NJ 07821

BUTERBAUGH, ARTHUR DALE, trust company executive; b. Pitts., Mar. 18, 1948; s. Charles Murray and Ida Mae (Matson) B.; m. Darlene Ruth Heinlein, Nov. 25, 1971; children: Ivy, Charles. MBA, Gannon U., 1980. Programmer, analyst Wheeling (W.Va.) Dollar Bank, 1970-72; v.p. info. tech. Marine Bank, Erie, Pa., 1972-80; v.p., mgr. info. systems Corestates Banking, Phila., 1980-84; sr. v.p. systems and communications Mfrs. and Traders Trust Co., Buffalo, 1984—; chief oper. officer First Ops. Resource, Inc. subs. Mfrs. and Traders Trust Co., Swedesboro, N.J., 1986—. Vol. corp. leadership United Way, Buffalo, 1986; bd. dirs. Manheim (Pa.) Cen. Schs., 1984-85. With U.S. Army, 1968-70. Mem. Masons. Republican. Methodist. Office: First Ops Resource Inc Beckett & Center Square Rds Swedesboro NJ 07085

BUTKI, ARNOLD, engineering company executive, educator; b. Detroit, Apr. 25, 1935; s. Julius Joseph and Clara Tillie (Sadowski) B.; B.S., U. Mich., 1960; M.B.A., Claremont Grad. Sch., 1968; m. Joanne Ruth Schumacher, July 22, 1961; children—Jay Michael, Ellen Kay, Scott Andrew. With Kaiser Steel Corp., Fontana, Calif., 1960—, supr. indsl. engring., 1968-70, div. indsl. engr., 1970—, div. supr. operating practices, 1976-78, asst. supt., 1979-83; chief proposal engr. Hunter Engring., Riverside, Calif., 1985-86; chief project engr. Cherry Textron Corp., Santa Ana, Calif., 1986—; asst. prof. mgmt. Calif. State U., Los Angeles, 1968—; asst. prof. engring. Calif. State Poly. U., Pomona, 1984—. Bd. dirs. YMCA Trail Blazers, 1976-80, dir., chief, 1968-71, 73-76; treas. Loma Linda Lopers, 1980—, Riverside Runners, 1981—, Jr. Achievement, 1986—. Served with U.S. Army, 1954-56. Registered profl. engr.; cert. plant engr. Mem. Am. Iron and Steel Engrs., Am. Inst. Indsl. Engrs. (pres. 1984-85), Iron and Steel Soc. AIME, Nat. Soc. Profl. Engrs., Calif. Profl. Engrs., Claremont Grad. Sch. Alumni Assn. (fin. v.p. council 1969-73, pres. 1974-76). Republican. Contbr. articles to profl. jours. Home: 2180 Buckskin Pl Riverside CA 92506 Office: 1224 E Warner Ave Santa Ana CA 92707-0157

BUTLER, DENNIS EUGENE, chamber of commerce executive; b. Lenox, Iowa, Feb. 9, 1940; s. Elliott Arthur and Elizabeth Eleanor (DeVoe) B.; m. Jean Marie Thorstenson, Aug. 8, 1981; children: Melissa, Sarah. BA, U. Mo., 1962; postgrad., U. Iowa, 1966-67, U. Nebr., Omaha, 1968-75, Iowa State U., 1975, Institutes for Orgnl. Mgmt., Boulder, Colo., 1979-84. Cert. Tchr. Iowa. Tchr. Council Bluffs Pub. Schs., Iowa, 1969-75; salesman life ins. Bankers Life of Iowa, Omaha, 1975-77; exec. v.p. Harlan C. of C., Iowa, 1977-79; exec. v.p., dir. econ. devel. Fergus Falls Area C. of C., Minn., 1979-81; exec. v.p. Williston C. of C., N.D., 1981-85, Devel. Corp. Ottumwa (Iowa) Area C. of C., 1985-87; life ins. salesman, fin. planner Beaty & Assocs., Ottumwa, 1987-88; pres., chief exec. officer Campbell County C. of C., Gillette, Wyo., 1988—; cons. Iowa Energy Policy Council, 1973, Community Vision, 1988—. Co-author: Instructional Manual in Environmental Problems, 1971. State rep. Iowa Gen. Assembly, 1973-74; mem. pub. relations com. Upper Mo. Valley Fair, Williston, 1982-83; vice chmn. Mont.-Dakota Utilities Adv. Com., Williston, 1983-84; area coordinator N.D. Transp. Week, 1983, 84; co-chmn. Williston Clean-Up Days, 1983-84; bd. dirs. Williams County Hist. Soc., Williston, 1984-85; sec. Hwy. 2 Assn., N.D., 1984. Served to lt. USN, 1962-66. Mem. Am. C. of C. Execs., Indsl. Devel. Assn. of N.d., N.D. co of C. Execs. (pres. 1982-83). Republican. Lodge: Kiwanis (bd. dirs. 1975-76, 78-79), Elks, Eagles. Home: PO Box 1461 Gillette WY 82717 Office: Beaty & Assocs 118 W 3d St Ottumwa IA 52501

BUTLER, GEORGE ANDREWS, banker; b. Westmont, N.J., Apr. 14, 1928; s. John T. and Kathryn B.; m. Barbara J. Thomas, June 17, 1950; children—Lynn B., William E. Thomas S., Pamela S. B.S. in Econs, U. Pa., 1950. With First Pa. Banking and Trust Co., 1950—, exec. v.p., 1968—, chief adminstrv. officer, 1976—; exec. v.p. First Pa. Corp., 1973-74, vice chmn., 1975—; also dir.; vice chmn., dir. First Pa. Bank, pres., chief operating officer, 1977—; chmn., pres., chief exec. officer First Pa. Corp., 1979—; dir. Gen. Accident Group Cos. Bd. dirs. Peirce Phelps. Served with AUS, 1946-47. Clubs: Union League, Mfrs. Golf and Country (Phila.). Home: Philadelphia PA Office: First Pa Bank PO Box 7558 Philadelphia PA 19101-7558

BUTLER, JAMES HENRY, chemical company executive; b. Grayling, Mich., Oct. 27, 1931; Arrived in Can., 1986.; m. Marriel Harriet Childs, Dec. 25, 1951; children: Sherry, Janet, Linda, Alan. BS in Chem. Engring., Mich. Technol. U., 1955; MBA, Cen. Mich. U., 1965. With Dow Chem. Co., Midland, Mich., 1955; various mgmt. assignments plastics mfg. Midland, 1960-72; pres. Rexene Polymers Co. subs. Dart Industries, Paramus, N.J., 1972-76; pres. div. Styro Products Co. subs. Dart Industries, Phoenix, 1976-77; v.p. Mobil Petrochems., N.Y.C., 1977-86; chmn., chief exec. officer Novacor Chems. Ltd., Calgary, Alta., Can., 1986—, Alta. Gas Ethylene Co. Ltd., Calgary, 1986—; pres. NOVA Corp. Alta., Calgary, 1988—; pres., chief exec. officer Polysar Ltd., Calgary, 1988—; holder of various exec. positions and directorships within Nova Group. With USAF, 1956-60. Office: Nova Corp Alta, 801 7th Ave SW, Calgary, AB Canada T2P 2N6

BUTLER, JAMES ROBERTSON, JR., lawyer; b. Cleve., May 29, 1946; s. James Robertson and Iris Davis (Welborn) B.; m. Laurie Jean Smith, June 26, 1979; 1 child, Brandy Valentine. AB magna cum laude, U. Calif., Berkeley, 1966, JD, 1969. Bar: Calif. 1970, U.S. Tax Ct. 1977, U.S. Supreme Ct. 1980. Sr. corp. and securities ptnr., chmn. Fin. Instns. Dept. Jeffer, Mangels , Butler & Marmaro, Los Angeles and San Francisco; speaker and panelist Robert Morris Assocs. Nat. Conf., Chgo., 1988; frequent TV appearances as expert on securities, real estate and banking, 1985-88. Author: Arbitration in Banking, A Robert Morris Associates State of the Art Book, 1988, Lending Liability: A Practical Guide, A BNA Special Report, 1987; editor Banking Law Report Capital Adequacy series, 1985, Calif. Law Rev.; co-chmn. adv. council Money and Real Estate: The Jour. of Lending, Syndication, Joint Ventures, and the Third Market; contbr. chpt., Mapping the

Minefield--Lender's Liability to book, The Workout Game, Solutions to Problem Real Estate Loans, 1987; contbr. articles to profl. jours. Mem. Am. Arbitration Assn., Comml. Arbitration Panel; founding dir. Liberty Nat. Bank; Charter Adv. bd. dirs., Adv. Council of the Banking Law Inst. Recipient Kraft Prize U. Calif., 1966; Bartley Cavenaugh Crum scholar U. Calif. Sch. Law, 1969. Mem. ABA (corp., banking and bus. law sect., taxation sect.), Los Angeles County Bar Assn., Beverly Hills Bar Assn., Calif. League of Savs. Instns. (chmn. arbitration com. 1987, 88), Order of Coif, Phi Beta Kappa, Pi Sigma Alpha. Office: Jeffer Mangels & Butler 2121 Ave of the Stars Los Angeles CA 90067 also: One Sansome St 12th Fl San Francisco CA 94104

BUTLER, JESSE LEE, banking consultant; b. Greenwood, S.C., Apr. 21, 1953; m. Jannie Connor, June 2, 1984; children: Christian Jarad, Garrison Jay. BA, Lander Coll., 1977; MA, Howard U., 1982. Bank examiner Fed. Res. Bank N.Y., N.Y.C., 1980-85; compliance audit officer, cons. First Fidelity Bancorp, Newark, 1985—; cons., instr. Am. Inst. Banking, Bloomfield, N.J., mem. speaker network; instr. N.J. Bank Audit Group, Bank Adminstrn. Inst. Grantee, Merrill Found., 1977. Mem. N.J. Bankers Assn., Am. Mgmt. Assn., North Jersey Compliance Officers Assn., Joint Ctr. Polit. Studies, Lander Coll. Alumni Assn., Howard U. Alumni Assn., Omega Psi Phi. Democrat. Baptist. Home: 20 Constantine Place Summit NJ 07901 Office: First Fidelity Bancorp 151 Centennial Ave PO Box 1351 Piscataway NJ 08855

BUTLER, JOHN MUSGRAVE, transportation company executive; b. Bklyn., Dec. 6, 1928; s. John Joseph and Sabina Catherine (Musgrave) B.; m. Ann Elizabeth Kelly, July 9, 1955; children: Maureen, John, Ellen, Suzanne. BA cum laude, St. John's U., 1950; MBA, NYU, 1951. CPA, N.Y. Sr. acct. Lybrand, Ross Bros. & Montgomery (CPAs), N.Y.C., 1953-59; sr. auditor ITT Corp., N.Y.C., 1959-62; asst. to controller Dictaphone Corp., Bridgeport, Conn., 1962-63; controller Dictaphone Corp., Bridgeport, Rye, N.Y., 1964-68; v.p. acctg. Chgo. & North Western Ry. Co., Chgo., 1968-69; v.p. fin. and acctg. Chgo. & North Western Ry. Co., 1969-72, Chgo. and North Western Transp. Co., Chgo., 1972-79; sr. v.p. fin. and acctg. Chgo. and North Western Transp. Co., 1979—, dir., 1976—, trustee, 1978-82; sr. v.p. fin. and acctg., dir. CNW Corp., 1985—. Served with USCGR, 1951-53. Mem. Assn. Am. R.R.s, Am. Inst. CPAs, Fin. Execs. Inst. Roman Catholic. Office: Chgo & N Western Transp Co 1 North Western Ctr Chicago IL 60606

BUTLER, JOHN PAUL, sales professional; b. Lexington, S.C., Sept. 6, 1935; s. Albert G. and Alma J. (Braswell) B.; m. Clare Vestal, Nov. 8, 1958 (div. 1978); children—Cathy, Tom, Frank. B.S.M.E. (NROTC scholar), U. S.C., 1957; M.B.A., U. Conn., 1965. Sr. engr. Pratt & Whitney Aircraft, East Hartford, Conn., 1960-65; engring. supr. Westinghouse Electric Corp., Pitts., 1966-70, mktg. supr., 1971-76; dir. sales and mktg. Morgan div. Amca, Alliance, Ohio, 1977-78; sales dir. Mid-East, Westinghouse Electric Corp., Orlando, Fla., 1979-84; pres. Butler Assocs., Orlando, 1984-86; mgr. Tandy Corp., Ft. Lauderdale, Fla., 1987—. Republican committeeman. Served to lt., USN, 1957-60. Mem. ASME. Methodist. Contbr. articles to profl. jours.; patentee in field. Home: 733 Riverside Dr Coral Springs FL 33071 Office: Tandy Corp 4368 N Federal Hwy Fort Lauderdale FL 33308

BUTLER, LESLIE RICHARD, banker; b. Camden, N.J., Mar. 21, 1940; s. Charles Harvey and Anne W. (Smith) B.; m. Geraldine Tepper, Aug. 8, 1981; children: Charles H., Lynda E. BA, Susquehanna U., 1962; postgrad., U. Va., 1963; MBA, Drexel U., 1970. Vice chmn., chief adminstrv. officer First Pa. Bank, NA, Phila., 1963—. Bd. dirs. First Pa. Bank, N.A., Susquehanna U., Opera Co. Phila.; ch. council St. James Luth. Ch., Pitman, N.J.; pres., mem. Pitman Bd. Edn., 1968-70. Mem. Phila. Clearing House Assn. (pres. 1987), Consumer Bankers Assn. (pres. 1978). Home: RR 3 PO Box 29 Sewell NJ 08080 Office: First Pa Bank 16th & Market Sts PO Box 7558 Philadelphia PA 19101

BUTLER, ROBERT LEONARD, sales executive; b. West Warwick, R.I., Aug. 8, 1931; s. Leonard Thomas and Henrietta Marie (Theroux) B.; m. Rosemarie Ann D'Ambra, Nov. 5, 1955; children: Robert Arthur, David Paul. MS in Fin. Services, Am. Coll., 1982, MS in Mgmt., 1985. Chartered fin. cons., CLU. With sales and dept. mgmt. Sears Roebuck & Co., Worcester, Mass., 1956-67; dir. investment, prodn., sales State Mut. Am., Worcester, 1976-86; asst. sec. SMA Life Assurance Co., Worcester, 1974-86; v.p. SMA Equities Inc., Worcester, 1976-86; sr. v.p. sales Phoenix Equity Planning Corp., Hartford, Conn., 1986—; speaker, workshop leader conf. Life Office Mgmt. Assn. Contbr. articles to ins. mags. Mem. Am. Soc. Life Underwriters, Internat. Assn. Fin. Planners, Ins. Affiliated Broker-Dealer Forum (chmn. 1978-81), Nat. Assn. Securities Dealers (dist. bus. conduct com.). Roman Catholic. Lodge: KC. Office: Phoenix Equity Planning Corp 100 Brights Meadow Blvd Enfield CT 06082-1989

BUTRIE, ANNA MARIE, hospital administrator; b. Palmerton, Pa., Oct. 23, 1956; d. Michael and Anna (Polivka) B. BS in Nursing, U. Pa., 1978; MS in Nursing, Columbia U., 1984, MPH, 1985. Cert. child and adolescent nurse, critical care nurse. Staff nurse Children's Hosp. of Phila., 1979-82, nursing supr., 1984-85; lectr., clin. instr. U. Pa., Phila., 1985; adminstrv. resident Hosp. of U. Pa., Phila., 1984-85, dir. preadmission testing program, 1985-86, sr. program dir., 1986-88; corp. mgr. quality assurance Universal Health Services, King of Prussia, Pa., 1988—; chmn. Louise Mellen Grad. Fellowship, 1985-87; PRO contact person U. Pa. Hosp., Phila.; member Blue Cross Short Procedure Unit Subcom., 1987-88. Instr. basic life support Am. Heart Assn., Phila., 1978—. Louise Mellen Grad. fellow in critical care nursing, 1982-84; Hattie M. Strong Found. scholar, 1983. Mem. Am. Coll. Health Care Execs., Am. Mgmt. Assn., Am. Pub. Health Assn., Am. Med. Peer Rev. Assn. (cert.), Hosp. Fin. Mgmt. Assn., Sigma Theta Tau. Home: 1000 Greystone Ln Newark DE 19711

BUTTERFIELD, BRUCE SCOTT, publishing company executive; b. N.Y.C., Feb. 4, 1949; s. Richard Julian and Mary (Hart) B.; m. Karin Lynn Wittlinger, June 20, 1986; 1 child, Elizabeth Holly. B.A. cum laude, Amherst Coll., 1971; M.A., Harvard U., 1972; M.B.A., U. Conn., 1977; advanced cert. in journalism and creative fiction, Newspaper Inst. Am, 1981. Adminstrv. asst. Golden Press div. Western Pub. Co., N.Y.C., 1972; editor, coordinator Golden Press div. Western Pub. Co., 1973-74, sr. editor, 1975-76, mng. editor, adminstr., 1977; gen. mgr. Decisions Publs., 1978; assoc. pub. Scholastic Inc., N.Y.C., 1979-80, v.p., pub., 1981-83; exec. v.p. Longman Inc., N.Y.C., 1984; pres. Longman Inc., 1985—, also bd. dirs.; officer Addison-Wesley/Longman Holdings Pub. Group Ltd.; bd. dirs. Pitman Pub. Inc., Longman Inc., Ind. Sch. Press, Angel Entertainment Inc. Author: Fantasy and the Free School Thought: E.B. White and His Literature for Children, 1971; A Plea for Fantasy, 1972; Our Real Work Can't Be Drudgery, 1979; editor various books including: ABC's Wide World of Sports, 1975; Buccaneers, 1975; Book of the Mysterious, 1976; Chroma-Schema, 1977; Calculator Games, 1977; Children's Bible Stories, 1978; Oh Heavenly Dog, 1980; The Watcher in the Woods, 1980. Named Most Valuable Pitcher, Bergen Highlanders, 1969, All New Eng. Amateur Baseball Pitcher, 1971, All Am. Amateur Baseball Pitcher, 1971; recipient Wall St. Jour. Achievement award, 1968; Nat. Fedn. Music award, 1963; J.F. Kennedy Brotherhood Essay award, 1967; Gardener Fletcher fellow, 1972; St. Clair Meml. fellow 1972; Amherst Coll. fellow, 1972. Mem. Am. Acad. Arts and Scis., Am. Acad. Polit. and Social Scis., Assn. Am. Pubs., Children's Book Council, M.B.A. Execs., Internat. Platform Assn., Beta Gamma Sigma, Phi Delta Kappa, Phi Delta Sigma. Republican. Christian Scientist. Clubs: Forum, Harvard (N.Y.C.). Home: 189 Parish Rd S New Canaan CT 06840 Office: Longman Inc Longman Bldg 95 Ch St White Plains NY 10601

BUTTERFIELD, CRAIG WILLS, engineer, contractor; b. Middlebury, Vt., Apr. 24, 1933; s. Darrell Douglas and Helen (Mudgett) B.; m. Elaine Nancy Peduzzi, Apr. 7, 1972; children: Dawn, Douglas. BCE, Norwich U., 1955. Registered profl. engr., Vt. Owner, mgr. Engring., Inc. of Vt., Burlington, Vt., 1958-75, Superior Asphalt, Inc., Mt. Dora, Fla., 1975—; bd. dirs. So. Bank, Mt. Dora, River Gem; mem. Lake County (Fla.) Home Bldg. Assn., 1980—. Pres. Ocean Beach II Homeowners Assn., 1985—; selectman Town Govt., Colchester, Vt., 1970. Served to capt. U.S. Army, 1956-58. Mem. Vt. Soc. Engrs., Vt. Soc. Surveyors. Republican. Baptist. Home: 1700 Buena Vista Rd Eustis FL 32726

BUTTERFIELD, DAVID HOMER, financial services company executive; b. East St. Louis, Ill., June 12, 1938; s. Homer James and Lois (Vancil) B.; m. Lois Mary Israelian, Jan. 31, 1960; children: L. Mindi, Lisa M. BS in Indsl. Mgmt., MIT, 1960; MBA, Washington U., St. Louis, 1962. Various positions IBM, New Eng., Mass., 1964-73; dir. systems Gillette Co., Boston, 1973-80; sr. dir. Prime Computer, Natick, Mass., 1980-82; pres., mng. dir. Fidelity Systems, Boston, 1982-84; exec. v.p. HCW, Inc., Boston, 1984-86; chmn., pres., chief exec. officer Internat. Heritage Corp., Boston, 1986—. 1st ltd. U.S. Army, 1962-64. Office: Internat Heritage Corp 101 Summer St Boston MA 02110

BUTTERMORE, BRADLEY SCOTT, financial executive; b. Detroit, Feb. 19, 1956; s. Joseph Carlisle and Betty Jeanette B.; m. Debra L. Aitchison, Feb. 13, 1989. BBA, Wayne State U., 1982. Various positions C.I.T. Fin. Services, Southeast, Mich., 1974-77; dealer specialist, credit analyst Chrysler Corp., Highland Park, Mich., 1977-80; div. comptroller, asst. v.p. Advance Mortgage Corp., Southfield, Mich., 1980-83; mgr. external reporting, v.p. fin. control Lomas & Nettleton Fin. Corp., Dallas, 1983-88; chief fin. officer Lomas Mgmt. Corp., Dallas, 1989—; mem. task force to strengthen automobile network through fin. mgmt. assistance during Chrysler Corp.'s return to profitability, 1978-79; developed, implemented fin. reporting package enabling systematic collection of fin. data from subs. of 6 billion dollar fin. services co. Mem. Am. Mgmt. Assn., Nat. Assn. Accts. Republican. Lutheran. Clubs: Exchange Athletic, 2001 (Dallas). Office: Lomas & Nettleton Fin Corp 2001 Bryan Tower Dallas TX 75201

BUTTLER, PETER HAVILAND, manufacturing executive; b. New Brunswick, N.J., Nov. 9, 1942; s. George Harold and Margaret Victoria (Peterson) B.; m. Irene Groteloh, Apr. 4, 1969; children: Jennifer, Kirsten. BSME, Carnegie Inst. Tech., 1964; MBA in Fin., U. Pitts., 1967; grad., Quality Coll., 1981. Project engr. Allied Chem. Corp., Moundsville, W.Va., 1964-66; asst. controller, fin. analyst Celanese Corp., N.Y.C., 1967-74, dir. mktg. strategies, 1974-75; venture mgr. Celanese Coatings & Specialties Co., N.Y.C., 1975-77; dir. strategic planning Celanese Corp., N.Y.C., 1977—; v.p. planning Celanese Polymer Specialties Co., Louisville, 1978-79; v.p. planning and bus. devel. Celanese Plastics & Specialty Co., Chatham, N.J., 1979-83; v.p. corp. devel. Bird, Inc., East Walpole, Mass., 1983-87; sr. v.p. fin. and adminstrn. Bird Machine Co., Inc., South Walpole, Mass., 1987—. Active Hemlock Farms Community Assn., Lords Valley, Pa. Republican. Home: 98 Pine St Medfield MA 02052 Office: Bird Machine Co Inc 100 Neponset St South Walpole MA 02071

BUTTREY, DONALD WAYNE, lawyer; b. Terre Haute, Ind., Feb. 6, 1935; s. William Edgar and Nellie Madaline (Vaughn) B.; children: Greg, Alan, Jason; m. Karren Lake, Mar. 23, 1985. B.S., Ind. State U., 1956; J.D., Ind. U., 1961. Bar: Ind. 1961. Law clk. to chief judge U.S. Dist. Ct. So. Dist. Ind., 1961-63; assoc. McHale, Cook & Welch, P.C., Indpls., 1963—, pres., 1986—; chmn. Cen. Region IRS-Bar Liaison Com., 1983-84. Editor Ind. Law Jour., 1960-61. Pres. Indpls. Athlectic Club Arts Found., 1987-89; chmn. Marion County Dem.Fin. Com., 1984-86. Served with AUS, 1956-58, Korea. Mem. ABA (taxation, real property, probate, trust sects.), Ind. Bar Assn. (chmn. taxation sect. 1982-83), Indpls. Bar Assn. (pres. elect 1989), 7th Cir. Bar Assn., Ind. Soc. Chgo., Highland Golf and Country Club, Columbia Club, Indpls. Athletic Club (bd. dirs. 1982-83), Phi Delta Phi, Theta Chi. Presbyterian. Office: McHale Cook & Welch PC 1100 C of C Bldg 320 N Meridian St Indianapolis IN 46204

BUTTROS, PETER ANTHONY, computer communications executive; b. Newark, Apr. 6, 1952; s. Paul Joseph Buttros and Margaret Louise (McMahon) Buttros-Russell; m. Susan Roberta Sherr; children: Lissa, Jacqueline, Ari, Danielle, Desiree. Student, County Coll. of Morris, 1979-81, NYU, 1981-82. Computer products specialist Arrow Electronics, Fairfield, N.J., 1982-84; ea. regional dir. Corvus Systems, San Jose, Calif., 1984-86; dir. network services RMK Enterprises, Flanders, N.J., 1986—. Author: (with others) Selecting a Local Network, 1986. Trustee Temple Shalom Brotherhood, 1985-87. Mem. Local Area Network Dealer Assn., Mensa (regional coord. 1987-88), Toastmasters, Alpha Beta Gamma. Home: 350 Lakeside Blvd Hopatcong NJ 07843 Office: RMK Enterprises 1 gold Mine Rd Flanders NJ 07836

BUTTS, ARTHUR EDWARD, electronics manufacturing executive; b. Melrose, Mass., Mar. 6, 1947; s. Arthur E. and Anne (Wallace) B.; m. Nancy E. Dias, Sept. 9, 1967; children: Catherine A., Jeffrey A. Student, Northeastern U., 1966-72. Mgr. H.K. Porter Inc., Somerville, Mass., 1964-72; v.p. Melville Corp., Somerville, 1972-82; nat. sale mgr. O'Sullivan Corp., 1982-84; chief exec. officer TRM, Inc., Manchester, N.H., 1984—. Trustee Longmedow Ch.; mem. Auburn Budget Com. Mem. Am. Mgmt. Assn. Republican. Home: 7 Rockhead Ter Auburn NH 03032 Office: TRM Inc 401 Kelley Ave Manchester NH 03061

BUYERS, JOHN WILLIAM AMERMAN, agribusiness and specialty foods company executive; b. Coatesville, Pa., July 17, 1928; s. William Buchanan and Rebecca (Watson) B.; m. Elsie Palmer Parkhurst, Apr. 11, 1953; children: Elsie Buyers Viehman, Rebecca Watson Buyers-Basso, Jane Palmer Buyers-Russo. B.A. cum laude in History, Princeton U., 1952; M.S. in Indsl. Mgmt., MIT, 1963. Div. ops. mgr. Bell Telephone Co. Pa., 1964-66; dir. ops. and personnel Gen. Waterworks Corp., Phila., 1966-68; pres., chief exec. officer Gen. Waterworks Corp., Phila, 1971-75; v.p. adminstrn. Internat. Utilities Corp., Phila., 1968-71; pres., chief exec. officer, dir. C. Brewer and Co., Ltd., Honolulu, 1975—, chmn. bd., 1982—; chmn. Calif. and Hawaiian Sugar Co., 1982-84, 86-88; pres. Buyco, Inc., 1986—; mem. Gov.'s Adv. Council on China Affairs, U.S. Army Civilian Adv. Group, Hawaii Joint Council Econ. Edn., Japan-Hawaii Econ. Council, Commn. on Jud. Discipline; bd. dirs. 1st Hawaiian Bank, IU Investment Corp. Pres., trustee U. Hawaii Found.; trustee Hawaii Prep. Acad., 1986—, Whitworth Coll., 1986—; bd. dirs. Research Corp. U. Hawaii, Pacific Aerospace Mus. Served with USMC, 1946-48. Sloan fellow, 1963. Mem. Hawaiian Sugar Planters Assn. (chmn. bd. dirs. 1980-82, dir.), C. of C. Hawaii (chmn. bd. dirs. 1981-82), Nat. Alliance Bus. (chmn. Hawaii Pacific Metro chpt. 1978). Presbyterian. Clubs: Cap and Gown (Princeton); Hilo Yacht, Oahu Country, Pacific, Waialae Country; Prouts Neck (Maine) Country. Home: 148 Poipu Dr Honolulu HI 96825 Office: Calif & Hawaiian Sugar Co PO Box 4126 Concord CA 94524-4126 also: C Brewer & Co Ltd PO Box 1826 Honolulu HI 96805 *

BUYOK, JOHN PAUL, agricultural engineer; b. Sheridan, Wyo., July 9, 1957; s. Paul N.M.I. and Helen Louise (Pratt) B.; m. Vanessa Ann Skurok, June 13, 1987. BS in Agrl. Engring., U. Wyo., 1979. Registered profl. engr., Wyo., Colo. Interstate streams engr. Wyo. State Engr.'s Office, Cheyenne, 1979-83; cons. engr., jr. ptnr. Western Water Cons. Inc., Sheridan, 1984—. Mem. ASCE (assoc.), Wyo. Engring. Soc., Am. Soc. Agrl. Engrs. (assoc.), Colo. River Water Users' Assn. (sec.-treas. 1983). Democrat. Lutheran. Home: 717 N Custer Sheridan WY 82801 Office: Western Water Cons Inc 2 N Main Ste 405 Sheridan WY 82801

BUYS, CLIFFORD RICHARDS, consultant; b. Wichita, Kans., Dec. 13, 1923; s. Ivan and Abbie Frances (Richards) B.; B.S. with honors in Banking and Fin., U. Ill., 1943; M.Bus. and Public Adminstrn., Southeastern U., 1978; m. Elva Catherine Quaglia, Nov. 20, 1945 (dec. 1969); 1 dau., Barbara Catherine Buys Fries; m. 2d, Jean Elizabeth Perryman Grande, Nov. 24, 1973. Acct., Am. Pres. Lines, Yokohama, Japan, 1946-51; dir. case analysis Wage Stblzn. Bd., Richmond, Va., 1951-53; mgr. automation Allied Chem. Corp., N.Y.C., 1953-64; gen. mgr. Frantzreb & Pray Assos., N.Y.C., 1964-66; dir. mgmt. systems Am. Trucking Assn., Washington, 1966-85; now pvt. practice cons., Vienna, Va.; adj. instr. Fairleigh Dickinson U., Madison, N.J., 1964-66; bd. dirs. Transp. Data Coordinating Com., Inc., 1971-85; bd. dirs. Data Interchange Standards Assn., Inc., 1986—. Served with USMC, 1943-46. Cert. data educator; cert. systems profl. Mem. Ret. Officers Assn., Beta Gamma Sigma, Phi Kappa Phi, Pi Kappa Alpha. Republican. Methodist. Clubs: Army and Navy (Washington); Westwood Country (Vienna). Author: Motor Carrier Management Systems, 1980, Motor Carrier/Shipper Electronic Data Exchange, 1985; editor: Handbook of Data Processing in the Motor Carrier Industry, 1969. Home and Office: 1709 Irvin St Vienna VA 22180

BUZZELL, ROBERT DOW, management educator; b. Lincoln, Nebr., Apr. 18, 1933; s. Dow Alan and Grace (Blomquist) B.; m. Edith F. Moser, June 5, 1953; children: Susan, Robert Dow, Barbara, William. A.B., George Washington U., 1953; M.S., U. Ill., 1954; Ph.D., Ohio State U., 1957. Grad. asst. Ohio State U., Columbus, 1953-54, instr., 1955-57, asst. prof., 1957-59, assoc. prof., 1960-61; asst. prof. bus. Harvard U., Boston, 1961-63, assoc. prof., 1963-67, prof., 1967—, chmn. area mktg., 1972-77; vis. prof. Inst. European d'Adminstrn. des Affaires, 1967; exec. dir. Mktg. Sci. Inst., 1968-72, trustee, 1968-81; trustee Strategic Planning Inst.; mem. nat. mktg. adv. ocm. U.S. Dept. Commerce, 1969-71; dir. Chelsea Industries, Inc., VF Corp., Gen. Nutrition, Inc., Hills Dept. Stores; cons. in field, 1960—. Author or co-author: Wholesaling, 1959, Mathematical Models and Marketing Management, 1964, Marketing: An Introductory Analysis, 1964, rev., 1972, Marketing Research, 1969, Marketing in An Electronic Age, 1985, Strategic Marketing, 1986, The PIMS Principles: Linking Strategy to Performance, 1987, Multinational Marketing Management: Cases and Readings, 1988. Mem. Am. Mktg. Assn., Phi Beta Kappa. Republican. Congregationalist. Office: Harvard U Sch Bus Soldiers Field Rd Rowler 23 Boston MA 02163

BYAM, SEWARD GROVES, JR., financial executive; b. Bridgeport, Conn., Jan. 9, 1928; s. Seward Groves and Marjorie W. (Cotton) B.; student Princeton U., 1949, U. Del., 1951; m. Constance Patricia Randell, Feb. 28, 1981; children—Pamela E. Byam Tinsley, John T. Mktg. exec. duPont Co., 1951-67; bus. mgr. Dow Badische Co., 1967-76; mktg. dir. Borg Textile Corp., 1976-79; v.p. Tower Securities Inc., 1979-81; pres., prin., Seward, Groves, Richard & Wells, Inc., 1985—; pres. Randell-Byam Assocs., Inc., Rye, N.Y., 1987—; mng. dir. Fiduciary Counsel Inc., 1981—, Econ. Analysts, Inc., 1983—. Chmn. Williamsburg (Va.) Sch. Bd., 1973-76. Served with USMC, 1946-47, USMCR, 1947-51. Mem. Mensa, SAR. Episcopalian. Clubs: Union League, Princeton (N.Y.C.); Nassau (Princeton, N.J.), Apawamis (Rye). Home: 472 Grace Church St Rye NY 10580 Office: Seward, Groves, Richard & Wells 40 Wall St New York NY 10005

BYARD, JAMES BERTON, JR., industrial engineer, consultant; b. Milan, Ind., Aug. 1, 1943; s. James Berton III and Jeanette Laverne (Volz) B.; m. Alysa Kay Rigsby, Sept. 3, 1977; children: James Berton (dec.), Jennifer Reneé, Julie Ann. Student, Ind. State U., 1963-64, Ind. U., 1964-75. Indsl. engr. Cummins Engine Co., Columbus, Ind., 1962-80; mgr., indsl. engr. Greenheck Fan Corp., Schofield, Wis., 1980-82; sr. indsl. engr. Oil Dynamics, Inc., Tulsa, 1982-85, Outboard Marine Corp., Rutherfordton, N.C., 1985—; cons., pres., owner Modern Mfg. Tech., Forest City, N.C., 1987. Author: Operator Process Instructions, 1981. Project dir. Jaycees, Columbus, 1977. Mem. Inst. Indsl. Engrs. (pres. 1988—), Soc. Mfg. Engrs. Republican. Office: Outboard Marine Corp PO Box 1060 Rutherfordton NC 28139

BYE, ALLAN FREDERICK, real estate and construction consultant; b. Elgin, Ill., Sept. 1, 1955; s. Allan Harold and Dorothy (Siffrar) B. AA, Broward Community Coll., 1977. Instr. scuba Profl. Assn. of Diving Instrs., Santa Ana, Calif., 1976-83; constrn. supr. All Trades, Pompano Beach, Fla., 1982—; diver Nuclear Power Plants, Crystal River, Fla., 1983; prin. Allan Frederick Bye Corp. Constrn. in Water Filteration, Pompano Beach, 1983—; owner real estate brokerage Home Equity Sales, Inc., Lighthouse Point, Fla., 1985—. With USCG, 1983—. Lodges: Masons, Shriners. Home and Office: PO Box 5994 Lighthouse Point FL 33074

BYE, JULIANNE, business executive; b. Mpls., Jan. 14, 1952; d. William D. and Margaret Jean (McInnes) B. B.A., Mont. State U., 1974; M.B.A., Coll. St. Thomas, St. Paul, 1985. Adminstrv. researcher Billings and Yellowstone County study commns., Mont., 1975-77; sr. planner Hennepin County, Minn., 1978-82; assoc. dir. corp. devel. Naegele Outdoor Advt., Mpls., 1982-83; corp. treas. Hawaii Benefits, Eden Prairie, Minn., 1984—, also bd. dirs.; exec. v.p. Nat. Benefits, Inc., Eden Prairie, 1983—, also bd. dirs. Mem. Mpls. Charter Commn., 1983, Mpls. Pay Equity Com., 1984, Eden Prairie Planning Commn. (sec. 1987), 1985. Mem. Eden Prairie C. of C. (chair edn. com. 1984, planning commn. 1988), Minn. Women's Consortium, Minn. Assn. Woman in Housing (pres. 1980-82, program chair 1979). Lodge: Rotary. Avocations: travel, reading, hockey, skiing, walking. Office: Nat Benefits PO Box 444029 Eden Prairie MN 55346

BYER, STEVEN DAVID, restauranteur; b. Hartford, Conn., June 1, 1955; s. Jonah Joseph and Cynthia (Greenberg) B.; m. Susan Van Horn, Sept. 20, 1986. BA, Tufts U., 1977. Founder, owner Saladalley Restaurants, Inc., Ardmore, Pa., 1978—, also chmn. bd. Office: Saladalley Restaurants Inc Suburban Sq Coulter Ave and Saint James St Ardmore PA 19003

BYERS, KENNETH VERNON, insurance company executive; b. Logan, Ohio, Apr. 6, 1940; s. Kenneth Vernon and Ruth Elizabeth (Klingel) B.; m. Diane Petty, Aug. 21, 1972; children: Juli, Kimberly, Jeffrey, Matthew, Kristine, Brandon. BA in Edn., U. Cin., 1962. CLU; chartered fin. cons. Football player N.Y. Giants then Minn. Vikings, 1962-67; pres. Ken Byers and Assocs., Cin., 1968—, Dolle Life Ins. Agy. Inc., Cin., 1987—; chmn. adv. council Gen. Am. Life Ins. Co., St. Louis, 1987—. Mem. NFL Alumni Assn. (bd. dirs. 1983—), Cin. Assn. Life Underwriters (pres. 1978), Gen. Agts. and Mgrs. Assn. (pres. 1976), Internat. Assn. Fin. Planners, Nat. Assn. Life Underwriters, Cin. C. of C. (mem. sports council 1987—). Republican. Episcopalian. Home: 782 Watch point Dr Cincinnati OH 45230 Office: Ken Byers & Assocs 49 E 4th St Ste 600 Cincinnati OH 45202

BYERS, TERRENCE CHARLES, aerospace executive; b. Cleve., Mar. 11, 1948; s. Harry Fountain and Erma Ellen (Behm) B.; m. Margaret Alberta Magill, Mar. 29, 1980; children: Kirsten Noel, Austin Chase. BS, George Washington, 1975. Dir. ops., new bus. devel. Bay Diving Assoc., Balt., 1969-78; regional mgr. Nat. Repeater Systems, N.Y.C., 1978-86; dir. new bus. devel. Spot Image Corp., Reston, Va., 1986—. Contbr. articles to profl. jours. 1st lt. U.S. Army. Mem. Tech. Mktg. Soc., Internat. Strategic Studies Assn. Home and Office: 1220 D Gemini Dr Annapolis MD 21403

BYERS, THEODORE ERNEST, health science consultant; b. June 10, 1923; s. Ernest and Suzanne Adelaide (Matson) B.; m. Virginia Kathryn Noell, July 1, 1960; 1 child, James Ethan. BS, Ohio u., 1950. Chemist FDA, Cin., 1950-54; dir. quality control Warren-Teed Products, Columbus, Ohio, 1954-57; chemist FDA, Cin., Washington, 1957-60; chief chemist FDA, N.Y.C., 1960-64, dep. dir., 1964-66; dir. div. case guidance FDA, Washington, 1966-69, dir. office of compliance, 1969-81; pres. Byers Enterprises, Alexandria, Va., 1981—; bd. dirs. Royce Labs., Miami, Fla., 1985—, InstaCool N.Am., Anaheim, Calif., 1986—; lectr. in field. Contbr. to profl. jours. and books. Sci. advisor Key Intermediate Sch., Fairfax County, Va., 1980—; judge Nat. Acad. Sci. fairs, Fairfax and Arlington Counties, Va., 1983—. Served with UAS, 1942-45, PTO. Superior Service grantee FDA, 1981; recipient award of merit FDA, 1963. Mem. Proprietary Assn. (Washington) (assoc.), Parenteral Drug Assn. (Phila.), Soc. Mfg. Engrs. (Dearborn, Mich.) (sr.). Republican. Home and Office: 6104 Beech Tree Dr Alexandria VA 22310

BYRD, HARRY FLOOD, JR., former U.S. senator, newspaper executive; b. Winchester, Va., Dec. 20, 1914; s. Harry Flood and Anne Douglas (Beverley) B.; m. Gretchen B. Thomson, Aug. 9, 1941; children: Harry, Thomas Thomson, Beverley. Student, Va. Mil. Inst., 1931-33, U. Va., 1933-35; hon. LL.D., L.H.D., D. Internat. Service. Editor Winchester Evening Star, from 1935; pub. Harrisonburg (Va.) Daily News-Record, 1937—; Pres., dir. Rockingham Pub. Co., from 1946; dir. A.P., 1950-66; v.p., mem. exec. com.; mem. Va. Senate, 1947-65; mem. U.S. Senate from Va., 1965-83. Author state automatic tax reduction law. Mem. Va. Democratic Central Com., 1940-66. Served to lt. comdr. USNR, 1942-46. Recipient Honor medal Freedoms Found. Mem. V.F.W., Am. Legion. Clubs: Rotarian, National Press, Army-Navy. Home: Winchester VA 22601 Office: Rockingham Pub Co Inc 2 North Kent St Winchester VA 22601

BYRD, JONATHAN EUGENE, restaurant executive; b. Franklin, Ind., Jan. 6, 1952; s. Carl Eugene Byrd and Lala Jean (Wethington) Isom; m. Virginia Beatrice Driver, Sept. 8, 1973; children: Jonathan E. II, David Noah. Student, Cornell U., 1969-70, Robert F. Sharpe Sch. Fin. Planning, 1974. Pres. Byrd Enterprises Inc., Greenwood, Ind., 1973—, Byrd Enterprises Advt. Agy., Greenwood, Ind., 1973—, Channel 29 TV Inc., Mpls.,

1981-84; treas. Jack Van Impe Crusades, Detroit, 1977-80; owner Jonathan Byrd's Cafeteria, Greenwood, 1988—; fin. cons. to various nat. ministries, 1976—. Exec. producer TV spls. Bd. dirs. Greenwood Little League, 1985—, Free Am. Polit. Action Com., Washington, 1988; county fin. chmn. campaign U.S. Congressman, Johnson County, Ind., 1986, 88. Recipient Championship award U.S. Auto Club, 1986, 87. Republican. Baptist. Office: Byrd Enterprises Inc PO Box 413 Greenwood IN 46142

BYRD, RICHARD HAYS, food company executive; b. Wheeling, W.Va., Apr. 26, 1939; s. Enoch Woodyard and Jean Matilda (Hays) B.; m. Sarah Foster Lyon, Apr. 30, 1966; children: Jennifer Anne, David Woodyard. BA, Mich. State U., 1960, MBA, 1961; cert., Dartmouth Coll., 1970. Indsl. salesman Dow Chem. Co., Chgo., 1964-66; regional credit mgr. Dow Chem. Co., Midland, Mich., 1966-75, corp. cash mgr., 1978-80; mgr. credit and fin. Dow Chem. Pacific, Hong Kong, 1975-78; asst. treas. Borden, Inc., Columbus, Ohio, 1980—. Chmn. bd. Better Bus. Bur. Cen. Ohio, 1987; trustee Perry Twp., Franklin County, Ohio, 1986—; sec., treas. Cen. Ohio Fire Mus., Columbus, 1982—. Served to 1st lt. U.S. Army, 1962-64. Mem. Columbus Area C. of C. (trustee Treas. Club 1985—), Box 15, Inc., Athletic Club. Republican. Methodist. Clubs: Box 15, Inc. (Columbus); Athletic of Columbus. Home: 7963 Green Side Ln Worthington OH 43235 Office: Borden Inc 180 E Broad St Columbus OH 43215

BYRD, RUSSELL AARON, association executive; b. Little Rock, Aug. 1, 1904; s. Erasmus Aaron and Clara Isabel (Alsbury) B.; m. Lillie Mae Hill, Jan. 27, 1949; children: Wesley Oliver, Jeannette Byrd Dahle, Evelyn Ray. Student, Leland Stanford Jr. U., 1931-32. With Greyhound Lines, 1929-31, Columbia Pacific Nite CoachLines, Inc., 1932-35, Santa Fe Transp. Co., 1935-68, Calif. Sightseeing Co., 1968-73, Las Vegas Travel Club, 1973-74; asst. to pres. Douglas Bus Lines, Inc., Long Beach, Calif., 1974-78; with Greyline Tours, 1979-82; chmn., chief exec. officer Piston Parking, Inc., Bakersfield, Calif., 1986—; exec. dir. Nat. Drivers Assn. Prevention of Traffic Accidents, Inc., Bakersfield, Calif., 1958—; dir. Space Parking, Inc.; pres. Green Byrd Assocs., Inc. Author: Russ's Bus, 1945, Driving to Live, 1948, Americanism, 1934, Highway Killers, 1978, Planet of Gold, 1983. Named admiral of Am. hwys., Bakersfield Jr. C. of C., 1956; recipient 5 Million Mile No Chargable Accident award U.S. Dept. of Transportation, 1979. Mem. Brotherhood R.R. Trainmen (past local pres.), United Transp. Union, World Safety Orgn. (co-chmn. internat. com. on transp.). Republican. Methodist. Clubs: Stanford Alumni (Bakersfield). Lodge: Masons. Office: Piston Parking Inc PO Box 604 Bakersfield CA 93302

BYRD, STEPHEN FRED, human resource consulting firm executive; b. Charleston, S.C., June 12, 1928; s. Paul Fred and Dorothy B.; m. Margaret A. McAulay, Apr. 15, 1955; children: Owen, Susan. Student, CCNY, 1945-48; LL.B., N.Y. Law Sch., 1951. Bar: N.Y. 1951. Corp. indsl. relations rep. Pan Am. Airways, 1957-62, Sinclair Oil Corp., 1962-64; v.p. employee relations indsl. chems. div. Allied Chem. Corp., 1964-68; v.p. indsl. relations and personnel Internat. Nickel Co., Ltd., 1968-72; sr. v.p. human resources Schering-Plough Corp., Madison, N.J., 1973-88; sr. v.p. Right Assocs., Parsippany, N.J., 1988—. Author: Front Line Supervisors Labor Relations Handbook, 1962, Management Strategy in Collective Bargaining, 1964. Bd. dirs. United Fund Morris County, N.J., Big Bros. Morris County, Morristown YMCA, 1962-63; chmn. Madison council Boy Scouts Am., 1975-76; trustee Drew U., Madison, N.J., 1976-80. Served with AUS, 1952-53, Korea. Mem. Indsl. Relations Research Assn., N.Y. Law Sch. Alumni Assn. Home: 23 Academy Rd Madison NJ 07940 Office: Right Assocs Gatehill I 1 Gatehall Dr Parsippany NJ 07054

BYRNE, GARY CECIL, banker; b. Upland, Calif., May 1, 1942; s. Cecil John Byrne and Verda Alice (Burgers) Frehe; m. Norma E. Elliott, Aug. 19, 1967; children: Silas Elliott, Tristan Oliver. BA, U. Redlands, 1965; PhD, U. N.C., 1969. Assoc. prof. San Diego State U., 1969-73; assoc. Arthur Young & Co., Washington, 1973-74; v.p. Orkand Corp., Silver Spring, Md., 1974-75; dir., ptnr. Miller and Byrne Inc., Washington, 1975-77; v.p. H.C. Elliott Inc., Sacramento, 1977-83; chmn. Meridian Nat. Bank, Concord, Calif., 1979—; chmn., pres., chief exec. officer Alex Brown Fin. Group, Sacramento, 1985—, Alex Brown Devel. Corp., Sacramento, 1986—, Bank of Alex Brown, Sacramento, 1987—; bd. dirs. Physicians Clin. Labs, Sacramento, Elliott Fin., Sacramento. Author: (with others) The Great American Convention, 1977; co-editor: Politics in Western Europe, 1972; contbr. articles to profl. jours. Trustee U. Redlands, Calif., 1983—, Sutter Hosps., Sacramento, 1983-86; bd. dirs. Boy Scouts Exec. Council, 1980-84. Grantee NSF, 1968; fellow Rotary Internat., 1965, NIMH, 1969. Mem. Am. Bankers Assn., Calif. Bankers Assn., Western Ind. Bankers Assn., Western Mobile Home Assn. (bd. dirs. 1982-84), Sutter Club, Capital Athletic Club. Office: Bank Alex Brown 1425 River Park Dr Sacramento CA 95815

BYRNE, JAMES WILLIAM, recruiting company executive; b. Glen Ridge, N.J., Mar. 9, 1953; s. Harry and Susan (Bart) Bobyack; m. Kathleen E. Morris, May 17, 1975; children: Kimberly, Jonathan, Kelly. BS, Montclair (N.J.) State Coll., 1974. Mgmt. trainee DeLuxe Check Printers, Clifton, N.J., 1974-76; ops. div. mgr. Allstate Ins. Co., Murray Hill, N.J., 1976-82; ops. mgr. Home Ins. co., Florham, N.J., 1982-85; v.p. Nat. Ins. Assn., Paramus, N.J., 1985-87; pres. Mgmt. Group of Am., Inc., Fairfield, N.J., 1987—; bd. dirs. Nat. Bus. Inst., Paramus. Pres. Holmehill Assn., Roseland, N.J., 1984-85. Mem. Am. Coll. Real Estate. Roman Catholic. Office: Mgmt Group of Am 31 Kulick Rd Fairfield NJ 07006

BYRNE, JOHN JOSEPH, JR., insurance executive; b. Passaic, N.J., July 11, 1932; s. John Joseph and Winifred (Mohr) B.; m. Dorothy M. Cain, July 22, 1958; children: John Joseph III, Mark James, Patrick Michael. B.S., Rutgers U., 1954; postgrad., Harvard Law Sch., 1957; M.S. in Meth., U. Mich., 1959; hon. degrees, U. Md., St. Anselm Coll., Rutgers U., Mt. St. Mary's Coll. C.L.U. With Lincoln Nat. Life Ins. Co., Ft. Wayne, Ind., 1959-63; exec. v.p. Mass. Life Ins. Co., Boston, 1963-67, Travelers Ins. Cos., Hartford, Conn., 1967-76; chmn. bd., chief exec. officer Geico, 1976-85, Fireman's Fund Corp., 1985—; dir. Martin Marietta, Potomac Electric Power Co. Chmn. Nat. Symphony Orch. Ann. Fund; bd. overseers Amos Tuck Sch. Bus. Adminstrn., Dartmouth Coll. Served to maj. USAF, 1954-57. Recipient Boss of Year award Jr. C. of C.; Community Service award United Way. Mem. Soc. Actuaries (assoc.), Ins. Inst. Am. (trustee), Am. Inst. Property and Liability Underwriters (trustee), Knights of Malta, Cap and Skull, Zeta Psi. Republican. Roman Catholic. Clubs: Univ. (Boston); Univ. (Washington); Burning Tree, Mid Ocean. Office: Fireman's Fund Corp PO Box 2604 Greenwich CT 06836-2604

BYRNE, JOHN N., food company executive; b. Newark, May 21, 1925; s. Owen Francis and Rose (Daly) B.; m. Audrey Helmers; children: John W., Andrew J., Kathleen A., Steven T., Eileen R., Gregory F. BSME, Stevens Inst., 1949, MS in Indsl. Mgmt., 1954. Engr. Thomas J. Lipton Inc., Hoboken, N.J., 1948-54; plant mgr. Thomas J. Lipton Inc., Suffolk, Va., 1954-61; dir. engring. Thomas J. Lipton Inc., Englewood Cliffs, N.J., 1961-64, dir. production and Engring., 1964-67, asst. v.p. mfg., 1967-72, v.p. engring. and planning, 1972-77, v.p. gen. mgmt. group, 1977-84, sr. v.p., 1984—, also bd. dirs. V.p. Tidewater Devel. Council, Norfolk, Va., 1960. Served to 1st lt. USAF, 1943-45, ETO. Mem. Am. Soc. Mech. Engrs., Suffolk C. of C. (pres. 1958). REpublican. Roman Catholic. Office: Thomas J Lipton Inc 800 Sylvan Ave Englewood Cliffs NJ 07632

BYRNE, MICHAEL JOSEPH, business executive; b. Chgo., Apr. 3, 1928; s. Michael Joseph and Edith (Lueken) B.; B.Sc. in Mktg., Loyola U., Chgo., 1952; m. Eileen Kelly, June 27, 1953; children—Michael Joseph, Nancy, James, Thomas, Patrick, Terrence. Sales engr. Emery Industries, Inc., Cin., 1952-59; with Pennsalt Chem. Corp., Phila., 1959-60; with Oakton Cleaners, Inc., Skokie, Ill., 1960-70, pres., 1960-70; pres. Datatax Inc., Skokie, 1970-74, Midwest Synthetic Lubrication Products, 1978—, Pure Water Systems, 1984—, Superior Tax Service, 1984—. Served with ordnance U.S. Army, 1946-48. Mem. A.I.M., VFW, Alpha Kappa Psi. Club: Toastmasters Internat. Home: 600 Grego Ct PO Box 916 Prospect Heights IL 60070

BYRNE, NOEL THOMAS, sociologist, educator; b. San Francisco, May 11, 1943; s. Joseph Joshua and Naomi Pearl (Denison) B.; m. Elizabeth Carla Rowlin, Nov. 5, 1966 (div.); 1 child, Ginger Butler. BA in Sociology, Sonoma State Coll., 1971; MA in Sociology, Rutgers U., 1975, PhD in Sociology, 1987. Instr. sociology Douglass Coll., Rutgers U., New Brunswick, N.J., 1974-76, Hartnell Coll., Salinas, Calif., 1977-78; research dir. mgmt. grads. survey projects Sonoma State U., Rohnert Park, Calif., 1983-86, 89, family bus. research project, 1987-88; from lectr. to assoc. prof. depts. sociology and mgmt. Sonoma State U., 1978—. Contbr. articles and revs. to profl. lit. Recipient Dell Pub. award Rutgers U. Grad. Sociology Program, 1976, Louis Bevier fellow, 1977-78. Mem. AAAS, Am. Sociol. Assn., Pacific Sociol. Assn., Acad. of Mgmt., N.Y. Acad. Sci., Soc. for Study Symbolic Interaction (rev. editor Jour. 1980-83), Soc. for Study Social Problems. Democrat. Club: Commonwealth. Home: 4773 Ross Rd Sebastopol CA 95472 Office: Sonoma State U Sch Bus and Econs Rohnert Park CA 94928

BYRNE, PATRICK FRANCIS, banker, international tax specialist; b. Bethlehem, Pa., Dec. 16, 1952; s. Francis James and Rose Marie (Casey) B.; m. Debra Kay Ritter, Aug. 22, 1975 (div. Apr. 1980); m. Heather Robertson Denton, Mar. 25, 1982; children: Charlotte Elizabeth, Andrew Patrick. AA in Gen. Edn., Northampton Coll., 1973; BBA, Pa. State U., Harrisburg, 1975; postgrad., Pacific Coast Banking Sch., 1987—. Auditor Fin. Am. Corp., Allentown, Pa., 1975-78; project mgr. systems Fin. Am. Corp., Allentown, 1978-81; internat. auditor Bank Am., London, 1981-82; sr. trust officer BankAm. Trust, Georgetown, Cayman Islands, 1982-85; asst. v.p. internat. pvt. banking Bank Am., San Francisco, 1985-86, v.p., 1986-87, also bd. dirs.; v.p./mgr. new internat. pvt. banking group Bank of Calif., San Francisco, 1987-89; with SVP/Equity Investments, Sonoma, Calif., 1989—. Republican. Lutheran. Home: 4582 Pressley Rd Santa Rosa CA 95404 Office: SVP/Equity Investments Principle 813 W Napa St Sonoma CA 95476

BYRNE, PATRICK JAMES, financial planner; b. Bklyn., Apr. 29, 1949; s. Patrick and Petronilla (Seymour) B.; m. Rose Marie Alice Bruno, Aug. 24, 1974; children: Patrick James Jr., Antonio Carl, Marie Rose. BA, Southwestern Coll., Winfield, Kans., 1970. CLU; cert. fin. planner. Service mgr. Mut. of Am., N.Y.C., 1973-77; life ins. agt. J.S. Sloane, Inc., Scarsdale, N.Y., 1977-78; assoc. Employee Incentive Plans Am., N.Y.C., 1978-79; fin. service advisor United Resources Inc., Torrance, Calif., 1979-85; dist. mgr. United Resources Inc., Santa Ana, Calif., 1986—; registered rep. Integrated Resources, N.Y.C., 1981—; equity coord. Equitable Life, N.Y.C., 1985-86. Mem. Internat. Assn. Fin. Planning., Am. Soc. CLUs, Am. Soc. CLU and ChFC, Inst. Cert. Fin. Planners. Republican. Roman Catholic. Home and Office: 739 E Fourth St Brooklyn NY 11218

BYRNE, PATRICK MICHAEL, management consultant; b. Dublin, Ireland, Sept. 18, 1952; came to U.S., 1955; s. Maureen (McQuire) B.; m. Karyn Anahad Ahigian, May 27, 1978; children; Ryan, Christopher. BBA, Kent State U., 1975; MBA, U. Wis., 1981. Distbn. mgr. George A. Hormel & Co., Austin, Minn., 1975-78; dir. transp. Schneider Nat., Inc., Green Bay, Wis., 1978-81; ptnr., dir., transp. cons. Ernst & Whinney, Washington, 1982—. Author: Implementing the Marketing Plan, 1986, Marketing Planning for Motor Carriers, 1984; co-author: Transportation Accounting and Control, 1983. Sgt. N.G., 1971. Mem. Nat. Acctg. and Fin. Council, Sales and Mktg. Council (ann. service award 1986), Am. Soc. Transp. and Logistics, Council Logistics Mgmt., Interstate Carriers Conf. Home: 2014 Spring Beach Dr Vienna VA 22180

BYRNES, DONALD J., consumer products company executive; b. Glendive, Mont., May 5, 1926; s. Charles Joseph and Amanda Marie (Halvorson) B.; m. Carol Jean Dana, Aug. 14, 1949; children—Donald, Karen, David, Ronald. B.B.A., U. Mont., Missoula, 1949. With phys. damange ins. dept. Gen. Motors Corp., Gt. Falls, Mont., 1949-57; mgr. mktg. Gen. Electric Co., Louisville, 1957-71; mgr. mktg. Evenflo Juvenile Products Co., Ravenna, Ohio, 1971-72, v.p. mktg., 1972-73; v.p. ops. Evenflo Juvenile Furniture Co., Los Angeles, 1973-77; pres. Questor Juvenile Furniture Co., Los Angeles, 1977-80, Los Angeles and Ravenna, 1980-81; sr. v.p., chief operating officer Questor Corp., Tampa, Fla., 1982-84; pres., chief operating officer Spalding and Evenflo Cos., Inc., Tampa, 1984—; dir. Spalding & Evenflo Cos., Tampa. Served with USN, 1944-46; PTO. Office: Spalding & Evenflo Cos Inc 5750-A N Hoover Blvd Tampa FL 33634

BYRNES, KATHLEEN ANN, financial services executive; b. Detroit, July 28, 1950; d. John Maurice and Maylou Ann (Babcock) Closs; m. Robert A. Byrnes, Jr., Sept. 20, 1975 (div. 1983); children: Michael R., Kelly E. Grad. high sch. With Mich. Consol. Gas Co., Detroit, 1969-76; owner, operator Am. Previously Owned, St. Clair Shores, Mich., 1977-80; rep. Detroit Bond & Mortgage Co., 1982-84, Fin. Intradated Svcs., Mt. Clemens, Mich., 1985-86, Mariner Fin. Svcs., Livonia, Mich., 1985—; owner, mgr. Village Fin. Svcs., Grosse Pointe, Mich., 1985—; with C.J. Duke Scrafano & Assocs., Southfield, Mich., 1982—. Fellow NAFE; mem. Internat. Assn. Fin. Planning. Republican. Office: Village Fin Svcs 16980 Kercheval Grosse Pointe MI 48230

BYRNES, ROBERT MICHAEL, diversified manufacturing company executive; b. Copenhagen, N.Y., June 15, 1937; s. Lawrence Thomas and Clara (Clark) B.; children from previous marriage: Robert, Larry, Melissa, Matthew; m. Donna A. De Capua; 1 child, Molly. BA, U. Notre Dame, 1959. Indsl. relations trainee St. Regis, N.Y.C., Fla. and Maine, 1960-61; personnel mgr. St. Regis, Tacoma, 1961-65; indsl. relations rep. St. Regis, N.Y.C., 1965-67, regional indsl. relations mgr., 1967-71, mgr. labor relations, 1971-78, dir. human resources, 1978-79, v.p., 1979-84; v.p. Champion Internat., Stamford, Conn., 1984-86; sr. v.p. Emhart Corp., Farmington, Conn., 1986—; mem. Machinery and Allied Products Inst. Human Relations Council I, Washington, 1986—. Vice chmn. Dominican Coll., Blauvelt, N.Y., 1981-86. Served with USN, 1959. Mem. Labor Policy Assn. (bd. dirs. 1983—). Republican. Roman Catholic. Home: 106 Woodford Hills Dr Avon CT 06001 Office: Emhart Corp 426 Colt Hwy Farmington CT 06032

BYWATER, WILLIAM HAROLD, labor union official; b. Trenton, N.J., Sept. 10, 1920; s. William Harold and Rose Ann Bywater; married; 2 children. Mem. Internat. Union Electronic, Elec., Salaried, Machine and Furniture Workers, Washington, 1941—, pres. dist. council 3, 1968-80, sec.-treas., 1980-82, dir. orgn., 1980-84, pres., 1982—; chief steward local 425 group Internat. Union Elec., Radio and Machine Workers, East Rutherford, N.J., 1941-46, v.p., 1947-49, pres., 1949-57; internat. rep. Internat. Union Elec., Radio and Machine Workers, AFL-CIO, East Rutherford, N.J., 1957-58; chmn. conf. bd. Sperry Rand Corp., 1958-67. Served with U.S. Army. Office: Internat Union Electronic Elec Salaried Machine & Furniture 1126 16th St NW Washington DC 20036

CABOT, JOHN GODFREY LOWELL, chemical manufacturing company executive; b. Rio de Janeiro, Brazil, Aug. 8, 1934; s. John Moors and Elizabeth (Lewis) C.; m. Carroll Lloyd Trimble, July 9, 1960; children: John Ridgeway, Andrew Lowell. AB, Harvard U., 1956, MBA, 1960. Various positions Cabot Corp., Boston, 1960-72, v.p., 1972-77, sr. v.p., 1977-85; exec. v.p. Cabot Corp., Boston and Waltham, Mass., 1985-88, vice chmn., 1988—, also bd. dirs.; bd. dirs. Hollingsworth & Vose Co., E. Walpole, Mass., Haynes Internat. Inc., Kokomo, Ind., Eaton Vance Corp. Trustee Tufts U., Medford, Mass., 1983—; overseer & gov. New Eng. Med. Ctr., Boston, 1981—; mem. of the corp., Mass. Gen. Hosp., Boston, 1982—; vice chmn., treas., dir. New Eng. Legal Found., Boston, 1977—; overseer WGBH Ednl. Found., Boston, 1988—. Office: Cabot Corp PO Box 9073 Waltham MA 02254-9073

CABOT, LOUIS WELLINGTON, chemical manufacturing company executive; b. Boston, Aug. 3, 1921; s. Thomas Dudley and Virginia (Wellington) C.; m. Mary Ellen Flynn de Pena Vera, Oct. 19, 1974; children by previous marriage: James Bass, Anne Cabot Alletzhauzer, Godfrey Lowell, Amanda Cabot Kjellerup, Helen Reuter. A.B., Harvard U., 1943, M.B.A., 1948; LL.D. (hon.), Norwich U., 1961. With Cabot Corp., 1948—, pres., 1960-69, chmn. bd., 1969-86, also bd. dirs.; chmn. Brookings Instn., Washington, 1986—; dir. Owens-Corning Fiberglas Corp., R.R. Donnelley & Sons Co., Wang Labs Inc., New Eng. Tel. & Tel., 1965-82, Fed. Res. Bank Boston, 1970-78, chmn., 1975-78; U.S. rep. 15th Plenary Session UN Econ. Commn. for Europe, 1960; mem. bus. ethics adv. council Dept. Commerce, 1961-63; dir., New Eng. chmn. Nat. Alliance Businessmen, 1970-72, Boston chmn., 1968-69; chmn. Sloan Commn. on Govt. and Higher Edn., 1977-80; mem. Pres.'s Blue Ribbon Commn. on Def. Mgmt., 1985-86; mem. Def. Sec.'s Commn. on Base Realignment and Closure, 1988. Overseer Harvard U., 1970-76; chmn. Harvard Coll. Fund Council, 1963-65; pres. Beverly (Mass.) Hosp., 1958-61; chmn. Com. Corp. Support Pvt. Univs., 1977-83; trustee Norwich U., 1952-77, Mus. of Sci., Boston; corp. mem. MIT; trustee Northeastern U., Nat. Humanities Ctr.. Fellow Am. Acad. Arts and Scis.; mem. C. of C. of U.S. (dir., exec. com. 1978-83), Nat. Coun. for U.S.-China Trade (dir. 1978-82), Bus. Coun., Conf. Bd., Coun. Fgn. Rels., Phi Beta Kappa, Sigma Xi. Clubs: Somerset (Boston), Commercial (Boston) (pres. 1970-72), Harvard (Boston); Metropolitan (Washington); Wianno (Osterville, Mass.); N.Y. Yacht, River. Office: Cabot Corp 950 Winter St PO Box 9073 Waltham MA 02254-9073 also: The Brookings Instn 1775 Massachusetts Ave NW Washington DC 20036

CABRINETY, PATRICIA BUTLER, software company executive; b. Earlville, N.Y., Sept. 4, 1932; d. Eugene Thomas and Helen Sylvester (Fulmer) Butler; m. Lawrence Paul Cabrinety, Aug. 20, 1955; children: Linda Anne, Margaret Marie, Stephen Michael. BS in Elem. Edn. and Music, SUNY, Potsdam, 1954. Cert. tchr. N.Y., Pa., Minn., Mass. Asst. tchr. music Hamilton (N.Y.) Cen. Sch., 1948-50; tchr. Cherry Lane Sch., Suffern, N.Y., 1954-56; instr. music, Towanda, Pa., 1960-63, Sayre, Pa., 1963-79; pres. Superior Software Inc., Mpls., 1981—; poet and illustrator, Edina, Minn., 1981—; cons. in field. Composer, artist numerous compositions; inventor: Musical for Computer, 1981; author monthly column on Boy Scouts, 1975-78, also more than 70 pub. poems and 35 pub. illustrations; author: CHARIS series; composer of "Pauletter Fry" and "Mi Cazone"; creator of The Professional Writers' MAIL-IT Kit and Name in Notes. Recipient Golden Poet award World of Poetry, 1985-88, Poet of Month award All Season's Poetry, 1986, Vantage Press Invitational award, 1985-88, Poet of Month award Editor's Desk, 1986, Internat. Poet award, 1986. Mem. Nat. Assn. Female Execs., Am. Soc. Profl. and Exec. Women, Nat. Assn. Bus. and Profl. Women, Nat. Writers Assn., Am. Mgmt. Assn., DAR, AAUW, Pioneers, Computer History Inst. for the Preservation of Software, Legion of Mary, Third Order Carmelite, Mpls. Music Tchrs. Forum, Edina C. of C., Worcester County Music Assn., Worcester County Poetry Assn. Avocations: philately, art, needlecraft, photography, outdoor activities. Home: 925 Pearl Hill Rd Fitchburg MA 01420

CACCIATORE, RONALD KEITH, lawyer; b. Donalsonville, Ga., Feb. 5, 1937; s. Angelo D. and Myrtice E. (Williams) C.; children—Rhonda, Donna, Rex. Student Spring Hill Coll., 1955-56; B.A., U. Fla., 1960, J.D., 1963. Bar: Fla. 1963, U.S. Supreme Ct. 1969. Asst. state atty. 13th Jud. Cir., 1963-65; pvt. practice, Tampa, Fla., 1967—; lectr. criminal law; mem. 13th Jud. Cir. Jud. Nominating Commn., 1976-80, chmn., 1980; mem. Fed. Judiciary Adv. Commn. Fla., 1987—. Trustee, Hillsborough Community Coll., 1979-83, chmn., 1982-83. Fellow Am. Coll. Trial Lawyers; mem. Hillsborough County Bar Assn. (pres. 1975-76, chmn. trial lawyers sect. 1983-85), Fla. Bar Assn. (chmn. criminal law sect. 1977-78), Fla. Coun. Bar Pres.'s (chmn. 1979-80), Fed. Bar Assn. (pres. Tampa Bay chpt. 1985-86), Palma Ceia Golf and Country Club, Tampa Club.

CADIEUX, PIERRE H., government official; b. Hudson, Que., Can., Apr. 6, 1948. Minister of labour Can., 1987-89, minister of Indian affairs and northern devel., 1989—. Office: House Commons, Parliament Bldg, Ottawa, ON Canada K1A 0A6 *

CADIGAN, PATRICK FINBAR, electronics company executive; b. Stoneham, Mass., Mar. 1, 1935; s. Dennis J. and Mary (O'Sullivan) C.; widowed; children: Ann K., David P., Maria A. BS, Boston Coll., 1957; MBA, Boston U., 1966; MA, Claremont Grad. SCh., 1978, PhD in Mgmt., 1980; postgrad., Harvard U., 1975. Product mgr. GTE/Slyvania Electronics Systems, Waltham, Mass., 1962-67; pres., chief exec. officer EECO Inc., Santa Ana, Calif., 1967-86; chmn. The Cadigan Co, Irvine, Calif., 1987—; bd. dirs. Beach Savs. Bank, FHP Inc., Gateway Communications Inc., Interface Products Inc., Media Systems Tech. Inc. Bd. dirs. U. Calif.-Irvine Found., bd. dirs. fin. com.; past bd. dirs., bd. fellows-trustees Claremont U. Ctr. and Claremont Grad. Sch. Mem. Cardinal and Gold Assn. Orange County (bd. dirs.), Mich. State U. Pres. Assn., Boston Coll. Alumni Assn., Boston U. Alumni Assn., Claremont Alumni Assn., Lincoln Club Orange County, Chancellor's Club. Home: 323 Morning Star Ln Newport Beach CA 92660 Office: The Cadigan Co 3 Corporate Pk Dr Ste 200 Irvine CA 92714

CADMAN, WILSON KENNEDY, utility company executive; b. Wichita, Kans., Sept. 7, 1927; s. Wilson K. and Ethel Louise (Wheeler) C.; m. Mary Roslyn Rowley, Nov. 22, 1950; children: Elizabeth Louise, Robert Wilson. AB, Wichita State U., 1951, postgrad., 1953; postgrad., Okla. State U., 1965. With Kans. Gas & Electric Co., Wichita, 1951—, mgr. Witchita div., 1967-70, v.p., 1970-79, pres., 1979—, chief exec. officer, 1981—, also chmn. bd. dirs.; bd. dirs. Edison Electric Inst., Bank IV of Wichita, Electric Power Research Inst. Bd. govs. Wichita State U. Endowment Assn.; bd. dirs. St. Frances Hosp., Wichita State U. Athletic Scholarship Orgn.; mem. Gov.'s Task Force on High Tech. Devel., Mayor's Econ. Adv. Council, Kans. Water Resources Council. Served with USN, 1945-46. Mem. Edison Electric Inst., Wichita Area Devel. (exec. com.), Wichita State U. Endowment Assn., Phi Lambda Phi. Clubs: Wichita, Wichita Country. Lodge: Kiwanis. Home: 3147 Keywest Ct Wichita KS 67204 Office: Kans Gas & Electric Co 120 E 1st Wichita KS 67202

CAFFEE, MARCUS PAT, computer consulting executive; b. Tulsa, Feb. 23, 1948; s. Malcolm Wesley and Martha Marjorie (Deming) C.; m. Virginia Maureen Gladden, May 31, 1975; 1 child, Katheryn Elizabeth. Student, Tulsa U., 1965-66, Okla. State U., 1966-67, 77-78. Pres. Computer Sales & Service, Tulsa, 1972-75; owner Data Mgmt. Systems, Tulsa and Houston, 1975-77; staff analyst Okla. State U., Stillwater, 1977-78; project leader Ranger Ins. Cos., Houston, 1979-80; group mgr. corp. and fin. services Am. Gen. Life Ins., Houston, 1980-82; mgr. systems devel. U. Tex. Health Sci. Ctr., Houston, 1982-84; owner Marcus Caffee, Cons., Conroe, Tex., 1984—; pres., chief exec. officer Emcee Systems Inc., 1989—; pvt. cons. ins. agy., cleaners/laundry/linen supply, mfg., med. field, builder, fin. inst., wholesale distbn., retail sales. Copyright computer operating system IBOL, 1972, integrated bus. software Office Master!, 1988, 89; author, editor small bus. newletter Read.Me, 1986, 89. Mem. Montgomery County Econ. Devel. Team, 1987; mem. adminstrv. bd. First United Meth. Ch., Conroe, 1987, instr. computer literacy, 1985-87. Served with USN, 1967-71. Mem. Conroe C. of C., Nat. Fedn. Ind. Bus., Lions. Republican. Lodge: Rotary (Conroe chpt., guest speaker 1988). Office: 409 N Loop 336 West Conroe TX 77301

CAFIERO, EUGENE A., manufacturing company executive; b. N.Y.C., June 13, 1926; s. Anthony and Frances (Lauricell) C. BA, Dartmouth Coll., 1946; MS, MIT, 1961; DSc (hon.), Wittenburgh U., 1976. Pres. Chrysler Corp., Highland Park, Mich., 1975-78, vice-chmn., 1978-79; pres. DeLorean Motor Corp., N.Y.C., 1979-81; pres., chief exec. officer Keene Corp., N.Y.C., 1982-86; chmn., pres., chief exec. officer KDI Corp., N.Y.C., 1986—. Lt. (j.g.) USNR, 1944-77. Named Internat. Exec. of Yr. Thunderbird Sch., Phoenix, 1977; Sloan fellow MIT, 1959. Office: KDI Corp 45 Rockefeller Pla New York NY 10111

CAGE, LEO SPAULDING, gas company executive; b. Shreveport, La., Feb. 23, 1934; s. Leo S. Cage and Nell (Rankin) Hamilton; m. Katie Vickers, Aug. 20, 1955 (div. 1987); children—Christopher L., Tracy M. B.S. Centenary Coll., 1959. With Arkla Gas Co., 1961—, asst. gen. sales mgr., Little Rock, 1974-76, gen. sales mgr., 1976-77: v.p. sales Arkla, Inc., Little Rock, 1977-85, v.p. mktg., 1985—. Loaned exec. United Way, Little Rock; bd. dirs. Am. Cancer Soc., 1985-86, Salvation Army, 1976-77; 1st v.p. Quapaw council Boy Scouts Am., 1984. Mem. Sales and Mktg. Execs. Assn. (bd. dirs. 1975-84, Pres.' award 1975-80), Am. Gas Assn. (mktg. com. 1980-84, communications com. 1983-84, Communication award 1984). Democrat. Episcopalian. Clubs: Little Rock Racquet, Westside Tennis (Little Rock), Capitol. Lodge: Rotary. Home: 7510 Indiana #10 Little Rock AR 72207 Office: Arkla Gas Co 400 E Capitol Little Rock AR 72202

CAGGIANO, JOSEPH, advertising executive; b. N.Y.C., Oct. 22, 1925; s. Daniel Joseph and Lucia (Gaudiosi) C.; m. Catherine Marie Gilmore, Aug. 28, 1948; children—Cathleen, Mary Yvonne. B.B.A., Pace Coll., 1953. Chief accountant Criterion Advt. Co., N.Y.C., 1947-57; treas. Emerson Foote, Inc., N.Y.C., 1957-67; became sr. v.p. Bozell & Jacobs, Inc. (now Bozell, Jacobs, Kenyon & Eckhardt Inc.), N.Y.C., 1967; exec. v.p. finance and adminstrn. Bozell & Jacobs, Inc. (now Bozell, Jacobs, Kenyon & Eckhardt Inc.), Omaha, 1971-74; vice chmn. bd., chief financial officer Bozell

& Jacobs, Inc. (now Bozell, Jacobs, Kenyon & Eckhardt Inc.), 1974—, also dir., mem. exec. com.; dir. Emerson Foote, Inc. Bd. dirs. St. Mary's Coll., Omaha Zool. Soc. Served with USNR, 1943-46, ETO, PTO. Mem. N.Y. Credit and Financial Mgmt. Assn., Omaha Zool. Soc. (dir.). Home: 9731 Fieldcrest Dr Omaha NE 68114 Office: Bozell Jacobs Kenyon & Eckhardt Inc 40 W 23rd St New York NY 10010

CAGGIANO, MICHAEL VINCENT, financial services company executive; b. Bronx, N.Y., Apr. 15, 1936; s. Vincent and Laura (Petti) C.; student pub. schs., Bronx; m. Carol Ann Marconelli, Feb. 3, 1962; children—Michael Peter, Stephen Vincent. With Bache Halsey Stuart, N.Y.C., 1954-69, v.p., 1969-74; chmn., pres., chief exec. officer Bradford Securities Processing Services, N.Y.C., 1975-77; chief exec. officer M.V. Caggiano Assos., N.Y.C., 1977-80; sr. v.p. First Wall St. Settlement Corp., N.Y.C., 1980-82; chief exec. officer Security Pacific Clearing Services, RMJ Securities Corp., N.Y.C., 1982-84; chmn., chief exec. officer SPC Securities Services Corp., N.Y.C., 1983—; exec. v.p., mng. dir. Security Pacific Nat. Bank, 1987. Mem. U.S. Senate Bus. Adv. Bd.; adv. bd. trustees Iona Coll., New Rochelle, N.Y. Served with U.S. Army, 1955-57. Republican. Roman Catholic. Club: Rockland Country (Sparkill, N.Y.). Office: Security Pacific Nat Bank PO Box 2097 Terminal Annex Los Angeles CA 90051

CAGLE-KRETLOW, MARY ANN, market research executive, financial planner; b. Peoria, Ill., June 30, 1943; d. George Earl and Maud Arlene (Davis) Jones); m. Thomas I. Cagle, Dec. 19, 1965 (div. 1982); 1 child, April Ann; m. Thomas Edgar Kretlow, Dec. 20, 1987. BS, So. Ill. U., 1965, MS, 1971; MBA, U. Okla., 1979. CLU; cert. broker. Tchr. Ottawa (Ill.) Pub. Schs., 1965-66, Del Rio (Tex.) Ind. Sch. Dist., 1966-67, Snelling (Calif.) Mercer Falls Sch., 1967-68; model, Riverside, Calif., 1970-74; prin., mgr. Mary Ann Cagle Pub. Rels., Marquette, Mich., 1974-78, Cagle Rsch. Svcs., Macon, Ga., 1978—. Mem. pub. rels. com. Ga. chpt. Am. Lung Assn., 1986-88. Mem. Am. Mktg. Assn., Market Rsch. Assn., Career Women's Network (mem. pub. rels. com. Macon chpt. 1983—), Advt. Club Cen. Ga. (mem. pub. rels. com. 1982-85), Ga. Bus. Owners (mem. edn. com. 1985—), LWV. Democrat. Methodist. Home: 890 Orange Terr Macon GA 31201 Office: Cagle Rsch Svcs PO Box 6810 Macon GA 31208

CAGNINELLI, GIOVAN BATTISTA, banker; b. Villa d'Ogna, Bergamo, Italy, Feb. 17, 1941; came to U.S., 1977; s. Giovanni and Anna Maddalena Cagninelli; m. Elizabeth Sarah Lively, June 4, 1977; children: Elizabeth, Julia. BBA in Acctg., Inst. Vittorio Emanuele II, Bergamo, 1961; diploma internat. trade and fin., U. Milziade Tirandi, Brescia, Italy, 1964; diploma bus. adminstrn., Dartmouth Coll., 1986. Bank ofcl. Credito Bergamasco, Bergamo, 1973-74; procurator Am. Express Bank, SpA, Rome, 1974-76, vice dir., 1976-77; asst. v.p. Am. Express Bank, N.Y.C., 1977-79, v.p., 1979-84, 1st v.p., 1984-86, sr. v.p., 1987—. Decorated Cavaliere Republicca di Italy. Mem. Bankers Assn. for Fgn. Trade, Italy-Am. C. of C. (exec. com., dir. chmn. banks, fin. investment and ins. com.), French-Am. C. of C., Brit.-Am. C. of C., Nigerian-Am. C. of C., Portugal-U.S. C. of C., U.S.-Austrian C. of C., Netherlands-Am. C. of C., German-Am. C. of C., Belgian-Am. C. of C., Hellenic-Am. C. of C., U.S. Yugoslav Econ. Coun., Turkish-Am. C. of C., Norwegian-Am. C. of C., Spain-U.S. C. of C., Finnish-Am. C. of C., U.S.-USSR Trade and Econ. Coun. Roman Catholic. Office: Am Express Bank World Fin Ctr New York NY 10285

CAHILL, GERARD ALBIN, electronics company executive; b. N.Y.C., Dec. 21, 1936; s. Albin G. and Susan E. (Maschenic) C.; BS in Elec. Engring., Manhattan Coll., 1958; MBA, City Coll. N.Y., 1962; PhD, NYU, 1973; m. Barbara Viator, July 5, 1969. With Western Electric Co. Inc., N.Y.C., 1959-67; div. controller Gen. Dynamics Corp., Orlando, Fla., 1967-68; corp. controller Liberty Equities Corp., Washington, 1968-69; v.p. HETRA Co., Melbourne, Fla., 1969-71, CODI Corp., Fairlawn, N.J., 1971-73; v.p. fin., treas. Cablecom-Gen. Inc., Denver, 1973-81; sr. v.p. Capital Cities Cable Inc., Bloomfield Hills, Mich., 1981-82; sr. v.p. Simmons Communications, Inc., Stamford, Conn., 1982-85; prof. Westfield (Mass.) State Coll., 1986-87; prof. Fla. Inst. Tech., 1987—; cons. in field. Ford Found. fellow, 1965. Registered profl. engr., N.Y. Mem. Nat. Soc. Profl. Engrs., Am. Mgmt. Assn., Am. Mktg. Assn., IEEE, N.Y. Athletic. Home: 575 Dawson Dr Melbourne FL 32940 Office: Fla Inst Tech Melbourne FL 32901

CAHILL, JEANNE TAYLOR, fitness systems company executive; b. Atlanta, Oct. 19, 1932; d. David Clifford and Wannie B. (Sweat) Taylor; m. William Alpheus Cahill, Aug. 14, 1959; children: William Alpheus Jr., Carol, Cary Taylor. Student, Berry Coll., 1949-51. Editor Atlanta Jour.-Constrn., 1962-64; pres. Cahill Properties Inc., Atlanta, 1965—; pres., chief exec. officer Advanced Fitness Systems, Inc., Atlanta, 1981—; exec. dir. Ga. Commn. on Status of Women, Atlanta, 1972-75; bd. dirs. Fitmar Assn., Columbus. Bd. dirs., mem. exec. com. Epilepsy Found Am., 1982—. Mem. Nat. Sporting Goods Assn., Nat. Sporting Goods Mfg. Assn., Buckhead Bus. Assn. (v.p., bd. dirs. 1984—), Friendship Force Internat. Democrat. Episcopalian. Home: 281 E Paces Ferry Atlanta GA 30305 Office: Advanced Fitness Systems Inc 281 E Paces Ferry Rd Atlanta GA 30305

CAHILL, WILLIAM JOSEPH, JR., utility company executive; b. Suffern, N.Y., June 13, 1923; s. William Joseph and Sophie A. (Scozzafava) C.; m. Edna Kiernan, Oct. 3, 1953; children: William E., Kathleen, Madeleine. B MechE, Poly. Inst. Bklyn., 1949. Registered profl. engr., N.Y., La., Tex. Engr. Consol. Edison, N.Y.C., 1949-54, 57-60, nuclear plant engr., 1961-68, v.p., 1969-80; engr. Knolls Atomic Power Lab., Schenectady, N.Y., 1954-56; sr. v.p. Gulf State Utilities Co., St. Francisville, La., 1980-88; cons. to pres. Tex. Utilities Co., Dallas, 1988; exec. v.p. TU Electric Co., Dallas, 1989—; chmn. safety and analysis task force Electric Power Research Inst., Palo Alto, Calif., 1978-80. Inventor, patentee nuclear reactor vessel, self-activated valve, triggerable fuse. Pres. Queens County Young Republicans, (N.Y.), 1952; bd. dirs. Rockland County Assn. for Retarded, 1966-67. Served with AUS, 1942-46. Mem. Am. Nuclear Soc. (dir. 1980-81, Walter H. Zinn award for outstanding contbns. to advancement nuclear power 1986), La. Nuclear Soc. (chmn. 1982—), ASME, Am. Soc. Registered Profl. Engrs., Knights Holy Sepulcher. Republican. Roman Catholic. Club: City (Baton Rouge, La.); Nat. Arts (N.Y.C.). Home: PO Box 1700 Saint Francisville LA 70775 Office: TU Electric Co 400 N Olive St LB 81 Dallas TX 75201

CAHN, STANLEY ERIC OLLENDORFF, stock exchange executive, financial planner; b. N.Y.C., May 15, 1939; s. Erich and Anny (Ollendorff) C.; m. Stefanie Sandra Dosik, Jan. 4, 1964; children: Melissa, Ethan Howard. BS, NYU, 1962. Sr. editor UPITN Corp., Washington, 1967-73; so. regional dir. B'nai B'rith Found., 1973-77; Washington rep. Zionist Orgn. Am., 1977-79; v.p. Legg Mason Wood Walker, Inc., Washington, 1979—; instr. Okla. Ctr. for Continuing Edn., Norman, 1973-75, Nat. Inst. Fin., Newark, 1985. Mem. Internat. Assn. Fin. Planning, Inst. Cert. Fin. Planners, Army Navy Club, Springfield (Va.) Golf Club (membership chair 1987), Rotary. Jewish. Home: 7012 Hundsford Ln Springfield VA 22153 Office: Legg Mason Wood Walker Inc 1747 Pennsylvania Ave NW Washington DC 20006

CAHNERS-KAPLAN, HELENE R., civic worker; b. Boston, Nov. 29, 1920; d. Sidney R. and Esther (Cohn) Rabb; AA, Westbrook Coll., 1940; student Mt. Holyoke Coll.; LLD (hon.), Northeastern U., 1974; m. Norman L. Cahners, May 15, 1941 (dec. Mar. 1986); children: Robert Merrill, Andrew Philip, Nancy Lynne; m. George I. Kaplan, Jan. 11, 1989. Former mem. trust bd. 1st Nat. Bank Boston; dir. Boston Edison Co., Berkshire Mut. Life Ins. Co., SYR Corp. Pres. women's aux. Beth-Israel Hosp., Boston, 1959-61 (hon. life trustee hosp.); co-chmn. Council of Friends Boston Symphony Orch., 1962-68, chmn. bd. overseers Orch., 1980-82, also trustee; pres. women's div. Combined Jewish Philanthropies, Boston, 1965-67, asst. sec., 1967-69, v.p., 1969-77, life trustee; bd. dirs. ladies com. New Eng. Med. Center, Boston 1965, Children's Med. Ctr., Boston, 1961—; trustee emerita Westbrook Coll. (Tower award 1966), chmn. bd., 1972-75; trustee Carroll Sch., 1971-86 , Boston Opera Assn., 1972-85, Mt. Holyoke Coll., 1970-80, Women's Ednl. and Indsl. Union, World Affairs Council, Wang Ctr., Boston; trustee Boston Mus. Sci.; mem. adv. bd. Colby Coll. Art Mus., 1970-76 , Mayor's Office of Cultural Affairs; bd. dirs. WGBH-TV, Boston, also vice-chmn.; bd. dirs. United Community Planning Corp.; bd. visitors Boston U. Sch. Social Work; hon. v.p. Boston Children's Svc.; mem. council on arts MIT; bd. visitors Sch. Social Work, Boston U.; numerous others. Named Tower Disting. Alumnae Westbrook Coll., 1966, Ralph Lowell Disting. Citizen, 1981; fellow Mt. Holyoke Coll., 1988. Home: 1500 S Ocean Blvd Boca Raton FL 33432

CAHOUET, FRANK VONDELL, banker; b. Cohasset, Mass., May 25, 1932; s. Ralph Hubert and Mary Claire (Jordan) C.; m. Ann Pleasonton Walsh, July 14, 1956; children: Ann P., Mary G., Frank V., David R. BA, Harvard U., 1954; MBA, U. Pa., 1959. Corp. loan asst. Security Pacific Nat. Bank, Los Angeles, 1960-66, v.p., 1966-69; sr. loan adminstr. Security Pacific Nat. Bank, Europe/Middle East/Africa, 1969-73; exec. v.p. Security Pacific Nat. Bank, 1978-80, vice chmn., 1980-84; exec. v.p. Security Pacific Corp., Los Angeles, 1973-80, vice chmn., 1980-84; chmn., pres. and chief exec. officer Crocker Nat. Bank, San Francisco, 1984-86; pres., chief operating officer Fed. Nat. Mortgage Assn., 1986-87; chmn., chief exec. officer Mellon Bank Corp., Pitts., 1987—; bd. dirs. Avery Internat. Corp., Los Angeles. Trustee Carnegie-Mellon U., Pitts., U. Pitts., Pa's. S.W.Assn., Pitts.; mem. bd. overseers Wharton Sch., U. Pa. Mem. Newcomen Soc. Clubs: Duquesne, Edgeworth, Laurel Valley Golf (Pitts.); California (Los Angeles); Pacific Union (San Francisco). Office: Mellon Bank Corp 1 Mellon Bank Ctr Pittsburgh PA 15258-0001

CAILLÉ, ANDRÉ, gas distribution company executive; b. Saint-Luc, Que., Can., Sept. 11, 1943; s. Jean-Paul C.; m. Lyse Senécal; children: Daniel, Guillaume, Marc-Vincent. BSc, U. Montreal, Que., Can., 1965, MSc, 1966, PhD, 1968, postdoctoral study in biophysics, 1969. Dir. Fed./Provincial Com. on St. Lawrence River, Quebec, 1975-76, Environ. Protection Services, Quebec, 1977-79; dep. minister Dept. Environ., Quebec, 1980-82; sr. v.p. adminstrn. and pub. affairs Gaz Metro., Montreal, 1983-85, exec. v.p., 1985-87, pres., chief exec. officer, 1987—, also bd. dirs.; bd. dirs. Sanivan, Montreal. Home: 345 Bloomfield, Outremont, PQ Canada H2V 3R7 Office: Gaz Métropolitain Inc, 1717 du Havre, Montreal, PQ Canada H2K 2X3

CAIN, PATRICIA JEAN, financial executive, accountant; b. Decatur, Ill., Sept. 28, 1931; d. Paul George and Jean Margaret (Horne) Jacka; m. Dan Louis Cain, July 12, 1952; children: Mary Ann, Timothy George, Paul Louis. Student, U. Mich., 1949-52, Pasadena (Calif.) City Coll., 1975-76; BS in Acctg., Calif. State U., Los Angeles, 1977, MBA in Acctg., 1978; M in Taxation, Golden Gate U., Los Angeles, 1988. CPA, Calif.; cert. personal fin. planner; cert. advanced fin. planner. Tax supr. Stonefield & Josephson, Los Angeles, 1979-87; chief fin. officer Loubella Extendables, Inc., Los Angeles, 1987—; participant program in bus. ethics U. So. Calif., Los Angeles, 1986. Bd. dirs. Sierra Madre Girl Scout Council, Pasadena, 1968-73, treas., 1973-75, elected nat. del., 1975; mem. Town Hall, Los Angeles, 1987—. Listed as one of top six tax experts in L.A. by Money mag., 1987. Mem. Am. Inst. CPAs (chairperson nat. tax teleconf. 1988), Am. Women's Soc. CPA's (bd. dirs. 1986-87, v.p. 1987—), Calif. Soc. CPAs (chairperson free tax assistance program 1983-85, high rd. com. 1985-86, chairperson pub. relations com. 1985-87, microcomputer users discussion group, taxation com., fin. com./speaker computer show and conf. 1987-88, planning com. and speaker San Francisco Tax and Microcomputer show 1988), Internat. Arabian Horse Assn., Beta Alpha Psi. Democrat. Episcopalian. Club: Wrightwood Country (Calif.). Home: 3715 Fairmeade Rd Pasadena CA 91107 Office: Loubella Extendables Inc 2222 S Figueroa St Los Angeles CA 90007

CAINE, STEPHEN HOWARD, data process executive.; b. Washington, Feb. 11, 1941; s. Walter E. and Jeanette (Wenborne) C.; student Calif. Inst. Tech., 1958-62. Sr. programmer Calif. Inst. Tech., Pasadena, 1962-65, mgr. systems programming, 1965-69, mgr. programming, 1969-70; pres. Caine, Farber & Gordon, Inc., Pasadena, 1970—; lectr. applied sci. Calif. Inst. Tech., Pasadena, 1965-71, vis. asso. elec. engring., 1976, vis. asso. computer sci., 1976-84. Mem. Pasadena Tournament of Roses Assn., 1976—. Mem. Assn. Computing Machinery, Nat. Assn. Corrosion Engrs., AAAS, Am. Ordnance Assn. Clubs: Athenaeum (Pasadena); Engrs. (N.Y.C.). Home: 77 Patrician Way Pasadena CA 91105

CAIRNS, RAYMOND ELDON, JR., chemical company executive; b. Troy, N.Y., Dec. 13, 1932; s. Raymond Eldon Sr. and Anne Marie (Kennedy) C.; m. Mae Friswell; children: Michael R., Marianne Cairns Katz. SB, MIT, 1954, SM, 1960, ScD, 1962. Metallurgist Westinghouse Co., Pitts., 1954, Nat. Research Corp., Boston, 1956-59; sr. metallurist E.I. DuPont De Nemours & Co., Wilmington, Del., 1962-69; supt. mfg. E.I. DuPont De Nemours & Co., Circleville, Ohio, 1969-74; mgr. engring. research E.I. DuPont De Nemours & Co., Wilmington, 1974-77, mgr. corp. planning, 1977-79, mng. dir. info. systems, 1979-85, v.p. info. systems, 1985—. Served to 1st lt. USAF, 1954-56. Home: 102 Santomera Ln Greenville DE 19807 Office: E I Du Pont de Nemours & Co 1007 Market St Wilmington DE 19898

CAIRNS, SHIRLEY ANN, financial planner; b. Hundred, W.Va., Sept. 26, 1937; d. John Martin and Thelma Irene Stiles; children: John Michael, Lyle Dennis, Glynis Ann. BS, W.Va. U., 1959, MA, 1964; MPA, Harvard U., 1989. Cert. fin. planner. Tchr. public schs., Alliance, Ohio, 1958-60, Morgantown, W.Va., 1960-61;tchr., head bus. edn. dept. Sutherlin (Oreg.) High Sch., 1964-80; registered rep. IDS, 1980-83; prin. Shirley A. Cairns & Assocs., 1983-88. Active Oreg. State Dem. 4th dist. Cen. Com., 1982, Oreg. Dem. Rules Com., Oreg. Dem. Exec. Com., 1985-88, Oreg. Dem. Cen. Com., 1982-89, Douglas County Tourist Adv. Com., Douglas County Dem. Cen. Com., 1980-88; del. Dem. Nat. Conv., 1984, mem. rules com., 1988; mem. Roseburg dist. adv. com. Bur. Land Mgmt., 1987-90; mem. Oreg. Port Adv. Com., 1988-89; bd. dirs. Calapooia Water Dist., March of Dimes; active Leadership Am., 1988. Mem. Nat. Women's Polit. Caucus, So. Oreg. Women's Polit. Caucus (v.p.). Oreg. Women's Polit. Caucus, Internat. Assn. Fin. Planners, Inst. Cert. Fin. Planners, Roseburg C. of C., Douglas County C. of C., AAUW, Lioness, Xi Tau. Home: 2460 Hwy 138W PO Box 76 Oakland OR 97462 Office: 1012 SE Oak Ste 330 Roseburg OR 97470

CAJIGAL, JOSEPH A., financial services executive; b. N.Y.C., Nov. 15, 1953; s. Jose and Frances (Cabezal) C.; m. Virginia E. Divers, May 2, 1983; 1 child, Joseph Neil. BA in Math. Econs., St. Peter's Coll., 1976. Sr. v.p. Fiduciary Trust Co. Internat., N.Y.C., 1976-87; pres. Fiduciary Fin. Services Corp., N.Y.C., 1987—, also bd. dirs., 1986—; allied mem. N.Y. Stock Exchange. Club: Downtown Athletic (N.Y.C.). Office: Fiduciary Fin Svcs Corp 2 World Trade Ctr New York NY 10048

CAJTHAML, MICHAEL JOSEPH, insurance and investment sales executive; b. Woodstock, Ill., Dec. 26, 1955; s. ALbert Anton and Ethel Virginia (Nykl) C.; m. Deborah Anne Pintozzi, June 2, 1979; 1 child, Michael Joseph Jr. Grad. high sch., McHenry, Ill., 1974. Owner, operator Cyscorp, McHenry, 1972-86; registered rep. Transamerica Fin. Resources, McHenry and Oak Brook Terrace, Ill., 1986—; owner Cyscorp Fin. Ins. and Investment Services, McHenry, 1986—; with SWANK Ins. Agy., Waukegan, Ill., 1989—. Chmn. Fiesta Days Festival, McHenry, 1984, Crimestoppers, McHenry, 1983-85, Village Sunnyside Plan Commn., 1988—. Named one of Outstanding Young Men Am., U.S. Jaycees, 1984; Life Underwriters Tng. Council fellow, 1988. Mem. Du Page County Life Underwriters, Nat. Assn. Life Underwriters (polit. action com. 1987—), McHenry Area C. of C. (chmn. pub. relations 1983, bd. dirs. 1983-85). Republican. Roman Catholic. Club: Toastmasters. Home: 4416 Mayfair Dr McHenry IL 60050 Office: Cyscorp Fin Ins and Investment Svcs 4416 Mayfair Dr McHenry IL 60050 also: 329 N Genesee St Waukegan IL 60079

CALABRO, JACK LOUIS, consumer products executive; b. N.Y.C., Sept. 7, 1941; s. Samuel Joseph and Pearl (Jacobs) C.; children: Rachel, Michael. BA, CCNY, 1963; MBA, U. Ill., 1969. Mgr. Inland Steel Co., Chgo., 1964-69; v.p. Maremont Corp., Chgo., 1969-80, Alusuisse of Am., Inc., N.Y.C., 1980-83, Helene Curtis Industries, Inc., Chgo., 1984—; dir. adminstrn. ITT, Skokie, Ill., 1983-84. Bd. dirs. Urban Gateways, Chgo., 1984—, chmn. com. 1985-88; bd. dirs. Am. Cancer Soc., Chgo., 1984-87. Mem. Human Resource Assn. (chmn. com. 1986), Fgn. Rels. Counc. Chgo., U. Ill. Alumni Assn. (bd. dirs. 1974-78), Econ. Club, Univ. Club (chmn. com. 1986-88). Office: Helene Curtis Industries Inc 325 N Wells St Chicago IL 60610

CALAFATI, PETER GABE, construction company executive; b. Newark, Feb. 25, 1957; s. Gabriel Raffele and Anna Lucia (Giliberti) C.; m. Lynn Marie Schoenrock, Jan. 14, 1978; children: Nicholas, Maria, Anna. BBA, U. Notre Dame, 1979. Field engr., carpenter Frank Briscoe Co., Inc., 1974-77, carpenter foreman, 1978; contract adminstr. Frank Briscoe Co., Inc., Roseland, N.J., 1982-84, project exec., 1985—, also bd. dirs.; sr. reliability engr. Gen. Motors, 1979-82. Mem. Woodbridge (N.J.) Environ. Commn., 1986-87, Woodbridge Planning Bd., 1986-87, Colonia Civic Assn., Bay View Shores Owners Assn.; exec. dir. Essex County council Boy Scouts Am., 1988—. Mem. Assn. Gen. Contractors, Bldg. Contractors Assn. N.J., N.J. Indsl. Devel. Agy, NCCJ, Eaglerock Club (Roseland), Compuserve (Columbus, Ohio). Roman Catholic. Home: 32 Claremont Ave Colonia NJ 07067 Office: Frank Briscoe Co Inc Briscoe Bldg Roseland NJ 07068

CALAMOS, JOHN PETER, SR., financial executive; b. Aug. 28, 1940; s. Peter and Mary (Kyriakopoulos) C.; m. Jackie Calamos, Aug. 15, 1962; children: John Peter Jr. and Laura Lynn. BS in Econs., Ill. Inst. Tech., 1963, MBA in Fin., 1965. Registered rep. DuPont Walston Co., Chgo., 1971-74, Loeb Rhoades Co., Chgo., 1974, Bache & Co., Chgo., 1974-75, Hornblower-Weeks Co., Chgo., 1975-76; sr. v.p. Woodlard & Co., Chgo., 1976-77; pres., mng. dir. Calamos Asset Mgmt., Inc., Oak Brook, Ill., 1977—; pres. Calamos Convertible Income Fund, Oak Brook, 1985—. Author: Investing in a Convertible Securities: A Guide to Their Risks and Rewards, 1988; contbr. articles to profl. jours. Served as maj. USAF, 1965-70, Vietnam. Mem. Am. Mgmt. Assn., Internat. Assn. Fin. Planners, Chgo. Assn. Commerce and Industry, Assn. Investment Mgmt. Sales Execs. Club: Sky Haven (Aurora, Ill.) (pres.). Office: Calamos Asset Mgmt Inc 2001 Spring Rd Ste 750 Oak Brook IL 60521

CALARCO, VINCENT ANTHONY, specialty chemicals company executive; b. N.Y.C., May 29, 1942; s. George Michael and Madeline C.; m. Linda Joyce Maniscalo, Apr. 10, 1971; children—David V., Christopher G. B.S., Poly. Inst., Bklyn., 1963; M.B.A., Harvard U., 1970. With Crompton & Knowles Corp, N.Y.C., pres., chief exec. officer, 1985—; chmn. bd. Crompton & Knowles Corp, 1986—; chmn. consultor com. Faculty of Chem. Engring. Manhattan Coll. Trustee Poly. U. Served with U.S. Army, 1966-68. Mem. Soc. Chem. Industry, Soc. de Chimie Industrielle, Chem. Mfrs. Assn. (bd. dirs.), The Chemists Club, Chem. Mfrs. Assn. Club: Harvard Bus. Sch. Office: Crompton & Knowles Corp 1 Station Pl Metro Ctr Stamford CT 06902

CALCAGNI, JOSEPH, treasurer, controller; b. Youngstown, Ohio, Apr. 10, 1956; s. Eugene James and Antonette Marie (Popio) C.; m. Cynthia Marie Moschella, May 28, 1980; children: Deana Marie, Joseph Michael, Anthony Thomas. BBA in Acctg., Youngstown State U., 1980. CPA, Ohio. Staff acct. Burns, O'Hare and Co., CPA's, Youngstown, 1980-83; sr. staff acct. Schroedel, Scullin and Bestic, Inc., CPA's, Youngstown, 1983-85; controller Graphic Svc. Co., Youngstown, 1985; asst. treas. Youngstown Rubber Products Co., Youngstown, 1987—. Mem. Nat. Assn. Accts. (bd. dirs.). Office: Youngstown Rubber Products Co 854 Mahoning Ave PO Box 1377 Youngstown OH 44501

CALDABAUGH, KARL, holding company executive; b. Salisbury, Md., Nov. 26, 1946; s. Harry Rahr and Eleanor (Long) C.; m. Kay Laws, May 27, 1978; children—Kevin, Kyle. B.A., W. Va. Wesleyan Coll., 1968; M.B.A., U. Ala., 1973. Asst. v.p. Jacksonville Nat. Bank, Fla., 1973-79; v.p., treas. Charter Oil Co., Jacksonville, 1979-81; v.p. corp. devel. The Charter Co., Jacksonville, 1981-84, sr. v.p. fin., 1984-86, exec. v.p., chief fin. officer, 1986-87; v.p., treas. LTV Corp., Dallas, 1987—. Mem. Leadership, Jacksonville, 1983. Mem. Fin. Execs. Inst., Mensa, Beta Gamma Sigma. Republican. Methodist. Club: Bent Tree. Home: 3108 Caruth Dallas TX 75225 Office: LTV Corp 2001 Ross Ave Dallas TX 75201

CALDICOTT, JACK RICHARD, electronics executive; b. Coventry, Warwickshire, Eng., Mar. 13, 1937; s. Oliver James and Violet Mary (Wells) C.; m. Cindy Amy Neal, Aug. 31, 1963; children: Ian Mark, Simon John. M in Mgmt., Northwestern U. Chartered profl. engr., Eng. Project engr. Hawker Siddelt Dynamics, Inc., Cheadle Hulme, Eng., 1963-69; mng. dir. Railweight Ltd., Stockport, Eng., 1969-78; v.p., dir. Railweight Ltd., Elm Grove, Ill., 1978-79; v.p. Streeter/Amet div. Mangood Corp., Grayslake, Ill., 1981-85; pres. Automatic Measurement Tech., Inc., Wauconda, Ill., 1985—. Patentee electronic circuits and weight-controlled loading systems. Mem. Can. Task Force on Motion Weighing, 1983-84. Served with Royal Elec. and Mech. Engrs. Mem. British Inst. Electronic and Radio Engrs. Home: 28461 West Kelsey Ct Barrington IL 60010 Office: Automatic Measurment Tech 1000 Rand Rd Bldg 111 Wauconda IL 60084

CALDWELL, BILLY RAY, geologist; b. Newellton, La., Apr. 20, 1932; s. Leslie Richardson and Helen Merle (Clark) C.; m. Carolyn Marie Heath, May 9, 1979; children—Caryn, Jeana, Craig. BA, Tex. Christian U., 1954, MA, 1970; Cert. petroleum geologist, Tex. Geologist, Geol. Engring. Service Co., Ft. Worth, Tex., 1954-60; sci. tchr. Ft. Worth and Lake Worth Sch. Dists., 1960-63; mgr. Outdoor Living, 1963-71; instr. geology Tarrant County Jr. Coll., Ft. Worth, 1971—; petroleum geologist cons., Ft. Worth, 1971—. Bd. dirs. Ft. Worth and Tarrant County Homebuilders Assn., 1973. Named Dir. of Yr., Ft. Worth Jaycees, 1966-67. Mem. Am. Inst. Profl. Geologists (cert.), Ft. Worth Geol. Soc., Am. Assn. Petroleum Geologists, Soc. Profl. Well Log Analysts, Geol. Soc. Am. Republican. Baptist. Avocations: traveling, gardening, ch. work. Home: 305 Bodart Ln Fort Worth TX 76108 Office: 101 Jim Wright Freeway Suite 402 Fort Worth TX 76108

CALDWELL, CATHERINE CAROLYN DI NARDO, construction company executive; b. Cokeburg, Pa., Jan. 26, 1938; d. Pietro and Paula Josephine (Intervartol) Di Nardo; m. James Wilson Caldwell Jr., Jan. 17, 1959; children: James Michael, Gregory Albert. Cert., Pa. Comml. Coll., Washington, 1957; student, Kane Modeling Sch., Butler, Pa., 1988—. Jr. acct. Chartiers Motor Co., Washington, Pa., 1957-60; with dept. warehouse control ctr. Joy Mfg. Co., Meadowlands, Pa., 1960-62; payroll clk. radio and TV div. Westinghouse, Edison, N.J., 1962-63; sec. Permacel div. Johnson & Johnson, New Brunswick, N.J., 1966-67; asst. v.p. Viking Erectors Corp., Butler, 1969—; asst. sec., treas. J&K Erection Co., Inc., Butler, 1971—, Delrose Constrn. Co., Butler, 1986—. Roman Catholic. Home: 153 Heather Dr Butler PA 16001 Office: Viking Erectors Corp 108 W McMurray Rd McMurray PA 15317

CALDWELL, CHARLES ANDERSON, banker; b. Amory, Miss., Sept. 4, 1942; s. William Stanley and Martha Frances (Wade) C.; m. Sandra Delores Leech, Dec. 17, 1961; children: Diana Leigh, Kimberly Frances, Charles Anderson II. BBA, U. Miss., 1965, postgrad., 1972-73; postgrad. in bank ops., U. Wis.-Madison, 1977. Asst. mgr. Retail Furniture Store, Amory, Miss., 1965-68; prodn. forecaster Rockwell Internat., Tupelo, Miss., 1968-70; ops. officer Bank of Miss., Tupelo, 1970-80, asst. v.p., loan officer, 1980—. Chmn. Monroe County Carmichael for Gov. campaign, 1976; vol. Heart Fund, Tupelo, 1975, Lee County United Neighbors, Tupelo, 1970-80. Mem. Common Cause, Internat. Platform Assn., Sierra Club, Amnesty Internat., Nature Conservancy, Greenpeace U.S.A., Greenpeace Southeast (activist com.), Univ. Miss. Alumni Assn. and Loyalty Found. Republican. Presbyterian. Clubs: Amory Country; Aberdeen Country. Lodge: Lions (pres. Nettleton, Miss. club 1982-83, treas. 1983—). Avocations: golfing, fishing, cooking. Home: 1221 Williamsburg Dr Amory MS 38821 Office: Bank of Miss PO Drawer B Nettleton MS 38858

CALDWELL, DONALD R., accountant, savings and loan executive; b. Boston, June 22, 1946; s. Donald Mitchell and Flora Agnes (Raymond) C.; m. Judith McGregor, June 10, 1972; children: Richard Carter, Marcy McGregor. BSBA, Babson Coll., 1967; MBA, Harvard U., 1973. CPA, N.Y. With Shawmut Bank, Boston, 1968-71; asst. to treas. InterAm. Devel. Bank, Washington, 1972; with Arthur Young & Co., N.Y.C., 1973-83, ptnr., co-chmn. fin. svcs. group, 1982-83; exec. v.p., chief operating officer, bd. dirs. Atlantic Fin., Bala Cynwyd, Pa., 1983-84, pres., chief exec. officer, 1984—; trustee Thomson McKinnon Investment Trust, 1983-86, Cash Accumulation Trust N.Y., 1983-86, The Windjammer Fund, 1987—, Com. for Econ. Devel., 1987—; bd. dirs. Fed. Home Loan Bank Pitts., Greater Phila. 1st. Corp. Contbr. articles to profl. jours. Task force project mgr. Pres. Reagan's Pvt. Sector Survey on Cost Control in Fed. Govt., 1982-83; trustee Com. for Econ. Devel., 1987—; bd. dirs. Phila. Orch. Assn., 1987—, The Union League of Phila., 1987—, Penjerdel Coun. of Phila., The Urban Affairs Partnership. Mem. AICPA, N.Y. State Soc. CPAs (com. for econ.

devel. 1987—), Greater Phila. C. of C. (bd. dirs. 1988—). Republican. Episcopalian. Clubs: N.Y. Racquet and Tennis; Phila. Racquet, Union League (Phila.), Merion Cricket (Haverford, Pa.). Home: 531 N Rose Ln Haverford PA 19041 Office: Atlantic Fin Fed 50 Monument Rd Bala-Cynwyd PA 19004

CALDWELL, JUDY CAROL, advertising executive, public relations executive; b. Nashville, Dec. 28, 1946; d. Thomas and Sarah Elizabeth Carter; m. John Cope Caldwell; 1 child, Jessica. BS, Wayne State U., 1969. Tchr. Bailey Mid. Sch., West Haven, Conn., 1969-72; editorial asst. Vanderbilt U., Nashville, 1973-74; editor, graphics designer, field researcher Urban Observatory of Met. Nashville, 1974-77; account exec. Holden and Co., Nashville, 1977-79; bus. tchr. Federated States of Micronesia, 1979-80; dir. advt. Am. Assn. for State and Local History, Nashville, 1980-81; dir. prodn. Mktg. Communications Co., Nashville, 1981-83; owner, pres. Ridge Hill Corp., Nashville, 1983—. Office: Ridge Hill Corp 4004 Hillsboro Rd Ste A-201 Nashville TN 37215

CALDWELL, RICHARD CLARK, banker; b. Ottawa, Ont., Can., July 28, 1944; came to U.S., 1945; s. Robert Ralston Chrisman and Patricia Ann (Clark) C.; m. Judith Ann Van Harn, Sept. 2, 1967; 1 child, Jennifer MacLean. A.B., Kenyon Coll., 1967; M.B.A., Emory U., 1972. Officer Harris Bank, Chgo., 1976, asst. v.p., 1977-79, v.p., 1979-82, sr. v.p., group exec. instl. trust adminstrn., 1982-86, exec. v.p., trust dept. exec., 1986—; bd. dirs. Harris Trust Bank Ariz. Treas. Travelers and Immigrants Aid, Chgo., 1982, hon. bd. dirs., 1986—; bd. govs. Ill. Council on Econ. Edn.; trustee Hadley Sch. for Blind. Served to 1st lt. U.S. Army, 1968-71, Vietnam. Decorated Bronze Star with v-device, Air medal with v-device; recipient Phoenix award Atlanta Advt. Club, 1972. Mem. Beta Gamma Sigma. Republican. Episcopalian. Clubs: University, Economic (Chgo.); Indian Hill (Winnetka, Ill.). Home: 1125 Spruce St Winnetka IL 60093 Office: Harris Trust & Savs Bank 111 W Monroe St PO Box 755 Chicago IL 60690

CALDWELL, ROBERT H., manufacturing company executive; b. Broofield, Mo., Nov. 17, 1930; s. Robert Dallas and Mary (King) C.; m. Adelaide Bailey, June 22, 1957; children: Kenneth, Allison. BS in Accountancy, U. Ill., 1953. With Armstrong World Industries, Lancaster, Pa., 1956—, various positions, 1956-74, v.p., gen. mgr., 1974-79, group v.p., 1979-83, exec. v.p., sr. exec. v.p., 1988—, also bd. dirs. Bd. dirs. Lancaster YMCA Found., 1982—. Served with USN, 1953-56. Mem. Lancaster Country Club (dir. 1977—), Hamilton Club. Office: Armstrong World Industries Inc 333 W Liberty St PO Box 3001 Lancaster PA 17604

CALDWELL, WILEY NORTH, distribution company executive; b. L.A., Apr. 24, 1927; s. Wiley North and Jean (Clarke) C.; m. Joanne Humphrey, Mar. 25, 1950; children: David, Wendy, Charles, Thomas. BSME, Stanford U., 1950; MBA, Harvard U., 1952. Mgr. prodn. control Waste King Corp., L.A., 1952-54; v.p., co-founder Poroloy Equipment, Inc., Van Nuys, Calif., 1954-58, dir. sales and mktg. Bendix Filter div., 1958-60; v.p. Jamieson Labs., Inc., Van Nuys, 1960-61; v.p. mktg., exec. v.p. McGaw Labs., Am. Hosp. Supply Corp., L.A., Chgo., 1961-69; v.p. internat. Am. Hosp. Supply Corp., Chgo., 1969-72, pres. Midwest Dental div., 1972-77; v.p. ops. distbn. group W.W. Grainger, Inc., Skokie, Ill., 1977-78, pres. distbn. group, 1978-81, exec. v.p., 1981-84, pres., 1984—, also bd. dirs.; bd. dirs. Kewaunee Sci. Corp., Wilmette, Ill, CBI Industries, Inc., Oak Brook. Bd. dirs. Evanston-Glenbrook Hosp., Evanston, Ill.; gov. bd. Ill. Coun. Econ. Edn. and Northwestern Univ. Assocs. With USN, 1945-46. Mem. Indian Hill Club, Chgo. Club. Home: 125 Woodstock Ave Kenilworth IL 60043 Office: W W Grainger Inc 5500 W Howard St Skokie IL 60077

CALESTINO, KAREN JOAN, construction company executive; b. Providence, R.I., Sept. 18, 1952; d. Astillodore and Maria (Micheletti) Diodati; m. Peter George Calestino, Apr. 11, 1976; children: Maria, Peter A. Student, R.I. Jr. Coll., Warwick, 1972. Notary Public. Exec. sec. A&D Constrn. Co., Inc., Cranston, R.I., 1974-87, asst. treas., 1980-87, also bd. dirs. Recipient Honor award Hist. Preservation Soc., Providence, 1983. Mem. Women in Constrn, Bldg. Trades Assn. Roman Catholic. Office: A&D Constrn Co Inc 116 Preston Dr Cranston RI 02910

CALFEE, JOHN BEVERLY, lawyer; b. Cleve., May 2, 1913; s. Robert M. and Alwine (Haas) C.; m. Nancy Leighton, Feb. 8, 1944; children—John Beverly Jr., David L., Peter H., Mark E. Grad., Hotchkiss Sch., 1931; B.A., Yale, 1935; LL.B., Western Res. U., 1938. Bar: Ohio bar 1939. Ptnr. Calfee, Halter & Griswold, Cleve., 1939—; retired Calfee, Halter & Griswold, 1986; Dir. Morrison Products Inc. Dir. civil def., Cleve., 1951; chmn. Cuyohoga County Rep. Fin. Com., 1978-81; mem. Ohio N.W. Ordinance Bicentennial Commn., 1986; trustee Ohio Hist. Soc., 1988. Maj. AUS, 1942-46. Mem. ABA, Ohio Bar Assn., Cleve. Bar Assn., Ohio Hist. Soc. (trustee 1988—), Soc. of Benchers, University Club (N.Y.C.), Mayfield Club, Union Club, Pepper Pike Club, Masons, Shriners, Rotary, Jupiter (Fla.) Hills Club. Presbyterian. Home: 4892 Clubside Dr Lyndhurst OH 44124 Office: 1800 Society Bldg Cleveland OH 44114

CALHOUN, JOHN COZART, financial and marketing executive; b. Ft. Oglethorpe, Ga., Aug. 6, 1937; s. James Paul and Geneva F. (Fortson) C.; LLB, Blackstone Sch. Law, 1970; BA, Eastern Nebr. Coll., 1972; LLD (hon.), Edward Waters Coll., 1975, Morris Brown Coll., 1976, Daniel Payne Coll., 1976; PhD (hon.), Va. Coll., 1976, PhD Clayton U., 1977, postgrad. U. East Asia, Macau. Intelligence analyst NATO, Izmir, Turkey, 1959; corr. Stars and Stripes, Dept. Def., 1959-60; newspaper editor, Ft. Myer, Va., 1961-63; news editor Sta. VUNC, Okinawa, 1963-64; public affairs rep. Dept. Def., Maine-N.H.-Vt., 1964-67; Tokyo public affairs rep. UN, 1967-68; chief community relations Mil. Dist. Washington, 1969-70; dir. public affairs Nat. Farmers Union, 1970-71; dir. minority communications Peace Corps, 1971-73; staff asst., dep. spl. asst. to Pres. for minority affairs, 1973-74; spl. asst. to Pres., also dir. for media relations The White House, Washington, 1975-76; chmn. bd. Aaken Calhoun Group; pres. Calhoun Assocs., Counselors, Internat. Law, Bus. and Internat. Relations; dir. Am.-Asian Trading Co., Am. Bionics Enterprises. Bd. dirs. Bel-Pre Civic Assn., 1973-76; communications adv. Republican Nat. Com.; mem. Nat. Adv. Council on Edn. for Disadvantaged Children, World Affairs Council Washington D.C. Served with U.S. Army, 1955-59. Decorated Army Commendation ribbon; recipient award Middle Atlantic Assn. Indsl. Editors, 1961; Clio award Am. TV and Radio Comml. Festival Group, 1971; Andy award Advt. Club N.Y., 1971; Nat. Man of Yr. award Nat. Inst. Rural Agrarian Life, 1976; Disting. Public Service award Prairie View A&M U., 1976. Mem. Internat. Communication Assn., Am. Mgmt. Assn., Acad. Polit. Sci., DAV (life), Am. Legion, Am. Assn. Retired People, Assn. Internat. Practical Tng. (bd. dirs. U.S. affiliate), Nat. Press Club, Capital Press Club (dir. 1969—), Rep. Nat. Com. Assos. Republican. Club: Capital Office: Box 70620 SW Sta Washington DC 20024

CALHOUN, JOHN P., manufacturing company executive; b. 1926; married. B.C.E., Clemson U., 1948; advanced mgmt. program, Harvard U., 1980-81. Sales engr. B.L. Montague Co., 1955-56; sales rep. Kieckhefer Container Corp., 1956-57; with Rexnord Co., Milw., 1957—, mgr. sales, 1957-68, div. mgr. mktg., 1968-70, pres. gear div., 1970-74; v.p. sales mktg. ECG-Rexnord Inc., Milw., 1974-79; pres. rotary components group Rexnord Inc., Milw., 1979-81, pres. mech. power div., 1981-82, v.p. sector exec., 1982-85, pres., chief operating officer, 1985-88, chmn. chief exec. officer, 1988—. Served with U.S. Army, 1944-46. Office: Rexnord Inc 350 N Sunny Slope Rd Milwaukee WI 53005

CALIGIURI, IRENE GLORIA, senior economist; b. Buenos Aires, Sept. 13, 1939; came to U.S., 1963; naturalized, 1969; d. Roque Nicolas and Angela (Andia) C. Student, U. Law, Argentina, 1960; BS in Fin. and Acctg., N.Y. Inst. Tech., 1978, MBA, 1985; postgrad., Ctr. for Profl. Advancement, 1980; NARUC regulatory studies program, Mich. State U., 1980. Asst. sr. economist Zinder Cos., Washington, 1965-69; tech. asst. to Dr. F.J. Leerburger, econs. and engring. cons. N.Y.C., 1969-70; exec. asst. Allan J. Schultz, N.Y.C., 1970-78; mgr. Power Authority State of N.Y., N.Y.C., 1978—. Mem. Delta Mu Delta. Home: 501 Eagle Bay Dr Ossining-on-Hudson NY 10562

CALISE, NICHOLAS JAMES, corporate lawyer; b. N.Y.C., Sept. 15, 1941; s. William J. and Adeline (Rota) C.; m. Mary G. Flannery, Nov. 10, 1965; children: James R., Lori K. AB, Middlebury Coll., 1962; MBA, LLB, Columbia U., 1965. Bar: N.Y. 1965, Conn., 1974, Ohio, 1986. Assoc., ptnr. Olvany, Eisner & Donnelly, N.Y.C., 1969-76; corp. staff atty. Richardson-Vicks Inc., Wilton, Conn., 1976-82; div. counsel, dir. planning and bus. devel. home care products div. Richardson-Vicks Inc., Memphis, 1982-84; staff v.p., sec., asst. gen. counsel The BFGoodrich Co., Akron, Ohio, 1984-89, v.p., sec., assoc. gen. counsel, 1989—. Mem. Flood and Erosion Control Bd., Darien, Conn., 1976, Rep. Town Meeting, Darien, 1977-78; chmn. Zoning Bd. Appeals, Darien, 1978-82; Justice of the Peace, Darien, 1982. Served to lt. USN, 1965-68, serves as capt. JAGC, USNR, 1984—. Mem. ABA, Am. Soc. Corp. Secs., N.Y. Bar Assn., Conn. Bar Assn., Ohio Bar Assn., Assn. of Bar of City of N.Y., Ohio Regional Group (treas. 1988-89), U.S. Naval Inst., Navy League, Judge Advocates Assn., Naval Reserve Assn. (life), Reserve Officers Assn. (life). Roman Catholic. Clubs: Cascade (Akron); Country of Hudson (Ohio). Home: 2731 Stonebridge Ct Hudson OH 44236 Office: BF Goodrich Co 3925 Embassy Pkwy Akron OH 44313

CALLAHAN, DANIEL JOSEPH, III, banker; b. Washington, May 7, 1932; s. Daniel Joseph and Anne Bailey (Scott) C.; m. Colleen Adrienne Mount, May 5, 1956; children: Daniel Joseph IV, Carey Scott, Caren Anne, Carolyn Patricia, Colleen Gerry. BA, Williams Coll., 1954. Trainee Riggs Nat. Bank, Washington, 1956-58; v.p. Chase Manhattan Bank, N.Y.C., 1958-69; exec. v.p. Hambro Am. Bank and Trust Co., N.Y.C., 1969-72; mng. dir. Merrill Lynch-Brown Shipley Bank Ltd., London, Eng., 1972-73; exec. v.p. Riggs Nat. Bank, Washington, 1973-76, pres., 1976-83; pres. Am. Security Bank, Washington, 1983-85, chmn., chief exec. officer, 1985—, also bd. dirs.; pres. MNC Fin., Inc., 1987—; bd. dirs. USLICO Corp., Md. Nat. Bank. Chmn. Mayor's Econ. Devel. Com., Washington, 1980-82; treas. Nat. 4-H Council; trustee Fed. City Council; chmn. bd. dirs. Meridian House Internat.; bd. dirs. Georgetown U., 1983—, Washington Area Convention and Visitors Assn., Atlantic Council, Washington. Served to capt. USAF, 1954-56. Mem. Assn. Res. City Bankers, Delta Kappa Epsilon. Republican. Roman Catholic. Clubs: Sunningdale, Overseas Bankers (London); Royal and Ancient Golf (Scotland); Alfalfa, Met. (Washington), Alibi, City; Chevy Chase; Burning Tree (Md.); Knickerbocker (N.Y.C.). Home: 4361 Westover Pl NW Washington DC 20016 Office: Am Security 730 15th St NW Washington DC 20013

CALLAHAN, HARRY LESLIE, civil engineer; b. Kansas City, Mo., Jan. 11, 1923; s. B. Frank and Myrtle Lou (Anderson) C.; m. V. June Yohn, Dec. 16, 1944; children: Michael Thomas, Maureen Lynn, Kevin Leslie. BS in Civil Engring, U. Kans., 1944; postgrad., UCLA. Exec. ptnr. Black & Veatch Co., Kansas City, Mo., 1946-89; ret. Black & Veatch Co.; dir. B & V Waste Sci. & Tech. Corp.; chmn. CCL Constrn. Cons., Overland Pk., Kans. Contbr. articles to profl. jours. 1st lt., inf. AUS, 1944-46, Japan. Recipient Mo. Design Excellence award 1st pl., 1972. Fellow ASCE, Am. Cons. Engrs. Council; mem. Am. Nuclear Soc., Nat. Soc. Profl. Engrs., Soc. Mil. Engrs., Am. Concrete Inst., Water Pollution Control Fedn., Combustion Inst., Kappa Sigma. Congregationalist. Clubs: Kansas City, Leawood South Country, Homestead, Chancellor, U. Kans., Sadelle & Sirloin, Rancho Viejo. Office: CCL Constrn Cons 4400 College Blvd Ste 150 Overland Park KS 66211

CALLAHAN, MICHAEL JOSEPH, food company executive; b. Detroit, Feb. 12, 1939; s. John William and Virginia (Allair) C.; m. Clare Breuer, Jan. 16, 1971; children—James Blair, Susan Allair. B.A., U. Mich., 1962, M.B.A. with distinction, 1967. Various positions Esso Ea., Inc., Tokyo, N.Y.C., Sydney, Australia, 1969-78; treas. Esso Ea., Inc., Houston, 1978-81; asst. gen. mgr. Exxon Co. U.S.A., Houston, 1981-82; chief fin. officer, sr. v.p. Quaker Oats Co., Chgo., 1982-88, exec. v.p. groceries specialties div., 1988—, also bd. dirs.; dir. LinBeck Corp., Houston. Pres., trustee Leukemia Soc. Ill., Chgo., 1985—, nat. trustee; bd. dirs. United Charitpies Chgo., 1984—. Served to lt. USN, 1962-65. Mem. Chgo. Commonwealth Club, Phi Kappa Phi, Beta Gamma Sigma. Roman Catholic. Clubs: Chicago, Exmoor Country (Chgo.). Home: 82 Locust Rd Winnetka IL 60093 Office: Quaker Oats Co PO Box 9001 Chicago IL 60604-9001

CALLAN, CHARLES VINCENT, management consultant; b. N.Y.C., Jan. 20, 1956; s. Charles Edward and Rita (Cicchetti) C.; m. Yolanda Maldonado, Oct. 26, 1980. AB in Econs. cum laude, Columbia U., 1978; MBA, Harvard U., 1982. Systems engr. IBM, N.Y.C., 1978-80, project adminstr., 1981; cons. Schubert Assocs., Cambridge, Mass., 1982; prin., mgmt. cons. Index Group, Cambridge, 1983—; new bus. devel. various banks and fin. svc. firms. Contbr. articles to fin. publs.; water safety instr. Fischel fellow ZBT Found., N.Y.C., 1973. Mem. Info. Industry Assn., Columbia Club New Eng. (recruiter). Office: Index Group 5 Cambridge Ctr Cambridge MA 02142

CALLANAN, ANNE MCGUIRE, financial analyst; b. Montclair, N.J., Jan. 25, 1958; d. Paul H. and Julia T. (Pressmar) McGuire; m. Neal E. Callanan, Sept. 20, 1980 (div. Apr. 1987). BS in Bus., Marymount Coll., 1983; postgrad. in fin., L.I. U., 1985. Office mgr. Dalbar Electric Co. Inc., Port Chester, N.Y., 1978-80; acctg. clk. Fits Systems Inc., White Plains, N.Y., 1980-81; accounts receivable clk. AMAX Chem. Corp., Greenwich, Conn., 1981-82; sr. benefits acctg. clk. AMAX Inc., Greenwich, Conn., 1982-84, benefits supr., 1984-85, fin. analyst, 1985-89; spl. projects mgr. Carteret (N.J.) Ops. AMAX Inc., 1989—. Mem. Delta Mu Delta. Office: AMAX Inc Carteret Ops 400 Middlesex Ave Carteret NJ 07008

CALLANAN, KATHLEEN JOAN, electrical engineer, airplane company executive; b. Detroit, Feb. 10, 1940; d. John Michael and Grace Marie (Kleehammer) C. BSE in Physics, U. Mich., 1963; postgrad. in physics Northeastern U., 1963-65; MSEE, U. Hawaii, 1971; diploma in Japanese lang. St. Joseph Inst. Japanese Studies, Tokyo, 1973; cert. in mgmt. Boeing Mil. Airplane Co. Employee Devel., 1985. Vis. scholar Sophia U., Tokyo, 1976-79; elec.-electronic components engr. Boeing Mil. Airplane Co., Wichita, Kans., 1979-83, instrumentation design engr., 1983-85, strategic planner for tech., 1985-86, research and engring. tech. supr., 1986-87; electromagnetic effects Avionics mgr., 1987—. Contbr. articles to profl. jours. Mem. Rose Hill Planning Commn., Kans., 1982-85; coordinator Boeing Employees Amateur Radio Soc., Wichita, 1982-83. Mem. Soc. Women Engrs. (sr. mem., sect. rep. 1981-83, sec. treas. 1985-86, regional bd. dirs. 1983-85, sect. pres. 1987-88), AIAA, Bus. and Profl. Women, Quarter Century Wireless Assn. (communications com. 1985-86). Lodge: Toastmasters (local pres. 1985-86, competent toastmaster 1985). Avocations: amateur radio, singing, bowling. Home: 1201 N West St Rose Hill KS 67133 Office: PO Box 7730 Wichita KS 67277-7730

CALLARD, DAVID JACOBUS, investment banker; b. Boston, July 14, 1938; s. Henry Hadden and Clarissa Cooley (Jacobus) C.; children: Owen Winston, Francis Jacobus, Anne Lloyd, Elizabeth Hadden, Samuel Porter. AB, Princeton U., 1959; postgrad., Union Theol. Sem., 1964-65; JD, NYU, 1969. With Morgan Guaranty Trust Co., N.Y.C., 1959-61, asst. v.p., 1965-69, v.p., 1970-72; ptnr. Alex Brown & Sons, Balt., 1972—; also bd. dirs. Alex Brown Inc., Balt.; bd. dirs., mem. exec. com. Waverly, Inc.; trustee Hotel Investors Trust. Bd. dirs. Home for Incurables, Balt.; trustee; Peabody Inst., Balt.; dep. exec. dir. Pres.'s Commn. on All Vol. Armed Force, 1969-70. Served to lt. USMC, 1971-74. Boothe Ferris fellow, 1964-65. Democrat. Episcopalian. Clubs: Union, Racquet and Tennis (N.Y.C.); Elkridge (Balt.). Home: 631 Colorado Ave Baltimore MD 21210 Office: 135 E Baltimore St Baltimore MD 21202

CALLARD, DONALD ERIC, school business administrator; b. San Diego, Jan. 6, 1936; s. Eric George and Winifred Mary (Hopkins) C.; m. Shirley Darlene Harris, Sept. 7, 1957; 1 child, Michelle Dawn. AA, Mesa Community Coll., 1965; BBA, U.S. Internat. U., 1971, MBA, 1972, D Bus. Adminstrn., 1984. Registered profl. engr., Calif.; registered sch. bus. adminstr. Calif. supr. Gen. Dynamics/Convair, San Diego, 1955-65; project quality engr. Teledyne Ryan, San Diego, 1965-70; fin. analyst San Diego Unified Sch. Dist., 1972-74; quality assurance adminstr. Gen. Atomic Co., La Jolla, Calif., 1974-76; asst. supt. bus. svcs. Encinitas (Calif.) Union Sch. Dist., 1976-88, Fallbrook (Calif.) High Sch. Dist., 1988—; adj. prof. Sch. Bus Webster Coll., Camp Pendleton, Calif., 1984—; county chmn. San Diego Workers Compensation Com., 1985-86; exec. officer Sch. Facilities Corp., Encinitas, 1988. Mem. Assn. Sch. Bus. Ofcls., Calif. Assn. Sch. Bus. Ofcls., Am. Soc. Quality Control, San Diego Fern Soc. (pres. 1986-88), Horseless Carriage Club, Rotary, Masons. Republican. Office: Fallbrook High Sch Dist 2100 Stagecoach Rd Fallbrook CA 92028

CALLENDER, ROBERT STEVENS, JR., data processing executive; b. Poughkeepsie, N.Y., Nov. 20, 1941; s. Robert Stevens Sr. and Wynnefred Audrey (Wadewitz) C.; m. Mary Sedgwick Sutro, Oct., 1983. BA, Yale U., 1965; MBA, U. Denver, 1970. Cert. adv. Montessori tchr. Security analyst, portfolio mgr. Colo. Nat. Bank, Denver, 1965-70; tchr. Old Colony Montessori Sch., Hingham, Mass., 1971-72; headmaster, founder The Montessori Community Sch., Scituate, Mass., 1973-78; headmaster The Whitby Sch., Greenwich, Conn., 1979-80; v.p., chief fin. officer PSS Inc., Greenwich, 1981-85; dir. MIS Exel Systems, Inc., Stamford, Conn., 1986—. Treas. Greenwood Good Govt. League, 1968. Served as petty officer 3d class, USNR, 1963-71. Mem. Data Processing Mgrs. Assn. Republican. Club: Yale (N.Y.C.); Rocky Point (Greenwich, Ct.). Home: 22 Sunset Rd Old Greenwich CT 06870 Office: Exel Systems Inc 83 Harvard Ave Stamford CT 06902

CALLIHAN, CLAYTON ARTHUR, marketing director; b. Uchitomari, Japan, Feb. 20, 1954; s. John Clayton and Wanda Faye (Smith) C.; m. Valerie Cage McKesson, June 9, 1979 (div. Apr., 1982). BS in Mktg., Syracuse U., 1975, BS in Advt., 1975. Asst. copywriter Muir, Cornelius, Moore, Inc., N.Y.C., 1976-78; writer, editor Gen. Electric, Syracuse, N.Y., 1978-81; freelance writer Callihan Communications, Houston, 1985—; assoc. editor Tunnell Publs., Houston, 1985-86; mktg. dir. Tri-Sen Systems, Inc., La Marque, Tex., 1986—; freelance writer Callihan Communications, Houston, 1986-88; mktg. dir. Stitt Spark Plug Co. Inc., 1988—. Served as sgt. U.S. Army, 1981-85. Recipient On Target award Mfrs. Assn. Cen. N.Y., 1978, award Best Overall Publ., Bus. Industry Communications Council of Cen. N.Y., 1978, 79. Mem. SAR. Republican. Home: 10810 Telephone Rd Lot 441 Houston TX 77075

CALLIS, BRUCE, insurance company executive; b. Sedalia, Mo., Dec. 4, 1939; s. George Elgin and Jo (Trigg) C.; m. Nancy Williams, Nov. 14, 1959; children: Cheryl, Kevin, Kimberly. B.S., U. Mo., 1961. Plant mgr. Boonslick Mfg. Co., Boonville, Mo., 1961-62; field claim rep. State Farm Mut. Automobile Ins. Co., Rolla, Mo., 1963; asst. personnel mgr. State Farm Mut. Automobile Ins. Co., Columbia, Mo., 1964-66; various personnel, sales positions State Farm Mut. Automobile Ins. Co., Bloomington, Ill., 1966-76, v.p., personnel, 1976-83, v.p. Office of Pres., 1983—; dir. State Farm Life & Annuity, State Farm Internat. Services. Mem. McLean County (Ill.) Bd., 1968-74; chmn. McLean County Republican Com., Bloomington, 1978—; bd. dirs. Brokaw Hosp., Normal, Ill., 1979-82. Recipient appreciation award Am. Compensation Soc., 1969. Mem. Am. Soc. for Personnel Adminstrn. (chmn. adv . com. 1976-83), Ins. Inst. for Hwy. Safety (personnel com. chmn. 1977-83), McLean County Assn. Commerce, Westminster Coll. Alumni Assn. (award 1986). Presbyterian. Home: 4 Tami Ct Bloomington IL 61701 Office: State Farm Mut Automobile Ins Co 1 State Farm Pla Bloomington IL 61701

CALLISON, JAMES W., airline executive, lawyer; b. Jamestown, N.Y., Sept. 8, 1928; s. J. Waldo and Gladys A. C.; m. Gladys I. Robinson, Oct. 3, 1959; children: Sharon Elizabeth, Maria Judith, Christopher James. AB with honors, U. Mich., 1950, JD with honors (Overbeck award 1952, Jerome S. Freud Meml. award 1953), 1953. Bar: D.C. 1954, Ga. 1960. Atty. Pogue & Neal, Washington, 1953-57; with Delta Air Lines, Inc., Atlanta, 1957—, v.p. law and regulatory affairs, 1974-78, sr. v.p., gen. counsel, 1978-81, sr. v.p., gen. counsel, corp. sec., 1981-88; sr. v.p. legal and corp. affairs, sec. Delta Air Lines, Inc., 1988—. Contbr. articles to legal jours.; asst. editor: Mich. Law Rev, 1952-53. Bd. dirs. S.E. Region NCCJ, Georgians for Better Transp.; bd. councilors Carter Presdl. Ctr., Atlanta. Recipient Papal Pro Ecclesia Et Pontifice award, 1966. Mem. ABA (vice chmn. internat. law sect. 1980-81, corp. law depts. com.), State Bar Ga. (chmn. corp. counsel sect. 1989—), Atlanta Bar Assn., Am. Corp. Counsel Assn., Corp. Counsel Assn. Greater Atlanta, Am. Soc. Corp. Secs. (chmn. southeast region 1986—), Order of Coif. Clubs: Atlanta Athletic, Atlanta Lawyers, Atlanta Commerce. Home: 130 Blenheim Pl Atlanta GA 30350 Office: Delta Air Lines Inc Hartsfield Atlanta Internat Airport Atlanta GA 30320

CALLOWAY, D. WAYNE, food and beverage products company executive; b. 1935. BBA, Wake Forest U., 1959. Exec. v.p., chief fin. officer Pepsico, Inc., Purchase, N.Y., 1983-85, pres., chief operating officer, 1985-86, chmn., chief exec. officer, 1986—; former chmn., pres., chief exec. and operating officer Frito-Lay, Inc. (subs. Pepsico, Inc.), Dallas. Office: PepsiCo Inc Anderson Hill Rd Purchase NY 10577 *

CALVANI, TERRY, government official, former law educator, lawyer; b. Carlsbad, N.Mex., Jan. 29, 1947; s. Torello Howard and Mary Virginia (Hawkins) C.; m. Mary Virginia Anderson, May 3, 1969; m. 2d, Judith Thompson, Aug. 28, 1980; children: Dominic Mario, Torello Howard. BA, U. N.Mex., 1969; JD with distinction, Cornell U., 1972. Bar: N.Mex. 1972, Calif. 1972, Tenn. 1978, U.S. Dist. Ct. N.Mex. 1972, U.S. Dist. Ct. (no. dist.) Calif. 1972, U.S. Dist. Ct. (mid. dist.) Tenn. 1978, U.S. Ct. Appeals (9th cir.) 1972, U.S. Ct. Appeals (6th cir.) 1977, U.S. Ct. Appeals (5th cir.) 1981, U.S. Ct. Appeals (11th cir.) 1981, U.S. Supreme Ct. 1985. Teaching fellow Stanford U. Law Sch., 1972-73; assoc. Pillsbury, Madison & Sutro, San Francisco, 1973-74; asst. prof. law Vanderbilt U. Sch. Law, Nashville, 1974-77, assoc. prof., 1977-80, prof., 1980-83; vis. prof. law U. Va., Charlottesville, 1981-82; of counsel Haskell Slaughter & Young, Birmingham, Ala., 1980-83; commr. U.S. FTC, 1983—; acting chmn., 1985-86. Author: (with John Siegfried) Economic Analysis and Antitrust Law, 1979, 2d edit., 1988; bd. editors Antitrust Bull., 1982—, Bur. Nat. Affairs RICO Report, 1986—. Mem. Am. Law Inst. (mem. adminstrv. law conf. U.S. 1985—, adv. bd.), ABA (chmn. spl. com. to study antitrust penalties and damages Antitrust Sect. 1979-82, chmn. Robinson-Patman com. antitrust sect. 1981-83, council mem. 1985-86), 6th Cir. Jud. Conf. (life), Adminstrv. Conf. U.S., Newcomen Soc. N.Am., Order of Coif. Republican. Roman Catholic. Clubs: The Club (Birmingham); Cumberland (Nashville). Office: FTC 6th St & Pennsylvania Ave NW Ste 540 Washington DC 20580

CALVANICO, THOMAS PAUL, corporate lawyer; b. Jersey City, Oct. 18, 1955; s. Emanuel Paul and Helen A. (Miller) C. AB in Polit. Sci., St. Peter's Coll., 1976; JD, N.Y. Law Sch., 1979. Bar: N.J. 1979, N.Y. 1986, U.S. Dist. Ct. N.J. 1979, U.S. Dist. Ct. (ea. and so. dists.) N.Y. 1985. Asst. prosecutor Hudson County, Jersey City, 1979-81; sole practice Jersey City, 1981-87; asst. corp. counsel Jersey City Law Dept., 1981-87; gen. counsel The Ryan Group, Middletown, N.J., 1987—; counsel, cons. Pathfinder Real Estate Devel., San Antonio, 1985. Counsel PJP Landfill Task Force, Jersey City, 1985-86, counsel to bd. dirs. Jersey City Pub. Library, 1985-86. Mem. N.J. Bar Assn., Hudson County Bar Assn., Profl. Liability Com. (assoc. 1987-88), N.J. Soc. Architecture. Democrat. Roman Catholic. Club: U.S. Power Squadron (Shrewsbury). Home: 156 Wharfside Manor Monmouth Beach NJ 07750 Office: The Ryan Group 1 Arin Park 1715 Hwy 35 Middletown NJ 07748

CALVIN, DONALD LEE, stock exchange executive; b. Mount Olive, Ill., Nov. 10, 1931; s. Mike H. and Mary Josephine (Salovich) C.; m. Louise Elinor Peterson, Mar. 28, 1952; children—Jane Calvin Palasek, Sally Anne, Calvin Salvaterra. Student Eastern Ill. U., 1950-54; LLB, U. Ill., 1956. Bar: Ill. 1956. Atty., Sec. of State, Ill., 1957-58, securities commr., 1959-62; syndicate mgr. A.C. Allyn & Co., Chgo., 1962-63; atty. F.I. DuPont & Co., Chgo., 1963-64; exec. asst. civic and govt. affairs N.Y. Stock Exch., N.Y.C., 1964-65, v.p., 1966-77, sr. v.p., 1977-79, exec. v.p. pub. affairs, 1979-85, exec. v.p. internat., 1986-87; chmn. Internat. Bus. Enterprises, Inc., 1987—; advisor to chmn. Chgo. Bd. Options Exch. and Geneva (Switzerland) Stock Exch., 1987—, adviser to pres. Fedn. International des Bourses de Valeurs (Internat. Fedn. Stock Exch., Paris 1989—); bd. dir. Depository Trust Co., 19880-86, N.Y.C., N.Y. Futures Exch., 1981-85, Right Mgmt. Cons., Inc., 1987—; mem. adv. bd. Securities Law Inst., U. Calif.-San Diego; lectr, in field. Bd. visitors U. Ill., Urbana, Mem. ABA, Internat. Bar Assn., Ill. State Bar Assn., Chgo. Bar Assn., Am. Law Inst. Clubs: Met., Stock Exch. Luncheon (N.Y.C.), Manhasset Bay Yacht (Port Washington, N.Y.), Stockbridge Golf (Mass.). Home: 4 Knolls Ln Manhasset NY 11030 Office: 60 Broad St 35th Fl New York NY 10004

CALVIN, DOROTHY VER STRATE, computer company executive; b. Grand Rapids, Mich., Dec. 22, 1929; d. Herman and Christina (Plakmyer)

Ver Strate; m. Allen D. Calvin, Oct. 5, 1953; children: Jamie, Kris, Bufo, Scott. BS magna cum laude, Mich. State U., 1951; MA, U. San Francisco, 1988. Mgr. data processing. Behavioral Research Labs., Menlo Park, Calif., 1972-75; dir. Mgmt. Info. Systems Inst. for Prof. Devel., San Jose, Calif. 1975-76; systems analyst, programmer Pacific Bell Info. Systems, San Francisco, 1976-81; staff mgr., 1981-84; mgr. applications devel. Data Architects Inc., San Francisco, 1984-86; pres. Ver Strate Press, San Francisco, 1986—. Instr., Downtown Community Coll., San Francisco, 1980-84, Cañada Community Coll., 1986—; mem. computer curriculum adv. council San Francisco City Coll., 1982-84. Vice pres. LWV, Roanoke, Va., 1956-58; pres. Bulliss Purissima Parents Group, Los Altos, Calif., 1962-64; bd. dirs. Vols. for Israel, 1986-87. Mem. NAFE, Assn. Systems Mgmt., Assn. Women in Computing. Democrat. Avocations: computing, gardening, jogging, reading. Office: Ver Strate Press 1645 15th Ave San Francisco CA 94122

CAMBI, JOSEPH ARMAND, food company executive; b. Springfield, Mass., Apr. 29, 1957; s. Georgio and Maria Ann (Perrone) C. BS in Mgmt., Babson Coll., 1979. Account exec. Sysco Corp., Houston, 1979-83; v.p. sales and mktg. Springfield Foodsvc. Corp., 1983-86, pres., chief exec. officer, 1986—; bd. dirs. CODE, Inc., Pitts., Domesticode Corp., St. Louis. Home: 359 Bliss Rd Longmeadow MA 01106 Office: Springfield Foodsvc Corp North Ctr Indsl Park PO Box 3024 Springfield MA 01101

CAMDESSUS, MICHEL (JEAN), French government official; b. Bayonne, France, May 1, 1933; s. Alfred and Madeleine (Cassembon) Camdessus; m. Brigitte d'Arcy, Dec. 7, 1957; children: Francois, Marie-Odile, Christine, Thibaut, Claire, Marie-Genevieve. Licencie en Droit, U. Paris, Diplome d'etudes superieures d'economie politique et de sciences economiques; Diplome de l'Institut d'etudes politiques; Ancien eleve de l'Ecole Nationale d'Administration (promotion Alexis de Tocqueville). Civil servant Treasury, French Ministry Fin., 1960-66, chief bur. indsl. affairs Treasury, French Ministry Econs. and Fin., 1969-70, dep. dir. treasury, 1974-82, dir. Treasury, 1982-84, gov. Bank of France, Paris, 1984-87; mng. dir. Internat. Monetary Fund, Washington, 1987—; fin. attache Permanent Representation, EEC, Brussels, 1966-69, mem. monetary com. EEC, 1978-84, pres. monetary com., 1982-84. Chmn. Paris Club, 1978-84. Decorated chevalier Nat., chevalier Légion d'Honneur, Order Merit; recipient Cross of Mil. Valor.

CAMERON, DONALD SEYMOUR, insurance agent; b. Rochester, N.Y., Nov. 5, 1931; s. Thomas Francis and Gertrude Joan (Lash) C.; m. Helen Marie Cameron, May 15, 1954; children: Anne, David, Susan Cameron Kausch. Salesman Swift Co., Rochester, 1952-57, N.Y. Life Ins. Co., Rochester, 1957-69; gen. agt. Nat. Life Vt., Rochester, 1969—; mem. adv. bd. N.Y. State Ins. Dept., 1987—; bd. dirs. Estate Planning Council, 1985-86. Contbr. articles to profl. jours. Bd. dirs. Hearing and Speech of Rochester, 1980—, Family Service or Rochester, 1980—, Rochester Area Multiple Sclerosis; chmn. Nazareth Coll. Deferred Giving. Served as cpl. with USMC, 1950-52, Korea. Mem. Rochester Sales Exec. and Market Assn., Rochester Gen. Agts. and Mgrs. Assn. (pres. 1975, 86), Rochester Life Underwriters (cert., pres. 1968), Chartered Life Underwriters (pres. 1976), N.Y. State Assn. Life Underwriters (regional v.p. 1973). Republican. Roman Catholic. Lodge: Rotary. Home: 104 Lake Lea Rd Rochester NY 14617 Office: Nat Life of Vt 19 W Main St Suite 500 Rochester NY 14614

CAMERON, JAMES M., resource company executive; b. Turner Valley, Alta., Can., June 30, 1928; s. Frederick J. and Evelyn G. Cameron; m. Charlotte Guterson, Sept. 25, 1954; children—Louise, Frederick, Jean-Marie. B.Commerce, U. Alta., 1950, LL.B., 1953. Legal advisor Can. Export Gas & Oil Co., Calgary, Alta., 1954-58; ptnr. Milner & Steer, Calgary, 1958-66; exec. asst. TransCan. PipeLines, Toronto, Ont., 1966-67, gen. counsel, 1967-68, v.p. and gen. counsel, 1968-72, group v.p., 1972-75; exec. v.p., gen. counsel TransCan. PipeLines, 1975-77; dir. TransCan. PipeLines, Toronto, Ont., 1977, exec. v.p. corp., 1980-83, exec. v.p., 1986-87, pres. pipeline div., 1988—, also bd. dirs.; chmn., chief exec. officer TCPL Resources Ltd., 1983-86; v.p., bd. dirs., TransCan. PipeLine USA Ltd.; vice chmn., bd. dirs. Wessely Energy Co., Gt. Lakes Gas Transmission Co., Trans Que. & Maritimes Pipeline, TCPL Resources Ltd., Calgary. Bd. dirs. Met. Toronto and Region Conservation Found., Queen Elizabeth Hosp. Clubs: Bayview Golf and Country (Thornhill, Ont.); Calgary Golf and Country, Ranchmen's (Calgary); Ontario (Toronto). Office: TransCan PipeLines, PO Box 54 Commerce Ct W, Toronto, ON Canada M5L 1C2

CAMERON, JOHN THURSTON, oil company executive; b. Greenville, Tex.; s. Hugh Alexander and Fannie May (Olive) C.; m. Colleen Cain, March 10, 1957; children: Laura, Sarah. BS in Petroleum Engring., Tex. A&M U., 1955, BS in Geol. Engring., 1955. Engr. various cos., 1958-75; unit supr. SACROC Chevron U.S.A. Inc., Snyder, Tex., 1975-78; div. supt. Chevron U.S.A. Inc., La Habra, Calif., 1978-80; gen. mgr. Chevron U.S.A. Inc., Denver, 1980-82, v.p. cen. region, 1982-84; v.p. western region Chevron U.S.A. Inc., San Ramon, Calif., 1984—; pres., bd. dirs. Western Oil and Gas Assn., L.A.; bd. dirs. Long Beach (Calif.) Oil and Devel. Co.; mem. Dean's Engring. Adv. Com., Calif. Poly. State U., San Luis Obispo. Bd. dirs. Contra Costa Devel. Assn. Mem. Soc. Petroleum Engrs., Am. Petroleum Inst. Office: Chevron USA Inc 6001 Bollinger Canyon Rd San Ramon CA 94583

CAMERON, NICHOLAS ALLEN, diversified corporation executive; b. Phila., Jan. 6, 1939; s. Nicholas Guyot and Katherine (Rogers) C.; m. Leslie Wood, Dec. 14, 1974; children: Christopher Wilson, Pamela Wilson. BS, Yale U., 1960. Treas. Allied Corp., Morristown, N.J., 1979-81, v.p. and treas., 1981-82, v.p. fin., 1982-83, v.p. planning and devel., 1983-85; sr. v.p. planning, devel. and adminstrn. Allied-Signal Inc., Morristown, N.J., 1985-86; sr. v.p. tech. and bus. devel. Bendix Aerospace-Allied-Signal, Inc., Arlington, Va., 1986-87; group pres. Allied-Signal Aerospace, 1988; sr. v.p. ops. services Allied-Signal, Inc., Morristown, N.J., 1988—. Treas., bd. dirs. United Way of Morris County, Morristown, N.J., 1980-86. Mem. Morris County C. of C. (bd. dirs. 1975-86), Tau Beta Pi. Republican. Episcopalian. Clubs: St. Elmo Soc. (New Haven); Morris County Golf. Home: Five Noe Ave Madison NJ 07940 Office: Allied-Signal Inc Columbia Rd and Park Ave Morristown NJ 07960

CAMERON, PETER ALFRED GORDON, corporate executive; b. Toronto, Ont., Can., Sept. 15, 1930; s. Alfred Gordon C. and Dorothy (Somerville) Hendrick; m. Suzanne M.S. Noble, Oct. 19, 1955; children: Ian, Janet, Patricia. B.Commerce, McGill U., 1953. Mgmt. trainee Ford Motor Co. Can., Windsor, Ont., 1954; asst. to advt. mgr. Brading Breweries, Toronto, Ont., 1954; sales rep. William B. Stewart & Sons Ltd., 1955; asst. advt. mgr. Warner Lambert Can. Ltd., Toronto, 1955, product mgr. Proprietaries div., 1956-58; account exec. MacLaren Advt. Co. Ltd., Toronto, 1958-60; account exec. Foster Advt. Co. Ltd., Toronto, 1960-62, group supr., 1962-65, v.p., 1965-69, group v.p., 1969; v.p. Can. Industries Ltd., Montreal, Que., 1970-78; pres., dir. Can. Corp. Mgmt. Co. Ltd., Toronto, 1978-87; chmn., chief exec. officer Chromalox, Inc., Rexdale, Ont., Can., 1987—; dir. Halifax Ins. Co., Halifax Life Ins. Co., Bank of Montreal Realty, Inc.; chmn. bd. Sunnybrook Med. Ctr. Inst., Toronto; co-chmn. Def. Indsl. Preparedness Adv. Coun. to Minister of Nat. Def. Immediate past chmn. bd. of govs. Appleby Coll., Oakville, Ont.; immediate past chmn. Task Force on Def. Policy Bus. Council on Nat. Issues, Ottawa. Served as lt. col. 48th Highlanders Can., 1967-70, comdr. Montreal Dist., 1974-78, brig. gen. & spl. projects officer res. council, 1983—. Clubs: York, Toronto, Toronto Golf, Toronto Racquet; Racquets, St. James, Hermitage (Montreal).

CAMERON, ROY EUGENE, scientist; b. Denver, July 16, 1929; s. Guy Francis and Ilda Annora (Horn) C.; m. Margot Elizabeth Hoagland, May 5, 1956 (div. July 1977); children: Susan Lynn, Catherine Ann; m 2d Carolyn Mary Light, Sept. 22, 1978. B.S., Wash. State U., 1953, 54; M.S., U. Ariz., 1958, Ph.D., 1961; D.D. (hon.), Ministry of Christ Ch., Delavan, Wis., 1975. Research scientist Hughes Aircraft Corp., Tucson, 1955-56; sr. scientist Jet Propulsion Lab., Pasadena, Calif., 1961-68, mem. tech. staff, 1969-74; dir. research Darwin Research Inst., Dana Point, Calif., 1974-75; dep. dir. Land Reclamation Lab. Argonne Ill. Nat. Lab., 1975-77, dir. energy resources tng. and devel., 1977-85; sr. staff scientist Lockheed Engring. and Scis. Co., Las Vegas, Nev., 1986—; cons. Lunar Recieving Lab. Baylor U., 1966-68, Ecology Ctr. Utah State U., Desert Biome, 1970-72, U. Alaska Tundra Biome, 1973-74, U. Maine, 1973-76, numerous others; mem. Nat. Agriculture Research and Extension Users Adv. Bd., 1986—. Contrb. articles to sci. books; participated in 7 Antarctic expdns. Served with U.S. Army, 1950-52, Korea, Japan. Recipient 3 NASA awards for tech. briefs, EPA award of Excellence for global climate program, 1988; Paul Steere Burgess fellow U. Ariz., 1959; grantee NSF, 1970-74; Dept. Interior, 1978-80. Mem. AAAS, Soil Sci. Soc. Am., Am. Chem. Soc., Am. Soc. Microbiology, Am. Soc. Agronomy, Antarctican Soc., Polar Soc. Am., Am. Scientist Affiliation, World Future Soc., Internat. Soc. Soil. Sci., Council Agrl. Sci. and Tech., Am. Inst. Biol. Sci., Am. Geophys. Union, Sigma Xi. Mem. Christian Ch.

CAMERON, WILLIAM DUNCAN, plastic company executive; b. Harrell, N.C., June 14, 1925; s. Paul Archiebald and Atwood (Herring) C.; m. Betty Gibson, Oct. 3, 1953; children—Phillip MacDonald, Colleen Kay. Student Duke U., 1945-49. Chmn. Reef Industries Inc., Houston, 1958—. Pres. bd. trustees Trinity Episcopal Sch., Galveston, Tex., 1981-82; trustee William Temple Found., 1987—. Served with U.S. Army, 1943-45. Mem. World Bus. Council, Houston C. of C. (chmn. mfg. com. 1967). Clubs: Rotary, Galveston Artillery, Bob Smith Yacht. Home: 2868 Dominique Dr Galveston TX 77551 Office: Reef Industries Inc 9209 Almeda-Genoa Rd Houston TX 77075

CAMISI, DOMENICK J., association executive; b. Phila., May 9, 1947; s. Domenick J. and Madeline Helen (Wroblewski) C.; BS, Rider Coll., 1969. children: Michael, Mark, Steven Paul; m. Laureen Martinelli, May 5, 1984; 1 child, Jodi. CPA, N.J. Acct. Peat, Marwick, Mitchell, Trenton, N.J., 1969-72; group sr. v.p., chief fin. officer, treas. N.J. Hosp. Assn., Princeton, 1972—; mem. N.J. State Uncompensated Care Adv. Com., adv. coms. to Dept. Health. Mem. AICPA, N.J. Soc. CPAs, Healthcare Fin. Mgmt. Assn. Office: NJ Hosp Assn 760 Alexander Rd CN-1 Princeton NJ 08540

CAMMA, PHILIP, accountant; b. Phila., May 22, 1923; s. Anthony and Rose (LaSpada) C.; m. Anna Ruth Karg, July 21, 1956 (dec. Aug. 1960); 1 child, Anthony Philip. BS, U. Pa., 1952. CPA, Ohio, Ky. Acct., Main and Co., CPA's, Phila., 1952-53; in-charge acct. Haskins & Sells, CPA's, Phila., St. Louis, Cin. and Columbus, Ohio, 1953-60; controller Marvin Warner Co., Cin., 1960-61, Leshner Corp., 1961-63; mng. ptnr. Camma & Patrick, CPA's, 1963-66; founder Philip Camma Co., CPA's, Cin., 1966—. Served with USAAF, 1942-45, ETO. Mem. Am. Inst. CPA's, Ohio Soc. CPA's, Ky. Soc. CPA's, Am. Acctg. Assn., Nat. Assn. Accts. Republican. Clubs: Cincinnati; University Pa.; Hamilton City. Home: Phelps Townhouse 506 E 4th St Cincinnati OH 45202 Office: 700 Walnut St Ste 603 Cincinnati OH 45202

CAMP, EHNEY ADDISON, III, mortgage banker; b. Birmingham, Ala., June 28, 1942; s. Ehney Addison and Mildred Fletcher (Tillman) C.; BA, Dartmouth Coll., 1964; m. Patricia Jane Hough, Sept. 17, 1966; children: Ehney Addison IV, Margaret Strader. Sr. v.p. Cobbs, Allen & Hall Mortgage Co., Inc., Birmingham, 1965-72; v.p., gen. mgr. The Rime Cos., Birmingham, 1972-75; pres. Camp & Co., Birmingham, 1975—; bd. dirs. AmSouth Corp., Birmingham. Bd. dirs. Community Chest/United Way Jefferson, Walker and Shelby Counties, Better Bus. Bur. of Gt. Birmingham, 1988; pres., trustee Civic Club Found, Inc.; bd. dirs. All Am. Bowl. Served with USAF, 1965, Ala. Air N.G., 1966. Mem. Am. Mortgage Bankers Assn. (income property com.), Ala. Mortgage Bankers Assn. (treas. 1985, sec. 1986, v.p. 1987, pres. 1988). Methodist. Clubs: Kiwanis (dir. 1977-78, 82-83, sec. 1983-84, v.p. 1985-86, pres. 1986-87); Mountain Brook (bd. govs. 1976-77, 89—); Birmingham Country; The Club (bd. dirs., fin. chmn. 1987-88), Wade Hampton Golf (Cashiers, N.C.); Downtown; Shoal Creek (bd. govs. 1983—). Home: 3510 Victoria Rd Birmingham AL 35223 Office: 3300 Cahaba Rd Ste 300 Birmingham AL 35223

CAMP, ROGER ALLEN, manufacturing executive; b. Guntersville, Ala., Aug. 4, 1939; s. Coy Allen and Evelyn (Bush) C.; m. Marilyn Bird, Feb. 2, 1963; children: Kimberly, Kristen. BS in Indsl. Mgmt., Ga. Inst. Tech., 1968, MBA in Fin., Ga. State U., 1971, M in Profl. Accountancy, 1974. Ops. analyst Space div. Chrysler Corp., Cape Kennedy, Fla., 1968-69; budget analyst Lockheed Aerospace Corp., Atlanta, 1969-71; office mgr. DeKalb County, Decatur, Ga., 1971-74; asst. contr. Presbyn. Ch. Hdqrs., Atlanta, 1974-75, Atlanta Hawks and Flames, 1975-76; chief fin. officer Motor Convoy and Auto Convoy, Inc., Decatur, 1976-88; treas. Asbury Ferst, Inc., Atlanta, 1988—; Contbr. articles to profl. jours. Treas. Presbyn. Ch., Marietta, Ga., 1981-84, elder, 1984-88, trustee 1988—. With USN, 1961-65. Southeastern chpt. Nat. Acctg. & Fin. Coun. (sec. 1982-83, v.p. 1983-84, pres. 1984-85, plaque award 1985). Democrat. Lodges: Kiwanis (Decatur bd. dirs. 1985-88, treas. 1985-88), Gideons Internat. (chaplain 1986). Home: 4309 Blackland Dr Marietta GA 30067 Office: Asbury Ferst Inc 3550 Industrial Blvd SW Atlanta GA 30354

CAMPANA, ANA ISABEL, architect; b. Banes, Oriente, Cuba, Jan. 16, 1934; came to U.S., 1967, naturalized, 1974; d. Abelardo Joaquin and Amparo (Cabrera) C. B.S., Instituto del Vedado, Havana, 1953; postgrad., Havana U., 1962, Albany (N.Y.) Inst. History and Art, 1970. Architect, Havana U., 1962, Ministry of Pub. Works, Havana, 1962-67; architect designer various firms, N.Y., 1967-74; sr. architect Gen. Electric Co., Schenectady, 1974—. Recipient 1st nat. award Nat. Mus. Com., Havana, 1948, 1st Province award, 1948, several international archtl. performance awards. Mem. AIA (assoc.). Roman Catholic. Home: 422 Sand Creek Rd Apt 506 Albany NY 12205 Office: LaBerge Group Ltd 4 Computer Dr W Albany NY 12205

CAMPBELL, ARTHUR RAYMOND, construction company executive; b. Penhook, Va., Mar. 17, 1938; s. G. Raymond and Virginia F. (Ferguson) C.; m. Judith C. Bousman, Aug. 26, 1960; children: Christopher R., Melanie L. Student, Va. Poly. and State U., 1957-58. Engr. supt. Sollitt Constrn. Co., Inc., South Bend, Ind., 1960-73; v.p. Cardinal Constrn. Co., Roanoke, Va., 1973-77; pres. Contractors Service, Inc., Parkersburg, W.Va., 1977-87; prin., owner United Constrn. Co., Inc., Vienna, W.Va., 1987—. Republican. Methodist. Club: Parkersburg Country. Lodges: Masons, Shriners, Moose, Elks. Home: 2 Oakwood Estates Parkersburg WV 26101

CAMPBELL, BERNARD PATRICK, banker; b. Providence, July 10, 1926; s. Bernard Christopher and Elizabeth (Kiernan) C.; m. Ruth Marie DiSaia, Oct. 14, 1950; children: Bernard G., David M., Maria P., Thomas J. Student, Providence Coll., 1943-44, 46-47; LLB, Boston U., 1950. Bar: R.I. 1950. Sole practice Providence, 1950-62; trust officer Citizens Trust Co., Providence, 1962-65, v.p., 1965-72, sr. v.p., 1972-86, exec. v.p., 1986—. Mem. Barrington Budget Com., 1959-62, Barrington Sewere Commn., 1976-77; dir. Sch. One, 1976-82; chmn. found. div. United Arts Fund, 1976-78; chmn. R.I. Heart Assn., Barrington and Bristol County, 1958-62; mem. investment com. Cath. Diocese R.I., 1983—; chmn. trust adv. com. Cath. Found. R.I., 1982—; solicitor United Way, Cath. Charity Fund, R.I. Philharm., others. Served with USN, 1944-46. Mem. R.I. Bar Assn. (v.p. Found. 1986—), Estate Planning Council (past pres.), Life Ins. Underwriters Assn. Club: Turks Head (Providence). Home: 265 New Meadow Rd Barrington RI 02806 Office: Citizens Trust Co 870 Westminster St Providence RI 02903

CAMPBELL, CALVIN ARTHUR, JR., mining and plastics molding equipment manufacturing company executive; b. Detroit, Sept. 1, 1934; s. Calvin Arthur and Alta Christine (Koch) C.; m. Rosemary Phoenix, June 6, 1959; 1 dau., Georgia Alta. AB in Econs, Williams Coll., 1956; SB in Chem. Engring., M.I.T., 1959; J.D., U. Mich., 1961. With Exxon Chem. Co., N.Y.C., 1961-69; chmn. bd., treas. John B. Adt Co., York, Pa., N.Y.C., 1969-70; pres., chief exec. officer Goodman Equipment Corp., Chgo., 1971—; chmn. Improved Blow Molding Equipment Co. Inc., Hudson, N.H.; pres. Improved Parts and Service (subs. Goodman Equipment Corp.), Chgo., 1979—; founder, chmn. Goodman Conveyor Co. Inc., Belton, S.C., 1984—; mem. exec. com. Econ. Devel. Commn., City of Chgo., 1980-86; co-chmn. labor mgmt. com. Ill. Devel. Bd., 1982-86; bd. dirs., mem. compensation and benefits com. Cyprus Minerals Co. Inc. Trustee Ill. Inst. Tech., 1986—; mem. Gov's. Commn. on Sci. and Tech., Pres.'s council Mus. Sci. and Industry, Build Ill. Com.; mem. Chgo. adv. bd. The Salvation Army; dir. Chgo. unit Am. Cancer Soc., chmn. Chgo. Trades and Industry, 1978; pres. 1320 North State St. Coop. Apts. Inc., 1984-86. Mem. ABA, N.Y. Bar Assn., Am. Mining Congress (gov. 1972—, chmn. bd. govs. mfrs. div. 1980-83, dir. 1980—, chmn. product liability com.), Ill. Mfrs. Assn. (dir. 1978-84, exec. and fin. coms., chmn. long range planning com. 1984, succession com. 1983), Am. Inst Chem. Engrs., Chief Execs. Orgn. Inc., World Bus. Council, Newcomen Soc. U.S., Chgo. Pres.'s Orgn. (bd. dirs. 1987—), Psi Upsilon, Phi Delta Phi. Clubs: Racquet, Chicago, Commonwealth, Economic, Commercial (Chgo.); Glen View (Ill.). Home: 1320 N State Pkwy Chicago IL 60610 Office: Goodman Equipment Corp 4834 S Halsted St Chicago IL 60609

CAMPBELL, CAROLINE KRAUSE, drug company executive; b. Praha, Tex., May 5, 1926; d. Charles Joseph and Mary Victoria (Havrde) Krause; student, U. N.Mex., 1958-63; diploma Alexander Hamilton Inst., 1966-69; m. Richard E. Campbell, Dec. 30, 1946; children—Richard E., Don Michael, Scott Gary, Jonathan Miles, Candace Kay. Survey researcher Winona Research Co., Mpls., 1953-54; merchandiser, buyer Campbell Drug Inc., Albuquerque, 1961-77, gen. mgr., 1978—, pres., 1978—, dir., 1978—. Mem. Nat. Assn. Corp. Dirs., Assn. Commerce and Industry of N.Mex., C. of C. Albuquerque (bd. dirs.), Small Business Roundtable, Nat. Assn. Retail Druggists (impaired pharmacist com.), Medicine/Bus. Coalition, N.Mex. Pharm. Assn., Internat. Platform Assn., Albuquerque Symphony Women's Assn. Republican. Clubs: Albuquerque Rose Soc., Italian Cultural. Lodge: Elks. Office: Campbell Drug Inc 8252 Menaul Blvd NE Albuquerque NM 87110

CAMPBELL, CHARLES ALTON, corporate executive; b. Brunswick, Ga., Mar. 10, 1944; s. Rayford Monroe and Cecelia Elizabeth (Camilla) C.; B Indsl. Engring., Ga. Inst. Tech., 1966; MBA, Harvard U., 1973; m. Mary Alla Traber, Aug. 15, 1970; children—Christine Beensen, Elizabeth Traber, Charles Traber. Mgr. ops. projects Camak Lumber Ops., ITT Rayonier, Thomson, Ga., 1974-75, mgr. ops. projects Wood Products Group, N.Y.C., 1975-77, dir. chems. devel. parent co., 1977-79, dir. operational planning and control, Seattle, 1979-80; pres. Fox Mfg. Co., Rome, Ga., 1980-81, Camtec, Inc., Rome, 1981-88; chmn. bd. Universal Ceramics, Inc., Adairsville, Ga., 1984-87; exec. v.p. Saunders, Inc., Birmingham, Ala., 1987-88, pres., chief operating officer, 1988—. Lt. C.E.C., USNR, 1967-69. Episcopalian. Club: Mountain Brook (Ala.) Swim and Tennis. Lodge: Rotary (Birmingham). Home: 3725 Briar Oak Circle Mountain Brook AL 35223 Office: 250 Office Park Dr Birmingham AL 35223

CAMPBELL, CHERIE LYNN, real estate development executive; b. Buffalo, July 15, 1950; d. Arthur Jerome and Margaret Ann (Wharton) C.; children: Ross Arthur, Wyatt Joseph. BA, Mills Coll., 1972; postgrad., U. Ariz., 1972-73. Asst. head planning dept. Jerry Jones & Assocs., Tucson, 1978-80; dir. planning and bus. devel. Johnson-Brittain & Assoc., Tucson, 1980-83; v.p. planning and devel., cons. Schomac Corp., Tucson, 1983—; cons. Nat. Self Storage, Tucson, 1987—. Mem. So. Ariz. Homebuilders Assn., Am. Planning Assn. Office: Schomac Corp 1790 E River #300 Tucson AZ 85718

CAMPBELL, CRAIG GARDNER, financial advisor; b. Fredericksburg, Va., Mar. 11, 1962; s. Herbert Everett Campbell and Marlene (Klein) Leslie. BS in Fin. Svcs. summa cum laude, San Diego State U., 1984. Cert. fin. planner, real estate broker, Calif. Casewriter Joel R. Baker, Inc., Solvang, Calif., 1984-85; fin. advisor, owner Campbell & Assocs., San Diego, 1985—; chief exec. officer, chief fin. officer Mindsight, Newbury Park, Calif., 1987—; owner Craig G. Realty, San Diego, 1988—. Bus. editor Ventura County Mag., 1986. Mem. Inst. Cert. Planners. Home: 4025-123 Porte La Paz San Diego CA 92122 Office: Craig G Realty 380 Stevens Ave Ste 210 Solana Beach CA 92012-0002

CAMPBELL, DAVID DOUGLAS, automotive company executive; b. Detroit, Dec. 2, 1929; s. Robert Richard and Lulu Ellen (Caddell) C.; m. Audrey Ann Peterson, June 2, 1951; children—Gary S., Barry J. B.S.M.E., Gen. Motors Inst., Flint, Mich., 1953; postgrad., Harvard U., 1977. Draftsman product engring. specifications Fisher Body div. Gen. Motors Corp., Mich., 1948-53, various supervisory positions, 1953-70, project mgr. air cushion restraints, 1970-71, dir. research and devel., 1971-76, chief engr., 1976-78, gen. dir. product engring., 1978-79, gen. mfg. mgr., 1979-83; exec. dir. mfg. and assembly ops. Adam Opel, A.G. subs. Fisher Body div. Gen. Motors Corp., 1983-84; group dir. ops. Chevrolet, Pontiac, GM of Can. Group Gen. Motors Corp., Warren, Mich., 1984—; officer, v.p. Gen. Motors Corp., Detroit, 1985—; dir. New United Motor Mfg., Inc., Fremont, Calif. Patentee in field (12). Chmn. United Found. Community Campaigns, Detroit, 1985-86; chmn. div. II Torch Drive United Way Mich., 1984; bd. dirs. ARC, Detroit, 1985. Served with U.S. Army, 1953-55. Recipient Safety award Nat. Hwy. and Safety Traffic Agy., 1978. Fellow Engring. Soc. Detroit; mem. Soc. Automotive Engrs., Am. Soc. Body Engrs., Tau Beta Pi. Republican. Home: 4833 W Wickford Bloomfield Hills MI 48013 Office: GM Corp Chevrolet Pontiac Car Group 30001 Van Dyke Ave Warren MI 48090

CAMPBELL, DAVID GWYNNE, petroleum executive, geologist; b. Oklahoma City, May 2, 1930; s. Lois Raymond Henager and La Vada (Ray) Henager Campbell; B.S., Tulsa U., 1953; M.S., U. Okla., 1957; m. Janet Gay Newland, Mar. 1, 1958; 1 son, Carl David. Geologist, Lone Star Producing Co., Oklahoma City, 1957-65; dist. geologist and geol. cons. Mid-Continent div. Tenneco Oil Co., Oklahoma City, 1965-77; exploration mgr. Leede Exploration, Oklahoma City, 1977-80; pres. Earth Hawk Exploration, Inc., Oklahoma City, 1980—; div. exploration mgr. PetroCorp., Oklahoma City, 1983—. Active Last Frontier council Boys Scouts Am., 1960-73, chmn. edn. com. Eagle dist., 1963-67, asst. scoutmaster Wiley Post dist., 1971-73, Oklahoma County rep. to Cherokee Nation, 1976-78, YMCA., Okla. City. Served with USNR, 1948-53, U.S. Army, 1953-55. Recipient cert. of recognition Okla.-Kans. Oil and Gas Assn., 1982. Mem. Am. Petroleum Inst., Am. Assn. Petroleum Geologists (infor. com. 1968 nat. conv., field trip chmn. 1978 conv., Ho. of Dels. 1980-83, 83-86, del. at large, 1987—, nat. chmn. Ho. of Dels. 1981-82, exec. com. 1981-82, found. trustee assoc. 1983—, mem. adv. council 1984-87, councillor mid-continent sect. 1984-87, nominating com. 1984-85, 86-87, astrogeology com. 1984—, chmn. liason subcom. astrogeology com. 1984, honors and awards com. 1984-85, 1985-86, adv. bd. Treatise of Petroleum Geology 1986—, Nat. Membership Adv. council 1987—, membership com., chmn. mid-continent sect., 1987-90, Disting. Svc. award, 1989), Okla. City Geol. Soc. (pub. rels. chmn. Speakers bur. 1963-64, chmn. stratigraphic code com. 1967-68, presdl. appointee 1969-70, advt. mgr. Shale Shaker 1969-71, rep. to AAPG Ho. of Dels. 1980-86, bylaws and incorp. rev. com. 1986), Ind. Petroleum Assn. Am. Petroleum Assn., Okla. Petroleum Assn., Tulsa Geol. Soc., Oklahoma City Assn. Petroleum Landmen, Oklahoma City Geol. Discussion Group (pres. 1975-76), Oklahoma City Petroleum Club (bd. dirs. 1987-91, sec. 1989), Internat. Assn. Energy Economists, Soc. Ind. Profl. Earth Scientists (pres. Okla. chpt. 1988, chmn. 1989), Soc. Profl. Well Log Analysts, AAAS, N.Y. Acad. Scis., U. Okla. Search Com., 1984—, U. Okla. Sch. Geology and Geophysics Alumni Adv. Coun. (bd. dirs. 1989-91), U. Okla. Found. Assoc., U.S. C. of C., Oklahoma City C. of C., Okla. Hist. Soc., Cherokee Nat. Hist. Soc. (chmn. solicitation com. of heritage council, mem. search com. 1987-90, devel. com. 1987—, bd. dirs. nat. soc. 1983—), Mus. of Cherokee Indian Assn., Thomas Gilcrease Mus. Assn., Okla. Pilots Assn., Exptl. Aircraft Assn., Sigma Xi, Pi Kappa Alpha. Contbr. articles to Jour. Cherokee Studies. Home: 6109 Woodbridge Rd Oklahoma City OK 73132 Office: Petro Corp 210 W Park Ave First Okla Tower Ste 3131 Oklahoma City OK 73102

CAMPBELL, DENNIS GEORGE, finance company executive; b. Phila., Apr. 20, 1949; s. George Reid and Bernice Patricia (Klatt) C.; m. Karen Ann Brown, June 18, 1971; children: Meghan, Alison, Christian. BA in Econs., Allentown (Pa.) Coll. St. Francis de Sales, 1971; MBA, Drexel U., 1976. Investment securities analyst Phila. Saving Fund Soc., 1971-76, comml. mortgage officer, 1976-80, asst. v.p. mortgage lending, 1980-82, v.p. residential mortgage lending, 1982-83; sr. asst. regional v.p. Fed. Nat. Mortgage Assn., Washington, 1983-85, v.p. mktg., 1985-87, sr. v.p. mktg., 1987—; instr. LaSalle Coll., Phila., 1977-83. Trustee Allentown Coll., 1986—, chmn. ann. fund, 1983-84, 88-89, chmn. com. fin. and budget, 1988—; mem. adv. bd. DeSales Sch. Theology, Washington, 1986—. Mem. Mortgage Bankers Assn. (lectr. 1982—), Fin. Analysts Fedn. (lectr. 1980—), Lambda Omega Chi. Democrat. Roman Catholic. Home: 3809 King William Dr Olney MD 20832 Office: Fed Nat Mortgage Assn 3900 Wisconsin Ave NW Washington DC 20016

CAMPBELL, DONALD GRAHAM, communications company executive; b. Toronto, Ont., Can., Aug. 14, 1925; s. James Lindsay and Margaret (Graham) C.; m. Audrey Irene Reid, Aug. 12, 1944; children: David, Reid, Marc, Craig (dec.), Scott. Chartered accountant, 1950. With Price Waterhouse, 1945-50; treas. Noma Lites Ltd., 1950-51; sec. treas. Atomic Energy Can. Ltd., Chalk River, 1952-57; with Maclean Hunter Ltd., Toronto, 1957—, contr. 1957-58, dir. 1958-60, v.p. 1960-69, exec. v.p. 1969-70, pres., chief exec. officer, 1970-76; chmn. bd., pres., 1976-77, chmn. bd., chief exec. officer, 1977-86; chmn. 1986—; also chmn. of number of MacLean Hunter subs. ops.; bd. dir. Toronto Dominion Bank, Can. Life Assurance Co., Interhome Energy Inc., Stelco Inc., Hunco Ltd., Toronto Sun Pub. Corp. Chmn. rsch. devel. corp. Hosp. for Sick Children Toronto; chmn. adv. com. Sch. Bus. Adminstrn. U. Western Ont. With RCAF, 1942-45. Mem. Toronto Golf Club, York Club. Avocations: Golf, tennis, skiing. Office: MacLean Hunter Ltd, 777 Bay St, Toronto, ON Canada M5W 1A7

CAMPBELL, DOUGLASS, banker; b. N.Y.C., Aug. 31, 1919; s. William Lyman and Helene (Underwood) C.; m. Marion Danielson Strachan, Jan. 13, 1962; step-children: Richard and Stephen Strachan. A.B., Yale U., 1941. With N.Y. Central System, 1939-67, timekeeper, traveling car agt., asst. train master, train master, asst. supt. asst. to freight traffic mgr., asst. to pres., supt. exec. rep., 1939-58; v.p. N.Y.C. R.R. (and subs.), 1958-67; also in charge pub. relations and advt. dept. N.Y.C. R.R. (and subsidiaries), 1960-67; also dir. N.Y.C. R.R. (affiliates and subsidiaries); chmn. pres. Bowater Paper Co., Inc., 1967-68; pres. Argyle Research Corp. (consultants), N.Y.C., 1968-83; v.p. Hambro Am., Inc., 1983-85; sr. v.p. Resource Holdings Ltd., N.Y.C., 1986—. Served as maj. AUS, 1942-46. Episcopalian. Clubs: Down Town Assn., River, Yale (N.Y.C.); Chagrin Valley Hunt (Cleve.); Saturn (Buffalo); Chgo. Racquet (Chgo.). Home: 3 E 71st St New York NY 10021 Office: Resource Holdings Ltd 10 E 53d St New York NY 10022

CAMPBELL, EDWARD CLINTON, violin maker; b. Scranton, Pa., May 24, 1929; s. Raymond Pyne and Mercedes Ruth (Simmons) C.; m. Mary Ringwald Dunfee, Sept. 1, 1954. BS in Engring., Pa. State U., 1955. Supr. order sect. Square D Electric Co., Inc., Detroit, 1955-59; propr., master violin maker Chimneys Violin Shop, Boiling Springs, Pa., 1960; operator Chimneys Sch. Violin Making; lectr. various colls. Contbr. articles to Viol mag., Violin Soc. Am. Jour. Pres. bd. trustees Amelia S. Given Library, Mt. Holly Springs, Pa. Served with USN 1946-50. Recipient Grand Prize (14), Gold medal (3), Cert. of Merit (11), Internat. Violin Makers Competition; violins made by Edward Campbell exhibited at Renwick Gallery, Smithsonian Instn., 1978-79 and Oberlin Mus., Oberlin U., Ohio, 1987-88. Mem. Violin Soc. Am. (bd. dirs.), Catgut Acoustical Soc., Ariz., So. Calif. Violin Makers Assns. (award for Outstanding Contbns. to Art of Violin Making 1985), Violin Makers Assn. Ariz. (bd. dirs.). Republican. Methodist. Clubs: Lions (pres. Mt. Holly Springs 1967-68, 85-86, 88—); Allenberry (pres. 1969) (Boiling Springs).

CAMPBELL, EDWARD DUDLEY, II, behavioral consultant, psychology educator; b. South Gate, Calif., Sept. 10, 1940; s. Edward Dudley and Blanche (Sokolow) C.; m. Candace Theresa, Sept. 4, 1965; 1 child, Tiffany Danielle. BA, UCLA, 1970; MA, Calif. State U., 1972; C.Phil. in Human Behavior, U.S. Internat. U., San Diego, 1980. With Lockheed Calif. Co., 1962-1970; prof. psychology Los Angeles Pierce Coll., 1972—; cons. Dudley Campbell & Assocs., Van Nuys, Calif., 1978—; honors program dir. Los Angeles Pierce Coll., 1987—; design and conduct tng. programs in areas of affirmative action, applied behavioral mgmt., effective managerial communication, equal employment opportunity, performance appraisal, leadership, motivation, organizational design, psychol. preparation for retirement, sex roles in the workplace, stress and time mgmt; also guest speaker in field numerous corps., spl. interest assns. and orgns., various cities, 1976—; honors program dir. Los Angeles Pierce Coll., 1987—. Author social psychology study guide Concepts and Applications, 1986. Chairperson adv. com. Dist. Transfer Edn. Los Angles Community Coll., 1980-82; com. mem. U. Calif., 1980-82, Acad. Affairs UCLA, 1980-82. Grantee Higher Edn. Act, 1976-78, NSF, 1983-84; recipient Outstanding Service award Affirmative Action Assn. for Women, 1983, Outstanding Tchr. award Alpha Gamma Sigma, 1987. Mem. Nat. Collegiate Honors Council, Western Regional Honors Council, Soc. for Indsl. Organizational Psychology, Soc. for Psychol. Study of Social Issues, AAAS, Am. Psychol. Assn., Internat. Assn. Applied Psychology, Western Psychol. Assn., World Future Soc.

CAMPBELL, GEORGE EMERSON, lawyer; b. Piggott, Ark., Sept. 23, 1932; s. Sid and Mae (Harris) C.; m. Joan Stafford Rule; children: Dianne, Carole. J.D., U. Ark., Fayetteville, 1955. Bar: Ark. bar 1955, U.S. Supreme Ct. bar 1971. Law clk. to judge Ark. Supreme Ct., 1959-60; assoc. Kirsch, Cathey & Brown, Paragould, Ark., 1955; mem. Rose Law Firm (P.A.), Little Rock, 1960—; Del. 7th Ark. Constl. Conv., 1969-70; regional v.p. Nat. Mcpl. League, 1974-86; mem. Ark. Ednl. TV Commn., chmn. 1980-82, 88—; bd. dirs. Ark. Ednl. TV Found., chmn. 1988—. Chmn. Pulaski County Law Library Bd., 1980—; bd. dirs. Ark. Symphony Orch. Soc., 1982-87, Ark. Capital Corp., The Downtown Partnership, Youth Home Inc. Mem. ABA, Ark. Bar Assn., Pulaski County Bar Assn., Am. Law Inst., Am. Judicature Soc. Office: Rose Law Firm PA 120 E 4th St Little Rock AR 72201

CAMPBELL, GILBERT GOULD, insurance company executive; b. Boston, June 4, 1945; s. Curtis and Eunice Gould (Murray) C.; BA, Trinity Coll., Hartford, 1967; MBA, Columbia U., 1969; m. Marriett Topping, Nov. 28, 1970; children: Craig Andrew, Emily Morrill, Laura Nelson, Curtis Price. Internat. banking account rep. Continental Bank, Chgo., 1969-70, comml. banking account rep., 1971-72; investment officer New Eng. Mut. Life Ins. Co., Boston, 1972-78; sr. investment analyst Union Mut. Life Ins. Co., Portland, Maine, 1978-83; asst. v.p. corporate fin. dept. Equitable Life Assurance Soc. U.S., N.Y.C., 1983-84, v.p., 1984-85, v.p., mng. dir. Equitable Capital Mgmt. Corp., N.Y.C., 1985—. Bishop, Mormon Ch., 1979—. C.L.U.; chartered fin. analyst. Mem. Fin. Analysts Fedn., Am. Soc. C.L.U.s. Republican. Home: 106 Glenside Rd Murray Hill NJ 07974 Office: 1285 Ave of Americas New York NY 10019

CAMPBELL, J. CAMERON, insurance brokerage executive; b. N.Y.C., Jan. 28, 1943; s. Thomas Robertson and Esther McKim (Brackbill) C.; m. Carol Anne Witte, Sept. 12, 1973; 1 child, Thomas Robertson II. BS in Commerce and Fin., Wilkes Coll., 1964. V.p. Johnson & Higgins, N.Y.C., 1964-75; sr. v.p. Johnson & Higgins of Tex., Inc., Houston, 1975-80; exec. v.p., br. mgr. Johnson & Higgins of Tex., Inc., Dallas, 1982—. Chmn. human resources com., bd. dirs. ARC Dallas chpt., 1987—; bd. dirs., fin. com. Dallas Arboretum and Botanical Soc.; mem. budget com. Dallas Mus. Art. With N.Y. Army N.G., 1965-70. Mem. N.Y. Yacht Club, India House, Tower Club, Dallas Petroleum Club. Republican. Episcopalian.

CAMPBELL, JAMES HOWARD, JR., banker; b. West Chester, Pa., Jan. 18, 1958; s. Eugene G. and Lorraine J. (Hinkle) Gillinger; m. Wendy A. Wiedemer, June 11, 1983. BA, U. Pitts., 1979; MA, Am. U., 1981. Cert. fin. planner. Acct. exec. The Copeland Cos., Harrisburg, Pa., 1983-87; trust officer Mid-State Bank and Trust Co., Altoona, Pa., 1987—; adj. facutly Mt. Aloysius Jr. Coll., Cresson, Pa., 1986-87, Washington Ctr. for Learning Alternatives, 1980; instr. Am. Inst. of Banking, 1989—; bd. dirs. Altoona Area Employees Fed. Credit Union, 1987—. Mem. Railroaders' Mus., Altoona, 1988; mem. Hollidaysburg Area Recreation Study Citizens Adv. Bd., 1988—. Mem. Rotary (bd. dirs. 1987—, bulletin editor 1985—), Pi Alpha Alpha. Home: 715 Garber St Hollidaysburg PA 16648 Office: Mid-State Bank and Trust Co 1130 12th Ave Altoona PA 16603

CAMPBELL, JEAN, retired, human services organization administrator; b. Fairhaven, Mass., Mar. 4, 1925; d. Elwyn Gilbert and Marion Hicks (Dexter) C. AA, Lasell Jr. Coll., Auburndale, Mass., 1944; BA, Brown U., 1946; MEd, U. Hartford, 1963. Field dir. Waterbury Area Council Girl Scouts, Inc., Waterbury, Conn., 1946-52; exec. dir. Manchester (Conn.) Girl Scouts, Inc., 1952-60; dist. dir. Conn. Valley Girl Scout Council, Inc., Hartford, 1961-63; dir. field services Plymouth Bay Girl Scout Council, Taunton, Mass., 1963-64, exec. dir., 1964-68; exec. dir. New Bedford (Mass.) YWCA, 1968-87; mem. adv. bd. Bay State Ctrs. for Displaced Homemakers, Southeastern Mass., 1982-87, Southeastern Mass. U. Women's Studies, North Dartmouth, Mass., 1987. Trustee Millicent Library, Fairhaven, 1970—; corporator Compass Bank for Savs., 1976—; bd. dirs. Greater New Bedford Concert Series, 1978—; hon. trustee St. Luke's Hosp. of New Bedford, 1986—; mem. adv. bd. Bierstadt Art Soc., New Bedford, 1987-88; com. mem., past pres. Interchurch Council of Greater New Bedford, 1976—. Recipient Sidney Adams Community Service award Interchurch Council of Greater New Bedford, 1984, AAUW Achievement award, 1987; named Woman of Yr., Internat. Women's Day Com., 1987. Mem. Delta Kappa Gamma Soc. (pres. Eta chpt. 1986-88). Clubs: YWCA Investment (advisor 1976—), Moneta Assocs. Investment (New Bedford) (pres. 1982-84, 86—).

CAMPBELL, JOHN DE VRIES, financial executive; b. Wheeling, W.Va., Jan. 28, 1949; m. Katherine Kincannon, July 1, 1972; children: Patrick Kincannon, Erin Maureen, John Murray. BS in Acctg., Va. Poly. Inst. and State U., 1972. CPA, D.C. Audit mgr. Deloitte Haskins & Sells, Washington, 1972-80; dir. audit div. ARC, Washington, 1980-86, dir. acctg. div., 1986-88, chief fin. officer, 1988—. Author: Standards of Accounting and Financial Reporting for Voluntary Health and Welfare Organizations, 3d ed., 1988. Mem. AICPAs, D.C. Inst. CPAs. Roman Catholic. Home: 9129 Fishermans Ln Springfield VA 22153 Office: ARC 17th and D Sta NW Washington DC 20006

CAMPBELL, LARRY E., ceramics company executive; b. Gas City, Ind., Feb. 21, 1941; s. Edwin L. Campbell and Ozetta (Maine) Albert; m. Nancy Sue Brunner, July 30, 1960 (div. 1970); children: Larry D., Derek, Bruce; m. Fay Lois Cooper, Oct. 28, 1972; children: Cailen G., Douglas G. B.S. in Chem. Engring., Purdue U., 1963, Ph.D., 1967. Research mgr. Corning Glassworks, Corning, N.Y., 1967-75; research mgr. Engelhard Corp., Iselin, N.J., 1975-78, gen. mgr. chem. catalysts, 1977-81, v.p. electronic materials, 1981-83, sr. v.p. electronics, 1983-88; pres., chief exec. officer Am. Matrix, Inc., Knoxville, Tenn., 1988—. Contbr. chpts. to books; patentee in field. Mem. Am. Inst. Chem. Engrs., Am. Ceramics Soc., Internat. Soc. Hybrid Micro Electronics, N.Am. Catalysis Soc., Omega Chi Epsilon, Tau Beta Pi. Republican. Methodist. Lodge: Masons. Home: 11033 Farragut Hills Blvd Knoxville TN 37922 Office: Am Matrix Inc Knoxville TN 37923

CAMPBELL, MARIA BOUCHELLE, banker, lawyer; b. Mullins, S.C., Jan. 23, 1944; d. Colin Reid and Margaret Minor (Perry) C. Student, Agnes Scott Coll., 1961-63; A.B., U. Ga., 1965, J.D., 1967. Bar: Ga. 1967, Fla. 1968, Ala. 1969. Practiced in Birmingham, Ala., 1968—; law clk. U.S. Circuit Ct. Appeals, Miami, Fla., 1967-68; assoc. Cabaniss, Johnston and Gardner, 1968-73; sec., counsel Ala. Bancorp., Birmingham, 1973-79; sr. v.p., sec., gen. counsel AmSouth Bancorp., 1979-84, exec. v.p., gen. counsel, 1984—; exec. v.p., gen. counsel AmSouth Bank, 1984—; lectr. continuing legal edn. programs; cons. to charitable orgns. Exec. editor Ga. Law Rev, 1966-67. Bd. dirs. St. Anne's Home, Birmingham, 1969-74, chancellor, 1969-74; bd. dirs. Children's Aid Soc., Birmingham, 1970—, 1st v.p., 1988—; bd. dirs. Positive Maturity, 1976-78, Mental Health Assn., 1978-81, YWCA, 1979-80, NCCJ, 1985—, Operation New Birmingham, 1985-87, personnel com., 1987—; bd. dirs. Soc. for the Fine Arts U. Ala., 1986—; commr. Housing Authority, Birmingham Dist., 1980-85, Birmingham Partnership, 1985-86, Leadership Birmingham, 1986—; mem. pres. adv. council Birmingham So. Coll, 1988—; trustee Ala. Diocese Episcopal Ch., 1971-72, 74-75, mem. canonical revision com., 1973-75, liturg. commn., 1976-78, treas., chmn. dept. fin., 1979-83, mem. council, 1983-87, chancellor, 1987—, cons. on stewardship edn., 1981—, dep. to gen. conv., 1985, 88. Mem. Am. Corp. Counsel Assn. (bd. dirs. Ala. 1984—), State Bar Ga., Fla. Bar, Am., Ala., Birmingham bar assns., Assn. Bank Holding Cos. (chmn. lawyers com. 1986-87). Club: Mountain Brook, Downtown. Lodge: Kiwanis. Home: 141 Camellia Circle Birmingham AL 35213 Office: AmSouth Bancorp PO Box 11007 Birmingham AL 35288

CAMPBELL, MARION LEE, financial executive; b. Shreveport, La., Nov. 1, 1930; d. William Raymond and Onie (Austin) F.; m. Max Richard Campbell, Feb. 4, 1966; children by previous marriage: Walter H. Harvey, H. Wayne Harvey. Bank teller Comml. Nat. Bank, Shreveport, 1949-51; artist Shreveport Times, 1946-48; acct. Hunter Engring. Corp., Bridgeton, Mo., 1953-63; sec. to pres. bd. Pak-A-Sak So. Stores, Shreveport, 1963-65; sec. to bus. mgr. E.Tenn. State U., Johnson City, 1965-78; fin. aid officer Coll. of Medicine, E.Tenn. State U., Johnson City, 1978—. Del. Dem. Party, Tenn., 1972; pres. U.S. Postal Council, Johnson City, 1980-82. Mem. Nat. Assn. Female Execs. (dir. 1978), So. Assn. Fin. Aid Adminstrs., Nat. Assn. Fin. Aid Adminstrs., Tenn. Assn. Fin. Aid Adminstrs., Am. Bus. Women's Assn. Democrat. Home: Rte 4 Box 3240 Elizabethon TN 37643 Office: East Tenn State U Coll of Medicine Box 19900A Johnson City TN 37614

CAMPBELL, MARY KATHLEEN, mortgage banker; b. Torrance, Calif., Aug. 5, 1944; d. David F. and Katherine I. (Norton) Shields; m. John Alan Campbell, Aug. 19, 1963; children—Lisa Marie Campbell Mitchell, John Andrew. B.B.A. in Acctg., Nat. U., San Diego, 1984. Head cashier Navy Exchange, San Diego, 1968-69; customer relations mgr. J.M. Fields, Norfolk, Va., 1970-72; acct. Hart Enterprises, San Diego, 1973-76; asst. treas. Midwest Pacific Fin., Inc., San Diego, 1976-80, treas., 1980-84, v.p., treas., 1984—; asst. sec. Midwest Fed. Savs. of Eastern Iowa, Burlington, 1978—, asst. v.p., 1985—; treas., dir. Burlington Fin., San Diego, 1984—. Vol. worker Girl Scouts U.S.A., San Diego, 1970-77, Boy Scouts Am., San Diego, 1972-79, Am. Cancer Soc., San Diego, 1978-82; student-family liaison Am. Field Service, Poway, Calif., 1983—. Mem. Fin. Mgrs. Soc., Assn. for Profl. Mortgage Women, Am. Bus. Women's Assn. (treas. 1980-81, Woman of Yr. Poway 1982). Office: Midwest Pacific Fin Inc 5405 Morehouse Dr San Diego CA 92121

CAMPBELL, MICHAEL LEONARD, controller; b. Des Moines, May 15, 1945; s. Ira Leonard and Sarah Elizabeth (Sorrick) C.; m. Catherine Anne Frankling, Nov. 30, 1968; children: Brian, Heather. AA, Grand View Jr. Coll., 1965; BSBA, Drake U., 1967; JD, Northwestern U., Chgo., 1972. CPA, Iowa; bar: Iowa 1975. Tax acct. Ernst & Whinney, Des Moines, 1972-73, Sidney B. Smith & Co., Des Moines, 1974-77; estate analyst Prin. Fin. Group, Des Moines, 1973-74; tax atty. Smith, Schneider & Stiles, Des Moines, 1977-78; tax mgr. Galinsky & Co., Des Moines, 1978-79; controller, corp. sec. Fareway Stores, Inc., Boone, Iowa, 1979—, also sec. bd. dirs. With U.S. Army, 1969-71. Mem. ABA, AICPA, Iowa State Bar Assn., Iowa Soc. CPA's, Am. Assn. CPA's and Attys. Avocations: computers, gardening, tennis, reading, travel. Home: 1627 Prairie Ave Boone IA 50036 Office: Fareway Stores Inc 2600 E 8th St Boone IA 50036

CAMPBELL, PATRICK J., union official; b. N.Y.C., July 22, 1918; s. Peter James and Mary (Clark) C.; m. Catherine Keane, May 19, 1940; children: Patrick M., Cynthia Campbell McGuire, Kevin. Organizer United Brotherhood of Carpenters and Joiners of Am., Washington, 1955-57, gen. rep., 1957-66, asst. to. gen. pres., 1966-69; gen. exec. bd. mem. 1st dist. United Brotherhood of Carpenters and Joiners of Am., N.Y.C., 1969-74; 2d gen. v.p. United Brotherhood of Carpenters and Joiners of Am., Washington, 1974-80, 1st gen. v.p., 1980-82, gen. pres., 1982—; dir. Urban Devel. corp., N.Y., 1971-74; v.p. bldg. and constrn. dept. AFL-CIO, Washington, 1982—, mem. exec. council, 1982—. Served with USAF, 1941-45, S. Pacific. Recipient Cert. Merit U.S. Dept. Labor, 1974; recipient Michael J. Quill award Hibernarian Soc., 1974, D. Russell Harlow award Bldg. Contractors Assn. N.Y., 1983; named Gael of Yr. United Irish Counties Assn., 1974. Mem. VFW, Holy Name Soc., KC. Roman Catholic. Home: 3445 Mt Burnside Way Woodbridge VA 22180 Office: UBC 101 Constitution Ave NW Washington DC 20001

CAMPBELL, REA BURNE, financial executive; b. Niceville, Fla., Aug. 13, 1954; s. Charles Burnette Campbell and Phyllis (Burgan) Campbell Patty. AA, SW Miss. Jr. Coll., 1974; BSBA in Fin., U. So. Miss., 1976. Mgmt. trainee Deposit Guaranty Nat. Bank, Jackson, Miss., 1976-77, credit analyst, 1977-80, asst. mgr. comml. loan ops., 1980-81, mgr. customer profl. analysis, 1981-83; mgr. acctg. Fred S. James & Co. Miss., Jackson, 1983-85; controller Fred S. James & Co. Ariz., Tucson and Phoenix, 1985-87; chief fin. officer James Benefits, San Francisco, 1987—. CPR inst. ARC, Jackson, 1985, San Francisco, 1989—. Club: Toastmasters. Home: 850 Powell #103 San Francisco CA 94108 Office: Fred S James & Co 600 Montgomery St 3rd Fl San Francisco CA 94111

CAMPBELL, RICHARD ALDEN, business consultant; b. Bend, Oreg., July 31, 1926; s. Corlis Eugene and Lydia Amney (Peck) C.; m. Edna Mary Seaman, June 12, 1948; children: Stephen Alden, Douglas Niall (dec.), Carolyn Joyce. B.S. in Elec. Engring., U. Ill., 1949, M.S. in Elec. Engring., 1950. With TRW Inc., Redondo Beach, Calif., 1954-86, exec. v.p., 1979-86; ptnr. Calif. Investment Assocs.; bd. dirs. Tylan Corp., Lombard Acquisition Corp. Patentee in radio communications. Trustee Nat. Multiple Sclerosis Soc.; bd. dirs. U. Ill. Found., Hugh O'Brien Youth Found. Served with USN, 1944-46. Recipient Alumni Honor award U. Ill. Coll. Engring. Mem. Am. Electronics Assn. (pres. 1969, dir. 1970), IEEE (sr.), Sigma Xi, Phi Kappa Phi, Tau Beta Pi, Eta Kappa Nu, Sigma Tau, Pi Mu Epsilon, Phi Eta Sigma. Republican. Clubs: Kiwanis (Palos Verdes, Calif.); Rolling Hills Country, Rancheros Visitadores, Los Caballeros. Office: TRW Electronics & Def Sector 1 Space Pk Bldg E-2 Redondo Beach CA 90278

CAMPBELL, RICHARD PARKER, JR., investment company executive; b. Louisville, Ky., Feb. 25, 1944; s. Richard Parker and Mildred (Poister) C.; m. Mary Breckinridge McGee, June 11, 1966; children: Douglas, Alexander. BA, U. Pa., 1966, MBA, 1968. Spl. asst. to Sec. of State Henry Kissinger State Dept., Washington, 1972-74; planning and analysis group dir. Pepsi Cola Co., Purchase, N.Y., 1974-75; v.p. fin. Pepsi Cola Bottling Group, Purchase, 1975-78; fin. mgmt. and planning corp. v.p. Pepsi Co., Inc., 1981-85; corp. services v.p. Wilson Sporting Goods, Chgo., 1978-81; exce. v.p., chief fin. officer PaineWebber Inc., N.Y.C., 1985-89; also bd. dirs; mng. dir., ptnr. Saugatuck Capital Co., Stamford, Conn., 1989—. With USN, 1968-72, Vietnam.

CAMPBELL, ROBERT AYERST, accounting company executive; b. Montreal, Que., Can., July 15, 1940; s. James Kenneth and Doris Victoria (Ayerst) C.; m. Cynthia Abbey, Aug. 17, 1963; children: Colin Ayerst, David Arthur, Sarah Reid. BBA, Clarkson U., 1961; MBA, U. Colo., 1966. CPA. Staff acct. Touche Ross, Montreal, 1961-63; mgr. Touche Ross, Rochester, N.Y., 1968-75; ptnr.-in-charge Touche Ross Internat., Tokyo, 1975-78; audit ptnr.-in-charge Touche Ross Internat., Milw., 1978-82; mng. ptnr. Touche Ross, Dallas, 1982—; asst. dir. admissions Clarkson U., Potsdam, N.Y., 1963-65, instr. acctg., 1966-68. Treas., dir. Am. Sch. in Japan, Tokyo, 1976-78; bd. dirs. Gaston Episc. Hosp., Dallas, 1988—, Boys Clubs Dallas, 1983—, Dallas United Way, 1987—, Baylor Inst. for Rehab., 1986—. Mem. AICPA, Tex. Soc. CPA's, Beta Gamma Sigma, Beta Alpha Pi, Milw. Country Club, Royal Oaks Country Club, Dallas Club. Republican. Presbyterian. Home: 4409 Larchmont Ave Dallas TX 75205 Office: Touche Ross & Co 2001 Bryan Tower Ste 2400 Dallas TX 75201-2170

CAMPBELL, ROBERT L., management consultant; b. Haverford, Pa., Jan. 6, 1944; s. Robert L. and I. Lee (Groah) C.; B.S. in Mktg., Loyola U., Chgo., 1964; M.M., Northwestern U., 1978; m. Elizabeth A. Powers, Dec. 20, 1975; 1 dau., Elisabeth. Mgmt. cons. Quirsfeld, Hussey & Manes, Chgo., 1964-70, Peat, Marwick, Mitchell & Co., Chgo., 1970-73, Booz, Allen & Hamilton, Chgo., 1973; founder, owner, mgr. Robert Campbell & Assocs., Chgo., 1973—; lectr. Loyola U., part-time, 1976—; Fin. Inst., part-time, 1972—. Bd. dirs. Youth Guidance Chgo., 1977—; bd. dirs., exec. com. Wyler Children's Hosp. U. Chgo.; bd. dirs. Mental Health Greater Chgo.; chmn. devel. com. Ill. Republican Com., 1970—. Mem. Assn. Bus. Economists, Am. Econometric Assn., Nat. Small Bus. Assn., Am. Prodn. and Inventory Control Soc., Am. Mktg. Assn., Northwestern U. Alumni Assn. (dir. 1978—). Clubs: Chgo. Yacht, University (Chgo.). Contbr. articles on labor econs. to profl. publs. Home: 470 Deming Pl Chicago IL 60614 Office: Robert Campbell & Assocs 18 S Michigan Ave Chicago IL 60603

CAMPBELL, ROBERT PATRICK, insurance company executive; b. East Orange, N.J., Jan. 31, 1956; s. Bernard Patrick and Evelyn Grace (Sommer) C.; m. Rina Ann Pappalardo, Mar. 23, 1985; 1 child, Scott Robert. BS in Econs. cum laude, U. Pa., 1978; MBA, U. Chgo., 1980. Investment analyst N.Y. Life Ins. Co., N.Y.C., 1980-82, sr. investment analyst, 1982-83, asst. v.p., 1983-85, investment v.p., 1985-88, v.p., 1988—. Mem. Am. Numismatic Assn., Am. Numismatic Soc. Presbyterian. Home: 100 Windsor Way Berkeley Heights NJ 07922 Office: NY Life Ins Co 51 Madison Ave New York NY 10010

CAMPBELL, ROBERT WALTER, real estate developer, real estate finance analyst; b. N.Y.C., July 23, 1934; s. Walter J. and Leonora J. (Daly) C.; m. Ann Catherine Boes, Sept. 3, 1955; children: Jean Gerhard, Kathleen, Barbara Wallace, George, Kerry. BCE, Poly. Inst. N.Y., 1958; postgrad., N.Y. Law Sch., 1960-65. Engr., project mgr. George A. Fuller Co., N.Y.C., 1955-62; prin., pres. Highland Const Corp., N.Y.C., 1962-67; contract adminstr. Allied Realty Corp., N.Y.C., 1967-72; v.p. McKee-Berger-Mansueto, N.Y.C., 1972-77; v.p. internat. ops. McKee Assocs., N.Y.C. and London, 1978-83; resident prin. officer, v.p. offices Brazil, Venezuela, Ireland, Saudi Arabia, Qatar; dir. devel. Solow Realty Corp., N.Y.C., 1983-84; exec. v.p., gen. mgr. Duro Devel. Corp., N.Y.C. and Washington, 1984—; participant Harvard Law Sch. negotiation programs. Author: Construction and Development in the Eastern Province of Saudi Arabia, 1974, Management Systems Related to Major School District Management, 1975, Management Information Control Systems, 1977. Retiring officer St. Vincent's Hosp., N.Y.C., 1977. Mem. Internat. World Congress Builders (founder Birmingham, Eng. chpt.), European Mgmt. Corp. (London), Real Estate Bd. N.Y., Am. Arbitration Assn. (comml. arbiter), Am. Mgmt. Assn. (lectr.). Republican. Roman Catholic. Club: Wykagyl Country (New Rochelle). Lodges: Friendly Sons St. Patrick, Ancient Order Hibernians. Office: Duro Devel Corp 23-25 Warren St New York NY 10007

CAMPBELL, ROGER D., utility company executive; b. Reading, Pa., Apr. 2, 1946; s. Richard J. and Thelma L. (Eberhart) C.; m. Christine Kehs, Sept. 6, 1969; children: Lynn Marie, Beth Anne. BBA, Bucknell U., 1968; MBA, Pa. State U., 1970. Sr. acct. Gilbert Assocs., Inc., Reading, 1971-74; asst. to v.p. Delmarva Power & Light Co., Wilmington, Del., 1974-76, asst. to sr. v.p., 1976-78, mgr. internal audit and prodn., 1978-79, asst. comptroller, 1979-80, gen. mgr. fin., 1981-82, gen. mgr. strategic planning and new bus. projects, 1982, gen. mgr. energy and fuels supply, 1982-84, v.p. chief fin. officer, 1984-85, treas., v.p., chief fin. officer, 1985-86, chief fin. officer, sr. v.p., 1985-87; pres. Delmarva Capital Investments, Inc., Wilmington, 1987—; mem. fin. com. Edison Electric Inst. Bd. dirs. Children's Home, Claymont, Del.; chmn. fund raising IHM Ch., Wilmington. Decorated Bronze Star. Mem. Fin. Exec. Inst., Fin. Analysts Fedn. Club: Rodney Sq. (Wilmington). Home: 1600 Turkey Run Rd Wilmington DE 19803 Office: Delmarva Power & Light Co 800 King St PO Box 231 Wilmington DE 19899

CAMPBELL, SCOTT ROBERT, food company executive, lawyer; b. Burbank, Calif., June 7, 1946; s. Robert Clyde and Genevieve Anne (Olsen) C.; m. Thersa Melanie Mack, Oct. 23, 1965; 1 son, Donald Steven. B.A., Claremont Men's Coll., 1970; J.D., Cornell U., 1973. Bar: Ohio 1973, Minn. 1976. Assoc. atty. Taft, Stettinius & Hollister, Cin., 1973-76; atty. Mpls. Star & Tribune, 1976-77; sr. v.p., gen. counsel, sec. Kellogg Co., Battle Creek, Mich., 1977—; U.S. del. ILO Food and Beverage Conf., Geneva, 1984. Mem. ABA, Ohio Bar Assn., Minn. Bar Assn., Grocery Mfrs. Assn. (exec. steering com.), Am. Soc. Corp. Secs. Office: Kellogg Co 1 Kellogg Sq PO Box 3599 Battle Creek MI 49016-3599

CAMPBELL, WILLIAM FOLEY, public relations executive; b. Mt. Vernon, N.Y., June 4, 1951; s. Joseph Peter Campbell and Patricia (Foley) Windman; m. Donna Campbell, July 8, 1978 (div. 1982). AB in English, Georgetown U., 1973. Copywriter Metro. Life Ins. Co., N.Y.C., 1973-74; editor mgmt. and labor Engring. News-Record, N.Y.C., 1974-79; v.p. Bozell Jacobs Pub. Relations Co., N.Y.C., 1979-82, Creative Systems Group, N.Y.C., 1982-84; dir. mktg. Adams & Rinehart, Inc., N.Y.C., 1984-87; sr. mng. dir. GreyCom Corp. Fin., N.Y.C., 1987—. Office: GreyCom Corp Fin 777 3rd Ave New York NY 10012

CAMPBELL, WILLIAM STEEN, magazine publisher; b. New Cumberland, W.Va., June 27, 1919; s. Robert N. and Ethel (Steen) C.; m. Rosemary J. Bingham, Apr. 21, 1945; children: Diana J., Sarah A., Paul C., John W. Grad., Steubenville (Ohio) Bus. Coll., 1938. Cost accountant Hancock Mfg. Co., New Cumberland, 1938-39; cashier, statistician Weirton Steel Co., W.Va., 1939-42; travel exec. Am. Express Co., N.Y.C., 1946-47; adminstr., account exec. Good Housekeeping mag., 1947-55; pub. Cosmopolitan mag., 1955-57; asst. dir. circulation Hearst Mags., N.Y.C., 1957-61; gen. mgr. Motor Boating mag., 1961-62; v.p., dir. circulation Hearst Mags., 1962-85; pres. Internat. Circulation Distbrs., 1978-81, Mags., Meetings, Messages, Ltd., 1986—; with Periodical Pubs. Svc. Bur. subs. Hearst Corp., Sandusky, Ohio, 1964-85, pres. Periodical Pubs. Srvc. Bur., 1970-85; dir. Audit Bur.

Circulations, 1974-86, Periodical Pubs. Svc. Bur., 1964-86, Nat. Mag. Co., Ltd., London, Randolph Jamaica Ltd., Omega Pub. Corp. Fla., Hearst Can. Ltd., 1964-86; former chmn. Central Registry, Mag. Pubs. Assn.; Chmn. bd. trustees Hearst Employees Retirement Plan, 1971-85; mem. president's council Brandeis U., 1974—; chmn. nat. corp. and found. com. U. Miami, 1979-85; dir. Broadway Assn., 1985—, v.p. 1988—. Served to lt. col. USAF, 1942-46, ETO. Recipient Lee C. Williams award Mag. Fulfillment Mgrs. Assn.; Torch of Liberty award Anti-Defamation League, 1979. Mem. Masons. Office: Mags Meetings Messages Ltd 240 Central Park South New York NY 10019

CAMPBELL-WHITE, ANNETTE JANE, venture capitalist; b. Dunedin, Otago, New Zealand, Jan. 28, 1947; came to U.S., 1975; d. Charles and Patricia Gwendolyn Ann (Pratt) C.; m. Ruediger Naumann-Etienne, Aug. 22, 1985. BSc in Chem. Engring., U. Capetown, Republic of South Africa, 1968, MSc in Phys. Chem., 1970. Market devel. exec. Brit. Oxygen, London, 1973-74; health economist SRI Internat.(formerly Stanford Rsch. Inst.), Menlo Park, Calif., 1975-76; prin. and owner ECCO Cons. Group, Berkeley, Calif., 1976-79; sr. analyst Hambrecht & Quist, San Francisco, 1979-81, gen. ptnr., 1981-83; spl. ltd. ptnr. L.F. Rothschild, Unterberg, Towbin, San Francisco, 1983-85; founder, mng. gen. ptnr. MedVenture Assoc., San Francisco, 1986—; dir. Apprise, Inc., Mountain View, Calif., Corus Med. Corp., Sunnyvale, Calif., Acoustic Imaging Techs. Corp., Tempe, Ariz., Devices For Vascular Intervention, Redwood City, Calif., Luconex, Inc., Foster City, Calif. Mem. adv. bd., chmn. capital com. Salvation Army, San Francisco, 1987—. Mem. Western Assn. Venture Capitalists. Office: MedVenture Assoc Pier 33 S 2d Fl San Francisco CA 94111

CAMPEAU, ROBERT, real estate development company executive; b. Sudbury, Ont., Can., Aug. 3, 1924; m. Ilse Luebbert; 6 children. Machinist Inco Ltd., Sudbury, Ont.; homebuilder from 1949; chmn., chief exec. officer, dir. Campeau Corp., Toronto, Ont., until 1969, then 1972—; chmn., chief exec. officer Allied Stores Corp., N.Y.C., 1987—; mem. adv. bd. Can. Bus. Health Research Inst., Guaranty Trust Co. Can.; bd. dirs. Great West Life Ins. Co. Bd. govs. Ashbury Coll., Ottawa, Ont. Clubs: Lambton Golf and Country, Donalda, Rideau, Ottawa Hunt and Golf; Mt. Royal; Rivermead Golf, Aylmer Country; Laval sur-le-lac, Jupiter Hills, Metropolitan, Granite. Office: Campeau Corp, Scotia Pla 40 King St W, Toronto, ON Canada M5H 3Y8 *

CANAKES, STEPHEN GEORGE, financial planner; b. Waterloo, Iowa, Sept. 12, 1950; s. Peter George and Dorothy (Charleton) C.; m. Constance Evelyn Wolff, June 17, 1969; 1 child, Stephanie Georgiana. Student, Faith Bapt. Coll., Ankeny, Iowa, 1974; MDiv., Grand Rapids Sem., 1978. Cert. fin. planner, 1984. With Key Fin. Services, Des Moines, 1984—, now pres.; br. mgr. Multi-Fin. Securities Corp.; mktg. dir. Security Benefit Life. Home: 1066 Belle Mar Dr West Des Moines IA 50265 Office: Key Fin Svcs Des Moines IA 50322

CANARDO, HERNANDO VICENTE, import and export company executive, lawyer; b. Buenos Aires, Argentina, Jan. 26, 1957; s. Vicente and Maria Dolores (Espina) C. Abogado, U. Catolica Argentina, Buenos Aires, 1981, JD, 1982. Bar: Corte Suprema de Justicia de la Nación, 1982, Colegio Póblico de Abogados Buenos Aires, 1986. Asst. prof. internat. law U. Catolica Argentina, 1982-84, asst. prof. legal ethics, 1985-87; mgr. Union Olivarera Canardo and Co., Buenos Aires, 1981—, Importadora and Exportadora Indian, Buenos Aires, 1986—; adj. prof. internat. law U. Catolica Argentina, 1988—. Official rep. to Second Argentine Congress of Internat. Law, 1985. Mem. Am. Soc. Internat. Law, ABA (internat. assoc.), Coll. Pub. Abogados Buenos Aires. Roman Catholic. Avocations: golf, swimming. Home: Paraguay 2421 7th Fl, Buenos Aires 1121, Argentina Office: Union Olivarera Canardo and Co, Sarmiento 3239, Buenos Aires 1196, Argentina

CANE, CHRIS FRANK, sales and marketing executive; b. N.Y.C., Oct. 30, 1938; s. John and Anne C.; m. Margaret Lisa, June 7, 1959; children: John, Joanne, Christine. Student, SUNY, 1968-69. With Westinghouse Lamp, 1959-84; regional sales mgr. Westinghouse Lamp, Chgo., 1975-79; nat. sales mgr. Westinghouse Lamp, Bloomfield, N.J., 1979-82, dir. mktg./sales, 1982-83; dir. nat. sales Philips Lighting, Bloomfield, 1983-86; v.p. mktg./sales Philips Lighting, Somerset, N.J., 1986—. With U.S. Army, 1957-59. Office: Philips Lighting 200 Franklin Sq Dr PO Box 6800 Somerset NJ 08875-6800

CANES, BRIAN DENNIS, employee benefits and systems consultant; b. London, July 14, 1945; came to U.S., 1982.; s. Jules Joel and Freda Rica (Gavronsky) C.; m. Melanie Maxine Segal, June 29, 1969; 1 child, David. B.Sc, U. Witwatersrand, Johannesburg, Republic of South Africa, 1967; student, Inst. Actuaries, London. Systems mgr. Shepley & Fitchett Consulting Actuaries, Johannesburg, 1968-75; asst. v.p. William M. Mercer Ltd., Toronto, Ont., Can., 1975-80; controller William M. Mercer Ltd., Toronto, 1980-82; prin. William M. Mercer-Meidinger-Hansen, N.Y.C., 1982-87; sr. cons. The Wyatt Co., N.Y.C., 1987—. Home: 162 Clarence Rd Scarsdale NY 10583-6318 Office: The Wyatt Co 99 Park Ave New York NY 10016-1580

CANFIELD, GRANT WELLINGTON, JR., educational association administrator; b. Los Angeles, Nov. 28, 1923; s. Grant Wellington and Phyllis Marie (Westland) C.; m. Virginia Louise Bellinger, June 17, 1945; 1 child, Julie Marie. BS, U. So. Calif., 1949, MBA, 1958. Personnel and indsl. relations exec., Los Angeles, 1949-55; employee relations cons., regional mgr. Mchts. and Mfrs. Assn. Los Angeles, 1955-60; v.p., orgnl. devel. cons. Hawaii Employers Council, Honolulu, 1960-75; pres., dir. Hawaiian Ednl. Council, 1969—, chmn., chief exec. officer, 1989; exec. v.p. Hawaii Garment Mfrs. Assn., 1965-75, Assn. Hawaii Restaurant Employers, 1966-75; exec. dir. Hawaii League Savs. Assns., 1971-78; exec. dir. Pan-Pacific Surg. Assn., 1980-81, exec. v.p., 1982-83; exec. dir. Hawaii Bus. Roundtable, 1983—; sec., treas. Econ. Devel. Corp. Honolulu, 1984-85; sec., treas. Hawaii Conv. Park Council, Inc., 1984-86, hon. dir., 1986-88. Co-author: Resource Manual for Public Collective Bargaining, 1973. Bd. dirs. Hawaii Restaurant Assn., 1974-76, bd. dirs. Hawaii chpt. Nat. Assn. Accts., 1963-67, nat. dir., 1965-66; bd. dirs. Vol. Service Bur. Honolulu, 1965-66, pres., 1966-68; bd. dirs. Vol. Info. and Referral Service Honolulu, 1972-75, Goodwill Vocat. Tng. Ctrs. of Hawaii, 1973-81, Girl Scout council Pacific, 1961-65, 71-72; bd. dirs. Hawaii Com. Alcoholism, 1962-71, co-chmn., 1964-68; pres., dir. Friends of Punahou Sch., 1972-75; mem. community adv. bd. Jr. League Hawaii, 1968-70; exec. bd. Aloha council Boys Scouts Am., 1962-65; bd. regents Chaminade U., 1983-85. Served to 1st lt. inf. AUS, 1943-46. Decorated Bronze Star, Purple Heart, Combat Inf. badge. Mem. Am. Soc. Assn. Execs. (cert. assn. exec.), Inst. Mgmt. Cons. (cert.), Am. Soc. Tng. and Devel., Am. Soc. Personnel Adminstrn., Pacific Club, Rotary, Masons. Home: 1950 W Dry Creek Rd Healdsburg CA 95448 Office: PO Box 4145 Honolulu HI 96812-4145

CANFIELD, HELEN J., utility company executive; b. Elmira, N.Y., Aug. 30, 1942; d. Ernest Harry and Julia Cora (Forker) Bowen; children—Tammy Austin, Timothy Canfield, Todd Canfield. Student Empire State Coll. Nurses aide Corning Hosp., N.Y., 1960-65; office mgr. L.J. Graham, M.D., Corning, 1966-76; customer acctg. clk. N.Y. State Electric & Gas Corp., Corning, 1976-80, resdl. rep., Monticello, N.Y., 1981-82, staff analyst, Binghamton, 1982-85, customer accounts mgr., Oneonta, N.Y., 1985-88, area mgr. customer svc., 1988—; pres. Speakers Club, 1985-86, info. center coordinator, 1984-86. Vol. ARC. Mem. Nat. Assn. Female Execs. Republican. Clubs: Zonta, Civic of Binghamton; Bus./Profl. Women's (Oneonta). Avocations: flying; golf; swimming; tennis. Home: Box 299 Southside Dr Oneonta NY 13820 Office: NY State Electric 65 Country Club Rd Oneonta NY 13820

CANION, JOSEPH ROD, computer company executive; b. Houston, Jan. 19, 1945. MSEE, U. Houston, 1967. With Tex. Instruments, Inc., Houston, 1968-81; pres., chief exec. officer Compaq Computer Corp., Houston, 1982—, also bd. dirs. Office: COMPAQ Computer Corp 20555 FM 149 Houston TX 77070 *

CANNADAY, LISA WOODSON, marketing professional; b. Roanoke, Va., June 22, 1962; d. Robert Wilbert Jr. and Gloria (Powell) W.; m. James Thomas Cannaday Jr., Nov. 14, 1987. BS magna cum laude, Ferrum Coll., 1986. Mktg. asst. Fralin & Waldron, Inc., Roanoke, 1986, mktg. assoc., 1986-88; corp. mktg. mgr. Van Scoyoc Assocs., Inc., Alexandria, 1988—. Republican. Episcopal. Home: 7803 Beard Ct Falls Church VA 22043 Office: Van Scoyoc Assocs Inc 1900 N Beauregard St #205 Alexandria VA 22311

CANNALIATO, VINCENT, JR., investment banker, mathematician; b. Bklyn., July 12, 1941; s. Vincent and Margaret (Mancuso) C.; BS in Math., Fordham U., 1963; MA in Math., CUNY, 1964; grad. cert. in system design U. Pa. Sch. Bus., 1970; m. June A. Marino, Apr. 8, 1967; children—Amy June, Kimberly Dawn, Douglas Vincent. Systems analyst N.Y. Telephone Co., N.Y.C., 1969-70; account exec. CIT Leasing Corp., N.Y.C., 1970-72; v.p. Kidder Peabody & Co., Inc., N.Y.C., 1972-80, head leasing and project financing group corp. fin. dept., 1977-80; sr. v.p., mng. dir., Smith Barney, Harris Upham & Co., Inc., dept. head leasing and project fin., corp. fin., 1980—; bd. dirs. Nortankers, Inc., 1989—; vis. instr. Southwestern Grad. Sch. Banking, 1976-77; speaker law jour. seminars equipment leasing industry, 1986-87; adv. bd. U.S. Mcht. Marine Acad., 1974—, chmn., 1977—; instr. math. U. Md., 1966-69; mem. maritime adv. com. Dept. Transp., 1982-84, chmn. fin. subcom. 1983-84. Exec. bd., curriculum chmn. Gifted Child Soc., 1975-82; nation chief Rampo Indian Guides and Princesses, Western Hills YMCA, 1980-83; mem. parish council St. Elizabeth Roman Cath. Ch., 1986-88, pres., 1987-88. Capt. AUS, 1963-69. Decorated Bronze Star. Mem. Am. Assn. Equipment Lessors (bd dirs. exec. and nominating coms., fed. legis. com. 1975-84, chmn. keyman com. 1978-83, chmn. membership com. 1982-83, chmn. academia awareness task force), Acad. Magical Arts, Inc. Roman Catholic. Clubs: Metropolitan (N.Y.C.); Indian Trail (Franklin Lakes, N.J.); Ocean City (N.J.) Yacht. Contbg. author: U.S. Taxation of International Operations, 1975, 77, 87; Oil and Gas Taxes/Natural Resources Service, 1979; World Leasing Yearbook, 1980, 81. Home: 501 Alexis Ct Franklin Lakes NJ 07417 Office: Smith Barney 1345 Ave of the Americas New York NY 10105

CANNAVO, SAL MICHAEL, chemical company executive; b. Staten Island, N.Y., Oct. 25, 1928; s. Emil E. and Jennie (Guercio) C.; m. Rose T. Massetti, Dec. 11, 1949; children: Michael E., Diane L. BS in Chemistry, Wagner Coll., 1961. Lab technician L.A. Dreyfus Co., Edison, N.J., 1946-51, jr. rsch. chemist, 1951-54, process control chemist, 1954-57, rsch. chemist, 1957-65, sr. rsch. chemist, 1965-69, asst. to pres., 1969-74, 1st v.p., 1974-75, exec. v.p., 1975, pres., 1975—; b. dirs. Malayan Guttas Pvt. Ltd., Singapore, Wrigley S.A., Biesheim, France. Mem. Nat. Assn. Chewing Gum Mfrs. (bd. dirs. 1976—), Am. Chem. Soc., Inst. Food Technologists. Roman Catholic. Office: LA Dreyfus Co 3775 Park Ave Edison NJ 08820

CANNIZZARO, PAUL PETER, food products executive; b. N.Y.C., Jan. 31, 1925; s. Pietro and Anna (Nicolini) C.; m. Dolores Cecile della Cella, Apr. 15, 1950; children: Diane, Linda, Peter. BS in Econs., U. Pa., 1948. Salesman Cannizzaro Wine Co., Inc., N.Y.C., 1948-50, dir. mktg., 1955-58; treas., gen. mgr. Continental Cigar Co., Inc., N.Y.C., 1951-54; treas. L. Della Cella Co., Inc., N.Y.C., 1959-62; pres. Mineola, N.Y., 1963—; proprietor Cordova Sales Co., Garden City, N.Y., 1970—; pres. G. Nino Bragelli, Inc., Mineola, 1974—. Pres. Italy-Am. C. of C., N.Y.C., 1984, bd. dirs., 1980-85; treas. Malvern, N.Y. chpt. Com. for Preservation of Neighborhood Schs., Inc., 1966. Served to lt. (j.g.) USN, 1943-46. Mem. Cheese Importers Assn. Am., Inc. (pres. N.Y.C. chpt. 1968-70, dir.-at-large 1971—), Beta Gamma Sigma. Republican. Roman Catholic. Club: Freeport (N.Y.) Yacht (vice-commodore 1979, commodore 1980). Home: 235 Brixton Rd Garden City NY 11530 Office: L Della Cella Co Inc 100 E Old Country Rd Mineola NY 11501

CANNON, CHRISTOPHER PERRY, human resource development executive; b. Drummondville, Que., Can., Jan. 22, 1953; s. Charles Christopher George and Mary Theresa (Davis) C.; m. Susan Caroline Middleton, July 17, 1978; 1 child, John Christian. BA, U. N.C., Charlotte, 1975; MS, Shippensburg State U., 1977. Asst. dean students Denison U., Granville, Ohio, 1977-79; personnel devel. coordinator Firestone Tire and Rubber, Akron, Ohio, 1979-81; dir. tng. Sheller-Globe Corp., Toledo, 1981-84, dir. edn., 1984-89; mgr. edn. and learning systems Libby-Owens Ford Co., Toledo, 1989—. Mem. Toledo area Small Bus. Assn. Tech. Task Force, 1983, Career Devel. Adv. Com. Toledo Pub. Schs., 1983, Youth Motivational Task Force, Ohio, 1984, Adv. Com. Tech. Coll. U. Toledo, 1986; advisor Northwest Ohio Jr. Achievement. Named ALCOA scholar, 1971; recipient Human Resource Devel. award, 1987. Mem. Am. Soc. Tng. and Devel. (bd. dirs., Pacesetter of Yr. award 1986), Human Resource Planning Soc., Internat. Assn. Quality Circles, Pi Kappa Phi (advisory com., pres. Greater Toledo alumni chpt.), Alpha Phi Omega. Republican. Presbyterian. Club: Brandywine Country (Toledo). Office: Sheller-Globe Corp 1505 Jefferson Ave Toledo OH 43097

CANNON, DANIEL WILLARD, lawyer; b. Pitts., Sept. 3, 1920; s. Edgar Carl and Violet Jessie (Burke) C.; m. Ann Marshall Price, Sept. 30, 1943; children—Susan Melchior, David, Judith Lillie, Barbara, Ann Finch. A.B., U. Pitts., 1941, J.D., 1968. Bar: Pa. 1948, D.C. 1952, U.S. Supreme Ct. 1952. Atty., U.S. Steel Corp., Pitts., 1947-50; sec., gen. counsel Bituminous Coal Operators Assn., Washington, 1951-58; dir. Indsl. Devel. and Natural Resources, NAM, N.Y.C., 1958-74, dir. environ. affairs, Washington, 1974-84, dir. program devel., 1984—; lectr. in field. Served to 1st lt. USAAF, 1942-46. Recipient Moot Ct. award, U. Pitts. Law Sch., 1947; Award of Appreciation, Water Quality Research Council, 1974. Mem. ABA, Fed. Bar Assn., Bar Assn. D.C., Allegheny County Bar Assn., Air Pollution Control Assn., Water Pollution Control Fedn., Order of the Coif. Republican. Episcopalian. Clubs: Univ., Army and Navy, Pa. Soc., Masons. Editorial adv. bd. Indsl. Wastes Mag., Air Quality Control, 1975; editor, Hazardous Waste Mgmt. Under RCRA: A Primer for Small Business, 1980; A Pollution Tax Won't Help Control Pollution, 1977; National Strength and the National Environmental Policy Act, 1972; Staying Out of Trouble: What You Should Know About the New Hazardous Waste Law, 1985; Preparing for Emergency Planning, 1987, Retroactive Emission Controls, 1987. Home: 637 E Capitol St SE Washington DC 20003 Office: 1331 Pennsylvania Ave NW Suite 1500 N Washington DC 20004-1703

CANNON, JOHN, III, lawyer; b. Phila., Mar. 19, 1954; s. John and Edythe (Grebe) C. BA, Denison U., 1976; JD, Dickinson Sch. Law, 1983. Bar: Pa. 1983, Hawaii 1986, U.S. Dist. Ct. (ea. dist.) Pa. 1983, U.S. Ct. Appeals (3d cir.) 1985. Account exec. PRO services, Inc., Flourtown, Pa., 1976-79, br. officer mgr., Pitts., 1979-80; law clk. Montgomery County Ct. of Common Pleas, Norristown, Pa., 1983-84; assoc. Rawle & Henderson, Phila., 1984-88; atty. CIGNA Corp., Phila., 1988— . Comments editor Dickinson Internat. Law Ann., 1983. Mem. Pa. Bar Assn., Phila. Bar Assn., Montgomery Bar Assn., ABA, Hawaii State Bar Assn., Kappa Sigma (pres. 1975-76), Gamma Xi (v.p., trustee 1982-86). Republican. Episcopalian. Office: CIGNA Corp 1600 Arch St Philadelphia PA 19103

CANNON, JOHN HAILE, retail executive; b. Hampton, Va., Mar. 27, 1942; s. Arthur Haile and Dorothy (Obrey) C.; m. Dorothy Gills, Aug. 1, 1964; children—Arthur, Paulus. B.S., Va. Poly. Inst., 1964, M.S., 1968. Asst. to treas. Burlington Industries, N.Y.C., 1972-73; assoc. mgr. investments Gen. Foods, White Plains, N.Y., 1973-76, mgr. banking, 1976-77, asst. treas., 1977-82; asst. treas. F.W. Woolworth, N.Y.C., 1982-83, v.p., treas., 1983—. Mem. Fin. Execs. Inst., Nat. Assn. Corp. Treas. Republican. Methodist. Home: 276 Greenley Rd New Canaan CT 06840 Office: F W Woolworth 233 Broadway New York NY 10279

CANNON, LINDA BYRD, computer systems analyst; b. Bath, Maine, Sept. 24, 1952; d. Jerry Edward and Kathryn Barbara (Shupert) Byrd; 1 child, Lawra Susan. BS in Math., Coll. Charleston, 1974. Programmer Med. U. S.C., Charleston, 1974-77, systems analyst info. resource mgmt., 1977-86, mgmt. info. systems mgr., 1986-87, assoc. dir., acting exec. dir., 1987, adminstrv. systems mgr. CSX Tech., 1987—. Mem. Coll./Univ. Machine Records Conf., 1986, 87, CAUSE, 1987—; charter mem. Med. U. S.C. Key 100, 1987—. Mem. Data Processing Mgmt. Assn., S.C. Assn. Data Processing Dirs., Epsilon Sigma Alpha Women Internat. (pres. local chpt. 1977-78, 80-81, woman of the yr. award 1978). Republican. Baptist. Club: YWCA Women's Breakfast (Charleston). Home: PO Box 30361 Charleston SC 29417 Office: Med U SC/CSX 171 Ashley Ave Charleston SC 29425

CANNON, LYNNE MARPLE, investment management company executive; b. Phila., Oct. 14, 1955; parents: John and Edythe (Grebe) C. BA, Ohio Wesleyan U., 1977. Employee PRO Services Inc., Flourtown, Pa., 1979-82; asst. sec. PRO Services Inc., Blue Bell, Pa., 1982-86; v.p. AMA Advisers Inc. (formerly PRO Services Inc.), Blue Bell, 1986—; v.p., sec. AMA Growth Fund Inc., AMA Income Fund Inc., Med. Tech. Fund Inc., AMA Money Fund Inc., Emerging Med. Tech. Fund Inc. Sec., vol. Plant Ambler Inc., Ambler, Pa., 1983—. Mem. No-Load Mut. Fund Assn. (sec. retail mktg. com. 1984—). Republican. Episcopalian. Home: 122 N Ridge Ave Ambler PA 19002 Office: AMA Advisers Inc 5 Sentry Pkwy W Ste 120 Blue Bell PA 19422

CANNON, MICHAEL DAVID, auditor; b. Amarillo, Tex., Mar. 30, 1947; s. Robert Clinton and Anne Viola (Juracek) c.; m. Linda Ann Thompson, Mar. 3, 1973; children: Angela Signe, Allison Victoria. Assoc. of Applied Sci. in Data Processing, St. Louis Community Coll., 1972; BS in Bus. Adminstrn., U. Mo., 1974; MBA, So. Ill. U., 1977. Systems analyst Gen. Am. Life Ins. Co., St. Louis, 1975-78; sr. auditor Kellwood Co., St. Louis, 1978-80; audit mgr. Boatmen's Bancshares, Inc., St. Louis, 1980—; lectr. U. Mo., St. Louis, 1983—, St. Louis Community Coll., 1983—, Washington U., St. Louis, 1983-85. Tchr. sunday sch. Trinity Luth. Ch., St. Louis, 1983—. Served with USAF, 1966-70. Mem. EDP Auditor's Assn. (pres. 1983-84), Computer Security Inst. Republican. Lutheran. Office: Boatmens Bancshares Inc 100 N Broadway St Saint Louis MO 63102

CANNON, ROBERT EMMET, consumer products manufacturing company executive; b. Greenville, Miss., Nov. 18, 1929; s. Robert Emmet and Louise (Hill) C.; m. Kathryn Gracey, Aug. 28, 1955; children: Katherine, Howard, Hall. B.M.E., Ga. Inst. Tech., 1951. With Procter & Gamble Co., 1954—; group v.p. Procter & Gamble Co., Memphis, 1981—. Pres. Chickasaw council Boy Scouts Am., 1978-80, bd. dirs., 1975—; bd. dirs. United Way Greater Memphis, Future Memphis, Inc., Lebonheur Children's Hosp.; mem. nat. adv. bd. Ga. Inst. Tech., mem. adv. bd. Sch. Mech. Engring.; pres., bd. dirs. Memphis Orchestral Soc.; officer Shady Grove Presbyn. Ch., Memphis. Served with USN, 1951-54. Mem. Am. Paper Inst. (chmn. pulp producers exec. bd. 1977-78), Can. Pulp and Paper Assn. (exec. bd.). Club: Chickasaw Country. Home: 445 Shady Grove Rd Memphis TN 38119 Office: Procter & Gamble Co 1001 Tillman St Memphis TN 38108

CANOSA, ALBERT ANTHONY, corporate finance officer; b. New Haven, Conn., Jan. 1, 1946; s. Albert and Beatrice Rose (Villano); m. Sharon Ann Good, Oct. 7, 1972; 1 child, Adam. BS in Acctg., Quinnipiac Coll., 1969. Fin. mgr. Olin Corp., Stamford, Conn., 1969-80; div. controller Raymark, Trumbull, Conn., 1980-85; v.p., corp. controller Raymark Corp., Trumbull, Conn., 1985-86; v.p., treas., chief fin. officer Ray Tech Corp., Trumbull, Conn., 1986—. Served to sgt. U.S. Army, 1966-72. Mem. North Haven Jaycees (v.p. 1973-76). Republican. Roman Catholic. Home: 12 Deer Path Rd Branford CT 06405 Office: Ray Tech Corp 100 Oakview Dr Trumbull CT 06611

CANTER, STEPHEN EDWARD, investment management company executive; b. Muncie, Ind., July 18, 1945; s. Floyd Martin and Marianna (McGarrell) C.; m. Carol Magovern, Apr. 19, 1969; children—Stephen Edward Jr., Marigrace, Joanna. A.B., Cornell U., 1967; M.B.A., Columbia U., 1969. Investment officer Chase Manhattan Bank, N.Y.C., 1970-72; v.p. Chase Investors Mgmt. Corp., N.Y.C., 1972-78; sr. v.p. Chase Investors Mgmt. Corp., 1978-80, pres., 1980-88; pres. Mitchell Hutchins Instl. Investors, N.Y.C., 1988—. Trustee Tuskegee (Ala.) Univ. Fellow Fin. Analysts Fedn.; mem. N.Y. Soc. Security Analysts (bd. dirs. 1980-82). Club: Econs. Office: Mitchell Hutchins Instl Investors 1285 Ave of the Americas New York NY 10019

CANTERBURY, JOHN JEFFERSON, III, real estate associate, director of corporate properties; b. Houston, Feb. 2, 1956; s. John Jefferson Jr. and Peggy Jane (Owen) C. BA, U. Tex., 1980; MBA, U. St. Thomas, 1984. Lic. real estate broker, Tex. Real estate broker Coldwell Banker Comml. Real Estate Sevices, Dallas, 1985—. Mem. The 500 Inc., Dallas, 1986—, Dallas Opera Guild, 1986—, Dallas County Rep. Men's Club, 1987—. Mem. Greater Dallas Bd. Realtor (comml. investment div.). Episcopalian. Office: The Assocs Corp NAm PO Box 660237 Dallas TX 75266-0237

CANTOR, ALAN BRUCE, management consultant, computer software developer; b. Mt. Vernon, N.Y., Apr. 30, 1948; s. Howard and Muriel Anita Cantor; m. Judith Jolanda Szarka, Mar. 1, 1987; BS in Social Scis., Cornell U., 1970; MBA, U. Pa., 1973. Mgmt. cons. M & M Risk Mgmt. Services, N.Y.C., 1974-78, nat. services officer, spl. projects div. Marsh & McLennan, Inc., 1978-80, asst. v.p., mgr. Marsh & McLennan Risk Mgmt. Services, Los Angeles, 1980-81; sr. v.p. sr. cons. prin. Warren, McVeigh & Griffin, Inc., 1981-82, sr. v.p., prin., 1982; founder, pres. Cantor & Co., 1982—; co-mgr. Air Travel Research Group, N.Y.C., 1977-79; instr. risk mgmt. program Am. Mgmt. Assn.; lectr. Risk and Ins. Mgmt. Soc. Conf., 1975-87; seminars How to Use Spreadsheets in Risk Mgmt., 1986-89. Cons., Vol. Urban Cons. Group, N.Y.C. Mem. Cornell Alumni Assn. N.Y.C. (bd. govs., program chmn.), Cornell Alumni Assn. So. Calif. Clubs: Wharton Bus. Sch. (N.Y.C.); Los Angeles, Wharton of Los Angeles (chmn., mem. adv. bd.) Los Angeles Athletic (Los Angeles). Copyright airline induatry model, 1975. Contbr. articles to profl. jours.; creator, developer, copyright RISKMAP risk mgmt. software products, 1982, 83, 84, 85, 86, 87, 88; copyright airline industry model, 1975, Exposure Base Mgmt. System (EBMS), 1985, 86, patient care monitoring system, 1985, 86, 87, 88, COLTS, corp. overall legal tracking system, 1983, hosp. risk info. mgmt. system, 1984, 86, 87, 89. Office: Cantor & Co 9348 Civic Ctr Dr Beverly Hills CA 90210

CANTOR, SAMUEL JAY, lawyer, real estate developer; b. Phila., Nov. 1, 1953; s. Edward Richard and Anita L. (Weinstein) C.; m. Sharon Bernice Rinehimer, Feb. 9, 1985. BA, Am. U., 1976; JD, Widener U., 1979. Bar: Pa. 1979, Fla. 1982; licensed real estate broker. Sole practice Phila., 1979-81; legal counsel Jane McDonough Realty Inc., Phila., 1980-81; v.p., corp. counsel Raben-Pastal, Coconut Creek, Fla., 1981-84; pres. Cantor and Rinehimer, Boca Raton and Tamarac, Fla., 1984—. Home: 2520 NE 48th St Lighthouse Point FL 33064 Office: Cantor and Rinehimer 7300 N Federal Hwy Ste 207 Boca Raton FL 33487

CANTRELL, WESLEY E., SR., office equipment company executive; b. 1935. Student, So. Inst. Tech. With Lanier Business Products, Inc., 1955-87, v.p., 1966-72, exec. v.p., 1972-77, pres., dir. 1977-87; pres., chief exec. officer Harris 3M, Atlanta, 1987— Office: Harris 3M 2300 Parklake Dr NE Atlanta GA 30345

CANTWELL, DENNIS MICHAEL, finance company executive; b. Milw., Apr. 21, 1943; s. Paul Frederick and Maureen Louise (Bolton) C.; m. A. Kathleen Gray, May 16, 1970; 1 child, Jennifer. BA, Marquette U., 1966; MBA, Northwestern U., 1968. Various acctg., systems and analysis positions Chrysler Corp., 1968-74; mgr. internat. systems Chrysler Fin. Corp., Troy, Mich. and Paris, 1975-77; dir. fin. Chrysler Fin. Corp. Subs., London, 1977-81; asst. treas. Chrysler Fin. Corp. Subs., Troy, 1982-85, v.p. strategic planning, 1985—. Office: Chrysler Fin Corp 901 Wilshire Dr Troy MI 48084

CAPABLANCA, FERNANDO AQUILES, banker; b. Havana, Cuba, Sept. 22, 1944; came to U.S., 1961; s. Felix Fernando and Eugenia Maria (Calienes) C.; m. Ana Maria Hernandez, Aug. 3, 1968; children: Katherine Ann, Christina Theresa, Fernando Aquiles Jr. BS, NYU, 1970; postgrad., Harvard U., 1977. Asst. treas. Chase Manhattan Bank, N.Y.C., 1963-70; asst. v.p. Am. Swiss Credit Co., N.Y.C., 1970-71; pres. WFC Corp., Miami, Fla., 1971-77; gen. mgr. Bank Tokyo Internat., Coral Gables, Fla., 1977-84; pres., chief exec. officer Gulf Bank, Miami, 1984-88; regional dir., gen. mgr., chief exec. officer Banco Exterior de Los Andes y de España, Miami, 1988—. Active citizens bd. U. Miami, Coral Gables Econ. Devel. Bd., Internat. Ctr. With U.S. Army, 1962-68. Named Disting. Citizen Kaufman & Roberts, Miami, 1987. Mem. Bankers Adv. Council (pres. Latin chamber 1988—), Fla. Bankers Assn. (bd. dirs. 1987—), Fla. Internat. Bankers Assn., Harvard Bus. Club So. Fla. (past pres., bd. dirs. 1980—), Greater Miami C. of C. (bd. dirs. 1987—), Rotary. Republican. Roman Catholic. Home: 1702 SW

103rd Pl Miami FL 33165 Office: Extebandes 701 Brickell Ave Miami FL 33131

CAPALDI, ANTHONY C., credit information company executive; b. Phila., Mar. 8, 1939; s. Charles C. and Rose A.; B.S., St. Joseph's Coll., 1961; postgrad. U. Pa., 1969; m. Carole L. Leix, Sept. 22, 1971. With Trans Union Credit Info. Co. (formerly Credit Info. Corp. of Phila./Trans Union System Corp. and Phila. Credit Bur.), 1953—, mgr. mortgage dept., 1961, mgr. sales promotional dept. 1962, dir. sales promotion, 1963-66, dir. Credit Info. Ctr., 1966, asst. gen. mgr., asst. treas., asst. sec., 1968-71; exec. v.p., gen. mgr., 1971-75, Eastern regional v.p. mktg., 1975-77, v.p. mktg. Phila. div., 1977-79, pres. Credit Reporting Corp. N.J., 1979-80, v.p., gen. mgr. Phila. and N.J. divs., 1980-84, v.p., gen. mgr. Phila div., 1985, regional v.p., Atlantic region, Phila., 1985—; pres. Credit Counseling Service of Delaware Valley, 1980-84; bd. dirs. Better Bus. Bur., 1984; bd. dirs. , v.p. Pa. Coalition to Prevent Shoplifting, 1977—; instr. fall semester Community Coll .Pa., 1966-69; bd. dirs. Associated Credit Burs. of Pa., 1976-83, pres. 1984-85. Assoc. to Pres. St. Joseph's U., 1982-86. Bd. dirs. Dist. XII Internat. Credit Assn. Named Mgr. of Yr., Trans Union Credit Info. Co., 1983, 84; recipient James D. Hays Leadership award Associated Credit Bur. Pa., 1984-85, Consumer Credit Men's Assn. award 1970, Medal of Merit, Republican Presdl. Task Force; named Ambassador for Pa. Gov. of Pa. Mem. Internat. Consumer Credit Assn. (exec. mem.), Consumer Credit Execs. Assn. Delaware Valley (dir. 1968-86, sec. 1971-75), Delaware Valley Retail Fin. Execs. Assn. (dir. 1970-84), Phila. Retail Controllers Assn. (chmn. 1976-78). Roman Catholic. Clubs: Vesper, Racquet (Phila.). Avocations: reading, sailing, swimming. Office: Trans Union Credit Info Co Atlantic Region 2401 Pennsylvania Ave Philadelphia PA 19130

CAPANI, PETER MICHAEL, systems representative; b. Binghamton, N.Y., Jan. 13, 1951; s. Peter Jr. and Helen Threas (Gonda) C.; m. Jayne Alice Post, Aug. 17, 1974; children: Nicholle Christine, Jennifer Brigette, Laurie Chantelle. AAS, Broome Community Coll., 1971; BSEE, Clarkson U., 1975, MEE, 1976. Lic. broadcast engr. IBM research fellow Cornell U., Ithaca, N.Y., 1981-86; project engr. Missile and Ordnance div. Tex. Instruments, Inc., Dallas, 1976-77; advanced weapons and communications engr. Fed. Systems div. IBM Corp., Owego, N.Y., 1977-79; advance test system engr. Systems Products div. IBM Corp., Endicott, N.Y., 1979-80; site research liaison Systems Tech. div. IBM Corp., Endicott, 1980-81; prin. researcher in compound semicondrs. Gen. Tech. div. IBM Corp., Endicott, 1981-85, dir. materials microcharacterization, 1983-86; systems rep. Southwest Mktg. div. IBM Corp., Dallas, 1986—; broadcast cons. 1969-74; communications cons. 1981—; invited speaker IBM Research Lab., Zurich, Switzerland, 1985, Max Planck Inst., Stuttgart, Fed. Republic Germany, 1985. Referee Jour. Vacuum Sci. and Tech., 1986-89; contbr. articles to profl. jour. Mem. Eta Kappa Nu, Sigma Pi Sigma, Sigma Xi. Office: IBM 1603 LBJ Freeway Ste 501 Dallas TX 75234

CAPEHART, HARRIET JANE HOLMES, economics educator; b. Springfield, Ill., Sept. 29, 1917; d. Walter Creager and Mary Gladys (Copeland) Holmes; m. Homer Earl Capehart Jr., June 17, 1950; children: Craig Earl, Caroline Mary, John. AB, Vassar Coll., 1938; MA, Harvard U., 1945, PhD, 1948; LLD (hon.), U. Indpls., 1986. Instr. Wheaton Coll., Norton, Mass., 1945-46, Wellesley (Mass.) Coll., 1947-48; assoc. prof. Western Coll. for Women, Oxford, Ohio, 1948-50; assoc. prof. econs. Butler U., Indpls., 1950-53; staff adult edn. div. U. Indpls. (formerly Indiana Cen. U.), 1973-75, adj. faculty, 1983—; lectr. summer sch. Butler U., 1948-50; bd. dirs. Indpls. Power and Light Co., IPALCO Enterprises Inc. Bd. trustees U. Indpls., 1969—; exec. bd. Women's Com. Indpls. Symphony Orch., 1964—; bd. dirs. Utility Women's Conf., 1986—; mem. Children's Mus. Guild, aux. Indpls. Day Nursery, others. Mem. Am. Econ. Assn., Econometric Soc., AAUP, Indpls. Mus. Art, Nat. Soc. Colonial Dames Am. (bd. mgrs. Ind.), Kappa Alpha Theta, Phi Beta Kappa. Republican. Clubs: Ind. Vassar (past pres.) Radcliffe of Ind. (past pres.). Home: 445 Pine Dr Indianapolis IN 46260 Office: IPL 25 Monument Circle PO Box 15958 Indianapolis IN 46206

CAPELL, ROBERT ASHBY, JR., chemical company executive; b. Mobile, Ala., Jan. 13, 1951; s. Robert Ashby Sr. and Jewell Irene (Griffith) C.; m. Cynthia Ann Schultze, Dec. 16, 1972; children: Laura Ashley, Brian Wesley. BS, Auburn U., 1973; MBA, U. South Ala., 1978. Project engr. Union Carbide Corp., Mobile, 1973-74, devel. engr., 1974-76, prodn. engr., 1976-78, tech. services engr., 1978-79, staff engr., 1979-81, prodn. supr., 1981-86, lab. and tech. service mgr., 1986—. Bd. dirs. Mobile Met. YMCA, 1985-87. Mem. Internat. Mgmt. Council (treas. 1982-84, v.p. 1984-85, pres. 1985-87), Tau Beta Pi, Phi Lambda Upsilon, Beta Gamma Sigma. Methodist. Home: 1275 Westchester Ct Mobile AL 36695 Office: Union Carbide Corp PO Box 11486 Chickasaw AL 36611

CAPEN, VICTOR LAWRENCE, computer company executive; b. Romulus, Mich., Sept. 19, 1943; s. Willard Capen and Josephine (Steck) Laurell; m. Akiko Irie, Jan. 10, 1964 (div. Oct. 1978); 1 child, Sheila Junko; m. Mary Ellen Torrecarion, Dec. 28, 1978; children: Maria Victoria, Corina Marie, Christine Mary, Candice Marion. AA, San Jose City Coll., 1970; BSBA, San Jose State U., 1972, MBA, 1974. Sr. field engr. EMR Computer Inc., Mpls., 1969-73; tech. advisor Itel Corp., Palo Alto, Calif., 1973-76; v.p. sales and mktg. Philipino Computer Group, Manila, 1976-78; internat. sales mgr. Nat. Semiconductor Corp., Santa Clara, Calif., 1978-79; gen. mgr. Zilog, Inc., Campbell, Calif., 1979-81; dir. world trade Onyx Systems Inc., San Jose, Calif., 1981-84; gen. mgr. Asia Corvus Systems Inc., San Jose, Calif., 1984-85; v.p. sales, chief fin. officer Info. Industry Cons. Corp., Campbell, 1985—; treas. EMW Technologies, Inc., Campbell, 1976—; bd. dirs. Corp. Networks Inc., Campbell, Uniware Corp., Inc., San Jose, Digital Repair Services, Inc., Campbell. With USAF, 1962-67, Japan. Republican. Roman Catholic. Office: EMW Technologies Inc PO Box 1027 Big Bear Lake CA 92315

CAPES, JOHN ROBERT, real estate broker; b. Covington, Ga., Jan. 12, 1934; s. John Zack and Inez (Johnson) C.; married; children: Barbara Pickens, Stephanie Dellinger. BA, Wofford Coll., 1956. Traffic mgr. So. Bell Tel.&Tel. Co., Spartanburg, S.C., 1957-64; sales mgr. Tom Jenkins Realty, Inc., Columbia, S.C., 1964-83; pres., chmn. bd. Bob Capes Realty, Inc., Columbia, 1983—. Lt. U.S. Army, 1956-57, capt. Res. Mem. Nat. Assn. Realtors, Nat. Homebuilders Assn., Columbia Bd. Realtors (pres. 1979), Network 50 (state chmn. 1985—), Exec. Assn. Columbia. Republican. Methodist. Home: 475 Greentree Ln Lexington SC 29072 Office: 300 Candi Ln Columbia SC 29210

CAPESTRANI, TIMOTHY JOHN, controller; b. Cleve., June 22, 1956; s. Joseph G. and Grace (Fabrizio) C. BBA, Cleve. State U., 1979, MBA, 1985. Staff acct. Parker Hannifin Corp., Cleve., 1979-82, sr. acct., 1982-84; supr. acctg. Parker Hannifin Corp., North Brunswick, N.J., 1985-86; asst. contr. R.C. Industries Inc., Linden, N.J., 1986-87, contr., 1987—. Republican. Roman Catholic. Office: RC Industries Inc 120 Jersey Ave New Brunswick NJ 08903

CAPLAN, AMY GAIL, security analyst; b. Balt., Aug. 14, 1960; d. Alvin G. and Helene Marsha (Segall) C. BA, Johns Hopkins U., 1982; diploma (hon.), Johns Hopkins U., Bologna, Italy, 1981. Chartered fin. analyt. Sec., research asst. Legg Mason, Balt., 1982-83, jr. analyst, 1983-86, chartered fin. analyst, 1986—; co-instr. Howard Community Coll., 1987—. Mem. Balt. Security Analysts Soc., Fin. Analysts Fedn. Office: Legg Mason 111 S Calvert St Baltimore MD 21203-1476

CAPLAN, L(AZARUS) DAVID, manufacturing company executive; b. Montreal, Que., Can., May 24, 1940. B in Commerce, McGill U., 1961; sr. mgrs. program, Harvard U., 1979. Articled for Riddell, Stead & Co., Chartered Accts., 1961-64; with Pratt & Whitney Can., Montreal, 1964—, v.p. fin. and adminstrn., 1976-80, exec. v.p., 1980-84, pres., chief operating officer, 1984-85, pres., chief exec. officer, 1985—. Mem. Can. Inst. Chartered Accts. Office: Pratt & Whitney Can Inc, 1000 Marie Victorin Blvd E, Longueuil, PQ Canada J4G 1A1

CAPONE, MARYANN, savings banker; b. N.Y.C., July 25, 1952; d. Patsy and Dorothy (Rizzo) C.; m. Donald W. Huebner, June 7, 1975. With F. Eberstadt and Co. Inc., N.Y.C., 1975-78; asst. v.p. Merrill Lynch Huntoon Paige, N.Y.C., 1978-82; asst. controller Res. Fund, Inc., N.Y.C., 1982; v.p. Integrated Resources, N.Y.C., 1982-85, Mid-Island Equities, N.Y.C., 1984-85, Am. Savs. Bank, N.Y.C., 1985-86; 2d v.p., mgr. mortgage servicing dept. Greater N.Y. Savs. Bank, N.Y.C., 1986—. Mem. Nat. Assn. Accts., Am. Soc. Women Accts., Savs. Bank Womens Assn., Am. Assn. Individual Investors. Roman Catholic. Office: Greater NY Savs Bank 211 Station Rd Mineola NY 11501

CAPONEGRO, ERNEST MARK, stock broker, financial planner; b. Hoboken, N.J., Feb. 8, 1957; s. Joseph Edmund and Anne (DiPietro) C.; m. Ida Teresa Russo, Aug. 23, 1987. BS in Econs., Fairleigh Dickinson U., 1983; cert. in fin. planning, Adelphi U., 1987. With corp. fin. E.F. Hutton, N.Y.C., 1980; investment broker Philiphs Appel and Waldin, N.Y.C., 1981; securities broker Prudential-Bache Securities, N.Y.C., 1982—. Republican. Roman Catholic. Home: 168 Cliff Rd Bricktown NJ 08723 Office: Prudential-Bache Securities 2 Penn Pla New York NY 10121

CAPONIGRO, RALPH ANGELO, beverage company executive; b. Des Moines, May 31, 1932; m. Barbara J. Paul; children: Joseph, John, Jeffrey, Cindy, James, Lisa. BBA, Drake U., 1954; MBA cum laude, Mich. State U., 1973. Mgr. credit and acctg. Gen. Mills Corp., Kankakee, Ill., 1954-59; U.S. controller Parker Pen Co., Janesville, Wis., 1959-67; treas., controller Am. Lincoln Corp., Toledo, 1967-69; sr. v.p. fin., treas. The Stroh Brewery Co., Detroit, 1969—; bd. dirs. Coca-Cola Bottlers, Detroit; mem. Protection Mut. Adv. Bd., Park Ridge, Ill., 1984—. Bd. dirs., treas. Greater Detroit Area Health Council, 1983—; bd. dirs., council, Boys Hope, Detroit, 1985—; adv. bd. The Salvation Army, Detroit, 1984—; mem. Pres. Club. Oakland U. Mem. Fin. Execs. Inst. (bd. dirs. Detroit chpt. 1986—), Mich. State Alumni Assn. (bd. dirs. Bus. Sch. 1986—). Roman Catholic. Clubs: Renaissance, Detroit Athletic. Home: 644 Bennington Dr Bloomfield Hills MI 48013 Office: Stroh Brewery Co 100 River Pl Detroit MI 48207

CAPORASO, FRAN ELLEN, sales executive; b. Bridgeport, Conn., Apr. 21, 1947; d. William Howard and Margeret (Toth) Frisbie; m. James H. Steinmetz (div. May 1978); m. John L. Caporaso; children: James, Christopher. Student, Housatonic Community Coll., Sacred Heart U., 1978. Staff coord. med. records Roncalli Health Ctr., Bridgeport, 1972-78; sales rep. John Hancock Ins., Stratford, Conn., 1978-80; mgr. Trumbull (Conn.) Liquor Ctr., 1980-83; mgr. import brand A Gallo Distbg., Danbury, Conn., 1983-86; dist. mgr. All Brand Importers, Hartford, Conn., 1986—. Democrat. Roman Catholic. Home: 214 Washington Pkwy Stratford CT 06497 Office: All Brand Importers 1 Colony Rd Jersey City NJ 07305

CAPPIO, JAMES, manufacturing company executive; b. Montpelier, Vt., July 24, 1941; s. Jildo Elmo and Anne (Bruce) C.; m. Claire McCorquodale, Sept. 9, 1967; children: James, Adam, Matthew, Clay. BA, Dartmouth Coll., 1963; MBA, U. Va., 1967. Mktg. dir. Richardson-Vicks Health Care Products, Wilton, Conn., 1973-79; pres. Richardson-Vicks Home Care Products, Memphis, 1979-85; v.p. mktg. Tenneco Automotive, Lincolnshire, Ill., 1985-87; pres. Ryobi Motor Products Div., Liberty, S.C., 1987—. Office: Ryobi Motor Products Div PO Box 35 Pickens SC 29671

CAPPITELLA, MAURO JOHN, architect; b. N.Y.C., July 11, 1934; s. Gaetano and Maria (D'Errico) C.; m. Christine Wilhelmine Otte, Oct. 11, 1964; children: Mark, Christina, Nicole. BS in Architecture, CCNY, 1956; postgrad., Columbia U., 1960-62; M in Urban Planning, NYU, 1967. Registered architect, N.Y., N.J.; cert. profl. planner, N.J. Designer Garfinkel & Marenberg, N.Y.C., 1956-57; architect Western Electric Co., Inc., N.Y.C., 1957-69; cons. architect Norwood, N.J., 1968-76, Upper Saddle River, N.J., 1976—. Served to 1st lt. U.S. Army, 1957-59. Mem. Am. Inst. Architects, N.Y. Soc. Architects, N.J. Soc. Architects (bd. dirs. 1983-84), Architects League No. N.J. (bd. dirs. 1980-83, sec. 1984-85, v.p. 1985, 1st v.p. 1986, pres.-elect 1987, pres. 1988, bd. dirs. 1989—, Dir. of Yr. 1981, 82), N.J. Soc. Architects (bd. dirs. 1987-89), Nat. Council of Archtl. Registration Bds., Soc. of the 3d Infantry Div. Republican. Roman Catholic. Club: Saddle River Tennis, Windham Ridge Resorts Swim and Tennis. Office: 332 E Saddle River Rd Upper Saddle River NJ 07458

CAPPO, JOSEPH C., publisher; b. Chgo., Feb. 24, 1936; s. Joseph V. and Frances (Maggio) Caeioppo; m. Mary Anne Cappo, May 7, 1967; children: Beth, John. B.A., DePaul U., 1957. Reporter, Hollister Publs., Wilmette, Ill., 1961-62; reporter Chgo. Daily News, 1962-68, bus. columnist, 1968-78; columnist Crain's Chgo. Bus., 1978-79, pub., 1979-89; v.p. Crain Communications, Inc., 1981-89, v.p. grp. pub. Crain Communications, Inc., 1989; daily bus. commentator Sta. WLOO-FM, Chgo.; dir. Assn. Area Bus. Publs., 1982—. Bd. dirs.: Off the Street Club, Chgo., 1981—, Chicago Advertising Club, Mus. of Broadcast Communications. Served with U.S. Army, 1959-61. Recipient award Ill. Press Assn., 1962, (with other Daily News staffers) Nat. Headliner award, 1966, Disting. Alumni award DePaul U., 1975, Page One award Chgo. Newspaper Guild, 1978, Peter Lisagor award Sigma Delta Chi, 1978, Outstanding Achievement award in Communication, Justinian Soc. Lawyers, 1979. Mem. Soc. Am. Bus. and Econ. Writers (bd. govs. 1984—), Ill. Small Business Advisory Commn., DePaul U. Alumni Assn. (bd. dirs. 1984—), Delta Mu Delta (hon.). Roman Catholic. Office: Crain Communications Inc 740 N Rush St Chicago IL 60611-2590 *

CAPPS, THOMAS EDWARD, holding company executive; b. Wilmington, N.C., Oct. 31, 1935; s. Edward S. Jr. and Agnes (Rhodes) C.; m. Jane Paden, Sept. 13, 1963; children: Ashley R., Leigh C. AB, U. N.C., 1958, JD, 1965. Bar: Fla. 1975, N.C. State Bar 1966. Sr. counsel Carolina Power & Light Co., Raleigh, N.C., 1970-74; v.p., gen. counsel Boston Edison Co., 1974-75; sr. ptnr. Steel Hector & Davis, Miami, Fla., 1975-84; exec. v.p. Va. Power, Richmond, 1984-86; pres. Dominion Resources, Inc., Richmond, 1986—; bd. dirs. Signet Banking Corp., Richmond, Signet Bank/Va., Richmond. Mem. bd. assocs. U. Richmond, 1984; chmn. Gov.'s Job Coordinating Council, State of Va., 1987; mem. bd. visitors U. N.C., Chapel Hill, 1985, trustee, 1987—; bd. dirs. Metro Richmond Blood Bank, 1986. Served to lt. USCG, 1959-62. Mem. ABA, Bd. of Bar Overseers, N.C. Bar Assn., N.C. Bar Assn., Fla. Bar Assn., Mass. Bar Assn. Episcopalian. Clubs: Union (N.Y.C.); Biscayne Bay Yacht (Miami, Fla.). Office: Dominion Resources Inc 701 E Byrd St PO Box 26532 Richmond VA 23219

CAPPUCCIO, RONALD JOSEPH, lawyer; b. Phila., Mar. 3, 1954; s. Anthony R. and Marie A. (Rigolizzo) C.; m. Sondra J. Lippi, Aug. 2, 1980; 1 dau., Sondra Nicole. B.S.F.S. in Internat. Econs., Georgetown U., 1974, LL.M. in Taxation, 1977; J.D., U. Kans., 1976. Bar: N.J. 1976, U.S. Dist. Ct. N.J. 1976, D.C. 1977, U.S. Tax Ct. 1977, U.S. Ct. Appeals, (3d cir.) 1984. Chief law clk. to judge, 1977-78; assoc. Lario & Nardi, Haddonfield, N.J., 1978-80; sole practice 1980—; solicitor Gloucester Twp. Planning Bd., 1981-82, Evesham Twp Planning Bd., 1982-83; adj. instr. dept. govtl. services Rutgers U., 1977-80. Mem. ABA, N.J. Bar Assn., Camden County Bar Assn. (chmn. tax com. 1987-88, trustee 1988—). Office: 1409 Kings Hwy N Cherry Hill NJ 08034

CAPRIA, FRANK ANTONIO, insurance company executive; b. Bklyn., Sept. 26, 1951; s. Alfonso and Josephine (Concolino) C.; m. Vita Capria, June 6, 1971; children: Christine, Frank, Justine. AAS, Kinsborough Community Coll., Bklyn., 1971; BBA, CUNY, 1977. Supr. acctg. Home Life Ins. Co., N.Y.C., 1971-76; asst. v.p. Ch. Pension Fund and Affiliates, N.Y.C., 1976-79; controller Amalgamated Life and Pension Fund Co., N.Y.C., 1979-82; pres., chief exec. officer Golden Eagle Mut. Life Ins. Corp., Bklyn., 1982—, also bd. dirs.; mem. Life Ins. Guarantee Corp., 1984—. Chmn. adv. bd., cons. econs. Bklyn. chpt. Jr. Achievement N.Y., 1986-88. Served with N.Y. N.G., 1971-77. Recipient Exemplary Service award Jr. Achievement N.Y., 1988. Mem. Life Ins. Council N.Y., Pres.'s Assn., Bklyn. C. of C. (bd. dirs. 1985—). Club: Bklyn. Office: Golden Eagle Mut Life Ins Corp 105 Court St Brooklyn NY 11201

CAPRON, JOHN CALVIN, accountant; b. Wells, Vt., Apr. 23, 1951; s. Bernard F. and Amelia L. (LaPerle) C.; m. Diane F. Green, July 15, 1978; children: Daniel William, Julie Anne. AA in Acctg. and Bus. Adminstrn., Albany Bus. Coll., 1973; BSBA in Acctg., Coll. St. Rose, 1981. Pres. C&C Acctg. and Tax Svc., South Bethlehem, N.Y., 1980; dist. acctg. mgr. Browning Ferris Industries, Latham, N.Y., 1987—; adj. instr. acctg., math and income tax Hudson Valley Community Coll., Troy, N.Y., 1985. Mem. Bethlehem Rep. Club, Phi Theta Pi. Roman Catholic. Office: Browning Ferris Industries 136 Sicker Rd Latham NY 12110

CAPSALIS, BARBARA DAMON, banker; b. Washington, Apr. 22, 1943; d. Wallace Carver and Gertrude Marie (Larson) Damon; m. John N. Capsalis, Aug. 7, 1965. B.S. cum laude in Math, Ohio U. Dep. commr. N.Y.C. Dept. Gen. Services; chief technology officer Chem. Banking Corp., N.Y.C. Recipient Catalyst Women of Yr. award, Woman of Achievement award YWCA. Office: Chem Bank 277 Park Ave 4th Fl New York NY 10172

CAPUTO, LUCIO, trade company executive; b. Monreale, Italy, May 22, 1935; s. Giuseppe and Gioacchina (Spinnato) C.; came to U.S., 1967; Law Degree, Palermo U., 1957, Journalism Degree, 1958, Degree in Polit. Sci., 1960, postgrad. economics, 1961; m. Maria Luisa Mayr, Oct. 5, 1967; 1 son, Giorgio. Journalist, Italy, 1950-65; admitted to Italian bar, 1961; asso. firm Studio Legale Caputo-Orlando, Palermo, Sicily, 1960-62; ofcl. Italian Fgn. Trade Inst., 1962-82, mkt. researcher, Libya, Cyprus, 1963, dep., London, 1964-67, dir. study mission SE Asia, 1967, Italian trade commr., Phila., 1967-71, N.Y.C., 1972-82; founder Italian Wine Promotion Center, N.Y.C., 1975—, Italian Tile Center, 1979—, Italian Fashion Center, 1980—, Italian Shoe Center, 1981—, Italian Trade Center, N.Y.C., 1981—; pres. Ital Trade USA Corp., 1982-86 ; pres. Italian Wine and Food Inst., 1984—; organizer ann. Italian Week on 5th Ave., N.Y.C.; exec. v.p., exec. com. Gruppo Esponenti Italiani, 1974—; adv. bd. Italy-Am. C. of C., 1972—; chmn. Internat. Trade Ctr., Inc., 1987—. Served to lt. Italian Air Force, 1959-61. Named Cavaliere Ufficiale all' Ordine del Merito della Repubblica Italiana, 1972, Commendatore, 1981. Mem. Italian Bar Assn., Italian Journalist Assn., Fgn. Consular Assn. Phila., Soc. Fgn. Consuls N.Y. Roman Catholic. Club: World Trade Center. Signer agreement between Italy and Peoples' Republic of China, 1967; editor trade mags.: Italy Presents, Quality (English, French, Spanish, German), 1962-64; contbr. articles to Italian mags. and newspapers. Office: 1 World Trade Ctr Suite 1513 New York NY 10019

CARANO, JOHN JOSEPH, JR, foundry products sales manager; b. Warren, Ohio, Oct. 19, 1954; s. John Joseph and Theresa Rose (Mattinat) C.; m. Teresa Helen Scott, Oct. 4, 1980. BS in Edn., Youngstown State U., 1979. Sales trainee Nat. Castings div. Midland Ross Corp., Sharon, Pa., 1979-80, coordinator mktg. services , sales rep. RR products, Chgo., 1980-81, sales rep. indsl. castings, Sharon, 1981-82, dist. sales mgr. mining and mill sales, Columbus, Ohio, 1982-86, regional sales mgr. Midwest sales, Nat. Castings, Inc., Columbus, 1986-87; dist. mgr. Columbia Steel Casting Co., Inc., Columbus, 1987—. Mem. Hubbard Vol. Fire Dept., Ohio, 1975-79; active Ohio Hist. Soc., Columbus, 1984—, Cat Welfare Assn., Misty Meadows Civic Assn., Northwest Civic Assn. Mem. Am. Foundrymen's Soc., Am. Acad. Polit. and Social Sci., Youngstown State U. Alumni Assn. Democrat. Roman Catholic. Clubs: Columbus Italian, Unity, Toastmasters (Columbus) (v.p. local chpt. 1984, pres. 1987—, Best Pub. Speaker award 1984-85, Pub. Debate speaker award 1984, Best Speaker Evaluator award 1985, Able Toastmaster award 1987). Avocations: running, book collecting, home repair and restoration. Home: 2667 Delcane Dr Columbus OH 43220-1712 Office: Columbia Steel Casting Co Inc 4663 Executive Dr Columbus OH 43220-3627

CARAS, CONSTANTINE GEORGE, service company executive; b. Steubenville, Ohio, June 20, 1938; s. George and Bess (Tsouris) C.; married; 1 child, Valerie Alexandra. BA, U. Pitts., 1962; LLB, U. Va., 1965. Atty. U.S. Maritime Adminstrn., Washington, 1967-72, gen. counsel, 1978-79; atty. Ogden Corp., N.Y.C., 1972-78; v.p. Ogden Corp., Washington, 1981-86, Lykes Bros. Steamship Co., New Orleans, 1979-80; exec. v.p., chief adminstrv. officer Ogden Allied Services Corp., N.Y.C., 1986—. Mem. ABA, Ohio State Bar Assn. Greek Orthodox. Office: Ogden Allied Svcs Corp 2 Pennsylvania Pla New York NY 10121

CARAS, RICHARD ALAN, investment executive; b. Brookline, Mass., Jan. 21, 1949; s. J. Sheldon and Adele (Salett) C. BA, Bowdoin Coll., 1971. Mgmt. trainee Shawmut Bank, Boston, 1971-72; acct. exec. Merrill Lynch, Boston, 1973-76, E.F. Hutton, Boston, 1976-77; asst. mgr., asst. v.p. E.F. Hutton, Salem, Mass., 1977-79; v.p., resident mgr. E.F. Hutton, Portland, Maine, 1979-82; v.p., resident mgr. E.F. Hutton, Chestnut Hill, Mass., 1982-87, 1st v.p., 1987-88; sr. v.p. Shearson Lehman Hutton, Chestnut Hill, 1988—; bd. dirs. Newton TriCentennial Corp, Newton Pride Corp. Mem. Boston Leadership Forum (charter), Boston C. of C. (chmn. membership com. 1972-73) (hon. life). Jewish. Home: 85 Grove St Chestnut Hill MA 02167 Office: Shearson Lehman Hutton Chestnut Hill Pla Chestnut Hill MA 02167

CARBERRY, MICHAEL GLEN, advertising agency executive; b. N.Y.C., Nov. 8, 1941; s. Glen Michael and Grace (Brennan) C.; m. Dianne Helen Riggs, Oct. 18, 1969; children—Glen, John, Catherine. BS, Manhattan Coll., 1963; MBA, Columbia U., 1968. Account exec. SSC&B, N.Y.C., 1968-69; account supr. Wells, Rich & Greene, N.Y.C., 1969-71; advt. mgr. U.S. Postal Svc., Washington, 1971-72; v.p., dir. Porter, Novelli & Assocs., Washington, 1972-79; pres. Henry J. Kaufman & Assocs., Washington, 1979—; adj. prof. Georgetown U., Washington, 1984—. V.p. exec. bd. Am. Cancer Soc., D.C. div., 1988—. 1st. lt. USMC, 1963-66, Vietnam, col. USMCR, 1968—. Mem. Marine Corps Res. Officers Assn. (nat. v.p. 1985-86), Marine Corps Assn. (bd. dirs. 1987—), N.Y. Athletic Club, Advt. Club Washington, Kenwood Country Club (Washington). Roman Catholic. Avocations: running, scuba diving. Office: Henry J Kaufman & Assocs 2233 Wisconsin Ave NW Washington DC 20007

CARBONE, RALPH JOHN, banker; b. N.Y.C., May 31, 1940; s. Ralph and Sophie (DeBellis) C.; m. Rose Ann Manfrini, Mar. 20, 1960; children: Ralph, Paul, Jennifer. BA, CUNY, 1972. Office mgr. First Nat. City Bank of N.Y., N.Y.C., 1958-63, Bank of N.Y., White Plains, 1963-79; sr. tng. officer Citibank of N.Y., Melville, 1979-86; v.p., dir. tng. AmSouth Bank of Fla., Pensacola, 1986—. Advisor Big Bros. of West Fla., U. West Fla., 1987—, Jr. Achievement, Pensacola, 1987—. Mem. Am. Inst. Banking (sr. intr. Westchester County, N.Y., 1970-79), Rotary, Lions. Roman Catholic. Office: AmSouth Bank of Fla 575 Navy Blvd Pensacola FL 32507

CARBONE, ROBERT CARLO, investment adviser; b. Berkeley, Calif., Apr. 16, 1942; s. John A. and Dorothy M. (Dahleen) C.; m. Mary L. Wootten, July 20, 1969; children: Kelly Ray, Jill Elizabeth. BA, U. Calif., Berkeley, 1967, MBA, 1968. Sr. security analyst Bank of Am., San Francisco, 1969-77; pres. Carbone Investment Mgmt. Corp., Paso Robles, Calif., 1978—. Editor, pub. Photovoltaic Investment Newsletter. Democrat. Office: Carbone Investment Mgmt Corp 7390 Creston Rd Paso Robles CA 93446

CARBONELL, ROBERT J., foods products company executive. married. Student, U. El Salvador, Purdue U., Columbia U. With Standard Brands, 1953-83; with Nabisco Brands, Inc., Hanover, N.J., 1983—, exec. v.p., 1984-85, vice chmn. bd., 1985—; pres., vice chmn. Nabisco Brands U.S.A., Winston-Salem, N.C., 1987; now chmn., chief exec. officer Del Monte Foods, Coral Gables, Fla. Office: Del Monte Foods 201 Alhambra Coral Gables FL 33145 *

CARDEN, JAMES MATTHEW, brokerage company executive; b. Chgo., Sept. 27, 1956; s. James Matthew and Azell (Christian) C.; m. Linda Faye Hentz, June 23, 1980; children: Nicole Elise, Monica Alexandra. BA, U. Miss., 1982, MBA in Fin., 1983; JD, Miss. Coll., 1987. CLU, ChFC, CFM. Gen. agt. Carden Ins. Agy., Oxford, Miss., 1980-83; asst. nat. bank examiner Office of Compt. of the Currency, U.S. Treasury, Jackson, Miss., 1983; fin. cons. Merrill Lynch Pierce Fenner & Smith Inc., Jackson, 1983—; adj. prof. Jackson State U., 1987—. With CAP, 1986. adm. Mensa (life). Club: MBA Breakfast (pres. 1986—). Lodge: Sertoma (life mem. Jackson chpt.). Home: Box 31323 Jackson MS 39206 Office: Merrill Lynch Pierce Fenner & Smith 111 E Capitol Ste 101 Jackson MS 39201-2198

CARDEN, ROBERT CLINTON, III, electrical engineer; b. Phila., Mar. 26, 1933; s. Robert Clinton and Mary Alice (Blanton) C.; B.E.E., Ga. Inst. Tech., 1955, M.S. in Elec. Engring., Ga. Inst. Tech., 1959; postgrad. UCLA, 1961-74, U. Calif.-Irvine, 1980-81; m. Mary Eleanore Clapp, Aug. 15, 1959; children—Robert Clinton IV, Linda Warren. Project engr. Bendix Radio div.

Bendix Aviation, Towson, Md., 1950-57; mem. tech. staff Space Tech. Labs. TRW, 1959-62, El Segundo, Calif.; mem. tech. staff Marshall Labs., Torrance, Calif., 1962-68; founder, dir. Time Zero Corp., Torrance, 1968-71; founder, dir., mgr. engring. Comtec Data Systems div. Am. Micro Systems, Cupertino, Calif., 1971-75; engring. mgr., prin. engr. Ball Corp., Gardena, Calif., 1975-80, staff cons. Ball Corp., Huntington Beach, Calif., 1980-83; sr. staff engr. TRW Inc., Redondo Beach, Calif., 1983—; cons. engr. digital systems, 1980—; instr. in field. Served with AUS, 1957. Mem. Am. Rocket Soc., IEEE, Computer Soc., Ga. Tech. Alumni Assn., Tau Beta Pi, Eta Kappa Nu, Scabbard and Blade, Chi Phi. Republican. Presbyterian. Research in digital space systems. Author, producer: Space for the Everday Man, 1978; contbr. articles to profl. jours. Home: 1217 N Kennymead St Orange CA 92669 Office: TRW Inc 1 Space Park 105/2810 Redondo Beach CA 90278

CARDIN, MEYER M., retired judge; b. Balt., July 14, 1907; s. Harris and Anna (Hersh) C.; m. Dora G. Cardin, Nov. 21, 1936 (dec. Dec. 1972); children: Howard L., Benjamin L.; m. Sylvia D. Cardin, July 14, 1976. LLB, U. Md. Chief justice magistrate Balt., 1955-57; chief justice Traffic Ct., Balt., 1957-58; chmn. Workman's Compensation Commn., 1958-61; supreme ct. bench justice State of Md., 1961-77. Office: B Green & Co Inc 3601 Washington Blvd Baltimore MD 21227

CARDINAL, ROBERT JEAN, benefit administration executive; b. Springfield, Mass., Dec. 24, 1935; s. Alexander Joseph Jr. and Alice Irene (Bellevance) C.; m. Lois Jane Perry, June 21, 1958 (div. 1979); children: David, Suzette, Amy; m. Jane Ellen Vandenburg, Mar. 13, 1981. BS, U.S. Coast Guard Acad., 1957; MS in Indsl. Engring., Ill. Inst. Tech., 1967. Registered profl. engr., Ill., Calif.; cert. mgmt. cons. Supervisory engring. adminstr. major systems RCA Corp., Moorestown, N.J., 1961-63; mgr. program control Lunar Module-Apollo Program Grumman Corp., Bethpage, N.Y., 1963-65; mng. assoc. L.B. Knight & Assocs., Chgo., 1965-67; v.p. L.B. Knight & Assocs., Chgo. and Washington, 1969-72, exec. v.p., 1973-79; div. v.p., gen. mgr. Walworth div. Aloyco, Greensburg, Pa., 1967-68; pres., chief oper. officer Mass. Ins. Adminstrs. and Cons., Inc., Chgo., 1979-84; dir. mgmt. cons. SRI Internat., Menlo Park, Calif., 1984-86; pres. Am. Benefit Plan Adminstrs. div. TPA Am. Inc., L.A., 1986-89; sr. v.p. TPA Am. Inc., 1986-89; pres., co-owner Benefit Adminstrn. Corp., Fresno, Calif., 1989—. Contbr. numerous articles to profl. jours. Bd. dirs. Am. Service Bur. Inc., Chgo., Jr. Achievement Chgo. and No. Ind., 1977-84, Chgo. Crime Commn., 1977-84; trustee Ill. Inst. Tech., Chgo., 1980-85, Boys Club Found. Union League Club Chgo., 1980-84. Lt. USCG, 1957-61. Mem. Internat. Found. Employee Benefit Plans, Soc. Profl. Benefit Adminstrs. (bd. dirs. 1982-84), Inst. Mgmt. Cons. (sr., bd. dirs. 1976-79), Am. Inst. Indsl. Engrs. (sr.), NSPE (ethics and practices com. Ill. chpt.), Am. Arbitration Assn., Union League Club (bd. dirs. 1983-84, admissions chmn.), Army-Navy Club (Washington). Office: Benefit Adminstrn Corp 1141 W Shaw Fresno CA 93711

CARDONA, ROSEMARY LYNN, stockbroker; b. Wabash, Ind., Oct. 17, 1947; d. George E. and Dorothy Jean (DuBois) Dershem; m. Michael Paul Cardona, May 15, 1971. BA in Polit. Sci. and History, Manchester Coll., 1969. Clk. McDonnell Douglas, Lomita, Calif., 1971; specialist asst. Daniel Reeves & Co., Los Angeles, 1971-74; floor trader Crowell Weedon & Co., Los Angeles, 1974-78, researcher, 1978-81; trust officer Security Pacific Bank, Los Angeles, 1980-81; stockbroker Seidler Amdec Securities, Los Angeles, 1981—; 1st woman market maker on Pacific Stock Exch., L.A., 1973. Subject of Sta. WNET spl. Woman Alive!, 1974. Office: Seidler Amdec Securities 515 S Figueroa Los Angeles CA 90071

CARDWELL, JAMES WILLIAM, human resource consultant; b. Seattle, Aug. 16, 1948; s. William H. and Mary Kay (Tapert) C.; m. Karla P. Norwood, Nov. 28, 1970; children: Michael James, Christine Michelle. BA in Speech magna cum laude, U. Wash., 1971; MA, U. Wis., 1973, MBA in Organizational Behavior, 1975. Asst. dir. orgn. devel. CUNA, Inc., Madison, Wis., 1974-76, dir. orgn. devel., 1976-78; with Ernst & Ernst, Cleve., 1978-83, mgr., regional/human resource cons., 1980-83; pres., chmn. Exec. Network Cons., Westlake, Ohio, 1983—; bd. dirs. Resource, cleve., 1982-83. Contbr. articles to profl. jours. Mem. Coun. Small Enterprise, Cleve., 1983—. Mem. Nat. Assn. Corp. Profl. Recruiters, Am. Soc. Tng. and Devel. (orgn. devel. div.), Nat. Assn. Corp. Dirs., Am. Compensation Assn., Clevelander Club, Phi Beta Kappa, Clevelander Club. Office: Exec Network Cons 1991 Crocker Rd Ste 220 Westlake OH 44145

CARETTI, RICHARD LOUIS, lawyer; b. Grosse Pointe, Mich., Dec. 17, 1953; s. Richard John and Doris Eleanor (Evans) C.; m. Nancy Louise Matouk, Oct. 14, 1983; children: Katherine Lynn, Kristin Doris. BA, Wayne State U., 1975; JD magna cum laude, Detroit Coll. Law, 1980. Bar: Mich. 1980, U.S. Dist. Ct. (ea dist.) Mich. 1980, U.S. Ct. Appeals (6th cir.) 1982, U.S. Supreme Ct. 1989. Assoc. Dickinson, Wright, Moon, Van Dusen & Freeman, Detroit, 1979-84, ptnr., 1985—. Mem. ABA, Detroit Bar Assn., Mich. Def. Trial Counsel, Assn. Def. Trial Counsel. Delta Theta Phi. Roman Catholic. Club: Detroit Athletic (club open raquetball champion). Home: 1380 Devonshire Grosse Pointe Park MI 48230 Office: Dickinson Wright Moon et al 800 First Nat Bldg Detroit MI 48226

CAREY, ANITA LESTER, accountant; b. Salina, Kans., Mar. 19, 1958; d. Louis Philip Rosenthall and Anita Lester Carey. BA, U. Colo., 1982; MBA, Babson Coll., 1987. Acct. Southwest Savs., Phoenix, 1983-85, Coopers & Lybrand, Boston, 1987—; sr. v.p., founder PBC Innovations, Boston, 1986—. Active Young Reps.; asst. treas. Jr. League, Boston, 1987—. Home: 20 Westgate Dr #105 Woburn MA 01801 Office: Coopers & Lybrand 1 Internat Pl Boston MA 02110

CAREY, EDWARD MARSHEL, JR., accounting co. exec.; b. Washington, Pa., June 12, 1942; s. Edward Marshel and Mildred Elizabeth (Bradley) C.; B.S. in Bus. Adminstrn., Greenville (Ill.) Coll., 1964; m. Naomi Ruth Davis, June 1, 1964; children—Martha Ann, Mary Louise. Acct., Gen. Motors Corp., Anderson, Ind., 1964-68, supr. accounting, 1968-70; staff accountant Carter, Kirlin & Merrill, C.P.A.s, Indpls., 1970-74, partner, 1974—, pres. CKM Mgmt., Inc., Indpls., 1985—, mng. ptnr., 1988—. Mem. Am. Inst. C.P.A.s (mgmt. of accounting practice com. 1976-80, chmn. com. 1978-80, mgmt. adv. services com. 1980-83, chmn. com. 1982-83, dir. Indpls. chpt. 1977-83, treas. 1978-79, pres. 1979-80), Nat. Assn. Accountants, Am. Mgmt. Assn., Inst. Internal Auditors (dir.), Greenville Coll. Alumni Assn. (dir., treas. Ind. chpt. 1980-82). Republican. Methodist. Club: Indpls. Athletic. Home: 215 Royal Oak Ct Zionsville IN 46077 Office: 9102 N Meridian St Indianapolis IN 46260

CAREY, EVANGELINE RUTH, writer; b. Laurel, Miss., Aug. 5, 1949; d. Samuel L. Smith and Girtha L. (Tate) Smith Bailey; m. Winston Carey, Mar. 1, 1969; children: Chanda Alicia, Winston Jr., Gina Danielle. BA in Sociology, Ind. U., Gary, 1974. Revenue officer IRS, Gary, 1974-75; transcriptionist U. Chgo., 1986—; caseworker Lake County Welfare Dept., Gary, 1987. Author numerous poems; contbr. articles to profl. jours.; editor newsletter 1st Ch. God, 1985—. Democrat. Home and Office: 1744 Waite St Gary IN 46404

CAREY, HUGH L., lawyer, former governor of New York; b. Bklyn.; s. Dennis and Margaret C.; m. Helen Owen, Feb. 27, 1947 (dec. Mar. 1974); children—Alexandria, Christopher, Susan, Peter (dec.), Hugh (dec.), Michael, Donald, Marianne, Nancy, Helen, Bryan, Paul, Kevin, Thomas; m. Evangeline Gouletas, Apr. 11, 1981; J.D., St. John's U. Mem. N.Y. Ho. of Reps., 1960-74, dep. whip; gov. N.Y., 1974-82; ptnr., mem. mgmt. com. Finley, Kumble, Wagner, Heine, Underberg, Manley, Myerson & Casey, N.Y.C., 1982-87; exec. v.p. W.R. Grace & Co., 1987—. Chmn. N.Y. State World Trade Council, 1984—. Served to col. in infantry N.Y.N.G., WWII, Decorated Bronze Star Medal, Croix de Guerre. Office: W R Grace & Co 1114 Ave of the Americas New York NY 10036 *

CAREY, JANE QUELLMALZ, printing company executive; b. Albany, N.Y., May 6, 1952; d. Henry and Marion Agar (Lynch) 1979. Student, Stephen's Coll., 1969-70; cert., Katherine Gibbs Sch., Boston, 1971. Sec. to headmaster St. Agnes Sch., Albany, 1971-72; exec. sec. Dwight Bldg. Co., Hamden, Conn., 1972-73; v.p. Q Corp., U.S. Agt. for WHO Publs., Albany, 1973-77, pres., 1978—. Bd. dirs. Next Step, Inc., Albany, 1976-79, Mohawk Hudson Humane Soc., Menands, N.Y., 1988—. Mem. Printing Industries East and Cen. N.Y. (bd. dirs. 1985—), Am. Assn. World Health (bd. dirs. 1977-78), Alumnae Assn. Doane Stuart Sch. (bd. dirs. 1988). Episcopalian. Clubs; Traffic (N.Y.C.), Hudson River (Albany). Home: 12 Strathmore Dr Loudonville NY 12211 Office: Boyd Printing Co Inc 49 Sheridan Ave Albany NY 12210

CAREY, JEAN LEBEIS, management consulting executive; b. Charleston, W.Va., June 2, 1943; d. Edward H. and Marian (Lendved) Lebeis; m. Robert W. Carey, Nov. 1971; 1 child, Megan Rose. BA, Pa. State U., 1965. Programmer Penn Mutual Life Ins., Phila., 1967-68; sr. analyst/programmer U. Pa., Phila., 1969-72; sr. systems analyst Acme Markets, Phila., 1972-74; programming mgr. Bryn Mawr Coll., Pa., 1976-77; project adminstr. Smith Kline Beckman, Phila., 1977-83; project mgmt. cons. Arco Chem. Co., Phila., 1983-88; chief exec. officer Carey Project Orgn., Ardmore, Pa., 1988—; chmn. Systems Methodology Users Mid-Atlantic, 1984-86, PMI Systems Tech. Papers, 1983; co-dir. Cobol project, U. Pa., Phila., 1969-72; Pa. Counc. on Children's Svcs., 1988—; lectr. in field. Contbr. articles to profl. jours. Bd. dirs. Scan/Child Abuse Treatment Ctr., Phila., 1983—, Danceteller/Dance Theater, Phila., 1985—, Family and Community Service of Delaware County; mem. Leadership, Phila. vol. svcs. group, 1985—. Recipient Excel award, Arco, 1986. Mem. Project Mgmt. Inst. Soc. of Friends. Home and Office: Carey Project Orgn 663 Cricket Ave Ardmore PA 19003

CAREY, JOHN ANDREW, investment company executive; b. Glendale, Calif., May 27, 1949; s. John Nelson and Dorothea Ruth (Bordwell) C.; m. Harriet Ruth Stolmeier, June 19, 1982; 1 child, Julia Scott. B.A., Columbia U., 1971; A.M., Harvard U., 1972, Ph.D., 1979. Chartered fin. analyst. Teaching fellow Harvard U., Cambridge, Mass., 1973-78; sr. council rep. Yankelovich, Skelly & White, Stamford, Conn., 1977-79; analyst Pioneering Mgmt. Corp., Boston, 1979-81, sr. analyst, 1981-83, v.p., 1983—; v.p. Pioneer Scout, Inc., Boston, 1984—, v.p. Pioneer Fund, 1987— . Author: Judicial Reform in France before the Revolution of 1789, 1981. Treas., Newton Hist. Soc., Mass., 1983—. Mem. Inst. Chartered Fin. Analysts, Fin. Analysts Fedn., Boston Security Analysts Soc., Am. Hist. Assn. Republican. Episcopalian. Clubs: Boston Athenaeum, Harvard of Boston, Bull Terrier of New Eng. Avocation: archtl. restoration. Home: 553 Walnut St Newtonville MA 02160 Office: Pioneer Group Inc 60 State St Boston MA 02109

CAREY, KATHRYN ANN, corporate philanthropy, advertising and public relations executive, editor, consultant; b. Los Angeles, Oct. 18, 1949; d. Frank Randall and Evelyn Mae (Walmsley) C.; m. Richard Kenneth Sundt, Dec. 28, 1980. BA in Am. Studies with honors, Calif. State U.-Los Angeles, 1971. Tutor Calif. Dept. Vocat. Rehab., Los Angeles, 1970; teaching asst. U. So. Calif., 1974-75, UCLA, 1974-75; claims adjuster Auto Club So. Calif., San Gabriel, 1971-73; corp. pub. relations cons. Carnation Co., Los Angeles, 1973-78; cons., adminstr. Carnation Community Service Award Program, 1973-78; pub. relations cons. Vivitar Corp.; sr. advt. asst. Am. Honda Motor Co., Gardena, Calif., 1978-84; exec. dir. Am. Honda Found., 1984—; mgr. Honda Dealer Advt. Assns.; cons. advt., pub. relations, promotions. Editor: Vivitar Voice, Santa Monica, Calif., 1978, Honda Views, 1978-84, Found. Focus, 1984—; asst. editor Friskies Research Digest; contbg. editor Newsbriefs, Am. Honda Motor Co., Inc. employees mag.; Calif. Life Scholarship Found. scholar, 1967. Mem. Advt. Club Los Angeles, Pub. Relations Soc. Am., So. Calif. Assn. Philanthropy, Council Founds. of Washington, Aircraft Owners and Pilots Assn., Ninety-Nines, Am. Quarter Horse Assn., Los Angeles Soc. for Prevention Cruelty to Animals, Greenpeace, German Shepherd Dog Club Am., Ocicats Internat., Am. Humane Assn., Elsa Wild Animal Appeal. Avocation: private pilot. Democrat. Methodist. Office: Am Honda Found 700 Van Ness Ave Torrance CA 90509-2205

CAREY, MICHAEL JOSEPH, business research company executive; b. Omaha, Mar. 26, 1947; s. Joseph Thomas and Mary Frances (O'Brien) C.; m. Barbara Christine Whidden, Jan. 1976; 1 child, Elizabeth Widden. BA, U. Portland, 1969; MA, U. Nev., 1972; PhD, U. Calif., Santa Barbara, 1977. Prof. polit. sci. Loyola Marymount U., L.A., 1976-82; v.p. mktg. Trans World Trading Co., Portland, Oreg., 1982-84; editor Asia Cable, Portland, 1984-86; owner, prin. Bus. Rsch. Counsel, Portland, 1986—; cons. Oreg. Bus. Counc., Portland, 1987, Spl. People Inc., Portland, 1987—; bd. dirs. Venture Communications, Inc., Portland. Author, editor: Food Politics, 1981; contbg. editor Pacific Bus. mag., 1982-84; editor GIS/CAD Mapping Solutions, 1987—. Cheif fgn. policy advisor U.S. Senate campaign D.K. Whitehurst, L.A., 1981-82; policy advisor Myllenbeck Re-election campaign, Portland, 1986; trade policy advisor Goldschmidt campaign, Portland, 1986—. Rsch. fellow U. Nev., 1972. Mem. Newsletter Assn., Anglers Club. Home: 8406 SE 8th Ave Portland OR 97202 Office: Venture Communications Inc PO Box 02332 Portland OR 97202

CAREY, THOMAS HILTON, advertising agency executive; b. Oak Park, Ill., Aug. 31, 1944; s. James Patrick and Caroline Hale (Hilton) C.; m. Barbara Lynn Hardy, Sept. 13, 1969; children: Christopher, Colleen, Jill. B.A., Holy Cross, 1966; M.S. in Journalism, Northwestern U., 1967. Account mgr. Benton & Bowles Inc., N.Y.C., after 1967; now sr. v.p., mng. dir. D'Arcy Masius Benton & Bowles, N.Y.C. Office: D'Arcy Masius Benton & Bowles Inc 909 3rd Ave New York NY 10022 *

CAREY, TOM MAX, oil company executive; b. Guthrie, Okla., Sept. 26, 1928; s. Glen T. and Ora Jo (Mitchell) C.; m. E. Joyce Derden, June 18, 1953; children—Ellen, Martha. B.S., Okla. State U., 1950; M.B.A., So. Meth. U., 1957. Acctg. mgr. Mobil Oil Co., Dallas, 1954-61; exec. v.p., chief fin. officer, dir. Koch Industries, Wichita, Kans., 1961-88, Koch Engring. Co., 1988—; dir. Matador Cattle Co., Koch Refining Co., Koch Chem. Co. Served to 1st lt. USAF, 1952-54. Home: 562 Brookfield St Wichita KS 67206 Office: Koch Engring Co 800 Tall Grass Exec Pk Wichita KS 67226

CAREY, WILLIAM JOSEPH, retired controller; b. N.Y.C., May 15, 1922; s. Cornelius Montague and Ellen Katherine (Gannon) C.; m. Barbara L. Garrison, Aug. 24,7 1946; children: Kathleen, Eileen, Christine, Robert. B.S., Rider Coll., 1949; postgrad., NYU, 1952-53. C.P.A., N.Y. Mgr. Ernst and Ernst, N.Y.C., 1949-59; controller Reynolds and Co., N.Y.C., 1959-61; exec. v.p. Bache and Co., N.Y.C., 1961-69; exec. ptnr. Goodbody and Co., N.Y.C., 1970-71; v.p. Paine Webber, N.Y.C., 1971-73; controller, treas., and chief fin. officer J. Henry Schroder Bank and Trust Co., Franklin Lakes, N.J., 1973-84; arbitration panel mem. Nat. Assn. Securities Dealers, N.Y.C. Trustee emeritus Rider Coll. Served with USN, 1942-45, PTO. Decorated Purple Heart. Mem. N.Y. State Soc. C.P.A.s, Am. Inst. C.P.A.s, Fin. Execs. Inst. (ops. com., internat. com). Clubs: Franklin Lakes, Indian Trail. Home: 237 Mountainview Terr Mahwah NJ 07430

CARFAGNO, ROBERT FRANCIS, financial executive; b. Norristown, Pa., Jan. 3, 1951; s. Charles L. and Anna M. (Santangelo) C.; m. Linda Modica, Jan. 27, 1973 (div. Feb. 1987); children: Robert, Renee. BS in Acctg., Villanova U., 1972; MBA in Fin., U. Pa., 1985. CPA, Pa. Sr. auditor Coopers and Lybrand, Phila., 1972-75; sr. fin. auditor Bell of Pa., Phila., 1975-76; controller Extracorporeal Med. Specialties, Inc., King of Prussia, Pa., 1976-78, Johnson & Johnson Cardiovascular, King of Prussia, Pa., 1978-85; v.p. fin. Geriatric and Med. Ctrs., Inc., Phila., 1985-89, sr. v.p. fin. and adminstrn., 1989—; assoc. prof. Montgomery County Community Coll., Blue Bell, Pa., 1980-85. Chmn. U.S. Savs. Bonds Johnson and Johnson Cardiovascular, King of Prussia, 1981. Mem. Am. Inst. CPA's, Pa. Inst. CPA's. Office: Geriatric Med Ctrs 5601 Chestnut St Philadelphia PA 19139

CARGILL, ROBERT LEE, JR., oil and gas company executive; b. Marshall, Tex., Sept. 11, 1934; s. Robert Lee and Pauline Elizabeth (Wood) C.; m. Linda Ann Sanders, Aug. 29, 1965 (div. 1976); children: William Robert, Thomas Oscar, Ann Hope; m. Katherine Joann Parker, Aug. 1, 1980. BA, Rice U., 1955; PhD, MIT, 1960. Rsch. fellow U. Calif., Berkeley, 1960-62; asst. prof., then assoc. prof. U. S.C., Columbia, 1962-73, prof. chemistry, 1973-80; v.p. R. Cargill & Co., Inc., Longview, Tex., 1980-82, pres., 1982-85; mng. ptnr. Cargill Interests, Ltd., Longview, 1982—; adj. prof. chemistry Rice U., Houston, 1980-84, mem. vis. com., 1988—; mem. vis. com. dept. chemistry U. Tex.-Austin, 1987—; bd. dirs. MRW Concepts, Inc., Houston, Chiron Press, Inc., N.Y.C. Patentee housefly sex attractant; contbr. articles to profl. publs. Mem., vice chmn. adv. bd. Longview City Library, 1983-87; bd. dirs. East Tex. Area council Boy Scouts Am., 1983—, Greater Longview Econ. Devel. Found., 1986—. Grantee NSF, 1962-80, Petroleum Rsch. Fund, 1962-80, NIH, 1962-80; recipient Russell Rsch. award U. S.C., 1974. Mem. Am. Chem.Soc., Tex. Ind. Producers and Royalty Owners, Ind. Petroleum Assn. Am. Office: Cargill Interests Ltd PO Box 992 Longview TX 75606-0992

CARIDAS, EVANGELINE CHRIS, sales executive; b. Houston, Sept. 4, 1950; d. Chris N. and Aglaia (Ioannidis) C. BA, U. Houston, 1978. Sales rep. Jones Bus. Products, Houston, 1980-81; sr. sales exec. Xerox Corp., Houston, 1981—. Fund raiser Charles Lindbergh Fund, Houston, 1985; mem. program com. March of Dimes Gala, Houston, 1988; fund raiser Houston Youth Symphony and Ballet, 1988. Mem. Houston Assn. of Neuro-Linguistic Programming (cert.). Home: 3223 Albans Rd Houston TX 77005 Office: Xerox Corp 1614 Fannin Houston TX 77002

CARISEO, DAVID JOSEPH, financial services executive; b. Syracuse, N.Y., Feb. 16, 1941; s. Joseph Anthony and Theresa Elizabeth (Clairmont) C.; m. Peggy Ann Coe, June 8, 1974; children: Amy, Elizabeth. BJ, Syracuse U., 1963. Owner Boca Raton (Fla.) Office Supply Inc., 1964-66; stockbroker Hayden Stone Inc., Boca Raton, 1966-69; v.p. Hayden Stone Inc., Cleve., 1969-70, Reynolds Securities Inc., Pompano Beach, Fla., 1970-74; sr. v.p. Reynolds Securities Inc., N.Y.C., 1974-78, Dean Witter Reynolds Inc., N.Y.C., 1978-80; exec. v.p. Dean Witter Reynolds Intercapital, N.Y.C., 1980-82; pres. Balcor Securities Co. Inc., Skokie, Ill., 1982-87; pres. Fidelity Investor Ctrs. Inc. Boston, 1987—; bd. dirs. Fidelity Brokerage Svcs. Inc., Boston. Staff sgt. USAFR, 1962-68. Republican. Home: 21 Livermore Rd Wellesley MA 02181 Office: Fidelity Brokerage Svcs Inc 161 Devonshire St Boston MA 02110

CARL, ROBERT DELROY, III, health care company executive, lawyer; b. Lancaster, Pa., Jan. 12, 1954; s. Robert Delroy and Mary Anne (McGarvey) C.; m. Anne Caroline Alexander Currie. BA, Franklin & Marshall Coll., 1975; JD, Emory U., 1978. Bar: Ga. 1977. Pvt. practice Decatur, Ga., 1978-81; v.p. Cardiopul Techs., Decatur, 1981-85; pres., chmn. Health Images, Inc., Atlanta, 1985—. Democrat. Home: 857 Hillwood Dr Marietta GA 30067 Office: Health Images Inc 8601 Dunwoody Pl Ste 200 Atlanta GA 30350

CARL, ROBERT E., marketing company executive; b. Independence, Mo., Sept. 1, 1927; s. Elmer T. Carl and Marion R. (Pack) C.; B.S., U. Kans., 1950; cert. in real estate So. Meth. U., 1965; certificate in investment analysis N.Y. Inst. Fin., 1967; m. Linda Arlene Sutton, Aug. 30, 1967; children—Melanie Ruth, Robert Brady, Camber Carleen. Vice pres. sales promotion Riverside Press, Inc., Dallas, 1951-54; pres., chief operating officer Jones-Carl, Inc., Dallas, 1954-62; v.p. mktg. communications Modern Am. Corp., Dallas, 1962-70; v.p. sales Dunn Properties of Tex., Inc., Dallas, 1970-71; sr. v.p. mktg. services Vantage Cos., Dallas, 1971-84; pres. Mktg. Mgmt. Systems, Dallas, 1984—; mem. Dallas Cable TV Bd., 1981-83. Recipient legion of honor degree Internat. Supreme Council of Order of De Molay, 1957; Silver Anvil award Pub. Relations Soc. Am., 1958. Mem. Sales and Mktg. Execs. Dallas (pres. 1976-77, Disting. Salesman's award 1954), S.W. Found. Free Enterprise (pres. 1975-76), Tex. Indsl. Devel. Council, Nat. Assn. Corp. Real Estate Execs., Sales and Mktg. Execs. Internat. (sr. v.p.), Nat. Assn. Indsl. and Office Parks. Republican. Baptist. Clubs: Big D. Toastmaster (pres. 1966), Press, Dallas, Masons, Shriners. Contbr. articles to profl. jours. Home: 4209 Gloster Rd Dallas TX 75220 Office: Mktg Mgmt Systems 8300 Douglas Ave Ste 800 Dallas TX 75225

CARLETON, BUKK GRIFFITH, lawyer, investment counsel; b. N.Y.C., May 30, 1909; s. Bukk G. and Clarice (Griffith) C.; A.B. magna cum laude, Harvard U., 1931, LL.B., 1934; m. Mary Elizabeth Tucker, June 16, 1934; children—Elizabeth Holland, Bukk Griffith. Bar: N.Y. 1935. Assoc. Larkin, Rathbone & Perry, N.Y.C., 1934-36; asst. counsel, asst. sec. Gen. Chem. Co., 1936-41; v.p., sec., dir. Perma-Bilt Homes, Inc., 1941-42; counsel RFC, 1942-44; head N.Y. law office Montgomery Ward & Co. 1944-46; mem. legal dept. Sinclair Refining Co., 1946-56; owner, investment counsel Griffith Carleton, 1946—. Pres., trustee Hicks-Stearns Mus. Mem. ABA, N.Y. Bar Assn., New Eng. Soc., Phi Beta Kappa. Quaker (com. nat. legis. 1957-58). Clubs: Met., Sleepy Hollow, Harvard (N.Y.C.); Woodway Country (Conn.); Quinnatisset Country (Conn.); R.I. Country; New Canaan Country, Harvard (New Canaan). Home: 61 Parade Hill Ln New Canaan CT 06840 Office: Bukkskin East Killingly CT 06243

CARLETON, DAVID, consumer products executive; b. Silver Spring, Md., Feb. 24, 1955; s. Henry and Barbara C.; m. Barbara Carleton, June 9, 1985. BS in Mktg., Ind. U., 1977; MBA in Mktg., Adelphi U., 1981. Dist. sales asst. Michelin Tire Corp., Lake Success, N.Y., 1977-79; sales merchandiser Duracell Battery co., Bethel, Conn., 1979, mgr. territory, 1979-80, regional sales trainer, 1980, mgr. area sales, 1981, mgr. dist. sales, 1982-84, mgr. regional sales, 1984-87; mgr. nat. sales automotive products Black & Decker, Hunt Valley, Md., 1987-88, mgr. nat. sales, mktg.-buck knives, 1988—. Mem. Am. Mktg. Assn. Office: Buck Knives 1900 Weld Blvd El Cajon CA 92020

CARLETON, PAUL HUNTER, investment banker; b. Jamestown, N.Y., Mar. 22, 1948; s. Bernard Lyon Carleton and Lillian (Hunter) Ducharme; m. Sheryl Arnold, June 18, 1971; children: Kelly, Drew, Meghan, Molly. BA, Baldwin-Wallace Coll., 1970; MBA, Northwestern U., 1972. With staff dept. comml. banking Harris Bank, Chgo., 1972-78; mng. dir. McDonald & Co. Securities, Inc., Cleve., 1978—; bd. dirs. Autodie Corp., Grand Rapids, Mich., Lesco Inc., Cleve., Primus Capital Fund, Cleve., McDonald & Co. Investments, Inc., Cleve. Trustee Health Hill Hosp., Cleve. Republican. Presbyterian. Clubs: Cleve. Athletic, Union (Cleve.). Home: 21306 Brantley Rd Shaker Heights OH 44122 Office: McDonald & Co Securities Inc 2100 Society Bldg Cleveland OH 44114

CARLIELL, KERRY A., manufacturing executive; b. Sheboygan, Wis., Sept. 8, 1946; d. Merlin and Ann (Suemnicht) Hueppchen; m. James L. Carliell, Oct. 20, 1965 (div. 1986). BSBA magna cum laude, Am. Internat. Coll., Springfield, Mass., 1988. Adminstrv. asst. Smith & Wesson, Springfield, 1974-80; buyer Tambrands, Inc., Palmer, Mass., 1980-82, mgr. consumer svcs., 1982—. Mem. Soc. Consumer Affairs Profls. in Bus., Grocery Mfrs. Assn. (consumer affairs com.), Bus. and Profl. Women. Home: PO Box 174 Three Rivers MA 01080 Office: Tambrands Inc PO Box 271 Palmer MA 01069

CARLIN, BENEDICT, automotive executive; b. Bklyn., Sept. 3, 1911; s. Jacob A. and Ida (Stavisky) C.; m. Gertrude Freundlich, June 21, 1936; children: Joan, Marilyn. PharmD with honors, Bklyn. Coll., 1935. Lic. pharmacist, N.Y.; CLU. Ins. agt. Met. Life Ins. Co., N.Y.C., 1937-45; asst. mgr. Met. Life Ins. Co., L.I., 1945-47, field tng. instr., 1947-48; v.p. C-F Sales Co., Jacksonville, Fla., 1948-50; prin. King Sales Co., Jacksonville, 1950-74, Patten Distbrs., Inc., Jacksonville, 1963-77; pres. King Auto Air, Inc., Jacksonville, 1963-66, 78-86, chmn. bd., 1986—; owner Auto Parts Export Corp. (Parts Fin., Inc.), 1977—. v.p. Jewish Family Services, 1982-86, bd. mem. 1982—; bd. mem. Jewish Temple, 1980-81; mem. Sales and Mktg. of Jacksonville, 1962—. Mem. Com. of 100, C. of C. Clubs: L.I. U. Pharm. Alumnus; Overseas Auto; Baymeadows Rocket. Lodge: B'nai Brith. Home: 7785 Las Palmas Way Jacksonville FL 32256 Office: King Auto Air Inc 4052 University Blvd S Jacksonville FL 32216

CARLIN, MICHAEL KEVIN, comptroller; b. Bklyn., Mar. 2, 1951; s. Michael Henry and Mary Kathleen (O'Brien) C.; married; children: Maureen, Michael. BBA in Acctg., Fairleigh Dickinson U., 1975, MBA in Fin., 1977. CPA, N.Y., N.J. Acct. Everlon Fabrics subs. Associated Products, Closter, N.J., 1972-78; asst. contr. Associated Poducts subs. Nabisco, N.Y.C., 1978-81; contr. Associated Products, 1981-85; regional contr. Am. Bldg. Maintenance, 1983-85; compt. Trans World Maintenance Svcs., 1985—. Trea. William Pat Schuber Election Com., N.J., 1983—; mem. Bogota Zoning Bd., 1984-86; pres. Rep. Club, Bogota, 1986. With USNG, 1970-76. Republican. Roman Catholic. Home: 27 Burton Ave Hasbrouck Heights NJ 07604 Office: Trans World Maintenance Svcs 110 W 27th St New York NY 10001

CARLINI, JAMES, management consultant; b. Berwyn, Ill., Aug. 27, 1954; s. Harvey Reno and Helen Dorothy (Stan) C.; m. Holly R. Haupin, Sept. 29, 1979. MusB, Roosevelt U., 1976, BS in Computer Sci., 1978; MBA in Mgmt. Info. Systems and Mktg., DePaul U., 1982. Info. systems designer Western Electric div. Bell Labs., Naperville, Ill., 1977-79; software engr. Motorola, Schaumburg, Ill., 1979-81; mgr. Ill. Bell, Chgo., 1981-83; dir. telecommunications and computer hardware cons. Arthur Young & Co., Chgo., 1983-86; pres. Carlini & Assocs., Inc., Evanston, Ill., 1986—; adj. prof. Technol. Inst. Northwestern U., Evanston, Ill., 1986—, grad. sch. of bus. DePaul U., Chgo., 1986—. Contbr. articles to profl. jours. Pres. Mental Health Bd., Berwyn, 1983. Mem. Info. Industry Coun., Data Processing Mgmt. Assn. (speaker's award), Intelligent Bldg. Inst. (chmn. definitions com.), DAV (citation 1979). Roman Catholic. Home: 6840 W 29th Pl Berwyn IL 60402 Office: Carlini & Assocs Inc 36 S Washington St Hinsdale IL 60521

CARLINO, GUY THOMAS, construction executive; b. N.Y.C., Sept. 2, 1928; s. Peter T. and Beatrice (Logerfo) C.; m. Berniece Ruth Horth, Sept. 28, 1952; children: Margaret M., Peter T., Sharon S., James C. Student, Columbia U., 1946-49. Designer DeLeuw, Cather & Brill, N.Y.C., 1952-54, Allen & Kelly, Indpls., 1954-58; sales engr. Hugh J. Baker Co., Indpls., 1958-65; sales mgr. Holcomb & Hoke, Inc., Indpls., 1965-68; mgr. constrn. Geupel DeMars, Inc., Indpls., 1968-73; v.p. engring. and constrn. Herman Devel., Inc., Indpls., 1973-75; pres. Carlino Corp., Indpls., 1975—. Pres. Producers' Council of Ind., Washington, 1964, Washington Twp. Sch. Found., Indpls., 1975, Indpls. Day Nursery Assn., 1982; treas. Day Nursery Found., Indpls.; bd. dirs. Salt Creek Realty. Sgt. U.S. Army, 1950-52, Fed. Republic Germany. Mem. Indpls. Athletic Club, Gyro Club (pres. 1986). Republican. Methodist. Home: 3737 E 71st St Indianapolis IN 46220 Office: Carlino Corp 151 N Delaware Indianapolis IN 46204

CARLISLE, DWIGHT L., JR., clothing manufacturing executive; b. Alexander City, Ala., Nov. 7, 1935; s. Dwight L. Carlisle; m. Sarah Wilbanks; children—Danice, Rebecca, Meredith. B.S. in Textile Engring., Auburn U., 1958. Asst. gen. supt. Russell Corp., Alexander City, Ala., 1968-70, gen. supt., 1970-71, v.p. mfg., 1971-80, exec. v.p., 1980-82, pres., chief operating officer, 1982—, pres., chief exec. officer, 1988—, also dir.; dir. First Nat. Bank, Alexander City. Bd. dirs. Russell Hosp., Alexander City, 1984—. Mem. Nat. Knitwear Mfrs. Assn. (chmn. 1988), Ala. C. of C. (bd. dirs.). Office: Russell Corp Lee St PO Box 272 Alexander City AL 35010

CARLISLE, RANDALL DEAN, banker; b. Belton, Tex., May 25, 1956; s. Larry Dean and Raye Elizabeth (Durham) C.; m. Sean Louise Burton, May 29, 1976 (div. 1987); 1 child, Brooke Elise. BBA, U. Tex., 1978. Mgmt. trainee 1st Fed. Savs. and Loan, Temple, Tex., 1978-81; asst. v.p. Peoples Nat. Bank, Belton, 1981-83, v.p., 1983-84; v.p. 1st Nat. Bank, Belton, 1984-87, pres., chief exec. officer, 1987—, also bd. dirs. Bd. dirs. Bell County Chpt. Am. Heart Assn., 1984-85, Bell County Rehab. Ctr., 1986—; pres., bd. dirs. Belton United Way, 1985—; city councilman City of Belton, 1985-87, mayor pro-tem, 1987—. Mem. Belton Area C. of C. (chmn. bd. 1987, bd. dirs. 1984—), Tex. Bankers Assn. (sec. installment div. 1984-85), Belton-Temple Home Builders Assn. (sec. 1984-85), Bell County U. Tex. Alumni Assn. (pres. 1988). Democrat. Baptist. Lodge: Rotary (bd. dirs. 1985-86). Home: 3024 Summit Dr Belton TX 76513 Office: 1st Nat Bank 300 E 1st St Belton TX 76513

CARLISLE, WOODSON STUDEBAKER, JR., corporate executive; b. South Bend, Ind., June 14, 1934; s. Woodson Studebaker and Mary Lorinda (Poindexter) C.; m. Nancy Jane Parmalee, 1967 (div. 1974); 1 child, Woodson Studebaker III. B.A., Yale U., 1957. Salesman Salomon Bros., N.Y.C., 1961-63; asst. treas. Clark Equipment Co., Buchanan, Mich., 1964-80; exec. v.p., treas. Clark Equipment Credit Corp., Buchanan, Mich., %, also dir.; treas. Sullair Corp., Michigan City, Ind., 1980-84; v.p. treas. Figgie Internat., Willoughby, Ohio, 1984—. Mem. Assn. Corp. Treas. Office: Figgie Internat 4420 Sherwin Rd Willoughby OH 44094

CARLL, PAUL LOUDON, chemical company executive; b. Elgin, Kans., July 1, 1920; s. James Lawrence and Ora Lee (Loudon) C.; Marian Elizabeth Heckathorne, June 6, 1944; children—Thomas Paul, Peggy Lee Carll Keene, William Floyd. B.S. in Chem. Engring., Case Inst. Tech., 1949. Gen. mgr. plants Lubrizol Corp., Houston, 1967-69, v.p. mfg., 1969-75, v.p. purchasing and distbns., 1975-83, v.p. adminstrn., asst. to the pres., Wickliffe, Ohio, 1983-86, dir., 1973-76. Served to capt. USAAF, 1941-46. Mem. Am. Inst. Chem. Engrs., Am. Chem. Soc., Alpha Chi Sigma. Republican. Lodge: Masons (32 deg.). Home: 31881 Meadowlark Way Pepper Pike Cleveland OH 44124 Office: Lubrizol Corp 29400 Lakeland Blvd Wickliffe OH 44092

CARLON, PATRICK J(OHN), accountant; b. Mitchell, S.D., May 15, 1947; s. John Patrick and Anne Marie (Menke) C.; m. Barbara Kathryn White, Nov. 24, 1973; children: Daniel, Leah. BS in Acctg., U. S.D., 1969. CPA, S.D. With audit dept., tax sr. Touche Ross & Co., Mpls., 1969-71, 72-75; mgr. Wohlenberg Gage & Co., Brookings, S.D., 1975-77; co-owner, shareholder Wohlenberg Cage & Co., Mitchell, 1977-82; prin. Patrick John Carlon, CPA, Mitchell, 1982-88; ptnr. Person, Thurman, Carlon & Co., Mitchell, 1988—. Treas. Mitchell Area Arts Coun., 1978-85; pres. Mitchell YMCA, 1985; councilman City of Mitchell, 1984-85. 1st lt. U.S. Army, 1970-71, Vietnam. Decorated Bronze Star. Mem. AICPA, S.D. CPA Soc., Minn. Soc. CPA, Am. Legion (fin. officer 1986—), Rotary. Republican. Roman Catholic. Office: Person Thurman Carlon & Co 403 N Lawler Ste 206 Mitchell SD 57301

CARLSON, ARNOLD R., manufacturing company executive; b. Worcester, Mass., Oct. 18, 1928; s. Arnold R. and Wanda (Racienska) C.; divorced; children: Susan, Judith, Roy; m. Ann. C. Woodcock, Aug. 17, 1968. BBA, Clark U., 1952; MBA, Northeastern U., 1957. Mgr. Carling Turbine Blower Co., Worcester, 1955-60, pres., 1960—. Mem. Hubbardston (Mass.) Planning Bd., 1972-75. With U.S. Army, 1946-48. Mem. Nat. Assn. Accts., Nat. Elec. Mfrs. Assn., Am. Petroleum Inst. Home: 2 Rawson Pl Shrewsbury MA 01545 Office: Carling Turbine Blower Co 8 Nebraska St Box 5048 Worcester MA 01615-0048

CARLSON, BYRON LEE, insurance company executive; b. Moline, Ill., Sept. 10, 1945; s. Karl Bloomberg and Ethel Lucille (Beckman) C.; m. Carol Lynn Asmus, Apr. 3, 1976; 1 child, Andrea Joyce. AA, Black Hawk Coll., 1966; BS in Bus., Western Ill. U., 1968, MBA, 1970. CLU. Asst. to agy. sec. Modern Woodmen Am., Rock Island, Ill., 1970-76; supr. tax sheltered div. Modern Woodmen Am., Rock Island, 1976-82, mgr. advanced underwriting, 1982-85, mgr. product research, 1985—. Pres. Orion (Ill.) Fall Festival, 1986. Mem. Rock Island County Life Underwriter's Assn., CLU & Certified Fin. Cons. (pres., dirs. Quad-City chpt. 1981-82), Nat. Assn. Fraternal Ins. Counselors, Life Ins. Mgmt. & Research Assn. (chmn. quality bus. com. 1988), Lions (pres. 1984). Home: PO Box 81 Orion IL 61273 Office: Modern Woodmen Am Miss River at 17th St Rock Island IL 61201

CARLSON, CHARLES A., data processing executive; b. Mpls., Jan. 28, 1933; s. Clifford and Loretta M. (Sengir) C.; m. Marlene G. Carlson, Nov. 1, 1969; children—Susan, Anne, Richard, Patricia, Andrew. B.A. in English, Coll. St. Thomas, St. Paul, 1954; postgrad., U. Iowa. Retail store mgmt. positions Sears Roebuck & Co., Mpls., 1955-66; dept. mgr. positions Sears Roebuck & Co., Chgo., 1966-76; territorial data processing mgr. Sears Roebuck & Co., Atlanta, 1976-80; nat. mgr. computers and communications Sears Roebuck & Co., Chgo., 1980-81, v.p. data processing and communications, 1981—. Bd. dirs. Jr. Achievement of Chgo., 1985—. Woodrow Wilson fellow, 1955. Mem. Nat. Retail Mchts. Assn. (bd. dirs. info. systems. div. 1981—). Republican. Lutheran. Home: 908 S Royal Blackheath Ct Naperville IL 60540 Office: Sears Roebuck & Co D-704X Sears Tower Chicago IL 60684

CARLSON, CURTIS LEROY, business executive; b. Mpls., July 9, 1914; s. Charles A. and Letha (Peterson) C.; m. Arleen Martin, June 30, 1938; children: Marilyn Carlson Nelson, Barbara Carlson Gage. B.A. in Econs., U. Minn., 1937. Salesman, Procter & Gamble Co., Mpls., 1937-39; founder, pres. Gold Bond Stamp Co., Mpls., 1938-84, pres., chmn. bd. dirs., 1938—; chmn. bd. dirs. Carlson Cos., Inc. (formerly Premium Service Corp.), 1972-84; pres. MIP Agy., Inc.; chmn. bd. Gold Bond Stamp Co., Radisson Hotel Corp., Radisson Group Inc., Radisson Mo. Corp., Radisson Raleigh Corp., Colony Resorts, Inc., Carlson Properties, Inc., Carlson Mktg. Group, Inc., Carlson Leasing, Inc., Carlson Tours, Inc., Jason Empire, Inc., TGI Friday's Inc., Dallas, CSA, Inc., Nordic-Am. Travel, Inc.; dir. Premiums Internat. Ltd., Can., Gold Bond Japan Ltd., Marquette Bank of Mpls., Bank Shares, Inc., Radisson Wilmington Corp.,. Sr. v.p. U. Minn. Found.; bd. dirs. Fairview Hosp.; chmn. Swedish Council Am.; bd. dirs., founder Boys Club Mpls.; bd. dirs. Minn. Orchestral Assn., Mpls. Downtown Council, Minn. Meetings; mem. adv. bd. U. Minn. Exec. Program, Curtis L. Carlson Sch. of Mgmt., U. Minn.; bd. dirs. U.S. Swedish Council; mem. Hennepin Ave. Meth. Ch. Mem. Trading Stamp Inst. Am. (dir., founder, pres. 1959-60), Mpls. C. of C. (exec. com.), Swedish-Am. C. of C. (dir.), U. Minn. Alumni Assn. (honors com.), Sigma Phi Epsilon. (nat. trustee). Clubs: Minneapolis, Minneapolis Athletic; Northland Country (Duluth); Minikahda, Woodhill Country; Ocean Reef Yacht (Key Largo); Palm Bay (Miami). Lodges: Masons, Shriners, Jesters. Office: Carlson Marketing Group Inc 12755 State Hwy 55 Minneapolis MN 55441

CARLSON, DAVID GILBERT, communications executive; b. Springfield, Ohio, July 31, 1961; s. Robert and Mildred (Gilbert) C.; m. Kristen A. Nicewander, Aug. 18, 1984. BA, Bethany Coll., 1983; MA in Internat. Mgmt., Am. Grad. Sch. Internat. Mgmt., 1985. Mgr. mktg. Echosphere Internat., Englewood, Colo., 1985-86, mgr. internat. ops., 1986-87; dir. European ops. Echosphere Internat., Rotterdam, Netherlands, 1987—. Presbyterian. Office: Echosphere Internat, Smirnoffweg 5a, 7604 BJ Almelo The Netherlands

CARLSON, DAVID MARTIN, retail executive; b. Marinette, Wis., July 15, 1940; s. Martin Algot and Ellen (Blom) C.; m. Sheri Phyllis Allen, Sept. 1, 1961 (div. Mar. 1970); 1 child, Kristin Elizabeth; m. Jean Marie Furniss, May 1, 1971; 1 child, Erik David. B.S. in Math., U. Mich., 1964, M.S. in Indsl. Adminstrn., 1966, Ph.D., 1975. Vice-pres. MIS Chatham Supermarkets, Inc., Warren, Mich., 1971-75; vice-pres. MIS Allied Supermarkets, Inc., Livonia, Mich., 1975-78; v.p. mktg. Data Terminal Systems, Inc., Maynard, Mass., 1978-83; pres., chief exec. officer Transaction Mgmt., Inc., Lexington, Mass., 1983-85; v.p. elec. merchandise systems Kmart Corp., Troy, Mich., 1985-86, v.p. corp. info systems, 1986-89, sr. v.p. info systems, 1989—. Served with U.S. Army, 1958-59, 61-62. Mem. Bus. Execs. for Nat. Security. Unitarian. Office: K Mart Corp 3100 Big Beaver Troy MI 48084

CARLSON, EDWIN THEODORE, computer company executive; b. Berwyn, Ill., Mar. 6, 1936; s. Theodore William and Edwina (Warner) C.; m. Melvie Sue Tidwell, June 15, 1964 (div. 1977); children: Gary Scott, Donna Sue; m. Janice Lynn Reed, April 28, 1983; children: Christian Alexandra, Garet William. BS in Engring., U.S. Naval Acad., 1961. Commd. 2d lt. USAF, 1961-63, resigned, 1963; nat. sales and mktg. mgr. Xerox Corp., El Segundo, Calif., 1969-78; v.p. sales Computer Sci. Corp., El Segundo, 1978-81; info. systems and service mgr. Control Data Group, Dallas, 1981-84; gen. mgr. Businessland Inc., Orange, Calif., 1984-86; sales exec. Metier Mgmt. Systems, Irvine, Calif., 1986-88; area mgr. AGS Info. Svcs. Inc., Houston, 1988—. Contbr. articles on computers to profl. jours. Mem. Naval Acad. Alumni Assn., Am. Mgmt. Assn. Republican. Lutheran. Home: 3 Meadow Fair Ct The Woodlands TX 77381 Office: AGS 1415 N Loop W Ste 260 Houston TX 77008

CARLSON, ORVILLE JAMES (SKIP), accountant, financial planner; b. Mpls., Sept. 20, 1944; s. Orville Harlan and Marguerite (Fleming) C.; m. Shirley A. Steele, Feb. 20, 1968; children: Orville J., Jr., Melissa. AA, U. Minn.; BS, St. Cloud (Minn.) State Coll. CPA. Minn. Staff acct. George M. Hansen, CPA, Mpls., 1972-75; sr. acct. J.K. Lasser & Co., CPA, Mpls., 1975-76, DeLaHunt Voto & Co., White Bear Lake, Minn.; founder O.J. Carlson & Assoc., Anoka, 1978; founding ptnr. Wingad Carlson Cos., Anoka, Minn., 1984—; bd. dirs., chmn. bd. Family Life Ctr., Anoka, 1988—; sec., treas. Flores do Mundo Inc., 1983; chief fin. officer, treas. Am.'s Floral Express, Inc., 1989—. Chmn. Utility Adv. Bd., Anoka, 1975-84; treas. Anoka, Blaine and Coon Rapids Outward Bound Found., Coon Rapids, Minn., 1984-86; bd. dirs. Anoka Bus. Assistance Network, Coon Rapids, 1985; mem. charter commn. City of Fridley, 1987; mem. assoc. staff Campus Crusade for Christ. With U.S. Army, 1966-70. Mem. Nat. Soc. Pub. Accts., Minn. Assn. Pub. Accts., Nat. Assn. Tax Preparers, Inst. Cert. Fin. Planners, Anoka County C. of C. (past pres-elect, bd. dirs., now pres.). Mem. Evang. Covenant. Lodge: Rotary (Anoka) (bd. dirs. 1979-85). Home: 1440 Windemere Dr Minneapolis MN 55421 Office: Wingad Carlson Cos O J Carlson & Assocs 229 Jackson St Ste 105 Anoka MN 55303

CARLSON, ROBERT FREDERICK, JR., manufacturing company executive; b. Glendale, Calif., Aug. 5, 1952; s. Robert Frederick Sr. and Nancy Leigh (Claybrook) C.; m. Margaret Ann Gray, Nov 21, 1987. BA, U. Calif., 1976; MBA, Harvard U., 1986. Corp. planner Channel Industries Inc., Santa Barbara, Calif., 1976-84, Beech Aircraft Corp., Wichita, Kans., 1985—; instr. dept. mgmt. Wichita State U., 1987—. Mem. Sch. Bd. Goleta (Calif.) Union Sch. Dist., 1977. Home: Box 78-1933 Wichita KS 67278-1933 Office: Beech Aircraft Corp PO Box 85 Wichita KS 67201-0085

CARLSON, ROBERT NILS, international management consultant; b. Indpls., Nov. 16, 1942; s. Clarence Nils and Barbara Helen (Weir) C.; m. Nancy Elizabeth Hinkel, Jan. 4, 1969; children: Russell Nils, Lisa Suzanne. BS in Indsl. Engring., Lehigh U., 1964; MBA, U. Pa., 1969. Vol. Peace Corps., Valdivia, Chile, 1964-66; mgmt. trainee Gen. Electric Co., 1969-71; mgr. inventory control, large AC motor div. Gen. Electric Co., Schenectady, 1971-73; plant mgr., med. systems div. Gen. Electric Co., Milw., 1973-75; mgr. market devel., food service equipment div. Gen. Electric Co., Chicago Heights, Ill., 1975-77; mgr. strategic planning component products group Gen. Electric Co., Carmel, Ind., 1977-79; pres. Harowe Servo Controls, Inc., West Chester, Pa., 1979-83; dir. St. Kitts (British West Indies) Enterprises Co. Ltd., 1979-83; pres. Robert Carlson Assocs., Inc., West Chester, 1983—. Bd. dirs. United Way of Chester County; vol. soccer Spl. Olympics, 1980-82; coach Little League, 1978-84; pres. bd. trustees, mem. pastor search com. First Presbyn. Ch., West Chester, 1985; mem. long range planning com. Delaware County Christian Sch., 1985—.; elder in charge of missions Christ Community Ch., West Chester, 1987—. Mem. Am. Mgmt. Assn., Internat. Mgmt. Council West Chester, Mfrs. Assn. Delaware Valley.

CARLSON, ROGER ALLAN, manufacturing company executive, accountant; b. Mpls., Dec. 12, 1932; s. Carl Albert and Borghild Amanda (Anderson) C.; m. Lois Roberta Lehman, Aug. 20, 1955; children: Gene, Bradley. BBA, U. Minn., 1954. CPA, Minn. Investment mgr. Mayo Found., Rochester, Minn., 1963-83; controller Luth. Hosp. and Homes Soc., Fargo, N.D., 1983-84; v.p., treas. Crenlo Inc., Rochester, 1984—, also bd. dirs.; instr. seminars, 1971, 82. Pres. Ability Bldg. Ctr., Rochester, 1974-75, United Way, Olmsted County, Minn., 1980; trustee Minn. Charities Rev. Council, Mpls., 1981-83. Served to capt. U.S. Army, 1955-57. Mem. Am. Inst. CPA's, Minn. Soc. CPA's, Nat. Assn. Accts. (pres. So. Minn. chpt. 1969). Methodist. Home: 1208 19th Ave NE Oakcliff Rochester MN 55904 Office: Crenlo Inc 1600 4th Ave NW Rochester MN 55901

CARLSON, ROLLAND SIGFRID, banker; b. Chgo., Apr. 15, 1932; s. Sigfrid and Esther (Peterson) C.; m. Gretchen J. Lindfelt, Mar. 17, 1956 (dec. Oct. 1986); children—Kristine, David, Karin; m. Janis L. Swanson, July 24, 1988. A.A., North Park Coll., 1952; B.A., Augustana Coll., 1954; M.B.A., U. Chgo., 1960. Cashier Harris Bank, Chgo., 1962-65, asst. v.p., 1965-68, v.p., 1968-76, sr. v.p., 1976-78, exec. v.p., 1978—; bd. dirs. Harris Bank, Barrington, Midwest Automated Clearing House Assn., Inc. Mem. pres.'s adv. council North Park Coll., Chgo.; bd. dirs. Swedish Covenant Hosp., Chgo., Evang. Covenant Ch. Am., United Negro Coll. Fund. Club: Union League. Office: Harris Trust & Savs Bank 311 W Monroe St PO Box 755 Chicago IL 60690

CARLSON, THEODORE JOSHUA, lawyer, retired utility company executive; b. Hartford, Conn., Jan. 4, 1919; s. John and Hulda (Larson) C.; m. Jacqueline L. Coburn, Apr. 25, 1953; children: Stephanie, Christopher J., Victoria, Antoinette. A.B., Montclair State Coll., 1940; J.D., Columbia U., 1948, A.M., 1951; postgrad., U. Chgo., 1942. Bar: N.Y. 1948. Assoc. Gould & Wilkie, N.Y.C., 1948-54, partner, 1954—, sr. partner, 1970—; dir. Central Hudson Gas & Electric Corp., Poughkeepsie, N.Y., 1968-89, chmn., 1975-89, prin. officer, 1975-86; mem., chmn. fin. and audit com. N.Y. State Energy Research Devel. Authority, 1980-88; dir. Empire State Electric Energy Research Corp., Edison Electric Inst., 1976-79; chmn. exec. com. Energy Assn. N.Y. State, 1976-77, 82-83, N.Y. Power Pool, 1977-78; dir., mem. exec. com. Mid-Hudson Pattern, Inc., Poughkeepsie, N.Y. Author: A Design For Freedom. Pres. United Fund Rockville Centre, N.Y., 1966; chmn. Westchester County (N.Y.) adv. bd. Salvation Army, 1977-80, N.Y. State adv. bd., 1977-83, Greater N.Y. adv. bd.; chmn. bd. trustees King's Coll. Capt. USAAF, 1942-46. Mem. Edison Electric Inst., Am., N.Y. bar assns., Bar Assn. City N.Y. (chmn. pub. utility sect. com. on post admissions-legal edn. 1970-73). Lodge: Rotary (hon.). Office: Gould & Wilkie 1 Wall St New York NY 10005

CARLSON, THOMAS LEE, auditor; b. Clam Center, Kans., Jan. 6, 1958; s. Wayne Robert and Bonnie Lou (Savage) C.; m. Anna Gayl, Sept. 1988. AA, Garden City (Kans.) Community Coll., 1978; BBA, Emporia State U., 1983. CPA, Tex. Staff auditor Touche Ross & Co., Oklahoma City, 1984-85; sr. internat. auditor Lone Star Industries, McKinney, Tex., 1985—. Mem. Tex. Soc. CPA's, Am. Inst. CPA's. Republican. Baptist. Office: Lone Star Industries Inc 555 Republic Dr #314 Plano TX 75074

CARLSON, WILLIAM D., financial executive; b. Bklyn., Apr. 7, 1945; s. William A. and Margaret D. (Lorentsen) C.; m. Melinda K. Strayer, May 26, 1976; children: David, Kenneth. BBS, Pace U., 1967. Cost acct. GTE Sylvania, York, Pa., 1969-71; internal auditor Unitec, York, 1971-72; tax mgr. Unitec/Campbell Chain, York, 1972-74; gen. acct., tax mgr. Studebaker Worthington, Inc. div. Campbell Chain, York, 1974-76, acctg. mgr., 1976-79; acctg. mgr. McGraw-Edison, Inc. div. Campbell Chain, York, 1979-80, controller, 1980-84; v.p. fin. Cooper Industries, Inc. div. Campbell Chain, York, 1985-86; dir. fin. and adminstrn. Cooper Industries div. Gardner-Denver Mining and Constrn., Roanoke, Va., 1986—. Scoutmaster Boy Scouts Am., York, 1970-84, dist. chmn., mem. council bd., 1984-87; treas. St. Stephen's United Ch. Christ, York, 1983-87. Sgt. U.S. Army, 1967-69. Decorated Bronze Star. Democrat. Office: Cooper Industries div Gardner- Denver Mining & Constrn 1700 Blue Hills Dr Roanoke VA 24012

CARLSTON, RICHARD CHARLES, aerospace engineer; b. San Francisco, May 17, 1929; s. Charles Oliver and Gertrude Madeline (Green) C.; m. Margaret Elizabeth Schoenborn, July 19, 1958; children: Donald, Elizabeth, Stuart. BS, U. San Francisco, 1951; MS, U. Mo., Columbia, 1954; PhD in Chemistry, U. Kans., Lawrence, 1957. Registered profl. engr., Calif. Sr. chemist Sperry Gyroscope Co., Great Neck, N.Y., 1957-60; research engr. Grumman Aircraft Co., Bethpage, N.Y., 1960-62; head solid state physics dept. Aerojet Gen. Corp., Azusa, Calif., 1962-64; physicist Office Naval Research, Washington, 1964-68; assoc. prof. metall. engring. Calif. Poly. State U., San Luis Obispo, 1968-72; research group leader EG&G Co., Santa Barbara, Calif., 1972-76; mgr. corrosion program for ICBMsystems TRW Def. and Space Systems Group, Redondo Beach, Calif., 1976—; mgr. The Trading Post and Serra Stamp Service (scout memorabilia and philately). Mem. editorial bd. Electrochem. Soc., 1967-72, chem. abstractor, 1960-65. Co-founder Plainedge (N.Y.) Pub. Library, 1961; active local Boy Scouts Am., mem. Jamboree staffs, Can., U.S., 1985; mem. Nat. Cath. Com. on Scouting, chmn. Area III Western region. Recipient Wood badge Boy Scouts Am. Fellow Washington Acad. Scis., Am. Inst. Chemists; mem. Nat. Assn. Corrosion Engr.s (chmn. TPC T-9), Air Pollution Control Assn., Am. Soc. Quality Control, Electrochem. Soc., Am. Soc. Metals, Am. Philatelic Soc., German Philatelic Soc., Philatelic Library of So. Calif., Sigma Xi. Republican. Roman Catholic. Clubs: Scandinavian, Collectors. Lodge: KC. Home: 3201 Flora St San Luis Obispo CA 93401 Office: Bldg DH5/2662 TRW Redondo Beach CA 90278

CARLTON-JONES, DENNIS, retired environmental management company executive; b. Colwyn Bay, North Wales, Wales, Dec. 11, 1930; came to U.S., 1964; s. Charles Richard and Amy (Slater) Carlton-J.; m. Anne Helen Nixon, Oct. 3, 1955; children: Christopher Richard, Michael John. B.Sc., U. London, 1951. Engr. George Wimpey & Co., London, 1954-57; asst. to v.p. George Wimpey & Co., 1957-60; mgr. Custodis Canadian Chimney Co., Ltd., Toronto and Montreal, 1961-64; mgr., v.p. sales and engring. Custodis Constrn. Co., Inc., Chgo., 1964-69, v.p., gen. mgr., 1969-71; v.p., gen. mgr. Hamon Cooling Tower div. Research-Cottrell, Inc., 1971-73, Air Control Group, 1973-77; pres. Environ. Cos. Research-Cottrell, Inc., 1977-82; pres., chief exec. officer Constructed Products Group of Research-Cottrell Inc., Somerville, N.J., 1983-87, chmn., 1987-88. Served with RAF, 1952-54. Mem. Instn. Civil Engrs., Air Pollution Control Assn. Episcopalian. Club: Raritan Valley Country, Fiddlesticks Country. Office: Rsch-Cottrell Inc PO Box 1500 Somerville NJ 08876

CARLUCCI, FRANK CHARLES, III, former secretary of defense; b. Scranton, Pa., Oct. 18, 1930; s. Frank Charles, Jr. and Roxanne (Bacon) C.; m. Marcia Myers, Apr. 15, 1976; children: Karen, Frank, Kristin. A.B., Princeton U., 1952; postgrad., Sch. Bus. Adminstrn., Harvard U., 1956; postgrad. hon. dr. degree, Wilkes Coll., Kings Coll., 1973. With Jantzen Co., Portland, Ore., 1955-56; fgn. svc. officer Dept. State, 1956; vice consul, econ. officer Dept. State, Johannesburg, S. Africa, 1957-59; second sec., polit. officer Dept. State, Kanshasa, Congo, 1960-62; officer in charge Congolese polit. affairs Dept. State, 1962-64; consul gen. Dept. State, Zanzibar, 1964-65; counselor for polit. affairs Dept. State, Rio de Janeiro, Brazil, 1965-69; asst. dir. Office Econ. Opportunity, Washington, 1969, dir., 1970; assoc. dir. Office Mgmt. and Budget, 1971, dep. dir., 1972; undersec. HEW, 1972-74; ambassador to Portugal, 1975-78; dep. dir. CIA, Washington, 1978-81; dep. sec. Def. Washington, 1981-82; pres. Sears World Trade, Inc., Washington, 1983-84, chmn., chief exec. officer, 1984-86; asst. to the Pres. Nat. Security Affairs, Washington, 1986-87; Sec. Def. Washington, 1987-89; vice chmn. Carlyle Group, Washington, 1989—. Served as lt. (j.g.) USNR, 1952-54. Recipient Superior Service award Dept. State, 1972, Superior Honor award, 1969, HEW Disting. Civilian Service award, 1975, Def. Dept. Disting. Civilian award, 1977, Disting. Intelligence medal, 1981, Nat. Intelligence Disting. Service medal, 1981, Presdl. Citizens award, 1983, Woodrow Wilson award, 1988, James Forrestal Meml. award, 1988. Office: Carlyle Group 1001 Pennsylvania Ave NW Washington DC 20004

CARMACK, COMER ASTON, JR., steel company executive; b. Phenix City, Ala., June 26, 1932; s. Comer Aston and Mary Kate (Mills) C.; AS, Marion Mil. Inst., 1951; BS, Ala. Poly. Inst., 1954; m. Blanche Yarbrough, Nov. 30, 1957; children—Comer Aston, Mary Kate. Project mgr. Muscogee Iron Works, Columbus, Ga., 1956-58, v.p. engring., 1958-73, pres., 1973—; pres. Universal Drives & Svcs., 1985-89; pres. M.K. Realty, Columbus, 1985—. Past bd. dirs. Better Bus. Bur. With USAF, 1954-56. Registered profl. engr., Calif. Mem. ASTM, Nat. Soc. Profl. Engrs., Ga. Soc. Profl. Engrs., Ga. Archtl. and Engring. Soc. (past pres., bd. dir. Columbus chpt.), Order of Engr., Chattahoochee Valley Safety Soc., Columbus Country Club. Methodist. Office: Muscogee Iron Works 1324 11th Ave Columbus GA 31902

CARMICHAEL, CHARLES WESLEY, industrial engineer; b. Marshall, Ind., Jan 18, 1919; s. Charles Wesley and Clella Ann (Grubb) C.; B.S., Purdue U., 1941; m. Eleanor Lee Johnson, July 2, 1948 (dec. 1984); 1 dau., Ann Bromley Carmichael Biada; m. Bernadine P. Carlson, Dec. 21, 1985. Owner, operator retail stores, West Lafayette, Ind., 1946-48, Franklin, Ind., 1950-53; mem. staff time study Chevrolet Co., Indpls., 1953-55; indsl. engr. Mallory Capacitor Co., Indpls., 1955-60, Greencastle, Ind., 1960-70, plant engr., 1970-81; contract cons. Northwood Assocs., 1981—; lectr. in field. Chmn. Greencastle br. ARC, 1962-63; bd. dirs. United Way Greencastle, 1976-79, 84-86. Served to capt., F.A., U.S. Army, 1941-46; ETO. Decorated Bronze Star, Purple Heart with oak leaf cluster. Mem. Greencastle C. of C. (dir. 1962-64), Am. Inst. Plant Engrs., Ind. Bd. Realtors (dir. 1983-85), Putnam County Bd. Realtors (pres. 1983-84), Ind. Hist. Soc, Am. Legion. Republican. Methodist. Clubs: John Purdue, Soc. Ind. Pioneers, Windy Hill Country. Lodges: Masons, Shriners, Kiwanis (past pres.). Home and Office: 3628 Woodcliff Dr Kalamazoo MI 49008-2513

CARMICHAEL, DONALD SCOTT, lawyer, business executive; b. Toledo, Feb. 19, 1912; s. Grey Thornton and Edna Earle (Jaite) C.; m. Mary Glenn Dickinson, May 28, 1940; children: Mary Brooke McMurray, Pamela Hastings Keenan. A.B., Harvard U., 1935, law student, 1935-37; LL.B., U. Mich., 1942. Bar: Ohio 1942. Staff dept. law City of Cleve. 1938-40; chief renegotiation br. Cleve. Ordnance Dist., War Dept., 1942-46; practiced in Cleve., 1946; asst. sec. Diamond Alkali Co., 1946-48, sec., 1948-57, gen. counsel, 1957-58; v.p.-gen. counsel Stouffer Corp., 1959-60, exec. v.p., 1960-64; practiced in Cleve., 1964-71; pres. Schrafft's div. Pet, Inc., N.Y.C., 1971-75, Sportservice Corp., Buffalo, 1975-80; pres. Del. North Cos., Inc., Buffalo, 1980-89, vice chmn., 1989—; officer, dir. various corps. Editor: F.D.R; Columnist, 1947; Contbr. to law revs. Mem. Cuyahoga County Charter Commn., 1959—; chmn.; mem. Cleve. Met. Services Commn., 1957-59, President's Task Force on War Against Poverty, 1964; Del. Democratic Nat. Conv., 1960, 64; mem. Cuyahoga County Dem. Exec. Com.; Chmn. bd. trustees Cuyahoga County Hosps., 1958-64, Urban League, Karamu House. Mem. Am., Ohio, Cleve. bar assns., Phi Gamma Delta. Clubs: Union (Cleve.), Chagrin Valley Hunt (Cleve.); Harvard, River (N.Y.C.); Buffalo; Crag Burn Golf (East Aurora, N.Y.). Home: Hardscrabble Rd Lyme NH 03768 Office: Del N Cos 1 Delaware N Pl Buffalo NY 14209

CARMODY, GEORGE EDWARD, lawyer, venture capitalist, financial advisor; b. Mt. Vernon, N.Y., June 16, 1931; s. George Edward and Florence Alba (Liccione) C.; divorced; children: Elizabeth, Susan, Matthew, David. BA, U. Conn., 1955; JD, Fordham U., 1960. Bar: N.Y. 1961, U.S. Dist. Ct. (so. and ea. dists.) N.Y. 1962. Securities analyst Merrill Lynch Pierce Fenner & Beane, N.Y.C., 1955-60, assoc. law dept., 1960-62; gen. counsel Van Alstyne, Noel & Co., 1962-64; ptnr. Stamer & Haft, N.Y.C. and London, 1964-70; prin. Carmody Law Office, N.Y.C. and Phila., 1970—; founder Telescis. Capital Corp., Marlboro, N.J.; bd. dirs. Leach Entertainment Enterprises, Inc., Danbury, Conn., Delta Switching Corp., Cherry Hill, N.J., The Ptnrs. Group, Inc., Dover, Del. Active Met. Art, Mus. Modern Art. Mem. Nat. Assn. Corp. Dirs., N.Y. Acad. Sci., Fgn. Policy Assn., Fordham Law Alumni Assn., Am. Assn. Arbitrators. Libertarian. Home and Office: 135 E 54th St New York NY 10022

CARMODY, ROBERT EDWARD, human resource information systems professional; b. N.Y.C., Dec. 13, 1942; s. Henry Adrian and Lucille Dorothy (Dorsey) C.; m. Sara Jane Morris, Oct. 4, 1969; children: Jon Andrew, Heather Brooke. BA in Psychology, U. Va., 1964. CLU. Personnel systems supt. State Farm Ins. Co., Bloomington, Ill., 1966-78; exec. project dir. Info. Sci. Inc., Chgo., 1978-79; dir. human resources systems CIGNA Corp., Phila., 1979-88, asst. v.p., human resources info. services, 1988—; founding mem. Ins. Personnel Systems Group, 1987—. Contbr. articles to profl. jours. Served with USNG, 1964-70. Mem. Am. Soc. Personnel Adminstrs., Am. Mgmt. Assn., Soc. Human Resource System Profls., Conf. Bd., Info. Industry Assn., Ins. Personnel Systems Group (founding mem. 1987). Home: 118 Oak Ave Haddonfield NJ 08033 Office: CIGNA Corp 1600 Arch St Philadelphia PA 19103

CARMODY, THOMAS ROSWELL, business products company executive; b. Cleve., May 18, 1933; s. Thomas R. and Mary (Farrell) C.; m. Grace Marie Wagner, Aug. 25, 1956; children—Thomas, John, Michael. B.B.A., John Carroll U., 1956. Adminstrv. mgr. Curtis 1000 Inc., Houston, 1962-68; div. mgr. Curtis 1000 Inc., Lawrence, Kans., 1969-75, regional exec. v.p., 1976-81; exec. v.p. Am. Bus. Products, Inc., Atlanta, 1982-84, pres., 1985—, also bd. dirs. Served to 1st lt. U.S. Army, 1957-59. Republican. Roman Catholic.

CARNAHAN, ROBERT DEAN, technology transfer and new business executive; b. Pontiac, Mich., June 14, 1931; s. Clarence A. and Lena Ann (Rose) C.; m. Judith L. Isola, Dec. 28, 1953; children: Michael, Patrick, Kirstina, Kevin. BS with honors in Metall. Engring., Mich. Tech. U., 1953; postgrad., U. Minn., 1957-59; PhD, Northwestern U., 1963. Registered profl. engr., Calif. With Honeywell Rsch., 1956-59; mgr. quality control lab. Honeywell Rsch., New Brighton, Minn., 1959; rsch. asso., teaching asst. Northwestern U., 1960-62; with Aerospace Corp., El Segundo, Calif., 1962-68; asst. dept. head Aerospace Corp., 1966-68; dir. materials sci. lab. Universal Oil Products Co., Des Plaines, Ill., 1968-73; dir. rsch. elec. electronics lab., dir. corp. office tech. devel. Gould Inc., Rolling Meadows, Ill., 1973-80; sr. v.p. sci. and tech. U.S. G. Corp., Chgo., 1980-87; pres., founder Partec, Inc., Park City, Utah, 1988—; mem. NATO spl. program panel for materials sci. NATO Sci. Com., 1982-85, chmn., 1983; rep. to Indsl. Rsch. Inst.; bd. dirs. Radius Engring. & Tooling, Inc., Salt Lake City, Spectrix Corp., Evanston, Ill. Patentee in field. Bd. dirs. Ill. Sci. Lectures Assn.; pres. Barrington (Ill.) Babe Ruth League, 1969-70; treas. Timberlake Civic Assn., 1970-71; bd. dirs. Northwestern U./Evanston (Ill.) Rsch. Park Inc., 1986—; trustee Mich. Tech. U., 1985—; exex. v.p., assoc. Univ. Sci. Ptnrs., Inc., Ann Arbor, Mich., 1988—. With USNR, 1953-56, Korea. Recipient Silver Medal Alumni award U. Mich., 1949; Alumni Silver medal Mich. Technol. U., 1984; Disting. Alumni Merit award Tech. Inst. Northwestern U., 1984. Mem. AAAS, ASM Internat., Blue Key, Tau Beta Pi, Sigma Xi. Lutheran. Office: Partec Inc PO Box 2051 Park City UT 84060

CARNER, WILLIAM JOHN, banker; b. Springfield, Mo., Aug. 9, 1948; s. John Wilson and Willie Marie (Moore) C.; m. Dorothy Jean Edwards, June 12, 1976; children: Kimberly Jean, John Edwards Carner. AB, Drury Coll., 1970; MBA, U. Mo., 1972, PhD, 1989. Mktg. rep. 1st Nat. Bank Memphis, 1972-73; asst. br. mgr. Bank of Am., Los Angeles, 1973-74; dir. mktg. Commerce Bank, Springfield, Mo., 1974-76; affiliate mktg. mgr. 1st Union Bancorp., St. Louis, 1976-78; pres. Carner & Assocs., Springfield, Mo., 1977—; instr. Drury Coll., 1975, 84-86, U. Mo., Columbia, 1986-88; asst. prof. SW Mo. State U., 1988—; dir. Ozark Pub. Telecommunications, Inc. 1982-88, sec., 1984-85, treas., 1985-86, vice chmn. 1986-87, chmn., 1987-88. Bd. dirs. Am. Cancer Soc., Greene County, Mo., 1974-82, crusade chmn., 1982-83, publicity chmn., 1974-78; bd. dirs. Springfield (Mo.) Muscular Dystrophy Assn., 1975-76, Greater Ozarks council Camp Fire Girls, 1980-81, Chameleon Puppet Theatre, 1988—, Downtown Springfield Assn., 1989—. Mem. Bank Mktg. Assn. (service mem. council 1985-88), Mo. Banker's Assn. (instr. Gen. Banking sch.), Fin. Instns. Mktg. Assn. (chmn. service mem. com.), Assn. MBA Execs., Drury Coll. Alumni Assn. (v.p. 1985-86, pres. 1986-87). Democrat. Mem. Christian Ch. (Disciples of Christ). Club: Hickory Hills Country. Lodges: Masons, Shriners. Home: 1500 S Fairway Ave Springfield MO 65804 Office: PO Box 50005 Springfield MO 65805

CARNES, DAVID JAMES, seafood company executive; b. Newton, Mass., Aug. 1, 1944; s. George D. and Jean Ellis (Anderson) C.; m. Roxane Howes Goodspeed, June 9, 1973; children: Kristen, Michael. Assocs., Monmouth Coll. Asst. mgr. wharf Chatham (Mass.) Seafood Coop., 1967-68, retail/wholesale mgr., 1971-76, gen. mgr., 1976-80; pres. Chatham Fish & Lobster Co., 1981—; treas., mgr. Chatham Weirs, 1981—. With U.S. Army, 1969-71, Vietnam. Republican. Office: Chatham Fish & Lobster Co 121 Commerce Park South Chatham MA 02659

CARNEY, PATRICIA, Canadian legislator; b. Shanghai, China, May 26, 1935; d. John James and Dora (Sanders) C.; two children. B.A. in Econs. and Polit. Sci., U. B.C., Can., 1960, M.A. in Comml. and Regional Planning, 1977. Econ. journalist various publs. 1955-70; owner, cons. Gemini North Ltd., Vancouver, B.C., Can., 1970-80, Yellowknife, N.W.T., Can., 1971, Alta., Can., 1971; mem. Can. Ho. of Commons, Ottawa, Ont., 1980—, minister of state, 1981, minister fin., 1983, minister energy, mines and resources, 1984-86, minister for internat. trade, 1986-88, pres. Treas. Bd., 1988-89; mem. planning and priorities com.; mem. fgn. def. cabinet com. Recipient Can. Women's Press award, 1968, 3 MacMillan Bloedel Ltd. awards. Mem. Assn. Profl. Economists B.C., Can. Inst. Planners. Office: House Commons, Parliament Bldgs, Ottawa, ON Canada K1A 0A6 *

CARNEY, PHILLITA TOYIA, marketing communications management company executive; b. Chgo., Apr. 18, 1952; d. Phillip Leon Carney and Margaret Clarice (Ewing) Brown. Student, U. Utah, 1971-74; BS in Bus., Westminster Coll., 1976. Corp. tng. dir. U&I Sugar Corp., Salt Lake City, also Moses Lake, Wash., 1976-77; program coordinator Div. on Aging, Seattle, 1977-78; bus. devel. officer Del Green Assoc., Foster City, Calif., 1978-79; regional v.p. Equitec Fin. Group, San Francisco, Irvine and Oakland, Calif., 1979-84, United Resources, Oakland, San Francisco, Nev., 1984-86; owner, mgr. Carney & Assocs., Oakland, 1986; regional v.p. Eastcoast Ops. Benefits Communications Corp. div. Great West Life Assurance Co., Washington, 1986-87; nat. dir. enrollment services, nat. plan adminstr. U.S. Conf. Mayors Fringe Benefits Program, MCW Internat., Ltd., 1988—; dir. Total One, San Francisco; corp. cons., advisor Am. Intermediation Services, San Francisco, 1986; nat. dir. communications and enrollment services for U.S. Conf. Mayor's flexible benefits plan MCW Internat., Ltd., 1988—; cons. Washington Literacy Council; sr. bus. cons., ptnr. Performance Strategies Inc., San Diego, 1986. Moderator, creator pub. affairs radio program, 1975-76 (Best Pub. Affairs Program award Nat. Pub. Radio 1976). Del. White House Conf. on Small Bus., Washington, 1986; mem., lobbyist Concerned Women for Am., 1987; dir. communications U.S. Conf. Mayors, MCW Internat., Nat. Adminstrs. Recipient award Am. Legion, 1970, DAR, 1970. Fellow Am. Biog. Inst. Research Assn. (assoc., nat. advisor); mem. Internat. Assn. Fin. Planning, Women Entrepreneurs, Internat. Biog. Ctr., Bus. and Profl. Women, Sales Mktg. Exec. Assn., Zonta Internat. (pres. 1985—). Avocations: jogging, swimming, reading, writing. Home: 10925 S Wood Chicago IL 60643

CARNEY, ROBERT ARTHUR, restaurant executive; b. Haddonfield, N.J., Aug. 20, 1937; s. George Albert and Margret (Hollworth) C.; B.A., Ursinus Coll., 1963; m. Patricia Louise Igo, July 15, 1983; children—Lynn Ann, Jeffrey Todd, Jill Christine, Jason Michael, Justin David, Jennifer Lynn. Procurement agt. Campbell Soup Co., Paris, Tex., 1963-69, mgr. procurement, Salisbury, Md., 1969-72, dir. procurement, Camden, N.J., 1972-78; v.p. procurement Burger King Corp., Miami, Fla., 1978-82; v.p. purchasing Pizza Hut Inc., Wichita, 1978—. Served to capt. U.S. Army, 1958-60. Mem. Nat. Restaurant Assn. Republican. Roman Catholic. Home: 412 Lauber Ln Derby KS 67037 Office: 9111 E Douglas Wichita KS 67201

CARNICERO, JORGE EMILIO, aeronautical engineer, business executive; b. Buenos Aires, Argentina, July 17, 1921; came to U.S., 1942, naturalized, 1950; s. Alberto and Ana (Sulimeau) C.; m. Jacqueline Joanne Damman, Feb. 22, 1946; children—Jacqueline Denise, Jorge Jay. Student, U. LaPlata, Argentina, 1939-41, Aero. Engr., Rensselaer Poly. Inst., 1945. Chief engr. Dodero Airlines, Argentina, 1945, Flota Aerea Mercante, Argentina, 1945-46; v.p. Air Carrier Service Corp., Washington, 1946, exec. v.p., 1947-55, chmn. bd., dir., 1955—; past chmn. bd. Dyncorp. (formerly Calif. Eastern Aviation then Dynalectron Corp.); chmn. bd., dir. Servair Corp., Calif., Servair Inc., Del., Servair Maintenance, N.Y., Solar Insulators Inc.; pres., dir. Blue Cove Inc., N.Y., Emerald Cove Inc., Del., Internat. Plate Corp., Del., Trans-Am. Aero. Corp., Del.; bd. dirs. Aneco Co., Ga., Aneco Power Co., Fla., Calif. Heavy Oil Upgrading Corp., CFE Services Inc., Del., DYN Constrn. Corp., Calif., HRI Inc., Del., Hydrocarbon Research Inc., Del., PAC ORD, Calif., Servair of Tex., Trans-DYN Control Systems Inc., Calif., Airtech Service Inc., Fla., Round Hill Devel. Ltd., Jamaica. Bd. visitors Sch. Fgn. Service, Georgetown U., Washington; mem. council Rensselaer Poly. Inst., Troy, N.Y. Assoc. fellow Royal Aero. Soc.; mem. Argentine-Am. C. of C. (dir.). Clubs: University; Metropolitan (N.Y.C.); Congl. Country, Georgetown Country (Washington). Home: 3949 52nd St NW Washington DC 20016 Office: DynCorp 1313 Dolley Madison Blvd McLean VA 22101

CARNOCHAN, JOHN LOW, JR., retired aluminum company executive; b. Hagerstown, Md., Oct. 19, 1918; s. John Low and Susan (Long) C.; m. Emily Kent Linton, July 3, 1943; children: John, David, Susan, Jean, Carol, Robert. AB, Western Md. Coll., 1940, MEd, 1947; EdD, Columbia, 1963. Tchr. pub. schs., Washington County, Md., 1941-53; vice-prin. schs., Hagerstown, Md., 1953-55; prin., Maugansville, Md., 1955-56, Williamsport, Md., 1956-61; ednl. TV project coordinator, Harrison, N.Y., 1961-62; asst. to state supt. schs. Md. Dept. Edn., Balt., 1962-63; asst. supt. county schs., Frederick Md., 1963-64, supt. county schs., 1964-76; mgr. community relations Eastalco Aluminum Co., Frederick, 1976-84; cons., 1984—; prin. Carnochan, Felton & Gardiner Ednl. and Communications Cons., 1986—; chmn. bd. dirs. Home Care Research, Inc. Past chmn. Md. Adv. Council Vocat. Tech. Edn. Served from pvt. to capt., AUS, 1941-46, lt. col. Res. (ret.). Danforth fellow, 1974. Mem. Am. Assn. Sch. Adminstrs., Md. Assn. Sch. Supts. (past pres. and legis. chmn.), Public Relations Soc. Am., Md. C. of C. (past v.p.), Frederick C. of C., Phi Delta Kappa, Delta Kappa Pi. Home: 4829 Round Hill Rd Frederick MD 21701

CARO, CHARLES CRAWFORD, microcomputer company executive, international consultant; b. Champaign, Ill., Feb. 15, 1946; s. William Crawford and Marian Dell (Heischmidt) C.; m. Sallye Simons, Dec. 18, 1977 (div. 1987); 1 child, Mark Christopher. BA, U. South Fla., 1973, MA, 1976. Program support specialist Bendix/Siyanco, Riyadh, Saudi Arabia, 1973-74; chmn., chief exec. officer Caro Internat. Trade and Relations Corp. (CITAR), Tampa, Fla. and Jeddah, 1976-79, dir., 1976-79; mng. dir. Architect Lee Scarfone Assocs. (ALSA), Al-Khobar, Saudi Arabia, 1979-80; exec. dir. Caro Research Assocs., Tampa, 1980—; pres., chief exec. officer C3DS, Inc., Tampa, 1987-88, Microfine, Inc., Tampa, 1983-84, also dir.; DIR., V.P. Chancelogic, Inc., Tampa and London, 1989—; dir. Action Cons. Services, Inc., Brandon, Fla., 1986. Editor Internat. Round Table, 1987—; contbr. articles to publs. in field. Mem. Hillsborough Democratic Exec. Com., Tampa, 1982—, Hillsborough County Minority Bus. Enterprise Citizen Part. Com., Tampa, 1988—; pres. Drug Abuse Awareness Group, 1987, Communities Against Substance Abuse, Inc., 1988— . Served with U.S. Army Security Agy., 1967-71. Mem. World Inst. Achievement (life), Assn. Computing Machinery (computers and soc. spl. interest group), Internat. Platform Assn., Phi Kappa Phi, Pi Sigma Alpha. Episcopalian. Club: Tiger Bay of Tampa Bay.

CAROLAN, DOUGLAS, retail company executive. BS, Western Mich. U., 1964. Store mgr. to dir. mktg. div. Nat. Tea Co., 1962-83; sr. v.p. Associated Wholesale Grocers, Inc., Kansas City, Kans., 1983-86, exec. v.p., sec., 1986—. BD. dirs. Kans. City area food bank Harvesters. Office: Associated Wholesale Grocers Inc 5000 Kansas Ave Kansas City KS 66106

CARON, BETH RENEE, household products manufacturing company executive; b. Balt., Aug. 23, 1957; d. Roger George and Lena Belle (Belton) C. BEE with honors, Duke U., 1979; MBA, East Carolina U., 1985. Mgr. shift team Procter & Gamble Co., Greenville, N.C., 1979-81, elec. mgr. oper. dept., 1981-83, mech. mgr., 1983-84, indsl. engr., 1984-85, mgr. computer dept., 1986-88, mgr. prodn. dept., 1988—. Armco Steel Corp. scholar, 1975-79. Mem. Beta Gamma Sigma, Zeta Tau Alpha (gen. advisor 1986—). Republican. Roman Catholic. Home: 309 Lindell Rd Greenville NC 27834

CAROSI, ALFRED CHARLES, JR., marketing executive; b. Boston; s. Alfred Charles and Mary (Sprague) C.; m. Jean F. Whalen, May 19, 1973; children: Derek A., Brendan J. BS in Indsl. Engring., Northeastern U., 1970; MBA, U. Mich., 1973. Systems analyst Foxboro Co., Mass., 1970-71; brand mgr. Procter & Gamble, Cin., 1973-74; dir. mktg. Anheuser-Busch, Inc., St. Louis, 1975-80, Shasta Beverages, Inc., Hayward, Calif., 1981-83; v.p. mktg. Hasbro, Inc., Pawtucket, R.I., 1984-88, corp. v.p. mktg. svcs., 1987-88; corp. sr. v.p. mktg. svcs. Playskool Industries div. Hasbro, Pawtucket, R.I., 1988—. Roman Catholic. Office: Hasbro Inc 1027 Newport Ave Pawtucket RI 02862

CAROUSO, NICHOLAS HARRY, mining executive; b. Oakland, Calif., Mar. 25, 1920; s. Victor Harry and Nina (Mitchell) C.: student St. Mary's Coll., 1946-47; B.A., U. Calif., 1950, M.S., 1959; postgrad. U. Nev., 1956-57, U. Ariz., 1968—; m. Barbara Elizabeth Stephenson, Feb. 2, 1952; children—Mark Nicholas, Joan Patricia, Valerie Elizabeth. Sr. research engr. Berkeley Research Co. (Calif.), 1957-59; geophys. engr. Phelps Dodge Corp., Douglas, Ariz., 1959; plant prodn. engr. Eitel-McCullough, Inc., San Bruno, Calif., 1959-61; concentrator, metall. engr. Kennecott Copper Corp., Hayden, Ariz., 1961-65; mgmt. supr., cons. Bonanza-MJV, Superior, Ariz., 1969-70; pres. Geo-Processing, Inc., Prescott, Ariz., 1971—, also bd. dirs.; v.p. mining Cherry Creek Gold Corp., 1985-86; mining cons. Ibex Keystone Mine, Nev., Gold Star, Inc., Ariz., 1985—; mineral exploration cons. Capt. Kearny (Ariz.) Vol. Fire Dept., 1964-65. Served with USNR, World War II. Mem. Am. Inst. Mining, Metall. and Petroleum Engrs., Ariz. Geol. Soc., Am. Radio Relay League. Republican. Episcopalian. Inventor distance calculator, 1955. Home: 2106 Nolte Dr Prescott AZ 86301

CARPENTER, ALVIN RAUSO, transportation executive; b. Berea, Ky., Jan. 24, 1942; s. Warren G. and Pauline G. Carpenter; m. Marilyn Rex; 1 dau., Dana. B.A., U. Cin., 1964. With Chessie Seaboard R.R., 1964—; sr. v.p. coal coordinations Cleve., 1982-85; pres. CSX Transp., Jacksonville, Fla.; bd. dirs. Monogahela Ry., First Union Nat. Bank, Fla., St. Vincent's Hosp., Meml. Hosp., Jacksonville. Bd. dirs. W. Va. Coll. Grad. Studies, St. Vincent's Hosp., Jacksonville, Meth. Hosp., Jacksonville, First Union Bank, Jacksonville, CSX Transp., Jacksonville Symphony. Mem. Nat. Freight Traffic Assn., U.S. C. of C., San Jose Country Club, Timuquana Country Club, Epping Forest Yacht Club (Jacksonville), University Club, River Club. Republican. Clubs: Laurel Valley Golf (Ligonier, Pa.); Balt. Country (Balt.); San Jose, San Jose Country, University, The River, Timuquana Country (Jacksonville). Home: 9403 Woodhaven Jacksonville FL 32217 Office: CSX Transp 500 Water St Jacksonville FL 32202

CARPENTER, C. DONALD, JR., land surveyor, title researcher; b. Ballston Spa, N.Y., Nov. 9, 1933; s. C. Donald and Carolyn (Male) C.; children: Ann M., Arthur D., Marilyn J., Catherine M., Duane D., John T., Scott C. Student, Rensselaer Poly. Inst., 1951-58. Designer medium motors dept. Gen. Electric Co., Schenectady, N.Y., 1955-57; hwy. designer J. Clarkeson Cons. Engr., Albany, 1957-62; computer programmer Rist-Frost Assocs., Glen Falls, N.Y., 1962-64; office mgr. Coulter McCormack Surveyors, Saratoga Springs, N.Y., 1964-66; dep. dir. Saratoga County Planning Bd., Ballston Spa, 1966-71, Saratoga County Real Property Tax, Ballston Spa, 1971-73; prin. C. Donald Carpenter, Galway, N.Y., 1973-84; pres. Carpenter Assocs., PC, Galway, 1984—; cons. in ancient land title and mcpl. boundry matters; expert witness land patent and boundary disputes. Author: Kayaderosseras Allotment Maps, 1964, A Comprehensive History of Kayaderosseras Patent; reconstructor land patent maps from original survey records. Active Greenfield Environ. Commn., 1972-76; committeeman Galway Conservative party, 1978—. Recipient Award of Merit Fedn. Hist. Svcs., 1988. Mem. N.Y. State Assn. Profl. Land Surveyors, Ea. N.Y. Soc. Profl. Land Surveyors (past bd. dirs.). Methodist. Lodge: Lions. Home and Office: Carpenter Assocs PC Old Mill Rd Galway NY 12074

CARPENTER, EDMUND MOGFORD, electronics company executive; b. Toledo, Dec. 28, 1941; s. Charles N. and Vivian (Mogford) C.; m. Mary Winterhoff, May 20, 1962; children: Susan, Edmund Mogford, Molly. BS in Indsl. Engring., U. Mich., 1963, MBA, 1964. Dist. plant mgr. Mich. Bell Telephone Co., Detroit, 1964-68; ptnr. Touche Ross & Co., CPA's, Detroit, 1968-74; pres. Fruehauf do Brasil, Sao Paulo, 1974-76; pres. auto truck group Kelsey-Hayes Co., Romulus, Mich., 1976-81; group gen. mgr. world wide automotive ops. ITT Corp., Southfield, Mich., 1981-83; v.p. ITT Corp., N.Y.C., 1983-85, pres., dir., 1985-88, also bd. dirs.; chief operating officer ITT Indsl. Products, N.Y.C., 1987-88; chmn., chief exec. officer Gen. Signal Corp., High Ridge Park and Stamford, Conn., 1988—, also bd. dirs. Mem. Soc. Automotive Engrs., Machinery and Allied Products Inst. (exec. com.). Office: Gen Signal Corp High Ridge Pk Stamford CT 06904

CARPENTER, MARGARET DUFFEY, stockbroker; b. N.Y.C., Dec. 7, 1937; d. Joseph E. and Mary K. (Zimmerman) Duffey; m. Brian John Pendleton, Sept. 1957 (div. 1972); children: Brian John, Barbara Pendleton Gniewek, Joseph Michael, David Hall; m. Robert Stearns Carpenter, Aug. 27, 1973; stepchildren: Craig Robert, Debra Lee Carpenter Richner. Student, Mt. Holyoke Coll., 1955-57; grad., Coll. Fin. Planning, Denver. Cert. fin. planner. Adminstrv. dir. Morris County Legal Aid Soc., Morristown, N.J., 1968-73; v.p., resident mgr. Shearson, Lehman, Hutton, Inc., Port Jervis, N.Y., 1976—; radio fin. corr. Sta. WDLC-WTS, Port Jervis, 1980—, Sta. WALL, Middletown, N.Y., 1983—, Sta. WSUL, Monticello, N.Y., 1986—, Sta. WSUS, Franklin, N.J., 1987—. Contbr. articles to local newspapers. Mem. adv. bd. Mercy Community Hosp., Port Jervis, 1985—; mem. vestry St. Mary's Ch., Sparta, N.J. Mem. Inst. Cert. Fin. Planners, Sparta C. of C., Lakeside Tennis, Lake Mohawk Golf Club. Republican. Episcopalian. Home: 34 Deire Dr Sparta NJ 07871 Office: Shearson Lehman Hutton Inc PO Box 1118 Port Jervis NY 12771

CARPER, FREDA SMITH, bank marketing director; b. Roanoke, Va., Aug. 19, 1953; d. Samuel E. and R. Violet (Wilson) Smith; m. Charles R. Carper, June 18, 1978. AAS in Mgmt., U. Ky., Prestonburg, 1980. Sales dir. Ramada Inn, Roanoke, 1975-76; account exec. mgr. Am. Hotel Mgmt., Raleigh, N.C., 1976-78; asst. v.p., mktg. dir. Pikeville (Ky.) Nat. Bank, 1980-83; v.p. mktg. dir. First Fed. Roanoke (name changed to CorEast Savs. Bank), 1983-88, Colonial Am. Nat. Bank, Roanoke, 1988—. Bd. dirs. Mt. Pleasant Civic League; chmn. YMCA membership com., Roanoke, local ARC adv. coun. Recipient Addy award Charleston/Huntington Ad Club, W.Va., 1982, 83. Mem. Sales Mktg. Execs. (pres. 1986-87), Sales Mktg. Execs. Internat. (regional bd. dirs. 1986-87), Advt. Fedn. Roanoke (treas. 1986-87, v.p. 1987-88, pres. 1989-90, Addy award 1984), Fin. Instn. Mktg. Assn. Democrat. Baptist. Office: Colonial Am. Nat Bank 10 Franklin Rd Roanoke VA 24011

CARPP, EDWARD DANIEL, manufacturing company executive; b. Derby, Conn., Jan. 5, 1952; s. Alex and Helena Antoinette (Danielecki) C.; m. Suzanne Burrage Wilson, Sept. 16, 1978; 1 child, Emilie. Student, Temple U., 1969-72, Pa. State U., 1974-75; BS, U. New Haven, 1975. Dispatcher Roadway Express, Akron, Ohio, 1976-77; supr. dock Yellow Freight Systems Inc., Scranton, Pa., 1977-79; supr. shipping Gen. Motors Corp., Warren, Ohio, 1979-81; prodn. planner Gen. Motors Corp., Warren, 1981-84; mgr. prodn. control Picker Internat., Highland Heights, Ohio, 1984-87; dir. materials mgmt. Gen. Machine Products Co. Inc., Trevose, Pa., 1987—; pres. Compucorp Inc., Seymour, Conn., 1986—. Mem. Charter Revision Commn., Seymour, 1972-73. Alpha Chi Nat. scholar, 1974. Mem. Am. Prodn. and Inventory Control Soc., Pa. State Alumni Assn. (life). Home: 41 Cottonwood Dr Holland PA 18966 Office: Gen Machine Products Co Inc 3111 Old Lincoln Hwy Trevose PA 19047

CARR, ARTHUR, electronic mfg. co. exec.; b. Newark, July 9, 1931; s. Michael Thomas and Gertrude A. (Levy) C.; grad. pub. schs.; m. Virginia Lea Merry, July 11, 1953; children—Karen, Vickie, William. Field tech. specialist Remington Rand Univac, Boston, 1955-61; dir. mktg. Computer Control div. Honeywell, Framingham, Mass., 1961-68; v.p. mktg. Codex Corp., Mansfield, Mass., 1968-70, pres., chief exec., 1970-82; also dir.; v.p. Motorola Inc., 1979-82, exec. v.p., gen. mgr. info. systems group, 1982-86, pres. Stellar Computer, Inc., Newton, Mass., 1986—; dir. Prime Computer Inc., 1972-82, Zymark Corp., 1984-87, StorageTech., 1984, Wellfleet Communications, 1987—. Mem. Recreation Com., Ashland, Mass., 1969, Federated Ch. (dir. 1964-69, 74-77), Dover Ch., 1984—; bd. dirs. Mass. Tech. Council, 1974—. Served with USN, 1951-55. Mem. Ind. Data Communications Mfrs. Assn. (v.p., dir. 1971-82). Home: 44 Donnelly Dr Dover MA 02030 Office: Stellar Computer Inc 100 Wells Ave Newton MA 02159

CARR, DAVID KENNETH, corporate executive; b. Erie, Pa., Sept. 28, 1950; s. Kenneth Reed and Elinor Mae (Friel) C.; m. Barbara Davies, May 29, 1976; children: Michael, Brian. BA, Pa. State U., 1972, MPA, 1973. Ptnr. Coopers & Lybrand, Washington. Cub master Boy Scouts Am., Franklin Farm, Va., 1988—. Mem. Am. Soc. Pub. Adminstrn., Air Force Assn., Naval Inst. Repblican. Home: 13107 Briargrove Ct Herndon VA 22071 Office: Coopers & Lybrand 1800 M St NW Washington DC 20036

CARR, ELLIOTT GRABILL, bank executive; b. Hanover, N.H., Sept. 24, 1938; s. Robert Kenneth and Olive (Grabill) C.; m. Susan Wheatley, July 6, 1968; children: Priscilla, Sarah. AB, Dartmouth Coll., 1960; postgrad., Princeton U., 1960-61; MBA, Harvard U., 1964. Treas., chief investment officer Mass. Indemnity and Life Ins. Co., Boston, 1964-69; pres. Savs. Bank Assn. Mass., Boston, 1969-82, Cape Cod Five Cents Savs. Bank, Orleans, Mass., 1982—; bd. dirs. Abington (Mass.) Mut. Ins. Co. Author: Better Management of Business Giving, 1969. Vice-chmn. Silver Lake Regional Sch. Commn., Kingston, Mass., 1973-79, chmn. bd. assessors, Pembroke, Mass., 1979-80, chmn., 1986-88; chmn. Capital Planning Com., Brewster, Mass., 1980—. With U.S. Army, 1961-67. Mem. Mass. Bankers Assn. (vice-chmn. 1988—), Nat. Coun. Thrift Inst. (mem. adv. coun. to bd. govs. of fed. res. 1984-86). Home: 46 Run Hill Rd Brewster MA 02631 Office: Cape Cod Five Cents Savs PO Box 10 West Rd Orleans MA 02653

CARR, HAROLD NOFLET, corporate executive; b. Kansas City, Kans., Mar. 14, 1921; s. Noflet B. and Mildred (Addison) C.; m. Mary Elizabeth Smith, Aug. 5, 1944; children: Steven Addison, Hal Douglas, James Taylor, Scott Noflet. B.S., Tex. A&M U., 1943; postgrad., Am. U., 1944-46. Asst. dir. route devel. Trans World Airlines, Inc., 1943-47; exec. v.p. Wis. Central Airlines, Inc., 1947-52; mem. firm McKinsey & Co., 1952-54; pres. North Central Airlines, Inc., Mpls., 1954-69; chmn. bd. North Central Airlines, Inc., 1965-79; chmn. Republic Airlines, Inc., 1979-84, chmn. exec. com., 1984-86; chmn. Carr and Assocs., 1986—; professorial lectr. mgmt. engring.

Am. U., 1952-62; dir. Dahlberg, Inc., Ross Industries, Inc., Governor's Sound, Ltd., Cayman Water Co., Metro Airlines, Inc., First Nat. Bank Bryan (Tex.), Cayman Mile, Ltd.; Mem. bd. nominations Nat. Aviation Hall of Fame; mem. exec. adv. council Nat. Register Prominent Americans and Internat. Notables. Trustee Tex. A&M Research Found., Internat. Inst. for Effective Communication; mem. devel. council Coll. Bus. Adminstrn., Tex. A&M U. (chancellor's century con.). Mem. Nat. Aero. Assn., World Bus. Council, Am. Mgmt. Assn., Nat. Trust Historic Preservation, Minn. Execs. Orgn., Nat. Def. Transp. Assn., Pine Beach Peninsula Assn., Am. Econ. Assn., Tex. A&M Former Students Assn., Beta Gamma Sigma. Episcopalian. Clubs: Nat. Aviation, Aero (Washington); Minneapolis; Aggie (dir.) (College Station, Tex.); Tex. A&M Century; Racquet (Miami); Gull Lake Yacht (Brainerd, Minn.); Wings (N.Y.C.); Stearman Alumnus (Wichita, Kans.); Briarcrest Country, Plaza (Bryan).

CARR, HOWARD ERNEST, retired insurance agency executive; b. Johnson City, Tenn., Oct. 4, 1908; s. William Alexander and Gertrude (Feathers) C.; BS, E. Tenn. State U., 1929; MEd, Duke, 1935; postgrad. U. N.C., 1938-39; m. Thelma Northcutt, June 11, 1937 (dec. Oct., 1972); 1 son, Howard Ernest. Supt., Washington Coll. (Tenn.), 1929-35; ednl. advisor U.S. Office Edn., Ft. Oglethorpe, Ga., 1935-37; prin. Greensboro (N.C.) city schs., 1937-42; dir. activities First Presbyn. Ch., Greensboro, 1946-47; with Jefferson Standard Life Ins. Co., Greensboro, 1947—, spl. rep., 1947-54, supr. agy. Greensboro, 1964, mgr., 1964-67; pres. Everett's Lake Corp. Chmn. Guilford County Bd. Edn., 1950-77; vice chmn. N.C. Gov's Com. Edn., 1956-60; N.C. rep. White House Conf. Edn., 1955. Mem. adv. com. Greensboro div. Guilford Coll., 1958—; head Guilford County Cancer Drive, 1956, bd. dirs. Cancer Soc., 1956—; v.p. N.C. State Sch. Bds. Assn., 1959-61; bd. dirs. Greensboro Jr. Mus., 1956-62, Sternberger Found. Lt. with USNR, 1942-46, asst. head motion picture dept., Washington; to capt., 1951-54, as head motion picture dept; ret. as capt., 1968. Recipient Nat. Quality award, Nat. Assn. Life Underwriters, 1948—; named Boss of the Year, Lou-Celin chpt. Am. Bus. Woman's Assn., 1967; W.H. Andrews, Jr. award, 1985; Named Man of Yr., 1988. Mem. Nat., N.C. (pres. 1964-65; Man of Year award 1969), Greensboro (pres. 1956-57) assns. life underwriters, N.C. Leaders Club, Greensboro C. of C. (chmn. edn. com. 1960-62). Presbyn. (elder). Mason (32 deg.), Kiwanian (pres. Greensboro 1951). Author: History of Higher Education in East Tennessee, 1935. Home: 3927 Madison Ave Greensboro NC 27410 Office: Jefferson Standard Life Ins Co 3101 N Elm Ste 400 Greensboro NC 27408

CARR, JACK RICHARD, candy manufacturer executive; b. Bancroft, Ia., Jan. 14, 1937; s. Alan Goodspeed and Ruth Mae (Stoddard) C.; m. Doris Jean Dall, Apr. 22, 1967; children: Sarah Beth, Jennifer Marie, Janet Marie. BS, Drake U., 1963. Auditor Touche Ross and Co., Kansas City, Mo., 1963-68; asst. treas. Russell Stover Candies Inc., Kansas City, 1968-75, treas., 1975—. Cpl. U.S. Army, 1954-57. Mem. AICPA, Tax Exec. Inst. Republican. Methodist. Office: Russell Stover Candies Inc 1000 Walnut St Kansas City MO 64106

CARR, JAMES T., transportation company executive; b. Jersey City, Nov. 24, 1924; s. James V. and Augusta E. (Stenecke) C.; m. Helen A. De Tore, Jan. 4, 1948; children: Elaine, James T. Jr., Pamela. BS, NYU, 1950. Notary pub., N.J. Dist. mgr. W.T. Cowan, Inc., Jersey City, 1947-78; terminal mgr. Transcon Lines, Clifton, N.J., 1978—. Trustee I.L.A. 1730 Pension-Welfare Fund, N.Y.C., 1970-78. With AUS, 1943-46, ETO. Mem. N.J. Motor Truck Assn. (chmn. ops. coun.), Delta Nu Alpha. Roman Catholic.

CARR, JESSE METTEAU, III, lawyer, engineering executive; b. Roanoke, Va., Sept. 3, 1952; s. Jesse Metteau Jr. and Martha Ann (Niday) C.; m. Amelia Kathryn Tynes, May 6, 1983 (div. Oct. 1985). BSEE, La. State U., 1974, JD, 1977. Registered profl. engr., Tex.; bar: La. 1978, Tex. 1979. Elec. engr. Southeastern Chem., Reserve, La., 1974-77; control systems engr. J.E. Sirrine Co., Houston, 1977-83; pvt. practice cons. Houston, 1983-84; control systems engr. Jacobs Engring., Houston, 1985-86; mng. gen. ptnr. Carr/Sperry Design, Houston, 1985-87, Tech. Ventures Group, Houston, 1987—; v.p. Intellex Corp., Houston, 1986—, also bd. dirs.; mng. gen. ptnr. Tech. Ventures Group, Houston, 1987—; bd. dirs. Mimics Inc., Houston, East Tex. Co., Washington, Ga. Cub Scout leader Boy Scouts Am., Houston, 1987—. Mem. ABA, La. Bar Assn., Tex. Bar Assn., IEEE, Instrument Soc. Am., Tau Beta Pi, Omicron Delta Kappa, Eta Kappa Nu. Republican. Methodist.

CARR, M(ARY) L(OIS), mental health professional; b. Quincy, Fla., May 13, 1948; d. J.T. and Clara Drucilla (Sexton) C.; m. Daniel J. Groothuis, Sept. 16, 1967 (div. Sept. 1977); children: Gregory David, Kristen Lea; m. Edward J. Scholl III, Oct. 24, 1987; 1 stepdaughter, Stacie Allen. AA, Pensacola (Fla.) Jr. Coll., 1969; BS, U. South Fla., 1981; MS, Nova U., 1988. Developer, dir. resource ctr. Girls Club of Sarasota, Fla., 1981-83, assoc. dir., 1983, exec. dir., 1983-86, also bd. dirs.; bd. dirs. Girls Club of Sarasota County Found., 1983-86, Sarasota County Youth Related Services Assn., 1983-85; creator, co-developer various Girls Club Programs; lectr. in field. Writer children's advice column, Kila, 1982; co-writer TV program Girls In Motion, 1982-83; writer local TV pub. service announcement for Girls Club of Sarasota County, Coast Update, 1985; Contbr. articles on children to popular mags. Active Sarasota County Drug Task Force, 1983; asst. dir. Community Health Edn. Council, 1982-83, Women's Support Group, Venice, Fla., 1982, Sarasota County Driving Under the Influence Panel, 1987; evaluator, program com. mem. Big Brothers, Big Sisters of Sarasota County, 1985; co-founder Venice chpt. Students Against Drunk Driving , 1984, fundraiser, 1986, advisor, 1987; mem. steering com. Resource co-chairperson project graduation Venice High Sch.; co-chmn. adv. bd. Make-A-Wish Found., Sarasota, 1988. Mem. Phi Kappa Phi. Republican. Roman Catholic. Home: 1729 Lakeside Dr Venice FL 34293

CARR, SHIRLEY G. E., trade union president; b. Niagara Falls, Ontario, Can.; d. John James Boutilier and Mary Geraldine (Wilson) Little; m. W. Bruce Carr, May 29, 1948. Student, Stamford Collegiate Vocat. Inst., Niagara Falls, Ont., Can., Niagara Coll. Applied Arts and Tech., Niagara Falls, Ont., Can.; LLD (hon.), Brock U., St. Catharines, Ont., 1981; D of Civil Laws (hon.), Arcadia U., Wolfville, N.S., Can., 1984; LLD (hon.), McMaster U., 1988; PhD (hon.), U. Western Ont., Can. Various positions at local, provincial and nat. levels Can. Union Pub. Employees, Niagara Falls, 1960-74; exec. v.p. Can. Labour Congress, Ottawa, Ont., 1974-84, sec.-treas., 1984-86, pres., 1986—. Chairperson bd. govs. Labour Coll. Can., Ottawa, 1986—; co-chairperson Can. Labour Market and Productivity Ctr., Ottawa; coun. mem. Amnesty Internat.; candidate New Dem. Party, Niagara Falls, 1971. Decorated office Order of Can., 1980; recipient Centennial medal Govt. Can., 1980; hon. fellow Ryerson Poly. Inst., Toronto, Ont., Can., 1987. Mem. Internat. Confedn. Free Trade Unions (v.p.), Commonwealth Trade Union Council (v.p., chairperson 1986—). Office: Can Labour Congress, 2841 Riverside Dr, Ottawa, ON Canada K1V 8X7

CARR, THOMAS JEFFERSON, JR., gaming executive; b. Memphis, Aug. 19, 1942; s. Thomas J. Sr. and Emily K. (Draper) C.; m. Jean N. Simpkins, May 10, 1984; children: Jeff, Tricia, Ashley. BBA, Memphis State U., 1967. C.P.A., Tenn. Asst. controller Holiday Corp., Memphis, 1965-81; v.p., controller Harrah's, Reno, 1981-85, v.p. devel., 1986, sr. v.p. devel., 1987—; mem. adv. bd. Arkwright Ins. Mem. AICPA, Tenn. C.P.A. Soc. Office: Harrahs 300 E 2nd St Reno NV 89520

CARR, WILLIAM ANTHONY, retail company executive; b. N.Y.C., Aug. 24, 1938; s. William and Catherine (Coyne) C.; m. Eileen Patricia O'Connor, Apr. 8, 1961; children: Jeanne, Coleen, William K. BS, Fordham U., 1960. CPA, N.Y. Sr. auditor Arthur Andersen & Co., N.Y.C., 1960-65; asst. to controller Mercantile Stores Co. Inc., N.Y.C., 1965-72, asst. controller, 1972-77, controller, asst. sec., 1977—. Served to capt. U.S. Army, 1960-61. Mem. N.Y. State Soc. CPA's. Roman Catholic. Office: Mercantile Stores Co Inc 128 W 38th St New York NY 10001

CARRAHER, DANIEL PETER, accountant; b. Hawthorne, Nev., Dec. 27, 1953; s. Martin William and Pernina (Cadwell) C.; student U. Nev., 1971-72; BS in Bus. Adminstrn., U. San Francisco, 1975; postgrad. Golden Gate U., 1978—; m. Pamela Marie Peterson, Mar. 22, 1975; children: Tiffin, Kyle, Alexandria. CPA, Calif. Adminstrv. asst. U. San Francisco, 1974-75; staff acct. Alexander Grant & Co., San Francisco, 1975-78; ptnr. Carraher & Carraher, Ltd., CPAs, Reno, 1978-81; pvt. practice, 1981-82; chief fin. officer Oiltech, Reno, 1982-85, sec., 1984-85; chief fin. officer Mushroom King, Inc., Santa Rosa, Calif., 1985-86; controller Marine Terminals Corp., San Francisco, 1986—; sec. Majestic Ins. Co., San Francisco, 1987—; instr. Western Nev. Community Coll., Reno, 1978. Treas., bd. dirs. John Mark Christian Sch., Santa Rosa, 1986—; mem. Healdsburg Community Band, 1985—. Recipient The Wall St. Jour. award, U. San Francisco, 1975. Mem. Ins. Accts. and Systems Assn., Calif. Soc. CPAs. Republican. Avocations: trumpet, chess, golf. Home: 36 Grande Paseo San Rafael CA 94903 Office: Marine Terminals Corp 289 Steuart St San Francisco CA 94105

CARRELL, TERRY EUGENE, heat exchanger company executive; b. Monmouth, Ill., July 1, 1938; s. Roy Edwin and Caroline Hilma (Fillman) C.; AB, Monmouth Coll., 1961; MBA, Calif. State U., Los Angeles, 1967; D of Bus. Adminstrn., U. So. Calif., 1970; m. Bonnie Lee Clements, July 11, 1964; children—Philip Edwin, Andrew David. Prin. engr. reconnaissance and communications N.Am. Aviation, 1963-67; mgr. avionics analysis and techs. B-1 div. Rockwell Internat., 1967-73, dir. engring. Morse Controls div., 1973-74; gen. mgr. Morse Controls div. Incom Internat. Inc., 1974-78, pres. indsl. div. Morse Controls, 1978-80, pres. Morse Controls, 1980-82; pres. Heim Bearings, 1982-85;gen. mgr. Stewart-Warner Corp., 1985-88; pres. Stewart-Warner South Wind Corp., 1988—; cons.; lectr. U. So. Calif., 1967-70. Mem. Hudson (Ohio) Econ. Devel. Com., 1979-82; bd. dirs., council commr. Boy Scouts Am., 1980-85, mem. nat. council, 1980-85; mem. service rev. panel United Way of Summit County, 1980. NDEA fellow, 1961-63. Mem. Hudson C. of C. (trustee 1976-78), Boating Industry Assn. (chmn. steering task force 1974-85), Am. Boat and Yacht Council (dir. 1980-88). Contbr. articles to profl. jours. Patentee in field. Club: Columbia. Lodge: Kiwanis.

CARRICO, HAROLD STEWART, II, real estate financier; b. Louisville, Jan. 19, 1950; s. Harold Stewart and Elizabeth Joyce (King) C.; m. Kathleen Gwen Tobin, Jan 8, 1972; children: Jacqueline Marie, H. Stewart III. BS in Zoology, Tex. Tech U., 1973, MS in Acctg., 1975. CPA, Tex. Staff acct. Arthur Young & Co., Dallas, 1975-78, sr. acct., 1979-80; sr. acct. Alford Meroney & Co., Dallas, 1978-79; asst. contr. Computer Lang. Rsch., Carrollton, Tex., 1980-84; chief fin. officer, v.p. Stephen S. McGinnis & Assocs., Dallas, 1984-86; chief fin. officer Charter House Group Holdings Ltd., Dallas, 1986—. Bd. dirs. Plano (Tex.) YMCA, 1987; bd. dirs., St. Mark Sch., Plano, 1982-88. Mem. Am. Inst. CPA's, Tex. Soc. CPA's. Roman Catholic.

CARRIER, GLASS BOWLING, JR., banker; b. Lexington, Ky., Sept. 2, 1931; s. Glass Bowling and Margaret (Sexton) C.; m. Dorothy Kay Olsen, June 15, 1957; children: Catherine Anne, David Bowling. B.S. in Bus, U.N.C., 1953. Supr. Allstate Ins. Co., Charlotte, N.C., 1956-61; div. supr. Allstate Ins. Co., St. Petersburg, Fla., 1961-62; with First Union Nat. Bank, Charlotte, 1962—; exec. v.p. investment div. head First Union Nat. Bank, 1968—. Bd. dirs. N.C. Municipal Council. Served with USNR, 1953-56. Mem. Bank Capital Markets Assn. (bd. dirs.), Am. Bankers Assn. (exec. com. investment div.). Presbyterian (elder). Home: 3300 Shillington Pl Charlotte NC 28210 Office: 1st Union Nat Bank NC First Union Pla Charlotte NC 28288

CARRIGG, JAMES A., utility company executive; b. 1933. Student, Union Coll., 1951-53; AAS in Electrical Engring. Tech., Broome Community Coll. Safety cadet N.Y. State Electric & Gas Corp., Ithaca, 1958, safety dir., 1958-61, personnel dir., 1961-63, supr. tng., 1963-64, local mgr., 1964-69, asst. to v.p., 1969-72, area mgr., 1972-73, gen. mgr., 1973-82; v.p. N.Y. Electric & Gas Corp., Binghamton, 1982-83, pres., dir., 1983-86, pres., chief operating officer, 1986-88, chmn., chief exec. officer, 1988—; bd. dirs. Security Mut. Life Ins. Co. N.Y., Endicott Trust Co., Home Mut. Ins., Co., Utilities Mut. Ins. Co.; pres. Empire State Electric Energy Research Corp. Bd. dirs. Found. of SUNY Binghamton, Broome County Community Charities, Inc.; bd. dirs. United Health Services Inc., N.Y. Bus. Devel. Corp.; adv. council Clarkson U. Sch. Mgmt. Served with U.S. Army 1954-55. Mem. Broome County C. of C. (former chmn.). Office: NY State Electric & Gas Corp 4500 Vestal Pkwy E Binghamton NY 13903

CARRIKER, RUSSELL LLOYD, real estate investment executive; b. Ord, Nebr., Dec. 29, 1932; s. Lloyd Franklin and Loye Goldie (Weber) C.; grad. in accounting Nat. Bus. Coll., Lincoln, Nebr., 1959; m. Jayne Elinor Wunderlich, Apr. 27, 1957; 1 son, Thomas Andrew. Engring. aide Nebr. Dept. Roads, Lincoln, 1951-57; dir. data processing Nat. Bus. Coll., Lincoln, 1959-61; co-founder, sch. dir. Automation Inst., Kansas City, Mo., 1961-69; sch. dir. Control Data Corp., Chgo., 1970-71, Manpower Bus. Tng. Inst., Manpower, Inc., St. Louis, 1971-73; with ITT Ednl. Services, Inc., 1973-84; sch. dir. Hammel-Actual Coll., Akron, Ohio, 1973-74, ITT Tech. Inst., Boston, 1974-75, Taylor Bus. Inst., L.I., N.Y., 1976-79, ITT Tech. Inst., Chelsea, Mass., 1980-84; dist. mgr. Wilfred Am. Ednl. Corp., 1984-87; now in pvt. practice real estate investments; past pres. Systems & Procedures Assn., Kansas City, Mo.; past pres. Mass. Pvt. Career Schs. Home: 26 Pine Ridge Rd North Reading MA 01864

CARROLL, ADORNA OCCHIALINI, real estate executive; b. New Britain, Conn., Aug. 24, 1952; d. Antonio and Mary Ida (Reney) Occhialini; m. Christoper P. Buchas, Sept. 7, 1974 (div. Nov. 1982); 1 child, Jenna Rebecca; m. John Francis Carroll, Oct. 15, 1983; children: Jordan Ashley, Sean William. BA in Philosophy, Cen. Conn. State U., 1974; cert., Grad. Realtors Inst., 1989. Lic. real estate broker, Conn. Dir. therapeutic recreation program Ridgeview Rest Home, Cromwell, Conn., 1974, Meadows Convalescent Home, Manchester, Conn., 1975, Andrew House Health Care, New Britain, 1976; owner, mgr. Liquor Locker, Newington, Conn., 1977-87; owner, broker A.O. Carroll & Co., Newington, 1985—; ptnr. Marco Realty & Devel. Co., Newington, 1978—. Mem. Nat. Assn. Realtors, Conn. Assn. Realtors (mem. polit. aciton com. 1988-89), Greater New Britain Bd. Realtors (sec. 1988, chmn. polit. affairs. 1988, pres. elect 1989, bd. realtors Greater New Brit., chairperson polit. affairs 1989, chairperson bd. programming 1989, mem. ednl. orientation com. 1989, mem. budget. com. 1989), Nat. Package Store Assn., Conn. Package Store Assn. (legis. lobbyist 1984-88, sgt.-at-arms 1983, 2d v.p. 1984, 1st v.p. 1985, pres. 1986-88, Disting. Svc. award 1985), Greater Hartford Package Store Assn. (pres. 1981-82), Newington C. of C. (bd. dirs. 1987, 88, 89, chmn. legis. 1988), New Britain C. of C. Home: 22 Hickory Hill Ln Newington CT 06111 Office: 976 W Main St New Britain CT 06053

CARROLL, ELIZABETH J., investment management consultant; b. Providence, Nov. 26, 1955; d. Robert Edward and Dorothy Mary (Desautels) Walker; m. Michael James Carroll, Feb. 12, 1978; children: Barton Joseph, Marina Jae. Student, U. R.I., 1976-77. Legal sec. Joseph B. Going, Esq., Newport, R.I., 1974-76; asst. adminstr. Forest Farm Health Care Ctr., Middletown, R.I., 1976-77; adminstrv. asst. Arboleda, Inc., Providence, 1977, treas., 1977-80; treas. ABANCO Mgmt. Corp., Newport, 1980, v.p., treas., 1980—; bus. mgr. 2d Story Theatre, Inc., Newport, 1978-84; cons. in field. Fundraiser Newport Co. Child & Family Svcs., 1982, various local charities. Named Career Woman of Yr., Bus. and Profl. Women of Newport Co., 1986. Mem. Newport Co. Bus. and Profl. Women (bd. dirs. 1984-87, treas. 1985-86). Democrat. Roman Catholic. Home: PO Box 537 Newport RI 02840

CARROLL, JAMES LAWRENCE, financial executive; b. Detroit, June 18, 1950; s. John W. and Virginia F. (Rozek) C.; m. Perry Bowen, Oct. 26, 1974; children: Christina, William. B.A. in Econs., Wayne State U., 1973, M.B.A. in Corp. Fin., 1976. Asst. v.p. Nat. Bank Detroit, 1974-81; v.p. Rotan Mosle, Inc., Houston, 1981-84; sr. v.p. Paine Webber, Inc., N.Y.C., 1985—; ptnr. St. Clair Properties, Inc., Grosse Pointe, Mich., 1987—. Named to All-Am. Research Team, Instl. Investor Mag., N. Y.C., 1983-88. Fellow Fin. Analyst Fed.; mem. Nat. Assn. Petroleum Investment Analysts, Inst. Chartered Fin. Analysts, N.Y. Soc. Security Analysts. Roman Catholic. Club: Middlesex (Darien, Conn.). Office: Paine Webber Inc 1285 Ave of the Americas New York NY 10019

CARROLL, JOHN B., financial executive; b. Oct. 3, 1935; m. Edith Dorothy Kovacs, Sept. 26, 1959; children: Theresa, Kevin, Bryan. BA, St. John's Coll., 1957. V.p. Chem. Bank, N.Y.C., 1973-84; v.p. investment mgmt. GTE Corp., Stamford, Conn., 1984—; exec. v.p. Evaluation Assn., Westport, Conn., 1981-84; mem. N.Y. Stock Exchange Mgrs. Com., 1988. Chmn. bd. dirs. Jessie Smith Noyes Found., 1982—. Office: GTE Corp One Stamford Forum Stamford CT 06904

CARROLL, LOREN KENNETH, oil company executive; b. Modesto, Calif., Aug. 31, 1943; s. Ray Eugene and Lores Ina (Turney) C.; m. Marilyn Hobbs, Nov. 27, 1965; children: Stacey, Dawn, Brian. BS, Calif. State U., 1965. CPA, Calif. With Arthur Andersen & Co., Costa Mesa, Calif., 1969-80, ptnr., 1980-84; mng. ptnr. Arthur Andersen & Co., Tucson, Ariz., 1984; sr. v.p., chief fin. officer Smith Internat., Inc., Newport Beach, Calif., 1984-88, exec. v.p., chief fin. officer, 1988—. Treas., chmn. fin. com., bd. dirs. Orange County council Girl Scouts U.S.; mem. urban devel. com. City of Yorba Linda. Served to 1st lt. U.S. Army, 1966-69. Mem. Am. Inst. CPA's, Calif. Soc. CPA's, Nat. Assn. Accts. (past pres., Man of Yr. 1979), Fin. Execs. Inst. Republican. Office: Smith Internat Inc 4075 Cassia Ln Yorba Linda CA 92686

CARROLL, MARY COLVERT, director non-profit organization; b. Milw., June 5, 1940; d. Frederick Rohlfing and Helen (McCall) Colvert; m. Andrew David Carroll; children: Sherri L. Oberg, Andrew DAvid Carroll III. BA mgna cum laude, U. Miami, Fla., 1966. Chmn. bd. Friends Independence Nat. Hist. Park, Phila., 1978-81; bd. dirs. Urban Affairs Partnership, Phila., 1979—; pres., founder Friends Conversation Hall, Phila., 1982-83; bd. dirs. Internat. House, Phila., 1982—; chmn., founder Nat. Parks Mid-Atlantic Council, Phila., 1982-87; vice chmn. bd. Nat. Parks and Conservation Assn., Washington, 1982-88; bd. dirs. Phila. First Econ. Devel. Coalition, 1983—; chmn., founder Hospitality Phil. Style, 1984-86, World Affairs Council, Phila., 1984—; bd. trustees Bryn Mawr (Pa.) Presby. Ch., 1984—; bd. dirs. Independence Hall assn., Phila., 1984—, Phila. Hist. Preservation Corp., 1986—; vice chmn. bd. Fort Mifflin on Del., Inc., Phila., 1986—; trustee William Penn Found., Phila., 1987—; co-dir. Pa 250 U. Pa., Phila., 1988; chmn. Nat. Park Trust, Washington, 1988; bd. dirs. Phila. Suburban Water Co., Bryn Mawr, 1979—, Phila. Suburban Corp., Bryn Mawr, 1981—. Active Century IV Com., Phila., 1980-82, Regional Adv. Com. Nat. Parks, 1982-84, Amb. Corps, Phila., 1984—. Recipient Civic Environ. award Found for Architecture, 1983, Conservation Service award U.S. Dept. Interior, 1978. Mem. Nat. Assn. Corporate Dirs., Merion Cricket Club, Faculty Club U. Pa. Republican. Presbyterian. Home: 603 Winsford Rd Bryn Mawr PA 19010

CARROLL, PATRICIA WHITEHEAD, computer company executive; b. Tallahassee, Fla., Oct. 20, 1954; d. Albert and Lucinda (Brown) Whitehead; m. Napoleon A. Carroll, May 28, 1979 (div. 1985). BS cum laude in Psychology, Bethune-Cookman Coll., 1977. Records supr. State Farm Ins. Co., Winter Haven, Fla., 1977-79; ins. agt. Pat Carroll Ins. Agy., Orlando, Fla., 1979-82; dir. mktg. Systems Support Corp., Washington, 1982-85, v.p., 1985—. Recipient Youth Day Appreciation award City of Titusville, 1976, Millionaire Club award State Farm Ins. Co., 1981, Million Dollar Round Table award State Farm Ins. Co., 1979, others. Mem. Nat. Assn. Female Execs., Am. Mgmt. Assn., Delta Sigma Theta. Democrat. Avocations: reading, coin and stamp collecting, outdoor sports. Office: Systems Support Corp 1140 Connecticut Ave NW Ste 1202 Washington DC 20036

CARROLL, PAULA MARIE, security company executive; b. Fresno, Calif., July 17, 1933; d. Paul Edward Mikkelsen and Helen Marie (Anderson) Mack; m. Herman S. Carroll Jr., April 25, 1954. V.p., co-owner Cen. Valley Alarm Co., Inc., Merced, Calif., 1963—; pres., co-owner Cen. Valley Alarm Co., Inc., Merced, 1988—. Author: Life Wish, 1986. Mem. Hospice of Merced and Mariposa Counties, Calif., 1979; pres., founder Consumers for Med. Quality Inc., Merced, 1981; chair Ombudsman, Merced, 1982-85. Recipient Celebrating Women award Merced County, 1987, Pres.'s award Calif. Trial Lawyers Assn., 1987; named Woman Distinction Soroptimist Internat., 1986; Consumers for Med. Quality grantee Calif. Trial Lawyers Assn., 1987. Mem. Western Burglar and Fire Alarm Assn., Soc. Law and Medicine, Hastings Ctr. Inst. of Soc., NAFE, Am. Biol. Inst. Rsch. Assn., Internat. Platform Assn., Beta Sigma Phi. Home: 3271 Alder Ave Merced CA 95340 Office: Cen Valley Alarm Co Inc 620 W 14th St Merced CA 95340

CARROLL, PHILIP JOSEPH, oil company executive; b. New Orleans, Sept. 24, 1937; s. Philip Joseph and Rosemary Agnes (McEntee) C.; m. Charlene Marie Phillips, Jan. 3, 1959; children: Philip III, Kenneth, Bruce. BS in Physics, Loyola U., New Orleans, 1958; MS in Physics, Tulane U., 1961. Petroleum engr. Shell Oil Co., New Orleans, Los Angeles, N.Y.C. and Midland, Tex., 1961-73, regional engr., mgr. so. exploration and production, 1974-75; div. mgr. prodn., western exploration and production Shell Oil Co., Houston, 1975-78, gen. mgr. prodn., western ops., 1978-79, gen. mgr. plans and integration, 1979, v.p. pub. affairs, 1979-85, sr. v.p. adminstrn., 1986-88, exec. v.p. adminstrn., 1988—; mng. dir. Shell Internat. Gas, London, Eng., 1985-86; dir. energy conservation pres.' exec. interchange program Dept. Commerce, Washington, 1973-74. Bd. trustees Houston chpt. Am. Leadership Forum, 1987-88, House Mus. Fine Arts, Houston, 1980-84, 88—, Found. for Bus., Politics and Econs., 1987—; bd. dirs. Central Houston, 1989—, Houston Grand Opera, 1980-83, Better Bus. Bur. Met. Houston, 1987—, Harris County Children's Protective Svcs. Found., Houston, 1987—, Bus. ArtsFund, 1988— , Tex. Med. Ctr., 1988—. 2d lt. U.S. Army, 1959. Mem. Am. Petroleum Inst. (bd. dirs. 1989—), 25 Yr. Club Petroleum Industry, Champions Golf Club, Houston, Tchefuncta Country Club, Covington, La. Office: Shell Oil Co 1 Shell Pla PO Box 2463 Houston TX 77252

CARROLL, THOMAS JOSEPH, accountant, investment services executive; b. Hartford, Conn., Aug. 30, 1941; s. Patrick Joseph and Mary Theresa (Jennings) C.; m. Gail Ruth Paterno, Feb. 5, 1963 (div. 1974); children: Thomas Jr., Cathy. BBA, U. Notre Dame, 1963. CPA, N.Y., Ga. Acct. Peat, Marwick, Mitchell and Co., Hartford, Conn., 1965-68; mgr. Peat, Marwick, Mitchell and Co., Schenectady, N.Y., 1969-72; ptnr. Peat, Marwick, Main and Co., N.Y.C., 1973; ptnr., nat. dir. investment services Peat, Marwick, Mitchell and Co., N.Y.C., 1975—. Contbr. articles to profl. jours. Participant Outward Bound Program, Denver, Colo., 1984-88. Served to lt. USN, 1963-65. Mem. Am. Inst. CPA's (stock brokerage acctg. com., 1984—), N.Y. State Soc. CPA's (cooperation investment bankers, stock exchanges com. 1985—), Securities Industry Assn. (internal audit div., treas. exec. com. 1981—), No-Load Mut. Fund Assn. (assoc.). Republican. Roman Catholic. Clubs: N.Y. Yacht, University (N.Y.). Home: 60 Sutton Pl S New York NY 10022 Office: Peat Marwick Main & Co 345 Park Ave New York NY 10154

CARROLL, WALLACE EDWARD, instruments and equipment manufacturing company executive; b. Taunton, Mass., Nov. 4, 1907; s. Patrick J. and Katherine (Feely) C.; m. Lelia Holden, Nov. 7, 1936; children: Wallace E. Jr., Denis H., Barry J., Lelia K.H. PhB, Boston Coll., 1928, LLD, 1957; postgrad., MIT, 1929; postgrad. in bus., Harvard U., 1930, NYU, 1933; postgrad., Northwestern U., 1936; LLD, DePaul U., 1966; HHD (hon.), St. Xavier Coll., 1986. With acctg. dept. N.Y. Telephone Co., 1930-33; indsl. engr. Reed & Barton, 1933-34; with sales dept. Fed. Products, 1934-40; chmn., bd. dirs. Wacker Sales, from 1940, Size Control Co., from 1941, Walsh Press & Die Co., from 1945; chmn., bd. dirs. Am. Gage & Machine Co., Elgin, Ill., 1948—, now also pres.; chmn., bd. dirs. Simpson Electric Co., from 1950; vice chmn. bd. dirs., chief exec. officer Katy Industries, Inc., Elgin, 1970-88, vice chmn., chmn. exec. com., 1988—; vice chmn., dir. Ludlow Typograph Co.; vice chmn. bd. dirs. M-K-T R.R., Dallas; treas., dir. G.M. Diehl Machine Co., Champion Pneumatic Machinery Co., 1957—; bd. dirs. numerous cos. including Binks Mfg. Co., Franklin Park, Ill., OEA, Inc., Denver, CRL, Inc., Denver, British LaBour Pump Co., London, Ruttonsha-Simpson Pvt. Ltd., Bombay, Bush Universal, Inc., N.Y.C., Mercantile Nat. Bank Chgo.; dir. metal-working equipment div. BDSA, Dept. Commerce, Washington, 1957; with U.S. Trade Mission to India, 1958-59, UAR, 1960, Ireland and Portugal, 1966, U.S. Council Commerce and Industry, 1973, U.S. Bus. Trade Mission Korea, 1974, Trade and Investment Mission Rep. China, 1975. Chmn. fed. agys. Community Fund drive, 1959; mem. citizen's com. Loyola U.; bd. dirs. Cath. Charities, 1962, Chgo. Boys Club, Chgo. Girls Club, Am. Irish Found., Gregorian U. Found., N.Y.; past bd. regents Boston Coll.; trustee Christine and Alfred Sonntag Found. Cancer Research, U. Chgo. Cancer Rsch. Found.; past trustee DePaul U. Served with U.S. Army Air Corps, 1929, with N.G., 1930-33. Recipient Civic award Loyola

U., 1965, Heinze/Winzeler award, 1982; named hon. mem. Chippewa Indian Tribe. Mem. Tool and Die Inst. (pres. 1952-53), U.S. C. of C. (econ. policy com. 1959-62), Nat. Machine Tool Builders Assn. (pres. 1962-63). Roman Catholic. Clubs: Chgo. Athletic, Chgo., Mid-Am., MIT, Harvard, Harvard Bus., Boston Coll., NYU (Chgo.); Burning Tree (Bethesda, Md.); Exmoor Country (Highland Park, Ill.); East Chop Beach, Martha's Vineyard, Edgartown Yacht (Mass.); Everglades, Bath and Tennis (Palm Beach, Fla.); Univ. (N.Y.C.). Office: Katy Industries Inc 853 Dundee Ave Elgin IL 60120

CARSON, EDWARD MANSFIELD, banker; b. Tucson, Nov. 6, 1929; s. Ernest Lee and Earline M. (Mansfield) C.; m. Nadine Anne Severns, Dec. 13, 1952; children: Dawn, Tod. BSBA, Ariz. State U., 1951; grad. in banking, Rutgers U., 1963. With First Interstate Bank of Ariz., Phoenix, 1951-85, exec. v.p., 1969-72, chief adminstrv. officer, 1972-75, vice chmn. bd., 1975-77, pres., chief exec. officer, 1977-85, also bd. dirs.; pres. First Interstate Bancorp, Los Angeles, 1985—, also bd. dirs.; bd. dirs. Inspiration Resources Corp., Ramada Inns, Inc., First Interstate Bank of Oreg. Bd. fellows Am. Grad. Sch. Internat. Mgmt. Recipient Service award Ariz. State U. Alumni Assn., 1968; named to Ariz. State U. Alumni Assn. Hall of Fame, 1977. Mem. Assn. Res. City Bankers, Assn. Bank Holding Cos. (bd. dirs.). Clubs: Paradise Valley Country, Thunderbirds, Los Angeles Country, Calif.; Phoenix Country. Office: 1st Interstate Bancorp 707 Wilshire Blvd Los Angeles CA 90017 *

CARSON, GINGER ROBERTS, financial consultant; b. Austin, Minn., Nov. 30, 1957; d. Sherbun Lee and Joyce Ellen (Lightly) R.; m. Randy Lynn Hanson, July 21, 1978 (div. July 1984); m. John M. Carson, Apr. 19, 1985. BS in Acctg., Mankato State U., 1979, postgrad., 1985—. Internal auditor Bretts Dept. Store, Mankato, Minn., 1977-78; staff acct. Morken & Andring, Mankato, 1978-79; tax acct. Morem Gearty, Austin, 1980-82; dir. bus. affairs Gerard of Minn. and Iowa, Austin, 1979-83, cons., 1983; fin. cons. Merrill Lynch Pierce Fenner & Smith, Rochester, Minn., 1983—; cons. Kessner Electric, Austin, 1982-83. Mem. Talented Women in Math Mentors Program; vol. Olmsted Couty United Way. Recipient Triple A Woman award Roch BPW, 1986. Mem. Nat. Assn. of Security Dealers, Bus. and Prof. Women of Austin and Rochester (Young Career Woman award 1981), Rochester C. of C. (diplomat). Mem. Democratic Farm Labor Party. Baptist. Lodge: Zonta. Avocations: skiing, raquetball, reading. Office: Merrill Lynch Ste 300 Marquette Bank Bldg Rochester MN 55904

CARSON, JAMES TYSON, automotive executive; b. Phila., Apr. 12, 1925; s. John Baker and Frances (Tyson) C.; m. Paula L. Hunter, Dec. 21, 1961 (div. 1965); 1 child, Paula J.; m. Patricia A.S. Noble, Nov. 30, 1984. BA in Econs., U. Pa., 1950. Sales corr. E.I. duPont Corp., Wilmington, Del., 1950-52; service instr. Ford Motor Co., Chester, Pa., 1952-56; founder Carson-Pettit, Inc., Devon, Pa., 1956, sec.-treas., 1956-84, pres., 1984—; Mem. tech. com. Automotive Service Excellence, 1973, Mercedes-Benz Nat. Dealer Council, 1972-73; chmn. Peugeot Nat. Dealer Council, 1977-78, vice-chmn. 1986. 1st v.p., Voyage House, Phila., 1980-85. Served with U.S. Army, 1943, ETO. Mem. Am. Internat. Automobile Dealers Assn. (bd. dirs. 1986). Home: Tyca Farm Newtown Square PA 19073

CARSON, KENT (LOVETT CARSON), paper company executive; b. White Plains, N.Y., June 24, 1930; s. Oswald B. and Frances (Buente) C.; m. Margaret J. Stroker, May 11, 1963; children: Ann Frances, Michael K. B.A., Williams Coll., 1952. Salesman Kimberly-Clark Corp., N.Y.C., 1954-59; with Andrews/Nelson/Whitehead div. Boise Cascade Corp., Long Island City, N.Y., 1959-78; mgr. book pub. Andrews/Nelson/Whitehead div. Boise Cascade Corp., 1969-74, div. gen. mgr., 1974-78; exec. v.p., gen. mgr. Ris Paper Co., Inc., N.Y.C., 1978-84; pres. Ris Paper Co., Inc., 1984—. Mem. Greenburgh Republican Town Com., N.Y. Served with arty. U.S. Army, 1952-54. Mem. The Navigators (pres. 1963-65), Paper Mchts. Assn. N.Y. (pres.), Paper Club N.Y. Presbyterian. Clubs: Williams, Orleans Yacht, Westchester Country. Home: 16 Old Farm Ln Hartsdale NY 10530 Office: Ris Paper Co Inc 45-11 33rd St Long Island City NY 11101

CARSON, WILLIAM CHARLES, sales and marketing manager; b. Palmyra, N.J., Nov. 9, 1924; s. William and Carrie (Forderer) C.; m. Jean Gingerich, Apr. 1, 1950; children: William Scott, Colleen Jean, Caroline Grace. BA, Gettysburg Coll., 1949. Sales rep. Nat. Sugar Refinery Co., Phila., 1949-60; account exec. Metal Edge Industries, Barrington, N.J., 1960-70, sales mgr., 1970-80; gen. mgr. Metal Edge div. Lydall, Inc., Hartford, Conn., 1980-83; mktg. and sales mgr. Mefco, North Wales, Pa., 1983—. Campaign chmn. United Way, Berkeley Heights, N.J., 1966, bd. dirs. Burlington County, N.J., 1985—, sec., bd. dirs. Moorestown, N.J., 1984—. Served to cpl. U.S. Army, 1943-45, ETO. Decorated Bronze Star with oak leaf cluster, Purple Heart; recipient Presdl. citation, U.S. Army. Mem. Am. Mgmt. Assn. (seminar chmn. 1972), Sales & Mktg. Execs. So. Jersey (v.p., bd. dirs. 1974-78), Am. Def. Preparedness Assn. (cons. 1984—, bd. dirs.), Def. Fire Protection Assn. (bd. advisors 1987—), Phi Kappa Psi (sec.). Republican. Home: 125 Somer Ct S Moorestown NJ 08057 Office: Mefco 337 W Walnut St North Wales PA 19454

CARSTEN, JACK CRAIG, semiconductor company executive; b. Cin., Aug. 24, 1941; s. John A. and Edith L. C.; m. Mary Ellis Jones, June 22, 1963; children: Scott, Elizabeth, Amy. B.S., Duke U., 1963. Mktg. mgr. Tex. Instruments, Dallas, Houston, 1965-71; integrated circuits gen. mgr. Tex. Instruments, Houston, 1971-75; v.p. sales and mktg. Intel Corp., Santa Clara, Calif., 1975-79, v.p., microcomputer gen. mgr., 1979-82, sr. v.p., components gen. mgr., 1982-87; gen. ptnr. U.S. Venture Ptnrs., Menlo Park, Calif., 1988—; dir. Cimatel, Inc., Paris. Contbr. articles to profl.jours. Mem. Semiconductor Industry Assn., Am. Mgmt. Assn.

CARSWELL, ROBERT DEAN, lawyer; b. Glasgow, Scotland, July 23, 1940; came to U.S., 1965; s. Robert and Helen Mary (Cowan) C.; m. Elizabeth Ann Turner, Sept. 7, 1967 (div.); children: Robbie, Ian, Lindsay. MA, U. Glasgow, 1962, LLB, 1965; postgrad., Cornell U., 1965-66. Assoc. Winthrop, Stimson, Putnam & Roberts, N.Y.C., 1966; asst. McGrigor, Donald & Co., Glasgow and Edinburgh, Scotland, 1967-70, ptnr., 1971-79; v.p., internat. counsel Gearhart Industries, Inc., Ft. Worth, 1980-85, v.p., gen. counsel, 1985—; bd. dirs. Gearhart Australia, Ltd., Brisbane. Contbr. articles to profl. jours. and chpts. to books. Fulbright Exch. fellow, 1965-66. Mem. ABA, Internat. Bar Assn., Law Soc. Scotland, Union Internat. des Avocats, Am. Corp. Counsel Assn., Tex. Soaring Assn. Office: Gearhart Industries Inc PO Box 1936 Fort Worth TX 76101

CARTEE, THOMAS EDWARD, JR., banker; b. Largo, Fla., Jan. 30, 1960; s. Thomas Edward and JoAnne (Todd) C.; m. Kathryn Armecia Stokes, Aug. 6, 1983; 1 child, Thomas Edward III. AB in Econs., Davidson Coll., 1982; MBA, U. N.C., 1984. Assoc. account rep. First Nat. Bank Chgo., 1984-85; credit analyst, account rep. Swiss Bank Corp., Chgo., 1985, asst. treas., head credit dept., 1986-87, asst. v.p., account officer, 1988—; assoc. Robert Morris Assocs., Chgo., 1986—. Treas. Clifton Place Condominium Assn., Chgo., 1985-86; mem. Lake Bluff Adv. Com., 1988—. Mem. U. N.C. Alumni Assn. Republican. Office: Swiss Bank Corp 3 1st National Pla Ste 2100 Chicago IL 60602

CARTER, ANDREW LAWRENCE, manufacturing company executive; b. Chgo., Dec. 20, 1944; s. David F. and G. Ann (Lenhart) C.; m. Karen S. Anderson, Aug. 28, 1968; children: Andrew L., Gregory T. BS in Indsl. Mgmt., Purdue U., 1968, MS in Indsl. Mgmt., 1969. Budget analyst Gruman Aerospace Co., Bethpage, N.Y., 1969-73; fin. analyst Assn. Fin. North Am., Dallas, 1973-77; with Cooper Industries, Inc., Dallas, 1977—; mgr. fin. planning and cost Pneutronics div., Grand Haven, Mich., 1977-80; controller Cooper Electronics div., Nashua, N.H., 1980-81; asst. controller Kirsch div., Sturgis, Mich., 1981-85; dir. fin. Apex div., Dayton, Ohio, 1985—. Mem. Assn. Prodn. Inventory Control Soc. Office: Cooper Industries Inc Apex Div 762 W Stewart St Dayton OH 45408

CARTER, CHARLES J., forest products company executive; b. June 4, 1922; married; 2 children. B.Sc. in Civil Enging. with honors, Queen's U., 1947. With Gt. Lakes Forest Products Ltd. (formerly Gt. Lakes Paper Co., Ltd.), Thunder Bay, Ont., Can., 1947—, successively design engr., asst. plant engr., chief engr., then v.p. engring., 1964-71; pres. Gt. Lakes Forest Products Ltd. (formerly Gt. Lakes Paper Co. Ltd.), Thunder Bay, Ont., Can., 1971—, chmn. bd., pres., 1978-86, chmn. and chief exec. officer, 1986—, also dir.; mem. Thunder Bay adv. bd. Royal Trust Corp. Can.; dir. Ormiston Mining & Smelting Co. Ltd., Forintek Can. Corp.; chmn. Ont. Forestry Council; chmn. bd. Ponderay Newsprint Co., Lake Superior Constrn. Inc. Mem., past mem. several hosp. bds. Fellow Lakehead U., 1987. Mem. Forest Enging. Research Inst. Can. (dir.), Can. Pulp and Paper Assn. (exec. bd.), Ont. Forest Industries Assn. (dir.), Assn. Profl. Engrs. Ont., Tech. Assn. Pulp and Paper Industry, Order St. John. Club: Ft. William Gyro. Lodges: Masons; Shriners. Office: Gt Lakes Forest Products Ltd, PO Box 430, Thunder Bay, ON Canada P7C 4W3

CARTER, GEORGE KENT, oil company executive; b. Toledo, Ohio, Nov. 5, 1935; s. Fred S. and Charlotte J. (Horen) C.; m. Louise Monica Mali, July 13, 1958; children—Caitlin, Seth. A.B., Stanford U., 1957, M.B.A., 1961. Various fin. positions Standard Oil of Calif., San Francisco, 1962-74, asst. treas., 1974, asst. comptroller, 1974-81; comptroller Chevron U.S.A., Inc., San Francisco, 1981-83, v.p. fin., 1986—; comptroller Chevron Corp. (formerly Standard Oil of Calif.), San Francisco, 1983-86. Mem. Stanford Bus. Sch. Assn., Fin. Execs. Inst., Stanford U. Alumni Assn. Clubs: Orinda Country (Calif.), Bankers. Office: Chevron USA Inc 575 Market St San Francisco CA 94105

CARTER, JOHN BERNARD, insurance company executive; b. Phila., Sept. 21, 1934; s. John Mein and Elise Hoban (Alexander) C.; m. Hope Elliot, Apr. 12, 1958; children: Hope, John, Helen, Charles, Henry, George, Charlotte, Ann, Katherine, Elizabeth, Richard. BA, Yale U., 1956; MBA, Harvard U., 1961; postgrad., Am. Coll., Bryn Mawr, Pa., 1967; LLD (hon.), Morehouse Coll., 1986. With Equitable Life Assurance Soc. U.S., 1960—, chief ins. officer, 1981-82, pres., chief operating officer, 1982-83, pres., chief exec. officer, 1983—; dir. Colgate-Palmolive Corp., Westinghouse Electric Corp. Trustee Marymount Coll., Tarrytown, N.Y., 1984—, Morehouse Coll., Atlanta, 1980—, Am. Coll., Bryn Mawr, Pa., chmn.; bd. dirs. Cath. Hist. Soc., Council for Fin. Aid to Edn., 1985—, N.Y.C. Partnership Inc., 1988—, Inner City Scholarship Fund, Dole Found., Found. for Children with Learning Disabilities, Com. Econ. Devel.; commr. Statue of Liberty Ellis Island Found., United Way of Tri State. Served with USN, 1956-59. Mem. Nat. Alliance Bus. (bd. dirs., chmn. bd.), Assocs. Harvard Bus. Sch. (bd. dirs.). Office: Equitable Life Assurance Soc US 787 7th Ave New York NY 10019

CARTER, LARRY ALEXANDER, securities brokerage firm executive; b. Joplin, Mo., Nov. 9, 1940; s. Samuel E. and Laura L. (House) C.; m. Jan. 24, 1962; children: Larry Vince, Donna Diane, Mitchell Alexander. Student, Cerritos Coll., Long Beach State Coll., UCLA, Calif. Orange Coast Coll. Police officer South Gate (Calif.) Police Dept., 1963-65; Long Beach (Calif.) police dept. narcotics expert 1965-75, pvt. practice constrn., 1975-76; v.p., office mgr. Diversified Securities, Inc., El Toro, Calif., 1976—; speaker in field. Recipient Calif. Commn. on Police Officer Standards and Tng. Advanced cert., 1974; named to Multimillion Dollar Club, 1982-88; named Top Ten Mem. Diversified Securities, Inc., 1976-88. Mem. Saddleback C. of C., Lake Arrowhead C. of C., Crestline C. of C., Narcotics Officers Assn. Republican. Baptist. Lodge: Rotary. Home: 396 Hartman Circle PO Box 3271 Crestline CA 92325 Office: 24028 Lake Dr Ste C PO Box 3271 Crestline CA 92325

CARTER, MANSON HILDRETH, clothing company executive; b. Newton, Mass., Nov. 12, 1923; s. Horace Ronald and Anne Margaret (Noble) C.; m. Barbara Hecker Replogle, Oct. 20, 1951; children: Deborah Carter Roman, Stephen William. BA, Colby Coll., 1949. Asst. product mgr. William Carter Co., Needham Heights, Mass., 1953-58, product mgr., 1958-62, clk., 1959-78, mgr. mdse., 1962-73, v.p., 1973-78, vice chmn., 1978-85, chmn., chief exec. officer, 1985—, also bd. dirs.; mem. nat. adv. com. for Flammable Fabrics Act Consumer Product Safety Commn., 1980-82; bd. dirs. Eliot Savs. Bank, Boston. Corporator New Eng. Deaconess Hosp., Boston, 1967—; mem. adv. bd. Greater Boston Salvation Army, 1981—; pres. Needham Cemetery Assn., Mass. Served with USN, 1943-46. Mem. Am. Apparel Mfrs. Assn. (bd. dirs. 1985—), Associated Industries Mass. (bd. dirs. 1986—). Republican. Methodist. Clubs: Brae Burn Country (West Newton, Mass.); Capitol Hill (Washington). Lodges: Masons (33 degree) (past master, past dist. dep.), Shriners. Home: 2 Buttercup Ln Dover MA 02030 Office: William Carter Co 963 Highland Ave Needham Heights MA 02194

CARTER, ORWIN, chemical executive; b. Geneseo, Ill., Aug. 22, 1942; s. O. Louis and Florence W.A. (Vogt) C.; m. Anita M. Ashdown, Aug. 20, 1966; children: Jeffrey L., Stephen S. BS, U. Iowa, 1964; MS, U. Ill., 1965, PhD, 1967; MBA, Rider Coll., 1975. Research analyst Rohm and Haas Co., Spring House, Pa., 1970-74; dir. prodn. devel. and regulatory affairs Micromedic Systems, Horsham, Pa., 1974-77; assoc. dir. immunodiagnostics Becton Dickinson Lab. Group, Rutherford, N.J., 1977-78; acting dir. Becton Dickinson Research Ctr., Triangle Park, N.C., 1978-79; v.p. div. planning Becton Dickinson Innumodiagnostics, Orangeburg, N.Y., 1979-80, v.p., gen. mgr., 1980-82; pres. Amersham Corp., Arlington Heights, Ill., 1982-86; chmn., pres., chief exec. officer IncStar Corp., Stillwater, Minn., 1986—. Served to capt., U.S. Army, 1967-70. Mem. Am. Chem. Soc., Am. Assn. Clin. Chemistry. Republican. Methodist. Office: Incstar Corp 1951 Northwestern Ave Stillwater MN 55082

CARTER, ROBERT EUGENE, JR., physician, oil company executive; b. Evansville, Ind., Sept. 29, 1932; s. Robert Eugene and Vera Lucille (Carnahan) C.; m. Kathi Lorene Griffin, Oct. 24, 1971; children: Kelley Jo, Christy Lynn. AB in Chemistry, U. Evansville, 1954; MD, Ind. U., 1957. Diplomate Am. Bd. Radiology. Chief of radiology Alliance (Ohio) City Hosp., 1976-88, also bd. trustees; pres. KLC Petroleum Co., Henderson, Ky., 1983—; pres. Alliance Radiology Assn., Inc., 1976-88. Capt. U.S. Army, 1961-63, Vietnam. Mem. AMA, Am. Bd. Radiology, Am. Coll. Radiology, Ky. Oil and Gas Assn. Republican. Lodge: Elks. Home: 9795 Gregory Rd Henderson KY 42420 Office: KLC Petroleum 9787 Gregory Rd Robards KY 42452

CARTER, ROBERT POWELL, III, financial executive; b. Balt., Sept. 30, 1957. BS in Acctg., U. Del., 1980. CPA, Pa., N.J. With tax dept. Price Waterhouse, Phila., 1979; audit sr. Coopers and Lybrand, Phila., 1980-83; chief fin. officer ORFA Corp. Am., Cherry Hill, N.J., 1984—. Mem. AICPA, Pa. Inst. CPAs, Inst. Mgmt. Accts., Beta Alpha Psi. Home: 45 Westminster Dr Voorhees NJ 08043 Office: ORFA Corp of America 51 Haddenfield Rd Cherry Hill NJ 08002

CARTER, THOMAS SMITH, JR., railroad executive; b. Dallas, June 6, 1921; s. Thomas S. and Mattie (Dowell) C.; m. Janet R. Hostetter, July 3, 1946; children: Diane Carter Petersen, Susan Jean, Charles T., Carol Ruth. B.S. in Civil Engring., So. Meth. U., 1944. Registered profl. engr., Mo., Kans., Okla., Tex., La., Ark. Various positions Mo. Kans. Tex. R.R., 1941-44, 46-54, chief engr., 1954-61, v.p. ops., 1961-66; v.p. Kansas City So. Ry. Co., La. and Ark. Ry. Co., 1966—; pres. Kansas City So. Ry. Co., 1973-86, also bd. dirs., chmn. bd., 1981—; pres. La. and Ark. Ry. Co., 1974-86, also bd. dirs., chmn. bd., 1981—, chief exec. officer, 1981—; dir. Kansas City So. Industries. Served with C.E. AUS, 1944-46. Fellow ASCE; mem. Am. Ry. Engring. Assn., Assn. Am. Railroads (dir. 1978—), Nat. Soc. Profl. Engrs. Clubs: Chgo, Kansas City, Shreveport. Home: 9319 W 92d Terr Overland Park KS 66212 Office: Kansas City So Ry 114 W 11th St Kansas City MO 64105

CARTER, WILLIAM ALLEN, accounting firm executive; b. Kokomo, Ind., Jan. 19, 1932; s. Virgil Glen and Edna Waneta (Edwards) C.; m. Carolyn Ann Miller, June 13, 1954; children: David, Matthew, Timothy, Joseph. BSBA, Ball State U., 1954. CPA, Ind., Calif. With Ernst & Whinney, 1953—; ptnr. in charge tax service Ernst & Whinney, Indpls., 1966-78; mng. ptnr. Indpls. office Ernst & Whinney, 1978-84; mng. ptnr Ind. practice Ernst & Whinney, Indpls., 1984-86; vice-chmn., mng. ptnr. Western region Ernst & Whinney, Los Angeles, 1986—. Bd. dirs. Regional Inst. So. Calif., Los Angeles, Music Ctr. Oper. Com.; chmn. fin. com. Los Angeles 2000 Com.; gen. campaign chmn. L.A. Music Ctr., 1988-89, bd. govs., mem. exec. com.; mem. Commn. for Downtown, Inc., 1984-86, treas., dir., mem. exec. com. Served with U.S. Army, 1954-56. Named to Hall of Fame, Sch. Bus., Ball State U., 1980, named Alumnus of Yr., 1983; named Vol. of Yr., Fund Raising Council Ind., 1984. Mem. AICPAs (governing council 1970-71, 73-76, mem. tax div. 1973-75), Ind. Soc. CPAs (pres. 1970-71), Calif. C. of C. (bd. dirs.), Rotary, Regency Club, Lincoln Club, Calif. Club., Beta Gamma Sigma, Beta Gamma Psi. Republican. Methodist. Home: 1750 Lombardy Rd Pasadena CA 91106 Office: Ernst & Whinney 515 S Flower St Ste 2700 Los Angeles CA 90071

CARTHEN, BILLY BURTON, real estate developer; b. Portsmouth, Va., Aug. 5, 1950; s. Roy Burton and Angilene (Gray) C.; m. Kim Diane Reasner, July 3, 1955; 1 child, Ryan Burton. AA, Valencia Community Coll., 1976; BS, Fla. So. Coll., 1979. Retail mgr. Federated Dept. Stores, Orlando, Fla., 1971-75; cons. Orange County Govt., Orlando, 1975-76; pres. Century 21/Carthen Realty Inc., Winter Park, Fla., 1977—; owner Carthen Ins. Agy., Winter Park, 1983—, Satellite Commn., Winter Park, 1983—; prin. Century 21 Securities Corp., Winter Park, 1983—; pres. Century Equity and Mortgage Inc., Winter Park, 1985—; pres., bd. dirs. Seminole Woods Assn., Winter Park, 1985—. Corp. sponsor Easter Seals, Winter Park, 1981—. Served with USN, 1968-71. Recipient Cert. of Excellence Nat. Stat. Research, 1981. Mem. Orlando Area Bd. of Realtors, Fla. Assn. Realtors, Nat. Assn. Realtors, Profl. Ins. Agts., Cen. Fla. Brokers Council (chmn. multiple listing service 1986—), Century 21 Investment Soc., Nat. Rifle Assn. (life). Republican. Baptist. Club: Greater Orlando Bowling (pres. 1981-85). Lodge: Kiwanis (v.p. Winter Park chpt. 1985). Office: Century 21/Carthen Realty Inc 2471 Aloma Ave Winter Park FL 32792

CARTIER, BRIAN EVANS, association executive; b. Providence, Apr. 12, 1950; s. Clarence Joseph and Mary Anna (Evans) C.; B.A., R.I. Coll., 1972; M.Ed., Springfield (Mass.) Coll., 1973. Exec. dir. Arthritis Found. Conn., Hartford, 1976-78, dep. exec. dir. N.Y. chpt., N.Y.C., 1979; exec. dir. Found. for Chiropractic Edn. and Research, Arlington, Va., 1979—. Cert. Am. Mgmt. Assn. Mem. Am. Soc. Assn. Execs, Greater Washington Soc. Assn. Execs., Moose. Democrat. Roman Catholic. Home: 7727 Whiterim Terr Potomac MD 20854 Office: Found for Chiropractic Edn and Research 1701 Clarendon Blvd Arlington VA 22209

CARTLAND, JOHN EVERETT, III, investment executive; b. Paterson, N.J., Dec. 11, 1944; s. John Everett Jr. and Klazina Dirk (Kuiken) C.; m. Lucy Anne Campbell, July 12, 1969; children: Kathryn Allerton, Elizabeth Fairgreives. BA, Bowdoin Coll., 1966; JD, Georgetown U., 1969; MBA, Harvard U., 1972. Assoc. Robinson & Cole, Hartford, Conn., 1972-74; atty Aetna Life & Casualty Co., Hartford, 1974-77, investment officer, 1977-80, asst. v.p., 1980-87, mng. dir., v.p., 1987—; dir. Hartford Capital Corp., Local Initiatives Mgmt. Assets Corp., N.Y.C. Trustee Grace Blass Trust, Hartford. Club: Hartford Golf. Office: Aetna Life & Casualty Co CityPlace Hartford CT 06156

CARTLEDGE, RAYMOND EUGENE, paper company executive; b. Pensacola, Fla., June 12, 1929; s. Raymond H. and Meddie (Brookins) C.; m. Gale Perry, June 30, 1962; children: John R., Perri Ann, Susan R. BS, U. Ala., 1952; postgrad., Harvard Bus. Sch., 1970. With Procter & Gamble Co., 1955-56; with Union Camp Corp., Wayne, N.J., 1956-71, 81—, v.p., gen. mgr. container div., 1981-82, exec. v.p., 1982-84, pres., chief operating officer, 1983-86, chmn., pres., chief exec. officer, 1986—, also bd. dirs.; pres., chief exec. officer Clevepak Corp., White Plains, N.Y., 1971-80. Served with U.S. Army, 1952-55. Office: Union Camp Corp 1600 Valley Rd Wayne NJ 07470

CARTWRIGHT, MICHAEL WAYNE, banker; b. Chattanooga, Feb. 1, 1962; s. Wayne Hulen and Cecile (Nichols) C.; m. Cynthia Mae Frazier, Mar. 2, 1985. Student, U. Tenn., Chattanooga, 1982-83; A in Bus. Sci. and Acctg., McKenzie Coll., 1984. Sales rep. Kennedy Wholesale, Chattanooga, 1981-82; pvt. practice fin. cons. Chattanooga, 1982-84; fin. cons. IDS Am. Express, Chattanooga, 1984-88, J.J.B. Hilliard, W.L. Lyons, Inc., Chattanooga, 1987-88; co-owner R&R Painting Contractors, 1988—; personal fin. officer First Fed. Savs. and Loan, 1988—; grad. asst. Dale Carnegie, Chattanooga, 1982. Named Rookie of Yr. IDS Fin. Services Dist., 1985. Mem. John Birch Soc. Republican. Baptist. Lodge: Kiwanis. Home: 105 Melrose Dr Chattanooga TN 37421

CARUSILLO, BRUCE EDWARD, accountant; b. Waterbury, Conn., Dec. 28, 1955; s. Elmer Thomas and Gloria Rose (Perugini) C.; m. Lori Ann Longo, Oct. 29, 1977. BS in Acctg. with honors, U. Conn., 1977; MS in Taxation with honors, U. Hartford, 1986. CPA, Conn. Sr. acct. Clairol, Inc., Stamford, Conn., 1977-79; supr. Peat, Marwick, Mitchell & Co., Hartford, Conn., 1979-83; supr./mgmt. Coopers & Lybrand, Hartford, Conn., 1983-86; treas. Wolcott (Conn.) Devel. Corp., 1986—; pres., chief exec. officer Bruce E. Carusillo, CPA, PC, Woodbury, Conn., 1986—. Com. mem. Waterbury Rep. Town Com., 1977-78. Mem. Am. Inst. CPA's, Conn. Soc. CPA's Nat. Assn. Accts., Post Coll. Tax Inst., Greater Waterbury C. of C., Delta Sigma Pi (life mem.). Republican. Roman Catholic. Lodge: Lions (Woodbury) (fin. chmn. 1985—). Office: Bruce E Carusillo CPA PC Cornerstone Profl Park Woodbury CT 06798

CARUSO, DAVID JOHN, securities company executive; b. Bay Shore, N.Y., June 6, 1959; s. John Anthony and Stella Barbara (Frasca) C.; m. Yasmin Antoinette Kaker, Mar. 24, 1985. BS, NYU, 1981, Diploma in Fin. Planning, 1986. Fin. svcs. mgr. Automatic Data Processing, N.Y.C., 1979-84; mgr. fin. Brokers Trust Clearing Corp., N.Y.C., 1984-85; supervising sr. examiner NYSE, N.Y.C., 1985-87; v.p. Oppenheimer & Co., N.Y.C., 1987—; pres. Personal Money Mgmt., East Stroudsburg, Pa., 1986-87. Mem. Nat. Assn. Accts., Internat. Assn. for Fin. Planning. Home and Office: 196 Penn Estates East Stroudsburg PA 18301

CARUSO, FRANK LAWRENCE, plant pathologist; b. Hackensack, N.J., Nov. 18, 1949; s. Victor Ernest and Ruby Ann (Akre) C.; m. Barbara Ann Steller, Dec. 27, 1975; children: Emily Weber, Nicholas Akre. BA, Gettysburg Coll., 1971; MS, U. Mass., 1974; PhD, U. Ky., 1978. Asst. prof. U. Maine, Orono, 1979-85; extension plant pathologist Cranberry Expt. Sta., East Wareham, Mass., 1985—. Contbr. articles to profl. jours. Mem. Am. Phytopathological Soc., Can. Phytopathological Soc., Am. Soc. Horticultural Sci., Sigma Xi. Home: 17 Freedom Rd Forestdale MA 02644 Office: Cranberry Exptl Sta PO Box 569 East Wareham MA 02538

CARUSO, NICHOLAS DOMINIC, fraud analyst; b. Wilmington, Del., Feb. 2, 1957; s. Nicholas Anthony and Philomena Marie (Pelaia) C. BA in Polit. Sci., U. Del., 1985; MA in Liberal Arts, Widener U., 1988. Sr. analyst Bank of N.Y., Newark, 1985—. With U.S. Navy, 1979-83. Mem. Nat. Intelligence Study Ctr., Internat. Assn. of Stategic Studies, Acad. of Polit. Sci. Democrat. Roman Catholic. Home: 1908 W 4th St Wilmington DE 19805 Office: Bank of NY 700 White Clay Ctr Newark DE 19714

CARUSO, RICHARD ERNEST, financial company executive; b. Atlantic City, May 12, 1943; s. Cono and Louise (Piroli) C.; m. Sally Feitig, Aug. 2, 1972; children: Jonathan, Peter. BS, Susquehanna U., 1965; MBA, Bucknell U., 1966. Auditor Price Waterhouse and Co., Phila., 1966-69; exec. v.p. LFC Fin. Corp, Radnor, Pa., 1969—, also bd. dirs.; bd. dirs. 202 Data Systems, Wayne, Pa., First Sterling Bank, Devon, Pa. Trustee Susquehanna U., Selinsgrove, Pa., 1983—, Baum Sch. Art, Allentown, Pa., 1986—. Mem. AICPA, Pa. Assn. CPAs, N.J. Inst. CPA, Delta Mu Delta. Roman Catholic. Office: LFC Fin Corp 3 Radnor Ctr Ste 400 Radnor PA 19087

CARUTHERS, JANE RHODES, corporation executive; b. Shreveport, La., Apr. 10, 1940; d. William Cecil and Catherine (Cobb) Rhodes; (div. Jan. 1979); m. John D. Caruthers Jr., Apr. 28, 1979; children: Thomas E. White IV, Morgan Elizabeth White. BS cum laude, Centenary Coll., 1962. Legal sec. John D. Caruthers, Jr. Atty., Shreveport, La., 1961-67; legal, oil and gas sec. John D. Caruthers, Jr. Atty., Shreveport, 1961-71, office mgr., 1971-81; sec., tres. Caruthers Operating Co., Inc., Shreveport, 1962—, Camelot Investment Corp., Shreveport, 1977—; v.p., sec. River Rose Boat Co., Inc., Shreveport, 1984-86; sec., tres. Caruthers Producing Co., Inc., Shreveport, 1982—, asst. to pres., 1982—. Sponsor Shreveport Summer Music Festival, 1985, 86. Mem. NAFE. Democrat. Methodist. Office: 1325 American Tower Shreveport LA 71101

CARVER, CHARLES LEONARD, banker; b. San Antonio, Aug. 9, 1956; s. Thurman DeLeon and Patricia Josephine (Vorce) C.; m. Susan Kay Leach, Mar. 17, 1984. BA, U. N. Colo., 1978. Utility asst. Mid States Bank, Denver, 1980-82; v.p. First Nat. Bank of Lakewood (Colo.), 1982-85; sr. v.p. Chaves Indsl. Bank, Denver, 1985; v.p. Met. Indsl. Bank, Denver, 1985-88; mgr. personal banking, dir. bus. devel. United Bank of Monaco, Denver, 1988—; pres. Capital Quest of Colo., Arvada, 1985—. V.p. Colfax on the Hill, Denver, 1987-88. Mem. Am. Inst. Mortgage Brokers, Colo. Assn. Mortgage Brokers (bd. dirs. 1988), Am. Soc. Profl. Appraisers, Nat. Assn. Real Estate Appraisers, Nat. Assn. Rev. Appraisers and Mortgage Underwriters. Republican. Presbyterian. Lodge: Kiwanis (Denver) (pres. 1988). Office: United Bank Monaco 1001 S Monaco Pkwy Denver CO 80224

CARVER, DENNIS WAYNE, lawyer, construction company executive; b. Caldwell, Idaho, Jan. 26, 1956; s. William Hoyt and Mary Frances (Mayhew) C. BA, BS in Constrn. Mgmt., Wash. State U., 1979; JD, Gonzaga U., 1983. Bar: Wash. 1983. Project engr. J.A. Jones Constrn. Svcs. Co., Richland, Wash., 1980-81, sr. engr., 1983-85, legal coord., 1985-87; assoc. Layman, Loft, Smythe & Arpin, Spokane, Wash., 1981-83; contract compliance mgr. J.A. Jones Constrn. Co., Charlotte, N.C., 1987—; trustee Wash., Idaho amd Mont. Carpenters' Pension Plan, 1985-87, Ea. Wash. Carpenters' Health and Welfare Plan, Spokane, 1985-87. Loaned exec. United Way, Richland, 1985; bd. dirs. Tri-Cities Residential Svs., Richland, 1986-87; corp. co-chmn. United Way, Charlotte, 1987. Mem. ABA, Wash. State Bar Assn., Nat. Contract Mgmt. Assn., Nat. Mgmt. Assn., Internat. Found. Employee Benefit Plans, Delta Sigma Phi (chpt. supr. 1980-83, pres. alumni control bd. 1983-85). Home: 13106 Indian Hills Ln Charlotte NC 28217 Office: JA Jones Constrn Co 6060 St Albans Charlotte NC 28287

CARVER, MARTIN GREGORY, manufacturing company executive; b. Davenport, Iowa, May 10, 1948; s. Roy James and Lucille Avis (Young) C. B.A. in Math, U. Iowa, 1970; M.B.A., U. Ind., 1972. Asst. treas. Consol. Foods Corp. now Sara Lee, 1975-79; regional v.p. heavy duty parts, then vice chmn. Bandag, Inc., Muscatine, 1979-81; chief exec. officer Bandag, Inc. (retreaded tires mfrs.), 1982—, chmn. bd., 1981. Chmn. bd. dirs. Augustana Coll., 1986—; bd. of visitors U. Iowa Sch. of Bus. Named Chief Exec. Officer of Yr., rubber and plastics industry, Fin. World, 1986, Chief Exec. Officer of Decade, 1989. Mem. Nat. Assn. Mfrs. (dir. 1987—). Clubs: 33, Chicago. Lodge: Rotary. Office: Bandag Inc Bandag Ctr Muscatine IA 52761

CARY, CORNELIUS ADAMS, marketing retail company executive; b. Balt., Dec. 2, 1949; s. William Kendrick and Georgia Mae (Shackleford) C.; m. Georgia Carol Powell, Mar. 28, 1968; children: Stephanie Lynn, Mathew Adam. Student, Brandywine Coll., 1967-79, Jones Coll., 1986—. Dist. mgr. Southland Corp., Dallas, 1967-76; zone mgr. Fast Fare Inc., Raleigh, N.C., 1976-83; exec. recruiter Coleman Lew & Assocs., Charlotte, N.C., 1983-85; sr. v.p. ops. Charter Mktg. Co., Jacksonville, Fla., 1985—. Served with USCGR, 1967-73. Mem. S.C. Convenience Store Assn. (pres. 1981-83, bd. dirs. 1979-81). Republican. Episcopalian. Club: Ponte Vedra (Jacksonville); Seminole (Jacksonville). Office: Charter Mktg Co 1 Charter Pla Box 4726 Jacksonville FL 32232-0036

CARY, ELTON MIKELL, banking and insurance company executive; b. Savannah, Ga., Jan. 28, 1929; s. Theron Elton Mikell and Nellie (Johnson) Walker; m. Ilene Joyce Cary; children: Mikell, James. BS, U. Ga., 1950; postgrad., Emory U., 1950-51. Ins. agt., chmn. Adae & Hooper, Miami Beach, Fla., 1950—; chmn. Gen. Ins. Co., Miami Beach, 1973—, Cary Marine, 1967-74, Wometco Enterprises Inc. and Wometco Cable TV Inc., Miami, 1983-84; dir., exec. com. Fin. Fed. Savs., Miami, 1983; chmn. bd. Fin. Fed. Savs & Loan Assn., 1986—. Trustee Papenicolaou Cancer Research Inst., Miami, 1975-79. Mem. Fla. Assn. Domestic Ins. Cos. (vice-chmn. 1978—). Democrat. Methodist. Home: 1 Palm Bay Towers Miami FL 33138 Office: Gen Ins Co Inc 1815 Purdy Ave Miami Beach FL 33139

CASAMENTO, CHARLES JOSEPH, pharmaceutical industry executive; b. Hoboken, N.J., June 8, 1945; s. Charles Vincent and Mary (Brignola) C.; m. Evelyn Ann Kenez, June 8, 1968 (div. 1983); children: Christopher Charles, Suzanne Marie; m. Doris Ann Mason, May 25, 1985. BS in Pharmacy, Fordham U., 1968; MBA in Mktg., Iona Coll., 1971. Registered pharmacist, N.J., N.Y. Mgr. Sandoz Pharm. Div., East Hanover, N.J., 1970-71, fin. planner, 1972-73, product coordinator, 1973-74, mgr. new product planning, 1974-75, mgr. new product planning and licensing, 1975-77; mgr. product devel. Hoffmann-La Roche, Nutley, N.J., 1977-79; dir. new products and acquisitions Johnson & Johnson, New Brunswick, N.J., 1979-83; v.p. bus. devel. Am. Critical Care div. Am. Hosp. Supply, Waukegan, Ill., 1983-86; sr. v.p., gen. mgr. Genzyme Corp., Boston, 1986—; lectr. in field. Campaign mgr. Rep. Com., Veron, N.J., 1976; coach Little League, Upper Saddle River, 1978-79, Little League, Basking Ridge, 1980-82, local Soccer League, Upper SAddle River, 1978-79; pres. Ch. Parrish Council, 1979. Mem. Licensing Exec. Soc., Am. Pharm. Assn., Comml. Devel. Assn., Assn. Corp. Growth, Cambridge Racquet Club. Episcopalian. Office: Genzyme Corp 75 Kneeland St Boston MA 02111

CASE, DOUGLAS MANNING, lawyer; b. Cleve., Jan. 3, 1947; s. Manning Eugene and Ernestine (Bryan) C.; m. Marilyn Cooper, Aug. 23, 1969. BA, U. Pa., 1969; JD, MBA, Columbia U., 1973. Bar: N.Y. 1974, N.J. 1975, Calif. 1980. Assoc. Brown & Wood, N.Y.C., 1973-77; corp. counsel PepsiCo Inc., Purchase, N.Y. and Irvine, Calif., 1977-83, Nabisco Brands Inc., N.Y.C., East Hanover, N.J. and London, 1983—. Chmn. Olde Colonial Dist.; active Morris-Sussex Area Council Boy Scouts Am., 1986-88; sec., trustee Marble Scholarship Com., N.Y.C., 1983-88. Mem. ABA, N.Y. State Bar Assn. Clubs: Morris County Golf (Convent Station, N.J.); Columbia Bus. Sch. (N.Y.C.) (pres. and bd. dirs. 1974-79). Office: Internat Nabisco Brands Ltd, 26 Mount Row, Mayfair, London W1Y 5DA, England

CASE, HADLEY, oil company executive; b. N.Y.C., Mar. 28, 1909; s. Walter Summerhayes and Mary Soule (Hadley) C.; m. Julie Marguerite Ill, June 8, 1935 (dec. Mar. 1975); children: Mary C. Durham, Julie Anne, Rosalie C. Clark, Deborah Joan; m. Elizabeth M. McCabe, Nov. 8, 1975. Student, Kent (Conn.) Sch., 1924-29, Antioch Coll., 1929-33. Geol. field work Australia, 1933-34, Tex., 1935-36; with geol. dept. Case, Pomeroy & Co., Inc., 1936-39, v.p., 1939-41, pres., chief exec. officer, dir., 1941-83, chmn. bd., chief exec. officer, 1983—; pres. chief exec. officer Felmont Oil Corp., 1952-72; chmn. bd., chief exec. officer Felmont Oil Corp. (merger Felmont and Homestake Mining Co.), 1972-84; dir. Homestake Mining Co., 1984—, Brown Bros. Harriman Trust Co. Fla., 1986—; bd. dirs. N.W. Airlines, Inc., 1957-78, Copper Range Co., 1966-77, Nashua Corp., 1965-81, Numac Oil & Gas Ltd., 1963-88; trustee Antioch U., 1987—. Trustee Kent Sch., 1959-75, Brewster Acad., 1956-63, Boys' and Girls' Camps, Inc., Boston, 1971-76; trustee Hosp. St. Barnabas, Newark, 1942-59, pres. bd. trustees, 1949-52; bd. dirs. Greenwich Boys Club Assn., 1957-73, hon. mem., 1974—; trustee Naples (Fla.) Community Hosp., 1985—; dir. of The Conservancy, Naples, 1985—; chancellor Kent Sch., 1982—, trustee, 1986—. Mem. Am. Inst. Mining and Metall. Engrs., Am. Petroleum Inst., Ind. Petroleum Assn. Am. (past v.p., dir.). Office: Case Pomeroy & Co Inc 529 Fifth Ave New York NY 10017

CASE, PAUL WATSON, JR., cable television company executive; b. Elmira, N.Y., Dec. 4, 1949; s. Paul Watson and Josephine Pharr (Pollock) C.; m. Laura Lee Moseley, Dec. 12, 1972; 1 child, Brian M. BA, U. Colo., 1971. Cert. computer programming Inst. Cert. Computer Profls., data processing Inst. Cert. Computer Profls. Programmer analyst Boulder (Colo.) Daily Camera, 1968-73; v.p. Mr. Steak Inc., Denver, 73-83, United Cable TV Corp., Denver, 1983—. Mem. Assn. Computer Machinery, Data Processing Mgmt. Assn. (cert.), Cable Data User Com. (chmn. 1986—). Home: 6561 N Pike Circle Larkspur CO 80118 Office: United Cable TV Corp 4700 S Syracuse Pkwy Denver CO 80237

CASE, WELDON WOOD, telephone company executive; b. Hudson, Ohio, Feb. 22, 1921; s. Harry Nelson and Alice (Wood) C.; m. Beatrice Kuhn, Jan. 3, 1942; children: Thomas W., William R. Student, Case Western Res. U., 1939-40, Ohio Wesleyan U., 1940-41. With Western Res. Telephone, Hudson, 1934-56; with Elyria Telephone Co., Ohio, 1956-60; pres. Mid-Continent Telephone Co., Hudson, 1960-83; chmn. Alltel Corp. formerly Mid-Continent Telephone Corp., Hudson, 1983—. Served to 2d lt. U.S. Army, 1942-46; ETO. Mem. U.S. Ind. Telephone Assn. (bd. dirs., past pres., Disting. Service medallion 1973), Ohio Ind. Telephone Assn. (past pres.). Republican. Congregationalist. Clubs: Royal Palm (Boca Raton, Fla.); Country (Pepper Pike, Ohio). Home: 1200 S Ocean Blvd Apt 17H Boca Raton FL 33432 Office: Alltel Corp 100 Executive Pkwy Hudson OH 44236

CASEBOLT, VICTOR ALAN, paper company executive; b. Spokane, Jan. 2, 1935; s. Victor Study and Elizabeth Marie (Sheffels) C.; m. Jo Elaine Beeson, Aug. 25, 1956; children: Victor Study, Mark Alan, Bryan Joseph, Elizabeth Virginia. A.B. in Econs, Stanford U., 1956; M.B.A., Harvard U., 1958. Sales and mktg. mgmt. positions Gen. Electric Co., 1958-66; mng. dir. De La Rue Bull Machines Ltd., London, 1966-67; dir. gen. adjoint Cie Bull-Gen. Electric, Paris, 1967-69; mgr. info. systems sales ops. Gen. Electric Co., Phoenix, 1969-70; gen. mgr. utility and process automation dept. Gen. Electric Co., Lynn, Mass., 1972-75; v.p. Tampa (Fla.) ops. Honeywell Inc., 1970-72; pres., chief operating officer, dir. Storage Tech. Corp., Louisville, Colo., 1975-77; gen. mgr. Internat. Container div. Internat. Paper Co., 1977-79; gen. mgr. Folding Carton & Label div. (Internat. Paper Co.), 1979-80; v.p., group exec., Splty. Packaging Group Internat. Paper Co., 1980-81, v.p., group exec. Indsl. Packaging Group,, 1981-85, sr. v.p. paperboard and packaging, 1985-86, sr. v.p. Kraft paper, board and packaging, 1986—; Chmn. Tampa Metro chpt. Nat. Alliance Businessmen, 1971-72; bd. dirs. Fourdrinier Kraft Bd. Group, Am. Paper Inst. Bd. dirs. Greater Tampa C. of C., 1971-72; chmn. troop com. Boy Scouts Am., 1980-83. Served with AUS, 1958. Episcopalian. Clubs: Harvard of N.Y, Masons. Office: Internat Paper Co 2 Manhattanville Rd Purchase NY 10577

CASEL, MARY LYNN, real estate broker; b. Carthage, N.Y., Jan. 16, 1943; d. Floyd Albert and Mary Frances (Schack) Neuroth; m. Ronald Anthony Casel, Nov. 28, 1963 (div. Nov. 1977); children—Mark, Steven, Glen. Grad. Harper Method, Rochester, N.Y., 1961. Lic. real estate broker. Owner M. L. Salon, Rochester, N.Y., 1962-72; specialty tchrs.-aide Broward County, Ft. Lauderdale, Fla., 1973-77; office mgr. Broward County Voter Registration, Margate, Fla., 1977-82; real estate salesperson Pelican Bay, Daytona Beach, Fla., 1982-84, broker, 1984-86, broker, sales mgr., 1986— owner C & F Shakemasters, Inc, 1989—. Mem. adv. bd. Democratic Club, Margate, Fla., 1977-82. Mem. Nat. Assn. Realtors, Fla. Home Builders Assn., Nat. Home Builders Assn., Daytona Beach Home Builders Assn., Daytona Beach Bd. Realtors, Ft. Lauderdale Bd. Realtors, Nat. Assn. Women in Constrn. (v.p. 1988—), Nat. Assn. Female Execs., Sales and Mktg. Council. Avocations: travel, dancing, theater, real estate investments. Democrat. Roman Catholic. Home: 825 Pelican Bay Dr Daytona Beach FL 32019 Office: Churl Corp 138 Seahawk Dr Daytona Beach FL 32019

CASEY, EDWARD PAUL, manufacturing company executive; b. Boston, Feb. 23, 1930; s. Edward J. and Virginia (Paul) C.; m. Patricia Pinkham, June 23, 1950; children: Patricia Estes Casey Shepherd,Tyler, Casey White, Jennifer Paul Casey Schwab, Sheila Pinkham Casey McManus, Virginia Louise. AB, Yale U., 1952; MBA, Harvard U., 1955. With Davidson Rubber Co., Dover, N.H., 1950-65; chief operating officer McCord Corp., 1965-78, dir., 1965-78; pres. McCord Corp., Detroit, 1965-78; chief operating officer Ex-Cell-O Corp., Troy, Mich., 1978-81; chief exec. officer, pres., dir. Ex-Cell-O Corp., Troy, 1981—; chmn. Ex-Cell-O Corp., Troy, Mich., 1983-86; vice chmn. Textron Inc., 1986-87; pres. E. Paul Casey Assocs., 1987—; mng. gen. ptnr. Metapoint Ptnrs., Salem, Mass.; dir. Mfrs. Nat. Corp., Norton Co., Worchester, Mass. Trustee Henry Ford Health Care Corp., Detroit, St. Mary's Hosp., West Palm Beach, Fla.; trustee Benetley Coll. Mem. Engring. Soc. Detroit, Soc. Automotive Engrs., Harvard Bus. Sch. Club So. Fla. Clubs: N.Y. Yacht (N.Y.C.), Yondotega (Detroit), Grosse Pointe; Country Club of Detroit (Grosse Pointe Farms, Mich.), Ea. Yacht (Marblehead, Mass.), Bath and Tennis (Palm Beach, Fla.), Wig and Pen (London, Eng.); Union (Boston); The Island Club (Hobe Sound, Fla.). Home: 330 S Beach Rd Hobe Sound FL 33455

CASEY, GEORGE EDWARD, JR., construction executive; b. Cohasset, Mass., July 15, 1946; s. George Edward and Dorothea Evelyn (Oliver) C.; m. Linda Lauraine Bail, Aug. 24, 1974; children: Peter, Matthew. BS in Environ. Engring., Rensselaer Poly. Inst., 1968; MBA, U. Pa., 1974. V.p. Charter Adv. Co., Jacksonville, Fla., 1974-76; owner, mgr. Casey & Co., Brunswick, Maine, 1976-79; project mgr. Toll Bros., Inc., Huntingdon Valley, Pa., 1979-81, v.p., 1981-84, sr. v.p., 1984—. Trustee Am. Boychoir Sch., Princeton, N.J., 1986-88. Lt. USN, 1968-72, Vietnam. Decorated Bronze Star. Mem. Urban Land Inst., Assn. MBA Execs., U.S. Yacht Racing Assn., Beta Gamma Sigma, Marlboro Yacht Club. Republican. Home: 3096 Comfort Rd New Hope PA 18938 Office: Toll Bros Inc 2425 Pennington Rd Pennington NJ 08534

CASEY, JANICE MARIE, financial analyst; b. Ames, Iowa, July 23, 1954; d. Donald J. and LaDeane (Olser) C. BA, Iowa State U., 1976; postgrad., Ariz. State U., 1984-86, Coll. Fin. Planning, 1987-89. Sales rep. Vet. Sales Ancom Norden, Smithe-Kline, Phoenix, 1976-77; sales mgr. D.V.M. Inc., Los Angeles, 1977-78; regional cons. mgr. Hospitex, San Jose, Calif., 1978-79; dir. mktg. Incentive Journeys, San Jose, 1979-83; leasing agt., gen. mgr., advt. dir. Granada Mktg. Mgmt., Phoenix, 1983-86; adminstrv. asst. fin. planner McCarthy & Assocs. Anchor Nat. Fin. Services, Inc., Phoenix, 1986-89; mgr. Sun State Fin. Svcs. Corp., Phoenix, 1989—. Vocal soloist Maria Goretti Cath. Ch., Scottsdale, Ariz., 1987—. Mem. Internat. Assn. Fin. Planners, Ariz. Vet. Med. Assn. (mem. bus. task force). Office: Sun State Fin Svcs Corp 4222 E Camelback Ste J-200 Phoenix AZ 85018

CASEY, JOHN PATRICK, public relations executive, political analyst; b. Syracuse, N.Y., July 19, 1928; s. Patrick Joseph and Ellen (Loftus) C.; m. Ursula Casey, Feb. 3, 1951 (div. 1975); children: Michael, Gretchen, John, Patrick; m. Mary Lou Butcher, May 2, 1982. BA, U. Toledo, 1958. Reporter Toledo Times, 1951-56; staff writer Detroit Free Press, 1951-56; spl. asst. to mayor City of Detroit, 1962-66; v.p. MG and Casey Communications Inc., Detroit, 1966-82; pres. Casey Communications Mgmt. Inc., Southfield, Mich., 1982—; polit. analyst Sta. WJR-Radio, Detroit, 1966—, Sta. WDIV-TV, Detroit, 1978-87. Contbr. articles on polit. topics; speaker on pub. relations and polit. analysis. Campaign mgr. Re-elect Mayor Cavanagh, Detroit, 1966; chmn. Commn. on Community Relations, City of Detroit, 1968-70. Served with U.S. Army, 1946-48. Recipient Page One awards Newspaper Guild, Detroit, 1957, 58; other awards for news coverage. Mem. Am. Assn. Polit. Cons., Pub. Relations Soc. Am. (pres. Detroit chpt. 1981-82, counselors acad., pub. affairs sect.), Adcraft Club of Detroit, Plum Hollow Golf Club, Detroit Press Club, Skyline Club, Arthur Page Soc. Democrat. Home: 4281 Echo Rd Bloomfield Hills MI 48013 Office: Casey Communications Mgmt Inc 17117 Nine Mile Rd Ste 700 Southfield MI 48075

CASEY, MICHAEL KIRKLAND, business executive, lawyer; b. Wheeling, W.Va., Jan. 24, 1940; s. Clyde Thomas and Joan Ferrell (McLure) C.; m. Mary Ann McCarten, Jan. 29, 1969; children—Michael Kirkland II, Mary Larkin, Colin McCarten. Student U. Notre Dame, 1957-58; B.S., W.Va. U., 1964; J.D., George Washington U., 1967. Bar: D.C. 1974, U.S. Dist. Ct. D.C., U.S. Ct. Appeals (D.C. cir.). Cons. to White House, Washington, 1977-81, handled overseas Presdl. missions in India, Western Europe, Brazil and Middle East; dir. White House Conf. on Small Bus., Washington, 1979-80; assoc. adminstr. for investment SBA, Washington, 1980-81; chmn. bd. MCW Internat. Ltd., Alexandria, Va., 1981—; nat. adminstr. fringe benefits program U.S. Conf. Mayors, 1984—. Advance man Kennedy for Pres. Com., 1968, spl. asst. Muskie for Pres. Com., 1972, asst. campaign mgr. Jackson for Pres. Com., 1976, campaign mgr. Carter-Mondale Reelection Com. in Mo. and Ill., 1980. Served with USMC, 1958-61, Mediterranean. Recipient Presdl. Cert., Pres. of U.S., 1977, 78, 79, plaque White House Commn. on Small Bus., 1980, Disting. Service award SBA, 1980. Mem. ABA, D.C. Bar Assn., Nat. Democratic Club, Nat. Conf. Democratic Mayors (founding). Roman Catholic. Club: Belle Haven Country (Alexandria). Home: 7105 Fort Hunt Rd Alexandria VA 22307 Office: MCW Internat Ltd 301 N Fairfax St Ste 110 Alexandria VA 22320

CASEY, PHILLIP EARL, steel company executive; b. Atlanta, Dec. 27, 1942; s. Frank Augustus and Nancy Drucilla (Hill) C.; m. Betty Zubiski Casey, Aug. 28, 1981. BBA in Fin., U. Ga., 1966; BA, MS in Internat. Mgmt., Am. Grad. Sch. Internat. Mgmt., 1971. Internal auditor Exxon, Esso Intern-Am., Coral Gables, Fla., 1971-74; asst. controller Exxon, Esso Brazil, Rio de Janeiro, 1974-80; chief fin. officer Oyx Typewriter div. Exxon, Lionville, Pa., 1980-81; asst. controller Exxon Office Systems Co., Stamford, Conn., 1981-85; exec. v.p., chief fin. officer Birmingham (Ala.) Steel Corp., 1985—; exec. v.p., sec., treas., bd. dirs. Birmingham Bolt Co., Birmingham Steel Corp., , Norfolk Steel, Salmon Bay Steel Corp., Barbary Coast Steel Corp. Served to 1st lt. U.S. Army, 1967-70, Vietnam. Republican. Baptist. Office: Birmingham Steel Corp PO Box 1208 Birmingham AL 35201

CASEY, THOMAS J., III, financial planner; b. Malden, Mass., Apr. 16, 1951; s. Thomas J. II and Muriel (Evans) C.; m. Linda Meyers, July 31, 1976; children: Ryan, Sharon. BSBA, Georgetown U., 1973; postgrad., Adelphi U., 1986. Advt. asst. Procter & Gamble Co., Cin., 1973-76; product mgr. Nestle Foods Corp., Purchase, N.Y., 1976-81, Cheesebrough-Pond's Inc., Greenwich, Conn., 1981-83; account exec. Majers Corp., Stamford, Conn., 1983-84; fin. planner Jefferson Fin. Svcs., Stamford, 1984-87; pres., chief fin. planner Salem Fin. Advisors Inc., Georgetown, Conn., 1988—. Vice chmn. ARC, Norwalk, 1987—; mem. exec. bd. Wilton (Conn.) Congl. Ch., 1988—. Mem. Inst. Cert. Fin. Planners (cert. fin. planners), Internat. Assn. Fin. Planning (v.p. 1985—), Registry Fin. Planning Practitioners, Weston Field Club, Roton Point Club. Republican. Mem. Christian Ch. Home: 215 Sturges Ridge Rd Wilton CT 06897 Office: The Salem Group 73 Redding Rd PO Box 628 Georgetown CT 06829

CASH, FRANCIS WINFORD, hotel and restaurant executive; b. Buena Vista, Va., Mar. 16, 1942; s. Winsford McKinley and Elsie E. (Yates) C.; m. Judith R. Robey, Dec. 27, 1962; children: Jeri Cash Colton, Lori, Robin, David, Kristine. B.S. in Acctg, Brigham Young U., Provo, Utah, 1965. C.P.A., D.C. With Arthur Andersen & Co. (C.P.A.s), Washington, 1965-74; v.p., corp. controller Marriott Corp., Washington, 1974-79; sr. v.p. corp. services Marriott Corp., exec. v.p. Roy Rogers, 1980-84, group v.p. food service mgmt. and Courtyard, 1983, exec. v.p., 1984; exec. v.p. Host Internat. and Lifecare divs., 1984, all Marriott restaurants, 1986-88; pres. Marriott Service Group, 1988—; dir. Sailors and Mchts. Bank and Trust. Pres. Hayfield Elem. Sch. PTA, Fairfax, Va., 1973-74; chmn. Washington area Boy Scouts Am. show, 1978; bd. advisers Sch. Accountancy, Brigham Young U., 1978-84; mem. Presdl. Commn. on White House fellowships, 1985. Recipient Service award Boy Scouts Am., 1978, Beta Alpha Psi Outstanding Alumnus award Brigham Young U., 1984. Mem. Fin. Execs. Inst. Mormon. Office: Marriott Corp 1 Marriott Dr Washington DC 20058 also: 10400 Fernwood Rd Bethesda MD 20058

CASHEL, WILLIAM S., JR., food products company executive; b. 1920. BA, Dartmouth Coll., 1941. With Bell Telephone Corp., 1946-60, 63-76; vice chmn., chief fin. officer AT&T, 1976-83; chmn. bd. Campbell Soup Co., Camden, N.J., 1984—. Served to maj. USMC, 1942-46. Office: Campbell Soup Co Campbell Pl PO Box 60A Camden NJ 08101 *

CASHEN, JOSEPH LAWRENCE, real estate broker; b. Kansas City, Mo., May 10, 1931; s. John Lawrence and Anna May (Sutcliffe) C.; m. Michele Ann Hayes, June 15, 1960; children: Michael, Patricia, Kelly. Student real estate U. Calif., Los Angeles, 1965-66. Sales cons. chems. Economics Lab., Los Angeles, 1954-64; broker Forest E. Olsen Realtors, Canoga Park, Calif., 1964-67; pres. Property World, Inc., Woodland Hills, Calif., 1967-71; pres. Century 21 Real Estate #1, Inc., Woodland Hills, 1971—; mem. Calif. State Senate Commn. on Franchises. Inventor in field. Pres. Police Activity League, Woodland Hills, 1975-80; dir., mem. adv. council Pierce Coll. Rotoract, 1974-75. Served with USMC, 1950-54. Mem. San Fernando Valley Bd. Realtors, Calif. Assn. Realtors, Nat. Assn. Realtors, Nat. Inst. Farm and Land Brokers, Nat. Assn. Home Builders, Aircraft Owners and Pilots Assn., Woodland Hills C. of C. (pres. 1976). Lodges: K.C., Rotary (pres. 1974-75). Office: 5959 Topanga Canyon Woodland Hills CA 91367

CASHMAN, JOHN WILLIAM, JR., accountant, financial planner; b. Worcester, Mass., July 7, 1956; s. John William Sr. and Corrine (Zellmer) C.; m. Gerogia Andrea Raneri, Oct. 9, 1982; children: Rachael, Monica. AS, Worcester Jr. Coll., 1976; BS, Bentley Coll., 1978; cert., Coll. Fin. Planning, 1987. CPA, Mass. Cost acct. Van Brodie Milling Co, Inc., Clinton, Mass., 1978-79; tax acct. Hutchinson & Picchi, P.C., Natick, Mass., 1979-84; tax mgr. Hutchinson & Picchi, P.C., Framingham, Mass., 1987—, Beers & Co., Inc., Framingham, 1984-87. Fellow Am. Inst. CPA's, mass. Soc. CPA's (fin., estate planning com. 1988—); mem. Mass. Assn. Pub. Accts., Inst. Cert. Fin. Planners. Home: 101 Bacon St Natick MA 01760 Office: Hutchinson & Picchi PC 555 Commonwealth Ave Newton MA 02159

CASHMAN, W. TIMOTHY, II, financial executive; b. Cleve., Nov. 20, 1929; s. Eugene R. and Pauline (Lenihan) C.; m. Diana C. Plumb, Feb. 27, 1960; children: W. Timothy, Sarah, John, Alison. B.S.B.A., Babson Coll., Wellesley, Mass., 1958. With Sears Roebuck Acceptance Corp., Wilmington, Del., 1960—; now sr. v.p. mktg. Sears Roebuck Acceptance Corp., Wilmington, also dir. Chmn. bd. St. Francis Hosp., Wilmington, 1981—; pres. Children's Home, Wilmington, 1977-80. Served with U.S. Army, 1953-55, ETO. Club: Wilmington (treas. 1978—). Office: Sears Roebuck Acceptance Corp PO Box 4680 Greenville DE 19807

CASKEY, WILLIAM JOSLIN, food products executive; b. Louisville, Oct. 12, 1949; s. William Rex and Sara Katherine (Joslin) C.; m. Kathy Lynn Caskey, Dec. 12, 1975; 1 child, Kristyn Leigh. BBA, Auburn U., 1971. Sales mgmt. trainee Carnation Co., Miami, 1974-75; sales supr. Carnation Co., Dallas, 1975-76; dist. sales mgr. Carnation Co., Jacksonville, Fla., 1976-78; reg. sales mgr. Carnation Co., Phila., 1978-81; gen. sales mgr. Carnation Co., Los Angeles, 1981-85; v.p., gen. mgr. Nestle Foods Corp., Purchase, N.Y., 1985—; bd. dirs. Culinary Inst. Am., Hyde Park. Mem. Strike Force United Way, Westchester County, N.Y., 1987. Served to lt. j.g. USN, 1971-73. Mem. Internat. Food Service Mfg.'s Assn. (bd. dirs.), Nat. Automatic Merchandising Assn., Nat. Coffee Service Assn., Nat. Restaurant Assn., Sigma Chi (Balfour award 1971). Republican. Episcopalian. Office: Nestle Foods Corp 100 Manhattanville Rd Purchase NY 10577

CASLER, VELTON STARLING, business machines company executive; b. Hereford, Tex., Apr. 30, 1941; s. Jerome Thomas and Nellie (Stephenson) C.; m. Murle L. Cushion, Feb. 13, 1965; children: Dhana, DeAnne, Debra, Darren, Dawn. BA in Math., U. North Tex., 1964; postgrad., U. Utah. Computer analyst Martin Marietta Corp., 1965; project leader URS Data Scis. Co., 1966-69; dir. European field offices, Fed. Republic Germany, 1969-70; owner, cons. Success Motivation Inst., Denton, Tex., 1970-71; with Evans and Sutherland, Salt Lake City, 1971—, mgr. cen. region sales, 1972-74, mgr. internat. sales, 1974-75, dir. mktg., 1975-76, dir. interactive systems and mktg., 1976-80, v.p., dir. interactive systems, 1980-81; pres. Cameo Electronics, Anaheim, Calif., 1981-82; v.p. mktg. computer systems div. Gould Inc., Plantation, Fla., 1982-84; pres., chief exec. officer, chmn. bd. dirs. Porta-Printer Systems, Inc., Largo, Fla., 1984-88; founder, pres., chief exec. officer Micro Palm Computers, Inc., Clearwater, Fla., 1988—; chmn. bd. dirs. Porta-Printer Systems, Inc., Largo; bd. dirs. Micro Palm Computers, Inc. Mem. Tech. Mktg. Soc. Am., Am. Mgmt. Assn., Assn. Computer Machinery, C. of C., Exchange Club. Mormon. Office: 13773 500 Icot Blvd Clearwater FL 34620

CASLOW, RICHARD WALKER, JR., manufacturing company executive; b. Cambridge, Ohio, May 7, 1933; s. Richard Walker and Esther (Strimatter) C.; m. Peggy Elaine Pressney, Aug. 31, 1968; children: Eric, Scott, Karen. BA, Case Western Res. U., 1955. Registered profl. engr., Calif. Engr. Gen. Tire, Wabash, Ind., 1959-60; engr. Mattel, Hawthorne, Calif., 1961-67, engring. mgr., 1967-80; dir. engring. Mattel, Hong Kong, 1976-80; v.p., gen. mgr. Mattel, Edison, N.J., 1980-83; sr. v.p. Orient Ops. Mattel, Hong Kong, 1983—. Served with U.S. Army, 1955-57. Home: 3-C Headland Rd, Repulse Bay Hong Kong Office: Mattel Inc 5150 Rosecrans Ave Hawthorne CA 90250

CASON, CAROL COLVARD, graphics and editing company executive; b. Asheville, N.C., Nov. 11, 1940; d. Dean Wallace and Martha (Lampkin) Colvard; m. Robert Benjamin Cason, Dec. 30, 1967; children: David Benjamin, Alexander Colvard. BA, Atlantic Chriistian Coll., 1963; postgrad., No. Va. Community Coll., 1975-80, Miss. State U., 1961. Tech. asst. Sta. WUNC-TV, Raleigh, N.C., 1958-59; sect. editor Raleigh Times, 1963-66; state editor St. Petersburg (Fla.) Times, 1967-68; freelance editor Washington,

1968-81; prodn. mgr. The Connection, newspaper, Reston, Va., 1980; art dir. Creative Types, Reston, 1983-85; pres. Graffica, Reston, 1985—. Mem. Reston Bd. Commerce (editor newsletter 1984-85). Office: Graffica 1462 Roundleaf Ct Reston VA 22090

CASON, MARILYNN JEAN, technological education institute executive; b. Denver, May 18, 1943; d. Eugene Martin and Evelyn Lucille (Clark) C.; married. BA in Polit. Sci., Stanford U., 1965; JD, U. Mich., 1969; MBA, Roosevelt U., 1977. Bar: Colo. 1969, Ill. 1973. Assoc. Dawson, Nagel, Sherman & Howard, Denver, 1969-73; atty. Kraft, Inc., Glenview, Ill., 1973-75; corp. counsel Johnson Products Co., Inc., Chgo., 1975-86, v.p., 1977-86; mng. dir. Johnson Products Co., Inc., Lagos, Nigeria, 1980-83; v.p. internat. Johnson Products Co., Inc., Chgo., 1986-88; v.p., gen. counsel DeVry, Inc., Chgo., 1989—. Bd. dirs. Ill. chpt. Arthritis Found., Chgo., 1979—, sec. 1989—; bd. dirs. Internat. House, Chgo., 1986, Ill. Humanities Coun., Chgo., 1987—. Mem. ABA, Nat. Bar Assn., Chgo. Bar Assn., Cook County Bar Assn. (pres. community law project 1986-88). Club: Stanford (Chgo.) (pres. 1985-87). Home: 322 Darrow Ave Evanston IL 60202 Office: DeVry Inc 2201 W Howard St Evanston IL 60202

CASPAR, GEORGE J., III, lawyer; b. 1933. BS, Ohio State U., 1954; LLB, U. Mich., 1957; LLM, NYU, 1958. Assoc., White & Case, 1962-65; asst. gen. counsel Heublein Inc., Farmington, Conn., 1965-69, sec., assoc. gen. counsel, 1969-71, sec., gen. counsel, 1971-72, v.p., sec., gen. counsel, 1972-84; sr. v.p. Travelers Corp., 1983-86, assoc. gen. counsel, corp. sec., 1986—. Office: Travelers Corp 1 Tower Sq Hartford CT 06183

CASPER, PAUL ALEXANDER, publishing company executive; b. N.Y.C., Sept. 28, 1947; s. Alex and Inez (Brindle) C.; m. Kathleen McNamee, Sept. 21, 1980; 1 child, Nicholas. BFA, Drake U., 1969. Creative dir. Woodall Pub. Co., Chgo., 1973-80; pres. Alexander Communications, Inc., Chgo., 1980-88, Macmillan Creative Svcs. Group, Chgo., 1988—. Mem. Am. Inst. Graphic Arts, Soc. Typographical Artists. Office: Macmillan Creative Svcs Group 212 W Superior St Chicago IL 60610

CASPERSEN, FINN MICHAEL WESTBY, financial company executive; b. N.Y.C., Oct. 27, 1941; s. Olaus Westby and Freda Caspersen; m. Barbara Caspersen, June 17, 1967. B.A. With honors in Econs., Brown U., 1963; LL.B. cum laude, Harvard U., 1966; LL.D., Hood Coll.; H.H.D., Washington Coll., Chestertown, Md. Bar: Fla. 1966, N.Y. 1967. Assoc. Dewey, Ballantine, Bushby, Palmer & Wood, N.Y.C., 1969-72; assoc. counsel Beneficial Mgmt. Corp., Wilmington, Del, 1972-75; v.p., dir., mem. exec. com. Beneficial Corp., 1975, vice chmn., mem. exec., fin. coms., 1975, chmn. bd., chief exec. officer, mem. exec. com., 1976—; bd. dirs., mem. exec. com. Beneficial Nat. Bank; chmn., bd. dirs. Beneficial Trust Co. Ltd.; bd. dirs. Beneficial Found., Inc. Wilmington, Westby Corp., Westby Mgmt. Corp.; chmn., bd. dirs. Harbour Island, Inc.; bd. dirs., pres. Tri-Farms Inc.; chmn. 35th Ann. N.J. Bus. Conf., Rutgers U. Grad. Sch. Mgmt. and Sales Execs. Club N.J., 1983; mem. adv. bd. Nat. Ctr. Fin. Services, U. Calif., Earl Warren Inst., Inferential Focus, N.Y.C.; bd. advisors Inst. Law and Econs. U. Pa., John M. Olin speaker; vice chmn. Am. Fin. Services Assn. Former trustee N.J. Coll. Fund Assn.; emeritus trustee Brown U.; trustee Camp Nejeda Found. for Diabetic Children, N.J. State Police Meml. Library & Mus. Assn.; mem. nominating com. Morristown Meml. Hosp.; past trustee Com. Econ. Devel.; former mem. N.J. Bd. Higher Edn.; bd. dirs. Shelter Harbor Fire Dist.; bd. dirs., v.p. O.W. Caspersen Found.; chmn. bd. trustees, mem. exec. com. Peddie Sch., Hightstown, N.J.; past chmn. bd. Drumthwacket Found.; chmn. Waterloo Found. for Arts. Inc.; charter mem. Ptnrship for N.J., New Brunswick; trustee James S. Brady Presdl. Found., The Savs. Forum; pres. Coalition of Service Industries,Inc., Washington; chmn. bd. trustees Gladstone Equestrian Assn. Inc.; mem. adv. com. to exec. bd. Morris-Sussex Area Council Boy Scouts Am.; mem. driving com. Am. Horse Shows Inc.; mem. corp. Cardigan Mountain Sch.; mem. bd. advisors Inst. for Law and Econs. U. Pa.; mem. Harvard Resources Com. Served to lt. USCG, 1966-69. Recipient President's medal Johns Hopkins U.; named Civic Leader of Yr. YMCA, 1982. Mem. Am. Fin. Svcs. Assn. (trustee, chmn. govt. affairs com., chmn. membership com., adminstrn. com., vice chmn., chmn.), ABA, Fla. Bar Assn., N.Y. Bar Assn., Conf. Bd. (reg.), Harbour Island Inc. (chmn.). Clubs: Harvard; Knickerbocker (N.Y.C.); Univ. (Sarasota and Tampa, Fla.); Wilmington (Del.). Office: Beneficial Corp 1100 Carr Rd Wilmington DE 19899

CASS, DAVID, economist, educator; b. Honolulu, Jan. 19, 1937; s. Phil and Muriel (Dranga) C.; m. Janice Vernon, Sept. 14, 1959 (div. July 1983); children—Stephen, Lisa. B.A., U. Oreg., 1958; Ph.D. in Econs. and Stats., Stanford U., 1965. From asst. to assoc. prof. Yale U., New Haven, 1964-70; prof. econs. Carnegie-Mellon U., Pitts., 1970-74; prof. econs. U. Pa., Phila., 1974-88, Paul F. and Warren S. Miller prof. econs., 1988—. Contbr. articles to profl. jours.; co-editor: Selected Readings in Macroeconomics from Econometrica, 1974; The Hamiltonian Approach to Economics, 1976. 1st lt. USAR, 1959-65. Guggenheim fellow, 1970-71; recipient Morgan prize U. Chgo., 1976; Sherman Fairchild Disting. Scholar Calif. Inst. Tech., 1978-79; NSF grantee, 1971—. Fellow Econometric Soc.; mem. Phi Beta Kappa. Office: U Pa Ctr Analytic Rsch in Econs & Social Scis 3718 Locust Walk CR Philadelphia PA 19104-6297

CASS, E. R. PETER, electronic publishing executive; b. La Porte, Ind., Nov. 21, 1941; s. Edward Smith and Shirley (Mazor) C.; m. Marilyn Brooks Cass, Apr. 1, 1967; children: Edward, Alexander. AB, Hamilton Coll., 1964; MBA, Syracuse U., 1970. Sr. v.p., gen. mgr. Travel Industry Assn. Am., Washington, 1974-78; gen. mgr., chief operating officer Tri County Met. Transp., Portland, Oreg., 1978-81; pres. Cablebus System Corp., Beaverton, Oreg., 1981-82; v.p. unregulated activities Pacific Telecom, Inc., Vancouver, Wash., 1982-83; chmn. bd. dirs., pres. Transax Data Corp., Falls Church, Va., 1983-85; pres. Transax/RATES, Falls Church, 1985—. Office: Transax RATES 5111 Leesburg Pike Ste 100 Falls Church VA 22041

CASS, ROBERT MICHAEL, lawyer, consultant; b. Carlisle, Pa., July 5, 1945; s. Robert Lau and Norma Jean (McCaleb) C.; BA, Pa. State U., 1967; JD, Temple U., 1971; m. Patricia Ann Garber, Aug. 12, 1967; children: Charles McCaleb, David Lau. Benefit examiner Social Security Adminstrn., Phila., 1967-68; mktg. rep. Employers Comml. Union Ins. Co., Phila., 1968-70; asst. sec. Nat. Reins. Corp., N.Y.C., 1970-77; admitted to N.Y. bar, 1974; asst. v.p. Skandia Am. Reins. Corp., N.Y.C., 1977-80; mgr. Allstate Reins. div., South Barrington, Ill., 1980-86; mgr. R.K. Carvill, Inc., Chgo., 1986-87; pres. R. M. Cass Assocs., Barrington, Ill., 1987—; v.p. Assurance Alliance, Inc., Crystal Lake, Ill., 1989—; lectr. Ins. Sch. Chgo. Mem. ABA (com. on internat. ins. law, self ins. and risk mgrs., ins. law, excess, surplus lines and reins. law, vice chmn., newsletter editor), N.Y. State Bar Assn., Soc. CPCUs, Soc. Ins. Research, Am. Arbitration Assn. (panel arbitrators). Home: 325 Old Mill Rd Barrington IL 60010 Office: PO Box 1362 Barrington IL 60011

CASSAGNE, GILBERT MICHAEL, soft drink company executive; b. Bay Shore, N.Y., Aug. 6, 1956; s. Gilbert Joseph and Frances Alice (Olander) C. BSBA magna cum laude, Boston U., 1978. Sales rep Procter & Gamble Co., Washington, 1978-79; from account mgr. to area field mgr. Procter & Gamble Co., Balt., 1979-81; assoc. area mgr. Procter & Gamble Co., Boston, 1981-82; regional v.p. Fountain/Foodservice div. Dr. Pepper Co., L.A., 1982-86; v.p. sales Dr. Pepper Co., Dallas, 1986-87; v.p.sales Fountain/Foodservice div. Dr. Pepper/Seven-Up Co., Dallas, 1987—. Mem. advance liaison com. Calif. Reps., 1984-85, advance com. Reagan-Bush Campaign, Long Beach, Calif., 1984-85, Rep. Congl. leadership com., 1988. Regents scholar State of N.Y., 1974. Mem. Soc. for Advancement Mgmt., Beta Gamma Sigma. Roman Catholic. Office: Dr Pepper/Seven Up Co 8144 Walnut Hill Ln Dallas TX 75231-8144

CASSANI, KASPAR V., information processing and business machines executive; married. With IBM Corp. Armonk, N.Y., 1951—, v.p. then sr. v.p., 1982-87, exec. v.p., 1987-88, vice-chmn., 1988—; dir. IBM World Trade Europe/Middle East/Africa Corp., White Plains, N.Y., v.p., 1978-80, pres., 1980-81, chmn., 1981—; also pres. IBM World Trade Corp., White Plains; chmn. IBM Europe. Office: IBM Switzerland, Postfuch, CH 8022 Zurich Switzerland *

CASSEL, JOHN ELDEN, accountant; b. Verden, Okla., Apr. 24, 1934; s. Elbert Emry and Erma Ruth (McDowell) C.; m. Mary Lou Malcom, June 3, 1953; children—John Elden, James Edward, Jerald Eugene. Plant mgr., also asst. gen. mgr. Baker and Taylor Co., Oklahoma City, 1966-71; paymaster, office mgr. Robberson Steel Co., Oklahoma City, 1971-76; pvt. investor, 1976—. Democrat. Methodist. Home: 2332 NW 118th St Oklahoma City OK 73120

CASSIDAY, DONALD MARION, bank executive; b. Clinton, Iowa, Jan. 15, 1935; s. Donald Marion and Ruth Abbey (Beil) C.; m. Rosalie J. Yeoman, Jan. 17, 1959; children: Karen Lynn, Terry Jane Cassiday Blood, Julie Anne. BA in History, Grinnell Coll., 1956; MS in Mgmt., Colo. U., 1968. Commd. 2d lt. USAF, 1956, advanced through grades to col., 1971, ret., 1977; dean Sch. Bus. Aurora (Ill.) U., 1977-85; v.p. corp. devel. Mchts. Bancorp. Inc., Aurora, 1985—. Co-author: Study of MBA Business Communication Course Needs, 1985; contbr. articles to profl. jours. Pres., bd. dirs. Aurora United Way, 1979-87; bd. dirs. Mercy Ctr. for Health Care Svcs., Aurora, 1985—; v.p., bd. dirs. Mental Health Bd., Aurora, 1983-86; dir. Two Rivers coun. Boy Scouts Am., St. Charles, Ill. 1988. Recipient Humanitarian award St. John's AME Ch., Aurora, 1988, Community Builders award Masons, Aurora, 1987. Mem. Bank Mktg. Assn., Air Force Assn., Ret. Officers Assn., Aurora U. Alumni Assn. (bd. dirs.), Am. Assn. Higher Edn., Am. Mgmt. Assn., Kiwanis (Aurora chpt. pres. 1986, lt. gov. 1987, recipient Disting. Pres. award, 1986, named Kiwanian of Yr., 1987), Assn. Individual Devel. (bd. dirs. 1988—). Republican. Methodist. Office: Mchts Bancorp Inc 34 S Broadway Aurora IL 60505

CASSIDY, ADRIAN CLYDE, telephone company executive; b. Polar, Wis., Jan. 27, 1916; s. William Thomas and Ethel (Jenkins) C.; m. Elizabeth Bevans, Mar. 24, 1945; children: David Bevans, Leigh Sheridan, Lynne Porter, Laurie Bevans. BA, U. Wis., 1939, LLB, 1942. Bar: Wis. 1945, N.Y. 1947, Minn. 1951, N.J. 1962. Atty. N.Y. Telephone Co., 1946-50, Am. Tel. & Tel. Co., 1950, 56-61; Minn. atty. Northwestern Bell Telephone Co., 1950-56; gen. atty. N.J. Bell Telephone Co., 1961-63, v.p., 1963-66; v.p. Pacific Tel. & Tel. Co., San Francisco, 1966-81, chief fin. officer, 1972-81; bd. dirs. Datron Systems, Inc., Clemente Global Growth Fund, Inc. Served to lt. USCGR, 1942-46. Mem. ABA., Am. Judicare Soc., Order of Coif. Clubs: Menlo Country (Woodside, Calif.), Bankers (San Francisco). Office: 525 University Ave Palo Alto CA 94301

CASSIDY, DONALD L., investment analyst; b. Cambridge, Mass., June 25, 1945; s. Francis Joseph and Ethel Dorothy (Lange) C. BS in Econs., U. Pa., 1967. Asst. to pres. Spear & Staff, Inc., Wellesley, Mass., 1973-74; sr. analyst Arthur D. Little Decision Resources, Cambridge, 1974-86; sr. research analyst Boettcher & Co., Inc., Denver, 1986; v.p. Boettcher & Co., Inc., 1987—. Umpire Little League Baseball, 1970—; chmn. bd. dirs. Citizens for Ltd. Taxation, Boston, 1978-84, author, drafter tax-limitation initiative ballot question, 1980. Served with U.S. Army, 1968-70. Libertarian. Office: Boettcher & Co Inc PO Box 54 Denver CO 80201

CASSIDY, JAMES JOSEPH, public relations counsel; b. Norwood, Ohio, Dec. 31, 1916; s. Martin D. and Helen (Johnston) C.; m. Rita Hackett, Oct. 18, 1941; children: Claudia, James. Student, U. Cin., 1934-38. Dir. spl. events, internat. broadcasts Crosley Broadcasting Corp., 1939-44, war corr., 1944-45, dir. pub. relations, 1946-50; war corr. NBC, 1944-45; account exec. Hill & Knowlton, Inc., N.Y.C., 1950-53; v.p. Hill & Knowlton, Inc., 1953-61, sr. v.p., 1961-66, exec. v.p., 1966-71, pres., chief operating officer, 1971-74, vice chmn., 1974-75; vice chmn. Burson-Marsteller, Washington, 1975-81. Trustee Cabrini Health Care Center and Columbus Hosp., N.Y.C. Recipient Variety award 1944; citation for reporting in combat areas Sec. War, 1945. Mem. Pub. Relations Soc. Am. (past pres. N.Y. chpt.), Aviation Writers Assn., Ohio Soc., Internat. Assn. Bus. Communicators, Profit Sharing Council Am. (past chmn. bd.). Clubs: George Town, 1925 F St, Nat. Press, Sky, Overseas Press; International (Washington). Home: 826 Heritage Village Southbury CT 06488

CASSIDY, JAMES MARK, construction company executive; b. Evanston, Ill., June 22, 1942; s. James Michael and Mary Ellen (Munroe) C.; B.A., St. Mary's Coll., 1963; m. Bonnie Marie Bercker, Aug. 1, 1964 (d. Dec. 1981); children—Micaela Marie, Elizabeth Ann, Daniel James; m. Patricia Margaret Mary Murphy, Sept. 15, 1984. Estimator, Cassidy Bros., Inc., Rosemont, Ill., 1963-65, project mgr., 1965-67, v.p., 1967-71, exec. v.p., 1971-77, pres., 1978—; trustee Plasterer's Health & Welfare Trust, 1971—. Arae fund leader constrn. industry salute to Boy Scouts Am., 1975; mem. pres.'s council St. Mary's Coll.; chmn. labor liaison com. Laborers Internat. Union N.Am. and Assn. Wall and Ceiling Industries, 1982-85, chmn. labor-mgmt. group, 1985-88; chmn. Chicagoland Assn. Wall and Ceiling Contractors' Carpenters Union Negotiating Team, 1983—. Served with U.S. Army, 1963-64, N.G., 1964-69. Mem. Chgo. Plastering Inst., Builder Uppers Club (pres. 1973-74), Chicagoland Assn. Wall and Ceiling Contractors (pres. 1976-79), Great Lakes Council, Internat. Assn. Wall and Ceiling Contractors (chmn. 1977), Constrn. Employers Assn. Chgo. (dir. 1976—, chmn. com. labor-mgmt. relations 1983—), Chicagoland Safety Council (dir. 1988—), Assn. Wall and Ceiling Industries (dir. 1978-81, 88—). Roman Catholic. Clubs: Abbey Springs Country (Fontana, Wis.); Park Ridge (Ill.) Country. Office: Cassidy Bros Inc PO Box 570 Rosemont IL 60018

CASSIDY, JOHN HAROLD, lawyer; b. St. Louis, June 18, 1925; s. John Harold and Jennie (Phillips) C.; m. Marjorie Blair, Nov. 26, 1947; children: Patricia, John, Brian. AB, Washington U., 1949, JD, 1951. Bar: Mo., U.S. Dist. Ct. (ea. dist.) Mo., U.S. Ct. Appeals (8th cir.), U.S. Supreme Ct. Atty. U.S. Govt., St. Louis, 1951-56; sole practice St. Louis, 1956-59; atty. Crown Zellerbach Corp., San Francisco, 1959-61; atty. Ralston Purina Co., St. Louis, 1961—, v.p., 1975-85, v.p., sr. counsel, 1985—. Served with U.S. Mcht. Marine, 1943-45. Mem. ABA, Mo. Bar Assn., St. Louis Bar Assn., Am. Soc. Corp. Secs. Republican. Presbyterian. Office: Ralston Purina Co Checkerboard Sq Saint Louis MO 63164

CASSIDY, MICHAEL STANLEY, banker; b. N.Y.C., May 9, 1938; s. Joseph Stanley and Alice Regina (McGurk) C.; m. Anne Barr Coventry, Feb. 3, 1968; children: Susan, Sean, Margaret, Pamela. B.A. in Econs., Holy Cross Coll., 1960; M.B.A. in Fin., Iona Coll., 1969. With Chase Manhattan Bank, N.Y.C., 1965—, sr. v.p., 1983—. Republican. Roman Catholic. Office: Chase Manhattan Corp 1 Chase Manhattan Pla New York NY 10081

CASSIDY, PATRICK EDWARD, chemist, educator; b. East Moline, Ill., Nov. 8, 1937; s. Bert Garfield and Ilene Vertha (Anderson) C.; m. Mary Jeanne Groover, June 24, 1984; children: Andrew P., Lacey M. Menzies, Melissa K. Menzies. BS in Chemistry, U. Ill., 1959; MS in Chemistry, U. Iowa, 1962, PhD in Chemistry, 1963. Fellow U. Ariz., Tucson, 1963-64; staff mem. Sandia Corp., Albuquerque, 1964-66; sr. scientist Tracor, Inc., Austin, Tex., 1966-71; prof. S.W. Tex. State U., San Marcos, 1971—; v.p. Tex. Rsch. Inst., Austin, 1975—; pres. TRI/TESSO, 1987—; bd. dirs. Actran Systems, Tex. Rsch. Inst.; cons. in field. Author: Thermally Stable Polymers, 1980; mem. editorial bd. Jour. Polymer Materials, 1987—; contbr. articles to profl. jours. Bd. dirs. Extend-A-Care, Austin, 1979-81. Fellow Tex. Acad. Sci.; mem. Am. Chem. Soc. (counselor 1978-83, Service award Cen. Tex. chpt. 1982), Soc. Plastics Engrs. Republican. Presbyterian. Home: 6102 Bend O'River Austin TX 78746 Office: Tex Rsch Inst 9063 Bee Cave Rd Austin TX 78733

CASSIDY, ROBERT JOSEPH, consumer products company executive; b. Hiawatha, Kans., Feb. 20, 1930; s. Joseph A. and Bertha (Fulton) C.; m. Ashby Miller Long, Jan. 8, 1955; children: Claire Sussman, Patricia Cassidy Devine. B.S., U. Kans., 1952. With Union Carbide Corp., 1954-86; dir. automotive mktg. Union Carbide Corp., N.Y.C., 1974-76, gen. mgr. automotive, 1976-77; v.p., gen. mgr. automotive products Union Carbide Corp., Danbury, Conn., 1977-86; exec. v.p. First Brands Corp., Danbury, 1986—. Served to 1st lt. USAF, 1952-54. Mem. Automotive Sales Council. Episcopalian. Club Fairfield County Hunt (Westport, Conn.). Office: 1st Brands Corp 83 Wooster Heights Rd Bldg 301 PO Box 1911 Danbury CT 06813-1911

CASSIDY, WILLIAM DUNNIGAN, III, telecommunications company executive; b. Bluefield, W.Va., Aug. 4, 1941; s. William D. Jr. and Josephine Elizabeth (Williams) C.; m. Beverly Ann Lisk, Nov. 25, 1967; children: William IV, Michael, Sean. BS, Hampden-Sydney (Va.) Coll., 1963; MS, George Washington U., 1966; PhD in Psychology, Clayton U., St. Louis, 1987. With human resources dept. ITT, N.Y.C., 1965-82; sr. v.p. adminstrn. Warburg, Paribas, Becker, N.Y.C., 1982-84; v.p. adminstrn. The Genlyte Group, N.Y.C., 1984-86, Penn Cen. Telecommunications Corp., Woodcliff Lake, N.J., 1986—; cons. Battalia & Assocs., N.Y.C., 1984. Elder West Side Presbyn. Ch., Ridgewood, N.J., 1986; trustee Arthur M. Hughes Trust, Ridgewood, chmn. bd. Mem. Nat. Assn. Corp. and Profl. Recruiters (bd. dirs.), The George Jr. Rep. Sch. of N.Y. (bd. dirs.), Union League (N.Y.C.). Republican. Home: 274 Phelps Rd Ridgewood NJ 07450 Office: Penn Cen Telecommunications 50 Tice Blvd Woodcliff Lake NJ 07675

CASSIN, WILLIAM BOURKE, lawyer; b. Mexico City, Sept. 11, 1931; s. William Michael and Elouise (Hall) C.; m. Kristi Shipnes, July 15, 1961; children: Clay Brian, Michael Bourke, Macy Armstrong. A.B., Princeton U., 1953; J.D., U. Tex., 1959. Bar: Tex. 1959. Law clk. Judge Warren L. Jones, Fifth Circuit U.S., 1959-60; atty. Baker & Botts, Houston, 1960-70; v.p., gen. atty. United Gas Pipe Line Co., Houston, 1970-73; sr. v.p., gen. atty. United Gas Pipe Line Co., 1973, group v.p., gen. counsel, dir., mem. exec. com., 1974-76; exec. v.p., gen. counsel, mem. exec. com. United Energy Resources, Inc., Houston, 1976-84, dir., 1976-86; of counsel Mayer, Brown & Platt, Houston, 1985-87; chmn., pres., chief exec. officer D2 Software, Inc., 1984-89; mem. Pub. Utility Commn., Austin, Tex., 1988—; gen. counsel Houston Grand Opera Assn., 1961-70, mem. governing coun., 1977-88 , also bd. dirs.; adj. prof. U. Houston Law Ctr., 1988. Contbr. articles to profl. jours.; editor-in-chief Tex. Law Rev, 1959. Gen. counsel Harris County Republican Exec. Com., 1963-64, 67-68; exec. vp. Tex. Bill Rights Found., 1967-68; mem. exec. com. Associated Reps. of Tex., 1976—, Landmark Legal Found., 1985—, Armand Bayou Nature Ctr., 1986—; bd. dirs. Iowa State Utility Regulatory Conf., 1986—, Legal Found. Am.; trustee Tex. Mil. Inst., Atwill Meml. Chapel; mem. vestry Christ Ch. Cathedral, 1970-72, 80-82, lay reader. Lt. Airborne Arty. AUS, 1953-57; capt. Res. ret. Fellow Tex. Bar Found. (life); mem. ABA, Tex. Bar Assn., Houston Bar Assn., Fed. Energy Assn., Fed. Bar Assn., Nat. Assn. Regulatory Utility Commrs., Order of Coif, Phi Delta Phi. Republican. Episcopalian. Clubs: Houston Country, Houston Met. Racquet, Bayou, Ramada, Allegro, Garwood Hunting; Argyle (San Antonio); Army and Navy (Washington); Northport Point (Mich.); Princeton (N.Y.C.); Princeton Terrace. Home: 1 S Wynden Dr Houston TX 77056 Office: Pub Utility Commn Tex 7800 Shoal Creek Blvd Suite 400 Austin TX 78757

CASSON, RICHARD FREDERICK, travel bureau executive; b. Boston, Apr. 11, 1939; s. Louis H. and Beatrix S. C. AB, Colby Coll., 1960; JD, U. Chgo., 1963. Bar: Ill. 1963, Mass. 1964. Ptnr. Casson & Casson, Boston, 1967-68; assoc. counsel, corporate sec. Bankers Leasing Corp., 1968-75; asst. gen. counsel, corp. sec. Commonwealth Planning Corp., 1975-76; assoc. gen. counsel, asst. sec. Prudential Capital Corp., 1976—; ptnr. Cities of Sea Cruise Cen., Travel Agency . Bd. dirs. Children's Speech and Hearing Found., Temple Ahavath Achim, Gloucester, Mass. Capt. JAGC U.S. Army, 1964-67. Decorated Bronze Star. Jewish. Club: B'nai B'rith (Gloucester) (v.p.). Home: Off Lowe Dr Magnolia MA 01930

CASTANEDA, ROBERTO RUDOLPH, accountant, Latin America consultant; b. Chgo., July 26, 1956; s. Roberto Castaneda and Jessita (Hernandez) Martinez; m. Dorothy Biel (div. July, 1978); m. Celina Hernandez, Nov. 10, 1979; children: Jacqueline, Bianca. BS in Commerce, DePaul U., 1980; postgrad. in Bus. Mgmt., Northwestern U., 1987—. CPA, Ill. Sr. auditor Arthur Andersen & Co., Chgo., 1980-84; licensee acctg. mgr. McDonald's Corp., Oak Brook, Ill., 1984—. Treas., bd. dirs. Mex. Fine Arts Ctr. Mus., 1981—. Mem. Am. Inst. CPAs, Ill. Soc. CPAs. Democrat. Roman Catholic. Home: 6519 S Rockwell Chicago IL 60629 Office: McDonalds Corp McDonalds Pla Oak Brook IL 60521

CASTEL, JOHN CHRISTOPHER, medical electronics company executive; b. Boston, July 6, 1954; s. John G. and Jane Ellen (Farris) C.; m. Dawn Sharon Graver, Aug. 28, 1982; children: Jacqueline, Jean Paul. Student, York U., 1969-73; PhD (hon.), Sci. Orgn. Alternative Medicine, Caracas, Venezuela, 1984. Pres., founder Intertronic Systems, Ltd., Toronto, Ont., Can., 1973-77; dir. neurologic div. Med. Research Labs., Inc., Lake Forest, Ill., 1979-83; chmn., exec. v.p. research and devel. Physio Tech, Inc., Topeka, 1983-85, exec. v.p. research and devel., 1983—; lectr. in field. Contbr. articles to profl. publs. Recipient award Can. Assn. Physicists, 1971; named Philips Young Scientist of the Yr. Youth Sci. Found. Physics award. Fellow N.Y. Acad. Scis.; mem. Am. Soc. Laser Medicine and Surgery, Am. Assn. Advancement Med. Instrumentation, Laser Inst. Am., Soc. Photo-optical Instrumentation Engrs. Office: Physio Tech Inc 1505 SW 42d St Topeka KS 66609

CASTELLANO, MICHAEL JOHN, accountant; b. Bklyn., May 17, 1946; s. Wilbur Paul and Mary Ellen (Quigley) C.; m. Kathleen Suzanne Nitka, Aug. 5, 1967; children: Susan Kathleen, Karen Elizabeth. BBA, Baruch Coll., 1967. CPA. Sr. acct. Deloitte Haskins & Sells, N.Y.C., 1970-74, mgr., 1974-80, ptnr., 1980—. Club: Raveneaux Country, Houston. Home: 106 Worths Mill Ln Princeton NJ 08540 Office: Deloitte Haskins & Sells 1 World Trade Ctr New York NY 10048-0601

CASTELLANOS, JULIO J(ESUS), banker; b. Havana, Cuba, Mar. 7, 1910; came to U.S., 1960, naturalized, 1967; s. Manuel de Jesus and Virginia (Justiniani) C.; B of Arts and Letters, De La Salle Coll., Havana, 1927; JD, Tulane U., 1933; DCL, U. Havana, 1934; student Fed. Res. System Examiner's Sch., 1964-65; m. Irene Machado, Dec. 27, 1976; children: Julio J., Maria, Ana Maria, Carlos. Bar: Cuba 1934. Tax commr. City of Havana, from 1934; sr. ptnr. Lopez Munoz & Castellanos, Havana; sec. gen. Banco de la Construccion, Havana, 1959-60; analyst Morgan Guaranty Trust Co. N.Y., N.Y.C., 1960-63; examiner Fed. Res. Bank N.Y., N.Y.C., 1963-66; v.p. Marine Midland Bank, N.Y.C., 1966-71; founder, organizer, sr. v.p., mgr. First Wis. Internat. Bank, N.Y.C., 1971-76; pres. Pan Am. Nat. Bank, Union City, N.J., from 1976; exec. rep. Banco de Intercambio Regional, N.Y.C., 1976-80; pres. Banco del Estado Holding Co. Inc., Atlanta, 1982-84; adviser Banco de Reservas de la Republica Dominicana, N.Y.C., 1982-84; N.Y.C. rep. Banco del Estado, Bogota, Colombia, 1978-84; N.Y. rep. Banco Hipotecario Dominicano, 1983-85; banking cons. law firm Reid & Priest, 1983-86; v.p. BHD Corp., real estate investments, 1984-86; pres., chief cons. Castellanos Cons. Group Inc., 1984—; v.p. IDOSA N.Y. Inc., 1984-85; cons. Remesa Universal Corp., N.Y., Centro Financiero Universal, Santo Domingo, Dominican Republic. Bd. dirs. Colombian-Am. Assn. Pan Am. Soc. of U.S., 1984-85 . Recipient retirement recognition diploma First Wis. Internat. Bank, 1976, pub. recognition diploma Dr. Guillermo Belt, former Mayor Havana, 1979. Republican. Address: 510 E 85th St New York NY 10028

CASTILLO, LUCY NARVAEZ, healthcare administrator; b. Guayaquil, Ecuador, June 25, 1943; came to U.S., 1965, naturalized, 1972; d. Jose N. and Teresa (Sanchez) Narvaez; Ph.D. in Psychology, Kensington U., 1981; m. Boris Castillo, Apr. 20, 1964 (div.); children—Sylvia, Boris M. corp. sec. Castillo Med. Assos., P.A., Panama City, Fla., 1972-74; mgr. Bell Med. Group Med. Clinic, Los Angeles, 1974-76; pres. Lunar Enterprises, Inc., import-export co., Daytona Beach, Fla., 1976-78; real estate broker Watson Realty, Inc., Ormond Beach, Fla., after 1978; owner, dir. Today's Fashions; pres. So. Med. Ctrs., Lucy Motors Cia. Lta. Recipient award of merit Challenge to Am., 1979; named Outstanding Female in Community, Camara de Comercid Latina, 1986. Republican. Author: (fiction) For Better or For Worse, 1979. Home: 3610 Yacht Club Dr #908 North Miami Beach FL 33180 Office: 21311 NW 2d Ave North Miami FL 33169

CASTILLO, MANUEL ARAGON, social services administrator; b. Albuquerque, July 24, 1951; s. George Limon and Rita (Aragon) C.; m. Marian Maestas, Sept. 4, 1980; 1 child, Arthur. AA in Sociology, Western Wyo. Community Coll., 1983; BSW, U. Wyo., 1985. Laborer, foreman Laborers Local Union, Green River, Wyo., 1974-80; outreach dir. PineRidge Outreach, Green River, 1985—; intern Dept. Pub. Assistance and Social Svcs., Rock Springs, 1984-85, S.W. Counseling, Rock Springs, 1984-85, Western Wyo. Community Coll., Rock Springs, 1984-85; Hispanic interpreter Vocat. Rehab., 1982-83. Organizer, pub. relations vol. Vietnam Vets., 1982-83; bd. dirs. Green River Pks. and Recreation Dept., 1986, Mayor's Com. for

Handicapped, Green River, 1986. Mem. Wyo. Assn. Addiction Specialists (cert., bd. dirs. 1986—). Home: 48 W 3d S Green River WY 82935

CASTLE, STEPHEN NEIL, oil company executive; b. Tyler, Tex., Apr. 14, 1952; s. Hamp Gossett and Adrah Janice (Hicks) C.; m. Kay Marie Salisbury, July 17, 1970; children: Suzanne Marie, David Howard, Andrew Stephen. BBA in Acctg., Angelo State U., 1974; MBA in Mgmt./Acctg., U. Denver, 1979. With Mobil Oil Corp., Midland, Tex., 1974-76; specialist, bus. planning TRW-Reda Pump Co., Bartlesville, Okla., 1976-77; with Mobil Oil Corp., Denver, 1977-80; controller, treas. Tom Brown, Inc., Midland, 1980-83; sec.-treas. Hanley Petroleum, Inc., Midland, 1983—; bd. dirs. Hanley Petroleum, Inc., Midland, Bernie Phillips Well Svc., Inc., Big Lake, Tex., Hanley Co., Inc., N.Y.C., Lexington Mgmt. Group, Inc., N.Y.C.; guest lectr., instr. U. Denver, U. Colo., Boulder, Arapahoe Community Coll., Littleton, Colo., 1979-80. Elder, deacon, dept. chmn. Meml. Christian Ch., Midland, 1980—; scoutmaster, com. chmn. Boy Scouts Am., Midland, 1963; coach, dir. Midland County Library Adv. Bd., 1986—. Recipient award Am. Legion, 1967. Mem. Council Petroleum Accts. Socs. (com. mem., bd. dirs. 1989—), Petroleum Accts. Soc. Permian Basin (dir., pres. 1974—), Delta Sigma Pi (alumni dir. 1978-80). Republican. Disciple of Christ. Club: Ranchland Hills Country (Midland). Home: 2814 Auburn Dr Midland TX 79705 Office: Hanley Petroleum Inc 1500 Wilco Bldg 415 W Wall St Midland TX 79701

CASTLE, VERNON CHARLES, recording company executive; b. Whitewater, Wis., May 17, 1931; s. Erwin Ellesworth and Anne Bertha (Nelson) C.; B.Ed., U. Wis., Whitewater, 1951; m. Mary Lou Hill, Mar. 19, 1983. Profl. entertainer, musician, 1956-65; pres. Castle Prodns., Inc., Lake Geneva, Wis., 1966-79, Castle Rec., 1972-78, Recreational Recs., Ltd., 1972-77, 81-82; leader Last Dance Band, 1980—; broadcast advt. cons., 1979—; controller Mary Castle Co. Ltd., 1986—. Served with Adj. Gen. Corps, U.S. Army, 1952-55. Office: Americana Lake Geneva Resort Hwy 50 Lake Geneva WI 53147

CASTLES, JOHN WILLIAM, financial consultant; b. Portland, Oreg., Dec. 13, 1947; s. James B. and Ruth (Lintz) C.; student U. Wash., 1966, 67, Linfield Coll., 1968; student Portland State U., 1969-72; m. Sarah E. Boylston, Dec. 27, 1985. Comml. loan officer, br. mgr. Oreg. Bank, Portland, 1972-76; mgr. fin. mgmt. div. Capital Consultants, Inc., Portland, 1976-80; fin. cons., Portland, 1981—; chmn. Oreg. Salmon, Inc., Portland, Oreg. Aqua-Foods, Inc., Touchstone Investment Group, Inc., Portland; bd. dirs. Atlas Telecom, Inc., Portland, Oreg. Resource and Tech. Devel. Corp., Portland; Clubs: Multnomah Athletic, West Hills Racquet. Home: 11430 SW Lynnvale Dr Portland OR 97225 Office: 200 SW Market Ste 978 Portland OR 97201

CASTRONOVO, THOMAS NICHOLAS, banker; b. Chgo., Apr. 3, 1959; s. Joseph James and Virginia Marie (Santoro) C.; m. Cynthia Louise Cunningham, Mar. 14, 1987. BA, Knox Coll., 1981; MBA, Ind. U., 1982; cert., Coll. Fin. Planning, Denver, 1988. Mgmt. trainee Ill. Regional Banks, St. Charles, 1983-84; fumds mgmt. officer Ill. Regional Banks, Elmhurst, Ill., 1984-86, fin. services officer, 1986-87, asst. v.p., 1987—; Instr. Am. Inst. Banking, 1989. Tchr. Jr. Achievement, Chgo., 1988. Mem. Internat. Bd. Cert. Fin. Planners, Assn. MBA Execs., Ind. U. Fin. Guild. Club: Rotary (sgt.-at-arms Batavia, Ill. club 1988). Office: Ill Regional Banks 105 S York Elmhurst IL 60126

CASWELL, JOHN ROSS, engineer; b. Boston, Feb. 11, 1928; s. John and Margaret Selden Kennedy (Ross) C.; m. Carol Bradley, Dec. 28, 1949; children: John B., Christopher K., Frederick M., William W. II, Carolyn B. AB in Phys. Sci., Harvard U., 1953; MS in Physics, UCLA, 1954. Registered profl. engr., Mass., lic. real estate broker. Student engr. Raytheon Co., Waltham, Mass., 1949-52; mem. tech. staff Hughes Aircraft Co., Fullerton, Calif., 1952-56, mgr. transmitter dept., 1956-58; engr. Raytheon Co., Bedford, Mass., 1958-62, mgr. transmitter dept., 1962-64; prin. engr. Raytheon Co., Wayland, Mass., 1964-67, mgr. Missile Site Radar, 1967-70, mgr. An/SPY-1 Transmitter, 1970-73; site mgr. Raytheon Co., Kwajalein Marshall Islands, 1973-75; mgr. Pave Paws program Raytheon Co., Wayland, 1975-81, mgr. NATO Seasparrow program, 1981—; cons., lectr. in traffic, municipal, regional planning, Lincoln Ctr., Mass., 1964—. Contbr. articles to profl. publs.; patentee in field. Dist. commr. Boy Scouts Am., Kwajalein; sr. warden St. Anne's Ch., Lincoln Mass., 1966, Episcopal Ch., Kwaljalein Marshall Island, 1975; selectman, chmn. Town of Lincoln, 1983-89; mem., chmn. Lincoln Planning Bd., 1971-80. Served to lt. USN, 1945-49, ret. lt. USNR, 1962. Mem. Am. Soc. Testing Materials, Indep. Microwave Power Inst. Republican. Episcopalian. Clubs: Wiscasset Yacht (Maine). Home: Po Box 98 Lincoln Center MA 01773 Office: Raytheon Co Post Rd Wayland MA 01778

CATABELLE, JEAN-MARIE HENRI, industrial firm executive; b. Mamers, Sarthe, France, Dec. 10, 1941; s. Christian Aristide and Annette Marie (Lemonnier) C.; children by previous marriage: Laurent, Christine, Diane; m. Michèle Archambaud, Sept. 1, 1987. Engr., Ecole Centrale des Arts et Manufactures, Paris, 1963-66; M.S. with honors, Yale U., 1967; M.B.A. with distinction, Harvard Bus. Sch., 1974. Dept. mgr. IBM France, Paris, 1969-72; asst. to controller IBM Am. Far East, White Plains, N.Y., 1973; ops. mgr. Raychem S.A., Pontoise, France, 1974-78; mktg. mgr. Europe Raychem, Pontoise, 1978-81; gen. mgr. Compagnie Franç aise des Isolants, France, 1981-82; mng. dir., chief operating officer DAV, Annemasse, France, 1982—; dir. ETUDOC, Annecy, France; chmn. bd. examiners LEP Profl. Sch., Annemasse, 1983—; dir. ASDTN, Annecy, 1983—; bd. dirs. French Nat. Edn. Com. Grenoble Acad., 1986—; chmn. edn. com. Employers Union (Haute Savoie). . Patentee in field. Contbr. articles to profl. jours. Trustee, LEP Profl. Sch., 1982; v.p. export sect. C. of C., Amiens, France, 1981. Served to lt. French Army, 1967-69. Fulbright fellow, 1966, 72; French Govt. fellow, 1972; Alliance Franç aise fellow, 1966. Mem. French Assn. for Tech. and Econ. Cybernetics, Ingenieurs and Scientifiques de France, Association Franç aise de l'Enseignement Technique (dir.), Ecole Centrale Alumni Assn. Roman Catholic. Clubs: Golf, Tennis. Lodge: Rotary. Avocation: travel. Home: 5 Impasse Des Champais, 74290 Veyrier Du Lac, Haute-Savoie France Office: DAV, Rue Jules Verne, Vetraz Monthoux, 74101 Annemasse France

CATACOSINOS, WILLIAM JAMES, utility company executive; b. N.Y.C., Apr. 12, 1930; s. James and Penelope (Paleologos) C.; m. Florence Maken, Oct. 16, 1955; children: William, James. BS, NYU, 1951, MBA, 1952, PhD, 1962. Asst. editor 20th Century-Fox, N.Y.C., 1951-52; asst. dir. bus. mgmt. and adminstrn. Brookhaven Nat. Lab., Upton, N.Y., 1956-69; pres. Applied Digital Data Systems, Inc., Hauppauge, N.Y., 1969-77; chmn. and chief exec. officer Applied Digital Data Systems, Inc., 1977-82; chmn., chief exec. officer L.I. Lighting Co., Hicksville, N.Y., 1984—, also bd. dirs., 1978—; adj. asst. prof. NYU, 1962-64; mgmt. counselor, 1962-69; chmn. bd. Corometrics Med., 1968-74; bd. dirs. Utilities Mut. Ins. Co., 1985—; bd. dirs. Ketema Inc., 1988—. Bd. dirs. Brookhaven Town Indsl. Commn., 1956-77, Suffolk County chpt. Am. Cancer Soc., 1969-77, Stony Brook Found., 1978-85; trustee Poly. Inst. N.Y., 1981-85; nat. chmn. Am. Soc. Prevention of Cruelty to Children, 1981-83. Home: Cleft Rd Mill Neck NY 11765

CATALANO, ELLEN JANE MOHR, writer, management consultant; b. Whidby Island, Wash., Jan. 5, 1953; d. Charles Henry and Wanda June (Regier) Mohr; m. Larry Michael Williams, May 25, 1978 (div. June 1981); m. Glenn Henry Catalano, Oct. 5, 1985. BA in Russian Language, Duke U., 1975; M in Orgn. Devel. Leadership, Leadership Inst. of Seattle, 1984. Translator Russian U.S. Army, Ft. Mead, Md., 1975-76, U.S. Army Fgn. Sci. and Tech. Ctr., Charlottesville, Va., 1976-78; trainer human rels. Community Action Agy., Roanoke, Va., 1978-81; biofeedback therapist U. Va., Charlottesville, 1981-86; writer New Harbinger Pubs., Oakland, Calif., 1986—; dir. tng. and devel. Mgmt. Resources, Staunton, Va., 1987-88. Author: Chronic Pain Control Workbook, 1987. Coach water ballet team, Charlottesville, 1981—. Mem. Nat. Soc. Tng. and Devel. (dir. membership com. Blue Ridge chpt. 1988—), Aerobics club (instr. 1987—. Democrat. Presbyterian. Office: Wilcoxson Cons Assocs 801 E High St Suite B Charlottesville VA 22901

CATALANO, GERALD, accountant, oil company executive; b. Chgo., Jan. 17, 1949; s. Frank and Virginia (Kreiman) C.; BS in Bus. Adminstrn., Roosevelt U., 1971; m. Mary L. Billings, July 4, 1970; children—James, Maria, Gina. Jr. acct. Drebin, Lindquist and Gervasio, Chgo., 1971; jr. acct. Leaf, Dahl and Co., Ltd., 1971-77, prin., 1978—, ptnr. 1980—; prin. Gerald Catalano, CPA, Chgo., 1982-83; ptnr. Barbakoff, Catalano & Assocs., 1983-87; pres. Barbakoff, Catachno & Caboor, Ltd., 1988—; v.p. Tri-City Oil, Inc., Addison, Ill., 1983—; corp. officer Bionic Auto Parts, Inc. Pres. Young Democrats, Roosevelt U., 1967-71; dir. Elmhurst Jaycees, 1976. CPA, Ill. Mem. Am. Inst. CPA's, Ill. CPA Soc., Theosophical Soc. Roman Catholic. Office: 1550 N Northwest Hwy Park Ridge IL 60068

CATALDO, ANTHONY JOSEPH, II, accountant; b. Tucson, Ariz., Sept. 12, 1957; s. Anthony Joseph Sr. and Angeline (Palumbo) C. BBA, U. Ariz., 1980, MS in Acctg., 1985. CPA, Ariz. Acct. Craig & Wendtland; div. contr. Reddington Investments Inc., Ruidoso, N.Mex., 1985-86; performance auditor Calif. Auditor Gen., Sacramento, 1986; cons., expert witness Fontana Group, Tucson, 1986-87; cons. A.J. Cataldo II, Tucson, 1987—; lectr. and expert witness in field. Served with USMC, 1975-76. Mem. AICPA, Ariz. Soc. CPA's, Nat. Assn. Acc.s., Inst. Cert. Mgmt. Accts. (cert.), No. Calif. Motor Car Dealers Assn. (assoc.). Republican. Roman Catholic. Home: 4334 N Radin Ave Tucson AZ 85705 Office: U Ariz Dept Fin Tucson AZ 85721

CATALFO, ALFRED (ALFIO), JR., lawyer; b. Lawrence, Mass., Jan. 31, 1920; s. Alfio and Vincenza (Amato) C.; m. Caroline Joanne Mosca (dec. Apr. 1968); children: Alfred Thomas, Carol Joanne, Gina Marie; m. Gail Varney, 1988. BA, U. N.H., 1945, MA in History, 1952; LLB, Boston U., 1947, JD (hon.), 1969; postgrad., Suffolk U. Sch. Law, 1955-56, Am. Law Inst., N.Y.C., 1959. Bar: N.H. 1947, U.S. Dist. Ct. 1948, U.S. Ct. Appeals 1978, U.S. Supreme Ct. 1979. Sr. ptnr. Catalfo, McCarthy & Catalfo, Dover, N.H., 1948—; county atty. Strafford County, Dover, N.H., 1949-50, 55-56; mem. bd. immigration appeals U.S. Dept. Justice, 1953—; football coach Berwick Acad., South Berwick, Maine, 1944, Mission Catholic High Sch., Roxbury, Mass., 1945-46. Author: Laws of Divorces, Marriages, and Separations in New Hampshire, 1962, History of the Town of Rollinsford, 1623-1973, 1973. Pres. Young Dems. of Dover, 1953-55; 1st vice-chmn. Young Dems., N.H., 1954-56; mem. Strafford County Dem. com., 1948-75; vice chmn. N.H. Dem. com., 1954-56, 1st chmn., 1956-58, chmn. spl. activities, 1958-60; del. Dem. Nat. Conv., 1956, 60, 76; chmn. N.H. Dem. Conv., 1958, conv. dir., 1960; mem. Dem. state exec. com., 1960-70; Dem. nominee for U.S. Senate, 1962; vice chmn. Dover Cath. Sch. Com., 1969-71; mem. Dover Bd. Adjustment, 1960-65. Served as pilot AC, USN, 1942-44; lt. comdr. USNR. Recipient keys to cities of Dover, Somersworth, Concord, Berlin and Manchester, N.H.; 5 nat. plaques DAV; 3 disting. svc. awards Am. Legion; Am. Legion Life Membership award; spl. recognition award Berwick Acad., 1985. Mem. ABA, N.H. Bar Assn., Strafford County Bar Assn. (v.p. 1966-67, pres. 1968-69), Assn. Trial Lawyers Am., N.Y. State Trial Lawyers Assn., Mass. Trial Lawyers Assn., N.H. Trial Lawyers Assn., Tex. Trial Lawyers Assn., Nat. Assn. Criminal Def. Lawyers, N.H. Assn. Criminal Def. Lawyers, Am. Judicature Soc., Phi Delta Phi, DAV (judge adv. N.H. dept. 1950-56, 57-68, 72—; comdr. chpt. 1953-54, comdr. N.H. 1956-57), Am. Legion (life, chmn. state conv. 1967, 77, 84), Navy League, N.H. Hist. Soc., Dover Hist. Soc., Rollinsford Hist. Soc. Clubs: Eagles (Somersworth, N.H.), Sons of Italy (Portsmouth, N.H.). Lodges: Lions, Elks, K.C. (grand knight 1975-77), Moose, Lebanese (Dover). Home: 20 Arch St Dover NH 03820 Office: 450 Central Ave Dover NH 03820

CATALLO, CLARENCE GUERRINO, JR., financial services company executive; b. Detroit, Feb. 1, 1940; s. Clarence Guerrino and Christine (Miozzi) C.; m. Sharron Ann Teschendorf, Apr. 24, 1965; children—Curt Gregory, Cara Lynn. A.A., Long Beach City Coll., 1961; B.A., U. Detroit, 1963; postgrad., U. Toledo, 1963, Wayne State U., 1964. Account exec., asst. mgr. E.F. Hutton, Detroit, 1965-67, regional commodity mgr., 1967-70; br. mgr. E.F. Hutton, Southfield, Mich., 1970-80; dist. mgr., sr. v.p. E.F. Hutton, Birmingham, Mich., 1979-85; sr. v.p., regional v.p. Gt. Lakes region E.F. Hutton, 1986-87, exec. v.p. dir., regional v.p. Gt. Lakes region, 1987-88; sr. v.p., dir. North Cen. Div., including state of Mich., Ohio, Ind., Ill., Wis., Minn., N.D. and S.D. PaineWebber Inc., Farmington Hills, Mich., 1988—. Trustee Mich. Opera Theatre, Detroit, 1984-88. Republican. Roman Catholic. Club: Renaissance, LaSalle. Home: 29 Buffalo Clarkston MI 48016 Office: PaineWebber Inc N Cen Div 210 S Woodward #250 Birmingham MI 48009

CATANIA, RONALD, loss prevention company executive; b. Hartford, Conn., Nov. 28, 1945; s. John and Angeline (Torza) C.; m. Donna Louise Langevin, Aug. 10, 1979; children: Anthony, Jennifer. AS, Manchester Community Coll., 1971; BS, Thomas Edison Coll., 1981; MBA, U. New Haven, 1984. Internal auditor Sage-Allen & Co., Inc., Hartford, 1971, asst. dir. security, 1971-72, dir. security, 1972-73, dir. safety and security, 1973-80, dir. loss prevention, 1980-84, v.p. loss prevention, 1984—. Author: Loss Prevention Awareness Training, 1988. Chmn. pers. rev. bd. Town of Rocky Hill, Conn., 1983—. Staff sgt. USAF, 1965-69, Vietnam. Mem. Am. Soc. Security, Conn. Police Chiefs Assn. (mem. pvt. security com. 1983—), Conn. Loss Prevention Assn. Democrat. Roman Catholic. Office: Sage-Allen & Co Inc 900 Main St Hartford CT 06103

CATANZANO, FRANK ALEXANDER, public relations executive, consultant; b. Pittsburgh, Feb. 21, 1947; s. Frank Severino and Gladys Evelyn (Stahl) C.; m. Michele Antoinette McTigue, Mar. 18, 1978; children: Alexis Michele, and Jon Michael. BA in Journalism, Point Park Coll., 1969. Editor, internal communications Duquesne Light Co., Pitts., 1969-72; photojournalist Gulf Oil Corp., Pitts., 1972-76; v.p. Burson Marsteller, Pitts., 1976-81; ptnr. Mangus/Catanzano, Inc., Pitts., 1981—; pub. rels. dir. Internat. Tech. Inst, Pitts., 1981—. Author mag. articles for United Way Campaign, 1970, 71 (Merit award 1970, 71); mng. editor: Pittsburgh Engineer Mag., 1983— (honorable mention 1984); contbr. articles to trade and bus. jours. Pub. rels. dir. Italian Cultural Heritage Soc., Pitts., 1985-86; bd. trustees Point Park Coll. Mem. IEEE, Engrs. Soc. of Western Pa. Home: 5090 Cole Rd Murrysville PA 15668 Office: Mangus Catanzano Inc Three PPG Pl Pittsburgh PA 15222

CATAPANO, JOSEPH JOHN, construction company executive; b. N.Y.C., Mar. 28, 1935; s. Pascal and Helen (Pasta) C.; B.S. in Accounting, Queens Coll., 1956; m. Joan A. Tanzola, Nov. 12, 1960; children—Dorothy, Joseph P., MaryJo. Sr. accountant Klein, Katcher & Schultheis, C.P.A.'s, N.Y.C., 1958-63; sr. v.p. fin. Slattery Assocs., Inc., Maspeth, N.Y., 1963—, Slattery Group Inc., Roslyn, N.Y., 1968—. Mem. Fin. Execs. Inst. (dir. 1975-77, chmn. tax com. N.Y.C. chpt. 1973-74), Am. Inst. C.P.A.s, N.Y. State Soc. C.P.A.s. Club: Huntington Yacht. Office: Slattery Group Inc 46-36 54th Rd Maspeth NY 11378

CATELL, ROBERT BARRY, gas utility executive; b. Bklyn., Feb. 1, 1937; s. Joseph Daniel and Belle (Mishkind) Cicatelli; m. Joan Katherine Weigand, June 25, 1971; children—Laura Ann, Erica Ann; children by previous marriage—Robert Edward, Carla Ann, Donna Theresa;. B.M.E., CCNY, 1958, M.M.E., 1964. Registered profl. engr. Asst. v.p. Bklyn. Union Gas Co., 1974-78, v.p., 1978-82, sr. v.p., 1982-84, exec. v.p., 1984-86, exec. v.p., chief operating officer, 1986—; trustee Independence Savs. Bank, Bklyn., 1984—; mem. adv. com. CCNY, 1986—. bd. dirs. Jr. Achievement N.Y., 1980—, Bklyn. Law Sch., 1985—. Served with U.S. Army, 1962. Mem. Am. Gas Assn., Soc. Gas Lighting. Office: Bklyn Union Gas Co 195 Montague St Brooklyn NY 11158

CATER, JAMES THOMAS, financial and investment planner; b. Beatrice, Ala., Oct. 30, 1948; s. LaFayette Sigler and Lula Dell (Knight) C.; m. Sarah Frances Crisman, Apr. 12, 1975 (div. Sept. 1980); 1 child, Elizabeth Anne. MusB, U. Ala., 1971; MusM, U. Mich., 1974. Ind. paino and organ salesman 1974-80; fin. planner John Hancock Fin. Services, Houston, 1981—. Dir. music, organist, St. Luke's Presbyn. Ch., Houston, 1983—. Recipient numerous ins. awards, John Hancock Fin. Service. Mem. Houston Assn. Life Underwriters, Nat. Assn. Health Underwriters (leading producers round table 1984), Phi Mu Alpha Sinfonia. Republican. Office: John Hancock Fin Svcs 720 N Post Oak Rd Ste 328 Houston TX 77024

CATHCART, SILAS STRAWN, investment banking firm executive; b. Evanston, Ill., May 6, 1926; s. James A. and Margaret (Strawn) C.; m. Corlene A. Hobbs, Feb. 3, 1951; children: Strawn, James A., Daniel and David (twins), Corlene. Student, U. Notre Dame, 1944-46; A.B., Princeton U., 1948. With Ill. Tool Works Inc., Chgo., 1948-87, v.p., 1954-62, exec. v.p., 1962-64, pres., 1964-72, chmn., 1972-86; chmn., chief exec. officer Kidder Peabody Group Inc., N.Y.C., 1987—; bd. dirs. Ill. Tool Works Inc. Bd. dirs. Northwestern Meml. Hosp., Chgo. Served as ensign USNR, 1944-46. Clubs: Chgo., Old Elm, Commercial, Chgo. Commonwealth, Econ. (Chgo.). Office: Kidder Peabody & Co Inc 10 Hanover Sq New York NY 10005

CATHEY, BONNIE MARIE, educator; b. Protection, Kans., Feb. 7, 1943; d. Lee S. and Viola L. (Smutz) Lemasters; m. Robert E. Cathey, Apr. 14, 1962; children: Gregory, Kimberly, Shannon. BEd, Wichita State U., 1968; MBA, East Tex. State U., 1980. Tchr. Garland (Tex.) Ind. Sch. Dist., 1975-80; mktg. instr. East Tex. State U., Commerce, 1980—; tax preparer H&R Block, Garland, 1983-85, advanced tax instr., 1984-85; fin. advisor Dallas North Flying Club, 1980-84. Mem. Sales and Mktg. Execs.

CATHEY, ROGER ALLEN, business manager; b. Port Lavaca, Tex., Feb. 2, 1956; s. James Philip and Mary Louisa (Bird) C.; m. Onnalisa Marie Knowles, Sept. 21, 1974; children: Joshua Wayne, Tricia Colene. BS, U. Ill., 1979. Mem. Soc. Research Adminstrs. Office: U Ill 1304 W Green Rm 201 Urbana IL 61801

CATHEY, WILLIAM BLAIR, geologist, oil and gas exploration consultant; b. Columbia, Tenn., Nov. 30, 1954; s. Cecil Blair and Mary Lou (Sawyer) C.; m. Victoria Ann Russell, Oct. 18, 1974. BA in Geology, U. Tenn., 1977, MS in Geology, 1980; postgrad. Tulane U., 1982-83; MS in Indsl. Engring., U. Tenn., 1989. Cert. profl. geologist. Coop geologist Union Carbide, Oak Ridge, Tenn., 1975-77; assoc. geologist Exxon Minerals, Denver, 1978; prodn. geologist Conoco, Inc., New Orleans, 1980-81; exploration geologist Shell Oil Co., New Orleans, 1981-83; supr. phosphate-aquisition Occidental Petroleum, Columbia, Tenn., 1984-87; pres. Tnread, Inc., Knoxville, Tenn., 1983-84; grad. asst. in geology U. Tenn., Knoxville, 1978; grad. research fellow Oak Ridge Assoc. Univs., Tenn., 1979. Recipient Tarr award U. Tenn., 1977. Mem. Am. Inst. Profl. Geologists, Am. Assn. Petroleum Geologists, Geol. Soc. Am., New Orleans Geol. Soc., Phi Kappa Phi, Sigma Gamma Epsilon (v.p. 1979-80). Methodist. Lodge: Kiwanis. Avocations: hiking, camping, hunting, fishing. Home: 460 Bear Creek Ln Knoxville TN 37922

CATSIMATIDIS, JOHN ANDREAS, retail chain executive, airline executive; b. Nissiros, Greece, Sept. 7, 1948; came to U.S., 1949, naturalized, 1950; s. Andreas John and Despina (Emmanulides) C. BS in Engring., NYU, 1970. Pres. Red Apple Cos. (Gristedes, Red Apple, Pantry Pride supermarkets), N.Y.C. and Ft. Lauderdale, Fla., 1970—; vice chmn., chief fin. office Capitol Airlines, Smyrna, Tenn., 1983-84; chmn., chief exec. officer United Refining Inc., Warren, Pa., 1985—; chmn., chief exec. officer Designcraft, N.Y.C. Recipient Humanitarian award NCCJ, 1978, Am. Jewish Com., 1982, Nat. Kidney Assn., 1986; Entrepreneurship award NYU Bus. Sch., 1987. Mem. Westside C. of C. (vice chmn. 1975—). Clubs: New York Univ., Wings, Young Men Philanthrapic League. Office: Red Apple Cos 823 11th Ave New York NY 10019

CATTANI, MARYELLEN BILLETTE, lawyer; b. Bakersfield, Calif., Dec. 1, 1943; d. Arnold Theodore and Corinne Marilyn (Kovacevich) C.; m. Frank C. Herringer, Feb. 11, 1989; 1 child by previous marriage: Sarah Cattani Mikell. AB, Vassar Coll., 1965; JD, U. Calif.-Berkeley, 1968. Bar: N.Y. 1969, Calif. 1969. Assoc. Davis Polk & Wardwell, N.Y.C., 1968-69; assoc. Orrick, Herrington & Sutcliffe, San Francisco, 1970-74, ptnr., 1975-81; v.p., gen. counsel Transam. Corp., San Francisco, 1981-83, sr. v.p., gen. counsel, 1983-89; ptnr. Morrison & Foerster, San Francisco, 1989—; mem. adv. com. U. San Francisco Inst. on Fin. Svcs., 1984-86; mem. vis. com. Golden Gate U. Sch. Law, San Francisco, 1983—; vice chairperson, bd. dirs. Transam. Found., 1987-89. Contbg. author: Corporate Counselor's Desk Book, 1982, Litigation for Non-Litigator, 1987. Mem. pvt. sector task force on juvenile justice Nat. Council on Crime and Delinquency, San Francisco, 1985-87; trustee Vassar Coll., 1985—, Women's Campaign Fund, 1988; bd. regents St. Mary's Coll. Calif., 1985—. Named Outstanding Woman Equal Rights Advocates, 1984, Oustanding Woman Women's Campaign Fund, 1988. Mem. ABA, State Bar Calif. (chmn. bus. law sect. 1980-81), Bar Assn. San Francisco, Calif. Women Lawyers, San Francisco C. of C. (bd. dirs. 1987—), Am. Corp. Counsel Assn. (bd. dirs. 1982-87), Women's Forum West (bd. dirs. 1984-87), The Exploratorium (bd. dirs. 1988—). Democrat. Roman Catholic. Office: Morrison & Foerster 345 California St San Francisco CA 94104

CATTARULLA, ELLIOT REYNOLD, oil company executive; b. Binghamton, N.Y., Sept. 27, 1931; s. Edward and Helen (Padeletti) C.; m. Karin Magda Hartell, Sept. 12, 1959; 1 child, John Edward. BChemE, Cornell U., 1954. Econ. analyst U.S. affiliate Exxon Corp., N.Y.C. and Linden, N.J., 1954-61; exec., dir. Middle East and Latin Am. affiliates Exxon Corp., N.Y.C., London, Fla., Saudi Arabia, Peru, 1961-71; mng. dir. Greek affiliate Exxon Corp., Athens, 1971-73; v.p. Middle East affiliate Exxon Corp., N.Y.C., 1973-76, dep. mgr. pub. affairs dept., 1976-82, exec. v.p. Middle East affiliate, 1982-85, v.p., sec., 1985-86, v.p. corp. and pub. affairs, sec., 1986—. Bd. dirs. Middle East Inst., N.Y.C., 1981-86, Lincoln Ctr. Inst., N.Y.C., 1981—, Alliance for the Arts, N.Y.C., 1979—; mem. adv. council Herbert F. Johnson Mus. Art Cornell U., Ithaca, N.Y., 1987—; trustee Teagle Found. Inc., N.Y.C., 1986—. Mem. Am. Soc. Corp. Secs., Pub. Relations Seminar, Tau Beta Pi, Phi Kappa Phi. Presbyterian. Clubs: Queens (London); Quogue (N.Y.) Field. Office: Exxon Corp 1251 Ave of the Americas New York NY 10020

CATTIE, EUGENE GERARD, loan authority executive; b. Phila., July 13, 1948; s. Joseph Pierre and Agnes Gail (Seidle) C.; m. Margaret Theresa Ezokas, Nov. 7, 1970; children—Sean, Eugene, Mark, Jason. B.S., LaSalle Coll., 1974. Asst. bursar LaSalle Coll., Phila., 1967-72, dir. fin. aid, 1972-77; pres. Va. Edn. Loan Authority, Richmond, 1977—. Served to sgt. USMC, 1966-72. Mem. Nat. Council Higher Edn. Loan Programs (treas. 1982-84, pres. 1987), Nat. Assn. Fin. Aid Adminstrs., Eastern Assn. Fin. Aid Adminstrs., So. Assn. Fin. Aid Adminstrs., Vir. Assn. Fin. Aid Adminstrs., Pa. Assn. Fin. Aid Adminstrn. (trainer 1974-76), Bond Club N.Y. Roman Catholic. Avocations: jogging; fishing. Office: Va Edn Loan Authority 737 N Fifth St Richmond VA 23219

CATTOI, ROBERT LOUIS, high technology avionics and telecommunications design, manufacturing and marketing company executive; b. Hurley, Wis., Apr. 18, 1926; s. Louis Charles and Anna (Dahl) C.; m. Mary Frances Obertone, Aug. 30, 1949; children—David, Carol, Robert. B.E.E., U. Wis., 1950. With Collins Radio Group, Rockwell Internat., Dallas, 1950-77; v.p. Collins Radio Group, Rockwell Internat., 1971-77; v.p. engring. Aerospace and Electronics ops. Rockwell Internat., 1977-78, corp. v.p. engring., 1978-84, sr. v.p. research and engring., 1984—. Past mem. devel. bd. U. Tex. at Dallas; past trustee Assn. Grad. Edn. and Research North Tex. Served with USAAF, 1944-46. Mem. IEEE, AIA (aerospace tech. council), Quadroto della Radio, Tau Beta Pi, Eta Kappa Nu, Phi Eta Sigma, Phi Kappa Phi. Clubs: Balboa Bay (Newport Beach, Calif.); Bent Tree Country (Dallas). Home: 7350 Paldao Dr Dallas TX 75240 Office: Rockwell Internat PO Box 568842 Dallas TX 75356-8842

CAUGHLIN, STEPHENIE JANE, futures company executive, metals company executive; b. McAllen, Tex., July 23, 1948; d. James Daniel and Betty Jane (Warnock) C. BA in Family Econs., San Diego State U., 1972, MEd, 1973; M. in Psychology, U.S. Internat. U., San Diego, 1979. Cert. secondary life tchr., Calif. Owner, mgr. Minute Maid Svc., San Diego, 1970-75; prin. Rainbow Fin. Svcs., San Diego, 1975-78; tchr. San Diego Unified Sch. Dist., 1973-80; mortgage broker Santa Fe Mortgage Co., San Diego, 1980-81; commodity broker Premex Commodities, San Diego, 1981-84; pres., owner Nationwide Futures Corp., San Diego, 1984-88; owner, sec. Nationwide Metals Corp.; owner gen. mgr. Seabreeze Organic Farm, 1984-88. Sec. Arroyo Sorrento Assn., Del Mar, Calif., 1978—. Mem. Greenpeace Nature Conservancy, DAR, Sierra Club. Republican. Avocations: horseback riding, swimming, skiing, gardening. Lodge: Jobs Daus. Home: 3909 Arroyo Sorrento Rd San Diego CA 92130

CAULDER, MARY MEZZANOTTE, bank training officer; b. Phila., Dec. 28, 1953; d. Antonio Joseph and Dora (Ciccozzi) Mezzanotte; m. Bruce Edward Caulder, Oct. 29, 1983; children: Heather, Bruce Jr. BS in Labor Relations, LaSalle U., Phila., 1983. Bank clk. Phila. Nat. Bank, 1971-76, tng. specialist, 1976-85; tng. officer Main Line Fed. Savs. Bank, Villanova, Pa., 1986—; instr. Inst. Fin. Edn., Bucks County Community Coll., 1987—. Mem. Am. Soc. for Tng. and Devel., Internat. Assn. Quality Circles (treas. 1983-85), Nat. Assn. Female Execs. Office: Main Line Fed Savs Bank Rt 320 and Lancaster Ave Villanova PA 19085

CAULO, RALPH DANIEL, publishing executive; b. Jan. 7, 1935; children: Andrew, Timothy, Penelope. BA, U. Redlands, 1956, MA, 1958. SW regional mgr. sch. dept. Harcourt Brace Jovanovich Inc., Orlando, Fla., 1974-75, mgr. gen. sales, 1975-78, dep. dir., 1978-79, v.p., 1979-81, sr. v.p., 1981-83, exec. v.p., 1983-88; pres., chief operating officer Harcourt Brace Jovanovich, Orlando, Fla., 1988-89, pres., chief exec. officer, 1989—; bd. dirs. sch. dept. Harcourt Brace Jovanovich Inc., Orlando, Fla. Office: Harcourt Brace Jovanovich Inc 6277 Sea Harbor Dr Orlando FL 32887

CAUNTER, HARRY ALLEN, electronics company executive; b. Cleve., Dec. 21, 1935; s. Harry Albert and Ruth Olive (Woollacott) C.; m. Nancy Isella Reyes, Sept. 17, 1983; children from previous marriage: Keith Allen, Christine Ann. BBA, Case Western Res. U., 1961. Various mgmt. positions Gould, Inc., Ohio, 1957-69; various plant and ops. mgmt. positions Gould, Inc., Bridgeport, Ohio, 1969-73; controller indsl. products div. Gould, Inc., Cleve., 1973-76, pres., gen. mgr. indsl. products div., 1976-77; group v.p. indsl. products div. Gould, Inc., Rolling Meadows, Ill., 1977-79, sr. v.p. adminstrn., 1979-80, exec. v.p., operating officer, 1980—; bd. dirs. Compagnie Francaise d'Electro Chimie, Paris, SPD Technologies, Phila., Mohawk Rubber Co., Akron. Republican. Episcopalian. Clubs: Inverness Country (Ill.); Meadow (Rolling Meadows). Office: Gould Inc 10 Gould Ctr Rolling Meadows IL 60008

CAUTHEN, CHARLES EDWARD, JR., retail food and department store executive; b. Columbia, S.C., Oct. 26, 1931; s. Charles Edward and Rachel (Macaulay) C.; BA, Wofford Coll., 1952; cert. Charlotte Meml. Hosp. Sch. Hosp. Adminstrn., 1956; MS in Bus. Adminstrn. and Labor Mgmt., Kennedy-Western U., 1986, PhD in Bus. Adminstrn., 1986; m. Hazel Electa Peery, June 13, 1959; children—Portia Cauthen White, Sara Rohrer, Rachel Macaulay, Sidney Peery. Asst. adminstr. Union Meml. Hosp., Monroe, N.C., 1956-58; adminstr. Lowrance Hosp., Inc., Mooresville, N.C., 1958-61; v.p., mgr. Va. Acme Market, Bluefield, W.Va., 1961-68; v.p. Acme Markets and A-Mart Stores, (name now Acme Markets of Tazewell, Va., Inc.), North Tazewell, Va., 1965-87 , exec. v.p., 1968-71, pres., 1971-87, provost King Coll., Bristol, Tenn., 1987—; dir. Bluefield Supply Co., W.Va., 1968-85; pres. Doran Devel. Corp., 1971-87, Big A Market, Inc., 1981-87. Author: Evaluation of the Small Company For Strategic Planning, Merger or Acquisition, 1987. Deacon, elder, trustee WFirst Presbyn. Ch., Bristol, Tenn.; provost King Coll., Bristol, Tenn. Served to 1st lt. AUS, 1952-54. Decorated Army Commendation medal, Combat Med. badge. Mem. W.Va. Assn. Retail Grocers (v.p., dir. 1968-82), Va. Food Dealers Assn. (dir. 1978), Bluefield Sales Exec. Club (dir. 1965-67). Republican. Lodge: Rotary (dir. 1966). Home: 1626 King College Rd Bristol TN 37620 Office: King Coll East State St Bristol TN 37620

CAVALIERE, MICHAEL V., ceramics and glass company executive; b. Bklyn., Aug. 7, 1957; s. Vincent and Laura Cavaliere; m. Virginia Radu, June 26, 1983; 1 child, Virginia Ann. BA in Econs., Bklyn. Coll., 1979. Mgr. ops. Weil Ceramics & Glass Inc., Carlstadt, N.J., 1984-85, contr., 1985-88; treas. Carlstadt, N.J., 1988—. Mem. Am. Mgmt. Assn. Office: Weil Ceramics & Glass Inc 303 Patterson Plank Rd Carlstadt NJ 07072

CAVALLETTI, GIACOMO M., banker; b. Florence, Italy, Oct. 15, 1928; came to U.S., 1952; s. Carlo Alberto and Guilia (Magherini) C.; m. Julia B. Grundy, May 16, 1968 (div. 1979); 1 child, Lorenzo Alessandro. BA, Badia Fiesolana Coll., Florence, 1947; Degree in Bus. Adminstrn., U. Florence, 1951. Sales exec. Pan Am. World Airways, N.Y.C., 1953-58; vice dir. sr. mgmt. Fiat Auto Spa, Turin, Italy, 1958-81; exec. comml. dept. BNL-Lavoro Bank, N.Y.C., 1982—. Author: Fiat Sales Manual, 1967. Mem. Nat. Rep. Com., Washington, 1983-87. Mem. Saddle Room Club (London). Roman Catholic. Home: 80 Castle Rd Chappaqua NY 10514 Office: BNL-Banca Nazionale Del Lavoro 25 W 51st St New York NY 10019

CAVANAGH, CARROLL JOHN, business advisor, lawyer; b. N.Y.C., Nov. 11, 1943; s. Carroll and Mona (Schmid) C.; m. Valerie Ives Mixter (div.); children: Dorothy, Carroll III. BA, Yale U., 1964; JD cum laude, U. Pa., 1970; cert., Hague (The Netherlands) Acad. Internat. Law, 1969. Bar: D.C. 1979, Conn. 1970, N.Y. 1970. Assoc. Sullivan & Cromwell, N.Y.C., 1970-79; sec., gen. counsel Nat. Gallery Art, Washington, 1979-85, mem. coun. trustees, 1984—; bus. advisor Paul Mellon, Upperville, Va., 1985—. Lt. USNR, 1964-71. Clubs: Metropolitan (Washington), Union (N.Y.C.). Home: 3407 Dent Pl NW Washington DC 20007 Office: Rokeby Farms 1729 H St NW 4th Fl Washington DC 20006

CAVANAGH, PETER ROBERT, health educator, researcher, academic facility executive; b. Wolverhampton, Staffordshire, Eng., July 31, 1947; came to U.S., 1972; s. John Joseph and Dorothy Ann (Stokes) C.; m. Magda Margalova, Dec. 21, 1968 (div. 1979); 1 child, Sasha; m. Ann Elizabeth Vandervelde, Apr. 18, 1981; children: Drew, Chris, Jennifer. BEd, U. Nottingham, Loughborough Coll., 1968; PhD, U. London, Royal Free Med. Sch., 1972. Rsch. asst. Royal Free Med. Sch., London, 1968-72; asst. prof. Pa. State U., 1972-75, assoc. prof., 1975-81, prof., 1981—, dir. Ctr. for Locomotion Studies, 1986—; cons. U.S. Olympic Com., Colorado Springs, Colo., 1984—, NASA, Houston, 1986—, various athletic shoe cos., U.S., Japan and Fed. Republic Germany, 1978—; expert witness. Author: The Running Shoe Book, 1980; co-author: Biomechanics and Physiology of Cycling, 1978; contbr. articles to profl. jours.; patentee in field. Fellow Am. Acad. Phys. Edn.; mem. Am. Soc. Biomechanics (pres. 1986-87), Am. Coll. Sports Medicine (trustee 1987, Wolffe lectr. 1987), Internat. Soc. Biomechanics (coun. 1987, Muybridge medal 1987), Am. Acad. Podiatric Sports Medicine (hon.), Orthopedic Rsch. Soc., Am. Diabetes Assn. Home: 1352 Deerfield Dr State College PA 16803 Office: Pa State U Ctr for Locomotion Studies University Park PA 16802

CAVANAGH, RICHARD EDWARD, academic administrator, consultant, writer; b. Buffalo, June 15, 1946; s. Joseph John and Mary Celeste (Stack) C. AB, Wesleyan U., Conn., 1968; MBA, Harvard U., 1970. Assoc. McKinsey & Co., Inc., Washington, 1970-77, sr. cons., 1979, ptnr., 1980-87; exec. dir. fed. cash mgmt. U.S. Office Mgmt. and Budget, Washington, 1977-79; exec. dean John F. Kennedy Sch. Govt., Harvard U., Cambridge, Mass., 1987—; mem. staff Carter-Mondale Policy Planning, 1976; cons. Carter-Mondale Presdl. Transition, 1976-77; domestic coordinator Pres.'s Reorgn. Project, The White House, Washington, 1978-79; mem. exec. com. Pres.'s Pvt. Sector Survey on Cost Control, Grace Commn., 1982-83; mem. bus. adv. com. advanced study program Brookings Instn., 1983-86; adviser to nat. govts., EEC, N.Y.C. Partnership, Am. Bus. Conf.; quoted on pub. issues in Time, Bus. Week, Nation's Bus., Inc., Fortune, Venture, AP, UPI. Co-author: (with Donald K. Clifford, Jr.) The Winning Performance, 1985; contbr. articles to Wall Street Jour., Mgmt. Rev., Fin. World., Planning Rev., N.Y. Times. Bd. judges Dively Award, Harvard U., 1984—; bd. visitors Georgetown U. Sch. Bus., 1985—; trustee Ctr. for Excellence in Govt., 1985, Wesleyan U., 1989—. With U.S. Army, 1968. Recipient Presdl. commendation, 1979, 80, 83; John Reilly Knox fellow, 1979, Clark fellow, 1979. Mem. Am. Soc. Pub. Adminstrn., Acad. Polit. Sci., Raimond Duy Baird Assn., Wesleyan U. Alumni Assn. (chmn. 1985-87), Beta Theta Pi. Democrat. Roman Catholic. Club: Harvard (N.Y.C.). Office: Harvard U John F Kennedy Sch Govt 79 John F Kennedy St Cambridge MA 02138

CAVANAGH, ROBERT TERRANCE, electronics company executive; b. Winnipeg, Man., Can., May 31, 1922; came to U.S., 1947; naturalized, 1957; s. Edgar L. and Margaret (Gillies) C.; m. Ethel A. Ball, June 28, 1948; children: Thomas, Richard, Joanne. BEE, U. Toronto, Can., 1945. Project engr. Cyclograph Svcs. Ltd., Toronto, Ont., Can., 1945-47; successively asst. to dir. rsch., chief engr. TV div., dir. cir. rsch. lab., gen. mgr. mil. ops. Allen B. DuMont Labs., Clifton, N.J., 1947-60; with North Am. Philips Corp., N.Y.C., 1960-87; past gen. mgr. Philips Electronic Instruments, 1960-67; v.p. North Am. Philips Co., Inc., 1967-72, PEPI, Inc., Philips Broadcast Equipment Corp., 1965-67; group v.p., v.p. corp. devel. and engring., sr. v.p. N.Am. Philips, 1967-87; ret. Philips Broadcast Equipment Corp., 1987. Mem. IEEE, AAAS, Am. Inst. Aeros. and Astronautics, Electron Microscopy Soc. Am., Ont. Soc. Profl. Engrs. Clubs: Sleepy Hollow Country; Union League (N.Y.C.). Home: 5 Birch Close Sleepy Hollow Manor North Tarrytown NY 10591 Office: N Am Philips Corp 100 E 42nd St New York NY 10017

CAVANAUGH, DENNIS MILES, railroad company executive; b. Los Angeles, Sept. 19, 1937; s. Edward and Louella (Olson) C.; m. Marilyn J. Scovil, Sept. 11, 1965; children—Ann Louise, Amy Denise. B.S., U. Minn., 1965. Yard clk. Soo Line R.R. Co., Mpls., 1955-57, 61-65, asst. trainmaster, 1965-67, indsl. engr., 1969-72, dir. transp. planning, 1972-73, asst. supt. central div., 1974, gen. supt., 1974-77, asst. to exec. v.p., 1977-78, gen. mgr. transp. and maintenance, 1978, v.p. ops., 1978-81, exec. v.p., 1981-83, pres., 1983—, chief oper. officer, 1983-84; chmn., chief exec. officer Soo Line Corp. and Soo Line R.R., 1989—; chmn., chief exec. officer, pres. Soo Line Corp., Mpls., 1987—; bd. dirs. Consol. Papers, Inc., Wis. Rapids, Wis., Minn. Bus. Partnership, Inc., Mpls., Soo Line Corp., Mpls., bd. dirs., mem. adv. bd. exec. com. Ctr. Transp. U. Minn. Carlson Sch. Mgmt. Served with USN, 1957-61. Mem. Am. Mgmt. Assn. Clubs: Midland Hills Country, Minneapolis, Minn. Alumni, Transp. Internat. Office: Soo Line Corp 800 Soo Line Bldg Box 530 Minneapolis MN 55440

CAVANAUGH, NEIL CHRISTIAN, equipment manufacturing executive; b. Newark, Feb. 1, 1940; s. James Joseph and Irene Marie (Nielsen) C.; m. Nancy Joan Smith, July 28, 1962; children: Roberta Ann, Richard Niel. BS in Acctg., U. Hartford, 1968. Cert. internal auditor. Auditor Colt Industries, N.Y.C., 1969-71, div. acctg. mgr., 1971-72, corp. audit mgr., 1972-75; v.p., controller Pratt & Whitney Machine Tool, West Hartford, Conn., 1975-78; controller N.R.M. Corp., Talmadge, Ohio, 1978-80; corp. controller Sandvik, Fairlawn, N.J., 1980-81; exec. v.p. planner Sandvik, Allendale, N.J., 1981-83; pres. The Bethlehem Corp., Easton, Pa., 1983—; chmn. bd. B. F. Gilmour Co., Inc., Bklyn., 1987—. Office: The Bethlehem Corp 25th & Lennox Sts PO Box 348 Easton PA 18042

CAVAZZA, FABIO LUCA, publishing executive; b. Bologna, Italy, May 24, 1927; s. Giulio and Marina M. (Rossi) C.; m. Adriana Cassarini, July 1, 1961; children: Federico, Marianna. JD, U. Bologna, 1950. Gen. mgr. Il Mulino Publishing House, Bologna, 1951-64, dir., 1964—; dir. La Stampa, Torino, Italy, 1969-71; mng. dir. Il Sole-24 Ore, Milan, 1972-78, editor-in-chief, 1978-80, dep. chmn., 1980-82; dir. Il Corriere della Sera, Milan, 1984-88; chmn., chief exec. officer Studi & Servizi Internazionali, Milan, 1986—; v.p. DGA Internat., Inc., Washington, 1988—; chmn. C&C Co., 1988—. Bd. dirs. Ist per gli Studi Storici Croce, Naples, 1986—. Roman Catholic. Home: 4 Via Tommaso Salvini, 20122 Milan Italy Office: C & C Co, Via Rossini 5, 20122 Milan Italy

CAVENEY, WILLIAM JOHN, pharmaceutical company executive, lawyer; b. Wheeling, W.Va., Aug. 5, 1944; s. James Joseph and Esther Virginia (Ackermann) C.; AB cum laude, W.Va. U., 1966; JD, Vanderbilt U., 1969; LLM in Taxation, NYU, 1977, Advanced Profl. Cert. in Fin., Grad. Sch. Bus. Adminstrn., 1979; m. Margaret Carol Serota, Sept. 18, 1971; children: Ryan Benjamin, Christine Joanna. Bar: N.Y. 1972, U.S. Supreme Ct. 1976. Tax mgr. Arthur Andersen & Co., N.Y.C., 1969-73; tax atty. Texaco, Inc., N.Y.C., 1973-76; mgr. tax planning Norton Simon, Inc., N.Y.C., 1976-78; dir. tax planning Warner-Lambert Co., Morris Plains, N.J., 1978-79, tax counsel, mem. tax planning com., 1979—; mem. Township Com., Millburn, N.J., Bd. Health , Millburn; lectr. Taxation and internat. fin. CPA, N.Y. Council mem., auditor The Short Hills Assn.; trustee Rep. Club of Milburn, Short Hills. Mem. N.Y. State Bar Assn. (mem. exec. com. tax sect.), ABA (com. fgn. activities of U.S. taxpayers), Am. Inst. CPA's, N.Y. State Soc. CPA's, Tax Execs. Inst., (chmn. internat. tax steering com.), World Trade Inst. Contbr. articles to profl. jours. Club: Beacon Hill (Summit, N.J.). Home: 88 Stewart Rd Short Hills NJ 07078 Office: 201 Tabor Rd Morris Plains NJ 07950

CAVICCHIO, DANIEL JOSEPH, JR., investment executive; b. Cambridge, Mass., Aug. 24, 1944; m. Brenda Carol Nicholson, June 2, 1985; children: Daniel III, Benjamin, John. BS in Math., Rensselaer Polytech. Inst., 1966; MS, U. Mich., 1968, PhD in Computer and Communication Scis., 1970. With tech. staff Aerospace Corp., El Segundo, Calif., 1970-73; mgr. McKinsey & Co., N.Y.C., 1973-78; dir. bus. devel. Am. Can Co., Greenwich, Conn., 1978-84; chmn. Greenwich Venture Ptnrs., 1984—, Commonwealth Sprague Capacitor, North Adams, Ma., 1986—. Home: 10 Terr Pl Pelham NY 10803 Office: Greenwich Venture Ptnrs 8 Sound Shore Dr Ste 100 Greenwich CT 06830

CAVILL, RONALD WILLIAM, financial advisor; b. Escanaba, Mich., July 8, 1944; s. Robert Hugh and Lorraine (Kondory) C. BA, U. Md., 1971. Cert. fin. planner. Regional v.p. Am. Gen. Corp., Houston, 1973-75; pres. Corp. Benefit Cons., Inc., Denver, 1975-80, Cavill and Co., Rockville, Md., 1980—; bd. advisors Tax Mgmt. Fin. Planning (BNA), Washington, 1985—. Pres. Jefferson County Assn. for Retarded Citizens, Denver, 1977; bd. dirs. Good Shepherd Life Care Ctr., Silver Spring, Md., 1985. Mem. Internat. Assn. Fin. Planning (v.p. nat. capital chpt. 1984-86), Mem. Inst. Cert. Fin. Planners. Office: Cavill & Co 1225 Eye St NW #1200 Washington DC 20005-3914

CAVOULACOS, PANOS E., management consultant; b. Athens, Greece, Apr. 1, 1957; came to U.S., 1976; s. Elias P. and Daisy E. (Pastou) C.; m. Alix de la Barre d'Erquelinnes, Dec. 15, 1984; children: Alexandra Daphne, Sophie Madeleine. BS in Nuclear Engring., MS in Nuclear Engring., MIT, 1980, MS in Mgmt., 1982, PhD in Energy Econs., 1987. Engr. Électricité de France, Paris, 1980; cons. Energy Rsch. Group, Inc., Waltham, Mass., 1981-82, Marsoft, Inc., Boston, 1983-84, Exeter Group, Inc., Cambridge, Mass., 1984; assoc. McKinsey and Co., Inc., Washington, 1985—. Contbr. articles to profl. jours. Henry Ford II scholar Ford Corp., 1981-82. Mem. Internat. Assn. Energy Economists, Athens Coll. Alumni Assn., Hellenic Students Assn. Harvard/MIT (exec. council 1979-80), Phi Beta Kappa, Sigma Xi, Alpha Nu Sigma. Office: McKinsey and Co Inc 1700 Pennsylvania Ave NW Washington DC 20006

CAWOOD, JAMES SCOTT, security professional; b. Lansing, Mich., May 6, 1956; s. James Humes and Joan Patricia Cawood; m. Anne Virginia Capron, Aug. 28, 1982. BA, U. Calif., Berkeley, 1978. Cert. protection profl. Security officer St. Francis Hotel, San Francisco, 1980-82; investigator W.J. Weaver Co., Hayward, Calif., 1982; dir. corp. security IMI, San Francisco, 1983; security ops. mgr. BankAmerica Data Ctr., San Francisco, 1984; pres. Factor One Security and Investigative Service, Inc., San Leanrdo, Calif., 1985—; instr. Golden Gate U., 1987—. Spl. asst. U.S. delegation UN, N.Y.C., 1977. Mem. Am. Soc. Indsl. Security, Calif. Assn. Licensed Investigators, Internat. Assn. Arson Investigators. Republican. Mem. Taoist faith. Office: Factor One Security and Investigative Service Inc PO Box 1772 San Leandro CA 94577

CAWTHORN, ROBERT ELSTON, health care executive; b. Masham, Eng., Sept. 28, 1935; came to U.S., 1982; s. Gerald P. and Gertrude E. (Longster) C.; m. H. Susan Marshall, Jan. 15, 1960; children: Amanda, Liza. B.A. in Agriculture, Cambridge U., 1959. Exec. v.p. Rorer Group, Inc., Fort Washington, Pa., 1982-84; pres. Rorer Group, Inc., 1984-85, pres., chief exec. officer, 1985-86, chmn., chief exec. officer, 1986—; pres. Rorer Internat. Corp., 1982-83; bd. dirs. Cytogen Corp., Princeton N.J., First Pa. Corp., Phila., Immune Response Corp., Greater Phila. First Corp. Chmn. Internat. Bus. Forum; trustee The Baldwin Sch., Bryn Mawr, Pa., 1984—, Universal Health Realty Income Trust, United Way Southeastern Pa.; bd. dirs. World Affairs Council Pa. Served to lt. Brit. Army, 1954-56. Mem. Pharm. Mfrs. Assn. (bd. dirs. 1985—), Greater Phila. C. of C. (bd. dirs. 1987—). Home: 50 Crosby Brown Rd Gladwyne PA 19035 Office: Rorer Group Inc 500 Virginia Dr Fort Washington PA 19034

CAYNE, JAMES E., investment banker; b. 1934. With Bonn Bush Mach, 1954-66, Lebenthal and Co., 1966-69; now pres., sr. mng. dir. Bear Stearns and Co. Inc., also bd. dirs. Office: Bear Stearns Co Inc 245 Park Ave 9th Fl New York NY 10167 *

CAYWOOD, JAMES ALEXANDER, III, transportation engineering company executive, civil engineer; b. Kona, Ky., Jan. 28, 1923; s. James Alexander and Mary Viola (Crawford) C.; m. Carol Ann Fries, Mar. 20, 1959; children: Daniel, Malinda, Elizabeth; children from previous marriage: Beverly, James. B.S.C.E., U.Ky., 1944. Registered profl. engr., 50 states. Asst. engr., sr. instrumentman Louisville & Nashville R.R., Ky., 1946-47; chief engr., gen. mgr. C & O-B R.R., 1961-64; pres., dir. Royce Kershaw Co., 1964-65; v.p., then exec. v.p. De Leuw, Cather & Co., Washington, 1965-78, pres., 1978—. Served to lt. USN, 1944-46. Inducted into Hall of Disting. Alumni U. Ky., Lexington, 1985. Mem. Am. Pub. Transit Assn., Am. Ry. Bridge and Bldg. Assn., Am. Ry. Engring. Assn., Am. Rd. and Transp. Builders Assn. (Guy Kelcey award 1978, chmn., Washington, 1982), ASCE (John I. Parcel - Leif J. Sverdrup Civil Engr. Mgmt. award 1978), D.C. Soc. Profl. Engrs., Inst. Transp. Engrs., Nat. Soc. Profl. Engrs., Roadmasters and Maintenance of Way Assn., Soc. Am. Mil. Engrs., The Moles. Clubs: University, Burning Tree (Washington). Office: De Leuw Cather & Co 1133 15th St NW Washington DC 20005-2701

CAYWOOD, JOHN MILLARD, electronics company executive; b. Chico, Calif., Oct. 27, 1941; s. John Marion and Doris Bernice (Mackey) C.; m. Pamela Ann Marlow, Dec. 17, 1967; children: Lisa, Carolyn. BS, Calif. Inst. Tech., 1963, MS, 1964, PhD, 1969. Rsch. fellow Calif. Inst. Tech., Pasadena, 1970-72; mem. tech. staff Tex. Instruments, Dallas, Tex., 1972-75; process devel. mgr. Fairchild Semiconductor, Palo Alto, 1975-76; mgr. reliability engr. Intel Corp., Santa Clara, Calif., 1976-80; v.p. tech. devel. and corp. product assurance Xicor, Inc., Milpitas, Calif., 1981—. Contbr. articles to profl. jours. Mem. IEEE, Böhmische Physickalische Gesellschaft, Sigma Xi. Office: Xicor Inc 851 Buckeye Ct Milpitas CA 95035

CAZEL, HUGH ALLEN, industrial engineer, educator; b. Asheville, N.C., Aug. 6, 1923; s. Fred Augustus and Agnes (Petrie) C.; B.S. in Indsl. Engring., N.C. State U., 1948, M. Indsl. Engring., 1972; m. Edna Faye Hawkins, Sept. 2, 1944; children—Audre Elizabeth, Hugh Petrie, Susan Margaret, Steven Sidney. Service mgr. Cazel Auto Service Co., Asheville, 1948-51; sales rep. Snap-On Tools Corp., Kenosha, Wis., 1951; estimator, cost acct. Standard Designers, Inc., Asheville, N.C., 1951-52; designer Robotyper Corp., Hendersonville, N.C., 1952-53; engr. Western Electric Co., Burlington, N.C., 1953-74; mgr. engring. So. Bell Telephone Co., Atlanta, 1974-79, ret., 1979; partner Engring. Unltd., 1963—; instr. math. Elon Coll., 1956-59; instr. engring. graphics and design Ga. Inst. Tech., 1977-87; instr. DeKalb Community Coll., 1981-87. Mem. Dekalb County (Ga.) Adv. Com., 1979-82; dir. Glendale Townhouses Assn., chmn., 1979-80; mem. adminstrv. bd. 1st United Methodist Ch., Decatur, 1976-86. Served with AUS, 1943-46. Registered profl. engr., N.C., Ga. Mem. Am. Inst. Indsl. Engrs., Nat. Soc. Profl. Engrs., Ga. Profl. Engrs. in Industry (chmn. 1976), AAAS, Ga. Soc. Profl. Engrs. (Ga. Engr. of Yr. in Industry 1976; energy com. 1979-86). Clubs: Rotary, Republican, Odd Fellows. Patentee ultra low frequency sound generator for deep sea, 1972. Home: 1469 Country Squire Dr Decatur GA 30033

CECIL, ROBERT SALISBURY, telecommunications company executive; b. Manila, Philippines, May 28, 1935; came to U.S., 1941; s. Robert Edgar and Susan Elizabeth (Jurika) C.; m. Louise Nuttal Millholland, Nov. 30, 1963; children: Scott Douglass, James Hilliard. BSEE, U.S. Naval Acad., 1956; MBA, Harvard U., 1962. Commd. 2d lt. USAF, 1956, advanced through grades to 1st lt., 1958, ret., 1960; dir. govt. programs IBM, Washington, 1976-77; corp. v.p. mktg. Motorola Inc., Schaumburg, Ill., 1977-84; pres. Cellular Group Lin Broadcasting, N.Y.C., 1984—. Mem. Aspetuck Valley Country Club. Republican. Episcopalian. Office: Lin Broadcasting Corp 1370 6th Ave New York NY 10019

CEDERBERG, JOHN EDWIN, accountant; b. Osceola, Nebr., Feb. 18, 1943; s. Carl Edwin and Bernita Irene (Burns) C.; m. Bonnie Louise Butler, June 20, 1970; children: Erika Kristine, Kevin Bradley. BA summa cum laude, Dana Coll., 1965; MA, U. S.D., 1967; postgrad., Georgetown U., 1967-68. CPA, Md. Mem. audit staff Arthur Andersen & Co., Washington, 1968-71, mem. tax staff, 1971-73, mgr. taxes, 1973-75; mgr. taxes Touche Ross & Co., Lincoln, Nebr., 1976-78, tax ptnr., 1979—; chair comml. banking industry tax specialization group Touche Ross & Co., 1979-89, ptnr. in charge tax tech. svcs. to comml. banks, 1988—, ptnr. in charge Nebr. state tax svcs., 1988—; mem. Nat. Tax Council, 1983-87; trustee Nebr. Tax Research Council, 1986—; mem. bd. advs. The Journal of Bank Taxation, 1988—. Mem. editorial com. Bank Tax Bulletin, 1986—; editorial bd. Federal Income Taxation of Banks and Financial Institutions, 1979—. Mem. adminstrv. bd. St. Marks United Meth. Ch. Mem. AICPA (mem. tax div. 1989—, sub-com. specialized entities 1985-87), Nebr. Soc. CPAs, Nebr. State C. of C. and Industry (tax comm. 1985—), Bank Tax Inst. (adv. bd. mem. 1979—), Lincoln C. of C. (mem. state legis. com. 1976—, chmn. fed. legis. com. 1980-81), Sons of Am. Legion, Newcomen Soc. Home: 1916 Devonshire Dr Lincoln NE 68506 Office: Touche Ross & Co 1040 NBC Ctr Lincoln NE 68508

CEGNAR, RONALD WILLIAM, food company executive; b. Caldwell, Idaho, Feb. 11, 1945; s. Lewis William and Ethel Agnes (Parr) C.; m. Eileen Marie Murphy, Apr. 24, 1971; children: Tim, Ann. BS, U. Idaho, 1967, MS, 1969; MBA, Boise State U., 1976. Mgr. McDonald's Corp., Oak Brook, Ill., 1972-79; v.p. Popeyes Famous Fried Chicken, New Orleans, 1979-84; sr. v.p. Jerrico, Lexington, Ky., 1984-89; pres. Lexington (Ky.) Equipment Co., 1986—; pres. Metro Industries, Lexington, 1986—, also bd. dirs. Served as 1st lt. U.S. Army, 1969-72, Vietnam. Mem. Nat. Restaurant Assn., Nat. Frozen Food Assn., Nat. Fishery Inst., Am. Mgmt. Assn., Young Pres.' Orgn., Alpha Zeta. Republican. Roman Catholic. Club: Covington (Ky.) Country (pres. 1982-83). Home: 2109 Broadhead Pl Lexington KY 40515 Office: Jerrico Inc PO Box 11988 Lexington KY 40579

CELAYA, AUGUSTINE, JR., industrial company executive; b. Brownsville, Tex., Oct. 22, 1926; s. Augustine and Carmen (Barreda) C.; m. Virginia Hillman, Sept. 10, 1962; children: Michael, Laura, Francisca. BS, Tex. A. and M. U., 1947. Rancher, farmer, Brownsville, 1948-55; asst. to mng. dir. N.Y. Potash Export Assn., Inc., N.Y.C., 1956-60; sales mgr. indsl. products Union Carbide Inter Am. Inc., 1960-62, gen. mgr., 1963-64; asst. v.p. Latin Am. Union Carbide Co., N.Y.C., 1965-66; gen. mgr. consumer products div. Union Carbide Mexicana, Mexico City, 1966-68; pres. UCC Colombia, UCC Ecuador, Bogotá, 1968-70; pres. UCC Argentina, Buenos Aires, 1971-73; chmn. bd., pres. Union Carbide P.R., San Juan, 1973-76; v.p. engring. and mfg. agrl. chem. div. Union Carbide Corp., N.Y.C., 1976-78, v.p. internat. div., 1978-79; v.p. internat. ops. Houbigant, Inc., 1979-89; ind. intertnat. bus. cons., 1989—. Served to 1st lt. USAF, 1945-46, 50-51, Korea. Recipient awards for conservation, commerce, sports. Roman Catholic. Clubs: New Canaan (Conn.) Country; N.Y. Yacht; Jockey (Buenos Aires); Bankers (P.R.). Home: 142 Bridle Path Ln New Canaan CT 06840 Office: 1135 Pleasantview Terr Ridgefield NJ 07657

CELENTINO, THEODORE, airline and computer executive; b. Tarrytown, N.Y., Feb. 8, 1938; s. James and Natalie (Buonacquista) A.; m. Valerie Kopa, Sept. 16, 1961; children: Christopher, Lisa, Theodore Jr. BA, Iona Coll., 1960. Acctg. clk. Chevorlet div. GM, Tarrytown, N.Y., 1960-62; programmer Systems Devel. Co., Paramus, N.J., 1962-64; mgr. Am. Airlines, Briarcliff Manor, N.Y., 1964-69; dir. TWA, Kansas City, Mo., 1969-84; v.p. Piedmont Airlines, Winston-Salem, N.C., 1984-89; pres. TPF Incs., Winston-Salem, N.C., 1988-89; bd. dirs. Arinc Cos., Annapolis, Md., AvSat, Annapolis. Mem. editorial adv. bd. Georgetown Jour. Law and Tech., 1987. Mem. Citizens Adv. Com., Tarrytown, 1960, Vol. Fire Dept., Tarrytown, 1965; pres. Dem. Club, Tarrytown, 1967; chmn. Mcpl. Housing Authority, Tarrytown, 1968. Mem. Airline Industry On-Line Group. Roman Catholic. Home: 4150 Grossman Ct Winston-Salem NC 27104 Office: TPF Inc 1001 S Marshall St Ste 85 Winston-Salem NC 27101

CELLA, FRANK G., finance company executive; b. West Pittston, Pa., Feb. 23, 1929. BA in Bus. Adminstrn. and Acctg., Muhlenberg Coll., 1982. Br. mgr. GAC, Allentown, Pa., 1956-62; auditor GAC, Allentown, 1962-64, regional personnel dir., 1964-68; exec. recruiter GAC Corp., Miami, Fla., 1968-71; v.p. Fin. Am. GAC Corp., Allentown, 1971-79; sr. v.p. adminstrn. Chrysler First, Inc., Allentown, 1979—. Bd. dirs. Muhlenberg Coll., Allentown, Sta. WLTV Channel 39, Allentown, Burn Found., Allentown Hosp., also bd. assocs. Staff sgt. U.S. Army, 1950-52, Korea. Recipient Outstanding Leadership award Community Music Sch., 1985, Allentown Literacy Council, 1987. Mem. Rotary (1st v.p. Liberty Bell chpt. 1987-88). Office: Chrysler 1st Inc 1105 Hamilton St Allentown PA 18101

CELLIERS, PETER JOUBERT, public relations specialist; b. Vogelfontein, S. Africa; s. Bartilimy and Elsie Blanche (Goldberg) C.; ed. Eng., Continent; m. Helen Rassaby, Sept. 10, 1949; children—Gordon A.J., Jennefer A.J. Editor, to 1959; cons. to fgn. govts., internat. corps. Peter J. Celliers Co., N.Y.C., 1958-68; chief fgn. press services Olympic Organizing Com., Mexico, 1968; dir. for N.Am., Mexican Nat. Tourist Council, 1962-72; owner Ellis Assos., N.Y.C., 1969—; tech. adviser internat. market devel. to UN, hotels, carriers, govts. Mem. Soc. Am. Travel Writers (past pres.), N.Y. Assn. Travel Writers, Am. Soc. Journalists and Authors. Clubs: Nat. Press (Washington); Overseas Press, Dutch Treat (N.Y.C.). Home: 240 Garth Rd Scarsdale NY 10583 Office: Ellis Assocs 41 Union Sq West Suite 420 New York NY 10003

CELLINI, WILLIAM QUIRINO, JR., electrical engineer; b. Ardmore, Pa., Mar. 12, 1951; s. Quirino and Clara (Ricciardi) C. BSEE, Drexel U., 1974; MBA, U. Pitts., 1975; postgrad., George Washington U., 1977-81. Registered profl. engr., Va. With Fleming Corp., Washington, 1986-87, Kidde Cons., Inc., Balt., 1987, MK Ferguson Co., Annapolis Junction, Md., 1987-88, Hill Internat., Washington, 1988; chief electrical engr. EACI, Amherst, Mass., 1988—; cons. European Acad. Scis. Arts and Humanities, Paris. Mem. World Affairs Council Washington; active friend Am. Mus. Natural History, Am. Film Inst. Mem. IEEE, ASHRAE, AAAS, Am. Soc. Elec. Engrs., Nat. Soc. Profl. Engrs., Assn. Energy Engrs., Computer Security Inst., Indsl. Electronics Soc., Internat. Assn. Elec. Inspectors, Soc. Am. Mil. Engrs., Internat. Platform Assn., Space Studies Inst., Planetary Soc., Nat. Space Soc., Cousteau Soc., Smithsonian Instn., Am. Legion, Nat. Trust for Hist. Preservation, Cath. Alumni Clubs Internat., Nat. Italian-Am. Found., Order of Sons of Italy in Am., Internat. AMIGO, Alpha Phi Omega. Home: 34 Dickinson St Apt 2N Amherst MA 01002 Office: EACI PO Box 723 49 S Pleasant St Amherst MA 01004

CENCI-MAROLDI, DEBORAH ANN, computer company executive; b. Hackensack, N.J., June 4, 1959; d. Armand and Dolores (Palma) Cenci; m. David Maroldi, Aug. 10, 1985. BA, Fairleigh Dickinson U., 1979. Pres. Cenci Systems, Paramus, N.J., 1984—. Mem. NAFE (bd. dirs. 1983-89), Am. Mgmt. Assocs. Home and Office: 431 Holly Ave Paramus NJ 07652

CENSITS, RICHARD JOHN, healthcare company executive; b. Allentown, Pa., May 20, 1937; s. Stephen A. and Theresa M. C.; m. Linda A. Malin, June 21, 1958; children: Debra, Mark, David. BS in Econs., U. Pa., 1958; MBA, Lehigh U., 1964. Sr. auditor Arthur Andersen & Co., 1958-62; mgr. acctg. Air Products & Chems., 1962-64; contr. Hamilton Watch Co., Lancaster, Pa., 1964-69; v.p., contr. IU Internat., Phila., 1969-75; v.p. fin. Campbell Soup co., Camden, N.J., 1975-86; pres., chief exec. officer Summit Health Group, Inc., Gibbsboro, N.J., 1986—; bd. dirs. Checkpoint Systems Inc., Travelers Mortgage Svc., Communications Group, Inc., Penny Plate Inc.; adv. bd. Lutroe Electronics, Inc. Trustee United Way Camden County, South Jersey March of Dimes Sports Award Dinner Com.; assoc. trustee U. Pa., bd. overseers Sch. Nursing; exec. bd. undergrad. adv. Wharton Sch. Mem. Am. Inst. CPA's, Pa. Inst. CPA's, N.J. Soc. CPA's, Fin. Execs. Inst., Greater N.J. C. of C. (bd. dirs.). Club: Tavistock Country. Home: 120 Partree Rd Cherry Hill NJ 08003 Office: Summit Health Group Inc 20 E Clementon Rd Ste 102 S Gibbsboro NJ 08026

CENTER, JOHN WILLIAM, engineer, educator; b. Berkeley, Calif., Aug. 4, 1946; s. William Cranford and Thelma May (Ammons) C.; m. Lois Ann Koopmeiners, Nov. 8, 1975; childen: James William, Olivia Ann. BS in Physics, U. Calif., Riverside, 1968; MS in Systems Engring., Calif. State U., Fullerton, 1973; MBA, Coll. St. Thomas, St. Paul, 1982. Registered profl. engr. Physicist USN, 1968-70, 72-73; engr. Control Data Corp., St. Paul, 1973-75; mgr. Medtronic Inc., Mpls., 1975-84; cons. Ctr. Assocs., St. Paul, 1984—; adj. prof. Coll. St. Thomas, St. Paul., 1983—. Served as sgt. U.S. Army, 1970-72. Mem. NSPE, IEEE, Assn. Computing Machinery, Ints. Mgmt. Sci. Office: Center Assocs 1006 Mercury Dr Saint Paul MN 55126

CEPPOS, JEROME MERLE, newspaper editor; b. Washington, DC, Oct. 14, 1946; s. Harry and Florence (Epstein) C.; m. Karen E. Feingold, Mar. 7, 1982. B.S. in Journalism, U. Md., 1969. Reporter, asst. city editor, night city editor Rochester Democrat & Chronicle, N.Y., 1969-72; from asst. city editor, to nat. editor, to asst. mng. editor The Miami Herald, Fla., 1972-81; assoc. editor San Jose Mercury News, Calif., 1981, mng. editor, 1983—; mem. adv. bds. to journalism depts. San Jose State U. and Santa Clara U. Mem. Am. Soc. Newspaper Editors, AP Mng. Editors, Sigma Delta Chi. Home: 14550 Pike Rd Saratoga CA 95070 Office: San Jose Mercury News 750 Ridder Pk Dr San Jose CA 95190

CERDÁN, RICHARD, management consultant; b. N.Y.C., June 12, 1943; s. Aurelio and Henriette (Sorries) C.; m. Esther Antonia Baettig; children: Frédéric, Isabelle, Constantin. BS, Georgetown U., Washington, 1966; postgrad. in bus. adminstrn. Instituto de Estudios Superiores de la Empresa, Barcelona, Spain, 1966-67; postgrad. in law and econs., U. Geneva, 1968. Personnel mgr. UN, Geneva and N.Y.C., 1969-73; assoc. cons. Kepner-Tregoe, Princeton, N.J. and Wiesbaden, W. Ger., 1973-74; personnel mgr. Gen. Telephone and Electronics, Geneva, 1974-75; mng. dir. Charles Barker, Frankfurt, W. Ger., 1975-78; sr. assoc. Heidrick & Struggles Internat., Frankfurt, 1979-80; v.p., Zurich, Switzerland, 1980-81; ptnr. Carré, Orban & Ptnrs., 1981-88; chief exec. officer, Artists Risk Mgmt. and Investment Co., London, 1988—. Mem. Georgetown U. Alumni Assn. (pres.), Union Internat. (Frankfurt/Main) (bd. dirs.), Baur au Lac., Rotary. Home: Aurorastrasse 65, 8032 Zurich Switzerland Office: Artists Risk Mgmt &, Investment Co, Rennweg 32, Zurich CH-8001, Switzerland

CERIELLO, NANCY DEE, business executive, management consultant; b. Glen Cove, N.Y., Oct. 19, 1951; d. Edward Derrick and Marjorie D. (Francis) Albertson; m. Franco P. Ceriello, Dec. 22, 1980; children: Margie, Giovanna Maria. Grad. high sch., Glen Head, N.Y. Auditor quality control Photocircuits Kolmorgan Corp., Glen Cove, 1977-81; divisional v.p. SKO Inc., Glen Head, N.Y., 1981-85; mgr. Williams Charles & Scott Ltd., Commack, N.Y., 1985—; collection cons. Acad. Aeros., Queens, N.Y., 1982—, N.Y. Inst. Tech., Greenvale, N.Y., 1982—, Millersville (Pa.) U., 1982—. Mem. N.Y. State Orgn. Bursars and Bus. Assocs. (assoc.). Republican. Office: Williams Charles & Scott Ltd 649 Commack Rd Commack NY 11725

CERNA, CHRISTINA MONICA, lawyer; b. Munich, Fed. Republic Germany, Oct. 9, 1946; came to U.S., 1951; d. Eduardo Joseph and Marija (Vogel) C. BA, NYU, 1967; MA, U. Munich, 1970; JD, Am. U., 1973; LLM, Columbia U., 1974. Bar: D.C., U.S. Ct. Appeals (D.C. cir.), U.S. Supreme Ct. With Fried, Frank Harris, Shriver and Kampelman, Washington, 1974; with solicitor's office U.S. Dept. Labor, Washington, 1976-79; human right specialist Inter Am. Commn. on Human Rights, OAS, Washington, 1979—. Mem. Am. Soc. Internat. Law. Democrat. Office: OAS 1889 F St NW Washington DC 20006

CERNUGEL, WILLIAM JOHN, personal products company financial executive; b. Joliet, Ill., Nov. 19, 1942; s. William John, Sr. and Catherine Ann (Piechowiak) C.; m. Laurie M. Kusnik, Apr. 22, 1967; children: Debra, James, David. B.S., No. Ill. U., 1964. C.P.A., Ill. Supervising sr. accountant Peat, Marwick, Mitchell & Co., Chgo., 1964-70; asst. corp. controller Alberto-Culver Co., Melrose Park, Ill., 1970-71, corp. controller, 1972-74, v.p. and controller, 1974-82, v.p. fin., controller, 1982—. Bd. govs., treas. Gottlieb Meml. Hosp., Melrose Park; bd. advisors Coll. Bus., No. Ill. U. Mem. Nat. Assn. Accountants, Am. Inst. CPA's, Ill. Soc. CPA's. Lodge: Lions. Home: 8111 Lake Ridge Dr Burr Ridge IL 60521 Office: Alberto-Culver Co 2525 Armitage Ave Melrose Park IL 60160

CERNY, DANIEL JOHN, information technology executive, consultant; b. Chgo., May 4, 1945; s. John Frederick and Josephine Wanda (Dzien) C. BSEE, Ill. Inst. Tech., 1967; cert. in computer sci., U. Ill., Chgo., 1972; MBA in Mktg. and Fin., U. Chgo., 1972. Staff engr. GTE, Northlake, Ill., 1967-72; group mgr. ITT-Delta Systems, Chgo., 1972-76; cons. A.T. Kearney, Chgo., 1976-79; mng. cons. N.W. Industries, Chgo., 1979-82; v.p. info. systems Arvey Corp., Chgo., 1982-86; v.p. ops. Score Group, Inc., Chgo., 1986—. Contbr. articles to profl. jours. Capt. USMCR, 1968-76. Mem. Soc. for Info. Mgmt. (program mgr.), Tau Beta Pi, Eta Kappa Nu. Republican. Roman Catholic. Office: Score Group 5948 W Lawrence Chicago IL 60630

CERRANO, ROBERT EDWARD, accountant; b. N.Y.C., Nov. 29, 1947; s. Edward F. and Mary M. (Audano) C.; m. Sherry L. Kibler, Jan. 31, 1970; children: Jason A., Anne M. BS in Acctg., Quincy Coll., 1969. Staff acct. Dancer, Fitzgerald, Sample, Inc., N.Y.C., 1969-70, Gray, Hunter, Stenn & Co., Quincy, Ill., 1970-72; pvt. practicw Quincy, 1972-78; mgr. fin. analysis Quincy Compressor div. Colt Industries, Inc., Quincy, 1978-85, mgr. gen. acctg., 1985—. Treas. Pamel Bedford Dance Theatre, Inc., Quincy, 1979; advisor Jr. Achievement, Quincy, 1980; mem. Adams County Bd., 1982084; allocations com. United Way of Adams County, Quincy, 1984-88; St. Francis Solanus Parish Sch. Bd., 1986-88. Mem. Nat. Assn. Accts., Am. Legion (fin. officer Quincy chpt. 1971-76). Republican. Roman Catholic. Office: Colt Industries Inc Quincy Compressor Div 36 Wismann Ln Quincy IL 62301

CERRITO, ORATIO ALFONSO, real estate investor, financial advisor; b. Cleve., Mar. 10, 1911; s. Carl and Lillian (DiVita) C.; m. Rita McCue, Oct. 9, 1931 (div. 1946); children: Lillian, Rita-Diane; m. Maria Capri, Dec. 18, 1947; children: Miriam, Linda, Claudia. BA, John Carroll U., 1935; LLB, Cleve. Law Sch., 1940. Bar: Ohio, 1941, U.S. Dist. Ct. (no. dist.) Ohio, 1950. Foreman Chase Brass and Copper Co., Euclid, Ohio, 1931-41; assoc. Sindell & Sindell, Cleve., 1941-42; law violations investigator Wage-Hour div. U.S. Dept. Labor, Cleve., 1942-44; price officer Allied Control Commn. of Allied Mil. Govt., Rome, 1944-45; hdqs. distbn. officer UNRRA, Athens, 1945-46; pres., gen. mgr. U.S. Store Fixture Co., Cleve., 1946-52; account exec. Research Inst. Am., Cleve., 1952-54, So. Calif., 1954-60; regional mgr. indsl. div. Marlin, So. Calif., 1960-81; fin. advisor, mgr. O.A. Cerrito Family Trust, Fountian Valley, Calif., 1981—. Home and Office: 18173 Santa Cecilia Circle Fountain Valley CA 92708

CERVONI, ROBERT ANGELO, financial executive, consultant; b. N.Y.C., Feb. 2, 1953; s. Paul and Maria (Capogna) C.; m. Diane Eileen Peters, May 29, 1976; children: Dana, Robert Ryan. BSin Acctg., L.I.U., 1975. CPA, N.Y. Audit mgr. Oppenheim Appel Dixon & Co., N.Y.C., 1975-82; contr. Trading Co. of the West, L.A., 1982-84; chief fin. officer Spear Securities, Inc., L.A., 1984-88, Spear Fin. Svcs., Inc., L.A., 1984-88, bd. dirs., 1988—; chief fin. officer Weeden & Co., L.P., 1986—; cons. Forstmann Leff Assocs., N.Y.C., 1982-84, Instinet Corp., N.Y.C., 1983-84. Mem. Am. Inst. CPA's, N.Y. State Soc. CPA's, Nat. Soc. Compliance Profls. Roman Catholic. Office: Weeden & Co Inc 180 Maiden Ln New York NY 10038

CESARZ, PAUL MICHAEL, clinical pharmacist; b. Milw., Mar. 24, 1956; s. Jerome Edward and Carol Ann (Hendricks) C.; m. Colette Ann Chartier, Sept. 29, 1979; 1 child, Claire Elizabeth. B in Pharm. Sci., U. Wis., 1979. Intern Laabs Inc., Milw., 1977-79; staff pharmacist Snyder Pharmacy, Milw., 1979-82; prin. Paul M. Cesarz Pharmacist, S.C., Greenfield, Wis., 1982—; mem. faculty and staff U. Wis. Sch. Pharmacy, Madison, 1985—; preceptor Pharmacy Internship Bd., Madison, 1986—; lectr. in field. Mem. Pharmacists Soc. Milw. County (bd. dirs. 1979—, pres. 1984-85), Wis. Pharmacists Assn. (mem. adminstrv. council 1986—), Am. Pharm. Assn., Wis. Pharmacy Alumni Assn. (life, pres.-elect 1989). Roman Catholic. Office: 7420 W Forest Home Ave Greenfield WI 53220

CESZKOWSKI, DANIEL DAVID, financial analyst; b. Geneva, Dec. 9, 1954; s. Ignaz Ceszkowski and Veronika Noemi (Goldstein) Blanc; m. Hayett Djoudi, Oct. 26, 1988. Lic. Sci. Commerce & Industry, U. Geneva, 1977; MBA, Internat. Mgmt. Devel. Inst., Lausanne, Switzerland, 1985. Systems engr. Honeywell Bull, Geneva, 1977-80; dir. Corinfo S.A., Geneva, 1980-81; systems analyst Hewlett Packard, Meyrin, Switzerland, 1981-84; fin. cons. Merrill Lynch Internat., Inc., Geneva, 1986—; pvt. practice in fin., investment advising Geneva, 1988—; bd. dirs. Mievda S.A., Geneva, 1974—.

CETERSKI, JOHN JOSEPH, transportation executive; b. Amsterdam, N.Y., July 14, 1948; s. Victor Edward and Esther Irene (Curtis) C. BS, Bemidji State U., 1971. Trackman Can. Nat. Railway, Baudette, Minn., 1972; claims examiner R.R. Retirement Bd., Chgo., 1973-75; contact rep. R.R. Retirement Bd., Fargo, N.D., 1975-85, dist. mgr., 1985—. Pub., editor newsletter Prairie Trails. R.R. restoration Fargo Park Dist., 1985—, Western Minn. Steam Thresherman, Rollag, 1983—. Mem. Nat. Railway Hist. Soc. (pres. Red River Valley chpt. 1982—), Minn. Transp. Mus., Siouxland Hist. R.R. Assn., Fed. Exec. Assn. Mem. Democratic Farm Labor Party. Roman Catholic. Home: 3029 S 16th Ave Moorhead MN 56560 Office: Railroad Retirement Bd 657 N 2nd Ave Box 383 Fargo ND 58107

CHABOT, PHILIP LOUIS, JR., lawyer; b. Coaldale, Pa., Mar. 23, 1951; s. Philip Louis and Dorothy Louise (Casselberry) C.; m. Karen Sue Pirko, June 6, 1970 (div. 1981); m. Lynne Marx, Nov. 23, 1985; children: Alexander, Elizabeth, Patrick. BA with high honors, U. Va., 1973, JD, 1976. Bar: Va. 1976, D.C. 1976, U.S. Ct. Claims 1978, U.S. Dist. Ct. D.C. 1976, U.S. Dist. Ct. (ea. dist.) Va. 1984, U.S. Ct. Appeals (1st, 2d, 4th, 5th, 8th, 9th and 10th cirs.), U.S. Ct. Appeals (D.C. cir.) 1976, U.S. Supreme Ct. 1979. Assoc. Northcutt Ely, Washington, 1976-77; prin. Duncan, Weinberg & Miller, P.C., Washington, 1978-84; pres. Philip Chabot, Chartered, Washington and Alexandria, Va., 1984-88; ptnr. Grad, Toothman, Logan & Chabot, P.C., Washington and Alexandria, Va., 1988—; aide U.S. Senator John V. Tunney, 1973, U.S. Senator William V. Roth, 1974-75; adj. prof. law Am. U., Washington, 1977-81; asst. to dir. com. on tech., transfer and utilization Nat. Acad. Engring., Washington, 1973-74; bd. dirs. Route One Corridor Housing, Inc., 1985-89. Editor: (newsletter) Stateline, 1983-85. Dem. candidate Va. Ho. of Dels., 44th House Dist., Va., 1983; state coordinator Va. Youth Coalition for Muskie, 1972; mem. Fairfax Com. 100, 1983—; mem. Mt. Vernon Dem. Com., 1982—; mem. Fairfax County Dem. Com., 1982—; mem. citizens adv. bd. Mt. Vernon Nursing Ctr., Fairfax, 1982—; trustee Va. Outdoors Found., 1982-86; trustee, vice chmn. Fairfax County Uniformed Retirement System Bd., 1982-86; nat. vice chief Order of Arrow Boy Scouts Am., 1968-70; pres. Sherwood Estates Citizens Assn., 1986—, co-chmn. Mt. Vernon Coun. of Citizens Assns., 1989—; bd. dirs. Fairfax County Fedn. Citizens Assn., 1988—. Recipient Eagle Scout award Boy Scouts Am., 1964. Mem. ABA, Va. State Bar Assn., Va. Trial Lawyers' Assn., D.C. Bar Assn., Mt. Vernon-Lee C. of C., Fairfax C. of C., Alexandria C. of C., Phi Beta Kappa. Avocation: sailing. Office: Grad Tootham Logan & Cabot 1990 M St NW #800 Washington DC 20036 other: 112 N Columbus St Alexandria VA 22314

CHABRAYA, KENNETH M., communications executive; b. San Jose, Calif., Oct. 25, 1957; s. Daniel M. and Helen Chabraya; m. Gail E. Davis, Nov. 7, 1976; children: Dawn M., David M. Field service engr. Micro Manipulator, Escondido, Calif., 1979-82; owner Chabraya Industries, Inc., San Jose, 1982-86, pres., 1986—; sales engr. Alessi Industries, Irvine, Calif., 1984-85; v.p. Am. Probe and Techs., San Jose, 1985-86; pres. Chabraya Industries, Inc., San Jose, 1986—. Office: Chabraya Industries Inc 1701-F Fortune Dr San Jose CA 95131

CHACKO, GEORGE KUTTICKAL, systems science educator, consultant; b. Trivandrum, India, July 1, 1930; came to U.S., 1953.; s. Geevarghese Kuttickal and Thankamma (Mathew) C.; m. Yo Yee, Aug. 10, 1957; children: Rajah Yee, Ashia Yo. MA in Econs. and Polit. Philosophy, Madras (India) U., 1950; postgrad. (Coll. scholar), St. Xavier's Coll., Calcutta, India, 1950-52; B in Commerce, Calcutta U., 1952; cert. postgrad. tng. (Inst. fellow), Indian Stat. Inst., Calcutta, 1951; postgrad. (SE Asia Club fellow), Princeton U., 1953-54; PhD in Econometrics, New Sch. for Social Research, 1959; postgrad. (Univ. fellow), UCLA, 1961. Asst. editor Indian Fin., Calcutta, 1951-53; comml. corr. Times of India, 1953; dir. mktg. and mgmt. research Royal Metal Mfg. Co., N.Y.C., 1958-60; mgr. dept. ops. research Hughes Semicondr. div. Calif., 1960-61; ops. research staff cons. Union Carbide Corp., N.Y.C., 1962-63; mem. tech. staff Research Analysis Corp., McLean, Va., 1963-65, MITRE Corp., Arlington, Va., 1965-67; sr. staff scientist TRW Systems Group, Washington, 1967-70; cons. def. systems, computer, space, tech. systems and internat. devel. systems; assoc. in math. test devel. Ednl. Testing Service, Princeton, N.J., 1955-57; asst. prof. bus. adminstrn. UCLA, 1961-62; lectr. Dept. Agr. Grad. Sch., 1965-67; asst. professorial lectr. George Washington U., 1965-68; professorial lectr. Am. U., 1967-70, adj. prof., 1970; vis. prof. def. systems Mgmt. Coll., Ft. Belvoir, Va., 1972-73; vis. prof. U. So. Calif., 1970-71, prof. systems mgmt., 1971-83, prof. systems sci., 1983—; sr. Fulbright prof. Nat. Chengchi U., Taipei, 1983-84, sr. Fulbright research prof., 1984-85; prin. investigator and program dir. Tech. Transfer Project/Taiwan Nat. Sci. Council, 1984-85; disting. fgn. expert lectr. Taiwan Ministry Econ. Affairs, 1986; sr. vis. research prof. for Taiwan Nat. Sci. Council Nat. Chengchi U., Taipei, 1988-89; v.p. program devel. Systems and Telecommunications Corp., Potomac, Md., 1987—; chief sci. cons. RJO Enterprises, Lanham, Md., 1988—. Author: 23 books in field, including Applied Statistics in Decision-Making, 1971, Computer-aided Decision-Making, 1972, Systems Approach to Public and Private Sector Problems, 1976, Operations Research Approach to Problem Formulation and Solution, 1976, Management Information Systems, 1979, Trade Drain Imperative of Technology Transfer-U.S. Taiwan Concomitant Coalitions, 1985, Robotics/Artificial Intelligence/Productivity-U.S.-Japan Concomitant Coalitions, 1986, Technology Management Applications to CorporateMarkets and Military Missions, 1988, Dynamic Program Management From Defense Experience to Commercial Application, 1989, The Systems Approach to Problem-solving from Corporate Markets to National Missions, 1989, Toward Expanding Exports Through Technology Transfer-IBM-Taiwan Concomitant Coalitions, 1989; contbr. articles to profl. publs.; editor, contbr.: 17 books, including The Recognition of Systems in Health Services, 1969, Reducing the Cost of Space Transportation, 1969, Systems Approach to Environmental Pollution, 1972, National Organization of Health Services—U.S., USSR, China, Europe, 1979, Educational Innovation in Health Services-U.S., Europe, Middle East, Africa, 1979; guest editor Jour. Research Communication Studies, 1978-79; assoc. editor Internat. Jour. of Forecasting, 1982-85. Active Nat. Presbyn. Ch., Washington, 1967-84, mem. ch. council, 1969-71, mem. chancel choir, 1967-84; chmn. worship com. Taipei Internat. Ch., 1984, chmn. membership com., 1985, chmn. Stewardship com., 1985; chmn. com. Christian Edn., 1989, Sunday Sch. Supt., 1989; mem. adult choir; co-dean Ch. Family Camp, 1977; coordinator Life Abundant Discovery Group, 1979; adult Sunday Sch. leader 4th Presbyn. Ch., Bethesda, Md., 1986—, mem. Sanctuary choir, 1985—, mem. Men's Ensemble, 1986—. Recipient awards, including Gold medal Inter-Collegiate Extempore Debate in Malayalam U. Travancore, Trivandrum, India, 1945, 1st Pl. Yogic Exercises Competition U.ravancore, 1946, 1st prize Inter-Varsity Debating Team Madras, 1949, NSF internat. sci. lectures award, 1982, Jr. Lectureship prize Physics Soc. U. Travancove, 1946; USIA sponsored U.S. Sci. emissary to Egypt, Burma, India, Singapore, 1987. Fellow AAAS (mem. nat. council 1968-73, chmn. or co-chmn. symposia 1971, 72, 74, 76, 77, 78), Am. Astronautical Soc. (v.p. publs. 1969-71, editor Tech. Newsletter 1968-72, mng. editor Jour. Astronautical Scis. 1969-75); mem. Ops. Research Soc. Am. (vice chmn. com. of representation on AAAS 1972-78, mem. nat. council tech. sect. on health 1966-68, editor Tech. Newsletter on Health 1966-73), Washington Ops. Research Council (trustee 1967-69, chmn. tech. colloquia 1967-68, editor Tech. Newsletter 1967-68), Inst. Mgmt. Scis. (rep. to Internat. Inst. for Applied Systems Analysis in Vienna, Austria 1976-77, session chmn. Athens, Greece 1977, Atlanta 1977), World Future Soc. (editorial bd. publs. 1970-71), N.Y. Acad. Scis. Democrat. Club: Kiwanis (Capital Dist. Div. One Internat. Disting. Service award 1968, 70, Friendship Heights Club Outstanding Service award 1972-73, 1st disting. dir. Taipei-Keystone Club 1978, spl. rep. of internat. pres. and counselor to dist. of Republic of China 1983—, pioneer premier project award Asia-Pacific Conf. 1986, Legion of Honor 1985, chmn. citizenship services, chmn. fund raising Bethesda Club 1986-87). Office: U So Calif Office 5510 Columbia Pike Arlington VA 22204

CHADER, PAUL BRUCE, human resource executive; b. Newton, Mass., June 9, 1941; s. Harold William and Barbara (Pease) C.; m. Charlotte L. Williams, Feb. 28, 1970; children: Jennifer Rebekah, Sarah Elizabeth. BA in Econs., Colby Coll., 1963; MBA in Mktg., U. Pa., 1969. Mktg. and planning analyst TWA, N.Y.C., 1969-71, sr. analyst, 1971-72, mgr. organizational planning, 1972-74, dir. organizational and pers. devel., 1974-76; area pers. exec. div. home furnishings Burlington Industries, N.Y.C., 1976-78, area pers. exec. Klopman div., 1978-80, dir. sales and prodn. forecasting div. menswear, 1981-81; dir. human resource devel. Philip Morris Internat., N.Y.C., 1981—. Capt. USAF, 1963-67. Mem. Human Resource Planning Soc., Am. Soc. Pers. Adminstrn. (exec. bd. N.Y. chpt.). Home: 28 Addison Terr Old Tappan NJ 07675 Office: Philip Morris Internat 120 Park Ave New York NY 10017

CHADSEY, WILLIAM LLOYD, III, business executive; b. Miami, Sept. 25, 1942; s. William Lloyd and Vivian (Hervig) C.; m. Mary Elizabeth Henschel, Feb. 2, 1980; children—Geoffrey, Gillian, Ian, Elisabeth. B.A. in Engring. and Applied Physics, Harvard U., 1964; M.S. in Physics, U. Pa., 1968. Physicist Gen. Electric Co., Phila., 1965-72; sr. v.p. Sci. Applications Internat. Corp., McLean, Va., 1972—; sci. advisor U.S. Air Force, 1981-83, Def. Nuclear Agy., Washington, 1984—. Republican. Episcopalian. Home: 12007 Canter Ln Reston VA 22091 Office: Sci Applications Internat Corp 1710 Goodridge Dr McLean VA 22102

CHADWELL, JAMES RUSSELL, JR., comptroller; b. Shelbyville, Ky., Dec. 29, 1948; s. James Russell and Martha (Cinnamond) C.; m. Caroline Meadows Taylor, Jan. 8, 1978; children: Cameron, Aaron. BS in Math., Ea. Ky. U., 1970; BBA in Acctg., U. Cen. Fla., 1975; MBA, U. Louisville, 1981. CPA, Ky. Auditor Ky. State Auditor's Office, Frankfort, 1975-80, audit mgr., 1981-84; comptroller Ky. Tchr.'s Retirement System, Frankfort, 1984—. Bd. dirs. Commonwealth Credit Union, 1988—. With U.S. Army, 1970-72, Vietnam. Mem. Assn. Govt. Accts. (pres. 1981-82, treas. 1983-84), Am. Inst. CPAs, Ky. Soc. CPAs, Govtl. Fin. Officers Assn., Sigma Chi. Democrat. Episcopalian. Office: Ky Tchrs Retirement System 479 Versailles Rd Frankfort KY 40601

CHADWELL, SUSIE, real estate broker; b. Jellico, Tenn., Aug. 26, 1940; d. Ross James and Irene (Jones) C.; m. Richard Rodriguez, May 30, 1957 (dec. Aug. 1965); children: Susan Denise, Richard. Student, U. Tampa, 1965-67, Midland Tech. Coll., 1972-73, Hillsborough Community Coll., 1975-78, Tampa Coll., 1982-83. Ordained to ministry Universal Life Ch.; licensed real estate broker, mortgage broker. Clk. Chad Supply, Tampa, 1977-78, sec., 1978-79; salesperson real estate Chadwell Homes, Seffner, Fla., 1979-82, Thonotossassa, Fla., 1984—; salesperson condominiums Eastfield Slopes, Thonotossassa, 1982-84; pvt. practice mortgage brokerage Susie Chadwell Assn., Thonotossassa, 1985—; cons., tchr. in field. Charter mem. Tampa Bay Performing Arts Ctr., 1987—. Mem. NAFE, Internat. Platform Assn., Brandon (Fla.) C. of C., Fla. Assn. Mortgage Brokers, 21st Century Women's Club, Beta Sigma Phi. Home and Office: 9540 Field View Cir Thonotossassa FL 33592

CHAFFIN, GARY ROGER, business executive; b. Satanta, Kans., June 6, 1937; s. Owen Charles and Leona Irene (Dale) C.; m. Charlotte Daisy Hawley, Aug. 17, 1958; children: Darcy Lea, Charla Cai, Darren Roger, Charles Dale. BA, U. Kans., 1960. Loan officer Limerick Fin., Lawrence, Kans., 1959-60; asst. mgr. Chaffin Grocery, Moscow, Kans., 1960-62; store mgr. Chaffin Inc. Gibson Discount Ctrs., 1962-68; gen. mgr. Chaffin Inc., Dodge City, Kans., 1968-85; pres. Chaffin, Inc., Dodge City, Kans., 1985—; pres. Great SW Ban Corp., Dodge City, Gibson Franchise Corp., Dodge City; chmn. bd. dirs. Bank SW, Dodge City. Republican. Methodist. Home: 510 Clover Dodge City KS 67801 Office: Chaffin Inc 100 Chaffin Industrial Park Dodge City KS 67801

CHAIKA, STEPHEN, sales executive; b. N.Y.C., Sept. 7, 1920; s. William and Mary (Fil) C.; m. Katherine Grace Olsen, July 20, 1944; children: Judith, Stephen William. BEE, CCNY, 1943. Design engr. Sperry Gyroscope Co., Garden City, N.Y., 1946-48; sales engr. Fed. Electric Products, Newark, 1949-50; v.p. sales Gen. Switch Corp., Bklyn., 1960-65; regional sales mgr. Zinsco Mfg., L.A., 1965-67; v.p. sales and mktg. Slater Electric Inc., Glen Cover, N.Y., 1967—. Lt. USN, 1940-46. Mem. Am. Soc. Photography, U.S. Power Squadrons Club. Republican. Roman Catholic.

Home: 73 Shaw Dr North Merrick NY 11566 Office: Slater Electric Inc 45 Sea Cliff Ave Glen Cover NY 11542

CHAING, LIEN HWA, finance company executive, financial planner; b. Seoul, July 20, 1946; s. Ki Hyoung and Ok Soon (Kim) C. BBA in Fin., Loyola Marymount U., 1978; MBA, U. Nev., 1981; diploma, Coll. for Fin. Planning, Denver, 1984. Cert. fin. planner. Chief fin. officer M.B. Dalitz, Las Vegas, Nev., 1979-82; sr. capital planner Rockwell Internat., El Segundo, Calif., 1982; master fin. planner Bretcourt Fin. Planning, Upland, Calif., 1982-84; pres. L.H. Chaing Fin. Cons., Inc., Woodland Hills, Calif., 1985—; mem. Internat. Bd. Standards and Practices for Cert. Fin. Planners. Mem. Inst. Cert. Fin. Planners (chmn. continuing edn. program San Francisco Valley chpt. 1987—). Republican. Home: 4551 Tam O'Shanter Dr Westlake Village CA 91362 Office: 5850 Canoga Ave Ste 500 Woodland Hills CA 91367

CHALEFF, CARL THOMAS, brokerage house executive; b. Inpls., Nov. 21, 1945; s. Boris Carl and Betty J. (Miller) C.; m. Carolyn F. Heath, Apr. 26, 1970 (div. Apr. 1985); children: Fritz, Eric; m. Darlene Finkel, Dec. 13, 1987. BS in Econs., Purdue U., 1969; MBA in Fin., Xavier U., 1976. Asst. v.p. Am. Can Corp., N.Y.C., 1969-70; sales mgr. Am. Can Corp., Cin., 1970-73; account exec. Merrill Lynch, Cin., 1973-76; v.p. Oppenheimer, Chgo., 1976-81; assoc. dir. Bear Stearns & Co., Chgo., 1981-87; sr. v.p., branch mgr. Oppenheimer & Co., Chgo., 1987—. Mem. Young Execs. Club, Chgo. Film Makers (bd. dirs. 1986), Chgo. Council on Fgn. Relations, Internat. Platform Assn., Chgo. Bond Club. Clubs: East Bank, Rainbows (Chgo.) (bd. dirs. 1984), Metro. Lodge: Rotary. Home: 55 W Goethe Chicago IL 60610

CHALFANT, JOSEPH SHAW, mangement consultant; b. Richmond, Ind., Apr. 12, 1936; s. Ray King and Margaret (Shaw) C.; B.S., Ind. U., 1958; postgrad. U. Louisville Sch. Law, 1959-62; m. Harriet Vaughan Strange, June 6, 1959; children—Martin Joseph, Matthew Christopher, Peggy. Sales, Colgate-Palmolive Co., 1958, merchandising rep., 1959-61; sales mgr. Mid-Continent Carton Corp., Louisville, 1961-72, pres., 1972—; pres. Shaw Internat., New Albany, Ind., 1972—; dir. various corp. and charity bds. Served with AUS, 1958-59. Cert. mgmt. cons. Mem. Sigma Alpha Epsilon, Alpha Delta Sigma. Republican. Methodist. Home: Trimingham Rd New Albany IN 47150 Office: Shaw Internat PO Box 375 New Albany IN 47150

CHAMBERLAIN, CHARLOTTE APPEL, corporate executive, economist; b. N.Y.C., Apr. 30, 1946; d. Henry and Marie (Lugscheider) Appel. Ph.D. in Econs., Cornell U., 1971. Prof. econs. Northeastern U., Boston, 1971-73; br. chief forecasting and modeling U.S. Dept. Transp., Cambridge, Mass., 1973-79; v.p., mgr. dept. econs. Glendale Fed. Savs. and Loan Assn. (Calif.), 1979-81; dir. Office of Policy and Econ. Research, Fed. Home Loan Bank Bd., Washington, 1981-83; sr. v.p. asset liability mgmt. Glendale Fed. Savs. (Calif.), 1983-85, exec. v.p. strategic planning and mktg., 1985—. Bd. dirs. Real Estate Ctr., U. Calif., Berkeley. Lehman fellow. Mem. Am. Econ. Assn., Nat. Assn. Bus. Economists, Western Econs. Assn., Phi Beta Kappa, Phi Kappa Phi. Editor Jour. Housing Fin. Office: Glendale Fed Savs 700 N Brand Blvd PO Box 1709 Glendale CA 91209

CHAMBERLAIN, DAVID HAROLD, research and development company executive; b. East Stroudsburg, Pa., Mar. 2, 1944; s. John Harold and Elizabeth Gertrude (Altemose) C.; m. Jeanne Marge Fleming, Aug. 22, 1966; children: Elizabeth, Mary, Dianne. BA, Cen. Coll., Pella, Iowa, 1976. Project engr. Stresau Lab., Spooner, Wis., 1967-74, gen. mgr., 1974-80, pres., 1980—. Contbr. numerous articles to profl. jours. Founding dir., officer Spooner Area Civic Ctr.; bd. dirs. Spooner Lake Dist. Mem. Am. Def. Preparedness Assn., Spooner Area Econ. Devel. Corp. Methodist. Home: 805 La Follette St Spooner WI 54801 Office: Stresau Lab Inc 1400 S River St PO Box 368 Spooner WI 54801

CHAMBERLAIN, DAVID M., consumer products company executive; b. Ft. Benning, Ga., 1943; m. Karin Chamberlain; children: Pamela, Katheryn. BS, U. Pa., 1965; MBA, Harvard U., 1969. With Quaker Oats Co., Chgo., 1969-74, v.p., gen. mgr., 1974-77, pres. frozen foods div., 1977-80; pres. margarine and desserts div. Nabisco Brands, Inc., N.Y.C., 1980-82; sr. v.p. Nabisco Brands, Inc., Toronto, Can., 1982-83; pres., chief op. officer Shaklee Corp., San Francisco, 1983-85, pres., chief exec. officer, 1985—. Bd. dirs. San Francisco Boys and Girls Club, San Francisco Opera, U.S. C. of C., Washington, Calif. Roundtable; pres. San Francisco C. of C. Served to 1st lt. U.S. Army, 1965-67. Mem. St. Francis Yacht Club, University Club, Apawamin Club, Larchmont (N.Y.) Yacht Club, Royal Canadian Yacht Club. Republican. Office: Shaklee Corp 444 Market St San Francisco CA 94111

CHAMBERLAIN, JILL FRANCES, financial services executive; b. Chgo., Mar. 25, 1954; d. Chester Emery and Mary Edythe (Hurd) C. B.A. in Math. with honors, Ill. State U., 1975; M.B.A., U. Chgo., 1981. Programmer, Arthur Andersen, Chgo., 1975-76; cons. Laventhol & Horwath, Chgo., 1976-77; fin. systems analyst U. Chgo. Hosp., 1978-80; v.p. CHI/COR Info. Mgmt., Inc., Chgo., 1980-87; systems designer GECC, Stamford, 1987-88; mgr. GE Capital Corp., 1988—; cons. RMS Bus. Systems, Chgo., 1976-77. Mem. Delaware Valley Disaster Recovery Info. Exch. Group, Nat. Assn. Female Execs. Libertarian. Methodist. Avocations: reading; traveling; needlework. Office: GECC 3003 Summer St Stamford CT 06901

CHAMBERLAIN, RONALD LEE, banker; b. Danville, Pa., July 10, 1941; s. John Wert and Vivian Geraldine (Fertig) C.; m. Eileen Kathleen Visotski, July 31, 1966; children: Ronald, Dee Ann. Degree in Pre-Standard and Standard Banking, Am. Inst. Banking, 1967; degree in Pa. Banking, Bucknell U., 1973; degree, Nat. Sch. Fin. and Mgmt., Fairfield, Conn., 1988. Teller Pa. Nat. Bank, Shamokin, 1959-61; asst. treas. No. Cen. Bank, Shamokin, 1961-80; v.p. Cen. Pa. Savs. Assn., Shamokin, 1980—. Past pres. Lower Anthracite United Way, Shamokin, bd. dirs. 1985—; past pres. Shamokin/Mt. Carmel ARC, bd. dirs. 1984. With U.S. Army 1964-70. Mem. Inst. Fin. Edn., Nat. Coun. Savs. Instns., Am. Inst. Banking (assoc. councilman dist. 3 1972-77, officer, bd. dirs. Black Diamond chpt. 1962-79), Pa. Savs. Instns. (ops. com.), Northeastern Pa. Savs. Assn., Cen. Pa. Savs. Assn. (pres., state com.), (Shamokin High Sch. Alumni Assn. (class rep. 1959—), Shamokin C. of C. (bd. dirs. 1984—), Rotary (past pres., bd. dirs. 1984—), Masons (32 degree). Republican. Home: RD 2 Box 166 Shamokin PA 17872 Office: Cen Pa Savs Assn 100 W Independence St Shamokin PA 17872

CHAMBERLAIN, WILLARD THOMAS, energy company exective; b. New Haven, Nov. 22, 1928; s. Thomas Huntington and Alice Irene (Daley) C.; m. Harriet Halbert Keck, Nov. 20, 1965; children: Huntington Wilson, Amy Thatcher. B.E., Yale U., 1950; postgrad., Ill. Inst. Tech., 1951-53. With Armour Research Found., Chgo., 1951-53; asst. to tech. mgr. Anaconda Brass div. Anaconda Corp., Waterbury, Conn., 1953-56, tech. supr., 1956-60; metall. mgr. Anaconda Brass div. Anaconda Corp., Torrington, Conn., 1960-61; mgr. devel. Anaconda Brass div. Anaconda Corp., Waterbury, 1961-62, lab. mgr., 1962-64, mgr. research-tech. ctr., 1964-67; mgr. Anaconda Brass div. Anaconda Corp., Valley Mills, 1967; mgr. Anaconda Brass div. Anaconda Corp., Ansonia, 1967-70, mgr. prodn. planning, 1970-71, v.p. mfg., 1971-72, exec. v.p. Brass div., 1972-74, pres., 1974-80; pres. Anaconda Industries, 1980; sr. v.p. Atlantic Richfield Co., 1980-82; pres. Arco Metals Co., 1982-85; sr. v.p. corp. affairs Atlantic Richfield Co., 1985-87; sr. v.p. govt. and pub. affairs ARCO, 1987—; mem. So. Calif. bus. com. Econ. Literacy Council Adv. of Calif. Mem. exec. bd. Waterbury Republican Town Com., 1964-70; commr. Waterbury Bd. Fin., 1966-67, chmn. charter revision com., 1966-67; mem. exec. bd. Mattatuck council Boy Scouts Am., 1965-72, Waterbury Assn. for Retarded Children, 1965-56; co-chmn. Clergy-Industry Conf., 1965-66; campaign chmn. Valley United Fund, 1970-71; bd. dirs. United Way, Central Naugatuck Valley, 1974, The Banking Ctr., 1974-81, Western Conn. Indsl. Council, 1974-81, Calif. State U. Found., Found. for Am. Communications, Los Angeles Arts Council; trustee Calif. Mus. Found., Harvey Mudd Coll.; bd. trustees Greater Los Angeles Partnership for the Homeless. Recipient Outstanding Civic Leader award, 1967. Mem. Copper Devel. Assn., Aluminum Assn. (dir.), Am. Soc. Metals, Yale Engring. Assn., Greater Waterbury C. of C. (bd. dirs. 1974), Alliance for Aging Research (bd. dirs.), Am. Petroleum Inst. (emerging issues task force), The Brookings Instn. (council mem.), Calif. State U. (Los Angeles) Found. (bd. dirs., compensation planning com., chmn. investment com.), Calif. State U. Bus. Assocs., Constl. Rights. Found. (bus. adv. council), Econ. Literacy Council Adv. Calif. (So. Calif. bus. com.), Found. for Am. Communications (dir.), Greater Los Angeles Partnership for the Homeless (trustee), Harvey Mudd Coll. (trustee, ednl. planning com., chmn. corp. com. and founding friends assocs.), Hugh O'Brian Youth Found. (bd. govs.), Joint Council Econ. Edn. (trustee, fin. and devel. com.), Los Angeles Urban League (exec. com., bd. dirs., chmn. fin. devel. com.), Los Angeles Philharmonic (bd. dirs.), Math., Engring. and Sci. Achievement (industry adv. bd.), Nat. Action Council for Minorities in Engring., Nat. Minority Supplier Devel. Council (bd. dirs.), Nat. Wetlands Policy Forum, Nat. Wildlife Fedn. (vice chmn. corp. conservation council), Town Hall, U.S. C. of C. (emerging issues subcom.), World Affairs Council. Presbyterian. Clubs: Copper, Plaza, Yale of Chgo., Meadow, University (Los Angeles), Founders, Music Ctr. (Los Angeles). Home: 721 Madre St Pasadena CA 91107 Office: ARCO 515 S Flower St Los Angeles CA 90071

CHAMBERLIN, JOHN STEPHEN, private investor, former cosmetics company executive; b. Boston, July 29, 1928; s. Stephen Henry and Olive Helen (McGrath) C.; m. Mary Katherine Leahy, Oct. 9, 1954; children—Mary Katherine, Patricia Ann, Carol Lynn, John Stephen, Liane Helen, Mark Joseph. A.B. cum laude, Harvard U., 1950, M.B.A., 1953. Lamp salesman Gen. Electric Co., N.Y.C., 1954-57, mgmt. cons., 1957-60; mgr. product planning TV receiver dept. Gen. Electric Co., Syracuse, N.Y., 1960-63; mgr. mktg., gen. mgr. radio receiver dept. Gen. Electric Co., Utica, N.Y., 1963-70; exec. v.p., dir. Lenox Inc., Trenton, N.J., 1970-71; v.p., gen. mgr. housewares div. Gen. Electric Co., Bridgeport, Conn., 1971-74, v.p., gen. mgr. housewares and audio div., 1974-76; pres., chief exec. officer, dir. Lenox Inc., Lawrenceville, N.J., 1976-81, chmn., chief exec. officer, 1981-85; pres., chief operating officer Avon Products, Inc., N.Y.C., 1985-88; pvt. investor N.Y.C., 1988—; bd. dirs. Travelers Companies, Prince Mfg. Co. Trustee Med. Ctr. at Princeton, Woodrow Wilson Nat. Fellowship Found.; bd. overseers Parson Sch. Design. Mem. Bedens Brook Club, Harvard Club (N.Y.C.), Union League Club (N.Y.C.). Home: 182 Fairway Dr Princeton NJ 08540

CHAMBERS, LOIS IRENE, insurance agency executive; b. Omaha, Nov. 24, 1935; d. Edward J. and Evelyn B. (Davidson) Morrison; m. Peter A. Mscichowski, Aug. 16, 1952 (div. 1980); 1 child, Peter Edward; m. Frederick G. Chambers, Apr. 17, 1981. Clk. Gross-Wilson Ins. Agy., Portland, Oreg., 1955-57; sec., bookkeeper Reed-Paulsen Ins. Agy., Portland, 1957-58; office mgr., asst. sec., agt. Don Biggs & Assocs., Vancouver, Wash., 1958-88, v.p. ops., 1988—; automation cons. Chambers & Assocs., Tualatin, Oreg., 1985—; chmn. adv. com. Clark Community Coll., Vancouver, 1979—. Mem. citizens com. task force City of Vancouver, 1976-78, mem. Block Grant rev. task force, 1978—. Mem. Ins. Women of S.W. Wash. (pres. 1978, Ins. Woman of Yr. 1979), Nat. Assn. Ins. Women, Nat. Users Agena Systems (charter; pres. 1987-88), Soroptimist Internat. (Vancouver)(pres. 1978-79, Soroptimist of the Year 1979-80, charter pres. 1987—). Democrat. Roman Catholic. Office: Don Biggs & Assocs 916 Main St PO Box 189 Vancouver WA 98666-0189

CHAMBERS, PATRICK JOSEPH, JR., utility company executive; b. Cleve., June 3, 1934; s. Patrick J. and Catherine (Green) C.; m. Nancy Carol Prock, June 3, 1956; children: Stephanie, Patrick, Michele. BSEE, Case Inst. Tech., 1961. Rate engr. E. Ohio Gas, Cleve., 1956-64; exec. cons. Commonwealth Svcs., Inc., N.Y.C., Washington, 1965-72; sr. v.p., chief fin. officer Orange and Rockland Utilities, Inc., Pearl River, N.Y., 1972—, also dir.; bd. dirs. MidLantic Nat. Bank North. V.p. fin. Boy Scouts Am., Rockland County, 1976-79, now trustee and mem. exec. bd.; bd. dirs., treas. Nyack (N.Y.) Hosp.; bd. dirs. United Way Bergen County, chmn. campaign, 1983; trustee Bullawa Trust Fund. Mem. Am. Gas Assn. (mem. fin. com. 1978—), Edison Electric Inst. (fin. com. 1978—). Roman Catholic. Club: Ridgewood Country (N.J.). Office: Orange & Rockland Utilities Inc 1 Blue Hill Pla Pearl River NY 10965

CHAMBERS, RAY WAYNE, security and loss control consultant; b. Cascade, W.Va., June 22, 1931; s. Robert and Mildred Ethel (Starrett) C.; m. Joan Roberta Tilley, Apr. 7, 1952; children: Rebecca H. Frase, Bonita I. Knight, Diana L. Sobalvarro. Cert. protection profl. Enlisted U.S. Army, 1949, advanced through grades to lt. col., 1971; U.S. Army, Republic of Korea, 1952-53, Europe, 1956-60, 62-65, 67-70, Socialist Republic of Vietnam, 1966-67; dep. chief staff, intelligence command U.S. Army, ret., 1973; v.p. loss prevention Little Gen. Store div. Gen. Host Corp., Tampa, Fla., 1973-84; pres. Assets Protection Systems Assocs., Inc., Largo, Fla., 1985—; loss control cons. JRB Investigations Inc., Largo, 1986-87. Contbr. articles to profl. jours.. Bd. dirs. Del Prado Imperial Assn., Largo, chmn. neighborhood watch com. 1983—. Decorated Bronze Star, Legion of Merit. Mem. Am. Soc. Indsl. Security (chmn. 1975-76, cert. 1976), Internat. Assn. Profl. Security Cons., Retail Grocers Assn. Fla. (chmn. crime prevention 1983-85), Pinellas Assn. Pvt. Investigators (pres. 1986), Fla. Crime Prevention Officers Assn., Nat. Assn. Convenience Stores. Republican. Home and Office: Assets Protection Systems Assoc Inc 11113 Bella Loma Dr Largo FL 34644

CHAMBLEE, JAMES ALLEN, finance company executive; b. Boaz, Ala., Aug. 13, 1946; s. John L. and Nellie (Battles) C.; m. Janice R. Hubbard, July 3, 1965; children: Jeff A., Tracy D. and Stacy J. (twins). Student, Auburn U., 1964, Jacksonville State U., 1981. Asst. mgr. Key Fin. Co., Birmingham, Ala., 1965-71; pres., mgr. Delta Fin. Co., Tuscaloosa, Ala., 1971-79; pres., chief exec. officer Family Loan, Inc., Anniston, Ala., 1979—; bd. dirs. J.A.C. Mgmt. Services Inc., Anniston, J.A.C. Fin. Co, Anniston; real estate salesman Realty World-McCrimmon Realty, Anniston, 1986—. Mem. steering com. Calhoun County Rep. Exec. Com., Anniston, 1987—. Mem. Ala. Lenders Assn. (v.p. 1986—), Anniston Credit Assn. (pres. 1988—). Republican. Mem. Assembly of God Ch. Lodge: Rotary. Home: 737 Hillyer High Rd Anniston AL 36201 Office: Family Loan Inc 20 W 13th St Anniston AL 36201

CHAMBERS, ROY ALLEN, data processing executive; b. St. Louis, Oct. 14, 1949; s. Roy C. and Bonnie M. (Poelker) C.; m. Regina M. Conte, Feb. 26, 1983. AA, St. Louis Community Coll., 1970. Data processing operator McDonnell Douglas Corp., St. Louis, 1968-76; sales rep. Morgan Svcs., Inc., 1977-80; gen. mgr. Lien Svcs. Co., 1980-83; mgr. sales ADP, 1983-84; br. mgr. Systems & Programming Resources, 1984—. Mem. Assn. for Systems Mgmt., Regional Commerce & Growth Assn. Home: 2021 Willow Trail Saint Charles MO 63303 Office: Systems & Programming Resources Inc 1810 Craig Rd Ste 203 Saint Louis MO 63146

CHAMPIE, ELLMORE ALFRED, historian, writer; b. Eden, Tex., Sept. 11, 1916; s. Sam Houston and Nora Louise (Sorrell) C.; student Tex. Coll. Mines and Metallurgy, 1941-42; BA with highest honors, U. Tex, Austin, 1947, MA (Univ. Scholar), 1948; PhD in History (Bayard Cutting Scholar), Harvard U., 1967; m. Rosemary Erter, Sept. 7, 1947 (dec. Nov. 1962); children—Ellmore Alfred, Nora Beatrice; m. 2d, Miriam Helene Boysen Mann, Aug. 28, 1971 (div. Oct. 1974). Archivist, Nat. Archives, 1952-55; historian U.S. Marine Corps Hdqrs., 1955-56, Joint Chiefs of Staff, U.S. Dept. Def., 1956-61; asso. agy. historian Fed. Aviation Agy., 1961-67; agy. historian FAA, Dept. of Transp., 1967-72; hist. researcher and writer, 1972—; mem. tech. com. on history U.S. Inst. of Aeros. and Astronautics, 1970-72; editorial cons. history of FAA and predecessor agys., 4 vols. With USN, 1936-40, 1st lt. USAAF, 1942-45. Mem. Am. Hist. Assn., Am. Soc. for Eighteenth-Century Studies, Am. Soc. for Pub. Adminstrn., Phi Beta Kappa. Democrat. Club: Harvard (So. Ariz.). Lodge: Masons. Author: The Federal Turnaround on Aid to Airports, 1926-38, 1973. Home: 7480 E Rio Verde Dr Tucson AZ 85715

CHAMPLIN, CHARLES DAVENPORT, editor, critic, writer; b. Hammondsport, N.Y., Mar. 23, 1926; s. Francis Malburn and Katherine Marietta (Masson) C.; m. Margaret Frances Derby, Sept. 11, 1948; children: Charles Jr., Katherine, John, Judith, Susan, Nancy. AB cum laude, Harvard U., 1947. Reporter Life mag., N.Y.C., 1948-49; corr. Life mag., Chgo., 1949-52, asst. editor, 1954-59; corr. Denver, 1952-54, Time mag., L.A., 1959-62, London, Eng., 1962-65; arts editor, columnist L.A. Times, 1965—, prin. film critic, 1967-80, book critic, 1981—; host-commentator Sta. KCET-TV, Los Angeles, ETV Network, 2 Channel Cable TV, 1969—; adj. prof. Loyola-Marymount U., L.A., 1969-86; adj. assoc. prof. U. So. Calif., 1986—. Author: (with C. Sava) How to Swim Well, 1960, The Flicks, 1977, rev. as The Movies Grow Up, 1981, Back There Where the Past Was, 1989; contbr. numerous articles to mags. and pubs. Trustee Los Angeles Film Tchrs. Assn., Jr. Student Film Festival. Cpl. U.S. Army, 1944-46, ETO. Decorated Purple Heart; recipient Order Arts and Letters, France, 1977. Mem. Nat. Soc. Film Critics, Nat. Book Critics Circle, L.A. Film Critics Assn., Nat. Soc. Journalists. Democrat. Office: LA Times Times-Mirror Sq Los Angeles CA 90053

CHAN, DEBORAH ROSARIO, investment banker; b. Mount Holly, N.J., Sept. 23, 1959; d. Pablo Kintanar and Angeles Rotea (Adolfo) C.; 1 child, Allison Elizabeth. BS in Econs., U. Pa., 1981. Corp. fin. analyst Dean Witter Reynolds, N.Y.C., 1981-82; corp. fin. assoc., asst. v.p. Butcher & Singer Inc., Phila., 1982-86, corp. syndicate asst. v.p., 1986—. Mem. St. Anthony Padua Ch. Choir, Ambler, Pa., Ambler Community Chorus. Republican. Roman Catholic. Office: Butcher & Singer Inc 211 S Broad St Philadelphia PA 19107

CHAN, WILLIAM HSIAO-LIEN, electrical engineer; b. Kiangsi, Republic of China, Sept. 30, 1939; came to U.S., 1966; s. Chung-Yen and Sheng-Chien (Wang) C.; m. May Lee, Aug. 31, 1968; children: Jean, David. BEE, Cheng Kung U., 1963; MEE, U. Kans., 1969, PhD, 1975. Engr. Chinese Govt. Radio Adminstrn., Taipei, Taiwan, 1964-66; research assoc. Ctr. for Research Inc. U. Kans., Lawrence, 1966-72, sr. research assoc. Ctr. for Research, Inc., 1973-75, instr., 1970-73; electronics engr. Naval Weapons Ctr., China Lake, Calif., 1975-83; assoc. prof. Naval Weapons Ctr., U. Calif., Northridge, 1978-80; sect./br. head Naval Weapons Ctr., China Lake, 1983-85, project mgr., 1985—; program monitor ESL, Ohio State U., Columbus, 1975-87, CRINC, U. Kans., 1978-79, U. Ill., Champaign, 1980-81, U. Tex., Arlington, 1984-87. Contbr. articles to profl. jours. Pres. Indian Wells Valley Swimming Team, China Lake, 1981-82. Mem. Sigma Xi. Home: 1209 S Norma Ridgecrest CA 93555 Office: Naval Weapons Ctr China Lake CA 93555

CHANCE, BRITTON, JR., naval architect; b. Phila., June 12, 1940; s. Britton Chance and Jane (Earle) Chance Lindenmayer; m. Dianne Lynn Reichel, Sept. 28, 1974 (div. 1983); 1 child, Tasmin M.L. Student, U. Rochester, 1958-61, Columbia U., 1964. Pres., chief naval architect Chance and Co., Inc., Essex, Conn., 1962—; mem. U.S. yachting team 1964 Olympics, U.S. Admiral's Cup team, 1977, U.S. Onion Patch team, 1981. Designer (5.5 meters yacht) Wasa, 1968 (Olympic gold medal 1968), (12 meter yacht) Intrepid '70, 1969 (Am.'s Cup winner 1970), (one-ton yacht) Resolute Salmon, 1975 (One-Ton Cup winner 1976); sr. designer (12 meter yacht) Stars & Stripes, 1986 (Am.'s Cup winner 1987). Recipient Outstanding Design award PM Mag., Helsinki, Finland, 1974, Outstanding Design award Chesapeake Bay Yacht Racing Assn., Anapolis, Md., 1987; named in presdl. proclamation, Washington, 1987; honored in congratulatory statements, Gov. Conn., Hartford, 1987, Pa. State Senate, Harrisburg, 1987. Mem. Soc. Naval Architects and Marine Engrs. (panel H13). Clubs: N.Y. Yacht (N.Y.C.), Dauntless (Essex). Office: Chance and Co Inc Pratt St Essex CT 06426

CHANCE, JAMES WILLIAM, communications company executive; b. Winter Haven, Fla., June 23, 1938; s. Broward Chance and Nell Clare (McDuffy) Chance Hicks; m. Janet June Proffitt, July 5, 1956; children: Janet J., Teresa L., Judith A., James W. Jr., Patricia N. Student, Cochise Coll., Sierra Vista, Ariz., 1976-77. Enlisted U.S. Army, 1955, served to sta. chief signal corps., 1969-76, ret., 1976; technician RCA, Galena, Alaska, 1977-78; field engr. Gen. Telephone Co., Los Angeles, 1978-85; owner, operator Calif. Communications Contractors, Buena Park, 1986—; pres. CEE Communications Inc., Buena Park, 1988—. Mem. Communications Workers Am. (trustee health and welfare fund 1987—). Lodge: Moose. Home: 8659 Carnation Dr Buena Park CA 90620 Office: Calif Communications Contractors PO Box 834 Buena Park CA 90621

CHANDLER, COLBY H., photographic equipment and materials manufacturing executive. married. B.S., U. Maine, 1950; postgrad., MIT. With Eastman Kodak Co., Rochester, N.Y., 1950—, mem. sales estimating council, then corp. asst. v.p., until 1972, exec. v.p., 1972-77, pres., 1977-83, chmn., chief exec. officer, 1983—, also dir.; exec. dir. Lincoln 1st Bank, Rochester.; dir. Continental Group, Inc., Ford Motor Co., J.C. Penney Co. Bd. dirs. Indsl. Mgmt. Council Rochester; bd. dirs. Congl. Award Com.; Bd. dirs. United Way of Greater Rochester; bd. dirs. Rochester-Monroe County Conv. and Visitors Bur., Nat. Orgn. on Disability; exec. dir. Rochester Civic Music Assn.; trustee Rochester Inst. Tech., Colgate Rochester Div. Sch., U. Rochester, Nat. 4-H Council, Internat. Mus. Photography at George Eastman House; mem. MIT Corp. Mem. Soc. Sloan Fellows (bd. govs. 1964, pres. 1966-68), Tau Beta Pi, Sigma Pi Sigma, Phi Kappa Phi, Beta Gama Sigma. Office: Eastman Kodak Co 343 State St Rochester NY 14650 *

CHANDLER, GEORGE ALFRED, manufacturing executive; b. Cleve., Aug. 15, 1929; s. George Alfred and Doris Beatrice (Datson) C.; m. Sally Jane Topping, Apr. 10, 1954; children: Nancy, David, James, Elizabeth. B.A., Princeton U., 1951; M.B.A., Harvard U., 1956. With brass div. Olin Corp., East Alton, Ill., 1956-67; v.p., gen. mgr. Aluminum Group Olin Corp., Stamford, Conn., 1967-71; pres. Winchester Group Olin Corp., New Haven, 1971-77; pres. Am. Productivity Ctr., Houston, 1978, Indsl. Products group Amstar Corp., N.Y.C., 1978-82; pres., chief exec. officer Am. Ship Bldg. Co., Tampa, Fla., 1983-85; pres., chief exec. officer Aqua-Chem, Inc., Milw., 1985—, also chmn. bd. dirs.; dir. The Allen Group, Melville, L.I., Advanced Aluminum Products, Hammond, Ind., Aqua-Chem, Inc. Mem. Alton Bd. Edn., Ill., 1963-67; mem. Darien Bd. Edn., Conn., 1969-72. Served to 1st lt. arty. U.S. Army, 1951-53, Korea. Republican. Episcopalian. Home: 8335 N Range Line Rd River Hills WI 53209 Office: Aqua-Chem Inc 210 W Capitol Dr Milwaukee WI 53209

CHANDLER, JAMES WENDELL, public relations and communications executive; b. Winnfield, La., Oct. 19, 1932; s. Wendell L. and Callie (Jones) C.; m. Jimmie Ruth Carter, Aug. 27, 1950; children—Steven Michael, Kay Lynne. Student Marietta Coll., 1956-57, W. Liberty State U., 1958-60. Reporter, Wheeling Intelligencer, 1957-59; editor Weirton Steel Co. div. Nat. Steel, 1959-64; mgr. communications Allegheny Ludlum Industries, Inc., 1964-71; dir. pub. relations Dayton Press, Inc., 1971-77; v.p. corp. communications NCNB Corp., Charlotte, N.C., 1977-83, v.p., dir. pub. relations, Tampa, Fla., 1984-88, v.p. pub. affairs and communication, 1988—. Contbr. articles to profl. jours. Served with USAF, 1951-55. Mem. Pub. Relations Soc. Am., Temple Terr. Golf and Country Club, Tampa Club. Home: 1724 Magdalene Manor Dr Tampa FL 33613 Office: NCNB Nat Bank PO Box 31590 Tampa FL 33631

CHANDLER, KARYLN DOROTHY, infosystems specialist; b. Pitts., Mar. 28, 1943; d. Wilbert and Theresa). (McClenny) Scott; m. James R. Chandler, Feb. 17, 1979; 1 child, Tina Marie. AS in Bus. Mgmt., Allegheny Community Coll., 1979. Name processor for city directory R.L. Polk Co., Cleve., 1966; keypunch operator Higbee Co., Cleve., 1968-69; keypunch operator Westinghouse Electric Corp., Forest Hills, Pa., 1970-76, sr. keypunch operator, 1976-80, fin. projects clk., 1980; supr. computer ops. Westinghouse Electric Corp., Pitts., 1980—. Mem. Assn. Female Execs. Office: Westinghouse Electric Corp 777 Penn Center Blvd Pittsburgh PA 15235

CHANDLER, LINDA CLINE, investment broker, financial consultant; b. Sioux Falls, S.D.; d. Lawrence Alphonse and Wilba Nell (Leatherwood) Dhaemers; m. Terence E. Chandler, Oct. 16, 1976. BS, Iowa State U., 1968, MA, 1972. Registered investment advisor. With Sutro & Co., San Jose, Calif., 1974—, assoc. v.p., 1977-78, v.p. investments, 1978—; pres., founder Chandler Roberts, Inc., Santa Clara, Calif., 1983—, Pacific Integrated Group, 1987—, pres., 1988—; sr. v.p. Morgan, Olmstead, Kennedy & Gardner, 1985—; assoc. gen. ptnr. Brichard Properties, Phoenix Portfolio; bd. advisors Rancon Securities; assoc. gen. ptnr. Rancon Pacific, 1988—; co-founder, pres. Uptown Properties of San Diego Inc., First Ptnrs. Corp.; contbg. personal fin. editor Sta. KCSM-TV; fin. commentator Sta. KPEN; speaker in field. Pub. Investment Monitor, 1989; contbr. articles to profl. jours. Bd. dirs. League of Women Friends. Named Fin. Planner of Yr., Am. Home Properties, 1981, 83, one of nations leading brokers Wall Street Transcript, 1982, Nation's Outstanding Fin. Planners, Consol. Capital, 1983, Number One Sales Performance Rancho Cons. Realty, 1983, 85, 86. Fin.

Planner of Yr., Brichard & Co., 1985-86, Outstanding Broker of Yr., Brichard & Co., 1986, Fin. Planner of Yr., Rancon Fin., 1986. UN fellow. Mem. Santa Clara County Profl. Brokers Assn., Santa Clara County Profl. Young Women, Internat. Assn. Fin. Planners (keynote conf. speaker, nat. speaker L.A. and Orlando, Fla. 1988), AAUW, Real Estate Securities and Syndications Inst. (nat. conv. speaker 1988), Phi Kappa Phi, Phi Delta Theta, Alpha Delta Pi. Methodist. Clubs: Sutro Century (pres.'s coun. 1978-81), Sutro Second Century, Sutro Pres. Office: 2880 Lakeside Dr Ste 115 Santa Clara CA 95054 Also: 2515 Camino Del Rio S Ste 328 San Diego CA 92018

CHANDLER, REUBEN CARL, packaging company executive; b. Lawrenceville, Ga., Oct. 25, 1917; s. Reuben C. and Florine (Doster) C.; m. Sarah Megee, Oct. 27, 1940; children: Carla Evalynee, Robert Megee, David Pratt, Craig D. Grad., Marist Coll., Atlanta, 1935; student, Ga. Inst. Tech., 1935-37; A.B., Emory U., 1941; student, Atlanta Law Sch., 1946-48; D.Sc. in Bus. Adminstrn. (hon.), Detroit Inst. Tech., 1960. Sales rep. Gen. Motors Acceptance Corp., Atlanta, 1941-42; asst. dir. tng. Southeastern Shipbldg. Corp., Savannah, Ga., 1942-43; prodn. mgr. Mead-Atlanta Paper Co., 1946-49; salesman Union Camp Corp. (formerly Union Bag & Paper Corp.), 1949-50; dist. sales mgr. Union Camp Corp. (formerly Union Bag & Camp Paper Corp.), Trenton, N.J., 1950-51; Eastern div. sales mgr. Union Camp Corp. (formerly Union Bag & Camp Paper Corp.), 1951-52; dir. corrugated container and bd. sales Union Camp Corp. (formerly Union Bag & Camp Paper Corp.), N.Y.C., 1952; v.p. sales Union Camp Corp. (formerly Union Bag & Camp Paper Corp.), 1952-55; chmn., chief exec. officer, chmn. exec., finance coms. Standard Packaging Co., N.Y.C., 1955-66; chmn. bd. Crowell-Collier Pub. Co., N.Y.C., 1957; ltd. partner Elliott & Co. (investment bankers), N.Y.C., 1960-62; chmn bd. J.D. Jewell, Inc., Gainesville, Ga., 1962-72; pres. J.D. Jewell, Inc., 1969—; also chmn. exec. com., dir.; pres. Identiseal Systems, Atlanta, 1972—, Perkins-Goodwin Mgmt. Services Co., N.Y.C., 1973—, Am. Resources Corp., 1973-75; chmn. bd. Lanier Mortgage Corp., Gainesville, Ga., 1973-75; pres., chief exec. officer Duncan & Copeland, Inc., 1976-79, Va. Packaging Supply Co., McLean, 1979-84; dir. Am. Agy. Life Ins. Co., Atlanta, Berry Steel Corp., Edison, N.J., Jones & Presnell, Charlotte, N.C. Trustee Detroit Inst. Tech., 1960—, Christ Ch. Sch., Short Hills, N.J., 1963—, Brenau Coll., 1968—, Emory U., Atlanta, 1972—, Ga. Found. for Ind. Colls., 1969—; bd. dirs. Am. Soc. Indsl. Security Found. Served as lt. (s.g.) USNR, 1943-46; Lt. col. aide de camp Gov.'s staff Ga. 1951-52, 70-72. Recipient Man of Year award Am. Jewish Com., 1964; Horatio Alger award, 1965; Achievement award Delta Tau Delta, 1966; Disting. Alumni award Marist Coll., 1985. Mem. Savannah Jr. C. of C. (v.p. 1942-43), Gainesville C. of C., Navy League (life), Def. Orientation Conf. Assn., Am. Pulp and Paper Mill Supts. Assn. (life), Emory U. Alumni Assn. (pres. 1965, Honor award 1968), Ga. Tech. Nat. Alumni Assn. (nat. adv. bd. 1964 —), Ga. Poultry Fedn. (mem. round table 1970—), Tenn. Wesleyan Coll. Parents Assn., U.S. Navy Supply Corps Assn. (trustee 1972—), Delta Tau Delta (life), Alpha Delta Sigma, Omicron Delta Kappa. Episcopalian. Clubs: Atlanta, Athletic (Atlanta); N.Y. Area Emory (pres. 1964), University, Economic (N.Y.C.). Home: 4101 Dunwoody Club Dr Apt 25 Dunwoody GA 30350

CHANDLER, ROBERT LESLIE, public relations executive; b. Phila., Mar. 3, 1948; s. Joel Leslie and Evelyn Laney (DeLaney) C.; A.S., Atlantic Community Coll., 1969; B.S., Bowling Green State U., 1971; M.S., Ohio U., 1972; M.B.A. in Hosp. Adminstrn., Wagner Coll., 1980; m. Maureen O'Keefe, Mar. 21, 1970. Dir. public relations Athens Mental Health Ctr., Ohio, 1972; internal communications editor, public affairs dept. Owens-Corning Fiberglas Corp., Toledo, 1972-74; dir. community relations Wyandotte Gen. Hosp., Mich., 1974-76; v.p. asst. adminstr. mktg./public affairs Meth. Hosp., Bklyn., 1976-82; sr. v.p. Burson-Marsteller Public Relations, N.Y.C., 1982—. Mem. budget com. United Way Mich., 1975-76. N.J. State scholar, 1969. Mem. Pub. Relations Soc. Am., Am. Soc. Hosp. Mktg. ans Pub. Rels., Am. Hosp. Assn., Hosp. Pub. Relations Soc. Greater N.Y., Sigma Delta Chi, Kappa Tau Alpha. Home: 2 Horatio St Apt 2M New York NY 10014 Office: Burson Marsteller Pub Rels 230 Park Ave S New York NY 10003

CHANDLER, WALLACE LEE, tobacco company executive; b. Oct. 18, 1926; m. Juanita Hodnett; children: Elizabeth Chandler Hallberg, Brenda Chandler Bell, Blair Chandler Grappone. AB, Elon (N.C.) Coll., 1949; D of Comml. Sci. (hon.), Elon Coll., 1983; LLB, Smithdeal Coll. of Law, 1953; LLD (hon.), James Madison U., 1983. With Universal Corp. (formerly Universal Leaf Tobacco Co.), Richmond, 1949, asst. sec., 1953, sec. and gen. counsel, 1963, dir., 1966, mem. exec. com., v.p., 1969, sr. v.p., 1974, exec. v.p., 1982, now vice chmn., also bd. dirs.; bd. dirs. Lawyers Title Ins. Corp., Regency Bank, Life of Va. Series Fund, Inc. Mem. bd. of visitors James Madison U., 1964-74, rector of bd., 1972-74, chmn. found.; bd. dirs., v.p. The Met. Found., Richmond; bd. advisors The Va. Home; former bd. dirs. Met. Richmond C. of C., Va. Soc. for Crippled Children and Adults, Richmond; trustee Elon Coll., 1967—, River Rd. Bapt. Ch., mem. bd. deacons, former chmn. bd. adminstrn. 1st lt. U.S. Army. Recipient Disting. Service award James Madison U., 1973, Chandler Hall named in his honor; recipient Disting. Alumni award Elon Coll., 1978, Wallace L. Chandler Hall named in his honor, 1982. Mem. Tobacco Assn. of U.S. (bd. govs.), Country Club of Va., Princess Anne Country, Commonwealth, Willow Oaks Country Club (former bd. dirs.), Focus, Richmond Gentry. Clubs: Country of Va., Princess Anne Country, Commonwealth, Willow Oaks Country (former bd. dirs.), Focus, Richmond Gentry. Home: 2 Raven Rock Rd Richmond VA 23229 Office: Universal Leaf Tobacco Co Inc Hamilton St at Broad Richmond VA 23230

CHANDLER, WILLIAM EVERETT, manufacturing executive; b. Chattanooga; s. Everett C. and Evelyn N. (Nalley) C.; m. Mary Elizabeth Bergman, June 27, 1969; children: Meghan, Amanda. BSBA, U. Fla., 1965. Various positions Gen. Electric Co., Fairfield, 1966-83; sr. v.p., chief fin. officer Parker Pen Co., Janesville, Wis., 1983-86, Household Mfg., Inc., Prospect Heights, Ill., 1986—. Mem. Fin. Execs. Insts., Abbey Springs Yacht Club, Janesville Country Club. Office: Household Mfg Inc 2700 Sanders Rd Prospect Heights IL 60070

CHANDRAMOULI, RAMAMURTI, electrical engineer; b. Sholinghur, Madras, India, Oct. 2, 1947; s. Ramamurti and Rajalakshmi (Ramamurti) Krishnamurti; m. Ranjani; 1 child, Suhasini. BSc, Mysore U., 1965, BE, 1970, MEE, Pratt Inst., 1972; PhD, Oreg. State U., 1978; m. Ranjani, Dec. 4, 1980. Instr., Oreg. State U., Corvallis, 1978; sr. engr. R & D group, mem. tech. staff spacecraft datasystems sect. Jet Propulsion Lab., Pasadena, Calif., 1978-81; staff engr., design automation group Am. Microsystems Inc., Santa Clara, Calif., 1982-83; staff software engr. corp. computer-aided design Intel, Santa Clara, 1983-86; project leader computer-aided design Sun Microsystems, Mountain View, Calif., 1986—; adj. lectr. Calif. State U.-Fullerton, 1987—. Sec., South India Cultural Assn., L.A., 1980-81; bd. dirs. Am. Assn. East Indians. Mem. IEEE, IEEE Computer Soc., Sigma Xi, Eta Kappa Nu. Home: 678 Tiffany Ct Sunnyvale CA 94087 Office: Sun Microsystems 2550 Garcia Ave Mountain View CA 94043

CHANDRU, G. A. See ADVANI, CHANDERBAN GHANSHAMDAS

CHANEY, JOHN DOUGLAS, financial executive; b. Mpls., May 19, 1950; s. Glen Jackson and Alien Marie (Currel) C.; m. Diane Ruth Winzer, July 1, 1972; children: Ruth, Jack, Mollie, Peter. BA in Computer Sci., Bus. Adminstrn., Econs., Principia Coll., 1972. Gen. mgr. Office Services, Inc., Houston, 1972-73, pres., 1973-78; pres., chmn., chief exec. officer TeleCheck Payment Services Co., Houston, 1976—; organizing dir. Westheimer Meml. Bank, Houston. Sponsor Blue Santa/Houston Police Dept., 1985-87. Served to 1st lt. USAF, 1971-74. Recipient John Rathbone Meml. award and other numerous awards TeleCheck Services, Inc. Mem. Young Pres.'s Orgn., TeleCheck Franchise Assn. (numerous offices including pres., v.p. and various chairmanships). Republican. Christian Scientist. Lodge: Rotary. Office: TeleCheck Payment Svcs Co 720 N Post Oak Rd Houston TX 77024

CHANG, BERTINA PANG LOH, industrial engineer; b. San Francisco, Sept. 10, 1957; d. Kuo-Liu and Ann Sun Fong (Chiang) C. BS in Indsl. Engring., Stanford U., 1979. Process engr. Hewlett-Packard Co., Santa Clara, Calif., 1979-82; sr. assoc. indsl. engr. IBM Corp., San Jose, Calif., 1982-86, staff indsl. engr., 1986-88; project mgr. Hewlett-Packard Co., Sunnyvale, Calif., 1988—. Speaker Youth Motivational Task Force, San Jose, 1984—. Mfg. Tech. Inst. scholar IBM Corp., 1986. Mem. Inst. Indsl. Engrs. (v.p. programs 1987—). Presbyterian. Office: Hewlett-Packard Co 974 E Arques Ave Sunnyvale CA 94086

CHANG, C. EUGENE, insurance executive; b. Taichung, Republic of China, June 16, 1938; came to U.S., 1965; s. Chang T. and Tsai (Chen) C.; m. Lucia S. Chen, Sept. 9, 1967; 1 child, Michael K. BBA, Chang Kung U., 1962; MS in Stats., Mich. State U., 1967. Chief actuary Chrysler Ins. Group, Troy, Mich., 1970-80; v.p. ITT Lyndon Ins. Group, St. Louis, 1980; asst. v.p. actuary Citizens Ins. Co. Am., Howell, Mich., 1980-85; pres., chief exec. officer Lake States Ins. Co., Traverse City, Mich., 1985—. Mem. Am. Acad. Actuaries, Soc. Actuaries (assoc.), Mich. Actuarial Soc. (pres. 1981-82), Internat. Actuarial Assn. Home: 6176 Singletree Dr Williamsburg MI 49690 Office: Lake States Ins Co 12935 W Bay Shore Dr PO Box 352 Traverse City MI 49685

CHANG, C. YUL, banker; b. Seoul, Korea, Feb. 21, 1934; came to U.S., 1958, naturalized, 1972; s. Insuk and Insook Chang; children: Edward W., Leonard W., Mira W. BS, Naval Acad., Korea, 1953; MA in Fin., U. Miami, 1961; postgrad., Columbia U., 1962; DD (hon.), Calif. Missionary Coll., 1984. Sr. fin. cons. Mobil Oil Corp., N.Y.C., 1963-74; gen. mgr. Chem. Bank, N.Y.C., 1974-86; chmn., chief exec. officer Hanam Capital Corp./SBIC, N.Y.C., 1986—; chmn. adv. bd. Capital Nat. Bank, N.Y.C., 1986-87; advisor Korean Businessmen's Assn., N.Y.C., 1982, Korean-Am. Credit Union, N.Y.C., 1985. Author: Automated Banking, 1968; also articles. Recipient Cert. of Commendation Korean Consulate Gen., 1982, Korean Assn. of N.Y., 1982, Korean Ch.'s Fedn., 1985. Mem. Nat. Assn. Investment Cos., Rotary (pres. Riverdale, N.Y. chpt. 1987-88). Republican. Presbyterian. Home: 5900 Arling Ave #20 K Riverdale NY 10471 Office: Hanam Capital Corp One Penn Plaza New York NY 10119

CHANG, DAVID Y., design engineer; b. Taipei, Taiwan, Republic of China, Nov. 7, 1953; s. Ya-Shang and Maio-Yan (Hsue) C.; m. Cecilia Fang, Aug. 16, 1982. BS, Tunghai U., Taiwan, 1976; MS, Stevens Inst. Tech., Hobroken, N.J., 1979; MBA, No. Ill. U., DeKalb, 1985. Research asst. Stevens Inst. Tech., Hobroken, 1978-79; sr. material engr. Honeywell, Inc., Freeport, Ill., 1979-84; sr. design engr. Barber-Coleman Co., Love Park, Ill., 1984-86; prin. engr. Honeywell, Inc., El Paso, Tex., 1986—. Mem. LSoc. Plastics Engrs. Republican. Office: Honeywell Inc 4171 N Mesa El Paso TX 79902

CHANG, HARRY, financial executive; b. Jiangyin, Jiangsu, China, Oct. 22, 1916; came to U.S., 1953; s. Yu-Mei and Chow Chang; m. Rebecca Chang, Jan. 7, 1943; children: David, Diana, Julia. Ba, Shanghai Coll. Commerce, 1941; MBA, NYU, 1954. Contr. Overseas Credit Corp., N.Y.C., 1954-59; from. treas,. v.p. to exec. v.p., sec. Deltec Group subs. Deltec Securities Corp., N.Y.C., 1959—. Republican. Lutheran. Home: 15 W 72d St New York NY 10023 Office: Deltec Securities Corp 101 E 52d St 12th Fl New York NY 10022

CHANG, JEONG-JA JOAN, banker; b. Kwangju, Korea, May 27, 1952; came to U.S., 1976; d. Yong-sun Lee and Jeong-soon Kee; m. Young-ook Chang, Feb. 26, 1976; children: Brian K., Rebecca H. BA, Ewha Women's U., Seoul, Rep. of Korea, 1974; MBA, U. Pitts., 1980. Trade specialist Chase Manhattan Bank, Seoul, 1974-76; credit mgr. Algemene Bank Nederland, Pitts., 1980-83; asst. v.p. Mellon Bank, Pitts., 1983—. Mem. Toastmasters. Home: 308 Rawley Dr Pittsburgh PA 15243 Office: One Mellon Bank Ctr Rm 873 Pittsburgh PA 15258

CHANG, NELSON, brokerage executive; b. Shanghai, China, July 17, 1923; s. Nai Chi and June (Zee) C.; m. Edith Hsi, Apr. 3, 1954; children: Phyllis, Edmund, Laurence. BS, MIT, 1948; postgrad. Wharton Sch. of Finance, 1947. Sales engr. Am. Cyanamid Co., Boundbrook, N.J., 1948-51; commodity futures brokerage Orvis Bros. & Co., N.Y.C., 1952-57; eastern sales mgr., commodity dept. Reynolds Securities, N.Y.C., 1957-63; commodity Futures broker Hayden Stone, Inc., N.Y.C., 1963-71, v.p., dir. commodity research and trading, 1971-73, sr. v.p., dir. commodity research and trading Shearson, Hayden Stone, N.Y.C., 1973-80; sr. v.p., dir. commodity research, dir. strategic planning Shearson Amex; pres. Hayden Commodities; bd. dirs. Shearson Amex Asia Ltd., 1980—; adv. dir. Shearson Lehman Amex, 1985—. Presbyterian. Home: Pratt Island Darien CT 06820 Office: Shearson Lehman Amex 2 Greenwich Pla Greenwich CT 06830

CHANG, ROBERT TIMOTHY, bank executive; b. N.Y.C., Nov. 17, 1958; s. T. Timothy and Mabel (Li) C. BS in Engring. and Econs., Calif. Inst. Tech., 1980; MS in Computer Sci., Poly. Inst. N.Y., 1982; postgrad., NYU, 1986—. Systems analyst Fed. Res. Bank N.Y., N.Y.C., 1980-85; mgr. Citibank N.A. subs. Citicorp, N.Y.C., 1985-87, asst. v.p., 1988—; systems officer Morgan Guaranty Trust Co. N.Y. subs. J.P. Morgan and Co. Inc., N.Y.C., 1987-88. Mem. Assn. for Computing Machinery, Computer Soc. IEEE. Home: 501 W 123d St #7E New York NY 10027-5009 Office: Citibank NA 111 Wall St New York NY 10043

CHANG-MOTA, ROBERTO, electrical engineer; b. Caracas, Venezuela, Dec. 28, 1935; s. Roberto W. and Mary C. (Mota) Chang; D.E.E., U. Central Venezuela, 1960; M.S., U. Ill., 1962; A.R., Harvard U., 1970; m. Alicia Santamaria-Gonzales, May 4, 1968; children—Roberto Ignacio, Roxana Ivette, Ricardo Ignacio. Dir. Sch. Elec. Engring., also prof. Central U., 1964-69; prof., dean Schs. Engring., Architecture and Sci., Simon Bolivar U., 1971-77; pres. Colegio de Ingenieros de Venezuela, 1974-79; dir. Venezuelan Power Co., 1974-79; pres. Latin Am. Orgn. Engring., 1977-79, Corporoil, 1981-85, Audio Interface Corp., 1983—; cons. in field. Spl. cons. Venezuelan Navy and Army, 1971-75, Venezuelan Congress, 1989—; mem. tech. com. Venezuelan Supreme Election Council, 1971-81, exec. dir., 1981-82, gen. dir., 1982-89; trustee Simon Bolivar U., 1985-88. Mem. Venezuelan Soc. Elec. and Mech. Engring. (pres. 1972-73), IEEE, Am. Soc. Engring. Edn., Instn. Elec. Engrs. Roman Catholic. Clubs: Puerto Azul, Playa Pintada, Caracas Racquet. Home: Quinta Cumana Calle Colon, Prados de Este Estado, Miranda Venezuela Office: Torres Centro Simon Bolivar, Consejo Supremo Electoral, Esq Pajarito, Caracas Venezuela

CHANNICK, HERBERT S., broadcasting corporation executive; b. Phila., Aug. 27, 1929; s. Maurice and Rose (Rosenberg) C.; m. Nancy Abarbanel Wolfe, Dec. 1, 1950; children: Joan D., Robert L. AB, U. Ill., 1951; JD, Yale Law Sch., 1954. Assoc. Antonow & Weissbourd, Chgo., 1957-59; ptnr. Met. Investment Co., Chgo., 1960—; chmn. Channick Broadcasting Corp., Chgo., 1979—; bd. dirs. Canisteo Valley Broadcasting Co., Hornell, N.Y., Crest Hill Broadcasting, Inc., Joliet, Ill. Bd. dirs. Ctr. for Psychosocial Studies, Chgo., 1977—, Monmouth (Ill.) Coll., 1973-75; mem. Highland Park (Ill.) Planning Commn., 1972-74, Ill. Racing Bd., Chgo., 1974-76. Capt. USAF, 1955-57. Office: Channick Broadcasting Corp 400 N Michigan Ave Chicago IL 60611

CHANT, DAVIS RYAN, real estate broker, consultant; b. Port Jervis, N.Y., Dec. 15, 1938; s. B. Ryall and Miriam C. (Cathy) C.; m. Judith E. Gahm, Nov. 6, 1982; children: Tamara, Holley. Constrn. materials salesman, architect service U.S. Gypsum Co., Chgo., 1960-62; chmn. bd. Davis R. Chant, Inc., realtors, Milford, Pa., 1962—; chmn. Davis R. Chant Assoc., Inc., realtors, Lords Valley, Pa., Davis R. Chant, Inc. Realtors N.J.; prin. DRC Group of Cos. Chmn., Econ. Devel. Council NE Pa.; mem. Pres.'s Com. on Leisure Housing. Bd. dirs. Pike County Conservation Dist.; trustee Milford Reservation, Inc. Recipient nat. award for advt. Nat. Assn. Real Estate Brokers, 1971. Mem. Nat. Assn. Review Appraisers, Nat. Time Share Council, Internat. Inst. Valuers, Am. Right of Way Assn., Nat., N.Y. assns. real estate bds., Nat. Inst. Real Estate Brokers, Pa. Vacation Land Developers Assn., Pa., N.Y. assns. Realtors, Internat. Real Estate Fedn., Sullivan County, Delaware County bds. Realtors, Pike County (past dir.), Wayne County, Port Jervis, N.Y. chambers commerce, Pike-Wayne County Bd. Realtors (past pres.), Pike Builders Assn., Urban Land Inst., Realtors Land Inst. (chmn. legis. com.), Am. Resort and Residential Devel. Assn., Am. Resort & Hosp. Devel. Assn., Nat. Assn. Home Builders, Pocono Mountain Vacation Bur., Community Assn. Inst. Am. (charter, dir.). Clubs: Masons, Lions. Home: Clove Rd Montague NJ 07827 Office: 106 E Harford St Milford PA 18337

CHAO, JAMES MIN-TZU, architect; b. Dairen, China, Feb. 27, 1940; s. T. C. and Lin Fan (Wong) C.; came to U.S., 1949, naturalized, 1962; m. Kirsti Helena Lehtonen, May 15, 1968. BArch, U. Calif., Berkeley, 1965. Cert. architect, Calif.; cert. instr. real estate, Calif. Intermediate draftsman Spencer, Lee & Busse, Architects, San Francisco, 1966-67; asst. to pres. Import Plus Inc., Santa Clara, Calif., 1967-69; job capt. Hammaberg and Herman, Architects, Oakland, Calif., 1969-71; project mgr. B A Premises Corp., San Francisco, 1971-79; constrn. mgr. The Straw Hat Restaurant Corp., 1979-81, mem. sr. mgmt., dir. real estate and constrn., 1981-87; pvt. practice architect, Berkeley, Calif., 1987—; pres. Food Service Cons., Inc., 1987—; pres., chief exec. officer Stratsac, Inc., 1987—; lectr. comml. real estate site analysis and selection for profl. real estate seminars; coordinator minority vending program, solar application program Bank of Am.; guest faculty mem. Northwest Ctr. for Profl. Edn. Patentee tidal electric generating system; author first comprehensive consumer orientated performance specification for remote banking transaction. Recipient honorable mention Future Scientists Am., 1955. Mem. AIA. Republican. Clubs: Encinal Yacht (dir. 1977-78).

CHAOUI, NABIL MICHEL, hotel executive; b. Damascus, Syria, Nov. 20, 1950; came to U.S., 1979; s. Michel Khalil and Violette (Masri) C. BA, Sacred Heart Coll., Beirut, Lebanon, 1968; grad., Hotel Mgmt. Sch., Beirut, Lebanon, 1972. Front office mgr. Phoencia Intercontinental Hotel, Beirut, 1972-74; asst. gen. mgr. Riyadh (Saudi Arabia) Intercontinental Hotel, 1974-79, Alamoana Americana Hotel, Honolulu, 1979-81, Hyatt Anaheim, Calif., 1981-82; gen. mgr. Holiday Inn, Downtown L.A., 1982-83, 86—; gen. mgr. West Covina, Calif., 1983-84, Denver, 1984-86, Milipitas, Calif., 1985-86; cons. East/West Hotel Mgmt., L.A., 1986—. Home: 6667 Burke Ct Chino CA 91710 Office: Holiday Inn LA Downtown 750 Garland Ave Los Angeles CA 90017

CHAPEL, R(AY) JOHN, JR., aerospace company executive; b. White Hall, Md., Feb. 13, 1943; s. Ray John Chapel Sr. and Eulalie (Killon) Delp; m. Virginia Ellen Todd, Dec. 23, 1967; children: Ray John III, Christopher Todd. BBA, Drexel U., 1967; postgrad., U. N.C., 1967-68. Project adminstr. Westinghouse D&ESD, Balt., 1968-73; gen. mgr. D&C Concrete Constrn. Co., Bel Air, Md., 1973-74; mgr. fin. TCOM-Westinghouse, Columbia, Md., 1975; bus. mgr. TCOM-Westinghouse, Lagos, Nigeria, 1976-79; mgr. pricing ATG Div. Sundstrand Corp., Rockford, Ill., 1979-83, dir. bus. planning, 1983-86; v.p., gen. mgr. Dowty Aerospace Corp., Sterling, Va., 1986-87, pres., 1987—. Contbr. articles to profl. jours. Mem. Dulles Task Force, Washington, 1986, bd. dirs. 1989—; bd. dirs. Oatlands Found., 1988—. Mem. Nat. Contracts Mgmt. Assn. (cert. 1983, fellow 1985—, v.p. 1985-86), Nat. Estimating Soc. (cert. 1983), Inst. Cost Analysis (cert. 1983), Air Force Assn., Sterling C. of C., Va. C. of C., U.S. C. of C. Republican. Baptist. Home: 11400 Fieldstone Ln Reston VA 22091 Office: Dowty Aerospace Corp PO Box 5000 Sully Rd Sterling VA 22170

CHAPIN, JOHN NETTLETON, JR., litigation and claims services executive; b. St. Louis, Dec. 26, 1933; s. John Nettleton and Dora Wooders (Burge) C.; m. Meryl Carolyn Schmidt, Dec. 23, 1955; children: Carolyn Chapin Strandberg, Sharon Chapin Crist. Student, DePauw U., 1951-53; BSBA, Washington U., St. Louis, 1955, MBA, 1960; postgrad., Rutgers U., Princeton, N.J., 1961. Dist. plant engr. AT&T Co., St. Louis, 1955-59, comml. rep., 1959-60; mktg. rep. IBM Corp., St. Louis, 1960-65; ind. rep. fin. IBM Corp., Chgo., 1966-67, mktg. mgr., 1968-73; br. mgr. Control Data Corp., Chgo., 1973-78; v.p. Nat. Sharadata Corp., Chgo., 1978-79; dir. litigation svcs. Coopers & Lybrand, Chgo., 1979-86, ptnr.-in-charge litigation, 1986—. Dir. Presbyn. Home, Evanston, Ill., 1978-82, Tamarack Townhouses Assn., Snowmass, Colo., 1969—; chmn. Dist. Rev. Com., New Trier Twp., Ill., 1979, avoca caucus Avoca Sch. Dist., 1971; bd. govs. Snowmass Resort Assn., 1988—. Mem. Am. Arbitration Assn. (panel arbitrators 1984), Inst. Mgmt. Cons. (v.p. 1986—, cert.), ABA (assoc.), Nat. Dist. Attys Assn., Nat. Assn. Securities Dealers, (bd. arbitration), Univ. Club, Skokie Country Club, Chgo. Curling Club (bd. dirs. 1981-86). Republican. Presbyterian. Home: 3040 Indian Wood Rd Wilmette IL 60091 Office: Coopers & Lybrand 203 N LaSalle St Chicago IL 60601

CHAPMAN, ALGER BALDWIN, finance executive, lawyer; b. Portland, Maine, Sept. 28, 1931; s. Alger Baldwin Sr. and Elizabeth (Ives) C.; m. Beatrice Bishop, Oct. 30, 1983; children: Alger III, Samuel P., Andrew I., Henry H. BA, Williams Coll., 1953; JD, Columbia U., 1956. Bar: N.Y. 1957. Pres. Shearson & Co., 1970-74, co-chmn., 1974-81; vice chmn. Am. Express Bank, 1982-85; chmn., chief exec. officer Chgo. Bd. Options Exchange, 1986—. Mem. N.Y. State Bar Assn. Clubs: Chgo., Racquet Club Chgo.; Metropolitan (N.Y.C.); Attic, Glenview. Home: 1500 N Lake Shore Dr Chicago IL 60610 Office: Chgo Bd Options Exch 400 S LaSalle St Chicago IL 60605

CHAPMAN, ALVAH HERMAN, JR., newspaper executive; b. Columbus, Ga., Mar. 21, 1921; s. Alvah Herman and Wyline (Page) C.; m. Betty Bateman, Mar. 22, 1943; children: Dale Page Chapman Webb, Chris Ann Chapman Hilton. B.S., The Citadel, 1942; hon. degree, Barry U., 1985, Fla. Internat. U., 1988. Bus. mgr. Columbus Ledger, 1945-53; exec. v.p., gen. mgr. St. Petersburg (Fla.) Times, 1953-57; pres., pub. Morning News and Evening Press, Savannah, Ga., 1957-60; pres. Savannah News-Press, Inc., 1957-60; exec. Knight-Ridder Newspapers, Inc., Miami, Fla., 1960—; exec. com. Knight-Ridder Newspapers, Inc., 1960—, exec. v.p., 1967-73, pres., 1973-82, chief exec. officer, 1976-88, chmn., 1982—; v.p., gen. mgr. Miami Herald, 1962-70, pres., 1970-82; lectr. Am. Press Insts., Columbia. Served from 2d lt. to maj. USAAF, World War II. Decorated D.F.C. with 2 oak leaf clusters, Air medal with 5 clusters U.S.; Croix de Guerre; named one of five outstanding young men in Ga., 1951, Outstanding Young Man Columbus Jr. C. of C., 1952, Dade County's Outstanding Citizen of 1968-69, Brigham Young U. Internat. Businessman of Year, 1984; recipient Citadel Palmetto award, 1985, Isaiah Thomas award Rochester Inst. Tech., 1986. Mem. Am. Newspapers Pubs. Assn. (chmn., pres.), So. Newspapers Pubs. Assn. (pres. 1976). Methodist. Home: 4255 Lake Rd Miami FL 33137 Office: Knight-Ridder Inc 1 Herald Pla Miami FL 33132-1693

CHAPMAN, EDWARD ARNOLD, JR., marketing professional; b. Ann Arbor, Mich., Apr. 20, 1933; s. Edward A. and Mary Alice (Moore) C.; m. Mary Tewksgury, Sept. 13, 1957 (div. 1979); children: Mary, Edward. BA, Dartmouth Coll., 1955. Various positions with N.Y. Telephone, N.Y.C., 1958-81; exhibit mktg. supr. AT&T, N.Y.C., 1981-86; pres. Sextant Communications, N.Y.C., 1987—. Author: The Candidates Guide, 1974, Exhibit Marketing, 1987. Campaign mgr. Gannon for Civil Ct., Staten Island, N.Y., 1968; planner Friends of the Rockefeller Team, 1970. Mem. Internat. Exhibitors Assn., Health Care Exhibitors Assn., Nat. Assn. Exposition Mgrs. Republican. Episcopalian. Club: Richmond County Yacht. Home and Office: 355 S End Ave 2L New York NY 10280

CHAPMAN, HUGH MCMASTER, banker; b. Spartanburg, S.C., Sept. 11, 1932; s. James Alfred and Martha (Marshall) C.; m. Anne Allston Morrison, Dec. 27, 1958; children: Anne Allston, Rachel Buchanan, Mary Morrison. B.S. in Bus. Adminstrn, U. N.C., 1955. With Citizens & So. Nat. Bank S.C., 1958—, pres., 1971-74, chmn. bd., 1974—; pres. Citizens & So. Corp., Atlanta, 1986—; bd. dirs. SCANA Corp, Inman Mills. Pres. Carolinas United Community Services, 1966; mem. S.C. Commn. on Higher Edn., 1971-75; trustee Presbyn. Coll., Clinton, S.C., 1973-82, Com. for Econ. Devel., Duke Endowment. Served to 1st lt. USAF, 1955-57. Mem. S.C. Bankers Assn. (pres. 1976-77). Office: Citizens & So Corp 35 Broad St PO Box 4899 Atlanta GA 30303

CHAPMAN, JAMES CLAUDE, marine equipment manufacturing executive; b. Detroit, Mar. 16, 1931; s. Claude Byrand and Madolin C. (Werstine) C.; m. Elizabeth Jane Quinley, May 1, 1954; children: Diane, Donna. BME cum laude, U. Detroit, 1956, MBA, 1966. Registered profl. engr., Mich. Plant mgr. Rockwell Internat. Corp., Marysville, Ohio, 1971-74; dir. facilities Rockwell Internat. Corp., Troy, Mich., 1974-78; dir. mfg. Outboard Marine Corp., Waukegan, Ill., 1978, v.p. mfg., 1978-85, pres., chief operating officer, 1985—. Pres. Northeast Ill. council Boy Scouts Am.; bd. dirs. Lake Forest Sch. of Mgmt., Ill., 1984. Served with USNR, 1950-58. Mem. Soc. Mfg. Engrs., Soc. Automotive Engrs., Waukegan-Lake County C. of C. (vice chmn. 1985), Glen Flora Country Club. Republican. Roman Catholic.

Home: 25310 W Hickory Antioch IL 60002 Office: Outboard Marine Corp 100 Sea Horse Dr Waukegan IL 60085

CHAPMAN, JAMES MONTGOMERY, financial executive, insurance underwriter; b. St. Louis, Nov. 25, 1946; s. John Robinson and Mary Ann (Stevens) C.; m. Linda Podas, Aug. 15, 1970; children: Caroline Victoria, Melissa Anne. BS, U. Ariz., 1968; cert., Coll. Fin. Planning, 1984. Field underwriter Home Life Ins. Co. N.Y., N.Y.C., 1969—; sole practice broker, ins. and securities agt. Santa Barbara, Calif., 1971—; pres. Planned Estate Service Inc., Santa Barbara, 1983—; prof. ins., fin. and banking Santa Barbara City Coll., 1986—. Served with USAR, 1968-74. Recipient Personal Service award Life and Health Ins. Insts., 1976. Mem. Assn. Advanced Life Underwriting, Million Dollar Round Table (mem. mktg. com. 1979-80, manuscript rev. com. 1982-83, sales idea com. 1987, divisional v.p. 1988, bottomline com. 1984-85), Nat. Assn. Life Underwriters (mem. fed. law and legis. com. 1982-83), Calif. Assn. Life Underwriters (past trustee region V, mem. state legis. com. 1980-81, fed. legis. com. chmn. 1981-83), Santa Barbara Assn. Life Underwriters (pres. 1975-76). Republican. Episcopalian. Office: Planned Estate Svc Inc 3868 State St Santa Barbara CA 93105

CHAPMAN, JOHN SUTHERLAND, retail executive; b. Chgo., Dec. 24, 1925; s. Charles Williamson and Flora Naomi (Findlay) C.; B.S. in Psychology, Ill. Inst. Tech., 1952, postgrad., 1952-54; postgrad. John Marshall Law Sch., 1964-66; m. Catherine M. Bobber, June 26, 1948; children—John Charles, Carl William, Mary Eileen. Asst. personnel mgr. Nabisco Inc., Chgo., 1948-53, personnel mgr., Atlanta, 1954-60, personnel mgr. Chgo. Mfg. Complex, 1961-71, regional personnel relations mgr., Naperville, Ill., 1971-74, regional personnel mgmt. cons., state govt. relations coordinator, 1975-81; corp. personnel mgmt. cons., area mgr. govt. relations Nabisco Brands U.S.A., 1982-83; ind. cons. on indsl. relations and mgmt. devel., 1984-86, also EEO; pres. Handy Hawware Inc., Chgo.; bd. agt. Ill. State Labor Relations Bd., 1984-88; program chmn., conf. leader Am. Mgmt. Assn., 1968—. Mem. Ill. Gov.'s Adv. Com., 1969-71, Ill. Gov.'s Com. on Workers Compensation, 1973. Served with USNR, 1944-46. Mem. Am. Soc. Safety Engrs., Am. Soc. Personnel Adminstrn. (accredited exec. in personnel, mem. nat. EEO com.), Personnel Mgmt. Assn. (v.p. Chgo. 1971-72, pres. 1972-73), Ill. Mfg. Assn., Ill. C. of C. (labor relations com. 1977-86), Assoc. Employers Ill. (bd. dirs., chmn. labor relations com. 1984-86), Chgo. Area Public Affairs Group, Psi Chi. Office: 10204 Cook Ave Oak Lawn IL 60453

CHAPMAN, JULIANN GAYLE, real estate executive; b. Waukesha, Wis., July 25, 1951; d. Glenn D. and Mary (Muhasky) C. BBA, Tex. Tech U., 1973; MBA, La. Tech. U., 1974. Tchr., bus. mgr., coach Dallas Ind. Sch. Dist., 1974-79; v.p. Superior Carpet Corp., Dallas, 1979-83, Gehan Investments, Inc., Irving, Tex., 1983—. Life mem. Tex. PTA, Dallas, 1979; bd. dirs. Dallas chpt. Am. Lung Assn., 1988. Named Woman of Yr., Dallas chpt. Am. Bus. Women's Assn., 1985. Mem. Nat. Assn. Realtors, Dallas Bd. Realtors (comml. investment div.). Republican. Methodist. Club: Toastmasters (pres. Dallas chpt. 1985). Home: 621 Raven Ln Coppell TX 75019 Office: Gehan Investments Inc 545 E John Carpenter Freeway Suite 101 Irving TX 75062

CHAPMAN, PETER HERBERT, merchant banker; b. Stockton, Calif., Mar. 6, 1953; s. Duff Gordon and Emalee (Sala) C.; m. Diane Clark; children: Charlotte Moseley, Alexander Clark. AB, Columbia U., 1977. V.p. Salomon Bros., Inc., N.Y.C., 1977-86, 1st Boston Corp., N.Y.C., 1986-88; dir. Girozentrale Vienna, N.Y.C., 1989—; bd. dirs. C.D. Stimson Co., Seattle. Mem. Am. Internat. Sch., Florence, Italy, 1982—. Mem. The Links Club, Racquet and Tennis Club, Downtown Assn. Republican. Office: 65 E 55th St New York NY 10022

CHAPMAN, RICHARD LEROY, public policy researcher; b. Yankton, S.D., Feb. 4, 1932; s. Raymond Young and Vera Everette (Trimble) C.; m. Marilyn Jean Nicholson, Aug. 14, 1955; children: Catherine Ruth, Robert Matthew, Michael David, Stephen Raymond, Amy Jean. BS, S.D. State U., 1954; postgrad., Cambridge (Eng.) U., 1954-55; MPA, Syracuse U., 1958, PhD, 1967. Profl. staff mem. com. govt. ops. Sec. of Def., 1958-59, 61-63, U.S. Ho. Reps., Executive Office of Pres. (Bur. of Budget), Washington, 1960-61, U.S. Ho. Reps., 1966; program dir. NIH, Bethesda, Md., 1967-68; sr. research assoc. Nat. Acad. Pub. Adminstrn., Washington, 1968-72, dep. exec. dir., 1973-76, v.p., dir. research, 1976-81; sr. research scientist Denver Research Inst., 1982-86; mem. adv. com. Denver Research Inst. U. Denver, 1984-86; ptnr. Milliken Chapman Rsch. Group Inc., Denver, 1986-88; prin., v.p. Chapman Rsch. Group, Inc., Denver, 1986-88; v.p. Chapman Research Group, Inc., Littleton, 1988—; cons. U.S. Office Personnel Mgmt., Washington, 1977-81, Denver, 1986—; cons. CIA, Washington, 1979, 80, 81, Arthur S. Fleming Awards, Washington, 1977-81. Contbr. articles to profl. jours. Mem. aerospace com. Colo. Commn. Higher Edn., Denver, 1982-83; chmn. rules com. U. Denver Senate, 1984-85; bd. dirs. S.E. Englewood Water Dist., Littleton, 1984-88, pres. 1986-88. Capt. U.S. Army, 1955-57, Korea. Brookings Inst. fellow, 1964-65. Mem. Tech. Transfer Soc. (bd. dirs.), Am. Soc. Pub. Adminstrn., AAAS, IEEE, Engring. Mgmt. Soc., Futures Soc. Republican. Lodges: Masons, Commandery, Order of DeMoley (Cross of Honor 1982). Office: Chapman Rsch Group 6631 S University Blvd Ste 212 Littleton CO 80121

CHAPMAN, ROGER STEVENS, JR., construction company executive; b. Hartford, Conn., Dec. 3, 1927; s. Roger Stevens and Katherine Marie (Willetts) C.; B.C.E., Cornell U., 1949; M.S. in Mgmt., Rensselaer Poly. Inst., 1970; m. Viola Mohl, Feb. 7, 1959; children—David, Ellen. Field engr. A.S. Wikstrom, Inc., Skaneateles, N.Y., 1949-54; project engr. Savin Constrn. Co., East Hartford, Conn., 1954-58; project mgr. Merritt-Chapman & Scott Corp., N.Y.C., 1958-62; supt., chief estimator, v.p. C.W. Blakeslee & Sons, Inc., New Haven, 1962-76; v.p., dir. Blakeslee Arpaia Chapman, Inc., Branford, Conn., 1976-86, pres., 1986—; v.p., dir. BAC Marine, Inc., Branford, 1977—. Bd. dirs. Southeastern Conn. Better Bus. Bur., 1980-86. Served with U.S. Army, 1951-53. Registered profl. engr. Fellow ASCE; mem. Am. Arbitration Assn., Conn. Constrn. Industries (dir. 1983—), Conn. Road Builders Assn. (v.p. 1985-88, pres. 1988—). Republican. Episcopalian. Patentee in field. Office: Blakeslee Arpaia Chapman Inc 200 N Branford Rd Branford CT 06405

CHAPNIK, ELISSA-BETH LYNDA, biomechanics and ergonomics executive; b. N.Y.C., Jan. 29, 1962; d. Arthur and June (Meltzer) C. m. Clifford Mark Gross, June 12, 1984; 1 child, Marielle Sophia. BBA in Math., Simmons Coll., 1983. Prodn. coord. Chapnik & Co., Inc., N.Y.C., 1983-84; sec., treas. Biomechanics Corp. of Am., Deer Park, N.Y., 1984-85, acting contr., 1985—, acting v.p., contr., 1986—. Contbr. articles to profl. jours. Mem. Simmons Club, Sid Jacobson's Y. Home: 1675 Northern Blvd Roslyn NY 11576 Office: Biomechanics Corp of Am 337 Skidmore Rd Deer Park NY 11729

CHAPPELL, TED JUDSON, JR., marketing executive; b. Raleigh, N.C., Dec. 28, 1942; s. Theodore Judson and Clara Bell (Worrell) C.; m. Frances Gail Frazier, Dec. 27, 1966; children: Heather, Shannon. BS in Liberal Arts, N.C. State U., 1966, BS in Elec. Engring., 1980. Mktg. rep. Carolina Power & Light Co., Raleigh, 1966-78, energy specialist, 1978-80, mktg. mgr., 1980-86; cons. Raleigh C. of C., 1986; mktg. mgr. Lennox Industries, Raleigh, 1986—. Served as 2nd lt. U.S. Army, 1966. Mem. Profl. Engrs. N.C., Raleigh C. of C. (life mem., Sales award 1980), N.C. Soc. Engrs. Republican. Presbyterian. Home: 3212 Stoneyford Ct Raleigh NC 27603

CHARLES, LYN ELLEN, marketing executive, commercial artist; b. Little Falls, N.Y., Sept. 1, 1951; d. Searle and Barbara (Yount) C. Student So. Conn. State U., 1969-70; B.A., U. Conn., 1970-73; student Lake Placid Sch. Art, 1975-76; A.I.S., Art Instrn. Schs., Inc., 1974-76. Student employee East Conn. State U., Willimantic, 1969, 70; research asst. Conn. State U., New Britain, 1974; comml. artist Conn. Community Colls., Hartford, 1978; market researcher Karen Assocs., Farmington Valley Mall, Avon, Conn., 1981; market research operator Consumer Surveys Telemarketing, Inc., Dedham, Mass., 1981-87; receptionist and file clerk Jobpro Temp. Services, 1987-88; field rep. Actnow, Westhampton Beach, N.Y., 1987-88; with Inventory Control Co., South Hasckensack, N.J., 1988—; freelance artist West Hartford Art League, 1978-81; artist, vol. Farmington Valley Arts, Avon, Conn., 1982-84; freelance artist Northwestern Conn. Art Assn., 1979-81, Wadsworth Atheneum, 1980-82. Vol. med. receptionist Hosp. and Clinical Info. Desk, U. Conn. Health Ctr., 1976-78, 75, Office Cultural Affairs, Pub. Survey to Select Artist for Art Work at Coliseum, Hartford Civic Ctr., 1979. Recipient Alice Collins Dunham prize, 69th Ann. Exhbn. of Conn. Acad. Fine Arts, 1980. Christian Ch. Avocations: hiking; swimming; bicycling; horseback riding; skiing; ballet; skating. Office: Inventory Control Co PO Box 23 South Hasckensack NJ 07606

CHARLEY, PHILIP JAMES, testing laboratory executive; b. Melbourne, Australia, Aug. 18, 1921; came to U.S., 1940, naturalized; 1948; s. Walter George and Constance Mary (Macdonald) C.; B.S., U. Wis., 1943; M.S. in Mech. Engring., U. So. Calif., 1947, Ph.D. in Biochemistry, 1960; m. Katherine Truesdail, Jan. 31, 1948; children—James Alan, Linda Kay, William John. Test engr. Gen. Electric Co., Schenectady, 1943-44; lectr. in engring. U. So. Calif., Los Angeles, 1947-49; project engr. Standard Oil of Calif., El Segundo, 1948-55; v.p. Truesdail Labs., Los Angeles, 1955-70, pres., 1970—. Served to lt. Royal Can. Elec. and Mech. Engrs., 1943-45. Recipient Dueul award U. So. Calif., 1960, research asso., 1960-65; registered profl. engr., Calif. Mem. AAAS, Am. Soc. Metals, ASTM, ASME, Am. Soc. Safety Engrs., Am. Chem. Soc., Sigma Xi, Tau Beta Pi, Beta Theta Pi. Republican. Club: Rotary. Home: 1906 Calle de los Alamos San Clemente CA 92672 Office: Truesdail Labs Inc 14201 Franklin Ave Tustin CA 92680

CHARNAS, (MANNIE) MICHAEL, packaging company executive; b. Cleve., Sept. 24, 1947; s. Max and Eleanor (Gross) C.; divorced; 1 child, Matthew. BBA, Ohio State U., 1969, MBA, 1971. Page Ohio Ho. of Reps.; Fin. analyst Addressograph-Multigraph, Inc., Cleve., 1971-73; asst. to pres., dir. planning and budget 1st Nat. Supermarkets, Inc. (Pick-N-Pay), Cleve., 1975-78; asst. to pres., v.p. planning and budgets 1st Nat. Supermarkets, Inc. (Pick-N-Pay), 1978-79, sr. v.p. fin., adminstr., 1979-81; sr. v.p., chief fin. officer, adminstrv. officer 1st Nat. Supermarkets, Inc. (Pick-N-Pay), Hartford, Conn., 1981-86; pres., owner Indsl. Pallet and Packaging Co., Beachwood, Ohio, 1986—; owner, v.p. Revere Electronics, 1988—. Jewish. Office: Indsl Pallet & Packaging Co 24700 Chagrin Blvd Ste 305 Beachwood OH 44122

CHARPIE, ROBERT ALAN, physicist; b. Cleve., Sept. 9, 1925; s. Leonard Asbury and Dorothy (McLean) C.; m. Elizabeth Downs, July 12, 1947; children: Richard Alan, Carol Elizabeth, David Wayne, John Robert. B.S. with honors, Carnegie Inst. Tech., 1948, M.S., 1949, D.Sc. in Theoretical Physics, 1950; D.H.L., Denison U., 1965; D.Sc., Alderson-Broaddus Coll., 1967; LL.D., Marietta Coll., 1975; D.Sc., Boston Coll., 1982. With Westinghouse Electric Corp., 1947-50; with Oak Ridge Nat. Lab., 1950-51, tech. asst. to research dir., 1952-54, asst. research dir., 1954-58, dir. reactor div., 1958-61; mgr. adv. devel. Union Carbide Corp., 1961-63, gen. mgr. devel. dept., 1963-64, dir. tech., 1964-66, pres. electronics div., 1966-68; pres. Bell & Howell Co., Chgo., 1968-69; pres. Cabot Corp., Boston, 1969-86, also. bd. dirs.; chmn. Cabot Corp., Waltham, Mass., 1986-88; trustee Mitre Corp., Boston, 1966-82, chmn., 1972-82; dir. Federated Dept. Stores, Inc., Cabot Corp., Campeau Corp., Champion Internat. Corp., Northwest Airlines, Inc., Ashland Coal, Inc.; sec. gen. adv. com. AEC, 1959-63; mem. Nat. Sci. Bd., 1969-76; sci. sec., editor-in-chief proc., also asst. U.S. mem. 7 nation adv. com. 1st Internat. Conf. Peaceful Uses Atomic Energy, 1955; coordinator U.S. fusion research exhibit, 2d Conf., 1958; chmn. invention and innovation panel U.S. Dept. Commerce, 1965-67. Gen. editor: Internat. Monograph Series on Nuclear Energy, 1955-60; editor: Progress Series in Nuclear Energy, 1955-60, Jour. Nuclear Energy, 1955-60. Mem. Oak Ridge Bd. Edn., 1957-61; pres. Byram Hills Central Sch. Dist., 1966-68; trustee Carnegie Inst. Tech., 1962—. Recipient Alumni Merit award Carnegie Inst. Tech., 1957. Fellow Am. Phys. Soc., Am. Nuclear Soc. (dir.); mem. N.Y. Acad. Sci., Nat. Acad. Engring., Sci. Research Soc. Am., Sigma Xi, Tau Beta Pi, Phi Mu Epsilon. Office: 1380 Lawrence St Ste 1100 Denver CO 80204

CHARRIER, MICHAEL EDWARD, investment banker; b. Columbia, S.C., July 6, 1945; s. Raymond Joseph and Anne Mary (Toth) C.; m. Elizabeth Andrea Alexandra Thyssen, June 17, 1967. BA, Columbia U., 1967, MA, 1968; postgrad., Harvard U., 1977, Yale U., 1988. With strategic planning and devel. div. TWA, N.Y.C., 1970-73; dir. devel. City Fed. Savs. Bank, Elizabeth, N.J., 1974-76; fin. cons. Pan Am., N.Y.C., 1976; chief fin. officer Jet Aviation Internat., N.Y.C., 1976, Hardwick, Wells & Winthrop, N.Y.C., 1978-84; also bd. dirs. Hardwick, Wells & Winthrop; cons. Columbia U., N.Y.C., 1985; sr. ptnr. Ardsley, Milbank & Co., Inc., N.Y.C., 1985—; also bd. dirs. Ardsley, Milbank & Co., Inc.; pres. Hamilton Sci. Corp., Greenwich, Conn. , N.Y.C., 1985—; also bd. dirs. Hamilton Sci. Corp.; pres. Hamilton Chem. Corp., N.Y.C., 1988—, also bd. dirs. Contbr. articles to mags. Bd. dirs. Jet Aviation, N.Y.C., 1976-78, Rep. Speakers Bur., N.Y.C., 1986; strategist Reagan-Bush Campaign, N.Y.C., 1984; mem. adv. bd. Def. Fire Protection Assn., 1987—; advisor Urban Design & City Planning, City of N.Y., 1973—; coach Yale Croquet Team, 1988—. Recipient Proclamation City of N.Y., 1978, Citation for Bus. Devel. City of N.Y., 1978, Medal of Merit Presdl. Task Force, Washington, 1983. Mem. Naval Inst., Navy League, N.Y. Acad. Scis., Am. Acad. Sci. & Tech., Global Econ. Action Com. Clubs: N.Y. Stock Exchange , Columbia U. Faculty, LeClub, New York Croquet (bd. dirs. 1989—), U.S. Croquet Assn. (Palm Beach, Fla.). Home: 1520 York Ave New York NY 10028 Office: Hamilton Chem Corp 230 Park Ave New York NY 10017

CHARVAT, DAVID ALLAN, accountant, auditor; b. Toledo, July 11, 1959; s. James Richard and Barbara Mae (Enck) C. BBA, U. Toledo, 1981, postgrad., 1982-86. CPA, Ohio. Trust tax analyst Ohio Citizens Bank, Toledo, 1981-85; audit officer Nat. City Corp., Toledo, 1985—; income tax preparer, Toledo, 1982—. Asst. scoutmaster Boy Scouts Am., Toledo, 1978—; treas. Grace Evang. Ch., Toledo, 1984-88, pres. 1988, trustee Found., 1987-88. Mem. Ohio Soc. CPA's, Beta Alpha Psi. Republican. Home: 5142 Oakridge Dr Toledo OH 43623 Office: Nat City Corp 405 Madison St Toledo OH 43603

CHASE, CYNTHIA ANN, financial executive; b. Kowloon, Hong Kong, Jan. 1, 1949; d. Arthur A. and Ilsa Yvonne (White) C.; m. Larry Mack Jeppesen, May 1, 1978; children: Karis Maile, Tambra Noelani. BA, Colo. Women's Coll., 1970; cert., Coll. Fin. Planning, 1982. Asst. to office mgr. D'Arcy-McManus Masius Advt. Co., San Francisco, 1970-72; traffic mgr. Hank Inouye Advt. Co., Honolulu, 1972-75; media buyer FoBreGaSa & Assocs. Advt. Co., Honolulu, 1975-76; account exec. Fawcett, McDermott & Cavanagh, Honolulu, 1976-78; fin. cons. Shearson Lehman Bros., Boise, Idaho, 1979-86; dir. mktg. services Pvt. Ledger Fin. Services, San Diego, 1986—; instr. Boise State U. Community Edn., 1983, Treasure Valley Community Coll., Ontario, Oreg., 1983, State Bd. Acctg., Boise, 1983-86, YWCA, Boise, 1981-86. Contbr. articles to newspapers, 1984-85. Speaker seminar Women in Mgmt., Boise, 1984; pres. Treasure Valley Estate Planning Council, 1984-85. Mem. Internat. Assn. Fin. Planning (v.p. local chpt. 1985-86), Inst. Cert. Fin. Planning (bd. dirs. local chpt. 1984-86), Soroptmist Internat. (chmn. pub. com. 1984-85). Democrat. Office: Pvt Ledger Fin Svcs 5871 Oberlin Dr San Diego CA 92121

CHASE, FRANCIS MICHAEL, manufacturing executive; b. Canton, Mass., Feb. 27, 1920; s. Francis G. and Mary A. (Griffin) C.; m. Barbara Ann Sullivan, Apr. 19, 1952; children—Francis G., Michael C., Anne L. B.S. in Civil Engring., U. N.H., 1941. Pres., chmn. bd. Chase & Sons, Inc., Randolph, Mass., 1947—; chmn., chief exec. officer Chase Corp., Braintree, Mass., 1971—; chmn. bd. Royston Labs., Inc., Pitts., 1973—; bd. dirs. Internat. Contacts Inc., Cohasset, Mass. Bd. dirs. Family Counseling and Guidance Ctrs., Braintree, World Affairs Council, Boston. Served as capt. U.S. Army, 1941-46, ETO. Decorated Bronze Star medal. Mem. World Bus. Council (founding), Chief Execs. Orgn. Republican. Roman Catholic. Clubs: Metropolitan (N.Y.C.); Orleans (Mass.) Yacht; Cohasset Golf. Office: Chase Corp 220 Forbes Rd Braintree MA 02184

CHASE, HELEN LOUISE, banker; b. Waukegan, Ill., Sept. 29, 1943; d. David William and Ruth Virginia (Sawyer) C. BA, U. Ill., 1965. Sec., exec. sec. Foote, Cone and Belding, Chgo., 1965-66; various positions Continental Bank, Chgo., 1966-73, internat. banking officer, 1973-76, 2nd v.p., 1976-77; Brazil rep. Continental Bank, Sao Paulo, 1977-80; 2nd v.p., sect. head Far East group Continental Bank Internat., N.Y.C., 1980-81; 2nd v.p. internat. div. Continental Bank, Chgo., 1981-83; v.p. N.Am. Union Trust Bank (now Signet Bank), Balt., 1983-84; v.p., mgr. internat. ops. Signet Bank, Balt., 1984—. Bd. dirs. Res Musica Baltimore, Inc. Mem. U.S. Coun. on Internat. Banking (nat collections com.). Clubs: Downtown Athletic, East Bank. Office: Signet Bank/Md 7 St Paul St 5th Fl Baltimore MD 21202

CHASE, ROBERT STEVEN, investment broker; b. Evanston, Ill., Aug. 13, 1945; s. Robert H. and Jean E. Chase; m. Susan E. Miller, Jan. 29, 1968; children: Ann, Owen. BA, U. Wis., 1968. Registered rep. Wayne Hummer & Co., Appleton, Wis., 1976-82, mgr., 1982—; fin. instr. U. Wis., Menasha, 1984—, Lakeshore Sch., Cleve., 1981-85. Vol., U. S. Peace Corps., Brazil, 1968-69; dir. Garrett Theol. Sem., Evanston, 1969-71; adminstrv. asst. Nat. Council Chs., Recife, Brazil, 1971-72; econ. devel. dir. Fox Cities C. of C., 1972-74; regional dir. Wis. Assn. Retarded Citizens, 1974-76; chmn. Fox Valley Interfaith Refugee Com., Appleton, 1977-80, Appleton Equal Opportunity Commn., 1981-82; sec. Gov. Commn. on U.N., Madison, 1982—; treas. Appleton Area Hunger Walk, 1983—. Democrat. Unitarian. Office: Wayne Hummer & Co 200 E Washington Appleton WI 54911

CHASTAIN, ROGER W., textile company executive; b. 1941; married. BS, U. S.C. With Riegel Textile Corp., Greenville, S.C., 1964—, chief indsl. engr., night supr., 1967-68, corp. dir. indsl. engring., 1968-69; plant mgr. consumer products div. Riegel Textile Corp., Lexington, 1969-70; mgr. ops. Aiken plant Riegel Textile Corp., 1970-74, v.p. ops., 1974-79, exec. v.p., 1979-80, pres. consumer goods group, 1980-82, corp. dir. consumer goods, 1982—, corp. v.p., 1982-85, pres., chief operating officer, 1985—; also exec. v.p. Mount Vernon Mills Inc., Greenville, S.C. Served with USAFR, 1967-74. Office: Mt Vernon Mills Inc Box 3478 Greenville SC 29602 *

CHATFIELD, CHERYL ANN, stock brokerage firm executive, writer; b. King's Park, N.Y., Jan. 24, 1946; d. William David and Mildred Ruth (King) C.; m. Gene Allen Chasser, Feb. 17, 1968 (div. 1979); m. James Bernard Arkebauer, Apr. 16, 1983 (div. 1987). BS, Cen. Conn. Coll., 1968, MS, 1972; PhD, U. Conn., 1976. Cert. gen. prin. securities. Tchr. Bristol East High Sch., Conn., 1968-77; adminstr. New Britain Schs., Conn., 1977-79; prof. Ariz. State U., Phoenix, 1979; stockbroker J. Daniel Bell, Denver, 1980-83, Hyder and Co., Denver, 1983-84; stockbroker, pres. Denari Securities, Denver, 1984—; tchr. investment seminars Front Range Community Coll., Denver, 1984-86; speaker women's groups, Denver, 1983-86. Author: Low-Priced Riches, 1985, Selling Low-Priced Riches, 1986, (newspaper columns) For Women Investors, 1982-84, Commentary, 1985-86; editor, founder (newsletter) Women in Securities . Project bus. cons. Jr. Achievement, Denver, 1986; trustee Orchestra of Santa Fe. Mem. Nat. Assn. Female Execs., Aircraft Owners and Pilots Assn., AAUW, N.Mex. Venture Capital Club (treas.), Kappa Delta Pi. Republican. Roman Catholic. Avocation: flying. Office: Chatfield Dean and Co 7935 E Prentice Ave Ste 300 Englewood CO 80111

CHATROO, ARTHUR JAY, lawyer; b. N.Y.C., July 1, 1946; s. George and Lillian (Leibowitz) C. BChemE, CCNY, 1968; JD cum laude, New York Law Sch., 1979; MBA with distinction, NYU, 1982. Bar: N.Y. 1980. Process engr. Standard Oil Co. of Ohio, various locations, 1968-73; process specialist BP Oil, Inc., Marcus Hook, Pa., 1974-75; sr. process engr. Sci. Design Co., Inc., N.Y.C., 1975-78; mgr. spl. projects The Halcon SD Group, N.Y.C., 1978-82; corp. counsel, tax and fin. The Lubrizol Corp., Wickliffe, Ohio, 1982-85; gen. counsel Lubrizol Enterprises, Inc., Wickliffe, 1985-89; sr. counsel spl. investment projects Lubrizol Corp., Wickliffe, 1989—. Mem. Met. Parks Adv. com., Allen County, Ohio, 1973. Mem. ABA, Am. Chem. Soc., Am. Inst. Chem. Engrs., N.Y. State Bar Assn., Cleve. Bar Assn., Jaycees (personnel dir. Lima, Ohio chpt. 1972-73), Omega Chi Epsilon, Beta Gamma Sigma. Club: Toastmasters. Home: 1 Bratenahl Pl Ste 705 Bratenahl OH 44108 Office: Lubrizol Enterprises Inc 29400 Lakeland Blvd Wickliffe OH 29400

CHAUHAN, JOSEPH HIRENDRA, magazine publisher; b. Kalol, Gujarat, India, Sept. 16, 1922; came to U.S., 1961; s. Purushottam D. and Jadiben Chauhan; m. Yvonne Joyce Fruitticher, June 10, 1972 (div.); 1 child, Mark. BA in History and Econs., Bombay U.; LLB, JD, John Marshall Law Sch.; M of Internat. Relations and Orgns., Am. U.; PhD in Internat. Studies, U. S.C. Editor, pub. Savannah mag., 1969-77, Columbia mag., 1977—; realtor, pres. Internat. Cultural Ctr., Columbia. Past mem. legis. com. Gen. Assembly Ga.; chmn. fgn. affairs com. ARC, Savannah, Ga.; bd. dirs. March of Dimes, Savannah, Human Relations Council, Epilepsy Found., Savannah chpt. Am. Heart Assn., Boy Scouts Am., Savannah, Richland County Heart Assn., Telfair Acad. Arts and Scis., Savannah, Savannah Symphony. Mem. Internat. Mgmt. Council Savannah, Savannah Hotels and Motels Assn. (chmn. publicity com.), Columbia Hotels and Motels Assn. (task force for degree program hotel, restaurant and tourism adminstrn. at U. S.C.), Columbia Bd. Realtors, S.C. Assn. Realtors, Nat. Assn. Realtors, Internat. New Town Assn., Investments Unltd. (pres.), Savannah C. of C. (bus. task force), Savannah Beach C. of C. (v.p.), LWV (chmn. budget com.). Hindu. Club: Inter-Cultural, Savannah Advt. Lodge: Masons. Home and Office: Columbia Mag 1120 Broad River Rd Columbia SC 29210

CHAVARRIA, ERNEST MONTES, JR., international trade, business and finance consultant; b. Laredo, Tex., May 9, 1955; s. Ernesto M. Sr. and Josefa M. C.; m. Sandra Mercado, Aug. 13, 1978. BA in Internat. Bus. and Mktg., U. Tex., 1977, postgrad. Cert. internat. financier. Pres., chief exec. officer ITBR, Inc., Austin, Tex., 1977—; elected del. Nat. White House Conf. on Small Bus., 1986, vice chmn., moderator Tex. delegation, chmn. internat. trade and investment coms.; issue leader for internat. trade and investment forums; bd. dirs. U.S. Small Bus. Adminstrn. Adv. Council for region 6, 1986—; mem. U.S. Small Bus. Adminstrn./San Antonio Dist. Internat. Trade Task Force, 1987—, U.S. Small Bus. Adminstrn./Hispanic Border Bus. Devel. Com., 1987—, U.S. Congl. Adv. Bd.; mem. steering com. Partnership Tex.-Small and Large Bus. and State Govt. United for Opportunity Gov.'s Task Force, 1987—; co-chmn. membership com. Austin Foreign Trade Council, 1986—; chmn., moderator Tex. Conf. Small Bus., 1987; moderator, speaker confs. in field; lectr. in field. Mem. minority adv. bd. Austin Am. Statesman newspaper, 1987—; author various newsletters. Participant Austin leadership, 1986-87; vice chmn. extension com. YMCA NW, Austin, 1986—; mem. steering com. Tex. Civil Justice League, Austin, 1987—; bd. dirs. Small Bus. Devel. Com. and Neighborhood Assn., Austin, 1986—, Austin Met. YMCA, 1987—, N.W. Area Council, Austin, 1986—, Econ. Devel Assessment Com. and 183 Roadway Plan, Austin, 1986—, Cedar Park (Tex.) Econ. Devel. Comm., 1986—, Austin Govtl. Relations Council, 1987—, Child Assault Prevention Program, Austin, 1987—, Tex. Civil Justice League, Austin, 1987—; fed. appt. to Industry Sector adv. com. on small and minority bus., U.S. Dept. Commerce, 1988. Recipient Am. award for Most Outstanding Bus. Cons. Co. in U.S.A., 1986, Internat. Award for Good Service and Quality, 1987; named Tex. Minority Advocate of Yr., U.S. Small Bus. Adminstrn., 1987, Exporter of Yr., U.S. Small Bus. Adminstrn., 1987; Ernesto Chavarria Day proclaimed by City of Austin, 1986. Mem. Nat. Assn. Profl. Cons., Am. Soc. Profl. Cons. (mem. bd. govs.), Profl. Bus. Cons. Assn. (mem. bd. govs.), U.S. C. of C., U.S. Hispanic C. of C. (bd. dirs., chmn. econ. devel. com. 1988, co-chmn. govt. relations com. 1988), Austin Hispanic C. of C. (cert. appreciation 1987), Am. C. of C. of Mex., Austin C. of C. (various coms. and councils), Internat. Traders Assn., Tex. Army N.G. Assn. Home: PO Box 160325 Austin TX 78716 Office: ITBR Inc 2 Cielo Ctr 3rd Fl 1250 Capital of Texas Hwy S Austin TX 78746

CHAWLA, MANTOSH KUMAR, manufacturing executive, engineer; b. Fazilka, Punjab, India, Oct. 4, 1946; came to U.S., 1977; s. Prem Nath and Parkash Wat (Narang) C.; m. Anil Arora, Feb. 8, 1973; children: Pooja, Aarti, Amit. B in Tech. with honors, Bradford (Eng.) U., 1971; MBA, John Carroll U., 1980. Registered profl. engr., Can. Various positions Hepworth & Grandage, Bradford, 1964-75; various quality and reliability positions Picker Internat., Cleve., 1976-83; quality mgr. Hughes Aircraft, El Segundo, Calif., 1983-84; v.p. Photo Acoustic Tech., Inc., Westlake Village, Calif., 1984-85, pres., chief exec. officer, 1985—. Sec. Hindu Cultural Soc., 1972-74. Mem. Am. Soc. Quality Control (sr.), Assn. Profl. Engrs. Ont. Office: Photo Acoustic Tech Inc 756 Lakefield Rd Unit G Westlake Village CA 91361

CHAYAMA, YUKIHIKO, commercial finance company executive; b. Himi City, Japan, Sept. 28, 1947; came to U.S, 1965; s. Hikoso and Midori C.; m. Yoshiko Ishii, Feb. 11, 1973; children: Yukiteru, Yukichika, Junko. BS in

Econs., Tokyo U., 1971; MBA, Harvard U., 1977. Asst. mgr. N.Y. agy. The Fuji Bank, Ltd., N.Y.C., 1977-82; mgr. corp. planning The Fuji Bank, Ltd., Tokyo, 1982-83, mgr. internat. planning, 1983-85; v.p. corp. planning and mktg. Heller Internat. Corp., Chgo., 1985-86, v.p. corp. planning and adminstrn., 1986—. Home: 486 Ravine Dr Highland Park IL 60035 Office: Heller Internat Corp 200 N LaSalle St Chicago IL 60601

CHAZEN, JEROME A., apparel company executive; b. N.Y.C., Mar. 21, 1927; s. David and Rose (Mark) C.; m. Simona Chivian, June 26, 1949; children: Kathy Ann, Louise Sharon Chazen Banon, David Franklin. BA, U. Wis.-Madison, 1948; MBA, Columbia U., 1950. Security analyst Sutro Bros., N.Y.C., 1950-51; salesman/mgr. Rhea Mfg. Co., Milw., 1951-52, buyer Milw. Boston Stores, 1952-54, Lit Bros., Phila., 1954-57; v.p. Winkelman Stores, Detroit, 1957-68; v.p. sales Westwood Textiles, N.Y.C., 1968-73, Eccobay Sports Wear, N.Y.C., 1973-77; chmn. bd. dirs., Liz Claiborne, Inc., N.Y.C., 1977—; bd. dirs. Fashion Inst. Tech., Shenkar Coll. Vice chmn. Internat. Peace Park/Jewish Nat. Fund, Israel, 1987; bd. dirs. Greater N.Y. council Boy Scouts Am., 1983-84, Rockland Ctr. for Arts, Nyack, N.Y., 1983—, Lupus Found., N.Y.C., 1984, Ednl. Found., Am. Craft Mus., 1989; bd. dirs., chmn., div. leader Fedn. United Jewish Appeal, N.Y.C., 1983-86. Served with USN, 1945-46. Jewish. Avocations: Jazz music, travel, boating, glass art collecting. Office: Liz Claiborne Inc 1441 Broadway New York NY 10018

CHBOSKY, FRED G., steel company executive; b. McKeesport, Pa., July 16, 1944; s. Stephen Frank and Anna (Klacik) C.; m. Lea Meyer, June 25, 1966; children: Stephen, Stacy. BS, Lehigh U., 1966. CPA, Pa. Audit mgr. Price Waterhouse & Co., Pitts., 1966-75; dir. fin. reporting Wheeling-Pitts. Steel Corp., 1975-76, asst. comptr., 1976-80, compt., 1980-83, v.p. purchasing traffic and raw materials, 1983-85, v.p. fin., 1985-86, v.p. fin., chief fin. officer, 1986—; bd. dirs. South Hills Health System, Pitts. Served with U.S. Army Res., 1966-72. Mem. Am. Inst. CPA's, Pa. Inst. CPA's. Democrat. Roman Catholic. Clubs: Montour Heights Country (Pitts.), Ft. Henry (Wheeling, W.Va.). Home: 295 Carmell Dr Pittsburgh PA 15241 Office: Wheeling-Pitts Steel Corp 1134 Market St Wheeling WV 26003

CHEATHAM, DANIEL E., insurance agency executive; b. Sioux Falls, S.D., Feb. 15, 1949; s. Arthur Richard and Evelyn Carolyn (Eichhorn) C.; m. Ann Maurine Funk, Aug. 16, 1970; children: Kimberly, Amanda, Kelli. BS in Fin. and Ins., Ill. Wesleyan U., 1971. Supr. customer svc. and assigned risk Horace Mann Ins. Co., Springfield, Ill., 1971-74, group sales rep., 1974-75; treas. Forsyth Ins. Agy., Inc., Springfield, 1975-78, v.p., 1979-82, exec. v.p., 1982—, also bd. dirs. Precinct committeeman Sangaman County Rep. Cen. Com., Springfield, 1976-80; mem. Gov.'s Planning Coun. on Devel. Disabilities, State of Ill., 1979-83; bd. trustees Jacksonville (Ill.) Assn. for Retarded Citizens Found., 1987—; regional sponsor Mathcounts Competition, Springfield, 1988; dir. Hope Sch. Multi Handicapped, Springfield, 1987—. Named Dist. 20 All-Star Nat. Assn. Intercoll. Athletics, 1970. Mem. Ind. Ins. Agts. Ill., Springfield Bd. Realtors, Masons. Republican. Mem. United Ch. Christ. Home: RR 1 Box 79P New Berlin IL 62670 Office: Forsyth Ins Agy Inc 1201 S 4th St Springfield IL 62703

CHECOTA, JOSEPH WOODROW, business executive; b. Watertown, Wis., May 6, 1939; s. Joseph Woodrow and Rachael Cecilia C.; m. Ellen McNamara, Sept. 7, 1963; children—Benjamin David, Nicholas Forbes. B.S., U. Wis., 1963. Wis. area coordinator Area Redevel. Adminstrn., U.S. Dept. Commerce, 1963-64; area supr. Econ. Devel. Adminstrn., Washington, 1965-66; co-founder, pres., dir. Am. Med. Bldgs., Inc., Milw., 1968-83; chmn. bd. Am. Med. Bldgs., Inc., 1975-83; chmn. bd., chief exec. officer The Am. Network, Inc., 1981-83; founder, chief exec. officer Universal Med. Bldgs. L.P., Milw., 1984—; dir. Mid-Continental Bancorp., Continental Bank & Trust Co., 1978-85. Treas. Wis. Democratic Party, 1969-70, chmn., 1979-81; v.p. Port of Milw. Bd. Harbor Commrs., 1978-80, pres., 1980-81; bd. dirs. Milw. Art Mus., 1983—, Pub. Policy Forum, 1979—. Office: Universal Med Bldgs LP 839 N Jefferson St Milwaukee WI 53202

CHEDGY, DAVID GEORGE, mining company executive; b. Bristol, Eng., July 6, 1939; came to U.S., 1962; s. Reginald and Winifred Joyce (Yeates) C.; m. Peggy Ann Young, Jan. 26, 1958 (div. Jan. 1983); children: Cheryl Ann, Dean. BS in Mining Engring., Norton Radstock Tech. Inst., Bristol, 1960; BS in Elec. Engring., City of Bath Tech. Inst., Eng., 1962. Mining engr. Welsh div. Nat. Coal Bd., Cardiff, 1958-62; v.p. ops. Robert & Schaefer Co., Chgo., 1962-79; regional mgr. Kaiser Engrs., Oakland, Calif., 1983-87; pres., chief operating officer CLI Corp., Pitts., 1987—, also bd. dirs. Author: Coal Preparation, 1977; contbr. numerous articles on coal and tech. processing to tech. publs. Mem. Instn. Elec. Engrs., Soc. Mining Engrs., Assn. Iron and Steel Engrs., AIME (best tech. paper award 1985, bd. dirs. 1986-87). Republican. Methodist. Home: 525 Reamer Dr Carnegie PA 15106

CHEEK, BARBARA, real estate broker, sales consultant; b. Detroit, Nov. 12, 1937; d. Joseph P. and Francis (Michoin) Wontroba; m. George Wesley Buzby, May 24, 1956 (div. 1967); children: Mark Alan, Paul Stuart. Student, Pasadena Community Coll., 1969-72; cert. in techniques of teaching indsl. edn., U. Calif., Fairfield, 1978. Lic. real estate agt., Calif. Personnel adminstr. Cushman & Wakefield Brokerage Co., L.A., 1971-73; cert. moving cons. Bekins Moving and Storage Co., Concord and Pasadena, Calif., 1973-78; sales agt. Vacaville (Calif.) Realty, 1978-80; regional mktg. mgr. Comfort Publs., Vallejo, Calif., 1980-82; leasing agt. Commerce Communities, San Jose, Calif., 1982-84; comml. broker Grubb & Ellis Brolerage, San Jose, 1984—; presenter seminars, workshops; cons. Sales Ter. Mgmt., San Jose, 1984—, Pacific Rim Cos.-Real Estate, San Jose, 1987—; rep. Osaka (Japan) Prefecture Govt., U.S.-Japan Tech. Trade Ctr., San Jose, 1987. Contbr. articles to profl. jours. Den mother Pasadena area Boy Scouts Am., 1966; bd. dirs. Concord Parents without Ptnrs., 1976; active Am. Cancer Soc. With USN, 1954-56. Mem. Assn. South Bay Brokers, Pasadena C. of C. (recipient awards 1973, 74, 75),Toastmaster (pres. 1988, San Jose chpt.). Roman Catholic. Home: 169 Park Dartmouth Pl San Jose CA 95136 Office: Grub & Ellis Comml Brokerage Co 224 Airport Pkwy Ste 150 San Jose CA 95136

CHEEK, JACK THOMAS, JR., wholesale food brokerage company executive; b. Augusta, Ga., Apr. 6, 1934; s. Jack Thomas and Geneva (Price) C.; m. Mary Beulah Cook, Nov. 27, 1952; children: Jan, Jack, Susan. BS, La Salle U., 1961. Asst. bakery technician Claussen Co., Augusta, 1952-54; from salesman to gen. mgr. market devel. Kingan Co. (now Hygrade Foods), Orangeburg, S.C. and Detroit, 1954-68; chmn., chief exec. officer Packer Sales (now Cooke's Plantation Foods), Palm Valley, Fla., 1968—; bd. dirs. Jack's Hi-Grade Foods, Jacksonville, Fla.; cons./bd. dirs. Prestige Aviation, St. Augustine, Fla., 1983-87, J. Cheek and Son, Ponte Vedra, Fla. Scoutmaster Boy Scouts Am., Jacksonville, 1965; sec. South Ponte Vedra Assn., 1984-85. Recipient Key to City of St. Augustine, 1985. Mem. Pilot's Assn. St. John's Co., Tournament Players Club (founder), River Club. Office: Cooks Plantation Foods PO Box 1879 Ponte Vedra FL 32082

CHEEK, LOGAN MCKEE, venture capital company executive, author; b. Glasgow, Ky., Sept. 21, 1938; s. Logan M. II, Kathleen Lowndes (Jarrett) C.; m. Pamela Louise Wilcox, Apr. 15, 1965; children: Christen, Ashby, Alexander R.W. AB, Cornell U., 1960, postgrad., 1961-63; postgrad., MIT, 1960-61. Supr. Rochester (N.Y.) Telephone, 1963; mgr. personnel research Charles Pfizer & Co., N.Y.C., 1968-69; assoc. McKinsey & Co., N.Y.C., 1969-71; mgr. group program Xerox Corp., Rochester, 1971-79; mng. prin. The Pittsford (N.Y.) Group, Inc., 1975—. Author: Zero Base Budgeting Comes of Age, 1977, Zero Base Budgeting: A Manual of Decision Packages, 1978. Capt. U.S. Army, 1964-68, Vietnam. Decorated Silver Star, Bronze Star. Mem. Farm Neck Golf Club (Martha's Vineyard, Mass.). Republican. Presbyterian.

CHEFITZ, HAROLD NEAL, investment banker; b. Boston, Jan. 5, 1935; s. David and Sadie (Bacalenick) C.; m. Charlotte Myra Goldfine, May 22, 1937; children: Robert, Amy, Lauren. BS, Boston U., 1955; postgrad., Harvard U., 1957; student, Boston Coll. Sch. Law, 1958-59. Sr. ptnr. James H. Oliphant, N.Y.C., 1969-75; v.p. Oppenheimer and Co., N.Y.C., 1975-81, Gintel and Co., N.Y.C., 1981-83; mng. dir. Swergold, Chefitz Inc., N.Y.C., 1983—; cons. Ethyl Corp., Richmond, Va., 1974—; bd. dirs., advisor Elan Pharm.,Inc., Athlone, Ireland, 1983—, O'Brien Pharm., Parsippany, N.J., 1986-88, Carondolet Rehab. Ctrs. Am., Culver City, Calif. Author: booklet, Chefitz Health Service Pharmaceutical Survey, 1968, 77. Mem. Dem. County Com., Livingston, N.J., 1980-87. Recipient Presidential citation Columbia U., 1976. Mem. Fin. Analyst Fedn. Club: Princeton, Chatham Squash. Office: Swergold Chefitz Inc 110 Wall St New York NY 10005

CHEH, HUK YUK, electrochemist, engineering educator; b. Shanghai, China, Oct. 27, 1939; s. Tze Sang and Sue Lan (Che) C.; m. An-li, July 26, 1969; children: Emily, Evelyn. B.A.Sc. in Chem. Engring, U. Ottawa, Can., 1962; Ph.D., U. Calif.-Berkeley, 1967. Mem. tech. staff AT&T Bell Labs., N.J., 1967-70; asst. prof. chem. engring. Columbia U., N.Y.C., 1970-73; assoc. prof. Columbia U., 1973-79, prof., 1979—, Ruben-Viele prof., 1982—, chmn. dept., 1980-86; program dir. NSF, 1978-79; vis. research prof. Nat. Tsinghua U., Taiwan, 1977. Mem. editorial adv. bd. Ency. of Phys. Sci. Tech.; mem. exec. adv. bd. Dictionary Sci. Tech.; contbr. articles to sci. jours. Recipient Harold C. Urey award, 1980, Electrodeposition Research award The Electrochem. Soc., 1988. Mem. Am. Inst. Chem. Engrs., N.Y. Acad. Scis., Electrochem. Soc., Am. Electroplaters Soc., Sigma Xi. Office: Columbia U New York NY 10027

CHELBERG, BRUCE STANLEY, holding company executive; b. Chgo., Aug. 14, 1934; s. Stanley Andrew and Josephine Marie (Mohn) C.; children—Stephen E., David M., Kimberly Anne. B.S. in Commerce, U. Ill., 1956, LL.B., 1958. Bar: Ill. 1958. Atty. Trans Union Corp., Chgo., 1958-64, asst. gen. counsel, 1964-68; pres. Getz Corp., San Francisco, 1968-71; v.p. Trans Union Corp., Chgo., 1971-78, pres., chief oper. officer, 1978-81; sr. v.p. Whitman Corp. (formerly IC Industries, Inc.), Chgo., 1982-85, exec. v.p., 1985—, also bd. dirs.; mem. adv. bd. Schwinn Bicycle Co., 1987—; bd. dirs. First Midwest Bank corp., Northfield Labs. Bd. dirs. Exec. Council on Fgn. Diplomats, N.Y.C., 1982—, Chgo. Crime Commn., 1983-87 , Arlington Heights Pub. Sch Dist 25, Ill., 1974-83; mem. bd. higher edn. State Ill., 1988—; mem. Internat. Exec. Service Corps, Stamford, Conn., 1980—. Mem. ABA, Ill. State Bar Assn. Clubs: Chicago, Metropolitan (Chgo.); World Trade (San Francisco).

CHELL, BEVERLY C., lawyer; b. Phila., Aug. 12, 1942; d. Max M. and Cecelia (Portney) C.; m. Robert M. Chell, June 21, 1964. BA, U. Pa., 1964; JD, N.Y. Law Sch., 1967; LLM, NYU, 1973. Bar: N.Y. 1967. Assoc. Polur & Polur, N.Y.C., 1967-68, Thomas V. Kingham, Esq., N.Y.C., 1968-69; v.p., sec., asst. gen. counsel, dir. Athlone Industries, Inc., Parsippany, N.J., 1969-81; asst. v.p., asst. sec., assoc. gen. counsel Macmillan Inc., N.Y.C., 1981-85, v.p., sec., gen. counsel, 1985—. Mem. Assn. Bar City N.Y., Am. Soc. Corp. Secs. Home: 9 Marsh Rd Westport CT 06880 Office: Macmillan Inc 866 3rd Ave New York NY 10022

CHELLGREN, PAUL WILBUR, petroleum company executive; b. Tullahoma, Tenn., Jan. 18, 1943; s. Wilbur E. and Kathryn L. (Berquist) C.; m. Shelia Mary McManus, Nov. 21, 1970; children: Sarah, Matthew, Jane. BS, U. Ky., 1964; MBA, Harvard U., 1966; diploma in Devel. Econ., Univ. Coll., Oxford, Eng., 1967. Assoc. McKinsey & Co., Washington and London, 1967-68; ops. analyst Office Sec. Def., Washington, 1968-70; adminstrv. asst. Boise Cascade Corp., Idaho, 1970-71; div. gen. mgr. Boise Cascade Corp., Los Angeles, 1971-72; pres. Universal Capital Corp., Kansas City, Mo., 1972-74; exec. asst. to chmn. Ashland (Ky.) Oil Inc., 1974-77; adminstrv. v.p. Ashland Chem. Co., Columbus, Ohio, 1977-78, group v.p., 1978-80; sr. v.p., group operating officer Ashland Oil Inc., 1980-88, sr. v.p., chief fin. officer, 1988—; chmn. bd. Ashland Coal Inc.; bd. dirs. Greater Ashland Found., Melamine Chems. Inc. Past pres., trustee Huntington (W.Va.) Mus. Art; chmn. bd. River Cities Cultural Council, Ashland; bd. dirs, sec., Am. Friends of Univ. Coll. Oxford Inc.; bd. dirs., trustee Nat. Found. Advancement in the Arts. Served to 1st lt. AUS, 1968-70. Mem. Am. Petroleum Inst., Nat. Petroleum Refiners Assn., Soc. Chem. Industry, Chem. Mfrs. Assn. (former dir.), Am. Indsl. Health Council (dir.), Univ. Ky. Fellows. Club: Bellefonte Country (Ashland). Home: 608 Sunset Dr Ashland KY 41101 Office: Ashland Oil Inc PO Box 391 Ashland KY 41114

CHEMEROW, DAVID IRVING, financial company executive; b. Washington, July 12, 1951; s. Ben-ami S. and Elynor (Pollay) C.; m. Doreen L. Conforti, Dec. 16, 1972. AB, Dartmouth Coll., 1973, MBA, 1975. Fin. analyst Primerica Corp., Greenwich, Conn., 1975-77; mgr. mergers and acquisitions Am. Can Co., Greenwich, 1977-78, dir. corp. fin., 1978-80, asst. treas., 1980-82, v.p., treas., 1982-85, v.p., corp. contr., 1985-87; sr. v.p., corp. contr. Am. Can Co., 1987, sr. v.p. ops., 1987-89; adv. bd. Conn. Nat. Bank. Bd. overseers Darmouth Inst., Darmouth Coll. Mem. Fin. Execs. Inst. Home: 77 Blackberry Dr Stamford CT 06903

CHEN, ARTHUR BERNARD, accountant; b. N.Y.C., Jan. 14, 1955; s. Kao and May (Yoh) C.; m. Eileen Yan Zhi Lin, May 6, 1985. Student, Lehigh U., 1974-76; BS in Fin. and Econs., Fairleigh Dickinson U., 1978; postgrad., Pace U., Rutgers U., 1982-85. Internal auditor Prudential Ins. Co., South Plainfield, N.J., 1978-79; reins. acct. Pinehurst Reins. Intermediary, Parsippany, N.J., 1979-81, Am. Internat. Group, N.Y.C., 1981-83; sr. acct. Federated Reins. Corp., Piscataway, N.J., 1983-84, Continental Ins. Co., Piscataway, 1985—; vis. lectr. modern acctg. and econ. principles Shanghai (People's Republic of China) Mech. Inst., 1985, Shanghai Fin. and Acctg. Inst., 1985. Mem. YMCA, Somerville, N.J.; sustaining mem. Nat. Rep. Com., Washington, 1984—. Mem. Nat. Assn. Accts., Nat. Soc. Accts. for Coops. Home: 6 Shawns Way Burlington NJ 08016 Office: Continental Ins Cos 2 Corporate Pl Piscataway NJ 08854

CHEN, HO-HONG H. H., industrial engineer, educator; b. Taiwan, Apr. 11, 1933; s. Shui-Cheng and Mei (Lin) C.; m. Yuki-Lihua Jenny, Mar. 10, 1959; children—Benjamin Kuen-Tsai, Carl Joseph Chao-Kuang, Charles Chao-Yu, Eric Chao-Ying, Charmine Tsuey-Ling, Dolly Hsiao-Ying, Edith Yi-Wen, Yvonne Yi-Fang, Grace Yi-Sin, Julia Yi-Jiun. Owner, Tai Chang Indsl. Supplies Co., Ltd., 1967—; pres. Pan Pacific Indsl. Supplies, Inc., Ont., Can., 1975—, Maker Group Inc., Md., 1986—, Wako Internat. Co., Ltd., Md., 1986—. prof. First Econ. U., Japan. Clubs: Internat. (Washington); Kenwood Golf and Country (Bethesda, Md.). Author: 500 Creative Designs for Future Business, 1961; A Summary of Suggestions for the Economic Development in Central America Countries, 1979; Access and Utilize the Potential Fund in Asia, 1980. Office: PO Box 5674 Friendship Sta Washington DC 20016

CHEN, KOK-CHOO, lawyer, educator; b. Hong Kong, Oct. 24, 1947; d. Chin Poo and Kim Suan (Lin) Tan; children: Shahn Y., Mei-Mei. Barrister-at-law, Inns of Ct., Eng., 1968. Bar: Calif., 1974. Assoc. Law Offices of Tan, Rajah and Cheah, Singapore, 1969-70; lectr. Nanyang U., Singapore, 1970-71; law clk. Sullivan and Cromwell, N.Y.C., 1971-74; assoc. Heller, Ehrman, White and McAuliffe, Calif., 1974-75; founding ptnr. Ding and Ding, Taipei, Taiwan, 1975-88, Ding, Ding and Chan, Calif., 1983-88; prin. Deacons & Chen, Taipei, Republic of China, 1988—; assoc. prof. Soochow U., Taipei, 1981—. Author: Licensing Technology to Chinese Enterprise (Chia Hsin Found. award), 1986. Named One of Ten Most Outstanding Women of Yr., Taiwan, 1982. Mem. Honorable Soc. of Inner Temple, Calif. Bar Assn., Zonta Internat. Office: Chen & Assocs, 602 Minchuan Rd E, Suite #824, Taipei Republic of China

CHEN, RICHARD LI-CHIA, oil company executive; b. Tientai, Zhejiang, China, Aug. 12, 1938; s. Kehfei and Rujun (Ma) C.; m. Chi-hong Betty Meng, Nov. 2, 1969; 1 child, Darin. BSEE, Nat. Taiwan U., Taipei, 1959; MSEE, U. Kans., 1962; postgrad. study of electrophysics, Poly. Inst. of N.Y., 1970. Equipment engr., computer systems coordinator Western Electric Co., N.Y.C., 1962-67; systems engr., adv. industry specialist IBM, N.Y.C. and N.J., 1967-79; dir. China affairs Occidental Petroleum Co., Los Angeles, 1979-83, v.p. Asian affairs, 1983—; conf. interpreter State Dept., 1979—. Editor (mag.) The Bridge, 1973-77; contbr. articles to profl. jours. Office: Occidental Petroleum Corp 10889 Wilshire Blvd Los Angeles CA 90024

CHENEY, RICHARD EUGENE, public relations executive; b. Pana, Ill., Aug. 30, 1921; s. Royal F. and Nelle E. (Henke) C.; m. Betty L. McCray, Oct. 17, 1943; children: R. Christopher, Elyn G. Cheney McInnis; m. 2d, Virginia B. Burns, Jan. 23, 1966; children: Benjamin, Anne. AB, Knox Coll., Galesburg, Ill., 1943; MA, Columbia U., 1960. Assoc. editor Tide Mag., 1953; dir. pub. relations Tri Continental Corp., 1953-55; asst. mgr. pub. relations dept. Mobil Corp., 1955-60; vice chmn. bd. Hill & Knowlton, Inc., N.Y.C., 1960-86, chmn. bd., 1987—; bd. dirs. Chattem Inc., Chattanooga, C.R. Gibson Co., Norwalk, Conn., Alphabet Inc., Warren, Ohio, Rowe Furniture. Served to lt. (j.g.) USNR, 1943-47, PTO. Clubs: University, Dutch Treat (N.Y.C.); Edgewood (Tivoli, N.Y.); Castalia (Ohio); Century Club (N.Y.C.). Home: 25 W 81st St Apt 5A New York NY 10024 Office: Hill & Knowlton Inc 420 Lexington Ave New York NY 10706

CHENEY, THOMAS WARD, insurance company executive; b. Union, Nebr., Dec. 17, 1914; s. Gilbert Ward and Vernie (Barnum) C.; m. E. Margaret Phillippe, Oct. 15, 1938; children—Patricia Kay Cheney Keim, Thomas Charles. B.S., U. Nebr., 1936; student, Life Ins. Mktg. Inst., U. Kans., 1950. With Modern Woodmen of Am., 1935-79; dir., asst. to pres. Modern Woodmen of Am., Rock Island, Ill., 1954-60; pres. Modern Woodmen of Am., 1960-79, also dir.; dir. 1st Nat. Bank of Quad Cities, mem. exec. com., 1974-87. Bd. dirs. Rock Island Community Chest, 1956-58, 65-66, YMCA, Rock Island, 1965-69; v.p. Blackhawk Indsl. Devel. Assn., Rock Island County, 1959; mem. bus. advisory com. Coll. Bus. U. Ill., 1969-81; bd. dirs. Augustana Coll., 1970-78, mem. exec. com., 1972-78, chmn. devel. com., 1972-78; bd. govs. Rock Island Found., 1967-76, Franciscan Med. Ctr. Found., 1986—; trustee, mem. exec. com. Rock Island Franciscan Med. Ctr., 1971-78, chmn. bd. trustees, 1974-75; mem. lay advisory bd. St. Anthony's Hosp., Rock Island, 1965-72. Served to lt. col. USAAF, 1941-46. Decorated Legion of Merit.; Recipient Distinguished Service award U.S. Jaycees, 1940. Mem. Fraternal Ins. Counsellors Assn., Life Underwriters Assn., Gen. Agents and Mgrs. Conf., Nat. Fraternal Congress Am. (mem. exec. com. 1961-62, pres. 1967-68), Ill. Fraternal Congress, Ill. (dir. 1966-72), Ill. Fraternal Congress (vice chmn. 1971-72); Ill. C. of C. (bd. dirs. 1966-72, vice chmn. 1970-72), Rock Island C. of C. (pres. 1965), Delta Upsilon. Republican. Presbyterian (elder, trustee, deacon). Club: Rock Island Arsenal Golf (bd. govs. 1975-81, pres. 1979, exec. com.). Home: 2205 22 1/2 Ave Rock Island IL 61201

CHENG, BEN, real estate broker, educator; b. Taipei, Taiwan, Dec. 15, 1953; came to U.S., 1966; s. Stanway and Lucy (Tai) C.; m. Peggy Choi, Oct. 23, 1983. BS, U. Calif., Berkeley, 1976. Cert. comml. real estate broker; cert. comml. investment mgr. Sales assoc. Herbert Hawkins Realtors, Alhambra, Calif., 1979-80; broker, assoc. East West Realty, Monterey Park, Calif., 1980-82, Cathay Realty, 1982-85; broker, owner Calif. Real Estate Profls., San Gabriel and Upland, Calif., 1985—; approved instr. Real Estate Seminar Am., Newport Beach, 1986-88, UCLA. Contbr. articles to profl. mags. Mem. Nat. Assn. Realtors, Calif. Assn. Realtors, Cert. Comml. Investment Mgrs. (pres.-elect L.A. chpt.). Office: Calif Real Estate Profls 401 E Valley Blvd Ste 101 San Gabriel CA 91776

CHENG, NOLAND, strategic operations officer, legal and education fund executive; b. Oakland, Calif., Apr. 14, 1957; s. Lu-I and Helen (Yu) C. BA in Econs., BS in Adminstrv. Sci., Yale U., 1979; MBA, NYU, 1985. Sr. auditor Coopers & Lybrand, N.Y.C., 1979-81; asst. v.p. fin. Drexel Burnham Lambert, N.Y.C., 1981-83, v.p. fin., strategic planning, 1983-84, asst. to pres., chief ops. officer, 1984-85, investment banker, mgr. ops. planning and analysis, 1986-87, 1st v.p., dir. ops., 1987—. Dir. Asian Legal Def. and Ednl. Fund, N.Y.C., 1982—. Mem. Securities Industry Assn., Internat. Ops. Assn. Club: Yale (N.Y.C.). Office: Drexel Burnham Lambert 60 Broad St New York NY 10004

CHENG, PAUL HUNG-CHIAO, civil engineer; b. China, Dec. 1, 1930; s. Yen-Teh and Shu-Yin (Tsou) C.; came to U.S., 1958, naturalized, 1973; BSCE, Nat. Taiwan U., 1951; MSCE, U. Va., 1961; m. Lucial Jen Chen, Aug. 1, 1964; children: Maria, Elizabeth, Deborah, Samuel. Structural engr. Swift & Co., Chgo., 1963-67; sr. structural designer P&W Engring., Inc., Chgo., 1967; sr. structural engr. A. Epstein & Son, Inc., Chgo., 1967-68; staff engr. Interlake, Inc., Chgo., 1968-71, supervising engr., 1971-73, chief structural engr., 1973-80, product engring. mgr., 1980-82, CAD/CAM devel. mgr., 1982-84; CAD/CAM System mgr. Continental Can Co., 1984-88; CAD/CAM System mgr. Continental Container system div. Figgie Internat., Inc., 1988—. Registered structural engr., Ill.; registered profl. civil engr., Calif. Mem. ASCE, Soc. Mfg. Engrs. (Computer and Automated Systems Assn.), Am. Mgmt. Assn. Home: 1869 Allen Ln Saint Charles IL 60174 Office: Continental Can Co 1700 Harvester Rd West Chicago IL 60185

CHENG, SAMSON, architect; b. Wu Chow, Kwong Si, China, Mar. 15, 1934; emigrated to Can., 1958; s. Wai Shun and Fong (Wong) C.; children—Colleen, Caron. B.Sc. in Architecture, Cheng Kung U., Tainan, Taiwan, 1957; B.Arch., U. Man., Winnipeg, Can., 1960, MArch., 1962. Planner Cen. Mortgage and Housing Corp., Ottawa, Ont., 1962-63; architect John B. Parkin Assoc., Bregman & Hammann, Toronto, Ont., 1963-67, Toronto Bd. Edn., 1967-73; self-employed architect, planner, 1973—; archtl. cons. cement industry, hotel industry, Venezuela, U.K., Far East and Can., 1974-77; cons. Ky. Fried Chicken Internat. image design, 1978—. Recipient Nat. House Design award Expo '67, Montreal, 1967. Mem. Ont. Archtl. Assn. Avocations: tennis, skiing, badminton, photography, writing poetry.

CHENOK, PHILIP BARRY, association executive, accountant; b. N.Y.C., Oct. 21, 1935; s. Irving and Anna C.; m. Judith Chenok, Aug. 4, 1972; children—David, Dan; stepchildren: Justin Jackson, Adam Jackson. Student, NYU, 1957; postgrad., Grad. Sch. Bus., 1962. Staff acct. Pogson, Peloubet & Co., 1957-61; mgr. spl. projects Am. Inst. C.P.A.'s, N.Y.C., 1961-63; pres. Am. Inst. C.P.A.'s, 1980—; partner Main Hurdman, N.Y.C., 1963-80. Mem. Am. Inst. C.P.A.'s, Conn. Soc. C.P.A.'s, N.Y. State Soc. C.P.A.'s, Am. Acctg. Assn. Office: Am Inst CPA 1211 Ave of the Americas New York NY 10036

CHENOWETH, ARLENE JOYCE, construction company executive; b. Cass City, Mich., Apr. 1, 1941; d. Robert Melvin and Geraldine Thelma (Bell) Milner; grad. Olivet Nazarene U., Kankakee, Ill., 1963; postgrad. U. Mich., 1963-65; m. Robert R. Chenoweth, Sept. 1, 1962; children: Timothy, Eric, Gregg. Tchr. bus. edn. Swartz Creek (Mich.) Sr. High Sch., 1963-67, Flushing (Mich.) Sr. High Sch., 1969-74; co-owner, exec. v.p. Chenoweth Constrn. Co., Inc., Fenton, 1974—; pres. Chenoweth Cons., 1988—; mem. alumni bd. Olivet Nazarene U., 1983—; mem. adv. bd. bus. adminstrn. Wept Baker Coll., 1989—; lectr. and freelance writer in field. Recipient O Alumni award Olivet Nazarene U., 1986. Founder Fenton Businesswomen's Breakfast Fellowship; dir. Eastern Mich. Dist., Women's Ministries, 1983-86; chairperson Ea. Mich. Dist. Nazarene Lay Retreat, 1986—. Mem. Am. Mgmt. Assn., Nat. Assn. Female Execs., Am. Soc. Tng. and Devel., Nat. Coun. Women Cons., Fenton Area Bus. and Profl. Women's Club (charter mem., treas. 1979). Nazarene. Clubs: University (Flint, Mich.); Spring Meadows Country. Home: 12050 White Lake Rd Fenton MI 48430 Office: Am Soc Tng and Devel 501 N Alloy Dr Fenton MI 48430

CHEPUCAVAGE, PETER JAMES, lawyer; b. Scranton, Pa., Sept. 9, 1947; s. Peter John and Mary Ann (Meikle) C.; m. Katherine Ann Connoly, Aug. 16, 1975; Thomas More, Michael Patrick. BS in Econs., U. Scranton (Pa.), 1969; JD, Cath. U., 1974; LLM, George Washington U., 1981. Law clk. to presiding justice D.C. Ct. Appeals, Washington, 1974-75; asst. gen. council Nat. Assn. Securities Dealers, Washington, 1975-84; gen. counsel Nomura Securities Internat. Inc., N.Y.C., 1984—. 1st lt. U.S. Army, 1969-71. Securities Industry Assn. (mem. fed. regulation com. 1987—). Democrat. Roman Catholic. Home: 104 Glenwood Rd Ridgewood NY 07450 Office: Nomura Securities Internat 180 Maiden Ln New York NY 10038

CHERESKIN, ALVIN, advertising executive; b. Bklyn., May 16, 1928; s. Benjamin and Jessie (Levine) C.; m. Susan Barocas, June 3, 1956; children—Jessica, Benjamin, Sara. Student, Pratt Inst., 1947-48, Parsons Sch. Designing, 1948, Art Students League, 1948-50. Asst. to Joseph Binder; art asst. Hockaday Assocs., Inc., 1950-55, v.p., creative dir., 1955-60, pres., 1960-65; established AC&R (wholly owned subs. Ted Bates Worldwide), 1965-87; vice chmn. AC&R/DHB & Bess Advt. Inc. formerly AC&R (wholly owned subs. Ted Bates Worldwide), 1987—. Active anti-smoking campaign Am. Cancer Soc., Jewish Fedn. Philanthropies, 1970; bd. dirs. United World Colls., Princeton, N.J., Merce Cunningham Dance Found. Served with AUS, 1945-47. Office: AC&R/DHB&BESS 16 E 32nd St New York NY 10016

CHERIS, SAMUEL DAVID, lawyer; b. Bklyn., Nov. 14, 1945; s. Hyman and Gertrude Eunice (Perlman) C.; m. Judith Lynn Jones, 1972 (div. 1976); 1 child, Aaron Joseph; m. Elaine Gayle Ingram, June 8, 1980. BS in Acctg., Bklyn. Coll., 1967; MBA, JD, Stanford U., 1971. Bar: Calif. 1972, Colo. 1973, U.S. Tax Ct. 1972, U.S. Ct. Appeals (fed. cir.) 1972. Law clk. to justice U.S. Ct. Appeals (fed. cir.), Washington, 1971-72; ptnr. Hall & Evans, Denver, 1972—; bd. dirs. Petrofiche, Inc. Author: (book) Estate Planning and Administration in Colorado, 1987; editor Stanford Jour. of Internat. Studies, 1970-71, Stanford Law Rev., 1968-71. Bd. dirs. U.S. com. Sports for Israel, Phila., 1982—, Internat. Hearing Dog., Henderson, Colo., 1981—; pres. of jury Fed. Internat. d'Escrime, Paris, France, 1980—; mem. Leadership com., Denver, 1987-88; del. U.S. Olympic Com., Colorado Springs, Colo., 1988—. Fellow Am. Coll. Probate Counsel, mem. ABA (com. chmn. real property probate and trust 1985—), Denver Estate Planning Council, Denver C. of C. (membership council 1986—, task force chmn. 1987-88), Am. arbitration Assn. (comml. arbitrator 1983—), Asia Pacific Lawyers Assn., U.S. Fencing Assn. (pres. 1988—), Cheyenne Fencing Soc. (pres. 1981—). Jewish. Home: 5730 Monview Blvd Denver CO 80207 Office: Hall & Evans 1200 17th St #1700 Denver CO 80202

CHERNIAWSKI, ANTHONY MICHAEL, insurance consultant; b. Caro, Mich., Aug. 9, 1950; s. Alex and Laura Betty (Rokita) C.; m. Suzanne Carol Palid, Aug. 26, 1972; children: Michael Anthony, Stefan Andrei, Christian Alexander, Claire Marie, David Joseph. BA, Mich. State U., 1972; postgrad., Mich. State U. Sch. Bus., 1972-73. CLU; chartered fin. cons. Agent Fidelity Union Life, Dallas, 1972-76; sr. agent Prin. Fin. Group, Des Moines, 1976—; pres., founder Benefits Design, Inc., Lansing, Mich., 1982—; reg. rep. Princor Fin. Svcs. Corp., Detroit, 1982-88; fin planner Principal Fin. Advisors, Inc., Lansing, 1984-88; registered rep. Princor Fin. Svcs. Corp., East Lansing, Mich., 1989—; Frequent guest speaker Sta. WKAR-FM on fin. and investments; fin. planner Prin. Fin. Advisors, Inc., 1989—. Chmn., founder Ednl. Trust Fund, Ch. of Resurrection, Lansing, 1984-88; trustee, treas. Greater Lansing Cath. Edn. Found., 1987-88; mem. Greater Lansing Estate Planning Council; pres. bd. pregnancy svcs. Greater Lansing, Abortion Alternatives, Inc., 1988-89; mem. Fellowship Christian Fin. Advisors. Recipient Nat. Quality award Nat. Assn. Life Underwriters, Washington, 1977-88, Nat. Sales Achievement award Nat. Assn. Life Underwriters, 1973-89; Named Agent of Yr. Gen. Agents and Mgrs. Assn., Grand Rapids, Mich., 1980, 81, 84, 87. Mem. Internat. Assn. Fin. Planning, Lansing Assn. Life Underwriters (bd. dirs. 1985—), Am. Soc. Chartered Life Underwriters (pres. cen. Mich. chpt. 1985-86), Life Ins. Leaders Mich. (pres., bd. dirs. 1980-81), Million Dollar Round Table. Roman Catholic. Home: 120 Marshall Lansing MI 48912 Office: Prin Fin Group 280 E Saginaw East Lansing MI 48823

CHERREY, GERALDINE LORRAINE, insurance agent; b. Towson, Md., May 4, 1957; d. Edward James and Eileen Mary (Dorzack) Rybak. Cert., Peabody Prep. Sch., 1978. Assoc. agt. SF&C Ins. Agy., Balt., 1982-84, dist. mgr., 1984-86, gen. agt., 1986—. Appeared as Lady Jane Patience Young, Victorian Opera Co., Balt., 1986, Queen Fairy Iolanthi, 1986, Katisha Mikado, 1988. Alto soloist Lovely Ln. United Meth. Ch., Balt., 1979—. Named Woman of Yr. Wis. Nat. Life Ins. Assn., Oshkosh, 1982-84, dist. Mgr. of Yr., 1984-85, Mgr. of Yr., 1985, 86, 88, Top Gen. Agt., 1988. Mem. Balt. Life Underwriters, Wis. Nat. Life Millionaries Club, Pres.'s. Coun. (life). Office: SF&C Assocs 7215 York Rd Ste 302 Baltimore MD 21212

CHERRY, CHARLES LEWIS, petroleum exploration company executive; b. Platteville, Colo., Mar. 5, 1926; s. Ernest Joseph and Mildred Helen (Hall) C.; m. Eleanor Marie Rasmussen, Dec. 22, 1946; children: Bryan Alan, Jilleen Marie Cherry Day. Student Colo. State Coll. Edn., 1946-47; BS, U. Wyo., 1950. Regional geologist Royal Resources Corp., Denver, 1969-71; pvt. practice cons. geologist, Littleton, Colo., 1971-78; staff geologist Natural Resources Corp., Denver, 1972-73; pres. Charles L. Cherry and Assocs., Inc., Fayette, Ala., 1978—. Author: (with others) Geology of the Paradox Basin, 1953. Mem. bd. dirs. Assn. for Retarded Citizens, 1987—. Served with USMC, 1943-45, PTO. Decorated Bronze Star, Purple Heart. Mem. Am. Assn. Petroleum Geologists, Rocky Mountain Assn. Geologists, Am. Petroleum Inst. (Warrior Basin chpt. bd. dirs. 1984), Fayette C. of C. (bd. dirs. 1985-86), Ala. Sight Conservation Assn. (bd. dirs. 1985-86), Internat. Platform Assn. Republican. Lodges: Lions (pres. 1981-82), Exchange Club. Avocations: fishing, hunting. Home: 1136 11th Ave NW Fayette AL 35555 Office: Charles L Cherry and Assocs 1600 Temple Ave N Fayette AL 35555

CHERRY, DIANE, lawyer; b. Chester, Pa., Mar. 8, 1961; d. Garland Delmont and Lucy (Varano) C. BA, NYU, 1983; JD, Temple U., 1988. Assoc. Fox, Rothschild, O'Brien & Frankel, Phila., 1988—. Republican. Home: 1931 Spruce St Philadelphia PA 19103 Office: Fox Rothschild O'Brien & Frankel 2000 Market St Philadelphia PA 19103

CHERRY, MARY JO, automobile dealership executive; b. Jefferson City, Tenn., May 29, 1960; d. Van Alton and Elizabeth Anna (Bryan) Sharpe; m. Todd Robert Cherry, Oct. 27, 1984. BS in Bus., Carson-Newman Coll., 1982. Staff acct. Duane Cline CPA, Morristown, Tenn., 1982-85; computer mgr. Farris Motor Co., Jefferson City, 1985-88, bus. mgr., 1988—. Republican. Methodist. Home: #5 Maple Crest Sq Jefferson City TN 37760

CHERRY, MURIEL ELIZABETH, human resource specialist; b. N.Y.C., July 17, 1947; d. Edward Murell and Inez Mae (Bloomfield) Britt; m. Arnold Cherry, Apr. 27, 1965; 1 child, Arnold Jr. B, CUNY, 1976. Cert. secondary educator. Exec. dir. Soul & Latin Theater, Inc., N.Y.C., 1970-72; human rights specialist N.Y.C. Commn. on Human Rights, 1976-78; asst. personnel dir. Urban Acad. for Mgmt., N.Y.C., 1978-79; affirmative action specialist N.Y. State Met. Trans. Authority, N.Y.C., 1980-81, asst. mgr. personnel, 1981-83, dir. recruitment and employee relations, 1984—; cons. Harmony, Opportunity, Mobility, Elevation and Equality, Inc., Bronx, 1980—, Harlem Communications, N.Y.C., 1986—; owner, designer The African Closet, Bklyn., 1987—. Author short story, 1979. Lectr. N.Y.C. women's prisons, 1985—. Baptist.

CHERRY, WENDELL, health care company executive; b. Riverside, Ky., BS, U. Ky., 1957, LLB, 1959. Bar: Ky., 1959. Founder Humana Inc., Louisville, Ky.; pres., chief operating officer, dir. Humana Inc., Louisville, 1969—. Named one of Outstanding Young Men Am. U.S. Jaycees, 1970. Home: Speed Ave & Sulgrave Rd Louisville KY 40205 Office: Humana Inc 500 W Main St PO Box 1438 Louisville KY 40201

CHESHIRE, SANDRA KAY, lawyer; b. Akron, Ohio, Sept. 4, 1958; d. Clarence and Pauline Patricia (Kriener) C. BA in History, Polit. Sci., Capital U., 1979; MBA, Ohio State U., 1982, JD, 1982. Bar: Ind. 1982, Ohio 1982, U.S. Dist. Ct. (no. and so. dists.) Ind. 1982, Nebr. 1988. CLU. Atty. gen. counsel Lincoln Nat. Corp., Ft. Wayne, Ind., 1982-87; assoc. gen. counsel Universal Assurors Inc, Omaha, 1987—; adj. faculty Ind.-Purdue U., 1983-87. Fellow Life Mgmt. Inst.; mem. ABA, Nebr. Bar Assn., Omaha Bar Assn. Lutheran. Home: 2405 S 165th St Omaha NE 68130 Office: Universal Assurors Inc 12809 W Dodge Rd Omaha NE 68154

CHESLEY, PHYLLIS DICKERSON, accountant; b. Paterson, N.J., Mar. 9, 1956; d. Philip Golden Jr. and Constance Cecelia (Berridge) Dickerson; m. James S. Cheeley Jr., May 22, 1982; children: Lorene Eva, Stephen Philip. BSBA in Acctg., Georgetown U., 1978. CPA, D.C., Md. Acct. FTC, Washington, 1978-80, Dept. of Energy, Germantown, Md., 1980-83, Immigration and Naturalization Service, Washington, 1985-87, Dr. James S. Chesley Jr., Clinton, Md., 1987—. Mem. Hillandale Citizens Assn., Hillandale Swim and Tennis Assn. (treas. 1987—). Democrat. Roman Catholic. Office: 7700 Old Branch Ave Ste B-106 Clinton MD 20735

CHESSER, DOUGLAS STANLEY, bank executive; b. Albany, N.Y., Jan. 19, 1948; s. Stanley F. and Betty (Jardine) C.; m. Carol Butler, Nov. 3, 1979; children: Ginger Rae, Geoffrey Ian. BS, SUNY, Albany, 1970; diploma, Rutgers U., 1980. Nat. bank examiner U.S. Treasury Dept., Washington, 1970-74; v.p. Wilber Nat. Bank, Oneonta, N.Y., 1974—; pres. Wilderness Properties Ltd., Oneonta, 1985—; mem. adv. com. Cen. Atlantic Sch. Comml. Lending Bucknell U., Lewisburg, Pa., 1984-87. Mem. N.Y. State Bankers Assn., Otsego County (N.Y.) C. of C. (pres. 1987), Kiwanis. Office: Wilber Nat Bank 245 Main St Oneonta NY 13820

CHESSER, KERRY ROYCE, accountant; b. Gallipolis, Ohio, July 18, 1956; s. Kenneth LaVerne and Hazel Louise (Steward) C. Student, Mountain State Coll., 1974-76; BA in Acctg., Mt. Vernon Nazarene Coll., 1979; MBA in Fin., Wright State U., 1982. CPA, W.Va. Jr. acct. Dayton (Ohio) Tire & Rubber, 1979-80; acct. K-P Acctg., Dayton, 1980-82; chief acct. FMRS Mental Health Council, Beckley, W.Va., 1983-86; fiscal services supr. Shawnee Hills Mental Health/Mental Research Ctr., Charleston, W.Va., 1986—; pres., chief exec. officer Royce Chesser Assoc., Beckley, W.Va., 1984—. Dir. fin. and audit coms., bd. dirs. Centerville (Ohio) Ch. of the Nazarene, 1979-81. Mem. Am. Inst. of CPA's. Home: PO Box 922 Beckley WV 25801 Office: Community MH/MR Ctr 511 Morris St Charleston WV 25301

CHESSON, REGINALD EUGENE, JR., communications company executive; b. Greer, S.C., July 27, 1953; s. Reginald Eugene and Sue (Clayton) C.; married; 2 children. BS, U. S.C., 1975. CPA, S.C. Sr. acct. Deloitte Haskins & Sells, Columbia, S.C., 1977-81; v.p., controller J.H. Mgmt. Co., Columbia, 1981-84; controller Telecommunications Systems, Inc. subs. SouthernNet, Inc., Columbia, 1984-87, SouthernNet, Inc. div. Telecom USA, Greenville, S.C., 1987—. Recipient Order of Palmetto Gov. S.C., 1971, Presdl. Commendation Pres. Nixon, 1971, Cert. Commendation ARC, 1971. Mem. Am. Inst. CPA's, S.C. Assn. CPA's. Republican. Baptist. Office: Southern Net Inc 728 N Pleasantburg Dr Greenville SC 29607

CHESTER, ALVIN MITCHELL, medical film producer, writer, director; b. Phila., June 10, 1931; s. Sigmund Silvan and Reba (Cossoy) C.; m. Rosanne Rothenberg, Feb. 27, 1955; children: Jeffrey, Pamela. BA in English Lit., Pa. State U., 1952. Film producer Smith Kline & French, Phila., 1965-70; dir. film dept. Sci. and Medicine, N.Y.C., 1970-76; v.p. MED Communications, Woodbridge, N.J., 1976-84; pres. Chester/Roth Communications, Inc., Hunt Valley, Pa., 1984—. Author: (drama) The Kohinoor, 1962 (W. Bellow Meml. award 1962); writer, producer: (films) Recognition of Narcotic Withdrawal Symptoms in New Born Infants, 1968 (EFLA Blue Ribbon award 1969), Resuscitation in the OR, 1970 (CINE Golden Eagle award 1972), Benzodiazepine Receptor, 1980 (CINE Golden Eagle award 1981), Hormone Receptors, 1980 (IFTV Gold award 1981); writer, producer, dir.: (films) The Sea Within Us, 1976 (J. Muir Gold award 1976), The Insidious Mite, 1984 (AMWA award for Excellence in Filmmaking 1985), Atherosclerosis: Mechanisms of Lipid Control, 1987 (CINE Golden Eagle award, AVC Bronze plaque), Hypertension Mosaic, 1988 (AVC award); producer, dir. (film) Post-Op Wound Care, 1977 (IFTV Gold award 1977); exec. producer: (films) Interferon Series, 1983 (IFTV Gold award 1983), Osteoporosis: A Silent Epidemic, 1983 (CINE Golden Eagle award 1984). Mem. Am. Med. Film Writers Assn. (bd. dirs.).

CHESTER, JOHN ERVIN, medical supplies company executive; b. N.Y.C., Nov. 9, 1932; s. John E. and Helen (Burns) C.; m. Arden J. Fuller, Sept. 20, 1952. Grad., USN Sch. Nursing, 1953; BSBA, Queens Coll., 1957; M in Internat. Bus., Columbia U., 1964; postgrad., Advance Mgmt. Program, Internat. Sch. Mgmt. V.p. corp devel. Weck div. E.R. Squibb Corp., Lawrenceville, N.J., 1959-75; mktg. dir. Am. Hosp Supply Corp., Evanston, Ill., 1975-79; v.p., gen. mgr. G.D. Searle Corp., Skokie, Ill., 1979-81; v.p., then pres. Unitek Corp. Div. Bristol-Myers Co., N.Y.C., 1981-85; pres., chief exec. officer Pilling Co., Ft. Washington, Pa., 1986—; guest lectr. Claremont Grad. Sch. Bus., St. Mary's Coll. Grad. Sch. Bus., Peter Drucker/Reed Powell Seminars; profl. papers presented in Australia, People's Rep. of China, U.K. and U.S. Contbr. articles to profl. jours.; 3 patents of surg. instruments. Served with USN, 1951-55. Mem. Health Industries Mfrs. Assn. Republican. Roman Catholic. Office: Pilling Co 420 Delaware Dr Fort Washington PA 19034

CHESTERFIELD, RHYDONIA RUTH EPPERSON, financial company executive; b. Dallas, Tex., Apr. 23, 1919; d. Leonard Lee and Sally E. (Stevenson) Griswold; m. Chad Chesterfield, Apr. 21, 1979. BS Southwestern U., 1952; BS, N. Tex. U., 1954, ME, 1956; PhD, Bernardean U., 1974, Calif. Christian U., 1974, LLD (hon.), 1974. Evangelist with Griswold Trio, 1940-58; tchr., counselor Dallas public schs., 1952-58, Los Angeles public schs., 1958-74; pres. Griswold-Epperson Fin. Enterprise, Los Angeles, 1974—; pres. GEC Enterprises, 1979—; guest speaker various schs., chs. and civic orgns. in U.S. and Can. Author: Little Citizens series, Cathedral Films; contbr. articles on bus. to profl. publs. Fellow Internat. Naturopathic Assn.; mem. Los Angeles Inst. Fine Arts, Assn. of Women in Edn. (hon.), Internat. Bus. and Profl. Women, Calif. C. of C., Los Angeles C. of C., Pi Lambda Theta (hon.), Kappa Delta Pi (hon.). Office: 10790 Wilshire Blvd 202 Los Angeles CA 90024

CHEVALIER, SAMUEL FLETCHER, banker; b. Islip, N.Y., Mar. 9, 1934; m. Elinor Louise Towell; children: David, Peter, Valerie. B.A., Northeastern U., 1957. Asst. sec. Irving Trust Co., N.Y.C., 1965-67, asst. v.p., 1967-70, v.p., 1970-77, sr. exec. v.p., 1982-84, now vice chmn., dir., 1984—; sr. v.p. Irving Bank Corp., N.Y.C., 1977-80, exec. v.p., 1980-82, pres., dir., 1984—. Bd. dirs. Greater N.Y. chpt. March of Dimes, 1984—. Served to 1st lt. U.S. Army, 1957-59. Office: Irving Bank Corp 1 Wall St New York NY 10005

CHEVINS, ANTHONY CHARLES, advertising agency executive; b. Frackville, Pa., Apr. 1, 1921; s. Charles A. and Mary (Swade) C.; m. Margaret Macy, Sept. 18, 1948; children: Cheryl L., Christopher M., Cynthia M. AB in Eng. and Advt. magna cum laude, Syracuse U., 1947; postgrad., Columbia U., 1948-49. Writer Batten, Barton, Durstine & Osborn (advt.), 1948-51; with Cunningham & Walsh, 1951-87, sr. v.p., 1959-61, creative dir., 1958-61, exec. v.p., 1961-68, pres., chief operating officer, 1968-84, chmn., chief exec. officer, 1984-87; chmn., chief exec. officer The C&W Group Inc., 1985-87; vice chmn. N.W Ayer Inc., 1987—, also bd. dirs.; cons. Meridien Capital Mgmt., San Diego, 1987—. Contbr. articles to mags. Mem. Nat. Advt. Rev. Bd.; mem. dean's adv. coun. Newhouse Sch.; bd. dirs. Medic Alert Found. Internat. Served to lt. USNR, 1941-45. Mem. Phi Beta Kappa, Alpha Delta Sigma. Clubs: Sky, Union League (N.Y.C.); Woodway Country (Darien, Conn.); Nat. Golf Links Am. (Southampton, L.I.); Ocean Reef, Card Sound (Key Largo, Fla.). Home: 10 South Rd Key Largo FL 33037 Office: NW Ayer 1345 6th Ave New York NY 10019

CHI, ROBIN LAI-PING, financial planner; b. Taipei, Republic of China, Mar. 18, 1958; came to U.S., 1980; parents: Fei and Yeong-Jeh (Kao) C. BA, Columbia U., 1983; MA, U. Chgo., 1984. Registered rep., mortgage broker; cert. fin. planner. Rep. 1st Investors Corp., Scarsdale, N.Y., 1984-85; asst. v.p. JSK Assocs. Inc., White Plains, N.Y., 1985-87; v.p. Finamax Planning Services, Inc., Tarrytown, N.Y., 1987—; fin. advisor Found. for Am.-Chinese Cultural Exchs., N.Y.C., 1985—. Mem. Nat. Assn. Life Underwriters, Inst. Cert. Fin. Planners (internat. bd. standards and practice), Gen. Agtss & Mgrs. Conf. Home: 198 Garth Rd Apt 1A Scarsdale NY 10583 Office: Finamax Planning Svcs Inc 555 White Plains Rd Tarrytown NY 10591

CHIA, PEI-YUAN, banker; b. Hong Kong, Jan. 27, 1939; came to U.S., 1962, naturalized, 1970; s. Dewey T.H. and Kitty C.; m. Frances T.C. Yen, Feb. 20, 1965; children: Katherine, Douglas, Candice. BA, Tunghai U., Taiwan, 1961; MBA, U. Pa., 1965. Products group mgr. Gen. Foods Corp., White Plains, N.Y., 1965-73; mktg. dir. Citibank (N.A.), N.Y.C., 1974-75; div. exec. Citicorp Savs., 1985; div. exec., mem. policy com. U.S. Card Products Group Citicorp, 1986-87, group exec., mem. policy com Comsumer Svcs. Group Internat., 1988—; head br. automation project Citibank (N.A.), 1976-77; mng. dir. Famibank, Belgium, 1978-80; pres., chief exec. officer Diner Club/Carte Blanche Corp., L.A., 1980, div. exec. devel., 1982-84. Office: Citibank 399 Park Ave New York NY 10043

CHIARAMONTE, STEVEN, corporate professional, consultant; b. San Jose, Calif., May 4, 1956; s. Philip John and Mary Elizabeth (Basso) C.; m. Joan Lizabeth Fajen, Mar. 21, 1981; children: Anthony, Francis. BS, Santa Clara U., 1978; MBA, Golden Gate U., 1985. CPA, Utah. V.p., chief fin. officer Atari Games, Milpitas, Calif., 1974-84; v.p. fin. Atari Internat., Sunnyvale, Calif., 1984-85; v.p. Internat. Ops. Wicat Systems, Inc., Orem, Utah, 1986-89, v.p. treas., chief fin. officer, 1985-89; pres. Clearmountain Assocs., Salt Lake City, 1989—; cons. Clearmountain; bd. dirs. Biometrics Inc., Fremont, Calif., 1984-86. Republican. Roman Catholic.

CHIARELLI, JOSEPH, accountant, banker; b. N.Y.C., Sept. 23, 1946; s. Biagio John and Mary Teresa (Cancellieri) C.; m. Eileen Mary Cook, Sept. 7, 1968; children: Claire Marie, Matthew Joseph, Christopher Joseph. BBA, Manhattan Coll., 1968; MBA, U. Hawaii, 1973. CPA, N.Y., Mont. Auditor Coopers & Lybrand, N.Y.C., 1973-77, audit mgr., 1977-81; asst. comptroller Morgan Guaranty Trust Co., N.Y.C., 1981-82, dep. comptroller, 1982-83; v.p., comptroller Morgan Bank Del., Wilmington, 1983-86, Morgan Securities Services Corp., N.Y.C., 1986—; chmn. adv. bd. acctg. dept. U. Del., Newark, 1985-87. Served to capt. USAF, 1968-73, maj. res. Named Outstanding Res. Officer of Yr., Air Force Audit Agy., 1980. Mem. Am. Inst. CPA's, N.Y. Soc. CPA's, Fin. Execs. Inst. (founding dir. Del. chpt. 1985-87. Roman Catholic. Home: 510 Farview Ave Wyckoff NJ 07481 Office: Morgan Securities Svcs Corp 37 Wall St New York NY 10015

CHIARO, A. WILLIAM, management consultant; b. Chgo., July 12, 1928; s. Anthony Joseph and Marie Anne (Bonario) C.; m. Lyne LaVerne Franke, Aug. 27, 1961; children: David Huntington, Caroline Elizabeth. BS, U. Ill., 1954. Cert. profl. bus. cons. Acct., IBM, Chgo., 1954-55; with Black & Skaggs Assocs., Chgo., 1955—, pres., 1978—; dir. P.M. Chgo., Inc. Contbr. articles to med. and profl. jours. Served with U.S. Army, 1946-47, USAF, 1950-52. Mem. Soc. Advancement Mgmt., Soc. Profl. Bus. Cons., Nat. Soc. Public Accts. Presbyterian. Office: PM Chgo Inc 717 Ridge Rd Wilmette IL 60091

CHIAT, JAY, advertising agency executive; b. N.Y.C., Oct. 26, 1931; s. Sam and Min (Kretchmer) C.; children: Debra, Marc, Elyse. BS, Rutgers U. Formerly v.p. Leland Oliver Co., Los Angeles; pres., chief exec. officer Jay Chiat & Assocs.; now chmn., chief exec. officer Chiat/Day Inc., N.Y.C. Served with USAF. Office: Chiat/Day Inc 79 Fifth Ave New York NY 10003 also: Chiat/Day Inc Advt 320 Hampton Dr Venice CA 90291 *

CHIAVERINI, JOHN EDWARD, construction company executive; b. Providence, Feb. 6, 1924; s. John and Sadie (Ginsberg) C.; m. Cecile Corey, Mar. 31, 1951; children—Caryl Marie, John Michael. Cert. advanced san. engring. U. Ill., 1945; B.S., U. R.I., 1947. Registered profl. engr., Mass., R.I. Project engr. Perini Corp., Hartford, Conn., 1950-51, project mgr., 1951-55, asst. project mgr., Pitts. and Que., 1955-61, v.p., Framingham, Mass., 1965-84, sr. v.p., San Francisco, 1984—; pres., dir. Compania Perini S.A., Colombia, 1961—; v.p., exec. mgr. Perini Yuba Assocs., Marysville, Calif., 1966-70, v.p. Western ops., 1970-78, 79-84, group v.p., 1978-79; sr. v.p. spl. projects Perini Corp., 1984—; dir. Perini Corp.; mem. U.S. com. Internat. Commn. on Large Dams. Served to 2d lt. USAAF, 1944-46. Recipient Golden Beaver award, 1989. Fellow ASCE; mem. Nat. Soc. Profl. Engrs., Calif. Soc. Profl. Engrs., Soc. Am. Mil. Engrs. (bd. dirs.), Beavers (bd. dirs.), Moles, Commonwealth Club of Calif. Democrat. Roman Catholic. Lodges: K.C., Rotary. Home: 37 Dutch Valley Ln San Anselmo CA 94960 Office: Perini Corp 75 Broadway San Francisco CA 94111

CHIEN, STEVEN FONG, computer company executive; b. Taipei, Taiwan, Nov. 1, 1965; came to U.S., 1969.; s. Yie Wen and Margaret Chin-Mei (Chung) C. BA, Rutgers U., 1986. Chief programmer Cocomp Internat., Roslyn Heights, N.Y., 1981-83; pres. Universal Systems Rsch., Inc., Great Neck, N.Y., 1983-87; v.p. rsch. and devel. ISYS Technology Corp., Totowa, N.J., 1987—. Office: ISYS Technology Corp 555 Preakness Ave Totowa NJ 07512

CHIERCHIA, MADELINE CARMELLA, management consulting company executive; b. Bklyn., Jan. 30, 1943; d. Lawrence Cataldo Carrozzo and Victoria Angel (Torchio) Carrozzo Petrisic; m. Jerry Chierchia, Oct. 3, 1959 (div. July 1975); children—Gertrude Chierchia Kraljic, Geraldine Rosalie Gorga. Student parochial schs. Bklyn. Personnel mgr. Argyle Personnel Agy., N.Y.C., 1976-77; clk. typist Atlantic Mut. Ins. Co., N.Y.C., 1977-78; sec. ARC, N.Y.C., 1978-82; mgr. D.F. King & Co. Inc. N.Y.C., 1982-89; asst. v.p., 1989—. Mem. Proxy Div. Securities Industry Assn., Nat. Assn. Female Execs., Reorganization Securities Industry Assn., Am. Soc. for Profl. and Exec. Women, Corp. Transfer Agts. Assn. Democrat. Roman Catholic. Avocations: bowling; chess; reading; old movies. Office: DF King & Co 77 Water St New York NY 10005

CHIERI, PERICLE ADRIANO C., retired educator, consulting mechanical and aeronautical engineer, naval architect; b. Mokanshan, Chekiang, China, Sept. 6, 1905; came to U.S., 1938, naturalized, 1952; s. Virginio and Luisa (Fabbri) C.; m. Helen Etheredge, Aug. 1, 1938. Dr Engring., U. Genoa, Italy, 1927; ME, U. Naples, Italy, 1927; Dr Aero. Engring., U. Rome, 1928. Registered profl. engr., Italy, N.J., La., S.C. chartered engr., U.K. Naval architect. mech. engr. research and exptl. divs., submarines and internal combustion engines Italian Navy, Spezia, 1929-31; naval architect, marine supt. Navigazione Libera Triestina Shipping Corp., Libera Lines, Trieste, Italy, 1931-32, Genoa, 1933-35; aero. engr., tech. adviser Chinese Govt. commn. aero. affairs Nat. Govt. Republic of China, Nanchang and Loyang, 1935-37; engring. exec., dir. aircraft materials test lab., supt. factory's tech. vocational instrn. SINAW Nat. Aircraft Works, Nanchang, Kiangsi, China, 1937-39; aero. engr. FIAT aircraft factory, Turin, Italy, 1939; aero. engr. and tech. sec. Office: Air Attache, Italian Embassy, Washington, 1939-41; prof. aero. engring. Tri-State Coll., Angola, Ind., 1942; aero. engr., helicopter design Aero. Products, Inc., Detroit, 1943-44; sr. aero. engr. ERCO Engring. & Research Corp., Riverdale, Md., 1944-46; assoc. prof. mech. engring. U. Toledo, 1946-47; assoc. prof. mech. engring., faculty grad div. Newark (N.J.) Coll. Engring., 1947-52; prof., head dept. mech. engring. U. Southwestern La., Lafayette, La., 1952-72; cons. engr. Lafayette, 1972—; research engr., adv. devel. sect., aviation gas turbine div. Westinghouse Electric Corp., South Philadelphia, Pa., 1953; exec. dir. Council on Environment, Lafayette, 1975—. Instr. water safety ARC Nat. Aquatic Schs., summers 1958-67; Bd. dirs. Lafayette Parish chpt. ARC. Fellow Royal Instn. Naval Architects London (life); assoc. fellow Am. Inst. Aeronautics and Astronautics; mem. Soc. Naval Architects and Marine Engrs. (life mem.), AAAS, AAUP (emeritus), Am. Soc. Engring. Edn. (life), Am. Soc. M.E., Soc. Automotive Engrs., Instrument Soc. Am., Soc. Exptl. Stress Analysis, Nat. Soc. Profl. Engrs., N.Y. Acad. Scis., La. Engring. Soc., La. Tchrs. Assn., AAHPER, La. Acad. Scis., Commodore Longfellow Soc., Cons. Engrs. Council La., Phi Kappa Phi., Pi Tau Sigma (hon.). Home: 142 Oak Crest Dr Lafayette LA 70503 Office: PO Box 52923 Lafayette LA 70505

CHIHOREK, JOHN PAUL, electronics company executive; b. Wilkes-Barre, Pa., June 22, 1943; s. Stanley Joseph and Caroline Mary C.; m. Christina Maria Marroquin, Dec. 28, 1968; children: Jonathan, David, Crista, Daniel. BSEE, Pa. State U., 1965; postgrad., Calif. State U., San Diego, 1970-71; MBA, Calif. State U., Sacramento, 1972. Officer program Hdqrs. Air Force Logistic Command, Dayton, Ohio, 1972-75; sr. engr. Hdqrs. Air Force Space Div., Los Angeles, 1975-78; mgr. software systems dept. Logicon Inc., San Pedro, Calif., 1978; mgr. software product assurance dept. Ford Aeronutronics, Newport Beach, Calif., 1978-85, mgr. software engring., 1985—, mgr. test equipment, facilities, 1989—; owner CMC Systems. Mem. Congl. Adv. Bd., 1980; active PTA, mem. Republican Nat. com. Served with USN, 1965-70, Vietnam. Decorated Bronze Star. Mem. IEEE, Air Force Assn., AAAS, Internat. Platform Assn. Roman Catholic. Clubs: Lions, Odd Fellows. Office: Ford Aeronutronics Ford Rd Newport Beach CA 92633

CHILCOTE, DAVID BONNELL, venture capitalist; b. Cleve., June 13, 1958; s. William August and Mary (Jones) C.; m. Nancy G. Antle, June 29, 1985; 1 child, Courtney. BA, Dartmouth Coll., 1980; MBA, Case-Western Res. U., 1984. Officer Nat. City Bank, Cleve., 1980-84; v.p. Capital Funds Corp.-Soc. Captial Corp., Cleve., 1985—; bd. dirs. Taprell Loomis, Orion Research. Mem. Assn. Corp. Growth, Ohio Venture Assn., Nat. Assn.

Small Bus. Investment Cos. Republican. Methodist. Office: Capital Funds Corp 800 Superior Ave 14th Fl Cleveland OH 44114

CHILCOTE, DAVID CHARLES, manufacturing company executive; b. Glendale, Calif., Apr. 26, 1951; s. Donald Gordon and Dorothy Marguerite (Squires) C.; m. Catherine Ann Rode, May 13, 1972; children: Timothy Michael, Amy Elizabeth. BS, MBA, San Jose State U., 1976; postgrad., Golden Gate U., 1981—. Supr. Lockheed Corp., Sunnyvale, Calif., 1977-84; mgr. material dept. Lockheed Missiles & Space Corp., Austin, Tex., 1984-86, mgr. mfg. dept., 1986-87, ops. program mgr., 1987—. Com. chmn. Boy Scouts Am., 1986-88. Served with U.S. Army, 1971-74. Mem. Nat. Mgmt. Assn. (v.p. 1986-89, spl. achievement award 1986, nat. dir. 1989—), Nat. Property Mgmt. Assn. (nat. rep., com. chmn. 1986, 87, 88), Soc. Logistics Engrs. (sr., chmn. 1980-81). Republican. Methodist. Home: 3314 Lost Oasis Hollow Austin TX 78739 Office: Lockheed Missiles & Space Co 6800 Burleson Rd Austin TX 78760

CHILCOTE, SAMUEL DAY, JR., association executive; b. Casper, Wyo., Aug. 24, 1937; s. Sam D. and Juanita C. (Cornelison) C.; m. Ellen Sheridan Spear, Nov. 11, 1966. B.S., Idaho State U., 1959. Adminstrv. asst. Continental Oil Co., Glenrock, Wyo., 1960-63; asst. supt. public instrn., dir. Wyo. Surplus Property Agy., Wyo. Sch. Lunch Program, Cheyenne Wyo. Dept. Edn., 1963-67; supr. N. Central region Distilled Spirits Inst., Denver, 1967-71; exec. dir., chief operating officer N. Central region Distilled Spirits Inst., Washington, 1971-73; exec. v.p., chief operating officer Distilled Spirits Council, Inc., Washington, 1973-77, pres., chief exec. officer, 1978-81; pres. Tobacco Inst., Washington, 1981—; mem. industry sect. adv. council consumer goods, Dept. Commerce. Pres. Sky Ranch Found. for Boys, 1975-81, pres. emeritus, 1981—; treas. Ford's Theatre, 1984-88, vice-chmn., bd. trustees, 1988—; bd. dirs., exec. com. Art Barn. Served to capt., U.S. Army, 1959-60. Recipient Profl. Achievement award, Idaho State U. Coll. Bus., 1986, Man of Yr. award, Anti-Defamation League, 1986. Mem. U.S. C. of C. Clubs: George Town, Congressional Country (past pres., exec. com., bd. govs.), Burning Tree; Nat. Press, Capitol Hill, City, F Street, TPC Avenel (Washington). Lodges: Masons, Elks, Shriners, Rotary. Office: Tobacco Inst 1875 I St Washington DC 20006

CHILD, ARTHUR JAMES EDWARD, food company executive; b. Guildford, Eng., May 19, 1910; s. William Arthur and Helena (Wilson) C.; m. Mary Gordon, Dec. 10, 1955. B.Commerce, Queen's U., 1931, LL.D., 1983; grad., Advanced Mgmt. Program, Harvard, 1956; M.A., U. Toronto, 1960, LL.D., 1984; LL.D., U. Calgary, 1984. Chief auditor Can. Packers Ltd., 1938-52, v.p., 1952-60; pres. Intercontinental Packers Ltd., 1960-66; chmn., chief exec. officer, dir. Burns Foods Ltd., Calgary, Alta., 1966—; chmn. bd., dir. Can. West Found. A.R. Clarke & Co. Ltd.; chmn. bd., dir. Scott Nat. Co., Ltd.; chmn. Ajex Enterprises Ltd.; pres. Jamar Inc.; bd. dirs. Newsco Investments Ltd., Canoe Cove Mfg. Ltd., Imperial Trust Co.; asso. prof. U. Sask., 1964-65. Author: Economics and Politics in United States Banking, 1965, (with B. Cadmus) Internal Control, 1953. Chmn. Can. West Found. Decorated Order of Can. Fellow Chartered Inst. Secs.; mem. Can. Meat Council (past pres.), Inst. Internal Auditors (past pres.), Am. Mgmt. Assn., Inst. for Strategic Studies. Office: Burns Foods Ltd, PO Box 2520 Sta M, Calgary, AB Canada T2P 3X4

CHILD, JOHN SOWDEN, JR., lawyer; b. Lansdale, Pa., July 22, 1944; s. John Sowden and Beatrice Thelma (Landes) C. B.S. in Polit. Sci., MIT, 1967; B.S. in Chem. Engring., 1967; J.D., U. Pa., 1973; B.Lit. in Politics, Oxford U., 1974. Bar: Pa. 1974, N.Y. 1977, U.S. Dist. Ct. (ea. dist.) Pa. 1978, U.S. Dist. Ct. (ea. dist.) N.Y. 1978, U.S. Patent and Trademark Office 1978, U.S. Ct. Appeals (2d cir.) 1978, U.S. Ct. Appeals (fed. cir.) 1981, U.S. Ct.Appeals (3d cir.) 1986. Assoc. Davis Hoxie Faithfull & Hapgood, N.Y.C., 1974-78; assoc. Synnestvedt & Lechner, Phila., 1978-88; of counsel Dann, Dorfman, Herrell and Skillman, Phila., 1988— ; arbitrator Pa. Ct. Common Pleas, Phila., 1979—, U.S. Dist. Ct., Ea. Dist.) Pa., Phila., 1983—. Firm coordinator United Way Southeastern Pa., 1983-88. Mem. Am. Intellectual Property Law Assn., N.Y. Patent, Trademark and Copyright Law Assn., Phila. Bar Assn., Phila. Patent Law Assn. (chmn. program com. 1981-85, editor, co-editor newsletter 1980—, gov. 1985-87, sec. 1987—), Mil. Order Fgn. Wars, Com. of Seventy, Soc. Colonial Wars, English Speaking Union, Colonial Soc. Pa., Phila. Oxford and Cambridge Soc. (sec. 1985—). Republican. Mem. Soc. of Friends. Clubs: Union League, Phila. Club., Cricket (Phila.). Home: 8221 Seminole Ave Philadelphia PA 19118 Office: Dann Dorfman Herrell & Skillman 3 Mellon Bank Center Ste 900 15th St and South Penn Sq Philadelphia PA 19102-2440

CHILDEARS, DON A., lawyer, bank executive; b. Monte Vista, Colo., Mar. 21, 1950; s. D. Marion and Myrtice B. (Pierson) C.; m. Dinah L. Lewis, Apr. 18, 1981. BSBA, Colo. State U., 1973; JD, U. Denver, 1981. Legis. asst. Congressman James P. Johnson, Washington, 1973-74; campaign coord. Johnson for Congress, Ft. Collins, Colo., 1974; asst. mgr., lobyist Colo. Bankers Assn., Denver, 1975-79, exec. v.p., 1980—; mem. exec. com. Am. Bankers Assn. State Assn. Div., Washington, 1982-87; pres. Cen. States Conf., Snowmass, Colo., 1983-84; bd. trustees Grad. Sch. Banking, Boulder, Colo., sec., 1980—, Madison, Wis., 1980—. Active U. Denver Fund Drive, 1986. Mem. Colo. Hist. Soc., Denver Athletic Club. Republican. Methodist. Office: Colo Bankers Assn 1225 17th St 240 Denver CO 80202

CHILDERS, JOHN HENRY, talent company executive, personality representative; b. Hoopston, Ill., July 26, 1930; s. Leroy Kendal and Marie Ann (Sova) C.; m. JoAnn Uhlar, July 27, 1956; children—Michael John, Mark Joseph. Sales rep. Universal Match Corp., Chgo., 1956-59; v.p. sales to pres. Sales Merchandising, Inc., Chgo., 1959-63; chmn. bd., chief exec. officer Talent Services, Inc. and Talent Network, Inc., Skokie, Ill., 1963—. Served as pilot USAF, 1950-56. Mem. Assn. Reps. of Profl. Athletes (v.p.); Internat. Wine and Food Soc., Chaine des Rotisseurs, Les Amis du Vin, Wine finders, Classic Car Club Am., Auburn-Cord-Dusenberg Club. Republican. Roman Catholic. Clubs: Knollwood Country; Big Foot Country; Lake Geneva Country, PGA Country. Home: 1299 Knollwood Circle Lake Forest IL 60045 Office: Talent Svcs Inc 5200 W Main St Skokie IL 60077

CHILDS, CLINTON LANGWITH, real estate investment consulatant; b. Honolulu, Sept. 14, 1922; s. Clinton Stibbs and Eleanor (Langwith) C.; m. Frances A. Johnston, Jan. 6, 1944; children: Candis L., Patrick J., Cristy S. BBA, U. Oreg., 1947. With Bishop Nat. Bank, 1946-51; asst. to v.p. Lihue Plantation Co., 1951-65; Kauai mgr. comml. land devel. Amfac Corp., 1965-68; pres. Kauai Helicopters, Inc., 1966-76, Clint Childs, Inc., Realtors, Hanamaulu, Hawaii, 1974-88; real estate investment cons., 1988—; mng. dir. Alii Travel, Inc., 1977-81, SRI & Assoc., Inc., 1980—. Mem. Hist. Hawaii Found. Served to capt. U.S. Army, 1944-46. Mem. Hawaii State C. of C. (pres. 1965), Kauai Bd. Realtors (pres. 1970-73), Hist. Hawaii Assn., Kauai Hist. Soc., Acad. of Arts, Punahou Alumni Assn. (dir.), Sigma Alpha Epsilon. Republican. Episcopalian. Office: PO Box 431 Lihue HI 96766

CHILDS, JOHN DAVID, computer hardware and services company executive; b. Washington, Apr. 26, 1939; s. Edwin Carlton and Catherine Dorothea (Angerman) C.; m. Margaret Rae Olsen, Mar. 4, 1966 (div.); 1 child, John-David. Student Principia Coll., 1957-58, 59-60; BA, Am. U., 1963. Jr. adminstr. Page Communications, Washington, 1962-65; account rep. Friden Inc., Washington, 1965-67; Western sales dir. Data Inc., Arlington, Va., 1967-70; v.p. mktg. Rayda, Inc., Los Angeles, 1970-73, pres., 1973-76, chmn. bd., 1976-84; sr. v.p. sales Exec. Bus. Systems, Encino, Calif., 1981—; sr. assoc. World Trade Assocs., Inc., 1976—. Pres. Coll. Youth for Nixon-Lodge, 1959-60, dir. state fedn.; mem. OHSHA policy formulation com. Dept. Labor, 1967. Served with USAFR, 1960-66. Mem. Assn. Data Ctr. Owners and Mgrs. (chmn. privacy com. 1975, sec. 1972-74, v.p. 1974). Democrat. Christian Scientist. Office: 15760 Ventura Blvd #700 Encino CA 91436

CHILTON, HORACE THOMAS, pipeline company executive; b. San Antonio, June 18, 1923; s. Horace Thomas and Lear Isabel (Word) C.; m. Betty Jane Gray, Oct. 18, 1947; children: Thomas G., William D. B.S. in Mech. Engring., U. Tex., 1947, B.A. in Bus. Adminstrn., 1947; grad., Advanced Mgmt. Program, Harvard U., 1958. Engr. Stanolind Pipe Line Co., Tulsa, 1947; div. chief engr. Service Pipe Line Co., Lubbock, 1950-52; supt. maintenance and constrn. Service Pipe Line Co., 1956-60, asst. gen. mgr., 1960; mil. pipe line cons. U.S. Govt., Paris, 1955; mgr. products pipelines, lake tankers and barges Amoco Oil Co., Chgo., 1963-68; mgr. transp. ops., v.p. Amoco Pipeline, 1969-71, gen. mgr. transp., pres., chief exec. officer, 1971-74; pres., chief exec. officer Colonial Pipeline, Atlanta, 1974—. Mem. U. Tex. Engring. Advisory Found. Bd., 1977—. Served with USN, 1944-46. Mem. Assn. Oil Pipe Lines (mem. exec. com. 1973—, chmn. 1983-84), Am. Petroleum Inst. (mem. gen. com. div. transp. 1971—, dir. 1975—), Nat. Petroleum Council, Beta Theta Pi. Presbyterian. Club: Cherokee Town and Country (Atlanta). Home: 8920 River Landing Way Atlanta GA 30338 Office: Colonial Pipeline Co 3390 Peachtree Rd NE PO Box 18855 Atlanta GA 30326

CHILVERS, DEREK, insurance company executive; b. Torquay, Eng., Feb. 7, 1940; came to U.S., 1962; s. Reginald Charles and Selina Adelaide (Adamson) C.; m. Elizabeth Anne Locke, Aug. 25, 1968 (div. 1983); m. Cheryl Baker, Apr. 14, 1984; 1 child, Justine. BA, Cambridge U., 1962, MA, 1962. With John Hancock Mut. Life Ins. Co., Boston, 1962—, v.p. internat., 1980-85, sr. v.p. internat., 1985—; bd. dirs. John Hancock Properties Inc., Boston; pres. John Hancock Internat. Holdings Inc., Boston; chmn. bd. John Hancock Internat. Services, S.A., Brussels, 1984—, John Hancock Internat. Services Hong Kong Ltd., 1986—; vice chmn. bd. P.T. Asuransi Pensiun Bumiputera John Hancock, Jakarta, Indonesia 1987—. Office: John Hancock Mut Life Ins Co PO Box 111 Boston MA 02117

CHIMPLES, GEORGE, lawyer; b. Canton, Ohio, Oct. 8, 1924; s. Mark and Katherine (Hines) C.; m. Margaret Joanna Cavalaris, July 31, 1949; children: Alicia Candace, Mark II, John Hines, Katherine Hines. AB, Princeton U., 1951; LLB, Harvard U., 1954. Permanent assoc. Phila. Mus. Art; life mem. Library Co. Phila. Served to capt. USSAF, 1942-46, ETO. Decorated D.F.C., Air medal with four oak leaf clusters, Air Force Commendation medal, Victory medal, four Battle Stars. Mem. Commanderie de Bordeaux. Clubs: Cannon (Princeton); Princeton (N.Y.); Army and Navy (Washington); Penn, Athenaeum Phila., Phila.; Merion Cricket, The British Officers (Phila.). Home: 1179 Lafayette Rd Wayne PA 19087 Office: Stradley Ronon Stevens & Young 2600 One Commerce Sq Philadelphia PA 19103

CHIN, JAMES YING, corporate executive; b. N.Y.C., Nov. 22, 1953; s. Bing Fon and Mung King (Chew) C.; m. Randy-Jo Gensler, June 28, 1981. AAS, Queensborough Community Coll., Queens, N.Y., 1973. Customer engr. IBM, Bklyn., 1973-83; systems ctr. rep. IBM, Gaithersburg, Md., 1983-86; field mgr. IBM, Reston, Va., 1986—. Democrat. Office: IBM 1850 Centennial Park Dr Reston VA 22091

CHIN, MARIA THERESA, advertising company executive; b. Barranquilla, Colombia, Apr. 10, 1959; came to U.S., 1971; d. Gen. and Siu Yong (Mony) C.; children: Li Ju, Li Ming. Student, North Harris County Coll., 1980-82. Exec. sec. Zeolla's Bros., Boston, 1978-79; receptionist Cooley & Shillinglaw, Inc., Houston, 1980-81, media buyer, 1981-82, prodn. mgr., 1982—. Office: Cooley & Shillinglaw Inc 5613 Star Ln Houston TX 77057

CH'IN, MICHAEL KUO-HSING, agricultural products company executive; b. Singapore, Sept. 19, 1921; s. Chin-cho and Wen-chih (Chang) C.; m. Edith Tzu-lin Fang; children: Lucy Wei-Tzu, May An-Tzu, Peggy Hsien-Tzu, Judy Pei-Tzu. BS, Yen Ching U., Cheng-tu, People's Republic of China, 1945. Asst. proctor's office Yenching U., Cheng-tu, People's Republic of China, 1945-46; asst. bur. of relief Chinese Nat. Rural Rehab., Nanking, People's Republic of China, 1946-48; statistician-in-charge, personnel-in-charge Nanking Phys. Rehab. Ctr., People's Republic of China, 1948-50; technician soil analysis Pub. Health Research Inst., Taipei, Taiwan, Republic of China, 1950-51; asst., jr. adminstrv. asst., adminstrv. asst. Sino-Am. Joint Commn. on Rural Reconstrn., Taipei, Taiwan, Republic of China, 1960-71; exec. officer Asian Vegetable Research and Devel. Ctr., Shanhua, Taiwan, Republic of China, 1971-83, dir. adminstrn., 1983—. Baptist. Home: #60 Yi-Min-Lao Shanhua, Tainan Hsien 74103, Republic of China Office: AVRDC, PO Box 42 Shanhua, Tainan Hsien 74199, Republic of China

CHINDAMO, MICHAEL LEONARD, financial planner; b. Queens, N.Y., Mar. 6, 1949; s. Michael Joseph and Lena (Seletti) C.; m. Claudia Lynn, Sept. 3, 1983; 1 child, Joey Michael. Cert. fin. planner. Registered rep. Paine Webber, Garden City, N.Y., 1978-80; registered rep., bond coordinator Merrill Lynch, Jericho, N.Y., 1980-81; fin. planner, cons. E.F. Hutton, Huntington, N.Y., 1981-86; pres. Sparta (N.Y.) Group, 1986—. Mem. Internat. Assn. Fin. Planners, Internat. Bd. Cert. Fin. Planners, Inst. Cert. Fin. Planners., Branchville Businessman's Club, Rotary (dir. vocat. svcs. 1986). Office: Sparta Group 17 Woodport Rd Sparta NJ 07871

CHING, LARRY FONG CHOW, construction company executive; b. Honolulu, Mar. 15, 1912; s. Dung Sen and Dai (Chong) C.; m. Beatrice Jook Yee Fong, Aug. 6, 1944; children: Randall Ming-Yu, Thalia Ping-Hsi-a. BCE, U. Hawaii, 1935; postgrad. in mining engring., U. Utah, 1938-39. Registered profl. engr., Hawaii. Instr. math. and engring. U. Yunan, Kunming, Peoples Republic of China, 1935-37; engr. Moses Akiona, Contractor, 1939-42, 45; supr. roads and airport constrn. U.S. Corps Engrs., 1942-44; mgr. Universal Contracting Co., 1945-47; supt. constrn. Associated Builders, 1948-49; pres., gen. mgr. Hwy. Constrn. Co., Ltd., Honolulu, 1949—; bd. dirs. Hawaii Franchise No-Joint Concrete Pipe, Hawaii Contractor's License Bd., 1960-63; pres., bd. dirs. Constrn. Industry Legis. Orgn., 1977-78; sub-chmn. design constrn. and maintenance Hawaii Hwy. Safety Council. Pres. Larry and Beatrice Ching Found; pres., dir. Hawaii Chinese History Ctr., 1971; pres. Hawaii Heritage Ctr., 1982-83; mem. Gov. Hawaii commn. commemorating Chinese Bicentnnial. Mem. Assn. Gen. Contractors Am. (bd. dirs., treas. 1983), Gen. Contractors Assn. Hawaii (pres. 1968, bd. dirs.), Hawaii C. of C. (bd. dirs.), Chinese C. of C. (bd. dirs., pres. 1971-72), Honolulu Better Bus. Bur., Friends of East-West Ctr., United Chinese Soc. (pres. 1980—), Tu Chiang Sheh (pres.). Home: 18 Kimo Dr Honolulu HI 96817 Office: Hwy Constrn Co 720 Umi St Honolulu HI 96819

CHING, LAWRENCE LIN TAI, retail executive; b. Hanalei, Hawaii, July 23, 1920; s. Young and Ah Har (Dang) C.; student St. Louis Coll., 1936-40; m. Jennie Kim Pang, Dec. 27, 1947; children—Steven L., Michael G. Clk., USAAF, Honolulu, 1942-44; dir. Kauai Realty, CKKS Corp.; pres., dir. Can Corp.; 1946—; owner, pres., mgr. Ching Young Store; bd. dirs. Na Pali Properties. Mem. Kauai Charter Commn., 1964-65. Served with AUS, 1944-46. Democrat. Buddhist. Address: PO Box 426 Hanalei HI 96714

CHING, PATRICK DOUGLAS, finance company executive; b. Honolulu, Jan. 18, 1957; s. Edward Tim and Lillian Y. Ching; m. Marybeth W.H. Wong, June 28, 1980; 1 child, Stephanie Erin. BBA, U. Wash., 1979; MBA, U. Hawaii, 1986. CPA, Hawaii, Wash. Tax mgr. Deloitte Haskins & Sells, Seattle and Honolulu, 1979-85; sr. v.p., treas. Servco Pacific, Inc., Honolulu, 1985—. Mem. AICPA, Tax Execs. Inst. (chmn. membership com. Honolulu chpt. 1987), Punahou Alumni Assn. (bd. dirs. 1986—), Pacific Club. Roman Catholic. Office: Servco Pacific Inc PO Box 2788 Honolulu HI 96803

CHISENA, ERNEST, III, financial consultant; b. Darby, Pa., Mar. 13, 1956; s. Ernest and Nancy Doris (Jacobson) C.; m. Carollynn Pepe, July 28, 1984; 1 child, Thomas Ernest. BS in Econs., U. Pa., 1978; MBA, Drexel U., 1981. Cert. fin. cons. Sr. credit analyst Bethlehem (Pa.) Steel Corp., 1981-83; fin. cons. CIGNA-IFS, King of Prussia, Pa., 1983-88; ptnr. Chisena & VanderWaal, Malvern, Pa., 1988—; mem. adv. bd. Pa. State Tech. Devel. Ctr., King of Prussia, 1987—. Mem. Internat. Assn. Fin. Planners, Phila. Assn. Life Underwriters, Nat. Assn. Life Underwriters, Wharton Club, Beta Gamma Sigma. Republican. Home: 965 W Miner St West Chester PA 19382 Office: Chisena & Vanderwaal 10 Valley Stream Pkwy Ste 290 Malvern PA 19355

CHISHOLM, TOMMY, utility company executive; b. Baldwyn, Miss., Apr. 14, 1941; s. Thomas Vaniver and Rube (Duncan) C.; m. Janice McClanahan, June 20, 1964; children: Mark Alan (dec.), Andrea, Stephen Thomas, Patrick Ervin. B.S.C.E., Tenn. Tech. U., 1963; J.D., Samford U., 1969; M.B.A., Ga. State U., 1984. Bar: Ala. 1969; Registered profl. engr., Ala., Fla., Ga., Miss., Del., N.C., S.C., Tenn., La., W. Va., Va., Ky., P.R., N.H., Pa., Tex., Ark. Civil engr. TVA, Knoxville, Tenn., 1963-64; design engr. So. Co. Services, Birmingham, Ala., 1964-69; coordinator spl. projects So. Co. Services, Atlanta, 1969-73; sec., house counsel So. Co. Services, 1977-82, v.p., sec., house counsel, 1982—; asst. to pres. So. Co., Atlanta, 1973-74; sec., asst. treas. So. Co., 1977—; mgr. adminstrv. services Gulf Power Co., Pensacola, Fla., 1975-77; sec. So. Electric Internat., Atlanta, 1981-82, v.p., sec., 1982—; sec. The So. Investment Group, 1985—. Mem. Am. Bar Assn., State Bar Ala., ASCE, Am. Soc. Corp. Secs., Am. Corporate Counsel Assn., Phi Alpha Delta, Beta Gamma Sigma. Home: 1611 Bryn Mawr Circle Marietta GA 30068 Office: The Southern Co 64 Perimeter Ctr E Atlanta GA 30346

CHISHOLM, WILLIAM DEWAYNE, contract manager; b. Everett, Wash., Mar. 1, 1924; s. James Adam and Evelyn May (Iles) C.; B.S. in Ch.E., U. Wash., 1949, B.S. in Indsl. Engring., 1949; M.B.A., Harvard U., 1955; m. Esther Troehler, Mar. 10, 1956; children—James Scott, Larry Alan, Brian Duane. Chemist, unit leader, tech. rep. The Coca-Cola Co., Atlanta and Los Angeles, 1949-59; contract adminstr. Honeywell Inc., Los Angeles, 1959-61, mktg. adminstr., 1961-64, contracts work dir., 1964-66, contracts mgr., Clearwater, Fla., 1966-73, contracts supr., 1973-75, sr. contract mgmt. rep., 1975-80, prin. contract mgmt. rep., work dir., 1980-82, contracts mgr., 1982—; chmn. bd. Creative Attitudes, Inc., 1987—; adj. faculty Fla. Inst. Tech. Contbr. articles to profl. jours. Trustee, John Calvin Found.; mem. budget adv. com. City of Clearwater, 1983-85; commr. to 196th gen. assembly Presbyterian Ch. (U.S.A.), 1984. Served with USN, 1944-46. Cert. profl. contracts mgr. Recipient Award of Distinction Fla. Inst. Tech. Grad. Ctr., 1987. Fellow Nat. Contract Mgmt. Assn. (chmn. S.E. region fellows 1985-87, past nat. dir., pres., v.p. Suncoast chpt.). Republican. Presbyterian (elder session mem. 1964-65, 73-76, 77-80, 81-84, 86—). Club: Breakfast Optimist of Clearwater (dir. 1982—, disting. sec.-treas. 1983-84, disting. pres. 1984-85). Home: 1364 Hercules Ave S Clearwater FL 34624 Office: Honeywell Inc 13350 US Hwy 19 S Clearwater FL 34624

CHISM, JAMES ARTHUR, data processor; b. Oak Park, Ill., Mar. 6, 1933; s. William Thompson and Arema Eloise (Chadwick) C.; AB, DePauw U., 1957; MBA, Ind. U., 1959; postgrad. exec. program U. Pa., 1984; postgrad. sr. exec. devel. program U. Notre Dame, 1988. Mgmt. engr. consumer and indsl. products div. Uniroyal, Inc., Mishawaka, Ind., 1959-61, sr. mgmt. engr., 1961-63; systems analyst Miles, Inc., Elkhart, Ind., 1963-64, sr. systems analyst, 1965-69, project supr., distbn. systems, 1969-71, mgr. systems and programming for corp. fin. and adminstrv. depts., 1971-73, mgr. adminstrv. systems and corp. staff svcs., 1973-75, group mgr. consumer products group systems and programming, 1975-79; dir. adminstrn. and staff svcs. Cutter/Miles, 1979-81, dir. advanced office systems and corp. adminstrn. 1982-84; dir. advanced office systems Internat. MIS and Adminstrn., 1984-85, dir. advanced office systems, tng. and adminstrn., 1985-87; exec. dir. Advanced Office Systems, Fin. and Adminstrn., 1987—. Bd. dirs. United Way Elkhart County, 1974-75. With AUS, 1954-56; amb. Associated Colls. of Ind. Fundraising, 1988—. Mem. Assn. Systems Mgmt. (chpt. pres. 1969-70, div. dir. 1972-77, Merit award 1975, Achievement award 1977, cert. systems profl. 1984, Disting. Svc. award 1986, 25 Yrs. Leadership award 1988), Dean's Assocs. of Ind. U. Sch. Bus.-Bloomington (mem. adv. coun.), Assn. Internal Mgmt. Cons., Fin. Execs. Inst., Office Automation Soc. Internat., Nat. Assn. Bus. Economists, DePauw U. Alumni Assn., Ind. U. Alumni Assn., Delta Kappa Epsilon, Sigma Delta Chi, Sigma Iota Epsilon, Beta Gamma Sigma. Republican. Episcopalian. Clubs: Morris Park Country (South Bend, Ind.); Delta Kappa Epsilon Club (N.Y.C.), Yale of N.Y.C., Vero Beach Country (Fla.); Coast (Melbourne, Fla.); Ind. Soc. of Chgo. Home: 504 Cedar Crest Ln Mishawaka IN 46545 Office: Miles Labs Inc 1127 Myrtle St PO Box 40 Elkhart IN 46515

CHISOLM, O(LIVER) BEIRNE, JR., investment advisor; b. Balt., Sept. 9, 1928; s. O. Beirne and Loti M. (Ficken) C.; m. Liliane Freya Gsell, Dec. 3, 1955; children—Freya, Melinda, Beirne, Gregg. B.A., Williams Coll., 1950. With Pan Am. World Airways, Cocoa, Fla., 1954-57; investment mgr. Kidder, Peabody, Inc., N.Y.C., 1957-61; v.p. Clark, Dodge, Inc., N.Y.C., 1962-73; pres. Clark Dodge Mgmt., N.Y.C., 1974-76; exec. v.p. Webster Mgmt., N.Y.C., 1976—; pres., dir. Webster Cash Res. Fund, N.Y.C., 1981—, Kidder, Peabody Premium Fund, N.Y.C., 1983—, Kidder, Peabody Govt. Money Fund, N.Y.C., 1983—; bd. dirs., trustee Kidder Peabody Govt. Income Fund., Kidder, Peabody Tax Exempt Money Fund., Kidder, Peabody Tax Exempt Income Fund., Kidder, Peabody Equity Income Fund, Kidder, Peabody Market Guard Appreciation Fund. Served as 1st lt. USAF, 1951-54. Republican. Episcopalian. Clubs: Am. Yacht (Rye, N.Y.); Broad St. (N.Y.C.). Home: 43 Halsted Pl Rye NY 10580 Office: Webster Mgmt 20 Exchange Pl New York NY 10005

CHITWOOD, HAROLD OTIS, food company executive; b. Gadsden, Ala., Aug. 5, 1930; s. Herman Otis and Demile (Hall) C.; m. Fern Nash, June 12, 1954; children: H. Wayde, G. Wesley, J. Weldon. BBA, U. Ala., 1955; postgrad. in advanced mgmt., Emory U., 1987; postgrad. in mgmt., Ga. State U., U. Mo. With Gold Kist Poultry Processing, Boaz, Ala., 1957-66; plant ops. mgr. Gold Kist Inc., Atlanta, 1966-71; div. mgr. Gold Kist NE Ala. div., Boaz, 1971-72; asst. mgr. Gold Kist Poultry, Atlanta, 1972-74; asst. group v.p. Gold Kist Inc.-Poultry Group, Atlanta, 1974-81, group v.p., 1981-84, exec. v.p., 1984—, mem. corp. planning com.; vice chmn., chief exec. officer Golden Poultry Co., Atlanta, 1982—; v.p., bd. dirs. Agri Internat. Inc., Atlanta, Luker Engring. Co., Atlanta; chmn. market news adv. com. Ga. Dept. Agriculture; bd. dirs. AgraTech Seeds, Atlanta, AgraTrade Fin., Atlanta. Mem. exec. bd. dirs., 2d v.p. Highland Exchange Service Co-op., Waverly, Fla., 1987—; deacon Mt. Vernon Bapt. Ch., Atlanta. Served to 1st lt. USAF, 1951-55, Korea. Mem. Nat. Broiler Council (chmn. bd. dirs. 1987—), Ga. Poultry Fedn. (pres. 1987—), Ga. Processor Assn. (past pres.), Ala. Processor Assn. (past pres.). Club: Cherokee Country (Atlanta). Lodge: Rotary. Office: Gold Kist Inc 244 Perimeter Center Pkwy PO Box 2210 Atlanta GA 30346

CHIZMADIA, STEPHEN MARK, lawyer; b. Perth Amboy, N.J., June 19, 1950; s. Stephen Thomas and Madeline Cecilia (Vojack) C.; m. Gail Farina, June 23, 1988; 1 child (stepson) Keith. BA in Econs., U. Pa., 1971; MS in Mgmt., N.J. Inst. Tech., 1975; JD with honors, N.Y. Law Sch., 1977. Bar: N.J. 1977, Fla. 1978, N.Y. 1980, U.S. Dist. Ct. (so. and ea. dists.) N.Y. 1981, U.S. Dist. Ct. N.J. 1977. Assoc., Hampson & Millet, P.C., Somerset, N.J., 1978, sole practice, New Brunswick, N.J., 1979-80; counsel Home Ins. Co., Short Hills, N.J., 1980-81; assoc. John M. Downing, P.C., N.Y.C., 1981-84, Schneider, Kleinick & Weitz, P.C., N.Y.C., 1984—; arbitrator Small Claims, N.Y.C. Civil Ct., 1986—, arbitrator U.S. Dist. Ct. (east dist.), N.Y., 1987—; lectr. legal topics profl. seminars; adj. instr. law and bus. mgmt. Middlesex County Coll., 1978-80. Dir. Raritan Bay (N.J.) Area YMCA, 1980-86, N.J. Inst. Tech. Alumni Council, 1987—. Recipient Am. Jurisprudence award, 1977, several community service awards. Mem. N.J. Bar Assn., N.Y. State Bar Assn., Fla. Bar Assn., Am. Judicature Soc., Internat. Platform Assn., Toastmasters Internat., N.J. Inst. Tech. Alumni Council. Home: 125 Sun Dance Rd Stamford CT 06905 Office: Schneider Kleinick & Weitz 11 Park Pl New York NY 10007

CHLEBOWSKI, JOHN FRANCIS, JR., financial executive; b. Wilmington, Del., Aug. 19, 1945; s. John Francis and Helen Ann (Cholewa) C.; m. Roxanne J. Decyk; children: J. Christopher, Lauren R. B.S., U. Del., Newark, 1967; M.B.A., Pa. State U., State College, 1971. Vice pres. planning Polumbus Co., Denver, 1977-78; asst. treas. W.R. Grace & Co., N.Y.C., 1978-83; v.p. fin. planning GATX Corp., Chgo., 1983-85, v.p. fin., chief fin. officer, 1985—. Bd. dirs. Chgo. Heart Assn., 1985—; bd. dirs. Travelers & Immigrants Aid Assn., 1987—. Served with USN, 1965-68. Leadership Greater Chgo. fellow, 1984-85. Mem. Beta Gamma Sigma. Roman Catholic. Clubs: Economic, River, McGraw Wildlife. Home: 55 W Goethe Townhouse #1254 Chicago IL 60610 Office: GATX Corp 120 S Riverside Pla Chicago IL 60606

CHMIEL, JOSEPH ANTHONY, JR., retirement and financial planner; b. Pitts., May 10, 1959; s. Joseph Anthony and Dorothy Eleanor (Vroble) C. BA, U. Pitts., 1981. Cert. secondary tchr., Pa. Instr. Pitts. Pub. Schs., 1981-85; retirement planner Aetna Life Ins. and Annuity Co., Pitts., 1987—; pub. speaker Aetna Life and Annuity Co., Pitts., 1988—. Producer TV program Smile! You're on Pittsburgh, 1983. One of Founding Fathers Tex. Children's Mus., Fredericksburg, 1985. Mem. Phi Delta Theta (treas. Iota Alumni Corp.). Democrat. Roman Catholic. Home: 741 Broughton St Shadyside PA 15213-1107 Office: Aetna Life Ins and Annuity Co 600 Two Chatham Ctr Pittsburgh PA 15219

CHMIELEWICZ, JOSEPH STANLEY, banker; b. Webster, Mass., Nov. 30, 1915; s. John Alexander and Stepania Mary (Skrzypek) C.; student pub. schs., Webster. With J.P. Ivascyn Ins. Co., 1936-42; sports editor Webster Times, 1940-55; mem. Webster Bd. Assessors, 1944-56, treas., 1957—; trustee Webster Five Cents Savs. Bank, 1968—, bd. investment, 1981—, v.p., 1984—; dir. Nichols Coll. Golf Course. Bd. dirs. ARC, Webster-Dudley Boys' Club, United Way, Hubbard Regional Hosp.; trustee Webster Contributory Retirement Bd., 1957—. Named Man Yr. Webster-Dudley-Oxford C. of C., 1986. Mem. Mass. Assessors Assn., New Eng. Fin. Officers Assn., Treas.'s Assn. U.S. and Can., Polish Am. Youth Fedn. (pres. 1960), Polish Nat. Alliance, Serra Internat. Democrat. Roman Catholic. Clubs: Polish Am. Citizens (Man of Yr. 1962), Elks (Man of Yr. Webster lodge 1982), Eagles, KC (4 deg.), Exchange. Home: 31 Morris St Webster MA 01570 Office: Webster Five Cents Savs Bank Town Hall Main St Webster MA 01570

CHMIELINSKI, EDWARD ALEXANDER, electronics company executive; b. Waterbury, Conn., Mar. 25, 1925; s. Stanley and Helen C.; m. Elizabeth Carew, May 30, 1946; children: Nancy, Elizabeth, Susan Jean. BS, Tulane U., 1950; postgrad. Colo. U., 1965. V.p., gen. mgr. Clifton Products, Litton Industries, Colorado Springs, Colo., 1965-67; pres. Memory Products div. Litton Industries, Beverly Hills, Calif., 1967-69, Bowmar Instruments, Can., Ottawa, Ont., 1969-73; gen. mgr. Leigh Instruments, Carleton Pl., Ont., 1973-75; pres., dir. Lewis Engring. Co., Naugatuck, Conn., 1975-85; pres., dir. Liquidometer Corp., Tampa, Fla., 1975-85; pres. Lewis div. Colt Industries, 1985—. Pres., Acad. Water Bd., 1963-65; bd. dirs. United Way, Colorado Springs, 1965-67; fellow Tulane U. Pres.'s Council. Served with USN, 1943-46. Mem. C. of C., Pres.'s Council, Nat. Mfrs. Assn., IEEE, Air Force Assn., Navy League, Nat. Aero. Assn., Am. Helicopter Soc., Nat. Bus. Aircraft Assn. Club: Sales Execs. of N.Y.

CHOATE, JOHN RICHARD, manufacturing company executive; b. Chgo., Aug. 20, 1946; s. John Milton and Mildred (Baxter) C.; m. Priscilla West, Sept. 8, 1972 (div. May 1975); m. Joann Hill, Feb. 11, 1989. BS in Rsch. Biology, Wash. State U., 1969; MS in Counseling Psychology, Troy State U., 1977; MBA in Exec. Program, Pepperdine U., 1986. Mgr. Program Info. Ctr. Corning Glass Works, Wilmington, N.C., 1979-81; sr. sales rep. Corning Glass Works, L.A., 1981; dir. materials Pacesetter Systems, Inc., Sylmar, Calif., 1981-83; program mgr. Diametrics, Van Nuys, Calif., 1983-84; mgr. material svcs. United Tech. Communications Co., Westlake Village, Calif., 1984-85; dir. support ops. Leach Corp., L.A., 1985—; also bd. dirs. Leach Corp.; chmn. supervisory com. Maxwell Credit Union, Montgomery, Ala., 1975-79. Capt. USAF, 1969-79. Mem. Am. Prodn./Inventory Control Soc., Nat. Assn. Purchasing Mgmt., Soc. Logistics Engrs., Am. Mgmt. Assn., Internat. Materials Mgmt. Soc. Home: 452 E Cypress St Apt C Burbank CA 91501

CHOATE, LESLEY JEANNE, accountant; b. Deer Island, Oreg., Mar. 10, 1935; d. Edward Leroy and Lesley Frances (Saunders) Howe; m. William Calvin Choate, Jan. 28, 1955; children: Julia Casandra Nettiecris, Jerome Vincent Alexander. Student, Pacific U., 1952-53; BSBA, U. Nev. Las Vegas, 1974; postgrad., Portland (Oreg.) State U., 1977-79. Jr. acct. Walter J. Frenz P.A., Portland, 1974-75, Holdner Backstrom & Co., Portland, 1975-76; acct. Portland Iron Works, 1976-78; staff acct. Tube Forgings Am., Portland, 1978-79; inventory cost supr. Bingham Internat., Inc., Portland, 1979-87; accounts payable supr., cost acct. Metra Steel Co., Portland, 1988—. Mem. Nat. Assn. Accts., Nat. Soc. Pub. Accts., Oreg. Assn. Pub. Accts. Republican. Lodge: Rebekahs. Office: Metra Steel Co 12219 N Burgard St Portland OR 97208

CHOATE, LEWIS DUANE, healthcare company executive; b. Baytown, Tex., Feb. 26, 1959; s. Walter Lewis and Lavora (Jackson) C.; m. Betsy Ann Sebesta, July 9, 1983. AA in Math. with hons., Lee Jr. Coll., Baytown, 1979; BBA in Acctg. cum laude, U. Houston, 1981. CPA, Tex. Supervising sr. auditor Peat, Marwick, Main, Houston, 1981-84; asst. contr. HMSS, Inc., Houston, 1984-88, contr., 1988—. Participant, Easter Seals and March of Dimes, Houston. Mem. Am. Inst. CPA's, Tex. Soc. CPA's, Houston chpt. of Tex. Soc. CPA's. Home: 4608 Country Club View Baytown TX 77521

CHOE, WON-GIL, electronics executive; b. Gang-Nung, Korea, Apr. 24, 1932; s. Chan-Jang and Sook-Ja (Shin) C.; came to U.S., 1957, naturalized, 1970; BS, Ariz. State U., 1960; MS, Stanford U., 1962, PhD, 1975; m. Mirang Wonne. children: Iliad, Christopher, Charlotte, Scott, Julia. Engr. Fairchild Semiconductor, 1962-64; project mgr. Memorex Corp., 1966; mgr. indsl. engring. Internat. Video Corp., 1967-68; v.p. ops. Dole Electro-Systems, Inc., Palo Alto, Calif., 1968-70; v.p. ops. Intellex Corp., Palo Alto, 1970-72; v.p. fin. Vacu-Blast Corp., Belmont, Calif., 1972-74, exec. v.p., 1977-79; pres. Tronic Corp., Belmont, 1973-79; v.p. Applied Implant Tech, Santa Clara, Calif., 1979-81; pres., chief exec. officer Video Logic Corp., Sunnyvale, Calif., 1982-87, v.p., chief fin. officer Mass Micro Systems, Inc., Sunnyvale, 1987-88; sr. v.p., chief exec. officer Televideo Systems Inc., San Jose, Calif., 1988—; bd. dir. EEI, Inc., TRI, Inc., Visidata, Inc., Adivan Tech, Inc., Chexel Internat., Inc., Gold Tech., Inc., PSI, Inc., Video Logic Corp. Mem. Am. Mgmt. Assn., Inst. Indsl. Engring. Assn. Republican. Presbyterian. Author: Quality of Profit in Non-Financial Companies, 1975. Home: 11 Cowell Ln Atherton CA 94025 Office: Televideo Systems Inc 550 E Brokaw Rd San Jose CA 95112

CHOHAN, SATISH MOHANSINGH, automotive industrial products manufacturing executive; b. Karachi, Pakistan, May 9, 1943; came to U.S., 1963; s. Madhav M. and Indumati (Verma) C.; m. Blanche V. Stack, Dec. 1964 (div.); children: Rajkumar, Rani; m. Shashi B. Singh, Apr. 5, 1983; 1 child, Rupa. BS with honors, Karachi U., 1962; MSME, Mich. Technol. U., Houghton, 1969; MBA, Northwestern U., 1976. Registered profl. engr., Ill. Estimating engr. Elcen Metal Products Co., Franklin Park, Ill., 1965-67; supr. advanced engring. Electro-Motive div. Gen. Motors Corp., McCook, Ill., 1969-80; mgr. engring. Gates Corp., Rockford, Ill., 1980—; pres. Technology Innovation, Inc., Rockford, 1987—. Patentee engine starting control circuit, auto quick-connect coupling; contbr. tech. papers to ASME Jour. Mem. ASME, Soc. Automotive Engrs., India Assn. Greater Rockford (pres. 1986). Hindu. Club: Rockford Racquet. Home: 2507 Saxon Pl Rockford IL 61111

CHOI, JOHNSON WING-KEUNG, financial executive; b. Hong Kong, July 15, 1955; s. Ping Fan and Pui Yee (Cheng) C.; m. Vinney S.M. Law, Dec. 20, 1978; children: Clara, Jonathan. BBA, U. Hawaii, 1977; MBA, Chaminade U., 1978. Asst. mgr. HMS Bounty Seafood Restaurant, Honolulu, 1975-78; gen. mgr. Aloha Waikiki Vacation Apartment, Honolulu, 1978-81; pres. J.W.K. Choi and Co. Inc. dba First Hawaiian Capital, Honolulu, 1981—; v.p. Four Season Inc., 1982—, Farco Inc., 1985—. Mem. Honolulu Bd. Realtors, Hawaii Assn. Life Underwriters, Nat. Assn. Security Dealers, Internat. Assn. Registered Fin. Planners, Soc. Chinese Profls., Asian Pacific Am. C. of C., Rotary, Hawaii Chinese Assn. Home: 1620 Keeaumoku St #705 Honolulu HI 96822 Office: First Hawaiian Capital 1001 Bishop St Pauahi Tower Ste 800 Honolulu HI 96818

CHOLAK, PAUL MICHAEL, financial services personnel executive; b. Cin., Nov. 28, 1941; s. Jacob and Etta (Simon) C.; m. Jane Meryl Steiner, Dec. 29, 1985; 1 child, Olivia; children from previous marriage: Karin, David. BA, U. Cin., 1963, MA, 1964. Various personnel positions Kaiser Aluminum and Chem. Corp., Oakland, Calif., 1966-76; v.p. employee relations R.H. Macy & Co., Inc., N.Y.C., 1976-81; sr. v.p. personnel and adminstrn. Columbia Pictures Industries, Inc., N.Y.C., 1981-85; sr. v.p. human resources Zale Corp., Dallas, 1985-86; exec. v.p. human resources Shearson Lehman Hutton, Inc., N.Y.C., 1986—. 1st lt. U.S. Army, 1964-66. Mem. Phi Beta Kappa, Omicron Delta Kappa. Home: 6 Woodsford's Bend Briarcliff Manor NY 10510 Office: Shearson Lehman Hutton Inc 2 World Trade Ctr 101st Fl New York NY 10048-0647

CHOLLET, JEAN-LOUIS, paper company executive; b. Quebec, Que., Can., June 29, 1930; s. Louis and Jeanne (Lacroix) C.; m. Renée Painchaud, Sept. 9, 1953; children: Denis, André, Caroline. BSCE, Laval U., 1953. Research chemist Anglo Paper Products Ltd., Quebec City, 1955-59, head pulping research, 1959-61; project coordinator overseas div. Reed Paper Group, Aylesford, Kent, Eng., 1961-64; tech. dir. Rolland Inc., St.-Jérôme, Que., 1964-67; v.p. research and tech. services Montreal, 1967-70; v.p. mfg. 1970-72, exec. v.p., 1972—. Athlone fellow Brit. Bd. Trade, 1953-55. Mem. Can. Pulp and Paper Assn. (chmn. tech. sect. 1985, F.G. Robinson award 1970), Tech. Assn. Pulp and Paper Industry, Order Profl. Engrs., Can. Mfrs. Assn. Home: 16 De La Marquise, Saint-Sauveur-des-Monts, PQ Canada J0R 1R0 Office: Rolland Inc, 2000 McGill College Ave, Montreal, PQ Canada H3A 3H3

CHOO, YEOW MING, lawyer; b. Johore Bahru, Malaysia, Aug. 1, 1953; s. Far Tong and Kim Fong (Wong) C.; LLB with honors (1st in class), U. Malaya, 1977; LLM, Harvard U., 1979; JD, Chgo.-Kent Coll., 1980. Admitted to Malaysia bar, 1977, Ill. bar, 1980; lectr. law U. Malaya Law Sch., Kuala Lumpur, Malaysia, 1977-78, Monash U. Law Sch., Melbourne, Australia, 1978; internat. atty. Standard Oil Co. (Ind.), Chgo., 1979-82; partner firm Anderson, Liu and Choo, Chgo., 1982-84; ptnr. Baer Marks and Upham, N.Y.C., 1984-85; ptnr. Winston and Strawn, Chgo., 1985-87; ptnr. Dorsey and Whitney, N.Y.C., 1987—; dir. Harvard Bros. Internat. Corp.; Boston; chmn. tax subcom. Nat. Council for US-China Trade, 1980-84. Mem. Am. Mining Congress (alt. mem. com. on law of sea 1980-82), ABA, Ill. Bar Assn., Chgo. Bar Assn., Malayan Bar Council, U.S. Chess Fedn., Harvard Law Sch. Alumni Assn. Club: Harvard. Office: Dorsey & Whitney 350 Park Ave New York NY 10022

CHOOKASZIAN, DENNIS HAIG, financial executive; b. Chgo., Sept. 19, 1943; s. Haig Harold and Annabelle (Kalkanian) C.; m. Karen Margaret Genteman, Mar. 18, 1967; children: Jeffrey, Michael, Kerry. BS in Chem. Engring., Northwestern U., 1965; MBA in Fin., U. Chgo., 1967; MS in Econs., London Sch. of Econs., 1968. CPA, Ill. Mgmt. cons. Touche Ross & Co., Chgo., 1968-75; chief fin. officer CNA Fin. Corp., Chgo., 1975—; chmn. Agy. Mgmt. Svcs., Boston. Pres. Wilmette Tennis Assn., Ill., 1986-88; bd. dirs. Chgo. Coun. Boy Scouts Am., scoutmaster, Wilmette, 1985-88; chmn. Found. for Health Enhancement, 1980—. Mem. Am. Inst. CPA's, Ill. Soc. CPA's, Beta Gamma Sigma, Westmoreland Country Club (Wilmette), East Bank Club (Chgo.). Republican. Home: 214 17th St Wilmette IL 60091 Office: CNA Fin Corp CNA Pla Chicago IL 60685

CHOQUETTE, PAUL JOSEPH, JR., construction company executive; b. Providence, July 24, 1938; s. Paul Joseph and Virginia Josephine (Gilbane) C.; m. Elizabeth Walsh, Aug. 18, 1962; children: Jeanne Marie, Denise Elizabeth, Suzanne, Christine Noell, Paul Joseph III. B.A., Brown U., 1960; LL.B., Harvard U., 1963. Assoc. firm Edwards & Angell, Providence, 1963-65; gov.'s legal counsel State of R.I., Providence, 1965-67; assoc. Edwards & Angell, 1967-69; gen. counsel Gilbane Bldg. Co., Providence, 1969-71, v.p., 1971-75, exec. v.p., 1975-81, pres., 1981—, dir.; bd. dirs. Fleet Bank, Fleet Fin. Group, Taco, Inc.; chmn. bd. Gilbane Properties Inc., Suga-loaf Mt. Group. Chmn. New Eng. Council, 1985. Nat. Football Found. scholar, 1959. Mem. Providence C. of C. (past pres., dir.). Roman Catholic. Clubs: Dunes, Hope, University. Home: 57 Forge Rd Warwick RI 02818 Office: Gilbane Bldg Co 7 Jackson Walkway Providence RI 02940

CHOQUETTE, WILLIAM H., construction company executive; b. Webster, Mass., Jan. 9, 1941; s. Paul J. and Virginia (Gilbane) C.; m. Lynn DeVaney, Aug. 12, 1967; children—William, Madeleine. B.A., U. Notre Dame, 1962; M.B.A., Columbia U., 1966. Field supt. Gilbane Bldg. Co., Providence, R.I., 1966-68, asst. adminstrv. mgr., 1968-71, mgr. sales engring., 1971-75, v.p. bus. devel., 1975-79; regional adminstrv. mgr. Gilbane Bldg. Co., Landover, Md., 1979-80, v.p., regional mgr., 1980-82, sr. v.p., regional mgr., 1982—. Co-chmn. United Way Prince George's County, Md., 1983, 84, Corp. heroes' chmn., 1985; mem. steering com. Greater Washington Bd. Trade, 1983, 84, co-chmn. planning and devel. com., 1986-87; bd. dirs. Wash. area chpt. Boy Scouts Am. Explorers div.; chmn. Nat. Capitol Area; mem. enterprise task force Greater Balt. Com., 1983. Served to 1st lt. Signal Corps, U.S. Army, 1962-64. Mem. Washington Bldg. Congress (bd. govs. 1982-88). Home: 7704 Glendale Rd Chevy Chase MD 20815 Office: Gilbane Bldg Co 8400 Corporate Dr Landover MD 20785

CHOR, JACK EDGAR, financial planner, consultant; b. Lebanon, Ill., Aug. 24, 1933; s. William Jennings and Mabel Irene (Papproth) C.; m. Anagene Browning, Jan. 9, 1955 (div. Feb. 1986); children: Jack E., Paula J., Marianne Chor Kasten, David. J., Jason R. Student, So. Ill. U., 1951-54, Washington U., St. Louis, 1954-56. With outside sales Sears, Roebuck & Co., St. Louis, 1954-57; with ins. sales Monarch LIfe Ins. Co., St. Louis, 1957-60; dist. mgr. Union Mut. Life, St. Louis, 1960-66; with pharm. sales Pitman Moore Co., St. Louis, 1960-64; pres. Capital Coordination Co., Belleville, Ill., 1966—; pres. Compensation Programs Inc., Belleville, 1973—; cons. Fin. One Inc., Belleville, 1981—. Author: Administrative Manual for Retirement Plan, 1974, chpt. Retirement Plan, 1974 (award 1985). Mem. Internat. Assn. Fin. Planners, Am. Soc. Pension Actuaries (assoc.), Registered Health Underwriters, Aircraft Owners & Pilots Assn., Mo. Athletic Club, Oak Hill Racquet Club (pres. 1980-86). Office: Capital Coordination Co 7 N 44th St Belleville IL 62223

CHORMANN, RICHARD F., banker; b. 1937. BS, Western Mich. U., 1959. With First Am. Bank Mich., Kalamazoo, 1959-80, sr. v.p., 1972-76, exec. v.p., 1976-80; pres. First Am. Bank Wayne Oakland, Detroit, 1980-84; exec. v.p. First Am. Bank Corp., Kalamazoo, 1984-85, pres., chief operating officer, 1985—. Office: 1st Am Bank Corp 108 E Michigan Ave Kalamazoo MI 49007

CHOU, MARK, importer; b. Peking, China, Apr. 1, 1910; came to U.S., 1949; M. European History, San Francisco U., 1950; postgrad. U. Calif., Berkeley; m. Florence Fong Ling Siu, Sept. 10, 1955; children—Raymond, Samuel, Theodore, Jadine. Pres., Mark Chou Gallery, Inc., Skokie, Ill., 1950—; appraiser Oriental arts and antiques; tchr. Chinese antiques, investment in Oriental antiques. Author: A Discourse on Hung Hsien Porcelain; Dictionary of Jade Nomenclature- an exculsive compilation of jade terms; contbr. articles on Chinese antiques to periodicals. Home and Office: 9024 Tripp Ave Skokie IL 60076

CHOU, RAYMOND H., architect; b. Chgo., Dec. 19, 1956; s. Mark and Florence (Siu) C.; m. Helen Nonnemacher, Aug. 31, 1979. BS, U. Ill., 1979; MArch, Harvard U., 1981. Registered architect, Mass. and Ill. Project architect Urban Investment & Devel. Corp., Cambridge, Mass., 1981-84; pres. R.H. Chou Co., Inc., Chgo., 1984—. Mem. AIA, Nat. Assn. Home Builders.

CHOW, GEORGE SHEUNG-KWAN, telecommunications plannner, engineer, consultant; b. Kun-Ming, China, May 21, 1948; came to U.S., 1966; s. Fu Cheng and Ming Che (Fan) C.; m. Martha L. Truax, June 13, 1971 (div. 1986); children: Sarah K., Simon L., Sonya J.; m. Priscilla Lau, June 23, 1986; 1 child, George Steven. BSEE, U. Wash., 1969, MSEE, 1971. Registered profl. engr., Wash. Switching engr. Western Union, Seattle, 1973-76; transmission engr. Pacific Northwest Bell, Seattle, 1976-79; mem. tech. staff Bell Labs, Whippany, N.J., 1979-82; dir. engring. Executone Inc., Jericho, N.Y., 1982-83; mem. sci. staff Bell Northern Rsch., Mountain View, Calif., 1983-86; founder, pres. Able Telecommunications Inc., Milpitas, Calif., 1986—. Mem. IEEE, Milpitas C. of C. Office: Able Telecommunications Inc 56 Corning Ave Milpitas CA 95035

CHOW, GREGORY CHI-CHONG, educator, economist; b. Macau, South China, Dec. 25, 1929; came to U.S., 1948, naturalized, 1963; s. Tin-Pong and Pauline (Law) C.; m. Paula K. Chen, Aug. 27, 1955; children: John S., James S., Jeanne S. BA, Cornell U., 1951; MA, U. Chgo., 1952, PhD, 1955; hon. doctorate, Zhongshan U., 1986. Asst. prof. MIT, 1955-59; assoc. prof. Cornell U., 1959-62, vis. prof., 1964-65; staff mem., mgr. econ. models IBM Research Center, Yorktown Heights, N.Y., 1962-70; prof. and dir. econ. research program 1970—; Class of 1913 prof. polit. economy Princeton, 1979—; adj. prof. Columbia U., 1965-70; vis. prof. Harvard U., 1967, Rutgers U., 1969; hon. prof. Fudan U. and Zhongshan U., 1985—. Author: Demand for Automobiles in the United States: A Study in Consumer Durables, 1957, Analysis and Control of Dynamic Economic Systems, 1975, Econometric Analysis by Control Methods, 1981, Econometrics, 1983; The Chinese Economy, 1985; co-editor: Evaluating the Reliability of Macro-Economic Models, 1982; Contbr. to: The Demand for Durable Goods, 1960; also articles to profl. jours. Fellow Econometric Soc., Am. Statis. Assn., Academia Sinica; mem. Am. Econ. Assn., Soc. for Econ. Dynamics and Control (pres. 1979-80). Home: 30 Hardy Dr Princeton NJ 08540 Office: Princeton U Econs Rsch Program Princeton NJ 08544

CHOW, STEPHEN Y(EE), lawyer; b. Cleve., Miss., Sept. 8, 1952; s. Chester H. and June (Eng) C.; m. Lynn Elin Anderson, May 4, 1981; children: Astrid Crockett, Augustus Stephen. AB cum laude, SM in Applied Physics, Harvard U., 1975; JD, Columbia U., 1979. Bar: N.Y. 1980, Mass. 1983, U.S. Supreme Ct. 1983, U.S. Patent Office 1984. Assoc. Donovan Leisure Newton & Irvine, N.Y.C., 1979-82, Gaston Snow & Ely Bartlett, Boston, 1982-85, Cesari and McKenna, Boston, 1985-88; ptnr. Nutter, McClennen & Fish, 1988—. V.p. Hawthorne Residents Assn., Boston, 1983—; trustee Hawthorne Place Condominium Trust, Boston, 1985—. Mem. ABA, IEEE, Boston Bar Assn., N.Y.C. Bar Assn. (com. on patent law 1987—, sec. com. on nuclear tech. and law 1982-85). Republican. Club: Harvard (N.Y.C.); Union Boat (Boston). Home: 9 Hawthorne Pl Boston MA 02114 Office: Nutter McClennen & Fish 1 International Plaza Boston MA 02110

CHOW, WINSTON, chemical engineer; b. San Francisco, Dec. 21, 1946; s. Raymond and Pearl C.; m. Lilly Fah, Aug. 15, 1971; children: Stephen, Kathryn. BSChemE, U. Calif., Berkeley, 1968; MSChemE, Calif. State U., San Jose, 1972; MBA with honors, Calif. State U., San Francisco, 1985. Registered profl. chem. and mech. engr.; instr.'s credential Calif. Community Coll. Chem. engr. Sondell Sci. Instruments, Inc., Mountain View, Calif., 1971; mem. research and devel. staff Raychem Corp., Menlo Park, Calif., 1971-72; supervising engr. Bechtel Power Corp., San Francisco, 1972-79; sr. project engr. water quality and toxic substances control program Electric Power Research Inst., Palo Alto, Calif., 1979—. Contbr. author Water Chlorination, vol. 4; contbr. articles to profl. publs. Pres., chief exec. officer Directions, Inc., San Francisco, 1985-86, bd. dirs. 1984-87, chmn. strategic planning com., 1984-85; mem. industry com. Am. Power Conf., 1988—; bd. dirs., treas. Calif. State 2 Alumni Assn., San Francisco, 1989—. Recipient Grad. Disting. Achievement award, 1985; Calif. Gov.'s Exec. fellow. Mem. Am. Inst. Chem. Engrs. (Profl. Devel. Recognition cert.), NSPE, Calif. Soc. Profl. Engrs. (pres. Golden Gate chpt. 1983-84, v.p. 1982-83, state dir.), Water Pollution Control Fedn., Calif. Water Pollution Control Assn., ASME, Calif. Alumni Assn., Beta Gamma Sigma. Democrat. Presbyterian. Office: Electric Power Rsch Inst 3412 Hillview Ave Palo Alto CA 94303

CHOYKE, PHYLLIS MAY FORD (MRS. ARTHUR DAVIS CHOYKE, JR.), ceiling systems company executive, editor, poet; b. Buffalo, Oct. 25, 1921; d. Thomas Cecil and Vera (Buchanan) Ford; m. Arthur Davis Choyke Jr., Aug. 18, 1945; children: Christopher Ford, Tyler Van. BS summa cum laude, Northwestern U., 1942. Reporter City News Bur., Chgo., 1942-43, Met. sect. Chgo. Tribune, 1943-44; feature writer OWI, N.Y.C., 1944-45; sec. corp. Artcrest Products Co., Inc., Chgo., 1958—, v.p., 1964—; pres. The Partford Corp., 1988—; founder, dir. Harper Sq. Press div., 1966—. Mem. Daughters Am. Revolution, 1988. Bonbright scholar, 1942. Mem. Soc. Midland Authors (treas. 1988, bd. dirs.), Mystery Writers Am. (assoc.), Chgo. Press Vets. Assn., Hist. Alliance of Chgo. Hist. Soc., Phi Beta Kappa. Clubs: Arts (Chgo.); John Evans (Northwestern U.). Author: (under name Phyllis Ford) (with others) (poetry) Apertures to Anywhere, 1979; editor: Gallery Series One, Poets, 1967, Gallery Series Two, Poets—Poems of the Inner World, 1968, Gallery Series Three—Poets: Levitations and Observations, 1970, Gallery Series Four, Poets—I am Talking About Revolution, 1973, Gallery Series Five/Poets—To An Aging Nation (with occult overtones), 1977; (manuscripts and papers in Brown U. Library). Home: 29 E Division St Chicago IL 60610 Office: Artcrest Products Co Inc 500 W Cermak Rd Chicago IL 60616

CHRIS, HARRY JOSEPH, architect, archtl. co. exec.; b. Beaumont, Tex., Sept. 13, 1938; s. Harry Adam and Lucille Helen (Junca) C.; BArch., Tulane U., 1961; MBA, Memphis State U., 1969. Registered architect, Colo., Fla., Ky., La., Mo., N.J., N.Y., Ohio, Tex. ; m. Jimmie Lea Bowen, Sept. 21, 1966; children—James, William, Mary Elizabeth, Mark, Lisa. Architect, Tex. State Bldg. Commn., Austin, 1966-68, Holiday Inn Am., Memphis, 1968-69; v.p. Club Corp. Am., Dallas, 1969-74, dir., 1972-74; pres. Architectural Designers, Inc., Dallas, 1969-74, RYA Architects, Inc., Dallas, 1974-78, H.J. Chris Architects Inc., Dallas, 1978—; pres., owner Park City Club, Inc., Dallas. Lt. comdr. USNR, 1961-66. Mem. Irving C. of C., AIA, Exec. Clubs of Am. Roman Catholic. Clubs: Lancers, Las Colinas Country (Dallas). Lodge: K.C. Home: 417 San Jose St Irving TX 75062 Office: 1520 W Airport Frwy Ste 200 Irving TX 75062

CHRISMAN, JAMES JOSEPH, management educator; b. Kansas City, Mo., Oct. 11, 1954; s. James John and Mildred Fay (Nelson) C. AA, Ill. Cen. Coll., 1977; BB, Western Ill. U., 1980; MBA, Bradley U., 1982; PhD, U. Ga., 1986. Machinst WABCO, Peoria, Ill., 1974-78; asst. prof. U. S.C., Columbia, 1986—. Assoc. editor: Case Research Jour., 1984-87, Strategic Planning Management, 1987-88; advt. and cirulation editor Am. Jour. of Small Business, 1986-88; promotion editor for Entretreneurship Theory and Practice, 1989—; author, numerous articles in field. Mem. North Am. Case Rsch. Assn. (v.p. publs., 1987, proceedings editor 1987, v.p. mem., 1988-89), Internat. Coun. for Small Bus. (competitive papers chair, 1988, v.p. programs 1989), U.S. Assn. for Small Bus. and Entrepreneurship (competitive papers chair, 1988, v.p. corp. entrepreneurship div. 1989), Acad. Mgmt. Republican. Roman Catholic. Office: U SC Coll Bus Adminstrn Columbia SC 29208

CHRIST, KATHY SCOTT, advertising executive; b. Hartford, Conn., July 6, 1951; d. Arthur Herman and Elizabeth M. (McCombe) C.; m. Paul J. Arnini, Jan. 17, 1969 (div. Apr. 1970); 1 child, June Elizabeth. Diploma, U. Conn., 1972. Asst. to v.p. adminstrn. Nat. Telephone Co., East Hartford, Conn., 1972-74; adminstrv. asst. Downtown Council, Hartford, 1974-76; exec. asst. to chmn. Imaginetics Internat., Unionville, Conn., 1977-78; mgr. sales and mktg. Info-Dial Corp., Bloomfield, Conn., 1979-80; mktg. dir. Southerby Prodns., Long Beach, Calif., 1982; account exec. to advt. sales mgr. King Videocable Co., Lake Elsinore, Calif., 1982—. Dir. pub. relations Hartford Easter Seals Rehab. Softball Marathon, 1980; mem. Students at Risk Adv. Com. Elsinore Union High Sch. Dist., 1987—; bd. dirs. Substance Abuse Council, SW Riverside County, 1987—; media coord. United Way telethon, 1989. Mem. Cable Advt. Bur., Bus. and Profl. Women, Lake Elsinore Valley C. of C., Temecula Valley C. of C., Greater Hartford Women's Softball Club (spokesman, mgr. 1978-80). Republican. Office: King Videocable Co PO Box 989 Lake Elsinore CA 92330

CHRIST, RONALD DUANE, manufacturing executive; b. Spencer, Iowa, Oct. 28, 1942; s. Clyde A. and Mildred E. (Karr) C.; m. Hedwig E. Christ, Mar. 11, 1987; children: David, Deborah, Richard, Erica, Heidi. BSBA, Drake U., 1965; MBA, Northwestern U., 1968. Div. contr. Baxter Travenol Labs., Deerfield, Ill., 1965-76; with fin. dept. Rockwell Internat., Houston, 1976-79; v.p. fin. and adminstrn. Ruska Instrument Corp., Houston, 1979—, also bd. dirs.; bd. dirs. Tele Electronic, Houston. Pres. Jaycees, Libertyville, Ill., 1974; active Jr. Achievement, Morton Grove, Ill., 1969. Sgt. USNG, 1965-71. Mem. Risk Ins. Mgrs. Soc., Nat. Assn. Accts., Fin. Planning Soc. Lutheran. Office: Ruska Instruments Corp 3601 Dunvale Houston TX 77063

CHRISTAKIS, ALEXANDER NICHOLAS, academic administrator, educator; b. Athens, Greece, Sept. 19, 1937; came to U.S., 1956; s. Nicholas Christos and Euridice (Kotsopoulos) C.; m. Lenna Sarantis, July 29, 1961 (div. 1978); children: Nicholas, Dimitri, John, Anna Katrina, Nora; m. Marjorie Pearl Ambirge, 1979. AB, Princeton U., 1959; MS, Yale U., 1961, PhD, 1965. Dir. rsch. Doxiadis Assocs., Washington, 1967-69; fellow Acad. for Contemporary Problems, 1971-75; rsch. leader Battelle Meml. Inst., 1975-79; prof. U. Va., Charlottesville, 1979-84; dir. George Mason U., Fairfax, Va., 1984—. Author: (with others) Technology Assessment, 1975, Creative Futures, 1980. Recipient Cert. of Appreciation USDA, 1984, Creative Teaching award NEA, 1984; Fulbright scholar U.S. Dept. State, 1956. Mem. Internat. Soc. for Gen. Systems Research (adv. council). Democrat. Home: 13558 Point Pleasant Dr Chantilly VA 22021 Office: George Mason U 4400 University Dr Fairfax VA 22030

CHRISTENSEN, BRUCE L., public broadcasting executive; b. Ogden, Utah, Apr. 26, 1943; s. LeRoy and Wilma (Olsen) C.; m. Barbara Lucelle Decker, June 17, 1965; children—Jennifer, Heather, Holly, Jesse. BA cum laude, U. Utah, 1968; MS, Northwestern U., 1969. Radio and TV news reporter KSL, Inc., Salt Lake City, 1965-68, state house corr., 1969-70; weekend sports writer WGN Radio and TV News, 1968-69; instr. U. Utah, 1969-70, adj. assoc. prof. broadcast regulation, 1980-81, gen. mgr. Sta. KUED-TV and KUER-FM, 1979-82, dir. media svcs., 1981-82; asst. to dir. univ. rels. Brigham Young U., 1970-72, asst. prof., 1971-79, dir. dept. broadcast svcs., 1972-79; pres. Nat. Assn. Pub. TV Stas., Washington, 1982-84, PBS, Washington, 1984—; bd. govs. Pacific Mountain Network, 1979-82, chmn., 1978-80; producer, writer Channel 5 Eye-Witness News, 1967-68. Producer numerous TV documentaries including the Great Dinosaur Discovery, 1973, A Time to Dance, 1976, Navajo, 1976, Christmas Snows, Christmas Winds, 1978 (Emmy award 1978). Bd. dirs. Utah Lung Assn., 1976-82, pres., 1978-80. Allen-Heath fellow Medill Sch. Journalism Northwestern U., 1969. Mem. Rocky Mountain Corp. for Pub. Broadcasting (bd. dirs.), Sigma Delta Chi (pres. U. Utah chpt. 1967-68), Kappa Tau Alpha. Office: PBS 1320 Braddock Pl Alexandria VA 22314

CHRISTENSEN, C. LEWIS, real estate developer; b. Laramie, Wyo., June 3, 1936; s. Raymond H. and Elizabeth C. (Cady) C.; m. Sandra Stadheim, June 11, 1960; children: Kim, Brett. BS in Indsl. Engring., U. Wyo., 1959. Mgmt. trainee Gen. Mills, Chgo., 1959, Mountain Bell, Helena, Mont., 1962-63; data communications mgr. Mountain Bell, Phoenix, 1964-66, dist. mktg. mgr., So. Colo., 1970-73; seminar leader AT&T Co., Chgo., 1966-68, mktg. supr., N.Y.C., 1968-70; land planner and developer Village Assocs., Colorado Springs, Colo., 1973, exec. v.p., 1975-77; v.p. Cimarron Corp., Colorado Springs, 1974-75; pres. Lew Christensen & Assocs., Inc.; ptnr., gen. mgr. Briargate Joint Venture, 1977—. Bd. dirs. Pikes Peak council Boy Scouts Am., Citizens Goals, Colo. Council on Econ. Edn., Cheyenne Mountain Zoo, 1987—; chmn. Colorado Springs Econ. Devel. Coun., 1989. Served with USAF, 1959-62. Mem. Colorado Springs Home Builders Assn. (bd. dirs.), Urban Land Inst., Colorado Springs C. of C. (bd. dirs. chmn. bd.). Republican. Presbyterian. Clubs: Broadmoor Golf, Colorado Springs Country (bd. dirs.). Developer of 10,000-acre New Town area, east of USAF Acad., Colorado. Home: 2948 Country Club Dr Colorado Springs CO 80909 Office: Lew Christensen & Assocs Inc 7710 N Union Blvd Colorado Springs CO 80920

CHRISTENSEN, DON M., general contractor, realtor; b. Hinckley, Utah, Jan. 3, 1929; s. Joseph M. and Lula (Payne) C.; m. Arda Jean Warnock, Oct. 8, 1953; children—Jean Larie, Jolene, Mary Kaye, Martin Don, Evan Warnock, Rachel, Glenn Leroy, Ruth Angela. Student agr. Utah State U., 1951-53, student bldg. Brigham Young U., 1955-56. Ptnr. Christensen Bros. Constrn. Co., Salt Lake City, 1956-59; pres. Constrn. Realty, Inc., Salt Lake City, 1959—, Don M. Christensen Constrn. Co., Salt Lake City, 1965—, Bountiful Constrn. Co., Salt Lake City, 1960-65, Advanced Reprodns., Inc., Salt Lake City, 1960-61, Land Investors, Inc., Salt Lake City, 1960-63. Co-author: Yours Can Be a Happy Marriage, 1983. Co-editor: Precious Testimonies, 1976. Bishop's counselor Ch. of Jesus Christ of Latter Day Saints, Salt Lake City, 1960-66, bishop, 1966-76, high councilman, 1976-85, counselor to stake pres., 1985—. Served with U.S. Army, 1954-55. Named Missionary of Yr., Mormon Finland Mission, 1951. Mem. Home Builders Assn. Republican. Home: 1630 Olive Dr Salt Lake City UT 84124 Office: Constrn Realty Inc 345 E 33d S Salt Lake City UT 84115

CHRISTENSEN, DONN WAYNE, insurance and management executive; b. Atlantic City, Apr. 9, 1941; s. Donald Frazier and Dorothy (Ewing) C.; BS, U. Santa Clara, 1964; m. Marshella Abraham, Jan. 26, 1963 (div.); children: Donn Wayne, Lisa Shawn; m. Mei Ling Fill, June 18, 1976 (div.); m. Susan Kim, Feb. 14, 1987; stepchildren: Don Kim, Stella Kim. West Coast div. mgr. Ford Motor Co., 1964-65; agt. Conn. Mut. Life Ins. Co., 1965-68; pres. Christensen & Jones, Inc., L.A., 1968—; v.p. Rsch. Devel. Systems Inc.; investment advisor SEC, 1985—. Pres. Duarte Community Drug Abuse Council, 1972-75; pres. Woodlyn Property Owners Assn., 1972-73; mem. L'ermitage Found., 1985-86, Instl. Rev. Bd. White Meml. Hosp., L.A., 1975—. Recipient Man of Yr. award L.A. Gen. Agts. and Mgrs. Assn., 1969, 72, 73, 75, 77. Mem. Nat. Life Underwriters Assn., Calif. State Life Underwriters Assn., Investment Co. Inst. (assoc.), Soc. Pension Actuaries, Foothill Community Concert Assn. (pres. 1970-73). Office: 709 E Colorado Blvd Ste 270 Pasadena CA 91101

CHRISTENSEN, ERIC DEAN, airline executive; b. Logan, Utah, Feb. 27, 1958; s. Rondo A. and Jeannine (Lunt) C.; m. Lichelle Langton, June 5, 1980; children: Shautel, Kristen, Marissa. BA in Acctg., Utah State U., 1981, MBA, 1982. CPA, Utah. Acct. Ernst and Whinney, Salt Lake City, 1982-85; dir. fin. Skywest Airlines, St. George, Utah, 1986-87; asst. to pres. Skywest Airlines, St. George, 1987—. Mem. AICPA, Utah Assn. CPAs. Mormon. Office: Skywest Airlines 50 E 100th St Ste 200 Saint George UT 84770

CHRISTENSEN, GUSTAV AMSTRUP, pharmaceutical executive; b. Haderup, Denmark, Aug. 23, 1947; came to U.S., 1974; s. Folmer and Vera (Madsen) C.; m. Vibeke Rathje, June 9, 1973; children: Sara, Daniel. MS, U. Aarhus, Denmark, 1973; MBA, Harvard U., 1976. Asst. to pres., dir. mktg. internat. div., gen. mgr. Travenol Lab Sweden, v.p. ops. Fenwall Labs. div. Baxter Travenol Labs., Deerfield, Ill., 1976-83; v.p. mktg. Genetics Inst., Cambridge, Mass., 1983-86, sr. v.p., 1986-88; pres., chief exec. officer ImmuLogic Pharm. Corp., Cambridge, 1988—; bd. dirs. Sensonix, Inc., Concord, Mass. Mem. regional bd. Dept. Mental Retardation, Boston, 1988. Office: ImmuLogic Corp One Kendall Sq Bldg 600 Cambridge MA 02139

CHRISTENSEN, HOWARD EVERETT, human resource executive; b. Wood, Wis., Jan. 3, 1937; s. Gilbert Oscar and Gertrude Bell (Wilson) C.; m. Beverly Elaine Nesbitt, May 27, 1966; 1 child, Megan; stepchildren: Mark, Lisa. BBA, U. Wis., 1963. Trainee employee relations Gen. Electric Co., Brockport, N.Y., 1965-67; trainee employee relations Gen. Electric Co., Louisville, 1967-68, union relations specialist, 1968-71; mgr. employee relations Gen. Electric Co., Columbia, Tenn., 1971-74, Shelbyville, Ind., 1974-78; mgr. plant and employee relations Gen. Electric Co., Syracuse, N.Y., 1978-81, mgr. human resources mil. electronic systems ops., 1981-83; dir. human resources Alliance Tool Corp., Rochester, N.Y., 1983-87; dir. partnership devel. Gleason Components Group, Rochester, 1987—. Pres. Girls Club, Shelbyville, 1975; bd. dirs. Shelbyville United Way, pres. 1976; bd. dirs. Jr. Achievement, Syracuse, 1983. 1st lt. U.S. Army, 1963-65. Mem. Delta Epsilon. Home: 80 Lynnwood Dr Brockport NY 14420 Office: Gleason Components Group 180 Willowbrook Office Park Fairport NY 14450

CHRISTENSEN, LYDELL LEE, telephone company executive; b. Walnut, Iowa, Nov. 16, 1934; s. Hans J. and Alma P. C.; m. Barbara M. Pearsall, June 1, 1974; children: Brent, Amy, Paul, Jeffrey. B.S., U. Nebr., Omaha, 1959; postgrad., Pace Coll. With Northwestern Bell Telephone Co., Omaha, 1959-80; asst. treas., then treas. Northwestern Bell Telephone Co., 1972-80; dir. fin. planning AT&T Co., N.Y.C., 1980-82, asst. treas., 1982-84, corp. v.p. plans, sec., 1984-87; v.p., treas. Pacific Telesis Group, San Francisco, 1987—; pres., bd. dirs. PacTel Capital Resources, San Francisco, 1987—, PacTel Capital Funding, San Francisco, 1989—; bd. dirs. PacTel Finance, PacTel RE Ins. Co. Inc. Bd. dirs., treas. Pacific Telesis Found., 1987—; bd. dirs. The Danish Immigrant Mus. Mem. Fin. Execs. Inst. (Com. on Investment of Employee Benefits Assets), Fin. Officers of No. Calif., Calif. Utilities Fin. Officers, N.Y. Stock Exchange Pension Mgrs. Adv. Com. Republican. Mem. United Ch. of Christ. Office: Pacific Telesis Group 130 Kearny St San Francisco CA 94108

CHRISTENSON, GREGG ANDREW, bank executive; b. Kalamazoo, Mich., June 11, 1958; s. Elmer J. and Marie E. (Durrstein) C.; m. Karen Peterson. BA, Mich. State U., 1980. CPA. Auditor Price Waterhouse, N.Y.C., 1980-82; with Bankers Trust Co., N.Y.C., 1982—, v.p., 1987—. Mem. Rep. Nat. Com. Mem. Internat. Platform Assn., Jr. Achievement Alumni Assn. (charter), Mich. State Alumni Assn., Phi Kappa Phi, Beta Gamma Sigma. Republican. Methodist. Office: Bankers Trust 1 Bankers Trust Pla New York NY 10015

CHRISTENSON, WENDY KAY, medical practice administrator; b. Ballston Spa, N.Y., Aug. 7, 1959; d. James August and Marilyn Yeuvonne (Pysher) C. BS in Health Planning and Adminstrn., Pa. State U., 1981; MBA, U. Pitts., 1983. Dir. mktg. and planning Cen. Med. Ctr. and Hosp., Pitts., 1983-85; adminstr. Eyesight Assocs. Middle Ga., Warner Robins, 1985—. Mem. Am. Soc. Ophthalmic Adminstrs., Leadership Warner Robins. Methodist. Home: 1620 Rembert Ave Macon GA 31201 Office: Eyesight Assocs Middle Ga 216 Corder Rd Warner Robins GA 31088

CHRISTIAN, CAROL PENDERGAST, interior designer; b. Thomasville, Ga., Oct. 3, 1948; d. Alvis Watson and Loette Hattie (Asbell) Pendergast; m. Joseph Lamar Fowler, Apr. 8, 1967 (div. 1972); 1 child, Rhonda Leigh; m. William Douglas Christian, Sept. 20, 1980. Student, Clayton Jr. Coll., 1968-70, Thomas Coll., 1966-67. Sec., mgr. Ramsey Devel., Atlanta, 1968-71; mgr. office IAMAW, Atlanta, 1971-75; owner Tara Answering Service, Atlanta, 1975-79; ptnr., mgr. Anserfone Services, Atlanta, 1979-81; mgr. sales Driggers & Assocs., Tampa, Fla., 1981-85; owner, pres. Carol Christian & Assocs., Inc., Tampa, 1985—. Contbr. articles to profl. jours. Active The Missing Children Help Ctrs., Tampa, 1985—, Adam Walsh Found., Ft. Lauderdale, Rational Living Therapy, Tampa. Mem. Greater Tampa Bay Homebuilders (assoc.), Carrollwood Area Bus. Assn. (assoc.), Westshore Devel. Assn. (assoc.). Democrat. Methodist. Office: 2805 W Busch Blvd Tampa FL 33618

CHRISTIAN, JAMES WAYNE, economist; b. Ft. Worth, Oct. 7, 1934; s. Nap B. and Daphne (Wright) C.; B.A., U. Tex., Austin, 1962, M.A. (univ. fellow), 1964, Ph.D. (NSF fellow), 1965; m. Jo June Maples, June 5, 1952; children—Amy Joella, Nicole Denise. Prof. econs. Iowa State U., 1965-74; dir. internat. div. Fed. Home Loan Bank Bd., Washington, 1972-74; sr. v.p., chief economist Nat. Savs. and Loan League, Washington, 1974-80; sr. v.p., chief economist U.S. League Savs. Instns., Chgo., 1980—; dir. Nat. Housing Conf., 1980—; cons. 15 developing country govts., 1970-80. Contbr. articles to fin. and econ. jours. Served with USN, 1952-55, USAF, 1955-59. Recipient Am. Legion award, 1949; Social Sci. Research Council grantee, 1968-69. Mem. Am. Econ. Assn., Am. Fin. Assn., So. Econ. Assn., Phi Beta Kappa, Omicron Delta Epsilon, Pi Sigma Alpha, Phi Kappa Phi. Club: Cosmos. Office: U S League Savs Insts 1709 New York Ave NW Washington DC 20006

CHRISTIAN, SUZANNE HALL, financial planner; b. Hollywood, Calif., Apr. 28, 1935; d. Peirson M. and Gertrude (Engel) Hall; children: Colleen, Carolyn, Claudia, Cynthia. BA, UCLA, 1956; Master's, Redlands U., 1979; cert. in fin. planning, U. So. Calif., 1986. Cert. fin. planner. Instr. L.A. City Schs., 1958-59; instr. Claremont (Calif.) Unified Schs., 1972-84, dept. chair, 1981-84; fin. planner Waddell & Reed, Upland, Calif., 1982—, sr. account exec., 1986; corp. mem. Pilgrim Place Found., Claremont; lectr. on fin., estate and tax planning for civic and profl. groups. Author: Steps in Composition, 1979. Recipient Silver Crest award Torchmark, 1985-87. Mem. Inst. Cert. Fin. Planners, Internat. Assn. Fin. Planners, Planned Giving Roundtable, Internat. Soc. Pre-Retirement Planners, Curtain Raisers Club of Gairison (pres. 1972-75), Kappa Kappa Gamma (pres. 1970-74). Home: PO Box 1237 Claremont CA 91711 Office: Waddell & Reed 545 N Mountain Ste 109 Upland CA 91786

CHRISTIANSEN, CHRISTIAN CARL, JR., banker; b. York, Pa., May 17, 1933; s. Christian Carl and Anna Marie C.; m. Nancy Louise Sheffer, Sept. 29, 1956; children: David, Melinda. B.S. in Bus. Adminstrn, Pa. State U., 1955. C.P.A., Pa. Auditor Ernst & Whinney, Pitts., 1955-56, 58-59; controller Sealtest Foods div. Kraft Foods, Washington, Phila. and N.Y.C., 1959-70, Bergen Record, Hackensack, N.J., 1970-72; v.p. Bankers Trust Co., N.Y.C., 1972-80, sr. v.p., 1980-82, gen. auditor, 1982—; mem. audit commn. Bank Adminstrn. Inst. Mem. Ramsey (N.J.) Bd. Edn., 1976-79. Served with U.S. Army, 1956-58. Mem. Fin. Execs. Inst. (dir., v.p., pres. N.Y.C. chpt.), Am. Inst. CPAs, N.Y. Soc. CPAs, Inst. Internal Auditors (bd. govs. N.Y.C. 1988—), Ramsey Golf and Country Club (pres. 1973-74), Brookside Racquet Club. Office: Bankers Trust Co 280 Park Ave New York NY 10017

CHRISTIANSON, STANLEY DAVID, corporate executive; b. Chgo., Dec. 8, 1931; s. Stanley Olai and Emma Josephine (Johnson) D.; m. Elin J. Ballantyne, July 25, 1959; children: Erica Joanna, David Ballantyne. BS, U. Ill., 1954; MBA, U. Chgo., 1960. Auditor Price Waterhouse & Co., Chgo., 1956-58; asst. to controller Miehle-Goss-Dexter, Inc., Chgo., 1960-67, v.p. adminstrn. Goss Div., 1967-69; dir. mgmt. systems MGD Graphics Systems-N.Am. Rockwell (formerly Miehle-Goss-Dexter), Chgo., 1969-70; v.p. fin. Duchossois/Thrall Group (formerly Thrall Car Mfg. Co.), Chicago Heights, Elmhurst, Ill., 1970-83; pres., bd. dirs. Thrall Enterprises, Inc., Chgo., 1983—; bd. dirs. Pubs. Equipment Corp., Dallas, Chamberlain Mfg. Co., Elmhurst, 1972-83. Bd. govs. Internat. House, U. Chgo., 1988—; mem. Hobart (Ind.) Plan Commn., 1986—, pres. 1988. Capt. U.S. Army, 1954-56. Home: 141 Beverly Blvd Hobart IN 46342 Office: Thrall Enterprises Inc 200 W Madison St Chicago IL 60606

CHRISTIE, DAVID GEORGE, insurance company executive; b. Glen Ridge, N.J., June 25, 1930; s. Francis Johnston and Catherine Fisher (Somes) C.; student Rutgers U., 1950-52; m. Diane Grace Wettyen, Mar. 23, 1950; children—Lindsey Diane, Mark Wettyen, Meredith Leigh. Asst. U.S. mgr. Union Re-ins. Co., Zurich, Switzerland, U.S. Br., 1956-64; v.p. Am. Re-Ins. Co., N.Y.C., 1964-71; v.p. Towers, Perrin Forster & Crosby Inc., N.Y.C., 1971-78; sr. v.p., dir. Duncanson & Holt Inc., N.Y.C., 1979-83; pres. Fothergill & Hartung Ltd., 1984—. Served with U.S. Army, 1953-54. Republican. Presbyterian. Clubs: Nassau (Princeton, N.J.); Wall St. Home: 3 Ober Rd Princeton NJ 08540 Office: 90 William St New York NY 10038

CHRISTIE, GEORGE NICHOLAS, economist; b. Wilmington, N.C., Nov. 2, 1924; s. Nicholas and Helen (Lymberis) C.; B.B.A., U. Miami, 1948; M.B.A., N.Y. U., 1956, Ph.D., 1963; m. Mary Danatos, July 22, 1951; children—Sultana Helen, Stephanie Hope, Susan Adrianne, Sandra Alicia, Gregory Nicholas. With Dun and Bradstreet, Inc., N.Y.C., 1949-61, staff bus. writer, 1959-61; asso. dir. Credit Research Found., asst. dir. edn. Nat. Assn. Credit Mgmt., N.Y.C., 1961-63; asst. sec. credit policy com., small bus. credit com. Am. Bankers Assn., N.Y.C., 1963-64, sec., 1964-67; v.p., dir. research Credit Research Found., 1967-80, sr. v.p., 1980-82, exec. v.p., 1983—; assoc. dir. Grad. Sch. Credit and Financial Mgmt., 1967-86, exec. dir., 1986-87; dir. Nat. Inst. of Credit, 1967-84. Instr. N.Y. Inst. Credit; lectr. Dartmouth, Stanford U.; asso. prof. L.I. U.; adminstr. 2d year banking course Stonier Grad. Sch. Banking, Rutgers U. Served with AUS, 1943-46. Mem. Am. Econ. Assn., Am. Fin. Assn., Fin. Mgmt. Assn. Contbr. articles to profl. publs. Home: 65 Nassau Rd Great Neck NY 11021 Office: Credit Rsch Found 3000 Marcus Ave Lake Success NY 11042

CHRISTIE, IAIN THORNTON, development banker; b. Glasgow, Scotland, June 23, 1941; came to U.S., 1962; s. Albert and Eva Ellen (Walker) C.; m. Stephanida Martysz, Oct. 1, 1967; children: Rebekka, Adam, Timothy. 1st class diploma, Strathclyde U., Glasgow, 1962; MBA, Mich. State U., 1966; MBA in Econs., NYU, 1972. Asst. prof., extension specialist Mich. State U., East Lansing, 1966-69; mgmt. cons. Laventhol & Horwath, N.Y.C., 1969-72; fin. analyst World Bank, Washington, 1972-80, dep. div. chief, 1980-86, chief infrastructure div. Asia country dept. 1, 1987—; assoc. prof. NYU, N.Y.C., 1970-72, No. Va. Community Coll., Alexandria, 1973-76; lectr. in field. Contbr. articles to profl. jours. Fellow Mich. State U., 1965-66. Mem. Bretton Woods Club (Germantown, Md.). Presbyterian. Office: World Bank 1818 H St NW Washington DC 20433

CHRISTIE, SCOTT GRAHAM, advertising account executive; b. Indpls., July 8, 1953; s. Bruce W. and Jane (Richardt) C.; m. Laurie E. Potter, Nov. 15, 1980. BA, Hanover Coll., 1975; M in Pub. Adminstrn., Ind. U., 1982. News sec. Friends of Dick Lugar, Indpls., 1976; caucus asst. Ind. House of Reps., Indpls., 1977-81; mgr. indsl. pub. relations Caldwell-Van Riper Advt., Indpls., 1981-85; exec. dir. Exec. Council on Fgn. Diplomats, Indpls., 1985-87; advt. acct. exec. Handley & Miller Advertising, Indpls., 1987—; freelance pub. relations writer, Indpls., 1985—. Contbr. articles to profl. jours. Mem. com. X Pan-Am. Games, Indpls., 1986; pres. chi chpt. Alumni Corp., Hanover, Ind., 1986—. Named one of Outstanding Young Men Am., U.S. Jaycees, 1978; recipient scholarship Hanover Coll., 1975. Mem. Indpls. Appaloosa Assn. (bd. dirs. 1988-89), Pub. Relations Society Assn., Sigma Chi (sec. Indpls. alumni chpt. 1978-79, 86). Republican. Episcopalian. Clubs: Columbia, Culver (Indpls.). Office: Handley & Miller 1712 N Meridian Ste 300 Indianapolis IN 46202

CHRISTIE, WALTER SCOTT, state official; b. Indpls., 1922; s. Walter Scott and Nina Lilian (Warfel) C. BS in Bus. Adminstrn., Butler U., 1948. CPA, Ind.; cert. fin. examiner. With Roy J. Pile & Co., CPAs, Indpls., 1948-56, Howard E. Nyhart Co., Inc., actuarial consultants, Indpls., 1956-62; with Ind. Dept. Ins., Indpls., 1962—, dep. commr., 1966-74, adminstrv. officer, 1974-79, sr. examiner, 1979-81, adminstrv. asst., 1981-82, chief auditor, 1982—; bd. dirs. Sr. Enterprises. Bd. dirs., treas. Delt House Corp., Butler U. Served with AUS, 1942-45. Named Ky. Col. Mem. Ind. Assn. CPAs, Soc. Fin. Examiners (state chmn.), Indpls. Actuarial Club, Nat. Assn. Ins. Commrs. (chmn. zone IV life and health com. 1970-75), Internat. Platform Assn. Episcopalian (assoc. vestryman 1948-60). Club: Optimist (dir.). Home: 620 E 53d St Indianapolis IN 46220 Office: Indiana Dept Ins 311 W Washington St Ste 300 Indianapolis IN 46204

CHRISTOFF, WENDELL LEE, food company executive; b. Grand Rapids, Mich., June 25, 1944; s. Clinton John and Dorothy Jean (Lampkin) C.; m. Helen Condurelis, Feb. 27, 1971; children: Nathan, Ryan. BS, Western Mich. U., 1967. Commd. 2d lt. USAF, 1968, advanced through grades to capt., 1971, resigned, 1974; from v.p. to treas. to pres. C.J. Christoff & Sons, Inc., Lowell, Mich., 1974—. Area dir. United Way, Grand Rapids, 1977—; bd. dirs. Jr. Achievement, Grand Rapids, 1983—; pres., v.p. Thornapple Assn., Cascade, Mich., 1985—. Republican. Mem. Evang. Free Ch. Lodge: Rotary (pres., v.p. 1974—, Paul Harris fellow 1984, Man of Yr. 1982). Home: 2731 Cascade Springs Grand Rapids MI 49506

CHRISTOFFERSEN, JON M., banker; b. Coeur d'Alene, Idaho, Sept. 18, 1942; s. Arne Birger and Mary Louis (Chaney) C.; m. B. Joan Bigley, Apr. 8, 1965; children—Eric Stephen, Lisa M. Student, Wash. State U., 1961; BA, U. Wash., 1964, MBA, 1969; postgrad. advanced mgmt., Harvard U., 1979. With Citibank, 1970-81; v.p. Citibank, Tokyo, 1970-71, Seoul, Republic of Korea, 1971-73, Taipei, Republic China, 1974-76; mng. dir. Citibank, Sydney, Australia, 1976-81; exec. v.p. Rainier Nat. Bank, Seattle, 1981-86, pres., 1986-88, also bd. dirs.; pres. Ranierbancorp., 1986-88, bd. dirs.; pres. Visa USA, San Mateo, Calif., 1988—; bd. dirs. Visa USA, San Mateo; chmn. Oreg. Bank. Portland. Mem. adv. bd. Grad. Sch. Bus. Adminstrn. U. Wash.; bd. dirs. United Way King County, Seattle, 1988. Capt. U.S. Army, 1964-68.

CHRISTOPHER, ALEXANDER GEORGE, transportation company executive; b. Melrose Park, Ill., Apr. 17, 1941; s. George Alexander and Ann (Gianoulis) C.; m. Susan Bernice Breitweiser, May 12, 1979; children: Anna Bernice, Jason Woodrow. BA in Econs., Elmhurst (Ill.) Coll., 1963; postgrad., DePaul U., 1963-64. Mgr. Dunn & Bradstreet, Chgo., 1965-67, various Chgo.-area currency exchs., 1967-71; v.p. Ill. Armored Car Corp., River Grove, 1971-82, dir.-in-exile, 1982-83; pres. Ill. Armored Car Corp., Broadview, 1983—; mem. adv. bd. fin. instns. sec. state, Ill. With USMCR, 1964-70. Mem. Ind. Armored Car Operators Assn. (pres. 1979-80, chmn. bd. 1980-81, chmn. legis. com. 1988—), Exec. Club. Greek Orthodox. Office: Ill Armored Car Corp 2001 W Cermak Rd Broadview IL 60153

CHRISTOPHER, FLOYD HUDNALL, JR., tobacco company executive; b. Franklin, Va., Dec. 9, 1933; s. Floyd Hudnall and Dorothy Eberwine (Ames) C.; m. Claire Penn Cannon, Feb. 11, 1961; children—John H., Ashley Penn, David Ames. B.Chem.Engring., U. Va., 1955; S.M., MIT, 1959. With R.J. Reynolds Industries, Inc., 1959; v.p. R.J. Reynolds Tobacco Co., Winston-Salem, N.C., 1976-79, sr. v.p., 1981-83, exec. v.p., 1983—, dir., 1981—; pres., chief exec. officer RJR Archer, Inc., 1979-81, dir., 1979—; mem. Northwest Regional Bd. Wachovia Bank & Trust Co., N.C.; mem. Council for Tobacco Research U.S.A., Inc.; bd. dirs. Planters LifeSavers Co., Winston-Salem Bus., Inc. Mem. Winston-Salem Found. Com., Winston-Salem/Forsyth County Utilities Commn.; bd. dirs. United Way Forsyth County, 1978—, chmn. 1986—; bd. dirs. Children's Ctr. Physically Handicapped, 1973-85; vice chmn. bd. visitors Wake Forest U., Winston-Salem, 1986—, chmn. bd. visitors, 1987—; bd. dirs. Reynolda House Mus. Am. Art. Served to lt. (j.g.) USN, 1955-57. Mem. Aluminum Assn. (dir. 1979-81), Winston-Salem C. of C. Republican. Episcopalian. Clubs: Old Town (Winston-Salem) (bd. govs.), Piedmont. Lodge: Rotary. Home: 2837 Reynolds Dr Winston-Salem NC 27104 Office: R J Reynolds Tobacco Co Box 2959 Winston-Salem NC 27102

CHRISTOPHERSON, JOHN HANDEL, banker; b. Scarborough, Eng., Oct. 30, 1932; came to U.S., 1961; s. John Fuller and Mabel (Fletcher) C.; m. Marguerite Davis, Apr. 19, 1954; children: Susan Heather, Peter John. Grad. pub. schs., Scarborough. Fgn. exchange trader Imperial Bank Can., Toronto, 1953-61, Continental Bank Internat., N.Y.C., 1961-67; chief trader, asst. v.p. Continental Ill. Bank, London, 1967-72; v.p., global mgr. fgn. exchange Bank Montreal, Que., Can., 1972-75; sr. v.p., global mgr. fgn. exchange United Calif. Bank, N.Y.C., 1975-76; v.p., mgr. fgn. exchange Chem. Bank, N.Y.C., 1976-82, Bank N.Y., N.Y.C., 1982-84; sr. v.p., treas. N.Am. Comml. Bank Kuwait, N.Y.C., 1984-88; v.p., treas. Banco Portugues do Atlantico, N.Y.C., 1988—. Pilot RAF, 1951-53. Mem. Fgn. Exchange U.S.A. (bd. dirs. 1977—, pres. 1979-82), Fgn. Assn. London (com. 1968-72), Fgn. Exchange Assn. Can. (pres. 1973-75). Republican. Episcopalian. Office: Banco Portugues do Atlantico 2 Wall St New York NY 10005

CHRISTOPHERSON, WESTON, banker; b. Walum, N.D., May 5, 1925; s. Carl and Ermie (Larsen) C.; m. Myrna Christensen, June 8, 1951; children: Mia Karen Kammerer, Mari Louisa Armour, Kari Marie. B.S., U. N.D., 1949, J.D., 1951. Bar: N.D. 1951, Ill. 1952. With Jewel Cos., Inc., Chgo., 1951-84; pres. Jewel Cos., Inc., 1970-80, chief exec. officer, 1979-84, also dir.; chmn. bd., chief exec. officer No. Trust Co., 1984—; chmn. bd., chief exec. officer No. Trust Corp., 1984—, also dir.; dir. Ameritech, GATX Corp., Quaker Oats Co. trustee U. Chgo., mem. Bus. Council. Presbyn. Clubs: Economic, Chicago, Onwentsia, Old Elm, Commercial, Commonwealth. Home: 200 N Green Bay Rd Lake Forest IL 60045 Office: No Trust Corp 50 S LaSalle St Chicago IL 60675

CHRISTOV, DRAGAN SPIROV, international executive, engineering consultant; b. Koutouguertzi, Bulgaria, Aug. 18, 1934; s. Spiro Stoyev and Jordanka (Angelova) C.; m. Euterpe-Terezinha Correia, Aug. 18, 1967; children: Virginia, Marco, Stefan, Daniel. Diploma technician, Technicum Ch. Botev, Sofia, Bulgaria, 1953; cert. in engring., Sofia High Sch. Engring., 1963; diploma engring., Inst. Bldg. and Constrn., Paris, 1964; cert. in gen. mgmt., La Sorbonne, Paris, 1966. Unit chief Regional Municipality of Kustindil, Bulgaria, 1953-55; regional supr. Governorat, Sofia, 1957-59; project engr. Ponts et Chaussees, Paris, 1964-66; chief engr. Ministry Constrn., Sofia, 1966-67; expert Internat. Labour Office ONU/ILO, Tunis, 1967-68; tng. mgr. Internat. Labour Office ONU/ILO, Geneva, 1968-74; dir. Internat. Labor Office, Dacca, Bangladesh, 1975-78; chief indsl. urban tng.div. Internat. Labor Office, Geneva, 1979—. Co-author: Training of Foreman in Building Industry, 1981. Mem. Bldg. and Constrn. Assn. Club: Diplomatic (Geneva).

CHRISTY, JOHN GILRAY, diversified company executive; b. Silver Creek, N.Y., Aug. 27, 1932; s. John Van Vlack and Ruth (Gilray) C.; children: Andrew, Jennifer. B.A., Dartmouth Coll., 1954; M.A. in Asian Studies, U. Calif., Berkeley, 1960. Loan officer U.S. Devel. Loan Fund, 1960-61; with AID, New Delhi and Washington, 1961-65; chief extended risk guaranty div. AID, 1965; with ITT, N.Y.C., 1965-72; treasury dept. ITT, 1965-68, v.p. internat. communications, 1968-69, asst. group exec. internat. communications, 1969-70; pres. ITT World Directories, Inc., N.Y.C., 1970-72; group v.p. land transp. IU Internat., Inc., Phila., 1972-76; exec. v.p. IU Internat., Inc., 1976-78; pres. and chief operating officer IU Internat. Corp., 1978-80, chmn., pres., chief exec. officer, 1982-85, chmn., chief exec. officer, 1985-88; chmn. Chestnut Capital Corp., Phila., 1988—; dir. Pennwalt Corp., 1st Fidelity Bancorp., Inc., Fidelity Bank, Echo Bay Mines Ltd., 1838 Bond Debenture Trading Fund, Phila. Contributorship. Trustee Colby Coll., Eisenhower Exchange Fellowships Inc.; bd. dirs. Phila. Orch. Served to lt. as aviator USNR, 1958. Recipient Disting. Service award AID, 1965. Office: Chestnut Capital Corp 320 Walnut St Philadelphia PA 19106

CHRISTY, ROBERT ALLEN, investment broker; b. Butler, Pa., Feb. 22, 1956; s. Allen B. and Jane (McMinn) C.; m. Diana Lynn Hinson, June 2, 1984; children: Kenneth Robert, Ashley Lynn. BA in Econs., Grove City (Pa.) Coll., 1978. Investment broker Bache, Halsey, Stuart & Shields, Charlotte, N.C., 1982-87; v.p. investments Prudential-Bache Securities,

Atlanta, 1987—. Served to capt. USMC, 1978-82. Mem. Am. Mgmt. Assn., Ga. Securities Dealers Assn., N.C. Securities Dealers Assn., Internat. Assn. Fin. Planning. Republican. Presbyterian. Lodge: Rotary (editor Charlotte chpt. 1984-85, Paul Harris fellow 1986). Office: Prudential-Bache Securities 14 Piedmont Ctr Ste 200 Atlanta GA 30305

CHRUNEY, JOHN, food company executive, systems developer-operational controller; b. Wilkes-Barre, Pa., Dec. 20, 1930; s. George and Mary (Watlack) C.; m. Marian Agnes Walsh, June 30, 1956; children—George, James, John, Jr., Jeffrey, Colleen. B.S. in Bus. Edn., Bloomsburg State Coll., 1956; postgrad. U. Pitts., 1956-57, Lehigh U., 1958, Syracuse U., 1959-62. Cert. tchr. bus. Mass., 1974, systems profl., 1985. Field auditor Liberty Mut. Ins., Syracuse, N.Y., 1956-62, sr. methods analyst, Boston, 1962-68; cons., project engr. Auerbach Corp., Phila., 1968-72; div. controller Dunkin Donuts, Inc., Randolph, Mass., 1972-76, dir. systems devel., 1976-88; lectr. mgmt. Northeastern U., Boston, 1970-81. Bd. dirs. Yorkshire Terr. Civic Assn., 1960-62; chmn. Indsl. Devel. Commn., Norfolk, Mass., 1965-68; chmn. Capital Budget Com., Norfolk, 1972-76; pres. Norfolk Youth Football Program, 1974-77; mem. Gov's. Mgmt. Engring. Task Force, 1965. Served to 1st lt. U.S. Army, 1951-54, Korea. Recipient Outstanding Service award Gov. Mass., 1965; Merit award Systems and Procedures Assn., 1968. Mem. Assn. for Systems Mgmt. (pres. chpt. 1966-67, Outstanding Service award 1966, Achievement award 1973, Distinguished Service award, 1988), Am. Mgmt. Assn., Pi Omega Pi. Roman Catholic. Club: King Phillip Sports (v.p. 1974-75). Avocation: antique auto restoration. Home: 283 Pleasant St Pembroke MA 02359 Office: Dunkin Donuts Inc Pacella Park Dr Randolph MA 02368

CHRYSSIS, GEORGE CHRISTOPHER, business executive; b. Crete, Greece, May 21, 1947; came to U.S., 1966; naturalized U.S. citizen; s. Christopher and Ourania (Kamisakis) C.; m. Margo Sayegh, May 21, 1978; children: Rania, Lilian, Alexander. AS in Elec. Engring., Wentworth Inst., 1969; BEE, Northeastern U., 1972, MEE, 1977. Electronic engr. Orion Rsch., Boston, 1977-78; sr. engr. Datel, Inc., Mansfield, Mass., 1978-79; co-founder, v.p. ops. and engring. Power Gen. Corp., Canton, Mass., 1979-85; pres., founder, chief fin. officer Intelco Corp., Acton, Mass., 1985—, also chmn. bd. dirs.; dir. nat. coun. Northeastern U. (mem. Pres. Club, 500 Club), Wentworth Inst. (mem. Pres. Coun., chmn. membership com.); mem. internat. bus. adv. bd. BSSC Boston U., Mass. High Tech. Coun. Author: High Frequency Switching Power Supplies, 1984; contbr. articles to profl. jours. Active bus. adv. bd. U.S. Senate; bd. dirs. St. Demetrios Ch., Weston, Mass.; fellow Orthodox Stuart of Boston Diocese. Served to 2d lt. Greek Army, 1973-75. Mem. Pancretan Assn. Am (pres. Boston chpt. 1987-89, co-chmn. 30th nat. conv. 1988, chmn. publicity com.), Northeastern U. Husky Assn., Orthodox Christian Assn. of Medicine, Psychology and Religion, Greater Boston C. of C., Execs. Club. Greek Orthodox. Office: Intelco Corp 8 Craig Rd Acton MA 01720

CHRYSTIE, THOMAS LUDLOW, investor; b. N.Y.C., May 24, 1933; s. Thomas Witter and Helen (Duell) C.; m. Eliza S. Balis, June 9, 1955; children: Thomas W., Alice B., Helen S., Adden B., James MacD. BA, Columbia U., 1955; MBA, NYU, 1960. With Merrill Lynch, Pierce, Fenner & Smith, Inc., N.Y.C., 1955-75, dir. investment banking div., 1970-75; sr. v.p. Merrill Lynch & Co., 1975-78, chief fin. officer, 1976-78; chmn. Merrill Lynch White Weld Capital Markets Group, 1978-81, Merrill Lynch Capital Resources, 1981-83; adv. on strategy Merrill Lynch & Co. Inc., 1983-88; pvt. practice Jackson, Wyo., 1988—; dir. Philips Industries, Titanium Industries, LSW. Trustee emeritus Columbia U.; trustee Presbyn. Hosp. Capt. USAF, 1955-58. Mem. Down Town Assn. Club: Short Hills. Home: PO Box 563 Snowridge I Teton Village WY 83025 Office: PO Box 3154 Jackson WY 83001

CHRZAN-SEELIG, PATRICIA ANN, corporate professional; b. Springfield, Mass., Mar. 3, 1954; d. Stanley Paul Jr. and Roberta Ann (Casey) Chrzan; m. Harold Cranmer Seelig, Nov. 5, 1977; children: H. Casey, Marguerite Andrea. BS in Human Devel., U. Mass., 1974. Dir. YWCA, Infant Day Care Ctr., Springfield, Mass., 1974-75, Tri-Cities Info. and Referral, Petersburg, Va., 1975-77; policy analyst Office of the Sec. Human Resources, Richmond, Va., 1977-78; data specialist Dept. Mental Health/Retardation, Richmond, Va., 1978-79; programmer Sands Internat., Oakton, Va., 1979-80; programmer analyst Carter Hawley Hale, Richmond, Va., 1980; v.p. Preferred Custom Software, Wilsons, Va., 1980-88; pres. Focused Systems, Inc., Wilsons, 1988—. Co-chmn. St. Jude's Hosp. (Bikeathon), Blackstone, Va., 1987. Mem. NAFE, Blackstone Woman's Club (v.p. 1985-86), Va., Blackstone Town, Hobby, and Garden Club (pres. 1987-88). Home and Office: Focused Systems Inc PO Box 157 Wilsons VA 23894

CHUBB, STEPHEN DARROW, medical corporation executive; b. Newton, Mass., Mar. 16, 1944; s. Phillip Darrow and Clarissa Stoddard (Nye) C.; m. Kathleen Alice Zimmerman, Mar. 24, 1973. BS, U.S. Naval Acad., 1965; MBA, Northwestern U., 1974. CPA, Ill. Commd. ensign USN, 1965, advanced through grades to lt., 1968, resigned, 1970; with Am. Can Co., 1970-73; with Baxter Travenol Labs., Deerfield, Ill., 1974-81, asst. to exec. v.p., 1978; also mem. chmn.'s sr. mgmt. com., pres. Hyland Diagnostics, 1978-81; pres., chief exec. officer, dir. Cytogen Corp., 1981-84, T Cell Scis., Inc., 1984-86, Matritech Inc., 1987—; advisor Pa. Ventures, Phila., 1987—; mem. adv. bd. First Stage Capital Fund, Cambridge, Mass.; bd. dirs. Clonetics, Inc., San Diego, Calif., Photo Dynamic Systems, Inc., Boston, Epoulon Inc. Bd. dirs. Sherwood Community Assn., 1978-79, v.p., 1979-80. Serves as capt., USNR, 1970—. Recipient Navy Achievement medal, Combat Action Ribbon, U.S. Navy. Mem. AICPAs, Northwestern U. Mgmt. Alumni Assn. (bd. dirs. 1980-81). Club: U.S. Naval Acad. Alumni Assn. Home: 21 Fairfield #4 Boston MA 02116 Office: Matritec Inc 763 Concord Ave Cambridge MA 02138

CHUCK, WALTER G(OONSUN), lawyer; b. Wailuku, Maui, Hawaii, Sept. 10, 1920; s. Hong Yee and Aoe (Ting) C.; m. Marian Chun, Sept. 11, 1943; children: Jamie Allison, Walter Gregory, Meredith Jayne. Ed.B., U. Hawaii, 1941; J.D., Harvard U., 1948. Bar: Hawaii 1948. Navy auditor Pearl Harbor, 1941; field agt. Social Security Bd., 1942; labor law insp. Terr. Dept. Labor, 1943; law clk. firm Ropes, Gray, Best, Coolidge & Rugg, 1948; asst. pub. prosecutor City and County of Honolulu, 1949; with Fong, Miho & Choy, 1950-53; ptnr. Fong, Miho, Choy & Chuck, 1953-58; pvt. practice law Honolulu, 1958-65; ptnr. Chuck & Fujiyama, Honolulu, 1965-74; ptnr. firm Chuck, Wong & Tonaki, Honolulu, 1974-76, Chuck & Pai, Honolulu, 1976-78; sole practice Honolulu, 1978-80; pres. Walter G. Chuck Law Corp., Honolulu, 1980—; dist. magistrate Dist. Ct. Honolulu, 1956-63; gen. ptnr. M & W Assocs., Tripler Warehousing Co., Kapalama Investment Co.; dir. Aloha Airlines, Inc., Honolulu Painting Co., Ltd., Negov Inc. subs. Volkswagen of Am. Inc. Chmn. Hawaii Employment Relations Bd., 1955-59; bd. dirs. Nat. Assn. State Labor Relations Bd., 1957-58, Honolulu Theatre for Youth, 1977-80; chief clk. Ho. of Reps., 1951, 53; chief clk. Hawaii senate, 1959-61; govt. appeal agt. SSS, 1953-72; mem. jud. council, State of Hawaii; exec. com. Hawaiian Open; dir. Friends of Judiciary History Ctr. Inc., 1983—; former bd. dirs. YMCA. Served as capt. inf. Hawaii Territorial Guard. Fellow Internat. Acad. Trial Lawyers (dir.); mem. ABA (chmn. Hawaii sr. lawyers div.), Hawaii Bar Assn. (pres. 1963), Am. Trial Lawyers Assn. (editor), U. Hawaii Alumni Assn. (Distinguished Service award 1967, dir., bd. govs.), Law Sci. Inst., Assoc. Students U. Hawaii (pres.), Am. Judicature Soc., Internat. Soc. Barristers, Am. Inst. Banking, Chinese C. of C. Republican. Clubs: Harvard of Hawaii, Waialae Country (pres. 1975), Pacific, Oahu Country. Home: 2691 Aaliamanu Pl Honolulu HI 96813 Office: Suite 1814 745 Fort St Honolulu HI 96813

CHUDOBIAK, WALTER JAMES, electronics company executive, electronics engineer; b. Gliechen, Alta., Can., Apr. 2, 1942; s. John and Clara (Suchy) C.; m. Mary Annetta Budarick, Oct. 11, 1969; children—Michael, Anne. B.Sc. in Elec. Engring., U. Alta., Edmonton, 1964; M.Eng. in Electronic Engring., Carleton U., Ottawa, Ont., Can., 1965, Ph.D. in Electronic Engring., 1969. Research officer Def. Research Bd., Ottawa, 1965-69; group leader, research scientist Communications Research Centre, Dept. Communications, Ottawa, 1969-75; assoc. prof. Carleton U., 1975-81; pres., founder Avtech Electrosystems Ltd., Ottawa, 1975—, also dir. U. Alta. scholar, 1960-64; Carleton U. scholar, 1964-65. Mem. IEEE, Assn. Profl. Engrs. (Ont.). Conservative. Contbr. numerous articles to profl. jours.; patentee in field; inventor nanosecond pulse circuits. Home: 12 Timbercrest Ridge, Nepean, ON Canada K2H 7V2 Office: 55 Grenfell Crescent, Ste 205, Nepean, ON Canada K2G 0G3

CHUDY, MARC CHRISTOPHER, controller; b. Northampton, Mass., Sept. 4, 1949; s. Tadeusz L. and Ruth Mary (Parker) C.; m. Cindy L. Wilkerson, June 24, 1972; children: Erica, Amanda, Rebecca. BBA in Acctg., U. Mass., 1971; MBA in Fin., Roosevelt U., 1979. Chief acct. Clow Corp., Oak Brook, Ill., 1973-76; staff acct. Signode Corp., Glenview, Ill., 1976-79, Furnas Electric Co., Batavia, Ill., 1979-83; acctg. mgr. Adams (Mass.) Print Works, Inc., 1983-84; staff acct. Stanhome, Inc., Easthampton, Mass., 1984-86; controller Tighe & Bond, Inc., Easthampton, 1986—; clk., treas. Chudy's Plainfield (Mass.) Tire Barn, Inc., 1983—. Assessor Town of Plainfield, 1983—. Methodist. Home: Jones Ave HC 70 Box 23 Plainfield MA 01070 Office: Tighe & Bond Inc 50 Payson Ave Easthampton MA 01027

CHUMLEY, NORRIS JEWETT, programming executive; b. Bloomington, Ind., Sept. 30, 1956; s. Norris Gary and Mary Ellen (Buskirk) C.; m. Catherine Morris Stine, Oct. 22, 1983; 1 child, Jack Hudson Morris. BFA magna cum laude, NYU, 1981. Lic. FCC Gen. Class Radiotelephone. Dir. Sta. WTTV-TV, Indpls., 1973-76; producer, dir. KPVI-TV, Pocatello, Idaho, 1977; engr. Sta. KMGH-TV, Denver, 1978; prodn. asst. Sta. WNET-TV, N.Y., 1979-81, producer writer, 1984-87; assoc. producer Arts and Entertainment Network, N.Y.C., 1981—; assoc. world liaison ABC Network 1984 Olympics, Los Angeles, 1984; founder, pres. Magnetic Arts, Inc., N.Y.C., 1987—; judge Emmy awards, Internat. Film/TV Festival, Monitor awards, Am. Women in Radio and TV, N.Y., Los Angeles. Producer, dir. Little Mike, 1984 (grand prize Am. Film Inst., Silver medal Internat. Film and TV Festival); producer, The Diaries of Adam and Eve for American Playhouse series; inventor telephone dial system, 1984. Com. chair Nat. Soc. Arts and Letters, N.Y.C., 1986-87. Grantee Conn. Pub. TV, Hartford, 1987; recipient Founder's award NYU, 1981. Mem. Writer's Guild of Am., Nat. Acad. TV Arts and Scis., Internat. Radio and TV Soc., Nat. Acad. Cable Programming, Am. Film Inst. Mem. Soc. of Friends. Office: Magnetic Arts Inc 20 Desbrosses St New York NY 10013

CHUN, SE-CHOONG, trading company executive; b. Mokpo, Chonnam, Republic of Korea, June 10, 1929; s. Chung-Pyo Chun and Yang-Duk Ko; m. Anita Kim; children: Josefine, Johan. B in Polit. Sci., Korea U., Seoul, 1971; diploma in social welfare, Stockholm U., 1974; PhD in Indsl. Mgmt., Pacific States U., Los Angeles, 1981. Acting mgr. Logistics Auto Works, Pusan, Republic of Korea, 1967; mgr. Logistics Machine Works, Pusan, Republic of Korea, 1968-72; vice advisor Logistics Hdqrs., Republic of Korea, 1972-73; owner Birkan Trading, Stockholm, 1977—; lectr. Stockholm U., 1983-84; researcher Tokyo U., 1985-86. Author: Social Welfare System, 1986 (pub. in Republic of Korea). Pres. Korean Residents Soc. in Sweden, 1975-76, advisor, 1981-84; dir. Korea Ctr. in Sweden, 1984—; Mem. Sweden chancellery, 1989. Served to lt. Q.M. Korean Army, 1953-56. Recipient UN medal, 1955. Social Democrat. Home: Lummergangen 39, 13535 Tyreso Sweden Office: Birkan, PO Box 168, 13523 Tyreso Sweden

CHUNG, JUNG GIT, aerospace engineer; b. Sun Wai, Moy Kok, Canton, China, Apr. 12, 1922; s. Pak Wing and Yow Fun (Dong) C.; m. Fay Yung Ma, May 3, 1951; 1 child, John Gingkeong. BAE, N.Y. U., 1949, MAE, 1951. With Fairchild Republic, Farmingdale, N.Y., 1951-86, design air loads engr. Boeing 757, Boeing Aircraft, Seattle, 1979, preliminary design and performance FRC/SAAB Transport, Swearingen Aviation, San Antonio, 1980, loads and dynamics engr. Grumman E-2C, Grumman Aircraft, Bethpage, 1981, preliminary design of aerial refueling tank, 1982, missile ejection and separation dynamics Grumman F-14, 1983, ASW-340 store carriage and separation, F-15 dispenser tech., 1984, A-10 performance maintenance, capacity acctg., interface mgmt., aircraft accident analysis, 1985, T-46 aeroperformance, quality control flying surfaces, 1986; faculty N.Y. Inst. Tech., 1969; instr. H&R Block, 1986. Vol. IRS Outreach Retired Sr. Vol. Program, Medicare/Medicaid Assistance Program, Sr. connections in Farmingdale; instr. Vol. Income Tax Assistance; coordinator and instr. Tax Counseling for the Elderly; mem. adv. bd. Sr. Connections Adelphi U. Sch. Social Work; 1st v.p. AARP Farmingdale chpt., 1988-89; program and membership chmn. Fairfield Republic Retirees, 1986-89. Mem. Met. Mus. Art, Mus. Natural History, Am. Fedn. Arts, U.S. Coast Guard Aux., CAP, AIAA, Data Processing Mgmt. Assn., Air Force Assn., AAAS, Am. Def. Preparedness Assn., N.Y. Acad. Sci., Nat. Assn. Tax Practitioners, Nat. Mgmt. Assn., Portrait Inst., Internat. Platform Assn. Republican. Presbyterian. Home: 17 Roberts St South Farmingdale NY 11735 Office: Sr Connections South Farmingdale Library Farmingdale NY 11735

CHUNG, TCHANG-IL, engineer; b. Seoul, Republic of Korea, Dec. 12, 1932; came to U.S., 1954; s. In-Taek and Yang-Rae (Rhee) C.; m. Pauline Lamarche, Sept. 16, 1958; children: Daniel, Christopher. BS, Seoul Nat. U., 1955; postgrad., Santa Rosa Jr. Coll., 1955; MS, U. Lowell, 1958; postdoctoral, MIT, 1958-59; PhD, Calif. Western U., 1982. Registered profl. engr., Calif., Mass. Mgr. mfg. engring div. Unitrode Corp., Salem, Mass., 1966-69, mgr. quality reliability assurance, 1969-72; product mgr. Unitrode Corp., Watertown, Mass., 1972-77; product line mgr. Unitrode Corp., Watertown, 5, 1977-81, mgr. subcontract, 1981—; mem. adv. bd. Electronics Internat. Adv. Panel, 1974-75. Mem. IEEE (sr.), Cert. Mfg. Engrs., Electrochem. Soc. Home: 35 Sonning Rd Beverly MA 01916 Office: Unitrode Corp 580 Pleasant St Watertown MA 02172

CHURCH, ABIAH A., broadcasting company executive, lawyer; b. St John's Park, Fla., Aug. 3, 1922; s. Harrison C. and Emile R. (Goss) C.; A.B. in Govt., George Washington U., 1948, J.D. with honors, 1950; m. Bety Morrison, Sept. 13, 1947; children—Harry, Susan, Sharon. Admitted to Fla. bar, 1950, D.C. bar, 1950; law clk. U.S. Ct. of Claims, Washington, 1950-51; atty. Nat. Assn. Broadcasting, Washington, 1951-54; staff atty. Storer Communications Inc Miami Beach, Fla., 1954-57, asst. sec., 1957-79, v.p. corp. law, sec., 1979-80, v.p., gen. counsel, sec., 1980—. Pres. Dade Assn. Retarded Citizens, Dade County, Fla., 1959-61. Served with USCG, 1942-45. Mem. Fla. Bar, Fed. Communications Bar Assn. Democrat. Presbyterian. Clubs: Surf (Miami Beach); Palm Bay (Miami, Fla.); Nat. Lawyers, (Washington). Office: SCI Holdings Inc 12000 Biscayne Blvd Miami FL 33261-8000

CHURCH, IRENE ZABOLY, personnel services company executive; b. Cleve., Feb. 18, 1947; d. Bela Paul and Irene Elizabeth (Chandas) Zaboly; children: Irene Elizabeth, Elizabeth Anne, Lauren Alexandria Gadd, John Dale Gadd II. Student pub. schs. Personnel cons., recruiter, Cleve., 1965-70; chief exec. officer, pres. Oxford Personnel, Pepper Pike, Ohio, 1973—, Oxford Temporaries, Pepper Pike, 1979—; guest lectr. in field, 1974—; expert witness for ct. testimony, 1982—. Troop leader Lake Erie council Girl Scouts Am., 1980-81; mem. Christian action com. Federated Ch., United Ch. Christ, 1981-85, sub-com. to study violence in rels. to women, 1983, creator, presenter programs How Work Affects Family Life and Re-entering the Job Market, 1981, mem. Women's Fellowship Martha-Mary Circle, 1980—, program dir., 1982-84, 87—; chpt. leader Nat. Coalition on TV Violence, 1983—; mem. The Federated Ch., United Ch. of Christ, Chagrin Falls, Ohio, program dir Mary-Martha Circle, 1982—, christian action com. 1981-85, mem. Mary-Martha Circle, Women's fellowship, 1980—; mem Better Bus. Bur., 1973-82. Mem. Nat. Assn. Personnel Cons. (cert., mem. ethics com. 1976-77, co-chairperson ethics com. 1977-78, mem. bus. practices and ethics com. 1980-82, mem. cert. personnel cons. soc. 1980-82, regional leader for membership 1987—, Pres.'s award 1989), Ohio Assn. Personnel Cons. (trustee 1975-80, 85—, sec. 1976-77, 85—, chairperson bus. practices and ethics com. 1976-77, 81-82, 1st v.p., chairperson resolutions com. 1981-82, chairperson membership com. 1985—, 2d v.p. 1987—, Outstanding Svc. award 1987, pres. 1988-89), Greater Cleve. Assn. Personnel Cons. (2nd then 1st v.p., 1974-76, state trustee 1975-80, pres. 1976-77, bd. advisor 1977-78, chairperson bus. practices and ethics com. 1974-76, chmn. nominating com., 1983-88, membership com. 1987—, arbitration com., 1980, 85-87, fundraising, 1980—, bd. dirs. 1980—, trustee 1985—, program chair 1987—, Vi Pender Outstanding Svc. award 1977), Euclid C. of C. (small bus. com. 1981, chairperson task force com. evaluating funding in social security and vet.'s benefits 1981), Internat. Platform Assn., Am. Bus. Women's Assn., Nat. Assn. Temp. Svcs., Chagrin Valley C. of C. (leader Chagrin Blvd./East chpt. 1987—, Pres.'s award for Outstanding Contbns. 1988), Greater Cleve. Growth Assn. Council Small Enterprises, Rotary (program com. 1987—, membership chairperson 1988—). Home: 8 Ridgecrest Dr Chagrin Falls OH 44022 Office: Oxford Personnel 2945 Chagrin Blvd Exec Commons 300 Pepper Pike OH 44122

CHURCH, JOHN ALFRED, college development executive, finance company executive; b. Cadillac, Mich., May 26, 1920; s. Felix M. and Eleanor (Baker) C.; B.A. in Journalism, Mich. State U., 1942; m. Hannah G. Baker, Feb. 20, 1946; children—John B., Mary E. Church Maier, Susan H. Church Schehl, William B., Sarah A. Church Kehr, Thomas B., James H., Margaret Ruth. With Dow Corning Corp., advt. dept., Midland, Mich., 1945-49; production mgr. Wagnitz Advt. Co. Midland, 1949-55, pres., 1954-55; pres. Church & Guisewite Advt., Inc., Midland, 1955-69, treas., 1955-69; exec. v.p., sec. C & G Graphics, Inc., Midland, 1958-77; pres. Heritage Arms, Inc., Midland, 1965—; dir. Midland Econ. Devel. Corp. (Mich.), 1963-75; mem. indsl. advt. com. Northwood Inst., Midland, 1963-69, sr. v.p., 1969-86, trustee, 1986—; dir. Midland Fed. Savs. & Loan Assn., 1957—, chmn. bd., 1976—, pres., 1980-88 . Mem. Midland Planning Commn., 1966-69; mem. Mich. Gov.'s Adv. Council on Water Safety, 1964-68, chmn., 1964-68; chmn. bldg. com. Pines council Boy Scouts Am., 1961-64; mem. deacon bd. Meml. Presbyterian Ch., 1960-63, trustee, 1983-86; bd. dirs. Coast Guard Found., 1969—, pres., 1977-81, dir. 1986—. Served as 2d lt., inf., U.S. Army, 1942-45. Mem. Midland C. of C. (dir. 1957-66, pres. 1962-64), Am. Assn. Advt. Agys. (bus. publs. operating com. 1966-69), Navy League U.S. (Mich. council 1968—), Model R.R. Assn. Republican. Presbyterian. Home: PO Box 1849 Midland MI 48641

CHURCH, JOHN FRANKLIN, JR., paper company executive; b. Chgo., Jan. 1, 1936; s. John Franklin Church and Josephine (Marks) Taylor; m. Catherine Neth, Apr. 10, 1974; children: John F. III, Jennifer Scribner, Jane Pitcock, Jessica S. AB, Colby Coll., 1959; BS, Carnegie Inst. Tech., 1961. Salesman Cin. Cordage and Paper Co., 1964-74, exec. v.p., 1974-76, pres., 1976—. Active in Leadership Cin., 1979; chmn. Jr. Achievement of Greater Cin., 1983-85,Quality of Life Steering Com., 1987. Capt. U.S. Army, 1961-64. Mem. Paper Found. (chmn. 1985—), Nat. Paper Trade Assn. (past chmn.1981-83, mem.adv. coun. 1984—), Nat. Assn. Wholesale-Distribrs. (sec. 1987, 2d vice chmn. 1988, 1st vice chmn. 1989—). Republican. Christian Scientist. Home: 116 Oak St Glendale OH 45246

CHURCH, JOHN TRAMMELL, retail stores company executive; b. Raleigh, N.C., Sept. 22, 1917; s. Charles Randolph and Lela (Johnson) C.; m. Emma Thomas Rose, Dec. 31, 1943; children: John Trammell, Elizabeth Church Bacon. Student, Catawba Coll., 1936-37; B.S., U. N.C., 1942. With Rose Co., Henderson, N.C., 1945—; asst. sec., dir. Rose Co., 1948-49, buyer several depts., 1949-54, v.p., sec., 1954-57; mdse. mgr. Rose's Stores Inc., 1957-63, sr. v.p., 1963-73, chmn. bd., from 1973, now chmn. bd. emeritus. Past mem. Tax Study Commn. N.C., Legis. Pay Commn., Exec. Residence Bldg. Commn., Legis. Svcs. Commn.; mem. State Art Mus. Bldg. Commn.; chmn. Kerr Reservoir Devel. Commn., 1967; mem. N.C.-Va. Water Resources Mgmt. Com.; sec. N.C. Ports Authority; pres. United Fund, 1955; trustee, mem. exec. com. Carolinas United, 1955-59; sec. Vance-Granville Community Coll.; mem. adv. bd. Salvation Army, 1959-65; v.p., mem. exec. bd. Occoneechee council Boy Scouts Am., 1955-69, pres., 1969-70; adv. bd. S.E. regional council; seal chmn. Tar River Lung Assn., 1976; Mem. Henderson City Council, 1965-66, N.C. Ho. of Reps., 1967-69, 77, 79, 81, 83, 85, 87, N.C. Senate, 1971; past chmn. N.C. Exec. Democratic Com.; past mem. Nat. Dem. Com.; chmn. bd. trustees Maria Parham Hosp., Henderson, N.C., chmn. doctors procurement com.; past trustee N.C. Symphony Soc.; bd. visitors, past trustee U. N.C. at Chapel Hill; past mem. Morehead Scholarship selection com.; bd. dirs. Bus. Found.; bd. dirs. Order of Tar Heel One Hundred, chmn. utilities study commn.; trustee Vance-Granville Community Coll.; past chmn. bd. visitors; trustee Peace Coll., Raleigh; vice chmn. bd. trustees Louisburg (N.C.) Coll. Capt., aviator USMCR, 1942-45. Decorated D.F.C. with 2 oak leaf clusters (3), Air medal (10); recipient Silver Beaver award, Disting. Citizen award Boy Scouts Am.; O.B. Michael Distinguished Alumnus award Catawba Coll., 1973; named Tarheel of Week, 1962; Man of Year Henderson-Vance County, 1977. Mem. N.C. Mchts. Assn. (pres. 1962, 64, dir., exec. com), Assn. Gen. Mdse. Chains (sec., exec. com.), N.C. Citizens Assn. (dir.), Am. Retail Fedn. (vice chmn. 1965), Am. Legion, 40 and 8, Henderson-Vance County C. of C. (dir. 1959-63, pres. 1976), Jr. C. of C. (pres. 1950-51), Nat. Retail Mchts. Assn. (past dir.), U. N.C. Alumni Assn. (dir., pres. 1980), Newcomen Soc. N.C., Mason, Shriners, Elk, Rotary (pres. Henderson club 1964-65), Henderson Country Club, (pres. 1956-57), Hound Ears Lodge and Club,, Grandfather Golf and Country Club, Sphinx Club, Capital City Club. Methodist (chmn. bd. trustees, past chmn. adminstrv. bd.). Home: 420 Woodland Rd Henderson NC 27536 Office: Roses Stores Inc PO Box 947 Henderson NC 27536

CHURCH, MARGARET RUTH, mortgage broker; b. Midland, Mich., Sept. 6, 1960; d. John Alfred and Hannah Gertrude (Baker) C. Diploma, Southeastern Acad., Kissimmee, Fla., 1979; AA in Bus. Mgmt., AA in Banking and Fin., Northwood Inst., 1983, BBA. Lic. mortgage broker. Sales clk. Mark Cross, Palm Beach, Fla., 1980-81; res. teller City Fed. Savs. & Loan, Lake Worth, Fla., 1985-86; loan closer Lakeland Mortgage, Pompano Beach, Fla., 1986-87; loan officer, prin. mktg. broker So. Floridabanc Fed. Savs. & Loan, Boca Raton, Fla., 1987-88; mortgage broker Jupiter (Fla.) Mortgage Corp., 1988, Mega Mortgage, Margate, Fla., 1988—. Republican. Presbyterian. Home: 2278 Saratoga Bay Dr West Palm Beach FL 33409 Office: Mega Mortgage 1303 N State Rd 7 Ste B6 Margate FL 33063

CHURCH, WALTER H., III, automotive parts company executive; b. Plattsburgh, N.Y., Oct. 20, 1946; s. Walter H. and Mary Anne (Sheehan) C.; m. Nancy J. Suway, July 9, 1977; 1 child, Mariette Ivy. BA in Polit. Sci., Siena Coll., 1968. Corp. asst. Plattsburgh Motor Svc., Inc., 1972-80, v.p., 1980-87, pres., 1987—. With U.S. Army, 1968-71. Mem. Rotary, Elks. Roman Catholic. Home: 4 Flaglar Dr Plattsburgh NY 12901 Office: Plattsburgh Motor Svc Inc 95 Bridge St Plattsburgh NY 12901

CHURCHILL, DANIEL WAYNE, management and marketing educator; b. Bloomington, Ind., Dec. 2, 1947; s. Warren L. and Mary Ellen (Boynton) C.; m. Jean F. McEnroe, Nov. 11, 1972. BBA, U. Mass., 1970, MBA, 1972. Lic. real estate broker, Mass. Internal auditor Liberty Mut. Ins. Co., Boston, 1972-73; site location analyst, mktg. researcher Zayre, Framingham, Mass., 1974-75; pres. Daniel W. Churchill Real Estate, South Easton, Mass., 1976-83; prof. mgmt. and mktg. Mt. Ida Coll., Newton, Mass., 1984—. Mem. exec. bd. Easton (Mass.) Field Authority, 1981-85, supt. screening com., 1988; mem. exec. bd. Easton Softball League, 1975-85, Camp Yomechas, Middleboro, Mass., 1978-82; chmn. Cable 2 Auction, Easton, 1986, Jim Craig Day Banquet, Easton, 1980, Easton Walkathon, 1979-81. Mem. Easton Jaycees (pres. 1981, Jaycee of Yr. award), Boston Computer Soc., Lions (pres. Easton chpt. 1988, Lion of Yr. award). Home: 16 Summer St North Easton MA 02356 Office: Mt Ida Coll 777 Dedham St Newton Centre MA 02159

CHURCHILL, GLEN D., electric company executive; b. Matoon, Ill., 1934. BBA, Tex. A&M U., 1956; postgrad., Harvard U., 1978. Mgr. Arthur Andersen & Co., 1956-64; chief fin. officer, exec. v.p. Cen. Power & Light Co., 1976-79; asst. to controller West Tex. Utilities Co., Abilene, 1964-65, asst. controller, 1965-72, chief account officer, 1966-72, v.p., treas., 1972-76, pres., chief exec. officer, 1979—, also bd. dirs. Served to capt. U.S. Army. Office: W Tex Utilities Co 301 Cypress St Abilene TX 79601

CHUTE, HAROLD LEROY, chemical company executive; b. Winnipeg, Man., Can., Sept. 4, 1921; came to U.S., 1949, naturalized, 1957; s. Kenneth Karl and Hilda Mae (Stoddart) C.; student N.S. Agrl. Coll., 1942-44, hon. asso., 1976; D.V.M., Ont. Vet. Coll., 1949; MS, Ohio State U., 1953; DVSc., U. Toronto, 1955; m. Marion B. Baker, Aug. 9, 1947; children—Pamela D., Hazel Lee, Cameron C. Poultry pathologist U. Maine, Orono, 1950-80, prof., 1949-76, dir. pullorum typhoid testing, 1958-68, dir. devel., 1967-76; pres. Chute Chem. Co., Bangor, Maine, 1977—; bd. dir. Blue Cross Blue Shield, Maine, 1988—, Key Bank of Eastern Maine. Bd. dirs. U. Maine Found.; trustee Grand Lodge Charity Fund; mem. Orono Town Coun., 1963-72; pres. Pine Tree 4-H Found., 1986—. Mem. Am. Assn. Avian Pathologists (past pres.), Am. Assn. Vet. Lab. Diagnosticians (past pres.), AVMA (del.), Maine Vet. Med. Assn. (past pres.). Republican. Lodges: Masons, Shriners (potentate Anah Shrine Temple, Bangor 1981), Order of DeMolay (exec. officer Maine 1971-80, grand master grand lodge of Maine 1968-70). Contbr. over 200 articles to profl. jours. Home: 432 Main St Orono ME 04473 Office: Chute Chem Co 233 Bomarc Rd Bangor ME 04401

CHUTORANSKY, PETER, JR., data processing executive, chemical engineer; b. Framingham, Mass., May 18, 1941; s. Peter and Mary Frances (Gudzinowicz) C.; B.S., Worcester Poly. Inst., 1963, Ph.D. (Exxon Research Grantee 1963-67), 1968; m. Jacquelyn Ann McPartlen, Sept. 7, 1963; children—Elizabeth Mary, Peter III, Alexandra Rachel. Engr., Pratt and Whitney Aircraft, East Hartford, Conn., 1963; research chem. engr. Mobil Research and Devel. Corp., Paulsboro Lab. (N.J.), 1967-77; asso. engr. Mobil Chem. Corp., Edison Labs. (N.J.), 1977-80; venture mgr. Mobil Adminstrv. Service Co., Northeast Computer Center, Princeton, N.J., 1980-81, mgr. strategic planning Corporate Computer Services, N.Y.C., 1981-85; mgr. Resource Planning Northeast Computer Ctr., Princeton, 1986; Resource Mgmt. and Planning, U.S. Computer Ops., 1987—; adj. asst. prof. Rutgers U., 1978-81. Pres. PTA, 1973-75, ch. council, 1973-75. Served to capt. U.S. Army, 1967-69. Mem. Am. Inst. Chem. Engrs. (chmn. So. Jersey Sect. 1974), Digital Equipment Corp. Users Soc., Sigma Xi, Alpha Tau Omega Alumni Assn. (treas. 1963-67). Roman Catholic. Contbr. articles on catalysis, kinetics, computers to profl. publs. Home: 12 Warner Dr Somerville NJ 08876 Office: US Computer Ops PO Box 1033 Princeton NJ 08540

CHYUNG, CHI HAN, management consultant; b. Seoul, Korea, Jan. 27, 1933; s. Do Soon and Boksoon (Kim) C.; came to U.S., 1954, naturalized, 1963, B.S., Kans. Wesleyan U., 1958; M.B.A., Mich. State U., 1960; postgrad. Mass. Inst. Tech.; m. Alice Yvonne Whorley, Dec. 23, 1961; children—Eric, Diana. Ops. analyst Chevrolet div. Gen. Motors Corp., Detroit and Flint, Mich., 1959-61; economist Internat. Harvester Co., Chgo., 1961-63; sr. analyst market div. Internat. Minerals & Chem. Corp., Skokie, Ill., 1963-66; mgr. market info. and planning Gulf & Western Industries, N.Y.C., 1966-68; dir. market planning and devel. Am. Standard, Inc., N.Y.C., 1968-71; pres. Oxytech Corp.; mgmt. cons., internat. market devel., Darien, Conn., 1971—; dir. Korea Hapsum Co.; cons. Govt. of Korea, Taisei Constrn. Co., Tokyo. Served with Korean Army, 1951-53. Mem. Inst. Mgmt. Scis., Am. Mktg. Assn., Ops. Research Soc., Am. Chem., N.Am. Corp. Planning Soc., Beta Gamma Sigma. Contbr. papers to profl. lit. Office: Oxytech Inc 433 Post Rd Darien CT 06820

CICCARONE, RICHARD ANTHONY, investment company executive; b. Akron, Ohio, June 15, 1952; s. Andrew and Marie Antoinette (Danzi) C.; m. Marilyn Douglas DeBorde, May 26, 1984. BA, Miami U., Oxford, Ohio, 1974; MA, U. Akron, 1978. Mcpl. bond analyst Harris Bank, Chgo., 1977-82, mcpl. research mgr., 1982-83; v.p., dir. rsch., sr. analyst Van Kampen Merritt Investment Adv. Corp. (formerly Am. Portfolio), Lisle, Ill., 1983—, dir. unit trust rsch. Contbr. articles to profl. jours. and fin. pubs. Named one of Outstanding Young Men of Am., 1980, 85, 88. Mem. Nat. Fed. Mcpl. Analysts (nat. chmn. 1984-85, Disting. Service award 1988), Chgo. Mcpl. Analysts Soc. (pres. 1984), So. Mcpl. Fin. Soc., Am. Soc. Pub. Adminstrn., Miami (Ohio) U. Alumni Assn. (pres. Chgo. chpt. 1988-89), Omicron Delta Kappa. Roman Catholic. Home: 513 Arlington Ave Naperville IL 60565 Office: Van Kampen Merritt Investment Adv Corp 1001 Warrenville Rd Lisle IL 60532

CICCHETTI, MARK ANTHONY, state official; b. Newark, Oct. 25, 1956; s. Salvatore and Carol Ann (Lombardi) C.; m. Pamela Denise Taylor, June 3, 1978; children: Michael Anthony, Matthew Anthony. BS, Fla. State U., 1980, MBA, 1981. Planning analyst Flagship Banks, Inc., Miami, Fla., 1982; fin. analyst Fla. Pub. Service Commn., Tallahassee, 1983-87, chief, bur. fin., 1987—. Served with USN, 1974-76. Recipient Competitive Papers award Pub. Utilities Reports Inc., 1986. Mem. Fin. Mgmt. Assn., Nat. Soc. Rate of Return Analysts, Toastmasters (pres. Tallhassee club 1988, Speech Contest award 1987, 88). Republican. Roman Catholic. Home: 3216 Black Gold Tr Tallahassee FL 32308 Office: Fla Pub Svc Commn 101 E Gains St Tallahassee FL 32399

CICERO, JERRY WAYNE, typesetting executive, plaque manufacturer; b. Pitts., May 23, 1944; s. Charles and Idabelle Rose (Anselene) C.; m. Pamelia Dell Mallory, June 10, 1967; children: Shane Christopher, Jennifer Summer. BS in Printing Tech., Pittsburg State U., 1967. Pres. Cicero Typographers, Merriam, Kans., 1967—. Served with USN, 1968-69. Named Outstanding Alumnus, Pittsburgh State U., 1977, Outstanding Young Man of Am., 1978. Mem. Advt. Club Kansas City (pres. 1975—), Typographic Assn. Kansas City (pres. 1976-77), Internat. Typographic Composition Assn. (bd. dirs. 1973), Ad II-Jr. Ad Club of Kansas City (past pres., treas., social chmn.), Advt. and Mktg. Club (pres. 1978), Advt. Typographers Assn., Art Dir.'s Club. Republican. Methodist. Home: 8941 Maple Dr Overland Park KS 66207 Office: Cicero Typographers 9003 W 51st Merriam KS 66203

CICET, DONALD JAMES, lawyer; b. New Orleans, May 24, 1940; s. Arthur Alphonse and Myrtle (Ress) C. BA, Nicholls State U., 1963; JD, Loyola U., New Orleans, 1969. Bar: La. 1969, U.S. Dist. Ct. (ea. dist.) La. 1972, U.S. Dist. Ct. (mid. dist.) La. 1978, U.S. Dist. Ct. (we. dist.) La. 1979, U.S. Ct. Appeals (5th cir.) 1972, U.S. Supreme Ct. 1972. Pvt. practice, Reserve, La., 1969-88, LaPlace, La., 1988—; staff atty. La. Legis. Coun., 1972-73; legal counsel Nicholls State U. Alumni Fedn., 1974-76, 78-80; spl. counsel Pontchartrain Levee Dist., 1976—; adminstrv. law judge La. Dept. Civil Svc., 1981—. Mem. St. John the Baptist Parish Emergency Planning Com., 1987—; bd. dirs. Boys' State of La. Inc., 1988—. Served with AUS, 1964, USNG, 1964-70. Recipient Am. Jurisprudence award Loyola U., 1968. Mem. 40th Jud. Dist. Bar Assn., (pres. 1985-87), La. Bar Assn. (ho. dels. 1973-77, 79-85), ABA, La. Trial Lawyers Assn., Assn. Trial Lawyers Am., Nicholls State U. Alumni Fedn. (exec. council 1972-76, 77-85, pres. 1982, James Lynn Powell award 1980), Am. Judicature Soc., K.C., Am. Legion (post comdr. 1976-77, dist. judge advocate, 1975—, mem. La. dept. comn. on nat. security and govtl. affairs, 1974—, chmn. 1977-78, 79-81, 85—, M.C. "Mike" Gehr Blue Cap award 1983). Roman Catholic. Home: 124 W 1st St Reserve LA 70084 Office: 176 Belle Terre Blvd PO Box 461 La Place LA 70069-0461

CIECHANOVER, JOSEPH, banker; b. Haifa, Israel, Oct. 1, 1933; m. Atara Pchor; children: Tamar, Dafna, Isaac. Magister juris, Hebrew U., Jerusalem, 1958, postgrad., 1961-62; LLM, U. Calif., Berkeley, 1967. Bar: Israel 1958, N.Y. 1982. Head adminstrn. Ministry Agr., Israel, 1957-60, gen. counsel, 1960-68; head Israel Def. Mission to U.S. and Can., 1974-78; dir. gen. Ministry Fgn. Affairs, Israel, 1979-80; vice chmn. Israel Discount Bank, N.Y.C., 1981-86; pres. PEC Israel Econ. Corp., N.Y.C., 1981-86; chmn. Israel Discount Bank Ltd., PEC Israel Econ. Corp., N.Y.C., 1986—; lectr. adminstrv. law and agrl. law Hebrew U., 1962-74. Recipient U.S. Dept. Def. medal, 1980. Office: Israel Discount Bank Ltd 511 Fifth Ave New York NY 10017

CIEPIELA, STEPHEN JOSEPH, financial services company executive; b. Chgo., Feb. 2, 1954; s. Valentine and Catherine (Foran) C.; m. Marian S. Smith, June 28, 1980; children: Adam, Annemarie, John. Student, U.S. Air Force Acad., 1972-73; BA, U. N.Mex., 1976, MBA, 1979; postgrad., Am. Coll. Grad. Sch. Fin. Services, 1987—. Cert. fin. planner. Grad. asst., football coach U. N.Mex., Albuquerque, 1975-76; investigator 2d jud. dist. State of N.Mex., Albuquerque, 1976-80; planner, assoc. Resources Fin. Co., Albuquerque, 1980-83; prin., pres. Charles Stephen Fin. Services Corp., Albuquerque, 1983—; adj. prof. Coll. for Fin. Planning, Denver, 1985-86. Bd. dirs. Morningstar, Albuquerque, 1986—. Named One of Best Fin. Planners in Am. Money mag., 1987. Mem. Inst. Cert. Fin. Planners (pres. Albuquerque chpt. 1986-87, Regional Cert. Fin. Planner of Yr. 1985), Internat. Assn. Fin. Planning (Regional Cert. Fin. Planner of Yr. Albuquerque chpt. 1985), U. N.Mex. Alumni Letterman Assn. (pres. 1987-88). Roman Catholic. Office: Charles Stephen Fin Group 4209 San Mateo NE Albuquerque NM 87110

CIFALDI, GERALD JAMES, investigations company executive; b. Paterson, N.J., Nov. 21, 1947; s. Carmine A. and Joel C. (Hutchinson) C.; m. Laura Ellen Zusi, Aug. 5, 1972 (div. 1980); m. Janice Gemma Karr, June 22, 1986; children: Michael, Dylan. BS in Criminal Justice, William Paterson Coll., 1981. Patrolman Paterson Police Dept., 1970-83; security cons., instr. King Khaled Airport, Riyadh, Saudi Arabia, 1983; pres. Cifaldi Investigations, Inc., Totowa, N.J., 1984—; security cons. Acme Courier Svcs., Inc., Hackensack, N.J., 1981-83. With USN, 1965-69. Mem. N.J. Police Pilots Assn., Police Honor Legion, N.Y. Transit Police Honor Legion, Adam Reiser Club. Democrat. Roman Catholic. Office: Cifaldi Investigations Inc 65 Scrivens St Totowa NJ 07511

CIHON, JOHN ALLEN, manufacturing executive, ceramic tile consultant; b. Dover, Ohio, Jan. 14, 1944; s. John Eugene and Marian M. (Kaiser) C.; m. Susan E. Welling, Sept. 3, 1966; children: Michael J., Jennifer L. BA in Ceramics Engring., Ohio State U., Columbus, 1967. Project engr. abrasives div. Bendix Corp., Jackson, Mich., 1968-71; tech. dir. MWA Corp., Owosso, Mich., 1971-73; chief ceramics engr. Am. Olean Tilt Co., Quakertown, Pa., 1973-75; dir. mfg. Cardinal Industries, Inc., Conshohocken, Pa., 1975-77; tech. dir. Robertson Am. Corp., Morrisville, Pa., 1977-81; chief ceramics engr. U.S. Ceramic Title Co., East Sparta, Ohio, 1981-82, plant mgr., 1982-83, v.p. mfg., 1983-85; product line mgr. GTE Enigineered Ceramics, Wellsboro, Pa., 1985-88; pvt. cons. 1988—. Active Can. U.S. Congress, Mich., 1970; chmn. 6th Congress Dist. Dems., Mich., 1971. Mem. Am. Ceramic Soc. (chmn. whitewares div. 1983-84), Nat. Inst. Ceramic Engrs. Roman Catholic. Home and Office: 154 Sutton Ave NE North Canton OH 44720

CIMINERO, GARY LOUIS, economist; b. Youngstown, Ohio, Dec. 16, 1943; s. Felix Louis and Rosalind Janet (Carano) C.; m. Anita Cecile Turgeon, Sept. 3, 1966; children: Steven, Sabina. BS, Case Inst. Tech., Cleve., 1965; MS, MIT Sloan Sch. Mgmt., 1972; postgrad., Harvard U., 1972. Sr. analyst Booz, Allen & Hamilton, Bethesda, Md., 1967-70; sr. research officer The Boston Co., Mass., 1970-75; dir. industry fin. service Data Resources, Inc., Lexington, Mass., 1975; sr. v.p., mgr. macro forecasting Merrill Lynch Econs., Inc., N.Y.C., 1975-82; sr. v.p., chief economist Fleet/Northstar Fin. Group, Providence, 1982—; mgr. R.I. econ. forecast New Eng. Econ. Project, Boston, 1982—, pres. New Eng. Econ. Project,1986—, appointed to exec. com. of gov.'s R.I. Workforce 2000 Council, 1988—. Designed (with others) Merrill Lynch Econs. Macroecon. Forecasting Model, 1979; Contbr. econ. forecasts to profl. jours. Mem. tax study com. of R.I. Pub. Expenditure Council, Providence, 1985—; appointed to exec. com. of govs. R.I. Workforce 2000 Council, 1988—. Sloan Found. scholar Case Inst. Tech., Cleve. 1962-65, Inst. scholar MIT-Sloan Sch. Mgmt., Cambridge, 1966-67. Mem. Nat. Assn. Bus. Economists, Eastern Econ. Assn., Am. Bankers Assn. (mem. econ. adv. com. 1985—). Home: 2 Bay Vista Pl Warwick RI 02886 Office: Fleet Nat Bank 111 Westminster St Providence RI 02903

CINA, CRAIG E., marketing professional; b. Biwabik, Minn., Oct. 9, 1949; s. Stanley George and Margaret Katherine (Bradach) C.; m. Patricia Anne Beckel Cina, Sept. 14, 1951; children: Michael Brent, Todd Anthony. BS, U. Utah, 1972; MCRP, Kans. State U., 1974. Planner City of Omaha, 1974-76; sr. mkt. analyst Federated Dept. Stores, Cin., 1976-81; mktg. mgr. Midland Affiliated Co., Cin., 1981-83; dir. mktg. Zale Corp., Dallas, 1983-85; dir. market planning Yellow Freight Systems, Inc., Overland Park, Kans., 1985—. Contbr. articles to profl. jours. Bd. dirs. United Way of Johnson County, Kans., 1986—; internal coordinator Yellow Freight United Way Campaign, Overland Park, 1985; account exec. United Way, Heartland of Am., Kansas City, 1986. Mem. Am. Mktg. Assn. (mem. long range. planning com., 1987—, bd. dirs. Kansas City chpt.), Am. Mgmt. Assn., Am. Trucking Assns. Sales & Mktg. Coun., KC. Roman Catholic. Office: Yellow Freight Systems Inc 10900 Roe Ave Overland Park KS 66207

CIOE, EILEEN, financial planner; b. Providence, Sept. 5, 1943; d. Joseph and Brigida Evelyn (Macerone) C. BS, Bryant Coll., 1969; MA, Memphis State U., 1973. Engring. technician R.I. Dept. Transp., Providence, 1976-79; gen. mgr. R.I. Pub. Transit Authority, 1979-81, M.A.R.T.A., Atlanta, 1981-84, Westinghouse Broadcasting Co., N.Y.C., 1984-86; fin. planner I.D.S. Fin. Svcs., Inc., Boca Raton, Fla., 1986—. Sec. Leukemia Soc. Am., 1987. Named Transp. Woman of Yr. Woman's Transp. Group, 1980, First Woman of R.I. State of R.I., 1980, Outstanding Alumni Bryant Coll., 1984. Mem. Am. Businesswomen's Assn. (pres. 1987-89), Am. Business Woman of Yr. 1988-89, Women of Yr. 1989), Torch Club. Roman Catholic. Home: 6461 NW 2d Ave Boca Raton FL 33487

CION, RICHARD M., investment banker, lawyer; b. Hartford, Conn., July 27, 1943; s. Irving and Anne (Miller) C.; m. Marjorie Baum; children: Stephanie Lee, Zachary Samuel. A.B., Princeton U., 1965; LL.B., Harvard U., 1968. Assoc., ptnr. Kaye, Scholer, Fierman, Hays & Handler, N.Y.C., 1968-81; v.p., gen. counsel Condec Corp., Old Greenwich, Conn., 1981-82, v.p. fin. and legal affairs, 1982-85, exec. v.p., chief fin. officer, 1985-88, dir., 1983-87; dir., exec. v.p., chief fin. officer Farley Ind., Fruit of the Loom, Inc., Farley Metals, 1985-88; mng. dir. Drexel Burnham Lambert Inc., 1988—. Home: 401 E 34th St #S 10 J New York NY 10016 Office: Drexel Burnham Lambert Inc 60 Broad St New York NY 10004

CIONI, JOSEPH ANTHONY, food products company executive; b. Cumberland, Md., July 20, 1939; s. Paul Thomas and Sara Margaret (Spoltore) C.; m. Susan Jane Cibelli, Aug. 3, 1963; children: Joseph Jr., Anastasia. BBA, Johns Hopkins U., 1962. CPA, N.Y. Audit mgr. Coopers & Lybrand, White Plains, N.Y., 1962-73; asst. treas. Amicor, Inc., Atlanta, 1973-76; v.p. fin. Italicor, Inc., Milan, Italy, 1976-77; treas. Combustion Equipment Assn. Inc., N.Y.C., 1977-80; sr. v.p., gen. mgr. Pollio Dairy Products Corp., Mineola, N.Y., 1981—. Mem. Fin. Execs. Inst. (pres. L.I. chpt. 1987-88), Garden City (N.Y.) C. of C. Roman Catholic. Home: 122 Stratford Ave Garden City NY 11530 Office: Pollio Dairy Products Corp 120 Mineola Blvd Mineola NY 11501

CIPRICH, SYBILLA BARRY, insurance agent, image consultant; b. Bryn Mawr, Pa., May 16, 1957; d. Meredith William and Sybilla Barry (Welles) Ruark; m. Steven Phillip Ciprich, Nov. 1, 1975 (div. 1988); children: Matthew S., Meredith L. Grad. high sch. Shop mgr. Jayne's Beauty Salon, Meshoppen, Pa., 1976-87; color cons. Beauticontrol, Meshoppen, 1985—; image cons. Profl. Image, Meshoppen, 1986-87; ins. agt. Hawk Agy., Tunkhannock, Pa., 1987—; cons. Image Impact, Tunkhannock, 1987—; seminar producer, 1987—. Mem. Am. Soc. Tng. and Devel., Toastmasters. Democrat. Roman Catholic.

CISLER, CYNTHIA MARIE, corporate recruiting company executive; b. Green Bay, Wis., Nov. 3, 1962; d. Alvin George and Rosalyn Elnore (Herlick) C. BA in Psychology, U. Wis., Whitewater, 1985. Cert. nat. task force in leadership & supervisory skills for women. Corp. recruiter Cap Gemini Am., Vienna, Va., 1985—. Contbr. computer profl. job guide for the Washington area. Mem. NAFE, Data Processing Mgmt. Assn., Renew Group. Home: The Carlton 4600 Four Mile Run Dr Unit 416 Arlington VA 22204 Office: CAP GEMINI AM 8381 Old Courthouse Rd Ste 300 Vienna VA 22182

CITRIN, HARVE, electronics company executive, lawyer; b. Bklyn., Feb. 2, 1935; s. Nathan William and Dorothy (Ragin) C.; m. Carol Pineles, Mar. 26, 1961. BEE, BME, CUNY, 1956, MEE, 1965; JD, Fordham U., 1976. Engr. Autonetics, Downey, Calif., 1956-57, GE, Utica, N.Y., 1957-59; engr. Sperry Corp., Gt. Neck, N.Y., 1959-74, with major subcontracts dept., 1978-84; assoc. Weil Gotshal & Manges, N.Y.C., 1974-78; procurement mgr. Paramax, Inc., Montreal, Que., Can., 1984-86; with subcontracts dept. Unisys Corp., Gt. Neck, 1986—. Author: The New York Dojo, 1974. Zone leader New Rochelle (N.Y.) Democratic Club, 1980—. Mem. IEEE, Nat. Assn. Contract Mgrs., Nat. Assn. Purchasing Mgrs. Jewish.

CIVELLO, ANTHONY NED, retail drug company executive, pharmacist; b. Pitts., Aug. 27, 1944; s. Joseph N. and Rose (Calbone) C.; m. Colleen M. McCarthy, July 26, 1969; 1 child, Erin Rose. BS, U. Pitts., 1967. Lic. pharmacist, Pa. Asst. store mgr. Thrift Drug Co., Pitts., 1968, store mgr., 1968-75, dist. mgr., 1975-80, v.p. loss prevention and security, 1980-85, v.p. facilities planning and constrn., 1985, sr. v.p. adminstrn., 1985-86, sr. v.p. ops., 1986-87, exec. v.p. retail ops., 1987—. Account exec. United Way, Pitts., 1982-85, chmn. retail sect., 1988; vol. Generations Together, Pitts., 1985—; mem. com. Fox Chapel Mini-Grant program com., Pitts., 1985— ; bd. dirs. Abraxas Found., Pitts., 1987, chmn. capital campaign, 1988—; mem. grad. sch. bus. U. Pitts. Assoc. Program, 1985—; bd. visitors Sch. Pharmacy U. Pitts., 1988. Mem. Am. Mgmt. Assn., Nat. Assn. Chain Drug Stores, Pitts. Field Club. Republican. Roman Catholic. Office: Thrift Drug Co 615 Alpha Dr Pittsburgh PA 15238

CIZIK, ROBERT, manufacturing company executive; b. Scranton, Pa., Apr. 4, 1931; s. John and Anna (Paraska) C.; m. Jane Morin, Oct. 3, 1953; children: Robert Morin, Jan Catherine, Paula Jane, Gregory Alan, Peter Nicholas. BS, U. Conn., 1953; MBA, Harvard U., 1958; LLD (hon.), Kenyon Coll., 1983. Acct. Price Waterhouse & Co. (C.P.A.s), N.Y.C., 1953-54, 56; fin. analyst Exxon U.S.A., N.J., 1958-61; exec. asst. Cooper Industries, Inc., Houston, 1961-63, treas., controller, 1963-69, exec. v.p., 1969-73, pres., chief exec. officer, 1973—, chmn. bd., 1983—, also dir.; bd. dirs. Harris Corp., Tex. Ea. Corp., Temple Inland Inc., Tex. Research League; bd. dirs., v.p. Machinery and Allied Products Inst. Bd. dirs. Cen. Houston, Inc., 1983—; co-chmn. Wortham Theater Found., 1981—; mem. Houston Bus. Com. for Arts, Tex. Strategic Econ. Policy Commn.; trustee Houston Grand Opera; trustee Com. Econ. Devel., The Conf. bd., 1979—; mem. Rice U. Assocs.; dir. Assocs. Harvard Bus. Sch., Boston, 1984—. 1st lt. USAF, 1954-56. Recipient Gen. Maurice Hirsch award Bus. Com. for the Arts, 1984, 1st place Bronze award Indsl. Equipment Cos., 1989; Chief Exec. Officer of Yr. Bronze award Fin. World Mag., 1987; named Best Chief Exec. Officer in Machinery Industry, Wall St. Transcript, 1987, Chief Exec. Officer of Decade, 1989. Mem. Elec. Mfrs. Club (bd. govs. 1984—), Bus. Roundtable, Houston C. of C. (bd. dirs. 1987—), Machine and Allied Products Inst. (bd. dirs., v.p., exec. com. 1976—), The Conf. Bd., Coronado Club, Houston Petroleum Club, River Oaks Country Club, Ramada Club, Forum of Houston (founding), Houston Ctr. Club. Office: Cooper Industries Inc 1001 Fannin Ste 4000 Houston TX 77002

CLABAUGH, ELMER EUGENE, JR., lawyer; b. Anaheim, Calif., Sept. 18, 1927; s. Elmer Eugene and Eleanor Margaret (Heitshusen) C.; m. Donna Marie Organ, Dec. 19, 1960 (div.); children: Christopher C., Matthew M. BBA cum laude, Woodbury U.; BA summa cum laude, Claremont McKenna Coll., 1958; JD, Stanford U., 1961. Bar: Calif. 1961, U.S. Dist. Ct. (cen. dist.) Calif., U.S. Ct. Apls. (9th cir.) 1961, U.S. Sup. Ct. 1971. Fgn. svc. staff U.S. Dept. State, Jerusalem and Tel Aviv, 1951-53; field staff Pub. Adminstrn. Service, El Salvador, Ethiopia, U.S., 1953-57; dep. dist. atty. Ventura County, Calif., 1961-62; pvt. practice, Ventura, Calif., 1962—; mem. Hathaway, Clabaugh, Perrett and Webster and predecessors, 1962-79, Clabaugh & Perloff, Ventura, 1979—; state inheritance tax referee, 1968-78. Bd. dirs. San Antonio Water Conservation Dist., Ventura Community Meml. Hosp., 1964-80; trustee Ojai Unified Sch. Dist., 1974-79; bd. dirs. Ventura County Found. for Parks & Harbors, Ventura County Maritime Mus. With USCGR, 1944-46, USMCR, 1946-48. Mem. Calif. Bar Assn., Am. Arbitration Assn., NRA, Safari Club Internat., Mason, Shriners, Phi Alpha Delta. Republican. Home: 241 Highland Dr Channel Island Harbor CA 93035 Office: 1st Nationwide Savs Bldg 1190 S Victoria Rd Suite 305 Ventura CA 93003

CLABBY, WILLIAM ROBERT, editor; b. Waterloo, Iowa, Feb. 12, 1931; s. James Francis and Pearl Marie (Bloes) C.; m. Joann Alma Carroll, Aug. 9, 1952; children—Theresa, Joseph, Dennis, Carolyn, Kathleen, Maureen, Timothy, Margaret, Brigid, Erin. Student, No. Iowa U., 1949-51; B.A., U. Iowa, 1953. With Dow Jones & Co., N.Y.C., 1953—; bur. mgr. Wall St. Jour., N.Y.C., 1966-71; mng. editor AP-Dow Jones, 1971-77; v.p. Dow Jones News Services, 1977—. Mem. Omicron Delta Kappa, Sigma Delta Chi. Roman Catholic. Home: 25 Tulip St Summit NJ 07901 Office: Dow Jones News Svc 200 Liberty St New York NY 10281

CLACK, DICK SCOTT, international trade consultant; b. Celina, Tex., Nov. 13, 1927; s. Clyde William and Tink (Blakemore) C.; BS in Wildlife Conservation, Okla. State U., 1952; postgrad. Hokkaido U., Sapporo, Japan, 1953-54, U. Hawaii, 1979; m. Yoshiko Eguchi, Oct. 1, 1955; children: Michael Bruce, Meiling Jade. Served as enlisted man U.S. Army, 1945-48, commd. 2 lt., 1952, lt. col., 1967, ret., 1970; asst. v.p. Makaha Surfside Devel. Co., Honolulu, 1970-72; pres. D. Clack Inc., pub. relations cons., Honolulu, 1972-74; v.p. PCO Inc., Honolulu, 1974-76; Chmn. of founding com., exec. trustee Hawaii Army Museum Soc., Honolulu, 1976-78, trustee, 1976-84; v.p., dir. mktg. Traders Pacifica Ltd., Honolulu, 1979-81; dir. Société Tahitienne de Developpement Agri-Industrielle et Touristique, Papeete, 1982-85; propr. C & S Imports, Honolulu, 1981-86, bd. dirs. C.S.W. Holdings, Nadi, Fiji, Kaikoo Devel. Co., Inc., 1983—; v.p. K.N. Devel. Co., 1983—; internat. rep. COPABAM, Moorea, Tahiti, 1982-83; dir. Pacific Trade and Devel. Decorated Legion of Merit, Army Commendation medal with 3 oak leaf clusters; named hon. mem. City Council Kumagaya (Japan), 1954; recipient cert. of commendation Gumma Prefectural Govt. Japan, 1955, Saitama Prefecture Govt. Japan, 1955; named Okla. Col., 1957, Ark. Traveler, 1962, La. Col., 1963, Hon. Citizen New Orleans, 1964. Mem. Assn. U.S. Army (exec. com. Hawaii chpt. 1967—), Navy League, Mil. Order World Wars, War Mus. Can., VFW (chief of staff Hawaii 1973), Regent Clan Buchanan Soc. Am., Caledonian Soc., Polynesian Voyaging Soc., Rotary (dir. public relations Dist. 500, 1974, 79, dir. internat. relations Dist. 500, 1980, mem. Internat. Yachting Fellowship chpt.), Adventurers Honolulu Club, Cook Island Game Fishing Club. Office: 1507 Kapiolani Ste 6 Honolulu HI 96814

CLADIANOS, PETE, JR., hotel executive; b. Reno, Nev., Dec. 19, 1929; s. Pete and Antonia Cladianos; divorced; children: Pete III, Antonia. BA in History, U. Nev., 1953. Pres. The Sands Regent Hotel Casino, Reno, 1965—. Mem. Elks. Republican. Greek Orthodox. Home and Office: Sands Regents Hotel Casino 345 N Arlington Ave Reno NV 89501

CLAIBORNE, LIZ (ELISABETH CLAIBORNE ORTENBERG), fashion designer; b. Brussels, Mar. 31, 1929; came to U.S., 1934; d. Omer Villere and Louise Carol (Fenner) C.; m. Arthur Ortenberg, July 5, 1957; 1 son by previous marriage, Alexander G. Schultz. Student, Art Sch., Brussels, 1947, Academie, Nice, France, 1948. Asst. Tina Lesser, N.Y.C., 1949-50, Omar Khayam, Ben Reig, Inc., N.Y.C., 1950-52; designer Juniorite, N.Y.C., 1952-54, Dan Keller, N.Y.C., 1955-60, Youth Guild Inc., N.Y.C., 1960-76; designer, pres. Liz Claiborne Inc., N.Y.C., 1976—; chmn. Liz Claiborne Cosmetics, 1985—; guest lectr. Fashion Inst. Tech., Parsons Sch. Design; bd. dirs. Council of Am. Fashion Designers, Fire Island Lighthouse Restoration Com. Recipient Designer of Yr. award Palciode Hierro, Mexico City, 1976, Designer of Yr. award Dayton Co., Mpls., 1978, Ann. Disting. in Design award Marshall Field's 1985, One Co. Makes a Difference award Fashion Inst. Tech., 1985, award Council of Fashion Designers, 1986. Mem. Fashion Group. Roman Catholic. Office: Claiborne Inc 1441 Broadway New York NY 10018 *

CLAIRE, THOMAS ANDREW, treasurer non-financial institution; b. Cleve., Feb. 13, 1951; s. William Henry and Dorothy Helen (Taylor) C. BA, Kenyon Coll., 1973; MA, Brown U., 1977; MBA, Columbia U., 1978. Account adminstr. Irving Trust Co., N.Y.C., 1978-80; dir. fin. planning and analysis W.R. Grace & Co., N.Y.C., 1980-83; asst. treasurer Harper & Row Publishers, Inc., N.Y.C., 1983-87; treas., asst. sec. Moët-Hennessy U.S. Corp., N.Y.C., 1987—. Mem. Greenwich Village Soc. for Hist. Preservation, N.Y.C., 1986-87. Recipient Fulbright scholar Acad. Coms., Paris, 1974-75, Nat. Merit scholar, Ohio, 1969-73. Mem. Phi Beta Kappa, Beta Gamma Sigma. Democrat. Roman Catholic. Clubs: Brown (N.Y.C.), Victorian Soc. of Am. (N.Y.C.). Home: 59 W 12th St New York NY 10011 Office: Moët-Hennessy US Corp 135 E 57th St New York NY 10022

CLANCY, JOHN PATRICK, real estate company executive; b. N.Y.C., Aug. 4, 1942; s. Joseph Edward and Rita Gertrude (Hass) C.; m. Carol Ann Furnari, May 26, 1962 (div. 1982); children—Laureen, Lisa, Janine; m. Maureen Kearney Rose, Oct. 1, 1988. B.B.A., St. John's U., 1965. C.P.A., N.Y Acct. McGrath, Doyle & Phair, N.Y.C., 1965-66; mgr. Ernst & Whinney, N.Y.C., 1966-81; exec. v.p., chief fin. officer Douglas Elliman Gibbons & Ives, Inc., N.Y.C., 1981—. Mem. Nat. Assn. Accts., Am. Inst. C.P.A.s, N.Y. State Soc. C.P.A.s. Office: Douglas Elliman Gibbons and Ives Inc 575 Madison Ave New York NY 10022

CLAPMAN, PETER CARLYLE, insurance company executive; b. N.Y.C., Mar. 11, 1936; s. Jack and Evelyn (Clapman); m. Barbara Posen, May 8, 1966; children: Leah, Alice. AB, Princeton U., 1957; JD, Harvard U., 1960. Bar: N.Y. State 1961, Conn. 1972. Assoc. Sage, Gray, Todd & Sims, N.Y.C., 1961-63; asst. counsel Stichman Commn., N.Y.C., 1964; legal cons.

OEO, Washington, 1965; assoc. counsel Equitable Life, N.Y.C., 1965-72; asst. counsel Tchrs. Ins. and Annuity of Am., Coll. Ret. Equities Fund, N.Y.C., 1972; counsel Tchrs. Ins. and Annuity of Am., Coll. Ret. Equities Fund, 1973-74, asst. gen. counsel, 1975, 2d v.p., assoc. gen counsel, 1976-78, v.p., assoc. gen. counsel, 1978-79, sr. v.p., assoc. gen. counsel, 1980—. Co-Author: Notre Dame U. Law Review, 1981, Role of Independent Director in Corporate Government, (handbook) Harcourt Brace. Bd. dirs. Scarsdale Greenacres Assn., 1981-83. With U.S. Army, 1960. Mem. ABA (mem. com. devels. in bus. financing), Assn. Life Ins. Counsel (bd. govs., chmn. investment sect.), Am. Coun. Life Ins. (chmn. securities investment commn.), Assn. of Bar of City N.Y. (mem. corp. law dept. com.), N.Y. State Bar Assn. Home: 3 Valley Rd Scarsdale NY 10583 Office: Tchrs Ins & Annuity Assn Am 730 3rd Ave New York NY 10017

CLAPP, ALLEN LINVILLE, electric supply and communications utility consultant; b. Raleigh, N.C., Oct. 8, 1943; s. Byron Siler and Alene Linville (Hester) C.; m. Anne Stuart Calvert, Dec. 18, 1966. BS in Engring. Ops., N.C. State U., 1967, M in Econs., 1973. Registered profl. engr., N.C., N.J. Asst. engr. Booth-Jones and Assocs., Raleigh, 1965-67; assoc., 1969-71; chief ops. analysis N.C. Utilities Commn., Raleigh, 1971-77, engring. and econs. advisor to commrs., hearing examiner, 1977-82; dir. tech. assessment N.C. Alternative Energy Corp., Research Triangle Park, 1982-85; mng. dir. Clapp Research Assocs., 1985—; pvt. practice electric safety cons., Raleigh, 1971—; chmn. Nat. Elec. Safety Code Com., 1984—; lectr. in field. Author: National Electrical Safety Code Handbook, 1984, 87, Assembly and Testing of Aerial Mines, 1968; contbr. to McGraw-Hill Standard Handbook for Electrical Engineers; contbr. articles to profl. jours. Co-chmn. Brookhaven/Deblyn Park Action Com., Raleigh. Served with U.S. Army, 1967-69. Recipient cert. of Recognition and Appreciation Aerial Mine Lab., 1969. Mem. NSPE, Profl. Engrs. N.C. (pres. 1980; Disting. Service award cen. Carolina chapt. 1978), N.C. Assn. Professions (pres. 1981), IEEE (mem. standards bd.), Power Engring. Soc., Nat. Safety Council, Am. Soc. Safety Engrs., Indsl. Applications Soc., Am. Nat. Standards Inst. Republican. Baptist. Avocations: competitive target shooting, photography, raising orchids. Home: 3206 Queens Rd Raleigh NC 27612 Office: Clapp Rsch Assocs 5540 McNeely Dr Ste 201 Raleigh NC 27612-0189

CLAPP, JOSEPH MARK, motor carrier company executive; b. Greensboro, N.C., July 29, 1936; s. Frederick Lawrence and Mary Beatrice (Flaherty) C.; m. Helen Grey Roberts, June 8, 1963; children: Kathryn Grey, Amy Elizabeth. B.S. in Bus. Adminstrn., U. N.C., 1958. Practitioner ICC. From mgmt. trainee to dir. safety, personnel Ryder Tank Line, Inc., Greensboro, N.C., 1959-66; asst. to pres. T.I. McCormack Trucking, Inc., Woodbridge, N.J., 1966-67; div. employee relations mgr. to sr. v.p. Roadway Express, Inc., Akron, Ohio, 1967-74; vice chmn. corp. services Roadway Services, Inc., Akron, 1985; pres., chief exec. officer Roadway Services, Inc., 1986—, chmn., 1987—; past chmn. Transp. Research Bd. of NRC. Mem. Nat. Motor Carrier Adv. Council, Washington, 1985; bd. trustees Akron City Hosp., 1985—; bd. dirs. St. Edwards Home, Fairlawn, Ohio, 1985. Served to staff sgt. USAFR, 1959-65. Mem. Am. Trucking Assn. (v.p. at large), Transp. Practitioners Assn., Regular Commn. Carrier Conf. (chmn. 1984). Roman Catholic. Clubs: Congl. Country (Bethesda, Md.); Fairlawn Country (Akron). Office: Roadway Svcs Inc care Gayle Frank 1077 Gorge Blvd PO Box 88 Akron OH 44309 *

CLAPP, KENNETH WAYNE, conference center executive; b. Greensboro, N.C., Mar. 16, 1948; s. James Ernest and Lillian (Hutchens) C. AB in Sociology, Catawba Coll., 1970; M of Divinity, Yale U., 1973; PhD, Lancaster (Pa.) Theol. Sem., 1989. Ordained to ministry Christian Ch., 1973. Minister edn. North Haven (Conn.) Congl. Ch., 1971-73; pastor Emanuel United Ch. of Christ, Lincolnton, N.C., 1973-79; exec. dir. Blowing Rock (N.C.) Assembly Grounds, 1979—; del. Gen. Synod-United Ch. of Christ, Washington, 1977-79; v.p. Market Art, Inc., Greensboro, 1972—; bd. dirs. nat. adv. com. Outdoor Ministries. Author: (book) Tried and Tested Retreats, 1976, Making Retreats Work, 1981; editor (curriculum) Confirmation Studies, 1975; composer Shalom For You and Me, 1975; creator (board game) Wilderness, 1973. Advancement chmn. Lincoln dist. Boy Scouts Am., 1976-78; bd. dirs. Mental Health, Lincolnton, 1978-79; mem. adv. com. Dunn Fund, Blowing Rock, 1981—. Mem. Assn. United Ch. Educators (regional rep. 1974-79). Republican. Lodge: Rotary (pres. Blowing Rock club 1985). Home: Goforth Rd Blowing Rock NC 28605 Office: Blowing Rock Assembly Grounds PO Box 974 Blowing Rock NC 28605-0974

CLAPS, NICHOLAS JOHN, insurance company executive; b. Bklyn., Mar. 15, 1946; s. Julius Dominick and Elsie Helen (Proies) C.; m. Mary Beth Mastin, Aug. 15, 1971. BS, U. Nebr., 1971. Cert. tchr. N.Y. Sci. tchr. Lafayette (N.Y.) High Sch., 1972-82, chmn. sci. dept., 1975-82; sales rep. Nationwide Ins. Co., Liverpool, N.Y., 1983-84; co-chmn. fin. planning Nationwide Ins. Co., Liverpool, 1986—; speaker on "Managing Your Time". Scoutmaster North Syracuse Area Boy Scouts Am., 1980-82. Grantee NSF, 1973. Mem. Am. Assn. Life Underwriters, Nat. Assn. Fin. Planning Agts. Republican. Roman Catholic. Home: 8059 Crockett Cr Clay NY 13041

CLARE, DAVID ROSS, pharmaceutical company executive; b. Perth Amboy, N.J., July 21, 1925; s. Robert Linn and Helen M. (Walsh) C.; m. Margaret Mary Corcoran, July 5, 1947; children: Lynne Clare Ferree, Carol Clare Brown, David Ross, Christopher E. B.S. in Mech. Engring., MIT, 1945. With Johnson & Johnson, New Brunswick, N.J., 1946—, pres. domestic operating co., 1970, corp. pres., 1976—, dir., 1971—, mem. exec. com., 1971—, chmn. exec. com., 1976—. Mem. corp. Mass. Inst. Tech.; bd. dirs. Overlook Hosp. Served as lt. (j.g.) USNR, 1944-46. Roman Catholic. Clubs: Echo Lake Country (Westfield, N.J.); Lost Tree (North Palm Beach, Fla.). Office: Johnson & Johnson 1 Johnson & Johnson Pla New Brunswick NJ 08933

CLARE, GEORGE, safety engineer; b. N.Y.C., Apr. 8, 1930; s. George Washington and Hildegard Marie (Sommer) C.; student U. So. Calif., 1961, U. Tex., Arlington, 1963-71, U. Wash., 1980; m. Catherine Saidee Hamel, Jan. 12, 1956; children: George Christopher, Kristine René. Enlisted man U.S. Navy, 1948, advanced through grades to comdr., 1968; naval aviator, 1951-70; served in Korea; comdr. Res., 1963-70; ret., 1970; mgr. system safety LTV Missiles and Electronics Group, Missiles div., Dallas, 1963—. Mem. Nat. Republican Com., Rep. Senatorial Com., Rep. Congl. Com., Tex. Rep. Com., Citizens for Republic. Decorated Air medal with gold star, others; cert. product safety mgr. Mem. AIAA, Am. Security Council, Internat. Soc. Air Safety Investigators, System Safety Soc., Am. Def. Preparedness Assn., Assn. Naval Aviation, Ret. Officers Assn., Air Group 7 Assn. (pres.). Roman Catholic. Home: 817 N Bowen Rd Arlington TX 76012 Office: LTV Missiles and Electronics Group Missiles Div PO Box 650003 Dallas TX 75265-0003

CLARENS, JOHN GASTON, investment executive; b. Bordeaux, France, July 16, 1924; s. Pierre Maurice and Cecile (Dupreuilh) C.; m. Francoise Legrand, Aug. 7, 1948. Engr., Ecole Polytechnique, Paris, 1948; MBA (Am. Field Service scholar), Harvard U., 1950. Chartered fin. analyst, N.Y. Vice-pres. Lepercq, de Neuflize & Co., Inc., N.Y.C., 1970-75; pres., chief exec. officer Lepercq, de Neuflize & Co., Inc., 1975-76; pres. Istel Fund, N.Y.C., 1975-76; chmn., pres. Clarens Assocs., Inc., N.Y.C., 1976—. Served to lt. French Army. Clubs: Knickerbocker, Harvard (N.Y.C.). Home: 51 Fox Run Rd Redding CT 06896 Office: Clarens Assocs Inc 1044 Madison Ave Penthouse New York NY 10021

CLARIDGE, THOMAS HOLMAN, automotive executive, geologist; b. St. Louis, Aug. 25, 1941; s. Robert Alexander and Vera Louise (Holman) C.; m. Janice Elizabeth Futch, Oct. 5, 1978. BS in Geology, Northeast La. U., 1964. Sales mgr. Fasson, Inc., Atlanta, 1970-73; pres. Gregg Motorcars, Jacksonville, Fla., 1973-78, BMC Corp., Santa Cruz, Calif., 1978-81, Claridge's Ltd., Fremont, Calif., 1981—; pres. Graymarket Commn., Calif., 1983—. Author: Geology of Sandhills, 1967, (book and map) Geology of Vietnam, 1969. Served as capt. U.S. Army, 1966-70, Vietnam. Decorated Army Commendation medal. Mem. Mercedes-Benz Dealer Council, Sigma Gamma (v.p. 1962-63). Republican. Home: 1663 Calera Creek Milpitas Hills CA 95035 Office: Claridge's Ltd 4300 Peralta Blvd Fremont CA 94536

CLARK, ARTHUR BRODIE, electrical equipment manufacturing company executive; b. Exeter, N.H., July 11, 1935; s. Leslie Clinton and Eva Jane (Proctor) C.; B.S., U. N.H., 1959; M.B.A., Lynchburg Coll., 1973; Degree in Engring., George Washington U., 1987; m. Mary Ann Maddox, June 15, 1974; children: Melanie, Belinda. With Gen. Electric Co., 1959—, sr. project/tech. unit leader mobile communications mfg. dept., sr. engr. U.S. mobile radio dept., Lynchburg, Va., 1973—. Adminstrv. bd. mem. Meth. Ch. Mem. Am. Soc. Mech. Engrs. (past chmn., Cert.), Pi Kappa Alpha. Methodist. Club: Elks. Home: 2312 Heron Hill Pl Lynchburg VA 24503 Office: Gen Electric Co Mountain View Rd Rm 1614 Lynchburg VA 24502

CLARK, BERNARD F., natural gas company executive; b. 1921; B.S., Fordham U., 1942; M.B.A., Harvard U., 1949. Chemist, Pan-Am. Refining and Transport Co., 1947-49; asst. v.p. sales Baker J.T. Chem. Co., 1949-51; asst. exec. v.p. Pan-Am. So. Corp., 1951-56; with Mitchell Energy & Devel. Corp., 1956—, asst. to pres., 1956-57, v.p., gen. mgr., 1957-63, exec. v.p., 1963-79, vice chmn., dir., 1979—. Served to maj. U.S. Army Air Corp, 1942-46. Address: Mitchell Energy & Devel Corp PO Box 4000 The Woodlands TX 77387-4000 *

CLARK, BILLY PAT, physicist; b. Bartlesville, Okla., May 15, 1939; s. Lloyd A. and Ruby Laura (Holcomb) C. BS, Okla. State U., 1961, MS, 1964; PhD, 1968. Grad. asst. dept. physics Okla. State U., 1961-68; postdoctoral research fellow dept. theoretical physics U. Warwick, Coventry, Eng., 1968-69; sr. mem. tech. staff Booz-Allen Applied Research, 1969-70; sr. mem. tech. staff field services div. Computer Scis. Corp., Leavenworth, Kans., 1970-73, sr. mem. tech. staff, field services div., Hampton, Va., 1973-76, head quality assurance engring. Landsat project Goddard Space Flight Center, NASA, Greenbelt, Md., 1976-77, quality assurance sect. mgr., 1977-79, sr. staff scientist engring. dept., 1979-80, sr. staff scientist image processing ops., 1980-82, sr. prin. engr./scientist GSFC sci. and application operation, system scis. div., 1982-83, sr. adv. staff CSC/NOAA Landsat Operation, 1983—; tech. rep. internat. Landsat Tech. Working Group (representing USA Landsat operation). Author tech. publs. Recipient undergrad. scholarships Phillips Petroleum Co., 1957-61, Am. Legion, 1957-58, Okla. State U., 1957-58. Mem. Am. Acad. Polit. and Social Sci., Internat. Platform Assn., Am. Phys. Soc., AAAS, N.Y. Acad. Scis., Soc. Photo Optical Instrumentation Engrs., Internat. Soc. for Photogrammetry and Remote Sensing, Am. Soc. for Photogrammetry and Remote Sensing, IEEE, Pi Mu Epsilon, Sigma Pi Sigma. Club: Victory Hills Golf and Country (Kansas City, Kans.), Crofton Country (Crofton, Md.). Home: 5811 Barnwood Pl Columbia MD 21044

CLARK, CARLETON EARL, tax consultant; b. North Easton, Mass., Apr. 5, 1942; s. Carleton Earl and Amy Ella (Toner) C.; m. Judy Carol Johnson (div. June 1983); children: Amy Laura, Carla Elaine. BS in Acctg., Bentley Coll., 1980. Asst. v.p. BayBank Norfolk, Dedham, Mass., 1967—; pvt. practice tax cons., Brockton, Mass., 1985—. Mem. Nat. Assn. Accts., Nat. Assn. Tax Preparers. Democrat. Congregationalist. Home: 670 Pearl St Brockton MA 02401 Office: EW Costa & Assocs Inc 706 Montello St Brockton MA 02401

CLARK, DAYLE MERITT, civil engineer; b. Lubbock, Tex., Sept. 5, 1933; s. Frank Meritt and Mamie Jewel (Huff) C.; B.S., Tex. Tech. U., 1955; M.S., So. Meth. U., 1967; m. Betty Ann Maples, Apr. 11, 1968; 1 dau., Alison. Registered profl. engr., pub. surveyor. Field engr. Chgo. Bridge & Iron Co., 1955; mgr. L.K. Long Constrn. Co., 1958-64; faculty U. Tex., Arlington, 1964—; cons. AID, 1966, NSF, 1967-68; expert witness in court cases. Served to capt. USAF, 1955-57. Mem. ASCE (pres. Dallas br. 1987). Club: Rotary (pres. Arlington-West 1986). Editor Tex. Civil Engr., 1967-71. Contbr. papers, reports to profl. jours. Office: Box 185 Arlington TX 76004

CLARK, DONALD CAMERON, financial services company executive; b. Bklyn., Aug. 9, 1931; s. Alexander and Sarah (Cameron) C.; m. Jean Ann Williams, Feb. 6, 1954; children: Donald, Barbara, Thomas. B.B.A., Clarkson U., 1953; M.B.A., Northwestern U., 1961. With Household Fin. Corp., Chgo., 1955—, sec., asst. treas., 1965-72, treas., 1972-74, dir., 1974, sr. v.p., office of chief exec. officer, 1974-76, exec. v.p., chief fin. officer, 1976-77, pres., 1977-81, also bd. dirs.; pres. holding co. Household Internat., Inc., Prospect Heights, Ill., 1981-88, dir., 1981, chief operating officer, 1982-88, chief exec. officer, 1982—, chmn., 1984—, also bd. dirs.; chmn. bd. dirs. Eljer Industries, Inc., Scotsman Industries, Inc., Schwitzer, Inc.; dir. Sq. D. Co., Warner-Lambert Co., Ameritech. Bd. dirs. Lyric Opera of Chgo.; trustee Clarkson U., Evanston Hosp., Com. Econ. Devel., Northwestern U. Lt. U.S. Army, 1953-55. Mem. Econ. Club Chgo. (dir., pres. 1985-87), Chgo. Council Fgn. Relations (dir.), Conf. Bd. Clubs: Chgo., Westmoreland Country, Mid-Am., Commercial (Chgo.). Office: Household Internat Inc 2700 Sanders Rd Prospect Heights IL 60070-2799

CLARK, DONALD MALIN, association executive; b. Buffalo, Feb. 11, 1929; s. Jack Merritt Malin and Louise Mary C.; m. Joan Marie Coyle, Dec. 27, 1958; children—Kevin Malin, Michael John, Elizabeth Anne. B.S. magna cum laude, Canisius Coll., Buffalo, 1950, M.A., 1952; Ed.D., SUNY, Buffalo, 1961; grad., U.S. Army Command and Gen. Staff Coll., 1969, U.S. Army War Coll., 1975. Administrv. asst. Traveler's Ins. Co., Buffalo, N.Y., 1950-51; faculty Orchard Park (N.Y.) Sr. High Sch., 1957-66; dir. Ctr. Econ. Edn. SUNY, Buffalo, 1966-70; exec. dir. Edn. Council Niagara Falls (N.Y.) Area Industry, 1970-79; pres., chief exec. officer Nat. Assn. Industry-Edn. Cooperation, Buffalo, 1979—; pres. Consumer Credit Counseling Service, Buffalo, 1973, edn. chmn.; radio and TV public info. news commentator, 1962-78. Author: Meeting the Challenge of a Free Society, 1965; also handbooks, articles, guides; producer film on industry-edn. cooperation. Mem. Nat. Adv. Council on Ednl. Research and Improvement, 1988—. Served with Army N.G.; to col. USAR, 1948—. Recipient Kazanjian Found. teaching award, 1968, Freedoms Found. medal, 1965; Presdl. Citation for Pvt. Sector Initiatives, 1985; fellow NAM, 1965. Mem. Western N.Y. Export Council (assoc.), U.S. Dept. of Commerce, Active Corps Execs., U.S. Small Bus. Adminstrn., Am. Soc. Tng. and Devel., Res. Officers Assn., Phi Delta Kappa. Republican. Roman Catholic. Club: Buffalo Tennis, Amherst Dance (pres. 1987-88). Home: 235 Hendricks Blvd Amherst NY 14226

CLARK, EARNEST HUBERT, JR., tool company executive; b. Birmingham, Ala., Sept. 8, 1926; s. Earnest Hubert and Grace May (Smith) C.; m. Patricia Margaret Hamilton, June 22, 1947; children: Stephen D., Kenneth A., Timothy R., Daniel S., Scott H., Rebecca G. BS in Mech. Engring, Calif. Inst. Tech., 1946, MS, 1947. With Baker Hughes, Inc. (formerly Baker Oil Tools, Inc.), L.A., 1947-89, v.p., asst. gen. mgr., 1958-62, pres., chief exec. officer, 1962-69, 75-79, chmn. bd., 1969-75, 79-89, chief exec. officer, 1979-87, chmn. bd., 1987-89, ret., 1989; chmn., chief exec. officer The Friendship Group, New Port Beach, Calif., 1989—; bd. dirs. CBI Industries, Inc., Honeywell Inc., Am. Petroleum Inst., Kerr-McGee Corp., Beckman Instruments Inc.; mem. Nat. Petroleum Coun. Bd. dirs. YMCA of U.S.A., YMCA for Met. L.A.; mem. nat. coun. YMCA; chmn. bd. trustees Harvey Mudd Coll. With USNR, 1944-46, 51-52. Mem. Am. Inst. M.E., Am. Petroleum Inst. (bd. dirs.), Petroleum Equipment Suppliers Assn. (bd. dirs.), Calif. C. of C. (mem. exec. com.), Tau Beta Pi. Office: Friends Group Newport W Tower #3000 5000 Birch St Newport Beach CA 92660

CLARK, EDGAR SANDERFORD, insurance broker, consultant; b. N.Y.C., Nov. 17, 1933; s. Edgar Edmund, Jr., and Katharine Lee (Jarman) C.; student U. Pa., 1952-54; B.S., Georgetown U., 1956, J.D., 1958; post-grad. INSEAD, Fountainbleau, France, 1969, Golden Gate Coll., 1973, U. Calif., Berkeley, 1974; m. Nancy E. Hill, Sept. 13, 1975; 1 dau., Schuyler; children by previous marriages—Colin, Alexandra, Pamela. Staff asst. U.S. Senate select com. to investigate improper activities in labor and mgmt. field, Washington, 1958-59; underwriter Ocean Marine Dept., Fireman's Fund Ins. Co., San Francisco, 1959-62; mgr. Am. Fgn. Ins. Assn., San Francisco, 1962-66; with Marsh & McLennan, 1966-72, mgr. for Europe, resident dir. Brussels, Belgium, 1966-70, asst. v.p., mgr. captive and internat. div., San Francisco, 1970-72; v.p., dir. Risk Planning Group, Inc., San Francisco, 1972-75; v.p. Alexander & Alexander Inc., San Francisco, 1975—; lectr. profl. orgns.; guest lectr. U. Calif., Berkeley, 1973, Am. Grad. Sch. Internat. Mgmt., 1981, 82. Served with USAF, 1956-58. Mem. Am. Mgmt. Assn., Am. Risk and Ins. Assn., Chartered Ins. Inst., Am. Soc. Internat. Law, Pub. Risk & Ins. Mgmt. Assn., Nat. League of Cities, Nat. Inst. Mcpl. Law Officers, Govt. Fin. Officers Assn., Internat. City Mgrs. Assn. Episcopalian. Clubs: Meadow (Fairfax, Calif.); World Trade (San Francisco). Editorial adv. bd. Risk Mgmt. Reports, 1973-76. Home: 72 Millay Pl Mill Valley CA 94941 Office: Alexander & Alexander Inc Ste 1280 Two Embarcadero Ctr San Francisco CA 94111

CLARK, EMORY EUGENE, financial planning executive; b. Opelika, Ala., Jan. 24, 1931; s. Bunk Henry and Dorothy (Bolt) C.; m. Jean F. Reed, Sept. 30, 1951; children— Steven E., Michale E. grad. pub. schs. CLU, Cert. fin. planner. With Mgrs. Life Ins. Co., 1956-74, agt. supr., Los Angeles, 1956-60, mgr. Hawaii br., 1960-65, Pitts. br., 1965-68, Houston br., 1968-74; with Jefferson Standard Life Ins. Co., Fort Worth, 1974-82; fin. planner E.F. Hutton & Co., Inc., 1983—. Served with AUS, 1950-56. Mem. Fort Worth Life Underwriters Assn., Am. Soc. Life Underwriters, Fort Worth Soc. Life Underwriters, Ft. Worth Securities Dealers Assn., Inst. Cert. Fin. Planners. Home: 8109 Meadowbrook Dr Fort Worth TX 76112 Office: 1320 S University Dr Ste 1000 Fort Worth TX 76107

CLARK, E(UGENE) ROGER, manufacturing executive; b. New Rochelle, N.Y., Jan. 10, 1947; s. Eugene A. and Beatrice T. (Ulsheimer) C.; m. Deborah E. Rohloff, Sept. 2, 1972; children: Christen E., Colin R. BSBA in mktg., Xavier U., 1969; MBA in Internat. Bus., George Washington U., 1972. Systems analyst Pfizer, N.Y.C., 1972-73; mktg. mgr. Avon Products, Inc., N.Y.C., 1973-79; from mktg. mgr. to pres. Kanthal Corp., Bethel Conn., 1979—; bd. dirs. Gateway Bank, Norwalk, Conn., U. Found. West Conn. Inc., Danbury, Conn. Served to 1st lt. U.S. Army, 1969-71. Mem. Danbury C. of C., W. Conn. 100 Soc., Washington Soc. Republican. Episcopalian. Office: The Kanthal Corp 119 Wooster St Bethel CT 06801

CLARK, FRED, legal writer, editor; b. Limón, Costa Rica, Dec. 12, 1930; came to U.S., 1968; s. Thomas and Irene (Penney) C.; m. Dorothy Hyacinth James, Aug. 4, 1956; children: Paul, Fred Jr., Lydia Ramona. Student Central Am. Acad., 1944-49; BLitt, U. Costa Rica, 1951; postgrad. Stafford Coll., 1956-57; barrister-at-law, Inner Temple, London, 1960. Bar: Eng., 1960, Jamaica, 1960; cert. in law Council Legal Edn. Master of langs. Merl Grove Sch., 1951-55; trust officer Govt. of Jamaica, 1960-61; individual practice law, Kingston, Jamaica, 1961-67; legal editor Corp. Trust Co., N.Y.C., 1968-69; sr. legal editor Prentice-Hall, Inc., Englewood Cliffs, N.J., 1969—; cons. commonwealth law. Editor: The Corp. Jour., 1968-69. Trustee, United Ch. of Christ, 1970-78; spl. adviser U.S. Congl. Adv. Bd.; mem. nat. adv. bd. Am. Security Council. Recipient Disting. Leadership award, 1984, Presdl. medal of Merit, 1986. Mem. Am. Mgmt. Assn., Internat. Platform Assn., Internat. Commn. Jurists, Am. Mus. Natural History, Nat. Geog. Soc., AAAS, N.Y. Acad. Scis., Am. Ballet Theatre, Met. Opera Guild, U.S. Naval Inst., Freeport Bus. Promotion (bd. dirs.), U.S. Power Squadron (asst. sec.), Inter-Am. Soc. Lodge: Rosicrucians. Home: 39 W 4th St Freeport NY 11520 Office: Prentice-Hall Inc Sylvan Ave Englewood Cliffs NJ 07632

CLARK, GEOFFREY, accountant; b. Blackpool, Eng., Feb. 2, 1946; came to U.S., 1946; s. Ernest and Lucy (Moss) C. AA, San Jacinto Coll., 1966; BBA, U. Houston, 1969. CPA, Tex. Pvt. practice acctg. Houston, 1970-74, 76-78, 80-82; acct. Weison & Kennedy, Houston, 1974-76, Alan D. Buck, Houston, 1978-80; assoc. Oscar Nipper & Co., Houston, 1982—. Judge Precinct 191, Pasadena, Tex., 1983—. Mem. Am. Inst. CPAs, Tex. Soc. CPA's (Houston chpt.), Nat. Conf. CPA Practitioners, Clear Lake Area Tax Forum, Univ. Houston Alumni Assn. Clubs: Plays and Players (Houston) (asst. acting chmn. 1983-87), The Forum. Lodges: Rotary (treas. Gulfway-Hobby Airport chpt. 1987—), Shriners, Woodmen of World (Am. Hist. award 1960). Home: 421 Brown Dr Pasadena TX 77506 Office: Oscar Nipper & Co 7654 Park Pl Houston TX 77087

CLARK, GERALD STUART, sales executive; b. Kansas City, Mo., July 10, 1956; s. Robert Stuart and Geraldine (McGee) C.; m. Glenda M. Norman, July 3, 1981; children: Melissa Butler, Justin. BS, SW Mo. State U., 1978; MA, Webster U., 1988. With Sunshine Racquet Club, Springfield, Mo., 1978-79, Pennzoil Products Co., Kansas City, Kans., 1979-82; sales rep. Pennzoil Products Co., Kansas City, 1982—. Recipient scholarship Sigma Tau Gamma, 1977, 78, athletic award, 1976. Mem. Mo. Tile Dealers Assn. Republican. Office: Pennzoil Products Co 2530 Bayard St Kansas City KS 66105

CLARK, HERBERT TRYON, JR., banker; b. Glastonbury, Conn., Jan. 7, 1913; s. Herbert Tryon and Alice (House) C.; B.S., U. Conn., 1934; m. Barbara Richmond, Aug. 1, 1936 (dec. June 10, 1980); children—Herbert Tryon, LeRoy Richmond, Marjorie Ann; m. 2d, Ruth Whitney Knox, Apr. 4, 1981. Asst. foreman assembly Royal-McBee Typewriter Co., Hartford, Conn., 1934-41; asst. plant mgr. Buffalo Arms Corp., 1941-44; procurement mgr. Gen. Ry. Signal Co., Rochester, 1945; purchasing agt. Frontier Industries div., Houdaille, Ind., 1946-49; pres. Geo. C. Field Co., Madison, Conn., 1949-78, Tuxis Lumber, 1957-68; pres. First Fed. Savs. & Loan Assn., Madison, Conn., 1957-64, chmn. bd., 1964-75; pres. Wildwood Properties Inc., 1965-78; arbitrator Am. Arbitration Assn., 1976—; dir. Coginchaug Devel. Corp. (now Lyman Farms, Inc.), 1967-78. Mem. Bd. Finance Madison, 1959-65, sec., 1962-65. Active Boy Scouts Am.; mem. Municipal Bldg. Study Com., 1967-69. Mem. Theta Sigma Chi. Congregationalist. Mason (32 deg.). Club: Exchange. Home: 23 Maplewood Ln PO Box 489 Madison CT 06443 Office: Am Arbitration Assn 107 Bradley Rd Madison CT 06443

CLARK, HOWARD LONGSTRETH, JR., financial executive; b. N.Y.C., Feb. 1, 1944; s. Howard Longstreth and Elsie (Dancaster) C.; m. Sandra Little, Aug. 27, 1966; 1 child, Howard Longstreth III. BSBA, Boston U., 1967; MBA, Columbia U., 1968. Exec. v.p., chief fin. officer Am. Express Co., N.Y.C., 1981—; bd. dirs. Fireman's Fund Corp., Gen. Devel. Corp., The Maytag Co., Stamford Capital Group, Inc. Episcopalian. Clubs: River, Racquet and Tennis, Round Hill, Blind Brook, Links. Home: 1112 Park Ave New York NY 10028 Office: Am Express Co Am Express Tower World Fin Ctr New York NY 10285

CLARK, JACK, hospital company executive, accountant; b. Munford, Ala., Feb. 23, 1932; s. Raymond E. and Ora (Camp) C.; m. Louise Omega Lackey, Jan. 30, 1951; 1 son, Terry Wayne. B.S., Springhill Coll., Mobile, Ala., 1960. Staff acct. Max E. Miller, C.P.A., Mobile, 1960-62; comptroller Mobile Gen. Hosp., 1962-67; assoc. adminstr. fin. Univ. Med. Ctr., Mobile, 1967-74; regional mgr. Humana Inc., Mobile, 1974-75, v.p., 1975-80, sr. v.p., 1980-84, exec. v.p., 1984—; trustee Mid-South region Humana Hosps., 1974-87, trustee Southeastern region, 1987—. Bd. dirs. Agape of S. Ala., Mobile, 1983. Served in USAF, 1952-56, Korea. Mem. Hosp. Fin. Mgmt. Assn. (assoc.), Am. Hosp. Assn., Ala. Hosp. Assn., Ala. Hosp. Assn. Accts. (pres. so. council, dir. 1967-68), Mobile C. of C. Democrat. Mem. Ch. of Christ. Home: 6449 Canebrake Rd Mobile AL 36609 Office: Humana Inc 1565 Hillcrest Rd Mobile AL 36609

CLARK, JOHN EARL, realtor, consultant; b. Columbus, Ohio, June 19, 1951; s. Earl W. and Juanita (Wolford) C.; m. Donna M. Weimann, June 12, 1971; children: Carol, Andrea. AA, Columbus Tech., 1971; cert. Am. Inst. Banking, 1977, Ohio Sch. Consumer Credit, Kent State U., 1978, Ohio Sch. Banking, Ohio U., 1984. Br. asst. City Loan Co., Newark, Ohio, 1969-74; asst. mgr. Credithrift of Am., Lancaster, Ohio, 1974-75; mgr. br. office Group One Realty Inc., Lancaster, 1975—; comml. realtor Group One Realty, Lancaster, 1988—; freelance photographer, Lancaster, 1977-84; pres. J.E. Clark & Assocs., Inc., Lancaster, 1984—; ptnr. C & E Devel., Gameboard Gallery, Lancaster, 1984—; pres. Lancaster Deli, Inc. Cons. Jr. Achievement, Lancaster, 1979-83, bd. dirs. 1983-86, pres. 1985-86; mem. sales com. Fairfield County Jr. Fair Bd. Recipient Gold award United Way, Lancaster, 1977, Citation of Service, Am. Diabetes Assn., 1983. Mem. Nat. Assn. Realtors, Ohio Assn. Realtors, Lancaster Downtown Merchants Assn., Ohio Bus. Brokers Assn., Fairfield County C. of C., Buckeye Lake C. of C. Baptist. Lodge: Lions (pres. 1984-85). Avocations: photography, fishing, antique collecting. Home: 333 W Fair Ave Lancaster OH 43130 Office: Group One Realty Inc 123 S Broad St Ste 207 Lancaster OH 43130

CLARK, J(OSEPH) PATRICK, dental supply company executive, legal consultant; b. Lewistown, Pa., Apr. 27, 1941; s. John Howard and Frances Lucille (Monaghan) C.; m. Betty Louise Weaver, Oct. 15, 1965 (div. Nov. 1972); 1 child, Joseph P.; m. Linda Elaine Dennis, Aug. 17, 1973; children:

Lisa A., Elizabeth. BBA in Acctg., Lehigh U., 1963; LLB, U. Md., 1967. Bar: Md. 1963, Pa. 1967. Asst. tax and ins. mgr. McCormick & Co., Inc., Balt., 1963-65, asst. treas., 1965-66; assoc. Wogan, Elsesser & Yost, York, Pa., 1967-71; asst. counsel Dentsply Internat. Inc., York, 1971-76, counsel, 1977-81, assoc. counsel, asst. sec., 1981-86, gen. counsel, sec., 1986—. Bd. dirs. ARC, York, 1970-73, Community Progress Coun., York, 1970-73, Am. Cancer Soc., York, 1974-79; pres. York County Blind Ctr., 1987. Mem. ABA, Pa. Bar Assn., York County bar Assn., Am. Corp. counsel Assn., Am. Soc. Corp. Secs., Outdoor Country Club. Democrat. Office: Dentsply Internat Inc 570 W College Ave York PA 17405

CLARK, KEITH ALLEN, lawyer, consultant; b. Reading, Pa., Sept. 18, 1945; s. Donald Earl and Betty Jane (Geiger) C.; child from previous marriage, Leah Marie. BA, Rutgers U., 1967; JD, Dickinson Sch. Law, 1970. Bar: Pa. 1970. Assoc. Shumaker, Williams & Placey, Harrisburg, 1970-72; pres. Shumaker William, P.C., Harrisburg, 1972—; solicitor Borough of Marysville, Pa., 1976-82, Indsl. Devel. Authority Cen. Pa., Harrisburg, 1979—; bd. dirs., past pres. Capital Region Devel. Corp., Camp Hill, Pa. Chmn. Tri-County Regional Planning Commn., Harrisburg, 1980-81, Perry County Planning Commn., Pa., 1976-81; organizational dir. West Shore Advanced Life Support Svcs., Camp Hill, 1985; mem. adv. com. Dauphin County Citizens Adv. Bd., Harrisburg, 1988—; past sec. com. Gen. Osteo Hosp. Found., Harrisburg; mem. exec. bd. Keystone area counc. Boy Scouts Am., Harrisburg, 1988—; mem. Adv. bd. Pa. State U., Harrisburg, 1988—. 1st lt. USAF, 1971-72. Recipient Comdr.'s award New Cumberland (Pa.) Army Depot, 1987. Mem. ABA, Pa. Bar Assn., Am. Arbitration Assn., Greater West Shore C. of C. (pres. 1985-86), Estate Planning Counc. Cen. Pa. (pres. 1983-84), Lions (v.p. Marysville club 1979-80). Republican. Office: Shumaker Williams PC PO Box 88 Harrisburg PA 17108

CLARK, KEVIN CRONIN, healthcare personnel executive; b. Redbank, N.J., June 21, 1960; s. Milton J. and Vera (Burnham) C.; m. Michelle Ferlise, Mar. 16, 1985; 1 child, Katheryn Anne. AA, U. Fla., 1980; BBA, Fla. Atlantic U., 1982. Account exec. E.F. Hutton, Inc., Ft. Lauderdale, Fla., 1983-84; v.p. Dean Witter, Reynolds, Inc., Ft. Lauderdale, 1984-86; co-chief exec. officer, v.p., chmn. bd. Cross Country Nurses, Inc., Boca Raton, Fla., 1986—; co-chief exec. officer, v.p., chmn. bd. Cross Country Therapists, Croos Country Tech.; cons. Jr. Achievement Fla.; co-chief exec. office, pres. Cross Country Healthcare Personnel. Active Young Reps. Club. Mem. Boca Raton Men's Rep. Club, Fla. Atlantic U. Pres.'s Club (found. mem.), Town Swim and Racquet Club. Roman Catholic. Office: Cross Country Healthcare Personnel Inc 1515 S Federal Hwy Ste 210 Boca Raton FL 33432

CLARK, LEONARD HANLEY, public relations and advertising executive; b. Buffalo, Aug. 23, 1921; s. Irving Elisha and Elizabeth (Hanley) C.; m. Elizabeth Evelyn Hughes, Sept. 6, 1947; children: Darcy Clark Bens, Elizabeth Lloyd. BS, Syracuse U., 1943. Cert. bus. communicator. Div. product line mgr. SPS Techs., Jenkintown, Pa., 1966-70, div. mktg. mgr., 1970-78, mgr. corp. advt. and pub. relations, 1978—. Served to lt. (j.g.) USN, 1943-46, PTO. Mem. Am. Mktg. Assn., Pub. Relations Soc. Am., Bus. Profl. Advt. Assn., Am. Soc. Metals, Nat. Investor Relations Inst. Republican. Episcopalian. Clubs: Mfrs. Golf and Country (Oreland, Pa.); Bachelors Barge (Phila.); Penllyn (Pa.). Home: 12 Bromley Dr Blue Bell PA 19422 Office: SPS Techs Corp Offices Newtown PA 18940

CLARK, LEONARD RAY, JR., lawyer; b. Jackson, Miss., Jan. 11, 1952; s. Leonard Ray and Marie (Glover) C.; m. Berry Stevens Lauderdale, Aug. 14, 1974; 1 child, Leonard Ray III. BS, U. Miss., 1975, JD, 1980; LLM in Taxation, U. Fla., 1981. Bar: Miss. 1980, U.S. Tax Ct. 1980. Law clk. Dossett Magruder & Montgomery, Jackson, 1980; assoc. Wise Carter Child & Caraway, Jackson, 1981-82; assoc. Magruder Montgomery Brocato, Jackson, 1982-86, ptnr., 1987; ptnr. Heidelberg Woodliff & Franks, Jackson, 1988—. Mng. editor Miss. Law Jour., 1979-80. Mem. ABA, Miss. Bar Assn., Fed. Bar Assn., U. Miss. Alumni Assn., Ole Miss. Assocs., Law Jour. Assn., Rebel Club, Jackson Country Club. Republican. Episcopalian. Office: Heidelberg Woodliff & Franks 125 S Congress St Ste 1400 Jackson MS 39201 also: PO Box 23040 Jackson MS 39225

CLARK, LOUIS MORRIS, JR., investment broker; b. Rochester, N.Y., Feb. 22, 1931; s. Louis Morris Sr. and Hazel Gertrude (Rudman) C.; m. Joan Alexandra Fenton, April 26, 1974; children: Elizabeth Johnston Kinglsey, Leisa Fenton Clark. BS, U. Rochester, N.Y., 1958. Sales engr. Comm. Controls Corp., Rochester, N.Y., 1958-60; br. mgr. Home Fed. Savs. and Loan, Canandaugua, N.Y., 1960-64; acct. exec. Frncis I. DuPont and Co., Rochester, 1964-76; fin. mgmt. advisor E.F. Hutton and Co., Rochester, 1976-78; assoc. v.p. Dean Witter Reynolds, Rochester, 1978-81; v.p. Tucker, Anthony and R.L. Day, Rochester, 1981-87; br. mgr. Sage, Rutty, and Co., Canandaugua, 1987—; owner Acorn Antiques; v.p., treas. Grovetown, Inc., 1966-70; v.p. Grove Place Assn., 1966-70; pres. Canandaugua Properties Corp., 1962-64. regular contbr. to The Upstate Bus. Jour. Patron Wood Library Assn., Granger Homestead Soc., F.F. Thompson Hosp. Guild, Ont. County Hist. Soc.; trustee Canandahgua Lake Pure Waters, Ltd., Ontario County Hist. Soc., and treas.; sec. Sonnenberg Gardens, also trustee; adv. bd. Salvation Army, Canadaigua, N.Y., ptnr. The Acorn. Served with U.S. Army, 1951-53, Korea. Republican. Episcopalian. Club: University (dir. 1968-72). Lodges: Masonic (trustee 1955-58), Elks (trustee 1961-63), Kiwanis (dir. 1961-64). Home: 4508 Bristol Valley Rd PO Box 1019 Canandaigua NY 14424 Office: Sage Rutty and Co 17 Chapin St PO Box 353 Canandaigua NY 14424

CLARK, L(UTHER) JOHN, consumer and industrial products retail and distribution executive; b. Eustis, Fla., Aug. 27, 1941; s. Eno Treverton and Opal (Johnson) C.; m. Judith Anne Dooley, Nov. 13, 1965; children: Sandra Faraday, James Treverton. BS in Econs. and Fin., U. Pa., 1963, MBA in Mktg. and Fin., 1968. Various positions The Singer Co., N.Y.C., 1968-78; v.p. The Singer Co., Stamford, Conn., 1978-81; v.p., pres. Europe, Africa, and Middle East The Singer Co., London, 1982-85; exec. v.p. VF Corp., Wyomissing, Pa., 1986-87; pres., chief operating officer Transnat. Capital Ventures Inc., 1988; pres., chief exec. officer Core-Mark Internat. Inc., 1988—; bd. dirs. Yale and Nutone Inc., Transnat. Capital Inc., Leath Furniture Inc., Coremark Internat. Inc. Bd. dirs. The Reformed Ch., Bronxville, N.Y., 1975—. Served to capt. USMC, 1963-66, Okinawa. Republican. Clubs: Annabel's (London); Bronxville Field; Lawrence Beach (N.Y.). Home: 22 Greenfield Ave Bronxville NY 10708

CLARK, MALCOLM DOWDLES, manufacturing company executive; b. Glasgow, Scotland, May 1, 1940; came to U.S. 1986; s. Joseph and Margaret (McFadyen) C.; m. Pamela Rugless, Dec. 18, 1965; children: Karen, Colin Joseph. Cert., Instn. Mech. Engrs., Glasgow, 1959; higher cert., Stow Coll. Engring., Glasgow, 1960. Design engr. Ford Motor Co., London, 1961-64; project engr., chief design engr. Ramcon div. of Hills McCanna, Chgo., 1964-68; dir. prodn. engring. Raymond Control Systems, St. Charles, Ill., 1968-71; gen. mgr. Ketstone Valve U.K. Ltd., Glasgow, 1971-74, mng. dir., 1974-85; pres., chief operating officer Keystone Internat. Inc., Houston, 1985—. Patentee in field. Mem. British Am. Bus. Assn. Office: Keystone Internat Inc 9600 W Gulf Bank Dr Houston TX 77040

CLARK, MARY JANE, mortgage company executive; b. Washington, Sept. 2, 1948; d. William Joseph and Virginia Rae (Whipp) Fearson; m. Ted Bonanno, Jan. 31, 1971 (div. Sept. 1, 1983); m. John Edmund Clark, Nov. 16, 1983; children: Angelina, Nino, Ashley. Grad. high sch., Rockville, Md. Loan rep. Wells Fargo Credit Corp., Silver Spring, Md., 1983-84; closing dept. supr. Weaver Bros., Inc., Chevy Chase, Md., 1984-87; office mgr. GMAC Mortgage Corp., Rockville, 1987—. Mem. Mortgage Bankers Assn., Inc. Democrat. Roman Catholic. Home: 10 Hibiscus Ct Gaithersburg MD 20878 Office: GMAC Mortgage Corp 7505 Standish Pl Rockville MD 20855

CLARK, MAXINE, retail executive; b. Miami, Fla., Mar. 6, 1949; d. Kenneth and Anne (Lerch) Kasselman; m. Robert Fox, Sept. 1984. B.A. in Journalism, U. Ga., 1971. Exec. trainee Hecht Co., Washington, 1971, hosiery buyer, 1971-72, misses sportswear buyer, 1972-76; mgr. mdse. planning and research May Dept. Stores Co., St. Louis, 1976-78, dir. mdse. devel., 1978-80, v.p. mktg. and sales promotion Venture Stores div., 1980-81, sr. v.p. mktg. and sales promotion Venture Stores div., 1981-83, exec. v.p. mktg. and softlines, 1983-85; exec. v.p. apparel Famous-Barr, St. Louis, 1985-86; v.p. mdsing. Lerner Shops div. Limited Inc., N.Y.C., 1986-88; exec. v.p. Venture Stores, St. Louis, 1988—. Sec., Lafayette Sq. Restoration Com., 1978-79. Mem. NAFE, St. Louis Women's Commerce Assn., Advt. Club Greater St. Louis, St. Louis Forum.

CLARK, MAXINE MARJORIE, real estate executive, small business owner; b. Southwest Harbor, Maine, Feb. 20, 1924; d. Leverett Sherman and Albra Marion (Staples) Stanley; m. John O. Clark Sr., May 6, 1955 (div. June 1983); children: Gary, Margery, Paul John O. Jr. Cert. real estate broker mgr., residential specialist. Owner Maxine M. Clark, Real Estate, Southwest Harbor, 1971—; owner, mgr. Island Watch Bed and Breakfast, Southwest Harbor, 1988—. Mem. warrent com. Town of Southwest Harbor, 1980-82, planning bd., 1983-84; bd. dirs. Harbor House Youth Ctr., Southwest Harbor, 1973-75. Mem. Nat. Assn. Realtors, Hancock Washington Bd. Realtors (pres. 1985), Nat. Mktg. Inst., Nat. Assn. Real Estate Appraisers (cert.). Republican. Club: Millay Study (Bass Harbor, Maine) (pres. 1954). Lodge: Order of Eastern Star (Grand Ruth). Office: Rte 102 Southwest Harbor ME 04679

CLARK, PAUL ALAN, accountant; b. Ft. Wayne, Ind., Nov. 15, 1943; s. Harold L. and C. Ruth (Kantzer) C.; m. Patricia L. Martin, Sept. 13, 1980. BS, Ind. U., 1967, postgrad., 1967-68. CPA, Ohio, Ind. Staff acct. Arthur Young & Co., Toledo, 1969-74; ptnr. Chastain, Due & Thomas, CPA's, Anderson, Ind., 1974-81; prin. Paul A. Clark, CPA, Anderson, 1981—. Bd. dirs. March of Dimes, 1975-76; treas. House of Hope, 1986-87. Mem. Am. Inst. CPA's, Ind. CPA Soc., Ohio Soc. CPA's, Ind. U. Alumni Assn. (life), Ind. Tax Practioners Assn., Evans Scholars Alumni, Nat. Rifle Assn. (life, cert. instr.), Alpha Kappa Psi. Lodges: Lions (local pres. 1985-86, dep. dist. gov. 1988-89), Elks. Office: 2527 E 10th St Anderson IN 46012

CLARK, PAUL NEWTON, pharmaceutical company executive; b. Fremont, Ohio, Jan. 3, 1947; s. Paul W. and Catherine (Newton) C.; m. Carolyn Champion, Sept. 4, 1971; children: Lindsay Noelle, Ashley Christine. BS in Fin., U. Ala., Tuscaloosa, 1969; MBA, Dartmouth Coll., 1971. Regional sales mgr. Sandoz Inc., Denver, 1979-80; asst. to the dir. CIA, Langley, Va., 1979-80; dir. mktg. Dorsey Labs. subs. Sandoz Inc., Lincoln, Nebr., 1980-81; exec. dir. mktg. pharm. div. Sandoz, Inc., East Hanover, N.J., 1981-83; v.p. mktg. and sales pharm. div. Marion Labs, Kansas City, Mo., 1984-85; exec. v.p. pharm. div. Abbott Labs, North Chicago, Ill., 1984-85, pres. pharm. div., 1985—; bd. dirs., vice-chmn. Nat. Pharm. Coun., Reston, Va. Bd. dirs. Am. Found. Pharm. Edn., N.Y.C., 1986—. 1st lt. U.S. Army, 1972. Republican. Presbyterian. Home: 555 Douglas Dr Lake Forest IL 60045 Office: Abbott Labs 1 Abbott Park Rd Abbott Park IL 60064

CLARK, PHYLLIS RHODA, financial executive; b. Montreal, Que., Can., Apr. 21, 1955; came to U.S., 1974; d. Hyman and Lily (Brustein) Borts; m. Craig N. Clark, Oct. 18, 1974; 1 child, Adam. BS, Drake U., 1978. Cost analyst Ruan Leasing Co., Des Moines, 1979, fin. analyst, 1980, sr. analyst, 1981, asst. dir. fin. analysis and planning, 1982; dir. fin. planning Heritage Communications Co., Des Moines, 1982-85, asst. treas., 1985-87, v.p. and treas., 1987—. Mem. Com. Golden Circle Devel. Corp., Des Moines, 1986—. Clubs: Consortium, Women's Breakfast. Office: Heritage Communications Inc 2195 Ingersoll Ave Des Moines IA 50312

CLARK, RICHARD J(AMES), electronics company executive; b. Cortland, N.Y., June 10, 1925; s. Elwyn Emmet and Marjorie Aileen (Snow) C.; m. Anita Frances Rutherford, Aug. 30, 1947; children: Sharon Lynne Clark Groff, Richard James Jr. BEE, Syracuse U., 1950. Engr. Gen. Electric Co., Syracuse, N.Y., 1950-61, sr. engr., 1961-70, cons. engr., 1970-82, mgr. design rev., 1982-88; pres. Integrated Tech. Svcs., Syracuse, 1988—; lectr. in field. Author: Handbook of Thick Film Technology, 1975; contbr. articles to profl. publs.; patentee optical device. With USN, 1943-46, PTO. Mem. Internat. Electronics Packaging Soc. (founder 1977, recipient numerous awards), IEEE, Internat. Electronics Packaging Soc. Baptist. Home: 106 David Dr North Syracuse NY 13212

CLARK, RICHARD LEFORS, systems research scientist; b. Aberdeen, S.D., Oct. 29, 1936; s. Robert Montgomery and Marion (Shook) C.; m. Barbara Louise Battersby, Mar. 28, 1980; 1 child, Robert James. BA, Pacific Western U., 1974, MS, 1975, PhD, 1978; BS in Engring. and Applied Sci., Jackson State Coll., 1968, MA in Bus. Mgmt., 1972. Technician Honeywell Co., 1957-58; quality assurance Martin Co., 1958-59, Remington Rand, 1959; engr. Gen. Dynamics/Electronics, 1959-68; supr. Graco, Inc., 1971-74; with Internat. Harvester, 1975-81, Caterpiller Tractor Co., 1981—, Solar Turbines subs. Caterpiller Tractor Co.; systems research in fusion power, parapsychology and physics, over unity elec. generators, archeol. research and gravity research, San Diego, 1975—; lectr. gravity/Maxwell-Faraday physics systems and devices. Inventor vortex fusion engine; author tech. papers. Served with U.S. Army, 1954-57.

CLARK, ROBERT HENRY, JR., holding company executive; b. Manchester, N.H., Mar. 4, 1941; s. Robert Henry and Elva C. (Stearns) C.; m. Rosalie Foster Case, Dec. 21, 1963; children: Robert Henry III, Hilary Eagan, Hadley Case. B.S. in Bus. Adminstrn., Boston U., 1964. Mcpl. bond underwriter Merrill Lynch, Pierce, Fenner & Smith, N.Y.C., 1964-70; v.p. Case, Pomeroy & Co., Inc., N.Y.C., 1971-75, exec. v.p., 1975-83; pres. Case, Pomeroy & Co., Inc., 1983—, also dir.; v.p. fin. Felmont Oil Corp., 1972-79, exec. v.p., 1979-84; bd. dirs. Essex Offshore, Inc., Homestake Mining Co., Itran Corp., Putnam Trust Co., Greenwich, Conn. Trustee Boston U., 1984-87. Mem. Sigma Alpha Epsilon. Clubs: Downtown Assn.; University (N.Y.C.); Leash; Bald Peak Colony (Melvin Village, N.H.); Round Hill; Bankers (San Francisco). Office: Case Pomeroy & Co Inc 529 Fifth Ave New York NY 10017

CLARK, RONALD MICHAEL, investment executive; b. Beaver Dam, Wis., July 8, 1947; s. John Lawrence and Velma Grace (Stienbach) C.; m. Ann Marie Holzen, Oct. 12, 1974; 1 child, Julie. BSIE, U. Wis., 1970, MBA, 1972. Chief investment officer North Am. Life & Casualty Co., Mpls., 1972-80; sr. v.p. Allianz Investment Corp., Dallas, 1980-83, pres., 1984—; bd. dirs. Allianz Investment Corp., Allianz Real Estate, Allianz of Am. Corp., Minn. Valley Bank, Mpls., Minn. Racetrack Inc., Mpls. Program chmn. United Way, Mpls., 1978. Mem. Mortgage Bankers Assn. Am., Nat. Assn. Rev. Appraisers, Phi Beta Sigma, Pi Tau Sigma. Roman Catholic. Office: Allianz Investment Corp 2323 Bryan St Ste 1890 Dallas TX 75201

CLARK, R(UFUS) BRADBURY, lawyer; b. Des Moines, May 11, 1924; s. Rufus Bradbury and Gertrude Martha (Burns) C.; m. Polly Ann King, Sept. 6, 1949; children: Cynthia Clark Maxwell, Rufus Bradbury, John Atherton. BA, Harvard U., 1948, JD, 1951; diploma in law, Oxford U., Eng., 1952; D.H.L., Ch. Div. Sch. Pacific, San Francisco, 1983. Bar: Calif. Assoc. O'Melveny & Myers, L.A., 1952-62, sr. ptnr., 1961—, mem. mgmt. com., 1983-89; bd. dirs. So. Calif. Water Co., Econ. Resources Corp., Brown Internat. Corp., Automatic Machinery & Electronics Corp., John Tracy Clinic, also pres. 1982-88. Editor: California Corporation Laws, 6 vols, 1976—. Chancellor Prot. Episcopal Ch. in the Diocese of L.A., 1967—, hon. canon, 1983—. Capt. U.S. Army, 1943-46. Decorated Bronze star with oak leaf cluster, Purple Heart with oak leaf cluster; Fulbright grantee, 1952. Mem. ABA (subcom. on audit letter responses, com. on law and acctg., task force on legal opinions), State Bar Calif. (chmn. drafting com. on gen. corp. law 1973-81, chmn. drafting com. on nonprofit corp. law 1980-84, mem. exec. com. bus. law sect., 1977-78, 84-87, sec. 1986-87), L.A. County Bar Assn., Calif. Club (L.A.), Harvard Club (L.A.), Chancery Club (L.A.), Alamitos Bay Yacht Club (Long Beach). Republican. Office: O'Melveny & Myers 400 S Hope St Los Angeles CA 90071-2899

CLARK, SANDRA MARIE, elementary school administrator; b. Hanover, Pa., Feb. 17, 1942; d. Charles Raymond Clark and Mary Josephine (Snyder) Clark Wierman. BS in Elem. Edn., Chestnut Hill Coll., 1980; MS in Child Care Adminstrn., Nova U., 1985. Cert. elem. tchr., Pa. Tchr. various elem. schs., Pa., 1962-75; asst. vocation directress Mt. St. Joseph Motherhouse, Chestnut Hill, Pa., 1975-76; tchr. St. Catharine's Sch., Spring Lake, N.J., 1976-77; asst. mgr. Jim's Truck Stop, New Oxford, Pa., 1977-81; adminstr. Little People Day Care Sch., Hanover, 1981-88, sec., treas. bd. dirs., 1985-86; coord. regional resource Magic Yrs. Child Care & Learning Ctrs., Inc., Hanover, 1987-88; prin. St. Vincent De Paul Sch., Hanover, Pa., 1988—; presenter Hanover Area Seminar for Day Care Employees, 1983-86. coord. sch. safety patrols St. Vincent's Sch., Hanover, 1969-75, vice-chmn. bd., 1982-84; multi-media instr. first aid ARC, Hanover, 1983-86, bd. dirs., 1984-88; exec. sec. of bd. of dirs. ARC, Hanover, 1988; 1st v.p. Hanover Area Coun. of Chs., 1988, pres., 1989; validator accredidation program Nat. Acad. Early Childhood Programs, Washington, 1987—; bd. dirs. Life Skills Unltd. Handicapped Adults, 1988—; facilitator Harrisburg Diocesan Synod, Hanover, 1985-88, parish del., 1988. Pa. Dept. Pub. Welfare tng. grantee, 1986. Mem. NAFE, Nat. Cath. Ednl. Assn. Democrat. Roman Catholic. Club: Internat. Assn. Turtles (London). Home: 348 Barberry Dr Hanover PA 17331 Office: Saint Vincent De Paul Sch Hanover PA 17331

CLARK, SARA JANE, accounting company executive; b. South Bend, Ind., Aug. 28, 1948; d. Robert F. and Maxine (Walker) Bennett; m. William H. Clark, Oct. 2, 1976; 1 child, Kristen Marie. Adminstrv. asst. Doherty Zable & Co., Chgo., 1975-77; gen. ptnr. Bennett Clark Co., Valparaiso, Ind., 1977—; mem. LaSalle St. Cashiers, Chgo., 1979-85, 87-88, outing com. chmn., 1982, correspondence com. chmn., 1987-88. Mem. Am. Soc. Profl. Women, Am. Inst. Profl. Bookkeepers, Nat. Assn. Female Execs. Republican. Presbyterian. Avocations: reading, traveling, needlework.

CLARK, THOMAS BRADBURY, brokerage executive; b. Dayton, Ohio, Dec. 20, 1954; s. William Bradbury and Clara Simrall (Lane) C.; m. Victoria Elizabeth Koehler, June 1, 1985. BA in Econs., Coll. of Wooster, 1980. Account exec. Dean Witter Reynolds, Greenwich, Conn., 1980-82; account exec. Merrill Lynch, Stamford, Conn., 1982-85, fin. cons., 1985, sr. fin. cons., 1986-87, asst. v.p., 1987-88, v.p. consumer markets, 1988—; mem. Pres.' Club, 1984-85, Merrill Lynch Execs. Club, 1983, Chmn.'s Club, 1988. Alumni rep. Sea Edn. Assn., Woods Hole, Mass., 1980—. Win Smith fellow, Merrill Lynch, 1985. Republican. Presbyterian. Clubs: Landmark (Stamford) (career rep. 1985—), Indian Harbor Yacht (Greenwich) (bd. dirs. 1985-86, fleet cpt. 1988—). Home: 2 Jofran Ln Greenwich CT 06830 Office: Merrill Lynch 5 Landmark Sq Stamford CT 06901

CLARK, WILLIAM JAMES, insurance company executive; b. Kansas City, Mo., Oct. 1, 1923; s. William LeRoy and Margaret (Theobald) C.; children: Holly Clark Perkins, Jane , Nancy Clark Mundel, Patricia Clark Midura; m. Elizabeth A. Smith, May 1, 1984. Student, Kansas City Jr. Coll., 1941-42; BS, U. Mo., 1947. With Mass. Mut. Life Ins. Co., Springfield, 1947—, v.p. sales, 1967-70, sr. v.p., 1971-74, pres., 1974-86, chief exec. officer, 1980-88, also chmn. bd. dirs.; dir. Bank of Boston, Bank of Boston Corp. Bd. dirs. Springfield Coll.; trustee Clarke Sch. for Deaf. Served to 1st lt. USAAF, 1943-45. Clubs: Longmeadow (Mass.) Country; Colony (Springfield). Home: 101 Woodsley Rd Longmeadow MA 01106 Office: Mass Mut Life Ins Co 1295 State St Springfield MA 01111

CLARK, WILLIAM KALAR, manufacturing company executive; b. Prairie Lee, Tex., Feb. 7, 1921; s. Archibald Fletcher and Bird Ella (Shanklin) C. BBA, U. Tex., Austin, 1942; MBA, Stanford U., 1948. Sales rep. Uvalde Rock Asphalt Co., San Antonio, 1948-52, sales mgr. Azrock div., 1952-59, v.p. sales, dir., 1959-67, exec. v.p., dir., 1967-74, pres., bd. chmn. (name changed to Azrock Industries, Inc.), 1974-86, chmn., chief executive officer, 1986—; dir. North Frost Bank, San Antonio, 1982—. Served to lt. comdr. USNR, 1942-48. Named to Hall of Fame Western Floors mag., 1960. Mem. Resilient Floor Covering Inst. (pres. 1968-70, dir. 1967—), Nat. Home Fashions League Found. (bd. chmn. 1977-80), Internat. Furnishings & Design Assn. Found. (dir. 1988—), Phi Gamma Delta, The Argyle Club (bd. govs., 1982-84), The German Club, Order of the Alamo, Tex. Cavaliers. Home: 4001 N New Braunfels #1404 San Antonio TX 78209 Office: Azrock Industries Inc PO Box 34030 San Antonio TX 78265

CLARK, WORLEY H., JR., specialty chemical company executive; b. Big Stone Gap, Va., June 18, 1932; s. Worley H. and Grace Ethel (Bledsoe) C.; m. Callie Anne Coughlin, Aug. 20, 1955; children: Caryl Smith, Cindy Clark. B.S. in Indsl. Engring., N.C. State U., 1956; student, Northwestern U.; postgrad., Cleve.-Marshall Law Sch.; grad. exec. program, Stanford U. Sales engr. Standard Oil Ohio, 1956-60; dist. rep. indsl. div. Nalco Chem. Co., Houston, 1960-64, area mgr., 1964-67; dist. mgr. Wis. dist. Nalco Chem. Co., 1967-68, dist. mgr. Mich. dist., 1968-71, sales mgr. water treatment chems. group, 1971-74, gen. mgr. water treatment chems. group, 1974-78, group v.p., pres. indsl. div., 1978-80, dir., 1980—, exec. v.p., 1982, pres., chief exec. officer, 1982—, chmn. bd., 1984—; dir. Chgo. Northwestern Transp. Co., No. Trust Corp., USG Corp. Governing bd. Ill. Coun. Econ. Edn.; mem. Northwestern U. Assocs.; trustee Rush-Presbyn. St. Lukes Med. Ctr., Field Mus., Mus. Sci. and Industry. Mem. TAPPI, Paper Industry Mgmt. Assn., Assn. Iron and Steel Engrs., Am. Petroleum Inst., Am. Inst. Chem. Engrs., Chem. Mfrs. Assn. (chmn. 1986-87), Soc. Chem. Industry (exec. com.), Conf. Bd. Clubs: Commercial; Hinsdale Golf; Butler Nat. Golf. Republican. Episcopalian. Office: Nalco Chem Co 1 Nalco Ctr Naperville IL 60566-1024

CLARKE, DAVID H., industrial products executive; b. 1941; married. Vice chmn. bd. Hanson Trust Pub. Ltd. Co., 1965-83; pres., chief exec. officer Hanson Industries N.Am., 1978—, also bd. dirs. Office: Hanson Industries Inc 100 Wood Ave S Iselin NJ 08830 *

CLARKE, JACK GRAEME, petroleum company executive; b. N.Y.C., Aug. 7, 1927; s. Jack Arnold and Jessie Alva (Murray) C.; m. Dorothea Jean Snyder, Feb. 3, 1951; children: David Dean, Douglas Graeme, Kathryn Alva. BA in Polit. Sci, Hofstra U., 1949; LLB, Cornell U., 1952; LLM in Internat. Law, Harvard U., 1953. Bar: N.Y. 1952. With Sullivan & Cromwell, N.Y.C., 1953-56; atty. Creole Petroleum Corp., N.Y.C., 1957, Venezuela, 1957-59; counsel Standard Oil Co. N.J., N.Y.C., 1959-65; dep. Middle East rep. Standard Oil Co. N.J., London, 1965-66, Middle East rep., 1966-68; asst. gen. counsel Standard Oil Co. N.J., N.Y.C., 1968-69, assoc. gen. counsel, 1969-72, gen. counsel, 1972-73; exec. v.p. Esso Europe Inc., London, 1973-75; sr. v.p. Exxon Corp., N.Y.C., 1975—, bd. dirs.; bd. dirs. Arabian Am. Oil Co.; vice chmn. U.S. Council for Internat. Bus.; mem. Earl Warren Legal Tng. Program. Bd. dirs. Am. Ditchley Found.; bd. dirs., assoc. mem. exec. com. NAACP Legal Def. and Ednl. Fund; chmn. Aspen Inst.; adv. bd. Ctr. Strategic and Internat. Studies; trustee Ednl. Testing Svc. Mem. Coun. on Fgn. Rels., Fgn. Policy Assn. (bd. dirs.). Office: Exxon Corp 1251 Ave of the Americas Rm 5107 New York NY 10020

CLARKE, MICHAEL BRADSHAW, cement company executive; b. Montreal, Que., Can., Aug. 29, 1946; s. Gordon Bradshaw and Elizabeth Mildred (Phillips) C.; m. Anne Christine Soutter, Feb. 21, 1970; 1 child, Lacey Christina. BS in Metal Engring., McGill U., 1969; MBA, Harvard U., 1973. Engr. Dofasco Steel Ltd., Hamilton, Ont., 1969-71; asst. to pres. Moore McCormack Resources, Stamford, Conn., 1973-74; v.p. fin. Moore McCormack Resources, Tampa, Fla., 1981-84; asst. v.p. Picklands Mather & Co., Cleve., 1974-81; pres., chief exec. officer Glens Falls (N.Y.) Cement Co., 1984—; bd. dirs. Glens Falls Nat. Bank, Arrow Bank Corp. Chmn. Caritas Hospice, Glens Falls, 1988; bd. dirs. United Way, 1984—. Mem. Portland Cement Assn., N.E. Cement Shippers Assn. (bd. dirs. 1986—), Adirondack Reg. C. of C. (chmn. econ. devel. adv. com.). Republican. Clubs: Glens Falls Country. Office: Glens Falls Cement Co 313 L Warren St Glens Falls NY 12801

CLARKE, PETER, university dean, communications educator; b. Evanston, Ill., Sept. 19, 1936; s. Clarence Leon and Dorothy (Whitcomb) C.; m. Karen Storey, June 4, 1962 (div. 1984); 1 child, Christopher Michael. B.A., U. Wash., 1959; M.A., U. Minn., 1961, Ph.D., 1963. Dir., asst. prof. Communication Research Ctr. U. Wash., Seattle, 1965-68, assoc. prof. sch. communications, 1967-72, dir. sch. communications, 1971-72; prof. dept. journalism U. Mich., Ann Arbor, 1973-74, chmn., prof. dept. journalism, 1975-78, chmn., prof. dept. communications, 1979-80; dean, prof. Annenberg Sch. Communications U. So. Calif., Los Angeles, 1981—; cons. for various fed. and state govt. commns. on mass media and social problems. Coauthor: (with Susan H. Evans) Covering Campaigns: Journalism in Congressional Elections, 1983; editor: New Models for Communication Research, 1973; co-editor: (with Susan H. Evans) The Computer Culture, 1985; contbr. articles to profl. jours. Grantee U.S. Office of Edn., 1967-69, NSF, 1973-78, ABC-TV, 1984, IBM, 1987, other granting agys. Mem. Am. Assn. for Pub. Opinion Research, Am. Sociol. Assn., Internat. Communication Assn., Am.

Polit. Sci. Assn., Internat. Assn. Mass Communication Research, Am. Psychol. Assn., Am. Statis. Assn., Assn. Edn. in Journalism (chmn. research com., mem. exec. com.), Am. Assn. Schs. and Dept. Journalism (exec. com.). Office: Annenberg Sch of Communications Univ So Calif 3502 South Hoover St Los Angeles CA 90089-0281

CLARKE, RICHARD ALAN, lawyer, electric and gas utility company executive; b. San Francisco, May 18, 1930; s. Chauncey Frederick and Carolyn (Shannon) C.; m. Mary Dell Fisher, Feb. 5, 1955; children: Suzanne, Nancy C. Stephen, Douglas Alan. AB Polit. Sci. cum laude, U. Calif., Berkeley, 1952, JD, 1955. Bar: Calif. 1955. Atty. Pacific Gas and Electric Co., San Francisco, 1955-60, sr. counsel, 1970-74, asst. gen. counsel, 1974-79, v.p., asst. to chmn., 1979-82, exec. v.p., gen. mgr. utility ops., 1982-85, pres., 1985-86, chmn. bd., chief exec. officer, 1986—; ptnr. Rockwell, Fulkerson and Clarke, San Rafael, Calif., 1960-69; bd. dirs. Potlach Corp.; dir. exec. com. Edison Elec. Inst., Invest in Am. Dir. exec. com. Bay Area Coun.; mem. Bay Area Econ. Forum, Calif. Bus. Roundtable; trustee Com. for Econ. Devel., Boalt Hall Trust-U. Calif.-Berkeley Sch. Law; bd. govs. San Francisco Symphony; exec. com. San Francisco Edn. Fund, United Way of Bay Area, Campaign Cabinet, 1988. Mem. State Bar Calif., Pacific Coast Elec. Assn., Pacific Coast Gas Assn., Edison Electric Inst. (dir., mem. exec. com.), Calif. C. of C. (past dir.), San Francisco C. of C. (past dir., v.p. econ. devel.), Pacific-Union Club, Marin Tennis Club. Office: Pacific Gas & Electric Co 77 Beale St San Francisco CA 94106

CLARKE, ROBERT BRADSTREET, publishing company executive; b. Mountainside, N.J., Oct. 31, 1928; s. Bert and Antoinette (Bartlett) C.; m. Roberta Powell, Aug. 26, 1950; children—William, Cynthia. Student, U. Miami (Fla.). Exec. v.p. Grolier Enterprises, Inc., 1960-67, pres., dir., 1967—; pres., dir. Am. Peoples Press, Westmont, Ill., 1965-70; v.p. mail order, then exec. v.p. Grolier Inc., N.Y.C., 1974-76; pres., chief exec. officer Grolier Inc., 1976-78, chmn., pres., chief exec. officer, 1978-87, chmn., chief exec. officer, 1987-89; mem. adv. bd. Union Trust Co., Stamford, Conn.; dir. Book Industry Study Group, 1985; mem. direct mktg. adv. bd. NYU, 1983-85. Trustee Danbury (Conn.) Hosp., 1974-78; vice chmn. Danbury United Way, 1972; bd. dirs. Western Conn. State U., Corp. Coll. Council, 1978—; trustee Direct Mktg. Assn. Ednl. Found., 1981—. Named Direct Mktg. Man of Year Direct Mktg. Day in N.Y., Inc., 1977; recipient Edward N. Mayer Jr. award Direct Mktg. Ednl. Found., 1988. Mem. Am. Mgmt. Assn. (trustee, v.p., chmn. gen. mgmt. council) Direct Selling Assn., Direct Mktg. Assn. (dir., past chmn.), Danbury C. of C. (past chmn.), Cousteau Soc (founding dir. 1974—), Assn. Am. Pubs. (bd. dirs. 1987—), Tower Fellows. Clubs: Saugatuck Harbor Yacht (past commodore), N.Y. Yacht, Pubs. Lunch. Home: 12 St John Pl New Canaan CT 06840 Office: Grolier Inc Sherman Turnpike Danbury CT 06816

CLARKE, ROBERT LOGAN, comptroller of currency; b. Tulsa, June 29, 1942; s. Ralph Logan and Faye Louise (Todd) C.; m. Jean Barrow Talbert, Sept. 23, 1967; 1 child, Logan Clarke. B.A., Rice U., 1963; LL.B., Harvard U., 1966. Bar: N.Mex. 1966, Tex. 1967. Assoc. Hinkle, Bondurant, Cox, Eaton & Hensley, Roswell, N.Mex., 1966; assoc., ptnr. Bracewell & Patterson, Houston, 1968-85, founder, head banking sect., 1972-85; comptroller of currency Washington, 1985—. Precinct chmn. Harris County Reps., 1970-74, 76-85, legal counsel, 1984-85; dist. chmn. Senatorial Dist. 15, 1978-80, del. numerous state and dist. Rep. convs., 1970-84; founding dir. Houston Rep. Club, 1982-85; mem. Assoc. Reps. Tex., 1975-85; bd. dirs. Houston Polit. Action Com., 1983-85; mem. adv. com. Harris County Reagan-Bush campaign, 1984; asst. scoutmaster local Boy Scouts Am.; deacon 1st Presbyterian Ch., sec., 1984; trustee Houston Ctr. for Photography, Mus. of N.Mex. Found., 1987—; bd. dirs. Houston Ballet Found., 1986—. Served to capt. U.S. Army, 1966-68. Mem. Rice U. Alumni Assn. (chmn. area clubs com. 1984-85, exec. bd. dirs. 1987—). Club: Tuesday Breakfast (pres. 1975-76). Lodge: Rotary (trustee Students' Ednl. Fund 1973—). Office: Treasury Dept 490 L'Enfant Pla E SW Washington DC 20219

CLARKE, ROGER GLEN, investment advisor, educator; b. Ogden, Utah, Aug. 9, 1948; s. Glen Wallace and Lulu Fern (Meyers) C.; m. Janet Rounds, Aug. 11, 1971; children: Angela, Stephanie, Mary Ann. BA, Brigham Young U., 1972, MBA, 1974; AM, Stanford U., 1977, PhD, 1978. Asst. prof. Brigham Young U., Provo, Utah, 1978-81, assoc. prof., 1981-85; sr. v.p. Trust Svcs. of Am., L.A., 1985-87, pres., chief investment officer, 1987, vice-chmn., chief investment officer, 1988—; bd. dirs. Nat. Applied Computer Tech., Orem, Utah; cons. in field. Author: Strategic Financial Management, 1988, Option Strategies for Institutional Investment Management, 1983; contbr. articles to profl. jours. Recipient Roger F. Murray award Inst. for Quantitative Rsch. in Fin., 1982, others. Mem. Am. Fin. Assn., Western Fin. Assn. (Treffetz award 1978), Fin. Mgmt. Assn. Republican. Mormon. Office: Trust Svcs of Am 700 Wilshire Blvd Los Angeles CA 90017

CLARKE, VAUGHN ANTHONY, media executive; b. Syracuse, N.Y., July 2, 1953; s. Hugh Anthony and Athea Grace (Anderson) C.; m. A. Shawn Jones, July 16, 1983; 1 child, Austin Myles. BA in Econs., Brown U., 1975; MBA in Fin., Cornell U., 1977. Asst. to officer Chem. Bank, N.Y.C., 1977-78, asst. mgr., 1978-79, asst. sec., 1979-80, asst. v.p., 1980-81; dir. corp. financing Gannett Co., Inc., Rochester, N.Y., 1981-86; asst. treas. Gannett Co., Inc., Arlington, Va., 1986—. Active exec. alumni council Johnson Grad. Mgmt., Cornell U., 1985—. Recipient Outstanding Service award Urban League Rochester, 1985; named One of Am.'s Best and Brightest Young Bus. and Profl. Men, Dollars Sense mag., 1987. Mem. Exec. Leadership Council (treas.), Brown U. Alumni Assn. Democrat. Roman Catholic. Office: Gannett Co Inc 1100 Wilson Blvd Arlington VA 22209

CLARKIN, JOHN FRANCIS, health care operations management executive; b. Atlantic City, Dec. 30, 1936; s. John Francis and Agnes (Winterholer) C.; B.S. in Bus. Adminstrn., Rider Coll., 1959; postgrad. Temple U.; m. Dorothy Louise Piffath; 1 son, John F. Mktg. rep. Scott Paper Co., Indpls., 1960-62; systems and mktg. rep. Burroughs Corp., Phila., 1962-67; dir. Mid-Atlantic health care ops. mgmt. practice Coopers & Lybrand, Phila., 1967—; lead instr. speaker numerous meetings and seminars. Mem. Grand Oak Run Civic Assn., 1970—. Served with U.S. Army, 1959. Rotary Club grantee, 1955-59; cert. mgmt. cons. Mem. Inst. Mgmt. Cons., Hosp. Mgmt. Systems Soc., Hosp. Fin. Mgmt. Assn., Med. Group Mgmt. Assn., Am. Hosp. Assn. Republican. Roman Catholic. Clubs: Vesper, Pickering Racquet. Author: Topics in Health Care Financing, 1982; (with others) Handbook of Health Care Accounting and Finance, 1982, 89; Billing Systems, 2 vols., 1982, 89; contbr. articles to profl. jours. Home: 1421 Grand Oak Ln West Chester PA 19300 Office: Coopers & Lybrand Eleven Penn Ctr Ste 2400 Philadelphia PA 19103

CLARKSON, ANDREW MACBETH, retail executive; b. Glasgow, Scotland, July 9, 1937; s. Robert Gibson and Josephine Abigail (Anderson) C.; m. Carole Frances Grant, June 4, 1966; children: Jennifer Mary, William MacBeth. B.A., Oxford (Eng.) U., 1960, M.A., 1980; diploma in agr., Mcgill U., 1961; M.B.A., Harvard U., 1966. Various positions to asst. v.p. First Nat. Bank, Chgo., 1966-72; corp. asst. treas. Gen. Foods Corp., White Plains, N.Y., 1972-78; fin. dir. Gen. Foods Ltd., U.K., 1978-80; asst. corp. controller and controller Gen. Foods Internat., 1980-81; v.p. and treas. F.W. Woolworth co., N.Y.C., 1981-83; sr. v.p. fin. and adminstrn., dir. Malone & Hyde, Memphis, 1983-88; sec., dir. AutoZone, Inc., Memphis, 1988—; bd. dirs. Auto Shack, Inc.; lectr. internat. fin. U. Conn., 1976. Treas., dir. Memphis Arts Coun., 1987—. Served to 2d lt. Brit. Army, 1955-57. mem. Fin. Execs. Inst. Clubs: Field (New Canaan), Crescent (Memphis). Office: AutoZone Inc 3030 Poplar Ave Memphis TN 38111

CLARKSON, CHARLES GERARD, business executive; b. N.Y.C., Feb. 13, 1953; s. Charles Thomas and Margaret Mary (Kennedy) C.; m. Marilyn Clark Clarkson, July 10, 1983; 1 child, Brooke Robbins. BS, Fordham U., 1975. Cons. Arthur Andersen & Co., N.Y.C., 1975-78; rsch. assoc. Fin. Acctg. Standards Bd., Stamford, Conn., 1979-80; dir. Barry Wright Corp., Newton, Mass., 1980—; bd. dirs. MCC Design Systems, Weston, Mass. Republican. Home: 131 Sherburn Circle Weston MA 02193 Office: Barry Wright Corp 1 Newton Exec Pla Newton MA 02163

CLARKSON, DAVID SCOTT, manufacturing executive; b. Corpus Christi, Tex., Aug. 29, 1946; s. Paul Howard and Vinita Ann (Scott) C.; m. Virginia Ann Colin, June 22, 1968; children: Paul Andrew, Alexander Scott. AA, El Camino Coll., 1970; BA, Calif. State U., Long Beach, 1973; postgrad., Drexel U., 1982-85; MBA, Case Western Res. U., 1988. Ops. supr. U.S. Steel Supply Div., Los Angeles, 1972-76; gen. mgr. Timet div., East Granby, Conn., 1976-79; sales mgr. Suisman & Blumenthal, Hartford, Conn., 1979-82; dir. mktg. and planning A. Johnson & Co., Lionville, Pa., 1982-85; v.p. sales and mktg. Astro div. Harsco, Wooster, Ohio, 1985-88; pres. VisionMark, Sidney, Ohio, 1988—; chmn. stats. com. Titanium Devel. Assocs., Dayton, Ohio, 1984-88. Contbr. articles to profl. jours. Served as cpl. USMC, 1964-68, Vietnam. Mem. Am. Mktg. Assn., Am. Soc. Metals, Nat. Assn. Corrosion Engrs., Titanium Devel. Assn. (chmn. stats. com. 1984—), Am. Inst. Mech. Engrs. (metall. soc.), Phi Sigma Tau, Alpha Gamma Sigma. Home: 4337 Fryman Dr Akron OH 44313 Office: VisionMark 2309 Industrial Dr Sidney OH 45365

CLARKSON, KENNETH WRIGHT, economics educator; b. Downey, Calif., June 30, 1942; s. William Wright and Constance (Patch) C.; m. Mary Jane Purdy, June 20, 1965; children: Steven Wright, Thomas David. A.B., Calif. State U., 1964; M.A., UCLA, 1966, Ph.D., 1971. Economist Office Mgmt. and Budget, Washington, 1971-72, assoc. dir., 1982-83; asst. prof. econs. U. Va., 1969-75; prof. econs. U. Miami, Coral Gables, Fla., 1975—, dir. Law & Econs. Ctr., 1981—; cons. in field; mem. Pres.'s Task Force on Food Assistance, 1983-84; mem. governing bd. Credit Research Ctr., Purdue U., 1981—; mem. research com. Fla. C. of C. Found., 1985—; mem. nat. adv. bd. Nat. Ctr. for Privatization, 1985—, Washington Legal Found., 1985—; mem. Fla. adv. com. U.S. Commn. Civil Rights, 1985—. Author: Food Stamps and Nutrition, 1975, Intangible Capital and Rates of Return, 1975; co-author: Correcting Taxes for Inflation, 1975, Distortions in Official Unemployment Statistics, 1979, Industrial Organization: Theory, Evidence and Public Policy, 1982, West's Business Law, 1980, 3d edit., 1986, The Federal Trade Commission Since 1970, 1981, Economics Sourcebook of Government Statistics, 1983, The Role of Privatization in Florida's Growth, 1987, Using Private Management to Foster Florida's Growth: Initial Steps, 1987, A Proposal for Medical Malpractice Insurance in Florida, 1987, Alternative Service Delivery Project: An Analysis of the City and County of Los Angeles, 1988; contbr. numerous articles to profl. jours. Mem. Regan-Bush Transition Team, Washington, 1980; mem. econ. adv. panel Fla. State Comprehensive Plan Com., 1986—; bd. dirs. Econs. Inst. for Fed. Adminstrv. Law Judges, 1982—. NSF grantee, 1972-74; Heritage Found. adj. scholar, 1977—. Mem. Am. Econ. Assn., Am. Bus. Law Assn., Western Econ. Assn., Mont Pelerin Soc., Phil. Soc., Sigma Xi. Home: 15925 SW 77th Ct Miami FL 33157 Office: U Miami 1541 Brescia Ave Coral Gables FL 33146

CLARNER, WALTER J., credit executive; b. N.Y.C., Aug. 8, 1947; s. George Christopher and Nora Winifred (Johansen) C. Student, Queens Coll., N.Y. Inst. of Credit. Collector for Crompton Richmond Factors, N.Y.C., 1969-71, James Talcott Factors, N.Y.C., 1971-74; collector for factoring div. Chemical Bank, N.Y.C., 1974-80; asst. sec. Security Pacific Bus. Credit, N.Y.C., 1980-84; asst. v.p. Century Bus. Credit, N.Y.C., 1984-86; asst. v.p., Ambassador Factors div. Fleet-Norstar Fin. Group, N.Y.C., 1986—. Mem. Contemporary Credit Club. Democrat. Roman Catholic. Office: Ambassador Factors 1450 Broadway New York NY 10018

CLARY, RONALD GORDON, insurance agency executive; b. Moultrie, Ga., May 2, 1940; s. Ronald Ward and Hazel Collins C. Student Young Harris Coll., 1958-60; BBA in Ins., U. Ga., 1963; LLB, Woodrow Wilson Coll. Law, 1966. Field rep. Comml. Union Ins. Cos., 1962-67; ind. ins. agt., 1967—; ins. agt., sec. of agy. Day, Reynolds & Parks, Gainesville, Ga., 1970—. Mem. Profl. Ins. Agts. Am., Ga. Assn. Ind. Ins. Agts., Gainesville Assn. Ind. Ins. Agts. (past pres.), Young Agts. Com. Ga. (past chmn.), Am. Legion. Republican. Baptist. Lodge: Elks. Home: 510 Bradford St Gainesville GA 30501 Office: Day Reynolds & Parks 611 Spring St Gainesville GA 30501

CLARY, ROSALIE BRANDON STANTON, timber farm executive, civic worker; b. Evanston, Ill., Aug. 3, 1928; d. Frederick Charles Hite-Smith and Rose Cecile (Liebich) Stanton; B.S., Northwestern U., 1950, M.A., 1954; m. Virgil Vincent Clary, Oct. 17, 1959; children: Rosalie Marian Hawley, Frederick Stanton, Virgil Vincent, Kathleen Elizabeth. Tchr., Chgo. Public Schs., 1951-55, adjustment tchr., 1956-61; faculty Loyola U., Chgo., 1963; v.p. Stanton Enterprises, Inc., Adams County, Miss., 1971—; author Family History Record, genealogy record book, Kenilworth, Ill., 1977—; also lectr. Leader, Girl Scouts, Winnetka, Ill., 1969-71, 78-86, Cub Scouts, 1972-77; badge counselor Boy Scouts Am., 1978-87 ; election judge Republican party, 1977—. Mem. Nat. Soc. DAR (Ill. rec. sec. 1979-81, nat. vice chmn. program com. 1980-83, state vice regent 1986-88, state regent 1989), Am. Forestry Assn., Forest Farmers Assn., North Suburban Geneal. Soc. (governing bd. 1979-86), Winnetka Hist. Soc. (governing bd. 1978—), Internat. Platform Assn., Delta Gamma (mem. nat. cabinet 1985—). Roman Catholic. Home: 509 Elder Ln Winnetka IL 60093 Office: Stanton Enterprises Inc PO Box 401 Kenilworth IL 60043

CLASSON, BRUCE DAVID, trust company executive; b. N.Y.C., Oct. 5, 1932; s. Lawrence Lazarus and Sylvia Lois (Miller) C.; m. Wilma Susan Fagin, Dec.28,1955; children: Gregory Bruce, Elizabeth Ann. BA cum laude, Dartmouth Coll., 1956; MBA, Harvard U., 1956. Asst. to pres. Tru Balance, Inc., N.Y.C., 1956-58; exec. v.p. James Talcott Factors, N.Y.C., 1958-70; v.p. James Talcott, Inc., N.Y.C., 1958-70; sr. v.p. adminstrn. Bankers Trust Co., N.Y.C., 1970—; bd. dirs. Venice Industries, Inc., N.Y.C., Standard Motor Products, L.I. City, N.Y. Author: Commercial Credit and Collection Guide, 1968. Mem. N.Y. Credit & Fin. Mgmt. Assn., N.Y. Inst. Credit (chmn. bd. trustees 1981), Nat. Comml. Fin. Conf. (bd. dirs., exec. com.), Esquire-Toppers Credit Club, Inc. (pres. 1971-72), Phi Beta Kappa. Jewish. Clubs: Yale (N.Y.C.), 475, Inc. Office: Bankers Trust Co 280 Park Ave PO Box 318 Church St Sta New York NY 10015

CLATSOFF, WILLIAM ADAM, financial consultant; b. Toronto, Ont., Can., Sept. 24, 1940; came to U.S., 1967; s. William and Audrey May (Martin) C.; m. Carole Jean Hopper, Jan. 9, 1967; children: Heather May-Jo, William Adam Jr. Student, St. Andrews Coll., Aurora, Ont., 1954-58. CLU; chartered fin. cons.; cert. fin. planner, reg. health underwriter. Restaurant mgr. Pilot Tavern Holdings Ltd., Toronto, 1961-69; ins. salesman John Hancock, North Miami, Fla., 1969-71; agy. mgr. Maccabees Mut., North Miami, 1971-73; ins. salesman Mut. of Omaha, Ft. Lauderdale, Fla., 1973-76; chief exec. officer, fin. cons. Adcahb Fin. Group, Coral Springs, Fla., 1976—. Mem. Commisioner's Life and Health Adv. Com. (by spl. appt., 1982—). Mem. Nat. Assn. Life Underwriters (Broward County chpt. bd. dirs. 1983-86), Am. Soc. CLU, Nat. Assn. Health Underwriters (Gold Coast chpt. bd. dirs. 1985-86), Internat. Assn. Fin. Planners (pres. Gold Coast chpt. 1984-86), Inst. Cert. Fin. Planners. Republican. Home: 8879 NW 21st St Coral Springs FL 33065 Office: Adcahb Fin Group Adcahb Centre 3000 NW 101 Ln Coral Springs FL 33065

CLAUER, CALVIN KINGSLEY, investment advisor, financial planner; b. South Bend, Ind., Dec. 18, 1926; s. Kenneth Kingsley and Edna Mae (Rose) C.; m. Emily Catherine Purcell, June 12, 1964. BS, Purdue U., 1949; MS, Stanford U., 1968, PhD, 1972. Cert. fin. planner; registered investment advisor. Engr. IBM, San Jose, 1957-84; owner, mgr. Clauer & Assocs., Los Gatos, Calif., 1984—. Treas., trustee Family Svc. Assn., Santa Clara Valley, 1972—; treas. Rinconada Hills Assn., Los Gatos, 1985-87. Mem. Inst. Cert. Fin. Planners, Internat. Assn. for Fin. Planning, Am. Assn. Individual Investors (pres. Silicon Valley chpt. 1986—).

CLAUSEN, ALDEN WINSHIP, banker; b. Hamilton, Ill., Feb. 17, 1923; s. Morton and Elsie (Kroll) C.; m. Mary Margaret Crassweller, Feb. 11, 1950; children: Eric David, Mark Winship. B.A., Carthage Coll., 1944, LL.D., 1970; LL.B., U. Minn., 1949; grad., Advanced Mgmt. Program, Harvard U., 1966. Bar: Minn. 1949, Calif. 1950. With Bank Am. (NT & SA), San Francisco, 1949-81, 1986—; v.p. Bank Am. (NT & SA), 1961-65, sr. v.p., 1965-68, exec. v.p., 1968-69, vice chmn. bd., 1969, pres., chief exec. officer, 1970-81, chmn., chief exec. officer, 1986—; pres. World Bank, 1981-86; now chmn., pres., chief exec. officer BankAmerica Corp.; past pres. Internat. Monetary Conf., San Francisco; Clearing House Assn. Past pres. Fed. Adv. Council, 1972; past chmn. Bay Area Council; past bd. govs. United Way of Am.; past chmn. United Way of Bay Area; past mem. Bus. Roundtable; mem. Bus. Council; past mem. Japan-U.S. Adv. Council; past bd. dirs. Conf. Bd., San Francisco Opera; past bd. dirs., mem. adv. council SRI Internat.; mem. adv. council Stanford U. Grad. Sch. Bus.; bd. dirs. Harvard Bus. Sch.; trustee Carthage Coll., Brookings Instn. Mem. Res. City Bankers Assn. (hon.), Calif. Bar Assn. Clubs: Bankers of San Francisco, Pacific Union, Burlingame Country; Bohemian, Links (N.Y.C.); Metropolitan (Washington); Chevy Chase (Md.). Office: BankAm Corp 555 California St San Francisco CA 94104 *

CLAUSON, SHARYN FERNE, consulting company executive, educator; b. Phila., Oct. 4, 1946; d. Eugene and Gertrud Jayn (Besser) C. BA in English, Temple U., 1968; MEd in Psychology, Beaver Coll., 1979; MBA, Drexel U., 1982; postgrad in law, Temple U. Market analyst Epstein Research, Bala, Pa., 1967-69; cons. Ednl. Testing Service, Princeton, N.J., 1979-80; chief exec. officer CCX, Narberth, Pa., 1978-79; tchr. Cheltenham Twp. Sch. Dist., Elkins Park, Pa., 1969-86; dir. Sharyn Clauson Bus. Communications, Narberth, Pa., 1975-85; pres. S. Clauson & Assocs., Inc., 1985—; dir. Execuwriter, 1985—; mem. adj. faculty Drexel U., Phila., 1979—, Phila. Coll. Textiles & Sci., Phila, 1985—, St. Joseph's U., Phila., 1986—, Phila. Ctr. of Great Lakes Coll. Assn., 1988—; talk show host Sta. WDVT-AM, Phila., 1985—; bd. dir. Site Selex, Inc., Jenkintown, Pa., dir. communications/pub. relations, 1988—. Editor: Curriculum for Optacon Music Reading, 1984; mem. editorial adv. bd. Bus. Communications and Concepts, 2d edit., 1985. Mem. com. Women's Polit. Caucus, Phila., 1982—; mem. Phila. Art Alliance; mem. exec. bd., arts and scis. alumni bd. Temple U. Women's Law Caucus. Mem. Am. Mktg. Assn., Internat. Platform Assn., Nat. Speakers Assn. (chair 1985), Nat. Assn. Profl. Saleswomen, (honoree 1982—), Nat. Council Tchrs. English, Del. Valley Writing Council, Wallenberg Communicators, Phi Delta Kappa. Home: 308 Oak Hill E Narberth PA 19072

CLAUSSEN, HOWARD BOYD, recruiting company executive; b. Kansas City, Mo., May 12, 1946; s. Harry Ben and Mary Loraine (Shipley) C.; m. Virginia Ione Nehf, July 21, 1973; children: Paul, Rebecca, Debora, Arienne, John, Jennifer. BA in Econs., Yale U., 1968. Systems engr. IBM Corp., 1969-70; salesman Sperry Corp., Kansas City, 1970-72; sr. salesman Honeywell Inc., Kansas City, 1972-73; dist. mgr. Singer Bus. Machines, Kansas City, 1973-75; pres. 'C' Cons., Inc., Kansas City and Terre Haute, Ind., 1975-80, 82—; nat. sales mgr. Delta Systems, Seattle, 1980-82; pres. Profile Source, Inc., Los Gatos, Calif., 1988—; cons. CBS, Inc., N.Y.C., 1976-80, Southwestern Bell Telephone Co. subs. AT&T, St. Louis, 1978-80, Convergent Tech., San Jose, Calif., 1983—, Multiflow Computer, Branford, Conn., 1986—. Mem. instructional adv. com. Vigo County Sch. Bd., 1984-87; v.p. Yale Club of Western Washington, 1983-84; coach Terre Haute Baseball Little League, 1986—, YWCA Basketball. Mem. AAAS, Nat. Trust Hist. Preservation. Republican. Methodist. Club: Yale of Ind. Home and Office: 4519 Park Ln Ct Terre Haute IN 47803

CLAWSON, HARRY QUINTARD MOORE, business executive; b. N.Y.C., Aug. 8, 1924; s. Harry Marshall and Marguerite H. (Burgoyne) C.; m. Annemarie Korntner, Dec. 1967 (dec. Apr. 1988). Student, NYU, 1951-52, New Sch. for Social Research, 1953. Supr. transp., liaison with U.S. Army ARC, 1945-46; asst. to dir. personnel UNESCO, Paris, 1947; resident rep. Tex. Co., Douala, French Cameroun, West Africa, 1948-50; asst. dir. overseas bus. service McGraw-Hill Pub. Co., 1951-58; dir. client services Internat. Research Assocs., N.Y.C., 1958-61; v.p., sec. Frasch Whiton Boats, Inc.; gen. mgr. Sailboat Tng. Facility; pres. Harry Q.M. Clawson & Co., Inc., N.Y.C., 1961-76, Charleston, S.C., 1978—; dir. planning and adminstrn. div., splty. chems. div. Essex Chem. Corp., 1976-78; pres. Trident Seafarms Co., Charleston, 1980-85. Contbr. articles to profl. jours. Served with U.S. Army, 1943-45, ETO. Decorated Bronze Star. Mem. Ex-Mems. Assn. Squadron A. Club: Carolina Yacht. Home: 1 King St Charleston SC 29401

CLAWSON, RAYMOND WALDEN, independent oil producer; b. San Jose, Calif.; s. Benjamin B. and Mae Belle (Names) C.; LL.B., Am. U., 1936; m. Barbara M. Robbins, 1965. Ind. operator, exploration and devel. oil properties, 1936—; pub. Los Angeles Mirror, 1945-47; pres. Ariz. Securities, Phoenix, 1947-50, Transcontinental Oil Co., Los Angeles, 1947-49; geophys. cons. in offshore drilling ops. Gulf of Mexico, 1963—, North Sea, 1970—; chmn., chief exec. officer Clawco Petroleum Corp., Newport Beach, Calif., 1979—. Clubs: Balboa Bay, Acapulco Yacht. Office: PO Box 2102 Newport Beach CA 92663

CLAY, HARRIS AUBREY, chemical engineer; b. Hartley, Tex., Dec. 28, 1911; s. John David and Alberta (Harris) C.; B.S., U. Tulsa, 1933; Ch.E., Columbia U., 1939; m. Violette Frances Mills, June 19, 1948 (dec. June 1972); m. 2d, Garvice Stuart Shotwell, Apr. 28, 1973. Pilot plant operator Phillips Petroleum Co., Burbank, Okla., 1939-42, resident supr. Burbank pilot plants, 1942-44, process design engr., Bartlesville, Okla., 1944-45, process engring. supr. Philtex Plant, Phillips, Tex., 1946-56, tech. adviser to pilot plant mgr., Bartlesville, 1957-61, chem. engring. assoc., 1961-74; cons. engr., 1974—; chmn. tech. com. Fractionation Research, Inc., 1966-71, mem. tech. com., 1972-73. Mem. dist. commn. Boy Scouts Am. Fellow Am. Inst. Chem. Engrs.; mem. Am. Chem. Soc., Electrochem. Soc. Presbyterian. Clubs: Elks, Lions. Contbr. articles to profl. jours. Patentee in field. Home: 1723 Church Ct Bartlesville OK 74006

CLAY, ORSON C., insurance company executive; b. Bountiful, Utah, July 26, 1930; s. George Phillips and Dorothy (Cliff) C.; m. Dianne Jones, June 13, 1961; children: Orson Cliff, Charles Kenneth, Elizabeth Temple. B.S., Brigham Young U., 1955; M.B.A. with distinction (Donald Kirk David fellow), Harvard U., 1959. With Continental Oil Co., various locations in, U.S.; mng. dir. Conoco A.G., Zug, Switzerland, 1962-63; dir. econs. div. Continental Oil Co. Ltd., London, Eng., 1964-65; gen. mgr. adminstrn. and ops. Continental Oil (U.K.) Ltd., London, 1965-66; asst. mgr. marine transp. N.Y.C., 1966-68; exec. asst. fin. Pennzoil United, Inc., Houston, 1968-70; exec. v.p. fin., treas. Am. Nat. Ins. Co., Galveston, Tex., 1970-73; sr. exec. v.p., treas. Am. Nat. Ins. Co., 1973-76, pres., 1977—, chief exec. officer, 1978—, also dir.; chmn. bd. dirs. Standard Life & Accident Ins. Co., Oklahoma City, Commonwealth Life & Accident Ins. Co., Am. Nat. Property & Casulty Co., Am. Nat. Gen. Ins. Co; adv. dir. First City Nat. Bank of Houston; chmn. bd., pres. Am. Nat. Life Ins. Co. of Tex., Galveston; v.p., bd. dirs. Am. Nat. Real Estate Mgmt. Corp.; mem. exec. com., bd. dirs. Securities Mgmt. & Research, Inc., Galveston; bd. dirs. Health Ins. Assn. Am., Galveston Indsl. Devel. Corp., Am. Printing Co. Bd. dirs. United Way Galveston; nat. adv. council sch. mgmt. Brigham Young U. 1st lt. USMCR, 1955-57. Mem. Tex. Life, Accident, Health and Hosp. Svc. Ins. Guaranty Assn. (chmn.), Tex. Life Ins. Assn. (exec. com., dir.), Tex. Rsch. League (dir.). Mem. Ch. of Jesus Christ of Latter-day Saints (missionary in Can. 1951-53). Home: 2619 Christopher Dr Galveston TX 77551 Office: Am Nat Ins Co 1 Moody Pla Galveston TX 77550

CLAY, W. ROBERT, chemical company executive; b. Old Hickory, Tenn., Apr. 16, 1932; s. Ernest and Effie (Jackson) C.; m. Judith Angstadt. BE in Chem. Engring., Vanderbilt U., 1954. Mktg. dir. E.I. du Pont de Nemours & Co., Wilmington, Del., 1974-76; dir. textile fibers Du Pont de Nemours Internat. S.A., Geneva, Switzerland, 1976-78; dir. indsl. fibers div. E.I. du Pont de Nemours & Co., Wilmington, 1978-80, gen. mgr. textile fibers, 1980-81, gen. mng. dir. internat., 1981-83; chmn. Du Pont de Nemours Internat., S.A., Geneva, 1983-85; v.p. internat. E.I. du Pont de Nemours & Co., Wilmington, 1985—. Patentee in field. Served to 1st lt. C.E., U.S. Army, 1955-57. Recipient Marketers award Elec. and Electronics Insulation Conf., 1979. Mem. U. S.C. Adv. Bd. Internat. Bus. Studies, Council of Americas (bd. dirs., exec. com. 1985—), Adv. Group Capital Devel. Mex. (U.S. Council Mex. and U.S. Bus.Com. 1986—). Republican. Episcopalian. Clubs: Wilmington Country; Linville Ridge Country; Grenelefe Country; Rodney Sq. Home: 627 Kilburn Rd Wilmington DE 19803 Office: E I Du Pont de Nemours & Co 4042 Du Pont Bldg Wilmington DE 19898

CLAYTON, BERNARD MILES, JR., insurance company executive; b. Ketchikan, Alaska, Jan. 26, 1953; s. Bernard Miles and June Ester (Thompson) C.; m. Elizabeth Harte Johnson, Mar. 12, 1982. AA in Bus. Adminstrn., El Camino Coll., 1974; BS in Bus. Adminstrn. cum laude, Calif. State U., Long Beach, 1976. Underwriter Gamble Alden Ins. Co., Century City, Calif., 1976-77; dir. mktg. Ruland and Mattingley, Irvine, Calif., 1977-83; v.p., gen mgr. Gen. Benefits Ins. Services Corp., Orange, Calif., 1983—; bd. dirs. So. Calif. (Tustin) Health Resources Ctr.; del. Orange County

Health Planning Council. Mem. Calif. Assn. Health Underwriters, Orange County Assn. Health Underwriters (exec. bd. dirs. 1987—), Orange County Employee Benefit Council (bd. dirs. 1988—). Republican. Office: Gen Benefits Ins Svcs Corp 333 City Blvd W #220 PO Box 1046 Orange CA 92668

CLAYTON, EVELYN WILLIAMS, company executive; b. Durham, N.C., Feb. 11, 1951; d. Virge and Inez Florence (Jordan) Williams; m. Archie L. Clayton, Mar. 1, 1972 (div. May 1975); 1 child, Dorel. Student Durham Tech. Inst., 1969-71, Durham Bus. Coll., 1971-72, U. N.C.-Chapel Hill, 1977-81; A.B.A., Durham Tech. Inst., 1971. Fiscal officer Durham County Health Dept. (N.C.), 1974-82; dir. fin. MedVisit Inc., Butner, N.C., 1982—; exec. dir., pres. EC & Assocs., fin. mgmt. and cons. firm, Durham, 1982—. Mem. Durham Com. on Affairs of Black People; cubmaster, Pack 442, Boy Scouts Am.; active congl. campaign Kenneth B. Spaulding, 1985. Mem. N.C. Assn. Home Care (treas. 1980-83), N.C. Public Health Assn., NAACP. Democrat. Baptist. Home: 36 Burgess Ln Durham NC 27707 Office: EC & Assocs 2514 University Dr Durham NC 27707

CLAYTON, RANDY JOE, financial executive; b. Charlotte, N.C., Sept. 17, 1954; s. Henry Clarence and Jean Henrietta (Johansen) C.; m. Sherry E. Binkley, July 3, 1976 (div. 1988); 1 child, Nicholas A. BA in Psychology, Washburn U., 1988. Agt. Ohio Nat. Life Ins. Co., Cin., 1976-82; pres. Clayton Fin. Services Inc., Topeka, 1982—; instr. Emporia State U., Kans., 1987—; co-host fin. radio program WIBW, topeka, 1987—. Bd. dirs. Topeka Peace Resource Ctr., 1987—, Kans. Citizen's Forum, Topeka, 1987—. Mem. Inst. Cert. Fin. Planners. Republican. Lutheran. Office: Clayton Fin Svs Inc 534 S Kansas 820 Topeka KS 66603

CLAYTON, WILLIAM L., investment banking executive; b. Tenafly, N.J., Oct. 27, 1929; s. Walter I. and Emily A. (Caverly) C.; m. Carol L. Farmer, June 23, 1951; children: Andrew L., Robin L., Kathleen L., Kevin L., Susan L., Christopher L. BS, Lehigh U., 1951, LLD (hon.), 1987; postgrad. in Bus., NYU, 1953-56. Asst. portfolio mgr. Marine Midland, N.Y.C., 1953-54; account exec. E.F. Hutton, N.Y.C., 1954-64, v.p., 1964-71, sr. v.p., 1971-81, exec. v.p., 1981—; dir. Stabler Cos., Harrisburg, Pa., Eastern Industries, Harrisburg, Pa. Trustee Lehigh U., 1980—, Blair Acad., 1984—, New Eyes for Needy, 1984—. Recipient Nat. Mktg. Club, 1980; named Outstanding Alumnus Lehigh U., 1971. Mem. Lehigh U. Alumni Assn. (pres. 1980—), Beta Gama Sigma, Chi Phi (treas. 1951). Clubs: Baltusrol (Springfield, N.J.); University (N.Y.C.). Lodge: Knights of Malta. Home: 1 Slope Dr Short Hills NJ 07078 Office: Shearson Lehman Hutton 599 Lexington Ave New York NY 10022

CLAYTOR, ROBERT BUCKNER, retired railroad executive; b. Roanoke, Va., Feb. 27, 1922; s. William Graham and Gertrude Harris (Boatwright) C.; m. Frances Tice, Sept. 25, 1943; children—Jane Gordon (Mrs. Samuel J. Webster), Robert Harris, John Preston. A.B. cum laude, Princeton U., 1944; J.D., Harvard U., 1948; L.H.D. (hon.), Hollins Coll., 1982. Bar: Mass. bar 1948, N.Y. bar 1949, Va. bar 1952. Atty. AT&T, 1948-51; solicitor Norfolk & Western, Roanoke, 1951-54, asst. gen. solicitor, 1954-56, asst. gen. counsel, 1956-60, gen. solicitor, 1960- 64, v.p. law, 1964-68, sr. v.p., 1968-70, exec. v.p., 1970-80, also chmn., pres., chief exec. officer, 1980-82; chmn., chief exec. officer Norfolk So. Corp., 1982-87, chmn. exec. com., bd. dirs., 1987—; bd. dirs. Richardson-Wayland Elec. Corp., Ga.-Pacific Corp., Ashland Coal Inc. Chancellor Episcopal Diocese Southwestern Va., 1969-74; trustee Hollins Coll., chmn. bd. 1972-82, Va. Theol. Sem. Bd.; Eastern Va. Med. Found., 1983; bd. visitors Va. Poly Inst.; chmn., bd. regents Mercersburg Acad.; chmn. Va. Found. for Ind. Colls., 1987—. Served to 1st lt. AUS, 1943-46. Mem. ABA, Va. Bar Assn., Roanoke Bar Assn., Norfolk Bar Assn., Va. Opera Assn. (bd. dirs.), Phi Beta Kappa. Episcopalian. Clubs: Princeton (N.Y.C.); Metropolitan (Washington); Harbor (Norfolk); Norfolk Yacht and Country; Shenandoah (Roanoke); Links (N.Y.C.). Home: 7300 Woodway Ln Norfolk VA 23505 Office: Norfolk So Corp Three Commercial Pl Norfolk VA 23510-2191

CLAYTOR, WILLIAM GRAHAM, JR., railroad executive; b. Roanoke, Va., Mar. 14, 1912; s. William Graham and Gertrude Harris (Boatwright) C.; m. Frances Murray Hammond, Aug. 14, 1948; children: Frances Murray, William Graham III. BA, U. Va., 1933; JD summa cum laude, Harvard U., 1936; LLD, U. Miami, 1985. Bar: N.Y. 1937, D.C. 1938. Law clk. U.S. Judge Learned Hand, 1936-37, Mr. Justice Brandeis, 1937-38; assoc. firm Covington & Burling, Washington, 1938-47; partner Covington & Burling, 1947-67, counsel, 1981-82; v.p. law So. Ry. Co., 1963-67, chief exec. officer, 1967-77, pres., 1967-76, chmn. bd., 1976-77; chmn. bd., pres. Nat. R.R. Passenger Corp., Washington, 1982—; former chief exec. officer, dir. various cos. comprising So. Ry. System; sec. Navy, Washington, 1977-79, acting sec. Transp., 1979, dep. sec. Def., 1979-81; bd. dirs. Assn. Am. R.R.s, 1967-77, 82—. Pres. Harvard Law Rev, 1935-36. Trustee Episcopal Home Children, Washington, 1960-65, v.p., 1960-63; trustee Ctr. for Strategic and Internat. Studies, 1987—; govs. Beauvoir Sch., Washington, 1958-61, St. Albans Sch., 1961-67; mem. adv. bd. Center for Advanced Studies, U. Va., 1974-80; trustee Eisenhower Fellowships, Inc., 1981—; mem. adv. com. Mt. Vernon (Va.) Ladies Assn. of the Union, 1980-86. Served to lt. comdr. USNR, 1941-46. Mem. Am. Bar Assn., Am. Law Inst., Am. Judicature Soc., Harvard Law Sch. Assn., Am. Soc. Corp. Execs. (asso. mem.). Democrat. Episcopalian. Clubs: Metropolitan (Washington), City Tavern Assn. (Washington) (bd. govs. 1961-64); Chevy Chase (Md.), Gibson Island (Md.); Shenandoah (Roanoke). Home: 2912 N St NW Washington DC 20007 Office: Nat RR Passenger Corp 400 N Capitol St NW Washington DC 20001

CLEAR, GEOFFREY POSSELT, financial executive; b. Bronxville, N.Y., Mar. 23, 1950; s. Albert Francis and Jeanne (Posselt) C.; m. Marjorie Philimina McKeever, Nov. 23, 1979; children: Allison Marie, Michael Edward. BA, Dartmouth Coll., 1972, MBA, 1974. CPA., N.Y. Sr. auditor Arthur Andersen & Co., N.Y.C., 1974-77; various positions fin. mgmt. W.R. Grace & Co., N.Y.C., 1977-82; controller div. W.R. Grace & Co., Lexington, Mass., 1982-86; chief fin. officer T Cell Scis. Inc., Cambridge, Mass., 1986-87; v.p., chief fin. officer T Cell Scis. Inc., Cambridge, 1987—. Mem. Mass. Soc. CPA's. Congregationalist. Office: T Cell Scis Inc 38 Sidney St Cambridge MA 02139

CLEARY, RAYMOND P., data processing executive; b. N.Y.C., July 14, 1939; s. James I. and Mary (Carr) C.; m. Carol M. Noonan, Apr. 7, 1945; children: Robert N., Jennifer L. AS in Bus., Rutgers U., 1971, BS in Bus., 1972; MBA, Fordham U., 1974; postgrad., New Sch. for Social Rsch., 1974-76. V.p. Comouter Info. Systems, Fairfield, N.J., 1973-75; dir. ea. sales United Computing systems, Kansas City, Kans., 1975-84; v.p. sales Compro Software, Inc., Norcross, Ga., 1984-87; dir. ops. Cappcomm Software, Inc., Jersey City, 1987—; cons. Dover Twp., N.J., 1980. Legis. aide Assemblyman Anthony Villana, State of N.J., 1977-78; aide Bi-State Commn. on Ocean Pollution, N.Y. and N.J. With USMC, 1959-63. Republican. Home: 3 Conover Ln Rumson NJ 07760 Office: Cappcomm Software Inc 26 Journal Sq Ste 1003 Jersey City NJ 07306

CLEARY, WILLIAM JOSEPH, JR., lawyer; b. Wilmington, N.C., Aug. 14, 1942; s. William Joseph and Eileen Ada (Gannon) C.; AB in History, St. Joseph's U., 1964; JD, Villanova U., 1967. Bar: N.J. 1967, U.S. Ct. Appeals (3d cir.) 1969, Calif. 1982, U.S. Ct. Appeals (9th cir.) 1983. Law sec. to judge N.J. Superior Ct. Jersey City, 1967-68; assoc. Lamb, Blake, H&D, Jersey City, 1968-72; dep. pub. defender State of N.J., Newark, 1972-73; 1st asst. city corp. counsel, Jersey City, 1973-76; assoc. Robert Wasserwald, Inc., Hollywood, Calif., 1984-86, 88—, Gould & Burke, L.A., 1986-87. Mem. ABA, N.J. State Bar, Calif. Bar Assn., L.A. County Bar. Democrat. Roman Catholic.

CLEGHORN, JOHN EDWARD, banker; b. Montreal, Que., Can., July 7, 1941; m. Pattie E. Hart; children: Charles, Ian, Andrea. B.Comm., McGill U., Montreal, 1962. Articled with Clarkson Gordon, chartered Accts., Montreal, 1962-64; sugar buyer and futures trader St. Lawrence Sugar Ltd., Montreal, 1964-66; with Merc. Bank of Can. (affiliate of Citibank) with assignments in N.Y., Montreal; mgr. Winnipeg br. and v.p. western div., Vancouver, 1966-74; joined Royal Bank of Can., 1974, asst. gen. mgr. project finance, 1975-76, dep. gen. mgr. corp. lending, 1976-78, v.p. nat. accounts, 1978-79, sr. v.p. planning and mktg. internat. div., 1979-80, sr. v.p. and gen. mgr. B.C., Vancouver, 1980-83; exec. v.p. Internat. Banking div. Royal Bank of Can., Toronto, 1983-86; pres. Royal Bank of Can., Montreal, 1986—; bd. dirs. Royal Bank Can., McDonald's Restaurants Can. Ltd. Mem. adv. council Faculty of Commerce and Bus. Adminstrn., U. B.C.; chmn. capital campaign Corp. of Bishop's U. Mem. Can. Inst. Chartered Accts. Clubs: Vancouver, Royal Canadian Yacht (Toronto); Mount Royal, Forest and Stream, Montreal Indoor Tennis. Office: care Camille Laperrière, Royal Bank Can Royal Bank Pla, 200 Bay St Pub Affairs Ste 935, Toronto, ON Canada M5J 2J5

CLEM, CASEY GALYEAN, real estate broker, accountant; b. Jacksonville, Tex., Mar. 2, 1954; s. Ross Albert and Genevieve Ruth (Keith) C. BBA, Baylor U., 1975. CPA, N.Mex. Adminstrv. asst. Major Brick Co., Henderson, Tex., 1970-75; acct. audit services Main Hurdman, Waco, Tex., 1976-78, Neff & Co., Albuquerque, 1978-79, Main Hurdman, Dallas, 1981-82; exec. ptnr. Clem Investments, Santa Fe, N.Mex., 1982—; gen. ptnr. Century House II, Santa Fe, 1982— , Clem Enterprises, Santa Fe, 1981—; chmn. Galyean Ltd., Santa Fe, 1978—; owner Casey G. Clem, CPA, Santa Fe; v.p. Houtman & Co., P.C., CPA's, 1984-86 . Mem. major gifts com. Ballet at Santa Fe, 1983. treas. N.Mex. AIDS Svcs. Inc., 1987—. Mem. AICPA, Tex. Soc. CPA's, N.Mex. Soc. CPA's. Republican. Episcopalian. Lodge: Kiwanis (Waco, Tex.). Office: 121 Sandoval St Santa Fe NM 87501

CLEMENS, T. PAT, manufacturing company executive; b. Hibbing, Minn., July 26, 1944; s. Jack LeRoy and Mildred (Coss) C.; m. Marianne Paznar, Oct. 1, 1966; children: Patrick Michael, Heather Kristen. BS in Econs. and Mgmt., St. Cloud State U., 1968, student of theology, Coll. St. Thomas, 1985-87. Sales adminstr. Transistor Electronics Co., Eden Prarie, Minn., 1969; head instnl. sales Chiquita Brands, Edina, Minn., 1970; dist. sales mgr. Menley & James Labs., Phila., 1971-75; owner, pres. T.P. Clemens Labs., Eagan, Minn., 1975—; instr community edn. Rosemount, Minn., 1977-78; bd. dirs. Rosemount Hockey, 1977-78, Relocation Assistance Assn. Am., 1984-85; v.p. Sch. Dist. #196 Booster Club, 1984-85; lectr. econs. to corps., high schs. and colls. in U.S., Scotland, Ireland, and Jamaica, 1979—. Author, editor: How Prejudice and Narcissism Control Economics of the United States and the World, 1979. Recipient letter recognition Dakota County Atty.'s Dept. Mem. Rosemont Community Edn. Bd., 1985, chmn. 1986-87; chmn. speakers bur. Citizens Steering Com., 1984-85; little League coach, 1970-82, 88; high sch. weight lifting coach, 1975—; vol. worker with comatose children. Mem. Internat. Platform Assn. Home and Office: 1276 Vildmark Dr Eagan MN 55123

CLEMENT, PHILIP A., electronics executive; b. Gary, Ind., Sept. 18, 1944; s. Earl Jr. and Bettee (Schutz) C.; m. Sue F. Wagner, Feb. 2, 1965; children: Philip Bradford, David Shane. BA, Western Mich. U., 1966; MBA, U. Chgo., 1970. V.p., gen. mgr. Sitka Corp. Jansport Div., Everett, Wash., 1973-79; v.p. adminstrn. and control Bell & Howell Co., Chgo., 1979-83; pres., chief exec. officer DeVry, Inc. subs. Bell & Howell Co., Evanston, Ill., 1983-87; pres., sr. v.p. adminstrn. Bell & Howell Co., Skokie, Ill., 1987-88, exec. v.p., chief fin. officer, 1988—. Dir. alumni Grad. Sch. Bus. U. Chgo., 1986; bd. dirs. Better Boys Found., Chgo., 1985; pres. Robert B. Huff Meml. Scholarship Fund., Wilmette, Ill., 1986; mem. Pres.'s Council Nat. Coll. Edn., Wilmette, 1986; v.p., bd. dirs. Chgo. Council Boy Scouts Am., 1987. Mem. Nat. Assn. Mfrs., Nat. Assn. Corp. Dirs., U. Chgo. Alumni Assn. (dir. 1986—). Office: Bell and Howell Co 5215 Old Orchard Rd Skokie IL 60077

CLEMMER, WILLIAM ALFRED, marketing professional; b. Hong Kong, Mar. 14, 1933; s. Raymond Moyer and Hazel Marcella (Grant) C.; m. Shirley Rebecca Ruleman, June 15, 1958; children: Kelly Blair, Brett Alan. BA, San Francisco State U.; student, Houghton (N.Y.) Coll., St. Paul (Minn.) Bible Coll. Tech. sales rep. 3M Co., Washington, 1962-66; registered rep. Ferris & Co., Washington, 1966-70; investment exec. Reynolds & Co., Washington, 1970-71; pres. F.I.M.S. subs. Info. Systems, Inc., Fairfax, Va. and Fla., 1971-72; v.p. Info. Systems, Inc., Fairfax, 1971-72; president, chief exec. officer Mariculture Growth Ind., Pensacola, Fla., 1972; v.p.-annuity mktg. Mass. Fin. Services Co., Boston, 1972-85; 1st v.p.-mktg. Integrated Resources, Inc., N.Y.C., 1985-88; exec. v.p., nat. sales mgr. J & W Seligman & Co. Mktg., Inc., N.Y.C., 1988—; lectr. in field; mem. Sales and Mktg. Com. Investment Co. Inst., Washington, D.C., 1988—; assoc. mem. I.A.F.D., Denver. Author: (manuals) Public Relations at State, 1964, Retirement Planning-Basics, 1987. Active staff, tchr., dir. Evangelism & Discipleship Ministries, 1975-85, Grace Chapel, Lexington, Mass., The Navigators, Inc., Washington, D.C., 1962-64. PFC with U.S. Army, 1952-54. Mem. World Trade Assn. (pres. San Francisco chpt. 1963-64, recipient Wilson award 1964), Securities Industry Assn., San Francisco Club. Republican. Home: 35 Dudley Rd Wilton CT 06897 Office: J & W Seligman & Co Mktg Inc 130 Liberty St New York NY 10006

CLENDENIN, JOHN L., telephone company executive; b. El Paso, Tex., May 8, 1934; s. Thomas Pipes and Maybelle Baumann C.; m. Margaret Ann Matthews, Aug. 30, 1954; children: Elizabeth Ann, Linda Susan, Mary Kathryn, Thomas Edward. B.A., Northwestern U., 1955. With Ill. Bell Telephone Co., 1955-78, v.p., 1975-78; v.p. ops. Pacific Northwest Bell, Seattle, 1978-79; v.p. AT&T, 1979-81; pres. So. Bell Tel. & Tel. Co., Atlanta, 1981-82, chmn. bd., 1982-84; chmn. bd., pres., chief exec. officer BellSouth Corp., Atlanta, 1984—, also dir., 1984—; dir. 1st Atlanta Corp., 1st Nat. Bank Atlanta., Nat. Service Industries Inc., Equifax Inc., Capital Holding Corp., RJR Nabisco, Inc., First Wachovia Corp.; Kroger Co., Coca-Cola Enterprises, Inc. Trustee Atlanta Arts Alliance; nat. chmn. Nat. Alliance Bus.; nat. treas. United Way Am.; bd. dirs. U.S. C. of C., nat. exec. bd. Boy Scouts Am., Jr. Achievements. Served with USAF, 1956-59. Presbyterian. Clubs: Commerce (dir.), Cherokee Town and Country, Piedmont Driving (Atlanta). Office: BellSouth Corp 1155 Peachtree St NE Atlanta GA 30367 *

CLERK, NORMAN JEFFREY, advertising agency executive; b. Oakland, Calif., Mar. 3, 1923; s. Ira and Winifred (Mastick) C.; m. Anne Linderman, Apr. 28, 1951; children: Norman G., Bradford L., Amyann M. Student Modesto Jr. Coll., 1942-43, Armstrong Coll., 1948-49, U. Calif. at Berkeley, 1949. Owner, N.J. Clerk & Asso., San Francisco, 1954-64; account exec. Kennedy, Hannaford & Dolman, Inc., Oakland, 1964-65, v.p., 1966-69; owner, pres. N.J. Clerk & Assos., Oakland, 1969—; instr. advt. Laney Jr. Coll., 1966-67. Contbr. articles to profl. jours. Club: Encinal Yatch (Alameda, Calif.). Lodge: Elks. Home and Office: Clerk & Assocs 6688 Brook Way Paradise CA 95969

CLEVETT, METON LLOYD (BUD), engineer; b. Allentown, Pa., Oct. 25, 1918; s. Merton L. and Lena R. (Wenger) C.; m. Hazel J. Satterwhite, Apr. 17, 1950 (div. 1973); children: Laura, Steve, Stan, Jim; m. Mildred L. McIntosh, July 20, 1974; children: Barbara, Linda, Laura, Brad. Student, Yale U., 1943; BSME, Purdue U., 1947; postgrad., MIT, 1954. Registered profl. engr., Ind., Calif., Mass., Colo. Research engr. U.S. Army Research Lab., Natick, Mass., 1950-56; owner, bd. dirs. Clevelab, Littleton, Colo., 1957—. Contbr. more than 60 articles to profl. jours. Over 50 patents in field. Served with U.S. Army, 1942-46. Recipient 47 indsl. awards. Home: 6121 S Logan Ct Littleton CO 80121

CLIFF, BARRY LEE, financial planner; b. Reading, Pa., Mar. 31, 1943; s. James Denton and Virginia Mae (Kelly) C. AAS, Capitol Inst. Tech., 1964; student in engring. econs., Iowa State U., 1967-68. Cert. in fin. planning. Dist. mgr. Equity Funding Securities Corp., Washington, 1969-73; br. mgr. Investors Fin. Services, Rockville, Md., 1973-74; co-founder, chief exec. officer, pres. Am. Fin. Cons., Silver Spring, Md., 1974—; mem. adj. faculty Coll. Fin. Planning. Served with USN, 1961-63. Named to Coll. Fin. Planning Hall of Fame, 1978; fellow Captitol Inst. Tech., 1987. Fellow Capitol Coll.; mem. Inst. Cert. Fin. Planners, Fin. Products Standards Bd. (chmn.), Internat. Assn. Fin. Planners, Registry of Fin. Planning Practitioners. Home: 10112 Kensington Pkwy Kensington MD 20895 Office: 8555 16th St Ste 701 Silver Spring MD 20910

CLIFF, STEVEN BURRIS, engineer; b. Knoxville, Tenn., Mar. 30, 1952; s. Edgar Burris and Otella (Patterson) C.; m. Sharon Grace Davis, Sept. 11, 1971 ; children: Sarah Elizabeth, Susan Rebecca, Steven John. BS in Engring. Sci., U. Tenn., 1974, MS in Engring. Sci., 1976; postgrad., So. Sem., 1974-75. Research asst. U. Tenn., Knoxville, 1972-75, asst. research prof., 1975-76; program analyst Oak Ridge (Tenn.) Nat. Lab., 1976-77, research engr., 1977-79; chief tech. officer Computer Concepts Corp., Knoxville, 1979-81; pres. Productive Programming Inc., Knoxville, 1981-82; v.p. research and devel. Control Tech. Inc., Knoxville, 1982—. Contbr. articles to profl. jours. Mem. exec. bd. Rocky Hill Parent-Tchr. Orgn., Knoxville, 1987; deacon West Knoxville Bapt. Ch., 1984-87, Loveland Bapt. Ch., Knoxville, 1976-82. U. Tenn. scholar, 1970. Mem. Soc. Mfg. Engrs., Nat. Electronic Mfg. Assn. (chmn. com. 1987—, seminar speaker 1988—). Home: 8210 Northshore Dr Knoxville TN 37919

CLIFFORD, STEWART BURNETT, banker; b. Boston, Feb. 17, 1929; s. Stewart Hilton and Ellinor (Burnett) C.; m. Cornelia Park Woolley, Apr. 26, 1952; children—Cornelia Lee Wareham, Rebecca Lyn Mailer-Howat, Jennifer Leggett Danner, Stewart Burnett. A.B., Harvard U., 1951, M.B.A., 1956. Asst. cashier Citibank, N.A., N.Y.C., 1958-60, asst. v.p., 1960-63; exec. v.p., gen. mgr. Merc Bank, Montreal, Que., Can., 1963-67, v.p. planning Overseas div.. exec. v.p., gen. mgr., 1967-68; v.p., adminstr. comml. banking group Citibank, N.A., N.Y.C., 1969-72; v.p. head world corp. dept. Citibank, N.A., London, 1973-75; sr. v.p. domestic energy Citibank, N.A., N.Y.C., 1975-80, sr. v.p., head pvt. banking and investment div., 1981-87; div. exec., head investment div. Citicorp, N.Y.C., 1987—; bd. dirs. Cititrust Ltd., Bahamas. Pres., 120 East End Ave. Corp., Woolley-Clifford Found.; life trustee Spence Sch.; bd. dirs. Horizon Concerts, Inc.; mem. Neighborhood Com. for Asphalt Green; elder, trustee Brick Presbyterian Ch.; trustee YWCA, N.Y.C. Served to 1st lt. arty. U.S. Army, 1951-54. Republican. Clubs: Pilgrims, Union, University (N.Y.C.); Duxbury Yacht (Mass.). Home: 120 Eastend Ave New York NY 10028 Office: Citibank NA 153 E 53d St New York NY 10043

CLINARD, JOSEPH HIRAM, JR., securities company executive; b. N.Y.C., Jan. 29, 1938; s. Joseph Sr. and Bertha (Feins) C.; m. Marcia Blyer, Sept. 1, 1958; children: Susan Clinard Jacobs, Robert. Cert., N.Y. Inst. Fin., 1962, Am. Coll., 1976, Adelphi U., 1980. Cert. fin. planner. Account exec. Merrill Lynch, N.Y.C., 1964-68; v.p. Shearson Lehman, N.Y.C., 1968-73; nat. dir. fin. planning Herzfeld & Stern, N.Y.C., 1974-78; v.p. Chem. Bank, N.Y.C., 1978-83; pres. DESCAP Securities, Inc., Hauppauge, N.Y., 1983—; adj. prof. Adelphi U., Garden City, N.Y., 1980—, asst. to dean, 1983-87; chief cons. Clinard Mgmt. Assocs., Huntington, N.Y., 1985—; exec. dir. L.I. Ctr. Fin. Studies, Hauppauge, 1986—. Author: Increasing Your Worth Through Personal Financial Planning, 1987. With USAF, 1956-59. Mem. L.I. Internat. Assn. Fin. Planning (pres. 1980-83, chmn. bd. dirs. 1983-88) (Appreciation award 1988), Adelphi Soc. Fin. Planners (v.p. 1985-86). Republican. Home: 3 Colyer Pl Greenlawn NY 11740 Office: DESCAP Securities Inc 200 Motor Pkwy Hauppauge NY 11788

CLINE, C. BOB, natural gas company executive; b. Oklahoma City, Nov. 30, 1946; s. David Brummitt and I. Fae (Dagenhart) C.; m. Anne Marie Marchand, Dec. 30, 1972; children: Beth, David. BSCE, U. Okla., 1969. Engr. Conoco Natural Gas Dept., Houston, 1972-75; dir. natural gas liquids Conoco, Houston, 1975-77; mgr. natural gas Conoco Ltd., London, 1977-79; mgr. engring. natural gas dept. Conoco, Houston, 1979-80; gen. mgr. bus. devel. Continental Pipeline Co., Houston, 1980-83, gen. mgr. ops., 1984; gen. mgr. strategic planning Conoco, Inc., Houston, 1983; sr. v.p. bus. devel. Parker Gas Co., Inc., Houston, 1984-85, pres., chief exec. officer, 1985—, also bd. dirs.; bd. dirs. Capitol Trenchers Corp., Austin. bd. dir. sales Houston Pin Oak Charity, 1985-87, YMCA Camp Cullen, 1989—. 1st lt. U.S. Army, 1969-71, Vietnam. Mem. Natural Gas Men Houston, So. Gas Assn., Young Pres' Orgn. (mem. Houston chpt.). Republican. Methodist. Clubs: Nottingham Country (Katy, Tex.), Houston Met. Raquet. Office: Parker Gas Cos Inc 1600 Smith St Ste 3800 Houston TX 77002

CLINE, CLEO RUTH, insurance consultant, broker; b. Hutchinson, Kans., Feb. 2, 1929; d. Earl Isaac and Lena (Little) Rounkles; m. Jack Byron Cline, Dec. 15, 1946. Grad. in ins. Am. Inst., 1977. Supr. Auto Club So. Calif., Los Angeles, 1947-54; underwriter Employees Mut. Des Moines, Wichita, Kans., 1954-56; various positions Crum Forster Co., Los Angeles, 1956-84; spl. acct. mgr. Indsl. Indemnity, Pasadena, Calif., 1979-84; ins. broker, instr., cons. Cleo Cline Cons., 1984-87. Cons., co-editor to The Umbrella Book, 1978. Mem. fund-raising com. Blind Sports, San Francisco, 1977. Named Calif. Ins. Woman of Yr., Profl. Ins. Assn., Los Angeles, 1977. Mem. Nat. Soc. CPCU's (risk mgmt. sect., internat. ins. sect., officer San Gabriel chpt., nat. dir. Western region 1986—, coordinator first satellite teleconf. nat. seminar, 1985), Internat. Soc. CPCU's (chmn. com. 1977-83), Nat. Assn. Ins. Women, San Marino Bus. and Profl. Women, Ind. and Profl. Ins. Agents Assn. Republican. Club: Los Angeles, University. Office: 1500 Hampton St PO Box 69 Columbia SC 29202

CLINE, GREGORY PAUL, business information systems consultant, market analyst; b. Port Huron, Mich., May 14, 1960; s. Roger Charles and Patricia Jean C. BA, BS with highest distinction, U. Maine, Orono, 1982; MS, Dartmouth Coll., 1986. Software engr. Digital Equipment Corp., Merrimack, N.H., 1982-87; cons. The Yankee Group, Boston, 1987—. Mem. Dartmouth Alumni Club, Phi Beta Kappa, Phi Kappa Phi, Alpha Phi Omega. Democrat. Home: 390 The Riverway #6 Boston MA 02115 Office: The Yankee Group 200 Portland St Boston MA 02114

CLINE, RICHARD GORDON, business executive; b. Chgo., Feb. 17, 1935; s. William R. and Katherine A. (Bothwell) C.; m. Carole J. Costello, Dec. 28, 1957; children: Patricia, Linda, Richard, Jeffrey. BS, U. Ill., 1957. With Jewel Cos., Inc., Chgo., 1963-85; pres. Osco Drug, Inc. subs., 1970-79, sr. exec. v.p., 1979, pres., chief oper. officer, 1980-84, chmn., pres., chief. exec. officer, 1984-85; pres. NICOR Inc., Naperville, Ill., 1985, chmn., pres., chief exec. officer, 1986-88, chmn., chief exec. officer, 1988—, also bd. dirs.; chmn., bd. dirs. No. Ill. Gas and subs.; bd. dirs. Whitman Corp., Pet Inc. and Hussmann Corp. Trustee Rush-Presbyn.-St. Luke's Med. Ctr.; gov. and former chmn. bd. Cen. DuPage Hosp.; bd. dirs. U. Ill. Found.; chmn. and gov. Ill. Council on Econ. Edn.; mem. Northwestern Univ. Assocs., Chicagoland United Way/Crusade of Mercy. Mem. Am. Gas Assn. (bd. dirs.), Econ. Club of Chgo., Chgo. Golf Club, Comml. Commonwealth Club. Office: NICOR Inc 1700 W Ferry Rd Naperville IL 60566

CLINE, ROBERT ALEXANDER, JR., banker; b. Cin., June 8, 1935; s. Robert Alexander Sr. and Martha (Kunkel) C.; m. Rosalen Ehemann, Sept. 30, 1978; children: John Emery, Christopher Raymond. BA, Williams Coll., 1957; MBA, Xavier U., 1965. Staff asst. Procter & Gamble Co., Cin., 1960-63; mktg. rep. IBM, Cin., 1963-66; sr. v.p. Fifth Third Bank, Cin., 1966-80; pres. Harley's Inc., Charleston, S.C., 1980-84; v.p. First Nat. Bank Commerce, New Orleans, 1984-85; group v.p. Fifth Third Bank, Cin., 1985—. Trustee Cin. Hist. Soc., St. Margaret's Hall, Cin., Cin. Theatrical Assn.; mem. adv. bd. Grad. Sch. Xavier U., Dan Beard Council Boy Scouts Am. Lt. USAF, 1957-58. Mem. Cin. Country Club, Commonwealth Club, Queen City Club, Charleston Country Club. Home: 4775 Miami Rd Cincinnati OH 45243 Office: Fifth Third Bank 38 Fountain Sq Cincinnati OH 45202

CLINE, ROBERT STANLEY, air freight company executive; b. Urbana, Ill., July 17, 1937; s. Lyle Stanley and Mary Elizabeth (Prettyman) C.; m. Judith Lee Stucker, July 7, 1979; children: Lisa Andre, Nicole Lesley, Christina Elaine, Leslie Jane. B.A., Dartmouth Coll., 1959. Asst. treas. Chase Manhattan Bank, N.Y.C., 1960-65; v.p. fin. Pacific Air Freight Co., Seattle, 1965-68; exec. v.p. fin. Airborne Freight Corp., Seattle, 1968-78, vice chmn., chief fin. officer, dir., 1978-84, chmn., chief exec. officer, dir., 1984—; bd. dirs. Rainier Bancorp, Rainier Nat. Bank. Trustee Seattle Repertory Theatre, 1974—, Children's Orthopedic Hosp. Found., 1983—, Corp. Council of the Arts, 1983—, Wash. Gives, 1983—; chmn. bd. Seattle Repertory Theatre, 1979-83; bd. dirs. Washington Roundtable, 1985—; chmn. bd. Children's Hosp. Found, 1987—. Served with U.S. Army, 1959-60. Home: 1209 39th Ave E Seattle WA 98112 Office: Airborne Freight Corp 3101 Western Ave PO Box 662 Seattle WA 98121

CLINGAN, MELVIN HALL, lumber executive, publisher; b. Atchison, Kans., July 12, 1929; s. Frank E. and Hazel Ellen (Hall) C.; B.S. in Bus. (Summerfield scholar), U. Kans., 1951; children—Sandra, Scott, Kimberly, Marcia. Pres., Holiday Homes, Inc. and Clingan Land Co., Olathe, Kans., 1956—; chmn. Johnson County Pubs., 1965—; former pub. Johnson County Herald, Gardner News, De Soto News, Spring Hill New Era; dir. R.L. Sweet Lumber Co. and subs., Kansas City, Kans., 1959—, exec. v.p., 1973-80, pres., 1981—. V.p. Westwood View Sch. Bd., 1965-68; Republican congl. dist. chmn., mem. state exec. com., 1966-72; bd. dirs. Johnson County Community Coll. Found., 1973-82. Served with USAF, 1951-55. Mem. Home Builders Assn. Greater Kansas City (past pres.), Home Builders Assn. Kans. (past pres.), Nat. Assn. Home Builders (nat. life dir.), Mission C. of C. (pres. 1971), Sigma Nu (grand officer 1961-68, ednl. found. 1980-85 , trustee 1982-85), Omicron Delta Kappa, Beta Gamma Sigma, Sigma Delta Chi. Republican. Presbyterian. Clubs: Mission Hills Country; Shadow Glen Golf (Olathe, Kans.); Eagle Creek Golf (Cave Creek, Ariz.). Home: 5345 Mission Woods Rd Shawnee Mission KS 66205

CLINGMAN, WILLIAM HERBERT, JR., managment consultant; b. Grand Rapids, Mich., May 5, 1929; s. William Herbert and Elizabeth (Davis) C.; BS with distinction and honors in Chemistry, U. Mich., 1951; MA, Princeton U., 1954, PhD, 1954; m. Mary Jane Wheeler, Feb. 6, 1951; children—Mary Constance, James Wheeler. Chemist, Am. Oil Co., Texas City, Tex., 1954-57, group leader, 1957-59; head thermoelectric sect. Tex. Instruments, Inc., Dallas, 1959-61, dir. energy research lab., 1961-62, mgr. corp. research and devel. mktg. dept., 1962-67; pres. W.H. Clingman Co., Inc., Dallas, 1967—; v.p., bd. dirs. Precision Measurement Inc., Dallas, 1985—; speaker, cons. SBA, 1967-70; mem. adv. com. on sci., tech. and economy Nat. Planning Assn., 1966-67. Mem. Am. Chem. Soc., IEEE, Assn. Computing Machinery, Sigma Xi. Club: Brook Hollow Golf (Dallas). Mem. editorial adv. bd. Jour. Advanced Energy Conversion, 1961-66. Home: 4416 McFarlin St Dallas TX 75205 Office: 700 N Pearl St Suite 300 Dallas TX 75201

CLINTON, JOHN PHILIP MARTIN, communications executive; b. Sheffield, Eng., Apr. 30, 1935; came to U.S., 1967; s. John A.T. and Phyllis Mary (Fowler) C.; m. Margaret Rosemary Morgan, Aug. 26, 1961; children: Alaric, Ivan, James. BA, Oxford U., 1959, MA, 1962. Mgr. computer systems Stanford (Calif.) U., 1967-70; v.p. systems devel. Computer Curriculum Corp., Palo Alto, Calif., 1970-79; exec. v.p. Captec, Inc., Santa Clara, Calif., 1979-80; mgr. product devel. Siltec Corp., Menlo Park, Calif., 1980-82; cons. Instructive Tech., Palo Alto, 1982-83; mgr. software devel. Voicemail Internat., Inc., Santa Clara, 1983-85, v.p. engring., 1985-87, sr. v.p. engring., 1987-88; pres. In-Gate Tech., Santa Clara, 1988—. Author: Begin Agol, 1966; editor (newsletter) Flat Tyre, 1982. Hastings scholar Queens Coll., Oxford U., 1955-59. Mem. Info. Industry Assn. (voice standards com. 1988—), Western Wheelers Bicycle Club (pres. 1983), Oxford and Cambridge Club (London), Oxford Soc. Home: 2277 Bryant St Palo Alto CA 94301 Office: In-Gate Tech 1333 Lawrence Expwy #440 Santa Clara CA 95051

CLOCK, PHILIP, lawyer, international affairs consultant; b. Redlands, Calif., Aug. 30, 1915; s. Charles Henry and Muriel Adelaide (Beamer) C.; m. Audrey Brumfield; children: Charles Philip II, Barbara Clock Allen, Frederic Timothy. Exchange student, Lingnan U., Canton, China, 1935-36; AB, Stanford U., 1937, Stanford U., 1938; JD, Stanford U., 1940; MA, U Malaya, Singapore, 1953; postgrad., Nat. War Coll., 1957-58. Bar: Calif. 1946. Joined Fgn. Svc. Dept. State, 1946; polit., legal officer Am. Legation, Budapest, 1947-49; polit. officer, officer in-charge rels. internat. ct. justice The Hague, 1951-52; counselor in charge fgn. and polit. affairs Am. Embassy, The Hague, Teheran, Iran, 1955-57; dep. chief mission, charge d'affairs Am. Embassy, Panama, 1960-62; counselor, in charge fgn. and polit. affairs Am. Embassy, Ankara, Turkey, 1962-65; dep. chief mission Am. Embassy, Monrovia, Liberia, 1965-69; engaged in devel. programs UN, Malaysia, Sabah, Sarawak, Brunei and Singapore, 1970-73; pvt. practice law, cons. internat., legal and fgn. affairs San Francisco, 1973—; cons. Internat. Ct. Justice, The Hague, The Netherlands, 1973—; fundraiser Stanford U., prep. schs.; advisor U.S. Mission UN, N.Y.C. Maj. transp. corps, U.S. Army, 1941-46, ETO, MTO. Decorated Bronze Star. Mem. Chevy Chase Club (Md.), Olympic Club, Sloane Club (London), numerous others in S.E. Asia, Middle East. Republican. Episcopalian. Home and Office: 2201 Sacramento St Unit 203 San Francisco CA 94115

CLOSE, DONALD PEMBROKE, management consultant; b. Orange, N.J., July 11, 1920; s. Charles Mollison and Simah Close; B.S. in Economics, Wharton Sch. U. Pa., 1942; m. L. Carolyn Reck, Apr. 22, 1950; children—Geoffrey Stuart, Cynthia Leigh, Sara Carolyn. Sales rep. IBM, Newark, 1946-47; asst. budget dir. L. Bamberger & Co., Newark, 1947-53; staff exec. Am. Express, N.Y.C., 1953; controller, sec. Ciba Co., Inc., N.Y.C., 1953-59; dir. fin. and control Avon Products Inc., N.Y.C., 1960-72; pres. Corp. Fin. Assos., Inc., N.Y.C., 1973-76; v.p. Nelson Walker Assos., N.Y.C., 1973-76, Internat. Mgmt. Advisors, Inc., N.Y.C., 1976-86, Deven Assocs. Internat. Inc., 1986—; mem. Pvt. Sector Study on Cost Control in Fed. Govt., 1982. Trustee, Morristown (N.J.) Beard Sch., 1974-77; pres. Jr. Essex Troop Cavalry, 1964-68. Served with AUS, 1942-46. Decorated Bronze Star with oak leaf cluster, Letter of Commendation. Mem. Fin. Execs. Inst., Am. Soc. Corp. Secs., Systems and Procedures Assn., Nat. Assn. Accts., Human Resources Planning Soc., Group for Strategic Organizational Effectiveness, St. Andrews Soc. of N.Y., Nat. Assn. Corp. and Profl. Recruiters, Phi Sigma Kappa (past sec.). Republican. Episcopalian. Clubs: University (N.Y.C.); Montclair Golf; Morristown; Wharton. Home: 6 Ridge Rd Gladstone NJ 07934 Office: Deven Assocs Internat Inc 1 Claridge Dr Verona NJ 07044

CLOSS, MAURICE JOSEPH, automotive company executive; b. Toronto, Ont., Can., Dec. 14, 1927; s. Wilfred Clinton and Kathleen Rose (Skelly) C.; children: Paul Maurice, Patricia Lynn. Student, U. Western Ont., Queen's U., Kingston, Ont., Wayne State U. With Gen. Motors, 1943-55, Ford Motor Co., 1955-59; with Chrysler Can., 1959—, exec. v.p., 1980, pres., 1980—; sales mgr. West Chrysler Corp., Detroit, 1979-80, v.p., 1981—; dir. Union Enterprises Ltd., Chrysler Credit Can. Ltd., Chrysler Ins. Can. Ltd., Lumonics, Inc., Nat. Bank Can. Clubs: Beach Grove Golf & Country, Windsor; Renaissance (Detroit). Office: Chrysler Can Ltd, 2450 Chrysler Ctr, Windsor, ON Canada N9A 4H6

CLOUD, BRUCE BENJAMIN, SR., construction company executive; b. Thomas, Okla., Feb. 15, 1920; s. Dudley R. and Lillian (Sanders) C.; m. Virginia Dugan, June 5, 1944; children: Sheila Marie Cloud Kiselis, Karen Susan, Bruce Benjamin, Deborah Ann Cloud McKenzie, Virginia Ann Cloud Treadwell. BCE, Tex. A. and M. U., 1940. Registered profl. engr., Tex. With H.B. Zachry Co., San Antonio, 1940-42, 55—; exec. v.p. H.B. Zachry Co., 1963-87, pres., 1987—; also dir.; partner Dudley R. Cloud & Son, constrn., San Antonio, 1946-55. Mem. adv. council Boysville Inc., 1978-79; bd. dirs. Tex. State Tech. Inst. Found., 1983—. Served to lt. col. C.E. AUS, 1942-46, ETO. Recipient Pro Deo Et Juventute award Nat. Council Catholic Youth. Mem. Tex. Assn. Gen. Contractors (dir. hwy. and heavy br. 1947-48, 72-76, pres. 1974), Am. Concrete Paving Assn. (v.p. 1970-74, dir. 1970—, 1st v.p. 1975-75, pres. 1976), Nat. Asphalt Paving Assn., Tex. Hotmix Paving Assn. (dir. 1972), Nat. Asso. Gen. Contractors (life dir. 1976—, mem. exec. com. 1978-79, chmn. heavy div. 1979), San Antonio Livestock Assn. (life), Nat., Tex. Socs. Profl. Engrs., Tex. Good Rds.-Transp. Assn. (dir. 1974-79, exec. com. 1975-81, 85—), AIM, Am. Mgmt. Assn., San Antonio C. of C. (chmn. better roads task force 1978-79, 85-86), Cons. Contractors Council Am. (chmn. 1989), Holy Name Soc. (v.p. 1962-63), Nocturnal Adoration Soc., Alpha Epsilon Chi. Lodge: K.C. (3 deg.). Home: 127 Cave Ln San Antonio TX 78209 Office: H B Zachry Co PO Box 21130 San Antonio TX 78285

CLOUD, SANFORD, JR., insurance company executive; b. Hartford, Conn., Nov. 27, 1944; s. Sanford Sr. and Inez (Morgan) C.; m. Diane Marie Brown, June 10, 1967; children: Adam, Christopher, Robin. BA, Howard U., 1966, JD, 1969. Bar: Conn., 1969. Research asst. Sen. Thomas J. Dodd's Office, Washington, 1965-67; atty. Aetna Life & Casualty Co., Hartford, 1969, counsel dept. law, 1978-83, cons., 1983-86, corp. v.p. pub. involvement, 1986—; ptnr. Robinson, Robinson & Cole, Hartford, 1975-76, Cloud & Ibarguen, Hartford, 1977-78; state sen. Conn., 1977-80; adj. lectr. Sch. Law U. Conn., West Hartford, 1980-86. State senator Conn., 1977-80; pres. New Samaritan Communications Corp., New Haven, 1983—; bd. dirs. Wadsworth Atheneum, Hartford, 1985—, United Ch. Christ Conn. Conf., Hartford, 1983—, Mt. Sinai Hosp., Hartford, 1980—. Recipient Charter Oak Leadership medal Greater Hartford C. of C., 1979, Disting. Service award Greater Hartford Jaycees, 1975; named Lay Person of Yr. Christian Activities Council, Conn., 1986, One of 11-Person Del. to Peoples Republic China Am. Council Young Polit. Leaders, 1980. Mem. ABA, Nat. Bar Assn. Conn. Bar Assn., Conf. Bd./Contribution Council, Assn. of Bar of City of N.Y., Farmington Country Club, University Club. Home: 24 Woodside Circle Hartford CT 06105 Office: Aetna Life & Casualty Co 151 Farmington Ave Hartford CT 06156

CLOUGH, CHARLES ELMER, corporation executive; b. Concord, N.H., Aug. 7, 1930; s. Harold Roland and Roelene (Sawyer) C.; m. Nancy Carter, July 18, 1985; children: Martha, John, David, Benjamin, Thomas. A.B., Dartmouth Coll., 1952, M.B.A., 1953. Mem. rectifier dept. GE, Lynn, Mass., 1956-57; with Nashua (N.H.) Corp., 1957—, budget dir., then asst. treas., then treas., then v.p., then exec. v.p., now pres., chmn. Served to lt. USN, 1953-56. Republican. Club: Dartmouth (N.Y.C.). Office: Nashua Corp 44 Franklin St Nashua NH 03061

CLOUGH, CHARLES MARVIN, electronics company executive; b. Chgo., Nov. 9, 1928; s. Charles Marvin and Margaret Cecile C.; m. Emma Marie Giachetto, Oct. 11, 1952; children—John, Susan, Margaret, Irene, Charles Marvin III, Melissa. B.S., U. Ill., 1951. Vice pres. mktg. Tex. Instruments, Dallas, 1955-82; pres. Wyle Electronics Mktg. Group, Irvine, Calif., 1982-85; pres., chief operating officer Wyle Labs., El Segundo, Calif., 1985-88, pres., chief exec. officer, 1988—, also bd. dirs.; dir. Farr Co., El Segundo. Served to 1st lt. USAF, 1950-55. Republican. Roman Catholic. Home: 15 Cherry Hills Ln Newport Beach CA 92660 Office: Wyle Labs 128 Maryland St El Segundo CA 90245

CLOUSE, JOHN DANIEL, lawyer; b. Evansville, Ind., Sept. 4, 1925; s. Frank Paul and Anna Lucille (Frank) C.; m. Georgia L. Ross, Dec. 7, 1978; 1 child, George Chauncey. AB, U. Evansville, 1950; JD, Ind. U., 1952. Bar: Ind. 1952, U.S. Supreme Ct. 1962, U.S. Ct. Appeals (7th cir.) 1965. Assoc. firm James D. Lopp, Evansville, 1952-56; pvt. practice law, Evansville, 1956—; guest editorialist Viewpoint, Evansville Courier, 1978-86, Evansville Press, 1986—, Focus, Radio Sta. WGBF, 1978-84; 2d asst. city atty. Evansville, 1954-55; mem. appellate rules sub-com. Ind. Supreme Ct. Com. on Rules of Practice and Procedure, 1980. Pres. Civil Service Commn. Evansville Police Dept., 1961-62, v.p. 1988; pres. Ind. War Memls. Com., 1963-69; mem. jud. nominating com. Vanderburgh County, Ind., 1976-80. Served with inf. U.S. Army, 1943-46. Decorated Bronze Star. Fellow Ind. Bar Found.; mem. Evansville Bar Assn. (v.p. 1972), Ind. Bar Assn., Selden Soc., Pi Gamma Mu. Republican. Methodist. Club: Travelers Century (Los Angeles). Home: 819 S Hebron Ave Evansville IN 47715 Office: 1010 Hulman Bldg Evansville IN 47708

CLOUTIER, ROGER R., II, financial executive, accountant; b. Des Moines, May 26, 1953; s. Roger R. and Gertrude C.; m. Janice L. Cloutier; children: Alyssa, Jennifer. BSBA, U. N.D., 1975. CPA., Minn., Iowa. Mem. audit staff Arthur Andersen & Co., Mpls., 1975-80, audit mgr., 1980-84; v.p., controller CVN Co., Inc. (formerly C.O.M.B. Co.), Plymouth Minn., 1984-85, sr. v.p., chief fin. officer, 1985—. Mem. Am. Inst. CPA's, Minn. Soc. CPA's, Fin. Execs. Inst. Office: CVN Cos 1405 Xenium Ln N Plymouth MN 55441

CLOW, GORDON HENRY, data processing executive; b. Washington, Jan. 5, 1942; s. James McLaren and Eleanor Seymour (Johnston) C.; m. Elizabeth Ann Childress, June 28, 1964 (div. 1975); children: Lori Ann, Michael Gordon; m. Holly Margaret Evans, Aug. 14, 1976. BS in Engring., U.S. Naval Acad., 1964; MBA, Am. U., 1975. Commd. ensign USN, 1964, resigned from active duty, 1969; account exec. Merrill Lynch, Pierce, Fenner & Smith, Inc., Washington, 1969-73; program mgr. Potomac Rsch., Inc., McLean, Va., 1975-79; exec. v.p. Vanguard Technologies Internat., Fairfax, Va., 1979-87, dir., 1979-88. Mem. Naval Res. Assn. Home: 721 SW Bay Pointe Circle Palm City FL 34990

CLOYD, MARSHALL PRESTON, engineering company executive, civil engineer; b. Dallas, Nov. 28, 1939; s. Marshall Sadler and Frances (Spears) C.; m. Carol Gilliland, June 28, 1968 (dec. Mar. 1977); m. Jeannette Singleton, Sept. 6, 1980; children: Marshall David, Catherine Anne, Gertrude Singleton. BS, So. Meth. U., 1964; MS, Stanford U., 1965; postgrad., Harvard U., 1965-66. Registered profl. engr., Tex., La. Rodman, instrumentman Brown and Root, Inc., New Roads, La., 1959-66; from field engr. to sr. v.p. Brown & Root, Inc., Houston, London, Singapore, Santa Barbara (Calif.), Anchorage, 1966-82; chmn. InterMarine Inc., Houston, 1982—; Class agt. Phillips Acad., Andover, Mass., 1976—. Contbr. articles to profl. jours. Bd. dirs. Houston Ballet Found., 1983-84. Mem. ASCE, AIME, Am. Petroleum Inst., Newcomen Soc. N.Am., Naval League U.S., U.S. Naval Inst., Met. Club N.Y., Houston Racquet Club, River Oaks Country (Houston), Brook Hollow Club, Dallas Country Club. Home: 8 Pinewood Circle Houston TX 77024 Office: InterMarine Inc 8552 Katy Freeway Suite 144 Houston TX 77024

CLYMER, JOHN MARION, finance company executive; b. Indpls., July 8, 1960; s. Richard Marion and Jean (Archibald) C. AB in Religion and Econs., Wabash Coll., 1982. Registered fin. planner. Mktg. rep. Springs Industries, Youngstown, Ohio, 1982-83, Grand Rapids, Mich., 1983-84; sr. mktg. rep. Springs Industries, Columbus, Ohio, 1984-85, Mpls., 1985; fin. cons. Indpls. Fin. Group, 1986—. Author: Escape!, 1981. Youth dir. Hudnut Mayoral Campaign, Indpls., 1975; mem. staff Ford Presdl. Campaign, 1976, Reagan Presdl. Campaign, 1980; Rep. precinct capt., Indpls., pct. comm., 1986-87; mem. dist. com. Boy Scouts Am.; mem. Ch. Coun. on Ministries. Named Eagle Scout, 1973, Outstanding Young Man of Am., 1987, 88. Mem. Nat. Assn. Life Underwriters, Ind. Assn. Life Underwriters, Econ. Club Indpls., Nat. Assn. Wabash Men (bd. dirs.), Phila. Soc., Phi Kappa Psi (vol. cons. to endowment fund). Republican. Methodist. Club: Indpls. Athletic. Office: Indpls Fin Group 400 Marott Ctr 342 Massachusetts Ave Indianapolis IN 46204-2161

COAKLEY, WILLIAM THOMAS, utilities executive; b. Dubuque, Iowa, Oct. 18, 1946; s. Harold Leo and Mary Margaret (Schwartz) C.; m. Deborah Dixon Leach, Nov. 25, 1971; children: Matthew David, Kenneth William. BA, Loras Coll., 1968; postgrad., Drake U., 1968-69, 71. Commd. U.S. Army, 1970, advanced through grades to capt.; co. exec. officer U.S. Army, Fort Bragg, N.C., 1971-73; brigade staff officer U.S. Army, Stuttgart, Fed. Republic of Germany, 1973-75; budget analyst U.S. Army Corps of Engrs., Frankfurt, Fed. Republic of Germany, 1975-77; budget officer U.S. Army Corps of Engrs., Riyadh, Saudi Arabia, 1977-80; resigned U.S. Army Corps of Engrs., 1980; budget and fin. officer Western Area Power Adminstrn., Billings, Mont., 1980-85, fin. mgr., 1985—. Author, editor Fiscal Procedures and Control of Funds, 1975. Committeeman fund campaign Billings United Way, 1984. Mem. Internat. Soc. Am. Mil. Engrs. (sec., treas. Frankfurt chpt. 1974-75), Yellowstone Country Club (bd. dirs. 1984-86), Rotary. Republican. Roman Catholic. Home: 5620 Walter Hagen Dr Billings MT 59106-1003 Office: Western Area Power Adminstrn 2525 N 4th Ave Billings MT 59106-1001

COATES, NORMAN, university professor; b. Haifa, Palestine, Mar. 25, 1931; came to U.S., 1963; s. William and Emilie (Gabriel) C.; m. Marie-Claude Sabourin; children: Norman, Jean-Pierre. BA, Sir George Williams U., Montreal, 1957; MS, Cornell U., 1959, PhD, 1967; cert., Am. Grad. Sch. Internat. Mgmt., Glendale, Ariz., 1968. Staff cons. Can. Nat. Hdqrs., Montreal, 1950-60; vis. prof. Nat. Inst. Mgmt. Devel., Cairo, 1961-63; teaching asst. Cornell U., Ithaca, N.Y., 1963-66; asst. prof. industry Wharton Sch. U. Pa., Phila., 1966-68; Ford Found. vis. prof. Inst. Estudios Superiores Administracion, Caracas, Venezuela, 1968-70; directing staff sr. exec. Nat. Def. Coll., Ottawa, Can., 1970-71; prof. mgmt. U. R.I., Kingston, 1971—; dir. Inst. Internat. Bus. U. R.I., 1988—, chmn. steering com., project dir. 1987—; coordinator internat. bus. Coll. Bus. Adminstrn., 1984—; cons. numerous govts. and corps. Contbr. chpts. to books, articles to profl. jours. Recipient numerous fellowships and grants, U. R.I. Mem. Acad. Mgmt., Acad. internat. Bus., Assn. Japanese Bus. Studies, Decision Scis Inst., Indsl. Relations Research Assn., Internat. Indsl. Relations Assn., Soc. Advancement Behavioral Econs., Strategic Mgmt. Soc. Home: 27 Wampum Rd Narragansett RI 02881 Office: Univ RI Coll Bus Adminstrn Kingston RI 02881

COBB, ALONZO FLOYD, JR., chemical company executive; b. N.Y.C., Jan. 12, 1947; s. Alonzo Floyd Sr. and Lorene (Brown) Cobb; m. Ernestine Mitchell (div.); children: Tarik Walden, Tammy Melissa. AS in Chemistry, Nassau Community Coll., 1976; BBA in Finance, Baruch Coll., 1979; MA in Econs. and Bus., Stanford U., 1983. Internal auditor Crocker Bank, San Francisco, 1979-80; fin. analyst Castle & Cooke, San Francisco, 1981-82; fin. planner Childers, Swan & Co., Fremont, Calif., 1983-85; mktg. analyst Pacific Bell Directory, San Francisco, 1985-87; sr. fin. analyst Pacific Bell, San Ramon, 1987-88; pres. Cobb Chemicals Société Privée À Résponsabilité Limitée, Kinshasa, Zaire, 1989—. Tutor San Francisco Sch. Vols., 1986—; com. mem. Corp. Action in Pub. Schs., 1986—. Served with U.S. Army, 1966-70. Republican. Adventist. Home: 537 16th Ave San Francisco CA 94118 Office: Cobb Chemicals SPRL, 10 B Ave, Bakongo Republic of Zaire

COBB, CAROLUS MELVILLE, science company executive, chemical researcher; b. Lynn, Mass., Jan. 22, 1922; s. Carolus Melville and Estelle Cecille (Snow) C.; 1 child, Carolus Melville III. SB, MIT, 1944, PhD, 1951. Rsch. chemist Tenn. Eastman Corp., Oakridge, 1944-46; sr. chemist Ionics, Inc., Cambridge, Mass., 1951-55, Allied Rsch. Assn., Boston, 1955-60; v.p., chief chemist Am. Sci. and Engring., Inc., Cambridge, 1960—, also bd. dirs. Mem. Am. Chem. Soc., Am. Phys. Soc., Combustion Inst., Internat. Acad. Dental Rsch., Maugus. Office: Am Sci and Engring Inc 40 Erie St Cambridge MA 02139

COBB, CAROLYN JANE, service executive; b. Harrisburg, Pa., Aug. 20, 1943; d. Edward John and Doris May (Magel) Swerk; m. Don Rickey Hall, June 1, 1961 (div. Dec. 1979); m. Phil Allison Cobb, July 10, 1981; children: Jon David, Allison C. Weaver. BFA cum laude, U. Tex., 1964. Tchr. NE Ind. Sch. Dist., San Antonio, 1964-66, Austin (Tex.) Ind. Sch. Dist., 1966-68; illustrator Tex. Employment Commn., Austin, 1968-77, instructional media technician, 1977-78, staff services asst., 1978-80, mgr. design/graphics, 1980—; v.p. Cruise Line Assocs., Inc., Austin, 1985—. Works adopted by Am. Greetings card co., 1981. Mem. Nat. Assn. Cruise Only Agencies (founding), Internat. Assn. Personnel in Employment Security (State award 1974), Nat. Assn. Female Execs., So. Watercolor Soc. (award 1983), Alpha Lambda Delta. Episcopalian. Home: 2610 Chowan Way Round Rock TX 78681 Office: Cruise Line Assocs Inc 9600 Great Hills Trail Ste 150-W Austin TX 78759

COBB, LESLIE DAVIS, utility executive; b. Beaumont, Tex., Jan. 4, 1935; d. Leslie Lethrage and Willie Sammie (Wiltshire) Davis; married; children: Terry W. Ogden, David Bryan Ogden. Student, Lamar U., public utility exec. program U. Mich. With Hall & Hall Ins., Beaumont, 1953-54; with Gulf States Utilities Co., Beaumont, 1955—; sec. to chmn. bd. Gulf States Utilities Co., 1974-79, corp. sec., 1979—. Mem. Am. Soc. Corp. Secs., Beaumont C. of C. Episcopalian. Clubs: Beaumont, Tower, Bus. and Profl. Men's. Office: Gulf States Utilities Co 350 Pine St Beaumont TX 77701

COBB, SHIRLEY ANN, public relations specialist, journalist; b. Oklahoma City, Jan. 1, 1936; d. William Ray and Irene (Fewell) Dodson; m. Roy Lampkin Cobb, Jr., June 21, 1958; children: Kendra Leigh, Cary William, Paul Alan. BA in Journalism with distinction, U. Okla., 1958, postgrad., 1972; postgrad., Jacksonville U., 1962. Info. specialist Pacific Missle Test Ctr., Pt. Mugu, Calif., 1975-76; corr. Religious News Service, N.Y.C., 1979-81; splty. editor fashion and religion Thousand Oaks (Calif.) News Chronicle, 1977-81; pub. relations cons., Camarillo, Calif., 1977—; sr. mgmt. analyst pub. info City of Thousand Oaks, 1983—. Contbr. articles to profl. jours. Trustee Ocean View Sch. Bd., 1976-79; pres. Pt. Mugu Officers' Wives Club, 1975-76; bd. dirs. Camarillo Hospice, 1983-85. Recipient Spot News award San Fernando Valley Press Club, 1979. Mem. Pub. Relations Soc. Am., Sigma Delta Chi, Phi Beta Kappa. Republican. Clubs: Las Posas Country, Town Hall of Calif. Home: 2481 Brookhill Dr Camarillo CA 93010 Office: 2150 W Hillcrest Dr Thousand Oaks CA 91320

COBB, SYLVIA ROSE, music publisher; b. Atlanta, Apr. 26, 1953; d. Alonzo Z. and George Mae (Butler) Rose; m. Lanza Kilmer Cobb, Apr. 26, 1980. AA, Southwestern Christian Coll., 1973; BA, Harding Coll., 1975. Mem. faculty Southwestern Christian Coll., Terrell, Tex., 1975-79, Luckett Christian Acad., Warren, Mich., 1981-85; pres. Srose Pub. Co., Detroit, 1985—. Author: A Guide to Effective Choral Singing, 1987; composer hymnal, Songs of Faith, 1985; arranger, composer numerous record albums and motivational cassette tapes. Bible tchr. Oakland Ch. of Christ, Southfield, Mich., 1985; bd. dirs. Luckett Christian Acad., 1987. Mem. Gospel Music Assn., Gospel Music Workshop Am., Nat. Acad. Recording Arts and Scis., NAFE, Gospel Song of Month Club Detroit. Home: 8866 Warwick St Detroit MI 48228 Office: Srose Pub Co 24801 Five Mile Rd Ste 22 Redford MI 48239

COBB, W. CECIL, JR., insurance and financial consultant; b. Decatur, Ala., Nov. 10, 1938; s. William C. and Ruby (Romine) C.; m. Judith Smith, July 17, 1959; children: Jack Alan, John Mark. BS in Psychology and Communication Arts, Xavier U., 1968; post-grad., U. Cin., 1970-72. Sr. analyst Proctor & Gamble Co., Cin., 1960-70; asst. dean U. Cin., 1970-72; salesman Bostitch-Textron, Inc., Cin., Toledo, Indpls., 1972-82; fin. services cons. Mass. Mut. Life Ins. Co., Seymour and Assocs., Inc., Toledo, 1982—. bd. dirs. Rolling Meadows Christian Acad., Toledo, 1982-84. mem. Nat. Assn. Life Underwriters, Nat. Mgmt. Assn. (bd. dirs. 1984—, mgmt. training dir. 1984—Toledo chpt.), Ohio Assn. Life Underwriters, Toledo Assn. Life Underwriters, Nat. Assn. Realtors, Toledo Bd. Realtors, Am. Numismatics Assn., Am. Power Boat Assn. (chief pit steward 1986), Internat. Assn. Fin. Planning. Mem. Ch. of Christ. Office: Seymour & Assocs Inc 3930 Sunforest Ct Toledo OH 43623

COBLE, WILLIAM CARROLL, computer engineer; b. Detroit, July 23, 1958; s. Haskin Frazier and Wilma Jolela (King) C.; m. Barbara Karen Smith, Aug. 22, 1987. BS in Physics, Morehouse Coll., 1981; BS in Elec. Engring., Ga. Inst. Tech., 1981; postgrad., U. Dayton, 1981-82, Ga. State U., 1983-84. Electronics engr. Dept. of Def., Dayton, Ohio, 1981-82; jr. computer engr. Ga. Power Co., Norcross, 1983-85; engr. info. systems Ga. Power Co., Atlanta, 1985-86, sr. engr., project leader, 1987—; pres. Masterplan Computers, Decatur, Ga., 1983—; with Distributed Mgmt. Systems, Norcross, 1983-85; cons. Sprull Products, Inc., Atlanta, 1987—; bd. advisors Rutledge Coll., Atlanta, 1988—. Pres. Springwoods Community, Decatur, 1986—. Mem. Data Processing Mgmt. Assn., Data Processing Assn., Info. Systems Cons. Assn., Nat. Soc. Black Engrs. (physics tutor Atlanta chpt. 1987—), Atlanta Exch. Home: 3408 Spring Circle Decatur GA 30032 Office: Ga Power Co Trans Info Systems 270 Peachtree St 8th Fl Atlanta GA 30303

COBLENTZ, GASTON, stockbroker; b. N.Y.C., June 8, 1918; s. Gaston and Lillian (Lashanska) C.; m. Zoubida Bentaieb, Jan. 22, 1982; m. Milosava Mikich, Jan. 16, 1952 (div. 1981); children: Andrea, Marina. Grad. cum laude Hotchkiss Sch., 1936; B.A. cum laude, Harvard Coll., 1939. Fgn. corr. N.Y. Herald Tribune, N.Y.C., 1946-63; ptnr., dir. Mitchell Hutchins & Co., Inc., N.Y.C., 1963-77; sr. v.p., dir. Paine Webber Mitchell Hutchins Internat., Inc., Paris, 1977-79; dir. Gaston Coblentz & Co. Ltd., St. Helier, Jersey, C.I., 1979-81, U.K. rep., 1982-88; dir. N.Am. Gen. & Mining Securities, Ltd., 1988—; cons. Golden Eagle Investments SA, 1983—, Lula 10100 Gold Mining N.V., 1985—. Co-author: Duel on the Brink, 1960. Served as maj. USAAF, 1941-45. Decorated D.F.C.; Croix de Guerre avec etoile de bronze (France); recipient Disting. Service in Journalism award Sigma Delta Chi, 1961. Clubs: Harvard, Overseas Press (N.Y.C.); Cercle de l'Union Interallie (Paris). Home: Morley Old Hall, Morley St Peter, Wymondham Norfolk NR18 9TT, England

COCHETTI, ROGER JAMES, international communications company executive; b. Albany, N.Y., Apr. 11, 1950; s. Roger Peter and Mary Ann (Bevelaqua) C. BS in Fgn. Svc., Georgetown U., 1972; MA in Internat. Rels., Johns Hopkins U., 1975; cert., Cambridge U., 1976, U. Va., 1986. Dir. Washington office UN Assn. of U.S.A., 1972-77; asst. dir. for legis. and pub. affairs U.S. Internat. Devel. Coop. Agy., Washington, 1978-81; dir. pub. and investor rels. Communications Satellite Corp., Washington, 1981-85, dir. investor and internat. rels., 1985-87, v.p. maritime bus. planning and devel., 1987—; cons. to John D. Rockefeller III, N.Y.C., 1975. Advisor Udall for Pres. Campaign, 1976. N.Y. State Regents scholar, 1968. Mem. Nat. Investor Rels. Inst., Am. Mgmt. Soc., Ctr. for Strategic and Internat.

Studies, Nat. Press Club (Washington), Princeton Club (N.Y.C.). Democrat. Roman Catholic. Office: Communications Satellite Corp 950 L'Enfant Pl SW Washington DC 20024

COCHRAN, DON WAYNE, systems industrial engineer; b. Mt. Gilead, Ohio, Sept. 25, 1952; s. Dean Merlin and Wilma Jean (Hesket) C.; m. Linda Ruth Guenthner, Aug. 23, 1975; children: David William, Amanda Marie. BS in Systems and Indsl. Engring., Ohio State U., 1975. Sales engr., mgr. distbn. div. Pressco, Inc., Cleve., 1975-78, v.p., sales mgr. distbn. div., 1978-82, dir. Am. Profl. Mktg., 1979-82, v.p. engring., gen. mgr. automation systems div., 1982-86, pres., chief exec. officer, chmn. bd., 1986—; v.p. mktg. and engring. Premier Products Co., Cleve., 1981-83; v.p. mktg. Am. Health & Safety Co., Willoughby, Ohio, 1982-84; mem. tech. adv. bd. Mr. Tune-Up, Inc., Willoughby, 1982-85. Mem. Soc. Mfg. Engrs., Beta Theta Pi. Republican. Office: Pressco Inc 145 Alpha Pk Cleveland OH 44143

COCHRAN, GEORGE CALLOWAY, III, banker; b. Dallas, Aug. 29, 1932; s. George Calloway and Miriam (Welty) C.; m. Jerry Bywaters, Dec. 9, 1961; children—Mary, Robert. B.A., So. Meth. U., 1954; J.D., Harvard U., 1957; cert., Sch. Banking, La. State U., 1969. Bar: Tex. 1957. Assoc. Leachman, Gardere, Akin and Porter, Dallas, 1960-62; various positions Fed. Res. Bank of Dallas, 1962-76, sr. v.p., 1976—; mem. adv. com. Bank Ops. Inst., East Tex. State U., Commerce, 1982—; mem. task force on truth in lending regulation Bd. Govs. of FRS, Washington, 1968-69; bd. dirs. Dallas chpt. Am. Inst. of Banking, 1986—. Mem. hist. landmark survey task force City of Dallas, 1974-78. Served to capt. USAF, 1958-60. Mem. ABA, State Bar Tex., Dallas Bar Assn., Phi Beta Kappa. Methodist. Club: Harvard (Dallas). Home: 3541 Villanova Dallas TX 75225 Office: Fed Res Bank of Dallas 400 S Akard St Dallas TX 75222

COCHRAN, JOSEPH EDWARD, II, financial executive; b. Boonville, Mo., May 7, 1952; s. Joseph Sr. and Patty (Sieckman) C. BBA, Culver-Stockton Coll., 1973; M in Internat. Mgmt., Am. Grad Sch. Internat. Mgmt., 1976. Pres., chief exec. officer JEC II Enterprises Ltd., Phoenix, 1978—, CETCOA, Phoenix, 1985—; v.p. adminstrn., dir. Provident Holding Corp., Phoenix, 1978—; v.p., chief fin. officer Refinery Mgmt. Co., Phoenix, 1983—; chief fin. officer, dir. AVM Hess Inc., Phoenix, 1987—. Republican. Episcopalian.

COCHRANE, JAMES LOUIS, economist; b. Nyack, N.Y., Aug. 31, 1942; s. Thomas and Anna (Yaroscak) C.; m. Katherine Prince Schirmer, Mar. 24, 1984; 1 child, Katherine Anne. BA, Wittenberg U., 1964; PhD, Tulane U., 1968. Instr. Tulane U., New Orleans, 1967-68; asst. prof. U. S.C., Columbia, 1968-70, assoc. prof., 1970-72, prof., 1972-77; sr. staff mem. NSC, Washington, 1978-79; directorate of intelligence CIA, Washington, 1980-83; sr. v.p., chief economist Tex. Commerce Bancshares Inc., Houston, 1984-88, N.Y. Stock Exch., 1988—; assoc. staff mem. Brookings Instn., Washington, D.C., 1972-74, 76-78; editorial bd. History of Polit. Economy Duke U., 1974-80, So. Econ. Jour. U. N.C., 1976-79; 1st v.p. So. Econ. Assn. U. N.C., 1976-77. Author: Macroeconomics Before Keynes, 1970, Macroeconomics Analysis and Policy, 1974, Industrialism and Industrial Man in Retrospect, 1977; editor: Multiple Criteria Decision Making, 1975. Mem. History of Econs. Soc. (treas. 1974-80), Asia Soc. (adv. dir. 1986). Home: 2019 Dunstan Houston TX 77005 Office: NY Stock Exch 11 Wall St New York NY 10005

COCKAYNE, ROBERT BARTON, retail company executive; b. Berkeley, Calif., Dec. 10, 1937; s. William Henry and Thelma (Cooper) C.; m. Hope Gaebl, May 23, 1964 (div.); 1 child, William Barton; m. Sally Frick, July 25, 1972; 1 child, Robin, stepchildren: Bruce, Vanessa, Kimberly. BS in Econs., Stanford U., 1959. Various positions from trainee to v.p., gen. mgr. Burdine's, Miami, Fla., 1960-74; pres., chief exec. officer Silverwood's, Los Angeles, 1974-75, May Cohens, Jacksonville, Fla., 1975-84, May Co., Cleve., 1984—. Active Downtown Devel. Authority, Jacksonville, 1981-83; mem. Young Pres.'s Orgn., Fla. chpt., 1980—; vestry St. Mark's Episc. Ch., Jacksonville, 1975-84, St. Paul's Episc. Ch., Cleveland Heights, Ohio, 1984-87; trustee United Way, Jacksonville, 1977-84, Cleve., 1986—. Served with U.S. Army N.G., 1960-66. Republican. Clubs: Mayfield Country, Union (Cleve.). Office: May Co 158 Euclid Ave Cleveland OH 44114

COCKBURN, JOHN F., banker; b. Everett, Wash., Apr. 8, 1928; s. Charles G. and Florence S. C.; m. Lynn F. Pierson, June 29, 1960; children—Steven, Matthew, Teresa, Patrick. BBA, U. Wash., Seattle, 1950. With Rainier Nat. Bank, Seattle, 1948—; exec. v.p. Rainier Nat. Bank, 1975—, mgr. pvt. banking, 1987—; pres. Pacific Coast Banking Sch., 1977-79; bd. dirs. Wash. Council Econ. Edn., 1979-81, fin. chmn., 1980-81. Trustee Forest Ridge Sch., Bellevue, Wash., Mcpl. League of Seattle and King County. Mem. Assn. Res. City Bankers. Congregationalist. Clubs: Rainier (Seattle) (trustee), Seattle Tennis (Seattle), Wash. Athletic (Seattle); Broadmoor Golf. Home: 1524 Shenandoah Dr E Seattle WA 98112 Office: Rainier Nat Bank 1301 5th Ave PO Box 3966 Seattle WA 98124

COCKFIELD, DAVID WELLINGTON, utility company executive; b. Toledo, Jan. 31, 1932; s. Edward George and Harriet (Wyandt) C.; m. Mary Winifred Davis, June 29, 1957 (div. 1977); children: Susan, William, John, James, Christopher; m. Dolores Rose Negri, May 22, 1980. BS, U.S. Naval Acad., 1955. Commd. ensign USN, 1955, advanced through grades to rear adm., 1982, ret., 1987; v.p. nuclear div. Portland (Oreg.) Gen. Electric Co., 1987—. Decorated 4 Legion of Merits. Republican. Office: Portland Gen Electric Co 121 S W Salmon St Portland OR 97204

COCKLIN, ROBERT FRANK, association executive; b. Lincoln, Nebr., Feb. 13, 1919; s. Frank Dietrich and Helen Catherine (Sampson) C.; m. Ruth Elizabeth Castner, June 25, 1942; children: John Andrew, Mary Collison (dec.). Student, U. Nebr., 1938-41, U.S. Army Command and Staff Coll., 1964, Army War Coll., 1969. Commd. 2nd lt. U.S. Army, 1941, advanced through grades to maj. gen., 1977; assoc. editor Field Arty. Jour., Washington, 1946-48; bus. mgr. N.G. Assn., Washington, 1948-50; dir. public affairs Assn. U.S. Army, Arlington, Va., 1950-77; exec. v.p. Assn. U.S. Army, 1977-88, sr. assoc., 1988—; dir. United Services Life Ins. Co., USLICO Corp. Author: Battery Duties, 1950, also pamphlets and articles. Trustee George C. Marshall Research Found. Decorated D.S.M., Bronze Star, Air medal, Purple Heart; recipient Disting. Civilian Svc. award, Disting. Svc. medal SSS, Disting. Svc. medal Nat. Guard Assoc. U.S. Fellow Inst. Land Warfare; mem. Air Force Assn., Army-Navy Club. Roman Catholic. Home: 1322 N Lynnbrook Dr Arlington VA 22201 Office: Assn US Army 2425 Wilson Blvd Arlington VA 22201

COCKRUM, WILLIAM MONROE, III, investment banker, consultant, educator; b. Indpls., July 18, 1937; s. William Monroe II C. and Katherine J. (Jaqua) Moore; m. Andrea Lee Deering, Mar. 8, 1975; children: Catherine Anne, William Monroe, IV. A.B. with distinction, DePauw U., Greencastle, Ind., 1959; M.B.A. with distinction, Harvard U., 1961. With A.G. Becker Paribas Inc., 1961-84, mgr. nat. corp. fin. div., 1968-71; mgr. pvt. investments A.G. Becker Paribas Inc., Los Angeles, 1971-84; fin. and adminstrv. officer A.G. Becker Paribas Inc., 1974-80, sr. v.p., 1975-78, vice chmn., 1978-84, also dir.; mem. faculty Northwestern U., 1961-63; vis. lectr. UCLA Grad. Sch. Mgmt., 1984-88, adj. prof., 1988—; dir. Knapp Communications Corp., Cinema Capital Mgmt., Inc. ; trustee Bruin-Trojan Superstar Classic. Mem. Delta Kappa Epsilon. Clubs: University (Chgo.); Monterey (Palm Desert, Calif); Deke (N.Y.C.); Alisal Golf (Solvang, Calif.).

COCKWELL, JACK LYNN, financial company executive; b. East London, Republic of South Africa, Jan. 12, 1941; s. William Henry and Daphne (Cound) C.; children: Linda, Lorie, Leslie, Tessa, Malcolm. M.Com., U. Cape Town, 1964, postgrad. with distinction, 1966. Chartered Acct. Mgr. Touche Ross & Co., Montreal, Que., Can., 1959-67; exec. v.p., chief operating officer Edper Enterprises Ltd., Toronto, Ont., Can., 1968—; also dir. Edper Enterprises Ltd.; exec. v.p., chief operating officer Brascan Ltd., Toronto, 1979—; also dir. Brascan Ltd.; vice chmn., dir. Hees Internat. Bancorp, Inc.; dir. Astral Bellevue Pathe Ltd., Bramalea Ltd., Brascade Resources Inc., Continental Bank of Can., Great Lakes Group Inc., Kerr Addison Mines Ltd., London Life Ins. Co., Noranda Inc., Noranda Forest, Inc., Trilon Fin. Corp., Trizec Corp. Ltd., Westmin Resources Ltd., M.A. Hanna Co., John Labatt Ltd., Norcen Energy Resources Ltd., Coscan Devel. Corp, Carena Bancorp Inc.; pres. Continental Bank of Can.; mem. adv. bd. The Fin. Post. Office: Brascan Ltd Commerce St W, Suite 4800, Toronto, ON Canada M5L 1B7

COCO, SAMUEL BARBIN, chemical company executive; b. Cottonport, La., Nov. 6, 1927; s. Samuel Barbin and Hattie Mae (Smith) C.; m. Hannalou John, June 25, 1957; children—Harvey Samuel, Caroline Shannon. B.S. in Mech. Engring., La. State U., 1950; postgrad., MIT, 1964. Plant engr. Cabot Corp., Ville Platte, La., 1950-52; with mfg. dept. Cabot Corp., Pampa, Tex., 1952-56; sales rep. Cabot Corp., Akron, Ohio, 1956-60; exec. asst. Cabot Corp., Boston, 1960-64, asst. gen. mgr. carbon black div., 1964-70, v.p., gen. mgr. carbon black div., 1970-77, sr. v.p., 1977-85, exec. v.p., 1985-89, pres., 1989—. Served with U.S. Army, 1946-47. Mem. Am. Chem. Soc. Club: Algonquin. Office: Cabot Corp 950 Winter St Waltham MA 02254

CODEN, MICHAEL HENRI, fiber optics and electronics manufacturing company executive; b. N.Y.C., Mar. 6, 1947; s. William and Ruth (Carmel) C. B.S. in Elec. Engring., MIT, 1967; M.S. in Bus., Columbia U., 1975; M.S. in Math, NYU, 1979. Engr., Hewlett Packard Co., Palo Alto, Calif., 1967-69; mktg. mgr. Digital Equipment Corp., Maynard, Mass., 1969-72; v.p. data processing Maher Terminals Co., Jersey City, 1972-75; div. mgr. Exxon Enterprises, Inc., N.Y.C., 1975-79; pres., chief exec. officer Codenoll Tech., Yonkers, N.Y., 1979—, also chmn. bd. Patentee compound semiconductor and communications equipment, computer local network equipment; contbr. articles to profl. jours. Mem. adv. bd. Polytech. U. of N.Y. Recipient Distinction cert. Laser Inst. Am., Am. Chem. Soc. Mem. IEEE (mem. tech. com. on computers and communications), Optical Soc. Am., N.Y. Acad. Sci., AAAS, Inst. Mgmt. Sci., Am. Electronics Assn. (mem. exec. coun.), Westchester County C. of C. (bd. dirs.), Beta Gamma Sigma. Jewish. Club: Columbia. Office: Codenoll Tech Corp 1086 N Broadway Yonkers NY 10701

CODY, ANDREA RHODARMER, financial planner; b. Waynesville, N.C., Sept. 8, 1958; d. Harold Cathey Rhodarmer and Rubena (Childers) Silver; m. Neal E. Cody Jr., Apr. 30, 1983. AS, Asheville-Buncombe Tech., 1978; BS, Western Carolina U., 1980; MA, Auburn U., 1982. Cert. fin. planner. Customer relations officer Am. Fed. Bank, Greenville, S.C., 1983; fin. planner Colton/Groome and Co., Asheville, N.C., 1983—. Literacy tutor Buncombe County Literacy Vols., 1987—. Mem. Internat. Assn. Fin. Planning, Am. Council Consumer Interests, Inst. Cert. Fin. Planners. Office: Colton/Groome and Co PO Box 2779 Asheville NC 28802

CODY, THOMAS GERALD, lawyer; b. N.Y.C., Nov. 4, 1941; s. Thomas J. Cody and Esther Mary Courtney; m. Mary Ellen Palmer, Nov. 26, 1966; children: Thomas Jr., Mark, Amy, Anne. BA in Philosophy, Maryknoll Coll., 1963; JD, St. John's U., 1967; LLD (hon.), Cen. State U., Wilberforce, Ohio, 1985. Bar: N.Y. 1967. Assoc. Simpson Thatcher & Bartlett, N.Y., 1967-72; asst. prof. law sch. St. John's U., N.Y., 1972-76; sr. v.p., gen. counsel, sec. Pan Am. Airways, N.Y., 1976-82; sr. v.p. law and pub. affairs Federated Dept. Stores, Cin., 1982-88, exec. v.p. legal & human resources, 1988—. Trustee Southwest Ohio Regional Transit Authority, Cin., Xavier U., Cin., Cen. State U., Dartmouth Inst.; bd. overseers Hanover, N.H. Mem. ABA. Roman Catholic. Clubs: Bankers (Cin.); Queen City (Cin.); Hyde Park Country (Cin.). Office: Federated Dept Stores Inc 7 W 7th St Cincinnati OH 45202

COE, MARVIN PARNICK, real estate broker; b. Benton, Tenn., Sept. 14, 1931; s. John Denton and Viola (Pettit) C.; m. Annie Ruth Compton, Apr. 8, 1950 (dec. Feb. 1987); children: Deloris Stephenson, Mary Evelyn. Graduate of Theology, Tenn. Temple U., 1962; BA, Belmont Coll., 1970; MA, Scarritt Coll., 1978. Constrn. carpenter Ga. and Tenn., 1951-69; constrn. supt. Culbert Constrn. Co., Nashville, 1971-79; salesman Owen Reese Realty & Auction, Franklin, Tenn., 1977-78, Realty and Assocs., Franklin, 1978-79, Inman Realtors, Franklin, 1980-82; owner Coe Realty & Auction Co., Franklin, 1983—; mission pastor 23 St. Baptist Ch., Chattanooga, Tenn., 1961-62; assoc. pastor 1st Baptist Cohutta, Ga., 1962-65; pastor Hillsboro Baptist Ch., Franklin, 1965-76, Harpeth Valley Baptist Ch., Franklin, 1984—. Mem. Nashville Baptist Assn. (student com. 1986), Williamson Coutny Bd. Realtors (Realtors Polit. Action Com. and benevolence com.), Nashville Bd. Realtors, Tenn. Bd. Realtors, Nat. Bd. Realtors, Tenn. Auctioneers Assn., Internat. Orgn. of Real Estate Appraisers. Office: Box 2030 Spring Hill Exit and I-65 Peytonsville Rd and Long Ln Franklin TN 37064

COFFIN, AUDRESS MARIE, financial executive; b. Montague, Mass., June 1, 1949; d. Lionel Arthur and Ella May (Aiken) Giard; m. Robert R. Ritacco, July 17, 1971 (div. Jan. 1981). A in Bus., Quinsigamond Community Coll., 1973; BS in Acctg., Assumption Coll., 1983. Jr. acct. Alfonso Puccio Pub. Acctg., Worcester, Mass., 1975-80; acct. Bay State Circuits, Northboro, Mass., 1980-81; asst. controller Northland investment Corp., Newton, Mass., 1981-86, Liberty Properties, Boston, 1985-86; registered rep. IDS Fin. Services, Inc., Westboro, Mass., 1986-89; founder, prin. Westborough Fin. Svcs., 1989—. Mem. Nat. Assn. Accts., Worcester Area C. of C., Westboro Civic Club. Republican. Roman Catholic. Office: Westborough Fin Svcs 5 E Main St Westborough MA 01581

COFFIN, DAVID LINWOOD, specialty chemicals and nonwoven materials manufacturing company executive; b. Windsor Locks, Conn., Dec. 15, 1925; s. Dexter Drake and Elizabeth (Dorr) C.; m. Marie Jeanne Cosnard des Closets, Sept. 15, 1973; children by previous marriage: Deborah Lee, David Linwood, Robert George. Student, Trinity Coll., Hartford, Conn., New Eng. Coll. With Dexter Corp., Windsor Locks, Conn., 1947—, asst. sec., asst. treas., asst. sales mgr., 1949-51, v.p., asst. treas., asst. sales mgr., asst. gen. mgr., 1951-52, v.p., asst. gen. mgr., sales mgr., 1952-55, v.p., gen. mgr., 1955-58, pres., chief exec. officer, from 1958, now chmn., chief exec. officer, also dir.; bd. dirs. Bank of New England Corp., Boston, Conn. Health Systems Agy., Hartford, Conn., Conn. Mut. Life Ins., Hartford, Life Technologies Inc., Gaithersburg, Md. Bd. dirs. Horace Bushnell Meml. Hall, Hartford, Conn. Hist. Soc., Hartford, Conn. Trust for Hist. Preservation, Hartford, The Inst. of Living, Hartford, Mystic Seaport Mus. and Stores, Mystic Conn. Served with USNR, World War II. Clubs: Hartford Golf (West Hartford, Conn.); Hartford; Lake Sunapee Yacht (N.H.); Links (N.Y.C.). Office: Dexter Corp 1 Elm St Windsor Locks CT 06096 *

COFFIN, DWIGHT CLAY, grain company executive; b. Evansville, Ind., Aug. 21, 1938; s. Dwight DeWitt and Ruth Robertson (Clay) C.; m. Carol Ann Elsaesser, Dec. 27, 1986; 1 child by previous marriage, John Charles. Student, DePauw U., 1959-61; BA, U. Pitts., 1963; MBA, NYU, 1970; postgrad. in bus., Harvard U., 1976. With Chase Manhattan Bank, N.Y.C., 1964-72, employee relations officer, 1971-72, mgmt. services officer, 1970-72; dir. employment and tng. Continental Grain Co., N.Y.C., 1972-73; dir. internat. personnel Continental Grain Co., Paris, 1973-75; v.p. personnel Continental Grain Co., N.Y.C., 1975-85, v.p., sec., 1985-86, v.p. human resources, 1986—; dir. internat. personnel Paris, 1973-75. Mem. cands. com. Citizens Union, N.Y.C., 1976—; mem. Conn. Peace and Justice Commn., Hartford, 1988. Mem. Orgnl. Devel. Network, Indsl. Relations Research Assn., Mgmt. Devel. Forum, Nat. Fgn. Trade Council (chmn. mgmt. resources com. 1984), World Bus. Adv. Council (bd. dirs. 1987), N.Y. Personnel Mgmt. Assn. (bd. dirs.), Human Resource Planning Soc. Republican. Episcopalian. Home: 11 Birch Ln Greenwich CT 06830 Office: Continental Grain Co 277 Park Ave New York NY 10172

COFFIN, JOHN DEVEREUX, investment banking executive; b. Elko, Nev., Apr. 17, 1937; s. J. Reginald and M. Margaret (Thompson) C.; m. Anne Gagnebin, Apr. 7, 1962; children: Samuel D., Thomas H. B.A., Williams Coll., 1959. With Bache Halsey Stuart, N.Y.C., 1960-72; mng. dir. Bache & Co. Ltd., London, 1972-76; exec. v.p., dir. The Drexel Burnham Lambert Group Inc. and Drexel Burnham Lambert Inc., N.Y.C., 1976—; dir. mem. exec. com. Commodity Exchange Inc., N.Y.C., 1979—; dir. Winchester Diversified Ltd., Bermuda. Clubs: University (N.Y.C.); Rumson Country (N.J.); Hurlingham (London). Home: 1192 Park Ave New York NY 10128 Office: Drexel Burnham Lambert Inc 60 Broad St New York NY 10004

COFFIN, WILLIAM SARGENT, business consultant; b. Pittsfield, Maine, Dec. 16, 1914; s. Carl Sargent and Grace (Summerbell) C.; A.B., Bates Coll., 1937; grad. Am. Inst. Banking; m. Amelia Amanda Moore, Sept. 7, 1945; children—Thomas Carl, William Sargent. Clk., First Nat. Bank, Pittsfield, Maine, 1939-41; credit mgr. Sears Roebuck Co., Augusta, Maine, 1947-53; clk. Electric Boat div. Gen. Dynamics Corp., Groton, Conn., 1953-55; examiner Dept. Banks and Banking, Augusta, Maine, 1955-58; exec. dir. Devel. Credit Corp. Maine, Augusta, 1958-75; owner, gen. mgr. W.S. Coffin & Assoc. Manchester, Maine, 1975—. Served to capt. AUS, 1941-46. Mem. Nat. Assn. Bus. Devel. Corps. (exec. v.p. 1973-82), Indsl. Devel. Council Maine, Maine Bankers Assn., Maine Mchts. Assn. Republican. Clubs: Masons. Order Eastern Star.

COFFMAN, DALLAS WHITNEY, financial planner; b. Louisville, Sept. 18, 1957; s. Lawrence DuWaine and Jean (Smith) C.; m. Deborah Joan Schneider, May 18, 1980 (div. July 1987); 1 child, Robert Smith; m. Francine R. Coffman, Dec. 26, 1987. AS in Bus. Mgmt., No. Essex Community Coll., Haverhill, Mass., 1977; BS in Mktg. Mgmt., Bentley Coll., 1979. CLU; chartered fin. cons.; regisisterd investment advisor. Mgr. McDonalds Corp., Westwood, Mass., 1975-79; fin. salesman Gold Assocs., Chestnut Hill, Mass., 1979-84; propr., fin. planner Whitman Fin. Services, Wakefield, Mass., 1984—; prin. gen. securities N.Y. Stock Exchange, 1987; adj. faculty Am. Coll., Bryn Mawr, Pa., 1986—, Northeastern U., Boston, 1986—, Coll. for Fin. Planning, Denver, 1986—; cons. to taxpayers for IRS, 1989. Pub. Who's Who in Life Ins., 1982-84; contbr. artices to profl. jours. Sponsor Wakefield Little League. Mem. Internat. Assn. for Fin. Planning, Registry Fin. Planning Practitioners, Boston Estate Planning Coun. Office: Whitman Fin Svcs 233 Albion St Wakefield MA 01880-3122

COFFMAN, GLEN EARL, toy manufacturing executive; b. Seattle, Aug. 4, 1943; s. Howard Earl and Geraldine May (Enberg) C.; m. Marjorie Dewester, July 3, 1965 (div. 1969); m. Carol Frances Dopkus, June 6, 1970; children: Brett, Ryan, Melodie. Student, Santa Clara U.; BSME, Mountlake Coll., 1966. Electronic technician Boeing Co., Seattle, 1961-65; pvt. practice cons. engr. Sunnyvale, Calif., 1966-70, Los Angeles, 1970-73; E/M engr. Woodward Gov., Ft. Collins, Colo., 1973-74; design engr. U.S. Navy, China Lake, Calif., 1974-76; pvt. practice cons. engr. Los Angeles, Sunnyvale, 1976-86; dir., v.p. engring. Video Research Inc., Sunnyvale, 1986—, also bd. dirs.; pres., chmn. bd. dirs. Intellitoy Inc., Sunnyvale, 1987—. Contbr. articles on pro sports to profl. jours.; inventor L.E.D. meters. League rep. Am. Soccer League, western U.S., 1981-82; commr. Boy Scouts Am., 1986-88; advisor Cogswell Coll. Inventors Program, Cupertino, Calif., 1988; explorer leader Boy Scouts Am., Thousand Oaks, 1970-71; mem. election staff John Mercer for Congress, Sunnyvale, 1986. Fin. grantee Playgroup Inc., Hong Kong, 1987; recipient Best in Show award IEEE, 1970. Mem. Am. Mgmt. Assn., Nat. Soccer Coaches Assn. (coach), Silicon Valley Entrepreneurs Club, Earthquakes Boosters Club (pres. 1988—), Lazers Boosters Club. Republican. Office: Intellitoy Inc 830 E Evelyn Ave Sunnyvale CA 94086

COFFMAN, ORENE BURTON, hotel executive; b. Fluvanna, Va., Mar. 13, 1938; d. John C. and Adele (Melton) Burton; m. John H. Emerson, Aug. 5, 1955 (div. 1972); 1 child, Norman Jay; m. Mack H. Coffman, Oct. 26, 1986. Degree in hotel and motel mgmt., Michigan State U., 1966-70. Cert. hotel mgr., Mich. State U., 1970. Telephone operator Colonial Williamsburg (Va.) Hotel, 1962-64; room clk. Colonial Williamsburg (Va.) Hotel, 1964-68; mgr. front office Colonial Williamsburg (Va.) Hotel, 1968-83; asst. mgr. Williamsburg Inn, 1983—; pres. Colonial Williamsburg Employees Fed. Credit Union, 1980-85. Mem. Am. Hotel Motel Assn. (nat. acctg. award 1970). Democrat. Baptist. Office: Williamsburg Inn PO Box B Williamsburg VA 23187

COGAN, JOHN FRANCIS, JR., lawyer; b. Boston, June 13, 1926; s. John Francis and Mary (Galligan) C.; m. Mary T. Hart, May 1, 1951 (div.); children: Peter G., Pamela E., Jonathan C., Gregory M. A.B. cum laude, Harvard U., 1949, LL.B., 1952. Bar: Mass. 1953. Since practiced in Bosto; ptnr. firm Hale and Dorr, 1957-80, mng. ptnr., 1976-83, chmn., 1983—; pres. Pioneer Fund, Inc., Boston, 1963—, Pioneer Group, Inc., Boston, 1963—, Pioneering Mgmt. Corp., Boston, 1963, Pioneer II, Inc., 1969—, Pioneer Bond Fund, 1978—, Pioneer Three, Inc., 1983—; chmn., dir. Teberebie Goldfields, Inc., 1986—, ICI Mutual Ins. Co., 1987—, Seatrain Lines, Inc., 1959-65; sec. Cabot, Cabot & Forbes Co., 1963-72, Ritz-Carlton Hotel Co., Boston, 1964-79; corporator Boston 5 Savs. Bank, 1961-79; chmn. exec. com., dir. Pioneer Western Corp., 1968-79; sr. v.p., dir. Western Res. Life Assurance Co., Ohio, 1968-79; dir. Scandia Trading Co., Inc. Treas. Lexington (Mass.) Counseling Service, 1964-69; chmn. bd. trustees Univ. Hosp., Boston, 1965—; treas. Friends of Harvard Track, 1964-66; mem. Lexington Capital Expenditures Com., 1967-73; mem. Mass. Demo. State Com., 1968-80; bd. dirs. Wendell P. Clark Meml. Assn., Walker Home for Children, Brigham Surg. Group, Inc., 1981—, The Med. Found., 1986—; trustee Boston U. Med. Ctr.; bd. govs. Investment Co. Inst., 1971-74, 75, 81, 82, chmn. bd. govs., 1978-80, 82-85, vice chmn., 1987—; overseer Boston Symphony Orch., 1984—; mem. Mass. Health and Ednl. Facilities Authority, 1985, Mass. Anti-Takeover Commn., 1988—; trustee, exec. com. Boston Ballet, 1986—; corporator Handel and Haydn Soc., 1986—. Served with USNR, 1944-46. Mem. ABA, Internat. Bar Assn., Internat.-Am. Bar Assn., Mass. Bar Assn., Boston Bar Assn. (past chmn. profl. services sect., mem. bench-bar com.), Boston Estate and Bus. Planning Council (past pres.), Boston Probate and Estate Planning Forum (sec. 1958-73), Nat. Assn. Security Dealers (gov. 1983-86, legal adv. com. 1988—). Home: 975 Memorial Dr Cambridge MA 02138 Office: Hale & Dorr 60 State St Boston MA 02109

COGAN, MARSHALL S., private industralist; b. Boston, 1937. Grad., Harvard U., 1959, M.B.A., 1962. With Carter Berlind Weill, 1962-67; vice chmn. Cogan Weill & Levitt, 1968-71, CBWL Hayden-Stone, 1973; chmn., chief exec. officer Knoll Internat. Holdings, Inc., N.Y.C. Office: Knoll Internat Holdings Inc 153 E 53 St Ste 5901 New York NY 10022

COGGESHALL, NORMAN DAVID, former oil company executive; b. Ridge Farm, Ill., May 15, 1916; s. Lester B. and Grace (Blaisdell) C.; m. Margaret Josephine Danner, Aug. 22, 1940; children: Nancy Ellen Von der Ohe, David M., M. Gwen Calabretta, Phillip A. BA, U. Ill., 1937, MS, 1938, PhD, 1942. Tcrh. physics U. Ill., 1942-43; scientist Gulf Oil Research, Pitts., 1943-50, asst. dir. physics div., 1950-55, dir. analytical sci. div., 1955-61, dir. phys. scis. div., 1961-67, v.p. process scis., 1967-70, v.p. exploration and prodn., 1970-76, v.p. tech. govt. coodination, 1976-81; pvt. investor and pvt. cons., Lynn Haven, Fla., 1981—. Contbg. author: Colloid Chemistry, 1946, Physical Chemistry of Hydrocarbons, 1950, Organic Analysis, 1953, Advances in Mass Spectrometry, 1963; contbr. articles to tech. jours.; patentee in field. Recipient Resolution of Appreciation, Am. Petroleum Inst., 1970. Fellow Am. Phys. Soc.; mem. Am. Chem. Soc. (award in chem. instrumentation 1970), Spectroscopy Soc. Pitts., Bay County C. of C. (mil. affairs com.). Republican. Clubs: St. Andrews Bay, Yacht (Panama City, Fla.). Lodge: Rotary. Home and Office: 701 Driftwood Dr Lynn Haven FL 32444

COGGINS, GEORGE MILLER, JR., aerospace company executive; b. Spartanburg, S.C., Sept. 23, 1939; s. George Miller and Inez (Caldwell) C.; m. Kathey Ann Allen, May 10, 1958; children: Rebecca, Leigh, Elisabeth, George III. BBA magna cum laude, Nat. U., 1981, MBA, 1983; D of Bus. Adminstrn., U.S. Internat. U., 1985. Mgr. logistics support B-2 div. Northrop Corp., Pico Rivera, Calif., 1985—; adj. prof. Nat. U., L.A., 1983—. Author: Excellence in the Military, 1985. Major USMC, 1961-65. Republican. Baptist. Home: 1502 S Longview Dr Diamond Bar CA 91765 Office: Northrop Corp Advanced Systems Div 8900 E Washington Pico Rivera CA 90660-3132

COGHLAN, ALAN, banker; b. Aylesbury, Eng., June 1, 1947; came to U.S., 1955; s. Johnny K. and Joan E. (Kibble) C. BS, U. Calif., 1969; M in Banking with honors, U. Va., 1988. Sr. area analyst Bank Am., San Francisco, 1969-80; v.p., mgr. retail banking research Union Bank (formerly Calif. First Bank), San Francisco, 1980—. Mem. U. Calif. Berkeley Bus. Alumni Assn. (scholar 1965). Home: 1834 Helena Dr Concord CA 94521 Office: Union Bank 350 Calif St San Francisco CA 94104

COHAN, LEON SUMNER, electric company executive, lawyer; b. Detroit, June 24, 1929; s. Maurice and Lillian (Rosenfeld) C.; m. Heidi Ruth Seelmann, Jan. 22, 1956; children: Nicole, Timothy David, Jonathan

Daniel. B.A., Wayne State U., 1949, J.D., 1952. Bar: Mich. 1953. Sole practice Detroit, 1954-58; asst. atty. gen. State of Mich., Lansing, 1958-61, dep. atty. gen., 1961-72; v.p. legal affairs Detroit Edison Co., 1973-75, v.p., 1975-79, sr. v.p., 1979—, gen. counsel, 1975—; bd. dirs. United Savings Bank, FSB. Chmn. State Bd. Ethics; trustee Mich. Cancer Found., Sinai Hosp. Detroit; bd. dirs. Orch. Hall; chmn. Mich. Coun. for Arts, Nat. Com. for Labor Israel-Histadrut; bd. govs. Jewish Welfare Fedn.; mem. Arts Commn. Detroit Inst. Arts; bd. dirs. Concerned Citizens for Arts in Mich., Internat. Visitors Coun. of Met. Detroit; mem. exec. bd. Friends of Detroit Pub. Libr.; mem. exec. com. Jewish Community Coun. Met. Detroit. With U.S. Army, 1952-54. Recipient Disting. Alumni award Wayne State U. Law Sch., 1972, Disting. Service award Bd. Govs., Wayne State U., 1973, Judge Ira W. Jayne award NAACP, 1987, Israel Histadrut Menorah award, 1987, Knights of Charity award Pontifical Inst. for Fgn. Missions, 1989, Fellowship award Am. Arabic and Jewish Friends of Met. Detroit. Mem. Am., Detroit bar assns., State Bar Mich., Mich. Gen. Counsel Assn., Am. Arbitration Assn. (mem. comml. panel). Democrat. Jewish. Club: Detroit. Home: 5324 Forest Way Bloomfield Hills MI 48013 Office: Detroit Edison Co 2000 2nd Ave Detroit MI 48226

COHEN, ALAN NORMAN, business executive; b. Clifton, N.J., Dec. 19, 1930; s. Samuel and Ida (Phillips) C.; m. Joan Meryl Fields, Nov. 25, 1953; children: Laurie Elizabeth, Gordon Geoffrey. Student, Dartmouth, 1948-49; AB, Columbia U., 1952, LLB, 1954. Bar: N.Y. 1954. Assoc. Cahill, Gordon, Reindel & Ohl, N.Y.C., 1954-55, Paul, Weiss, Goldberg, Rifkind, Wharton & Garrison, N.Y.C., 1957-63; ptnr. Paul, Weiss, Goldberg, Rifkind, Wharton & Garrison, 1964-70, 78-80; pres. Andal Corp., N.Y.C., 1980—, also bd. dirs.; exec. v.p., dir., mem. exec. com. Warner Communications, Inc., N.Y.C., 1970-74; pres., chief exec. officer, dir., mem. exec. com. Madison Sq. Garden Corp., N.Y.C., 1974-77; chmn. N.J. Nets, 1978-83; vice chmn., treas., dir. Boston Celtics Ltd. Partnership, 1986—; dir. Steve's Homemade Ice Cream, Inc., 1986—; dir., chmn. The Franklin Corp., 1986—; bd. govs. NBA, 1978—. Bd. overseers Grad. Sch. Mgmt. and Urban Professions, New Sch. Social Research; Bd. dirs. others; mem. bd. govs. NBA, 1978—, chmn., 1986-88. Served with AUS, 1955-57. Named to Jewish Sports Hall of Fame, 1988; recipient John Jay award Columbia Coll., 1988, John Jay award, Columbia Coll., 1988; trustee Internat. Ctr. Photography, 1988—. Office: Andal Corp 560 Lexington Ave New York NY 10022

COHEN, ALBERT DIAMOND, merchandising executive; b. Winnipeg, Man., Can., Jan. 20, 1914; s. Alexander and Rose (Diamond) C.; m. Irena Kankova, Nov. 6, 1953; children: Anthony Jan, James Edward, Anna Lisa. LLD (hon.), U. Man., 1987. Pres. Gendis Inc., Winnipeg, 1953-87; chmn., chief exec. officer Gendis, Inc., Winnipeg, 1987—; chmn. exec. com. Met. Stores of Can., Ltd., Winnipeg, 1961—, Greenberg Stores Ltd.; dir. Saan Stores Ltd.; chmn., chief exec. officer Sony of Can. Ltd., Saan Stores Ltd. Author: The Entrepreneurs (Cert. of Merit Nat. Bus. Book award 1986). Pres. Winnipeg Clin. Research Inst., 1975-80, Paul H.T. Thorlakson Research Found., 1978-80.; hon. chmn. St. John's Ravenscourt Sch., 1984. Served with Royal Can. Navy, 1942-45. Recipient Internat. Disting. Entrepreneur award U. Manitoba, 1983, Order of Can., 1984. Office: Gendis Inc, 1370 Sony Pl, Winnipeg, MB Canada R3C 3C3

COHEN, CARY, consulting executive, writer; b. Bklyn., Oct. 11, 1935; s. Isaac and Lillian (Cohen) C.; m. Eleanor Hirsh, Nov. 19, 1957; children: Andrew, Douglas. BS in Applied Sci., CUNY, 1966; BBA, CCNY, 1970; JD, U. San Gabriel Valley, Pasadena, Calif., 1983. Cert. profl. contract mgr. Corp. mgr. Burns and Roe, Inc., Oradell, N.J., 1968-76; v.p. Wm. A. Pope Co., Chgo., 1976-77; dir. contracts Va. Electric, Richmond, 1977-84; pres. Caldwell Cons. Assocs., Richmond, Va., 1977—; mem. adj. faculty J. Sargeant Reynolds Community Coll., Richmond, 1985—, Fla. Inst. Tech. Grad. Sch., Ft. Lee, Va., 1986—; instr. minority bus. office Dept. Commerce, Washington, 1970-80. Author: 8 bus. texts including Federal Contract Management; producer bus. videos PBS, Fed. Publs. Inc., Fortune 500 firms. Coach Cub Scouts of AM., Caldwell, N.J., 1968-74; mem. band boosters Mills E. Godwin High Sch., Richmond, 1980-83. Fellow Nat. Contract Mgmt. Assn. (chpt. pres. 1968-70, nat. dir., Blanche Witte Meml. award 1972), mem. Authors Guild Am., Inc., Dramatists Guild, Actors Equity Assn., Internat. TV and Video Assn., Assn. Govt. Accts., Nat. Assn. Purchasing Mgmt., Am. Soc. Tng. and Devel. Office: Caldwell Cons Assocs PO Box 10141 Richmond VA 23240

COHEN, DEVON MICHAEL, finance company executive; b. Paterson, N.J., Dec. 17, 1957; s. Bernard and Eileen (Fish) C.; m. Erica Cohen, Dec. 27, 1981. BS, SUNY, Binghamton, 1979. CPA, N.Y. Sr. acct., fin. industry specialist Peat, Marwick, Mitchell & Co., N.Y.C., 1979-81; supr. gen. acctg. Merrill Lynch Mortgage Corp., Stamford, Conn., 1981-82, mgr. fin. ops., 1982-84; v.p. fin. Goldome Realty Credit Corp., Williamsville, N.Y., 1984-86, chief fin. officer, 1986—, sr. v.p., 1987—; adj. prof. Sacred Heart U., Bridgeport, Conn. V.p. Mineola Vol. Ambulance Corp., 1980; bd. dirs. Mercy Flight, 1988—. Mem. N.Y. Soc. CPA's, Am. Inst. CPA's, Mortgage Bankers Assn. (internal mgmt. com. 1986—, Willis Bryant award 1987), Pi Kappa Delta. Office: Goldome Realty Credit Corp 205 Park Club Ln Williamsville NY 14221

COHEN, EDWARD, civil engineer; b. Glastonbury, Conn., Jan. 6, 1921; s. Samuel and Ida (Tanewitz) C.; m. Elizabeth Belle Cohen, Dec. 19, 1948 (dec. June 1979); children: Samuel, Libby M. Wallace, James; m. Carol Simon Kalb, Jan. 11, 1981; stepchildren: Anne Kalb Bronner, Paul Kalb. BS in Engring., Columbia U., 1945, MS in Civil Engring., 1954. Registered profl. engr., N.Y., Conn., Fla., Ga., Md., N.J., La., Mass., Mich., Pa., D.C., Okla., Va., Wis., Del.; chartered civil engr., Gt. Britain; lic. land surveyor, N.Y., Conn., Mass., N.J. Engring. aide Conn. Hwy. Dept., 1940-42; asst. engr. East Hartford Dept. Pub. Works, 1942-44; structural engr. Hardesty & Hanover, N.Y.C., 1945-47, Sanderson & Porter, N.Y.C., 1947-49; lectr. architecture Columbia U., 1948-51; with Ammann & Whitney, N.Y.C., 1949—; ptnr. Ammann & Whitney, 1963-74, sr. ptnr., 1974-77, mng. ptnr., 1977—, dir. co. work as engrs. of record restoration of Statue of Liberty, West Face of U.S. Capitol Bldg. and Roebling Del. Canal Bridge; exec. v.p. Ammann & Whitney, Inc., 1974-77, in charge bldg., transp., communications, mil. and hist. preservation projects, chmn., chief exec. officer, 1977—; v.p. Ammann & Whitney Internat. Ltd., 1963-73; pres. Safeguard Constrn. Mgmt. Corp., 1973-77, chmn., chief exec. officer, 1977—; cons. RAND Corp., Santa Monica, Calif., 1958-72, Dept. Def., 1962-63, Hudson Inst., Croton-on-Hudson, N.Y., 1967-71, World Bank, 1984, TVA, 1987; Stanton Walker lectr. U. Md., 1973, Henry M. Shaw lectr. N. Carolina State U., 1987; deptl. adv. com. Urban and Civil Engring. U. Pa., 1978-84, Rutgers U., 1984—; mem. engring. council Columbia U., 1975—, vice chmn., 1985-86; mem. adv. bd. Dept. Civil Engring. and Engring. Mechs. Ctr. for Infrastructure Studies, 1987—. Mem. adv. bd. Jour. Resource Mgmt. and Tech., 1981—; co-editor: Handbook of Structural Concrete, 1983; contbr. more than 100 articles to profl. jours. and govt. manuals on structural, seismic, hardened design, wind forces, dynamic analysis, ultimate strength and plastic design guyed towers and shell structures. Mem. Nat. Endowment for Arts (chmn. engring. com. 1st presdl. awards for design excellence 1985); commr. Bklyn. Bridge Centennial Commn., 1981-83; spl. adv. N.Y. State Statue of Liberty Centennial Commn., 1985; bd. dirs. Cejwin Youth Camps, 1972—, Com. of 100 Trailblazer Summer Camp for Underprivileged Children, 1985—; trustee Hall of Sci., N.Y.C., 1976—; mem. exec. com. March of Dimes Transp. Award Luncheon, 1983—; mentor in engring. N.Y. Alliance for Pub. Schs., 1986—; N.Y. area chmn. engring. sect. Orgn. for Rehabilitation through Tng., 1983— (Sci. and Tech. award 1987), nat. dir. 1989—. Recipient Illig medal in Applied Sci. Columbia U., 1946, Patriotic Civilian Svc. award Dept. of Army, 1973, Egleston medal Columbia U., 1981, Goethals medal for Engring. Achievement Soc. Am. Mil. Engrs., 1985, Mayor's Award of Honor for Sci. and Tech., N.Y., 1988, U.S. Presdl. Design Excellence award NEA, 1988; Best of Program award for Achievement in Arc Welded Design Engring. and Found., Bronze award James F. Lincoln Arc Welding Found., 1988; Nat. Historic Preservation award for engring. U.S. Capitol restoration U.S. Dept. Interior and Adv. Coun. Historic Preservation, 1988. Fellow Am. Cons. Engr. Council (Grand award for Engring. Excellence 1986), Inst. Civil Engrs. (Gt. BRitain); Hon. mem. ASCE (chmn. com. design loads for bldgs. and other structures A58, 1968—, chmn. reinforced concrete research council 1980—, met. sect. v.p. 1978-79, pres. 1980, Ridgeway award 1946, Civil Engring. State-of-the-Art award 1974, Raymond Reese award 1976, Ernest Howard Gold Medal 1983, Met. Civil Engr. of Yr. award 1986, Service to People award 1987); mem. N.Y. Assn. Cons. Engrs. (bldg. code adv. com., bd. dirs. 1981-82, 85—), N.Y. Acad. Scis. (hon. life, Laskowitz Aerospace research gold medal 1970, chmn. 1977-79), Am. Concrete Inst. (hon. mem., dir. 1966-76, v.p. 1970-72, pres. 1972-73, chmn. com. bldg. couirements for reinforced concrete 1963-71, Wason medal 1956, Delmar Bloem award 1973), Nat. Acad. Engring. (elected 1975), N.Y. Concrete Industry Bd. (dir. 1976—, pres. 1978-79), Columbia U. Sch. Engring. Alumni Assn. (bd. dirs. 1985-86), N.Y. Concrete Constrn. Design Inst. (pres. tall bldgs. council 1975-80), NSPE (Outstanding Engring. Achievement award 1987), N.Y. State Soc. Profl. Engrs. (Engr. of Yr. 1987, Nassau chpt. Engr. of Yr. 1987), Internat. Bridge and Turnpike Assn., Internat. Assn. Bridge and Structural Engrs., Am. Welding Soc., U.S. Dept. Interiors and Adv. Coun. Hist. Preservation (Nat. Hist. Preservation award for engring U.S. Capitol restoation 1988), Comite European de Beton (specialist mem.), Moles, Century Assn., Sigma Xi, Chi Epsilon, Tau Beta Pi. Clubs: Engrs. N.Y.C. (dir. 1974-75), Wings, Club at World Trade Ctr. Lodge: B'nai Brith. Home: 56 Chestnut Hill Roslyn NY 11576 Office: Ammann & Whitney 96 Morton St New York NY 10014

COHEN, EDWARD HERSCHEL, lawyer; b. Lewistown, Pa., Sept. 30, 1938; s. Saul Allen and Barbara (Getz) C.; m. Arlene Greenbaum, Aug. 12, 1962; children: Fredrick, James, Paul. AB, U. Mich., 1960; JD, Harvard U., 1963. Bar: N.Y. 1964. Assoc. Rosenman and Colin, N.Y.C., 1963-72, ptnr., 1972—, counsel, 1987; v.p., gen. counsel, sec. Phillips-Van Heusen Corp., N.Y.C., 1987. Republican. Jewish. Club: Fenway Golf (Scarsdale, N.Y.). Home: 21 Sycamore Rd Scarsdale NY 10583 Office: Rosenman & Colin 575 Madison Ave New York NY 10022

COHEN, GLORIA ERNESTINE, educator; b. Bklyn., July 6, 1942; d. Victor George and Marion Theodosia (Roberts) C. BS in Edn., Wilberforce U., 1965; MA in Elem. Edn., Adelphi U., 1975; Profl. Diploma in Ednl. Adminstrn., L.I. U., 1984; M.S. in Edn., Bklyn. Coll., 1986. Tchr. Bd. Edn., Bklyn., 1965—; case worker Dept. Welfare, Bklyn., 1965—. Mem. Northwest Civic Assn., Freeport, N.Y., 1973—, Roosevelt-Freeport Civic Assn., Freeport, 1984—. Mem. NOW, Assn. for Supervision and Curriculum Devel., Nat. Alliance of Black Sch. Educators, Inc., Bklyn. Reading Coun. of Internat. Reading Assn., N.Y. State Reading Assn., Assn. Black Educators of N.Y., NAFE, Inc., Zeta Phi Beta, Kappa Delta Pi. Democrat. Roman Catholic. Clubs: FSO Internat. (Jamaica, N.Y.); Freeport Indoor Tennis. Avocations: tennis, skiing, swimming. Home: 4 Sterling Pl Freeport NY 11520 Office: Bd Ed PS 149 700 Sutter Ave Brooklyn NY 11207

COHEN, GORDON S., health products executive; b. N.Y.C., May 18, 1937; s. Leon Lewis and Irene (Lipton) C.; m. Marjorie Rennick, June 12, 1960; children: Terri Susan, Lisa Michelle, Bonnie Lynne. AB, Brown U., 1959; MD, Yale U., 1963. Diplomate Am. Bd. Pathology, Anatomic Pathology and Clin. Pathology. Instr. dept. pathology Yale U., New Haven, 1967-70, asst. prof. pathology, 1970-71, asst. clin. prof. pathology, 1971-78; pres. Jeneric Industries, Wallingford, Conn., 1975-86; chmn. Pentron Corp., Wallingford, 1977-87; pres. Jeneric/Pentron, Inc., Wallingford, 1987—; chmn. Customedix Corp., Wallingford, 1987—; attending pathologist Yale-New Haven Hosp., 1970-71, Hosp. St. Raphael, New Haven, 1971-76; pathologist The Charlotte Hungerford Hosp., Torrington, Conn., 1967-70. Author numerous articles in field. Sr. edn. officer Milford (Conn.) U.S. Power Squadron, 1987; mem. Congressman DeNardis's Small Bus. Adv. Com., 1982. Capt. USAR, 1964-70. Mem. Internat. Acad. Pathology, N.Y. Acad. Scis., Milford Yacht Club, Phi Beta Kappa, Sigma Xi, Alpha Omega Alpha. Office: Jeneric/Pentron Inc 53 N Plains Industrial Rd Wallingford CT 06492

COHEN, IRA D., financial executive; b. N.Y.C., May 30, 1951; s. Victor and Elaine (Groder) C. BS in Acctg., CUNY, 1973. CPA, N.Y., N.J. CPA, Laventhol & Horwath, N.Y.C., 1971-78; dir. internal audit MetPath Inc., Teterboro, N.J., 1978-79; v.p., chief fin. officer Hi-G, Inc., Windsor Locks, Conn., 1979-84; v.p., chief fin. officer Sci/Med Advances Corp, N.Y.C., 1984; v.p., treas., chief fin. officer USC Co. (formerly CGA Computer, Inc.), Holmdel, N.J., 1984-87; pres. Updata Group Inc., Holmdel, 1986—. Mem. Am. Inst. CPA's, N.Y. State Soc. CPA's. Home: 300 Gorge Rd Cliffside Park NJ 07010 Office: Updata Group Inc 960 Holmdel Rd Holmdel NJ 07733

COHEN, IRWIN, economist; b. Bronx, N.Y., Feb. 29, 1936; s. Samuel and Gertrude (Levy) C.; B.S. in Accounting, N.Y. U., 1956, M.B.A. in Finance, 1964, M.A. in Econs., 1969; B.S. in Math., CCNY, 1970. Financial analyst U.S. SEC, N.Y.C., 1965-67, Fed. Res. Bank N.Y., N.Y.C., 1967-72, Prudential Ins. Co. Am., 1973-74, SEC, N.Y.C., 1974—. Life Fellow Internat. Biog. Assn., Am. Biog. Inst. Research Assn. (dep. gov.), World Acad. Scholars, World Literary Acad., World Inst. Achievement; mem. Internat. Biographical Ctr. (dep. dir. gen.), Internat. Platform Assn (life), Math. Assn. Am., Am. Finance Assn., Econ. History Assn. Home: 372 Central Park Ave Apt 2K Scarsdale NY 10583

COHEN, JAY ADAM, investment banker; b. Los Angeles, Feb. 14, 1962; s. Leonard and Jean (Hide) C. BA in Econs., U. Calif., 1984; MA in Mgmt., Northwestern U. J.L. Kellogg Sch. Mgmt., Evanston, Ill., 1988. CPA. Sr. acct. Peat Marwick Mitchell & Co., Los Angeles, 1984-86; assoc. Merrill Lynch & Co., N.Y.C., 1988; dir. L&J Cohen Inc., Los Angeles, 1981—. Mem. Omicron Delta Epsilon. Jewish.

COHEN, JUDITH LYNNE, healthcare consultant, accountant; b. N.Y.C., July 25, 1951; d. Everett Herbert and Rose (Schulman) C. BS with distinction, Simmons Coll., 1973; MBA, NYU, 1984. CPA, N.Y. Staff and research therapist NYU Med. Ctr., 1974-79; clin. specialist U. Mich. Med. Ctr., Ann Arbor, 1979-81; audit staff Ernst & Whinney, N.Y.C., 1984-85; cons. Peat, Marwick, Mitchell & Co., N.Y.C., 1985-86; healthcare cons. Loeb & Troper, Inc., N.Y.C., 1986—. Mem. Am. Hosp. Assn., Healthcare Fin. Mgmt. Assn., Am. Inst. CPA's, N.Y. Soc. CPA's, Beta Gamma Sigma. Home: 2185 Lemoine Ave Fort Lee NJ 07024 Office: Loeb & Troper 270 Madison Ave New York NY 10016

COHEN, LARRY STEVEN, metal processing executive; b. Nashville, Oct. 29, 1951; s. Julius Bernard and Shirley (Cohen) C.; m. Laura Chakoff, Aug. 16, 1975; children: Heather, Marcie, Eric. BS, Bradley U., 1973; MA, U. Tenn., 1975; MBA, Vanderbilt U., 1982. Grad. research asst. U. Tenn., Knoxville, 1973-75; grad. teaching asst. Cornell U., Ithaca, N.Y., 1975-76; v.p. M. Cohen Iron and Metal Co., Nashville, 1976-86, pres., 1986—. Mem. Inst. Scrap Recycling Industries (v.p. S.E. chpt. 1986-88, pres. 1989—). Jewish. Lodge: B'nai B'rith. Home: 235 Vaughns Gap Rd Nashville TN 37205 Office: M Cohen Iron & Metal Co 724 S 2d St Nashville TN 37213

COHEN, LEONARD, hospital management company executive; b. 1925; married. BS, UCLA, 1948; LLB, Loyola U., 1951. Ptnr. Ervin, Cohen & Jessup, 1952-68; with Nat. Med. Enterprises, Los Angeles, 1968—, pres., chief operating officer, 1983—, now also vice-chmn., dir. With U.S. Army, 1942-46. Office: Nat Med Enterprises Inc 11620 Wilshire Blvd Los Angeles CA 90025

COHEN, LOIS WOLK, stock brokerage company official, travel agency company official; b. Bklyn., Mar. 5, 1934; d. Harry and Ruth (Lindenbaum) Wolk; divorced; children: Ruth Ellen Cohen Chadick, James M. BA, Bklyn. Coll., 1955; MS, Queens Coll., 1973. Cert. fin. planner. Tchr. Hicksville (N.Y.) Schs., 1955-59, Port Washington (N.Y.) Schs., 1969-87; fin. planner Michael Philips Securities, Roslyn, N.Y., 1987; account exec. Dean Witter Reynolds Inc., Jericho, N.Y., 1987—; outside sales travel agt. Here's Joanie Travel, Merrick, N.Y., 1981—. Mem. Internat. Assn. for Fin. Planning (v.p. membership 1987), Inst. Cert. Fin. Planners. Home: 2734 Clubhouse Rd Merrick NY 11566 Office: Dean Witter Reynolds Inc Two Jericho Pla Jericho NY 11753

COHEN, MARSHALL, beverage company executive. Formerly lawyer Canadian govt.; with fin. dept. Olympia and York Devels. Ltd., exec. v.p., to 1988; pres., chief operating officer Olympia and York Enterprises Corp., to 1988; chmn. Gulf Can. Resources Ltd., to 1988; pres., chief exec. officer GW Utilities Ltd., to 1988; now pres., chief exec. officer Molson Cos., Toronto, Ont., Can., 1988—. Office: Molson Cos Ltd, 2 International Blvd, Toronto, ON Canada M9W 1A2 *

COHEN, MARTIN, communications company executive; b. N.Y.C., Jan. 8, 1932; s. I.R. and J.D. C.; m. Nancy L. Young, May 15, 1960; children: Edward M., Jonathan S., George D. A.B., Brown U., 1953; M.B.A., Wharton Sch., U. Pa., 1957. C.P.A., D.C. Tax cons., mgr. Price Waterhouse, Washington, 1957-64; tax advisor U.S. Treasury Dept., Washington, 1964-66; various exec. positions The Washington Post Co., 1966—, v.p., dir., 1975—; dir. Internat. Herald Tribune, S.A., Paris, Bowater Mersey Paper Co. Ltd., Liverpool, N.S., Can. Mem. corporate bd., chmn. audit com. Childrens Hosp. Nat. Med. Ctr., Washington, 1973—. Served to lst lt. USMC, 1953-55. Recipient Meritorious Service award U.S. Treasury Dept., 1965. Mem. Am. Inst. C.P.A.s, Fin. Execs. Inst. Club: Woodmont Country (Rockville, Md.) (v.p. 1983, pres. 1987). Home: 5024 Baltan Rd Bethesda MD 20816 Office: Washington Post Co 1150 15th St NW Washington DC 20071

COHEN, MELVYN DOUGLAS, securities company executive; b. Newtonards, Northern Ireland, Nov. 29, 1943; came to U.S., 1972; s. Arnold Ernest and Clara (Praeger) C.; m. Rosita Nahum, May 9, 1974; children: Suzanne, Cary. AA, Miami Dade Community Coll., 1975; BBA, Fla. Internat. U., 1977, MS in Mgmt., 1981. Cert. fin. planner. With Merrill Lynch, Miami, 1977—; v.p., mgr. sales Merrill Lynch, N.Y.C., 1986-88; v.p., resident mgr. Merrill Lynch, Coral Springs, Fla., 1988—; fin. mgr. Donald Regan Sch. Fin. Planning. Mem. Jaycees (pres. Miami chpt. 1982). Jewish. Office: 3300 University Dr Coral Springs FL 33065

COHEN, MICHAEL NORMAN, sales executive; b. Newark, Mar. 22, 1960; s. Jack Louis and Rachel (Dubiecki) C.; m. Theodora Worth Sala, May 11, 1985; 1 child, Kara Theresa. BS, U. Pa., 1982. Sales rep. ASI Computer Systems, Waterloo, Iowa, 1982-84, sales mgr., 1984-86, nat. sales mgr., 1986—. Contbr. articles to profl. jours. and mags. Mem. Toastmasters (pres. Gulph Mills chpt. 1987-88). Home: 1580 Sheldrake Dr Paoli PA 19301 Office: ASI Computer Systems 1120 Wheeler Way Langhorne PA 19047

COHEN, MORLEY MITCHELL, chain store executive; b. Winnipeg, Man., Can., Jan. 2, 1917; s. Alexander and Rose (Diamond) C.; m. Rita Lillian Stober, Nov. 4, 1957; children: Joanne (Mrs. Barry Goldmeir), Donna Susan (Mrs. Graeme Low). Ed., St. John's Tech. Sch.; Ph.D., Haifa U., 1985. Pres. Saan Stores, Ltd., Winnipeg, 1954-57; exec. v.p. Gen. Distbrs., Ltd., Montreal, 1958-63, Met. Stores of Can., Ltd., Montreal, 1964-68; pres. Met. Stores of Can., Ltd., 1969—, chmn., 1979—; chmn. Hineni of Can., 1984—; dir. Gen. Distbrs., Ltd., Montreal Bd. Trade, 1973-75. Chmn. Combined Jewish Appeal, Montreal, 1970, mem. campaign cabinet, 1980; treas. YMHA and YWHA, Montreal, 1971, chmn. capital fund drive, 1980, bd. trustees, 1986-87; treas. United Israel Appeal, 1970-71; chmn. Arthritis Soc., Que., 1981; bd. dirs., v.p. Jewish Community Fund Found., 1980; bd. dirs. Jewish Gen. Hosp., Montreal, Que. Safety League; chmn. Univ. Grad. Employment Agy.-Jewish Vocat. Service, 1984; chmn. capital campaign sect. Montreal Gen. Hosp., 1986-87, mem. bd. govs., 1988. Served with RCAF, 1940-45. Mem. Internat. Golf Soc. (founder). Clubs: B'nai B'rith (Montreal), Elmridge Golf and Country (Montreal) (past pres.), Montefiore (Montreal).

COHEN, MORRIS, economist; b. Phila., Mar. 2, 1919; s. Meyer and Bella (Furman) C.; m. Kathleen Shanahan, July 20, 1950; children: Barbara, Mark. BA, U. Pa., 1939; MA, Pa. State U., 1941; MPA, Harvard U., 1952, PhD, 1958. Sr. economist The Conf. Bd., N.Y.C., 1953-60; assoc. editor Fortune Mag., N.Y.C., 1960-67; prof. econs. and fin. L.I. U., Bklyn., 1967-80; chief economist Schroder, Naess & Thomas, Bklyn., 1969-80; pres. Morris Cohen & Assocs., Hackensack, N.J., 1980—. Sgt. Med. Service Corps U.S. Army, 1942-46, PTO. Mem. Nat. Assn. Bus. Economists. Office: 946 Main St Hackensack NJ 07601

COHEN, PETER, retail company executive. Exec. v.p. Circle K Convenience Stores Inc., Phoenix. Office: Circle K Convenience Stores Inc PO Box 52084 Phoenix AZ 85072 *

COHEN, PETER A., financial services company executive; b. N.Y.C., Aug. 20, 1946; s. Sidney and Florence Cohen; m. Karen Cohen; 2 children. BS, BA, Ohio State U., 1968; MBA, Columbia U., 1969. With Reynolds Securities Inc., 1969-70; with Shearson Hayden Stone Inc., 1971-78, Republic Nat. Bank, 1978-79; v.p., chief adminstrv. officer Shearson Lehman Bros. Inc. (formerly Shearson Am. Express), N.Y.C., 1979-83, chmn., chief exec. officer, 1983—; also bd. dirs. Shearson Lehman Bros Inc (formerly Shearson Am. Express), N.Y.C.; bd. dirs. Societe Generale de Belgique, Andover Togs Inc. Office: Shearson Lehman Bros Inc Am Express Tower 200 Vesey St New York NY 10285 *

COHEN, PHILIP HERMAN, accountant; b. Bklyn., Dec. 4, 1936; s. David J. and Toby (Jaeger) C.; m. Susan Rudd; children: Davina Ellen, Tobias Samuel Dory. BS, NYU, 1957. Acct. Touche Ross & Co., N.Y.C., 1957-64, supr., 1965, mgr., 1966-69, ptnr., 1969-81; exec. v.p. fin., chief fin. officer Integrated Resources, Inc., N.Y.C., 1981-86, sr. exec. v.p. fin., chief fin. officer, 1986—; dir. W.J. Schafer & Assocs., ALI Equipment Mgmt. Corp., ALI Capitol Corp., ALI Leasing Svc., Fin. Svc. Clearing Corp.; lectr. in field. Bd. dirs. Alpha Epsilon Pi Found., Inc., Nat. Interfrat. Conf., 1975-86, Jewish Bd. Family and Children's Svc.; bd. dirs., fin. sec. Sutton Pl. Synagogue; bd. dirs. joint purchasing com. Fedn. Jewish Philanthropies, 1977-78; N.Y. bd. govs. State of Israel Bonds. Recipient State of Israel Bond Peace award 1983, Accts. Bankers and Fin. award Am. Jewish Congress. Mem. Found. Acctg. Edn., Am. Inst. CPA's (real estate com. 1987—), N.Y. State Soc. CPA's (admissions com. 1968-69, chmn. fin. and leasing com. 1972-74, com. on rels. with the bar 1974-76, com. on real estate acctg. 1976-79, com. ins. 1980-81, fin. acctg. standards com. 1983-86, chmn. mem.-in-industry com. 1981-83, chief fin. officers com. 1984-86, furtherance com. 1986, annual conf. com. 1985-87, com. on ops. 1987-88, bd. dirs. 1983-86, v.p. 1985-86, Outstanding CPA in Industry award 1986), Fin. Execs. Inst., Am. Acctg. Assn., Nat. Assn. Accts., Soc. Ins. Accts., Alpha Epsilon Pi (supreme gov. 1966-73, nat. pres. 1974-76, mem. fiscal control bd. 1977-81, vice chmn. 1981—), Beta Alpha Psi, Areopagus. Jewish. Club: N.Y. Alumni of Alpha Epsilon Pi. Lodge: Masons. Home: 30 Beekman Pl New York NY 10022 Office: Integrated Resources Inc 666 3d Ave New York NY 10017

COHEN, RICHARD, grocery company executive; b. Worcester, Mass., July 25, 1952; s. Lester and Norma (Russem) C.; m. Janet Lee, May 26, 1974; children: Perry, Jill, Rachel. BA in Econs., U. Pa., 1974. V.p. fin. C&S Wholesale, Worcester, Mass., 1977-81; gen. mgr. C&S Wholesale, Brattleboro, Vt., 1981-83, pres., chief exec. officer, 1983—. Jewish. Office: C & S Wholesale Grocery Inc Old Ferry Rd PO Box 821 Brattleboro VT 05301

COHEN, RICHARD STEVEN, utility executive, lawyer; b. N.Y.C., Nov. 23, 1942; s. Harold B. and Adele (Hartman) C.; m. Devorah Kanter, Oct. 8, 1972. AB, Rutgers U., 1968, JD, 1971. Bar: N.J. 1971. Assoc. Rosen & Weiss, Newark, 1971-73, Krugman, Chapnick & Grimshaw, Paterson, N.J., 1973-74; atty. Jersey Cen. Power & Light Co., Morristown, N.J., 1974-77, sr. atty., 1977-81, gen. atty., 1981-86, sec., corp. counsel, 1986—. 1st lt. U.S. Army, 1964-67, Vietnam. Mem. ABA, N.J. Bar Assn. (bd. consultors pub. utility law sect. 1986—), Am. Corp. Counsels Assn. Office: Jersey Cen Power & Light Co Madison Ave at Punch Bowl Rd Morristown NJ 07960

COHEN, ROBERT HARRIS, communications executive; b. Milw., Oct. 30, 1962; s. Arthur Albert and Reha (Laserstein) C. BA in Broadcasting, Bradley U., Peoria, Ill., 1985. On-air talent Sta. WLIU (Pub. Broadcasting System), L.I., N.Y., 1985-86, Sta. WMVS (Pub. Broadcasting System), Milw.; producer, host Sta. WTVP (Pub. Broadcasting System), Peoria, Ill., 1982-83; reporter Sta. WMFG-FM, Milw., 1982-83; producer Sta. WPEO, Peoria, 1983-84; reporter, producer Sta. WHOI-TV, Peoria, 1983-84; reporter Viacom Cable, Milw.; news dir. Sta. WAUK-FM, Milw.; dir. Radio Fin. Cons. Network Sta. FCN, N.Y.C., 1988—; now with Shearson Lehman Hutton, N.Y.C. Office: Shearson Lehamn Hutton World Fin Ctr Am Express Tower C New York NY 10285

COHEN, ROGER J., financial executive; b. Bklyn., July 5, 1950; married. BS, Bklyn. Coll., 1971; MS, U. Pa., 1972. CPA, N.Y. Chief fin. officer Garvin Guy Butler Corp., N.Y.C., 1982—, Garban Ltd., N.Y.C., 1984—; pres. Garban Securities, N.Y.C., 1987—. Fin. dir., sec. Congregation Anshe Emeth, South River, N.J., 1987—. Mem. N.Y. State Soc. CPAs, Am. Inst. CPAs. Office: Garvin Guy Butler Corp 120 Broadway New York NY 10271

COHEN, RONNA, investment executive; b. Troy, N.Y., July 19, 1955; d. Louis Arthur and Elaine Esther (Schiff) C.; m. Howard Kanner, Nov. 23, 1984. BS cum laude, Coll. Forestry, 1977; JD, Syracuse U., 1983, MBA, 1983. Exec. dir. N.Y.-N.J. Trail Conf., N.Y.C., 1976-77; dir. edn. Appalachian Mt. Club, Boston, 1977-80; broker, analyst Lazard Freres and Co., N.Y.C., 1983-85; investment mgr. P. Oppenheimer and Assoc. Inc., N.Y.C., 1986—; mem. fin. com. N.Y.-N.J. Trail Conf., 1987—. Contbr. articles to mags. Instr. Darien (Conn.) YMCA, 1988; bd. dirs. Entrepreneurial Network of Fairfield County. Mem. NAFE, N.Y. State Bar Assn., N.Y. State Wilderness Guide Assn. Democrat. Jewish. Office: P Oppenheimer and Assocs Inc 489 5th Ave 34th Floor New York NY 10017

COHEN, SHERMAN SHEPARD, attorney; b. Clinton, Mass., Oct. 27, 1919; s. Harry and Rae (Verstein) C.; m. Helen Adele Falk, July 12, 1943. children: Harrison, Julia. A.B., U. of Rochester, 1941; JD, Columbia U., 1948; LLM., NYU, 1949. Atty. CAB, ICC, Salary Stabilization Bd., Wash., D.C., 1949-52; pvt. practice Washington, 1952—; prof. Chase Law Sch., Lewis Univ. Sch. of Law, Okla. U. Sch. of Law, Washington, 1969-78; Author: Businessperson's Guide To Government Advice and Information, 1952, Journals - Tax, 1952-85. With USAAF, 1942-45. Mem. D.C. Bar Assn., ABA, Am. Bus. Law Assn., Am. Arbitration Assn. Home: 499 Wellesley Ave Cincinnati OH 45224 Office: No Ky U Highland Heights KY 41076

COHEN, STEPHEN DAVID, economics educator; b. Balt., June 10, 1942; s. Leon W. and Ella C.; m. Linda R. Forman, June 30, 1968; children: Sondra Lynn, Marc R. BA, Am. U., 1963; MA, Syracuse U., 1964, PhD, 1969. Internat. economist U.S. Dept. Treasury, Washington, 1964-67; chief economist U.S.-Japan Trade Council, Washington, 1969-73; mem. profl. staff Commn. on Orgn. of Govt. for Conduct of Fgn. Policy, Washington, 1974-75; internat. economist Washington Analysis Corp., 1975—; prof. econ. Sch. Internat. Service Am. U., Washington, 1975—; presenter testimony on econs. concerns to U.S. Congress, 1977, 78, 79, 80, 83. Author: International Monetary Reform, 1964-69; The Political Dimension, 1970, The Making of United States International Economic Policy-Principles, Problems, Proposals for Reform, 1977, 2d edit., 1981, 3rd edit., 1988, U.S. International Economic Policy in Action: The Diversity of Decision Making (with others), 1982, International Economic Handbook of the World (with others), 1981, Uneasy Partnership: Competition and Conflict in U.S.-Japanese Trade Relations, 1985 (published in Japan as Trade Frictions Between the United States and Japan, 1985); author monographs; contbr. articles and essays to numerous publs.; contbg. editor Bus. View Mag., Tokyo, 1981-84. Research fellow Rockefeller Found., 1975-76, Fulbright-Hays Found., 1981-82. Mem. Nat. Assn. Bus. Economists. Office: Am U Sch Internat Service Washington DC 20016

COHEN, WILLIAM ALAN, marketing educator, author, lecturer, consultant; b. Balt., June 25, 1937; s. Sidney Oliver and Theresa (Bachman) C.; m. Janice Dawn Stults, Jan. 3, 1963 (div. Jan. 1966); 1 child, William Alan II; m. Nurit Kovnator, May 28, 1967; children—Barak, Nimrod. BS, U.S. Mil. Acad., 1959; MBA, U. Chgo., 1967; MA, Claremont Grad. Sch., 1978, PhD, 1979. Registered profl. engr., Israel. Project mgr. Israel Aircraft Industries, 1970-73; mgr. research and devel. Sierra Engring. Co., Sierra Madre, Calif., 1973-76; pres. Global Assocs., 1973—; mgr. advanced tech. mktg. McDonnell-Douglas Co., Huntington Beach, Calif., 1976-78; prof. mktg. Calif. State U.-Los Angeles, 1979—, dir. Bur. Bus. and Econ. Research, 1979-83, chmn. mktg. dept., 1986—; dir. Small Bus. Inst.; cons. Fortune 500 cos. Author: The Executives Guide to Finding a Superior Job, 1978, 83, Principles of Technical Management, 1980, Successful Marketing for Small Business, 1981, How To Sell To Government, 1981, The Entrepreneur and Small Business Problem Solver, 1983, Direct Response Marketing, 1984, Building a Mail Order Business, 1982, 85, Making It Big as a Consultant, 1985, Winning on the Marketing Front, 1986, High Tech Management, 1986, Developing A Winning Marketing Plan, 1987, The Students Guide To Finding A Superior Job, 1987, The Practice of Marketing Management, 1988; contbr. numerous articles to profl. jours. Served to maj. USAF, 1959-70, col. Res. Decorated D.F.C. with 3 oak leaf clusters, Air medal with 11 oak leaf clusters ; recipient Ministry Def. award State of Israel, 1976, Outstanding Service award Nat. Mgmt. Assn., 1979, Pres.'s award West Point Soc., 1982, Outstanding Prof. award Calif. State U.-Los Angeles, 1983, Chgo. Trib Gold Medal, George Washington medal Freedoms Found at Valley Forge, 1986; numerous grants. Fellow Acad. Mktg. Sci.; mem. Direct Mktg. Assn. (fellow 1980, 83) bd. World Mktg. Congress (del. N.S. 1983), Direct Mktg. Club So. Calif. (bd. dirs. 1980—, grantee 1981), Am. Mktg. Assn. (award 1982), West Point Soc. (pres., bd. dirs. 1981-82). Republican. Jewish. Office: Calif State U Sch Bus and Econs Los Angeles CA 90032

COHN, IAN J., architect; b. Phila., Jan. 9, 1950; s. Isidore and Jacqueline (Heymann) C., Jr.; m. Vicki Hertzberg, June 23, 1973; children: Kevin Aton, Adrian Kirrin. Grad. The Gunnery, Washington, Conn.; BA, Washington U., St. Louis, 1971, MArch., 1974. Registered architect, N.Y. Staff architect Howell, Killick, Partridge & Amis, London, 1974-76; staff architect, George Nelson & Co., N.Y.C., 1977; assoc. Perkins & Will, N.Y.C., 1977-80; founding ptnr. Ian/Aaron Architects, N.Y.C., 1980—, Ian/Aaron Architects, Internat. (in assn. with Sheehan & Barry, Dublin, Ireland), 1985—; prin. Diversity: Architecture & Design, 1989; young artist-in-residence The Gunnery Sch., 1989—. Author: Structures: A Rule of Thumb Handbook, 1973; designs exhibited in mus. and mags. Mem. The Gunnery Alumni Assn. Democrat. Jewish. Avocations: photography, tennis, traveling, wine, gourmet food. Office: Ian/Aaron Architects 77 Lexington Ave New York NY 10010

COHN, MILTON SEYMOUR, business executive; b. N.Y.C., Oct. 11, 1920; s. Max B. and Dorothy (Zucker) C.; m. Lucille Sanders, May 20, 1945; children: Bonnie L., Judd M. B.S. cum laude, NYU, 1941, J.D. cum laude, 1950. Bar: N.Y. 1950. With Cerro Wire & Cable Co., Queens, N.Y., 1945-81; pres. Cerro Wire & Cable Co., 1955-81, ret., 1981; dir. CCX, Inc., Bridgewater, N.J., Condec Corp., Old Greenwich, Conn., 1955-84; dir., chmn. exec. com. United Aircrafts Products, Inc., Dayton, Ohio, 1972-86. Trustee Beth Israel Med. Ctr., Ohr Torah Inst.; dir., sec., treas. Max B. Cohn Family Found. Mem. Beta Gamma Sigma. Clubs: City Athletic, NYU Fin. Office: 445 Park Ave New York NY 10022

COHN, THEODORE, management consultant; b. Newark, June 15, 1923; s. Julius H. and Bessie R. (Einson) C.; m. Dina Berkson, Nov. 28, 1946 (dec. July 4, 1985); children: Don Jonathan, Jordan Ellis, Karen Jane; m. Alice Ginott, Aug. 26, 1986. BA, Harvard U., 1943; MA, Columbia U., 1948. With J.H. Cohn & Co. (C.P.A.s), Newark, 1951-74; mng. partner J.H. Cohn & Co. (C.P.A.s), 1963-74; mgmt. cons., specializing in problems and opportunities of family owned cos. 1975—. Co-author: Operations Auditing, 1972, How Management Is Different in Small Companies, 1972, Practical Personnel Policies for Small Business, 1984, Survival and Growth: Management Strategies for the Small Firm, 1974, Compensating Key Executives in the Smaller Company, 1979, The Marketing Book for Growing Companies that Want to Excel, 1986; Mem. editorial adv. bd.: Jour. of Accountancy, 1973; Contbr. articles to profl. jours. Mem. AICPA (head task force on HRA 1973-74), N.J. Soc. CPAs, N.Y. Socs. CPAs, Am. Mgmt. Assn., Am. Psychol. Assn. (assoc.). Home and Office: 923 Fifth Ave 4A New York NY 10021

COHRS, WILLIAM MICHAEL, investment banker; b. Midland, Mich., Oct. 9, 1956; s. William E. and Lois Ellen. (Gremel) C.; m. Arlene Ines Cebollero-Catanchi, June 16, 1984. AB, Harvard U., 1976, MBA, 1981. Producer Hasty Pudding Theatricals, Cambridge, Mass., 1974-75; pres. HSA, Inc., Cambridge, 1974-75; assoc. Goldman, Sachs & Co., N.Y.C., 1981-85, v.p., 1985—. Mem. sr. profl. staff Presdl. Task Force on Market Mechanisms, N.Y.C., 1987-88; mem. jr. com. N.Y.C. Opera, 1986. Named leader in Fin. between Japan and U.S., Japan Econ. Jour., 1985. Club: Delphic (Cambridge). Home: 1170 5th Ave New York NY 10029 Office: Goldman Sachs & Co 85 Broad St New York NY 10004

COKE, ALFRED MACK, real estate construction firm executive, consultant; b. Sulphur Springs, Tex., Sept. 8, 1941; s. Buster Mack and Willie Louise (Wilburn) C.; m. Anne Rector, Sept. 19, 1987; children: Corey Lynn, Dane Shelby. BS in Geology, U. So. Miss., 1963; MS in Adult Edn., Kans. State U., 1977; MA in Human Resources Mgmt., Pepperdine U., 1979; MBA, PhD in Organizational Devel., Columbia Pacific U., 1981. Registered organizational development consultant. Commd. officer U.S. Army, 1963; advanced through grades to lt. col., inf. U.S. Army, Germany, Korea, Vietnam, U.S.A, Panama; retired U.S. Army, 1983; sr. cons. Synergistic Systems, Denham Springs, La., 1975—; ptnr. Leah Investments, Walker, La., 1985—; lectr. The Pres.'s Assn., N.Y.C., 1983—; pres., owner Pelican Properties, Denham Springs, La., 1985-86; prin. Chosen Frozens Co.; cons. Am. Mgmt. Assn., N.Y.C., 1982—, Fairfield Cons. Group, Denham Springs, 1985-87; trainer Associated Mgmt. Inst., Fairfield, Calif., 1984-86. Contbr. articles and book chpts. on mgmt. Mem. Internat. Mgmt. Council, Retired Officers Assn., Internat. Registry of Orgn. Profls. Republican. Baptist. Home and Office: 8134 Hermitage Dr Denham Springs LA 70726

COKE, C(HAUNCEY) EUGENE, consulting company executive, scientist, educator, author; b. Toronto, Ont., Can; s. Chauncey Eugene and Edith May (Redman) C.; m. Sally B. Tolmie, June 12, 1941. B.Sc. with honors, U. Man., M.Sc. magna cum laude; M.A., U. Toronto; postgrad., Yale U.; Ph.D., U. Leeds, Eng., 1938. Dir. research Courtaulds (Can.) Ltd., 1939-42; dir. research and devel. Guaranty Dyeing & Finishing Co., 1946-48; various exec. research and devel. positions Courtaulds (Can.) Ltd., Montreal, 1948-59, dir. research and devel.; mem. exec. com. Hart-Fibres Co., 1959-62; tech. dir. textile chem. Drew Chem. Corp., 1962-63; dir. new products fibers div. Am. Cynamid Co., 1963-68, dir. applications devel., 1968-70; pres. Coke & Assoc., Cons., Ormond Beach, Fla., 1970-78, chmn., 1978—; pres. Aqua Vista Corp. Inc., 1971-74; vis. research prof. Stetson U., 1979—; internat. authority on man-made fibers; guest lectr. Sir George Williams Coll., Montreal, 1949-59; chmn. Can. adv. com. on Internat. Standards Orgn. Tech. Com. 38, 1951-58; mem. Can. Standards Assn., 1958-59; del. Textile Tech. Fedn. Can., 1948-57, bd. dirs., 1957-59. Contbr. articles to profl. jours. Vice chmn. North Peninsula adv. bd. Volusia County Council, 1975-78; mem. Halifax Area Study Commn., 1972-74, Volusia County Elections Bd., 1974—; bd. dirs. Council of Assns. N. Peninsula, 1972-74, 76-77. Served from 2d lt. to maj. RCAF, 1942-46. Recipient Bronze medal Can. Assn. Textile Colourists and Chemists, 1963. Fellow Royal Soc. Chemistry (Gt. Britain life), Textile Inst. (Gt. Britain), Soc. Dyers and Colourists (Gt. Britain), Inst. Textile Sci. (co-founder, 3d pres.), Chem. Inst. Can. (life, mem. council 1958-61), AAAS, N.J. Acad. Sci., Am. Inst. Chemists; mem. Am. Assn. Textile Tech. (life, past pres. Bronze medal), Can. Assn. Textile Colourists and Chemists (hon. life, past pres.), N.Y. Acad. Scis. (life), Fla. Acad. Scis., U.S. Metric Assn. (life). Clubs: Greater Daytona Beach Republican Men's (pres. 1972-75), Rep. Pres.'s Forum (pres. 1976-78, v.p. 1978-81), The Chemist's. Home: 26 Aqua Vista Dr Ormond Beach FL 32074 Office: Coke & Assoc Cons Ormond by the Sea Ormond Beach FL 32074

COKER, CHARLES WESTFIELD, diversified manufacturing company executive; b. Florence, S.C., 1933; married. BA, Princeton U., 1955; MBA, Harvard U., 1957. With Sonoco Products Co., Hartsville, S.C., 1958—, v.p. adminstrn., 1961-67, v.p. gen. mgmt., corp. planning and fin., from 1967, exec. v.p., 1966-70, pres., chief exec. officer, 1970—, also bd. dirs.; bd. dirs. Bank of Hartsville, Carolina Power and Light Co., NCNB Corp., Springs Industries Inc., Sara Lee Corp. Served to 2d lt. USAR, 1957-63. Office: Sonoco Products Co N 2nd St Hartsville SC 29550 *

COKER, CLAUDIA GERMAINE, savings and loan executive; b. Walnut Ridge, Ark., Jan. 6, 1953; d. Zack Tiley and Germaine Marie (Piantoni) C. BS, Ark. State U., 1975. Cashier Harps Supermarket, Walnut Ridge, 1972-73, Rorex Supermarket Hoxie, Ark., 1973-74; office mgr. Higginbotham Burial Ins., Walnut Ridge, 1975; clk. typist Crane Co., Jonesboro, Ark., 1975-76; savs. and loan examiner Fed. Home Loan Bank Bd., Little Rock, 1976-85; Savs. and loan examiner Fed. Home Loan Bank, Dallas, 1985-87; v.p., regulatory compliance officer, United Fed. Savs. and Loan, Jonesboro, Ark., 1987—. Mem. Leadership Jonesboro 1988. Recipient Civil Services Beta award Fed. Home Loan Bank Bd., 1978. Bd. dirs. United Way, Jonesboro; bd. trustees United Way Craighead County. Mem. Assn. Bus. Profl. Women (1st v.p. Downtown Jonesboro chpt. 1988-89), Fin. Mgrs. Soc., Nat. Assn. Female Execs. Baptist. Clubs: Altrusa (Jonesboro), Confederate Air Force (security detachment) (Harlingen, Tex.); Razorback Wing (security detachment)(Pine Bluff, Ark.). Avocations: counted cross stitch, knitting, needlepoint, reading, collecting depression-era glass. Home: 2106 Wind Cove Jonesboro AR 72401 Office: United Fed Savs and Loan 515 West Washington Jonesboro AR 72401

COKER, DONALD WILLIAM, banker; b. Mobile, Ala., Nov. 26, 1945; s. William Mack and Gloria Antoinette (Croker) C.; m. Linda Carol Sandlin, July 12, 1969; children: Caroline Tiffany, Brittany Blair. BA, U. Ala., 1968, postgrad., 1968. Trust mortgage officer AmSouth Bank, Mobile, 1968-72; sr. loan officer Gibraltar Savs., Houston, 1972-73; mortgage officer Citicorp Real Estate, Houston, 1973-74; comml. loan officer M Bank-Houston, 1974-77; regional mgr. Comml. Credit Co., Houston, 1977-83, Ford Motor Credit, Houston, 1983-84; sr. v.p. First Fed. Savs., San Antonio, 1984-85; exec. v.p. Home Savs., Houston, 1985-86; also bd. dirs. Home Savs.; supr. banking Tex. Savs. & Loan Dept., Houston, 1986-88; chmn. Fin. Inst. Mgmt. Svcs., Mobile, Ala., 1988—; cons. in field. Author: Complete Guide to Income Property Financing, 1984, Self-Management, 1985; editor: Complete Real Estate Computer Workbook, 1986, The Complete Loan Officers Handbook, 1989. Trustee Katy Ind. Sch. Dist., Houston, 1987; treas. Nottingham Country Civic Club, Houston, 1980. Served with U.S. Army, 1968. Mem. Nat. Assn. of State Savs. and Loan Suprs., Mortgage Bankers' Assn. Republican. Episcopalian. Clubs: Sweetwater Country. Home: PO Box 91182 Mobile AL 36691

COKER, L.N. (JIM), manufacturing executive; b. Anson, Tex., Aug. 16, 1930; s. H. Wardell and A. Avenell (Nevill) C.; m. W. Jean Barclay, June 12, 1953; children: Lynette Coker Davis, Debra Ann Singleton. AA in Bus., Odessa Coll., Tex., 1955; student, La Salle Coll., Chgo., 1964. Landman Shell Oil Co., Midland, Tex., 1953-57; area mgr. Drilco Oil Tools, Midland, 1957-64; product mgr. Drilco Indsl., Midland, 1964-72, ops. mgr., 1972-76, gen. sales mgr., 1982-85, dir. sales, 1985-87, v.p., 1987—; owner, pres. Jackson Hill Marina, Inc., Broaddus, Tex., 1976-82. Sgt. USMC, 1949-53, Korea. Mem. Inst. Shaff Drilling Tech., Soc. Mining Engrs., Nat. Water Well Assn., Midland Lions (pres., Tex. zone chmn.). Home: 1910 County Rd 130 W Midland TX 79703 Office: Drilco Indsl PO Box 3135 Midland TX 79702

COKER, ROBERT HILTON, construction executive; b. Pensacola, Fla., May 19, 1947; s. Robert H. and Billie (Bennett) C. BS, Fla. State U., 1969. Pers. analyst Shell Oil Co., New Orleans, 1969-72; v.p. Coker Industries, Miami, Fla., 1972-74; pers. mgr. Lehigh Portland Cement, Miami, 1974-76; mgr. sales and pers. Hertz Equipment Rental Corp., Tampa, Fla., 1976-78; regional sales mgr. Gelco Space, Tampa, 1978-79, div. v.p., 1979-83; exec. v.p. Gelco Space, Phila., 1983—. With USAFR, 1970-76. Mem. Modular Office Assn. Democrat. Baptist. Home: 2020 Walnut St #21H Philadelphia PA 19103 Office: Gelco Space Two Bala Pla 800 Bala Cynwyd PA 19004-0943

COLANTUONO, FRANK JOHN, insurance executive; b. Phila., Nov. 3, 1948; s. Carl George and Catherine Sarah (Doherty) C.; m. Kathleen Shannon Paulus, June 5, 1971 (div. 1981); 1 child, James. BS in Fin., Gannon U., 1971; MBA, SUNY, Buffalo, 1977. Dist. mgr. Gen. Nutrition Ctrs., Buffalo, 1971-73; terr. mgr. Ross Labs., Buffalo, 1973-75; with mgmt. Ind. Health Assn., Buffalo, 1976-79, v.p. fin. and planning, 1979-84, pres., chief exec. officer, 1984—. Cons., bd. dirs. Jr. Achievement, Buffalo, 1986—; treas. Allentown Community Ctr., Buffalo, 1986—; bd. dirs. Studio Arena Theater, Buffalo, 1987—; pres., bd. dirs. Hallwalls Art Gallery, Buffalo, 1987—. Democrat. Roman Catholic. Club: Buffalo Yacht. Office: Ind Health Assn 4510 Main St Buffalo NY 14226

COLARUSSO, JOSEPH RICHARD, electronics company executive; b. N.Y.C., July 18, 1931; s. James Vincent and Rachel (Carjullo) C.; m. Alfina Joy Borgese, Dec. 18, 1954; children: James Vincent, Linda Joy, Robert Joseph. Student, Fordham U., 1948-50; BA, St. Michaels Coll., 1950-52; postgrad., Columbia U., 1956-57, NYU, 1957-58. V.p. communications, detection, identification Hazeltine Corp., Greenlawn, N.Y., 1973-74, v.p. mil. systems, 1974-75, v.p. industry products div., 1975-82, sr. v.p. bus. devel., 1982-86, sr. v.p. C3I, 1986-87, exec. v.p., 1987—; cons. Dept. of Def., Washington, 1974-75. Served to lt. (j.g.) USN, 1953-56, Korea. Republican. Roman Catholic. Home: 39 Lawrence Ln Bay Shore NY 11706

COLASACCO, TONY, bank executive; b. Capestrano City Aquila, Abruzzi, Italy, Dec. 10, 1953; came to U.S., 1969; s. Gildo Alberto and Maria Elena (DiGregorio) C.; m. Maria Clara Spagnolo, June 12, 1975; children: Giovanni, Tony, Melissa. Student, Computer Processing Inst., 1973, 76, Manchester Community Coll. Baker Modern Pastry, Hartford, Conn., 1973-75; computer operator Conn. Bank & Trust, Hartford, 1975-79, computer programmer, 1979-87, check processing mgr., 1987—. Lodge: Elks. Office: Conn Bank & Trust 99 Founders Pla East Hartford CT 06108

COLBERT, ANNETTE DARCIA, silver company executive; b. Tulsa, Oct. 24, 1959; d. Buel and Bonnie Helen (Pickens) C.; 1 child, Siobhan Nicole. Student, Devry Inst., Dallas, 1979, Oklahoma City U., 1986. Tech. rep. Xerox Corp., Oklahoma City, 1979-80; field engr. NCR Corps., Oklahoma City, 1980; chief exec. officer Silver Merchants Ltd., Oklahoma City, 1981—; exec. dir., cons. Embassy, Inc., Oklahoma City, 1987—. Fund raiser U.S. C. of C., Oklahoma City, 1985-86; project dir. Embassy Inc., Oklahoma City, 1986-87. Mem. Am. Mgmt. Assn., Am. Metal Assn., Gold and Silver Inst. Republican. Home: 7501 S Sherwood #2 Oklahoma City OK 73159 Office: Silver Merchants Ltd 6161 N May #25W Oklahoma City OK 73112

COLBERT, LESTER LUM, JR., technology company executive; b. Detroit, Feb. 6, 1934; s. Lester Lum Sr. and Daisy (Gorman) C. AB, Princeton U., 1955; MBA, Harvard U., 1961. V.p., dir. Reichhold Chemicals, Inc., White Plains, N.Y., 1961-72; chmn., pres., chief exec. officer Xidex Corp., Palo Alto, Calif., 1972-87, chmn., 1987-88; with Am. Indsl. Ptnrs., San Francisco, 1988—. Bd. dirs. Castle Convertible Fund, N.Y.C., 1974—. Served to lt. (j.g.) USN, 1955-57. Mem. Phi Beta Kappa. Clubs: Bohemian (San Francisco); Knickerbocker (N.Y.C.). Office: care Am Indsl Ptnrs 1 Maritime Pla 23rd Fl San Francisco CA 94111

COLBERT, ROBERT REED, JR., real estate developer; b. Ithaca, N.Y., June 13, 1949; s. Robert Reed and Barbara Jane (Schaefer) C.; B.S., Cornell U., Ithaca, 1971; m. Mary Elizabeth Murrin, Oct. 4, 1980; children: Katharin Murrin, Christopher Reed. Dir. property mgmt. Pyramid Cos., DeWitt, N.Y., 1971-73; pres. Concept Property Mgmt. Group, Ithaca, 1973—; lectr. Architecture Coll., Cornell U., 1977-78. Bd. dirs. Blind Work Assn. Central N.Y. Roman Catholic. Clubs: Ithaca Yacht (dir.), Cornell, Quadrangle. Home: 304 Highgate Rd Ithaca NY 14850 Office: Concept Property Mgmt Group 105 N Tioga St PO Box 697 Ithaca NY 14850

COLBERT, VIRGIS WILLIAM, brewery company executive; b. Jackson, Miss., Oct. 13, 1939; s. Quillie and Eddie C.; grad. Exec. Inst., Earlham Coll., 1974; B.S., Central Mich. U., 1974. With Toledo Machining Plant, Chrysler Corp., 1966-79, foreman, 1968-70, gen. foreman, 1970-73, mfg. supt., 1973-77, gen. mfg. supt., 1977-79; asst. to plant mgr. Miller Brewing Co., Reidsville, N.C., 1979-80, prodn. mgr., Ft. Worth, Tex., 1980-81, plant mgr. Milw. Container Plant, 1981-87, asst. dir. can mfg., 1987-88, dir. container and support mfg., 1988—. Active Youth program Nat. Alliance Businessmen, NAACP, Black Execs. Program of Nat. Urban League; bd. dirs. Mental Health Assn. Milw. County, Planned Parenthood Wis., Inc.; mem. adv. bd. Milw. Pub. Libr.; mem. adv. com. indsl. tech. program div. bus. So. U. at New Orleans; mem. accreditation team Jackson State U. Indsl. Tech. Program. Mem. Am. Mgmt. Assn., Nat. Urban League's Black Exec. Exchange Program, Omega Psi Phi. Club: Frontiers Internat. Lodges: Masons, Shriners. Home: 1811 E Fox Ln Fox Point WI 53217 Office: Miller Brewing Co 3939 W Highland Blvd Milwaukee WI 53201

COLBURN, GENE LEWIS, insurance and industrial psychology consultant; b. Bismarck, N.D., July 12, 1932; s. Lewis William and Olga Alma (Feland) C.; PhD, UCLA, 1982. Pres., gen. mgr. Multiple Lines Ins. Agy., Auburn, Wash., 1953-79; ins. and risk mgmt. cons., Auburn, Wash., 1980—; pres. Feland Safe Deposit Corp.; bd. dirs. Century Service Corp. sub. Capital Savs. Bank, Olympia, Wash.; mem. exec. com. Great Republic Life Ins. Co., Portland, Oreg., 1971-75; mem. Wash. State Ins. Commrs. Test Devel. Com., 1986—. cons. indsl. risk mgmt. and psychology. Councilperson Auburn City, 1982-85; mayor-pro tem, City of Auburn, 1984; co-incorporator, chmn. bd. SE Community Alcohol Ctr., 1971-75; mem. Wash. State Disaster Assistance Council, 1981—, founding mem.; pres. Valley Cities Mental Health Center, 1980; mem. instn. rev. com. Auburn Gen. Hosp., 1978—; prin. trustee Dr. R. B. Bramble Med. Research Found., 1980—; bd. dirs. Wash. Assn. Chs. (Luth. Ch. in Am.), Asian Refugee Resettlement Mgmt. div., 1981-83, Columbia Luth. Home, Seattle, 1985—, Wash. Law Enforcement Officers and Fire Fighter's Pension Disability Bd., Auburn, 1980-84. Cert. ins. counselor, 1978. Recipient Disting. Alumni award Green River Community Coll., 1982. Fellow Acad. Producer Ins. Studies (charter); mem. Internat. Platform Assn. Lodge: Auburn Lions (past pres.). Office: 201 A St NW Auburn WA 98002

COLBURN, KENNETH HERSEY, investment banker; b. Melrose, Mass., Jan. 8, 1952; s. Warren Edward and Mabelle (Hersey) C.; married. AB, Brown U., 1975; MPPM, Yale U., 1978. Assoc. First Boston Corp., N.Y.C., 1978-83, v.p., 1983-88, mng. dir., 1988—. Mem. adv. bd. sch. orgn. and mgmt. Yale U., New Haven, 1986—. Mem. Yale Club, Watch Hill Yacht Club. Office: 1st Boston Corp Park Avenue Pla New York NY 10055

COLBY, LEWIS JAMES, JR., manufacturing company executive; b. Seattle, Jan. 22, 1934; s. Lewis James and Della (Danielson) C.; m. Harriett Lane Wright, Aug. 23, 1958 (div. 1986); children: Cheryl Layne Colby Bartels, Steven James. AA, Santa Rosa Jr. Coll., 1953; BS, U. Calif., Berkeley, 1955; PhD, Purdue U., 1960. Prof. Purdue U., West Lafayette, Ind., 1959-60; research specialist Atomics Internat., 1960-65; staff phys. chemist AEC, 1966-69; div. dir. Gen. Atomic Co., 1969-75; exec. v.p. Allied Nuclear Co. div. Allied Chem. Corp., 1975-77; pres. Nuclear Services div. Allied Chem. Corp., 1976-77, Allied Chem. Nuclear Products div. Allied Chem. Corp., 1977; group v.p. Allied Chem. Corp., 1977-79; sr. v.p. Allied-Signal Inc. (formerly Allied Corp.), Morristown, N.J., 1979—; bd. dirs. Maxwell Labs. Inc., San Diego, Identitech, Livingston, N.J. Mem. Am. Chem. Soc. Office: Allied Signal Inc Columbia Rd & Park Ave Morristown NJ 07960

COLE, AUBREY LOUIS, forest products company executive; b. Wichita Falls, Tex., Dec. 29, 1923; s. Aubrey Mizell and Lila Ellen (Burge) C.; m. Dorothy Jeanne Wilson, Dec. 27, 1944; children—Melissa Ann, Gordon Louis. B.B.A., U. Tex., 1949. Asst. controller Tex. div. Champion Papers Co., Pasadena, 1950-59; corporate controller Champion Papers Co., Hamilton, Ohio, 1959-65; v.p. mgmt. info. systems Champion Papers Co., 1966-69; v.p. planning and control U.S. Plywood-Champion Papers, N.Y.C., 1969-73; v.p. mgmt. info. Champion Internat., Stamford, Conn., 1973-74; sr. v.p. control Champion Internat., 1974-85; vice chmn., dir. Champion Internat. Corp., 1985—; Mem. dirs. assos. U. Tex.; mem. Econ. Policy Council, UN Assn.; participant Ctr. for Strategic and Internat. Studies; mem. employee rels. com. The Bus. Roundtable. Mem. bus. adv. council Coll. of Bus. Adminstrn. at U. Tex. Served with USNR, 1942-45. Mem. Fin. Execs. Inst., Nat. Assn. Accountants, Alpha Kappa Psi. Office: Champion Internat Corp 1 Champion Pla Stamford CT 06921

COLE, CAROLYN JO, brokerage company executive; b. Carmel, Calif.; d. Joseph Michael, Jr., and Dorothea Wagner (James) C.; A.B., Vassar Coll., 1965. Mgr. tech. services Aims Group, N.Y.C., 1965-67; editor Standard & Poor's Corp., N.Y.C., 1968-74; sr. v.p. PaineWebber, Inc., N.Y.C., 1975—; guest lectr. Harvard U. Bus. Sch. Mem. N.Y.C. Commn. on Status of Women. Named to YWCA Acad. Women Achievers. Mem. N.Y. Soc. Security Analysts (bd. dirs.), Fin. Analysts Fedn., Soc. Fgn. Analysts, Aspen

Inst. Humanistic Studies, Fin. Women's Assn., Women's Econ. Roundtable, Econ. Club N.Y., Women in Need (chmn. fin. com.), NOW, DAR. Democrat. Episcopalian. Club: Vassar (N.Y.C.). Contbr. to Ency. Americana. Office: Paine Webber Inc 1285 Ave of the Americas New York NY 10019

COLE, CLYDE LEONARD, defense contractor; b. Bath, N.C., Nov. 4, 1932; s. Elmer L. and Hallie Blanche (Kernodle) C.; m. Debra Kay Heater, Dec. 27, 1979. Enlisted USN, 1951, resigned, 1955, commd. to USAF, 1959, served to master sgt., Vietnam, ret. 1973; tech. services Jackson & Church Electronics, Inc., Melbourne, Fla., 1973—; cons. Jacox Inc., 1975, 77; v.p. Video Applications Co., Inc., Melbourne, 1978-85; quality engr. Dept. Def. at Hughes Aircraft, Forest, Miss., 1986—. Lodge: Masons. Home: 121 Prescott Dr Brandon MS 39042 Office: Hughes Aircraft Corp Rt 5 Box 9 Forest MS 39074

COLE, DOY FRED, business executive; b. Tulsa, Mar. 6, 1940; s. Roy Edwards and Ellen Louise (Levernz) C.; m. SuzAnne C. Cole, June 29, 1963; children: Bradley, Wesley, Mike. BS in Chem. Engring., U. Tulsa, 1962, MS in Chem. Engring., 1963; student sr. exec. program, London Bus. Sch., 1982. Registered Chem. Engr., Calif. Project mgr. Pritchard Corp., Kansas City, Mo., 1970-72, regional sales mgr., 1972-74; regional sales mgr. The McKee Corp., Houston, 1974-78; v.p. acquisitions The McKee Corp., Cleve., 1977-78; v.p., gen. mgr. Davy McKee, St. Louis, 1978-81; sr. v.p. sales Davy McKee, Houston, 1981-84; v.p. western hemisphere sales The M.W. Kellogg Co., Houston, 1984-87, v.p. European ops., 1987-89; v.p. ops. M.W. Kellogg Ltd., Houston, 1989—; mng. dir. M.W. Kellogg Ltd., London, 1987-89. Indsl. adv. bd. U. Tulsa, 1988—. Mem. Am. Inst. Chem. Engrs., Houston City Club. Republican. Presbyterian. Office: MW Kellogg Ltd #3 Greenway Pla Houston TX 77046-0395

COLE, GREGORY CLAYTON, electrical engineer; b. McKeesport, Pa., Jan. 21, 1963; s. W. Clayton and Sara Susan (Leiter) C. BSEE, Ga. Inst. Tech., 1985. Elec. engr. 1 Sci.-Atlanta, Norcross, Ga., 1985-86; elec. engr. 2 Sci.-Atlanta, Norcross, 1986-87, sr. engr., 1987—; mem. panel Ga. Inst. Tech., Atlanta, 1988; presenter in field. Mem. IEEE. Lutheran. Office: Sci-Atlanta 4311 Communications Dr Norcross GA 33093

COLE, JACK NEWCOMBE, computer consulting company executive; b. Little Rock, Feb. 10, 1947; s. Jack Newcombe and Jeanette Dolores (Gardiner) C.; m. Lynn Crow, Aug. 13, 1976; children: Meredith Allison, Taylor Gardiner. BA, Cath. U., 1968; MA in Teaching, Wayne State U., 1970; PhD, U. Md., 1977. Tchr. Hartford County Bd. Edn., Bel Air, Md., 1970-72; instr. U. Md., Collge Park, 1976-77; coordinating supr. Prince George's County Pub. Schs., Upper Marlboro, Md., 1977-84; pres. Computer Mgmt. Services, Columbia, Md., 1985—. Editor (guide) Basic Study Skills, K-12, 1981. Chmn. legis. com. Md. Reading Assn., 1982-84; adv. bd. Howard County Pub. Sch. Tchrs. Ctr., Columbia, 1984—. Mem. Data Processing Mgrs. Assn., Am. Mktg. Assn., Howard County C. of C. Republican. Roman Catholic. Lodge: Rotary.

COLE, JAMES DEAN, financial executive; b. Asheville, N.C., Mar. 3, 1958; s. William G. Shelby (McIntosh) C.; m. Mary Ann Alley, Sept. 17, 1983; children: April, Andrew. BS in Acctg., Va. Inst. Tech., 1980. CPA, Va. Staff acct. Brown Edwards & Co., Roanoke, Va., 1980; audit mgr., asst. recruiting coordinator Ernst & Whinney, CPA's, Roanoke, 1980-84; dir. acctg. Va. Tech. Found., Ind., Blacksburg, 1984-85; asst. treas. Va. Poly. Inst. and State U., Blacksburg, 1985—. Active Montgomery County (Va.) Bus. Edn. Adv. Council, 1986—. Recipient Meritorious Service award Beta Alpha Psi, 1980. Mem. AICPA, Nat. Assn. Accts. (bd. dirs. Roanoke chpt. 1981-83, 88), Ea. Assn. Coll. and Univ. Bus. Officers, Fin. Officers Colls. and Univs., Shawsville (Va.) Athletic Boosters, Masons, Ruritan (pres. 1983-85). Methodist. Home: PO Box 5 Shawsville VA 24162 Office: Va Poly Inst 233 Burress Hall Blacksburg VA 24061

COLE, JOHN STERLING, II, communications company executive; b. Bennington, Vt., June 5, 1954; s. Charles Sterling and Lorna (Bass) C.; m. Sue Parrott, July, 21, 1979; children: Kristen Elizabeth, John Sterling III. BS in Acctg., Bentley Coll., 1976; MBA, U. Notre Dame, 1982. Cert. internal auditor, fin. analyst, Conn., Minn. Auditor United Parcel Svc., Greenwich, Conn., 1976-77; mgr. acctg. United Parcel Svc., Neuss, Federal Republic Ger., 1977-79; nat. auditor United Parcel Svc., Greenwich, 1979-80; sr. auditor Cowles Media Co., Mpls., 1982-83, asst. treas., 1983-85, treas., 1985—; bd. dirs. Cowles Media Found. Mem. Rotary. Office: Cowles Media Co 329 Portland Ave Minneapolis MN 55415

COLE, JOSEPH EDMUND, specialty retail company executive; b. Cleve., Jan. 4, 1915; s. Solomon and Sarah (Miller) C.; m. Marcia Newman, Oct. 31, 1937; children: Jeffrey, Stephan. Student, Ohio State U., 1932, Fenn Coll., Cleve., 1933. Salesman Waldorf Brewing Co., 1933-35; office mgr., then gen. mgr. Nat. Key Shops, Inc., 1935-44; partner, sales dir. Curtis Industries, 1944-50; pres., now chmn. Cole Nat. Corp., Cleve., 1950—; past chmn. Shelter Resources Corp.; past dir. BancOhio Nat. Bank, Cleve. Past pub. The Cleveland Press. Active Jewish Welfare Fund, Cleve., 1963-64; Chmn. Ohio Citizens for Kennedy, 1960; chmn. Hubert Humphrey for Pres., 1972; mem. Cuyahoga County Democratic Exec. Com., 1960—; chmn. finance com. Dem. Nat. Com., 1973-74; Bd. dirs. Jewish Community Fedn., Cleve., Notre Dame Coll., Playhouse Sq. Found., Cleve., Palm Beach Ctr. for the Performing Arts, Fla.; past trustee Cleve. State U.; past chmn. scholarship fund Ohio State Coll.; life mem. Brandeis U. Mem. Cleve. C. of C. Jewish (trustee temple). Clubs: Masons (32 deg.), Shriners, Oakwood Country City (Cleve.); Standard (Chgo.); Palm Beach (Fla.) Country. Office: Cole Nat Corp 5915 Landerbrook Dr Cleveland OH 44124

COLE, NANCY C., mortgage banker; b. Buffalo, Dec. 11, 1952; d. Norman R. and Helen L. (Latza) C. BA in Econs. summa cum laude, Ohio State U., 1973; MBA, Xavier U., 1979. Mgr. Huntington Nat. Bank, Columbus, Ohio, 1974-76; mgr. admissions Ohio State U., Columbus, 1976-78; v.p. BancOhio Mortgage Co., Columbus, 1978-83, Goldome Realty Credit Corp., Buffalo, 1983—. Mem. com. allocations Buffalo United Way, 1988. Mem. Mortgage Bankers Assn. Am., Western N.Y. Mortgage Bankers Assn. Office: Goldome Realty Credit Corp 205 Park Club Ln Buffalo NY 14221

COLE, PATRICIA ANN, financial executive, consultant; b. Indpls., Aug. 24, 1953; d. Jessie and Luella (Gadis) C. BS in Bus., Ind. U., 1981; postgrad., Ind. U.-Purdue U., Indpls., 1985-86, 88. Supr. U.S. Postal Svc., Indpls., 1982-83; region computer analyst U.S. Postal Svc., Chgo., 1984; coordinator logistics U.S. Postal Svc., Indpls., 1984, mgmt. trainee, 1984-86; postmaster U.S. Postal Svc., McCordsville, Ind., 1985; mgr. office svc. U.S. Postal Svc., Indpls., 1986, sr. fin. analyst, 1986—; paralegal; salesperson real estate. Author: (poetry collection): Who Am I?, 1978. Active Women in Community Svc., Indpls., Indpls. United Way. Merit scholar Ind. U., 1971. Mem. Am. Bus. Women's Assn., NAFE, Am. Assn. Engrs., Nat. Phoenix Assn. (sec. 1986-88, Edn. award 1987), Indpls. Profl. Assn., Nat. Coun. Negro Women (exec. bd.). Office: US Postal Svc 125 W South St Indianapolis IN 46206-9521

COLE, PAUL LEON, material handling company executive, marketing engineer, consultant; b. Lansing, Mich., June 25, 1946; s. Leslie Arthur and Alice Margaret (LeBoeuf) C.; m. Candace Ann Denhof, June 15, 1968; children. BSE, U. Mich., 1970; MBA, U. Mont., 1975. Registered profl. engr., Mich. Engr., Brunswick Corp., Muskegon, Mich., 1967-70; product planner, crane and hoist ops. Dresser Industries Inc., Muskegon, 1976-78, mgr. product planning, 1978-82; product mgr. Shaw Walker Co., 1983-87, mgr. mktg., planning and devel., 1987-88; v.p. sales and market devel. Pipp Mobile Systems, Grand Rapids, Mich., 1988—; cons. The Cole Group. Capt. USAF, 1970-76. Mem. Nat. Soc. Profl. Engrs., Mich. Soc. Profl. Engrs., Soc. Mfg. Engrs. (sr.). Home: 4283 Carolyn Dr Muskegon MI 49444

COLE, RICHARD HENRY, construction company executive; b. Franklin, N.H., July 4, 1926; s. Harry Michael and Mabel (Mott) C.; m. Lois I Willson, Apr. 1, 1952; children: Susan, Stephen, Nancy, Michael, Kathryn. Grad. summa cum laude, Tilton (N.H.) Sch., 1948; BS in Civil Engring., New Eng. Coll., 1951. Civil engr. Mass. Hwy. Dept., Beverly, 1951-52, Metcalf & Eddy Co., Thule, Greenland, 1952; project engr. N.H. Dept. PUb. Works and Hwys., Concord, 1952-57; pres., treas. E.D. Swett, Inc., Concord, 1957—. Trustee New. Eng. Coll., Henniker, N.H. and Arundel, Sussex, Eng., 1974—, treas., 1977—; active N.H. Good Rds. Assn., 1952—, Gov.'s Com. of N.H., 1974—. Served with USAAF, 1944-46. Mem. Assn. Gen. Contractors Am. (pres. 1974, exec. bd. 1970—, nat. committeeman 1975—, nat. dir., nat. hwy. bridge com.). Home: 17 Surry Coach Ln Bow NH 03301 Office: Ed Swett Inc Box 586 Concord NH 03301

COLE, ROBERT BATES, lawyer; b. Scarborough, Eng., Feb. 9, 1911; s. William and Mary Elizabeth (Bates) C.; brought to U.S., 1911, naturalized, 1914; A.B., U. Fla., 1932, J.D., 1935; m. Frances Lee Arnold, June 23, 1937; children—Charles Robert, George Thomas, Richard Phillip. Admitted to Fla. bar, 1935, since practiced in Miami; mem. firm Mershon, Sawyer, Johnston, Dunwody & Cole, Miami, Fla., from 1946, now of counsel; sec., dir. Major Appliances, Inc., Miami, 1953—; sec., dir. Lennar Corp., Miami, 1969—, chmn. exec. com., gen. counsel, 1984— . Pres. 200 Club Greater Miami, 1986. chmn. bd. trustees Bapt. Hosp. Miami, Inc., 1985—. Mem. Nat. Assn. Coll. and Univ. Attys., Am., Dade County bar assns., Fla. Bar, Phi Kappa Phi, Sigma Chi. Baptist. Clubs: Miami; Riviera Country (past pres.) (Coral Gables, Fla.). Home: 2301 Alhambra Circle Coral Gables FL 33134 Office: Lennar Corp 700 NW 107th Ave Miami FL 33172

COLE, ROBERT LEROY, broadcast advertising specialist, musician; b. St. Louis, Dec. 7, 1958; s. LeRoy and Barbara Louise (Keller) C.; m. Rose Marie Waller, Apr. 15, 1978; 1 child, Justin LeRoy. Grad. high sch., Jefferson City, Mo. Mgr. Music Works, Columbia, Mo., 1984—. Producer (radio advertising) Return of Widdley, 1987 (award 1987), Video Bop (award 1987); writer, producer Larry Klein New Location Round-Up, 1987. Mem. Communicators of Mid-Am. (award 1987). Office: Music Works 165 E Hoedown Columbia MO 65203

COLE, THOMAS COURTNEY, retail executive; b. Mt. Vernon, Ohio, Feb. 25, 1957; s. Charles Morton Cole and Shirley Ann (Goudy) H.; m. Deborah Ann Cole, June 22, 1979; children: Courtney Ann, Phillip Thomas. Student, U. Miami, 1975-79. Mgr. sales United Liquors, Memphis, 1979-81; mgr. wine sales Fla. Beverage Corp., Jacksonville, 1981-84; gen. mgr. Duval Spirits, Jacksonville, 1984—. Mem. Chaine des Rotisseurs, Somelier Guild, Wine and Spirits Wholesale Assn. Republican. Episcopalian.

COLE, TODD G., retired financial company executive, consultant; b. Coushatta, La., Mar. 5, 1921; s. Ira and Lucie (Triche); m. Inez Hamilton, Feb. 9, 1953 (div. 1974); children: Michael H., Diane Cole Janusz; m. Josephine Giovanetti, Oct. 1974 (dec. 1985); children: Paola Smith, Leda Sanford; m. Pamela Wilds, Mar., 1987. Student, La. State U., 1935-37; LL.B., Woodrow Wilson Coll., 1947. C.P.A. With Delta Airlines, 1940-63, dir., exec. v.p. adminstrn., 1959-63; sr. v.p. finance and adminstrn., dir. Eastern Airlines, 1963-67, vice chmn., chmn. finance com., dir., 1967-69; v.p., asst. to pres. C.I.T. Financial Corp., N.Y.C., 1969; v.p. fin. C.I.T. Financial Corp., 1969-71, mem. exec. com., 1970—, exec. v.p., 1971-73, pres., chief adminstrv. officer, 1973-80, pres., chief operating officer, 1980-83, pres., chief exec. officer, 1984-86; dir. Emery Air Freight, Carlisle Retailers, Inc., Frontier Air Lines, Primerica Corp., Nacre Corp.; trustee DR Equity Fund. Mem. Ga. Bar Assn. Address: 636 Steamboat Rd Greenwich CT 06830

COLE, WILLIAM FRANCIS, real estate executive; b. Cheverly, Md., Feb. 15, 1955; s. Hal Edwin and Patricia Ann (Horne) C.; m. Monica Annette Johnson, Nov. 24, 1979; children: Heather Annette, Blake William. BSBA, U. Richmond, 1977. Commd. 2d lt. U.S. Army, 1977, advanced through ranks to capt., 1981, resigned, 1985; investment broker A.G. Edwards & Sons, Inc., Dothan, Ala., 1985-88; owner Stoutamire-Proctor, Inc., Enterprise, Ala., 1988—. Sect. chmn. United Way, Dothan, 1985, employee chmn. 1986, campaign chmn. 1988—; employee chmn. Boy Scouts Am., 1986; youth choir asst. 1st Bapt. Ch., Enterprise, Ala. Mem. Internat. Assn. Fin. Planners, Assn. U.S. Army, Ducks Unltd., Army Aviation Assn. Am. Republican. Baptist. Lodge: Lions. Home: 813 S Ouida St Enterprise AL 36330 Office: Stoutamire-Proctor Inc Realtors PO Box 1616 Enterprise AL 36330

COLEMAN, ALAN BROUSE, financial management educator; b. San Francisco, Jan. 11, 1929; s. Alan Brouse and Hazel Virginia (Deane) C.; m. Janet M. Saville, July 4, 1953; children—Kathleen, Frances Jennifer. BA, U. San Francisco, 1952; MBA, Stanford U., 1956, PhD, 1960. Mem. faculty Grad. Sch. Bus. Harvard U., 1958-62, Stanford U., 1962-70; dean ESAN, Lima, Peru, 1963-66; v.p., treas. U.S. Natural Resources, Inc., 1970-71; pres., chief exec. officer Yosemite Park and Curry Co., Calif., 1971-73; pres., chief adminstrv. officer Sun Valley Co., Idaho, 1973-74; Caruth Prof. fin. mgmt. So. Meth. U., Dallas, 1974-81, pres., chief exec. officer S.W. Sch. Banking Found., 1980—, dean Edwin L. Cox Sch. Bus., 1975-81, pres. Southwestern Grad. Sch. of Banking Found., 1980—; cons. Treas., trustee Family Svc. Assn. Mis-Peninsula; mem. adv. bd. East Palo Alto br. Bank Am.; bd. dirs. Stanford Credit Union; mem. adv. bd. Amigos de las Americas, Houston; treas. Dallas United Nations Assn.; active Salvation Army, Dallas; mem. adv. coun. Dallas Community Chest Trust Fund; adv. dir. Army and Air Force Exch. Svc. World Hdqrs., Dallas. 1st lt. U.S. Army, 1952-54. Recipient Palmas Magisteriales, Orden de Commendador (Peru); Ford Found. fellow, 1956-57; Am. Numis. Soc. fellow, 1980—. Mem. Fin. Mgmt. Assn., Fin. Execs. Inst., Am. Fin. Assn., Beta Gamma Sigma. Author: (with Hempel and Simonson) Bank Management: Text and Cases, 1983, (with Robichek) Management of Financial Institutions, 1967, 77, (with Vandell) Case Problems in Finance, 1962, (with Marks) Cases in Commerical Bank Management, 1962. Office: 6211 W Northwest Hwy #2906 Dallas TX 75225 Office: 6211 W NW Hwy Dallas TX 75225

COLEMAN, BRYAN DOUGLAS, lawyer, corporate executive, educator; b. Texarkana, Tex., Aug. 16, 1948; s. William Bryan and Armeda (Crawford) C.; m. Tommye Lou Bettis, Jan. 31, 1984; children: Douglas Patrick, Sarah Elizabeth. AS, Texarkana Coll., 1968; BS in Bus. Adminstrn., Stephen F. Austin U., 1970; postgrad. Rice U., 1971-73; JD (E.E. Townes award, Am. Jurisprudence award), South Tex. Coll. Law, 1973; grad. JAG Sch., U.S. Army, 1978. Bar: Tex. 1973, U.S. Dist. Ct. (so. dist.) Tex. 1974, U.S. Tax Ct., 1987, U.S. Ct. Appeals (11th cir.) 1982, U.S. Ct. Appeals (5th cir.) 1975; cert. Fellow Life Mgmt. Inst. Quality control insp. Lone Star Ammunition Plant, Texarkana, 1966-68; law clk. Fulbright & Jaworski, Houston, 1970-71, Boswell, O'Toole, Davis & Pickering, Houston, 1971-72, Helm, Pletcher & Hogan, Houston, 1972-73; assoc. Law Office Gus Zgourides, Houston, 1973-76, Ray & Coleman, P.C., Houston, 1976—; dir. Med. Assurance Group, Houston, 1978—; counsel Gt. SW Life Ins. Co., Houston, 1983—, First Columbia Life Ins. Co., Dallas, 1987—; instr. U. Houston, 1979-81. Mem. Republican Nat. Com., 1983—. Served to comdr. Army ROTC, 1972-73, to 1st lt. U.S. Army, 1973-79. Mem. ABA, State Bar Tex. (founder law student div. 1973, chmn. grievance com. 1979-81), Am. Judicature Soc., Houston Bar Found., Houston Bar Assn., Alpha Kappa Psi (sec. 1969-70), Alpha Phi Omega (pledge trainer 1970) Delta Theta Phi. Home: 3510 Saratoga Ln Houston TX 77088 Office: Ray & Coleman PC 1314 Tex Ave 500 Great SW Bldg Houston TX 77002

COLEMAN, CATHERINE AMELIA, customer technical support professional; b. Augusta, Ga., Mar. 12, 1963; d. Thomas Gerald and Carole (Garrett) C. Student, Livingston U., 1981-84, U. South Ala., 1987—. Fin. advisor Citicorp Retail Services, Mobile, Ala., 1985-86; mktg. specialist QMS Inc., Mobile, 1986-88, Beta/ISV specialist, 1988—. Home: 701 University Blvd #186S Mobile AL 36609 Office: QMS Inc One Magnum Pass Mobile AL 36618

COLEMAN, CLARENCE WILLIAM, banker; b. Wichita, Kans., Mar. 24, 1909; s. William Coffin and Fanny Lucinda (Sheldon) C.; m. Emry Regester Ingham, Oct. 2, 1935; children—Rochelle, Pamela, Kathryn Sheldon. Student, U. Kans., 1928-32; DHL, Friends U.; D. Laws, Ottawa U. bd. dirs. Union Blvd. Nat. Bank, 1987—. With Coleman Co., Inc., Wichita, 1932—; v.p. charge mfg. Coleman Co., Inc., 1944, dir., 1935—, asst. gen. mgr., 1951-54; pres. Union Nat. Bank, Wichita, 1957-72; vice chmn. bd. Union Nat. Bank, 1972—; chmn. bd. dir. Cherry Creek Inn, Inc., Denver, 1961-69, Kans. Devel. Credit Corp.; bd. dirs. Union Blvd. Nat. Bank. Bd. dirs. Inst. Logopedics, 1940-74, chmn. bd., 1947-48; bd. dirs. Wichita Symphony Soc.; trustee Wichita Symphony Soc. Found.; bd. dirs. Found. for Study of Cycles, Irvine, Calif., chmn., 1988; bd. dirs. Wichita Mental Health Assn., 1956-74, United Fund Wichita and Sedgewick County, 1957-74, Friends U., 1956-74; bd. dirs. Wichita Crime Commn., 1953-74, pres., 1958; mem. Nat. Budget Com., 1952; chmn. State Mental Health Fund Kans., 1953; Trustee Peddie Sch., Hightstown, N.J., chmn. bd. trustees, 1972-76, chmn. emeritus, 1981. Mem. Mid-Ark. Valley Devel. Assn. (treas.), Wichita C. of C. (pres. 1956, dir. 1947-74), Rotary, Phi Kappa Psi. Office: Union Nat Bank 1005 Union Ctr Wichita KS 67202 also: Coleman Co Inc 250 N St Francis Ave Wichita KS 67202

COLEMAN, DARRELL GLENN, forecast analyst; b. Clarksville, Tenn., May 17, 1953; s. Lathie Lee and Mattie Erlene (Harvey) C.; m. Delores Ruth Pendley, July 4, 1975; children: Eric Brent, Kristen Elaine. BS, Austin Peay State U., 1975. Territory mgr. Burroughs Corp., Chattanooga, Tenn., 1975-77; field underwriter N.Y. Life Ins. Co., Chattanooga, 1977-79; mgr. Acme Boot Co., Clarksville, 1979-86; master scheduler, forecast analyst Hartmann Luggage Co., Lebanon, Tenn., 1986—. Mem. Am. Prodn. and Inventory Control Soc. Baptist. Office: Hartmann Luggage Co Hartmann Dr Lebanon TN 37087

COLEMAN, DEBORAH ANN, computer company executive; b. Providence, Jan. 22, 1953; d. John Austin and Joan Mary Coleman. BA, Brown U., 1974; MBA, Stanford U., 1978; PhD in Engring. (hon.), Worcester (Mass.) Poly., 1987. Prodn. supr. metals and controls Tex. Instruments, Attleboro, Mass., 1974; fin. mgmt. tng. program Gen. Electric, Providence, 1974-76; gen. acctg. supr., fin. system analyst components group Hewlett-Packard, Cupertino, Calif., 1978-79, cost acctg. supr. instrument group, 1980, fin. mgr. tech. computer group, 1981; controller Macintosh project Apple Computer, Cupertino, 1981-82, div. controller Macintosh project, 1982-83, sr. fin. controller Apple 32 product group, 1983-84, ops. mgr. Macintosh div., 1984, dir. ops. Macintosh div., 1985, v.p. ops., 1986-87, chief fin. officer, v.p. fin., 1987—; dir. worldwide mfg. Apple Computer, Fremont, Calif., 1985, v.p. worldwide mfg., 1985-86; v.p. ops. Apple Computer, Fremont, 1986-87, chief fin. officer, v.p. fin., 1987—; bd. dirs. Claris Software, Mountain View, Calif. Advisor Harvard U. Bus. Sch.; bd. dirs. Resource Ctr. for Women, Palo Alto, Calif., 1986—. Mem. Stanford Inst. Mfg. and Automation (indsl. advisor 1985-87), Com. 200, APICS. Democrat. Roman Catholic. Office: Apple Computer Inc 20525 Mariana Ave Cupertino CA 95014

COLEMAN, DENIS PATRICK, JR., investment banker; b. N.Y.C., Jan. 6, 1946; s. Denis Patrick and Muriel (Clark) C.; m. Annabelle Giellerup, Sept. 15, 1972; children: Denis P. III, Nicholas A., Timothy W., Matthew T. BSBA, Georgetown U., 1967. Exec. v.p. Bear Stearns Cos. Inc., N.Y.C., 1967—. Bd. dirs. Covenant House, N.Y.C., Canterbury Sch., New Milford, Conn. Mem. Mcpl. Bond Club N.Y., Bond Club N.Y. Roman Catholic. Home: PO Box 1328 Southampton NY 11969 Office: Bear Stearns Cos Inc 247 Park Ave New York NY 10067

COLEMAN, GEORGE WILLARD, financial consultant; b. June 11, 1912; married. B.A., U. Ariz., 1934; M.A., Washington U., St. Louis, 1935, Ph.D., 1939. Asst. in econs. Washington U., St. Louis, 1935-39; lectr. econs. Grad. Sch., 1955-59; economist Merc. Trust Co., St. Louis, 1939-66; econ. adviser Am. Bankers Assn., 1966-67, dep. dir., 1967-74; cons. bd. govs. Fed. Res. System, 1974-76; adviser IMF, 1975-80; internat. fin. cons. to various cos. and banks, 1980—. Mem. long-term planning com. Greater St. Louis council Girl Scouts U.S.A., 1962-66. Contbr. articles to publs. in fields of econs. and banking. Mem. Artus, Phi Beta Kappa, Pi Sigma Alpha. Home: 607 Sunset Towers 11 Sunset Dr Sarasota FL 34236

COLEMAN, GERALD CHRISTOPHER, business executive; b. Boston, Sept. 27, 1939; s. Gerald Christopher and Anna Rose (Dubanevich) C.; m. Kathleen Louise Dolan, June 3, 1967; children—Lisa, Emily, Craig, Mary. AB, Boston Coll., 1964; MBA, Dartmouth Coll., 1966. Asst. nat. retail sales mgr. photog. products Sears Roebuck & Co., Chgo., 1966-68, asst. nat. buyer calculators, 1968-69, staff asst. to v.p., 1969-70, nat. buyer, product mgr. bedding products, 1970-72, nat. retail sales mgr. toy products, 1972-73, nat. retail mktg. mgr. furniture products, 1973-74; v.p. Wilson, Haight & Welch, Inc., Boston, 1974-77; sr. v.p. N.W. Ayer, Inc., Chgo., 1977-83, N.Y.C., 1983-87; corp. v.p. New Eng. Devel. & Mgmt., Inc., Newton, 1987—; dir. Allied Fin. Instns. Inc., Boston. Rep.-at-large Kenilworth Citizens Adv. Com., Ill., 1982. Mem. Am. Mktg. Assn. (officer, chpt. bd. dirs. 1983-84). Roman Catholic. Clubs: Economic of Chgo.; Dartmouth, N.Y. Athletic (N.Y.C.); Middlesex (Darien, Conn.). Home: 9 Sherry Ln Darien CT 06820 Office: New Eng Devel & Mgmt Inc 1 Wells Ave Newton MA 02159

COLEMAN, JAMES JULIAN, JR., real estate executive, lawyer; b. New Orleans, May 7, 1941; s. James Julian Sr. and Dorothy Louise (Jurisich) C.; m. Carol Campbell Owen, Dec. 19, 1970 (dec. Sept. 1979); 1 child, James Owen; m. Mary Olivia Cochrane Cushing, Oct. 12, 1985. BA, Princeton U., 1963; postgrad. in law, Oxford (Eng.) U., 1963-65; JD, Tulane U., 1968. Bar: La. 1969, U.S. Supreme Ct. 1969. Chmn. Internat.-Matex Tank Terminals, New Orleans, 1969—; pres. Coleman Devel. Co., New Orleans, 1969—; ptnr. Coleman, Dutrey & Thomson, New Orleans, 1972—; chmn. DownTown Parking Service, New Orleans, 1978—; pres. City Ctr. Properties, New Orleans, 1980—; Trustee Loving Found., New Orleans, R.L. Blaffer Found., Houston. Author: Gilbert Antoine de St. Maxent: The Spanish Frenchman of New Orleans, 1975. Mem. Princeton U. History Council, 1982—. Named H.M. Hon. Brit. Consul for La., Brit. Consulate, New Orleans, 1975—, to Order of Brit. Empire, Queen Elizabeth II, London, 1986. Mem. ABA, La. State Bar Assn. Republican. Mem. Ch. of Christ Scientists. Clubs: N.Y. Yacht, Union League (N.Y.). Office: Coleman Devel Co 321 St Charles Ave 10th Fl New Orleans LA 70130

COLEMAN, JOHN JOSEPH, telephone company executive; b. Boston, Aug. 2, 1937; s. Martin Joseph and Anna Veronica (Leonard) C.; B.S. cum laude in Bus. Adminstrn., Boston Coll., 1964; postgrad. Harvard U. Bus. Sch., 1970; m. Carol Ann Holmes, May 6, 1961; children—Mark Christopher, Cara Romaine. With New Eng. Telephone Co., 1955—, various supervisory positions in plant and acctg. depts., Mass., R.I., now v.p., Boston; dir. Merchants Nat. Bank, Manchester. Bd. dirs. United Way of Greater Manchester, chmn., 1980; chmn. Gov.'s Mgmt. Rev., 1981; chmn. fundraising campaign, Manchester Crimeline, Inc., 1982; bd. dirs. Boston Mcpl. Research Bur., 1984-86, Mass. Taxpayers Found. Inc., 1984-86; mem. New Spirit in Boston Com., 1984-85. Served with USN, 1956-58. Mem. Bus. and Industry Assn. of N.H. (dir.), N.H. Safety Council (adv. bd.), Am. Automobile Assn. Mass. (mem. adv. bd.), Greater Boston C. of C. (chmn. pub. safety com. 1985-86). Office: 101 Huntington Ave Ste 2100 Boston MA 02199

COLEMAN, KENNETH WILLIAM, publishing company executive; b. Phila., Apr. 22, 1930; s. George Craig Coleman and Catherine Estelle (Irwin) Cohen; m. Seraphine Elizabeth Rinaudo, Aug.9, 1952; 1 child, Catherine Coleman Chambers Little. BA in History, Calif. State U., Los Angeles, 1957; MS in Ednl. Psychology, Calif. State U., Long Beach, 1975. Cert. tchr., Calif. Tchr. Los Angeles city schs., 1957-75; chief exec. officer Seraphim Press, Carlsbad, Calif., 1978—. Author and pub.: The Misdirection Conspiracy, 1982, 2d rev. ed. 1983, U.S. Financial Institutions in Crisis, 1982, 4th rev. ed. 1986, America's Endangered Banks, 1984, 2d rev. ed. 1986, Reality Theory, 1982—, The Fed Tracker, 1984—, dir. Am. Monetary Found., 1987—, fin. editor Mobilehome News, Santa Ana, Calif., 1983-84; regular contbr. Am. Assn. Fin. Profls. mag., Orange County Bus. Jour., Smart Money Investor mag. Bus. and fin. adv. com., Chet Wray for Calif. Assembly, Cerritos, Calif., 1978-84; consumer affairs com., Richard Robinson for Calif. Assemby, Garden Grove, Calif., 1986—; pres. Chansall Mut. Water Co., Bell, Calif. 1961-65. Served with U.S. Army, 1945-47. Lodge: Elks. Home and Office: 4805 Courageous Ln Carlsbad CA 92008

COLEMAN, LESTER EARL, chemical company executive; b. Akron, Ohio, Nov. 6, 1930; s. Lester Earl and Ethel Angeline (Miller) C.; m. Kathleen A. Liptak, Sept. 9, 1988; children by previous marriage: Robert Scott, Kenneth John. B.S., U. Akron, 1952; M.S., U. Ill., 1953, Ph.D., 1955. With Goodyear Tire & Rubber Co., Akron, 1951-52; with Lubrizol Corp., Cleve., 1955—; asst. to pres. Lubrizol Corp., 1972, v.p. internat. ops., 1973, exec. v.p., 1974-76, pres., 1976-83, chief exec. officer, 1978—, chmn. bd., 1983—, also dir.; bd. dirs. Norfolk (Va.) So. Corp., Harris Corp., Melbourne, Fla. S.C. Johnson & Son, Inc., Racine, Wis., Gencorp, Akron, Ohio. Contbr. articles to profl. jours.; patentee in field. Mem. nat. exec. bd. Boy Scouts Am.; chmn. bd. trustees The Lubrizol Found. Capt. USAF, 1955-57. Mem. Am. Chem. Soc. (local chmn. 1973), Chem. Mfrs. Assn. (bd. dirs.), Sigma Xi, Alpha Chi Sigma, Phi Lambda Upsilon, Phi Delta Theta. Methodist. Office: Lubrizol Corp 29400 Lakeland Blvd Wickliffe OH 44092

COLEMAN, LEWIS WALDO, bank executive; b. San Francisco, Jan. 2, 1942; s. Lewis V. and Virginia Coleman; m. Susan G.; children: Michelle, Gregory, Nancy, Peter. B.A., Stanford U., 1965. With Bank Calif., San Francisco, 1963-73; with Wells Fargo Bank, San Francisco, 1973-86, exec. v.p., chmn. credit policy com., until 1986; vice chmn. Bank Am., San Francisco, 1986—.

COLEMAN, LINDA R., financial executive. BA, U. Md., 1970; MBA, Seton Hall U. Various positions Johnson & Johnson, 1972-77; sr. product mgr. toiletry products div. Richardson-Vick, 1978-79; sr. products mgr. Chesebrough-Ponds Inc., 1980-82, mgr. mktg., 1982-84; v.p. product planning and mktg. N.Y. Stock Exch., N.Y.C., 1984-86, v.p. corp. mktg., 1986-87, v.p. strategic planning, mktg. and bus. devel., 1987-88; exec. v.p. planning and devel. Boston Stock Exch., 1988-89. Home: 71 Aiken St #Q-14 Norwalk CT 06851

COLEMAN, MARION LESLIE, insurance company executive; b. Mobile, Ala., Mar. 20, 1925; s. Luther Woodward and Carrie (Lockler) C.; student pub. schs.; m. Joyce Kelley, Aug. 29, 1944; children—Connie, Woodward L. and Franklin M. (twins). Agt., Life Ins. Co. Ga., Mobile, 1946-55, dist. mgr., El Dorado, Ark., 1955-56, Hattiesburg, Miss., 1957-60, Meridian, Miss., 1960-64; v.p., agy. dir. Nat. Preferred Life Ins. Co., Atlanta, 1964-65; v.p. tng. Found. Life Ins. Co., Atlanta, 1965—; v.p. Kelley-Blakely Land Corp., Mobile; pres. Yamaha Sports World, Meridian, Melco Ltd. Custom Tailors, Meridian, Meridian Motors, Buddy Coleman Enterprises, Meridian, Triple C Corp.; div. mgr. Jefferson Standard Life Ins. Co., Meridian; v.p. Merchandizers Inc. (Gibson Discount Center), Meridian; dir. Gulf Cascade Investment Properties, Inc., Long Beach, Miss. Served with USNR, 1943-46. Mem. Life Underwriters Assn., Sales and Mktg. Execs. Club. Home and Office: 2100 23d Ave Meridian MS 39301

COLEMAN, MARY LEE RONNOW, real estate development executive; b. Las Vegas, Nev., Mar. 12, 1937; d. Charles Leland and Mary Almeda (West) Ronnow; m. Gary Edwin Coleman, Apr. 23, 1960; children: Christopher, Michael, Daryle. BS, U. So. Calif., 1959; MBA, Nat. U., 1982. Pres. Coleman Enterprises, San Diego; bd. dirs. Nev. Power Co., Las Vegas. Treas. Children's Hosp. Aux., San Diego, 1982-84; mem. San Diego Zool. Soc., San Diego Art Assn., San Diego Hist. Soc. Mem. Nat. Assn. Corp. Dirs. (sec. 1985-87), Assn. Women Utility Dirs., La Jolla C. of C., San Diego Venture Club, Trojan League (v.p.). Home: 6216 Camino de la Costa La Jolla CA 92037 Office: Coleman Enterprises 7385 Mission Hills Dr Las Vegas NV 89113

COLEMAN, MARY LOUISE, medical laboratory administrator; b. Harrison, Miss., Dec. 1; d. Clyde and Mattie (Smith) Cadney; m. Clarence Ray Coleman, Feb. 12, 1972; 1 child, Shani Rashida. Student So. U., Baton Rouge, 1966-70; diploma in cytotech. Mount Sinai Hosp., Chgo., 1971. Registered Cytotechnologist. Cytotechnologist Pathology lab. Meml. Hosp., Gulfport, Miss., 1971-74, Meth. Hosp., Memphis, 1974-76, Mercy Hosp., Vicksburg, Miss., 1977-79; founder, lab. supr. So. Lab., Fayette, Miss., 1980—; asst. adminstr. Medgar Evers Home Health, Fayette, 1983-85. Trustee Copiah-Jefferson Regional Library, Fayette and Hazlehurst, 1985; campaign mgr. Sammy White for chancery clk. Jefferson County, 1983. Mem. So. Assn. Cytotechnologists, Miss. Soc. Cytopathologists, Am. Soc. Clin. Pathologists, Am. Entrepreneurs Assn., Am. Mgmt. Assn. Democrat. Roman Catholic. Avocations: tennis; dancing; traveling; sewing. Office: So Lab Inc 414 Rodney Rd Fayette MS 39069

COLEMAN, NORMAN ARTHUR, insurance company executive; b. New Philadelphia, Ohio, Mar. 4, 1923; s. Harrison Arthur and Margaret Ersman (Campbell) C.; B.S., Northwestern U., 1947; postgrad. U. Ky., 1947-48; m. Yvonne Lou Cotterman, Apr. 7, 1956; 1 son, Matt Arthur. Salesman, Youngen Ins. Agy., New Philadelphia, 1949-59; pres. CBS Ins., Colorado Springs, Colo., 1959—; dir. Air Acad. Nat. Bank. Trustee U.S. Naval Acad. Found. Served to rear adm. USNR. Mem. Soc. Chartered Property Casualty Underwriters, Ret. Officers Assn. Clubs: Broadmoor Golf, Garden of the Gods. Home: 142 Miramar Dr Colorado Springs CO 80906 Office: PO Box 1900 Colorado Springs CO 80901

COLEMAN, PAUL JEROME, JR., physicist, educator; b. Evanston, Ill., Mar. 7, 1932; s. Paul Jerome and Eunice Cecile (Weissenberg) C.; m. Doris Ann Fields, Oct. 3, 1964; children: Derrick, Craig. BS in Engring. Math., U. Mich., 1954, BS in Engring. Physics, 1954, MS in Physics, 1958; PhD in Space Physics, UCLA, 1966. Research scientist Ramo-Wooldridge Corp. (now TRW Systems), El Segundo, Calif., 1958-61; instr. math. U. So. Calif., L.A., 1958-61; mgr. interplanetary scis. program NASA, Washington, 1961-62; research sci. Inst. Geophysics and Planetary Physics UCLA, 1962-66, prof. geophysics, space physics Inst. Geophysics and Planetary Physics, 1966—; pres. Univs. Space Rsch. Assn., Columbia, Md., 1987—; bd. dirs. Lasertechnics Inc., Albuquerque, Applied Electron Corp., Santa Clara, Univ. Tech. Transfer, Inc., L.A., others; mem. adv. bd. The Space Found., Houston, 1986—, West Coast U., L.A., 1986—; trustee Univs. Space Research Assn, Columbia, Md., 1981—; vis. scholar U. Paris, 1975-76; vis. scientist Lab. for Aeronomy Ctr. Nat. Research Sci., Verrieres le Buisson, France, 1975-76; asst. lab. dir., mgr. Earth and space scis. div., chmn. Inst. Geophysics and Planetary Physics Los Alamos (N.Mex.) Nat. Lab., 1981-86; com. mem. numerous scientific and ednl. orgns., cons. numerous fin. and indsl. cos. Co-editor (books) Solar Wind, 1972, Pioneering the Space Frontier, 1986; mem. editorial bd. Geophysics and Astrophysics Monographs, 1970—; assoc. editor Cosmic Electrodynamics, 1968-72; contbr. reviews to numerous profl. jours. Appointed Nat. Commn. on Space, Pres. U.S., 1985; mem. Fraternity of Friends of the Los Angeles Music Ctr., 1987—, Los Angeles County Mus. Nat. History, 1980—, Los Angeles County Mus. Art, 1968; bd. dirs. St. Matthew's Sch., Pacific Palisades, Calif., 1979-82, v.p. 1981-82. 1st lt. USAF, 1954-56, Korea. Recipient Exceptional Sci. Achievement Medal NASA, 1970, 1972, spl. recognition for contributions to the Apollo Program, 1979; Guggenheim fellow 1975-76, Fulbright scholar, 1975-76, Research grantee NASA, NSF, Office Naval Research, Calif. Space Inst., Air Force Office Sci. Research, U.S. Office Geol. Survey. Mem. AAAS, AIAA, Am. Geophys. Union, Am. Phys. Soc., Soc. Exploration Geophysicists, Internat. Acad. Astronautics, Bel Air Bay Club (L.A.) Birnam Wood golf Club (Santa Barbara, Calif.), Cosmos Club (Washington), Explorers Club (N.Y.C.), Tau Beta Pi, Phi Eta Sigma. Home: 1323 Monaco Dr Pacific Palisades CA 90272 Office: UCLA Inst Geophysics and Planetary Physics 405 Hilgard Ave Los Angeles CA 90024-1567

COLEMAN, ROBERT FEASTER, III, education administrator; b. Whiteville, N.C., Oct. 25, 1945; s. Robert Feaster Jr. and Leanna (Koonce) C. A.B., U. N.C., 1968, MAT, 1971. Cert. tchr., N.C. Tchr. Charles L. Coon Jr. High Sch., Wilson, N.C., 1968-69, John T. Hoggard High Sch., Wilmington, N.C., 1969-72; tchr., adminstr. Cape Fear Acad., Wilmington, 1972-78, headmster, 1978-87; bus. mgr. Forsyth Country Day Sch., Lewisville, N.C., 1987—. Active Cape Fear United Way, 1979-85; pres. S.E. Ind. Conf., 1980-86; treas. Olde Vineyard Homeowners Assn., 1988—; bd. dirs. Lower Cape Fear Hist. Soc., 1982-86. Mem. N.C. Assn. Ind. Schs. (bd. dirs. 1980-87, asst. treas. 1988—), Phi Delta Kappa (treas. Cape Fear chpt. 1981-86, pres. 1986-87). Democrat. Methodist. Home: 239 Olde Vineyard Ct Winston-Salem NC 27104 Office: Forsyth Country Day Sch 5501 Shallowford Rd Winston-Salem NC 27023

COLEMAN, ROGER W., institutional food distribution company executive; b. Newark, Mar. 30, 1929; s. Bernard Simpson and Evelyn (Bornstein) C.; m. Ruth Rykoff (div. Apr. 1982); children—William, Wendy, Paul, Eric; m. Francesca Marie Wessilius, Sept. 1983. B.S., UCLA, 1950. Gen. mgmt. positions Rogay Food Supply div. S. E. Rykoff & Co., Los Angeles, 1951-58; purchasing and gen. mgmt. positions S.E. Rykoff & Co., Los Angeles, 1958-63, gen. mgr., 1963-67, pres., chief exec. officer, 1967-86; pres., chief exec. officer John Sexton Inc., 1983-86, Rykoff-Sexton, Inc., 1986—. Bd. dirs. Los Angeles Conv. Ctr., Reiss-Dis Child Study Ctr., Los Angeles, ARC (Los Angeles chpt.). Mem. Nat. Inst. Food Service (bd. dirs.), L.A. C. of C. (bd. of dirs.). Clubs: Los Angeles Athletic, Hillcrest Country, Regency, Met., Carlton, World Trade and Stock Exchange, Pebble Beach, Beach and Tennis of Pebble Beach, La Costa Country. Home: 515 Homewood Rd Los Angeles CA 90049 Office: Rykoff-Sexton Inc 761 Terminal St Los Angeles CA 90021

COLEMAN, SHARETTA LITTLE, accountant; b. Pikeville, Ky., Nov. 25, 1949; s. Cecil Warren and Villa (Tackett) L.; m. Dwight E. Coleman, May 25, 1968; children: Jill, Melinda. BBA, Ea. Ky. U., 1973. CPA, Ky. Acct. Linton & Co., Pikeville, Ky., 1974-79; v.p., auditor Pikeville Nat. Bank & Trust, 1979-85, v.p. acctg., 1985—. Mem. Am. Inst. CPA's, Ky. Soc. CPA's. Republican. Baptist. Home: HC 83 Box 20 Virgie KY 41572 Office: Pikeville Nat Bank & Trust 208 N Mayo Trail Pikeville KY 41501

COLEMAN, SHELDON C., JR., outdoor equipment company executive; b. 1953; married. BS, U. Kans., 1975; MBA, Calif. State U., 1978; postgrad., Harvard U., 1984. Prodn. mgr. O'Brien Internat., 1981; with Coleman Co. Inc., Wichita, Kans., 1981—, asst. to pres., 1983-84, gen. mgr., then v.p., 1984-87, pres., chief operating officer, now pres., chief exec. officer, 1987—, also bd. dirs. Office: Coleman Co Inc PO Box 1762 Wichita KS 67201 *

COLEMAN, WALTER NORMAN, consumer products company executive; b. Paterson, N.J., May 26, 1946; s. Walter Robert Coleman and Madeline (Maynard) Heines; m. Patricia Ann Alnor, Sept. 2, 1967; children: Colleen Ann, Todd. BS cum laude, Seton Hall U., 1969, MBA, 1974. CPA, N.J. Audit mgr. Peat Marwick Co., N.Y.C., 1969-79; mgr. exec. office Short Hills, N.J., 1975-77; dir. internal audit Ingersoll-Rand, Woodcliff Lake, N.J., 1979-83; staff v.p. for audit RCA N.Y.C., 1983-86; v.p., gen. auditor Nabisco Brands, Inc., East Hanover, N.J., 1986-87, RJR Nabisco, Inc., Atlanta, 1987—. Pres., bd. dirs. Hawthorne (N.J.) Jaycees, 1974-75; mem. bus. adv. bd. Rider Coll., Lawrenceville, N.J., 1985-87. With USMC, 1965-66. Named hon. alumni Seton Hall U., 1987. Mem. Am. Inst. CPAs, N.J. Soc. CPAs, Inst. Internal Auditors (trustee rsch. found.). Office: RJR Nabisco Inc 300 Galleria Pkwy Atlanta GA 30339

COLEY, HARVEY TURNER, JR., communications executive; b. Rocky Mount, N.C., Oct. 3, 1942; s. Harvey Turner Sr. and Jean (Ledbetter) C.; m. Gayle Morris, Apr. 6, 1969; children: Christa Michelle, Camden Turner. Degree in Bus., U. N.C., 1961-65. Asst. cashier Northwestern Bank, Winston-Salem, N.C., 1965-66; writer sales promotion Integon Corp., Winston-Salem, 1966-75, mgr. communications, 1975-77, asst. v.p. communications, 1977-79, v.p. communications, 1979, v.p. corp. communications, 1986—; mem. com. pub. relations Am. Council Life Ins., Washington, 1985—; mng. trustee Integon Found., Winston-Salem, 1987—. Chmn. Contact USA, Harrisburg, Pa., 1983-86; sr. warden St. Paul's Episcopal Ch., Winston-Salem, 1986-87; mem. com. fin. United Way Forsyth County, Winston-Salem, 1985-86. Mem. So. Roundtable Life Advertisers (chmn. 1979-80). Democrat. Office: Integon Corp PO Box 3199 Winston-Salem NC 27152-0502

COLEY, ROBERT BERNARD, software company executive, management consultant; b. Bethesda, Md., Aug. 10, 1951; s. Robert L. and Anne M. (Antrum) C.; m. Denise Elena Bolden, July 4, 1976; children: Robert Jr., Elena. AB, Harvard U., 1973; JD and MBA, Stanford U., 1977. Mgmt. cons. McKinsey and Co., N.Y.C., 1976, Am. Mgmt. Systems, Foster City, Calif., 1977-79; adminstrv. mgr. ISD ADPAC Corp., San Francisco, 1979-80; pres., chief exec., fin. officer Avalanche Prodns., Inc., Palo Alto, Calif., 1980-83, PRIMS, Inc., Redwood City, Calif., 1984-86, PSMG, Inc., Palo Alto, 1986—; prin. RBC and Assocs., 1974—; bd. dirs., chief exec. officer RBC Acquisitions Corp., 1982—, Palo Alto. Dir. St. Elizabeth Seton Sch. bd., Palo Alto, 1984-87, chmn. fin., 1985-88; bd. dirs., fin. com. Palo Alto YMCA, 1988—; asst. coach Palo Alto Little League, 1986—; coach Little League Basketball, 1986-89, area coord., 1987—; fundraiser YMCA, 1988. Phillip Morris fellow Stanford Grad. Sch. Bus., 1975; recipient Achievement Award for Excellence in Tech. Mgmt. Nat. Tech. Assn., 1987; numerous other acad. awards. Mem. Nat. Assn. Corp. Dirs., Stanford Bus. Sch. Alumni Assn., Nat. Tech. Assn. (Achievement award for Excellence in Tech. Mgmt. 1987), Fundraising Exhibitors Assn. (steering com. 1987-88). Democrat. Baptist. Office: PSMG Inc 2124 Clarke Ave Palo Alto CA 94303

COLI, GUIDO JOHN, chemical company executive; b. Richmond, Va., Sept. 12, 1921; s. Guido and Rena (Pacini) C.; m. Vonda L. Coli; children: Pamela, Patricia, Deborah, Richard. B.S., Va. Poly. Inst., 1941, M.S., 1942, Ph.D., 1949. Registered profl. engr., N.Y., Va. Asst. engr. Va. Health Dept. bur. indsl. hygiene, 1941; assoc. chemist Naval Research Lab., 1942-43; instr. chem. engring. Va. Poly. Inst., 1947-48; chem. engr. Mobil Oil Co., Paulsboro, N.J., 1949-50; with Allied Chem. Corp., N.Y.C., 1950-72, group v.p. corp., 1968-72, dir., 1970-72; pres. Am. Enka Co., Enka, N.C., 1979-82; dir. Akzo Am. Inc., 1979-86, pres., chief exec. officer, 1982-86; chmn., chief exec. officer Armira, Inc., Asheville, N.C., 1986—; dir. NCNB Nat. Bank of N.C. Mem. Gov. Va. Commn. to Establish Urban Univ. in Richmond Area, 1966-67; mem. adv. council Coll. of Engring., Va. Poly. Inst.; bd. dirs. St. Joseph's Hosp., Asheville, N.C.; chmn. St. Joseph's Health Services Corp., Asheville, 1986—. Served to lt. USN, 1943-46. Fellow Am. Inst. Chemists; mem. Am. Chem. Soc. (chmn. Va. 1957), Am. Inst. Chem. Engrs., Sigma Xi, Phi Lambda Upsilon, Tau Beta Pi, Phi Kappa Phi, Alpha Kappa Psi. Clubs: University (N.Y.C.); Country of Asheville. Home: 314 Town Mountain Rd Asheville NC 28804 Office: Armira Inc PO Box 192 Bolivar TN 38008

COLIN, KIM RENEE, financial advisor; b. Hardin, Mont., Oct. 7, 1957; d. Raymond and Doris C. Student, Wash. State U., 1976-77. Cert. fin. planner. Registered rep. Investor's Diversified Services, Honolulu, 1978-79, Portland, Oreg., 1979-80; registered rep. Waddell & Reed, Inc., Portland, 1980-81; fin. advisor, pres. Diversified Fin. Planning, Inc., Beaverton, Oreg., 1981—; registered prin. PFG Securities, Inc., Beaverton, 1987—, Titan Capital Corp., Beaverton, 1981-87; tech. cons. Money Mag., Parent Mag., Working Mother, Oregonian Newspaper, Self Mag., USA Today newspaper; continuing edn. tchr. Portland State U., 1987; with KMS Fin. Svcs., Inc., Beaverton, 1989—, PFG Securities, Inc., Beaverton, 1987-88.. Author, editor Fin. Perspectives, 1987—. Named One of 200 Top Fin. Planners, Money Mag., 1987. Mem. Inst. Cert. Fin. Planners (pres. Oreg. 1988-89, exec. dir. regional coun.), Internat. Assn. Fin. Planning (v.p. pub. relations Portland chpt. 1986-87). Office: Diversified Fin Planning 8196 SW Hall Ste 202 Beaverton OR 97005

COLKER, JAMES, venture capital executive; b. Pitts., Feb. 18, 1928; s. Benjamin and Dorthy (Swartz) C.; m. Janice Seiner, Aug. 17, 1950; children: David, Harold, Ruth, Sarah. BS in Physics, U. Pitts., 1949. Engr. Union Switch and Signal Co., Pitts., 1953-57; chief engr. J.W. Fecker, Pitts., 1957-64; exec. v.p. Goerz Optical Co., Pitts., 1964-68; pres. Goerz-Inland, Pitts., 1968-74; chmn., pres. Contraves Goerz Corp., Pitts., 1974-88; mng. gen. ptnr. CEO Venture Fund, Pitts., 1985—; dir. Dravo Automation Scis., Inc., Pitts., Duquesne Systems, Pitts., Blue Cross Western Pa., Pitts. Contbr. articles to tech. publs. Trustee Penn South West Assn., Pitts., 1983—; bd. dirs. Magee Hosp., Pitts., 1986—, Pa. Econ. Devel. Ptnrship, Harrisburg, 1986—; mem. exec. bd. Allegheny Conf. Community Devel., 1987—. Mem. IEEE, French-Am. C. of C. (bd. dirs.), Pitts. High Tech. Council (pres. 1983—), Pitts. Athletic Assn. Republican. Jewish. Club: Duquesne (Pitts.). Office: CEO Venture Fund 4516 Henry St Pittsburgh PA 15206

COLLAZO, JOSE ANTONIO, computer company executive; b. P.R., Dec. 29, 1943; s. Jose Antonio and Maria Luisa (Marti Tellado) C.; m. Brigitte Collazo Ayers; children: Dan Donley, Randy. BSc, Northrop U., 1965; MBA, Pepperdine U., 1979. Pres. internat. div. Computer Scis. Corp., El Segundo, Calif., 1975-84, pres. infto. network svcs. bus. unit, 1984-87; pres., chmn. chief exec. offier Infonet Svc. Corp., El Segundo, 1987—; bd. dirs. Computer Scis. Can. Ltd., Interpac France, Interpak Sweden. Home: 2928 Via La Selva Palos Verdes CA 90279 Office: Infonet Svcs Corp 2100 E Grand Ave El Segundo CA 90245

COLLEY, TERRY BLAKE, economic redevelopment executive; b. Austin, Tex., Oct. 4, 1957; s. Joseph Benjamin and Eleanor Ann (Kimmons) C.; m. Jennifer Lynn Landes, Aug. 20, 1983. BBA, Southwest Tex. State U., 1983; postgrad., Southwestern Bapt. Theol. Sem., Ft. Worth. Ordained to ministry, 1987. Downtown revitalization mgr. City of San Marcos, Tex., 1984-86; exec. dir. Muskogee (Okla.) Unlimited Inc., 1986-88; Main St. dir. City of Grapevine, Tex., 1988—; lectr. in field. Contbr. articles to profl. jours. Bd. dirs. Muskogee Performing Arts Inc., 1987—; mem. Historic Preservation Commn., Muskogee, 1988—; mem. Juarez (Mex.) Mission team, 1981—. Mem. Greater Muskogee Area C. of C., Nat. Trust for Historic Preservation, Urban Land Inst., Internat. Downtown Assn., Rotary, Exchange Club. Baptist. Home: 617 Reed St Roanoke TX 76262 Office: City of Grapevine PO Box 729 Grapevine TX 76051

COLLIER, BOYD DEAN, finance educator, management consultant; b. Waco, Tex., Jan. 16, 1938; s. Denis Lee and Anne Alice (Berry) C.; m. Barbara Nell Joseph, June 20, 1966; children: Diedra Michelle, Christopher Boyd. BBA, Baylor U., 1963, MS, 1965; PhD, U. Tex., 1970. CPA, Tex. Asst. prof. U. N.C., Greensboro, 1969-72, asst. dean, 1970-72; assoc. prof. U. Houston, 1972-73; chief ops. auditor Glastron Boat Co., Austin, Tex., 1973; prof. bus. econs., dean Ctr. for Bus. Adminstrn. St. Edward's U., Austin, 1974-83; prof. fin., head dept. acctg. and fin. Tarleton State U., Stephenville, Tex., 1983—; co-owner Vranich, Collier Co., CPA's, Austin, 1974-83; v.p. fin. Execucom Systems, Austin, 1979; sr. lectr. U. Tex., Austin, 1980-83; bd. dirs. Acctg. Info. Systems, Houston, 1974-78; advisor Office of Atty. Gen., State of Tex., Austin, 1986, Office of Comptroller, State of Tex., Austin, 1986. Author: Measurement and Environmental Deterioration, 1971; editorial advisor Jour. Accountancy, N.Y.C., 1982—; contbr. articles to profl. jours. Faculty advisor Coll. Reps. of Tex., Stephenville, 1984—. With USN, 1955-59. Fellow Earhart Found., Ann Arbor, Mich., 1963, 68, NSF, Washington, 1966; recipient Sargent Americanism award Innovative Collegiate, 1989. Mem. Nat. Acctg. Assn. (v.p. 1978-83, Outstanding Service award 1983), Am. Acctg. Assn., AICPA, Tex. Soc. CPA's, Southwestern Fin. Assn., U. Tex. at Austin Ex-Students Assn. (life). Republican. Baptist. Avocations: tennis, hiking, collecting coins and walking canes. Home: 930 Charlotte St Stephenville TX 76401 Office: Tarleton State U 1603 W Washington Box T-459 Stephenville TX 76402

COLLIN, ROBERT WILLIAM, planning educator; b. Potsdam, N.Y.; s. Frank Carroll and Marilyn (Griggs) C. JD, Albany Law Sch., 1981; MSW, M Planning, Columbia U., 1983; LLM, U. Mo., 1984. Bar: Mo. 1984. Assoc. dir. Legis. Drafting Bur., Coll. Law Tulane U., New Orleans, 1984-86; prof. Cleve. State U., 1986-87; prof. Sch. Planning U. Va., Charlottesville, 1987—; cons. Planned Parenthood, N.Y.C., 1983, Kansas City (Mo.) Redevel. Authority, 1984, Loyola U. Sch. Law, New Orleans, 1985, Loudoun (Va.) Inst. Contbr. chpt. Creditor's Remedies on Municipal Default, 1987; contbr. articles on homelessness to various publs. Bd. dirs. L'Chaim Goup Home, New Orleans, 1985. Von Horne fellow, 1980, Kinne fellow, 1983, John B. Gage fellow, 1984. Mem. Planners Network, Urban Affairs Assn., ABA, Am. Planning Assn., Urban Land Inst. Office: U Va Sch Planning Charlottesville VA 22903

COLLINGS, ALBERT FREDERICK, insurance company executive; b. Springfield, Mass., July 15, 1941; s. Albert, Jr. and Ina Agnes (Kennedy) C.; m. Kathleen M. St. Marie, July 18, 1964; children—Peter Frederick, Lynn Kathleen. B.S. in Bus. Adminstrn., Am. Internat. Coll., 1964. Sr. acct. Lybrand, Ross Bros. & Montgomery, Springfield, Mass., 1964-68; controller Gray Supply Co., Springfield, 1968-69; v.p. Aetna Life & Casualty Co., Hartford, Conn., 1969—. Mem. Am. Inst. C.P.A.s, Nat. Assn. Accts. (dir. 1968-76), Fin. Execs. Inst. Served with USAR, 1964-71. Home: 23 Colorado Dr Somers CT 06071 Office: Aetna Life & Casualty Co 151 Farmington Ave Hartford CT 06156

COLLINGS, CHARLES LEROY, supermarket executive; b. Wewoka, Okla., July 11, 1925; s. Roy B. and Dessie L. C.; m. Frances Jane Flake, June 28, 1947; children—Sandra Jean, Dianna Lynn. Student, So. Methodist U., 1943-44, U. Tex., 1945. Sec., contr., dir. Noble Meat Co., Madera, Calif., 1947-54; chief acct. Montgomery Ward & Co., Oakland, Calif., 1954-56; with Raleys, Sacramento, 1956—; sec. Raleys, 1958—, pres., 1970—, also dir. Bd. dirs. Pro Athlete Outreach, Youth for Christ. With USNR, 1943-46. Mem. Calif. Grocers Assn. (dir., officer, past chmn.), Calif Retailers Assn. (bd. dir.). Republican. Baptist. Home: 6790 Arabela Way Sacramento CA 95831 Office: Raleys 500 W Capitol Ave Broderick CA 95605

COLLINS, CHRISTOPHER CARL, manufacturing executive; b. Schenectady, N.Y., May 20, 1950; s. Gerald Edward and Constance (Messier) C.; m. Margaret Elizabeth Busby Cox, May 20, 1972 (div. Apr. 1978); 1 child, Carly Elizabeth; m. Mary Sue Kuhn, Jan. 9, 1988. BS in Mech. Engring., N.C. State U., 1972; MBA, U. Ala., 1975. Registered profl. engr., Ala., N.Y. Sales engr. Westinghouse Elec. Corp., Birmingham, Ala., 1972-76; market rsch. analyst Westinghouse Elec. Corp., Buffalo, 1976-77, mgr. market planning, 1978-79, mgr. gearing div., 1980-82; pres., chmn., chief exec. officer Nuttall Gear Corp., Niagara Falls, N.Y., 1983—. Bd. dirs. Kenmore Mercy Hosp., 1986—; mem. ho. of dels. United Way, Buffalo, 1986—. Mem. Young Pres.'s Orgn. (chmn. edn. com. 1987-88, chpt. chmn. 1988—), Brookfield Country Club. Republican. Roman Catholic. Home: 8 Ransom Oaks Dr East Amherst NY 14051 Office: Nuttall Gear Corp PO Box 1032 Niagara Falls NY 14302

COLLINS, FRANK CHARLES, JR., industrial and service quality specialist; b. El Paso, Tex., Oct. 29, 1927; s. Frank Charles Sr. and Lucile Ellen (Reynolds) C.; m. Esther Frances Shiell, Aug. 16, 1948; children: Lucile Frances Collins Silveira, Sue Ellen Collins Hekman, Francene C. Collins Newman, Virginia Ann Collins Friesen, Melissa Esther Collins Murphy, Laura Beth Collins Leach, Frank Charles III. BA in Sociology, La. State U., 1949; postgrad., Naval War Coll., 1966, UCLA, 1976-77. Enlisted USNR, 1945-46, commd. ensign, 1951, advanced through grade to rear adm., 1951-78; comdr. U.S.S. LSS(L) 65, 1953-54, U.S.S. Saline CTY LST 1101, San Diego, 1957-59, U.S.S. John A. Bole DD 755, 1967-69; ops. officer Naval Support Activity, Danang, Vietnam, 1966-67; comdr. COMDESRON Nine, San Diego, 1974-76, Devel. and Tng. Center/Fleet Maintenance Assistance Group, Pacific, San Diego, 1976-78; chief Navy Sect., Army Mission, Mil. Assistance Adv. Group, Iran, 1978-79; dir. logistics planning Office Chief of Naval Ops., Washington, 1979-81; exec. dir. quality assurance Def. Logistics Agy., 1981-83; ret. 1983; v.p. quality ops. Textron, Inc. (formerly AVCO Corp.), Providence, 1983-86; pres. Frank Collins Assocs. Survival Twenty-One, Alexandria, Va., 1987—; chmn. bd. Quality Printing and Graphics Internat. Inc., Chula Vista, Calif. Author: Quality-The Ball in Your Court, Fifteen Steps in Establishing a Quality Improvement Process; contbg. author: Energy and Sea Power, 1981, Vietnam: The Naval Story, 1986; contbr. articles to profl. jours. Mem. exec. bd. Iran Am. Friendship Found., Washington, 1985—; bd. dirs. Malcolm Baldrige Nat. Quality Award Consortium, Milw., 1988—, Nat. Found. Inc. (bd. dirs.), Washington; vice-chmn. emeritus Grace Christian Reform Ch. Coun., Burke, Va., 1987—. Decorated Legion of Merit (2), Bronze Star, Navy Commendation medal (all with Combat V), Def. Superior Service medal, Def. Meritorious Service medal., Def. Disting. Service medal. Mem. Am. Soc. for Quality Control (chmn. aerospace and def. div. 1987-88), Assn. for Quality and Participation, Ret. Officers Assn., U.S. Naval Inst., Navy League, Nat. Security Indsl. Assn. Republican. Home and Office: 5819 Colfax Ave Alexandria VA 22311

COLLINS, GARY DEAN, accountant, religious foundation administrator; b. Rolla, Mo., Nov. 1, 1951; s. Eugene and Fern (Schlup) c.; m. Carol Ann Schultz, Jan. 30, 1972; 1 child, Cari Deon. BS, S.W. Mo. State U., 1973, MBA, 1976. CPA, Mo. Acct. Fox & Co., CPA, Springfield, Mo., 1977-80; dir. income maintenance Mo. Dept. Social Services, Springfield, 1980-81; dir. bus. services Mo. Bapt. Conv., Springfield, 1981-86; exec. dir., treas. Mo. Bapt. Found., Springfield, 1986—; commr. Stewardship Commn. SBC, Nashville, 1987—; bd. dirs. Waynesville (Mo.) Security Bank. Chmn. budget com. United Way, Jefferson City, 1986; chmn. bus. campaign Am. Heart Assn., Jefferson City, 1988—. Mem. Mo. Soc. CPA's, C. of C. (chmn. conv. and visitors com. 1985-86), Jefferson City Country Club, Rotary (pres.-elect Jefferson City chpt. 1988). Office: Mo Bapt Found 400 E High St Jefferson City MO 65101

COLLINS, GARY WALTER, computer consulting executive; b. Tulsa, Nov. 23, 1938; s. Howard David and Ernestine Louemma (Dunning) C.; m. Cornelia Elizabeth Warkentin, Aug. 12, 1965; children: Lisa Marie, David Winston. BS, Stanford U., 1962, MS, 1964; student, Fuller Theol. Sem., Pasadena, Calif., 1967. Registered profl. engr., Calif., Colo. Assoc. engr. IBM Corp., San Jose, Calif., 1964-66; design engr. Jet Propulsion Labs., Pasadena, 1968-70; devel. engr. Magnavox Research Lab., Torrance, Calif., 1970-72, Calcomp Inc., Anaheim, Calif., 1973-76; sr. engr. Storage Tech. Co., Louisville, Colo., 1976-84; prin. Collins Computer Cons., Boulder, Colo., 1984—; cons. computer disk life Library Congress, Washington, 1985-86. Contbr. articles to profl. jours.; patentee in field. Mem. bd. 1st Presbyn. Ch., Boulder, 1984-86. Mem. Optical Disk Standards Com., Inst. Noise Control Engrs. Republican. Lodge: Elks. Home and Office: Collins Computer Cons 5259 Idylwild Tr Boulder CO 80301

COLLINS, GERARD JAMES, accountant; b. Bklyn., Mar. 1, 1949; s. Gerard Robert and Anne Kathryn (Diver) C.; BA, Cath. U. Am., 1972; MSA, George Washington U., 1981, cert. mgmt. acct., 1982; m. Catherine Holt Collins; children: Melissa Leigh Phillips, Meghan Devon Collins. Research analyst Cath. U., Washington, 1972-74; sr. statis. analyst Blue Cross & Blue Shield Assn., Washington, 1974-77, mgr. statis. analysis and reporting, 1977-79, sr. mgr. govt. audits, 1979-82, dir. audit services, 1982—. Dir. swim program Montgomery County Assn. Retarded Citizens, 1972-74; mem. audit com. Montgomery Village Found., 1983-84. Mem. Nat. Assn. Accts. (dir. Montgomery-Prince Georges chpt. 1983-84, v.p. 1984-85. dir. No. Va. chpt. 1986-88), Inst. Cert. Mgmt. Accts., Inst. Internal Auditors, Nat. Assn. Sports Ofcls., No. Va. Football Ofcls. Assn. Office: Blue Cross Blue Shield 1615 L St NW Ste 800 Washington DC 20036

COLLINS, GROVER, real estate executive, insurance broker, auctioneer; b. Lewisburg, Tenn., Jan. 2, 1945; s. Algie Lee and Willie Mae Collins; m. Peggy Ann Payne, June 1967; children: Andrew, Matthew, Lee Ann, Christopher. BS, Mid. Tenn. State U., 1967, MS, 1970. Pres., bd. dirs. Grover Collins Real Estate, Inc., Lewisburg, 1974—; ptnr. Collins & Murrey Ins., Lewisburg, 1980—; bd. dirs. Sovran Bank, Lewisburg. Mem. devel. coun. David Lipscomb Coll., 1980—, Marshall County Bd. Edn., 1982-86; Sunday sch. tchr. Mem. Nat. Bd. Realtors, Tenn. Bd. Realtors, Tenn. Auctioneers Assn., Marshall County C. of C. (bd. dirs. 1974-76), Lewisburg C. of C. (pres. 1976), Quarterback Club (treas. 1989), Masons, Shriners, Rotary (bd. dirs. Lewisburg club 1977-80, pres. 1980), Kiwanis (pres. 1989). Democrat. Mem. Ch. of Christ. Office: Collins & Murrey Ins 1103 Nashville Hwy Lewisburg TN 37081

COLLINS, HARRY DAVID, mechanical engineer, construction claims consultant, expert witness, retired army officer; b. Brownsville, Pa., Nov. 18, 1931; s. Harry Alonzo and Cecelia Victoria (Morris) C.; B.S. in Mech. Engring., Carnegie Mellon U., 1954; M.S., U.S. Naval Postgrad. Sch., 1961; postgrad. George Washington U., 1971-72; MS in Physics; postgrad. Exptl Physics; m. Suzanne Dylong, May 11, 1956; children—Cynthia L., Gerard P. Commd. 2d lt. C.E., U.S. Army, 1954, advanced through grades to lt. col. 1969; comdr. 802d Heavy Engr. Constrn. Bn., Korea, 1972-73; dep. dist. engr. and acting dist. engr. Army Engr. Dist., New Orleans, 1973-75; ret., 1975; v.p. deLaureal Engrs., Inc., New Orleans, 1975-78; v.p. Near East mktg. Kidde Cons., Inc., 1978-82; dir. new bus. devel. for Middle East, Am. Middle East Co., Inc., 1982-84; sr. cons. Wagner, Hohns, Inglis, Inc., 1984—. Decorated Legion of Merit, Bronze Star with oak leaf cluster, Meritorious Service medal; registered profl. engr., Miss., La. Mem. ASME, Am. Soc. Mil. Engrs. (past pres. La Post), La. Engring. Soc., N.Y. Acad. Scis., NSPE, Am. Nuclear Soc., AAA, Internat. Platform Assn., Sigma Xi. Home: 2024 Audubon St New Orleans LA 70118

COLLINS, J. BARCLAY, II, lawyer, oil company executive; b. Gettysburg, Pa., Oct. 21, 1944; s. Jennings Barclay and Golda Olevia (Hook) C.; m. Janna Claire Fall, June 25, 1966; children: J. Barclay III, L. Christian. AB magna cum laude, Harvard U., 1966; JD magna cum laude, Columbia U., 1969. Bar: N.Y. 1969. Law clk. to presiding judge U.S. Ct. Appeals (2d cir.), N.Y.C., 1969-70; assoc. Cravath, Swaine and Moore, N.Y.C., 1970-78; v.p., asst. gen. counsel City Investing Co., N.Y.C., 1978-84; sr. v.p., gen. counsel Amerada Hess Corp., N.Y.C., 1984—, also bd. dirs. Trustee Bklyn. Hosp.-Caledonian Hosp., Plymouth Ch. of the Pilgrims, Bklyn.; bd. dirs. United Hosp. Fund N.Y., John Milton Soc. for Blind; gov. Bklyn. Heights Assn. Mem. ABA, N.Y. Bar Assn. Clubs: Heights Casino (Bklyn.); Harvard N.Y.C. Home: 2 Montague Terr Brooklyn Heights NY 11201 Office: Amerada Hess Corp 1185 Ave of the Americas 40th Fl New York NY 10036

COLLINS, JAMES ARTHUR, fast food company executive; b. Huntington Park, Calif., Dec. 20, 1926; s. Albert Preston and Lucile Marie (Riglesberger) C.; m. Carol Elizabeth Leonard, July 15, 1950; children: Cathleen E., Kelly L., Michael J., Melissa L. B.S. in Civil Engring., UCLA, 1950. Civil engr. Thiesen Constrn. Co., Pasadena, Calif., 1950-52; owner, operator Airport Village Hamburger Handout, Culver City, Calif., 1952-68; chmn., chief exec. officer Collins Foods Internat., Inc., Los Angeles, 1968-87; chmn. bd. dirs. Collins Foods Internat., Inc., Sizzler Restaurants Internat., Inc. Chmn. bd. dirs. YMCA Met. Los Angeles; past chmn. bd. mgrs. Westside Los Angeles YMCA; chmn., past pres. U. Calif. at Los Angeles Found.; past regent U. Calif. Served with USN, 1944-46. Named Foodservice Operator of Yr. Internat. Foodservice Mfrs. Assn., 1977; recipient Univ. Service award UCLA, 1977, Profl. Achievement award UCLA, 1981, Alumnus of Yr. award UCLA, 1982, Operator of Yr. award Multi-Unit Food Service Operators, 1986, Horatio Alger award, 1987. Mem. Nat. Restaurant Assn. (bd. dirs.), Calif. Restaurant Assn. (dir., past pres.), Chief Execs. Orgn. (bd. dirs.), U. Calif. at Los Angeles Alumni Assn. (past pres.), Young Pres. Orgn. (past chmn. Los Angeles chpt.). Republican. Methodist. Club: Rotary (pres. 1962-63). Office: Collins Foods Internat Inc 12655 W Jefferson Blvd Los Angeles CA 90066

COLLINS, JAMES DAVID, III, industrial engineer; b. Madison, Wis., Jan. 4, 1960; s. James David and Margret Ann (Weber) C. BS in Indsl. Engring., Iowa State U., 1983; MBA, St. Thomas Coll., St. Paul, 1988. Registered profl. engr., Minn. Indsl. engr. intern Eaton Corp., Eden Prairie, Minn., 1980; integration engr.Cummins Engring. div. Onan Corp., Mpls., 1983—. Fundraiser Jr. Achievement, Mpls., 1985; mem. Big Bros., 1989. Named Young Indsl. Engr. of Yr. award for Twin Cities, 1988. Mem. Nat. Soc. Profl. Engrs. (chpt. sec. 1984), Inst. Indsl. Engrs. (v.p. 1985, treas. 1984, dir. Twin City chpt. 1989, Young Engr. of Yr. 1988)), Soc. Mfg. Indsl. Engrs. Republican. Home: 1322 7th St SW New Brighton MN 55112 Office: Onan Corp 1400 73rd Ave NE Minneapolis MN 55432

COLLINS, JAMES ODELL, investment management company executive; b. Rock Hill, S.C., Aug. 26, 1934; s. Jesse Odell and Bernice (Seymoure) C.; m. Lynne Nichols, June 9, 1962; children: Leslie Chase, Ashley Michelle, Christy Camille. BEE, Ga. Inst. Tech., 1956; MBA, Harvard U., 1963; cert., Pacific Coast Banking Sch., 1979. Chartered fin. analyst. Vice-pres. Capital Cons., Inc., Portland, Oreg., 1972-77; v.p. Wells Fargo Bank, San Francisco, 1977-81, Pacific Investment Mgmt. Co., Newport Beach, Calif., 1981-82; sr. v.p. San Diego Trust & Savs. Bank, 1982-83; chmn., chief exec. officer Insight Capital Mgmt., Inc., Moraga, Calif., 1983—, also bd. dirs.; bd. dir. Pacific Basin Telecommunications, Ltd., Moraga, Data Base Mgmt., Inc., Walnut Creek, Calif.; former bd. dirs. Vadic Corp., Mountain West Airlines. Served to lt. (j.g.) USN, 1955-58. Mem. Inst. Chartered Fin. Analysts. Republican. Presbyterian. Club: Commonwealth (San Francisco). Home: 426 Springfield Pl Moraga CA 94556 Office: Insight Capital Mgmt Inc 1600 School St Ste 105 Moraga CA 94556

COLLINS, JOHN PATRICK, oil company executive, lawyer; b. Evanston, Ill., July 5, 1942; s. John Allen and Rosalie Elizabeth (Grossenkemper) C.; m. Gretta O'Connell, June 4, 1974; 1 child, Courtney Ellen. A.B., Marquette U., 1966; J.D., Georgetown U., 1970; LL.M., Harvard U., 1972. Bar: D.C. 1970, Mass. 1972, N.Y. 1975. Vis. prof. Law Sch., Ind. U., Indpls., 1970-71; assoc. Debevoise & Plimpton, N.Y.C., 1973-79; pres., chief exec. officer Plains Resources Inc., Oklahoma City, 1979—. Editor-in-chief Law and Policy in Internat. Bus., 1969-70. Nat. Commn. on Marijuana and Drug Abuse grantee, 1972. Mem. Assn. Bar City N.Y., D.C. Bar Assn. Roman Catholic. Clubs: Union of City N.Y., Racquet and Tennis, Harvard of N.Y.C. (N.Y.C.). Home: 423 Hunterwood Houston TX 77024 Office: Plains Resources Inc 1600 Smith St #1500 Houston TX 77002

COLLINS, JOHN ROGER, aerospace company executive; b. Tulsa, Jan. 13, 1941; s. John Leland and Velma (Jones) C.; m. Mary Susan Lanphier, Aug. 29, 1964; children: John Burkett, Stephanie Lanphier, Elizabeth Arnold. AB, Princeton U., 1963; MBA, U. Chgo., 1967. Officer trainee Continental Ill. Nat. Bank, Chgo., 1963-65; economist Skelly Oil Co., Tulsa, 1967-70, asst. treas., 1970-72; exec. v.p. Vanply, Inc., Tulsa, 1972-76; v.p. adminstrn. Parker Drilling Co., Tulsa, 1976-79, sr. v.p., 1979-86; dir. econ. devel. NORDAM, Tulsa, 1987—; bd. dirs. Community Bank, Bristow, Okla., Bank of Lakes, Langley, Okla., Relvue Royalty Corp.; pres. Collins Energy Corp., Tulsa, 1980—. Author: The Vision of a Creature, 1963. Vice chmn. Tulsa Area United Way, 1975; trustee Hillcrest Med. Ctr., Tulsa, 1979-86, 87—; mem. alumni council Princeton (N.J.) U., 1979-85; bd. dirs. Tulsa Opera, Inc., 1980, Tulsa Internat. Visitors Council, 1981, Tulsa area Campfire Girls, 1978. Democrat. Presbyterian. Clubs: Princeton N.Y. (N.Y.C.); Tulsa. Home: 1754 E 30th Pl Tulsa OK 74114

COLLINS, JOHN WENDLER, consumer products company executive; b. Rutherford, N.J., Nov. 7, 1930; s. Nelson Haley and Agnes Lucinda (Maier) C.; m. Martha E. Raiff, Oct. 26, 1952; children: Bruce, Nancy, Susan; m. Janet Doyle, July 17, 1975. B.A., Dartmouth Coll., 1952. V.p. Procter & Gamble Co., Cin., 1955-76; group v.p. Clorox Co., Oakland, Calif., 1976—, exec. v.p. ops., 1984, exec. v.p., chief operating officer, 1985-86, pres., chief operating officer, 1986—, dir., 1983—. Trustee East Oakland Youth Devel. Ctr., Oakland, 1976—; com. mem. United Way, Bay Area, 1976—. Served to lt. USNR, 1952-55. Mem. Phi Beta Kappa. Democrat. Home: 19 Honey Hill Rd Orinda CA 94563 Office: Clorox Co 1221 Broadway Oakland CA 94612 *

COLLINS, KATHLEEN ELIZABETH, pharmaceutical company official; b. Rock Island, Ill., Jan. 14, 1951; d. A. Phillip and Henrietta (Zeis) C.; m. David Mark Hasenmiller, June 23, 1973 (div. June 1975). Fgn. student degree, U. Grenoble, 1970; student, Barat Coll., 1968-70, U. Wis., 1970-71; BA in French and English, St. Ambrose Coll., Davenport, Iowa, 1972; postgrad. secondary edn., Augustana Coll., Rock Island, 1975, U. Iowa, 1979, 84. Sales clk. Scharff's Dept. Store, Bettendorf, Iowa, 1970-72; teller Moline (Ill.) Nat. Bank, 1972-73; mgr. Music Box, Rock Island, 1973-74, Disc Records, Moline, 1974-75; with quality assurance dept. U.S. Army, Savanna, Ill., 1975-76; sales rep. Burroughs Wellcome Co., Rsch. Triangle Park, N.C., 1976-81; vol. nutritionist Peace Corps, Niger, 1981-82; sales rep. Phil Collins Co., Rock Island, 1982-85; med. rep. Lederle Labs., Overland Park, Kans., 1985-88; sales rep. Summit (N.J.) Pharms. Co., 1988—. vol. Big Bros./Big Sisters, Moline, 1984-85, Pathway Hospice, Luth. Hosp., Moline, 1984-86, 88. Mem. Quad Cities Pharm. Assn. (treas. 1978, 86, v.p. 1979, sec. 1987, sec./treas. 1988), Jr. League Quad Cities. Roman Catholic. Clubs: Davenport, Outing (Davenport). Home: 3649 Cedarview Ct Bettendorf IA 52722 Office: Summit Pharms care Ciba Geigy 556 Morris Ave Summit NJ 07901

COLLINS, LOU, management consultant; b. Meremac, Okla., Feb. 29, 1936; s. Hoyal and Doris (Dilley) C.; m. Cheryl Pottorff, May 31, 1975; children: Colleen, Heidi, Jaime, Andrew. Degree in Theol. Counseling, Freelandia Inst., 1980. Field ops. mgr., supt. foreman various contracting firms, Calif., Okla., Oreg., N.Mex., 1957-76; owner, chief exec. officer C&L Developers, Central Point, Oreg., 1976-81; ops. mgr. LoLo (Mont.) Springs Resort, 1981-84; property mgr. Hyder & Co., Solana Beach, Calif., 1984-87; ops. mgr. housing Calif. State Poly. U., Pomona, 1987—. Served as sgt. 1st class U.S. Army, 1953-57. Mem. Cachuho, Acuho, Nat. Geographic Soc., Nat. Audubon Soc., Smithsonian Inst., Am. Mgmt. Assn., NRA, Am. Legion. Democrat. Home: 2530 Balboa Ave Ontario CA 91761 Office: Calif State Poly U 3801 W Temple Ave Pomona CA 91768

COLLINS, PAUL JOHN, banker; b. West Bend, Wis., Oct. 26, 1936; s. Curtis Alvin and Adele (Stopenbach) C.; m. Carol Lee Hoffmann, May 8, 1965; children: Ronald Alvin, Julia Downing. B.B.A., U. Wis., 1958; M.B.A., Harvard U., 1961. With Citibank, N.Y.C., 1961—; investment analyst, portfolio mgmt. Citibank, 1961-70, sr. v.p., chmn. investment policy com., 1970-75, sr. v.p., head dept. corporate planning, 1976-77, sr. v.p., head fin. div., 1977-79, exec. v.p. acctg. and control, 1980-81, group exec. investment br., 1982-85, sr. corp. officer N.Am., 1985-88, vice chmn., 1988—, also bd. dirs.; bd. dirs. Citicorp, Kimberly Clark Corp. Trustee U. Wis. Found.; mem. coun. econ. devel. N.Y. Philharm. Republican. Congregationalist. Club: River (N.Y.C.). Home: 29 Wilton Crescent, London SW1, England Office: Citibank House, 336 Strand, London WC2, England

COLLINS, RICHARD MATTHEW, municipal official; b. Perth Amboy, N.J., July 27, 1954; s. John James and Jean Shirley (Bohlen) C.; m. Donna Diane Pendley, July 9, 1988; 1 child, Christopher David. AA, Antelope Valley Coll., 1977; BA in Polit. Sci. with honors, Calif. State U., Northridge, 1979; postgrad., Southwestern U. Law, Los Angeles, 1982. Adminstrv. intern City of Lancaster, Calif., 1979-80, planning intern, 1980-81, code enforcement officer, 1981-87, code enforcement supr., 1987—; pres. Antelope Valley Council on Alcoholism and Drug Dependency, Lancaster, 1983-85. Pres. Antelope Valley Young Reps., Lancaster, 1979; v.p. Antelope Valley Rep. Assembly, Lancaster, 1980; ofcl. Calif. Rep. Party, Sacramento, 1985; mem. Antelope Valley Health Planning Council, Lancaster, 1981—, Rep. Nat. Party, Washington, 1985, Antelope Valley Safety Profl. Assn., campaign com. Antelope Valley United Way, Statue of Liberty-Ellis Island Found. Named one of Outstanding Young Men Am., Jaycees, 1983; recipient Disting. Leadership award for excellence Am. Biog. Inst., 1988. Mem. So. Calif. Assn. Code Enforcement Officers, Mcpl. Mgmt. Assn., Am. Planning Assn., Calif. Hist. Soc., Internat. Platform Assn., Am. Assn. Code Enforcement. Episcopalian. Home: 1835 W Ave K-10 Lancaster CA 93534 Office: Lancaster City Hall 44933 N Fern Ave Lancaster CA 93534

COLLINS, THOMAS MERRIGAN, video company executive; b. N.Y.C., Jan. 14, 1926; s. William Charles and Roscrana (Merrigan) C.; m. Ann Louise Servey; children: Thomas Jr., Peter, Kathryn. BS, U.S. Merchant Marine Acad., 1947; MBA, NYU, 1959. 3d officer Moore McCormick Lines, N.Y.C., 1947; 2d officer W.R. Grace Steamship Lines, N.Y.C., 1947-48; with sales, customer service Whittaker Clark & Daniels, Inc., N.Y.C., 1949; sales rep. Borden Chem. Div., N.Y.C., 1949-50, Gen. Aniline and Film Ansco Div., N.Y.C. and Phila., 1951-53; mgr., chief buyer photo service U.S. Army, Nuremburg, Fed. Republic Germany, 1953-56; sales rep. spl. markets bus. systems div. Eastman Kodak Co., N.Y.C., 1956-62, market research analyst, 1962-65, sales engr. motion picture div., 1966-83; pres. Collins Mktg., Inc., Westport, Conn., 1983—, pres. Access Video div., 1985—; mktg. cons. VCA Teletronics, Inc., Leonia, N.J., 1987—; cons., bd. dirs. Union Carbide Video and Photo Services, Danbury, Conn., 1986-88. Selectman Town of Weston, Conn., 1971-73. Served to lt. USN, 1944-47, ETO, PTO, USNR, 1947-56. Mem. Soc. Motion Picture and TV Engrs. Republican. Roman Catholic. Home: 280 Georgetown Rd Weston CT 06883 Office: Collins Mktg Inc PO Box 2510 Westport CT 06880

COLLINSON, JOHN THEODORE, former railroad company executive; b. Pitts., July 29, 1926; s. John Gordon and Katherine (Bichy) C.; m. Patricia Ann Davison, Nov. 15, 1947; children: John G. II, Donald L., Nancy Ann. B.S. in Civil Engring., Cornell U., 1946. Project engr. Dravo Corp., Pitts., 1946; various engring. positions Balt. & Ohio R.R. Co., Pitts., 1946-65, Newark, 1946-65, Akron, Ohio, 1946-65; chief engr. Balt. & Ohio R.R. Co., 1965; with Chessie System, Inc., Cleve., 1965-88, v.p. ops., 1973-76, exec. v.p., 1976-78; pres., chief exec. officer C & O Ry., Balt. & Ohio R.R., Cleve., 1978-85; vice chmn. CSX Corp., Richmond, Va., 1985-88, also bd. dirs.; chmn. Chessie System & Seaboard R.R.s, 1985—; bd. dirs. Nat. Mine Service, Nat. City Bank, RFBP Corp. Served to lt. (j.g.) USN, 1943-46. Republican. Presbyterian. Clubs: Country of Cleve.; Quail Creek (Naples, Fla.). Lodges: Masons, Shriners. Home: 4301 Gulf Shore Blvd N Naples FL 33940 Office: Chessie System Inc 1126 Terminal Tower Cleveland OH 44113 Other: CSX Corp 901 E Cary St Richmond VA 23219

COLLIS, KAY LYNN, banker; b. Dallas, July 15, 1958; d. Martin Edward and Norma June (Hall) C. A.A., Tyler Jr. Coll., 1978; B.B.A., Sam Houston State U., 1982. Mgr., World Finance Corp., Bryan, Tex., 1978-81; ops. analyst Republic Bank Dallas, 1983-85; asst. v.p. MBank, Dallas, 1985-87; asst. v.p., dept. mgr. Murray Savings, 1987—; cons. Collis Cons. Co., Sulphur Springs, Tex., 1983—. Vol., speaker for local chpt. Arthritis Found., 1983—. Mem. Nat. Assn. Female Execs., Nat. Assn. Bank Women (Dallas Group sec. 1987-88, v.p. 1988—), Am. Bus. Womens Assn. Republican. Episcopalian. Home: 5018 N Hall St Dallas TX 75235-8814 Office: Murray Savs 5550 LBJ Fwy Ste 675 Dallas TX 75240

COLLISHAW, ROBERT JAMES, banker; b. Suffern, N.Y., Aug. 14, 1934; s. James Albert and Dorothy (Conover) C.; m. Jacquelyn Jarrett, June 18, 1955; children: Daniel, Thomas, Robert, Karen, Stacey. BA, Colgate U., 1955. With exec. tng. Chem. Bank, N.Y.C., 1955-57, asst. sec. to regional v.p. nat. div., 1957-71, sr. v.p. metro div., 1971-77, sr. v.p. govt. affairs, 1977-87, sr. v.p., asst. to chmn., 1987—. Trustee Valley Hosp., Ridgewood, N.J., 1987—. Mem. Bus. Council N.Y. State (dir. 1972-82). Republican. Presbyterian. Home: 130 Mahwah Rd Mahwah NJ 07430 Office: Chem Bank 277 Park Ave New York NY 10172

COLLISON, CURTIS LEE, JR., processed food and beverage company executive; b. Providence, Feb. 3, 1940; s. Curtis Lee and Sue Elizabeth (Peterson) C.; m. Jean Ann Brown, Apr. 27, 1963; children: Curtis III, Eric, Jeff. BBA, Syracuse U., 1961. Sales and systems engr. IBM Corp., Natick, Mass., 1961-63; mktg. rep. Atlantic Richfield Corp., East Hartford, Conn., 1963-65; dir. employee relations Honeywell Info. Systems, Waltham, Mass., 1965-73; v.p. adminstrn. Cambridge Memories Inc., Bedford, Mass., 1973-75; dir. personnel Martha's Vineyard Hosp., Oak Bluffs, Mass., 1975-80, Digital Equipment Corp., Merrimack, N.H., 1980-82; v.p. human resources Ocean Spray Cranberries Inc., Plymouth, Mass., 1982-85, sr. v.p. corp. services, 1985—. Served with USCG, 1962-64. Fellow Am. Soc. Personnel Adminstrn., Employment Assn., Nat. Food Processors Assn. Home: PO Box 170 Pawkechatt Way Marion MA 02738 Office: Ocean Spray Cranberries Inc 1 Ocean Spray Dr Lakeville-Middleboro MA 02349

COLLISON, DIANE WITTROCK, communications executive; b. Carroll, Iowa, May 11, 1939; d. Michael August and Alberta Ernestine (Marcucci) Wittrock; m. David Michael Collison, Nov. 28, 1959 (div.); children: Christopher, Lucia, Charles, Nicholas, Paul, Michael. BA, Iowa State U., 1979, postgrad., 1979-80. Dir. communications and orgn. Rep. State Cen. Com, state, gubernatorial, nat., presdl. polit. campaigns Rep. Party Iowa, 1979-85; arts mgmt. Denver Symphony Orch., 1985-87, Boulder Philharm. Orch., Boulder, Colo., 1985-87; bus. communications specialist US West Communications, Denver, 1987-89; dir. pub. rels. Internat. Guide Acad., Denver, 1989—; coord. career edn. program Regis Coll., Denver; presenter in field; pub. speaker, 1983—. Pres. Am. Field Service Foreign Exchange Program, Iowa, 1977; regional rep. Ames Internat. Orch. Fest. Assn., 1977-78; mem. Colo. steering com. Dole Presdl. Campaign, 1987-88; mem. Rep. Nat. Com., 1980—; bd. dirs. Am. Lung Assn. of Iowa, 1978-79. Recipient award Arion Found. Mem. Internat. Platform Assn. Roman Catholic. Office: Internat Guide Acad 3003 Arapahoe St Ste 101 Denver CO 80205

COLLMER, RUSSELL CRAVENER, data processing executive, educator; b. Guatemala, Jan. 2, 1924; s. G. Russell and Constance (Cravener) C.; B.S., U. N.M., 1951; postgrad. Calif. Inst. Tech., 1943-44; M.S., State U. Iowa, 1955; m. Ruth Hannah Adams, Mar. 4, 1950; 1 son, Reed Alan. Staff mem. Mass. Inst. Tech., Lincoln Lab., Lexington, 1955-57; mgr. systems modeling, computer dept. Gen. Electric, Phoenix, 1957-59; mgr. ARCAS Thompson Ramo Wooldridge, Inc., Canoga Park, Cal., 1959-62; asso. mgr. tech. dir. CCIS-70 Bunker-Ramo Corp., 1962-64; sr. asso. Planning Research Corp., Los Angeles, 1964-65; pres. R. Collmer Assos., Benson, Ariz., 1965—; pres. Benson Econ. Enterprises Corp., 1968-69. Lectr. computer scis. Pima Community Coll., Tucson, 1970—. Served with USAAC, 1942-46, to capt. USAF, 1951-53. Mem. IEEE, Am. Meteorol. Soc., Assn. for Computing Machinery, Phi Delta Theta, Kappa Mu Epsilon. Republican. Baptist. Office: R Collmer Assocs PO Box 864 Benson AZ 85602

COLLOMB, BERTRAND PIERRE, cement company executive; b. Lyon, France, Aug. 14, 1942; came to U.S., 1985; s. Charles and Helene (Traon) C.; m. Marie Caroline Wirth, June 31, 1967; children: Cedric, Alex, Stephanie. Engring. student, Ecole Poly., Paris, 1960-62; engring. degree, Ecole des Mines, Paris, 1963-66; law degree, U. Nancy, France, 1968; PhD in Mgmt., U. Tex., 1971. Mining engr. Ministry of Industry, France, 1966-73; spl. asst. to Minister of Edn. Paris, 1974-75; v.p., then prin. Ciments Lafarge, Paris, 1975-82; exec. v.p. Lafarge-Coppee, Paris, 1983-88, vice-chmn., chief ops. officer, 1989—; chmn. Orsan, Paris, 1983—; pres. and chief exec. officer Gen. Portland, Inc., Dallas, 1985-87; vice chmn., chief exec. officer LaFarge Corp., Dallas, 1987-88; chmn. bd. dirs. LaFarge Corp., 1989—; research dir. Ecole Poly., 1972-74; bd. dirs. Ciments Lafarge. Served as lt. French Cav., 1962-63. Mem. Portland Cement Assn. (bd. dirs. 1985-88). Home: Lyme Kiln Farm Leesburg VA 22075 Office: Lafarge Corp 11130 Sunrise Valley Dr Ste 300 Reston VA 22091

COLLOPY, CHRISTOPHER STEPHEN, clothing company executive; b. San Francisco, Sept. 26, 1952; s. George Francis and Dorothy (Rose) C.; m. Mary Catherine Collopy, Apr. 26, 1986; 1 child, Tristan Connor. BA, San Jose State U., 1977. With Brookhurst Inc.; counselor Options House, Hollywood, Calif., 1981-86. Instr. Jr. Achievement, Redondo Beach, Calif., 1982-86; bd. commr. City of Redondo Beach. Recipient Vol. Service award City of Los Angeles, 1984, Mater Dei award Archdiocese of San Fancisco, 1979. Mem. Sierra Club. Democrat. Roman Catholic. Home: 2009 Marshallfield Ln Redondo Beach CA 90278 Office: Brookhurst Inc 3751 S Hill St Los Angeles CA 90007

COLNETT, RONALD H., advertising executive; b. Toronto, Ont. Can., June 25, 1929; came to U.S., 1966; s. Harry Elson and Lily (Skidmore) C.; m. Patricia Crofts (div. 1970); m. Linda Gail Sanders, Sept. 20, 1976; children: Pamela Jane, Paul Ronald. V.p., mgmt. supr. Vickers and Bronson, Toronto, Ont., Can., 1949-65; chief exec. officer, chmn. bd. Wilton, Loomiss & Condor, San Francisco, 1966-84; chmn. Saatchi & Saatchi DFS/Pacific (formerly Dancer, Fitzgerald, Sample), San Francisco, 1984—, also chief oper. officer. Club: Olympic (San Francisco). Office: Saatchi & Saatchi DFS 1010 Battery St PO Box 7166 San Francisco CA 94120 *

COLODNY, EDWIN IRVING, airline executive; b. Burlington, Vt., June 7, 1926; s. Myer and Lena (Yett) C.; m. Nancy Dessoff, Dec. 11, 1965; children: Elizabeth, Mark, David. AB, U. Rochester, 1948; LLB, Harvard, 1951. Bar: N.Y. 1951, D.C. 1958. With Office Gen. Counsel, GSA, 1951-52, CAB, 1954-57; with Allegheny Airlines, Inc. (now USAir, Inc.), 1957—, exec. v.p. mktg. and legal affairs, 1969-75; pres., chief exec. officer Allegheny Airlines, Inc. (now USAir Inc.), 1975—, chmn. bd. dirs., 1978—; bd. dirs. PNC Fin. Corp., Martin Marietta Corp. dir. Martin Marietta Corp; mem. bd. trustees U. Rochester. Served to 1st lt. AUS, 1952-54. Recipient James D. McGill Meml. award U. Rochester. Mem. ABA, U.S. C. of C. (bd. dirs.), U. Rochester (bd. trustees). *

COLOMBARI, GIUSEPPE, steel company executive; b. Gemmano, Italy, Dec. 13, 1922; came to U.S., 1959; s. Alfredo and Quinta (Mancini) C.; m. Margaret Jean Pelton, May 18, 1957; children—Thomas P., Michael J., Brian D. Comml. Scis. degree U. Bologna, Italy, 1946; postgrad. in exec. mgmt. Columbia U., 1960. From topographer to asst. gen. supt. Orinoco Mining Co. subs. U.S. Steel Corp., Venezuela, 1950-64; from gen. mgr. to v.p. Navios Corp. subs. U.S. Steel, Bahamas, 1964-72; v.p. U.S. Steel Internat., N.Y.C. and Pitts., 1972-75, pres. Navios Corp., Bahamas, 1975-76; v.p. resource devel. USX, Pitts., 1976-79, v.p., gen. mgr. ores, 1979-84, sr. v.p. related resources, 1984-87, pres. U.S. Steel Internat. Inc., 1988—. Served as lt. Italian Army, 1940-44. Mem. Am. Iron and Steel Inst., AIME. Roman Catholic. Clubs: Duquesne, St. Clair Country (Pitts.). Office: USX Corp 600 Grant St Rm 6142 Pittsburgh PA 15230

COLON, DENISE CASSANDRA, telecommunications executive; b. N.Y.C., Feb. 1, 1952; d. Isaac Tillman and Julia (Simmons) Jackson; (div. 1988); children: Denise Regina, Lana Autumn Schupbach. Student, Marymount Coll., N.Y., 1982. Cons. telecommunications various co., N.Y.C., 1980-82; pres., chief exec. officer Colón Tele-Consultants Inc., N.Y.C., 1982—; cons. U.S. Dept. Labor U.S., 1986-87, Permanent Mission Guinea to UN. H.E.M. Saliou Coumbassa, 1985-87. Author: Controlling Corporate Telecommunications Costs, 1985. Mem. Am. Mgmt. Assn.,

Pres.'s Assn., Soc. Telecommunications Cons., Nat. Assn. Female Execs., Double Image Theatre (patron). Democrat. Roman Catholic.

COLONEY, WAYNE HERNDON, civil engineer; b. Bradenton, Fla., Mar. 15, 1925; s. Herndon Percival and Mary Adore (Cramer) C.; m. Anne Elizabeth Benedict, June 21, 1950; 1 child, Mary Adore. B.C.E. summa cum laude, Ga. Inst. Tech., 1950. Registered profl. engr. and surveyor, Fla., Ga., Ala., N.C., also Nat. Council Engring. Examiners. Project engr.S.A. Constructora Gen., Venezuela, 1948-49; project engr. Fla. Rd. Dept., 1950-55; hwy. engr. Gibbs & Hill, Inc., Guatemala, 1955-57; project mgr. Gibbs & Hill, Inc., Tampa, Fla., 1957-59; project engr., then assoc. J.E. Greiner Co., Tampa, 1959-63; ptnr. Barrett, Daffin & Coloney, Tallahassee, 1963-70; pres. Wayne H. Coloney Co., Inc., Tallahassee, 1970-78, chmn., bd. chief exec. officer, 1978-85; pres., sec. Tesseract Corp., 1975-85; chmn. bd., chief exec. officer Coloney Co. Cons. Engrs., Inc., 1978—; dep. chmn. Howden Airdynamics Am., Tallahassee, 1985—; v.p., dir. Howden Coloney Inc., Tallahassee, 1985—; chmn. adv. com. Area Vocat. Tech. Sch., 1965-78; pres. Retro Tech. Corp., 1983—, Profl. Mgmt. Con. Group, 1983-87, pres., bd. dirs. Internat. Enterprises Inc, 1967-73. Patentee roof framing system, dense packing external aircraft fuel tank, tile mounting structure, curler rotating device, bracket system for roof framing; contbr. articles to profl. jours. Pres. United Fund Leon County, 1971-72; bd. dirs. Springtime Tallahassee, 1970-72, pres., 1981-82; bd. dirs. Heritage Found., 1965-71, pres., 1967; mem. Pres.'s Adv. Council on Indsl. Innovation, 1978-79; bd. dirs. LeMoyne Art Found., 1973, v.p., 1974-75; bd. dirs. Goodwill Industries, 1972-73, Tallahassee-Popoyan Friendship Commn., 1968-73; mem. Adv. Com. for Hist. and Cultural Preservation, 1969-71, Better Bus. Bur. Served with AUS, 1943-46. Fellow ASCE; mem. Am. Def. Preparedness Assn., NSPE, Fla. Engring. Soc. (sr.), Nat. Acad. Forensic Engrs. (diplomate), Fla. Inst. Cons. Engrs., Fla. Soc. Profl. Land Surveyors, Tallahassee C. of C., Anak, Koseme Soc., Am. Arbitration Assn., Fla. Small bus. Assn. (pres. 1981), Sales & Mktg. Execs. (1983—), Phi Kappa Phi, Omicron Delta Kappa, Sigma Alpha Epsilon, Tau Beta Pi. Episcopalian. Clubs: Governor's, Killearn Golf and Country, Met. Dinner (past pres.). Home: 3219 Thomasville Rd Apt 1-D Tallahassee FL 32312 Office: Coloney Co Cons Engrs Inc PO Box 668 Tallahassee FL 32302

COLOSIMO, ROBERT, labor relations executive; b. Thunder Bay, Ont., Can., Dec. 25, 1929; s. Henry and Ann Marie (Dolce) C.; m. Marilyn June MacKay, Nov. 3, 1954; children: James Mark, Joy Melanie. Grad., Selkirk High Sch., Thunder Bay. Spl. rep. CP Rail, Montreal, Que., Can., 1961-66, supr. personnel and labor relations, 1966-68, asst. mgr. labor relations, 1968-69, mgr. labor relations, 1969-77, asst. v.p. indsl. relations, 1977-81, v.p. indsl. relations, 1981—. Mem. Ry. Pers. Assn. (pres. 1985-86, exec. com. 1981—), Am. Mgmt. Assn., C. of C. (employer-employee rels. com.), Can. Mfrs. Assn., Can. Occupational Projection System (nat. adv. com.), Federally Regulated Employers—Transp. and Communication, Internat. Bus. Coun. Can. (bd. dirs.), Mgmt. Coun. for Responsible Employee Rels., Ry. Assn. Can. (labor rels. com.), Montreal Bd. Trade, Conf. Bd. of Can. (coun. of indsl. rels. execs.), Can. Labour Market and Productivity Centre (bd. dirs.), Railway Club (Montreal). Roman Catholic. Home: 173 King's Rd, Pointe Claire, PQ Canada H9R 4H6 Office: CP Rail, 910 Peel St PO Box 6042, Montreal, PQ Canada H3C 3E4

COLOVIC, ALEX JOHN, florist; b. Lubeck, Germany, Aug. 14, 1947; came to U.S., 1953, naturalized, 1959; s. John Daniel and Mary Colovic; student Marquette U., 1965-67; UCLA, 1968-69, U. Calif.-Northridge, 1969-70; m. Goldi Tolliver, May 4, 1978. Asst. oral pathology dept. Marquette U., 1963; clk. Kroger Co., Milw., 1964-66; asst. Chinese chef, Milw., 1965-67; clk. Fedco Foods, Inc., Van Nuys, Calif., 1967-70; sales rep. Symmar Dist., Vernon, Calif., 1971; sales rep. Kennedy Wholesale, Glendale, Calif., 1971-73; owner, operator Plantasia, Glendale, 1973—. Served with Calif. N.G., 1970-76. Mem. Cactus and Succulent Soc., Begonia Soc., Fern Soc., Glendale C. of C., U.S. C. of C. Democrat. Eastern Orthodox. Inventor self humidifying pottery, resin clothing plant stands. Office: Plantasia 2840 N Verdugo Rd Glendale CA 91208

COLPRON, MERLYN DALLAS, insurance executive; b. Newfolden, Minn., June 25, 1933; s. Ismael Charles and Freda Olivia (Nesterud) C.; m. Patricia Rose Gilbert, May 26, 1960; children: Cynthia Jean, David Allen. AA in Bus. Adminstrn., Lower Columbia Jr. Coll., 1953; BA in Fin., U. Wash., 1955. CPCU Ins. mgr. United Grocers Inc., Portland, Oreg., 1970-75; bur. chief Idaho Bur. Risk Mgmt. Boise, 1975-76; v.p., cons. Diversified Risk Mgmt. Services Inc., Boise, 1976-80; sec. Assoc. Loggers Mgmt. Corp., Boise, 1979—; v.p. Bayly, Martin & Faye Inc., Boise, 1980-82; pres. U.S. Risk Mgmt. Services Inc., Boise, 1982-86; pres. North/South Ins. Cons., Inc., Miami/Boise, 1986; risk mgr., cons. Stein-McMurray Ins. Svs., Boise, Idaho, 1986—; dir. Assoc. Loggers Exchange, Boise, 1979—. With U.S. Army, 1955-57. Mem. Soc. CPCU. Methodist. Home: 4014 Kingswood Dr Boise ID 83704

COLTON, ROY CHARLES, management consultant; b. Phila., Feb. 26, 1941; s. Nathan Hale and Ruth Janis (Baylinson) C.; B.A., Knox Coll., 1962; M.Ed., Temple U., 1963. With Sch. Dist. of Phila., 1963-64; systems analyst Wilmington Trust Co., 1967-69; exec. recruiter Atwood Consultants Inc., Phila., 1969-71; pres. Colton Bernard Inc., San Francisco, 1971—; occasional lectr. Fashion Inst. Tech., Phila. Coll. Textiles and Scis. Served with AUS, 1964-66. Mem. San Francisco Fashion Industries, San Francisco C. of C., Calif. Exec. Recruiter Assn., Nat. Assn. Exec. Recruiters, Am. Apparel Mfrs. Assn., Am. Arbitration Assn. (panel arbitrators), Am. Mgmt. Assn. Office: Colton Bernard Inc 417 Spruce St San Francisco CA 94118

COLTON, STERLING DON, lawyer, business executive; b. Vernal, Utah, Apr. 28, 1929; s. Hugh Wilkens and Marguerite (Maughan) C.; m. Eleanor Ricks, Aug. 21, 1954; children: Sterling David, Carolyn, Bradley Hugh, Steven Ricks. BS in Banking and Fin., U. Utah, 1951; JD, Stanford U., 1954. Bar: Calif. 1954, Utah 1954, D.C. 1967. Ptnr., Van Cott, Bagley, Cornwall & McCarthy, Salt Lake City, 1957-66; gen. counsel Marriott Corp., Washington, 1966—, sr. v.p., 1974—; also bd. dirs.; bd. dirs., v.p. Colton Ranch Corp., Vernal, 1987-88; bd. dirs. Nat. Litigation Ctr. Bd. dirs. Polynesian Cultural Ctr., 1988—, Nat. Litigation Ctr., 1988—; chmn. nat. adv. council U. Utah, Ballet West, nat. adv. counsel. Served to maj. JAG, U.S. Army, 1954-57. Mem. ABA, Calif. Bar Assn., Utah Bar Assn., D.C. Bar Assn., Washington Met. Corp. Counsel Assn. (former pres. dir.), Sigma Chi. Republican. Mormon. Office: Marriott Corp Marriott Dr Washington DC 20058

COLUMBUS, ROBERT HOWARD, sales executive; b. Olean, N.Y., Oct. 4, 1952; s. Howard Cletus and Elizabeth Jane (Anderson) C.; m. Jane Helen Plutat, May 20, 1980; children: Douglas Arthur, Natalie Marie. AAS, Erie Community Coll., Buffalo, 1976; BS, SUNY, Buffalo, 1978. Sales trainee Ingersoll-Rand, Nashua, N.H., 1978-79; mgr. terr. Beloit Corp., Dalton, Mass., 1979-80; regional sales mgr. Disogrin Industries, Manchester, N.H., 1980-86; nat. sales mgr. Daiichi Jitsugyo/Niigata, Elk Grove Village, Ill., 1986—. With USN, 1970-74. Lutheran. Home: 17 University Circle Hawthorn Woods IL 60047 Office: Daiichi Jitsugyo Am 1533 Elmhurst Rd Elk Grove Village IL 60007

COLUSSY, DAN ALFRED, service executive; b. Pitts., June 3, 1931; s. Dan and Viola E. (Andreis) C.; m. Helene Graham, June 6, 1953; children: Deborah, Jennifer. B.S. U.S. Coast Guard Acad., 1953; M.B.A., Harvard U., 1965. Applications engr. Jet Propulsion div. Gen. Electric Co., 1956-63; dir. ops. Am. Airlines, N.Y.C., 1965-66; v.p. mktg. N.E. Airlines, Boston, 1966-69; v.p. Wells, Rich, Green Advt. Agy., N.Y.C., 1969-70; v.p. mktg. devel. Pan Am. World Airways, N.Y.C., 1970-72, v.p. passenger mktg., 1972-74, sr. v.p. passenger mktg., 1974, sr. v.p. field ops., 1974-75, sr. v.p. mktg. and services, 1975-76, exec. v.p. mktg. and services, dir., 1976-78, pres., chief operating officer, mem. exec. com., 1978-80; chmn., chief exec. officer Columbia Air, Balt., 1980-82; pres., chief exec. officer, mem. exec. com. Can. Pacific Air, Vancouver, B.C., 1982-84, chmn., 1985-86, now bd. dirs.; mem. exec. com. Can. Pacific Hotels, 1983-84; pres., chief exec. officer, chmn. exec. com. UNC Inc., Annapolis, Md., 1985—, also bd. dirs.; mem. Anne Arundel County Exec.'s Bus. Roundtable. Mem. bd. visitors Coll. of Bus. and Mgmt. U. Md., bd. dirs. Nat. Aquarium in Balt., Hist. Annapolis, Inc. Served to lt. USCG, 1953-56. Mem. Md. C. of C. (bd. dirs.), Md. Econ. Growth Assocs. (bd. dirs.), Campaign Cabinet, U.S. Naval Inst., Am. Bus. Conf. Clubs: Royal Vancouver Yacht, Larchmont Yacht, Annapolis Yacht, Harvard. Lodge: Order of St. John. Office: UNC Inc 175 Admiral Cochrane Dr Annapolis MD 21401

COLWELL, BRYAN YORK, investment banker; b. Atlanta, Feb. 10, 1961; s. Olin Bryan and Betty Rose (York) C. BA magna cum laude, Harvard U., 1983; MBA, Columbia U., 1986; postgrad., U. Pa., 1985. Strategic planner SmithKline Beckman Corp., Phila., 1983-85; assoc. Goldman, Sachs and Co., N.Y.C., 1985—. Author: The Public-Private Partnership, 1983. Co-chmn. program com. N.Y. Rep. State Fin. Com. Forum 500, 1989—. Named Outstanding Young Am., WSB-Radio-TV Network, Atlanta, 1979; recipient Young Scholar award Harvard Club of Atlanta, 1979, Outstanding Student cup Atlanta Jour., 1979. Mem. Am. Fin. Assn. (v.p. 1985-86), Columbia Bus. Sch. Alumni Assn., Harvard U. Inst. of Politics, World Affairs Council, Harvard Architecture Soc. (pres. 1980), Phila. Art Alliance, Boys Club N.Y. (jr. com.), Youth Counseling League Club (jr. com.). Clubs: Owl, Hasty Pudding (Cambridge, Mass.) (v.p. 1981-83, grad. bd. 1984—); Harvard of N.Y.; Harvard of Boston; Harvard of Phila. Home: 1060 Park Ave New York NY 10128 Office: Goldman Sachs and Co 85 Broad St 26th Floor New York NY 10004

COLYER, RALPH JOSEPH, telephone directory company executive; b. Newark, June 2, 1935; s. Ralph Mitchell and Violet May (Kreideweis) C.; BS, Rutgers U., 1964; m. Grace Margaret Smith, Dec. 21, 1957; children: Donna Marie, Ralph Joseph, Lisa Rose. V.p. fin., treas. Nat. Telephone Dir. Corp., Union, N.J., 1972-88, ret. 1988. Served with U.S. Army, 1954-56; ETO. CPA, N.J. Mem. N.J. Soc. CPA's, Am. Inst. CPA's, Nat. Assn. Accts. Episcopalian. Home: 314 McKinley Ave Edison NJ 08820 Office: Nat Tel Directory Corp 1050 Galloping Hill Rd Union NJ 07083

COMAN, EDWARD JOHN, real estate and finance executive; b. Chgo., Dec. 7, 1939; s. Edward John and Agnes Marie (Martin) C.; m. Maxine Margaret Mikols, Dec. 29, 1962; children: Martin Edward, Daniel Gerard, Timothy Joseph, Amy Marie. BS in Acctg., Walton Sch. Commerce, 1961; postgrad., U. Ill., 1964, MIT, 1967; MBA, U. Chgo., 1969. CPA, Ill. Mgr. Glen Ingram & Co., Chgo., 1961-64; fin. exec. Jewel Co., Melrose Park, Ill., 1964-69; pres. Edward J. Coman & Assocs., Lombard, Ill., 1969—, also chmn. bd. dirs.; pres. Real Estate Mgmt. Co., Lombard, 1981-88, also chmn. bd. dirs.; pres. Bus. Loans Co., Lombard, Ill., 1989—; also chmn. bd. dirs. Bus. Loans Co., Lombard; acct. prof. U. Ill., 1970-73. Author: How To Make Money Doing Tax-Free Exchanges of Real Estate, 1987, How To Make Money Giving Real Estate To Charity, 1987. Bd. dirs. Raintree Homeowner's Assn., Glen Ellyn, Ill., 1987-89. Served with USNG, 1961. Mem. Lombard C. of C. (bd. dirs. 1978-80), Rotary (bd. dirs. 1979-81, pres. 1980). Roman Catholic. Home: 555 Prince Edward Rd Glen Ellyn IL 60137 Office: Edward J Coman and Assoc 1100 S Main St Lombard IL 60148

COMANN, TYLER KENT, investment banker; b. Chgo., Sept. 14, 1950; s. Richard Kent and Marilyn Day (Crosby) C.; m. Cynthia Blees, Dec. 20, 1975 (div. 1981). BA, Stanford U., 1972; MBA, Harvard U., 1978. Sr. assoc. Booz, Allen & Hamilton, San Francisco, 1978-82; dir. Golden West Fin. Corp., Oakland, Calif., 1982-83; v.p. Crocker Nat. Bank, San Francisco, 1983-86; ptnr. Comann, Howard & Flamen, San Francisco, 1986—; instr. sophomore seminar program Stanford U., 1982-85. Lt. USNR, 1972-75. Mem. San Francisco Tennis Club, Olympic Club, Guardsmen of San Francisco. Office: Comann Howard & Flamen 2 Embarcadero Ctr Ste 1780 San Francisco CA 94111

COMBE, IVAN DEBLOIS, drug company executive; b. Fremont, Iowa, Apr. 21, 1911; s. Louis Abel and Elsie (Mange) C.; m. Mary Elizabeth Deming, Dec. 10, 1938; children—Diana M. Combe McDermott, Juliette M. Combe Larson, Christopher Bryan. BS, Northwestern U., 1933, postgrad. Law Sch., 1933-35. Salesman, sales promotion exec. Nat. Dairy Products, Chgo., 1935-36; div. sales mgr. Wilbert Products Co., N.Y.C., 1936-40; merchandising account exec. Young & Rubicam, Inc., N.Y.C., 1940-43; v.p. sales and advt. Pharmacraft Corp. (subs. Seagram Distillers), N.Y.C., 1944-49; pres., founder Combe Inc., White Plains, N.Y., 1949-70; chmn., 1970—. Chmn. Council on Family Health, N.Y.C., 1972-79; bd. dirs. White Plains Hosp. Med. Ctr., 1962—; trustee Northwestern U., 1968—, life trustee, 1979—, life regent. Recipient Alumni Service award Northwestern U., 1962, Merit award, 1971. Mem. U.S. Proprietary Drug Mfrs. Assn. (bd. dirs., exec. com. 1958—, chmn. 1964-66), World Fedn. Proprietary Medicine Mfrs. (bd. dirs., exec. com. 1977—, chmn. 1977-79), Met. Club (N.Y.C.), Blind Brook Club (Purchase, N.Y.), Country Club of Fla. (Delray), Ekwanok Country Club, (Manchester, Vt.), Svc. Club, Rotary, Alpha Delta Phi. Home: 25 Wilshire Rd Greenwich CT 06831

COMBS, AUSTIN OLIN, real estate and insurance broker; b. Harr, Tenn., Aug. 5, 1917; s. Clyde Harmon and Bess (Widner) C.; 1 child by previous marriage, Hope; m. Marjorie Thayer Mason, Dec. 28, 1947; 1 child, Carolyn; adopted children: Dianne, Marjorie, Duncan Dowling III. Student Stetson Bus. Coll. V.p. Kipp & Combs, Inc., 1952-54; ptnr. Combs-Sibley, 1954; pres. Austin O. Combs, Inc., Daytona Beach, Fla., 1954—; airplane pilot. Trustee Volusia County Heart Assn., 1955-56, pres., 1965; trustee, chmn. bd. visitors Embry-Riddle Aero. U.; bd. dirs. YMCA; bd. dirs., pres. Fla. Internat. Festival Com. Served with USAAF, 1944-46, Air Def. Command, Air Res. Adv. Bd., 1946-47. Mem. Flying Realtors, Fla. Aero Club, Aircraft Owners and Pilots Assn., Daytona Beach C. of C., Tomoka Gems and Minerals Soc. (past pres.), Internat. Platform Assn., Quiet Birdmen, UN Assn. U.S., Internat. Order Characters, Silver Wings, Soc. for the Preservation and Enrichment of Barber Shop Quartet Singing in Am. (past judge, bd. dirs. Daytona Beach chpt.). Clubs: Elinor Village Country (past pres., bd. dirs.), Dayton Beach Yacht; Miami Springs Exec.; Oceanside Country, Pelican Bay Country. Lodges: Masons, Shriners, Jesters, Elks, Moose, Rotary (past pres.). Home: 3756 Cardinal Blvd Daytona Beach FL 32019 Office: 2008 S Atlantic Ave Daytona Beach FL 32018

COMBS, CHARLES DONALD, academic administrator; b. Levelland, Tex., Mar. 28, 1952; s. Harold Bloyd and Emma Laura (Cole) C.; m. Pamela Quattlebaum, Mar. 31, 1983. BA with high honors, Tex. Tech U., 1972, MA, 1974; PhD, U. N.C., 1980. Instr. polit. sci. Tex. Tech U., Lubbock, 1973-76, Elton (N.C.) Coll., 1973-76; instr. pub. adminstrn. N.C. Cen. U., Durham, 1976-77; sr. program assoc. Robert Wood Johnson Found., Chapel Hill, N.C., 1977-79; adminstr. Surry (Va.) Family Health Group, 1978-81; program dir. Ea. Va. Med. Sch., Old Dominion U., Norfolk, 1980-85; asst. v.p. adminstrn. and svcs. Med. Coll. Hampton Rds., Norfolk, 1985-87, assoc. v.p. instl. advancement, 1987-88, v.p. instl. advancement, 1988—; cons. numerous health and human svc. orgns., Va., N.C., Tex.; chmn. exec. com. Va. Statewide Health Edn. Adv. Com., 1982-88. Contbr. articles to profl. jours. Grantee City of Durham, 1976, Kresge Found., 1979, Dept. Health and Human Svcs., 1981-85, Champus Mental Health Demonstration Program, 1986—. Mem. Am. Assn. Univ. Adminstrs., Coun. Advancement and Support of Edn., Am. Hosp. Assn., Am. Mgmt. Assn., Am. Pub. Health Assn., Am. Soc. Pub. Adminstrs., Hampton Rds. C. of C. (mem. regional legis. affairs com. 1985—). Democrat. Methodist. Home: Rte 1 Box 167 Earlysville VA 22936 Office: Med Coll Hampton Rds PO Box 1980 Norfolk VA 23501

COMBS, DOUGLAS LEE, management consultant; b. Cin., Dec. 16, 1946; s. Francis G. and Nellie Marie (Lauterwasser) C.; married. B.S. with honors in Advt., U. Fla., 1972; M.B.A., U. Ala., 1979. Dir., Combs & Assocs., Gainesville, Fla., 1971; communications dir. Gainesville C. of C., 1972; dir. public relations Blount Bros. Corp., Montgomery, Ala., 1973-77; dir. promotions So., Living, Decorating & Craft Ideas, Progressive Farmer mags., Birmingham, 1977-82; circulation dir. Omega Group, Ltd., Boulder, Colo., 1982-84; sr. ptnr. William K. Douglas Co., Los Angeles, 1984—. Bd. dirs. United Appeal, 1975—. Served with Intelligence Corps, U.S. Army, 1964-68; Vietnam. Mem. Pub. Relations Soc. Am., Direct Mail Mktg. Assn., Soc. Profl. Journalists, Am. Soc. Personnel Adminstrs., Assn. MBA Execs., Alpha Delta Sigma. Republican. Office: William K Douglas 375 S El Molino Pasadena CA 91101

COMBS, EDDIE CONLEY, business executive; b. Jackson, Ohio, Dec. 21, 1951; s. Eddie Conley and Betty Berniece (Hayes) C.; m. Sabrina Diane King, Dec. 13, 1977; children: Clifford Conley, Rachel Elizabeth. BBA, W. Ga. Coll., 1978. Material scheduler Sewell Mfg., Bremen, Ga., 1974-78; fin. analyst Southwire Co., Carrollton, Ga., 1978-79; inventory/cost acct. Del/Mar subs. Triangle Pacific, Atlanta, 1979-80; gen. mgr. Triangle Pacific, Morristown, Tenn., 1980—. Avocations: farming, golf, swimming. Office: Triangle Pacific 1007 Trade St Morristown TN 37814

COMBS, JANET LOUISE, sales and advertising company executive; b. Houston, Jan. 13, 1959; d. James Lee and Mary Lynn (Woolley) Combs. B.S. in Bus. Adminstrn., U. Ark., 1981. With Exxon Chem. Co., Houston, 1981-82; account exec. Promotional Products Co., Houston, from 1982, asst. v.p., 1982-86, v.p., 1986—. Mem. Houston Young Profl. Reps. Mem. Spring Branch Meml. C. of C., Girls' Cotillion, Mortar Bd., Blue Key, Houston C. of C., Kappa Alpha Theta (Founder's Meml. scholar 1980-81), Beta Gamma Sigma, Alpha Mu Alpha, Omicron Delta Kappa. Republican. Methodist. Home: 12611 Trail Hollow Houston TX 77024 Office: Promotional Products Co 1700 W Belt N Houston TX 77043

COMBS, THOMAS NEAL, lawyer; b. Dallas, Nov. 30, 1942; s. Thomas James and Edith (Gibson) C.; m. Dorothy Elaine Bell, Mar. 12, 1965; children—Thomas Neal, James, John. J.D. with honors, So. Meth. U., 1968. Bar: D.C. 1968, U.S. Supreme Ct. 1975, Mich. 1976. Assoc. Alston, Miller & Gaines, Washington, 1968-70, Marmet & Webster, Washington, 1970-73; from assoc. to ptnr. Webster, Kilcullen & Chamberlain, Washington, 1973-75; v.p., gen. counsel, sec. Fruehauf Corp., Detroit, 1975-85, exec. v.p. fin. and legal, chief fin. officer, sec., 1985-86, pres., chief adminstrv. and fin. officer, 1986-88, vice chmn., chief exec. officer, 1988—, also bd. dirs.; bd. dirs. Fruehauf Corp., Fruehauf Internat. Ltd.; lectr. various tax insts., 1968—. Contbr. articles to profl. publs. Bd. visitors So. Meth. U. Sch. Law. Mem. ABA, Mich. Bar Assn., Bar Assn. D.C., Fin. Exec. Inst., Order of Coif. Clubs: Metropolitan (Washington); Detroit Athletic, Country of Detroit. Home: 169 Stephens Rd Grosse Pointe Farms MI 48236 Office: Fruehauf Corp 10900 Harper Ave Detroit MI 48213

COMBS, WILLIAM G., pharmaceutical company executive; b. Alameda, Calif., Nov. 24, 1930; s. Burton John and Elsie Gertrude (Hammond) C.; m. Norma Louise Fraser, Mar. 17, 1951; children: Steve, Bob, Donald, Kathy. AA, City Coll. San Francisco, 1952. Store mgr. Longs Drug Stores, Walnut Creek, Calif., 1954, office mgr., 1955-61, corp. treas., 1961-76, v.p., treas., 1976-80, v.p. adminstrn., treas., 1980—, also bd. dirs.; bd. dirs. John Muir Med. Ctr., Walnut Creek. Councilman City of Moraga, Calif., 1974-86, vice mayor, 1974, 76, 80, 83, mayor 1975, 79, 85. Named Citizen of Yr. Town of Moraga Contra Costa Sun newspaper, 1984-85. Mem. Calif. Taxpayers Assn. (pres. bd. dirs. 1988—), Calif. Retailers Assn. (bd. dirs. 1988—, exec. com.). Republican. Office: Longs Drug Stores Calif Inc 141 N Civic Dr Walnut Creek CA 94596

COMER, BARBARA ANN, financial planner; b. New Haven, Nov. 19, 1940; d. Clyde Joseph and Alice Elizabeth (Farren) Auger; m. Thomas H. Comer Sr., Feb. 14, 1957; children: Colleen, Thomas Jr., Robert. Grad. high sch., Branford, Conn. Cert. fin. planner; registered fin. planning practicioners. Indsl. salesman Indian Head Lubricants Inc., Branford, 1972-81; fin. planner CIGNA Fin. Services, New Haven, 1981—; bd. dirs. Civitan, New Haven. Mem. Bridgeport (Conn.) Bus. Council, 1987—. Mem. Inst. Cert. Fin. Planners, Internat. Assn. Fin. Planning (pres. 1987-88), Bus. and Profl. Women (rec. sec., pres. local chpt., chmn. task force on women in the workplace, Woman of the Yr., 1987). Roman Catholic. Home: 192 Nortontown Rd Madison CT 06443 Office: Nutmeg Fin Svcs 11 Woodland Rd Madison CT 06443

COMER, CLARENCE C., oil, gas and cement company executive; b. 1948; married. BBA, Lamar U, 1971. Auditor Arthur Andersen & Co., 1971-75; controller Stratford of Tex., Inc., 1975-77; v.p. fin. Southdown Sugars Inc., 1977-79; treas. Southdown Inc., Houston, 1979-80, controller, then v.p., 1980-85, exec. v.p., 1985-86, pres., 1986—, chief operating officer, from 1986, chief exec. officer, 1987—. Office: Southdown Inc 1200 Smith St Ste 2200 Houston TX 77002

COMER, JAMES PIERPONT, psychiatrist; b. East Chicago, Ind., Sept. 25, 1934; s. Hugh and Maggie (Nichols) C.; m. Shirley Ann Arnold, June 20, 1959; children: Brian Jay, Dawn Renee. AB, Ind. U., 1956; MD, Howard U., 1960; MPH, U. Mich., 1964; DSc (hon.), U. New Haven, 1977; LittD (hon.), Calumet Coll., 1978; LHD (hon.), Bank St. Coll., N.Y.C., 1987. Served with USPHS, Washington and Chevy Chase, Md., 1961-68; intern St. Catherine's Hosp., East Chicago, 1960-61; resident Yale Sch. Medicine, 1964-67; asst. prof. psychiatry Yale Child Study Center and dept. psychiatry, 1968-70, assoc. prof., 1970-75, prof., 1975-76, Maurice Falk prof. psychiatry, 1976—; assoc. dean Yale Med. Sch., New Haven, 1969—; dir. pupil services Baldwin-King Sch. Project, New Haven; dir. sch. devel. program Yale Child Study Ctr.; dir. Conn. Energy Corp.; trustee Conn. Savs. Bank; cons. Joint Commn. on Mental Health of Children, Nat. Commn. on Causes and Prevention of Violence, NIMH; mem. nat. adv. mental health council HEW; Henry J. Kaiser Sr. fellow Center for Advanced Study in the Behavioral Scis., Stanford, 1976-77. Author: Beyond Black and White, 1972, Black Child Care, 1975, School Power, 1980, Maggie's American Dream, 1988; Editorial bd.: Am. Jour. Orthopsychiatry, 1970-76, Youth and Adolescence, 1971-87, Jour. Negro Edn.; columnist: Parents mag; Contbr. articles to profl. jours. Bd. dirs. Dixwell Soul Sta. and, Yale Afro-Am. House, Field Found., 1981—, Nat. Council for Effective Schs., 1985—; bd. dirs., profl. adv. bd. Children's TV Workshop; trustee Wesleyan U.; mem. profl. adv. council Nat. Assn. Mental Health; mem. ad hoc adv. com. Conn. Research commn.; adv. council Nat. Com. for Citizens in Edn.; nat. adv. council Hogg Found for Mental Health, 1983-86; adv. com. adolescent pregnancy prevention Children's Def. Fund. Recipient Child Study Assn.-Wel-Met Family Life book award, 1975; Howard U. Disting. Alumni award, 1976; John and Mary Markle Found. scholar, 1969—; Rockefeller Public Service award, 1980; Media award NCCJ, 1981; Community Leadership award Greater New Haven C. of C., 1983; Disting. Fellow award Conn. chpt. Phi Delta Kappa, 1984; Elm and Ivy award New Haven Found., 1985; Disting. Service award Conn. Assn. Psychologists, 1985; Disting. Educator award Conn. Coalition of 100 Black Women, 1985; Whitney M. Young Jr. Svc. award Boy Scouts Am., 1989; Outstanding Leadership award Children's Def. Fund, 1987. Mem. AMA, Nat. Med. Assn., Am. Psychiat. Assn. (Agnes Purcell McGavin award 1985), Am. Orthopsychiat. Assn., Am. Acad. Child Psychiatry, Black Psychiatrists of Am., NAACP, Black Coalition of New Haven, Greater New Haven Black Family Roundtable, Alpha Omega Alpha, Alpha Phi Alpha. Office: Yale Child Study Ctr 230 S Frontage Rd New Haven CT 06510

COMER, RUSSELL WAYNE, banker; b. Scottsburg, Ind., Sept. 10, 1959; s. Robert Gene and Ruth Ann (Bartle) C.; m. Bonnie Turner, Aug. 6, 1988. BS, Purdue U., 1982. Substitute tchr. Scott County Sch. Dist. 2, Scottsburg, 1980-82; asst. v.p. Scott County State Bank, Scottsburg, 1982—; ptnr. 4-R Comer Farms, Scottsburg, 1981—. Leader 4-H Club, Scottsburg, 1982-87; bd. edn. Bethel Baptist Ch., 1987—, trustee, 1983-86. Named one of Outstanding Young Men of Am., Jaycees, 1986. Mem. Ind. Young Bankers Assn., (bd. dirs. Indpls. chpt., 1987—), Scottsburg C. of C. (bd. dirs. 1984—, treas. 1987—), Purdue Alumni (pres. 1985—). Democrat. Lodge: Masons. Office: Scott County State Bank 125 W McClain Ave Scottsburg IN 47170

COMER, WAYNE ARTHUR, real estate investment executive; b. Somers Point, N.J., Feb. 14, 1953; s. Willard Arthur and Mary Dorothy (Schroeder) C.; m. Michele Susan Mandel, Oct. 2, 1983. AB, Princeton U., 1973; MSc, London Sch. Econs., 1975; MBA, U. Pa., 1983. Mgmt. cons. Strategy Research Assocs., Ltd., London, 1979-81, The Mac Group, Cambridge, Mass., 1983-84; dir. research Mellon Real Estate Investment Mgmt., Inc., N.Y.C., 1984-85, investment mgr., 1985-87; v.p., sr. investment officer J.P. Morgan Investment Mgmt., Inc., N.Y.C., 1987—. bd. dirs. Cranbury Landmarks, Inc., N.J., 1985—. Mem. Urban Land Inst., Pension Real Estate Assn., N.Y. Real Estate Bd., Young Mortgage Bankers Assn. Democrat. Club: Princeton (N.Y.C.). Office: JP Morgan Investment Mgmt 522 Fifth Ave New York NY 10036

COMEY, J. MARTIN, pharmaceutical company executive; b. N.Y.C., Feb. 7, 1934; s. John J. and Anna May (McCann) C.; m. Margaret A. Doyle, Jan. 17, 1957; children—Rita, James, Peter, Deirdre, Louise, Anne, Christopher,

Margaret. B.S. in Acctg., Fordham U., 1957; M.B.A. in Corp. Fin, NYU, 1965. Auditor Eckes & Dean, C.P.A.s, N.Y.C., 1957-60; tax acct. Sperry Rand Corp., N.Y.C., 1960-62; tax mgr. Pet, Inc., St. Louis, 1962-66; tax dir. Schering-Plough Corp., Kenilworth, N.J., 1966-75; treas. Schering-Plough Corp., 1976—, v.p., 1979—; mem. bd. mgrs. Provident Savs. Bank, Jersey City. Trustee Coll. of St. Elizabeth, Convent Station, N.J. Mem. Am. Inst. C.P.A.s, N.J., N.Y. socs. C.P.A.s, Fin. Execs. Inst. Office: Schering-Plough Corp 1 Giralda Farms Madison NJ 07940

COMFORT, TED PAUL, savings and loan association executive; b. N.Y.C., Oct. 5, 1950; s. Albert and Claire (Jaeger) C.; m. Maria Gonzalez, Feb. 13, 1988. AB, Harvard U., 1972; MBA, Fla. Atlantic U., 1975; grad., Mortgage Bankers Am. Sch., 1975, Northwestern Sch. Mortgage Banking, 1976. Loan officer, asst. br. mgr. Fin. Fed. Savs., Miami Beach, Fla., 1972-77; asst. v.p. Am. Savs. Mortgage Corp., Del Ray Beach, Fla., 1977-79; regional v.p. Am. So. Mortgage Corp., Houston, 1979-81; regional v.p. Gibraltar Savs., Houston, 1981-83, Dallas, 1983-84; sr. v.p. real estate devel. Nev. Savs. & Loan Assn., Las Vegas, 1984-85, sr. exec. v.p., chief landing officer, 1985-89; sr. exec. v.p., chief landing officer PriMerit Bank, Fed. Savs Bank (formerly Nev. Savs. & Loan Assn.), Las Vegas, 1989—; chmn. Western States Real Estate Cons., Inc., Las Vegas, 1987-88. Mem. Nev. Devel. Authority, 1987, 88; mem. memberhsip com. Nev. Dance Theatre, Las Vegas, 1987, United Way So. Nev., Las Vegas, 1988—. Mem. Mortgage Bankers Am., So. Nev. Homebuilders Assn., Prospectors (C. of C.) (membership com. 1987-88). Jewish. Office: Nev Savs & Loan Assn 3300 W Sahara Ave Las Vegas NV 89102

COMMACK, WILLIAM EARL, insurance company executive; b. St. Louis, Mar. 24, 1929; s. Earl Wilfred Commack and Leona (Voigt) Messerla; m. Marietta Bartlett (dec. 1967); children: Kim Michelle, Cathy Lane; m. Alice Marie Briedenbach, Sept. 13, 1975. BS and BS in Edn., N.E. Mo. State U., 1952. Salesman Liberty Mut. Ins. Co., St. Louis, 1954-56, dist. sales mgr., 1956-62; dist. mgr. Liberty Mut. Ins. Co., Kansas City, Mo., 1962-69, St. Louis, 1969-76; div. sales mgr. Liberty Mut. Ins. Co., Dallas, 1976-81, asst. v.p., asst. div. mgr., 1981-83, v.p., div. mgr., 1983-85; exec. v.p. Liberty Mut. Ins. Co., Boston, 1985—; bd. dirs. Liberty Ins. Corp., Delaware, 1985, Liberty Northwest, Portland, Oreg., 1987; pres. Helmsman Ltd., Boston, 1987. Cpl. USMC, 1946-48. Mem. Weston (Mass.) Country Club. Office: Liberty Mut Ins Co 175 Berkeley St Boston MA 02117

COMMES, THOMAS A., manufacturing company executive; b. 1942; married. BA, Coll. of St. Thomas, 1964. With Gould Inc., 1968-75; controller, treas., v.p., chief fin. officer W.T. Grant Co., 1975-76; v.p., controller Saks Fifth Ave., 1976-79; chief fin. officer, sr. v.p. Sherwin-Williams Co., 1979-86, pres., chief operating officer, 1986—, also bd. dirs.; bd. dirs. Society Nat. Bank, Centerior Energy Corp. Office: Sherwin-Williams Co 101 Prospect Ave NW Cleveland OH 44115 *

COMMINS, ERNEST ALTMAN (ERNIE), certified financial planner; b. Charleston, S.C., Feb. 13, 1946; s. John Commins and Marie Edna (Crosby) Jenkins; m. Nancy Palmer Redd, May 11, 1968; children: Scott Palmer, Ashley Redd. BS in Indsl. Mgmt., Clemson U., 1968; MBA, Wichita State U., 1972. Cert. fin. planner, Colo.; registered stock broker. Broker Mick, Stack & Smartt Investors, Wichita, Kans., 1971-72; div. mgr. Ortho Pharm. Corp., Raritan, N.J., 1972-82; dist. mgr., fin. planner IDS/Am. Express, Mpls., 1982-87; fin. planner Ctr. for Fin. Planning, Inc., Pensacola, Fla., 1987-88; registered investment advisor Money Profls. Group, Inc., Pensacola, 1988—; bd. dirs. Cordova Sq. Owners Assn., Pensacola. Coach YMCA, Pensacola, 1984-87, Youth Basketball League, Pensacola, 1987—, Men's Softball League, Pensacola, 1983—; vol. U. West Fla. Found. Fund Drive, Pensacola, 1983-84. Capt. USAF, 1968-72. Mem. Internat. Bd. Cert. Fin Planners, Internat. Assn. Fin. Planners, Pension Profls. NW. Fla. (pres. 1987-88), Pensacola C. of C., Gulf Coast Econ. Club. Republican. Presbyterian. Office: Money Professionals Group Inc 4400 Bayou Blvd Ste 32 Pensacola FL 32503

COMO, VITA PALMA, oil company executive; b. N.Y.C., Apr. 18, 1947; d. Anthony and Palma Blanche (Yannolo) C. BA, CUNY, 1968; MBA, Columbia U., 1972; postgrad., U. Houston, 1988. Legal adminstr. Foreman and Dyess, Houston, 1976-81; oil co. exec. Ptnrs. Oil Co., Houston, 1981-82; corp. sec. Oxoco Inc., Houston, 1982—, Am. Nat. Petroleum, Houston, 1986—. Bd. dirs. Bus. Vols. for Arts, Houston, 1980—, Severals Dancers Corp., Houston, Atlanta, 1986—, Ctr. Attitudinal Healing, Houston, 1987—. Mem. State Bar of Tex., Invester Relations Inst., Houston Legal Asst. Assn. Office: Am Nat Petroleum Co 1717 St James Pl Ste 200 Houston TX 70056

COMOTTO, ROBERT PAUL, entrepreneur; b. Queens, N.Y., Dec. 16, 1948; s. Robert and Mary Elizabeth (Repak) C.; m. Dorothy Adele Romano, July 22, 1984; 1 stepchild, Andrew J. Haase Jr. Diploma, Acad. Aeronautics, Queens, 1970. V.p. Town and Country Cycle Inc., White Plains, N.Y., 1971-74; adminstr. New Era Designs, Armonk, N.Y., 1975-76; mgr. Kalajian Pontiac, Mt. Kisco, N.Y., 1976-77, Crestwood RV Ctr., Tuckahoe, N.Y., 1977-80, Nassau Campers, Bethpage, N.Y., 1980-82; lead salesman Am. Specialty, Hauppauge, N.Y., 1982—; v.p. B.A.D. Enterprises Inc., Lake Ronkonkoma, N.Y., 1988—; sr. cons. Wheel Estate Cons., Lake Ronkonkoma, 1987—. Contbg. editor, columnist Leisure Traveler News, 1980-82. Active Lake Ronkonkoma Hist. Soc., 1988-88; coord. ann. event Lighthouse, White Plains, 1973; instr. St. Elizabeth Ann Seton, Lake Ronkonkoma, 1988-89. Recipient Leadership award Quality Circles, Hauppauge, 1985. Mem. Automotive Hall of Fame. Roman Catholic. Home: 10 Hill St Lake Ronkonkoma NY 11779 Office: Motormedia 2145 Rte 112 Medford NY 11763

COMPTON, RONALD E., insurance and financial services executive; b. 1933; married. B.S., Northwestern U., 1954. With Aetna Life & Casualty Co., 1954—; sr. v.p. Am. Re-Ins. Co., N.Y.C., 1980-81, exec. v.p., 1981-83; pres., dir. Am. Re-Ins. Co. unit Aetna Life and Casualty Co., N.Y.C., from 1983; corp. sr. v.p. Aetna Life and Casualty Co., 1987-88, exec. v.p., 1988—, now pres., chief operating officer; sr. v.p., exec. asst. to chmn. Aetna Life Ins. Co., 1986-87, exec. v.p., 1987; with Aetna Casualty and Surety Co., 1954-80, 1987—, sr. v.p., 1987-88, exec. v.p., office of chmn., 1988—. Office: Aetna Life & Casualty Co Corp Hdqrs 151 Farmington Ave Hartford CT 06156 *

COMPTON, WALTER A., manufacturing company executive. BS, Princeton U., 1933; MD, Harvard U., 1937. With Miles, Inc., Elkhart, Ind., 1938—, v.p. research med. div., 1946-61, exec. v.p., 1961-64, chief exec. officer, 1964-81, pres., 1964-73, chmn. bd. dirs., 1973-81, hon. chmn. bd. dirs., 1981—. Served to lt. col. AUS, 1942-46. Office: Miles Inc 1127 Myrtle St Elkhart IN 46517

COMPTON, WILLIAM THOMAS, computer consulting firm owner; b. Bedford, Ind., Dec. 1, 1945; s. Thomas Franklin and Dorothy Jane (Smith) C.; m. Nancy Marie Radocchia, Sept. 13, 1969; children: Kimberly Dawn, Lindsay Ann. BS in Mgmt., MIT, 1968, Postgrad., 1968-70. Cert. data. processing. Sr. systems analyst First Nat. Bank Boston, 1970-73; systems analyst Gen. Computer Systems, Wellesley, Mass., 1973-76; bus. systems analyst Fram Corp., East Providence, R.I., 1976-78; v.p. Span Mgmt. Systems, East Providence, 1978; project leader Prime Computer Inc., Natick, Mass., 1979-81; owner Computer Software Solutions, Tiverton, R.I., 1981—; prodn. foreman Trillotson Rubber Co., Inc., Fall River, Mass., 1988—. Author several computer software programs, 1982-85. Loaned officer United Fund Boston, 1970. Mem. Data Processing Mgmt. Assn. (cert. data processing instr. 1985-86). Republican. Methodist. Lodge: Kiwanis (local v.p. 1985, pres. 1985-86). Home and Office: Compton Software Solutions 23 Jennifer Ln Tiverton RI 02878

COMSTOCK, ROLLIE WALTER, utility executive, lawyer; b. Mankato, Minn., May 14, 1930; s. Walter T. and Vera E. (McCarron) C.; m. Margaret J. Oswald, Aug. 21, 1952 (div. Sept. 1975); children: Brett, Dana; m. M. Jane Cooper, June 25, 1977. BS, Mankato State U., 1956; JD, U. Minn., 1957. Bar: Minn.1957. Sole practice, Mpls., 1957-58; atty. No. States Power Co., Mpls., 1958-65, asst. to pres., 1966, dir. pub. relations planning, 1967-68, dir. environ. affairs, 1969-71, dir. communications, 1972-74, v.p. communications, 1974-77, v.p. pub. affairs, 1978-83; sr. v.p. Ruhr/Paragon Inc., Mpls., 1984-86; sr. v.p. corp. affairs United Illuminating, New Haven, 1986—. Author: The Future of Housing in Minnesota, 1975; co-author: Energy Crisis or Opportunity, 1976, The Public Affairs Handbook, 1980. Bd. dirs. Stress Resource Inst., Mpls., Schubert Theater, New Haven. Mem. Pub. Relations Soc. Am., Edison Electric Inst. (exec. adv. coum.), New Eng. Power Pool (pub. info. com.). Lutheran. Home: 42 Oak Ridge Dr Bethany CT 06525 Office: United Illuminating Co 80 Temple St New Haven CT 06506

CONABLE, BARBER B., JR., international agency administrator; b. Warsaw, N.Y., Nov. 2, 1922; s. Barber B. and Agnes G. (Gouinlock) C.; m. Charlotte Williams, Sept. 13, 1952; 4 children. AB, Cornell U., 1942, LLB, 1948. Bar: N.Y. 1948. Sole practice Buffalo, 1948-50, Batavia, N.Y., 1952-64; U.S. senator from N.Y. 1963-64; mem. 89th-98th congresses from 30th N.Y. dist., 1965-85, Pres. Reagan's Commn. on Defense Mgmt., from 1985; prof. U. Rochester, N.Y., 1985-86; pres. Internat. Bank for Reconstrn. and Devel. (World Bank), Washington, 1986—; sr. fellow, Am. Enterprise Inst., 1985. Editor: Cornell U. Law Quar., 1947-48. Mem. sr. adv. com. Kennedy Inst. Politics; trustee U.S. Capitol Hist. Soc., Mus. Am. Indian. Served with USMCR, 1942-46, 50-51. Republican. Lodge: Rotary (pres. Batavia chpt.). Office: Internat Bank for Reconstrn & Devel 1818 H St NW Washington DC 20433 *

CONANT, HERBERT D., construction executive; b. 1924; married. BSME, Steven's Inst. Tech., 1950. V.p. Turner Constrn. Co., 1965-68, sr. v.p., 1968-79, exec. v.p., 1979-84, pres., 1984-85, chmn., pres., dir., 1985—; chief exec. officer Turner Corp., 1984—, also chmn. bd. Office: Turner Corp 633 3rd Ave New York NY 10017 *

CONANT, JEFFREY SCOTT, marketing educator; b. Buffalo, Apr. 5, 1955; s. Howard Somers Conant; m. Carol Susan Conant; 1 child, Danielle Christine. BA in Polit. Sci., NYU, 1977; MBA, U. Ariz., 1979; PhD in Mktg., Ariz. State U., 1986. Fin. analyst Ford Aerospace and Communications Corp., Newport Beach, Calif., 1979-80; grad. programs advisor U. Ariz., Tucson, 1980-81; asst. prof. mktg. Tex. A&M U., College Station, 1986—. Ad hoc mem. editorial rev. bd. Jour. Health Care Mktg., 1988—; contbr. articles to profl. jours. Mem. Am. Mktg. Assn., Western Mktg. Educators Assn., Acad. Mktg. Sci., Am. Acad. Mgmt., Alpha Mu Alpha. Home: 4706 Huntington Dr Bryan TX 77802-5901 Office: Tex A&M U Dept Mktg College Station TX 77843-4112

CONARY, DAVID ARLAN, investment company executive; b. South Paris, Maine, Mar. 3, 1937; s. Wilfred Grindle and Arline (Whitney) C.; m. Frances Jane Harrison, June 8, 1957; children: Lee Harrison, Neil Whitney. AB, Bowdoin Coll., 1959; postgrad. Northeastern U., 1965-66, Mass. Inst. Tech., 1966-67; Boston U., 1967. Securities trader H.C. Wainwright & Co., Boston, 1959-60; securities trader May & Gannon, Boston, 1960-65, v.p., 1968-71; securities analyst, adminstr. The Boston Co., Boston, 1965-68; mgr. instl. trading Fahnestock & Co., Boston, 1971-72; resident mgr. G.A. Saxton & Co., Boston, 1972-75; instl. trader Baker, Weeks & Co., N.Y.C., 1975; equities trader State St. Research & Mgmt. Co., Boston, 1976-87; v.p. Howard, Weil, Inc., 1987-88; sr. v.p. Boettcher & Co., Inc., Denver, 1989—; dir. Astra Corp., Security 1 Specialists, Inc.; pres., chmn. Granite Solid State, Inc., Conifer Holding Corp., Inc.; lectr. in field. Dist. dir. Mass. Bay United Fund, 1966. Mem. Nat. Security Traders Assn., Boston Securities Traders Assn. (gov. 1972-73, 81-82), Boston Investment Club (pres. 1985-89), Bowdoin Club of Boston (dir. 1965-66, dir. 175th anniversary campaign 1973-74), Mensa, Theta Delta Chi. Club: Weymouth Sportsmen's (sec. 1965-66, 71-72). Republican. Home: 79 Atlantic Ave North Hampton NH 03862 Office: Boettcher & Co Inc 828 17th St Denver CO 80201

CONCEVITCH, BILL BYRON, retail executive, training specialist; b. N.Y.C., Jan. 29, 1958; s. John Edwin and Mary Catherine (Kuehl) C.; m. Sharon Patricia Kurtz, July 29, 1979; 1 child, Heather Lynne. Student, Allentown Coll. St. Francis de Sales, 1988. Cert. audio engr. Dir. human rels., pub. Wall to Wall Sound and Video, Inc., Phila., 1977-87; corp. tng. specialist Dale Carnegie Tng., 1987-88; dir. franchise sales and tng. Megavideo, Inc., Easton, Pa., 1988—. Editor, pub. (newsletter) Outstanding Performance. Home: 1727 Elm St Bethlehem PA 18017 Office: Megavideo Inc 25th & Butler Sts Easton PA 18042

CONDELLO, RUSSELL ANTHONY, accountant, information systems company official; b. Buffalo, Nov. 26, 1958; s. Dominick and Marilyn T. (Martin) C.; m. Carol Louise Gatti, Mar. 25, 1958. Cert. in Bank Mgmt., Am. Inst. Banking, 1980; BS in Acctg., St. John Fisher Coll., 1980; MBA, Tex. Christian U., 1986. CPA, Tex. Acctg. clk. Lincoln 1st Bank, Rochester, N.Y., 1976-80; acct. D.J. Andrews, Inc., Rochester, 1980-81, supr. acctg., 1982; assoc. systems engr. data systems div Gen. Dynamics Co., Ft. Worth, 1982; software engr. Data Systems div. Gen. Dynamics Co., Ft. Worth, 1983, sr. fin. analyst, 1984-85, adminstrv., fin. specialist, 1985-88; contract proposal estimator Ft. Worth div. Gen. Dynamics Co., 1989—; instr. Am. Inst. Banking, 1988. Mem. Nat. Assn. Accts., Am. Inst. Cert. Pub. Accountants. Republican. Roman Catholic. Home: 5012 Bridgewater Dr Arlington TX 76017 Office: Gen Dynamics Co Ft Worth Div General Dynamics Blvd PO Box 748 Fort Worth TX 76108

CONDICT, EDGAR RHODES, medical electronics, aviation instrument manufacturing executive, medical health care executive, inventor; b. Boston, Apr. 27, 1940; s. Clinton Adams and Elizabeth May (Lane) C.; m. Judith Pond, June 9, 1962; children: Edgar Rhodes, Robert Adams, Carolyn Helen. BS, Bucknell U., 1962. Chmn. bd., pres. Bio-Tronics Research, Inc., 1962—, Kearsarge Healthcare, Inc., 1978—, Kearsarge Rehab. Hosp., Inc., Condict Instruments, Inc., 1985—; pres. Medel Corp., patent devel. investment, 1965—; cons. U. Tex. Med. Sch., 1968-70; cons. in med. electronics, electronics, biophysics, biofeedback, telecommunications, environ. health and welfare. Chmn., Mantowa dist., exec. bd. Daniel Webster council Boy Scouts Am., 1979-84. Recipient various grants in neuro-brain scis.; numerous med. awards from fgn. countries. Mem. Sigma Chi. Baptist. Author: A Theory of Anesthesia, Feedback Anesthesia, Electronic Pain-Killing Devices, others. Patentee in med. electronics, telecommunications fields. Address: Rural Rt 2 Box 475 Main St New London NH 03257

CONDIT, LINDA FAULKNER, economist; b. Denver, May 30, 1947; d. Claude Winston and Nancy Isabelle (McCallum) Faulkner; BA, U. Ark., 1969; MA, U. Wis., 1970; postgrad. U. Minn., 1974-77; m. John Michael Condit, Dec. 20, 1970; 1 child, David Devin. Economist, St. Louis Fed. Res. Bank, 1971-73; ops. analyst No. States Power Co., Mpls., 1973-76; energy economist, 1976-78; economist Pennzoil Co., Houston, 1978-79, sr. economist, 1979-81, mgr. econ. research dept., 1981-84, dir. corp. planning and econs. dept., 1984-86; dir. treasury ops., 1986—; research asst. U. Wis., 1969-70; econ. cons. Jr. Achievement, 1983. Recipient Alumni award U. Ark., 1969. Mem. Internat. Assn. Energy Economists (pres., v.p., treas.), Nat. Assn. Bus. Economists, Internat. Bus. Council (v.p.), Am. Econ. Assn., N. Am. Soc. Corp. Planners, Harvard Discussion Group Indsl. Economists, Phi Beta Kappa, Mortar Bd., Kappa Alpha Theta. Republican. Unitarian. Clubs: Forest, River Oaks Women's Breakfast (v.p., pres.), Toastmasters. Home: 10115 Inwood Dr Houston TX 77042 Office: Pennzoil Co PO Box 2967 Houston TX 77001

CONDON, BREEN O'MALLEY, lawyer; b. Boston, Mar. 24, 1944; s. William Jospeh and Dorothy (Murphy) C.; m. Bernadette Fogel, Dec. 18, 1972 (div.). A.B., Georgetown U., 1966; J.D., Fordham U., 1971. Assoc. White & Case, N.Y.C., 1971-80; v.p. and gen. counsel Hardee's Food Systems, Inc., Rocky Mount, N.C., 1980-82; sr. v.p., gen. counsel, sec. Imasco USA, Inc./Hardee's, Rocky Mount, 1982—. Editor: Fordham Law Rev., 1969-71. Served to 1st lt. USAR, 1966-68. Mem. ABA. Roman Catholic. Clubs: N.Y. Athletic; Benvenue Country (Rocky Mount). Office: Hardee's Food System Inc 1233 Hardee's Blvd Rocky Mount NC 27804

CONDON, DONALD STEPHEN, real estate investor and developer, broker, consultant; b. Bklyn., Dec. 26, 1930; s. Joseph Francis and Helen (Carboy) C.; m. Cristina Maria Basarrate, Sept. 27, 1969; children: Gregg, Mark, Brian, Alexander, Kevin. Student Oberlin Coll., 1949-50; BA, Northwestern U., 1953; postgrad. U. Detroit, 1956. Mem. sales and mktg. dept. Owens-Corning Fiberglas, 1955-63; v.p., gen. mgr. Howard T. Keating Co., Birmingham, Mich., 1963-65; chief exec. officer Condon Investment & Devel. Corp., Bloomfield Hills, Mich., 1965-69; pres. Condyne, Inc., N.Y.C., 1969-74; chmn., dir. Parr, O'Mara, Condon & Assocs., Inc., N.Y.C. and Palm Beach, Fla., 1974-81; pres., chief exec. officer The Condon Corp., Palm Beach, Fla., 1981—; lectr. Practising Law Inst., 1970-71. Served with Signal Corps, U.S. Army, 1953-55. Contbr. articles to House and Home, Profl. Builder mag., Bus. week, Instn. Investor, others. Recipient Sales Builder award Owens-Corning Fiberglas, 1959, Am. Home Builders award for design, 1964, Practical Builders Top Merchandising award, 1966, Mktg. Mgr. of Yr. award Nat. Assn. Home Builders, 1967, Product of Year award Mich. C. of C., 1968, Assn. Indsl. Mgmt. award, 1972; Oberlin Coll. scholar, 1949-50, Northwestern U. scholar, 1953. Mem. Internat. Platform Assn., Phi Gamma Delta. Clubs: N.Y. Athletic; Birmingham Athletic; The Beach (Palm Beach). Home: 255 Bahama Ln Palm Beach FL 33480 Office: The Condon Corp 204 Brazilian Ave Palm Beach FL 33480

CONDON, VERNER HOLMES, JR., retired utility executive; b. Bloomington, Ill., June 26, 1926; s. Verner Holmes and Lucille (Dennis) C.; m. Ann Garman, Sept. 3, 1949; children—Martha, Nancy. B.S., Pa. State U., 1948; M.B.A., Northwestern U., 1949. Securities analyst Harris Trust & Savs. Bank, Chgo., 1949-51; with Ford Motor Co., 1951-68, controller tractor div., 1961-62, marketing mgr., 1962-68; sr. v.p., chief fin. officer AMBAC Industries, Inc., Garden City, N.Y., 1968-78; exec. v.p., chief fin. officer Gen. Public Utilities Corp., Parsippany, N.J., 1979-87; fin. com. Edison Electric Inst., Washington, 1978-87. V.p. Harding (N.J.) Civic Assn. Served with USNR, 1944-46. Mem. Fin. Execs. Inst. Republican. Episcopalian. Club: Bright Creek Park. (bd. dirs.). Home: Box 116 Young's Rd Basking Ridge NJ 07920

CONDOS, JAMES ALEXANDER, mortgage banker; b. San Antonio, Nov. 19, 1959. BA, U. Tex., 1981; MBA, U. Chgo., 1984. Lic. real estate broker, Tex., Ill. Devel. exec. Condos and Rhame, San Antonio, 1982; pres. Solitaire Corp., San Antonio, 1982—, also bd. dirs.; sr. real estate investment officer Lomas Fin. Corp., Chgo., 1984-88; pres. Alexander Condos Real Estate, San Antonio, 1989—. Mem. Chgo. Real Estate Council, Internat. Council Shopping Ctrs.

CONE, EDWARD CHRISTOPHER, newspaper publisher; b. Montclair, N.J., Mar. 29, 1937; s. Edward della Torre and Patricia Clapp (Laurence) C.; married; children: David Christopher, Jennifer Lynn. BA, Princeton U., 1958. Missionary Holy Cross Mission, Bolahun, Liberia, 1958-63, commissary, 1984—; asst. to editor West Essex County Tribune, Livingston, N.J., 1963-68, mng. editor, 1968-80, pub., 1980—; cons. Vols. in Tech. Assistance, Washington, 1964—, Assn. Episc. Colls., 1985—. Author: Automotive Operation and Maintenance, 1973. Trustee North Essex United Way, Montclair, N.J., 1982—, Livingston Symphony Orch., 1978—; sole sponsor Korea-Vietnam Veterans Meml., Livingston, 1987; sponsor Occupational Ctr. Sheltered Workshop, Livingston, 1981; tech. mgr. Studio Players Theater, Montclair, 1963-68. Mem. N.J. Press Assn. (editorial com. 1968—, bd. dirs. 1988—), Nat. Newspaper Assn., Livingston C. of C. (bd. dirs. 1981—). Republican. Episcopalian. Office: West Essex Tribune 495 S Livingston Ave PO Box 65 Livingston NJ 07039

CONEYRS, SUE ANN, small business owner; b. Detroit, Dec. 4, 1942; d. Albert P. and Zella B. (Stevens) Latendresse; m. Dudley Matson Coneyrs, Oct. 7, 1963; children: Christine Anne, Robert Matson. BS, Mich. State U., 1964. Field staff dir. YWCA, Lansing, Mich., 1964-65; asst. office mgr. UAW Union, Lansing, Mich., 1965-66; exec. sec. Miami Beach (Fla.) First Nat. Bank, 1970-71; sales mgr. Sunburst Farms Inc., Miami, 1971-75; pres., chief exec. officer Southern Rainbow Corp., Miami, 1975-79, World Flowers Inc., Miami, 1979—. Mem. Nat. Assn. Women Bus. Owners, Miami Importers Credit Assn. (pres. 1985-87), Assn. of Floral Importers (bd. dirs. 1981—), Alliance of Floral Importers (pres. 1986-88). Roman Catholic. Office: World Flowers Inc 9450 NW 12 St Miami FL 33172

CONGER, HARRY MILTON, mining company executive; b. Seattle, July 22, 1930; s. Harry Milton, Jr. and Caroline (Gunnell) C.; m. Phyllis Nadine Shepherd, Aug. 14, 1949; children: Harry Milton IV, Preston George. E.M., Colo. Sch. Mines, 1955; hon. degrees, S.D. Sch. Mines, Colo. Sch. Mines. Registered profl. engr., Ariz., Colo. Shift foreman Asarco, Inc., Silver Bell, Ariz., 1955-64; mgr. Kaiser Steel Corp. Eagle Mountain Mine, 1964-70; v.p., gen. mgr. Kaiser Resources, Ltd., Fernie, B.C., Can., 1970-73, Consolidation Coal Co. (Midwestern div.), Carbondale, Ill., 1973-75; v.p. Homestake Mining Co., San Francisco, 1975-77; pres. Homestake Mining Co., 1977-78, pres., chief exec. officer, 1978-82, chmn., pres., chief exec. officer, 1982-86, chmn., chief exec. officer, 1986—; also bd dirs.; bd. dir. CalMat, Inc., ASA Ltd., Pacific Gas & Electric Co., Baker Hughes Inc., Am. Mining Congress, chmn. 1986; chmn. Am. Mining Congress., 1986-89. Bd. dirs. Bay Area Council; trustee Calif. Inst. Tech. Served with C.E. U.S. Army, 1956. Recipient Disting. Achievement medal Colo. Sch. Mines, 1978. Mem. Am. Inst. Mining Engrs. (distinguished), Mining and Metallurgy Soc. Am., Mining Club; sr. mem. Conf. Bd. Republican. Episcopalian. Clubs: Bohemian, Commonwealth, Pacific Union, Bankers, World Trade, Diablo Country. Office: Homestake Mining Co 650 California St San Francisco CA 94108

CONKLIN, RICHARD ALLAN, management consultant; b. Syracuse, N.Y., Dec. 16, 1939; s. George William and Beatrice Anne (Weeks) Conklin. BA, Pacific Coll., Fresno, Calif., 1964; postgrad., Cornell/Hofstra U., 1978-80. Asst. mgr. Weinstein Holding Corp., Commack, N.Y., 1967-73; ops. mgr. Allan Tire Ctrs., Selden, N.Y., 1973-77; zone mgr. Vogue Tire Co., Bayside, N.Y., 1977-81; personnel mgr. United Cerebal Palsy Assn., Roosevelt, N.Y., 1981-86; assoc. ptnr. R.J. Carroll Co., Springfield, Pa., 1986-88; dir. human resources Daughters of Jacob Geriatric Ctr., Bronx, N.Y., 1988—; adj. prof. Cornell U.; instr. U. Pa., Hofstra U., N.Y. Inst. Tech.; cons. N.Y. State Senator Levy, Albany, 1980-86; Nassau County Bd. Cooperative Edn. Service, Westbury, N.Y., 1982-85; Inst. Internat. Med. Edn., N.Y.C., 1982-84; Goodwill Industries, L.I. City, N.Y., 1986—. Recipient Pres. Sports award, 1979; Repub. Pres. Task Force Medal of Merit, 1984. Mem. Research Inst. Am., Soc. Personnel Adminstrn., Am. Personnel Guidance Assn., Alpha Psi Omega (bd. dirs. 1976—). Roman Catholic. Home: 32 Barnum Ave Plainview NY 11803

CONLEY, ELTON BOHANNAN, manufacturing company executive; b. South Norwalk, Conn., Apr. 29, 1907; s. Walter Frederick and Leila Frances (Pitzer) C.; m. Norma Neal, Dec. 7, 1947 (div. 1960); children: Elton Bohannan Jr., Jane, Donald, Dawn; m. Dorothy Gertrude Lonsdale, Oct. 28, 1976. BS in Indsl. Engring., U. Bridgeport, 1954; MS in Mech. Engring., Hamilton State U., 1956. Asst. to pres. Electric Splty. Co., Stamford, Conn., 1947-50; v.p., gen. mgr. Allied Internat. Corp., N.Y.C., 1950-54; ea. mgr. Electra Motors Inc., Anaheim, Calif., 1954-58; dist. mgr. Janette Elec. Co., Skokie, Ill., 1958-60; asst. v.p. sales Richardson-Allen Corp., College Point, N.Y., 1960-65; sales mgr. William P. Little Inc., Fairfield, Conn., 1965-71; owner, prin. Packaged Power Co., Darien, Conn., 1971-74; pres. E.B. Conley Assocs., Inc., Port Richey, Fla., 1975—, also chmn. bd. dirs. Vol. Salvation Army, Port Richey. Mem. Instrument Soc. Am. (sr.), Moose, Elks. Republican. Episcopalian. Home: 9025 Shallow Ford Ln Port Richey FL 34688 Office: EB Conley Assocs Inc PO Box 264 Port Richey FL 34673

CONLEY, GLEN TAYLOR, corporation executive; b. Wanette, Okla., Dec. 28, 1923; s. Taylor and Pearl (Waddle) C.; m. Hazel Carla Sandrini, Oct. 3, 1956; 1 son, Kelly Ugo. Student, Bakersfield Jr. Coll., (Calif.). Foreman Bechtel Corp., San Francisco, 1952-53; supt. Fluor Corp., Los Angeles, 1953-56; v.p. Paul Hardeman, Inc., Los Angeles, 1956-64; pres. Conley Contractors, Montebello, Calif., 1964-66; pres. Fischbach & Moore, Internat., Dallas, 1966-80, chmn. bd., 1981—; chmn. bd. Fischbach & Moore, Inc., Dallas, 1986—. Served to tech. sgt. U.S. Army, 1943-46, Japan. Decorated Presdl. Citation Combat Infantryman's Badge with 6 gold stars. Roman Catholic. Lodges: Beavers, Elks. Office: Fischbach & Moore Inc 11030 Ables Ln Dallas TX 75229 *

CONLEY, JAMES PATRICK, accountant; b. Boston, Oct. 26, 1938; s. James and Eleanor Dorothy (Lewis) C.; m. Christine Zanone, July 14, 1973; 1 child, Peter J. BSBA, Northeastern U., 1961. CPA, Mass. Sr. mgr. Ernst & Whinney, Boston, 1968-72, ptnr., 1972-86; ptnr. Ernst & Whinney, Cleve., 1986—. Bd. dirs. Morgan Meml. Goodwill Industries, Boston, 1979-85.

Mem. Nat. Assn. Accts. (bd. dirs. 1980-82, pres. Boston chpt. 1979-80), Am. Inst. CPA's, Mass. Soc. CPA's. Home: 15900 S Woodland Rd Shaker Heights OH 44120 Office: Ernst & Whinney 1300 Huntington Bldg Cleveland OH 44115

CONLEY, JOHN MICHAEL, business consultant; b. Denver, Oct. 1, 1953; s. Elry Jackson and Edna Odell (Martin) C. BS in Bus., U. Colo., 1982; BS in Computer Sci., Met. State Coll., Denver, 1984. Lic. real estate agt., Ga. Sr. acct. Stearns-Rogers Mfg., Denver, 1980-83; contr. Enstrupan, Denver, 1983-85; tchr. pvt. schs. Tokyo, 1985-87; chief fin. officer Maxicenters USA, Atlanta, 1987-88; pres. Bus. Systems and Svcs., Denver and Atlanta, 1980—. Contbr. articles to profl. jours. Instr. ARC, Denver, 1983-84, Fulton County Recreation Ctr., Atlanta, 1987, others. Mem. Atlanta C. of C., Mensa, Intertel, Masons.

CONLEY, PATRICK O'ROURKE, software company executive; b. L.A., Dec. 2, 1956; s. Arza and Joy C. Student, Orange Coast Coll., 1970-72; BS in Physics, Calif. State U., Fullerton, 1972-76; postgrad., U. Portland, 1980-84. Researcher Chevron Rsch. Co., La Habra, Calif., 1970-75, Digital Euipment Corp., Portland, Oreg., 1976-80, Tektronix Co., Beaverton, Oreg., 1981-84; pres. Abraxas Software Inc., Portland, 1984—. Vol. rescuer Mountain Rescue, Portland. Mem. IEEE, Assn. Computing Machinery. Home: 8712 SW Terwilliger Blvd Portland OR 97219 Office: Abraxas Software Inc 7033 SW Macadam Portland OR 97219

CONLON, PETER JOHN, JR., financial consultant; b. S.I., N.Y., Aug. 24, 1951; s. Peter John and Alice Virginia (Berk) C.; m. Tina Diane Schiller, Dec. 28, 1974 (div. 1981); m. Nancy Louise Elliott, Nov. 16, 1986. BS in Mktg., Syracuse U., 1973; MBA, U. Tex., Arlington, 1978. Mfrs. rep. Warner Electric/Red Lion, Ft. Worth, 1979-85; fin. cons. Shearson Lehman Bros., Ft. Worth, 1985-88; retirement planning specialist Rotan Mosle/Paine Webber, Ft. Worth, 1988—, registered fin. planner, 1989—. Pres. Wellington Pl. Homeowners Assn., Arlington, 1981-88. With USAF, 1973-79. Mem. Ft. Worth Security Dealers, Res. Officers Assn. (v.p. Ft. Worth chpt. 1987-88), Arlington City Club (com. chmn. 1986-87). Republican. Roman Catholic. Office: Rotan Mosel/Paine Webber 301 Commerce St 28th Fl Fort Worth TX 76102

CONN, ROBERT HENRY, government official, former naval officer; b. Boonton, N.J., June 8, 1925; s. Henry Hammond and Violet (Doremus) C.; m. Virginia Inness-Brown, July 6, 1946; children: Portia Conn Hirschman, Judith Conn Bell, Robert H., Patricia, Catherine Conn Cort. B.B.A., U. Miss., 1955; M.S., U. Rochester, 1962; D.B.A., Ind. U., 1965; student, U.S. Naval War Coll., 1963. Commd. ensign U.S. Navy, 1946, advanced through grades to capt., 1967; asst. dir. budgets and reports Office Navy Comptroller (U.S. Navy), Washington, 1969-72; ret. Office Navy Comptroller, 1972; mgr. fed. liaison div. Arthur Andersen & Co., Washington, 1972-81; comptroller of the navy Dept. Navy, Washington, 1981—; asst. prof. naval sci. U. Rochester, N.Y., 1959-62; lectr. Armed Forces Indsl. Coll., Nat. War Coll., Naval War Coll.; dir. Clipper Belt Lacer Co. Author: Financial Management Systems for Political Campaigns, 1972. Bd. dirs. Navy Mut. Aid Soc., 1970-72. Decorated Legion of Merit; decorated Meritorious Service medal; recipient Nat. Pres. award Am. Soc. Mil. Comptrollers, 1985, Disting. Pub. Service award, Dept. Navy, 1987. Fellow Sigma Iota Epsilon; mem. Am. Soc. Mil. Comptrollers (Pres.' award 1985), N.Y. Yacht Club, Army-Navy Club, Indian Creek Yacht Country Club. Republican. Episcopalian. Office: Compt of Navy Dept Navy Rm 4E 768 Pentagon Washington DC 20350

CONN, WILLIAM JOHN, investment banker; b. Bacchus Marsh, Victoria, Australia, Apr. 10, 1946; s. William and Kathleen Mary (Grieve) C.; m. Janice Edyth Armstrong, Apr. 26, 1968; children: Ashley, Cecilia, Jonathan, Michael. B of Commerce with honors, U. Melbourne, Australia, 1967; MBA, Columbia U., 1971. Mining analyst Potter Ptnrs. Ltd., Melbourne, 1968-70, with corp. fin. advisory dept., 1972-78, head corp. fin. advisory dept., 1980-86; dep. chief exec. Potter Ptnrs. Group Ltd., Melbourne, 1986, chief exec., 1987—; mem. Corp. Affairs Adv. Bd., Melbourne, 1985—. Mem. bd. mgmt. Royal Children's Hosp., Melbourne, 1986—; bd. dirs. Nat. Gallery Victoria Art Found., Melbourne, 1985—. Mem. Securities Inst. Australia (assoc.), Australian Soc. Accts. Clubs: Royal Melbourne Golf, Athenaeum (Melbourne). Office: Potter Ptnrs Group Ltd, 325 Collins St, Melbourne, Victoria 3000, Australia

CONNELL, GROVER, food company executive; b. N.Y.C., Apr. 12, 1918; s. Grover Clevel and Violet Regina (Connell) C.; m. Patricia Day, July 31, 1940; children—Ted, Terry, Toni. B.S. in Bus. Adminstrn, Columbia, 1939. With Connell Rice & Sugar Co., Inc., Westfield, N.J., 1939—; pres. Connell Rice & Sugar Co., Inc., 1950—. Served to lt. USNR, 1942-46. Democrat. Presbyterian. Home: 207 Watchung Fork Westfield NJ 07090 Office: Connell Rice & Sugar Co Inc 45 Cardinal Dr Westfield NJ 07092

CONNELL, HUGH P., vintner, lawyer; b. Bethlehem, Pa., May 7, 1931; s. Joseph B. and Mary (McFadden) C.; m. Susan Richardson Hobbs, July 2, 1965; children: Hugh Richardson, Andrew Warfield, Edward William. A.B., Moravian Coll., 1953; LL.B., U. Pa., 1956; student, Hague Acad. Internat. Law, 1959; LL.M., U. London, Eng., 1960. Bar: Pa. 1956, N.Y. 1963. Lectr. internat. law U. London, Eng., 1960-62; with firm Coudert Bros., N.Y.C., 1962-65; gen. counsel J. Walter Thompson Co., N.Y.C., 1966—; v.p. J. Walter Thompson Co., 1967-73, sec., 1972—, sr. v.p., 1973, exec. v.p., 1974—, dir., 1974—; exec. v.p., dir. JWT Group, Inc., 1980-86; founder, owner, operator Crosswoods Vineyards, Inc., North Stonington, Conn., 1981—; also bd. dirs. Crosswoods Vineyards, Inc. Trustee Nat. Soc. to Prevent Blindness, 1972-86; chmn. bd. trustees Jackson Lab., Bar Harbor, Maine; trustee Moravian Coll., Plimoth Plantation, Plymouth, Mass. Served with AUS, 1956-58. Mem. Am. Soc. Internat. Law, Soc. Pub. Tchrs. Law (U.K.), Pilgrims of U.S. Club: Union (N.Y.C.); Wadawanuck (Stonington, Conn.). Home: PO Box 276 Boca Grande FL 33921

CONNELL, JOSEPH EDWARD, insurance executive; b. Niagara Falls, N.Y., Oct. 8, 1930; s. George Kerr and Katharine Elsa (Vodra) C.; m. Patricia Jane Parsons, Aug. 22, 1953; children: Douglas Edward, Marjorie Elsa. BA, Antioch Coll., 1954; postgrad., George Washington U., 1956-58. CPA, Mich., Tex. With Coopers & Lybrand (C.P.A.s), 1958-74; ptnr., SEC specialist Coopers & Lybrand (C.P.A.s), Detroit, 1958-62, Mpls., 1962-73, Des Moines, 1973-74; exec. v.p., chief fin. officer Am. Gen. Group Ins. Co. (formerly Republic Nat. Life Ins. Co.), Dallas, 1974—. Served to lt. USNR, 1955-58. Fellow Life Mgmt. Inst.; mem. Am. Inst. C.P.A.s, Nat. Assn. Accts., Fin. Execs. Inst. Unitarian. Clubs: Canyon Creek Country, White Rock Marathoner. Home: 422 Fall Creek Dr Richardson TX 75080 Office: Box 660238 Dallas TX 75266-0238

CONNELL, PHILIP FRANCIS, food industry executive; b. Hamilton, Ont., Can., Jan. 20, 1924; s. Maurice W. and Kathleen (Richardson) C. BA, McMaster U., Can., 1946. Chartered acct. With Clarkson Gordon & Co., Hamilton and Toronto, 1946-57; comptroller Canadian Westinghouse Co. Ltd., Hamilton, 1957-67; controller Domtar Ltd., Montreal, 1967-68; v.p. fin. George Weston Ltd., Toronto, Ont., 1968-75, Loblaw Cos., Ltd., Toronto, Ont., 1972-75; sr. v.p. fin., dir. Oshawa Group Ltd., 1976—; dir. Acklands Ltd. Mem. Fin. Execs. Inst. (pres. Hamilton chpt. 1966-67), Ont. Inst. Chartered Accts. Clubs: Hamilton, National. Home: 400 Walmer Rd Apt 2510, Toronto, ON Canada Office: Oshawa Group Ltd, 302 East Mall, Toronto, ON Canada M9B 6B8

CONNELL, TED, food products company executive; b. N.Y.C., Dec. 31, 1946; s. Grover and Patricia (Day) C.; m. Eileen Connell, Mar. 2, 1983; children: Lisa, Sean; children from previous marriage: Shane, Duane. BA, U. Miami, Coral Gables, 1969; MBA, NYU, 1971. Exec. v.p. Connell Rice & Sugar Co., Westfield, N.J. Office: Connell Rice & Sugar Co Inc 45 Cardinal Dr Westfield NJ 07091

CONNELL, TERRY, agricultural products company executive; b. N.Y.C., May 28, 1950; s. Grover and Patricia (Day) C. BS, Ursinus Coll., 1972; MBA, Coll. William and Mary, 1975. CPA, N.Y., N.J. Computer audit mgr. Arthur Young & Co., N.Y.C., 1977-83; sr. v.p., treas. Connell Rice & Sugar Co., Inc., Westfield, N.J., 1983—. Office: Connell Rice & Sugar Co Inc 45 Cardinal Dr Westfield NJ 07092

CONNELL, WILLIAM FRANCIS, diversified company executive; b. Lynn, Mass., May 12, 1938; s. William J. and Theresa (Keaney) C.; m. Margot C. Gensler, May 29, 1965; children: Monica Cameron, Lisa Terese, Courtenay Erin, William Christopher, Terence Alexander, Timothy Patrick. B.S. magna cum laude, Boston Coll., 1959; M.B.A., Harvard U., 1963. Controller Olga Co., Inc., Van Nuys, Calif., 1963-65; asst. treas. Litton Industries, Inc.; also pres. div. Marine Tech., Inc., 1965-68; treas. Ogden Corp., N.Y.C., 1968-69; v.p., treas. Ogden Corp., 1969-71, sr. v.p., 1971-72, exec. v.p., 1980-85; chief exec. officer, chmn. bd. Ogden Leisure, Inc.; chmn. bd., chief exec. officer Ogden Food Service, Inc., Ogden Recreation, Inc., Ogden Security, Inc., Ogden Services Inc.; dir. Ogden Corp., various Ogden subs., 1969-85; chmn., chief exec. officer, pres. Avondale Industries, Inc. 1985-87; chmn., chief exec. officer Connell Ltd. Partnership, 1987—. Active fund raising Boston Coll., trustee, 1974-86, 88—, chmn. bd. trustees, 1981-84; trustee St. Elizabeth Hosp., Boston, Boston 200 Corp. Served to 1st lt. AUS, 1959-61. Mem. Greater Boston C. of C. (chmn. bd. dirs. 1988—), Beta Gamma Sigma, Alpha Sigma Nu, Alpha Kappa Psi. Roman Catholic. Clubs: Algonquin, Univ. (Boston); Tedesco Country, Knights of Malta. Home: 111 Ocean Ave Swampscott MA 01907 Office: Connell Ltd Partnership 1 Mass Tech Ctr PO Box 22 Boston MA 02128

CONNELLEY, EARL JOHN, JR., water and waste treatment company executive; b. Covington, Ky.; s. Earl John and Grace (Muzzio) C.; B.S., U. Cin., 1947, M.S., 1948; m. Eileen L. O'Connor, Feb. 20, 1965; children—Ann Lloyd, Carol Jeanne, Cynthia Jane. Research engr. Eckey Research Labs., Cin.; process engr. Permutit Co. subs. Zurn Corp., N.Y.C., sales engr., East Orange, N.J., Chgo., dist. engr., Cin., regional mgr., Chgo., 1948-66, sales mgr., Paramus, N.J., 1966-78; dir. Havens & Emerson Cons. Environ. Engrs., Saddle Brook, N.J., 1978-84; pres. Multi Area Cons., environ. engrs., Ramsey, N.J., 1984—; exec. v.p. Joint Cons., W.B.E. Cons. Engrs., Ramsey, 1984—; instr. U. Cin., 1947-48; mem. industry com. Ann. Am. Power Conf. Registered profl. engr., Ohio, Ill., N.J., Ind., N.Y., Pa., Mass., Mich., Mo., Wis., Ky., Iowa, Tex., Minn. Mem. Am. Water Works Assn. (desalination com.), Waste Pollution Control Fedn., Alpha Chi Sigma, Phi Kappa Theta, Scabbard and Blade. Roman Catholic. Contbr. articles to profl. jours. Home: 8 Split Rock Rd Upper Saddle River NJ 07458 Office: Interstate Ctr Ste 110 PO Box 366 Ramsey NJ 07446

CONNELLY, JOHN FRANCIS, manufacturing company executive; b. Phila., Mar. 4, 1905; m. Josephine O'Neill, Apr. 1938; children: Josephine, Emily, John, Thomas, Judith, Christine. LLD (hon.), LaSalle Coll., Villanova U., 1958. Dir. Crown Cork & Seal Co., Phila., 1956—, pres., 1957-76, chmn. bd., 1957—, chief exec. officer, 1979—; chmn. bd. Connelly Containers, Inc. Chmn. Archbishop's laity com. Office: Crown Cork & Seal Co 9300 Ashton Rd Philadelphia PA 19136 *

CONNELLY, RICHARD, accountant; b. Chgo., Sept. 30, 1951; s. James H. and Elizabeth (Hoffart) C.; m. Cheryl L. Batelli, Aug. 18, 1973. BS, U. Ill., Urbana, 1973; MS, U. Tex., Dallas, 1988. Audit mgr. Ernst & Whinney, Chgo., 1974-79; cost acctg. mgr. Tex. Instruments, Houston, 1980-83; div. controller Tex. Instruments, Dallas, 1983-85; chief fin. officer Photomatrix Corp., Dallas, 1985-87; dir. acctg. Sterling Software, Inc., Dallas, 1987—. Mem. Nat. Assn. Accts., Am. Inst. CPA's, Tex. Soc. CPA's, Phi Sigma Pi Alumni Assn. Republican. Roman Catholic. Office: Sterling Software Inc 8080 N Central Ste 1100 Dallas TX 75206

CONNELLY, WILLIAM JOSEPH, marketing and public relations executive; b. Pottsville, Pa., Sept. 29, 1931; s. Joseph Thomas and Marie Cecelia (Ryan) C.; m. Margaret Ann Scanlan Carl, Oct. 6, 1951; children: Margaret Marie, William Joseph, Colleen; m. 2d, Ellen Marie Bufe, May 20, 1972; 1 son, Sean Ryan. AB, King's Coll., Wilkes-Barre, Pa., 1966; postgrad. U. Scranton, 1965-66, St. Louis U., 1968-70. Profl. broadcaster and journalist, 1949-66; radio continuity and comml. copywriter, 1951-53; corp. communications specialist Mgmt. Cons., Kingston, Pa., 1958-63; cons. to pres. ednl. radio/TV King's Coll. Wilkes-Barre, Pa., 1963-66; dir. pub. rels. St. Louis U. Med. Ctr., 1967-71; dir. pub. affairs Chgo. State U., 1971-74; dir. pub. rels. Schwab Rehab. Hosp., Chgo., 1974-76; mgr. advt. copywriting Bankers Life and Casualty Co., Chgo., 1976-78, dir. mktg. pub. rels., 1978-80, dir. mktg. communications and pub. rels. Underwriters Labs. Inc., Northbrook, Ill., 1980-83; sr. cons. JN Co., 1983-85; prin. Bufe, Connelly & Ryan, Mktg. & Pub. Rels., 1985—; adj. prof. journalism Chgo. State U., 1973-74. Executive producer, screenwriter (ednl. film) "Let's Keep in Touch:, 1979 (numerous awards); writer, dir., narrator (radio documentary) "Watchman on the Wall), 1964. Active Boy Scouts Am., 1946-62, Suburban Cook County-Du Page County Health (Planning) Systems Agy., 1984-87. With USAF, 1950-51. Mem. Pub. Rels. Soc. Am. Democrat. Roman Catholic.

CONNER, JOHN RICHARD, financial planner; b. Indpls., June 26, 1961; s. Richard Floyd and Janetnelle (Wierick) C.; m. Julie Sendelweck, Aug. 29, 1987. BSBA, Ball State U., 1987. Cert. fin. cons., fin. planner. Fin. planner Century Co. of Am., Indpls., 1987-88; pres. Conner Fin. Group, Inc., Indpls., 1989—. Republican. Protestant. Home and Office: 4730 E 77th St Indianapolis IN 46250

CONNERS, JOHN BRENDAN, insurance company executive; b. Boston, Oct. 6, 1945; s. Stephen Edward and Josephine (McMahon) C.; m. Jean Marie McLean, June 15, 1968; children: James, Michael, Colleen. AB Boston Coll., 1967. Cert. casualty actuary. Actuarial asst. Liberty Mut. Ins. Co., Boston, 1969-70, actuarial analyst, 1970-73, asst. actuary, 1973-75, assoc. actuary, 1975-79, asst. v.p., assoc. actuary, 1979-80, v.p., assoc. actuary, 1980, v.p., actuary, 1980-82, v.p., mgr. personal risks, 1982-83, sr. v.p., mgr. personal market, 1983-87, exec. v.p. personal market, 1987—. Chmn. All Industry Research Adv. Council, 1982; chmn. bd. dirs. Hwy. Loss Data Inst., Washington, 1987. Mem. Casualty Actuarial Soc. (bd. dirs. 1983-85), Casualty Actuaries New Eng. (pres. 1980). Roman Catholic. Office: Liberty Mut Ins Co 175 Berkeley St Boston MA 02117

CONNOLLY, CHARLES HASTINGS, corporate communications executive; b. N.Y.C., Dec. 17, 1934; s. Charles Bernard and Grace Ann (Hastings) C.; m. Elise Lillian Meyer, Jan. 9, 1960; children: Douglas, Evan, David, Melissa. AB, Fordham U., 1957; postgrad., Columbia U., 1958. Editor office mag. Met. Life Ins. Co., N.Y.C., 1958-61; corp. communications mgr. Columbia Records div. CBS, N.Y.C., 1961-64; dir. pub. affairs, planning and rsch. Chrysler Corp., Detroit, 1964-82; v.p. corp. communications Whitman Corp., Chgo., 1982—. Author: Air Pollution and Public Health, 1972. Chmn. Chgo. Council on Urban Affairs, 1987; trustee St. Xavier Coll., Chgo., 1989—; deacon Chgo. United Ch., 1987—. Mem. Pub. Relations Soc. Am., Chgo. Athletic Assn. Home: 450 Hamilton Wood Homewood IL 60430 Office: Whitman Corp 111 E Wacker 27th Fl Chicago IL 60601

CONNOLLY, EUGENE B., JR., industrial mineral company executive; b. N.Y.C., Mar. 31, 1932; s. Eugene B. and Charlotte (Boquet) C.; m. Dorothy E. O'Brien, June 5, 1954; children—Kathleen, Jennifer, Patrick, Michael, Amy, Daniel. B.S. in Mgmt., Hofstra U., Hempstead, N.Y., 1954, M.B.A. in Mktg., 1964. With USG Corp. (formerly U.S. Gypsum Co.), Chgo., 1958—; group v.p. U.S. Gypsum Co., Chgo., 1983-85, pres., chief operating officer, 1985-87, also bd. dirs.; exec. v.p. USG Corp., 1987—; pres., chief exec. officer DAP, Inc., Chgo., 1988-89; also bd. dirs. USG Interiors, Chgo.; pres., chief exec. officer DAP, Inc., 1988—, also bd. dirs. Mem. adv. bd. St. Mary of Nazareth Hosp., Chgo., 1985—, Good Shepher Hosp., Barrington, 1987—. Office: USG Corp 101 S Wacker Dr Chicago IL 60606

CONNOLLY, J. WRAY, food manufacturing executive; b. Pitts., Jan. 8, 1934; m. Shirley Betz, Sept. 3, 1955; children: Paul, Mark, Christopher, Claire, Michael. AB, St. Vincent Coll., 1955; JD, U. Pitts., 1958. Atty. H.J. Heinz Co., Pitts., 1961-65, asst. sec., 1965-67, treas., 1973-76; v.p. Ore-Ida subs. H.J. Heinz Co., Boise, Idaho, 1968-71; pres., chief exec. officer Hubinger Co. subs. H.J. Heinz Co., Keokuk, Iowa, 1973-79; exec. v.p. Heinz U.S.A. div. H.J. Heinz Co., Pitts., 1979-80, 1979-80, pres., chief exec. officer, 1980-85; sr. v.p. Europe H.J. Heinz World Hdqrs., Pitts., 1985—; also bd. dirs. H.J. Heinz World Hdqrs.; bd. dirs. Consol. Natural Gas Co., Pitts. Bd. visitors, trustee U. Pa., Pitts. ; bd. dirs. Eye and Ear Inst. Pitts., 1983—. Mem. Pa. Bar Assn. Republican. Roman Catholic. Clubs: Duquesne (Pitts.), Allegheny Country (Pa.). Home: RD #3 Backbone Rd Sewickley PA 15143 Office: H J Heinz Co 600 Grant St Pittsburgh PA 15219

CONNOLLY, JOSEPH MICHAEL, banker, lawyer; b. New Orleans, July 29, 1933; s. George Charles Sr. and Clare (Walsh) C.; m. Brenda Duhe Connolly, Oct. 10, 1959; children: Collen Connolly Switzer, Nancy L., Brenda A., Celeste L. BBA, Loyola U., New Orleans, 1955, JD, 1960. Bar: La. 1960, U.S. Ct. Mil. Appeals 1968, U.S. Supreme Ct. 1970. Chmn. First Nat. Bank (formerly Century Bank), New Orleans, 1972-87; vice chmn. First Nat. Corp., Covington, New Orleans, La., 1988—; state chmn. U.S. savings bonds div. U.S. Treasury Dept., 1983—. Mem. pres.'s council Loyola U. of the South, New Orleans, 1979—; bd. dirs. Associated Cath. Charities, New Orleans, 1981—; trustee Mercy Hosp., New Orleans, 1985—. Capt. USAR, 1955-57. Mem. ABA, Am. Bankers Assn. (pres. 1983-84, bd. dirs. 1978-85, mem. adv. bd. community bankers div. 1978-81, mem. community bankers council 1984-86), La. State Bar Assn., Conf. State Bank Suprs. (state rep. 1983—, sr. rep. 1985—), La. Bankers Assn. (pres. 1983-84, bd. dirs. 1978-85), Blue Key Honor Soc., Delta Sigma Pi. Democrat. Roman Catholic. Home: 5925 Canal Blvd New Orleans LA 70124 Office: First Nat Bank 3801 Canal St New Orleans LA 70119

CONNOLLY, MICHAEL JOSEPH, III, state official; b. West Roxbury, Mass., Apr. 20, 1947; s. Michael Joseph and Florence C.; m. Lynda Murphy, Aug. 14, 1971; children: John Ronan, Justin, Allison, Lauren. A.B., Holy Cross Coll., 1969; J.D., New Eng. Sch. Law, 1976. Tchr. math. Boston Latin Sch., 1972; mem. Mass. Ho. of Reps., 1973-79, chmn. spl. legis. com. on commuter traffic, 1973-79; sec. of state Commonwealth of Mass., 1979—; Chmn. Mass. Hist. Commn.; chmn. Archives Adv. Commn. Mem. Marriage Encounter. Mem. Mass. Bar Assn., Nat. Assn. Secs. of State. Club: Holy Cross (Boston). Office: State House Rm 337 Boston MA 02133

CONNOLLY, RONALD CAVANAGH, financial services executive; b. Boston, May 22, 1932; s. Edmund Jerome and Norah Francis (Cavanagh) C.; m. Marie Elizabeth Hynes, July 9, 1955; children: Marie Elizabeth, Judith, Susan, Lisa. AB, Tufts U., 1955. Trainee Conn. Gen. Life, Hartford, 1957-59; salesman IBM Corp., N.Y.C., 1959-65; v.p. Greyhound Leasing and Fin. Corp., Phoenix, 1965-69; exec. v.p. Finserv Corp. subs. Studebaker-Worthington, N.Y.C., 1969-70, Commonwealth Edison Co., Chgo., 1970-72; 1st v.p. Halsey, Stuart & Co., Inc., Chgo., 1972-77; exec. v.p. Connell Rice & Sugar Co., Inc., Westfield, N.J., 1977—. Served to 1st lt. USMCR, 1953-63. Roman Catholic. Office: Connell Rice & Sugar Co Inc 45 Cardinal Dr Westfield NJ 07092

CONNOLLY, THOMAS EDWARD, lawyer; b. Boston, Nov. 7, 1942; s. Thomas Francis and Catherine Elizabeth (Skehill) C.; A.B., St. John's Sem., Brighton, Mass., 1964; J.D., Boston Coll., 1969. Admitted to Mass. bar, 1969; assoc. Schneider & Reilly, Boston, 1969-73; ptnr. Schneider, Reilly, Zabin, Connolly & Costello, P.C., Boston, 1973-85, Connolly & Leavis, Boston, 1986—; instr. law Northeastern Law Sch., Boston, 1975-76. Mem. governing council Boston Coll. Law Sch. Alumni Council, 1980—. Mem. ABA (vice chmn. products liability sect. 1978—), Am. Trial Lawyers Assn. (nat. gov. 1977-80), Mass. Acad. Trial Lawyers (gov. 1976—), Am. Coll. of Trial Lawyers. Democrat. Roman Catholic. Club: Univ. (Boston). Home: 15 Vincent Rd Roslindale MA 02131 Office: Connolly & Leavis 168 Milk St Boston MA 02109

CONNOLLY, WALTER JUSTIN, JR., banker; b. Boston, Aug. 3, 1928; s. Walter Justin and Helen Agnes (Cavanagh) C.; m. Paulina Quilty, Apr. 14, 1951; children: Timothy J., Kevin A., Mary-Elise, Walter Justin III, Paulina, Sarah D. B.A. in History, Yale U., 1950. With Hartford Ins. Group, 1955-58; with Hornblower & Weeks, Hartford, Conn., 1958-61; with Conn. Bank & Trust Co., Hartford, 1961-85, dir. investment ops., 1961-65, dir. mktg., 1965-66, sr. v.p., 1966-68, exec. v.p., dir. adminstrv. staff, 1968-70, pres., 1970-77, chief exec. officer, 1977-80, chmn. bd., chief exec. officer, 1980-85; chmn. Bank of New England Corp., Boston, 1985—; dir. Conn. Mut. Life Ins. Co., Dexter Corp. Bd. dirs. Greater Hartford Arts Council, St. Francis Hosp., Kingswood/Oxford Sch. Served with USMC, 1952-55. Mem. Am. Bankers Assn., Assn. Res. City Bankers, Conn. Bankers Assn., Greater Hartford C. of C. (dir.). Clubs: Hartford, Hartford Golf, Hyannis Port Yacht. Office: Bank New Eng Corp 28 State St Boston MA 02109 *

CONNOR, GERALD RAYMOND, business executive, portfolio manager; b. Aurora, Ill., Jan. 12, 1946; s. Roy Lewis and Beatrice Susan (Walt) C.; m. Carla Lynn Galbrecht, June 17, 1967; children: Gregory, Trevor, Grant. BA, DePauw U., 1968. Head ops. duPont Glore Forgan, Toronto, Ont., Can., 1968-70, account exec., 1970-72; account exec. Baker Weeks & Co., Toronto, 1972-77; pres. Connor, Clark & Co. Ltd., 1977—. Mem. Fin. Analysts Assn., Young Pres. Orgn., Granite Club, Cambridge Club, Rosedale Country Club, Devils Glen Country Club, Nat. Club. Address: Scotia Pla, 40 King St W, Ste 5110, Toronto, ON Canada M5H 3Y2

CONNOR, JAMES ALOYSIUS, lawyer; b. Manchester, N.H., Sept. 28, 1936; s. Beatrice (Bisson) C.; m. Joan M. Connor; children: Sean, Jamie Justin. AB with honors, Holy Cross Coll., 1958; LLB, Boston Coll., 1961. Bar: N.H. Asst. atty. Hillsborough (N.H.) County, 1965-68, atty., 1968-74; sole practice Manchester, N.H., 1974—. Mem. Hillsborough County Crime Commn., Gov.'s Commn. on Cts.; mem. Audubon Soc., N.H. Soc. for Preservation of Forests, N.H. Inst. Arts and Scis.; state chmn. N.H. Heart Fund, 1978; bd. dirs. Odyssey House; del. Dem. Convs.; co-chmn. Hillsborough County Muskie for Pres.; democratic primary candidate for Gov., 1976. Mem. ABA, Manchester Bar Assn., U.S. Dist. Ct. Bar Assn., N.H. Bar Assn. (chmn. constrn. and by-laws com. 1980-82), Nat. Dist. Attys. Assn., Hillsborough County Law Enforcement Assn., Jolliet Club, 100 Club, Rye Beach Club.

CONNOR, JOHN THOMAS, JR., lawyer; b. N.Y.C., June 16, 1941; s. John Thomas and Mary (O'Boyle) C.; m. Susan Scholle Connor, Dec. 18, 1965; children: Seanna, Marin, John. BA cum laude, Williams Coll., 1963; JD, Harvard U., 1967. Bar: N.Y. 1968, D.C. 1980. Assoc. Cravath, Swaine & Moore, N.Y.C., 1967-71; dep. dir. Office Econ. Policy and Case Analysis, Pay Bd., Washington, 1971-72; dep. dir. Bur. E.-W. Trade, U.S. Dept. Commerce, Washington, 1972-73; sr. v.p. U.S.-USSR Trade and Econ. Coun., Moscow, 1973-76; assoc. Milbank, Tweed, Hadley & McCloy, N.Y.C., 1976-79; ptnr. Curtis, Mallet-Prevost, Colt and Mosle, Washington, 1980-82; v.p., gen. counsel, sec. PHH Corp., 1982-88; v.p., govt. affaris counsel Prudential Ins. Co. Am., Newark, 1988—. Bd. dirs. Micros Systems, Inc. Exec. dir. Dem. party N.J., 1969-70; trustee St. Mary's Coll., Com. Nat. Security. Fulbright tutor Ferguson Coll., Poona, India, 1963-64. Mem. ABA, N.Y. State Bar Assn., D.C. Bar Assn., Coun. Fgn. Rels., Am. Law Inst., Phi Beta Kappa. Clubs: Met. (Washington); Union (N.Y.C.); Chevy Chase (Md.). Home: 12 Primrose St Chevy Chase MD 20815 Office: Prudential Ins Co Am 745 Broad St 21st Fl Newark NJ 07101

CONNOR, JOSEPH ANDREW, electronic security company executive; b. Dublin, Ireland, Sept. 23, 1952; came to U.S., 1955; s. Joseph Andrew and Devota (Mullen) C.; m. Carol Stafford McDonald, Oct. 14, 1979; children: Jessica, Kerianne, Patrick. BS, Georgetown U., 1975; MBA, JD, Northwestern U., 1979. Please give bar admissions, if applicable. Dir. devel. Mark Controls Corp., Evanston, Ill., 1976-79, asst. to chmn., 1979-80, dir. mktg., 1980-81, v.p. mktg., 1981-82; pres. Rubicon Inc., Westfield, Mass., 1982-84; gen. mgr. ADT Security Systems, Salt Lake City, 1984-86; v.p. ADT Security Systems, Long Beach, Calif., 1986-88, sr. v.p., 1988—; bd. dirs. ADT Ariz., Phoenix. Bd. dirs. Angel Gate Cultural Ctr., San Pedro, Calif., 1987. Austin scholar Northwestern U., 1976; named Boss of Yr. Women in Bus., 1985. Mem. Am. Soc. Indsl. Security Mgrs., Phi Beta Kappa. Office: ADT Security Systems Inc 1984 Obispo Long Beach CA 90804

CONNOR, JOSEPH E., accountant; b. N.Y.C., Aug. 23, 1931; s. Joseph E. C.; m. Cornelia B. Camarata, Apr. 17, 1958 (dec. Oct. 11, 1983); children: Anthony, Cornelia, David; m. Sally A. Mierson, June 12, 1988. A.B. summa cum laude, U. Pitts.; M.S. in Bus., Columbia U. Joined Price Waterhouse & Co., N.Y.C., 1956; ptnr. Price Waterhouse & Co., 1967—; mng. ptnr. Western region Price Waterhouse & Co., Los Angeles, 1976-78; chmn. policy bd. U.S. Price Waterhouse & Co., 1978-88, chmn. World Firm, 1988—; cons. fgn. direct investment program U.S. Dept. Commerce; project adv. research study AICPA; lectr. in field.; mem. adv. council Columbia U. Grad. Sch. Bus.; bd. visitors U. Pitts. Grad. Sch. Bus., Georgetown U. Sch. Bus.; chmn. U.S. Council for Internat. Bus., 1987—; mem. Pres.'s Mgmt. Adv. Council, Pres.'s Pvt. Sector Survey on Cost Control. Contbr. articles to profl. jours.

Trustee YMCA Greater N.Y.; bd. overseers Meml. Sloan Kettering Inst.; bd. dirs. Georgetown U.; mem. council Brookings Instn. Served to 1st lt. U.S. Army, 1954-56. Mem. N.Y. State Soc. CPAs (chmn. internat. ops. com., mem. acctg. and auditing com., real estate acctg. com.), Calif. Soc. CPAs (legis. com.), U.S. C. of C., Internat. C. of C. (v.p., exec. bd. 1989—). Clubs: Met. (Washington); Links, George Town, Board Room, Greenwich Country, Seaview Country. Office: Price Waterhouse & Co 1251 Ave of the Americas New York NY 10020

CONNORS, JOHN MICHAEL, JR., advertising agency executive; b. Boston, June 9, 1942; s. John Michael and Mary (Horrigan) C.; m. Eileen Marie Ahearn; children: John, Timothy, Susanne, Kevin. Grad., Boston Coll., 1963. Mktg. rep. Campbell Soup Co., Boston, 1963-65; account exec. Batten, Barton, Durstine & Osborne, New York and Boston, 1965-68; pres. Hill, Holliday, Connors, Cosmopulos, Inc., Boston, 1968—. Trustee Boston Coll., 1979—. Named one of Boston's Ten Outstanding Young Leaders Jaycees, 1972. Mem. Advt. Club Greater Boston (past pres.), Am. Assn. Advt. Agys., New Eng. Broadcasting Assn. (past pres.), Longwood Cricket Club, Dennis Yacht Club, Badminton and Tennis Club, Braeburn Country Club, Algonquin Club, Univ. Club. Roman Catholic. Office: Hill Holliday Connors Cosmopulos Inc 200 Clarendon St Boston MA 02116

CONNORS, LEO GERARD, financial executive; b. Mahanoy City, Pa., July 2, 1927; s. Leo V. and Regina C. (Klitsch) C.; m. Ann Seydel, Oct. 18, 1952; children: Kevin, Deirdre, Christopher, Carl, Leo, John, Maura, Miriam, Stacey, Matthew. BSBA, St. Joseph's Coll., 1951. CPA, Pa. Sr. acct. Frank Vallei CPA Firm, Phila., 1952-55, Peat, Marwick, Mitchell & Co., Phila., 1955-61; asst. controller Chrysler First Inc. (formerly Fin. Am. Corp.), Allentown, Pa., 1961; asst. v.p. Chrysler First Inc. (formerly Fin. Am. Corp.), Allentown, 1964, v.p., 1971, sr. v.p., 1977—; bd. dirs. Sacred Heart Hosp., Allentown, vice-chmn. 1987—, chmn., 1988. Pres. Indian Mountain Lake Civic Assn., Monroe County, Pa., 1985-88, treas., 1988—, bd. dirs. 1984—. With U.S. Army, 1945-47. Mem. AICPA, Nat. Accts. Assn., Pa. Inst. CPAs (coun. mem. 1982-84), Fin. Execs. Inst. (pres. local chpt. 1985). Republican. Roman Catholic. Office: Chrysler First Inc 1105 Hamilton St Allentown PA 18101

CONNORS, ROBERT LEO, city official; b. Kings County, N.Y., June 11, 1940; s. John Leo and Emma Mae (Bayers) C.; m. Elaine Roscoe, July 21, 1979; children: Anne, Laura, Kathleen. B. Profl. Studies, Pace U., 1974, MS in Indsl. Labor Relations, 1976. Police officer, trustee, fin. sec. exec., 1st v.p. Patrolmen's Benevolent Assn., N.Y.C. Police Dept., 1965-77; dep. commr., dir. labor relations Dept. Gen. Services City of N.Y., 1977-83; dir. personnel adminstrn. City of Fall River, Mass., 1984-85, city adminstr., 1985—; lectr. in field. Co-author: Comprehensive Reorganization of Municipal Government, 1986. Mem. Fall River Regional Task Force, 1984—. Served with USAF, 1957-61. Recipient Community Relations Service award, U.S. Justice Dept., Boston, 1985. Mem. Am. Mgmt. Assn., Nat. League of Cities, Internat. City Mgmt. Assn., Greater Fall River Personnel Council, Internat. Personnel Mgmt. Assn., Soc. of Profls. in Dispute Resolution. Democrat. Lodge: Masons. Home: 4980 N Main St Fall River MA 02720 Office: City of Fall River One Government Ctr Fall River MA 02722

CONOBY, JOSEPH FRANCIS, chemist; b. Albany, June 12, 1930; s. Joseph Francis and Helen Emma (Brucker) C.; B.S., Union Coll., 1952; m. Mary Joan A. Ryan, June 21, 1958; children—James Francis, Mark Joseph. Sr. tech. service engr. Allied Chem. Corp., Syracuse, N.Y., 1956-66; research chemist Conversion Chem. Corp., Rockville, Conn., 1966-69; environ. engr., indsl. hygienist, mgr. environ. and health engring. Honeywell Bull, Billerica, Mass., 1969-87, mgr. environ. engring. Bull HN Worldwide Info. Systems, 1987—; mem. adv. bd. Mass. Water Resources Authority Sewer Use (rules and regulations, policy and procedures, and facilities planning task forces); cons. exptl. project course Mass. Inst. Tech., 1977-78. Served to lt. USN, 1952-56. Mem. Am. Electroplaters Soc. (chmn. project com.), Am. Electroplaters Soc. (pres. Merrimack br.), Am. Indsl. Hygiene Assn. Patentee in field, U.S., Germany. Contbr. articles to profl. jours. Home: 5 Samuel Parlin Dr Acton MA 01720 Office: Bull H N Worldwide Info Systems Billerica MA 01821

CONOLE, CLEMENT VINCENT, corporate executive; b. Binghamton, N.Y., Sept. 29, 1908; s. P.J. and Briget (Holleran) C.; m. Marjorie Anable, Sept. 26, 1931; children—Barbara (Mrs. Francis B. McElroy), Marjorie (Mrs. Marjorie A. Hargrave), Richard, Jacalyn (Mrs. John N. Harman III). B.S.C.E., Clarkson Coll. Tech., Potsdam, N.Y., 1931; postgrad., Cornell U., N.Y. U., Yale U.; M.B.A., Fla. Atlantic U. Licensed profl engr. and land surveyor, N.Y., Pa. Engr. City of Binghamton, also N.Y. State, 1930-32; ptnr. Richmeyer, Harding and Conole, 1932-33; engr. Dept. of Interior, 1933-35; dist. dir. Fed. Works Adminstrn.; dist. supt. N.Y. Unemployment Ins. Div., 1936-37; asst. state indsl. commr. N.Y., 1937-39; dep. indsl. commr. 1939-43; dir. indsl. bur. C. of C. Bd. of Trade of Phila., 1943-44, operating mgr., 1945-46, exec. v.p., 1946-52; also editor, pub. Greater Phila. mag., 1945-50; v.p. Bankers Securities corp., 1952-55; pres. Municipal Publs., Inc., 1947-50; pub. relations cons. Phila.-Balt. Stock Exchange, 1947-52; chmn. bd., pres., dir. Hearn Dept. Stores, Inc., N.Y.C., 1952-54; dir., chmn. bd. James McCutcheon & Co., 1956-57; chmn. bd., dir. Bus. Supplies Corp. Am., Skytop, Pa., 1962-65; chmn. bd. dir., pres. Tabulating Card Co., Inc., Princeton, N.J., 1955-62; chmn. bd. dir. Am. Bus. Mgmt. Co., 1955-62, Whiting Paper Co., Inc., 1959-62, Sky Meadow Farms, Inc., 1965-68, Am. Bus. Machines Co., 1958-65, Data Processing Supplies Co., 1959-65, Am. Bus. Execs. Co., 1960-65, Am. Bus. Investment Co., 1958-62, Gen. Bus. Supplies Corp., 1965-70; prof. adminstrn. Fla. Atlantic U., 1972-74; now chmn. bd. trustees, pres. Am. Coll. Adminstrs. Execs. Mgrs., Laguna Hills, Calif.; dean Sch. Adminstrn., Coll. Boca Raton; exec. head. mgmt. engring. div. S.D. Leidesdorf & Co., 1954-55; dir. City Stores Corp., City Stores Merc. Co., Inc., City Splty. Stores Co., Inc., Oppenheim Collins & Co., Franklin Simon Co., N.Y.C., R.H. White Co., Boston, Wise Smith & Co., Hartford, Conn. Mem. Broome County Planning Commn., 1936-38, Pa. War Manpower Commn.; chmn. War. Emergency Bd. N.Y. State, 1941; industry mem. appeals com. Nat. War Labor Bd., 1943-45; cons. HOLC and FHA, 1936-39; chmn. Armed Forces Regional Council, Pa. and Del., 1950-52; mem. adv. com. 2d Army, 4th Naval Dist.; pres. 175th Anniversary of the Signing of the Declaration of Independence, 1951, Phila. Conv. and Visitors Bur., 1953; chmn. United Com. Fund, Princeton; apptd. mem. State Commn. to reorgn. Govt. City N.Y., 1953; apptd. mem. Mayor's Adv. Council, chmn. com. on city mgmt. and adminstrn., 1954; Citizens Com. to Keep N.Y. Clean, 1955, Citizens Com. on Cts., 1955; pres. Quiet City Campaign, 1956; vice chmn., sec. Phila. Parking Authority.; Trustee William Shelton Harrison Found., Hun School, Princeton, N.J., Clarkson Coll. of Tech. Mem. Am. Mgmt. Assn., A.I.M. (president's council, charter mem. adv. bd.), Nat. Retail Research Inst. (dir.), Bronx Bd. Trade (dir. 1954-64), Ave. of Americas Assn. (dir. 1952-55), Soc. for Advancement Mgmt., Nat. Assn. Cost Accountants, Commerce and Industry Assn. N.Y. (treas., dir., mem. exec. com. 1954-58), Lambda Iota (pres.), Delta Upsilon (trustee), Phi Beta Lambda. Clubs: Midday (Phila.), Philadelphia Country (Phila.), Lake Placid (N.Y.) Skytop (Pa.), Merion Cricket, Racquet, Poor Richard, Pen and Pencil (Phila.); Economic (N.Y.C.), Union League (N.Y.C.); Nat. Golf Links of Am. (Southampton, L.I.); Uptown; Springdale Golf (Princeton, N.J.), Rotary (Princeton, N.J.), Nassau (Princeton, N.J.); Laguna Hills (Calif.) Golf, Boca Raton, Pinehurst Country, Royal Palm Yacht and Country (gov.), Mission Viejo Country, El Niguel Country (Calif.), P.G.A. National Golf, Calif. Office: Executive Center PO Box 2704 Laguna Hills CA 92653

CONOLE, RICHARD CLEMENT, professional athletics executive; b. Binghamton, N.Y., Dec. 7, 1936; s. Clement V. and Marjorie E. (Anable) C.; student U. Pa., 1955, 1960, Clarkson Coll., 1956-57; children—Margaret Ann, Allen, Linda Elizabeth Fandel; m. Sharyn Stafford, Apr. 18, 1969; 1 dau., Samantha Erin. Data processing dept. Campbell Soup Co., Inc., Camden, N.J., 1954; draftsman Gannett, Fleming, Corddry & Carpenter, Inc., Ardmore, Pa., 1955-56; plant mgr., office mgr. Tabulating Card Co., Inc., Princeton, N.J., 1957-59, asst. to pres., asst. sec.-treas., sec. 1959; pres., dir. Data Processing Supplies Co., Inc., Princeton, 1959; sec., dir. Whiting Paper Co., Inc., Princeton, 1959, pres. 1961-62; pres., dir. Mercer-Princeton Realty Co., Inc., Princeton, 1959-61; pres. Am. Bus. Investment Co., Inc., Princeton, 1960; pres., dir. Business Supplies Corp. Am., Skytop, Pa., 1962-65, Gen. Bus. Supplies Corp., Ardmore, 1965-71; chmn. bd. Nat. Productive Machines, Inc., Elkridge, Md., 1965-71; v.p., chmn. finance com., dir. Pocono Internat. Raceway Inc., 1964-74; pres. Gen. Automotive Supplies Co., 1971-72; pres., dir. Autoberfest, Inc., 1973—, Promotional Printing Ltd., 1973; pres. The World Series of Auto Racing Corp., 1973-78, Tex. World Speedway Inc., 1976—, Speedway Mgmt. Corp., 1978—; pres., chief exec. officer Gt. Tex. Truckstop, Tex. World Affordable Homes; sales cons. Hess & Barker, 1972-76; mem. competition com. U.S. Auto Club, 1976—; treas., chmn. fin. com. Tex. Pvt. Sch. Found., Inc.; trustee Allen Acad. Founder Tex. 500, Tex. Grand Prix, Tex. Race of Champions. Mem. Am. Mgmt. Assn., Tex. Manufactured Housing Assn., Phila. Dist. Squash Racquets Assn. (life), U.S. Squash Racquets Assn., Nat. Greyhound Assn., Tex. Greyhound Assn., Tex. Horse Race Assn., Texas Thoroughbred Breeders Assn. Clubs: Skytop (Skytop, Pa.); Phila. Country, Merion Cricket (Haverford, Pa.); Manor (Pocono Manor, Pa.). Patentee magnetic printing cylinder. Home: Box 9191 College Station TX 77842 Office: Autoberfest Inc PO Box 11000 College Station TX 77842

CONOMIKES, GEORGE SPERO, management consultant executive; b. Canastota, N.Y., Oct. 8, 1925; s. Spero P. and Mary (Pappas) C.; children: Melanie, Spero. AB with honors, Middlebury Coll., 1950; AM in Econs., U. Chgo., 1956. Research assoc., project dir. Indsl. Relations Ctr., U. Chgo., 1951-55; dir. Dept. of Commerce, U. Chgo., 1955-57; pres. Bus. Forum, Inc., Chgo., 1958-69; pres. Conomikes Assocs., Inc., Greenwich, Conn., 1969-74, Marina del Ray, Calif., 1974—; lectr. in econs. U. Chgo., 1955-58; guest lectr. Purdue U., NYU, Loyola U., Chgo., U. So. Calif., UCLA, U. Tex., Tufts U., U. Puerto Rico, U. Iowa, U. Tenn., U. Minn., Georgetown U., Marquette U., U. Md., Temple U., U. Oreg., Emory U. Contbg. editor: Stock Market Handbook, 1969; editor, pub. Conomikes Reports, 1982—. Served with USAAF, 1943-45. Mem. Soc. of Tchrs. of Family Medicine. Republican. Club: Marina City (Marina del Rey, Calif.). Office: Conomikes Assocs Inc 6033 W Century Blvd Ste #990 Los Angeles CA 90045-6418

CONRAD, DONALD GLOVER, insurance executive; b. St. Louis, Apr. 23, 1930; s. Harold Armin and Velma Glover (Morris) C.; m. Stephania Sanzone, Feb. 8, 1980; 1 stepdau., Alexa Sanzone; children by previous marriage: Marcy Conrad Tramont, Suzanne, Mark. Student, Wesleyan U., 1948-49; B.S., Northwestern U., 1952; M.B.A., U. Mich., 1957. With Exxon Co., 1957-70; fin. adv. Exxon Co. (Esso Natural Gas), The Hague, Netherlands, 1965-66; treas. Exxon Co. (Esso Europe), London, 1966-70; sr. v.p. Aetna Life & Casualty Co., Hartford, Conn., 1970-72; exec. v.p. Aetna Life & Casualty Co., 1972-88, also dir.; vice chmn. Ind. Energy Co., 1989—; bd. dirs. MBIA Corp., N.Y.C., Comml. Union Ins. Cos., Chevy Chase Savs. Bank; chmn., owner Hartford Whalers Hockey Club. Bd. govs. Nat. Hockey League; chmn. mem. exec. com. Am. Council for Arts, Greater Hartford Arts Council; chmn. Downtown Council, Hartford; corporator Hartford Hosp.; bd. dirs. Inst. of Living, Hartford; elector Wadsworth Atheneum. Served to lt. USNR, 1952-55. Clubs: Hartford (dir.), Watch Hill Yacht, Windermere Island.

CONRADES, GEORGE HENRY, information systems company executive; b. St. Louis, Feb. 26, 1939; s. Ralph Andrew and Elizabeth (Quermann) C.; m. Patricia Ruth Belt, Feb. 9, 1963; children: Elizabeth, Laura, George, Mary Emma, Anna. BA in Physics and Math., Ohio Wesleyan U., 1961; MBA, U. Chgo., 1972. With IBM Corp., 1961—; pres. data processing div. IBM Corp., White Plains, N.Y., 1980-82; corp. v.p. IBM Corp., Armonk, 1981-86, pres. nat. accounts div., 1982-83; corp. v.p., asst. group exec. Info. Systems and Tech. Group IBM Corp., Harrison, N.Y., 1983-84; corp. v.p., group exec. Asia/Pacific Group IBM Corp., Tokyo, 1984-86, sr. v.p., group exec. Info. Systems and Products Group, 1986-87; corp. sr. v.p. IBM Corp., Armonk, 1986—; gen. mgr., Personnel Systems, White Plains, N.Y., 1988, US Mkgt. & Services, IBM Corp, White Plains, 1988—; mem. IBM's Corp. Mgmt. Bd.; bd. dirs. First Am. Bank of N.Y., Finevest Foods, Inc. Vice chmn. bd. trustees Ohio Wesleyan U., Delaware, Ohio. Mem. U. Chgo. Grad. Sch. Bus. Alumni Assn. Office: IBM 1133 Westchester Ave White Plains NY 10601

CONROY, DENNIS JOSEPH, management consultant; b. N.Y.C., Jan. 31, 1945; s. Dennis J. and Margaret M. (Sheehy) C.; m. Gail A. Sheridan, Nov. 30, 1974; children: Bridget Anne, Devin Sheridan. BS in History, Iona Coll., 1987. Cert. mgmt. cons. Sales profl. SCM Corp., N.Y.C., 1968-69, Lanier Bus. Prodn., Inc., N.Y.C., 1969-71; communications cons. N.Y. Telephone Co., N.Y.C., 1971-75; regional dir. MCI Communications Corp., N.Y.C., 1975-77; sr. assoc. Booz, Allen & Hamilton, Inc., N.Y.C., 1977-82; ptnr. Coopers & Lybrand, N.Y.C., 1982—; Contbr. articles to mags. and profl. jours. Contbr. articles to profl. jours. Chmn. fin. com. Immaculate Conception Ch. and Sch., Tuckahoe, N.Y., 1987-88; vice-chmn. Citizen's Adv. Com. on Cable TV, Eastchester, N.Y., 1984-86; v.p. Calif. Ridge Civic Assn., Eastchester, 1988. Sgt. USMC, 1963-67, Vietnam. Mem. Inst. Mgmt. Cons., Soc. Telecommunications Cons., N.Y. Athletic Club, Westchester Country Club. Republican. Roman Catholic. Home: 6 Columbus Circle Eastchester NY 10709 Office: Coopers & Lybrand 1251 Ave of the Americas New York NY 10020

CONROY, ROBERT JOHN, lawyer; b. Newark, Feb. 17, 1953; s. Michael John and Frances (Goncalves) C.; m. Mary Catherine McGuire, June 7, 1975; children: Caitlin Michaela, Michael Colin. BS, St. Peter's Coll., 1977; M in Pub. Adminstrn., CUNY, 1981; JD, N.Y. Law Sch., 1981; MPH, Harvard U., 1985. Bar: N.Y. 1981, N.J. 1981, U.S. Dist. N.J. 1981, Calif. 1982, U.S. Dist. Ct. (so. and ea. dists.) N.Y. 1982, U.S. Ct. Appeals (2d and 3d cirs.) 1982, Fla. 1984, D.C. 1984, U.S. Supreme Ct. 1984. Asst. corp. counsel City of N.Y., 1981-83, dep. chief med. malpractice unit, 1983, chief med. malpractice unit, 1984; assoc. Jones, Hirsch, Connors & Bull, N.Y.C., 1985-88; counsel Kern & Augustine, P.A., Morristown, N.J., 1988—; spl. counsel pro bono med. malpractice research project, City of N.Y., 1985-88. Solomon scholar, N.Y. Law Sch., 1979. Mem. ABA (chmn. govt. mgmt. com. 1984-86, mgr. products media bd. 1985—, chmn. document retrieval com. 1985-86, vice-chmn. ins. and malpractice com. 1986—, econs. of law practice sect.), N.J. Bar Assn. (dir. health hosp. sect.), Soc. Health Care Risk Mgmt. N.J. (chmn. legis. com.), San Diego County Bar Assn., Assn. of Bar of City of N.Y., Harvard Club N.J., Pi Alpha Alpha. Home: 69 Sandy Hill Rd Westfield NJ 07090 Office: Kern & Augustine PA 82 Speedwell Ave Morristown NJ 07960

CONROY, STEPHEN MARTIN, internal audit manager; b. Geneva, N.Y., Dec. 28, 1959; s. Martin Ambrose and Patricia Ann (Rayno) C.; m. Sheryl Anne LaSpina, May 25, 1985. BBA, U. Notre Dame, 1981. CPA, Pa. Staff acct. Price Waterhouse, Phila., 1981-83; sr. auditor Dow Jones & Co., Inc., Princeton, N.J., 1983-85; audit supr. Commonwealth Land Title Ins. Co., Phila., 1985-86, asst. gen. auditor, 1986-88, asst. v.p., gen. auditor, 1988—. Mem. AICPA, Pa. Inst. CPA's, Notre Dame Club of Phila. Home: 805 Litwa Ln Aston PA 19014 Office: Commonwealth Land Title Ins Co 8 Penn Ctr Philadelphia PA 19103

CONSIDINE, FRANK WILLIAM, container corporation executive; b. Chgo., Aug. 15, 1921; s. Frank Joseph and Minnie (Regan) C.; m. Nancy Scott, Apr. 3, 1948. PhB, Loyola U., Chgo., 1943, LLD (hon.), 1986; LHD (hon.), Northwestern U., 1987. Owner F. J. Hogan Agy., Chgo., 1945-47; asst. to pres. Graham Glass Co., Chgo., 1947-51; owner F.W. Considine Co., Chgo., 1951-55; v.p. Metro Glass div. Kraftco, Chgo., 1955-60; v.p., dir. Nat. Can Corp. (now Am. Nat. Can. Co.), Chgo., 1961-67, exec. v.p., 1967-69, pres., 1969-88, chief exec. officer, 1973-88, chmn., 1983—; vice chmn. Triangle Industries, Inc. (parent corp.), New Brunswick, N.J., 1985-88; dir. Allis Chalmers Corp., Ency. Britannica, 1st Chgo. Corp., 1st Nat. Bank Chgo., Helene Curutis Industries, Inc., Ill. Power Co., Schwitzer, Inc., Scotsman Industries, Internat. Minerals & Chem. Corp., Maytag Co., Tribune Co., IMC Fertilizer Group Inc.; mem. bd. govs. Midwest Stock Exch., Chgo. Past chmn. U.S. sect. Egypt Bus. Coun.; trustee, mem. exec. com. Mus. Sci. and Industry Chgo.; bd. dirs. Can Mfrs. Inst., Evanston Hosp., Lyric Opera of Chgo., Field Mus. Natural History, Jr. Achievement Chgo., Loyola U., Chgo. Lt. USNR, 1943-46. Named to Chgo. Bus. Hall of Fame, 1985. Mem. Econ. Club Chgo., Chgo. Assn. Commerce and Industry (past pres.). Clubs: Econ., Chgo., Comml., Mid-Am., Glen View (Golf, Ill.), Old Elm. Office: Am Nat Can Co 8770 W Bryn Mawr Chicago IL 60631 *

CONSOLACION, FRANCO HERMINIA, accounting executive; b. Philipines, Dec. 11, 1938; s. Jose De Los Santos and Coleta Sanchez (Herminia) C.; m. Lourdes Siazon Ancheta, May 14, 1966; children—Franco, Rosavilla, Garry. A.C.S., U. of the E., 1959; B.B.A., 1962; M.B.A., John F. Kennedy U., 1977. CPA, Phillipines, Calif., Tex.; cert. teacher. Sr. bank examiner Central Bank Phillipines, Manila, 1967-73; sr. acct. U. Calif.-San Francisco, 1973-81; gen. mgr. C&C Profl. Cons. Co., San Francisco, 1981-82; pres., gen. mgr. Consolacion & Partible C.P.A.s, Inc., 1982-87; mng. ptnr. Consolacion, Partible and Vasquez, 1987—; prof. Nat. Hispanic U., 1986—, U. of East, Manila, 1966-73; instr. City Coll. San Francisco, 1980; lectr. San Francisco State U., 1980-81, Golden Gate U., 1981-82; auditor Filipino-Ams. of Contra Costa, Inc. Regional dir. Congress of Filipino-Am. Citizens; mem. Cursillos in Christianity; mem. human relations com. Richmond Unified Sch. Dist. Bd. Edn. Recipient Outstanding leadership award San Francisco Bd. Suprs., 1981; Pub. Service award as Most Outstanding Filipino Acct. Phillipine Consul Gen., 1981; named Outstanding Filipino Acct. of Decade, Supr. Carol Ruth Silver, 1981; cited for Outstanding Leadership Calif. State Bd. Acct., 1983, Calif. Legislature, 1983; spl. commendation Calif. Assembly, 1983, cert. of recognition on behalf Filipino-Am. Accts., 1984, FIL-AM. Council of San Francisco, 1986; Top Awardee Ten Outstanding Filipinos in Am. Community & Vol. Service, 1984. Mem. Am. Inst. C.P.A.s, Filipino Accts. Assn. (founder, pres. 1974-82, chmn. bd., Outstanding Leadership plaque of Appreciation. 1982), Soc. Calif. Accts. (pres. East Bay chpt. 1988—). Republican. Roman Catholic. Lodge: K.C. Home: 1835 Hoke Ct Pinole CA 94564 Office: Consolacion Partible Vasquez 833 Market St Ste 508-510 San Francisco CA 94103

CONSTANT, CLINTON, chemical engineer; b. Nelson, B.C., Can., Mar. 20, 1912; came to U.S., 1936, naturalized, 1942; s. Vasile and Annie (Hunt) C.; m. Margie Robbel, Dec. 5, 1965. B.Sc. with honors, U. Alta., 1935, postgrad., 1935-36; Ph.D., Western Res. U., 1939. Registered profl. engr. Devel. engr. Harshaw Chem. Co., Cleve., 1936-38, mfg. foreman, 1938-43, sr. engr. semi-works dept., 1948-50; supt. hydrofluoric acid dept. Nyotex Chems., Inc., Houston, 1943-47, chief devel. engr., 1947-48; mgr. engring. Ferro Chem. Co., Bedford, Ohio, 1950-52; tech. asst. mfg. dept. Armour Agrl. Chem. Co. (name formerly Armour Fertilizer Works), Bartow, Fla., 1952-61, mfg. research and devel. div., 1961-63, mgr. spl. projects Research div. (co. name changed to USS Agri-Chems 1968), 1963-65, project mgr., 1965-70; chem. adviser Robert & Co. Assocs., Atlanta, 1970-79; chief engr. Almon & Assocs., Inc., Atlanta, 1979-80; project mgr. Engring. Service Assocs., Atlanta, 1980-81; v.p. engring. ACI Inc., Hesperia, Calif., 1981-83; sr. v.p., chief engr. MTI (acquisition of ACI), Hesperia, 1983-86; engring. cons. San Bernardino County APCD, Victorville, Calif., 1986—. Fellow AAAS, Am. Inst. Chemists, Am. Inst. Chem. Engrs., N.Y. Acad. Scis., AIAA (assoc.); mem. Am. Chem. Soc., Am. Astron. Soc., Astron. Soc. Pacific, Royal Astron. Soc. Can., NSPE, Am. Water Works Assn., Calif. Water and Pollution Control Assn., Air Pollution Control Assn., Soc. Mfg. Engrs., Calif. Soc. Profl. Engrs. Author tech. reports, sci. fiction; patentee in field.

CONSTANTINI, LOUIS ORLANDO, financial consultant, stock broker; b. Columbus, Ga., Jan. 12, 1948; s. Louis T. and Edna G. (Spears) C.; m. Mary Ann Jennings, Feb. 9, 1974; children: Rachel J., Emily J. BA, U. Fla., 1972. Cert. fin. planner, N.Y. Intelligence officer CIA, Washington, 1972-76; fin. cons. Merrill Lynch & Co., El Paso, Tex., 1976-84; fin. cons. Merrill Lynch & Co., Las Cruces, N.Mex., 1984-88, v.p., 1988—. Chmn. El Paso Estate Planning Coun., 1982. Decorated Bronze Star, Combat Infantryman Badge, Cross of Gallantry with Gold Star (Republic of Vietnam). Mem. Sigma Phi Epsilon. Home: 1837 Regal Ridge Las Cruces NM 88001 Office: Merrill Lynch & Co 880 Telshor Blvd Las Cruces NM 88001

CONTI, CARL JOSEPH, electronics executive; b. Ravenna, Ohio, Oct. 12, 1937; s. Sebastian Galenti and Carmella (Triscori) C.; m. Marjorie Alberta Ruehr, June 6, 1959; children: Christopher, Thomas, Andrew. BS, Case Inst. Tech., 1959. Engr. IBM, Poughkeepsie, N.Y., 1959-62; engring. mgr. IBM, Poughkeepsie, 1963-72; dir. application systems devel. IBM, Mohansic, N.Y., 1973-75; dir. logic and package devel. IBM, East Fishkill, N.Y., 1975-77; dir. Endicott Lab. IBM, Endicott, N.Y., 1978-79, site gen. mgr., div. v.p., 1980-81; site gen. mgr., div. v.p. IBM, Poughkeepsie, 1982-83; pres. data systems div. IBM White Plains, N.Y., 1984-85, v.p., group exec., 1985-88; sr. v.p., gen. mgr. IBM Enterprise Systems, Somers, N.Y., 1988—; mem. corp. mgmt. bd. IBM, Armonk, N.Y., 1985—. Contbr. articles to profl. jours. Trustee Clarkson U., Potsdam, N.Y., 1985-86, Case Western Reserve U., Cleve., 1986—; bd. mem. Syracuse (N.Y.) Engring. Coll. Adv. Bd., 1982-85, Case Inst. Tech. Adv. Bd., Cleve., 1984—, Scenic Hudson Adv. Com., Poughkeepsie. Commencement speaker Case Western Res. U., 1986. Mem. IEEE, NRC (bd. telecommunications computer applications 1986—). Office: IBM Corp PO Box 100 Somers NY 10589

CONTILLO, LAWRENCE JOSEPH, financial consultant; b. Washington, Mar. 3, 1960; s. Lawrence and Kathleen Grace (O'Neil) C. BS in Acctg. and Fin., U. Md., 1981; MBA, George Washington U., 1982. CPA, Md. Financial analyst Fed. Home Loan Mortgage Corp., Washington, 1982-83; budget analyst Am. Security Bank, 1983-84; mgr. MCI, Arlington, Va., 1984-86; cons. Laventhol & Horwath, Washington, 1986-87; mgr. Watkins, Meegan, Drury& Co., Bethesda, Md., 1987—. Mem. Md. Assn. CPAs (com. mem.). Office: Watkins Meegan Drury & Co One Bethesda Ctr 4800 Hampden Ln Bethesda MD 20814

CONTRERAS, PHILLIP A., lawyer, manufacturing company executive; b. El Paso, Tex., Oct. 2, 1934; s. Felipe and Margaret (Edgar) C.; m. Carolyn E. Ahnert, Aug. 24, 1962 (div. Dec. 1982); children: Kimberly, Kelly, Kaysi. B.S. in Civil Engring, Seattle U., 1958; LL.B., So. Meth. U., 1965. Bar: Tex. 1966. Engr. trainee Boullion, Griffith & Christofferson, Seattle, 1955-58; hydraulic engr. U.S.C.E., Dallas, 1961-66; mgr. properties for Latin Am. Braniff Internat., Dallas, 1966-68; legal counsel, asst. sec. Mohawk Airlines, Utica, N.Y., 1968-71; v.p. legal internat. White Motor Corp., Eastlake, Ohio, 1971-75; asst. gen. counsel, sec. White Motor Corp., 1975-79; also dir., pres. WMISA, 1975-79; dir. numerous subs. White Motor Corp.; v.p., gen. counsel Ferro Corp., 1979—. Bd. dirs. Cosmopolitan Community Center, Utica, N.Y., 1968-71; bd. trustees Greater Cleve. Neighborhood Ctrs. Assn., Community Neighborhood Assn., 1988—. 1st lt. U.S. Army, 1958-61. Mem. Tex. Bar Assn., ABA, Am. Soc. Internat. Law, Am. Soc. Corp. Secs., Tex. Soc. Profl. Engrs., Ohio Fgn. Commerce Assn., Greater Cleve. Internat. Lawyers Club. Roman Catholic. Club: Fun Country Soaring. Home: 11419 Snow White Dr Dallas TX 75229 Office: Ferro Corp 100 Lakeside Ave Cleveland OH 44114

CONVERTI, VINCENZO, computer engineering executive; b. Roseto, Italy, Nov. 27, 1925; came to U.S., 1949; s. Rocco and Maria Antoinette (Russo) C.; m. Marjorie Ruth Pefley, Sept. 12, 1951; children: Mark, David, Paul, Cathy. B.S. in E.E., U. Ariz.-Tucson, 1952, M.S. in E.E., 1956. Research engr. Ariz. Computer Research, Phoenix, 1955-59; systems engring. supr. Ariz. Pub. Service, Phoenix, 1959-67, systems engring. mgr., 1967-75, computer service mgr., 1975-85, computer systems mktg. dir., 1985—. Contbr. in field. Fellow IEEE (chmn. power system engring. com. 1980-81). Republican. Home: 7039 N 14th St Phoenix AZ 85020 Office: Ariz Pub Svc PO Box 21666 Phoenix AZ 85020

CONWAY, CASEY ANTHONY, petroleum company executive; b. Portland, Oreg., Mar. 11, 1953; s. James William and Wanna Donna (Caspers) C. AA, Orange Coast Coll., 1974; BA in Bus. Adminstrn., Calif. State U.-Fullerton, 1976; MS in Safety, U. So. Calif., 1978. Cert. instr./trainer in surface/underground mine safety; cert. mine foreman surface uranuim; cert. Colo. audiometric technician; lic. amateur radio operator (extra class). Safety and environ. technician energy mining div. Union Oil Co. Calif., 1979, Rawlins, Wyo., safety trainer, 1979-80, safety supr., 1980-82; regulatory compliance coordinator oil shale ops., Parachute, Colo., 1983-85; safety supr. UNOCAL Los Angeles Refinery, Wilmington, Calif., 1986; supr. regulatory compliance, refining and mktg. div. UNOCAL, Los Angeles, 1986—; vol. examiner FCC amateur radio lics. Mem. Am. Soc. Safety Engrs. (membership chmn. Wyo. chpt. 1981-82, Wyo. safety congress com. 1982, sec. 1982-83, Western Slope chmn. 1983-86), Am. Petroleum Inst. (hazard communication and labeling issues group), Western Oil and Gas Assn. (chmn. occupational health and safety subcom.), Nat. Safety Mgmt. Soc., Am. Mgmt. Assn., Am. Radio Relay League (asst. dir. SW Div. 1986—) Soc. Advancement Mgmt. (Outstanding mem. 1975; v.p. membership 1976), Carbon County Amateur Radio Assn. (pres. 1980), Grand Mesa Contesters (sec.-

treas. 1985), South Orange Amateur Radio Assn., So. Calif. Contest, Cactus Radio.Roman Catholic. Lodge: Elks. Home: 310 Driftwood Rd Corona Del Mar CA 92625 Office: Unocal Refining and Mktg Div PO Box 7600 911 Bldg Los Angeles CA 90051

CONWAY, E. VIRGIL, banker, lawyer; b. Southhampton, N.Y., Aug. 2, 1929; m. Elaine Wingate, June 28, 1969; children by previous marriage: Allison, Sarah. BA in Philosophy and Religion magna cum laude, Colgate U., 1951; LLB cum laude, Yale U., 1956. Bar: N.Y. 1956. Assoc. firm Debevoise & Plimpton, N.Y.C., 1956-64; 1st dept. supt. Banks of State N.Y., 1964-67; sec. N.Y. State Banking Bd., 1964-67; exec. v.p. Manhattan Savs. Bank, N.Y.C., 1967-68; vice chmn., bd. dirs. Seamen's Corp.; pres., chmn. The Seamen's Bank for Savs., 1969—, also bd. dirs.; bd. dirs. Union Pacific Corp., chmn. exec. compensation com., mem. exec. com.; bd. dirs. J.P. Stevens & Co., Inc., 1974-88 ; dir. mut. funds managed by Nat. Securities and Rsch. Corp.; trustee, mem. exec. com. Atlantic Mut. Ins. Co.; trustee, chmn. fin. com., mem. exec., exec. personnel and pension nominating, exec. budget and contracts coms. Consol. Edison Co. of N.Y.; N.Y. rep. Conf. of State Bank Suprs., 1970-77, mem. adv. coun., 1973-74, mem. adv. com. to N.Y. State Supt. Banks, 1967-70. Editor: Yale Law Jour. Chmn. Temporary State Commn. on Water Supply Needs of Southeastern N.Y., 1970-75; mem. Audit Com. N.Y.C., 1982—, Mayor's Mgmt. Adv. Bd., N.Y.C., 1975-77; del. Republican State Conv. N.Y., 1962, 66; pres. N.Y. Young Rep. Club, 1962-63; bd. mgrs. Seaman's Ch. Inst. N.Y. and N.J.; mem. adv. bd. N.Y. U. Real Estate Inst.; bd. dirs. Realty Found. N.Y.; bd. dirs., chmn. audit, fin., exec. coms. Josiah Macy, Jr. Found.; trustee, former vice chmn., mem. exec. com. Citizens Budget Commn.; trustee N.Y.C. Police Found., Pace U., N.Y.C., Colgate U., 1970-76; trustee N.Y. coun. Boy Scouts Am.; trustee devel. com. South Street Seaport Mus.; bd. govs., pres. Fed. Hall Meml. Assos., Inc., 1981-84; bd. dirs., vice chmn, treas., mem. audit and fin., compensation, project planning and rev. policy com. N.Y.C. Partnership, Inc. With USAF, 1951-53; capt. Res. Recipient Humanitarian award Jewish Hosp. and Rsch. Ctr., Denver, 1977, Good Scout award Greater N.Y. couns. Boy Scouts Am., 1980, Spl. Recognition award NAACP, 1980, Disting. Svc. to Higher Edn. medal Brandeis U., 1976, Urban Leadership award NYU, 1981, Hundred Yr. Assn. Gold Medal award, 1986, Eagle Scout award, 1988; named Man of Yr. Realty Found. N.Y., 1978. Mem. ABA, Nat. Assn. Mut. Savs. Banks (past dir.), Savs. Banks Assn. N.Y. State (pres. 1978-79, past dir. and chmn. legis.), N.Y. C. of C. and Industry (bd. dirs., exec. com., sec.-treas., chmn. mission rev. com. 1985), Real Estate Bd. N.Y. (bd. govs. 1976-79), Assn. of Bar of City of N.Y., N.Y. State Bar Assn., Newcomen Soc., Econ. Club N.Y., Econ. Devel. Coun. N.Y.C., Knights o St. Patrick, Union League Club, Links Club, Down Town Assn. Club, Fort Orange Club (Albany, N.Y.), Siwanoy Country Club, Phi Beta Kappa. Office: 30 Wall St New York NY 10005

CONWAY, JAMES WALTER, accountant; b. Berwyn, Ill., May 1, 1955; s. Raymond J. and Hettie (McMillan) C.; m. Pamela A.M. Feige, Oct. 25, 1980; children: Kathleen Ann, Brendan Paul. BS in Acctg., U. Ill., 1979; MS in Taxation, DePaul U., 1984. CPA, Ill.; cert. tax acct.; registered fin. planner. Acct. Pritzker & Pritzker Co., Chgo., 1978-79; sr. acct. Ronald J. Borden & Co., Chgo., 1980-83; controller Callaghan Paving, Inc., Orland Park, Ill., 1983-85; ptnr. Moticka & Ralph, Inc., Brookfield, Ill., 1985—. Mem. AICPA (fin. planning div.), Ill. Soc. CPA's (pres. Fox Valley chpt.), Wis. CPA Soc. (personal fin. planning com.), Am. Assn. Personal Fin. Planners, Internat. Assn. Fin. Planners, Ind. Accts. Assn. Ill., Nat. Soc. Pub. Accts., Nat. Soc. Tax Profls., Inst. Tax Cons., Internat. Platform Assn., U. Ill. Alumni Assn., U.S. Naval Inst. Office: Moticka & Ralph Inc 9040 W Ogden Ave Brookfield IL 60513

CONWAY, JOHN THOMAS, utility company executive, lawyer, engineer; b. N.Y.C., May 10, 1924; s. John Joseph and Johannah (Stanley) C.; m. Priscilla Harris, Sept. 13, 1947 (div. 1978); children: John, Daniel, Sean, Thomas, Christopher, Johannah; m. Virginia McLaughlin, Mar. 17, 1989. B.N.S., Tufts U., 1945, B.S. in Engring., 1947; J.D., Columbia U., 1949. Bar: N.Y. 1949, U.S. Supreme Ct. 1952. Spl. agt. FBI, Washington, 1950-56; asst. dir. U.S. Congress Joint Com. on Atomic Energy, Washington, 1956-62, exec. dir., 1962-68; exec. asst. to chmn. Consol. Edison, N.Y.C., 1968-78, exec. v.p., 1982—; pres. Am. Nuclear Energy Council, Washington, 1978-82, chmn. bd., 1983—; bd. dirs. Empire State Energy Research Com., N.Y., 1970-76, Atomic Indsl. Forum, 1976-78; mem. oversite com. U.S. Com. Energy Awareness, Washington, 1982—. Bd. dirs. Americans for Energy Independence, Youth for Energy Independence, Washington, 1982—, Assn. For A Better N.Y., 1982—, N.Y. Fire Safety Found., 1984—; mem. N.Y.C. Mayor's Com. for Sci., 1969-76. Served to lt. j.g. USN, 1943-46. Mem. Fed. Bar Assn., Bar Assn. City N.Y., Am. Nuclear Soc., Assn. for a Better N.Y. Democrat. Roman Catholic. Clubs: University, Democratic (Washington). Office: Consol Edison Co NY Inc 4 Irving Pl New York NY 10003

CONWAY, MORNA HELEN, marketing company executive; b. Edinburgh, Scotland, Apr. 1, 1945; came to U.S., 1971; d. Wilfred Ormiston and Helen Douglas (Linton) Trotter. MA, U. Edinburgh, 1966, Diploma in Gen. Linguistics, 1967; MEd, Loyola Coll., Balt., 1980; PhD, U. Md., 1986. Lectr. Fourah Bay Coll., Freetown, Sierra Leone, 1967-68; dir. Internat. Sch., Saigon, Vietnam, 1968-70; mgr. sales promotion Waverly Press, Inc., Balt., 1971-75; pres. Morna Conway, Inc., Taneytown, Md., 1975—; v.p. mktg. EPS Group, Balt., 1984; sr. v.p. mktg. U. Support Svcs., Washington, 1987-89; adj. faculty Loyola Coll., 1987—, Western Md. Coll., 1986. Author: Integrated Course for English in Vietnam, 1978; contbr. article to profl. jours. Vol. Johns Hopkins Hosp., 1979, Edinburgh Royal Infirmary, 1962. Mem. Council Biology Editors (presenter workshop 1978, 86-89, membership chmn. 1978), Soc. Scholarly Pubs., Advtg. Assn. Balt. (v.p. 1978). Home and Office: 4785 Baptist Rd Taneytown MD 21787

CONWAY, ROBERT MICHAEL, investment banker; b. Rochester, Minn., Apr. 22, 1944; s. Robert Martin and Margaret (Olsen) C.; m. Lois Karch, Mar. 1968; children: Rebecca, Caroline. BA, U. Notre Dame, 1966; MBA, U. Chgo., 1968; MA, U. Louvain, Belgium, 1969. Assoc. Goldman, Sachs & Co., N.Y.C., 1970-73, v.p., 1973-78, ptnr., 1978—; also bd. dirs. Goldman Sachs Internat. Corp., London; adv. council coll. arts and letters U. Notre Dame, 1987—; adj. prof. grad. sch. bus. Columbia U., 1978-83. Office: Goldman Sachs & Co 85 Broad St New York NY 10004 Also: Goldman Sachs & Co 85 Broad St New York NY 10004

CONWAY, THOMAS J., grocery store company executive. V.p. Safeway Stores Inc., Oakland, Calif. Office: Safeway Stores Inc 201 4th St Oakland CA 94660 *

CONYERS, GAYLE UTSEY, real estate mortgage owner; b. Jacksonville, Fla., Nov. 13, 1936; d. George Emmett and Hazel (Tyler) Utsey; divorced; children: Harrison Edward III, William Emmett. BA in Fashion Merchandising, Fla. State U., 1958. Advt. mgt. Davison's, Augusta, Ga., 1958-59; with advt. dept. Sears, Roebuck & Co., 1959-60, mgr. sportswear/swimwear dept., 1960-63; officer mortgage loans George E. Utsey Sr., Jacksonville, 1963-84, owner, mgr., 1984—. Leader prayer chpt. Concerned Women Am., Jacksonville, 1985—; mem. Rep. Nat. Com., Washington, 1986—; mem. exec. com. Rep. Party, Jacksonville, 1987—. Mem. Timuquana Country Club, Capitol Hill Women's Club. Avocations: pro-family, pro-Am. ch. activities. Office: 3575 St Johns Ave Jacksonville FL 32205

COOGLE, JOSEPH MOORE, JR., advertising agency executive; b. Louisville, Jan. 13, 1933; s. Joseph Moore and Dorothy Virginia (Miller) C.; m. Maryhelen Doty, Jan. 27, 1957; children: Suzanne Grace, Virginia Louise. B.S., U. Ky., 1957; M.B.A., U. Chgo., 1958. Grocery products salesman Pillsbury Co., Mpls., 1958-59; marketing research up to sr. research analyst Pillsbury Co., 1959-62, up to marketing mgr., grocery products marketing dept., 1962-65; account exec. Ketchum, MacLeod & Grove, Pitts., 1965-66; account supr. Ketchum, MacLeod & Grove, 1966-68, v.p., account mgr., 1968-70, v.p., dir. marketing, research and media planning, 1970-72, sr. v.p., 1972-77, dir. ops. planning, 1975-77; dir. mktg. Ketchum, MacLeod & Grove, N.Y.C., 1977-79; exec. v.p. Ketchum, MacLeod & Grove, 1978-79; pres. Ketchum Internat., Inc. div. Ketchum Communications Inc., Pitts., 1979-84, exec. v.p. ops. and planning, dir., 1984-88, exec. v.p. specialized services group, 1988—; dir. MCS, Inc. Former chmn. Pitts. chpt. Am. Assn. Advt. Agys.; Trustee Pressley Ridge Sch.; bd. dirs. Sewickley Valley Hosp., Three Rivers Shakespeare Festival, Pitts. Dance Council. Served with AUS, 1953-55. Mem. Am. Mktg. Assn., Am. Mgmt. Assn., Beta Gamma Sigma. Lutheran. Clubs: Duquesne (Pitts.); Edgeworth (Sewickley, Pa.); Erie Yacht (Pa.); West River Sailing (Galesville, Md.), Allegheny Country, Edgeworth. Home: Sewickley PA 15143 Office: Ketchum Communications Inc 6 PPG Pl Pittsburgh PA 15222

COOK, ALBERT THOMAS THORNTON, JR., financial advisor; b. Cleve., Apr. 24, 1940; s. Albert Thomas Thornton and Tyra Esther (Morehouse) C.; m. Mary Jane Blackburn, June 1, 1963; children: Lara, Thomas, Timothy. BA, Dartmouth Coll., 1962; MA, U. Chgo., 1966. Asst. sec. Dartmouth Coll., Hanover, N.H., 1972-77; exec. dir. Big Brothers, Inc., N.Y.C., 1977-78; underwriter Boettcher & Co., Denver, 1978-81; asst. v.p. Dain Bosworth Inc., Denver, 1981-82, Colo. Nat. Bank, Denver, 1982-84; pres. The Albert T.T. Cook Co., Denver, 1984—; arbitrator Nat. Assn. Securities Dealers, N.Y.C., 1985—, Mcpl. Securities Rulemaking Bd., Washington, 1987—. Pres. Etna-Hanover Ctr. Community Assn., Hanover, N.H., 1974-76; mem. Mayor's Task Force, Denver, 1984; dir. Rude Park Community Nursery, Denver, 1985-87; trustee The Iliff Sch. Theol., Denver, 1986—. Mem. Dartmouth Alumni Council (exec. com., chmn. nominating and trustee search coms. 1987-89), Delta Upsilon. Congregationalist. Clubs: University, Cactus (Denver); Dartmouth of N.Y.C., Yale. Lodge: Lions (bd. dirs. Denver chpt. 1983-85, treas. 1986-87, pres. Denver Found., 1987-88). Home: 7099 E Hinsdale Pl Englewood CO 80112 Office: 1225 Seventeenth St 23rd Floor Denver CO 80202

COOK, ALEXANDER TROWBRIDGE, real estate executive; b. Greenwich, Conn., May 1, 1955; s. Daniel Carrington and Katherine Skinner (Warner) C.; m. Sharon Lee Andrews, June 18, 1988. BA in Econs., U. Pa., 1977; (hon.), Young Mktg. Bankers Assn., 1984. Mgr. credit Fidelity Bank, Phila., 1977-79; asst. v.p. Mfrs. Hanover Bank, N.Y.C., 1979-84, Cushman and Wakefield Fin. Services, N.Y.C., 1984-85; pres. Hist. Cons., Phila., 1986—, Restoration Cons., Phila., 1986—; lectr. U. Pa., 1985—; bd. govs. St. Anthony, 1988. Contbr. articles to profl. jours. Chmn. Saunders Zoning Com., Phila, 1986—; vol. Spruce Hill Hist. Dist., 1986-87. Mem. Greater Phila. C. of C., Nat. Trust, Delta Alumni Assn. Republican. Presabyterian. Club: St. Anthony. Home: 424 N 39th St Philadelphia PA 19104 Office: Restoration Cons 424 N 39th St Philadelphia PA 19104

COOK, BRIAN MCCAMMAN, banker; b. Landstuhl, Fed. Republic of Germany, Aug. 21, 1958; s. Calvin Raymond and Betty (Esmoil) C.; m. Ann Arthur, Aug. 10, 1985. Student, Princeton U., 1979; BA with honors, Bowdoin Coll., 1980. Asst. treas. European Am. Bank and Trust Co., N.Y.C., 1980-83; v.p., mgr. N.Y. br. BHF Bank, N.Y.C., 1983—. Republican. Episcopalian. Club: Met. (N.Y.). Office: BHF Bank 55 E 59th St New York NY 10022

COOK, BRUCE EDWARD, I, insurance company executive; b. Muskegon, Mich., Aug. 21, 1944; s. Marshall DeBois and Francis Alberta (Cady) C.; m. Kathryn Joyce Sneer, June 8, 1967; children: Shelley Ann, Hope Lynn, Bruce Edward II. AA, Mt. Hood Coll., Gresham, Oreg., 1971; BS, Portland State U., 1972. CLU. Group rep. Equitable Life Assurance Co., Portland, 1972-74; owner Bruce Cook & Assocs., Portland, 1974-86, Group Benefits Systems, Inc., Sandy, Oreg., 1986—; pres. Life Leaders Oreg., Portland, 1980-81. Councilman City of Sandy, 1978-82, chmn. dept. parks, 1981; mem. Pvt. Industry Council, Oregon City, 1988—. Served as sgt. U.S. Army, 1968-70, Vietnam. Decorated Purple Heart, Combat Inf. citation. Mem. Nat. Assn. Security Dealers, Oreg. Life Underwriters, Portland Life Underwriters, Portland CLU's, Million Dollar Round Table (life), Sandy C. of C., VFW (project chmn. Sandy chpt. 1987-88). Republican. Clubs: Mt. Hood Golf (Wemme, Oreg.) (pres. 1988); Gresham (Oreg.) Exec. Lodge: Elks. Office: Group Benefits Systems Inc 38776 Proctor Box 520 Sandy OR 97055

COOK, CHARLES BECKWITH, JR., securities company executive; b. Buffalo, July 14, 1929; s. Charles Beckwith Cook and Elaine Satterfield; m. Barbara Welch, May 11, 1942; children: Deborah Legge, Charles B. III, Rachel, Andrew. BA, Yale U., 1952. Trainee exec. 1st Nat. City Bank, N.Y.C., 1954-56; pres., chmn. Hoppin Watson Inc., N.Y.C., 1956-82; vice chmn. Janney Montgomery Scott, N.Y.C., 1982—, also bd. dirs.; bd. dirs. Am. Maize-Prod Co., Stamford, Conn., Am. Fructose Co., Stamford, Westbury (N.Y.) Fed. Savs. & Loan. 1st lt. arty. U.S. Army, 1952-54, Korea. Republican. Episcopalian. Clubs: Adirondack League (Old Forge, N.Y.); Weston Gun (Westport, Conn.). Lodge: Moose.

COOK, CHARLES EDWARD, JR., editor, political analyst; b. Shreveport, La., Nov. 20, 1953; s. Charles Edward and Mary Elizabeth (Hudgens) C.; m. Lucy Gerald, Apr. 17, 1982. Student Georgetown U., 1972-77. Research dir. Democratic Senatorial Campaign Com., Washington, 1977-79; so. regional desk person Kennedy for Pres. Campaign, Washington, 1979-80; public opinion analyst, polit. cons. William R. Hamilton & Staff, Washington, 1980; asst. dir. for polit. affairs Nat. Assn. of Home Builders, Washington, 1981-82; mem. profl. staff Senate Democratic Policy Com., 1982-84; editor, The Cook Polit. Report (formerly The Nat. Polit. Rev.), Washington, 1984—; polit. analyst Hill and Knowlton Pub. Affairs, Worldwide (formerly Govt. Research Corp.), 1986-88, v.p. strategic and econ. analysis div., 1988—. Election night analyst, commentator for Cable-Satellite Pub. Affairs Network, 1986; election night analyst C-Span, 1986, 88, NBC News, 1988; columnist weekly newspapaer Roll Call. Methodist. Home: 4002 East-West Hwy Chevy Chase MD 20815 Office: Washington Harbour 901 31st St NE Washington DC 20007

COOK, CHARLES FRANCIS, insurance executive; b. Hackensack, N.J., Mar. 23, 1941; s. John Cooper and Emily (Morse) C.; m. Barbara Ann Dotter, Sept. 8, 1962; children: Melanie, Tammy, Cynthia. AB, Princeton U., 1963; MBA, St. Mary's of Tex., 1974. Asst. actuary Continental Ins. Cos., N.Y.C., 1965-68; actuary Gen. Accident, Phila., 1968-70; v.p., actuary USAA, San Antonio, 1970-75; sr. v.p. Am. Internat. Underwriters, N.Y.C., 1975-80, N.H. Ins. Co., Manchester, 1980-83; pres. Am. Universal Group, Providence, 1983-88; pvt. cons. practice in actuarial and ins. mgmt. Barrington, R.I., 1988—; bd. dirs. Casualty Actuarial Soc. Contbr. articles to profl. jours. Pres. St. John and St. Matthew Emanuel Luth. Ch., Bklyn., 1978-80; bd. dirs. United Way of Southeastern New Eng., Providence, 1985—. Fellow Casualty Actuarial Soc. (bd. dirs 1971-74, 85, gen. chmn. exam com., recipient Woodward Fondiller Prize 1968); mem. Am. Acad. Actuaries, Soc. CPCU's (cert.), Internat. Assn. Actuaries. Home and Office: 5 Spinnaker Dr Barrington RI 02806

COOK, DEBORAH CHUNN, accountant; b. Columbia, S.C., Oct. 4, 1961; d. Matthew Locke III and Carolyn (Faile) Chunn; m. Brian Lee Cook, Mar. 1, 1986. BBA, Coll. Charleston, S.C., 1983. CPA, S.C. Jr. staff acct. McKnight, Frampton & Buskirk, Charleston, 1983-84; jr. staff acct. Thiem, Jackson & Pace, Charleston, 1984-85, sr. staff acct., 1985-88; fin. office Berkeley-Charleston-Dorchester Coun. of Govts., S.C., 1988—. Mem. AICPA, S.C. Assn. CPAs, Phi Mu (chpt. fin. advisor 1987-88), Phi Mu Alumnae Assn. Office: Berkeley-Charleston-Dorchester Coun of Govts 701 E Bay St BTC Box 1120 Charleston SC 29403

COOK, DORIS MARIE, accountant, educator; b. Fayetteville, Ark., June 11, 1924; d. Ira and Mettie Jewel (Dorman) C. BS in Bus. Adminstrn., U. Ark., 1946, MS, 1949; PhD, U. Tex., 1969. CPA, Okla., Ark. Jr. acct. Haskins & Sells, Tulsa, 1946-47; instr. acctg. U. Ark., Fayetteville, 1947-52, asst. prof., 1952-62, assoc. prof., 1962-69, prof., 1969-88, Univ. prof. and Nolan E. Williams lectr. in acctg., 1988—; mem. Ark. State Bd. Pub. Accountancy, 1987—; apptd. Nolan E. Williams lectrship in acctg., 1988—. Contbr. articles to profl. jours. Mem. Ark. Bus. Assn. (editor newsletter 1982-85), Am. Acctg. Assn. (chair nat. membership 1982-83, chair Arthur Carter Scholarship com. 1984-85, chair membership Ark. 1985-87), Am. Inst. CPA's, Am. Women's Soc. CPA's, Ark. Soc. CPA's (v.p. 1975-76, pres. NW Ark. chpt. 1980-81, sec. Student Loan Found. 1981-84, treas. Student Loan Found. 1984—, chair pub. relations 1984-88), Acad. Acctg. Historians (trustee 1985-87, mem. review bd. 1984—), Ark. Fedn. Bus. and Profl. Women's Clubs (treas. 1979-80), Mortar Bd., Beta Gamma Sigma, Beta Alpha Psi (editor nat. newsletter 1973-77, nat. pres. 1977-78), Phi Gamma Nu, Alpha Lambda Delta, Delta Kappa Gamma (sec. 1976-78, pres. 1978-80), Phi Kappa Phi. Club: Fayetteville Bus. and Profl. Women's (pres. 1973-74, 75-76, Woman of Yr. 1977). Home: 1115 Leverett St Fayetteville AR 72703 Office: U Ark Dept Acctg Fayetteville AR 72701

COOK, ERNEST EWART, oil company executive; b. Stratton, Wiltshire, Eng., Mar. 23, 1926; came to U.S., 1946; s. Edgar John and Dorothy May (Wiltshire) C.; m. Concepcion Fernandina Cairo, Sept. 23, 1953 (div. Apr. 1982); 1 child, Julia Ann; m. Marian Frances Miller, June 24, 1985. BA, U. Cambridge, Eng., 1946; MA, U. Cambridge, 1950. Geophysicist Cia Shell de Venezuela, Maracaibo, 1947-56; chief geophysicist Pakistan Shell Oil Co., Karachi, 1956-57; chief geophysicist Signal Oil and Gas Co., L.A., 1957-66, internat. exploration mgr., 1966-67; v.p. Seismic Computing Corp., Houston, 1968-70; chmn. Invent Inc., Houston, 1971-78; pres. Zenith Exploration Co., Houston, 1978-83; chmn. Barsdall Geo-Techs. Inc., Houston, 1983-84; pres. Enjay Enterprises Inc., Houston, 1984—; bd. dirs. Triton Energy Corp., Dallas, Triton Europe PLC, London, Input/Output Inc., Houston; treas. Interam. Affiliates Inc., Houston. Contbr. articles in field to profl. jours. Fellow Geol. Soc. London; mem. Am. Assn. Petroleum Geologists, Soc. Exploration Geophysicists, European Assn. Exploration Geophysicists, Soc. Petroleum Engrs., Marine Tech. Soc., United Oxford and Cambridge U. Club. Office: Enjay Enterprises Inc 12200 Northwest Frwy Ste 682 Houston TX 77092

COOK, GARY MORRIS, energy corporation executive; b. Lincoln, Nebr., Apr. 11, 1942; s. Eugene E. and Mary Margaret (Morris) C.; m. Diane Grafe, Sept. 3, 1966 (div. Feb. 1989); children: Christian M., Lauren S. BA in Econs. with honors, Wesleyan U., Middletown, Conn., 1964; JD (hon.), Harvard U., 1967. Mgmt. cons. McKinsey & Co. Inc., N.Y.C., 1967-70; spl. asst. to sec., dep. asst. sec. HEW, Washington, 1970-72; dep. asst. sec., acting dir. Bur. Domestic Commerce, Dept. Commerce, Washington, 1972-74; sr. v.p. Agrico Chem. Co., Tulsa, 1974-78; chmn. Trend Constrn. Corp., Tulsa and Oklahoma City, 1978-82; pres., chief operating officer Barringer Resources Inc., Golden, Colo., 1983-84; mng. dir. Gary M. Cook Interests., Denver, 1980—; mng. ptnr. Kimbrel & Cook Inc., Tulsa and Denver, 1985—; pres. chief exec. officer, dir. Kimce Energy Corp., Dallas, Denver, 1987—; vice-chmn. OECD Industry Com., Paris 1973-74. Contbr. articles to profl. jours. Mem. Council on Fgn. Relations. Clubs: Sankaty Golf (bd. dirs 1982), Sankaty Casino (Nantucket); Harvard (N.Y.); University (Washington), Denver Club. Home: 7355 E West Kentucky Dr Lakewood CO 80226 Office: Kimco Energy Corp 1801 Broadway Suite 300 Denver CO 80202

COOK, GEORGE HENRY, JR., manufacturing company executive; b. Chgo., Feb. 3, 1951; s. George Henry and Ruth (Van Auken) C.; m. Pamela Jean Rintoul, June 14, 1975; children: Elizabeth, Philip, Leslie, Grace. BS in Fin. and Acctg., S. Ill. U., 1973; MBA, No. Ill. U., 1978. CPA, Ill. Internal auditor McGraw-Edison Co., Elgin, Ill., 1973-74, audit mgr., 1974-75, dir. corp. acctg., 1975-77, dir. fin. analysis, 1977-78, controller comml. equipment group, 1978-79, controller foodservice equipment div., 1979-80; dir. fin. service div. McGraw-Edison Co., Columbus, Ohio, 1980-83; controller Worthington div. McGraw-Edison Co., BAsking Ridge, N.J., 1983-85; v.p. fin. CR Industries, Elgin, 1985-89; sr. v.p., chief fin. officer Boulevard Bancorp, 1989—. Instr. Jr. Achievement Elgin, 1975. So. Ill. U. Academic scholar, 1972-73. Mem. AICPA, Ill. Soc. CPAs, Fin. Execs. Inst. Republican. Roman Catholic. Home: 2255 Pebble Creek Dr Lisle IL 60532 Office: CR Industries 900 N State St Elgin IL 60123

COOK, HAROLD RODNEY, military officer, medical facility administrator; b. Sterling, Colo., Feb. 13, 1944; s. Harold E. Cook and Adelaide Cook; m. Shirley Carnel; 1 child, Dawn. BS in Bus., Psychology and Sociology, Kearney State Coll., 1973, MA in Psychology, 1974; MHA, Baylor U., 1985. Commd. 2d lt. U.S. Army, 1974, advanced through grades to maj., 1986; med. adminstr. U.S. Gen. Hosp., Nürnberg, Germany, 1975-78; comdr. 560th Ambulance Co., Korea; chief ops. med./surg. div. Acad. of Health Sci., Ft. Sam Houston, Tex., 1980-83; with health care adminstrn. Baylor U., Waco, Tex., 1983-85; surgery adminstr. Fitzsimons Army Med. Ctr., Aurora, Colo., 1985—; exec. dir., pres. Colo. Petrolon Inc., 1986-88; regional v.p. Petrolon Inc., 1988—. Mem. Am. Coll. Hosp. Adminstrs., Am. Soc. Mgmt., Nat. Assn. Collegiate Vets. (exec. bd.), Fitz Alpine Club (pres. 1985-87), Pantera Club. Home: 40 Plaza Sq Ste 202 Saint Louis MO 63103 Office: 1520 Market St Ste 2457 Saint Louis MO 63103

COOK, JAMES, editor; b. Schenectady, N.Y., Nov. 9, 1926; s. Harold James and Ruth May (Turner) C.; m. Claire Rose Kehrwald, Sept. 12, 1953; children—Karen Louise, Cassandra Claire. A.B., Bowdoin Coll., 1947; A.M., Columbia U., 1948. Instr. English Yankton (S.D.) Coll., 1948-49, Ohio U., 1949-52; editor Popular Publs., N.Y.C., 1952-53; mng. editor Railroad mag., 1953-55; assoc., sr. editor Forbes mag., N.Y.C., 1955-76; exec. editor Forbes mag., 1976—; reviewer Forbes Restaurant Guide, 1970-71; editor Forbes in Arabic, 1975-76. Home: 200 W 16th St New York NY 10011 Office: Forbes Inc 60 Fifth Ave New York NY 10011

COOK, JAY MICHAEL, accounting company executive; b. N.Y.C., Sept. 16, 1942; s. Gerald Cook and Mary Elizabeth (McGill) Totten; m. Mary Anne Griffith, July 11, 1964; children—Jennifer Lynn, Angela Marie, Jeffrey Thomas. B.S. in Bus. Adminstrn. cum laude, U. Fla., 1964. C.P.A., N.Y., Fla. Staff acct. Deloitte, Haskins & Sells, Fort Lauderdale, Fla., 1964-70; mgr. Deloitte, Haskins & Sells, Miami, Fla., 1970-74; ptnr. Deloitte, Haskins & Sells, N.Y.C., 1974-81; ptnr.-in-charge Deloitte, Haskins & Sells, Miami, 1981-83; mng. ptnr. Deloitte, Haskins & Sells, N.Y.C., 1983-86, chmn., 1986—; advisor SEC Reporting Inst., U. So. Calif., Los Angeles, 1982—; advisor Sch. Bus., U. Fla., Gainesville, 1981—. Author: Retained Earnings and Dividends, 1975; contbr. articles to profl. jours. Trustee Pace U., N.Y.C., 1984-85, Cen. Park Conservancy; pacesetter United Way of Tri-State; bd. dirs. N.Y.C. Ballet; mem. dean's adv. council Columbia Bus. Sch.; bd. dirs. Assocs. Harvard Bus. Sch. Mem. Am. Inst. C.P.A.s (chmn. SEC regulations 1980-83, mem. council 1983—, vice chmn. 1985-86, chmn. 1986-87), Am. Acctg. Assn., Conf. Bd., U.S. C. of C. (commerce services industries council), Advt. Council (industries adv. com.). Republican. Methodist. Clubs: Greenwich Country (Conn.); Sky, Princeton (N.Y.C.); City (Miami), Links. Home: 980 Lake Ave Greenwich CT 06830 Office: Deloitte Haskins & Sells 1114 Ave of the Americas New York NY 10036-7778

COOK, JOHN ALVIN, feed company executive; b. Danville, Pa., May 9, 1952; s. Alvin R. and Rheta J. (Teitsworth) C.; m. Deborah Lambert, Aug. 24, 1974; Kristen Joy, Ian Andrew, Collin Robert, Evan Stanley. BA in Bus. and Econs., The King's Coll., 1974. Mgmt. trainee Glyco Chem. Inc., Greenwich, Conn., 1974-76; acct. controller McDowell & Walker, Delhi, N.Y., 1976-78, treas., 1978-83; sec., treas. McDowell & Walker, Delhi, 1983—, C.E. Kiff, Inc., Delhi, %. Republican. Club: Fit for Life Internat. (Birmingham, Mich.). Office: McDowell & Walker Inc 4 Depot Delhi NY 13753

COOK, LEWIS H., manufacturing company executive; b. Phila., Mar. 17, 1943; s. Lewis and Kathryn (Harmstad) C.; children: Stephanie E., Russell L. BA in Econs., Denison U., 1965. Various positions to v.p. Young Windows Inc., Conshohocken, Pa., 1965-70, pres., 1970—. Mem. Mfg. Assn. Del. Valley, Robotics Inst., Mfg. Assn. Conshohocken. Republican. Episcopalian. Home: 689 N Valley Rd Paoli PA 19301 Office: Young Windows Inc Brook & Colwell Rds Box 387 Conshohocken PA 19428

COOK, LODWRICK MONROE, petroleum company executive; b. Grand Cane, La., June 17, 1928; married. B.S., La. State U., 1950, B.S. in Petroleum Engring., 1955; M.B.A., So. Meth. U., 1965. Petroleum engr. Union Producing Co., 1955-56; with Atlantic Richfield Co., Los Angeles, 1956—; engring. trainee Atlantic Richfield Co., Inc., Los Angeles, 1956-61, adminstrv. asst., 1961-64, sr. personnel dept., then personnel mgr., 1964-67, labor reins. con., 1967-69, mgr. labor reins. dept., 1969-70, v.p., gen. mgr. product div. Western area, 1970-72, v.p. mktg. products div., 1972-73, v.p. corp. planning div., 1973-74, v.p. products div., 1974-75, v.p. transp. div., 1975-77, sr. v.p. transp. div., 1977-80, exec. v.p., dir., 1980-85, pres., chief exec. officer, 1985, chmn., chief exec. officer, 1986—. Chmn. bd. dirs. Nat. Jr. Achievement; bd. regents Pepperdine U., La. State U. Found; bd. govs. Music Ctr. Los Angeles. Served to 1st lt. U.S. Army, 1950-53. Mem. Bus. Roundtable, Nat. Petroleum Council, Am. Petroleum Inst. (dir.). Office: Atlantic Richfield Co 515 S Flower St Los Angeles CA 90071 *

COOK, MICHAEL ANTHONY, financial services executive; b. Kingston, Jamaica, Jan. 10, 1956; came to U.S., 1979; s. Noel Keith and Edna Elaine (Walsh) C.; m. Maida E. Riviera, June 7, 1985; 1 child, Yvette. Diploma, Coll. Arts, Scis. and Tech., Kingston, 1976; BS, CUNY, 1982; MBA, Baruch Coll., 1984. Registered profl. engr., N.J., Jamaica. Transmitter engr. Radio Jamaica Ltd., Kingston, 1976-79; acct. South Bklyn. Health Ctr., 1981-83; fin. cons. Tri-Star Fin. Svcs., Queens, 1983-85; fin. planner John Hancock, Queens, 1985-87; chief exec. officer M.A.C. Assocs., Queens, 1987—; cons. Tri-Star Fin. Svcs., 1985—; bd. dirs. Scudder's Trucking, Inc., Bronx, Expressways, Inc., Bklyn. Inventor high voltage, high frequency isolating transformer. Recipient Econs. award Am. Econs. Assn., 1982. Mem. Internat. Assn. for Fin. Planners, Inst. Cert. Fin. Planners, Nat. Soc. Pub. Accts., N.Y. Soc. Ind. Accts., IEEE, Masons, Rosicrucian. Home: 85-12 169th St Jamaica NY 11432 Office: MAC Assocs 89032 210th St Queens Village NY 11428

COOK, NOEL ROBERT, manufacturing company executive; b. Houston, Mar. 19, 1937; s. Horace Berwick and Leda Estelle (Houghton) C.; student Iowa State U., 1955-57; B.S. in Indsl. Engring., U. Mich., 1960; children—Laurel Jane, David Robert. Engr. in tng. Eaton Mfg., Saginaw, Mich., 1960-61; mgr. mfg. and contracting J. N. Fauver Co., Madison Heights, Mich., 1961-65; pres. Newton Mfg., Royal Oak, Mich., 1965—; soc. Indsl. Piping Contractors, Birmingham, Mich., 1969-75; pres. RNR Metal Fabricators, Inc., Royal Oak, Mich., 1974-78; chmn. bd. Kim Internat. Sales Co., 1978—; pres. Newton Sales Co., Royal Oak, 1978—, Power Package Windsor Ltd., Windsor, Ont., Can., 1981—. Served with U.S. Army, 1960-61. Registered profl. engr., Mich. Mem. Fluid Power Soc., Nat. Fluid Power Assn., Birmingham Jr. C. of C. (past bd. dirs.). Patentee in field. Home: 4481 W Cherry Hill Dr Orchard Lake MI 48033 Office: Newton Mfgs 4249 Delemere Blvd Royal Oak MI 48073

COOK, NORMA BAKER, consulting company executive; b. North Wilkesboro, N.C.; d. Charles Chauncey and Mildred (Bates) Baker; m. Jerry A. Cook (div. 1981). BA in Bus. and Econs., Meredith Coll., 1963; student, Alliance Francaise, N.Y.C., 1980-83, N.Y. Sch. Interior Design, 1980-83. Cert. tchr., N.C. Pres., owner John Robert Powers Sch. Fashion Careers, Raleigh, N.C., 1971-87, NBC of Raleigh, Inc., 1979—; mem. adv. com. N.C. Pvt. Bus., Trade and Corr. Schs., 1986. Author articles on fashion and success motivation for women. Establisher Norma Baker Cook Art Scholarship at Meredith Coll., Raleigh, 1989. Recipient Svc. award Am. Cancer Soc., 1978. Mem. The Fashion Group, Inc., AFTRA, Greater Raleigh C. of C. (arts com.), North Raleigh Civitans, Capital City Club, Raleigh Racquet Club, Longboat Key Club (Fla.).

COOK, OWEN THOMAS, printing executive; b. Springfield, Ill., Aug. 30, 1926; s. Owen Thaddius and Opal (MacDonald) C.; m. Gail Ann Maize, June 12, 1963; children: Thomas G., James V. BS in Printing Mgmt., Carnegie Mellon U., 1950. Mgr. plant Acme Printing Co., Pitts., 1950-55; supt. plant William G. Johnston Co., Pitts., 1955-62; pres. ABC Press, Inc., Monroeville, Pa., 1962-81, Assocs. Litho, Inc., Pitts., 1981—; instr. Printing Industry Pitts., 1957-58. Lt. Monroeville Vol. Fire Dept. 4, Pa., 1970-73; pres. bd. dirs. Monroeville Pub. Library, 1981-87; troop leader Boy Scouts Am., Monroeville, 1975-85. Recipient Albert Gallatin Bus. award Zurich-Am. Co., 1972. Mem. Printing House Craftsmen, Monroeville Area C. of C. (pres. bd. dirs. 1965-75). Republican. Presbyterian. Lodge: Masons. Home: 215 College Park Dr Monroeville PA 15146 Office: Assocs Litho Inc 325 32d St Pittsburgh PA 15201

COOK, PAUL M., chemical manufacturing company executive; b. Ridgewood, N.J.. B.S. in Chem. Engring, M.I.T., 1947. With Stanford Research Inst., Palo Alto, Calif., 1949-53, Sequoia Process Corp., 1953-56; with Raychem Corp., Menlo Park, Calif., 1957—, former pres., now chmn., chief exec. officer, bd. dirs. Recipient Nat. Medal Tech., 1988. Office: Raychem Corp 300 Constitution Dr Menlo Park CA 94025 *

COOK, PETER SMITH, company executive; b. Cheyenne, Wyo., Mar. 28, 1927; s. William Lincoln and Margaret (Bentson) C.; m. Carrell DeFrance, Aug. 25, 1963; children: Ginger V., Scot S. BA, U. Colo., 1951. With P.S. Cook Co., Cheyenne, Wyo., 1950—, pres.; bd. dirs. First Wyo. Bank, Cheyenne. Chmn., mem. adv. bd. Mil. Affairs Com., Cheyenne, 1988—; bd. dirs. Cheyenne Airport Bd., 1988—. Served with AC, USN, 1944-46, PTO. Mem. Am. Inst. Banking, Newcomen Soc. U.S., Cheyenne C. of C., Sigma Alpha Epsilon. Republican. Lodges: Rotary, Masons. Office: PS Cook Co 400 W 15th St Cheyenne WY 82001

COOK, ROBERT DONALD, business executive; b. Chicago Heights, Ill., Nov. 1, 1929; s. Webster Warren and Gladys (Miner) C.; m. Maxine Jensen, Nov. 11, 1950; children: Carolyn Jean, Robert Donald II. B.S. in Bus. U. Md., 1956; grad. advanced mgmt. program, Harvard U., 1973. C.P.A., Md. Audit mgr. Arthur Andersen & Co. (CPAs), Washington, 1956-63; comptroller Peoples Drug Stores, Washington, 1963-68; v.p., controller Booz, Allen & Hamilton, Inc., Chgo., 1968-72; pres. Cookemper Rentals, Inc., Barrington, Ill., 1971-73; controller Esmark, Inc., Chgo., 1973-77; pres., chief operating officer Castle & Cooke, Inc., San Francisco, 1977-86; chmn. R.D. Cook Mgmt. Corp., 1986—. Served with USNR, 1948-52. Mem. Inst. C.P.A.s, Fin. Execs. Inst., Beta Alpha Psi. Clubs: Masons (32 deg.), Shriners. Home and Office: RD Cook Mgmt Corp 75 Rolling Hills Rd Tiburon CA 94920

COOK, ROBERT WILLIAM, financial executive; b. Sulligent, Ala., Mar. 11, 1943; s. Murray Ray and Millie Grace (Allman) C.; m. Lenore Y. Pinckney, Aug. 28, 1965; children—Miranda J., Adrienne S.; m. Deborah L. Holmes, Mar. 11, 1982; 1 dau., Nina L. B.A. in Econs. cum laude, Rutgers U., 1970, M.B.A. in Acctg., 1971. Cost acctg. clk. Permacel div. Johnson & Johnson, New Brunswick, N.J., 1968-69; staff acct. Arthur Young & Co., C.P.A.s, N.Y.C., 1971-73; fiscal mgr. Opportunities Industrialization Ctrs., Phila., 1973; mgr. adminstrn. Zion Investment Assocs., Phila., 1973-76; sr. acct., then asst. controller Unified Industries, Inc., Springfield, Va., 1976-79, controller, 1979-82; controller PolyTech, Inc., Cleve., 1982-85, pres. CMDI Engrs., 1985-87; v.p. fin. and personnel Summit Technologies, Springfield, Va., 1987-89; prin., chief exec. officer Breil Cons., Arlington, Va., 1989—; cons. in field. Served with USAF, 1964-68. Rutgers U. Bd. Govs. scholar. Mem. Nat. Assn. Accts. Home: 9060 Gavelwood Ct Springfield VA 22153 Office: Breil Cons 2708 S Nelson St Arlington VA 22206

COOK, RONALD DEAN, lawyer, consultant; b. Cherry Point, N.C., Nov. 9, 1963; s. Stephen Cole and Patricia Ellen (Tingle) C.; m. Celisa Walls, July 27, 1985. BS, U. Fla., 1984; JD, Stetson U., 1987. Bar: Fla. 1987, U.S. Dist. Ct. (mid. dist.) Fla. 1987. Assoc. Throp, Reed & Armstrong, Sarasota, Fla., 1987-89, Nelson Hesse Cyril, et al, Sarasota, 1989—; bd. dirs. Stetson U. Moot Ct., St. Petersburg. Contbr. articles to profl. jours. Pres. devel. com. Sarasota County Library, 1988-89; advisor Mote Marine Lab. Council, Sarasota, 1988-89, Sarasota County Arts Council; bd. dirs. Friends of the Selby Pub. Libr., Sarasota, 1987-88. Recipient 1st pl. Ctr. Computer Law, 1987, 1st pl. Intram. Neg. Acad. Trial Lawyers, 1986. Mem. ABA, Fla. Bar Assn., Sarasota County Bar Assn., Computer Law Assn., Data Processing Mgmt. Assn., Tiger Bay Club. Republican. Office: Nelson Hesse Cyril et al 2070 Ringling Blvd Sarasota FL 43237

COOK, SAM BRYAN, banker; b. Jefferson City, Mo., Oct. 27, 1951; s. Sam B. and Lois (McAdam) C. BA in Econs., Washington and Lee U., 1974; MA, U. Mo., 1976, MBA, 1977, PhD, 1980. Assoc. Interfirst Bank Dallas, 1980-82, officer, 1982; fin. mgr. Interfirst Corp., Dallas, 1982-83; asst. v.p. investments Cen. Bank, Jefferson City, Mo., 1983; sr. v.p. Cen. Bancompany, Jefferson City, 1985-87, exec. v.p., 1987—; also bd. dirs. Cen. Bancompany; exec. v.p. Cen. Bank, 1989—. Trustee William Woods Coll., Fulton, Mo.; com. chair Jefferson City United Way, 1987. Mem. Mo. Bankers Assn. (chmn. mgmt. com. 1986-88), Columbia C. of C., Old Warson Country Club (St. Louis), Country Club Mo., Jefferson County Country Club, Rotary. Office: Cen Bank 238 Madison St Jefferson City MO 65101

COOK, STANTON R., newspaper publisher; b. Chgo., July 3, 1925; s. Rufus Merrill and Thelma Marie (Borgerson) C.; m. Barbara Wilson, Sept. 23, 1950. BS in Mech. Engring., Northwestern U., 1949. Dist. sales rep. Shell Oil Co., 1949-51; prodn. engr. Chgo. Tribune Co., 1951-60, asst. prodn. mgr., 1960-65, prodn. mgr., 1965-67, prodn. dir., 1967-70, dir. ops., 1970, gen. mgr., 1970-72, pub., 1973—, v.p., 1967-70, exec. v.p., dir., 1970-72, pres., 1972-74, chief officer, 1974-76, chmn., 1974-81; dir. Tribune Co., 1972—, v.p., 1973-74, pres., chief exec. officer, 1974-88, chmn., chief exec. officer, 1989—; dir. AP, 1975-84, 2nd vice chmn., 1979-84, Newspaper Advt. Bur., 1987—; former dep. chmn. and dir. Fed. Res. Bank of Chgo., 1980-83, chmn. 1984-85. Trustee, U. Chgo., 1973-87, Mus. Sci. and Industry, Chgo., 1973—, Field Mus. Natural History, Chgo., 1973—, Robert R. McCormick Trusts and Founds., 1979—, Gen. Douglas MacArthur Found., 1979—, Northwestern U., 1987—, Shedd Aquarium Soc., 1987—. Mem. Am. Newspaper Pubs. Assn. (trustee Found. 1973-82; dir. 1974-82), Chgo. Council Fgn. Relations (dir. 1973—). Clubs: Commercial (past pres.), Economic (past pres., life mem.) (Chgo.).

COOK, STEPHEN BERNARD, insurance company executive; b. Balt., June 26, 1947; s. Allen Bernard and Evelyn Naomi (Thomas) C.; m. Marlena Marie Sapia, Dec. 27, 1969; children—Geoffrey Matthew, Katherine Marie. B.S. in Acctg., Loyola Coll., Balt., 1969. C.P.A., Md. Audit mgr. Ernst & Whinney, Balt., 1977-81; v.p., treas. U.S. Fidelity and Guaranty Co., Balt., 1982-85, v.p., controller, 1985—. Fellow Life Mgmt. Inst.; mem. Am. Ins. Assn. (chmn. fin. reporting principles com. 1988—), Md. Assn. C.P.A.s, (chmn. ins. co. 1980-85, outstanding com. chmn. award 1984-85), Ins. Acctg. and Systems Assn. (v.p. Mid.-Atlantic chpt. 1982-83, pres. 1983-84), Nat. Assn. Accts. (bd. dirs. Balt. chpt. 1978-81). Roman Catholic. Club: Hillendale Country (treas., bd. govs. 1985—). Home: 1 Norwick Circle Baltimore MD 21093 Office: US Fidelity & Guaranty Co 100 Light St PO Box 1138 Baltimore MD 21202

COOK, STEVEN GERALD, computer software company executive; b. Portland, Oreg., Feb. 16, 1960; s. Keith Earl and Geraldine Marion (Altman) C.; m. Wendy Sue James, Aug. 19, 1984. Student pub. schs., Portland. Computer programmer Osborne/McGraw-Hill, Berkeley, Calif., 1979-80, tech. editor, 1980-82; tech. editor PC mag., San Francisco, 1982; tech. editor PC World Communications, San Francisco, 1982-83, tech. mgr., 1983-84; mgr. software acquisitions Paperback Software Internat., Berkeley, 1984-86, v.p. acquisitions and product devel., 1986-88, pres., 1988—. Author: (with others) The Apple II Users Guide, 1981, Business System Buyers Guide, 1981, Your Atari Computer, 1982; contbg. editor PC World mag., 1984—, editor column, 1984-87; contbr. articles to profl. jours. Home: 50 Buckeye Ave Oakland CA 94618 Office: Paperback Software Internat 2830 9th St Berkeley CA 94710

COOK, VICTOR JOSEPH, JR., marketing educator, consultant; b. Durant, Okla., June 25, 1938; s. Victor Joseph and Athelene Ann (Arduser) C.; m. Linda Lee Potter, June 6, 1960 (div. 1971); children: Victor Joseph III, William Randall, Christopher Phelps. BA, Fla. State U., 1960; MS, La. State U., 1962; Ph.D., U. Mich., 1965. Rsch. assoc. Mktg. Sci. Inst., Phila., 1965-68, assoc. rsch. dir., Boston, 1968-69; asst. prof. U. Chgo., 1969-75; pres., dir. Mgmt. & Design, New Orleans, 1975-78; prof. Freeman Sch. Bus. Tulane U., 1978—; cons. Ford Motor Co., Dearborn, Mich., 1964-67, IBM, N.Y.C., 1968-72, Sears, Roebuck & Co., Chgo., 1975-77, STC/ICL, London, 1981—, The DuPont Co., Wilmington, 1986—, SAMI/Burke, Inc., Cin., 1986—. Author: Brand Policy Determination, 1967; designer, patentee furniture, Sud Möbel, 1976. Mem. Rep. Presdl. Task Force, Washington, 1981—. Mem. Am. Mktg. Assn., Am. Econ. Assn., Inst. Mgmt. Scis., Assn. for Consumer Rsch., Ops. Rsch. Soc. Am., Beta Gamma Sigma, Phi Beta Kappa. Republican. Methodist. Avocations: golf, drawing, art collecting, travel. Office: Tulane U AB Freeman Sch Bus New Orleans LA 70118

COOK, VINCENT N., information processing and business machinery company executive; BA U. Ala., MA Am. U., student Harvard U. With IBM Corp., 1960—, asst. to pres. Fed. Systems div., 1971-71, div. mgr. Morris Plains, N.J., dir. worldwide mil. command & control systems, dir. complex systems control command and surveillance programs, 1974-77, v.p. Fed. Systems div., 1977-81, v.p. def. & space systems Fed. Systems div., then pres. Fed. Systems div. from 1981, corp. v.p. 1982-89. Office: IBM Corp Fed Systems Div 6600 Rockledge Dr Bethesda MD 20817 *

COOK, WALTER BLACKWELL, oil company executive; b. La Crosse, Va., Dec. 8, 1930; s. James Byran and Maude Doma (Moseley) C.; m. Grace Azilee Tumlin, Apr. 27, 1957; children: Walter Blackwell, James Crawford, Beth. B.S. in Econs., Furman U. Southeastern sales rep. Quaker State Oil Refining Co., Oil City, PA., 1956-61; div.mgr. Quaker State Oil Refining Co., Columbus, Ohio, 1961-66; supr. div. sales Quaker State Oil Refining Co., Oil City, Pa., 1966-70, sales mgr., 1970-73, v.p. brand sales, 1973-75, v.p. mktg., 1975-76, exec. v.p., dir., 1977—; bd. dirs. Truck-Lite, Jamestown, Quaker State Inc./Can.; trustee Clarion U. Bd. dirs. Oil City Sch. Authority, Pa., 1981-85; mem. council of trustees Clarion U. Pa. Served with U.S. Army, 1952-54. Mem. Am. Petroleum Inst., Pa. Grade Crude Oil Assn., Nat. Petroleum Refiners Assn., 25-Yr. Club of Petroleum Industry. Republican. Clubs: Wanango Country (Reno, Pa.), Oil City, Poinsett (Greenville, S.C.). Home: 516 W 3d St Oil City PA 16301 Office: Quaker State Corp 255 Elm St PO Box 989 Oil City PA 16301

COOK, WILLIAM ROBERT, business consultant; b. Sacramento, Mar. 4, 1925; s. George Barker and Albertina (Nuenke) C.; m. Jeanne Mari Allen, Feb. 14, 1947; children: David Allen, Robert Scott. Student, U. Calif., Berkeley, 1943, U. Redlands, 1944-45, Marine Corps Schs., Quantico, Va., 1945, 50, Internat. Acct. Soc., Chgo., 1967. Cert. tax preparer. Prin. William R. Cook, Cons., Walnut Creek, Calif., 1976—; bd. dirs., sec. Miller & Jones, Inc., Pleasanton, Calif.; gen. ptnr. C&M Enterprises, Pleasanton, 1980—, The Bridge Group, Mpls., 1984—. Served with USMCR, 1943-46, 1950-51. Republican. Presbyterian. Club: Rossmoor Golf and Country (Walnut Creek, Calif.). Lodge: Masons.

COOKE, A. CURTS, business executive; b. Clifton, N.J., Oct. 18, 1936; s. Albert Curts and Gertrude (Wenting) C.; m. Geraldine Campbell, Aug. 8, 1959; children—Albert, David, Jeffery, Kenneth. B.S., Lehigh U., 1958. C.P.A., N.J. Mgr., sr. auditor Price Waterhouse, 1958-68; audit supr. Gen. Foods, 1968-70; controller, dir. planning Burger Chef Systems, 1970-73; contr. Beacham Inc. W.H. div., Clifton, N.J., 1973-77; v.p. fin., adminstrv. gen. mgr. Beacham Inc., W.H. div., Clifton, 1977-82; chief fin. officer, exec. v.p. adminstrn. Russ Berrie, Oakland, N.J., 1982—. Trustee Upper Saddle River Libr., 1975-88; mem. bd. edn., Upper Saddle River, 1978-84; bd. dirs. U.S.R. Baseball Assn., Upper Saddle River, 1978-79. Served with U.S. Army, 1959-65. Mem. Lions (bd. dirs. Upper Saddle River club 1976-78). Office: Russ Berrie & Co Inc 111 Bauer Dr Oakland NJ 07436

COOKE, JOSEPHINE GLORIA, mortgage company executive; b. Phila., May 5, 1931; d. Harry Elzy Cooke and Marion Elethia (Teal) Holloman; m. Joseph Robinson Jr., Sept. 1954 (div. Jan. 1968); 1 child Tracey Marion Robinson-Harris. Student, Va. Union U., 1951-53, Cheyney State Tchrs. Coll., Pa., 1953-55; cert., Northwestern U. Sch. Mortgage Banking, Evanston, Ill., 1973. Tchr. adult edn. Phila. Bd. Edn., 1965-67; v.p. secondary mktg. The Colwell Co., Los Angeles, 1969-83; sr. v.p. Cypress Fin. Corp., Pasadena, Calif., 1983—; instr. Calif. Mortgage Banking Sch., Los Angeles, 1983-84. Mem. Tenth Dist. Women's Steering Com., 1976—, v.p. 1983-84; dir. Vols. Am. Los Angeles, 1981-84. Recipient Service award City of Los Angeles, 1983. Mem. Mortgage Bankers Assn. Am., Calif. Mortgage Bankers Assn., Mid City C. of C., Zonta Internat. (pres. L.A. chpt. 1980-82, dist. sec. Chgo. chpt. 1982-84, area 3 dir. Chgo. chpt. 1984—, lt. gov. 1984, gov. dist. IX 1988—). Democrat.

COOKE, MERRITT TODD, banker; b. Phila., Mar. 20, 1920; s. Merritt Todd and Beatrice (Crawford) C.; m. Mary T. Cooke, Sept. 24, 1949 (dec.); children—Mary Marshall, Merritt Todd; m. Margaret S. Groome, Dec. 4, 1965. B.A., Princeton, 1942; M.C.P., Mass. Inst. Tech., 1947. Exec. dir. Del. County Planning Commn., Media, Pa., 1951-55; v.p. W.A. Clarke Mortgage Co., Phila., 1956-60; asst. v.p. First Pa. Bank, Phila., 1961-65; with The Phila. Saving Fund Soc., 1966—, pres., 1971—, chmn., chief exec. officer, 1979-86, vice chmn., 1986-87, also bd. dirs.; trustee Mut. Assurance Co., Phila.; dir. Provident Mut. Ins. Co. Pres. United Fund Phila., 1974-76; bd. dirs. Pa. Hosp., Phila., chmn., 1969-75; v.p. United Way Phila., 1976-85; bd. dirs. Greater Phila. Partnership, Phila. Urban Coalition, Ctr. Phila. Devel. Corp., former pres. Phila. Orch. Assn., chmn., 1989—; trustee Phila. Mus. Art. Served with AUS, 1942-46. Mem. Phi Beta Kappa, Lambda Alpha. Home: Greenlands Newtown Street Rd Media PA 19063 Office: PSFS Bldg 1212 Market St Philadelphia PA 19107

COOKE, PANDORA MORGAN, insurance company executive; b. Dalton, Ga., July 8, 1952; d. Edwin Marshall Morgan and Winnie Elizabeth (Harkins) Stone; m. Robert G. Cooke, Jan. 30, 1973; 1 child, Robert Gene Jr. AA in Merchandising, Massey Jr. Coll., 1972; grad., Ala. Real Estate Inst., 1975; BS, Samford U., 1986. CLU; Chartered Fin. Cons.; registered investment advisor, fin. planner. Mgr. Ups n Downs, Atlanta, 1971-73; co-owner Pandora's Sewing Box, Sylacauga, Ala., 1973-78; pres. Diversified Plans, Inc., Sylacauga, 1976—; bd. dirs. Occupational Services, Inc., Sylacauga. Bd. dirs. Sylacauga City Sch. Found. Named Sylacauga's Young Career Woman, 1974. Mem. Soc. for CLU's, Internat. Assn. Fin. Planners, Ala. Assn. Life Underwriters (v.p. Sylacauga 1985-86, bd. dirs. LUPAC 1987—), Women's Life Underwriters Confedn., Bus. and Profl. Women's Club (pres. Sylalauga chpt. 1974-86). Democrat. Baptist. Office: Diversified Plans Inc PO Box 2130 Sylacauga AL 35150

COOL, KIM PATMORE, retail executive, needlework consultant; b. Cleve., Feb. 1, 1940; d. Herman Chester Earl and Eva (Geneau) Patmore; m. Kenneth Adams Cool Jr., Mar. 12, 1963; 1 child, Heidi Adams. BA in Econs., Sweet Briar Coll., 1962; postgrad., Case Western Reserve U., 1962-63. Test adminstr. Pradco, Cleve., 1962-63; pvt. needlework cons. Cleve., 1970-72; retail v.p., treas., custom designer And Sew On, Inc., Cleve., 1973—, exec. v.p., treas., 1982—; tchr. Wellesley Coll. Continuing Edn. Program, 1986; pub. Fredericktown Rress, Md. Artist collector quality custom hand-painted canvases; co-author: How to Market Needlepoint—The Definitive Manual, 1988. Rep. committeeman Cuyahoga County, Shaker Heights, Ohio, 1964-72. Regional Curling champion, 1987-88. Mem. Nat. Needlework Assn. (lectr. seminar on mktg. needlepoint, charter assoc. retail, conductor of senimars on buying and merchandising 1988—), Embroiderers Guild of Cleve. (bd. dirs. 1980-82), Am. Profl. Needlework Retailers, S.E. Yarncrafters Guild (conductor merchandising seminars 1989—), Nat. Standards Coun. Am. Embroiderers, U.S. Figure Skating Assn. (nat. judge gold and senior competitions 1967—, sect. precision judge), Sweet Briar Coll. Alumnae Assn. (nat. bd. dirs. upper Midwest region 1965-66, class sec. 1988-89), Cleve. Skating Club, Mayfield Country Club. Baptist. Home: 14500 Washington Blvd University Heights OH 44118 Office: And Sew On Inc 2243 Warrensville Ctr University Heights OH 44118

COOLEY, MARIE SZPIRUK, financial company executive; b. Gnezno, Poland, Dec. 20, 1935; came to U.S., 1950; d. Pavlo and Taisia (Bohdaniw) Szpiruk; m. Victor Cooley, Sept. 19, 1954; children: George, Oleg, Paul. Student, CUNY, 1955-56, Montgomery Coll., 1975, Am. U., 1975-77; BS, U. Md., 1982. Purchase clk. Am. U., Washington, 1975-77; asst. internal auditor Citizens Savs. Bank, Silver Spring, Md., 1977-83; asst. v.p., sec., treas. First Citizens Mortgage Corp., Silver Spring, 1984—; pres. Ukrainian Washington Fed. Credit Union, 1984-86, treas., 1986—. Mem. Dumka Choir, N.Y.C., 1953-55; v.p. St. Olga's Sisterhood, Washington, 1970; instr. Ukrainian Easter Eggs White House Exhibits, 1975-80. Mem. Millennium of Ukrainian Orthodoxy, Ukrainian Assn. of Washington, The Smithsonian Assn. Ukranian. Office: First Citizens Mortgage Corp 12501 Prosperity Dr Ste 200 Silver Spring MD 20904

COOLEY, RICHARD PIERCE, banker; b. Dallas, Nov. 25, 1923; s. Victor E. and Helen (Pierce) C. B.S., Yale, 1944. With Wells Fargo Bank, San Francisco, 1949-82; exec. v.p. Wells Fargo Bank, 1965-66, pres., chief exec. officer, 1966-79, chmn. bd., chief exec. officer, 1979-82, also dir.; chmn., chief exec. officer, pres. Seattle-1st Nat. Bank (now Seafirst Corp.),, 1983-86, chmn., chief exec. officer, 1986—; chmn. bd., chief exec. officer, dir. Wells Fargo & Co., 1968-83; dir. UAL, Inc., Howmett Turbine Components Corp., Pechiney Ugine Kuhlmann Corp. Trustee Children's Hosp., San Francisco, Rand Corp., Calif. Inst. Tech., Pasadena. Served to 1st lt. Armed Services. Decorated Air medal. Mem. Assn. Res. City Bankers, Smithsonian Instn. Nat. Assn. (bd. dirs.), Calif. C. of C. (bd. dirs.). Office: Seafirst Corp PO Box 3977 Seattle WA 98124 also: Bank of Amer Nat Trust & Savs Bank of America Ctr San Francisco CA 94104 *

COOLIDGE, LAWRENCE, private trustee; b. Boston, Mar. 2, 1936; s. Lawrence Coolidge and Victoria (Tytus) Steward; m. Nancy Rich, June 22, 1963 (div. July 1985); children: David S., Edward W., Elizabeth A.; m. Nancy G. Myers, Sept. 7, 1985. AB, Harvard U., 1958, MBA, 1962. Pvt. trustee Loring, Wolcott & Coolidge, Boston, 1962—; chmn. Seven Islands Land Co., Bangor, Maine; bd. dirs. Big Sandy Coal Co., Inc., Boston, Hollingsworth & Vose Co., Walpole, Mass. Dir., treas. Boston Athenaeum, 1984—. Home: 85 Mt Vernon St Boston MA 02108 Office: Loring Wolcott & Coolidge 230 Congress St Boston MA 02110

COOMBE, GEORGE WILLIAM, JR., lawyer, banker; b. Kearny, N.J., Oct. 1, 1925; s. George William and Laura (Montgomery) C.; A.B., Rutgers U., 1946; LL.B., Harvard, 1949; m. Marilyn V. Ross, June 4, 1949; children—Susan, Donald William, Nancy. Bar: N.Y. 1950, Mich. 1953, Calif. 1976, U.S. Supr. Ct. Practice in N.Y.C., 1949-53, Detroit, 1953-69; atty., mem. legal-staff Gen. Motors Corp., Detroit, 1953-69, asst. gen. counsel, sec., 1969-75; exec. v.p., gen. counsel Bank of Am., San Francisco, 1975—. Served to lt. USNR, 1942-46. Mem. Am., Mich., Calif., San Francisco, Los Angeles, N.Y.C. bar assns., Phi Beta Kappa, Phi Gamma Delta. Presbyterian. Home: 2190 Broadway #2E San Francisco CA 94115 Office: BankAm Corp Bank Am Ctr 555 California St San Francisco CA 94104

COON, JULIAN BARHAM, energy company executive; b. Jackson, Miss., Nov. 16, 1939; s. Morris Galloway and Dru Etta (Camp) C.; m. Barbara Schultz, Aug. 30, 1961; children: Julianne, Robert. BS in Physics, Tex. A&M U., 1961; PhD, La. State U., 1966. Asst. prof. physics U. Houston, 1968-73; with Conoco Inc., Houston, 1973-88, mgr. mining and research, 1978-81, mgr. exploration research, 1981-84, v.p. research and devel., 1984-88, gen. mgr. Worldwide Exploration Tech., 1988—. Contbr. articles to profl. jours. Patentee in field. Mem. Soc. Exploration Geophysicists, Am. Assn. Petroleum Geologists, Soc. Petroleum Engrs., Phi Kappa Phi, Sigma Xi, Phi Eta Sigma, Sigma Pi Sigma. Republican. Episcopalian. Lodge: Rotary. Avocation: tennis. Home: 19926 Sky Hollow Ln Katy TX 77450 Office: Conoco Inc PO Box 2197 Houston TX 77252

COONEY, JOAN GANZ, broadcasting executive; b. Phoenix, Nov. 30, 1929; d. Sylvan C. and Pauline (Reardan) Ganz; m. Timothy J. Cooney, 1964 (div. 1975); m. Peter G. Peterson, 1980. BA, U. Ariz., 1951; hon. degrees, Boston Coll., 1970, Hofstra U., Oberlin Coll., Ohio Wesleyan U., 1971, Princeton U., 1973, Russell Sage Coll., 1974, U. Ariz., Harvard U., 1975, Allegheny Coll., 1976, Georgetown U., 1978, U. Notre Dame, 1982, Smith Coll., 1986, Brown U., 1987. Reporter Ariz. Republic, Phoenix, 1953-54; publicist NBC, 1954-55, U.S. Steel Hour, 1955-62; producer Channel 13/WNET; pub. affairs documentaries Channel 13/WNET, N.Y.C., 1962-67; TV cons. Carnegie Corp. N.Y., N.Y.C., 1967-68; exec. dir. Children's TV Workshop (producers Sesame Street, Electric Company, others), N.Y.C., 1968-70; pres., trustee Children's TV Workshop (producers Sesame Street, Electric Company, others), 1970—; trustee Channel 13/Ednl. Broadcasting Corp.; dir. Xerox Corp., Johnson & Johnson, Chase Manhattan Corp., Chase Manhattan Bank N.A., Met. Life Ins. Co. Mem. Pres.'s Commn. on Marijuana and Drug Abuse, 1971-73, Nat. News Council, 1973-81, Council Fgn. Relations, 1974—, Pres.'s Commn. for Agenda for 80's, 1980-81, Adv. Com. for Trade Negotiations, 1978-80; mem. Gov.'s Commn. on Internat. Yr. of the Child, 1979, Carnegie Found. Nat. Panel on High Sch., 1980-82. Recipient numerous awards for Sesame Street and other TV programs including Nat. Sch. Pub. Relations Assn. Gold Key 1971; Disting. Service medal Columbia Tchrs. Coll., 1971; Soc. Family Man award, 1971; Nat. Inst. Social Scis. Gold medal, 1971; Frederick Douglass award N.Y. Urban League, 1972; Silver Satellite award Am. Women in Radio and TV; Woman of Yr. in Edn. award Ladies Home Jour., 1975; Woman of Decade award, 1979; NEA Friends of Edn. award; Kiwanis Decency award; NAEB Disting. Service award; 5th Women's Achiever award Girl Scouts U.S.A.; Stephen S. Wise award, 1981; Harris Found. award, 1982; Ednl. Achievement award AAUW, 1984; Disting. Service to Children award Nat. Assn. Elem. Sch. Prins., 1985; DeWitt Carter Reddick award Coll. Communications, U. Tex.-Austin, 1986. Mem. NOW, Nat. Acad. TV Arts and Scis., Nat. Inst. Social Scis., Internat. Radio and TV Soc., Am. Women in Radio and TV. Office: Children's TV Workshop 1 Lincoln Pla New York NY 10023 *

COONEY, JOHN THOMAS, business executive; b. Mpls., Apr. 17, 1921; s. John Thomas and Helen (Bork) C.; BBA, U. Minn., 1943; postgrad. advanced mgmt. program Harvard U., 1971; m. Margaret Frances Bonner, Oct. 30, 1948; children—Mary, John Thomas, Patricia Bell, David, Stephen, Michael, Thomas. Pub. rels. M & O Paper Co., Mpls., 1946-49; ter. mgr. Univis, Inc., Ft. Lauderdale, Fla., 1949-52, regional sales mgr., 1952-57, product mgr., 1957-59, gen. sales mgr., 1959-61, v.p. mktg., 1961-68, group v.p. mktg. and distbn., 1968-71, exec. v.p., 1971-72; v.p. mktg. and distbn. Itek Vision Optical div. Itek Corp., Boston, 1972-74, pres. div., 1974-75; pres. Jack Cooney & Assocs., Ft. Lauderdale, 1975—. Bd. dirs. Boys' Clubs Broward County; Broward chpt. NCCJ, United Way, Broward Workshop, Boy Scouts Am., So. Fla. Maj. U.S. Army, 1943-46. Decorated Silver Star, Bronze Star, Legion of Honor, Crown of Leopold. Mem. Sales and Mktg. Execs. Ft. Lauderdale (past pres., bd. dir.), Beta Theta Pi. Roman Catholic. Clubs: Quail Ridge Country (bd. trustees). Home: 10451 Coralberry Way Boynton Beach FL 33436 Office: Jack Cooney & Assocs 2601 E Oakland Park Blvd Fort Lauderdale FL 33306

COONEY, THOMAS MICHAEL, greeting card company executive; b. N.Y.C., Feb. 7, 1926; s. Michael Joseph and Ellen Florence (McIntyre) C.; m. Mary Lynn Sullivan, Dec. 26, 1953; children—Michael, Thomas, William, John. B.S., U. Va., 1945; LL.B., Columbia U., 1949; M.B.A., NYU, 1959. Group v.p. Pfizer, Inc., N.Y.C., 1955-71, Am. Home Products, N.Y.C., 1971-74; exec. v.p., chief exec. officer Fairmont Foods Co., Des Plaines, Ill., 1974-78; pres., chief exec. officer Gibson Greetings, Inc., Cin., 1978-86, chmn., chief exec. officer, 1986-87, chmn. bd., 1986-89; dir. exec. com., pres. Gibson Found., Cin., 1989—; dir. Genovese Drug Stores, Inc., Melville, L.I., N.Y., Cin. Region Adv/ Bd. AmeriTrust Corp.; chmn. bd. Stark Candy Co., Pewaukee, Wis. Dir. Drug Alcohol Rehab. Edn., N.Y.C. Office: Gibson Found Inc 4221 Malsbary Rd Ste 207 Cincinnati OH 45242

COONEY, WILLIAM JOSEPH, JR., communications company executive; b. Pottstown, Pa., Sept. 4, 1951; s. William Joseph Sr. and Lilie May (Endy) C.; m. Frieda Elizabeth DeGiorgio, July 6, 1974; children: Natalie, William, Veronica. BS in Mktg./Acctg., Drexel U., 1974; MBA, George Washington U., 1983. With Martin Marietta Corp., 1972-78; cost/consolidations acct. Martin Marietta Corp., Bethesda, Md., 1976-78; controller Data Processing Div. Penril Corp., Rockville, Md., 1978-83; dir. fin. and adminstrn. Telecommunications Techniques Corp., Gaithersburg, Md., 1983-84; v.p. fin./adminstrn. Telecommunications Techniques Corp., Gaithersburg, 1984-88, sr. v.p., 1988—. dir. Bldg. Blocks Day Care Ctr., Poolesville, Md., 1976-84. Recipient Nat. Arians Found. award, 1965. Mem. Nat. Assn. Accts., Pi Kappa Phi. Roman Catholic. Home: 4015 Tranquility Ct Monrovia MD 21770

COONROD, RICHARD ALLEN, agricultural products company executive; b. Mahaska, Kans., Mar. 30, 1931; s. Orville R. and Nell (Eversole) C.; m. Phyllis Clark, Jan. 7, 1960; children—Amy Ginette, Wade Allen, Paul Nelson. B.S., Kans. State U., 1953. With Pillsbury Co., Mpls., 1956-85, v.p., gen. mgr. commodity merchandising, 1975-77, v.p., gen. mgr. agri-products div., 1977-78, group v.p., gen. mgr., 1978-79, exec. v.p., 1979-81, pres. agri-products, 1981-85; pres., chief exec. officer Am. Grain and Related Industries, Des Moines, 1985-86; pres. Coonrod Agriprodn. Corp., Mpls., 1985—; chmn., chief exec. officer Terra Agribus., Mpls., 1986; pres., chief exec. officer St. Louis Ship, 1988; bd. dirs. Alter Co., Davenport, Iowa, Portland (Oreg.) Food Products, Mchts. Grain & Transp., St. Louis, Zapata-Haynie, Hammon, La., Benson-Quinn, Mpls. Campaign chmn. Minn. United Negro Coll. Fund, 1979; bd. dirs. Mpls. Jr. Achievement, Urban Coalition, Art Inst. Mpls.; trustee Minn. 4-H Found., 1981-84. Served to capt. USAF, 1954-56. Mem. Millers Nat. Fedn. (exec. com.), St. Louis Grain Exchange (pres. 1973-74), Chgo. Bd. Trade. Clubs: Mpls; Interlaken Country (Edina, Minn.). Office: Coonrod Agriprodn Corp 121 S 8th St Ste 1335 Minneapolis MN 55402

COONS, ELDO JESS, JR., manufacturing company executive; b. Corsicana, Tex., July 5, 1924; s. Eldo Jess and Ruby (Allison) C.; student engring. U. Calif., 1949-50; m. Beverly K. Robbins, Feb. 6, 1985; children by previous marriage—Roberta Ann, Valerie, Cheryl. Owner C & C Constrn. Co., Pomona, Calif., 1946-48; sgt. traffic div. Pomona Police Dept., 1948-54; nat. field dir. Nat. Hot Rod Assn., Los Angeles, 1954-57; pres. Coons Custom Mfg., Inc., Oswego, Kans., 1957-68; chmn. bd. Borg-Warner Corp., 1968-71; pres. Coons Mfg., Inc., Oswego, 1971-84; pres. E.B.C Mgmt. Cons., Grove, Okla., 1984—. Mem. Kans. Gov.'s Adv. Com. for State Architects Assn. Served with C.E., AUS, 1943-46. Named to Exec. and Profl. Hall Fame, Recreational Vehicle/Mobile Homes Hall of Fame; recipient Paul Abel award Recreation Vehicle Industry Assn., 1978, 1st Ann. New Product award Kans. Gov.'s Office and Kans. Engring. Soc. 1982-83. Mem. Oswego C. of C. (dir.), Nat. Juvenile Officers Assn., Municipal Motor Officers Assn., Am. Legion, AIM (fellow pres.'s council), Young Pres.'s Orgn. Mason (K.T., Shriner), Rotarian (pres. Oswego 1962-63). Originator 1st city sponsored police supervised dragstrip. Home and Office: EBC Mgmt Cons Rt 4 Box 246 Grove OK 74344

COONS, MARION MCDOWELL, retail food stores executive; b. Macedonia, Iowa, Apr. 11, 1915; s. Lindsey D. and Luella May (McDowell) C.; m. Margaret Lorrene McReynolds, June 23, 1940; children: Kenton Richard, Kenneth Lee. BSC, U. Iowa, 1938. Tax acct. F.L. Ellis, Council Bluffs, Iowa, 1938-40; acct. Hyde & Vredenburg, Inc., Lamoni, Iowa, 1940-43; sr. v.p. and chief fin. officer Hy-Vee Food Stores Inc., Chariton, Iowa, 1943—, also bd. dirs.; bd. dirs. Iowa Transfer Systems; bd. dirs. Perishable Dists. of Iowa; sec., treas., bd. dirs. Chariton Storage Co.; treas., bd. dirs. Iamo Realty Co.; treas. Hy-Vee Found. Inc.; chmn. bd. dirs. Nat. Bank and Trust. Councilman, Chariton City Council, 1954-60; active Chariton Community Sch. bd., 1961-70; chmn. Lucas County Reps., 1961-81. Recipient Citizen of Yr. award City of Chariton, 1971, Silver Beaver award Boy Scouts Am., Des Moines, 1974. Mem. Fin. Exec. Inst. Republican. Methodist. Lodges: Rotary (pres. 1955, fellow 1986), Masons (master 1945), Shriners. Office: Hy-Vee Food Stores Inc 1801 Osceola Ave Chariton IA 50049

COOPER, ALCIE LEE, JR., insurance executive; b. Gadsden, Ala., Aug. 3, 1939; s. Alcie Lee and Jettie Merle (Farabee) C.; A.B., Asbury Coll., 1961; B.D., St. Paul Sch. Theology, 1966; postgrad., 1979; m. Audrey May MacAuslan, Sept. 3, 1976. Claims adjuster Sentry Ins. A Mut. Co., St. Louis, 1967-69, claim supr., Kansas City, Kans., 1969-72, regional claims supr., Dallas, 1972-77; home office workers compensation cons. Houston Gen. Ins. Co., Ft. Worth, 1977-79, asst. claims mgr., 1979-82, worker's compensation claims mgr., 1982-85; dir. Field Claim Ctr.; asst. v.p. claims, 1986—; partner Al Cooper & Assos., distbrs. Amway products, Ft. Worth, 1977—; instr. Workers Compensation Sch. Mem. Republican Presdl. Task Force; bd. dirs. Am. Heart Assn., Tarrant County, Tex., 1983. Mem. Amway Distbrs. Assn., U.S. Senatorial Club. Home: 4125 Alicante Ave Fort Worth TX 76133 Office: Field Claim Ctr 4055 International Plaza Fort Worth TX 76113

COOPER, CAROL DIANE, publishing executive; b. Williamsport, Pa., Aug. 14, 1953; d. Ray Calvin and Norma Jane (Steiger) C. BA, Colgate U., 1975; cert. in pub., Radcliffe Coll., 1977; MA, Syracuse (N.Y.) U., 1977. Editorial and promotion asst. St. Martin's Press, N.Y.C., 1977-78, sales rep., 1978-79; dir. sales, v.p. Clearwater Pub. Co., Inc., N.Y.C., 1979-80, dir. mktg., 1980-81, v.p., 1981-83; exec. v.p. K.G. Saur Inc., N.Y.C., 1983-88; v.p., pub. R.R. Bowker Co., N.Y.C., 1988—; bd. dirs. Bouker-Saur and K.G. Saur Verlag, Reed Pub. U.K. Mem. ALA (com. microform standards rsch. and tech. standards div. 1986). Office: RR Bowker Co 245 W 17th St New York NY 10011

COOPER, CHARLES BYRON, life insurance company executive; b. Seattle, May 5, 1938; s. Byron Soren and Helen Geraldine (Lamb) C.; m. Judith Lorain Whitver, Mar. 18, 1961 (div. 1982); children: Cathleen, Charles; M. Kathy Bolt, Jan. 30, 1987. B.A. in Econs., U. Wash., 1960, J.D., 1963. Bar: Wash. 1963, Pa. 1967. Asst. sec. Koppers Co. Inc., Pitts., 1966-70; v.p. Commonwealth Life, Louisville, 1970-73; exec. v.p. Ga.Internat. Life, Atlanta, 1973-75; sr. v.p. Am. Income Life Ins. Co., Waco, Tex., 1975-76, exec. v.p., 1976-77; pres. Am. Income LIfe Ins. Co., Waco, Tex., 1977—; bd. dirs. Action Industries, Inc., Pitts. Pres. United Way, Waco, 1981, Contbrs. Rev. com., 1983, Waco-McLennan Library Found., 1985-88; mem. City Library Commn., Waco, 1985. Fellow Life Mgmt. Inst. Office: Am Income Life Ins Co 1200 Wooded Acres Dr Waco TX 76710

COOPER, CHARLES G., toiletries and cosmetics company executive; b. Chgo., Apr. 4, 1928; s. Benjamin and Gertrude Cooper; m. Miriam Meyer, Feb. 11, 1951 (dec. Oct. 17, 1984); children: Debra, Ruth, Janet, Benjamin; m. Nancy Cooper. B.S. in Journalism, U. Ill., 1949. With sales promotion dept. Maidenform Co., N.Y.C., 1949-51; with circulation promotion dept. Esquire mag., Chgo., 1951-52; with Helene Curtis Industries Inc., Chgo., 1953—, pres. salon div., 1971-75, pres. consumer products div., 1975-82, corp. exec. v.p., 1982-85, exec. v.p., chief operating officer, 1985—. Served with AUS, 1952-53. Mem. Nat. Wholesale Druggists Assn., Nat. Assn. Chain Drug Stores. Club: Mid-Am. (Chgo.). Office: Helene Curtis Industries Inc 325 N Wells St Chicago IL 60610

COOPER, CHARLES GORDON, insurance consultant; b. Providence, May 31, 1927; s. Irving and Helen Christina (Skog) C.; m. Barbara Caroline Termohlen, June 17, 1950; 1 dau., Marie Suzanne. B.A., Ohio Wesleyan U., 1949. C.L.U. Group rep. Washington Nat. Ins. Co., 1949-53, asst. mgr., 1953-58, mgr., 1958-63, dir. assn. field services, 1963-65, asst. sec., 1965-67, 3d v.p., 1967-72, 2d v.p., 1972-77, v.p., 1977-79, sr. v.p., 1979-83; exec. v.p. Washington Nat. Ins. Co., Evanston, Ill., 1983-85; dir., mem. exec. com. Washington Nat. Ins. Co., 1979-85; sr. v.p.-mktg. Washington Nat. Corp., parent co. Washington Nat. Ins. Co., Evanston, 1983-85; cons. Washington Nat. Corp., parent co. Washington Nat. Ins. Co., 1985—; dir. Washington Nat. Trust Co., 1974-85, chmn. exec. com., 1979-85; chmn., dir. Washington Nat. Fin. Services, Inc., 1979-85; pres., dir. Washington Nat. Equity Co., 1973-85, chmn. bd., 1983-85. Bd. dirs. North Shore Assn. for Retarded, Evanston, 1983—. Served with USNR, 1945-46, PTO. Mem. Am. Coll. Life Underwriters, Chartered Life Underwriters, Nat. Assn. Life Underwriters, Chgo. Life Underwriters Assn., Nat. Assn. Health Underwriters, Chgo. Health Underwriters. Republican. Club: Thorngate Country (Deerfield, Ill.). Lodges: Masons, Shriners.

COOPER, DENNIS RICHARD, manufacturing executive; b. Grand Rapids, Mich., May 8, 1947; s. Joseph Richard and Teresa Mary (Troy) C.; m. Dee Ann Antvelink, Apr. 4, 1970; children: Jeanene, Kristine, Brett. BBA, Aquinas Coll., 1969. Acct. Rapistan, Grand Rapids, 1969-72; budget dir. Leigh Products, Inc., Coopersville, Mich., 1972-74; controller Harrow Products Inc., Coopersville, 1974-79; pres. W.C.M. div. Harrow Products Inc., Miami, Fla., 1984—; v.p. Robco Products, INc., Youngstown, Ohio, 1979-84. Republican. Roman Catholic. Home: 2625 NW 114th Ave Coral Springs FL 33065 Office: Harrow Products Inc 3443 NW 107th St Miami FL 33167

COOPER, E. CAMRON, oil company executive; b. Redlands, Calif., Apr. 14, 1939; d. Jack and Ekla (Scott) C. B.A., Stanford U., 1960. Research asst., registered rep. Smith, Barney & Co., Inc., N.Y.C., 1960-62; investment analyst Bank of Am., Los Angeles, 1962-63; asst. mgr. research dept. Lester, Ryons & Co., Los Angeles, 1963-67, dir. sales tng. program, sales analyst for spl. situations, asst. to sales ptnr., 1967-68, dir. research, 1968-69; sr. investment analyst Hornblower & Weeks-Hemphill, Noyes, 1969-72; registered rep. Loeb, Rhoades & Co., Los Angeles, 1972-74; mgr. investor relations Atlantic Richfield Co., Los Angeles, 1974-75, investment officer, 1975-78, treas., 1978—, v.p., 1983-87, sr. v.p., treas., 1987—; bd. dirs. Inland Steel Co. Trustee, bd. dirs. Seaver Inst.; vice chmn. bd. Greater Los Angeles Zoo Assn.; trustee Los Angeles County Mus. Natural History. Mem. Stanford U. Alumni Assn., Cap and Gown. Republican. Home: 620 Busch Garden Ln Pasadena CA 91105 Office: Atlantic Richfield Co 515 S Flower St Los Angeles CA 90071

COOPER, FREDERICK EANSOR, lawyer; b. Thomasville, Ga., Jan. 18, 1942; s. Martin Milner and Margeret (Philips) C.; m. Helen Dykes, Dec. 10, 1966; children: Frederick Eansor, Johnson Joseph. B.A., Washington and Lee U., 1964; J.D., U. Ga., 1967. Bar: Ga. Partner firm Herndon & Cooper, Thomasville, 1972-73; gen. counsel Flowers Industries, Inc., Thomasville, 1973-74; gen. counsel, sec. Flowers Industries, Inc., 1974—, corp. v.p., 1978-83, exec. v.p., 1983-84, pres., 1984—, vice chmn., 1986—, dir., 1975—. Chmn. Ga. Republican Com., 1981—. Served with JAGC AUS, 1967-72; mem. Res. Presbyterian. Club: Rotary. Home: 203 Junius St Thomasville GA 31792 Office: Flowers Industries Inc US Hwy 19 S PO Box 1338 Thomasville GA 31799

COOPER, GORDON MAYO, manufacturing company executive; b. Waterbury, Conn., Dec. 11, 1925; s. George Leslie and Margaret Mercedes (Reed) C.; B.S. in Mech. Engring., U. Conn., 1950; postgrad. Harvard U., 1970; m. Edna A. George, June 15, 1948; children—Jan-Louise, Gordon Mayo. Chief engr. Timex Corp., Middlebury, Conn., 1951-66, pres. Timex Industries, 1972-76; v.p. mfg. and engring. Shuron/Continental div. Textron Inc. Rochester, N.Y., 1966-68, pres., 1968-72; exec. v.p. energy products group Gulf & Western Inc., Oakbrook, Ill., 1976-78; pres., chief exec. officer Broan Mfg. Co., Inc., Hartford, Wis., 1978-87; exec. v.p. Nortek Inc., Providence, 1987—; adv. bd. Milw. Sch. Engring., 1980—. Trustee, Post Coll., Waterbury, 1974-76, Waterbury Hosp., 1974-76. Served as pilot USAAF, 1943-45. Named Most Disting. Alumni U. Conn., 1986. Registered profl. engr., Conn.; cert. mfg. engr. Mem. Am. Mgmt. Assn., Soc. Mfg. Engrs., Nat. Soc. Profl. Engrs., Nat. Rifle Assn. (life), Home Ventilating Inst. (pres. 1982—), Waterbury C. of C. (dir. 1974-76). Episcopalian. Clubs: Country of Waterbury, Ozaukee Country, Mason, KT. Office: Nortek Inc 50 Kennedy Pla Providence RI 02903

COOPER, JOHN EDWARD, financial planner; b. Oak Hill, W.Va., Aug. 30, 1945; s. Elwood O. and Lee (Boyd) C.; m. Linda Vaughan Smith; children: Robert John, Christopher Brandon. BA, U. Va., 1967; MS in Mgmt., Troy State U., 1978. Rep. Paine Webber & Co., Phila., 1978-82, Motley, Pa., 1982-84; dir. estate and fin. planning Am. Soc. CLU and Chartered Fin. Cons., Bryn Mawr, Pa., 1984-86; fin. planning officer Provident Nat. Bank, Phila., 1986—. Editor audio tape series Fin. Planning Forum, 1984-86. Capt. USAF, 1967-78, Vietnam, ETO. Mem. Internat. Assn. Fin. Planners, Va. Club. Republican. Baptist. Office: Provident Nat Bank 1235 Westlakes Dr Malvern PA 19312

COOPER, JOHN JOSEPH, lawyer; b. Vincennes, Ind., Oct. 20, 1924; s. Homer O. and Ruth (House) C.; m. Nathalie Brooke, 1945. A.B., Stanford, 1950, LL.B., 1951; LL.M., U. So. Calif., 1964. Bar: Calif. 1952. Practice in San Francisco, 1951-54, Los Angeles, 1954-61, Palo Alto, 1961—; gen. counsel, v.p. Varian Assos., 1970—, also bd. dirs.; lectr. Am. Law Inst.-Am. Bar Assn., Seattle, 1964, Kansas City, 1965, 66; moderator Trademark and Copyright Inst., George Washington U., 1968; participant Tokyo Conf., U.S.-Japanese Patent Licensing Symposium, U. Wash.-Japanese Inst. Internat. Bus. Law, 1968; speaker Mid-Am. World Trade Conf., Chgo., 1971. Contbr.: chpt. to Patent and Know-How Licensing in Japan and the United States; also law rev. articles and profl. jours. Served with USNR, 1942-45. Mem. ABA, Calif. Bar Assn. (speaker Conf. Corp. Counsel 1969), Am. Corp. Counsel Assn. (past pres., bd. dirs. San Francisco chpt.), Bay Area Gen. Counsels Group, Peninsula Assn. Gen. Counsels, Santa Clara Bar Assn. Republican. Home: 191 Ramoso Rd Portola Valley CA 94025 Office: Varian Assocs Inc 611 Hansen Way Palo Alto CA 94303

COOPER, LEON EARL, JR., banker; b. Roanoke, Ala.; s. Leon Earl Sr. and Flora Evelyn (Bonner) C.; BS, U. Ala., 1965, JD, 1967; MBA, Harvard U., 1973; m. Mary Patricia A. Wood, Aug. 20, 1977; children: William E. Whitmel, Patricia E. Fitzsimmons, Henry Elgin B., John F. H. Bar: Ala. 1967. With Blyth Eastman Dillon & Co., Inc., N.Y.C., 1973-80, v.p., 1976, 1st v.p., 1977-79, sr. v.p., 1980; mng. dir., v.p. Dean Witter Reynolds, Inc., N.Y.C., 1980-83; mng. dir., chief exec. officer Elmsmere Co., 1983—, Delapré Co., 1986—, E. Co. Leasing, 1985—. Trustee Cooper Trust, 1988—, Pi Trust, Cooper Edn. Trust, Cooper Med. Trust, Cooper Art Trust, Cooper Sci. and Tech. Inst. Capt. JAGC USAF, 1968-71. Mem. Jasons, Omicron Delta Kappa, Kappa Alpha. Home: 210 Sasco Hill Rd Southport CT 06430 Office: 109 E 73d St 4A New York NY 10021

COOPER, LIDA ELAINE, accountant; b. Goltry, Okla., May 18, 1932; d. Jesse Earl and Mildred Mabel (Secord) Wayman; m. Lloyd Gene Cooper, Aug. 4, 1956; children—Nancy Laine, Cammy Jean. A.A., Central Coll., 1952; B.A., Seattle Pacific U., 1954. C.P.A., Tex. Tchr. Sequim pub. schs., Wash., 1954-56; tax preparer J.T. Williams, Vacaville, Calif., 1967; pvt. practice acctg., Vacaville, 1968-70; prin. Cooper's Tax Service, Schertz, Tex., 1971—. Mem. Cibolo Valley C. of C. Republican. Presbyterian. Avocation: Painting. Home: 140 Cloverleaf Dr Schertz TX 78154 Office: Cooper's Tax Svc 204 Mill St Schertz TX 78154

COOPER, LISA RENÉE, data processing executive; b. Rockville, Md., Aug. 20, 1962; d. Joseph David and Virginia Dare (Payton) C. AA, Montgomery Coll., 1985; BA in Econs., U. Md., 1988. Data entry clk. Tracor Inc., Rockville, 1982-83; computer operator Computer Sci. Press, Rockville, 1983-84; specialist logistics support M/A Com Info. Systems Inc., Rockville, 1984-86; computer specialist Bur. Labor Stats., Washington, 1987-88; analyst ERC Internat., Fairfax, Va., 1988—. Democrat. Roman Catholic. Home: 205 Ashley Ave Rockville MD 20850

COOPER, MARY ADRIENNE, publishing executive; b. Bklyn., Jan. 27, 1927; d. James H. and Helen (Hofeditz) C. BSBA, SUNY, Albany, 1948; postgrad. in bus., NYU, 1949-50, Columbia U., 1976. With McGraw Hill, Inc., N.Y.C., 1953—, asst. v.p. corp. fin. ops., 1973-75, v.p. corp. fin. ops., 1975-76, v.p. adminstrv. services, 1976-84, v.p. fin. services, 1984-85, sr. v.p. adminstrv. services, 1985-86, sr. v.p. corp. affairs, exec. asst. to Chief Exec. Officer, chmn., 1986—. Mem. Fin. Execs. Inst. (com. on govt. liaison N.Y.C. chpt., bd. dirs. 1986—). Roman Catholic. Avocations: golf, biking, reading, travel. Office: McGraw-Hill Inc 1221 Ave of the Americas New York NY 10020

COOPER, MELVIN, financial planner; b. New Haven, June 19, 1936; s. Abraham and Mary (Schrieberg) C.; m. Zelda A. Molaver, June 29, 1958; children: Susan, Lawrence, Allan. BS in Bus., U. Conn., 1958; cert., Nat. Assn. Seurity Dealers Inst. Fin., N.Y.C., 1969; cert. fin. planner, Coll. for Fin. Planning, Denver, 1985. Cert. fin. planner; registered investment advisor. Prin., cons., now pres. Cooper Fin. Services, Inc., Hamden, Conn. Named to Hall of Fame, Integrated Resources Equity Corp., 1984, 85, 86, 87, 88. Mem. Internat. Assn. Fin. Planners, Inst. Cert. Fin. Planners, Registra Fin. Planning Practitioners, Alumni Assn. U. Conn., Assn. for Retarded Persons, Probus (Hamden, pres. 1972, past holder various offices), AF & AM.

COOPER, ROGER HARVEY, sales executive, educator; b. Hackensack, N.J., Feb. 14, 1941; s. George Manning and Hazel (Rainey) C.; BA in Bus., Econs. and Sociology, Drury Coll., 1963; m. Vicki Lynn Vantrease, Feb. 12, 1961; children: Douglas, Deborah, Denise, Davie. With Standard Oil Co., 1957-63; mgr. Queen Anne Apts., 1962-63; self-employed salesman, 1963-72; founder, pres., chmn. bd. Ozark Ry. Supplies, Inc., Nixa, Mo., 1973-83; pres., chmn. bd. Ozark Properties of Nixa, Inc., 1979-84, chmn. bus. dept.; prof. bus. adminstrn., econs. and fin. Bapt. Bible Coll., Springfield, Mo., 1983—; chmn. bus. dept. Bapt. Bible Coll. 1983—; tchr. seminars, 1977-79. Bd. deacons, lay ch. worker Parkcrest Bapt. Ch. Mem. Roadmasters Assn., Am. Ry. Bridge and Bldg. Assn., Ill. Ry. Club, St. Louis Ry. Club. Club: Rotary. Designer Ozark Spike Re-Cla-Mer. Home and Office: Bart Bible Coll 1953 E Nottingham Ln Springfield MO 65804

COOPER, RONALD R., engineer; b. Center, Mo., July 5, 1947; s. Clarence C. and Margaret (Crane) C.; m. Madonna Rose Emmack, Dec. 23, 1967; children: Rae Marie, Timothy Scott. BS in Physics, Cen. State U., Edmond, Okla., 1976. Engr. Xerox Corp., Oklahoma City, 1971—. Pres. Found for Exceptional Children, Okla., 1980-83. Served with U.S. Army, 1967-71. Home: 7900 Maehs Circle Oklahoma City OK 73162 Office: Xerox Corp 50 Penn Pl Oklahoma City OK 73118

COOPER, ROWLAND, III, financial planner, insurance agent; b. Jamaica, N.Y., Oct. 2, 1951; s. Rowland Jr. and Evelyn C. (Bruland) C.; m. Rita Ann Stumpf, July 8, 1972; children: Jennifer, Kirsten. BS, SUNY, 1989. CLU, ChFC. Sales. rep. Met. Life, Fitchburg, Mass., 1973-75, sales mgr., 1975-79, sales rep., 1979-86; fin. planner MetLife Securities, Inc., Fitchburg, 1987—. Capt. USAR, 1970—. Mem. Montachusett Assn. Life Underwriters (pres. 1984-85, v.p. 1982-84, sec. 1980-81), Nat. Assn. Life Underwriters, Met. Life New Eng. Sales Adv. Counc., Jaycees (v.p. Pepperell club 1974-76), Mass. Assn. Life Underwriters (chmn. satet edn. 1985-86), Rotary. Lutheran.

COOPER, THEODORE, pharmaceutical company executive, physician; b. Trenton, N.J., Dec. 28, 1928; s. Victor and Dora (Popkin) C.; m. Vivian Cecilia Evans, June 16, 1956; children—Michael Harris, Mary Katherine, Victoria Susan, Frank Victor. B.S., Georgetown U., 1949; M.D., St. Louis U., 1954, Ph.D., 1956. USPHS fellow St. Louis U. Dept. Physiology, 1955-56; clin. asso. surgery br. Nat. Heart Inst., Bethesda, Md., 1956-58; faculty St. Louis U., 1960-66; prof. surgery, 1964-66; prof., chmn. dept. pharmacology U. N.Mex., Albuquerque, 1966-68, on leave, 1967-69; assoc. dir. artificial heart, myocardial infarction programs Nat. Heart Inst., Bethesda, 1967-68; dir. Nat. Heart and Lung Inst., 1968-74; dep. asst. sec. for health HEW, 1974-75, asst. sec. health, 1975-77; dean Med. Coll., Cornell U., N.Y.C., 1977-80; provost for med. affairs Cornell U., 1977-80; exec. v.p. Upjohn Co., Kalamazoo, 1980-84; vice chmn. bd. Upjohn Co., 1984-87, chmn. bd., chief exec. officer, 1987—; mem. USPHS Pharmacology and Exptl. Therapeutics Study Sect., 1964-67; Bd. overseers Meml. Sloan-Kettering Cancer Center. Author: (with others) Nervous Control of the Heart, 1965, Heart Substitutes, 1966, The Baboon in Medical Research, Vol. II, 1967, Factors Influencing Myocardial Contractility, 1967, Acute Myocardial Infarction, 1968, Advance in Transplantation, Prosthetic Heart Valves, 1969, Depressed Metabolism, 1969; Editorial bd.: Jour. Pharmacology and Exptl. Therapeutics, 1965-68, 77—, Circulation Research, 1966-71; editor: Supplements to Circulation, 1966-71; sect. co-editor for: Jour. Applied Physiology, 1967-73; contbr. numerous articles med. jours.; discoverer new techniques of denervating heart which have helped delineate role of nerves in heart, on its ability to function under a wide variety of circumstances, and on its ability to respond to drugs. Bd. govs. ARC, 1980. Recipient Borden award, 1954; Albert Lasker Spl. Public Service award, 1978; Ellen Browning Scripps medal, 1980; medal for Disting. Pub. Service, Dept. Def., 1985. Mem. Am. Soc. Pharmacology and Exptl. Therapeutics, Am. Physiol. Soc., Soc. Exptl. Biology and Medicine, Am. Soc. Clin. Investigation, Am. Fedn. Clin. Research, Am. Soc. Artificial Internal Organs, Internat. Cardiovascular Soc., Am. Coll. Chest Physicians, AAUP, Am. Coll. Cardiology, AAAS, Sigma Xi. Home: 3656 Woodcliff Dr Kalamazoo MI 49008 Office: Upjohn Co 7000 Portage Rd Kalamazoo MI 49001

COOPER, WILLIAM ROBERT, mining company executive; b. Calgary, Alta., Can., July 12, 1933; s. Ralph Blain and Audrey (Hamilton) C.; m. Joan Gladys Cooper, Aug. 24, 1955; 1 child, Carmen. BSc in Petroleum Engring., U. Okla., 1957. Sales mgr. Schlumberger of Can., Calgary, 1968-70, ops. mgr., 1973-75; mgr. Schlumberger of Can., Edmonton, Alta., Can., 1975-81; sales devel. engr. Schlumberger Well Survey Corp., Houston, 1971-72; sr. v.p. exploration and prodn. Asamera Oil (U.S.) Inc., Denver, 1981-82; sr. v.p. oil and gas Asamera Inc., Calgary, 1982-83, exec. v.p., chief operating officer, 1987-88; pres. Asamera Indonesian Group of Cos., Jakarta, 1983-87; pres. Asamera Minerals, Calgary, 1988—, also dir.; bd. dirs. Lovitt Mining Co., Wenatlhee, Wash. Home: 610 Stratton Terr SW, Calgary, AB Canada T3H 1M6

COOPERSMITH, FREDRIC S., financial planning executive; b. N.Y.C.; s. Phillip and Ruth L. (Brown) C.; divorced; children: Lisa, Jeffrey, Steven. BS, NYU, MBA. Cert. life underwriter; cert. fin. planner; chartered fin. cons. Cons. fin. planning Englewood, N.J., 1961—; adj. prof. fin. Rutgers U., New Brunswick, N.J., NYU. Contbr. articles to profl. jours. Lt. U.S. Army. Named Man of Yr., Nat. C. of C.; recipient Man in Fin. award Finance Club (N.Y.C.). Mem. Internat. Assn. Fin. Planners, Nat. Council Fin. Planners, Nat. Assn. Estate and Fin. Planners, Duke U. Met. Alumni Club. Club: NYU (N.Y.C.). Lodge: Masons. Office: Fredric S Coopersmith & Assocs 145 Cedar Ln Englewood NJ 07631

COORS, JEFFREY H., brewery company executive; b. Denver, Feb. 10, 1945; s. Joseph Coors. B.Chem. Engring., Cornell U., 1967, M.Chem. Engring., 1968. With Coors Porcelain Co., 1968-70; with Adolph Coors Co., Golden, Colo., 1970—; pres. Adolph Coors Co., 1985—. Office: Adolph Coors Co Golden CO 80401 *

COORS, JOSEPH, brewery executive; b. 1917; m. Holly Coors; children: Jeff, Peter, Joseph Jr., Gover, John. Grad., Cornell U., 1939. With Adolph Coors Co., Golden, Colo., v.p., from 1947, vice chmn., 1975, pres., 1977-85, vice chmn., 1982—, chief operating officer, 1982-87. Former regent U. Colo. Office: Adolph Coors Co Golden CO 80401 *

COORS, PETER HANSON, beverage company executive; b. Denver, Sept. 20, 1946; s. Joseph and Holly (Hanson) C.; m. Marilyn Gross, Aug. 23, 1969; children: Melissa, Christien, Carrie Ann, Ashley, Peter, David. B.S. in Idsl. Engring., Cornell U., 1969; M.B.A., U. Denver, 1970. Prodn. trainee, specialist Adolph Coors Co., Golden, Colo., 1970-71, dir. fin. planning, 1971-75, dir. market research, 1975-76, v.p. self distbn., 1976-77, v.p. sales and mktg., 1977-78, sr. v.p. sales and mktg., 1978-82, div. pres. sales, mktg. and adminstrn., 1982-85, now pres. brewing div.; pres. Coors Distbn. Co., 1976-82, 1976-81, chmn., from 1981, dir.; dir. Adolph Coors Co., 1973—, asst. sec.-treas., 1974-76; dir. CADCO, 1975-85. Bd. dirs. Nat. Wildlife Fedn., 1978-81, Wildlife Legis. Fund, 1987—; hon. bd. dirs. Colo. Spl. Olympics Inc., 1978—; trustee Colo. Outward Bound Sch., 1978—, Adolph Coors Found., Pres.'s Leadership Com., U. Colo., 1978—; chmn. Nat. Commn. on the Future of Regis Coll., 1981-82, chmn. devel. com., 1983—, now trustee. Mem. Nat. Indls. Adv. Council, Opportunities Ctrs. of Am., Young Pres.' Orgn., Ducks Unlimited (nat. trustee 1979, sr. v.p., mem. mgmt. com., exec. com. 1982—, dir. Can. 1982—, pres. 1984-85, chmn. bd. 1986—). Club: Met. Denver Exec. (dir 1979, pres. 1981—). Office: Adolph Coors Co Golden CO 80401 *

COORS, WILLIAM K., brewery executive; b. Golden, Colo., 1916. Chmn. bd. Adolph Coors Co., Golden, Colo. Office: Adolph Coors Co Golden CO 80401 *

COOVER, HARRY WESLEY, manufacturing company executive; b. Newark, Del., Mar. 6, 1919; s. Harry Wesley and Anna (Rohm) C.; m. Muriel Zumbach, Sept. 17, 1941; children—Harry Wesley, Stephen R., Melinda Coover Paul. B.S. in Chemistry (Southerland prize 1941), Hobart Coll., Geneva, N.Y., 1941; M.S., Cornell U., 1942, Ph.D., 1944. Research chemist Eastman Kodak Co., Rochester, N.Y., 1944-49; sr. research chemist Tenn. Eastman Co., Kingsport, 1949-54; research asso. Tenn. Eastman Co., 1954-63, head polymers div., 1963-65, dir. research, 1965-73, v.p., 1970-73, exec. v.p., 1973-81; v.p. Eastman Kodak Co., Kingsport, 1981-84; internat. mgmt. cons. Kingsport, 1984-85; pres. New Bus. Devel. Loctite Corp., Newington, Conn., 1985—. Author; patentee in field. Recipient Chem. Pioneers award, 1986. Mem. Internat. Union Pure and Applied Chemistry, Am. Chem. Soc. (So. Chemist award 1960, Speaker of Year award N.E. Tenn. sect. 1962), AAAS, Am. Assn. Textile Tech., Am. Inst. Chemists, Assn. Research Dirs., Dirs. Indsl. Research, Indsl. Research Inst. (pres. 1981-82), Soc. Chem. Industry, Soc. Plastics Industry, Textile Research Inst. (trustee), N.Y. Acad. Scis. Presbyterian. Lodges: Lions, Masons. Office: 1101 Eastman Rd PO Box 3866 Kingsport TN 37664 also: Loctite Corp 705 N Mountain Rd Newington CT 06111

COPANAS, THOMAS M., financial services executive; b. Oct. 6, 1944; s. Franklin W. and Nancy B. (Childress) C.; m. Sondra Lee Hodgson, Dec. 17, 1966; children: Tanya, Tamra, Tara. BS in Indsl. Mgmt., U. Cin., 1968; MBA in Fin., Cornell U., 1971. Indsl. engr. IBM Corp., Endicott, N.Y., 1968-71; with strategic planning and sales Owens-Ill., Toledo, 1971-74; co. planning mgr. The Andersons, Maumee, Ohio, 1974-79, mgr. planning and human resources, 1979-83, gen. ptnr.-mgr. adminstrv. services, 1983-88, exec. v.p. fin and adminstrv. services, 1988—. Chmn. personnel com., mem. exec. com. Riverside Hosp., Toledo, 1986—; chmn. U. Toledo Com. Investment Corp., Toledo, 1987—. Mem. Rotary Club. Club: Sylvania Country. Office: The Andersons 1200 Dussel Dr Maumee OH 43537

COPANS, KENNETH GARY, accountant; b. Stamford, Conn., Dec. 6, 1946; s. Lawrence W. and Rosaline (Davidoff) C.; m. Jo Ellen Silbert, Apr. 25, 1972; children: Scott David, Richard Harris, Mark Adam. BS in Acctg., Bucknell U., 1968. CPA, N.Y. With Arthur Andersen & Co., N.Y.C., 1968; with Copans, Copans & Piccone, N.Y.C., 1971-74, ptnr., 1974-84, mng. ptnr., 1984—; instr. Long Island U., Found. for Acctg. Edn. Bd. dirs. Congregation Aqudas Israel, Newburgh, N.Y., 1980—. Served with U.S. Army, 1968-70. Mem. Am. Inst. CPA's, N.Y. State Soc. CPA's, Am. Assn. Personal Fin. Planners. Republican. Lodge: Rotary (local bd. dirs. 1980-84). Home: 43 Parkhill Dr New Windsor NY 12550 Office: Copans Copans & Piccone 540 Gidney Ave Newburgh NY 12550

COPE, ALFRED HAINES, political scientist, educator; b. Oakbourne, Pa., May 29, 1912; s. Joseph and Ellen (Fussell) C.; m. Ruth Balderston, Aug. 23, 1937; 1 child, Joan. AB, Earlham Coll., 1934; PhD, U. Pa., 1948. Agt. Equitable Life Ins. Co., 1934-36; dir. Am. Friends Service Co., Chgo., 1936-38, War Relief Adminstrn., Spain, 1938-39; adminstrv. asst. U. Pa. Inst. Local and State Govt., 1940-42, instr., 1946-48; sr. adminstrv. aid. U.S. CSC, Phila., 1942-43; asst. prof. Syracuse (N.Y.) U., 1948-51, assoc. prof., 1951-56; asst. dean Coll. Liberal Arts, 1960-70, prof. citizenship, 1965-75, prof. polit. sci., 1962-75, prof. emeritus, 1975—, registrar, mgr. student data systems, 1970-74; asst. dean, prof. citizenship Utica Coll., 1956-60. Author: Administration of Civil Service in Cities of the Third Class in Pennsylvania, 1948; (with Fred Krinsky) Franklin Roosevelt and the Supreme Court, 1952, rev. edit., 1969; Current Defense of the U.S., 1954; (with E.E. Palmer) The Dixon Yates Contract and the National Power Policy, 1955; The Basis for a New Legal System, 1973; Managing World Resources, 1975. Pres. bd. dirs. Child and Family Services, 1963-66; arbitrator Syracuse Better Bus. Bur.; trustee Oakwood Sch., Poughkeepsie, N.Y., 1974—, treas., 1977-84, chmn. fin. com., 1984—, pres. bd. mgrs., 1987—; chmn. fin. com. Friends World Com., sect. of Ams., 1976-81, mem. world fin. group, 1975-81, del. triennial meeting Gwatt, Switzerland, 1980; Friends Assn. for Higher Edn.; co-clerk Task Force on Peace Studies, 1985-88; mem. cen. com. Friends Gen. Conf., 1978-84; chmn. devel. com., mem. exec. personnel and advancement coms.; mem. gen. services com. N.Y. Yearly Meeting, Religious Soc. Friends, 1978-81, chmn. com. sharing of world resources, 1981-85; mem. gen. bd. Pendle Hill, Wallingford, Pa., 1982—; treas., trustee Syracuse Friends Meeting; trustee Lindley Murray Fund, 1984—. Served to capt. AUS, 1943-46. Fellow AAAS; mem. Am. Acad. Polit and Soc. Sci., Friends Assn. Higher Edn. (assoc.), Acad. Polit. Sci., Am. Judicature Soc., Friends Hist. Soc., Geneol. Soc. Pa., Chester County Hist. Soc. (life), Pi Gamma Mu, Phi Delta Kappa. Club: Torch (Syracuse) (pres. 1969-70). Home: 201 Houston Ave Syracuse NY 13224

COPE, LAURENCE BRIAN, utilities rate analyst, economic consultant; b. White Plains, N.Y., May 28, 1951; s. Lawrence Lyndon and Dorothea Anne (Herrick) C.; m. Ana Virginia Ambrosini, June 7, 1986. BS, Fla. So. Coll., 1974; MS in Govt. and Pub. Adminstrn., So. Ill. U.-Edwardsville, 1980; postgrad. in Econs., George Washington U., 1982. Mgr. cost estimating Potomac Electric Power Co., Washington, 1974-77, systems and tng. specialist, 1977-82, project mgr., 1982-84, mem. speakers bur., 1978-84; utilities rate analyst Nat. Rural Utilities Coop. Fin. Corp., Washington, 1984—; econ. cons. Cope Assocs., Washington, 1978-84; chmn. budget com. Oakton Condominium Assn., 1986-88. Author articles in field. Co-chmn. Christian Young Adults Group, Washington, 1983. Mem. Am. Soc. Pub. Adminstrn. (budget and fin. div.), Am. Soc. Tng. and Devel. (reporter chpt. organ The Torch 1977, 78), Nat. Economists Club (rapporteur, 1985—), Nat. Soc. Rate of Return Analysts, Cath. Alumni Club of Washington. Roman Catholic. Home: 10170 Oakton Terr Rd Oakton VA 22124 Office: Nat Rural Utilities Coop Fin Corp 1115 30th St NW Washington DC 20007

COPELAND, ALVIN CHARLES, fast food company executive; b. New Orleans, Feb. 2, 1944; s. William Allen and Augustine Marie (Comeaux) C.; m. Patty White, Nov. 4, 1977; children: Alvin, Bonnie, Chris Ali, Charli. Pres. Popeyes Famous Fried Chicken, Copeland Enterprises, Inc., New Orleans, 1972—, chmn., chief exec. officer, Church's Fried Chicken Inc., 1989—; adviser La. Gov. Edwin Edwards, 1975. Bd. dirs. Contemporary Arts Ctr., New Orleans. Recipient Brit. Harmsworth Trophy, 1982; holder U.S. Powerboat Record Fastest Average Course Speed, 1982; winner Detroit Stroh Light Challenge Pan American Championship, 1982, Chrysler Classic, 1983, Bud Warmington Grand Prix 1983, Popeyes Offshore Prix, 1984, Lee County Regatta, 1984, Stroh/Downriver Challenge Cup, 1984. Mem. Am. Mktg. Assn. (Marketer of Yr. 1977), Am. Power Boat Assn., Nat. Restaurant Assn., Internat. Franchise Assn. Roman Catholic. Club: Marid Gras Krewes. Home: 5001 Folse Dr Metairie LA 70002 Office: A Copeland Anterprises 1333 S Clearview Pkwy Jefferson LA 70121 *

COPENHAVER, ELMER RANDALL, consultant, real estate investment executive; b. Waco, Tex., Oct. 11, 1931; s. Elmer Randall and Margie Belle (Chadwick) C.; m. Maria DelRosario Chavarria, Nov. 12, 1959 (div. 1976); children: Edward, David, Janice; m. Marina Escalante Borges, Sept. 26, 1987. BA, Tex. A&I Coll., 1952; BS, MBA, UCLA, 1965; PhD, Polyglot Inst., Kuwait, 1982, U. Alta., Edmonton, Can., 1982. Registered chartered property and casualty underwriter. Surety underwriter Fidelity & Casualty Co., N.Y.C, Los Angeles, f1954-58; surety mgr. Continental Casualty Co., Los Angeles, 1958-62; v.p. Nat. Auto & Casualty Ins., Los Angeles, 1962-65; pres. Copenhaver Cons. Ltd., Edmonton, 1979-83, also bd. dirs.; bd. dirs. Copenhaver Cons. S.A., San Jose, Costa Rica; chmn. bd. dirs., chief exec. officer Copenhaver Cons. Inc., Montebello, Calif., 1965—; bd. dirs. Western Tech Labs., Ltd., Edmonton. Mem. Housing Mediation Bd., City of Montebello, 1985—. Served to sgt. USAF, 1952-54. Republican. Methodist. Home: Box 83 1345 Manzanita Way Lake Arrowhead CA 92352 Office: Copenhaver Cons Inc PO Box 5423 Hacienda Heights CA 91745

COPLEY, WILLIAM MCKINLEY, III, mental health counselor, human relations consulting company executive; b. Orlando, Fla., July 10, 1943; s. William McKinley Jr. and Dorothy (Rathbun) C.; m. Suzanne Howard Montgomery, June 14, 1985. BA, East Carolina U., 1966; MA, Ball State U., 1971; AS, Fla. Community Coll., 1976. Dir. aftercare Univ. Hosp., Jacksonville, Fla., 1972-80; exec. dir. Orange County Crisis Unit, Orlando, 1980-81, Hillcrest House, Inc., Orlando, 1981-83; dir. CSP Mental Health Svcs. Orange County, Orlando, 1983-85; mng. ptnr. Montgomery, Copley & Assocs. Inc., Jacksonville, 1985—. Mem. Jacksonville Community Council, Inc., 1986—, Leadership Jacksonville, 1987-88; bd. dirs. Vol. Jacksonville, 1988—. With U.S. Army, 1967-70. Mem. Am. Assn. for Counseling and Devel., Mental Health Assn. (bd. dirs. 1989, chmn. adv. com.). Republican. Episcopalian. Office: Montgomery Copley & Assocs Inc 1812 Atlantic Blvd Jacksonville FL 32207

COPLIN, THOMAS HARLAND, physical therapist, company executive; b. Wichita, Kans., July 17, 1944; s. Raymond Eugene and Alma Louise (Thomas) C.; m. Jacque Kaye Hess, Dec. 30, 1965 (div. 1981); children: Tac, Wade; remarried, Oct. 28, 1984. BA in Edn., Macalester Coll., 1966; BS in Phys. Therapy, U. Minn., 1969. Registered phys. therapist; cert. athletic trainer. Athletic trainer Macalester Coll., St. Paul, 1965-80; research therapist U. Minn. Hosp., Mpls., 1969-72; v.p. Orthopedic Phys. Therapy, St. Paul, 1972-81; pres. Coplin Phys. Therapy, Inc., St. Paul, Mpls. and Bloomington, Minn., 1981—; phys. therapist Minn. North Stars Profl. Hockey Club, Bloomington, 1981—; cons. in sports medicine Mpls., St. Paul Pub. High Schs., 1981—; exec. dir. Second Wind Sports Medicine Ctr.of Mt. Sinai Hosp., Mpls.; phys. therapist Minn. N. Stars Profl. Hockey Orgn., Bloomington, Minn., 1981—, cons. Cambridge (Minn.) Sports Medicine, 1986—. Author sports medicine column, 1984-88; hosted numerous TV sports segments, 1985; frequent guest Minn. radio sports medicine talk show, 1986—. Coach Irondale Basketball Assn., New Brighton, Minn., 1972-87. Mem. Nat. Athletic Trainers Assn., Am. Phys. Therapy Assn. (v.p. Minn. chpt. 1980-82), Am. Coll. Sports Medicine, Mpls. C. of C., St. Paul C. of C. Office: Coplin Physical Therapy Assocs Inc 1550 E 79th St Bloomington MN 55425

COPPER, JAMES ROBERT, manufacturing company executive; b. St. Louis, Aug. 19, 1939; s. Charles Alva and Cora Imogene (Shifley) Copper; m. Patricia Leeper, Aug. 12, 1961; children: Susan, Robin, Julie. A.B., Culver-Stockton Coll., 1961; M.S., U. Tenn.-Knoxville, 1969. Tchr. Mo. Mil. Acad., Mexico, 1961-63; mgr. applications analysis Nuclear div. Union Carbide, Oak Ridge, Tenn., 1963-69; mgr. corp. mgmt. scis. Coca-Cola Co., Atlanta, 1969-76; v.p. strategic planning and analysis Pillsbury Co., Mpls., 1976-80; v.p. strategic planning IC Industries, Inc., Chgo., 1980-86, sr. v.p. corp. planning and devel., 1986-88; pres., chief oper. officer Pet, Inc., St. Louis, 1988, pres., chief exec. officer, 1989—; council mem., v.p. Inst. Mgmt. Scis., Providence, 1970—. Mem. Mgmt. Sci. Roundtable, Chgo. Council Fgn. Relations. Club: Optimist. Home: 1121 Kinsic St Naperville IL 60540

COPPER, JOHN FREDERICK, financial planner; b. Wilmington, Del., Oct. 18, 1944; s. James Albert Frederick and Kathryn (Atwell) C.; m. Freda Bernice Sharp, Mar. 22, 1969. BS in Indsl. Mgmt., Ga. Inst. Tech., 1967. Cert. fin. planner, registered fin. planner. Sr. systems analyst ALCOA, Alcoa, Tenn., 1967-73; salesman Mut. Benefit Life, Pitts., 1973-76, salesman, supr., 1979-82; employee benefit cons. Marsh & Mclennan, Pitts., 1976-79; registered rep. Cardell & Assocs., Pitts., 1982-86; owner, br. mgr. John F. Copper/Titan Capital, Pitts., 1986—. Mem. Inst. Cert. Fin. Planners, Registered Fin. Planners, Am. Soc. CLUs, Internat. Assn. Fin. Planners, Life Underwriters Assn. Republican. Methodist. Home and Office: Titan Capital 542 Sangree Rd Pittsburgh PA 15237

COPPERSMITH, W. LOUIS, lawyer; b. Johnstown, Pa., July 19, 1928; s. Samuel George and Bella (Glosser) C.; m. Bernice Evans (dec. Oct. 1976); children: Samuel, Susan, Beth; m. 2d, Marian Ungar. AB, U. Pa., 1950; JD, Harvard U., 1953. Asst. dist. atty. County of Cambria, Ebensburg, Pa., 1956-67; senator State of Pa., Harrisburg, 1969-80; gen. counsel Glosser Bros. Inc., Johnstown, 1961—, corp. sec., 1986—, also bd. dirs.; chmn. pub. health and welfare com. Pa. State Senate, 1971-80; commr. Pa. Pub. TV Network, Harrisburg, 1979-80. Bd. dirs. Keystone chpt. ARC, Johnstown, 1962—, Pub. TV Bd., Harrisburg, 1978-80; trustee U. Pitts., 1977—. Mem. ABA, Pa. Bar Assn. Democrat. Jewish. Home: 900 Parkview Dr Johnstown PA 15905 Office: Margolis & Coppersmith PO Box 69 Johnstown PA 15905

COPPETT, JOHN IRVIN, marketing educator; b. Texarkana, Tex., Aug. 25, 1936; s. Irvin Oliver and Catherine Ezell (Evans) C.; m. Mary Florence Villerett, July 2, 1961; children: Philip Kyle, Katherine Elizabeth. BS, So. Ark. U., 1958; MBA, U. Houston, 1965; PhD, U. Ark., 1973. Credit analyst Exxon, Houston, 1963-66; asst. prof. Iowa State U., Ames, 1969-78; assoc. prof. Drake U., Des Moines, 1978-80; mgr. mktg. AT&T, Bedminster, N.J., 1980-85; assoc. prof. U. Houston, 1986—; cons. AT&T, 1979-80, Am. Airlines, Tulsa, 1987. Contbr. articles to profl. jours. Lt. USNR, 1958-63. Mem. Bay Area Purchasing Assn. (acad. advisor), So. Mktg. Assn. (s.w. mktg.). Methodist. Home: 15706 Lake Lodge Dr Houston TX 77062 Office: U Houston 2700 Bay Area Blvd Houston TX 77058

COPPIE, COMER SWIFT, federal agency administrator; b. Washington, Oct. 19, 1932; s. John Lee and Marion (Peck) C.; m. Judith Ann Wright, Apr. 29, 1961; children: Cynthia, Sean, Scott. AB, Hamilton Coll., 1955; M in Pub. Adminstrn., Syracuse U., 1959. Budget analyst Bur. of Budget, State of Md., Balt., 1958-62; exec. dir., trustee Md. State Colls., Balt., 1963-68; dep. budget dir. Govt. of D.C., Washington, 1968-69; dir. Office of Budget and Mgmt. Systems, Washington, 1969-78; exec. dir. N.Y. State Fin. Control Bd., N.Y.C., 1978-86; chief fin. officer U.S. Postal Service, Washington, 1986—; bd. dirs. Lionel Corp., N.Y.C., 1985—, Univ. Support Services, Inc., Washington, 1988. Served with USN, 1955-57. Recipient Gold medal Fin. Officers Assn. of U.S. and Can., 1978. Mem. Cosmos Club. Episcopalian. Office: US Postal Svc 475 L'Enfant Pla SW Washington DC 20260-5000

COPPOLA, BETTE MARIE, accountant; b. Camden, N.J., Apr. 2, 1959; d. Joshua Ashley and Doris Annette (Saunders) Tobey; m. Michael Jeffery Coppola, July 30, 1983. BS with honors in Acctg., Pa. State U., 1981. CPA, Conn. Staff acct. Ernst and Whinney, Hartford, Conn., 1981-83; sr. mgr. Peat Marwick Main and Co., Phila., 1983—. Mem. AICPA, Penn State Club (Bucks County, Pa.), Beta Gamma Sigma, Beta Alpha Psi, Phi Mu. Republican. Methodist. Office: Peat Marwick Main 1600 Market St Philadelphia PA 19103

COPULSKY, WILLIAM, chemical company executive; b. Zhitomir, Russia, Apr. 4, 1922; s. Boris and Betty (Bruman) C.; came to U.S., 1923, naturalized, 1929; B.A., N.Y. U., 1942, Ph.D., 1957; m. Ruth B. Brody, Dec. 26, 1948; children—Stephen, Jonathan, Lewis. Chemist, Ammeco Chem. Co., Rochester, N.Y., 1942; asst. research dir. J.J. Berliner Co., N.Y.C., 1946-48; research dir. R. S. Aries and Assos., N.Y.C., 1948-51; comml. dir. W.R. Grace and Co., N.Y.C., 1951-74, v.p. operations services group, 1974-86; prof. mktg. Baruch Coll., City Univ., N.Y., 1987—. Served with AUS, 1942-46. Mem. Am. Chem. Soc., Chemists Club, Beta Gamma Sigma. Author: Marketing Chemical Products, 1948; Forecasting Chemical Commodity Demand, 1962; Practical Sales Forecasting, 1970; Entrepreneurship and the Corporation, 1974. Home: 23-35 Bell Blvd Bayside NY 11360 Office: Baruch Coll Mktg Dept 17 Lexington Ave New York NY 10010

CORBALLY, JOHN EDWARD, educator; b. South Bend, Wash., Oct. 14, 1924; s. John Edward and Grace (Williams) C.; m. Marguerite B. Walker, Mar. 12, 1946; children—Jan Elizabeth, David William. B.S., U. Wash., 1947, M.A., 1950; Ph.D., U. Calif.-Berkeley, 1955; LL.D., U. Md., 1971, Blackburn Coll., 1972, Ill. State U., 1977, Ohio State U., 1980; Litt.D., U. Akron, 1979. Tchr. Clover Park High Sch., Tacoma, 1947-50; prin. Twin City High Sch., Stanwood, Wash., 1950-53; asst. prof. edn., assoc. prof. Ohio State U., Columbus, 1955-60, prof., 1960-69, dir. personnel budget and exec. asst. to pres., 1960-64, v.p. adminstrn., 1964-66, provost, v.p. acad. affairs, 1966-69; chancellor, pres. Syracuse (N.Y.) U., 1969-71; pres. U. Ill., Chgo. and, Urbana-Champaign, 1971-79; pres. emeritus U. Ill., 1979—; disting. prof. higher edn. U. Ill., Urbana-Champaign, 1979-82, disting. prof. emeritus, 1982—; pres., dir. John D. and Catherine T. MacArthur Found., 1979—; dir. Ill. Bell Telephone Co.; mem. Commn. on Govt. Relations, Am. Council on Edn., 1972-76; bd. visitors Air U., 1974-80; mem. governing bd. Ill. Council Econ. Edn., 1972-80; bd. dirs. Ill. Ednl. Consortium, 1973-78; chmn. Nat. Council on Ednl. Research, Nat. Inst. Edn., 1973-79; bd. dirs. Council for Fin. Aid to Edn., 1973-79, Found. for Teaching Econs., 1978-85. Author: Introduction to Educational Adminstration, 6th edit, 1983, Educational Administration: The Secondary School, 2d edit, 1965, School Finance, 1962. Trustee Joint Council on Econ. Edn., Lincoln Acad. Ill., 1971-83; trustee Mus. Sci. and Industry, 1971-79; mem. Gov.'s Task Force Med. Malpractice, 1985; chmn. Ill. Bd. Edn. Commn. Curricular Outcome, 1985-86; chmn. Chgo. Sch. Reform Authority, 1988—. Served to lt. (j.g.) USNR, 1943-46. Recipient Centennial medal U. Calif. Alumni Assn. and Sch. Edn. Alumni Soc., 1976, Disting. Eagle award Boy Scouts Am., Disting. Service award U. Ill. Alumni Assn., 1986, Van Miller award Ill. Assn. Sch. Adminstrs. and Ednl. Adminstrn. Alumni Assn. U. Ill., 1986, Humanitarian award No. Ill. U., 1986, Disting. Alumnus award Coll. Edn. U. Wash., 1987; named Alumnus Summa Laude Dignatus U. Wash., 1988; named Laureate Lincoln Acad. Ill., 1989. Mem. Phi Beta Kappa, Phi Kappa Sigma, Phi Kappa Phi, Omicron Delta Kappa, Chi Gamma Iota, Beta Gamma Sigma, Alpha Phi Omega. Clubs: Tavern, Wayfarers, Chicago, Economic, Mid-Day (Chgo.); Useless Bay Country (Wash.). Office: 140 S Dearborn #700 Chicago IL 60603

CORBER, ROBERT JACK, I, lawyer; b. Topeka, June 29, 1926; s. Alva Forrest and Katherine (Salzer) C.; m. Joan Irene Tennal, July 16, 1949 (dec. July 1987); children: Janet, Suzanne, Wesley Sean, Robert Jack II; m. Deborah Perkins Corkey, Jan. 7, 1989. B.S. in Aero. Engring, U. Kans., 1946; J.D. cum laude, Washburn U., 1950; postgrad., U. Mich., 1950-51. Bar: Kans. bar 1950, D.C. bar 1951, U.S. Supreme Ct. bar 1964. Asso. firm Steptoe & Johnson, Washington, 1951-57; partner Steptoe & Johnson, 1957-75, 80—; commr. ICC, Washington, 1975-76; partner firm Conner, Moore & Corber, Washington, 1977-80. Author: Motor Carrier Leasing and Interchange Under the Interstate Commerce Act, 1977; contbr. legal and polit. articles to various publs. Chmn. Arlington (Va.) Republican Com., 1960-62; chmn. Va. 10th Congl. Dist. Rep. Com., 1962-64; state chmn. Rep. Party of Va., 1964-68. Served to lt. (j.g.) USNR, 1944-47. Mem. ABA (chmn. motor carrier com. pub. utility sect. 1983-86), Bar Assn. D.C. (chmn. adminstrv. law sect. 1978-79, chmn. continuing legal edn. com. 1979-83), Transp. Lawyers Assn., Assn. Trans. Practitioners. Methodist. Clubs: Met. (Washington), Capitol Hill (Washington), Washington Golf and Country (Washington).

CORBETT, JAMES ROBERT, market professional; b. Chgo., Apr. 11, 1945; s. Roy Robert and Elinor Catherine (Haberzettle) C.; m. Nancy Marie Glomb, Apr. 20, 1968; children: Michael, Jennifer. AA, Ill. Benedictine Coll., 1972. Sr. planner Kendall, Chgo., 1966-70; product mgr. Kendall div. Bauer and Black, Chgo., 1971-73; sr. product mgr. Kendall div. Bike Athletic Co., Boston, 1974-75, Southern Athletic div. Bike Athletic Co., Knoxville, Tenn., 1975-76; dir. mktg. Bike Athletic Co., Knoxville, 1976-85, pres., 1985—. Trustee Knoxville Cath. High Sch.; bd. dirs. Boy Scouts of Am. Mem. Sporting Goods Mfrs. Assn. Republican. Roman Catholic. Club: Fox Den Country (Farragut, Tenn.). Office: Bike Athletic Co PO Box 666 Knoxville TN 37901

CORBETT, JOHN RICHARD, metals company executive; b. Chgo., Apr. 28, 1928; s. William Fred and Minnie Frances (Heitmann) C.; m. Nancy Reese, June 28, 1952 (div. June 1987); children: Scott R., Douglas R., Mark R., Peter R.; m. Ellen Smith Liesching, Oct. 22, 1988. B.S., U. Wis., 1950, postgrad. U. Wis. Law Sch., 1950-51, 54-55; J.D., Columbia U., 1956. Atty., ASARCO Inc., N.Y.C., 1955-60, asst. dir. indsl. relations, 1960-64, dir. labor relations, 1964-83, v.p. indsl. relations, 1983-84, v.p. indsl. relations and personnel, 1984—; bd. dirs. N.Y.-NJ. Arbitration Group, N.Y.C., Inter-Am. Safety Council, Englewood, N.J., Unemployment Benefits Assn., Washington. Served to lt. (j.g.) USNR, 1951-54. Mem. Nat. Assn. Mfrs. (indsl. relations commn.), Am. Mining Congress (indsl. relations commn.). Presbyterian. Clubs: Wall Street, City Mid-day (N.Y.C.). Office: Asarco Inc 180 Maiden Ln New York NY 10038

CORBETT, MICHAEL ALAN, corporate treasurer; b. New Rochelle, N.Y., Dec. 19, 1951; s. William John and Lois Ruth (Amy) C.; m. Catherine Ann Lyon, June 11, 1977; children: William John II, Carolyn Elizabeth. BA, U. Miss., 1974; MBA, Emory U., 1981. Calling officer Mfrs. Hanover Trust Co., N.Y.C., 1974-78; sr. fin. analyst West Point (Ga.) Pepperell, 1978-86; treas. Purolator Courier Corp., Basking Ridge, N.J., 1986-87, Macmillan, Inc., N.Y.C., 1987—. Bus. dir. West Point United Fund, 1984-86; bd. dirs. Albrook Sch., Basking Ridge, 1987—. Office: Macmillan Inc 866 3rd Ave New York NY 10022

CORBETT, MICHAEL DERRIK, accountant; b. Galway, Ireland, Sept. 17, 1929; s. John Patrick and Mary (O'Connor) C.; m. Margaret Veronica Pitcher, June 27, 1957; children: Margaret, Catherine. BA, Nat. Univ. Ireland, 1951; postgrad., Columbia U., 1961-62. Chartered acct. Controller Carroll Industries, Inc., Dublin, 1959-66, fin. dir., 1967-71, 75-87; chief exec. officer Brooks Watson Group, Ltd., Dublin, 1971-75; chmn. Norwich-Union Ins. Group, Ireland, 1981—; mem. Irish Govt. Decimal Currency Bd., Dublin, 1968-71, Dublin Port and Docks Bd., 1973-74. Mem. Inst. Chartered Accts. Ireland, Confedn. Irish Industry (nat. council 1968-80). Roman Catholic. Clubs: Royal Irish Yacht, Milltown Golf. Home: 5 Green Park, Dublin 14, Ireland

CORBETT, PETER GERALD, lawyer; b. Shanghai, June 2, 1935; s. Peter Andrew and Martha Laurie (Gilmour) C.; m. Margaret Sacco; 3 children. Student Stonyhurst Coll. Eng., 1948-52; B.A., U. B.C. 1957, LL.B., 1958; LL.M., Harvard U., 1959. Bar: N.Y. 1964, U.S. Dist. Ct. (so. dist.) N.Y. 1966, U.S. Dist. Ct. (ea. dist.) N.Y. 1966, U.S. Ct. Appeals (2d cir.) 1966. Atty., Allied Chem. Corp., N.Y.C., 1959-61; assoc. Olwine Connelly Chase O'Donnell & Weyher, N.Y.C., 1961-66; assoc. Regan Goldfarb Powell & Quinn, N.Y.C., 1966-70, ptnr., 1970-72; atty. Western Electric Co., N.Y.C., 1972-83, AT&T Technologies, Inc., 1984-85, gen. atty. AT&T, 1985-86, AT&T Tech. Systems, 1987-88, gen. atty. AT&T Microelectronics, 1988—. Mem. Republican Presdl. Task Force, 1981; mem. Rep. Nat. Com., 1980; mem. U.S. Congl. Adv. Bd., 1983; Served with Can. Army, 1954-58. Harvard Law Sch. fellow, 1958-59; U. B.C. scholar. Mem. Am. Arbitration Assn. (nat. panel 1971—), ABA, N.Y. State Bar Assn. Roman Catholic. Home: 4 Chimneys Farm Pequest Rd Oxford NJ 07863 Office: 2 Oak Way 5 SC 11 Berkeley Heights NJ 07922

CORBETT, ROBERT THOMAS, investment banker; b. Albany, N.Y., June 24, 1944; s. Robert Wilson and Ethel (Messina) C.; m. Maureen W. Lewis, Apr. 12, 1970; children: Colleen Anne, Robert Milton, Maureen Clare. BA, Georgetown U., 1966; MS in Fin., Syracuse U., 1968. V.p. Merrill Lynch Capital Markets, N.Y.C., 1878-83; sr. v.p., head leverage buyout group Dean Witter Reynolds, Inc., N.Y.C., 1983-87; mng. ptnr. Crimson Capital Co., Hackensack, N.J., 1987—. Mem. bd. govs. Georgetown U., Washington, 1980—; mem. Archbishop's Council Lay Advisers, Newark, 1984—. Served as cpl. U.S. Army, 1969-70. Mem. N.Y. Soc. Security Analysts, Georgetown U. Alumni Assn. Clubs: Hackensack Golf; Georgetown of N.Y. Office: Continental Pla Tower II 4111 Hackensack Ave Hackensack NJ 07601

CORBIN, HERBERT LEONARD, public relations executive; b. Bklyn., Mar. 30, 1940; s. H. Dan and Lillian C.; m. Carol Heller, June 2, 1963; children: Jeffrey, Leslie Faith. BA, Rutgers U., 1961. Staff corr. Newark News, 1961-63; asst. dir. pub. relations Rutgers U. News Service, New Brunswick, N.J., 1963-65; account exec. A.A. Schechter Assocs., N.Y.C., 1965-66, Barkis & Shalit, Inc., N.Y.C., 1965-66; sr. account exec. Daniel J. Edelman, Inc., N.Y.C., 1967-69; founder, pres., mng. ptnr. Kanan, Corbin, Schupak & Aronow, Inc., N.Y.C., 1969—. Bd. dirs., sec. Altro Health and Rehab. Services; chmn. pub. relations com. White Plains Pub. Access Cable TV Commn. Mem. Pub. Relations Soc. Am., Sigma Delta Chi. Clubs: Williams Coll., Old Oaks Country. Home: 31 Hathaway Ln White Plains NY 10605 Office: KCS&A Pub Rels 820 2nd Ave New York NY 10017

CORBIN, KRESTINE MARGARET, manufacturing company executive, author, fashion designer, columnist; b. Reno, Apr. 24, 1937; d. Lawrence Albert and Judie Ellen (Johnston) Dickinson; m. Lee D. Corbin, May 16, 1959 (div. 1982); children: Michelle Marie, Sheri Karin. BS, U. Calif., Davis, 1958. Asst. prof. Bauder Coll., Sacramento, 1974—; columnist Sacramento Bee, 1976-81; owner Creative Sewing Co., Sacramento, 1976—; pres., chief exec. officer Sierra Machinery Inc., Sparks, Nev., 1984, bd. dirs. 1980—; nat. sales and promotion mgr. Westwood Retail Fabrics, N.Y.C., 1985—; bd. dirs. F.S.C. Mgmt. Svcs. Ltd., No. Internat. Bank, England, Exim Factors, Ltd.; cons. in field. Author: Suede Fabric Sewing Guide, 1973, Creative Sewing Book, 1978, (audio-visual) Fashions in the Making, 1974; producer: (nat. buyers show) Cream of the Cream Collections, 1978—, Style is What You Make It!, 1978-83. Named Exporter of Yr. State of Nev., 1989. Mem. Crocker Art Gallery Assn., 1960-78, Rep. Election Com., Sacramento, 1964, 68. Mem. Home Economists in Bus., Am. Home Econs. Assn., Internat. Fashion Group, Women's Fashion Fabrics Assn., Nat. Tool Builders Assn., Nat. Fluid Power Assn., Nev. World Trade Coun., Omicron Nu. Address: PO Box 435 Reno NV 89504 Office: Sierra Machinery Inc 1651 Glendale Rd Sparks NV 89431

CORBIN, RICHARD HENRY, business development consultant; b. Cleve., Dec. 21, 1936; s. Milford H. and Miriam (Eshner) C.; m. Eileen Richards; children: Philip, Caroline, Peter. B.A., Lehigh U., 1958. Project mgr. St. Regis Paper Co., N.Y.C., 1963-65; dir. New products Kayser Roth, N.Y.C., 1965-67; mem. sr. mgmt. staff Helena Rubinstein/Faberge, N.Y.C., 1967-75; cons. Richard Corbin Assocs., Westport, Conn., 1975-77; sr. v.p. Innotech Corp., Trumbull, Conn., 1977-82; v.p., ptnr. Glendinning Assocs., Westport, 1982-86; mng. dir., prin. Westport Cons. Group Inc., 1986—; sr. cons. Advanced Mgmt. Research, N.Y.C., 1977-79; lectr. Am. Mgmt. Assn., N.Y.C., 1973-77, Bus. Week, N.Y.C., 1984—, Frost & Sullivan, Eng., 1986—. Contbr. articles to bus. jours. Served to lt. (j.g.) USNR, 1959-62. Home: 8 Indian Point Ln Westport CT 06880

CORBOY, JAMES MCNALLY, investment banker; b. Erie, Pa., Nov. 3, 1940; s. James Thomas and Dorothy Jane (Schluraff) C.; BA, Allegheny Coll., 1962; MBA, U. Colo., 1986. m. Suzanne Shaver, July 23, 1965; children: Shannon, James McNally. Sales staff Boettcher & Co., Denver, 1964-70; sales staff Blyth Eastman Dillon, Denver and Chgo., 1970-74; sales staff William Blair & Co., Chgo., 1974-77; mgr. corp. bond dept. Boettcher & Co., Denver, 1977-79; ptnr. in charge William Blair & Co., Denver, 1979-86; first v.p. Stifel, Nicolaus & Co., 1986-88; pres., chief exec. officer J.M. Corboy, Inc., 1988—; gen. ptnr. Corboy & Co., L.P. Served with USMC, 1962-67. Mem. Securities Industry Assn., Nat. Assn. Securities Dealers (bd. arbitrators). Republican. Presbyterian. Clubs: The Attic (Chgo.), Glenmoor Country, Metropolitan. Home: 60 Meade Ln Englewood CO 80110-6024 Office: 4643 S Ulster St Ste 1120 Denver CO 80237

CORBY, FRANCIS MICHAEL, JR., manufacturing company executive; b. Chgo., Feb. 2, 1944; s. Francis M. and Jean (Wolf) C.; m. Diane S. Orselli, Aug. 5, 1972; children: Francis Michael III, Brian A., Christopher S. B.A., St. Mary of the Lake, 1966; M.B.A., Columbia U., 1969. With Chrysler Corp., 1969-80; treasury mgr. Chrysler Peru S.A., Lima, 1973-74; fin. dir. Chrysler Wholesale Ltd., London, 1974-76; mng. dir. Chrysler Comml. S.A. de C.V., Mexico City, 1976-77; v.p., treas. Chrysler Fin. Corp., Troy, Mich., 1977-80; treas. Joy Mfg. Co., Pitts., 1980-83; controller Joy Mfg. Co., 1983-86, v.p., 1984-86; sr. v.p. fin., chief fin. officer Harnischfeger Industries, Inc., Milw., 1986—; dir. Syscon Corp. Mem. Fin. Execs. Inst. Club: Westmoor Country. Office: Harnischfeger Industries 13400 Bishop's Ln Brookfield WI 53005

CORDARO, MATTHEW CHARLES, utility executive, energy developer, engineer/physicist; b. N.Y.C., July 25, 1943; s. Matteo C. and Josephine (Picone) C.; m. Janet Chick, June 24, 1967; children: Anne Marie, Allison; m. Martha Warnock, July 18, 1987. B.S., C.W. Post Coll., 1965; M.S. in Nuclear Engring., NYU, 1967; Ph.D. in Engring.and Physics, Cooper Union, 1970. Asst. engr. L.I. Lighting Co., Hicksville, N.Y., from 1966, successively assoc. engr., nuclear physicist, sr. environ. engr., mgr. environ. engring., 1978-84, v.p. engring., 1978-84; v.p. engring. and adminstrn. L.I. Lighting Co., 1984-85, sr. v.p. elec. ops. and engring., 1985-87, pres., 1988; sr. v.p. Long Lake Cogeneration Corp., N.Y.C., 1988—; guest research assoc. Brookhaven Nat. Lab., 1968-71; adj. assoc. prof. nuclear engring. Poly. Inst. N.Y., 1979-80; adj. asst. prof. engring. C.W. Post Coll., 1968-72; bd. dirs. ctr. for energy studies Adelphi U. Contbr. articles to profl. jours. Council overseers C.W. Post Coll.; mem. community adv. bd. Sta. WLIW pub. TV, Garden City, N.Y. AEC fellow, 1965-66. Mem. Am. Nuclear Soc., Health Physics Soc. Office: Long Lake Cogeneration Corp 420 Lexington Ave New York NY 10170

CORDELL, JOE B., diversified corporation executive; b. Daytona Beach, Fla., Aug. 4, 1927; s. Joe Wynne and Ada Ruth (Wood) C.; m. Joyce Hinton, June 16, 1951; children: Joe B., Coleman Wynn, Lauren. Student, Yale U., 1945-46, Fla. So. Coll., 1946-47; B.S. in Bus. Adminstrn, U. Fla., 1949. C.P.A. Intern Price Waterhouse Corp., N.Y.C., 1948-49, staff acct., 1949-50; audit mgr. Price Waterhouse Corp., Atlanta, 1950-58; v.p. Jim Walter Corp., Tampa, Fla., 1958-70, sr. v.p., treas., 1970-74, pres., 1974—, chief operating officer, from 1974; also chief exec. officer Walter Industries Inc. (formerly Jim Walter Corp.), Tampa, Fla., bd. dirs.; bd. dirs. Royal Trust Bank of Tampa, Gen. Instrument Corp., Fla. Steel Corp. Past pres., trustee U. Fla. Found.; trustee bus. adv. council U. Fla. Served with USNR, 1945-46. Mem. Am. Inst. C.P.A.s, Ga. Inst. C.P.A.s, Fla. Inst. C.P.A.s, Greater Tampa C. of C., Com. of 100, Alpha Kappa Psi, Alpha Tau Omega. Methodist. Clubs: Tower of Tampa, Tampa Yacht and Country, Palma Ceia Golf and Country, Wildcat Cliffs Country, University of Tampa, Ye Mystic Krewe of Gasparilla. Office: Walter Industries Inc 1500 N Dale Mabry Hwy Tampa FL 33607 *

COREY, CLAYNE IRA, small business owner; b. Idaho Falls, Idaho, Nov. 2, 1959; s. Richard Ira and Thelma (Waters) C.; m. Tracy Ann Olson, Sept. 1, 1979; children: Kristen, Janelle, Emily, Rebecca, Marissa. BS in Fin. and Acctg. with honors, U. Utah, 1986, postgrad. Owner, founder, mgr. Child Co., Salt Lake City, 1982—. Mem. Assn. Collegiate Entrepreneurs, Beta Sigma. Home: 1720 Yale Ave Salt Lake City UT 84108 Office: Child Co 2007 S 1300 E Salt Lake City UT 84105

COREY, DONALD LEE, manufacturing company executive, accountant; b. Louisburg, Kans., Mar. 26, 1932; s. Paul Clifford and Gladys Marie (Whitaker) C.; m. Phyllis Jo Goodman, Aug. 16, 1954; children: Dawn Denise, Kevin Lee, Kay Lynette, Sonya Jo. BS, Kans. State U., 1954. CPA, Mo.; Cert. internal auditor. Acct. Price Waterhouse & Co., St. Louis, 1957-63; controller Miss. River Corp., St. Louis, 1963-70; asst. controller Pet, Inc., St. Louis, 1970-74; controller Talley Industries Inc., Phoenix, 1974-76, v.p., treas., 1976-82, v.p. corp. devel., 1982—; bd. dirs., treas. Talley Internat., Phoenix, 1976—; bd. dirs., v.p. Talley Metals, Florence, S.C., 1983—; bd. dirs. Talley Subs. Author articles on internal auditing. Served to 1st lt. USAF, 1954-57. Mem. Am. Inst. CPA's (bd. dirs.), Inst. Internal Auditors (bd. dirs. 1966-70, pres. 1969-70), Assn. Corp. Growth, Fin. Execs. Inst. (v.p.). Republican. Clubs: Talley Pac, Arizona Biltmore Country. Home: 5421 E Mariposa Phoenix AZ 85018 Office: Talley Industries Inc 2800 N 44th St Phoenix AZ 85008

COREY, RAYE W., financial executive; b. Moline, Ill., Mar. 9, 1941; d. Raymond W. Corey and Maye (Louise) Stablein; m. James R. Pappas, Sept. 8, 1962 (div.); children: Deborah Lynn, James R. Jr.; m. Cyril Barlow, Jan. 2, 1986; 1 child, Joanna Elizabeth. BA, Webster Coll., Webster Groves, Mo., 1961. Ins. mgr. Booz, Allen & Hamilton, Florham Park, N.J., 1975-79; pres. Corey Fin. Group, Ft. Lauderdale, Fla., 1979—, Pension & Benefit Cons., Ft. Lauderdale, 1984—; benefit mgr. Pantry Pride, Ft. Lauderdale, 1980-81; asst. v.p. Wolper Ross, Miami, Fla., 1981-82; assoc. cons. Herget & Co., Ft. Lauderdale, 1982-84; exec. v.p. Pension & Benefit Cons., Ft. Lauderdale, Fla., 1984—. Mem. Nat. Assn. Female Execs., Nat. Assn. Tax Practicioners, Network Connection, So. Fla. Employees Benefits Council, Sales and Mktg. Execs. Office: Pension & Benefit Cons 1280 S Powerline Rd Ste 5 #407 Pompano Beach FL 33069

CORK, EDWIN KENDALL, business and financial consultant; b. Toronto, Ont., Can.; m. Eve Slater, Dec. 31, 1960; children: Sarah, John, Peter, Mary. B in Commerce, U. Toronto, 1954. With Noranda Inc., Toronto, 1959-88; sr. v.p., treas., dir. Sentinel Assocs. Ltd., Toronto, 1988—; bd. dirs. Bank of N.S., E.-L Fin. Corp., United Corp.; mem. Can. Inst. Internat. Affairs, 1975—; governing council U. Toronto, 1979-88. Recipient Disting. Bus. Grad. prize U. Toronto, 1987. Christian Scientist. Clubs: National, Caledon Ski, Hart House.

CORLESS, HARRY, chemical company executive; b. Coppull, Eng., Oct. 6, 1928; s. Albert and Edith (Cheetham) C.; m. Jean Houghton, Jan. 24, 1953; children: John Timothy, Victoria Elizabeth, James Anthony. B in Eng., U. Liverpool, 1949. With Imperial Chem. Industries, Ltd. (various locations), 1953—; sr. v.p. ICI Americas Inc., Wilmington, Del., 1976-79, exec. v.p., 1979-82, pres., chief exec. officer, 1982-86, chmn., 1986—, also bd. dirs.; bd. dirs. Del. Trust Co. Trustee, bd. dirs., mem. exec. com. Med. Ctr. of Del., 1980—. Served to 2d lt. Brit. Army, 1951-53. Mem. Soc. Chem. Industry, Nat. Assn. Mfrs. (bd. dirs. 1984). Office: ICI Am Inc New Murphy & Concord Pike Wilmington DE 19897

CORLEY, RALPH RANDALL, electrical engineer; b. Eldorado, Ark., July 22, 1941; s. Leander Gene and Vallie (Patterson) C.; m. Sharron Jeane Denney, Sept. 16, 1961; children: Ralph Randall Jr., Richard Clinton, Chad Justin. BSEE, So. Meth. U., 1964. Registered profl. engr., Tex. Elec. engr. Alcoa, Point Comfort, Tex., 1964-68; chief elec. engr. Cavalier Constrn. Co., Kwinana, West Australia, 1968-72; project elec. engr. Alcoa, Pitts., 1972-74, corp. safety engr., 1978-80; chief elec. engr. Alcoa, Mobile, Ala., 1974-78; elec. maintenance supt. Alcoa, Warrick County, Ind., 1980-87, reliability and systems supt., 1987—. Contbr. articles to profl. mags. Mem. IEEE, Aircraft Owners and Pilots Assn. Methodist. Home: 8099 Marywood Dr Newburgh IN 47630 Office: Alcoa Warrick Ops PO Box 10 Newburgh IN 47630

CORLEY, THOMAS BENNETT, III, sales executive; b. Columbus, Ga., Nov. 17, 1938; s. Thomas Bennett Jr. and Ida Amerzell (Ingram) C.; m. Harriett Evelyn Zediker, Aug. 13, 1960; children: Philip Preston, Thomas Bennet IV. Student, Gulf Coast Jr. Coll., 1958-59; BS in Bus., Fla. State U., 1962. Sales rep. Lever Bros. Co., Columbus, 1963-70, sr. sales rep., 1970-79; dist. field asst. Lever Bros. Co., Atlanta, 1980; area sales mgr. Ala., Ga. and NW Fla., 1980—. Bd. dirs. Lakewood Golf Course, Phenix City, Ala., 1965-71; exec. dir. Dixie Majors Baseball, Phenix City, 1980-82. Mem. Phenix City Jaycees (pres. 1968-69), Columbus Sales Club (founding mem., charter pres. 1978—), Atomic Investment Club (founder, pres.). Republican. Methodist. Home: 4010 Lakewood Dr Phenix City AL 36867 Office: Lever Bros Co 100 Crescent Ctr Pkwy Ste 1220 Tucker GA 20084

CORLEY, WILLIAM JOSEPH, JR., financial executive; b. Evergreen Park, Ill., Nov. 6, 1953; s. William Joseph and Anna Mae (Hennigan) C.; m. Denise Ann Letourneau, Dec. 15, 1973; children: Julie Ann, Kerrie Elizabeth, William Joseph III., Margaret Ann. BA in Acctg. and Bus. Econs., Ill. Benedictine Coll., 1975. Mgr. dist. billing Rapistan Inc., Oak Brook, Ill., 1976-79; plant controller Celanese Plastics and Specialties Co., Bridgeview, Ill., 1979-81; mgr. cost and budget Hysan Corp., Chgo., 1981-84, asst. controller, 1984-86; controller, sec. Hysan Corp., Des Plaines, Ill., 1986—. Active in Congressman Marty Russo's Small Bus. Adv. Com., Chgo., 1986. Mem. Nat. Assn. Accts., Ill. Mfrs. Assn. Taxation Com., Chgo. Area C. of C. Roman Catholic. Office: Hysan Corp 1400 E Touhy Des Plaines IL 60018

CORN, JACK W., oil company executive; b. Coff County, Ga., Oct. 8, 1929; s. Ezra and Sarah (Pruitt) C.; m. Ann McConnel; children: Dana Corn Crissey, William E., Beth Ann. BBA, U. Ga., 1953. Pres., chief exec. officer Corn Bros., Inc. subs. Quaker State Corp., Smyra, Ga., 1974-86; from vice chmn. to pres. and chief exec. officer Quaker State Corp., Oil City, Pa., 1988—; mem. emeritus Smyra Bank and Trust Co. Active 1st Bapt. Ch., Marietta, Ga. With USAF, 1953-56. Mem. Am. Petroleum Inst. (bd. dirs.), Allegheny Mountain Health Systems, Marietta Country Club, Georgian Club, Oil City Club, Wanango Country Club. Home: 9 Shady Oak Ln Oil City PA 16301 Office: Quaker State Corp 255 Elm St Oil City PA 16301

CORNA, MARK STEVEN, construction company executive; b. Columbus, Ohio, July 21, 1949; s. Albert and Ann Elizabeth (Amicon) C.; m. Margaret Ann Igoe, July 18, 1970 (div. Apr. 1986); children: Joshua Daniel, Sophia Ann. With Corna and DiCesare Builders, Inc., Columbus, 1970-76; pres. The M.S. Corna Co., Columbus, 1976-85, Corna and DiCesare Construction Co., Columbus, 1985—; mem. Gov.'s Blue Ribbon Com. to Investigate Delays in Bldg. Plan Approval, State of Ohio, 1980. Coach soccer Immaculate Conception Sch., Columbus, 1982-83, basketball, 1983-85, com. chmn. Mem. Associated Gen. Contractors (bd. dirs. 1980-87, pres. 1986), Builders Exchange Cen. Ohio (bd. dirs. 1981—, pres. 1989), Athletic Club, Columbus Italian Club, Capital Club of Columbus. Democrat. Roman Catholic. Office: Corna & DiCesare Constrn Co 2500 Harrison Rd Columbus OH 43204

CORNELISSEN, MICHAEL ADRIAAN, trust company executive; b. Durban, Republic of South Africa, June 1, 1943; s. Marinus and Koos (Van der Hoeven) C.; m. Catriona Butcher, Jan. 1967; 2 children. C.A., U. Natal, 1965; M.B.A., U. Capetown, 1970. Audit supr. Touche Ross and Co., 1961-69; dir., v.p. fin. Rennies Consol. Holdings Ltd., 1971-75; v.p. Edper Investments Ltd., 1976; exec. v.p., chief operating officer Trizec Corp. Ltd., 1977-83, now dir.; pres., chief exec. officer, dir. Royal Trustco Ltd., Toronto, Ont., Can., 1983—; dir. Trilon Fin. Corp., Hees Internat. Corp. Inc., London Life Ins. Co., Royal LePage Ltd., Trizec Corp. Ltd. Chmn. United Way Greater Toronto, 1984; bd. govs. Appleby Coll., Oakville; chmn. capital campaign Nat. Ballet Sch.; chmn. Can.'s Challenge for Am.'s Cup; bd. dirs. The Chamber Players of Toronto, The Toronto symphony. Conservative. Clubs: Toronto, York, Royal Can. Yacht, Oakville Yacht Squadron. Office: Royal Trustco Ltd, PO Box 7500, Toronto, ON Canada M5W 1P9 *

CORNELIUS, JAMES MILTON, pharmaceutical company financial executive; b. Oct. 28, 1943, Kalamazoo; s. Charles D. and Eleanor F. (Short) C.; m. Kathleen McGovern; children: Andrew, Lindsay. BA in Acctg., Mich. State U., 1965, MBA in Fin., 1967. Assoc. accountant Eli Lilly & Co., Indpls., 1967, fin. planning analyst, 1969-73, adminstr. corporate finance, 1973-75, mgr. econ. studies, 1975-78, dir. health care bus. planning, 1978-80, corp. treas., 1982-83, v.p. fin., chief fin. officer, 1983—, also bd. dirs.; pres. IVAC Corp. subs. Eli Lilly & Co., San Diego, 1980-82; bd. dirs. Ind. Nat. Bank, Ind. Bell Telephone Co. Inc. Contbg. author: The CFO's Handbook, 1986. Treas. Children's Mus., Indpls., 1983—, Noyes Found., Indpls., 1983—; mem. adv. bd. bus. corp. Mich. State U., 1983—; bd. dirs. Mcpl. Recreation, Inc., 1982—. Served to 1st lt. U.S. Army, 1967-69. Mem. Fin. Execs. Inst., Pharm. Mfg. Assn., Ind. C. of C. (bd. dirs. 1982—, exec. com. 1983—). Republican. Roman Catholic. Avocations: tennis, reading, jogging. Office: Eli Lilly & Co Lilly Corporate Ctr Indianapolis IN 46285

CORNELIUS, KARLA MARIE, land developer, architect; b. Stamford, Conn., Jan. 17, 1945; d. Walter G. and Janet Elaine (Martin) Wirthwein; m. James B. Moore, 1964 (div. 1968); m. Harry A. Cornelius, Aug. 2, 1975. BA, Miami U., Oxford, Ohio, 1966; grad., Real Estate Inst. Lic. real estate broker; state permitted land developer. Copywriter Internat. Promotions Co., Chgo., 1972-75; free-lancer in mktg. communications Chgo. and Burlington, Vt., 1975-77; owner, land developer Countryside and Pinnacle Ridge, Waterbury, Vt., 1978—; pres. Blush Hill Constrn. Co., Waterbury, 1979—; architect Waterbury, 1978—; real estate broker The Blush Hill Co., Waterbury, 1984—; cons. in field, Waterbury, 1982—. Scheduling and advance vol. McGovern for Pres., Chgo., 1971. Mem. Nat. Assn. Realtors. Home: Blush Hill Rd Waterbury VT 05676 Office: The Blush Hill Co Blush Hill Rd Waterbury VT 05676

CORNELIUS, KENNETH CREMER, JR., finance executive; b. Plainwell, Mich., Sept. 7, 1944; s. Kenneth Cremer and Hollie Jane (Tupper) C.; m. Mary Patricia Hagen, Aug. 19, 1967; children: Kari, Jay, Lee Ann. BA, Carleton Coll., 1966; MBA, U. Mich., 1967. Mgr. acctg. div. Maremont Corp., Nashville, 1972-74, mgr. regional acctg. div., 1974-75, div. controller, 1975-79, corp. controller, 1979-80; v.p., chief fin. officer Maremont Corp., Chgo., 1980—. Served to capt. USAF, 1968-72. Mem. Phi Beta Kappa. Home: 6201 Sleepy Hollow Lisle IL 60532 Office: Maremont Corp 250 E Kehoe Carol Stream IL 60188

CORNELIUS, MARK RICHARD, real estate executive, venture capitalist; b. Salt Lake City, Aug. 20, 1953; s. Richard Lowell and Dolores Marie Cornelius; m. CHeri Ellingson, May 24, 1980; children: Brittany, Adam, Megan. BA in Acctg., U. Utah, 1978, MBA, 1980. Assoc. Golden Corp., Houston, 1980-81; v.p. Regency Securities, Wilmington, Del., 1982—, Advanced Holographics, Salt Lake City, 1987—, Holographic Films, Salt Lake City, 1988—, Regency Biotech, Wilmington, 1988—; real estate broker, Tes., Utah, 1982—; cons. in field. Chmn. Young Adults Bi-Centennial, Salt Lake City, 1975-76; del Rep. State Conv., Salt Lake City, 1976. Republican. Mormon. Club: Rodney Square (Wilmington). Office: Regency Securities 2469 E 7000 S 108 Salt Lake City UT 84121

CORNELIUS, WILLIAM EDWARD, utilities company executive; b. Salt Lake City, Sept. 6, 1931; s. Edward Vernon and Gladys (Bray) C.; m. Mary Virginia Bunker, June 13, 1953; children: Mary Jean, Linda Anne. B.S., U. Mo., 1953; M. Liberal Arts, Washington U., St. Louis, 1983. C.P.A., Mo. Mgr. Price Waterhouse & Co., St. Louis, 1955-62; asst. comptroller Union Electric Co., St. Louis, 1962-64, dir. corporate planning, 1964-67, exec. v.p., 1968-80, pres., 1980-88, chief exec. officer, chmn., 1988—, also bd. dirs.; bd. dirs. Boatmen's Bancshares, Gen. Am. Life Ins. Co., McDonnell Douglas Corp., INTERCO, Inc. Bd. dirs. St. Louis Children's Hosp., Mcpl. Theater Assn.; trustee Washington U. Served to 1st lt. AUS, 1953-55. Mem. Mcpl. Theater Assn. (bd. dirs.), Beta Theta Pi. Clubs: Bellerive Country, St. Louis, Log Cabin. Home: 2 Dunlora Ln Saint Louis MO 63131 Office: Union Electric Co PO Box 149 Saint Louis MO 63166

CORNELL, HARRY M., JR., mattress company executive; b. 1928; married. Grad., U. Mo., 1950. With Leggett & Platt, Inc., 1950—, salesman, 1950-53, gen. mgr., 1953-55, v.p., 1955-60, pres., gen. mgr., from 1960; now chmn., chief exec. officer Leggett & Platt, Inc., Carthage, Mo. Office: Leggett & Platt Inc 1 Leggett Rd PO Box 757 Carthage MO 64836 *

CORNELL, JOHN WALLACE, accountant, marketing professional; b. Alexandria, Va., Jan. 22, 1956; s. John Evans and Faye Alice (Wallace) C.; m. Debbie Lee, Dec. 28, 1982; 1 child, John Wallace II. BS in Fin., San Diego State U., 1978. With sales Aqua-Ben Chem., Santa Ana, Calif., 1978-79, Calgon Corp., Pitts., 1979-85; with mktg. Sweetwater Techs., El Toro, Calif., 1985—. Mem. AWWA. Republican. Home: 25481 Grissom Laguna Hills CA 92653 Office: Sweetwater Techs 22642 Lambert St #406 El Toro CA 92630

CORNELSEN, PAUL FREDERICK, manufacturing and engineering company executive; b. Wellington, Kans., Dec. 23, 1923; s. John S. and Theresa Albertine (von Klatt) C.; m. Floy Lila Brown, Dec. 11, 1943; 1 son, John Floyd. Student, U. Wichita, 1939-41, 45-46; BS in Mech. Engring, U. Denver, 1949. With Boeing Airplane Co., 1940-41, Ralston Purina Co., St. Louis, 1946—; v.p. internat. div. Ralston Purina Co., 1961-63, adminstrv. v.p., gen. mgr. internat. div., 1963-64, v.p., 1964-68, dir., 1966—, exec. v.p., 1968-78, vice-chmn. bd., chief operating officer, 1978-81, pres. internat. group, 1964-77; pres., chief exec. officer Moehlenpah Industries Inc., St. Louis, 1981-82, Mitek Industries (formerly Moehlenpah), St. Louis, 1982—; bd. dirs. DeKalb (Ill.) Genetics Co., Sunmark Capital Corp., St. Louis, Petrolite Corp., St. Louis; founding mem. Latin Am. Agribus. Investment Corp., 1970—; founding mem. industry coop. program UN Agys., Rome. Mem. Nat. 4-H Coun. Adv. Com.; trustee Ill. Coll., Jacksonville. 1st Lt. AUS, World War II, AUS, Korean War. Decorated Silver Star. Home: 506 Fox Ridge Rd Saint Louis MO 63131 Office: 11710 Old Ballas Rd Creve Coeur MO 63141

CORNER, HAROLD LEROY, manufacturing company executive; b. Mercer, Pa., Oct. 19, 1934; s. Edward Harold and Gladys (Rice) C.; m. Allene Adele Ashcraft, Apr. 30, 1955; children: Daniel L., Douglas H. Grad. high sch. Co-founder, chief exec. officer, chmn. bd. C&J Industries Inc., Meadville, Pa., 1962-78; owner, developer, mgr. Renroc Mobile Home Pk., Meadville, Pa., 1962-78; bd. dirs. Meadville City Hosp., Alliance Coll., Cambridge Springs, Pa. Mem. exec. bd. Rep. Party Crawford County, Pa., 1979-81, fin. com., 1977-80, chmn. spl. fund-raising projects, 1977-80. With U.S. Army, 1955-57. Mem. ASME, Am. Soc. Metals, Am. Ordinance Assn., Am. soc. Quality Control, Nat. Tooling & Machining Assn. (pres. 1981-82, chmn. polit. action com. 1985-87; L.A. Somer award 1986), Amateur Trapshooting Assn. Am., Meadville Sportsmen's, Black Ash Sportsmen's, Meadville Field Archers, Elks, Masons, Scottish Rite, Shriners. Home: PO Box 4990 Meadville PA 16335 Office: C&J Industries Inc 760 Water St Meadville PA 16335

CORNISH, LARRY BRIAN, lawyer, corporate executive; b. Kingston, N.Y., July 13, 1946; s. Harry Preston and Beverly Mae (Schmidt) C. B.A., George Washington U., 1968, J.D., 1973. Bar: Calif. 1974, N.Y. 1974. Mem. legis. counsel U.S. Ho. of Reps., Washington, 1973-74; dir. fed. affairs Am. Speech & Hearing Assn., Washington, 1974-76; asst. counsel Pres. Ford Com., Washington, 1975-76; exec. dir., gen. counsel Irwin Lehrhoff Ph.D. & Assocs., Beverly Hills, Calif., 1976-78; counsel, dir. legal affairs Beverly Enterprises, Inc., Pasadena, Calif., 1978-79, 79-82, v.p., gen. counsel, sec., 1982-84, sr. v.p., sec., chief legal officer, 1984—; sec., Beverly Investment Properties Inc., Pasadena, Calif., 1985-88; counsel Calif. Speech Pathologists and Audiologists in Pvt. Practice, San Jose, 1976-88. Served with U.S. Army, 1969-70; Vietnam. Decorated Bronze Star, Air medal. Mem. ABA, Nat. Health Lawyer's Assn. Republican. Mem. Dutch Reformed Ch.

CORNISH, SCOTT CHARLES, publishing company executive; b. Canandaigua, N.Y., May 4, 1960; s. Claude Samuel and Marilyn Jean (Button) C. BS, Rochester Inst. Tech., 1982. Quality assurance asst. USA Today, Arlington, Va., 1982-84, mgr. color imaging, 1986—; quality assurance asst. Gannett Co., Inc., Arlington, 1984-85; guest speaker numerous profl. confs. Mem. Am. Soc. Quality Control, Graphic Arts Tech. Found., Am. Numismatic Assn., Nat. Computer Graphics Assn., Toastmasters. Republican. Methodist. Home: 6917-H Victoria Dr Alexandria VA 22310 Office: USA Today 1000 Wilson Blvd Arlington VA 22209

CORNYN, JOHN EUGENE, accounting company executive; b. San Francisco, Apr. 30, 1906; s. John Eugene and Sara Agnes (Larkin) C.; B.S., St. Mary's Coll., 1934; M.B.A., U. Chgo., 1936; m. Virginia R. Shannahan, Sept. 10, 1938 (dec. May 1964); children—Virginia R., Kathleen R. Cornyn Arnold, John Eugene, Madeleine A. Cornyn Shanley, Carolyn G. Cornyn Clemons; m. 2d, Marian C. Fairfield, Aug. 21, 1965. Partner, John E. Cornyn & Co., C.P.A.s, Winnetka, Ill., 1951-73; pres. John E. Cornyn & Co. Ltd., 1973—. Exec. sec. North Shore Property Owners Assn., 1953—. C.P.A., Ill. Mem. Am. Inst. C.P.A.s, Ill. Soc. C.P.A.s, Am. Acctg. Assn., Am. Tax Assn., Fellowship Cath. Scholars. Catholic (Byzantine Rite). Home: 126 Bertling Ln Winnetka IL 60093-4299

CORONADO, SHIRLEY JEANNE, personnel administrator; b. Pontiac, Mich., Sept. 28, 1948; d. Leonard and Hazel Elaine (Monroe) Slade; m. Reyes Coronado, Apr. 27, 1968. B in Gen. Studies, Wayne State U., 1987. With GM, Pontiac, 1966—, adminstr. personnel, 1988—. Office: GM Personnel Ctr 359 Enterprise Ct Bloomfield Hills MI 48013

CORONEL, GUSTAVO RAFAÉL, development banker; b. Caracas, Venezuela, Aug. 23, 1933; s. Jesus M. and Filomena (García) C.; m. Marianela Criollo; children: Gustavo Jr., Corina, Ana. BS in Geology, U. Tulsa, 1955; postgrad., U. Cen., Caracas, 1958, Johns Hopkins U., Washington,

1987. Cert. geologist. Petroleum geologist Shell Venezuela/Shell Indonesia, Maracaibo and Djakarta, 1955-65; exploration mgr. Venezuelan Petroleum Corp., Caracas and Maracaibo, 1965-67; sr. rsch. geologist Phillips Petroleum, Bartlesville, Okla., 1967-69; mgr. mktg. Shell Petroleum Co., Caracas, 1969-74; chief ops. officer Meneven, 1979-81; fellow Harvard U., Cambridge, Mass., 1981-83; hydrocarbons advisor Interam. Devel. Bank, Washington, 1983—; del. OPEC, 1966-69. Author: Nationalization of the Venezuelan Oil Industry, 1983; (with others) Political Risk Analysis, 1986; mem. editorial bd. Jour. S.Am. Geology, 1987—; contbr. articles to profl. jours. Trustee U. Tulsa, 1987—. Named to Engring. Hall Fame, U. Tulsa, 1980, Disting. Alumnus, 1981. Mem. Venezuelan Engring. Coll. Home: 8205 Kenfield Ct Bethesda MD 20817 Office: Interam Devel Bank 1300 New York Ave Washington DC 20577

CORPREW, JAMES CROSBY, electronics company executive; b. Norfolk, Va., Sept. 8, 1942; s. John Elmer Sr. and Dorothy Ruth (Outlaw) C. BSBA, Old Dominion U., 1969, MBA, 1970; DBA, Miss. State U., 1973; M in Decision Scis., Ga. State U., 1974. Research asst., teaching asst. Miss. State U., 1970-73; instr. quantitative methods and postdoctoral studies Ga. State U., 1973-74; asst. prof. mgmt. Va. Commonwealth U., 1974-75; asst. prof. gen. adminstrn. Cleve. State U., 1975-77; mgr. prin. Case & Co., Inc., Stamford, Conn., 1977-83; mgmt. cons., mgr. Fenvessy & Schwab, Inc., N.Y.C., 1983-84, KPMG Peat Marwick, N.Y.C., 1984-87; prin. Fairfield Assocs., Bethel, Conn., 1987-88; mgr. ops. div. microelectronics Sharp Electronics Corp., Mahwah, N.J., 1988—. Contbr. articles to profl. jours. Served with AUS, 1964-68. Mem. Acad. Mgmt., Decision Scis. Inst., Inst. Mgmt. Scis., Inst. Mgmt. Cons., Alpha Iota Delta, Beta Gamma Sigma. Presbyterian. Home: PO Box 759 Bethel CT 06801-0759

CORR, D. JOSEPH, air transportation company executive; b. 1941; married. Grad., Western Ill. U., 1963, Harvard U., 1981. With Morris-Knudsen Co. Inc., Boise, Idaho, 1963-77; from mgr. sales to v.p., mgr. ACF Industries Inc., Hazelwood, Mo., 1977-84, pres., 1984-86, vice chmn., 1986—, also bd. dirs.; pres., chief operating officer Trans World Airlines Inc., N.Y.C., 1987-88; chmn., chief exec. officer Continental Airlines Inc., 1988—. Office: Continental Airlines Corp PO Box 4607 Houston TX 77019 also: ACF Industries Inc 3301 Rider Trail S Earth City MO 63045 *

CORRADO, FRED, food company executive; b. Mt. Vernon, N.Y.; s. Anthony Edward and Rose (Capone) C.; m. Josephine Ann Gonda, July 4, 1962; children: David, Paul, Christopher. B.B.A. in Acctg, Manhattan Coll., 1961; grad. Advanced Mgmt. Program, Harvard U., 1983. C.P.A., N.Y. Sr. auditor Arthur Andersen & Co., N.Y.C., 1961-65; controller Romney Cosmetics Co. div. Pfizer Co., Stamford, Conn., 1966-68; with ITT Corp., 1968-69, Kenton Corp., 1969-73, Nabisco Brands USA (name formerly Standard Brands Inc.), 1973-84; pres. Planters div. Nabisco Brands USA, East Hanover, N.J., 1980-84; exec. v.p., chief operating officer Nabisco Brands Ltd., Toronto, 1984-85, pres., chief operating officer, 1985-86, also bd. dirs.; exec. v.p., chief fin. officer Great Atlantic and Pacific Tea Co., Inc., Montvale, N.J., 1987—. Mem. Fin. Execs. Inst., Am. Inst. C.P.A.s, Planning Execs. Inst. Home: 9 Coventry Ct Croton-on-Hudson NY 10520 Office: Gt Atlantic & Pacific Tea Co Inc 2 Paragon Dr Montvale NJ 07645

CORREIA, ALBERTO ABRANTES, sales executive; b. Milford, Mass., Nov. 16, 1956; s. Alberton Filipe and Julia Abrantes (Simones) C.; m. Sharon Ann Haaf; 1 child, alexis Abrantes. BS, Coll. Holy Cross, Worcester, Mass., 1978. With Genex, Milford, Mass., 1976-77, sales rep., 1978-79, sales mgr., 1980; dir. sales Millipore Co., Paris, 1981-84, Xydex Techs., Inc., Bedford, Mass., 1985-87, Genex Co., Gaithersburg, Md., 1988—. Home: 216 Bristol Downs Dr Gaithersburg MD 20877 Office: Genex 16020 Industrial Dr Gaithersburg MD 20877

CORRIE, ROBERT DONALD, financial analyst; b. West Hempstead, N.Y., Apr. 29, 1931; s. George Wilson and Edith (Vega) C.; m. Ann McLean Cameron, Sept. 19, 1959; children: Suzanne Louise, Jean Elizabeth, Carolyn Jane. BA in History, Cornell U., 1953; MBA in Fin., U. Pa., 1957. V.p., dep. controller Nat. Westminster Bankq, N.Y.C., 1957-85; corp. risk mgr. Fidata Corp., N.Y.C., 1985-86; ins. mgr. Merrill Lynch, N.Y.C., 1986-88; v.p., bd. dirs. Lyric Found., N.Y.C., 1978—. Treas. Community Fund of Garden City, N.Y.; trustee Garden City Adv. Com. on Edn., 1976-80. Served to 1st lt. U.S. Army, 1953-55. Mem. Risk Ins. Mgmt. Soc., Kappa Delta Rho (Outstanding Alumni 1987). Republican. Methodist. Club: Cornell of Nassau County (treas. 1966-76). Home: 10 Ash St Garden City NY 11530 Office: Fidata Corp 1 State St Pla 35th Fl New York NY 10004

CORRIGAN, KEAN WESLEY, advertising executive; b. Moscow, Idaho, May 21, 1960; s. Donald Kean and Nancy Dionne (Daley) C. BA in Art, Calif. State U., 1985. Mktg. assoc. Clear Images, Long Beach, Calif., 1983-84; account exec. Stolrow Advt., Costa Mesa, Calif., 1985-86; prin. K. Wesley Hall Advt., Fountain Valley, Calif., 1986—; instr. Calif. State U., Long Beach, 1986—; cons. Cover Technologies, Norwalk, Calif., 1987—; lectr. Am. Mktg. Assn., 1988—. Mem. Nat. Pool and Spa Inst., Nat. Ski Patrol, Kiwanis. Republican. Roman Catholic. Home: 111 10th St #1 Seal Beach CA 90740 Office: K Wesley Hall Advt 10231 Slater Ave #202 Fountain Valley CA 92708

CORRINGTON, RICHARD FITCH, brokerage house executive; b. Evanston, Ill., June 10, 1931; s. John William and Aileen (Fitch) C.; m. Frances Elizabeth Boal, Dec. 23, 1953; children: Richard Fitch Jr., William B., James F., Frances. BA, Pomona Coll., Claremont, Calif., 1953; MBA, Stanford U., 1955. Broker Paine Webber Inc., Chgo., 1958-65, ptnr., 1965-71; nat. instl. mgr. Paine Webber Inc., N.Y.C., 1968-71, v.p., dir. mktg., 1971-74, v.p., dir. fin. planning, 1974-77; v.p., br. mgr. Paine Webber Inc., Roanoke, Va., 1977—; pres. Lime Kiln Arts, Inc., Lexington, Va., 1986—. Served to lt. USNR, 1955-58. Mem. Farmington Club, Hunting Hills Club, Sheandoah Club. Republican. Presbyterian. Office: Paine Webber Inc 600 Colonia Plaza Roanoke VA 24011

CORRO, PRUDENCIO CHU, otolaryngologist, medical facility executive; b. Bulan, Philippines, Apr. 28, 1940; came to U.S., 1964; s. Leocadio Corro and Kim Cio Chu; m. Carol Curry, Feb. 25, 1967; children: John, Robert, Kathryn, Christina. MD, Far Eastern U., Manila, 1963. Intern Nassau Med. Ctr., East Meadow, N.Y., 1964-65; resident in surgery N.Y. Polyclinic, N.Y.C., 1965-66; resident in otolaryngology Bronx (N.Y.) Mcpl. Hosp. Ctr., 1966-69; otolaryngology fellow Albert Einstein Coll. Medicine, Bronx, 1969-70; pvt. practice Beckley, W.Va., 1976—; pres. Raleigh Hearing Ctr., Beckley, 1976—. Fellow ACS, Am. Acad. Otolaryngologic Allergy, A, Am. Acad. Otolaryngology-Head and Neck Surgery. Democrat. Roman Catholic. Home: Box 128 Coolridge WV 20825 Office: Rte 4 Box 630 Stanaford Rd Beckley WV 25801

CORRY, CHARLES ALBERT, steel company executive; b. Wyoming, Ohio, Feb. 14, 1932; s. Charles Albert and Rella Marie (Ulrich) C.; m. Margaret Anna Stuve, Dec. 9, 1961; children: Lynne, Diane, Elizabeth. BA, U. Cin., 1955, JD, 1959. Bar: Ohio 1959. Tax atty. U.S. Steel Corp. (now USX Corp.), Pitts., Cleve. and N.Y.C., 1959-70, asst. comptroller Am. Bridge div., Pitts., 1970-71, mgr. acctg.-steel, parent co., Homestead, Pa., 1972-73, comptroller, treas. USS Engrs. & Cons., Pitts., 1974, gen. mgr. taxes U.S. Steel Corp., Pitts., 1975-78, asst. comptroller, 1978, v.p. corp. planning, 1979-82, sr. v.p. corp. planning, comptroller, 1982-86, pres. USX Diversified Group, 1987—, corp. pres., dir., 1987—, also chmn., chief exec. officer, 1989—. Bd. dirs. Jr. Achievement SW Pa., Pitts., 1983. Served to capt. USAF, 1955-57, Europe. Mem. ABA, Ohio Bar Assn., Fin. Execs. Inst., Machinery and Allied Products Inst. (fin. council), Am. Iron and Steel Inst., N.Am. Soc. Corp. Planning, Pa. C. of C. (bd. dirs. 1982—). Lutheran. Clubs: Duquesne, St. Clair Country (Pitts.). Office: USX Corp 600 Grant St Pittsburgh PA 15230 *

CORSON, THOMAS HAROLD, manufacturing company executive; b. Elkhart, Ind., Oct. 15, 1927; s. Carl W. and Charlotte (Keyser) C.; m. Dorthy Claire Scheide, July 11, 1948; children: Benjamin Thomas, Claire Elaine. Student, Purdue U., 1945-46, Rennsselaer Poly. Inst., 1946-47, So. Meth. U., 1948-49. Chmn. bd. Coachmen Industries, Inc., Elkhart, Ind., 1965—; also chmn. bd. Coachmen Industries, Inc. (numerous subs. cons.); bd. dirs. First State Bank, Middlebury, Canton Drop Forge Co. (Ohio), Olofsson Corp., Lansing, Mich., R.C.R. Scientific Inc., Goshen, Ind.; chmn., sec. Greenfield Corp., Middlebury. Adv. coun. U. Notre Dame; past trustee Ball State U.; vice chmn. Interlochen (Mich.) Arts Acad. and Nat. Music Camp. Served with USNR, 1945-47. Mem. Ind. Mfrs. Assn. (dir.), Elkhart C. of C. (past dir.), Ind. C. of C. (bd. dirs.), Capitol Hill Club, Imperial Golf Club, Elcona Club (past dir.), Masons, Shriners. Methodist. Home: PO Box 504 Middlebury IN 46540 Office: Coachmen Industries Inc 601 E Beardsley Ave Box 3300 Elkhart IN 46515

CORTELLESSA, DOMINICK RALPH, information systems executive; b. Mt. Vernon, N.Y., Mar. 30, 1943; m. Dorothy Piccininni, Apr. 1, 1967; two children. BS, Villanova U., 1965; MBA, Iona Coll., 1981. Programmer IBM, White Plains, N.Y., 1966-68; systems engr. IBM, N.Y.C., 1968-70, mktg. rep., 1970-74, fin. analyst, 1974-76, adminstrv. asst., 1976-78, mktg. mgr., 1978-80; sr. planning adminstr. IBM, White Plains, 1980-82, planning mgr., 1982-83; sr. v.p., pres. Ins. Services Office Inc., N.Y.C., 1983-84, exec. v.p., pres., 1984—. Bd. dirs. Mt. Pleasant Library, 1980-84. Served with USMCR. Mem. Data Processing Mgmt. Assn., Am. Mgmt. Assn. Republican. Roman Catholic. Lodge: KC. Office: Ins Scs Office Inc 2 Blue Hill Pla Pearl River NY 10965-8750

CORTES, WILLIAM PATRICK, telecommunications executive; b. Ellenville, N.Y., Apr. 23, 1955; s. Robert Paul and Joan Helen (Whitstock) C. AB, Stanford U., 1977; MBA, U. Wash., 1983, JD, 1984. Bar: Wash. 1984; CPA, Wash. Accts. payable mgr. Cen. Distbrs., Inc., Portland, Oreg., 1977-78; fin. instr. Sch. Bus. Adminstrn. U. Wash., Seattle, 1980-83; strategic planning analyst Burlington No., Inc., Seattle, 1982, 83; sr. cons. Ernst & Whinney Telecommunications Group, Tacoma, 1985-86; fin. mgr. spec. projects US WEST NewVector Group Inc., Bellevue, Wash., 1986-88, dir. investor rels. and bus. fin. analysis, 1988—. Treas. Erxleben for State Rep. Campaign, Bellevue, 1982. Mem. ABA, AICPA, Wash. State Bar Assn., Fed. Communications Bar Assn., Wash. Soc. CPA's, U. Wash. Grad. Sch. Bus. Adminstrn. Alumni Assn. (bd. dirs. 1985-87). Democrat. Roman Catholic. Office: US WEST NewVector Group Inc 3350 161st Ave SE Bellevue WA 98008

CORUM, CAROLINE FERGUSON, trust administrator; b. Madisonville, Ky.; d. William Montgomery and Frances (Ferguson) C. BS, Am. U., 1987. Dir. bookkeeping, fin. records Corum Farms, Madisonville, 1979—; fin. planner Waddell & Reed Fin. Svcs., Washington, 1987—; asst. mut. funds adminstr. trust dept. Riggs Nat. Bank, Washington, 1987—; cons. in field. Rep. alumnae admissions Sweet Briar Coll., 1987—. Mem. Kappa Alpha Theta Alumnae Assn. Home: 1121 Arlington Blvd Ste 246 N Arlington VA 22209

CORWIN, HENRY HOBART, communications company executive; b. Jackson, Mich., Feb. 2, 1944; s. Frederic William and Marian Elizabeth (Clark) C.; m. Paula Elizabeth Ayotte, Aug. 21, 1971; children: Leslie, Stephanie. BA, Williams Coll., 1966; MBA, U. Pa., 1973. CPA, Ga. Mktg. rep. IBM, Waltham, Mass., 1970-71; sr. acct. Peat Marwick Mitchell, Atlanta, 1973-77; v.p. fin. Superior Trucking Co., Atlanta, 1977-83; v.p. fin., treas. Advanced Telecommunications Corp., Atlanta, 1983—. Lt. USNR, 1966-70, Vietnam. Mem. Ga. Soc. CPA's, Am. Inst. CPA's. Office: Advanced Telecommunications Corp 148 International Blvd Ste 500 Atlanta GA 30303

CORZINE, JON STEVENS, investment banker; b. Taylorville, Ill., Jan. 1, 1947; s. Roy Allen and Nancy June (Hedrick) C.; m. Joanne Dougherty, Sept. 8, 1968; children: Jennifer, Jeffrey, Joshua. B.A., U. Ill., 1969; M.B.A., U. Chgo., 1973. Bond officer Continental Ill. Nat. Bank, Chgo., 1970-73; asst. v.p. BancOhio Corp., Columbus, 1974-75; with Goldman, Sachs & Co., N.Y.C., 1975—; v.p. Goldman, Sachs & Co., 1977, pntr., 1980—, mem. mgmt. com., 1985—, co-head fixed income div., 1988—. Served USMC, 1969-70. Mem. Pub. Securities Assn. (vice chmn. 1985, chmn. 1986). Office: Goldman Sachs & Co 85 Broad St New York NY 10004

COSAR, AHMET, accountant, telecommunications company executive; b. Mersin, Turkey, May 17, 1952; s. Ibrahim and Fatma Cosar; m. Ayla Yilmaz, July 19, 1977; children: Bala, Irem. Student, Toros Coll., Mersin, 1970; BS in Fin., Acad. Econs. and Comml. Sci., Istanbul, Turkey, 1977; MS in Bus. Adminstrn., Faculty Adminstrn. in Bus. Adminstrn., Istanbul, 1980. Cost acct. Elmet A.S., Inc., Istanbul, 1975-77; mgr. acctg. Kurtkaya Holding, Inc., Istanbul, 1977-80; acctg. controller Hisar Fgn. Trade Co., Istanbul, 1980-82; asst. gen. mgr. Delta Fgn. Trade Co., Istanbul, 1981-83; fin. and acctg. dir. Teletas Telecommunications Co., Istanbul, 1983-88; gen. mgr. Türktelekom Endüstri ve Ticaret A.S., 1988—; lectr. internat. forum Euromoney Leasing Digest, Istanbul, 1988, Banking and Ins. Inst. Marmara U., 1988, Bosphorous U.; privatization coord. Teletas/Chase Manhattan Corp., London, 1987-88. Mem. Turkish Assn. Acct. Experts. Moslem. Lodge: Lions. Office: Türktelefon Ticaret Ve Sanayi, AS Venicarsi Caddesi Biltez Han, 40 Galatassaray Istanbul Turkey

COSBY, GEORGE HARRIS, III, management consulting executive, holding company executive; b. Sept. 8, 1932. BS, Trinity Coll., 1954. Analyst audit and systems dept. Warner Lambert Pharmaceutical Co., Morris Plains, N.J., 1957-58; trainee Travelers Ins. Co., Bklyn., 1958-59; various positions Travelers Ins. Co., 1959-66; asst. mgr. casualty/property Travelers Ins. Co., Detroit, 1966-67; underwriting mgr. casualty/property Travelers Ins. Co., Richmond, Va., 1967-70; asst. v.p. Johnson and Higgins of Va. Inc., Richmond, 1970-74; pres. Alexander and Alexander of Va. Inc., Richmond, 1973-74; v.p. Rollins Burdick and Hunter Co., Richmond, 1974-77; pres., owner Tuxford Corp., Richmond, 1975-77, Cosby and Assocs. Inc., Richmond, 1977-80, Risk Adminstrs. Inc., Richmond, 1980—, Riad Equities Inc., Richmond, 1987—; pres. Riad Group, Richmond, 1989—. Capt. USAF, 1954-57. Home: 11632 E Briarpatch Dr PO Box 727 Midlothian VA 23113

COSENZA, VINCENT JOHN, accountant; b. Bklyn., Aug. 12, 1962; s. Vincent James and Rosalie Theresa (Ferraro) C. BS in Acctg., NYU, 1984. CPA, N.Y. Mgr. fin. adminstrn. Jr. Achievemnt N.Y. Inc., N.Y.C., 1984-85; staff acct. Rosenshein, Neiman & Weiss, CPA's, N.Y.C., 1985-87, Pepper, Gelbord, Roth & Co., N.Y.C., 1987—; assoc. acct. Sheldon Plotnick, Bklyn., 1986—. Mem. Citizens' Choice. Democrat. Roman Catholic. Home: 1393 E 53d St Brooklyn NY 11234-3226 Office: Pepper Gelbord Roth & Co 605 3d Ave 17th Fl New York NY 10158

COSGROVE, HOWARD EDWARD, JR., utility executive; b. Phila., Apr. 12, 1943; s. Howard Edward and Margaret (May) C.; m. Roberta Joyce Olewine, Apr. 19, 1965; children—Pamela Joyce, Susan Ann. B.S. in Mech. Engring, U. Va., 1966; M.B.A., U. Del., 1970. Registered profl. engr., Del. With Delmarva Power Co., Wilmington, Del., 1966—, mgr. fin., 1979, v.p., chief fin. officer, 1979—, exec. v.p., 1984—. Mem. Nat. Soc. Profl. Engrs., Fin. Execs. Inst. Home: 8 Fox Ln Newark DE 19711 Office: Delmarva Power & Light Co 800 King St Wilmington DE 19899 *

COSGROVE, WILLIAM JEROME, lawyer; b. Lancaster, Pa., July 28, 1909; s. Jerome A. and Laura (Baumann) C.; student Franklin and Marshall Coll., 1926-27, Columbia, 1927-29; LLB, St. John's Law Sch., 1932; m. Agatha Hagen, Oct. 25, 1933. Bar: N.Y. 1934. Practiced in Bklyn.; ptnr. Wrenn & Schmid, 1947-79, counsel, 1979—; acting city judge, Glen Cove, 1950-51; mem. adv. bd. Kings Lafayette Bank, 1973, Republic Nat. Bank N.Y., 1974-76. Pres., Glen Cove Community Chest, 1953; mem. Glen Cove Urban Renewal Com., 1956-65; pres. Glen Cove Lincoln Settlement, Inc., 1958-62; mem. Glen Cove Housing Auth., 1958-66. With U.S. Army, 1943-45. Mem. Bklyn. Bar Assn. Home: 170 SW Garden St PO Box 1218 Keystone Heights FL 32656 Office: 26 Court St Brooklyn NY 11242

COSSIN, ALEXANDER IRA, lawyer; b. N.Y.C., July 8, 1944; s. Louis Barney and Tessie (Connor) C.; m. Phyllis Linda Ettinger, July 25, 1976; children: Tracy, Robert. BS, L.I. U., 1965; JD, St. Johns U., 1973; cert. pub. mgmt. edn., Cornell U., 1977. Bar: N.Y. 1974, N.J. 1985, U.S. Supreme Ct. Chemist U.S. FDA, Bklyn., 1965-74, compliance officer, 1974-77; asst. counsel Faberge Inc., N.Y.C., 1978-85; corp. counsel Barr Labs Inc., Northvale, N.J., 1985-88, Taro Pharm. Inc., 1988—. Mem. Regulatory Affairs Profl. Soc., Bar Assn. Rockland County, Rotary. Jewish. Home: 4 Fox Hollow Pomona NY 10970 Office: Barr Labs Inc 2 Quaker Rd Pomona NY 10970

COSTA, PAT VINCENT, automation sciences executive; b. Cambridge, Mass., Sept. 4, 1943; s. Vincent James and Mary Florence (Mercurio) C.; m. Kathleen Ann Valachovic, Aug. 9, 1975; children: Jessica Kate, Hannah Pat. BSEE, Northeastern U., 1966; SM, MIT, 1969; MBA, Harvard U., 1977. Exec. v.p. GCA Corp., Bedford, Mass., 1977-84; pres., chief exec. officer, chmn. Robotic Vision Systems, Inc., Hauppauge, N.Y., 1984—. Mem. Automated Vision Assn. (chmn. bd.), Machine Vision Assn., Soc. Mech. Engrs., Robotic Industries Assn., Navy League of U.S. Office: Robotic Vision Systems Inc 425 Rabro Dr E Hauppauge NY 11788

COSTA, WALTER HENRY, architect; b. Oakland, Calif., July 2, 1924; s. Walter H.F. and Mamie R. (Dunkle) C.; m. Jane Elisabeth Ledwich, Aug. 28, 1948; 1 dau., Laura. B.A., U. Calif., Berkeley, 1948, M.A., 1949. Designer Mario Corbett (architect), San Francisco, 1947-48, Ernst Born (Architect), San Francisco, 1949; draftsman Milton Pflueger, San Francisco, 1950-51; designer Skidmore, Owings & Merrill, San Francisco, 1951-57, participating asso., then asso. partner, 1957-69, gen. partner, 1969—. Bd. dirs. East Bay Regional Park Dist., 1977-87, pres., 1984-85; mem. city council, Lafayette, Calif., 1972-76, mayor, 1973. Served with USSNR, 1943-46. Fellow AIA. Clubs: Olympic (San Francisco), Univ. (San Francisco). Home: 1264 Redwood Ln Lafayette CA 94549 Office: Skidmore Owings & Merrill 333 Bush St San Francisco CA 94104

COSTANZO, PHILIP R., JR., advertising executive, consultant; b. Scranton, Pa., Aug. 9, 1944; s. Philip R. Sr. and Francis (Bonadio) C. AS in Bus., Lackawanna Jr. Coll., 1964; BBA, U. Scranton, 1967, MBA in Fin., 1973. Contr. Acme Fast Freight, Inc., Scranton, 1972-74; sec., treas. United Gilsodite Labs., Scranton, 1974-80; sec., treas., v.p. adminstrn. Leshore Calgift Corp., Archibald, Pa., 1980-86; pres. Davoc United Cons., Archibald, 1986—. With U.S. Army, 1966-68, Vietnam. Mem. Pa. Assn. Accts., Am. Mgmt. Assn. Home: 1271 Short Ave Scranton PA 18508

COSTELLESE, LINDA E. GRACE, banker; b. Providence, Mar. 22, 1950; d. Lawrence A. and Lucy R. (Fiore) Grace; m. Dennis P. Costellese, May 8, 1971. AS in Bus. Adminstrn., Bryant Coll., 1981; cert., Sch. Bank Mktg., Colo., 1982; BS in Organizational Behavior, Lesley Coll., 1985, MS in Applied Mgmt., 1988. Sec. R.I. Hosp. Trust Nat. Bank, Providence, 1969-78, adminstrv. asst., 1978-80, br. adminstrv. officer, 1980-81, community mktg. officer, 1981-82, retail sales officer, 1982-84, asst. v.p., 1984-85, v.p., 1985-87, regional mgr., 1986-87, 1st v.p., dept. mgr. retail banking, 1987—. Vol. Spl. Olympics, Providence, United Way Southeastern R.I., Providence; mem. St. Frances de Sales Women's Guild, Save-the-Bay. Named Woman of Yr., North Kingstown Bus. and Profl. Women's Club, 1987. Mem. Nat. Assn. Bank Women, R,I, Bankers Assn. (pub. rels. and mktg. com.), New Eng. Bank Mktg. Assn. (sec. 1987-88, 1st v.p. 1988-89), Bank Mktg. Assn. (schs. adv. coun.). Office: RI Hosp Trust Nat Bank 1 Hospital Trust Pla Providence RI 02903

COSTELLO, ALBERT JOSEPH, business executive; b. N.Y.C., Sept. 4, 1935; s. John and Lena (Compiani) C.; m. Barbara Theresa Antolotti, May 31, 1958; children: Gregory A., Peter M., Albert Joseph. B.S., Fordham U., 1957; M.S., NYU, 1964. With Am. Cyanamid Co., 1957—; asst. mng., mng. dir. Am. Cyanamid Co., Mexico City, Madrid, Spain, 1974-77; div. v.p. Am. Cyanamid Co., Wayne, N.J., 1977-82, pres. agrl. div., 1982, group v.p., 1982-83, exec. v.p., 1983—. Patentee in field. Served with U.S. Army, 1959-61. Mem. Nat. Agrl. Chems. Assn. (dir. 1982—, chmn. 1984-85). Office: Am Cyanamid Co 1 Cyanamid Pla Wayne NJ 07470 *

COSTELLO, JAMES JOSEPH, electrical manufacturing company executive; b. Boston, Feb. 15, 1930; s. James Joseph and Jennie Theresa (Boyle) C.; m. Mary Virginia Bird, May 7, 1960; children: James, Susan, Maureen, Thomas, Daniel. B.S. in Bus. Adminstrn, Northeastern U., 1953. With Gen. Electric Co. (various locations), 1956—; div. fin. mgr. Gen. Electric Co. (AC Motor div.), Schenectady, 1971-76; group fin. mgr. Gen. Electric Co. (Components and Materials group), Pittsfield, Mass., 1976-77; staff exec. Gen. Electric Co. (Tech. Systems and Materials sector), Fairfield, Conn., 1977-79; v.p., comptroller Gen. Electric Co., 1979—; Dir. nat. council Northeastern U., 1980-81. Served as officer U.S. Navy, 1953-56. Mem. Fin. Execs. Inst., Fin. Acctg. Standards Bd. (subcom. on measurements). Office: GE 3135 Easton Turnpike Fairfield CT 06431

COSTELLO, JOHN H., III, marketing executive; b. Akron, Ohio, June 2, 1947; s. John H. and Lia C.; m. Margaret Heil, Oct. 5, 1974; children: Michael, Jeffrey, Matthew. BS in Indsl. Mgmt., Akron U., 1968; MBA, Mich. State U., 1970. Mktg. dir. Procter & Gamble Co., Cin., 1971-84; sr. v.p. Pepsi-Cola USA, Purchase, N.Y., 1984-86; exec. v.p. Wells, Rich & Greene, Inc., N.Y.C., 1986-88; pres. Nielsen Mktg. Rsch. U.S.A., Chgo., 1988—; sr. mktg. execs. panel Conf. Bd., N.Y.C., 1985-87; featured conv. speaker Nat. Soft Drink Assn.'s, L.A., 1985—. Strategy mgr. to various Rep. campaigns, 1980-84; fund raiser Hamilton County Reps., Cin., 1980-84; group coord. United Appeal of S.W. Ohio, Cin., 1983; mem. nat. mktg. fundraising com., bd. dirs. Nat. Multiple Sclerosis Soc., N.Y.C., 1986—. Mem. La Racquet Club, Beta Gamma Sigma. Episcopalian. Home: 34 Hoyt Farm Rd New Canaan CT 06840 Office: A C Nielsen Nielsen Pla Northbrook IL 60062

COSTELLO, RICHARD NEUMANN, advertising agency executive; b. Phila., Sept. 2, 1943; s. Joseph Neumann and Katherine Cash (Birkhead) C.; m. Ann M. Dodds, Oct. 24, 1970; children—Brian Stuart, Gregory Scott. B.A. in English, U. Pa., 1965, M.B.A. in Mktg, 1967. Account mgr. Ogilvy & Mather, Inc., N.Y.C., 1967-71; v.p. Rosenfeld, Sirowitz & Lawson, Inc., N.Y.C., 1971-73; pres. Baron, Costello & Fine, Inc., N.Y.C., 1973-77, TBWA Advt., Inc., N.Y.C., 1977—; internat. bd. dirs. TBWA Advt., Inc., 1984—, chief operating officer, 1987—. mem. Young Pres.'s Orgn. Office: TBWA Advt Inc 292 Madison Ave New York NY 10017

COSTENBADER, CHARLES MICHAEL, lawyer; b. Jersey City, Dec. 9, 1935; s. Edward William and Marie Veronica (Danaher) C.; m. Barbara Ann Wilson, Aug. 1, 1959; children: Charles Michael Jr., William E., Mary E. BS in Acctg., Mt. St. Mary's Coll., 1957; JD, Seton Hall U., 1960; LLM in Taxation, NYU, 1968. Bar: N.J 1960; U.S. Tax Ct. 1961, U.S. Ct. Appeals (3d cir.) 1973, U.S. Supreme Ct. 1983. Trial atty. office regional counsel IRS, N.Y.C., 1961-69; tax assoc. Shanley & Fisher, Newark, 1969-76; tax ptnr. Stryker, Tams & Dill, Newark, 1976—. Mem. N.J. State and Local Expenditure and Revenue Commn., 1985-88; bd. policy advisors Pub. Affairs Rsch. Inst. N.J. Mem. ABA, N.J. Bar Assn. (chmn. taxation sect. 1984-85), N.J. State C. of C. (chmn. cost of govt. com. 1988—), Am. Coll. Tax Counsel, Essex Club. Republican. Roman Catholic. Home: 8 Neptune Pl Colonia NJ 07067 Office: Stryker Tams & Dill 33 Washington St Newark NJ 07102

COSTIGAN, EDWARD JOHN, investment banker; b. St. Louis, Oct. 31, 1914; s. Edward J. and Elizabeth Keane; m. Sara Guth, Mar. 30, 1940; children—Sally, Ed Jr., James, Betsy, Robert, David, Louise. A.B., St. Louis U., 1935; M.B.A., Stanford U., 1937. Analyst, v.p. Whitaker & Co., St. Louis, 1937-43; ptnr. Edward D. Jones & Co., 1943-72; sr. v.p. Stifel Nicolaus & Co. Inc., St. Louis, 1972-74, pres., 1974-79, vice chmn., 1979-83, emeritus, 1983; gov. Nat. Assn. Securities Dealers, 1967-70, Investment Bankers Assn., 1968-69, Midwest Stock Exchange, Chgo., 1962-64. Trustee Calvary Cemetery Assn., St. Louis, 1956—. Republican. Roman Catholic. Clubs: Bellerive, Mo. Athletic, Noonday. Office: 500 N Broadway Saint Louis MO 63102

COSTIGAN, JOHN MARK, lawyer, consumer products executive; b. Newark, Aug. 2, 1942; s. Dennis Aloysius and Claire (Reilly) C.; m. Emily Anne Lincoln, July 2, 1966; children—Elizabeth Anne, Catherine Lynn, Matthew David, Daniel John. B.A.in English, Fordham U., 1964; LL.B., Columbia U., 1967; M.B.A., U. Chgo., 1978. Bar: N.Y. 1968, Ill. 1973. Atty. Bigham, Englar, Jones & Houston, N.Y.C., 1967-70; atty. Kraft, Inc., Glenview, Ill., 1970-74, gen. atty., 1974-76, sr. atty., 1976-79, asst. gen. counsel, 1979-81; sr. corp. counsel Dart & Kraft, Inc., Northbrook, Ill., 1981-82, v.p. investor relations, 1982-84, v.p., assoc. gen. counsel, 1985-86;

sr. v.p., gen. counsel Premark Internat. Inc., Deerfield, Ill., 1986—. Mem. ABA, Chgo. Bar Assn., Northwestern Corp. Counsel Ctr. (adv. bd.), N. Shore Gen. Counsel Assn., N. Shore Country Club (Glenview, Ill.). Home: 671 Newcastle Dr Lake Forest IL 60045 Office: Premark Internat Inc 1717 Deerfield Rd Deerfield IL 60015

COSTLEY, GARY EDWARD, food company executive; b. Caldwell, Idaho, Oct. 26, 1943; s. Donald Clifford and Verna C.; m. Cheryl J. Zesiger, Dec. 21, 1963; children: Angela I., Chad D. B.S., Oreg. State U., M.S., Ph.D. in Nutrition-Biochemistry. With Kellogg Co., Battle Creek, Mich.; formerly dir. nutrition, dir. public affairs, v.p. public affairs, v.p. and asst. to pres. Kellogg Co., sr. v.p. corp. devel., sr. v.p. sci. and quality, exec. v.p. sci. and tech.; currently exec. v.p. Kellogg Co. and pres. U.S. food products div. Trustee Miller Found., Battle Creek, YFU Internat. Exch.; dir. St. Joseph's U. Acad. Food Mktg. Mem. Am. Inst. Nutrition. Democrat. Lutheran. Office: Kellogg Co 1 Kellogg Sq PO Box 3599 Battle Creek MI 49016

COSTON, ROBERT GENE, controller; b. Moultrie, Ga., Mar. 13, 1944; s. Jesse and Sara (Posey) C.; m. Kitty Randall, May 20, 1967; children: Stuart Randall, Blake Douglas. BS, Fla. State U., 1969, MBA, 1971; MS in Acctg., Nova U., 1987. Fin. trainee Ford Motor Co., Dearborn, Mich., 1971-73; plant analyst Celanese Corp., Greenville, S.C., 1974-75; sr. fin. analyst Celanese Corp., Greenville, 1975-77; mgr. fin. adminstrn. Celanese Corp., N.Y.C., 1997-79, internat. fin. mgr., 1979-81; mgr. fin. analysis DWG Corp., Miami Beach, Fla., 1981-83; corp. planning mgr. Coulter Corp., Hialea, Fla., 1983-86; controller diagnostics div. Coulter Corp., Hialea, 1986—. Served to 1st lt. U.S. Army, 1966-68, Vietnam. Mem. Am. Mgmt. Assn. Republican. Home: 5180 SW 21st St Plantation FL 33317 Office: Coulter Diagnostics Div 740 W 83d St Hialeah FL 33014

COTE, DANIEL ROBERT, financial planner; b. Pittsfield, Mass., Oct. 13, 1950; s. Bernard Joseph and Doris Lucille (Cloutier) C.; m. Jane Lucille Benson, Aug. 7, 1971; children: Catrina Anne, Benjamin Daniel, Melanie Jane. AA, Blinn Coll., 1976; BBA, Sam Houston State U., 1977, MBA, 1979. CPA, Wash. Forecasting analyst Tex. Eastern Transmission, Houston, 1977-79; sr. budget analyst Mitchell Energy and Devel., Houston, 1979-81; profit planning coordinator Dailey Oil Tools, Inc., Houston, 1981-83; profit planning supr. Thousand Trails, Inc., Bellvue, Wash., 1983-85; fin. ops. mgr. Am. Adventure, Inc., Kirkland, Wash., 1985-87; fin. planning mgr. Audio Environments, Inc., Seattle, 1987-88; owner Fin. Forecasts, Woodinville, Wash., 1988—. Treas., Boy Scouts Am., Woodinville, Wash., 1984-87; pres. Raintree Homeowners Assn., Woodinville, 1984. Grad. fellow Sam Houston State U., 1977. Mem. Wash. Soc. CPAs. Lutheran. Home and Office: Fin Forcasts 18310 194th Ave NE Woodinville WA 98072

CÔTÉ, PIERRE, petrochemical and fiber manufacturing company executive; b. Quebec, Que., Can., ; s. Jules H. and Andrée (Fortier) C.; chmn., Celanese Can. Inc., Montreal, Que.; chmn. Can. Devel. Corp., Toronto; bd. dir. Can. Tire Corp., CAE Industries, Ltd., Consolidated Bathurst, Inc., Polysar, Inc., Savin Corp., Guarantee Co. of North Am., Hoechst Can., Inc., Bank of Montreal, Bombardier, Inc., Canron Inc., Mut. Life Assurance Co. Can.; past pres. Que. C. of C. Office: Celanese Can Inc, 800 Rene Levesque Blvd W, Montreal, PQ Canada H3B 1Z1 also: Can Devel Corp, 444 Yonge St, Toronto, ON Canada M5B2H4 *

COTE-WILKIN, PAULA ANN, health administrator, nurse; b. Newton, Mass., Dec. 3, 1942. Diploma in nursing, Mercy Hosp. Sch. Nursing, 1964; BS in Nursing, U. N.H., 1975; MS in Nursing, Boston U., 1981, postgrad., 1983. RN, N.H., Mass. Head nurse med.-surg. unit Alexander-Eastman Hosp., Derry, N.H., 1972-74; instr. acute clin. care sch. nursing Cath. Med. Ctr., Manchester, N.H., 1975-81; dir. nursing edn. Nashua (N.H.) Meml. Hosp., 1981, dir. edn. and tng., 1981-87, dir. health and wellness, 1987—; adj. assoc. prof. U. N.H., Durham, 1984—. Bd. dirs. Community Hospice Greater Nashua, 1983—. Mem. Am. Soc. Healthcare Edn. and Tng. (rep. region I bd. 1987—, pres. No.-N.E. chpt. 1986, bd. dirs. 1982—, Educator of Yr. 1987). Roman Catholic. Home: 36 Copperfield Dr Nashua NH 03062 Office: Nashua Meml Hosp 8 Prospect St CS 2014 Nashua NH 03061

COTHRAN, ANNE JENNETTE, advertising sales executive; b. Buffalo, Nov. 28, 1952; d. Raymond John and Thelma Lorraine C. BA in English, Gordon Coll., 1975; MBA in Specialization Mktg., U. Chgo., 1989. Mgr. 1776 House, Salem, Mass., 1974-75; dept. mgr. Goldblatt's Dept. Store, Chgo., 1975-77; sales rep. Sta. WWMM, Arlington Heights, Ill., 1977-79, Sta. WYEN, Des Plaines, Ill., 1979-81; coop. mgr. Southtown Economist Newspapers, Chgo., 1981-83, div. sales mgr., 1983-88; retail advt. mgr. Lansing (Mich.) State Jour., 1988—. Bd. dirs. Cabrini Green Legal Aid Clinic, Chgo., 1981-83. Mem. U. Chgo. Women's Bus. Group (bd. dirs., chair 1987), Am. Mktg. Assn. (exec.), Women's Ad Club Chgo., Chgo. Ad Club, Women in Mgmt., Oak Park Village Players (chair workshop com. 1987). Office: Lansing State Jour 120 E Lenawee Lansing MI 48919

COTMAN, JOHN MARTIN MATTHEW, accountant; b. Cleve., June 10, 1953; s. John Joseph and Gertrude Irene (Tomosko) C.; m. Joyce Ann Bill, Aug. 6, 1977. BBA, Cleve. State U., 1975, MBA, 1979, M in Accountancy and Fin. Info. Systems, 1981. CPA, Ohio; cert. mgmt. acct. Sr. acct. NOACA, Cleve., 1977-79; fin. analyst APCOA, Cleve., 1979-80; asst. dir. Greater Cleve. Hosp. Assn., Cleve., 1981-86; fin. mgr. Univ. Hosp., Cleve., 1986—; cons. Ctr. Hosp. Services, Cleve., 1984—, Hosp Fin. Corp., Cleve., 1985—. Fin. coordinator Jerry Lewis Telethon, Cleve. 1971-77; mem. allocations panel Children & Youth Services United Way Cleve., 1987—. Mem. AICPA, Nat. Assn. Accts., Ohio Soc. CPAs. Democrat. Roman Catholic. Home: 5070 Hampton Dr North Olmsted OH 44070 Office: Univ Hosps of Cleve 2074 Abington Rd Cleveland OH 44106

COTT, BURL GENE, transportation company executive; b. Wichita, Kans., Dec. 2, 1940; s. T. Otho and Leona F. (Binford) C.; m. Marsha J. Thomason, Dec. 27, 1975; 1 son, John. B.A., Wichita State U., 1963. Mgr. Arthur Andersen and Co., Kansas City, Mo., 1963-75; controller Terminal Transport Co., Atlanta, 1975-77; v.p., treas. Am. Freight System Inc., Overland Park, Kans., 1977-80; pres. Sioux Falls Service Ctr. Inc., S.D., 1982—; sr. v.p. Am. Carriers Inc., Overland Park, Kans., 1980—; dir. Am. Freight System Inc., Overland Park, Sioux Falls Service Ctr. Inc. Mem. Am. Trucking Assn. (nat. acctng. finance council), Am. Inst. C.P.A.s. Office: Am Carriers Inc 9393 W 110th St Overland Park KS 66210

COTTER, DANIEL A., diversified company executive; b. Duluth, Minn., Dec. 26, 1934. B.A., Marquette U., 1957; M.B.A., Northwestern U., 1960. With Cotter & Co., Chgo., 1959—, pres., chief executive officer. Office: Cotter & Co 2740 N Clybourn Ave Chicago IL 60614 *

COTTER, ERNEST ROBERT, III, finance company executive; b. Chattanooga, Sept. 18, 1951; s. Ernest Robert II and Adelene (Alverson) C.; m. Susan Cochran, Aug. 23, 1975; children: Hadley, Ernest Robert, Lauren, Brian. AB in Econs., Princeton U., 1973; MBA, Harvard U., 1977. Mng. dir. First Boston Corp., N.Y.C., 1977—; bd. dirs. Atlantic Monthly Press, N.Y.C. Office: 1st Boston Corp Park Avenue Pla New York NY 10055

COTTER, GARY WILLIAM, financial company executive, consultant; b. White Plains, N.Y., Nov. 19, 1947; s. Edgar Richard and Frances Ray (Sturm) C.; m. Shirley Ann Pereira, Dec. 11, 1982. BA, U. Corpus Christi, 1970; MS, SUNY, 1973; postgrad., U. S.Fla., 1988—. Cert. fin. planner. Assoc. dir. admissions Bard Coll., Annandale-on-Hudson, N.Y., 1970-74; dir. admissions Carroll Coll., Waukesha, Wis., 1974-76, Eckerd Coll., St. Petersburg, Fla., 1976-77; mgr. dist., fin. planner Investors Diversified Services, St. Petersburg, 1978-81; mgr. br. Investors Diversified Services, Corpus Christi, Tex., 1981-83; fin. planner E.F. Hutton & Co., Corpus Christi, 1983-84; registered prin. Planner's Securities Group Inc., Atlanta, 1985-89, DeRand, Pennington& Bass, Inc., Arlington, Va., 1989—; pres., chmn. Cotter & Cotter Risk Mgmt. Corp., Corpus Christi, 1985—, Cotter & Cotter Fin. Cons. Inc., Corpus Christi, 1984—; panelist Fin. Profl. Adv. Panel, 1985; commentator fin. Sta. KIII-TV (ABC affiliate), Corpus Christi, 1987—, KEYS Radio, 1440 AM; writer grants Our Lady Star of Sea Parish, Corpus Christi, 1986. Mem. fin. columnist Corpus Christi Bus. Jour.; contbr. articles to Corpus Christi Monthly, Today, Senior News, Corpus Christi Caller-Times. Precinct del. Nueces County Republican Conv., Corpus Christi, 1988; mem. fin. coun., lay reader Corpus Christi Cathedral. Named Outstanding Young Man Am., 1977. Mem. Inst. Cert. Fin. Planners, Internat. Assn. Fin. Planning (pres. Corpus Christi chpt. 1988—, dir. 1986-87, S.W. regional council rep. 1987-88), Jackson's Landing Owners' Assn. (pres. 1985-87), Corpus Christi C. of C., Corpus Christi State U. Alumni Assn. (dir. 1983-86). Office: Cotter & Cotter Fin Cons 705 MBank Ctr N Corpus Christi TX 78471-0801

COTTER, GEORGE LOUIS, JR., automotive manufacturing executive; b. Pitts., May 29, 1932; s. George Louise Cotter and Lillian Laura (Kerr) Miller; m. Lois Jean Dyer, Oct. 19, 1957; children: Patricia Cotter Wilson, Diane B., George L. III. BS in MechE, U. Mich., 1954; MBA, Harvard U., 1956. Trainee Eaton Corp., Cleve., 1956-57, mgr. factory, 1957-69, asst. gen. mgr. heater div., 1969-71, gen. mgr. climate control div., 1971-79, gen. mgr. axle div., 1979-83; gen. mgr. axle and brake div. Eaton Corp., Galesburg, Mich., 1983—. Mem. Soc. Automotive Engrs., Tau Beta Pi, Pi Tau SIgma, Phi Eta Sigma. Republican. Mem. United Ch. Christ. Office: Eaton Corp PO Box 4008 Kalamazoo MI 49003

COTTER, JOHN M., diversified company executive; b. 1904. With Dayton's Bluff Hardware Co., 1916-23; salesman Raymer Hardware Co., 1923-28; gen. ptnr. Kohloop Hardware, 1928-31; gen. mdse. mgr. Kelly-How-Thompson Co., 1933-42; v.p., gen. mgr. Oakes & Co., 1942-48; with Cotter & Co., Chgo., 1948—, chmn. bd., dir., 1978—. Officer: Cotter & Co 2740 N Clybourn Ave Chicago IL 60614 *

COTTER, JOSEPH FRANCIS, retired hotel chain executive; b. Brockton, Mass., May 18, 1927; s. Joseph and Sarah (Thornell) C.; m. Catherine Sullivan, 1950 (dec.); m. Barbara Tribou Salter, 1986. B.S. cum laude, Boston Coll., 1949. C.P.A., Mass., N.Y. Accountant Price Waterhouse & Co., N.Y.C., 1949-67; v.p., controller Howard Johnson Co., Braintree, Mass., 1967-70; exec. v.p., comptroller, dir. Sheraton Corp., Boston, 1970-85, exec. v.p. planning and devel., 1985-87. Former vice chmn. bd. trustees Boston Coll.; former chmn. bd. dirs. Greater Boston YMCA.; trustee Dana-Farber Cancer Research Inst. Mem. AICPA, N.Y. Soc. C.P.A.s, Mass. Soc. C.P.A.s, Am. Hotel and Motel Assn., Boston Coll. Alumni Assn. (past pres.), Greater Boston C. of C. (v.p. 1989—). Club: Executives (pres.). Home: 35 Beacon St Boston MA 02108

COTTER, VINCENT PAUL, foods company executive; b. Boston, June 18, 1927; s. John J. and Margaret (O'Hara) C.; m. Lillian Agnes Carroll, Oct. 4, 1952; children: Charles E., Mary A., Paul J., Jeanne M., Kathleen. BSBA, Northeastern U., 1952, MBA, 1965. Office mgr. Wilson Foods Corp., Oklahoma City, 1954-68, treas., 1968-87, v.p., treas., 1969-85, sr. v.p., treas., 1985-87, exec. v.p., chief fin. officer, 1987—; bd. dirs. Century Bank N.A., Oklahoma City. Chmn. bd. trustees Oklahoma County Fin. Authority, 1986—; pres. bd. dirs. Bishop McGuinness High Sch., Oklahoma City, 1983-85, Mt. St. Mary High Sch., Oklahoma City, 1980-84. Served with USN, 1945-46. Recipient Award of Yr. Notre Dame Club Oklahoma City, 1985, Silver Beaver award and Boy Scouts Am., 1978, Dist. award of Merit Boy Scouts Am., 1976, Last Miler award Last Frontier Council, 1982. Mem. Okla. C. of C. (chmn. fin. com. 1987—), Econ. Club (bd. dirs.), K.C. Home: 8016 Lakehurst Dr Oklahoma City OK 73120 Office: Wilson Foods Corp 4545 N Lincoln Blvd Oklahoma City OK 73105

COTTER, WAYNE BILLINGS, state agency administrator; b. Bridgeport, Conn., Sept. 9, 1949; s. Edward William and Sonya Viola (Billings) C.; m. Susanne Carolyn Olson, Nov. 24, 1973; children: Eric Edward, Timothy Billings. BA in Econs., Gettysburg Coll., 1971; MBA in Econ. Theory, St. John's U., 1985. Sr. economist, researcher N.Y. State Dept. Labor, Hicksville, N.Y., 1979, assoc. economist, researcher, 1979-82; asst. dir. rsch. and statistics N.Y. State Dept. Ins., N.Y.C., 1982-87, dir. rsch. and statistics, 1987—. Contbr. articles to profl. publs. Mem. Omicron Delta Epsilon, Pi Lambda Sigma, Pi Delta Epsilon, Alpha Tau Omega (pres. 1970-71). Democrat. Lutheran. Office: NY State Ins Dept 160 W Broadway New York NY 11703

COTTERILL, DAVID LEE, banker; b. Rochester, N.Y., May 7, 1937; s. Henry John and Ethel May (Townsend) C.; m. Joan Elizabeth Royer, July 1, 1961; children—Jonathan David, Susan Elizabeth. B.S. in Indsl. Psychology, Pa. State U., 1960. Trainee Mellon Nat. Bank & Trust Co., Pitts., 1961-64; pres. First Wachovia Student Fin. Svcs., Inc. (formerly Wachovia Svcs., Inc.) subs. Wachovia Corp., Winston-Salem, 1964-68, 70-72, 78—; dir. electronic data processing Wachovia Bank & Trust Co. N.A., Winston-Salem, 1968-70, sr. v.p. ops., 1972-79, exec. v.p., head adminstrn. div., 1979-88, exec. v.p., head operational svcs. div., 1985-88; pres. First Wachovia Trust Svcs. Inc. subs. First Wachovia Corp., 1988—; organizer N.C. Payments System, Inc., 1973-74, dir., chmn. systems-ops. subcom., 1975, chmn. bd., 1975-77; mem. ops. adv. com. 5th Fed. Res. Dist., 1978-82; chmn., bd. dirs. Video-Fin. Services, Inc.; mem. bd. advisors Bankers Mag.; instr. Sch. Banking of South, also profl. courses. Contbr. articles to profl. jours. Bd. dirs. Child Guidance Ctr. of Forsyth County, Inc., Forsyth Country Day Sch., 1979-82; mem. citizens adv. group Oncology Research Ctr. Served with USNR, 1954-62. Mem. Bank Adminstrn. Inst. (industry systems commn. 1974—, chmn. 1977-78, mem. exec. com. 1979-80, chmn. banking svcs. steering com. 1979-80, dir.-at-large 1986—), Am. Bankers Assn. (exec. com. ops./automation div. 1981-83), N.C. Bankers Assn. (ops. and automation com. 1981-83), Am. Nat. Standards Inst., Internat. Standards Orgn., Rotary, Sigma Nu. Home: Box 595 Bermuda Run NC 27006 Office: 1st Wachovia Corp PO Box 3099 MC 32114 Winston-Salem NC 27150

COTTING, JAMES CHARLES, manufacturing company executive; b. Winchester, Mass., Oct. 15, 1933; s. Edward L. and Mary Ellen (Worrell) C.; m. Marjorie A. Kirsch, Feb. 8, 1963; children: James Charles, Steven Robert, Brenda Ann-Marie. BA cum laude, Ohio State U., 1955. Acctg. supr. U.S. Steel Corp., Pitts., 1959-61; mgr. profit analysis Ford Motor Co., Dearborn, Mich., 1961-63; mgr. devel. planning A.O. Smith Corp., Milw., 1963-66; asst. contr. Gen. Foods Corp., White Plains, N.Y., 1966-71; v.p. planning Internat. Paper Co., N.Y.C., 1971-76, v.p., contr., 1976-79; sr. v.p. fin. and planning, chief fin. officer Navistar Internat. Corp. (formerly Internat. Harvester Co.), Chgo., 1979-82, exec. v.p. fin., 1982-83, vice chmn., chief fin. officer, 1983-87, chmn., chief exec. officer, 1987—, also bd. dirs.; mem. The Mid-Am. Com., Chgo. Com., Conf. Bd., Officer's Conf. Group, Pres. Reagan's Task Force on Market Mechanisms; bd. dirs. ASARCO Inc., USG Corp., Interlake Corp., Navistar Fin. Corp., Harbour Assurance Co. of Bermuda; mem. adv. com. bd. N.Y. Stock Exchange. Trustee Jr. Achievement of Chgo., Adler Planetarium; mem. vis. com. grad. sch. of bus. Fordham U.; mem. coun. Grad. Sch. Bus., U. Chgo. Lt. USN, 1955-58. Mem. Comml. Club Chgo., Econ. Club Chgo., Montclair Golf Club, Barrington Hills Country Club, Mid-Am. Club, Chgo. Club, Phi Beta Kappa, Alpha Tau Omega. Office: Navistar Internat Corp 401 N Michigan Ave Chicago IL 60611

COTTINGHAM, RICHARD SUMNER, paper company executive; b. Columbus, Ohio, May 7, 1941; s. Robert E. and Lee Alice (Gasaway) C.; B.A. in History, Ohio State U., 1964; m. Sheila L. Robertson, Dec. 20, 1980. Pres., Cottingham Paper Co., Columbus, Ohio, 1968—. Chmn. bd. Network Services Co., 1986-88. Served as lt. (j.g.) USN, 1964-67; Vietnam. Mem. Nat. Paper Trade Assn. (young exec. com. 1976), Am. Mgmt. Assn., Nat. Assn. Wholesale Distbrs., Internat. Sanitary Supply Assn., Columbus C. of C., Ohio C. of C. Republican. Club: Worthington Country. Address: Cottingham Paper Co 324 E 2d Ave PO Box 622 Columbus OH 43216

COTTINGHAM, STEPHEN KENT, real estate development executive, researcher; b. Denver, Dec. 28, 1951; s. Miles Dixon and Ruth (Skeen) C.; m. Susan Kay Kelfer, Aug. 11, 1984. Student, So. Oreg. Coll., 1970-71; BBA, So. Meth. U., 1974; ThM, Dallas Theol. Sem., 1984. V.p. Cottingham Constrn. Co., Dallas, 1974-79; project mgmt. Avery Mays Constrn. Co., Dallas, 1981-82; asst. v.p. Pacific Realty Corp., Dallas, 1983-85, v.p., 1985-86, exec. v.p., 1986-88; devel. exec. Paragon Group, Dallas, 1988—; mem. presdl. exec. bd. Guaranty Service Corp. and Pacific Realty Corp., 1986—; adj. tchr. N.W. Bible Ch. Coll. Class, Dallas, 1981-83; student leader, counselor Young Life Internat., Dallas, 1974-76. Charter mem. Rep. Nat. Com., Washington, 1985—. Named one of Outstanding Young Men of Am., Montgomery, Ala., 1986; So. Meth. U. Scholar, 1972-74. Mem. Urban Land Inst. (assoc.), Evang. Theol. Soc., Phi Gamma Delta (treas.), Phi Beta Lamda. Republican. Mem. Protestant Episcopal Ch. Office: Paragon Group 7557 Rambler Rd Suite 1200 Dallas TX 75231

COTTON, KATHLEEN LAURA, financial planner; b. Camas, Wash., Dec. 20, 1940; d. Charles Herschel Miller and Gladys Louise (Bundy) Miller Coffey; m. David Cotton, July 15, 1970 (div. 1979); children: Laura Suzanne Nelson, Stephen Ross Nelson, Thomas Charles. BS, City U., Bellevue, Wash., 1981. Cert. fin. planner. Fin. planner Painter Fin. Group, Bellevue, 1982-83; owner, fin. planner MoneyWorks, Bellevue, 1983-85; fin. cons. Old Stone Savs. & Loan, Seattle, 1985-86; adj. faculty City U., 1985—; instr. Inst. Bus. and Profl. Devel., Seattle, 1987—. Author: Financial Planning for the Not Yet Wealthy, 1987. Chair bus. adv. com. Seattle Community Coll., 1988-89. Mem. Internat. Assn. Fin. Planning (pres. 1988-89), Inst. Cert. Fin. Planners., Rotary. Episcopalian. Office: Cotton and Hefflefinger 2200 6th Ave Ste 424 Seattle WA 98121

COTTRELL, G. WALTON, financial executive; b. Auburn, N.Y., Sept. 26, 1939; s. George H. and Eleanor H. (Day) C.; m. Jean H. Springer, June 15, 1963; children: Lisa, Lori. BSME, Cornell U., 1962, MBA, 1963. Various positions Owens-Ill., Inc., Toledo, 1965-85, treas., 1980-83, v.p. corp. planning, 1984-85; dir. fin. Europe Owens-Ill. Internat., Geneva, 1976-80; v.p. fin. The Allen Group, Inc., Melville, N.Y., 1986; v.p., treas. Squibb Corp., Princeton, N.J., 1987-88; v.p. fin., chief fin. officer Carpenter Tech. Corp., Reading, Pa., 1989—. Dir. Jr. Achievement NW Ohio, Toledo, 1980-86, Planned Parenthood NW Ohio, Toledo, 1982-86. Served to lt. USNR. 1963-65. Mem. Fin. Execs. Inst. (bd. dirs. 1982-85), Nat. Assn. Corp. Treas. Republican. Presbyterian. Home: 46 Colfax Rd Skillman NJ 08558 Office: Carpenter Tech Corp 101 W Bern Reading PA 19612-4662

COTTRELL, MARY-PATRICIA TROSS, banker; b. Seattle, Apr. 24, 1934; d. Alfred Carl and Alice-Grace (O'Neal) Tross; m. Richard Smith Cottrell, May 17, 1969. BBA, U. Wash., 1955. Systems service rep. IBM, Seattle, also Endicott, N.Y., 1955-58, customer edn. instr., Endicott, 1958-60, 62-65, edn. planning rep., San Jose, Calif. and Endicott, N.Y., 1960-62; cons. data processing, Stamford, Conn., 1965-66; asst. treas. Union Trust Co., Stamford, 1967-68, asst. v.p., 1969-76, v.p., 1976-78, v.p., head corp. services, 1978-83; v.p. corp. fin. services Citytrust, Bridgeport, Conn., 1983—. Bd. dirs. Family and Children's Aid of Greater Norwalk (Conn.), chmn. 1986-87, Gaylord Hosp., 1986—, Bridgeport Housing Services, New Eng. Network, Inc., Bank Mktg. Assn., 1988—; trustee New Money Inst., Washington. Mem. Electronic Funds Transfer Assn. (vice chmn., bd. dirs., chmn. bd. dirs. 1983-84), Fairfield County Bankers Assn. (dir., pres. 1984-85), West Norwalk Assn. (bd. dirs.). Republican. Roman Catholic. Club: Grad. Office: Citytrust 961 Main St Bridgeport CT 06601

COUCH, JOHN CHARLES, diversified company executive; b. Bremerton, Wash., May 10, 1939; s. Richard Bailey and Frances Harriet (Gilmore) C. BS in Engring., U. Mich., 1963, MS, 1964; MBA, Stanford U., 1976. With Ingalls Shipbldg. div. Litton Industries, 1967-74; exec. v.p. Alexander and Baldwin Inc., Honolulu, 1976-85; asst. to sr. v.p. engring. and marine ops. Matson Navigation Co. subs. Alexander and Baldwin., San Francisco, 1976-84, exec. v.p., chief operating officer, 1984; pres., chief operating officer Alexander and Baldwin Inc., Honolulu, 1985—, Matson Navigation Co., 1985; dir. A&B Devel. Co., Calif., A&B Properties, Inc., Alanui Corp., East Maui Irrigation Co., Ltd., Kahului Trucking & Storage, Inc., McBryde Sugar Co., Ltd., Ohanui Corp., Princess Orchards, Wailea Devel. Co., Inc., Wailea Realty Corp., Calif., Hawaiian Sugar Co., First Hawaiian Bank, Hawaiian Sugar Transp. Co., Inc., Hawaiian Western Steel, Ltd., Pacific Resources, Inc. Bd. dirs. Kauai Econ. Devel. Bd., 1985—, Maui Econ. Devel. Bd., 1986—; mem. exec. bd. Aloha coun. Boy Scouts Am., 1986—; bd. dirs., mem. exec. com. Aloha United Way, 1988, chmn., 1988. Mem. Hawaiian Sugar Planters' Assn. (bd. dirs. 1985—), C. of C. of Hawaii (bd. dirs. 1986—), Hawaii Bus. Roundtable, Inc., Hawaii Maritime Ctr. (vice-chmn. 1988), Honolulu Club, Oahu Country Club, Plaza Club. Office: Alexander & Baldwin Inc 822 Bishop St Honolulu HI 96813

COUGHLAN, GARY PATRICK, food corporation executive; b. Fresno, Calif., Feb. 14, 1944; s. Edward Patrick and Elizabeth Claire (Ryan) C.; m. Mary Cary Kelley, Dec. 21, 1967; children: Christopher, Sarah, Laura, Claire, Moira. B.A., St. Mary's Coll., 1966; M.A. in Econs., UCLA, 1967; M.B.A., Wayne State U., 1971. Sr. fin. analyst Burroughs Corp., Detroit, 1969-72; with Dart Industries, Los Angeles, 1972-81, group v.p. field services, 1978-81, v.p. ops. services, 1981; v.p. ops. services Dart & Kraft Inc., Northbrook, Ill., 1981-82, v.p. fin., controller, 1984-85, sr. v.p. fin. affairs, 1985-86, sr. v.p., chief fin. officer, 1986—; v.p. fin. retail food group Kraft Inc., Glenview, Ill., 1982-84, sr. v.p., chief fin. officer, 1986-88; sr. v.p. Kraft Gen. Foods, Glenview, 1989—; instr., prof. fin. Extension Program UCLA, 1974-80; dir. Boulevard Bank, Chgo. Mem. Fin. Execs. Inst., Conf. Bd. Council Fin. Execs. Republican. Roman Catholic. Club: Economic Chgo. Home: 1135 Central Rd Glenview IL 60025 Office: Kraft Inc Kraft Ct Glenview IL 60025

COUGHLIN, CORNELIUS EDWARD, accounting company executive; b. Boston, Sept. 9, 1927; s. Cornelius Stephen and Mabel Josephine (McMahon) C.; BBA with honors, Northeastern U., 1956; student Bentley Coll., 1948-50; m. Rosemarie Toppi, Sept. 5, 1954; children: William, Brian, Stephen, Christopher, Maureen, Michael. Office mgr. Trim Alloys, Inc., Boston, 1952-57; controller Form-A-Lite Inc., Northbridge, Mass., 1957-59; sales adminstr. Reiss Assos., Inc., Lowell, Mass., 1959-61; ops. mgr. GPS Instrument Co., Newton, Mass., 1961-65. Computer Products, Newton, 1965-67; partner McShane & Coughlin, Milton, Mass., 1967-74; owner, mgr. C.E. Coughlin & Co., Acton, Mass., 1974-78; pres. Coughlin, Sheff & Assocs., Acton, 1979—. Mem. auditcom. Town of Acton. Served with USN, 1945-48, 50-51. Mem. Mass. Soc. CPAs, Mass. Assn. Public Accts. (pres. 1989—), Am. Inst. CPAs, Nat. Soc. Public Accts., Nat. Assn. Accts., Small Business Assn. N.E. Democrat. Roman Catholic. Lodge: Rotary. Home: 98 Summer St Acton MA 01720 Office: Coughlin Sheff & Assocs 289 Great Rd Acton MA 01720

COUGHLIN, TIMOTHY CRATHORNE, bank executive; b. Evanston, Ill., June 1, 1942; s. Laurence and Mary (Crathorne) C.; m. Laura Jane Philipp, June 10, 1967; children: Elisabeth A., Timothy C. Jr., Mary Blair, John C. BA, Brown U., 1964; MBA, NYU, 1969. With spl. devel. program Chase Manhattan Bank, N.Y.C., 1964-67, asst. treas., 1967-69, 2d v.p., 1969-71, v.p., 1971-74, v.p., dist. exec., 1974-78; sr v.p., dep. gen. mgr. Banque Paribas, N.Y.C., 1978-83; exec. v.p. Riggs Nat. Bank Washington, 1983-85, pres., chief operating officer, 1985—, also bd. dirs.; bd. dirs. AP Bank Ltd., Pizza Nat. Corp. Treas. John F. Kennedy Ctr. for the Performing Arts, Washington, 1986—; bd. dirs. Greater Washington Bd. Trade, 1986—; vestryman St. Alban's Parish, Washington, 1986—; bd. dirs. Boys and Girls Clubs Greater Washington, 1987—; mem. governing bd. St. Albans Sch., Washington, 1987—. Mem. Assn. Res. City Bankers. Episcopalian. Clubs: Columbia Country, Skytop. Office: Riggs Nat Bank 800 17th St NW Washington DC 20006

COULSON, NORMAN M., savings and loan executive; b. Hilt, Calif.; m. Helen; children—Virginia Coulson Bullard, Maria, Edward, Michael. B.S. in Mgmt., Long Beach State Coll., 1957; M.B.A., Pepperdine U., 1973; postgrad. exec. program UCLA, postgrad. in exec. devel. U. Wash. With 1st Fed. Savs. San Pedro (Calif.), 1957-59; with Glendale Fed. Savs. and Loan Assn. (Calif.), 1959—, successively v.p., group v.p., exec. v.p., sr. exec. v.p. and gen. mgr. Calif. div., pres., chief executive officer, chmn., dir. 1984—, also vice-chmn., pres., chief exec. officer, Glenfed Inc.; instr. Inst. Fin. Edn., Community Coll. Accreditation. Mem. council communication div. Pepperdine U.; past chmn. adv. bd. Kennedy High Sch., Granada Halls, Calif.; bd. dirs. Citizens for Law and Order, Glendale, Glendale Adventist Med. Ctr. Found.; bd. govs. Inst. Fin. Edn., Los Angeles; bd. dirs., mem. exec. com., chmn. communications com. Am. Heart Assn., Los Angeles. Served with USCG. Mem. Downey-Studio City C. of C. (bd. dirs.), Stonewood Mchts. Assn. (pres.), Calif. Savs. and Loan League (com. mem.), U.S. League Savs. Assn. (mem. savs. account adminstrn. com.), Nat. Council Savs. Instns. (state dir. 1984-85), Newcomen Soc. U.S. Clubs: Lakeside Country, Verdugo (Glendale); Rotary (Los Angeles). Office: GLENFED Inc 700 N Brand Blvd Glendale CA 91203

COULSON, ZOE ELIZABETH, food processing executive; b. Sullivan, Ind., Sept. 22, 1932; d. Marion Allan and Mary Ann (Thompson) C. B.S., Purdue U., 1954; A.M.P., Harvard Bus. Sch., 1983. asst. dir. home econs. Am. Meat Inst., Chgo., 1954-57; account exec. J. Walter Thompson Co., Chgo., 1957-60; creative consumer dir. Leo Burnett Co., Chgo., 1960-64; mag. editor-in-chief Donnelley-Dun & Bradstreet, N.Y.C., 1964-68; food editor Good Housekeeping Inst., N.Y.C., 1968-76, dir., 1976-81; v.p. Campbell Soup Co., Camden, N.J., 1981—; dir. Rubbermaid Inc., Campbell Sales Co. Author: Good Housekeeping Illustrated Cookbook, 1981; Good Housekeeping Cookbook, 1972. Trustee Cooper Hosp./Univ. Med. Ctr., 1982—. Named Disting. Alumna, Purdue U., 1971. Mem. Women's Econ. Bus. Alliance (bd. govs.), Kappa Alpha Theta Alumnae Assn. Republican. Presbyterian. Avocation: meso-Am. archaeology. Home: 220 Locust St Philadelphia PA 19106 Office: Campbell Soup Co Campbell Pl Camden NJ 08103-1799

COULTER, BARBARA CLARE, telecommunication company professional; b. N.Y.C., Nov. 10, 1950; d. Francis Thomas and Mary Catherine (Hall) C.; m. Jay E. Pultz; May 7, 1978; children: Jude Elliott, Mary Margaret Anna Coulter-Pultz. BS in Physics and Math., Georgian Ct. Coll., 1972; MS in Ops. Research, Poly. Inst. N.Y., 1977; MBA, Pace U., 1984. Research asst. Oak Ridge (Tenn.) Nat. Labs., 1971; sr. tech. asst. Bell Labs., Whippany and Holmdel, N.J., 1972-74; mem. tech. staff Holmdel, 1974-78; staff mgr. tariffs and costs AT&T, Basking Ridge, N.J., 1978-79, bus. case dist. mgr., 1980-81; dist. mgr. fin. planning, market planning and strategic planning AT&T, Morristown, N.J., 1982-85; product mgr. Spirit Communications Systems AT&T, Parsippany, N.J., 1985-87; div. mgr. facsimile product mgmt. Parsippany, N.J., 1987—.

COULTER, DEBORAH ANN, building official; b. Seattle, Oct. 11, 1952; d. Arthur Bernard and Jean Judith (Campbell) C. Supply specialist U.S. Dewline Ops. Maintenance Service, Barter Island, Alaska, 1973-74; div. mgr. Prudhoe Bay A&P-Griswold Expeditors, Inc., Fairbanks, Alaska, 1974-76; constrn. coordinator Saudi Devel. & Comml. Co., Jeddah, Saudi Arabia, 1977-78, Star Machinery Co., Seattle, 1979-80; constrn. inspector, field rep. Seattle Housing Authority, 1980-83; building official, fire marshal City of Fife (Wash.), 1983-85; building official, code adminstr. City of Issaquah, Wash., 1985-87; bldg. official Yakima County, Wash., 1987-88; dep. state fire marshall State of Wash., 1988—. Election, re-election campaign mem. Seattle Mayoral Race, 1980-84. Mem. Internat. Conf. Bldg. Officials, Wash. Assn. Bldg. Officials (chmn. legisl. state liaison com. 1986-87), Nat. Assn Women in Constrn. Home: PO Box 891 Mercer Island WA 98040 Office: Dept Community Devel Fire Protection Services Div 3600 S Graham St Seattle WA 98118

COULTER, JACK BENSON, JR., financial planner; b. Louisville, Jan. 30, 1947; s. Jack Benson and Mary Belle (Roby) C.; m. Mary Llew Browne, July, 1977. BS, Fla. State U., 1967, MBA, 1969. CPA, Fla. Staff acct. Arthur Andersen & Co., Miami, Fla., 1971-73; sales rep. Commerce Clearing House, Inc., Miami, 1973-80; pres. First Fin. Planners, Jupiter, Fla., 1980—. Capt. U.S. Army, 1969-71. Mem. Inst. Cert. Fin. Planners (cert., nat. bd. dirs. 1986—), Registry Fin. Planning Pracitioners, Fla. Inst. CPAs. Republican. Office: First Fin Planners Inc 825 S US One Ste 370 Jupiter FL 33477

COUNTRYMAN, GARY LEE, insurance company executive; b. South Bend, Wash., July 30, 1939; s. William T. and Vernela K. (Stewart) C.; m. Sally Ann Mathews, Aug. 16, 1958; children: Christopher John, Susan Michelle, Sherry LeeAnn, Stefanie May. B.S., U. Oreg., 1961, M.S., 1963. With Liberty Mut. Ins. Co., Boston, 1963—, pres., 1981—, pres., chief exec. officer, 1986—; dir. Liberty Mut. Ins. Group, Bank of Boston Corp., 1st Nat. Bank of Boston, Boston Edison Co., Neiman Marcus Group, Dennison Mfg. Co.; bd. dirs. Ins. Services Office, Inc., Alliance Am. Insurers. Trustee Northeastern U. H.T. Miner fellow, 1962-63. Mem. Am. Inst. Property and Liability Underwriters. Club: Algonquin (Boston). Office: Liberty Mut Ins Co 175 Berkeley St Boston MA 02117

COUPER, WILLIAM, banker; b. N.Y.C., May 3, 1947; s. John Lee and Margery (Beemer) C.; m. Elise Marie Palma, Oct. 4, 1969; children: Elise, Margery, Dorothy. BS in Commerce, U.Va., 1968; cert., Coll. Fin. Planning, 1986. Trainee Am. Security Bank, N.A., Washington, 1972, asst. treas., asst. br. mgr., 1972-76, asst. v.p., mgr. main office, 1976-77, v.p., regional mgr., 1977-80, v.p. strategic planning, 1981-83, v.p. retail banking devel., 1983-84, sr. v.p. retail banking, 1984-89; sr. v.p. Md. Nat. Bank, Greenbelt, 1989—. Loaned exec. Nat. Alliance Businessmen, Washington, 1974, United Way, Washington, 1979; bd. dirs. Better Bus. Bur., Washington, 1986—. Served with USN, 1968-72. Mem. Inst. Cert. Fin. Planners, Greater Washington Fin. Instns. Assn., Greater Washington B. Trade. Republican. Episcopalian. Home: 9008 Maritime Ct Springfield VA 22153 Office: Md Nat Bank 7474 Greenway Ctr Dr Ste 1200 Greenbelt MD 20770

COURSEN, CHRISTOPHER DENNISON, lawyer; b. Mpls., Dec. 6, 1948; s. Richard Dennison and Helen Wilson (Stevens) C.; m. Pamela Elizabeth Lynch, June 3, 1978; children: Cameron Dennison, Matthew Ashbolt, Madeline Messurier. BA, Washington & Lee U., 1970; JD, The George Washington U., 1975. Bar: D.C. 1975, U.S. Dist. Ct. D.C., 1976, U.S. Ct. Appeals (D.C. Cir.) 1976, U.S. Ct. Mil. Appeals 1976, U.S. Supreme Ct. 1978. Sole practice, Washington, 1975-78; assoc. Dempsey & Koplovitz, Washington, 1978-80; communications counsel U.S. Senate Com. Commerce, Sci., and Transportation, Washington, 1980-83; ptnr. O'Connor & Hannan, Washington, 1983-87; pres. The Status Group, Washington, 1988—; adj. prof. law The George Washington U., Washington, 1983. Team mem. Pres.-Elect Reagan's Transition Team, Washington, 1980; atty. adv. Reagan-Bush 1984, Washington; telecommunications adviser Bush/Quayle presdl. campaign, 1988. Mem. ABA, Fed. Communications Bar Assn., D.C. Bar Assn. Roman Catholic. Club: Chevy Chase (Md.). Home: 5006 Nahant St Bethesda MD 20816 Office: The Status Group The Army & Navy Club Bldg 1627 Eye St NW Suite 525 Washington DC 20006

COURSON, JOHN A., mortgage banker; b. Vincennes, Ind., May 21, 1942; s. Addison J. and Virginia K. (Klingler) C.; m. Marica Heidel, June 5, 1963; children—Melissa A., Christopher J. Student Monmouth Coll., 1960-67; BS in Bus., U. Colo., 1964. Vice pres. Kassler & Co., Denver, 1967-68; v.p. Westwood Mortgage Corp. (formerly Ft. Wayne Mortgage Co.), Denver, 1968-70, sr. v.p., 1970-72, exec. v.p., Birmingham, Mich., 1972-78, pres., chief exec. officer, Dallas, 1978-85; pres. Criterion Fin. Corp., Dallas, 1985—; pres. Southmark Mortgage Corp., Dallas; dir. Devel. Dynamics Group, St. Louis. Mem. bd. cons. Ea. Mich. U., Ypsilanti, 1979-82, allocation com. United Fund, Detroit, 1982—; pres. Detroit Inst. for Children, 1980-83; chmn. Teke Ednl. Found., Indpls., 1985—; elder 1st Presbyn. Ch., Birmingham, Mich., 1980-83. Mem. Mortgage Bankers Assn. Am. (bd. govs. 1982—), Mortgage Bankers Assn. Mich. (pres. 1979-80, Mortgage Banker of Yr. 1982), Real Estate Industries Council (bd. dirs. 1987—), Dallas Mortgage Bankers Assn. (pres. 1988—), Tau Kappa Epsilon (nat. pres. 1981-83). Clubs: Orchard Lake Country (Detroit); Bent Tree Country (Dallas). Avocations: jogging, golf. Home: 7120 Cliffbrook Dr Dallas TX 75240 Office: Southmark Mortgage Corp 13800 Montfort Dr Dallas TX 75240

COURTENAY, ADRIAN HENRY, III., publishing executive; b. Rockville Centre, N.Y., July 6, 1942; s. Adrian Henry and Judith (Clark) C.; m. Elisabeth Van Gulik. Student, Hamilton Coll., Clinton, N.Y., 1959-62. Founder, pres. Mill Hollow Corp., N.Y.C., 1972—; founder, pub. Laundry News, N.Y.C., 1974—, DM News, N.Y.C., 1979—, Catalog Bus., N.Y.C., 1986—. Home: 106 Franklin St New York NY 10013 Office: Mill Hollow Corp 19 W 21st St New York NY 10010

COURTER, JAMES ANDREW, lawyer; b. Lansing, Mich., May 21, 1936; s. John L. and Melba (Olsen) C. Ph.B., U. Detroit, 1954-58, LL.B., 1958-61. Staff attorney Ford Motor Co., Dearborn, Mich., 1961-67; sr. atty. Ford of Europe, Warley, Brentwood, Essex, England, 1967-69; asst. sec. Ford Motor Co., Dearborn, Mich., 1969-71, corp. counsel, 1971-72, asst. gen. counsel, 1972-74, assoc. gen. counsel, 1974-87, assoc. gen. counsel, sec., 1987—. Captain U.S. Army, 1961-67. Mem. ABA, Mich. Bar Assn. Office: Ford Motor Co The American Rd Dearborn MI 48121

COURTNEY, DON RUSSELL, advertising executive; b. Chattanooga, Feb. 18, 1929; s. James D. and Elna (Russell) C.; m. Doris Anita Schobert, Dec. 22, 1951; children—Kathryn Ann, Sharon Elaine. B.B.A., U. Okla., 1952. Sales rep. Eaton Labs., Norwich, N.Y., 1958-64, sales promotion mgr., 1964-65; account supr. McCann Erickson, N.Y.C., 1965-72; sr. v.p. Frank J. Corbett, Inc., Chgo., 1972—. Author: The Literate Smoker's Guide to Quitting, 1984; (film) Time Factors (Golden Eagle award 1977); contbr. articles to profl. jours. Served with U.S. Army, 1952-54. Recipient awards for advt. achievements. Mem. Am. Soc. Microbiology, Midwest Pharm. Advt. Council. Home: 391 N Valley Ct Barrington IL 60010 Office: Frank J Corbett Inc $S1211 E Chicago Ave Chicago IL 60611

COURTRIGHT, LEE FLIPPEN, financial planner; b. Elkhart, Ind., May 22, 1937; s. Harold Franklin and Norma (Gibbs) C.; m. Kay Louise Custer, Oct. 3, 1958; children: Laura Jo Courtright Matteson, Beth Elaine. BSBA, U. Nebr., Omaha, 1961. CLU, chartered fin. cons., cert. fin. planner. Spl. agt. Prudential Ins. Co. Am., 1961-66; life ins. cons. Overland-Wolf Inc., 1966-67; sales supr. Life Ins. Co. N.Am., 1967-71; ind. ins. broker Don Peterson & Assocs., Fremont, Nebr., 1971-72; mgr. life and health sales Sentry Life Ins. Co., Stevens Point, Wis., 1972-74; dir. mktg. Sentry Life Ins. Co., Stevens Point, 1974-80, dir. market devel. and rsch., 1981-87; assoc. markets devel. Nationwide Life Ins. Co., Columbus, Ohio, 1980-81; pres. Courtright Adv. Ltd., Stevens Point, Wis., 1986—; br. mgr. Fin. Network Investment Corp., Torrance, Calif., 1988—. Mem. Life Ins. Mktg. and Rsch. Assn. (com. 1983-86), Internat. Assn. Fin. Planning, Am. Soc. CLU's and Chartered Fin. Cons. (bd. dirs.), Nat. Ctr. Fin. Edn., Inst. Cert. Fin. Planners (sec., v.p. 1987-88), Golden Sands Home Builders Assn., Stevens Point/Plover Area C. of C., Am. Assn. Individual Investors, Stevens Point County Club, Kiwanis, Elks. Republican. Methodist. Office: Courtright Adv Ltd 3118 Post Rd Ste 1 Stevens Point WI 54481

COUSINS, KENNETH EDDLEMAN, corporate executive; b. Louisville, Aug. 25, 1939; s. David Dunnington and Louise (Eddleman) C.; m. Betsy Dunton Shreaves, June 25, 1966; children: Kimberly, Kevin, David. BS, U. Richmond, 1961. Accountant Robertshaw Controls Co., Richmond, Va., 1963-64, internal auditor, 1964-68, computer systems analyst, 1968-72, asst. to treas., 1972-82, asst. treas., 1982-87, treas., 1987—. Served to 1st lt. U.S. Army, 1961-63. Mem. Risk Ins. Mgmt. Soc., Cash Mgmt. Assn. Republican. Presbyterian. Home: 221 Farnham Dr Richmond VA 23236 Office: Robertshaw Controls Co 1701 Byrd Ave Richmond VA 23230

COUTU-MELKA, NANCY GRACE, financial planner; b. Chgo., Mar. 10, 1953; d. Hugh Park and Lucy (Marsh) Coutu; m. Robert K. Reed, May 1, 1976 (div. 1985); m. Steven J. Melka, Mar. 10, 1986. AA, Triton Coll., 1979; BS, Mundelein Coll., 1982. Cert. fin. planner. Sales rep. Trans Union Credit Info. Co., Chgo., 1970-78, First Nat. Bank Chgo., 1978-79, Robert F. White & Co., Chgo., 1979-81; mgr. dist. sales IDS Fin. Svcs., Oakbrook Terrace, Ill., 1981-87; prin., fin. planner Money Mgrs. Ltd., Oak Brook, Ill., 1987—; presenter seminars, ednl. programs. Contbr. articles to profl. jours. Mem. Internat. Assn. Fin. Planners, Internat. Assn. Registered Fin. Planners, Women Mgmt., The Savoy Co., Phila. Graphic Arts Golf Club. Methodist. Office: Money Mgrs Ltd 1301 W 22nd St Ste 308 Oak Brook IL 60521

COUTURE, PHILLIP QUINN, financial executive; b. Pleasant Ridge, Mich., Jan. 15, 1946; s. Joseph J. and Ardis (Ward) C.; m. Kathleen Gay Branstetter, Aug. 28, 1964 (div. 1981); children: M. Lance, Troy M.; m. Sandra Gail Rinchich, Dec. 6, 1986. Cert. fin. planning, Coll. Fin. Planning, 1985; cert. fin. adviser, Sierra U., 1986. V.p. James Ins. Agy., Westchester, Calif., 1974-77; pres. Couture & Assocs. Inc, Newport Beach, Calif., 1977-87; pres. Ameritrust Fin. Services Inc., Irvine, Calif., 1986—, investment adviser, 1983—; instr. Orange Coast Coll., Cost Mesa, Calif., 1982, 83, 87, 88, Sierra U., Newport Beach, 1986; mem. bd. advisers Fin. Profl. Adv. Panel, Newport, 1985, Chapman Coll., Orange, Calif., 1988. Recipient Honored Service award Ch. of Religious Sci., 1984. Mem. Internat. Assn. Fin. Planners, Inst. Cert. Fin. Planners, Registry Fin. Planning Practitioners. Republican. Mem. Religious Sci. Ch. Office: Ameritrust Fin Svcs 19700 Fairchild Ste 240 Irvine CA 92715

COUTURIER, RONALD LEE, services company executive, consultant; b. Toledo, Ohio, Mar. 18, 1949; s. James Carl and Caroline Betty (Chiles) C.; m. Rebecca Lohnas; children: Scott James, Aimee Colette, Renee Leigh. BBA cum laude, U. Toldeo, 1972; MBA, U. N.H., 1981; postgrad., U. Toledo. Intern, Owens-Ill., Inc., Toledo, 1969-71, planning analyst, 1969-72; mgr. mgmt. info. systems div. McCord Corp., Cedar Rapids, Iowa, 1972-75; mgr. group mgmt. info. systems Carborundum Co. subs. Standard Oil of Ohio, Niagara Falls, N.Y., 1975-80; dir. mgmt. info. systems Kennecott Engineered Systems subs. Standard Oil of Ohio, Niagara Falls, 1980-82; dir. worldwide computer tech. Pfaudler div. Standard Oil of Ohio, Rochester, N.Y., 1982-86; v.p. New Tech. div. Meszaros Assocs., Inc., Buffalo, 1986-87; founder, pres. Amsys Inc., 1988—; bd. dirs. FP Techs., Ltd., Advanced Computer Techs., Biznet Info. Svcs. Corp.; mem. adv. council Applied Data Research Princeton, N.J., 1984-86; cons. Rod Williams Assocs., Rochester, 1984—, Coca-Cola Consol., 1985-88, Cordis Corp., Contel Corp., Ga. Fed. Bank, Duke Power Co., Touro Infirmary, Upstate Milk Coops., Buffalo, Moog Inc., 1986-87, Buffalo, Guilford County, N.C., Parmed Pharmaceuticals, Inc., 1986-87, Niagara Falls, N.Y., Rochester Telephone Co., 1986-87, Hanes Corp., Agway Data Services, Syracuse, N.Y., 1986-88, Citibank, N.Y.C., 1988, GTE, Tampa, Fla., 1988, Cordis Corp., 1988—, Ga. Fed. Bank, 1988—, Duke Power Co., 1988—, BellSouth Enterprises, Atlanta, 1988—, Freddie Mac, Reston, Va., 1988—, Sony Corp. of Am., Montvale, N.J., 1989—. Contbg. author to various profl. jours. Mem. Rochester Philharm. Orch. Assn., 1984-86, Geva Theatre, Rochester, 1984-86; dist. exec. Standard Oil of Ohio Polit. Action Com., Washington, 1984-85; mem. Republican Nat. Com., Washington, 1981—. Mem. Assn. for Systems Mgmt. (cert.), Charlotte C. of C., Assn. for Data Processing Service Cos., Assn. for Inst. for Cert. of Computer Profls., ASME, Beta Gamma Sigma. Roman Catholic. Avocations: theatre, electronics; skiing; woodworking.

COUZENS, FRANK, JR., banker; b. Detroit, Jan. 18, 1924; s. Frank and Margaret (Lang) C.; m. Joan Marie Ulrich, Aug. 9, 1947; children: Joan Marie Couzens Cliff, Margaret Mary Couzens Crandall, Anne Marie, Mary Carol Couzens Marantette, Frank III, William Ulrich, John Manning. B.S., U. Detroit, 1948. With Mfrs. Nat. Bank Detroit, 1951—, officer, 1955, 2d v.p., 1956-60, v.p., 1960-64, v.p. adminstr., 1964-67, sr. v.p., 1967-71, sr. v.p., sr. trust officer, 1971-77, exec. v.p., 1977—; pres., trustee Oakland Housing Inc., Birmingham, Mich.; dir., chmn. orgn. and nominating com. Jacobson Stores Inc., Jackson, Mich. Trustee, vice chmn. Children's Hosp. Mich., 1973—, chmn. fin., 1976—; trustee United Community Services, 1971, v.p., 1974, pres., 1975-76, chmn. bd., 1977-81; mem. exec. com. Greater Detroit Area Health Council, 1974—, mem. budget and fin. com., 1980—, chmn. Project Health Care, 1982-84; mem. Citizens' Com. Higher Edn.; trustee Henry Ford Hosp./Maplegrove Ctr; mem. fin. com. Detroit Med. Ctr.; trustee Mich. Cancer Found. Served with USNR, 1942-46. Recipient Ser. Recognition Citizens Com. Higher Edn.; Silver Beaver award Detroit area council Boy Scouts Am., Knight of Charity award PIME Missionaries, 1987. Mem. Greater Detroit C. of C. Roman Catholic. Clubs: Economic (Detroit), Detroit Athletic (Detroit), Country (Detroit), Hundred (Detroit), Cardinal (Detroit). Home: 66 Lothrop Rd Grosse Pointe Farms MI 48236 Office: Mfrs Nat Corp Mfrs Bank Tower 100 Renaissance Ctr Detroit MI 48243

COVACEVICH, ANTHONY, county governmental official; b. Weslaco, Tex., Sept. 30, 1954; s. Jesus and Josefina (Alvarado) C.; m. Leticia Garza, Nov. 25, 1976; children: Anthony Christopher, Maria Christina, Andres Raul. BS in Polit. Sci., Pan Am. U., 1976; postgrad., Bucknell U., 1980-81. City mgr. intern City of Weslaco, Tex., 1973-74, asst. city mgr., 1981-87; circuit city mgr. Assn. City/County Econ. Devel. Corp., Edinburg, Tex., 1975-77; community devel. dir. City of Mercedes, Tex., 1977-80; asst. city mgr. City of Weslaco, Tex., 1981-87; urban county dir. Hidalgo County, Tex., 1987—. Pres. Roosevelt Sch. PTO, Weslaco, 1984-85; trustee Weslaco Sch. Bd., 1988—. Nat. Urban fellow, 1980; recipient Devel. Concept award Valley AIA, 1983. Mem. Nat. Community Devel. Assn. (com. mem. 1979-80), Nat. League of Cities (research panel 1980-81), Tex. City Mgrs. Assn., Tex. Indsl. Devel. Corp. Democrat. Roman Catholic. Lodge: KC (editor local chpt. 1983—). Office: County of Hidalgo PO Box 1356 Edinburg TX 78540

COVENY, RICHARD GRIFFIN, graphic arts company executive, consultant; b. Wheeling, W.Va., July 26, 1958; s. William B. and Marie (Piccolo) C. BBA, Ga. State U., 1980. Sales rep. Litton Industries, Beverly Hills, Calif., 1980-81; v.p. Williams Group, Atlanta, 1981—; agt. Random House Vintage Contemporaries. Mem. Soc. Photographers and Artist Rep. (pres. N.Y.C. 1985-86). Republican. Roman Catholic. Home: 820 Piedmont Ave #2 Atlanta GA 30308

COVERDALE, GLEN EUGENE, life insurance company executive; b. Trafalgar, Ind., Jan. 9, 1930; m. Laurel Larson, Mar. 21, 1951; children: Beth Karen, Anne Christine. A.B. cum laude, Franklin (Ind.) Coll., 1951; M.B.A., Ind. U., 1952. With Met. Life Ins. Co., 1954—; exec. v.p. charge real estate and agrl. investments Met. Life Ins. Co., N.Y.C., 1978—, mem. corp. mgmt. office; mem. adv. bd. Real Estate Inst. NYU; chmn. Housing Partnership Mortgage Corp.; bd. dirs. Realty Found. N.Y. Trustee Urban Land Inst.; mem. dean's council Ind. U. Bus. Sch.; pres. exploring div. Greater N.Y. councils Boy Scouts Am., also bd. dirs. Served with AUS, 1952-54. Decorated Commendation medal; Brandeis U. fellow. Fellow Life Office Mgmt. Assn. Inst.; mem. Real Estate Bd. N.Y. (bd. govs.), Sigma Alpha Epsilon, Beta Gamma Sigma, Phi Alpha Theta. Home: 355 Heights Rd Ridgewood NJ 07450 Office: Met Life Ins Co 1 Madison Ave New York NY 10010

COVERDALE, WATSON SHALLCROSS, JR., computer company official; b. Milw., Nov. 22, 1932; s. Watson Shallcross and Ada Margueritte (Sheridan) C.; student Washington and Lee U., 1951-53, Ursinus Coll., 1956-61; m. Carolyn Lucille Mumby, Apr. 6, 1963; children: Watson Shallcross III, Carter Sheridan. Regional mgr. fed. mktg. Mohawk Data Scis., Washington, 1971-72, dist. mgr., N.Y.C., 1977-81; dir. nat. sales, product and systems div. Lockheed Electronics, Plainfield, N.J., 1972-74; br. mgr. Four Phase System Co., Rochelle Park, N.J., 1974-77; regional mgr. OEM sales WICAT Systems, N.Y.C., 1981-83; Eastern regional mgr. Xerox Imaging Systems, 1983—. First v.p. bd. dirs. Haystack Ski Ednl. Found., 1978-80; bd. dirs. Chimney Hill Owners Assn., 1981-87. Served with USMC, 1954-56. Mem. Md. Soc. of Pa. (bd. of govs. 1985—). Episcopalian. Club: Downtown (Phila.). Home: 8 Parkview Ave Bell Island Rowayton CT 06853 Office: 2050 Center Ave Fort Lee NJ 07024

COVERT, CALVIN C., manufacturing company executive; b. 1924. With Woodward Governor Co., Rockford, Ill., 1942—; supr. green house and ground, asst. sec. 1970-75, chmn. bd., chief exec. officer, 1976—, pres., 1982—. Office: Woodward Gov Co 5001 N 2nd St Rockford IL 61125

COVERT, MICHAEL HENRI, hospital executive; b. Chgo., Apr. 7, 1949; s. Leonard and Shirley Gladys (Jeffe) C.; m. Robyn McClay, Feb. 22, 1975; children: Jason, Tiffany, Brienn. BS in Bus., Washington U., St. Louis, 1970, M in Health Adminstrn., 1972. Adminstrv. asst. St. Agnes Hosp., White Plains, N.Y., 1969; adminstrv. resident Hillcrest Med. Ctr., Tulsa, 1971-72, asst. adminstr., 1972-73, adminstr., 1973-80; exec. v.p., chief operating officer St. Francis Regional Med. Ctr., Wichita, Kans., 1980-85; chief exec. officer Ohio State Univ. Hosps., Columbus, 1985-88; sr. v.p. Physician Corp. of Am., Wichita, Kans., 1988—; bd. dirs., U. Hosp. Consortium, Chgo., 1985-88, Lifeline of Ohio Organ Procurement, Columbus, 1985-88; pres.-elect, Franklin County Hosp. Council, Columbus, 1987-88. Fellow Am. Coll. Healthcare Execs. (commr. to accreditation, commn. for Grad. Edn. in Health Care Adminstrn. 1988—, chmn. various coms.); mem. Ohio Hosp. Assn. (bd. dirs. 1988, pres.-elect cen. dist. 1987-88). Lodge: Rotary. Home: 747 Linden Ct Wichita KS 67206 Office: Physician Corp Am 151 N Main St Wichita KS 67202

COVEY, FRANK MICHAEL, JR., lawyer, law educator; b. Chgo., Oct. 24, 1932; s. Frank M. and Marie B. (Lorenz) C.; m. Patricia Ann McGill, Oct. 7, 1961; children: Geralyn, Frank Michael III, Regis Patrick. BS with honors, Loyola U., Chgo., 1954, JD cum laude, 1957; SJD, U. Wis., Madison, 1960. Bar: Ill. 1957, U.S. Supreme Ct. 1965. Research assoc. Wis. Gov.'s Com. on Revision Law of Eminent Domain, 1958; law clk. Ill. Appellate Ct., 1959; assoc. Belnap, Spencer, Hardy & Freeman, Chgo., 1959-60; assoc. McDermott, Will & Emery, Chgo., 1960-64, ptnr., 1965-88, mem. exec. com., 1979-81, mgmt. com., 1979-82, of counsel, 1988—; instr. Northwestern U. Sch. Law, 1958-59, Loyola U. Coll., 1958-69, 79-80; prof. law Loyola U., Chgo., 1988—; assoc. gen. counsel Union League Civic and Arts Found., 1967-69, v.p., 1969-72, 73-75, pres., 1972-73, mng. dir., 1975-80; co-dir. Grant Park study team Nat. Commn. on Causes and Prevention of Violence, 1968. Author: Roadside Protection Through Access Control, 1960, (with others) Federal Civil Practice in Illinois, 1974, 6th edit., 1987, Business Litigation I: Competition and Its Limits, 1978, Class Actions, 1979, 2d edit., 1986, Architect and Engineer Liability; Claims Against the Design Professional, 1987; contbr. articles to profl. jours. Mem. bd. athletics Loyola U., 1970-72, mem. estate planning com., 1969-81, mem. com. on the future of the law sch., 1975-76, trustee, 1979-88, mem. citizens bd., 1979—; bd. dirs. Chgo. Bldg. Congress, 1978-82, sec., 1982-84; mem. revenue adv. com. Chgo City Council, 1983-84; mem. Spl. Commn. on Adminstrn. Justice in Cook County, 1984-88; chmn. bd. trustees St. Viator High Sch., Arlington Heights, Ill., also chair, 1988—; dir. Met. Chgo. Air Force Community Coun., 1988—. Recipient Conf. on Personal Fin. Law award, 1955, Founders Day award Loyola U., 1976, Disting. Service award Loyola U. Dept. Polit. Sci., 1979, Disting. Service award Loyola U. Dept. Socio-legal Studies, 1980, Excellence medal Loyola U. Law Sch., 1979. Fellow Ill. Bar Found. (charter), Chgo. Bar Found.; mem. ABA, Ill. State Bar Assn. (Lincoln award 1963, Bd. Govs. award 1986), Chgo. Bar Assn., Fed. 7th Circuit Bar Assn., Catholic Lawyers Guild, Chgo. Council Lawyers, Am. Judicature Soc., Howard T. Markey Inn of Ct., Acad. Polit. Sci., North Shore Bd. Realtors (affiliate), Internat. Assn. Defense Counsel, Def. Research Inst., Ill. Hist. Soc., Air Force Assn., U.S. Navy League, Loyola U. Alumni Assn. (pres. 1965-66), Loyola U. Law Sch. Alumni Assn. (chmn. alumni fund campaign 1967-68, v.p. alumni 1968-69, pres. 1969-70, chmn. Thomas More Club 1973-75; award 1957), Western Soc. Engrs. (assoc.), Chgo. Architecture Found., Acad. Polit. Sci. (Howard T. Markey Inn of Ct), The Forum for Architecture, Blue Key, Phi Alpha Delta, Alpha Sigma Nu, Pi Gamma Mu, Delta Sigma Rho. Clubs: Union League (Chgo.) (bd. dirs. 1977-80, chmn. house com. 1977-80, 2d v.p. 1988-89, 1st v.p. 1989—), Legal (Chgo.), Law (Chgo.). Home: 1104 W Lonnquist Blvd Mount Prospect IL 60056 Office: Loyola U Chgo Sch Law 1 E Pearson St Chicago IL 60611

COVEY, HAROLD DEAN, insurance company executive; b. Clinton, Ill., Sept. 8, 1930; s. Elmer Lloyd and Nora (Fittro) C.; m. Margaret F. Thompson, Mar. 25, 1951; children: Cheryl Covey Ramsey, Philip H. B.S. in Bus. Adminstrn., Ill. Wesleyan U., Bloomington, 1956. Various underwriter positions State Farm Mut. Auto. Ins. Co., Bloomington, 1950-64; div. mgr. State Farm Mut. Auto. Ins. Co., Greeley, Colo., 1964-69; exec. asst. State Farm Mut. Auto. Ins. Co., Bloomington, 1969-71; dep. regional v.p. State Farm Mut. Auto. Ins. Co., Santa Ana, Calif., 1971-72; v.p. underwriting Bloomington, 1972-86; v.p., chief adminstrv. officer State Farm Fire and Casualty Co., Bloomington, 1987—; dir. Nat. Industry Com., N.Y.C., 1974-78, chmn., 1976; bd. govs. S.C. Reins. Facility, Columbia, 1973-79; trustee Md. Auto Ins. Fund, Annapolis, 1976-86, chmn., 1984-85; dir. Conf. Casualty Ins Cos., Indpls., 1978-87, pres., 1981-82; dir. N.J. Auto Ins. Assn., Trenton, 1983—. Bd. dirs. United Way of McLean County, Bloomington, 1973-86, pres., 1980-81; bd. dirs. Ill. Wesleyan U. Assocs., 1975-80, 84-87. Served with USN, 1952-54. Mem. Soc. C.P.C.U.s, Soc. C.L.U.s, Kiwanis (bd. dirs. 1973-74), Masons, Shriners. Republican. Presbyterian. Home: 4 Lucille Lane Normal IL 61761 Office: State Farm Fire & Casualty Co 112 E Washington Bloomington IL 61701

COVEY, RONALD HARRY, JR., banker; b. Manchester, N.H., May 16, 1956; s. Ronald H. and Elaine Rita (Guerrette) C.; m. Maryjo McKenney, Aug. 7, 1983; children: Shana, Dwire. BS in Bus. Adminstrn., U. N.H., 1978; MBA in Acctg., N.H. Coll., 1982. Comml. credit analyst BankEast, Manchester, N.H., 1978-80, comml. loan officer, 1982-85, v.p. comml. lending, 1982-85; sr. v.p. sr. loan officer Numerica Savs. Bank, Manchester, 1985—; bd. dirs. Granite State Econ. Devel., Portsmouth, N.H., 1983—; prof. continuing edn. N.H. Coll., Manchester, 1983-86. Bd. dirs. The Mental Health Ctr. of Greater Manchester. Mem. Am. Inst. Banking (bd. govs.

Manchester chpt. 1983—), Robert Morris Assocs., Am. Bankers Assn., Manchester C. of C. Republican. Roman Catholic. Home: 11 Camelot Dr Hooksett NH 03106 Office: Numerica Savs Bank 1155 Elm St Manchester NH 03105

COVINGTON, CALVIN BLACKWELL, agricultural association administrator; b. Winston-Salem, N.C., Sept. 24, 1955; s. Calvin Roger and Ruth (Walker) C.; m. Lorraine Simms, Mar. 29, 1980. BS, N.C. State U., 1977. Area rep. Am. Jersey Cattle Club, Columbus, Ohio, 1977-78, equity specialist, 1978-82, exec. asst., 1982-84, asst. sec., 1984—, treas., 1985—; gen. mgr. Am. Jersey Cattle Club, Columbus, 1988—; lectr. on milk mktg. to groups in U.S. and abroad; participant in Ohio State U. Agr. Leadership Edn. and Devel. program. Contbr. articles to profl. jours. Mem. World Jersey Bur., Dairy Shrine, N.C. State Wolfpack Club, N.C. State Alumni Assn., Wis. Jersey Breeder Assn. (Disting. Service award 1987), Reynoldsburg C. of C. Republican. Methodist. Office: Am Jersey Cattle Club 6486 E Main St Reynoldsburg OH 43068

COVINGTON, DONALD KINGSLEY, JR., plywood sales executive; b. Newport News, Va., May 28, 1920; s. Donald Kingsley and Jessie Alexandria (MacNeill) C.; B.S. in Aero. Engring., Parks Coll., St. Louis U., 1941; postgrad. U. Md., 1942; m. Minnie Virginia Seay, Mar. 13, 1943; children: Donald Kingsley III, Duncan Seay. Cert. Sales Exec. Engring. draftsman to project flight test engr. Glenn L. Martin Co., Balt., 1942-48; successively asst. sales mgr., sales mgr., gen. sales mgr., dir. and sec., pres. Harbor Sales Co., Inc., Balt., 1948—. Bd. dirs. YMCA Greater Balt. Area, 1963-78; trustee Md. Masonic Homes, 1982-85, 88-90; pres. Sales Exec. Council of Balt. Assn. Commerce, 1958. Lic. mechanic; cert. pvt. pilot. Mem. Sales and Mktg. Execs. Internat. (v.p., dir., Outstanding Service award 1981, 86), Sash and Door Jobbers Assn. (dir.), Forest Products Research Soc., Exptl. Aircraft Assn., Sales and Mktg. Execs. Balt. (hon., trustee Accreditation Inst. 1988—), Sales Execs. Council Balt. (past pres.), Research Inst. Am. (charter), So. Sash and Door Jobber Assn. (past dir.), Ponderosa Pine Woodwork Assn., AIAA, Inst. Aero. Scis. (past sec. Balt. sect.), Balt.-Washington Lumber Sales Club, numerous others. Republican. Methodist. Clubs: Salmagundi, Masons (past master, past pres. Knights of Mecca, sr. grand warden Grand Lodge of Md.). Office: 1401 Russell St Baltimore MD 21230

COWAN, CARY L., publishing company executive; b. Bklyn., Nov. 8, 1936; s. Sanford R. and Sylvia M. (Lichtenberg) C.; m. Edith Buchter, July 3, 1960; children: Scott, Robin, Michael. Student, N.Y.C. Prodn. mgr., v.p. Cowan Publishing Corp., N.Y.C., 1959-81; prodn. mgr. Tech. Pub., Port Washington, N.Y., 1981-86, PennWell Pub., Port Washington, 1987—. Mgr. Little League, Great Neck, N.Y., 1959-60, Bayside, N.Y., 1960-65, Stony Brook, N.Y., 1966-85. 2d class petty officer USN, 1956-59. Home: 4 Parish Ct Stony Brook NY 11790 Office: PennWell Pub 14 Vanderventer Ave Port Washington NY 11050

COWAN, DEBORAH ANN, chemical engineer; b. Sacramento, June 26, 1955; d. Donald Raymond and Genevieve Marie Wilson; m. Robert John Cowan, Apr. 15, 1978; children: Elizabeth Marie, Natalie Joy. BS in Chem. Engring., Calif. Inst. Tech., 1977. Registered profl. engr., Calif. Engr. C.F. Braun & Co., Alhambra, Calif., 1977-79, sr. engr., 1980-85; engr. Ralph M. Parsons, Pasadena, 1979-80; v.p. software Lost Voltigeur Enterprises, San Dimas, Calif., 1985—; mgmt. systems spl. sr. Gen. Dynamics, Pomona, Calif., 1986—; registered VAR, Ashton-Tate, Torrance, Calif., 1985—. Choir mem. LaVerne Heights Presbyn. Ch., Calif., 1984—. Mem. Am. Inst. Chem. Engrs. Republican. Christian Ch.

COWAN, WALLACE EDGAR, lawyer; b. Jersey City, Jan. 28, 1924; s. Benjamin and Dorothy (Zunz) C.; m. Ruth Daitzman, June 8, 1947; children: Laurie, Paul, Judith. BS magna cum laude, NYU, 1947; JD cum laude, Harvard U., 1950. Ptnr. Stroock, Stroock & Lavan (attys.), N.Y.C., 1950—; sec., dir. Ametek, Inc., N.Y.C. ; sec. Marshall Cavendish Corp., Freeport, N.Y., H.S. Stuttman Inc., Westport, Conn. Mem. Teaneck (N.J.) Adv. Bd. on Parks, Playgrounds and Recreation, 1966—, chmn., 1974—; pres. No. Valley Commuters Assn.; v.p., trustee Congregation Beth Sholom, Teaneck. Served to 1st lt. USAF, 1942-45, ETO. Decorated Air medal with silver cluster. Mem. Am. Bar Assn., N.Y. State Bar Assn., Beta Gamma Sigma. Home: 499 Emerson Ave Teaneck NJ 07666 Office: Stroock Stroock & Lavan 7 Hanover Sq New York NY 10004

COWELL, JOE BARRIE, material handling company executive; b. Rice Lake, Wis., May 21, 1935; s. Robert E. and Winifred R. (Dunbar) C.; m. Carol L. Cronin, Sept. 12, 1958 (div. Sept. 1970); children: Dagny C., Danielle C.; m. Valorie Ann Lucas, Nov. 20, 1971; 1 child, Christopher S. B in Mining Engring., U. Minn., 1959, postgrad., 1960. Cert. material handling engr. With Kimberly Clark Corp., N.Y.C. and Neenah (Wis.), 1961-63; plant supr. Crown Zellerbach Corp., Carthage, N.Y., 1963-64; indsl. engr. Am. Can Co., N.Y.C., 1964-67; sr. indsl. engr. Am. Can Co., San Francisco, 1967-71; plant supr. Am. Can Co., Rochester, N.Y., 1971-72; mgr. material handling and packaging systems Am. Can Co., Greenwich, Conn., 1972-79; maj. account sales mgr. Cascade Corp., Portland, Oreg., 1979-83, sales mgr., 1983—. Contbr. articles to profl. jours. Mem. Nat. Account Mktg. Assn. (bd. dirs. 1984—, pres. 1988—, Chpt. Chmn. award 1984, 85), Warehouse Edn. and Research Council, Inst. Indsl. Engrs., Sales Execs. Club N.Y. Republican. Club: Danbury Yacht. Lodge: Lions. Office: Cascade Corp PO Box 20187 Portland OR 97220

COWEN, BRUCE DAVID, environmental services company executive; b. Springfield, Mass., Jan. 19, 1953; s. Irving Abraham and Pearl (Glushien) C.; m. Judith Paterson, July 2, 1983. BS in Bus. Adminstrn., Am. Internat. Coll., 1974. Audit mgr. Price Waterhouse & Co., Hartford, Conn., 1974-79; controller TRC Environ. Cons., Inc., East Hartford, Conn., 1979-85; treas., sec. TRC Cos., Inc., East Hartford, 1980—; sr. v.p., chief fin. officer TRC Cos., Inc. and TRC Environ. Cons., Inc., 1985—; pres., chmn. bd. Alliance Techs. Corp., Bedford, Mass., 1987—; dir. TRC Cos., Inc., Halcyon, Ltd., Hartford, Conn., Synergistic Capital Inc., 1984; Chmn. Sammy Davis, Jr. Greater Hartford Open PGA Golf Tournament, 1984; mem. Conn. Gaming Policy Bd., 1987—; commr. Conn. Cen. Commn. for Statue of Liberty and Ellis Island, 1985—. CPA, Conn. Mem. Am. Inst. CPAs, Nat. Assn. Accts., Nat. Assn. Security Dealers (info. com. of bd. govs.), Hartford Jaycees. Republican. Jewish. Home: 117 Knob Hill Rd Glastonbury CT 06033 Office: 800 Connecticut Blvd East Hartford CT 06248

COWEN, DAVID SIMON, software consultant, musician; b. Chgo., July 20, 1950; s. Harold Allen and Augusta (Greenspan) C.; m. Wendy Joan Segal, July 13, 1986; 1 child, Leah Shoshanah. BA in English Lit., Yale U., 1972; BSME with high hons., U. Ill., Chgo., 1977; MBA, U. Chgo., 1984. Cellist Chgo. Civic Symphony, 1972-73; energy researcher U. Ill., Chgo., 1976-77; energy analyst Inst. Gas Tech., Chgo., 1977-81; sr. assoc. A.T. Kearney, Inc., Chgo., 1981-82; prin. Strategic Decisions, Chgo., 1985-87; cellist The Mostly Haydn Trio, Chgo., 1986—; lectr. Northwestern U., 1988—; pres. Ariel Cons., Chgo., 1984—; cellist in concert series Civic Theatre, Chgo., 1986—. Author software programs; contbr. articles to profl. jours. Mem. Chgo. Area Relational Database Users Group (sec.), Musicians' Union. Democrat. Jewish. Home and Office: 7446 N Hoyne Ave Chicago IL 60645

COWGILL, F(RANK) BROOKS, insurance company executive; b. Huntington Park, Calif., Mar. 16, 1932; s. Frank H. and Henriette J. (Dickey) C.; m. Mary Lucena Hanna, Dec. 22, 1954; children: David B., Ann M. A.B., Stanford U., 1954, M.B.A., 1956. Analyst treas.'s dept. Exxon Corp., N.Y.C., 1958-61; sr. analyst treas.'s dept. WR Grace Co., Cambridge, Mass., 1961-62; with New England Mut. Life Ins. Co., Boston, 1962—; v.p., treas. New England Mut. Life Ins. Co., 1979—. Served to 1st lt. U.S. Army, 1956-58. Mem. Inst. Chartered Fin. Analysts, Boston Security Analysts Soc. Clubs: Boston Econ. (Boston), Treasurers (Boston). Office: New Eng Mut Life Ins Co 501 Boylston St Boston MA 02117

COWIE, ROBERT ARTHUR, manufacturing company executive; b. N.Y.C., Aug. 14, 1933; s. Robert A. and Lenore Cowie; m. Vanne Shelley, Apr. 23, 1960; children: Anne, Robert, Ronald. BME, Cornell U., 1956, MBA, 1957; postgrad. Advanced mgmt. program, Harvard U., 1977. Registered profl. engr., N.Y., Pa. Systems engr. Sperry Gyroscope, Great Neck, N.Y., 1957-59; pres. C&M Spring Co., Long Island, N.Y., 1959-71; instr. mgmt. devel. Pa. State U., Univ. Park, 1968; gen. mgr. Chassis Products div. Dana Corp., Toledo, Ohio, 1971-75; v.p., gen. mgr. Spicer F.D.S. div. Dana Corp., Toledo, 1976-79; v.p. pub. affairs Dana Corp., Toledo, 1979—. Vice chmn. Cornell U. Exec. Com., trustee Cornell U. Bd. Dirs., Ithaca, N.Y., 1973—; chmn. Indiana U. Bd. Visitors, Sch. Pub. and Environ. Affairs, Bloomington, Ind., 1980—; com. mem. Lucas County United Way, 1981—; chmn. Pub. Affairs Council Machinery and Allied Products Inst., Washington, 1987-88, 88-89; trustee Parkview Hosp., Toledo, 1984—. Mem. Soc. Automotive Engrs. Republican. Home: 2521 Underhill Rd Toledo OH 43615 Office: Dana Corp PO Box 1000 Toledo OH 43697

COWLES, ED BURTON, tax company executive; b. Roseburg, Oreg., May 20, 1935; s. Earl C. Cowles and Florence Talcott. Student, Clark Coll., 1965-67. Owner, mgr. Adjust Your Debts Inc., Vancouver, Wash., 1964-69, Space Age Fiber Enterprise, Vancouver, 1966-78, CMS Tax & Bookkeeping, Vancouver, 1966—; ptnr. Quick Tune, Vancouver, 1975-77. Author: Business Preview, 1976. Served with U.S. Army, 1958-59. Mem. Toastmasters (past pres.). Home and Office: CMS Tax & Bookkeeping 6501 NE St Johns Rd Vancouver WA 98661-1296

COWLEY, SAMUEL PARKINSAN, utility company executive, lawyer; b. Washington, Mar. 29, 1934; s. Samuel Parkinson and Lavon (Chipman) C.; m. Carole Cook, June 9, 1958; children: Samuel, Christina, Nicole, Peter, Mathias. BS, U. Utah, 1958; JD, George Washington U., 1962. Bar: Utah 1962, U.S. Dist. Ct. Utah 1962, Nev. 1964, U.S. Dist. Ct. Nev. 1964, Mo. 1974, U.S. Dist. Ct. (we. dist.) Mo. 1975, U.S. Supreme Ct. 1980. V.p., gen. counsel Nev. Power Co., Las Vegas, 1965-74; asst. gen. counsel Kans. City (Mo.) Power and Light Co., 1974-77, gen. counsel, 1977-79, v.p., corp. sec., 1979-83, sr. v.p., corp. sec., chief legal officer, 1983—; bd. dirs. Wymo Fuels Inc., Kansas City, Red Hill Coal Co., Gillette, Wyo, Utility Fuel Co., Wichita, Kans. Mem. Homestead Country, Sigma Nu. Republican. Mormon. Club: Kansas City. Office: Kans City Power & Light Co 1330 Baltimore Ave Kansas City MO 64105

COWLEY, WILLIAM EUGENE, manufacturing company executive; b. Stithton, Ky., May 29, 1909; s. William G. and Emma Grooms (Henderson) C.; m. Margaret Ruth Baron, Jan. 25, 1944; children: William E., Margaret A., Claire E., Michael Thomas, John P., James K. B.S. in Mech. Engring, U. Ky., 1934. Mech. enr. Detroit Lubricator Co., 1934-40; mech. engr. Am. Elevator & Machinery Co., Louisville, 1946-48; chief engr. Am. Saw and Tool Co., Louisville, 1948-58; v.p engring. Vt. American Corp., Louisville, 1958-71, exec. v.p. engring., 1971-87, also dir. Served to lt. col. AUS, 1940-46. Decorated Legion of Merit. Democrat. Baptist. Club: Jefferson. Office: Vt Am Corp 715 E Gray St Louisville KY 40202

COWMAN, EDWARD FLOYD, insurance company executive; b. Des Moines, Mar. 16, 1942; s. Harlan Floyd and Eva Mae (deHaai) C.; m. Judith Ann Waddle, June 15, 1962; children: Jeffrey Edward, Darla Judith, Brent Nelson, Shaun Eric. BA, U. Iowa, 1964. With Bankers Life, Des Moines, 1965-71; systems analyst Preferred Risk Life, West Des Moines, 1971-73, systems actuary, 1977-79; v.p., actuary Bankers Mut. Life, Freeport, Ill., 1979-82; exec. v.p., actuary Bankers Mut. Life, Freeport, 1982-83, pres., actuary, 1983—. Bd. dirs. United Way of Freeport, 1984—. Mem. Soc. Actuaries (editorial bd. of the Record 1984—, com. on continuing edn. 1987—), Am. Acad. Actuaries, Rotary, Phi Beta Kappa. Republican. Home: 1344 Empire Ct Freeport IL 61032 Office: Bankers Mut Life 500 W South St Freeport IL 61032

COWSERT, THEO DALE, electronics executive; b. Jackson, Miss., Aug. 18, 1943; s. Theo Robert and Jimmy Faye (West) C.; m. Meadrith Jewel Kirby, Sept. 18, 1974; children: Jason, Jessica. AS, Perkinson Jr. Coll., 1963; BS, U. So. Miss., 1983. Pres. Robotics Tech., Inc., Grand Prairie, Tex., 1981-88, Gulfport, Miss., 1988—. Contbr. articles to profl. jours. Mem. Spokesman's Club (pres. Biloxi, Miss. chpt. v.p. 1988—). Office: Robotics Tech Inc 1412 35th Ave Gulfport MS 39501

COX, ALLAN J., management consultant; b. Berwyn, Ill., June 13, 1937; s. Brack C. and Ruby D. C.; m. Jeanne Begalke, 1961 (div. 1966); 1 child, Heather; m. Bonnie Lynne Welden, 1966; 1 child, Laura. B.A., No. Ill. U., 1961, M.A., 1962. Instr. Wheaton (Ill.) Coll., 1963-65; assoc. Case and Co., Inc., Chgo., 1965-66, Spencer Stuart & Assos., Inc., Chgo., 1966-68; v.p. Westcott Assos., Inc., Chgo., 1968-69; founder, pres. Allan Cox & Assocs., Inc., 1969—; adj. staff Ctr. for Creative Leadership, Greensboro, N.C. Author: Confessions of a Corporate Headhunter, 1973, Work, Love and Friendship, 1974, The Cox Report on the American Corporation, 1982, The Making of the Achiever, 1985, The Achiever's Profile, 1988; also articles. Chmn. bd. Ctr. for Ethics and Corp. Policy; elder Fourth Presbyterian Ch. of Chgo. Mem. Am. Sociol. Assn., N.Am. Soc. Adlerian Psychology, Human Resources Mgmt. Assn. of Chgo., ASTD, Midwest Human Resources Planners Group, Am. Group Psychotherapy Assn., Alpha Kappa Delta. Presbyterian. Clubs: Chgo.; University (N.Y.C.). Office: 400 N Michigan Ave Chicago IL 60611

COX, ANDREW PAUL, JR., data systems company executive; b. Balt., Aug. 27, 1937; s. Andrew Paul and Laura (Streett) C.; m. Trudy Ann Forsythe, June 27, 1959; children—Michael P., Julie A., Daniel P. B.S. in Elec. Engring., Johns Hopkins U., 1959; M.S., 1970. Registered profl. engr., Md. Sr. engr. Westinghouse Electric Corp., Balt., 1960-68; mgr. mktg. IBM, Richmond, Va., 1968-80; pres., chief exec. officer Data Systems Corp., Richmond, 1980—, dir. Data Systems Holding Co. Patentee efficient computer device, 1968. Vice-pres. Lake Patrick Henry Civic Assn., Midlothian, Va., 1979. 1st lt. AUS, 1959-62. Mem. Assn. Info. Mgrs. (v.p. 1983-84, pres. 1984-85, bd. dirs. 1981-87). Republican. Presbyterian (deacon 1983-86). Clubs: Midlothian Rotary (pres. 1985., bd. dirs. 1984-87, Paul Harris fellow 1986), Salisbury Country (bd. dirs., past v.p.). Home: 2821 W Brigstock Rd Midlothian VA 23113 Office: Data Systems Corp 8827 Staples Mill Rd Richmond VA 23228

COX, ARCHIBALD, JR., investment banker; b. Framingham, Mass., July 13, 1940; s. Archibald and Phyllis (Ames) C.; m. Cornelia Sharp, Aug., 1962 (div. July 1977); children: Suzanne, Archibald III; m. Jean Inge, Aug. 20, 1977; 1 child, Christopher. AB, Harvard U., 1962, MBA, 1964. Assoc. Morgan Stanley & Co., Inc., N.Y.C., 1964-70, v.p., 1971-72, mng. dir., 1973-88; mng. dir. Morgan Stanley Internat., London, 1977-88. Mem. Internat. Primary Market Assn. (vice chmn. 1984-86), Securities & Investments Bd. Ltd. (bd. dirs. 1986-88). Clubs: N.Y. Yacht, Piping Rock (Locust Valley, N.Y.). Home: Annfield Rt 3 Box 5325 Berryville VA 22611

COX, BENJAMIN VINCENT, electrical engineer; b. Chgo., Jan. 25, 1934; s. Benjamin and Lorretta Deloris (Jozwiak) C.; BS in Elec. Engring., U. Utah, 1963, MS, 1969, PhD, 1979; m. Mary Patricia Mitchell, Apr. 18, 1959; children: Linda Marie, Stephen Martin. With Sperry Univac Co. (now UNISYS), 1963-73, 74—, staff engr., 1974-78, engring. mgr., advanced research and devel., dir. advanced tech., Salt Lake City, 1978—; engring. dir. Naval Civil Engring. Lab., Port Hueneme, Calif., 1973-74; adj. prof. U. Utah. Served with U.S. Army, 1954-57. Recipient Utah Gov.'s medal for Sci. and Tech., 1987, Unisys fellow award, 1988. Mem. AIAA (council Utah chpt. 1980-81), IEEE, Am. Def. Preparedness Assn., Air Force Assn., Assn. Old Crows. Author papers, reports in field. Home: 2760 E Blue Spruce Dr Salt Lake City UT 84117 Office: Sperry Univac Co 640 N Sperry Way Salt Lake City UT 84116-2988

COX, CHARLES C., federal official; b. Missoula, Mont., May 8, 1945. BA, U. Wash., 1967; AM, U. Chgo., 1970, PhD, 1975. Asst. prof. econs. Ohio State U., Columbus, 1972-80; asst. prof. mgmt. Tex. A&M U., College Station, 1980-82; chief economist SEC, Washington, 1982-83, commr., 1984—. Nat. fellow Hoover Institution, 1977-78. Office: SEC 450 5th St NW Washington DC 20549

COX, DAVID CARSON, media company executive; b. Orange City, N.J., July 31, 1937; s. Earl Byron and Ruth Elinor (Carson) C.; m. Vicki Bever, Aug. 29, 1958; children: Brian Bever, Carson Burns. AB magna cum laude with honors in Econs., Stanford U., 1959; MBA, Harvard U., 1961. V.p., gen. mgr. Lawry's Foods, Inc., Los Angeles and Paris, 1962-75, Litton Microwave Co., Mpls., 1975-79, Toro Co., Mpls., 1979-81; exec. v.p., chief operating officer Cowles Media Co., Mpls., 1981-85, pres., chief operating officer, treas., 1984-85; pres., chief exec. officer Cowles Media Co., 1985—, corp. sec., 1983-84, dir., 1982—; bd. dirs. Nat. Computer Systems, Mpls., Northwestern Nat. Life Ins. Co., Mpls., Industry Square Devel. Co., Mpls. Bd. dirs. Spring Hill Ctr., 1981—; bd. dirs. Guthrie Theater, 1977-86, v.p., 1982, pres., 1983-85, chmn., 1985—; bd. dirs. Minn. Bus. Partnership, Inc., 1985—, Bus. Execs. for Nat. Security, 1988—. Lt. U.S. Army, 1962-64. Mem. Am. Newspaper Publishers Assn. (telecommunications com. 1985—), Greater Mpls. C. of C. (bd. dirs. 1981—, exec. com. 1985, 1st vice chmn. 1986, vice chmn. transp. div. 1986—, chmn. 1987), Council Fgn. Relations Mpls., Harvard Bus. Sch. Club, Stanford Alumni Club, Mpls. Club. Club: Minneapolis. Office: Cowles Media Co 329 Portland Ave Minneapolis MN 55415

COX, DOUGLAS LYNN, financial corporation executive; b. Des Moines, Dec. 13, 1945; s. Carol Eugene and Maribelle (Harter) C.; B.S., U. Pa., 1968, M.B.A., 1973; m. Janice C. Kuchka, Nov. 15, 1969; children: David Michael, Kristen Anne. With IU Internat. Corp., Phila., 1974-88 , treasury assoc. long term fin., 1974-76, sr. treasury assoc. internat. fin., 1976-77, mgr. internat. fin., 1977-79, dir. treasury planning, 1979-80, asst. treas., 1980-85, v.p. and treas., 1985-88; sr. v.p. fin., chief fin. officer Pennwalt Corp., Phila., 1988—. Class gift chmn. U. Pa.; bd. dirs. Big Bros., Big Sisters; treas. Old Pine St. Presbyn. Ch.; bd. govs. Pa. Econ. League. With USCG, 1969-72. Decorated Gallantry Cross (S. Vietnam). Club: Phi Kappa Sigma (pres. bd. trustees Alpha chpt.) Home: 1220 Rodman St Philadelphia PA 19147 Office: Pennwalt Corp 3 Parkway Philadelphia PA 19102

COX, GLENN ANDREW, JR., petroleum company executive; b. Sedalia, Mo., Aug. 6, 1929; s. Glenn Andrew and Ruth Lonsdale (Atkinson) C.; m. Veronica Cecelia Martin, Jan. 3, 1953; children: Martin Stuart, Grant Andrew, Cecelia Ruth. BBA, So. Meth. U., 1951. With Phillips Petroleum Co., Bartlesville, Okla., 1956—; asst. to chmn. operating com. Phillips Petroleum Co., Bartlesville, 1973-74, v.p. mgmt. info. and control, 1974-80, exec. v.p., 1980-85, dir., 1982—, pres., chief operating officer, 1985—. Pres. Cherokee Area coun. Boy Scouts Am., 1977-82, S. Cen. Region, 1987—, mem. nat. exec. bd. 1987—; bd. curators Cen. Meth. Coll., Fayette, Mo., 1984-88, trustee, 1988—; trustee Philbrook Mus. Art, 1987—. Served as pilot USAF, 1951-55. Mem. Am. Petroleum Inst. (bd. dirs.), Nat. Assn. Mfrs. (bd. dirs.), Bartlesville Area C. of C. (pres. 1978), Hillcrest Country Club. Methodist. Office: Phillips Petroleum Co 4th & Keeler Bartlesville OK 74004

COX, HOWARD ELLIS, JR., venture capitialist; b. N.Y.C., Feb. 1, 1944; s. Howard Ellis and Anne Delafield (Finch) C.; m. Julia Bolton Dempsey, Oct. 31, 1970. BA, Princeton U., 1964; JD, Columbia U., 1967; MBA, Harvard U., 1969. Bar: N.Y. 1967. Co-mng. ptnr. Greylock, Boston, 1971—; bd. dirs. Arbor Health Care, Lima, Ohio, Rehab. Systems, Camp Hill, Pa., BMR Fin., Atlanta, Greylock Mgmt. Corp., Boston, Lunar, Madison, Wis., Summation, Kirkland, Wash., Stryker, Kalamazoo. bd. dirs. Preuss Found., San Diego, 1986—; trustee Dana Farber Cancer Inst., 1987—; v.p., trustee Assn. Relief of the Elderly, N.Y.C., 1985—. Served to capt. U.S. Army, 1969-71. Mem. New England Venture Capital. Assn. (pres. 1986—), Bus. Assocs. Club, Boston (pres. 1979-80). Episcopalian. Home: 225 Sargent Rd Brookline MA 02146 Office: Greylock Mgmt Corp One Federal St Boston MA 02110

COX, JAMES CARL, JR., chemist, researcher, consultant; b. Wolf Summit, W.Va., June 17, 1919; s. James Carl and Maggie Lillian (Merrells) C.; m. Alma Lee Tenney, Sept. 8, 1945; children: James Carl III, Joseph Merrells, Alma Lee, Elizabeth Susan Cox Unger, Albert John. BS summa cum laude, W.Va. Wesleyan Coll., 1940; MS in Organic Chemistry, U. Del., 1947, PhD in Phys. Organic Chemistry, 1949; postgrad. in law Am. U., summer 1953, George Washington U., summer 1954; JD with honors, U. Md., 1955. Bar: Md. 1955. Registered profl. sanitarian, Tex. Rsch. chemist E.I. duPont de Nemours Corp., Belle, W.Va., 1940-43; grad. instr. chemistry U. Del., Newark, 1946-49; prof. chemistry, head dept. chemistry Wesleyan Coll., Mason, Ga., 1949-51; prof. U.S. Naval Acad., Annapolis, Md., 1951-55; prof., rsch.dir. Lamar U., Beaumont, Tex., 1955-65; prof., head dept. chemistry, dir. div. sci. and math. Oral Roberts U. Tulsa, 1965-68; prof., head dept. chemistry Wayland Baptist U., Plainview, Tex., 1968-76; v.p., rsch. dir. Agrl. & Indsl. Devel., Inc., Plainview, 1976-79; environ. health expert Tex. Dept. Health, Plainview, 1979-84; mem. W. Tex. indsl. planning commn., commdr. 19th dist. Dept Tex.; cons. in field; vis. prof. organic chemistry Middle Tenn. State U., Murfreesboro, summer 1950, U. Baghdad, Iraq, 1956-57. Author: Lives of Splendor, 1970; Patterson's German-English Chemical Dictionary, rev. edit., 1985; contbr. articles to profl. jours., also abstracts. Editor The Condenser, 1957-65. Precinct chmn. Hale County Rep., Plainview, 1983-84; bd. dirs. Plainview chpt. ARC, 1969-73, United Way, Plainview, 1972-75. Served to cpl. Combat Engrs., U.S. Army, 1943-45, ETO. Named Outstanding Prof., Lamar U., 1963-64, Wayland Bapt. U., 1971-74; fellow DuPont Endowment Found., 1947-49, Carnegie Found., 1949-51, State of Tex., 1957-59. Fellow Tex. Acad. Sci.; mem. Am. Chem. Soc., AAAS, AAUP, Tex. Pub. Health Assn., Tex. Environ. Health Assn. (governing council 1982-84), Am. Legion (adj.) DAV (chmn. Americanism, judge adv.), VFW (vice commdr.). Methodist. Lodge: Rotary (pub. relations officer 1969-84). Current work: Novel fuels for industry; agricultural chemicals. Subspecialties: Organic chemistry; Polymer chemistry.

COX, JOHN LEE, security management consultant; b. El Paso, Tex., May 5, 1944; s. Edwin Lee and Dorothy (Bissell) C.; m. Darlene Marie Allen, Aug. 6, 1966 (div. Dec. 1976); children: Shawn, Andrew, Bret; m. Karen Hern, July 8, 1978; stepchildren: Dawn, Amy, Robert Porter. BS, Pacific So., 1972, MS, 1974. Police officer City of Blythe (Calif.), 1965-69; police detective City of Palm Springs (Calif.), 1969-75; mgr. internat. graphics Div. Moore Bus. Forms, Portland, Oreg., 1978-80; owner Cox Agy., Palm Springs, 1975-78; chief exec. officer F.S.M.G., Inc., Portland, 1978—. 1st lt. USAF, 1962-64, Vietnam. Republican. Mormon. Home: 1833 NE 148 Portland OR 97230 Office: FSMG Inc 4187 SE Division St Portland OR 97202

COX, JOSEPH MERRELLS, II, chemical company executive; b. Macon, Ga., Dec. 18, 1949; s. James Carl Jr. and Alma Lee (Tenney) C.; m. Nancy Parker, June 5, 1971; children: Catherine G., Elizabeth M. BSChemE, Vanderbilt U., 1971; MS in Engring. Mgmt., Boston U., 1974; MBA, U. Houston, 1986. Registered profl. engr., Tex., Va.; cert. fin. planner. Prodn. engr. Clorox Co., Houston, 1977; project-process engr. Brown & Root Inc., Houston, 1977-81; project engr. Foster Wheeler, Houston, 1981-82; sr. project engr. Matthew Hall Engrs., Houston, 1982; account exec. Dean Witter Reynolds Inc., Houston, 1983-88; project mgr. Allstates Design & Devel. Co. subs. DuPont Co., Houston, 1988—. Maj. U.S. Army, 1971-77. Mem. Am. Chem. Soc., Am. Inst. Chem. Engrs., Kiwanis (pres. local chpt. 1987—). Home: 3207 Flaming Candle Spring TX 77388

COX, LESTER LEE, broadcasting executive; b. Springfield, Mo., Nov. 6, 1922; s. Lester Edmund and Mildred Belle (Lee) C.; m. Claudine Viola Barrett, Jan. 19, 1946; 1 son, Lester Barrett. A.B. in Econs., Westminster Coll., 1944, LL.D., 1974; postgrad., U.S. Mil. Acad., 1944-46; M.B.A., Drury Coll., 1965. Pres. Springfield TV, Inc. (KYTV), 1952-79, K.C. Air Conditioning, North Kansas City, 1968-85; Pres., Mid-Continent Telecasting, Inc. (KOAM-TV), Pittsburg, Kans., 1958-85, Pittsburg Broadcasting Co. (KOAM); Pres., Ozark Motor & Supply Co., Springfield, Modern Tractor & Supply Co.; bd. dirs. Commerceshares, Inc., Kansas City, Mo., TWA.; chmn. Ozark Air Lines, 1972-86. Mem. Mo. Bd. Health, 1968-73, past chmn.; mem. Commn. on Higher Edn. for Mo., 1977-83; pres. Ozark Empire council Boy Scouts Am., 1960; chmn. bd. Lester E. Cox Med. Ctr.; bd. dirs. Westminster Coll., 1949-79, Drury Coll., 1965-79, Midwest Research Inst., Kansas City. Served with AUS, 1943-46, to; capt. 1951-53. Recipient Silver Beaver award Boy Scouts Am., 1961; named Hon. col. Gov. of Mo., 1960-64, 68-72. Mem. Central States Shrine Assn. (pres. 1970). Club: Hickory Hills Country. Lodges: Masons, Shriners. Office: Ozark Airlines INc Lambert Field Saint Louis MO 63145

COX, MARSDEN HAIGH, III, insurance agent; b. Dillon, S.C., Aug. 14, 1950; s. Marsden Haigh Jr. and Lavinia Merle (Bethea) C.; m. Mary Boyle

Haselden, June 28, 1975; children: Mary Kristen, Marsden Haigh IV. BBA, The Citadel, 1972; postgrad. in law, U. S.C., 1972-73, MS in Accountancy, 1974; cert., Coll. Fin. Planning, 1987. Acct. Pee Dee Oil Co., Inc., Latta, S.C., 1975-76, v.p., 1977-82; acct. C.C. McGregor and Co., Columbia, S.C., 1976-77; pres. Service Ins. Agy., Inc., Latta, 1982—. Named one of Outstanding Young Man of Am., 1978. Mem. Inst. Cert. Fin. Planners, Carolinas Assn. Profl. Ins. Agts., Latta Merchants Assn. (pres. 1984, 85), Rotary, Mason. Methodist. Home: PO Box 144 106 Highland Dr Latta SC 29565 Office: Svc Ins Agy Inc 110 E Main St Latta SC 29565

COX, MARVIN M., JR., finance executive, corporate officer; b. Kingman, Kans., Nov. 19, 1953; s. Marvin M. Sr. and Willa J. (Huddleston) C.; m. Barbara J. Bodecker, Oct. 6, 1979; 1 child, Andrew Michael. BBA, U. Kans., 1975. Mem. dept. acctg. First Securities Co. Kans. Inc., Wichita, 1975-76, cashier, 1975-76, account rep., 1976—, v.p., 1982-87, also bd. dirs., v.p., corp. sec., 1984-87, exec. v.p., corp. sec., 1987—. Mem. Wichita Art Assn., Wichita Symphony Orch., Wichita Salvation Army; chmn., precinct capt. Rep. Cen. Com.; chmn. various coms. City of Wichita, 1980—. Mem. Fin. Analysts Fedn., Wichita C. of C., U. Kans. Alumni Assn., Wichita Downtown Club, Tallgrass Country Club. Office: First Securities Co 100 N Main Ste 200 Wichita KS 67202

COX, RONALD FREY, educator, academic administrator; b. Lebanon, Pa., Aug. 15, 1938. BBA, Pa. State U., 1969; MBA, Ohio U., 1971; PhD, U.S. Internat. U., 1978. CPA, Pa. With Laventhol and Horwath, Harrisburg, Pa., 1964-70; asst. prof. hospitality mgmt. Bryant Coll., Smithfield, R.I., 1972-76; asst. prof. bus. Providence Coll., 1978-80; assoc. prof. bus. U.S. Internat. U., London and Africa, 1980-82; assoc. prof. hospitality mgmt. Purdue U., West Lafayette, Ind., 1982-83; dir. hospitality mgmt. Bethune Cookman Coll., Daytona Beach, Fla., 1983-88, N.Mex. State U., Las Cruces, 1988—; cons. in field. With USN, 1956-60. Mem. ASTD, Hotel and Restaurant Assn., Council Hotel and Restaurant Trainers, Las Cruces C. of C. Office: N Mex State U Box 3HTS Las Cruces NM 88003

COX, TERRENCE GUY, manufacturing automation executive; b. Revere, Mass., Feb. 29, 1956; s. Thomas Ambrose and Jennie Constance (Meli) C.; m. Therese Marie Paone, Sept. 15, 1979. BS in Fin. cum laude, Babson Coll., 1976, MBA, 1977. Asst. to pres. Standard Bldg. Systems, Inc., Point of Rocks, Md., 1977-80; sr. fin. analyst Nortek, Inc., Cranston, R.I., 1980-82; mgr. new bus. devel. Compo Industries, Waltham, Mass., 1982-83; founder, v.p., chief fin. officer, treas. CAD/CAM Integration, Inc., Woburn, Mass., 1983—, also bd. dirs.; treas., bd. dirs. Encode, Inc., Nashua, N.H. Founder Revere track league, 1974, pres., 1974-77; coach Revere little league, 1969-77; bd. dirs. Revere Parks and Recreation Commn., 1972-74, Boy's Club of Revere, 1974-77. Roman Catholic. Office: CAD/CAM Integration Inc 80 Winn St Woburn MA 01801

COX, TIMOTHY C., service executive; b. Kingstree, S.C., July 11, 1946; s. Theron C. and Ora Lee (Tanner) C.; m. Elizabeth Motte, Dec. 25, 1984; 1 child, Angelia Dian. AA, Palmer Coll., Columbia, S.C., 1969; BS, Francis Marion Coll., Florence, S.C., 1982. Programmer Infitronics, Charlotte, N.C., 1969-71; programmer, operator Santee Electric Coop., Kingstree, 1971-72; sr. programmer S.C. Dept. Social Services, Columbia, 1972-75; host, coordinator Sta. WKSP-Radio, Kingstree, 1979-80; instr. Florence-Darlington Tech. Coll., 1983-85; owner, pres. Exec. Services of the Pee Dee, Florence, 1986—. Bd. dirs. Crimestoppers of the Pee Dee, Florence, 1987—; mem. Handicapped, S.C., 1988. Recipient Mayor's Trophy for Handicapped Citizen of Yr., Florence, 1988. Mem. Am. Diabetes Assn., Jaycees (named Outstanding Jaycee S.C. chpt. 1978). Republican. Club: Civitan (Florence). Office: Exec Svcs of the Pee Dee 256 S Irby St Florence SC 29501

COXE, THOMAS C., III, gas company executive; b. Florence, S.C., Sept. 1, 1930; s. Thomas C. Jr. and Emily Wood (Badham) C.; m. Mary Marshall Ragland; children: Thomas C. IV, Campbell D., E. Ragland, Miles B. BBA, U. N.C., 1952. V.p. Coxe Lumber Co., Darlington, S.C., 1952-70; mgr. forest products div. Sonoco Products Co., Hartsville, S.C., 1970-74, v.p. spl. products div., 1974-77, v.p. corp. devel., 1977-79, sr. v.p. corp. devel., 1979-83, sr. v.p., 1983-85, exec. v.p., 1985—, also bd. dirs.; bd. dirs. S.C. Nat. Bank, Columbia, Peoples Natural Gas Co., Florence, 1st Fed. Savs. and Loan, Darlington. Lay reader St. Matthew's Episc. Ch., Darlington, 1967—. Republican. Home: 601 Cashua Ferry Rd Darlington SC 29532 Office: Sonoco Products Co N 2nd St Hartsville SC 29550 *

COY, DOUGLASS EDWARD, management consultant, restaurant chain executive; b. Mpls., June 23, 1934; s. Craig Leon and Evelyn Adela (Seydel) C.; m. Rahcel Joan Sitter, Aug. 19, 1955; children: Robin Lynn, Wendy Lee. BA, U. Minn., 1956. Br. mgr. Rentco div. Fruehauf Co., Mpls., 1965-67; dist. mgr. Rentco div. Fruehauf Co., Los Angeles, 1967-69; exec. v.p. Transport Body, Inc., Mpls., 1969-72; exec. v.p. Phoenix, Inc., Mpls., 1972-78, chief exec. officer, 1978-82; chief exec. officer Minn. Truck Ctr., Mpls., 1983-84, Griffin Tire, Inc., Mpls., 1984-85, Pfau Tire, Inc., Denton, Tex., 1985-87, Bridgeman's Restaurant, Denton, 1987—, Sternco, Inc., St. Louis Park, Minn., 1987—. Capt. U.S. Army, 1958-68. Mem. Am. Quarter Horse Assn. (bd. dirs. Amarillo chpt. 1980—). Office: Sternco Inc 6009 Wayzata Blvd Ste 113 Saint Louis Park MN 55416

COYLE, ANNE FRANCES, marketing consultant; b. Roscommon, Ireland, July 6, 1942; d. William Francis and Anne Frances (Naughton) C. BA in English, Mt. St. Mary's Coll., Los Angeles, 1971; MA in English, U. So. Calif., Los Angeles, 1974, MS in Edn., 1974, PhD in Edn., 1977. Dist. sales mgr. Tratec-McGraw Hill, Los Angeles, 1981, v.p. devel., 1981-82, v.p. sales, 1982-83; v.p. sales McGraw Hill Tng. System, Del Mar, Calif., 1984-86, v.p. mktg., 1986-87; ind. cons. San Diego, 1987—. Mem. San Diego Zoo Soc., San Diego Mus. of Man. Recipient Product Enhancement award McGraw-Hill Corp., 1984, Best Product Design award Tratec, Inc., 1976-77, Best Product award NSPI L.A. chpt., 1987; named Top Salesperson, Tratec McGraw-Hill, 1980. Mem. Am. Soc. Tng. Dirs., Phi Delta Kappa. Democrat. Roman Catholic. Clubs: Bus. (founder 1984), Toastmasters. Home: 2911 Nutmeg St San Diego CA 92104

COYLE, MARTIN ADOLPHUS, JR., lawyer; b. Hamilton, Ohio, June 3, 1941; s. Martin Adolphus and Lucille Baird C.; m. Sharon Sullivan, Mar. 29, 1969; children: Cynthia Ann, David Martin, Jennifer Ann. BA, Ohio Wesleyan U., 1963; JD summa cum laude, Ohio State U., 1966. Bar: N.Y. 1967. Assoc. Cravath, Swaine & Moore, N.Y.C., 1966-72; chief counsel securities and fin. TRW Inc., Cleve., 1972-73; sr. counsel, asst. sec. TRW Inc., 1973-75, asst. gen. counsel, asst. sec., 1976, asst. gen. counsel, sec., 1976-80, v.p., gen. counsel, sec., 1980—; sec. TRW Found., 1975-80, trustee, 1980—. Co-inventor voting machine. Pres. Judson Retirement Community, 1986-88, trustee; nat. chmn. Ohio Wesleyan U. Assocs., 1987-89; chmn., sec. Martin A. Coyle Found.; trustee Berea Coll., 1989—. Mem. ABA, Am. Soc. Corp. Secs. (pres. Ohio regional group 1978-80, nat. dir. 1981-87, nat. chmn. 1985-86), Assn. Gen. Counsel, Ohio Bar Assn., Bar Assn. Greater Cleve., Cleve. Skating Club, Mayfield Country Club, Union Club. Home: 23175 Laureldale Rd Shaker Heights OH 44122 Office: TRW Inc 1900 Richmond Rd Cleveland OH 44124

COYNE, JAMES KITCHENMAN, III, engineering executive; b. Farmville, Va., Nov. 17, 1946; s. James Kitchenman Jr. and Pearl Beatrice (Black) C.; m. Helen Biddle Mercer, Oct. 24, 1970; children: Alexander, Katherine, Michael. BS, Yale U., 1968; MBA, Harvard U., 1970; LLD (hon.), Spring Garden Coll., 1984. Pres. Coyne Chem. Co., Phila., 1981-83; mem. 97th Congress from 8th Pa. dist. 1981-83; spl. asst. to Pres. White House, Washington, 1983-85; chief exec. officer Am. Cons. Engring. Coun., Washington, 1985-86; pres., founder Am. Tort Reform Assn., Washington, 1986-88; v.p. regional mgr. Roy F. Weston, Inc., Washington, 1988—; lectr. U. Pa., Phila., 1974-78; chmn. Energy Mgmt. Svcs., Phila., 1976-78; bd. dirs. P.B.&S. Chem. Co., Henderson, Ky., Rsch. and Mgmt. Found., Washington; vice chmn. Environ. Study Com., Washington, 1982. Contbr. articles to profl. jours. Del., mem. platform com. Rep. Nat. Conv., Dallas, 1984. Recipient Boy Scout of Yr. award Boy Scouts Am., 1982, Outstanding Pvt. Sector award Am. Legion Exch. Coun., 1986, Disting. Svc. award Am. Tort Reform Assn., 1988. Mem. Former Mem. Congress Assn. (bd. dirs. 1984—), Union League Phila., World Affairs Coun. (bd. dirs. Phila. chpt. 1983-85), Yale Club, Washington Club, Pine Valley Country Club. Office: Roy F Weston Inc 958 L'Enfant Pla SW 6th Fl Washington DC 20024

COZAD, JAMES W., oil company executive; b. Huntington, Ind., Feb. 10, 1927; s. Emmett and Helen (Motz) C.; m. Virginia E. Alley, Nov. 25, 1948; children: J. Michael, Catherine L., W. Scott, Jeffrey A., Amy Jo. BS in Acctg., Ind. U., 1950, LLD (hon.), 1982. With Peat, Marwick, Mitchell, Detroit, 1950-57; treas. Hygrade Food Products, Detroit, 1957-67, Philip Morris, Inc., N.Y.C., 1967-69; v.p., fin. Amoco Oil Co., Chgo., 1969-71; various exec. positions Standard Oil Co. Ind., Chgo., 1971-83; vice chmn. Amoco Corp., Chgo., 1983—, also bd. dirs.; bd. dirs. Continental Bank Corp., Continental Bank, Eli Lilly and Co., GATX Corp., Whitman Corp., USG Corp. Active United Way, Crusade of Mercy, Chgo.; chmn. adv. bd. INROADS, Chgo., Inc.; bd. dirs. Chgo. Med. Sch., Ind. U. Found., Ind. U. Grad. Sch. Bus. Dean's adv. coun., U. Chgo. Coun. on Grad. Sch. of Bus., Lyric Opera of Chgo., Nat. Merit Scholarship Corp., Northwestern Meml. Hosp, Nat. Jr. Achievement, Inc. Served with USN, 1944-46. Clubs: Chgo., Mid-Am., Comml., Glen View, Old Elm Club, Shoreacres. Home: 1205 Central Rd Glenview IL 60025 Office: Amoco Corp 200 E Randolph Dr Chicago IL 60601

COZZOLINO, SALVATORE JAMES, manufacturing company executive; b. New Haven, Sept. 1, 1924; s. Salvatore and Sophia F. (Lungo) C.; m. Rheta Dawn Troostwyk, Apr. 11, 1947; children—Nancy Trewhella, Patricia Whigham, Roger, Peter, Carol Dole. BBA, St. John's U., Bklyn., 1950. Auditor Arthur Andersen & Co., N.Y.C., 1951-56; asst. controller Congoleum Industries, Kearney, N.J., 1956-63, v.p., treas., 1966-70; mktg. rep. IBM, Rochester, N.Y., 1963-66; with Colt Industries, Inc., N.Y.C., 1970—; now exec. v.p., chief fin. officer Colt Industries, Inc.; dir. Mariner Instl. Funds, Inc., N.Y.C., Mariner Tax-Free Instl. Funds, Inc., N.Y.C. Served to 2d lt. USAF, 1943-45. Roman Catholic. Office: Colt Industries Inc 430 Park Ave New York NY 10022

CRACRAFT, MARY MILLER, lawyer; b. Cape Girardeau, Mo., Aug. 29, 1946; d. Sherman Cooper and Elizabeth Marie (Blackwell) C.; 1 child, Geoffrey Lee Rosser. EdB, U. Mo., 1968, JD, 1975. Bar: Mo. 1975, U.S. Dist. Ct. (we. dist.) Mo. 1975. Clk. Mo. Supreme Ct., Jefferson City, 1975-76; assoc., then ptnr. Gage & Tucker, Kansas City, Mo., 1981-86; assoc NLRB, Washington, 1986—. Office: NLRB 1717 Pennsylvania Ave NW Washington DC 20570 *

CRAFT, DONALD BRUCE, fuel oil distribution company executive; b. White Plains, N.Y., Jan. 19, 1935; children: Joan, Elizabeth, Kinson, Courtney, Leslie. BS, NYU, 1954; MBA, Columbia U., 1956. Sr. v.p. Wyatt Energy, Inc., New Haven, 1959—. Mem. fin. com. Conn. Republican party, 1969-79. Mem. New Eng. Fuel Inst. (bd. dirs. 1974—, chmn. bd. dirs. 1972-74, Disting. Achievement award 1975), Conn. Petroleum Assn. (pres. 1970-72, bd. dirs. 1972—, named Oilman of Yr. 1972), Ind. Conn. Petroleum Assn. (bd. dirs. 1970—), Petroleum Marketers Assn. Am. Office: Wyatt Energy Inc 900 Chapel St New Haven CT 06510

CRAFTON-MASTERSON, ADRIENNE, real estate executive; b. Providence, Mar. 6, 1926; d. John Harold and Adrienne (Fitzgerald) Crafton; m. Francis T. Masterson, May 31, 1947 (div. Jan. 1977); children: Mary Victoria Masterson Bush, Kathleen Joan, John Andrew, Barbara Lynn Wickes. Student, No. Va. Community Coll., 1971-74. Mem. staff Senator T.F. Green of R.I., Washington, 1944-47, 54-60, U.S. Senate Com. on Campaign Expenditures, 1944-45; asst. chief clk. Ho. Govt. Ops. Com., 1948-49, clk. Ho. Campaign Expenditures Com., 1950; asst. appointment sec. Office of Pres., 1951-53; with Hubbard Realty, Alexandria, Va., 1962-67; owner, mgr. Adrienne Investment Real Estate, Alexandria, 1968-73; pres. AIRE, Ltd., 1973—; pres. AIRE-Merkli developers, 1988—. Mem. adv. panel Fairfax County (Va.) Council on the Arts; founder, pres. Mt. Vernon/Lee Cultural Ctr. Found., Inc., 1984—; pres. Mt. Vernon/Lee Choral Soc., 1988. Mem. Nat. Assn. Realtors, No. Va. Bd. Realtors (chmn. comml. and indsl. com. 1981-82, community revitalization com. 1983-84), Va. Assn. Realtors, Internat. Orgn. Real Estate Appraisers (sr.), Alexandria C. of C., Mt. Vernon Lee C. of C., Friends of Kennedy Ctr. (founder). Home: 1200 Olde Towne Rd Alexandria VA 22307 Office: 6911 Richmond Hwy Ste 450 Alexandria VA 22306

CRAGER, BRUCE LEE, underwater service company executive; b. Lubbock, Tex., Nov. 11, 1952; s. Ted Jack and Ada Ruth (Hilburn) C.; m. Karen Sue Persall, Dec. 23, 1973; children: Chad, Autumn, Zachary. BS in Ocean Engring., Tex. A & M U., 1975; MBA, U. Houston, 1979. Registered profl. engr., Tex. Design engr. The Offshore Co. (Sonat), Houston, 1975-80; project engr. Seaflo Systems, Houston, 1980-83; project engr. Hughes Offshore, Houston, 1983, plant mgr., 1983-84, project mgr., 1984, gen. mgr., 1985-86; ops. mgr. Vetco Gray, Inc., Houston, 1987; v.p. Ocean Systems Engring., Houston, 1988—. Contbr. articles to profl. jours.; patentee in field. Chmn. deacons First Bapt. Ch. of Spring Br., Houston, 1986-88. Mem. Am. Petroleum Inst. Com. 17 (sec. 1984—), Tau Beta Pi. Republican. Baptist. Home: 12819 Corona Ln Houston TX 77072 Office: Ocean Systems Engring 1441 Park Ten Blvd Houston TX 77084

CRAIG, ANNA MAYNARD, financial educator, consultant; b. Columbus, Ohio, Sept. 2, 1944; d. David Stuart and Ann (Armstrong) C.; m. John D. Hogan, Nov. 26, 1976. BA cum laude, Smith Coll., 1966; MA, U. Wis., 1970, PhD, 1972. Chartered fin. analyst; cert. fin. planner. Asst. prof. U. Ill., Chgo., 1971-75; vis. asst. prof. Ohio State U., Columbus, 1974-76; asst. prof. Cen. Mich. U., Mt. Pleasant, 1976-79; cons. Am. Productivity Ctr., Houston, 1979-81; adj. prof. Houston Bapt. U., 1980-86, Jones Grad. Sch. Adminstrn., Rice U., Houston, 1986; adj. prof. dept. fin. U. Ill., Champaign-Urbana, 1987—; bd. advisors Assn. for Internat. Exchange Students in Econs. and Commerce, U. Ill., 1987—; outstanding prof. fin. commerce council, 1987-88. Editor: (with John D. Hogan) Dimensions of Productivity Research, Vol. 1, 1980, Vol. II, 1981. Bd. dirs. Champaign-Urbana Symphony, 1987—; mem. trust mgmt. com. Univ. YWCA, Champaign, 1987—. Ford fellow, U. Wis., 1970-72, NSF fellow, Stanford U., 1972; Fulbright scholar, 1966-67; named Outstanding Prof. Fin. U. Ill. Commerce Coun., 1987-88. Mem. Inst. Chartered Fin. Analysts, Internat. Assn. Cert. Fin. Planners, Nat. Assn. Enrolled Agts., Am. Econ. Assn., Fin. Analysts Fedn., Investment Analysts Soc. Chgo., Smith Coll. Alumnae Assn. (chmn. spl. gifts com., class fund agt. 1984—), Fulbright Alumni Assn., Phi Beta Kappa. Club: Lincolnshire Fields Country (Champaign). Office: U Ill Dept Fin 1206 S 6th St Urbana IL 61820

CRAIG, ANTHONY L., computer industry executive; b. Belfast, Northern Ireland, Aug. 19, 1945; s. Robert Hyslop and Millicent (Luke) C.; m. Jane Elizabeth Macey, Aug. 31, 1968; children: Tamara, Alexandra. BS in Math. and Physics, Dalhousie U., Halifax, N.S., Can., 1966. Salesperson IBM Can., Montreal and Halifax, 1966-68; product mgr. IBM Can., Toronto, 1968-74, systems engr. mgr., 1978-79; product line mgr. IBM Europe, Paris, 1974-78; mem. corp. mktg. staff IBM Corp., Armonk, N.Y., 1979-81; with IBM Info Systems, White Plains, N.Y., 1981-83; internat. sr. v.p. Gen. Electric Info. Services, London, United Kingdom, 1983-86; pres. Gen. Electric Info. Services, 1986-88; v.p. Gen. Electric Corp., until 1988; exec. v.p. Prime Computer Inc., Natick, Mass., 1988, chief operating officer, 1988, now pres., chief exec. officer, 1988—. Mem. Am. Mgmt. Assn. Office: Prime Computer Inc Prime Pk M515-13 Natick MA 01760 *

CRAIG, CHARLES SAMUEL, business educator; b. Atlantic City, May 6, 1943; s. Charles Hays and Catherine Sara (McMullen) C.; m. Elizabeth Anne Coyne, Aug. 10, 1985. BA, Westminster Coll., 1965; MS, U. R.I., 1967; PhD, Ohio State U., 1971. Mktg. rep. IBM, Providence, 1966-68; asst. dir. Mechanized Info. Ctr., Columbus, 1971-73; asst. prof. lib. adminstrn. Ohio State U., Columbus, 1971-73, asst. prof. mktg., 1972-74; asst. prof. mktg. Grad. Sch. Bus. and Pub. Adminstrn., Cornell U., Ithaca, N.Y., 1974-77, assoc. prof., 1977-79; vis. assoc. prof. mktg. Stern Sch. of Bus., N.Y.U., 1979-81, assoc. prof. mktg., 1981-84, prof. mktg., 1984-88, assoc. dean acad. affairs, 1984-88, prof. mktg. internat. bus., 1988—; dir. Presbyn. and Reformed Pub. Co., Phila., 1973—; mem. exec. bd. Jour. Retailing, 1985—. NDEA fellow, 1969-71. Mem. Am. Mktg. Assn., Assn. Consumer Rsch., Phi Kappa Phi, Omicron Delta Epsilon, Psi Chi. Presbyterian. Co-author: Consumer Behavior: An Information Processing Perspective, 1982; International Marketing Research, 1983; co-editor: Personal Selling: Theory, Research and Practice, 1984, The Development of Media Models in Advertising, Repetition Effects over the Years, The Relationship of Advertising Expenditures to Sales, 1986; mem. editorial bd. Jour. Mktg. Research, 1978-85, Jour. Retailing, 1980-85; contbr. articles to profl. jours. Home: 100 Bleecker St Apt 28-B New York NY 10012 Office: NYU 100 Trinity Pl New York NY 10006

CRAIG, CHRIS PAUL, airlines executive; b. Phila., Dec. 28, 1954; s. Frank Charles and Marie (Hart) C. BA in Spanish, Loyola U., 1979. Mgr. dist. cargo sales Mexicana Airlines, Phila., 1980-89, Chgo., 1989—. coordinator N.E. Ams. for Internat. Aid, Phila., 1982—. Mem. Phila Air Cargo Assn. (bd. dirs. 1982-84). Roman Catholic. Democrat. Office: Mexicana Airlines 55 E Monroe Ste 1608 Chicago IL 60603

CRAIG, DAVID CLARKE, economics and finance educator; b. Ft. Smith, Ark., Oct. 23, 1955; s. Earl Lewis Craig and Shirley Ann (Clarke) Shepherd; m. Dana Jane Thompson, Dec. 19, 1980; 1 child, Lauren Elizabeth. BBA, U. Ark., 1978, MBA, 1979; postgrad., U. Tex., 1983-88, U. Ark., 1988—. Mktg. officer Merchants Nat. Bank, Ft. Smith, 1979-81; instr. fin. and econs. Westark Community Coll., Ft. Smith, 1981—, faculty chairperson, 1987-88; asst. to pres. Richland Coll., Dallas, 1985; cons. rate study to advt. agy., Ft. Smith, 1982, bus. etiquette to med. ctr., Ft. Smith, 1984; treas. Bost Human Devel. Services, Inc., Ft. Smith, 1982-84; faculty chmn. Westark Community Coll., 1988-89, sec. faculty senate, 1987-88, faculty tenure rev. com., 1987—, chmn. faculty assn. constitional revision com., 1984, assn. sec., 1985-86, group ins. com. 1984, sec. curriculum com., 1983-84, social com., 1985-86; telephone installation, etiquette trainer, 1987; sec. self study com. faculty sect. North Cen. Accreditation of Colls. and Univs., 1983; appt. by Gov. Bill Clinton to Bd. of Ark. Student Loan Authority, 1988—. Pres. Am. Cancer Soc., 1988-89; mem. Pub. Awareness Com., Ft. Smith, 1985—; pres. Interfaith Community Ctr., Ft. Smith, 1982-84; co-residential chmn. Am. Cancer Soc., Ft. Smith, 1985-87, v.p. local bd., 1987-88; vol. Ft. Smith Art Ctr. Auction, 1987; mem. Noon Civics Club Ft. Smith, 1987; sponsor Harding U. Invitational Bus. Games, 1986, 87. Named one of Outstanding Young Men Am., 1983-84. Mem. Am. Inst. Banking (v.p. Ft. Smith chpt. 1981), Ark. Two Yr. Coll. Assn., Nat. Assn. Bus. Economists, Ark. State Council on Econ. Edn., Nat. Bus. Edn. Assn., So. Bus. Edn. Assn., Ark. Bus. Assn., Ft. Smith C. of C. (mem. ednl. com. 1987-88), Blue Key Nat. Hon. Soc., Kappa Delta Pi, Alpha Kappa Psi (sec. 1977-78), Phi Delta Kappa (Kappan of Month, 1985), Phi Beta Lambda (co-advisor 1986—). Office: Westark Community Coll 5210 Grand Ave Fort Smith AR 72904

CRAIG, DELENE JONES, trucking company executive; b. Ripley, Tenn., Mar. 21, 1934; d. Elmer Eldredge and Willie Mae (Walker) Jones; m. Stewart L. Craig, Nov. 14, 1952; 1 child, Kathie Lynn Craig Cepparulo. Grad. high sch., Ripley. Bookkeeper J.M. Morris & Sons, Ripley, 1954-56; sec. 1st Bapt. Ch., Ripley, 1958-64; sec., office mgr. Tenn. 16th Jud. Dist., Ripley, 1966-78; sec.-treas. D & L Trucking, Inc., Ripley, 1973—; cons. Mary Kay. Mem. Nat. Fedn. Ind. Bus., U.S. C. of C., Ripley C. of C., Ripley-Lauderdale County Jr. Aux. (pres. 1988—), Ripley High Sch. Band Boosters. Home: 120 Thompson Dr Ripley TN 38063 Office: D&L Trucking Inc Rte 4 Box 16D Ripley TN 38063

CRAIG, DOUGLAS WARREN, food service executive; b. Woodbury, N.J., Nov. 22, 1942; s. John Galbraith Craig and Vivian (Rundquist) Morris; m. Carolyn Louise McCans, Nov. 22, 1964 (div. Oct. 1984); children: Carl Douglas, Jeffrey Alan, Eric John; m. Helen Mae Reisner, June 29, 1985; 1 child, Whitney Reisner. BA, Gettysburg Coll., 1964; MBA, Loyola Coll., Balt., 1982. With Servomation Corp., N.Y.C., 1960-75, regional v.p., 1972-75; pres. Food Services Internat. Inc., Ft. Lauderdale, Fla., 1975-77; div. v.p. Marriott Corp., Washington, 1977-88; pres. Whitco Corp., Alexandria, Va., 1988—; sec.-treas., dir. Chesapeake Computer Solutions, Inc., Middleburg, Va., 1985—. Fin. sec. Good Shepherd Luth. Ch., Reston, Va., 1983-85, treas., 1985-87; mem. Nat. Assn. Coll. and Univ. Bus. Officers, Nat. Assn. Coll. Aux. Services, Loyola Coll. Exec. Alumni Assn. (pres. 1985-88), Am. Philatelic Soc. Republican. Avocation: philately. Home and Office: 608 Oronoco St Alexandria VA 22314

CRAIG, GEORGE ARTHUR, retired marketing and sales executive; b. Buffalo, July 22, 1923; s. Roy Vincent and Margaret (Connors) C.; m. Rittchell Marion Peterson, Aug. 27, 1949; children: Rittchell Anne, Scott Roy, Sandra Lynn. B.A., Knox Coll., 1949; A.M.P., Harvard U., 1959. Commerce agt., gen. agt., dir. indsl. devel. Chgo. & Eastern Ill. R.R., Chgo., 1951-58, v.p. traffic, 1958-61; v.p. mktg. Tex. & Pacific R.R., Dallas, 1961-65; asst. v.p. sales Mo. Pacific R.R., St. Louis, 1965-77; v.p. Mo. Pacific R.R., Houston, 1977-82, sr. v.p. mktg., 1982-83; sr. v.p. mktg. and sales Union Pacific R.R., Omaha, 1983-87. Served with USAAF, 1942-45. Mem. Nat. Freight Transp. Assn., Nat. Def. Transp. Assn. Republican. Presbyterian. Home: 13322 Fairfield Sq Chesterfield MO 63017 Office: Union Pacific RR 345 Park Ave New York NY 10154

CRAIG, GEORGE DENNIS, economics educator, consultant; b. Geneva, Ill., Sept. 14, 1936; s. George S. and Alice H. (Childs) C.; m. Lelah Price, Aug. 21, 1984; children—R. Price Coyle, R. Nolan Coyle, Deborah L. Craig, W. Sean Coyle. A.B., Wheaton Coll., 1960; M.S., U. Ill., 1962, Ph.D., 1968. Asst. prof. econs. La. State U., Baton Rouge, 1965-69; assoc. prof. sch. bus. No. Ill. U., Dekalb, 1969-82; prof. econs., chmn. Oklahoma City U., 1982—; cons. AT&T, Oklahoma City, 1984—. Contbr. articles to profl. jours. Mem. Am. Econs. Assn., So. Econs. Assn. Nat. Assn. Bus. Economists, Internat. Inst. of Forecasting. Avocation: tennis. Home: 6915 Avondale Ct Oklahoma City OK 73116 Office: Oklahoma City U Dept Econs NW 23rd at N Blackwelder Oklahoma City OK 73106

CRAIG, GREGORY LEWIS, personal computing company executive; b. Rochester, N.Y., Jan. 25, 1961; s. Albert Burchfield and Sybil (Smart) C. BA in Polit. Sci. and Econs., U. Rochester, 1983. Sec. of corp. Logical Ops., Rochester, 1983—, support svcs. mgr., 1983-85, tng. ctr. mgr., 1985-86, publs. dir., 1986-87; v.p. pub. Logical Tng. Systems, Inc., Rochester, 1987—. Inventor Datapouch, 1983. Mem. Data Processing Mgmt. Assn. Home: PO Box 40028 Rochester NY 14604 Office: Logical Tng Systems Inc 240 East Ave Rochester NY 14604

CRAIG, JOHN GRANT, finance management executive; b. Windsor, Ont., Canada, Aug. 14, 1942; s. Jarmin Grant and Kathleen Edith (Netherway) C.; m. Evelyn Doreen Pascal; children—Randall, Kelly, Melanie, David. Honors Bus. Adminstrn., U. Western Ont., 1964. Chartered acct., Canada. Controller, sec., treas. Multiple Access, Toronto, Ont., Canada, 1969-74; sec., treas. Multiple Access, Montreal, Que., Canada, 1974-76; v.p. fin., adminstrn. Global Communications Ltd., Toronto, Canada, 1976-81; v.p. fin., sec. Southam Inc., Toronto, Canada, 1981-85, sr. v.p. fin., sec., 1985—; chmn. fin. taxation com. Can. Daily Newspaper Pubs. Assn. Chmn. Presdl. Investment Adv. Com. U. Toronto. Mem. Fin. Execs. Inst. Can., Ont. Inst. Chartered Accts., Inst. Newspaper Fin. Officers (dir.). Club: Bayview Country (pres., bd. dirs.). Office: Southam Inc, 150 Bloor St W, Toronto, ON Canada M5S 2Y8

CRAIG, JOHN LEROY, financial planner; b. Saratoga, Wyo., May 5, 1949; s. James D. and Audrey (West) C.; m. Mary Ann Ricketts, May 2, 1975; children: William Skylar, Torri Sunol. Grad. high Sch., Bergman, Ark. Personal fin. planner IDS Fin. Svcs., Casper, Wyo., 1983—. Actor video Bowhunting Pronghorn Antelope, 1987. State judge Wyo. State Forincs Tournament, Casper, 1987. With USAF, 1967-69. Mem. Am. Assn. Women CPA's, Pioneer 97 Toastmasters Club, Optimist. Avocations: bowhunting, fishing, golf. Home: 950 Waterford St Casper WY 82609 Office: IDS Fin Svcs 123 W 1st St Ste C-90 Casper WY 82601

CRAIG, MAX DEAN, food products company executive; b. Garden City, Kans., Nov. 7, 1953; s. Richard L. and Vernadene (Piland) C.; m. Diana Kay Webb, Sept. 1, 1974; children: Kimberly, Stephanie, Jeffrey. BBA, Southwestern Coll., 1975; MBA, U. Kans., 1976. Supr. cost analyst Ford Motor Co., Dearborn, Mich., 1977-80; sr. dir. fin. PepsiCo Food Services Internat., Dallas, 1980-86; v.p. bus. planning Taco Bell Corp., Irvine, Calif., 1987—. Home: 24862 Buckboard Laguna Hills CA 92653 Office: Taco Bell Corp 17901 Von Karman Irvine CA 92714

CRAIG, ROBERT JAMES, healthcare marketing executive; b. Newport, R.I., Oct. 27, 1958; s. James E. and Shirley A. (Terry) C.; m. Rebecca T. Thurmond, May 26, 1985; 1 child, Sean Michael Craig. BS cum laude,

Indiana U. Pa., 1981; M in Health Adminstrn., Duke U., 1983. Adminstrv. resident Meth. Hosps., Memphis, 1983-84, spl. projects coord., 1984; adminstrv. asst. Meth. Health Systems, Memphis, 1984-85; v.p. mktg. Lancaster (Ohio)-Fairfield Community Hosp., 1985—; sec. Home Health Resources, Inc., Lancaster, 1986-87, Zane Properties, Inc., Lancaster, 1987—. Bd. dirs. Info. and Crisis Fairfield County, Lancaster, 1987—; mem. com. Forward Lancaster, 1987. Named Outstanding Young Man of Am., 1984. Mem. Am. Coll. Healthcare Planning and Mktg., Cen. Ohio Healthcare Adminstrs. Assn., Lancaster-Fairfield C. of C., Rotary. Republican. Roman Catholic. Office: Lancaster Fairfield Community Hosp 401 N Ewing St Lancaster OH 43130

CRAIG, THOMAS, management consultant; b. Vienna, Austria, Dec. 6, 1954; (parents American citizens); s. John Tucker and Ruth Doris (Weiler) C.; m. Jennifer Christine Lenox, Oct. 18, 1986; 1 child, Michael Tucker. AB, Princeton U., 1976; MBA, Harvard U., 1979. Scuba diver Tropical Fish Exports, Haiti, 1976; research asst. Nat. Econ. Research Assn., Washington, 1976-77; faculty Harvard Bus. Sch., 1979-80; cons., v.p. Agribus. Assn., Wellesley, Mass., 1980-83; prins./cons. Monitor Co., Cambridge, Mass., 1983—; bd. dirs., trustee Monitor Co. Europe, London, 1985—. Baker scholar Harvard U., 1979. Office: Monitor Co 124 Mt Auburn Cambridge MA 02138

CRAIG, WILLIAM AMES, banker; b. Lynn, Mass., Apr. 15, 1942; s. William Ames and Constance (Lauzon) C.; m. Margaret Mary Mazza, Jan. 29, 1977; children: Stephen, David. BA, U. Md., 1973; MS in Indsl. Personnel Mgmt., George Washington U., 1977. Personnel supr. Giant Food Inc., Landover, Md., 1963-78; v.p. personnel Woodward and Lothrop, Washington, 1978-83; sr. v.p. human resources Perpetual Savs. Bank, Alexandria, Va., 1983—. Pres., Monticello Community Assn., Bethesda, Md., 1986—; chmn. elect Nat. Capitol Area Health Care Coalition, 1987—; mem. Greater Washington Bd. of Trade, 1987; bd. dirs D.C. Assn. Retarded Citizens, 1987. Mem. Greater Washington Fin. Insts. Assn. (personnel com. 1986—), Washington Personnel Assn. Republican. Roman Catholic. Office: Perpetual Savs Bank 2034 Eisenhower Ave Alexandria VA 22314

CRAIGHEAD, GEORGE PALMER, publisher; b. Indpls., Oct. 22, 1929; s. George Vankirk and Janet Louise (Palmer) C.; m. Peggy Ann Walters, Aug. 16, 1958; children: Scott, Bradford, Catherine. AB, Yale U., 1952; MBA, Harvard U., 1956. Sales rep. GE, Bridgeport, Conn., 1956-59; dir. mktg. rsch. C.H. Masland & Sons, N.Y.C., 1959-61; dir. mktg. cons. svcs. Touche Ross & Co., Detroit, 1961-66; exec. v.p. William H. Clark Assos., Inc., N.Y.C., 1967-77; pres. Egon Zehnder Internat., Inc. (U.S.A.), N.Y.C., 1977-83; prin. Craighead Assocs. Inc., Stamford, Conn., 1983-86; pres. Craighead Pubs. Inc., Darien, Conn., 1987—; pub. Craighead's Internat. Exec. Travel and Relocation Svc. Served with M.I. U.S. Army, 1953-55. Mem. Assn. Exec. Recruiting Cons. (pres. 1974-76), Woodway Country Club, Yale Club. Home and Office: Craighead Pubs 6 Fox Hill Ln Darien CT 06820

CRAIGHILL, SHERRY PERKINS, manufacturing executive; b. Richmond, Va., May 27, 1957; d. William Samuel and Patsy (Kinker) Perkins; m. Lloyd Langhorne Craighill, Jr., Sept. 26, 1981; children: Christopher Langhorne, William Peyton. BS in Acctg., Va. Polytech. Inst. and State U., 1979. CPA, Va. Internal auditor Burlington Industries, Greensboro, N.C., 1979-81; plant acct. Russel Stover Candies, Clarksville, Va., 1981-82; controller Allied Piping Products, Norristown, Pa., 1982-84, Williamsburg (Va.) Motors, 1984-85, Franz Windows, Newport News, Va., 1985-87, Groupe Andre Perry Ltd., Washington, 1988—. Rep. Com. to Prevent Child Abuse, Richmond, Va., 1986; treas. Jr. Women's Club of Williamsburg, 1986-87. Mem. AICPA (mem. tax com. 1988-89). Republican. Episcopalian. Home: 2123 Salt Kettle Way Reston VA 22091 Office: Groupe Andre Perry Ltd 1155 21st St NW Washington DC 20036

CRAIN, C. WILLIAM, apparel company executive; b. Bloomington, Ill., Mar. 12, 1941; s. Charles W. and Helen (Powell) C.; m. Sharon Cheek, Sept 2, 1961; children: C. Wesley, W. Eric, Tamara. BA, Duke U., 1963; MBA, Stanford U., 1965. Various mktg. and mgmt. positions Gen. Mills Inc., Mpls. and Cin., 1965-70; pres. Questor Ednl. Products Co., Bronx, N.Y., 1971-78, Buxton Inc., Agawam, Mass., 1979-86, Lee Apparel Co., Merriam, Kans., 1986-88; group v.p. VF Corp., Wyomissing, Pa., 1988—; bd. dirs. ProGroup Inc., Ooltewah, Tenn., Accessories Enterprises Inc., Wilbraham, Mass. Chmn. campaign drive United Way Pioneer Valley, Springfield, Mass., 1985; trustee Am. Internat. Coll., Springfield, 1979-86. Mem. Duke U. Alumni Assn. (bd. dirs. 1988), Apawamis Club. Democrat. Office: VF Corp 1047 N Park Rd Wyomissing PA 19610

CRAIN, RANCE, publishing company executive. Pres. Crain Communications, Inc., Chgo., N.Y.C.; also editor-in chief Crain's New York Business, N.Y.C., 1984—. Office: Crain Commmunications Inc 740 Rush St Chicago IL 60611 also: Crain Communications Inc 220 E 42nd St New York NY 10017 *

CRAMER, GEORGE BENNETT, estate management executive; b. Swampscott, Mass., Aug. 15, 1903; s. Stuart Warren and Rebecca Warren (Tinkham) C.; m. Elizabeth Crooks, Jan. 28, 1947; children: George Bennett, Richard Warren. Student, U. N.C., 1921-22; BS, Harvard U., 1926. Dir. Cramerton Mills, Inc., N.C., 1927-47, sec., 1927-46, asst. treas., 1927-31, treas., 1931-46; mill rep. Galey & Lord, N.Y.C., 1929-32; ptnr. Cramer & Cramer Investments and Estate Mgmt., Charlotte, N.C., 1947—; mem. adv. bd. Liberty Mut. Ins. Co., Charlotte, 1934-46; chief of textile div. Econ. Cooperation Adminstrn., Dept. State, Paris, 1949-51. Mem. Cramerton Sch. Bd., 1933-38; bd. dirs. Charlotte Symphony Orch., 1955-58, United Community Service Found., Charlotte, Charlotte United Community Fund, Charlotte Alcoholism Info. Ctr.; v.p. Mint Mus. Art, Charlotte, 1930-40. Served from lt. to maj. USAF, 1940-46, ETO. Decorated Bronze Star. Mem. Charlotte C. of C. (aviation, fgn. trade and edn. com. 1968—), Soc. Mayflower Descs., SAR, Sons Colonial Wars, English Speaking Union (founding pres. Charlotte 1958-62), N.C. Hist. Assn., Soc. of Four Arts, Am. Legion. Republican. Episcopalian. Clubs: N.C. Wildlife, Rifle and Pistol, Charlotte Country, Quail Hollow Country, Myers Park Country, Charlotte City (Charlotte); Mchts., Harvard, Univ., Columbia Yacht (N.Y.C.); Palm Beach Yacht, Palm Beach Rifle and Pistol, Everglades, Bath and Tennis, Beach, Sailfish (Palm Beach); Hurlingham (London); Nantucket Yacht; Army and Navy, University (Washington); Interllié (Paris). Home: Midwood 2733 Country Club Ln Charlotte NC 28205 Office: Cramer & Cramer Investments 6407 Idlewild Rd Charlotte NC 28212

CRAMER, JOHN SCOTT, retired banker; b. Charlotte, N.C., Dec. 10, 1930; s. Stuart Warren, Jr. and Julia (Scott) C.; m. Nancy Arnott, Aug. 9, 1952; children: Julia Baxter, Alice Arnott. AB, U. N.C., 1953. With Wachovia Bank & Trust Co., CHarlotte, 1955—, asst. v.p., 1958-61, v.p., 1961-64, sr. v.p., bd. mgrs., 1964-71; exec. v.p., head banking div. Wachovia Bank & Trust Co., Winston-Salem, N.C., 1971-74; vice chmn. bd., head fiduciary div. Wachovia Bank & Trust Co., Winston-Salem, 1974-88; ret. Wachovia Bank & Trust Co., 1988, also bd. dirs.; vice chmn. bd., dir. The Wachovia Corp.; exec. v.p. First Wachovia Corp., 1986; pres. First Wachovia Trust Services, Inc., 1987; dir. Shadowline, Inc., Linville Resorts, Inc. Mem. Arts and Scis. Bd., U. N.C.-Chapel Hill; mem. cen. selection com. J. Motley Morehead Found., active numerous civic, ednl. and svc. orgns. 1st lt. USAF, 1953-55. Mem. Newcomen Soc. Am. (chmn. N.C. com.), Linville Golf Club (N.C.), Old Town Club, Piedmont Club, Sigma Alpha Epsilon. Home: 16 Graylyn Place Ln Winston-Salem NC 27106

CRAMER, LEE H., accountant, treasurer; b. Pitts., Nov. 18, 1945; s. Walter C. and Eleanor J. Cramer, Jr.; m. Kathryn M. Martin, July 24, 1971; children: Julie, James. BS in Acctg., Pa. State U.; MBA in Acctg., So. Meth. U. CPA, Pa. Treas. Rockwell Internat. Corp., Pitts., from 1981, now v.p. and treas., 1988—.

CRAMER, RICHARD A., manufacturing company executive. Chmn., chief exec. officer Fisher Scientific Group Inc., La Jolla, Calif.; bd. dirs. City Nat. Bank, City Nat. Corp., Henley Group Inc. Office: Fisher Sci Group Inc 11255 N Torrey Pines Rd La Jolla CA 92037 *

CRAMP, LORI ANGELL, hotel executive; b. Kansas City, Mo., Apr. 17, 1955; d. William Greenleaf and Arline (Mullaney) Angell; m. John Stitzer, Aug. 13, 1977; children: Jeffrey William, Chelsea Angell. BA, Franklin & Marshall Coll., 1977; MBA, Harvard U., 1979. Mgmt. cons. Coopers & Lybrand Co., Washington, 1979-80, supr. mgmt. cons., 1980-81; supr. internal cons. Marriott Corp., Washington, 1981-82, mgr. internal cons., 1982-83, mgr. corp. fin., 1983-85, dir. corp. fin., 1985-86, v.p. corp. fin., 1987—. Treas. Churchill Sq. Homeowners Assn., Falls Church, Va., 1983. Mem. Harvard Bus. Sch. Club, Phi Beta Kappa, Pi Gamma Mu. Office: Marriott Corp One Marriott Dr Washington DC 20058

CRANDALL, DREW MARTIN, sales and marketing professional; b. Bridgeport, Conn., Dec. 19, 1955; s. Robert D.L. and Jeanne (Whittaker) C.; m. Dawn Celeste Martel, June 21, 1986. BA, U. Conn., 1977. Percussionist Walt Disney World, Lake Buena Vista, Fla., 1976; rsch. mgr. MBD Assocs., Washington, 1977; dir. mem. rels. Am. Music Conf., Chgo., 1977-79; nat. sales mgr. Star Instruments, Stafford Springs, Conn., 1979-81; v.p. Marcom, East Windsor, Conn., 1981-88; pres. Keep In Touch, Tolland, Conn., 1988—. Author: The Role of Music in the Life of Man, 1977; contbr. articles to profl. jours. Percussionist Govs. Foot Guard, Hartford, Conn., 1982-86; vol. Big Bros., Storrs, Conn. and Chgo., 1976-83; asst. scoutmaster Boy Scouts Am., Vernon, Conn., 1981-84; drum instr. Rockville High Marching Band, Vernon, 1983—; pub. info. mgr. Am. Cancer Soc., 1988—. Mem. Bus. Profl. Advt. Assn., Direct Mktg. Assn., Better Bus. Bur., Christian Businessmen's Fellowship. Office: Keep In Touch 45 Industrial Park Rd W Tolland CT 06084

CRANDALL, JOHN LYNN, insurance company executive; b. Chgo., Apr. 17, 1927; s. Paul Bertram and Olga (Bliech) C.; m. Irene Anze Ruenne, Dec. 26, 1973; children by previous marriage: Deborah Crandall Schmude, Jeffrey, Lynne Crandall Blais; stepchildren: George Ruenne, Helgi Ruenne Beckler. BS in Fire Protection Engring., Ill. Inst. Tech., 1951. CPCU; cert. in gen. ins. Highly protected risk inspector FIA, Chgo., 1951-53, asst. engring. supr., 1953-56, engring. supr., 1956-59, underwriting supr., special agt., 1959-65; HPR engr., underwriter Kemper Group, Chgo., 1965-67, HPR sales specialist, 1967-71; asst. to dir. underwriting Protection Mutual Ins. Co., Park Ridge, Ill., 1971-73, v.p. underwriting, 1973-78, v.p., dir. underwriting, 1978—. Served with USN, 1945-46. Mem. Soc. Fire Protection Engrs. (charter), Soc. CPCU (chpt. pres. 1980-81, nat. dir. 1987—). Republican. Lutheran. Home: 24 Lambert Dr Schaumburg IL 60193 Office: Protection Mut Ins 300 S Northwest Hwy Park Ridge IL 60068

CRANDALL, ROBERT LLOYD, airline executive; b. Westerly, R.I., Dec. 6, 1935; s. Lloyd Evans and Virginia (Beard) C.; m. Margaret Jan Schmults, July 6, 1957; children: Mark William, Martha Conway, Stephen Michael. Student, Coll. William and Mary, 1953-55; B.S., U. R.I., 1957; M.B.A., Wharton Sch., U. Pa., 1960. With Eastman Kodak Co., Rochester, 1960-62, Hallmark Cards, Kansas City, Mo., 1962-66; asst. treas. TWA Inc., N.Y.C., 1966-70; v.p. systems and data services TWA Inc., 1970-71, v.p., controller, 1971-72; sr. v.p., treas. Bloomingdale Bros., N.Y.C., 1972-73; sr. v.p. fin. Am. Airlines, Inc., N.Y.C., 1973-74, sr. v.p. mktg., 1974-80, pres., 1980—, chmn., chief exec. officer, 1985—, also dir., 1976—; bd. dirs. Republic Bank Corp., Halliburton Co., Recognition Equipment, Inc. Bd. dirs. Boy Scouts Am. Served with Inf. U.S. Army, 1957. *

CRANDELL, K(ENNETH) JAMES, management and planning consultant; b. Ajax, Ont., Can., July 12, 1957; s. James Bauder Butterill and Barbara Joy Gillard; m. Christine Josephine McElhenney, July 28, 1984. B in Adminstrn. and B in Commerce, U. Ottawa, 1980; MBA, Fla. Atlantic U., 1982. CPA, Fla. Assoc. dir. entrepreneurial services Arthur Young & Co., Ft. Lauderdale, Fla., 1982-88; pres. NBS Cons. Group, Inc., Pompano Beach, Fla., 1988—. Writer, co-producer TV series Florida Business Advisor, 1988; contbr. articles to mags. Mem. AICPA, Fla. Inst. CPA's, Am. Assn. Accts. (MAS div.), Nat. Assn. Accts. (bd. dirs. Ft. Lauderdale chpt. 1983, pres. 1988-89, bus. planning com. 1987-89), Inst. Bus. Appraisers, Internat. Inst. Forecasters, Internat. Soc. Financiers, Gold Coast Venture Capital Club (v.p. bd. dirs., treas. 1987—, exec. com. Forum 1986—, editor newsletter 1987—), Ft. Lauderdale C. of C. (chair venture capital activities 1986—, small bus. task force 1985—), Fla. Atlantic U. MBA Assn. (pres. 1981), Beta Gamma Sigma, Phi Kappa Phi. Home: 3120 NW 66 St Fort Lauderdale FL 33309 Office: NBS Cons Group Inc 1000 W McNab Rd Pompano Beach FL 33069

CRANE, EDWARD J., airline executive; b. 1928; m. Margaret Struif; children: Steven, Edward J., Mary Ann, John. Grad., St. Louis U. Sch. Commerce and Fin., 1951. Acctg. dept. comptroller Ozark Air Lines, Inc., St. Louis, 1951-60, v.p., comptroller, 1960-65, v.p., treas., 1965-68, exec. v.p., treas., 1968-71; pres., chief exec. officer Ozark Air Lines, Inc. (acquired by TWA Inc., 1986), St. Louis, 1971-87; vice-chmn. TWA, N.Y.C., 1986—, also bd. dirs.; dir. Bank of St. Louis, Valley Industries, Gen. Bancshares Corp. Mem. pres.'s council, trustee St. Louis U.; bd. dirs. United Way, 1977-83, Regional Commerce and Growth Assn. St. Louis, St. Louis Council Boy Scouts Am.; trustee Incarnate Word Hosp. Served with USMC, World War II. Mem. Assn. Local Transport Airlines (past chmn., bd. dirs.), Air Transport Assn. (bd. dirs.), Air Conf. (bd. dirs.). Office: Ozark Airlines Inc PO Box 10007 Lambert Field Saint Louis MO 63145 *

CRANE, KENT BRUCE, management services executive; b. North Hornell, N.Y., July 25, 1935; s. Willard L. and Elizabeth (Ewart) C.; BA cum laude, Dartmouth Coll., 1957; postgrad. in internat. econs. Am. U., 1958; divorced;children—Jeffery Stuart, James Andrew. Third sec. polit. sect. U.S. Embassy, Jakarta, Indonesia, 1960-62; with U.S. Dept. State, Washington, 1963-64; vice consul in charge econ. sect. U.S. Consulate, Zanzibar, 1964-65; 2d. sec. polit. sect. U.S. Embassy, Accra, Ghana, 1965-67; sr. research asso. for fgn. affairs, sec. to task force on conduct of fgn. relations, Republican Nat. Com., 1967-68; spl. asst. to Senator George Murphy, 1968-69; nat. security affairs adv. to v.p. of U.S., 1969-72; asst. dir. for East Asia and Pacific, USIA, 1972-74; adminstrv. asst. to Rep. Peter H.B. Frelinghuysen, 1974-75; project dir. U.S. Commn. on Orgn. of Govt. for Conduct of Fgn. Policy, 1974-75; chmn. bd. Crane Pub. Co., Ridgewood, N.J., 1975-80; co-chmn. Africa subcom. Rep. Nat. Com., 1978-80; pres., mng. dir. Crane Group Ltd., Washington, 1978—; pres. Ranch Devel. and Mgmt., Inc., Tex., 1980—; officer, dir. various cos. U.S. and abroad including Corona Co., Harrow Corp., Belize-Orient Corp.; real estate joint ventures U.S., N.Z., Spain, Africa. Served to 1st lt. U.S. Army, 1957-59, to capt. USAR. Mem. Inst. Strategic Studies (London), Nat. Rifle Assn. (dir.), Explorers Club, Game Conservation Internat. Clubs: Met. (N.Y.C.); Internat., Capitol Hill (Washington); Internat. Economists, Mt. Kenya Safari, Safari Internat. Office: PO Box 25535 Washington DC 20007

CRANE, LAWRENCE L., JR., food store franchise company executive; b. 1938. BS, Fairfield U., 1960. Salesman Addressograph-Multigraph Corp., 1960-62; gen. mgr. Quality Stamp Co., from 1962, pres., 1968; with Malone & Hyde Inc., 1962—, now v.p.; now also pres. Piggly Wiggly Corp., Memphis. Office: Piggly Wiggly Corp 3030 Poplar Ave Memphis TN 38111 *

CRANE, LEO STANLEY, retired railroad executive; b. Cin., Sept. 7, 1915; s. Leo Vincent and Blanche Gottlieb (Mitchell) C.; m. Joan McCoy, Sept. 3, 1976; children by previous marriage: Pamela Blanche, Penelope Ann. BSE, George Washington U., 1938. With So. Ry. Co., Washington, 1937-63, 65-80, engr. of tests, 1948-56, mech. rsch. engr., 1956-59, v.p. engring. and rsch., 1965-70, exec. v.p. ops., 1970-76, pres., chief adminstrv. officer, 1976-77, pres., chief exec. officer, 1977-79, chmn., 1979-80; chmn., chief exec. officer, dir. Consolidated Rail Corp. (known as Conrail), Phila., 1981-88, ret., 1988. Trustee George Washington U. Fellow ASTM (past pres.), ASME; mem. Nat. Acad. Engring., Soc. Automotive Engrs., Am. Ry. Engring. Assn., Am. Soc. Traffic and Transp. Clubs: Metropolitan, Burning Tree, Phila. Country, Union League (Phila.); Gulph Mills Golf (King of Prussia, Pa.). Home: 1351 Monk Rd Gladwyne PA 19035

CRANE, ROBERT FRANKLIN, utility company executive; b. N.Y.C., Apr. 11, 1936; s. Elmer Leach and Helen Marie (Higbee) C.; m. Carol Cleone Hardman, May 30, 1960; children: Neal, Janine, Douglas, Raymond, Monica. BCE, Manhattan Coll., 1957; MCE, NYU, 1964. Mgmt. intern Consol. Edison Co. N.Y., Inc., N.Y.C., 1960-63, chief project engr., 1970-72, chief civil engr., 1972-78, asst. v.p., 1978-82, v.p., 1982—. Bd. dirs. Cath. Youth Orgn., Blauvelt, N.Y., 1970-80, Queens (N.Y.) Cancer Soc., 1981-83; pres. 14th St. Local Devel. Corp., N.Y.C., 1984—; mem. Rockland County Solid Waste Com., New City, N.Y., 1984-86, Town of Orangetown (N.Y.) Solid Waste Com., 1987—. Mem. N.Y. Hall Sci. (bd. dirs. 1982—), West Side Assn. (bd. dirs. 1984—), 6th Ave. Assn. (bd. dirs. 1984—), KC. Republican. Office: Consol Edison Co NY Inc 4 Irving Pl New York NY 10017

CRANFORD, EULA FORREST, health science administrator, retired; b. Stanly County, N.C., Sept. 24, 1923; d. Claude Columbus and Gertie Ann (Chandler) Forrest; m. John Henry Cranford, July 4, 1942; children: Brenda C. Couick, Barbara Gail Childers. Cert., Vocat. Rehab. Tng. Sch., Cleve., 1967, Stanly Tech. Coll., Albemarle, N.C., 1975; cert. in human svcs., Cen. Piedmont Coll., 1974. Acting dir. Stanly County Vocat. Workshop, Inc., Albemarle, 1966-67, exec. dir., 1967-85; dir. adult day program Assn. for Retarded Citizens, Inc., Albemarle, 1985-87. Pres. N.C. Shelter Workshops, Inc., 1977, treas., 1973, pres. adminstrv. practice div., 1976, sec., treas., 1974; vol. Albemarle Cancer Soc., Heart Fund, Cystic Fibrosis Soc., Spl. Olympics, Assn. for Retarded Citizens, 1988—; mem. N.C. Easter Seal Soc., bd. dirs. 1976-77, adv. com. 1976-77; pres. Albemarle United Methodist Women, 1988, dist. coord. Christian Social Concerns, 1988-89; pres. chpt. I N.C. Rehab. Assn. Facility, 1977. Recipient VIP award N.C. Easter Seal Soc., 1978, Citation of Merit award, 1973. Mem. Stanly County C. of C. (Community Svc. award). Democrat. Methodist. Lodge: Civitan (Stanly Actioneers chpt. v.p. 1985-86, pres. 1986-87, Citizen of Yr. award 1970, 71). Home: 1623 W Park Ave Albemarle NC 28001 Office: Assn for Retarded Citizens Inc 730 Greenwood St PO Box 68 Albemarle NC 28002-0068

CRANKSHAW, JOHN HAMILTON, mechanical engineer; b. Canton, Ohio, Aug. 29, 1914; s. Fred. Weir and Mary (Lashels) C.; m. Wilma Chaffee Thurlow, June 5, 1940; children: Wilma Jean, John H., Geoffrey Thurlow. B.S. in Mech. Engring., Mass. Inst. Tech., M.S., 1940. Rotating engr. Gen. Electric Co., 1940-41, sect. engr., mech. design sect. Motor Engr. div. Locomotive Car Equipment, Erie, Pa., 1946-52; exec. engr. J.A. Zurn Mfg. Co., Am. Flexible Coupling Co., 1952-54; v.p. engring., 1954; exec. v.p., dir. Zurn Industries, Inc., mng. dir. Zurn Research and Devel. Div., until 1957; pres., dir. Dynetics, Inc., Erie, 1957—, Dynetic Systems, Inc., Erie, 1970—. Mem. adv. council Gannon Coll.; chmn. Erie Sewer Authority. Served to maj. Ordnance Dept., AUS, 1941-46. Registered profl. engr., Pa. Mem. ASME, Soc. Automotive Engrs., Assn. Iron and Steel Engrs., Soc. Exptl. Stress Analysis, Soc. Naval Architects and Marine Engrs., Am. Soc. Metals, ASTM, Am. Soc. Lubricating Engrs. Erie Engring. Socs. Council (pres. 1955-57), Pa. Soc. Profl. Engrs., Sigma Xi. Clubs: M.I.T. (N.Y.); Erie. Author several tech. papers. Patentee; inventor, designer main propulsion clutches and couplings for nuclear powered submarines and surface ships. Home: 439 Shawnee Dr Erie PA 16505 Office: Dynetics Inc Rm 1315 Daniel Baldwin Bldg Erie PA 16501

CRANNELL, DAVID JOHN, distribution company executive; b. Schenectady, N.Y., July 28, 1949; s. John David and Elaine (Howarth) C.; m. Sue Bransford Weathers, July 11, 1970; children: Scott, Chloe. BS in Indsl. Engring., Ga. Inst. Tech., 1969. Pres., chief exec. officer Safety Equipment Co., Tampa, Fla., 1974—. Pres. Temple Terrace (Fla.) Soccer Assn, 1988—. Lt. USN, 1969-74. Mem. Am. Soc. Safety Engrs. (exec. com.), Am. Indsl. Hygiene Assn., Nat. Indsl. Glove Distbrs. Assn. (pres.), Safety Equipment Distbrs. Assn. (bd. dirs.), Tampa Club, Temple Terrace Golf Club, Masons. Office: Safety Equipment Co 6507 N Harney Rd Tampa FL 33610-9501

CRANSTON, HOWARD STEPHEN, lawyer, management consultant; b. Hartford, Conn., Oct. 20, 1937; s. Howard Samuel and Agnes (Corvo) C.; m. Karen Youngman, June 16, 1962; children: Margaret, Susan. BA cum laude, Pomona Coll., 1959; LLB, Harvard U., 1962. Bar: Calif. 1963, U.S. Dist. Ct. (cen. dist.) Calif. 1966, U.S. Dist. Ct. (no. dist.) Calif. 1973, U.S. Dist. Ct. (so. dist.) Calif. 1976, U.S. Supreme Ct. 1972. Assoc. MacDonald & Halsted, Los Angeles, 1964-68; ptnr. MacDonald, Halsted & Laybourne, Los Angeles, 1968-82, of counsel, 1982-86; pres. Knapp Communications, Los Angeles, 1982-87; pres. S.C. Cons. Corp., 1987—; bd. dirs. Wood Knapp & Co., Cambridge Mfg., St. Clair & Co., Accurate, Inc. 1st lt. U.S. Army, 1962-64. Mem. Assn. Corp. Growth, Conf. Bd., San Gabriel Country Club, Harvard Club. Republican. Episcopalian. Author Handbook for Creative Managers, 1987, Management Decision Mag., 1988—. Office: SL Cons Corp 2233 Huntington Dr San Marino CA 91108

CRANTS, DOCTOR ROBERT, JR., entrepreneur; b. Salamanca, N.Y., Nov. 17, 1944; s. Doctor Robert and Dorothy May (Snyder) C.; m. Shirley Jean Moravec, July 2, 1966; children: Doctor R. III, Jeffrey Thomas, Jennifer Ashley. BS in Engring., U.S. Mil. Acad., 1966; MBA, Harvard U., 1974, JD, 1974. V.p. fin. Town Properties Inc., Nashville, 1974-75; sr. v.p. 1st Am. Nat. Bank, Nashville, 1975-77; pres. Doctor Grants & Assocs., Nashville, 1977-79; founder, chief exec. officer Broadcast Mgmt. Svcs. Inc., Nashville, 1979-83; founder, treas. Corrections Corp. Am., Nashville, 1983-87, pres., chief exec. officer, 1987—; pres. Tri Ins. Inc., Nashville, 1985—; bd. dirs. Sahara Resorts. Assoc. producer theatrical movie Bat-21, 1988. Capt. U.S. Army, 1966-70, Vietnam. Decorated Air medal with 1 oak leaf cluster, Bronze Star with 1 oak leaf cluster. Mem. Am. Correctional Assn., West Point Soc. Mid. Tenn. (pres. 1987—). Methodist. Office: Corrections Corp Am 28 White Bridge Rd Ste 206 Nashville TN 37205

CRASSARIS, LEONIDAS GEORGE, pharmaceutical products executive, researcher; b. Alexandria, Egypt, Mar. 23, 1935; s. George P. and Helen (Vakirtzi) C.; m. Valentina-Victorovna Erascova, Aug. 4, 1962; children: George, Alexios-Victor. BS in Medicine, Faculty of Medicine, 1960, PhD in Pharmacology, 1978. Salesperson Squibb AEBE, Athens, Greece, 1961-63, mgr. sales, 1963-66, dir. mktg., 1966-79, chmn., chief exec. officer, 1979—. Contbr. articles to profl. jours. Mem. Med. Assn. Athens, N.Y. Acad. Sci., Am. Soc. Microbiology, Brit. Soc. for Venereal Diseases, Assn. Greek Pharm. Industry (bd. dirs. Athens chpt. 1982—, v.p. 1988), Greek Working Group Pharm Mfg. Assn. (chmn. 1982—), Greek-Am. C. of C. (bd. dirs. 1982—). Clubs: Propeller (Porto Piraeus); Athenian (Athens). Home: 52-54 Vas Sophias Str, 153 41 Aghia Paraskevi Greece Office: Squibb AEBE, Messohgion Ave, 67 Tzavela Str, 152 31 Halandri Greece

CRAUGH, JOSEPH PATRICK, JR., lawyer, insurance company executive; b. Yonkers, N.Y., Oct. 21, 1934; s. Joseph Patrick and Lucille Maxine (Gruber) C.; m. Ellen Maria Roesser, Sept. 5, 1959; children: Joseph Patrick III, Elizabeth. BS, Coll. of Holy Cross, 1956; LLB, Syracuse U., 1959. Bar: N.Y. 1961, N.H. 1971. Counsel Inter-County Title Guaranty Co., White Plains, N.Y., 1959-61; dist. claims mgr. Utica (N.Y.) Mut. Ins. Co., 1961-70; staff lawyer Nat. Grange Mut. Ins. Co., Keene, N.H., 1970-75, gen. counsel, v.p., bd. dirs., 1975-81; v.p., sec., gen. counsel Harleysville (Pa.) Mut. Ins. Co., 1981—; instr. profl. courses. Chmn. Cheshire County Republican Com., 1979. Mem. N.Y. State Bar Assn., N.H. Bar Assn., Internat. Assn. Def. Counsel, Am. Corp. Counsel Assn., Fedn. Ins. Counsel, Assn. CPCU, Am. Soc. Corp. Secs., Am. Arbitration Assn., K.C. Republican. Roman Catholic. Home: 236 Elm Dr Lansdale PA 19446 Office: Harleysville Mut Ins Co 355 Maple Ave Harleysville PA 19438

CRAVEN, DONALD NEIL, former finance company executive; b. Springfield, Mass., Aug. 18, 1924; s. C.S. and Edna B. (Blanchard) C.; m. Betty L. Rodda, July 16, 1947; 1 dau., Patricia Craven Matheson. Student, Williams Coll., 1942-43, Grad. Sch. Bus., Columbia U., 1967. Advt. sales staff Springfield Newspapers, 1946-51; fin. br. mgr. Assos. Investment Co., South Bend, Ind., 1951-62; br. mgr. Ford Motor Credit Co., Boston, 1962-64; br. mgr., then regional mgr. Chrysler Fin. Corp., 1964-69; v.p. Eastern U.S., 1969-80; dir. Indsl. Components Corp., Wilbraham, Mass. Bd. dirs., mem. fin. com. Springfield chpt., N.E. Regional Blood Svcs., dist. rep. for Mass. ARC; mem. S.C.O.R.E. Served with USMC, 1943-46, 50-51. Clubs: Landmark (Stamford, Conn.); Dennis (Mass.) Yacht. Lodges: Masons, Shriners. Home: 18 Manchester Terr Springfield MA 01108

CRAVEN, HOMER HENRY, JR., pilot, aviation consultant; b. Seattle, Jan. 31, 1925; s. Homer Henry and Juanita Normah (Briscoe) C.; student S.W. Tex. State Coll.; m. Mary Kathleen Weaver, May 3, 1945 (dec. Feb. 1985); children—James Michael, Scott Marshall, Anne Elizabeth Craven McDonald. With Boeing Airplane Co., Seattle, 1946-48, Smith Aviation,

Renton, Wash., 1948-52; pilot Northwest Orient Airlines, Seattle, 1952-85, B-747 capt., 1976-85; aviation cons. 19—. Served with USAAF, 1943-45; PTO. Decorated Air medal. Mem. Am. Soc. Aerospace Edn., Nat. Aero. Assn., Exptl. Aircraft Assn., Aircraft Owners and Pilots Assn., 14th Air Force Assn., Northwest Captain's Club, Confederate Air Force. Episcopalian. Author research papers on fuel conservation. Home: 2005 180th Ct NE Redmond WA 98052 Office: Northwest Airlines Sea-Tac Airport Seattle WA 98001

CRAVEN, JOHN MICHAEL, manufacturing executive; b. Cin., Feb. 20, 1948; s. John Robert and Rose Marie (Hoffman) C.; m. Noreen Farrell, July 24, 1971; children: John Michael Jr., Keri Marie. BBA, U. Cin., 1970; MS, St. Francis Coll., Ft. Wayne, Ind., 1973. Acct. Magnavox, Ft. Wayne, 1970-73; v.p. fin. Brighton Corp., Cin., 1973-87; chief fin. officer Keystone Gen. Inc., Cin., 1987—; treas. J's, Cin., 1987—; mem. adv. bd. Midwest Assessment Cons., 1987—. Co-chmn. Mercy Hosp., Hamilton, Ohio, 1984—, audit and budget com., 1984—. Mem. Assn. MBA Execs., Nat. Assn. Accts., Queen CIty Racquet Club (Cin.). Republican. Roman Catholic. Club: Queen City Racquet (Cin.). Home: 1805 Lockbourne Cincinnati OH 45240 Office: Keystone Gen Inc 11495 Deerfield Rd Cincinnati OH 45242

CRAVER, WILLIAM EVERETT, JR., finance, manufacturing, real estate and shipping executive; b. Columbus, Ga., Aug. 14, 1922; s. William Everett and Myrtle (Ivey) C.; m. Jane Honour McDonald, Oct. 19, 1946; children: Virginia St. Clair Craver Good, Ellen Lloyd Craver Young, Jane Honour Craver Izard, William III. Student, George Washington U., 1940-43; BS, U.S. Mcht. Marine Acad., 1945. Adminstrv. asst. OPM, WPB, Washington, 1940-43; founder, ptnr. Bradham-Craver Co., 1946-49; founder, owner, ptnr. Craver & Co. pub. accts., Charleston, S.C., 1948-58; founder, dir., pres. So. Gen. Corp., Charleston, 1949-83, Carolina Gen. Corp., Charleston, 1952-82, Universal Fin. Corp., Charleston, 1962—; founder, pres. Coastal Investers, Inc., 1955-56, Craver Indsl. Park, Inc., 1963-67, Beautyguard Mfg. Corp., 1962-67, Leasemasters, Inc., 1968-88, Fin. Resources Corp., 1973—; ptnr. Atlantis Hotel, Atlantic City. Patentee metal forming equipment and device field. Vice-chmn. Charleston Cancer Crusade, 1965; mem. Charleston County Aviation Authority, 1970—, chmn., 1971-88, chmn. emeritus, 1988—; bd. dirs. Airport Ops. Coun. Internat., 1987—; mem. parent's adv. coun. Converse Coll., 1965-74, chmn., trustee, 1972-74; bd. dirs. Patriots Point Found., 1977—, v.p., 1979-82, pres. 1982—. Lt. USNR, 1945-46, PTO, ETO. Recipient Outstanding Bus. Achievement award U.S. Mcht. Marine Acad. Alumni, 1960, Meritorious Alumni award, 1970. Mem. Am. Soc. Metals, Hibernian Soc. (founding trustee Hibernian Soc. Found. 1976—, v.p. 1977-80, 81-83, pres. 1983-85), Navy League (pres. Charleston coun. 1971-73, nat. exec. com. 1971-75, nat. dir. 1977-80, 81-88, life), Soc. First Families S.C. 1670-1700 (life), Charleston Trident C. of C., U.S. Mcht. Marine Acad. Alumni Assn. (pres. Charleston charter chpt. 1964-65, regional gov. 1965-71, life), Carolina Yacht Club, Charleston Country Club, Albemarle Club (pres. 1965-66), Propeller Club Charleston, Sertoma, Pi Kappa Alph. Democrat. Presbyterian. Home: 55 South Battery Charleston SC 29401 Office: Universal Fin Corp PO Box 1014 Charleston SC 29402

CRAWFORD, CHRISTOPHER M(ILLER), gas distributing company executive; b. Indpls., Dec. 24, 1942; s. Willard John and Beryl (Blossom) C.; m. Phyllis Ann Corn, Jan. 25, 1964; children: John, Andrew, Anne, Jane. BS, Purdue U., 1965; MBA, Butler U., 1968. Programmer analyst Ind. Gas Co. Inc., Indpls., 1967-68, systems analyst, 1969-70, mgr. data processing, 1970-74, dir. data processing, 1974-80, v.p. adminstrv. services, 1980—. Author, editor: Sponsoring Olympic Canoeing Sprint Races, 1987; contbr. articles to profl. jours. Pres. Eagle Creek Park Found., Indpls., 1986, Arsonal Tech. Adv. Com., Indpls., 1977-81; chmn., founder Indpls. Canoe Racing Council Inc., 1987. Named Vol. of Yr., Am. Canoe Assn., 1987; recipient Leisure Leaders award City of Indpls., 1986, Service award Internat. Canoe Fedn., 1987. Mem. Am. Gas Assn. (chmn. info. systems com. 1979), U.S. Canoe/Kayak Team Inc. (Heinz Wahl Meml. award 1986). Republican. Presbyterian. Clubs: Hoosier Canoe, Model A Ford (Indpls.).

CRAWFORD, HOMER, retired lawyer, paper company executive; b. St. Louis, Nov. 28, 1916; s. Raymond S. and Mary (Homer) C.; m. Esther Wilkinson, Oct. 4, 1944 (div. 1949); 1 dau., Candace C.; m. Sara E. Twigg, May 3, 1952; children: Georgiana, William Twigg. A.B., Amherst Coll., 1938; LL.B., U. Va., 1941. Admitted to N.Y. bar, 1942; assoc. firm LeBoeuf, Lamb, Leiby & MacRae, 1942-54, partner, 1954-56, v.p., sec. St. Regis Paper Co., 1956-82, gen. counsel, 1981, now ret. Mem. Am., N.Y. State bar assns., Am. Soc. Corp. Secs. (dir. 1965-68), Theta Delta Chi. Republican. Presbyterian. Home: 11 Laurel Heights PO Box 1057 Old Lyme CT 06371

CRAWFORD, JOHN JOSEPH, finance company executive; b. East Cleveland, Ohio, Feb. 9, 1948; s. Loman Blackburn and Sophia (Slunski) C. Student, Howard U., 1966-68, Colo. State U., 1968-70; M in Pub. Adminstrn., U. Colo., 1976. Adminstrv. budget officerjudiciary dept. State of Colo., Denver, 1973-78; dir. corp. First Fin. Securities, Aurora, Colo., 1980-84; analyst small bus. Churchill Tech. Co., Lakewood, Colo., 1984-87; dir. corp. fin. Pro Quest, Inc., Englewood, Colo., 1986—. Bd. dirs. Colo. Mt. Vineyards, Palisade, Colo. sect. Cystic Fibrosis Found., 1978-81, March of Dimes, 1981-85; chmn. fundraising Art Reach Found., 1985. Mem. Mensa, Rocky Mt. Flute Assn. (treas. 1982-84), Colo. St. Andrews Soc. (bd.-at-large 1988—). Republican. Presbyterian. Office: Internat Med Systems 6400 S Fiddlers Green Ste 1700 Englewood CO 80111

CRAWFORD, LESTER MILLS, JR., veterinarian; b. Demopolis, Ala., Mar. 13, 1938; s. Lester Mills and Susan Doris (Mitchell) C.; m. Catherine Walker, July 27, 1963; children: Catherine Leigh, Mary Stuart. D.V.M., Auburn U., 1963; Ph.D., U. Ga., 1969. Pvt. practice vet. medicine Meridian, Miss. and Birmingham, Ala., 1963-64; research and devel. staff Agrl. div. Am. Cyanamid Co., Princeton, N.J., 1964-66; also cons. Am. Cyanamid Co.; assoc. prof. pharmacology, assoc. dean Coll. Vet. Medicine, U. Ga., 1970-75; dir. Bur. Vet. Medicine, FDA, HEW, Rockville, Md., 1978-80, 82-85; assoc. adminstr. food safety and inspection service USDA, Washington, 1986-87, adminstr., 1987—; head dept. physiology-pharmacology U. Ga., 1981-82; cons. pharm. industry, agribus. FDA, WHO. Contbr. sci. articles to profl. jours. Lay speaker Methodist Ch., 1970—; bd. dirs.; Ga. div. Am. Cancer Soc. U. Ga. Faculty Club, Athens Acad. Recipient Alpha Psi Nat. Council award Am. Coll. Vet. Pharmacology and Therapeutics, 1977; A.M. Mills award; K.F. Meyer award; named Outstanding Sr. Auburn U. Sch. Vet. Medicine, 1963; Commr.'s spl. citation FDA; award of merit FDA, 1983. Mem. AVMA (Aux. award), Ga. Vet. Med. Assn., D.C. Vet. Med. Assn., AAAS, Sigma Xi, Phi Zeta, Phi Kappa Phi. Republican. Club: Athens (Ga.) Country. Home: 5815 Highland Dr Chevy Chase MD 20815 Office: Bur Vet Medicine FDA 5600 Fishers Ln Rockville MD 20857

CRAWFORD, ROGER BRENTLEY, real estate executive; b. Roswell, N.Mex., Jan. 15, 1951; s. Oscar Fay and Marie Elizabeth C.; student N.Mex. Mil. Inst., 1970, Eastern N.Mex. U., 1971, N.Mex. State U., 1972, U. N.Mex., 1973; married; children: Mariesha, Joshua, Jordan. Pres. Sundoxa Corp., Roswell, 1977-80; pres. The Berrendo Co., Roswell, 1980-82, Diamond Braich Ltd.-Internat. Properties; chmn. bd. CitiGas Corp., The New Energy Co., Midland, Tex., 1982-83, New Energy Oil & Gas Corp., 1982—, Jordache Investment Co., 1982-86; chmn. bd., pres., and chief exec. officer Citigas Corp., Midland and Dallas, 1986—; dir. Berrendo Co., Roswell, Braich Devel. Co., Roswell, Townes Energy Co., Barclay Resources, N.Mex. Gas Co., Internat. Communications, Inc. Mem. Internat. Real Estate Fedn., Farm and Land Inst., Am. Real Estate Exchange, Nat. Assn. Realtors, Realtors Nat. Mktg. Inst., Inst. Valuers (Zurich), Ind. Petroleum Assn., Am. Gas Processors Assn., Internat. Petroleum Exchange, Am. Mgmt. Assn., Realtors Assn. N.Mex. Office: 6 Desta Dr Ste 2700 Midland TX 79705

CRAWFORD, WARREN JAY, mechanical engineer; b. Ft. Bragg, N.C., June 11, 1950; s. Bernard Lee and Anne Catherine (Van Hassell) C. BSME, Valparaiso U., Ind., 1974. Designer Mason Cumberlain, Richmond, Ky., 1977; tool design engr. Standard Products, Lexington, Ky., 1977-78; mfg. engr. Multi-Metals, Louisville, 1978-79; process engr. Genesco, Nashville, 1979-80; machine design engr. U.S. Tobacco Co., Nashville, 1980-84, dir. mfg. engring, 1984—. Mem. ASME, Soc. Mech. Engrs. Home: 914 Steeplecupse Dr Brentwood TN 37027 Office: US Tobacco Co 905 Harrison St Nashville TN 37203

CRAWFORD, WILLIAM WALSH, consumer products company executive; b. Clearwater, Fla., Oct. 7, 1927; s. Francis Marion and Frances Marie (Walsh) C. B.S., Georgetown U., 1950; LL.B., Harvard, 1954. Bar: N.Y. 1955, Ill. 1972. Assoc. firm Sullivan & Cromwell, N.Y.C., 1954-58; counsel Esso Standard Oil, N.Y.C., 1958-60; partner Alexander & Green, N.Y.C., 1960-71; v.p. Internat. Harvester Co., Chgo., 1971-76; v.p., gen. counsel, sec. 1976-80; sr. v.p. gen. counsel Kraft, Inc., Glenview, Ill., 1980-81; sr. v.p., gen. counsel, sec. Dart & Kraft, Inc., 1981-86; sr. v.p., gen. counsel, sec. Kraft, Inc., 1986-88, sr. v.p., sec., 1988—. Mem. ABA, Ill. Bar Assn., Assn. of Bar of City of N.Y., Am. Judicature Soc., Am. Law Inst., Am. Soc. Corp. Secs., Assn. Gen. Counsel. Clubs: Saddle and Cycle, Chicago.; Chgo. Golf (Wheaton, Ill.); Chgo. Office: Kraft Inc Kraft Ct Glenview IL 60025

CRAWN, LINDEN RALPH, aerospace company executive; b. Newark, Jan. 19, 1923; s. Lester R. and Mathilda E. (Schmidt) D.; div. 1984; children: Lynn C., Richard L., Sandra L. Student, Oreg. State U., 1943-44; BA in Accountancy, Pace U., 1948. Staff pub. acct. Various firms, Newark and Los Angeles, 1948-52; supr. contract adminstrn. Charles Engelhard, Inc., East Newark, N.J., 1952-55; chief acct. Curtiss-Wright Corp., N.J. and Pa., 1955-61; asst. to treas., contracts adminstr. Lummus Corp., N.Y.C., 1961-62; mgr. project control, combustion engring. Lummus Corp., Bloomfield, N.J., 1967-68; asst. controller, materials mgr. UNIVAC Corp., Phila., 1962-64; dir. prodn. control ITT Fed. Labs., Clifton, N.J., 1964-67; mgr. material Weston Instruments Co., Newark, 1968-71; mgr. ops. control Lockheed Electronics Corp., Plainfield, N.J., 1971—. Pres. Pine Glen (Pa.) Civic Assn., 1958-60; mem. Pine Glen Sch. Bd., 1960-61; bd. dirs., bldg. and grounds com. Bald Eagle (Pa.) Jointure Sch. Bd., Wingate, 1961. Served as sgt. USAF, 1942-46, Guam. Mem. Inst. Cert. Mgrs. (cert. mgr.), Am. Prodn. and Inventory Control Soc. (internat. dir. ednl. policies 1964-66, chpt. bd. dirs. 1963-64), Systems and Procedures Assn. Am. (chpt. treas. 1956-57), Nat. Mgmt. Assn., Am. Legion. Lodge: Elks. Office: Lockheed Electronics Corp 1501 US Hwy 22 Plainfield NJ 07061

CRAY, CLOUD LANOR, JR., grain products company executive; b. Detroit, Nov. 7, 1922; s. Cloud Lanor and Edna (Reinoehl) C.; m. Sara Jane Hunter, Feb. 12, 1944; children: Karen Lee Cray Seaberg, Susan Hunter Cray Robbins, Cathy Lynn Cray Freund. BS in Chemical Engring., Case Inst. of Tech., Cleve., 1943; Hon. Dr. of Indsl. Arts, Benedictine Coll., Atchison, 1984. Dir. Midwest Grain Products, Inc., Atchison, Kans., 1947—, pres., 1962-80, chmn. bd., 1980—, chief exec. officer, 1980-88; dir. City Nat. Bank of Atchison, Atchison, 1955-83, Union Terminal Railway Co., Atchison; pres. Atchison Leather Products Co., 1980-86, Midwest Grain Asset Co., Inc., 1980-88; dir. Commerce Bank of Kans. City, 1981-84; pres. Cray Med. Rsch. Found., 1981—; bd. dirs. Kans. Power and Light Co., Security Benefit Life Ins. Co., Commerce Bancshares, Kans. diabetes Adv. Coun. bd. dir. Unified Dist. #409 Sch. Bd., 1967-75, trustee Coll. of Emporia, Kans., 1962-1973; fin. chmn., 1970-73; chmn Million Dollar Endowment Fund, 1968-71; bd. dir. Y.M.C.A., Atchison, 1963-72; v.p. of Bd., 1970, pres. 1971, Dir. of the Bldg. Fund Dr., 1980; trustee Atchison Hosp. Assn., 1966—; chmn. Rep. Fin. Commn, Atchison County, 1966; state dir. Kans. Day Program, 1972; pres. Kans Day, 1975; treas. 2nd Congl. Dist., 1973-74; exec. dir. Rep Kans. Leadership Club, 1975-76; chmn. rs, 1976. Republican. Presbyterian. Office: Midwest Grain Products Inc 1300 Main St Atchison KS 66002

CRAZE, STEVEN LEE, heating and air conditioning company executive; b. Oak Ridge, Tenn., Oct. 2, 1950; s. Leroy and Hazel (Watkins) C.; m. Julia Elizabeth Haislip, July 31, 1982. BA, U. Tenn., 1974. Mem. staff Craze Bros. Air Conditioning, Oliver Springs, Tenn., 1968-77; dist. mgr. sales Assoc. Equipment Co. Inc., Huntsville, Ala., 1977-83; dist. mgr. sales Assoc. Equipment Co. Inc., Knoxville, Tenn., 1983-87, supr. sales, 1987—. Mem. Tennessee Valley Heat Pump Tng. Assn., Million Dollar Sales Club, Two Million Dollar Sales Club. Home: 703 Banbury Rd Knoxville TN 37922 Office: Assoc Equipment Co Inc 300 E Depot Knoxville TN 37917

CREAMER, WILLIAM HENRY, III, insurance company executive; b. Narberth, Pa., Mar. 24, 1927; s. William Henry and Stella Elizabeth (McShane) C.; m. Anne Tyson Greer, Sept. 20, 1952; children: William Henry IV, Anne McSherry Creamer Gregg, Mary Greer Conyack. B.S. in Econs, Villanova U., 1951. C.L.U. With N.Y. Life Ins. Co., 1951—; gen. mgr. N.Y. Life Ins. Co., Towson, Md., 1957-60; regional supt. tng. N.Y. Life Ins. Co., 1960-62; gen. mgr. N.Y. Life Ins. Co., Scranton, Pa., 1962-66, Arlington, Va., 1966-69; supt. agencies N.Y. Life Ins. Co., N.Y.C., 1969-70; regional v.p. N.Y. Life Ins. Co., Mpls., 1970-74; v.p. N.Y. Life Ins. Co., N.Y.C., 1974-83; sr. v.p. N.Y. Life Ins. Co., 1983-85; in charge office fed. affairs N.Y. Life Ins. Co., Washington, 1986-89. Served with USN, 1945-46. Mem. Nat. Assn. Life Underwriters, Am. Soc. C.L.U.s, U.S. Power Squadron (past comdr. Shrewsbury squadron), Estate Planning Council (past dir.). Republican. Roman Catholic. Clubs: Shrewsbury River Yacht, George Town, Capital Hill. Lodge: Kiwanis (past pres. Scranton chpt., past dir.). Home: 3 Wardell Ave Rumson NJ 07760 Office: NY Life Ins Co 51 Madison Ave New York NY 10010

CREAN, JOHN C., housing and recreational vehicles manufacturing company executive; b. Bowden, N.D., 1925; married. Founder Fleetwood Enterprises, Inc., Riverside, Calif., 1951, pres., 1952-70, chmn., chief exec. officer, 1970—, also dir. Served with USN, 1942; with U.S. Mcht. Marines, 1944-45. Office: Fleetwood Enterprises Inc 3125 Myers St Riverside CA 92523 *

CREANGE, PETER MILES, securities trader; b. Chgo., June 3, 1945; s. Arthur Creange and Leone (Brinkley) Mitchell; m. Jo Moya, Oct. 23, 1966; children: Melissa, Traci. Cert. in fin. planning, Coll. Fin. Planning, Denver, 1984. Asst. v.p., adminstrv. mgr. Merrill Lynch, Albuquerque, 1967—. Pres. Vis. Nurse Service, Albuquerque, 1977. Served with U.S. Navy, 1967-70. Mem. Inst. Cert. Fin. Planners. Republican. Roman Catholic. Lodge: Kiwanis (pres. 1978-79). Office: Merrill Lynch PO Box 3030 Albuquerque NM 87110

CREASON, GARY WAYNE, engineer; b. Excelsior Springs, Mo., Apr. 2, 1948; s. Wayne Thomas and Thelma Grace (Payne) C.; m. Janet Sue Hoyle, May 11, 1974. BSCE, U. Mo., Rolla, 1971; MBA, Rockhurst Coll., 1984. Constrn. engr. Sangamo Constrn., Springfield, Ill., 1971-73; hydraulic engr. U.S. Army C.E., Kansas City, Mo., 1973-79; project engr. Burns & McDonnell, Kansas City, 1979-85, mgr. project devel., 1985—. Admissions ambassador U. Mo. Rolla, 1987—; chmn. com. Riverfront Redevel. Inc., Kansas City, 1987; mem. com. Task Force on Quality, Kansas City, 1988. Mem. ASCE, NSPE, Mo. Soc. Profl. Engrs. Republican. Methodist. Office: Burns & McDonnell Engring Co 4800 E 63d St Kansas City MO 64130

CRECELIUS, ROBERT ALLEN, financial consultant; b. Princeton, Ind., Apr. 10, 1927; s. Henry and Maude Muller (Miley) C.; m. Sylvia Ann Cribb, Nov. 12, 1966; children: Beth Ann, Robert Allen Jr. BS in Bus. Stats., Ind. U., 1950; postgrad., N.Y. Inst. Fin., 1967. Cert. fin. planner. Agt. gen. ins. various agys., 1950-67; account exec. Hayden, Stone Inc., 1967-69; regional mgr. Westam. Fin. Corp., Princeton, Inc., 1969-86; sec.-treas Wealth Concepts Inc., Princeton, 1984—; regional mgr. Anchor Nat. fin. Services iNc., Princeton, 1986—; pres., sec., treas. Coordinated Ins. Ctr., Inc., Princeton, 1982—; cons. Nat. Ctr. Fin. Edn., San Francisco, 1987—. Treas. Rep. party Fla., Miami, 1967, del. Nat. Conv., 1968; mem. Temple Christina Acad. Fin. Com., Princeton. Mem. Internat. Assn. Fin. Planners, Inst. Cert. Fin. Planners, Ind. Soc. Pub. Accts., Masons. Home: Lake Rd RR 2 Princeton IN 47670 Office: The Fin Ctr 1250 W Broadway Princeton IN 47670

CREEDON, JOHN J., insurance company executive; b. N.Y.C., Aug. 1, 1924; s. Bartholomew and Emma (Glynn) C.; m. Vivian Elser, Aug. 17, 1947 (dec. 1981); children: Juliette, Michele, John, David; m. Diane Ardouin, 1983; children: Jean Philippe, Genevieve. B.S. magna cum laude, N.Y.U., 1952, LL.B. cum laude, 1955, LL.M., 1962. Bar: N.Y. State 1955, U.S. Supreme Ct. 1960. With Met. Life Ins. Co., N.Y.C., 1942—; v.p., asso. gen. counsel Met. Life Ins. Co., 1970-73, sr. v.p., gen. counsel, 1973-76, exec. v.p., 1976-80, pres., dir., 1980-83, pres., chief exec. officer, 1983—; chmn. bd. Met. Property & Liability Ins. Co., 1979-80, dir., 1986; adj. prof. law NYU Law Sch., 1962-72; bd. dirs., pres. Am. Bar Found., 1980-82; chmn. bd. Met. Life Found.; trustee Practicing Law Inst. NYU, 1968-81, NYU Law Ctr. Found.; mem. legal adv. com. N.Y. Stock Exchange, 1978-83; chmn. Life Ins. Council N.Y., 1977-78; chmn. Am. Council of Life Ins., 1986-87; bd. dirs. NYNEX Corp., Union Carbide Corp., Albany Assurance Co., Ltd., Banco Santander, Melville Corp., Rockwell Internat. Corp., Sonat Inc., State St. Research and Mgmt. Co., Met. Property and Liability Ins. Co. Editor: The Bus. Lawyer, 1973-74; contbr. articles to profl. jours. Served with USNR, 1943-46. Mem. ABA (assembly del. 1972-75, chmn. sect. corp. banking and bus. law 1975-76), N.Y. State Bar Assn., Assn. Bar City N.Y., Assn. Life Ins. Counsel (pres. 1977-78), Am. Law Inst., Bus. Council N.Y. State (chmn. 1987-88), N.Y. State C. of C. and Industry, Alliance for Free Enterprise. Office: Met Life Ins Co 1 Madison Ave New York NY 10010

CREIGHTON, JOHN DOUGLAS, newspaper publisher; b. Toronto, Ont., Can., Nov. 27, 1928; s. Stanley Dixon and Ethel Grace (Armstrong) C.; m. Marilyn June Chamberlain, June 20, 1953; children: Scott, Bruce, Donald. Grad., Humberside Collegiate, Can., 1948. With Toronto Stock Exchange, 1948; reporter Toronto Telegram, 1948-62, asst. city editor, 1962-65, sports editor, 1965-67, city editor, 1967-69, mng. editor, 1969-71; pub. Toronto Sun, 1971-84; pres. Sun Pub. Co., 1984—; mem. Nat. Newspaper Awards Com.; bd. dirs. McDonald's Restaurant of Can. Ltd., CAE Industries Ltd., Colonia Life Ins. Co. Active Big Bros. of Can., 1969—, also past pres.; bd. dirs. Heart and Stroke Found. Ont.; mem. Premier's Adv. Com. on Exec. Resources; mem. nat. council of Duke of Edinburgh's Award in Can. Mem. Toronto Men's Press Club (pres. 1959), Nat. Press Club. Anglican. Clubs: Lambton Golf and Country (Toronto); Albany; Les Ambassadeurs, Mark's, Annabel's (London); River Oaks Country (Houston). Office: Toronto Sun Pub Corp, 333 King St E, Toronto, ON Canada M5A 3X5

CREIGHTON, JOHN W., JR., manufacturing company executive; b. 1932; married. BS, Ohio State U., 1954, JD, 1957; MBA, U. Miami, 1965. With Arthur Andersen and Co., 1957-59, Arvida Corp., 1959-66; exec. v.p. Mortgage Cons. Inc., 1966-70; with Weyerhaeuser Co., 1970—, v.p., then exec. v.p., now pres.; pres. Weyerhaeuser Real Estate Co.; chmn. bd. dirs. Fed. Home Loan Bank Seattle; bd. dirs. Nat. Corp. Houston Partnership; trustee Puget Sound Mutual Savs. Bank. With U.S. Army, 1954-56. Office: Weyerhaeuser Co Tacoma WA 98477 *

CREIGHTON, JOHN WALLIS, JR., former management educator, consultant; b. Yeung Kong, China, Apr. 7, 1916; s. John Wallis and Lois (Jameson) C.; m. Harriet Harrington, June 30, 1940; children: Carol (Mrs. Brian LeNeve), Joan (Mrs. Christopher B. Martin). Student, Wooster Coll., 1933-36; B.S., U. Mich., 1938; A.B., Hastings Coll., 1939; Ph.D. in Wood Tech. and Indsl. Engring., U. Mich., 1954. Operator, sawmill Cayahoga Falls, Ohio, 1939-41; mem. staff U.S. Bd. Econ. Warfare, Ecuador, 1941-43; asst. gen. mgr. R.S. Bacon Veneer Co., Chgo., 1943-44; gen. mgr., v.p. Bacon Lumber Co., Sunman, Ind., 1943-45; mem. faculty Mich. State U., Lansing, 1945-54; prof. wood tech. Mich. State U., 1945-54; asst. to gen. mgr., v.p. Baker Furniture Inc., Grand Rapids, Mich., 1954-58; pres. Creighton Bldg. Co., Santa Barbara, Calif., 1958-65; prof. mgmt. Colo. State U., Fort Collins, 1965-67, U.S. Naval Postgrad. Sch., Monterey, Calif., 1967-86; emeritus prof. U.S. Naval Postgrad. Sch., 1986—, chmn. dept., 1967-71; cons. to govt. Assoc. editor: Jour. Tech. Transfer, 1975-88; author papers in field. Mem. Forestry Commn., Carmel, Calif. Recipient various research grants in lumber mfg., research and orgn. studies for U.S. Navy and U.S. Forest Service. Mem. Tech. Transfer Soc. Presbyterian. Home: 8065 Lake Pl Carmel CA 93923

CRENNA, JAMES ALAN, brokerage executive; b. St. Paul, Nov. 14, 1950; s. Angelo William and Margret Elizabeth (Anderson) C.; m. Pamela Kaye Timm, Nov. 3, 1978; 1 child, Randi Kristina. BS, St. Cloud State U., 1973; postgrad., Securities Industry Inst., 1989. Cert. fin. planner. Real estate salesman Internat. Resources, Alexandria, Va., 1973-75; stockbroker Merrill Lynch, Duluth, Minn., 1975-77; stockbroker John G. Kinnard & Co., Mpls., 1977-82, mgr. options dept., 1982—, br. office mgr., 1983—. Mem. Presdl. Task Force, Washington, 1980—; contbr. Rep. Nat. Com., Washington, 1980—. Mem. I.A.F.P., T.C.A.F.P. (house ops. com.), Mpls. Athletic Club, S.I.A. Inst. Republican. Lutheran. Office: John G Kinnard & Co 600 S State Hwy 169 Ste 1960 Saint Louis Park MN 55426

CRENSHAW, CARLTON BOYD, software company executive; b. Kansas City, Mo., Mar. 18, 1945; s. Clarence Albert and Sarah Elizabeth (Bloom) C.; m. Andrea Cecile Crenshaw, Dec. 31, 1966 (div. July 1986); children: Collette, Christine, Catherine; m. Janet Marie Servadio, Dec. 27, 1986; children: Alison, Justin. BBA, So. Meth. U., 1966; MBA, NYU, 1970. Fin. analyst Mobil Oil Corp., N.Y.C., 1970-71; fin. analyst Sperry Corp., N.Y.C., 1971-72, staff v.p. investor relations, asst. treas., 1972-79, treas., 1979-83, v.p. strategic planning, 1984-85; v.p. fin. and adminstrn., chief fin. officer Software AG Systems Inc., Reston, Va., 1985—. Served to capt. USMC, 1966-69, Vietnam. Decorated Bronze Star with combat V, Purple Heart with oak leaf cluster; Vietnamese Cross of Gallentry with silver star, bronze star, gold leaf cluster; recipient Excellence in Investor Relations award Computer Industry Analysts, 1979. Mem. Fin. Execs. Inst. Home: 1233 Gilman Ct Herndon VA 22070

CRENSHAW, GORDON LEE, tobacco company executive; b. Richmond, Va., Jan. 19, 1922; s. Walter and Hattie (Ready) C.; m. Deubre Anne Roper, May 12, 1945; children—Clarke Hutchins, Gordon Lee. BA in Econs., U. Va., 1943. With Universal Leaf Tobacco Co., Inc., Richmond, 1946—, v.p., 1958-65, pres., 1965-88, chmn., chief exec. officer, 1988, chmn., 1989—; chmn., chief exec. officer Universal Corp. (holding. co. formed with Universal Leaf Tobacco Co., Inc. and subs.), Richmond, 1988, chmn., 1989—; bd. dirs. Crestar Fin. Corp., Lawyers Title Ins. Corp. (sub. Universal Corp.). Bd. dirs. Jr. Achievement, Va. Found. for Ind. Colls., Va. Port Authority, Va. Inter-Gov. Inst., Richmond Eye Hosp., Va. Bus. Council; bd. govs. Va. Home for Boys; trustee Richmond Meml. Hosp. Lt. USNR, 1943-46. Mem. NAM (bd. dirs.), Tobacco Assn. U.S. (gov., past pres.), Commonwealth Club, Country Club of Va. Episcopalian. Office: Universal Corp Hamilton St at Broad PO Box 25099 Richmond VA 23230

CRENSHAW, PARIS EVANS, JR., retail company executive; b. Albemarle County, Va., June 14, 1936; s. Paris Evans Sr. and Margaree (Birckhead) C.; m. Betty Gibson, June 14, 1958; children: Wanda Kelen Andrews, Paris Evans III. AA, Mars Hill Coll., 1956; BA, U. Va., 1959. Sales rep. Fidelity Union Ins. Co., Charlottesville, Va., 1959-60, Met. Ins. Co., Charlottesville, Va., 1960-61; buyer Leggett Stores, Charlottesville, Va., 1961-69, div. mgr., 1969-73, asst. store mgr., 1973-79; corp. credit mgr. Leggett Stores, Lynchburg, Va., 1979—; bd. dirs. credit div. Nat. Retail Mchts. Assn., Lynchburg Retail Mchts. Assn. Bd. dirs. Carter Glass Heritage Edn. Found., Lynchburg, 1987—. Mem. Piedmont, Peakland Swim Club, Rotary. Baptist. Office: Leggett Credit Union Ctr 1014 Church St Lynchburg VA 24505

CRESWELL, DONALD CRESTON, management consultant, marketing specialist; b. Balt., Mar. 28, 1932; s. Carroll Creston and Verna Moore (Taylor) C.; student Johns Hopkins U., 1951-52; M.B.A., U. Dayton, 1966; postgrad. bus. Stanford U., 1975; m. Terri Sue Tidwell, Dec. 28, 1958; 1 son, Creston Lee. Cons. engr. A.D. Ring & Assocs., Washington, 1956-58; sales and mktg. mgr. Ampex Corp., Redwood City, Calif., 1959-68; dir. mktg., magnetic products div. RCA Corp., N.Y.C., 1968-71; staff v.p. sales and advt. Pan Am. World Airways, N.Y.C., 1971-74; mktg. v.p. Rocor Internat., Palo Alto, Calif., 1975; v.p., chief operating officer, gen. mgr., Am. AmBuCar Services, Inc., San Francisco, 1976; prin. mgmt. cons., dir. mktg. services Stanford Research Inst., Menlo Park, Calif., 1977-86 ; v.p. and gen. mgr. Strategic Decisions Group-Decisions Systems, 1987—; bd. dirs. Rogerson Aircraft Controls, 1981-85, Jets Cybernetics; lectr. planning and mktg. mgmt. Am. Mgmt. Assn., 1968-69; program chmn. Grad. Bus. Assn., 1965; rep. to Electronics Industries Assn., 1968-71, to Internat. Air Transport Assn., 1971-74. Bd. dirs. Peninsula Youth Soccer Club, 1981-82; nat. dir. referee assessment, mem. referee com. U.S. Soccer Fedn., 1986-88; regional chief referee San Carlos Am. Youth Soccer Orgn., 1981-85; State dir. assessment Calif. Soccer Assn., 1982-85 ; mem. Los Angeles Olympics Organizing Com., 1983-84; ofcl. N. Am. Soccer League, 1983-84. Mem. Am. Mktg. Assn. (exec. mem.), Am. Theatre Organ Assn. (bd. dirs. 1978-79), Nat. Intercollegiate Soccer Ofcls. Assn., Charles Lindbergh Found., U.S. Soccer Fedn. (cert. soccer referee). Republican. Club: Wings. Home: 8 Pyrola Ln San Carlos CA 94070 Office: SDG Decision Systems 2440 Sand Hill Rd Menlo Park CA 94025-6900

CRESWELL, DOROTHY ANNE, computer consultant; b. Burlington, Iowa, Feb. 6, 1943; d. Robert Emerson and Agnes Imogene (Gardner) Mefford; m. John Lewis Creswell, Aug. 28, 1965. AA, Burlington Community Coll., 1963; BA in Math., U. Iowa, 1965; MS in Math., Western Ill. U., 1970; postgrad., Iowa State U., 1974—. Computer programmer Mason & Hanger, Silas Mason Co., Inc., Burlington, Iowa, 1965-74; systems programmer Contractor's Hotline, Ft. Dodge, Iowa, 1974; dir. data processing Iowa Cen. Community Coll., Ft. Dodge, 1975-80; systems programming mgr. Norand Corp., Cedar Rapids, Iowa, 1980-82; spl. svcs. mgr. Pioneer Hi-Bred Internat., Inc., Cedar Rapids, 1982-87; owner, pres. D.C. Cons., Ankeny, Iowa, 1987—; computers-in-edn. del. to People's Rep. China, People to People Internat., Kansas City, Mo., 1987. Contbr. articles, papers to profl. publs. Mem. Data Processing Mgmt. Assn. (bd. dirs. 1986-87, v.p. 1988), Adminstrv. Mgmt. Soc. (v.p. 1986-88, sec. 1985-86, merit award 1987), Assn. Computing Machinery, Hawkeye Personal Computer Users (pres. 1985-86), Macintosh Users, DEC Users Group (v.p. eastern Iowa chpt. 1981-82). Democrat. Methodist. Office: DC Cons PO Box 195 Ankeny IA 50021

CREUZIGER, DONALD PHILLIP, professional services company executive, former army officer; b. Racine, Wis., Aug. 22, 1927; s. Charles Melford and Iva Hazel (Brandt) C.; m. Mary Louis Larsen, July 15, 1950; children—Karen; John. B.S., U.S. Mil. Acad., 1950; M.S., U. So. Calif., 1963. Lic. comml. helicopter pilot. Commd. 2d lt. U.S. Army, 1950, advanced through grades to col., 1970; staff officer Joint Chiefs of Staff, Washington, 1969-70; chief firepower div. Dept. Chief of Staff, Ops., Dept Army, Washington, 1971-72; chief of staff 1st Armored Div., Ansbach, Fed. Republic Germany, 1973-75; dep. asst. Sec. of Army, Washington, 1975-76; asst. v.p. Jaycor, Alexandria, Va., 1977-79; chief exec. officer XMCO Inc., Reston, Va., 1979—. Decorated Legion of Merit with bronze oak leaf cluster, Air medal with 2 bronze oak leaf clusters. Mem. Nat. Trust Hist. Preservation, U.S. Senatorial Club, Fairfax C. of C., Assn. U.S. Army, Am. Def. Preparedness Assn., U.S. Armor Assn. (sec. 1978-82). Republican. Lutheran. Club: River Bend. Lodge: Masons. Avocations: golf; woodworking. Home: 10531 Brinham Rd Great Falls VA 22066 Office: XMCO Inc 11150 11150 Sunrise Valley Dr Reston VA 22091

CREVELING, ROBERT NORMAN, mortgage banking executive; b. Harvey, Ill., Dec. 27, 1947; s. Norman D. Creveling and Margaret E. (Hollett) Mullin.; m. Nhuong T. Nguyen, May 28, 1972; 1 child: Norman C. From asst. mgr. to sr. mgr. Fireside Thrift, Santa Rosa, Calif., 1972-79; mgr. real estate loan dept. Fireside Thrift, Redwood City, Calif., 1980-81; credit adminstr. ILS Funding, San Jose, Calif., 1979-80; from v.p. production to sr. v.p. ops. ILS Funding, San Mateo, Calif., 1981-84; sr. v.p. ops. Unified Mortgage Co., Cupertino, Calif., 1984-87; v.p. mortgage lending bus. line Barclays Bank, San Jose, Calif., 1987-88; sr. v.p. mortgage banking div. Barclays Bank, San Jose, 1988—. Served to sgt. U.S. Army, 1969-72, Vietnam. Decorated Bronze Star, Purple Heart, Air medal. Mem. Mortgage Bankers Assn., Calif. Mortgage Bankers Assn. Republican. Home: 20 Tissiack Ct Fremont CA 94539 Office: Barclays Bank 2 N Market St San Jose CA 95150

CREVELT, DWIGHT EUGENE, computer company executive; b. Kansas City, Mo., Jan. 16, 1957; s. James Robert and Louise Gwendolynn (Wolchek) C.; m. Jean Anne Cassens, Aug. 11, 1979; children: William Michael, Michelle Anne, Matthew Henry. Student U. Las Vegas, 1973-74, U.S. Naval Acad., 1975-77; BS in Computer Engring., Iowa State U., 1979. Computer engr., cons., Las Vegas, Nev., 1972-73; software engr. Gamex Industries, Las Vegas, 1973-74, United Audio Visual, Las Vegas, 1977; computer engr. Sircoma, Las Vegas, 1979-80; dir. research Mills-Jennings, Las Vegas, 1981; pres., chmn. Crevelt Computer, Las Vegas, 1977-88; mgr. design and devel. Electronic Data Techs., 1988—. Corr. sec. Clark County Rep. Party; del. Rep. Nat. Conv., 1988. Author (computer programs): CDC160/NCR310 Disassembler, 1971; Computer Networking, 1983; Telephone Access Control, 1984; Fiber Optic Network, 1984; (co-author) Slot Machine Mania. Mem. Nat. Eagle Scout Assn., U.S. Congl. Adv. Bd.; del. Rep. Nat. Conv., 1988. Mem. Soc. Naval Engrs., Sales Mktg. Execs. Assn., Am. Philatic Soc., U.S. Naval Acad. Alumni Assn. (sec.), USN League, U.S. Naval Inst., Las Vegas Exchange Club (bd. dirs.). Office: Electronic Data Techs 2950 S Highland Las Vegas NV 89102

CREVIER, ROGER L., banker; b. Holyoke, Mass., May 14, 1939; s. Gabriel and Justine (Gagnon) C.; m. Sandra Boyer, Nov. 18, 1966 (dec. Jan. 1976); children—Justin, Christopher; m. May Sadaka, May 5, 1979; children—Rana, Petra. B.S., Rensselaer Poly. Inst., 1961; M.S., Yale U., 1964; M.B.A., Harvard U., 1967. Asst. treas. Chase Manhattan Bank, N.Y.C., 1968-70, 2d v.p., 1970-72, v.p., 1972-83, sr. v.p., 1983-87; exec. dir. Investcorp Internat. Inc., N.Y.C., 1987—. Republican. Club: Harvard (N.Y.C.). Home: 220 E 72nd St Apt 7F New York NY 10021 Office: Investcorp Internat Inc 280 Park Ave 37th Fl New York NY 10017

CREW, KERMIT RAY, credit company executive; b. Parsons, W.Va., Apr. 20, 1952; s. Kermit and Katie (Cross) C.; m. Mary Elizabeth Piers, Jan. 4, 1975 (div. 1982); 1 child, Kermit Todd; m. Allene Susan Darnell, May 7, 1983; 1 child, Jesse Colin. BFA, Western Ky. U., 1975. Credit mgr., then. asst. mgr. Norwest Fin., Pensacola, Fla., 1976-79; br. mgr. Norwest Fin., Tuscaloosa, Ala., 1979-85; sales mgr. Credit Bur. Tuscaloosa, 1985-86; v.p., CSD mgr. Credit Bur. Muscle Shoals, Florence, Ala., 1986-88, v.p., gen. mgr., 1989—. Bd. dirs. Helen Keller Festival. Mem. Assn. Credit Burs., Credit Bur. Inc., Med.-Dental-Hosp. Burs. Am. (bd. dirs., nat. seminar speaker 1987—), Am. Collectors Assn., Florence Exchange Club (chmn. 1987-88), Greater Shoals Area C. of C. Home: 617 Windover Rd Florence AL 35630 Office: Credit Bur Muscle Shoals 205 W College Florence AL 35630

CREWS, JOHN ERIC, rehabilitation administrator; b. Marion, Ind., Aug. 4, 1946; s. Odis Earl and Beatrice True (Wright) C.; m. Nancy J. Murphy, Aug. 9, 1975; 1 dau., Katherine. B.A. in English, Franklin Coll., 1969; M.A. in English, Ind. U., 1971; M.A. in Blind Rehab. with honors, Western Mich. U., 1977, postgrad in pub. adminstrn., 1983—. Mem. English faculty Ball State U., Muncie, Ind., 1971-73, S.W. Mo. State U., Springfield, 1973-76, Western Mich. U., Kalamazoo, 1976-77; rehab. tchr. Mich. Commn. for the Blind, Saginaw, 1977-80, program mgr. Sr. Blind Program, Saginaw, Southeastern Mich. Ctr. for Ind. Living, Detroit, 1980—; program mgr. Ind. Living Rehab. Program, 1986—; v.p. bd. Midland County Council on Aging, 1982-84; bd. dirs. Saginaw Valley Spl. Needs Vision Clinic, 1981—; mem. adv. bd. rehab. continuing edn. program So. Ill. U., Carbondale, 1985—; sec. Statewide Ind. Living Council, 1987—. Mem. editorial bd. Jour. Visual Impairment and Blindness, 1984—. Contbr. to book and profl. publs. Recipient Grant award Ind. Living Services for Older Blind Rehab. Services Adminstrn., 1986; grantee Ctr. Ind. Living U.S. Dept. Edn., 1980, 82, Ind. Living for Elderly Blind, 1986; All-Univ. grad. research and creative scholar Western Mich. U., 1988. Mem. Nat. Council Aging, Assn. Retarded Citizens (pres. Midland 1981-87; Ann. Appreciation award 1981). Methodist. Home: 5502 Whitehall Midland MI 48640 Office: Mich Commn for the Blind 411-G E Genesee Saginaw MI 48607

CRIBBS, JEFFREY SCOTT, SR., educational administrator; b. Meadville, Pa., Sept. 6, 1945; s. Paul and Marian Marden (Mohney) C.; m. Peggy Lynn Judy, Nov. 12, 1967; children: Jeffrey Scott Jr., Megan Lynn, Sarah Elizabeth. BS, Chaminade U. of Honolulu, 1970; M of Commerce, U. Richmond, 1975. Material contr. Talon Div., TEXTRON, Inc., Meadville, Pa., 1966; funds mgr. USAF, Honolulu, 1966-70; budget examiner State Dept. Planning and Budget, Richmond, Va., 1970-72; coordinator fin. planning and rsch. State Coun. Higher Edn., Richmond, 1972-76; univ. budget dir. Va. Commonwealth U., Richmond, 1976-80, assoc. v.p. planning and budget, 1980—. Contbr. articles to profl. jours. Sch. bd. vice chmn. Chesterfield County Pub. Schs., Va., 1982-88; edn. com. chmn. Va. Congress of Parents and Tchrs., 1981; pres., sec. Civic Assn., Hanover County, Va., 1974-76; bd. mem. Regional Math-Sci. Ctr., Richmond, 1983-87. Mem. Soc. for Coll. and Univ. Planning (state coordinator 1987—), Nat. Assn. Coll. and Univ. Bus. Officers, Am. Assn. Higher Edn., Am. Assn. Med. Colls., Assn. for Institutional Rsch. Methodist. Home: 1801 Hollingsworth Dr Richmond VA 23235 Office: Va Commonwealth U 914 W Franklin St Richmond VA 23284

CRIDEN, MARK ALAN, banker, lawyer; b. Buffalo, June 20, 1952; s. Henry I. and Lois R. (Hoffman) C.; m. Nicole S. Urdang, Mar. 1, 1980; children: Madelaine, Maxwell. BA, Boston U., 1974; JD, George Washington U., 1978. Bar: Conn. 1978, N.Y. 1982, U.S. Dist. Ct. 1978, U.S. Tax Ct. 1979, U.S. Ct. Claims 1979. Assoc. Pinney Payne, Danbury, Conn., 1978-80, Bergman, Horowitz, Reynolds, New Haven, 1980-81; ptnr. Saperston & Day, Buffalo, 1981-85; prin. Goldome Strategic Investments, Inc., Buffalo, 1985—; mem. adv. bd. SUNY, Buffalo, 1984—; speaker tax topics various forums, 1978-85. Contbr. articles to profl. jours. Mem. ABA, N.Y. State Bar Assn., Erie County Bar Assn., Western N.Y. Fin. Planners., Assn. Corp. Growth, Internat. Merger and Acquisition Cons.

CRIM, JACK C., diversified industry executive; b. 1930. B.S., Purdue U., 1954. With Economy Regulator, 1956-62; v.p. ops. Textron Inc., 1962-68; pres. Cuno div. AMF Inc., 1968-73, group v.p. exec. recreation vehicles, 1970-73; group v.p. Textron Inc., 1982-83, pres. Townsend div., 1981-82; exec. v.p., chief oper. officer Talley Industries Inc., 1982-83, pres., chief oper. officer, 1983—, also bd. dirs. Office: Talley Industries Inc 2800 N 44th St Phoenix AZ 85008

CRIMMINS, ALFRED STEPHEN, JR., manufacturing company executive; b. Bayonne, N.J., Dec. 6, 1934; s. Alfred Stephen and Agnes Veronica (Corcoran) C.; m. Catherine Lechner, June 11, 1960; children: Karen, Douglas, Jennifer, Michael. B.B.A. cum laude, CCNY, 1960. C.P.A., N.Y. With Price Waterhouse & Co. (C.P.A.'s), 1960-65; mgr. profit analysis Trans World Airlines, Inc., 1965-68; v.p. fin. Bairnco Corp., N.Y.C., 1968-80; exec. v.p. fin., dir. Collins & Aikman Corp., N.Y.C., 1980-84; pres. Collins & Aikman Corp., 1984-86, chief operating officer, 1986-87, chief executive officer, 1987-88; pres., chief exec. officer Knoll Internat. Holdings, Inc., N.Y.C., 1988-89, also bd. dirs. Served with USNR, 1955-56. Mem. Fin. Execs. Inst., Am. Inst. C.P.A.s, N.Y. State Soc. C.P.A.s, Beta Gamma Sigma. Clubs: Union League, Upper Ridgewood Tennis. Home: 703 Belmont Rd Ridgewood NJ 07450

CRIMMINS, SEAN T(HOMAS), oil company executive; b. Pitts., Sept. 2, 1945; s. John Michael and Catherine Lucille (O'Malley) C.; m. Cynthia Ann Floyd, Aug. 21, 1971 (div. May 1985); 1 child, Brendan J. BA, U. Notre Dame, 1967, JD, 1972. Assoc. Mayer, Brown & Platt, Chgo., 1972-77; mgr. tax reorgn. Gulf Oil Co., Pitts., 1978-84; dir. tax planning Ashland (Ky.) Oil, Inc., 1984-88, v.p., gen. tax counsel, 1988—. Mem. Ill. Bar Assn., Pa. Bar Assn., Ky. Bar Assn., Boyd County Bar Assn., Bellefonte Country Club. Home: 2350 Hickory Ridge Rd Ashland KY 41101 Office: Ashland Oil Inc 1000 Ashland Dr Russell KY 41169

CRISLER, RICHARD CARLETON, brokerage executive; b. Cin., Nov. 30, 1907; s. Carleton Graves and Elizabeth Page (Cropper) C.; m. Helen Orrick, June 12, 1934 (div. 1940); m. Lucy Cash Hagin Howard, June 10, 1948; 1 child, Richard C. Jr. PhB, Yale U., 1929. Sales rep., office mgr. Guaranty Trust co., N.Y.C. and Cin., 1929-32; sales mgr. Western & Southern Indemnity Co. and Western & Southern Fire Ins. Co., Cin., 1932-35; v.p. corp. securities Field Richards & Co., Cin., 1935-46; pres., major stockholder R.C. Crisler & Co. Inc., Cin., 1951—; dir. So. Ohio Bank, 1984. V.p. Cincinatus Assn., 1940-41; campaign mgr. Cin. Charter Com., 1951, 53; trustee Yale Devel. Bd., 1951-70; found. bd. No. Ky. U. Served to capt. USAF. Mem. Investment Bankers Assn. (regional chmn. 1939-41), Am. Angus Assn. Home: 2444 Madison Rd Cincinnati OH 45208 Office: RC Crisler Co Inc 600 Vine St Cincinnati OH 45202

CRISPIN, JAMES HEWES, engineering and construction company executive; b. Rochester, Minn., July 23, 1915; s. Egerton Lafayette and Angela (Shipman) C.; A.B. in Mech. Engring., Stanford U., 1938; M.B.A., Harvard U., 1941; grad. Army Command and Gen. Staff Sch., 1943; m. Marjorie Holmes, Aug. 5, 1966. With C.F. Braun & Co., Alhambra, Calif., 1946-62; treas. Bechtel Corp., San Francisco, 1962-73, v.p., mem. fin. com., 1967-75, mgr. investment dept., 1973-75, ret.; personal investments, 1976—. Served to lt. col. Ordnance Corps, AUS., 1941-46. Registered profl. mech. engr., Calif. Mem. Mil. Order World Wars, S.R., Soc. Colonial Wars Calif., Baronial Order Magna Carta, Mil Order Crusades, Am. Def. Preparedness Assn., World Affairs Council No. Calif. (trustee 1968-75), Santa Barbara Mus. Art (trustee 1979—, pres. 1986-88), Calif. Hist. Soc. (trustee 1979-86), Beta Theta Pi. Republican. Clubs: Valley of Montecito (Santa Barbara) (pres. 1987—, bd. dirs. 1981—); Calif. (Los Angeles); St. Francis Yacht, San Francisco Golf, Pacific-Union, World Trade (pres. 1977-78, dir. 1971-78) (San Francisco). Home: 1340 E Mountain Dr Santa Barbara CA 93108 Office: La Arcada Bldg 1114 State St Ste 220 Santa Barbara CA 93101

CRISWELL, CHARLES HARRISON, analytical chemist, evironmental and forensic consultant and executive; b. Springfield, Mo., Jan. 9, 1943; s. John Philip and Elba Anne (Denton) C.; m. Joyce LaVonne Louth, Apr. 26, 1968; 1 child, Christina Rachel. AB in Chemistry and Biology, Drury Coll., 1967; postgrad., U. Mo., 1967-68. Cert. hazardous materials and waste specialist; registered profl. sanitarian. Dir. Water Pollution Control Labs City of Springfield, 1968-72, chief Water Pollution Sect., 1972-80; pres., chmn. bd. dirs. Consulting Analytical Services Internat., Springfield, 1979—; assoc. Environ. Planning Assocs., Inc., 1985—; appointed by gov. mem. Mo. Hazardous Waste Mgmt. Commn., 1978; mem. Mo. Joint Commn. on Hazardous Waste Mgmt. Legis., statewide Ad-hoc Com. on Regulations; speaker in field nationwide. Contbr. numerous articles to profl. jours. Active Springfield Employees Activities Club, ARC, Friends of Zoo; ruling elder First & Calvary Presby. Ch., elected for life 1974, bd. deacons, sr. high youth advisor, active numerous coms.; permanent judicial commn. John Calvin Presbytery, 1977-85, treas., 1975—, mem. spl. adminstrv commns., Presbytery Synod Gen. Assembly Inter-judicatory Consultation on Long Range Ch. Fin., various clerk positions and other offices. Fellow Am. Biog. Inst.; mem. Am. Inst. Biol. Scis., Am. Chem. Soc. (com. environ. analytical methodology, charter mem. Ozarks sect.), Assoc. Industries of Mo. (environ. com., hazardous waste task group), Mo. Acad. Sci., Mo. Water and Sewerage Conf. (sect. pres. 1975), Mo. Water Pollution Control Assn. (pres. 1979, exec. com. 1977-83, chmn. 1979-80, newsletter editor, chmn. numerous coms., chmn. confs.), Water Pollution Control Fedn. (chmn. ann. nat. conf. 1982, 83, asst. chmn. 1980, 81, 84, active numerous other coms. 1976—, Arthur Sidney Bedell award); mem. Am. Mensa, Ltd., Beta Beta Beta, Phi Mu Alpha. Republican. Office: Cons Analytical Services Internat 2804 E Battlefield Rd Springfield MO 65804

CRISWELL, KIMBERLY ANN, public relations executive, dancer; b. L.A., Dec. 6, 1957; d. Robert Burton and Carolyn Joyce (Semko) C. BA with honors, U. Calif.-Santa Cruz, 1980. Instr., English Lang. Services, Oakland, Calif., 1980-81; freelance writer Gambit mag., New Orleans, 1981; instr. Tulane U., New Orleans, 1981; instr., editor Haitian-English Lang. Program, New Orleans, 1981-82; instr. Delgado Coll., New Orleans, 1982-83; instr., program coord. Vietnamese Youth Ctr., San Francisco, 1984; dancer Khadra Internat. Folk Ballet, San Francisco, 1984—; dir. mktg. communications Centram Systems West, Inc., Berkeley, Calif., 1984-87; communications coord.Safeway Stores, Inc., Oakland, 1985; dir. corp. communications TOPS, div. Sun Microsystems, Inc, 1987-88; pres. Criswell Communications, 1988—. Vol. coord. Friends of Haitians, 1981, editor, writer newsletter, 1981; dancer Komenka Ethnic Dance Ensemble, New Orleans, 1983; mem. Contemp. Art Ctr.'s Krewe of Clones, New Orleans, 1983, Americans for Nonsmokers Rights, Berkeley, 1985. Mem. Internat. Assn. Bus. Communicators, Sci. Meets the Arts Soc. (founding), NAFE, Dance Action, Bay Area Dance Coalition, Oakland Mus. Assn., Mus. Soc. Democrat. Avocations: visual arts, travel, creative writing.

CRITCHLOW, SUSAN MELISSA, public relations executive, advertising and printing consultant; b. Gainesville, Fla., Dec. 24, 1950; d. James Carlton and Mildred Estelle (Pringle) Barley; m. Warren Hartzell Critchlow, Jr., Aug. 18, 1973. BA, U. South Fla., 1972, MA in Speech Communication with honors, 1973. Asst. dir. pub. relations Goodwill Industries of N. Fla., Inc., 1973-74; dir. pub. relations St. Luke's Hosp., Jacksonville, Fla., 1974; dir. informational services Greater Orange Park Community Hosp., Orange Park, Fla., 1974-82; pres. Susan Critchlow & Assocs., SC&A Pub. Co., Inc., Orange Park, 1976—. Mem. bd. dirs. Children's Haven. Named N.E. Fla. Bus. Communicator of Month, 1975, 78. Mem. Fla. Hosp. Assn. (bd. dirs. pub. relations council 1976-78, Gold award 1975, Silver award 1976, 78), Jacksonville Hosp. Pub. Relations Council (chmn. 1975-77), Fla. Pub. Relations Assn. (Golden Image award 1975-83), Pub. Relations Soc. Am., Jacksonville Advt. Fedn. (Addy award 1982-86). Democrat. Episcopalian. Office: 1580 Wells Rd Ste 15 Orange Park FL 32073

CRITSER, GARY LEE, chemical company executive; b. Henderson, Ky., Nov. 1, 1949; s. Gordon Charles and Mildred Vernita (Jones) C.; m. Charlotte Kaye Preston, Nov. 6, 1976; children: Bart, Logan, Corey. BA, Ky. Wesleyan Coll., 1973. Admissions counselor Ky. Wesleyan Coll., Owensboro, 1973-75, assoc. dir. admissions, 1975-76; fuels acct. Big Rivers Elec. Utility, Henderson, Ky., 1976-77; sales rep. PB&S Chem. Co., Nashville, 1977-78; br. mgr. PB&S Chem. Co., Bowling Green, Ky., 1978-80, St. Albans, W.Va., 1980-81; br. mgr. PB&S Chem. Co., Chattanooga, 1981-84, asst. div. mgr., 1984-85, reg. mgr., 1985—. Coach Spl. Olympics, Henderson, 1975-77; vol. fund drives, sch. Sunday tchr. St. Timothy Episcopal Ch. Recipient Key Man award Henderson Jaycees, 1976. Mem. Nat. Assn. Chem. Distbrs. (regional sec. 1985-87), Chattanooga Area C. of C., Chattanooga Mfg. Assn., Signal Mt. Country Club. Home: PO Box 367 Signal Mountain TN 31377 Office: PB&S Chem Co 317 Old Wauhatchie Pike Chattanooga TN 37419

CRITTENDEN, EUGENE DWIGHT, JR., chemical company executive; b. Syracuse, N.Y., Feb. 27, 1927; s. Eugene Dwight and Meltina Ester (Feldkamp) C.; m. Sarah Ann Rogers, June 23, 1951; children: Sarah Ann Crittenden D'Alonzo, Susan Gray Crittenden Chambers. BS, Purdue U., 1947; MS, U. Pa., 1949, PhD, 1951. With Hercules, Inc., 1951—, sr. engr. Research Ctr., Wilmington, Del., 1951-53, asst. to dir. devel. Naval Stores Dept., 1953-55, sr. chem. engr., Brunswick, Ga., 1955-56, Wilmington, 1956-57, tech. asst. to devel. dir., 1957-60, sr. tech. rep., N.Y.C., 1960-62, asst. dir. devel. synthetics dept., Wilmington, 1962-63, asst. to gen. mgr. internat. dept., 1963-64, dir. Hercules Europe, Brussels, 1965-66, dir. sales organic chem. div., synthetics dept., Wilmington, 1966-67, asst. gen. mgr. synthetics dept., 1967-68, gen. mgr. new enterprise dept., 1968-72, indsl. systems dept., 1972-77, v.p. adminstrn. and pub. affairs, 1977-82, div. v.p. ops., corp. dir., mem. exec. and mgmt. com., 1982, corp. v.p. internat., 1983-87, pres. chief exec. officer, Aqualon Group, 1987—; corp. dir. Hercules Inc., Wilmington, 1982—. Bd. dirs. City of Wilmington and New Castle County YMCA, 1968—, pres. 1977-82; trustee Eleutherian Mills-Hagley Found., 1981—; bd. dirs. World Affairs Council, 1981—; trustee, bd. dirs. Med. Ctr. of Del., 1978—; Del. met. chmn. Nat. Alliance of Bus., 1981-82; mem. Gov.'s Internat. Trade Council, 1984—; mem. Del. and Eastern Pa. Dist. Export Council, 1984—, Del. Econ. and Fin. Adv. Council, 1977—. Served with USN, 1945-46. Yerger fellow in chem. engring., 1949-51. Mem. AAAS, Am. Chem. Soc., Am. Inst. Chem. Engrs., Sigma Xi. Republican. Episcopalian. Clubs: Hercules Country (bd. govs. 1979-82), Wilmington Country (bd. govs.), Wilmington, Vicmead Hunt, Pine Valley Golf. Avocations: piano, golf, tennis. Office: The Aqualon Group Little Falls Centre One 2711 Centerville Rd Wilmington DE 19850-5417

CROCKER, ALBERT RUDOLPH, emergency management consultant; b. Higganum, Conn., May 28, 1914; s. Albert Nathan and Laura (Gundlach) C.; m. Gertrude Elizabeth Jewell Crocker; children: Jewell Ann, James Albert, Jonathan Alan, Jane Alice. BS, NYU, 1936, MS, 1937; postgrad., Inst. Nuclear Studies, 1949-53. Registered profl. engr., Calif. Exptl. test engr. Pratt & Whitney Aircraft Co.,, East Hartford, Conn., 1938-40; asst. chief engr. Propeller div. Engr. and Research Co., Riverdale, Md., 1941-48; chief exptl. engring, nuclear engring. propulsion aircraft Fairchild, Oak Ridge, Tenn., 1949-51; mgr. mech. devel. aircraft nuclear propulsion Gen. Electric Co., Cin., 1951-53; mgr. test ops. Gen. Electric Co., Idaho Falls, 1953-61; program mgr. radiation effects ops. Gen. Electric Co., Syracuse, N.Y., 1961-64; mgr. advanced systems engring. Gen. Electric Co., Bay St. Louis, Miss., 1964-72; program mgr. internat. Gen. Electric Co., N.Y.C., 1972-74; emergency mgmt. cons.; cons. N.Y. State Atomic Research and Devel. Authority, 1964. Contbr. articles to profl. jours. Vol. cons. disaster Ea. N.Y. Territory ARC, Albany, 1983—; exec. bd. Teton Peaks Council Boy Scouts Am., Idaho Falls, 1954-61; v.p. N.Y. State Assn. Conservation com., Syracuse, 1980-83; exec. com. Onondaga Co. Environ. Mgmt. Council, Syracuse, 1980-82; mem. tng. team N.Y. State Emergency Mgmt. Office, Albany, 1983-87. Recipient Silver Beaver award, Boy Scouts Am., 1961. Fellow AIAA (assoc.) (chmn. instrumentation and communications com. 1960-61); mem. Tau Beta Pi, Sigma Pi Sigma. Home: PO Box 44 Memphis NY 13112

CROCKER, FREDERICK GREELEY, JR., manufacturing company executive, controller; b. Boston, June 26, 1937; s. Frederick Greeley and Mary Jane (Bigelow) C.; m. Laura D. Case, Nov. 22, 1959 (div. 1977); children: Frederick Greely, Stephen Chase, Marian Dennison; m. Rebecca C. Bennett, Jan. 19, 1980. BA cum laude, Harvard U., 1959; MBA, Columbia U., 1964. Fin. analyst Norton Co., Worchester, Mass., 1964-66, mgr. fin. planning, 1966-69, dir. bus. devel., 1969-70, controller grinding wheel div., 1970-73, v.p., gen. mgr. safety products div., 1973-82, v.p., controller parent co., 1982—; bd. dirs. Siebe North, Inc., Bank New Eng., Worcester. Pres. trustee Bancroft Sch., Worchester, 1979-81; treas. Holden (Mass.) Dist. Hosp., 1967-70; trustee Worchester Found. Exptl. Biology, 1973-75; trustee, bd. dirs. Worchester County Mechanics Assn., 1982; bd. dirs. U. Mass. Hosp., 1984. Served to lt. (j.g.) USNR, 1959-62. McKinsey scholar Columbia U., N.Y.C., 1964; recipient Profl. Acctg. prize Columbia U., 1964. Mem. Beta Gamma Sigma. Republican. Episcopalian. Home: 10 Surrey Ln Worcester MA 01609 Office: Norton Co 120 Front St Worcester MA 01606

CROCKER, GARY LAMAR, research corporation executive; b. Salt Lake City, Oct. 13, 1951; s. LaMar E. and Aenona (Mayhew) C.; m. Ann Taylor Sorenson, June 11, 1975; children: Julie Ann, Jared, Derek, Jonathan, Charisse. BS, Harvard U., 1976, MBA, 1978. Internal analyst Baxter Travenol Labs., Chgo., 1978-79; internat. sales mgr. Sorenson Research Co. div., Abbott Labs., Salt Lake City, 1979-80, dir. mktg., dir. bus. devel., 1980-83; pres., chief exec. officer Research Industries Corp., Salt Lake City, 1983—; bd. dirs. Sorenson Devel., Inc., 1986—, U. Utah Research Inst., Salt Lake City, 1987—, MSI, Inc. 1989—. V.p. Harvard Club of Utah, 1980-85, pres. 1985—; mem. adv. com. Utah State Ctrs. of Excellence, 1986—. Harvard nat. scholar, 1974. Republican. Mormon. Club: Exchange of Salt Lake. Lodge: Rotary. Office: Rsch Industries Corp 1847 W 2300 South Salt Lake City UT 84119

CROCKER, MALCOLM JOHN, mechanical engineer, noise control engineer, educator; b. Portsmouth, Eng., Sept. 10, 1938; came to U.S., 1963, naturalized, 1975; s. William Edwin and Alice Dorothy (Mintram) C.; m. Ruth Catherine, July 25, 1964; children: Anne Catherine, Elizabeth Claire. B.Sc. in Aeros. with honors, Southampton (Eng.) U., 1961, M.Sc. in Noise and Vibration, 1963; Ph.D. in Acoustics, Liverpool (Eng.) U., 1969. Co-op. apprentice, Vickers scholar Brit. Aerospace Co., Weybridge, Surrey, Eng., 1957-62; research asst. Southampton U., 1962-63, vis. research fellow, 1976; scientist Wyle Labs. Research, Huntsville, Ala., 1963-66; research fellow U. Liverpool, 1967-69; assoc. prof. mech. engring. Purdue U., West Lafayette, Ind., 1969-73; prof. Purdue U., 1973-83; asst. dir. acoustics and noise control Herrick labs., 1977-83; head dept. mech. engring. Auburn U. (Ala.), 1983—; vis. prof. U. Sydney, Australia, 1976; cons. to industry, speaker in field; gen. chmn. acoustics confs. including Inter-Noise 72, Washington, 1972, Noise-Con 79 Nat. Conf. Noise Control Engring., West Lafayette, 1979; cons. and lectr. in field. Author: Noise and Noise Control, 2 vols, 1975, 82, Benchmark Papers in Acoustics: Noise Control, 1984; editor: Noise and Vibration Control Engineering, 1972, Reduction of Machinery Noise, 1974, rev. edit., 1975, others; editor-in-chief: Noise Control Engineering Jour., 1973—; mem. editorial bd.: Archives Acoustics, Warsaw, Poland, 1979—; contbr. numerous articles to profl. jours. Grantee NSF, 1972-74, 75-77, U.S. Dept. Transp., 1972-73, 79-81, EPA, 1976-80, NASA, 1980-83, 84—, Dept. Def., 1984—, others; Acoustical Soc. India hon. fellow, 1985. Fellow Acoustical Soc. Am.; mem. Inst. Noise Control Engring./U.S.A. (dir., v.p. for communications, pres. 1981), Inst. Acoustics (London), Am. Soc. Engring. Edn. (chmn. engring acoustics & vibration 1986-88), ASME, Am. Nat. Standards Inst. (com. chmn.). Home: 454 Pinedale Dr Auburn AL 36830 Office: Auburn U Dept Mech Engring Auburn AL 36849

CROCKETT, BRUCE LARMOUR, communications company executive; b. Rochester, N.Y., Mar. 31, 1944; s. Colin Moore and Gladys Anne (Larmour) C.; m. Gail Ethel Freiday, June 21, 1969; children—Scott Colin, Drew Freiday. A.B., U. Rochester, 1966; M.B.A., Columbia U., 1971; B.S., U.

Md., 1978. Sr. cons. Chem. Bank, N.Y.C., 1971-72; asst. to pres. Ford Products Corp., Valley Cottage, N.Y., 1972-74; dir. fin. planning Martin Marietta Corp, Bethesda, Md., 1975-76; asst. treas. Martin Marietta Corp, 1976-78; treas. Martin Marietta Aluminum, Bethesda, 1979-80; v.p., chief fin. officer Communications Satellite Corp., Washington, 1980-86, v.p., gen. mgr. intelsat satellite services, from 1986, now pres. World Systems div.; dir. CIGNA High Yield Fund, Inc., Hartford, Conn., INA Investment Securities, Inc., Hartford; mem. fin. adv. bd. Columbia U. Grad. Sch.; mem. bus. adv. council Marymount Coll. Va. Served to 1st lt. U.S. Army, 1966-69. Mem. U.S. C of C. (econ. policy com.). Republican. Home: 906 Frome Ln McLean VA 22102 Office: Communications Satellite Corp 950 L'Enfant Pla SW Washington DC 20024 *

CROFT, EDWARD STOCKTON, III, investment banker; b. Columbia, S.C., Sept. 12, 1942; s. Edward Stockton and Irene (Weston) C.; m. Susan Bronson, June 20, 1964; children—Stockton, Gabrey. B.A., Washington and Lee U., 1964; M.B.A., Wharton Grad. Sch., U. Pa., 1969. Corp. fin. assoc. White, Weld & Co., N.Y.C., 1969-71; corp. fin. officer Robinson-Humphrey Co., Inc., Atlanta, 1971-82; mng. dir. Robinson-Humphrey Co., Inc., 1982—; dir. Computer Products, Inc., Ft. Lauderdale, Fla., The Tensar Corp., Atlanta; mem. Hosp. Authority of Fulton County (Northside Hosp.), Atlanta, 1982—; Chmn., Bridge Family Center of Atlanta, 1978—. Served as 1st lt., U.S. Army, 1964-66. Republican. Episcopalian. Clubs: Piedmont Driving, The Nine O'Clocks, Commerce, Homosassa Fishing, The Buckhead Club. Home: 500 Argonne Dr Atlanta GA 30305 Office: Robinson Humphrey Co 3333 Peachtree Rd NW Atlanta GA 30326

CROFT, LEONARD MATHIUS, toy company executive; b. Toronto, Ont., Can., Apr. 27, 1930; came to U.S., 1984; s. Frank Dudley and Elizabeth Ann (Fitz) C.; m. Elizabeth Ann Bastedo, Sept. 17, 1953 (div.); children: Karen, Kim, Sheila, Neil, Lincoln. BA, Sir George Williams U., Montreal, Que., Can., 1965. Sales rep. The Walker Press Ltd., Toronto, 1953-58; advt. mgr. Mil-ko Food Products, Hamilton, Ont., Can., 1958-60; product dir. Johnson & Johnson, Montreal, 1960-64, product group dir., 1964-68; v.p. mktg. Brooke Bond Foods Ltd., Montreal, 1968-74; pres. Pillsbury Can. Ltd., Toronto, 1974-76; mng. ptnr. Croft Palmer Inc., Toronto, 1976-81; pres. Mattel Can. Inc., Toronto, 1981-84; sr. v.p. Americas Mattel Inc., Hawthorne, Calif., 1984—. Office: Mattel Inc 5150 Rosecrans Ave Hawthorn CA 90250

CROFWELL, JAMES B., stock exchange executive. BSBA, Stonehill Coll., 1973. Staff acct. Boston Stock Exchange, 1974-77, internal auditor, 1978-82, v.p., 1983-84, sr. v.p., 1983-86, exec. v.p., treas., 1987—. Mem. Security Industry Assn. (div. data mgmt.), Treas.'s Club Boston.

CROISANT, EUGENE R., banker; b. Chgo., Aug. 2, 1937; s. Edward H. and Alice R. C.; m. Barbara Byczek; children: Thomas D., Cynthia. B.S.C., Loyola U., Chgo., 1959, M.S., 1966; postgrad., Nat. Assn. Bank Audit Control Sch. U. Wis., summers 1964-66. With Continental Ill. Nat. Bank and Trust Co., Chgo., 1959—, electronics officer, 1966-67, 2d v.p., 1967-69, operating rep., 1969-70, v.p., 1970-74, sr. v.p., 1974-81, exec. v.p., from 1981, now chief oper. officer; now chief oper. officer Continental Ill. Corp., Chgo.; dir. Continental Ill. Venture Corp., Continental Ill. Equity Corp.; lectr. in field. Mem. com. cabinet selection Ill. Gov., 1977; mem. Ill. Commn. to Investigate Welfare Fraud; trustee, chmn. fin. and devel. coms. Loyola U.; assoc. Chgo. Rehab. Inst. Served to 1st lt. U.S. Army, 1959-61. Mem. Am. Mgmt. Assn. (v.p.), Am. Bankers Assn. Office: Continental Ill Corp 231 S LaSalle St Chicago IL 60697 *

CROKE, JOSEPH VAETH, real estate developer; b. Colorado Springs, Colo., Mar. 18, 1957; s. Autrey Raymond and Paricia Jean (Vaeth) C.; m. Debi Dianne Handley, Dec. 29, 1982; children: Tyler Autrey, Erin McShea, Teagan Marie. BA in History and Polit. Sci., Colo. Coll., 1979; postgrad., Western U., 1982. Legal aide Law Office Paul Newberry, La Jolla, Calif., 1980-82; project mgr., counsel Sammis Properties, San Diego, 1982-85; owner, pres. La Jolla Devel., Colorado Springs, Colo., 1985—; cons. MCO Holdings, Inc., L.A., 1987; bd. dirs. Am. for Reagan Agenda, Washington, 1983, Found. for the Pvt. Sector, Washington, 1984. Mem. Urban Land Inst., Cheyenne Mountain Club. Office: La Jolla Devel Co PO Box 1561 Colorado Springs CO 80901

CROLL, ROBERT FREDERICK, educator, economist; b. Evanston, Ill., Feb. 3, 1934; s. Frederick Warville and Florence (Campbell) C.; m. Sandra Elizabeth Bell, June 15, 1968; 1 child, Robert Frederick. BSBA, Northwestern U., 1954; MBA (Burton A. French scholar) with high distinction, U. Mich., 1956; DBA, Ind. U., 1969; DLitt, John F. Kennedy Coll., 1970. Instr. Ind. U. Sch. Bus., Bloomington, 1956, researcher in bus. econs., 1960-62; mng. dir. Motor Vehicle Industry Research Assocs., Evanston, 1962-63; personal asst. to speaker Ill. Ho. of Reps., 1963-65; asst. prof. bus. adminstrn. Kans. State U., 1965-66; asst. prof. Inst. Indsl. Relations, Loyola U. Chgo., 1966-70; assoc. prof. Sch. Bus. Adminstrn., Central Mich. U., 1970-76, prof., 1976—. Mem. platform committee Ind. Republican Com., 1958; Ind. del. Young Rep. Nat. Conv., 1959; nat. chmn. Youth for Goldwater Orgn., 1960-61; chmn. coll. clubs Young Rep. Orgn. Ill., 1960-62; treas. Young Rep. Orgn. Ill., 1963-65; asst. chief page Rep. Nat. Conv., 1964; mem. Mt. Pleasant City Charter Commn., 1973-76. Trustee estate of F.W. Croll, Chgo., 1959—; bd. govs. Clarke Hist. Library, 1986—. Recipient Grand prize Gov. of Ind., 1958. Accredited personnel diplomate Am. Soc. Personnel Adminstrn. Accreditation Inst. Mem. Soc. Automotive Engrs., Am. Inst. Mgmt., Soc. Advancement Mgmt., Am. Econ. Assn., Mt. Pleasant C. of C., Young Ams. for Freedom (founder 1960, vice chmn. 1962-63), Phila. Soc. (founder 1964), Beta Gamma Sigma, Delta Sigma Pi Key, Phi Delta Kappa, Phi Kappa Phi, Pi Sigma Alpha, Delta Mu Delta, Sigma Pi, Alpha Kappa Psi, Sigma Iota Epsilon, Phi Chi Theta, Pi Omega Pi. Episcopalian. Clubs: Little Harbor (Harbor Springs, Mich.); Mount Pleasant Country. Author: Fall of an Automotive Empire: A Business History of the Packard Motor Car Company, 1945-1958, others. Contbr. articles to profl. jours. Address: 1224 Glenwood Dr Mount Pleasant MI 48858

CROM, THOMAS LEROY, financial executive; b. Compton, Calif., Oct. 3, 1955; s. Thomas L. Jr. and Joyce A. (Bonner) C.; m. Debora L. Wellman, Oct. 17, 1985. BS, Santa Clara U., 1977; MS, Golden Gate U., 1983. CPA, Calif.; cert. mgr. acct. Mgr. Hamilton & Bradshaw, San Jose, Calif., 1977-80; v.p. Scott Enterprises, Aptos, Calif., 1980-83; chief fin. officer Gold Group, San Bruno, Calif., 1983-89, North Lily Mining Co., San Bruno, 1989—; bd. dirs. Am. 2000, Atlanta, N.Am. Investors, Miami, Fla., Dragon Mining. Co., San Bruno. Mem. Nat. Assn. Accts., Am. Inst. CPA's. Republican. Home: 407 Roberts Rd Pacifica CA 94044 Office: North Lily Mining Co 851 Traeger St Ste 320 San Bruno CA 94066

CROMER, ROBERT JOHN, lawyer, finance company executive; b. Bonne Terre, Mo., Dec. 27, 1949; s. Charles Felix and Sybil May (Rodbourn) C.; m. Judith Lee Wiser, June 20, 1970; children: Rebecca Lee, John Benjamin, Michael Robert. BA summa cum laude, U. Pitts., 1974, JD, 1977. Bar: Pa. 1977, U.S. Dist. (we. dist.) Pa. 1977. Assoc. Jones, Talland & Bailey, Murrysville, Pa., 1977-80; staff atty. Dollar Bank, F.S.B., Pitts., 1980-83, counsel, 1984-88; sec., counsel, dir. Dollar Fin., Inc., Wilmington, Del., 1985—; bd. dirs. Security Savs., Mortgage Corp., Canton, Ohio. Treas. DOLPAC, Pitts., 1984—; bd. dirs. United Meth., Found., Pitts., 1985—; chmn. Trafford (Pa.) Zoning Bd., 1985-88; solicitor Tafford Borough, 1989—. Mem. Pa. Bar Assn., Ohio Bar Assn., Allegheny County Bar Assn., Rotary (pres. Penn-Trafford chpt. 1987-88), Elks (presiding justice Norwin chpt. 1987—). Republican. Methodist. Office: Dollar Fin FSB Three Gateway Ctr 9S Pittsburgh PA 15222 also: 315 5th St Trafford PA 15085

CROMLEY, JON LOWELL, lawyer; b. Riverton, Ill., May 23, 1934; s. John Donald and Naomi M. (Mathews) C. BS, U. Ill., 1958; JD, John Marshall Law Sch., 1966. Bar: Ill. 1966. Real estate title examiner Chgo. Title & Trust Co., 1966-70; admitted to Ill. bar, 1966; pvt. practice, Genoa, Ill., 1970—; mem. firm O'Grady & Cromley, Genoa, 1970—; bd. dirs. Genoa State Bank, Kingston Mut. Ins. Co., Genoa Day Care Center, Inc. Mem. ABA, Am. Judicature Soc., Am., Ill. State Bar Assn., Chgo. Bar Assn., DeKalb County Bar Assn. Home: 130 Homewood Dr Genoa IL 60135 Office: O'Grady & Cromley 213 W Main St Genoa IL 60135

CROMWELL, OLIVER DEAN, investment banker; b. Cleve., Sept. 19, 1950; s. Oliver and Mildred Jeanette (Galko) C.; m. Sheila Lea Terry, May 19, 1984; 1 child, Ashley Melissa. A.B., Brown U., 1972; M.B.A., Harvard U., 1976. Chartered fin. analyst, 1980. Trust adminstr. Bankers Trust, N.Y.C., 1973-74; assoc. Donaldson, Lufkin & Jenrette, N.Y.C., 1976-79, v.p., 1980-84, sr. v.p., 1985-87; sr. v.p. Oppenheimer & Co. Inc., N.Y.C., 1987-88; 1st v.p. Paine Webber, N.Y.C., 1988—. Mem. exec. com., bd. dirs. Associated Alumni Brown U., 1985-87, bd. govs., 1987-88, co-head class agt. ann. fund, 1983—, mem. steering com. 5-yr. reunion fund, 1976-77, 10-yr. reunion fund, 1981-82, 15-yr. reunion fund, 1986-87. Mem. Investment Assn. N.Y., Inst. Chartered Fin. Analysts, N.Y. Soc. Security Analysts, Fin. Analysts Fedn., Securities Industry Assn. N.Y. (exec. com. 1987—), Aston Martin Owners Club-East, Maserati Club Am., Empire Jaguar Club N.Am., Brown Univ. (treas. 1984-88, v.p. 1988—, bd. dirs. 1983—). Home: 4 Eastway Bronxville NY 10708 Office: Paine Webber Investment Banking Div 1285 Ave of the Americas New York NY 10019

CROMWELL, ROGER JAMES KISSEL, banker; b. N.Y.C., Mar. 4, 1931; s. Jarvis and Barbara (Kissel) C.; m. Anne Marie Reid, Apr. 25, 1975 (div. 1987); children: Jarvis II, Katharine Eleonora. AB, Brown U., 1950-54. Asst. sec. Hanover Bank, N.Y.C., 1966-73; asst. v.p. Marine Midland Bank and Trust Co., N.Y.C., 1965-73; v.p. State Nat. Bank, Bridgeport, Conn., 1974-78; pres. The Cromwell Group, Inc., Fairfield, Conn., 1978—. Editor Jour. Search, 1974—. Served to sgt. U.S. Army, 1954-56, Korea. Republican. Episcopalian. Club: New Canaan Country. Lodge: Masons. Home and Office: The Cromwell Group 1696 Orchard Hill Rd Cheshire CT 06410

CRONAN, PHILIP FRANCIS, banker; b. N.Y.C., Dec. 11, 1941; s. John and Marion (McSweeny) C.; m. Mary Irene Barrows, Sept. 4, 1965; 1 child, Patrick. BA, St. Michaels Coll., Winnoski Park, Vt., 1964. Sales account mgr. Burroughs Corp., N.Y.C., 1964-67; nat. sales mgr. Efficient Leasing Co., Ft. Lee, N.J., 1967-73; also bd. dirs. Efficient Leasing Co., Ft. Lee; pres. 1st Leasing Corp., Englewood, N.J., 1973-74; sr. v.p. Mfrs. Hanover Leasing Co., N.Y.C., 1974-85; country mgr. Mfrs. Hanover Leasing Co., P.R., 1975-77; sr. v.p. Mfrs. Hanover Leasing Co., N.Y.C., 1975-85; regional exec. Chase Manhattan Leasing Co., Chgo., 1985—. Bd. dirs. Cystic Fibrosis Found., Chgo., 1987-88; councilman Archtl. Rev. Bd., Glen Ellyn, Ill., 1987-88; mem. adv. bd. counsel Chgo. Opera Theater, 1988, Chgo. Shakespearean Found., 1988. Mem. Am. Assn. Equipment Lessors. Home: 393 Montclair Glen Ellyn IL 60137 Office: Chase Manhattan Leasing Co 440 S La Salle St 30th Floor Chicago IL 60605

CRONE, JOHN ROSSMAN, pharmacist; b. Franklin, Pa., Apr. 11, 1933; s. Wilmer Jennings and Lydia Juanita (Rossman) C.; m. Shirley Mae Parker, July 27, 1955; children: Michael John, David Jennings, Alan Parker. BS in Pharmacy, U. Pitts., 1955. Pharmacist King's Drug Store, Clarion, Pa., 1955-56; pharmacist, mgr. Cowdrick's Drug Stores, Inc., Philipsburg, Pa., 1956-57; pharmacist Warren, Pa., 1959-80, pharmacist, mgr., 1980-88; prin., pharmacist Crone's Drug Store, Warren, 1988—. Mem. adv. bd. Salvation Army, Warren, 1984—; bd. dirs. Warren County United Way, 1983—. Served with U.S. Army, 1957-59. Mem. Am. Pharm. Assn., Pa. Pharm. Assn., Warren County Pharm. Assn., Nat. Assn. Retail Druggists, Warren County C. of C. Republican. Methodist. Lodge: Lions (pres. Warren chpt. 1965-66, dist. gov. 1969-70, bd. dirs. Sight Cons. and Eye Research Found. 1970-79, Hearing Research Found. 1981—). Home: 605 Madison Ave Warren PA 16365 Office: Crone's Drug Store 212-214 Liberty St Warren PA 16365

CRONE, RICHARD KENNETH, consultant; b. Montbello, Calif., Feb. 2, 1957; s. Kenneth Richard and Carole Ann (Ainilian) C.; m. Heidi Ann Liebenguth, Mar. 34, 19845. BSBA, U. So. Calif., 1979, MBA, 1987. Mktg. mgr. Unisys, Los Angeles, 1979-87; sr. cons. Peat Marwick Main & Co., Los Angeles, 1988—. contbr. articles to profl. jours. bd. dirs., commerce assocs. U. So. Calif., 1988—. Beta Gamma Sigma. Club: Los Angeles Athletic. Home: 1330 Carmen Dr Glendale CA 91207 Office: Peat Marwick Main & Co 725 S Figueroa St Los Angeles CA 90017

CRONENWORTH, CHARLES DOUGLAS, manufacturing company executive; b. Mohawk, Mich., Aug. 7, 1921; s. Jacob and Margaret (Therien) C.; m. Lorraine Evelyn DeBruyne, May 18, 1946; children: Carol, Linda, Mary, Charles. B.S. in Mech. Engring., Mich. Tech. U., 1944. Registered profl. engr., Mich. Design engr. Chrysler Corp., Detroit, 1946-47; project engr. Gen. Foods, St. Clair, Mich., 1947-50; plant mgr. Diamond Crystal Salt Co., St. Clair, Mich., 1950-68, gen. mgr. prodn., 1968-75, pres., chief exec. officer, 1975-85, vice chmn., 1985-86; founder, pres. Mohawk Plastics, 1987—; bd. dirs. Comml. & Savs. Bank, St. Clair, Maritek Corp., Corpus Christi, Tex., Worldwide Protein Bahamas, Nassau, Diamond Crystal Salt, St. Clair, Seaway Fin. Corp., St. Clair; chmn. bd. dirs. Charles Corp., Marine City, Mich.. Mem. chmn. Mich. Mineral Well Adv., Lansing, Mich., 1970-78; mayor City of St. Clair, 1962-63, councilman, 1955-58. Recipient Silver medal Mich. Tech. U., 1976. Mem. Mich. Soc. Profl. Engrs. (alt. dir. 1958-62), Nat. Soc. Profl. Engrs., Nat. Assn. Mfrs. (dir. 1980—). Republican. Roman Catholic. Lodge: Rotary Internat. (St. Clair pres. 1979-80, St. Clair dir. 1976-82). Home: 129 E Meldrum Circle Saint Clair MI 48079 Office: Mohawk Plastics Inc 867 DeGurse St Marine City MI 48039

CRONICAN, RICHARD ALAN, computer company manager; b. Yonkers, N.Y., Sept. 5, 1943; s. John G. Sr., and Josephine M. (Ness) C.; student U. Ariz., 1966-74; m. Dana S. Yarian, July 3, 1965; children—Kimberly and Kelly (twins), Timothy Alan. Patrolman, police dept. City of Tucson, 1966-69, detective, 1969-70, programmer, analyst dept. fin., 1970-73, sys/prog supr., 1973-74, dir. dept. computer services, 1974-81; exec. dir., regional mgr., gen. mgr. Systems & Computer Technology Corp., Malvern, Pa., 1981-87, sr. prin. Am. Mgmt. Systems Inc., Arlington, Va., 1987— ; guest lectr. U. Ariz., 1970—, Pima Coll., 1970—, Western Mich. U.; cons. City of Lincoln, Lancaster County, Nebr., Oakland County, Mich., Union County, N.J., Fresno County, Calif., City of Phoenix, S. Tucson, Shelby County, Tenn., Maricopa County, Ariz., City and County of San Francisco, City of Mpls., Minn. Community Coll. System, Peoria County, Equitable Life Ins., Md. Nat. Bank, Gen. Dynamics EBD, PYA/Monarch Corp. Ordained deacon, Roman Catholic Ch., 1976; bd. dirs. Armory Park Found., 1977—, AMIGOS Bibliog. Council, Dallas, 1979-80; chmn. Diocese of Tucson Pastoral Council, 1977-81, also adult religious instr.; mem. advisory council Pima Coll., Tucson, 1975-81. Served with USAF, 1961-65. Mem. Am. Mgmt. Assn., Adminstrv. Mgmt. Soc., Internat. Assn. Chiefs of Police, Lincoln C. of C., Urban and Regional Info. Systems Assn. (chmn. DP mgmt. spl. interest group), Data Processing Mgmt. Assn. Clubs: Rotary, Kiwanis. Home: 5344 Forrest Ct Warrenton VA 22186 Office: Am Mgmt Systems Inc 1777 N Kent St Rd Arlington VA 22209

CRONIN, JOHN JOSEPH, advertising company executive; b. Charleville, Ireland, Oct. 10, 1931; came to U.S., 1986; s. Edmund J. and Bridget (McMahon) C.; m. Patricia C. O'Connor, Oct. 29, 1955; children: Mark, Jonathan, Shane, Paul, Conor, Jacqueline. Student, Sacred Heart Coll., 1940-45; higher learning cert., Oxford and Cambridge (Eng.) Univs., 1945-50. Reporter Canadian Press News Agy., Montreal, Can., 1953-55; with pub. relations dept. Great-West Life Ins. Co., Winnipeg, Man., Can., 1955-60; copy chief, creative dir. Cockfield, Brown Advt., Winnipeg, Man., Can., 1960-63; from sr. copy writer to creative dir. J. Walter Thompson, Montreal, 1964, mng. dir., 1971; pres., chief operating officer of Can. Co. J. Walter Thompson, Toronto, 1977, chief exec. Can., 1977; pres., chief exec. officer Europe J. Walter Thompson, London, 1980-86; vice chmn. J. Walter Thompson Co., N.Y.C., 1986-88, chief advertising officer, 1987-88. Head writer for documentary musical TV series, Red River Jamboree, 1960-63. Mem. Inst. Can. Advt. Agys. (vice chmn.), European Assn. Advt. Agys. (council mem.), Internat. Com. Am. Assn. Advt. Agys. Club: Sky (N.Y.). Office: J Walter Thompson Co 466 Lexington Ave New York NY 10017 *

CRONIN, KATHLEEN ANNE, executive search consultant; b. Oak Park, Ill., Sept. 17, 1933; d. Brendan C. and Rose J. (Mangini) Powell; B.A., DePaul U., 1977; m. Richard Cronin, May 29, 1954; children—Anne, Patrick, Richard, Edward, John, Michael, Eileen. Sec., credit asst. Hills Bros. Coffee, 1951-53; estimator Alpha Portland Cement, 1953-54; v.p. adminstrn. and research Hodge-Cronin & Assos., Inc., Rosemont, Ill., 1977—; cons. Office Cath. Edn. Ar . Mem. Human Relations Com., City of Des Plaines, 1971-72, St. Mary Pastoral Coun., 1984-88, chmn., 1986-88; pres. St. Mary Sch. Bd., Des Plaines, 1969-71; conciliator Archdiocese Chgo. Office Conciliation and Arbitration, 1970-74. Cert. CPR instr. Mem. Assn. Exec. Search Cons., Ill. Center Parapsychol. Research, Nat. Assn. Corp. and Profl. Recruiters. Clubs: Meadow, Plaza. Home: 1450 Harding Ave Des Plaines IL 60016 Office: Hodge Cronin & Assocs One O'Hare Centre 6250 N River Rd #4040 Rosemont IL 60018

CRONIN, ROBERT BARRINGTON, personnel executive, consultant; b. Harvre de Grace, Md., Nov. 23, 1926; s. Robert Clinton and Ethel (Bernshouse) C.; m. Ruth Elisabeth Stang, May 29, 1963; children: Claudia Cronin Victor, Cynthia Johnson Jones, Jan Cronin Deleu, Deborah Johnson Schwebert, Susan Johnson Karlix. BS in Marine Engring., U.S. Mcht. Marine Acad., 1946. Operating engr. Matson Navigation Co., San Francisco, 1946-49; indsl. engr. Deere & Co., Moline, Ill., 1949-55; sr. indsl. engr. Deere & Co., Moline, 1955-63, adminstrv. asst. in engring., 1967-70, mgr. employee benefits, 1970—; chief indsl. engr. Killefer works Deere & Co., L.A., 1963-67; lectr. bus., Marquette U., Madison, Wis., 1956; vis. lectr., St. Mary's Coll., South Bend, Ind., 1978. Crusade chmn. Rock Island County chpt. Am. Cancer Soc., Moline, 1983-84, dist. chmn. 1985. Mem. Coun. on Employee Benefits (co-chmn. ann. mem. conf. 1987), Conf. Bd. (rsch. coun. on employee benefits 1983—), Rock Island Arsenal Golf Club (trustee 1987—), Elks. Republican. Roman Catholic. Home: 3016 26th St Moline IL 61265 Office: Deere & Co John Deere Rd Moline IL 61265

CRONIN, THOMAS FRANCIS, JR., public utilities executive; b. N.Y.C., Mar. 6, 1939; s. Thomas Francis Sr. and Louise (Nesbitt) C.; m. Kathleen M. Hanig, Sept. 3, 1966; children: Thomas, Kathleen, Colleen, Kevin, William, Helen, Carol. BS in Social Sci., Fordham U., 1960. Bond underwriter Fireman's Fund Ins. Co., N.Y.C., 1962-65; sr. contract bond underwriter Chubb & Co., N.Y.C., 1965-68; mgr. contract bond dept. Charles H. Carmen Inc., N.Y.C., 1968-69; exec. asst. to congressman U.S. Congress, Washington and N.Y.C, 1969-75; mgr. steam ops. Consol. Edison Co. N.Y., N.Y.C., 1975-78, div. mgr., 1978-81, dir. risk mgmt., 1981—. Mem. exec. com. N.Y. State Conservative Party, N.Y.C., 1970—, chmn. Bronx County Com., 1970-75; vice chmn. Bayside Gables (N.Y.) Civic Assn., 1980-81; pres. Sacred Heart Cath. Youth Orgn., Bayside, 1981-87; bd. dirs. Bayside Gables Holding Corp., 1981—. Recipient Disting. Citizen award Bronx County Conservative Com., 1976, Civic Leadership award Michael Dolan Club, 1981. Mem. Risk and Ins. Mgmt. Soc. Inc., Edison Electric Inst. (chmn. risk mgmt. subcom. boiler and machinery 1984-86, subcom. nuclear task force), Midtown Ins. Buyers Assn., Union League, Bayside Conservative Club (vice chmn. 1985—). Office: Consol Edison Co NY 4 Irving Pl New York NY 10003

CRONIN, TIMOTHY CORNELIUS, III, computer manufacturing executive; b. Manchester, N.H., Sept. 26, 1927; s. Timothy Cornelius and Ann Frances (Meaney) C.; m. Gloria Mara, June 8, 1949 (dec. Sept. 1984); children: Gloria Ann, Constance, Timothy, Barbara, Mary, Thomas. BS, U.S. Mil. Acad., 1949; MBA, Ohio State U., 1952. Commd. 2d lt. USAF, 1949, advanced through grades to capt., 1956, resigned, 1956; mgr., v.p. Honeywell, Inc., Mpls. and Wellesley, Mass., 1956-71; v.p. Addressograph Multigraph, Cleve., 1971-74; chmn., chief exec. officer Inforex, Inc., Burlington, Mass., 1974-79; cons. in field Waltham, Mass., 1980-82; v.p. Wang Labs., Lowell, Mass., 1983-87; pres., chief exec. officer Wang Fin. Info. Services Corp., N.Y.C., 1987—. Decorated Legion of Merit. Mem. Computer Industries Assn. (exec. com. 1975—), Assn. Industries Mass. (bd. dirs. 1976—). Republican. Roman Catholic. Club: Manchester. Home: 31 Shaw Dr Bedford MA 03102 Office: Wang Fin Svcs Corp 120 Wall St New York NY 10005

CROOK, TROY NORMAN, geophysicist, consultant; b. Wall, Tex., May 24, 1928; s. Otis Allen and Callie Viola (Aylor) C.; m. Ruby Mae Keel, June 5, 1949; children: David Preston, Larry Norman. BEE, Tex. A&M U., 1949; BS in Geology, U. Houston, 1961. Seismic operator Humble Oil & Refining Co., Miss., Ala., Fla., La., 1949-54; rsch. geophysicist Humble Oil & Refining Co., Houston, 1955-64, asst. div. geophysicist, 1968-69, div. geophysicist, 1969-71; supr. rsch. Esso Prodn. Rsch. Co., Houston, 1965-67, mgr. basic geophysics, 1967-68; mgr. exploration systems div. Exxon Prodn. Rsch. Co., Houston, 1971-75, mgr. div. stratigraphic exploration, 1975-84, mgr. long-range rsch., 1984-86; prin. T. Norman Crook Cons., Houston, 1986—. Contbr. numerous articles to profl. jours.; patentee in field. Mem. Bethel Ind. Presbyn. Ch. Mem. IEEE, Am. Assn. Petroleum Geologists, European Assn. Exploration Geophysicists, Soc. Exploration Geophysicists (pres. 1978-79), Geophys. Soc. Houston. Home: 5527 Sylmar Houston TX 77081

CROOKE, JAMES S., United Nations executive. m. Nancy Crooke; 3 children. BS in Mech. Engring., U.S. Mcht. Marine Acad.; MA in Mgmt. and Econs., Columbia U. Resident industry officer U.S. Dept. State, Cairo, and Karachi, Pakistan; various sr. fin., engring. and managerial positions Union Carbide Corp., N.Y. Telephone Co., M.W. Kellogg Co., Mobil Oil Corp.; with U.N. Indsl. Devel. Orgn., N.Y.C., now dir. Asst. sec.-treas. Internat. Indsl. Devel. Found.; active numerous community orgns. Mem. Inst. Indsl. Engrs. (past pres. Met. N.Y. chpt.; rep. Engring. Manpower Commn. of Am. Assn. Engring. Socs.). Office: UN Indsl Devel Orgn 1 United Nations Pla New York NY 10017

CROOKS, WILLIAM HOWARD, JR., manufacturing company executive; b. Pitts., Aug. 30, 1949; s. William Howard and Helen Louise (Reitz) C.; m. Cynthia Ann Shaw, May, 7, 1977. BSME, U. Pitts., 1971. Gen. mgr. Glenfield Supply Co., Inc., Pitts., 1971—. Council mem. Twp. of O'Hara, Pa., 1975—, pres., 1984—; cert. lay speaker United Meth. Ch.; bd. dirs. Allegheny County Local Govt. Acad., 1988—. Mem. Soc. Mfg. Engrs., Nat. Rifle Assn. (life), Pa. Rifle & Pistol Assn. (life), Pitts. and Suburban Rifle League (bd. dirs. 1974—, pres. 1987—). Republican. Clubs: Rosedale (Pa.) Sportsmen's (sec. 1988—), Murrysville (Pa.) Sportsmen's. Lodge: Rotary. Home: 721 Midway Dr Pittsburgh PA 15215 Office: Glenfield Supply Co Inc 1935 Main St Pittsburgh PA 15215

CROOM, JOHN HENRY, III, utility company executive; b. Fayetteville, N.C., Dec. 12, 1932; s. John Henry and Mary Dalice (Howard) C.; m. Verna Arlene Willetts, June 21, 1953; children: Mary, Karen, Elizabeth, John. BSME, N.C. State Coll., 1954. Engr. United Fuel Gas Co., Charleston, W.Va., 1954-69; indsl. sales mgr. Charleston Group Cos., 1969-73; indsl. utilization mgr. Columbia Distbn. Cos., Columbus, Ohio, 1973-74, v.p. engring. and planning, 1974-79; sr. v.p. Columbia Gas System, Wilmington, Del., 1979-80, exec. v.p., dir., 1981-82, pres., bd. dirs., 1982-84, chmn., pres., chief exec. officer, 1984—; chmn., pres., chief exec. officer Columbia Gas System Inc., Wilmington, 1984—. Bd. dirs. Opportunities Ctr. Inc., Wilmington, YMCA of Del., Del.-Md.-Va. council Boy Scouts Am.; chmn. bd. Gas Research Inst., Chgo. Served with AUS, 1954-56. Mem. NSPE. Presbyterian. Home: PO Box 4175 Greenville DE 19807 Office: Columbia Gas System Inc 20 Montchanin Rd Wilmington DE 19807 *

CROPPER, WILLIAM A., utility company executive; b. Beaumont, Tex., Nov. 15, 1939; s. Joseph Wilfred and Julia Mary (Sonnier) C.; m. Genon Oliver, June 17, 1967; children: William A. Jr., Jenna C., Ryan T. BBA, Tex. A&M U., 1961; MBA, Lamar U., 1972. Asst. purchasing agt. Gulf States Utilities, Beaumont, 1969, market research analyst, 1969-73, fin. analyst, 1973-76, sr. fin. analyst, 1976-77, supr. long term financing, 1977-78, asst. treas., 1978-79, treas., 1979; dir. fin. Mid S. Utilities Co., New Orleans, 1979-83; dir. corp. fin. Panhandle Ea. Corp., Houston, 1983; v.p., treas. Houston Lighting & Power Co., 1983-86, Houston Industries Inc., 1986—; Mem. mgmt. com. Paragon Communications, 1986—; bd. dirs. Innovative Controls Inc., Houston, KBLCOM Inc., Houston, Houston Industries Fin. Inc. Coach Little League Football and Baseball, Beaumont and New Orleans, 1976-82; city chmn. March of Dimes, Beaumont, 1974; bd. dirs., v.p. Council Camp Fire Girls, Beaumont, 1979. Mem. Nat. Assn. Corp. Treas., Fin. Execs. Inst., Edison Elec. Inst., Nat. Investor Relations Inst., Beaumont Jaycees (bd. dirs. 1973). Republican. Roman Catholic. Office: Houston Industries Inc PO Box 4567 4300 Post Oak Pkwy Houston TX 77027

CROSBY, BENJAMIN GRATZ, electronics executive; b. Lexington, Ky., May 9, 1936; s. Ben Gratz Crosby and Myra (Smith) Brooking; m. Susan

Lee Nichols, Nov. 21, 1962 (div. June 1978); children: Alex Russell, Ben R., Elise M., Joanna D., Dawn N.; m. Jane White Firestone, Feb. 2, 1984. BS in Engring., U.S. Mil. Acad., 1958; cert., Armed Forces Staff Coll., 1972. Cert. fin. planner. Commd. 2d lt. U.S. Army, 1958, advanced through grades to lt. col., 1973, retired, 1978; v.p. F.L. Putnam & Co., Boston, 1978-81; pres. Blue Cactus Mining Corp., Las Vegas, 1981-84; exec. Oneac Corp., Libertyville, Ill., 1984—. Mem. Rep. Inner Circle, Washington, 1985—; bd. dirs. Citizen Scholarship Found., St. Paul, 1980—. Decorated two Silver Stars, four Bronze Stars, two Legions of Merit. Mem. Am. Fedn. Hosps., Am. Hosp. Assn., Hosp. Engring. Soc., Inst. Cert. Fin. Planners, Am. Inst. Ultrasound in Medicne, Assn. Advancement of Med. Instrumentation. Republican. Episcopalian. Office: Oneac Corp 27944 N Bradley Rd Libertyville IL 60048

CROSBY, EVALIE MUNROE, accountant; b. Northampton, Mass., Nov. 13, 1959; d. Richard Presson and Barbara Ann (Daykins) Munroe; m. David Marshall Crosby, Sept. 11, 1982. BA, Tufts U., 1980; MS in Acctg, Northeastern U., 1982. CPA, Mass. Staff auditor Bankers Trust Co., N.Y.C., 1980-81; sr. acct. Deloitte Haskins & Sells, Boston, 1981-85; pvt. practice acctg. Melrose, Mass., 1985-87, Amherst, Mass., 1987—. Mem. adminstrv. fin. com. Am. Bapt. Chs., Mass., 1987—. Mem. Nat. Assn. Accts., Mass. Sco. CPAs, Beta Gamma Sigma. Baptist. Home and Office: 337 Pelham Rd Amherst MA 01002

CROSBY, JOHN GRIFFITH, investment banker; b. Bayshore, N.Y., Feb. 10, 1943; s. Gordon Josiah and Ruth Louise (Plante) C.; m. Joan Louise Kelly; July 10, 1965; children—Bruce, Brian, David. Grad. Wm. Penn Charter Sch., 1961; A.B. with distinction, Lafayette Coll., 1965; M.B.A., Harvard U., 1969. Vice pres., stockholder, dir. Kidder, Peabody & Co. Inc., N.Y.C., 1969-80; mng. dir. Merrill Lynch & Co., N.Y.C., 1980—. Author: Private Placement Market Review, 1975-81. Class fund mgr. Lafayette Coll., 1969—; bd. deacons Presbyterian Ch., Madison, N.J., 1972; campaign chmn. Madison YMCA, 1975; coach Little League, 1977-84; treas. Troop 125, Boy Scouts Am., 1984-87; bd. dirs., asst. treas. Am. Coun. for Arts. Served to 1st lt. U.S. Army, 1965-67, Vietnam. Decorated Bronze Star medal. Mem. Bond Clubof N.Y., Securities Industry Assn. (chmn. corp. fin. com. 1984-85). Clubs: Noe Pond, Madison Golf. Office: Merrill Lynch World Hdqrs Fin Ctr N Tower 26th Fl New York NY 10281

CROSBY, MICHAEL JAMES, transportation executive; b. Dec. 6, 1939; s. Lawrence Eugene and Marcella Mary (Fishwick) C.; m. Yolanda Arlene Granger, June 10, 1961; children: Stephanie J., Jessica J., Michael G. BS in Mech. Engring., Case Western U., 1962, MS in Engring., 1967. Rsch. engr. NASA, Cleve., 1962-68; mgr. aerodynamic compatibility div. Gen. Electric, Evendale, Ohio, 1968-70; sr. rsch. assoc. Lord Corp., Eris, Pa., 1970-71, mgr. system dynamics and control div., 1971-74, mgr. vehicle products div., 1974-75, mgr. product market div., 1975-77, gen. mgr., 1977-78, v.p., 1978-88; pres., chief exec. officer Acadia Polymers Inc., Roanoke, Va., 1988—; bd. dirs. Corcap Inc., Hartford, Conn.; auditor Fairview Twp., Pa., 1988. Mem. Rep. fin. com., Erie County, Pa., 1987—. Mem. Am. Helicopter Soc. (bd. dirs. 1984-85), Soc. Automotive Engrs., Hunting Hills Country Club, Jefferson Club. Home: 3285 Winterberry Dr Roanoke VA 24018 Office: Acadia Polymers Inc 1420 Coulter Dr Roanoke VA 24012

CROSS, BETTY FELT, small business owner; b. Newcastle, Ind., Jan. 8, 1920; d. Frank Ernest and Olive (Shock) Felt; m. Paris O. Cross, July 14, 1939 (div.); children—Ernest, Betty J., Robert D., Paris, Toni, Frank; m. John B. Gatlin, 1976. Owner, mgr. Salon D'Or, Indpls., 1956-74; owner Bejon, Madison, Ind., 1974-78, Brass & Things, Madison, 1978—, Silver City USA I, Madison; pres. Felts Mfg., Inc., 1966—. Mem. Nashville C. of C. Avocation: collecting dolls, gold and silver coins, art objects, antique jewelry. Office: Silver City USA Olde Towne Village Madison TN 37115

CROSS, DENNIS WARD, insurance company executive; b. Santa Barbara, Calif., Sept. 22, 1943; s. Ward H. and Durith Ann (Stonner) C.; BS, Ill. Wesleyan U., 1965; MBA, Ind. U., 1967; CLU, Am. Coll., 1972; m. Judith M. Marston, Feb. 5, 1967; 1 child, Kimberly. Dir. consultation projects Life Ins. Mktg. and Rsch. Assn., Hartford, Conn., 1970-75; asst. v.p. sales USAA Life Ins. Co., San Antonio, 1975-78, v.p. sales, 1978-80, sr. v.p. sales, 1980-81, sr. v.p. mktg., 1981-86, sr. v.p. mktg., fin. svcs. div., 1986—, also dir.; pres. USAA Life Gen. Agy.; v.p. USAA Life Series Fund; sr. v.p. USAA Retirement Communities, bd. dirs. USAA Life Ins. Co.; instr., hon. faculty Army Logistics Mgmt. Center, Ft. Lee, Va., 1968-70; guest instr. U. Tex., San Antonio, 1970—, San Antonio Coll., 1978-81, St. Mary's U., 1981—. Mem. Cattle Barrons Steering com.; bd. dirs., v.p. Am. Cancer Soc.; bd. dirs., Jr. Achievement of South Tex.; with mktg. task force, United Way of San Antonio; bd. trustees Humana Hosp., San Antonio. Capt. U.S. Army, 1967-70. Fellow Life Office Mgmt. Assn.; mem. Am. Soc. CLUs, Life Advertisers Assn., Life Ins. Mktg. and Rsch. Assn. (bd. dirs., nominating and market rsch. coms., past chmn. direct response mktg. com., bd. dirs. 1986—), Direct Response Mktg. Ins. Council (Exec. of Yr. 1987), Am. Advt. Fedn., Army Res. Assn., Mutual Fund Ednl. Alliance (bd. govs. 1987—, v.p.), Oak Hills Country Club. Office: USAA Life Ins Co 9800 Fredericksburg Rd San Antonio TX 78288

CROSS, GLENN LABAN, development consultant, engineering executive; b. Mt. Vernon, Ill., Dec. 28, 1941; s. Kenneth Edward and Mildred Irene (Glenn) C.; m. Kim Lien Duong, Aug. 30, 1968 (div. Oct. 1975); m. Tran Tu Thach, Dec. 26, 1975; children—Cindy Sue, Cristy Luu; BA, Calif. Western U., 1981, MBA, 1982. Hosp. adminstr. pub. health div. AID, Dept. State, Washington, 1966-68; pers. mgr. Pacific Architects and Engrs., Inc., L.A., 1968-70, contract adminstr., 1970-73, mgr. mgmt. svcs., 1973-75; contracts adminstr. Internat. Svcs. div., AVCO, Cin., 1975-77; sr. contract adminstr. Bechtel Group, Inc., San Francisco, 1977-80, Arabian Bechtel Co. Ltd.; contract adminstrv. supr. Jubail Industrial City, Saudi Arabia, 1980-85; cons. Bechtel Western Power Corp., Jakarta, Indonesia, 1985—; with Pacific Engrs. & Constructors, Ltd., Jakarta, Indonesia. Author: Living With a Matrix: A Conceptual Guide to Organizational Variation, 1983. Served as sgt. 1st spl. forces group, airborne, AUS, 1962-65; Okinawa, Vietnam. Decorated Combat Infantryman's Badge. Mem. Internat. Pers. Mgmt. Assn., Assn. Human Resource Systems Profls., Human Resource Planning Soc., Assn. MBA Execs., Am. Mgmt. Assn., Am. Arbitration Assn., Internat. Records Mgmt. Council, Adminstrv. Mgmt. Soc. Republican. Avocations: swimming, reading. Home: 2841 Cottingham St Oceanside CA 92054 Office: Pacific Engrs & Constructors Ltd, PO Box 381/KBY, Jakarta 12790, Indonesia

CROSS, JEREMY LADD, aviation company executive; b. Lawrence, Mass., Mar. 23, 1939; s. Jerome Whitman and Margaret (Bain) C.; m. Beverly Brown, Sept. 12, 1964 (div. 1970); 1 child, Malcolm Tyler; m. Erlinda Kalinga, Sept. 14, 1970; children: Wynn, José, Kristine, Sarah, David John. BSA, Bently Coll., 1965; MBA, Boston Coll., 1967. V.p. fin., controller Winthrop Sterns Co., Philippines and Japan, 1969-71; cons. Sarmiento Enterprises, Philippines, 1971-72; v.p. fin., controller Dynatics Inc., Philippines, 1972-76; v.p. fin. Systrol Mfg. Inc., Philippines, 1976-78; chmn. ATS Aviation Inc., Manila, 1978-80, also bd. dirs.; bd. dirs. Systrol Mfg. Inc. Cons. Christian Unity Helps Fellowship, 1981. Served with USMC, 1957-60. Clubs: Manila Polo, Manila Yacht; Alabang Country. Office: ATS Aviation Inc, PO Box 1803 MCC, Makati, Manila Philippines

CROSS, LAURA ELIZABETH, lawyer; b. Lathrop, Mo.; d. Pross T. and Nina (Peel) C.; A.B., Lindenwood Coll., 1923; B.Litt., Columbia Sch. Journalism, 1925; J.D., George Washington U., 1939. Bibliog. research Library of Congress, Washington, 1931-42; admitted to D.C. bar, 1940; atty. Office Chief of Engrs., U.S. Army, 1942-73; practiced in Washington, 1973-—. Mem. ABA, Fed., D.C. bar assns., Am. Judicature Soc., Women in Communications, Kappa Beta Pi, Theta Sigma Phi. Home: 2500 Wisconsin Ave NW Apt 709 Washington DC 20007

CROSS, LOUISE PORTLOCK, manufacturing company executive; b. Norfolk, Va., Jan. 20, 1907; d. William Seth and Mary Louise (Fanshow) Portlock; m. James Byron Cross, July 17, 1929; 1 child, Blanche Louise. Grad. high sch. With J.B. Cross Inc., Norfolk, 1952—, exec. pres., 1959-60, then pres., chief exec. officer, from 1960, now pres., treas., agt. Mem. Audeubon Soc., Nature Conservancy, Heritage Found., Va. Beach Maritime Hist., Order Eastern Star, Ladies Oriental Shrine N.Am. Home and Office: Mayflower Seaside Towers 205-34th St Apt 1601 Virginia Beach VA 23451

CROSS, RALPH HERBERT, III, civil engineer; b. Oakland, Calif., Aug. 17, 1938; s. Ralph Herbert Jr. and Cecil (Terkelson) C.; m. Robin Nichols, June 27, 1959; children: Ralph H. IV, Geoffrey James. BS, U. Calif., Berkeley, 1961, MS, 1962, PhD, 1966. Asst. prof. civil engring. MIT, 1966-71; dir. environ. programs Alpine Geophys. Assocs., Norwood, N.J., 1971-74; asst. v.p. Woodward Clyde Cons., Oakland, 1974—. Contbr. articles to profl. jours.; patentee in field. Mem. ASCE, Phi Beta Kappa, Tau Beta Pi, Chi Epsilon. Republican. Home: 2365 Dapplegray Ln Walnut Creek CA 94596 Office: Woodward Clyde Cons 500 12th St Ste 100 Oakland CA 94607

CROSS, ROBERT WILLIAM, lawyer, computer company executive; b. Balt., Oct. 9, 1937; s. Rosamond and Mildred (Fowler) C.; m. Deanna Louise Deerr, Feb. 7, 1965; children Ann Elizabeth, Robert William II. BSBA, Washington U., St. Louis, 1962; JD, Washington U., 1964. Bar: N.Y. 1964. Assoc. Winthrop, Stimson, Putnam & Roberts, N.Y.C., 1964-68; gen. counsel Electronic Data Systems Corp., Dallas, 1968-69; pres. R.W. Corss & Co., Dallas and N.Y.C., 1970—; chmn., chief exec. officer World Computer Corp., Dallas, 1971-72; counsel Carter, Ledyard & Milburn, N.Y.C., 1981-82; pres., chief exec. officer Columbia (Md.) Data Products, 1984-85; chmn., chief exec. officer Delta Data Systems Corp., Columbia, 1986—, also bd. dirs. With USMC, 1957-59. Mem. Assn. of Bar of City of N.Y., University Club, Down Town Assn., Omicron Delta Kappa. Republican. Home: 349 Pondfield Rd Bronxville NY 10708 Office: Delta Data Systems Corp 7175 Columbia Gateway Dr Columbia MD 21046

CROSS, STEVEN JASPER, professor of finance; b. Hohenwald, Tenn., Apr. 19, 1954; s. Thomas Edward and Eula Mae (Mealer) C.; m. Martha Ellen Bradshaw, Aug. 23, 1974. B.S., Middle Tenn. State U., 1976, M.A.T., 1980, D.A., 1984. Sales rep. University Ford Inc., Murfreesboro, Tenn., 1976; ins. underwriter Continental Ins. Inc., Nashville, 1976-77; credit rep. SunAm., Inc., Murfreesboro, 1977-78; instr. mgmt. Dyersburg (Tenn.) State Community Coll., 1980-81; instr. Motlow State Community Coll., Tullahoma, Tenn., 1981-83, asst. prof. econs. 1983-85; assoc. prof. fin. Delta State U., 1985-88, prof., chmn. div. of econ. and fin., 1988—. Contbr. articles to profl. jours. Mem. Am. Econ. Assn., Nat. Assn. Bus. Economists, Am. Fin. Assn., Eastern Fin. Assn., So. Fin. Assn., Southwestern Fin. Assn., Midsouth Acad. Econs. and Fin., Midwest Econs. Assn., Sigma Rho, Phi Beta Lambda, Delta Mu Delta. Home: 25 Memorial Dr Boyle MS 38730 Office: Delta State U Sch Bus div Econs and Fin Cleveland MS 38733

CROSS, THOMAS GARY, insurance executive; b. Bayonne, N.J., July 17, 1947; s. Louis F. Jr. and Muriel B. (Burnett) C.; m. Lynda A. Armitage, June 15, 1968; children: Brian T., Jason S., Jonathan A. BA, Seton Hall U., 1969. CLU. Mgmt. trainee Chem. Bank, N.Y.C., 1969-70; sales mgr. Met. Life Ins., Hillside, N.J., 1970-74; employee benefits cons. Corroon & Black, N.Y.C., 1974-77; asst. v.p. Bayley Martin & Fay, N.Y.C., 1977-78; mktg. specialist Merrill Lynch, N.Y.C., 1978; sr. v.p., corp. life specialist Rollins Burdick Hunter, Roseland, N.J., 1978-87; v.p. exec. planning svcs. Alexander & Alexander, N.Y.C., 1987-88; pres. T.G. Cross Assocs., Inc., Bridgewater, N.J., 1988—. Asst. coach Long Valley (N.J.) Soccer Assn., 1982-84. Served with U.S. Army, 1969-75. Home: 15 Falcon Ln Long Valley NJ 07853 Office: TG Cross Assocs Inc 245 Union Ave Ste 2-C Bridgewater NJ 08807

CROSSEN, FRANK MARVIN, construction products manufacturing company executive; b. Dallas, 1923. BA, So. Meth., 1949; grad., Rutgers U., 1951. V.p. Preston State Bank, Dallas, 1940-55; v.p. Centex Corp., Dallas, from 1958, chmn., co-chief exec. officer, 1971-85, vice-chmn., 1985—, also dir. Trustee So. Meth. U.; bd. dirs. Lomas & Nettleton Fin. Corp., InterFirst Corp., Dallas. Office: Centex Corp 3333 Lee Pkwy Box 19000 Dallas TX 75219 *

CROSSLAND, SAMUEL HESS, lawyer, heavy construction company executive; b. Tulsa, Aug. 30, 1929; s. Samuel Hess and Louise (Weaver) C.; student U. Tulsa, 1947-48, 52-53; B.A., U. Okla., 1955, LL.B., 1957; m. Yolonda Phillips, Sept. 18, 1958; 1 child, Julia Allison. Bar: Okla., D.C. Pros. atty., Tulsa County, Okla., 1957-59; chief legal counsel to gov. of Okla., 1959-62; ptnr. Stuart, Symington, Hollings & Crossland, Washington, 1962-64; atty. Morrison-Knudsen Co., Inc., 1964—, corp. sec., counsel, 1968-73, v.p., sec., gen. counsel, 1973-89, sr. v.p., spl. asst. to chmn., 1989—. Served with USNR, 1948-52. Mem. ABA, Okla. Bar Assn., D.C. Bar Assn., Am. Soc. Corp. Secs., Phi Alpha Delta. Clubs: Hillcrest Country, Arid (Boise). Office: Morrison Knudsen Corp PO Box 73 Boise ID 83707

CROSSLEY, MARK LARRY, statistician, quality engineer, consultant; b. Little Rock; s. Mark and Betty Louise (Reynolds) C.; m. Betty Rice, Nov. 2, 1962; children: Brett, Brooke. BS in Chemistry and Math., U. N.C., 1969. Pres. Quality Mgmt. Assocs., Salisbury, N.C., 1984—. Bd. advisors Rowan Tech. Coll., Salisbury, 1981—. Petroleum research fellow Nat. Petroleum Inst., 1970. Mem. Am. Soc. Quality Control (sr., mem. nat. cert. com. 1964—, cert. quality engr., cert reliability engr.), Am. Statis. Assn., Mensa (exec. com. Charlotte 1985). Republican. Methodist. Home and Office: Quality Mgmt Assocs 5 Scottsdale Salisbury NC 28144

CROSSMAN, WILLIAM WHITTARD, retired communications executive; b. Mineola, N.Y., Aug. 10, 1927; s. Homer Danforth and Emily May (Whittard) C.; m. Mary DeJesu, Dec. 6, 1952; children: William Whittard, Lindsay Maria, Michael DeJesu. BS in Engring. Sci., U. Miami, 1949. West coast mgr., gen. mgr. HiTemp Wires div. Simplex Wire & Cable Co., 1955-69; pres. surprenat div. ITT Corp., 1969-74; pres. royal electric div. ITT Corp., Pawtucket, R.I., 1974-77; group gen. mgr. ITT Corp., N.Y.C., 1977-85, v.p., 1979-87; chmn. and group exec. communications and info. svcs. ITT Corp., Secaucus, N.J., 1985-88; sr. v.p. ITT Corp., Secaucus, 1987-88; ret. ITT Corp., 1988; bd. dirs. Hudson Internat., Corp., 1988. With USNR, 1945-46, USAF, 1951. Mem. IEEE, Wire Assn. Republican. Episcopalian. Clubs: Owls Head Harbor, San Remo. Home: 24 White Oak Shade Rd New Canaan CT 06840

CROTTY, LEO WILLIAM, textile leasing company executive; b. Detroit, Aug. 11, 1927; s. Fergus and Evelyn (Thorn) C.; BS in Bus. Adminstrn., U. Dayton, 1952; m. Marilyn Ann Hauer, Apr. 18, 1953; children: Kathleen, Daniel, Kevin, Robert, Shane, James, Brian. Service mgr. Van Dyne-Crotty, Inc., Dayton, Ohio, 1948-55, v.p. sales, 1955-63, pres., 1963—, chmn. bd., chief exec. officer, 1977—; dir. Third Nat. Bank & Trust Co., Xyovest Inc. Bd. dirs. U. Dayton. Served with USMC, 1946-48, U.S. Army, 1952-53. Mem. Young Pres.'s Orgn., Inc., Pres.'s Assn., Inc., Inst. Indsl. Launderers, Kex Nat. Assn., World Bus. Council, Dayton Area C. of C. (dir. 1974-77), U. Dayton Alumni Assn. (dir. 1965-71), Dayton Racquet Club, Moraine Country Club, Rotary. Roman Catholic. Home: 5503 Tall Trees Dayton OH 45429 Office: Van Dyne-Crotty Inc 903 Brandt St Box 442 Dayton OH 45401

CROUSE, JOSEPH ROBERT, lawyer, banker; b. Hudson, N.Y., Apr. 24, 1946; s. Robert Aloysius and Natalie Clair (McNamara) C.; m. Laura Anne Riley, Dec. 24, 1977; children—Jeffrey Robert, Jared William, Alexandra Natalie. B.A., St. Bonaventure U., 1968; J.D., SUNY-Buffalo, 1971. Bar: N.Y., D.C., Md. Atty. Fed. Res. Bd., Washington, 1975-77; chief counsel comsumer banking Md. Nat. Bank, Balt., 1977-80; bank commr. State of Md., Balt., 1980-83; sr. v.p., gen. counsel Equitable Bancorp., Balt., 1983—. Contbr. articles to profl. jours. Mem. adv. bd. Md. State Use Industries, Annapolis, 1984-87. Served to capt. JAG, USMC, 1972-75. Mem. ABA (lectr.), Md. Bankers Assn. (chmn. govt. relations com. 1985-87), Md. Bar Assn., D.C. Bar Assn. Roman Catholic. Home: 4017 Starrwreath Way Ellicott City MD 21043 Office: Equitable Bancorp Equitable Bank Ctr 100 S Charles St Baltimore MD 21201

CROUTHAMEL, THOMAS GROVER, SR., pharmaceutical consultant; b. Berkeley, Calif., Sept. 10, 1930; s. Martin Luther and Elizabeth (Grover) C.; m. Madalene Donati, Sept. 6, 1954; children: Thomas Grover Jr., Annalise. BS, Thiel Coll., 1953. Sr. drug investigator U.S. FDA, L.A. and Edison (N.J.), 1958-81; pres. Thomas G. Crouthamel, Inc., Bradenton, Fla., 1981—; ptnr. Crouthamel & Crouthamel, Brandenton, 1983—; treas. Crouthamel Enterprises, Inc., Liberty Hill, Tex., 1986—. Author: Auditing EtO, 1982, It's OK, 1986, A History of Trailer Estates, 1987; contbr. articles to profl. jours. Cubmaster Boy Scouts Am., Pomona, Calif., 1963, committeeman, Spotswood, N.J., 1968-76, adult adviser explorer post, 1976-79; trustee Spotswood Library Bd., 1970-79; co-leader Compassionate Friends, Sarasota, 1984—. Cpl. U.S. Army, 1953-54. Mem. Parenteral Drug Assn., Internat. Narcotics Officers Assn., Toastmasters (pres. 1969-71), Masons (high priest local chpt. 1967).

CROW, EDWARD R., marketing professional; b. Murphysboro, Ill., July 7, 1949; s. Olen L. and Mary T. (Schneider) C.; m. Janice M. Hustedde, Sept. 7, 1973; children: Timothy P., Shawn B., Erin K. BS in Recreation and Psychology, So. Ill. U., Edwardsville, 1975, Master's in City and Regional Planning, 1982. City and regional planner Southwestern Ill. Met. & Regional Planning Commn., Collinsville, 1974-85; bus. devel. mgr. Poettker Constrn. Co., Breese, Ill., 1985-86, v.p. mktg. and bus. devel., 1986-88. Asst. cubmaster Okaw Valley council Cub Scouts, 1986—, asst. den leader, pack com. mem. Served with USAF, 1967-71. Mem. Soc. Mktg. Profl. Services, Am. Legion, Genealogy Soc. So. Ill., So. Ill. U. Alumni Assn. Roman Catholic. Office: Poettker Constrn Co County Hwy 7 & 4th St Breese IL 62230

CROW, JOHN WILLIAM, banker; b. London, 1937; s. John Cornell and Mary Winifred (Weetch) C.; m. Ruth Kent, 1963; children—Rebecca, Jonathan. B.A., Oxford U., 1961. Economist Western Hemisphere dept. Internat. Monetary Fund, 1961-67, asst. chief Cen. Am. div., 1967-70, chief N.Am. div., 1970-73; dep. chief research dept. Bank of Can., Ottawa, 1973-74, chief research dept., 1974-79, adviser, 1979-81, dep. gov., 1981-84, sr. dep. gov., 1984-87, gov., 1987—. Office: Bank Can, 234 Wellington St, Ottawa, ON Canada K1A 0G9

CROW, MICHAEL RAY, savings and loan executive, accountant; b. Oklahoma City, Mar. 15, 1947; s. Melvin B. and Helen L. (Rand) C.; m. Leta M. Campbell, Jan. 25, 1969 (div. May 1977); m. Cody Jan Glasser, Apr. 20, 1979; 1 child, Rhonda Lynne. BBA, Tex. Tech U., 1969, MBA, 1970; grad. Southwest Sch. Banking, So. Meth. U., 1979. CPA, Tex. Staff acct. Arthur Anderson & Co., Ft. Worth, 1970-72; exec. v.p., chief fin. officer 1st City Nat. Bank Houston, 1972-83; sr. exec. v.p., chief fin. officer United Savs. Assn. Tex., Houston, 1983—; also bd. dirs. United Savs. Assn. Tex. Treas., bd. dirs. Houston chpt. ARC, 1981—. Republican. Methodist. Office: United Savs Assn Tex 5718 Westheimer Rd Ste 2200 Houston TX 77057

CROWDER, RICHARD THOMAS, food products executive; b. Baskerville, Va., Aug. 3, 1939; s. George Thomas and Estelle (Morgan) C.; m. Margaret Rainey, Sept. 4, 1960; children: Richard, Matthew. BS, Va. Poly. Inst. and State U., 1960, MS, 1962; PhD, Okla. State U., 1967. Staff economist Exxon USA, Houston, 1966-68; dir. econ. analysis Wilson & Co., Inc., Oklahoma City, 1968-75; sr. v.p. The Pillsbury Co., Mpls., 1975-89; asst. to sec. of agr. for internat. affairs and commodity programs USDA, Washington, 1989—; advisor Spl. Trade Representation, Washington, Office of Tech. Assessment, Washington; exec. v.p. Pillsbury Restaurant Group, 1987-89. Rep. precinct vice chmn. Hennepin County. Capt. U.S. Army, 1962-64. Mem. Am. Agrl. Econs. Assn. (bd. dirs. 1975-78, assoc. editor 1983-86). Mthodist. Lodge: Rotary (Mpls.). Office: USDA Office Sec Agr for Internat Affairs Washington DC 20250

CROWE, JAMES JOSEPH, shoe company executive; b. New Castle, Pa., June 9, 1935; s. William J. and Anna M. (Dickson) C.; m. Joan D. Verba, Dec. 26, 1959. B.A., Youngstown State U., 1958; J.D., Georgetown U., 1963. Bar: Va. bar 1963, Ohio bar 1966. Atty. SEC, Washington, 1964-65, Gen. Tire & Rubber Co., Akron, Ohio, 1965-68; sr. atty. Eaton Corp., Cleve., 1968-72; sec., gen. counsel U.S. Shoe Corp., Cin., 1972—; v.p. U.S. Shoe Corp., 1975—. Chmn. div. Fine Arts Fund, 1976; trustee Springer Ednl. Found., 1978-84, Cin. Music Festival Assn., 1980-86, Invest in Neighborhood Inc., 1982-89, pres. 1984-86; group chmn. United Appeal, 1980; mem. pres.'s council Coll. Mt. St. Joseph, 1985-88; trustee Tennis for Charity Inc., 1986—. 2d lt. U.S. Army, 1958-59. Mem. Ohio Bar Assn., Va. Bar Assn., Cin. Bar Assn., Am. Soc. Corp. Secs., Cin. C. of C. Clubs: Cin. Country (Cin.), Queen City (Cin.). Office: US Shoe Corp One Eastwood Dr Cincinnati OH 45227

CROWE, JOHN CARL, airline company executive; b. Harrisburg, Pa., Jan. 10, 1937; s. James Carl and Marion (Scholl) C. AB, Harvard U., 1959; MBA, U. Pa., 1966. Mgr. TWA, Inc., N.Y.C., 1967-70, dir., 1970-74, staff v.p., 1974-78, 81-86; staff v.p. TWA, Inc., Kansas City, Mo., 1978-81; corp. v.p. TWA, Inc., N.Y.C., 1986—. Mem. Harvard Club. Republican. Presbyterian. Home: 421 W Lyon Farm Dr Greenwich CT 06831 Office: TWA Inc 110 S Bedford Rd Mount Kisco NY 10549

CROWE, JOHN T., lawyer; b. Cabin Cove, Calif., Aug. 14, 1938; s. J. Thomas and Wanda (Walston) C.; m. Marina Protopapa, Dec. 28, 1968; 1 dau., Erin Aleka. BA, U. Santa Clara, 1960, JD, 1962. Bar: Calif. 1962, U.S. Dist. Ct. (no. dist.) Calif. 1964, U.S. Dist. Ct. (ea. dist.) Calif. 1967. Practiced in Visalia, Calif., 1964—; ptnr. firm Crowe, Mitchell & Crowe, 1971-85; referee State Bar Ct., 1976-82; gen. counsel Sierra Wine, 1986—. Bd. dirs. Mt. Whitney Area council Boy Scouts Am., 1966-85, pres., 1971, 72; bd. dirs. Visalia Associated In-Group Donors (AID), 1973-81, pres., 1978-79; mem. Visalia Airport Commn., 1982—. Served to 1st lt. U.S. Army, 1962-64; col. Res. Decorated Meritorious Service Medal with 2 oak leaf clusters, Army Commendation Medal; named Young Man of Yr., Visalia, 1973; Senator, Jr. Chamber Internat., 1970; recipient Silver Beaver award Boy Scouts Am., 1983. Mem. ABA, Tulare County Bar Assn., Nat. Assn. R.R. Trial Counsel, State Bar Calif., Visalia C. of C. (pres. 1979-80). Republican. Roman Catholic. Clubs: Rotary (pres. 1980-81); Downtown (Fresno, Calif.). Home: 3939 W School Ave Visalia CA 93291

CROWE, RONALD WAYNE, accountant, tax advisor; b. Rome, Ga., July 27, 1954; s. Willie Algin and Myra Ann (Vines) C. Student, U. Ga., 1973-75, BA, 1980; student, U. Tenn., Chattanooga, 1978-80. CPA, Tenn. Acct. fixed assets Coronet Industries Inc., Dalton, Ga., 1980-82, gen. acct., 1982-83; fin. analyst Blue Cross Blue Shield Tenn., Chattanooga, 1983-85, mgr. cost and budget payroll, 1985—. Mem. com. Rep. Exec. Com., Ga., 1984-87, nominating com. 7th Dist. Rep. Conv., Marietta, Ga., 1984; chmn. precinct Walker County Rep. Com., Lafayette, Ga., 1984. Mem. AICPA, Toastmasters (v.p. Chattanooga chpt. 1984-85), Pachyderm Club (nominating com. 1986). Home: 409 Cameron Circle Apt 2006 Chattanooga TN 37402 Office: Blue Cross and Blue Shield Tenn 801 Pine St Chattanooga TN 37402

CROWELL, OHMER OREAL, insurance company executive; b. Pulaski, Va., Oct. 2, 1924; s. Ohmer Oreal and Thelma Irene (Repass) C.; m. Patsy Helen Miller, June 12, 1948; children: James Douglas, Susan Patricia, Katherina Ann. B.S., Va. Poly. Inst., 1949. With Nationwide Ins. Co., 1949—; field underwriter Nationwide Ins. Co., Farmville, Va., 1949-50; audit supr. Nationwide Ins. Co., Columbus, Ohio, 1950-52; underwriting service mgr. Nationwide Ins. Co., Canton, Ohio, 1952-54; regional underwriting mgr. Nationwide Ins. Co., Lynchburg, Va., 1954-59; regional underwriting mgr., regional adminstrn. mgr. Nationwide Ins. Co., Lynchburg, 1959-60; dir. appraisals Nationwide Ins. Co., Columbus, 1960-62; regional mgr. Nationwide Ins. Co., Trenton, 1962-66; 2d v.p. Medicare Nationwide Ins. Co., Columbus, 1966-68, v.p. Medicare, 1968-69, v.p. personnel, 1969-77, v.p. central bus. ops., 1977-81, sr. v.p. bus. ops., 1981-82, sr. v.p. mktg., 1983—; mem. bd. commrs. Grievances and Discipline Supreme Ct. State Ohio; pres. Peoples Travel Service. Bd. dirs. Met. YMCA, Better Bus. Bur., Central Ohio, Inc.; bd. dirs., pres. Columbus Cancer Clinic. Served with U.S. Army, 1943-45; to 1st lt. U.S. Army, 1950-52. Mem. Am. Soc. C.L.U.s, Soc. Chartered Property and Casualty Underwriters. Lutheran. Lodges: Kiwanis; Masons; Elks. Home: 3430 Sunningdale Way Columbus OH 43221 Office: Nationwide Mut Ins Co 1 Nationwide Pla Columbus OH 43216

CROWL, R(ICHARD) BERN, aluminum company executive; b. New Brunswick, N.J., Aug. 10, 1931; s. Richard Bernard Crowl and Ella Marie (Hermann) Clarke; m. Lydia Canonico, Aug. 15, 1953 (div. June 1981); children: Joan M. Crowl Matri, Barbara, Robert; m. Katherine Alice Sparks, Dec. 11, 1981; stepchildren: Lauren E. Albrecht, Beth S. Albrecht. Student,

U. Notre Dame, 1950-51, Am. U., 1952-53; BBA, Rutgers U., 1955; grad. advanced mgmt. program, Harvard U., 1971. Treas. dept. Amax, Inc., Greenwich, Conn., 1955-81, exec. v.p., chief fin. officer, 1981-83; exec. v.p. Reynolds Metals Co., Richmond, Va., 1983-84, exec. v.p., chief fin. officer, 1984—. Served with USAF, 1951-52. Roman Catholic. Office: Reynolds Metals Co 6601 W Broad St Richmond VA 23261

CROWLEY, ANTHONY WILLIAM, JR., banker; b. Salem, Ill., Feb. 23, 1945; s. Anthony William Sr. and Lilyan (Griffin) C.; m. Karlene Linxweiler, Dec. 3, 1983; children: Kaila Christine, Sean William. BA, U. Notre Dame, 1967; MBA, U. Miami, 1972. Lending officer S.E. Bank, Miami, Fla., 1972-77, v.p., 1977-81, sr. v.p. nat. accounts div., 1981-83, sr. v.p. corp. banking div., 1983-86, mgr. capital markets group, 1986—, also bd. dirs. Chmn. com. United Way, Miami, 1981; mem. citizens adv. bd. U. Miami, 1981; mem. citizens adv. bd. U. Miami, 1985. With U.S. Army, 1967-70, Vietnam. Mem. Bankers Assn. for Corp. Fin. (chmn. pvt. placement com. 1986), Exec. Assn., Riviera Country Club, City Club. Republican. Roman Catholic. Office: SE Bank One Southeast Fin Ctr Miami FL 33131

CROWLEY, JAMES FARRELL, investment banker; b. Washington, Dec. 16, 1946; m. Martha Moore, Sept. 29, 1973; children—William, Farrell, Marjorie. B.S., B.A., Villanova U., Pa., 1972; M.B.A., U. Pa., 1976. Investment banker Smith Barney, N.Y.C., 1976-84; head investment banking N.Am., mng. dir., dir. Prudential-Bache Securities Inc., N.Y.C., 1984—, mem. exec. com., 1985—; chmn. Prudential Global Funding, N.Y.C., 1984—; bd. dirs. Prudential-Bache Interfunding, PB Capital Ptnrs. Clubs: Larchmont Yacht, N.Y. Athletic (N.Y.C.), N.Y. Yacht, Manhattan Yacht, Sandonana Sporting. Home: 121 Brookside Dr Greenwich CT 06830 Office: Prudential-Bache Securities 199 Water St New York NY 10292

CROWLEY, JAMES WORTHINGTON, lawyer; b. Cookville, Tenn., Feb. 18, 1930; s. Worth and Jessie (Officer) C.; m. Laura June Bauserman, Jan. 27, 1951; children—James Kenneth, Laura Cynthia; m. Joyce A. Goode, Jan. 15, 1966; children—John Worthington, Noelle Virginia; m. Carol Golden, Sept. 4, 1981. B.A., George Washington U., 1950, LL.B., 1953. Bar: D.C. bar 1954. Underwriter, spl. agt. Am. Surety Co. of N.Y., Washington, 1953-56; adminstrv. asst., contract adminstr. Atlantic Research Corp., Alexandria, Va., 1956-59; mgr. legal dept., asst. sec., counsel Atlantic Research Corp., 1959-65, sec., legal mgr., counsel, 1965-67; sec., legal mgr., counsel Susquehanna Corp. (merger with Atlantic Research Corp.), 1967-70; pres., dir. Gen. Communication Co., Boston, 1962-70; v.p., gen. counsel E-Systems, Inc., 1970-, sec., 1976—; v.p., asst. sec., dir. Air Asia Co. Ltd., Tainan, Taiwan, Republic China, 1975-87; dir. Cemco, Inc., Continental Electronic Systems, Inc.; v.p., dir. TAI, Inc., Serv-air, Inc., Greenville, Tex.; mem. adv. bd., sec. Internat. and Comparative Law Ctr., Southwestern Legal Found. Mem. Am. Soc. Corp. Secs. (nat. dir. 1989—, pres. Dallas regional group 1988-89, nat. dir. 1989—), Inf. Mus. Assn., ABA, Nat. Security Indsl. Assn., Machinery and Allied Products Inst. (mem. law coun.), Omicron Delta Kappa, Alpha Chi Sigma, Phi Sigma Kappa. Republican. Baptist. Home: 16203 Spring Creek Rd Dallas TX 75248 Office: E-Systems Inc PO Box 660248 Dallas TX 75266

CROWLEY, MARK, investment company executive; b. Portland, Maine, June 1, 1933; s. Mark Crowley and Catherine Matilda (Tibbetts) Murtha; m. Carol Johnson, Aug. 31, 1953 (div. 1975); children: John Stephen, Diane, Lisa; m. Florence Anita Valukas, Jan. 31, 1976. B in Marine Scis., Maine Maritime Acad., 1954. CLU. Ins. agt. N.Y. Life Ins. Co., Portland, Maine, 1955-57; gen. mgr. N.Y. Life Ins. Co., numerous locations, 1960-76; supt. agys. N.Y. Life Ins. Co., N.Y.C., 1976-78; regional v.p. N.Y. Life Ins. Co., Boston, 1978-81; v.p. N.Y. Life Ins. Co., N.Y.C., 1981-83, sr. v.p., 1983-86; pres., chief exec. officer NYLIFE Securities, Inc., N.Y.C., 1986; pres., chief exec. officer, trustee MacKay-Shields MainStay Fund Group, N.Y.C., 1986—; bd. dirs. N.Y. Life Internat. Investment Inc. Mem. N.H. Assn. Life Underwriters (pres. 1975), Gen. Agts. and Mgrs. Assn. N.H. (pres. 1974). Republican. Episcopalian. Home: 140 N Bald Hill Rd New Canaan CT 06840 Office: NY Life Ins Co 51 Madison Ave New York NY 10010

CROWLEY, NEELY DOWALL, broadcasting executive; b. Abington, Pa., Mar. 10, 1950; d. Robertson L. and Martha (Groome) Dowall; m. Michael E. Crowley, May 10, 1975; children: Kate Elizabeth, Megan Lynn. Student, High Point Coll., 1968-71. Field rep. Zeta Tau Alpha Nat. Frat., Indpls., 1972-74; account exec. Sta. WFPG/WIIN-Radio, Atlantic City, 1974-80; pres., SMC Inc., serving as gen. mgr. Sta. WSLT/WIBG-Radio, Ocean City, N.J., 1980—; pub. The Sun Newspaper, Ocean City, 1980—. Chairperson Ocean City Tourism Devel. Commn., 1983—, Families for Freedom of Choice, Ocean City, 1986; mem. N.J. Gov.'s Mgmt. Improvement Study Program, 1984; bd. dirs. Ocean City Task Force on Child Care, 1984—; youth coach Ocean City Recreation Dept., 1985—; mem. Mayor's com. Econ. Devel., 1988, Atlantic County 2001 Task Force. Recipient Cert. of Merit, 1975, Honor Ring, 1976 Zeta Tau Alpha, Media award N.J. Foster Parents Assn., 1986; named among People to Watch in '83 Atlantic City Mag., 1983. Mem. Alliance, The Women's Network (former bd. dirs. Atlantic City), Humane Soc. Ocean City (v.p., bd. dirs. 1986—), Ocean City C. of C. (v.p., bd. dirs. 1987—, named Citizen of Yr. 1988, pres. 1989—). Office: Sta WSLT/WIBG 957 Asbury Ave Ocean City NJ 08226

CROWLEY, ROBERT DALE, menswear direct mail company executive; b. Olean, N.Y., Dec. 30, 1949; s. William Charles and Marie (Richardson) C.; m. Barbara Jean Cook, Dec. 27, 1975; children: Gabrielle Marie, Veronica Jean. BS, St. Bonaventure U., 1971. Vice pres. New Process Co., Warren, Pa. Treas. Friends of Warren Basketball, 1986-88. Mem. Conewango Club. Republican. Roman Catholic. Office: New Process Co 229 Hickory St Warren PA 16366

CROWLEY, THOMAS B., marine transportation company executive; b. 1914; married. With Crowley Maritime Corp., San Francisco, 1935—, now chmn., pres., dir. Recip. Vice-Admiral Jerry Land Medal, Soc. Naval Architects and Marine Engrs., 1985. Office: Crowley Maritime Corp 101 California St San Francisco CA 94117 *

CROWN, FREDERICK SMITH, JR., financial analyst; b. Mobile, Ala., Jan. 18, 1949; s. Frederick Smith and Molly Erwin (Inge) C.; m. Renee Marie Mascoe, Sept. 1, 1973; children: Benjamin Pape, Rebecca Ellen. BA with hons., U. Ala., 1971; postgrad., U. S. Ala., 1972-73; grad., Stonier Grad. Sch. Banking, New Brunswick, N.J., 1981. Chartered fin. analyst. Mgmt. trainee Merchants Nat. Bank, Mobile, Ala., 1972-75, asst. v.p. bond dept., 1975-80, v.p., portfolio mgr., 1980-82; v.p., portfolio mgr. Lee, Robinson and Steine Inc., Nashville, 1982-88, pres., 1988—. Treas. Project Return Inc., Nashville, 1987—. With USAR, 1972. Fellow Fin. Analysts Fedn.; mem. Nashville Soc. Fin. Analysts, Phi Beta Kappa. Presbyterian. Office: Lee Robinson and Steine Inc 315 Deaderick St Nashville TN 37238-0035

CROWN, LESTER, manufacturing company executive; b. Chgo., June 7, 1925; s. Henry and Rebecca (Kranz) C.; m. Renee Schine, Dec. 28, 1950; children: Arie, James, Patricia, Daniel, Susan, Sara, Janet. BS in Chem. Engring., Northwestern U., 1947; MBA, Harvard U., 1949. Instr. math. Northwestern U., 1946-47; v.p., dir., chem. engr. Marblehead Lime Co., 1950-56, pres., 1956-66; v.p., dir. Material Service Corp. subs. Gen. Dynamics Corp., Chgo., 1953-66, pres., 1970-83, chmn., 1983—, also dir.; exec. v.p. Gen. Dynamics Corp., St. Louis, 1960-66, 77—, dir., 1974—, mem. exec. com., from 1982; pres., dir. Henry Crown & Co., Chgo., from 1969; dir. TW Services, Inc., Chgo. Pacific Corp.; ptnr. N.Y. Yankees Partnership, from 1973. Trustee Northwestern U., Michael Reese Hosp. and Med. Center; bd. dirs. John Crerar Library, Lyric Opera Chgo., Cradle Soc., Children's Meml. Hosp.; bd. advisors Chgo. Zool. Soc.; chmn. bd. overseers Jewish Theol. Sem. Mem. Harvard Bus. Sch. Alumni Assn., Tau Beta Pi, Pi Mu Epsilon, Phi Eta Sigma. Clubs: Lake Shore Country, Northmoor Country, Standard, Economic (dir. 1972), Chicago, Commercial, Mid-America (Chgo.); Carleton; Marco Polo (N.Y.C.); John Evans (Northwestern U.). Office: Material Svc Corp 222 N LaSalle St Chicago IL 60601-1090 also: Gen Dynamics Corp Pierre Laclede Ctr Saint Louis MO 63105 *

CROXSON, JEREMY P.G., oil industry executive. Formerly pres. BP Pipelines Inc., N.Y.C.; now mgr. Alaskan pipelines BP Pipelines (Alaska) Inc., Cleve. Office: BP Pipelines (Alaska) Inc 200 Public Sq 21J3801 Cleveland OH 44114-2375 *

CROZIER, WILLIAM MARSHALL, JR., bank holding company executive; b. N.Y.C., Oct. 2, 1932; s. William Marshall and Alice (Parsons) C.; m. Prudence van Zandt Slitor, June 20, 1964; children: Matthew Eaton, Abigail Parsons, Patience Wells. B.A. in Econs., Yale U., 1954; M.B.A. with distinction, Harvard U., 1963. With Hanover Bank, N.Y.C., 1954-61; asst. sec. Hanover Bank, 1959; with BayBanks, Inc., Boston, 1964—; asst. treas. BayBanks, Inc., 1965, asst. v.p., 1968, v.p., sec., 1969, sr. v.p., sec., 1973, chmn. bd., chief exec. officer, 1974—, pres., 1977—, dir., 1974—; bd. dirs. BayBank, Boston, 1978. Trustee Boston Symphony Orch., Commonwealth Energy System; overseer Boston Mus. Fine Arts. Served with U.S. Army, 1955-57. Mem. Boston Econ. Club. Episcopalian. Clubs: Comml.-Mchts. (Boston), Union (Boston), Harvard (Boston); Yale (N.Y.C.). Office: BayBanks Inc 175 Federal St Boston MA 02110

CRUFT, EDGAR FRANK, mining company executive; b. London, Eng., Feb. 8, 1933; s. William Frank and Rosina Jane (Edgar) C.; B.Sc., Durham U., Eng., 1954; Ph.D., McMaster U., Can., 1962; postdoctoral fellow, Pa., State U., 1962-63; m. Yvonne Odile Corne, Aug. 1952; children—Nicole Yvonne, Deborah Jane, Stephen Edgar; m. 2d, Geraldine Anne Monola, July 9, 1968; children—John Stuart, Elizabeth Rose. Mining and exploration geologist, S. and Central Am., 1954-57, Can., 1957-62; asst. prof., assoc. prof. U. N.Mex., 1963-73; chmn. Nord Resources Corp., Ohio, 1968—; chmn. Sierra Rutile Ltd., Sierra Leone, West Africa; dir. Nord Mining Co. Ltd., Australia, Trans Air S.W. Inc., Mond Aviation Inc., Nord Resources (Pacific) Pty. Ltd., Recipient Walker Mineral. award Can., 1964, NSF prin. investigator research grants, 1964-67. Cominco fellow Can., 1963. Fellow Inst. Mining and Metallurgy London; mem. Soc. Econ. Geologists, Geol. Soc. Am., Geochem. Soc., Soc. Exploration Geochemists. Contbr. articles to profl. jours. Home: 2850 Refugio Santa Ynez CA 93460 Office: 2963 Grand Ave Los Olivos CA 93441

CRUIKSHANK, THOMAS HENRY, corporation executive; b. Lake Charles, La., Nov. 3, 1931; s. Louis James and Helene L. (Little) C.; m. Ann Coe, Nov. 17, 1955; children: Thomas Henry, Kate Martin, Stuart Coe. B.A., Rice U., 1952; postgrad., U. Tex. Law Sch., 1952-53, U. Houston Law Sch., 1953-55. Bar: Tex.; C.P.A., Tex. Accountant Arthur Andersen & Co., Houston, 1953-55, 58-60; mem. firm Vinson & Elkins, Houston, 1961-69; v.p. Halliburton Co., Dallas, 1969-72, sr. v.p., 1972-80, exec. v.p., 1980, pres., chief exec. officer subs. Otis Engring. Corp., 1980-81, pres., 1981-83, pres., chief exec. officer, 1983-89, chmn., 1989—, dir., 1977—; bd. dirs. Goodyear Tire & Rubber Co. Pres. Jr. Achievement, Dallas, 1974-76, chmn., 1976-78, mem. nat. bd., 1976—. Served to lt. (j.g.) USNR, 1955-58. Mem. Am., Tex. socs. C.P.A.s, Am., Tex. bar assns. Clubs: Dallas Petroleum, Dallas Country (gov. 1977-79, 86—); River Oaks Country (Houston); Pine Valley (N.J.) Golf. Home: 3508 Marquette Dallas TX 75205 Office: Halliburton Co 3600 Lincoln Pla 500 N Akard St Dallas TX 75201-3391 *

CRULL, TIMM F., food company executive; b. 1931; married. BA, Mich. State U., 1955. Chief operating officer Norton Simon Inc., 1977-79; with Carnation Co., Los Angeles, 1955-77, 80—, exec. v.p., 1980-83, pres., 1983—, chief exec. officer, 1985—, vice chmn., dir. Office: Carnation Co 5045 Wilshire Blvd Los Angeles CA 90036 *

CRUM, DAVID HAROLD, electrical supply distributor; b. Hot Springs, S.D., Nov. 9, 1944; s. David N. and C. Lorraine (Cummings) C.; m. Mary M. Payne, June 28, 1968; children: David. M., Stacy J. BEE, U. Wyo., 1967. Sales engr. Cutler Hammer, Inc., Denver, 1971-76; chief exec. officer Crum Electric Supply Co., Inc., Casper, Wyo., 1976—; bd. dirs. 1st Interstate Bank of Casper. Pres. Casper United Way, 1984. Names Wyo. Small Businessman of Yr., SBA, 1982. Mem. Nat. Assn. Elec. Distbrs. (bd. dirs. 1986—), Instrument Soc. Am., Casper Country Club, Lions. Republican. Roman Catholic. Office: Crum Electric Supply Co Inc 460 Circle Dr Casper WY 82601

CRUM, DONALD JAY, aerospace company executive; b. East St. Louis, Ill., Jan. 29, 1947; s. George Luke and Sophia Pauline (Miller) C.; m. Belinda Dee Lasher, July 8, 1972; children: Shelby Susann, Eric Martin. BS in Accountancy, U. Ill., 1969. CPA, Ill.; cert. cost analyst. Auditor Haskins & Sells, St. Louis, 1972-74; mgr. gen. acctg. Affiliated Hosp. Products, Inc., St. Louis, 1974-77; contr. Entronic Co., St. Louis, 1977-78; cost account mgr. Boeing Mil. Airplane Co., Wichita, Kans., 1978-80, gen. acctg. mgr., 1980-81, chief auditor, 1981-86; dir. cost control Boeing Co., Seattle, 1987—. Mem. Rose Hill (Kans.) Bd. Edn., 1985-86. Capt. USMC, 1969-72. Mem. AICPA, Inst. Cost Analysis. Office: Boeing Co MS 1l-20 PO Box Seattle WA 98100

CRUM, JOHN KISTLER, association executive; b. Brownsville, Tex., July 28, 1936; s. John Mears and Mary Louise (Kistler) C. B.S., U. Tex., 1960, Ph.D., 1964; grad. Advanced Mgmt. Program, Harvard U., 1975. Research fellow Robert A. Welch Found., 1962-64; asst. editor Am. Chem. Soc., Washington, 1964-65; asso. editor Am. Chem. Soc., 1966-68, mng. editor, 1969-70, group mgr. jours., 1970, dir. books and jours. div., 1971-75, treas., chief fin. officer, 1975-80, dep. exec. dir. and chief operating officer, 1981-82, exec. dir., 1983—; chmn. bd. Centcom, Ltd.; mem. U.S. nat. com. Internat. Union Pure and Applied Chemistry; mem. Nat. Com. for Edn. in Space. Contbr. articles to profl. jours. Fellow Washington Acad. Scis.; mem. Chem. Soc. (London), N.Y. Acad. Scis., Am. Chem. Soc., Council Engring. and Sci. Soc. Execs., Assn. Sci. Soc. Editors, Sigma Xi, Phi Theta Kappa. Republican. Clubs: Cosmos, City, University (Washington). Home: 1701 N Kent St Arlington VA 22209 Office: Am Chem Soc 1155 16th St NW Washington DC 20036

CRUMP, FRANCIS JEFFERSON, III, lawyer; b. Alexandria, Va., Dec. 4, 1942; s. Ross Gault and Pauline (DeVore) C.; BS in Math., Va. Mil. Inst., 1964; JD, Ind. U., 1967; m. Nancy Jo Burkle, Aug. 20, 1966; children: Tom, Laura, Elizabeth. Admitted to Ind. bar, 1967, U.S. Dist. Ct. (so. dist.) Ind. 1967; gen. ptnr. firm Jewell, Crump & Angermeier, Columbus, Ind., 1971—; pres. Bonaventure Corp.; lectr. on estate planning and legal aspects of child abuse and neglect; bd. dirs., sec., treas. Hawpatch Corp.; past pres., bd. dirs. Columbus Boys' Club, Girls Club/Boys Club Found. Youth, Inc., Babe Ruth Baseball, Inc., sr. v.p. 1983-88; past deacon, elder 1st United Presbyn. Ch. of Columbus, 1972-75, 1977-80; founding bd. dirs. Y Columbus Family Fitness Ctr., YMCA; pres. Dowtown Columbus Antique Mall, Inc. Served with U.S. Army, 1968-70, lt. col. USAR. Mem. Ind. State Bar Assn. (mem. Ho. of Dels.), Bartholomew County Bar Assn. (pres. 1983), Columbus Coin Club, Inc. (pres.), Phi Alpha Delta. Republican. Home: PO Box 1061 Columbus IN 47202 Office: Jewell Crump & Angermeier PO Box 1061 Columbus IN 47202

CRUMPTON, GARY GENE, comptroller; b. Birmingham, Ala., Aug. 9, 1955; s. Elton Gene Crumpton and Glendora (Hopper) Hodges; m. Cheri Huffstutler, March 29, 1979. AA, Jefferson State U., 1977. Mgr., officer SouthTrust Bank of Ala., Birmingham, 1979-85; comptroller Glenn & Wright, Inc., Birmingham, 1985—. Office: Glenn & Wright Inc PO Box 100339 Birmingham AL 35210

CRUSOE, EDWIN EDGAR, IV, master mariner; b. Lakeland, Fla., Mar. 23, 1938; s. Edwin Edgar and Muriel Valerie (Christian) C. B.S. in Nautical Sci., Calif. Maritime Acad., 1960; M.A. in Bus. Mgmt., Central Mich. U., 1983. Served as lt. j.g. U.S. Navy, 1960-62; served from 3d mate to master U.S. Mcht. Marines, 1962-72; bar and harbour pilot Port of Key West, Fla., 1972—, harbor master, 1980-86; marine surveyor, cons.; chmn. Monroe County Port Authority Adv. Com.; past mem. Key West Port and Transit Authority; pres. Key West Bar Pilots. Past chmn. Monroe County Career Service Council; past campaign chmn. Monroe County Democratic Party, 1976; mem. Monroe County Dem. Exec. Com., 1976-78. Mem. Masters, Mates and Pilots, Am., Fla. pilots assns., Propeller Club of Key West (past pres., commendation), Navy League, U.S. Naval Inst., Key West C. of C., Nat. Assn. Marine Surveyors (life), Key West Art and Hist Soc. Club: Wiccan Circle. Lodges: Masons; Shriners; Elks; Arcane Order, Jesters. Author: (poetry) Wanderings, 1970. Home: Route 2 Box 306 Summerland Key FL 33042 Office: Port of Key West PO Box 848 Key West FL 33040

CRUTCHER, JOHN WILLIAM, federal agency commissioner; b. Ensign, Kans., Dec. 19, 1916; s. Otto Wilson and Orpha (French) C., m. Edith Virginia Colvard, Dec. 19, 1971. BS, U. Kans., 1941. Pres. Hutchinson (Kans.) Investment Co., 1955-70; lt. gov. State of Kans., Topeka, 1965-69; dir. state and local govt. OEO, Washington, 1969-74; adminstrv. asst. to Sen. Robert Dole U.S. Senate, Washington, 1974-75; dir. Bur. Outdoor Recreation, Washington, 1975-76; with govt. affairs dept. Nat. Transp. Commn., Washington, 1977-79; office mgr. Dole/Reagan Policiy Coms., Washington, 1979-81; commr. U.S. Postal Rate Commn., Washington, 1982—; sen. State of Kans., 1953-57; lectr. Associated Clubs, 1959-70. Contbr. articles to newspapers, profl. publs. Bd. govs. Kans. Cancer Soc., 1965-68, Kans. Heart Assn., 1966-69, Nat. Council State Govt., 1960; pres. ARC, Reno County, Kans., 1960. Capt. USN, 1943-76, PTO, Korea. Mem. Assn. for Navy Aviation, Res. Officers Assn., Navy Res. Officers Assn., Masons. Republican. Methodist. Home: 700 New Hampshire Ave NW #517 Washington DC 20037-2413 Office: Postal Rate Commn 1333 H St NW Ste 300 Washington DC 20268

CRUTCHFIELD, EDWARD ELLIOTT, JR., banker; b. Detroit, July 14, 1941; s. Edward Elliott and Katherine (Sikes) C.; m. Nancy Glass Kizer, July 27, 1963; children: Edward Elliott, III, Sarah Palmer. BA, Davidson Coll., 1963; MBA, U. Pa., 1965. With First Union Nat. Bank, Charlotte, N.C., 1965—, head retail bank services group, 1970-72, exec. v.p. gen. adminstrn., 1972-73, pres., 1973-84, vice chmn., from 1984; pres. First Union Corp. (parent), Charlotte, 1983-86, chief exec. officer, 1984—, now also chmn., bd. dirs.; bd. dirs. Bernhardt Industries, Inc., Charlotte, 1983—. Bd. deacons Myers Park Presbyn. Ch.; bd. dirs. United Community Services, Salvation Army, Charlotte Bd., Charlotte Latin Sch.; trustee Mint Mus. Art, N.C. Nature Conservancy; bd. mgrs. Charlotte Meml. Hosp.; bd. visitors Davidson Coll. Mem. Charlotte C. of C., Assn. Res. City Bankers, Am., N.C. bankers assns., Am. Textile Mfrs. Assn., Young Pres.'s Orgn. Clubs: Charlotte City, Charlotte Country, Linville (N.C.) Golf. Office: 1st Union Corp First Union Pla Charlotte NC 28288 *

CRUTSINGER, ROBERT KEANE, diversified food wholesale company executive; b. St. Louis, Sept. 2, 1930; s. Robert Matthews and Gertrude (Keane) C.; m. Mary Lou Hopkins, Feb. 2, 1957; children—Cary Anne, Robert H., Kathryn P. B.S. in Bus. Adminstrn., Quincy Coll., 1955. With Nat. Cash Register Corp., 1956-70, div. mgr. corp. accounts, 1970; owner, operator IGA food store, 1965-69; with Wetterau Inc., Hazelwood, Mo., 1970—, exec. v.p., 1974-78, pres. food services div., 1978-79, pres., chief operating officer, 1979-88, also dir., vice chmn., chief adminstrv. officer, 1988—; chief exec. officer, chmn. bd. Wetterau Properties Inc., Hazelwood; dir. Centerre Bank of Florissant, Mo. Trustee Quincy Coll., 1985—. Served with U.S. Army, 1952-54. Mem. Am. Mgmt. Assn., Nat. Am. Wholesale Grocers Assn., Knights of Cauliflower Ear. Club: Bellerive Country. Office: Wetterau Inc 8920 Pershall Rd Hazelwood MO 63042

CRYSTAL, JAMES WILLIAM, insurance company executive; b. N.Y.C., Oct. 9, 1937; s. I. Frank and Evelyn G. Crystal; B.S., Trinity Coll., 1958; m. Jean Crystal; children—James F., Sanford F., Jonathan F. With Royal Globe Ins. Group, N.Y.C., 1956; underwriter Home Ins. Co., N.Y.C., 1957, spl. agt., San Francisco, 1958-59; pres., chief exec. officer Frank Crystal & Co. Inc., N.Y.C., 1960—; dir. Gt. Am. Industries, Inc., F.F.H. Ins. Co., Northeast Ins. Co. Bd. dirs. Gar Reichman Found.; trustee Mt. Sinai Hosp., N.Y.C. Mem. Nat. Assn. Casualty and Surety Agts. Republican. Clubs: Harmonie, Century Country. Home: 33 E 70th St New York NY 10021 Office: Frank Crystal & Co 40 Broad St New York NY 10004

CSENDES, ERNEST, chemist, corporate and financial executive; b. Satu-Mare, Romania, Mar. 2, 1926; s. Edward O. and Sidonia (Littman) C.; came to U.S., 1951, naturalized, 1955; m. Catharine Vera Tolnai, Feb. 7, 1953; children: Audrey Carol, Robert Alexander Edward. BA, Protestant Coll., Hungary, 1944; BS, U. Heidelberg (Ger.), 1948, MS, PhD, 1951. Rsch. asst. chemistry U. Heidelberg, 1950-51; rsch. assoc. biochemistry Tulane U., New Orleans, 1952; fellow Harvard U., 1953; rsch. chemist organic chems. dept. E. I. Du Pont de Nemours and Co., Wilmington, Del., 1953-56, elastomer chems. dept., 1956-61; dir. rsch. and devel. agrl. chems. div. Armour & Co., Atlanta, 1961-63; v.p. corp. devel. Occidental Petroleum Corp., 1963-64, exec. v.p. rsch., engring. and devel., 1964-68, also mem. exec. com.; exec. v.p., dir. Occidental Rsch. and Engring. Corp., 1964-68; pres., chief exec. officer Tex. Rep. Industries, Inc., 1968-84, pres., chief exec. officer TRI Group, 1971-84; chmn., chief exec. officer Micronic Techs., Inc., 1981-85; mng. ptnr. Inter-Consult Ltd., Pacific Palisades, Calif., 1984—. Contbr. articles to profl. jours.; patentee in field. Recipient Pro Mundi Beneficio medal Brazilian Acad. Humanities. Fellow AAAS, Am. Inst. Chemists, Royal Soc. of Chemistry (London); mem. Am. Chem. Soc., German Chem. Soc., N.Y. Acad. Sci., Am. Inst. Chem. Engrs., Acad. Polit. Sci., Global Action Econ. Inst., Am. Mgmt. Assn., AIAA, Am. Def. Preparedness Assn., Sigma Xi. Rsch. in area of elastomers, rubber chemicals, dyes and intermediates, organometallics, organic and biochemistry, high polymers, phosphates, plant nutrients, pesticides, process engring. and design of fertilizer plants, sulfur, potash and phosphate ore mining and metallurgy, coal burning and acid rain, coal utilization, environ grinding for solids, petrochemicals; also acquisitions, mergers, internat. fin. related to leasing, investment and loans, trusts and ins.; regional devel. related to agr. and energy resources. Home: 514 Marquette St Pacific Palisades CA 90272

CUDDAHY, EDWARD FRANCIS, manufacturing company executive; b. Leominster, Mass., Oct. 21, 1959; S. Walter Edward and Mary Jane (Brooks) C. BBA, Nichols Coll., 1981. Ops. mgr., v.p. G Products Co., Inc., Stow, Mass., 1982-85; owner, pres., treas. Fiber Tech Industries-Princeton Boat Works, Fitchburg, Mass., 1986—. Assoc. mem. parking garage com. City of Leominster, 1986-87. Republican. Roman Catholic. Home: 8 Marita St Leominster MA 01453 Office: Fiber Tech Industries Patriot Circle Jytek Park Leominster MA 01453

CUDLIPP, ALICE VERNER, healthcare executive; b. Richmond, Va., Nov. 1, 1941; d. Joseph Henry and Mary Irene (Mills) C. BA, Bridgewater (Va.) Coll., 1962; MA, U. Richmond, 1968; postgrad. U. Va., Nova U. Tchr., dept. head Chesterfield (Va.) County Pub. Schs., 1967-71, Nansemond County Pub. Schs., Va., 1962-67; instr. Va. Commonwealth U., 1968-71; lectr. in residence, U. Va., 1973-74; v.p. Smithdeal-Massey Coll., Richmond, 1975-78; instr. J. Sargeant Reynolds Coll., Richmond, 1982-84; asst. to v.p. patient services Columbia Hosp., Milw., 1982-84; pres., chief exec. officer Med. Placement Services Inc., Milw., 1984—; pres. Cons. Resources, Inc., Richmond, 1974-81; gen. ptnr. Courtland Ltd., Richmond, 1981—; pres., chief exec. officer Shafer Rand Assocs., Inc., Glendale, Wis., 1987—; dir. David A. Linney, Inc., Milwaukee, 1987—; cons. and lectr. in field. Dir. Interfaith Programs, Milw.; v.p., bd. dirs. Shoreline Interfaith Outreach To The Elderly, Shorewood, 1988—. Mem. Clovernook Homeowners Assn.; ruling elder North Shore Presbyn. Ch., Shorewood, Wis., 1988—. Named one of Outstanding Young Women of Am., U.S. Jaycees, 1974; Nat. Sci. Found. fellow Longwood Coll., 1964; DuPont fellow U. Va., 1972. Mem. Columbia Coll. Nursing Alumni Assn. (chmn. 1984-85), Nat. League Nursing, Southeastern Wis. Home Health Assn., Assn. Profl. Saleswomen, Am. Mgmt. Assn., Nat. Assn. for Home Care, Wis. Home Care Orgn., NAFE, Am. Pub. Health Assn., Wis. Women Entrepreneurs, Wis. Assn. of Healthcare Staffing (pres. 1989), Rotary, Phi Delta Epsilon, Alpha Psi Omega, Delta Kappa Gamma. Office: Med Placement Services Inc 710 N Plankinton Ave Milwaukee WI 53203

CUDWORTH, ALLEN L., insurance company executive, researcher; b. Tuscaloosa, Ala., Jan. 2, 1929; s. James Rowland and Emily (Latham) C.; m. Cynthia Leach, Dec. 11, 1954; children: Ann, Lindsay, James. B.S. in E.E., U. ALa.-Tuscaloosa, 1949; M.S. in E.E., MIT, 1952; Sc.D. in Environ. Health, Harvard U., 1967. Cert. Am. Bd. Indsl. Hygiene; registered profl. engr., Mass. Mem. research staff MIT, 1949-55; acoustical engr. Liberty Mut. Ins. Co., Hopkinton, Mass., 1955-62, dir. research, 1967-72, v.p., dir. research, 1972—; dir. Ins. Inst. Hwy. Safety, Washington, 1980—. Author: Industrial Noise Control, 1974. Fellow Acoustical Soc. Am.; mem. Bd. Cert. Safety Profls. (pres. 1984-85), Am. Indsl. Hygiene Assn., Am. Acad. Indsl. Hygiene (chmn. accreditation com. 1980—), Inst. Noise Control Engrs. (bd. dirs. 1987—), Joint Council Safety and Health Edn. and Accreditation (pres. 1986), Tau Beta Pi. Club: Wellesley Country (Mass.). Office: Liberty Mut Ins Co 175 Berkeley St Boston MA 02117

CUELLAR, ROBERT ALEMAN, management consultant; b. Fresnillo, Zacatecas, Mex., Oct. 28, 1939; naturalized Am. citizen, 1963; s. Manuel R. and Lidia (Aleman) C.; m. Sylvia Cobos, Feb. 3, 1968 (div. 1988); children: Martin Edward, Mark Andrew. BA, N. Tex. State U., 1967, MA, 1969; postgrad. doctorate U. Tex. Cert. cons. Tchr. pub. schs. Mesquite (Tex.) Inds. Sch. Dist., 1967-68; asst. registrar N. Tex. State U., Denton, 1968-69; nat. dep. dir. Jobs for Progress, Inc., Angeles, 1969-74; pres., chief exec. officer R.A. Cuellar & Assocs. Inc., El Paso, Tex., 1974-75, Adcom Assocs., Inc., Phoenix, 1974-79; pres., chief exec. officer Cuellar Advt., El Paso, 1979—; bd. dirs. Nuestro Publs., Washington. Author: A History of Mexican Americans in Texas, 1976. Served with USAF, 1962-66. Mem. Am. Mgmt. Assn., Am. G.I. Forum of U.S., Southwestern Hist. Soc. Democrat. Roman Catholic. Research on national marketing potential of Spanish-speaking population. Home: 1420 Murchison El Paso TX 79902 Office: RA Cuellar & Assocs Inc 1477 Lomaland El Paso TX 79935

CUFF, WILLIAM, IV, food company executive; b. Stamford, Conn., Mar. 31, 1942; s. William III and Jean (Grant) C.; m. Judith Ann Watkins, Aug. 29, 1964 (div. Nov. 1976); children: Lisa Ann Zoellin, William David; m. Erin Ann Quinn, Dec. 1, 1978. BA, Yale U., 1964; MBA, Columbia U., 1966. Mgr. mktg. Gen. Foods, White Plains, N.Y., 1966-77; v.p. bus. devel. Standard Brands, N.Y.C., 1977-79; v.p. specialty foods Liddy subs. Nestle Co., Chgo., 1979-86; pres. The Bachman Co., Reading, Pa., 1986—. Republican. Office: The Bachman Co PO Box 15053 Reading PA 19607-5053

CUIL DE STRATCLUT, ALECSANDR See **KYLE, ALASTAIR (BOYD)**

CULBERTSON, DOOLEY EWELL, holding company executive; b. Albany, Ga., June 29, 1936; s. Erwell Robert and Gertrude (Shemwell) C.; m. Ann Marcesta Frick, Apr. 2, 1937; children—Keith, Kay. BS in Mech. Engring., Auburn U., 1958; various positions Morton Thiokol, 1958-68; v.p. mktg. Teledyne Brown Engring., 1968-72; group exec. product devel. staff Teledyne Corp., San Diego, 1972-74; pres. Pacemaker Corp., Egg Harbor City, N.J., 1974-78, Fuqua Homes, Arlington, Tex., 1978-84; exec. v.p. Fuqua Industries, Atlanta, Ga., 1986-89, chmn., chief exec. officer Inter-Redec, Richmond Hill, Ga., 1989; pres. Am. Seating Co., Grand Rapids, Mich., 1985-86. Mem. Rotary. Republican. Episcopalian. Office: Fuqua Industries Inc 4900 Ga-Pacific Ctr Atlanta GA 30303

CULBREATH, HUGH LEE, JR., electric utility company executive; b. Tampa, Fla., May 11, 1921; s. Hugh Lee and Daphne (Jackson) C.; m. Betty King, June 8, 1944; children: Betty Kay, Hugh Lee III. B.S., U.S. Naval Acad., 1944. Commd. officer USN, 1944, resigned, 1954; with Tampa Electric Co., 1957—, v.p. fin., sec., treas., 1966-71, exec. v.p., sec., treas., 1971, pres., 1971—, chief exec. officer, 1972-88; chmn., pres., dir. TECO Energy, Inc., Tampa, 1988—, chmn., dir. parent co.; dir. Transco Energy Co., Houston., NCNB Corp., Charlotte. Mem. Greater Tampa C. of C. (pres. 1972-73), Sigma Alpha Epsilon. Episcopalian (vestryman 1963-65, 67-69, treas. 1967). Clubs: Tampa Yacht and Country (Tampa) (commodore 1963), University (Tampa), Exchange (Tampa) (pres. 1961), Palma Ceia Golf and Country (Tampa), Ye Mystic Krewe of Gasparilla (Tampa). Office: TECO Energy Co PO Box 111 Tampa FL 33601

CULLEN, JAMES DOUGLAS, banker, finance company executive; b. N.Y.C., Jan. 26, 1945; s. Eugene Richard and Anna Marie (Constantine) C.; m. Wendy Stephens, May 24, 1969; children: John W., Anne T. B.S.B.A., U. Denver, 1968. Mgmt. trainee Wells Fargo Bank, San Francisco, 1968-69, credit officer, 1969-72, asst. v.p., 1972-77, v.p., 1977-82; v.p. Rainier Nat. Bank (named changed to Security Pacific Bank Wash. 1989), Seattle, 1982, sr. v.p., 1982-85, sr. v.p., mgr. internat. div., mem. mgmt. com., 1985, exec. v.p., mgr. internat. div., 1986; pres. Rainier Nat. Bank (name changed to Security Pacific Bank Wash. 1989), N.Y.C., 1987, exec. v.p., mgr. corp. banking div., 1987—; also bd. dirs. Rainier Bank Internat., N.Y.C.; pres. Rainier Internat. Bank, Los Angeles, 1987—; pres., bd. dirs. Rainier Internat. Trading Co.; bd. dirs., chmn. Rainier Leasing Co., Inc.; bd. dirs., mem. exec. com. C.D. Stimson Co., Seattle. Mem. exec. com. Wash. State China Rels. Coun., 1986—; trustee, mem. exec. com. Seattle Opera. Clubs: Seattle Tennis, Wash. Athletic (Seattle); Tanglin, Cricket (Singapore); Royal Hong Kong Yacht, Ladies Recreation (Hong Kong). Home: 1320 Lexington Way E Seattle WA 98112 Office: Security Pacific Bank Wash PO Box 3966e Seattle WA 98124

CULLEN, JAMES PATRICK, international trading company executive; b. Balt., Nov. 28, 1944; s. James Patrick and Frances Ann (Lanza) C. Cert., U. Madrid, 1964; BA, Johns Hopkins U., 1966; LLB, U. Pa., 1969. Bar: D.C., 1971. Trust officer First Am. Bank, N.A., Washington, 1970-74; spl. counsel U.S. Securities & Exchange Commn., Washington, 1974-80; corp. sec. COMSAT Gen. Corp., Washington, 1980-83; pres. Universal Export Ltd., Balt., 1983—. Author: The Fieldstone Affair, 1988; inventor hand-held computer, 1987. Mem. World Trade Inst., Md. Club, Met. Club., City Tavern Club. Home: 109 Thicket Rd Baltimore MD 21212 Office: Universal Export Ltd PO Box 27606 Baltimore MD 21285

CULLEN, JOHN B., food products company executive; b. 1911; married. With King Kullen Grocery Co. Inc., 1930—, sr. v.p., 1980—, chief exec. officer, also chmn. bd. Served with AUS, 1940-46. Office: King Kullen Grocery Co Inc 1194 Prospect Ave Westbury NY 11590 *

CULLENS, WILLIAM SCOTT, manufacturing company executive; b. Stirling, Scotland, Jan. 10, 1930; came to Can. 1953.; s. James and Laura (Scott) C.; m. Elizabeth Stewart Brewster, Mar. 18, 1953; children: B. Kim, E. Gail, Laura L., Jane. B.S. in Civil Engring., Glasgow U., Scotland, 1951. Registered profl. engr., Can. Group v.p. structural and mech. ops. Canron Inc., Toronto, Ont., Can., 1970-76; exec. v.p. Canron Inc., Toronto, 1976, chief exec. officer, 1977-80, dir., 1980—, pres., 1981—, chief exec. officer, 1982—; dir. Kamyr Inc. Mem. Can. Inst. Steel Constrn. (hon. bd. dirs., former chmn.), Can. Welding Bur. (former chmn.), Profl. Engrs. Ont., Profl. Engrs. Que. Presbyterian. Clubs: Toronto, Toronto Golf. Office: Canron Inc Box 134, 1 First Canadian Pl #3400, Toronto, ON Canada M5X 1A4 *

CULLIGAN, JOHN WILLIAM, corporate executive; b. Newark, Nov. 22, 1916; s. John J. and Elizabeth (Kearns) C.; m. Rita McBride, Feb. 19, 1944; children: Nancy, Mary Carol, Elizabeth, Sheila, Jack, Neil. Student, U. Utah, U. Chi, Philippine U. With Am. Home Products Corp., N.Y.C., 1937—; also bd. dirs. Am. Home Products Corp.; chmn. bd. dirs. Am. Home Products Corp., N.Y.C., 1981-86, chmn. exec. com., 1986-88; chmn. bd. dirs. Calif. Biotechnology Inc., 1987—; bd. dirs. Harvard Industries. Bd. dirs., v.p. Council on Family Health; bd. dirs. Am. Found. for Pharm. Edn., Valley Hosp. Found., Ridgewood, N.J.; adv. bd. St. Benedict's Prep. Sch., Newark; co-chmn. Archbishop's Com. of Laity, Newark. Served with AUS, 1943-46. Mem. Proprietary Assn. (hon. v.p.). Clubs: N.Y. Athletic, Sky, Union League (N.Y.C.), Hackensack Golf. Lodges: Knights of Malta, Knights of St. Gregory, Friendly Sons of St. Patrick. Office: Am Home Products Corp 685 3d Ave New York NY 10017

CULLINANE, CHARLES JUSTIN, manufacturing executive; b. Chgo., May 26, 1947; s. Charles S. and Concetta (Zappia) C.; m. Patricia Ann Cirocco, July 12, 1969; children: Michael J., Tina Ann. BA, U. Pitts., 1969; MBA, Fairleigh Dickinson U., 1975. Cert. prodn. inventory mgmt. Gen. mgr. pet products div. Seton Co., Newark, 1972-78; plant mgr. Whitestone Prodn., Piscataway, N.J., 1978-79; dir. mfg. Bretford Mfg., Schiller Park, Ill., 1979—. Served as sgt. U.S. Army, 1969-71. Mem. Am. Prodn. and Inventory Control Soc. (cert.), Midwest Indsl. Mfrs. Assn. (mfg. exec. round table). Republican. Roman Catholic. Home: 940 S Bodin St Hinsdale IL 60521 Office: Bretford Mfg Inc 9715 Soreng Ave Schiller Park IL 60176

CULLINGWORTH, LARRY ROSS, residential and commercial real estate developement company executive; b. Toronto, Ont., Can., Sept. 26, 1939; s. Allan Joyce and Ethel Alexandra (Davis) C.; m. Betty Kathleen Hughes, July 9, 1966; children: Lisa, Kevin. B.A.Sc., U. Toronto, 1963, P. Eng., 1965; M.B.A., York U., Toronto, 1972. Cons. engr. Proctor & Redfern, Toronto, 1963-68; regional mgr. George Wimpey Can. Ltd., Toronto, 1968-72; mgr. corp. devel. Coscan Devel. Corp. (formerly Costain Ltd.), Toronto, 1973-74, v.p. fin., sec., 1975-78, sr. v.p., chief fin. officer, sec., 1979, exec. v.p., chief fin. officer, sec., 1980-82, pres., chief operating officer, 1983-85, pres., chief exec. officer, 1986—; bd. dirs. Coscan Devel. Corp. Bd. dirs. RP Eye Rsch. Found., Consolidated Carma Corp., Can. Inst. Pub. Real Estate Cos. Mem. Assn. Profl. Engrs. Ont., National Club, Bayview Club, Granite Club (Toronto). Home: 23 York Valley Crescent, Willowdale, ON Canada M2P 1A8 Office: Coscan Devel Corp Box 428, 2 First Canadian Pl #2200, Toronto, ON Canada M5X 1H9

CULLMAN, EDGAR MEYER, diversified consumer products company executive; b. N.Y.C., Jan. 7, 1918; s. Joseph F. Jr. and Frances Nathan (Wolff) C.; m. Louise Bloomingdale, Aug. 28, 1938; children: Lucy (Mrs. Frederick M. Danziger), Edgar M. Jr., Susan C. Kudlow.). B.A., Yale U., 1940. With Underwriters Trust Co., 1940-42; with Office of Alien Pub. Custodian, Washington and N.Y.C., 1942-44; sr. v.p. tobacco and investments Cullman Bros., Inc., N.Y.C., 1944-62; ptnr. Cullman Bros., 1946-65; dir. Gen. Cigar Co., Inc. (now Culbro Corp.), N.Y.C., 1961—, pres., chief exec. officer, 1962; now chmn. bd., chief exec. officer Gen. Cigar Co., Inc. (name now Culbro Corp.), N.Y.C., 1981—; bd. dirs. Bloomingdale Properties, Inc.; former dir. Mut. Omaha Ins. Co., Studebaker-Worthington, Inc., Companion Life Ins. Co. Trustee, treas. Mt. Sinai Med. Ctr., Mt. Sinai Sch. Medicine, CUNY, Mt. Sinai Hosp.; vice chmn. exec. com. Yale Devel. Bd.; pres. Hotchkiss Sch. Bd. Trustees. Mem. Cigar Assn. Am. (hon. dir.), Restigouche Riparian Assn. (pres.). Clubs: India House, Century Country, Turf and Field, Steeplechase and Hunt Assn., Doubles, Yale (N.Y.C.). Office: Culbro Corp 387 Park Ave S New York NY 10016 *

CULLMAN, HUGH, retired tobacco company executive; b. N.Y.C., Jan. 27, 1923; s. Howard S. and Elsie (Gottheil) C.; m. Nan Alva Ogburn, May 12, 1951; children: Katherine Victoria, Hugh Jr., Alexandra Miriam. B.S., U.S. Naval Acad., 1945. With Benson & Hedges, 1949-54, mgr. research, 1952-54; with Philip Morris Inc., 1954—, treas., 1959-60, v.p., asst. chief ops., 1960-64, exec. v.p. ops., 1966— , also dir.; exec. v.p. Philip Morris Internat., 1965, pres., 1967-78, also bd. dirs.; group exec. v.p. Philip Morris Inc., 1978-84; chief exec. officer Philip Morris U.S.A., 1978-84; vice chmn. Philip Morris Cos. Inc., 1985-88. Sr. trustee, mem. exec. com. U.S. Council for Internat. Bus.; bd. dirs. United Negro Coll. Fund Inc. Served to lt. USN, 1945-47, PTO, 1951-52, Europe. Office: Philip Morris Inc 100 Park Ave New York NY 10017

CULLOM, HALE ELLICOTT, investment company executive; b. Nashville, Jan. 6, 1935; s. Hale Ellicott and Mildred (Holmes) C.; m. June Elizabeth Cauley, Mar. 11, 1978; children—Hale III, William, Scott, Cauley. B.A., Vanderbilt U., 1957. Comml. mgr. South Bell Telephone & Telegraph, Huntsville, Ala., 1959-62; br. mgr. Trulock & Co., Huntsville, 1962-63; account exec., br. Kohlmeyer & Co., Huntsville, 1963-70; br. mgr., div. v.p. Reynolds Securities, Atlanta and Houston, 1970-77; exec. v.p. Paine Webber Inc., N.Y.C., 1977—, dir.; also pres. Rotan Mosle Inc.; dir. Paine Webber Properties, Rotan Mosle Inc. Served to capt. Mil. Intelligence, U.S. Army, and USAR, 1957-61. Clubs: Sugar Creek Country (Houston); Bent Tree Country (Dallas); Conn. Gold (Fairfield). Office: Rotan Mosle Inc 4100 Louisiana Houston TX 77002 *

CULLUM, CHARLES GILLESPIE, retail food chain executive; b. Dallas, Aug. 26, 1916; s. Ashley Wilson and Eloise (Brooks) C.; m. Garland Mae Chapman, May 6, 1938; 1 child, Lee Brooks. BS, So. Methodist U., 1936; LLD, Tex. Coll., 1982. Reporter Dallas News, 1936-37; advt. mgr. Adolphus Hotel, 1937-38; salesman Cullum Cos., Inc., Dallas, 1938-43; v.p. Cullum Cos., Inc., 1946-53, pres., 1953-76, chmn., from 1976, chief exec. officer, 1976-85, chmn. exec. com., 1987—; bd. dirs. Republic Bank of Dallas. Mem. Dallas City Council, 1965-69, mayor, 1967-69; bd. dirs. Dallas Found., State Fair Tex., Cotton Bowl Council, Goals for Dallas, Internat. Linguistic Ctr., Dallas, Assn. Higher Edn., Dallas; mem. Dallas Alliance Ednl. Task Force. Served with USN, 1942-46, PTO. Recipient Newton D. Baker award, 1969, Disting. Alumnus award So. Meth. U., 1970, Entrepreneur of Yr. award, 1981. Mem. Tex. Employers Ins. Assn. (bd. dirs.), Food Mktg. Inst. (bd. dirs.), Dallas C. of C. (chmn.). Methodist. Office: Cullum Cos Inc 14303 Inwood Rd Dallas TX 75240 *

CULP, JOE C(ARL), electronics executive; b. Little Rock, July 23, 1933; s. Charles Carl and Doris Evelyn (Jackson) C.; m. Norma Carol Kennan, Jan. 26, 1954; 1 dau., Karen Gay Culp Ashorn. B.S.E.E., U. Ark., 1955. Staff asst. to exec. v.p. Collins Radio, Dallas, 1967-68; with Rockwell Internat., Dallas, 1968-88, dir. data systems mktg., 1968-71, dir. mktg. trans systems div., 1971-78, v.p. Latin Am., 1978-80, v.p., gen. mgr. trans systems div., 1980-82, pres. telecommunications group, 1982-88; pres., chief exec. officer Lightnet, Rockville, Md., 1988—. Chmn. engring. bd. U. Tex., Arlington, 1984; bd. advisors Coll. Engring. U. Ark., Fayetteville, 1982. Named Disting. Grad., Coll. Engring. U. Ark., 1981, Disting. Engr., U. Tex., Arlington, 1984. Mem. Electronic Industry Assn. (bd. govs. 1984-88), U.S. Telephone Suppliers Assn. (dir. 1984-88), Ind. Telephone Pioneers. Republican. Methodist. Office: Lightnet 600 E Jefferson St Rockville MD 20852

CULVER, DAVID M., aluminum company executive; b. Winnipeg, Man., Can., Dec. 5, 1924; s. Albert Ferguson and Fern Elizabeth (Smith) C.; m. Mary Cecile Powell, Sept. 20, 1949; children: Michael, Andrew, Mark, Diane. B.Sc., McGill U., 1947; M.B.A., Harvard U., 1949. Joined Alcan Aluminum Ltd., 1949; serving on staff of Centre d'Etudes Indsls. (now Internat. Mgmt. Inst.) Alcan Aluminum Ltd., Geneva; then mgr. sales office Alcan Aluminum Ltd., N.Y.C.; has since held various sr. mgmt. positions culminating with pres. and chmn. Alcan Aluminum Ltd., 1977, chmn., chief exec. officer, since 1979, also bd. dirs.; bd. dirs. Am. Express Co., Shearson Lehman Hutton Holdings Inc., Am. Cyanamid Co., Seagram Co. Ltd., C.D. Howe Inst.; chmn. Bus. Council on Nat. Issues; mem. Internat Council of Morgan Guaranty Trust Co. of N.Y.; mem. adv. council Ctr. of Can. Studies at Johns Hopkins U. Sch. Advanced Internat. Studies, Washington; gov. Joseph H. Lauder Inst. Mgmt. and Internat. Studies, U. Pa.; until 1988 Can. chmn. of Can.-Japan Businessman's Cooperation Com. Companion of the Order of Can. Office: Alcan Aluminum Ltd, 1188 Sherbrooke St W, Montreal, PQ Canada H3A 3G2 *

CULVER, JAMES, food wholesaler; b. 1939; married. With Fox Grocery Co., Belle Vernon, Pa., 1971—, now pres., gen. mgr. Office: Fox Grocery Co PO Box 29 Belle Vernon PA 15012 *

CULVER, WALTER JULIUS, computer sciences corporation executive; b. Bronx, N.Y., Nov. 28, 1937; s. Stanley Frederick and Christine Olga (Ferracci) C.; m. Sylvia Jean Rinke; 5 children. BEE, U. Detroit, 1960; MSEE, Case Inst. Tech., 1961, PhD, 1963. Teaching fellow Case Inst. Tech., Cleve., 1960-63; mgr. analysis Westinghouse Electric Corp., Balt., 1963-68; tech. advisor Computer Scis. Corp., Falls Church, Va., 1968-70, program mgr., ops. dir., 1970-77, pres. def. systems div., 1977-84, pres. systems div., 1984-87, corp. v.p. systems integration, 1988—. Pres. Fairfax County (Va.) Pub. Schs. Edn. Found., 1986—; trustee Meml. Hosp., Burlington County, N.J., 1979-84. Named Most Valuable Player 3d Anti-Submarine Warfare War Game Naval War Coll., Newport, R.I., 1981; recipient E.L. Patterson Edn. award No. Va. br. Washington Urban League. Office: Computer Scis Corp 3160 Fairview Park Dr Falls Church VA 22042

CUMMIN, ALFRED S(AMUEL), chemist; b. London, Sept. 5, 1924; came to U.S., 1940, naturalized, 1948; s. Jack and Lottie (Hainesdorff) C.; m. Sylvia E. Smolok, Mar. 24, 1945; 1 dau., Cynthia Katherine. B.S., Poly. Inst. Bklyn., 1943, Ph.D. in Chemistry, 1946; M.B.A., U. Buffalo, 1959. Research chemist S.A.M. labs, Manhattan Project, Columbia U., 1943-44; plant supr. Metal & Plastic Processing Co., Bklyn., 1946-51; research chemist Gen. Chem. div. Allied Chem. & Dye Corp., N.Y.C., 1951-53; sr. chemist Congoleum Nairn, Kearny, N.J., 1953-54; supr. dielecs-advance devel. Gen. Elec. Co., Hudson Falls, N.Y., 1954-56; mgr. indsl. products research dept. Spencer Kellogg & Sons, Inc. (Textron), Buffalo, 1956-59; mgr. plastics div. Trancoa Chem. Corp., Reading, Mass., 1959-62; asso. dir. product devel. service labs. chem. div. Merck & Co., Inc., Rahway, N.J., 1962-69; dir. product devel. Borden Chem. div. Borden Inc., N.Y.C., 1969-72; tech. dir. Borden Chem. div. Borden Inc., 1972-73; tech. dir. Borden Inc., 1973-78, v.p. product safety and quality, 1978-81, v.p. sci. and tech., 1981-89, sr. v.p. sci. and tech., 1989—; mem. exec. com. Food Safety Council, 1976-81, trustee, chmn. membership com., 1976-81; bd. dirs. Formaldehyde Inst., 1977-86, vice chmn., 1982-86, mem. exec. com., 1981-86, mem. med. com., 1977-86, steering com., 1977-86; bd. dirs. Internat. Life Scis. Inst., 1986—, Nutrition Found., 1986—, Risk Assessment Inst., 1986—, Rsch. Inst., 1986—; instr. Poly. Inst. Bklyn., 1946-47; asst. prof. Adelphi Coll., 1952-54; prof. math. sci. U.S. Merchant Marine Acad., 1954; seminar leader Am. Mgmt. Assn.; prof. mgmt. N.Y. U. Sch. Mgmt., 1968—. Contbr. articles to profl. jours. Recipient cert. award Fedn. Socs. Paint Tech., 1965. Mem. Am. Chem. Soc. Fedn. Coatings Tech., Inst. Food Tech., ASTM, Synthetic Organic Chems. Mfg. Assn. (dir. 1977-84), Paint Research Inst., Delta Sigma Pi, Gamma Sigma Epsilon, Beta Gamma Sigma, Phi Lamda Upsilon.

CUMMING, JOHN BATTIN, insurance company executive; b. South Orange, N.J., Sept. 9, 1936; s. James Coale and Elsie (Battin) C.; m. Marianne Loftus, June 14, 1958 (div. 1983); children—Joseph Loftus, James Hamilton; m. Valerie Farnham, Apr. 12, 1986. A.B., Princeton U., 1958; M.A., NYU, 1965. C.L.U.; chartered fin. cons. Field rep. N.Y. Life Ins. Co., Poughkeepsie, 1958; group underwriter N.Y.C., 1959-61; mgr. Coopers & Lybrand, N.Y.C., 1961-65; v.p. Equitable Life Assurance, N.Y.C., 1965-83; sr. v.p., chief actuary Home Life Ins. Co., N.Y.C., 1983-86, Penn Corp. Fin. Inc., Santa Monica, Calif., 1986—; chmn. com. actuaries N.Y. State Life Guaranty Corp., N.Y.C., 1979-86; adviser N.Y. State Ins. Dept., Albany, 1979-83; bd. dirs. Mass. Indemnity and Life Ins. Co., Pa. Life Ins. Co. Fellow Soc. Actuaries; mem. Health Ins. Assn. (chmn. com.), Am. Acad. Actuaries. Republican. Presbyterian. Club: Nassau (Princeton). Home: 4816 Patrae St Los Angeles CA 90066 Office: Penn Corp Fin Inc 3130 Wilshire Blvd Santa Monica CA 90406

CUMMINGS, ALBERT ALEX, real estate executive; b. Mesa, Ariz., June 21, 1927; s. Alexander John and Sofia (Carrillo) C.; m. Barbara Sue Warson, Sept. 1, 1956 (div. Mar. 1970); children: Jennifer, Alan, David; m. Carroll Ann Woods, June 10, 1970. Student, U. Ariz., 1952-76. Lic. real estate broker, ins. agt., gen. bldg. contractor. Salesman So. Ariz. Realty & Ins., Tucson, 1957-58, Greer B. Nelson, Realtor, Tucson, 1958-59, Charles P. Roberts Real Estate, Tucson, 1959-60; co-owner Hamilton & Assocs., Tucson, 1959-60; owner, mgr. Cummings Realty & Trust Co., Tucson, 1960-70, pres., 1970—; bd. dirs. Title Security Agy. Ariz, 1972-85; mem. adv. com., securities div. Ariz. Corp. Commn., 1983-85. Local pres. Sertoma Internat., Tucson, 1961-62, governor Ariz. dist., 1968-69; pres. John B. Wright PTA, Tucson, 1969-70, El Oasis Neighborhood Assn., Tucson, 1985-88. Mem. Farm and Land Inst. (Man of Yr. Ariz. chpt. 1978, regional v.p. 1979), Tucson Bd. Realtors (pres. 1972, Realtor of Yr. 1973), Ariz. Assn. Realtors (pres. 1983, grad. Realtors Inst., Realtor of Yr. 1984), Nat. Inst. Real Estate Brokers (pres. Ariz. 1977, cert. comml. investment mem.), Realtors Land Inst. (pres. Ariz. 1977, accredited land cons.), Real Estate Securities and Syndication Inst. (pres. Ariz. 1982-83, specialist in real estate securities), Nat. Assn. Realtors (Omega Tau Rho award 1979), Ariz. Real Estate Ednl. Found. (past. pres.). Home: 2324 N Madelyn Circle Tucson AZ 85712 Office: Cummings Realty & Trust Co Inc 1661 N Swan Rd Ste 100 Tucson AZ 85712

CUMMINGS, BYRON GREGORY, hospital executive; b. Wichita Falls, Tex., Dec. 9, 1957; s. Kermit Clyde Jr. and Betty Jo (Pierce) C.; m. Vicki Saxon, April 16, 1979; children: Elizabeth Ann, Justin David, Brian Charles. BS in Acctg., La. State U., 1980. CPA, La. Staff acct. Payne, Moore and Herrington, CPA's, Alexandria, La., 1980-83, Rapides Gen. Hosp., Alexandria, 1983-84; chief fin. officer Beauregard Meml. Hosp., DeRidder, La., 1984—. Treas. Beauregard Community Concerns, DeRidder, 1987—. Mem. Am. Inst. CPA's, Soc. La. CPA's, Healthcare Fin. Mgmt. Assn. Republican. Methodist. Home: 34 Mustang DeRidder LA 70634 Office: Beauregard Meml Hosp 600 S Pine St DeRidder LA 70634

CUMMINGS, GORDON ERIC MYLES, food products executive; b. Montreal, Que., Can., Sept. 15, 1940; s. Gordon Myles and Phyllis Myrtle (Bennell) C.; m. Barbara Marvel Therese Bodin, Nov. 4, 1961; children: Lesley Erica Louise, Gordon Gregory David. B.Commerce, Concordia U., Montreal, 1964; M.B.A., McMaster U., Hamilton, Ont., 1969. Prodn. planner Gillette of Can., Montreal, Que., 1960-62; indsl. acct. Continental Can Co., Montreal and Toronto, 1962-68; controller Bundy of Can., Bramalea, Ont., 1968-69; assoc. Woods Gordon, Toronto and Montreal, 1969-74; ptnr. Woods Gordon, Toronto and Montreal, Can., 1974-84; pres. Nat. Sea Products Ltd., Halifax, N.S., Can., 1985—; bd. dirs. Cobi Foods, Inc.; chmn. Pacific Aqua Foods Ltd., Vancouver. Riding pres. Que. Liberal party, 1977-80; bd. dirs. IWK Hosp. for Children Found., Jr. Achievement Can., Nat. Inst. for Nutrition, Ottawa. Fellow Soc. Mgmt. Accts. Can. (nat. exec. 1984-89); mem. Corp. Mgmt. Accts. Que. (pres. 1976-78), Soc. Mgmt. Accts. N.S. Club: Ashburn Golf (Halifax).

CUMMINGS, RANDALL RAY, biotechnologist; b. San Antonio, Oct. 3, 1956; s. John Robert and Patricia Ann (Shaw) C.; m. Diana Lynn Begley, July 27, 1985. BS in Biology, Stanford U., 1979; MA in Biochemistry, Harvard U., 1981; MBA, U. Calif., Berkeley, 1986. Sr. rsch. assoc. Armos Corp., South San Francisco, Calif., 1981-82; product mgr. Creative BioMolecules, Inc., South San Francisco, 1982-83, mgr. corp. planning, 1983-84; dir. bus. devel. Codon Corp., South San Francisco, 1984—. Mem. Am. Assn. Pharm. Scientists, Am. Fin. Assn., Calif. Indsl. Biotech. Assn. (co. rep.), Aircraft Owners and Pilots Assn., San Francisco C. of C. (co. rep.), Phi Beta Kappa, Beta Gamma Sigma. Home: 1608 Valley View Ave Belmont CA 94002 Office: Codon Corp 213 E Grand Ave South San Francisco CA 94080

CUMMINS, EVELYN FREEMAN, social agency administrator; b. Beatrice, Nebr., Mar. 24, 1904; d. John Allen and Irene (Townsend) Freeman; student Nebr. Wesleyan, 1920-23; B.A., U. Nebr., 1928; postgrad. U. Chgo., 1934-36, 41; M.S., Columbia, 1946; m. Paul Otto Cummins, Oct. 8, 1927 (dec. Sept. 1943); 1 dau., Beverly Anne (Mrs. Cummins Spangler). Tchr. rural Gage County, Nebr., 1921-22, Wilber, Nebr., 1923-25, Lincoln, Nebr., 1925-27; sch. social worker Lincoln, 1930-36; supr. Fla. Dept. Pub. Welfare, Orlando, 1936-42, dist. dir., 1942-45; dir. Nebr. Gov.'s Com. to Study Services to Blind, Lincoln, 1946-47; field rep. Fla. Dept. Pub. Welfare, Jacksonville, 1948-51, appeals officer, 1950-51; exec. dir. Community Council Oklahoma City Area, 1952-61; exec. dir. spl. projects Chgo. Community Fund, 1962-63; exec. dir. Family Service Assn. La Porte County (Ind.), 1964—; lectr. social problems Purdue North Central; participant rsch. seminar Non-Profits and Taxation NYU, 1988-89; field supr. Valparaiso U., Loyola U., Jane Addams Sch. Social Work, Chgo. Del. Area II Adv. Council on Aging, 1976-80; mem. housing com. Mayor of Michigan City (Ind.), 1973; pres. Community Service Council Michigan City, 1966-68; chmn. residential campaign United Way Michigan City, 1966-68. Diplomate Conf. Advancement Pvt. Practice in Social Work. Mem. Nat. Assn. Social workers, Acad. Certified Social Workers, Council Social Work Edn., Ind. Council Family Service Assns., Ind. Home Service Agys. Assn., Ind. Conf. on Social Concerns, Internat. Platform Assn., Nat. Network Social Work Mgrs., Inc., Women in Mgmt., Michigan City C. of C., LaPorte County Council on Aging (pres. 1978). Democrat. Methodist. Home: 1317 Washington St Michigan City IN 46360 Office: Ste 228 Warren Bldg Michigan City IN 46360

CUMMINS, PAUL ZACH, II, insurance company executive; b. Fitchburg, Mass., May 1, 1936; s. Paul Z. and Camille M. (Hook) C.; B.S., U.S. Naval Acad., 1958, M.S., 1964; children—Paul Zach II, Colleen Elizabeth. Mgr., engring. liaison Carrier Corp., Syracuse, N.Y., 1969-73; mgr. systems, mfg. group Republic Steel Corp., Youngstown, Ohio, 1973-74, mgr., bus. planning, 1974-76; dir. administrn. planning Republic Builders Products Corp., Atlanta, 1976-77; dir. corporate strategy and devel. Blue Cross/Blue Shield of Md., 1978—; instr. U.S. Naval Acad., Annapolis, 1964-65. Stratex Study mem. Dept. Def., 1967-68; chmn. Md. Gov.'s Vietnam and Disabled Vets. Bus. Resource Council. Served with USN, 1958-69. Decorated Joint Service Commendation medal. Mem. Planning Forum, U.S. Naval Acad. Alumni Assn., Am. Legion. Methodist. Club: Kiwanis (past pres. Liverpool, N.Y., past pres. Camillus, N.Y.). Home: 16933 Flickerwood Rd Parkton MD 21120 Office: 700 E Joppa Rd Baltimore MD 21204

CUNIN, JOHN RAYMOND, industrial distributing company executive; b. Akron, Ohio, Sept. 11, 1924; s. Earl Augusta and Mary Elizabeth (McAlonan) C.; m. Marilyn Ann McGuigan, Aug. 30, 1952; children: John M., Mary Catherine, Thomas K., Jane D., William E. Student, John Carroll U., Cleve., 1946-47, Akron U., 1947-48, Gen. Motors Inst., 1967. With Bearings, Inc., Cleve., 1948—; dist. mgr., then gen. sales mgr. Bearings, Inc.,

1972-80, pres., chief operating officer, after 1980, chmn., chief exec. officer, 1980—, also dir. Mem. adv. bd. Our Lady of the Wayside Homes for the Handicapped, Avon, Ohio, 1968; bd. dirs. Cleve. State U. Devel. Found.; trustee St. Vincent Charity Hosp. and Health Ctr., Cleve. Tomorrow; chmn. adv. bd. sch. bus. John Carroll U.; v.p., dir. Midtown Corridor; pres. Cleanland Cleve. Served with USAAF, 1942-45, ETO. Decorated D.F.C., Air medal. Mem. Power Transmission Distbrs. Assn., Associated Industries Cleve. (bd. dirs.), Bearing Specialist Assn. (bd. dirs.), Greater Cleve. Growth Assn. (bd. dirs.). Democrat. Clubs: Rotary, Univ, Caterpillar. Office: Bearings Inc 3600 Euclid Ave PO Box 6925 Cleveland OH 44101 *

CUNNING, JOE DAVID, fibers company research executive; b. Mount Ayr, Iowa, May 31, 1936. BSChemE, Iowa State U, 1958, MSChemE, 1962, PhD, 1965. With Du Pont Co., 1965—; research dir. Du Pont Co., Wilmington, Del., 1982—. Mem. Am. Inst. Chem. Engrs., Am. Chem. Soc., Textile Inst., Sigma Xi. Republican. Presbyterian. Office: Du Pont Co TF Dept 2068 Maple Run Pla Wilmington DE 19880-0721

CUNNINGHAM, C. SETH, investment company executive; b. N.Y.C.; s. Thomas Donald Jr. and Louise (Mills) C.; m. Sarah Peyton Gardner, May 10, 1986; 1 child, Julia Elizabeth. AB, Harvard U., 1979. V.p. Morgan Guaranty Trust Co. N.Y., N.Y.C., 1979-86, J.P. Morgan & Co., N.Y.C., 1986—. Office: JP Morgan & Co 23 Wall St New York NY 10015

CUNNINGHAM, CHARLES BAKER, III, manufacturing company executive; b. St. Louis, Oct. 1, 1941; s. Charles Baker C. and Mary Blythe (Cunningham); m. Georganne Rose, Sept. 17, 1966; children: Margaret B., Charles B. IV. B.S., Washington U., St. Louis, 1964; M.S., Ga. Inst. Tech., 1966; M.B.A., Harvard U., 1970. Dir. fin. The Cooper Group, Raleigh, N.C., 1972-75, v.p. adminstrn., 1975-77; v.p. devel. Cooper Industries Inc., Houston, 1977-79, v.p. ops., 1980-82, exec. v.p., 1982—; pres. Indsl. Equipment Group Cooper Industries Inc., 1979-80. Dir. Sam Houston council Boy Scouts Am., Houston, 1981—. Served to 1st lt. U.S. Army, 1966-68, Iran. Decorated Army Commendation medal. Office: Cooper Industries Inc PO Box 4446 Houston TX 77210 *

CUNNINGHAM, EDWARD PRESTON, JR., food manufacturing company personnel executive; b. Hammond, Ind., Sept. 24, 1945; s. Edward Preston and Louise Catherine (Kohler) C.; B.B.A., U. Wis., Madison, 1968, M.B.A., 1969; m. Julie Cunningham; children—Scott, Jennifer. Personnel supr. Quaker Oats Co., Rockford, Ill., 1972-75, employee relations mgr., 1975-79, employee and community relations mgr., Lawrence, Kans., 1979—. Met. bd. dirs. Nat. Alliance Bus., 1976-78; bd. dirs. U. Kans. Concert Series, 1980—, Lawrence chpt. ARC, 1983—, Douglas County Vis. Nurses, 1983—; chmn. commerce and industry unit Lawrence Multiple Sclerosis, 1981—; bd. dirs. Cotttonwood Inc. Served to capt. U.S. Army, 1969-72; Vietnam. Decorated Bronze Star; named Outstanding Young Man Am., U.S. Jaycees, 1981. Mem. Ill. Employment Service, Midwest Indsl. Mgmt. Assn. (instr. 1978-79), Am. Soc. for Tng. and Devel., Lawrence C. of C. (chmn. edn. com. 1980), Lawrence Personnel Club. Republican. Congregationalist. Club: Cosmopolitan. Home: 1593 El Dorado Dr Lawrence KS 66044 Office: 727 Iowa St Lawrence KS 66044

CUNNINGHAM, GORDON ROSS, financial executive; b. Toronto, Ont., Can., Nov. 15, 1944; s. Wendell Carson and Catherine Ann C.; m. Patricia Dorothy Westheuser, Dec. 12, 1966; children: Kristyn Catherine, Kaleigh Ann, James Gordon. BA, U. Toronto, 1966; LLB, Trinity Coll., 1969. Bar: Ont. 1971. With Tory, Tory DesLaurers & Bimmington, Toronto, 1971-76; ptnr. Tory, Tory Deshaurers & Bennington, Toronto, 1977-84; exec. v.p., chief oper. officer Trilon Fin. Corp., Toronto, 1985-88, pres., chief operating officer, 1988—, also bd. dirs.; sr. v.p. Brascan Lt., 1984—; chmn. Eurobrokers Investment Corp., Trilon Bancorp Inc.; dep. chmn. Wellington Ins. Co.; pres. Fairmoor Holdings Inc.; pres., chief exec. officer Royal LePage Holdings Ltd.; bd. dirs. Bardview Inc., China-Can. Investment Devel. Corp., Domco Foodsvcs. Ltd., Dome Consortium Inc., Edper Equities Ltd., Edper Holdings Ltd., Fidelity Standard, Gt. Lakes Investments Ltd., London Life Ins. Co., Lonvest Corp., Penstock Inns Ltd., Royal Trust Corp. Can., Royal Trustco Ltd., Security First, Shaw and Begg Ltd., Spraybake (Can.) Ltd., The Holden Group, The Optimum, The Royal Trust Co., Triathlon Leasing Inc., Trilon Equities Ltd., Trilon Holdings Ltd., Trivest Ins. Network Ltd., Westmin Holdings Ltd. Nat. chmn. Diabetes Can.; appointee Fed. Govt. Sectoral Adv. Group for Fin. Svcs.; bd. dirs. Juvenile Diabetes Found.; nat. chmn. Diabetes Can. Mem. Can. Bar Assn., Upper Can. Law Soc., Atlantic Salmon Fedn., Rosedale Golf Club, Univ. Club (past pres.), Granite Club, Devil's Glen Ski Club. Home: 164 Glencairn Ave, Toronto, ON Canada M5R 1N2 Office: Trilon Fin Corp Royal Trust Tower, Toronto-Dominion Ctr #3800, Toronto, ON Canada M5K 1G8

CUNNINGHAM, JAMES EVERETT, energy services company executive; b. Iowa, Apr. 14, 1923; s. James Franklin and Julia (Connors) C.; BS in Chem. Engring., U. Ala., 1946; m. Delores Ann Foytik, Jan. 31, 1959; children: Sharon Lee, Sandra Dee, Matthew Joseph, Susan Elizabeth, Michael James, Marc David. With Fluor Corp., Houston, 1947-54; pvt. practice oil bus., 1955-58; with J. Ray McDermott & Co., Inc., New Orleans, 1958—, treas., 1964-67, exec. v.p., 1967-78, vice chmn. fin. and adminstrn., 1978, vice chmn., chief exec. officer, 1979, chmn., chief exec. officer, 1979-88; dir. Reading & Bates Corp., The Greyhound Corp. Mem. president's council Loyola U.; vice chmn. Ctr. Internat. Bus.; bd. dirs. Bus. Task Force on Edn. Served with USNR, World War II. Mem. NAM (former vice chmn., so. div., mem. exec. com.), Conf. Bd. (policy com.), New Orleans C. of C. (econ. devel. council, dir.). Office: McDermott Internat Inc PO Box 61961 New Orleans LA 70161 *

CUNNINGHAM, JEFFREY MILTON, publishing executive; b. Rome, Aug. 25, 1952; s. Allen Hamilton and Nina (Gertzovsky) C.; m. Elizabeth Anne Moir, Sept. 17, 1983; children: Kimberly Anne, James Hamilton, Benjamin William. BA, SUNY, Binghamton, 1974. Auditor Bus. Pubs. Audit, N.Y.C., 1974-76; dist. mgr. McGraw-Hill Pubs., N.Y.C., 1976-80; mgr. agy. relations Forbes mag., N.Y.C., 1980-85, dir. advt., 1988—; regional advt. dir. Bus. Week, N.Y.C., 1985-86; pub. Am. Heritage mag., N.Y.C., 1986-88; sales dir. worldwide advt. Forbes mag., 1988—. Republican. Mem. Dutch Reformed Ch. Clubs: Siwanoy Country (Bronxville, N.Y.), N.Y. Atheletic, Sandanona Hunt, (Millbrook, N.Y.), Nat. Golf Links (Southampton, N.Y.). Office: Forbes Mag 60 Fifth Ave New York NY 10011

CUNNINGHAM, RALPH SANFORD, oil company executive; b. Albany, Ohio, Oct. 16, 1940; s. Harold Sanford and Julia Marie (Lasch) C.; m. Deborah Elaine Brookshire, Dec. 23, 1976; children: Ralph Sanford, Susan Ellen, Stephen Earl, Jennifer Marie. BS in Chem. Engring., Auburn (Ala.) U., 1962; MS, Ohio State U., 1962, PhD, 1966. With Exxon Co. U.S.A., Benicia, Calif., 1966-80, mgr. refinery, 1977-80; exec. v.p. Tenneco Oil Processing and Mktg., Houston, 1980-81, pres., 1982—, also bd. dirs.; exec. v.p. Tenneco Oil Co.; bd. dirs. IT Corp. Chmn. United Way Solano-Napa Counties, Calif., 1979; exec. council, v.p. Silverado council Boy Scouts Am., 1978-79. Mem. Am. Inst. Chem. Engrs., Am. Petroleum Inst., Sigma Xi. Republican. Presbyterian. Office: Tenneco Oil Co PO Box 2511 Houston TX 77001 *

CUNNINGHAM, RAYMOND CLEMENT, glass company executive; b. Toledo, Oct. 6, 1931; s. Raymond Clement Sr. and Mary Margrite (Stalker) C.; m. Dorothy Deborah, Oct. 5, 1957; children—Deborah Susan Cunningham Rigsby, John Raymond. B.S., Northwestern U., 1953, postgrad., 1953, 56. Mgr. sales promotion and tng. Lincoln-Mercury, Dearborn, Mich., 1966-70; advt. and merchandising mgr. Philco Ford, Phila., 1970-73; mgr. mktg. and prodn. planning Ford Glass Div., Detroit, 1973-81; speciality sales and mktg. mgr. Ford Glass Div., 1981-83; exec. v.p. AFG Inds., Inc., Kingsport, Tenn., 1983—; pres. Auto Glass Inc., AFG, 1987—. Mem. exec. bd. Kingsport Area Bus. Council on Health Care, Inc., Kingsport, 1985, Boy Scouts Am., 1985; mem. adv. bd. Jr. League; chmn. Fun Fest Exec. Com., Kingsport, 1985. Mem. Sealed Insulating Glass Assn. (named Man of Yr. 1978, 85), Kingsport C. of C. Roman Catholic. Clubs: Ridgefields Country, Village (Birmingham). Home: 1306 Watauga St Kingsport TN 37660 Office: AFG Industries Inc PO Box 929 Kingsport TN 37662 also: AFG Industries Inc 301 Commerce St Fort Worth TX 76102 *

CUNNINGHAM, TIMOTHY WHITE, venture capitalist; b. Murfreesboro, Tenn., Sept. 5, 1952; s. John Thomas and Shirley (Burke) C.; m. Ann Barkhuff, Nov. 26, 1975; children: Christopher W., William A. BA magna cum laude, Williams Coll., 1974; MS with honors, Am. Grad. Sch. Internat. Mgmt., Glendale, Ariz., 1976. Asst. buyer Gimbel Bros., N.Y.C., 1974; sales rep. Bucyrus-Erie Co., South Milwaukee, Wis., 1976-79, mgr. parts sales, 1979-81; gen. mgr. Bucyrus-Chile Co. subs. Bucyrus-Erie Co., Santiago, 1981-83; v.p. Keystone Venture Capital Mgmt. Co., Phila., 1983—; gen. ptnr. Butcher Venture Ptnrs., Phila., 1987—; bd. dirs. Am. Med. Imaging Corp., Doylestown, Pa., Ansoft, Inc., Pitts., Ind. Products, Inc., West Point, Pa., Integrated Cir. Systems, Inc., King of Prussia, Pa., Mothers Work, Inc., Phila., AM Communications, Inc., Quakertown, Pa. Mem. Delware Valley Venture Group, N.E. Venture Capital Group (founder 1987). Office: Keystone Venture Capital Mgmt Co 211 S Broad St Philadelphia PA 19107

CUNYUS, GEORGE MARVIN, oil company executive; b. Dallas, Jan. 13, 1930; s. George Grady and Ruby Gordon (King) C.; m. Mary Ellen Faust, Apr. 24, 1952 (dec. 1987); children: Bruce, Stuart, John. B.A., Rice U., 1951; J.D., So. Meth. U., 1956. Bar: Tex. 1956. With Hunt Oil Co., Dallas, 1956—; sr. v.p., gen. counsel Hunt Oil Co., 1962—, corp. sec., 1976—, dir., mem. exec. com.; chmn. bd, exec. com. E. Tex. Salt Water Disposal Co.; chmn. bd. Brooks Well Servicing, Inc. Trustees Disciples Found. of Dallas.; dir. Thai Christian Found. Served with U.S. Army, 1951-53. Mem. Mid-Continent Oil and Gas Assn. (dir. La. div.). Republican. Club: Dallas Petroleum. Home: 5634 Ledgestone Dr Dallas TX 75214 Office: Hunt Oil Co 1401 Elm St Dallas TX 75202

CUOCO, DANIEL ANTHONY, lawyer; b. N.Y.C., Oct. 19, 1937; s. Angelo and Mary (deGeso) C.; m. Joanne C. Colavita, July 8, 1961; children: Dana, Mark, Susan, Victoria. AB summa cum laude, Iona Coll., 1959; JD, Columbia U., 1962. Bar: N.Y. 1962, U.S. Supreme Ct. 1965. Assoc. Dewey Ballantine Bushby Palmer & Wood, N.Y.C., 1962-71; v.p., asst. gen. counsel Squibb Corp., N.Y.C., 1971-82; sec., sr. v.p., gen. counsel Squibb Corp., Princeton, N.J., 1982—, also bd. dirs.; trustee Food and Drug Law Inst., Washington. Trustee The Hun Sch., Princeton, N.J. Mem. ABA, N.Y. State Bar Assn., Bar Assn. City N.Y. Republican. Club: Univ. (N.Y.C.). Home: 28 Edgerstoune Rd Princeton NJ 08540 Office: Squibb Corp PO Box 4000 Princeton NJ 08543-4000

CURCIO, JAMES FRANCIS, oil company executive; b. Hornell, N.Y., Nov. 30, 1937; s. Thomas and Margaret (Milanese) C.; m. Jill Linnae Rocker, Feb. 2, 1963; children: Brian James, Bradley Allen. BBA, U. Notre Dame, 1960. Credit rep. Internat. Harvesters Co., Madison, Wis., 1962-67; dis. credit supr. Internat. Harvesters Co., Milw., 1967-69; office mgr. Gary Steel Products, Gary, Ind., 1969-76; asst. contr. Welsh Oil Inc., Merrillville, Ind., 1976-79; treas., asst. sec. Welsh Oil Inc., Merrillville, 1979—; treas. Aspen Inc., Merrillville, 1981—; sec., treas. Pyramid Oil, Benton Harbor, Mich., 1980—. Pres. Merrillville Sports Assn., 1983.; Northwest Ind. Forum; mem. Pres. Round Table Meth. Hosp., Rep. Nat. Senatorial Com.; pres. Merrillville CHamber Advancement Found., 1986—. With USMC, 1960-66. Mem. Am. Mgmt. Assn., Serra Club (local pres. 1975, Pres. award 1976), Notre Dame Alumni Assn. (local pres. 1976, Man of Yr. award 1980), Merrillville C. of C. (bd. dirs. 1984-86), Serra Club (local pres. 1975, Pres. award 1976), Notre Dame Quarterbacks Club, Edward Frederick Sorin Soc. Club. Roman Catholic. Home: 464 Wexford Rd Valparaiso IN 46383

CURCIO, JOHN BAPTIST, truck manufacturing company executive; b. Hazleton, Pa., May 29, 1934; s. John B. and Bridget (Slattery) C.; m. Rosemary J. Kutash, Aug. 28, 1954; children: Mary Beth, John W., Kris Ann. LL.B., LaSalle Coll., 1963. Pres., chief exec. officer Montone Mfg. Co., Hazleton, 1954-67; v.p. Mack Trucks Inc., Allentown, Pa., 1967-73, exec. v.p., 1976-80, pres., chief operating officer, 1980-84, pres., chief exec. officer, 1984—, chmn., 1986—; pres., chief exec. officer Crane Carrier Co., Tulsa, 1973-76. Served with USNR, 1951-54, Korea. Decorated Bronze Star, Purple Heart. Mem. Soc. Automotive Engrs. (nat. chmn. 1976). Club: Lehigh Valley Country. Office: Mack Trucks Inc 2100 Mack Blvd Box M Allentown PA 18105

CURFEW, JAMES V., engineer; b. McCamey, Tex., Dec. 22, 1946; s. James and Bennie Gordon (Cross) C.; m. Kathie Jeannean Dewbre, June 3, 1967; children: James Everett, John Michael. BME, Tex. Tech U., 1969. Engr. Atlantic Richfield Co., Midland, Tex., 1970-71, Roswell, N.Mex., 1971-72; ops., analytical engr. Atlantic Richfield Co., Ardmore, Okla., 1972-75; sr. engr. Atlantic Richfield Co., Anchorage, 1975-78; sr. staff engr. Atlantic Richfield Co., Dallas, 1978-80; area engr. Atlantic Richfield Co., Hobbs, N.Mex., 1980-82; dist. engr. Atlantic Richfield Co., Bakersfield, Calif., 1982-85; sr. area engr. Atlantic Richfield Co., Midland, 1985—. Author: (tech. tng. manual) Emulsion Treating and Well Testing, 1980. Mem. Civic Action Program, 1975—; advisor Aunt Cherries Home, Bakersfield, 1985—. Mem. Crane (Tex.) Jaycees (Citizenship award 1965), Soc. Petroleum Engrs., Pi Tau Sigma, Tau Beta Pi, Phi Kappa Phi. Republican. Lodge: Toastmasters. Office: ARCO Oil and Gas Co PO Box 1610 Midland TX 79702

CURKENDALL, BRENDA IRENE, business owner, consultant; b. Mesa, Ariz., Dec. 20, 1954; d. Arthur Blatt and Dorothy June (Goodnight) Dalton; m. James Patrick Monagle (div.); m. Christopher Lee Curkendall; 1 child, Chad Michael. Student, Edison Jr. Coll., 1971-72; BS in History, Fla. State U., 1976. Registered investment advisor. Realtor Harold A. Allen Co. Realtors, Tacoma, 1983; salesperson Computerland, Bellevue, Wash., 1983-84; systems analyst for contract labor Boeing Computer Svcs., Tukwila, Wash., 1985; fin. cons. Shearson Lehman Bros., Tacoma, 1985-87; cons. Curkendall Fin. Programs, Puyallup, Wash., 1988—; instr. Pierce Coll., Tacoma. Contbr. articles to profl. jours. Capt. U.S. Army, 1976-82, Korea. Mem. Apt. Assn. Pierce County (pres. 1988), Ft. Hood Flying Club (pres. 1980). Office: Curkendall Fin Programs 12303 Meridian S Ste 200 Puyallup WA 98373

CURLER, HOWARD J., business executive; b. Mosinee, Wis., Apr. 11, 1925; (married). B.S. in Chem. Engring, U. Wis., 1948. With research dept. Marathon Corp., 1948-58; pres. Curwood Inc., 1958-68; corp. v.p. Bemis Co. Inc., 1965-76, exec. v.p., chief operating officer, 1976, pres., chief operating officer, 1977, pres., chief exec. officer, 1978-87, chmn., chief exec. officer, 1987—. Office: PO Box 1154 Appleton WI 54912 also: Bemis Co Inc 800 Northstar Ctr 625 Marquette Ave Minneapolis MN 55402 *

CURLEY, JOHN FRANCIS, JR., securities company executive; b. Wollaston, Mass., July 24, 1939; s. John Francis and Ann (Omar) C.; m. Loretta Mae O'Keeffe, Oct. 20, 1962; children—William Laurance, Edward Reid, David Neil. Grad., Phillips Acad.; A.B., Princeton U., 1960; M.B.A., Harvard U., 1962. With Paine, Webber, Jackson & Curtis, Inc., N.Y.C., 1964—, gen. ptnr., 1969-72, exec. v.p., 1972-77, pres., 1977-80, chmn. fin. com., 1980-82; vice-chmn. bd. Legg Mason, Inc., Balt., 1982—, Legg Mason Wood Walker, Inc., Balt., 1982—; pres., dir. Legg, Mason Value Trust, Inc., 1982—; gov. Investment Co. Inst.; dir., ICI Mutual Ins. Co., Western Asset Mgmt. Co. Served to 1st lt. AUS, 1962-64. Mem. Securities Industry Assn. (dir., exec. com. 1978-80), Investment Assn. N.Y. (past pres.), Bond Club N.Y.C., Bond Club Balt. Clubs: Sleepy Hollow (Scarborough, N.Y.), Princeton (N.Y.C.), Center; L'Hirondelle, Maryland. Office: Legg Mason Wood Walker Inc 111 S Calvert St Baltimore MD 21202

CURLEY, JOHN J., diversified media company executive; b. Dec. 31, 1938; married. Reporter, editor AP, 1963-69; with Gannett Co. Inc., Washington, 1969—, former pres. Mid-Atlantic newspaper group, sr. v.p., 1982-84, pres., 1984—, chief operating officer, 1984-86, chief exec. officer, 1986—, chmn., 1989—, also bd. dirs. Office: Gannett Co Inc PO Box 7858 Washington DC 20044 also: Dem & Chronicle 55 Exchange Blvd Rochester NY 14614 *

CURLOOK, WALTER, mining company executive; b. Coniston, Ont., Can., Mar. 14, 1929; s. William and Stephanie (Acker) C.; m. Jennifer Burak, May 28, 1955; children: Christine, William Paul, John Michael, Andrea. BA in Sci., U. Toronto, 1950, MA in Sci., 1951, Ph.D., 1953; D.Sc. hon., Laurentian U., 1983. Postdoctoral fellow Imperial Coll. Sci. and Tech., London, 1954; rsch. metallurgist Inco, Sudbury, Ont., Can., 1954-59; supr. rsch. sta. Inco, Port Colborne, Ont., 1959-60; supr. rsch. Inco, Copper Cliff, Ont., 1960-64, asst. to gen. mgr., 1964-69; v.p. adminstrv. and engring. svcs. Inco, Copper Cliff, 1973-74; v.p. Inco, N.Y.C., 1974-77; sr. v.p. prodn. Inco Metals Co., Toronto, 1977-80, pres., chief exec. officer, 1980-82; exec. v.p. Inco Ltd., Toronto, 1982—; dir. Inco Ltd., 1989; pres. Inco Gold Co., Toronto, 1987—; dir. Technique of Cofimpac, Paris, 1969-72, v.p. adminstrn., 1972-73; bd. dirs. Great-West Life Assurance Co., Winnipeg., Man.; mem. Nat. Adv. Com. on Mining Industry, 1980—; chmn. Northern Ont. Hydro Adv. com., 1987—. Patentee in field. Bd. dirs. Foundation Cambrian Found., Sudbury, 1983; first chmn. bd. Cambrian Coll. Applied Arts and Tech., Sudbury, Ont., 1980. Fellow Can. Acad. Engring.; mem. Assn. Profl. Engrs. of Ont., Metall. Soc. of Can. Inst. Mining and Metallurgy (Airey 1979), AIME, Mining Assn. Can. (bd. dir. and past chmn.), Sci. North (hon. life Sudbury chpt. 1988), Ont. Mining Assn. (past pres. Toronto). Roman Catholic. Club: Board of Trade (Toronto). Home: 25 Cluny Dr, Toronto, ON Canada M4W 2P9 Office: Inco Ltd, Royal Trust Tower, Toronto-Dominion Ctr, Toronto, ON Canada M5K 1N4

CUROTTO, RICKY JOSEPH, lawyer, corporate executive; b. Lomita Park, Calif., Dec. 22, 1931; s. Enrico and Nora M. (Giusso) C.; m. Lynne Therese Ingram, Dec. 31, 1983; children: Dina L., John F., Alexis J. BS cum laude, U. San Francisco, 1953, JD, 1958. Bar: Calif. 1959. Assoc. Peart, Baraty & Hassard, San Francisco, 1958-60; sr. counsel, asst. sec. BHP Utah Internat. Inc., San Francisco, 1960—; of counsel Curotto Law Offices, San Francisco and Sacramento, Calif., 1984—, Calif. Loan Counsel, Crossland Mortgage Corp.; counsel, sec. Ross Valley Homes, Inc., Greenbrae, Calif.; dir. Ross Valley Homes, Inc., Garden Hotels Investment Co. Trustee, U. San Francisco; pres., dir. Shorebird Homeowners Assn. Served to 1st lt. U.S. Army, 1954-56. Named to U. San Francisco Athletic Hall of Fame, 1985, Alumnus of Yr. U. San Francisco, 1989; recipient Bur. Nat. Affairs award, 1958, Disting. Service award U. San Francisco, 1981, Alumnus of Yr., U. San Francisco, 1989. Mem. ABA, State Bar Calif., San Francisco Bar Assn., Am. Arbitration Assn. (nat. panel arbitrators), Am. Corp. Counsel Assn., Commonwealth Club of Calif. Republican. Roman Catholic. Contbr. articles to law revs. Office: BHP Utah Internat Inc 550 California St Ste 800 San Francisco CA 94104

CURRID, CHERYL CLARKE, information systems executive, technical writer; b. Newark, July 21, 1950; d. Charles McAleer and Evelyn (Agusta) Clarke; m. Raymond E. Currid Jr., Nov. 17, 1979; children: Raymond E. III, Justin Clarke. BA in Psychology, George Mason U., 1972, postgrad. in systems, 1976-77. Sales rep. R.J. Reynolds Co., Annandale, Va., 1975-78; sales mgr. M&M Mars Co., Annandale, 1978-82; systems mgr. Coca-Cola Foods, Houston, 1983—; bd. dirs. Connectivity Solutions 88 Personal Computer expo, Englewood Cliffs, N.J., 1987—. Author: The Power User Guide to R: Base, 1989; author regular column PC Week Newspaper; contbr. articles to profl. jours. Mem. Software Assocs. Group (pres. 1979-82), Capital Personal Computer Users Group, Houston Area League of Personal Computer Users, Microcomputer Mgrs. Assn., Netware In Common. Republican. Home: 818 Herdsman Houston TX 77079 Office: Coca-Cola Foods 2000 St James Pl Houston TX 77056

CURRIE, DEAN WINN, university official; b. Austin, Tex., Sept. 29, 1947; s. David Mitchell and Marguerite (Winn) C.; m. Carol Carlander, June 5, 1969; children: David Carlander, Sarah Winn. AB, Harvard U., 1969, MBA, 1973. Dir. admissions and fin. aid Bus. Sch., Harvard U., Cambridge, Mass., 1973-77, asst. dean ednl. affairs, 1977-80, assoc. dean adminstrn. and policy planning, 1980-88; v.p. fin. and adminstrn. Rice U., Houston, 1988—; bd. dirs. Stirrup Ranch Cattle Co., Canyon City, Colo., China Internat. Trade Assn., Atlanta. Democrat. Presbyterian. Home: 2616 Amherst Houston TX 77005 Office: Rice U PO Box 2666 Houston TX 77252

CURRIE, EARL JAMES, transportation company executive; b. Fergus Falls, Minn., May 14, 1939; s. Victor James and Calma (Hammer) C.; m. Kathleen E. Phalen, June 3, 1972; children: Jane, Joseph. BA, St. Olaf Coll., 1961; cert. in transp., Yale U., 1963; P.M.D., Harvard U., 1974. With Burlington No. Inc., 1964-85; asst. v.p. St. Paul, 1977-78, Chgo., 1978-80; v.p., gen. mgr. Seattle, 1980-83; sr. v.p. Overland Park, Kans., 1983-85; pres. Camas Prairie R.R., Lewiston, Idaho, 1982-83, Longview Switching Co., Wash., 1982-83, Western Fruit Express Co., 1984-85; exec. v.p. op. Soo Line R.R. Co. & Rail Units, 1985—; bd. dirs. Belt Ry. Co. Chgo., Ind. Harbor Belt Ry., Gibson, MT Properties Inc., St. Paul, Kansas City (Mo.) Terminal R.R. Bd. dirs. United Way, King County, Wash., 1980-83; bd. dirs. Corp. Council for Arts, Seattle, 1980-83, Jr. Achievement, 1980-82; trustee St. Martins Coll., Lacey, Wash., 1982-83; mem. Mpls. Neighborhood Employment Network. Mem. Am. Assn. R.R. Supts. (bd. dirs. 1979-80), Seattle C. of C. (dir. 1980-83, Interlachen Golf and Country Club, Mpls. Athletic Club. Republican. Roman Catholic. Home: 5921 Dewey Hill Rd Edina MN 55435 Office: Soo Line RR Co 105 S 5th St Minneapolis MN 55440

CURRIE, JAMES BARKER, lawyer, corporate secretary; b. Evanston, Ill., Mar. 1, 1948; s. James Edward and Miriam (Barker) C.; m. Mary Cecelia Currie, Jan. 31, 1981; children: James Arthur, Matthew Austin. Student, U. Iowa; BA, Miami U., 1970; JD, Ill. Inst. Tech., 1975. Bar: U.S. Dist. Ct. Ill. 1975, U.S. Supreme Ct. 1979. Sr. counsel Sears, Roebuck and Co., Chgo., 1975-83, dir. acquisitions, 1981-82, mgr. bus. devel., 1983-84, assoc. dir. strategic planning, 1984-86; v.p., sec., gen. counsel Coldwell, Banker & Co., Chgo., 1986—, Coldwell Banker Real Estate Group, Inc., Chgo., 1986—. Served to sgt. USAR, 1970-76. Mem. ABA, Ill. Bar Assn., Chgo. Bar Assn. Republican. Office: Coldwell Banker & Co 55 W Monroe St Suite 3100 Chicago IL 60603

CURRIE, JAMES DENNIS, systems analyst, consultant; b. Wenatchee, Wash., Oct. 11, 1928; s. David Lindsay and Ruth May (Richardson) C.; m. Barbara Mar Calder, Dec. 2, 1950; children: Paul Douglas, Matthew Robert, Sarah Marie. BS in Biosci. and Chemistry, Bemidji State Tchrs. Coll., 1955. Electronics engr. Air Tech. Intelligence Ctr., Wright-Patterson AFB, Ohio, 1956-62; sr. rsch. engr. N. Am. Aviation Co., Columbus, Ohio, 1962-64; electronics engr. fgn. tech. div. U.S. Air Force, Wright-Patterson AFB, 1964-84; tech. editor Sci. Applications Internat. Corp., Dayton, Ohio, 1984-85; sr. mem. adv. staff Computer Scis. Corp., Dayton, 1985-87; sr. engr. Corvus Systems, Inc., Fairborn, Ohio, 1987-88, Alphasci., Dayton, 1988—. Formerly active Boy Scouts Am., Springfield and Urbana, Ohio. With U.S. Army, 1950-52, Korea. Recipient Silver Beaver award Boy Scouts Am., 1984. Mem. Astronomical Soc. The Pacific, Assn. Lunar and Planetary Observiers. Republican. Roman Catholic. Home: 197 W Routzong Dr Fairborn OH 45324 Office: Alphascience 1020 Woodman Dr Dayton OH 45432

CURRIE, MALCOLM RODERICK, scientist, aerospace and automotive executive; b. Spokane, Wash., Mar. 13, 1927; s. Erwin Casper and Genevieve (Hauenstein) C.; m. Sunya Lofsky, June 24, 1951; children—Deborah, David, Diana; m. Barbara L. Dyer, Mar. 5, 1977. A.B., U. Calif. at Berkeley, 1949, M.S., 1951, Ph.D., 1954. Research engr. Microwave Lab., U. Calif. at Berkeley, 1949-52, elec. engring. faculty, 1953-54; lectr. U. Calif. at Los Angeles, 1955-57; research engr. Hughes Aircraft Co., 1954-57, v.p., 1965-66; head electron dynamics dept. Hughes Research Labs., Culver City, Calif., 1957-60; dir. physics lab. Hughes Research Labs., Malibu, Calif., 1960-61, asso. dir., 1961-63, v.p., dir. research labs., 1963-65, v.p., mgr. research and devel. div., 1965-69; v.p. research and devel. Beckman Instruments, Inc., 1969-73; undersec. research and engring. dept. Office Sec. Def., Washington, 1973-77; pres. missile systems group Hughes Aircraft Co., Canoga Park, Calif., 1977-83, exec. v.p., 1983-88, chief exec. officer, chmn. bd., 1988—, also bd. dirs.; pres., chief exec. officer Delco Electronics Corp., 1986-88, also bd. dirs.; bd. dirs. GM Hughes Electronics Co., group exec. def. ops., 1986; chmn., chief exec. officer Hughes Aircraft Co., 1988—; mem. Def. Sci. Bd. Contbr. articles to profl. jours.; patentee in field. Mem. adv. bd. U. Calif., Berkeley, UCLA, U. Tex.; trustee U. So Calif., UCLA Found. Served with USNR, 1944-47. Decorated comdr. Legion of Honor France; named nation's outstanding young elec. engr. Eta Kappa Nu, 1958, one of 5 outstanding young men of Calif. Calif. Jr. C. of C., 1960. Fellow IEEE, AIAA; mem. Nat. Acad. Engring., Am. Phys. Soc., Phi Beta Kappa, Sigma Xi, Lambda Chi Alpha. Club: Cosmos. Home: 28780 Wagon Rd Agoura CA 91301 Office: Hughes Aircraft Co 7200 Hughes Terr Los Angeles CA 90045

CURRIE, RICHARD JAMES, food store chain executive; b. St. John, N.B., Canada, Oct. 4, 1937; s. Hugh O'Donnell and Agnes Coltart (Johnstone) C.; m. Beverly Trites, Sept. 15, 1962; children: Jennifer Lee, Bryn Margaret,

Elizabeth Gay. B in Engring., Tech. Univ. N.S., 1960; MBA, Harvard U., 1970. Process engr. Atlantic Sugar Refineries, 1960-63, refining supt., 1963-68; sr. assoc. McKinsey & Co., 1970; v.p. Loblaws Cos. Ltd., Toronto, Ont., Can., 1972-74, exec. v.p., 1974-76, pres., from 1976; food distbg. group parent co. George Weston Ltd., Toronto, to 1986, sr. v.p., 1986—, also bd. dirs.; chmn. Nat. Tea Co., from 1981. Mem. bd. regents Mt. Allison U.; bd. govs. Bishop Strachan Sch. Clubs: York, Rosedale Golf, Granite. *

CURRIVAN, JOHN DANIEL, lawyer; b. Paris, Jan. 15, 1947. s. Gene and Rachel (Marash) C.; m. Mary Lou Janicki, Aug. 20, 1969; children: Christopher, Melissa. BS with distinction, Cornell U., 1968; MS, U. Calif.-Berkeley, 1969, U. West Fla., 1971; JD summa cum laude, Cornell Law Sch., 1978. Bar: Ohio 1978. Mng. ptnr. Southwest Devel. Co., Kingsville, Tex., 1971-76; note editor Cornell Law Review, Ithaca, N.Y., 1977-78; prosecutor, Naval Legal Office, Norfolk, Va., 1978-79, chief prosecutor, 1979-81; sr. atty. USS Nimitz, 1981-83; trial judge Naval Base, Norfolk, 1983-84; tax atty. Jones, Day, Reavis & Pogue, Cleve., 1984-88, ptnr., 1989—. Served to commdr. USN, 1969-84. Recipient Kerr prize Cornell Law Sch., 1977, Corpus Juris Secundum award West Pub. Co., 1978, Younger Fed. Lawyer award Fed. Bar Assn., 1981. Mem. ABA, Ohio State Bar Assn., Nat. Assn. Bond Lawyers, Order of Coif, Tau Beta Pi, Eta Kappa Nu, Phi Kappa Phi. Home: 2842 Sedgewick Rd Shaker Heights OH 44120 Office: Jones Day Reavis & Pogue 901 Lakeside Ave Cleveland OH 44114

CURRY, ALAN CHESTER, insurance company executive; b. Columbus, Ohio, Oct. 15, 1933; s. Harold E. and Martha (Dew) C.; children: Diane, Thomas, Timothy, Jeffrey, Barry. Student, U. Ill., 1951-52; EdB, Ill. State U., 1957. Various actuarial positions State Farm Mut. Automobile Ins. Co., Bloomington, Ill., 1952-70, v.p., actuary, 1970—. Mem. bd. indsl. advisors Rose-Hullman Inst. Tech. Fellow Casualty Actuarial Soc. (dir. 1970-73, 87—); mem. Am. Acad. Actuaries (dir. 1977-80), Midwestern Actuarial Forum (pres. 1972-73), Am. Risk and Ins. Assn., Am. Statis. Assn., Pi Gamma Mu, Pi Omega Pi, Kappa Delta Pi. Lodge: Shriners. Home: 7 Canterbury Ct Bloomington IL 61701 Office: State Farm Mut Automobile Ins Co 1 State Farm Pla Bloomington IL 61710

CURRY, CLARENCE F., JR., business executive, educator, consultant; b. Hampton, Va., Aug. 16, 1943; s. Clarence F. and Sadie (Mann) C.; m. Agnes A. Mason, Nov. 26, 1966; children: Clarence III, Candace. BSMetE, Lafeyette Coll., 1965; MBA, U. Pitts., 1971; MS in Indsl. Adminstrn., Carnegie-Mellon U., 1973. Engr. Westinghouse Electric Co., 1965-70; instr. U. Pitts., 1974—; dir. Small Bus. Devel. Ctr., 1979—; cons. in field. Contbr. articles to profl. jours. Mem. Am. Arbitration Assn., Beta Gamma Sigma, Alpha Phi Alpha. Lodge: Elks. Office: U Pitts Small Bus Devel Ctr 343 Mervis Hall Pittsburgh PA 15260

CURRY, DANIEL ARTHUR, lawyer, corporation executive; b. Phoenix, Mar. 28, 1937; s. John Joseph and Eva May (Wills) C.; m. Joy M. Shallenberger, Sept. 5, 1959; children: Elizabeth Marie, Catherine Jane, Peter Damien, Jennifer Louise, Julia Maureen, David Gordon. B.S., Loyola U., Los Angeles, 1957, LL.B., 1960; postgrad., U. So. Calif. Law Center, 1964-65; postgrad. exec. program, Grad. Sch. Bus., Stanford U., 1980. Bar: Calif. 1961, U.S. Ct. Mil. Appeals 1963, U.S. Customs Ct. 1968, Hawaii 1972, U.S. Ct. Appeals (9th cir.) 1972, U.S. Dist. Ct. (cen. and no. dists.) Calif. 1972, U.S. Dist. Ct. Hawaii 1972, N.Y. 1988. Assoc. Wolford, Johnson, Pike & Covell, El Monte, Calif., 1964-65, Demetriou & Del Guercio, Los Angeles, 1965-67; counsel, corporate staff divisional asst. Technicolor, Inc., Hollywood, Calif., 1967-70; v.p., sec., gen. counsel Amfac, Inc., Honolulu, 1970-78; sr. v.p., gen. counsel Amfac, Inc., San Francisco, 1978-87; v.p., gen. counsel Times Mirror, L.A., 1987—; Bd. dirs. L.A. Oncologic Inst.; bd. regents Loyola Marymount U., Chaminade U. (hon.). Served to capt. USAF, 1961-64. Mem. ABA (com. corp. law depts.), Sigma Rho, Phi Delta Phi. Clubs: The Family Club (San Francisco), St. Francis Yacht (San Francisco); 1925 F Street (Washington), The California (L.A.). Office: Times Mirror Times Mirror Sq Los Angeles CA 90053

CURRY, JAMES TRUEMAN, JR., mining company executive; b. Nevada City, Calif., June 12, 1936; s. James Trueman and Nancy (Sherwin) C.; m. Barbara Hartman, June 21, 1958; children—James Trueman, Jennifer, Steven John. B.S. in Civil Engring, U. Calif. at Berkeley, 1959; M.B.A., Stanford, 1962. With Utah Internat. Inc., San Francisco, 1962-87; adminstrv. asst. to pres. Utah Internat. Inc., 1962-65; asst. to mgr. Navajo (N.Mex.) Mine, 1965-66, adminstrv. mgr., 1966-68; adminstrv. mgr. Australian operations Utah Devel. Co., subsidiary, 1969-70; treas. Utah Internat. Inc., 1970-72, v.p., treas., 1972-75, fin. v.p., 1975-82; pres., mng. dir. Utah Devel. Co. subs., 1982-85, exec. v.p., 1985-87, also bd. dirs.; chief exec. officer minerals group Broken Hill Pty. Ltd.ernat., Melbourne and San Francisco, 1987—; also bd. dirs. BHP-Utah Minerals Internat. Served with AUS, 1959-60. Clubs: Burlingame Country, Pauma Valley Country, Bohemian, Pacific Union, Meblourne, Australian. Office: BHP-Utah Internat Inc 550 California St San Francisco CA 94104

CURRY, KELLY EDWIN, finance executive; b. Owensboro, Ky., Jan. 19, 1955; s. Martha (Fogle) C.; m. Susan Marie Miller, July 23, 1977; 1 child, Natalie Marie. BS, U. Ky., 1977. CPA, Ky. Sr. auditor Touche Ross & Co. CPA's, Louisville, 1977-79, Humana Inc., Louisville, 1979-82; dir. internal audit H.M.A. Inc., Naples, Fla.; dir. reimbursement H.M.A. Inc., Naples, 1983-84, hosp. ops. cons., 1984-85, v.p. fin. ops., 1985-87, sr. v.p. fin., chief fin. officer, 1987—. Mem. Ky. Soc. CPAs, Fla. Soc. CPAs, Am. Inst. CPAs. Republican. Baptist. Office: HMA Inc 800 Laurel Oak Dr Ste 500 Naples FL 33963

CURRY, MARY ANN KEMPER, data processing executive, bookstore manager; b. Spring Grove, Pa.; d. Ralph Leroy and Mabel Ann (Moul) Kemper; m. Thomas F. Curry, July 2, 1949; children: Bostick, Thomas Lee, Ruth Ann, David, Laurie, Clinton. BA in Edn., Pa. State U., 1948; postgrad. in acctg. and fin., Syracuse U. Sch. Bus., 1963-65. Secondary sch. tchr. Mechanicsburg, Pa., 1948-50; sec., treas. CML, Inc., Syracuse, N.Y., 1963-65; libr. asst. Va. Poly. Inst. and State U., Reston, Va., 1973-74; adminstrv. asst. to v.p. Applied Rsch. Lab. div. of M/S, Inc., Vienna, Va., 1974-75; mgr., acct. coll. textbook store Va. Tech., U. Va., Falls Church, Va., 1976—; sec., treas. C-Systems, Inc., Oakton, Va., 1975—. Vol. area pub. schs.; pres., treas. local PTA; active local Girl Scouts U.S. Mem. AAUW (charter, past pres. McLean br., chairperson fed. legis. program 1976-78; Fellowship awards 1971, 85), No. Va. Coord. Gt. Books Program, Leadership Tng. Program, Bus. and Profl. Women's Club (fellowship chairperson), Va. Coll. Stores Assn. (scholarship chair nomination com.), Nat. Assn. Coll. Stores, DAR, LWV, Pi Lambda Theta (life), Phi Delta Kappa, (charter; past rec. sec., past historian, awards com. chairperson, chpt. Mem. of Yr. award 1986), Delta Zeta (life). Club: Hunter Mill Swim & Racquet (Vienna). Office: C-Systems Inc PO Box 310 Oakton VA 22124

CURTIN, GENE LAWRENCE, retailing executive; b. Glen Rock, N.J., Mar. 17, 1948; s. Gene Lawrence and Barbara Anne Boland C. BA in Math., Iona Coll., 1970; MBA, Pepperdine U., 1981. Systems analyst Port Authority of N.Y. and N.J., N.Y.C., 1970-72; mgr. stores systems JC Penney Co., Inc., N.Y.C., 1972-80; mgr. retail systems Levi Strauss & Co., Inc., San Francisco, 1980-84; dir. merchandising systems Montgomery Ward, Chgo., 1984—. Mem. steering com. Council on Fgn. Relations, San Francisco, 1983-84. Mem. Chgo. Retail Exec. Assn., Chgo. Council on Fgn. Relations, Nat. Retail Mcht. Assn. Democrat. Roman Catholic. Office: Montgomery Ward 535 W Chicago Ave Chicago IL 60671

CURTIS, ALBERT BRADLEY, II, financial planner, tax specialist; b. Oklahoma City, Dec. 17, 1957; s. William Clyde Jr. and Ava Rene (Sewell) C.; m. Linda Lee Ford, May 29, 1982; children: A. Bradley III, Patrick Troy. BS in Bus., Oklahoma City U., 1981. CPA, Okla. Cost acct. Macklangurg-Duncan Corp., Oklahoma City, 1976-81; sr. auditor, tax acct. Ephraim, Sureck & Miller, CPA's, Oklahoma City, 1981-83; tax mgr., mem. joint com. Ward Petroleum Corp. & Associated Entities, Enid, Okla., 1983—. Fundraiser profl. div. United Way, Oklahoma City, 1981-83, 86-88; registrar Enid Voter Registration Campaign, 1986. Mem. AICPA, Okla. Soc. CPA's. Home: 126 S Burdel Ln Enid OK 73703 Office: Ward Petroleum Corp 502 S Fillmore Enid OK 73703

CURTIS, CORY ROMNEY, sales executive; b. Salt Lake City, July 13, 1953; s. Marvin Raine and Carrol (Romney) C.; m. Arwella Pierce, June 1, 1978; children: Shane Mathew, Jordan Romney, Tres Alexander, Brin Celeste. Student, Ricks Coll., Rexburg, Idaho, 1972-73, U. Utah, 1975-76. Sales exec. Medirec, Salt Lake City, 1979-81; mktg. dir., mgr. Wasatch Med. Supply, Salt Lake City, 1981-84; sales exec. Am. Expresss, Salt Lake City, 1984-85, Discover Card Svcs., Salt Lake City, 1985—; prin., pres. Telecash, Inc., Salt Lake City, 1986-87. Mem. Nat. Panel of Consumer Arbitrators (arbitrator 1987—), Better Bus. Bur. (arbitrator 1987—). Mormon. Home and Office: Discover Card Svcs 4284 Albright Dr Salt Lake City UT 84124

CURTIS, DAVID WAYNE, art director, design consultant; b. Lincoln, Nebr., Dec. 25, 1960; s. Marion Thomas Curtis and Earline Esther (Loper) Oma. BA in Environ. Design, N.C. State U., 1983. Founder, exec. art dir. D.C. Designs, Raleigh, N.C., 1983—; lectr. N.C. State U. Sch. Design, Raleigh, 1984—, Meredith Coll., 1987, Enloe High Sch., Raleigh, 1987. Mem. Indsl. Design Soc. Am. Democrat. Baptist. Office: DC Designs 5519 Alderbrook Ct Ste 208 Rockville MD 20851

CURTIS, GREGORY DYER, investment and philanthropic company executive; b. Mechanicsburg, Ohio, Jan. 14, 1947; s. Vernon L. and Jean (Dyer) C.; m. Lynne Everett, June 29, 1968; children: Sarah E., Alice D. AB cum laude, Dartmouth Coll., 1969; JD cum laude, Harvard U., 1974. Bar: Pa. 1974, U.S. Dist. Ct. (we. dist.) Pa. 1974. Assoc. Reed, Smith, Shaw & McClay, Pitts., 1974-79; counsel Roldiva, Inc., Pitts., 1979-81, v.p., bd. dirs., 1981-83; fin. adv. C.S. May Family Interests, Pitts., 1983—; pres. Laurel Found., Pitts., 1983—; pres., bd. govs. Laurel Assets Group, Pitts., 1983—; pres. C.S. May Assocs., Pitts., 1983—; bd. dirs. Clark Techs., Inc., Boulder, Enrecon, Inc., Golden, Colo., L.C. Holdings, Inc., Boulder, Phoenix Technologies, Inc., Denver, Water Resources Am., Tulsa, Western Water Reserves, Inc., Boulder, Sewickley Heights Estates, Inc., Pitts., Tenir, Inc., Pitts., Winding River Properties, Inc., St. George, Utah. Mem. legal com. ACLU, Pitts., 1974-78; bd. dirs. Neighborhood Legal Svcs. Assn., Pitts., 1976-79, The Ellis Sch., 1987—; bd. dirs. Grantmakers Western Pa., Pitts., 1986—, pres. 1989. Sgt. U.S. Army, 1970-72. Mem. ABA, Allegheny County Bar Assn., Duquesne Club (Pitts.), Rolling Rock Club (Ligonier). Home: No 8 Dunmoyle Pl Pittsburgh PA 15217 Office: Laurel Found 3 Gateway Ctr-6 N Pittsburgh PA 15222

CURTIS, JAMES THEODORE, lawyer; b. Lowell, Mass., July 8, 1923; s. Theodore D. and Maria (Souliotis) Koutras; B.A., U. Mich., 1948; J.D., Harvard, 1951; Sc.D. (hon.), U. Lowell, 1972; m. Kleanthe D. Dusopol June 25, 1950; children: Madelon Mary, Theodore James, Stephanie Diane, Gregory Theodosius, James Theodore. Admitted to Mass. State bar, 1951; asso. Adams & Blinn, Boston, 1951-52; legal asst., asst. atty. gen. Mass., 1952-53; pvt. practice law, Lowell, 1953-57; sr. partner firm Goldman & Curtis, and predecessors, Lowell and Boston, 1957—. Chmn. Lowell and Greater Lowell Heart Fund, 1967-68; mem. adv. bd. Salvation Army, sec., 1956-58; mem. Bd. Higher Edn. Mass., 1967-72; mem. Lowell Charter Commn., 1969-71; del. Democratic Party State Convs., 1956-60; trustee U. Lowell, 1963-72, chmn. bd., 1968-72; bd. dirs. U. Lowell Research Found., 1965-72, Merrimack Valley Health Planning Council, 1969-72. Served with AUS, 1943-46. Decorated Knight Order Orthodox Crusade Holy Sepulcher. Mem. Am., Mass., Middlesex County, Lowell bar assns., Am., Mass. trial lawyers assns., Mass. Acad. Trial Lawyers, Am. Judicature Soc., Harvard Law Sch., U. Mich. alumni assns., Lowell Hist. Soc., DAV, Delta Epsilon Pi. Democrat. Greek Orthodox. Clubs: Masons, Harvard of Lowell (pres. 1969-71, dir.). Home: 111 Rivercliff Rd Lowell MA 01852 Office: 144 Merrimack St Lowell MA 01852

CURTIS, JO DEE, accountant; b. Washington, Ind., Apr. 5, 1964; d. Matthew Leo and Carolyn (Thompson) Arvin; m. Kenneth Mathew Curtis, May 25, 1986. BS, U. Evansville, 1985. CPA, Ind. Acct. George S. Olive & Co., Evansville, 1985—. Vol. United Way. Mem. AICPA, Ind. CPA Soc., Chi Omega. Republican. Roman Catholic. Office: George S Olive & Co PO Box 628 14 NW Third St Evansville IN 47704

CURTIS, LISA BECKETT, publisher; b. Greeley, Colo., Mar. 21, 1960; d. Arnold Raymond and Karen Denise (Wetig) Napoleon; m. John William Curtis, Sept. 21, 1985. BSBA summa cum laude, Ariz. State U., 1983. Assoc. account exec. DBG&H Mktg., Advt., Phoenix, 1983-84; advt. rep. Ind. Newspapers, Inc., Phoenix, 1984-85, advt. mgr., 1985-86, mktg. dir., 1986-88, publ., gen. mgr., 1988—. Mem. Phoenix Advt. Club (bd. dirs. 1988—), Scottsdale C. of C., Paradise Valley C. of C. (bd. dirs. 1989—). Republican. Office: Ind Newspapers Inc 11000 N Scottsdale Rd Ste 210 Scottsdale AZ 85254

CURTIS, LUTHER CULLENS, lawyer; b. Atlanta, Sept. 7, 1946; s. Edward Alton and Corinne (Cullens) C.; m. Kathleen Blair Moore, Aug. 9, 1969; children: Karen Alice, Cullen Edward. BA, Furman U., 1968; JD, U. Ga., 1971. Bar: Ga. 1972. Assoc. Kelly, Champion, Denney & Pease, Columbus, Ga., 1971-73; ptnr. Cofer, Beauchamp & Hawes, Atlanta, 1973-85, Glass, McCullough, Sherrill & Harrold, Atlanta, 1985—. Active Downtown YMCA, Atlanta. Capt. USAR, 1971-73. Mem. Lawyers Club of Atlanta. Methodist. Club: Cherokee Country. Home: 2781 Atwood Rd NE Atlanta GA 30305 Office: Glass McCullough Sherrill & Harrold 1409 Peachtree St NE Atlanta GA 30309

CURTIS, NEVIUS MINOT, utility executive; b. Holyoke, Mass., Aug. 16, 1929; s. Frederick A. and Janet H. (Nevius) C.; m. Muriel Acheson, Nov. 9, 1957; children: Jeffrey, Janet. B.A. in Econs. cum laude, Haverford (Pa.) Coll., 1951; M.B.A. in Fin., Stanford U., 1956. With acctg. dept. Calif.-Oreg. Power Co., Medford, Oreg., 1956-58; asst. to pres. Holyoke Water Power Co., 1958-65; asst. to comptroller Central Maine Power Co., Augusta, 1965-67; from asst. comptroller to sr. v.p. fin., dir. Central Maine Power, 1967-77; v.p. Detroit Edison Co., 1977-78; sr. v.p. fin. Delmarva Power & Light Co., Wilmington, Del., 1978-79, pres., 1979—, chief operating officer, 1979-80, chief exec. officer, 1980-83, chmn. bd., chief exec. officer, 1984—; dep. chmn. bd. Fed. Res. Bank Phila.; pres. Wilmington Econ. Devel. Corp. Served with USNR, 1952-55. Mem. Phi Beta Kappa. Home: PO Box 953 Wilmington DE 19899 Office: Delmarva Power & Light Co 800 King St PO Box 231 Wilmington DE 19899 *

CURTIS, ROBERT JOSEPH, financial advisor; b. Trenton, N.J., Aug. 30, 1945; s. Robert and Eleanor (Schannen) C; m. Susan Stone, July 29, 1978; 1 child, Terresa Lorraine. BBA, U. Miami, Coral Gables, Fla., 1970; MBA, U. Pa., 1971. Sr. acct., cons. Peat, Marwick, Main Co., Trenton, 1971-74; treas., chief fin. officer Crest Ultrasonics, Inc., Trenton, 1974-76; v.p., chief fin. officer Winterset, Inc., Princeton, N.J., 1976-77; mgr. valuation svcs. Am. Valuation Cons. Inc., Des Plaines, Ill., 1977-81; dir. valuation svcs. Arthur D. Little Valuation, Inc., Woodland Hills, Calif., 1981-84, v.p., 1984—. Bd. dirs. Mercer St. Friends, Trenton, 1974. Bache & Co. scholar, 1970. Mem. Am. Inst. CPA's, N.J. Soc. CPA's, Nat. Acctg. Assn., Inst. Mgmt. Accts., Am. Acctg. Assn., Inst. Bus. Appraisers. Republican. Mem. Christian Ch. Home: 21 Ivanhoe Dr Robbinsville NJ 08691 Office: Arthur D Little Valuation Inc 399 Thornall St 3d Floor Edison NJ 08837

CURTISS, GREGORY ALAN, financial executive, consultant; b. Renton, Wash., Nov. 25, 1954; s. Howard Adams and Eva Mae (Sandquist) C. BS in Acctg., Fin., U. Colo., 1976, JD, 1984. Bar: Colo. 1984; CPA, Colo. Treas. Willard Owens Assoc. Inc., Wheat Ridge, Colo., 1978-83; pres. Curtiss Simmons Capital Resources, Inc., Englewood, Colo., 1984—, Funding Research, Inc., Englewood, Colo., 1985—, Caspian Ventures, Inc., Englewood, 1986; bd. dirs. Rockies Venture Club, Denver. Author: Venture Capital In Colorado: 1987, 1987. Republican. Office: Curtiss Simmons Capital Resources Inc 8101 E Prentice Ave Ste 602 Englewood CO 80111

CURTISS, JEFFREY EUGENE, recreational products company executive; b. Plainview, Nebr., Aug. 23, 1948; s. Eugene Herbert and Jan Beverly (Jeffrey) C.; m. Margaret Mary Karpowicz, Apr. 10, 1976; children: Anthony, Gene. BSBA, U. Nebr., 1970, JD, 1971; LLM in Taxation, Washington U., St. Louis, 1975. Bar: Nebr. 1972, Colo. 1973, Mo. 1973, Ill. 1981; CPA, Colo., Ill.; lic. real estate broker, Ill. Acct. Peat, Marwick & Mitchell, Denver, 1970-71; assoc. Nelson & Harding, Lincoln, Nebr., 1971-73; mgr. tax, treasury Monsanto Co., St. Louis, 1973-79; various positions including v.p. fin. G.D. Searle & Co., Skokie, Ill., 1979-88; sr. v.p., chief fin. officer, treas. The Coleman Co., Inc., Wichita, Kans., 1988—. Pres. bd. advisors Countryside Montessori Schs., Northbrook, Ill., 1985-87; sec. coun. Boy Scout Am.; bd. dirs. United Way Wichita. Mem. Fin. Execs. Inst., Econs. Club of Chgo. Club: Econs. (Chgo.). Home: 1601 Gatewood Wichita KS 67206 Office: Coleman Co Inc 250 N St Francis Ave Wichita KS 67202

CURTISS, TRUMBULL CARY, banker; b. Buffalo, May 30, 1940; s. Colman and Frances Rochester (Wheeler) C.; m. Leslie Fisher, July 18, 1964; children: Cullen, Meredith, Emily. BA in Am. Studies, Yale U., 1963; PMD, Harvard Bus. Sch., 1982. Dir. advt. Mfrs. and Traders Trust, Buffalo, 1963-68; asst. v.p. First Wis. Nat. Bank, Madison, 1968-69; v.p. Bank of Commonwealth, Detroit, 1969-70, BayBank Middlesex, Waltham, Mass., 1970-75; v.p. BayBanks, Inc., Boston, 1975-79, sr. v.p. mktg., 1979-80; pres, chief exec. officer BayBank Merrimack Valley N.A., Andover, Mass., 1980-85, BayBank Norfolk, Dedham, Mass., 1986—. Trustee Bradford (Mass.) Coll., 1980—. Served with USMCR, 1959-60. Clubs: Weston (Mass.) Golf, North Andover (Mass.) Country. Home: 54 Hundreds Rd Wellesley MA 02181 Office: BayBank Norfolk 858 Washington St Dedham MA 02026

CURZIO, FRANCIS XAVIER, finance company executive; b. N.Y.C., Feb. 19, 1944; s. Frank Americana and Rose (Pascale) C.; m. Jean Evelyn Darling, May 28, 1965; children: Christine, Nicholas, Francis II. AAS, N.Y. City Coll., 1972; postgrad., Pace U., Long Island U., Computer Programming Inst. Supr. of accts. Lone Star Ins., N.Y.C., 1970-72; pres., chmn., chief exec. officer FXC Investors Corp., Queens, N.Y., 1974—. Cited by the Wall St. Jour. and Wash. Post for accurately predicting the 1987 Stock Mkt. Crash. Catholic. Home: 65-09 68th Ave Queens NY 11385 Office: FXC Investors Corp 62-19 Cooper Ave Glendale Queens NY 11385

CUSANO, CARRIE MARIE, corporate professional; b. N.Y.C., Aug. 28, 1924; d. Carmine and Marie Josephine (Scrocca) Falcone; m. Angelo Andy Cusano, June 30, 1947 (dec. 1966); children: Frank Allen, Robert Paul. Student, Whitney Secretarial Sch., 1942-43, So. Conn. State U., 1969, 72, Quinnipiac Coll., 1975. With So. Conn. State U., New Haven, 1967—, purchasing asst., 1977-82, purchasing agt., 1982—. Past pres. so. chpt. Trinity, St. Rita's Rosary Soc., also historian, dist. deputy; active Mentally Retarded and Hospice charity. Mem. Conn. Assn. Purchasing Mgmt., Nat. Assn. Purchasing Mgmt., So. Conn. State U. Alumni Assn., Parents Without Ptnrs. (past pres. New Haven chpt.), Cath. Coun. Women, Fr. Kavanaugh Columbiettes (pres.). Home: 249 Circular Ave Hamden CT 06514 Office: So Conn State U 501 Crescent St New Haven CT 06515

CUSHING, DAVID ALBERT, II, landscape architect; b. Bucks County, Pa., July 10, 1960; s. Thomas Cushing and Deloreos Jeanette (Young) Cushing Wolfskiel; m. Gail Irene Adams; 1 child, Matthew Kristopher. A. in Landscape Constrn., Catawba Valley Community Coll., Hickory, N.C., 1981. Registered landscape architect, Va., S.C. Designer Kelley Green Garden Ctr., Gastonia, N.C., 1981; foreman Charter Oak Farms, Charlotte, N.C., 1981-82; landscape architect Jordan Design Collaborative, Charlotte, N.C., 1982. Dan Boone scholar, 1981. Mem. Am. Soc. Landscape Architects (publs. com. chmn. 1986-88), Exec. Assn. Greater Charlotte, YMCA. Office: Jordan Design Collaborative 127 Brevard Ct Charlotte NC 28202

CUSHING, STEVEN, computer science educator, consultant; b. Brookline, Mass., June 25, 1948; s. Alfred Edward and Evelyn (Kaufman) C. SB, MIT, 1970; MA, UCLA, 1972, PhD, 1976. Research asst. MIT, 1967-70, UCLA, 1973-74; instr. U. Mass., Boston, 1974-75; Roxbury Community Coll., Boston, 1975-77; research staff Higher Order Software Inc., Cambridge, Mass., 1976-82; research assoc. Rockefeller U., N.Y.C., 1979; lectr. Northeastern U., Boston, 1983-86; master lectr. Boston U., 1986—; research fellow NASA-Ames Research Ctr., Moffet Field, Calif., 1987-88, Stanford U., Palo Alto, Calif., 1987-88; asst. prof St. Anselm Coll., Manchester, N.H., 1983-85, Stonehill Coll., North Easton, Mass., 1985—; mem. bd. editorial commentators The Behavioral and Brain Scis., 1978—; chmn. software design Internat. Conf. System Scis., Honolulu, 1978; participant workshops. Author: Quantifier Meanings: A Study in the Dimensions of Semantic Competence, 1982; contbr. articles to profl. jours. Mem. nat. exec. council Nat. Ethical Youth Orgn., 1965-66; violist Brockton (Mass.) Symphony Orch. Recipient New Eng. Regional award Future Scientists of Am., 1965; NSF grantee, 1965, 70-71, NIMH grantee, 1970-71, NDEA grantee, 1970-73; Woodrow Wilson Found. fellow, 1970-71, NASA Summer Faculty fellow, 1987-88; research affiliate MIT, 1978-79; Boston U., 1986-88. Mem. AAAS, N.Y. Acad. Scis., Linguistic Soc. Am., Assn. Symbolic Logic, Assn. Computing Machinery, Am. Math. Soc., Am. Assn. for Applied Linguistics, Internat. Council Psychologists (profl. affiliate), Assn. for Computers and Humanities, Cognitive Sci. Soc., Math. Assn. Am., Assn. Computational Linguistics, Internat. Pragmatics Assn. Home: 90 Bynner St #4 Jamaica Plain MA 02130 Office: Stonehill Coll Dept Math and Computer Sci North Easton MA 02357

CUSHMAN, AARON D., public relations executive; b. Chgo., Aug. 29, 1924; s. Harry A. and Eva (Sternberg) C.; m. Doris Silverman, Mar. 8, 1948; children: Gary, Amy, Pamela. B.A., U. Ill., 1947. Publicity dir. Chgo. Lake Front Fair, 1950; pres. Aaron D. Cushman & Assos., Inc., Chgo., 1952—; mem. bus. adv. counsel LWV; bd. dirs. Chgo. White Sox. Mem. Adv. Council Kendall Coll.; mem. pub. relations com. Crusade of Mercy, Boy Scouts Am.; bd. dirs. Easter Seal Found., Columbia Coll., Am. Sch. of Needlecraft; v.p. bd. dirs. Variety Club of Ill. Served with USAF, 1943-45, 50-52. Mem. Pub. Relations Soc. Am. (past pres. counsellors sect. Chgo. chpt., Silver Anvil award), Am. Coll. Radio Arts, Crafts and Scis. (regent), Welfare Pub. Relations Forum, Assn. Pub. Relations Round Table, Indsl. Editors Soc. (v.p.), Am. Acad. TV Arts, Crafts and Scis., Nat. Sci. Writers Assn., Nat. Assn. Real Estate Editors, Soc. Am. Travel Writers, Publicity Club of Chgo. (past. pres.), Execs. Club, Green Acres Country Club (dir.). Jewish. Clubs: Green Acres Country (dir., v.p.), Chgo. Publicity (past pres.). Office: Aaron D Cushman & Assocs Inc 35 E Wacker Dr Chicago IL 60601

CUSTER, FELIPE ANTONIO, corporate professional; b. Lima, Peru, May 27, 1954; came to U.S., 1985; s. Jacques Richard and Julia Caroline (Hallett) C.; m. Isabel Edwards, Dec. 29, 1979; children: Felipe, Isabel Carolina, Malu. BA cum laude, Harvard U., 1976, MBA, 1979. Asst. mgr. Envases Comerciales, SA, San Jose, Costa Rica, 1979-80; mgr. planning and devel. Derivados del Maiz, Lima, 1980; nat. sales mgr. Famesa, Lima, 1980-82; gen. mgr. Arco, SA Camisas Arrow, Lima, 1983-84; pres. Swiss Am. Enterprises, Inc., Miami, Fla., 1985—; v.p. Inversiones, Guayacan, Ecuador. Composer, lyricist: Elegy to R. Butler, The Feb. 5th Nightmare, 1976. Trustee Ctr. for Fine Arts, Miami, Fla. ESAN Sch. of Bus., Lima; founder, pres. Found. for Victims of Terrorism, Lima; dir. Civilian Police Support Group, Lima. Mem. Swiss-Peruvian C. of C., Coral Gables C. of C., Greater Miami C. of C., Ft. Pierce C. of C. Clubs: Nacional (Lima), Lima Golf, Paracas (Peru) Yacht, Riviera Country (Miami), Harvard (N.Y.C.), The Owl (Cambridge, Mass.), LeCercle Foch (Paris), The Wine Soc. (N.Y.), Antique Collectors (Eng.). Office: Swiss Am Enterprises 2655 LeJeune Rd Ste 611 Coral Gables FL 33134

CUTCHINS, CLIFFORD ARMSTRONG, III, banker; b. Southampton County, Va., July 12, 1923; s. Clifford Armstrong Jr. and Sarah (Vaughan) C.; m. Ann Woods, June 21, 1947; children: Clifford Armstrong IV, William Witherspoon, Cecil Vaughan. B.S. in Bus. Adminstrn, Va. Poly. Inst. and State U., 1947; grad., Stonier Grad. Sch. Banking, 1953. From asst. cashier to pres., dir. Vaughan & Co., bankers, Franklin, Va., 1950-62; pres., cashier dir. Tidewater Bank & Trust Co., Franklin, 1962-63; (bank merged with Va. Nat. Bank), Norfolk, 1963; sr. v.p., dir., exec. v.p. (bank merged with Va. Nat. Bank), 1965-69, pres., 1969-80, chmn. bd., chief exec. officer, dir., 1980-83; chmn. bd., chief exec. officer, dir. Sovran Bank, N.A., Norfolk, 1983-86, Sovran Fin. Corp., Norfolk, 1983—; pres., dir. Va. Nat. Bankshares, Inc., 1972-80, chmn. bd., chief exec. officer, dir., 1980-83; dir. Franklin Equipment Co., Pulaski Furniture Corp. Bd. dirs. Camp Found., Franklin, 1962—; bd. dirs., trustee Sentra Health System; trustee Va. Found. Ind. Colls.; bd. visitors Va. Poly. Inst. and State U. Served to capt. AUS, World War II, PTO. Mem. Assn. Bank Holding Cos. (bd. dirs.), Assn. Reserve City Bankers (bd. dirs.). Baptist. Clubs: Commonwealth (Richmond); Norfolk Yacht and Country, Virginia, Harbor, Town Point (Norfolk); Princess Anne

Country (Virginia Beach, Va.); Cypress Cove Country (Franklin, Va.). Home: 7320 Glenroie Ave Norfolk VA 23505 Office: Sovran Fin Corp 1 Commercial Pl Norfolk VA 23510

CUTHBERT, WILLIAM R., consumer goods manufacturing company executive; b. Ogdensburg, N.Y., 1919. Student, Kenyon Coll. With Newell Co., Freeport, Ill., 1962—, chmn. bd. dirs., 1976—. With USAF, 1943-46. Office: Newell Co 29 E Stephenson St Freeport IL 61032 *

CUTHBERTSON, RICHARD WILEY, advertising company executive; b. Warren, Pa., Oct. 21, 1935; s. James and Virginia C.; m. Margaret Ann Samson, Aug. 1962; children: James, Jane, Craig. B.S., Rider Coll., 1961. C.P.A., N.Y., Ill. Mgr. audit and tax depts. Arthur Andersen & Co., N.Y.C., Tokyo, 1961-75; controller Foote, Cone & Belding, Chgo., 1975-80; exec. v.p. FCB Internat. Inc., Chgo., 1980—. Served to sgt. USMC, 1953-57, Korea, Japan. Mem. Am. Inst. C.P.A.'s, Fin. Execs. Inst., Tau Kappa Epsilon (pres. 1960-61). Roman Catholic. Club: Adventurers (Chgo.). Home: 83 Eaton Terrrace, London SW1, England Office: FCB Europe, 82 Baker St, London W1M 2AE, England *

CUTILLETTA, THOMAS PAUL, paper company executive; b. Chgo., July 5, 1943; s. Santo and Benedetta (Falzone) C.; m. Bernadine Paluch, Apr. 16, 1966; children—Sheryl, Laura, Jennifer. BS in Acctg., U. Ill., 1965; MBA, Northwestern U., 1966. CPA, Ill. Fin. analyst Amoco Corp., Chgo., 1966-70, supr. div. level, 1970-72, supr. corp. level, 1973-74; dir. profl. planning Norlin Industries-Gibson Div., Lincolnwood, Ill., 1974-75, v.p. and controller, 1975-80; corp. controller Stone Container Corp., Chgo., 1980-83, v.p., corp. controller, 1984—. Mem. bus. adv. council Walter E. Heller Coll. Bus. Adminstrn., Roosevelt U., Chgo., 1986—. Tuition scholar Northwestern U., 1966. Mem. AICPA, Fin. Execs. Inst., Rotary Club Chgo. Club: Plaza (Chgo.). Office: Stone Container Corp 150 N Michigan Ave Chicago IL 60601

CUTLER, ALEXANDER MACDONALD, manufacturing company executive; b. Milw., May 28, 1951; s. Richard Woolsey and Elizabeth (Fitzgerald) C.; m. Sarah Lynn Stark, Oct. 11, 1980; children: David Alexander, William MacDonald. BA, Yale U., 1973; MBA, Dartmouth Coll., 1975. Fin. analyst Cutler-Hammer, Milw., 1975-77, bus. group controller, 1977-79; controller custom distbn. and control div. Eaton Corp., Atlanta, 1979-80, plant mgr. custom distbn. and control div., 1981-82, mgr. custom distbn. and control div., 1982-83; mgr. power distbn. div. Eaton Corp., Milw., 1984-85, gen. mgr. indsl. control and power distbn., 1985-86; pres. controls group Eaton Corp., Cleve., 1986—. Class agt. alumni fund Loomis Chaffee Sch., Windsor, Conn., 1969—; bd. dirs. alumni fund Yale U., New Haven, 1974—; v.p. bd. trustees The Cleve. Play House, 1987—; bd. trustees Great Lakes Mus. Inc. Mem. Nat. Electrical Mfrs. Assn. (bd. govs. 1987—, indsl. automation div. 1986—). Club: Chagrin Valley Hunt (Gates Mills, Ohio). Office: Eaton Corp 1111 Superior Ave Eaton Ctr Cleveland OH 44114

CUTLER, ARNOLD R., lawyer; b. New Haven, Mar. 20, 1908; s. Max Nathan and Kate (Harder) C.; m. Hazel Lourie, Apr. 8, 1942; 1 son, David. B.A., Yale U., 1930, J.D., 1932; LLD, Brandeis U., 1984. Bar: Conn. 1932, Mass. 1946. Mem. staff Office Gen. Counsel Pub. Works Adminstrn., Washington, 1933-36; chief counsel Pub. Works Adminstrn., Wash., 1937-38; spl. asst. to chief counsel IRS, 1939-42, trial counsel New Eng. div., 1945-47; ptnr. Lourie & Cutler, Boston, 1947—; lectr. on taxation. Contbr. to books articles to legal jours. Trustee Beth Israel Hosp.; trustee emeritus Brandeis U.; trustee, past mem. exec. com. Combined Jewish Philanthropies Greater Boston; past. bd. dirs. Nat. Jewish Welfare Bd.; past pres. Brookline, Brighton and Newton Jewish Community Ctr.; past. treas. Associated Jewish Community Ctrs. of Greater Boston; past chmn. bd. Yale Law Sch. Fund; chmn. bequest com. Yale Law Sch. Lt. comdr. USCG, 1942-45. Fellow Am. Coll. Tax Counsel, Mass. Bar Found.; mem. ABA (com. on govt. submissions 1987—, past chmn. spl. adv. exempt orgns. com. tax sect.), Mass. Bar Assn., Boston Bar Assn. (past chmn. fed. tax com., past mem. council), Am. Law Inst. Clubs: New Century (past pres.), Greater Boston Brandeis (past pres.), Yale, Harvard, Wightman Tennis, Rotary (past bd. dirs.). Office: Lourie & Cutler 60 State St Boston MA 02109

CUTLER, FRANK CHARLES, accountant; b. Hart, Mich., Aug. 19, 1949; s. Douglas Richard and Pauline Hope (Ferry) C.; m. Terrell Kaye Haycook, Aug. 7, 1971; children: Douglas Charles, David John, Sara Ann. BBA magna cum laude, Cen. Mich. U., 1971. CPA, Mich, Colo., Wyo. Staff acct. Arthur Andersen & Co., Detroit, 1971-72, Washington, 1973-74; sr. staff acct. Arthur Andersen & Co., Milan, 1974-77; audit mgr. Arthur Andersen & Co., Grand Rapids, Mich., 1977-81; audit mgr. Arthur Andersen & Co., Denver, 1981-84, ptnr., 1984—. Active in Boy Scouts Am., Englewood, Colo. Mem. Assn. for Corp. Growth, Am. Inst. CPA's, Colo. Soc. CPA's, Phi Eta Sigma, Omicron Delta Epsilon, Phi Kappa Phi. Club: Denver Athletic. Office: Arthur Andersen and Co 717 17th St Suite 1900 Denver CO 80202

CUTLER, NORMAN BARRY, funeral service executive; b. Chgo., Mar. 5, 1942; s. Jerome and Hannah (Feinberg) C.; m. Gail Weinstein, June 30, 1965; children: Brett, Rebecca. BSBA, Northwestern U., 1964, MBA, 1965. Mgmt. trainee First Nat. Bank of Chgo., 1965-66; with Weinstein Bros., Inc., Wilmette, Ill., 1966—, pres., 1972—; pres. Levitt-Weinstein, Inc., North Miami Beach, Fla., 1979—; exec. v.p. Beth David Meml. Gardens, Hollywood, Fla., 1985—; gen. ptnr. Wilmette Computer Assocs., Dixie Ptnrs., N.M.B. Assocs.; faculty Worsham Coll., Skokie, Ill., 1981-82. Bd. dirs. North Suburban Jewish Community Ctr., 1975—, also past pres.; gen. co-chmn. Channel 11 Pub. TV Auction, 1974-75; bd. govs., v.p., pres., 1986-88, Congregation Am Shalom, Glencoe, Ill. Mem. Jewish Funeral Dirs. Am. (pres. 1985-86, bd. govs.), Acad. Profl. Funeral Svc. Practice (pres. 1988-87), B'nai B'rith (v.p.). Office: 111 Skokie Blvd Wilmette IL 60091

CUTMORE, ROSS HERBERT JAMES, steel company executive; b. Peterborough, Ont., Can., July 24, 1929; s. George Herbert Cutmore and Ruby Agnes Young; m. Glenda Llewellyn Hewett, Sept. 2, 1956; children—Timothy, Jennifer, Rebecca, Murray, Rachel. B.A. in Bus. Adminstrn., U. Western Ont., London, Can., 1951. Chartered acct. Devel. acct. Algoma Steel Corp. Ltd., Sault Ste. Marie, Ont., Can., 1955-59, asst. to v.p. fin., 1959-66, comptroller, 1966-72, v.p. fin., 1972-77, v.p. acctg., 1977-83, v.p. fin. and acctg., 1983—. Pres. United Way, Sault Ste. Marie, 1983-84. Mem. Can. Inst. Chartered Accts., Am. Iron and Steel Inst. Anglican. Home: Anglican Church Rd, RR 2, Goulais River, ON Canada P0S 1E0

CUTRIE, SHERRI ANN, social services administrator; b. Trenton, N.J., June 21, 1948; d. Joseph Cutry and Ruth (Gonzalez) M. Adminstrv. supr. Dept. Human Svcs.-Adult Mentally Retarded, Trenton, 1970-80; owner, adminstr. Lic. Skill Devel. Home-Mentally Retarded, Trenton, 1981—; program cons. for homeless woman House of Ruth Shelters, Washington, 1985-86, asst. dir., 1986-87, interim exec. dir., 1987; v.p. Design Programming Assoc., Inc., Trenton, 1988—; cons. various local human svc. agencies, Trenton, 1981-85, Echo Elderly, Trenton, 1982, Opportunities for Older Ams., Washington, 1987, Dept. Devel. Disabilities (sponsorship recognition 1988), Trenton, 1980—; bd. dirs. D.P.A., Inc., Delaware, Trenton, 1988—. Mem. West Trenton Fire Co. Ladies Auxillary, 1969; vol. United Way, Trenton, 1982, Community Food Svc. to Elderly, Trenton, 1982-83. Mem. NAFE, N.J. Bd. Realtors, N.J. Mentally Retarded Assn. Democrat. Home and Office: 239 Chestnut Ave Trenton NJ 08609

CUTRONE, LEE DAVID, JR., banker; b. Fairmont, W.Va., May 19, 1947; s. Lee David and Beatrice Rose (Israel) C.; m. Patricia Ann Pasco, Nov. 26, 1969; children—Christopher Lee, Cameron Michael. BA, Fairmont State Coll., 1969; MPub and Internat. Affairs, U. Pitts., 1974. Internat. banking officer Citizens & So. Nat. Bank, Atlanta, 1974-77; asst. v.p. First Nat. Bank, Mpls., 1977-80; v.p., mgr. Pitts. Nat. Bank, 1980-83, sr. v.p., mgr. internat. banking div., 1983—; chmn. PNC Internat. Bank, 1983—; adv. bd. mem. Pvt. Export Funding Corp. Bd. trustees Pitts. Council Internat. Visitors; bd. dirs. Parent and Child Guidance Ctr., Pitts., 1985, Pitts.-Wuhan Friendship Com., Inc.; bd. visitors grad. sch. pub. and internat. affairs U. Pitts.; internat. bus. adv. bd. U. S.C. Served to capt. U.S. Army, 1971-74. Mem. Lending/Fin. div. Coun. Robert Morris Assocs., Bankers' Assn. Fgn. Trade (dir.), World Affairs Coun., Robert Morris Assn. Republican. Roman Catholic. Clubs: Duquesne, St. Clair Country (Pitts.). Avocations: skiing; reading; fishing. Office: Pitts Nat Bank 5th & Wood St Pittsburgh PA 15265

CUTRONE, LUIGI CUTRONE, chemist; b. Ielsi, Italy, May 18, 1950; s. Pasquale and Giovanna (Passarelli) C.; m. Maria Teresa Maiorano, Aug. 8, 1976; children: Giovanna, Pasquale, Annarita. BSc in Chemistry, Loyola Coll., Montreal, Can., 1974; MS in Organic Chemistry, McGill U., Montreal, Can., 1980. Research and devel. chemist M.F. Paints 1972, Laval, Que., Can., 1977-81; application devel. Tioxide Can. Inc., Tracy, Que., 1981-85; section. mgr. Tioxide UK Ltd, Stockton-on-Tees, Eng., 1985-87; tech. service mgr. Tioxide Italia, Scarlino, 1987—. Contbr. articles to profl. jours. Fellow Oil and Colour Assn.; mem. Fedn. Coating Soc. Roman Catholic. Office: Tioxide Italia SPA, Contrada Casone CP 113, 58022 Follonica Italy

CUTTING, MARY DOROTHEA, audio and audio-visual communications company executive; b. N.Y.C., Feb. 20, 1943; d. Elliotte Robinson and Mary Dorothea (Clarke) Little; m. James H. B. Cutting, July 18, 1964; children—Gwendolyn Louise, Laura Elizabeth. Student Whitman Coll., 1960-62; B.A. in English Lit., U. Wash., 1964. Tchr. English, Severna Park High Sch., Md., 1965-66; remedial reading substitute tchr. St. Patrick's Day Sch., Washington, 1976-77; v.p. mktg. The Cutting Corp., Washington, 1978—, also dir. Editor children's cassettes: Fisher-Price Toys Spellbinder Series, 1983 (Consumer Com. of Ams. for Democratic Action award for being one of nation's 6 best toys for under $5 1983). Vol. chmn., bd. dirs. Washington Assn. for TV and Children, 1977. Mem. Internat. Assn. Bus. Communicators, Jr. League Washington (bd. dirs. 1977). Republican. Episcopalian. Office: 4940 Hampden Ln Ste 300 Bethesda MD 20814

CUZZETTO, CHARLES EDWARD, accountant, educator; b. Tacoma, Wash., Nov. 1, 1954; s. Edward Ralph and Bernice Almira (Schmidt) C. AA, Tacoma Community Coll., 1975; BA in Acctg., U. Wash., 1977; MBA, City U., Bellevue, Wash., 1982. CPA, Wash.; cert. internal auditor. Auditor Chevron Corp., San Francisco, 1977-79, Union Oil Corp., Seattle, 1980-83; owner, operator Cuzzetto Enterprises Restaurant, Tacoma, 1981-83; auditor Alaska Airlines, Seattle, 1983-85; dir. auditing Tacoma Pub. Schs., 1985—; instr. bus. and acctg. City U., Bellevue, 1985—. Contbr. articles to profl. jours. Active Freighthouse Theatre, Tacoma, treas., 1984; hon. mem. Seattle Ind. Comedy Co-Op, 1983—; chmn. supervisory com. Ednl. Employees Credit Union, 1987—. Mem. Assn. Sch. Bus. Ofcls. (vice chmn. rsch. internal audit), Wash. Assn. Sch. Bus. Officials, Inst. Internal Auditors (Internat. Gold Medal 1986), Christopher Columbus Soc. (treas. 1983—). Home: 1123 North Whitman Tacoma WA 98406 Office: Tacoma Pub Schs PO Box 1357 Tacoma WA 98401

CUZZOLINA, MICHAEL JOSEPH, financial executive; b. Pitts., Nov. 4, 1945; s. Michael Joseph and Thelma Effie (Alleman) C.; m. Brenda Joyce Gise, July 24, 1965; children: Jason, Brian. BS in Acctg., Susquehanna U., 1967. Sr. auditor Arthur Andersen & Co., Phila., 1967-71; mgr. budget and cost acctg. Air Products & Chemicals Inc., Allentown, Pa., 1971-74; with UGI Corp., 1974—; dir. fin. planning UGI Corp., Valley Forge, Pa., asst. treas.; v.p. fin. UGI subs. AmeriGas Inc., Valley Forge, Pa.; treas. UGI Corp., Valley Forge, Pa., v.p. acctg. & fin. control. Elder Ch. of the Saviour, Wayne, Pa., 1988—. Mem. Am. Inst. CPA's, Pa. Inst. CPA's, Waynesborough Country Club. Republican. Home: 17 Raven Ln Kennett Square PA 19348 Office: UGI Corp Box 858 Valley Forge PA 19482

CYMBLER, MURRAY JOEL, corporate professional; b. Germany, July 20, 1948; came to U.S., 1949; s. Harry and Adele C.; m. Carol Horowitz, Nov. 23, 1972; children: Adam, Robyn. BA, Hunter Coll., 1970. Tchr. N.Y. Bd. Edn., Bronx, 1970-71; contract analyst The Equitable Life Assurance Soc., N.Y.C., 1972-86; chmn., chief exec. officer Astro-Stream Corp., Levittown, N.Y., 1986—. Inventor Orbi Sport-toy, 1985. Office: Astro-Stream Corp 3000 Hempstead Turnpike Ste 301 Levittown NY 11756

CYR, J. V. RAYMOND, telecommunications and management holding company executive; b. Montreal, Que., Can., Feb. 11, 1934; s. Armand and Yvonne (Lagace) C.; m. Marie Bourdon, Sept. 1, 1956; children: Helene, Paul Andre. Student, Ecole Poly.; BASc., U. Montreal, 1958; postgrad. studies in engring., Bell Labs., N.J., Nat. Def. Coll., 1972-73; LLD (hon.), Concordia U. With Bell Can., 1958—, engr., 1958-65; staff engr. Bell Can., Montreal, 1965-70; chief engr. Bell Can., Quebec City, 1970-73; v.p. ops. staff region Bell Can., Montreal, 1973-75, v.p., 1975; exec. v.p. Bell Can., Quebec, 1975-79, v.p. adminstrn., 1979-83; pres. Bell Can., Montreal, 1983-85, chmn., pres., chief exec. officer, 1985-87, chmn. bd., 1987-88; pres. BCE (formerly Bell Can. Enterprises), Montreal, 1987-88; pres., chief exec. officer BCE Inc. (formerly Bell Can. Enterprises), Montreal, 1988—, also bd. dirs.; bd. dirs. No. Telecom Ltd., Steinbergs Inc., Banque Nationale de Canada, Bell-No. Rsch. Ltd., Confederation Life Assurance Co. of Can., Dominion Textiles, Centre de development technologique de l'Ecole Polytechnique, TransCanada PipeLines, Quebecor Inc. Dir. Quebec Arthritis Soc.; chmn. Mus. Contemporary Art of Montreal; chmn. Centre Inst. for Tech., Montreal; assoc. gov. U. Montreal; vice-chmn. Jr. Achievement of Can. Decorated Officer Order of Can.; recipient Can. Engrs. Gold Medal award, 1987, Ordre du Merite des Diplomes, U. Montreal, 1988. Mem. C.D. Howe Inst. (Quebec com.), Ordre des Ingenieurs du Que., U. Montreal (bd. govs.), Can. C. of C., Internat. Bus. Coun. of Can., St. Denis Club, Mount Royal Club, St. James Club, Mt. Bruno Golf Club, Islemere Club. Roman Catholic. Office: BCE Inc, 2000 McGill College Ave, Ste 2100, Montreal, PQ Canada H3A 3H7 also: Bell Can, 1050 Beaver Hall Hill, Montreal, PQ Canada H2Z 1S4

CYR, LEO PAUL, JR., small business owner; b. Boyd, Wis., Nov. 1, 1928; s. Leo Paul and Neva May (Soper) C.; m. Audrey LaVone Gerrits, Apr. 24, 1954; children: Rodney, Daryl, Keith, Rene, Gordon, Jill, Kyle, Melanie, Michelle, Lee, Curtis, Philip, Jeffery. Grad. high sch., Boyd. Foreman Seaman Andwall Co., 1955-58; founder, pres. Cyrgus Co., Inc., Omaha, 1960—; ind. bus. owner 1958-60. Producer videotape series on dissection and study, 1988. Election inspector City of Omaha, 1972-86. With USAF, 1950-53, Korea. Mem. Nat. Biol. Tchrs. Assn. Republican. Roman Catholic. Office: Cyrgus Co Inc 3823 Leavenworth Omaha NE 68105

CYRUS, MARGARET ANN, accountant; b. New Orleans, Nov. 6, 1963; d. Louis Ignatius and Marguerite Frances (De George) C. BS in Acctg., U. New Orleans, 1985. CPA. Sr. tax acct. NICOR Nat. Inc., New Orleans, 1986—. Mem. AICPA, La. Soc. CPA's, Carnival Revelers (capt. 1986— New Orleans). Roman Catholic. Home: 6680 Bellaire Dr New Orleans LA 70124 Office: NICOR Nat Inc 3201 General de Gaulle Dr 2d Fl New Orleans LA 70114

CYTRAUS, ALDONA ONA, insurance company executive; b. Hanau, Federal Republic of Germany, Dec. 16, 1947. BFA, U. Cin., 1970, MBA, 1978. CPA, Ohio. Art tchr., chmn. art dept. Seton High Sch., Cin., 1970-76; audit supr. Coopers & Lybrand, Cin. and Cleve., 1979-85; mgr. forecasting and data devel. Blue Cross/Blue Shield Ohio, Cleve., 1985—; sec., treas. Triatic Enterprises, Euclid, Ohio, 1986—; mem. exec. com. Assn. Home Care Agys., Cin., 1982-84. Fin. planning com. ARC, Cin., 1983. Mem. Am. Inst. CPA's, Ohio Soc. CPA's (chmn. members in industry com. 1988—), Am. Assn. Individual Investors, Internat. Platform Assn. Home: 60 Lake Edge Dr Euclid OH 44123

CZAJA, J. E., petroleum company executive. Exec. v.p. Shell Can. Ltd., Calgary, Alta. Office: Shell Can Ltd, PO Box 100 Sta M, Calgary, AB Canada T2P 2H5 *

CZAJKA, JAMES VINCENT, architect; b. Lackawanna, N.Y., Dec. 6, 1950; s. Joseph Martin and Livia Maria (Jengo) C. BS in Art and Design, MIT, 1972, MArch, 1975. Registered architect, N.Y. Asst. prof. architecture SUNY, Buffalo, 1975-79; architect Ehrenkrantz Group Architects and Planners, N.Y.C., 1979-84; architect Beyer, Blinder, Belle Architects and Planners, N.Y.C., 1984—, assoc., 1987—, studio dir., 1988—. Prin. works include Baird Point Amphitheater, SUNY, Buffalo, 1978, Social Security Adminstrn. Bldg., Queens, N.Y., 1982, Paul Klapper Hall Queens Coll., 1986. Mem. AIA, NCARB (cert.). Home: 303 E 84th St Apt 2F New York NY 10028 Office: Beyer Blinder Belle 41 E 11th St New York NY 10003

CZAPOR, EDWARD P., automobile company executive; b. 1926. BSEE U. Pitts., 1948. With Gen. Motors Corp., 1948—, exptl. engr. Delco Products div., 1951-53, design engr., 1953-55, sales engr., 1955-59, market & product mgr. Delco Products div., 1959-61, Delco Products div. new product planning and market research, 1961-66, chief engr., 1966-70, gen. mgr. Delco Products div., 1970-74, gen. mgr. Delco Remy div., 1974-78, gen. mgr. Delco Electronics div., 1978-81, corp. v.p. & group exec. elec. components group from 1981, now v.p. quality & reliability. Office: GM Gen Motors Bldg 3044 W Grand Blvd Detroit MI 48202 *

CZEKALSKI, LONI RAVEN, air transportation systems executive; b. Atlantic City, Aug. 24, 1948; d. Zigman Stanley Czekalski and Eleanor Frieda (Schnegelberger) Raven. BA in Math., Glassboro State Coll., 1970; M in Aviation Mgmt., Embry Riddle U., 1984. Mathematician data processing div. FAA Dept. Transp., Atlantic City, 1970-71, mathematician enroute systems div., 1971-74, mathematician terminal sect., 1974-76, mathematician systems sect., 1976-78, computer specialist, 1978-81, supr. mathematician, tech. program mgr., 1981-83, 1983-84, spl. asst. for programs Office of Dir., 1984-85, operations research analyst Office Sci. and Advanced Tech., 1985-88, asst. mgr. ind. operational test and evaluation div., mgmt. and control svc., 1988—. Contbr. articles to profl. jours. Jehovah's Witness. Office: FAA Atlantic City NJ 08405

DAAB-KRZYKOWSKI, ANDRE, pharmaceutical and nutritional manufacturing company administrator; b. Warsaw, Poland, May 16, 1949; came to U.S., 1973, naturalized, 1981; s. Aleksy Czeslaw crest Polkozic and Zofia (Dyszkiewicz crest Kudrys) Krzykowski; m. Susan Elizabeth Read, June 26, 1987. MSChemE, Tech. U. Warsaw, 1973; MBA, Memphis State U., 1979. Research chemist Schering-Plough, Memphis, 1974-77; process control mgr. Ralston Purina Co., Memphis, 1977-80; dir. Pharm. projects indsl. div. Bristol Myers, Bristol-Myers Co., Mayaguez, P.R., 1980—. Served to 2d lt. Polish Army Res. Mem. Am. Mgmt. Assn., Am. Chem. Soc. Republican. Lutheran. Club: Toastmasters (pres. local chpt. 1986). Avocations: sailing, scuba diving, karate. Office: Bristol Myers Indsl Div PO Box 897 Mayaguez PR 00709

DAANE, JAMES DEWEY, banker; b. Grand Rapids, Mich., July 6, 1918; s. Gilbert L. and Mamie (Blocksma) D.; m. Blanche M. Tichenor, Apr. 28, 1941 (div. 1952); 1 dau., Elizabeth Marie Daane Mallek; m. Onnie B. Selby, Jan. 23, 1953 (dec. Dec. 1961); m. Barbara W. McMann, Feb. 16, 1963; children—Elizabeth Whitney, Olivia Quartel. AB magna cum laude, Duke U., 1939; M in Pub. Adminstrn., Harvard U., 1946, D in Pub. Adminstrn. (Littauer fellow), 1949. With Fed. Res. Bank, Richmond, Va., 1939-60, asst. v.p., 1953-57, v.p., 1957-60, also cons. to pres. bank; adviser to pres. Fed. Res. Bank, Mpls., 1960; asst. to sec. treasury 1960-61, dep. undersec. treasury for monetary affairs, 1961-63; mem. bd. govs. Fed. Reserve System, Washington, 1963-74; vice chmn. bd. dirs. Commerce Union Bank, now Sovran Bank/Cen. South, Nashville, 1974-78; chmn. internat. policy com. Commerce Union Corp., 1978-87; chmn. internat. policy com Sovran Fin. Corp., Nashville, 1988; chmn. money market com. Commerce Union Bank, 1974-87; chmn. money market com. cen. S. Sovran Bank, 1988—; asso. economist Fed. Open Market Com., 1955-56, 58-59; chief IMF Fiscal Mission to Paraguay, 1950-51; vice chmn. Tennessee Valley Bancorp, Inc., 1975-78; Frank K. Houston prof. banking and fin. Owen Grad. Sch. Mgmt., Vanderbilt U., 1974-85, Valere Blair Potter prof. banking and fin., 1985—; dir. Whittaker Corp., Los Angeles, 1974—, Chgo. Bd. Trade, 1979-82, Nat. Futures Assn., 1983—. Bd. advisers Patterson Sch. Diplomacy and Internat. Commerce, U. Ky. Mem. J.F. Kennedy Sch. Govt. Assn. of Harvard U., Am. Econ. Assn., Am. Finance Assn. Home: 102 Westhampton Pl Nashville TN 37205 Office: Sovran Bank/Cen South One Commerce Pl Nashville TN 37219

DABERKO, DAVID A., banker; b. Akron, Ohio, 1945. Grad., Denison U., 1967, Case Western Res. U., 1970. Formerly exec. v.p., now dep. chmn. Nat. City Corp., Cleve.; pres., dir. BancOhio Nat. Bank, Columbus, 1985-87; pres. Nat. City Bank, Cleve., 1987—; dep. chmn. Nat. City Corp. Office: Nat City Bank 1900 E 9th St Cleveland OH 44114

DABNEY, ROY IRWIN, JR., banking executive; b. Washington, Apr. 23, 1942; s. Roy Irwin D.; m. Ruth Henrietta Lockett, Sept. 1965; children: Roy I. III, Claudia M.A. Grad. high sch., Washington. With 1st Am. Bank Md., Silver Spring, 1966—, asst. v.p. community banking, 1980-83, asst. v.p., br. mgr., 1983-87, v.p. bus. devel., comml. lending, 1987—. Pres. Prince George's County United Cerebral Palsy, 1980-85; mem. Prince George's County Council, 1980-82; mem. selection bd. Service Acad. Selection Com., office of Congressman Steny H. Hoyer, 1983—; trustee 1st Bapt. Ch., Glenarden, Md., 1975—. Served as sgt. USAF, 1960-66. Mem. Prince George's Bankers Assn. (pres. 1986), NCCJ (chmn. exec. bd. 1979-80, 83—), mem. regional bd. dirs. 1985—), Prince George's C. of C. (pres. 1977-78). Office: 1st Am Bank Md 9201 Basil Ct Andover MD 20785

DABOLL, EVELYN LOUISE KENYON, tax and financial consultant; b. Old Mystic, Conn., Feb. 22, 1927; d. Anson Surber and L. Maude (Tinker) Kenyon; student Jackson (Miss.) Sch. Law, 1954; m. H. Merle Witt, Oct. 29, 1945 (div. Apr. 1956); m. 2d, Frederick A. Daboll, Feb. 9, 1962. Instr. traffic dept. So. New Eng. Telephone Co., New Britain, Conn. and Mystic, Conn., 1943-45; residential designer Frank Kincannon, AIA, Tupelo, Miss., 1949-51; chief dep. Chancery clk. Chancery Clk's Office, Tupelo, 1951-54; jr. partner Sadler Oil Co., Jackson, Miss., 1954-61; owner, operator Witt Enterprises, bookkeeping and secretarial services, 1961-62; adminstr. asst. Copp, Brenneman & Tighe, attys., New London, Conn., 1961-62; owner, operator Daboll Enterprises, Noank, Conn., 1963—; bd. dirs. Hobo Line Inc. Moderator, Town of Groton Rep. Town Meeting, 1969-70, rep., 1968-70; mem. Bd. Selectmen Groton, 1980-81. Mem. Nat. Assn. Tax Preparers, VFW Aux. Democrat. Baptist. Lodge: Kiwanis. Avocations: photography, painting, needlework. Office: Daboll Enterprises 393 Gold Star Hwy Groton CT 06340

DACEY, JUDITH ELAINE, CPA, consultant; b. Ashland, Ohio, Apr. 13, 1946; d. Cyril R. and Coral Lillian Betty (Obetz) Robertson; m. William Perkins, Dec. 24, 1965 (div. July 1979); m. Raymond E. Dacey, Mar. 21, 1981; 1 child, Jennifer Lee. BBA, U. Cen. Fla., 1980; MBA, U. North Fla., 1986. CPA. Credit analyst Sears Roebuck & Co., Mansfield, Ohio, 1966-69; dir. mktg. Am. Venture Enterprises, Orlando, Fla., 1969-75; owner J. Perkins Tax Acct., Orlando, 1975-80; acct. fin. mgmt. Blue Cross and Blue Shield of Fla., Jacksonville, 1980-86; owner Dacey & Assocs., P.A., Jacksonville, 1986—; cons. Blue Cross and Blue Shield Assn., Chgo., 1985—. Author: Telemarketing for the Entertainment Industry, 1975. Active mem. Mandarin (Fla.) Community Club, 1982—; sem. leader Small Bus. Devel. Ctr., Jacksonville, 1987—. Mem. Fla. Inst. CPA's (chmn. 1987—, Svc. award 1987-88), Nat. Assn. Accts. (v.p. 1986-87), Mandarin (Fla.) Bus. Assn., Tall Club (founder 1980, Jax chpt.). Home: 4352 Walnut Bend Jacksonville FL 32257 Office: Dacey & Assocs PA 11018-112 Old St Augustine Rd Jacksonville FL 32257

DACHOWITZ, HENRY MOSES, investment research analyst; b. Jan. 22, 1956; s. Pincus and Seyma Anne (Sacksner) D.; m. Mary-Jane Moskowitz, May 1, 1983. BS, Bklyn. Coll., 1977; MBA, Harvard U., 1980. CPA, Md., N.Y. Founder, owner, pres. Tutoring Referral Service, Bklyn., 1974-77; auditor Coopers & Lybrand, N.Y.C., 1977-78; trader and gen. mgr. Empire Steel Trading Co., N.Y.C., 1980-82; v.p. fin. IGI Biotech., Inc., Columbia, Md., 1982-84; sr. mgmt. cons. Touche Ross & Co., N.Y.C., 1984-87; investment research analyst Sanford C. Berstein & Co., Inc., N.Y.C., 1987—; tchg. fellow in acctg. Harvard Coll., Cambridge, Mass., 1979-80; bus. mgr. Kingsman Newspaper, Bklyn., 1976-77; speaker Md. Assn. CPA's, Columbia, 1982-84. Adv. Inst. Politics Harvard U., Cambridge, 1979-80. Recipient Innovation award Touche Ross Fin. Services Ctr., 1986; Louis P. Goldberg scholar, Bklyn. Coll., 1977, N.Y. State Regents scholar, 1973. Mem. Am. Inst. CPA's, N.Y. State Soc. CPA's (fin. planning and control com.), Am. Mgmt. Assn., Internat. Platform Assn., Mensa. Republican. Jewish. Club: Century Club (Harvard). Home: 2 Salem Ln Port Washington NY 11050 Office: Sanford C Bernstein & Co 767 Fifth Ave New York NY 10153

DACHOWSKI, PETER RICHARD, financial executive; b. Hillingdon, Middlesex, Eng., June 2, 1948; came to U.S., 1969; s. Teodor and Mary

(Stracey) D.; m. Victoria Kaplan Ortiz, May 1, 1977. MA in Econs., Queens' Coll., Cambridge, Eng., 1969; MBA, U. Chgo., 1971. Fin. analyst Exxon Corp., 1971-73; mgr. Boston Cons. Group, 1973-76; asst. treas. CertainTeed Corp., Valley Forge, Pa., 1976-78; asst. to chief exec. officer CertainTeed Co., Valley Forge, Pa., 1979-80, v.p. planning and devel., 1980-81, v.p., treas., 1981-83, v.p., comptroller, 1983-85, v.p., pres. Shelter Materials group, 1985—, pres. vinyl bldg. products div., 1987—; pres., chief exec. officer Wolverine Tech. Inc., Valley Forge, 1988—; corp. devel staff Compagnie de Saint Gobain, Paris, 1978-79; dir. Mexalit S.A., Air Vent Inc. Recipient Wall St. Jour. award Dow Jones-Chgo., 1971. Mem. Fin. Mgmt. Assn., Fin. Execs. Inst., Newcomen Soc., U. Chgo. Grad. Sch. Bus. Alumni Assn. (bd. dirs. 1986-88—), Beta Gamma Sigma. Home: 321 Woodmont Circle Berwyn PA 19312 Office: CertainTeed Corp PO Box 860 Valley Forge PA 19482

DADA, NAYYAR ALI, architect; b. Delhi, India, Nov. 11, 1943; s. S. Anwar Ali and Kaneez Fatima; children: Reza Ali, Amir Ali. Diploma in architecture, Nat. Coll. Arts, Lahore, Pakistan, 1963. Mng. ptnr. Nayyar Dada Assocs., Lahore, 1974—; owner pvt. art gallery Lahore; sr. lectr. Nat. Coll. Arts, 1972-77, fellow, 1973, mem. bd. govs., 1985, bd. dirs 1987-88; mem. bd. govs. Punjab Council Arts, 1984-87; advisor Lahore Environ. Com. Prin. works include Quaid-e-Azam Library, Open Air Theater Lahore, Nishtar Hall Deshawar, Free Mason Hall Bldg., Shakir Ali Mus., Alhamra Arts Ctr., Nat. Meml., Hotel Sheraton Lahore, Holiday Inn Lahore, Lahore Zoo, Performing Art Ctr., Peshawar, Oil and Gas Devel. Corp. Bldg., Islamabad. Recipient Environ. award for pub. bldgs. Environ. mag., 1981-82; Nat. Coll. Arts fellow, 1973. Mem. Pakistan Inst. Architects (mem. council), Pakistan Council Architects (vice chmn.), Lahore Conservation Soc. (founder, treas.), Punjab Club. Home: 0 2 Habitat Housing Jail Rd, Shadman-II, Lahore Punjab, Pakistan Office: 8-F/3 New Muslim Town, Lahore Punjab, Pakistan

DADD, ROBERT FREDERICK, planning systems agency executive; b. Cumberland, Md., Nov. 30, 1947; s. William Frederick and Dorothy Evelyn (Goetz) D.; B.S., U. Md., 1970, M.B.A., 1975, C.D.P., 1981; m. Phyllis Lena Guralnick, Dec. 30, 1983; 1 son, Robert. Econ. analyst Tri-County Council for So. Md., Waldorf, 1970-73, mgmt. analyst, 1974-76, systems analyst, 83—; systems analyst Fairfax County, Fairfax, Va., 1973-74; dir. fin. and data adminstrn. So. Md. Health Systems Agy., Clinton, 1976-83; cons. Info. Systems, 1973—; treas. Phyllis, Inc., Kensington, Md., 1979—. Mem. Urban Regional Info. Systems Assn., Ops. Research Soc. Am., Washington Ops. Research and Mgmt. Sci. Council. Home: 9721 Connecticut Ave Kensington MD 20895 Office: PO Box 1634 Chalotte Hall MD 20622

DADISMAN, LYNN ELLEN, marketing executive; b. Los Angeles, Mar. 1, 1946; d. Orlan Sidney and Erna Lou (Harris) Friedman; m. Kent Dadisman, May 1973 (div. 1974). Student UCLA, 1963-65, 71-72, Willis Bus. Coll., 1965-66, Fin. Schs. Am., 1982, Viewpoints Inst., 1970-71. Office mgr. Harleigh Sandler Co., Los Angeles, 1965-67; customer svc. Investors Diversified Svcs., West Los Angeles, Calif., 1968-76; exec. sec. McCulloch Oil Corp., West Los Angeles, 1976; mgr. publs. Security 1st Group, Century City, Calif., 1976-80; office mgr. Morehead & Co., Century City, 1980-81; dir. mktg., mgr. customer svc. Ins. Mktg. Services, Santa Monica, Calif., 1981-82; v.p. Decatur Petroleum Corp., Santa Monica, 1982-83; asst. v.p., broker svcs., dir. Angeles Corp., L.A., 1984-87; asst. to pres. Pacific Ventures, Santa Monica, 1988—. Mem. Nat. Assn. Securities Dealers, Internat. Assn. Fin. Planning, NAFE, Migi Car Am. Club (sec., newsletter editor). Fin. and ins. writer; contbr. poetry to UCLA Literary Mag., 1964. Home: 3442 Centinela Ave Apt 15 Los Angeles CA 90066

DAERR, RICHARD LEO, JR., construction management company executive, lawyer; b. Victoria, Tex., Aug. 13, 1944; s. Richard Leo and Rosemary Jane (Dolesh) D.; m. Karin Birgitta Holmen, Aug. 13, 1975; children—Richard Jason, Carl Justin. B.S., Tex. A&M U., 1966; M.B.A., George Washington U., 1972; J.D., U. Tex., 1971. Bar: Tex. 1971. Legal intern antitrust div. Dept. Justice, Washington, 1970; trial atty Dept. Justice, Washington and Dallas, 1972-76; assoc. counsel Dresser Industries, Inc., Dallas, 1976-79; exec. v.p. CRS Sirrine, Inc., Houston, 1979—; Mem. Emergency Com. for Am. Trade, Washington, 1978-79. Editor: Symposium on Internat. Protection of Environment, 1971; articles editor Tex. Internat. Law Jour., 1970, 71; contbr. articles to profl. publs. Served to 1st lt. USMC, 1966-68, Vietnam. Decorated Cross of Gallantry (Vietnam), 1967; Found. fellow George Washington U., 1971; recipient Asst. Atty. Gen.'s Achievement commendation Dept. Justice, 1976, Outstanding Performance award Dept. Justice, 1975, Pres.' award Outstanding Community Achievement of Vietnam Era Vets., 1979. Mem. Tex. Bar Assn., ABA, Am. Corp. Counsel Assn. Republican. Roman Catholic. Club: El Cortez (Port Aransas, Tex.) (pres. 1979-84). Office: CRS Sirrine Inc 1177 W Loop S #900 Houston TX 77027

DAGGETT, BRADLEY D., sales executive; b. Omro, Wis., Sept. 15, 1964; s. David Bradley and Kathleen (Morrissey) D. BBA, U. Wis., 1987. Mktg. intern Ohmeda Med. Engring., Norcross, Ga., 1986; mkt. researcher Madison (Wis.) Interviewing Svc., 1986—; sales rep. Black & Decker, Sioux Falls, S.D., 1987-88; account exec. consumer products Black & Decker, Milw., 1988—. Republican. Methodist. Home: 1460 Carriage Ln #14 New Berlin WI 53151 Office: Black & Decker 10424 W Bluemound Wauwatosa WI 53226

DAGGETT, ROBERT SHERMAN, lawyer; b. La Crosse, Wis., Sept. 16, 1930; s. Willard Manning and Vida Naomi (Sherman) D.; m. Lee Sullivan Burton, Sept. 16, 1961; children: Ann Sherman, John Sullivan; m. Helen Ackerman, July 20, 1976. A.B. with honors in Polit. Sci. and Journalism, U. Calif.-Berkeley, 1952, J.D., 1955. Bar: Calif. 1955, U.S. Supreme Ct. 1967. Assoc. firm Brobeck, Phleger & Harrison, San Francisco, 1958-66, ptnr., 1966—; counsel Calif. Senate Reapportionment Com., 1972-73; adj. prof. evidence and advocacy Hastings Coll. Law, 1982—; instr. No. Dist. Fed. Practice Program, 1982—, mem. teaching com., 1983—; demonstrator-instr. Nat. Inst. for Trial Advocacy, 1981—, Hastings Ctr. for Trial and Appellate Advocacy, 1981-88, mem. adv. bd., 1983-88; vol. pro tempsmall claims judge San Francisco Mcpl. Ct., 1981-88; arbitrator San Francisco Superior Ct., and pvt. comml. arbitration, 1984—; instr. No. Dist. Fed. Practice Program, 1982—, mem. teaching com., 1983—. Bd. editors: Calif. Law Rev., 1953-55; contbr. articles to profl. jours. Rep. Pacific Assn. AAU, 1973; bd. dirs. San Francisco Legal Aid Soc.; bd. visitors Coll. V U. Calif.-Santa Cruz. Served to 1st lt. JAGC U.S. Army, 1958-62. Walter Perry Johnson scholar, 1953. Mem. ABA, State Bar Calif. (chmn. local adminstrv. com. 1964-65), San Francisco Bar Assn. (past dir.), Am. Judicature Soc., Am. Law Inst., Order of Golden Bear, Bohemian Club, Commonwealth Club, Commercial Club (bd. dirs. 1989—), Phi Delta Phi, Theta Xi. Republican. Office: Brobeck Phleger & Harrison Spear St Tower 1 Market Pla San Francisco CA 94105

D'AGOSTINO, JAMES SAMUEL, JR, financial executive; b. Balt., July 4, 1946; s. James Samuel and Betty Ann (List) D'A.; m. Diane Martin Greener, Sept. 25, 1971; children: James Martin, Ann Diestel. BS in Econs., Villanova U., 1968; JD, Seton Hall Sch. Law, Newark, 1974. Bar: N.J. 1974, Tex. 1979. Trust officer Fidelity Union Trust Co., Newark, 1968-73; asst. treas. The Chase Manhattan Bank, N.A., N.Y.C., 1973-76; v.p. Citibank/Citicorp, Houston, 1976-86; v.p., treas. Am. Gen. Corp., Houston, 1986-88, sr. v.p., treas., 1988—. Republican. Presbyterian. Office: Am Gen Corp 2929 Allen Pkwy Houston TX 77019

D'AGOSTINO, VINCENT RALPH, marketing executive; b. N.Y.C., Sept. 27, 1954; s. Vincent Francis and Rita Maria (Filarsi) D'A.; m. Nicolys Arden Hessleman, May 16, 1981; children: Rachel, Clifford. BS in Math., MS in Stats., Rensselaer U., 1981. Sr. systems analyst Arthur Anderson & Co., N.Y.C., 1976-79; sr. v.p. mktg. svcs. Comp-U-Card Internat., Stamford, Conn., 1981—. Office: CUC Internat 707 Summer St Stamford CT 06904-2049

DAHL, DANIEL HUELSTER, banker; b. Grand Rapids, Mich., June 6, 1935; s. Eric William and Sarah Alice (Huelster) D.; m. Mary Barbara Rue, Aug. 24, 1957; children: Nancy Marie, Daniel Steven, Stephen Rue. BBA, U. Mich., 1957, MBA, 1958. Mgr. investment Prudential Ins. Co. Am., Mpls., Detroit and Atlanta, 1958-69; v.p. corp. fin. Paine Webber Jackson & Curtis, Detroit, 1969-72; exec. v.p. NBS Fin. Corp., Southfield, Mich., 1972-74; v.p. corp. fin. Mfrs. Nat. Bank Detroit, 1974—. Mem. Detroit Athletic Club, Orchard Lake Country Club. Republican. Methodist. Office: Mfrs Nat Bank Detroit 100 Renaissance Ctr Detroit MI 48243

DAHL, HARRY WALDEMAR, lawyer; b. Des Moines, Aug. 7, 1927; s. Harry Waldemar and Helen Gerda (Anderson) D.; m. Bonnie Sorensen, June 14, 1952; children: Harry Waldemar, Lisabeth (dec.), Christina. BA, U. Iowa, 1950; JD, Drake U., 1955. Bar: Iowa 1955, U.S. Dist. Ct. (no. and so. dists.) Iowa 1955, U.S. Supreme Ct 1965, Fla. 1970, Nebr. 1983, Minn. 1984. Assoc. Steward & Crouch, Des Moines, 1955-59; Iowa dep. indsl. commr. Des Moines, 1959-62, commr., 1962-71; pres., prin. Law Offices of Harry W. Dahl, P.C., 1972—; of counsel Underwood, Gillis and Karcher, Miami, 1972-77; adj. prof. law Drake U., Des Moines, 1972—; exec. dir. Internat. Assn. Indsl. Accident Bds. and Commns., 1972-77; pres. Workers Compensation Studies, Inc., 1974—, Workers' Compensation Services, Inc., 1978—, Hewitt, Coleman & Assocs. Iowa, Inc., 1975-79; mem. adv. com. Second Injury Fund, Fla. Indsl. Relations Commn. Author: Iowa Law on Workmen's Compensation, 1975; editor: ABC Newsletter, 1964-77. Served with USNR, 1945-46. Recipient Adminstrs. award Internat. Assn. Indsl. Accident Bds. and Commns., 1967. Mem. Am. Trial Lawyers Assn. (chmn. workers' compensation sect. 1973), ABA (chmn. workers' compensation com. 1974-76), Iowa Bar Assn. (chmn. workers' compensation com. 1984—), Fla. Bar (bd. govs. 1988—), Nebr. Bar Assn., Minn. Bar Assn., Internat. Bar Assn., Am. Soc. Law and Medicine (council 1975-82), Iowa Assn. Workers' Compensation Lawyers (co-founder, past pres.), Def. Research Inst., Coll. of Workers Compensation Inc. (co-founder, regent), Swedish Pioneer Hist. Soc., Am. Swedish Inst., Des Moines Pioneer Club, East High Alumni Assn. (pres. 1975-76), Order of Coif. Lutheran. Lodges: Masons, Shriners, Sertoma (chmn. bd. dirs. 1974-75). Home: 3005 Sylvania Dr West Des Moines IA 50265 Office: 974 73 St #16 Des Moines IA 50312

DAHL, HENRY LAWRENCE, JR., human resource director; b. Topeka, Mar. 5, 1933; s. Henry and Emiline Ruth (Holtz) D.; m. Gayle Beggs, Oct. 2, 1952; children: Henry III, Richard W., Dorothy G., William J., John L., Lorna A. BBA, U. Minn., 1955. Personnel staff The Upjohn Co., Kalamazoo, 1957, mgr. employment, 1966, mgr. manpower planning, 1969, dir. corp. employee devel. and planning, 1972; lectr. to var. groups on improving human resources. Producer motion pictures Me! & You!, Me! & We! (recipient Cine Golden Eagle award for both pictures); author: Measuring and Improving the Return on Investment in Human Resources. Pres. Immanuel Luth. Ch., Kalamazoo, 1972; v.p. Kalamazoo Valley Intermediate Sch. Dist., 1976; mem. Kalamazoo 2000 Com., 1980, Whitehouse Conf. on Productivity, 1984; v.p. YMCA, Kalamazoo, 1984-85 pres., 1986-87, trustee, 1989—. Served to 1st lt. USAF, 1955-57. Recipient Upjohn award The Upjohn Co., 1976. Mem. Am. Soc. Tng. and Devel., Am. Soc. Personnel Adminstrn. (bd. dirs. 1986-87, v.p.), Midwest Human Resource Planning Group, Kalamazoo Personnel Assn. Republican. Home: 4109 Canterbury Kalamazoo MI 49007 Office: The Upjohn Co 7000 Portage Rd Kalamazoo MI 49001

DAHLBERG, CARL FREDRICK, JR., investment banker; b. New Orleans, Aug. 20, 1936; s. Carl Fredrick and Nancey Erwin (Jones) D.; BS in Civil Engring., Tulane U., 1958; MBA, Harvard U., 1964; m. Constance Weston, Dec. 30, 1961; children: Kirsten Erwin, Catherine Morgan. Regional mgr. bond dept. E.F. Hutton & Co., Inc., New Orleans, 1965-67; chmn. exec. com. Dahlberg, Kelly & Wisdom, Inc., New Orleans, 1967-71; pres. C.F. Dahlberg & Co., Inc., New Orleans, 1971—; co-organizer, dir. Charter Med. Corp., 1969-72; bd. dirs. Rathborne Cos., 1985—, Asgard Corp., 1987—; EuroBasins Petroleum, Ltd., 1987—; Internat. Trade Mart, 1974—, mem. exec. com. 1981-84, treas., 1983-84; consul gen. of Monaco, New Orleans, 1981—. Trustee, Metairie Park Country Day Sch., New Orleans, 1976-85; treas., 1980-82, chmn., 1982-84; trustee, Eye, Ear, Nose and Throat Hosp., New Orleans, 1980—, mem. exec. com., 1980-83; trustee Eye, Ear, Nose and Throat Found., 1980-83, U. of South, Sewanee, Tenn., 1984—; vestryman Christ Ch. Cathedral, New Orleans, 1981-85. Served with U.S. Army, 1958-59. Registered profl. engr., La.; registered land surveyor, La. Mem. ASCE, Fin. Mgmt. Assn., New Orleans Council Bus. Economists, Nat. Assn. Corrosion Engrs., Am. Soc. Venerable Order Hosp. of St. John of Jerusalem, Mil. and Hospitaller Order St. Lazarus. Republican. Episcopalian. Clubs: New Orleans Country, Pickwick; Knickerbocker (N.Y.C.); American (London). Co-author: Hydrochloric Acid Pickling, 1979. Home: 199 Audubon Blvd New Orleans LA 70118 Office: 601 Poydras St New Orleans LA 70130

DAHLE, STANLEY JAMES, manufacturing company executive; b. N.Y.C., Apr. 26, 1937; s. Earling and Jenny (Johansen) D.; m. Sherry Joan Pierce, June 7, 1958; children: Michael S., Bradford J., Jennifer A. BA in Econs., SUNY, Binghamton, 1959. Div. dir. United Fund Greater N.Y., N.Y.C., 1963-67; v.p. Ralf Shockey & Assocs., N.Y.C., 1967-68; pres. Stan Dahle & Assocs., N.Y.C., 1968-76, Metal Arts Co. Inc., Rochester, N.Y., 1976—, Bastian Co., Inc., Rochester, 1981—; bd. dirs. Metalbanc Corp., Miami, Fla., Metal Resources Corp., Miami. Sgt. U.S. Army, 1959-63. Mem. Sleepy Hollow Club (Scarsborough, N.Y..). Republican. Home: 32 Farm Rd Briarcliff Manor NY 10510 Office: Metal Arts Co 1600 N Clinton Ave Rochester NY 14621

DAHLKE, WAYNE THEODORE, civil engineer, corporate executive; b. Birmingham, Ala., Jan. 6, 1941; s. Hugo Theodore and Josephine (Huber) D.; m. Annette Riddle, May 19, 1984; children: Jeffrey, Jill, Jennifer Colie, Brad Colie. BSCE, U. Ala., 1965; postgrad., Emory U., 1983, Harvard U., 1985. Registered profl. engr., Ga. Jr. design engr. Ga. Power Co., Atlanta, 1965-71, asst. mgr. Wansley plant, 1971-76, project gen. mgr., 1976, asst. to sr. v.p., 1976-79, project gen. mgr. Wallace Dam, 1979-80, project gen. mgr. Scherer plant, 1980-82, v.p., gen. mgr. fossil and hydro projects, 1983-86, v.p. indsl. mktg., 1986-87, v.p. east metro div., 1987; v.p. design engring. So. Co. Svcs., Inc., Birmingham, Ala., 1987-89; sr. v.p. Ga. Power Co., Atlanta, 1989—. Unit chmn. Atlanta United Way drive. Lt. USNR, 1966-69. Fellow U. Ala., 1989. Mem. ASCE (assoc.), Am. Soc. Mil. Engrs. (assoc.), NSPE. Lutheran. Home: 2030 Country Ridge Pl Birmingham AL 35243 Office: So Co Svcs Inc PO Box 2625 Birmingham AL 35202

DAHM, ALFONS GEORGE, oil company executive, educator; b. N.Y.C., July 4, 1942; s. Alfonse and Berta (Schmider) D.; m. Jacqueline Ann Jones, June 27, 1965; 1 child, Jeremy Matthew. BA, Hunter Coll., 1964; MBA, Baruch Coll., 1973. Cert. fin. planner. Acct. United Parcel Service, N.Y.C., 1965-67; fin. analyst, adminstr. RCA Corp, N.Y.C., 1967-69; with Mobil Corp., N.Y.C., 1969—, sr. fin. systems cons., 1981-83, mgr. systems and computer services, records services, 1983—; assoc. prof. CUNY, N.Y.C., 1973—; chief exec. officer, bd. dirs. Kildare Adminstrv. Services Co., Inc., N.Y.C., 1986—; bus. advisor INROADS, Inc., NYC, 1986—. Solicitor United Way, N.Y.C., 1983-86, campaign organizer, 1986-87. Served with USAR, 1965-71. Recipient Disting. Service award CUNY, 1988. Mem. Inst. Cert. Fin. Planners, Assn. for Image and Info. Mgmt., Assn. Records Mgrs. and Adminstrs., Am. Mgmt. Assn. Roman Catholic. Home: 118 Kildare Rd Garden City NY 11530 Office: Mobil Corp 150 E 42d St New York NY 10017

DAHOD, AARIF MANSUR, service executive; b. Bombay, Apr. 9, 1952; came to U.S., 1970; s. Mansur M. and Rubab M. (Gandhi) D.; m. Cheryl Aline Rager, June 22, 1975; children: Micah, Sara. BS, SUCB, Buffalo, 1974; cert. in indsl. security, Princeton U., 1985. Cert. protection profl. Dist. mgr. Wackenhut Corp., Coral Gables, Fla., 1974-80; pres. Spectrum Mgmt. Svcs. Inc., Southfield, Mich., 1980-83, Risk Mgmt. Svcs. Inc., Marlboro, Mass., 1983-85; sr. v.p. sales and ops. Sahlen & Assocs. Inc., Deerfield Beach, Fla., 1985-86, exec. v.p. corp. devel. and mktg., 1986—; cons. Am. Soc. Indsl. Security, Detroit, 1980-81. Fund raiser Young Shin Won Orphanage, Republic Korea. Fellow Am. Soc. Indsl. Security, Young Execs. Am.; mem. Young Reps., N.Y. Roadrunners. Office: Sahlen & Assocs Inc 600 W Hillsboro Blvd Ste 601 Deerfield Beach FL 33441

DAIDONE, LEWIS EUGENE, financial company executive; b. Perth Amboy, N.J., Aug. 6, 1957; s. Eugene John and Gertrude Rose (Sawyer) D.; m. Kathleen Eleanor Ward, May 11, 1985; 1 child, Eugene Jospeh. BA, Rutgers U., 1979, MBA, 1980. CPA, N.Y., N.J. Sr. acct. Ernst & Whinney, N.Y.C., 1980-82; asst. controller Reserve Group, N.Y.C., 1982-84; mgr. commodity acctg. Dean Witter Reynolds, N.Y.C., 1984; v.p., treas. Cortland Distbrs., Inc., Hackensack, N.J., 1984—, also bd. dirs., 1984—; sr. v.p., chief fin. officer Cortland Fin. Group, Inc., Hackensack, N.J., 1984—; v.p., treas. Cortland Trust, Hackensack; cons. in field. Trustee Wyndmoor Condominium Assn., Woodbridge, N.J. Named one of Outstanding Young Men Am., U.S. Jaycees, 1979. Fellow N.J. State Soc. CPA's; mem. AICPA, N.Y. State Soc. CPA's, Woodbridge Racquet and Fitness Club, Beta Gamma Sigma. Office: Cortland Fin Group Inc 3 University Pla Hackensack NJ 07601-6208

DAIGNEAULT, MARILYN YVONNE, meeting planner, consultant, association executive; b. Atlanta, Apr. 18, 1935; d. Charles Frederick and Gaynell Edith (Teem) Eichwurtzle; m. William Lawrence Stephenson, June 17, 1955 (div. 1960); children: Beverly, Mark, Douglas; m. George Arthur Daigneault, Jan. 21, 1962; children: Ruth, Susan, Joseph, David; stepchildren: Rachelle, Michael. BA in Journalism, Maine U., 1957. Adminstrv. asst. H.B. Atkinson Co., Washington, 1963-66; free lance proofreader, Washington, 1970-75; meeting and incentive planner, corps. and assns., Washington, 1975—; dir. D&D Assocs., Rockville, 1982—; exec. dir. Assn. Ind. Meeting Planners, 1986—; editor-in-chief The Ind. Meeting Planner, 1986—. Active Nat. Fedn. Republican Women, 1983-86; sponsor GOP Victory Fund, 1984-87. Mem. Nat. Assn. Female Execs. (network dir. 1985-87), Am. Soc. Assn. Execs., Am. Soc. Writers, Nat. Assn. Women Bus. Owners, Am. Assn. Profl. Cons., The Cons. League, Epsilon Delta Chi. Republican. Avocations: writing, research, teaching meeting planning, traveling.

DALBY, ALAN JAMES, pharmaceutical company executive; b. Glasgow, Scotland, Jan. 15, 1937; s. William J. P. and Elizabeth Jean (McKenzie) D.; children: A. Royce, Mark. B.S., Paisley Coll., 1958. Analytical chemist Smith Kline & French Labs., Can., 1958; mgmt. trainee SK&F, Phila., 1960-61; gen. mgr. consumer products div. Menley & James Labs., Can., 1963-65; dir. mktg. SK&F, Can., 1966-71; v.p. comml. devel. Worldwide Pharms., Phila., 1971-72; v.p. Worldwide Pharms., Europe, Africa, India, Brussels, 1972-75; v.p. internat. Worldwide Pharms., Phila., 1975-80; pres. Worldwide Pharms., from 1980; exec. v.p. therapeutics products group Smith Kline Corp. (now SmithKline Beckman Corp.), Phila., 1980-87; pres. SmithKline and French Labs., Phila., 1980-87; pres., chief exec. officer Cambridge Neurosci. Research Inc., Cambridge, Mass., 1987—; dir. Westmoreland Coal Co., Reckitt & Colman. Republican. Episcopalian. Club: Aronomink Golf (Newtown Sq., Pa.). Office: Cambridge Neurosci Rsch 1 Kendall Sq Bldg 700 Cambridge MA 02139 *

DALE, JOHN DENNY, economist, business executive; b. N.Y.C., May 16, 1916; s. Francis Colegate and Imogen Hall (James) D.; m. Louise Boyd Lichtenstein, Oct. 22, 1938 (dec.); children: Anne Boyd (dec.), John Denny Jr.; m. 2d, Madeline Houston McWhinney, June 23, 1961; 1 child, Thomas Denny. AB, Hamilton Coll., 1936; MBA, NYU, 1954, PhD, 1962. Div. mgr. Am. Steel Export Co., N.Y.C., 1936-40; asst. to pres. Charles Hardy Inc., N.Y.C., 1940, v.p., sec., treas., 1941-45, pres., 1945-55; tech. dir. Charles Hardy Ltd., London, 1946-63; chmn. Mfrs. Mktg. Co., N.Y.C., 1949-50; pres. Dale Elliott & Co. Inc., N.Y.C., 1955-65, 71-76, chmn., 1976—; fin. economist Litton Industries Inc., Beverly Hills, Calif., 1965-68; fin. economist Am. Export Industries, Inc., N.Y.C., 1968-70; v.p. Litton Industries Leasing Corp., Beverly Hills, 1965-68; economist Dept. Labor and Industry, State of N.J., Trenton, 1976-82; advisor to WPB, 1941, to Gov. N.Y., 1948-51, to Chief Ordnance U.S. Army, 1952-55, Gov. Monmouth Med. Ctr., 1954-71, to Port Authority N.Y./N.J., N.Y.C., 1985-86. Author: Managerial Accounting in a Small Company, 1961. Trustee Mannes Coll. Music, 1957-69; mem. adv. bd. Root Art Ctr., Whitney Mus. Am. Art; advisor mgmt. dept. Brookdale Coll., Holmdel, N.J., 1983—; bd. dirs. Hudson River Conservation Soc., 1936-83, Internat. Schs. Services, Princeton, N.J., 1985—, NYU Alumni Council, Hamilton Coll. Alumni Council, 1948-52, 86—. Served to maj. AUS, 1942-45, ETO, 1951-52, Korea, to col. Res. (ret.). Decorated Legion of Merit; recipient Conspicious Service medal Gov. State N.Y., 1948, Alumni Merit Service award NYU Alumni Fedn., 1962. Mem. Am. Def. Preparedness Assn. (past pres., bd. dirs.), Order St. John, Knights Malta, Soc. Mayflower Descendants, Soc. Colonial Wars, Soc. War of 1812, Huguenot Soc., Mil. Order Fgn. Wars (past comdr.-gen. U.S.), Vet. Corps Arty., Soc. Am. Wars, S.R. St. Nicholas Soc., Res. Officers Assn., The Pilgrims, Psi Upsilon. Republican. Episcopalian. Clubs: University Glee, Racquet and Tennis, N.Y. Athletic (N.Y.C.), Rumson (N.J.) Country. Lodge: Masons. Home: 24 Blossom Cove Rd Red Bank NJ 07701 Office: PO Box 458 Red Bank NJ 07701

DALE, LARRY HUSTON, financial association executive; b. Charleston, W.Va., Feb. 9, 1946; s. Robert Frederick and Lois Jean (Huston) D.; m. Marilyn Mangels, Nov. 25, 1966; children: Brian H., Craig S., Andrew L. BS, Cornell U., 1968; M in Polit. Sci., Syracuse U., 1969. Various positions U.S. Dept. HUD, Washington, Phila., 1971-81; pres. Mid-City Fin. Corp., Bethesda, Md., 1981-83; v.p. Newman and Assocs., Denver, Washington, 1983-87; sr. v.p. multifamily Fed. Nat. Mortgage Assn., Washington, 1987—. Contbr. to profl. publs. Coach jr. sports programs, Bethesda, 1975-85; pres. Carderock Swim and Tennis Club, Bethesda, 1981-84; mem. PTA, Bethesda. Recipient numerous academic awards and fellowships. Mem. Nat. Housing Conf. (2d v.p., bd. dirs.), Nat. Leased Housing Assn. (v.p., bd. dirs.), Nat. Housing and Rehab. Assn. (past pres., bd. dirs.), Housing Devel. Reporter (bd. dirs.). Democrat. Office: Fed Nat Mortgage Assn 3900 Wisconsin Ave NW Washington DC 20016

DALE, LEON ANDREW, educator, arbitrator; b. Paris, May 9, 1921; m. Arlene R. Dale; children: Glenn Roy, Melinda Jennifer. B.A., Tulane U., 1946; M.A., U. Wis., 1947, Ph.D., 1949. Grad. asst. in econs. U. Wis., 1946-48; Asst. prof. labor econs. U. Fla., 1949-50; internat. economist AFL, Paris, 1950-53; AFL rep. at nat. labor convs. Greece, 1951, Naples, Italy, 1951, Switzerland, Sweden, Norway, Belgium, Austria, Luxembourg, Gt. Britain, 1950-53; cons. U.S. Govt., 1954-56; internat. economist U.S. Dept. Labor, Washington, 1956-59; chief econ. sect. Embassy of Morocco, Washington, 1959-60; prof., chmn. dept. mgmt. and indsl. relations, dir. internat. ctr., coordinator courses for fgn. students U. Bridgeport, Conn., 1960-69; prof. mgmt. and human resources Calif. State Poly. U., Pomona, 1969—; acting chmn. bus. mgmt. dept. Calif. State Poly. U., summer 1973, coordinator internat. activities Sch. Bus. Adminstrn., 1969-77; lectr. Internat. Confedn. Tree Trade Unions Summer Sch., Wörgl, Austria, 1951; lectr. on Am. labor UN, Stockholm, 1952; lectr. U. Wis., Milw., 1960; vis. prof. Columbia U., 1966, 67, Bernard Baruch Sch. Bus. and Pub. Adminstrn., 1966-69; cons., arbitrator, fact-finder State of Conn., 1964-69; Am. del., speaker 3d Internat. Symposium on Small Bus., Washington, 1976, 4th Internat. Symposium on Small Bus., Seoul, Korea, 1977, 5th Internat. Symposium on Small Bus., Anaheim, Calif., 1978, 6th Internat. Symposium on Small Bus., Berlin, 1979; also mem. U.S. steering com. Internat. Symposium on Small Bus.; sr. cons. Am. Grad. U., Covina, Calif., 1981-82; adj. prof. econs. Nat. U., San Diego, 1981-89, Pepperdine U., 1986; discussion leader Calif. Inst. Tech. Internat. Conf. on Combining Best of Japanese and U.S. Mgmt., Anaheim, 1981; lectr. on indsl. relations to execs. Miller Brewing Co., Irwindale, Calif., 1983; cons. Agy. Internat. Devel., N'Djamena, Republic of Chad, 1987; cons. to Minister for Planning, Republic of Chad; cons., instr. behavior courses U. Chad.; instr. mgmt. internat. ctr. Calif. State Poly. U., Pomona, 1988. Author: Marxism and French Labor, 1956, A Bibliography of French Labor, 1969; video tape Industrial Relations and Human Resources, 1982, Labor Relations in Crisis, 1989; contbr. articles to profl. jours. Served with U.S. Army, 1942-45. Recipient U. Bridgeport Faculty Research and Experimental Fund grant, 1962, fellowship econs. U. Wis., 1949; named one of Outstanding Educators of Am., 1972-73. Mem. Am. Arbitration Assn. (nat. panel arbitrators, nat. public employment disputes settlement panel), Indsl. Relations Research Assn., Am. Acad. Polit. and Social Sci., Soc. Profls. Dispute Resolution (charter). Club: Racing-Club de France. (Paris). Home: 30 S La Senda Laguna Beach CA 92677 Office: Calif State Poly U Pomona CA 91768

DALE, MARTIN ALBERT, investment banking consultant; b. Newark, Jan. 3, 1932; s. Philip D. and Lucie M. (Mintz) D.; BA, Princeton, 1953; postgrad. (Fulbright fellow) U. Strasbourg (France), 1953-54; MA in Internat. Econs. with honors, Tufts U., 1955; m. Joan C. Dale, Apr. 3, 1954 (div. 1977); children: Charles, W. Gregory, Pamela, Eric; m. Berteline Baier, Nov. 21, 1980. Fgn. svc. officer U.S. Dept. State, 1955-60; pvt. counsellor, econ. adviser Prince Rainier III of Monaco, 1960-64; v.p., exec. asst. to pres.

Grand Bahama Port Authority Ltd., Freeport, 1965-67; sr. v.p. fin., adminstrn. and ops. Revlon Internat. Corp., N.Y.C., 1967-72; corporate sr. v.p., dir. office strategic projects W.R. Grace & Co., N.Y.C., 1972-82; investment banking cons., 1983—; dir. Henkel of Am., Inc., Biotherapeutics, Inc; chmn. bd. of trustees Lycée Francais de N.Y., Princeton Club (South Fla.). Republican. Home: 6061 Collins Ave Apt 16-F Miami Beach FL 33140

DALE, ROBERT GORDON, business executive; b. Toronto, Ont., Can., Nov. 1, 1920; s. Gordon McIntyre and Helen Marjorie (Cartwright) D.; m. Mary Austin Babcock, Apr. 3, 1948; children: Robert Austin, John Gordon. Ed., U. Toronto Schs., 1930-39, Trinity Coll.; student, U. Toronto, 1939-40. Cert. in bus. adminstrn., 1946. With Maple Leaf Mills, Ltd., Toronto, 1947—; plant mgr. Maple Leaf Mills, Ltd., 1957-61, gen. product mgr., 1961-65, asst. to pres., 1965-67, exec. v.p., 1967-68, chmn., pres., chief exec. officer, 1968-86, dir., cons., 1986—; bd. dirs. Nat. Life Assurance Co. Can., ULS Capital Corp., Thornmark Corp. Mgmt. Inc., Standard Chartered Bank Can., Manpower Services (Ont.) Ltd.; chmn. Can. Exec. Service Orgn., ULS Capital Corp. Mem. adv. bd. Bloorview Children's Hosp.; past pres. Air Cadet League Can.; past chmn. Ont. Provincial Com.; trustee United Community Fund Greater Toronto; bd. govs. Can. Corps Commissionaires; bd. dirs. Sunnybrook Med. Cen. Served with RCAF, 1940-45. Decorated D.F.C., Can. Forces Decoration, Disting. Service Order. Mem. Can. Nat. Millers Assn. (dir., past chmn.), Grocery Products Mfrs. Can. (dir.), Air Cadet League Can. (hon. pres.), Phi Kappa Pi. Conservative. Anglican. Clubs: Rosedale Golf, Nat, Badminton and Raquet, Bd. of Trade, Empire. Office: ULS Internat, 49 Jackes Ave, Toronto, ON Canada M4T 1E2

DALE-DERKS, CHARLES EUGENE, mechanical engineer; b. Palo Alto, Calif., Oct. 19, 1960; s. Dickson Edward Krebs; adopted s. Herbert Lee and Virginia Ann (Keller) Derks; m. Lisa Kaye Dale, May 26, 1984. Student, U.S. Air Force Acad., 1979-81; BSME, U. Mo., 1983. Design engr. H.O.K. Engrs., St. Louis, 1984-85; v.p. RamAir Products Co., Fenton, Mo., 1985-88; mech. engr. Sigma Chem. Co., St. Louis, 1988—. Mem. ASHRAE (chmn. Heating, Refrigeration and Tech. Edn. com. 1987-88, Energy and Tech. Affairs com.), Nat. Soc. Profl. Engrs., Mo. Soc. Profl. Engrs. Republican. Methodist. Home: 1001 Sugar Creek Ct Saint Charles MO 63303 Office: Sigma Chem Co PO Box 14508 Saint Louis MO 63178

DALENBERG, ROBERT VAN RAALTE, lawyer, utility company executive; b. Chgo., Nov. 1, 1929; s. John R. and Helene (Van Raalte) D.; m. Diane Curtis, June 19, 1954; children: Douglas, Donald, Betsy. Student, Morgan Park Jr. Coll., 1947-49; J.D., U. Chgo., 1953. Bar: Ill. 1956, Calif. 1973. Assoc. firm Essington, McKibben, Beebe & Pratt, Chgo., 1955-58; assoc. firm Schuyler, Stough & Morris, Chgo., 1958-64, ptnr., 1964-67; gen. atty. Ill. Bell Telephone Co., Chgo., 1967-72; assoc. gen. counsel Pacific Tel. & Tel. Co., San Francisco, 1972-76, v.p., gen. counsel, 1976-82; exec. v.p., gen. counsel, sec. Pacific Telesis Group and Pacific Bell, 1983-88; of counsel Pillsbury, Madison and Sutro, San Francisco, 1988—. Served to lt. USCGR, 1953-55. Mem. Am., Ill., Chgo., Calif. bar assns., Am. Judicature Soc., Phi Kappa Psi, Legal Club Chgo., Law Club Chgo. Office: 225 Bush St San Francisco CA 94120

DALEY, FRANCIS DARNALL, JR., manufacturing company executive; b. Altoona, Pa., Mar. 9, 1938; s. Francis Darnall and Helen M. (Miller) D.; B.E.S. in Elec. Engring., Johns Hopkins U., 1960; postgrad. in elec. engring. U. Md., 1965-68; m. M. Ernestine Geist, Dec. 30, 1957; children—Francis Darnall, Christopher Michael. Design engr. Westinghouse Electric Co., Balt., 1960-65; sr. design engr. Martin Co., Balt., 1965-67; project engring. mgr. Electronic Modules Corp., Cockeysville, Md., 1967-70, sales engring. mgr., 1970-73; dir. adminstrn. Wolfe & Mann Mfg. Co., Balt., 1973-76, gen. mgr., 1976-77; dir. ops. Randolph operation Exide Electronics Inc. subs. Inco, Ltd., Randolph, Mass., 1977-81, dir. ops. Randolph and Mississauga, 1981-82; dir. ops. Willson Safety Products div. WGM Safety Corp., 1982-83; owner Power Solution Tech., 1983-84; v.p. ops. Pa. Optical div. BMC Industries, Reading, 1985-86; mfg. mgr. Arrow Precision Products, Inc., Reading, 1986—. Scoutmaster, Boy Scouts Am., 1969-77, asst. dist. commr., 1978, dist. commr., 1979, asst. council commr., 1982-84, v.p. Hawk Mountain council, 1985, council commr., 1986—. Mem. IEEE, Am. Prodn. and Inventory Control Soc. (cert. fellow). Republican. Mem. United Ch. Christ. Patentee digital linearization methods. Home: 1751 Garfield Ave Wyomissing PA 19610 Office: Arrow Precision Products Hill & George Aves Reading PA 19610

DALEY, PETER EDMUND, business and human resources company executive; b. Washington, Mar. 28, 1943; s. Edmund Frances and Marie (Herbert) D.; BS, Wheeling Coll., 1966; MBA, U. Md., 1968; JD, U. Balt., 1975; m. Alexandra Stanish, June 27, 1970; children: Peter, Gina, Milissa, Angela, Thomas, Paul, Alexis, Kara. With Westinghouse Electric Co., Balt., 1970-75, Pitts., 1975-77; corp. mgr. compensation benefits PHH Group, Hunt Valley, Md., 1977-78, corp. mgr. human resources, 1978-79, dir. human resources, 1979-81; dir. employee relations Fairchild Industries, 1981-83; v.p. human resources and adminstrv. services Fairchild Space and Fairchild Communications and Electronics Cos., 1983-84; pres. Harbor Cons. Group, 1985-88; pres., chief exec. officer P.M.A. Inc., 1988—; pres., prin. Yaffe and Co., 1988—. Bd. dirs. Girl Scouts U.S.A. Central Md., 1978-81; mem. exec. adv. com. indsl. relations and labor studies U. Md., mem. Naval Indsl. Facilities Adv. Panel. Mem. Md. Bar Assn., ABA, Am. Mgmt. Assn., Am. Assn. Personnel Adminstrs., Greater Balt. Personnel Assocs., Am. Compensation Assn. Home: 411 Deaconbrook Circle Reisterstown MD 21136

DALEY, ROBERT EDWARD, utility executive; b. Boston, Sept. 7, 1939; s. John R. and Mildred B. (Flavin) D.; m. Angela Basile, Sept. 26, 1970; children—Meghan A., Brandon R., Sean C. AB, Boston Coll., 1964; MBA, St. John's U., 1972. Supr., Equifax, Boston, 1964-68; auditor Goodbody/E.F. Hutton, N.Y.C., 1968-72; asst. treas. CIT Fin., N.Y.C., 1972-78, UNC Resources, Falls Church, Va., 1978-80; fin. analyst office chrysler fin. U.S. Treasury Dept., Washington, 1980-81; v.p. and treas. (chief fin. officer) Equitable Resources Inc., Pitts., 1981—. Mem. Fin. Execs. Inst. (dir. Pitts. chpt.), Nat. Investor Relations Inst., Am. Gas Assn. Roman Catholic. Home: 219 King Richard Dr McMurray PA 15317 Office: Equitable Resources Inc 420 Blvd of the Allies Pittsburgh PA 15219

DALHOUSE, WARNER NORRIS, banker; b. Roanoke, Va., June 4, 1934; s. Jefferson William and Gay-Nell (Henley) D.; m. Barbara Ann Dalhouse, Dec. 27, 1984. Student, Roanoke Coll., 1952-54; B.S. in Commerce, U. Va., 1956. Vice pres. 1st Nat. Exchange Bank, Roanoke, Va., 1967-69, sr. v.p., 1969-73, exec. v.p., 1973-77, pres., chief adminstrv. officer, 1977-81; exec. v.p., chief adminstrv. officer Dominion Bankshares Corp., Roanoke, Va., 1977-81, pres., chief exec. officer, 1981—. Pres. Roanoke Pub. Library Found., Va.; chmn. Ctr.-In-The-Sq. ; trustee, mem. exec. com. Roanoke Coll.; trustee Nat. Ctr. for the Humanities; bd. dirs. Washington Dulles Task Force. Office: Dominion Bankshares Corp PO Box 13327 Roanoke VA 24040

DALKOFF, MORRIS SIDNEY, retailer executive; b. Moline, Ill., Apr. 13, 1948; s. Leonard and Lisa (Barmak) D.; m. Ytta Gliksman, June 12, 1983. BS in Social Sci., Chadron State Coll., 1971. Care worker Covenant Children's Home, Princeton, Ill., 1971-73; mgr. Lensey Corp, Rock Island, Ill., 1971-76, exec. v.p., 1976—, exec. corp sec., 1980—; pres. Video House Rock Island, Rock Island, 1986—. Creator in field. Republican. Jewish. Office: Video House Corp 2720 18th Ave Rock Island IL 61201

DALLAS, THOMAS ABRAHAM, utility company executive; b. Natchez, Miss., Oct. 30, 1923; s. Freely Skyles and Virginia (Walton) D.; m. Billye Haskins, Nov. 16, 1952; children: Virginia Hilton, Thomas Walton, Sue Ellen Dallas Shepard. BEE, Miss. State U., 1948. Registered profl. engr., Miss. Engr. Miss. Power & Light Co., Brookhaven, 1948-56; mgr. Miss. Power & Light Co., Indianola, 1956-62; mgr. Miss. Power & Light Co., Jackson, 1962-80, v.p., chief engr., 1980-85, sr. v.p., 1985-88; ret. 1988; chmn. South Cen. Electric Cos., 1982-87. Served to 1st lt. USAAF, 1943-45, ETO. Recipient Pub. Service award Nat. Weather Service, 1973. Mem. Nat. Soc. Profl. Engrs. Republican. Methodist. Lodge: Kiwanis (pres. Jackson club 1981). Home: 5376 Farnsworth Dr Jackson MS 39211 Office: Miss Power & Light Co PO Box 1640 Jackson MS 39211

DALLMAN, STEVEN ROBERT, school business executive; b. Milw., Dec. 22, 1954; s. Robert Arthur and Betty Mae (Molden) D.; m. Bethany Marie Richards, Oct. 18, 1975; children: Amy, Rebekah, Karen, Todd. Student, Martin Luther Coll., New Ulm, Minn., 1973-75; BBA, LaSalle Extension U., 1981; postgrad., Century U., Beverly Hills, Calif., 1985—. Mgmt. trainee Grossman's Lumber Co., Milw., 1975-77; adminstr. coordinator Mortgage Guaranty Ins. Co., Milw., 1977-79; bus. mgr. Mich. Luth. Sem., Saginaw, 1979—; coach volleyball, football, softball Mich. Luth. Sem., 1979—. State ranking chmn. for volleyball, 1988-89, bd. dirs., 1988-89; dir. AAU Saginaw Area Volleyball Club, 1989. Mem. Assn. Sch. Bus. Ofcls. (personnel com. 1980—), Mich. Assn. Sch. Bus., Christian Mgmt. Assn., Mich. Football Coaches Assn., Mich. Volleyball Coaches Assn. (ranking com. 1985—), U.S. Volleyball Assn. Republican. Lutheran. Home: 1423 Bay St Saginaw MI 48602 Office: 2777 Hardin Ave Saginaw MI 48602

DALLOW, PHYLLIS FLORENCE, realtor; b. N.J., Nov. 17, 1924; d. Harry and Pauline (Isaacson) Lash; student Coll. City N.Y., 1944; m. Theodore J. Dallow, July 30, 1944; children—Ellen Poor, Richard Dallow, Constance Dallow. Vice pres., relocation dir., chief real estate mgmt. dept. Theo. J. Dallow Inc., Farmingdale, N.Y., 1952-82; pres. Century 21 Dallow Realty, Inc., 1982—. Pres., Levittown South-North Wantagh Republican Club, 1972-73; Rep. committeewoman, 1964-79. Recipient hon. service award Mademoiselle mag., 1944. Mem. L.I. Bd. Realtors, Nat. Assn. Realtors, Inst. Real Estate Mgmt., Internat. Real Estate Fedn. Club: Order Eastern Star. Home: 1370 S Ocean Blvd #2408 Pompano Beach FL 33062 Office: 3000 Hempstead Turnpike Levittown NY 11756 also: 392 Conklin St Farmingdale NY 11735

D'ALOIA, G(IAMBATTISTA) PETER, multinational corporation executive, lawyer; b. Sao Paulo, Brazil, Jan. 10, 1945; s. John and Rosali (Picarelli) D'A.; m. Marguerite Ann Fuccello, Aug. 3, 1946; children: Jonelle, Tara. BS, NYU, 1966, LLM, 1976; JD, St. John's U., 1969. Bar: N.Y. 1969. Tax atty. Arthur Young and Co., N.Y.C., 1969-72, Allied Chem. Co., Morristown, N.J., 1972-79; chief tax counsel Allied Corp., Morristown, 1979-81, dir. taxes, 1981-83; v.p. taxes Allied-Signal Inc., Morristown, 1983-88, v.p., treas., 1988—. Mem. Bd. Edn., Mendham, N.J., 1977-80. Mem. ABA, Assn. of Bar City of N.Y., N.Y. State Bar Assn. Roman Catholic. Home: 11 Kerby Ln Mendham NJ 07945 Office: Allied-Signal Inc Columbia Rd & Park Ave Morristown NJ 07960

DALTON, DICK NEWTON, communications executive; b. Piggott, Ark., Sept. 12, 1937; s. W.R. Dalton and L. Adele (Gowen) McIlroy; m. Beverly J., Mar. 26, 1959; children: Mark, Eric, Michelle. BSME, U. Miss., 1959; cert. in mgmt., Wash. U., 1966. Registered profl. engr., Miss. Project engr. Emerson Electric, St. Louis, 1963, dir. quality control, 1964, plant supt., 1965, asst. to pres., 1965-69, asst. v.p., 1969-76; v.p. Wetterau Inc., St. Louis, 1976-82, 1st v.p., 1982-86, sr. v.p., 1986—; bd. dirs. NIRI, St. Louis, 1976—. Bd. dirs., v.p. North County, Inc., St. Louis, 1983—; dir. Young Audiences, St. Louis, 1984—, Cancer Care, St. Louis, 1988. With USN, 1959-63, USNR, 63-65. Mem. Media Club. Republican. Baptist. Home: 24 Jamestown Acres Saint Louis County MO 63034 Office: Wetterau Inc 8920 Pershall Rd Saint Louis MO 63042

DALTON, EDWARD ALOYSIUS, JR., telecommunications company executive; b. Jersey City, Nov. 2, 1938; s. Edward Aloysius and Catherine Margaret (Lavin) D.; m. Jane McLaughlin, May 16, 1964; 1 child, Christopher. B in Mech. Engring., Stevens Inst. Tech., 1960, MS, 1964; MBA, Harvard U., 1966. Advt. supr. N.Y. Telephone, N.Y.C., 1968-70, planning mgr., 1972-77, div. mgr. corp. planning, 1977-81; mktg. supr. AT&T, N.Y.C., 1970-72; dir. strategic planning AT&T Internat., Basking Ridge, N.J., 1981-83; div. mgr. market assessment Bell Communications Research, Livingston, N.J., 1983-86; dir. technol. adminstrn. NYNEX, White Plains, N.Y., 1986, dir. external affairs, 1986-88, corp. dir. spl. project, 1988—. Pres., Jersey City Boys Club, 1978-84; chmn. Jersey City Planning Bd., 1974-77, Jersey City Incinerator Authority, 1972-74, Edwin A. Stevens Soc., 1984-86. Recipient Silver Keystone award Boys Club Am., 1985, Stevens Alumni award, 1982. Mem. Stevens Alumni, Delta Tau Delta. Roman Catholic. Clubs: Ridgewood Country, Stevens Met. Office: NYNEX 1113 Westchester Ave White Plains NY 10604

DALTON, JAMES EDWARD, business executive, retired air force officer; b. N.Y.C., Oct. 17, 1930; s. Edward A. and Marion (Conway) D.; m. Betty Jane Irwin, Nov. 29, 1958; children: Christopher, Stephanie, Todd. B.S., U.S. Mil. Acad., 1954; M.S.E. in Instrumentation Engring, U. Mich., 1960, M.S.E. in Aero./Astronautical Engring, 1960; grad. with distinction, Air Command and Staff Coll., 1965, Indsl. Coll. Armed Forces, 1970. Commd. 2d lt. U.S. Air Force, 1954, advanced through grades to gen., 1983; served in numerous operational and research assignments 1954-73; comdr. 39th Aerospace Rescue and Recovery Wing, Eglin AFB, Fla., 1973-75, Air Res. Personnel Center, Denver, 1975-76; dep. dir. concepts Hdqrs. USAF, Washington, 1976-77; dep. dir. Force Devel. and Strategic Plans, Plans and Policy Directorate, Office Joint Chiefs of Staff, Washington, 1977-78; vice dir. Joint Staff, 1978-80; commandant Indsl. Coll. of Armed Forces, Washington, 1980-81; dir. Joint Staff, 1981-83; chief of staff SHAPE, 1983-85; pres. R & D Assocs.; corp. v.p. Logicon. Decorated Def. Disting. Service medal with two oak leaf clusters, Legion of Merit with 1 oak leaf cluster, D.F.C., Bronze Star, Air medal with 5 oak leaf clusters, Meritorious Service medal with 2 oak leaf clusters, Air Force Commendation medal. Mem. Air Force Assn., Assn. Grads. U.S. Mil. Acad., Council Fgn. Relations. Roman Catholic. Home: 61 Misty Acres Rd Rolling Hills Estates CA 90274

DALTON, JOHN HOWARD, financial consultant; b. New Orleans, Dec. 13, 1941; s. William Carl and Jaunice Dalton (Davenport) Winterrowd Dalton. BS, U.S. Naval Acad., 1964; MBA, U. Pa., 1971. Commd. ensign USN, 1964, advanced through grades to lt., resigned, 1969; investment bank trainee Goldman, Sachs & Co., N.Y.C., 1971-72; with security sales sect. Goldman, Sachs & Co., Dallas, 1972-77; pres. Govt. Nat. Mortgage Assn., Washington, 1977-79; nat. treas. Carter/Mondale Presdl. Campaign, Washington, 1979; chmn., mem. Fed. Home Loan Bank Bd., Washington, 1979-81; pres. real estate div. Gill Cos., San Antonio, 1981-84; chmn., pres. Seguin Savs. Assn., San Antonio, 1984-88; chmn., chief exec. officer Freedom Capital Corp., San Antonio, 1984-88; chmn. fin. inst. adv. com. Fed. Res. Bank Dallas; bd. dirs. AmeriMac, Cupertino, Calif., Lomas Mortgage Corp.; adv. dir. 1st Liquidity. Trustee Ecumenical Ctr. Religion and Health, San Antonio, 1983—, Mental Health Assn. Tex., Austin, 1986—, YMCA, San Antonio, 1984—; chmn. World Affairs Council, San Antonio, 1987. Democrat. Episcopalian. Clubs: Club Giraud, Oak Hills Country (San Antonio). Lodge: Elks. Home: 112 Sheffield St San Antonio TX 78213 Office: Freedom Captial Corp 1802 NE Loop 410 Ste 100 San Antonio TX 78217

DALTON, RICHARD L., biotechnology company executive; b. Wentzville, Mo., Aug. 24, 1927; s. Warren R. and Evelyn (Chauncey) D.; m. I. Virginia Griewing, Oct. 20, 1946; children: Richard L. Jr., Mark A., James R., Diane V., John W. AB, Central Coll., Fayette, Mo., 1948; MS, U. Ill., 1949, PhD, 1951. Research chemist E.I. duPont de Nemours & Co., Wilmington, Del., 1951-54, research supr., 1954-65; devel. and service rep. E.I. duPont de Nemours & Co., Chgo., 1965-66; with sales mgmt. dept. E.I. duPont de Nemours & Co., Wilmington, 1966-76; v.p. mktg. Endo Labs. subs. DuPont, Garden City, N.Y., 1976-80; dir. adminstrn. and planning Pharm.-DuPont, Wilmington, 1980-82; bus. cons. Biotechnica Internat. Inc., Cambridge, Mass., 1984-85, v.p. affiliates and contracts, 1985—; pres. Biotechnica Diagnostics Inc., Cambridge, Mass., 1985-86. Contbr. articles to sci. publs.; patentee in field. Mem. Am. Chem. Soc., Sigma Xi, Phi Lambda Upsilon, Alpha Chi Sigma. Presbyterian. Lodge: Masons. Home: 269D S Lindsey Rd Old Monroe MO 63369 Office: Biotechnica Internat Inc 85 Bolton St Cambridge MA 02140

DALY, BRIAN PATRICK, financial consultant; b. Phila., Apr. 3, 1961; s. Joseph John Daly and Eleanor Mary (Owens) Frederick; m. Deborah Anne Markert, Nov. 19, 1983; 1 child, Stephen Patrick. BS, Glassboro State Coll., 1983. Agt. Prudential Ins. Co., Cherry Hill, N.J., 1983-84; account exec. Dean Witter Reynolds Ins. Co., Cherry Hill, 1984-88, RTD Fin. Advisors Inc., Phila., 1988-89; sr. fin. cons. Mellon Bank, Blue Bell, Penn., 1989—. Active mem. Marlton Rep. Club, Young Rep. of Burlington County. Mem. Inst. Cert. Fin. Planners, Del. Valley Soc. Inst. Cert. Fin. Planners, N.J. State and Fin. Planning Coun. Republican. Home: 23 Marsham Dr Marlton NJ 08053 Office: Mellon Bank 660 Sentry Pkwy Sentry Pk Blue Bell PA 19422

DALY, CHRISTOPHER THOMAS, financial executive; b. N.Y.C., Mar. 6, 1955; s. Joseph Sabestian and Audrey Dorthey (Sinton) D.; m. Joan Mary Brunner, Nov. 12, 1977; children: Christopher Patrick, Eileen Mary, Erin Catherine. BSBA, Manhattan Coll., 1977. CPA N.J., Pa. Sr. acct. Touche Ross & Co., Newark, 1977-81; dir. fin. controls Brodart Industries, Williamsport, Pa., 1981-83; asst. controller Brodart Co., Williamsport, Pa., 1983-84, treas., chief fin. officer, 1984-86, v.p., chief fin. officer, 1986—. Pack leader Lycoming County council Boy Scouts Am., 1987. Mem. Am. Inst. CPA's, N.J. Soc. CPA's. Republican. Roman Catholic. Home: 1141 Country Club Dr Williamsport PA 17701 Office: Brodart Co 500 Arch St Williamsport PA 17705

DALY, GEORGE GARMAN, economist, educator; b. Painesville, Ohio, Oct. 5, 1940; s. George Ferdinand and Helen May (Garman) D.; m. Barbara Leigh Anthony, Mar. 13, 1977. A.B., Miami U., Oxford, Ohio, 1962; M.A., Northwestern U., 1965, Ph.D., 1967. Asst. then assoc. prof. Miami U., Oxford, 1965-69; asst. prof. U. Tex., Austin, 1969-70; asst. prof., then prof. U. Houston, 1971-77, dean Coll. Social Sci., 1979-83; dean Coll. Bus. U. Iowa, Iowa City, 1983—; asst. dir. Inst. Defense Analysis, Arlington, Va., 1977-79; sr. economist Exec. Officer Pres., Washington, 1974; economist Fed. Energy Agy., Washington, 1975-76; adv. bd. Ctr. Pub. Policy, Houston. Mem. Am. Econs. Assn., Public Choice Soc., Phi Beta Kappa, Beta Gamma Sigma. Home: 14 The Woods Iowa City IA 52240 Office: U Iowa Coll Bus Adminstrn Iowa City IA 52242

DALY, GERALDINE VERONICA, financial services executive; b. Bklyn., July 4, 1956; d. James Patrick and Charlotte Jean (Reilly) D. AA in Humanities, Brookdale Community Coll., 1976; BA in Journalism, U. Richmond, 1978; MBA in Mktg., Loyola Coll., Balt., 1986. Admissions counselor U. Richmond, 1978-80, asst. dir. devel., 1980-81, dir. annual giving, 1981-82; dir. of capital resources Loyola Coll., Balt., 1982-84, dir. devel., 1984-86; dir. mktg. Legg Mason Wood Walker, Balt., 1986-89, assoc. v.p., 1989—. Mem. Greater Balt. Com., 1987-88; fundraising chmn. Xi-amen-Balt. Sister Cities Program, 1986-87. Named one of Outstanding Young Women of Am., 1981. Mem. U. Richmond Alumni Assn. (pres. Balt. chpt. 1984—), Bond Club (Balt.). Republican. Roman Catholic. Home: 229 Stanmore Rd Baltimore MD 21212 Office: Legg Mason Wood Walker 111 S Calvert St Baltimore MD 21203

DALY, JOHN FRANCIS, engineering company executive; b. N.Y.C., Dec. 13, 1922; s. John F. and Caroline (Pohl) D.; m. May Ann Avis, Mar. 20, 1943 (dec. Dec. 1950); m. Casilda Mary Boyd, July 16, 1953; children: Jo-Ann, Avis Ann, Carol Lilian, Peter Boyd, Alexia. BSME, Rensselaer Poly. Inst., 1942; D of Humanities (hon.), Siena Heights Coll., Adrian, Mich., 1971. Exec. v.p. Hardie Mfg. Co., Hudson, Mich., 1946-55; v.p. Internat. Steel Co., Evansville, Ind., 1955-58; exec. v.p. Universal Wire Spring, Solon, Ohio, 1958-60; v.p. Hoover Ball and Bearing, Ann Arbor, Mich., 1960-66, exec. v.p., 1966-67, pres., chief operating officer, 1967-72; chmn., pres., chief exec. officer Hoover Universal (previously Hoover Ball & Bearing), Ann Arbor, Mich., 1972-86; vice chmn. Johnson Controls, Ann Arbor, 1986-87; bd. dirs. Johnson Controls, Comerica Inc., Detroit, Cross and Trecker, Detroit, Handleman Co., Detroit. Dir. Citizens Rsch. Council, 1982—; trustee Siena Heights Coll., 1969—. Capt. USAAF, 1942-45, PTO. Mem. Indsl. Tech. Ins.t (chmn. 1986—), Ednl. Found. (chmn. 1984-86), Winged Foot Country Club, Barton Hill Country Club. Home: 18 Southwick Ct Ann Arbor MI 48105 Office: Johnson Controls Inc PO Box 1005 Ann Arbor MI 48106

DALY, JOSEPH RAYMOND, advertising executive; b. N.Y.C., May 14, 1918; s. William C. and Mary (Hendrick) D.; m. Elizabeth R. Schulte, Apr. 19, 1947 (div.); children: Dorothy E., Suzanne J., Peter J., Timothy J., Mark, Andrew, Jennifer; m. Kathy Cristy, Nov. 5, 1988. A.B., Fordham U., 1940. With John A. Cairns (advt.), 1946-49; with DDB Needham Worldwide, Inc. (formerly Doyle Dan Bernbach Internat.), N.Y.C., 1949—, sr. v.p., mgmt. supr., 1959-69, pres., 1968-74, chmn. bd., 1974-86, chmn. exec. com., 1986-88; chmn. Vitafort Internat. Corp., N.Y.C., 1986—. Served to lt. comdr., Air Corps USNR, 1940-46, PTO. Decorated Navy Cross, Purple Heart, Air medal. Clubs: Rockefeller Ctr. Luncheon, Turf and Field (N.Y.C.); Marco Polo, Ocean Reef. Office: DDB Needham Worldwide Inc 437 Madison Ave New York NY 10022

DALY, JUDITH MARIE, retail executive; b. Cedar Rapids, Iowa, Dec. 2, 1950; d. Elmer Frederick and Lucille Magdalen (Bousek) Vorhies; m. James Francis Daly, Sept. 3, 1970 (div. 1979); children: Jonathan W., Jaime B. Student, U. No. Iowa, 1970, Ind. U. N.W., 1988—. Head cashier Home Hardware Co., St. Charles, Ill., 1972-73, dept. mgr., 1973-74, buyer, merchandiser, 1974-79; head buyer Home Hardware Co., West Chicago, Ill., 1979-81, v.p. purchasing, 1982-86; sr. v.p. Home Hardware Co., Portage, Ind., 1987—; also bd. dirs. Home Hardware Co., Marengo, Ill.; pres. Nationwide Wholesale Supply, Portage, Ind., 1984—. Mem. Nat. Assn. Female Execs. Avocation: golf. Home: 156 Southport Dr Valparaiso IN 46383 Office: Nationwide Wholesale Supply 6044 Central Ave Portage IN 46368

DALY, ROBERT ANTHONY, film executive; b. Bklyn., Dec. 8, 1936; s. James and Eleanor D.; m. Nancy MacNeil, Oct. 7, 1961; children: Linda Marie, Robert Anthony, Brian James. Student, Bklyn. Coll. From dir. bus. affairs to v.p. bus. affairs, to exec. v.p. CBS TV Network, 1955-80; pres. CBS Entertainment Co., 1977—; chmn., chief exec. officer Warner Bros., Inc., Burbank, Calif., 1981—; Bd. dirs. Am. Film Inst. Trustee Am. Film Inst.; bd. dirs. Nat. Conf. Christians and Jews. Mem. Acad. Motion Picture Arts and Scis., Nat. Acad. TV Arts and Scis., Hollywood Radio and TV Soc., Motion Picture Pioneers. Roman Catholic. Club: Bel Air Country. Office: Warner Bros Inc 4000 Warner Blvd Burbank CA 91522 •

DALY, THOMAS FRANCIS, retired lawyer; b. N.Y.C., Dec. 30, 1902; s. Thomas F. and Josephine (Walsh) D.; m. Isabel Hope, Apr. 12, 1933 (dec. 1964); m. Virginia Barrett Melniker, June 16, 1966 (dec. Feb. 1988). Bar: N.Y., 1928, N.J., 1947. Student William and Mary Coll.; LLB, Columbia U., 1927. Assoc., ptnr. firm Lord, Day & Lord, N.Y.C., 1927-75, now of counsel; practiced in N.J., 1947; mem. Atty. Gen.'s Nat. Com. To Study Antitrust Laws; mem. N.Y. Supreme Ct. Med. Malpractice Panel, 1971—. Bd. dirs. Monmouth County Soc. for Prevention Cruelty to Animals, 1955-69 , Monmouth County chpt. ARC; trustee Monmouth Mus., 1974-88; mem. Rumson (N.J.) Sch. Bd., 1960-69. Fellow Am. Bar Found., N.Y. Bar Found., Am. Coll. Trial Lawyers; mem. ABA, N.Y. Bar Assn., N.J. Bar Assn., Guild Catholic Lawyers (gov. 1969-71). Clubs: Rumson (N.J.) Country; Root Beer and Checker (Red Bank, N.J.). Home: 70 East River Rd Rumson NJ 07760 Office: 25 Broadway New York NY 10004

DAMAN, ERNEST LUDWIG, mechanical engineer; b. Hannover, Germany, Mar. 14, 1923; came to U.S., 1940, naturalized, 1944; s. Fritz and Ruth Edith (Meyer) Dammann; m. Jan. 20, 1945 (div.); children: Diane Cathrine, Cynthia Ruth, Bruce Hershey; m. Dorothy Russo, June 21, 1980; stepchildren: Christopher Walsweer, Jonathan Walsweer. B.S. in Mech. Engring, Poly. Inst. Bklyn., 1943. With Foster Wheeler Corp., Livingston, N.J., 1947—, dir. research, 1960-73, v.p., 1973-81, sr. v.p., 1981-88; chmn. Foster Wheeler Devel. Corp., Livingston, N.J., 1977-88, chmn. emeritus, 1988—; chmn., chief exec. officer HDS Fibers Inc., 1986—; dir. Foster Wheeler Solar Devel. Corp.; chmn. Nat. Materials Property Data Network, Inc., 1986—; lectr. Patentee in field. Chmn. Westfield (N.J.) Democratic Com., 1956-60, Westfield Area Com. for Human Rights, 1962-68; mem. Westfield Charter Study Commn., 1964. Served with U.S. Army, 1944-46. Decorated Bronze Star. Fellow ASME (pres.-elect 1987, pres. 1988-89), Instn. Mech. Engrs.; mem. AAAS, Inst. Fuel (U.K.), Welding Research Council (chmn. 1985), Nat. Acad. Engring., Pi Tau Sigma. Club: Westfield Tennis. Home: 435 Wychwood Rd Westfield NJ 07090 Office: Foster Wheeler Corp Perryville Corp Pk Clinton NJ 08809

D'AMATO, ANTHONY S., chemical company executive; b. Brooklyn, N.Y., 1930. BSChE, Poly. Inst. of Brooklyn, 1952. Exec. vice pres. Borden Inc., New York, 1985—; pres. Borden Chem. Div., Columbus, Ohio, 1985—. Office: Borden Inc Chem Div 277 Park Ave New York NY 10172 •

D'AMBRISI, JOSEPH VINCENT, oil company executive; b. Phila., Apr. 19, 1928; s. James and Angelina (Gaudiosi) D'A.; m. Frances Margaret Farrell, Oct. 2, 1954; children: Michael Peter, James Joseph, Joseph James, Mary Frances. BSChemE, Villanova U., 1950, ScD (hon.), 1986. With Mobil Oil Corp., 1950—; tech., mgmt. positions various locations, 1950-67; mgr. ops. research and computer applications N.Y.C., 1967-69, mgr. ops., 1969-70; mgr. Joliet (Ill.) refinery 1970-74; mgr. service and coordination, Saudi Arabia N.Y.C., 1974-77, gen. mgr. projects coordination, Saudi Arabia, 1977-80, gen. mgr. Middle East Dept., 1980-83, v.p. Middle East coordination and marine transp., 1983-85; v.p. research and engring., pres. Mobil Research and Devel. Corp. Princeton, N.J., 1985—. Conf. pres. Boy Scouts Am., Joliet, 1970-74; chmn. United Fund, Joliet, 1973. Mem. Am. Inst. Chem. Engrs., Am. Petroleum Inst., Coordinating Research Council. Republican. Roman Catholic. Clubs: Nassau (Princeton), Springdale (Princeton); Sky (N.Y.C.). Office: Mobil R & D Corp Pennington-Rocky Hill Rd Pennington NJ 08534

D'AMBROSIO, HENRY A., publishing executive; b. N.Y.C., Jan. 20, 1946; s. Alfred Henry and Viola Emily Campione D.; m. Barbara Mary Roeder, Sept. 1, 1968; children: Lori, Alfred, Amanda. BBA, St. John's U., 1967; MBA, Pace U., 1970. Fin. analyst Norden div. United Techs., Norwalk, Conn., 1968-71; sr. fin. analyst McGraw Hill Info. System Co., N.Y.C., 1971-72; mgr. adminstrn. Bell & Howell Co., White Plains, N.Y., 1972-79; nat. mgr. adminstrn. Bell & Howell Co., Chgo., 1979-81, group mgr. human resources, 1981-84, nat. mgr. services ops., 1984-86, v.p. adminstrn., 1986—. Home: 1614 N Haddow Arlington Heights IL 60004 Office: Bell & Howell 5215 Old Orchard Rd Skokie IL 60077

DAMERON, LARRY WRIGHT, sales executive; b. Athens, Tex., Jan. 29, 1949; s. Leonard Wright and Ellen Louise (Cole) D.; m. Kathleen Adele Mittag, July 17, 1971; children: Greg, Mark, Jessica. BBA, U. Tex., 1970. Salesman Monroe Systems Litton Corp., Austin, Tex., 1972-74; sales mgr. Monroe Systems Litton Corp., Phoenix, 1974-76; br. mgr. Monroe Systems Litton Corp., Lubbock, Tex. and Columbus, Ohio, 1976-83; major accounts mgr. Victor Techs., Columbus, 1983; cen. region mgr., ea. regional mgr., dir. domestic distbn., v.p. sales CXI Corp., Columbus, 1984-88; v.p. sales-communications products div. Novell (formerly CXI Corp.), Columbus, 1988-89, mgr. strategic bus. devel., 1989—. Recipient Centurion awards Litton, 1974, 78, Pres.'s award, 1976, various top sales awards for region CXI Corp., 1984-86. Republican. Methodist. Office: Novell Inc 1631 NW Professional Pla Columbus OH 43220

DAMES, TRENT RAYSBROOK, engineering company executive; b. Bklyn., Oct. 6, 1911; s. Frank and Alice (Trent) D.; m. Phoebe Laura Rubins, 1934 (dec.); children: Melissa, Joyce, Roger; m. Carolyn Nancy Means (dec.). B.S., Calif. Inst. Tech., 1933, M.S., 1934. Registered profl. engr., Ariz., Calif., Guam, Ill., La., Mo., Nev., N.J., N.Y., Tex., Utah. Engr. Labarre & Converse, Los Angeles, 1934-35; engr. R.V. Labarre, Los Angeles, 1936-38; jr. engr. U.S. Bur. Records, Denver, 1935-36; co-founder Dames & Moore, Los Angeles, 1938—, now founding ptnr., mem. exec. com. Contbr. articles to profl. publs.; patentee in field. Trustee Mills Coll.; fin. chmn. engring. industry Com. for Econ. Devel., 1975; mem. So. Calif. regional adv. council Calif. Inst. Tech., 1975;. Named Constrn. Man of Yr., Los Angeles C. of C., 1975. Fellow Am. Inst. Cons. Engrs., Am. Cons. Engrs. Council; mem. ASCE (nat. and Los Angeles sect.), Seismol. Soc. Am., Cons. Engrs. Assn. So. Calif., Structural Engrs. Assn. So. Calif., Assocs. of Calif. Inst. Tech., Sigma Xi, Tau Beta Pi. Club: California. also: Dames & Moore 911 Wilshire Blvd Los Angeles CA 90017 *

DAMHOLT, RONALD JAMES, organ manufacturing executive; b. Racine, Wis., July 11, 1951; s. Einar Kristian and Edith Marie (Hansen) D.; m. Sharon Ann Colby, Sept. 6, 1975 (div.); children: Kristian, Alisa. BA, U. Wis., 1975; postgrad,, Gordon-Conwell Theol. Sem., S. Hamilton, Mass., 1975-78, Seabury-Western Theol. Sem., 1988-89. Apprentice organbuilder Prairie Organ Co., Evanston, Ill., 1978-81; v.p. Bradford Organ Co., Evanston, 1981—; minister of youth St. Augustine's Episcopal Ch., Wilmette, Ill., 1988—. Democrat.

D'AMICO, JOSEPH THOMAS, corporate professional; b. N.Y.C., Jan. 16, 1930; s. Stanislao and Mary (Maniscalo) D'A.; m. Lucille Smith, Dec. 30, 1966. BS in Mgmt., Fordham U., 1951; postgrad., Fairfield U., 1965. Dir. material Loral Electronics Corp., Yonkers, N.Y., 1952-65, Philco-Ford Corp., Blue Bell, Pa., 1965-70; v.p. material Varadyne Industries, Santa Monica, Calif., 1970-80; dir. material Superior IndustriesInc., Van Nuys, Calif., 1981-84, v.p. material, 1984—. Mem. Nat. Purchasing Mgmt. Assn. Home: 521 Muskingum Ave Pacific Padisades CA 90272 Office: Superior Industries Inc 7800 Woodley Ave Van Nuys CA 91406

D'AMICO, VINCENT JOSEPH, manufacturing company executive; b. N.Y.C., Oct. 18, 1929; s. Antonio and Josephine (Schepis) D'A.; m. Angela Maria Panzarino, Feb. 23, 1963; childrlen: Anthony Vincent, Joseph Rocco. BEE, Manhattan Coll., 1952; MBA, Adelphi U., 1965. Design engr. Bendix Aviation Corp., Teterboro, N.J., 1952-55; supr. elec. lab. Bulova Watch Co., Astoria, N.Y., 1955-58; quality control mgr. Arma div. Am. Bosh Arma Corp., Garden City, N.Y., 1958-66; plant mgr. Olivetti Corp of Am., Hauppauge, N.Y., 1966-73; mgr. ops. Olivetti Corp of Am., N.Y.C., 1973-78; gen. mgr. Powers Chemco Corp., Glen Cove, N.Y., 1978-82; v.p. Winston Network, Inc., N.Y.C., 1982—. Com. chmn. Farmingdale Council Boy Scouts Am., 1980-82, scoutmaster, 1982-88; asst. dist. commr. Nassau County Council Boy Scouts Am., N.Y., 1988—. Republican. Roman Catholic. Office: Winston Network Inc 275 Madison Ave New York NY 10016

DAMMERMAN, DENNIS DEAN, financial executive; b. Fairfield, Iowa, Nov. 4, 1945; s. Morris Melvin and Mary Louise (Watson) D.; m. Patricia Anne Bryk, July 9, 1967; children: Dwight David, Heather Lynne. B.S., U. Dubuque, 1967. Fin. mgmt. trainee Gen. Electric Co., 1967-69, corp. auditor, 1969-74, mgr. acquisitions analysis, lighting bus. group, 1974-76, mgr. ops. analysis, consumer products and services sector, 1976-78; v.p., comptroller Gen. Electric Credit Corp., Stamford, Conn., 1978-81; dir. Trafalgar Developers, Inc., Miami, Fla., 1979—; v.p. Real Estate Fin. Services div. Trafalgar Developers, Inc., 1981-84; sr. v.p. fin. Gen. Electric Co., 1984—. Mem. Council Fin. Execs., Fin. Execs. Inst., Officers Conf. Group. Republican. Home: 21 Bellevale Dr Monroe CT 06468 Office: GE 3135 Easton Turnpike Fairfield CT 06431

DAMOOSE, CAROL SWEENEY (CARI), commercial real estate broker; b. Pascagoula, Miss., Oct. 10, 1942; d. James Augustus and Leonora (Bixby) S.; m. George Lynn Damoose; children: Alison, George C. BS in Bus. Adminstrn., U. So. Calif., 1964; MBA, San Diego State U., 1978. Security analyst Mitchum Jones & Templeton, Los Angeles, 1966-70; prin. Cari S. Damoose, San Diego, 1970-75; sr. mktg. cons. Grubb & Ellis Co., San Diego, 1978—. Author: Residential Downzoning, 1978; contbr. articles to newspapers. Trustee La Jollans, Inc., La Jolla, Calif., 1974-77. Mem. San Diego Women in Comml. Real Estate (founding dir., pres. 1984-85), Charter 100, Bus. Alumni Assn. San Diego State U. (bd. dirs. 1986-88), Council Comml. Real Estate (founding dir. 1984-85), Urban Land Inst. (assoc.), Beta Gamma Sigma. Club: La Jolla Beach & Tennis. Office: Grubb & Ellis Co 2299 Camino del Rio S San Diego CA 92108

DAMOTTA, LORRAINE, controller; b. Hartford, Conn., Dec. 16, 1957; d. Edward I. and Anne E. (Wilkinson) DaM. BS in Acctg., Cen. Conn. State Coll., 1979. Asst. controller Sheraton Corp., Hartford, N.Y.C., Washington and Pasadena, Calif., 1980-86; hotel controller Morrison House, Alexandria, Va., 1986; assoc. Fin. Placement Network, Washington, 1986-87; asst. regional controller Beacon Hotel Corp., Washington, 1987—. Mem. NAFE, Cousteau Soc. Roman Catholic. Home: 5300 Holmes Run Pkwy Alexandria VA 22304 Office: 2101 L St NW Washington DC 20037

DAMSEL, RICHARD A., transportation company executive; b. 1942; married. BSBA, John Carroll U., 1964. Audit mgr. Deloitte Haskins and Sells, to 1974; with Leaseway Transp. Corp., Cleve., 1974—, mgr. fin. analysis, then treas., 1975-80, v.p. fin., treas., 1980-83, sr. v.p. fin. adminstrn., 1983-88, chmn., chief exec. officer, 1988—; bd. dirs. Midwestern Distbn. Inc., Fort Scott, Kans., Leaseway Personnel Corp., Cleve. Office: Leaseway Transp Corp 3700 Park E Dr Cleveland OH 44122 *

DANCEWICZ, JOHN EDWARD, investment banker; b. Boston, Mass., Feb. 12, 1949; s. John Felix and Teresa Sophia (Lewandowski) D.; m. Barbaragail Jarrett, Jan. 23, 1971; children: John Lawrence, Jill Elizabeth, Jenna Gail. BA in Econs., Yale U., 1971; MBA, Harvard U., 1973. Project adminstr., cons. Nat. Shawmut Bank Boston, 1972-73; v.p., mgr. U.S. investment banking Continental Ill. Nat. Bank Chgo., 1973-82; sr. mng. dir., mgr. corp. fin. Bear Stearns & Co. Inc., Chgo., 1982—; bd. dirs. Standard Havens, Inc., Kansas City, Mo. Contbr. articles to profl. jours. Active Yale U. Schs. Com., Spl. Gifts Com.; sec. Harvard Bus. Sch. sect. Mem. Mid. Am. Com., Assn. for Corp. Growth, Scholarship and Guidance Assn. (bd. dirs., treas. 1982—). Clubs: Economic, University, East Bank, Mid-America (Chgo.). Home: 969 E Spring Ln Lake Forest IL 60045 Office: Bear Stearns & Co Inc 3 First Nat Pla Chicago IL 60602

D'ANDRADE, HUGH A(LFRED), pharmaceutical company executive, lawyer; b. Metuchen, N.J., Nov. 7, 1938; s. Herman and Lucille (Peticolas) D'A.; m. Nancy K. Koyen (div.); 1 dau., Janine; m. Mary T. Bohner. B.A. in Econs., Rutgers U., 1961; LL.B. cum laude, Columbia U., 1964. Bar: N.J. 1964. Law sec. to assoc. justice N.J. Supreme Ct., 1964-65; assoc. Toner, Crowley, Woelper & Vanderbilt, Newark, 1965-68; gen. atty. CIBA Corp., Summit, N.J., 1968-70; counsel to pharms. div. CIBA-GEIGY Corp., Summit, 1970-75, v.p. and counsel pharms. div., 1975-77; sr. v.p. and counsel for planning and adminstrn. dept. CIBA-GEIGY, Summit, 1980-81; sr. v.p. adminstrn. Schering-Plough Corp., Kenilworth, N.J., 1981-84; exec. v.p. adminstrn. Schering-Plough Corp., Madison, N.J., 1984—; dir. Molecular Devices Corp., Palo Alto, Calif. Bd. overseers Found. at N.J. Inst. Tech., Newark; bd. trustees Drew U. Mem. ABA, N.J. Bar Assn., Indsl. Biotech. Assn. (dir.). Office: Schering-Plough Corp 1 Giralda Farms Madison NJ 07940

DANFORTH, DOUGLAS DEWITT, manufacturing company executive; b. Syracuse, N.Y., Sept. 25, 1922; s. Dewitt Ward and Ruth Cordellia (Ward) D.; m. Janet Mae Piron, May 15, 1943; children: Barbara Lee Danforth Osburn, Susan Jean Danforth Sutcliffe, Debra Lynn and Douglas Dewitt (twins). Student, Fenn Coll., Cleve., 1940-41; B.M.E., Syracuse U., 1947. Supt. planning Easy Washer Machine Co., Syracuse, N.Y., 1942-46; v.p., gen. mgr. in Mex. Internat. Gen. Electric Co., 1947-53; plant mgr. Gen. Electric Co., Balt., 1953-55; exec. v.p., gen. mgr. Industria Electrica De Mex., 1956-61; v.p. Westinghouse Electric Corp., Pitts., 1962-65, group v.p., 1965-69, exec. v.p., 1969-74; pres. Industry Products Co., Westinghouse, 1974-78, vice chmn., chief operating officer, 1978-83, chmn., chief exec. officer, 1983-88; chmn., chief exec. officer Pitts. Pirates baseball club, 1988—; dir. Pitts. Nat. Corp., PPG Industries, Inc., Whirpool Corp., Standard Oil, Nat. InterGroup. Trustee Carnegie Mellon U., Allegheny Health, Edn. and Research Corp; chmn. Allegheny Conf.; bd. dirs. United Way Allegheny County. Clubs: Duquesne (Pitts.), Longue Vue (Pitts.); Laurel Valley (Ligonier, Pa.), Rolling Rock (Ligonier, Pa.). Home: 272 Justabout Rd Venetia PA 15367 Office: Pitts Pirates PO Box 7000 Pittsburgh PA 15212

DANGLER, DAVID WALLER, health center executive, former banker; b. Chgo., Nov. 14, 1915; s. David and Lucy Alexander (Knott) D.; B.A., Yale U., 1937; postgrad. Northwestern U., 1939-40. With No. Trust Co., Chgo., 1938-79, v.p. trust dept., until 1979, ret., 1979. Pres. Johnston R. Bowman Health Center for the Elderly, Chgo., 1979-89, hon. pres., 1989—; former pres. bd. trustees Allendale Assn.; life trustee Rush Presbyn., Newberry Libr.; trustee St. Luke's Med. Center; bd. dirs. Erie Neighborhood House; former elder 1st Presbyn. Ch., Lake Forest, Ill. Club: Univ. (Chgo.).

DANGLER, RICHARD REISS, corporate service companies executive, entrepreneur; b. N.Y.C., Mar. 6, 1940; s. Edward and Gertrude (Reiss) D.; B.A., N.Y.U., 1962; LL.B., Bklyn. Law Sch., 1965, J.D., 1967; m. Lisa Frant, Feb. 1, 1968; children—Ellen Susan, Justin Todd. Asst. to pres. Bogue Electric Mfg. Co., Paterson, N.J., 1965-68; sr. contracts adminstr., mgr. export licensing ITT, N.Y.C., 1968-70; sr. v.p. N.Y.C. Off-Track Betting Corp., 1970—; pres., chmn. bd. Westwind Restorations Ltd., 1981—. Sponsor exec. internship program Human Resources Adminstrn., N.Y.C., 1972-76, sponsor internship program Bd. Edn., N.Y.C., 1981. Recipient Norman P. Hefley award, 1968; Blanche White award Nat. Contract Mgmt. Assn., 1974; Outstanding Achievement award United Fund N.Y., 1975; Partner in Edn. award N.Y.C. Bd. Edn., 1982. Fellow Nat. Contract Mgmt. Assn.; mem. ASME, Practising Law Inst., U.S. Naval Inst., Assn. Old Crows, Nat. Wildlife Fedn., Internat. Game Fish Assn. Clubs: Hist. Car of Pa., Chrysler 300, Walter P. Chrysler, Sea Horses Rod and Gun (pres. 1973-75); Admirals. Contbr. articles to profl. jours.; judge Antique Automobile Assn. Home: Crow Hill Path Mount Kisco NY 10549

DANIEL, DAVID RONALD, management consultant; b. Hartford, Conn., Feb. 26, 1930; s. David Richard and Marion (Ingalls) D.; m. Sally Storrs, June 20, 1953 (div. Aug. 1980); children—David, Peter, Stephen; m. Ana Jones, Sept. 20, 1980; 1 stepchild, Amanda Loud. BA, Wesleyan U., Middletown, Conn., 1952; MBA, Harvard U., 1954, LHD (hon.). Assoc. McKinsey & Co. Inc., N.Y.C., 1957-63, prin., 1963-68, dir., 1968—, mng. dir. N.Y. office, 1970, mng. dir. firm, 1976-88. Contbr. articles to profl. jours. Chmn. emeritus Wesleyan U.; bd. dirs., treas. Lincoln Ctr. for Performing Arts, Inc., N.Y.C.; bd. dirs. N.Y.C. Ballet, Am. Inst. for Contemporary German Studies, Washington, Brookings Instn.; bd. visitors Duke U.; adv. council Grad. Sch. Bus. Adminstrn. Stanford U.; mem. Commn. on Admission to Grad. Mgmt. Edn., exec. com. U.S. Golf Assn.; bd. dirs. Brookings Instn., mem. Coun. Fgn. Rels. Lt. (j.g.) USNR, 1954-57. Home: 146 Central Park W New York NY 10023 Office: McKinsey & Co Inc 55 E 52nd St New York NY 10022

DANIEL, ELEANOR SAUER, economist, real estate executive; b. N.Y.C., Feb. 8, 1917; d. Charles Peter and Elsie Edna (Dommer) Sauer; m. John Carl Daniel, Dec. 31, 1952; children: Victoria Ann, Charles Timothy. BA magna cum laude (Bardwell fellow), Mt. Holyoke Coll., 1936; MA (Perkins fellow), Columbia U., 1937. Economist, U.S. Steel Co., N.Y.C., 1938; lectr. econs. Bklyn. Coll., 1939-40; with Mut. Life Ins. Co. N.Y., N.Y.C., 1940-74, asst. v.p., 1972-74, sr. econ. adviser, 1972-74; economist Fed. Home Loan Bank, N.Y.C., 1974-75; v.p., dir. Daniel Realty Cos., N.Y.C., 1975—; pres. Midtown Daniel; former dir., chmn. fin. com. Atlantic City Electric Co.; past chmn. fin. com. Atlantic Energy, Inc.; former mem. bd. mgrs. U.S. Savs. Bank Newark; mem. Pres's. Task Force Fed. Credit Programs, 1968-69; mem. N.J. Gov's. Econ. Recovery Com., 1975-76; mem. econ. adv. bd. U.S. Sec. Commerce, 1971-73; mem. bus. research adv. council U.S. Bur. Labor Statistics, 1966-86. Author: (with J.J. O'Leary and S.F. Foster) Our National Debt and Our Savings; contbr. articles to profl. jours. Former trustee Blue Shield of N.J., trustee fellow Mt. Holyoke Coll., also past vice chmn., mem. fin. com., trustee. Mem. Am. Econ. Assn., Am. Fin. Assn. (past dir.), Phi Beta Kappa. Home: 34 North Dr East Brunswick NJ 08816

DANIEL, JAMES RICHARD, accountant, data processing excutive; b. Chgo., June 26, 1947; s. Elmer Alexander and June B. (Bush) D.; m. Marsha Ruth Stone, Nov. 8, 1969; children: Jennifer Rae, Michael James. BS in Acctg., U. Ill., 1970; MBA, Loyola U., 1974. CPA, Ill., La. Dir. fin. Baxter Travenol Labs., Chgo., 1974-79; corp. controller Bio-Rad Labs. Inc., Richmond, Calif., 1979-81; v.p., treas., controller Lykes Bros. Steamship Co. Inc., New Orleans, 1981-84; chief fin. officer SCI Systems Inc., Huntsville, Ala., 1984—. Served with U.S. Army, 1970-73. Mem. Am. Inst. CPA's. Republican. Home: 302 Jeff Rd Huntsville AL 35806

DANIEL, LARRY DARDEN, accountant; b. Franklin, Ga., Dec. 14, 1953; s. Darden and Grace A. (Hall) D.; m. Maria Ann Thompson, Aug. 9, 1974; 1 child, Ashley. AS in Bus., Abraham Baldwin Agrl. Coll., 1978; BBA in Acctg., Valdosta State Coll., 1980. CPA, Ga.; cert. fin. planner. Acct. J.K. Boatwright and Co. PC, CPA's, La Grange, Ga., 1980—. With U.S. Army, 1972-75. Mem. AICPA, Inst. Cert. Fin. Planners (cert.), Ga. Soc. CPA's. Republican. Methodist. Home: 2577 Antioch Rd La Grange GA 30240 Office: J K Boatwright and Co PC PO Box 1107 17 N Lafayette Sq La Grange GA 30241

DANIEL, MARK D., accountant, controller; b. Portsmouth, Ohio, May 26, 1950; s. Ralph E. and Rosemary K. Daniel; m. Kathy Schneider, Jan. 16, 1971; children: Aimee, Tadd, Christopher. BS, Wright State U., 1975; MS, Lesley Coll., 1985. Jr. acct. Gem City Savs., Dayton, Ohio, 1972-74; auditor AMF Electrosystems Div., Vandalia, Ohio, 1974-76; plant controller Lau Industries div. Phillips Industries, Dayton, 1976-77; gen. acctg. mgr., mgr. cost acctg. div. St. Regis Paper Co. div. L&CP, Troy, Ohio, 1977-80; mgr. acctg. Amcast Indsl. Corp., Dayton, 1980-82; div. controller Amcast Indsl. Corp. subs. Belcher, Easton, Mass., 1982-85; mgr. acctg. div., corp. controller Sigma Industries Div., Braintree, Mass., 1985-88; dir. fin. Weymouth, Mass., 1988—. Office: Pacific Sci Co Sigma Instruments Div 90 Libbey Pkwy Weymouth MA 02189

DANIEL, RICHARD JOEL, management consultant; b. Bethlehem, Pa., Sept. 16, 1945; s. John and Elizabeth (Lisy) D.; m. Carol Anne Joy, July 1, 1967; 1 child, Elizabeth Joy. BA, Muhlenberg Coll., 1967; postgrad., George Mason U., 1968-70. Dir. pers. adminstrn. Fla. Fed. Savs. and Loan, St. Petersburg, 1970-73; dir. pers. Cone Mills Corp., Greenville, S.C., 1973-75; corp. mgr. pers. Bigelow Sanford div. Sperry & Hutchinson, Greenville, 1975-78; div. dir. pers. Sperry & Hutchinson Furniture, High Point, N.C., 1978-81; group dir. indsl. rels. Dan River Inc., Danville, Va., 1981-82; pres., chief exec. officer Employers Assn., Charlotte, N.C., 1982—; mem. adj. faculty High Point Coll., 1978-81; bd. dirs. Key Risk Mgmt. Svcs. Inc., Greensboro, N.C., NCAI Svcs. Corp., Raleigh, N.C., N.C. Associated Industries, Raleigh, TEA Svc. Corp., Charlotte. Editor: North Carolina Employers Desk Manual, 1986. Mem. Commn. on Alcohol and Drug Abuse, Greenville, 1975-78, Mecklenburg County Pers. Commn., Charlotte, 1986—; chmn. bduget com. United Way, Greenville, 1975-78, Mayors Summer Youth Program, Charlotte, 1987—, Greenville Labor Forum, 1974-78; bd. dirs. ARC, Greenville, 1977-78, Worker Plans Luth. Ch.-Mo. Synod, St. Louis, 1986—, Open House Inc., Charlotte, 1984-89, Mercy Hosp., Charlotte, 1985—, Presbyn. Heath Svcs. Corp., Charlotte, 1985—, Luth. Svcs. for Aged, Salisbury, N.C., 1985—; chmn. Charlotte Pvt. Industry Coun., 1984-88. Staff sgt. U.S. Army, 1967-70. Mem. Am. Soc. Assn. Execs., Am. Soc. Pers. Adminstrs., Nat. Assn. Mgrs. (exec. com. 1985—, vice chmn. 1988, chmn.-elect 1989), Greenville Area Pers. Assn. (pres. 1977-78). Republican. Office: Employers Assn 8848 Red Oak Blvd Charlotte NC 28217

DANIEL, RICHARD NICHOLAS, fabricated metals manufacturing company executive; b. Bklyn., Sept. 18, 1935; s. Louis V. and Jean (D'Andrea) D.; m. Elaine E. Sherman, Sept. 24, 1966; children: Matthew, Jeffrey. B.B.A., St. John's U., 1957; M.B.A., U. Pa., 1959. C.P.A., Tex. Planning assoc. Mobil Oil Corp., N.Y.C., 1962-70; v.p. fin. Laird Enterprises Inc., N.Y.C., 1970-71; v.p. ops. Wheelabrator-Frye, N.Y.C., 1971; v.p., controller Handy & Harman, N.Y.C., 1971-76, v.p.-fin., 1977-78, group v.p., 1978-79, pres., chief operating officer, 1979-83, pres., chief exec. officer, 1983-87, chmn., pres., chief exec. officer, 1988—, also dir. Home: 91 Hawthorn Pl Briarcliff Manor NY 10510 Office: Handy & Harman 850 3d Ave New York NY 10022

DANIEL, ROYAL THOMAS, III, utility engineer; b. Portsmouth, Va., July 30, 1956; s. Royal Thomas Jr. and Lillian Martha (Miller) D. BS in Nuclear Engring., N.C. State U., 1978, MS in Indsl. Mgmt., 1980; MS in Acctg., Bentley Coll., 1985, MS in Computer Info. Systems, 1986; postgrad., Suffolk U. Law Sch., 1987—. Registered profl. engr., Mass.; CPA, Md.; cert. mgmt. acct., data processor, systems profl., paralegal. Sr. proposal engr. Combustion Engring. Power Systems, Inc., Windsor, Conn., 1979-80; coordinating specialist Boston Edison Co., 1980-85, power supply coordinator, 1985—. Mem. Am. Mgmt. Assn. (assoc.), Am. Inst. Indsl. Engrs., NSPE, Am. Inst. for Cert. of Computer Profls., Order St. Patrick, Phi Delta Phi, Tau Beta Pi. Baptist. Home: 18 Franklin Pl PO Box 149 Beverly MA 01915 Office: Boston Edison Co P222 800 Bolyston St Boston MA 02199

DANIELL, ROBERT F., diversified manufacturing company executive; b. Milton, Mass., 1933; married. Grad., Boston U. Coll. Indsl. Tech., 1954; DSc (hon.), U. Bridgeport; LLD (hon.), Trinity Coll., Boston U. With Sikorsky Aircraft, Stratford, Conn., 1956-82, design engr., from 1956, program mgr., 1968-71, comml. mktg. mgr., 1971-74, v.p. comml. mktg., 1974-76, sr. v.p. mktg., 1976-77, exec. v.p., 1977-80, chief exec. officer, 1980-82, pres., 1981-82; with United Technologies (parent co.), Hartford, Conn., 1982—, v.p., 1982-83, sr. v.p. def. systems, 1983-84, pres., chief operating officer, dir., 1984—, chief exec. officer, 1986—, chmn. bd. dirs., 1987—; bd. dirs. The Travelers Corp., Hartford, Conn., Shell Oil Co., Houston. Bd. trustees Boston U., Naval Aviation Mus. Found., Inc., Falcon Found.; corporator Inst. of Living. Served with U.S. Army, 1954-56. Fellow U. Bridgeport. Mem. Wings Club (pres.). Office: United Techs Corp United Technologies Bldg Hartford CT 06101

DANIELS, AARON MARTIN, broadcasting executive; b. Holyoke, Mass., May 11, 1935; s. Henry Chaning and Marie (Hurwitz) D.; m. Judy Lynn Friedman, Nov. 22, 1937; children: Gregory Martin, Alexander M. BA, Dartmouth Coll., 1957; grad. advanced mgmt. program, Harvard U., 1986. Salesman N.Y. Telephone Co., N.Y.C., 1957-58, Anchor Hocking Glass Co., N.Y.C., 1959-62, McCall Corp., N.Y.C., 1962-64; advt. dir. Davis Publs., N.Y.C., 1964-65; acct. exec. Sta. WPAT Capital Cities, N.Y.C., 1965-69, advt. dir. Fairchild Group, 1969-70, gen. sales mgr. Sta. WPAT, 1970-80; pres., gen. mgr. Sta. WPRO Capital Cities, Providence, 1980-85; pres. radio network Capital Cities/ABC, Inc., N.Y.C., 1986—. Mem. Radio Network Assn. (vice chmn. 1986—), Internat. Radio & TV Soc. (bd. dirs. 1987—). Club: East Hampton (N.Y.) Tennis (bd. dirs. 1980-82, 87—). Home: 1095 Park Ave New York NY 10182 Office: ABC Radio Network 1330 Ave of the Americas New York NY 10019 also: WPRO(AM) 1502 Wampanoag Trail East Providence RI 02915 *

DANIELS, ADELE WATKINS, banker; b. Farmville, Va., July 20, 1948; d. John Marshall and Adele (Hutchinson) Watkins; m. Frank Borden Daniels, Aug. 18, 1968 (div.); children: Adele, Frank, Marguerite. BA in Econs., Randolph Macon Women's Coll., 1983. Mgmt. trainee Cen. Fidelity Bank, Lynchburg, Va., 1983-85, loan officer, 1985-87, retail credit adminstrv. mgr., asst. v.p., 1987—. Trustee Seven Hills Sch., Lynchburg, 1983—; mem. Jr. League of Lynchburg, Inc., 1974—, Lynchburg Hist. Found., 1986—; Sunday sch. tchr. First Presbyn. Ch., Lynchburg, 1983—; mem. adv. bd. Lynchburg Mus. System; mem. cabinet bd. Cen. Va. United Way, 1988; bd. dirs. Point of Honor Mus. Mem. Va. Bankers Assn., Greater Lynchburg Retail Mchts. Assn. (bd. dirs.), DAR, Randolph Macon Women's Coll. Alumni (sec. 1984-86). Office: Cen Fidelity Bank 828 Main St Lynchburg VA 24503

DANIELS, DORIA LYNN, manufacturing executive; b. Kent, Ohio, Apr. 22, 1951; d. Eli and Henrietta (Johnson) D. BBA, Kent State U., 1973; postgrad., Old Dominion U., 1975-76, Akron U., 1984-86. Mgmt. trainee Cardinal Fed. Savs., Cleve., 1973-74; acctg. mgr. People Savs. and Loan, Hampton, Va., 1974-77; ins. agt. John Hancock Mut. Life Ins., Hampton, 1977-79; prodn. planner Little Tikes Mfg., Hudson, Ohio, 1979—; pres., co-founder Thomas Anderson Devel. Corp., 1986. Mem. Kent (Ohio) Bd. Edn., 1987, Shade Tree Commn. Kent City Council, 1987; candidate ward 3 council seat Rep. Party, Kent, 1969, co-founder and chmn. Thomas-Anderson Devel. Corp. Kent, 1986—; mem. bd. advisors Portage County Human Services Dept., 1988. City of Kent scholar, 1969; recipient Gov.'s Recognition award Gov. of Ohio, 1986, commendation from Ohio Ho. of Reps., 1987, Ohio House of Reps. State Commendation for record service to the Kent community, 1987, Kent Edn. Assn. awards, 1988. Mem. NAACP (life, polit. advisor), Am. Prodn. Inventory Control Soc., Nat. Assn. Female Execs., Internat. Platform Assn., Nat. Council Negro Women. Baptist. Home: 234 Dodge St Kent OH 44240 Office: Little Tikes Mfg 2180 Barlow Rd Hudson OH 44236

DANIELS, KAREN LYNNE, insurance company executive; b. Ft. Bragg, N.C., July 5, 1959; d. Thomas Jefferson and Julia Lina (Frye) D. AA, Mt. San Antonio Coll., 1979; BA, Calif. Poly. U., 1981. Night mgr. Alpha Beta Grocery Store, Covina, Calif., 1977-85; with Hartford Ins. Co., Van Nuys, Calif., 1985-87, claim supr., 1986-87; claim supr. Hartford Ins. Co., Covina, 1987—. Democrat. Baptist. Home: 15030 Victory Blvd #205 Van Nuys CA 91411 Office: Hartford Ins Co 1369 E Center Court Dr Covina CA 91724

DANIELS, MICHAEL ALAN, lawyer; b. Cape Girardeau, Mo., Mar. 6, 1946. B.S. in Speech, Northwestern U., 1968, M.A. in Polit. Sci., 1969; J.D., U. Mo., 1973. Bar: Fla. 1974, U. S. Supreme Ct. 1983. Spl. asst. for polit. sci. research Office Naval Research, Washington, 1969-71; legal aid Edwards, Seigfried, Runge and Hodge, Mexico, Mo., 1972-73; corp. atty. CACI, Inc., Washington, 1974-77; exec. v.p. gen. counsel Datex, Inc., Washington, 1977-78; chmn. bd., pres. Internat. Pub. Policy Research Corp., Falls Church, Va., 1978-86; v.p. Sci. Applications Internat. Corp., Washington, 1986—; pres. U.S. Global Strategy Council. Mem. Republican Nat. Com., Internat. Affairs Council, Nat. Security Adv. Council; mem. investment policy adv. com. Office U.S. Trade Rep., 1982-87. Recipient Outstanding Fed. Securities Law Student award U. Mo., 1973. Mem. ABA (chmn. working group on law, nat. security and tech., standing com. law and nat. security 1984—), Fla. Bar Assn., Fed. Bar Assn. (chmn. internat. law com. 1979-86), Internat. Studies Assn. Office: SAIC 1710 Goodrich Dr McLean VA 22102

DANIELS, RICHARD MARTIN, marketing communications company executive; b. Delano, Calif., Feb. 24, 1942; s. Edward Martin and Philida Rose (Peterson) D.; m. Kathryn Ellen Knight, Feb. 28, 1976; children: Robert Martin, Michael Edward. A.A., Foothill Coll., 1965; B.A., San Jose State U., 1967; M.A., U. Mo., 1971. News reporter Imperial Valley Press, El Centro, Calif., summers 1963-66, San Diego (Calif.) Evening Tribune, 1967-68, Columbia Daily Tribune (Mo.), 1969-70; nat. news copy editor Los Angeles Times, 1966-67; staff writer San Diego Union, 1971-74, real estate editor, 1974-77; v.p. pub. relations Hubbert Advt. & Pub. Relations, Costa Mesa, Calif., 1977-78; ptnr. Berkman & Daniels Mktg. Communications, San Diego, 1979—; lectr. various bus. groups and colls. Chmn. bd. dirs. March of Dimes San Diego County, mem. Nat. Council Vols. Served with USN, 1959-62. Recipient Excellence award Communicating Arts Group San Diego, 1981. Mem. Pub. Relations Soc. Am., Building Industry Assn. San Diego County, Nat. Assn. Office and Indsl. Parks (b.d dirs. San Diego Chpt.), Sigma Delta Chi. Republican. Home: 9080 Oviedo St San Diego CA 92129 Office: 1501 Fifth Ave San Diego CA 92101

DANIELS, TERRENCE DAVID, business executive; b. St. Louis, Jan. 11, 1943; s. Edgar M. and Mary Jane (Phelan) D.; m. Courtnay Sylvan, July 24, 1966; children: Courtnay Phelan, Catherine McDuffie, Charles Page, Christopher Channing. BA in History, U. Va., 1966, MBA, 1970. With corp. fin. dept. W.R. Grace & Co., N.Y.C., 1970-72, asst. to chmn. of bd. and chief exec. officer, 1972-75, v.p. devel., consumer services group, 1975-77, exec. v.p. Office of Chief Exec., 1982-86, vice chmn., 1986—, also bd. dirs.; v.p. corp. devel. Mattel, Inc., 1977-79; chmn., pres., chief exec. officer Western Pub. Co., 1979-82; bd. dirs. Faber-Castell Corp., Taco Villa, Inc., Universal Furniture Co. Served to lt. U.S. Army, 1966-68. Roman Catholic. Clubs: Somerset Hills Country, N.Y. Racquet. Office: W R Grace & Co 1114 Ave of the Americas New York NY 10036 *

DANIELS, TRICIA, television program producer; b. N.Y.C., Sept. 14, 1961; d. Irwin and Helen Daniels. Student, Queens Coll., 1979-80, Fashion Inst. Tech., 1980-81. Prodn. asst. Sta. WPIX-TV, N.Y.C., 1977-78; researcher News Close-Up ABC, N.Y.C., 1978, World News Tonight, N.Y.C., 1978-80; segment coordinator Good Morning Am., N.Y.C., 1978-85, assoc. producer, 1985-86, producer, 1986-88; cons. 20/20 Show, N.Y.C., 1978-79; co-producer celebrity stories Late Night News ABC-TV, L.A., 1987-88; mng. producer VH-I-TV, N.Y.C., 1988—; cons. Delilah Films, N.Y.C., 1982-83. Mem. Nat. Assn. Female Execs., Hollywood Women's Press Club, Greater Los Angeles Press Club. Republican. Office: VH-I TV Network 1775 Broadway New York NY 10019

DANIELSON, BETTY, cash manager; b. Manitowoc, Wis., Dec. 1, 1940; d. George and Bernadette M. (Foley) D. BS, U. Wis., 1963. Various positions First Nat. Bank, Chgo., 1963-76; corp. cash mgr. A.C. Nielsen Co., Chgo., 1977-85; assoc. mgr., treas. ops. Dun & Bradstreet, N.Y.C., 1985-89; asst. treas. Thomas Cook Travel, Inc., N.Y.C., 1989—. Mem. Nat. Corp. Cash Mgmt. Assn. (bd. dirs., pub. com. chmn. 1986-87), N.Y. Cash Mgmt. Assn. Home: 237 S Valley West Orange NJ 07052 Office: Thomas Cook Travel Inc 2 Penn Pla New York NY 10121

DANIELSON, THOMAS, sales professional; b. Teaneck, N.J., Sept. 19, 1958; s. William Joseph and Margaret (Kuehn) D. BA, The Citadel, 1980, postgrad., currently. Sales rep. Carolina Distbg. Co., Inc., Columbia, S.C., 1981-88; network account exec. AT&T Info. Systems, Columbia, 1988—. Hon. mem. Rep. Congl. Com., Washington, 1983—. Capt. Intelligence Agy. USAFR, 1980—. Mem. Am. Mgmt. Assn., Res. Officer's Assn., Air Force Assn. Episcopalian. Club: Assn. Citadel Men (Charleston, S.C.). Home: 340 E Sandpiper Dr Mount Pleasant SC 29464 Office: AT&T 120 Main St Columbia SC 29202

DANIERO, JOSEPH JAMES, financial executive; b. Smock, Pa., Oct. 31, 1938; s. Joseph and Sophia Ann (Spiranac) D.; m. Virginia Marie Coney, June 6, 1978; children: James Joseph, Christine Marie. BS in Econs., U. Pa., 1963. Computer programmer Provident Mut. Ins. Co., Phila., 1964-65; systems analyst Richardson-Merrell Inc., Phila., 1965-66; systems cons. Levin-Townsend Svc. Co., Phila., 1966-68; systems mgr. Delaware Mgmt. Co., Phila., 1968-74, computer svcs. officer, 1974-78, asst. v.p. EDP, 1978-81, v.p. EDP, 1981-85, exec. v.p., 1985-88, pres., 1988—; cons. Micromation Scis. Corp., Phila. Mem. Internat. Assn. Fin. Planning, Am. Mgmt. Assn., Inst. Cert. Computer Profls., Data Processing Mgmt. Assn. Republican. Roman Catholic. Home: 10 Crestview Dr Cherry Hill NJ 08003 Office: Delaware Svc Co Inc 10 Penn Ctr 14th Fl Philadelphia PA 19103

DANIS, JULIE MARIE, management consultant; b. Dayton, Ohio, Aug. 19, 1955; d. Charles Wheaton and Elizabeth Jane (Sliter) D. BS, Northwestern U., 1977; AM, U. Chgo., 1979, MBA, 1984. Juvenile justice planner Ill. Law Enforcement Commn., Chgo., 1979-80; prin. budget analyst City of Chgo., 1980-82; account mgmt. intern Foote, Cone & Belding, Chgo., 1983; product mgr. Frito-Lay, Inc., Dallas, 1984-87; advt. account exec. Leo Burnett Co, Chgo., 1987-88; mgmt. cons. Everest Group, Chgo., 1988—. Cons. United Way of Chgo., 1980. Mem. Nat. Assn. Female Execs., U. Chgo. Women's Bus. Group, Pi Beta Phi. Roman Catholic. Clubs: Ad-Net, Jr. League. Avocations: theater, dance, aerobics, tennis, travel. Home: 626 W Grace St #2E Chicago IL 60613 Office: Everest Group 310 S Michigan Ave Ste 2000 Chicago IL 60604

DANKMEYER, THEODORE ROGNALD, mining company executive; b. Balt., Mar. 15, 1938; s. Theodore Rognald and Anne Virginia (Burrier) D.; m. Juliet Foster Cooper, Aug. 17, 1963; children: Ingrid Elizabeth, Erica Anne. AB, Williams Coll., 1960; LLB, Harvard U., 1963. Bar: Md. 1964, D.C. 1966, Calif. 1974. Assoc. Niles, Barton & Wilmer, Balt., 1963-66, Covington & Burling, Washington, 1966-73; assoc. counsel nuclear energy bus. Gen. Electric, San Jose, Calif., 1973-78, counsel, 1978-81; v.p., gen. counsel BHP-Utah Internat. Inc., San Francisco, 1981-85, sr. v.p., gen. counsel, 1985—. With Md. Air N.G., 1963-69. Republican. Club: University (San Francisco). Office: BHP-Utah Internat Inc 550 California St San Francisco CA 94104

DANN, NORMAN, venture capitalist; b. Cleve., Apr. 27, 1927; s. Morris and Stella (Weiss) D.; married, 1951; children: Marlane, Bonnie, Mitchell, Janet. Student, U. Mo., 1945-46; BS in Indsl. Engring., Pa. State U., 1949. Project engr. Designers for Industry, Cleve., 1950-59; pres. The Dann Co., Cleve., 1960-70; sr. v.p. Medtronic, Mpls., 1971-77; cons. Pathfinder Cons., Mpls., 1977-81; ptnr. Pathfinder Venture Capital Funds, Mpls., 1981—. Home: 5285 Howards Point Shorewood MN 55331 Office: Pathfinder Venture Capital Fund 7300 Metro Blvd Minneapolis MN 55435

DANNEMAN, EDWARD CARL, bank executive; b. Fairfield, Calif., Jan. 1, 1959; s. Robert E. and Joye M. (MacDowell) D.; m. Patricia A. Gutierrez, Sept. 17, 1983; 1 child, Steven Earl. Student, Lewis and Clark Coll., 1977-79, U. Oreg., 1979-82; BS, SUNY, Albany, 1983. Office mgr. Beneficial Fin. Co., Olympia, Wash., 1982-86; 2d v.p. Capital Savs. Bank, Olympia, 1986-87; adminstrv. officer, loan trainer Gt. Am. First Bank, Federal Way, Wash., 1987—; underwriter Gt. Am. Ins. Co., San Diego, 1986—. Home: 33217 33d Ave SW Federal Way WA 98023 Office: Great Am Bank 31620 23d Ave S Federal Way WA 98063-9711

DANNEMILLER, JOHN C., transportation company executive; b. Cleve., May 17, 1938; s. John Charles and Jean I. (Bage) D.; m. Jean Marie Sheridan, Sept. 22, 1962; children—David, Peter. B.S., Case Western Res. U., 1960, M.B.A., 1964; postgrad., Stanford U., 1975, Columbia U., 1974, Tuck Exec. program Dartmouth Coll., 1976. Vice pres. foods div. Diamond Shamrock, 1978-81, dir. planning, 1981-83; v.p. SDS Biotech Corp., Cleve., 1984-85; group v.p. leasing group Leaseway Transp., Cleve., 1984-85, pres., chief operating officer, 1985-88, also dir.; exec. v.p. Bearings Inc., Cleveland, 1988—; dir. Bearings, Inc., Cleve. Bd. dirs., advisor Jr. Achievement, Cleve., 1962-64; fund raiser United Way, Cleve. and St. Louis. Mem. Am. Trucking Assns., Beta Gamma Sigma. Republican. Presbyterian. Clubs: Cleve. Athletic, Lakewood Country, Firestone Country. Office: Bearings Inc 629 Euclid Ave Dr Cleveland OH 44114 *

DANNEMILLER, NICHOLAS STEPHEN, association executive; b. Akron, Ohio, Dec. 11, 1961; s. Walter Nicholas and Clara (Usner) D. BA in Econs. and Bus. Administrn., Westmont Coll., 1984. Mgr. fin. Worldteam Inc., Coral Gables, Fla., 1984-85; chief fin. officer Worldteam Inc., Coral Gables, 1985—, dir. ops., 1988—. Active Rep. Nat. Com. Mem. Christian Ministries Mgmt. Assn. (chpt. dir. 1987—). Presbyterian. Clubs: Pelican Bay Country, South Seas Plantation, Silverlake Country. Office: Worldteam Inc 1607 Ponce de Leon Blvd Coral Gables FL 33134

DANNER, RAYMOND L., restaurant and franchise company executive; b. 1925; married. With T & D Market, 1947-49; with Bowling Cellay, 1949-50; ptnr. Moonlite Dreue, Inc., 1950-52; with Commonwealth Realty Co., 1956-58; with Shoney's Inc., Nashville, 1958—, former pres., chief exec. officer, now chmn., dir. Served with U.S. Army, 1944-47. Office: Shoney's Inc 1727 Elm Hill Pike Nashville TN 37210 *

DANSON, STEPHEN MICHAEL, brokerage firm executive; b. N.Y.C., Mar. 31, 1943; s. Irving Samuel and Beatrice (Mach) D.; m. Emily Stark, Apr. 13, 1969 (div. Sept. 1980); children: Christopher Stark, Melissa Stark; m. Margaret Kessler, May 15, 1983. Student, Princeton U., 1962-66. Registered rep., asst. to sr. ptnr. Herzfeld & Stern, N.Y.C., 1968-70, head mcpl. bond dept., 1970-74, ltd. ptnr., 1974-78, gen. ptnr., 1978-84; pres. S.M.D. Assocs., Inc., Hastings-on-the-Hudson, N.Y., 1984—. Trustee Beth Isreal Hosp., N.Y.C., 1976—. Clubs: Tiger Inn (Princeton, N.J.); St. Andrews Country (Hastings-on-Hudson, N.Y.); Palm Beach Polo and Country. Office: 1 Lincoln Pl #22S New York NY 10023

D'ANTONIO, FRANCIS MICHAEL, management consultant; b. Berwyn, Pa., Sept. 11, 1942; s. Russell Angelo and Lillian Maria (Nicoline) D'A.; m. Miclene Ann Machnicki; children: Maria, Angela, Francis Jr. AA, Compton Coll., 1963; BS in Indsl. Tech., U. Calif., Long Beach, 1973. Tool maker Houdaille-Burgmaster div. Houdaille Industries, L.A., 1963-65, mgr. mfg. engring., 1968-74; v.p. mfg. Houdaille Hydraulics div. Houdaille Industries, Buffalo, 1974-78, pres., 1978-84; gen. mgr. div. circuit breakers BBC Brown Boveri, Columbia, S.C., 1985-87; mgmt. cons. Inst. Mgmt. Resources, Westlake Village, Calif., 1987—. Home: 10 Turnberry Ct Columbia SC 29223 Office: Inst Mgmt Resources 2659 Townsgate Rd Ste 203 Westlake Village CA 91361

DANTRO, FRANCIS JAMES, marketing executive; b. Lancaster, Pa., July 28, 1941; s. Frank Peter and Elizabeth Marie (Clerico) D.; m. Virginia Louise Griggs, Feb. 2, 1972; children: Jacqueline Ann, Jamie Brett. BS, Milw. Sch. Engring., 1962. V.p. Dantro Inc., Lancaster, 1962-70; mgr. mktg. Am. Pubs. Co., Chgo., 1970-82; v.p. Am. Media Corp., Milw., 1982—. Mem. exec. bd. Boy Scouts Am., Montgomery, Ala., 1985—. Recipient Silver Beaver award Boy Scouts Am., 1988. Republican. Roman Catholic. Home: 600 Noble Rd Tallassee AL 36078 Office: Am Media Corp 219 N Milwaukee St Milwaukee WI 53202

DANZIG, SHEILA RING, marketing and direct mail executive; b. N.Y.C., Mar. 18, 1948; d. David and Yetta Ring; m. William Harold Danzig, Aug. 11, 1968; children: David Scott, Gregory Charles. BS, CUNY, 1968. Tchr. N.Y.C. Bd. Edn., 1968-71; treas. Nat. Success Mktg. Inc., Sunrise, Fla., 1969—; pres. Innovative Communications Market Cons., Plantation, Fla., 1984-87; cons. Crush Softball Team, Hollywood, Fla., 1986-87, The Eye Ctr., Sunrise, 1986-87, Bus. Expo., Plantation, 1987. Author: You Deserve to be Rich, 1972, (tng. manual) A Better Medical Practice, 1986; contbr. articles to trade publs. Coordinator Day Out program Mills Boys' Shelter, Ft. Lauderdale, Fla., 1985, 87, Put Seat Belts on Sch. Buses program Broward County Sch. Bd., 1986; vol. Miami Children's Hosp.; campaign dir. Help the Handicapped Keep Their Parking Spots, 1987. Mem. Mail Order Bus. Bd., Am. Med. Writers Assn., Plantation Bus. and Profl. Women's Assn., Mothers Against Drunk Drivers. Office: Nat Success Mktg 2574 N University Dr Sunrise FL 33322

DANZIG, WILLIAM HAROLD, management executive; b. Bklyn., Feb. 24, 1947; s. Sidney and Beatrice (Reiss) D.; m. Sheila Ring, Aug. 11, 1968; children: David Scott, Gregory Charles. BS in Acctg., Baruch Coll., 1969; MS in Edn., Long Island U., 1971. Acct. JK Lasser, N.Y.C., 1972; tchr. N.Y.C. Bd. Edn., Queens, 1969-74; pres. Nat. Success Mktg. Inc., Ft. Lauderdale, Fla., 1969—; sponsor Coop. Bus. Edn., Broward County, Fla., 1986; participant Bus. Expo, Ft. Lauderdale, 1985; cons. Mail Market Monitor, Ft. Lauderdale, 1988—, Gulfstream Pub., Ft. Lauderdale, 1988—. Co-author: You Deserve to be Rich, 1975, Play to Win, 1982. Mem. Mail Order Bus. Bd., Greater Ft. Lauderdale C. of C., Bnai Brith (chpt. bd. dirs. 1976). Republican. Jewish. Office: Nat Success Mktg Inc 2574 No University Dr #201 Sunrise FL 33324

DAO, TOM CHING SHUO, chemical company executive; b. Shanghai, China, Oct. 26, 1934; came to U.S., 1951, naturalized, 1966; s. Q.L. and S.J. (Yang) D.; m. Elizabeth Shao, Nov. 8, 1959; children: Erica, Mark. AA, Compton City Coll., 1956; BS in Chem. Engring., U. Calif., Berkeley, 1958. Sr. rsch. engr. Stauffer Chem. Co., Westport, Conn., 1958-65, asst. chief engr. licensing tech., 1965-69, area mgr. Far East devel., 1969-72, regional mgr. S.E. Asia, 1972-77, sr. bus. analyst corp. planning, 1977-78; pres. Cen. Pacific Ex-Im Corp., Houston, 1978—; dir. CPAC Trading Co., Hong Kong, Black Mesa Pipeline, Inc.; chmn. Proserve Inc., Memphis, 1982—, Cen. Pacific Timber Products, Seattle, 1985—; advisor CIC Corp., Stanford, Calif., 1983—. Patentee thin film evaporation, tar removal process. Charter mem. Rep. Presdl. Task Force, 1984; permanent mem. Rep. Nat. Senatorial Com.; pres. Chinese-Am. Voters League, Houston. Mem. Am. Inst. Chem. Engrs., Am. Mgmt. Assn., The Pres. Assn. Phi Lambda (mgr. 1959, 66, 76, 84), Houstonian Club, Assoc. Internat. Presbyterian (deacon). Office: Cen Pacific Ex-Im Corp 1400 Post Oak Blvd Houston TX 77056

DAOUD, GEORGE JAMIL, hotel and motel consultant; b. Beirut, Oct. 20, 1948; came to U.S., 1958, naturalized, 1970; s. Jamil G. and Shafika E. Daoud; B.S., N.Y.U., 1967; M.P.S., Cornell U., 1969; m. Barbara A. Fisco, Apr. 30, 1972; 5 children. Gen. mgr. Holiday Inn, New London and Groton, Conn., 1974-75, Gentle Winds Beach Resort, St. Croix, V.I., 1975-78; pres., cons. Motor Inn Mgmt., Inc., Dayton, Ohio, 1973—; pres. Central Services Group, Inc., First Group, Inc., Host Mgmt., Inc., The Inn Group, Inc., , 1981—, Metro Markets, Inc., Triad Ventures, Inc. (all Dayton), 1980-86; v.p. V.I. Hotel and Motel Assn., 1976. Mem. Am. Hotel and Motel Assn. (mem. Ednl. Inst., cert. hotel adminstr.), Ohio Hotel and Motel Assn., Nat. Assn. Rev. Appraisers, Cert. Real Estate Rev. Appraisers. Republican. Roman Catholic. Club: Masons. Office: Host Mgmt Inc 18 W 1st St Ste 100 Dayton OH 45402

DAOUD, MOHAMED, physicist; b. Tunis, Tunisia, Mar. 31, 1947; came to France, 1964; s. Hassen Daoud and Beya (Bahri) D. Maitrise, Ecole Normale Superieure, Saint Cloud, 1968-70, D.E.A., 1972, (hon.) Agregation, 1971; These, U. Paris VI, 1977. Research assoc. Commissariat äl Energie Atomique, C.E.A. Saclay, 1974-78, physicist, 1980—; physicist Boston U., 1978-80. Recipient Grand Prix, Groupement Français de Polymers, 1978, prix Commissariat d l'Energe Atomique, 1986. Mem. Societe Française de Physique, Am. Phys. Soc. Office: CEN Saclay, Lab Leon Brillouin, 91191 Gif-Yvette France

DAOUST, DONALD ROGER, pharmaceutical and toiletries company executive, microbiologist; b. Worcester, Mass., Aug. 13, 1935; s. G. Arthur and Alice Anne (Lavalee) D.; m. Johanna K. Kalinoski, May 30, 1959; children: Donna Jean, Stephen Michael, Sandra Marie. BA, U. Conn., 1957; MS, U. Mass., 1959, PhD, 1962. Sr. research microbiologist Merck Sharp & Dohme, Rahway, N.J., 1962-70, research fellow, 1970-72; mgr. biol. quality control Merck Sharp & Dohme, West Point, Pa., 1972-75; dir. quality control Armour Pharm. Co., Kankakee, Ill., 1975-76; v.p. quality assurance and regulatory compliance Armour Pharm. Co., Phoenix, 1976-78; v.p., quality control Carter-Wallace, Inc., Cranbury, N.J., 1978—. Contbr. articles to profl. jours., chpts. to books; patentee in field. Mem. Borough Council, South Plainfield, N.J., 1970-72; treas. George Washington council Boy Scouts Am., 1981-84, pres., 1984-87, area v.p., bd.dirs. NE region U.S., 1987—. Recipient Disting. Service award S. Plainfield Jaycees, 1969; named Outstanding Young Man, N.J. Jaycees, 1970. Mem. AAAS, Am. Soc. Microbiology, Am. Soc. for Quality Control, Pharm. Mfrs. Assn. (adminstrn. com. 1979-82, adv. bd. 1982—, rec. sec. 1986-88, vice chmn. 1988—). Roman Catholic. Club: Bedens Brook (Skillman, N.J.). Home: 8 Fairway Dr Cranbury NJ 08512 Office: Carter-Wallace Inc PO Box 1001 Cranbury NJ 08512

DAPRON, ELMER JOSEPH, JR., advertising executive; b. Clayton, Mo., Jan. 14, 1925; s. Elmer Joseph and Susanna (Kruse) D.; m. Sharon Kay Neuling, Feb. 22, 1977 (dec. Apr. 1987). Employed in constrn. bus., Fairbanks, Alaska, 1947-48; tech. writer-editor McDonnell-Douglas Corp., St. Louis, 1948-57; free-lance writer, Paris, France, 1957; with Gardner Advt. Co., St. Louis, 1960-78, v.p. 1969-78; sr. v.p. Kenrick Advt. Inc., 1978—; pres. Cornucopia Communications, Inc., 1979—. Producer syndicated radio and TV show Elmer Dapron's Grocery List; advt. and mktg. cons. to govt. and industry; daily commentator The Grocery List Armed Forces Radio Network (world wide). Mem. Nat. Dem. Com. Served with USMCR, 1943-45; PTO; 50-51; Korea. Recipient advt. awards including New Filming Techniques award Internat.-Film Festival. Hon. fellow Harry Truman Library Inst. Mem. Nat. Agrl. Mktg. Assn. (v.p. 1970—, trustee Miss. Valley Farm Mktg. (Man of Yr. 1974), Assn. R.R. Advt. and Mktg. (nat. membership chmn.) , Marine Corps League (nat. vice comdt. 1967-69). Clubs: Media, Presidents, St. Louis Track. Democrat. Contbr. articles to publs. Home: 300 Mansion House Center St Louis MO 63102 Office: 319 N 4th St Saint Louis MO 63102

DAQUI, PAUL JOSEPH, real estate developer; b. Bklyn., Feb. 1, 1942; s. Joseph Paul and Eugenia (Scida) D.; BS, N.Y. Inst. Tech., 1965; MBA, Western New Eng. Coll., 1971; m. Camille Mercurio, Aug. 18, 1968; children—Paula, Heather. Corp. fin. specialist Bank of N.Y., 1971-73; area dir., portfolio mgr. Conn. Gen. REIT, Hartford, 1973-79; pres. DaQui Belding Ptnrs., Inc., Hartford, 1979—; adj. faculty U. Hartford, 1975-79; comdr. USAF Acad. and ROTC admission program, Conn., 1974-88; bd. dir. Hartford Despatch; elector Wadsworth Atheneum; mem. adv. bd. art sch. U. Hartford; bd. dirs., exec. com. Rideshare, Inc., Hartford's Downtown Coun. With USAF, 1965-71. Decorated D.F.C., Air medal, Air Force Commendation medal. Mem. Nat. Assn. Indsl. and Office Parks (pres. Conn. chpt., dir. nat. chpt.), Urban Land Inst., Conn. Nat. Bank (adv. bd.), Greater Hartford C. of C. (internat. affairs com.), Nat. Assn. Corp. Real Estate Execs. Republican. Roman Catholic. Clubs: Hartford, Hartford Golf. Office: 795 Brook St I-91 Tech Ctr Rocky Hill CT 06067

DARANY, MICHAEL ANTHONY, financial executive; b. Detroit, Sept. 10, 1946; s. Sam and Betty Darany; m. Deborah Collins; 1 child, Danielle. Cert. fin. planner. Debit agt. Met. Life Ins. Co., Coral Gables, Fla., 1968-71; pres. Darany, Malagon & Assocs. Ins. Agy., Miami, Fla., 1970-71; loan appraiser Mortgage Corp. Am., Miami, Fla., 1971-72; loan officer J.I. Kislak Mortgage Co., Miami, Fla., 1973-74, Midwest Mortgage Co., Miami, Fla., 1973-74; pres. Consortium Group (subs. D&R Internat.), Miami, Fla., 1974-76; staff mgr. Peninsular Life Ins. Co., Miami, Fla., 1976-78; asst. to mgr. Sun Life Can., Miami, Fla., 1978-82; pres. Consortium Group(subs. D&R Internat.), Miami, Fla., 1982—. Co-author: The Expert's Guide, 1988; contbr. articles to profl. pubs. First v.p. Unico Nat., Coral Gables, 1975-76, sec. 1978-79, pres., 1980-81. Served with USN, 1963-67, Vietnam. Recipient Man of Yr. award Sun Life Can., 1978-81. Mem. Inst. Cert. Fin. Planners, Internat. Assn. Fin. Planners, Nat. Assn. Life Underwriters, Registry Fin. Planning, Nat. Fin. Adv. Panel. Republican. Episcopalian. Home and Office: 7501 SW 176th St Ste 106 Miami FL 33157

DARAZSDI, JAMES JOSEPH, food processing executive; b. Bethelehem, Pa., Feb. 13, 1949; s. George Edward and Anna (Venanzi) D.; B.S., Fairleigh Dickinson U., 1971; postgrad. Ga. State U., 1972-74; m. Janet Beth Hughes, Aug. 29, 1970. CPA, Md., Va.; cert. mgmt. acct. Sr. acct. Texaco Inc., Atlanta, 1971-77; gen. acctg. mgr. Georgetown Tex. Steel, Beaumont, 1978-79; asst. corp. controller Perdue Inc., Salisbury, Md., 1980-81; v.p. fin. Rocco Enterprises, Harrisonburg, Va., 1982-84, exec. v.p., 1984—; bd. dirs. Dominion Bank. Bd. dirs. James Madison U. Mem. Am. Inst. C.P.A.s, Va. Soc. C.P.A.s, Nat. Assn. Accts., Exec. Planning Inst., Am. Mgmt. Assn., Va. Mfrs. Assn. (taxation com.), Va. C. of C. (polit. action com.). Home: 209 Flint Ave Harrisonburg VA 22801 Office: Rocco Enterprises Inc PO Box 549 Harrisonburg VA 22801

DARCHUN, LINO AUKSUTIS, realtor; b. Chgo., Mar. 4, 1942; s. Joseph and Ursula (Shimkus) D.; m. Patricia Marcy Sobel, Sept. 1, 1978 (div. Sept. 1979); m. Mary Lynn Burchette, Nov. 11, 1983; 1 child, Matthew. Student, So. Ill. U., 1960-62, 65, U. Ill., Chgo., 1966. Agt. Ea. Airlines, Chgo., 1967-68; sta. mgr. World Airways, Oakland, Calif., 1968-71; mgr. The Bulls Restaurant-Nightclub, Chgo., 1971-73, pres., 1977-88; v.p. Leber-Darchun, Inc., Chgo., 1973-74; adminstr. dept. aviation City of Chgo., 1974-77; assoc. realtor Palormo Realty, Chgo., 1987-88, realtor, 1988—, dir. sales. Chmn. com. Old Wicker Park, Chgo., 1972-73; vol. Grant Hosp., Chgo.; v.p. Lincoln Park Inter-Agy. Council, 1988; mem. adv. bd., bd. dirs. Friends of Lincoln Park/Lakeview Schs., The Commons Theatre; mem. adv. bd. Acapulco (Mex.) Children's Home. Served to sgt. U.S. Army, 1962-65. Mem. Nat. Assn. Realtors, Chgo. Bd. Realtors, Lincoln Park C. of C. (chmn. human services com. 1987—, bd. dirs.), Lincoln Park Zool. Soc., Lincoln Park Conservation Assn. (1st v.p. 1988, bd. dirs.), Chgo. Pub. Schs. Alumni Assn. Democrat. Unitarian. Home: 3100 N Sheridan Rd Chicago IL 60657 Office: Palormo Realty 734 W Fullerton Chicago IL 60614

DARDIS, STAN KEITH, financial executive; b. Dickinson, N.D., Aug. 4, 1949; s. Thomas A. and Carolyn J. (Kowis) D.; m. Sharon Anne Wenko, Aug. 28, 1970; children: Jason, Christopher, Jennifer. BS with honors, N.D. State U., 1971; postgrad., U. Wis., 1982, Multi-Co. Mgmt. Sch., 1983-84. Loan officer Northwestern Bank Corp., Aberdeen, S.D., 1975-77; v.p. 1st Nat. Bank, Bowman, N.D., 1977-81; sr. v.p. Norwest Bank, Fargo, N.D., 1981-83, exec. v.p., 1983-86; exec. v.p. Met. Fin. Corp., Fargo, 1986—, chmn., 1987—; chmn. N.D. Bankers Mgmt. Com., Bismark, 1984-85. Vice chmn. Dakota Med. Found., Fargo, 1987—; bd. dirs. United Way, Fargo, 1983, N.D. State U. Teammakers, Fargo, 1988. Capt. USAF, 1971-75. Mem. N.D. State U. Alumni Assn., Rotary. Republican. Roman Catholic. Home: 72 Prairiewood Dr Fargo ND 58103 Office: Met Fin Corp 1600 Radisson Tower Fargo ND 58108

D'ARGENIO, RAYMOND, technology company public relations executive; b. Paterson, N.J., May 2, 1930; s. Maurice and Emilia (Berneri) D'A.; m. Barbara Ann Curtice, Nov. 5, 1955; children—David, Claudia. B.S., Georgetown U., 1950; M.A., George Washington U., 1951. Editorial writer Exxon Co., N.Y.C., 1957-63; mgr. editorial services, 1960-63; mgr. govt. and pub. relations Mobil Oil Co., Paris, 1963-68, dir. internat. pub. affairs, N.Y.C., 1968-73, dir. pub. relations, 1973-76; sr. v.p. United Technologies Corp., Hartford, Conn., 1976—; dir. Insilco, Meriden, Conn. Mem. adv. council Ctr. for Contemporary Arab Studies, Washington, 1979—; pres. Greater Hartford Arts Council, 1984-85; pres. United Way Greater Hartford, 1979; chmn. capital campaign Hill-Stead Mus., Farmington, Conn., 1983; trustee Cesare Barbieri Ctr., Hartford, 1980—. Served as lt. USN, 1952-57. Named Communications Exec. of Yr., Corp. Communications Report, 1981. Clubs: Tancanhoosen, Blackledge (Conn.). Office: United Techs Corp United Technologies Bldg Hartford CT 06101 *

DARKE, RICHARD F., corporate lawyer; b. Detroit, June 17, 1943; s. Francis Joseph and Irene Anne (Potts) D.; m. Alice Mary Renger, Feb. 14, 1968; children: Kimberly, Richard, Kelly, Sean, Colin. BBA, U. Notre Dame, 1965; JD, Detroit Coll. Law, 1969. Atty. AAA, Detroit, 1969-72;

assoc. Oster & Mollett P.C., Mt. Clemens, Mich., 1972-73; ptnr. Small, Darke, Oakes P.C., Southfield, Mich., 1973-77; v.p., gen. counsel, sec. Fruehauf Corp., Detroit, 1977—. Mem. ABA, Mich. Bar Assn., Detroit Bar Assn., Machinery and Allied Products Inst. (counsel), Mich. Gen. Counsel Group. Roman Catholic. Club: Essex Country (Windsor, Ont., Can.). Home: 1038 Audubon Grosse Pointe Park MI 48230 Office: Fruehauf Corp 10900 Harper Ave Detroit MI 48213

DARLING, GARY LYLE, carpet and furniture cleaning company executive; b. Passaic, N.J., Nov. 29, 1941: s. Earle Wallace and Lottie Anne (Shefcik) D.; B.A. in Bus. Adminstrn., Boston U., 1963; postgrad. Columbia U. Law Sch., 1963-64; m. Jane Constance Higgiston, Aug. 24, 1964; children—Susan Jane, Debra Ann, Eric Wallace. Data processing sales rep. Service Bur. Corp. subs. IBM, Boston, 1964-66; owner, pres. Renotex Corp., N.Y.C., 1966—. Mem. Assn. Interior Decor Specialists (pres. 1979-80), Carpet and Upholstery Cleaning Assn. (pres. 1974-76), Assn. Specialists in Cleaning and Restoration (treas. 1986—), N.Y. Rug Cleaners Inst. (dir. 1974—), Nat. Fedn. Ind. Bus., C. of C., Better Bus. Bur. Club: Englewood Field. Office: Renotex Corp 229 10th Ave New York NY 10011

DARLINGTON, DAVID WILLIAM, management consultant; b. Boston, Oct. 3, 1945; s. Horace and Maude Beatrice (Pfalzgraf) D.; B.S., Babson Coll., 1974, M.B.A., 1976; postgrad. Northeastern U., 1977-80; m. Stacey A. Mitchell, May 24, 1986; children—Elizabeth Joy, Christine Rebecca. Planning engr. Stone & Webster Engring. Corp., Boston, 1974-75; project adminstr. Northrop Corp., Norwood, Mass., 1975-80; mgr. program adminstrn. internat. systems div. Sanders Assos., Inc., Nashua, N.H., 1980-82; cons., program mgr. Arthur D. Little, Program Systems Mgmt. Co., Cambridge, Mass., 1982—Served with USN, 1964-71. Mem. Am. Prodn. and Inventory Control Soc. (cert.), Am. Assn. Cost Engrs., Inst. Cost Analysis (cert.), Performance Mgmt. Assoc. (sec.), Beta Gamma. Club: Appalachian Mountain. Home: 378 Charles Bancroft Hwy Litchfield NH 03103 Office: Acorn Park Cambridge MA 02140

DARLINGTON, HENRY, JR., investment broker; b. N.Y.C., Jan. 8, 1925; s. Henry and Dorothy (Stone-Smith) D.; m. Frances Elizabeth Richardson, June 5, 1948 (div. Feb. 1965); children: Henry Darlington III, Elizabeth Aldrich, Victoria Wilde; m. Dorothea Fiske Page, July 1965 (div. Dec. 1973). Student pvt. schs.; BA, Columbia U., 1949, LHD (hon.) St. Paul's Coll., Lawrenceville, Va., 1987. Salesman IBM, 1949-52; security salesman Cosgrave, Miller & Whitehead, 1952-55; gen. ptnr. Hill, Darlington & Co., 1955-62; registered rep. Cruttenden, Podesta and Miller, 1962; with syndicate dept. Loeb, Rhoades & Co., 1962-64, br. office adminstr., 1964-67, v.p., 1967-71, registered rep., 1972-79; investment exec. Shearson Loeb Rhoades, Inc., (now Shearson Lehman Hutton), 1980—; v.p., bd. dirs. B. J. Van Ingen & Co., Inc., 1956-59; bd. dirs. Energy Resources Corp., 1963-83, chmn. bd. dirs., 1975-76. Trustee Hoosac Sch., Hoosick, N.Y., 1968-75, Ch. Heavenly Rest Day Sch., N.Y.C., 1968-74, Search and Care, N.Y.C., 1972-87; bd. dirs. Fedn. Protestant Welfare Agys., 1962—, asst. treas., 1971-79; bd. dirs. Episcopal Mission Soc., 1979—, St. Paul's Ch., Rome, St. James' Ch., Florence, Italy; trustee Bd. Fgn. Parishes; vestryman Ch. Heavenly Rest, 1969-75; warden Eglise Francaise du Saint Esprit, 1984-88. With USNR, 1943-46, lt. Res., 1946-65. Mem. St. Nicholas Soc. (pres. 1976-78), S.R., SAR, St. Andrews Soc., The Huguenot Soc. (pres. 1986-89), Soc. Colonial Wars, Mil. Order World War, N.Y. Soc. Mil. and Naval Officers World War, Navy League U.S. (past sec., treas. Western Conn. Coun.), Naval Order, Pilgrim Soc., Delta Psi (trustee Alpha chpt. 1953-58). Clubs: Union, Univ. (N.Y.C.); Everglades (Palm Beach, Fla.); Piping Rock (Locust Valley, N.Y.). Home: 1115 Fifth Ave New York NY 10028 Office: 3 Corporate Park Dr N White Plains NY 10604

DARNALL, ROBERT J., steel company executive. married. BA in Math., DePauw U., 1960; BSCE, Columbia U., 1962; MBA, U. Chgo., 1973. With Inland Steel Co., Chgo., 1962—; gen. mill foreman Inland Steel Co., East Chicago, Ind., 1967-68, asst. supt., 1969-1970, supt., 1971-75, then asst. to v.p. steel mfg., 1975-77, asst. gen. mgr. flat product mills, 1977-79, gen. mgr., 1979, v.p. engring and corp. planning, 1981; exec. v.p. Inland Steel Co., Chgo., 1982, pres., 1984-86, chief operating officer integrated steel segment, 1984-86; pres., chief operating officer Inland Steel Industries, Inc., Chgo., 1986—, also bd. dirs.; bd. dirs. Household Internat. Active Flossmoor (Ill.) Community Ch. ; assoc. Northwestern U.; bd. dirs., United Way, Crusade of Mercy, United Way Suburban Chgo.; trustee DePauw U., Glenwood Sch. for Boys. Mem. Am. Iron and Steel Inst., Assn. Iron and Steel Engrs., Ill. Mfrs. Assn. (bd. dirs.). Office: Inland Steel Industries Inc 30 W Monroe St Chicago IL 60603

DARR, JOHN, insurance company executive; b. Balt., Oct. 9, 1951; s. Jack E. and Mary (Wurdack) D.; m. Sue Brezler, Jan. 5, 1980; children: Adrienne, Elena. BS, Towson State U., 1974; MBA, Loyola Coll., Balt., 1979. CPA, Md., Ill. Mgr. acctg. Md. Casualty Co., Balt., 1974-77; asst. to pres. First Federated Life Ins., Balt., 1977-80; mgr. fin. reporting RLI Ins. Co., Peoria, Ill., 1980-82; regional controller, v.p. Am. Internat. Underwriters, N.Y.C., 1982-83; asst. mgr. fin. reporting Royal Ins. Co., N.Y.C., 1983-84; v.p., treas. Seaboard Surety Co., N.Y.C., 1984—, also bd. dirs. Advisor Jr. Achievement, Balt., 1975. Mem. Am. Inst. CPA's, Soc. Ins. Accts. Home: 560 N Chestnut Westfield NJ 07090 Office: Seaboard Surety Co Burnt Mills Rd and Rte 206 Bedminster NJ 07921

DARR, JOHN KEITH, finance executive; b. Indiana, Pa., Aug. 17, 1944; s. Robert H. and Florabelle (Black) D.; m. Linda Electa Allison, Dec. 26, 1976; children: Joshua Keith, Christopher Allison. AB in Econs., Lafayette Coll., 1966; cert., U. Mich., 1976, Advanced Mgmt. Program Harvard Bus. Sch., 1987. Asst. v.p. investments Western Pa. Nat. Bank, Pitts., 1970-73; v.p., treas. Fed. Home Loan Bank San Francisco, 1973-78; sr. v.p., chief fin. officer No. Calif. Savs., Palo Alto, Calif., 1978-80; exec. v.p. fin. and adminstrn. Student Loan Mktg. Assn., Washington, 1980-84; vice chmn., chief adminstrv. and fin. officer City Fed. Fin. Corp. and City Fed. Savs. Bank, Bedminster, N.J., 1984—. Served to lt. USN, 1967-69, Vietnam. Republican. Presbyterian. Office: City Fed Savs Bank Bedminster 1 Rtes 202-206 Bedminster NJ 07921 also: CityFed Fin Corp 293 S County Rd PO Box 2872 Palm Beach FL 33480 *

DARRAGH, JOHN K., printing company executive; b. Cin., 1929. BS, Ariz. State U., 1959. Account auditor Arthur Andersen and Co., 1959-64; v.p. fin. Sorg Paper Co., Middletown, Ohio, 1964-74; with Standard Register Co., Dayton, Ohio, 1974—, treas., 1974-80, v.p. fin., 1976-80, exec. v.p., 1980-83, chief fin. officer, 1980-81, chief operating officer, 1981-83, pres., chief exec. officer, 1983—. Served to lt. USAF, 1950-56. Office: Standard Register Co PO Box 1167 Dayton OH 45401 *

D'ARRIGO, STEPHEN, JR., agricultural company executive; b. Stockton, Cal., Mar. 8, 1922; s. Stephen and Constance (Piccioto) D'A.; B.S., U. Santa Clara, 1943; m. Rosemary Anne Murphy, Aug. 20, 1949; children—Stephen III, Kathleen Anne, Joanne Marie, Michael Andrew, Dennis Patrick, Patrick Shane. Sec.-treas., D'Arrigo Bros. Co. of Calif., San Jose, 1946-62, Salinas, 1962-83, ret., 1983; sec.-treas. Santa Cruz Farms (co. merged with D'Arrigo Bros. 1970), Eloy, Ariz., 1947-52, pres., gen. mgr. 1952-70, dir. 1947-70. Mem. nat. adv. bd. Am. Security Council; mem. Nat. Def. Exec. Res. Served from pvt. to 2d lt., AUS, 1943-46. Decorated Bronze Star, Combat Inf. Badge, Belgian Fouragere; recipient Distinguished Service award Santa Clara Heart Assn. Mem. Nat. Rifle Assn. (life), Springfield Armory Mus. (life), Smithsonian Assos. (nat. charter), Mil. Order World Wars, Assn. U.S. Army, Co. Mil. Historians, Am. Soc. Arms Collectors, Tex. Gun Collectors Assn., Nat. Hist. Soc. Club: Commonwealth. Home: 2241 Dry Creek Rd San Jose CA 95124

DARROW, WILLIAM RICHARD, pharmaceutical company executive; b. Middletown, Ohio, Sept. 7, 1939; s. Richard William and Nelda Virginia (Darling) D.; B.A., Ohio Wesleyan U., 1960; M.D., Western Res. U., 1964; Ph.D. in Pharmacology, Case-Western Res. U., 1969; m. Janet Elizabeth Swan, June 20, 1964; children—James William, Susan Elizabeth, Margaret Ellen. Intern, Univ. Hosps., Cleve., 1964; sr. clin. research assoc. CIBA Pharm. Co., 1969, asst. dir. clin. pharmacology, 1969-70; dir. clin. pharmacology CIBA-GEIGY Corp., 1970-75, exec. dir. clin. research, 1975-76; sr. v.p. research, med. dir. Wallace Labs. div. Carter Wallace, Inc., Cranbury, N.J., 1976-80; med. dir. Schering Labs. div. Schering-Plough Corp., Kenilworth, N.J., 1980, v.p. med. and regulatory affairs, 1981-82, sr. v.p. med. ops., 1982—. Chmn. research com. N.J. Health Scis. Group, 1973-76, mem. exec. com., 1973-74, 76-86, treas. 1977-80, v.p., 1980-86, Bernards Twp. Bd. Health; 1979—, v.p., 1980, pres., 1981-85, 86—, PMA med. sect. steering com., 1985—, program chmn., 1987-89, vice chmn. 1989—. Roche award, 1962; USPHS postdoctoral fellow, 1965-69. Mem. AMA, Drug Info. Assn., N.J. Acad. Scis., Phi Gamma Delta, Phi Rho Sigma, Omicron Delta Kappa, Pi Delta Epsilon. Republican. Presbyterian. Home: 42 Palmerston Pl Basking Ridge NJ 07920 also: 521 E Lake Rd Penn Yan NY 14527 Office: Galloping Hill Rd Kenilworth NJ 07033

DARWIN, FRED ARRANTS, business consultant; b. Chattanooga, May 28, 1913; s. Fred Perry and Alexandra Allen (Arrants) D.; m. Hope Genung Sparks, Sept. 30, 1939 (dec. 1987); children—Fred Arrants, Hope Darwin Beisinger. Student, U. Chattanooga, 1929-31; BS U.S. Naval Acad., 1935; MS, Harvard U., 1936. Registered profl. engr. Sr. supr. traffic dept. Western Union Telegraph Corp., Chgo., 1936-41; asst. dir. engring. Hazeltine Electronics Corp., N.Y.C., 1946-49; exec. dir. com. guided missiles research and devel. bd. Dept. Def., Washington, 1949-54; mgr. guided missiles Crosley div. Avco Mfg. Corp., Cin., 1954-56; mgr. missile electronics McDonnell Aircraft Corp., St. Louis, 1956-61, gen. mgr. electronic equipment div., 1961-63; asst. to pres. Librascope group Gen. Precision, Inc., 1963-65; bus. counselor, owner Gen. Bus. Services, Dallas, 1966—; mem. spl. com. radio tech. commn. for aeros. Dept. State, Dept. Navy, 1946; cons. del. UN Provisional Internat. Civil Aviation Orgn., 1946; mem. Stewart spl. com. Nat. Guided Missiles Program, 1950, Gardner spl. com., 1953. Contbr. articles to profl. jours.; originator word transponder; inventor multiple-coincidence mixer used in pulse-train coding. Served to comdr. USNR, 1941-46. Recipient citations Sec. Navy, USAAF. Mem. IEEE, Aero. Weights Engrs., Harvard Grad. Soc., E. Dallas C. of C., Naval Acad. Alumni Assn., Alpha Lambda Tau. Democrat. Presbyterian. Club: Harvard. Home: 11805 Neering Dr Dallas TX 75218

DASBURG, JOHN HAROLD, hotel company financial executive; b. N.Y.C., Jan. 7, 1944; s. Jean Henry and Alice Etta Dasburg; AA, U. Miami, 1963; BS in Indsl. Engring., U. Fla., 1966, MBA, 1971, JD, 1973; m. Mary Lois Diaz, July 6, 1968; 1 child, John Peter. Admitted to Fla. bar, 1974. CPA, Fla., Md. Mem. staff Peat Marwick Mitchell & Co., Jacksonville, Fla., 1973-78, tax partner in charge, 1978-80; v.p. tax Marriott Corp., Washington, 1980-82, v.p. fin. 1982-84, sr. v.p., 1984-85, exec. v.p., chief fin. officer, 1985—, now also chief real estate officer. Bd. dirs. U. Fla. Found. Served to lt. (j.g.) USN, 1966-69; Vietnam. Mem. ABA, Urban Land Inst., Am. Inst. CPA's, Fla. Inst. CPA's, Md. Inst. CPA's, Fla. Bar Assn. Republican. Lutheran. Contbr. numerous articles on tax law and tax acct. to Jour. Taxation and Jour. Accountancy. Home: 10609 Alloway Dr Potomac MD 20854 Office: Marriott Corp 1 Marriott Dr Washington DC 20058

DASHER, DONOVAN FRANCIS, financial planning company executive; b. Valdosta, Ga., Sept. 10, 1936; s. Donovan O. and Fannie (Wisenbaker) D.; m. Lucia Gay Philips, Dec. 21, 1957; children: Kathryn Dasher Zanardo, Donovan Francis Jr., Kenneth Alan. B in Chem. Engrin., Ga. Inst. Tech., 1960; postgrad. exec. program in fin., Pa. State U., 1981; cert., Coll. for Fin. Planning, Denver, 1985. Foods rsch. and devel. engr. Procter and Gamble Co., Cin., 1959-62, coffee rsch. and devel. group leader, 1962-67; supt. instant coffee plant Folgers Coffee div. Procter and Gamble Co., South San Francisco, Calif., 1967-69; prodn. dir. Albany (Ga.) Plant M&M/Mars, 1969-74; quality control/tech. svc. dir. M&M/Mars, Chgo., 1974-76, prodn. dir., 1976-79; v.p. mfg. Snackmaster div. Mars Inc., Albany, 1979-81, v.p. svc. and fin., 1981-82; pres., owner Fin. Advisors Inc., Albany, 1982—; br. mgr. FSC Securities Corp., Albany, 1982-85, Pilot Fin. Svcs., Albany, 1985-86, PlanVest Capital Corp., Albany, 1986-87; mng. exec. Integrated Resources Equity Corp., Albany, 1987—. Patentee peanut butter stabilizers. Deacon Cardinal Dr. Ch. of Christ, Rolling Meadows, Ill., 1975-78, elder, 1978-79; chmn. bd. South Ga. Christian Acad., Albany, 1984-86; treas. Thronateeska Heritage Found., Albany, 1987—.8. Mem. Internat. Assn. for Fin. Planning, Inst. Cert. Fin. Planners (cert.), Albany Estate Planning Council, Kiwanis (pres. 1988—, treas. 1985-86). Home: 2205 E Doublegate Dr Albany GA 31707 Office: Fin Advisors Inc 2549 Lafayette Plaza Dr Ste A Albany GA 31707

DASSLER, RICHARD DETTMAR, defense supply company executive; b. Phila., July 13, 1938; s. Walter Dettmar and Alice May (Moore) D.; m. Rachelann Cecelia Assetto, Oct. 7, 1967; children: Rebecca, Richard. BS, Phila. Coll. Textiles and Scis., 1972. Credit investigator Phila. Nat. Bank, 1960-62; caseworker Pa. Dept. Pub. Welfare, Norristown, Pa., 1963-66; contract specialist Def. Indsl. Supply Ctr., Phila., 1966—; pres. Bayland Corp., Phila., 1970-82, Overbrook Child Care Ind., Bala Cynwyd, Pa., 1982-88. With U.S. Army, 1959-60. Mem. Phila. Ski Club, Masons. Home: 126 Derwen Rd Bala Cynwyd PA 19004 Office: 700 Robbins Ave Philadelphia PA 19111

DASTUR, KERSY B., real estate company executive; b. Bombay, July 27, 1946; came to U.S., 1969; s. Behram C. and Amy (Bilimoria) D.; m. Delna Sethna, June 5, 1971; children: Shahroukh, Ayesha, Laila. B of Commerce, U. Bombay, 1966; MBA, U. Pa., 1971. Chartered acct., 1969. V.p., regional mgr. Am. Mgmt. Systems Inc., Arlington, Va., 1971-82; sr. v.p. planning and devel. Suburban Bank, Bethesda, Md., 1982-86; exec. v.p., chief fin. officer Nat. Corp. for Housing Partnerships, Washington, 1986—. Mem. Planning Forum (program dir. 1985-86), Zoroastrian Assn. (hon. treas. 1986-87), Westwood Country Club (Vienna, Va.). Home: 1222 Raymond Ave McLean VA 22101 Office: Nat Corp for Housing Partnerships 1225 Eye St NW Washington DC 20005

DATELLE, ELIZABETH LOOMIS, health care marketing executive; b. Hartford, Conn., Nov. 3, 1945; d. Henry Simmons and Mary Dillon (Callahan) Loomis; m. H.R. Datelle, Nov. 17, 1967 (div. 1972); children: Marc Joseph, Lisa Marie. RN, St. Francis Hosp., Hartford, 1966; Cert. Nurse Practitioner, U. Ga., 1976; cert. in nursing mgmt., UCLA, 1981. Nurse various hosps., 1966-74; nurse practitioner Athens (Ga.) Neighborhood Health Ctr., 1974-78; dir. nurse recruitment Med. Coll. Ga., Augusta, 1978-79; recruiter, mgmt. cons. Am. Med. Internat., Atlanta, 1979-83; nursing adminstr. R.T. Jones Meml. Hosp., Canton, Ga., 1983-84; account exec. Observer TV, Athens, Ga., 1984-85; dir. mktg. Atlanta Rehab. Inst., 1985-88; mktg. assoc. New Medico Combined, Atlanta, 1988—; provider coun. Nat. Head Injury Found., 1987-88. Contbr. articles to profl. jours. Sec., bd. dirs. Country Place Condominiums, Alpharetta, Ga., 1987—; bd. dirs. Ga. Abortion Rights Action League, Atlanta, 1978-80, Athens Rape Crisis Line, 1976-78, Athens area for ERA, 1978. Mem. Nat. Assn. Nurse Recruiters (chair legis. com. 1978-80, sec. 1980-82, v.p. 1982-84), Ga. Assn. Rehab. Nurses (scholar 1988, chair legis. com. 1987-88, bd. dirs. 1986-88), Pvt. Rehab. Suppliers Ga. (bd. dirs. 1987-88, chair legis. com. 1986-88), Ga. Head Injury Found. (chmn. ann. fund raising and publicity 1987-88). Democrat. Roman Catholic. Office: New Medico Head Injury Systems 43 Country Place Ct Alpharetta GA 30201

DATOO, BASHIR AHMED, marketing consultant, researcher; b. Zanzibar, Tanzania, July 12, 1941; s. Ahmed Abdulrasul and Kulsum Ahmed (Lakha) D.; m. Marzia M.L. Esmail, June 25, 1979; children: Ahmed, Fatima. BA with honors, London U., Kampala, Uganda, 1964; PhD, London Sch. Econs. and Polit. Sci., 1968. Asst. prof. U. Dar-es-Salaam, Tanzania, 1968-72, assoc. prof., 1973-76; dir. rsch. project Total Rsch. Corp., Princeton, N.J., 1977-82, dir. quantitative rsch., 1982-87, head strategic rsch. support and devel. group, 1987—; vis. scholar U. Minn., Mpls., 1972, Princeton U., 1976-77. Author: Port Development in East Africa, 1975; contbr. articles to profl. jours. Mem. Am. Mktg. Assn. (speaker in agribus.), Bank Mktg. Assn., Am. Chem. Soc. Home: 3 Wellesley Ct Princeton Junction NJ 08550 Office: Total Rsch Corp 5 Independence Way Princeton NJ 08540

DAUCH, RICHARD E., automobile manufacturing company executive. BS, Purdue U., 1964. With Gen. Motors Corp., 1964-75; group v.p. mfg. Volkswagon of Am., 1976-80; v.p. Chrysler Corp., 1980, exec. v.p. diversified ops., 1980-81, exec. v.p. stamping assembly diversified ops., 1981-84, exec. v.p. mfg., 1984—. Recip. Eli Whitney Meml. Award, Soc. Mfg. Engrs., 1987. Office: Chrysler Motors Corp 12000 Chrysler Dr Highland Park MI 48288 *

DAUER, DONALD DEAN, investment executive; b. Fresno, Calif., June 1, 1936; s. Andrew and Erma Mae (Zigenman) D.; m. LaVerne DiBuduo, Jan. 23, 1971; children: Gina, Sarah. BS in Bus. Adminstrn.; postgrad., U. Wash., 1964. Loan officer First Savs. and Loan, Fresno, 1961-66, v.p., 1966-71, sr. v.p., 1971-81, exec. v.p., 1978-81; pres. Uniservice Corp., Fresno, 1976-81, Don Dauer Investments, Fresno, 1981-85; pres., chief oper. officer, dir. Riverbend Internat. Corp., Sanger, Calif., 1985—; bd. dirs. Univ. Savs. and Loan. Chmn. bd. dirs. City of Fresno Gen. Services Retirement Bd., 1973-83, West Fresno Econ. and Bus. Devel. Program Bd., 1980-83; pres., bd. dirs. Cen. Calif. United Cerebral Palsy Assn., 1979-82; chmn. found. Valley Children's Hosp., Fresno, 1984—; trustee Valley Children's Hosp., 1987—; bd. dirs. Youth for Christ USA, 1988—. Mem. Soc. Real Estate Appraisers (past pres.). Office: Riverbend Internat Corp 15749 E Ventura Ave Sanger CA 93657

DAUGHERTY, RAYMOND EDWARD, electronics company executive; b. Phila., May 21, 1946; s. Robert Edward and Hazel (Shuster) D.; m. Sherry Stebbins Daugherty, May 9, 1970; children: Scott Michael, Randy Edward. BE, Stevens Inst. Tech., 1968; MBA, N.Y. Inst. Tech., 1981. Mgr. bus. Hazeltine Corp., Greenlawn, N.Y., 1968-75, program mgr., 1976-80, dir. programs, 1981-83, dir. E3A Enhance, 1984-85, v.p. C3I programs, 1985-88, v.p., gen. mgr. C3I products, 1988—. Dir. Ft. Salonga (N.Y.) Civic Assn. Mem. Assn. U.S. Army. Presbyterian. Home: 14 Susan Dr Fort Salonga NY 11768 Office: Hazeltine Corp 450 E Pulaski Rd Greenlawn NY 11740

DAUGHTREY, ZOEL WAYNE, accounting educator, tax consultant; b. Sulphur Springs, Tex., June 30, 1940; s. Jewel D. and Hazel J. (Kostris) D.; m. Jackie E. Burch, Dec. 18, 1965; 1 child, Heather. BS, Tex. Tech. U., 1963, MS, 1982; MS, Okla. State U., 1966; PhD, N.C. State u., 1970. CPA, Tex., Miss. Materials analyst Tex. Hwy. Dept., Paris, 1963-64; instr. Okla. State U., Stillwater, 1964-66; agronomist N.C. Dept. Agr., Raleigh, 1966-70; prof., head dept. agr. Northwestern State U., Natchitoches, La., 1970-77; agronomist Tex. Agrl. Extension Svc., Lubbock, 1977-79; instr. Tex. Tech. U., Lubbock, 1980; tax mgr. Peat Marwick Mitchell and Co., Lubbock, 1981-82; prof. acctg. Miss. State U., Mississippi State, 1982—; dir. tax policy Watkins Ward and Stafford, CPAs, West Point, Miss., 1987—. Author tax update seminar, 1986—; mem. bd. advisors Jour. Agrl. Taxation and Law, N.Y.C., 1986—; editor Farm Mgmt. Tax Tips, 1983—, Taxpayers Digest, 1987—; contbr. articles to profl. jours. Mem. AICPA, Tex. Soc. CPAs, Miss. Soc. CPAs, Am. Acctg. Assn., Am. Taxation Assn., Starkville C. of C. (agr. com.). Methodist. Home: 302 Greenbriar Starkville MS 39759 Office: Miss State U PO Drawer EF Mississippi State MS 39762

DAUNER, JACK RHODES, marketing and management educator; b. Milw., Mar. 22, 1924; s. Wilson Walter and Pauline Ann (Rhodes) D.; m. Carolyn Lee Wells, May 12, 1947. BS, U. Iowa, 1947, MS, 1965; PhD in Bus. Adminstrn., St. Louis U., 1970. Various positions mng. trade assns. Davenport and Dubuque, Iowa, and Madison, Wis., 1947-53; v.p. adminstrn. Nat. Sales Execs. Assn., N.Y.C., 1953-56; mng. dir. Sales and Mktg. Execs. St. Louis, 1961-62; instr. mktg. St. Louis U., 1965-69; assoc. prof. U. Detroit, 1969-70, U. Akron, Ohio, 1970-76; prof. mktg. and mgmt. Fayetteville (N.C.) State U., 1976-88; pres. Jack R. Dauner Assocs., Pinehurst, N.C., 1960—. Author: Salesmen's Compensation: Plans, Policies and Trends, 1970; contbr. over 100 articles to profl. jours. Served to cpl. inf. U.S. Army, 1943-46, ETO. Grantee IBM, Assoc. Am. Collegiate Schs. of Bus., 1975, Kleid Found., 1971. Mem. Sales and Mktg. Execs. Internat. (v.p. Akron 1975-76, N.C. 1976-78, internat. dir. 1978-82), Acad. Mgmt., Am. Mktg. Assn. Clubs: Country of N.C., Pinehurst. Office: Jack R Dauner Assocs PO Box 1828 Pinehurst NC 28374

DAUSSMAN, GROVER FREDERICK, consulting engineer; b. Newburgh, Ind., May 6, 1919; s. Grover Cleveland and Madeline (Springer) D.; student U. Cin., 1936-38, Carnegie Inst. Tech., 1944-45, George Washington U., 1948-56; B.S. in Elec. Engring., U. Ala., 1963, postgrad., 1963-64, 77; postgrad. Indsl. Coll. Armed Forces, 1955, 63; Ph.D. (hon.), Hamilton State U., 1973; m. Elli Margrite Kilian, Dec. 27. 1941; children—Cynthia Louise Daussman Quinn, Judith Ann, Margaret Elizabeth Daussman Davidson Cooper. Coop. engr. Sunbeam Elec. Mfg. Co., Evansville, Ind., 1936-38; engr., draftsman Phila. Navy Yard, 1941-42; resident engr., supr. shipbldg. USN, Neville Island, Pa., 1942-45; engr. Pearl Harbor Navy Yard, 1945-48; sect. head Bur. Ships, USN, Washington, 1948-56; head guidance and control tech. liaison Army Ballistic Missile Agy., Huntsville, Ala., 1956-58, chief program coordination Guidance and Control Lab., 1958-60; chief program coordination Astrionics Lab., Marshall Space Flight Center (Ala.), 1960-63, dir's staff asst. for advanced research and tech., 1963-70; engring. cons., 1970—; project dir. fallout shelter surveys Mil Dept. Tenn., 1971-73; head drafting dept. Alverson-Draughon Coll., Huntsville, 1974-77; instr. Ala. Christian Coll., 1977-79; engring. draftsman Reisz Engring., 1979; chief engr. Sheraton Motor Inn, 1979; sr. engr. Sperry Support Services, 1980; asso. Techni-Core Profls., Huntsville, 1980-81; elec. engr. Reisz Engring., Huntsville, 1981-86; tutor in mathematics, scis. and engring. North Ala. Ednl. Opportunity Ctr., Huntsville, 1986—. Chmn. community spl. gifts com. Madison County Heart Assn., 1965; mem. Population Action Council. Recipient cert. of recognition, 1945, cert. of service USN, 1946; performance award cert. U.S. Army, 1960; certs. of appreciation AIEE, 1960, 61, 62, Ala. Soc. Profl. Engrs., 1982; IEEE Centennial Medal, 1984, IEEE Honor Role of Outstanding Vols., 1986, IEEE Ednl. Activities Award, 1987, award for disting. services Huntsville sect. IEEE, 1964; award for contbn. to successful launch of 1st Saturn V, George C. Marshall Space Flight Center, 1967, also award of achievement for contbn. to 1st manned lunar landing, 1969; Apollo achievement award NASA, 1969; named Engr. of Yr., 1968, 69, 82. Registered profl. engr., Ala., Va., D.C.; cert. fallout shelter analyst, Dept. Def. Fellow Explorers Club, Redstone Arsenal Officers Club; mem. Planetary Soc. (charter), Hellenic Profl. Assn. Am. (hon.), U. Ala. Alumni Assn., Ala. (state dir. 1962-65, 68-71, 85—, chpt. pres. 1966-67, coordinator), Nat. Socs. Profl. Engrs., AARP, Am. Inst. Urban and Regional Affairs, The Cousteau Soc., IEEE (life, sr. mem., sect. chmn. N. Ala. sect. 1961-62; founder and chmn. engring. mgmt. chpt. 1964-65, mem. Region 3 exec. com. 1969-79, mem. inst. research com. 1965-67, mem. adminstv. com. of engring. mgmt. soc. 1966-86, sec. soc. 1968-85, regional del.-dir. S.E. region, mem. inst. bd. dirs. 1972-73), Am. Def. Preparedness Assn. (post dir. Tenn. Valley 1963-66), AAAS, Internat. Platform Assn., AIAA, Nat. Assn. Retarded Children, Huntsville Assn. Tech. Socs. (founder; sec. 1969-70; v.p. 1970-71), Am. Soc. Naval Engrs., U.S. Naval Inst., Assn. U.S. Army, Missile, Space and Range Pioneers (life), Nat. Assn. of Retired Fed. Employees, NASA Retirees Assn. (v.p. 1973-74, pres. 1974—). Democrat. Mem. United Ch. of Christ (treas. 1959-61, ch. council 1964-66; sec. ch. council, program com. chmn. ch. council 1965-66; vice moderator Ala.-Tenn. assn. 1965-68; bd. dirs. Southeast conf. 1965-66, mem. budget and finance com. 1965-66). Hon. mem. editorial adv. bd. Am. Biog. Inst., 1975—. Home: 1910 Colice Rd SE Huntsville AL 35801 Office: 2205 University Dr Ste G Huntsville AL 35805

D'AVANZO, THOMAS ANTHONY, investment banker; b. Hartford, Conn., Oct. 31, 1944; s. Thomas A. and Julia M. (Piccolo) D'A.; m. Mary Lord Lawson, Apr. 28, 1972; children: Erica, Benjamin. BA, Amherst Coll., 1966; MS in Profl. Acctg., U. Hartford, 1975. Fin. planner Conn. Gen. Life Ins. Co., Hartford, 1966-68; trust investments analyst Conn. Bank & Trust Co., Hartford, 1968-70; co-developer Forum Apts., Hartford, 1970-72; mgr. fin. services Conn. Devel. Authority, Hartford, 1973-77; exec. dir. Mass. Indsl. Mortgage Ins. Agy./Mass. Indsl. Fin. Agy., Boston, 1977-81; investment banker B.L. McTeague & Co. Inc., Hartford, 1981-82; mng. dir., prin. Parker Benjamin, Inc., Farmington, Conn., 1983—; dir. Donahue, Inc., Hartford; mem. task force U.S. Dept. Treasury, 1978; adviser to State of Maine, State of Ky., 1978-79. treas., bd. dirs. Conn. Halfway House, Inc., Hartford, 1969-70; bd. dirs., treas. Seventh Day Adventist Ch., 1988—. Republican. Home: 9 Meadow Crossing Simsbury CT 06070 Office: Parker Benjamin Inc 160 Farmington Ave Farmington CT 06032

DAVENPORT, DONALD LYLE, engineering and real estate company executive; b. Eau Claire, Wis., Oct. 9, 1930; s. Douglas Benjamin and Leona Margaret (Fairbanks) D.; B.A. in Social Studies, Coll. St. Thomas, St. Paul, 1955; children—Ann, Martin, John, Donna, Jennifer. Adminstrv. asst. to regional mgr. Butler Mfg. Co., Mpls., 1955-58; corp. sec., gen. mgr. Spencer Corp., Eau Claire, 1958-60; sales mgr. Russell Structures Co., Madison, Wis., 1960; former pres. Bldg. Systems, Inc., Middleton, Wis., from 1960; pres. D Davenport Ltd., Madison, 1980—; Former chmn. bd., pres. Jr. Achievement.

Served with USAF, 1950-54. Registered profl. engr., Wis.; lic. real estate broker, Wis. Mem. Metal Bldg. Dealer Assn. (pres. 1971), Profl. Engrs. in Constrn., Wis. Soc. Profl. Engrs. (former pres. practice sect.), Johns Manville Dealer Council (chmn.), ARMCO Steel Corp. Dealer Council. Republican. Roman Catholic. Club: Exchange. Office: 2320 Darwin Rd Madison WI 53704

DAVEY, BRUCE JAMES, insurance company executive; b. Montclair, N.J., Nov. 17, 1927; s. Reginald and Ellen Louis (Bragg) D.; m. Julia B. Twyford, June 21, 1958; children: Lynn Kathrine, Laurie Ellen, Bruce James. Suzanne Elizabeth. B.A., Colgate U., 1950. With Chem. Bank, N.Y.C., 1951-58; with N.Y. Life Ins. Co., N.Y.C., 1958—, asst. treas., 1960-76, treas., 1976-82, v.p., treas., 1982—. Episcopalian. Home: 499 Harding Rd Fair Haven NJ 07701 Office: NY Life Ins Co 51 Madison Ave New York NY 10010 *

DAVID, GEORGE, psychiatrist, economic theory lecturer; b. N.Y.C., Feb. 19, 1940; s. Norman and Jennie (Danziger) D. BA, Yale U., 1961; MD, NYU, 1965. Intern Children's Hosp., San Francisco, 1965; resident in psychiatry Colo. Psychiat. Hosp., Denver, 1965-66; practice medicine specializing in psychiatry San Francisco; staff Mt. Zion Hosp., San Francisco, 1966-67, San Mateo County (Calif.) Mental Health Svcs., 1968-71; lectr. on application of econ. theory to personal decision making. Mem. San Francisco Clin. Hypnosis (v.p. 1973-74). Libertarian. Home: 2334 California St San Francisco CA 94115 Office: 3527 Sacramento St San Francisco CA 94118

DAVID, GEORGE ALFRED LAWRENCE, elevator company executive; b. Bryn Mawr, Pa., Apr. 7, 1942; s. Charles Wendell and Margaret (Simpson) D.; m. Barbara Osborn, Sept. 4, 1965; children—Eliza Pell, Hannah Lawrence, Henry Gibb. BA, Harvard U., 1965; MBA, U. Va., 1967. Asst. prof. fin. and acctg. U. Va., Charlottesville, 1967-68; v.p. The Boston Cons. Group, 1968-75; sr. v.p. corp. planning and devel. Otis Elevator Co., N.Y.C., 1975-77, sr. v.p., gen. mgr. Latin Am. ops., West Palm Beach, Fla., 1977-81, sr. v.p., pres. N.Am. ops., Farmington, Conn., 1981-85, pres., chief exec. officer Otis Elevator Co., 1985—; sr. v.p. United Techs. Corp., 1988—. Chmn. Greater Hartford chpt. ARC, 1985-87; trustee Wadsworth Atheneum, Hartford, 1984—. Republican. Episcopalian. Clubs: Union, N.Y. Yacht (N.Y.C.). Home: 62 Westwood Rd West Hartford CT 06117 Office: Otis Elevator Co 10 Farm Springs Rd Farmington CT 06032 also: United Techs Corp United Techs Bldg Hartford CT 06101

DAVID, IRWIN T., accountant; b. Chgo., Mar. 7, 1937; s. Jack and Gertrude (Goldsmith) D.; m. Jerri-Ann Pollak, Mar. 18, 1962; children: Debra, Douglas, Donald, Jonathan. BS in Chemistry, U. Ill., 1958; MS in Indsl. Adminstrn., Carnegie-Mellon U., 1960. CPA, D.C., Md., Va., Ill., Mich. Various positions Touche Ross, Chgo., 1950-69, ptnr., 1969—; nat. dir. pub. sector svcs. Touche Ross, Washington and Chgo., 1982—; ptnr.-in-charge Touche Ross Washington Svc. Ctr., 1986—; chmn. Govt. Rels. Com., Privatization Coun., Washington, 1988—. Co-author: How to Evaluate/Improve Internal Controls in Governmental Units, 1983, TR Government Executive Guide to Select Small Computer, 1984, author: Financing Infrastructure in America, 1985, Privatization in America, 1987; contbr. articles to profl. jours. Mem. Leadership Washington; chmn. Jewish Info. and Referral Svc. United Jewish Fedn., mem. budget and planning com.; bd. dirs., com. chmn. Coun. Jewish Elderly; bd. dirs. Jewish Inst. Nat. Security Affairs; pres., bd. edn. Sch. Dist. 109; bd. dirs., mem. several coms. Washington Ballet. Recipient Elija Watts Silver medal Ill. Soc. CPAs, 1963. Mem. AICPA (mem., chmn. several coms.), Assn. Govt. Accts., Govt. Fin. Officers Assn. U.S. and Can. (Achievement cert.), Indian Springs Country Club (Md.), Briarwood Country Club (v.p., com. chmn.), City Club (Washington). Office: Touche Ross & Co 1900 M St NW Ste 400 Washington DC 20036-3564

DAVID, JAMES DONALD, tax accountant; b. Ithaca, N.Y., July 25, 1957; s. Michael and Betty (Besemer) D.; m. Maria Coakley, Sept. 3, 1983; children: Kristin, Shannon. BS, Cornell U., 1979; MBA, Coll. William and Mary, 1983; postgrad. in taxation, Georgetown U., 1988—. CPA, Va. Sr. acct. Grant Thorton, Washington, 1982-84, Pannell Kerr Forster, Alexandria, Va., 1984-85; sr. tax cons. Price Waterhouse, Washington, 1985-88, Kenneth Leventhal & Co., Washington, 1988—. Mem. Am. Inst. CPA's, Cornell Soc. Hotelmen. Roman Catholic. Club: Washington Golf and Country. Home: 3408 N Buchanan St Arlington VA 22207 Office: Kenneth Leventhal & Co 2000 K StNW Washington DC 20006

DAVID, LYNN ALLEN, banking executive; b. Greeneville, Tenn., Nov. 14, 1948; s. Clayton Cunningham and Lenora Mildred (Scott) D. BS in Bus. Adminstrn., U. Ark., 1970; MS in Commerce, St. Louis U., 1973; cert., Stonier Grad. Sch. Banking, 1981, Nat. Comml. Lending Sch., 1984. Asst. v.p. Fed. Res. Bank St. Louis, 1970-84; v.p., dir. corr. banking Gen. Bank, St. Louis, 1984-86; v.p. ops. Cen. Bank Systems, Inc., Granite City, Ill., 1986-87; sr. cons., supr. Deloitte Haskins & Sells, St. Louis, 1987; mgr. Peat Marwick Main & Co., St. Louis, 1987—; sec. Pres. Conf., First V.P. Conf., Fed. Res. System, 1982. Recipient Status Cymbal award Mo. Bankers Assn., Jefferson City, 1985. Mem. Bank Adminstrn. Inst., Bank Mgmt. Assn. Republican. Presbyterian. Home: 12704 St Lazare Ln Saint Louis MO 63127 Office: Peat Marwick Main & Co 1010 Market St 18th Fl Saint Louis MO 63101

DAVID, PHILIP, finance and investments executive; b. N.Y.C., Sept. 1, 1931; s. Morris and Sylvia (Mantel) D.; m. Hilary Jane Knight-Revel (1977); children: Mark Jonathan, James Andrew-Watson. AM, Columbia U., 1953; MBA, Harvard U., 1953, D in Bus. Adminstrn., 1963. V.p., asst. to pres. Webb & Knapp Inc., N.Y.C., 1955-59; prof., rsch. fellow Grad. Sch. Bus Adminstrn. Harvard U., Cambridge, Mass., 1959-71; prof. bus. adminstrn. MIT, Cambridge, 1971-87; cons., chmn. investments and audit coms. Banner Industries Inc., N.Y.C., 1986—, also bd. dirs.; v.p. Godchaux Sugar Co. Inc., New Orleans 1957-60; vice chmn., treas. Advanced NMR Systems Inc., Woburn, Mass., 1984—; vice chmn. Sunresorts Ltd., St. Maarten, Antilles, 1986-87; cons. sec. Dept. Treasury, Washington, 1966, HUD, 1973, World Bank, 1971-72, pres. govt. Indonesia, Jarkarta, 1971-74; advisor to Pres. U.S. Nat. Urban Growth Policy, 1971-72; bd. dirs. Transcontinental Svcs. Group, Curacao, Netherlands Antilles. Author: Urban Land Development, 1971. Baker scholar Harvard U., 1955. Mem. Harvard Club (N.Y.C., Boston). Home: 1060 Fifth Ave New York NY 10128 Office: Banner Industries 110 E 59th St New York NY 10022

DAVIDOFF, HOWARD, investment banker, venture capitalist; b. Bklyn., June 8, 1956; s. Robert George and Esther Sarah (Schneier) D.; m. Lisa Jane Klein, Apr. 5, 1987. BBA, Boston U., 1978; MBA, NYU, 1980. Corp. loan officer Chase Manhattan Bank, N.Y.C., 1981-82, asst. treas., 1982-83, 2d v.p., 1983-85, v.p., 1985-86; v.p. Carl, Marks & Co. N.Y., N.Y.C., 1986—; bd. dirs. Aerodyne Products, Billerica, Mass., Rugtime, Inc., Boca Raton, Fla., Pressure Systems Inc., Hampton, Va., Collectors Guild Internat., N.Y.C. Mem. Assn. for Corp. Growth, N.Y. Venture Capital Assn., Beta Gamma Sigma. Republican. Jewish. Office: CMNY Capital Co 77 Water St New York NY 10005

DAVIDOW, GLENN ROBERT, financial planning executive; b. Winnipeg, Man., Can., Aug. 8, 1958; s. Harold Charles and Corrine Lou (Trester) D.; m. Laura Cheryl Droker, Nov. 6, 1988. Cert. fin. planning, Coll. Fin. Planning-U. So. Calif., 1987. Dist. asst. Equitable Life Assurance Soc., Burbank, Calif., 1979-82; pres., owner Davidow Fin. Svcs., Encino, Calif., 1982—; Senate commr. on Life and Health Ins., Sacramento, Calif., 1988—. Mem. Inst. Fin. Planners, Internat. Assn. Fin. Planning, Nat. Assn. Life Underwriters, Nat. Assn. Health Underwriters, Calif. Assn. Health Underwriters (chmn. fund raising for polit. action com.), L.A. Assn. Health Underwriters (bd. dirs.). Office: Davidow Fin Svcs 16633 Ventura Blvd Ste 725 Encino CA 91436

DAVIDOW, ROBERT, insurance company executive; b. Scranton, Pa., Aug. 3, 1947; s. Solomon and Margaret (Lang) D.; m. Hiroko Nakata, Dec. 13, 1981; children: Juliet Youko, Alexander Sho. BS in Econs., U. Pa., 1969; MBA, Columbia U., 1973. Trust examiner Fed. Reserve Bank Phila., 1970-71; fin. analyst I.T.T., N.Y.C., 1972-73; asst. to pres. Waddell and Reed, Kansas City, Mo., 1973-74; sr. engagement mgr. McKinsey & Co., Inc., N.Y.C., 1974-81; pres. Robert Davidow & Assocs. Inc., Greenwich, Conn., 1981-86; sr. v.p. group pension Mut. Benefit Life Ins., Newark, 1986-88; pres. Robert Davidow & Assocs., Inc., Greenwich, Conn., 1988—. Contbr. articles to profl. jours. Served with U.S. Army N.G., 1969-75. Recipient Profl. Acctg. prize Columbia U., 1973. Mem. Beta Gamma Sigma. Republican. Jewish. Home and Office: 367 Stanwich Rd Greenwich CT 06830

DAVIDSON, CARL B., oil company executive; b. Trenton, N.J., Apr. 17, 1933; s. Jack O. and Pearl (Watkins) D.; m. Lois Greenwald, June 28, 1959; children—Andrew William, Jane Hope. A.B., Rutgers U., 1954, LL.B., 1957. Bar: D.C. 1957, N.Y. 1960. Asst. to gen. mgr. Koret Inc., N.Y.C., 1957-58; field atty. NLRB, N.Y.C., 1958-65; with Texaco Inc., N.Y.C. and Westchester, N.Y., 1965—; asst. to v.p., then asst. sec. Texaco Inc., 1971-74, corp. sec., 1974-87, v.p., corp. sec., 1987—. Office: Texaco Inc 2000 Westchester Ave White Plains NY 10650

DAVIDSON, CHARLES MICHAEL BIRNIE, management consultant; b. Colombo, Sri Lanka, Nov. 2, 1944; came to U.S., 1979; s. Charles Alexander Birnie and Grace Louise (Gibson) D.; married Carol Anne Farmiloe, Dec. 13, 1969; children: Claire, Simon, Gail, James. MA in Math. with honors, Cambridge U., Eng., 1966; MS in Bus. Studies with distinction, London U., 1973. Mgr. organizational and pers. planning Ford of Britain, Brentwood, Eng., 1966-73; cons. Boston Cons. Group, London, 1973-76; staff exec. operational strategy Continental Group, Stamford, Conn., 1976-84; spl. advisor on strategic mgmt. Arthur Young, N.Y.C., 1985—; pres. Mike Davidson Assocs., New Canaan, Conn., 1984—; chmn. Strategos, New Canaan, Conn., 1988—. Presbyterian. Home: 36 Deacons Way New Canaan CT 06840

DAVIDSON, CHARLES TOMPKINS, construction company executive; b. Washington, Apr. 10, 1940; s. James S. Jr. and Lida R. (Moyer) D.; m. Joanne Clabaugh; children: Robert C., Jennifer L., Bonnie R. BCE, Lehigh U., 1962. Registered profl. engr., D.C. Field and office engr. Charles H. Tompkins Co., Washington, 1964-70; supt., project mgr. J. A. Jones Constrn. Co., Charlotte, N.C., 1970-76, pres., 1986—; v.p., mgr. Metric Constructors, Charlotte, 1976-79; pres. Tiber Constrn. Co., Fairfax, Va., 1979-86. Served to 1st lt. U.S. Army, 1962-64. Mem. Chi Epsilon. Episcopalian. Clubs: Quail Hollow Country (Charlotte); Moles, Beaver. Home: 3908 Moorland Dr Charlotte NC 28226 Office: J A Jones Constrn Co 6060 St Albans St Charlotte NC 28287 *

DAVIDSON, DAN D., brokerage house executive; b. Fla., Feb. 19, 1948; s. Edward J. and Lois (Aplin) D.; m. Aronda Register, Aug. 23, 1971; 1 child, Robert Michael. Student, Tallahassee Community Coll., Fla. State U. Fin. investigator State of Fla., Tallahassee, 1980-84; exec. v.p. Barry Fin. Group, Inc., Boca Raton, Fla., 1984—; pres. Asset Mgmt. Securities Corp., Boca Raton, 1984—. Sgt. U.S. Army, 1969-70, Vietnam. Mem. Internat. Assn. for Fin. Planners (bd. dirs., treas. Gold Coast chpt. 1987-88). Office: Barry Fin Group Inc 40 SE 5th St Ste 600 Boca Raton FL 33432

DAVIDSON, DONALD MATTHEW, credit union executive; b. Cleve., June 28, 1958; s. Donald Alan and Mary Ann (Diemer) D.; m. Tamara Anne Swartz, Oct. 18, 1980; children: Hilary Anne, Mallory Susan. BS in Acctg., Miami U., Oxford, Ohio, 1980; MBA in Fin. and Econs., Xavier U., 1987. CPA, Ohio. Acct. Hausser and Taylor, CPA's, Cleve., 1980-82; internal auditor Gold Circle Stores, Columbus, Ohio, 1982-83; acct. Ary and Earman, CPA's, Columbus, 1983-85, Accuray Corp., Columbus, 1985-87; supt. Ohio Div. Credit Unions, Columbus, 1987—; trustee Nat. Inst. State Credit Union Edn., Washington, 1987—. Editor: Div. Credit Unions Newsletter. V.p. Woodbridge Civic Assn., Columbus, 1987—. Mem. Nat. Assn. State Credit Union Suprs. (bd. dirs. 1988—), AICPA's, Ohio Soc. CPA's. Roman Catholic. Home: 7868 Saddle Run Powell OH 43065 Office: Dept Commerce Ohio Div Credit Unions 2 Nationwide Pla Columbus OH 43266-0544

DAVIDSON, FRANK PAUL, macro-engineer, lawyer; b. N.Y.C., May 20, 1918; s. Maurice Philip and Blanche (Reinheimer) D.; m. Izaline Marguerite Doll, May 19, 1951; children: Roger Conrad, Nicholas Henry, Charles Geoffrey. BS, Harvard U., 1939, JD, 1948, DHL (hon.), Hawthorne Coll., 1987. Bar: N.Y. 1953, U.S. Dist. Ct. (so. dist.) N.Y. 1953. Dir. mil. affairs Houston C. of C., 1948-50; contract analyst Am. Embassy, Paris, 1950-53; assoc. Carb, Luria, Glassner & Cook, N.Y.C., 1953-54; pvt. practice law, N.Y.C., 1955-70; rsch. assoc. MIT, Cambridge, 1970—, also chmn. system dynamics steering com. Sloan Sch. Mgmt., coord. macro-engring. Sch. Engring.; pres. Tech. Studies, Inc., N.Y.C., 1957—; vice chmn. Inst. for Ednl. Svcs., Bedford, Mass., 1980-84; Nat. Acad. Scis. del. to Renewable Resources Workshop, Katmandu, Nepal, 1981; governing bd. Channel Tunnel Study Group, 1957—; co-founder Channel Tunnel Study Group, London and Paris, 1957. Author: Macro: A Clear Vision of How Science and Technology Will Shape our Future, 1983, Macro: Big Is Beautiful, 1986; editor series of AAAS books on macro-engring. including Tunneling and Underground Transport, 1987; mem. editorial bd. Interdisciplinary Sci. Revs., 1985—; mem. adv. bd. Tech. in Soc., 1979—, Mountain Research and Development, 1981—, Project Appraisal, 1986—. Bd. dirs. Internat. Mountain Soc., Boulder, Colo., 1981—; trustee Norwich (Vt.) Ctr., 1980-83; mem. steering com. Am. Trails Network, 1986-88; bd. dirs. Am. Trails. Washington, 1988—. Capt. RCAC, 1941-46, ETO. Decorated Bronze Star; recipient key to City of Osaka, Japan, 1987; Lewis Mumford fellow Rensselaerville Inst., 1982. Mem. ABA, Internat. Assn. Macro-Engring. Socs. (bd. dirs. 1987—), Am. Soc. Macro-Engring. (bd. dirs. 1982—, vice chancellor 1983—), Assn. Bar of City of N.Y. (internat. law com. 1959-62). Clubs: Knickerbocker (N.Y.C.); St. Botolph (Boston). Home: 140 Walden St Concord MA 01742 Office: MIT E40-294 Cambridge MA 02139

DAVIDSON, GEORGE A., JR., utility company executive; b. Pitts., July 28, 1938. BS, U. of Pitts., 1960. Chmn., chief exec. officer, dir. Consol. Natural Gas Co., Pitts. Office: Consol Natural Gas Co 4 Gateway Ctr Pittsburgh PA 15222 *

DAVIDSON, HARVEY JUSTIN, university dean; b. Gentryville, Ind., Nov. 15, 1930; s. Harvey Harrison and Dorothy (Eberhardt) D.; m. Shirlee Jean Ploeger, Sept. 4, 1954; children: Charles Justin, John Clinton, James Christopher, Mary Jennifer. B.S. in Indsl. Mgmt, Carnegie-Mellon U., 1952, M.S. in Math. Econs, 1955; C.P.A. Staff asst. Ops. Evaluation Group, U.S. Navy-Mass. Inst. Tech., 1955-56; economist Arabian-Am. Oil. Co., 1956-58; mgmt. cons. Touche Ross & Co., 1957-64; partner 1964-69; dean Grad. Sch. Bus. and Pub. Adminstrn., Cornell U., 1969-79, Coll. Bus., Ohio State U., Columbus, 1979—; bd. dirs. Lukens, Inc., UNC Inc., Hubbell Inc. Co-author: Statistical Sampling for Accounting Information, 1962, The Future of Accounting Education, 1961. Served to 1st lt., C.E. AUS, 1952-54. Decorated Bronze Star. Mem. Am., Pa. insts. C.P.A.s, Ill. Soc. C.P.A.s, Mich. Assn. C.P.A.s, Inst. Mgmt. Sci., Am. Statis. Assn. Unitarian. Home: 306 E Sycamore St Columbus OH 43206 Office: Ohio State U Sch Bus Columbus OH 43210 *

DAVIDSON, JAMES W., controller; b. Evansville, Ind., Nov. 1, 1939; s. John and Lilian Ann (Effinger) D. BS, U. Colo., 1961. CPA, Colo. Staff acct. Harcourt, Tanner & McEwen, Denver, 1961; sr. acct. Harcourt, Tanner & Co., Denver, 1965-67; audit mgr. Coopers & Lybrand, Denver, 1968-74; asst. v.p. acctg. Midland Fed. Savs., Denver, 1974-78; controller Holland & Hart, Attys., Denver, 1978—; treas., bd. dirs. credit union Denver Bar Assn., 1979—. With U.S. Army, 1962-64. Mem. Am. Inst. CPA's, Colo. Soc. CPA's, Arapahoe Acres Homeowners Assn. (treas., bd. dirs. 1974—), KC. Republican. Roman Catholic. Office: Holland & Hart 555 17th St Ste 2900 Denver CO 80202

DAVIDSON, KAREN SUE, computer software designer; b. Chgo., July 24, 1950; d. Woodrow Wilson and Velma Louise (Dickinson) D. BS in Communications, U. Ill., 1972; MBA, De Paul U., 1977. News producer Sta. WIND, Westinghouse Broadcasting Co., Chgo., 1973-75; mktg. rep. div. data processing IBM, Chgo., 1977-80, process industry specialist, 1980; industry applications specialist IBM, White Plains, N.Y., 1981-83; sr. sales rep. Wang Labs., Chgo., 1983-84; ptnr. KDA-K Davidson & Assocs., Centralia, Ill., 1984—; pres. KDA Software Inc., Centralia, 1988—; cons. desktop pub. Greater Centralia C. of C., 1987-88. Author/designer software programs; contbr. articles to profl. pubs. Mem. Soc. Profl. Journalists, Ind. Computer Cons. Assn., Ill. Software Assn., Chgo. High Tech. Assn., Assn. St. Louis Info. Systems Trainers (v.p. 1988), Centralia Cultural Soc., Zeta Tau Alpha. Democrat. Methodist. Office: KDA Software Inc 315 E Third St PO Box 1163 Centralia IL 62801

DAVIDSON, PHILIP HAROLD, banker, planning consultant; b. East Grand Rapids, Mich., Aug. 20, 1944; s. Harold E. and Jeanne Elizabeth (Ulrich) D.; m. Kay Marie Heikkinen, Nov. 25, 1966; 1 child, Matthew Philip. AB, U. Mich., 1966; MBA, Western Mich. U., 1967; PhD, U. Ill., 1971. Economist Fed. Res. Bank, Richmond, Va., 1970-73; v.p. Signet Banking Corp., Richmond, 1974-81, sr. v.p., 1982-86, exec. v.p., 1987—. Co-author: Banking Tomorrow, 1978; contbr. articles to profl. jours. Pres. Housing Opportunities Made Equal, Richmond, 1977-80, Richmond Ballet; chmn. task force Chief Justice's Commn. on Future Va.'s Jud. System, 1987-88; active Richmond Renaissance, 1982-88; bd. dirs. Leadership Met. Richmond, 1985—, Richmond Ballet, 1987—; mem., chmn. task force Chief Justice's Commn. on Future Va.'s Jud. System, 1987-88. Recipient Sallie Peak Fair Housing award Housing Opportunities Made Equal, Richmond, 1985. Mem. Am. Econ. Assn., Nat. Assn. Bus. Economists, Am. Bankers Assn. (chmn. exec. com. corp. planning 1981-82), Econ. Forum, Capital Club, Hermitage Country Club. Home: 303 Cyril Ln Richmond VA 23229 Office: Signet Banking Corp 7 N 8th St Richmond VA 23219

DAVIDSON, RALPH PARSONS, performing arts facility executive; b. Santa Fe, Aug. 17, 1927; s. William Clarence Davidson and Doris Parsons Stanton; m. Lou Hill; children: William A., R. Andrew, Ross H., Scott H., Sydney E., Mary Elizabeth. BA in Internat. Relations, Stanford U., 1950; postgrad., Alliance Française, Paris, 1951. With CIA, 1952-54; advt. salesman Life mag., 1954-56; European advt. dir. Time mag., London, 1956-62; mng. dir. Time-Life Internat., N.Y.C., 1967-78; pub. Time mag., 1978-87; chmn. Time Inc., Kennedy Ctr. for the Performing Arts, Washington, 1988—; bd. dirs. Allied-Signal Co., First Interstate Bancorp. Trustee Phoenix Ho. drug prevention program. Served with USNR, World War II. Mem. Stanford U. Alumni Assn. (pres. 1972-73), Explorers Club. Clubs: River (N.Y.C.); American (London). Office: J F Kennedy Ctr Performing Arts Washington DC 20566

DAVIDSON, ROBERT C., JR., manufacturing executive; b. Memphis, Oct. 3, 1945; s. Robert C. Sr. and Thelma (Culp) D.; m. Alice Faye Berkley, Jan. 5, 1978; children: Robert III, John Roderick, Julian. BA, Morehouse Coll., 1967; MBA, U. Chgo., 1969. V.p. Urban Nat. Corp., Boston, 1972-74, Avant Garde Enterprises, Los Angeles, 1974-76; pres. Surface Protection, Industries, Los Angeles, 1976—. Bd. dirs. Pasadena Art Workshop, 1986—; planning commr. City of Pasadena, 1986—. Mem. Young Pres. Orgn. Club: 100 Black Men (Los Angeles). Office: Surface Protection Industries Inc 3411 E 15th St Los Angeles CA 90023

DAVIDSON, ROBERT GAGE, trust banker; b. Charlotte, N.C., Feb. 12, 1940; s. Chalmers Gaston and Alice Graham (Gage) D.; m. Jane Thompson, Jan. 25, 1964; children: Robert G., Jane Brandon. BA, Davidson Coll., 1962; MBA, U. N.C., Chapel Hill, 1965. Retail officer Signet Bank, Richmond, Va., 1966-70; product mgr. Sovran Bank, Richmond, 1970-75; v.p., mktg. dir. Bank of N.C., Raleigh, 1975-76; v.p., trust officer S.C. Nat. Bank, Columbia, 1976—; adj. faculty Va. Commonwealth U., Richmond, 1970-73, U. S.C., Columbia, 1978-82. Bd. dirs., treas. Hist. Columbia Found.; bd. dirs. Hammond Acad., Columbia; treas. Hammond Found.; deacon First Presbyn. Ch., Columbia, 1986—. Capt. U.S. Army, 1962-64. Mem. So. Pension Conf. (bd. mem. steering com. 1980-88), Lower Richland Soc. Execs. Assn. Greater Columbia, St. Andrew's Soc., Soc. Cin. (asst. treas. 1984-85), Wildewood Club, Springdale Hall, Beta Theta Pi. Presbyterian. Home: 1650 Milford Rd Columbia SC 29206 Office: SC Nat Bank 1401 Main St Columbia SC 29226

DAVIDSON, THOMAS MAXWELL, electronics company executive; b. N.Y.C., Dec. 14, 1937; s. Alfred Edward and Claire Helen (Dreyfus) D.; m. Ruth Elizabeth Bovenkerk, Dec. 8, 1962; children: Douglas Edward, Anne Elizabeth. B.A., Vanderbilt U., 1959; M.B.A., Columbia U., 1961. Mgr. Ford Motor Co., Dearborn, Mich., 1963-72; dir. credit ops. White Motor Corp., Eastlake, Ohio, 1972-73, v.p., treas., 1976-77; sr. v.p., chief ops. officer White Motor Credit Corp., Cleve., 1973-75, pres., chief exec. officer, 1975-77, also bd. dirs.; sr. v.p. fin., chief fin. officer, dir. Tex. Gas Transmission Corp., Owensboro, Ky., 1977-81; exec. v.p., chief fin. officer Arrow Electronics, Inc., N.Y.C., 1981-87; exec. v.p. Greenwich, Conn., 1987—, also bd. dirs. Served with U.S. Army, 1959. Mem. Inst. Mgmt. Scis. Clubs: N.Y. Athletic, Wall Street, Metropolitan. Home: 131 Doubling Rd Greenwich CT 06830 Office: Arrow Electronics 60 Arch St Greenwich CT 06830

DAVIDSON, WILLIAM G(EORGE), III, lawyer, accountant, financial and management consultant; b. Ft. Benning, Ga., Oct. 28, 1938; s. William George and Dorothea Kathryn (Wright) D.; B.S., U.S. Naval Acad., 1960; M.B.A. in Fin., U. Pa., 1970; J.D., Suffolk U., 1974. Bar: Ohio 1975, Md. 1980, D.C. 1981, U.S. Tax Ct. 1980, U.S. Ct. Claims 1983, U.S. Ct. Appeals (D.C. cir.) 1983, U.S. Supreme Ct. 1980, Va. 1985; C.P.A., Md. Electronics engr., systems analyst Phila. Naval Shipyard, 1968; fin. analyst Allied Chem. Corp., N.Y.C., 1969; fin. analyst, staff acct. Dennison Mfg. Co., Framingham, Mass., 1969-74; corp. controller Premix, Inc., North Kingsville, Ohio, 1974-78; owner, mgr. W.G. Davidson and Assocs., Inc., mgmt. and fin. cons., Rockville, Md., 1978-87; mem. faculty Lake Erie-Garfield Coll., Painesville, Ohio, 1977-78, Washington, 1981-87, Benjamin Franklin U., 1981-87, Montgomery Coll., 1983—; head. dept. acctg. and taxation, Southeastern U, Washington, 1981—; del. White House Conf. on Small Bus., 1980. Active Vols. in Tech. Assistance, 1970-75; mem. fiscal affairs com. Montgomery County, Md., 1983-84. Served to lt. comdr., USN, 1960-67. Mem. ABA, Am. Inst. C.P.A.s, Md. Bar Assn., Bar Assn. Montgomery County; Fairfax Bar Assn., Va. State Bar Assn., Rockville C. of C., Fin. Execs. Inst., Nat. Assn. Accts., U.S. Naval Acad. Alumni Assn., Naval Res. Assn., Suffolk Law Sch. Assn. Washington. Roman Catholic. Lodges: Kiwanis (past dir. Ashtabula, Ohio); Civitan (Rockville).

DAVIDSON, WILLIAM M., diversified company executive; b. 1921; divorced. LL.B., Wayne State U.; B.B.A., U. Mich. Pres. chief exec. officer Guardian Glass Co., Northville, Mich., 1957-68; pres., chief exec. officer, dir. Guardian Industries Corp., Northville, Mich., 1968—. Served with USN. Office: Guardian Industries Corp 43043 W Nine Mile Rd Northville MI 48167 *

DAVID-WEILL, MICHEL ALEXANDRE, investment banker; b. France, Nov. 23, 1932; came to U.S., 1977; s. Pierre Sylvain and Berthe Marie (Haardt) David-W.; m. Helene Lehideux, July 20, 1956; children: Beatrice David-Weill Stern, Cecile David-Weill de la Baume, Natalie Merveilleux du Vignaud, Agathe. Ed., Inst. Scis. Politiques, 1953. Ptnr. Lazard Freres & Co., 1961-65; ptnr. Lazard Freres & Cie, 1965—, sr. ptnr., 1975—; dir. Lazard Bros. & Co., Ltd., 1965—; sr. partner Lazard Freres & Co., N.Y.C., 1977—, also chmn., 1984—; chmn. bd., dir. Eurafrance, 1972—; vice chmn. BSN-Gervais-Danone, 1970—; bd. dirs. ITT, Dannon Co. Inc. Bd. govs. Soc. of N.Y. Hosp.; trustee Met. Mus. Art, 1985—. Mem. Academie des Beaux-Arts (mem. inst.). Clubs: Brook (N.Y.C.), Knickerbocker (N.Y.C.). Office: Lazard Freres & Co 1 Rockefeller Pla New York NY 10020

DAVIE, RONALD B., corporate realty executive; b. Grand Prairie, Tex., Jan. 9, 1934; s. Waldo Enis and Lyda Mae (Busby) D.; m. Jo Ann Mayo, Feb. 9, 1951; children: guy Wayne, Mark Edward, Kyle Busby. BEE, U. Tex., 1959. From field engr. to edn. mgr. IBM, 1959-70; br. mgr., sales and svc. Comma Corp., Dallas, 1970, dist. mgr., 1971-73; successively personnel mgr. svc. div., personnel devel. and ops. mgr. svc. div., v.p. telex svc. co., sr. v.p., pres. telex svc. co. Telex Computer Products, Inc., Tulsa, 1973-81, sr. v.p. and gen. mgr., svc. support div., 1982-86; v.p. corporate realty Memorex Telex Corp., Tulsa, 1987—; bd. dirs. Pvt. Industry Tng. Council, Tulsa; mem. Midwest adv. bd. Arkwright Mut. Ins. Co., Schaumburg, Ill., 1988—; mem. bd. trustees, v.p. Tulsa Vo-Tech Edn. Found., 1984—. Mem. steering com. Metro Tulsa C. of C., 1985—, econ. devel. div. 1986—; bd. dirs. Goodwill Industries of Tulsa, Inc., 1988—; mem. tech. adv. bd. Okla. State U., Okmulgee, 1987—. Home: 9148 S 33d Ave Tulsa OK 74132

DAVIES, JOHN DALE, finance company executive; b. Indpls., Apr. 5, 1927; s. John Miles and Lucile Matilda (Spurry) Miles Davies; m. Margaret Jean Sullivan, Dec. 21, 1947; children—Nancy Davies Davis, John Richard. B.S., Butler U., 1949. With Gen. Motors Acceptance Corp., various locations, 1949—, control br. mgr., St. Louis, 1967-71, regional mgr., Kansas City, 1971-77, v.p., Detroit, 1977—. Mem bus. adv. council Butler U., Indpls., 1982-83. Republican. Methodist. Clubs: Wabeek Country (Bloomfield Hills, Mich.); Birchwood Farm Country (Harbor Springs, Mich.). Office: GMAC 3044 W Grand Ave Detroit MI 48202 *

DAVIES, PAUL LEWIS, JR., retired lawyer; b. San Jose, Calif., July 21, 1930; s. Paul Lewis and Faith (Crummey) D.; m. Barbara Bechtel, Dec. 22, 1955; children: Laura (Mrs. Segundo Mateo), Paul Lewis III. A.B., Stanford U., 1952; J.D., Harvard U., 1957. Bar: Calif. 1957. Assoc. Pillsbury, Madison & Sutro, San Francisco, 1957-63, ptnr., 1963-89; of counsel Chevron Corp., 1984-89; bd. dirs. FMC Corp., FMC Gold Co., Indsl. Indemnity Co. Hon. trustee Calif. Acad. Scis., trustee, 1970-83, chmn., 1973-80; pres. Herbert Hoover Found.; bd. overseers Hoover Instn., chmn., 1976-82; bd. regents U. of Pacific. 1st lt. U.S. Army, 1952-54. Mem. State Bar Calif., ABA, San Francisco Bar Assn., Phi Beta Kappa, Pi Sigma Alpha. Republican. Clubs: Bankers, Bohemian, Pacific-Union, Villa Taverna, World Trade (San Francisco); Claremont Country, Lakeview (Oakland, Calif.); Cypress Point (Pebble Beach, Calif.); Sainte Claire (San Jose, Calif.), Collectors, Explorers, Links (N.Y.C.); Met., 1925 F St. (Washington); Chgo., Mid-Am. (Chgo.). Office: 50 Fremont St Ste 3825 San Francisco CA 94105

DAVIES, ROBERT ABEL, III, consumer products company executive; b. Englewood, N.J., Sept. 10, 1935; s. Robert Abel and Lillian Louise (Vila) D.; m. Marilyn Jean Doering, June 16, 1957; children: Bruce Gregory, Mark Richard, Eric Doering, Nancy Louise. A.B., Colgate U., 1957; M.B.A., Columbia U., 1963. Salesman Proctor & Gamble Co., Cin., 1960-61; product mgr. Colgate Palmolive Co., N.Y.C., 1963-66; group product mgr. Boyle-Midway div. Am. Home Products, N.Y.C., 1966-69; v.p. mktg. Church & Dwight Co. Inc., Princeton, N.J., 1969-76, v.p., gen. mgr., 1976-81, pres., chief operating officer, 1981-84, also dir., 1981-84; pres., chief exec. officer Calif. Home Brands Inc., Terminal Island, Calif., 1985—; chmn. Church & Dwight Ltd., Toronto, Can., 1981-84. Served to lt. (j.g.) USNR, 1957-60. Mem. Columbia Bus. Sch. Alumni Assn. (dir. 1981-84). Presbyterian. Home: 298 Nassau St Princeton NJ 08540 Office: Calif Home Brands Inc 772 Tuna St Terminal Island CA 90731

DAVIES, STEPHEN, computer executive; b. London, Apr. 4, 1951; came to U.S., 1986; s. Alex Ferris and Enid Elizabeth (Seaber) F.; m. Elisabeth Ann Palmer, July 17, 1971; children: Matthew Richard, Catherine Elizabeth. M in English Lit., Oxford U., Eng., 1973. Mgr. Barclays Bank, London, 1973-80, asst. v.p., 1980-83, asst. to group chmn., 1983-84, v.p., 1984-86; pres. U.S. Computer Group, Bellmore, N.Y., 1986—. Mem. Inst. Bankers. Office: US Computer Group 2647 Grand Ave Bellmore NY 11710

DAVIES, WILLIAM D., JR., executive management consultant; b. Greenwich, Conn., Mar. 9, 1928; s. William D. and Helen (Eastwick) D.; m. Helena Frances White, Apr. 19, 1952; children: Sandra Dawn, Peter Eastwick, William DeAth. BA, Yale U., 1950. Mng. dir. Squibb Proprietary, Ltd., Australia, 1958-61; v.p., gen. mgr. E.R. Squibb & Sons, Philippines, 1961-63; dir. mktg. and supply Squibb Internat., N.Y.C., 1963-67; pres. Squibb Pacific, Tokyo, 1967-70; corp. v.p. comml. devel. Squibb Corp., N.Y.C., 1970-72; sr. v.p., pres. internat. Lanvin-Charles of the Ritz (subs. of Squibb Corp.), N.Y.C., 1972-75; pres. Norwick Eaton Internat. div. Morton Norwich, Inc., N.Y.C., 1975-81; assoc. Heidrick and Struggles, N.Y.C., 1981-82; ptnr., corp. dir. Hedrick and Struggles, N.Y.C., 1982—. Lt. U.S. Army, 1952-54. Republican. Episcopalian. Home: 15 Ridgeview Ave Greenwich CT 06830 Office: Heidrick and Struggles 104 Field Point Rd Greenwich CT 06830

DAVIESS, JOHN HOWARD, mechanical designer; b. Terre Haute, Ind., Apr. 15, 1923; s. William Henry Sr. and Lulu Edyth (Jenkins) D.; m. Clementine N. Chapman; Jan. 28, 1945; children: Pamela Lynn Dean, Timothy Warren, Lisa Carol. Student, Purdue U., 1950. Layout and tech. illustrator Allison Div. GM, Indpls., 1952-60; mech. designer RCA, Indpls., 1961-66, 1974; mech. designer Magnavox Systems, Inc., Urbana, Ill., 1966-71; drafting supr. AM Monitor Corp., Indpls., 1971-74; chief draftsman Stewart-Warner Corp., Indpls., 1975—; instr. Ivy Tech. Coll., Indpls., 1981. Staff sgt. USAF, 1942-45. Mem. Masons. Republican. Baptist. Home: 4007 Westover Dr Indianapolis IN 46268 Office: Stewart-Warner Corp South Wind Div 1514 Drover St Indianapolis IN 46221

DAVILA, WILLIAM S., supermarket chain executive; b. 1931; married. AA, Los Angeles City Coll. Produce clerk Von's Grocery Co., El Monte, Calif., 1948-56; produce mgr. Von's Grocery Co., El Monte, 1956-59, with advt. dept., 1959-65, asst. advt. mgr., 1965-67, advt. mgr., 1967-73, mgr. sales promotion, 1973-75, v.p. sales, 1975-77, group v.p. mktg. sales, 1977-80, sr. v.p. supermarkets, 1980-84, exec. v.p., from 1984, now pres., chief operating officer, also bd. dirs. Served with USAF, 1951-54. Office: Von's Co Inc 10150 Lower Azusa Rd El Monte CA 91731 *

DAVIS, ALFRED LEWIS, manufacturing company executive; b. Chelsea, Okla., Oct. 2, 1941; s. Harold Lee and Irene (Burchett) D.; m. Linda Louise Layton, Aug. 19, 1962; children: Anissa Jolyn, Cherlyn Jodawn, Lindsay Jolane. From union foreman to plant mgr. Certain-Teed Corp., Kansas City, Kans., 1962-74; plant mgr. No. Fiber Products, Holland, Mich., 1974-80; gen. mgr., exec. v.p. So. Fiber Products, Thomson, Ga., 1980-85; plant mgr. Sheller-Globe, Thomson, 1985—. Patentee in field. Sgt. U.S. Army, 1965-67, Vietnam. Republican. Baptist. Home: Huntington II Rte 3 Box 298 Thomson GA 30824 Office: Sheller-Globe Warrenton Hwy Thomson GA 30824

DAVIS, AUDREY LANITA, association executive, decorating company executive; b. Tuskegee, Ala., July 8, 1941; d. John Lee and Willa Mae (Tyner) D.; m. Frank J. James, Apr. 6, 1968 (div. 1972); 1 child, Christopher A. BA, LeMoyne-Owen Coll., 1964; postgrad., Western Mich. U, Morraine Valley Coll., Northwestern U., U. Chgo. Tchr. Chgo. Pub. Schs., 1968-87; founder, pres. A Davis Decorating Svcs., Chgo., 1983—, Ill. Assn. Black Women Bus. Owners, Chgo., 1985—. Editor Career Alternatives for Tchrs., 1979-82. Organizer Women's Network for Washington, Chgo., 1983; del. Nat. Dem. Conv., 1984, White House Conf. on Small Bus., 1986; mem. Operation PUSH, Chgo. Named to Chgo. Women's Hall of Fame, 1988. Mem. Nat. Coalition Minority Women in Bus., Am. Assn. Black Women Intrepreneurs, NOW, Nat. Congress Black Women, League Black Women, NAACP, Nat. Polit. Congress Black Women. Home and Office: 1130 S Michigan Ave Apt 1609 Chicago IL 60605

DAVIS, CLAUDE-LEONARD, lawyer, educational administrator; b. Augusta, Ga., Feb. 16, 1944; s. James Isaac and Mary Emma (Crawford) D.; m. Margaret Earle Crowley, Dec. 30, 1965; 1 child, Margaret Michelle. BA in Journalism, U. Ga., 1966, JD, 1974. Bar: Ga. 1974. Broadcaster Sta. WKLE Radio, Washington, Ga., 1958-62; realtor Assocs. Realty, Athens, Ga., 1963-66; bus. cons. Palm Beach, Fla., 1970-71; asst. to dir. Ga. Coop. Extension Service, Athens, 1974-81; atty. U. Ga., Athens, 1981—; cons. numerous agrl. chem. industry groups nationwide, 1977—, Congl. Office of Tech. Assessment, Washington, 1978-79, USDA, Washington, 1979-80; del. Kellogg Nat. Leadership Conf., Pullman, Wash., 1980. Editor and contbr. Ga. Jour. of Internat. and Comparative Law, 1972-74; contbr. articles on agr. and fin. planning to profl. jours.; author and editor: DAWGFOOD: The Bulldog Cookbook, 1981, Touchdown Tailgates, 1986. Del. So. Leader Forum, Rock Eagle Ctr., Ga., 1976—; trainer Ga. 4-H Vol. Leader Assn., 1979—; vol. Athens United Way, 1980—; coordinator U. Ga. Equestrian Team, Athens, 1985-87; mem. Clarke County Sheriff's Posse, 1985—. Capt. U.S. Army, 1966-70. Chi Psi Scholar, 1965; Recipient Outstanding Alumnus award Chi Psi, 1972, Service to World Community award Chi Psi, 1975. Mem. ABA, Nat. Assn. Coll. Univ. Atty.'s, NRA, Disabled Am. Vets., Chi Psi (advisor and bd. dirs. 1974). Baptist. Clubs: The Pres.'s, City (Athens). Lodge: Gridiron Secret Soc. Home: 365 Westview Dr Athens GA 30606 Office: U Ga Peabody Hall Ste 3 Athens GA 30602

DAVIS, CRAIG ALPHIN, lawyer, manufacturing company executive; b. Oakland, Calif., July 28, 1940; s. Alphin Craig and Joyce Ida (Nevers) D.; m. Betty Rankin, July 13, 1963; children: Chelsea Alyson, Channing MacLaren. A.B. in Polit. Sci, U. Calif., Berkeley, 1964, J.D., 1967. Bar: Calif. 1968. Assoc. Heller, Ehrman, White & McAuliffe, San Francisco, 1968-71; counsel Aluminum div. AMAX Inc., San Mateo, Calif., 1971-74; dir. law Alumax Inc., San Mateo, 1974, gen. counsel, sec., 1974-84, v.p., 1978-82, group v.p., gen. counsel, 1982-84, sr. v.p., 1984-86, exec. v.p., 1986—. Mem. editorial bd., research editor: Hastings Law Jour, 1966-67. Mem. ABA, State Bar Calif. Office: Alumax Inc 400 S El Camino Real San Mateo CA 94402

DAVIS, CRAIG CARLTON, aerospace company executive; b. Gulfport, Miss., Dec. 14, 1919; s. Craig Carlton and Helen Lizette (Houppert) D.; B.S., Ga. Inst. Tech., 1941; J.D., Harvard U., 1949; children—Kimberly Patricia, Craig Carlton. Instr. aeros. Escola Tecnica de Aviacao, Sao Paulo, Brazil, 1946; contract adminstr. Convair, Fort Worth, 1949-51; mgr. contracts and pricing, atomics internat. and autonetics divs. N.Am. Aviation, Anaheim, Calif., 1954-62, asst. corp. dir. contracts and proposals, El Segundo, Calif., 1963-70; dir. contracts Aerojet Electro Systems Co., Azusa, Calif., 1971-81, v.p., 1982—. Served with AUS, 1941-45; USAF, 1951-53, to col. res., 1953-66. Mem. ABA, Fed. Bar Assn., D.C. Bar Assn., Res. Officers Assn., Harvard U. Alumni Assn., Ga. Tech. Alumni Assn. Republican. Episcopalian. Club: Harvard. Home: 10501 Wilshire Blvd Apt 1208 Los Angeles CA 90024 Office: Aerojet Electro Systems Co 1100 W Hollyvale St Azusa CA 91702

DAVIS, DONALD WALTER, manufacturing company executive; b. Springfield, Mass., June 10, 1921; s. Donald Walter and Laura (Mansfield) D.; m. Mary Virginia Cooper, Aug. 2, 1947; children: Randall C., Deborah Davis Curtiss, Donald Walter III, Palmer R., Jennifer Davis Heard, Ruth. A.B., Pa. State U.; M.B.A., Harvard U. Various positions Stanley Works, New Britain, Conn., 1948-62, exec. v.p., 1962-66, pres., chief exec. officer, 1966-77, chmn. bd., 1977—, chief exec. officer, 1977-87, also dir.; dir. N.E. Utilities, Berlin, Conn., Dexter Corp., Windsor Locks, Conn., Pitney Bowes, Inc., Stamford, Conn., Conn. Mut. Life Ins., Hartford, Allied-Signal Inc., Morristown, N.J. Bd. dirs. New Britain Gen. Hosp., 1966—; vice chmn. bd. of regents U. of Hartford. Served to lt. USN, 1943-46. Mem. NAM (vice chmn. 1986, chmn. 1987). Office: Stanley Works 1000 Stanley Dr New Britain CT 06053 *

DAVIS, E. HAROLD, manufacturing company executive; b. Scottsburg, Ind., Oct. 31, 1939; s. Elzie and Fannie (Creech) D.; m. Martha F. Malcomb, Dec. 22, 1963; 1 child, Brooke Lizabeth. BS in Bus. Adminstrn. and Acctg., Ind. U., 1961; MBA in Fin. and Internat. Bus., Harvard U., 1968. With Cummins Engine Co., Columbus, Ind., 1961—, v.p. fin. adminstrn., 1975-76, v.p. planning, 1976-79, v.p. planning and cont., 1979-86, v.p. info. systems and product mgmt., 1986—. Mem. Ind. Commn. for Higher Edn., Indpls., 1983-86, vice chmn., 1987-88, chmn. 1988—. Served to 1st lt. U.S. Army, 1961-63. Mem. Ind. U. Alumni Club, Trout Unlimited (Vienna, Va. bd. dirs. 1979-84, pres. 1985-86, chmn. 1987-88). Club: New Britton Hunt (Spencer, Ind.). Office: Cummins Engine Co Inc PO Box 3005 Columbus IN 47201

DAVIS, EDGAR GLENN, pharmaceutical company executive; b. Indpls., May 12, 1931; s. Thomas Carroll and Florence Isabelle (Watson) D. m. Margaret Louise Alandt, June 20, 1953; children: Anne-Elizabeth Davis Polestra, Amy Alandt, Edgar Glenn Jr. AB, Kenyon Coll., 1953; MBA, Harvard U., 1955. With Eli Lilly and Co., Indpls., 1958—, mgr. budgeting and profit planning, 1963-66, mgr. econ. studies, 1966-67, mgr. Atlanta sales dist., 1967-68, dir. market research and sales manpower planning, 1968-69, dir. mktg. plans, 1969-74, exec. dir. pharm. mktg. planning, 1974-75, exec. dir. corp. affairs, 1975-76, v.p. corp. affairs, 1976—; vis. fellow health policy rsch. and edn. div. Kennedy Sch. Govt., Harvard U., 1981—; pres. Eli Lilly and Co. Found., 1976-88; vis. fellow div. Health Policy Rsch. and Edn., Kennedy Sch. Govt., Harvard U., 1981—; mem. Inst. Ednl. Mgmt., Harvard U. Grad. Sch. Edn., 1987—; chmn. staff Bus. Roundtable Task Force on Health, 1981-85; U.S. rep. UN Indsl. Devel. Orgn. Conf., Lisbon, 1980; participant UNIDO meeting of experts on pharms., 1981; rep. to UN Commn. on Narcotic Drugs, Vienna, 1981; UN Econ. and Social Council, N.Y.C., 1981; UN Indsl. Devel. Orgn. conf. Casablanca, 1981, Budapest, 1983, Madrid, 1987. Contbr. articles to profl. jours. Pres., chmn. bd. Indpls. Health Inst.; trustee Kenyon Coll. Gambier, Ohio; bd. dirs. Martha's Vineyard Hist. Preservation Soc., Inc.; bd. advisors Christian Theol. Sem.; bd. dirs. Carnegie Council on Ethics and Internat. Affairs, Goodwill Industries Found. Cen. Ind., Inc., Sta. WFYI Pub. TV, Indpls., Indpls. Mus. of Art, Am. Symphony Orch. League, Nat. Health Council, Pub. Affairs Council, Washington, Nat. Fund for Med. Edn.; chmn. bd. dirs. Ind. Repertory Theatre, 1979-85; bd. visitors Bishops Sch., La Jolla, Calif.; vice chmn., mem. exec. com., bd. dirs. Indpls. Symphony Orch. and Ind. State Symphony Soc., 1977—; chmn. task force on fine arts, Commn. for Future of Butler U.; chmn. exec. com. Pan Am.. Econ. Leadership Conf., 10th Pan Am. Games, Indpls; bd. visitors N.C. Sch. of Arts; mem. Chgo. Council on Fgn. Relations; trustee Eiteljorg Mus. Am. Indian and Western Art. Served to lt., USN, 1955-58. Adj. sr. fellow The Hudson Inst., Indpls.; mem. Inst. Medicine, Nat. Acad. Scis., N.A.M. (bd. dirs., vice-chmn. health policy com.). Clubs: Capitol Hill, Met. (Washington); Overseas Press (N.Y.C.); Edgartown Yacht (trustee), Sheriffs Meadow Conservation Found. (trustee) (Mass.); Yacht (Chgo.); Woodstock, Univ., Contemporary, Lambs, Crooked Stick Golf (Indpls.), Traders Point Hunt; Harvard (Boston, N.Y.C.); Reform of London; Skyline Club (bd. govs.). Office: Eli Lilly and Co Lilly Corp Ctr Indianapolis IN 46285

DAVIS, EMERY STEPHEN, food wholesaling company executive; b. Kansas City, Mo., Dec. 31, 1940; s. Vernon Albert and Berneice Marie (Brenner) D.; m. Hildegarde Retzer; children—Angelica, Matthew, Nicholas. Student, Met. Coll., Stanford U. Exec. Program. Mgr. distbn. Fleming Cos., Fremont, Calif., 1972-75; dir. warehousing Fleming Cos., Topeka, 1975-77; dir. distbn. eastern region Fleming Cos., Phila., 1977-79; v.p. distbn. Fleming Cos., Oklahoma City, 1979-82, sr. v.p. distbn., 1982-85, exec. v.p. distbn., 1985—. Served with U.S. Army, 1962-63. Recipient Profl. Achievement award Traffic Mgmt. Publ., 1980. Mem. Nat. Council Phys. Distbn. Mgmt. Home: 404 N Crown Colony Rd Edmond OK 73034 Office: Fleming Cos 6301 Waterford Blvd Oklahoma City OK 73126

DAVIS, ERROLL BROWN, JR., utility executive; b. Pitts., Aug. 5, 1944; s. Erroll Brown and Eleanor Margaret (Boykin) D.; m. Elaine E. Casey, July 13, 1968; children—Christopher, Whitney. E.E., Carnegie-Mellon U., 1965; M.B.A. in Fin., U. Chgo., 1967. Mem. corp. fin. staff Ford Motor Co., Detroit, 1969-73; mem. corp. fin. staff Xerox Corp., Rochester, N.Y., 1973-78; v.p. fin. Wis. Power & Light Co., Madison, 1978-82, v.p. fin & pub. affairs, 1982-84, exec. v.p., 1984-87, pres., 1987, pres., chief exec. officer, 1988—; bd. dirs. WPL, Sentry Ins., Wis. Utilities Assn., 1989—. Commr. Madison Police and Fire Commn., 1982-89—; mem. Selective Service Bd. Madison, 1982—; bd. regents U. Wis., 1987—; bd. dirs. United Way Dane County, 1984-89—, chmn. 1987, Competitive Wis., 1989—, Wis. Utilities Assn., 1989—. Lt. U.S. Army, 1967-69. Mem. Am. Assn. Blacks in Energy, Wis. Assn. Mfrs. and Commerce (treas. and bd. dirs. 1986—). Club: Madison. Lodge: Rotary. Home: 501 San Juan Trail Madison WI 53715 Office: Wis Power & Light Co 222 W Washington Ave Madison WI 53703

DAVIS, FRANCES M., lawyer, corporate executive; b. 1925. Grad., UCLA, 1946; JD, U. Calif., Berkeley, 1953. Bar: Calif. 1954. Ptnr. LeProhn & LeProhn, 1960-67; asst. dean Earl Warren Legal Ctr. Calif. Coll. Trial Judges, 1968-72; assoc. Pillsbury, Madison & Sutro, 1972-75; v.p., gen. counsel Potlach Corp., San Francisco, 1975—; mem. Pvt. Industry Council of San Francisco. Bd. overseers U. Calif., San Francisco; mem. adv. bd. Sta. KOIT, San Francisco. Office: Potlatch Corp 1 Maritime Pla PO Box 3591 San Francisco CA 94111

DAVIS, FRANK ISAAC, entertainment company executive, lawyer; b. Beallsville, Md., Feb. 18, 1919; s. Frank Isaac and Susie Boyd (Griffith) D.; m. Virginia Elizabeth Battle, July 2, 1949; children—Richard, Battle, Elizabeth, Randolph. B.A., U. Md., 1941; LL.B., Harvard U., 1948. Bar: N.Y., 1948. Assoc. Donovan Leisure Newton Lumbard & Irvine, N.Y.C., 1948-51; v.p., pres. The Selznick Co., N.Y.C., 1951-56; v.p. Famous Artists Corp., Beverly Hills, Calif., 1956-62, Geo. Stevens Prodns., Culver City, Calif., 1962-66; v.p. bus. affairs Metro-Goldwyn-Mayer, Culver City, Calif., 1966-84; sr. v.p. bus. affairs MGM/UA Entertainment Co., Culver City, Calif., 1984—. Served to maj. U.S. Army, 1941-46 Mem. exec. com., bd. dirs. Motion Picture and TV Fund. Mem. Acad. Motion Picture Arts and Scis. Democrat. Episcopalian.

DAVIS, GEORGE ALFRED, financial executive; b. Montclair, N.J., Feb. 26, 1928; s. Robert Greener and Ruth (Conroy) D.; m. Maria Nekos, June 30, 1956; children—Stephen Greener, Carol Elizabeth, Leslie Ann. A.B. cum laude, Dartmouth Coll., 1952; M.B.A. with distinction, Amos Tuck Sch., 1953. C.P.A., N.J. Acct. Arthur Andersen & Co., N.Y.C., 1953-59; with Thomas J. Lipton, Inc., 1960-72, controller, 1965-72; controller Good Humor Corp., Continenal Foods, Inc., Good Humor Food Service, Inc., 1965-72; treas. C.R. Bard, Inc., Murray Hill, N.J., 1972-78, v.p., treas., from 1979-83, v.p. fin., chief fin. officer, 1983-87, exec. v.p., chief fin. officer, 1987—, also bd. dirs. Mem. corps. com. Fairleigh Dickinson U.; Trustee, v.p. Tenafly Community Chest, 1969-71; trustee, treas. Mary Fischer Home, Tenafly, N.J. Served with AUS, 1946-48. Mem. Am. Inst. C.P.A.'s, Fin. Execs. Inst., Nat. Assn. Accts., N.J. Soc. C.P.A.s. Episcopalian (vestryman, treas. 1966-68). Clubs: Canoe Brook Country, Dartmouth of Bergen County (trustee, treas. 1965-68). Office: CR Bard Inc 731 Central Ave Murray Hill NJ 07974

DAVIS, GEORGE EDWARD, industrial designer; b. Hugo, Okla., July 3, 1928; s. Silas William and Florence Elva (White) D.; student U. Tex., Austin, 1946-49; B.A., Art Center Coll. Design, Los Angeles, 1956; m. Betty Sue Walker, July 21, 1951; children—Susan Elizabeth, Laura Ellen. Staff designer Friedrich Refrigeration Co., San Antonio, 1957; design dir. comml. div. Woodarts Co., Houston, 1958-59; staff designer Brede, Inc., Houston, 1960-61; designer, co-founder Concept Planners and Designers, Houston, 1962-64; mgr. archtl. dept. Lockheed-Calif. Co., NASA Manned Spacecraft Center, Clear Lake, Tex., 1965-66; staff designer Litton Industries, office products div., Austin, San Antonio, 1967-68; staff designer Clegg Design Group, San Antonio, 1969-76; ind. design cons., San Antonio, 1977—; dir. Systemics, Inc., San Antonio, Christian Bookmark, Inc., San Antonio, 1972-88. Trustee, San Antonio Christian Sch., 1973-82, chmn. bd., 1979-80; bd. elders Christ Presbyterian Ch., San Antonio, 1982-85; mem. Zoning Commn., City of Castle Hills, 1983—. Served with USAF, 1950-54. Decorated D.F.C., Air medal with 3 oak leaf clusters. Mem. AIA, Tex. Soc. Architects (award of merit 1968). Home: 205 Wisteria Dr Castle Hills TX 78213 Office: PO Box 13385 San Antonio TX 78213

DAVIS, GEORGE LINN, banker; b. Des Moines, July 9, 1934; s. James Cox and Elizabeth (Linn) D.; m. Anne Roberts, May 1955 (div. Jan. 1967); children: James, Elliott, George Linn; m. Mary Elizabeth Graham, Apr. 27, 1968; children: Stephen, Thomas. B.A., Yale U., 1956; M.B.A., Harvard U., 1958. Sr. v.p. Citibank NA, N.Y.C., 1958-81; exec. v.p. First Chgo. Corp., Chgo., 1981-87; Citicorp/Citibank group exec. N.Am. Fin. Group, N.Y.C., 1987—; bd. dirs. Wyndham Foods. Mem. bus. com. N.Y. Zool. Soc. Mem. Robert Morris Assocs., Assn. Equipment Lessors (dir. 1974-76). Republican. Clubs: Chicago, Glenview, Sleepy Hollow Country. Office: N Am Fin Group 399 Park Ave New York NY 10043

DAVIS, HENRY BARNARD, JR., lawyer; b. East Grand Rapids, Mich., June 3, 1923; s. Henry Barnard and Ethel Margaret (Turnbull) D.; m. Margaret Lees Wilson, Aug. 27, 1946; children—Caroline Dellenbusch, Laura Davis Jackson, George B. B.A., Yale U., 1945; J.D., U. Mich., 1950; LL.D., Olivet Coll., 1983. Bar: Mich. 1951; U.S. Dist. Ct. (we. dist.) Mich. 1956, U.S. Ct. Apls. (6th cir.) 1971, U.S. Supreme Ct. 1978. Assoc. Allaben, Wiarda, Hayes & Hewitt, 1951-52; ptnr. Hayes, Davis & Dellenbusch, Grand Rapids, 1952—. Mem. Kent County Bd. Commrs., 1968-72, Community Mental Health Bd., 1970—, past chmn.; trustee, sec. bd. Olivet Coll., 1965—; chair Grand Rapids Historic Preservation Com., 1977-79. Republican. Trustee, East Congregational Ch., 1979-81. Served with USAAF, 1943-46; Philippines. ABA, Mich. Assn. Professions, Mich. Bar Assn., Grand Rapids Round Table (pres. 1969). Lodge: Masons. Home: 30 Mayfair Dr NE Grand Rapids MI 49503 Office: 535 Fountain St NE Grand Rapids MI 49503

DAVIS, HENRY RICHARD, commercial real estate company executive; b. Pahokee, Fla., Oct. 3, 1948; s. Henry Albert and Greta (Blechschmidt) D.; A.A., Palm Beach Jr. Coll., 1968; B.A., Fla. Atlantic U., 1969; m. Gail Ann Hayford, Oct. 28, 1972; children—Kyle Taylor, Brad Geoffrey. Merchandiser Walden Book Co. div. Carter Hawley Hale Stores, Inc., Stamford, Conn., asst. buyer, 1969-70, buyer, 1970-72, regional mgr., 1972-73, asst. dir. store ops., 1973-74, asst. dir. real estate, 1975-76, dir. real estate, 1976-79; v.p. leasing Pembrook Mgmt., N.Y.C., 1979-84; v.p., dir. leasing Corp. Property Investors, 1985—. Mem. exec. bd. Ridgefield Jaycees, 1976-77; mem. Ridgefield Republican Town Com., 1975-77, chmn. orgn. com., treas., 1976-77; justice of peace State of Conn., 1977-81; mem. bd. dirs. Norwalk Jr. Soccer Assn.; mem. Fla. Atlantic U. Found. Mem. Internat. Council Shopping Centers, Am. Mgmt. Assn., Urban Land Inst., Order Ky. Cols., Phi Alpha Theta. Baptist. Club: Silvermine Golf. Home: 6 Cricklewood Ln Norwalk CT 06851 Office: 3 Dag Hammarskjold Pla New York NY 10017

DAVIS, JAMES GRANVILLE, manufacturing company executive; b. Syracuse, N.Y., May 25, 1935; s. Willis E. and Thelma (Lakins) D.; student Syracuse U., 1953-57, Univ. Coll., Syracuse, 1957-60; cert. of completion sales and mktg. mgmt. program Syracuse U., 1979; m. Edith Jo Eichelberger, July 2, 1956 (div. Dec. 1962); children—Jen G., Jill G., Jody G., Jefferson G.; m. 2d, Bonnie Ann Byington, Aug. 23, 1969 (div. Jan. 1976); children—Matthew Richard, Stephen Patrick; m. 3d, Diane McColl, Feb. 20, 1976; children—Elizabeth McColl, Catherine Manroe. New bus. rep. 1st Deposit and Trust Co., Syracuse, 1956-61; asst. mgr. sales Stone Machinery Co., Manlius, N.Y., 1962; mgr. sales Trippe Mfg. Co., Chgo., 1967; gen. sales mgr. Fed. Sign & Signal Corp., Blue Island, Ill., 1967-71; v.p. Fed. Sign & Signal Internat., Ltd., 1971-72; regional sales mgr. Graver Tank & Mfg., East Chicago, Ind., 1972-73, mgr. mktg. and sales, 1973-78, dir. power generation markets, 1979-81; v.p. Power Generation Markets, 1979-81; pres., owner Corp. Constructs, Michigan City, Ind., 1981—; v.p., gen. mgr. Fiber Bond Corp., 1982—. Mem. Jr. C. of C. (past state v.p.), Internat. Trade Club, Psi Upsilon. Home: 2510 Roslyn Trail Long Beach Michigan City IN 46360 Office: 110 Menke Rd Michigan City IN 46360

DAVIS, JAMES HOWARD, new ventures executive; b. Columbus, Ohio, Jan. 23, 1955; s. Howard Calvin and Pauline Ann (Polasky) D.; m. Sarah Lynn Wynkoop, Mar. 6, 1982; 1 child, Zachary Howard. BS in Bus. and Communications, Ohio U., 1977. Dir. enterprise devel. and pub. affairs Appalachian Regional Commn., Cambridge, Ohio, 1978-79; mgr. new ventures and mktg. projects Battelle Meml. Inst., Columbus, Ohio, 1979-82; dir. Entrepreneurship Inst., U.S. Entrepreneurs Network, Columbus, 1983-88; mgr. div. Advt. Checking Bur. Inc., Columbus, 1988—. Rep. fed. govt. Ohio Tourism Council, Columbus, 1978-79; mem. White House Council on Appalachia, Washington, 1978-79. Recipient Venus Gold medal in bus. Internat. Festival Ams., 1982. Mem. Assn. Bus. Communicators (v.p. 1981-82). Office: Advt Checking Bur Inc 4500 E Broad St Columbus OH 43213

DAVIS, JAMES MCCOY, real estate executive; b. Columbus, Ohio, Oct. 19, 1914; s. James McCoy and Laura Victoria (Smith) D.; m. Phyllis Ruth Rowe, Jan. 24, 1948; children: Perine Davis Ceperley, Linda Davis Bryson, Carol Davis Meador, Paul, Jamie. BBA, Ohio State U., 1937; postgrad., Union Theol. Sem., N.Y.C., 1937-39; BD, Oberlin Grad. Sch. Theol., 1942; MA, Columbia U., 1947, EdD, 1952; MDiv (hon.), Vanderbilt U., 1973. Lic. real estate broker, Calif. Minister First Congl. Ch., Ravenna, Ohio, 1939-42; field exec. Congl. Christian Com. War Victims and Services, N.Y.C., 1942-43; counselor for internat. services U. Wash., Seattle, 1948-54; dir., assoc. prof. U. Mich., Ann Arbor, 1954-64; v.p. Inst. Internat. Edn., N.Y.C., 1964-67; provost U.S. Internat. U., San Diego, 1967-70; pres. Northwestern Mich. Coll., Traverse City, 1970-73; realtor assoc. Klaus Radelow Realtor, San Diego, 1973-74; realtor James M. Davis, San Diego, 1974-77; pres. James M. Davis Inc. & Assocs., San Diego, 1977—. Contbr. articles to profl. jours. Pres. World Affairs Council San Diego, 1981-83; chmn. bd. Consumer Credit Counselors, San Diego, 1988-89; mem. U. Calif. San Diego Faculty Club, 1988—. Served to capt. U.S. Army, 1943-46. Decorated Bronze Star with oak leaf cluster. Mem. Nat. Assn. Fgn. Student

Affairs (life), Calif. Assn. Realtors (dir. 1978-79, 88), San Diego Bd. Realtors (com. chmn. 1978-79, 88), Self Service Storage Assn., Nat. Assn. Realtors. Republican. Presbyterian. Club: U. Calif San Diego Faculty. Home: 4906 Pacifica Dr San Diego CA 92109 Office: James M Davis Inc & Assocs 4365 Mission Bay Dr Ste 6 San Diego CA 92109

DAVIS, JAMES MINOR, JR., utility company executive, mechanical engineer; b. Raeford, N.C., May 9, 1936; s. James Minor and Betsy S. (Sessoms) D.; m. Patsy Ann McLean, July 19, 1958; children: Martha Jeanette, James Owen, Julie Ann. B.S. in Mech. Engring., N.C. State U., 1958. Registered profl. engr., N.C. Test engr. Pratt & Whitney Aircraft Co., East Hartford, Conn., 1961-65; with Carolina Power & Light Co., Raleigh, N.C., 1965—, mgr. rates and regulation dept., 1976-79, v.p. fuel and materials mgmt. group, 1979-80; sr. v.p. fuel and materials mgmt. group Carolina Power & Light Co., 1980-83, sr. v.p. ops. support, 1983-86, sr. v.p. fossil generation and power transmission group, 1986—. Pres. Episcopal Laymen, Diocese of N.C., 1972-75; vestryman St. Michael's Episc. Ch., Releigh, 1973-76. Served with USAFR, 1958-61. Mem. N.C. Soc. Engrs., Profl. Engrs. N.C., Nat. Soc. Profl. Engrs., Am. Nuclear Soc., Health Physics Soc., Raleigh Engrs. Club. Republican. Lodge: Kiwanis. Office: Carolina Power & Light Co 411 Fayetteville St Raleigh NC 27602

DAVIS, JEFFREY STANFORD, real estate developer; b. Cleve., July 20, 1949; s. Larry and Lois Joann (Robinson) D.; m. Marcia Laven, Nov. 16, 1976 (div. June 1978). Associate's degree, Northwood Inst., Midland, Mich., 1970, student, 1971. V.p. Larry Davis Constrn. Co., Cleve., 1971-86; pres. Davis Devel. Group, Inc., Cleve., 1986—. Trustee Cleve. Internat. Film Festival, 1988, Jewish Community Housing, Cleve., 1986. Mem. Internat. Assn. Real Estate Exec., Nat. Assn. of Office and Indsl. Parks (local bd. 1983-85). Republican. Jewish. Office: Davis Devel Group Inc 32000 Solon Rd Solon OH 44139

DAVIS, JERRY DONALD, lawyer, construction and engineering company executive; b. Minden, La., Sept. 6, 1938; s. Dean P. and Alice G. D.; m. Beryl Hutchings, Jan. 25, 1964; 1 child, Elizabeth Ann. B.B.A., U. Tex., 1961, J.D., 1964. Bar: Tex. 1964. Adminstrv. asst., in house gen. legal work McCollough Tool Co., Houston, 1964-67; gen. legal work Gibson & Tatum, Houston, 1967-71; asst. gen. counsel Raymond Internat. Inc., Houston, 1971-78, v.p., sec., gen. counsel, 1979-83, sr. v.p., sec., gen. counsel, 1983-86; sr. v.p., sec., gen. counsel Raymond Internat. Co., Houston, 1986—; v.p., sec. Raymond Internat. Builders, Houston, 1978—. Mem. Tex. Bar Assn., Am. Soc. Corp. Secs., Houston C. of C. Home: 11626 Cypresswood St Houston TX 77070

DAVIS, JERRY RAY, railroad company executive; b. Sylvan Grove, Kans., June 30, 1938; s. Ralph Jacob and Clara Willamine (Jennsen) D.; m. Patricia L. Stauffer, Sept. 12, 1958; children: Richard, Roger, Anthony, Randall. MS in Mgmt., MIT, 1976. Telegrapher Union Pacific R.R., Salina, Kans., 1957-59; telegrapher, dispatcher Kans., Colo., 1959-65; asst. supt. safety and courtesy Union Pacific R.R., Kansas City, 1968; trainmaster Utah div. Union Pacific R.R., Salt Lake City, 1969-71; trainmaster Idaho div. Union Pacific R.R., Idaho Falls, 1971-73; asst. to gen. supt. transp. Union Pacific R.R., Omaha, 1973; asst. supt. Oreg. div. Union Pacific R.R., Portland, 1973-74; supt. Utah div. Union Pacific R.R., Salt Lake City, 1974-75; asst. gen. supt. transp. Union Pacific R.R., Omaha, 1976-78, gen. supt. eastern dist., 1978, asst. v.p. ops., 1979-81, v.p. ops., 1981-86, exec. v.p. ops., 1986—. Bd. dirs. Omaha Safety Coun., Luth. Med. Ctr., Omaha, Henry Doorly Zoo, Omaha. Mem. Am. Assn. R.R. (operating transp. com., chmn.), Am. Assn. R.R. Supts., Ry. Fuel and Operating Officers Assn. Republican. Lutheran. Clubs: The Omaha, Omaha Press, Highland Country (Omaha). Lodges: Masons, Omaha Consistary, Shriners (Tangier Temple). Home: 6501 Stones Throw Dr Omaha NE 68152 Office: Union Pacific RR 1416 Dodge St Rm 1206 Omaha NE 68179

DAVIS, JOHN CHARLES, market analyst; b. Rochester, N.Y., Nov. 10, 1944; s. Harry I. and Mary Pauline Davis; married; 1 child, Daniel. BA, BS in Chem. Engring., Bucknell U., 1967; MBA, NYU, 1978. Process engr. Mobil Oil Corp., Paulsboro, N.J., 1967-69; editor Chem. Engring. Mag. of McGraw-Hill Inc., N.Y.C., 1969-78, mng. editor, 1978-79; market rsch. assoc. PPG Industries Inc., Pitts., 1979-84, indsl. markets analyst, 1984—; pres. Davis Data Co., Pitts.; sr. cons. Probe Econs. Inc., Mt. Kisco, N.Y., 1985-87, cons. Kline & Co., Fairfield, N.J., 1984—. Mem. Chem. Mktg. Rsch. Assn., Comml. Devel. Assn. Pitts. Office: U Pitts Applied Rsch Ctr 645 William Pittway Pittsburgh PA 15238

DAVIS, JOHN EDWARD, manufacturing operations administrator; b. Topeka; s. Edward M. and Betty J. (Johnson) D.; m. Mona Jean Howell, Dec. 22, 1969; children: John, Laura, Rebecca. BEE, Ga. Inst. Tech., 1971. Div. engr. Kans. Power & Light Co., Salina, 1971-74; design engr. Butler Mfg. Co., Salina, 1974-75; asst. plant engr. TRW Wire & Cable Co., Lawrence, Kans., 1976, area mgr., 1976-77; plant engr. Ethyl VisQueen, Terre Haute, Ind., 1977-79; mgr. engring. and maintenance, plant mgr. Clopay Corp., Augusta, Ky., 1979-84, dir. mfg., 1984-85; v.p. ops. Clopay Corp., Cin., 1985—; mem. exec. com. Assocs. Clopay Europe, Leige, Belgium, 1988. Mem. Tech. Assn. Pulp and Paper Industry, Soc. Plastics Engrs. Office: Clopay Corp 101 E 4th St Cincinnati OH 45202

DAVIS, JOHN H., publishing company executive; b. Marion, Ill., Nov. 21, 1927; s. Chester Barnet and Sophia (Baker) D.; m. Anne Denise Neville, Mar. 3, 1956; children: Christopher, Alan; m. Melinda Wallace Williams, Jan. 24, 1981; children: Emory, John S.W. BS, U. Ill., 1951. Editor-in-chief Prentice-Hall Inc., Englewood Cliffs, N.J., 1970—; pres. coll. div. Prentice-Hall Inc., 1980—; pres. higher edn. group Simon & Schuster Pub. Co., 1985; pres., chief ops. officer Internat. Thomson Pub., Teaneck, N.J., 1988-89, pres., chief exec. officer, 1989—. Served with AUS, 1946-47. Home: Overlook Rd Alpine NJ 07620 Office: Internat Thomson Pub Glenpointe Ctr W Teaneck NJ 07666

DAVIS, JOHN KING, optics scientist; b. Webster, Mass., Nov. 30, 1913; s. Joseph Benjamin and Bertha C. (Rowell) D.; m. Lucy L. McNutt, Nov. 2, 1940; children: John M., Robert B. Student, Bowdoin Coll., 1932-33; AB, Clark U., 1937. Lens designer Am. Optical Corp., Southbridge, Mass., 1939-48, head geometric optics rsch., 1948-62, lens devel. mgr., 1962-71, chief ophthalmic scis., 1971-75; assoc. prof. physiol. optics Pa. Coll. Optometry, Phila., 1975-79, adj. prof., 1979—; cons. in optics Gentex Corp. and Gentex Optics Corp., Dudley, Mass., 1977—. Contbr. articles to profl. publs.; patentee in field. Mem., chmn. Woodstock Bd. Edn., 1955-63; chmn. subcom. Z80.3 Am. Nat. Standards Inst., 1971. Mem. Nat. Acad. Opticianry (life, bd. dirs. 1976-83, Beverly Myers Nelson Achievement award 1976), Sunglass Assn. Am., Acad. Optometry, Optical Soc. Am. Republican. Congregationalist. Home: Prospect St East Woodstock CT 06244 Office: Gentex Corp Dudley MA 02000

DAVIS, JOSEPH ALBERT, banker; b. Stanton, Tex., Aug. 9, 1937; s. Joseph E. and Rosalie (Prevo) D.; m. Susan Mae Caldwell, Aug. 7, 1959; children: Michael Joe, Larry Steven. AA, Tarleton State U., 1958; BA, U. Okla., 1960; MA, U. Tulsa, 1963. Pres. 1st Bank Holding Co., Ruston, Wash., 1974-80, 1st Computer Service, Ruston, La., 1976-80; sr. bank cons. Banking Systems, Dallas, 1980-83, Computer Task Group, Buffalo, 1983—. Contbr. articles to profl. jours. Mem. Am. Banker's Assn., Data Processing Mgmt., Assn. Republican. Mem. Disciples of Christ Ch. Office: Computer Task Group 1321 Greenway Dr Irving TX 75038

DAVIS, JOSEPH EDWARD, supermarket chain executive; b. Los Angeles, May 7, 1926; s. Joseph Edward and Myrtle Dorothy (Longstreet) D.; m. Marjorie Ann Mier, Mar. 27, 1953; children: Theresa, Sally, Victoria, Joseph. B.A., Occidental Coll., Los Angeles, 1949; M.B.A., U. Calif., Berkeley, 1951. C.P.A., Calif. Staff acct. Arthur Andersen & Co., C.P.A.s, Los Angeles, 1951-59; with Alpha Beta Co., La Habra, Calif., 1959-83; controller Alpha Beta Co., 1961-69, v.p., 1969-83, v.p. fin., 1973-83; v.p. fin. Stater Bros. Markets, Colton, Calif., 1983—. Treas. Museum Assn. North Orange County, 1975-83, Fullerton-Morelia Sister City Assn., 1975-85. Served with AUS, 1945-46. Mem. Am. Inst. C.P.A.s, Calif. Soc. C.P.A.s, Fin. Execs. Inst. Republican. Presbyterian. Club: Alta Vista Country. Office: 21700 Barton Rd Colton CA 92324

DAVIS, JOSEPH SAMUEL, department store executive; b. Chgo., Jan. 27, 1930; s. Joseph and Elizabeth (Cowen) D.; m. Martha Louise Gries, June 18, 1955; children: Elizabeth Louise, Katherine Ann, Mark Bennett, James Lincoln. B.A., Columbia U., 1951; M.B.A., Harvard U., 1953. From mgmt. trainee to buyer May D & F Co., Denver, 1956-61; from asst. div. mdse. mgr. to exec. v.p. Kaufmann's, Pitts., 1961-75; pres. G. Fox and Co., Hartford, Conn., 1975-79; pres., chief exec. officer M. O'Neil Co., Akron, Ohio, 1979-83; pres., chief exec. officer May D&F, Denver, 1983-89, chief exec. officer, 1989—; cons. dir. Banc-Ohio Nat. Bank, Akron, 1980-83; dir. Ohio Edison, 1982-83; adv. bd. Sch. Bus., Duquesne U., Pitts., 1974-79, Sch. Bus., U. Conn., 1977-79; trustee Colo. Nat. Bank. Bd. dirs. Hartford Symphony Soc., 1977-79, Downtown Denver, Inc., 1983-86, Nat. Jewish Ctr., from 1984; adv. bd. Akron Symphony, 1980-83, Jr. League Akron, 1979-83; trustee Akron Gen. Med. Center, 1980-83, Akron Art Mus., 1980-83, Akron Regional Devel. Bd., 1980-83, Denver Art Mus., 1984-87, Colo. Alliance Bus., 1985—. Served as officer USN, 1953-56. Mem. Harvard Bus. Sch. Club Colo. Clubs: Denver, Brown Palace. Office: May D&F 16th at Tremont Denver CO 80202

DAVIS, JUNE FIKSDAL, medical facility administrator, designer; b. Alexandria, Minn., June 18, 1944; d. Mads and Gladys Lillian Katherine (Engstrom) Fiksdal; m. Merrill Nathaniel Davis III, June 20, 1971; adopted children—Kim Geoffrey, Marc Lee. Cert. with highest honors, Am. Sch. Floral Arts, Chgo., 1965. Floral designer Fiksdal Flowers, Rochester, Minn., 1960-70; prin. floral designer, nat. design tchr. Retail Florists, Kansas City, Mo., also Houston, 1970-81; pres. owner, founder The Gables Found., Inc., Rochester, 1982—; floral designer, 1981—. Author: Floral Design (Am. Inst. Floral Design award 1974), 1973. Cellist Rochester Symphony Orch., 1960-69; bd. dirs., fin. planner United Way, 1974; real estate placement Riverplace Devel., 1980; bd. dirs. Rochester Ballet, 1975; mem. Rochester PTA; chair Symphony Ball, Rochester Symphony, 1975; coordinator music program, new pipe organ, harpsichord Unitarian Ch., 1975-81 (Outstanding Service award 1977), project pres. Walden Hill Bach Soc., 1975-82. Mem. Am. Inst. Floral Design, Bus. and Profl. Women, P.E.O. Avocations: gourmet cooking, water sports, winter sports, skiing, European travel, camping, music. Office: Gables Found Inc 300 3d Ave SE Rochester MN 55904

DAVIS, KATHLYNE MARY ELIZABETH, corporate financial planning executive; b. Oxnard, Calif., Mar. 23, 1954; d. Charles William Skillas and Patricia (Martin) Thurber; m. Bruce Herron Hadley, June 21, 1981 (div. Oct. 1985); m. Robert Kerth Davis, Sept. 6, 1987; 1 child, Anna Michelle. BA summa cum laude in Econs., U. N.H., 1976; MBA with high distinction, Babson Coll., 1980. Chartered fin. analyst, 1987; cert. mgmt. acct., 1983. Various analyst positions in regional econs. and enegry forecasting Pub. Service Co. of N.H., Manchester, 1976-78, various analyst positions in fin. planning, 1979-81, mgr., fin. planning & analysis, 1982-84, asst. treas., 1985—. Mem. Boston Security Analysts Soc. Office: Pub Svc Co NH 1000 Elm St Manchester NH 03105

DAVIS, KATHRYN LEOLA, labor union administrator; b. Muskogee, Okla., Apr. 23, 1954; d. Hershall Alvin and Jwell Juanita (Hale) Brown; m. Larry Dewayne Workman, Aug. 7, 1970 (div. Oct. 1978); 1 child, Tracy L. AS in Quality Control Tech., U. Tulsa; BS in Indsl. Technology, Northeastern State U., 1985, M in Indsl. Technology, 1987; postgrad., Tulsa U. Coll. Law, 1988. Cert. union counselor United Way Labor Community Services, 1979; lic. in airframe and powerplant, FAA. Machine operator Swan Hose Co., Stillwater, Okla., 1972-73; quality control inspector Dorsett Electronics/Labarge, Inc., Tulsa, Okla., 1973-74; mechanic Cessna Aircraft Co., Wichita, Kans., 1974-75; quality control lab. technician Red Devil, Pryor, Okla., 1975; mechanic McDonnell Douglas Corp., Tulsa, 1975-78, inspector, 1978-80, quality control analyst, 1980-86, structures and installations planner, 1986—; Mem. exec. bd., recording sec. UAW Local 1093, Tulsa, 1978-84, chair women's com., 1978-86, voting del. polit. action com., 1978—, voting del. community action com., 1978—, fin. sec., 1986—. Mem. community service com. Camp Fire Girls, Tulsa, 1978—, Claremore, Okla., 1980-82, Claremore Christian Fellowship Ch. Mem. Am. Soc. for Quality Control, Coalition of Labor Union Women (del. convention 1982-86, 88), Local Union Press Assn., Epsilon Pi Tau, Phi Alpha Delta. Democrat. Lodge: Eastern Star. Home: 201 W 20th St Owasso OK 74055 Office: UAW Local 1093 1414 N Memorial Tulsa OK 74112

DAVIS, KATHRYN WASSERMAN, foundation executive, writer, lecturer; b. Phila., Feb. 25, 1907; d. Joseph and Edith (Stix) Wasserman; m. Shelby Cullom Davis, Jan. 4, 1932; children: Shelby M. Cullom, Diana Davis Spencer, Priscilla Alden (dec.). BA, Wellesley Coll., 1928; MA, Columbia U., 1931; D Es Polit. Sci., U. Geneva, 1934. Researcher Coun. on Fgn. Rels., N.Y.C., 1934-36, State of Pa., Phila., 1936-37; writer and lectr. on fgn. affairs N.Y., 1937—; ptnr. Shelby Cullom Davis & Co., N.Y.C., 1985—; pres. Shelby Cullom Davis Found., N.Y.C., 1985—. Author: Soviets at Geneva, 1934. Trustee Wellesley Coll., 1983—; v.p. Women's Nat. Rep. Club, 1976—, chmn. internat. affairs com.; bd. govs. Harvard U., mem. vis. com. Russian studies, 1986—. Mem. LWV (pres.), Cosmopolitan Club (com. fgn. visitors). Club: Cosmopolitan (fgn. visitor's com.) (N.Y.C.). Home: 193 Wilson Park Dr Tarrytown NY 10591 Office: Shelby Cullom Davis & Co 70 Pine St New York NY 10270

DAVIS, KENNETH ALAN, mental health facility executive; b. Boston, Aug. 12, 1948; s. Saul and Shirley (Kaplan) D.; m. Diane L. Croft, Sept. 13, 1981; children: John M., James M., Ruben D. Nursing diploma, PBBH Hosp., Boston, 1972; grad., No. Essex Coll., 1976; EdM in Adminstrn. and Planning, Harvard U., 1979. Dir. Hope Cottage-Mclean Hosp., Belmont, Mass., 1976-79; exec. dir. NEWW Ctr. Inc., Newton, Mass., 1979-82; dir. adminstrn. and fin. MetroWest Mental Health Assn., Framingham, Mass., 1982-87, exec. dir., 1987—; sr. ptnr. Franken Assocs., Belmont, Mass., 1984—; fin. cons. East Boston Health Ctr., 1985; bd. dirs. Carroll Ctr. for the Blind, Newton, 1980-84; faculty Boston Coll., 1987—. Bd. dirs. Greater Boston Epilepsy Found., 1986—. Mem. Mass. Assn. Patient Account Mgrs., Meeting Planners Internat. Democrat. Jewish. Lodge: Kiwanis. Home: 50 Vincent Ave Belmont MA 02178 Office: MetroWest Mental Health Assn 88 Lincoln St Framingham MA 01701

DAVIS, KENT R., finance executive; b. Elmhurst, Ill., Jan. 23, 1933; s. William S. and Helen R. (Raymond) D.; m. Donna L. Farrar, May 30, 1980; children: Stephan, Gregory, Scott, Elizabeth, Francene, Rodney. BS in Mktg., U. Ill., 1954. Owner K. Davis and Assocs., Lombard, Ill., 1954-66; chief fin. officer Furnival Machinery, Phila., 1966-70; v.p. fin. and securities Rivinius Inc., Eureka, Ill., 1970-76; v.p. fin., adminstrn. Relco Equipment, Joliet, Ill., 1976-80; exec. v.p. and chief operating officer Utilities and Industry, Neponset, Ill., 1980-84; chief fin. officer Resource Tech. Inc. (name changed to PAL Health Techs. 1989), Peoria, Ill., 1985—. Trustee Village of Lombard, 1964-66, mem. planning commn., 1963. Republican. Protestant. Lodge: Kiwanis (v.p. 1961-66). Office: Resource Tech 124 SW Adams Peoria IL 61602

DAVIS, LAWRENCE, medical company sales and marketing executive, healthcare consultant; b. New Haven, July 9, 1945; s. David Denton and Josephine (Molloy) D.; m. Barbara Kulpa, Aug. 22, 1975 (div. 1980); 1 child, Courtney Anne. BA, Duquesne U., 1967. Account exec. Saalfield Pub. Co., Akron, Ohio, 1969-72; dist. mgr. Renauld Internat. Ltd., N.Y.C., 1972-76; spl. account mgr. Bausch & Lomb Inc., Rochester, N.Y., 1976-78; nat. account mgr. Bausch & Lomb Inc., Rochester, 1978-80, ea. sales mgr., 1980-82; dir. mktg. U.S. Sales Corp., Virginia Beach, Va., 1982-84; dir. sales and mktg. Med. Plus Corp., Boston, 1984—. With U.S. Army, 1967-69. Mem. Am. Mktg. Assn., Silver City Striders Club (v.p. 1985). Roman Catholic. Home: 48 Granite Rd Guilford CT 06437 Office: Med Plus Corp 52 Commercial Wharf Boston MA 02110

DAVIS, LESTER WILLIAM, JR., retired travel executive; b. Indpls., Dec. 12, 1924; s. Lester W. and Geraldine (Gregory) D.; B.S., Eastern Ill. U., 1947; m. Virginia M. Smith, Feb. 2, 1943; children—Shirley Ann Davis Casey, Debra Diann Davis Babbitt. Radio, TV announcer-news dir. WLBH, Mattoon, Ill., WPRS, Paris, Ill., WFRL, Freeport, Ill., WREX-TV, Rockford, Ill., 1947-57; del. leader dir. coordinator People to People Travel Program, Winnebago, Ill., Maupintour, Lawrence, Kans., 1957-87; trustee People to People, 1975—. Served with Paratroop Corps, U.S. Army, 1942-45. Mem. VFW. Republican. Presbyterian. Clubs: Lions, Elks, Moose, Masons, Shriners, Am. Legion, Footlighters. Home and Office: PO Box 128 306 N Elida St Winnebago IL 61088 also: 124 S Island Golden Beach FL 33160

DAVIS, LOURIE IRENE BELL, computer systems specialist; b. Las Vegas, N.Mex., Apr. 8, 1930; d. Currie Oscar and Minnie I. (Rodgers) Bell; m. Robert Eugene Davis, Aug. 21, 1950; children: Judith Anne, Robert Patrick, (adopted) Jaime Alleyn, Flint Christopher. BS, West Tex. U., 1959; student Ea. N.Mex. U., 1947-49. Cert. systems profl.; cert. data processing profl. Programmer/analyst Blue Cross/Blue Shield Okla., Tulsa, 1972-75, mgr. systems, 1977-81, dir. info. systems, 1981-82, mgr. project control, 1982-83, mgr. info. ctr., 1984-85, mgr. profl. cons. and tng., 1985-87; ind. profl. cons., Tulsa, 1987; faculty devel. coord. CAID Okla. State U., Okmulgee, 1987—; systems curriculum coord. Tulsa Jr. Coll., 1975-76, mem. computer sci. adv. bd., 1976-83; mem. steering com. U.S. Senate Bus. Adv. Bd., 1981. Mem. budget panel United Way Tulsa, 1981-87, Allocations Exec. Com. Appreciation award, 1987; mem. U.S. Presdl. Task Force, 1982—. Mem. Assn. Systems Mgmt. (regional dir. 1985-86, chpt. membership chair 1982-84; internat. awards 1980, 84), NAFE, AAUW, Tulsa Area Systems Edn. Assn. (recorder 1980-81), Alpha Chi, Mensa, Higher Edn. Assn. Colls. Okla., Intertel (nat. acceptance com. chair 1978, dir. region VIII 1987—). Republican. Mem. Unity Ch. of Christianity. Home: 2403 W Oklahoma Tulsa OK 74127 Office: OSUTBO 444 S Mission Okmulgee OK 74447

DAVIS, MARTIN S., diversified company executive; b. N.Y.C. With Samuel Goldwyn Prodns., N.Y.C., 1947-55, Allied Artists Pictures Corp. N.Y.C., 1955-58; with Paramount Pictures Corp., N.Y.C., 1958-69, v.p., 1962-66, exec. v.p., chief operating officer, mem. exec. com., dir., 1966-69; sr. v.p. Gulf & Western Inc., 1969-74, exec. v.p., mem. exec. com., from 1974, chmn. and chief exec. officer, 1983—, also dir.; bd. dirs. N.Y.C. Ptnrship. Bd. dirs. RJR Nabisco Inc., Nat. Multiple Sclerosis Soc., John Jay Coll. Criminal Justice; bd. trustees Carnegie Hall, Fordham U. Served with AUS, 1943-46. Club: Economic (N.Y.) (bd. trustees). Office: Gulf & Western Inc 1 Gulf & Western Pla New York NY 10023 *

DAVIS, MARVIN ARNOLD, manufacturing company executive; b. St. Louis, Nov. 16, 1937; s. Sam and Pauline (Neuman) D.; m. Trudy Brenda Rein, Aug. 11, 1968; children: Julie, Jeffrey. BS in Chem. Engring., WashingtonU., St. Louis, 1959; MBA in Fin.and Mktg., WashingtonU., 1966. Lead engr. Standard Oil Calif., San Francisco, 1962-64; product mgr. Shell Chem. Co., N.Y.C., 1966-69; group controller Pfizer, Inc., N.Y.C., 1969-75; exec. v.p. Good Hope Industries, New Orleans, 1975-77; pres., chief exec. officer Reed Industries, Inc., Stone Mountain, Ga., 1978—; pres. Sentrex Ltd., Atlanta, 1977-82; v.p. Sentry Ins., 1982-84; cons. Grisanti Galef Goldress, 1984—; instr. Fairleigh Dickinson U., 1968-71; lectr. Washington U., 1966, 77; also cons. Author: The Profit Prescription, 1985, Turnaround, 1987. Active Seville Recreation Assn. Served to lt. USNR, 1959-62. Recipient scholarship Washington U., 1959, fellow, 1968. Mem. DeKalb C. of C., Beta Gamma Sigma, Alpha Chi Sigma. Jewish. Club: Horseshoe Bend Country. Office: 19701 Hamilton Ave Torrance CA 90502-1335

DAVIS, MINNIE DELORES, consultant; b. Laurens, S.C., Oct. 27, 1945; d. John Ed and Minnie Florie (Watts) D. BA, No. Ill. U., 1967; MBA, U. Chgo., 1973. Tchr. pub. schs., Chgo., 1967-72; internal auditor Container Corp. Am., Chgo., 1973-74; sr. corp. auditor NCR Corp., Dayton, Ohio, 1974-76; project specialist J.I. Case Co., Racine, Wis., 1976-79, sr. fin. analyst, 1979-81; dir. strategic planning Peoples Gas Co., Council Bluffs, Iowa, 1981-84; sr. cons. Arthur D. Little Inc., Washington, 1984-88; owner Watts Jendy Cons., 1988—; vis. prof. Black Exec. Exchange Program. Chmn. family services com. United Way, Omaha, 1984, steering com. 1983-84; bd. dirs. Racine area United Way, 1979-81; mem. Foster Care Rev. Bd., Racine County, 1978-80, Ft. Valley Coll. Bus. Adv. Bd., Ga., 1979-81. Awarded key to city Office of the Mayor, Daytona Beach, Fla., 1979. Mem. Nat. Council Negro Women, The Planning Forum (bd. dirs. capital chpt. 1987—), Soc. Exec. and Profl. Women, Nat. Assn. Female Execs., Strategic Mgmt. Soc., Black MBA Assn., Eta Phi Beta Gamma. Baptist. Club: SouthEast Service. Home: 2701 Park Ctr Dr B1009 Alexandria VA 22302 Office: Arthur D Little Inc 955 L'Enfant Pla SW Ste 4200 Washington DC 20024

DAVIS, MULLER, lawyer; b. Chgo., Apr. 23, 1935; s. Benjamin B. and Janice (Muller) D.; m. Jane Lynn Strauss, Dec. 28, 1963; children: Melissa Jane, Muller, Joseph Jeffrey. Grad. with honors, Phillips Exeter (N.H.) Acad., 1953; B.A. magna cum laude, Yale U., 1957; J.D., Harvard U., 1960. Bar: Ill. 1960, U.S. Dist. Ct. (no. dist.) Ill. 1961. Practice law Chgo., 1960—; assoc. Jenner & Block, 1960-67; ptnr. Davis, Friedman, Zavett, Kane & MacRae, 1967—; lectr. continuing legal edn., matrimonial law and litigation Legal adviser Michael Reese Med. Research Inst. Council, 1967-82. Contbr. articles to law jours.; author (with Sherman C. Feinstein) The Parental Couple in a Successful Divorce; mem. editorial bd. Equitable Distbn. Jour., 1984—. Bd. dirs. Infant Welfare Soc., 1975—, pres., 1978-82. Capt. U.S. Army, Ill. N.G., 1960-67. Fellow Am. Acad. Matrimonial Lawyers, Am. Bar Found.; mem. Fed. Bar Assn., ABA, Ill. Bar Assn., Chgo. Bar Assn. (matrimonial com., sec. civil practice com. 1979-80, vice chmn. 1980-81, chmn. 1981-82), Chgo. Estate Planning Council, Law Club Chgo. Republican. Jewish. Clubs: Tavern, Lake Shore Country. Home: 1020 E Westleigh Rd Lake Forest IL 60045 Office: 140 S Dearborn St Chicago IL 60603

DAVIS, ORVAL CLIFTON, diversified energy company executive; b. Rosiclare, Ill., May 7, 1920; s. Luther and Elizabeth (St. John) D.; m. Gaye Lovett, Mar. 21, 1987; children (by previous marriage): Henry T., Jon F. B.S. in Mech. Engring., Tex. A&M U., 1947. Area mgr. Thompson, Starrett & Co., N.Y.C., 1942-43; various engring. positions Natural Gas Pipeline Co. of Am., Chgo., 1947-61, asst. v.p., 1962-63, v.p., 1963-66, exec. v.p., 1966-69, pres., 1969-73; pres. Peoples Gas Co., Chgo., 1973-77, chmn. bd. dirs., 1977-81; chmn., pres., chief exec. officer Peoples Energy Corp., Chgo., 1980-81; chmn., chief exec. officer MidCon Corp., Lombard, Ill., 1981-88, pres., 1981-85, 87-88; exec. v.p. Occidental Petroleum Corp. (parent), Los Angeles, 1986—, also bd. dirs., 1987—; bd. dirs. Amsted Industries Inc., Chgo., Continental Bank Corp., Chgo., Continental Bank, Chgo.; chmn. Inst. Gas Tech., Chgo. Served to capt. USAF, 1942-46, ETO. Mem. Northwestern Univ. Assocs., Am. Gas Assn. (ex-officio), Am. Inst. Mining & Metall. Engrs. Republican. Clubs: Economic (Chgo.). Office: MidCon Corp 701 E 22nd St Lombard IL 60148

DAVIS, PAUL, health administrator; b. Springfield, Mass., Feb. 14, 1951; s. A. Paul Davis and Lorraine M. (Miller) Dean; m. Jane Brackley, Dec. 20, 1975; 1 child, Kristen. BS in Analytical Mgmt., U.S. Naval Acad., 1974; BS in Health Care Mgmt., Med. Coll. Va., 1976; MBA, U. Richmond, 1977. Commd. 2d lt. USMC, 1969, resigned, 1975; adminstrv. officer VA Med. Ctr., Richmond, 1977-79; exec. dir., sec., treas. Univ. Internal Medicine Found., Richmond, 1979-85; adminstr. Dedman (Mass.) Med. Assocs., 1985-88; chief exec. officer, adminstr. Harbin Clinic, Rome, Ga., 1988—; bd. dirs. Harvard Community Health Plan, Boston, MultiGroup Health Plan, Boston, Univ. Internal Medicine Found., Richmond. Mem. Med. Group Mgmt. Assn., Am. Coll. Med. Group Adminstrs., Phi Kappa Phi. Republican. Roman Catholic. Home: 12 Rockridge Rd Rome GA 30161 also: PO Box 6187 Rome GA 30162 Office: Harbin Clinic 1825 Martha Berry Blvd Rome GA 30161

DAVIS, PETER, research center director; b. Doncaster, Yorkshire, Eng., May 1, 1944; came to U.S., 1966; s. Douglas and Joan Florence (Scott) D.; M.A., Cambridge U., 1965; M.Sc., London Sch. Econs., 1966; Ph.D., U. Pa., 1972; m. Ellen Ruth Bear, Jan. 7, 1967; children—Andrew Scott, Jonathan Michael. Sr. cons. Arthur D. Little Inc., Cambridge, Mass., 1972-75; asst. prof. Wharton Sch., U. Pa., 1975-80; dir. Busch Center, Wharton Sch., 1979-80, dir. Wharton Applied Research Center, from 1980, now dir. Entrepreneurial Ctr. Wharton Sch.; dir. Spitz Space Systems Inc., Phila., LaBarge Inc., St. Louis; Progress Investment Assocs. Inc., Phila.; Phila. Export Network, Phila. Mariette and Douglass Russell fellow Wharton Sch., 1967; recipient J. Parker Bursk award U. Pa., 1969. Co-author: Designing a National Scientific and Technological Communication System, 1976; contbr. articles to profl. jours. Home: 508 Manor Rd Wynnewood PA 19096 Office: 3508 Market St Philadelphia PA 19104 also: Wharton Sch U Pa Entrepreneurial Ctr Vance Hall 3733 Spruce St Rm 427 Phila PA 19104 *

DAVIS, R. W., chemical company executive; b. 1924; married. M.S., MIT, 1950; M.B.A., Northwestern U., 1966. With Chevron Chem. Co., 1951—, pres., chief exec. officer, 1982—, also dir. Office: Chevron Chem Co 575 Market St San Francisco CA 94105 *

DAVIS, RICHARD DAVID, manufacturing company executive; b. Decatur, Ill., Mar. 7, 1934; s. Newton David and Anna Josephine (Vest) D.; B.S. in Indsl. Engring., Millikin U., 1963; m. Sue Ann Willoughby, Dec. 18, 1955; children—Richard David, Brandon Wells. mfg. engr., numerical control coordinator Interlake Steel Co., Chgo., 1963-67; numerical control coordinator Trans Union, East Chicago, Ind., 1967-69; plant mgr. Metalmation, South Bend, Ind., 1969-70; mgr. mfg. engring. Pneumo Dynamics Machine Tool Group, Windsor, Vt., 1970-72, Colt Firearms, Hartford, Conn., 1972-77; adv. mfg. engr. Web Press div. Harris Corp., Westerly, R.I., 1977-79; v.p. engring. and mfg. Stoffel Grinding Systems, Inc., Tuckahoe, N.Y., 1979-81, v.p., gen. mgr. Stoffel Polygon Systems, Inc., 1981-84; cons. flexible mfg. systems-corp. engring. and mfg. Gen. Electric Co., 1984-86, mgr. precision mfg. ordnance systems div., 1986-88; advanced mfg. engr. GE Gas Turbine Div., 1988—. Served with USN, 1953-57. Mem. ASME, CASA, Soc. Precision Engring. Home: 11 Botany Dr Greenville SC 29615 Office: 100 Plastics Ave Bldg 59 Pittsfield MA 01201

DAVIS, RICHARD EDWARD, communications specialist; b. Akron, Ohio, July 10, 1963; s. Richard Edward and Mariann Lee (Fleischer) Paluagasi. BS in Communications, Ohio U., 1985. With R.H. Macy, Atlanta, 1985—, control mgr., 1987—; loan officer Macy's Atlanta Employee Credit Union, 1987—. Mem. Delta Tau Delta (sec. 1984-85). Republican. Baptist. Home: 6024 Old Town Pl Norcross GA 30093 Office: RH Macy 4400 Ashford Dunwoody Atlanta GA 30346

DAVIS, RICHARD RALPH, lawyer; b. Houston, July 28, 1936; s. William Ralph and Virginia (Allison) D.; m. Christina R. Zelkoff, June 1, 1974; 1 dau., Virginia Lee Allison. B.A., Yale U., 1962, LL.B., 1965; M.B.A., Columbia U., 1965. Bar: N.Y. 1966. Law clk. FAA, Washington, 1964; assoc. Chadbourne & Parke, N.Y.C., 1965-73, ptnr., 1974-83; sr. v.p., gen. counsel Inspiration Resources Corp., N.Y.C., 1983—, also dir. Served with U.S. Army, 1956-59. Mem. ABA. Home: 1185 Park Ave Apt 6-G New York NY 10128

DAVIS, ROBERT D., grocery store chain executive; b. 1931; married. Grad., U. Fla., 1953. With Winn-Dixie Stores, Inc., Jacksonville, Fla., 1955—, asst. treas. and sec., 1961-65, v.p. fin., from 1965, vice-chmn., 1982-83, chmn., chief fin. officer, 1983-88, also bd. dirs., vice-chmn., 1988—. Served with U.S. Army, 1953-55. Office: Winn-Dixie Stores Inc 5050 Edgewood Ct Jacksonville FL 32203 *

DAVIS, ROBERT EDWIN, industrial executive; b. Madison, Ill., July 15, 1931; s. Harry Earl and Bernice (Prusak) D.; m. Shirley M. Krumbholz, Sept. 4, 1954; children: Tom, Barbara, Sue Ann. BSChemE, U. Mo., 1953. With Mobil Oil Co., St. Louis and Chgo., 1953-54, 56-57, with petrochem. sales dept., 1953-54, dist. sales rep., 1956-57; dist. sales rep. Nalco Corp., Chgo. and Cleve., 1957-58; with Thiokol Corp., Newtown, Pa., 1958—, group v.p. gen. products, 1968-70, pres., 1970-82, chief exec. officer, 1973-82, chmn. bd., 1977-82; tech. dir. Thiokol Corp., Dayton, 1958-60; Eastern dist. mgr. Thiokol Corp., Washington, 1960-64, v.p. aerospace mktg., 1964-68; pres., chief operating officer Morton Thiokol, Inc., 1982-83; pres., chief operating officer Sequa Corp. (formerly Sun Chem. Corp.), N.Y.C., 1983—, also bd. dirs.; mem. Pres.'s Commn. on Personnel Interchange 1976-79; bd. dirs. H & R Block, Inc., Materials Research Corp. Himont, Inc. Bd. dirs. Pennsbury Scholarship Fund. Served with USAF, 1954-56. Mem. Am. Mgmt. Assn. Clubs: Burning Tree, Congressional; St. Andrews (Boca Raton, Fla. and Scarsdale, N.Y.), Marriott Seaview. Office: Sequa Corp 200 Park Ave New York NY 10166

DAVIS, ROGER BEDE, real estate corporation executive; b. Balt., Dec. 1, 1937; s. J. Roger and Rachel R. (Palmer) D.; m. Mary Carol Levickas, Feb. 5, 1966; children: Rebecca, Mark. BA, U. Md., 1968; MBA, Loyola Coll., Balt., 1981. CPA, Md. Br. mgr. Equitable Bank, Balt., 1964-71, acctg. officer, 1971-72; v.p., chief fin. officer Realty Growth Investors, Towson, Md., 1972-81, Calvert Telecommunication Inc., Timonium, Md., 1981-84; gen. mgr. Comcast Cablevision of Md., Timonium, Md., 1984-85; v.p. treas., chief fin. officer McCormick Properties Inc., Hunt Valley, Md., 1985—; bd. dirs. McCormick Properties, Inc., McCormick Constrn. Co., Inc., Hunt Valley. With U.S. Army, 1960-63. Mem. Fin. Execs. Inst. (chmn. publicity 1987—). Democrat. Office: McCormick Properties Inc. 11011 McCormick Rd Hunt Valley MD 21031

DAVIS, ROGER EDWIN, lawyer; b. Lakewood, Ohio, Dec. 29, 1928; s. Russell G. and Irma (Aboline) D.; m. Eva Grace Keeler, July 25, 1953 (div. Feb. 1980); children: Susan Lee, Lisa Ann, Steven Russell; m. Yvonne L. Berich, June 1, 1980. A.B., Harvard U., 1950; LL.B., U. Mich., 1953. Bar: Mich. 1953. Practice in Detroit 1955—; asso. Langs, Molyneaux & Armstrong, 1955-60; counsel Avis Enterprises, 1961-62; with legal dept. S.S. Kresge Co. (now Kmart Corp.), 1963-70, v.p., gen. counsel, sec., 1970-85, sr. v.p., gen. counsel, sec., 1985—. Trustee Arnold Home. Served with AUS, 1953-55. Mem. State Bar Mich., Fla. Bar, ABA, Am. Soc. Corp. Secs. Club: Pine Lake Country. Home: 3234 Pine Lake Rd Orchard Lake MI 48033 Office: K Mart Corp 3100 W Big Beaver Rd Troy MI 48084

DAVIS, RONALD VERNON, beverage products executive; b. Mobile, Ala., Jan. 26, 1947; s. Oliver V. and Lena A. (Minogue); m. Judith L. Walton, July 19, 1970; children: Bryce V., Lauren K. BA, Calif. State U., Fullerton, 1969; MBA, U. So. Calif., 1973. Sales mgr. Gen. Foods Corp., Anaheim, Calif., 1969-74; product mgr. Gen. Foods Corp., White Plains, N.Y., 1974-75, sr. product mgr., 1975-76, group product mgr., 1977-79; v.p. mktg. The Perrier Group, Greenwich, Conn., 1979-80, pres., chief exec. officer, 1980—. Vice chmn. bd. trustees western chpt. Multiple Sclerosis Soc.. Internat. Bottled Water Assn. (pres. Washington dept. 1984-85). Clubs: Innis Arben (Old Greenwich, Conn.) (bd. govs.), Winged Foot (Mamaroneck, N.Y.). Office: The Perrier Group 777 W Putnam Ave Greenwich CT 06830

DAVIS, RONALD WILLIAM, marketing professional; b. St. Louis, Nov. 17, 1946; s. Ronald William Sr. and Lorraine Mari (O'Brien) D.; m. Marsha E. Nieland, April 4, 1970; children: Christopher John, Jennifer Suzanne. BS, William Jewell Coll., 1969. Mfg. engr. Numerical Control, Inc., St. Louis, 1969-74, mktg. rep., 1974-77, mfg. engr. mgr., 1977-79; adv. mfg. engr. mgr. Cleve. Pneumatic Co., 1979-81, mgr. airframe sales, 1981-83; dir. mktg. Engineered Air Systems, Inc., St. Louis, 1983-84, v.p. mktg., 1984—. Mem. Am. Def. Preparedness Assn. Roman Catholic. Office: Engineered Air Systems Inc 1270 N Price Rd Saint Louis MO 63132

DAVIS, RONNIE DALE, property manager, consultant; b. Louisville, Jan. 15, 1957; s. Geneva Edward and Myrna Mae (Bratcher) D.; m. Rosalie Ann Davis (div.); m. Jeanette Sue Thompson, Sept. 4, 1982; 1 child, Sarah Nicole. Grad. high sch., Louisville. With Medford Property Co., Louisville, 1977-83; with mktg. staff, then community dir. Woodsmill Apts., Louisville, 1981-83; mgr. McArthur Park Apts., Raintree Properties, Louisville, 1983-84; ltd. ptrn. Woodcrest Apts., Louisville, 1984—; mgr. Mayfair Apt. Homes, Jeffersonville, Ind., 1984—. Active Empty Stockings Fund Christmas toy drive, Jeffersonville, 1987—. Named to Hon. Order Ky. Cols. Mem. Louisville Apt. Assn. (bd. dirs. 1987—, chair various coms.), Inst. Real Estate Mgmt. Club: Blue Grass Dems. Lodge: Optimists. Office: HFH Realty and Devel 7001 Bronner Ct Ste 2 Louisville KY 40218

DAVIS, SALLY JO, sales executive; b. Pitts., Nov. 22, 1957; d. Raymond Anthony and Rita Ann (Marsh) Dobosh; m. Jeffery Gerard Davis, Aug. 12, 1978; 1 child, Jessica Joann. Mgr. Dobosh Svc. Ctr., Pitts., 1975-86, 1987—; pres. Lawn Mowers & More, McMurray, Pa., 1986-87. Mem. Nat. Equipment Servicing Dealer's Assn. (v.p. 1987-88), Outdoor Power Equipment Servicing Dealers Assn. (past pres.). Democrat. Roman Catholic. Home: 2826 Stanley St Library PA 15129 Office: Dobosh Svc Ctr 5167 Brownsville Rd Pittsburgh PA 15236

DAVIS, SCOTT LIVINGSTON, banker, lawyer; b. Boston, Jan. 23, 1941; s. William Francis and Marion Livingston (Morrison) D.; BA, U. Calif., Berkeley, 1961; MBA, UCLA, 1965; JD, Columbia U., 1968; m. Christina Williams, June 10, 1968; 1 son, Scott Livingston. Admitted to N.Y. bar, 1969; assoc. firm Dewey Ballantine Bushby Palmer & Wood, N.Y.C., 1967-72; gen. counsel, v.p. Electro Audio Dynamics, Inc., Gt. Neck, N.Y., 1972-77, v.p. corp. devel. and legal affairs, 1978-80, group v.p. Consumer Products div., 1980-82, exec. v.p., 1982-84; vice chmn. Technodyne, Inc., 1984; pres., chief exec. officer IKC Internat., Inc., Canoga Park, Calif., 1980-83; pres., chief exec. officer KLH Research and Devel. Corp., Westwood, Mass., 1976-78; sr. v.p., gen. counsel Eastview Co., 1984-87; gen. ptnr., CSD Holdings, 1985—; pres. The Selzer Group, Inc., 1987—; pres., chief exec. officer River Oaks Industries Inc., 1988—; pres. Hanover Capital Corp., 1989— Home: 389 Stewart Ave Garden City NY 11530 also: 21 Bears Crossing Dover VT 05356 Office: 150 E 58th St 27th Fl New York NY 10155

DAVIS, SHELBY CULLOM, investment banker, former ambassador; b. Peoria, Ill., Apr. 1, 1909; s. George Henry and Julia Mabel (Cullom) D.; m. Kathryn Edith Waterman, Jan. 4, 1932; children: Shelby Moore Cullom, Diana Cullom, Priscilla Alden (dec.). Student, Lawrenceville (N.J.) Sch., 1924-26; A.B., Princeton U., 1930; A.M., Columbia U., 1931; D. Polit. Sci., U. Geneva, 1934. Spl. corr., also asso. with Columbia Broadcasting Co., Geneva, 1932-34; economist Investment Corp. Phila., 1934-37; treas. Delaware Fund, Inc., 1937-39; econ. adviser Thomas E. Dewey, 1940; presdl. campaigns; mem. N.Y. Stock Exchange, 1941—; chief fgn. requirements sect. WPB, Washington, 1942; chief div. statistics and research WPB, N.Y., No. N.J., 1943; 1st dep. supt. ins. N.Y. State, 1944-47; mng. partner Shelby Cullom Davis & Co. (investment bankers), N.Y.C., 1947-69, 75—; U.S. ambassador to Switzerland, Bern, 1969-75; dir. Value Line Funds, Frankona Am. Re, Stella Re, Plimoth Plantation; chmn. history adv. council Princeton U.; bd. dirs. Hoover Instn., Fletcher Sch. Diplomacy, Rockford Coll.; chmn. Heritage Found., Nat. Right to Work. Author: Your Career in Defense, 1942, others; former bus. editor: Current History and Forum mags; contbr. articles to several jours. Mem. Fin. Analysts Assn. (pres. 1955-56), Gen. Soc. SR, Soc. Colonial Wars (gov.), Mayflower Soc. Republican. Clubs: Knickerbocker, Univ., Sleepy Hollow Country, Princeton, Players (N.Y.C.); Hartford; Harbor (Maine); Down Town Assn., Charter (Princeton); Everglades (Palm Beach, Fla.). Home: 193 Wilson Park Tarrytown NY 10591 Office: Shelby Cullom Davis & Co 70 Pine St New York NY 10270

DAVIS, STUART, Savings and loan association executive; b. Santa Monica, Calif.; s. William Arthur and Ida Mae (Hanson) D.; children—Lynn Fatti, Richard Edward. B.S., St. Mary's (Calif.) Coll., 1938. Vice chmn. Gt. Western Financial Corp., Los Angeles; Chmn. bd. Gt. Western Savs. & Loan Assn., Los Angeles, 1964-81; chmn. exec. com. Gt. Western Savs. & Loan Assn., 1981—. Trustee Pomona Coll. Recipient Alumnus of Yr. award St. Mary's Coll., 1964. Mem. U.S. League Savs. Assns. (chmn. legis. com. 1980-82, v.p. 1977, pres. 1978), Calif. Savs. and Loans League (pres. 1956), Savs. and Loan Found., Calif. C. of C. (past pres.). Clubs: St. Francis Yacht, Los Angeles Country, California, Thunderbird Country. Office: Gt Western Fin Corp 8484 Wilshire Blvd Beverly Hills CA 90211

DAVIS, SUSAN DENISE, transportation company executive; b. Alameda, Calif., Oct. 2, 1954; d. H.T. and Anna Jean (Perry) Waits; m. Danny R. Davis Sr., Mar. 3, 1971 (div. Feb. 1978); 1 child, Danny Ray Jr.; m. Richard Herbert Spencer, Dec. 6, 1986; 1 child, Kevin Levi. Student, Wayne Community Coll., Goldsboro, N.C., 1984-87. Owner, entertainer Variety USO Bank, Phillipines, 1975-77; office mgr. Thurston Motor Lines, Goldsboro, 1977-81; owner, dispatcher Cross Country Transpn., Goldsboro, 1981-84; pres. Datrans Express Inc., Goldsboro, 1984—. Vol. ARC, Phillipines, 1975-77, local Rep. Com., Goldsboro, 1984. Mem. NAFE, U.S. C. of C., Wayne County C. of C., Coastal Plain Traffic Club, Goldsboro C. of C. (leadership award 1986, chmn. Ambassadors 1986-87, chmn. exec. dialogue 1987). Office: Datrans Express Inc 1427 W Grantham St Goldsboro NC 27530

DAVIS, WALTER STEWART, lawyer; b. Evanston, Ill., Mar. 31, 1924; s. Walter Stewart Sr. and Nina Louise (Nixon) D.; m. Betty May Grede, Apr. 19, 1947; children: Walter Stewart, Susan L. Davis Daigneau, Thomas W., Judith A. Davis Pequet, Robert J. BS, Northwestern U., Evanston, 1947; JD, Northwestern U., Chgo., 1950. Bar: Ill. 1950, Wis. 1953, U.S. Ct. Appeals (4th, 6th, 7th and D.C. cirs.), U.S. Supreme Ct. 1964. Gen. atty. Butler Bros., Chgo., 1950-51; ptnr. Davis & Kuelthau, Milw., 1952—; bd. dirs. Grede Foundries, Milw., Park Banks, Milw., Thomas Industries, Louisville, Milw. Seasoning, Germantown, Wis. Grucon Corp., Milw. Trustee Village of Elm Grove, Wis., 1958-64, George Williams Coll., Downers Grove, 1980—; bd. dirs. YMCA Met. Milw., 1964—, Congl. Home, Brookfield, Wis., 1970-80, 87—. Served to 1st lt. USAF, 1942-45, 51-52, ETO. Decorated Air medal with 2 oak leaf clusters. Mem. ABA, Milw. Bar Assn., Wis. Bar Assn., Internat. Bar Assn., Acad. Basic Edn. (bd. dirs. 1962—). Republican. Congregationalist. Clubs: Bluemound (Wauwatosa, Wis.) (pres., bd. dirs. 1968-76); Greater Milw. Country Assn. (bd. dirs., pres. 1975-77). Office: Davis & Kuelthau 111 E Kilbourn Ave Milwaukee WI 53202

DAVIS, WILLIAM DOYLE, JR., real estate appraiser; b. Kansas City, Mo., Sept. 24, 1934; s. William D. Sr. and Lindalou (Turner) D.; m. Mary Camille Bronaugh, Jan. 1, 1983. BS, U. Mo., 1956, MS, 1957. Ptnr. Appraisal Assocs., Kansas City, 1957—; pres. Farm Mgmt. Assocs., Kansas City, 1981—. Served as 1st lt. U.S. Army, 1956-57. Mem. Mo. Soc. Farm Mgrs. and Rural Appraisers, Agrl. Hall of Fame (pres., chmn. bd. 1976-81), Am. Inst. of Real Estate Appraisers (pres. local chpt. 1971), soc. Real Estate Appraisers (pres. local chpt. 1971-72), Internat. Assn. Assessing Officers, Am. soc. Real Estate Counselors. Mem. Christian Ch. Lodge: Masons: (York Rite, Ararat Shrine). Home: 1400 NE 76th Terr Kansas City MO 64118 Office: Appraisal Assocs 1009 Baltimore Suite 316 Kansas City MO 64105

DAVIS, WILLIAM HARRY, manufacturing company executive; b. Louisville, Dec. 26, 1925; s. Harry S. and Ruth (Hughes) D.; m. Mary A. Moothart, May 20, 1951 (dec. June 1985); children: Diane Davis Oxendale, Marcia Davis Bergren. BEE, U. Louisville, 1949. Registered profl. engr. Various mktg and mgmt. positions Allis Chalmers Corp., Cin. and Milw., 1949-67; gen. mgr. paper machine div. Allis Chalmers Corp., Appleton, Wis., 1967-69; gen. mgr. hydroelectrical products div. Allis Chalmers Corp., York, Pa., 1969-70; dep. group exec. Allis Chalmers Corp., Pitts., 1970-71; pres. E.L. Wiegard div. Emerson Electric Co., Pitts., 1971-75, group v.p., 1975—. Served with USN 1944-46. Recipient Profl. Engring. award U. Louisville, 1985. Republican. Presbyterian. Clubs: Duquesne (Pitts.), Pitts. Field, Rolling Rock (Ligonier, Pa.), Bellerive Country (St. Louis). Office: Emerson Electric Co 641 Alpha Dr Pittsburgh PA 15238

DAVIS, WILLIAM HOWARD, financial planner; b. Manassas, Va., July 3, 1942; s. Howard T. and Agnes E. (Beaver) D.; m. Yvonne I. Lindlow, Sept. 21, 1963; children: William P., Scott J. AA, Santa Ana (Calif.) Coll., 1980; BA, U. Wash., 1982. Enlisted USMC, 1960, advanced through grades to 1st sgt., ret., 1980; ptnr. Fin. Planners Equity Corp., Kent, Wash., 1982-87; prin. Davis & Assocs., Kent, 1987—. Pres. Kent Valley Youth Svcs., 1987-88. Mem. Inst. Cert. Fin. Planners, Fleet Reserve Assn. (bd. dirs. Br. 18), Kent C. of C. (chmn. 1986-87). Lodge: Rotary. Office: Davis & Assocs 505 Washington Ave S Kent WA 98032

DAVISON, M(ARY) JO, environmental research laboratory executive, educator, writer; b. Middletown, Ohio, Nov. 8, 1935; d. Harry Edmund and Marie Angeline (Caswell) D. BS, Miami U., Oxford, Ohio, 1957; MA in Sci. Edn., Environ. Studies, Counseling & Guidance, W.Va. U., 1974. Cert. high sch. sci. tchr., W.Va., Ohio. Sci. tchr. Los Angeles Schs., 1958-61; with sales, advt. and pub. relations staff Bell and Gen. Telephone, Columbus, Ohio and Long Beach, Calif., 1962-69; sci. tchr. Summers County (W.Va.) Schs., 1970-76; sci. and environ. edn. specialist Fayette County (W.Va.) Schs., 1976-84; pres., research dir. Lambda Group, Inc., Columbus, Ohio, 1984—, Lambda of Am., Inc., Columbus, 1984—; pres., owner Lambda Environ. Tech., Morgantown, W.Va., 1987—; pres. Lambda Prodn. Corp., Dayton, Columbus, Ohio, 1987—; environ. edn. cons. Columbus City Schs., 1984—; mem. Acid Rain Adv. Com.—U.S. and Can.; exec. council mem. Tech. Alliance Cen. Ohio. Author: The Colony Trilogy, 1974, Against The Odds, 1978; contbr. articles to sci. jours.; inventor coal and water cleaning processes, microbial delivery system, process for bioremediation of acid mine water and reversal of acid rain damaged aquatic ecosystems. Advisor Women's Outreach, Columbus, 1983—; adv. com. W.Va. Dems. in State Sen. and Ho.of Reps., Oak Hill and Charleston, 1979-84; dist. rep. W.Va. Conservation Edn. Council, Oakhill, 1979-84. Recipient several Sci. and Environ. Educator of Yr. awards, 1973-84; Dept. of Energy grantee, 1985-86. Mme. Nat. Assn. Biologist, Am. Assn. Scientists, Ohio Acad. Sci. (sci. fair judge, 1983—), W.Va. Acad. Sci., Sierra Club, Nature Conservancy, NOW, Nat. Orgn. Female Execs. Home: 1709 Hickory Creek Ln Columbus OH 43229 Office: Lambda Group Inc 1445 Summit St Columbus OH 43201

DAVISON, STANLEY MARTIN, banker; b. Enderby, C., Can., Sept. 12, 1928; s. Ronald and Janet Grace (Livingstone) D.; m. Bette Irene Rusconi, June 12, 1957; children: Loreen Joyce, Diane Janine, Ronald James. Grad., Banff Sch. Advanced Mgmt., 1967, Sch. Advanced Mgmt., Harvard U., 1980. With Bank of Montreal, 1947—, sr. v.p. Man. and Sask. div., 1968-71, exec. v.p. domestic banking, 1971-73, exec. v.p., gen. mgr. domestic banking, 1973-74, exec. v.p., gen. mgr. credits and investments, 1974-76, exec. v.p., chief gen. mgr., 1976-80; vice chmn., dir. Bank of Montreal, Calgary, 1980—. Clubs: Toronto; Petroleum (Calgary, Alta., Can.). Home: 3125 Linden Dr SW, Calgary, AB Canada Office: 1st Canadian Pl, 1st Bank Tower PO Box 1, Toronto, ON Canada M5X 1A1 *

DAVIT, FRANK TORINO, accountant; b. Rockford, Ill., June 20, 1961; s. Torino and Ernestina (Mazzoli) D. BS in Accountancy, No. Ill. U., 1983. CPA. Managerial acct. Ingersoll Engrs., Inc., Rockford, 1984-88, ptnr. in charge acct. and fin. svcs., 1988—. Mem. Nat. Assn. Accts. (Rockford chpt.). Republican. Roman Catholic. Home: 1732 Trainer Rd Rockford IL 61108 Office: Ingersoll Engrs 707 Fulton Ave Rockford IL 61103

DAWKINS, CHARLES N., insurance company executive; b. 1932. Student, Harvard U., 1953. With aerospace industry, L.A., 1955-60; dir. rsch. Bank of Am., San Francisco, 1960-67; investment officer Univ. Calif., San Francisco, 1967-70; v.p. fin. div. Aetna Life and Casualty Co.; v.p. investments Aetna Life Ins. and Annuity Co., 1970—, also bd. dirs. Office: Aetna Life & Casualty Co 151 Farmington Ave Hartford CT 06156 *

DAWLEY, DONALD LEE, data processing educator; b. Amanda, Ohio, Feb. 21, 1936; s. Stanley Bernel and Alice Opel (Santee) D.; m. T. Jane Bokay, Nov. 24, 1957; children: Donald Wayne, Douglas Lee, Denise Jane. BS in Edn., Kent State U., 1959; AA in Bus., U. Calif., Victor Valley, 1966; MBA in Bus., U. Hawaii, Far East div., 1968; MS in Logistics Engring., Air Force Inst. Tech., Dayton, Ohio, 1970; D in Bus. Adminstrn., George Washington U., 1980-81. Cert. systems profl., data processor. Enlisted USAF, 1959, advanced through grades to lt. col.; with data processing and logistics inspection Hdqrs. USAF, Washington, 1973-75; with data processing plans Def. Logistics Agy., Washington, 1973-75, Air Force Logistics, Dayton, 1978; resigned USAF, 1979; from instr. to assoc. prof. decision scis. Miami U., Oxford, Ohio, 1979—, asst. chair Mgmt. Info. Systems, 1985—; cons. J.M. Smucker Co., Orville, Ohio, 1982, McCullough-Hyde Hosp., Oxford, 1986—; pres. Internat. Bus. Schs. Computer Users Group; speaker in field. Author: Auditor Data Processing Knowledge Requirements, 1984; also articles. Decorated Medal of Honor (foreign), Bronze Star. Mem. Data Processing Mgmt. Assn. (internat. com., sec./treas. 1987, bd. dirs. 1988—), Internat. Bus. Schs. Computers Users Group (pres. 1988—, bd. dirs. 1984-88), Assn. for Systems Mgmt., Assn. for Ednl. Data Systems, Soc. Data Educators, Assn. Computing Machinery, Ohio Mgmt. Info. Systems Dirs. Assn. (founder, past pres.), Beta Gamma Sigma, Omnicron Delta Kappa. Baptist. Home: 323 Sandra Dr Oxford OH 45056 Office: Miami Univ Decision Scis Dept 221 Culler Oxford OH 45056

DAWSON, ANNIE L., state agency administrator; b. Sumter, S.C., Sept. 29, 1953; d. Wallace Roland Dawson and Nettie Dorothy (Baldwin) Kinsey; m. Algie Winslow Cuffee, Nov. 25, 1972 (div. 1984), Henry August Jr., Aug. 27, 1988. AS, Pierce Jr. Coll., 1973; BS, LaSalle U., 1983. Billing clk. Atlantic Richfield Co., Phila., 1969-71; stockbroker's aide Sade & Co., Phila., 1971-72; data entry supr. U.S. Computers, Inc., Tacoma, 1972-74; claims adjuster Equitable Life Assurance Soc., Phila., 1975-77; auditor marine payroll Keystone Shipping Co., Phila., 1980-82; maintenance acctg. technician Dept. Army, Edgemont, Pa., 1982-85; intern automotive maintenance mgmt. Southeastern Pa. Transp. Authority, Phila., 1985-86, quality assurance adminstr., 1985—. Pres. block com., North Phila., 1985—; tchr., instr. Phila. Mayor's Literacy Program, 1985—. Mem. Nat. Assn. Black Accts. (Outstanding Mem. award 1983, sec. 1986-87), Nat. Assn. Female Execs., Conf. Minority Transp. Offls. (pres. 1987—), Am. Passenger Transport Assn. (subcom. 1986—), Progressive Network Inc. Club (treas. Phila. chpt. 1985—). Democrat. Office: Southeastern Pa Transit Authority 200 W Wyoming Ave Philadelphia PA 19140

DAWSON, BETTY COX, sales executive; b. New Bern, N.C., Oct. 14, 1954; d. James Cortez and Alene (Garrell) Cox; m. Haywood Sim Dawson Jr., Mar. 14, 1981 (dec. May 1987); children: Crystal Lynn, Jonathan Sim. Grad. high sch., New Bern; student echocardiography tech., Owen Brown Sch., Chgo., 1979. Technician/nurse's aide various hosps., 1974-82; prin. Dawson Cleaning Svc., Raleigh and New Bern, N.C., 1983-84; sales rep. Electrolux, New Bern, 1985, dist. sales mgr., 1985—. Republican. Mem. Assemblies of God Ch. Office: Electrolux PO Box 847 Williamston NC 27892

DAWSON, DENNIS RAY, lawyer, manufacturing company executive; b. Alma, Mich., June 19, 1948; s. Maurice L. and Virginia (Baker) D.; m. Marilynn S. Gordon, Nov. 26, 1971; children—Emily Lynn, Brett Thomas. A.A., Gulf Coast Coll., 1968; A.B., Duke U., 1970; J.D., Wayne State U., 1973. Bar: Mich. 1973, U.S. Dist. Ct. (ea. dist.) Mich. 1973, U.S. Dist. Ct. (we. dist.) Mich. 1975. Assoc., Watson, Wunsch & Keidan, Detroit, 1973-75; mem., Coupe, Ophoff & Dawson, Holland, Mich., 1975-77; staff atty. Amway Corp., Ada, Mich., 1977-79; corp. counsel Meijer, Inc., Grand Rapids, Mich., 1979-82; sec., corp. counsel Tecumseh (Mich.) Products Co., 1982—; exec. com. Bank of Lenawee, Adrian, Mich., 1984—, also bd. dirs.; adj. prof. Aquinas Coll., Grand Rapids, 1978-82; govt. regulation and litigation com. Outdoor Power Equipment Inst. Inc., Washington, 1982—. Trustee Herrick Meml. Hosp., Tecumseh Civic Auditorium, 1986-89; mem. adv. council St. Joseph's Acad., Adrian, 1987—. Mem. ABA, Mich. State Bar Assn., Am. Soc. Corp. Secs., Am. Corp. Counsel Assn., Mich. Mfrs. Assn. (lawyers com. 1987—). Club: Tecumseh Country. Office: Tecumseh Products Co 100 E Patterson Tecumseh MI 49286

DAWSON, EDWARD JOSEPH, merger and acquisition executive; b. Rochester, Pa., Apr. 1, 1944; s. Ralph Edward and Evelyn May (Riggle) D.; B.S. in Indsl. Mgmt., Carnegie Inst. Tech., 1966; M.B.A. in Fin., U. Chgo., 1968; m. Lynda Sue Weir, 1975; 5 children. Computer systems analyst, corporate fin. analyst, Tex. Instruments Corp., Dallas, 1968-70, product planning mgr. digital systems div., 1970-72, mgr. comml. equipment bus. objective, 1972-74, mgr. mktg. electronic watch div., 1975-76, mgr. mktg. home video systems, 1976-77; sr. v.p. ops. and mktg. Capital Alliance Corp., Dallas, 1977-80, exec. v.p. merger ops., 1980-81, chmn. bd., pres., 1981—. Pres., coach Coppell Elem. Sch. Basketball Team, Tex., 1975-78; pres. Marina del Rey Homeowners Assn., 1982-84. Lic. security broker/dealer, real estate broker. Mem. Omicron Delta Kappa, Beta Theta Pi. Mem. Church of Christ. Home: 1634 Choteau Grapevine TX 76051 Office: Capital Alliance Corp 1111 W Mockingbird Ln Ste 737 Dallas TX 75247

DAWSON, GARY LYNN (BOB), banking executive; b. Washington, Dec. 22, 1948; s. Harry Samuel and Gladys (Avey) D.; m. Carol Ann Heidegger, Oct. 13, 1967; children: Kimberlie Yvonne, Christopher Erin. Student Abilene Christian U., 1966-68, Southwestern State Coll., 1969-70; B of Liberal Sci., U. Okla., 1982; MBA, U. Houston, 1984. Photographer Altus Times Democrat, Altus, Okla., 1968-72; mgr. ops. GC Services Corp., Houston, 1972-75, nat. mktg. mgr., 1975-78, mktg. v.p., 1978-86; v.p., risk mgr. Bank Am., 1986-88, v.p., credit risk mgr., 1988—; v.p. Montgomery County Health Devel. Corp., Woodlands, Tex., 1983-86 . Hosp. Commr. Montgomery County Tex., 1982-86; v.p. Med. Ctr. Hosp. Bd., 1982-84, pres. 1984-85, finance and exec. com., 1982-86; bd. dirs. Birnamwood Homeowners Assn., Spring, Tex., 1978; mem. adv. bd. Sam Houston State U., 1984-86. Recipient 1st place award for photography USAF, 1977, Dept. Def., 1972; named Ky. Col.; numerous photography awards Okla. Press Assn., 1971. Mem. Am. Bankers Assn., Hosp. Fin. Mgmt. Assn., Am. Coll. Med. Adminstrs., Tex. Hosp. Assn., Am. Hosp. Assn., Houston Area Apple

Users Group, Gamma Beta Sigma. Republican. Mem. Church of Christ. Home: 297 Montaire Pkwy Clayton CA 94517 Office: Bank Am Credit Risk Mgmt 180 Montgomery St #3407 San Francisco CA 94103

DAWSON, JAMES AMBROSE, printing industry executive; b. N.Y.C., Apr. 27, 1937; s. James J. and M. Margaret (Gatheral) d.; m. Elizabeth M. Murphy, Sept. 10, 1966; children: Margaret Mary, James Bernard, Kate Cronin, Elizabeth Ann, John Hartington. AB in English Lit., Holy Cross Coll., Worcester, Mass., 1958; MBA, NYU, 1966. With St. Regis Paper Co., N.Y.C., 1960-72, asst. mgr. ea. sales, 1965-68, asst. mgr. gen. sales, 1968-72; with World Color Pres., N.Y.C., 1972—, v.p. ea. sales, 1972-75, sr. v.p. sales, 1983-87; pres., chief exec. officer World Color Pres., N.Y.C. and Effingham, Ill., 1987—. Served with USAR, 1959-60. Roman Catholic. Home: 83 Stonehenge Dr New Canaan CT 06840 Office: World Color Press 485 Lexington Ave New York NY 10017

DAWSON, MIMI (WEYFORTH), government official; b. St. Louis, Aug. 31, 1944; d. Francis Griffin and Jeanne (Gething) Weyforth; m. Rhett Brewer Dawson, Jan. 15, 1976; 2 children: Elizabeth Stuart, Andrew Brewer. AB, Washington U., St. Louis, 1966. Legis. asst. Rep. Richard Ichord, Mo. Dist., 1969-72, 73; press sec., legis. asst. to Rep. James Symington, Mo. Dist., 1973; pres. sec., adminstrv. asst., chief staff, legis. dir. Sen. Bob Packwood, Oreg., 1973-81; commr. FCC, Washington, 1981-87; dep. Sec. U.S. Dept. of Transportation, Washington, DC, 1987—; Trustee Am. Council Young Polit. Leaders. Republican. Roman Catholic. Office: Transp Dept 400 7th St SW Washington DC 20590

DAY, CASTLE NASON, foods company executive; b. Springfield, Mass., July 24, 1933; s. Chauncey Castle and Anne Frances (Nason) D.; m. Patricia Jarko, Feb. 1, 1956; children: Robert Castle, Anne Wilson. B.A., Williams Coll., 1955; M.S., MIT, 1957. Exec. v.p. McCall Pattern Co., N.Y.C., 1970-72; v.p. Norton Simon Inc., N.Y.C., 1973-74; exec. v.p. Max Factor Inc., Los Angeles, 1975-77; v.p. fin. Can. Dry Corp., N.Y.C., 1978-81; exec. v.p. Am. Bakeries Co., N.Y.C., 1982-88; dir. Am. Bakeries Co., 1985-88. Home: 39 Driftway Ln New Canaan CT 06840 Office: Am Bakeries Co 4 Landmark Sq Stamford CT 06901

DAY, DONALD JOSEPH, transportation executive, consultant; b. Cleve., July 24, 1929; s. Everett A. and Vera D. (Boyer) D., m. Evelyn Kay Vaughan, Aug. 8, 1953; children: David, Ronald Alan. BS, Kent State U., 1955, MBA, 1967. Traffic mgr. Glastic Corp., Cleve., 1956-61; asst. to gen. traffic mgr. Glidden Co., Cleve., 1961-65; so. region traffic mgr. Durkee Foods div. Glidden Co., Louisville, 1965-69; transp. mgr.foods SCM Corp., Cleve., 1969-73, mgr. corp. transp. ops., 1973-77; dir. transp. Carlon div. TBG, Inc., Cleve., 1977-86; transp. cons. Donald J. Day & Assocs., Cleve., 1986-87; gen. traffic mgr. Airco Carbon div. BOC Group, Inc., Pitts., 1987—. Served with USAF, 1948-51. Mem. Nat. Freight Transp. Assn., Am. Soc. Transp. and Logistics, Nat. Indsl. Transp. League, Soc. Global Trade Execs., Guild Am. Transp. Specialists, Cleve. Traffic Club, Pitts. Traffic Club, Pine Brook Country Club, Venango Tr. Club. Republican. Methodist. Home: 2292 Salem Dr Franklin Park PA 15237

DAY, JAMES EDWARD, public relations executive; b. Alva, Okla., Sept. 6, 1940; s. Joe R. and Helen Dale (Nevitt) D. BA, U. Pa., 1962. Editor, writer Standard & Poor's Corp., N.Y.C., 1962-66; assoc. editor Fin. World mag., N.Y.C., 1966-68; account exec. Ruder & Finn, N.Y.C. and Dallas, 1968-71; dir. corp. communications Recognition Equipment, Inc., Dallas, 1971-74; account exec. Bozell & Jacobs Advt./Pub. Relations, Dallas, 1974-75; v.p., mgr. pub. relations First City Bancorp. of Tex., Houston, 1975—. Pres., bd. dirs. Stages Theatre, Houston, 1983—; bd. dirs. Armand Bayou Nature Ctr., Houston, 1978—, Tex. Council on Econ. Edn., 1980—. With USNG, 1963-69. Mem. Tex. Pub. Relations Soc., Pub. Relations Soc. Am. (pres., bd. dirs. fin. isnstns. sect. 1980-81). Home: 3530 Yupon Houston TX 77006 Office: First City Bancorp Tex PO Box 2557 Houston TX 77252

DAY, JOHN DENTON, wholesale industrial sales company executive, cattle and horse rancher, trainer; b. Salt Lake City, Jan. 20, 1942; s. George W. and Grace (Denton) Jenkins; student U. Utah, 1964-65; BA in Econs. and Bus. Adminstrn. with high honors, Westminster Coll., 1971; m. Susan Hansen, June 20, 1971; children: Tammy Denton, Jeanett. Riding instr., rangler Uinta wilderness area, U-Ranch, Neola, Utah, 1955-58, YMCA Camp Rodger, Kans.; with Mil. Data Cons., Inc., L.A., 1961-62, Carlseon Credit Corp., Salt Lake City, 1962-65; sales mgr. sporting goods Western Enterprises, Salt Lake City, 1965-69, Western rep. PBR Co., Cleve., 1969-71; dist. sales rep. Crown Zellerbach Corp., Seattle and L.A., 1971-73; pres. Dapco paper, chem., instl. food and janitorial supplies, Salt Lake City, 1973-79; owner, pres. John D. Day, mfrs. reps., 1972—; dist. sales mgr. Surfonics Engrs., Inc., Woods Cross, Utah, 1976-78, Garland Co., Cleve., 1978-81; rancher, Heber, Utah, 1976—, Temecula, Calif., 1984—; sec. bd. Acquadyne. Group chmn. Tele-Dex fund raising project Westminster Coll. With AUS, 1963-64. Recipient grand nat. award Internat. Custom Car Show, San Diego, 1962, Key to City, Louisville, 1964, Champion Bareback Riding award, 1957, Daily team roping heading and heeling champion, 1982. Mem. Internat. Show Car Assn. (co-chmn. 1978-79), Am. Quarter Horse Assn. (high point reining champion 1981, sr. reining champion 1981, working cowhorse champion 1982), Utah Quarter Horse Assn. (champion AMAT reining 1979, 80, AMAT barrel racing 1980), Profl. Cowhorseman's Assn. (world champion team roping, heeling 1986, 88, high point rider 1985, world champion stock horse rider 1985-86, 88, world champion working cowhorse 1985, PCA finals open cutting champion, 1985-88, PCA finals 1500 novice champion 1987, PCA finals all-around champion 1985-88, inducted into Hall of Fame 1988, first on record registered Tex. longhorn cutting contest, open champion, founder, editor newsletter 1985-89, pres. 1985-89), Intermountain Quarter Horse Assn. (champion AMAT reining 1979-81). Contbr. articles to jours. Home and Office: 76 Dgts #2 PO Box 1297 Temecula CA 92390 also: Rockin D Ranch #1 Box 4 Heber City UT 84032 also: Ranch #2 John D Day Tng Ctr 39935 E Benton Rd Temecula CA 92390

DAY, JOHN W., automotive company executive; b. Chgo., Feb. 25, 1933; s. John W. and Gay (Potters) D.; m. Barbara Cline, 1955; children: Lisa, Karen. BS in Bus., Northwestern U., 1955. Mgr. acctg. missile div. tech. applications USAF, 1957-61, mgr. fin. tech. applications, 1961-63; successively mgr. acctg. and audit, dir. fin., mng. dir., group dir., v.p. European div., pres. French div., group v.p. diversified ops. Chrysler Internat., 1963-79; v.p., controller Chrysler Corp., 1979-81; exec. v.p. Internat. Chrysler Corp., 1981-84; pres. Bendix group Allied-Signal Corp., 1984-88; pres. automotive div. Allied Signal, Southfield, Mich., 1989—. Bd. dirs. William Beaumont Hosp., Mich. Opera Theater. Capt. USMC, 1955-57. Mem. Mich. Mfrs. Assn. (bd. dirs.), Soc. Automotive Engrs., Detroit Athletic Club, Bloomfield Hills Country Club. Office: Allied Signal Inc 20650 Civic Center Dr PO Box 5029 Southfield MI 48086-5029

DAY, MELVIN SHERMAN, information company executive; b. Lewiston, Maine, Jan. 22, 1923; s. Israel and Frances (Goldberg) D.; m. Louisa Walker; children: Cynthia Day Solganick, Wendy Day Johnson, Robert Marshall. BS, Bates Col., 1943; postgrad. U. Tenn., 1953-54. Chemist, Metal Hydrides Inc., Beverly, Mass., 1943-44, Tenn. Eastman Corp., Oak Ridge, 1944-46; sci. analyst AEC, Oak Ridge, 1946-48, asst. chief tech. info. svc. extension, 1950-56, chief, 1956-58, dir. tech. info. div., Washington, 1958-60; dep. dir. Tech. Info. and Ednl. Programs Office, NASA, Washington, 1960-61, dir. Sci. and Tech. Info. div., 1961-67, dep. asst. adminstr. tech. utilization, 1967-70; head Office Sci. Info., NSF, Washington, 1970-72; dep. dir. Nat. Libr. Medicine, HEW, Bethesda, Md., 1972-78; bd. dir. Nat. Tech. Info. Svc. Dept. Commerce, 1978-82; v.p. Info. Tech. Group, 1982-84; v.p. Rsch. Publs., Arlington, Va., 1984-86; sr. v.p. Herner & Co., 1986-88; pres. M. Day Cons. Internat., Inc., Arlington, Va., 1988—; cons. Internat. Atomic Energy Agy., 1960; adviser OECD, 1970, 75; U.S. mem. info. policy group; U.S. mem. NATO Tech. Info. Panel, 1960-70, 79-82, chmn., 1970; chmn. com. on sci. and tech. info. Fed. Coun., 1970-72, chmn. com. on intergovtl. sci. rels., 1969-70; chmn. Sci. Info. Exch. Adv. Bd., 1963-69, mem. Chem. Abstracts Adv. Bd., 1964-68; mem. Fed. Libr. Com., 1968-78, chmn. exec. bd., 1973-75; U.S. mem. adv. com. on librs., documentation and archives UNESCO; pres. abstracting bd. Internat. Coun. Sci. Unions, 1977-83; bd. dirs. Internat. Coun. for Sci. and Tech. Info., 1983—, Inst. for Internat. Info. Programs, 1985—, del. numerous panels, also cons., adviser, lectr. in field. Mem. editorial bd. Health Communications and Informatics. Bd. visitors U. Pitts. Grad. Sch. Info. Sci., 1977-83; trustee Found. Ctr., 1974-78, trustee Engring. Info. Inc., 1981-84. With U.S. Army, 1944-46. Recipient Sustained Superior Performance award AEC, 1960, Exceptional Svc. medal NASA, 1971, Superior Svc. award USPHS, 1976. Fellow Am. Soc. Advancement Sci.; mem. Am. Soc. Info. Sci. (chmn. internat. rels. com. 1972-75, pres. 1975-76, coun. 1975-77, editorial bd. bull.), Am. Chem. Soc., N.Y. Acad. Sci., Spl. Libr. Assn., Am. Soc. Cybernetics (bd. dirs. 1975-79), Am. Libr. Assn., Venezuelan Acad. Scis. (hon. corr.), Internat. Coun. Sci. and Tech. Info. (hon.). Home and Office: 4309 Chesapeake St NW Washington DC 20016

DAY, NERINE CAROLYN, brokerage house executive; b. Watertown, S.D., Sept. 12, 1942; d. Clinton H. and Helen (Bender) Parliament; m. C. Michael Day, Nov. 26, 1977; 1 child, Ronald. Student, S.D. State U., 1960-62. Investment broker A.G. Edwards & Sons, Alexandria, La., 1972-78, v.p., br. mgr., 1978—; adjunct investment instr. La. Coll., Pineville, 1976-80. Trustee La. Econ. Edn. Council, 1988—; chmn. bd. dirs. Progress Alliance, Alexandria, 1986; participant nat. security forum AirWar Coll., 1988. Named One of Outstanding Young Women La., La. Jaycee Jaynes, 1976; recipient Community Service award, Alexandra Jr. League, 1986. Mem. Cen. L.A. C. of C. (pres. 1985), La. Bus. and Industry Assn. (bd. dirs. 1986—). Republican. Episcopalian. Home: 3132 Elliott St Alexandria LA 71301 Office: A G Edwards & Sons Inc 3700 Jackson St Ste 102 Alexandria LA 71303

DAY, ROBERT JENNINGS, mineral company executive; b. 1925. B.A., Pa. State U., 1947. With U.S. Gypsum Co., 1950—, dist. sales mgr., 1956, mktg. mgr. steel products, 1958, staff mktg. mgr. plastering materials, 1960, mdse. mgr., 1961, dir. product mgmt., 1966; div. gen. mgr. western div. U.S. Gypsum Co., Los Angeles, 1969; corporate v.p. mktg. U.S. Gypsum Co., 1974-77, sr. v.p., 1977-79, exec. v.p., 1979-81, pres., chief operating officer, 1981-85, also dir.; chmn., chief exec. officer USG Corp, 1985—; bd. dirs. Fed. Res. Bank Chgo., 1983—, chmn. bd. dirs., 1986—; bd. dir. BPB Industries, Plc, London, CBI Industries, GATX Corp., Can. Gypsum Co. Bd. dirs. Chgo. Lyric Opera, Great Books Found.; trustee Robert Crown Ctr., Hinsdale, Ill. Capt. USAFR, 1943-45, 51-53. Office: USG Corp 101 S Wacker Dr Chicago IL 60606

DAY, RONALD ELWIN, banker; b. Randolph, Vt., Dec. 15, 1933; s. John Ellis and Esther Murle (Tabor) D.; A.A., Pasadena City Coll., 1958, student, 1958-59; B.A., U. Calif., Santa Barbara, 1961; M.B.A., UCLA, 1962; m. Elizabeth Jean McKeage, June 26, 1955; children—Gary Alan, Kathi Ellen, Judy Anne, Jeffrey Evan. Internal auditor North Am. Aviation, Downey, Calif., 1962-64; systems and procedures mgr. Proto Tool Co., Los Angeles, 1964-65; computer programmer First Nat. Bank, Boston, 1966-67; project mgr., 1967-73, systems analyst 1974-77, system planning com. chmn., trust div., 1977—, trust info. mgmt. system adminstr., 1977—. Served with USAF, 1952-56. Mem. Soc. Advancement of Mgmt., Inst. Internal Auditors, Nat. Geog. Soc., Indsl. Mgmt. Club, Boston Computer Soc., Assn. Systems Mgmt., Alpha Gamma Sigma. Republican. Clubs: U.S. Ski Assn., Indian Guides. Home: 2 Bigham Rd North Reading MA 01864 Office: 1st Nat Bank Boston 100 Federal St Boston MA 02105

DAY, RONALD RICHARD, financial executive; b. York, Pa., Nov. 14, 1934; s. Russell Aldinger and Rosa Ellenora (Reever) D.; m. Patricia Glee Duncan, Nov. 24, 1956. BS in Econs., Lebanon Valley Coll., Annville, Pa., 1956; postgrad. U.S. Army Fin. Sch., Indpls., 1957, Lehigh U., 1961. Mgr. cost control and systems Mack Trucks, Inc., Allentown, Pa., 1963-67; mgr. cost acctg. Am. Chain div. Acco Babcock Co., York, 1967-70; div. controller, 1970-82, v.p. fin. and acctg., Chain & Lifting Prods. div.; committeeman York County Republican party, 1972-74; sec. Optimist Internat., York, 1973. Served to 1st lt. U.S. Army, 1957-59. Mem. Nat. Assn. Accts. (bus. planning bd.), Exec. Club Central Pa., York Area C. of C., Mfrs. Assn. York, Internat. Platform Assn., Rotary, Lafayette Club, Outdoor Country (York) Club, Masons, Shriners, Order of De Molay (mem. adv. bd. 1975—). Lutheran. Avocations: golf, hunting, fishing, boating, travel. Home: 2430 Ramblewood Rd York PA 17404 Office: Acco Babcock Inc 76 Acco Dr York PA 17402

DAYMAN, CRAIG RYAN, bank official; b. Pasadena, Calif., Jan. 2, 1961; s. Bain and Evelyn Mills (Waggener) D.; m. Frances Chiang, July 22, 1989. AA, Pasadena City Coll., 1981; BA in Psychology, U. Redlands, 1983; postgrad., Calif. State Poly. U. Pomona, 1986—. Teller Crocker Nat. Bank, Monrovia, Calif., 1984-86; new accounts rep. First Fed. Savs. & Loan San Gabriel Valley, Arcadia, Calif., 1986-87; human resources technician Home Savs. Am., Irwindale, Calif., 1987—. Republican. Mem. Congregational Ch. Club: Toastmasters. Home: 684 W Sierra Madre Blvd Sierra Madre CA 91024

DAYTON, BRUCE MCLEAN, finance executive; b. Bklyn., Jan. 24, 1934; s. George Henry and Agnes (Callendar) D.; m. Gracia Parkhill, Oct. 13, 1956; children: Heather, Jon, Gregory. BA, Williams Coll., 1956; postgrad., San Francisco State Coll., 1957-60. CLU; chartered fin. cons. Mgmt. trainee Wall Street Jour., N.Y.C., 1956-57; dir. personnel and pub. relations Atlee Corp., Waltham, Mass., 1960-61; co-founder, chmn., treas. Multi-Fin. Services, Inc., Weston, Mass., 1970—; bd. dirs. Chancellor Corp., Boston. Editor: (tax newsletter) Money Management, 1970—. Pres., bd. dirs. Twilight Cottagers, Haines Falls, N.Y., 1983-88; chmn. council Pilgrim Ch., Lexington, Mass., 1972-74, chmn. endowment and investment com., 1986—. Served with USNR, 1957-60. Mem. Am. Soc. CLU's and Chartered Fin. Cons. (pres., bd. dirs. Boston chpt. 1973-74, inst. fellow 1975, 86), Mass. Soc. Lic. Ins. Advisors, Internat. Assn. for Fin. Planning (sec. 1977-87), Greater Boston Fin. Services Consortium (chmn., convenor com. dels. 1987—), Boston Estate and Bus. Planning Council (exec. com. 1975-79), Boston Life Underwriters (chmn. ethics com. 1981), Smaller Bus. Assn. New Eng., Million Dollar Round Table (life, charter), Golden Key Soc., Chi Psi (mem. exec. council 1970-73, trustee emeritus ednl. found., Disting. Service award 1973). Republican. Congregationalist. Home: 1 Adams St Lexington MA 02173 Office: Multi-Fin Svcs Inc 30 Colpitts Rd Weston MA 02193

DEA, MARGARET MARY, wholesale school supplies company executive; b. St. Albans, Vt., Feb. 8, 1946; s. Ralph Homer and Irene Mae (Trombly) Wilson; m. Eugene Michael Dea, Aug. 26, 1967; children—Francesca Meredith, Vanessa Laurel. B.A., U. Vt., 1967; student Art Students League, 1972-77, Sch. Visual Arts, 1975-77. Tchr. French, Hun Sch., Princeton, N.J., 1968-70; tchr. French, Spanish, Newark Acad., Short Hills, N.J., 1970-71; dir. reading, research and edn. Park Sch., Indpls., summers, 1968-71; exec. tng. personnel Bloomingdale's, N.Y.C., 1972-74; commn. portrait artist, Englewood, N.J., Lake Forest, Ill., 1974-79; pres. Service Plus, Inc., Fort Myers, Fla., 1979—, United So., Inc., 1983—; art designer E.M. Dea & Assocs., Inc., Fort Myers, 1984—; pres. Margaret Dea Graphics Studio, Fort Myers, 1986—. Editor, author Bloomingdale's employee mag. Faces, 1972-74. Mem. Portrait Soc. Am., Nat. Assn. Female Execs., Portrait Inst., Womens Network, Lee County Alliance Arts, Mensa (chpt. South by Southwest). Republican. Roman Catholic. Club: Jr. League Bergen County. Avocations: piano; needlework; drawing; photography. Office: Service Plus Inc 30 Mildred Dr Fort Myers FL 33901

DEAKINS, JOHN DAVID, manufacturing executive; b. Kansas City, Mo., Sept. 12, 1942; s. John A. and Mary Phyllis (Mast) D.; m. Beth L. Beamer, June 5, 1965; children: Derrick, David, Jennifer. BSME, U. Kans., 1965; MSME, U Kans., 1966; MBA, U. Pa., 1972. CPA, Tex.; registered profl. engr., Tex. Mgr. treasury ops. Cameron Iron Works, Inc., Houston, 1975-80, v.p. fin., 1980-82, sr. v.p. fin., chief fin. officer, 1982—. Trustee Cypress-Fairbanks Ind. Sch. Dist., Houston, 1982-85. Mem. Fin. Execs. Inst. (dir. Houston chpt. 1979-81), Am Inst. CPA's, Tex Soc. CPA's (membership com. 1983—), Tex. Soc. Profl. Engrs., Soc. Petroleum Engrs., Tax Research Assn. (bd. dirs. 1985—), Tex. Research League (bd. dirs. 1986—). Methodist. Office: Cameron Iron Works Inc 13013 NW Freeway Houston TX 77040

DEAL, ERNEST LINWOOD, JR., banker; b. Florence, Ala., Jan. 5, 1929; s. Ernest Linwood and Nell W. (Willingham) D.; m. Mary Cooper, Dec. 27, 1952; children: Theresa Lynn, Sarah Street, Matthew Cooper, Jennifer Willingham. Student, Florence State Coll., 1947-49; B.S., U. Ala., 1952; postgrad., Southwestern Grad. Sch. Banking, So. Meth. U., 1961. V.p. Tex. Commerce Bank, Houston, 1956-65; sr. v.p. Capital Nat. Bank, Houston, 1965-71; pres., chief exec. officer Fannin Bank, Houston, 1971-82, chmn., chief exec. officer, 1982; chmn., chief exec. officer InterFirst Bank, Houston, 1983; chmn., chief exec. officer First City Nat. Bank, Houston, 1984-88, exec. v.p., 1988—; sr. chmn. bd. First City Bank-Dallas, 1988—; bd. dirs. Cherokee Resources Corp., N.Y. Mem. bd. visitors M.D. Anderson Hosp., Houston, 1971—; past chmn. Houston Parks Bd.; chmn. Local Organizing Com. U.S. Olympic Festival, 1986; chmn. bd. trustees Kinkaid Sch.; trustee Southwestern Grad. Sch. Banking. Served to lt. (j.g.) USNR, 1952-55. Mem. U. Ala. Alumni Assn., Houston C. of C. (dir., exec. com.), Am. Bankers Assn. (governing council, state v.p., govt. relations council 1977-82, v.p. 1978-79), Tex. Bankers Assn. (dir.), Assn. of Res. City Bankers, Phi Gamma Delta, Delta Sigma Pi, Omicron Delta Kappa. Republican. Presbyterian. Clubs: Houston Country, Ramada (treas.), Petroleum, Tower (Dallas). Office: 1st City Nat Bank 1001 Main St PO Box 2557 Houston TX 77252

DEAL, GEORGE EDGAR, corporate executive, management consultant; b. Marion, Ind., July 31, 1920; s. Harold Everett and Esther Victoria (Kendall) D.; m. Ruth Florence McFarland, Nov. 4, 1945; children: Joan Deal Eklund, Georgia Deal Ashcraft, Sharon Deal Ferdyiwek, Frank Kendall, Susan Deal Holton, Marylise Tobin. Student, Ind. Wesleyan U., 1937-39; B.S. with high distinction, Ind. U., 1941, M.S., 1942; postgrad., Am. U., 1942, Harvard U., 1943, Columbia U., 1948; D.B.A., George Washington U., 1970. Indsl. specialist WPB, 1942; dept. mgr. Macy's, N.Y.C., 1947-49; supt. Bloomingdale's, N.Y.C., 1949-53; v.p. The Kroger Co., Washington, 1953-63; asst. to pres. Bionetics Research Labs., Falls Church, Va., 1964-67; dir. Grad. Mgmt. Sch., Am. Mgmt. Assn., Saranac Lake, N.Y., 1967-69; sr. research assoc. Logistics Mgmt. Inst., Washington, 1969-70; pres. Mgmt. Factors Orgn., McLean, Va., 1970—; pres., chmn. San Luis Aurum, Inc., McLean, Va., 1984—; chmn. Canones de Oro, S.A. dec.V., Ensinada, B.C. Norte, Mex., 1987—; bd. advisors Nat. Grad. U., Coll. Democracy; chmn. sec. navy's adv. bd. edn. and tng., 1972-75; spl. asst. to dir. LIFE Internat.; mem. internat. faculty Cen. Mich. U.; cons. The World Bank. Author; contbr. articles to profl. jours. Mem. Greater Washington Health and Welfare Council, 1966-67; mem.-at-large Nat. council Boy Scouts Am.; bd. dirs. Nat. Women's Symphony. Capt. USNR, 1942-47, 50-52. Fellow Washington Acad. Scis.; mem. Nat. Council Assns. in Policy Scis. (steering com.), Councils Retail Mchts. (dir. Tenn. and Ala. councils 1954-60), Inst. of Mgmt., AAAS, Ops. Rsch. Soc. Am. (assoc. editor 1969-73, alt. U.S. rep. for NATO confs. on ops. rsch.), Acad. Mgmt., Strategic Mgmt. Soc., World Future Soc., Soc. for Internat. Devel., Am. Inst. Mgmt., Internat. Inst. Strategic Studies, Cath. Acad. Scis. (v.p.), Order St. George the Martyr, Order St. Basil the Gt., Order Knights of the Holy Sepulchre, Beta Gamma Sigma. Republican. Roman Catholic. Lodges: Masons (Scottish Rite). Home and Office: 6245 Park Rd McLean VA 22101

DEAL, THERRY NASH, college dean; b. Iredell County, N.C., Apr. 21, 1935; d. Stephen W. and Betty (Sherrill) Nash; m. J.B. Deal, July 10, 1954; children: Melaney Dawne, J. Bradley. BS in Home Econs., U. N.C., 1957, MS, 1961, PhD, 1965; postgrad., Harvard U., 1964, 87. Instr. pub. schs. Iredell County, N.C., 1959-61; instr. U. N.C., Greensboro, 1961-65; prof. U. Ga., Athens, 1965-72; dept. chair Ga. Coll., Milledgeville, 1972-82, dir. continuing edn. and pub. svcs., 1982-84, dean continuing edn. and pub. svcs., 1984—; bd. dirs. Pvt. Industry Coun., Baldwin Co., 1985—. Author numerous poems. Mem. Am. Home Econs. Assn., Nat. Coun. Adminstrs. of Home Econs., Nat. Assn. Edn. of Young Children, Milledgeville/Baldwin County C. of C., DAR. Democrat. Methodist. Office: Ga Coll Clark St Milledgeville GA 31061

DE ALMEIDA, ROBERT ANTHONY, executive financial controller; b. Balt., Sept. 8, 1954; s. Anthony B. and Lydia (Gertrudes) De A.; m. Joyce Ecker, May 15, 1982. AB in Acctg., Loyola Coll., Balt., 1976; MS in Econs., U. Balt., 1985. Asst. mgr. acctg. Brehm Savs. & Loan Assn., Balt., 1976-79; internal auditor First Fed. Savs. & Loan of Annapolis,, Md., 1979-80, fin. mgr., 1980-81; controller Wyman Pk. Fed. Savs. & Loan Assn., Lutherville, Md., 1981-87, exec. v.p., 1987—. Mem. Home Builders Assn. Mem. Fin. Mgrs. Soc., Soc. Real Estate Appraisers, United Meth. Men.'s Lodge. Lodge: Rotary. Home: 8824 Baker Ave Baltimore MD 21234 Office: Wyman Pk Fed Savs & Loan 11 W Ridgely Rd PO Box 505 Lutherville MD 21093

DEALY, JOHN FRANCIS, management consultant, lawyer, educator; b. Bklyn., May 4, 1939; s. John Edward and Marie Agnes (Jones) D.; m. Nana Louise May, Oct. 7, 1967; children: Anne Louise, Marian Jones. BS, Fordham U., 1961; LLB, NYU, 1964. Bar: N.Y. 1964, Md. 1974. Atty., advisor Office Sec. USAF, Washington, 1964-67; gen. counsel Fairchild Industries, Germantown, Md., 1967-74, exec. v.p., chief fin. officer, 1974-76; pres. Fairchild Industries Inc., Germantown, Md., 1976-82; chmn., chief exec. officer Am. Satellite Corp., Rockville, Md., 1977-80; cons. mgmt., mergers and acquisitions Washington, 1982—; sr. counsel Shaw, Pittman, Potts and Trowbridge, Washington, 1982—; disting. prof. Georgetown U., Washington, 1982—; bd. dirs. First Md. Bancorp, Balt.; adv. dir. Greenhorne and O'Mara, Greenbelt, Md., 1985—; sr. advisor Orion Network Systems Inc., Rockville, Md., 1987—, Oppenheimer-Palmieri Group, N.Y.C., 1986—, Atlantic Rsch. Corp., Alexandria, Va., 1989—. Co-inventor improvements to M-16 semi-automatic weapon; contbr. articles to profl. jours. Mem. Econ. Adv. Council, Rockville, 1978—; chmn. Gov.'s Com. on High Tech., Annapolis, Md., 1981-82; mem. High Tech. Roundtable, Annapolis, 1982-86, Gov.'s Com. on Excellence in Higher Edn., Annapolis, 1986-87; bd. dirs. Montgomery County High Tech. Council, 1987—, chmn. adv. bd., Annapolis, 1989—. Served to capt. USAF, 1964-67. Bus. exec. fellow Brookings Instn., 1982—; named one of Outstanding Young Men of Am., NYU, 1971; recipient Disting. Service award Georgetown MBA Program, 1987. Mem. ABA, Fed. Communications Bar Assn. Roman Catholic. Club: Georgetown (Washington). Office: Shaw Pittman Potts & Trowbridge 2300 N St NW Washington DC 20037

DEAN, CAROL CARLSON, accountant, educator; b. Ft. Worth, Aug. 1, 1944; d. Virgil Harry and Katherine Augusta (Staring) Carlson; m. William Franklin Dean, June 17, 1966; children: William Carlson, Kelly Meredith Carlson. BBA in Acctg., Midwestern State U., Wichita Falls, Tex., 1966, MBA, 1987. Acct. Parkland Meml. Hosp., Dallas, 1966-67; mortgage intern, acct. Fed. Nat. Mortgage Assn., Dallas, 1967-69; acct., bus. mgr. Wichita Falls Cardiovascular Assocs., 1984-87; instr. Midwestern State U., Wichita Falls, 1987—. Co-editor Texas Medical Association Auxilary Mag., 1988—. Mem. adv. bd., TEXPAC rep. Wichita County Med. Soc. Aux., 1979-80, pres., 1983-84; bd. dirs. YMCA, Wichita Falls, 1980-87, chmn. ann. membership and sustaining fund drive, 1988; chmn. Archer County Reps., Tex., 1984-87; apptd. to Com. for Health Care Reimbursement Alternatives for Tex., Mil. Acad. Appointment Com., Congl. Dist. 13, Tex. Republican. Roman Catholic. Office: Midwestern State U Div Bus Adminstrn 3400 Taft Blvd Wichita Falls TX 76308

DEAN, CHARLES HENRY, JR., government official; b. Knoxville, Tenn., Oct. 22, 1925; s. Charles Henry and Helen (Ford) D.; m. Lottie Lavender, Dec. 30, 1947; children: Helen, James Miles, Camille. Student, U. Tenn., 1943-44; B.S., U.S. Naval Acad., 1947. Sales rep. Knoxville Fertilizer Co., Dean-Planters Warehouses, 1950-59; with Knoxville Utilities Bd., 1959-81, gen. mgr., 1971-81; chmn. bd. TVA, 1981-88, bd. dirs., 1988—. Past pres. Knoxville Tourist Bur.; past chmn. Chancellors' Assos., U. Tenn.; bd. dirs. Electric Power Research Inst. Served with USMC, 1947-50. Recipient Profl. Mgrs. Citation Soc. Advancement Mgmt., 1972, Eminent Engr. award Tau Beta Pi, 1983. Mem. Am. Public Power Assn. (past dir.), Nat. Soc. Profl. Engrs., Tenn. Valley Public Power Assn. (past pres.). Republican. Presbyterian. Clubs: Civitan (past pres.), Racquet (past pres.) (Knoxville); LeConte (bd. govs.). Office: TVA 400 W Summit Hill Dr Knoxville TN 37902

DEAN, HARVEY RAY, catalog company executive; b. Pauls Valley, Okla., Dec. 16, 1943; s. George and Oleta Fern (Wallen) D.; m. Sharon Kay Terrell, July 3, 1963; childre: Barry, Krista, Jered. BS, East Cen. State U., 1965; MS, Pitts. State U., 1970; EdD, U. Ark., 1985. Instr. Weleetka (Okla.) Pub. Schs., 1965-69; dir. rsch. Kans. Dept. Edn., Topeka, 1971-74, facilitator, 1974-75; chief exec. officer, pres. PITSCO, Inc., Pittsburg, Kans., 1975—; dir. Ctr. for Tech. Transfer, Pitts. Author: Manufacturing: Industries and Careers, 1975, Numerical Control, 1982. Adv. coun. Pitts. State U. Sch.

Tech., 1985—; bd. dirs. Tourette Syndrome Assn., Bayside, N.Y., 1988—, pres., 1988—. Recipient Meritorious Service award Am. Indsl. Arts Studies Assn., 1980, Presdl. award Tech. Edn. Collegiate Assn., 1988. Mem. Optimist (lt. gov. 1973-74). Republican.

DEAN, HELEN BARBARA, sales executive; b. Roanoke, Va., Apr. 10, 1945; d. George William and Hestenia B. (Motley) Ferguson; m. Robert L. Dean, June 1972. BS, Knoxville Coll., 1967. Tchr. Hart Jr. High Sch., Washington, 1967-69; system analyst IBM, Indpls., 1969-72; adminstv. aide Ind. U., Bloomington, 1972-74; with sales mktg. dept. Redactron, Indpls., 1974-75; trainer Xerox, Chgo., 1975-77, mgr. branch support, 1977-79; mgr. nat. support Xerox, Dallas, 1979-82; mgr. regional sales Xerox, Chgo., 1982-85; sr. v.p. Thomson Fin. Network, Newton, Mass., 1985—. Democrat. Presbyterian. Home: 236 Congress St Milford MA 01757 Office: Thomson Fin Networks 85 Wells Ave Newton MA 02159

DEAN, HOWARD M., JR., food company executive; b. 1937; married. B.B.A., So. Meth. U., 1960; M.B.A., Northwestern U., 1961. With Dean Foods Co., Inc., Franklin Park, Ill., 1955—, internal auditor, 1965-68, asst. to v.p. fin., 1968-70, pres., 1970-89, also dir., chief exec. officer, 1987—, chmn., 1989—. Served to lt. (j.g.) USN, 1962-65. Office: Dean Foods Co 3600 N River Rd Franklin Park IL 60131 *

DEAN, JACK PEARCE, insurance company executive; b. Shreveport, La., Aug. 26, 1931; s. James Albert and Nina (Smith) D.; m. Elizabeth Anne Tillman, June 5, 1952; children—Linda Susan Dean Ratchford, Cynthia Anne Dean Thomas, James David. B.S. in Bus. Adminstrn., Acctg., La. Tech. U., Ruston, 1951. C.P.A. Audit supr. Peat, Marwick, Mitchell & Co., C.P.A.s, New Orleans and Jackson, Miss., 1958-63; treas. Lamar Life Ins. Co., Jackson, 1963-64, v.p., treas., 1964-68, sr. v.p., treas., 1968-73, pres., 1973—, also dir.; v.p. Lamar Life Corp., 1972-73, pres., 1973-83, chmn. bd., 1983-88; dir. Am. Council of Life Ins., Washington, 1978-81. Pres. United Way of Capital Area, Jackson, 1975, v.p., 1974, campaign chmn., 1973; pres. Goodwill Industries of Miss., Jackson, 1972; chmn. Life Ins. Polit. Action Com., 1981-84. Named Outstanding Alumnus of Yr., Coll. of Adminstrn. and Bus., La. Tech. U., 1974; recipient Service to Humanity award Miss. Coll., 1978, Vol. Activist award D.H. Holmes/Germaine Monteil, 1987. Mem. Am. Inst. CPA's, Soc. La. CPA's, Miss. Soc. CPA's, Jackson C. of C. (pres. 1986, bd. dirs. 1974-76, 1981-87), Health Ins. Assn. Am. (bd. dirs. 1985-88), Miss. Life & Health Ins. Guaranty Assn. (chmn. 1986-88). Baptist. Clubs: University, Capital City Petroleum, Newcomen Soc. Miss. (Jackson). Lodge: Rotary (Jackson). Home: 2241 Wild Valley Dr Jackson MS 39211 Office: Lamar Life Ins Co PO Box 880 Jackson MS 39205

DEANE, FREDERICK, JR., banker; b. Boston, Aug. 5, 1926; s. Frederick and Julia (Coolidge) D.; m. Dorothy Legge, Dec. 21, 1948; children: Dorothy Porcher, Eleanor Dodds, Frederick III. MBA with distinction, Harvard U., 1951. With Signet Bank/Va. (formerly Bank of Va.), 1953—, now chmn. bd. dirs.; chmn. bd. dirs. Signet Banking Corp.; bd. dirs. CSX Corp., Marriott Corp.; mem. fed. adv. council Fed. Res. System. Bd. dirs. Va. Mus. Found., Va. Found. Ind. Colls., United Way Greater Richmond, Chesapeake Bay Found., VA. Diocesan Ctr.; co-chmn. Richmond, Nat. Conf. Christians and Jews. Mem. Assn. Res. City Bankers, Assn. Bank Holding Cos. (chmn. 1979-80), Richmond Soc. Fin. Analysts, Conf. Bd. (chmn. So. regional council), Bank Capital Markets Assn. (vice chmn. com. competitive securities markets). Republican. Episcopalian. Clubs: Harvard of Va, Harvard Bus. Sch. of Va; Hasty Pudding-Inst. 1770, Delphic (Harvard); Commonwealth, Country of Va. (Richmond); Harvard, Brook (N.Y.C.); Mid Ocean (Bermuda); Burning Tree (Bethesda, Md.); Metropolitan (Washington); Country of Fla. Home: 4807 Lock Green Circle Richmond VA 23226 Office: Signet Banking Corp 7 N 8th St PO Box 25970 Richmond VA 23260

DEANGELIS, JOSEPH ANTHONY, personnel director; b. Greenfield, Mass., Mar. 22, 1955; s. Joseph John and Shirley (Aldrich) DeA.; m. Cynthia Jaye Horn, June 24, 1978. BS cum laude, Springfield Coll., 1977, MEd, 1978. Mgr. human resources GTE Comml. Electronics Corp., Waltham, Mass., 1979-81; mgr. western region human resources GTE Products Corp., Glendale, Calif., 1981-84; mgr. div. human resources GTE Products Corp., Manchester, N.H., 1984-85; sr. v.p. human resources First N.H. Banks, Inc., Manchester, 1985—. Chmn. Friends of Odyssey, Hampton, N.H., 1987—. Mem. Am. Mgmt. Assn., Greater Manchester Personnel Assn., Currier Gallery of Art, Psi Chi. Republican. Roman Catholic. Club: Manchester Country. Lodge: Elks. Home: 5 Sutton Pl Londonderry NH 03053 Office: First NH Banks Inc 1000 Elm St Manchester NH 03105

DEARMON, THOMAS ALFRED, automotive industry financial executive, life insurance executive; b. Montgomery, Ala., Dec. 28, 1937; s. Thomas A. and Rose (Giardina) D.; m. Leigh Caroline Smith, Dec. 28, 1963; children—Jacob Thomas, Joshua Carter. B.B.A., U. Okla, 1961; J.D., Oklahoma City U., 1968. Bar: Okla. 1968. C.P.A., Okla. Audit mgr. Arthur Andersen & Co., Oklahoma City, 1961-68; account exec. F.I. DuPont, Oklahoma City, 1968-73; v.p., sec. Fred Jones, Inc. and Fred Jones Mfg. Co., 1973—; v.p., sec. FOLIC, Inc. and First Okla. Life Ins. Co., 1987—; pres., bd. dirs. Century Mgmt. Co., Century Life Assurance, Oklahoma City, 1983—, Century Property and Casualty Ins. 1987—, Century Producers Life Ins., 1988—; mem. investment com. Fred Jones Industries, a Ltd. Partnership, Oklahoma City, 1985—; sec., bd. dirs. Hist. Preservation Inc., Oklahoma City, 1984—. Served with U.S. Army, 1963. Mem. Okla. Bar Assn., Okla. Soc. CPA's, Fin. Execs. Inst. Democrat. Methodist. Lodge: Downtown Lions (pres. 1985-86). Office: 123 S Hudson St Oklahoma City OK 73102

DE ARMOND, DAVID LEE, stress management company executive; b. San Mateo, Calif., May 7, 1955; s. Gene Vincent and Gerda (Hundevadt) De A. MA, Maharishi Internat. U., 1979, MBA, 1985. Exec. gov. Maharishi Internat. U., Fairfield, Iowa, 1977-82; v.p. The Purusha Group, Washington, 1982-84, pres., 1984-86; chief exec. officer Stress Mgmt. Assocs., Livingston Manor, N.Y., 1986—; bd. dirs. World Plan Exec. Council, Washington; cons. Corp. Devel. Program, Washington, 1985-86, Ayurvedic Products, Stoneham, Mass., 1986-88, Global Trading Group, N.Y.C., 1987—. Editor: Collected Papers, 1977; contbr. articles to various publs. Mem. AAAS, Creative Intelligence (pres. 1974-77), Inst. Advanced Research (bd. dirs. 1986—). Republican. Home: PO Box 370 Livingston Manor NY 12758

DEARTH, ROBERT ALFRED, JR., food processing executive; b. Birmingham, Ala., July 15, 1944; s. Robert Alfred and Regina (Miller) D.; m. Barbara Jane Nacci, June 22, 1968; children: Matthew Louis, Christopher Miller. BA, Wesleyan U., Middletown, Conn., 1966; MBA, U. Va., 1968. Office asst. Adam Opel Ag. (div. of Gen. Motors), Russelsheim, Fed. Republic Germany, 1965; engr., change control clk. Ford Motor Co., Dearborn, Mich., 1966, market survey analyst, 1967, cost analyst, 1968-70, budget analyst fin. staff, 1970-71, treasury analyst, 1971-72, treasury supr., 1972-73, supr. controllers dept., 1973-75; mgr. fin. planning and analysis Getty Refining and Mktg., N.Y.C., 1975-77; dir. fin. analysis United Brands Co., N.Y.C., 1977-79, asst. treas., 1979-82; v.p., chief adminstrv. officer United Brands Co., Cin., 1988—; sr. v.p., chief fin. officer John Morrell & Co., Northfield, Ill., 1983-88; mem. regional adv. bd. Arkwright Mut. Ins. Co., Boston, 1987—. Trustee Chi Psi Ednl. Trust, Ann Arbor, Mich., 1985—; treas. Boy Scouts Am., Winnetka, Ill., 1986-87. Home: 2900 Grandin Rd Cincinnati OH 45208

DEASY, THERESA, law firm financial executive; b. N.Y.C., May 19, 1958; d. Thomas Edward Deasy and Dorothy Beatrice (Federico) Deasy Cox; m. Dennis James Stanton, May 29, 1983. BS in Commerce, DePaul U., 1981; postgrad. Keller Grad. Sch. Bus. Acctg. clk. Kirkland & Ellis, Chgo., 1977-80; fin. div. clk. Talman Home Fed. Savs. & Loan, Chgo., 1980-81; staff acctg. Sachnoff Weaver & Rubenstien, Chgo., 1981-83, asst. controller, 1984-86, controller, 1987—. Vol. dir., treas. The Commons of Evanston, 1985-87; leader Ravenswood Hosp. Mental Health Ctr., Chgo., 1984 . Mem. Assn. Legal Adminstrs., Am. Soc. Women Accts., Digital Equipment Corp. Users Soc., Nat. Assn. Female Execs., Chgo. Council Fgn. Relations, Ill. Notaries Assn., Assn. Legal Adminstrn., Law Office Mgrs. Assn. Avocations: travel, photography, skiing, racquetball. Home: 1408 W Norwood Chicago IL 60660 Office: Sachnoff Weaver & Rubenstein Ltd 30 S Wacker Dr 29th Fl Chicago IL 60606

DEASY, WILLIAM JOHN, corporate executive; b. N.Y.C., June 22, 1937; s. Jeremiah and Margaret (Quinn) D.; m. Carol Ellyn Lemmons, Feb. 1, 1963; children: Cameron, Kimberly. B.S. in Civil Engring, Cooper Union, 1958; LL.B., U. Wash., 1963. With Morrison Knudsen Corp., Boise, Idaho, 1964-88, v.p. N.W. region, 1972-75, v.p. mining, 1975-78, group v.p. mining, 1978-83, exec. v.p. mining, shipbuilding and mfg., 1983-84, pres., chief operating officer, 1984-85, dir., chmn., pres., chief exec. officer, 1985-88; bd. dirs. Moore Fin. Group, Boise. Mem. adv. bd. Sch. Bus. Boise State U.; trustee, bd. dirs. St. Luke's Med. Ctr. Mem. Soc. Mining Engrs., Soc. Mil. Engrs., Beavers, Moles. Home: 4611 Hillcrest Dr Boise ID 83705 Office: 1st Interstate Ctr 877 W Main St Boise ID 83702

DEATON, TAMMIE LYNN, investment company representative; b. Arkadelphia, Ark., Jan. 24, 1964; d. Max Wyndell and Joyce Elaine (Brown) D. BSBA, U. Ark., 1986. Sec. Belva Deramus, Mena, Ark., 1982; tchr. asst. U. Ark., Fayetteville, 1982-85; personnel coordinator Dunhill Personnel, Little Rock, 1986; adminstrv. asst. Fidelity Investments, Dallas, 1987—. Mem. NAFE. Baptist. Office: Fidelity Investments 400 E Las Colinas Blvd Irving TX 75039

DEBARDELABEN, LOLA ALICE, accountant, consultant; b. Chgo., June 12, 1945; d. Loren Curtis and Anna Mae (Neason) Morris; m. James C. DeBardelaben, Sept. 3, 1966 (div. Aug. 1973); children: Sean, James. BS, DePaul U., 1979. Asst. controller Playboy Hotels, Chgo., 1974-76; acct. Sportsman's Inn, Chgo., 1976-78, Drexel, Burnham, Lambert, Chgo., 1979-82, Triangle Service Co., Chgo., 1982-84, On The Scene, Inc., Chgo., 1984—. Chairperson 21st Ward Women's Aux. Com., Chgo., 1984—. Mem. Nat. Assn. for Female Execs. Club: Chgo. Idlewilders. Home: 9608 S Emerald Chicago IL 60628 Office: On the Scene 505 N LaSalle St Ste 550 Chicago IL 60610

DEBARDELEBEN, JOHN THOMAS, JR., insurance company executive; b. Ft. Benning, Ga., Aug. 28, 1926; s. John Thomas and Erin Gautier (Howard) DeB.; m. Martha Evelyn Graves, Sept. 24, 1946; children: John T. III, Charles G., Eve Lamar. B.A., Vanderbilt U., 1947. C.L.U., Am. Coll., 1963. Agt., asst. mgr. N.Y. Life Ins. Co., Nashville and Chattanooga, 1951-56; gen. mgr. N.Y. Life Ins. Co., Knoxville, Tenn., Savannah, Ga. and Montgomery, Ala., 1957-70; regional v.p. N.Y. Life Ins. Co., Chgo., 1971-76; v.p. N.Y. Life Ins. Co., N.Y.C., 1976-78, sr. v.p., 1978-82, exec. v.p., 1982—; bd. dirs. N.Y. Life & Health Ins. Co., N.Y. Life Internat. Investments, N.Y. Life Found., Hillhouse Assocs., Austin, Tex., Madison Benefit Adminstrs., Charlotte, N.C., Sanus Corp. Health Systems, N.Y.C.; chmn. bd. dirs. Corp. Med. Mgmt., Dublin, Ohio. Mem. Republican County Com., Montgomery, Ala., 1963-64; active Crusade of Mercy, Chgo., 1972-75, United Way of Tri-State, N.Y.C., 1979-81. Mem. Nat. Assn. Life Underwriters, Am. Soc. C.L.U.s, Gen. Agts. and Mgrs. Conf., Montgomery, Chgo. chambers of commerce. Office: NY Life Ins Co 51 Madison Ave New York NY 10010

DEBEAUCHAMP, JOSEPH LOUIS, investment company executive; b. Seattle, Feb. 5, 1949; s. Robert Louis and Barbara (Mabee) DeB.; m. Deborah Sue Dec. 20, 1980; 1 child: Michelle Marie. BS, U. Nev., 1970, MS, 1972. Cert. Fin. Planner, 1988. Pvt. practice investments Las Vegas, Nev., 1972-79; v.p. investments Wedbush Securities Inc., Las Vegas, 1979—; mgmt. asst. council Wedbush Noble Cooke Inc., Los Angeles, 1979—, due diligence council, 1981—; v.p. mktg. Wedbush Noble Cooke Inc., Seattle, 1986, registered prin., 1986. Named Man of Yr. PLM, Jamaica, 1984-86, Man of Yr. Wedbush, Los Angeles, 1983-86, Man of Yr. Bogert, Okla., 1985-86; named to Leader Council Oppenheimer, N.Y., 1980-86. Mem. Fin. Profl. Adv. Panel, Profl. Ins. Assn., Nat. Assn. Profl. Accts., Internat. Assn. Fin. Planners, IAPF (fin. profl. adv. panel, legal regulatory com.), Nat. Assn. Pub. Accts., Seattle Fin. Analysts Soc., Internat. Fin. Analysts Assn. Republican. Congregationalist. Club: Short Wave Listeners (local pres. 1980—). Home: 801 Deercliff Rd Banbridge Island WA 98110 Office: Wedbush Inc 1001 Fourth Ave Suite 3040 Seattle WA 98154

DEBENEDICTIS, NICHOLAS, JR., chamber of commerce executive; b. Lansdowne, Pa., Sept. 15, 1945; s. Nicholas Sr. and Mildred (Caggiano) DeB.; m. Eileen Marie Sweeney, Mar. 20, 1969; children: Dana, Bret. BSBA, Drexel U., 1968, MS in Environ. Engring. and Scis., 1969, D of Bus. Adminstrn., 1987; DSc (hon.), Widener U., 1987. Supr. engring. U.S. EPA, Phila., 1972-76, dir. internal relations, 1976-80, asst. regional adminstr., 1980-81; exec. dir. Gov.'s Econ. Devel. Com., State of Pa., 1981-83, sec. dept. environ. resources, 1983-86; pres. Greater Phila. C. of C., 1986—; mem. Corp. Lobbying Com.; pres. policy com. City of Phila.; pres. Convention and Visitors Bur., Phila., 1986—, Greater Phila. 1st Corp.; mem. adv. bd. Drexel U. Sch. Civil Engring., U. Pa. Sch. Engring. and Applied Scis.; bd. dirs. Civil Service Nominating Com., Pa. Environ. Council, Inc., Pa. Resources Council, Pa. State Job Tng. Coordinating Council, Pa. Area Labor Mgmt. Com., Phila. Surburban Water Co. Pres. PhilaPride, The Pride of Phila., Phila. Indsl. Devel. Corp., Phila. Port Corp., Greater Phila. Econ. Devel. Coalition, Delaware Valley Regional Planning Commn., Pvt. Industry Council, Inc., 1986-88; mem. Pa. Polit. Action Com.; ex-officio Internat. Visitors Ctr. Phila.; bd. dirs. Boy Scouts Am., Cen. Phila. Devel. Corp., Coombs Coll. Music, 1986—, Nat. Conf. Christians and Jews, Ctr. City Office Space Rev. Com., Opportunities Industrialization Ctr., Inc., Phila. Health Mgmt. Corp., 1987—, Fairmount Park Commn. Adv. Com., 1987-88, West Chester Univ. Adv. Council, 1988—, Water Resources Assn. of Delaware River Basin. Mem. Am. Soc. Mil. Engrs., Pa. Soc., Greater Phila. Internat. Network, Inc. (bd. dirs.), Union League of Phila. Home: 4145 Apalogen Rd Philadelphia PA 19144 Office: Greater Phila C of C 1346 Chestnut St Ste 800 Philadelphia PA 19107

DEBERGE, GARY ALAN, metal processing company executive; b. Elgin, Ill., Sept. 16, 1947; s. Roy P. and Grace S. (Strom) DeB.; m. Ellen Kay Harrison, June 14, 1969; children: Timothy, Steven, Julie. BA, Ill. Wesleyan U., 1969. With Pre Finish Metals Inc., Elk Grove Vilage, Ill., 1969—; sales mgr. Pre Finish Metals Inc., Elk Grove Vilage, 1978, mktg. mgr., 1979-80, v.p. sales, 1981—. Coach Barrington (Ill.) Little League, 1980-83, Barrington Pony League, 1984-86; v.p. Barrington High Sch. Quarterback Club, 1985-88. Mem. Nat. Coil Coaters Assn., Inverness Club, Chgo. Soc. Clubs. Office: Pre Finish Metals Inc 2300 E Pratt Blvd Elk Grove Village IL 60007

DE BLASIO, MICHAEL PETER, electronics company executive; b. N.Y.C., Jan 15, 1937; s. Louis Leonard and Helen Virginia (Pomidoro) De B.; m. Kathleen Elizabeth O'Reilly, Oct. 20, 1962; 1 dau., Deirdre Noel. B.B.A. cum laude, St. Francis Coll., 1958; postgrad. CCNY, 1966-68. C.P.A., N.Y. Mgr. Touche, Ross & Co., N.Y.C., 1959-68; v.p., treas. Elgin Nat. Industries, Chgo., 1968-73; sr. v.p.-fin. Loral Corp., N.Y.C., 1973—, v.p., dir. subs. Conic Corp., San Diego, 1976—, Frequency Sources, Boston, 1980—, Narda Microwave, N.Y.C., 1983—, Loral Electo-Optics, Los Angeles, 1983—. Recipient Acctg. gold medal Archdiocese N.Y., 1958. Mem. N.Y. State Soc. C.P.A.s (chmn. various coms.), Fin. Execs. Inst., Am. Inst. C.P.A.s, Nat. Assn. Accts. Republican. Roman Catholic. Clubs: Westchester Country (N.Y.); Pinacle (N.Y.C.). Home: Park Dr S Rye NY 10580 Office: Loral Corp 600 3rd Ave New York NY 10016

DEBOCK, FLORENT ALPHONSE, corporation controller; b. LaLouviere, Belgium, Feb. 3, 1924; came to U.S., 1954, naturalized, 1959; s. Benoit and Elvire (Verbeke) DeB.; m. Mary C. Murray, July 2, 1960; 1 child, Mark Steven. Tchr. diploma, Inst. Ste. Marie, Arlon, Belgium, 1944; Accountant diploma, Inst. Professionel Superieur de Belgique, 1953; postgrad., La Salle Extension U., Chgo., 1956. CPA, D.C. Govt. auditor U.S. Army Audit Agy., Engr. Procurement Center, Europe, 1946-54; auditor Touche, Ross, Bailey & Smart, N.Y.C., 1954-61; controller Armor Elevator Co. (and affiliates), Queens, N.Y., 1962-64; controller subsidiary of Eaton, Yale & Towne, Dusseldorf, Germany, 1964-67; group controller bus. furnishings group Litton Industries, N.Y.C., 1967-68; controller Levitt & Sons, homebldg. div. ITT, Lake Success, N.Y., 1969-71, Intermodulex NDH Corp., White Plains, N.Y., 1971-74, Watch Case Corp. div. Zale Corp., Long Island City, N.Y., 1974-82; corp. controller Am. Gemsmiths, Inc., N.Y.C., N.Y., 1982-86; controller Loren Rings, Inc., N.Y.C., 1986—, Budoff Inc., Secaucus, N.J., 1986—. Served with inf. Belgian Army, 1945-46. Decorated War of 1940-45 Commemorative medal, 1940-45 Vol. medal. Mem. Am. Inst. CPA's, N.Y. State Soc. CPA's, Nat. Assn. Accountants. Home: 123 99th St Brooklyn NY 11209 Office: Budoff Inc 1375 Paterson Plank Rd Secaucus NJ 07094

DEBOIS, JAMES ADOLPHUS, lawyer; b. Oklahoma City, Dec. 23, 1929; s. James D. and Catherine (Bobo) DeB.; m. Mary Catherine Watkins, Aug. 4, 1951; children—James Adolphus Jr., Catherine Cecile, Annette Marie. B.A. in Liberal Arts, Okla. State U., 1951; LL.B., Okla., U., 1955. Bar: Okla. 1954, U.S. Dist. Ct. (ea. dist.) Okla. 1955, U.S. Dist. Ct. (we. dist.) Okla. 1959, Mo. 1963, N.Y. 1965, U.S. Ct. Appeals (8th cir.) 1969, Calif. 1971, U.S. Ct. Appeals (9th cir.) 1971, U.S. Ct. Appeals (D.C. cir.) 1975, U.S. Supreme Ct. 1976. Atty. Southwestern Bell Telephone Co., Oklahoma City, 1959-63, St. Louis, 1963-64, gen. atty., Oklahoma City, 1965-67, gen. solicitor, St. Louis, 1967-70; atty. AT&T, N.Y.C., 1964-65, gen. atty., 1976, gen. atty., Basking Ridge, N.J., 1976-78, assoc. gen. counsel, 1978-83, corp. v.p. law, 1985—; v.p. legal dept. Pacific Telephone and Telegraph Co., San Francisco, 1970-71, v.p., gen. counsel, 1971-76; v.p., gen. counsel, sec. AT&T Info. Systems Inc. (formerly Am. Bell Inc.), Morristown, N.J., 1983-85. Served to lt. USAF, 1951-53, Korea. Mem. ABA (chmn. pub. utility law sect. 1985-86), Calif. Bar Assn., San Francisco Bar Assn. (sect. chmn. corp. law dept. 1975). Episcopalian. Club: Baltusrol (bd. govs. Springfield, N.J. 1982-88). Office: AT&T Techs Inc 1 Oak Way Rm 4ED118 Berkeley Heights NJ 07922

DEBREU, GERARD, educator, economist; b. Calais, France, July 4, 1921; came to U.S., 1950, naturalized, 1975; s. Camille and Fernande (Decharne) D.; m. Françoise Bled, June 14, 1945; children: Chantal, Florence. Student, Ecole Normale Supérieure, Paris, 1941-44, Agrégé de l'Université, 1946; DSc, U. Paris, 1956; Dr. Rerum Politicarum honoris causa, U. Bonn, 1977; D. Scis. Economiques (hon.), U. Lausanne, 1980; DSc (hon.), Northwestern U., 1981; Dr. honoris causa, U. des Scis. Sociales de Toulouse, 1983, Yale U., 1987, U. Bordeaux I, 1988. Research assoc. Centre Nat. De La Recherche Sci., Paris, 1946-48; Rockefeller fellow U.S., Sweden and Norway, 1948-50; research assoc. Cowles Commn., U. Chgo., 1950-55; assoc. prof. econs. Cowles Found., Yale, 1955-61; fellow Center Advanced Study Behavioral Scis., 1960-61; vis. prof. econs. Yale U., fall 1961; prof. econs. U. Calif. at Berkeley, 1962—, prof. math., 1975—, Univ. prof., 1985—; Guggenheim fellow, vis. prof. Center Ops. Research and Econometrics, U. Louvain, 1968-69, vis. prof., 1971, 72, 88; Erskine fellow U. Canterbury, Christchurch, New Zealand, 1969, 87, vis. prof., 1973; Overseas fellow Churchill Coll., Cambridge, Eng., 1972; vis. prof. Cowles Found. for Research in Econs., Yale U., 1976; vis. prof. U. Bonn, 1977; research assoc. CEPREMAP, Paris, 1980; faculty research lectr. U. Calif. Berkeley, 1984-85, univ. prof., 1985—; Class of 1958 chair U. Calif., Berkeley, 1986—; vis. prof. U. Sydney, Australia, 1987. Author: Theory of Value, 1959, Mathematical Economics: Twenty Papers of Gerard Debreu, 1983; Assoc. editor: Internat. Econ. Rev, 1959-69; mem. editorial bd.: Jour. Econ. theory, 1972—, Games and Econ. Behavior, 1989—; mem. adv. bd.: Jour. Math. Econs, 1974—. Served with French Army, 1944-45. Decorated chevalier Légion d'Honneur; recipient Nobel Prize in Econ. Scis., 1983, Commandeur de l'Ordre du Merite, 1984; sr. U.S. Scientist awardee Alexander von Humboldt Found. Fellow AAAS, Econometric Soc. (pres. 1971), Am. Econ. Assn. (disting. fellow 1982, pres.-elect 1989); mem. NAS (com. human rights 1984—), Am. Philos. Soc., French Acad. Scis. (fgn. assoc.). Office: U Calif Dept Econs Berkeley CA 94720

DEBRUNNER, GERALD JOSEPH, accounting firm executive; b. Cin., Nov. 1, 1937; s. Richard Joseph and Alberta B. (Naberhaus) DeB.; m. Nancy Karen Schlie, Oct. 5, 1963; children: Anne, David, Katharine, Mark, Mary. BSBA, Xavier U., 1959. CPA, Ohio. Staff acct. DeLoitte Haskins & Sells, Cin., 1959-67, mgr., 1967-73, ptnr., 1973-79, 1979-85, area mng. ptnr., 1985-86, vice chmn., regional mng. ptnr., 1986—; bd. trustees Xavier U., Ohio. Chmn. Jr. Achievement, Cin., 1981-82, Greater Cin. Ctr. for Econ. Edn., 1986—; pres. Downtown Council, Cin., 1987—. Served as sgt. USAR, 1960-66. Mem. Am. Inst. CPA's, Ohio Soc. CPA's, Queen City Club. Roman Catholic. Clubs: Kenwood Country (Cin.) (bd. dirs. 1985-86), Cin. Country. Home: 11275 Ironwood Ct Cincinnati OH 45249 Office: Deloitte Haskins & Sells PO Box 85340 Cincinnati OH 45201-5340

DEBS, RICHARD A., investment banker, government official; b. Providence, Oct. 7, 1930; s. Abraham George and Madge (Fatool) D.; m. Barbara Knowles, July 19, 1958; children: Elizabeth Anderson, Nicholas. B.A. summa cum laude, Colgate U., 1952; postgrad. (Fulbright scholar), Cairo U., 1952-53; M.A., Princeton U., 1956, Ph.D., 1963; LL.B., Harvard U., 1958, grad. Advanced Mgmt. Program, Harvard U. Grad. Sch. Bus. Adminstrn., 1973. Bar: N.Y. 1960. Researcher joint project Harvard-Princeton, 1958-59; with Fed. Res. Bank of N.Y., N.Y.C., 1960-76; legal dept. Fed. Res. Bank of N.Y., 1960-64, asst. counsel, 1964-69, sec. of bank, 1965-69, v.p. govt. bonds and securities, 1969-72, v.p. loans and credits, 1969-72, v.p. open market ops., 1972, sr. v.p., 1973, 1st v.p., chief adminstrv. officer, 1973-76; alt. mem. Fed. Open Market Com., 1973-76; mng. dir. Morgan Stanley & Co., Inc., 1976-87; pres. Morgan Stanley Internat. Inc., 1976-87; chmn. R.A. Debs & Co., 1987—; adv. dir. Morgan Stanley Group, 1987—; chmn. The Malaysia Fund Inc., 1987—; bd. dirs. IBJ Schroder Bank & Trust Co., 1987—; advisor Bank Julius Baer, 1987—, United Gulf Group (Kuwait), 1987—; chmn. com. fiscal agy. ops. Fed. Res. System, 1969-76; mem. Fed. Res. Steering Com. on Payments Mechanism, 1973-76, Fed. Res. Steering Com. on Internat. Banking, 1973-76; allied mem. N.Y. Stock Exchange, also chmn. adv. com. internat. capital markets; mem. com. multinat. enterprises U.S. council Internat. Bus.; mem. internat. capital markets adv. com. Fed. Res. Bank of N.Y.; mem. Nat. Commn. on Pub. Service (The Volcker Commn.); mem. Overseas Devel. Council; mem. Take Stock in Am. Com., 1973-76; mem. Egypt-U.S. Bus. Council.; mem. adv. council Near Eastern program Princeton U.; mem. N.Y. State Savs. Bond Com., 1973-76; adv. council Am. Inst. Banking, 1973-76. Contbr. articles on internat. banking to profl. publs. Chmn. emeritus, trustee Carnegie Hall; bd. dirs. Fedn. Protestant Welfare Agys.; trustee Carnegie Endowment for Internat. Peace, Am. Univs. Field Staff; trustee Am. U., Beirut, vice chmn., from 1981; bd. dirs. Am. Council on Germany; mem. vis. com. Middle East Center Harvard U., 1976-82, mem. vis. com. Ctr. for Internat. Affairs; mem. Group of 30; also mem. exec. com. Bretton Woods Com.; mem. bus. steering com. U.S.-Saudi Joint Econ. Commn. Mem. ABA (com. Middle Eastern law), Assn. Bar City N.Y., Council Fgn. Relations, C. of C. U.S. (internat. policy com., chmn. subcom. on internat. econ. devel. 1979-87), Egyptian Am. C. of C. (chmn.), N.Y. C. of C. and Industry, Japan Soc., Asia Soc., Fgn. Policy Assn. (bd. govs.), Phi Beta Kappa Assocs. Clubs: Economic, Century Assn. (N.Y.C.); Larchmont Yacht (N.Y.).

DEBUS, ELEANOR VIOLA, business management company executive; b. Buffalo, May 19, 1920; d. Arthur Adam and Viola Charlotte (Pohl) D.; student Chown Bus. Sch., 1939. Sec., Buffalo Wire Works, 1939-45; home talent producer Empire Producing Co., Kansas City, Mo., sec. Owens Corning Fiberglass, Buffalo; public relations and publicity Niagara Falls Theatre, Ont., Can.; pub. relations dir. Woman's Internat. Bowling Congress, Columbus, Ohio, 1957-59; publicist, sec. Ice Capades, Hollywood, Calif., 1961-63; sec. to controller Rexall Drug Co., Los Angeles, 1963-67; bus. mgmt. acct. Samuel Berke & Co., Beverly Hills, Calif., 1967-75; Gadbois Mgmt. Co., Beverly Hills, 1975-76; sec., treas. Sasha Corp., Los Angeles, 1976—; bus. mgr. Dean Martin, Shirley MacLaine, Debbie Reynolds; pres. Tempo Co., Los Angeles, 1976—. Mem. Nat. Assn. Female Execs., Nat. Notary Assn., Nat. Film Soc., Am. Film Inst. Republican. Lodge: Order Eastern Star. Contbr. articles to various mags. Office: Tempo Co 1900 Avenue of Stars #1230 Los Angeles CA 90067

DE CARBONNEL, FRANÇOIS ERIC, management consultant; b. Paris, Dec. 7, 1946; s. Charles Eric and Elizabeth (Chevreux) De C.; diploma Ecole Centrale, Lyon, France, 1970; M.S. in Indsl. Adminstrn. (Smith award), Carnegie-Mellon U., 1972; m. L. Vercambre, Feb. 16, 1968; children—Geoffroy, Antoine, Thomas, Matthieu. With Boston Cons. Group, 1972-81, v.p., dir., Chgo., 1979-81; exec. v.p., chief operating officer Strategic Planning Assos., Inc., Washington, 1981-83, pres., 1983—. Mellon fellow 1971. Author: Les Mecanismes Fondamentaux de la Competitivite, 1980, La Victoire de Reagan, 1984. Office: 2300 N St NW Washington DC 20037

DE CASTRO, EDSON D., computer manufacturing corporation executive; b. Sept. 14, 1938; married. Grad., Lowell Technol. Inst., 1960. Engring. positions Digital Equipment Corp., 1961-68; with Data Gen. Corp., Westborough, Mass., 1968, pres., 1986—, chief exec. officer, dir., 1986—, chmn., 1986—. Office: Data Gen Corp 4400 Computer Dr Westborough MA 01580 *

DECESARE, JAMES CHARLES, pharmaceutical company executive; b. Orange, N.J., Apr. 4, 1931; s. James Charles and Sally Junita (Ray) D.; m. Gloria Brown, May 23, 1953; children: Dahmen Ray, James Charles III. BA, Syracuse U., 1953; postgrad., U. Pa., 1956-57. Mktg. trainee Merck & Co., Inc., Rahway, N.J., 1957-58; sales rep. Merck & Co., Inc., Denver, 1959-63; purchasing and materials mgmt. supr. Merck & Co., Inc., Danville, Pa., 1964-65; product mgr. Merck & Co., Inc., Rahway, 1965-66; corp. planning mgr. Schering Corp., Bloomfield, N.J., 1966-68; products mktg. mgr., Animal Health div. Schering Corp., Kenilworth, N.J., 1968-69; gen. sales mgr. Schering Corp., Kenilworth, 1970-75; v.p. mktg. Bayvet div. Cutler Labs. Inc., Kenilworth, 1975-78; pres. Bayvet div. Miles Lab., Inc., Kenilworth, 1978-84; v.p., gen. mgr. Animal Health div. Mobay Corp., Kenilworth, 1984-86; pres. Boehringer Ingelheim Animal Health Inc., St. Joseph, Mo., 1986—. Team capt. United Way, Johnson County, Kans., 1984; mem. Econ. Devel. Steering Com., St. Joseph, 1988; chmn. Kans. Legis. Affairs Com., Kansas City, Mo., 1985-86. Mem. Animal Health Inst. (exec. com. 1983-86, chmn. 1985, bd. dirs. 1980-82), St. Joseph Country Club, Barhegat Light Yacht Club. Home: 6 Eastwood Dr Saint Jospeh MO 64506 Office: Boehringer Ingelheim Animal Health Inc PO Box 999 Saint Joseph MO 64502

DECESARE, PAULA DOREEN, small business owner; b. Berlin, N.H., June 29, 1936; d. William Briry and Mildred Victoria (Sloan) Raymond; m. William Joseph DeCesare, Feb. 16, 1957; children: Jay Raymond, Mark William, Brett Patrick. Student, Jackson Coll., 1954; AA in Communication, Leland Powers Sch. Broadcasting and Speech, 1955-57. Copy writer, salesperson Sta. WHVW Radio, Hyde Park, N.Y., 1963-67; mgr. real estate Mobile Home Park, Hudson, N.Y., 1967—; pres., sole incorporator Alice in Videoland Ltd., Kingston, N.Y., 1983—; mgr. real estate numerous comml. holdings, 1967—; sales agt. Equitable Life Assurance, N.Y.C., 1975-77; account exec. sales Sta. WKIP Radio, Poughkeepsie, N.Y., 1977-83. Episcopalian. Home: 36 Roosevelt Rd Hyde Park NY 12538

DECHERD, ROBERT WILLIAM, newspaper and broadcasting executive; b. Dallas, Apr. 9, 1951; s. Henry Benjamin Jr. and Isabelle Lee (Thomason) D.; m. Maureen Healy, Jan. 25, 1975; children: William Benjamin, Audrey Maureen. BA cum laude, Harvard U., 1973. Mgmt. trainee, then asst. to exec. editor Dallas Morning News, 1973-78, exec. v.p., 1980-83; v.p. corp. adminstrn. A.H. Belo Corp., Dallas, 1978-80, exec. v.p., 1981-84, pres., chief operating officer, 1985-86, chmn., chief exec. officer, 1987—, also bd. dirs. Pres. Dallas Symphony Assn., 1979-80, Dallas Symphony Found., 1984-86; trustee St. Mark's Sch., Tex., 1979—, chmn. exec. com., 1983-85; chmn. Dallas Parks Found., 1985-87; mem. Trilateral Commn.; trustee Com. on Econ. Devel.; pres. Dallas Soc. Profl. Journalists, 1978; incorporator, pres. Freedom. of Info. Found. Tex., 1978. Office: A H Belo Corp Communications Ctr Young & Houston Sts Dallas TX 75265

DECHERT, MICHAEL SALVATORE ALFRED, architect; b. Bologna, Emilia, Italy, Aug. 18, 1958; s. Charles Richard and Anna Maria Pia (Leone) D. BS in Architecture, Cath. Univ. Am., 1979, MArch, 1981, PhD in Architecture, 1984. Registered architect, Md. Architect Architects Design Group, Lockington, Derbyshire, Eng., 1979; staff architect Arthur Cotton Moore Assocs., P.C., Washington, 1984-85, Hellmuth, Obata, Kassabaum, P.C., Washington, 1985-87; ptnr. Stowell-Dechert Assocs., P.C., Harpers Ferry, W.Va., Indian Head, Md., 1988—. Fulbright Rsch. grantee, 1987-88; U. Trento and Istituto Storico fellow, 1987-88. Mem. AIA (security desigh task force, archtl. preservation com.), ASCE, Soc. Arch. Historians. Roman Catholic. Home: 2 Rison Dr Rte 1 Indian Head MD 20640 Office: Stowell-Dechert Architects 769 Washington St Harpers Ferry WV 25425

DECKER, JAMES LUDLOW, management consultant; b. Batavia, N.Y., Nov. 5, 1923; s. James Ludlow and Ruth Adeline (Peard) D.; B.Aero.Engring., Rensselaer Poly. Inst., 1944; postgrad. Textron Advanced Mgmt. Program, Harvard U., 1974; m. Dorothy Belle Boone, Aug. 20, 1948. With The Martin Co., Balt., 1944-67; dep. mgr. Lunar Module, Apollo Office, NASA, Houston, 1963; program mgr. surface effect ship program U.S. Navy, Washington, 1967-72; v.p., gen. mgr. Bell Aerospace Can., Grand Bend, Ont., 1972-74; prin. J.L. Decker, Cons., Potomac, Md., 1974—; guest lectr. AIAA, 1972-79, Can. Aeros. and Space Inst., 1973-79, George Washington U., 1974, Royal Aero. Soc., 1972; cons. USN, Maritime Adminstrn., USCG, NRC Can., Can. Coast Guard, various corps., 1972—. Pres., Greenbrier Community Assn., 1956-57; regional chmn. Rensselaer Fund, 1982; mem. Congl. Subcom. to Rev. NASA Adv. Com. Utilization, 1987. Buffalo Alumni scholar, 1941-44; N.Y. State Regents scholar, 1941-44; registered profl. engr., Md. Mem. AIAA (asso. fellow), Soc. Naval Architects and Marine Engrs., Am. Soc. Naval Engrs., Rensselaer Soc. Engrs., N.Y. Acad. Sci., Patroons of Rensselaer, Sigma Xi, Tau Beta Pi. Republican. Presbyterian. Club: Towson Golf and Country. Contbr. articles to profl. jours.; patentee in field. Address: 12613 Newgate Rd Potomac MD 20854

DECKER, KURT HANS, lawyer, educator, researcher; b. Phila., Sept. 23, 1946; s. Hans Emil and Gertrude Elsa (Nestler) D.; m. Hilary McAllister, Aug. 13, 1973; children—Kurt Christian, Allison McAllister. B.A. in History, Thiel Coll., 1968; M.P.A., Pa. State U., 1973; J.D., Vanderbilt U., 1976; LL.M. in Labor, Temple U., 1980. Bar: Pa. 1976, U.S. Tax Ct. 1977, U.S. Ct. Internat. Trade 1977, U.S. Ct. Claims 1979, U.S. Dist. Ct. (mid. dist.) Pa. 1976, U.S. Dist. Ct. (ea. dist.) Pa. 1980, U.S. Ct. Appeals (3d cir.) 1980, U.S. Supreme Ct. 1980. Asst. atty. gen. Gov.'s Office, Pa. Bur. Labor Relations, Harrisburg, 1976-79; counsel Stevens & Lee, Reading, Pa., 1979—; adj. asst. prof. Indsl. Relations St. Francis Coll., Pa., 1985—; seminar speaker Reading/Berks Area C. of C., 1980—, Dickinson Sch. Law, 1983, Reading Area Community Coll., 1985—, Gov.'s Conf. on Small Bus., 1988; researcher in field. Author: A Manager's Guide to Employee Privacy: Law, Procedures, and Policies, 1989, Employee Privacy: Law and Practice, 1987, Employee Privacy Forms and Procedures, 1988, Employment Privacy: Law, Procedures, and Policies, 1989; adminstrv. editor Vanderbilt Jour. Transnat. Law; bd. editors Jour. Collective Negotiations in Pub. Sector, 1982—; contbr. chpts. to books, articles to profl. jours. Served with U.S. Army, 1968-72. Decorated Army Commendation medal. Mem. ABA (sect. labor and employment law), Pa. Bar Assn. (sect. labor and employment law, News Media award 1985), Phila. Bar Assn., Berks County Bar Assn., Am. Soc. Personnel Adminstrn., Am. Soc. Pub. Adminstrn., Indsl. Rels. Resch. Assn., Internat. Personnel Mgmt. Assn., Sigma Phi Epsilon, Phi Alph Delta. Lutheran. Office: Stevens & Lee 607 Washington St Reading PA 19601

DECONCINI, JOHN CYRUS, labor organization executive; b. Phila., Sept. 14, 1918; s. Frank and Lillian DeConcini; children: John, Thomas, Robert, Margaret Mary, Matthew. Student pub. schs., Kulpmont, Pa. With Bakery, Confectionery and Tobacco Workers Internat. Union, AFL-CIO, CLC, Washington, 1937—; successively mem. exec. bd., sec.-treas., exec. v.p., internat. rep., internat. v.p. Bakery, Confectionery and Tobacco Workers Internat. Union, AFL-CIO, CLC, 1951-57, internat. pres., 1957—. Chmn. bd. regents New Direction, Inc. Served to 1st lt. AUS, 1941-46. Democrat. Roman Catholic. Club: D.C. Friends of Ireland. Office: Bakery Confectionary & Tobacco Workers Union 10401 Connecticut Ave Kensington MD 20895

DECOSTA, LALER COOK, II, insurance company executive; b. Orangeburg, S.C., Aug. 10, 1958; s. Laler C. and Geraldine (Stevenson) D.; m. Delithe Christine Coleman, Sept. 20, 1988. BS, U. S.C., 1980. Mgmt. trainee Security Fed. Savs. & Loan, Columbia, S.C., 1980-81, loan officer, 1981-83; field rep. Equitable Life Assurance Soc., N.Y.C., 1983-84; asst. dir. prodn. Equitable Real Estate Investment Mgmt., Atlanta, 1984-87, dir. prodn. Mem. Nat. Assn. Indsl. and Office Parks (treas. 1988—). Home: 166 Plantation Trace Woodstock GA 30188 Office: Equitable Real Estate 5775 E Peachtree Dunwoody Rd Atlanta GA 30043

DE COTRET, ROBERT RENE, Canadian government official; b. Ottawa, Ont., Can., Feb. 20, 1944; m. Diane Chenier; children: Lynne, Marc, Michel. BA, U. Ottawa, 1964; MBA, U. McGill, 1966; CPh, U. Mich., 1969. Teaching fello; sr. economist to Pres. U.S. Washington; with Conf. Bd. Can., 1972-78; minister industry and commerce Govt. Can., 1979; 1st v.p., dir. gen., exec. v.p. internat. affairs Nat. Bank Can., Montreal, Que., 1979-84; pres. Treasury Bd. Can., Ottawa, Ont., 1984-87, 89—; minister regional indsl. expansion, minister of State for sci. and tech. Govt. Can., Ottawa, 1987—. Office: House Commons, Parliament Bldgs, Ottawa, ON Canada K1A 0A6

DECOY, JOHN TERRANCE, controller; b. Bellaire, Ohio, Dec. 3, 1949; s. Angelo and Margaret Ann (Flanagan) DeC.; m. Rosemary Batdorf, June 5, 1976; children: Angela Marie, Brian Matthew, Katherine Lee. BS in Fin., Miami U., Oxford, Ohio, 1972. Cert. Mgmt. Acct. Pa., Miss., Ga. Cost acct. Lithonia Lighting, Conyers, Ga., 1972-76; plant controller Masonite Corp., Meridian, Miss., 1976-78; supr. cost acctg. Fisher Controls, Coraopolis, Pa., 1978-81; fin. auditor Joy Mfg., Pitts., 1981-82; controller Gateway Rehab. Ctr., Aliquippa, Pa., 1982—; instr. Robert Morris Coll., Pitts., 1987—. Lector Our Lady of Peace Ch., Conway, Pa., 1984—, chmn. fin. com., 1987—; umpire Am. Softball Assn., Beaver County, Pa., 1987—. Mem. Inst. Mgmt. Acctg., Healthcare Fin. Mgmt. Assn. Roman Catholic. Home: 917 5th St Baden PA 15005 Office: Gateway Rehab Ctr RR 2 Moffett Run Rd Aliquippa PA 15001

DE CRAENE, JACQUES MARIA, plastics company executive, retired judge, arbitrator; b. Gent, Belgium, May 16, 1929; s. Robert and Marthe (Rosez) de C.; m. Marie-Thérèse Claes, Feb. 24, 1954; children: Guido, Erik, Kristin. Cert. Latin-Greek, Sint-Lievenscollege, Antwerp, Belgium, 1948. Commr. Vlaams Verbond der Katholieke Scouts, Belgium, 1956; founder, owner de Craene Plastics Engring., Monaco, 1983—; RIGI Ltd., Antwerp, 1948—, RIGI-OMNIA Ltd., Antwerp, 1986—, RIGI-MEDIA, Inc., Antwerp, 1975—, Profl. Info. Media Ltd., St. Héllier, C.I., 1985—; judge Social Ct., Antwerp, 1974-82. Pub. Plastics Bull., 1972—; contbr. articles to profl. jours.; speaker in field. Mem. Soc. Plastics Engrs. (founder Benelux Sect. 1972, pres. 1978-80, exec. com. and v.p. internat. affairs 1982-88, award for meritorious services 1979), Pres.'s Cup, Plastics Engrs Arbitration Council Internat. (pres. 1982—). Roman Catholic. Home: Leopoldslei 56, B2130 Brasschaat Belgium Office: RIGI Ltd, Noorderlaan 33, B2030 Antwerp Belgium

DECRANE, ALFRED CHARLES, JR., petroleum company executive; b. Cleve., June 11, 1931; s. Alfred Charles and Verona (Marquard) DeC.; m. Joan Elizabeth Hoffman, July 3, 1954; children: David, Lisa, Stacie, Stephanie, Sarah, Jennifer. B.A., U. Notre Dame, 1953; J.D., Georgetown U., 1959. Bar: Va. bar 1959, D.C. bar 1959, Tex. bar 1961, N.Y. bar 1966. Legal dept. Texaco, Inc., Houston, 1959-64, N.Y.C., 1964-66; asst. to vice chmn. bd. Texaco, Inc., 1965-67, asst. to chmn. bd., 1967-68, gen. mgr. producing dept. Eastern hemisphere, 1968-70, v.p., 1970-76, sr. v.p., gen. counsel, 1976-77, sr. v.p., dir., 1977-78, exec. v.p., 1978-83, pres., 1983-86, chmn. bd. dirs., 1987—; dir. CIGNA Corp. Trustee Council for Econ. Devel. Served to lt. USMCR, 1954-55. Mem. ABA (sect. sec. 1964-67, co-founder Natural Resources Law Jour. mineral law sect., council mem. minerals sect.). Home: 55 Valley Rd Bronxville NY 10708 Office: Texaco Inc 2000 Westchester Ave White Plains NY 10650

DEDDENS, JAMES CARROLL, utilities company executive; b. Louisville, Mar. 25, 1928; s. Carl John and Elizabeth Jane (Bickett) D.; m. Mary Lee Wright, June 23, 1953 (dec. Jan. 1977); children: John, Robert, Elizabeth, Lee. BSME, U. Louisville, 1952, MSME, 1953, MS in Engring., 1972. Registered profl. engr. Va., La. Engr. Babcock & Wilcox Co., Lynchburg, Va., 1954-66; mgr. svcs. sect. Babcock & Wilcox Co., Lynchburg, 1966-74, mgr. project mgmt., 1978-80, mgr. bus. adminstrn. and integration, 1980-83; v.p. River Bend Nuclear Group Gulf States Utilities Co., St. Francisville, La., 1983-86; sr. v.p. River Bend Nuclear Group, St. Francisville, 1987—; trustee Am. Tech. Inst., Memphis, 1987—. Contbr. articles to profl. jours. Bd. dirs. United Way of Cen. Va., Lynchburg, 1981-82; pres. Ch. Parish Council, Lynchburg, 1976-77, PTA, Lynchburg, 1965. Recpient Engr. Yr. award, Nat. Soc. Profl. Engrs., 1978. Mem. ASME, Am. Nuclear Soc., Camelot Club, The Bluffs Country Club. Office: Gulf States Utilities Co Hwy 61 & North Access Rd PO Box 220 Saint Francisville LA 70775

DEDERICK, ROBERT GOGAN, economist; b. Keene, N.H., Nov. 18, 1929; s. Frederic Van Dyck and Margaret (Gogan) D.; m. Margarida N. Magalhaes, Aug. 24, 1957; children: Frederic, Laura, Peter. A.B., Harvard U., 1951, A.M., 1953, PhD., 1958; postgrad., Cornell U., 1953-54. Econ. research mgr. New Eng. Mut. Life Ins. Co., Boston, 1957-64; assoc. economist No. Trust Co., Chgo., 1964; v.p., asso. economist No. Trust Co., 1965-69, v.p., economist, 1969-70, sr. v.p., economist, 1970-81, exec. v.p., chief economist, 1983—; mem. econ. adv. bd. U.S. Commerce Dept., 1968-70, 75-76, 83-85, asst. sec. commerce for econ. affairs, 1981-82, under sec. commerce for econ. affairs, 1982-83. Fellow Nat. Assn. Bus. Economists (pres. 1973-74, governing council 1969-76); mem. Conf. Bus. Economists (sec.-treas. 1980-81, chmn. 1984-85), Harvard Discussion Group Indsl. Economists, Am. Statis. Assn., Am. Econs. Assn., Nat. Economists, Am. Finance Assn., Asso. Harvard Alumni (dir. 1980-82). Clubs: Bankers, Economic, Executives, Chgo. Harvard; Chgo. Hinsdale Golf. Home: 113 S County Line Rd Hinsdale IL 60521 Office: No Trust Corp 50 S LaSalle St Chicago IL 60675

DEDEURWAERDER, JOSE JOSEPH, automotive executive; b. Brussels, Dec. 31, 1932; s. Louis and Philippine (Pater Not) D.; m. Nelly Antoinette Clemens, May 15, 1954; 1 child, Joelle Cabassol. Grad. in tech. engring, Ecole Technique Moyenne Superieure, Belgium, 1953. Mfg. dir. Renault, Belgium, 1958-67; indsl. dir. Renault, Argentina, 1967-73; chief exec. officer Renault Mexicana, Mexico, 1973-76; plant dir. Renault, Douai, France, 1976-81; exec. v.p. Am. Motors Corp., Detroit, 1981-82, pres., chief operating officer, 1982-84; pres., chief exec. officer Am. Motors Corp., Southfield, Mich., 1984-86, vice chmn., chmn. exec. com., 1986—. Served as officer Belgium Navy, 1952-53. Mem. Automotive Hall of Fame (bd dirs.). Office: Am Motors Corp 27777 Franklin Rd Southfield MI 48034 *

DEDONA, FRANCIS ALFRED, technology industry executive; b. Buffalo, N.Y., Apr. 29, 1924; s. Henry Joseph and Angela Agnes (Maggio) D.; m. Jacquelin Dalton, Apr. 14, 1956; children: Gregory Philip, Paul Francis, Andrea Grace, Daniela Angela. BS, U. Calif., Berkeley, 1949; DSc (hon), Northrop U., 1987. Engr. Northrop Aircraft Corp., Hawthorne, Calif., 1951-52; dir. fin. planning analysis Hughes Aircraft Co., Culver City, Calif., 1952-56; asst. dir., computer systems labs Litton Industries, Inc., Beverly Hills, Calif., 1956-61; exec. v.p., co-founder The Scionics Corp., Northridge, Calif., 1961-69; exec. v.p. U.S. Electro-Optical Systems Corp., L.A., 1969-72; pres., chief exec. officer The Scionics Corp, L.A., 1972-78; pres., co-owner chief ops. officer Arrowsmith Industries, Inc., L.A., 1978-85, also dir; vice-chmn., co-owner KDT Industries, Inc, Austin, Tex., 1985-87; also dir. KDT Industries, Inc, Austin; pres., owner Nortel and Nortel PTE, LTD, Sherman Oaks, Calif., 1970—; pres. Nortel Consultancy, import-export, Sherman Oaks, Calif., 1970—; dir. Pertron Controls Corp., Chatsworth, Calif., 1978—, AFCOA Corp., Chatsworth, 1968-69, Nat. Security Indsl. Assn., Los Angeles, 1979—. Inventor in technology field. Trustee, chmn. devel. com., Northrop U., Los Angeles, 1981—; fund raiser, advisor Boy Scouts Am., Los Angeles, 1960—; fund raiser campaign organizer, Senate campaign T.A. Bruinsma, Los Angeles, 1984. Lt. (J.G.) USN, 1943-46. Mem. Dist. export Coun. (US Dept. of Commerce), Exports Mgrs. Assn. of Calif., Nat. Security Indsl. Assn., Am. Defense Preparedness Assn., Am. Ordnance Assn., Soc. of Mfg. Engrs., Am. Metal Stamping Assn., Nat. Machine Tool Builder's Assn., Nat. Tool and Spl. Machine Assn., ASME-UCLA Engring. Adv. Coun., Inst. Mgmt. Scis., Railway progress Inst., Assn. Computing Machinery, Assn. Corp. Growth, The Newcomen Soc., Univ. Tech. Transfer, Inc (v.p.), The Regency Club, Los Angles Athletic Club. Republican. Home: 3553 Scadlock Ln Sherman Oaks CA 91403 Office: PO Box 5747 Sherman Oaks CA 91403

DEEG, EMIL WOLFGANG, manufacturing company executive; b. Selb, Germany, Sept. 20, 1926; s. Fritz and Trina (Poehlmann) D.; came to U.S., 1967, naturalized, 1975; Dipl. Physiker, U. Wuerzburg, 1954, Dr. rer. nat., 1956; m. Hedwig M.S. Kempf, Aug. 25, 1953; children—Wolfgang, Martin, Bernhard, Renate. Research asst. Max Planck Inst., Wuerzburg, 1954-59; mem. tech. staff Bell Telephone Labs., Allentown, Pa., 1959-60; research assoc. Jenaer Glaswerk Schott U. Gen., Mainz, Germany, 1960, dir. research, 1960-65; asso. prof. physics and solid state sci. Am. U., Cairo, 1965-67; mgr. ceramic research Am. Optical Corp., Southbridge, Mass., 1967-71, mgr. materials research, 1971-73, dir. process and materials research, 1973-75, dir. inorganic materials research and devel., 1975-77, tech. adviser, 1977-78; sr. scientist Anchor Hocking Corp., Lancaster, Ohio, 1978-79, mgr. materials research and devel., 1979-80; mgr. glass tech. Bausch & Lomb, Rochester, N.Y., 1980-82; mgr. glass and fiber devel. Mead Office Systems, Richardson, Tex., 1982-84; project mgr. AMP, Inc., Harrisburg, Pa., 1984—; mem. Internat. Commn. on Glass, 1963-81. Pres., PTA, Woodstock, Conn., 1970-71; committeeman Mohegan council Boy Scouts Am., 1967-73; trustee Woodstock Acad., 1971-78; overseer Old Sturbridge Village, Inc.; chmn. Optical Info. Center, Southbridge, 1976-77. Served with German Army, 1944-45. Fellow Am. Ceramic Soc.; mem. Optical Soc. Am., Nat. Inst. Ceramic Engrs., Tech., Soc. Advancement Materials and Process Engring, Lions (pres. Woodstock chpt. 1975; zone chmn. dist. 23 C, Lions Internat. 1976-78), Contbr. chpts. to books, articles to profl. jours. Author: (with H. Richter) Glas im Laboratorium, 1966. Patentee in field. Home: 501 Ohio Ave Lemoyne PA 17043 Office: 2901 Fulling Mill Rd Middletown PA 17057

DEEGAN, DEREK JAMES, transportation executive; b. Verdun, Que., Can., Feb. 5, 1940; m. Gail Lawson, Feb. 5, 1966; children: Christopher, Patrick, Alanna. Grad. high schs., Montreal, Can., 1956; also courses in mgmt., acctg. and transp. logistics. From jr. clk. to supr. bd. documentation Can. Pacific Ltd., Montreal, 1956-72, asst. sec., then sr. asst. sec., 1972-84, corp. sec., 1984-86, v.p. and sec., 1986—. Mem. Am. Soc. Corp. Secs., Chartered Can. Inst. Secs., Mt. Stephen Club. Home: 108 Yonge Crescent, Pointe Claire, PQ Canada H9R 2L9 Office: Can Pacific Ltd, PO Box 6042 Sta A, Montreal, PQ Canada H3C 3E4

DEEIK, KHALIL GEORGE, economist, financing company executive; b. Bethlehem, Palestine, Nov. 12, 1937; s. George Said Diek and Wadiea (Jalil) Lama; m. Jalileh Mary Marzouka, Aug. 22, 1965; children—George, Ramzi, Nader. B.A., Sacramento State U., 1961, M.A., 1964; Ph.D., U. So. Calif., 1972. Prin., adminstr. Manzinata Sch., Hyampom, Calif., 1964-65; mgr. Gen. Trading Co., Alkhobar, Saudi Arabia, 1966-69; program dir., instr. Krebs Coll., North Hollywood, Calif., 1969-72; mng. dir., v.p., sr. advisor, exec. asst. to chmn. Olayan Saudi Investment Co., Olayan Financing Co., Jeddah, Saudi Arabia, 1973—, Olayan Group of Cos.; bd. dirs. Saudi Polyester Products Co., Jeddah, 1984—; exec. com. mem. Saudi Arabian Constrn. and Repair Services Co., Jeddah, 1984—; hon. lectr. King Abdulaziz U., Saudi Arabia, 1979; faculty mem., program coordinator Century U., Calif., 1978—. Mem. Internat. Educators Assn. (v.p. 1970-72), Phi Delta Kappa, Phi Delta Epsilon. Club. Marquis (U.S.A.). Office: Olayan Fin Co, PO Box 8772, Riyadh 11492, Saudi Arabia

DEER, JAMES WILLIS, lawyer; b. Reading, Pa., Mar. 14, 1917; s. Irvin E. and Rosemary (French) D.; m. Marion M. Hawkinson, July 31, 1943 (dec. 1987); 1 child, Ann Marie. AB, Oberlin Coll, 1938; JD, U. Mich., 1941. Bar: Ohio 1941, N.Y. 1948. Legal staff SEC, 1942-45; practice in N.Y.C., 1945—; mem. firm Holtzmann, Wise & Shepard, 1954—; bd. dirs. Arts Way Mfg. Co., Inc., Selvac Corp., Am. Diversified Enterprises, Inc., Techsci. Industries, Applied DNA Sytems, Inc., Allegheny & Western Energy Corp. Mem. Am., N.Y. State bar assns., Phi Beta Kappa, Phi Alpha Delta. Home: 611 Shore Acres Dr Mamaroneck NY 10543 also: Barr Terr 50 East Dr Delray Beach FL 33483 Office: 745 Fifth Ave New York NY 10151

DEETS, HORACE, association executive. Exec. dir. Am. Assn. of Retired Persons, Washington, D.C. Office: Am Assn Ret Persons 1909 K St NW Washington DC 20049 *

DEFABIS, MARK VINCENT, real estate developer; b. San Juan, P.R., July 31, 1955; s. Michael and Jean Marie (Meyer) DeF.; m. Joan Stuart Ketterman, June 10, 1978; children: Michael Clark, Laura Marie. BS, Purdue U., 1977; JD, Ind. U., 1983. Adminstrv. asst. dept. met. devel. City of Indpls., 1977-79, dep. adminstr. econ. and housing div., 1979-81, adminstr. econ. and housing devel. div., 1981-83; pres. Indpls. Econ. Devel. Corp., 1983-85; v.p. Kosene & Kosene Devel. Co., Indpls., 1985—; bd. dirs. Indpls. City Market Corp. Mem. Penrod Soc., Indpls., 1985; bd. dirs. Greater Fgn. Trade Zone, Indpls., 1984, Indpls. Humane Soc., 1987, Greater Indpls. Rep. Fin. Com., 1988. Mem. ABA, Urban Land Inst., Internat. Council Shopping Ctrs., Highland Country Club, Kiwanis. Roman Catholic. Office: Kosene & Kosene Devel Co 8840 Commerce Park Pl Ste E Indianapolis IN 46268

DEFAZIO, THOMAS C., finance executive; b. Geneva, N.Y., Aug. 24, 1941; s. Carmen J. and Mary P. (Sarratori) DeF.; m. Kathleen White, July 1, 1961. BS, Syracuse U., 1967. V.p., contr. SCM Corp., N.Y.C., 1963-86, Gen. Instrument Corp., Lyndhurst, N.J., 1986-88; v.p. fin., chief exec. officer Gen. Instrument Corp., N.Y., 1988—. Mem. Am. Mgmt. Assn. (fin. coun. 1986). Office: Gen Instrument Corp 767 Fifth Ave New York NY 10153

DEFFEYES, ROBERT JOSEPH, manufacturing company executive; b. Oklahoma City, Aug. 16, 1935; s. Joseph Alfred and Hazel (Stover) D.; m. Ethel Black, Aug. 2, 1958; children: Joan Elizabeth, Suzanne Carol. BS, Calif. Inst. Tech., 1957. Devel. engr. Dow Chem. Co., Pittsburg, Calif., 1957-63; mgr. tech. svcs. Memorex Co., Santa Clara, Calif., 1963-69; sr. v.p. tech. Graham Magnetics, Graham, Tex., 1969-77; pres. Graham Magnetics, Fort Worth, 1978-84, Carlisle Cos., Inc., Cin., 1985-88, Carlisle Memory Products Group, North Richland Hills, Tex., 1988—. Patentee in field. Served with U.S. Army, 1958. Home: 2102 English Oak Dr Arlington TX 76016 Office: Carlisle Memory Products Group 6625 Industrial Park Blvd North Richland Hills TX 76180

DEFLURI, RICHARD FRANK, financial executive; b. Hazleton, Pa., Apr. 23, 1950; s. Frank Leonard and Anne E. (Davis) DeF.; m. Lori Ann Foor, Sept. 15, 1955; 1 child, Blake Justin. BS, Pa. State U., 1974. Sr. assoc. Pa. Fin. Group, State College, Pa., 1974—; dir. Nittany Health Care Services, Hazleton, AquaPenn Spring Water Co., State College, Zero Stage Capital Co., State College, PFG Capital Corp., State College; spkr. in field. Fund raiser Am. Cancer Soc., State College, 1986. Recipient Leading Producer award Provident Mut. Ins. Co., 1987, 88, Pa. Fin. Group, 1980—. Mem. Internat. Assn. Fin. Planning, Assn. Pvt. Pension and Welfare Plans, Small Bus. Assn., Nat. Spkrs. Assn. Methodist. Office: Pa Fin Group Inc 270 Walker Dr PO Box 259 State College PA 16801 Home: 1209 Haymaker Rd State College PA 16801

DEFRANCESCO, JAMES JOSEPH, JR., banker; b. New Haven, Feb. 24, 1948; s. James Joseph Sr. and Josephine Elizabeth (Malick) DeF.; m. Ann Elizabeth Alberino, May 18, 1968 (div. Feb. 1984); children: Anthony Joseph, Lisa Ann; m. Laurie Beth Cattaruzza, Jan. 18, 1986; 1 child, Michael James. BS in Fin., Quinnipiac Coll., 1980. Credit analyst Dun & Bradstreet, Inc., New Haven, 1967-69; supr. Boston, 1969-70; mgr. Portland, Maine, 1970-71; sr. v.p. Am. Nat. Bank, Hamden, Conn., 1972-85, 1st Constn. Bank, New Haven, 1986—; bd. dirs. Bank Credit Exchange, Bridgeport, Conn., 1976-80. Mem. Walter Camp Found., New Haven, 1978—; bd. dirs. Notre Dame High Sch., West Haven, Conn., 1982—. Mem. New Haven C. of C. (bd. dirs. 1985—). Republican. Roman Catholic. Clubs: Amity, Quinnipiac (New Haven). Home: 23 Marion Ave Hamden CT 06518 Office: 1st Constn Bank 80 Elm St New Haven CT 06510

DEFRANCISCO, ANNE ELIZABETH, accountant; b. Cut Bank, Mont., July 14, 1944; d. Earl Banks and Lois Edith (Strong) Horsell; student U. Puget Sound, 1962-65; diploma Internat. Accts. Soc., 1973; MBA, U. Portland, 1979. CPA, Wash.; m. Dale W. West, Jan. 4, 1988; children—Kimberlie, Nicholas. Staff acct. Halvor Knudtzon & Assocs., CPA's, Longview, Wash., 1973-76, ptnr., 1976-77; ptnr. DeFrancisco, Leber & Co., CPA's, Longview, 1977-79; owner, chief exec. officer Anne E. DeFrancisco, CPA, Longview, 1979-84; shareholder, tax mgr. Monroe, Lance & DeFrancisco P.S., CPA's, Longview, 1984—; seminar lectr.; instr. Lower Columbia Coll., SBA; speaker on tax and fin. planning to community orgns. Bd. dirs. Adult Devel. Ctr., 1978—, treas., 1980—; bd. dirs., treas. Emergency Support Shelter, 1981-84; mem. fin. com. Columbia Theatre Task Force, 1982; bd. dirs., treas. Residential Resources Assn., 1983—; bd. trustees Synod of Alaska N.W., 1987, treas., 1988—. Mem. Am. Inst. CPA's, Wash. State Soc. CPA's. Office: 200 Old Nat Bank Bldg Longview WA 98632

DE FREITAS, ROSEANN, accountant; b. Newark, July 2, 1953; d. José and Edith (Rodriguez) de F.; children: Cassandra Telenko, Andrea Telenko. BS in Econs., U. Pa., 1980. Bookkeeper John A. Steer Co., Phila.,

1973-76, 78-80; staff Asher & Asher, Phila., 1976-78, Goldenberg/Rosenthal, Phila., 1980-82; pvt. practice in acctg. Upper Darby, Pa., 1982—. Bd. dirs. Olde City Children's Ctr., Phila., 1988—; vol. Community Accts., Phila., 1985—. Mem. Am. Inst. Cert. Pub. Accts., Phila. Inst. Cert. Pub. Accts.

DEGAVRE, ROBERT THOMPSON, medical electronics company executive; b. Oxford, Eng., Oct. 31, 1940; came to U.S., 1949; s. Robert Thompson and Teresa (Cameron) deG.; m. Angela Jane Hulse, Feb. 28, 1966; children: Teresa, Timothy. BA, Princeton U., 1962, MPA, 1968; Degre Moyen, Pau (France) U., 1966. Fin. analyst treas. dept. Exxon Corp., N.Y., 1968-69, ESSO Kekiyu K.K., Tokyo, 1970-71, Exxon Corp., Tokyo, 1970-72; sr. fin. analyst treas. dept. ESSO Chem. Co., N.Y., 1971-72; project fin. mgr. treas. dept. Inco Ltd., N.Y., 1972-77; treas. Inco Ltd., N.Y.C., 1977-82; v.p., treas. Squibb Corp., Princeton, N.J., 1982-86; sr. v.p., chief fin. officer Westmark Internat., Seattle, 1987—; bd. dirs. Schafer Value Trust, N.Y.C., 1986—, Toronto Dominion Trust Co. N.Y., 1981-86; mem. adv. coun. dept. econs., Princeton U. Trustee Wetlands Inst., Stone Harbor, N.J.; bd. dirs. Schafer Value Trust. Lt. USN, 1962-66. Mem. Phi Beta Kappa. Office: Westmark Internat Inc 701 5th Ave Ste 6800 Seattle WA 98104-7001

DEGENER, HELEN MACDONALD ZOTTOLI, banker; b. Worcester, Mass., Oct. 25, 1941; d. Albert and Jenny Elizabeth (MacDonald) Zottoli; m. J. Michael Degener, July 23, 1973. BA in Econ., Lake Erie Coll., 1963; postgrad. U. Copenhagen, Denmark, 1961-62; postgrad. Clark U., 1964, Worcester State Coll., 1964, NYU, 1965, NYU , 1967, 68. Tchr. Goshen Sch., Va., 1964-66; security analyst Glore Forgan William P. Staats, N.Y.C., 1966-69, Clark Dodge & Co., N.Y.C., 1969-70; security analyst, asst. trust officer Mfgs. Hanover Trust, N.Y.C., 1970-76; v.p. Istel Fund, Lepercq de Neuflize, N.Y.C., 1976-81; v.p. Morgan Guaranty Trust Co., N.Y.C., 1981—. Bd. dirs. Greater N.Y. coun. Girl Scouts U.S., N.Y.C., 1985—, treas., 1988, 89. Recipient Tchr. of Yr. award Rockbridge County Jr. C. of C., 1966, Outstanding Young Woman of Yr., 1970, 71. Congregationalist. Club: Colony (N.Y.C.). Home: 151 E 83d St New York NY 10028 Office: Morgan Guaranty Trust Co 9 W 57th St New York NY 10019

DEGNER, ROBERT LOUIS, market research educator; b. Malone, Tex., Jan. 20, 1942; s. Louis William and Frances Olga (Strauch) D.; m. Nancy Lou Ballew, June 2, 1962 (div. Jan. 1972); children: Clifford, Clinton; m. Janet Louise Dunphy, May 29, 1976; children: Kelly, Travis. AA, Navarro Jr. Coll., Corsicana, Tex., 1961; BS, Tex. A&M U., 1963, MS, 1970, PhD, 1974. Asst. county agrl. agt. Tex. Agrl. Extension Service, Dallas, 1965-66, assoc. county agrl. agt., 1966-67; research assoc. Tex. A&M U., College Station, 1971-74; asst. prof. Tex. A&M U., Weslaco, 1974-76; asst. prof. U. Fla., Gainesville, 1976-81, assoc. prof., 1981-86, prof., 1986-87, prof., dir. Fla. Agrl. Market Research Ctr., 1987—. Contbr. articles to profl. jours. Hon. dir. Fla. Dairy Products Assn. 1985—. Recipient Def. Found. Edn. fellowship, 1967-71. Mem. Am. Mktg. Assn., Food Distbn. Research Soc. (pres. 1986-87), Am. Agrl. Econs. Assn., So. Agrl. Econs. Assn. Democrat. Lutheran. Home: 2842 NW 28 Pl Gainesville FL 32605 Office: U Fla 1083 McCarty Hall Gainesville FL 32611

DEGRIJS, LEO CHARLES, banker; b. Batavia, Java, 1926; came to U.S.,; married. Grad. Vrijzinning Christelijk Lyceum, The Hague, Netherlands, 1943. With Netherlands Post Tel & Tel Co., 1943-45, Netherlands-Indies Civil Adminstrn., 1945-49, Nederlandsche Handel-Maatschappij, bankers, Amsterdam, 1951-63, Continental Ill. Nat. Bank and Trust Co., Chgo., 1963—; internat. banking dept., 2d v.p. and head Continental Ill. Nat. Bank and Trust Co., Tokyo and Osaka, 1964; v.p. Continental Ill. Nat. Bank and Trust Co., Chgo., 1967; head Far East group Continental Ill. Nat. Bank and Trust Co., 1968; with Continental Devel. Bank SAL, Beirut, Lebanon, 1970; head Asia Pacific and Africa-Middle East groups, 1973, sr. v.p., 1974, head internat. banking dept., 1976, head internat. banking services dept., 1980, exec. v.p., 1981—, chmn. country exposure com., head sovereign risk mgmt., 1983—. Office: Continental Bank Corp 231 S LaSalle St Chicago IL 60697

DEGROFF, RALPH LYNN, JR., investment banker; b. Balt., Oct. 23, 1936; s. Ralph Lynn and Marion (Day) D.; m. Marion Parsons Sinwell, Feb. 4, 1989; AB, Princeton U., 1958; MBA, U. Va., 1960. With Dillon, Read & Co. Inc., N.Y.C., 1961-81, v.p., 1970-74, sr. v.p., 1974-81; sr. v.p. Donaldson, Lufkin & Jenrette, 1981—; past dir. The Ryland Group, Inc.; trustee Holland Soc. N.Y. With U.S. Army, 1960-61. Mem. Soc. of the Cin. Colonial Wars, Downtown Assn., Md. Club, Rockaway Hunting Club, Elkridge Club. Presbyterian. Home: 7 Gracie Sq New York NY 10028 Office: 140 Broadway 49th Fl New York NY 10005

DEGRUCHY, ALAN B., engineer; b. Bklyn., Oct. 4, 1932; s. William C. and Ethne L. deGruchy; IE, Indsl. Mgmt. Inst., 1956; degree in Bus. Adminstrn., Temple U., 1958. Apprentice, E.G. Budd Co., 1954-58; quality control mgr. Cutler Metal Products Co., 1958-62; plant mgr. Falco Products Co., 1962-63; chief engr. Met-Pro, Inc., 1963-66; project engr. Day & Zimmerman, Inc., 1966-72; corp. cons. engr. C.S.I., Bridgewater, N.J., 1972—; mng. dir. Thermalite, Inc., Rocky Mount, N.C., 1987—. Mem. Am. Inst. Indsl. Engrs., Am. Soc. Quality Control, Masons. Inventor automatic process and assembly machines. Office: Thermalite Inc 500 S Church St Rocky Mount NC 27803

DEHON, MELANIE PORTER, manufacturers representative; b. Athens, Ga., June 15, 1957; d. Neil Derrick and Rheumell (Frosteen) Porter; m. Kenneth Michael Dehon, Oct. 24, 1987. AS in Bus. Mgmt., Midlands Tech. Coll., Columbia, S.C., 1976; BA i Mktg., U. South Fla., 1984. Lic. real estate salesman, Fla. Computer programmer S.C. Fed. Savs. & Loan, Columbia, 1976-80; sr. flight attendant Air Fla. Airlines, Miami, Fla., 1981-82; installation mgr. Triad System, Ft. Myers, Fla., 1982-83; real estate agt. Bay Area Real Estate, Tampa, Fla., 1983-84; account exec. Info. System AT&T, Orlando, Fla., 1984-87; mfrs. rep. Melanie's Specialties, Ft. Myers, 1987—. Scholar U. Fla., 1984; named one of Outstanding Alumni Midland Tech. Coll., 1976. Mem. Am. Mktg. Assn., Am. Bus. Women's Assn., U.S. Fla. Alumni Club, Omicron Delta Kappa, Beta Gamma Sigma, Phi Beta Lambda. Republican. Mem. Christian Ch. Home and Office: 1729 SW 54 Lane Cape Coral FL 33914

DEICHMANN, BERNHARD ERNST, manufacturing company executive; b. Willoughby, Ohio, July 25, 1935; s. Walter Otto and Liesel (Ernst) D.; m. Joan Ellen Van Emburgh, Aug. 26, 1961; children: Walter, Evelynn, Robin, Holly. BSME, Princeton U., 1958; MBA, Drexel Inst. Tech., 1964. With Delaval Turbine Inc., Trenton, N.J., 1959-71; mgr. application engring., gen. sales mgr. Delaval Stork V.O.F., Hengelo, The Netherlands, 1971-76; mng. dir. Delaval Stork V.O.F., Hengelo, 1976-80; v.p. mktg. and sales Transam. Delaval Inc., Lawrenceville, N.J., 1980-86; v.p. strategic planning Transam. Delaval Inc., Lawrenceville, 1986-87; gen. mgr. Delaval Hydro Pump (div. Imo Delaval Inc.), Trenton, 1988—. 1st lt. USAR, 1958-59. Mem. ASME, Friends of Del. Canal Inc., Rotary Club. Republican. Lutheran. Home: 8 Devon Dr New Hope PA 18938 Office: Imo Delaval Inc Delaval Hydro Pump Div 853 Nottingham Way Trenton NJ 08638

DEIHL, RICHARD HARRY, savings and loan association executive; b. Whittier, Calif., Sept. 8, 1928; s. Victor Francis and Wilma Aileen (Thomas) D.; m. Billie Dantz Beane, Mar. 24, 1952; children: Catherine Kent, Michael, Victoria, Christine. A.B., Whittier Coll., 1949; postgrad., UCLA, 1949, U. Calif.-Berkeley, 1949-50. With Nat. Cash Register Co., Pomona, Calif., 1955-59; trainee Rio Hondo Savs. & Loan, Calif., 1959-60; loan cons. Home Savs. & Loan Assn. (now Home Savs. Am., A Fed. Savs. & Loan Assn.), Los Angeles, 1960-63; loan agt., supr., v.p. Home Savs. & Loan Assn. (now Home Savs. Am., A Fed. Savs. & Loan Assn.), 1964, loan service supr., 1964, v.p. ops., v.p. loans, 1965, exec. v.p., 1966, pres., 1967-84, chief exec. officer, 1967-84, chmn., 1984—, also dir.; chief exec. officer, dir. H.F. Ahmanson Co., 1984—, chmn., also pres., 1989—; bd. dirs. Fed. Home Loan Bank, Atlantic Richfield Good Samaritan Hosp. Contbr. articles to profl. jours. Served to 1st lt. USAF, 1951-55. Decorated D.F.C., Air medal with three clusters. Republican. Club: Fairbanks Ranch Country (Rancho Santa Fe). Office: H F Ahmanson & Co 3731 Wilshire Blvd Los Angeles CA 90010 also: Home Savs of Am 4900 Rivergrade Rd Irwindale CA 91706 *

DEINES, HARRY J., agricultural and livestock company executive; b. Loveland, Colo., Nov. 5, 1909; s. John and Mary (Maseka) D.; B.M.E., U. Colo.; grad. Advanced Mgmt. Program, Harvard; m. Eleanor Vrooman, 1932; children: Gretchen Deines Langston, Mark, Katrina, Stephen. Advt. mgr. Gen. Electric Co., 1930-45; v.p. Fuller & Smith & Ross, 1945-49; gen. advt. mgr. Westinghouse Electric Corp., 1949-53; v.p. J. Walter Thompson, N.Y.C., 1953-56, Fuller & Smith & Ross, N.Y.C., 1956-59; exec. v.p., dir. Campbell, Mithun, Inc., Mpls., 1959-71; mng. partner Deines Agr. & Livestock Co., Ft. Collins, Colo., 1971—; pres. Collectors' Books Ltd. Home and Office: 1852 Edna Pl Bainbridge Island WA 98110

DEITCHER, HERBERT, financial executive; b. Cohoes, N.Y., Oct. 27, 1933; s. John and Etta (Carr) D.; m. Barbara Judith Goldberg, Sept. 1, 1958 (dec. 1986); children: Janet Lee, Steven Robert. B.B.A., Siena Coll., 1955; M.B.A., Boston U., 1960. With Raytheon Co., 1958—; asst. treas. fin. planning and controls Raytheon Co., Lexington, Mass., 1967-69, asst. treas. ops., 1970-73, dir. internat. financing, 1973-78, v.p. internat. financing, 1979-83, v.p., treas., 1983—; instr. fin. Northeastern U., 1967-73; dir. Baybank Middlesex. Bd. dirs., treas. Lynnfield Inst. for Elderly (Mass.), 1982-83; bd. dirs., officer Temple Beth Shalom, Peabody, Mass., 1973-83. Fellow Planning Execs. Inst. (nat. v.p. 1964-72); mem. Fin. Execs. Inst. (internat. liason and Policy com. 1970—), Soc. Mfg. Engrs. (fin. com. 1986—), Aerospace Industries Assn. Am. (interant. fin. group 1973—), Govt. Contract Mgmt. Assn., Beta Gamma Sigma, Delta Epsilon Sigma. Jewish. Home: 9 Longbow Circle Lynnfield MA 01940 Office: Raytheon Co 141 Spring St Lexington MA 02173

DEITCHLE, GERALD WAYNE, restaurant company executive; b. Lockbourne AFB, Ohio, Sept. 19, 1951. BBA, Tex. A&M U., 1973; MBA, U. Tex., San Antonio, 1975. CPA, Tex. Div. controller Church's Fried Chicken Inc., San Antonio, 1978-80; asst. controller W. R. Grace and Co., San Antonio, 1980-84; v.p., controller Jerrico Inc., Lexington, Ky., 1984-87, sr. v.p. fin., 1987—. With USAF, 1974-78. Mem. AICPA, Tex. Soc. CPA's, Fin. Execs. Inst., Nat. Assn. Accts., Inst. Mgmt. Acctg., Nat. Assn. Securities Dealers Automated Quotations. Office: Jerrico Inc 101 Jerrico Dr Box 11988 Lexington KY 40509

DEKAT, JOSEPH CARROLL FRANCIS, financial planner; b. Biloxi, Miss., July 10, 1952; s. Carroll Joseph and Carlene Gertrude (Straub) D.; m. Carol Louise Retzer, June 9, 1973; children: Joseph R., Carlina L., Stephen L., Katherine E. BA, U. Dallas, 1974. Cert. financial planner, Denver, 1983. Mgr. Continental Audio Corp., Dallas, 1975-76; gen. ops. mgr. Sirco Internat., Dallas, 1976-77; tng. mgr. CBS Specialty Stores, Arlington, Tex., 1977-79; salesman T and W Sales, Dallas, 1979-80, Gen. Electric Mobile Communications, Dallas, 1980; dist. mgr. Waddell and Reed, Topeka, 1980-83; sr. planning ptnr. Santaularia and Assocs., Topeka, 1983-86; pres. Fin. Planning Ptnrs. Ltd., Mission, Kans., 1986—; adj. faculty Coll. Fin. Planning, Denver. Dir. youth activities Optimist Club, Topeka, 1985; com. mem. Topeka C. of C., 1985. Mem. Registry Fin. Planning Practitioners, Inst. Cert. Fin. Planners, Internat. Assn. Fin. Planning. Republican. Roman Catholic. Home: 20103 Nall Stilwell KS 66085 Office: Fin Planning Ptnrs Ltd 6950 Squibb Rd Ste 302 Shawnee Mission KS 66202

DEKRUIF, ROBERT M., financial services company executive. Vice chmn. bd. H.F. Ahmanson & Co., Los Angeles; dir. Home Savs. of Am. FA, Irwindale, Ca. Office: H F Ahmanson & Co 3731 Wilshire Blvd Los Angeles CA 90010 *

DELACOUR, YVES JEAN CLAUDE MARIE, technology information executive; b. Pamiers, Ariege, France, June 24, 1943; s. Jacques and Marie-Louise (Rambaud) D.; m. Elisabeth Peu-Duvallon; children—Thibault, Gauthier. Engr. French Naval Acad., 1965; B.S. in Econs., Fin., Institut d'Etudes Politiques, 1972; M.B.A., Stanford U., 1975. Commd. ensign, 1965, advanced through grades to lt. de Vaisseau, 1971; naval officer Helicopter Carrier Jeanne d'Arc, French Navy, 1965-69; in charge of communications dept. Destroyer, Toulon, 1966-69; staff mem. Navy Dept., Paris, 1969-73; credit officer Banque de l'Indochine et de Suez, Paris, 1975-77; pres. Transasia Corp., Paris, 1978—, pres. Internat. Data Group, France, 1980-86, v.p. Frau Internat. Data Group, Inc., 1986—. Home: 22 rue de la Federation, 75015 Paris France Office: IDG France, 12 Ave George V, 75008 Paris France

DELAGO, JOSEPH THOMAS, instrument company executive; b. Elizabeth, N.J., May 21, 1923; s. James Vincent and Rose Anne (Sarullo) DeL.; m. Louise Furia, May 30, 1949; children: Donna M. DeLago Rowe, Joseph T. Jr., Candida M. DeLago Schwartz. BME, Villanova U., 1947. Sr. tech. writer Chase Aircraft Co., West Trenton, N.J., 1947-52; sr. publs. engr. DeLaval Stem Turbine Co., Trenton, 1952-55; head tech. publs. Fischer & Porter Co., Warminster, Pa., 1955-57; mgr. engring. services, asst. sec. Fischer & Porter Co., 1957-80, asst. sec., v.p., 1980-84, v.p., sec., 1984—; dir. Furlong Promotions, Warminster, Fischer & Porter Research, Inc., Warminster, Fapico, Claremont., Calif. Active youth athletic assns. Served with U.S. Army, 1944-46. Mem. Instrument Soc. am., Am. soc. Corp. Secs. Republican. Roman Catholic. Home: 44 Fountain Rd Levittown PA 19056

DELAHANTY, EDWARD LAWRENCE, management consultant; b. South Bend, Ind., Feb. 17, 1942; s. Edward Lawrence and Rosemary Margaret (DeVreese) D.; m. Rebecca A. Paczesny, June 22, 1963; children: David Edward, Debra Ann. BS in Math., U. Notre Dame, 1963. Enrolled actuary. Asst. actuary Aetna Life & Casualty Co., Hartford, Conn., 1963-70; mng. ptnr. Hewitt Assocs., Mpls., 1971-85 , mem. exec. com., 1981-87; southeast region mng. ptnr., Hewitt Assocs., Atlanta, 1986—; v.p., sec.-treas., bd. dirs. CMI Stores Inc., 1983-85; bd. dirs. Brandt Barringmann Inc., 1981-84. Fellow Soc. Actuaries; mem. Am. Acad. Actuaries, So. Pension Conf., Am. Compensation Assn., Atlanta City Club, Atlanta Nat. Golf Club, Ashford Club, Georgian Club, Vinings Club. Home: 5710 Winterthur Ln NW Atlanta GA 30328 Office: 2100 Riveredge Pkwy 900 Atlanta GA 30328

DELAND, DIANE O. AMMONS, business executive; b. Redding, Calif., Jan. 3, 1940; d. Mark T. and Lucille I. (Wissert) Ammons; m. Maurice Graham DeLand, Feb. 19, 1966 (div. 1974); 1 child, Charles Maurice DeLand. B.A., U. Calif.-Berkeley, 1961; Cert., Goethe Inst., Berlin, 1961; postgrad. Am. U., 1969-71. Economist, AID, U.S. Dept. State, Washington, 1962-70; sr. economist U.S. EPA, Washington, 1970-73, PBGC, Washington, 1974-76; rep. U.S. Govt. Inter-Agy. Task Force, Washington, 1978; dir. tech. programs Pension Benefit Guaranty, Washington, 1976-79; pres. Pension Corp., Los Angeles, 1979—; cons. and lectr. in field. Co-author: (tech. booklet) Guidelines on Plan Termination, 1977; Syllabus on Pension Plans, 1981. Headmaster council Indian Mountain Sch., Conn., 1984—. Named Life mem. Calif. Scholastic Soc., 1957, U.S. Pres.'s Govt. exchange scholar, 1978-79. Mem. Women in Bus., Nat. Assn. Female Execs., Am. Soc. Pension Actuaries (assoc.), Jr. League. Avocations: Painting; reading; skiing; tennis; travel. Office: Pension Corp PO Box 32297 Washington DC 20007

DELANEY, ANDREW, retired insurance company executive, consultant; b. Vienna, Ohio, Aug. 2, 1920; s. John David and Elizabeth L. (Wurstner) D.; m. Wynelle Shellhouse, Apr. 5, 1947; 1 dau., Janet Lynn; m. Pauline Mills, July 31, 1982. B.A., Oberlin Coll., 1942; B.S., NYU, 1942. Actuarial trainee Equitable Life Assurance Co., N.Y.C., 1946-49; asst. actuary Union Central Life Ins. Co., Cin., 1949-54; v.p. actuary Am. Gen. Life Ins. Co., Houston, 1954-68, sr. v.p., 1968-76, sr. v.p., chief investment officer, 1976-82, vice chmn. bd., chief investment officer, 1982-85; ret. Am. Gen. Life Ins. Co., 1985; fin. cons. Fireman's Fund Corp., 1985—; bd. dirs. Cullen Ctr. Bank & Trust, Houston, Fireman's Fund. Corp., Novato, Calif., AOA Corp., Dallas. Life bd. dirs. Big Bros., Houston, 1969—; trustee Found. for Retarded, 1982—, Oberlin Coll., 1981—; past chmn. bd. trustees Emerson Unitarian Ch., Houston. Served to capt. USAF, 1942-46. Fellow Soc. Actuaries (bd. govs.), Houston Racquet Club, Ramada Club, Braeburn Club. Republican. Home: 2205 Pelham Houston TX 77019 Office: 2727 Allen Pkwy Ste 830 Houston TX 77019

DELANEY, EDWARD NORMAN, lawyer; b. Chgo., Sept. 16, 1927; s. Frederick E. and Wynifred (Ward) D.; m. Carole P. Walter, May 31, 1950; children: Deborah Delaney Rogers, Kathleen Delaney Langan, Edward Norman II, Dorian A. LLB, Loyola U., Chgo., 1951; LLM, NYU, 1959. Bar: Ill. 1952, Minn. 1961, U.S. Supreme Ct. 1963, Mo. 1974, D.C. 1975. Staff Office Chief Counsel IRS, N.Y.C., 1955-60; atty. Investors Diversified Svcs., Inc., Mpls., 1960-73, v.p., gen. counsel investment adv. group, 1968-73; sr. v.p., gen. counsel Waddell & Reed and United Investors Life Ins. Co., Kansas City, Mo., 1974; ptnr. firm Bogan & Freeland, Washington, 1975-81; prin. Delaney, Bitonti & Wilhelm, Chartered, Washington, 1981—; chmn. tax com. Investment Co. Inst., 1963-74; mem. bus. adv. com. SEC Inter-Agy. Task Force Offshore Funds, 1970-71. Active fundraiser Ctr. for Performing Arts, Kansas City, Mo., 1974; mem. lawyers com. Washington Performing Arts Soc.; bd. dirs. Civic Orch., Mpls., 1963-68, pres., 1966-68. With USMCR, 1945-46. Fellow Am. Bar Found.; mem. ABA (coun. tax sect. 1974-77, vice chmn. tax sect. 1978-81, chmn. tax sect. 1983-84), Fed., Minn., Hennepin County, Mo., D.C. Bar Assns., Am. Law Inst., Am. Coll. Tax Counsel, Congl. Country Club, Univ. Club, Georgetown Club. Clubs: Congl. Country, Univ., Georgetown, Capitol Hill (Washington). Home: 9405 Tobin Circle Potomac MD 20854 Office: Delaney Bitonti & Wilhelm 1629 K St NW Washington DC 20006

DELANEY, PHILIP ALFRED, banker; b. Chgo., Nov. 18, 1928; s. Walter J. and Kathryn M. (McWilliams) D.; m. Patricia O'Brien, June 21, 1952; children—Sharon Ann, Philip A., Nancy, Mary Beth. BS magna cum laude, U. Notre Dame, 1950; MBA, U. Chgo., 1956; grad., U. Wis. Grad. Sch. Banking, 1960. Trainee A.G. Becker & Co., Chgo., 1950; broker/dealer A.G. Becker & Co., 1951-52; dir. cen. area com. Harris Trust & Savs. Bank, Chgo., 1952—; exec. v.p., chief credit officer Harris Trust & Savs. Bank, 1980-84, pres., 1984—; pres. holding co. Harris Bankcorp, Inc., Chgo., 1984—, also bd. dirs.; prin. Chgo. United; prin. Chgo. United; bd. dirs. DeSoto, Inc., Des Plaines, Ill., Bankmont Fin. Corp., Robert Morris Assocs., Harris Brokerage Services, Inc., Evanston Hosp., Chgo; mem. Chgo. Cen. Area Bd. Dirs. Bd. dirs. Cath. Charities Chgo., Chgo. Conv. and Visitors Bur., Evanston Hosp.; mem. Chgo. Com., Chgo. Council Fgn. Relations; assoc. Northwestern U.; Chief Crusader United Way/Crusade of Mercy; mem. adv. council Chgo. Urban League; mem. citizens bd. Loyola U., Chgo. Served to 2d lt. USMC, 1951. Mem. Am. Bankers Assn., Am. Inst. Banking, Am. Mgmt. Assn., Assn. Res. City Bankers, Bankers Club Chgo., Chgo. Assn. Commerce and Industry, Chgo. Club, Comml. Club of Chgo., Commonwealth, Econ. Club of Chgo., Mid Am. Com., Notre Dame Club of Chgo., North Shore Country Club, Nortwestern U. (assoc.), U. Chgo. Alumni Assn. Roman Catholic. Office: Harris Bankcorp Inc 111 W Monroe St PO Box 755 Chicago IL 60603

DELANEY, ROBERT VERNON, management consultant, distribution executive; b. Passaic, N.J., Mar. 16, 1936; s. Edward Aloysius and Helen Margaret (Gauthier) D.; m. Elissa Ornato, June 15, 1963; children: Edward, James. BBA, NYU, 1963, MBA, 1966; postgrad., St. Louis U., 1967-69, Am. U., 1971-72. Registered practitioner ICC. Transp. mgr. Nabisco, N.Y.C., 1958-62; distbn. mgr. Monsanto Co., St. Louis, 1963-70; dir. phys. distbn. Md. Cup Corp., Owings Mills, 1970-74; mgr. internal cons. Pet Inc., St. Louis, 1974-78; mgr. distbn. planning Internat. Paper Co., N.Y.C., 1978-83; sr. v.p. Leaseway Transp. Co., Cleve., 1983-87; practice leader for transp. Arthur D. Little, Inc., Cambridge, Mass., 1988—; founder Warehousing Edn. and Research Council, Oak Brook, Ill., 1977; bd. dirs. Pvt. Carrier Conf., Inc.; faculty Acad. Advanced Traffic, 1966; guest lectr., frequent speaker ednl. and profl. orgns. Co-author Transportation Strategies for the Eighties, 1982, The Distribution Handbook, 1984; mem. editorial rev. bd. Jour. Bus. Logistics, Internat. Jour. Phys. Distbn. and Materials Mgmt.; contbr. articles to newpapers and bus. pubs. Mem. transp. com. The New Eng. Council, Boston, 1978-82. St. Louis Regional Commerce & Growth Assn., 1975-78; bus. advisor Norman Thomas High Sch., N.Y.C., 1979-82. Staff sgt. U.S. Army, 1953-56. Recipient Salzberg Medallion award for transp., Syracuse U., 1988. Mem. Am. Soc. Transp. and Logistics (cert.), Council of Logistics Mgmt. (exec. com. 1977-82, sec. 1963—, Disting. Service award 1981), Nat. Council Phys. Distbn. Mgmt. (John Drury Sheahan Disting. Service award 1981). Republican. Club: Nat. Press (Washington). Home: 24 Lincoln Dr Acton MA 01720 Office: Arthur D Little Inc Logistics Unit Acorn Pk Cambridge MA 02140

DELANO, LESTER ALMY, JR., advertising executive; b. New Bedford, Mass., Nov. 28, 1928; s. Lester A. and Beatrice (Thomas) D.; m. Margaret Dent (div.); 1 child, Leslie Ann; m. Helaine Shipper; children: Oliver Evan, Peter Franklin. Student, Amherst Coll., Brown U.; M.A., U. Chgo. Mktg. cons. Chgo., 1950-54; v.p. North Advt., Inc., Chgo., 1955-60; pres. Dodge & Delano, Inc., N.Y.C., 1961-71, Tinker, Dodge & Delano, Inc., 1971-76; chmn., chief exec. officer Tinker, Campbell-Ewald Inc., N.Y.C., 1976-77; pres. Campbell-Ewald Internat., London, Eng., 1977-80, Marschalk Campbell-Ewald Worldwide, N.Y.C., 1980-85; chmn. exec. com. Lowe Marschalk Worldwide, 1986-87; exec. dir. Lowe Howard-Spink & Bell plc, N.Y.C., 1987—. Author: Creative Advertising Planning. Served with USN, 1945-48. Home: 115 Central Pk W New York NY 10023 Office: Lowe Howard Spink & Bell 1345 Ave of the Americas New York NY 10105 also: Lowe Howard-Spink & Bell PLC, Bowater House, 68-114 Knightsbridge, London SW1X 7LT, England

DELANY, R. EMMET, lawyer; b. White Plains, N.Y., Feb. 20, 1956; s. Robert Emmet and Frances (Shea) D.; m. Nora Catriona Tully, Dec. 27, 1980; children: Maura Brigid, Erica Shannon. BA in History, Fordham U., 1978, JD, 1982. Bar: N.Y. 1983. Assoc. Golenbock & Barell, N.Y.C., 1983-86; sole practice Mamaroneck, N.Y., 1986—. Mem. ABA, N.Y. State Bar Assn., Westchester Bar Assn., Friendly Sons of St. Patrick. Roman Catholic. Home: 93 Buttery Rd New Canaan CT 06840 Office: 875 Mamaroneck Ave Mamaroneck NY 10543

DELAPLAINE, GEORGE BIRELY, JR., newspaper editor, cable television executive; b. Frederick, Md., Dec. 9, 1926; s. George B. and Ruth (Carty) D.; m. Elizabeth Barker, Aug. 12, 1955; children: George III, James, Edward, John. BBA, Johns Hopkins U., 1948. From reporter to publisher Frederick News-Post, 1949—; v.p. Frederick Brick Works, Inc.; bd. dirs. Farmers and Mechanics Nat. Bank, Frederick; pres. Cablevision Inc., GS Communications, C/R TV Cable. Named Honorary Am. Farmer Nat. Future Farmers Am., 1987. Mem. Kiwanis, Elks, Jaycees, Masons. Republican. Episcopalian. Office: Frederick News-Post 200 E Patrick Frederick MD 21701

DELARYE-GOLD, ANN ELIZABETH, corporate conference executive; b. Chgo., Apr. 11, 1955; d. William Lloyd and Marjorie Mae (Davis) DeLarye; m. Michael Aleck Gold, Aug. 7, 1977. Student, Northwestern U., 1973-76, New Sch. for Social Research, 1976-78. Free-lance writer Chgo., 1982-84; dir. communications Cen. Ednl. Network, Chgo., 1984-86; v.p. Inst. for Internat. Research, N.Y.C., 1986—; planner confs. Mike Gold Media Services, Chgo., 1976-86, field producer, 1982-84, vocal trainer, 1985-86. Contbr. articles to Chgo. Tribune, 1982-84. Chmn. tech. and tng. com., commr. Evanston (Ill.) Cable TV Regulatory Com., 1982-86. Mem. Nat. Assn. for Female Execs. Home: 2 Naples Ave East Norwalk CT 06855 Office: Inst for Internat Rsch 331 Madison Ave 6th Fl New York NY 10017

DE LAS HERAS, GONZALO, banker; b. Madrid, Spain, Jan. 16, 1940; came to U.S., 1984; s. Antonio and Mary (Milla) de las H.; m. Kathleen Anne Devitt; children: Elizabeth, Stephen, James. B.A., Cambridge U., 1960; LL.D., Madrid U., Spain, 1965; postgrad in bus. and econs., U. So. Calif. Exec. dir. B.V.H.A. Ltd., London, Eng., 1971-76; exec. v.p. Banco Urquijo, Madrid, Spain, 1976-77; v.p., gen. mgr. Morgan Guaranty Bank & Trust Co., Madrid, 1978-84; sr. v.p. Morgan Guaranty Bank & Trust Co., N.Y.C., 1984—. Contbr. articles on internat. econs., fin. to London, Madrid jours. Home: 350 Long Hill Dr Short Hills NJ 07078 Office: Morgan Guaranty Bank & Trust Co 23 Wall St New York NY 10015

DELASHMET, GORDON BARTLETT, newsprint executive; b. Moss Point, Miss., Dec. 19, 1928; s. Thomas Lewis and Ione (Broome) DeL.; m. Barbara Harris, Sept. 11, 1971; 1 child, Katherine Casey; children by previous marriage: Gordon Bartlett Jr., W. Premble. BA, U. Miss., 1950. Salesman Internat. Paper, Montreal, Que., Can., 1955-63, regional mgr., Atlanta, 1963-68; exec. v.p. Claredon Paper Sales, Atlanta, 1968-73; v.p. sales Abitibi Newsprint Corp., Atlanta, 1973-77; sr. v.p. Abitibi-Price Sales Corp., N.Y.C., 1977-80, exec. v.p., 1980-88; asst. to pres. Southeast Paper Mfg. Co., Marietta, Ga., 1989—. Patron South Africa Air Force Mus., Adv. Bd. Found. for Africa's Future. Capt. U.S. Army, 1950-54, prisoner of war,

Korea. Recipient Fred Hoyt award Atlanta Rotary, 1976. Mem. Am. Paper Inst., Sigma Chi (Award of Excellence 1983, Significant Sig 1987). Republican. Clubs: Commerce, Wee Burn Country, Capital City, Tournament Players. Lodge: Masons (Knight Comdr. Ct. of Honor 1987). Avocations: golfing, goose and duck hunting, salmon fishing. Home: 10 Granaston Ln Darien CT 06820 also: 2850 Delk Rd Apt 35-I Marietta GA 30067

DEL BEL, PAUL THOMAS, marketing research executive; b. Buffalo, Apr. 11, 1949; s. Peter Joseph and Doris Marie (Jank) Del B.; m. Ljubica L. Luksic, Nov. 15, 1980; children: Brandon L., Matthew L. BA, Canisius Coll., 1971; MSW, Tulane U., 1976; M of Internat. Mgmt., Am. Grad. Sch. Internat. Mgmt., Glendale, Ariz., 1982. Sr. counselor Buffalo Gen. Community Mental Health Ctr., 1972-75; sr. planner Navajo Health Systems Agy., Window Rock, Ariz., 1977-79; project analyst Cen. Ariz. Health Systems Agy., Phoenix, 1979-80; cons. mktg. research, Phoenix, 1982—; research coordinator Mktg. Innovations, Phoenix, 1983-84; market research analyst Del E. Webb Devel. Co., Phoenix, 1984-86; corp. mgr. market research Del E. Webb Corp., Phoenix, 1986—. Author mktg. news stories. Mem. Am. Mktg. Assn., Am. Demographics Inst., Drachman Inst. Roman Catholic. Club: Toastmasters (pres. Phoenix chpt. 1987). Home: 6036 W Hearn Rd Glendale AZ 85306

DEL CASTILLO, JEANNE LOUISE TAILLAC, oil industry executive; b. New Orleans, May 15, 1933; d. Roland Jean and Louise (Schwall) Taillac; m. Roberto Eduardo del Castillo (div.); children: Esther, Jeanne, Roberto, Eduardo, Tammy. Nursing student, Charity Hosp., New Orleans, 1951-52; student, various bus. mgmt. courses, 1952-86. Asst. office mgr. Ray Merc. Co., New Orleans, 1958-64; consul, maritime comml. officer Consulate Gen. Panama, New Orleans, 1964-72; mgr. McDermott Internat., Inc., New Orleans, 1972—; pres., owner Kiddie Kare Train'n Sta.; cons. Consulates of Panama, Houston, New Orleans, 1972—; coordinator Panama Maritime Licensing, 1985—. Co-chmn. Jerry Lewis Telethon, New Orleans, 1977; fundraising co-chair Annual Hanicapped Children's Easter Parade, bd. dirs. La. Sch. for Deaf, Baton Rouge, 1985—, Sta. WNNR-Radio, 1972-74, New Orleans Soccer Assn., 1969-73; pres. Costa Rica Soccer Assn., 1969-72; fundraiser Bayside Vol. Fire Dept., Bay St. Louis, Miss., 1986—; co-chmn. State Sex Edn. Handicapped Children Comn., Baton Rouge, 1986—; chmn. Handicapped Children Christmas Program; coord. various Christmas programs for sick, elderly and needy; mem. Hancock County Humane Soc. Recipient merit award Bayside Fire Dept., Bay St. Louis, 1987, New Orleans Soccer Leagues merit award, 1971. Mem. Panama Maritime Adv. Com., Panama C. of C. and Industry, U.S. C. of C. in Panama, Miss. C. of C. Republican. Roman Catholic. Home: 4413 Senac Dr Metairie LA 70003

DELEHANTY, PETER MICHAEL, marketing executive; b. Manchester, N.H., Mar. 8, 1954; s. Robert Henry and Mary (Woodhead) D.; m. SueAnn Louise, Apr. 16, 1983; children: Erin Ashley, Robert William. BS in Speech Communications, U. Oreg., 1975; postgrad., Coll. Fin. Planning. Registered rep. Smith, Barney, Harris & Upham, Medford, Oreg., 1976-77; underwriter N.Y. Life Ins. Co., Eugene, Oreg., 1977-79; dist. mgr. Pat Ryan & Assocs., Chgo., 1979-81; with sales & mktg. Clayton Brown & Assocs., Chgo., 1981-86; with mktg. and trading Unit Trust & Mut. Fund Dept. Oppenheimer Serurities, Chgo., 1986-87; mgr. mktg. Murphey Favre Securities, Composite Mut. Fund Group, Seattle, 1987—. Mem. Rep. Presdl. Task Force, Washington, 1984. Mem. Am. Mgmt. Assn., Investment Co. Inst. (sales force mktg. com.), Interat. Assn. Fin. Planning, Sigma Chi. Roman Catholic. Home: 4613 174th Pl SE Issaquah WA 98027 Office: Murphey Favre Inc 1000 Second Ave Ste 2700 Seattle WA 98104

DELEON, ARTHUR EUGENE, oil company executive; b. Houston, Aug. 25, 1942; s. Walter Calhoun and Mary Louise (Robertson) DeL.; m. Mary Jane Sidenblad, Jan. 12, 1963; children: Sheryl Lynne, Elizabeth Katherine, Mary Jeanne, Samuel Eugene. Student, San Jacinto Coll., 1967. Journeyman electrician Nat. Forge, Houston, 1967-69, Proler Steel, Houston, 1967-69, Petro-Tex Chem., Houston, 1970-75; owner DeLeon Constrn., Houston, 1975-79; elec. supr. Chevron Overseas Petroleum Inc., Cabinda, Angola, 1979—; owner A&D Electric Co., The Woodlands, Tex., 1974-76, Recycle Am. Co., 1988—. Mem. Garden Oaks Civic Club, Houston, 1981-86, Houston Police Patrolman's Assn., 1985; booster mem. Tex. State Troopers' Assn., Houston, 1986. Served with USN, 1961-65; trustee Garden Oaks Baptist Ch. Named to Eagle Scout, Order of Arrow Boy Scouts Am. Mem. Ind. Builders and Contractors Assn., Internat. Brotherhood Elec. Workers, Internat. Platform Assn., Gideons Internat., Am. Legion, Greater Heights Area C. of C. Baptist. Lodge: Masons, Shriners. Home: 1434 Chippendale Houston TX 77018 Office: Chevron Overseas Petroleum PO Box 7137 San Francisco CA 94120-7137

DEL GENIO, ROBERT M., publisher; b. Chgo., Dec. 5, 1945; s. Edward Rocco and Virginia Mary (Duffey) Del G.; m. Anita L. Sosa, Feb. 12, 1972 (div. 1986); 1 child, Laura. BA, St. Thomas Coll., 1967; MA, Northwestern U., 1968, MBA, 1972. Editor Commerce Clearing House Inc., Chgo. and Tampa, Fla., 1968-80, Enterprise Pub. Inc., Wilmington, Del., 1980, Newsletter Mgmt. Corp., Boca Raton, Fla., 1981-84; dir. product devel. Longman Group USA, Chgo., 1984-85; v.p. product devel. Practice Devel. Inst. Ltd., Chgo., 1985-87; editor/pubr. CPA Mktg. Group, Ltd., Oak Brook, Ill., 1987—, Cosmopolitan Pubs., Inc., Chgo., 1987—; mktg. cons. Cosmopolitan Nat. Bank, Chgo., 1987—, Surcom Internat., Chgo., 1988—. Editro/Pubr.: Businesslines, 1988, Briefs on the Practice of Law, 1987—, Pulse on Practice Management, 1987—; author: Complete Book of Corporate Forms, 1980. Home: 922 North Blvd #802 Oak Park IL 60301 Office: Cosmopolitan Pubs Inc 801 N Clark St #300 Chicago IL 60610

DELGREGO, ANDREW AUGUST, banker; b. Meriden, Conn., Feb. 7, 1942; s. Andrew and Nellie (Bukowski) DelG.; m. Susan Ann Tremper, July 31, 1965; children: Jamie, Scott, Mark. BBA, Bucknell U., 1964; MBA, Butler U., 1967; cert. in advanced mgmt. program, Harvard U., 1983. Sr. v.p. First Bank, New Haven, 1967-79; pres., chief exec. officer New Britian (Conn.) Bank & Trust, 1979-84; exec. v.p. Conn. Savs. Bank, New Haven, 1984-87; pres., chief exec. officer Lafayette Bank & Trust Co., Bridgeport, Conn., 1987—. Pres. United Way Conn., Hartford; former bd. dirs., treas. Rehab. Ctr., New Haven; bd. dirs. United Way Ea. Fairfield County, Bridgeport, Greater Bridgeport Bus. Coun. 1st lt. U.S. Army, 1965-67. Home: 294 Argyle Rd Cheshire CT 06410 Office: Lafayett Bank & Trust Co 1087 Broad St Bridgeport CT 06601

DEL GUERCIO, LOUIS RICHARD MAURICE, surgeon, educator, company executive; b. N.Y.C., Jan. 15, 1929; s. Louis and Hortense (Ardengo) Del G.; m. Paula Marie Helene de Vautibault, May 18, 1957; children: Louis, Francsca, Paul, Catherine, Maria, Michelle, Christopher Anthony. B.S., Fordham U., 1949; M.D., Yale U., 1953. Diplomate: Am. Bd. Surgery, Am. Bd. Thoracic Surgery. Intern Columbia-Presbyn. Med. Center, N.Y.C., 1953-54; resident St Vincent's Hosp., N.Y.C., 1954-58, Cleve. City Hosp., 1958-60; practice medicine specializing in thoracic surgery 1960—; mem. faculty Albert Einstein Coll. Medicine, N.Y.C., 1960-71; assoc. prof. Albert Einstein Coll. Medicine, 1966-70, prof. surgery, 1970-71, dir. Clin. Research Center-Acute, 1967-71; dir; clin. prof. surgery N.J. Coll. Medicine, Newark, 1971-76; prof. surgery N.Y. Med. Coll., N.Y.C., 1976—; chmn. dept. N.Y. Med. Coll., 1976—; chief surgery Westchester County Med. Center, 1976—; cons. surgeon other hosps.; mem. surg. study sect. NIH, 1970-74; mem. com. on shock NRC-Nat. Acad. Scis., 1969-71; mem. merit rev. bd. VA, 1971-74; mem. health care tech. study sect. Dept. HHS, 1980-84; cons. Nat. Ctr. Health Services Research, 1980-84; chmn. bd. dirs. Daltex Med. Scis., Inc. Author: (with B.G. Clarke) Urology, 1956, The Multilingual Manual for Medical History Taking, 1972, (with S.G. Hershey, R. McConn) Septic Shock in Man, 1971; editor-in-chief: Critical Care Monitor, 1980-85; contbr. articles to med. jours.; patentee in field. Served with Mcht. Marine, 1946-47; served with AUS, 1949-51. Recipient award in medicine Fordham U. Alumni Assn., 1974, Gold award Am. Acad. Pediatrics, 1973, Alpha Omega Alpha Faculty award N.Y. Med. Coll., 1982; Am. Thoracic Soc fellow, 1959-60; grantee Health Research Council N.Y., 1965-71; grantee NIH, 1962-71. Fellow A.C.S.; mem. Am. Trauma Soc. (founding mem.), Soc. Critical Care Medicine (founding mem., pres. 1976), Am. Surg. Assn., Am. Physiol. Soc., Soc. Univ. Surgeons, Equestrian Order of Holy Sepulchre of Jerusalem. Home: 14 Pryer Ln Larchmont NY 10538 Office: NY Med Coll Munger Pavilion Valhalla NY 10595

DELISLE, PETER ANDREW, human resources executive; b. Glen Cove, N.Y., Sept. 12, 1949; s. Leo Aime and Edith Joan (Murray) DeL.; m. Janice Louise Braem, Aug. 12, 1972; children: Amanda Edith, Margaret Ann (twins). BA, U. Conn., 1971; MS, Cen. Conn. State U., 1973. Dir. community corrections Colo. Dist. Ct., 1979; mgr. personnel Hewlett-Packard Co., Colorado Springs, 1979-85; v.p. Convex Computer Corp., Richardson, Tex., 1985-89; with The Ananda Co., Richardson, 1989—. Mem. adv. bd. Leadership Richardson, 1986—; trustee Town of Green Mountain Falls, Colo., 1978, Ch. in Wildwood, Green Mountain Falls, 1980; bd. dirs. Urban League Pikes Peak Region, Colorado Springs, 1983-85, Citizens Goals Colorado Springs, 1984-85. Capt. U.S. Army, 1971-79. Reciepient Recognition for Contbrn. award, Urban League Pikes Peak, 1984, Leadership Richardson award, 1987. Mem. Richardson C. of C. (bd. dirs. 1986-87, adv. bd. 1986—, higher edn. com. 1987—), Tex. Assn. Continuing Educators, Tex. Assn. Continuing Higher Edn. (cons. 1987—). Home: 2105 Rising Star Ct Plano TX 75075 Office: The Ananda Co 2201 Waterview Dr Richardson TX 75081

DELK, IRA EDWIN, utilities and diversified company executive; b. Weldon, Iowa, Jan. 21, 1930; s. Charles Wesley and Berniece Luela (Butler) D.; m. Barbara Jean Grovier, Oct. 20, 1951; children: Steven M., Linda J. Delk Rubel. BA, Drake U., 1951; JD, U. Iowa, 1958; MBA, U. S.D., 1977. Atty. Iowa Pub. Service Co., Sioux City, 1958-75, assoc. counsel, 1975-77, assoc. gen. counsel, 1977-82, gen. counsel, 1982-86; v.p., gen. counsel Midwest Engergy Co./Iowa Pub. Service Co., Sioux City, 1986—. V.p. Sioux City Lions Club, 1964-82; pres. Boys & Girls Home and Family Service, 1966-74; chmn. right-of-way com. Sioux City Plan and Zoning Commn., Sioux City, 1966-74. Served to staff sgt. USAF, 1951-55. Republican. Office: Midwest Energy Co 401 Douglas St Sioux City IA 51101

DELL, ERNEST ROBERT, lawyer; b. Vandergrift, Pa., Feb. 6, 1928; m. Karen D. Reed, May 8, 1965; children: Robert W., John D., Jane C. B.S., U. Pitts., 1949, M.Litt., 1953; J.D., Harvard U., 1956. Bar: Pa. 1957, U.S. Supreme Ct. 1961; C.P.A., Pa. Ptnr. firm Reed Smith Shaw & McClay, Pitts., 1956—; adj. prof. law Duquesne U. Law Sch., Pitts., 1960-86; bd. dirs. Atty's. Liability Assurance Soc. Inc., Chgo., Atty's. Liability Assurance Soc. (Bermuda) Ltd. Mem. ABA, Fed. Bar Assn., Pa. Bar Assn., Allegheny County Bar Assn., Pa. Inst. CPA's, Am. Inst. CPA's. Home: 119 Riding Trail Ln Pittsburgh PA 15215 Office: Reed Smith Shaw & McClay 435 6th Ave Mellon Sq Pittsburgh PA 15219

DELLA FEMINA, JERRY, advertising agency executive; b. Bklyn., July 22, 1936; (married); three children. Former advt. copywriter; former pres., now chmn. bd., chief exec. officer Della Femina, Travisano, & Partners Inc. (now Della Femina McNamee WCRS Inc.), 1967—. Author: (1970.) From Those Wonderful Folks Who Gave You Pearl Harbor. Named Advt. Exec. of Year, 1970. Office: Della Femina McNamee WCRS Inc 350 Hudson Ave New York NY 10014 *

DELLAS, ROBERT DENNIS, investment banker; b. Detroit, July 4, 1944; s. Eugene D. and Maxine (Rudell) D.; m. Shila L. Clement, Mar. 27, 1976; children—Emily Allison, Lindsay Michelle. B.A. in Econs., U. Mich., Ann Arbor, 1966; M.B.A., Harvard U., Cambridge, 1970. Analyst Burroughs Corp., Detroit, 1966-67, Pasadena, Calif., 1967-68; mgr. U.S. Leasing, San Francisco, 1970-76; pres., dir. Energetics Mktg. & Mgmt. Assn., San Francisco, 1978-80; sr. v.p. E.F. Hutton & Co., San Francisco, 1981-85; prin. founder Capital Exchange Internat., San Francisco, 1976—; gen. ptnr. Kanland Assocs., Tex., 1982, Claremont Assocs., Calif., 1983, Lakeland Assocs., Ga., 1983, Americal Assocs., Calif., 1983, Chatsworth Assocs., Calif., 1983, Walnut Grove Assocs., Calif., 1983, Somerset Assocs., N.J., 1983, One San Diego Assocs., Calif., 1984. Bd. dirs. Found. San Francisco's Archtl. Heritage. Mem. U.S. Trotting Assn., Calif. Harness Horse Breeders Assn. (Breeders award for Filly of Yr. 1986, Aged Pacing Mare, 1987, 88), Calif. Golf Club San Francisco. Home: 1911 Sacramento St San Francisco CA 94109 Office: care Shearson Lehman Hutton Inc 580 California St San Francisco CA 94104

DELLA SERRA, VIRGINIA ANN, savings and loan association executive; b. Morristown, N.J., Oct. 17, 1934; d. Walter Frederick and Margaret Ann (McGowan) Schmidt; m. Raymond Harry Della Serra, Jan. 30, 1954; children: Raymond, Mary, Susan, Daniel, Linda. Grad., Internat. Corr. Sch., 1988. Asst. mgr. Korvettes, Watchung, N.J., 1974-80; head teller 1st Atlantic Savs., Scotch Plains, N.J., 1981-82, asst. br. mgr., 1986—; customer svc. rep. 1st Atlantic Savs., South Plainfield, N.J., 1982-86. Recipient Cert. of Appreciation Scotch Plains-Fanwood High Sch., 1988. Republican. Methodist. Home: 191 Stirling Rd Warren NJ 07060 Office: 1st Atlantic Savs 1922 Westfield Ave Scotch Plains NJ 07076

DELLIS, FRÉDY MICHEL, car rental company executive; b. Frasnes-lez-Gosselies, Hainaut, Belgium, Aug. 11, 1945; s. Ernest and Josée (Bailly) D.; m. Agnes A. Parms, July 20, 1984; children: Jennifer Sarah, Nelson Charles. Student, Sorbonne, Paris, 1968-69; grad. advanced mgmt. program, Harvard U., 1985. Chief acct. Hertz Luxembourg, Brussels, 1969-70; sales mgr. Hertz Belgium, Brussels, 1971-74, regional mgr., 1975; gen. mgr. Hertz Scandinavia, Stockholm, 1976-77, Europcar France, Paris, 1977-78; asst. v.p. ops. Hertz Corp., Dallas, 1978; gen. mgr. Hertz Benelux, Amsterdam, The Netherlands, 1979-80; v.p. ops. Hertz Europe, London, 1980-82; pres. Hertz Europe, Middle East, Africa, London, 1982-84; exec. v.p. Hertz Corp., N.Y.C., 1984-87; pres. Hertz Internat., London, 1987—; bd. dirs. Axus S.A., Brussels. Roman Catholic. Office: Hertz Corp 225 Brae Blvd PO Box 713 Park Ridge NJ 97656 also: Hertz Internat, 700 Bath Rd, Cranford, Middlesex England TW5 9TW

DELLOMO, FRANK A., banker; b. Bklyn., Nov. 24, 1933; s. Anthony E. and Veronica K. (Jenson) D.; m. Pat Turvey, Oct. 24, 1962; children: Tracey, Alysen. Grad., Bklyn. Coll., 1957; postgrad., Brown U., 1963-66, Amherst Coll., 1968-69. Vice pres. Bklyn. Savs. Bank, 1968-72, sr. v.p., 1972-75, exec. v.p., 1975-81, pres., 1981—; sr. exec. v.p. Met. Savs. Bank, 1982-84; vice chmn. Crossland Savs. Bank, 1985—; mem. faculty Grad. Sch. Banking Brown U. Trustee Bklyn. Bur. Community Svc., Bklyn. Hosp., St. Vincent's Svcs.; mem. exec. com. N.Y. div. Am. Cancer Soc., 1981; bd. dirs. The Holy Child Sch. of Old Westbury. Mem. Savs. Instns. Mktg. Soc. Am. Clubs: Creek, N.Y. Athletic. Office: Crossland Savs 211 Montague St Brooklyn NY 11201

DELL'OSSO, LUINO, JR., energy and natural resources executive; b. Galveston, Tex., Oct. 25, 1939; s. Luino Sr. and Mary (Celli) Dell'O.; m. Margaret Ann Brougher, June 10, 1967; children: L. David, Scott B. BS, U. Notre Dame, 1961; PhD, Rice U., 1966. Various positions Conoco, Inc., various locations, 1968-73; project mgr. El Paso Alaska Co., Houston, 1973-75, Washington, 1975-77; gen. mgr. El Paso Long Terminal Co., Houston, 1977-79; dir. corp. planning and econs. The El Paso Co., Houston, 1979-82, v.p., 1982-83, sr. v.p., 1983-84; sr. v.p. and chief fin. officer Burlington No. Inc., Seattle, 1984-89; sr. v.p., chief fin. officer Burlington Resources, Inc., Seattle, 1989—; bd. dirs. Portal Pipeline Co., Dallas, Plum Creek Timber Co., Seattle, Nat. Exch., Inc., McLean, Va., vis. com. coll. engrng. U. Wash., Seattle, 1985—. Trustee Mus. History and Industry, Seattle, 1986—. Capt. U.S. Army, 1966-68. Recipient Top Chief Fin. Officer Industry award Instl. Investor, 1986. Mem. Chief Fin. Officers Task Force (coun. pvt. sector 1986—), Columbia Tower Club, Seattle Yacht Club. Roman Catholic. Home: 4591 E Mercer Way Mercer Island WA 98040 Office: Burlington Resources Inc 999 3rd Ave Seattle WA 98104-4097

DELMHORST, ARTHUR MCGILL, real estate consultant; b. Bklyn., Aug. 12, 1938; s. Berton J. and Margaret (McGill) D.; m. Wynne Paffard, July 11, 1964; children: Dwight, Frederic. BA, Columbia U., 1960, MBA, 1964. Sr. v.p. Landauer Assocs., N.Y.C., 1973—; lectr. NYU, 1984, 85. Contbr. articles to profl. publs. Vice chmn., dir. YMCA Greater N.Y., N.Y.C., 1985—; treas., bd. dirs. Columbia U. Club Found., N.Y.C., 1985—. Served to lt. USNR, 1960-62. Mem. Real Estate Bd. N.Y., Indsl. Devel. Research Council, Ave. of Ams. Assn. (pres., bd. dirs. 1988—). Office: Landauer Assocs 335 Madison Ave New York NY 10017

DEL MURO, RAUL, sales executive; b. Chgo., July 10, 1931; s. Rosalio and Guadalupe (Quezada) del M. BSEE, U. Ill., 1958; postgrad., Calif. Inst. Tech., 1962-64, Santa Clara U., 1966-69. Sr. staff mem. rsch. and devel. Lockheed Missile and Space Corp., Sunnyvale, Calif., 1964-68; mktg. program mgr. Gen. Electric Co., Washington, 1968-70; regional sales mgr. Advanced Systems, Inc., Los Angeles, 1970-73; nat. account mgr. Hughes Aircraft Co., Carlsbad, Calif., 1973-74; sales and mktg. mgr. Gerber/Camsco, Inc., San Diego, 1974-79; regional account exec. Auto-Trol Tech. Corp., San Diego, 1980-82; regional sales mgr. McDonnell Douglas Automation Co., Westminster, Calif., 1982-84, Computervision Corp/OIR, San Diego, 1984-85; nat. sales mgr. Teledyne Brown Engring, Costa Mesa, Calif., 1985—. Mem. IEEE, Nat. Computer Graphics assn., Sales Mktg. and Exec. Assn., Am. Mgmt. Assn. Office: IDM Assocs SA PO Box 2988 La Jolla CA 92038

DELPH, THOMAS LEE, publishing executive; b. Anderson, Ind., June 26, 1933; s. Everett William and Marjorie Isabelle (Cookman) D.; m. Sandra Lee Ford, June 20, 1961 (div. 1969); children: Deborah Lynn Delph Ellsworth, Stephanie Jane Delph Haroldson, Angela Kay; m. Marylu Merrell Freeman, June 13, 1970; children: Sara Elizabeth Freeman Gifford, Carol Lynn Freeman Crays, Kimberly Susan Freeman, William Thomas Delph. BS, Ind. U., 1955. Assoc. editor Nat. Retail Hardward Assn., Indpls., 1958-61, mng. editor, 1961-64, sales promotion mgr., 1964-66, mktg. mgr., 1966-68, gen. sales mgr., 1968-73, dir. sales and mktg., 1973-80, assoc. pub., 1980-84; pub. Chilton Co. div. ABC Cap Cities, Radnor, Pa., 1985-88, group pub., 1988—. Precinct del. Indpls. Rep. Party, 1961-64; mem. speakers bur. Indpls. United Fund, 1962-64. With U.S. Army, 1956-58. Mem. German Shepard Dog Club Am., Ind. U. Varsity Club. Methodist. Home: 331 N Woodmont Dr Downingtown PA 19335

DELSACK, KATHERINE LANDEY, lawyer; b. N.Y.C., Mar. 28, 1955. BA, Clark U., 1980; JD, U. Dayton, 1982; LLM in Tax, Georgetown U., 1983. Bar: D.C. 1983, Calif. 1986. Assoc. Kutak, Rock & Campbell, Washington, 1983-85; pres., chief exec. officer Plan Care, Inc., Irvine, Calif., 1985-88; ptnr. Polack & Landey, Irvine, 1985-86, Finley, Kumble, Wagner et.al., Newport Beach, Calif., 1986-88, Sheppard, Mullin, Richter & Hampton, Newport Beach, 1988-89, Delsack & Delsack, Newport Beach, 1989—; adj. prof. law U. So. Calif., 1986—, U. Calif., Irvine, 1988—. Contbr. articles on taxation and comml. law to profl. jours. Mem. ABA (chmn. internat. law com. of gen. practice sect., 1986—), Orange County Bar Assn., Nat. Assn. Women Lawyers (chmn. bankruptcy com., 1983—), Nat. Assn. Women Execs., Newport Beach (Calif.) C. of C. Republican. Club: Dolphins. Home: 25 Mainsail Dr Corona Del Mar CA 92625 Office: Delsack & Delsack 620 Newport Ctr Dr Ste 320 Newport Beach CA 92660

DEL SANTO, LAWRENCE A., retail merchandising company executive; b. 1934; married. B.S., U. San Francisco, 1955. With Household Merchandising Inc., Des Plaines, Ill., from 1957, with advt. dept. subs. Vons Grocery Co., 1957-58, asst. advt. mgr., 1958-61, advt. mgr., 1961-68, mgr. sales and mdse., 1968-71, sr. v.p., 1971-73, pres., chief exec. officer, 1973-75, corp. sr. v.p., 1975-79, exec. v.p., from 1979, also bd. dirs.; exec. v.p. Lucky Stores Inc., Dublin, Calif., to 1986, pres., 1986—, also bd. dirs. Served with U.S. Army, 1955-57. Office: Lucky Stores Inc 6300 Clark Ave Dublin CA 94568 *

DE LUCA, PETER J., lawyer, corporate executive; b. N.Y.C., Oct. 15, 1927; s. Thomas A. and Madeline (Insard) De L.; m. Marie Joan Macchia, Sept. 18, 1954; 1 child, David Laurence. LL.B. cum laude, N.Y. Law Sch., 1953. Bar: N.Y. With Cravath, Swaine & Moore, 1953-59; with Pepsi Co., Inc., N.Y.C., 1959-71, v.p., 1963-65, v.p., gen. counsel, sec., 1965-71; sr. v.p. for corp. affairs, gen. counsel, dir. Revlon, Inc., 1971-73; sr. v.p., gen. counsel Gen. Foods Corp., N.Y.C., 1973—, also bd. dirs. Mem. Gov. Carey's Com. on Appointee Standards; bd. dirs. Heart Found.; vice chmn. Burke Rehab. Hosp., N.Y. Foundling Com., NAACP Legal Def. and Edn. Fund; bd. dirs., chmn. Coun. of Better Bus. Bur.; trustee Food and Drug Law Inst., Fortune Soc., N.Y. Law Sch.; bd. visitors Pace U. Law Sch. With U.S. Mcht. Marine USNR, 1945-47. Mem. ABA, N.Y. State Bar Assn., Assn. Bar City N.Y., Delta Theta Phi, Sigma Pi Phi. Democrat. Clubs: Univ, Westchester Country. Home: 360 E 72d St New York NY 10021 Office: Gen Foods Corp 250 North St White Plains NY 10625

DELUCA, RONALD, advertising agency executive; b. Reading, Pa., Oct. 28, 1924; s. Nicola and Grace (Carabello) DeL.; m. Lois Ann Hall, Nov. 27, 1952; children: Christine, Diane, Patricia, Maria, Lisa, Nicholas. Certificate comml. art, Pratt Inst., 1949; B.F.A., Syracuse U., 1951; B.A., New Sch. Social Research, 1966. Art dir. Roy S. Durstine (advt.), N.Y.C., 1954-56, Kenyon & Eckhardt (advt.), N.Y.C., 1956-66; head creative group Grey Advt., N.Y.C., 1966-67; with Kenyon & Eckhardt Advt., N.Y.C., 1967-85; exec. v.p., vice chmn. Kenyon & Eckhardt Advt., 1976-85; pres. Bozell Jacobs, Kenyon & Eckhardt, N.Y.C., 1986—. Artist, J.C. Penney, N.Y.C., 1951-52; designer, Remington Rand, N.Y.C., 1952-53. Served with USAAF, 1942-46. Methodist (chmn. pastor parish relations com.). Home: Larchmont St Ardsley NY 10502 Office: Bozell Jacobs Kenyon & Eckhardt Inc 40 W 23rd St New York NY 10010

DE LUCIA, ROBERT (EDWARD), hospital finance executive; b. Chgo., Apr. 22, 1943; s. Donald Arthur and Angela (Galotta) De L.; m. Claudia Ann Johnson, Feb. 1969 (div. Nov. 1977); children: Laurie Catherine, Cheryl Lynn; m. Rose Marie Farkas, June 23, 1979 (div. Jan. 1984); children: Russell (dec.), Ronald, Rachel. AA, Thornton Community Coll., South Holland, Ill., 1978, cert. bus. mgmt., 1978. Cost acct. Royal Electric Mfg. Co., Chgo., 1962-64; data processing supr. Nat. Cert. Interviews, Chgo., 1964-66; project leader, programmer Rush-Presbyn. St. Luke's Med. Ctr., Chgo., 1966-69, systems mgr., 1969-73, dir. fin. systems, 1973-86; systems cons. Chgo. Osteopathic Health Systems, Inc., 1986—; chmn. Admissions, Discharges, Transfers/Med. Info. Systems devel. project Rush-Presbyn. St. Luke's Med. Ctr., 1977-80; project dir. outpatient system, 1978-86, payroll system, 1982-83, Uniform Bill-82 devel., 1983—. Mem. Electronic Computing Health Oriented, Ill. Uniform Bill-82 Implementation Task Force. Republican. Roman Catholic. Lodge: Elks.

DELWICHE, LYLE D., manufacturing executive; b. Rosierre, Wis., Apr. 27, 1934; s. Herman J. and Lucy (Naze) D.; m. Gail Cramer, Dec. 22, 1958 (div. Feb. 1973); m. Johanna A. Van Nunen, Feb. 1, 1974; children: Jeffrey Scott, Kimberly Cramer, Phillip Jason. BSBA, Lawrence U., 1956. Contract mgr. Honeywell, Mpls., 1958-59; market coord. Tennant Co., Mpls., 1959-62, product mgr., 1962-66, asst. div. mgr., 1966-68; European mgr. Tennant Co., Rotterdam, The Netherlands, 1968-72; internat. sales mgr. Tennant Co., Mpls., 1972-75, v.p. internat dept., 1975-85, sr. v.p., 1985—; dir. Fuji-Tennant, Tokyo, 1975—, Tennant NU, Uden, The Netherlands, 1975—, Tennant Maintenance Systems, London, 1984—; pres. Contract Application Inc., Mpls., 1985—; internat. chmn. MAPI, Washington, 1988—. Advisor Jr. Achievement, Mpls., 1963-64; mem. Consular Corps Consul of The Netherlands, Mpls., 1984—; trustee St. Mary's Coll., Winona, Minn., 1988—. With USN, 1956-58. Mem. Am. Assn. The Netherlands, The Netherlands C. of C. Republican. Methodist.

DELY, STEVEN, aerospace company executive; b. N.Y.C., July 16, 1943; m. Kristine Jon Kolbe, June 7, 1975. BBA, CCNY, 1966; JD, Bklyn. Law Sch., 1968; postgrad., Harvard U., 1979. Bar: N.Y. 1972, U.S. Supreme Ct. 1983. Corp. counsel, dir. personnel services Grumman Allied Industries Inc., Garden City, N.Y., 1971-75, gen. counsel, sec., 1976-78; v.p. human resources Melville, N.Y., 1979-82; dir. human resources Grumman Corp., Bethpage, N.Y., 1982-85; v.p. resources and adminstrn. Grumman Electronics Systems div., Bethpage, 1985-86; v.p., asst. to pres. Grumman Corp., Bethpage, 1986-88, v.p., asst. to chmn. bd., 1988—. Office: Grumman Corp 1111 Stewart Ave Bethpage NY 11714

DEMANN, MICHAEL MARCUS, industrial psychologist; b. Mpls., June 1, 1932; s. George S. and Mary Hazel (Short) DeM.; B.A., U. Minn., 1955, M.A., 1958, Ph.D., 1960; m. Carol L. Knutson, Feb. 10, 1961; children—James G., Susan M., John P. Staff mem. VA Hosp., Mpls., 1960-61; cons. psychologist Rohrer, Hibler and Replogle, Mpls., 1961-65; cons. psychologist in pvt. practice, Mpls., 1965—; dir. Internat. Graphics Corp., Mpls., 1967—; cons. Social Security Adminstrn., Mpls., 1966-67. Bd. dirs. Opportunity Workshop, Mpls., 1962-69; bd. govs. St. Mary's Jr. Coll., Mpls., 1973. Served with M.C., U.S. Army, 1950-52. Mem. Am. Psychol. Assn., Minn. Psychol. Assn. (exec. council 1971-73), Am. Legion. Episcopalian. Home: 6513 Stauder Circle Edina MN 55436 Office: 6750 France Ave S Minneapolis MN 55435

DEMARCO, RALPH JOHN, real estate developer; b. N.Y.C., Mar. 22, 1924; s. Frank and Mary (Castriota) DeM.; BA, Claremont Men's Coll., 1956; m. Arlene Gilbert, July 1, 1945; children: Sheryl DeMarco Grahn, Stephen, Laura DeMarco Wilson. Asso. John B. Kilroy Co., Riverside, Calif., 1960-64, also mgr. ops. Riverside, San Bernardino counties, 1960-64; v.p. Marcus W. Meairs Co., 1964-67; pres. Diversified Properties, Inc., Riverside, 1967-72; v.p. Downey Savs. & Loan Assn. (Calif.), 1972-75; exec. v.p. DSL Svc. Co., 1972-75; pres. Interstate Shopping Ctrs., Inc., Santa Ana, Calif., 1975-87; exec. dir. comml. devel. Lewis Homes Mgmt. Corp., Upland, Calif., 1987—. Mem. City of Riverside Planning Commn., 1955-59, Airport Commn., 1960-70; mem. Urban Land Inst. 1st lt. USAF, 1942-45. Mem. Internat. Coun. Shopping Ctrs. Home: 245 E Foothill Blvd #184 Upland CA 91786 Office: 1156 N Mountain Ave Upland CA 91786

DEMARCO, ROLAND R., foundation executive; b. Mt. Morris, N.Y., July 21, 1910; s. Marion and Mary (Scalzette) DeM.; m. Lydia Hees, June 23, 1934; children—Richard, Ronald, Lynn. Diploma, Geneseo State Tchrs. Coll., 1930; B.S., N.Y. State Coll. Tchrs., 1934; A.M., Columbia U., 1937, Ph.D., 1942; student, U. Munich, Germany, 1937, Shrivenham Am. U., Eng., 1945, Officers Candidate Sch., 1944, Air Intelligence Sch., 1944; LL.D., Chungang U., Seoul, Korea, 1959; D.Litt., Sung Kyun Kwan U., Seoul, 1969, Hanyang U., Seoul, 1974. Instr. Gowanda Pub. Schs., 1930-34; dir. social studies East Islip High Sch., N.Y., 1934-38; instr. social scis. Coll. Charleston, 1939; instr. social scis. Columbia U., 1939-40, vis. prof., 1946-47; prof. history, head dept. social scis. Ala. State Tchrs. Coll., 1940-46, pres. dept., dean, 1949, adminstrv. head, 1949-50, pres., 1950-52; pres. Finch Coll., 1952-70, pres. emeritus, cons., 1970-75; chmn., chief exec. officer Internat. Human Assistance Programs, Inc., N.Y.C., 1973-82, hon. chmn., 1982-84, 85—, pres., chief exec. officer, 1984-85; head history dept. Finch Jr. Coll., 1947-49; curriculum cons. Jackson County Schs., Ala., 1940-43; mem. Nat. Adv. Council Edn. Disadvantaged Children, 1971-73; exec. vice chmn., chmn. ednl. adv. com. Am.-Korea Found., 1953-64, pres., 1964-68, 71-73, hon. chmn., 1968-71, chmn., chief exec. officer, 1973-75. Author: The Italianization of African Natives, 1943, The Comeback Country, Vol. I: Light of the East, an Insight into Korea, 1972. Contbr. articles to profl. jours. Trustee Allen Stevenson Sch. Boys, pres., 1956-58; bd. dirs., treas. Council Higher Ednl. Instns., N.Y.C.; pres. All Am. Open Karate Championships, 1965-80, Karate Championships North Am., 1967-80; v.p. World Taekwan Do Fedn., 1973-82; trustee Universidad Politecnica de P.R., San Juan, 1974-85; bd. dirs. Am. Behavioral Scis., 1967-80. Served to 1st lt. USAAF, 1943-46. Decorated Order Cultural Merit Nat. medal (Korea); named hon. citizen of Seoul, 1964; knight officer Order of Merit (Italy); recipient Disting. Alumni award SUNY, 1969, Disting. Alumni award Coll. Arts and Sci. at Geneseo, 1971. Mem. Am. Acad. Polit. and Social Sci., NEA, Nat. Council Social Studies, N.Y. Assn. Deans and Guidance, Soc. Advancement Edn., Acad. Polit. Sci., Academia Tiberna, Internat. Sports Fedn., Phi Delta Kappa, Kappa Delta Pi (scholar 1939-40). Club: N.Y.C. Univ. Club, Rochester Univ. Home: 1400 East Ave Rochester NY 14610 also: Avoca NY 14809 Office: Internat Human Asst Programs Inc 360 Park Ave S New York NY 10010

DE MARGITAY, GEDEON, acquisitions and management consultant; b. Budapest, Hungary, Mar. 6, 1924; s. Joseph and Anne (de Bessenyei) de M.; came to U.S., 1953, naturalized, 1958; student U. Budapest Grad. Sch. Econs., 1941-44, Ecole des Scis. Politiques, Paris, 1946-48; m. Virginia Varet Martin, Dec. 30, 1963. With N.Y. Times, 1947-50, European info. div. Mut. Security Agy., 1950-53; with N.Y. Times, 1954-61; chief exec. Magnum Photos, Inc., N.Y.C., 1961-63; with Time Inc., 1964-75, dir. mktg. services Time/Life TV, 1975; dir. broadcast and corp. planning NBC, 1975-78; acquistions and mgmt. cons., N.Y.C., 1978—. Mem. The Planning Forum, Assn. for Systems Mgmt., Internat. Radio-TV Soc., World Future Soc., Am. Acad. Polit. and Social Sci. Republican. Presbyterian. Co-author: Broadcasting: The Next Ten Years, 1977. Address: 65 E 96th St New York NY 10128

DEMARKEY, DAVID LAWRENCE, marketing executive, consultant; b. Greenwich, Conn., Aug. 9, 1950; s. Joseph Dominic and Geraldine (Kennedy) DeM.; m. Debra King, Oct. 12, 1974 (div. Nov. 1980). B of Gen. Studies, U. Mich., 1972; MS in Mgmt., Marylhurst Coll., 1986. Site mgr. Techni Co-op, Inc., Stamford, Conn., 1972-73; property mgr. FCH Services, Inc., Washington, 1973-74; asst. chpt. mgr. Nat. Electric Contractors Assn., Washington, Portland (Oreg.), 1975-77; account exec. Pacific Northwest Bell, Portland, 1978-82; marketer Glackamas County Employment, Tng. and Bus. Services, Marylhurst, Oreg., 1983-84; dist. mgr. Research Inst. Am., Portland, 1984-85; mktg. cons. Internat. Refugee Ctr. Oreg., Portland, 1985-87; dir. sales and mktg. Hocks Labs., Portland, 1988; cons. 1988—. Author: Small Business Marketing, 1987; contbr. articles to profl. publs. Pres. Lents Edn. Ctr., Portland, 1980-83; mem. advt. and promotion com. Hollywood Boosters, Portland, 1987. Recipient Community Vol. award Multnomah County Commrs., 1983, Sam Chapman award Hollywood Boosters, 1987; State of Conn. scholar, 1968-71. Mem. Am. Mktg. Assn. (chpt. v.p. 1985-88). Democrat. Roman Catholic. Home and Office: 4653 NE 32d Ave Portland OR 97211

DEMENT, DONALD KEITHLEY, engineering executive; b. Phila., Nov. 30, 1936; s. George Earl and Beulah Louise (Buchanan) D.; m. Keren Sue Davison, June 24, 1972; 1 child, Margot. BSEE, Drexel U., 1959; postgrad., George Washington U., 1962-66. Engr. Nat. Security Agy., Ft. Meade, Md., 1955-63, div. chief, 1963-75; mgr. adv. commn. research NASA, Washington, 1976-80, dir. communications rsch. program, 1980-81; pres., founder Novacom, Inc., Annapolis, Md., 1981—; v.p. engring. Advanced Communications Corp., Little Rock, 1984—; v.p. communications Ardak, Inc., McLean, Va., 1985; sr. dir. Aero. Radio, Inc., Annapolis, 1986-88; bd. dirs. UEK Corp., Annapolis, Advanced Communications Corp., Little Rock, Advanced Communications Engring., Inc., Redondo Beach, Calif. Author: Direct Broadcasting Satellite Systems, 1984; contbr. articles to profl. jours. Mem., instr. USCG Aux., Annapolis, 1978-88. 1st lt. with U.S. Army, 1960-62. Fellow: AIAA (assoc.); mem. IEEE (sr.), Soc. Satellite Profls. Office: Novacom Inc 1568 Ritchie Ln Annapolis MD 21401

DEMERE, ROBERT HOUSTON, oil company executive; b. Savannah, Ga., Feb. 15, 1924; s. Raymond McAllister and Josephine Elizabeth (Mobley) D.; m. Mary Elizabeth Bullock, Sept. 21, 1946; children—Robert H., John B., Raymond S., Sims B., Anne E. Econs. student, Yale U. Chmn. bd. Colonial Oil Industries, Savannah, Ga., 1958—; pres., dir. Interstate Stas., Inc., Savannah, Ga., 1964—, Chatham Towing Co., Inc., Savannah, Ga., 1952—, Colonial Terminals, Inc., Savannah, Ga., 1977—; bd. dirs. 1st Union Bank Savannah, 1st Union Corp. Ga. Bd. dirs. YMCA of Savannah. Served to lt. (j.g.) USN, 1942-45. Named Indsl. Man of Yr., Internat. Mgmt. Council, Savannah, 1972. Mem. Ind. Fuel Terminal Operators Assn. (v.p. 1986—), Ind. Liquid Terminal Operators Assn., Nat. Oil Jobbers Assn., S.C. Petroleum Marketers Assn., N.C. Oil Jobbers Assn., Ga. Oilmen's Assn., World Bus. Council, Sea Edn. Assn. (trustee 1982—). Clubs: Savannah Yacht, Century, Chatham, Cotillion, Oglethorpe.

DEMETRIOU, MICHAEL, lawyer; b. N.Y.C., Nov. 4, 1927; s. Peter and Esther (Finkelstein) D.; m. Koula Rapton, Oct. 28, 1951; children: James P., Theodore, Diantha K., Paul. BS, NYU, 1948, MBA, 1952; JD, St. John's U., 1951; LLM, Bklyn. U., 1965. Bar: N.Y. 1953. Life ins. cons. Met. Life, N.Y.C., 1953-58; pvt. practice real estate mgmt. and investments cons. N.Y.C., 1948—; ptnr. Demetriou and Demetriou, N.Y.C., 1953-79, Demetriou & Demetriou Law Offices, N.Y.C., 1979—; counsel, dir. Queenschpt. ARC, Flushing , N.Y., 1986—; bd. mgrs. Long Island City YMCA, 1979—; adv. council paralegal studies N.Y. Inst. Tech., 1987—; adv. council Am. Title Ins. Co., 1984—, Long Island U. C.W. Post, 1985-86; judge Village of Brookville, N.Y., 1973—. Mem. adv. coun. C.W. Post Coll. L.I. U., 1985-86, devel. adv. com. Fiorello H. LaGaurdia Community Coll., 1989; Scoutmaster Boy Scouts Am., Troop 23, N.Y.C., 1945-51, chmn. bd. dirs. Troop 346, N.Y.C., 1965-69; counsel St. Demetrios, Asoria, N.Y., Holy Trinity, Hicksville, N.Y., Holy Cross, Whitestone, N.Y. Mem. Borough of Queens C. of C., N.Y. County Lawyers Assn., Queens County Bar Assn., Nassau County Bar Assn., Rotary, Parthenon F & AM, Ahepa. Republican. Greek Orthodox. Home: 20 Rolling Dr Brookville NY 11545 Office: Demetriou and Demetriou 29-14 Queens Pla East Long Island NY 11101

DE MEUSE, DONALD H., paper products manufacturing executive; b. 1936. With Ft. Howard Paper Co., Green Bay, Wis., 1959—; v.p. ops. 1977-79, exec. v.p., from 1979, now pres., dir. Office: Ft Howard Corp 1919 S Broadway Box 19130 Green Bay WI 54307 *

DE MICHELE, O. MARK, utility company executive; b. Syracuse, N.Y., Mar. 23, 1934; s. Aldo and Dora (Carno) De M.; m. Faye Ann Venturin, Nov. 8, 1957; children: Mark A., Christopher C., Michele M., Julianne; m. Barbara Joan Stanley, May 22, 1982. B.S., Syracuse U., 1955. Mgr. Seal Right Co., Inc., Fulton, N.Y., 1955-58; v.p., gen. mgr. L.M. Harvey Co. Inc., Syracuse, 1958-62; v.p. Niagara Mohawk Power, Syracuse, 1962-78; v.p. Ariz. Pub. Svc., Phoenix, 1978-81, exec. v.p., 1981-82, pres., chief exec. officer, 1982—, also bd. dirs.; bd. dirs. Am. West Airlines. Pres. Jr. Achievement, Syracuse, 1974-75, Phoenix, 1982-83, United Way of Central N.Y., Syracuse, 1978, Ariz. Opera Co., Phoenix, 1981-83, Phoenix Symphony, 1984-86, United Way of Phoenix, 1985-86, Ariz. Mus. of Sci. and Tech., 1988—; chmn. Valley of Sun United Way, 1984-86, Phoenix Commn. on Ednl. Excellence, 1987—, Ariz. Arts Stabilization Fund. Named Outstanding Young Man of Yr. Syracuse Jaycees, 1968. Mem. Phoenix C. of C. (chmn. bd. 1986-87). Republican. Clubs: Phoenix Country, Ariz. (Phoenix). Home: 77 E Missouri Ave Phoenix AZ 85012 Office: Ariz Pub Svc Co 411 N Central Ave Phoenix AZ 85036

DEMING, FREDERICK WILSON, economist, banker; b. St. Louis, Dec. 29, 1935; s. Frederick Lewis and Corinne Inez (Wilson) D.; m. Lynne Eve Anken, Mar. 24, 1960; children: Susanne Lyn, Frederick Lawrence. B.A., Princeton U., 1957; M.A., Yale U., 1958. With Fed. Res. Bank of N.Y., 1961-71; sr. staff economist Council Econ. Advisers, 1968; exec. dir. Commn. Mortgage Interest Rates, 1969; spl. asst. to Sec. of HUD, 1970-71; sr. v.p., economist Chem. Bank, N.Y.C., 1971—. Home: 24 Colt Rd Summit NJ 07901 Office: Chem Bank 277 Park Ave New York NY 10172 *

DEMOND, JEFFREY STUART, cable television company executive; b. Morristown, N.J., June 27, 1955; s. Marvin Harry DeMond and Lois Ann (Worrell) Kramer. BS, U. Ala., 1978. CPA, N.Y. Sr. mgr. Peat, Marwick, Mitchell & Co., N.Y.C., 1978-85; v.p., chief fin. officer Bresnan Communications Co., White Plains, N.Y., 1985—; lectr., adj. prof. Hunter Coll., N.Y., 1984-85. Composer various popular music, 1974—; performer Sailcat record album Cathouse, 1976. Named an Outstanding Musician, Nat. Assn. Jazz Educators, 1978, Outstanding Jazz Soloist, Stan Kenton Orch., 1978. Mem. Broadcast Fin. Mgmt. Assn., Am. Inst. CPA's, N.Y. State Soc. CPA's, Beta Gamma Sigma. Office: Bresnan Communications Co 709 Westchester Ave White Plains NY 10604

DEMONE, ROBERT STEPHEN, hotel company executive; b. Dartmouth, N.S., Can., June 13, 1932; s. Urban Roy and Effie Elfreda (Meisner) DeM.; B.Com., Dalhousie U., Halifax, N.S., Can., 1952; Dipl. Bus. Mgmt., U. Western Ont. (Can.), London, 1970; m. Jean Valerie Snedden, June 26, 1954 (dec. June 1984); children—Susan Liane, Jill Carol; m. Joanna Stefania Tchorek, Mar. 22, 1985. Corp. tax assessor Revenue Can., Halifax, N.S., 1955-56; works acct. Can. Rock Salt Co. Ltd., Pugwash, N.S., 1956-62; comptroller Ben's Ltd., Halifax, 1962-67; with Can. Pacific Ltd., Montreal, Que., 1967-77, Toronto, Ont., 1977-79, asst. v.p. fin. and acctg., dir. acctg.; chmn., chief exec. officer Can. Pacific Securities Ltd., Toronto, 1977-81; v.p. fin. and acctg. Can. Pacific Enterprises Ltd., Toronto, 1979-81; pres., chief operating officer Maple Leaf Mills Ltd., Toronto, 1981-83, pres., chief exec. officer, 1984-85, pres., chief exec. office, chmn. bd., 1985-87; chmn., pres., chief exec. officer Can. Pacific Hotels Corp., Toronto, 1987—. Mem. Can. Inst. Chartered Accts., Que. Order Chartered Accts., Ont. Inst. Chartered Accts., Nat. Club, Canadian Club, Masons. Anglican. Office: Can Pacific Hotels Corp, 1 University Ave Ste 1400, Toronto, ON Canada M5J 2P1

DEMOREST, JOAN FLORENCE, accounting analyst; b. Framingham, Mass., July 30, 1947; d. William Alfred and Blanche Viola (Milliken) Schenker; m. John Robert Schunder, Sept. 7, 1968 (div. 1972); m. David Robert Demorest, Sept 20, 1986; 1 child, William Arthur. BSBA, U. San Francisco, 1977. CPA, Wash. Programmer, analyst New England Power Service Co., Westboro, Mass., 1965-75; cons. Am. Mgmt. Systems, Arlington, Va., 1976-80; ind. contractor Seattle, 1981—; v.p. acctg. systems devel. Omnisoft Corp., Tri-Cities, 1983-85; sr. systems programmer, analyst Accts. Microsystems, Inc., Seattle, 1986-88. Co-author computer manuals. Home and Office: 4272 Whitman N Seattle WA 98103

DE MOUCHY, DUCHESSE, corporate executive; b. N.Y.C., Jan. 31, 1935; arrived in Luxembourg, 1967; d. Clarence Douglas and Phyllis Chess (Ellsworth) Dillon; m. James Brady Mosely (annuled 1963); 1 child, Joan Dillon Moseley Bryan; m. His Royal Highness Prince Charles of Luxembourg (dec. 1977); children: Princess Charlotte, Prince Robert; m. Philippe de Noailles Duc de Mouchy, Aug. 3, 1978. Diploma, Foxcraft Coll., 1952; postgrad., Vassar. Asst. editor The Paris Rev., 1958-65; pres. Domaine Clarence Dillon S.Am., Paris, 1975—, Infirmes des Moteurs Cerebraux-Kräzbierg, Dudelange, Luxembourg, 1977—; pres. Union Banques Suisses, Luxembourg, 1977-82. V.p. Les Auis Francais de Blérancourt, 1984—. Mem. Am.-Luxembourg Soc. (pres. 1967-78). Club: Inner-Wheel (Luxembourg) (pres. 1968-78). Office: Domaine Clarence Dillon SA, Chateau Haut Brion, 26 Rue de la Pepiniere, 75008 Paris France

DEMPSEY, F(RANCIS) BURKE, investment banker; b. Rockville, Conn., Mar. 15, 1962; s. Richard Edward and Mary Jane (Burke) D.; m. Elizabeth Gates Hallahan. BS in Applied Earth Sci., Stanford U., 1984. Assoc. Kidder, Peabody and Co. Inc., N.Y.C., 1985-87, Shearson, Lehman Bros. Inc., N.Y.C., 1987—; cons. Databeam Systems Inc., Hartford, Conn., 1984. L.F. Bissell scholar, Hartford Found. for Giving, 1980. Republican. Club: Downtown Athletic (N.Y.C.). Home: 455 E 86th St New York NY 10028 Office: Shearson Lehman Bros Inc 200 Vesey St World Fin Ctr New York NY 10285

DEMPSEY, JERRY EDWARD, service company executive; b. Landrum, S.C., Oct. 1, 1932; s. Adolphus Gerald and Willie Ceyattie (Lee) D.; m. Harriet Coan Calvert; children: Jerrie E., Harriet R., Margaret. BS, Clemson U., 1954; MBA, Ga. State Coll., 1968. With Borg-Warner Corp., Chgo., 1956-84, gen. mgr. York div., 1972-77, exec. v.p., 1977-79, pres., chief operating officer, 1979-84, also bd. dirs.; vice-chmn. Waste Mgmt. Inc., Oak Brook, Ill., 1984—; also bd. dirs. Waste Mgmt. Inc., Oak Brook; pres., chief exec. officer Chem. Waste Mgmt., also bd. dirs.; bd. dirs. The Brand Co., Navistar. Mem. dean's adv. council, bd. visitors and devel council Sch. Engring Clemson U.; mem. dean's adv. bd. Grad. Sch. Bus. Ga. State U.; chmn., bd. dirs. Adler Planetarium, Mid-Am. Com. Served to 1st lt. U.S. Army, 1954-56. Mem. ASHRAE, Univ. Club (bd. dirs.), Chgo. Club, Econ. Club, Butterfield Country Club, Melrose Club, Greenville Country Club, Oak Brook Execs. Breakfast Club (bd. dirs.). Clubs: Univ. (bd. dirs.), Chgo., Econ. (Chgo.); Butterfield Country; Melrose (Daufauskie Island); Greenville (S.C.) Country, Thornblade Country (Greenville). Office: Chem Waste Mgmt 3001 Butterfield Rd Oak Brook IL 60521

DEMPSEY, LOUIS F(RANCIS), III, banker; b. Morristown, N.J., Apr. 19, 1926; s. Louis F. and Clara V. (Lade) D.; m. Patricia Ann Fox, May 29, 1954; children: Maryann, Patricia, Kathleen, Louis, Thomas. BS, Georgetown U., 1948; postgrad. in banking, Rutgers U., 1966. Auditor Chase Manhattan Bank, Hong Kong and P.R., 1948-56; exec. v.p. No. Trust Co., Chgo., 1956-84, Chem. Bank, N.Y.C., 1984—; sr. advisor Brown Bros. Harriman & Co., 1987—; bd. dirs. China Trust Bank, N.Y. Mem. visitors com. Sch. Fgn. Svc., Georgetown U., Washington; mem. Cardinal's com. of laity Archdiocese of N.Y.; bd. dirs. Woodstock Theol. Ctr. Washington. With USMC, 1943-46. Mem. Am. Swiss Assn. (bd. dirs.). Home: 30 Beekman Pl New York NY 10022 Office: Brown Bros Harriman & Co 59 Wall St New York NY 10005

DEMPSEY, NEAL, III, data processing executive; b. Butte, Mont., Mar. 20, 1941; s. Neal and Katherine Spring (Shea) D.; m. Janet Rae Weiss, Nov. 17, 1967; children: Sean Christian, Heather Katherine. BA, U. Wash., 1964. Sales promotion coord. Gen. Tel./Electronics, San Carlos, Calif., 1965-67; asst. advt. mgr. Memorex Corp., Santa Clara, Calif., 1967-69; sales mgmt. positions Electronic Memories Inc., Hawthorne, Calif., 1969-73; nat. sales mgr. Intertel Inc., Burlington, Mass., 1973-74; Western regional mgr. Sanders Data Systems Group div. Sanders Assocs. (acquired by Harris Corp. 1977), L.A., 1974, nat. sales mgr., Nashua, N.H., 1976-77, dir. sales Harris Data Communications, Inc., 1977-79, v.p. sales data communications div., Dallas, 1979-80, v.p. mktg. data communication div., 1980-82, group v.p. mktg. info. terminals group Harris Corp., 1982-83; sr. v.p. mktg. Zentec Inc., Santa Clara, Calif., 1983-84; pres., chief exec. officer Envision Tech. Inc., San Jose, Calif., 1984-85; chief exec. officer QuBix Graphic Systems Inc., San Jose, 1985—; chmn. bd. dirs. Microserv, Inc., Bellevue, Wash., 1986—; adv. bd. U. Wash. Sch. Bus. Adminstrn., 1987—. Bd. dirs. Eastfield Found. Eastfield Children's Ctr., Campbell, Calif., 1985. 1st lt. U.S. Army N.G., 1964-70. Mem. Spring Park Swim and Racquet Club (chmn. bd. dirs. 1981-82, Richardson, Tex.). Republican. Roman Catholic. Home: 15976 Grandview Ave Monte Sereno CA 95030

DEMPSEY, RAYMOND J., banker; b. Yonkers, N.Y., Mar. 4, 1935; s. John Raymond and Ruth D.; m. Jill L. Kingdon; children: Christopher, Elizabeth. B.A., Colgate U., 1957. With Bankers Trust Co., N.Y.C., 1957-78; exec. v.p. Bankers Trust Co., 1975-78; chmn., pres. Fidelcor, Inc. and The Fidelity Bank, Rosemont, Pa., 1978-84; chmn., chief exec. officer European Am. Bancorp, N.Y.C., 1984—; pres. European Am. Bank, N.Y.C., 1984—; dir. Sunshine Mining Co. Served in USAR, 1958-64. Office: European Am Bank EAB Pla Long Island NY 11555

DEMSKI, BERNARD JOHN, personnel director; b. Balt., Jan. 12, 1932; m. Suzanne Woodall, Aug. 21, 1955; children: Gregory, Kevin, B. Thomas, Susanna, Allison. BS in Bus., U. Balt., 1968. Personnel asst. Proctor & Gamble, Balt., 1950-62; v.p., gen. mgr. Dixie Bread and Cake Co., Charlottesville, Va., 1962-64; personnel asst. Teledyne Avionics, Earlysville, Va., 1964-66; indsl. relations mgr. Stromberg-Carlson, Charlottesville, 1966-79; dir. indsl. relations O'Sullivan Corp., Winchester, Va., 1979-88; pres. B.D. Assocs. Human Resource Cons., Winchester, 1988—. Mem. Shenandoah Coll. Bus. Mgmt. adv. com. Served with U.S. Army, 1955-57. Mem. Am. Soc. Personnel Adminstrs., Winchester C. of C. (bd. dirs. 1986—), Northwestern Workshop (pres. 1987). Roman Catholic. Club: Rotary (bd. dirs. 1987—) (Winchester). Office: BD Assocs 3614 Forest Ridge Rd Winchester VA 22601

DEMSKI, DAVID MICHAEL, food products executive; b. Toledo, Dec. 30, 1957; s. Gerald Vincent and Maxine C. (Martin) D.; m. Lori A. Morgott, May 30, 1980 (div. Dec. 1987). BBA, U. Mich., 1980. CPA, Mich. Sr. supr. Peat, Marwick, Mitchell & Co., Detroit, 1980-83; mgr. fin. reporting Perry Drug Stores, Inc., Pontiac, Mich., 1983-85; dir. ops., mgr. distbrn. ctr. Domino's Pizza Ditbrn. Corp., Ann Arbor, Mich., 1985—; regional controller Northeastern U. Home: 25 Catamaran Lake Saint Louis MO 63367 Office: DNC Demski Mo 1 Cermak Blvd Saint Peters MO 63376 also: 17788 Vacri Ln Livonia MI 48152

DENAHAN, JOSEPH ANTHONY, financial executive; b. Trenton, N.J., Apr. 6, 1936; s. Eugene A. and Isabelle (Magyar) D.; m. Elaine Menszak, June 30, 1962; chidren: Joseph R., Linda M. BS with highest honors, Rider Coll., 1961. CPA, N.J. Auditor/cons., mgr. Peat, Marwick, Main & Co., Short Hills, N.J., 1961-71; controller, sr. v.p. fin. Engelhard Industries, Iselin, N.J., 1971-84; exec. v.p., chief fin. and adminstrv. officer Sunshine Mining Co., Dallas, 1984—, also bd. dirs. Served with U.S. Army, 1954-57. Mem. Am. Inst. CPA's, N.J. Soc. CPA's, Fin. Execs. Inst. Roman Catholic. Home: 5507 Bent Trail Dallas TX 75248 Office: Sunshine Mining Co 300 Crescent Ct 15th Fl Dallas TX 75201

DENBY, PETER, lawyer; b. Phila., Dec. 15, 1929; s. Charles and Rosamond (Reed) D.; m. Peggy Ann O'Hearn, May 19, 1956; children: Charles, Peter, Lee Curtis Marshall. A.B., Princeton U., 1951; J.D., Harvard U., 1954. Bar: N.Y. 1957, Pa. 1960. Assoc. Davis Polk & Wardwell, N.Y.C., 1954-59; assoc. Reed Smith Shaw & McClay, Pitts., 1959-62, ptnr., 1962—. Trustee Pressley Ridge Sch., Pitts., 1962-77, pres., 1965-72; bd. dirs. Western Pa. Sch. for Blind Children, 1965—, pres., 1970-82; term trustee Carnegie Inst. Fine Arts Com., Pitts., 1965-72; trustee Sarah Scaife Found., Pitts, 1969—, Pitts. Plan for Art, 1970-73; mem. exec. com. Western Pa. Golf Assn., 1976—, sec., 1978-86, 88—; bd. dirs. Pitts. Regional Planning Commn., 1971—; pres. Pitts Regional Planning Commn., 1974—; mayor, Borough of Edgeworth, Pa., 1989—. Mem. ABA, Allegheny County Bar Assn. Home: 518 Irwin Dr Sewickley PA 15143 Office: Reed Smith Shaw & McClay 435 6th Ave James H Reed Bldg Pittsburgh PA 15219

DENEGALL, JOHN PALMER, JR., insurance company executive; b. Tarrytown, N.Y., Mar. 21, 1959; s. John P., Sr. and Edna D. (Kirkaldy) D.; m. Johnnie Lou Jarrett, Feb. 27, 1982; children: John P. III, Revisa Taylor. Student, Westchester Community Coll., Vahalla, N.Y., 1977-80. Mgr. Elmsford (N.Y.) Raceway Inc., 1976-80, Radio Shack, Yorktown Heights, N.Y., 1980-81; ins. claims adjuster Liberty Mut. Ins. Co., N.Y.C., 1981-85; sr. ins. claims rep. Crum & Forster Comml. Ins., N.Y.C., 1985—; arbitrator Ins. Arbitration Forum, N.Y.C., 1986—; pres. Denegall Properties, Inc. Democrat. Presbyterian.

DE NEVERS, ROY OLAF, retired aerospace company executive; b. Strasburg, Sask., Can., Dec. 30, 1922; s. Edouard Albrecht V.V. and Christy Helen (Hunt) de N.; divorced; children Gregory Frank (dec.), Sara Dianne. BS in Econs., U. London, 1963; BA in Econ. History, U. Winnipeg (Can.), 1971. Served to lt. comdr. Royal Can. Navy, 1946-67; chief contract adminstr., aircraft repair and overhaul Bristol Aerospace Ltd., Winnipeg, MB, Can., 1968-83; originator co. operating procedure Bristol Aerospace Ltd., Winnipeg, Man., Can., 1983-86. Editor aero. mag., 1956-60. Served to flight lt. Royal Can. Air Force, 1941-45. Decorated DFC, 1945, Aircrew Europe Star, 1945, France and Germany Clasp, 1945, Def. medal, 1945. Mem. Can. Aeoros. and Space Inst. (assoc. fellow). Mem. Adventist Ch. Clubs: Royal Air Force (London), Fleet Air Arm Officers (London). Address: Group 2 Box 9 Route 1, Anola, MB Canada R0E 0A0

DENICOLA, ELLEN, banker; b. N.Y.C., Feb. 6, 1953; d. Arthur Pattison Jr. and Norma (Fisher) Davis; m. Nino Christopher, July 6, 1978; 1 child, Christopher. BA, Williams Coll., 1975; MBA, Wharton Sch. U. Pa., 1977. Mgmt. trainee, account offficer Citibank, N.Y.C., 1977-79; asst. treas. Chase Manhattan, N.Y.C., 1979-81; chief fin. officer Greens Farm Acad., Westport, Conn., 1981-84; v.p., head dept. comml. real estate Nat. Westminster Bank, U.S.A., Stamford, 1984-86; v.p. Nat. Westminster Bank, U.S.A., White Plains, N.Y., 1986—; asst. prof. microecons. U. Pa., Phila., 1976-77; adj. prof. U. Conn., Stamford, 1986. Vol. Jr. League Stamford-Norwalk, Conn., 1982-86; bd. dirs. Stamford YMCA, 1985-86. Wharton Pub. Policy fellow Wharton Sch. U. Pa., 1976. Mem. Southweston Area Commerce Assn. of Conn., Nat. Assn. Corp. Real Estate Execs., Nat. Assn. Indsl. and Office Parks, Real Estate Bd. N.Y. Office: Nat Westminster Bank USA 244 Westchester Ave White Plains NY 10604

DE NICOLA, PETER FRANCIS, holding company executive; b. N.Y.C., Oct. 28, 1954; s. Louis Joseph and Nancy Eleanor (Maddi) DeN.; B.S., NYU, 1976, M.B.A., 1978. Pres., founder P.F. DeNicola, Inc., N.Y.C., now Stamford, Conn., 1976-84; acct. Main Hurdman, N.Y.C., 1978-81; tax mgr. Gen. Signal Corp., Stamford, 1981-83; tax mgr. Emery Air Freight Corp., Wilton, Conn., 1983-85; dir. taxes A.I. Internat. Corp., N.Y.C., 1985—. Author: Legal Liability of Tax Return Preparers, 1978; contbr. articles to tax and investment periodicals. Recipient Ferdinand W. Lafrentz acctg. award, 1977 C.P.A., Conn., N.Y. Mem. Tax Soc. NYU, Assn. M.B.A. Execs., Am. Mgmt. Assn., Stamford Tax Assn. (sec.-treas. 1988—), Nat. Assn. Accts., NYU Commerce Alumni Assn. (dir. 1978—, corr. sec. 1978-79, rec. sec. 1979-81, chmn. budget com. 1987-88, chmn. Annual Bus. Conf. 1988, chmn. alumni admissions coun. 1989—), AICPA (fed. tax and tax acctg. coms. 1984—), N.Y. Soc. C.P.A.s (fed. and state tax com. 1983-85, depreciation and investment tax credit com. 1986-87), Conn. Soc. C.P.A.s, Tax Execs. Inst., Round Table Assn. of U.S. (co-founder 1986, nat. treas. 1987-88, nat. pres. 1988—, del. to internat. convention, 1987), Estate Planning Council Westchester County, Round Table 3 of Greenwich (Conn.) (dir. 1984—, v.p. 1985-86, pres. 1986-88), Internat. Platform Assn. Republican. Roman Catholic. Clubs: NYU, Rockefeller Ctr. (N.Y.C.), Landmark, Long Ridge (Stamford); Saw Mill River Racquet (Mt. Kisco, N.Y.); Lakeover Country (Bedford Hills, N.Y.); St. James's (Antigua). Home: PO Box 4637 Stamford CT 06907 Office: A I Internat Corp 650 Fifth Ave New York NY 10019

DENISE, ROBERT PHILLIPS, financial executive; b. Montreal, Que., Can., Nov. 13, 1936; s. Warren Edward and Lorena Hyacinth (Patterson) D.; m. Margaret Ellen Maloney, June 30, 1937; children: Robert Phillips, William Joseph, Christopher Andrew. A.B., Duke U., 1959; postgrad., Northeastern U., Boston, 1970-71. Various mgmt. positions Gen. Electric Co., 1959-77; treas. Hoffman-LaRoche Inc., Nutley, N.J., 1978-82, controller, 1982-85; v.p., treas. Becton Dickinson & Co., Franklin Lakes, N.J., 1985—; mem. Mid-Atlantic adv. bd. Arkwright-Boston Ins. Co., 1985—. Twp. committeeman, Millburn, N.J., 1981-86, vice chmn., dep. mayor, 1983-84, Mayor, chmn. twp. com., 1984-86; mem. Planning Bd., 1979-80; v.p., bd. dirs. Nat. Soc. to Prevent Blindness-N.J., 1980—; chmn. Permanent Com. on Municipal Improvements, Ashland, Mass., 1971; active Boy Scouts Am. Served with U.S. Army, 1960-62. Republican. Office: Becton Dickinson & Co 1 Becton Dr Franklin Lakes NJ 07417

DENIUS, FRANKLIN WOFFORD, lawyer; b. Athens, Tex., Jan. 4, 1925; s. S.F. and Frances (Cain) D.; m. Charmaine Hooper, Nov. 19, 1949; children: Frank Wofford, Charmaine. B.B.A., LL.B., U. Tex. Bar: Tex. 1949. Practiced in Austin 1949—; past sec.-treas., dir. Telcom Corp.; pres., chief exec. officer, chmn. bd. So. Union Co.; dir. Tex. Commerce Bank-Austin; past legal counsel Austin Better Bus. Bur. Chmn. spl. schs. div. United Fund, 1960, Pacesetters div., 1961, Schs. div., 1964; 1st v.p. United Fund; chmn. steering com. sch. bond campaign, past trustee Austin Ind. Sch. Dist., 1964; past pres. Young Men's Bus. League Austin; past pres., exec. council Austin Ex-Students Assn. U. Tex.; co-chmn. LBJ U Tex. Library Found.; mem. chancellor's council, pres.'s assos. U. Tex.; bd. dirs. Tex. Research League; advisory trustee Schreiner Coll. Decorated Silver Star medal with four oak leaf clusters, Purple Heart; recipient Outstanding Young Man of Austin award Jr. C. of C., 1959. Mem. ABA, Tex., Travis County bar assns., Tex. Philos. Soc. Presbyterian (deacon, elder). Clubs: Longhorn (past pres.), West Austin Optimists (past dir.), Headliners (pres., sec. bd. trustees, mem. exec. com.). Lodge: Masons. Home: 3703 Meadowbank Dr Austin TX 78703 Office: Tex Commerce Bank Bldg Ste #700 700 Lavaca Austin TX 78701-3102 also: So Union Co 1800 Renaissance Tower Dallas TX 75270

DENLEA, LEO EDWARD, JR., insurance company executive; b. N.Y.C., Mar. 7, 1932; s. Leo Edward Sr. and Teresa (Carroll) D.; m. Nancy Burkley, Aug. 16, 1959; children: Leo Edward III, Thomas, Gregory, Kathryn, Nancy, Rita, Philip. B.S. in Econs., Villanova U., 1954; M.B.A., U. Pa., 1959. Group v.p. fin. services Internat. Basic Economy Corp., N.Y.C., 1966-74; v.p., treas. Pacific Lighting Corp., Los Angeles, 1974-81; sr. v.p. fin. Farmers Group, Inc., Los Angeles, 1981-85, pres., 1985—, chief operating officer, 1985-86, chief exec. officer, chmn. bd., 1986—, also bd. dirs.; Bd. dirs. Alexander and Baldwin, Inc. Served to lt. (j.g.) USN, 1954-57. Club: California; Wilshire Country. Home: 2798 McConnell Dr Los Angeles CA 90064 Office: Farmers Group Inc care Jeffrey C Beyer 4680 Wilshire Blvd Los Angeles CA 90010 *

DENMAN, JOE CARTER, JR., forest products company executive; b. Lufkin, Tex., Sept. 30, 1923; m. Ginia Beth Cox, Jan. 10, 1948; children: Joe Carter, III, Elizabeth Anne, Ginia Geanette. B.Arch., Tex. A&M U., 1950. Registered profl. engr., Tex. With Temple Industries, Diboll, Tex., 1950—; corporate v.p. Temple Industries, 1964-66, exec. v.p., 1966-72, pres., 1972-77; exec. v.p. Temple-Eastex, Inc., Diboll, Tex., 1974-77, pres., chief exec. officer, 1977—, chmn. bd., 1983—; exec. v.p. Temple-Inland, Inc., 1984—; v.p. Time, Inc., 1976-78, group v.p., 1978-84, dir., 1979-84; v.p., dir. AFCO Industries, Inc., Diboll, Tex., 1978—; dir. Diboll State Bank, CRS Sirrine, Inc., Houston, Pineland Bank (Tex.), Lumbermens Investment Corp., Austin, Tex., Sunbelt Ins. Co., Tex., Tex. South-Eastern R.R. Co., Diboll, Temple-White Co., Inc., Topaz Oil Co., Angelina Free Press Inc., Diboll., Inland Container Corp., Indpls.; v.p., dir. Sabine Investment Co., Diboll, Scotch Investment Co., Diboll, Great Am. Reserve Ins. Co., Dallas; dir. Nat. Fidelity Life Ins. Co., Kansas City, Ga. Kraft Co., Rome, Temple Assocs., Inc., Diboll, Inland-Orange Inc., Orange, Tex., First Bank of Conroe, NA. (Tex.). Pres. Diboll Booster Club, 1952, Quarterback Club, Diboll, 1952; mem. Diboll Sch. Bd., 1960-62; dir. Angelina County Community Fund, Inc., 1960-61, chmn. indsl. fund, 1965; pres., bd. dirs. Temple Industries Employees Fed. Credit Union, 1963-64; v.p. Angelina County Water Control and Improvement Dist. 2, 1963-68; trustee Temple Pension Trust, 1964—, Meml. Hosp., Lufkin, 1978—, Angelina Coll., 1980—, Tex. Forestry Assn. Mus., Lufkin; past mem. adv. bd. Salvation Army, Lufkin.; mem. devel. council Coll. Agr., Coll. Architecture and Environ. Design Tex. A&M U. Served to lt. (j.g.), A.C. U.S. Navy, 1942-46. Named Disting. Alumnus Tex. A&M U., 1981. Mem. Nat. Forest Products Assn. (dir. 1968—), So. Forest Products Assn. (pres. 1969-70, dir. 1954—), Tex. Forest Products Mfrs. Assn. (pres. 1967-69, past dir.), Tex. Soc. Profl. Engrs., So. Pine Inspection Bur. (adv. bd.), So. Pines Plywood Standard (advisory com. 1961-64), Forest Products Research Soc. (dir. 1959-60), Am. Plywood Assn. (trustee 1973-74), Angelina County C. of C. (dir. 1966-68), Tau Beta Pi. Office: Temple-Inland Inc 303 S Temple Diboll TX 75941

DENNEEN, JOHN PAUL, lawyer; b. N.Y.C., Aug. 18, 1940; s. John Thomas and Pauline Jane (Ludlow) D.; m. Mary Veronica Murphy, July 3, 1965; children—John Edward, Thomas Michael, James Patrick, Robert Andrew, Daniel Joseph, Mary Elizabeth. B.S., Fordham U., 1963; J.D., Columbia U., 1966. Bar: N.Y. 1966, U.S. Ct. Appeals (2d cir.) 1974, U.S. Dist. Ct. (so. and ea. dists.) N.Y. 1975, Mo. 1987. Assoc. Seward & Kissel, N.Y.C., 1966-75; sr. v.p., gen counsel, sec. GK Techs., Inc., Greenwich, Conn., 1975-83; exec. v.p., gen. counsel, sec. Chromalloy Am. Corp., St. Louis, 1983-87; ptnr. Bryan, Cave, McPheeters & McRoberts, St. Louis, 1987—. Mem. ABA, Internat. Bar Assn., N.Y. State Bar Assn., N.Y.C. Bar Assn., Bar Assn. Met. St. Louis. Office: Bryan Cave McPheeters & McRoberts 500 N Broadway Saint Louis MO 63102

DENNING, MICHAEL MARION, computer company executive; b. Durant, Okla., Dec. 22, 1943; s. Samuel M. and Lula Mae (Waitman) D.; m. Suzette Karin Wallance, Aug. 10, 1968 (div. 1979); children—Lila Monique, Tanya Kerstin, Charlton Derek; m. Donna Jean Hamel, Sept. 28, 1985; 1 child, Caitlin Shannon. Student USAF Acad., 1963; B.S., U. Tex., 1966; B.S., Fairleigh Dickinson U., 1971; M.S., Columbia U., 1973. Mgr. systems IBM, White Plains, N.Y., 1978-79, mgr. service and mktg., San Jose, Calif., 1979-81; nat. market support mgr. Memorex Corp., Santa Clara, Calif., 1981, v.p. mktg., 1981-82; v.p. mktg. and sales Icot Corp., Mountain View, Calif., 1982-83; exec. v.p. Phase Info. Machines Corp., Scottsdale, Ariz., 1983-84; exec. v.p. Tricom Automotive Dealer Systems Inc., Hayward, Calif., 1985-87; pres. ADS Computer Services, Inc., Toronto, Ont., Can., 1985-87; pres. Denning Investments, Inc., Palo Alto, Calif., 1987—. Served with USAF, 1962-66; Vietnam. Mem. Phi Beta Kappa, Lambda Chi Alpha (pres. 1965-66). Republican. Methodist. Home: H-1030 Parkwood Way Redwood City CA 94061 Office: Denning Investments Inc O-525 University Ave Ste 203 Palo Alto CA 94301

DENNIS, PATRICIA DIAZ, government official, lawyer; b. Santa Rita, N.Mex., Oct. 2, 1946; d. Porfirio Madrid and Mary (Romero) Diaz; m. Michael John Dennis, Aug. 3, 1968; children: Ashley Elizabeth, Geoffrey Diaz, Alicia Sarah Diaz. A.B. in English, UCLA, 1970; J.D., Loyola U., Los Angeles, 1973. Bar: Calif. 1973, D.C. 1984. Law clk. Calif. Rural Legal Asst., McFarland, Calif., 1971; assoc. Paul, Hastings, Janofsky & Walker, Los Angeles, 1973-76; atty. Pacific Lighting Corp., Los Angeles, 1976-78; atty., asst. gen. atty. ABC, Hollywood, Calif., 1978-83; mem. NLRB, Washington, 1983-86; commr. FCC, Washington, 1986—. Exec. editor: Loyola Law Rev., 1972-73. Com. mem. Coro Found. Hispanic Leadership Program, Los Angeles, 1981-82; U.S. del. UN Commn. on Status Women, 30th session Econ. and Social Council, Vienna, Austria, 1984, World Conf. UN Decade for Women, Nairobi, Kenya, 1985; bd. dirs. Resources for Infant Educarers, 1981-83, Nat. Network Hispanic Women, Los Angeles, 1983—; mem. exec. com., nat. adv. bd. Leadership Am., Found. for Women's Resources, 1987—. Recipient cert. of achievement YWCA, Los Angeles, 1979, Woman of Yr. award of merit Mex. Am. Opportunity Found., 1984, Recognition for Outstanding Achievements award Nat. Council Hispanic Women, 1986, Woman of Achievement award City Club of Cleve., 1986, Friend of the Family award The Family Place, 1987; named one of 100 Influentials, Hispanic Bus. mag., 1987. Mem. Mex.-Am. Bar Assn. (sec. 1980-81, trustee 1979-80, 81-82), Los Angeles County Bar Assn. (child abuse subcom. chmn. barristers sect. 1980-81, exec. com. barristers sect. 1980-82), Hispanic Bar Assn. D.C., ABA (com. labor arbitration and the law of collective bargaining agreements, labor law sect. 1979-82). Democrat. Roman Catholic. Office: FCC 1919 M St NW Ste 832 Washington DC 20554

DENNIS, RICHARD IRWIN, company executive; b. Columbus, Ohio, Dec. 5, 1934; s. Russell Irwin and Mary Elizabeth (Ferguson) D.; m. Helen Emily Mandt, June 23, 1962; children—Julie Elizabeth, Amy Marie. B.S., Ohio State U., 1957. Retail sales rep. Copco Papers, Inc., Columbus, Ohio, 1957-62, indsl. sales rep., 1962-69, sales mgr., 1969-73; v.p. Copco Papers, Inc., Lansing, Mich., 1973-80; v.p., gen. mgr. Copco Papers, Inc., Columbus, 1980—. Home: 862 Bluffview Dr West Worthington OH 43085 Office: Copco Papers Inc PO Box 597 Columbus OH 43085

DENNIS, SHIRLEY MAE, federal agency administrator; b. Omaha, Feb. 26, 1938; d. Millard and Iantha (Hall) Haynes; m. William D.C. Dennis, Dec. 28, 1968; children: Pamela Peoples, Robin, Sherrie. Student Cheyney State Coll., 1955-56; A.S. in Bus. Adminstrn., Temple U., 1985; J.D. (hon.), Lincoln U., 1986. Sales and office mgr. Tucker and Tucker, Phila., 1961-67; equal opportunity specialist Redevel. Authority Phila., 1967-68; housing dir. Urban League of Phila., 1969-71; pub., founder Infill mag., Phila., 1972-79; mng. dir. Housing Assn. Delaware Valley, Phila., 1971-79; sec. Pa. Dept. Community Affairs, Harrisburg, 1979-86; dir. Women's Bur., U.S. Dept. of Labor, Washington, 1986—; chairperson Pa. Housing Fin. Agy., 1979-86, Pa. Martin Luther King, Jr. Holiday Commn., Local Govt. Records Com.; mem. Pa. Gov.'s Econ. Cabinet; sec. Pa. Indsl. Devel. Authority. Mem. sustaining adv. bd. Abington Meml. Hosp., 1981-82; bd. dirs. Abington Meml. Health Care Corp., 1983—; mem. Crestmont Bapt. Fed. Credit Union, 1970—; pres. Willow Grove br. NAACP, 1972-80, mem. exec. bd. Pa. State Conf. br., 1976-86; mem. Coalition of 100 Black Women, Phila. Tribune Charities. Recipient Assn. Black Journalists award, 1978, Nat. Freedom award, 1980, Pub. Service award Pa. Fedn. Bus. and Profl. Women's Clubs, 1980, Woman of Yr. award Black Women's Collective, 1981, Community Service award Nat. Assn. Negro Bus. and Profl. Women, 1981, Leadership award Pa. Tribune Charities. Mem. Community Info. Exchange, Nat. Conf. Women Execs in State Govt. (bd. dirs. 1985), Nat. Conf. State Housing Fin. Chairpersons (exec. com. 1983-85), Council of State Community Affairs Agys. (exec. bd. 1980-85). Republican. Baptist. Columnist Phila. Tribune, Phila. Daily News, 1974-75; author HADV housing series, Phila. Daily News, 1974; producer film Floodplain: The Path of Nature's Power, 1984 (award). Home: 1656 Easton Rd Willow Grove PA 19090 Office: Dept Labor Women's Bur 200 Constitution Ave NW Washington DC 20210

DENNIS, STEVEN PELLOWE, food company executive; b. Orange, N.J., Feb. 17, 1960; s. William Francis and Patricia Ann (Terhune) D.; m. Nancy Helen Pellowe, July 23, 1988. BA in Econs., Tufts U., 1982; MBA, Harvard U., 1984. Assoc. Booz Allen and Hamilton Inc, Chgo., 1984-86; mgr. strategic planning Nutra Sweet Co., Skokie, Ill., 1986-87, dir. bus. devel., 1987-88, dir. bus. ventures group, 1988—. Mem. Harvard Bus. Sch. Club of Chgo. Office: Nutra Sweet Co 1419 Lake Cook Rd Deerfield IL

DENNISON, STANLEY SCOTT, retired lumber company executive, consultant; b. Mitchelville, Md., Sept. 1, 1920; s. Ralph Stanford and Cora Adeline (Scott) D.; m. Sharon Lee Johnson, June 1, 1983; children by previous marriage: Judith Dennison Tucci (dec.), Joan Dennison Daffron, Joyce D. Dennison Bischoff. Ed., Columbia Union Coll.; B.S., M.B.A., Calif. Western U., Ph.D., 1982. Operative builder Dennison Co., 1939-43; traffic rep. U.P. R.R., 1943-49; v.p. Arlington Millwork, Va., 1949-52, Internat. Filling Machine Co., Petersburg, Va., 1952-57, Atlanta Oak Flooring Co., 1957-62; regional mgr. Ga.-Pacific Corp., Portland, Oreg., 1962-70; v.p. Ga.-Pacific Corp., 1970-78, sr. v.p., 1978-82, exec. v.p., 1982-85; exec. mgmt. cons. 1985—. Bd. regents U. Portland; bd. advisors Calif. Western U. Mem. Western Forestry Assn. (charter), Alpha Kappa Psi. Democrat. Roman Catholic. Clubs: Capital City (Atlanta), Commerce (Atlanta). Home: 2575 Peachtree Rd NE Apt 14-C Atlanta GA 30305 Office: 133 Peachtree St NE Atlanta GA 30303

DENNISTON, WARREN KENT, JR., financial executive, consultant; b. Jacksonville, Fla., Aug. 18, 1939; s. Warren Kent and Mary E. (McCleskey) D.; m. Linda Burgess, Dec. 14, 1963 (div. Nov. 1979); m. Pamela Boggs, Mar. 20, 1980; children: Warren Kent III, Julia Marie, Edward Allen, I. Scott. Student, U. Ariz., 1958-60. Asst. br. mgr. Borg-Warner Acceptance, Tucson, 1963-65; br. mgr., San Diego, 1965-72; regional mgr., Atlanta, 1972-75; div. mgr., Kansas City, Mo., 1975-76, area v.p., 1977-78; gen. mgr. Borg-Warner Leasing, Chgo., 1979; group v.p. Borg-Warner Comml. Fin., Chgo., 1980-85; corp. v.p. planning Trans Am. Comml. Fin., Chgo., 1986—. Commr. Downers Grove (Ill.) Liquor Commn., 1983-86; chmn. bd. Downers Grove YMCA, 1982—. Sgt. U.S. Army, 1960-63. Mem. East Bank Club. Republican. Episcopalian.

DENNON, GERALD BURDETTE, media executive; b. Astoria, Oreg., Sept. 18, 1938; s. Elmer Burdette and Wilma Elaine (Looney) D.; m. Anne Vining , Aug. 25, 1962; children: Elizabeth, Daniel. Pres. Jerden Music, Inc., Seattle, 1964-69, Jerden Industries, Inc., Seattle, 1969-82, First Am. Records, Inc., Seattle, 1977-82, Bainbridge Communications, Seattle, 1986—, The Montcalm Corp., Seattle, 1983—; cons. The Weyerhaeuser Co., Seattle, 1977, Union Carbide Corp., Seattle, 1976. Author: The Salmon Cookbook, 1978; editor, publ. (Newsletter) The Aquaculture, 1973-75; producer (record) Louie Louie, 1963-64. Mem. Nat. Assn. Broadcasters, Wash. State Broadcasters Assn., Oreg. Assn. Broadcasters, Nat. Assn. Media Brokers. Republican. Episcopalian. Clubs: Rainer (Seattle), Wash. Athletic (Seattle). Office: The Montcalm Corp 801 2nd Ave 1410 Norton Bldg Seattle WA 98104

DENNY, GREGG R., business executive; b. Syracuse, N.Y., Dec. 18, 1956; s. Neil Joseph and Mary Ruth (Livingston) D.; m. Patricia Ann Matro, Sept. 26, 1981; children: Stephanie Jean, Samantha Lynn. BS in Acctg., Clarkson U., 1979. CPA, N.Y. Mem. tax staff Price Waterhouse, Syracuse, 1979-82; tax mgr. Oneida (N.Y.) Ltd., 1982-86, asst. treas., 1986—. Mem. Tax Execs. Inst. (pres.). Office: Oneida Ltd Kenwood Ave Oneida NY 13421

DENNY, JAMES MCCAHILL, retail executive; b. Mpls., Oct. 25, 1932; s. Charles and Mary (McCahill) D.; m. Catherine Mary Florance, Aug. 19, 1961; children: James, Philip, Sarah, Matthew, Catherine, William. Student, Princeton U., 1950-54; AB, U. Minn., 1957; LLB, Georgetown U., 1960. Assoc. Dewey Ballantine, N.Y.C., 1960-68; treas. Firestone Tire and Rubber Co., Akron, Ohio, 1968-78; exec. v.p., chief fin. and planning officer G.D. Searle & Co., Skokie, Ill., 1978-85; sr. v.p., chief fin. officer Sears, Roebuck & Co., Chgo., 1986—; bd. dirs. Gen. Binding Corp., Northbrook, Ill., Sears, Roebuck & Co., Chgo. Trustee Ravinia Festival Assn., Highland Park, Ill., 1985—. Served to cpl. U.S. Army, 1954-56, Korea. Mem. ABA, Am. Soc. Internat. Law, Assn. Bar City N.Y., Fin. Execs. Inst. Republican. Roman Catholic.

DENNY, WILLIAM MURDOCH, JR., investment management executive; b. Schenectady, N.Y., June 10, 1934; s. William Murdock and Ione Elizabeth (Lundy) D.; ScB in Chemistry, Brown U., 1958; MBA in Fin., Drexel U., 1974; m. Delores Gay Shillady, June 11, 1966; children: Ellen Gay, Nancy Beth, Linda Ann. Mem. mgmt. staff chem. specialities div. Pennwalt Corp., Phila., 1961-73; pres. Denny Fin. Enterprises, Paoli, Pa., 1974—; chmn. mgmt. com. Houston-Leon County Coal Co. Interests, Crockett, Tex., 1987—. Bd. dirs. United Way of North Central Chester County, 1980-83. Served to lt. comdr. USN, 1959-61. Mem. Fin. Analysts Fedn., Fin. Analysts Phila., Navy League U.S., Corinthians (Phila. fleet), Phi Kappa Psi. Episcopalian. Clubs: Brown U. (pres. 1979-81) (Phila.); Aronimink Golf (Newtown Square, Pa.); Yacht of Hilton Head Island (S.C.); Sea Pines. Home: 6 Anthony Dr Malvern PA 19355

DENOTO, JOANNE, infosystems specialist; b. Cleve., Dec. 5, 1953; d. Charles Anthony and Angelina (Bompiede) DeNoto. BS, Cleve. State U., 1976. Tchr. St. Charles Elem. Sch., Parma, Ohio, 1976-77, Cleve. Pub. Schs., 1977-78; programmer Lamson & Sessions, Cleve., 1979-80; programmer analyst Sohio, Cleve., 1980-82; programmer analyst Soc. Nat. Bank, Cleve., 1982-84, I/S tng. coordinator, 1984-86; I/S tng. mgr. Progressive Corp., Cleve., 1986-88; owner, cons. JMD Cons., Cleve., 1988—. Mem. Am. Mgmt. Assn., Am. Soc. Tng. Devel, Ind. Computer Cons. Assn. Office: JMD Cons 3917 Skyview Dr Brunswick OH 44212

DENOVIO, SUSAN WILLIAMS, advertising agency executive; b. Phila., Feb. 9, 1948; d. William Clinton and Catherine Irene (Currie) Williams; m. Carl James DeNovio, Aug. 9, 1969 (div. 1982); 1 child, Nicole Marie. BA Journalism, Rider Coll., 1969. Coordinator publications Ocean County Coll., Toms River, N.J., 1969-72; pub. info. officer Burlington County Coll., Pemberton, N.J., 1972-73, asst. to pres. for pub. info., 1973-75; freelance copywriter, Yardley, Pa., 1978-80; mng. editor Ad World, Inc., Levittown, Pa., 1980-83; founder, pres. Catalyst Communications, Inc., Newtown, Pa., 1983-88, Vista Communications Inc., Newtown, 1988—; mktg. cons. Mercer County Small Bus. Devel. Ctr., Trenton, N.J., 1983-84; instr. continuing edn. Bucks County Community Coll., Newtown, 1985-87. Editor, contbg. author: Bucks' Fortune, 1983. Bd. dirs. YWCA of Bucks County, Langhorne, Pa., 1984—, recording sec., 1984-86. Recipient Outstanding Service award Bd. Trustees Burlington County Coll., 1975; cert. of Recognition Bucks County Community Coll., 1985; Addy award Phila. Club Advt. Women, 1985, Neographics Silver award Greater Del. Valley Graphic Arts Assn., 1986. Mem. Lower Bucks County C. of C., Greater Phila. C. of C., Pi Delta Epsilon. Republican. Roman Catholic. Office: Vista Communications Inc Newtown Indsl Commons 111 Pheasant Run Newtown PA 18940

DENT, ERNEST DUBOSE, JR., pathologist; b. Columbia, S.C., May 3, 1927; s. E. Dubose and Grace (Lee) D.; student Presbyn. Coll., 1944-45; M.D., Med. Coll. S.C., 1949; m. Dorothy McCalman, June 16, 1949; children—Christopher, Pamela; m. 2d, Karin Frehse, Sept. 6, 1970. Intern U.S. Naval Hosp., Phila., 1949-50; resident pathology USPHS Hosp., Balt., 1950-54; chief pathology USPHS Hosp., Norfolk, Va., 1954-56; asso. pathology Columbia (S.C.) Hosp., 1956-59; pathologist Columbia Hosp., S.C. Baptist Hosp., also dir. labs., 1958-69; with Straus Clin. Labs., Los Angeles, 1969-72; staff pathologist St. Joseph Hosp., Burbank, Calif., Hollywood (Calif.) Community Hosp., 1969-72; dir. labs. Glendale Meml. Hosp. and Health Ctr., 1972—. Diplomate clin. pathology and pathology anatomy Am. Bd. Pathology. Mem. Am. Cancer Soc., AMA, Los Angeles County Med. Assn. (pres. Glendale dist. 1980-81), Calif. Med. Assn. (councillor 1984—), Am. Soc. Clin. Pathology, Coll. Am. Pathologists (assemblyman S.C. 1965-67; mem. publs. com. bull. 1968-70), Los Angeles Soc. Pathologists (trustee 1984-87), Los Angeles Acad. Medicine, S.C. Soc. Pathologists (pres. 1967-69). Lutheran. Author papers nat. med. jours. Home: 1526 Blue Jay Way Los Angeles CA 90069 Office: 1420 S Central Ave Glendale CA 91204

DENTINGER, RONALD LEE, comedian, speaker; b. Milw., Feb. 14, 1941; s. William Cassel and Kathryn Faye (Ritzman) D.; m. Kaylee Ann Kasten, Aug. 28, 1965; children: Ronald Lee Jr., Joann Jean. Officer Milw. Police Dept., 1962-67; dist. mgr. Am. Automobile Assn., Madison, Wis., 1967-71; gen. mgr. Don Q Inn, Dodgeville, Wis., 1971-85; comedian, speaker, Dodgeville, 1976—; humorist quoted in comedy mags., books; jokes sold to Rodney Dangerfield, 1980—, Joan Rivers, The Tonight Show, Saturday Night Live, 20/20 Show, Time Mag. Pres. Hidden Valley Tourism Region, Wis., 1984. Named Funniest Person in Wis., Showtime-TV Network, 1985. Mem. Nat. Speakers Assn., Wis. Profl. Speakers Assn., Dodgeville C. of C. (pres. 1984). Home and Office: PO Box 151 Dodgeville WI 53533

DENTON, ARNOLD EUGENE, food company executive; b. Remington, Ind., Mar. 18, 1925; s. Alvin James and Gertrude M. (Schwartz) D.; m. Catherine Maxine Bruner, Sept. 6, 1950; children—James, Gregory, David. B.S., Purdue U., 1949, DAgr., 1986; M.S., U. Wis., 1950, Ph.D., 1953. Head pet food div. Swift and Co., Chgo., 1953-56, head biochemistry, 1956-58; dir. basic research Campbell Inst. Food Research, Camden, N.J., 1958-66, v.p. basic research, 1966-70; v.p. tech. adminstrn. Campbell Soup Co., Camden, 1970-73, 75-78; v.p. internat. div., pres. Campbell Soup Internat. Campbell Soup Co., 1973-75, v.p. research and tech., 1978-83, pres. Campbell Inst. Research & Tech., 1978-88, sr. v.p., 1983—; mem. adv. bd. Food Research Inst. Mem. Moorestown Zoning Bd., N.J., 1968-69; pres. United Way, Moorestown, 1966-68. Served to 1st lt. USAAF, 1943-46. Mem. Inst. Food Technologists, Am. Chem. Soc., Am. Inst. Nutrition, AAAS, Food Processors Inst. (trustee 1983-85), Nat. Assn. Food Processors (chmn. sci. affairs council 1983-86, bd. dirs., exec. com.). Republican. Presbyterian. Club: Internat. (Washington). Home: 6 Walnut Ct Moorestown NJ 08057 Office: Campbell Soup Co Campbell Pl Camden NJ 08101

DENTON, DAVID ALAN, banker; b. Richmond, Va., Nov. 22, 1951; s. Benjamin and Estelle (Poncy) D.; m. Paula Duncan, Mar. 2, 1984; children: Brian, Matthew. BA in English, U. Richmond, 1974. Ops. officer 1st and Merchants Bank, Richmond, 1978-82; v.p. Bankers Trust S.C., Columbia, 1982-83; asst. v.p. Barnett Banks Fla., Miami, 1983-84; v.p. bank ops. Investors Savs. Bank, Richmond, 1984—; instr. Fin. Inst., Richmond, 1986-87. Patentee storage miser for automobiles. Active Fed. Res. Ops. Adv. Com., 1987—, Va. Automated Clearinghouse Edn., 1985—. Mem. U.S. League Ops. and Automation. Republican. Episcopalian. Office: Investors Savs Bank 9201 Forest Hill AVe Richmond VA 23235

DENTON, ELWOOD VALENTINE, economist; b. Peoria, Ill., Feb. 14, 1912; s. George Washington and Nina (Brown) D.; B.S. in Bus., Miami U., Oxford, Ohio, 1934; M.B.A., Case Western Res. U., 1948; diploma Stonier Grad. Sch. Banking Rutgers U., 1955; m. Sara Reinartz, Sept. 17, 1938; 1 son, Elwood Valentine, II. Statistician, Armco Steel Corp., Middletown, Ohio, 1935-40; econ. analyst, asst. cashier Fed. Res. Bank, Cleve., 1940-59; adminstr. Central Nat. Bank, Cleve., 1960-65; v.p. Nat. Bank of Jackson (Mich.), 1965-69; salary adminstr. Consumers Power Co., Jackson, 1969-71, corp. economist, 1971-77, ret., 1977; econ. cons. Downtown Devel. Authority, Jackson, 1978-79; mem. Jackson Ofcls. Compensation Commn., 1971-79; chmn. Council on Econ. Edn. for Mich., 1976-77; mem. advisory council on econ. edn. Olivet Coll., 1971-78; mem. Chgo. Economists Group, Fed. Res. Bank Chgo., 1971-77; 1st v.p., sec., dir. 1st Walnut Creek Mut., Rossmoor-Walnut Creek, Calif., 1987-88. Pres. Family Service Assn. Jackson County (Mich.); dir., sec. Golden Rain Found., Rossmoor-Walnut Creek, 1985-87. Lt. commdr. Supply Corps, USNR, 1942-45. Decorated Navy Commendation ribbon. Mem. Nat. Assn. Bus. Economists, Econ. Soc. Mich. (governing bd. 1973-79, treas. 1977-79), Family Service Assn. Cleve. (life), Phi Beta Kappa, Beta Theta Pi. Republican. Lutheran. Club: Kiwanis (pres. Bay Village, Ohio, club 1963-64). Author: What Is a Social Worker Worth?, 1957. Home: 1540 Golden Rain Rd #2 Walnut Creek CA 94595

DENTON, JERE MICHAEL, oil company executive; b. Horton, Kans., Apr. 4, 1947; s. Alvin Norwin and Ferne (Moore) C.; m. Sheila Marie Creeden, Sept. 7, 1974; children: Christina Marie, Alexandra Leigh. BS in Bus., U. Colo., 1969. Fin. analyst Samsonite Corp., Denver, 1969-73; dir. planning Aztec Oil and Gas, Dallas, 1973-76; exploration mgr. Southland Royalty, Ft. Worth, 1976-81; v.p. Hawaiian ops. Thermal Power Co., Honolulu, 1981-84; mgr. corp. devel. Diamond Shamrock, Dallas, 1984-86; sr. v.p. corp. devel. Kaneb Services Inc., Dallas, 1986; gen. chmn. internat. meeting Geothermanl Resources Council, Kona, Hawaii, 1985; bd. dirs. Energy Storage Terminals Inc., Fin. Subs. Inc., Kaneb Holding Inc., Petroleum Ops. and Support Services Inc., Kaneb Exploration Inc., Sugar Land, Tex., Kaneb Pipe Line Co., Wichita, Kans., Kecsub Inc., Sugar Land, Mecklenburg Coal and Mining Inc., Somerset, Ky., Security Inc., Bryan, Tex.; pres. bd. dirs. Kanvest Enterprises Inc., Dallas. Contbr. articles to profl. jours. Roman Catholic. Office: Kaneb Svcs Inc 2400 Lakeside Blvd Richardson TX 75082

DENTON, RAY DOUGLAS, insurance company executive; b. Lake City, Ark., May 16, 1937; s. Ray Dudney and Edna Lorraine (Roe) D.; B.A., U. Mich., 1964, postgrad., 1969-70; J.D., Wayne State U., 1969, postgrad., 1964-65; m. Cheryl Emma Borchardt, Mar. 9, 1964; children—Ray D., Derek St. Clair, Carter Lee. Claims rep. Hartford Ins. Co., Crum & Forster, Detroit, and Am. Claims, Chgo., 1962-73; partner Chgo. Metro Claims, Oak Park, Ill., 1974-75; founder, pres. Ray D. Denton & Assocs., Inc., Hinsdale, Ill., 1975—. Mem. Pi Kappa Alpha, Phi Alpha Delta. Home: 4532 Howard Western Springs IL 60558 Office: 930 N York Ste 1 Hinsdale IL 60521

DENTON, ROBERT WILLIAM (PETE), financial executive; b. Wilmington, Del., May 27, 1944; s. William R. and Margaret L. (Mitchell) D.; m. Donna Hughes, Dec. 20, 1978; children: Dyanna, Rhett, Whitney. BBA, U. S.C., 1966, M in Accountancy, 1973, EdD, 1980; postgrad., U. Ky., 1975, Harvard U., 1985; MBA, Harvard U., 1967. Registered real estate broker, S.C.. With U. S.C., Columbia, 1967—, asst. v.p. fin., 1976-77, v.p. fin.,

1977-81, system v.p. fiscal affairs, 1981-83, sr. v.p. bus. and fin., 1983-88, treas., exec. v.p. bus. and fin., 1988-89; bd. dirs. Faculty House Carolina, Columbia, Dominion Fin. Svcs. Corp., Columbia; ptnr. Lockhart Car Wash Chain, S.C. Contbr. articles to profl. jours. Bd. dirs. U.S.C. Aux. Svc. Found.; bd. dirs., treas. Columbia Better Bus. Bur. Named Ky. Col. Mem. Nat. Assn. Colls. and Univ. Bus. Officers, Nat. Assn. State Univs. and Land Grant Colls., So. Assn. Coll. and Univ. Bus. Officers, So. Assn. Colls. and Schs. (accreditation com.), S.C. Pub. Colls and Univs., Univ. Assocs., U.S.C. Alumni Assn., Ducks Unlimited, Beta Alpha Psi, Beta Gamma Sigma, Omicron Delta Epsilon, Omicron Delto Kappa, Phi Delta Kappa, Kappa Sigma. Home: 109 Old Arms Ct Columbia SC 29212 Office: U SC System 201 Osborne Columbia SC 29208

DE NUCCIO, RAYMOND ADOLPH, plastics manufacturing company executive; b. Lawrence, Mass., July 29, 1933; s. Pasquale Pasco and Genoffa (Ferraro) De N.; m. Jeanette L. Mignanelli, Apr. 25, 1954; children—Raymond, Patricia, Randall, Robert. B.A., Merrimack Coll., 1962; B.S., Lowell Inst. Tech., 1960. With Vulcan Corp., Cin., 1967-74, div. pres., 1968-74; pres. Plastronic Engring. Co., Haverhill, Mass., 1974—. bd. dirs. Plastronic Engring Co., Inc., Br. Industries div., Hooksett, N.H., Smith Edwards div., Amherst, N.H. Adv. mem. Modern Plastics, N.Y.C., 1984-85. Mem. Methuen Town Meeting, Mass., 1962-64. Served with U.S. Army, 1953-56. Mem. Soc. Plastic Engrs. (sr.), DAV, Soc. Mech. Engrs, Sons of Italy. Democrat. Roman Catholic. Lodge: K.C. (4th deg.). Office: Plastronic Engring Co Inc 35 Walnut St Haverhill MA 01830

DENYSYK, BOHDAN, business executive; b. Kornberg, Fed. Republic Germany, Feb. 13, 1947; came to U.S., 1949; s. John and Maria (Zelenewich) D.; m. Halina Bubela, June 28, 1969; children: Maria H., Danya L., Adrienne Y., Alexis M. B.S., Manhattan Coll., 1968; M.S., Cath. U. Am., 1971; Ph.D., Union Exptl. Colls. and Univs., 1981. Project mgr. Naval Weapons Lab., Dahlgren, Va., 1968-72; scientist Naval Med. Research Inst., Bethesda, Md., 1972-75; program mgr. Naval Surface Weapons Ctr., Dahlgren, 1975-78; dept. head E.G. & G. Inc., Rockville, Md., 1978-81; dep. asst. sec. U.S. Dept. Commerce, Washington, 1981-83; dir. civil programs IBM Corp., 1983-86; pres. DLR Assocs., Arlington, Va., 1972-80, 83—; sr. v.p. Global U.S.A., 1986—, also bd. dirs.; mem. Congl. Adv. Panel on China, 1985—. Contbr. articles to profl. jours. Mem. Presdl. Transition Team, Washington, 1981; regional dir. Rep. Nat. Com., 1980; dir. pub. relations Ukranian Nat. Info. Service, 1976-80; mem. Pres.'s Export Council, 1981—, Presdl. Awards Commn., 1986-87; exec. dir. Md. Reagan-Bush Campaign, 1984; pres. Phi Mu Alpha Sinfonia, 1967-68; nat. dir. for coalitions Dole for U.S Pres. campaign. Navy fellow, 1969-72; Regents scholar, 1964-68. Mem. AIAA, AAAS, Am. Def. Preparedness Assn., Am. Phys. Soc. Republican. Roman Catholic. Office: Global USA Inc 2121 K St NW Washington DC 20037

DEOUL, NEAL, electronics company executive; b. N.Y.C., Feb. 27, 1931; s. George and Pearl (Hirschfield) D.; B.S. in Physics, Coll. City N.Y., 1952; postgrad. Rutgers U., 1954-55; LL.B., Bklyn. Law Sch., 1959; m. Bernice Kradel, Dec. 25, 1955 (div.); children: Cara Jan, Stefani Neva, Evan Craig; m., Kathleen B. Davis, June 20, 1982; 1 child, Shannon Rae. Engr., Signal Corps, U.S. Army, Evans Signal Lab., Belmar, N.J., 1952-55; engr. Airborne Instruments Lab., Deer Park, N.Y., 1955-56; sales mgr. FXR, Inc., Woodside, L.I., 1956-60; admitted to N.Y. State bar, 1960; pres. Microwave Dynamics Corp., Plainview, L.I., 1960-61, Paradynamics, Inc., Huntington Station, N.Y., 1961-64; mgr. Servo Corp. Am., Hicksville, N.Y., 1964-66; v.p. Trio Labs., Inc., Plainview, N.Y., 1966-69; exec. v.p. Microlab/FXR, Livingston, N.J., 1969-74; pres. Neal Deoul Assocs., Owings Mills, Md., 1974—. Mem. IEEE (sr.), N.Y. State Bar Assn., Md. Bar Assn., Young Pres.'s Orgn., Profl. Group Engring. Mgmt., Am. Arbitration Assn. Home and Office: 3104 Caves Rd Owings Mills MD 21117

DE PALMA, DANIEL P., advertising executive; b. Mt. Vernon, N.Y., July 8, 1934; married; children: Carla, Mark, Denise. AB, Columbia Coll., 1955, MS, 1956; LLB, N.Y. Law Sch., 1958. Exec. v.p. Rumrill-Hoyt, Inc., N.Y.C., 1980-81; pres. De Palma & Hogan, Inc., White Plains, N.Y., 1981—. Capt. USMC, 1958-61. Mem. Vis. Nurses Assn. (dir. Plainfield, N.J. chpt.). Republican. Roman Catholic. Home: 88 Hunter Ave Fanwood NJ 07023 Office: De Palma & Hogan Inc 3 Barker Ave White Plains NY 10601

DEPAOLIS, POTITO UMBERTO, food company executive; b. Mignano, Italy, Aug. 28, 1925; s. Giuseppe A. and Filomena (Macchiaverna) deP.; Vet. Dr., U. Naples, 1948; Libera Docenza, Ministero Pubblica Istruzione (Rome, Italy), 1955; m. Marie A. Caronna, Apr. 10, 1965. Came to U.S., 1966, naturalized, 1970. Prof. food service Vet. Sch., U. Naples, Italy, 1948-66; retired, 1966; asst. prof. A titre Benevole Ecole Veterinaire Alfort, Paris, France, 1956; vet. inspector U.S. Dept. Agr., Omaha, 1966-67; sr. research chemist Grain Processing Corp., Muscatine, Iowa, 1967-68; v.p., dir. product devel. Reddi Wip, Inc., Los Angeles, 1968-72; with Kubro Foods, Los Angeles, 1972-73, Shade Foods, Inc., 1975—; pres. Vegetable Protein Co., Riverside, Calif., 1973—, Tima Brand Food Co., 1975—, Dr. Tima Natural Foods, 1977—. Fulbright scholar Cornell U., Ithaca, N.Y., 1954; British Council scholar, U. Reading, Eng., 1959-60; postdoctoral research fellow NIH, Cornell U., 1963-64. Mem. Inst. Food Technologists, Italian Assn. Advancement Sci., AAAS, Vet. Med. Assn., Biol. Sci. Assn. Italy, Italian Press Assn., Greater Los Angeles Press Club. Contbr. articles in field to prol. jours. Patentee in field. Home: 131 Groverton Pl Bel Air Los Angeles CA 90077 Office: 8570 Wilshire Blvd Beverly Hills CA 90211 also: 6878 Beck Ave North Hollywood CA 91605

DE PFYFFER, ANDRE, lawyer; b. Lucerne, Switzerland, Nov. 3, 1928; s. Leodegar and Anna (Carvalho) de P.; Baccalaureat, U. Berne, 1947; postgrad. U. Geneva, 1947-50, 54; married; children: Corinne, Francois. Admitted to Geneva Lawyers Assn., 1952, since practiced in Geneva; ptnr. firm Mes. de Pfyffer, Argand, Troller & Assocs.; dir. IC Industries (Internat.) S.A., Volvo Suisse S.A., Cederroth Internat. S.A., Banque Paribas (Suisse) S.A., Groupe Bruxelles Lambert, (chmn.) Banque Scandinave en Suisse S.A.; vice chmn. Pargesa Holding, S.A. Mem. Internat. Law Assn., Circle de la Terrasse. Home: 41 Quai Wilson, Geneva Switzerland Office: 6 Rue Bellot, Geneva Switzerland

DE POKOMANDY, GABRIEL, lawyer: b. Oroshaza, Hungary, July 7, 1944: s. Alexander and Irene (Csizmadia) De P.; BA Coll. de Levis (Que., Can.), 1965; lic. in Law, Laval U., 1968; s. Louise Sirois, Dec. 11, 1971; children—Erik, Alexandra. Atty. Rouleau, Carrier & Assos., Baie Comeau, Que., 1968-72; crown prosecutor, Sept Iles, Que., 1973; sr. ptnr. De Pokomandy, Besnier & Assocs., Sept-Iles, 1974—; tchr. bus. law Regional Coll., 1972-79; legal adviser Fedn. des Jeunes Chambres du Can. Francais, 1978-83. V.p., Jeune Chambre de Baie-Comeau, 1971-72; pres. Jeune Chambre de Sept-Iles, 1973-74, Mcpl. Environ. Com., Sept-Iles, 1976-78; pres. Conseil de Gestion Scout-Guide, Sept-Iles Inc., 1983-84; pres. local com. P.Q. Hearth Found., Sept-Iles, 1979-80; v.p. Sept-Iles Mus., 1976-79, pres. 1985-89; mem. adminstrn. bd. Gallix Alpine Ski Team, treas. 1987-89. Mem. Barreau Du Que., Can. Bar Assn., Que. Bar Assn. (pres. north shore sect. 1984-86). Roman Catholic. Club: Richelieu, Gourmand Gourmet. Home: 11 Pampalon, Sept Iles, PQ Canada G4R 1T9 Office: 865 Laure, Sept Iles, PQ Canada G4R 1Y6

DEPPE, HENRY A., insurance company executive; b. S.I., N.Y., July 1, 1920; s. Herman and Marie Deppe; student Cornell Sch. Hotel Adminstrn., 1943; m. Florence Chieffo, Aug. 8, 1943; children: Katherine, Marlaina, Lynda. Agt. Travelers Life Ins. Co., White Plains, N.Y., 1946-49; dist. mgr. Mass. Life Ins. Co., White Plains, 1949-57; gen. agt. Guardian Life Ins. Co., White Plains, 1956-87 ; pres. Nat. Pension Service, Inc., White Plains, 1957-85, chmn. bd., chief exec. officer, 1985—; chmn. bd. Nat. Pension Service Inc.; bd. dirs. YOREC Corp.; mem. faculty C.L.U. Inst.; guest lectr. N.Y. State Trial Lawyers Assn., Fairleigh Dickinson Pension Inst., IRS, C.W. Post Tax Inst., various other profl. assns. and ednl. instns.; bd. dirs. Nat. Bank Stamford. Pres., Young Republicans Club of Westchester County (N.Y.), 1954-55, Ossining (N.Y.) PTA, 1963-64, Multiple Sclerosis Soc. Westchester, 1964, 65; pres. Estate Planning Council of Westchester; founder Tax Inst., Iona Coll., co-chmn. inst., 1976-78; bd. dirs. ARC, Westchester County, N.Y., 1984-88, Boy Scouts Am., Westchester County, 1988—; pres., bd. dirs. N.Y. Fertility Research Found. Served to lt., inf., U.S. Army, 1942-46. Recipient Nat. Sales Achievement award, 1966; Fred E. Hamilton award, 1975; David Ben Gurion Friendship award, 1975; Guest of Honor award United Jewish Appeal Fedn., 1978; Leadership award State of Israel, 1979; Disting. Citizen award, Westchester-Putnam Council Boy Scouts Am., 1986. Mem. Assn. Advanced Life Underwriters, Internat. Assn. Fin. Planners, Am. Pension Conf., Am. Soc. Pension Actuaries, Am. Soc. C.L.U.s, Life Underwriters Assn. Westchester (pres. 1949-50), Nat. Assn. Pension Cons. and Adminstrs. (treas.), Fertility Research Assn. (pres. bd. dirs. 1982-83), Nat. Assn. Health and Welfare Plans, Million Dollar Round Table (life and qualifying), Golden Key Soc. (founder), Top of Table, Ten Million Dollar Forum, Research Agys. Group, White Plains C. of C., Sleepy Hollow Country Country, Boca Raton Hotel and Country Club. Home: 1500 S Ocean Blvd Boca Raton FL 33432 Office: Nat Pension Svc 1025 Westchester Ave White Plains NY 10601

DEPPELER, JAMES GREGORY, management consultant agency executive; b. N.Y.C., Feb. 10, 1946; s. John Howard, Jr. and Muriel Dolores (Hecker) D.; B.Engring., Stevens Inst. Tech., 1968, M.Mgmt. Sci., 1971, postgrad., 1971—; m. Wende Cyrille Somers, June 9, 1979; children—James Gregory Jr., Hillary Somers. Engr., Jersey Central Power and Light Co., Asbury Park, N.J., 1968-71; internal cons. Gen. Pub. Utilities Corp., Morristown, N.J., 1971-73; sr. cons. Fantus Co., South Orange, N.J., 1973-77; v.p. Bus. Mktg. Corp., N.Y.C., 1977-80; chmn. Deppeler Assos., Manasquan, N.J., 1980—; dir. Econ. Geography Assos., Marlton, N.J., World Trade Services, Portland, Maine. Environ. commr. Borough of Brielle (N.J.), 1973-81, mem. bd. adjustment, 1979—, chmn. 1986—. Mem. Am. Soc. Metals, AIME, Am. Soc. Profl. Cons., Am. Assn. Econ. Developers (dir. 1979—), Barnegat Bay Yacht Racing Assn. (rep. 1985—), Squan Tri Sail Offshore Racing Assn. (pres. 1984—, bd. dirs. 1980—). Club: Manasquan River Yacht (Brielle) (trustee 1974—, sec. 1980-81, rear commodore 1982-83, vice commodore 1984, commodore 1985—). Researcher urban devel. problems of major cities, geographically variable costs for corp. facilities. Home: 519 Harris Ave Brielle NJ 08730

DE PREE, MAX O., furniture manufacturing company executive; b. 1924. BA, Hope Coll., 1947. With Herman Miller Inc., Zeeland, Mich., 1947—, exec. v.p., sec., 1962-71, chmn. bd. dirs., 1971-80, 82, 87, chief exec. officer, 1980-87, pres., 1982-87, chmn., 1987—, also bd. dirs. Office: Herman Miller Inc 8500 Byron Rd Zeeland MI 49464 *

DEPUE, BOBBIE LEE, management consultant; b. Cooper, Tex., July 22, 1938; d. Carl Benson and Mary Mozelle (Gatlin) Hewitt; m. Ronald Earl DePue, Nov. 12, 1954; children—Michael Allen, David Anthony, Gregory Scott. B.A. in Bus. Mgmt., Prescott Coll., Ariz., 1985. Food service sales mgr. Pepsi Cola Bottling Group, Phoenix, 1978-79; dist. sales mgr. Pepsi Cola Co., Ariz., N.Mex., Nev., West Tex., 1979-82, div. devel. mgr., western div., Phoenix, 1982-88, Weber Mgmt. Cons., 1988—. Mem. Corp. Bus. and Profl. Women, Nat. Assn. Female Execs. Republican. Home and Office: 326 E Paradise Ln Phoenix AZ 85022

DERAMUS, WILLIAM NEAL, III, railroad executive; b. Pittsburg, Kans., Dec. 10, 1915; s. William Neal and Lucile Ione (Nicholas) D.; m. Patricia Howell Watson, Jan. 22, 1943; children: William Neal IV, Patricia Nicholas Fogel, Jean Deramus Wagner, Jill Watson Dean. AA, Kansas City Jr. Coll., 1934; AB, U. Mich., 1936; LLB, Harvard U., 1939. Transp. apprentice Wabash R.R. Co., St. Louis, 1939-41; asst. trainmaster Wabash R.R. Co., 1941-43; asst. to gen. mgr. K.C.S. Ry. Co., Kansas City, Mo., 1946-48; asst. to pres. C.G.W. Ry. Co., Chgo., 1948; pres., dir. C.G.W. Ry. Co., 1949-57, chmn. exec. com., 1954-57; pres., dir. M.-K.-T. R.R., 1957-61; chmn. bd. MAPCO, Inc., Tulsa, 1960-73, chmn. exec. com., 1973-81, now dir.; pres., dir. Kansas City So. Lines, Mo., 1961-73; chmn. bd. Kansas City So. Lines, 1966-80; pres. Kansas City So. Industries, Inc., Mo., 1962-71, chmn. bd., 1966—; dir. Bus. Men's Assurance Co., Kansas City, Kansas City Royals. Capt. to maj. Transp. Corps, Mil. Ry. Svc. AUS, 1943-46, overseas, India. Mem. Beta Theta Pi. Clubs: Chgo.; Kansas City, River (Kansas City), Mission Hills Country (Kansas City), Mercury (Kansas City). Lodge: Rotary (Kansas City). Home: 37 LeMans Ct Prairie Village KS 66208 Office: Kans City So Industries Inc 114 W 11th St Kansas City MO 64105

DERAN, TIMOTHY MICHAEL, industrial executive; b. Tiffin, Ohio, Oct. 1, 1951; s. Robert Charles and Marjorie Ann (Distel) DeR.; m. Susan Elaine Bunce, Apr. 27, 1979 (div. Sept. 1983); 1 child, Aaron Timothy; m. Patricia Ann Davey, Sept. 30, 1983: children: Jeffrey Scott, Michael Anthony, Sean Bradley. BS in Edn., Bowling Green (Ohio) State U., 1976; MS in Edn., U. Toledo, 1983. Tchr. Cen. Local Sch. Dist., Sherwood, Ohio, 1976-77; foreman Strydel-Emenee Inc., Stryker, Ohio, 1977-79; case mgr. Quadco Inc., Stryker, 1978-81, plant mgr., 1981-84; indsl. relations mgr. Sheridan Mfg. Co. div. Sheller-Globe Corp., Wauseon, Ohio, 1984-85; dir. workshop Hocking Valley Industries Inc., Logan, Ohio, 1985-87; industries dir. Coshocton Co., Hopewell Industries Inc., Coshocton, Ohio, 1987—. Adv. panel YWCA. Coshocton, 1988—. Mem. K.C., Kiwanis (sec., treas. Coshocton club 1988—). Democrat. Roman Catholic. Home: 1007 Highland Blvd Coshocton OH 43812 Office: Hopewell Industries Inc 637 Chestnut St Coshocton OH 43812

DERBES, DANIEL WILLIAM, corporate executive; b. Cin., Mar. 30, 1930; s. Earl Milton and Ruth Irene (Grauten) D.; m. Patricia Maloney, June 4, 1952; children: Donna Ann, Nancy Lynn (dec.), Stephen Paul. B.S., U.S. Mil. Acad., 1952; M.B.A., Xavier U., Cin., 1963. Devel. engr. AiResearch Mfg. Co., Phoenix, 1956-58; with Garrett Corp., 1958-80; v.p., gen. mgr., then exec. v.p. Garrett Corp., L.A., 1975-80; dir. Garrett Corp., 1976-87; pres. Advanced Tech. Group, Signal Cos., Inc., La Jolla, Calif., 1980-85; pres. Allied-Signal Internat. Inc., 1985—; exec. v.p. Allied-Signal, Inc., Morristown, N.J., 1985-88; bd. dirs. Allied- Signal Can., Inc., San Diego Gas & Electric Co., WD-40 Co. V.p. nat. council Boy Scouts Am., 1981—; trustee U. San Diego, 1981—; mem. adv. bd. U. S.C., 1986—. Served with AUS, 1952-56. Republican. Roman Catholic. Office: Allied-Signal Inc 11255 N Torrey Pines Rd La Jolla CA 92037

DERCHIN, MICHAEL WAYNE, investment banker, financial analyst; b. N.Y.C., Aug. 17, 1942; s. James and Rose (Minenberg) D.; m. Dary Ingham, Dec. 29, 1970. B.A., Bklyn. Coll., 1964; M.B.A., CCNY, 1966; postgrad. Syracuse U., 1966-69. Sr. analyst Am. Airlines, N.Y.C., 1969-70; dir. mktg. Pan Am. World Airways, N.Y.C., 1970-74; dir. mktg. Am. Airlines, N.Y.C., 1974-79; v.p. Oppenheimer & Co. Inc., N.Y.C., 1979-82, First Boston Corp., N.Y.C., 1982-88; mng. dir. Drexel Burnham Lambert, N.Y.C., 1988—; columnist Travel Weekly, N.Y.C., 1984—; spl. guest Wall St. Week, Owings Mills, Md., 1982-88, guest MacNeil Lehrer Newshour, N.Y., 1985; expert witness U.S. Senate Aviation subcom., 1984; lectr. Travel Research Assn., N.Y.C., 1981-84. Named to first team All Am. analysts Instnl. Investor Mag., 1983. Mem. N.Y. Soc. Security Analysts, N.Y. Airline Analysts Soc. (chmn. membership com. 1985, pres. 1986-87), Wings Club Travel Tourism Research Assn. Club: Nat. Arts, University (N.Y.C.). Avocations: tennis; photography; reading. Office: Drexel Burnham Lambert 60 Broad St New York NY 10004

DERDENGER, PATRICK, lawyer; b. Los Angeles, June 29, 1946; s. Charles Patrick and Drucilla Marguerite (Lange) D.; m. Jo Lynn Dickins, Aug. 24, 1968; children: Kristin Lynn, Bryan Patrick, Timothy Patrick. BA, Loyola U., Los Angeles, 1968; MBA, U. So. Calif., 1971, JD, 1974; LLM in Taxation, George Washington U., 1977. Bar: Calif. 1974, U.S. Ct. Claims 1975, Ariz. 1979, U.S. Ct. Appeals (9th cir.) 1979, U.S. Dist. Ct. Ariz. 1979, U.S. Tax Ct. 1979, U.S. Supreme Ct. 1979. Trial atty. honors program U.S. Dept. Justice, Washington, 1974-78; ptnr. Lewis and Roca, Phoenix, 1978—; adj. prof. taxation Golden Gate U., Phoenix, 1983—; mem. Ariz. State Tax Ct. Legis. Study Commn. Author: Arizona State and Local Taxation, Cases and Materials, 1983, Arizona Sales and Use Tax Guide, 1986, Advanced Arizona Sales and Use Tax, 1987, Arizona Sales and Use Tax Handbook, 1988; author: (with others) State and Local Taxation, Arizona Sales and Use Tax, 1989. Bd. dirs. North Scottsdale Little League. Served to capt. USAF, 1968-71. Recipient U.S. Law Week award Bur. Nat. Affairs, 1974. Mem. ABA (taxation sect., various coms.), Ariz. Bar Assn. (taxation sect., various coms., chmn. state and local tax com., chmn. continuing legal edn. com.), Maricopa County Bar Assn., Nat. Assn. Bond Lawyers, Inst. Property Taxation, Inst. Sales Taxation, Inst. Sales Taxation, Phoenix Met. C. of C., Ariz. C. of C. (tax com.), U. So. Calif. Alumni Club (bd. dirs., pres.-elect), Phi Delta Phi, Sereno Soccer (bd. dirs.). Home: 9501 N 49th Pl Paradise Valley AZ 85253 Office: Lewis and Roca 100 W Washington St 2200 First Interstate Bank Pla Phoenix AZ 85003

DERMODY, MICHAEL CRAIG, real estate developer; b. Reno, Nev., June 9, 1950; s. John Arthur and Martha Sue (Deck) D.; m. Paula Anne Smith, Oct. 21, 1985; 1 child, Michael Craig II. BA, U. Colo., 1972; LLB, Gonzaga U., 1976. Treas. Dermody Properties, Reno, 1976-80, pres., chief exec. officer, 1980—. Chmn. bd. dirs., trustee Children's Cabinet, Reno; bd. dirs. Econ. Devel. Authority, Reno, 1985—, Boys Club Truckee Meadows, Reno, 1981—. Mem. Reno-Sparks C. of C. (bd. dirs. 1982-85), Young. Pres. Orgn. Nev. Democrat. Office: Dermody Properties 1200 Financial Blvd Reno NV 89502

DE ROES, NANDA YVONNE, banker; b. Rotterdam, The Netherlands, Apr. 12, 1945; m. Anthony G. De Roes, Jan. 27, 1973 (dec.). Kandidaats, U. Leiden, The Netherlands, 1972. Asst. sec. Mitsui Mfrs. Bank, Los Angeles, 1979-81, Am. Savs. and Loan, Beverly Hills, Calif., 1981-83; sec. First Charter Fin. Corp., Am. Savs. and Loan, Beverly Hills, 1983, Fin. Corp. Am., Los Angeles, 1983-85; v.p., sec. Am. Savs. and Loan, Los Angeles, 1985; sr. v.p., sec. Fin. Corp. Am., Am. Savs. and Loan, Irvine, 1985-88, Am. Savs. Bank F.A., Irvine, Calif., 1989—. Mem. Am. Soc. Corp. Secs. Republican. Office: Am Savs Bank 18401 Von Karman Ave 5th Fl Irvine CA 92715

DE ROSE, LOUIS JOHN, financial services executive; b. Elizabeth, N.J., Mar. 2, 1952; s. Ralph Anthony and Mary Rose (Di Leo) DeR.; m. Alejandrina Oriol, Jan. 20, 1982; children: Daniel A., Sandra M., Ralph A. III. AAS, Union Coll., 1972; BS, Rutgers U., 1980; postgrad., Pace U., 1980-84. Tax acct. U.S. Trust Co. N.Y., N.Y.C., 1972-79; tax acct. Fiduciary Trust Co., Inc., N.Y.C., 1979-80, asst. tax officer, 1979-84, tax officer, 1980-83; asst. v.p., dept. head Fiduciary Trust Co., Inc., Jersey City, 1983-86; v.p. Fiduciary Spl. Services, Inc., Jersey City, 1986—; mem. com. on banking instns. on taxation. Coach Rahway (N.J.) Youth Soccer Assn., 1984—. Mem. Nat. Soc. Notaries. Democrat. Roman Catholic. Office: Fiduciary Spl Svcs Inc Journal Sq Pla II Jersey City NJ 07306

DERR, KENNETH T., oil company executive. m. Donna Mettler, Sept. 12, 1959; 3 children. BME, Cornell U., MBA. With Chevron Corp. (formerly Standard Oil Co. of Calif.), San Francisco, 1960—, v.p., 1972-85; pres. Chevron U.S.A., Inc. subs. Chevron Corp., San Francisco, 1978-84; head merger program Chevron Corp. and Gulf Oil Corp., San Francisco, 1984-85; vice-chmn. Chevron Corp., San Francisco, 1985-88, chmn., chief exec. officer, 1989—; bd. dirs. Citicorp. Trustee Cornell U., The Conf. Bd. Mem. Am. Petroleum Inst. (dir.), Bus. Roundtable, Nat. Petroleum Coun., San Francisco Golf Club, Orinda Country Club, Pacific Union Club. Office: Chevron Corp 225 Bush St San Francisco CA 94104

DERR, THOMAS BURCHARD, manufacturing executive; b. Reading, Pa., Dec. 31, 1929; s. William Thomas and Clara Constance (Burchard) D.; m. Jane Lynette Ruppert, May 30, 1952; children: Jeffrey Allen, Kathy Jo Taylor. AA, WPI, Reading, 1955; BS in Indsl. Engring., Pa. State U., 1960, MS in Indsl. Engring., 1961. Project engr. Ordnance Research Lab., State College, Pa., 1960-61; indsl. engr. Textile Machine Works, Reading, 1961-62, personnel mgr., 1962-63, dir. employee relations, 1963-68; dir. indsl. relations Rockwell Standard Corp., Detroit, 1968-69, N.Am. Rockwell Auto. Div., Detroit, 1969-70; v.p., gen. mgr. Metlmex Corp., Lewistown, Pa., 1970-73, pres., 1973—; pres. Big John Corp., Lewistown, 1978—. Patentee convection oven. Pres., bd. dirs. Camp Fire Girls, Reading, 1962-66; pres. Mfrs. Assn. Berks County, Reading, 1962-65; hon. chmn. Mifflin County March of Dimes, Lewiston, 1981; chmn. annual fund Coll. Engring. Pa. State U., 1984-86. Mem. Am. Inst. Indsl. Engrs., Pa. State Engring Soc. (past pres.), Alpha Pi Mu, Sigma Tau. Republican. Presbyterian. Club: Centre Hills State Coll. (bd. dirs. 1980-86). Lodge: Elks. Home: 1366 Greenwood Circle State College PA 16803 Office: Big John Corp Box 250 Pleasant Gap PA 16823

DERRICKSON, WILLIAM BORDEN, business executive; b. Milford, Del., May 30, 1940; m. Patricia Jean Hayes, Feb. 1, 1964; children—Stephen Russel, Michael Scot. B.S.E.E., U. Del., 1964; diploma, Harvard Bus. Sch., 1979. Registered profl. engr. Supr. elec. maintenance Delmarva Power, Salisbury, Md., 1964-68; instrumentation engr. Hercules, Inc., Wilmington, Del., 1968-69, Sun Shipbldg., Chester, Pa., 1969-70; dir. project Fla. Power & Light Co., Juno Beach, Fla., 1970-84; sr. v.p. Pub. Service Co. N.H., Manchester, 1984-85; pres. New Hampshire Yankee Electric Co., Seabrook, 1985-87; pres., chief ops. officer WPD Assocs., Inc., 1986-88; chmn. bd., chief exec. officer Quadrex Corp., Campbell, Calif., 1989—; Nuclear advisor Tenn. Valley Authority Bd. Dirs., 1987; pres., chief operating officer Quadrex Corp., Campbell, Calif., 1988-89, chmn. bd., chief exec. officer, 1989—. Contbr. articles to profl. publs. Named Constrn. Man of Yr. ENR/McGraw-Hill Publs., 1984. Mem. Am. Nuclear Soc., Project Mgmt. Inst., Nat. Soc. Profl. Engrs., N.H. Soc. Profl. Engrs. Republican. Home: PO Box 1017 North Hampton NH 03862 Office: Quadrex Corp 1700 Dell Ave Campbell CA 95008-6986

DERRICO, GEORGIA SANTANGELO, banker; b. N.Y.C., Oct. 6, 1944; d. George M. and Rose Mary (Rao) Santangelo; B.A., St. Mary's Coll., Notre Dame, Ind., 1966; degree in internat. affairs Johns Hopkins U., Bologna, Italy, 1969; M.Internat. Affairs, Columbia U., 1970; postgrad. exec. seminar Harvard U., 1977; m. R. Roderick Porter, Feb 6, 1982. Various positions including lending officer, dist. head corp. div., chief adminstrv. and credit officer multinat. div. Chem. Bank, N.Y.C., 1971—, sr. v.p., 1982-84 , dir. corp. affairs, 1982-84, chmn. So. Fin. Fed. Savs. Bank, 1985—; bd. dirs. Oneida, Ltd. Bd. dirs. Nat. Dance Inst. Mem. Assn. M.B.A. Execs. Contbr. article to profl. publs. Office: So Fin Fed Svs Bank 362-364 Elden St Herndon VA 22070

DERSH, RHODA E., management consultant, business executive; b. Phila., Sept. 10, 1934; d. Maurice S. and Kay (Wiener) Eisman; m. Jerome Dersh, Dec. 23, 1956; children: Debra Lori, Jeffrey Jonathan. BA, U. Pa., 1955; MA, Tufts U., 1956; MBA, Manhattan Coll. Sch. Bus., 1980. Interpreter, Consul of Chile, 1954-57; various teaching and staff positions Albright Coll., Mt. Holyoke Coll., Amherst Coll., Marple Newtown Sch., 1957-64; systems designer Systems Inc., Reading, Pa., 1964-67; pres., chief exec. officer Profl. Practice Mgmt. Assocs., Reading, 1976—; pres., chief exec. officer Pace Inst.; chief exec. officer Pace Inst., Reading, 1981—; pres., chief exec. officer Pace Mgmt., Inc., 1983—, chief exec. officer Pace Microcomputers Internat., 1986—; pres. Wordserv, 1984—, State Bd. Pvt. Lic. Schs., 1987—; cons. dir. pub. sch. budget study project City of Reading, 1967-78, chmn. comprehensive community plan task force, 1973-75, chmn. pub. service cons. project, 1980—; panel chmn. budget allocations United Way, 1974-76; del. White House Conf. on Children Youth, 1970; co-founder World Affairs Council, Reading and Berks County, 1963-65; chmn. Berks County Com. for Children Youth, 1968-72; commr. Trial Ct. Nominating Commn. of Berks County (Pa.), 1982-84; bd. dirs. United Way of Berks County, 1984-87; chmn. programs Leadership Berks; mem. Bd. of Pvt. Lic. Schs., Pa., 1987—. Recipient grant AAUW Ednl. Found.; Outstanding Womens award Jr. League Reading; Trendsetter award YWCA, 1985; accredited ind. cons. Mem. Inst. Community Affairs (exec. com. 1975-79), Pa. Assn. Pvt. Sch. Bus. Adminstrs. (bd. dirs. 1985—), LWV, Berks County C. of C. (bd. dirs. 1983-86, chmn. edn. com. 1983-85), Pa. Chamber of Bus. and Industry, AAUW, Am. Mgmt. Assn., Am. Acad. Ind. Cons. (pres. 1978-80), Nat. Com. Citizens in Edn., Am. Acad. Polit. Social Sci., Nat. Assn. Female Execs., Reading and Berks C. of C (bd. dirs., chmn. edn. com., Entrepreneur of Yr. 1985). Lodge: Rotary (Reading, Pa., chpt.). Author: The School Budget is Your Business, 1976, Business Management for Professional Offices, 1977, The School Budget: It's Your Money, It's Your Business, 1979, Improving Public School Management Practices, 1979, Part-Time Professional and Managerial Personnel: The Employers View, 1979; contbr. articles to profl. jours. Office: 606 Court St Reading PA 19601

DERUCHER, KENNETH NOEL, civil engineering educator; b. Messina, N.Y., Jan. 24, 1949; s. Kenneth John and Verna May (MacDougall) D.; m. Barbara Eileen Frick, Apr. 15, 1978; 1 son, Kenneth James. AA, Erie County Tech. Coll., Buffalo, 1969; BCE, Tri-State U., Angola, Ind., 1971; MS, U. N.D., 1973; PhD, Va. Poly. Inst., 1977. Asst. prof. civil engring. U. Md., Coll. Park, 1976-79; rsch. cons. Civil Design Corp., Laurel, Md., 1979-80; assoc. prof., Stevens Inst. Tech., Hoboken, N.J., 1980-82, head dept. civil engring., 1982-89, prof., 1985-89, dean grad. sch., 1989—; rsch. cons. various govt. orgns.; cons. engr. 1983. Author: Structural Analysis and Design, 1980, Materials for Civil and Highway Engineering, 1981, 2d rev. edit., 1987, others; contbr. numerous articles to profl. jours. Pres. Marcel Lake Property Owners Assn., 1986—. Mem. ASCE (bd. dir. N.J. sect. 1981-82, awards chmn. N.J. br. 1980-83, v p. 1981-82, pres. 1983-84, Educator of Yr. local student chpt. 1981), Sigma Xi (sec. Stevens Inst. Tech. chpt. 1977-79). Office: Stevens Inst Tech Grad Sch Castle Point Station NJ 07030

DERVAES, CLAUDINE LUCIENNE, publisher; b. Tampa, Fla., July 23, 1954; d. Jules Camille and Lisette Elaine (DeWaele). BA in Sociology, U. South Fla., 1977. Cert. transp. tchr., Fla. Travel counselor Automobile Assn. Am., St. Petersburg, Fla., 1976-78, Tampa, Fla., 1978-79; asst. mktg. dir. Sanborn Tours, Austin, Tex., 1979-81; travel instr. Erwin Vocat. Tech. Ctr., Tampa, 1981-87; author, pub. Solitaire Pub. Co., Tampa, 1984—; pres. Travel Profl. Assoc., Tampa, 1987—. Author, pub.: The Travel Agent Training Workbook, 1984, 85, 87, The Travel Dictionary, 1985, 86, 88. Mem. Soc. Travel and Tourism Educators, Am. Soc. Travel Agts., North Tampa C. of C. Republican. Roman Catholic. Home: 216 S Bungalow Park Ave Tampa FL 33609 Office: Solitaire Pub Co PO Box 14508 Tampa FL 33690

DERWIN, JORDAN, lawyer, consultant, actor; b. N.Y.C., Sept. 15, 1931; s. Harry and Sadie (Baruch) D.; m. Barbara Joan Concool, July 4, 1956 (div. 1969); children: Susan Lee, Moira Ellen; m. Joan Linda Wolfberg, May 6, 1973. BS, NYU, 1953, JD, 1959. Bar: N.Y. 1959, U.S. Dist. Ct. (so. and ea. dists.) N.Y. 1960, U.S. Ct. Appeals (2d. cir.) 1960, U.S. Supreme Ct. 1962. Arthur Garfield Hays research fellow NYU, 1958-59, research assoc. Duke U. Sch. of Law, Durham, N.C., 1959-60; assoc. Brennan, London, Buttenwieser, N.Y.C., 1960-64; sole practice Jordan Derwin, N.Y.C., 1964-70; gen. counsel N.Y.C. Off Track Betting Corp., 1970-74; assoc. gen. counsel Gen. Instrument Corp., N.Y.C., 1974-79; cons., 1980—. Author (with F. Hodge O'Neal), Expulsion or Oppression of Business Associates: Squeeze Outs in Small Business, 1960; actor in various films, TV programs, comms. 1980—; contbr. articles to prof. jours. Served to lt. j.g., USNR, 1953-56, Korea, Vietnam. Mem. Am. Soc. of Mag. Photographers, SAG (dir. nat. bd. 1982—, sec. N.Y. br. 1983-87, 12th nat. v.p. 1984-87, 4th nat. v.p. 1987—, 1st v.p. N.Y. br. 1987—), AFTRA (dir. N.Y. local bd. 1980-83, 87—, dir. nat. bd. 1981—), Motion Picture Players Welfare Fund (trustee 1987—), Actors Equity Assn., Associated Actors and Artistes Am. AFL-CIO (del. internat. bd.), Phi Delta Phi. Home and Office: 305 E 86 St New York NY 10028

DESAI, SURESH VITHOBA, trading company executive; b. Margao, India, Mar. 13, 1950; s. Vithoba Ganesh and Rukminibai Vithoba (Rukminibai) D.; m. Maya Suresh, Feb. 17, 1984; 1 child, Dipti. BSc, Bombay U., 1973. Ptnr. Goa Trade Link Service, Margao, 1975—; ptnr. M/S Success Enterprises, Cuncolim, Philippines, 1979, M/S Shobsan Mktg. Agys., 1987—; bd. dirs. Desai Trade Well Mktg. Agys. Adv. com. Cuncolim Ednl. Soc., 1988—. Mem. Mahatma Gandhi Market Shop Owners Assn. (pres. 1981-86), Navelim Villagers Union (life), Alem de Margao (sec. 1985-86), Lions (pres. Margao club 1988-89). Office: Goa Trade Link Svc, Martires Dias Rd Opp New Era High Sch, Margao 403 601, India

DE SAINT PHALLE, FRANÇOIS, brokerage house executive; b. Phila., Mar. 26, 1946; s. Pierre and Virginia (Wall) de Saint P.; m. Susan de Saint P., Sept. 27, 1969 (div. July 1988). BA, Columbia Coll., N.Y.C., 1968. Assoc. Lehman Bros., N.Y.C., 1968-76, ptnr., 1976, mng. dir., 1977-84; sr. exec. v.p. Shearson Lehman Bros., N.Y.C., 1984—; also bd. dirs. Mem. Columbia Coll. Bd. of Visitors, N.Y.C., 1988. Mem. Internat. Adv. Bd. N.Y. Stock Exchange, 1988—, Deepdale Golf Club (Manhasset, N.Y.). Office: Shearson Lehman Hutton Inc Am Express Tower World Fin Ctr New York NY 10285

DESANTIS, DONALD ANTHONY, financial executive; b. Pitts., Aug. 15, 1950; s. Oswald Thomas and Mary Elizabeth (Wagner) DeS.; m. Mary Kathryn Mey, Apr. 27, 1979. BS magna cum laude, Case Western Res. U., 1972. Staff acct. Arthur Andersen & Co., Cleve., 1972-75, sr. acct., 1975-77, audit mgr., 1977-79; v.p. corp. services First Nat. Supermarkets, Inc., Cleve., 1979; v.p., controller First Nat. Supermarkets, Inc., Hartford, Conn., 1979-85, group v.p. fin., corp. controller, 1985; v.p., chief fin. officer, treas. Brands Corp., Danbury, Conn., 1986—. Mem. Am. Inst. CPA's, Ohio Soc. CPA's, First Fin. Execs. Inst. (bd. dirs. Y Western Conn.). Roman Catholic. Office: 1st Brands Corp 83 Wooster Heights Rd Bldg 301 PO Box 1911 Danbury CT 06813-1911 Home: 288 Keeler Dr Ridgefield CT 06877

DESAUTELLE, WILLIAM PETER, financial executive; b. N.Y.C.; s. Alfred F. and Nora T. D.; m. Joan H. Hryharrow, Sept. 7, 1963; children: Christopher, W.P., Mark, Jill. B.A. in Math., Fairfield U., 1961; M.B.A., U. Conn., 1970. Mgr. fin. and adminstrn. Burndy Corp., Norwalk, Conn., 1967-71; group controller, treas. Smith & Wesson, Springfield, Mass., 1971-78; v.p., treas. Kaman Corp., Bloomfield, Conn., 1979—. Office: Kaman Corp Blue Hills Ave Bloomfield CT 06002

DESDIER, STEVEN ROSS, financial planner; b. San Diego, Calif., Oct. 11, 1952; s. Dominic Jose Dupont and Audree Laverne (Leischner) D. BA summa cum laude, U.S. Internat. U., 1970. Cert. in taxation, 1986; CFP, 1986. Buyer men's wear Miller's West Dept. Store, San Diego, 1970-77; pres. Desdier, Inc., San Deigo and San Francisco, 1977—; ins. agt. life and disability Home Life Ins., San Diego, 1976-78; securities rep. Am. Pacific Securities, San Diego, 1982-89; acct. San Francisco AIDS Found., 1985-87. Mem., officer, treas. San Diego Citizens Scholar Found., 1982-84. Mem. Calif. Assn. Ind. Accts. (pres. 1988-89, pres.-elect 1987-88, v.p. 1985-87), Greater San Diego Bus. Assn. (treas. 1980-84, pres. 1984-85), Golden Gate Bus. Assn., (v.p. admistrn. 1985-86), Nat. Assn. Bus. Councils (treas. 1982-84). Republican. Lutheran. Office: Desco 584 Castro St #441 San Francisco CA 94114

DESHEROW, JAMES DARTMOUTH, food products executive; b. Chgo., Apr. 30, 1940; s. M. James and Anna Marie (Swank) D.; m. Dorothy Louise Babiak, Nov. 26, 1960; children: Edward James, Victoria Dawn, Douglas Keith, Deborah Kay, Robert James, Michael Paul. BBA, Okla. U., 1962; MBA, UCLA, 1964; postgrad., Harvard U., 1976-77. Cost acct. Pabst Brewing Co., Chgo., 1962-64; corp. acct. mgr. Gillette Co., Chgo., 1964-71; corp. controller Swift and Co., Chgo., 1971-74, v.p. fin. and treas., 1974-75; exec. v.p. Peer Foods, Chgo., 1975-77; dir. food service ops. Wilson Foods Corp., Oklahoma City, 1977-82, sr. v.p. foodservice, 1986—; pres., chief exec. officer Parklane Hosiery Co., New Hyde Park, N.Y., 1982-86. Mem. Oak Tree Country Club, Harvard Alumni Assn., Okla U. Alumni Assn., Ambucs. Office: Wilson Foods Corp 4545 Lincoln Blvd Oklahoma City OK 73105

DE SHON, ARTHUR EDWARD, bank executive; b. Oak Park, Ill., Feb. 27, 1946; s. Arthur Edward and Harriet (Wencel) DeSh.; m. Mary Jane McCann, July 11, 1970. B in Theology, San Lorenzo Sem., 1968. Programmer/analyst Alberto Culver Co., Melrose Park, Ill., 1968-71; sr. systems analyst Bell & Howell, Lincolnwood, Ill., 1971-73, Lake View Trust, Chgo., 1973-77; sr. programmer/analyst NW Gen. Data, Northbrook, Ill., 1977-78; dir. Heritage Bancorp., Hillside, Ill., 1978-81; group mgr. First Chgo. Data Corp., 1981-82; sr. v.p. Glenview State Bank, Glenview, Ill., 1982—. Ski instr. Am. Blind Skiing Found., Mt. Prospect, Ill., 1979-86. Roman Catholic. Office: Glenview State Bank 800 Waukegan Rd Glenview IL 60025

DESHPANDE, VIJAY DATTATRAYA, financial consultant; b. Bombay, India, Sept. 28, 1949; came to U.S., 1976; s. Dattatraya B. and Usha (Lanke) D.; m. Smita Gole, July 4, 1976; children: Raina, Reshma. BA in Acctg., Bombay U., 1971, diploma in gen. law, 1975. Registered investment advisor, chartered fin. cons.; lic. real estate broker; CLU. Mgr. Aviraj & Co., Bombay, 1971-76; cons. John Hancock Fin. Svcs., East Brunswick, N.J., 1977-88, N.Y. Life Ins. Co., East Brunswick, 1988—; owner Creative fin. Planning. Mem. Internat. Assn. Fin. Planners, Nat. Assn. Life Underwriters (polit. action com.), Million Dollar Round Table (Knight Found.). Home: 27 Van Hise Ct East Brunswick NJ 08816 Office: NY Life Ins Co 1 Aver Ct Ste B East Brunswick NJ 08816

DESIDERIO, FRED LEWIS, real estate broker; b. Reno, Nev., July 26, 1924; s. Luigi and Anna (Ferrari) D.; m. Lorraine Hamsa, Oct. 2, 1962; children: Denise A., Fred Lewis, John P. BSBA, U. Nev., 1949. Cert. property mgr., Nev. Pres. Fred L. Desiderio, Cert. Property Mgr., Reno, 1962-84, Sierra Nev. Ins. Inc., Reno, 1973-85; owner Desiderio Properties, Reno, 1971—. Commr. Reno Housing Authority, 1978. Mem. Reno Bd. Realtors (pres. 1966-67, named Realtor of Yr. 1968), Nev. Assn. Realtors (pres. 1970-71), Inst. Real Estate Mgmt. (pres. no. Nev. chpt. 1981), Elks, Druids, Sigma Alpha Epsilon. Republican. Roman Catholic. Office: Desiderio Properties 1750 Locust St Ste D Reno NV 89509

DE SILVA, COLIN, business executive, author, actor; b. Ceylon, Feb. 11, 1920; came to U.S., 1962, naturalized, 1972; s. John William and Rose Mary (Weerasinghe) de S.; children: Devayani, Cherine-Parakrama Chandrasoma. With Ceylon Civil Service, 1945-56, asst. sec. def., 1949-53, commr. nat. housing, 1953-56; diplomatic service 1953; mng. dir. Colombo Agencies, Ltd., also Colombo Indsl. Agencies, Ltd., 1957-62; exec. dir. Ceylon Mineral Waters, Ltd., 1957-62; dir. Vavasseur Trading Co., Ltd., 1957-62; pres., dir., owner Bus. Investment, Ltd., Honolulu, 1964—, West Coast Bus. Investment, Ltd., Portland, Oreg., 1970—, Econ. Devel. and Engring. Cons., Inc., Honolulu, 1965—; chmn. Gen. Mgmt. Corp., Honolulu, 1973—; pioneer in condominium devel., 1963—; chmn., dir. Condominium Mgmt., Inc.; lectr., cons. Peace Corps, 1962-66; econ. and fin. cons. nat. tourism studies. Del. Commonwealth Prime Ministers Conf., 1949, UN Housing Conf., 1955; chief liaison officer Commonwealth Fgn. Ministers Conf., 1949; pres. Ceylon Assn. Iron and Steel Mchts., 1956-62. Past chmn. bd. Opera Players of Hawaii; exec. com. Internat. C. of C., Ceylon, 1958-62; chmn. gen. importers com., mem. gen. council Ceylon Nat. C. of C., 1958-62; dir., past pres. McCully Bus. and Profl. Assn.; past dir. Waikiki Improvement Assn.; Trustee Kandyan Art Assn., 1946-49, Hawaii Pacific Coll., 1968-70. Mem. Screen Actors Guild, Honolulu, Portland chambers commerce, Smithsonian Instn. Home: 1040 Kealaolu Ave Honolulu HI 96816 Office: 1001 Bishop St Ste 2700 Pacific Tower Honolulu HI 96813

DE SILVA, DEEMATHIE WILHELMINA, university adminstrator, consultant; b. Galle, Sri Lanka, Apr. 27, 1939; came to U.S. 1977; d. Peter and Wilhelmina (Silva) Dantanarayana; m. Dharma de Silva, Apr. 11, 1962; children: Mrs. Harshini de Silva, Mahinda, Duminda, Lathika. Grad., Govt. Tchrs. Coll., Colombo, Sri Lanka; MA, Stanford U., 1964; PhD, Columbia Pacific U., 1988. Cert. tchr., Kans. Testing coordinator women's equity program Wichita State U., 1977-78, research assoc. coll. bus., 1979-81, lectr. biology, 1980, instr. anthropology, 1982-83, dir. student support svcs., 1985—; pres. Transcultural Mktg. Communication, Wichita, 1985—. Author: Mosquito, 1968, A Teacher's Guide for Effective Science Education, 1975; dir., scriptwriter video tapes, 1981. Fulbright scholar, 1963-64, NSF fellow, 1964, AAUW fellow, 1975-76, Nat. Sci. Council Sri Lanka grantee, 1977. Mem. Mo.-Kans.-Nebr. Assn., Mo.-Kans.-Nebr. Exec. Bd. Dirs., Internat. Soc. for Intercultural Edn. and Research, Mid Am. Assn. Ednl. Opportunity Program Personnel (exec. bd. dirs.), World Trade Council, World Trade Council Wichita, Sri Lanka Assn. for Advancement Sci., NAFE, Ind. Scholars Asia (dir., bd. dirs. southeast region 1985—). Home: 4917 E 24th St N Wichita KS 67220 Office: Operation Success Student Support Svcs 1845 N Fairmount Campus Box 81 Wichita KS 67208-1595

DE SIO, ANTHONY WILLIAM, communications executive; b. N.Y.C., Feb. 2, 1930; s. Oresto Joseph and Concetta (Curci) D.; children: Douglas, Darcy. BSEE, U. Conn., 1958; BA, U. Santa Clara, 1970. Mgr. Lockheed Missile and Space Co., Sunnyvale, Calif., 1958-71; staff asst. Exec. Office of the Pres., Washington, 1971-72; mgr. Gen. Electric Co., King of Prussia, Pa., 1972-74; dep. v.p. Western Union Space Commn., Upper Saddle River, N.J., 1974-77; dir. Linkabit Corp., San Diego, 1977-78; pres., chief exec. officer Mail Boxes Etc., San Diego, 1979—; bd. dirs. Mail Boxes Etc., San Diego, Just Security Corp., Pleasant Hill, Calif., Global Imaging Corp., Solana Beach, Calif. Advisor Interfaith Shelter Network, San Diego, 1988—, Brother Benn's Kitchen, Oceanside, Calif., 1988—. Recipient Outstanding Achievement award Pres. Nixon, 1972. Mem. Pres. Exec. Interchange Assn., Pres. Round Table, Nat. Assn. of Corp. Dirs. Lodge: Rotary. Office: Mail Boxes Etc 5555 Oberlin Dr San Diego CA 92121

DESJARDINS, PAUL ALFRED, fire communication company executive; b. Ft. Fairfield, Maine, June 27, 1945; s. Alfred Joseph and Ellen Marie (Ouellette) D.; m. Agnes T. Welschen, July 12, 1969; children: Jon, Jean. Assoc. Degree, Suffolk County Community Coll., 1975. Engring. aide Amperex, Hicksville, N.Y., 1969-70; test engr. Altec Lansing, Port Washington, N.Y., 1970-71; project engr. Comml. Radio-Sound, Inc., N.Y.C., 1971-74, Fire Controls, Inc., Woodside, N.Y., 1974-78; dir. engring. Firecom, Inc., Woodside, 1978-85, dir. R & D, 1980-85, v.p. R & D, 1985-88; v.p. engring. R & D Firecom/Auth, Deer Park, N.Y., 1986-89; pres. Protection Environ. Svcs. Inc., Long Island City, N.Y., 1989—; cons. N.Y. Stock Exchange, 1981-82. Contbr. articles to profl. jours. Patentee (4) in field. Mgr., asst. Commack Little League, N.Y., 1980-86; asst. cub master Commack council Boy Scouts Am.,1981-83; mem. Tulipwood Civic Assn. Served with USN, 1964-68. Mem. Nat. Fire Protection Assn. Lodge: KC. Home: 6 Old Pine Ln Commack NY 11725 Office: Protection Environ Svcs Inc 24-16 Bridge Pla S Long Island City NY 11101

DESJARDINS, RAOUL, medical association administrator, financial consultant; b. Montreal, Quebec, Can., Oct. 8, 1933; came to U.S., 1962; s. Elso and Blanche (Lemieux) D.; m. Regina Turgeon, Oct. 10, 1961; children: Bryan-Claude, Andrew-John. BA, U. Montreal, 1953, MD, 1958; MS, Baylor U., 1964, PhD, 1966. Diplomate Am. Bd. Medicine. Chief intern, resident St. Joan of Arc Hosp., Montreal, 1958-59; med. dir. Candiac (Can.) Med. Clinic, 1953-62, Ortho Research Found., Raritan, N.J., 1966-72; pres. Raoul Desjardins Assocs. Inc., Mendham, N.J., 1972-83, Research Cons. Inc., Mendham, 1983—; med. dir. Iroquois Class Co., Candiac, 1959-62; asst. prof. Hahneman Hosp. and Univ., Phila., 1976-80; vis. prof. pharmacology Chung U., Seoul, 1976—; bd. govs. Internat. Medicines Exchange and Devel., Georgetown, Ga., 1976—. Recipient Excellence Philosophy Bronze medal Gov. Gen. of Can., 1953, Accomplishment in Sci. Bronze medal Lt. Gov. of Quebec, 1953, Physician's Recognition award Am. Med. Assn., 1969. Fellow Am. Coll. Angiology, The Royal Soc. of Health, Am. Coll. Clin. Pharmacology, N.Y. Acad. of Medicine. Roman Catholic. Club: Doctor's (Houston); Med. Execs. (N.Y.C.). Home: 135 Talmage Rd Mendham NJ 07945 Office: Rsch Cons Inc Mendham NJ 07945

DES MARAIS, PIERRE, II, communications holding company executive; b. Montreal, Que., Can., June 2, 1934; s. Pierre and Rolande (Varin) Des M; m. Lise Blanchard, Jan. 21, 1956; children: Suzanne, Lison, Pierre III, Jean, Danielle, Stéphanie, Sophie, Phillipe, Anik. BA, Coll. St. Marie, 1954; grad. graphics arts course, Toronto, 1954; HEC in Bus. Adminstrn., U. Montreal, 1958. Pres. Pierre Des Marais Inc., 1954—; pres., chief econ. officer. Unimedia Inc., Montreal, 1987—; vice chmn. Can. Devel. Investment Corp. (CDIC); dir., former chmn. Carling O'Keefe Ltd., dep. chmn. 1987; former chmn. Canadair, Ltd., 1986; bd. dirs. Imperial Oil Ltd., Rothman's Inc., Hollinger Inc., Ouimet-Cordon Bleu Inc., Mfrs. Life Ins. Co.; chmn. Corp. de l'Hôpital Maisonneuve-Rosemont. Mem. PQ Adv. Bd., Central Trust; bd. dirs. Univ. de Montreal. Named hon. mem. Order of St. John, Que. Fellow Royal Geog. Soc. Clubs: Advt. & Sales Execs.; St. Denis; Mt. Royal; Forest & Stream. Office: 6125 Côte de Liesse, Saint Laurent, PQ Canada H4T 1C8 also: Unimédia Inc, 600 de Maisonneuve W, Ste 3200, Montreal, PQ Canada H3A 3J2

DESMOND, LOUIS, construction executive; b. Washington, Pa., Oct. 24, 1922; s. Joseph and Mary Ellen (Gallo) D.; m. Mary Ann Manfredi, June 2, 1946. Grad. high sch., Washington, Pa. Insp. Jessop Steel, Washington, Pa., 1942-53; propr., gen. contractor Louis Desmond Gen. Contractor, Washington, Pa., 1953—. Served with U.S. Army. Lodge: Elks. Home: 280 Glenwood Dr Washington PA 15301

DE SOFI, OLIVER JULIUS, data processing executive; b. Havana, Cuba, Dec. 26, 1929; s. Julius A. and Edith H. (Zsuffa) DeS.; B.S. in Math. and Physics, Ernst Lehman Coll., 1950; postgrad. in agronomy U. Havana, 1952, B.S. in Aero. Engring., 1956; came to U.S., 1956, naturalized, 1961; m. Phyllis H. Dumich, Feb. 14, 1971; children—Richard D., Stephen R., Kerri L. Dir. EDP tech. services and planning Am. Airlines, N.Y.C., 1968-70; dir. Sabre II, Tulsa, 1970-72; v.p. data processing and communications Nat. Bank of N. Am., Huntington Station, N.Y., 1972-76, sr. v.p. data processing and communications, 1976-78, sr. v.p. systems and ops., 1978-79, sr. v.p. adminstrn., N.Y.C., 1979-80, exec. v.p. adminstrn. group, 1980-83; exec. v.p. data processing methodologies and architecture Anacomp, Inc., Ft. Lee, N.J. and Sarasota, Fla., 1983-84; v.p. corp. devel. Computer Horizons Corp., N.Y.C., 1984-86; pres., chief exec. officer Coast to Coast Computers Inc., Sarasota, 1986—; lectr. program for women Adelphi Coll. Mem. Data Processing Mgmt. Assn., Computer Exec. Round Table, Am. Mgmt. Assn., Sales Execs. Club, Bank Adminstrn. Inst., AAAS, Internat. Platform Assn., Nat. Rifle Assn. Republican. Club: Masons (Havana).

DESSALET, SAMUEL ROBERT, treasurer; b. York, Pa., Apr. 14, 1932; s. Jack Rose and Ethel (Werner) D.; B.S. in Commerce, Rider Coll., 1957; m. Nancy Lee Ashmore, Jan. 29, 1953; children—Deborah Lee, Sharon Lynne, Theresa Louise, Samuel Robert. Staff acct. Price Waterhouse & Co., Newark, 1957-61; mem. controller's staff Remington Rand Systems Div., N.Y.C., 1961; sr. bus. analyst, asst. sect. head Bayonne and Bayway Refineries, Humble Oil & Refining Co., Bayonne and Linden, N.J., 1961-65; chief acct., tax mgr. Bro Dart Industries, Newark, 1965-67; dir. corp. acctg. No. Natural Gas Co., Omaha, 1967-68; controller Nat. Poly Products div. No. Petrochem. Co., Mankato, Minn., 1968-83; treas.-sec. Nat. Poly Products, Inc., Mankato, Minn., 1983-86, chief fin. officer, 1986—. bd. dirs. Winland Electronics, Inc., Playtronics Inc. Loaned exec. Mankato Area United Way, 1978; trustee Centenary United Methodist Ch., Mankato, 1972-81, treas., 1977-81; bd. dirs. Multi-Ch. Found., Inc., 1974-81, chmn. bd., 1978-81. Served with AUS, 1952-54. C.P.A., Minn., N.J., Nebr. Mem. Am. Inst. C.P.A.s, N.J. Soc. C.P.A.s, Nebr. Soc. C.P.A.s, Minn. Soc. C.P.A.s. Nat. Assn. Accts. (pres. South Central Minn. chpt. 1976-77, nat. dir. 1978-80, del. Minn. Council). Republican. Club: Mankato Exchange (1st v.p. 1973). Home: 10 N Hill Ct Rt 5 Mankato MN 56001 Office: 2111 3d Ave PO Box 1180 Mankato MN 56001

DE STEFANO, F. DENNIS, investment advisor, financial planner, tax consultant; b. Ft. Smith, Ark., Nov. 17, 1943; s. Frank F. and Josephine (Cardin) De S.; m. Katherine L. Elsen, Nov. 22, 1978. BS in Bus. Adminstrn. and Acctg., Bradley U., 1965; cert., Coll. for Fin. Planning, Denver, 1985. CPA, Ill., Hawaii; registered investment advisor. Ptnr. Bansley and Kiener, CPAs, Chgo., 1965-82, Moore Stevens & Co., CPAs, London, 1980-82; pres., owner Maui Planning Cons., Wailuku, Hawaii, 1982—; instr. entrepreneurial tng. program Maui C. of C. Contbr. articles to mags. and profl. publs. Mem. Am. Assn. Individual Investors, AICPA (tax div., personal fin. planning div.), Hawaii Soc. CPAs, Ill. Soc. CPAs, Inst. Cert. Fin. Planners (cert.), Nat. Assn. Personal Fin. Advisors, Am. Assn. Personal Fin. Planners, Internat. Assn. for Fin. Planning, Maui Estate Planning Coun. (treas.). Republican. Office: Maui Planning Cons 2145 Wells St Ste 101A Wailuku HI 96793

DESTEFANO, STEVEN, retail executive; b. Carle Place, N.Y., Aug. 10, 1960; s. Stephen Peter DeStefano and Georgene Charlate (Pino) Cohen. Grad. high sch., Elwood, N.Y. Carpenter Hugh F. Timms Constrn., Huntington, N.Y., 1976-83; owner, mgr. Innovative Creations, East Northport, N.Y., 1983—; supr. Dairy Barn Stores, Inc., East Northport, N.Y., 1986—. Mem. Rep. Nat. Com., 1983—. Roman Catholic. Home: 54 Amuxen Ct Islip NY 11751 Office: Dairy Barn Stores Inc 544 Elwood Rd East Northport NY 11731

DETERS, JAMES RAYMOND, manufacturing and services company executive; b. Cin., June 18, 1937; s. Joseph Gerard and Elsie Marie (Murphy) D.; m. Jacklyne Florence Eaton, Feb. 20, 1960; children—James, Deborah. B.S.C., Ohio U., 1959; M.B.A., Ohio State U., 1963. Acctg. mgr. Procter & Gamble Co., Cin., 1963-66; asst. controller Boise Cascade Corp., Mpls., 1967; controller Lindsay div. TransUnion Corp., Mpls., 1968-69; group controller Borg-Warner Corp., Chgo., 1970-72; asst. corp. controller Borg-Warner Corp., 1973-75, corp. controller, 1975-82, v.p. human resources, 1982-85, v.p. fin., 1985-87; sr. v.p., chief adminstrv. officer Material Scis. Corp., 1988—; exec. in residence Purdue U., 1976; dir. Material Scis. Corp. Pres. Kidney Found. Ill., 1974-77; bd. dirs. Chgo. Youth Centers, 1974-76; trustee Grant Hosp., Chgo., 1978-85, Barat Coll., Lake Forest, Ill., 1978-82; chmn. Lake Forest Sch. Mgmt., 1985-87; adv. bd. U. Ill., 1983—; mem. Leadership Council for Chgo. Open Communities, 1983-88. Served to capt. AUS, 1960-63. Mem. Fin. Execs. Inst., Machinery and Allied Products Inst. (fin. council), Ill. C. of C. (trustee 1980-82), Delta Tau Delta. Republican. Roman Catholic. Clubs: Economic, Union League, Onwentsia Country. Home: 1300 Loch Ln Lake Forest IL 60045 Office: Borg Warner Corp 200 S Michigan Ave Chicago IL 60604

DETHERO, J. HAMBRIGHT, banker; b. Chattanooga, Jan. 2, 1932; s. Jacob Hambright and Rosalie Frances (Gasser) D.; m. Charlotte Nixon Lee, Sept. 19, 1959; children: Dinah Lee, Charles Drew. B.S. in Bus. Adminstrn., U. Fla., 1953; B.F.T., Am. Grad. Sch. Internat. Mgmt., Phoenix, 1958. With Citibank, N.Y.C., P.R., Caracas, Venezuela, San Francisco, 1958-69; mgr. First Nat. City Bank (Internat.), San Francisco, until 1969; v.p. internat. div. Crocker Nat. Bank, San Francisco, 1969-75; sr. v.p. London, 1976-80, San Francisco, 1980-84; sr. v.p. Bank America World Trade Corp., San Francisco, 1984-85; 1st v.p. Security Pacific Nat. Bank, Los Angeles, 1986-87; sr. v.p. Exec. Resources Internat., Walnut Creek, Calif., 1987-88; regional mgr. Calif. Export Fin. Office, Calif. State World Trade Commn., San Francisco, 1988—. Mem. adv. bd. Sch. Internat. Mgmt., Golden Gate U., San Francisco; mem. exec. adv. com. U. Calif.-Berkeley Extension; bd. dirs. Calif. Council Internat. Trade, 1972-77, pres., 1974-76; trustee World Affairs Council No. Calif.; chmn. Dist. Export Council No. Calif. Served with USN, 1953-57. Mem. Nat. Fgn. Trade Council, U.S. C. of C. Club: Orinda (Calif.) Country. Home: 694 Old Jonas Hill Rd Lafayette CA 94549 Office: Calif State World Trade Commn World Trade Ctr Ste 250-S San Francisco CA 94111

DETLEFS, DALE RALPH, management consultant; b. Stickney, S.D., Jan. 12, 1927; s. William Frederick and Anna Caroline (Peterson) D.; m. Claire McIntosh, Aug. 29, 1953 (div. 1975); children: Paul Steven, Ann, William Frederick; m. Doris Goodknight, Mar. 18, 1978. BA, U. Nebr., 1947; JD, U. Iowa, 1950; BS in Commerce, U. Louisville, 1961, MBA, 1968. Bar: Iowa 1950, Ky. 1957. Rsch. editor Bur. of Analysis, Davenport, Iowa, 1950-51; sales rep. Prentice-Hall, Inc., Davenport, 1951-55; asst. dir. indsl. rels. Bendix Aviation, Inc., Davenport, 1955-56; pers. dir. Am. Air Filter Co., Inc., Louisville, 1956-74; ptnr. Mercer-Meidinger-Hansen, Inc., Louisville, 1974—; com. chmn. Assn. Pvt. Pension and Welfare Plans, Washington, 1980-82. Author: (booklets) Guide to Social Security, 1975, 89, Medicare Booklet, 1985, 89. Lt. comdr. USNR, 1944-68. Mem. Iowa Bar Assn., Ky. Bar Assn., Louisville Pers. Assn. (pres. 1966-67), Hurstbourne Country Club (pres. 1970), Rotary (pres.-elect 1988, pres. 1989-90). Republican. Home: 9001 Peterborough Ct Louisville KY 40222 Office: Mercer-Meidinger-Hansen Inc 1500 Meidinger Tower Louisville KY 40202

DETMAR-PINES, GINA LOUISE, school system administrator; b. S.I., N.Y., May 3, 1949; d. Joseph and Grace Vivian (Brown) Sargente; m. Michael B. Pines, Sept. 11, 1988. BS in Edn., Wagner Coll., 1971, MA in Edn., 1972; MA in Urban Affairs and Policy Analysis, The New Sch. for Social Research, 1987; post grad. studies in Bus. Adminstrn., Baruch Coll. City U., 1987—. Tchr. pub. schs. N.Y.C., 1971-82; coordinator spl. projects, pub. affairs N.Y.C. Bd. Edn., 1982, spl. asst. to exec. dir. pupil services, 1983, asst. to the chancellor, 1983-84; dir. Tchr. Summer Bus. Industry Program, Bklyn., 1984—; liaison for the Tchr. Industry Program, N.Y.C. Ptnrship., 1985—. Mem. Com. to re-elect Borough pres. Lamberti, S.I., 1985. Recipient Mayor's scholarship City of N.Y., 1984—. Mem. Fgn. Lang. Instrs. Assn., U.S. Seaplane Pilot's Assn., Internat. Orgn. for Licensed Women Pilots, Chinese-Am. Soc., Am. Mgmt. Assn. Democrat. Episcopalian. Club: Cambridge Flying Group. Office: NYC Bd Edn 65 Court St Brooklyn NY 11201

DETTMER, ROBERT GERHART, soft drink company executive; b. Parsons, Kans., Sept. 11, 1931; s. Ira Gerhart and Dema (Hinze) D.; m. Patricia Isabel York, Aug. 20, 1955; children: Stephanie, Constance, Robert Brantley. Student, U.S. Naval Acad., 1949-52; B in Bus. and Engring. Adminstrn., MIT, 1955; MBA, Harvard U., 1957. Engr. Lincoln Electric Co., Cleve., 1957-60; assoc. Booz, Allen & Hamilton, Cleve., 1960-64; propr. Robert G. Dettmer, Investment Mgmt., Cleve., 1964-66; v.p. ops. Tasa

Corp., Pitts., 1966-68; pres. Scott Aviation div. A-T-O, Lancaster, N.Y., 1968-70, George J. Meyer Mfg. div., Milw., N.Y., 1970-72, N.Am. Van Lines subs. PepsiCo, Inc., Fort Wayne, Ind., 1973-76; v.p. fin. mgmt. and planning parent co. N.Am. Van Lines subs. PepsiCo, Inc., Purchase, N.Y., 1976-79; pres. Pepsi Cola Bottling Group subs., Purchase, N.Y., 1979-86; exec. v.p., chief fin. officer PepsiCo., Purchase, N.Y., 1986—; bd. dirs. Pantesote, Inc., 1978. Chmn. bd. Am. Movers Conf., 1974-76; trustee Miss Porter's Sch., 1978-84, Manhattanville Coll., 1986—, chmn. bd. trustees, 1988—. Served with USN, 1949-52. Mem. MIT ALumni Assn., Harvard Bus. Sch. Alumni Assn., U.S. Naval Acad. Alumni Assn., Delta Tau Delta, Tau Beta Pi. Clubs: Harvard Bus. Sch. of Westchester-Fairfield County (chmn. bd. 1977-80), Harvard Bus. Sch. of Greater N.Y. (chmn. bd. 1982-83). Lodge: Masons. Home: 80 Round Hill Rd Greenwich CT 06831 Office: Pepsico Inc Purchase NY 10577

DETTWEILER, JACK H(ENRY), JR., real estate developer; b. Washington, Nov. 21, 1945; s. John Henry Dettweiler Sr. and Mary Camilia (Calnan) Sterner. Student, St. Louis U., Mo., 1963-64; grad., U. N.Mex., 1964-68. Stockbroker Doherty & Co., Albuquerque, 1968-70; real estate broker Albuquerque, 1971-77; broker Berger-Briggs, Albuquerque, 1978-84; owner Jack Dettweiler Comml. Real Estate Interests, 1984—; pres. Equity Securities, Albuquerque, 1982—; faculty Am. Savs. and Loan Inst., Albuquerque, 1973-76; founder, chmn. Real Estate Exchangors, Albuquerque, 1981; pres. U.S. Fiduciary Svcs. Corp. Chmn. NFL Celebrity Golf tourney for Cystic Fibrosis, 1987, 88, 89. Mem. Albuquerque Bd. Realtors (bd. dirs. 1983-84, Exchangors award 1982-83), Sigma Chi, Top 100 Club (bd. dirs. 1983). Democrat. Roman Catholic. Home: PO Box 8341 Albuquerque NM 87110 Office: 4004 Carlisle #C Albuquerque NM 87107

DEUTSCH, BARRY JOSEPH, management development company executive; b. Gary, Ind., Aug. 10, 1941; s. Jack Elias and Helen Louise (La Rue) D.; B.S., U. So. Calif., 1969, M.B.A. magna cum laude, 1970; m. Gina Krispinsky, Feb. 20, 1972. Lectr. mgmt. U. So. Calif., L.A., 1967-70; pres., founder The Deutsch Group, Inc., mgmt. cons. co. tng. upper and middle mgmt., L.A., 1970—, chmn. bd., 1975—; founder, chief exec. officer, chmn. bd. Investment Planning Network, Inc., 1988—; dir. Red Carpet Corp. Am., 1975-77, United Fin. Planners, 1984-86. Chmn. bd. govs. Am. Hist. Ctr., 1980—. With M.I., U.S. Army, 1964-66. Mem. Am. Mgmt. Assn., Am. Soc. Bus. and Mgmt. Cons.'s, Am. Soc. Tng. and Devel., Internat. Mgmt. by Objectives Inst. Author: Leadership Techniques, 1969, Recruiting Techniques, 1970, The Art of Selling, 1973, Professional Real Estate Management, 1975, Strategic Planning, 1976, Employer/Employee: Making the Transition, 1978, Managing by Objectives, 1980, Conducting Effective Performance Appraisal, 1982, Advanced Supervisory Development, 1984, Managing A Successful Financial Planning Business, 1988. Home: 4509 Candleberry Ave Seal Beach CA 90740

DEVANEY, CYNTHIA ANN, real estate broker, teacher; b. Gary, Ind., Feb. 6, 1947; d. Charles Barnard and Irene Mae (Nelson) Burner; m. Harold Verne DeVaney, Nov. 23, 1974 (dec. 1981). BS, Ball State U., 1970, MS, 1972; postgrad., Ind. U., Gary, 1974-76. Cert. real estate broker, Ind. Real estate broker Century 21 McColly Realtors, Merrillville, Ind., 1979-86; real estate broker Better Homes and Gardens McColly Realtors, Merrillville, 1986—, with Pres.' Coun.; tchr. Merkley Elem. Sch., Highland, Ind., 1969—. Active Schubert Theater Guild, Chgo. Mem. Calumet Bd. Realtors (bd. dirs., Million Dollar Club), Nat. Bd. Realtors, Jr. Ind. Hist. Soc., Pres. Club, Innsbrook Country Club, Match Point Tennis Club. Democrat. Methodist. Home: 607 E 78th Pl Merrillville IN 46410 Office: McColly Better Homes & Gardens 9143 Indianapolis Blvd Highland IN 46322

DEVASSIE, TERRY LEE, publishing executive; b. Columbus, Ohio, Oct. 27, 1939; s. Robert William and Laura Belle (VanOrsdel) DeV.; m. Lola Faye Sandifer, June 21, 1964; children: Trevor Lane, Thad Lamont. BA in Indsl. Design, Ohio State U., 1964. Clk., sta. mgr. Columbus Dispatch, 1957-70, div. mgr., 1970-71, asst. to circulation dir., 1971-77, state circulation mgr., 1977-79, circulation mgr., 1979-81, asst. circulation dir., 1981—; owner, designer TLD Design, Columbus, 1964-69; architect-designer Eagle Real Estate/Builders, Columbus, 1968-70; extrusion designer Plaskolite, Inc., Columbus, 1968-69. Pub. speaker in field; designer newspaper vending machine. Bd. dirs. St. Anthony Mercy Hosp., Columbus, 1987—, St. Anthony Med. Ctr., Columbus, 1987—, Shriners Hosps. Burns Ctr., Cin., 1986—. Mem. Ohio Circulation Mgrs. (pres. 1982, founder Pres.'s award 1982, Pres.'s award 1986), Ohio Newspaper Assn. (chmn. conv. 1983, Pres.'s award 1984), Internat. Circulation Mgrs. Assn. (chmn. Internat. Newspaper Carrier Day 1982-84), Press Club Ohio (pres. 1983-84), Charity Newsies, Masons, Shriners. Republican. Methodist. Home: 5808 La Paz Pl Westerville OH 43081 Office: Columbus Dispatch 34 S 3d St Columbus OH 43215

DE VEAU, ROBERT EUGENE, financial executive; b. Malden, Mass., Apr. 23, 1960; s. Robert Joseph and Clare Rita (Fournier) De V. AS, Fisher Jr. Coll., Boston, 1985; BS, U. Mass., Boston, 1988. Accounts mgr. Boston Soc. Architects, 1985—; cons. The Archtl. Bookshop, Boston, 1986—. Mem. Boston Computer Soc., Am. Mgmt. Assn. Home: 37 Massachusettes Ave Middletown RI 02840 Office: Boston Soc Architects 305 Newbury St Boston MA 02115

DEVENDITTIS, GLORIA-CORTINA, office manager; b. New London, Conn., Sept. 11, 1941; d. Antonio and Clementina Marie (Silva) Cortina; m. Paul James Devenditis, Oct. 21, 1961; children: Louie Paul, Monte Anthony. Student, U. Conn., 1959-60, U. Hartford, 1960. Legal sec. Gruskin and Gruskin, New London, 1957-59; sec. receptionist Sponsored Rsch. Acctg. U. Mich., Ann Arbor, 1961-63; floor sec. U. Rochester (N.Y.) Med. Ctr., 1963-65; ophthalmic med. asst. to Chief of Ophthalmology Jericho, N.Y., 1977-78; asst. to office mgr., bookkeeper Real Estate Mgmt., Jericho, N.Y., 1978-79; mgr. Non-Traditional Jobs for Women, Mineola, N.Y., 1979-80; office mgr., asst. to pres. Quality Tree Svc. Inc., Roslyn Heights, N.Y., 1980—. Author: Mama's Kitchen Goes to College, 1988. Treas. Duncan Estates Civic Assn.; active Women's Info. Exchange, Greenpeace, N.Y. Pub. Interest Rsch. Group, Neighbor to Neighbor, The Arts Council at Freeport, New Community Cinema; convener and officer South Nassau NOW, 1980-82. Mem. L.I. Country Music Assn. Democrat. Home: 16 Primrose Ln Hempstead NY 11550 Office: Quality Tree Svc Inc PO Box 1321 Roslyn Heights NY 11577

DEVENOW, CHESTER, manufacturing executive; b. Detroit, Mar. 3, 1919; s. Samuel and Bessie (Aronoff) D.; m. Marilyn Fruchtman, Apr. 20, 1947 (div. Feb. 1977); children: Mark F., Jeffrey A., Sara Devenow Abrams, Susan P.; m. Maudette Shapiro, Dec. 18, 1978. B.A., NYU, 1941; postgrad., Harvard Law Sch., 1941-42; D.B.A. (hon.), Siena Heights Coll., Adrian, Mich., 1977. Pres. Globe Wernicke Industries, Toledo, 1954-67; pres. Sheller-Globe Corp., Toledo, 1967-72; chmn., chief exec. officer Sheller-Globe Corp., 1972—, also bd. dirs.; bd. dirs. Toledo Edison, Toledo Trust Co., Toledo Trustcorp., Centerior Energy Corp., Knoll Internat. Holding, Inc. Bd. dirs. Tech. and Productivity Ctr. Ohio, Columbus, 1982—; trustee, chmn. bd. trustees Ohio State U., Columbus, 1972-82; mem. Labor-Mgmt. Citizens Com., Toledo, 1972; chmn. bd. Blue Cross NW Ohio, 1975-82. Served to 1st lt. U.S. Army, 1942-45. Recipient Heritage award Yeshiva U., 1971, Gov.'s award State of Ohio, 1981; named Hon. Prof., Ohio State U., 1982. Mem. Toledo Area C. of C. (pres. 1976, sr. council), Soc. Automotive Engrs., Nat. Energy Found. (bd. dirs.). Clubs: Renaissance (bd. govs. 1974—), Economic (Detroit); Toledo; Jockey (Miami, Fla.). Office: Sheller-Globe Corp 1505 Jefferson Ave Toledo OH 43697 *

DEVEREUX, LAWRENCE HACKETT, industrial executive; b. N.Y.C., Aug. 14, 1929; s. Philip L. and Agnes (Hackett) D.; m. Alice Fraser, Nov. 17, 1956; children—Lawrence, Elizabeth, Alison. AB, Holy Cross Coll., 1951; MBA, N.Y. U. Grad. Sch. Bus., 1958. Asst. treas., asst. contr. Hewitt Robins, 1956-65; asst. compt. Ingersoll Rand Corp., 1965-68; v.p., contr. Amerace Corp. (name formerly Amerace Esna Corp.), N.Y.C., 1968-72, v.p. adminstrn., treas., 1972-77; v.p. fin. Bell & Howell Co., Chgo., 1977-80; sr. v.p., chief fin. officer CF Industries, Inc., Long Grove, Ill., 1980—. 1st lt. USMC, 1951-53. Mem. Fin. Execs. Inst., Chgo. Economic Club. Home: 69 Indian Hill Rd Winnetka IL 60093 Office: CF Industries Inc Salem Lake Dr Long Grove IL 60047

DEVINE, BRIAN KIERNAN, retail furniture executive; b. Washington, Mar. 1, 1942; s. William John and Rita Marie (Kiernan) D.; m. Silvija Viktorija Kutlets, June 13, 1964; children—Brian Jr., Brooke. B.A., Georgetown U., Washington, 1963; postgrad., Am. U., Washington, 1964-65, Yale U., 1965. Statis. adv. USPHS, Washington, 1963-70; with Toys "R" Us, 1970-88; gen. mgr. San Jose, Calif., 1970-75; regional gen. mgr. Chgo., 1975-77; v.p. Saddle Brook, N.J., 1977-82; sr. v.p. Rochelle Park, N.J., 1982-88; pres. of furniture mfr./retailer Krause's Sofa Factory, Fountain Valley, Calif., 1988—. Contbr. articles to profl. publs. Democrat. Roman Catholic. Home: 16911 S Pacific Ave PO Box 469 Sunset Beach CA 90742 Office: 18430 Pacific Ave Fountain Valley CA 92708

DEVINE, CHARLES V., JR., retail real estate executive; b. Pitts., Feb. 1, 1948; s. Charles V. and Anna (LeDonne) D.; m. Carol Lynn Hunt, Jan. 3, 1971; children: Kerry L., Brian C., Katie L., Kristy G. BA in Math., Duquesne U., Pitts., 1970. Real estate mgr. Grand Union, Elmwood Park, N.J., 1971-73, Dunkin' Donuts, Inc., Edison, N.J., 1973-79; real estate dir. Tenneco Inc., Deerfield, Ill., 1979-80; mgr. leasing F.W. Woolworth Co., N.Y.C., 1980-83; v.p. real estate, corp. officer Shoe Town, Inc., Totowa, N.J., 1983-85, Consumers Distbg., Edison, 1985-86; pres. Devine Realty Cons., Washington Twp., N.J., 1986—; Chmn. bd. Retailers Only Invited, Totowa, 1983—; cons. Dress Barn, Shoe Town. Contbr. articles to profl. jours. Pres. Twp. Council, Washington Twp., N.J., 1986—, Wayne Robertson Charity Fund, Washington Twp., 1986-87; chmn. Zoning Bd., Washington Twp., 1982-85; advisor Colleen Giblin Charity Fund, 1986. Served to capt. U.S. Army, 1970-71. Decorated Medal of Heroism, U.S. Army. Mem. Nat. Assn. Corp. Real Estate Execs. (v.p. 1984-85), Internat. Council Shopping Ctrs., Nat. Mail Monitor Conf. (adv. com.), Mfrs. Idea Exchange. Republican. Roman Catholic. Lodge: K.C. Office: Devine Realty Cons 285 Pascack Rd Washington Township NJ 07675

DEVINE, DONALD JOHN, entrepreneur; b. Phila., Apr. 29, 1939; s. Daniel J. and Beatrice (Foster) D.; student Case Inst. Tech., 1960-61; B.A., U. Pa., 1964; m. Pamela F. White, Dec. 30, 1967; children—Douglas J., Laura Ann. Various positions Ins. Co. N.Am., Phila., 1957-66; a founder, v.p. Trilog Assos., Inc., Phila., 1966-72, pres., chief exec. officer, 1972-77, also dir.; pres. Trilog div. COMSHARE, Inc., 1977-78, group v.p. COMSHARE, Inc., Ann Arbor, Mich., 1978-83; owner, chief exec. officer TRILOG, Inc., Phila., 1983-85; founder, owner, chief exec. officer Digitax, Inc., Ann Arbor, 1982—; speaker at meetings of profl. orgns. Contbr. articles to profl. jours. Active Boy Scouts Am., 1957-68, 77-84. Mem. Assn. Data Processing Services Orgns. (pres. sect. 1983, 86, chmn. software protection com. 1984, v.p. govt. affairs 1985), Data Processing Mgmt. Assn. (cert. data processing 1963, pres. Phila. chpt. 1974-75), Am. Anthrop. Assn., Conf. Data Systems Langs. (chmn. systems com. 1966-67), Union League Phila., Phi Kappa Psi, Alpha Phi Omega. Home: 1375 Fairlane Ann Arbor MI 48104

DEVINE, PATRICK JAMES, psychology educator, consulting management psychologist; b. Milw., Mar. 11, 1952; s. Donald H. and Dee L. D.; m. Mary Ann Nancy Steck, Jan. 8, 1977. B.A. in Psychology, John Carroll U., 1974; M.Ed. in Counseling Psychology, Ga. State U., 1975; Ph.D. in Indsl.-Organizational Psychology, Ill. Inst. Tech., 1980. Lic. applied psychologist, Ga. Indsl.-organizational and sports psychologist, Atlanta, 1977—; mgmt. cons. Donald Shepherd and Assocs., Chgo., 1978-80; asst. prof. psychology Kennesaw State Coll., Marietta, Ga., 1980—; cons. psychologist Devine and Assocs., Atlanta, 1980—, Nat. Employer Assistance Services, Milw., 1984—. Chmn. study group program Leadership Cobb, Marietta, 1984-85; mem. program com. Leadership Cobb, Marietta, 1985-87; bd. dirs. Children's Shelter, Marietta, 1988—. Mem. Atlanta Soc. Applied Psychology (exec. com., treas. 1986—), Ga. Psychol. Assn., Am. Psychol. Assn., Southeastern Psychol. Assn., Soc. Indsl.-Organizational Psychology, Southeastern Indsl.-Organizational Psychol. Assn., Cobb C. of C. Roman Catholic. Lodge: KC. Avocations: athletics; model railroading; stained glass; theatre; reading. Home: 640 Holyroad Way Alpharetta GA 30201 Office: Kennesaw State Coll Dept Psychology Marietta GA 30061

DEVINEY, MARVIN LEE, JR., chemical company research scientist, administrator; b. Kingsville, Tex., Dec. 5, 1929; s. Marvin Lee and Esther Lee (Gambrell) D.; B.S. in Chemistry and Math., S.W. Tex. State U., San Marcos, 1949; M.A. in Phys. Chemistry, U. Tex. at Austin, 1952, Ph.D. in Phys. Chemistry, 1956; cert. profl. chemist; m. Marie Carole Massey, June 7, 1975; children—Marvin Lee III, John H., Ann-Marie K. Devel. chemist Celanese Chem. Co., Bishop, Tex., 1956-58; research chemist Shell Chem. Co., Deer Park, Tex., 1958-66; sr. scientist, head group phys. and radiochemistry Ashland Chem. Co., Houston, 1966-68, mgr. sect. phys. and analytical chemistry, 1968-71, mgr. sect. phys. chemistry div. research and devel., Columbus, Ohio, 1971-78, research assoc., supr. applied surface chemistry, Ashland Ventures Research and Devel., 1978-84, supr. electron microscopy, advanced aerospace composites, govt. contracts, 1984—; adj. prof. U. Tex., San Antonio, 1973-75. Mem. sci. adv. bd. Am. Petroleum Inst. Research Project 60, 1968-74. Mem. ednl. adv. com. Columbus Tech. Inst., 1974-84, Central Ohio Tech. Coll., 1975-82. Served to lt. col., USAR. Humble Oil Research fellow, 1954. Fellow Am. Inst. Chemists (pres. Ohio Inst. 1978-82); mem. Ohio, Tex. acads. scis., Am. Def. Preparedness Assn., Electron Microscopy Soc. Am., Materials Research Soc., SAMPE Composite Soc., N.Am. Catalysis Soc., Am. Soc. Composites, Am. Chem. Soc. (chmn. chpt. exec. bd. 1969, bus. mgr. nat. div. Petroleum Chemistry, 1986—, Best Paper award rubber div. 1967, 70, Hon. Mention awards 1968, 69, 73; symposia co-chmn., co-editor books on catalysis-surface chemistry 1985, carbon-graphite chemistry 1975), Engr.'s Council Houston (sr. councilor 1970-71), Sigma Xi, Phi Lambda Upsilon, Alpha Chi, Sigma Pi Sigma. Coauthor govt. research contract reports; contbr. numerous articles to profl. jours.; patentee in field. Home: 6810 Hayhurst Worthington OH 43085 Office: Box 2219 Columbus OH 43216

DEVINNEY, TIMOTHY MICHAEL, management educator; b. Pitts., Oct. 6, 1956; s. Donald James and Johann Rose (Farina) D.; m. Sandra L. Brandt, Apr. 16, 1977. BS with honors, Carnegie-Mellon U., 1977; MA, U. Chgo., 1979, MBA, 1981, PhD, 1984. Prof. Owen Grad. Sch. Mgmt. Vanderbilt U., Nashville, 1982—; cons. in field; vis. prof. U. Ulm, Fed. Republic Germany, 1985, U. Hamburg, 1987. Author: Rationing in a Theory of Banking, 1986; editor: Issues in Pricing, 1988; assoc. editor Mgmt. Sci. mag.; contbr. articles to profl. jours. Mem. Am. Econ. Assn., Am. Fin. Assn., Econometric Soc., Inst. Mgmt. Scis., Psi Chi. Roman Catholic. Home: 1603 18th Ave S Nashville TN 37212 Office: Owen Grad Sch Mgmt Vanderbilt U Nashville TN 37203

DE VISSCHER, FRANCOIS MARIE, investment banker; b. Louvain, Belgium, Sept. 24, 1953; s. Michel and Jacqueline (Velge) deV.; m. Maura Michaela Nicholson, Oct. 4, 1980; children: Patrick Michel. BA in Applied Econs., U. Louvain, 1975; MBA, Rutgers U., 1977. CPA, N.Y. Staff asst. Coopers & Lybrand, Brussels, 1975-76; staff acct. Coopers & Lybrand, N.Y.C., 1977-79, sr. acct., 1979-80, supr. audit, 1980; assoc. Smith Barney Harris Upham, N.Y.C., 1981-82, 2d v.p., 1983-84, v.p., 1985-88, mng. dir., 1988—. Mem. Nat. Assn. Securities Dealers (registered rep.), Am. Inst. CPA's, N.Y. Soc. CPA's, Belgian Am. C. of C. (bd. dirs.). Clubs: Larchmont Yacht (N.Y.); Westchester Country (Rye, N.Y.); Univ. (N.Y.C.); Sandanona (Millbrook). Office: Smith Barney Harris Upham 1345 Ave of the Americas New York NY 10105

DEVITO, CARMEN SAMUEL, petroleum and chemical company executive; b. Bridgeton, N.J., Aug. 2, 1954; s. Carmen Samuel and Lucy (Balestrieri) DeV.; m. Susanne Lee Castiglia, July 11, 1977; children: Christopher David, Brian Paul. BS in Commerce and Engring. Mgmt., Drexel U., 1977, BS in Mech. Engring., 1978, MS in Mech. Engring., 1980. Cert. engr. in training, Pa. Research engr. E.I. DuPont, Wilmington, Del., 1980-82, Seaford, Del., 1982-84; computer engr. supr. E.I. DuPont, Brevard, N.C., 1984-87; area supr. prodn. E.I. Dupont, Towanda, Pa., 1988—. Mem. Internat. Mgmt. Council, Am. Soc. Mech. Engrs. (local treas. 1983-84), Instrument Soc. Am., Highland Sports Car Club (fund raiser Asheville, N.C. 1985, Sylva, N.C. 1986, pres. 1986—). Club: Sports Car Am. Home: 5 Ann St Towanda PA 18848 Office: EI Dupont New James St Towanda PA 18448

DEVITO, FRANCIS JOSEPH, advertising agency executive; b. N.Y.C., July 13, 1938; s. Basil and Mary (Mincielli) DeV.; m. Lynn R. Brauneiss; children: Christopher F., Anthony P. B.F.A., Pratt Inst., 1961. Asst. art dir. Batton, Barton, Dursteen & Osborne, N.Y., 1965-67; art dir. Young & Rubicam, N.Y.C., 1967-73, creative supr., 1973-76, v.p. assoc. creative dir., 1976-80, sr. v.p. group creative dir., 1980-83; exec. v.p., co-creative dir. Young and Rubicam, N.Y.C., 1983-84; pres., dir. creative services Lintas: New York, 1984—. Served to capt. U.S. Army, 1961-65. Home: 20 Harbor Hill Rd Huntington NY 11743 Office: Lintas Worldwide 1 Dag Hammarskjold Pla New York NY 10017 *

DEVLIN, MICHAEL GERARD, lawyer; b. N.Y.C., Aug. 6, 1947; s. Hugh R. and Gertrude J. (Raubach) D.; B.S. in Mktg., St. John's U., 1970, J.D. (Thomas More scholar 1971-74), 1974; m. Eleanor Cathrine Barnett, Feb. 6, 1971; children—Kathleen Anne, Thomas Fitzmichael, Patrick Fitzmichael, Sean Fitzmichael, Gregory Fitzmichael. Bar: N.Y. 1975, U.S. Tax Ct. Supervising tax specialist Coopers & Lybrand, N.Y.C., 1974-78; tax mgr. Dow Corning Europe, Brussels, 1978-84; mgr. tax planning-Europe, Levi Strauss & Co., Brussels, 1984-86; dir. taxes Albany (N.Y.) Internat. Corp. Dep. police commr. Village of Centre Island (N.Y.), 1977-78; pres. bd. trustees Midland Montessori Sch., 1978-80; trustee St. John's Internat. Sch., Waterloo, Belgium. Served with USMCR, 1970-76. Mem. Internat. Bar Assn., N.Y. State Bar Assn., N.Y. County Lawyers Assn., Am. Bar Assn., Am. C. of C. (legal and tax com.). Home: 112 Newell Ct Menands NY 12204

DEVNEW, LYNNE ELISABETH, software development executive; b. Hartford, Conn., June 21, 1945; d. Stuart Douglas and Elizabeth (Lecrenier) D. BS, Simmons Coll., 1967; MS, Columbia U., 1978. Programmer, programming mgmt. IBM, White Plains, N.Y. and Bethesda, Md., 1967-76; fin. and bus. planning IBM, Armonk, N.Y. and San Jose, Calif., 1977-85; lab. mgr. Applications Systems div. IBM, Bethesda, 1985—. Pres. bd. dirs. Big Bros./Big Sisters, San Jose, 1981; v.p. allocations United Way, Greenwich, Conn., 1984. Office: IBM 10421 Fernwood Rd Bethesda MD 20817

DEVORE, KIMBERLY K., sales executive; b. Louisville, June 19, 1947; d. Wendell O. and Shirley F. DeV.; student, Xavier U., 1972-76; AA, Coll. Mt. St. Joseph, 1979. Patient registration supr. St. Francis Hosp., Cin., 1974-76; cons., bus. mgr. Family Health Care Found., Cin., 1976-77; exec. dir. Hospice of Cin., Inc., 1977-80; pres. Micro Med, 1979-86; v.p. Sycamore Profl. Assn., 1979-86; ptnr. Enchanted House, 1979-86, sec., 1979-80, treas. 1980-83; dist. sales rep. Control-O-Fax, 1986, dist. sales mgr., br. sales mgr., 1987, nat. dealer devel. rep., 1987—, computer specialist, 1988—; bd. dirs. Nat. Hospice Orgn., 1979-82, chmn. long-term planning com., fin. com., ann. meeting com., 1979-82, sec., 1980-81. treas., 1981-82; bd. dirs. Hospice of Miami Valley, Inc., 1982-86, also chmn. personnel com., by-laws com. Mem. Greater Cin. Soc. Fund Raisers, Better Housing League; Mem. service and rehab. com. Hamilton County Unit, Am. Cancer Soc., 1977-78. Mem. Ohio Hospice Assn. (co-founder, state chmn., pres., 1978-83), Nat. League for Nursing, Ohio Hosp. Assn., Nat.Fedn. Bus. and Profl. Women's, Ohio Fedn. Bus. and Profl. Women's, Cin. Bus. and Profl. Women's (pres. 1973-75).

DEVOS, RICHARD MARVIN, network marketing company executive; b. Grand Rapids, Mich., Mar. 4, 1926; s. Simon C. and Ethel R. (Dekker) DeV.; m. Helen J. Van Wesep, Feb. 7, 1953. Student, Calvin Coll., 1946; LL.D. (hon.), Oral Roberts U., 1976, Grove City (Pa.) Coll., Northwood Inst., Midland, Mich., 1977, Dickinson Sch. Law, Carlisle, Pa., 1980, Pepperdine U., 1980, Lubbock Christian Coll., 1981; D.Litt. (hon.), Hope Coll., 1982. Partner Wolverine Air Service, 1945-48; co-founder, pres. Ja-Ri Corp., 1949, Amway Corp., 1959—, Amway Communications Corp.; pres. Amway Hotel Corp., Amway Global, Inc., Ada, Mich., Amway Internat., Inc., Ja-Ri Corp.; co-chmn. bd. Nutrilite Products Inc., Buena Park, Calif.; bd. dirs. Old Kent Fin. Corp.; chmn. bd. Reference Map Internat. Author: Believe!. Chmn. Gospel Films, Muskegon, Mich.; bd. dirs., chmn. Midwest region BIPAC; bd. dirs. past pres. Grand Rapids Jr. Achievement, 1966-67; past mem. bd. control Grand Valley State Coll.; past bd. dirs. United Way Kent County; bd. dirs. Robert Schuller Ministries, Nat. Legal Center for Public Interest; trustee Butterworth Corp., Grand Rapids, Gerald R. Ford Found.; past chmn. New Grand Rapids Com.; spl. advisor Pres. Council on Physical Fitness and Sports; mem. Am.-Australian Bicentennial Found. Bd.; mem. Close-Up Found. Hon. State Bd. Adv.; mem. council trustees Freedoms Found. Served with USAAF, 1944-46. Recipient Alexander Hamilton award Econ. Edn. from Freedoms Found.; Disting. Salesman of Year award Grand Rapids Sales and Mktg. Assn.; Bus. Leader of Yr. award Religious Heritage Am.; Industry Week Excellence in Mgmt. award; Thomas Jefferson Freedom of Speech award Kiwanis Internat.; Mich. Week Vol. Leadership award; Mktg. Man of Yr. award West Mich. chpt. Am. Mktg. Assn.; Am. Enterprise Exec. award Nat. Mgmt. Assn.; Golden Plate award Acad. of Achievement; George Washington Honor Medal award Freedoms Found.; Free Enterprise award Americanism Ednl. League; Am. Enterprise Exec. award Nat. Mgmt. Assn., Patron award Mich. Found. for the Arts, 1982. Mem. NAM (past dir.), Direct Selling Assn. (past chmn., dir., Champion of Free Enterprise and Knights of Royal Way awards, Hall of Fame award), Newcomen Soc., Round Table, Omicron Delta Kappa (hon.). Mem. Christian Reformed Ch. (elder, chmn. fin. com.; past pres. missionary soc.). Clubs: Economic (Grand Rapids) (dir.), Rotary (Disting. Service award) (Grand Rapids); Pillars bd. dirs. Home: Grand Rapids MI Office: Amway Corp 7575 E Fulton Rd SE Ada MI 49355 *

DE WETTER, HERMAN PETER, healthcare management executive; b. New Rochelle, N.Y., Jan. 28, 1920; s. Herman and Louise (Hurlbutt) deW.; m. Margaret Belding, Aug. 7, 1943; children: Charles, David, Robert. Grad., Phillips Exeter (N.H.) Acad., 1939. Pres., chmn. bd. OK Van & Storage Co., Las Cruces, N.Mex., 1961-71; pres., chief exec. officer Bekins Co., Tex., 1973-79; exec. v.p. Nat. Med. Enterprises Inc., Los Angeles, 1979—, also bd. dirs.; mem. adv. bd. Nat. Alliance Businessmen, Los Angeles, 1973; pres. So. Calif. council Invest in Am., Los Angeles, 1977; bd. dirs. Thomas J. Lipton Inc., Englewood Cliffs, N.J. Mayor City of El Paso, 1969-71; chmn. bd. Civil Service Commn., El Paso, 1966-69; mem. adv. council Am. Heart Assn., Los Angeles, 1975—; mem. adv. council Town Hall Calif., Los Angeles, bd. govs., 1975-78; mem. exec. com. Boy Scouts Am., Los Angeles, 1984—, Citizens for Better Transp., Los Angeles, 1974; mem. nat. adv. bd. Goodwill Industries Am., Los Angeles, 1975—, bd. dirs. So. Calif. chpt., 1973-75, pres. El Paso chpt., 1966, bd. dirs. El Paso, 1962-70; chmn. banquet com. NAACP, Los Angeles, 1974; pres. El Paso Girl Scouts U.S. council, Rio Grande, Tex., 1958-60, El Paso Council Govts., 1965; bd. dirs., trustee City of Hope, Los Angeles, 1974—, Univ. Ams. Found., Pueblo, N.Mex., 1972-74; trustee Constl. Rights Found., 1975-79, Filmex, Los Angeles, 1981-83, Orthopaedic Hosp., Los Angeles, 1976-80, Sch. Theology Claremont (Calif.) Coll., 1973-75; corp. bd. dirs. Western region United Way Inc., Los Angeles, 1982—; bd. dirs., sec. John Douglas French Found. for Alzheimer's Disease, Los Angeles, 1984—; bd. dirs., v.p. YMCA Met. Los Angeles, 1972—; bd. dirs. NCCJ So. Calif. chpt., Los Angeles, 1971—, Urban League Los Angeles, 1975-77, El Paso Indsl. Devel. Council, 1968-69, So. Calif. Bldg. Funds, Los Angeles, 1972-79, Jr. Achievement, El Paso, 1969. Served to maj. U.S. Army, 1942-45, ETO. Decorated Bronze Star; recipient Thanks Badge Girl Scouts U.S., 1965, Leadership award West Tex. C. of C., 1969, Outstanding Community Service award, 1970, Humanitarian award NCCJ, 1981; named to Hon. Bd. Trustees, Am. Acad. Achievement, 1969-71. Mem. Mchts. and Mfrs. Assn. (bd. dirs. 1973—), Los Angeles Area C. of C. (v.p., bd. dirs. 1975-81), Newcomen Soc. N.Am., Order Cin., SAR. Clubs: California, Lincoln, 100, Twilight (Los Angeles); City (San Marino, Calif.); Valley Hunt (Pasadena, Calif.). Lodge: Rotary (bd. dirs. Los Angeles 1987—). Office: Nat Med Enterprises Inc 11620 Wilshire Blvd Los Angeles CA 90025

DEWEY, BARBARA LYNN, retail executive; b. Boston, Sept. 1, 1947; d. Robert Eugene and Mary Ellen (Sim) D.; m. James Bosmans Mercier (div.). BS, Upsala U., 1975. Cert. tchr., N.J. Vol. VISTA, Washington, 1968-69; tchr. East Orange and Orange (N.J.) Pub. Schs., 1969-75; supr. Koret of Calif., San Francisco, 1975-77; cons. Alexander Proudfoot, Chgo., 1977-80, Dewey Enterprises, San Francisco, 1980-81; analyst Finnigan Corp., San Jose, Calif., 1981-84; prin. Childrenswear Outlet, Lincoln, Nebr., 1985-88, Dewey's for Kids Ltd., Lincoln, 1988—. Treas. Lincoln Civic Orch. and Chorus; vol. leader Charlie Brown's Kids, Lincoln, 1987—. Democrat. Office: Dewey's for Kids 400 N 48th St #B-9 Lincoln NE 68504

DEWEY, DONALD WILLIAM, magazine editor and publisher, writer; b. Honolulu, Sept. 30, 1933; s. Donald William and Theckla Jean (Engeborg) D.; m. Sally Rae Ryan, Aug. 7, 1961; children: Michael Kevin, Wendy Ann. Student, Pomona Coll., 1953-55. With Pascoe Steel Corp., Pomona, Calif., 1955-56, div. Reynolds Aluminum Co., Los Angeles, 1956-58, Switzer Panel Corp., Pasadena, Calif., 1958-60; sales and gen. mgr. Western Pre-Cast Concrete Corp., Ontario, Calif., 1960-62; editor, pub. R/C Modeler Mag., Sierra Madre, Calif., 1963—, Freshwater and Marine Aquarium Mag., Sierra Madre, 1978—; pres., chmn. bd. R/C Modeler Corp., Sierra Madre, 1963—. Author: Radio Control From the Ground Up, 1970, Flight Training Course, 1973, For What It's Worth, Vol. 1, 1973, Vol. 2, 1975; contbr. articles to profl. jours. Sustaining mem. Rep. Nat. Com., 1981—; charter mem. Nat. Congl. Club, 1981—; mem. Rep. Presdl. Task Force, 1981—, U.S. Senatorial Club, 1983—, 1984 Presdl. Trust, Conservative Caucus, Nat. Tax Limitation Com., Nat. Conservative Polit. Action Com.; assoc. Meth. Hosp. of Southern Calif. Served with Hosp. Corps, USN, 1951-53. Mem. Oceanic Soc., Internat. Oceanograpnic Found., Internat. Assn. Aquatic Animal Medicine, Fedn. Am. Aquarium Socs., Am. Philatelic Soc., Am. Topical Assn., Marine Aquarium Soc., APS Writers Unit 30, Nat. Trust for Historic Preservation, Am. First Day Cover Soc., United Postal Stationery Soc., Confederate Stamp Alliance, Am. Air Mail Soc., Bur. Issues Assn., Am. Revenue Assn., C.Z. Study Group, Pitcairn Islands Study Group, Pet Industry Joint Adv. Council, Sierra Madre Hist. Soc., Friends of Sierra Madre Library, Internat. Betta Congress, Nat. Fisheries Assn., Am. Killifish Assn., Am. Catfish and Loach Assn., Am. Wildlife Fedn., Greater Los Angeles Zoo Assn., Am. Indian Heritage Found., Los Angeles County Arboretum Assn., Calif. Hist. Soc., Internat. Platform Assn. Republican. Episcopalian. Home: 410 W Montecito Ave Sierra Madre CA 91024 Office: 144 W Sierra Madre Blvd Sierra Madre CA 91024

DEWEY, JOHN BYRON, financial executive; b. Columbus, Ohio, Feb. 16, 1950; s. John Byron and Kathryn (Rheinfrank) D.; m. Sherrie R. Doten, Oct. 17, 1975; children: Benjamin, Christopher, McKenzie. Student, U.S. Mil. Acad., 1968-69; BS, U. Minn., 1972; MS, Mankato (Minn.) State U.; cert., Denver Coll. Fin. Planning, 1985. Tchr., coach St. Louis Park (Minn.) Sch. System, 1972-75, Wyzata (Minn.) Sch. System, 1975-80; football coach Normandale Jr. Coll., Bloomington, Minn., 1975-81; area mgr. Franklin Fin. Svcs., Bloomington, 1980—. Contbr. articles to profl. jours. Pres. Bass Lake Homeowners Assn., Plymouth, Minn., 1977-78; mem. Bus. Edn. Exch., 1987—; deacon Woodland Hills Bible Ch., Minnetonka, Minn., 1984—. Mem. Nat. Assn. Realtors, Nat. Assn. Life Underwriters, Inst. Cert. Fin. Planners (cert.), Million Dollar Round Table, Bloomington C. of C. Republican. Office: Franklin Fin Svcs 9031 Penn Ave S Bloomington MN 55431

DEWEY, RICHARD LEE, telephone company executive; b. Dayton, Ohio, Dec. 23, 1929; s. William C. and Juanita (Lee) D.; children: Douglas L., Deborah G., Ronald S.; m. Beverly J. Lipscomb, Nov. 12, 1971. BS in Bus., Miami U., Oxford, 1952. Various line and staff positions Cin. Bell Inc., 1952-67, div. commerce mgr., 1968-69, gen. planning supr., 1969-70, asst. sec., asst. treas., 1970-82, treas., asst. sec., 1982-85, sec., treas., 1985—; dist. mgr. AT&T, N.Y.C., 1967-68. Served to sgt. U.S. Army, 1952-54. Mem. Nat. Assn. Corp. Treas., Am. Soc. Corp. Secs. Republican. Presbyterian. Lodges: Masons (master 1960-61), Shriners. Home: 7984 Kimbee Dr Cincinnati OH 45244 Office: Cin Bell Inc 201 E 4th St Cincinnati OH 45202

DEWEY, ROBERT MANSON, JR., investment company executive; b. Bronxville, N.Y., July 1, 1931; s. Robert Manson and Helen (Sjoblom) D.; m. Rowena Bauer, Sept. 20, 1958 (div. 1970); children: Robert Manson III, Grant G., Bradley M.; m. Harriet Blees, Dec. 19, 1981. B.A. in History, Yale U., 1953. Adminstrv. asst. Citicorp, N.Y.C., 1954-59; v.p. State Nat.Bank Conn., Stamford, 1959-64; sr. v.p., dir. Laird Inc., N.Y.C., 1964-72, F.S. Smithers & Co., N.Y.C., 1972-74; mng. dir. Donaldson Lufkin & Jenrette, Inc., N.Y.C., 1974—; dir. Donaldson Lufkin & Jenrette Securities Corp.; dir. Telecredit Inc., Los Angeles. Served with USNR, 1953-54. Mem. New Canaan C. of C. (pres. 1962-63). Republican. Club: New Canaan (Conn.). Office: Donaldson Lufkin & Jenrette Inc 140 Broadway New York NY 10005

DEWILDE, DAVID MICHAEL, executive search consultant, lawyer, financial services executive; b. Bridgeton, N.J., Aug. 11, 1940; s. Louis and Dorothea (Donnelly) deW.; m. Katherine August, Dec. 30, 1984; children: Holland Stockdale, Christian DuCroix, Nicholas Alexander. AB, Dartmouth Coll., 1962; LLB, U. Va., 1967; MS in Mgmt., Stanford U., 1984. Bar: N.Y. 1968, D.C. 1972. Assoc. Curtis, Mallet-Prevost, Colt & Mosle, N.Y.C., 1967-69; assoc. gen. counsel HUD, Washington, 1969-72; investment banker Lehman Bros., Washington, 1972-74; dep. commr. FHA, Washington, 1974-76; pres. Govt. Nat. Mortgage Assn., Washington, 1976-77; mng. dir. Lepercq DeNeuflize & Co., N.Y.C., 1977-81; exec. v.p. policy and planning Fed. Nat. Mortgage Assn., Washington, 1981-82; pres. deWilde & Assocs., Washington, 1982-84; mng. dir., dir. fin. svcs. Boyden Internat., San Francisco, 1984-88, also bd. dirs.; chief exec. officer Chartwell Ptnrs. Internat., San Francisco, 1989—; bd. dir. Strategic Mortgage Investors, Glendale, Calif. Editor-in-chief Va. Jour. Internat. Law, 1966-67. Lt. USN, 1962-64. Republican. Club: Meadowood, Belvidere Tennis. Office: Chartwell Ptnrs Internat Citicorp Ctr 1 Sesame St San Francisco CA 94104

DEWITT, KATHERINE LOUISE, bank executive; b. Cleve., Mar. 25, 1948; d. DeMarquis Dale and Leonora Louise Wyatt; 1 child, Christina. V.p. Govt. Services S.L., Bethesda, Md., 1969-80, Md. Nat. Bank, Balt., 1980-86; chief exec. officer, pres. Republic Fed. Savs. Bank, Rockville, Md., 1987—; bd. dirs. exec. com. Nat. Savs. Loan League, Washington, 1974-80; chmn. standing com. Md. Savs. Loan League, Balt., 1972-79. Trustee Newport Schs. Wheaton, Md., 1984—; bd. dirs. Bethesda Chevy Chase C. of C., 1976-80; commr., v.p., pres., Montgomery County Commn. Women, Rockville, 1976-79; mem. steering com. womens' council Dem. Nat. Com., Washington, 1976-82. Mem. Women in Housing & Fin., Network, Nat. Assn. Bank Women, Women Advt. & Mktg., Nat. Forum Exec. Women (chmn. bd. dirs. 1974-80). Democrat. Unitarian.

DE WOODY, CHARLES, lawyer; b. Chgo., Oct. 18, 1914; s. Charles and Oneta (Ownby); student U. Fla., 1931-33, U. Mich., 1933-35, Columbia U., 1935-36, Western Res. U., 1936-38; m. Nancy Tremaine, June 15, 1940; children—Charles, Nancy. Office atty. Oglebay, Norton & Co., Cleve., 1939-43; ptnr. Arter, Hadden, Wykoff & Van Duzer, 1943-61; sole practice, 1961—; dir. Nat. Extruded Metal Products Co., Ferry Cap and Set Screw Co., Meteor Crater Enterprises, Inc.; gen. partner Bar-T-Bar Ranch, Mem. Am., Ohio, Cleve. bar assns., Cleve. Law Library Assn. Clubs: Rancho Santa Fe Tennis; Chagrin Valley Hunt (Gates Mills, Ohio). Home: El Mirador Box 1169 Rancho Santa Fe CA 92067

DEXHEIMER, HENRY PHILLIP, II, insurance agency executive; b. Dayton, Ohio, Sept. 16, 1925; s. Henry Phillip and Helene Francis (Veach) D.; BS in Commerce, U. So. Calif., 1952; children: James Phillip, Jana Helene; m. Maria DaGraca Fernandes, Nov. 21, 1988. Sales account exec. with various cos. and newspapers, 1946-51; broadcasting sales exec. Sta. KBIG, KTLA-TV, Los Angeles, 1952-58; broadcasting sales exec. Sta. KFXM, San Bernardino, Calif., 1956-57, pres., 1956-57; founder, owner, pres. Dexheimer Co., Los Angeles, 1958—. Served with inf. and adj. gen.'s dept. U.S. Army, 1943-46; PTO. Recipient Sammy award Los Angeles Sales Execs. Club, 1955; Silver Sales trophy Radio Advt. Bur. N.Y., 1955; named Agt. of Year, Los Angeles office Travelers Ins. Cos., 1978, 83-88, Nat. Agt. of Yr. Travelers Ins. Cos., 1983; Hal Parsons award, 1978, 83-88. C.L.U. Mem. Am. Soc. C.L.U.s (nat. dir. Travelers chpt. 1972-73, 80-81), Am. Coll. Life Underwriters, Advt. Assn. West, Radio and TV Soc. Hollywood, Life Ins. and Trust Council Los Angeles, Los Angeles Life Underwriters Assn. (dir. 1963-65, v.p. 1967-69), Million Dollar Round Table (life, honor roll), World Affairs Council Los Angeles, Internat. Assn. Fin. Planners, Am. Art Council, Decorative Art Council of Los Angeles County Art Mus., Alpha Delta Sigma, Phi Kappa Tau. Republican. Presbyterian. Clubs: Town Hall (Los Angeles); Beverly Hills Men's (Calif.); Masons (32 degree), Shriners, Legion of Honor. Office: Dexheimer Co Marina Bus Ctr 13160 Mindanao Way Ste 222 Marina del Rey CA 90292

DEXTER, MARILYN LOUISE, real estate executive; b. Eustis, Maine, Apr. 26, 1940; d. Eric Jonathan LeBlanc and Dorothy May (Seavey) Langley; m. Paul Wayne Allen, Apr. 21, 1962 (div. 1973); m. Douglas Stanley Dexter, Nov. 27, 1981; children: Christopher W., Kimberly J., Jeffrey P. Diploma, Carnegie Inst., Boston, 1961; BA, Bridgewater State Coll., 1978; MS in Media Edn., Boston State Coll., 1982. Med. asst. Children's Hosp., Boston, 1960-62; media specialist Braintree (Mass.) Pub. Schs., 1978-81, Easton (Mass.) Pub. Schs., 1981-83; sales mgr. Cadtronix Ltd., Greenwich, Conn., 1983-86; officer, asst. v.p. fin. svcs. BRT Corp., Danbury, Conn., 1986-87; real estate agt. Roach Bros. Realtors, West Chester, Pa., 1987—. Mem. Main St. Hist. Preservation, Kennett Square, Pa., 1987—; mem. Kennett Square Archtl. Rev. Bd., 1987—. Mem. Pa. Bd. Realtors, Millionaires in Making, Kennett Square Country Club, Kappa Delta Pi. Republican. Home: 359 N Union St Kennett Square PA 19348 Office: Roach Bros Realtors 1205 West Chester Pike West Chester PA 19380

DEYOUNG, E(DWARD) DONALD, securities company executive; b. Chgo., Mar. 24, 1940; s. Edward and Helen C. DeY. Student U. Chgo., 1958-60, DePaul U., 1961-62. Pres. Hornblower & Weeks/Hemphill Noyes Ins. Agy. Ill., Chgo., 1969-71; v.p. sales E.F. Hutton, Chgo., 1971-74; v.p. Dean Witter, Chgo., 1974-78; exec. v.p. Anchor Nat. Fin. Services, Phoenix, 1978-83; exec. v.p. N. Am. Coin & Currency, Phoenix, 1983-84, currently dir.; pres., chief exec. officer Am. Gen. Securities Inc., Houston, 1984-88. Served with USAF, 1962-68. Mem. Internat. Assn. Fin. Planning (past v.p. Phoenix chpt.), Chartered Life Underwriters. Roman Catholic. Home: 2100 TangleWilde #551 Houston TX 77063 Office: 2727 Allen Pkwy Houston TX 77019

DE YOUNG, STEPHEN PAUL, envelope manufacturing company executive; b. Kalamazoo, Nov. 19, 1953; s. Harold Everett and Reanetta Jane (Klepper) De Y.; m. Ruth Ann Lemmer, May 21, 1976; children: Nicholas Paul, Zachary Lucas. BS, Western Mich. U., 1975. Salesman Hoekstra Roofing Co., Kalamazoo, 1975; asst. to dir. instnl. rsch. Western Mich. U., Kalamazoo, 1975-79; mgr. data processing I.E. Products, Inc., Kalamazoo, 1979-80, mgr. acctg. computer svcs., 1980, mgr. fin. svcs., 1980-82; contr. MCE Inc., Kalamazoo, 1982-85; contr. Ill. Envelope, Inc., Kalamazoo, 1982-85, treas., 1985—, v.p., bd. dirs., 1988—; bd. dirs., asst. treas. Papermakers Credit Union, Kalamazoo, 1984—. Treas. Westwood Christian Ref. Ch., Kalamazoo, 1982-84, 88—, Christian edn. endowment fund, 1985—. Mem. Kalamazoo C. of C. Home: 927 Nichols Rd Kalamazoo MI 49007-2808 Office: Ill Envelope Inc 400 Bryant St Kalamazoo MI 49001-2996

DEYTON, CATHERINE ELIZABETH, banking administrator; b. Anchorage, Aug. 2, 1957; d. Robert Guy and Yvonne (Schweistris) D. BA, Duke U., 1979; cert., Southeastern Trust Sch., 1982. Staff auditor Planters Nat. Bank, Rocky Mount, N.C., 1980-82, sr. staff auditor, 1982, asst. auditor, 1983, mktg. research and devel. analyst, 1983-85; asst. v.p., ops. officer Planters Nat. Bank, Wilmington, N.C., 1985-88; br. mgr. First Fed. Savs. and Loan Assn. of Pitt County, Greenville, N.C., 1988—. Treas. Nash County Reps., Rocky Mount, 1985; mem. bd. govs. U. N.C. Wilmington MBA Assn. Bd. Mem. Am. Inst. Bankers, Bank Mktg. Inst., Tar River Jaycees (treas. 1985, first place award for fighting child abuse 1983). Presbyterian.

DHAINAUT CRÉMER, MICHEL EUGÉNE PIERRE, international agricultural trader; b. Bueno Aires, Argentina, Sept. 10, 1927; arrived in Spain, 1963.; s. Donatien and Thérése (Crémer) D.; m. Marie-France Audit; children: Caroline, Florence, Jean-Michel. Degree in Econs., U. Argentina, 1949. Trader Am. Sohr, Buenos Aires, 1945-48; purchasing mgr. Inteco-Etam, Buenos Aires, 1984-54; owner Garchel Soc. Responsabilidad Ltd., Buenos Aires, 1954-57; trader La Plata Cereal Co. SA, Buenos Aires, 1957-61, André & Co. SA, Lausanne, Switzerland, 1961-63; mgr. Silor SA, Madrid, 1963—; councillor Transcatalana S.A., Barcelona, Spain. Served with the Argentinian Army, 1946-48. Mem. French C. of C. Club: Real, Puerta de Hierro (Madrid). Home: Ave Miraflores 46 Bis, 28035 Madrid Spain Office: Silor SA, Gen Pardiñas 114, 7B, 28006 Madrid Spain

DIABLE, FREDERICKA HAWKINS, paralegal; b. Utica, N.Y., Oct. 10, 1934; d. Frederick Barket and Julia Jenny (Abbott) Barket-Foster; m. Paul C. Hawkins, Aug. 25, 1952 (div. Mar. 1980); children: Paula C. (dec.), Mitchell P., Christopher F.; m. Ray N. Diable, Aug. 27, 1983. Student, Mohawk Valley Community Coll.; legal asst. degree, Syracuse U., 1987. Cert. legal asst., tchrs. aide. Claims rep. Liberty Mutual Ins. Co., Utica, 1964-67; tchrs. aide, counsel Westmoreland (N.Y.) Cen. Sch., 1967-71; asst. fin. mgr. Westmoreland (N.Y.) Malleable Iron Co., 1971-76; officer in charge fins. and support Centrex Clin. Lab., Utica, 1977-79; asst. adminstr. Oneida County Indsl. Devel. Corp., Oriskany, N.Y., 1980-81, Spl. Metals Corp., New Hartford, N.Y., 1980-81; office adminstr., fin. cons. Pohl's Feedway, Vernon, N.Y., 1982-87; estate adminstrn., specialist Marine Midland Bank, Utica, 1987-88, semi-ret., 1988—. Co-author, editor: August 9, 1970, Cuzco, Peru. Mem. Smithsonian Assocs., Audubon Soc. Syrian Orthodox. Home: PO Box 231 Vernon NY 13476 also: 40 Verona St Vernon NY 13476

DI ADDEZZIO, FREDERICK JOHN, JR., banker, lawyer; b. Bryn Mawr, Pa., July 27, 1947; s. Frederick John and Eva Marie (De Felice) Di A.; m. Nancy Ann Gabriel, June 2, 1973; children: Christina Michele, Frederick John III. BA, Haverford Coll., 1975; JD, Villanova U., 1978. Bar: Pa. 1978, Fed. 1978. Mktg. dir. The Am. Coll., Bryn Mawr, 1978-84; product mgr. Nat. Liberty Mktg., Valley Forge, Pa., 1985-86; v.p. retail mktg. Provident Nat. Bank, Phila., 1986—. With USAF, 1968-72. Mem. Bank Mktg. Assn. Republican. Roman Catholic. Office: Provident Nat Bank 100 S Broad St Philadelphia PA 19110

DIAL, RONALD OWEN, financial company executive; b. Visalia, Calif., Oct. 10, 1950; s. Oran Lee and Stella I. (Westmoreland) D.; m. Jeannine Kathleen Lage, Jan. 20, 1986. BS in Econs., Calif. State U., 1972, M in Pub. Adminstrn. and Fin., 1986. Police officer City of Inglewood, Calif., 1970-72; risk mgr. City of Visalia, Calif., 1972-85; group dir. Equitec Fin. Group, Inc., Oakland, Calif., 1985—; cons., ptnr. Exec. Services, Visalia, 1981-83; cons. Execucomp, Visalia, 1981-85, Execucomp, Pleasant Hill, Calif., 1985—. Sustaining sponsor Boy Scouts Am., Visalia, 1981-85; mem. Rep. Nat. Com., Visalia, 1984-88. Served with USMC, 1969-70. Mem. Risk and Ins. Mgmt. Soc., Calif. Pub. Risk and Ins. Mgmt. Assn. (v.p. 1984-85), Cen. San Joaquin Valley Risk Mgmt. Authority (v.p. 1984-85), Soc. for Preservation and Encouragement of Barber Shop Quartet Singing in Am. (pres. Visalia chpt. 1980-82). Mem. First Christian Ch. Home: 400 Brandywine Ln Pleasant Hill CA 94523 Office: Equitec Fin Group 7677 Oakport Oakland CA 94614

DIAMOND, HARVEY JEROME, machinery manufacturing company executive; b. Charlotte, N.C., Dec. 7, 1928; s. Harry B. and Jeanette (Davis) D.; m. Betty L. Ball, May 22, 1953; children: Michael, Beth, David, Abby. BS, U. N.C., 1952. Sales mgr. Dixie Neon Supply House, Charlotte, 1950-61; pres., gen. mgr. Plasti-Vac, Inc., Charlotte, 1961—; pres., gen. mgr. Diamond Supply, Inc., 1971-84, chmn. bd. dirs., 1984—; pres. Plastic Prodn., Inc., 1973—, PVI Internat. Corp., 1980—; mem. dist. export council Dept. Commerce, 1979—; del. White House Conf. on Small Bus., 1980; bd. dirs. U.S. Free Trade Zone No. 57, 1983. Author: (manual) Introduction to Vacuum Forming, 1976; patentee inverted clamping frame system for vacuum forming machines, process of vacuum forming plastics with vertical oven. Chmn. Mecklenburg Dem. Party, 1974-75, treas., 1972-74; del. Dem. Nat. Conv., 1972; bd. advisors Pfeiffer Coll., Misenheimer, N.C., 1977—; participant White House Conf. on Small Bus., 1978, White House Conf. on anti-inflation initiatives, 1978. Served with U.S. Army, 1952-54. Recipient award for Activity in U.S. Trade Mission to S.Am., Dept. Commerce, 1967, March of Dimes award, 1966, Excellence in Exporting award N.C. Trade Club, 1981. Mem. Soc. Plastic Engrs., Soc. Plastics Industry, So. States Sign Assn. (bd. dirs. 1983—), Nat. Electric Sign Assn. Metrolina World Trade Assn. (v.p. 1982-83), Metrolina World Trade Club (pres. 1983-84), N.C. World Trade Assn. (bd. dirs. 1983-86, gen. chmn. ann. conv. 1984). Jewish. Lodge: Masons. Home: 9400 White Hemlock Ln Matthews NC 28105 Office: PO Box 5543 Charlotte NC 28205

DIAMOND, KIMBERLEY SUE, securities investment executive; b. Houston, Oct. 4, 1955; d. Louis Elliott II D. and Tommy Sue Smith. Student. U. Tex., 1975; BA magna cum laude, San Francisco State U., 1979. Lic. securities registered rep. Stockbroker Dean Witter Reynolds, Inc., Los Angeles, 1979-80, Smith Barney, Harris Upham and Co., Inc., Newport Beach, Calif., 1980-81; mktg. dir. Wall St. Cons. Group, Inc., Newport Beach, Calif., 1981-82; fin. counselor CIGNA Fin. Services Co., Newport Beach, Calif., 1982-83; account exec. E.F. Hutton and Co., Inc., Long Beach, Calif., 1983-84; investment exec. Bank America Capital Markets Group, Los Angeles, Calif., 1984—. Mem. Nat. Assn. Female Execs., Women of Wall St. (v.p. 1983-84), Delta Gamma. Home: PO Box 3249 Long Beach CA 90803

DIAMOND, LINDA BARBARA, information systems director; b. Queens, N.Y., Feb. 18, 1943; d. Irving Jerome and Sylvia (Heiser) Klein; m. Barry S. Diamond, Dec. 24, 1962; children—Brian, Robert, Sean. B.A. in Edn. and Math., Queens Coll., 1964. Tchr., Patchoque, L.I., N.Y., 1964-66; programmer Capac, Ridgefield, Conn., 1975-77; sr. tech. rep. Gen. Electric Info. Services, Stamford, Conn., 1977-80, sr. account mgr., 1980-82; sr. systems engr. Datapoint Corp., Stamford, 1982-85; dir. info. systems Direct Mktg. Assn., N.Y.C., 1985—. Mem. Assn. Info. Systems Profls., Nat. Computer Graphics Assn., Direct Mktg. Computer Assn., Nat. Assn. Exec. Women, Am. Soc. Profl. and Exec. Women. Jewish. Office: Direct Mktg Assn 6 E 43rd St New York NY 10017

DIAMOND, RICHARD EDWARD, publisher; b. S.I., N.Y., May 24, 1932; s. Joseph H. and Gertrude (Newhouse) D.; m. Alice W. Blach., July 27, 1963; children: Caroline. Alison. Richard Edward. Student, Cornell U., 1953. With S.I. Advance, 1953—; publisher 1979—; bd. dirs. Newspaper Advt. Bur. Trustee. S.I. Acad., 1967—, pres. bd. dirs., 1977-87; bd. dirs. S.I. Hosp., 1978—. Recipient Disting. Citizens award Wagner Coll., S.I., 1976. Mem. Am. Newspaper Pubs. Assn. Jewish. Office: SI Advance 950 Fingerboard Rd Staten Island NY 10305

DIAMOND, ROBERT STEPHEN, publishing company executive; b. Phoenix, Jan. 9, 1939; s. Bert A. and Rose (Garfinkle) D.; m. Susan E. Arnsberg, May 30, 1964. B.A., Claremont Mckenna Coll., 1961; M.S. in Journalism, Columbia U., 1967. Staff writer Ariz. Republic, Phoenix, 1962-64, Los Angeles Times, 1964-66; asso. editor Fortune mag., N.Y.C., 1967-70; v.p. Reliance Group, Inc., N.Y.C., 1970-75; v.p., dir. public relations Chase Manhattan Corp., N.Y.C., 1975-77; sr. v.p. corp. communications Dun & Bradstreet Corp., N.Y.C., 1977—; sec. polit. action com. Dun & Bradstreet Corp., 1980—. Bd. dirs. Reading is Fundamental, Washington; mem. president's adv. council Claremont McKenna Coll., 1975—. Mem. Sigma Delta Chi. Club: Quaker Ridge. Home: 5 Carstensen Rd Scarsdale NY 10583 Office: Dun & Bradstreet Corp 299 Park Ave New York NY 10171

DIAMOND, STEVEN JAY, utility company executive; b. Bklyn., July 29, 1952; s. Milton and Phyllis (Jacobs) D.; m. Mae Tucker, May 16, 1982. BS in Chemistry and Engring., U.S. Naval Acad., 1974; postgrad., Naval Nuclear Power Sch., 1975; MBA, Lehigh U., 1984. Registered profl. engr., Pa. Commd. ensign USN, 1974, advanced through grades to lt., 1978; nuclear ops. engr. Pa. Power & Light, Allentown, 1979-82, project mgr., 1982-87, internal cons., 1987—; pub. speaker Pa. Power & Light, Allentown, 1980; mgmt. cons., Allentown, 1984. Mem. Rotary. Republican. Home: 3361 Lindberg Ave Allentown PA 18103 Office: Pa Power & Light 2 N 9th St Allentown PA 18101

DIAMONDSTONE, LAWRENCE, paper company executive; b. N.Y.C., Mar. 27, 1928; s. Harry A. and Sally (Margulies) D.; B.S., U. Ill., 1950; m. Helen O'Connor, Dec. 8, 1984; 1 child, Cynthia Ann. Founder, pres., chief exec., chmn. bd., officer Newbrook Paper Div., N.Y.C., 1958—, Cottonwood Converting Div., Memphis, 1971—, Garden State Converters Div., Bayonne, N.J., 1973—, Triangle Mktg. Corp., N.Y.C., 1975—. Home: 2 Beekman Pl New York NY 10022 Office: 32 Bleecker St New York NY 10012

DIASIO, RICHARD LEONARD, president power transmisson company; b. Bridgeport, Conn., Nov. 25, 1937; s. Daniel Joseph and Rose Sarah (Agasi) D.; m. Julia Ann Krhla, Oct. 14, 1961; children: Richard J., Laura L., Christopher S. AS in Mech. Engring., Bridgeport Engring. Inst., 1965. Engr. U.S. Elec. Motors, Milford, Conn., 1962-64; sales profl. Reliance Electric, Hamden, Conn., 1964-66; sales mgr. Dynamatic div. Eaton Corp., Fairfield, N.J., 1966-72; mgr. regional sales Harnischfeger Corp., Woodbridge, N.J., 1972-74; mgr. nat. sales Kanematsu-Gosho, South Plainfield, N.J., 1974-77; dir. mktg. Ind. Gear Works, Indpls., 1977-78, gen. mgr., 1978-80; pres. Ind. Power Transmission Systems, Inc., Indpls, 1980—. With USAF, 1955-59. Mem. Soc. Mfg. Engrs. (sr.), Dramatists Guild, Authors League Am. Republican. Roman Catholic. Home: 665 Nottingham Ct Carmel IN 46032 Office: Ind Power Transmission Systems Inc 7776 Moller Rd Indianapolis IN 46268

DIAZ-VERSON, SALVADOR, JR., ins. co. exec.; b. Cuba, Dec. 31, 1951; came to U.S., 1959, naturalized, 1966; s. Salvador Diaz-Verson and Metodia Perez; B.A. in Fin., Fla. State U., 1973; m. Patricia Floyd, Apr. 24, 1976; children: Salvador, Patricia Elizabeth. Chief investment officer Am. Family Life Assurance Co., Columbus, Ga., 1978-81, also dir.; pres. Am. Family Corp., Columbus, 1983—, also dir.; bd. dirs. Total System Svcs., Com. Publicly Owned Cos. Sec. Am. Family Polit. Action Com.; bd. dirs. United Way, 1980—. Named Boss of Year Am. Bus. Women's Assn., 1982. Mem. Columbus C. of C. (bd. dirs.). Roman Catholic. Clubs: Green Island Country, Phi Gamma Delta. Home: 6433 Warm Springs Rd Columbus GA 31909 Office: 1932 Wynnton Rd Columbus GA 31904

DIBIANCA, JOSEPH P., financial executive, consultant; b. Phila., Apr. 8, 1954; s. N. Joseph and Anna M. (Spadaro) D.; m. Susanne L. Canosa, June 21, 1954; children: Joseph, Michael, Laura. BA in Acctg., Drexel U., 1975; MS in Taxation, Widener U., 1983. CPA, Pa. Audit supr. Peat Marwick Main, Phila., 1975-79, tax mgr., 1979-83; pres. Capital Mgmt., Valley Forge, Pa., 1983-85; fin. analyst Ecolaire, Malvern, Pa., 1985-87; dir. taxes Joy Mfg. Co., Pitts., 1987; dir. taxes and benefit funding Joy Techs., Pitts., 1988—; fin. cons. Pasta Bakery, Inc., Valley Forge, 1983—. Mem. Pa. Inst. CPA's (tax div., speaker com.). Republican. Roman Catholic. Home: 2509 Acorn Ct Wexford PA 15090 Office: Joy Mfg Co 3d and Grant St Pittsburgh PA 15219

DIBONA, CHARLES JOSEPH, association executive; b. Quincy, Mass., Feb. 26, 1932; s. Guido Ralph and Helen Elizabeth (Pangraze) DiB.; m. Evelyn Rauch, July 2, 1959; children—Caroline Anne, Charles J. B.S., U.S. Naval Acad., 1956; M.A. (Rhodes scholar), Oxford U., Eng., 1962. Pres., chief exec. officer Center for Naval Analyses, 1967-73; spl. cons. to Pres. U.S., dep. dir.; White House Energy Policy Office, 1973-74; exec. v.p., chief operating officer Am. Petroleum Inst., Washington, 1974-78; pres., chief exec. officer Am. Petroleum Inst., 1979—; vice chmn. U.S. nat. com. World Petroleum Congress; bd. dirs. U.S. Navy Meml. Found.; mem. Fed. City Council. Served to lt. comdr. U.S. Navy, 1956-67. Mem. UN Assn. of U.S.A. (bd. dirs.), Am. Council for Capital Formation. Roman Catholic. Clubs: Cosmos, F Street, City Tavern, Met. Home: 9306 Georgetown Pike Great Falls VA 22066 Office: Am Petroleum Inst 1220 L St NW Washington DC 20005

DIBONA, JAMES RICHARD, corporation executive; b. Quincy, Mass., Apr. 4, 1934; s. Guido Ralph and Helen Elizabeth (Pangraze) DiB.; m. Ann Olga Brigalli, Nov. 27, 1958; children: Helen, James, Hope, Anne. BBA, Boston U., 1959. With Gen. Electric Co., various locations, 1959-76; pres., chief exec. officer Internat. Stanley Co., Omaha, 1976-78; group controller Internat. Paper Co., N.Y. C., 1978-79, corp. auditor, 1979-82, corp. controller, 1982-86; v.p. fin. Quincy Industries Inc., 1986—; also bd. dirs. AC Label Co., Fremont, Calif.; bd. dirs. Quincy Industries, Inc., Fremont, Calif.; chmn. bd. dirs. Nat. Label Systems, Cin. Served to sgt. U.S. Army, 1953-55. Mem. Fin. Execs. Inst. Home: 1482 Brookside Dr Fairfield CT 06430 Office: 47690 Westinghouse Dr Fremont CA 94539

DIBRELL, LOUIS NELSON, III, tobacco company executive; b. Clarksville, Tenn., Feb. 20, 1945; s. Louis Nelson Jr. and Susan (Day) D.; m. Angela Carlin Dibrell. BA in Econs., U. Va., 1961. Salesman Dibrell Bros., Inc., Danville, Va., 1967-70, asst. v.p., 1970-75, v.p., 1975-84, sr. v.p., 1984—; bd. dirs. Tobacco Assocs., Raleigh, N.C. Bd. dirs. German Club, Danville, 1975-79. Served as sgt. U.S. Army, 1966-72. Methodist. Home: 444 Dogwood Dr Danville VA 24541 Office: Dibrell Bros Inc 512 Bridge St Danville VA 24543

DIBUONO, ANTHONY JOSEPH, lawyer, business executive; b. N.Y.C., Oct. 13, 1930; s. Sylvio and Rose (Pontolillo) diB.; m. Cecelia Marie La Penne, Feb. 11, 1956; children—Paul Jude, Mark Christopher, Ann Cecelia. B.A. in Econs., St John's U., 1951, LL.B., 1954, LL.M., 1955. Bar: N.Y. 1955, Calif. 1966, U.S. Supreme Ct. 1960. Clk. N.Y. Ct. Appeals, Albany, 1957-58; atty. NLRB, Newark, 1958; dep. chief counsel Marshall Space Flight Ctr. NASA, Huntsville, Ala., 1958-62; asst. div. counsel Gen. Dynamics Corp., San Diego, 1963-67; asst. sec. Gen. Dynamics Corp., N.Y.C., 1967-69; asst. gen. counsel Colt Industries Inc., N.Y.C., 1969-82, v.p., dep. gen. counsel, 1982-83, v.p., gen. counsel, 1983-85, sr. v.p., gen. counsel, sec., 1985—. Editor-in-chief St. John's U. Law Rev., 1953. Recipient Performance award Marshall Space Flight Ctr., 1962. Mem. ABA. Roman Catholic. Club: University (N.Y.C.). Office: Colt Industries Inc 430 Park Ave New York NY 10022

DICAMILLO, GARY THOMAS, manufacturing company executive; b. Niagara Falls, N.Y., Dec. 10, 1950; s. Joseph John and Olga Marie (Parenti) DiC.; m. Susan Christine Whitaker, Sept. 13, 1975; children: David, John, Benjamin. BSChemE, Rensselaer Poly. Inst., 1973; MBA, Harvard U., 1975. Brand mgr. Procter & Gamble, Cin., 1975-80; mgr. Mckinsey & Co., Chgo., 1980-83; v.p., gen. mgr. Culligan Internat. Co., Northbrook, Ill., 1983-86; pres. US. Power Tools Black & Decker Corp., Hunt Valley, Md., 1986—. Bd. govs. Goodwill Ind.; commr. Md. Pub. Broadcasting Commn.; trustee St. Paul's Sch. Recipient Livingston Houston Prize, Rensselaer Poly. Inst., 1973; Buffalo Alumni scholar Buffalo area Rensselaer Poly. Inst. Alumni, 1969; Chirurg Advt. fellow, 1974. Mem. Water Quality Assn. (bd. dirs. 1985-86), Md. Acad. Scis. (mem. bus. leadership com., mktg. com.), Rensselaer Poly. Inst. Club (bd. dirs. 1987-88), Rensselaer Alumni Assn. (bd. dirs.), Harvard Bus. Sch. Club, Skokie Country Club, Hillendale Country Club, Ctr. Club, Md. Club. Republican. Episcopalian. Home: 1001 St George's Rd Baltimore MD 21210 Office: Black & Decker 10 N Park Dr Hunt Valley MD 21030

DICE, BRUCE BURTON, exploration company executive; b. Grand Rapids, Mich., Dec. 24, 1926; s. William and Wilma (Rose) D.; children—Karen, Kevin, Kirk. BS in Geology, U. Mich., 1950; MS in Geology, Mich. State U., 1956. With El Paso Natural Gas, Tex., 1956-62, Drilling and Exploration Co., 1962-63; chief geologist Ocean Drilling and Exploration, New Orleans, 1963-75; pres. Transco Exploration Co., Houston, 1975-82, Dice Exploration Co., Inc., Houston, 1982—; bd. dirs. Maxus Energy Corp., Dallas, cons. in field; bd. dirs. Maple Corp., Denver. Elder Northwoods Presbyn. Ch., Houston; mem. Republican Com., Houston. Mem. Am. Assn. Petroleum Geologists, Houston Geol. Soc. Club: Forum (Houston). Home: 715 Loire Ln Houston TX 77090 Office: Dice Exploration Co Inc 1907 Grand Valley Ste 203 PO Box 73507 Houston TX 77090

DICHTER, BARRY JOEL, lawyer; b. Brookline, Mass., Feb. 19, 1950; s. Irving Melvin and Arlene Dichter; m. Judith Rand, Oct. 22, 1972; children: Rebecca Lynn, Jason Benjamin. AB magna cum laude, Harvard U., 1972, JD cum laude, 1975. Bar: Mass. 1975, N.Y. 1976, U.S. Dist. Ct. (so. and ea. dists.) N.Y. 1976, D.C. 1980, U.S. Dist. Ct. D.C. 1980, U.S. Ct. Appeals (D.C. cir.) 1985. Assoc. Webster & Sheffield, N.Y.C., 1975-82; assoc. Cadwalader, Wickersham & Taft, N.Y.C., 1983-84, ptnr., 1984—; lectr. in field. Vice chmn. Harvard Law Sch. Fund, Cambridge, Mass., 1984-88; class agt., 1988—. Mem. Assn. of Bar of City of N.Y. (bankruptcy com.), N.Y. UJA Fedn. (exec. com., bankruptcy and reorgn. group of lawyers div. of N.Y.). Office: Cadwalader Wickersham & Taft 100 Maiden Ln New York NY 10038

DICK, HAROLD L., manufacturing executive; b. Wichita, Kans., Oct. 24, 1943; s. Harold G. and Evelyn (Spines) D.; m. Jeanne Marie Luczai, Aug. 25, 1973; children: Harold Campbell, Edward Latham. BA, Washburn U., 1966; MBA, Harvard U., 1968. Exec. asst. to treas. Skelly Oil Co., Tulsa, 1968-70; mgmt. cons. McKinsey & Co. Inc., Chgo., Dallas, Houston, 1970-77; dir. planning Frito-Lay Inc., Dallas, 1977-80; v.p. Norton Simon Inc., N.Y.C., 1980-83; founder Summit Ptnrs., Wichita, Kans., 1983-85; pres., chief exec. officer Doskocil Cos. Inc., Hutchinson, Kans., 1985-88; founder, pres. The Summit Group, Hutchinson, 1988—; adv. bd. dirs. Garvey Industries, Wichita, 1987—. Mem. Washburn U. Alumni Assn. (bd. dirs. 1986—), Washburn Pres. Search Com., Assn. Corp. Growth. Republican. Episcopalian. Office: The Summit Group 405 First Nat Ctr Hutchinson KS 67501

DICK, KENNETH JOHN, financial analyst, real estate broker; b. St. Paul, Nov. 13, 1950; s. Willard Kenneth and Audrey Lee (Rauch) D.; m. Bonnie Marie Burnette, Nov. 27, 1970; children: Jonathan Michael, Nathan Allen. Student, San Jose City Coll., 1968-69, Coll. Fin. Planning, Denver, 1984. Assoc. broker Gibson Bowles Inc., Portland, Oreg., 1977-84; prin. fin. planner Fin. Network Investment Corp., Portland, 1983—; prin. broker real estate Asset Mgmt. Group, Portland, 1984—. Mem. Nat. Assn. Realtors, Realtors Nat. Mktg. Inst., Internat. Assn. for Fin. Planners, Inst. for Cert. Fin. Planners, Oreg. Assn. Realtors (legis. com. 1980-82), Oreg. Realtors Inst. (dean, bd. govs. 1978-83), Portland Million Dollar Club (past pres.), Christian Bus.Adv. Coun. (past chmn.), Rotary. Republican. Home: 102 NE Paloma St Gresham OR 97030 Office: 250 Willamette Wharf 4640 SW Macadam Portland OR 97201

DICK, NEIL ALAN, architecture executive; b. Cleve., June 15, 1941; s. Harvey L. and Rose (Flom) D.; B.Arch., Ohio State U., 1965; M.B., Cleve. State U., 1966; m. Bonnie M. Natarus, Sept. 3, 1967; 1 dau., Rory D. Exec. v.p. J.R. Hyde & Assos., Pitts., 1967-70; dir. tech. and market devel. Stirling Homex Corp., Avon, N.Y., 1970-72; sr. housing coordinator Nat. Housing Corp., Cleve., 1972-74; fin. and estate analyst Conn. Gen. Corp., Cleve., 1974-76; sr. v.p., dir. mktg. Cannon Design Inc., Grand Island, N.Y., 1976-82, also dir.; exec. v.p. Greiner, Inc. (formerly Daverman, Inc.), subs. Greiner Engring. Inc., Grand Rapids, Mich., 1983-88, Foth & Van Dyke, div. G.M., Green Bay, Wis., 1988—; bd. dirs. West Mich. Telecommunications Found., AIDS Found. Kent County; mem. bd. trustees Kendall Coll. Art & Design, Grand Rapids Art Mus., Grand Rapids C. of C. Found. (bd. dirs.), treas., Amherst (N.Y.) Democratic Com.; zone chmn., county fin. chmn., mem. exec. com. Erie County Dem. Com.; mem. Mich. Dem. State Com.; treas. Mich. 5th Congl. Dist. Dem. Com. Recipient Service award Erie County Dem. Com., 1979, Mem. Soc. Mktg. Profl. Services (regional coordinator), Buffalo Area C. of C., Green Bay C. of C. (chair planning taskforce), Rotary, Am. Hosp. Assn., Nat. Trust Hist. Preservation, Ohio State U. Alumni Assn., Mich. C. of C., Buffalo Mus. Sci., Albright Knox Art Gallery, Alpha Rho Chi. Jewish. Clubs: Economic, Peninsular, Cascade Hills. Lodge: Rotary (Grand Rapids). Address: care Foth & Van Dyke 2737 S Ridge Rd Green Bay WI 54307-9012

DICKELMAN, JAMES HOWARD, retail chain executive; b. Sheboygan, Wis., Oct. 21, 1947; s. Howard C. and Dorothy J. (Finkler) D.; m. Marilyn D. Lucchesi, May 10, 1947; children: David, Kerri, Kathleen, Cynthia. BA, Marquette U., 1969; MBA, U. Ariz., 1970. Sales rep. Phillip Morris, Cleve., 1970-72; dist. rep. No Nonense Panty Hose, St. Louis, 1972-73; mgr. nat. sales promotion Kayser-Roth, N.Y.C., 1973-74; v.p., mgr. merchandising Schultz Sav-O Stores, Inc., Sheboygan, 1974-77, exec. v.p., 1978-84, pres., chief exec. officer, 1984—, chmn. bd., 1988—. Roman Catholic. Office: Schultz Sav-O Stores Inc 2215 Union Ave Sheboygan WI 53081

DICKERMAN, ALLEN BRIGGS, business executive; b. Mt. Dora, Fla., Oct. 22, 1914; s. M. Marcellus and Emma (Dickerman) Javens; A.B., Hamilton Coll., 1936; M.B.A., Harvard U., 1941; Ph.D., Syracuse U., 1956; m. Stella M. Brower, May 15, 1943; children—Elizabeth (Mrs. Peter L. Thompson), Joanna (Mrs. Owen Parsons), Laura; m. Luise E. Peake, July 23, 1985. Instr., Harvard Bus. Sch., 1941-42; instr. U. Rochester, 1946-49; asso. prof. bus. adminstrn. Syracuse U., 1949-74, Internat. Bus. Research fellow, 1971, dir. internat. mgmt. devel. dept., 1960-74; prof. internat. bus., dir. Internat. Devel., Coll. Bus. Adminstrn., U. S.C., Columbia, 1974-85; pres. Carolina Internat. Devel. Assocs., Inc., Columbia, 1985—; advisor to univs., Colombia, Brazil, Philippines, Costa Rica, Venezuela, Indonesia. Mem. S.C. Dist. Export Council, 1976-81. Served with USNR, 1942-46. Mem. Acad. Internat. Bus., Delta Upsilon, Greater Columbia C. of C. Republican. Episcopalian. Author: Training Japanese Managers, 1974. Home: 4828 Citadel Ave Columbia SC 29206 Office: PO Box 11486 Columbia SC 29211

DICKERSON, FRANK SECOR, III, energy company executive; b. Ithaca, N.Y., June 19, 1939; s. Frank Secor, Jr. and Mary Louise (Pierson) D.; m. Leslie J. Parker, Nov. 22, 1961 (div. Mar. 1984); children—Wendy, David; m. Lynda Stucker, Apr. 14, 1984. B.A., Amherst Coll., 1962; J.D., U. Mich., 1966; grad. advanced mgmt. program, Harvard U., 1984. Assoc. Cravath, Swaine & Moore, N.Y.C., 1966-72; atty. Bethlehem Steel Corp., Pa., 1973-75, gen. atty., 1975-82, asst. sec., 1979-83, asst. gen. counsel, 1982-83, treas., 1983-86, v.p., treas., 1986-87; sr. v.p., chief fin. officer MAPCO Inc., 1987—. Bd. dirs., exec. com., treas. Tulsa chpt. ARC, bd. trustees endowment fund; trustee Tulsa Jr. Coll. Found. . Mem. ABA, Pa. Bar Assn., Fin. Execs. Inst. Clubs: Oaks Country, Summit, Tulsa. Office: 1800 S Baltimore Ave PO Box 645 Tulsa OK 74101-0645

DICKERSON, LAWRENCE RICHARD, drilling company executive; b. Cambridge, Eng., Dec. 11, 1952; s. Lamar Ronsell and Nancy Jane (Lawrence) D.; BBA with honors, U. Tex., 1976; m. Marcela E. Donadio, Feb. 17, 1981. Staff auditor Arthur Young & Co., Houston, 1976, audit sr., 1977-79; asst. controller Diamond M. Co., Houston, 1979-80, mgr. planning, 1980-81, controller, 1981-82, v.p., 1983-85, v.p. adminstrn., 1986—. Served with U.S. Army, 1972-74. CPA, Tex. Mem. Am. Inst. CPA's, Internat. Assn. Drilling Contractors (chmn. fin. com.). Episcopalian. Office: PO Box 4557 Houston TX 77210

DICKEY, DAVID DALE, communications executive; b. Williamston, N.C., July 27, 1927; s. Charles Hadley and Billie Irene (Hall) D.; m. Edith Cecile Bradley, June 19, 1955 (div. 1969); children: Frances Hall, Charles Bradley, Diana Dale. BA in Eng., U. Tenn., 1950. Advt. copywriter Gen. Electric Co., Schenectady, N.Y., 1950-52; reporter, feature writer Knoxville News-Sentinel, Tenn., 1952-57; exec. v.p. Home Builders Assn. of Greater Knoxville, 1957-60; dir. area devel. Greater Knoxville C. of C., 1960-70; exec. dir. Blount County Indsl. Devel. Bd., Maryville, Tenn., 1970-76; pres. PR Assocs., Knoxville, 1976—. Contbr. articles to mags. Dist. chmn. Knox County Rep. Exec. Com., 1960s; sec. Knox County Indsl. Devel. Bd., 1966-70; pres. Tenn. Indsl. Devel. Council, 1969-70; bd. dirs. East Tenn. Devel. Dist., 1967-75. With U.S. Army, 1946-47. Mem. Internat. Commerce Club (bd. dirs. 1967-70), Gt. Smoky Mountains Conservation Assn. (bd. dirs. 1958—), Southeast Outdoor Press Assn. (pres. 1967-68), Great Smoky Mountains Natural History Assn. (bd. dirs. 1984-86). Republican. Office: PO Box 11831 Knoxville TN 37939

DICKEY, THOMAS DALE, oil company executive; b. Sioux City, Iowa, June 15, 1952; s. David Arthur and Dorothy Belle (Nieuhenhaus) D.; m. Linda-Sue Dones, Sept. 14, 1974; children: Avery-Lynn, Seth, Merideth. BA, Houston Baptist U., 1974. Sales rep. Shell Oil Co., Dallas, 1974-75, Seattle, 1976-77; dist. mgr. Shell Oil Co., New Orleans, 1978-82; v.p., dir. Brock Exploration Corp., New Orleans, 1982—; also bd. dirs. Brock Exploration Corp. Deacon Ch. of Faith, Slidell, La., 1987—. Mem. Petroleum Landmen Assn. New Orleans, Alpha Tau Omega (v.p. 1973). Republican. Home: 802 Jefferson Ct Slidell LA 70458

DICKINSON, JAMES GORDON, editor; b. Melbourne, Australia, Nov. 13, 1940; came to U.S., 1974, naturalized, 1983; s. David Rushbrook and Lorna Aida (Anderson) D.; m. Carol Rosslyn McBurnie, Sept. 7, 1963; children: Craig, Peter (dec.), Samantha; m. Sheila Laraine Ferguson McManus, Aug. 20, 1982. Student Melbourne U., 1960-63. Cadet reporter Hobart Mercury, 1957-59, Melbourne Age, 1959-63; reporter Melbourne Herald, 1963-64, TV Channel O, Melbourne, 1964-66; cons. Internat. Public Relations Pty. Ltd., 1966-68; editor, pub. Australian Jour. Pharmacy, 1968-74; asst. exec. dir. Am. Pharm. Assn., Washington, 1975; sr. editor FDC Reports Inc., Washington, 1975-78; founder, editor Washington Drugwire, 1978-79; Washington bur. chief Drug Topics, Med. Econs. Co., 1978-83; Washington corr. Scrip, Clinica World Med. Device News, Animal Pharm World Vet. News (U.K.), 1978-85, Pharm. Tech., Pharm. Exec., N.Z. Pharmacy, Brit. Pharm. Jour., Drug News & Perspectives mag. (Spain), Med. Device and Diagnostic Industry mag., Washington; pres., chief exec. officer Ferdic Inc., 1982—; editor, pub. Dickinson's FDA and Dickinson's PSAO industry newsletters, 1985—; columnist syndicated all state pharm. jours., 1986—; cons. to drug industry; pres. Australian Monthly Newspapers and Periodicals Assn., 1972-74; founding sec. Melbourne Press Club, 1971-74. Editor: Weekly Pharmacy Reports, 1975-78. Mem. Australian Liberal Party, 1971-74; pres. Lee Forest Civic Assn., 1977-79. Mem. Periodical Corrs. Assn. Club: Nat. Press (Washington). Home and Office: 477 Winsley St Morgantown WV 26505

DICKINSON, JOANNE WALTON, lawyer; b. Windsor, N.C., Nov. 17, 1936; d. John Odell and Lois (King) Walton; m. Charles Cameron Dickinson III; children: Richard E.P. Eaton, John W.T. Eaton, Edward V.H. Eaton. Student Wake Forest Coll., 1961-62; BA, W.Va., U., 1975, JD, 1978. Bar: W.Va. 1978. Actress, W.Va., 1968-78; contbg. editor Victorian Poetry W.Va. U., Morgantown, 1970-75; assoc. Love, Wise, Robinson & Woodroe, Charleston, W.Va., 1978-82; adj. prof. U. Charleston, 1982-85 ; prof. Hebei Tchrs. U., Shijiazhuang, Hebei Province, People's Republic China, 1983-84; lectr. Erikson Ctr./Harvard Med. Sch., 1985-88; lead articles editor W.Va. Law Rev., Morgantown, 1977-78; asst. editor Mountain State Press, Charleston, 1980-83. Contbr. articles to profl. jours. Bd. dirs. Women's Health Ctr., Charleston, 1980-81; bd. dirs. Legal Aid Soc., Charleston, 1980-81. Recipient 1st prize Nathan Burkan Competition ASCAP, W.Va., 1977. Fellow Royal Soc. Arts; mem. W.Va. State Bar Assn., ABA, University Club, Harvard Club, Athenaeum Club, Harvard Am. Club Paris, Phi Beta Kappa, Home: 2100 Santa Fe #903 Wichita Falls TX 76309 Office: 1111 City National Bldg Wichita Falls TX 76301-3309

DICKINSON, RICHARD HENRY, accountant; b. Long Beach, Calif., June 16, 1944; s. Everett I. and Gertrude T. (Frear) D.; B.S., U. Wis.; B.B.A., Siena Coll., 1973; m. Georgette M. Turner, Jan. 27, 1968; children—Eric, Christine, Brent. Asso. accountant Alexander Varga, C.P.A., Catskill, N.Y., 1973; controller Hocker Power Brake Co., Inc., Evansville, Ind., 1974; dep. controller Watervliet (N.Y.) Arsenal, Dept. Def., 1975-76; auditor Melvin I. Weiskopf, C.P.A., Saratoga Springs, N.Y., 1977; owner, prin. Richard H. Dickinson, C.P.A., Ballston Spa, N.Y. and Saratoga Springs, N.Y., 1978-83; owner Dickinson & Co., C.P.A.s, Saratoga Springs, 1984—; lectr. Siena Coll., Loudonville, N.Y., 1983—. Served with U.S. Army, 1967-70. Decorated Silver Star, Bronze Star; C.P.A. Mem. Am. Inst. C.P.A.s, Nat. Assn. Accts., Am. Inst. Corporate Controllers, Delta Epsilon Sigma, Alpha Kappa Alpha. Republican. Lutheran. Clubs: Masons, Rotary (pres. Ballston Spa chpt. 1979). Home: 4 Ritchie Pl Saratoga Springs NY 12866 Office: 439 Maple Ave Saratoga Springs NY 12866

DICKINSON, RICHARD RAYMOND, oil company executive; b. Orange, Calif., Jan. 28, 1931; s. Raymond Russel and Florence Marie (Jacobson) D.; m. Barbara Jean Morrison, June 16, 1957; children: Roderick, Christine. B.S., Calif. Inst. Tech., 1952; M.S., U. So. Calif., 1960. Chem. engr. Los Angeles Refinery Texaco, 1952-68; gen. mgr. supply and distbn. Texaco, London, 1968-76; plant mgr. Eagle Point plant Texaco, Westville, N.J., 1976-79; gen. mgr. alternate energy group Texaco, White Plains, N.Y., 1979; v.p. strategic planning Texaco, 1979-82; sr. v.p. U.S. refining, mktg., supply and transp. Texaco, Houston, 1982-87; v.p. tech. Texaco, Inc., White Plains, N.Y., 1988—; bd. dirs. Nat. Petroleum Refiners Assn. Served with USNR, 1955-58. Home: 17 Crane Rd Darien CT 06820 Office: Texaco Inc 2000 Westchester Ave White Plains NY 10650 *

DICKSON, ALAN T., mill and holding company executive; b. 1931; married. B.S., N.C. State Coll., 1953; M.B.A., Harvard U., 1955. With Ruddick Corp., Charlotte, N.C., 1968—; now pres., dir. Ruddick Corp.; pres. Am. and Efird Mills, Inc. (subs.), Mount Holly, N.C., 1957-69; chmn. Am. and Efird Mills, Inc. (subs.), 1969, also dir.; dir. NCNB Corp., Chatham Mfg. Co., N.C. Textile Found., Sonoco Products Co., Harris-Teeter Super Markets. Trustee John Motley Morehead Found.; trustee, dir. Central Piedmont Community Coll. Served with U.S. Army, 1955-57. Office: Ruddick Corp 2000 Two First Union Ctr Charlotte NC 28282 *

DICKSON, FREDERIC HOWARD, financial executive; b. Balt., Jan. 6, 1946; s. Frederic Harold and Clio Edith (Russell) D.; m. Linda Elisabeth Makosky, Mar. 23, 1968; children: Katherine, Barbara. BS, Pa. State U., 1967; MBA, SUNY, Buffalo, 1973. Mktg. research supr. Gen. Foods Corp., White Plains, N.Y., 1970-73; v.p. research Goldman, Sachs & Co., N.Y.C., 1973-82; chief investment officer SHAREINVEST, Ridgefield, Conn., 1982-87; v.p., sr. portfolio mgr. Mgmt. Asset Corp., Westport, Conn., 1987—; sr. lectr. N.Y. Inst. Fin., N.Y.C., 1978—. Contbr. articles to profl. jours. Named disting. educator N.Y. Inst. Fin., 1982, disting. alumni, Pa. State U. Coll. Bus. Adminstrn., University Park, 1983. Mem. Market Technicians Assn. (pres. 1983-84, v.p. 1982-83, treas. 1981-82). Republican. Mem. United Ch. Christ. Home: 13 Tannery Hill Rd Ridefield CT 06877-2525 Office: Mgmt Asset Corp 253 Post Rd W Westport CT 06881

DICKSON, HERBERT JACKSON, finance company executive; b. Boston, Sept. 24, 1925; s. J. Herbert and Katie Lou (Bowen) D.; m. Louise P., Nov. 23, 1979; one child, Bradford. Student, U. Miami, 1946-47; BS, Ga. State U., 1949; student, Harvard U., 1964. Exec. v.p. Citizens and So. Nat. Bank, Atlanta, 1947-69; pres. Venture Industries, Inc., Atlanta, 1970-72, Counsins Mortgage and Equity Investments, Atlanta, 1972-73, Cousins Properties Inc., Atlanta, 1973-77; vice chmn. Farmbest Food Inc., Jacksonville, Fla., 1977-78; vice chmn., pres. Munford Inc., Atlanta, 1978-81; exec. v.p., chief exec. officer Watkins Assocs. Industries, Atlanta, 1982; mgmt. cons. Atlanta, 1982-87; chmn., chief exec. officer Fortune Fin. Services Inc., Atlanta, 1987—; bd. dirs. AM. BUs. Products Inc., Blount Inc., Deltona Corp., Munford Inc., Martin Industries Inc. Served with USCG, 1943-46, PTO. Republican. Presbyterian. Office: Fortune Fin Svcs Inc 2801 Buford Hwy Ste T60 Atlanta GA 30329

DICKSON, JEFFREY LEE, financial consultant; b. Framingham, Mass., June 27, 1962; s. William Robert and Patricia Ann (Lingley) D. BS in Mgmt., Babson Coll., 1984; postgrad., MIT, 1988—. Cert. fin. planner. Fin. analyst Intergrated Fin. Corp., Newton, Mass., 1983-84, mgr. equity dept., 1984-85; portfolio cons. Profl. Planners, Boston, 1985—; cons. Dickson Assocs., Framingham, 1987—; researcher MIT, Cambridge, 1987—; tchr. high sch. fin. planning program Coll. Fin. Planning, Framingham, 1988. Mem. Inst. Cert. Fin. Planners, Internat. Assn. Fin. Planners, Alpha Kappa Psi (chpt. v.p. 1983-84), Omicron Delta Epsilon. Republican. Roman Catholic. Home: Singletary Ln Farmingham MA 01701 Office: Profl Planners 4565 Prudential Tower Boston MA 02199

DICKSON, JOHN H., utilities executive; b. Cambridge, Mass., Jan. 16, 1943; s. John H. and Mary C. (Arsenault) D.; m. Nancy C. Oatt, Aug. 27, 1966; children: Michael, Brian, Andrew. BS, Boston Coll., 1965. Supr. Coopers & Lybrand, Boston, 1965-73; mgr. internal audit New Eng. Power Service Co., Westborough, Mass., 1973-77, controller, 1977-84, v.p., 1979—, treas., 1985—; controller New Eng. Energy, Inc., Westborough, 1977-83, v.p., 1982—, treas., 1984—, also bd. dirs., 1978—; treas. New Eng. Electric System, Westborough, 1985—, also bd. dirs., 1985—; treas. Mass. Electric Co., Westborough, 1985—, New Eng. Power Co., Westborough, 1987—. Office: New Eng Elec System 25 Research Dr Westborough MA 01582

DICKSON, JOHN R., food products company executive, dairy products company executive; b. 1930. BA, Ashland Coll., 1954. With Loblaw Co., Buffalo, 1954-63, Colonial Foods Inc., 1963-71, Shoprite Foods Inc., Arlington, Tex., 1971-76, Fox Grocery Co., Pitts., 1976-81, Wetterau Inc., St. Louis, to 1986; pres., chief exec. officer Roundy's Inc., Pewaukee, Wis., 1986—. Office: Roundys Inc 13000 Roundy dr Pewaukee WI 53072 *

DICKSON, MARKHAM ALLEN, wholesale company executive; b. Shreveport, La., June 10, 1922; s. Claudius Markham and Marjorie (Fields) D.; m. Margaret Shaffer, Sept. 4, 1943 (div. Mar. 1981); m. June Baldwin Dickson, Apr. 19, 1981; children: Louise Dickson Cravens, Claudius Markham, Markham Allen, Paul Meade. BS, MIT, 1947; MS, Calif. Inst. Tech., 1952. Registered profl. engr., La.; ordained priest Episcopal Ch., 1973. Prodn. engr. Brewster Co., Shreveport, 1948-51; pres. Shreveport Druggists, 1951-52, Morris & Dickson Co. Ltd., Shreveport, 1952—. Served to capt. USAAF, 1941-46. Recipient Conservationist of Yr. award DAR. Mem. Nat. Wholesale Druggists Assn., La. Wholesale Drug Distbrs. (pres. 1981—), La. Bd. Wholesale Drug Distbrs. (chmn. bd. 1988—), Kappa Alpha, Shreveport Club, Masons. Office: Morris & Dickson Co Ltd 410 Kay Ln Shreveport LA 71115

DICKSON, RUSH STUART, holding company executive; b. Charlotte, N.C., Aug. 18, 1929; s. Rush Smith and Lake (Simpson) D.; m. Joanne Shoemaker, Oct. 12, 1951; children: Rush Stuart, Thomas Walter, John Alexander, Laura Lake. Grad., Davidson Coll., 1951. With Am. & Efird Mills, Mt. Holly, N.C., 1951, Goldman, Sachs & Co., N.Y.C., 1951-52; pres. R. S. Dickson & Co., Charlotte, 1952-68; chmn. bd. Ruddick Corp., Charlotte, 1968—; dir. Am. & Efird Mills, Harris-Teeter Supermarkets, PCA Internat., Inc., Textron Inc., Jordan Graphics Inc., First Union Corp., Kings Entertainment Co. Chmn. Charlotte-Mecklenburg Hosp. Authority; bd. dirs. The Dickson Found., Found. U. N.C., Charlotte, Found. for Carolinas, N.C. Inst. Medicine; trustee Arts and Sci. Council, Heineman Found., Wake Forest U.; bd. visitors Johnson C. Smith U.; trustee U. N.C.-Charlotte, Davidson Coll., Queens Coll. Served with USAR. Mem. Charlotte C. of C. (dir.), Newcomen Soc. N.C., Boston Club, Charlotte City Club, Charlotte Country Club, Quail Hollow Country Club, Capital City Club, Country Club of N.C., Grandfather Golf and Country Club, Linville (N.C.) Country Club, Oakland Club, Tower Club, Wachesaw Plantation Club. Democrat. Office: Ruddick Corp 2000 Two First Union Ctr Charlotte NC 28282

DICKSON, THOMAS WALTER, textile company executive; b. Charlotte, N.C., Aug. 17, 1955; s. Rush Stuart and Joanne (Shoemaker) D.; m. Billie Cecelia Seddinger, Sept. 22, 1984; children: William Thomas, Michael Alan. BA in Econs., U. Va., 1977, MBA, 1980. Project mgr. spinning div. Am. & Efird, Inc., Mount Holly, N.C., 1980-81; project mgr. internat. Am. & Efird, Inc., Manchester, Eng., 1981-82; plant mgr. spinning div. Am. & Efird, Inc., Gastonia, N.C., 1982-84; mgr. Far East ops. Am. & Efird, Inc., Hong Kong, 1984-87; v.p. internat. ops. Am. & Efird, Inc., Mount Holly, 1987—; bd. dirs. Am. & Efird (Hong Kong) Ltd., Am. & Efird Mills Singapore, Am. & Efird (Great Britain) Ltd. Bd. dirs. Dickson Found., Charlotte, 1983—. Mem. Charlotte Country Club, Linville Golf Club. Republican. Baptist. Office: Am & Efird Inc PO Box 507 Mount Holly NC 28120

DIECKAMP, HERMAN M., retired utilities corporation executive; b. Jacksonville, Ill., 1928. B.S., U. Ill., 1950. With Rockwell Internat., 1950-73, pres. Atomics Internat. div., to 1973; v.p. Gen. Pub. Utilities Corp., Parsippany, N.J., 1973-74, pres., chief operating officer, 1974-88, also dir.; pres., chief operating officer GPU Service Corp., 1974-88; dir. Met. Edison Co., GPU Nuclear Corp., Jersey Central Power and Light Co., Pa. Electric Co. Office: Gen Pub Utilities Corp 100 Interpace Pkwy Parsippany NJ 07054

DIEDERICH, J(OHN) WILLIAM, newspaper executive; b. Ladysmith, Wis., Aug. 30, 1929; s. Joseph Charles and Alice Florence (Yost) D.; m. Mary Theresa Klein, Nov. 25, 1950; children: Mary Theresa Diederich Evans, Robert Douglas, Charles Stuart, Michael Mark, Patricia Anne Diederich Irelan, Donna Maureen (dec.), Denise Brendan, Carol Lynn Diederich Weaver, Barbara Gail, Brian Donald, Tracy Maureen, Theodora Bernadette, Tamara Alice, Lorraine Angela. Ph.B., Marquette U., Milw., 1951; M.B.A. with high distinction (Baker scholar), Harvard U., 1955. With Landmark Communications, Inc., Norfolk, Va., 1955—, v.p., treas., 1965-73, exec. v.p. fin., 1973-78, exec. v.p. community newspapers, 1978-82, exec. v.p., chief fin. officer, 1982—, also dir.; chmn. bd. dirs. Landmark Community Newspapers, Inc., 1977-88; pres. Exec. Productivity Systems, Inc., 1982-88; instr. Boston U., 1954, Old Dominion U., 1955-59. Bd. dirs. Landmark Charitable Found. Served as officer USMCR, 1951-53; lt. col. Res. (ret.). Mem. Internat. Newspaper Fin. Execs., Nat. Assn. Accts., Am. Numismatic Assn., S.A.R., Nat. Geneal. Soc., Wis. Geneal. Soc., Pa. Geneal. Soc., Sigma Delta Chi. Roman Catholic. Club: Town Point (Norfolk). Home: 3751 Little Neck Point Virginia Beach VA 23452 Office: Landmark Communications Inc 150 W Brambleton Ave Norfolk VA 23501

DIEFFENBACH, CHARLES MAXWELL, emeritus law educator, lawyer; b. Westfield, N.Y., July 9, 1909; s. Arthur Warren and Mary Bertha (Meyer) D.; m. Gladys Ethel Gray, June 29, 1935; children—Gretchen Dieffenbach Gehlbach, Roxann Huschard. B.S. in Civil Engring., U. Ala., 1934; postgrad. Bus. Sch., Harvard U., 1934-35; M.A. in Econs., U. Cin., 1948; J.D., Ohio No. U., 1957. Bar: Ohio 1957. Meat packing exec. H.H. Meyer Packing

Co., Cin., 1935-55; from asst. prof. to prof. law Chase Coll. Law, Cin., 1957-65; prof. bus. adminstrn. N.Mex. State U., Las Cruces, 1965-68; prof. law Chase Coll. Law, No. Ky. U., Highland Heights, 1968-79, prof. law emeritus, 1980—; vis. prof. law Detroit Coll. Law, 1979-80. Served to maj. U.S. Army, 1942-46, ETO. Republican. Episcopalian. Club: University (Cin.). Home: 710 Ivy Ave Cincinnati OH 45246 Office: No Ky U Chase Coll Law 508 Nunn Hall Highland Heights KY 41076

DIEHL, DANIEL JAMES, small business owner; b. Milford, Del., Apr. 20, 1959; s. David Duane and Rena Francis (Geofrey) D.; m. Patricia Louise Skinner, Feb. 28, 1987; children: Tanya, Jason, Aaron. Grad. high sch., Holyoke, Mass. Auto mechanic Northhampton (Mass.) Volkswagen BMW, 1977-79; siding applicator U.S. Siding, Springfield, Mass., 1979-80; auto mechanic Dover (Del.) Volkswagen, 1980-81; working supr., tng. instr. Superior Siding, Dover, 1981-87; owner, Diehl & Son, The Siding Experts, Dover, 1988—; founder Pro-found Inc., Dover, 1988—. Home and Office: RD 4 Box 461 Dover DE 19901

DIEHM, RUSSELL CHARLES, comptroller; b. Reading, Pa., Dec. 22, 1946; s. Russell Charles and Mary Helen (Ott) D.; m. Sherry Diane Kilburn, July 20, 1968; 1 child, Jacquline. BBA, Temple U., 1968, MBA, 1970. Staff acct. Boscov's Dept Store, Inc., Reading, 1971-79, acctg. mgr., 1979-82, asst. controller, 1982-88, comptroller, 1988—. Chmn. supervisory com. Boscov's Employee Credit Union, 1981-86. Mem. Agrl. and Horticultural Soc. Berks County (treas. 1979—). Office: Boscovs Dept Store Inc 4500 Perkiomen Ave Reading PA 19606

DIENER, ROYCE, health care services company executive; b. Balt., Mar. 27, 1918; s. Louis and Lillian (Goodman) D.; m. Jennifer S. Flinton; children: Robert, Joan, Michael. BA, Harvard U.; LLD, Pepperdine U. Comml. lending officer, investment banker various locations to 1972; pres. Am. Med. Internat., Inc., Beverly Hills, Calif., 1972-75, pres., chief exec. officer, 1975-78, chmn., chief exec. officer, 1978-85, chmn. bd., 1986-88, chmn. exec. com., 1986—; bd. dirs. Calif. Econ. Devel. Corp., Advanced Tech. Venture Funds, Am. Health Properties, AMI Healthcare Group, plc. Author: Financing a Growing Business, 1966, 3d edit., 1978. Bd. visitors Grad. Sch. Mgmt., UCLA; mem. governing bd., UCLA Med. Ctr.; mem. vis. com. Med. Sch. and Sch. Dental Medicine, Harvard U.; trustee Andrus Gerontol. Inst., U. So. Calif.; bd. dirs. L.A. Philharm. Assn., L.A. chpt. ARC, Heritage Sq. Mus., Santa Monica. Served to capt. USAF, 1942-46, PTO. Decorated D.F.C. with oak leaf cluster. Mem. L.A. C. of C. (bd. dirs.), Calif. C. of C. (bd. dirs.), Calif. Bus. Round Table (bd. dirs.), Harvard Club, Regency Club, Calif. Yacht Club, Riviera Country Club (L.A.), Marks Club (London). Office: Am Med Internat Inc 414 N Camden Dr Beverly Hills CA 90210

DIERKERS, JOSEPH ANDREW, automotive company executive; b. Cin., Nov. 12, 1930; s. Joseph Henry and Margaret Ann (Braun) D.; m. Joan Christina Wagner, May 12, 1956; children: Margaret, Marcia, Mark, Donna, Anthony, Elizabeth. BA in Math. and Engring., Ohio State U., 1954; postgrad., U. Cin., 1967-69. Engr. RCA, Cin., 1956-59, mgr. engring., 1959-70; pvt. practice engring. cons. Cin., 1971; asst. plant mgr. Stearns Foster, Cin., 1972; with Ford Motor Co., Cin., 1972—, supr. prodn. control, 1976-87, mgr. material control, 1988—. Pres. parish coun. Our Lady Sacred Heart, Reading, Ohio, 1968-72, 85-88; v.p. Archdiocesan Coun. Laity, Cin., 1973-75; mem. sch. bd. Mt. Notre Dame High Sch., Reading, 1976-77. With U.S. Army, 1954-56. Mem. Purcell Alumni Assn., Ohio State U. Alumni Assn. Republican. Office: Ford Motor Co 3000 Sharon Rd Sharonville OH 45241

DIERSEN, MICHAEL LARRY, financial planner, teacher; b. Louisville, Ky., Oct. 3, 1954; s. Kenneth Raymond and Eva May (Caffee) D. BSBA, U. Nev., 1984, MBA, 1988. Ops. engr. Stauffer Chem. Corp., Las Vegas, 1980-82; computer programmer, researcher EPA, Las Vegas, 1982-84; fin. planner Wedbush Securities, Las Vegas, 1984—, ins. coordinator, 1986—, spl. products coordinator, 1985—; instr. investment classes U. Nev., Las Vegas, 1985—; arbitrator Nat. Assn. Securities Dealers, Las Vegas, 1987—; lectr. Dow Jones Corp. and U. Nev., Las Vegas, 1985-86. Author (newsletter) The Income Investor. Promotor Council for Econ. Edn., Las Vegas, 1987. Named Ky. Col. Gov. Ky., 1982. Mem. Internat. Assn. Fin. Planners. Republican. Roman Catholic. Office: Wedbush Securities 2000 E Flamingo Rd Ste B Las Vegas NV 89119

DIETRICH, BRUCE N(EAL), treasurer; b. Roseburg, Oreg., July 6, 1956; s. William Benjamin and Lorena May (Updegrave) D.; m. Dolly Cathleen Cutchall, Aug. 15, 1982. BS in Acctg. Adminstrn., Pacific Union Coll., 1980; MBA, Andrews U., 1982. CPA, Calif. Staff auditor Gen. Conf. Auditing Service, Westlake Village, Calif., 1982-85; asst. prof. Andrews U., Berrien Springs, Mich., 1985-87; assoc. treas. Pacific Union Conf., Westlake Village, Calif., 1987—; audit supr. Raymond D. Roberts, CPA, Berrien Springs, 1985-87. Mem. Am. Inst. CPA's, Delta Mu Delta (sponsor 1985-86), Calif. Soc. CPA's. Seventh-day Adventist. Home: PO Box 6922 Thousand Oaks CA 91359-6922

DIETRICH, GEORGE CHARLES, chemical company executive; b. Detroit, Feb. 5, 1927; s. George Sylvester and Catherine Elizabeth (Cable) D.; B.S., U. Detroit; children—Linda Marie, Elizabeth Ann, George Charles. Field sales mgr. Allied Chem. Co., Chgo., 1960-64; dir. sales Aerosol Research Co., North Riverside, Ill., 1964—; pres. Aeropres Corp., Chgo., 1964-65, Diversified Chems. & Propellants Co., Westmont, Ill., 1965—, also dir.; chmn. bd. ChemSpec Ins. Ltd.; dir. Am. Nat. Bank, De Kalb, Ill., Diversified CPC Internat., Anaheim, Calif., Klockner CPC Internat.; bd. dirs., chmn. Consumers Specialties Ins. Co., Montpelier, Vt., Expert Mgmt. Systems, Phoenix; pres., chief exec. officer Gen. Energy Internat. Served with USNR, 1945-46. Mem. Chem. Splty. Mfrs. Assn. (gov., chmn. bd.), Chgo. Drug and Chem. Assn., Chgo. Perfumery Soap and Extract Assn., Nat. Paint and Coatings Assn., World Univ. Roundtable, Internat. Platform Assn., Econs. Club Chgo., Execs. Club Chgo. Roman Catholic. Clubs: Butler Nat. Golf; Boca Raton (Fla.) Hotel and Club; Butterfield Country. Home: 505 N Lakeshore Dr Apt #5111 Chicago IL 60611 Office: Diversified CPC Internat Durkee Rd PO Box 490 Channahon IL 60410-0490

DIETZ, CHARLTON HENRY, lawyer; b. LeMars, Iowa, Jan. 8, 1931; s. Clifford Henry and Mildred Verna (Eggensperger) D.; m. Viola Ann Lange, Aug. 17, 1952; children: Susan (Mrs. Jay Kakuk), Robin (Mrs. Jack Mayfield), Craig. B.A., Macalester Coll., 1953; J.D., William Mitchell Coll. Law, 1957. Bar: Minn. 1957. Mem. public relations staff 3M, St. Paul, 1952-58, atty., 1958-70, asso. counsel, asst. sec., 1970-72, asst. gen. counsel, sec., 1972-75, gen. counsel, sec., 1975-76, gen. counsel, v.p. legal affairs, 1976-88, sr. v.p., 1988—, also dir.; bd. dirs. Eastern Heights State Bank, chmn., 1981—; bd. dirs. State Bond and Mortgage Co., St. Paul Lowertown Redevel. Corp.; instr. William Mitchell Coll. Law, 1960-74, trustee, 1974-86, 87—, pres., 1980-83. Bd. dirs. St. Paul Area YMCA, 1973-80, chmn., 1978-80; bd. dirs. Minn. Citizens Council on Crime and Justice, 1976-88, pres., 1982-84; trustee United Theol. Sem., 1976-82; bd. dirs. St. Paul United Way, 1980—, v.p., 1988—; bd. dirs. Ramsey County Hist. Soc., 1979-86, St. Paul Lowertown Redevel. Corp., 1988—; mem. Conferees of Minn. Citizens Conf. on the Cts., 1981-82, Minn. U.S. Bicentennial Com., 1988—; trustee Macalester Coll., 1983—; bd. dirs. Indian Head council Boy Scouts Am., 1985—. Fellow Am. Bar Found.; mem. ABA, Fed. Bar Assn., Minn. Bar Assn., Ramsey County Bar Assn., Am. Soc. Corp. Secs., Assn. Gen. Counsel. Republican. Mem. United Ch. of Christ. Clubs: Mason (Shriner, Jester), St. Paul Athletic, North Oaks, Minn. Home: 1 Birch Ln North Oaks MN 55127 Office: Minn Mining & Mfg Co 3M Ctr Bldg 220-14W-07 Saint Paul MN 55144

DIETZ, PHILIP JOHN, JR., engineering executive; b. Balt., June 1, 1943; s. Philip J. and M. Geraldine (McKenzie) D.; m. Sallie L. Burguieres, May 10, 1975; children: Caroline, Christiane, Geoffrey. BS, Loyola Coll., 1964; MEE, U. S.C., 1966. Assoc. engr. Fed. Systems div. IBM Corp., Gaithersburg, Md., 1966-69; mem. tech. staff TRW, Inc., McLean, Va., 1969-71; project engr. Mechanics Rsch., Inc., McLean, 1971-77; mgr. Washington ops. Adams-Russell Co., Silver Spring, Md., 1977-82; dir. advanced tech. E-Systems, Inc., Fairfax, Va., 1982—; cons. NRC, Washington, 1971. Treas. Kings Manor Homeowners Assn., McLean, 1978-84; bd. dirs. McLean Citizens Assn., 1982--84; pres. McLean Country Estate Homeowners Assn., 1986—. Mem. IEEE (sr. mem., bd. dirs. No. Va. sect. 1985-87), Assn. Old Crows, Tau Beta Pi, Eta Kappa Nu, Langley Club (McLean). Republican. Roman Catholic. Home: 8198 Hunting Hill Ln McLean VA 22102 Office: E Systems Inc 7700 Arlington Blvd Falls Church VA 22046

DIFFENDAFFER, GARY LEE, financial executive; b. Scottsbluff, Nebr., May 20, 1946. BS, U. Nebr., 1968, MA, 1972. Cert. fin. planner. Ops. and credit analyst Fed. Intermediate Credit Bank, Omaha, 1973-76; info. analyst, bank rels. mgr., sr. cons., sr. rsch. specialist Farm Credit Corp. Am., Denver, 1976-87; fin. planner Fin. Network Investment Corp., Denver, 1987-89; fin. con. Capital Allocation and Mgmt. Inc., Englewood, Colo., 1989—; instr. U. Denver Ctr. Mgmt. Devel., 1988, local high schs., 1988. Precinct chmn. Rep. Party, Arapahoe County, Colo., 1987-88; mem. regional fin. com. Am. Bapt. Ch., Denver, 1988—; del. Rep. Party, 1987. Staff sgt. USAF, 1968-72. Mem. Inst. Cert. Fin. Planners, Internat. Assn. Fin. Planners, Planning Forum, U. Nebr. Alumni Assn., Colo. Soc. Inst. Cert. Fin. Planners (bd. dir. 1988—). Home: 7462 E Costilla Ave Englewood CO 80112 Office: Allocation and Mgmt Inc 5299 S DTC Blvd Ste 960 Englewood CO 80111

DIGGS, CHARLES EDWARD, real estate officer; b. Bessmer, Ala., Dec. 4, 1949; s. Albert Mills and Juanita Mills; m. Cheryl Elise Buford, June 26, 1971; children: Tina, Nikki, Charles Jr. Grad., Sinclair Coll., 1988; postgrad., 1977, 86-87. Designer, craftsman Frigidaire div. GM, Dayton, Ohio, 1973-76; sr. comml. artist GM, Dayton, 1976-80, reliability engr. Truck/Bus. Group div., 1980—; auditor GM; pres., chief exec. officer Diggs, Charles Edward, Real Estate Broker, 1985—; pres. Pro Tech. Illustrations, 1978-80. Bd. dirs. Gard Ave. Ch. of Christ, Dayton, 1988. Mem. Soc. Automotive Engrs., Dayton Area Bd. Realtors, Genesis Universal Artist (v.p. , cert. 1974, 77). Democrat. Home: 3638 Hermosa Dr Dayton OH 45416 Office: 4505 N Main St Ste 5 Dayton OH 45405

DIGIACOMO, MICHAEL D., investment banker; b. N.Y.C., Feb. 20, 1946; s. Michael P. and Dorothy K. DiGiacomo. AB, Yale U., 1968; JD cum laude, Fordham U., 1974. Bar: N.Y. 1975, U.S. Dist. Ct. (so. and ea. dists) N.Y. 1975, U.S. Ct. Appeals (2d cir.) 1975. Law clk. to Hon. William H. Mulligan U.S. Ct. of Appeals, 2d cir., N.Y.C., 1974-76; assoc. Dewey, Ballantine, Bushby, Palmer & Wood, N.Y.C., 1977-83; asst. v.p. Citicorp Capital Markets, N.Y.C., 1983-84; v.p., shareholder Kidder, Peabody & Co., Inc., N.Y.C., 1984—. Lt. (j.g.) USN, 1968-71. Republican. Roman Catholic. Clubs: Racquet and Tennis, N.Y.C., St. Moritz (Switzerland) Tobogganing. Home: 250 Bronxville Rd Bronxville NY 10708 Office: Kidder Peabody & Co Inc 10 Hanover Sq New York NY 10005

DIGIAMARINO, MARIAN ELEANOR, zoning and code specialist; b. Camden, N.J., July 23, 1947; d. James and Concetta (Biancosino) DiG. BS in Mgmt., Rutgers U., 1978. Clk. stenographer transp. div. Dept. of Navy, Phila., 1965-70, sec., 1970-73, realty asst. Profl. Devel. Ctr.. program, 1973-75, realty specialist, 1975-81, supervisory realty specialist, head acquisition and ingrant sect., 1981-85, supervisory realty specialist, mgr. ops. br., 1985—; instr. USNR, Phila., 1983, 88. Contbr. articles to profl. jours. Mem. AAUW, Soc. Am. Mil. Engrs., Nat. Assn. Female Execs., Phi Chi Theta (pres. Del. Valley chpt. 1984-86, nat. councillor 1984, nat. fundraising com., pres. and corr. sec. (Alpha Omega chpt. 1976-78). Office: Dept of Navy No Div Naval Facilities Engring Command Real Estate Div US Naval Base Philadelphia PA 19112

DIGIOVANNI, ELEANOR ELMA, scaffold installation company executive; b. Long Island City, N.Y., May 14, 1944; d. Charles and Josephine (Laureni) DiG. Student Queensboro Coll. Collector Atlas/Re/Sun Ins. Co., N.Y.C., 1965-69; instr. Oak Manor Equitation, Weyers Cave, Va., 1970-76; dispatcher, salesperson Safway Steel Products, Long Island City, N.Y., 1977-83; ops. mgr. York Scaffold, Long Island City, 1983—. Mem. Mus. Natural History, Nat. Assn. Female Execs., Women in Constrn., Internat. Platform Assn. Democrat. Roman Catholic. Avocations: reading, horseback riding, needlepoint. Home: 14-34 30th Rd Astoria NY 11102 Office: York Scaffold Equipment Corp 37-20 12th St Long Island City NY 11101

DIGMAN, LESTER ALOYSIUS, management educator; b. Kieler, Wis., Nov. 22, 1938; s. Arthur Louis and Hilda Dorothy (Jansen) D.; m. Ellen Rhomberg Pfohl, Jan. 15, 1966; children: Stephanie, Sarah, Mark. BSME, U. Iowa, 1961, MSIE, 1962, PhD, 1970. Registered profl. engr., Mass. Mgt. cons. U.S. Ameta, Rock Island, Ill., 1962-67; mgmt. instr. U. Iowa, Iowa City, 1967-69; head applied math. dept. U.S. Ameta, Rock Island, Ill., 1969-74, head managerial tng. dept., 1974-77; assoc. prof. mgt. U. Neb., Lincoln, 1977-84, dir. grad. studies in mgmt., 1982—, prof. mgt., 1984-87; Leonard E Whittaker Am. Charter disting. prof. mgmt. U. Nebr., Lincoln, 1987—; cons. various orgns., 1963-72; sec. treas. Mgmt. Svcs. Assocs. Ltd., Davenport, Iowa, 1972-77; owner L.A. Digman and Assocs., Lincoln, 1977—; gen. ptnr. Letna Properties, Madison, Wis., 1978—. Author: Strategic Management, 1986, 2nd edit., 1989, Network Analysis for Management Decisions, 1982; conbtr. articles to profl. jours. Recipient Dist. award SBA, 1980, Certs. of Appreciation Dept. of Def., 1972. Mem. Decision Scis. Inst. (charter) (assoc. program chmn. 1985-86, program chmn. 1986, pres. 1987-88, coord. doctoral consortium 1989), Strategic Mgmt. Soc. (founding), Acad. of Mgmt. The Planning Forum, Pan Pacific Bus. Assn., Inst. Mgmt. Scis., Ops. Rsch. Soc. Am., Hillcrest Country Club, Lincoln U. Club. Roman Catholic. Home: 7520 Lincolnshire Rd Lincoln NE 68506 Office: U Nebr 222 CBA Lincoln NE 68588

DILENSCHNEIDER, ROBERT LOUIS, public relations company executive; b. N.Y.C., Oct. 21, 1943; s. Sigmund J. and Martha (Witucki) D.; m. Janet Hennessey, Sept. 6, 1969. B.A. in Communication Arts, U. Notre Dame, 1965; M.A. in Journalism, Ohio State U., 1967. Account supr. Hill & Knowlton, Inc., N.Y.C., 1967-70, v.p., 1970-73, sr. v.p., 1973-80; exec. v.p. Hill & Knowlton, Inc., Chgo., 1980-84, pres, chief operating officer, 1984-86; pres., chief exec. officer Hill & Knowlton, Inc., 1986—; mem. adv. bd. Emory U. Sch. Bus. Admin., U.S.-Japan Bus. Council; mem. adv. bd. Adv. Council for Coll. Bus. Adminstrn. Notre Dame U. Past bd. dirs. United Charities, Chgo.; mem. adv. bd. N.Y. Hosp.-Cornell Med. Ctr. Served with USAR, 1965-66. Recipient Big Apple award N.Y.C. Jaycees, 1978. Mem. Internat. Pub. Relations Assn., Pub. Relations Soc. Am. (mem. adv. bd.). Clubs: Tavern, Chicago, Executives, Economic (N.Y.C. and Chgo.) Wisemen; Sky. Office: Hill & Knowlton Inc 420 Lexington Ave New York NY 10017

DILGARD, ROBERT CARL, financial executive, accountant; b. Waterloo, Ind., June 3, 1932; s. Carl Wilbur and Imogene (Mills) D.; m. Cynthia R. Corlen, July 26, 1957 (div. 1979); children: Leigh Ann, Lynda Dawn; m. Frieda K. King, May 17, 1987. BSc, Internat. Coll., 1952; BA magna cum laude, David Lipscomb Coll., 1956. CPA, Tenn. Tchr. Cen. High Sch., Ashland City, Tenn., 1956-57; dir. acctg. Cullom & Ghertner Co., Nashville, 1957-64, Genesco Inc., Nashville, 1964-84; v.p. fin. and adminstrn. Greif Cos., Allentown, Pa., 1984—. Bd. dirs. March of Dimes, Allentown, 1988. Recipient bronze award Am. Mgmt. Assn., 1972, Silver Plate award United Way, 1987. Mem. AICPA, Tenn. Soc. CPA's (bd. dirs. CPA's in industry 1972—), Nat. Assn. Accts., Am. Payroll Assn. (cert. 1984). Mem. Ch. of Christ. Home: 2898 Whitemarsh Pl Macungie PA 18062 Office: Greif Cos 939 Marcon Blvd Allentown PA 18001

DILGARDO, ROBERT CARL, financial executive; b. Waterloo, Ind., June 3, 1932; s. Carl Wilbur and Imogene (Mills) D.; m. Cynthia R. Corlew, July 26, 1957 (div. 1979); children: Leigh Ann, Lynda Dawn, m. Frieda K. King, May 17, 1987. BS, Internat. Coll., 1952; BA magna cum laude, David Lipscomb Coll., 1956. CPA, Tenn. Tchr. Cen. High Sch., Ashland City, Tenn., 1956-57; dir. acctg. Cullom & Ghertner Co., Nashville, 1957-64, Genesco Inc., Nashville, 1964-84; v.p. fin. and adminstrn. Greif Cos., Allentown, Pa., 1984—. Bd dirs. March. of Dimes, Allentown, 1988. Recipient Bronze award Am. Mgmt. Assn., 1972, Silver Plate award United Way, 1987. Mem. AICPA, Tenn. Soc. CPA's (bd. dirs. CPA's in Industry 1972—), Nat. Assn. Accts., Am. Payroll Assn. (cert. 1984). Mem. Ch. of Christ. Home: 2898 Whitemarsh Pl Macungie PA 18062 Office: Greif Cos 939 Marcon Blvd Allentown PA 18001

DILIBERTO, ROY THOMAS, financial planner; b. Phila., Apr. 21, 1940; s. Anthony and Anna (Monzo) D.; m. Rita Delores DiGiovanni, Sept. 7, 1963 (div. Sept. 1979); children: Lisa, Anthony; m. Peggy Ann Muckley, Nov. 6, 1987. BS in Bus. Adminstrn., Temple U., 1962. CLU. Ins. agt. John Hancock Ins., Phila., 1964-70; gen. agt. John Hancock Ins., Trenton, N.J., 1970-77; v.p. John Hancock Ins., Atlanta, 1977-82; pres., chief exec. officer RTD Fin. Advisors, Inc., Phila., 1982—. Named as one of Best 200 Fin. Planners in Am. Money Mag., 1987. Mem. Inst. Cert. Fin. Planners, Internat. Assn. Fin. Planning (bd. dirs. 1986—), Registry Fin. Planning Practitioners, Phila. Estate Planning Coun., Soc. CLU's (past pres.). Republican. Roman Catholic. Office: RTD Fin Advisors Inc 1500 Walnut St Ste 501 Philadelphia PA 19102

DILL, CHARLES ANTHONY, manufacturing company executive; b. Cleve., Nov. 29, 1939; s. Melville Reese and Gladys (Frode) D.; m. Louise T. Hall, Aug. 24, 1963 (dec. Sept. 28, 1983); children: Charles Anthony, Dudley Barnes; m. Mary M. Howell, Jan. 17, 1987. B.S. in Mech. Engring, Yale U., 1961; M.B.A., Harvard U., 1963. With Emerson Electric Co., 1963—, corp. v.p. internat., 1973-77; pres. subsidiary A.B. Chance Co., 1977-80; corp. group v.p. Emerson Electric, St. Louis, 1980-82; sr. v.p. Emerson Electric, 1982-88; pres. AVX Corp., Great Neck, N.Y., 1988—; bd. dirs. Stout Industries. Republican. Presbyterian. Club: St. Louis Country. Home: 807 S Warson Saint Louis MO 63124 Office: AVX Corp 60 Cutter Mill Rd Great Neck NY 11021

DILL, CHARLES GEORGE, construction executive; b. N.Y.C., Mar. 8, 1930; s. George and Dora (Müeller) D.; m. Rita Birssner, Dec. 29, 1951; children: Ellen, Jeffrey. BA, Mich. State U., 1957; MBA, Wagner Coll., 1966; postgrad., Pace U., 1982. Service mgr. Harrison div. GM, Buffalo, 1956-68; mfr. mgr. Gen. Cable Corp., N.Y.C., 1968-74, Thomas Industry, Lakewood, N.J., 1975-77; div. v.p. Burnham Corp., Irvinoson, N.Y., 1978-84; sr. v.p. English Greenhouse Products, Camden, N.J., 1984—; cons. United Rsch., Morristown, N.J., 1974-75. Lt. (j.g.) USNR, Korea. Republican. Home: 4B Dorchester Cranbury NJ 08512 Office: English Greenhouse Products 1501 Admiral Wilson Blvd Camden NJ 08109

DILL, JOHN FRANCIS, publishing company executive; b. Hempstead, N.Y., May 3, 1934; s. Samuel Leland and Jeanne Marie (Dorsch) D.; m. Joan Eileen Shipps, Aug. 22, 1959 (div. 1973); m. Virginia Rae Dapson, Nov. 23, 1973; children—Patricia, Diane, Kevin, Catherine, Glenn. B.A., Oberlin Coll., 1957; M.B.A., NYU, 1963. Mgmt. trainee Mut. Life Ins., N.Y.C., 1959-63; mgr. McGraw Hill Book Co., N.Y.C., 1963-68, dir. mktg., 1969-77, pub., gen. mgr., 1977-81; pres., chief exec. officer Year Book Med. Pubs., Chgo., 1981—, CRC Press Inc., Boca Raton, Fla.; dir. Mosby Can. Ltd., 1982—, Blackwell Year Book, Oxford, Eng., 1983—; chmn. Wolfe Med. Pub., London. Advisor Nat. Lekotek Ctr., originator toy lending libraries for handicapped children, Evanston, Ill., 1982—; former dep. chmn. devel. com. Providence St. Mel High Sch., Chgo., 1985. Served to 1st lt. U.S. Army, 1957-59. Mem. Am. Med. Pubs. Assn. (pres. 1987-88), Am. Assn. Pubs. (chmn. profl. div. 1981, chmn. libraries com. 1979). Clubs: University. Home: 950 N Michigan Ave Chicago IL 60611 Office: Yearbook Med Pubs Inc 200 N LaSalle St Chicago IL 60601

DILLARD, JAMES BORDEN, insurance executive; b. Aliceville, Ala., Oct. 7, 1937; s. Chester Austin and Annie Lee (Adams) D.; m. Mildred Hearn, June 1, 1963; children: Brian, Beth, Bonnie. BA, Howard Coll., 1956-60; student, So. Bapt. Theol. Sem., 1960-61, Southwestern Bapt. Theol. Sem., 1963; cert., Purdue U. Life Ins. Inst., 1971. Ordained to ministry Bapt. Ch. Agt. Pilot Life Ins. Co., Greenville, S.C., 1969-76; regional sales mgr. Am. Heritage Life Ins. Co., Greenville, 1980-83; dist. rep. Presbyn. Ministers' Fund, Greenville, 1985-88; exec. sales dir. Surety Capital Assocs., Greenville, 1983—; pres., cons. Surety Capitol Assocs., Greenville, 1988—; pres., cons. Southeastern Mktg. Assocs., 1984—. Assoc. chaplain St. Francis Hosp., Greenville, S.C., 1989—. Mem. Life Underwriters Assn. Home: 313 Poplar Ln Mauldin SC 29662 Office: Surety Capital Assocs 100 Executive Ctr Dr B156 Ste 225A Greenville SC 29615

DILLARD, JOAN HELEN, financial executive; b. Balt., June 12, 1951; d. Anthony Joseph and Frances Helen (Waclawski) Bartynski; m. Gordon Earl Dillard, Apr. 21, 1984; 1 child, Valerie Kay. A.A., Anne Arundel Community Coll., Md., 1973; B.A., U. Md., 1977; M.B.A., U. Balt., 1984. Instr. music Acad. Music, Glen Burnie, Md., 1972-77; cash mgr. Johns Hopkins Hosp., Balt., 1979-83, Md. Casualty Co., Balt., 1983-85; v.p., asst. treas. Am. Gen. Corp., Houston, 1985-89; v.p., treas. Am. Gen. Fin., Evansville, Ind., 1989—. Mem. Nat. Corp. Cash Mgmt. Assn., Houston Cash Mgmt. Assn. (v.p. 1986, pres. 1987), Nat. Assn. Corp. Treas. Office: Am Gen Fin 601 NW 2d St Evansville IN 47708

DILLARD, RODNEY JEFFERSON, real estate broker; b. Short Hills, N.J., Jan. 1, 1939; s. Albert Jefferson and Anne E. (Willingham) D.; m. Anne Palfrey Lanston, June 10, 1961 (div. 1985); children: Courtney Lanston, Carter Jefferson; m. Carole Baker Douglass, Apr. 14, 1989. BA, Rollins Coll., 1961. With A.M. Kidder Co., N.Y.C., 1961-62; with Previews, Inc., N.Y.C., 1962-63; with Previews, Inc., Palm Beach, Fla., 1963-79, regional v.p., 1967-70, v.p., 1970-79; pres., chmn. bd. Illustrated Properties, Inc., Palm Beach, Fla., 1976—; v.p., dir. Sotheby's Internat. Realty Corp., 1979—. Mem. Internat. Real Estate Fedn. Clubs: Sailfish, Bath and Tennis (Palm Beach), Palm Beach Yacht, Travelers (Paris). Home: 675 N Lake Way Palm Beach FL 33480 Office: Sotheby's Internat Realty Inc 440 Royal Palm Way Palm Beach FL 33480

DILLARD, WILLIAM, II, department store executive; b. 1945; married. Grad., U. Ark.; M.B.A., Harvard U. With Dillard Dept. Stores, Little Rock, 1967—, exec. v.p., 1973-77, pres. and chief operating officer, 1977—, also dir. Office: Dillard Dept Stores Inc 900 W Capitol Ave Box 486 Little Rock AR 72203 *

DILLARD, WILLIAM T., department stores company executive; b. Mineral Springs, Ark., 1914. B.B.A., U. Ark., 1935; M.S., Columbia U., 1937. Pres. Dillard Dept. Stores Inc., Little Rock, until 1977, chmn. bd., chief exec. officer, 1977—; chmn. bd. Frederick Atkins, Inc., N.Y.C.; mem. nat. adv. bd. First Comml. Bank, Little Rock. Mem. Nat. Retail Mchts. Assn. (dir.). Office: Dillard Dept Stores Inc 900 W Capitol Ave Box 486 Little Rock AR 72203 *

DILLE, EARL KAYE, utility company executive; b. Chillicothe, Mo., Apr. 25, 1927; s. George Earl and Josephine Christina (Kaye) D.; m. Martha Virginia Merrill, Sept. 8, 1951; children—Thomas Merrill, James Warren. B.S., U.S. Naval Acad., 1950; M.S., St. Louis U., 1961. With Union Elec. Co., St. Louis, 1957—, pres., 1988—, 1988—, also bd. dirs.; dir. Elec. Energy, Inc., Union Colliery Co., Merc. Bank, Merc. Bancorp. Inc.; pres. Asso. Industries Mo., 1974-76. Mem. adv. council Coll. Engring., U. Mo.; mem. exec. bd. St. Louis Area council Boy Scouts Am.; bd. dirs. Bethesda Hosps. and Homes, chmn., 1987—; bd. dirs. Webster U., Regional Commerce and Growth Assn. Served with USN, 1950-57; comdr. Res. Recipient Disting. Service in Engring award U. Mo., 1973, Alumni Merit award St. Louis U., 1974, Outstanding Engr. in Industry award Mo. Soc. Profl. Engrs., 1976, Silver Beaver award Boy Scouts Am., 1987. Mem. IEEE, Engrs. Club St. Louis (pres. 1977-78), Mo. Hist. Soc. (pres. 1987-89), Sigma Xi. Episcopalian. Clubs: Mason. (Grand master Mo. 1982-83), Bellerive Country, St. Louis.

DILLER, BARRY, entertainment company executive; b. San Francisco, Feb. 2, 1942; s. Michael and Reva (Addison) D. Vice pres. feature films and movies of week ABC, 1971-73, ABC (prime time TV), 1973-74; chmn. bd. Paramount Pictures Corp., 1974-84; pres. Gulf & Western Entertainment Group, 1983-84; chmn., chief exec. officer Twentieth Century Fox Film Corp., Los Angeles, 1984—, Fox, Inc., 1985—. Office: Fox Inc PO Box 900 Beverly Hills CA 90213 *

DILLER, CHARLES HERBERT, JR., corporate professional; b. Carlisle, Pa., Feb. 24, 1945; s. Charles Herbert Diller and Edith (Bruce) McConnell; m. Jane Elaine Eagle, Dec. 2, 1973; 1 child, Michael Charles. AA, Chaffey Coll., Alta Loma, Calif., 1966; BS in Acctg., Calif. Poly. U., Pomona, 1968. CPA, Md. Audit mgr. Peat, Marwick, Main & Co., Balt., 1971-77; sr. v.p., chief fin. officer, dir. JLG Industries, Inc., McConnellsburg, Pa., 1977—; bd. dirs. JLG Industries U.K. Ltd., Cumberland, Scotland, 1985—, Port McQuarie, Australia, 1987—. Mem. bus. adv. com. Shippensburg U., 1984.

Served to capt. USMC, 1968-71, Vietnam. Mem. Am. Inst. CPA's, Fin. Exec. Inst., Md. Assn. CPA's, Cen. Pa. Corp. Relations Soc. Republican. Home: 52 Obsidian Dr Chambersburg PA 17201 Office: JLG Industries Inc JLG Dr McConnellsburg PA 17233

DILLETT, GREGORY CRAFT, financial executive; b. Phila., Dec. 25, 1943; s. Robert Marshall and Jean Agnes (Craft) D.; m. Lynne Esther Reif, Oct. 17, 1964; children—Patrick, Alexis, Allison. BS in Acctg., St. Joseph's Coll., 1966. CPA, Pa. Staff acct., sr. supr. Arthur Young & Co., Phila., 1968-72, audit mgr., 1972-74; comptroller, gen. auditor Phila. Nat. Corp., 1974-76, v.p., comptroller, 1976-79, sr. v.p., comptroller, 1979-83; exec. v.p., chief fin. officer CoreStates Fin. Corp., Phila., 1983-86, vice chmn. fin. and adminstrn., 1986—, pres., dir.; bd. dirs. Phila. Internat. Bank, N.Y.C., Phila. Nat. Ltd., Hamilton Bank, Lancaster, Pa., CoreStates Enterprise Fund, Phila., Pa. Economy League. Mem. AICPA, Pa. Inst. CPA's, Fin. Execs. Inst., Bank Adminstrn. Inst., Huntingdon Valley Country Club. Republican. Roman Catholic. Home: 2600 Paper Mill Rd Huntingdon Valley PA 19006 Office: CoreStates Fin Corp NE Corner Broad & Chestnut Sts PO Box 7618 Philadelphia PA 19107

DILLING, KIRKPATRICK WALLWICK, lawyer; b. Evanston, Ill., Apr. 11, 1920; s. Albert W. and Elizabeth (Kirkpatrick) D.; m. Betty Ellen Bronson, June 18, 1942 (div. July 1944); m. Elizabeth Ely Tilden, Dec. 11, 1948; children—Diana Jean, Eloise Tilden, Victoria Walgreen, Albert Kirkpatrick. Student, Cornell U., 1939-40; B.S. in Law, Northwestern U., 1942; postgrad., DePaul U., 1946-47, L'Ecole Vaubier, Montreux, Switzerland; Degre Normal, Sorbonne U., Paris. Bar: Ill. 1947, Wis., Ind., Mich., Md., La., Tex., Okla., U.S. Ct. Appeals (2d, 3d, 5th, 7th, 8th, 9th, 10th, 11th, D.C. cirs.), U.S. Supreme Ct. Ptnr. Dilling and Dilling, Chgo., 1948—; gen. counsel Nat. Health Fedn., Cancer Control Soc.; dir. Dillman Labs.; v.p. Midwest Medic-Aide, Inc.; spl. counsel Herbalife (U.K.) Ltd., Herbalife Australasia Pty., Ltd.; lectr. on pub. health law. Contbr. articles to profl. publs. Bd. dirs. Nat. Health Fedn., Adele Davis Found. Served to 1st lt. AUS, 1943-46. Mem. ABA, Ill. Bar Assn., Chgo. Bar Assn., Assn. Trial Lawyers Am., Cornell Soc. Engrs., Am. Legion, Air Force Assn., Pharm. Advt. Club, Delta Upsilon. Republican. Episcopalian. Clubs: Rolls Royce Owners', Tower, Cornell U., Chicago. Home: 1120 Lee Rd Northbrook IL 60062 also: Casa Dorado Indian Wells CA 92260 Office: 150 N Wacker Dr Chicago IL 60601

DILLINGHAM, ROBERT BULGER, publishing executive; b. Buffalo, June 7, 1932; s. William O. and Loretta (Bulger) D.; m. Katherine A. Hunting, June 18, 1955; children: Katherine, Diane, Susan, Nancy, Carol. BA, Columbia U., 1955. Sales rep. Sports Illustrated, N.Y.C. and Chgo., 1958-67; divisional mgr. Sports Illustrated, Cleve. and Detroit, 1967-72; divisional ad mgr. Sports Illustrated, N.Y.C., 1972-77, ea. ad mgr., 1977-79, assoc. advt. dir., 1979-81; ad dir. U.S. News and World Report, N.Y.C., 1981-85; pub. Insight Mag., N.Y.C. and Washington, 1985—. With USAF, 1955-58. Mem. Silver Springs Country (Ridgefield, Conn.), Sky (N.Y.C.). Republican. Presbyterian. Office: Insight Mag 200 Park Ave Ste 1502 New York NY 10166

DILLMAN, GEORGE FRANKLIN, management and economic consultant, investor, financial executive; b. Coronado, Cal., Sept. 5, 1934; s. Wilbur Mitchell and Meadie (Ables) D.; m. Virginia Gayle Yeary, Sept. 1, 1961; children: Leesa Gayle, Mitchell Lynn, Virginia Louise, Laura Lynne. Student Abilene Christian Coll., 1952; BS, BBA U. Tex., 1958. Mng. ptnr. Dillman & Assocs., Dallas, 1968—; chmn., chief exec. officer Caprock Savs. and Loan Assn., 1982—;chmn., pres. Great West Bancshares, 1985—; cons., v.p. planning and devel. Friedrich Group of Wylain, Inc., 1977-82; chmn. exec. com. Preferred Properties Corp., 1982-83; pres. Geneva Basin Ski Corp., 1981-82; cons. govt. agys., fin. instns., mfg. cos., 1968—. Contbr. articles in field to profl. and ch. jours. Mem. univ. bd. Pepperdine U., Los Angeles, 1966-76, devel. bd. Abilene Christian U.; exec. com. Gov.'s Commn. on Physical Fitness, 1985—, Mayor's Criminal Justice Task Force; past chmn. bd. dirs. Tex. Tourist Devel. Agy.; trustee Southwestern Christian Coll., 1969—; chmn. Dallas Citizens/Police Review Bd., 1982—; Chmn. Dallas County Child Welfare Bd., 1982-88; bd. dirs. Community Council of Greater Dallas. Served with USNR, 1952-55. Democrat. Mem. Ch. of Christ. Home: 13809 Rockbend Pl Dallas TX 75240

DILLON, DAVID BRIAN, retail grocery executive; b. Hutchinson, Kans., Mar. 30, 1951; s. Paul Wilson and Ruth (Muirhead) D.; m. Dee A. Ehling, July 29, 1973; children: Jefferson, Heather, Kathryn. BS, U. Kans., 1973; JD, So. Meth. U., 1976. V.p. Fry's Food Stores of Ariz. Inc. div. Dillon Cos. Inc., Phoenix, 1978-79, exec. v.p., 1979-83; v.p. Dillon Cos. Inc., Hutchinson, 1983-86, pres., 1986—; bd. dirs. 1st Nat. Bank Hutchinson. Chmn. Leadership Hutchinson, 1986-87, Leadership Kans., 1988. Mem. ABA, U. Kans. Alumni Assn., Order of Coif, Sigma Chi (Balfour award 1973). Republican. Presbyterian. Office: Dillon Cos Inc 700 E 30th Ave Hutchinson KS 67502

DILLON, DENNIS FRANCIS, contract adminstrator; b. Phila., Apr. 5, 1947; s. Dennis Francis and Josephine Rita (Wawrzyniak) D.; m. Suzanne Marie Fitzpatrick, Sept. 13, 1969; children: Dennis Francis, Andrew David, Patrick William. BS, Pa. State U., 1973. Asst. contract adminstr. Transam. DeLaval, Inc., Trenton, N.J., 1975-78; contract adminstr. ChemPump div. Crane Co., Warrington, Pa., 1978-80; sr. contract adminstr. Stearns Catalytic Corp., Phila., 1980-85; mgr. contract adminstrn. SPS/Techs., Inc./Hartman Systems, Hatfield, Pa., 1985-88, Hercules Aerospace Display System, Inc., Hatfield, Pa., 1988—. Served with USNR, 1966-72. Mem. Nat. Contract Mgmt. Assn. Democrat. Roman Catholic. Home: 1121 Jeffrey Ln Langhorne PA 19047 Office: Hercules Aerospace Display System Inc 2321 Topaz Dr Hatfield PA 19440

DILLON, FRANCIS PATRICK, human resources executive, management consultant; b. Long Beach, Calif., Mar. 15, 1937; s. Wallace Myron and Mary Elizabeth (Land) D.; B.A., U. Va., 1959; M.S., Def. Fgn. Affairs Sch., 1962; M.B.A., Pepperdine U., 1976; m. Vicki Lee Dillon, Oct. 1980; children: Cary Randolph, Francis Patrick Jr., Randee, Rick. Traffic mgr., mgr. personnel svcs. Pacific Telephone Co., Sacramento and Lakeport, Calif., 1966-69; asst. mgr. manpower planning and devel. Pan-Am. World Airways, N.Y.C., 1969-71; mgr. personnel and orgn. devel. Continental Airlines, Los Angeles, 1971-74; dir. personnel Farwest Svcs., Inc., Irvine, Calif., 1974; dir. human resources Bourns, Inc., Riverside, Calif., 1974-80; dir. employee and community relations MSI Data Corp., 1980-83; pres. Pavi Enterprises, 1983—; mgmt. cons., 1983—; pres., chief exec. officer Personnel Products & Svcs., Inc., 1984—; pres. Meditrans Inc. Bd. dirs. Health Svcs. Maintenance Orgn., Inc., Youth Svcs. Ctr., Inc.; vol. precinct worker. Served to lt. comdr. USN, 1959-66; asst. naval attaché, Brazil, 1963-65. Recipient Disting. Svc. award Jaycees, 1969; Jack Cates Meml. Vol. of Year award Youth Svc. Ctr., 1977. Mem. Assn. Internal Mgmt. Cons.'s, Am. Soc. Personnel Adminstrn., Personnel Indsl. Relations Assn., Am. Soc. Tng. and Devel., Am. Electronics Assn. (human resources com., chmn. human resources symposium). Republican. Episcopalian. Clubs: Mission Viejo Sailing, YMCA Bike, Mission Viejo Ski, Caving, Toastmasters (pres. 1966-67), Have Dirt Will Travel. Office: Personnel Products & Svcs Inc 27331 Via Amistoso Mission Viejo CA 92692

DILLON, GARY G., manufacturing company executive; b. Eaton, Ohio, May 21, 1934; s. M.H. and E.L. (Clensy) D.; m. Beverly Mulholland, Jan. 2, 1954; children: Kristen, Deborah, Kirk. BSBA, Miami U., Oxford, Ohio, 1955. With Philip Carey Corp., Cin., 1955-57, Pillsbury Co., Mpls., 1957-78; exec. v.p., chief operating officer, Chgo. office King-Seeley Thermos Co. subs. Household Internat., Prospect Heights, Ill., 1978-81, pres., chief exec. officer, 1981-82; pres., chief exec. officer Household Mfg. Inc. subs. Household Internat., Prospect Heights, 1982-89, Schwitzer Inc., Deerfield, Ill., 1989—; also bd. dirs. Schwitzer Inc., Deerfield; bd. dirs. Household Internat. Office: Schwitzer Inc 1020 Milwaukee Ave Deerfield IL 60015

DILLON, GEORGE CHAFFEE, manufacturing company executive; b. Kansas City, Mo., Oct. 29, 1922; s. Edward J. and Mary (Coon) D.; m. Joan Alamo Kent, Sept. 11, 1948; children: Kent, Courtney, Emily. BS, Harvard U., 1944, MBA, 1948. Adminstrv. asst. J. A. Bruening Co., Kansas City, Mo., 1948-51; with Butler Mfg. Co., Kansas City, Mo., 1951-86, treas., from 1960, v.p., 1961-63, exec. v.p., 1963-67, pres., 1967-78, chmn. bd., chief exec. officer, 1978-86; chmn. Manville Corp., Denver, 1986—; bd. dirs. Johns Manville Corp., Phelps Dodge Corp., Newhall Land and Farming Co., Astec Industries, Chattanooga. Past. chmn. bd. trustees Midwest Research Inst., Kansas City, Mo.; trustee Mayo Found., Rochester, Minn., Children's Mercy Hosp., Kansas City, Mo.; bd. overseers Harvard U., 1980-86. Lt. USNR, 1943-46. Home: 5045 Wornall Rd Kansas City MO 64112 Office: Manville Corp 5045 Wornall Rd PO Box 5108 Denver CO 80127

DILLON, GREGORY RUSSELL, hotel executive; b. Chgo., Aug. 26, 1922; s. Gregory Thomas and Margaret Moore (Russell) D.; m. Nancy Jane Huntsberger, Nov. 8, 1969; children: Michael Gregory, Patricia Jean, Margaret Esther, Richard Thomas, Daniel Russell. Student, Elmhurst Coll., Ill., 1941-43, 45-46; JD, DePaul U., Chgo., 1948. Bar: Ill. Sole practice Chgo.; ptnr. Friedman Mulligan Dillon & Urist, Chgo., 1950-63; asst. to pres. Hilton Hotels Corp., Beverly Hills, Calif., 1963-65, v.p., asst. sec., 1965-71, sr. v.p., asst. sec., 1971-80, exec. v.p., also bd. dirs., 1980—; pres. Conrad Internat. Hotels, 1986—, also bd. dirs.; trustee Wells Fargo Mortgage & Equity Trust, San Francisco, 1975—; bd. dirs. Jupiters Mgmt. Ltd., Surfers Paradise, Queensland, Australia. Served to 1st lt. USAAF, 1943-46, ETO. Mem. Urban Land Inst. (trustee 1980—, trustee found. 1981—), ABA, Ill. Bar Assn., Chgo. Bar Assn., Nat. Realty Com. (chmn. exec. com. 1979), Am. Hotel and Motel Assn. Republican. Roman Catholic. Clubs: Chicago Athletic (Chgo.); Bel-Air Country (Los Angeles); Marco Polo (N.Y.C.). Office: Hilton Hotels Corp 9336 Civic Ctr Dr Beverly Hills CA 90210

DILLON, JACK DUDLEY, retail executive; b. South Bend, Ind., June 3, 1924; s. Russell D. and Mary Pauline (Cripe) D.; m. Jean Boller, Oct. 5, 1946; children: John, Mark, Matthew. BS in Bus. Adminstrn. and Personnel Mgmt., Ind. U., 1949. Control buyer R.F.W. Spiegel Inc., Oak Brook, Ill., 1949-52; buyer children wear R.F.W. Spiegel Inc., Oak Brook, 1952-63, buyer, 1963-72, sr. buyer R.F.W., 1972-78, merchandise mgr., 1978-85, v.p. G.M.M., mem. Strategic Long Range Planning Com., 1985—. Charter mem. Rep. Presdl. Task Force, Washington, 1982, trustee, 1983; mem. Nat. Rep. Conressional Com., 1984; sponsor G.O.P. Victory Fund, Washington, 1983. Lt. USAF, 1942-46. Decorated Disting. Flying Cross, Air Medal with 3 clusters, Purple Heart. Mem. Midlothian Country Club, John D MacArthur Country Club. Republican. Home: 5221 W Oak St Oak Lawn IL 60453 Office: RFW Spiegel Regency Towres Oak Brook IL 60522-9009

DILLON, JOHN ROBERT, III, communications executive; b. Valdosta, Ga., Oct. 7, 1941; s. John Robert and Mary (Murphey) D.; m. Joyce F. Dillon, Sept. 2, 1967 (div. 1978); 1 child, John Robert, IV; m. 2d, Ann Hudgins, Apr. 17, 1982; children—Philip Jones, Ansley Jones, Jennifer Jones. B.E.E., Ga. Inst. Tech., 1963; M.B.A., Harvard U., 1968. Gen. mgr. cable div. Sci. Atlanta, Inc., 1970-74, treas., 1978-81; exec. v.p. Fuqua Nat., Inc., Atlanta, 1974-78, pres., 1981-82; v.p. fin. Cox Communications, Inc., Atlanta, 1982-85; v.p., chief fin. officer Cox Enterprises, Inc., Atlanta, 1985, also bd. dirs. Served as 1st lt. U.S. Army, 1964-66. Mem. Broadcast Fin. Mgmt. Assn., Fin. Execs. Inst. (dir. 1983-84). Presbyterian. Clubs: Cherokee Town and Country, Ravinia (Atlanta); Wade Hampton Golf (Cashiers, N.C.). Lodge: Rotary. Home: 115 E Chambord Dr NW Atlanta GA 30327 Office: Cox Enterprises Inc 1400 Lake Hearn Dr Atlanta GA 30319

DILLON, PAUL WILSON, supermarket chain executive; b. Hutchinson, Kans., Aug. 4, 1926; s. Clyde Wilson and Flora L. (Jones) D.; m. Ruth Muirhead, Aug. 19, 1949; children—David B., Elizabeth Ann Dillon Ramseyer, Mary M. Dillon Esau. B.S. in Bus. U. Kans., 1950. With Dillon Cos., Inc., Hutchinson, 1950—; sec.-treas. Dillon Cos., Inc., 1965-80, sr. v.p., 1980—, also dir. Dir. First Fed. Savs. & Loan Assn., Hutchinson.; Active local Boy Scouts Am., 1955—; trustee, treas. Wesley Towers Methodist Retirement Home, 1970; trustee First Presbyn. Ch. of Hutchinson Hosp. Served with USNR, 1944-45. Mem. Am. Soc. Corp. Secs., Hutchinson C. of C. (bd. dirs.), Am. Legion, VFW, Phi Kappa Psi. Republican. Presbyterian. Club: Elks. Home: 207 Kisiwa Pkwy Hutchinson KS 67501 Office: Dillon Cos Inc 700 E 30th Ave Hutchinson KS 67501

DILLON, RAY E., JR., supermarket company executive; b. 1924; married. Student, Kans. U. With Dillon Cos., Hutchinson, Kans., 1946—, pres., chief exec. officer, 1969-72, chmn., 1972—, also dir.; dir. The Kroger Co., Cin. Office: Dillon Cos Inc 700 E 30th Ave PO Box 1266 Hutchinson KS 67501 •

DILLON, RAY WILLIAM, engineering technician; b. China Lake, Calif., Aug. 8, 1954; s. Duane L. and Audrey J. (Amende) D.; m. Kathy M. Shrum , Sept. 3, 1980; 1 child, Stephanie. Student, U. Okla., 1976-78, Oklahoma City Comm. Coll., 1986; BA, So. Nazarene U., Bethany, Okla., 1987. Shop foreman Arch/Mill Fixture Co., Oklahoma City, 1977-79; sr. design tech. B&B Fire Protection, Oklahoma City, 1979-80; lead design tech. Grinell Fire Protection, Oklahoma City, 1980-82; gen. mgr. A.L. Fire Protection, Oklahoma City, 1982-87; store mgr. Master Systems Ltd., Oklahoma City, 1987—. Mem. Nat. Inst. Cert. Engring. Technicians (cert.), Oklahoma City IBM-PC Users Group, Okla. Fire Protection Contractors Assn. (sec. 1986-87, chmn 1987). Republican. Baptist. Office: Master Systems Ltd 230 S Quadrum Oklahoma City OK 73108

DILLON, ROBERT MORTON, association executive; b. Seattle, Oct. 27, 1923; s. James Richard and Lucille (Morton) D.; m. Mary Charlotte Beeson, Jan. 6, 1943; children: Robert Thomas, Colleen Marie Dillon Brown, Patrick Morton. Student, U. Ill., 1946-47; BArch., U. Wash., 1949; MA in Architecture, U. Fla., 1954. Registered architect, Fla. Designer-draftsman Williams and Longstreet (Architects), Greenville, S.C., 1949-50, William G. Lyles, Bissett, Carlisle & Wolff (Architects), Columbia, S.C., 1949-50, Robert M. Dillon and Wm. B. Eaton (Architects), Gainesville, Fla., 1952-55; staff architect Bldg. Rsch. Adv. Bd., Nat. Acad. Scis.-NRC, Washington, 1955-56; project dir. Bldg. Rsch. Adv. Bd., Nat. Acad. Scis.-NRC, 1956-58, exec. dir., 1958-77; exec. sec. U.S. nat. com. for Conseil Internat. du Batiment, 1962-74: Sec. U.S. Planning Com. 2d Internat. Conf. on Permafrost, Yakutsk, USSR, 1972-74; exec. asst. to pres. Nat. Inst. Bldg. Scis., Washington, 1978-81, v.p., 1982-84, acting contr., 1983-84; exec. v.p. Am. Coun. Constrn. Edn., Washington, 1984—; Asst. prof. architecture Clemson Coll., 1949-50; instr., asst. prof. architecture U. Fla., 1950-55; lectr. structural theory and design Cath. U. Am., 1956-62; guest lectr. Air Force Inst. Tech., Wright-Patterson AFB, 1964-65; disting. faculty Acad. Code Adminstrn. and Enforcement, U. Ill., 1972, profl. ctr. engring. George Washington U., 1973-77, 81-82; vis. prof. architecture U. Utah, 1978; vis. prof. Coll. Environ. Design, U. Okla., 1984, adj. assoc. prof. bldg. sci., 1985-87. Author: (with S.W. Crawley) Steel Buildings: Analysis and Design, 1970, 3d edit., 1983; contbg. author: Funk and Wagnall's New Ency, 1972; editor-in-chief Guide to the Use of NEHRP Provisions in Earthquake Resistant Design of Bldgs., 1987; contbg. author Encyclopedia of Architecture, 1989. Cons. Ednl. Facilities Labs., N.Y.C., 1958-71; Mem. adv. com., low-income housing demonstration program HUD, Washington, 1964-67; mem. working groups U.S.-USSR Agreement on Housing and Other Constrn., 1975—; mem. subpanel on housing White House Panel on Civilian Tech., Washington, 1961-62; mem. advs. to the F. Stuart Fitzpatrick Meml. Award Trustee, 1969-84 , chmn., 1974-78; mem. adv. panel Basic Homes Program OEO and HUD, 1972-77; mem. Nat. Adv. Coun. on Rsch. in Energy Conservation, 1975-78; mem. adv. com. Coun. Am. Bldg. Ofcls., 1976-86; mem. tech. coun. on bldg. codes and standards Nat. Conf. of States, 1977-78. With USNR, 1942-45. Mem. AIA (mem. com. on rsch. for architecture 1962-67, chmn. 1969, chmn. com. archtl. barriers 1967-68, mem. nat. housing com. 1970-72, 84-85), Nat. Acad. Code Adminstrn. (trustee 1976-80, mem. exec. com. 1978-82, mem. new bd. dirs. 1980-82, 83-84, sec.-treas. 1981-82, life mem.), Md. Soc. Architects, ASCE (task com. on cold regions 1977-79, tech. coun. on codes and standards, exec. com. 1976-81, sec, tech. coun. on codes and standards, exec. com. 1977-78, mem. tech. coun. on cold regions engring., exec. com. 1976-84, vice-chmn. 1980-81, chmn. 1981), Am. Inst. Steel Constrn. (profl.), Am. Inst. Constructors, Sigma Lambda Chi. Home: 811 Arrington Dr Silver Spring MD 20901 Office: 1015 15th St NW Ste 700 Washington DC 20005

DILLON, W. MARTIN, retired steel and wire manufacturing executive; b. Sterling, Ill., Mar. 19, 1910; s. Paul Washington and Crete (Blackman) D.; m. Helene Reynolds, June 20, 1931; children—Peter W., Margo, Gale (Mrs. Philip Inglee). Grad., Culver Mil. Acad., 1929; student, Babson Inst., 1929-30; H.H.D., DePaul U., U. Chgo., U. Dubuque, Iowa. Asst. to pres. Northwestern Steel & Wire Co. (name formerly Northwestern Barb Wire Co.), 1939-48, pres., 1951-80, chmn. bd., 1980-86, chmn. emeritus, 1986-88. Bd. dirs. Sterling-Rock Falls Community Trust. Mem. Assn. Iron and Steel Engrs., C. of C., Am. Iron and Steel Inst. (dir.), NAM, Cum Laude Soc. (Culver Mil. Acad.). Club: Union League (Chgo.). Home: PO Box 537 Sterling IL 61081 Office: Dillon Found 2804 W LeFevre Rd Sterling IL 61081

DILWORTH, ANN EVANS, publishing company executive; b. Cleve., Jan. 1, 1947; d. Edmund Randall and Dorothy Monica (Potts) Dilworth. BS, Northwestern U., 1969, MS, 1970. Freelance writer San Francisco, 1971-73; instr. San Francisco State U., 1973-74; editor Addison-Wesley Pub. Co., Reading, Mass., 1975-77, editor-in-chief, 1977-80, gen. mgr., 1980-83, exec. v.p., 1983-88, pres. Gen. and Internat. Pub. Group, 1988—. Author: Working Free, 1972. Mem. Am. Assn. Pubs. (bd. dirs. 1988, exec. council 1987), Corp. Bd. Resource. Episcopalian.

DILWORTH, GRACE DOROTHY, health products company executive; b. N.Y.C., May 7, 1930; d. George Weldon and Martha Ruth (Ehleben) D. RN, L.I. Coll. Hosp., 1951; BS in Nursing, Incarnate Word Coll., 1963; postgrad., Trinity U., San Antonio, 1972-73. Staff nurse L.I. Coll. Hosp., Bklyn., 1951-55, pediatric supr., 1955-57; pediatric supr. Robert B. Green Hosp., San Antonio, 1957-63; dir. nurses Santa Rosa Children's Hosp., San Antonio, 1964-72; assoc. adminstr. San Antonio Community Hosp., 1973-78, St. Luke's Luth. Hosp., San Antonio, 1978-79; v.p. Am. Healthcare Mgmt., Dallas, 1979-82, sr. v.p., 1982—. Mem. Am. Nurses Assn., Tex. Hosp. Assn. (bd. dirs. 1973-78, 79—). Republican. Office: Am Healthcare Mgmt Inc 14160 Dallas Pkwy Ste 900 Dallas TX 75240

DIMAIO, VIRGINIA SUE, gallery owner; b. Houston, July 6, 1921; d. Jesse Lee and Gabriella Sue (Norris) Chambers; AB, U. Redlands, 1943; student U. So. Calif., 1943-45, Scripps Coll., 1943, Pomona Coll., 1945; m. James V. DiMaio, 1955 (div. 1968); children: Victoria, James V. Owner, dir. Galeria Capistrano, San Juan Capistrano and Santa Fe, N.Mex., 1979—; founder Mus. Women in Arts, Washington; cons., appraiser Southwestern and Am. Indian Handcrafts; lectr. Calif. State U., Long Beach; established ann. Helen Hardin Meml. scholarship for woman artist grad. Inst. Am. Indian Art, Santa Fe, also ann. Helen Hardin award for outstanding artist at Indian Market, S.W. Assn. on Indian Affairs, Santa Fe. Recipient Bronze Plaque Recognition award Navajo Tribal Mus., 1977. Mem. Indian Arts and Crafts Assn., S.W. Assn. Indian Affairs, Heard Mus., San Juan Capistano C. of C. Republican. Roman Catholic. Office: 31681 Camino Capistrano San Juan Capistrano CA 92675 also: 409 Canyon Rd Santa Fe NM 87501

DI MANTOVA, WALTER DARIO, educational administrator; b. N.Y.C., Nov. 8, 1958; s. Anthony John and Gloria Connaught (Woods) Di M.; m. Polly Carter Paulson, June 12, 1982; 1 child, Caitlin Emma. BA summa cum laude, U. Colo., 1981; MA in Anthropology, U. Mich., 1982. Spl. cons. dept. health County of Washtenaw, Ann Arbor, 1986-87; pres. Corp. Culture Cons., Ann Arbor, 1987—; vis. lectr. anthropology, assoc. dir. corp. edn. ctr. programs Ea. Mich. U., Ypsilanti, 1986—, project co-dir. UAW-Chrysler Paid Ednl. Leave. Author: (manual) Smoking in Work, 1986. Chmn. conf. com. Visitor and Conv. Bur., Ypsilanti, 1986-87; sec. Washtenaw AIDS Edn. Network, Ann Arbor, 1987—, v.p. strategic planning and mgmt. forum. Mem. Inst. Organizational Risk Reduction (founding). Democrat. Home: 1007 Arborview Ann Arbor MI 48103 Office: Corp Edn Ctr 119 Pearl Ypsilanti MI 48197

DI MARCO, GABRIEL ROBERT, tobacco company executive; b. Camden, N.J., July 31, 1927; m. Mary Senisch, June 12, 1949; children: Ann Marie, Lynn Mary, Robert Louis, Diane Maria, David Michael. BS, Rutgers U., 1954, PhD in Plant Pathology, 1959. Prof. food sci. Rutgers U., New Brunswick, N.J., 1959-74, chmn. dept. food sci., 1963-74, hon. prof. food sci., 1975—; group dir. basic and health scis. Cen. Research, Gen. Foods, White Plains, N.Y., 1975-77, dir., 1977-82; v.p. Research & Devel., R.J. Reynolds Tobacco Co., Winston-Salem, N.C., 1982-85, sr. v.p., 1985—; mem. White House adv. com. Sci. and Edn. Research Grants, Washington, 1982—; mem. Council for Tobacco Research Bd., N.Y.C., 1982—; mem. Agrl. Research Inst. Nat. Acad. Sci., 1964-75; bd. govs. Food Update, Food & Drug Law Inst., Washington, 1973; mem. Pa. State Agrl. Sci. Feasibility Study Group, 1986, AMA Food Ind. Liaison Adv. Panel, Nat. Research Council Adv. Bd. Mil. Personnel Supplies. Tech. editor Meat Sci., 1961-64; sci. editor Meat Processing mag., 1964-66. Fellow Inst. Food Technologists (bd. dirs. 1970-75, vice chmn. 1972-73); mem. Sigma Xi, Phi Tau Sigma, Alpha Zeta.

DIMARTINO, JOSEPH SALVATORE, investment company executive; b. Bklyn., Oct. 2, 1943; s. Raymond and Celia (Mecurio) DiM.; m. Linda Jeanne Rappa, Oct. 21, 1967; children: Joseph James, Jennifer Lynne. B.S. in Econs., Manhattan Coll., 1965; postgrad., NYU, 1966-68. Credit analyst Dun and Bradstreet, N.Y.C., 1965-66; investment officer Chase Manhattan Bank, N.Y.C., 1966-70, 2d v.p., 1971; investment officer, dir. various mut. funds The Dreyfus Corp., N.Y.C., 1973—; pres., chief operating officer The Dreyfus Corp., 1982—. Office: Dreyfus Corp 767 Fifth Ave 35th Fl New York NY 10153 •

DIMARZIO, PATRICIA ELIZABETH, small business owner; b. Leominster, Mass., Apr. 24, 1941; d. Raoul Arthur and Eleanor Mae (English) Brisson; m. Robert Christopher DiMarzio, Ju. 19, 1958; children: John Raoul, Steven Robert, Julie Louise, Robert Dean, James Richard. Grad. high sch., Leominster. Sec. E.R. Carpenter Co., Leominster, 1978-81; mgr. office James Monroe Wire and Cable, Sterling, Mass., 1981-82, Gateway Products Corp., Leominster, 1982-85; treas., clk., owner, bd. dirs. J.D. Industries Inc., Fitchburg, Mass., 1985—. Roman Catholic. Home: 62 Dupont Cir Leominster MA 01453 Office: JD Industries Inc 145 Authority Dr Fitchburg MA 01420

DI MEDIO-REIHER, ANGELA MARIA, personnel specialist; b. Bryn Mawr, Pa., Feb. 7, 1955; d. Angelo Marino and Maria (D'Eramo) DiMedio; m. Leonard DiMartino (div. 1988); m. John F. Reiher, 1988. BE, Cabrini Coll., 1977; cert., St. Charles Sem., Phila., 1978. Tchr. elem. sch. St. Callistus Sch., Archdiocese of Phila., 1977-83; personnel asst. Bryn Mawr Trust, 1983-84, mgr. personnel, 1984-85, personnel officer, 1985-86, v.p. personnel, 1986-88, v.p. tng. and devel., 1987-88; regional dir. Careers USA, Wilmington, Del., 1988—. Bd. dirs. Wellness Coun. Delaware Valley, Norristown, Pa., 1985—; vote tallier Haverford (Pa.) Rep. Party, 1987—. Mem. Am. Soc. Personnel Adminstrs., Nat. Assn. Banking Women, Am. Bankers Assn., Am. Inst. Banking, Internat. Nat. Employee Recreation Assn., Assn. Personnel Women (v.p. fin. and adminstrn. 1987—, pres. southeastern Pa. chpt. 1986-87), Llanerach Country Club. Home: 1539 Villa Rd Wilmington DE 19809 Office: Careers USA 711 Market St Wilmington DE 19809

DI MINO, ANDRÉ ANTHONY, manufacturing executive, consultant; b. Bklyn., Aug. 24, 1955; s. Alfonso and Nancy (Zarbo) DiM.; m. Jenny DiCapua, May 30, 1981. BS in Indsl. Engring., Fairleigh Dickinson U., 1978, MBA in Fin., 1981. Engr. ADMTronics Inc., Emerson, N.J., 1977-79; dir. tech. ADMTronics Inc., Emerson, 1979-82; sec./treas. ADMTronics Inc., Northvale, N.J., 1982-86; exec. v.p. and dir. ADMTronics Inc., Northvale, 1986—; ptnr., cons. Tech. Mgmt. Consulting, Woodcliff Lake, N.J., 1978—; dir. Am. Doctor's Fin. Corp., Summit, N.J, 1987—; v.p. and dir. Sonotron Med. Systems Inc., Northvale, 1988—; VET-Sonotron Systems Inc., Northvale, 1988—. Inventor in field. Councilman Council Borough of Woodcliff Lake, 1984—, pres. 1987-88. Republican. Roman Catholic. Office: ADMTronics Inc 224-S Pegasus Ave Northvale NJ 07647

DIMITRIADIS, ANDRE C., health care executive; b. Istanbul, Turkey, Sept. 29, 1940; s. Constantine N. and Terry D. B.S., Robert Coll., Istanbul, 1964; M.S., Princeton U., 1965; M.B.A., NYU, 1967, Ph.D., 1970. Analyst Mobil Oil Internat., N.Y.C., 1965-67; mgr. TWA, N.Y.C., 1967-73; dir. Pan Am. Airways, N.Y.C., 1973-76; asst. treas. Pan Am. Airways, 1976-79; v.p., chief fin. officer Air Calif., Newport Beach, 1979-82; exec. v.p. fin. and adminstrn., chief fin. officer Western Airlines, Los Angeles, 1982-85; dir. Western Airlines; sr. v.p. (fin) Am. Med. Internat., from 1985, chief fin. officer, 1985—, exec. v.p., 1988—, also dir. Democrat. Greek Orthodox. Office: Am Med Internat Inc 414 N Camden Dr Beverly Hills CA 90210

DIMITRIOU, THEODORE, data processing executive; b. Dayton, Ohio, Aug. 31, 1926; s. George and Evangelia (Kessis) D.; m. Chrissoula Economides, Sept. 1, 1950; children: Kristy, Constantine, Andrew, James, Gregory. BA, Kings Point, 1947, Miami U., 1950. Tech. researcher Standard Register Co., Dayton, 1952-59; with quality control Wallace Press, Chgo., 1959-60; plant mgr. Wallace Bus. Forms, Clinton, Ill., 1960-64, New Brunswick, N.J., 1964-67; v.p. mfr. East coast Wallace Bus. Forms, Luray, Va., 1967-68; v.p. mfg. corp. Wallace Bus. Forms, Chgo., 1968-70, exec. v.p., 1971-74; pres., chief exec. officer Wallace Bus. Forms, Hillside, Ill., 1974—; chmn. Wallace Computer Svcs., Hillside, 1979—, also bd. dirs.; bd. dirs. Walgreens Inc., Deerfield, Calumet Industries, Chgo. Served to lt. j.g., 1950-52. Recipient Gold award Wall Street Transcript, 1983, 84, 85, 87, 88; named to Printing Industry Hall of Fame. Mem. Ill. Mfg. Assn. (bd. dirs.), Thorngate Club. Greek Orthodox. Home: 63 A Saint Marys Rd Mettawa IL 60048 Office: Wallace Computer Svcs Inc 4600 Roosevelt Rd Hillside IL 60162

DIMLING, JOHN ARTHUR, research executive; b. Pitts., Apr. 9, 1938; s. John Arthur and Elizabeth (Powell) D.; m. Marilyn Jean O'Connor; children: Courtney O'Connor, Meredith O'Connor. A.B., Dartmouth Coll., 1960; M.S., Carnegie Mellon U., 1962; J.D., George Washington U., 1977. Bar: Md. 1977, D.C. 1978. Group mgr. Spindletop Rsch. Corp., Lexington, Ky., 1965-69; v.p. rsch. analysis Nat. Assn. Broadcasters, Washington, 1969-79; dir. planning & policy Corp. Pub. Broadcasting, Washington, 1979-82; exec. dir., chief exec. officer Electronic Media Rating Council, N.Y.C., 1982-85; sr. v.p. A.C. Nielsen Co., N.Y.C., 1985-88, exec. v.p., 1988—; chmn. Coltram, N.Y.C., 1969-79; asst. treas. Broadcast Rating Coun., N.Y.C., 1971-79; cons. Western Broadcasting Corp., Missoula, Mont., 1981; sec., treas. Electronic Media Rating Coun., N.Y.C., 1970-72. Author: (with others) The Role of Analysis in Regulatory Decision Making-- The Case of Cable Television, 1973; contbr. articles to profl. jours., book. Bd. dirs. Advt. Rsch. Found., 1989—. Lt. U.S. Army, 1963-65. Mem. ABA, Radio-TV Rsch. Coun., Ardsley Country (bd. govs. 1987—), Dartmouth (N.Y.). Home: 198 Judson Ave Dobbs Ferry NY 10522 Office: AC Nielsen Co 1290 Ave of Americas New York NY 10104

DIMOND, THOMAS, investment advisory company executive; b. Scarsdale, N.Y., Jan. 24, 1916; s. George A. and Jessie (Kennedy) D.; B.A. magna cum laude, Princeton U., 1939; M.B.A., Harvard U., 1941. Mem. faculty Wharton Sch. Fin., U. Pa., 1948; economist, account mgr. Lionel D. Edie & Co., 1948-50; economist, mgr. comml. research Youngstown Sheet and Tube Co. (Ohio), 1951-56; sr. account mgr., security analyst deVegh & Co., N.Y.C., 1956-60; pres. Humes-Schmidlapp Assos., N.Y.C., 1960—; dir. Mercer Mgmt. Corp., co-mgr. Mercer Fund, 1963-67; dir. Scudder Spl. Fund, 1967-72, Scudder Duv-Vest, 1968-71; gen. partner HS Spl. Fund. Trustee, Humes Found., 1963—. Served to capt. USAAF, 1941-46. Mem. N.Y. Soc. Security Analysts. Episcopalian. Clubs: Racquet and Tennis, Down Town Assn. (N.Y.C.). Contbr. articles to profl. publs. Home: 200 E 66th St New York NY 10021 Office: 345 Park Ave New York NY 10154

DIMSDALE, PARKS B., marketing educator; b. Atlanta, Nov. 23, 1934; s. Parks and Eugenia Paris Dimsdale; m. Bonnie M. Trinka, July 25, 1974. B.B.A., Ga. State U., 1961; M.B.A., Emory U., 1962; Ph.D., U. Fla., 1970. Cert. mgmt. cons. Assoc. prof. La. State U., Baton Rouge, 1969-71; exec. v.p. Purcell Cons., Decatur, Ga., 1971-73; prin. Dimsdale Assocs., Atlanta, 1973-78; dir. bus. programs U. W. Fla., Panama City, 1978-82; chmn. mktg. dept., 1982-87 , prof., 1985—; assoc. dean 1987; prof. and dean coll. bus., Pensacola, 1988—; cons. Bapt. Hosp., Pensacola, Ch. of Commerce, Okaloosa Guidance Clinic, Gulf Coast Community Coll., MDS Imaging, Atlanta, Dimsdale Assocs., Gulf Breeze, Fla., 1982—. Author: A History of Cotton Producers Association, 1971; (with John Wright) Pioneers in Marketing, 1974. Vice pres., bd. dirs. Atlanta Assn. Retarded Citizens, 1975-78; campaign coordinator Mary Hitt for Lt. Gov. of Ga., 1974. Served with USN, 1956-58. Recipient Outstanding Prof. award U. W. Fla., 1980, 81, Disting. Service award U. W. Fla. Mem. Am. Mktg. Assn. (v.p. 1986-88), N.W. Fla. Mktg. Assn. (founder, pres. 1984-86), Pensacola C. of C. (com. chmn. 1983—), So. Mktg. Assn., Acad. Mktg. Sci. Republican. Avocations: travel; biking. Office: U West Fla Coll Bus Pensacola FL 32514-5752

DIMUN, ANTHONY JOHN, accountant, financial company executive; b. Trenton, Apr. 6, 1943; s. George and Mae Daria (Gross) D.; BS in Acctg., Rider Coll., 1965; postgrad. Rutgers U., 1973; m. Bonnie Widelock, July 1, 1967; children—Amy, Ross. Staff acct. L.H. Linowitz & Co., 1964-67; mgr. Ernst & Whinney (former S.D. Leidesdorf & Co.), N.Y.C., 1967-76; ptnr. Goldstein Golub Kessler & Co., P.C., N.Y.C., 1976-87; exec. v.p., chief fin. officer Vital Signs Inc., 1987—, also bd. dirs.; founder, mng. dir. merger and acquisition adv. firm Strategic Concepts, Inc. Bd. dirs. ICor AB Acquisition Corp. With USAF, 1968-70. CPA, N.Y., N.J. Mem. Am. Inst. CPA's, N.Y. Soc. CPA's (mem. various coms.), Assn. for Corp. Growth. Writer speeches and articles Found. for Acctg. Edn. N.Y. Inst. Fin. and Robert Morris Assocs. Home: 3 Queens Rd East Brunswick NJ 08816 Office: 599 Lexington Ave New York NY 10022

DINAPOLI, THOMAS JOHN, furniture company executive; b. N.Y.C., Apr. 17, 1943; s. Joseph A. and Angela B. (Costantino) DiN.; m. Shan Paula Bowen, May 30, 1970. BBA, Pace U., 1964. Fin. analyst Am. Can Co., Greenwich, Conn., 1966-70, Martin Marietta Inc., Bethesda, Md., 1971-77; v.p. adminstrn. Marietta Resources Inc., Bethesda, 1978-80; v.p. fin. and adminstrn. Atelier Internat. Ltd., Plainview, N.Y., 1981-85, exec. v.p. fin. and ops., 1986—. Treas. Harbour Point at Northport Home Owners Assn., 1985—. Served with U.S. Army N.G., 1964-70. Republican. Roman Catholic. Clubs: Lloyd Harbour Yacht, North Shore Ski. Home: 71 E 77th St New York NY 10021 Office: Atelier Internat Ltd 235 Express St Plainview NY 11803

DINARDO, LUELLA KAY, bookkeeper; b. Montrose, Colo., May 3, 1948; d. William Edgar and Evelyn Ruth (Carlson) Bray; m. Monte Talbot, Aug. 22, 1970 (div. May 1972); m. John Nicholas Di Nardo, Sept. 25, 1976; 1 child, Nicholas John. BS, Colo. State U., 1970. With accounts payable and receivable dept. Beaver Mesa Exploration, Denver, 1976-79; pres. Ind. Bookkeeping Svcs., Denver, 1986—. Charter mem. Rep. Presdl. Task Force, 1981—; mem. Nat. Fedn. Rep. Women, 1983—. 2d lt. USAF, 1973-75. Mem. NAFE, Women Bus. Owners Assn., Beta Epsilon. Congregationalist. Avocations: reading, aerobic dance. Home and Office: 4927 S Eagle Circle Aurora CO 80015

DINEEN, ROBERT JOSEPH, diversified manufacturing company executive; b. Cin., Dec. 3, 1929; s. Thomas Leo and Stella Patricia (Finnegan) D.; m. Marilyn Kamp, May 4, 1957; children: Brian, Lynn, Erin, Kerrie, Kevin, Mary Shannon, Patricia. B.E.E., U. Cin., 1952. With Allis-Chalmers Corp., Milw., 1951—; group exec., v.p. power generation and transmission group Allis-Chalmers Corp., 1971-76; pres. Allis-Chalmers Power Systems, Inc., Fiat-Allis Constrn. Machinery Inc., Deerfield, Ill., 1976—; pres., chief exec. officer White Farm Equipment Co., 1981—; pres., chief operating officer Marley Co., 1984-86, chief exec. officer, 1986—, also bd. dirs.; bd. dirs. Kansas City Power & Light Co. Trustee Midwest Research Inst., 1987—. Served with AUS, 1952-54. Recipient Disting. Alumnus award U. Cin., 1971. Mem. Nat. Elec. Mfrs. Assn. (gov.), Constrn. Industry Mfrs Assn. (2d v.p.), Nat. Assn. Mfrs. (bd. dirs.). Office: Marley Co 1900 Shawnee Mission Pkwy Mission Woods KS 66205

DINGELDEY, PETER EDWARD, executive search consultant; b. Buffalo, Oct. 18, 1943; s. Edward F. and Kathryn S. (Bower) D.; m. Beatrice J. Buchhold, Aug. 22, 1964; children: Karen E., Amy B., Matthew E. BS, Fla. State U., 1966; MBA, Harvard U., 1973. Commd. ensign USN, 1966, advanced through grades to lt. comdr., 1975, served with supply corp, 1966-77; capt. USNR; ptnr. Thorndike Deland Assocs., N.Y.C., 1977-82; dir. exec. placement Carter Hawley Hale Stores, Inc., L.A., 1982-84; exec. dir. Russell Reynolds Assocs., Inc., L.A., 1984-85; pres. Dingeldey & Assocs., Rolling Hills Estates, Calif., 1986—; bd. dirs. Navy Supply Corps Assn. Mem. Naval Res. Assn., Res. Officers Assn., Harvard Bus. Sch. Assn. So. Calif. (v.p., bd. dirs.), Navy League U.S., Supply Corps, Binnacle Club, Harvard Club, Delta Sigma Pi. Office: Dingeldey & Assocs 710 Silver Spur Rd #201 Rolling Hills Estates CA 90274

DINGMAN, MICHAEL DAVID, industrial company executive; b. New Haven, Sept. 29, 1931; s. James Everett and Amelia (Williamson) D.; m. Jean Hazlewood, May 16, 1953 (div.); children: Michael David, Linda Channing (Mrs. Michael S. Cady), James Clifford; m. Elizabeth G. Tharp, Apr. 13, 1984; children: James Tharp, David Ross. Student, U. Md. Various mgmt. positions Sigma Instruments, Inc., Braintree, Mass., 1954-64; gen. and ltd. ptnr. Drexel Burnham Lambert, Inc. (formerly Burnham & Co.), N.Y.C., 1964-70; pres., chief exec. officer, bd. dirs. Wheelabrator-Frye, Inc., Hampton, N.H., 1970-83; chmn. bd. Wheelabrator-Frye Inc., Hampton, N.H., 1977-83; pres., bd. dirs. The Signal Cos., Inc., La Jolla, Calif., 1983-85, Allied-Signal Inc., Morristown, N.J., 1985-86; chmn. bd., chief exec. officer The Henley Group, Inc., La Jolla, 1986—; bd. dirs. Ford Motor Co., Time Inc. Trustee John A. Hartford Found. Mem. IEEE (mem. adv. bd.). Clubs: Links, Bd. Room, N.Y. Yacht (N.Y.C.); Union (Boston); Cruising of Am. (Conn.); Bohemian (San Francisco), Fairbanks Ranch Country; Lyford Cay (Nassau); La Jolla Country, San Diego Yacht. Office: Henley Group Inc Liberty Ln Hampton NH 03842

DINGMAN, ROBERT J., manufacturing company executive; b. Kingston, N.Y., Oct. 15, 1941; s. Eldoras and Irene Marie (Ritter) D.; m. Martha Dalzell Trainer, May 25, 1968; children: Kimberly Gamble, Jeffrey Ritter. BS, St. Lawrence U., Canton, N.Y., 1963. Mgr. selection and placement Koppers, Pitts., 1968-71, mgmt. mgr., 1972-77, v.p., gen. mgr. Arch. Bldg. Prod. div., 1978-83; southwest div. mgr. Trus Joist, Anaheim, Calif., 1983-84; v.p. Micro=Sam LVL div. Trus Joist, Boise, Idaho, 1984-86, v.p. western ops., 1986—. Bd. dirs. Hampton Sch. Bd., Pitts., 1981-83, Planned Parenthood, Boise, 1986—. Lt. U.S. Army, 1964-66. Republican. Home: 1410 Knights Dr Boise ID 83712 Office: Trus Joist Corp PO Box 7982 Boise ID 83705

DINKELSPIEL, PAUL GAINES, investment banking and public financial consultant; b. San Francisco, Feb. 12, 1935; s. Edward Gaines and Pauline (Watson) D.; A.B., U. Calif.-Berkeley, 1959. Gen. ptnr. Stone & Youngberg, San Francisco, 1961-71; 1st v.p. Shearson/Lehman and predecessor firms, San Francisco, 1971-79; pres., chmn. bd. dirs. Dinkelspiel, Belmont & Co., Inc., investment banking and pub. fin. cons., San Francisco, 1979—. With AUS, 1959-60. Mem. Mcpl. Fin. Officers Assn., Am. Water Works Assn., San Francisco Mcpl. Forum, Pub. Securities Assn. (public fin. com.), San Francisco Comml. Club, Commonwealth Calif. Club, Mcpl. Bond Club, N.Y. World Trade Club, Calif. Waterfowl Assn., Ducks Unltd., Sigma Chi. Home: PO Box 727 Stinson Beach CA 94970 Office: One California St San Francisco CA 94111

DINNIMAN, ANDREW ERIC, history educator, academic program director; b. New Haven, Oct. 10, 1944; s. Harold and Edith (Stephson) D.; B.A., U. Conn., 1966; M.A., U. Md., 1969; Ed.D., Pa. State U., 1978; m. Margo Portnoy, June 8, 1969; 1 dau., Alexis. Student personnel worker U. Md., 1969-71, U. Denver, 1971-72; mem. faculty West Chester (Pa.) State U., 1972—, asso. prof. history, 1972—; dir. Ctr. for Internat. Programs, 1986—. Chmn. Chester County Dem. Com., 1979-85; mem. Pa. Dem. State Com., 1982—, mem. exec. com., 1984—; chmn. Eastern Pa. Dem. County Chmn. Assn., 1982-85; mem. Dem. Nat. Com., 1984—; v.p. Downington Area (Pa.) Sch. Bd., 1975-79; mem. Central Chester County Vocat.-Tech. Sch. Bd., 1978-79. Recipient Bicentennial award Pa. Sch. Bds. Assn., 1976, Outstanding Acad. Service award Commonwealth Pa., 1977, Human Rights award W. Chester State U. chpt. NAACP, 1980. Mem. Orgn. Am. Historians, Chester County Hist. Soc., Pa. Soc. Jewish. Author: Book of Human Relations Readings, 1980; also articles. Home: 467 Spruce Dr Exton PA 19341 Office: West Chester State U Dept History West Chester PA 19383

DINSMOOR, KIM OWEN, service executive; b. Omaha, Mar. 11, 1954; s. Gordon W. Dinsmoor and Lorraine Daneau; m. Rhonda Lynn Libby, July 18, 1986. BBA in Mgmt., U. Tex., Arlington, 1977. Cert. hotel adminstrn. Dir. sales Adolphus Hotel, Dallas, 1977-80, Lincoln Radisson Hotel, Dallas, 1979-80; dir. mktg. Marriott Hotel, Corpus Christi, Tex., 1981; corp. dir. mktg. Vista Host Mgmt., Corpus Christi, 1982-85; gen. mgr. Denver Inn, 1986; dir. mktg. Resort Group, Denver, 1987; gen. mgr. Ascutney Mountain Resort, Brownsville, Vt., 1988—; instr. Edn. Inst. Am. Hotel Mgmt., Denver, 1987-88. Counselor, Circle K Internat., Tex.-Okla. dist., 1977-83. Fellow So. Meth. U., Dallas, 1987. Mem. Meeting Planner Internat. (chpt. pres. 1980), Hotel Sales/Mktg. Assn. (state dir. 1981-82), Soc. Incentive Travel Execs. (mem. edn. com. 1988). Republican. Mem. Bible Ch. Clubs: Mustang, Buff. Lodge: Kiwanis. Home: 1009 Flameleaf Ct Lewisville NC 27023 Office: Ascutney Mountain Resort PO Box 129 Brownsville VT 05037

DINSMORE, DAVID ALLEN, financial planner; b. Dayton, Ohio, Aug. 31, 1951; s. Donald D. and Grace Arlene (Libecap) D.; m. Vickie Kay McLaughlin, Aug. 12, 1972; children: Amanda Jayne, Erin Elizabeth. BS, Ball State U., 1973; cert., Coll. for Fin. Planning, Denver, 1987. Registered fin. planner, investment advisor. Tchr. math, sci. Tipp City (Ohio) Exempted City Schs., 1973-76, Randolph So. Schs., Lynn, Ind., 1976-78; sales rep. Horace Mann Ins. Co., Springfield, Ill., 1978-81, Variable Annuity Life Ins. Co., Houston, 1981-86, Aetna Life and Annuity Co., Hartford, Conn., 1986-88, Fin. Care Corp./Integrated Resources, Cin., 1987; owner, mgr. Dinsmore Fin. Svcs. Agy., Hamilton, Ohio, 1986-87, David A. Dinsmore CFP RFP fee only fin. planning firm, Hamilton, Ohio, 1988—; founding bd. dirs., treas. Am. Benefits Adminstrv. Agy., Columbus, Ohio, 1987. Fellow Inst. Cert. Fin. Planners, Miami Valley Inst. Cert. Fin. Planners, Internat. Assn. Registered Fin. Planners, Nat. Assn. Tax Practitioners. Republican. Mem. Ch. of Christ. Home and Office: 1005 Haldimand Ave Hamilton OH 45013

DION, PHILIP JOSEPH, consumer products and services, real estate and construction company executive; b. Chgo., Nov. 30, 1944; s. Philip J. and Loretta (Loftus) D.; B.A., St. Ambrose Coll., 1966; M.B.A., Loyola U., Chgo., 1968; m. Patricia Ann Reichert, June 24, 1967; children—Philip Joseph, David, Jaime. Cons. Booz, Allen & Hamilton, Chgo., 1966-68; pres., gen. mgr. Cocrema Inc., Lorenzo DeMexico, Chgo., 1968-70; with Armour-Dial Inc., Phoenix, 1970-82, pres. subs., 1970-82; sr. v.p. fin. Del Webb Corp., Phoenix, 1982-83, exec. v.p., 1983-87, pres., 1987; chmn. bd., chief exec. officer, 1987—; mem. Allendale Adv. Bd. Phoenix 40; bd. dirs. Boy's Hope. Mem. Assn. Corp. Growth, Paradise Valley Country Club. Office: Del Webb Corp 2231 E Camelback Rd Phoenix AZ 85038

DIONNE, JOSEPH LEWIS, publishing company executive; b. Montgomery, Ala., June 29, 1933; s. Antonio Ernest Joseph and Myrtle Mae (Armstrong) D.; m. Joan F. Durand, June 12, 1954; children: Marsha Joan Dionne Guerin, Gary Joseph, Darren Durand. B.A., Hofstra U., 1955, M.S., 1957; Ed.D., Columbia U., 1965. Guidance counselor L.I. Public Schs., 1956-61; asst. prof. Hofstra U., Hempstead, N.Y., 1962-63; dir. instrn., project dir. Ford Found. Sch. Improvement grant Brentwood (N.Y.) Pub. Schs., 1963-66; v.p. research and devel. Ednl. Developmental Labs., Huntington, N.Y., 1966-68; v.p., gen. mgr. CTB/McGraw-Hill, Monterey, Calif., 1968-73; sr. v.p. corp. planning McGraw-Hill, Inc., N.Y.C., 1973-77; pres. McGraw-Hill Info. Systems Co., N.Y.C., 1977-79; exec. v.p. ops. McGraw Hill, Inc., 1979-81, pres., 1981-88, chief exec. officer, 1983-88; chairman McGraw-Hill Inc, 1988—; bd. dirs. Equitable Life Ins. Co. Am., United Telecommunications Inc. Past moderator, alumni council Tchrs. Coll., Columbia U., now trustee; elder Presbyn. Ch. of New Canaan; past pres. Soc. To Advance Retarded; chmn. bd. trustees Hofstra U. 2d lt. AUS, 1955-56. Mem. Phi Alpha Theta, Kappa Delta Pi, Phi Delta Kappa. Clubs: Woodway Country (Darien, Conn.), Blind Brook Club, Inc. (Purchase, N.Y.). Home: 198 N Wilton Rd New Canaan CT 06840 Office: McGraw-Hill Inc 1221 Ave of the Americas New York NY 10020

DIPALMA, BARBARA ANN, financial planner; b. N.Y.C., July 24, 1939; d. Walter Strockbine and Marion Arlene (Lenz) Schuessler; m. Alphonse G. DiPalma, Nov. 21, 1959; children: Christopher G., Dina A. Student, Orange County Community Coll., Coll. for Fin. Planning. Cert. fin. planner. Announcer Sta. WTBQ-Radio, Warwick, N.Y., 1973-77; news reporter Advertizer Photo News, Monroe and Warwick, N.Y., 1970-77; sec. Chemtrol Lawn Service, Fla. and N.Y., 1977-78; v.p. Gary Goldberg & Co Inc., Suffern, N.Y., 1978—. Chmn. Woodbury Archtl. Rev. Bd., 1974-80; bd. dirs. Am. Cancer Soc., Orange County, N.Y., 1978-80, Pengiun Repertory Co., StonyPoint, N.Y., 1984-86; bd. elections Woodbury Archtl. Rev. Bd., 1974-80; sec. Woodbury Reps., 1974-76. Recipient Service award Monroe Lions Club, 1976, Woodbury BiCentennial, 1976, K.C., 1977, Congl. cert. Rep. Congl. Campaign, 1984. Mem. Internat. Assn. Fin. Planners, Inst. Cert. Fin. Planners, Nat. Assn. Female Execs., Adelphi U. Soc. Fin. Planners. Club: Women of Woodbury (pres. 1973-74). Avocations: travel, slimnastics, exercise. Home: PO Box 404 Overlook Dr Highland Mills NY 10930 Office: Gary Goldberg & Co Inc 75 Montebello Rd Suffern NY 10901

DI PAOLO, NICHOLAS, corporate executive, real estate investor; b. Garfield, N.J., Sept. 16, 1941; s. Nicholas and Nancy (DeRosso) Di P.; m. Patricia Anne Schaper, Jan. 22, 1966; children: Nicole, David. BS in Econs., Rutgers U., 1963. Dir. ops. Manhattan Industries, N.Y.C., 1964-72, Lawvin, Charles Ortha Ritz, N.Y.C., 1972-75; pres., chief exec. officer Villagar Industries, N.Y.C., 1976-85; pres., chief oper. officer Salanr Corp., N.Y.C., 1985—.

DIPIAZZA, MICHAEL CHARLES, insurance company executive; b. N.Y.C., Aug. 22, 1953; s. Carmelo and Grace (Vassallo) DiP.; m. Lillian Dugan, Dec. 21, 1979. CLU. Asst. v.p. sales Nat. Benefit Life Ins. Co., N.Y.C., 1975-79, asst. v.p. product devel., 1979-81; pres. Wm. B. Smith Agy., N.Y.C., 1979; cons. Ins. Sales Support Systems, Piscataway, N.J., 1981-82; asst. v.p. merchandising MONY, N.Y.C., 1982-86; v.p. merchandising Home Life Ins. Co., N.Y.C., 1986—. Mem. Nat. Assn. Life Underwriters, Am. Soc. Chartered Life Underwriters, Nat. Model Railroad Assn.

DIPIETRO, RALPH ANTHONY, marketing and management consultant, educator; b. N.Y.C., Oct. 27, 1942; s. Joseph and Marie (Borelli) DiP. BBA, CUNY, 1964, MBA, 1966; PhD, NYU, 1972. Mem. faculty Montclair State Coll., Upper Montclair, N.J., 1972—, prof. mktg., mgmt., 1971—, chmn. dept., 1971-76, chmn. mktg. Sch. Bus., 1979—; adj. prof. mgmt. NYU, 1976—; mgmt. tng. dir. Inst. Retail Mgmt., N.Y.C., 1976-86; cons. Mfrs. Hanover Trust, N.Y.C., 1979-85, Sharp Electronics, N.Y.C., 1980—, Battus Corp., N.Y.C., 1982-85; program dir. Bally of Switzerland, N.Y.C., 1981—, Fortunoff's, N.Y.C., 1984-86. Author: Managerial Effectiveness: A Review and an Empirical Testing of a Model, 1973; contbr. articles to profl. jours. Grantee Temple U., Phila., 1972-74, Montclair State Coll., 1976-79, 83. Mem. Am. Acad. Mgmt. (vice chmn. 1973), Am. Mktg. Assn., Internat. Assn. Applied Psychology, Omicron Delta Epsilon. Home: 361 Greenbrier Ct Mountainside NJ 07092

DIRACLES, JOHN MICHAEL, JR., financial executive; b. San Marcos, Tex., Aug. 15, 1944; s. John Michael Sr. and Louise (Hanzlik) D.; m. Marcia McKinney, July 5, 1975; 1 child, David Hampton. AB, Dartmouth Coll., 1966; MBA, Columbia U., 1972. Mgr. corp. fin. W.R. Grace & Co., N.Y.C., 1972-75; v.p., treas. Motel 6 Inc. (subs. City Investing Co.), Santa Barbara, Calif., 1976-80; v.p., treas., chief fin. officer Sambo's Restaurants Inc. (subs. City Investing Co.), Santa Barbara, 1979-82; prin. John M. Diracles & Co., Scarsdale, N.Y., 1982-86; v.p., treas. Carlson Cos., Mpls., 1986—. Bd. dirs., treas. Am. Heart Assn., Minn. chpt. 1986—, chmn. fin. and budget com., Mpls., 1988; bd. dirs. United Arts Twin Cities, 1986—. Served with U.S. Army, 1967-70. Decorated Bronze Star. Mem. Fin. Execs. Inst. (bd. dirs. Twin Cities chpt. 1988—). Home: 155 Homedale Rd Hopkins MN 55343 Office: Carlson Cos Inc 12755 State Hwy 55 Minneapolis MN 55441

DIRUSCIO, LAWRENCE WILLIAM, business executive; b. Buffalo, Jan. 2, 1941; s. Guido Carmen and Mabel Ella (Bach) DiR.; m. Gloria J. Edney, Aug. 19, 1972; children—Lawrence M., Lorie P., Darryl C., Teresa M., Jack D. With various broadcast stas. and instr., adminstr. Bill Wade Sch. Radio and TV, San Diego, San Francisco, Los Angeles, 1961-69; account exec. Sta. KGB Radio, San Diego, 1969, gen. sales mgr., 1970-72; pres. Free Apple Advt., San Diego, 1972—, Fin. Mgmt. Assocs., Inc., San Diego, 1979-84, Self-Pub. Ptnrs., San Diego, 1981—, Media Mix Assocs. Enterprises, Inc., 1984-86; pres. Press-Courier Pub. Co., Inc., 1985-86; pres. Media Mix Advt. and Pub. Relations, 1985—; lectr., writer on problems of small bus. survival. Served with USN, 1958-60. Five Emmy nominations for T.V. commercial writing and prodn. Mem. Nat. Acad. TV Arts and Scis. Democrat. Roman Catholic. Office: Free Apple Advt 726 W Kalmia St San Diego CA 92101

DIRVIN, GERALD VINCENT, consumer products company executive; b. Phila., Mar. 28, 1937; s. Vincent A. and Mary (Fitch) D.; m. Polly Burnett, June 27, 1959; children: John, David, Barbara. B.A., Hamilton Coll., Clinton, N.Y., 1959. With Procter & Gamble Co., 1959—, sales mgr., then v.p. coffee div., 1975-80; group v.p. Procter & Gamble Co., Cin., 1980—; dir. Procter & Gamble Co., 1981—. Mem. exec. bd. Dan Beard council Boy Scouts Am.; trustee Cin. Med. Ctr. Fund, Hamilton Coll., Cin. Zoo, Johnny Bench Scholarship Fund; mem. Xavier U. Bus. Sch. Adv. Bd. Republican. Roman Catholic. Clubs: Commonwealth, Camargo, Queen City, Pine Valley Golf. Office: Procter & Gamble Co 1 Procter & Gamble Pla Cincinnati OH 45202

DISBROW, ARTHUR RAY, aerospace manufacturing executive; b. Kaleva, Mich., June 26, 1932; s. Alan Stacy and Elsie Ruth (Fuller) D.; m. Vivian Childress, May 24, 1958; children: Michael Ray, Russell Paul, Colleen Lynn, Jennifer Mary. BSME, Mich. Tech. U., 1955; MBA with honors, Mich. State U., 1971. Machine designer AC Spark Plug div. Gen. Motors Co., Flint, Mich., 1955-57; lead engr. Missile div. Chrysler Corp., Sterling Heights, Mich., 1957-60; mech. process dept. head Mfg. Devel. div. Gen. Motors Co., Warren, Mich., 1960-74; mfg. engring. mgr. Compressor Comp. div. TRW Inc., Cleve., 1974-81; v.p., div. mgr. Hartzell Propeller Products div. TRW. Inc., Piqua, Ohio, 1981-87; pres. Hartzell Propeller Inc., Piqua, Ohio, 1987—, also bd. dirs.; bd. dirs. Miami County Am. Automobile Assn., Piqua. Co-inventor patent on electrical discharge machining, 1961. Campaign chmn. Piquarea United Fund, 1986, bd. dirs. 1984-88; adv. bd. Salvation Army, Piqua, 1984—; co-chmn. JVS Levy Campaign; trustee Upper Valley Med. Ctr., Piqua, Ohio, 1984—; pres. Piquarea United Way, 1989. Served to 2d lt., U.S. Army, 1955-58. Mem. Nat. Aviation Hall of Fame, Gen. Aviation Mfrs. Assn. (bd. dirs. 1981—), Nat. Aero. Assn., Army Aviation Assn., Am. Def. Preparedness Assn., Piqua C. of C. (bd. dirs. 1984-87). Lodge: Rotary. Home: 2940 Broken Woods Dr Troy OH 45373 Office: Hartzell Propeller Inc One Propeller Pl Piqua OH 45356

DISBROW, MICHAEL RAY, aerospace supplier company executive; b. Highland Park, Mich., June 12, 1959; s. Arthur Ray and Vivian (Childress) D.; m. Lynn Marie Lodyga, July 14, 1984. BSME, Purdue U., 1981; MBA, Harvard U., 1986. Co-op. assoc. BFGoodrich Co., Akron, Ohio, 1978-81; axle engr. Bendix Automotive Brake Systems div. Allied Signal, Inc., South Bend, Ind., 1982-83, research and devel. engr., 1983-84, disc brake engr., 1984, mgr. strategic planning, 1986-87, mgr. Far East bus. planning, 1987-88, mgr. N.Am. joint venture programs, 1988; internal cons. Fram div. Allied Signal, Inc., East Providence, R.I., 1985; dir. service ctr. Hartzell Propeller Inc., Piqua, Ohio, 1988—. Prodn. advisor Jr. Achievement of Michiana, South Bend, 1982-83, exec. advisor, 1983-84. Named Prodn. Advisor of Yr. Jr. Achievement of Michiana, 1983; fellow The Little Family Found., 1984, 85, Allied Signal, Inc., 1984-86. Mem. Nat. Mgmt. Assn., Soc. Automotive Engrs. (assoc.), Tau Beta Pi. Republican. Methodist. Home: 1760 Normandy Ln Troy OH 45373 Office: Hartzell Propeller Inc One Propeller Pl Piqua OH 45356

DISBROW, RICHARD EDWIN, utility executive; b. Newark, Sept. 20, 1930; s. Milton A. and Madeline Catherine (Segal) D.; m. Patricia Fair Warner, June 27, 1953 (div. Sept. 1972); children: John Scott, Lisa Karen; m. Teresa Marie Moser, May 12, 1973. B.S., Lehigh U., 1952; M.S. in Elec. Engring., Newark Coll. Engring., 1959; M.S. in indsl. mgmt., MIT, 1965. With Am. Electric Power Service Corp., N.Y.C., 1954-80; with Am. Electric Power Service Corp., Columbus, Ohio, 1980—, transmission and distbn. mgr., 1967-70, controller, 1970-71, v.p., controller, 1971-74, exec. v.p., 1974-75, vice chmn. bd., 1975-79, pres., chief adminstrv. officer, 1979-84, pres., chief operating officer, 1985—, dir.; pres., dir. Am. Electric Power Co.; dir. Banc Ohio Nat. Bank, 1986; instr. Newark Coll. Engring., 1959-64; mem. N.J. Engrs. Com. For Student Guidance, 1960-64; indsl. commr., Piscataway, N.J., 1960-64; vice-chmn. Franklin U.; bd. visitors N.J. Inst. Tech; v.p., bd. dirs. Columbus So. Power Co., Ind. Mich. Power Co., Wheeling Electric Co., Windsor Coal Co. Bd dirs. Ohio Found. Ind. Colls. 1st lt. USAF, 1952-54. Sloan fellow MIT. Mem. Edison Electric Inst. (dir.), Columbus Athletic Club, Worthington Hills Country Club, Breakers West

Country Club, Psi Upsilon, Eta Kappa Nu. Office: Am Electric Power Co Inc 1 Riverside Pla PO Box 16631 Columbus OH 43215

DISNEY, DIANE MARIE, management and career consultant; b. Louisville; d. Aubrey Hamilton and Norma Garnet (Masden) D. B.A., Stetson U., 1963; M.A. in Teaching, Duke U., 1965; M.B.A., U. R.I., 1977; PhD Brandeis U., 1989. Tchr., curriculum developer N.C. and N.Y. high schs., Fla. community colls., 1963-67; advt. analyst, bus. devel. coordinator, two divs. of Interpublic Group of Cos., N.Y.C., 1967-69; research coordinator Career Edn. Project, Edn. Devel. Ctr., Providence, 1972-73, dir. communications, 1973-76; acting dir. Opportunities for Women, Providence, 1977-78; mktg., mgmt. and career devel. cons., Providence, 1971—; pres. Disney Lightfoot Lee Ltd., Providence, 1978—; exec. dir. R.I. State Council on Arts, 1980-82; research assoc. Urban Inst., Washington, 1982-87 ; faculty mgmt. U. R.I., 1982-86, 88—,; cons. R.I. Small Bus. Devel. Ctr., 1983-85; research assoc. Heller Sch., Brandeis U., Waltham, Mass., 1986-88; adj. lectr., 1987—. Bd. dirs. Vols. in Action, 1973-86, v.p., 1976-78, treas., 1978-80, pres., 1980-83; bd. dirs. Opportunities for Women, 1975-78, pres., 1977-78; bd. dirs. Alternate Learning Project, 1971, sec., 1971; bd. dirs. Women's Devel. Corp., 1981-85, 88—, pres., 1981-83; bd. dirs. Women's Opportunity Realty Corp., 1986—, pres., 1986-88; bd. dirs. Nickerson House, 1974-80, Urban League R.I., 1979-82, New Eng. Found. for Arts, 1980-82; bd. dirs. Samaritans of R.I., 1978-87 , v.p., 1980-82, pres., 1982-83; bd. dirs. SER-Jobs for Progress, 1980—, treas., 1980—; chmn. nat. coordinating council Samaritans U.S.A., 1979-80; bd. dirs., 1985-87 , chmn. mgmt. com., 1986-87; chmn. adv. council Edn. Info. Centers Program; mem. corp. Blue Cross-Blue Shield R.I.; mem. R.I. Legis. Com. on Citizen Participation in Govt., 1979-80; mem. R.I. Legis. Com. on Gifted Edn., 1981-83; coordinator Vols. in Cultural Instns., 1979-80; mem. steering com. R.I. Folklife Project; mem. R.I. Com. for the Humanities, 1983—, chmn. media subcom., 1984-86, treas., 1986—; bd. dirs. R.I. Parks Assn., 1985-86,trustee, 1986—; bd. dirs. Greater R.I. chpt. ARC, 1986-88, chmn. strategic planning, 1987; Vol. Services for Animals, 1985—, chmn. nominating com., 1986— ; mem. adv. com. Urban Edn. Ctr., 1978-79; mem. R.I. Adv. Commn. on Women, 1978, pub. relations subcom. 1980-82, women in bus. com. 1984-85; mem. bldg. fund com. John Hope Settlement House, 1980-82, bd. dirs., 1983—, chmn. bylaws com. 1984—; judge essays & speech R.I. Acad. Decathlon, 1985—; trustee Community College of R.I. Found., 1980—, mem. nominating com. 1982-84, treas., 1985-87, v.p., 1987-88, chmn. nominating com., 1986—; mem. community involvement com. R.I. Industry-Edn.-Labor Council, 1977-78; mem. steering com. community edn. project R.I. Dept. Edn., 1978-81; active United Way Southeastern New Eng., 1974—, chmn. budget panel, 1977-80, chmn. evaluation com., 1980-82; mem. budget com. R.I. Hist. Soc., 1980-81, long-range planning com. 1983-85; bd. dirs. New Fedn. Humanities, 1985-86, 88, co-chmn. finance com. 1988—, v.p., 1989—; vice chmn. R.I. Arts and Tourism Commn., 1985—; mem. curriculum com. Heller Sch., Brandeis U., 1985—, R.I. Arts Advocates, 1986—. Recipient Nat. Vol. Activist award, 1977; Wall Street Jour. fellow, 1965; Ford Found. fellow, 1963; Duke U. fellow, 1964; Stetson U. scholar, 1959-63. Mem. Am. Soc. for Tng. and Devel., Am. Ednl. Research assn., Acad. Polit. Scis., AAUP, Nat. Assn. Parliamentarians, R.I. Conf. Social Work (nominating com. 1980-82), Indsl. Relations Research Assn., Zeta Tau Alpha, Beta Gamma Sigma, Kappa Delta Pi, Sigma Pi Kappa, Sigma Tau Delta. Home: 39 Langham Rd Providence RI 02906

DISNEY, ROY EDWARD, broadcasting company executive; b. Los Angeles, Jan. 10, 1930; s. Roy Oliver and Edna (Francis) D.; m. Patricia Ann Dailey, Sept. 17, 1955; children: Roy Patrick, Susan Margaret, Abigail Edna, Timothy John. B.A., Pomona Coll., 1951. Guest relations exec. NBC, Hollywood, Calif., 1952; apprentice film editor Mark VII Prodns., Hollywood, 1942; asst. film editor, cameraman prodn. asst., writer, producer Walt Disney Prodns., Burbank, Calif., 1954-77, dir., 1967—; pres. Roy E. Disney Prodns. Inc., Burbank, 1978—; chmn. bd. dir. Shamrock Broadcasting Co., Hollywood, 1979—; chmn. bd. dir., founder Shamrock Holdings Inc., Burbank, 1980—; trustee Calif. Inst. Arts, Valencia, 1967—; vice chmn. Walt Disney Co., Burbank. Author: novelized adaptation of Perri; producer movie: Pacific High; writer, dir., producer numerous TV prodns. Bd. dirs. Big Bros. of Greater Los Angeles; mem. adv. bd. dirs. St. Joseph Med. Ctr., Burbank; mem. U.S. Naval Acad. Sailing Squadron, Annapolis, Md.; fellow U. Ky. Recipient Acad. award nomination for Mysteries of the Deep. Mem. Dirs. Guild Am. West, Writers Guild Am. Republican. Clubs: 100, Confrerie des Chevaliers du Tastevin, St. Francis Yacht, Calif. Yacht, San Diego Yacht, Transpacific Yacht, Los Angeles Yacht. Office: Walt Disney Co 500 S Buena Vista St Burbank CA 91521 *

DISSTON, HARRY, author, business executive, horseman; b. Red Bank, N.J., Nov. 23, 1899; s. Eugene John Kauffmann and Frances Matilda Disston; A.B., Amherst Coll., 1921; m. Valerie Ivy Duval, Mar. 26, 1930 (dec. 1951); children—Robin John Duval, Geoffrey Whitmore (dec.); m. Catherine Sitler John, Aug. 26, 1960. With N.Y. Telephone Co., 1921-32, with AT&T, N.Y.C., 1932-60, exec. tng. student, dist. traffic supt., sales engr., dist. mgr., adv. staff engr., adv. staff exec. ind. co. relations, 1951-60; coordinator devel. activities, placement dir. Grad. Sch. Bus. Adminstrn., U. Va.; v.p. Equine Motion Analysis, Ltd., 1979-82; sr. v.p., dir. leasing Equivest Fin. Services Corp., Charlottesville, Va., 1986-88; pres. Harwood Corp., Ltd.; dir. AMVEST Horse Leasing Co., Charlottesville, Aide-de-camp to gov. Va.; chmn. Louisa County Electoral Bd.; mem. Va. Bd. Mil. Affairs; chmn. fin. com. Republican party Va.; chmn. Louisa County Rep. Com.; v.p. pres., dir. Park Ave. Assn.; mem. exec. com. Episcopal Diocese of Va., also pres. council, region 15; trustee Grant Monument Assn., Va. Outdoors Found.; bd. dirs. Atlantic Rural Expn.; bd. dirs., treas. Lee-Jackson Found.; chmn., bd. dirs. Charlottesville-Albemarle Clean Community Commn., 1978-84. Served from maj. to col., cav. and gen. staff corps, 1941-46; PTO; comdg. officer 107th Regtl. Combat Team, N.Y.N.G., 1947-57; brig. gen. ret. Awarded Legion of Merit, Bronze Star with oak leaf cluster; comdr. Order of Boliver; Philippine Liberation Medal; Medal of Merit with Swords, Free Poland. Mem. Am. Horse Shows Assn. (judge, steward, tech. del.), Vets. 7th Regt., N.Y. Soc. Mil. and Naval Officers World Wars (past pres.), Vet. Corps Arty., Mil. Order Fgn. Wars, Mil. Order World Wars, Am. Legion, Res. Officers Assn. (chpt. pres.), St. Georges Soc., St. Andrews Soc., Va. Thoroughbred Assn., U.S. Pony Clubs (gov.), Phi Beta Kappa, Phi Kappa Psi. Clubs: Torch (past pres. Charlottesville-Albermarle); Union; Amherst; Church of New York; Farmington Country, Greencroft, Jack Jouett Bridle Trails (pres.) (Charlottesville, Va.); Pilgrims of U.S.; Keswick Hunt, Keswick of Va. Author: Equestionnaire, 1947; Riding Rhymes, 1951; Know About Horses, 1961; Young Horseman's Handbooks, 1962; Elementary Dressage, 1971; Beginning Polo, 1973; Beginning the Rest of Your Life, 1980; columnist Daily Progress, Cen. Virginian; several mag. articles on mil., equine and bus. subjects; contbr. to Ency. Brit. Home: Hidden Hill Farm Keswick VA 22947 Office: 2955 Ivy Rd Suite 302 Charlottesville VA 22901

DISTEFANO, PETER ANDREW, insurance executive; b. N.Y.C., Nov. 26, 1939; s. Peter Julian and Marie Antoinette (Onorato) D.; student City Coll. San Francisco, 1965, Costa Mesa (Calif.)-Orange Coast Coll., 1975; cert. enrolled employee benefits, Wharton Sch., U. Pa., 1980; cert. profl. ins. agt., 1987; children: Diane, Daniel, Donald. Agt., Mut. N.Y., San Francisco, 1971-73; regional mgr. Hartford Ins. Group, Santa Ana, Calif., 1972-77; v.p. Lachman & Assos., Inc., ins., Lafayette, Calif., 1977-80; pres., owner Distefano Ins. Services, Benicia, Calif., 1980—; lectr., cons. risk mgmt., employee benefits. Pres. Contra Costa/Solano County Easter Seal Soc. Served with USNR, 1957-62. Recipient various ins. sales awards, Cert. Profl. Ins. Agt. Designation award, 1987; registered profl. disability and health ins. underwriter. Fellow Acad. Producer Ins. Studies; mem. Nat. Assn. Health Underwriters, Nat. Assn. Life Underwriters, Soc. Registered Profl. Health Underwriters, Nat. Assn. Security Dealers, Internat. Found. Employee Benefit Plans, Profl. Ins. Agts. Calif./Nev. Soc. (cert.), Oakland/East Bay Assn. Life Underwriters. Greek Orthodox. Office: Distefano Ins Svcs Inc 827 First St PO Box 696 Benicia CA 94510

DISTELHORST, GARIS FRED, association executive; b. Columbus, Ohio, Jan. 21, 1942; s. Harold Theodore and Ruth (Haywood) D.; m. Helen Cecilla Gillen, Oct. 28, 1972; children: Garen, Kristen, Alison. B.Sc., Ohio State U., 1965. Cert. assn. exec. Vice pres. Smith, Bucklin & Assocs., Washington, 1969-80; exec. dir. Nat. Assn. Coll. Stores, Oberlin, Ohio, 1980—; pres. NACSCORP Inc.; mem. exec. council Internat. Booksellers Fedn., Vienna, Austria; bd. dirs. Lorain County Bank Corp. Bd. dirs. Washington Choral Arts Soc., 1975-76, Oberlin Early Childhood Ctr., 1986-87; treas. Old Mill Community Council, Alexandria, Va., 1977-79; commr. Citizens Cable TV commn., Oberlin, Ohio, 1982-83; chmn. Sesquicentennial com., Oberlin, 1983; pres. Oberlin Community Improvement Corp., 1985-88; bd. dirs. Leadership Lorain County, 1988—. Served to lt. USN, 1965-69. Decorated USN Achievement medal, 1969. Mem. Inst. Assn. Mgmt. Cos. (treas. 1979-80 award merit), Am. Soc. Assn. Execs. (dir. 1981-84, vice chmn. 1985, Key award 1984), U.S. C. of C. Assn. Com. (assn. com. 1986—), Oberlin Area C. of C. (pres. 1987—), Greater Cleve. Soc. Assn. Execs., Trade Show Bur. Republican. Presbyterian. Lodge: Rotary (dir. 1982-84, 1986—) (Oberlin). Office: Nat Assn of Coll Stores 528 E Lorain Oberlin OH 44074

DITMORE, ROBERT KEITH, health care management company executive; b. Okemah, Okla., Mar. 12, 1934; s. Glen James and Etta Mae (Casady) D.; m. Lynne Lucille Denton, June 13, 1953; children: Robert S., Tracy E. Ditmore Clark, Brian C. BA, San Jose State U., 1959. Successively mgr. profl. employment, adminstrv. mgr., mgr. bus. ops. Stanford (Calif.) Rsch. Inst., 1959-70; successively v.p. fin. and adminstrn., dir. HMO Mgmt. div., corp. treas. InterStudy, Mpls., 1970-74; pres., chief exec. officer. dir. Share Health Plan of Minn., Mpls., 1973-82; vice chmn. bd. Share Health Plan of Minn., St. Paul, 1984—; pres., chief exec. officer Share Devel. Corp., Bloomington, Minn., 1982-85, also chmn. bd.; pres., chief ops. officer United HealthCare Corp., Minnetonka, Minn., 1985—, also bd. dirs.; Cons. Dept. HEW, Dept. Health and Human Svcs., 1972-85. Office: United HealthCare Corp 300 Opus Ctr 9900 Bren Rd E Minnetonka MN 55343

DITTMER, JAMES HAROLD, retail food company manager; b. Cook County, Ill., July 9, 1951; s. Harold and Petro (Einersen) D.; student So. Ill. U., 1969-70; B.S. in Bus. Edn., Western Mich. U., 1974; M.B.A., 1983; Ph.D., 1984; adopted children—Jeff, Harry, Terry, Tim. Public adminstr. Dundee (Ill.) Park Dist., 1974-75; v.p., gen. mgr. Interstate GMC, Elgin, Ill., 1975-76; pres., founder J. H. Dittmer & Co., Daytona Beach, Fla., 1976—; retail mgr. Super Foods, Inc., Orlando, Fla., 1981-82; retail grocery mgr. Gt. So. Foods, Inc., Titusville, Fla., 1982-83; Super's Food and Drugs, 1983-85; part-owner Destry's Inc., 1983-85; retail grocery mgr. Cert. Retail Store subs. Southland Corp., Daytona Beach, 1985—; pres., founder Computer Listings Co., Daytona Beach, Fla., 1983; bar and restaurant design and constrn. cons. Sustaining mem. Rep. Nat. Com., 1977—. Recipient Eagle Scout award Boy Scouts Am., 1967; Service award YMCA, Athletic Letters award, AAU, 1972. Mem. Nat. Grocer's Assn., Retail Grocer's Assn. Episcopalian. Home: 145 Orchid Ln Port Orange FL 32019

DITTRICH, RAYMOND JOSEPH, medical device company executive; b. Wichita, Kans., Feb. 17, 1932; s. Raymond Joseph and Helen Sue (Sheehan) D.; m. Paula Ann Makielski, Feb. 20, 1954; children: Lisa Ann, Claire Louise, David Thomas, Mark Alan. A.B. magna cum laude, U. Notre Dame, 1953; LL.B., U. Mich., 1958. Bar: Minn. bar 1958, Fla. bar 1973. Atty. Cargill, Inc., Mpls., 1958-71; v.p., gen. counsel, sec. Burger King Corp., Miami, Fla., 1971-74; v.p., gen. counsel Pillsbury Co., Mpls., 1974-80; sec. Pillsbury Co., 1977-80; v.p., gen. counsel Ga. Pacific Corp., 1980; v.p., sec., gen. counsel Medtronic, Inc., Mpls., 1980—. Mem. Charter Commn., Minnetonka, Minn., 1968-70; bd. dirs., pres. Mpls. Aquatenniel Assn., 1984. Served with USMCR, 1953-55; lt. col. Res. Mem. ABA, Fla. Bar Assn., Minn. Bar Assn. (v.p., dir. corporate counsel sect.), Food and Drug Law Inst. (trustee), Phi Alpha Delta. Republican. Roman Catholic. Clubs: Royal Palm Tennis (Miami); Wayzata Country, Minneapolis. Home: 4775 Bayswater Rd Shorewood MN 55331 Office: Medtronic Inc 7000 Central Ave NE Minneapolis MN 55432

DIX, DENNIS, JR., investment banker; b. Greenville, Miss., July 30, 1944; s. Dennis and Phyllis Ruxton (Heppenheimer) D.; m. Constance Griffith, Dec. 27, 1966; children: Eleanor Alden, Heather Evans, Dennis III. BA, Trinity Coll., Hartford, Conn., 1966; MBA in Fin., U. Conn., 1974. Credit analyst Hartford Nat. Bank, 1969-71, asst. mgr. Newington br., 1971-72, with mcpl. fin. dept., 1972-79; with corp. fin. dept. Advest Inc., Hartford, 1977-79; with mcpl. fin. dept. Conn. Nat. Bank, Hartford, 1979—. Mem. Towpath PTO, Avon, Conn., 1972-76, treas., 1975-76; chmn. Avon Econ. Devel. Commn., 1974-76; mem. Avon Bd. Edn., 1982-87. Served to 1st lt. U.S. Army, Vietnam. Mem. Govt. Fin. Officers Assn. Republican. Episcopalian. Club: Golf of Avon. Office: Conn Nat Bank 777 Main St MSN 223 Hartford CT 06115

DIXON, ANDREW DOUGLAS, real estate investment executive; b. Ithaca, N.Y., Nov. 18, 1958; s. Kenneth Earl and Helen Carleda (Carlson) D.; m. Debra Sue Montner, June 3, 1984. BS, Cornell U., 1981. Asst. controller Houragency, Inc., Ithaca, 1979-81; asst. fin. dir. Stonehenge Capital Corp., N.Y.C., 1981-83; syndication analyst, asset mgr. The Patrician Group, Inc., N.Y.C., 1983-85; sr. investment analyst fin. and systems The ITD Group, Inc., Stamford, Conn., 1985—; sr. analyst fin. and systems Retirement Ctrs. Network, Inc., Stamford, 1985-88; pres. A.D. Dixon & Co., Norwalk, Conn., 1988—. Contbr. articles to profl. jours. Active Small Bus. Council Tompkins County, Ithaca, 1980. Mem. Tompkins County C. of C., Cornell Club (v.p.) of Fairfield County. Office: ITD Group Inc 986 Bedford St Stamford CT 06905 also: 97 Ledgebrook Dr Norwalk CT 06854

DIXON, GEORGE FRANCIS, JR., manufacturing company executive; b. Jersey City, Feb. 24, 1918; s. George F. and Frances (Martin) D.; m. Lottie Ivy Carter, Dec. 1, 1950; children: George Francis III, Richard Elliott, Marshall Lawrence, Charlotte Ivy. B.S., U.S. Mil. Acad., 1940; M.S., Cornell U., 1947; D.Eng., Grenoble U., France, 1949. Dist. engr. Vicksburg Dist. Corps Engrs., 1949-53; pres. Dart Truck Co., Kansas City, Mo., 1955-57; also dir.; with Carlisle Corp., Pa., 1954—; pres., chief exec. officer Carlisle Corp., 1957-70, chmn. bd., 1970—, also dir.; dir. Dauphin Deposit Trust Co., Harrisburg, Pa., CDI Corp., Phila.; Chmn. Pa. Div. Trauma. Trustee Dickinson Sch. Law; trustee Gettysburg Coll. Served at lt. col. AUS, World War II; div. engr., comdg. officer 65th Engrs., 25th Inf. Div. Mem. ASCE, Assn. Grads. U.S. Mil. Acad. (trustee, pres.), Soc. Automotive Engrs., Soc. Am. Mil. Engrs. Home: Box 6 Boiling Springs PA 17007 Office: Carlisle Corp 250 E 5th St Cincinnati OH 45202

DIXON, JO-ANN CONTE, management consultant; b. Orange, N.J., Aug. 5, 1942; d. Rocco Louis and Antoinette (DeRosa) Conte; student Paterson State Coll., 1960-63; AA, Thomas A. Edison Coll., 1976, BA, 1978; m. Michael Eugene Dixon, July 26, 1964; children: Christopher Michael, Peter Eugene. Tchr., St. Raphael's Sch., Livingston, N.J., 1963-68; owner Orgn. Unltd., Glen Ridge, N.J., 1972-78; adminstr. corp. tng. dept. Rapidata, Inc., Fairfield, N.J., 1978-80, mgr. corp. tng. dept., 1980—; pres., prin. cons. Q, Inc., Essex Fells, N.J.; dir. alumni relations N.J. Inst. Tech., Newark 1981-83; dir. mgmt. devel. Rutgers U. Grad. Sch. Mgmt., 1983-84; dir. alumni affairs/devel. officer Seton Hall Law Sch., Newark, 1984-85; chmn. bd. trustees Nat. Inst. for Orgnl. and Mgmt. Research, Essex Fells, N.J., 1987—; bd. trustees, exec. dir. Nat. Inst. for Orgn. and Mgmt. Research; bd. dirs. Chmn. bd., sec. Passaic River Coalition, Basking Ridge, N.J., 1976-83, vice chmn. bd., 1983—, regional coordinator, 1971-76; chmn. mayor's com. on environment, Glen Ridge, 1974-75; mem. N.J. Gov.'s Task Force for Passaic River, 1976-78; mem., pres. Home and Sch. Bd., Glen Ridge, 1978-79. Nat. Trust Hist. Preservation scholar, 1977; citation Borough of Glen Ridge, 1975; Kiwanis award for excellence in citizen involvement, 1974. Mem. Am. Soc. Tng. and Devel. (v.p. communications, profl. excellence award 1980), LWV, Knights of Malta-Order St. John of Jerusalem (Dame of Malta 1986), Glen Ridge Hist. Soc. (founder), West Essex C. of C. (bd. dirs.), N.J. Women's Polit. Action Com. (v.p.). Roman Catholic. Home and Office: 97 Lane Ave West Caldwell NJ 07006

DIXON, JOHN KENT, computer scientist; b. Detroit, Sept. 1, 1934; s. Leonard John and Laura (Kyro) D.; m. Alice Coveyou, June 18, 1959 (div.); children: Bruce, Katherine, Laurie; m. Carolyn Good, Dec. 1, 1979; children: Andy, Bethany. BS in Elec. Engring., Lawrence Inst. Tech., 1957; MBA, Wayne State U., 1964; MS in Physics, U. Calif., Livermore, 1967, PhD in Computer Sci., 1970. Registered profl. engr., Mich. Electronics engr. Chrysler Missile Co., Warren, Mich., 1957-59, Bendix Rsch. Lab., Southfield, Mich., 1959-65; rsch. asst. Lawrence Radiation Lab., Livermore, 1965-68; computer scientist NIH, Bethesda, Md., 1968-74, Naval Rsch. Lab., Washington, 1974-86, Gould Electronics, Fairfax, Va., 1986-88, System Planning Corp., Rosslyn, Va., 1988—. Contbr. articles to profl. jours. Mem. IEEE, Assn. for Computing Machinery, Am. Assn. for Artificial Intelligence, World Population Soc. (v.p. 1972-75). Home: 17 Arthur Dr E Fort Washington MD 20744

DIXON, LAWRENCE PAUL, insurance company executive; b. N.Y.C., Oct. 23, 1938; s. Clinton DeForge and Frances Margaret (Van Deusen) D.; BS, Fordham, U., 1960; m. Barbara Carell, June 18, 1960; children—Laurie Jean, Gregory, Linda, Kenneth; m. Zelen Wilde, July 3, 1981. Lic. captain. Sr. underwriting officer Chubb & Son, Inc., Short Hills, N.J., 1960-73; sr. v.p. Contractors Coverage Corp., Great Neck, N.Y., 1973-76; v.p., ptnr. Global Planning Corp., Great Neck, 1976-78; pres. Dixon Brokerage, Inc., Melville, N.Y., 1978—, Ledd Co. Inc., Melville, 1987—; bd. dirs. Ebony Internat.; pres. Tiburn Services Ltd., Melville. Mem. U.S. Congl. Adv. bd., mem. The Pres.'s Com., Rep. Presdl. Task Force, Rep. Nat. State Elections Com., Am. Security Council Found.; pres. Fathers Club LaSalle Mil. Acad., chmn. Beef-o-Rama, 1982; trustee USMMA. Served with USCG. Mem. Profl. Ins. Agts., Ind. Ins. Agts., Am. Subcontractors Assn., Subcontractors Trade Assn., Assn. Gen. Contractors, Advancement Commerce and Industry, Old Chester Hills Civic Assn., Gen. Contractors Assn. Republican. Clubs: Northport Yacht, Drug and Chem., Huntington Yacht, Green Turtle Yacht, North Palm Beach Yacht, Familiares (bd. dirs.), Ducks Unltd. (sponsor). Home: 35 Bunkerhill Dr Huntington NY 11743 Office: 150 Broadhollow Rd Melville NY 11747

DIXON, RICHARD CRESSIE, natural gas company executive; b. Guymon, Okla., Mar. 24, 1929; s. Homer E. and Esta (Hayes) D.; m. Georgianna Sweet, Aug. 27, 1950; children—Richard Phillip, James Douglas, Daniel Kent. B.S. in Petroleum Engring, Okla. U., 1952. With Panhandle Eastern Pipe Line Co. (and subs. cos.), 1952—; mgr. gas purchase Panhandle Eastern Pipe Line Co. (and subs. cos.), Liberal, Kans., 1952-66; v.p. Anadarko Prodn. Co. subs., Liberal, 1961-65; pres. Anadarko, Ft. Worth, 1968-71; v.p., prodn. and gas supply divs. Panhandle Eastern Pipe Line Co., Kansas City, Mo., 1966-68; sr. v.p. Panhandle Eastern Pipe Line Co., Houston, 1971-85, group v.p., 1985—; group v.p. Panhandle Eastern Corp., Houston, 1988—. Mem. Am. Petroleum Inst., Ind. Petroleum Assn. Am., Mid-Continent Oil and Gas Assn., Soc. Petroleum Engrs., Ind. Natural Gas Assn. Republican. Presbyn. Clubs: Petroleum, University, Lakeside Country (Houston). Home: 334 Fawnlake Dr Houston TX 77079 Office: Panhandle Ea Corp PO Box 1642 Houston TX 77251

DIXON, SHARON PRATT, utility company executive; b. Washington, Jan. 30, 1944; d. Carlisle and Mildred (Petticord) Pratt; m. Arrington Dixon (div.); children: Aimee Arrington, Drew Arrington. BA, Howard U., 1965, JD, 1968. Bar: D.C. 1970, U.S. Dist. Ct. D.C. 1970, U.S. Ct. Appeals (D.C. cir.) 1970, U.S. Tax Ct. 1970. Assoc. Pratt & Queen, P.C., Washington, 1971-76; lawyer, prof. Antioch Sch. Law, Washington, 1972-76; assoc. gen. counsel Potomac Electric and Power Co., Washington, 1976-79, dir. consumer affairs, 1979-83, v.p. consumer affairs, 1983-86, v.p. pub. policy, 1986—. Chmn. Ea. regional caucus Dem. Nat. Com., Washington, 1976-85, treas., 1985—; nat. committeeperson D.C. State Com., Washington, 1977—. Recipient Disting. Svc. award Fedn. Women's Clubs, 1986, Nat. Assn. Black Women Attys., 1987, 88, Presdl. award NAACP, 1983, Disting. Leadership award United Nego Coll. Fund, 1985. Mem. Women's Rsch. and Ednl. Inst. (bd. dirs. 1986-88), D.C. Unified Bar, D.C. Bar Assn., Links Club, Jack & Jill Club. Home: 8227 W Beach Terr NW Washington DC 20012 Office: Potomac Electric Power Co 1900 Pennsylvania Ave NW Washington DC 20068

D'LUHY, JOHN JAMES, investment banker; b. Passaic, N.J., Sept. 18, 1933; s. John George and Leonora (Fila) D'L.; m. Gale Rainsford, Dec. 7, 1968; children: Amanda, Pamela. AB, Trinity Coll., 1955; MBA, U. Pa., 1959. Lic. amateur radio operator K2EXI, pvt. pilot. Jr. exec. trainee Merrill Lynch, N.Y.C., 1956-58, with over-the-counter research dept., 1959-60; assoc. syndicate dept., investment mgmt., investment banking Lazard Freres & Co., N.Y.C., 1960-68; sr. v.p., ptnr., dir. money mgmt. and venture capital divs. R.W. Pressprich & Co., N.Y.C., 1968-72; dir. money mgmt. and pvt. placements Wood Walker & Co., N.Y.C., 1972-73; pres. U.S. Oil Co., 1973-83, founder, pres., 1983-84; registered rep. Dominick & Dominick, Inc., Manasquan, N.J., 1986—; investment broker Dominick & Dominick, Inc., 1988—; adviser Hampshire Coll., Mass; trustee Collier Services Found., Marlboro, N.J., 1986—; pvt. investor, 1983-86. Hon. usher St. Patrick's Cath., N.Y.C., 1969—, chief hon. usher, 1975-76; founding mem. U.S. Naval War Coll. Found., Newport, R.I. Served with USNR, 1955. Fellow Frick Mus.; mem. Internat. Platform Assn., Investment Assn. N.Y. (bd. dirs. 1967, chmn. capital and money markets com.), Bond Club of N.Y., N.Y. Soc. Security Analysts (sr. analyst), Am. Radio Relay League, Aircraft Owners and Pilots Assn. Roman Catholic. Clubs: University (council exec. com., treas. 1979-83), Thursday Evening (N.Y.C.); Spring Lake (N.J.) Bath & Tennis, Bond. Home: 115 Ludlow Ave Spring Lake NJ 07762 Office: Dominick & Dominick Inc Valley Park 2517 Rt 35 Bldg D-101 Manasquan NJ 08736

DOBBINS, BETTY YARBOROUGH, savings and loan executive; b. Elkin, N.C., May 28, 1926; d. Andrew Frithey and Mary (Hudson) Yarborough; m. Stephen Glenn Dobbins Sr., Sept. 29, 1944; children: Stephen Glenn Jr., Pamela D. Keesee. Student, Draughn's Bus. Coll., 1943-44; cert., Associated Credit Burs. Am., 1952, N.C. Savs. and Loan League, 1986. Office clk. Firestone Co., Winston-Salem, N.C., 1944; with acctg. dept. May Co., Denver, 1945—; sec. Elkin Mchts. Assn., 1949-52; v.p., asst. sec. Mut. Fed. Savs. and Loan Assn., Elkin, 1954—, internal auditor, trainer, cons., 1960—, dir. mortgage and lending dept., 1973-84. Dir. choir Friendship Bapt. Ch., Elkin, 1958-76; dir. music Bethel Bapt. Ch., Ronda, N.C., 1976—; tchr. Sunday sch. for many yrs. Recipient Disting. Service award N.C. League of Savs. Instns., 1985. Democrat. Office: Mut Fed Savs and Loan Assn 201 W Main St Elkin NC 28621

DOBBINS, ROBERT HELM, banker; b. Louisville, June 6, 1951; s. John Dunlap and Sara (Helm) D.; m. Leslie MacNeil. BS with distinction, U. Va., 1973; M.B.A., Dartmouth Coll., 1978. With Mellon Bank, N.A., Pitts., 1973-76, Morgan Guaranty Trust Co., N.Y.C., 1977; v.p. nat. div. Liberty Nat. Bank, Louisville, 1978-81, sr. v.p. U.S. banking div., 1981—. Bd. dirs. Jr. Achievement, Leadership, Louisville, 1986—; bd. dirs., treas. Bellewood Presbyn. Children's Home, Louisville, Louisville Ballet; mem exec. com. Bellewood Homes, chmn. fin. com.; mem. Louisville Com. on Fgn. Relations. Presbyterian. Clubs: Pendennis, Louisville Country, River Valley, Filson (Louisville); Princeton (N.Y.C.). Home: 213 Travois Rd Louisville KY 40207 Office: PO Box 32500 Louisville KY 40232

DOBBS, DONALD EDWIN ALBERT, public relations executive; b. Ft. Wayne, Ind., Oct. 8, 1931; s. Edmund F. and Agnes (Stempnick) D.; B.S., Marquette U., 1953; m. Beatrice A. Spieker, July 27, 1957; children: Margaret L. Howard, Christopher E.J., Laura C. Pribe. Reporter Cath. Chronicle, Toledo, 1953; with pub. relations dept. Nat. Supply Co., Toledo 1955-59; employee communications exec. Prestolite Co., an Eltra Co., Toledo, 1959-61, public relations dir., 1961-80, dir. communications, 1980-83; mgr. external affairs Allied Electronic Components Co., an Allied Corp. Co.; pres. Dobbs & Assocs. Pub. Realtions and Advt., 1984—. Past chmn. Maumee Valley Hosp. Sch. Nursing Com.; pres. Internat. Inst., Toledo, 1970-73; past chmn. Child Nutrition Center, Toledo; past mem. Ohio Adv. Council Vocat. Edn.; vice chmn. Mayor's Citizen Devel. Forum; chmn., past pres. Mercy Hosp. adv. bd.; past pres. bd. dirs. Crosby Gardens; past pres. Ohio Friends of Library; past chmn. Salvation Army; past pres. Toledo Council of World Affairs, Toledo Hearing and Speech Center, Friends of Toledo/Lucas County Library; past pres. bd. dirs. Internat. Park; v.p. Toledo Opera Assn.; bd. dirs. Ohio Libr. Found. Served with AUS, 1953-55. Mem. Marquette U. Alumni Assn. N.W. Ohio (past pres., area dir.), Soc. Profl. Journalists, Public Relations Soc. Am. (past pres. N.W. Ohio), Automotive Public Relations Council (past pres.), Cath. Interracial Council (past pres.). Democrat (past nat. com. Wis. Young Dems.). Roman Catholic. Lodge: Kiwanis (past pres. Toledo, Mid-City Athletic League, Youth Found.; lt. gov. 1974-75). Home: 2433 Meadowwood Dr Toledo OH 43606 Office: PO Box 2964 Toledo OH 43606

DOBBS, JAMES FREDERICK, marketing professional; b. Dallas, Sept. 26, 1945; s. James Fred and Maureen Viola (McCrae) D.; m. Elizabeth Rutherford, Feb. 9; children: Meredith Leigh, Christine Elizabeth. BBA, U. Tex., Arlington, 1969. Pres. Dobbs-Stanford Corp., Dallas, 1970—.

patentee magnetic tape cassette. With USAR, 1966-72. Mem. Isthmus Inst., Pi Sigma Epsilon (pres. 1967-68). Episcopalian. Avocations: magic, writing. Office: Dobbs-Stanford Corp 2715 Electronic Ln Dallas TX 75220

DOBELLE, GLADYS KLEINMAN, public affairs executive; b. N.Y.C., Feb. 15, 1943; d. Irving and Sally Kleinman; m. William H. Dobelle, Dec. 31, 1972 (div.). B.A. with honors, Hunter Coll., 1964; postgrad. Harvard Inst. Arts Adminstrn., 1971. Mem. faculty Cambridge Ctr. for Adult Edn. (Mass.), Boston Ctr. for Adult Edn., 1968-72; asst. to pub. Boston After Dark, 1968-69; asst. to dir. Newport Romantic Music Festival (R.I.), summer 1969; exec. dir. Harvard Ind. newspaper, Cambridge, 1969-70; pub. relations dir. Boston Ctr. for Arts, 1970-72, Ballet West, Salt Lake City, 1973, San Francisco Opera, 1974, San Francisco Symphony, 1975; pres. Glad Tidings, pub. affairs cons., N.Y.C., 1976—; mem. faculty New Sch. Social Research, N.Y.C., 1977-80, NYU, 1979-81; cons. Boston Globe, Harvard Inst. Arts Adminstrn., Fine Arts Devel., America's Cup Races, 1970; chmn. Dialogue: A Working Woman's Seminar, 1977-79. Mem. Citizen's Com. for N.Y.C., Assn. for a Better N.Y., Landmark, Westpride; aux. patrol officer Manhattan; coordinator West 63rd/West 64th St. Block Assn.; chmn. Who Owns the Sunshine campaing; co-chmn. East Side/West Side Story; mem. Parks Coun., Landmarks Conservancy; mem. arts and landmarks com. Community Bd. 7, Bus. Execs. for Nat. Security; mem. young leadership bd. Jewish Mus.; mem. Am.-Israel Pub. Affairs Com., women's aux. Congregation Emanu-El; bd. dirs. Bus. Coun. for UN, Bus. and Profl. Women's Div. and Pub. Policy Com. United Jewish Appeal, Dance Library of Israel, Lincoln Sq. Community Council, Rapp Arts Ctr. Fellow Mcpl. Art Soc.; mem. Pub. Relations Soc. Am., Regional Plan Assn., Am. Women in Radio and TV, Women in Communications, LWV, Am. Jewish Congress (met. div.), Nat. Council Jewish Women, Women's Campaign Fund Fgn. Policy Assn., Roundtable (polit. action com.), Central Park Community Council, Westside C. of C., others. Editor: Getting into Ink and Print and On the Air, 1971. Democrat. Jewish. Clubs: City N.Y., Women's City N.Y., Road Runner N.Y. Avocations: sailing, aerobics. Home: One Lincoln Pla New York NY 10023 Office: Glad Tidings 20 W 64th St New York NY 10023

DOBES, IVAN RASTISLAV, computer executive; b. Bratislava, Czechoslovakia, Feb. 12, 1937; came to U.S., 1970; s. Jiří Dobeš and Hana (Hrčková) Kolínková; m. Ivana Schneiderová, Sept. 10, 1960 (div. 1982); children: Zuzana, Katerina, Nele; m. Jindra Divišová, June 19, 1983; 1 child, Nele. MS in Elec. Engring., Czech Tech. U., Prague, Czechoslovakia, 1960. Researcher Research Inst. Math. Machines, Prague, 1960-68; mem. tech. staff ICL, Ltd., Kidsgrove, Eng., 1968-70, NCR, Dayton, Ohio, 1970-73, Macrodata Co., Woodland Hills, Calif., 1973-77; cons. engr. Digital Equipment Corp., Maynard, Mass., 1977-83; sr. engring. mgr. Digital Equipment Corp., Marlboro, Mass., 1987—; dir. research and devel., chief scientist Omnicad Corp, Rochester, N.Y., 1983-87; lectr. Charles U., Prague, 1962-68; vis. scientist Leuven (Belgium) U., 1980-81. Contbr. articles to profl. jours.; editor books in field. Mem. IEEE, Assn. for Computing Machinery, Am. Assn. for Artificial Intelligence. Home: 62 Robert Rd Stow MA 01775 Office: Digital Equipment Corp 290 Donald Lynch Blvd Marlborough MA 01752

DOBIN, MICHAEL H., financial services executive; b. N.Y.C., Nov. 27, 1949; s. Alvin Dobin and Joyce (Wetzler) Tannenbaum; m. Deborah Sue Mordetsky, Sept. 24, 1970; children: Bradley Eric, David Benjamin, Alex Joshua. BS, Manhattan Coll., 1974. Asst. exec. cashier Thomson McKinnon Securities, Inc., N.Y.C., 1967-79; sr. v.p. and adminstrv. mgr. equity trading Shearson-Lehman Bros., Inc., N.Y.C., 1979—. With USAR, 1970-76. Mem. Security Industry Assn. (hon.), Security Traders Assn. N.Y., Nat. Assn. Security Dealers Arbitration Com. Club: Temple Sharri Emeth Men's (Englishtown, N.J.). Lodge: KP. Home: 141 Micki Dr Morganville NJ 07751 Office: Shearson Lehman Huison Inc World Fin Ctr New York NY 10285-0600

DOBMEIER, CLARENCE JOSEPH, JR., operations manager of employment and training; b. Redwood Falls, Minn., Nov. 21, 1952; s. Clarence Joseph Sr. and Agnes Josephine (Knutson) D.; m. Nancy Lynn Steele, Sept. 18, 1982; children: Brett Clarence, Brittany Steele. BA, Bemidji State U., 1974, postgrad., 1975—. Work tng. coordinator Rural Minn. Concentrated Employment Program, Bemidji, 1975-78; team leader Rural Minn. Concentrated Employment Program, Fergus Falls, 1978-79; ops. mgr. Rural Minn. Concentrated Employment Program, Alexandria, 1979—; mgmt. evaluator Minn. Dept. Edn., Post-secondary schs.; chmn., bd. dirs., fin. com. West Cen. CAP, Elbow Lake, treas. 1987, vice-chmn. 1988, chmn. bd., 1989, Minn.; chmn. bd. dirs., treas. Young Peoples Place, Alexandria. Mem. Handicapped Vocat. Task Force, 1985, local Congl. Awards Steering Com., 1985, Early Childhood Edn. Steering Com., 1984; clerk, vice chmn. Dist. 206 Alexandria Sch. Bd., 1983—; co-founder, troop leader mentally handicapped Boy Scouts Am., Alexandria, 1981-83; chmn. pub. relations Douglas County Cancer Soc., Alexandria, 1981-83; solicitor, div. leader, drive chmn. Heart of Lakes United Way, Alexandria, 1983—, now bd. dirs.; co-chmn. fundraising effort Alexandria Vocat. Sch. Found.; commr. Alexandria Housing and Redevelopment Authority, 1987—; trustee Alexandria Student Ctr. Found. Trust & Scholarship Fund, 1987—; bd. dirs. Alexandria Adult Edn. Bd., 1982—; 1982—; alt. del. Region 23 Minn. Sch. Bd. Assn.; mem. task force Douglas County AIDS Edn., 1988—; mem. adv. com. Alexandria Community Edn., 1988; chmn. Alexandria Police Civil Svc. Commn., 1989. Named one of Ten Outstanding Young Minnesotans, Jaycees, 1986, one of Outstanding Young Men Am., 1981. Mem. Alexandria Jaycees (pres., chmn. bd. dirs., dist. dir. 1979—, Disting. Service award, 1985. Episcopalian. Lodge: Lions (local bd. dirs. 1981-83, 85, 87—). Home: 1201 Douglas Alexandria MN 56308 Office: Rural Minn CEP Inc 700 Cedar Ste 266 Alexandria MN 56308

DOBRIN, BERNARD ROBERT, financial executive; b. Chgo., June 25, 1937; s. Max and Sophie (Schuman) D.; m. Marlene Joy Kempner, June 18, 1961; children: Lisa Diane, Jordan Eliot. AB, U. Chgo., 1961, MBA, 1962. CPA. Staff acct. Ernst & Ernst, Chgo., 1961-66; contr. Eckmar Corp., Chgo., 1966-69, Hoffman Rosner Corp., Hoffman Estates, Ill., 1969-73; pvt. practice fin. cons., Stamford, Conn., 1973-78; v.p. fin. Sirco Internat. Corp., Mt. Vernon, N.Y., 1978-82; sr. v.p. fin. and adminstrn. Morse/Diesel, Inc., N.Y.C., 1982-87; v.p. adminstrn., sec. Ogden Allied Abatement Svc., Inc., N.Y.C., 1988—. Mem. Fin. Execs. Inst., AICPA, Ill. CPA Soc. Home: 7 Cobblefield Ln White Plains NY 10605 Office: 2 Penn Pla New York NY 10121

DOBSON, BRIDGET MCCOLL HURSLEY, television executive and writer; b. Milw., Sept. 1, 1938; d. Franklin McColl and Doris (Berger) Hursley; m. Jerome John Dobson, June 16, 1961; children: Mary McColl, Andrew Carmichael. BA, Stanford U., 1960, MA, 1964; CBA, Harvard U., 1961. Assoc. writer General Hospital ABC-TV, 1965-73, headwriter General Hospital, 1973-75; producer Friendly Road Sta. KIXE-TV, Redding, Calif., 1972; headwriter Guiding Light CBS-TV, 1975-80, headwriter As the World Turns, 1980-83; creator, co-owner Santa Barbara NBC-TV, 1983—, headwriter Santa Barbara, 1983-86, exec. producer Santa Barbara, 1986-87. Recipient Emmy award Nat. Acad. TV Arts and Scis., 1988. Mem. Acad. TV Arts and Scis. (mem. com. on substance abuse 1986-88, Emmy nomination 1986), Writers Guild Am., Am. Film Inst. (mem. TV com. 1986-88). Office: 2121 Avenue of the Stars Suite 656 Century City CA 90067

DOBSON, GAVIN RICHARD, investment company executive; b. Wuppertal, Fed. Rep. Germany, Feb. 1, 1951; came to U.S., 1980; s. James Richard Easton and Dorothy Margaret (Ritchie) D. MA, Dundee U., Scotland, 1972; LLB, Edinburgh U., Scotland, 1974. Qualified Scottish lawyer, 1976. Solicitor Shepherd & Wedderburn, Edinburgh, 1974-76; mcht. banker Kleinwort Benson, London, 1977-80; dir., v.p. Kemper-Murray Johnstone Internat., Chgo., 1980—, also bd. dirs.; v.p. Kemper Internat. Fund, Chgo., 1981—, also bd. dirs. Contbr. articles to profl. jours. 2nd lt. Royal Scots TAVR infantry, 1974-76. Mem. Scottish Law Soc., Met. (Chgo.), Order Ky. Cols. Presbyterian. Home: 175 E Delaware Pl Apt 5714 Chicago IL 60611 Office: Kemper-Murray Johnstone Internat 120 S LaSalle St Chicago IL 60603

DOBSON, HOWARD RICHARD, JR., financial planner; b. Cedar Rapids, Iowa, Aug. 3, 1957; s. H. Richard and M. Jean (Marks) D. BA in Bus., U. Northern Iowa, 1981; cert. fin. planning, Coll. for Fin. Planning, 1985. Cert. fin. planner; registered investment advisor. Rep. Investors Profl. Services, Cedar Falls, Iowa, 1980-84; dir. annuity sales Profl. Brokerage Services, Cedar Falls, Iowa, 1984—; v.p. Am. Fin. Mgmt., Cedar Falls, Iowa, 1984—; bd. dirs. Investors Profl. Services, Cedar Falls, 1985—; instr. continuing edn.; with Iowa Ins. Dept.; Life Insurance Selling mag. Contbr. articles to Life Insurance Selling mag. Alumni advisor Pi Kappa Alpha (Theta Zeta chpt.), 1983—. Mem. Internat. Assn. Fin. Planners, Inst. of Cert. Fin. Planners, Nat. Assn. of Life Underwriters. Republican. Methodist. Office: Am Fin Mgmt 6003 University Ave Ste C Cedar Falls IA 50613

DOBSON, TERRANCE JAMES, banker; b. Odessa, Wash., Aug. 16, 1940; s. Leon C. and Dorothy (Armstrong) D.; m. Judith Kaye Blaesi, June 12, 1965; children: Terrance James Jr., Tad Jeremy. BA, Wash. State U., 1964; MBA, Mich. State U., 1969. Venture analyst Gen. Mills, Mpls., 1969-71; v.p., mgr. First Nat. Bank of Mpls., 1971-77; v.p. First Bank System, Inc., Mpls., 1977-78; exec. v.p. Old Nat. Bank of Wash., Spokane, 1978-87; sr. v.p. U.S. Bancorp, Portland, Oreg., 1987, exec. v.p., 1987—. Chmn. YMCA Inland Empire, Spokane, 1979-86; mem. bus. adv. council Wash. State U., 1980—; bd. dirs. Sisters of Holy Names, 1983-87. Capt. USAF, 1964-68. Mem. Am. Automobile Assn. (bd. dirs. 1978-88), Hayden Lake Country Club (bd. dirs. 1986-87), Oswego Lake Country Club, Rotary. Home: 17960 Ridge Lake Dr Lake Oswego OR 97034 Office: US Bancorp 111 SW Fifth Ave PO Box 8837 Portland OR 97208

DOCKERY, THOMAS HARLOWE, accountant; b. Asheville, N.C., Apr. 9, 1930; s. Grover William and Grace Wagner (Gorenflo) D.; B.S., U. S.C., 1955; postgrad. Jacksonville U., Fla. Jr. Coll.; m. Laverna Rebecca Robinson, May 19, 1951; children—Dorothy K. Dockery Wilder, V. Joanne Dockery Block, Jill C. Dockery Forrest, Robin K. Dockery Minton. Acctg. supr. U.S. Fidelity & Guaranty Co., Columbia, S.C., 1955-60, Jacksonville, Fla., 1960-63; acct. Duval Motor Co., Jacksonville, 1960-63; pres. Acctg. & Bus. Service Inc., 1962-77; self-employed acct., Jacksonville, 1963-72, Keystone Heights, Fla., 1972-77; comptroller Smoky Mountain Enterprises, Inc., Buck Stoves, Inc., Asheville, N.C., 1977-79; pvt. practice acctg., as Thomas H. Dockery & Co., Asheville, 1979—; ptnr. Lake Lure (N.C.) Art Supplies; owner Aaron Printing Industries, Allegro Pub. Co.; tchr. taxation Fla. Jr. Coll., Jacksonville, 1972, N.C. State U. Extension. Pres., PTA, Sherwood Elem. Sch., 1962. Served with USMC, 1948-52. Cert Nat. Soc. Pub. Accts. in Acctg. and Taxation. Mem. Fla. Accts. Assn. (pres. N.E. chpt. 1971), Jacksonville C. of C. (chmn. com. better bus. div. 1970-72), Clay County C. of C. (dir., treas. 1973), Asheville C. of C., Hickory Nut Grove C. of C. (treas.), Asheville Better Bus. Bur., (services com.), N.C. Soc. Accts. (sec.-treas., tax seminar speaker), Nat. Soc. Public Accts., Lee H. Edwards High Sch. Alumni Class (treas.), Toastmasters (v.p. 1961), Lions (officer Chimney Rock club.). Home and Office: PO Box 199 Lake Lure NC 28746

DOCKSON, ROBERT RAY, savings and loan executive; b. Quincy, Ill., Oct. 6, 1917; s. Marshall Ray and Letah (Edmondson) D.; m. Katheryn Virginia Allison, Mar. 4, 1944; 1 child, Kathy Kimberlee. A.B., Springfield Jr. Coll., 1937; B.S., U. Ill., 1939; M.S. in Fgn. Service, U. So. Calif., 1940, Ph.D., 1946. Lectr. U. So. Calif., 1940-41, 45-46, prof., head dept. mktg., 1953-59; dean U. So. Calif. (Sch. Bus. Adminstrn.); and prof. bus. econs. 1959-69; vice chmn. bd. Calif. Fed. Savs. & Loan Assn., Los Angeles, 1969-70; pres. Calif. Fed. Savs. & Loan Assn., 1970-77, chmn., 1977-88, chief exec. officer, 1973-83; chmn. CalFed Inc., 1984-88, chief exec. officer, 1984-85, also dir.; instr. Rutgers U., 1946-47, asst. prof., 1947-48; dir. Bur. Bus. and Econ. Research, 1947-48; economist Western home office Prudential Ins. Co., 1948-52, Bank of Am., San Francisco, 1952-53; econ. cons., 1953-57; dir. McKesson Corp., IT Corp., Pacific Enterprises Corp., Transam. Capital Fund, Inc., Transam. Income Shares, Inc., Internat. Lease Fin. Corp., Computer Scis. Corp. Am. specialist for U.S. Dept. State; mem. Town Hall, 1954—, bd. govs., 1963-65, hon. bd. govs., 1965—, pres., 1961-62; Trustee John Randolph Haynes and Dora Haynes Found., Rose Hills Meml. Park Assn., Com. for Econ. Devel., Calif. Council for Econ. Edn.; trustee, pres. Orthopedic Hosp.; bd. councilors Grad. Sch. Bus. Adminstrn., U. So. Calif.; bd. regents, chmn. univ. bd. Pepperdine U.; chmn. housing task force Calif. Roundtable. Served from ensign to lt. USNR, 1942-44. Decorated Star of Solidarity Govt. of Italy.; Recipient Asa V. Call Achievement award; Disting. Community Service award Brandeis U.; Whitney M. Young Jr. award Urban League, 1981, Albert Schweitzer Leadership award; Man of Yr. award Nat. Housing Conf., 1981; Industrialist of Yr. award Calif. Mus. Sci. and Industry, 1984. Mem. Calif. C. of C. (pres. 1980, dir. 1981-86), Los Angeles C. of C. (dir.), Am. Arbitration Assn., Newcomen Soc. North Am., Hugh O'Brian Youth Found., Phi Kappa Phi (Diploma of Honor award 1984), Beta Gamma Sigma. Clubs: Bohemian, California, Los Angeles Country, One Hundred, Silver Dollar, Birnam Wood Golf, Thunderbird Country. Office: CalFed Inc 5670 Wilshire Blvd Los Angeles CA 90036

DOCKSTADER, EMMETT STANLEY, construction company executive; b. Elmira, N.Y., Nov. 7, 1923; s. Roy S. and Gertrude (Everts) D.; B.C.E. cum laude, Syracuse U., 1947; m. Ruth Norma Emery, May 11, 1946; children—Deborah Ruth, David Stanley. Engr., Am. Bridge Co., Elmira, 1948-50; field engr. Sessinghaus & Ostergaard, Inc., Erie, Pa., 1950-53, project mgr., 1953-58, v.p., 1958-69; gen. mgr. constrn. div. H.H. Robertson Co., Ambridge, Pa., 1969-71; sr. v.p., sec. Sessinghaus & Ostergaard, Inc., Erie, 1972-79; constrn. exec. Gilbane Bldg. Co., Providence, R.I., 1979-84; pres., dir. Sessinghaus & Ostergaard Inc., Erie, 1984-86; pres. Dockstader Constrn. Assocs., 1986—; dir. Promac Corp., Research Triangle, N.C. Mem. Erie Port Commn., 1967-69. Bd. govs. Pastoral Counseling Center of Greater Providence, corporator Boston Seaman's Friend Soc., Inc. Served with USNR, 1944-46. Registered profl. engr., R.I., Pa., W.Va., Ga., N.C. Mem. Nat. Soc. Profl. Engrs., Nat Railway Hist. Soc. (bd. dirs. Lakeshore chpt.), Erie Mannerchor, SAR. Mem. Ch. of the Covenant (trustee). Mason (32 deg.), Rotarian. Clubs: Erie Yacht, Y Mens (past pres.). Home: 125 Lincoln Ave Erie PA 16505 Office: 2221 Peninsula Dr Erie PA 16506

DODD, JOE DAVID, safety engineer, consultant, administrator; b. Walnut Grove, Mo., Jan. 22, 1920; s. Marshall Hill and Pearl (Combs) D.; m. Nona Bell Junkins, Sept. 17, 1939; 1 dau. Linda Kay Dodd Helmick. Student SW Mo. State U., 1937-39, Wash. U., 1947-55. Cert. profl. safety engr. Calif. Office asst. retail credit co., Kansas City, Mo., 1939-42; bus driver City of Springfield (Mo.), 1945-47; ops., engring., and personnel positions Shell Oil Co., Wood River (Ill.) Refinery, 1947-66; health and safety dept. mgr. Martinez Mfg. Complex, Calif., 1966-83, retired 1983; exec. dir. Fire Protection Tng. Acad., U. Nev.-Reno; rep. Shell Oil Co., Western Oil and Gas Assn., 1970-81. Mem. Republican Presdl. Task Force. Served with USMC, 1942-45. Decorated Presdl. Citation. Mem. Western Oil and Gas Assn. (Hose Handler award 1972-81, Outstanding mem. award), Am. Soc. Safety Engrs., Veterans Safety, State and County Fire Chiefs Assn., Peace Officers Assn., Nat. Fire Protection Assn. Presbyterian (elder). Established Fire Protection Tng. Acad., U. Nev.-Reno, Stead Campus.

DODD, ROBERT WARREN, lawyer; b. Springfield, Ill., Jan. 20, 1938; s. Warren F. and Florence C. (Mueller) D.; m. Joyce M. Rowley, May 30, 1971; children: Cathy, Stephen, Joan, Jean, Brenda, James. AB, Josephinum Coll., Columbus, Ohio, 1960; JD, U. Ill., 1974. Bar: Ill. 1974, U.S. Dist. Ct. (cen. dist.) Ill. 1974; ordained priest Roman Cath. Ch., 1964. Sole practice Champaign, Ill., 1975-81; ptnr. Zimmerly, Dodd, Ansel & Stout, P.C., Champaign, 1981-82; sr. ptnr. Dodd, Beyers & Reeves, P.C., Champaign, 1982—; dep. mayor City of Champaign, 1981-83, mayor, 1983-87. Councilman City of Champaign, 1974-83; founder, v.p. Strategic Planning Com. Champaign Downtown Devel. Corp., 1986, cons., 1987—. Fellow Ill. Bar Assn.; mem. Champaign County Bar Assn., Ill. Bar Assn., Assn. Trial Lawyers Am. Roman Catholic. Club: Am. Bus. (Champaign). Lodge: Rotary. Home: 2120 Seaton Ct Champaign IL 61821 Office: Dodd Beyers & Reeves PC 303 S Mattis Ave Ste 201 Champaign IL 61821-3051

DODD, ROGER JAMES, lawyer; b. Sewickley, Pa., Sept. 15, 1951; s. Carl Roger and Dorothy Maude (Barley) D.; m. Emily Elizabeth Lilly, June 9, 1974; children: Matthew A., Andrew J. BA in Econs., Bucknell U., 1973; JD, U. Pitts., 1976. Bar: Ga. 1976, Fla. 1977, U.S. Ct. Appeals (5th cir.) 1976, U.S. Dist. Ct. (mid. dist.) Ga. 1976, U.S. Ct. Appeals (11th cir.) 1981, U.S. Dist. Ct. (no. dist.) Ga. 1983, U.S. Dist. Ct. Fla. 1983, U.S. Supreme Ct. 1987, U.S. Ct. of Mil. Appeals, 1987. Ptnr. Blackburn, Bright, Edwards, Dodd & Joseph, Valdosta, Ga., 1976-87; prin. Roger J. Dodd & Assocs., P.C., Valdosta, 1987—; spl. asst. atty. gen. State of Ga., 1979-85; mem. faculty Nat. Coll. Criminal Def., 1986—, Ga. Inst. Trial Advocacy, 1986—; bd. dirs. Ga. Inst. Trial Advocacy, 1986—; guest lectr. sch. law Mercer U., Ga. State U., mem. family law sect. exec. com., 1985-88, criminal law sect. Contbr. articles to profl. jours., newspapers. Bd. dirs. Lowndes Country Assn. Retarded Citizens, Valdosta, 1977, Valwood Sch., Valdosta, 1984-86. Fellow Am. Acad. Matrimonial Lawyers, The Ga. Bar Found; mem. Ga. Assn. Criminal Def. Lawyers (v.p. 1982-83, bd. dirs. 1982—, Pres.'s award 1982, exec. v.p. 1984, pres. 1986), State Bar Ga. (mem. exec. com. family law sect., 1986, sec. criminal law section, 1987—, Named Outstanding Law Day Chmn. 1977), Ga. Trial Lawyers Assn. (contbr. articles), Assn. Trial Lawyers Am., Nat. Assn. Criminal Def. Lawyers, Valdosta Bar Assn. (sec.-treas. 1977-78), Ga. Assn. Sch. Bd. Attys., MENSA, Nat. Inst. Trial Advocacy (Advance Trial Advocacy Skills 1985), Internat. Platform Assn. Libertarian. Presbyterian. Clubs: William Pitt (Pitts.), William Bucknell Assn. Lodge: Elks. Home: 1415 Williams St Valdosta GA 31601 Office: PO Box 1066 613 N Patterson St Valdosta GA 31603

DODGE, DOUGLAS WALKER, banker; b. Nyack, N.Y., July 1, 1932; s. James Walker and Ethel (Schaab) D.; m. Faith Drake; children: Kimberly A., Lisa H. AB, Dartmouth U., 1954; MBA, NYU, 1960. Lending officer Hanover Bank, N.Y.C., 1956-71; v.p. Merc.-Safe Deposit & Trust Co., Balt., 1971-77; exec. v.p. Deposit & Trust Co., Balt., 1977-83, pres., dir., 1983—; bd. dirs. Monumental Gen. Ins., Monumental Life Ins. Co., Balt., 1984—; vice chmn., dir. Merc. Bankshares Corp., Balt., 1984. Bd. dirs. United Way Cen. Md., Balt., 1983—, Union Meml. Hosp., Balt., 1984—, Goucher Coll., Balt., 1984—, Balt. Symphony Orch., 1984—. Served to lt. (j.g.) USN, 1954-60. Mem. Md. Bankers Assn. (pres. Balt. 1985), Robert Morris Assocs. (pres. Phila. 1983), Center Club, Balt. Office: Merc-Safe Deposit & Trust Co 2 Hopkins Pla PO Box 1477 Baltimore MD 21203

DODGE, THEODORE AYRAULT, geological mining consultant, drilling company executive; b. Chgo., Jan. 17, 1911; s. Robert Elkin Neil and Katherine Eleanor (Staley) D.; m. Isabelle Stebbins, June 15, 1935; children—Eleanor Dodge Gray, Janet, Richard Neil, Thomas Marshall. A.B. in Geology, Harvard Coll., 1932; A.M. in Geology, Harvard U., 1935, Ph.D. in Geology, 1936; M.A. in Geology, U. Wis., 1933. Registered geologist, Ariz. Geologist, sr. geologist Cerro de Pasco Copper Corp., Morococha, Peru, 1935-38; geologist, petroleum engr. various cos., 1939-41; geologist Anaconda Copper Mining Co., Las Cruces, N.Mex., 1941-42; geologist, acting chief geologist Cananea Consol. Copper Co., Cananea, Mexico, 1942-45; cons. geologist various companies, Ariz. and Mex. 1946-70; mgr. Christmas div. Inspiration Consol. Copper Co., Christmas, Ariz., 1971-75; pres. Hoagland & Dodge Drilling Co., Inc., Tucson, 1976—; instr. geology U. So. Calif., Los Angeles, 1940. Contbr. articles to profl. jours. Fellow Geol. Soc. Am., Mineral. Soc. Am.; mem. Ariz. Geol. Soc. (pres. 1955), Soc. Econ. Geologists, Am. Inst. Mining Engrs., Phi Beta Kappa, Sigma Xi. Baha'i. Club: Mining of the Southwest (Tucson). Home and Office: 1770 N Potter Pl Tucson AZ 85719

DODGE, WILLIAM DOUGLAS, diversified conglomerate executive; b. Savannah, Ga., Sept. 26, 1937; s. Kenneth Douglas and Bettie Wilbur (Sadler) D.; m. Sue M. Penny, Dec. 27, 1958 (div. 1976); children: Gregory D., Phillip C., Warren D., Andrew L.; m. Marian Elizabeth Monroe, Apr. 2, 1983. BS, Ga. Inst. Tech., 1959; MBA, Ga. State U., 1966. CPCU. Underwriter Liberty Mutual Ins. Co., Atlanta, 1960-66; ins. adminstr. Lockheed Corp., Marietta, Ga., 1966-78; risk mgr. Schlumberger Ltd., Atlanta, 1978-79; v.p. ins. Fuqua Industries, Inc., Atlanta, 1979—; pres. Fuqua Ins. Co. Ltd., Hamilton, Bermuda, 1980—; bd. dirs. N.Y. Ins. Exchange, N.Y.C., 1983—; adv. bd. Risk Mgmt. Inc., N.Y.C., 1978—, instr. 1974-79; chmn. bd., mem. investment com. J&H WF Syndicate B., N.Y., 1984-86. Co-author: The Hold Harmless Agreement, 1968. Mem. Exec. Com. Reorganization and Mgmt. Improvement State of Ga., 1971, Agents Licensing Examination Revision Bd. State Ga., 1970; bd. dirs. Ednl. Found., 1980—. Mem. Risk and Ins. Mgmt. Soc. Republican. Methodist. Clubs: Atlanta City; Oceanwoods (Hilton Head Island, S.C.) (bd. dirs.). Home: 7 W Ferry Ct NE Atlanta GA 30319 Office: Fuqua Industries Inc 4900 Georgia Pacific Ctr Atlanta GA 30303

DODGIN, BILL ARTHUR, fuels company executive; b. Nocona, Tex., Apr. 3, 1930; s. Elmer Clinton and Vera A. (Browning) D.; m. Mary Sue Foster, Oct. 22, 1949; children: Rebecca, Bill Clinton. Grad., Vega High Sch., Tex., 1947. Home builder Dodgin Home Builders, Amarillo, Tex., 1950-72; owner Dodgin Service, Amarillo, 1953-59; v.p. Affiliated Mgrs., Inc., Amarillo, 1960-72; pres. Beef Bds. of Amarillo, Inc., 1968-73; owner Dodgin Farms, Vega and Dalhart, Tex., 1972—; v.p., gen. mgr. High Plains Minerals, Amarillo, 1976-79; gen. mgr. Tri-State Minerals, Amarillo, 1978—; pres. Energiant, Inc., Amarillo, 1981—, Renewable Fuels Mng. Corp., Amarillo, 1984—; dir. Midwest Exploration, Inc., Oklahoma City, 1987—. Republican. Mem. Ch. of Christ. Home: Rte 1 Box 485 Amarillo TX 79102

DODSON, D. KEITH, engineering and construction company executive; b. Greenville, Tex., Nov. 2, 1943; s. Durwood R. and Louise (Amos) D.; m. Johnette Foster, Aug. 31, 1968; children: J. Marshall, Chandos A. B in Bus. and Engring., U. Tex., 1966; postgrad. in bus., U. Houston. Various positions leading to pres. internat. land ops. div. Brown & Root Inc., Houston, 1966-88; pres., chief exec. officer petroleum and chems. U.S.A. Davy McKee Corp., Houston, 1988—; mem. adv. com. dept. civil engring., U. Tex., Austin. Mem. exec. com. Constrn. Industry Inst., Austin, Tex., 1981-84; group chmn. Houston area United Way, 1983. Mem. Am. Inst. Chem. Engrs. (exec. bd. dirs. engring. and constrn. conf. 1985—), Houston Engring. and Scientific Soc. Club: Petroleum (Houston). Home: 10302 Holly Springs Houston TX 77042 Office: Davy McKee Corp 2925 Briarpark Houston TX 77042

DODSON, DONALD MILLS, cafeteria executive; b. Shamrock, Tex., Nov. 2, 1937; s. Freeman Mills and Marvie Hazel (Rives) D.; m. Sharon Jane Webb, Feb. 6, 1961; children—Randal, Stephanie, Kendal. Student, Tex. Tech. Trainee Furrs Bishops Cafeteria, Odessa, Tex., 1958, asst. mgr., 1958-59; mgr. Furrs Cafeteria, Odessa, Lubbock, Tucson, Denver, 1959-68; dist. mgr. Furrs Cafeteria, Lubbock, Tex., 1968-75, v.p. region, 1975-77, v.p. personnel devel., 1977-82, exec. v.p. ops., 1982—, sr. exec. v.p. ops., chief operating officer support depts., 1987—. Mem. Nat. Restaurant Assn., Tex. Restaurant Assn.

DODSON, THOMAS HAL, JR., oil company executive, accounting policy executive; b. Dallas, Aug. 24, 1934; s. Thomas Hal and Mildred Julia (Dunbar) D.; m. Jean Helen Burman, Sept. 7, 1954; children: Karen Lynn Dodson Arrington, Kathleen Diane Dodson Taylor, Brian Wayne. BBA, U. Tex., 1955, MBA, 1956. CPA, Tex. Various acctg. positions Humble Oil and Refining Co., 1956-68; refining controller Exxon USA, Houston, 1968-69; mgr. fin. reporting Exxon Corp., N.Y.C., 1969-71; asst. controller Exxon Internat., N.Y.C., 1971-72, Esso Europe, London, 1972-77; mgr. planning, budgets Exxon Corp., 1978-80, mgr. acctg. policy, 1980—; mem. acctg. adv. council U. Tex., Austin, 1970-72; mem. acctg. adv. roundtable U. Tenn., Knoxville, 1983-86. Pres. council Am. Ch. in London, 1974-76; clk. of session Presbyn. Ch., New Providence, N.J., 1985-88. Mem. Fin. Acctg. Standards Bd. (task force consols. project 1982—, pensions acctg. implementation group 1985-86, adv. group on joint ventures 1987—), Fin. Execs. Inst. (com. on corp. reporting 1982—), AICPAs. Home: 78 Hansell Rd New Providence NJ 07974 Office: Exxon Corp 1251 Ave of the Americas New York NY 10020

DOE, BURDELL FRANK, financial planner, tax preparer; b. Worthington, Minn., July 13, 1936; s. Frank William and Rose (Popken) D.; m. Janice Ruth McCord, Sept. 24, 1960; children: Denise, Darby, Alicia. BS, U.S. Navy Postgrad. Sch., 1964; MBA in Fin. Mgmt., George Washington U., 1974. Commd. ensign U.S. Navy, 1958, advanced through grades to comdr., 1971, retired, 1977; rep. Linsco, Alexandria, Va., 1977-78; exec. v.p. Manna Fin. Planning Corp., Fairfax, Va., 1978-86; v.p. Dondero and Assocs. Ltd., Alexandria, 1986-88; pres. Planning Assocs. Ltd., Alexandria, 1988—. Contbr. articles to profl. jours. Mem. Internat. Assn. for Fin. Planning (v.p. ethics Washington 1985-86), Inst. Cert. Fin. Planners, Nat. Assn. Tax Practitioners. Republican. Presbyterian. Home: 3204 Cunningham Dr Alexandria VA 22309 Office: Planning Assocs Ltd 209 Madison St Ste 335 Alexandria VA 22314

D'OENCH, RUSSELL GRACE, JR., editor; b. N.Y.C., Feb. 16, 1927; s. Russell Grace and Dorothie (Sharp) D'O.; m. Ellen Gates, Sept. 10, 1949; children: Peter, Ellen, Russell Grace III. Reporter Berkshire Eagle, Pittsfield, Mass., 1947-52; pub., editor Sunnyvale (Calif.) Standard, 1952-56; pres. Sagamore Press, Inc., N.Y.C., 1956-58; editor, chmn. bd. dirs. Middleton (Conn.) Press, 1959—; dir. Middleton adv. bd. Conn. Nat. Bank, chmn. adv. bd., 1982-86; vis. lectr. Wesleyan U., 1967-71; corporator Farmers and Mechanics Savs. and Loan, Middleton; bd. dirs. Middlesex Meml. Hosp., past chmn. bd. dirs.; bd. dirs. Middlesex Mut. Assurance Co. Active Bd. Govs. for Higher Edn., chmn. 1983-85; dir. Conn. Council on Freedom of Info., Goodspeed Opera Found., Conn. Pub. Expenditure Council, 1965-67, 87, Middlesex United Way, Conn. Student Loan Found.; past dir. Conn. Humanities Council; pres. Middleton Found. for the Arts; appointed mem. Commn. to Study Higher Edn., Gov.'s Commn. on Higher Edn. and Economy; past chmn. Conn. Joint Com. Ednl. Technology. With USMC, 1945-46. Mem. Am. Soc. Newspaper Editors, New Eng. Soc. Newspaper Editors (pres. 1965), Sigma Delta Chi (past sec.). Home: Phedon Pkwy Middleton CT 06457 Office: Middleton Press 2 Main St Middleton CT 06457

DOERFLER, RONALD JOHN, communications company executive; b. Jersey City, July 15, 1941; s. Louis S. and Ann E. (Dubiak) D.; m. Beatrice Mary Corbett, Jan. 4, 1942; children: Stephanie, Nicholas. BS, Fairleigh Dickinson U., MBA. CPA, N.Y. Fin. analyst ITT, N.Y.C., 1966-69; asst. controller Capital Cities Communications, N.Y.C., 1969-76, treas., 1977-80, v.p., 1980-83, sr. v.p., 1983-85, chief fin. officer, 1980-85; sr. v.p., chief fin. officer Capital Cities/ABC, N.Y.C., 1986—. Mem. Am. Inst. CPA's, Internat. Radio and TV Soc., Inst. Newspaper Fin. Execs., Broadcast Fin. Mgmt. Assn. (pres. 1979-80). Office: Capital Cities/ABC Inc 24 E 51st St New York NY 10022

DOERR, HOWARD P., telephone company executive; b. Lincoln, Nebr., June 3, 1929; s. Julius Henry and Kathryn (Kister) D.; m. ArVella Florence Stroh, Sept. 10, 1950; children: Cathleen K., Steven B., David S. B.S. in Bus. Adminstrn, U. Nebr., 1950. With Northwestern Bell Telephone Co., Omaha, 1950—, asst. v.p. ops., 1966-69; v.p., gen. mgr. Nebr. area Northwestern Bell Telephone Co., 1969-72, v.p. revenues, 1972-78; sr. v.p. fin. Northwestern Bell Telephone Co., Omaha, 1978-81; sr. v.p. fin. and external affairs Northwestern Bell Telephone Co., 1981-84; chief fin. officer, exec. v.p. U.S. West Inc., Englewood, Colo., 1984—; dir. Northwestern Nat. Bank, Omaha. Trustee Omaha Indsl. Found., Nebr. Ind. Coll. Found., Luth. Med. Center, Omaha; bd. dirs. Urban Housing Found., Park East, Inc., Gt. Plains council Girl Scouts U.S.A. Served to lt. USAF, 1951-52. Mem. Nebr. Assn. Commerce and Industry (dir.). Lutheran. Office: US West Inc 7800 E Orchard Rd Englewood CO 80111 *

DOGRA, BAL RAJ, retail stores executive; b. Sialkot, Punjab, India, Mar. 8, 1937; came to U.S., 1959; s. Sadhu Ram and Laj Wanti (Sharma) D.; children: Pamela Jayne, David Raj. BBA, Southeastern U., 1964, MBA, 1967. Store mgr. Safeway Stores, Inc., Washington, 1965-69; dist. mgr. Safeway Stores, Inc., Balt., 1970-80; adminstrv. coordinator Safeway Stores, Inc., Washington, 1980; dir. Casa Ley Safeway Stores, Inc., Cullican, Mex., 1981-82; dir. mktg. Safeway Stores, Inc., Los Angeles, 1983-84; v.p., div. mgr. Safeway Stores, Inc., El Paso, Tex., 1985-87; sr. v.p., div. mgr. Furr's Inc. Safeway Stores, Inc., El Paso, 1987—. Commr. Jr. League, Potomac, Md., 1977-78; bd. dirs. Sun Bowl, El Paso, 1986-87. Mem. El Paso C. of C. (adv. bd., bd. dirs. 1986-87). Republican. Home: 4750 Vista Del Monte El Paso TX 79922 Office: Safeway Stores Inc 9730 Railroad Dr El Paso TX 79924

DOHANIAN, JOYCE, mental health counselor; b. Cambridge, Va., Mar. 18; d. Armen and Rachel (Koumerian) D. BS, Boston U., 1977; MA, George Washington U., 1979. Lic. profl. counselor; cert. rehab. counselor; cert. ins. rehab. specialist, Va. Pvt. practice mental health counseling Arlington and Manassas, Va., 1980—; rehab. counselor Washington Area Hemophilia Ctrs., 1979-81, Commonwealth of Va., Alexandria, 1979-84; rsch. cons. Nat. Inst. Handicapped Rsch. and Rutgers U., 1984-86; ind. examiner Va. Bd. Profl. Counselors, Va. Dept. Health Regulatory Bds., 1986, 87; co-host, coproducer TV program Met. mag./Counselors at Large, 1985—. Mem. Consistory Bethel United Ch. of Christ, Arlington, 1984. Mem. Nat. Rehab. Counseling Assn. (Nat. Rehab. Counselor of Yr. award 1987), Va. Rehab. Counseling Assn. (pres. 1984), Nat. Rehab. Assn., Va. Rehab. Assn. (chmn. membership com. 1987-88), Am. Assn. for Counseling and Devel., Am. Rehab. Counselor Assn., Va. Head Injury Found., Assn. for Labor Mgmt. and Cons. on Alcoholism, Assn. Employee Asst. Program Practitioners, Bus. and Profl. Womens Assn. (Young Career Woman of Yr. award 1984). Office: PO Box 6085 Arlington VA 22206

DOHENY, DONALD ALOYSIUS, lawyer, business exec.; b. Milw., Apr. 20, 1924; s. John Anthony and Adelaide (Koller) D.; m. Catherine Elizabeth Lee, Oct. 25, 1952; children: Donald Aloysius, Celeste Hazel Doheny Kennedy, John Vincent, Ellen Adelaide, Edward Lawrence II, William Francis, Madonna Lee. Student U. Notre Dame, 1942-43; BME, Marquette U., 1947; JD, Harvard, 1949; M in Indsl. Engring. Washington U., St. Louis, 1956. Bar: Wis. 1949, Mo. 1949, U.S. Supreme Ct. 1970; registered prof. engr., Mo. Asst. to civil engr. Shipbuilding div. Froemming Bros., Inc., Milw., 1942-43; draftsman, designer The Heil Co., Milw., 1944-46; assoc. Igoe, Carroll & Keefe, St. Louis, 1949-51; asst. to v.p. and gen. mgr., chief prodn. engr., gen. adminstr., dir. adminstrn. Granco Steel Products subsidiary Granite City Steel, Granite City, Ill., 1951-57; asst. to pres. Vestal Labs., Inc., St. Louis, 1957-63; exec. v.p., dir. Moehlenpah Engring., Inc., Hydro-Air Engring., Inc., 1963-67; pres. dir. Foamtex Industries, Inc., St. Louis, 1967-75; exec. v.p., dir. Seasonal Industries, Inc., N.Y.C., 1973-75; sole practice, St. Louis, 1967-81; ptnr., Doheny & Doheny, Attys., St. Louis, 1981—, Doheny & Assocs. Mgmt. Counsel, St. Louis, 1967—; pres., dir. Mktg. & Sales Counsel, Inc., St. Louis, 1975—; pres., dir. Mid-USA Sales Co., St. Louis, 1976—; pres., bd. dirs. Profl. Bus. Exchange, Inc., St Louis, 1988—, Prestige Offices and Properties, Inc., St. Louis, 1987—; dir. St. Louis Airport Area Devel. Corp., 1988—; sec., bd. dirs. St. Louis Airport Area Devel. Corp., St. Louis, 1988—; lectr. bus. orgn. and adminstrn. Washington U., 1950-74; lectr. Grad. Sch. Bus., St. Louis U., 1980—. Served with AUS, 1943-44; 1st lt. res., 1948-52. Mem. ABA, Am. Judicature Soc., Am. Marketing Assn. (nat. membership chmn. 1959), Mo. Bar Assn., Wis. Bar Assn., Fed. Bar Assn., Bar Assn. St. Louis (gen. chmn. pub. relations 1955-56, vice chmn., sec.-treas. jr. sect. 1950, 51), Marquette Engring. Assn. (pres. 1946-47), Engring. Knights, Am. Legion, Tau Beta Pi, Pi Tau Sigma. Clubs: Notre Dame (pres. 1955, 56), Marquette (pres. 1961), Harvard (St. Louis); Stadium, Engineers, Mo. Athletic. Office: 11960 Westline Industrial Dr 12000 Bdlg Ste 330 Saint Louis MO 63146 also: 408 Olive St Mchts Laclede Bldg Ste 400 Saint Louis MO 63102

DOHERTY, EVELYN MARIE, data processing consultant; b. Phila., Sept. 26, 1941; d. James Robert and Virginia (Checkley) D. Diploma, RCA Tech. Inst., Cherry Hill, N.J., 1968. Freelance data processing programmer N.J., 1978-81; data processing cons. ednl., banking, transp., mfg., medical, pub., food wholesaling and brokerage community, project mgmt., contract mgmt., personal computer reseller, N.J., 1981—; lectr. data processing Camden County (N.J.) Coll. Contbr. articles in field. Chairwoman Collingswood (N.J.) Dems.. founder Babe Didikson Collingswood Softball Team for Women. Mem. Data Processing Mgmt. Assn. (chairperson, mem. ednl. com., bd. dirs. N.J. chpt., 1980—), Internat. Platform Assn., NAFE. Roman Catholic. Office: PO Box 3780 Cherry Hill NJ 08003

DOHERTY, WARREN L., industrial developer; b. Columbia, Miss., June 28, 1954; s. Jerry and Mary Ann (Taylor) D.; m. Patricia Elaine Sexton, Aug. 19, 1978. BS, U. So. Miss., 1984, MS, 1988. Tchr. Escuela Anaco, Venezuela, 1981-83; exec. dir. Stone County Econ. Devel. Found., Wiggins, Miss., 1985-86; exec. v.p. Marion County C. of C., Columbia, Miss., 1986—. Trustee First United Meth. Ch., Columbia, 1987—; adv. council Columbia/Marion County Votech. Tng., 1987—, Columbia Literacy Plus U.S., 1986—; co-founder Cultural Devel. Com., 1988. Served with USAF, 1975-79. Recipient Munro Petroleum award, 1985. Mem. Marion County Forestry Assn. (bd. dirs. 1986—), Miss. Assn. C. of C. Execs. (bd. dirs. 1987—), So. Indsl. Devel. Council, U.S. C. of C., Miss. Indsl. Devel. Council, So. Assn. C. of C. Execs., Rotary. Office: Marion County C of C 200 2nd St Columbia MS 39429

DOHMEN, FREDERICK HOEGER, retired wholesale drug company executive; b. Milw., May 12, 1917; s. Fred William and Viola (Gutsch) D.; BA in Commerce, U. Wis., 1939; m. Gladys Elizabeth Dite, Dec. 23, 1939 (dec. 1963); children: William Francis, Robert Charles; m. Mary Alexander Holgate, June 27, 1964. With F. Dohmen Co., Milw., 1939-82, successively warehouse employee, sec., v.p., 1944-52, pres., 1952-82, dir., 1947—, chmn. bd., 1952-82. Bd. dirs. St. Luke's Hosp. Ednl. Found., Milw., 1965-83, pres., 1969-72, chmn. bd., 1972-73; bd. dirs. U. Wis., Milw. Found., 1976-79, bd. vis., 1978-88, emeritus mem. 1988—; assoc. chmn. Nat. Bible Week, Laymen's Nat. Bible Com., N.Y.C., 1968-82, council of adv., 1983—. Mem. Nat. Wholesale Druggists Assn. (chmn. mfr. relations com. 1962, resolutions com. 1963, mem. of bd. control 1963-66), Nat. Assn. Wholesalers (trustee 1966-75), Druggists Service Council (dir. 1967-71), Wis. Pharm. Assn., Miss. Valley Drug Club, Beta Gamma Sigma, Phi Eta Sigma, Delta Kappa Epsilon, University Club, Town Club (Milw.). Presbyterian. Home: 3903 W Mequon Rd 112 N Mequon WI 53092

DOHNAL, WILLIAM EDWARD, retired steel company executive, consultant, accountant; b. Cleve., May 25, 1912; s. Frank and Anna (Florian) D.; children: David, Dennis. Grad. Cleve. Coll., 1940. CPA, Ohio. Auditor, Lybrand, Ross Bros. and Montgomery, 1942-45; acting auditor Cleveland-Cliffs Iron Co., Cleve., 1946-47, auditor, 1947-53, asst. treas., 1953-58, compt., 1958-63, v.p., compt., 1963-64, v.p. internat., 1964-73, sr. v.p., from 1973, now ret.; internat. bus. cons. Mem. Count. World Affairs. Mem. Am. Soc. CPA's, Ohio Soc. CPA's. Clubs: Clevelander; Weld (Perth, Australia). Home: PO Box 516 Safety Harbor FL 34695 Home: 1710 Lake Cypress Dr Safety Harbor FL 34695

DOI, MASAYUKI, credit card company executive; b. Amagasaki, Japan, Aug. 1, 1933; s. Masaharu and Tae (Shimizu) D.; m. Kazuko Yamamoto, Dec. 7, 1962; children: Masataka, Yasuhiro. BA in Econs., Kwansei Gakuin U., Nishinomiya, Hyogo, 1957. Various positions The Sumitomo Bank Co., Ltd., Osaka, Japan, 1957-73, br. mgr., 1973-83; mng. dir. The Sumitomo Credit Service Co., Ltd., Osaka, 1983—; adv. internat. risk Visa Internat. Service Assn., San Francisco, 1987. Office: The Sumitomo Credit Svc Co Ltd, 5 2 10 Shinbashi, Minato-ku, Tokyo 105, Japan

DOJNY, RICHARD FRANCIS, publishing company executive; b. Norwalk, Conn., Apr. 24, 1940; s. Francis Joseph and Mary (Ross) D.; m. Brooke Maury, July 16, 1966; children: Matthew, Maury. B.A., Dartmouth Coll., 1962. Sales rep. McGraw-Hill Book Co., N.Y.C., 1964-69, editor, 1969-73, field mgr., 1973-76, regional mgr., 1976-77, dir. mktg., 1977-79, v.p., gen. mgr., 1979-84; v.p. mktg. Macmillan Pub. Co., N.Y.C., 1984-85, v.p., dir. trade sales, 1985-86, v.p. adult trade pub., 1986-87, v.p. gen. pub. sales and mktg., 1987—. 1st lt. U.S. Army, 1962-64. Mem. Assn. Am. Publishers (head com. 1981-84). Roman Catholic. Home: 39 Burr Farms Rd Westport CT 06880 Office: Macmillan Pub Co 866 3d Ave New York NY 10022 *

DOLAN, BEVERLY FRANKLIN, diversified company executive; b. Augusta, Ga., 1927; married. Grad., U. Ga., 1952; grad. Advanced Mgmt. Program, Harvard U., 1969. Pres., co-founder E-Z Go Car Corp., 1954-60; with Textron Inc., Providence, 1960—, pres. Homelite div., 1976-79, corp. exec. v.p. ops., 1979-80, pres., 1980—, chief operating officer, 1980-85, chief exec. officer, 1985—, chmn., 1986—, also dir.; dir. First Union Corp., Allendale Mut. Ins. Co. Served with AUS, 1952-54. Office: Textron Inc 40 Westminster St Providence RI 02903 *

DOLAN, CATHERINE ELLEN, financial executive; b. N.Y.C., June 26, 1942; d. Thomas Michael and Margaret Mary (O'Neill) D.; B.A. cum laude, Newton Coll. of Sacred Heart, 1964. Statis. analyst Drexel, Harriman, Ripley, Inc., N.Y.C., 1966-68; mgr. Statis. Dept., Laird, Inc., N.Y.C., 1968-70; asst. treas. Old Lyme Corp., N.Y.C., 1970-78, treas., 1979-84; treas. Tru-Die, Inc., Franklin Park, Ill., 1976-84; asst. treas. Fabco-Air, Inc., 1981-84, Moore-Handley, Inc., 1982-84; v.p. Lyon & Stubbs, Inc., 1984-88 . Mem. U.S. C. of C., Fin. Women's Assn., Women's Econ. Roundtable. Home: 1030 Lions Ridge Loop #303 Vail CO 81657

DOLAN, JAMES T., JR., holding company executive; b. N.Y.C., Sept. 11, 1926; s. James T. and Mary C. (McBrien) D.; m. Hilda Johnson, Dec. 27, 1953; 1 child, Marian. BBA, Manhattan Coll., 1949. Labor relations asst. Nat. Lead Co., N.Y.C., 1951-62; from dir. personnel to sr. v.p. N.J. Natural Gas Co., Wall, 1962-78, pres., chief exec. officer, 1978-87; chmn. N.J. Resources Corp., Wall, 1987—; bd. dirs. Midlantic Nat. Bank N.J. Mem. Ocean County College Found., Pres.' Adv. Council Monmouth (N.J.) Coll.; bd. dirs., past pres. Monmouth-Ocean Devel. Council; pres. Tri-State Area Irish Youth Fund; active United Way, ARC, NCCJ. Recipient Clara Barton award ARC, 1979, Good Scout award Monmouth Council Boy Scouts Am., 1984. Mem. Am. Gas Assn. (nat. chmn. 1987-88), N.J. Utilities Assn. (bd. dirs., past pres.), Deal (N.J.) Country Club, Spring Lake (N.J.) Country Club, Metedeconk Country Club (Jackson, N.J.). Home: 1540 Ocean Ave Unit #23 Sea Bright NJ 07760 Office: NJ Resources Corp 1415 Wyckoff Rd Wall NJ 07719

DOLAN, JOHN JUDE, banker; b. Wheeling, W.Va., July 31, 1956; s. William Joseph and Mary Claire (Johnson) D.; m. Kimberly Ann Robbins, Sept. 9, 1978; children: David Michael, Robert William, Elizabeth Ann. BSBA, West Liberty State Coll., 1978. Jr. acct. Barnes, Saly & Co., Johnstown, Pa., 1978-80; with Nat. Bank of the Commonwealth, Indiana, Pa., 1980-85; v.p., contr. First Commonwealth Fin. Corp., Indiana, Pa., 1985-87, v.p., compt., chief fin. officer, 1987—; compt., chief fin. officer Commonwealth Trust Credit Life Ins. Co., Phoenix, 1989—; propr. Dolan Assocs., Indiana, Pa., 1981—. Bd. dirs. YMCA, Indiana, Pa. Mem. Indiana Area Jaycees. Republican. Roman Catholic. Club: Incovest Enterprise. Home: 110 Rural Gardens Ct Indiana PA 15701 Office: First Commonwealth Fin Corp 22 N 6th St Indiana PA 15701

DOLAN, RAYMOND BERNARD, insurance executive; b. Chgo., Feb. 13, 1923; s. Christopher P. and Florence M. (Taylor) D.; m. Theresa, May 25, 1946; children—Paul, Ronald, Donald, Sharon. Student, No. Mich. U., 1942; D.Arts and Scis. (hon.), Mt. Marty Coll., Yankton, S.D., 1980. With Equitable Life Assurance Soc. U.S., 1946—; v.p., chief line ops. Equitable Life Assurance Soc. U.S., N.Y.C., 1971-74; sr. v.p. corp. communications Equitable Life Assurance Soc. U.S., 1974-79, exec. v.p., chief agy. officer, 1979—; chmn. bd. Equitable of Del., 1985—; Inst. Life Ins. prof. in residence, econs. dept. St. Olaf Coll., 1975; dir. Equitable Variable Life Ins. Co., Equitable Capitol Mgmt. Corp., Equitable Life Leasing Corp., Equico Securities Corp., Donaldson, Lufkin & Jennette Inc. Vice chmn. Holy Spirit Ch. Parish Council, Stamford, Conn., 1968-71; chmn. Stamford dist. Boy Scouts Am., 1970-73; trustee Teledaga Coll., Ala.; chmn. bd. dirs. Nat. Council Better Bus. Burs. Served to lt. col. USAF, 1942-45, 51-52, 61-62. Decorated D.F.C., Air medal with 4 oak leaf clusters. Mem. Nat. Assn. Life Underwriters, C.L.U.'s N.Y., Nat. Guard Assn. (life), Consumer Council, Am. Council Life Ins., Res. Officers Assn., Conf. Bd., Pub. Affairs Research Council. Republican. Roman Catholic. Club: K.C. (4th deg.). Home: 5 Kings Grant 377 S Main St New Canaan CT 06840 Office: Equitable Life Assurance Soc US 1285 Ave of the Americas New York NY 10019

DOLAN, RONALD VINCENT, insurance company executive; b. Charleroi, Pa., Aug. 27, 1942; s. James L. and Kathryn (Stopp) D.; m. Mary Jane Tousignant, 1978; children—Gina, Ronalee, Mark, Craig, Samantha. B.A., St. Vincent Coll., Latrobe, Pa., 1964. Mgr. El Bent Supply, Pa., 1964-67; actuarial assoc. Penn Mut. Ins., Phila., 1967-72; pres. First Colony Life, Lynchburg, Va., 1973—; dir. Central Fidelity Bank, Richmond, Va., Va. Bapt. Hosp., Barclay Group Inc., Ft. Washington, Pa. Bd. dirs. The Sheltered Workshop, Lynchburg, Va., 1979—. assoc. Soc. of Actuaries; mem. Am. Acad. Actuaries. Home: Box 3152 Lynchburg VA 24503 Office: 1st Colony Life Ins Co PO Box 1280 Lynchburg VA 24505

DOLAN, THOMAS IRONSIDE, manufacturing company executive; b. Hastings, Mich., Mar. 31, 1927; s. Clifford and Katherine (Ironside) D.; m. Barbara Jane Sisson, June 11, 1948; children—Nancy, Sarah. B.S. in Indsl.-Mech. Engring, U. Mich., 1949. Pres. Kelvinator, Inc., Grand Rapids, Mich., 1969-75; sr. group v.p. White Consol. Industries, Inc., Cleve., 1975-80; sr. v.p. A.O. Smith Corp., Milw., 1980-82, pres., dir., 1982-84, chmn., chief exec. officer, 1984-89, chmn., 1984—, also dir. subs.; trustee Northwestern Mut. Life Ins. Co. Corp. mem. Milw. Sch. Engring; bd. dirs. Med. Coll. Wis. Mem. Met. Milw. Assn. Commerce (bd. dirs., chmn. 1988—), Machinery and Allied Products Inst. (exec. com.), Soc. Automotive Engrs., Hwy. Users Fedn. (trustee), Internat. Exec. Service Corps. (council), Bus. Council. Clubs: Milwaukee, Milw. Country, Milw. University. Lodge: Rotary.

DOLAN, WILLIAM FRANCIS, JR., utilities company executive, comptroller; b. Jersey City, Nov. 14, 1933; s. William Francis and Anna (Kurey) D.; m. Margaret Rose Leishman, Mar. 25, 1973; children: William F. III, Susan M., David M., Craig William, Scott Vincent. BS, Rutgers U., 1965. From clk. auditing asst. Pub. Service Elec. & Gas Co., Newark, 1956-72, asst. mgr. budget, 1972-74, asst. comptroller, 1974—; mem. acctg. research com. Edison Elec. Inst., Washington, 1978—. Mem. citizens adv. com. Middletown Twp. Solid Waste and Recycling, St. Vincent De Paul Soc. St. Mary's Ch. Mem. Am. Gas Assn. (chmn. acctg. prins. com. 1987—, vice chmn. 1985-87, mgmt. com.), N.J. Utilities Assn. (chmn. acctg./tax com. 1986-87), Nat. Assn. Accts., N.J. Assn. Pub. Accts. Republican. Roman Catholic. Lodge: Elks. Home: 5 Tournament Dr Leonardo NJ 07737

DOLBEN, DAVID H., financial executive; b. Arlington, Mass., May 8, 1935; m. Jean Dolben, July 4, 1956. AB, Dartmouth Coll., 1956; MBA, Columbia U., 1958. Asst. treas., comptroller, v.p. fin. Time Inc., N.Y.C., 1963—. Office: Temple-Inland Inc PO Drawer D Diboll TX 75941

DOLE, ROBERT PAUL, appliance manufacturing company executive; b. Freeport, Ill., Nov. 12, 1923; s. Herman Walter and Louise Marie (Bornemeier) D.; m. Joyce Lindsay, Mar. 14, 1947; 1 child, Luanne Dole Cloyd. BA, Cornell Coll., Mt. Vernon, Iowa, 1948. Personnel mgr. Green Giant Co., Lanark, Ill., 1948-50; controller Green Giant Co., 1951-52; asst. treas. Henney Motor Co., Inc., Freeport, 1952-53, Eureka Williams Corp., Bloomington, Ill., 1954-62; v.p. and asst. gen. mgr. The Eureka Co., Bloomington, 1962-79; sr. v.p. The Eureka Co., 1980, pres., 1980-88; exec. v.p., dir. parent co. Nat. Union Electric Corp., 1980-84, pres., dir., 1980-85, chmn. bd., pres., dir., 1985-88, chmn. bd., 1985—; group v.p., dir. Dometic Inc., Bloomington, Ill., 1984-86; group pres., dir. White Consol. Industries, Cleve., 1987-88; trustee Internat. Assn. Machinists Nat. Pension Fund, 1972-80. Served in U.S. Army, 1943-46. Republican. Lodges: Masons, Elks. Office: Nat Union Electric Corp 1201 E Bell St Bloomington IL 61701

DOLE, S. R., JR., retail executive; b. Emporia, Kans., Aug. 24, 1937; s. S. R. and Mary D. Student, San Bernadino Jr. Coll.; BA, San Diego U., 1960. With Spendee Mart, 1960-64; zone mgr. 7-Eleven, L.A., 1966-69, ops. mgr. no. Calif., 1969-70, mgr. western div., 1970-85; from franchise v.p., to v.p. stores group, sr. v.p., then exec. v.p. 7-Eleven, Dallas, 1985—. Office: Southland Corp 2828 N Haskell Ave Dallas TX 75204

DOLEZAL, DALE FRANCIS, truck manufacturing company executive; b. Ronan, Mont., Apr. 9, 1936; s. Henry Lewis and Regina Marie (Nedjelski) D.; B.S. in Indsl. Engring., Mont. State U., 1961; student Program for Mgmt. Devel., Bus. Sch., Harvard U., 1974; m. Patricia Louise Johnson, Aug. 27, 1960 (div. Dec. 1980); children—Craig, Kelly, Kathleen, Kari. Indsl. and methods engr. Westinghouse Electric Corp., Sunnyvale, Calif., 1961-63; chief indsl. engr. Clarke Equipment Corp., Spokane, Wash., 1963-65; mgr. materials Freightliner Corp., Portland, Oreg., 1965-67; with International Harvester Co., 1967—, dir. purchasing and inventory mgmt., Chgo., 1977-80, dir. materials and ops. planning, 1980-81; gen. mgr. parts and retail Indsl. Trucks div. Eaton Corp., Phila., 1981-84, pres. Modern Group, Phila., 1984-86, group v.p., gen. mgr. Holland Hitch Co., whitehouse Sta., N.J., 1986—; dir. Real Am. Corp.; mem. bd. bus. and indsl. advisers U. Wis., Madison; bd. dirs. Ops. Tng. Inst. Mem. parents adv. bd. Naperville (Ill.) Central High Sch., 1977—; mem. adv. bd. Sch. Dist. 203, Naperville, 1978—; mem. New Hope (Pa.) Solebury Sch. Bd., 1982-87 . Served with USMC, 1954-57. Registered profl. engr., Oreg. Mem. Am. Inst. Indsl. Engrs., Am. Prodn. and Inventory Control. Soc. (pres. 1968-74), Am. Soc. Indsl. Engrs. Republican. Roman Catholic. Clubs: Rotary (bd. dirs. 1988—), K.C. (pres.), Harvard (Chgo.). Contbr. articles to trade jours. Avocatons: golf, hunting, fishing. Home: 31 Greenbriar Ln Annandale NJ 08801 Office: Holland Group Ridge Rd Whitehouse Station NJ 08889

DOLGOW, ALLAN BENTLEY, consultant; b. N.Y.C.; BIE, NYU, 1959, MBA, 1972; m. Nina Kim; children: Nicole, Marc, Ginger, Kimbie. with, Republic Aviation Corp., Farmingdale, N.Y., 1959-60; mgr. Internat. Paper Co., N.Y.C., 1960-73; project mgr. J.C. Penney Co. Inc., N.Y.C., 1973-76; dir. mfg. and planning Morse Electro Products, N.Y.C., 1976-77, exec. mgr. Morse Electrophonic Hong Kong Ltd., 1976-77; internat. project mgr. Revlon Inc., Edison, N.J., 1977-79: mgmt. cons. SRI Internat., Menlo Park, Calif., 1979—. With U.S. Army, Germany. Office: 333 Ravenswood Ave Menlo Park CA 94025

DOLIN, JOEL DAVID, electronics executive, engineer; b. N.Y.C., Jan. 10, 1932; s. Irving and Carrie (Schwartz) D.; m. Lea Sharon Pruitt, June 14, 1969; children: Jennifer Lea, Claudia Martine. BA, Columbia Coll., 1953, BS, 1954, MS, 1955. Project adminstr. Loral Electronics, N.Y.C., 1958-59; engr. Ampex Corp., Redwood City, Calif., 1959-60; systems engr. McCarthy Assn., Menlo Park, Calif., 1960-62; pres. Leasametric, Foster City, Calif., 1962-80; pres. Target Fin. Corp., Foster City, 1981—. Served to lt. (j.g.) USN, 1955-58. Republican. Jewish. Home: 145 Fallenleaf Dr Hillsborough CA 94010 Office: Target Fin Corp 1153C Triton Dr Foster City CA 94404

DOLINER, NATHANIEL LEE, lawyer; b. Daytona Beach, Fla., June 28, 1949; s. Joseph and Asia (Shaffer) D.; m. Debra Lynn Simon, June 5, 1983. BA, George Washington U., 1970; JD, Vanderbilt U., 1973; LLM in Taxation, U. Fla., 1977. Bar: Fla. 1973, U.S. Tax Ct. 1973, U.S. Dist. Ct. (mid. dist.) Fla. 1974. Assoc. Smalbein, Eubank, Johnson, Rosier & Bussey, P.A., Daytona Beach, Fla., 1973-76; vis. asst. prof. law U. Fla., Gainesville, 1977-78; assoc. Carlton, Fields, Ward, Emmanuel, Smith & Cutler, P.A., Tampa, Fla., 1978-82, ptnr., 1982—, chmn. tax, corp. and securities dept., 1984—, treas. 1985-86, bd. dirs., 1983-87, 88-89. Bd. dirs. Big Bros./Big Sisters of Greater Tampa, Inc., 1980-82., dist. commnr. Gulf Ridge council Boy Scouts Am., 1983; bd. dirs. Child Abuse Council, Inc. 1986—, treas. 1988-89, pres.-elect 1989—; bd. dirs. Am. Heart Assn. (bd. dirs. Hillsborough County chpt. 1987-88, asst. treas. 1987-88, treas. 1988—), Fellow Am. Bar Found.; mem. ABA (vice chmn. continuing legal education com. tax sect. 1986-88, chmn. 1988—, chmn. subcom. on sales and exchanges, partnership com. ABA Tax Sect. 1986-88; com. on negotiated acquisitions bus. law sect.), Fla. Bar Assn. (mem. exec. com. tax sect. 1980-83, tax cert. com. 1987-88, vice chair 1988—); Greater Tampa C. of C. (chmn. Ambassadors Target Task Force of Com. of 100, 1984-85, 87-88, chair geographic task force, 1989—, vice chmn. govt. finance & taxation coun. 1987-88, chmn. 1988-89), Anti-Defamation League (regional bd. mem. 1986—, exec. com. 1987—), Tampa Jewish Fedn. (chmn. community relations com. 1986-87, bd. dirs. 1986-89). Clubs: Tampa Rotary (bd. dirs. 1986-88), The Tampa Club (bd. dirs., sec. 1987-89). Home: 3207 Tarabrook Dr Tampa FL 33618 Office: Carlton Fields Ward et al 777 S Harbour Island Blvd 5th Fl Tampa FL 33602

DOMBROWSKI, CHESTER JOHN, state agency administrator, political science educator; b. Chgo., June 24, 1938; s. Chester Stanley and Mary Jeanette (Wilczynski) D.; m. Melba Jean Cornish, May 26, 1962 (div. 1984); children: Debra Susan, Dana Lynn, Gregory John. BS in Mktg., No. Ill. U., 1961; MA in Polit. Sci., U. Tex., Arlington, 1983. Mgmt. trainee Packaging Corp. Am., Youngstown, Ohio, 1964-66; prodn. mgr. All-Steel Equipment Inc., Aurora, Ill., 1966-68; ins. agt. Washington Nat. Ins. Co., Dallas, 1968-72; owner, mgr. Little Kingdom Day Care Ctr., Plano, Tex., 1972-77; editor, publisher Child Care Reporter, Plano, 1973-74; ops. and fiscal mgr. Service Master, Ft. Worth, 1977-82; budget examiner Legis. Budget Bd., Austin, Tex., 1983-85, 1988—; dir. support service Collin County, McKinney, Tex., 1985-88; adj. instr. govt. Collin County Community Coll., McKinney, 1987—; polit. cons., McKinney, 1985-87. Precinct del. Dem. party, Austin, 1984. Served to commdr. USNR, 1961-82. Mem. Am. Soc. Pub. Administrs., U.S. Naval Inst., Naval Reserve Assn. Home: 2627 Baxter Dr Austin TX 78745 Office: Legis Budget Bd Box 12666 Capitol Sta Austin TX 78711

DOME, LAWRENCE ARTHUR, brokerage executive, underwriter; b. Cleve., July 25, 1946; s. Wilfred John and Agnes (Osicka) D.; m. Susan Sinclair, Oct. 5, 1968; children: Lawrence Arthur Jr., Kenneth John. BSBA, Bowling Green U., 1968. Appraiser trainee N.Y. Life Ins. Co., Cleve., 1968-71; appraiser II N.Y. Life Ins. Co., Washington, 1972-73, grade III, 1973-74, grade IV, 1974-76; regional appraiser N.Y. Life Ins. Co., N.Y.C., 1976-78, asst. chief appraiser, 1978-80, 2d v.p., chief appraiser, 1980-86, nat. underwriter, 1984-86; v.p. Goldman Sachs & Co., N.Y.C., 1986—. With U.S. Army, 1969-71. Mem. Am. Inst. Real Estate Appraisers (cert.), Mortgage Bankers Assn., Urban Land Inst. Office: Goldman Sachs & Co 85 Broad St 30th Fl New York NY 10004

DOMEIER, DAVID JOHN, controller; b. Washington, Apr. 17, 1953. CPA, Calif. Auditor DeLoitte, Haskins & Sells, San Francisco, 1975-79; v.p., controller Robert A. McNeil Corp., San Mateo, Calif., 1979-82; controller Cambridge Plan Internat., Monterey, Calif., 1982-83; div. mgr. corp. acctg. and adminstrn. Safeway Stores Inc., Oakland, Calif., 1983-88; v.p., controller Safeway Stores Inc., Oakland, 1988—. Mem. Fin. Execs. Inst., Calif. Soc. CPA's., Am. Inst. CPA's. Republican. Roman Catholic. Office: Safeway Stores Inc 201 4th St Oakland CA 94660

DOMIKE, ARTHUR LOUIS, financial services executive; b. Santa Monica, Calif., Jan. 19, 1926; s. Arthur Louis and Veneta Marie (McCarthy) D.; m. Joan Leslie Ronder, Mar. 3, 1950; children: Zachary Ronder, Steffi Ronder, Julie Ronder. BA, UCLA, 1948; MS in Agrl. Econs., U. Wis., 1953, PhD, 1961. Cooperative agt. Dept. Agrl. Econs., U. Minn., St. Paul, 1953-55; assoc. prof. Dept. Natural Resource Econs., U. R.I., Kingston, 1955-61; economist USDA, Washington, 1961-62, Orgn. of the Am. States, Buenos Aires, 1962-64; regional officer Food and Agr. Orgn., Santiago, Chile, 1964-68; coordinator, cooperative program Food and Agr. Orgn., Washington, 1968-76; research dir. Ctr. on Transnat. Corps., UN, N.Y.C., 1976-81; tech. dir. Ctr. for Internat. Tech. Cooperation, Am. U., Washington, 1981-83; corp. v.p. Developing Systems Ltd., Washington, 1983—, also bd. dirs.; consulting economist Office of the Pres. Mexico, Mexico City, 1981-83, Office of State Treas. Calif., Sacramento, 1986, Ford Found., Buenos Aires, 1965; adj. prof. Am. U., Washington, 1973. Author: Transnational Corporations in Food and Beverage Processing, 1980, Land Tenure Conditions and Socio-Economic Development of Argentina, 1966; contbr. articles to profl. jours. Served with USN, 1944-46, PTO. Research fellow USDA, 1961. Mem. Am. Econ. Assn., Am. Agrl. Econs. Assn., Latin Am. Studies Assn., Washington Economists Club. Club: Gypsy Trail. Office: Developing Systems Ltd 5225 Wisconsin Ave NW Washington DC 20016

DOMINIONI, ANGELO MARIA FRANCESCO, import-export company executive; b. Naples, Italy, Jan. 31, 1932; came to U.S., 1968; s. Giacinto Enrico and Jole (Vuturo) D.; student U. Messina (Italy), 1950-56; m. Valerie Ann Morrone, Aug. 25, 1971; 1 dau., Silvana Laura. With Securities Dept., Banco Di Sicilia, Milan, 1958-62; with SFI S.p.A., Milan, Italy, 1962-66; with Galbani S.p.A., Milan, Italy, 1966—, pres. Bel Paesesales Co. Inc. div., Galbani Inc., Brick, N.J., 1981—, also dir.; mktg. cons. Mem. Am. Mgmt. Assn., Nat. Cheese Inst., Nat. Assn. Specialty Trade. Republican. Club: Metedeconk River Yacht. Home: 47 Mizzen Rd Brick Town NJ 08723 Office: 445 Brick Blvd Ste 203 Brick Town NJ 08723

DOMKE, KERRY LYNN, controller; b. Marion, Kans., Dec. 3, 1950; s. Fredrick and Edna Marie (Bentz) D.; m. Judy Marie Iiams, Aug. 16, 1970; children: Ethan Brock, Nicolas Lynn. BS in Bus., Emporia State U., 1973. Acct. Nat. Coop. Refinery Assn., McPherson, Kans., 1973-75, budget dir., 1975-84, asst. contr., 1984-88, contr., 1988—; mem. supervisory com. McPherson Coop. Credit Union, 1976-79; bd. dirs., pres., 1980-85. Mem. Leadership McPherson, 1987, Leadership McPherson Alumni Group, 1988—; bd. dirs., treas. children's choir McPherson Arts Coun., 1988—. Mem. Nat. Assn. Accts., Contr. Coun., Am. Petroleum Credit Assn., Am. Petroleum Inst. Republican. Lutheran. Home: 1236 E Hulse McPherson KS 67460 Office: Nat Coop Refinery Assn 2000 S Main St PO Box 1404 McPherson KS 67460

DOMPKE, NORBERT FRANK, photography studio executive; b. Chgo., Oct. 16, 1920; s. Frank and Mary (Manley) D.; m. Marjorie Gies, Dec. 12, 1964; children: Scott, Pamela. Grad. Wright Jr. Coll., 1939-40; student Northwestern U., 1946-49. Cost comptroller, budget dir. Scott Radio Corp., 1947; pres. TV Forecast, Inc., 1948-52, editor Chgo. edit. TV Guide, 1953, mgr. Wis. edit., 1954; pres. Root Photographers, Inc., Chgo., 1955—. Adv. com. photography & audiovisual tech., So. Ill. U., 1980-81; adv. bd. Gordon Tech. High Sch., 1979-86. Co-founder TV Guide, 1947. With USAAC, 1943-47. CPA, Ill. Mem. United Photographers Orgn. (pres. 1970-71), Profl. Photographers Am., Profl. Sch. Photographers Am. (v.p. 1966-67, 87-88, sec.-treas. 1967-69, pres. 1969-70, dir. 1971-78, treas. 1985-86, sec. 1986-87, pres. 1988-89), Ill. Small Bus. Men's Assn. (dir. 1970-73), Chgo. Assn. Commerce and Industry (edn. com. 1966—), NEA, Nat. Sch. Press Assn., Ill. High Sch. Press Assn., Nat. Collegiate Sch. Press Assn., North Cen. Assn. (visitation com. 1986), Chgo. Bible Soc. (bd. advisors), Ill. C. of C., Barclay Club, International, Tonquish Creek Yacht. Home: 990 N Lake Shore Dr Chicago IL 60611 Office: 1131 W Sheridan Rd Chicago IL 60660

DOMRES, DAVID GORDON, real estate corporation officer; b. Milw., Apr. 3, 1959; s. Gordon Frederick and Amydee (Carr) D.; m. Nancy Elizabeth Rassmann, Oct. 23, 1982; children: Michael, Laura. BArch, Iowa State U., 1982. Resident asst. Iowa State Dept. Residence, Ames, 1981-82; property mgr. Blue Ridge Enterprises, Inc., Milw., 1982-84; mgr. Nat. Realty Mgmt., Inc., Wauwatosa, Wis., 1984-85; v.p. property mgmt. Sidney Kohl Co., Milw., 1985-87; dir. property ops. Nat. Realty Mgmt., Inc., Wauwatosa, 1987-88; v.p. Odgen & Co., Inc., Milw., 1988—. Exec. dir. The Pines Found., Waupaca, Wis., 1987—; com. mem. Pine Lake Camp, Inc., Waupaca, 1984—; mem. council Holy Cross Luth. Ch., 1984-87; asst. scoutmaster Boy Scouts Am., Milw., 1986—. Mem. Apt. Assn. Milw. (pres. 1987—), Inst. Real Estate Mgmt., Bldg. Owners and Mgrs., Nat. Apt. Assn. Republican. Office: Ogden E Co Inc 1550 N Prospect Ave Milwaukee WI 53202

DONAHUE, DONALD JORDAN, mining company executive; b. Bklyn., July 5, 1924; s. John F. and Florence (Jordan) D.; m. Mary Meyer, Jan. 20, 1951; children: Mary G., Judith A., Donald Jordan, Thomas, Nicholas P. B.A., Georgetown U., 1947; M.B.A., NYU, 1951. With Chem. Corn Exchange Bank, N.Y.C., 1947-49; with Am. Metal Climax Inc. (name changed to AMAX, Inc.), N.Y.C., 1949-75; treas. Am. Metal Climax Inc. (name changed to AMAX, Inc.), 1957-67, v.p., 1963-65, exec. v.p., 1965-69, pres., 1969-75, also dir., 1964-75; vice chmn. Continental Can Co., Inc. (name changed to Continental Group, Inc.), N.Y.C., 1975-84; chmn. KMI Continental Can Co., Inc. (formerly Continental Group, Inc.), 1987, Magma Copper Co., San Manuel, Ariz., 1987—; dir. Nat. Starch & Chem. Co., Northeast Utilities, Inc., Counsellors Cash Res. Fund, Counsellors Tandem Securities Fund; vice chmn. Greenwall Fedn. Chmn. bd. regents Georgetown U.; v.p., trustee ICD Research Center. Served with AUS, 1943-46. Mem. Greenwich Country Club, Blindbrook Country Club, University (N.Y.C.), Jupiter Hills (Fla.) Golf Club. Home: Meads Point Greenwich CT 06830 Office: Magma Copper Co Inc 99 Indian Field Rd Greenwich CT 06830

DONAHUE, JAMES A., JR., business development company executive; b. Boston, Apr. 30, 1929; s. James A. and Carolyn (Castonia) D.; m. Helen Marie Baker, June 27, 1957; children: James III, Michael, George, Stephen, Ann Marie. BS in Pharmacy, Mass. Coll. Pharmacy, 1952, MS in Pharmacy, 1956. Analyst R.A. Gosselin & Co., Boston, 1954-56, mgr. spl. project, 1956-58, v.p., gen. mgr., 1959-61, exec. v.p., 1962-71, pres., 1972; v.p. Lea, Inc., Ambler, Pa., 1973, IMS Am., Ltd., Ambler, 1974-79; group v.p. IMS Am., Ltd., Ambler and Plymouth Meeting, Pa., 1980—. Active Glenside Pa. Toen Watch. Cpl. U.S. Army, 1954-56. Mem. Am. Pharmacists Assn., Am. Soc. Hosp. Pharmacists, Mfrs. Golf and Country Club. Roman Catholic. Home: 406 Abington Ave Glenside PA 19038 Office: IMS Am Ltd 660 W Germantown Pike Plymouth Meeting PA 19462

DONALD, PAUL AUBREY, retired insurance company executive; b. Prince Frederick, Md., July 6, 1929; m. Anne Harris, Nov. 5, 1966; children: Cynthia Binz, Jan Donald, Glenn White, Mike Donald, Ken Donald, Steve Donald. B.Com., U. Balt., 1956. CLU; CPCU. V.p., regional mgr. Nationwide Ins., Lynchburg, Va., 1975-79; v.p. property casualty mktg. Nationwide Ins., Columbus, Ohio, 1979-80, v.p. western devel., 1980-81, v.p., adminstrv. asst. to pres., 1981, pres., gen. mgr., asst. exec. officer, 1981-89, also dir., 1981-89; chmn. bd. Neckura Life Ins. Co., Auto Direkt Ins. Co.; vice-chmn. Employers Ins. of Wausau; Beaver Pacific Corp., Colonial Ins. Co., Scottsdale Ins. Co.; vice chmn. Farmland Ins. Co., Farmland Life Ins. Co.; pres. Nationwide Found., Nationwide Transport, Inc.; trustee Ins. Svcs. Office, 1986—; dir. Farmland Mut. Ins. Co., NECKURA, numerous subs. and affiliates. Pres. United Way of Franklin County, Inc., Columbus, 1984-85, trustee, 1982-88; trustee Columbus Symphony Orch., 1982-88, Meth. Theol. Sch., Delaware, Ohio, 1983-88, Franklin U., 1986, INROADS/Columbus, Inc., 1986; officer Council for Study of Ethics and Econs., Columbus, 1983-86. Mem. Nat. Assn. Health Underwriters, Am. Soc. CLUs, Soc. CPCUs. Methodist. Home: 737 Old Oak Trace Worthington OH 43235 Office: Nationwide Mut Fire Ins Co 1 Nationwide Pla Columbus OH 43216 *

DONALDSON, GEORGE BURNEY, chemical company executive; b. Oakland, Calif., Mar. 16, 1945; s. George T. and L.M. (Burney) D.; m. Jennifer L. Bishop, Feb. 16, 1974; children: Dawn Marie, Paul Matthew. AS in Criminology, Porterville Coll., 1972. Police officer City of Lindsay (Calif.), 1966-67; distbn. mgr. Ortho div. Chevron Chem. Co., Lindsay, 1967-73; safety specialist Wilbur-Ellis Co. Fresno, Calif., 1973-77, safety dir., 1977-79, dir. regulatory affairs, 1979—; industry rep. to White House Inter-Govtl. Sci. Engring., and Tech. Adv. Panel, Task Force on Transp. of Non-Nuclear Hazardous Materials, 1980; industry rep. Transp. Rsch. Bd.'s Nat. Strategies Conf. on Transp. of Hazardous Materials and Wastes in the 1980's, NAS, 1981, Hazardous Materials Transp. Conf., Nat. Conf. of State Legislatures, 1982; chair industry/govt. task force for unique on-site hazardous waste recycling, devel. task force for computerized regulatory software and data base system, devel. task force modifying high expansion foam tech. for fire suppression; hazardous materials adviser, motor carrier rating com. Calif. Hwy. Patrol, 1978-79. With U.S. Army, 1962-65. Mem. Western Agrl. Chems. Assn. (past chmn. transp., distbn. and safety com., outstanding mem. of year 1981, govtl. affairs com.), Nat. Agrl. Chems. Assn. (past chmn. transp. and distbn. com., occupational safety and health com., environ. mgmt. com., state affairs com.), Am. Soc. Safety Engrs., Calif. Fertilizer Assn. (transp. and distbn. com., environ. com.), Fresno City and County C. of C. (agrl. steering com., govt. affairs com.), Calif. C. of C. (environ. policy com.), Am. Legion, Elks. Republican. Office: 191 W Shaw Ave Ste 107 Fresno CA 93704

DONALDSON, JOHN CECIL, JR., consumer products company executive; b. Bklyn., Dec. 8, 1933; s. John Cecil and Josephine (Greason) D.; m. Marilyn J. Smith, Aug. 29, 1959; children: Susan, John III. AB, Brown U., 1956; postgrad., Bentley Sch. Acctg., 1957, LaSalle Law Sch., 1959; MBA, Wharton Sch., U. Pa., 1959; student, Bentley Sch. of Acctg., Boston, 1957, LaSalle Law Sch., Chgo., 1959. Various positions Gen. Motors Corp., Flint, Mich., 1960-71; zone mgr. Gen. Motors Corp., Buffalo, 1971-76; zone mgr. Gen. Motors Corp., Newark, 1976-77, mgr. forward product planning, 1977-78; from dir. sales and mktg. to v.p. Corbin Ltd., 1979-85; exec. v.p. and gen. mgr. TMG Corp., N.Y.C., 1986—; pres. Gen. Motors Exec. Club, Newark, N.J., 1977-78. Mem. Am. Mktg. Assn. Republican. Home: 36 Nottingham Way Millington NJ 07946

DONALDSON, JONATHAN DOUGLAS, biotechnology company executive; b. Boston, July 14, 1949; s. Gordon Alcock and Elizabeth (Craighead) D.; m. Nancy Beals, June 28, 1980; children: Lindsay Sheaffer, Kate Wayland. BA, Harvard U., 1971; MBA, Amos Tuck U., 1977. Ptnr. Harbridge House, Boston, 1980-86; pres., chief oper. officer MedChem Products, Inc., Woburn, Mass., 1986—, also bd. dirs.; bd. dirs. BioChem Products, Inc., San Juan P.R. Mem. Harvard Club, Union Boat Club. Office: MedChem Products Inc 444 Washington St Woburn MA 10154

DONALSON, JAMES RYAN, real estate broker; b. Kansas City, Mo., Jan. 7, 1945; s. Joseph Elmer and Betty Lee (Cousins) D.; B.S. (Mo. Real Estate Assn. scholar), U. Mo., 1967; m. Sandra Lynn Yockey, Dec. 26, 1964; children—Kimberly Kay, Debra Lynn, Jennifer Lee. Loan officer City Wide Mortgage Co., Kansas City, 1967; interviewer personnel Panhandle Eastern Pipe Line Co., Kansas City, 1968; partner Donalson Realtors, Kansas City, 1969—; pres. Classic Homes, Kansas City, 1973—, Donalson Devel. Co., 1980—, Diversified Investments (formerly Donalson & Assos. Realtors), 1980—; bd. dirs. Multiple Listing Service Greater Kansas City, 1971-75, treas., 1972-73. Bd. dirs. Platte County unit Am. Cancer Soc., 1973-75. Mem. Nat. Assn. Real Estate Bds., Mo. Assn. Realtors (dir. 1974-75), Real Estate Bd. Kansas City (dir. 1978-80), Platte County Bus. and Profl. Men's Assn., U. Mo. Alumni Assn., Homebuilders Assn. Greater Kansas City. Baptist. Lion (dir. 1974-76).

DONATO, ALFRED VIRGIL, electrical engineer, consultant; b. N.Y.C., Feb. 8, 1917; s. Philip and Mary (Tafuri) D.; m. Josephine Louise Marsiglia, Sept. 7, 1947; 1 child, Beverly. BS Elect. Engring. NYU, 1940; MS in Electric Ship Propulsion, Poly., Inst., 1943. Cert. profl. engr., Md. Elec. engr. marine Gibbs & Cox, N.Y.C., 1940-45, Gen. Elec., Schenectady, N.Y., 1945-47, Bethleham Steel Ship Building, Balt., 1947-50, Gen. Services Adminstrn., Washington, 1950-53; interdisciplinary supervisory elec. engr. Dept. of Army Corps of Engrs. New Dist., N.Y.C., 1953—; cons. elec., Bklyn., 1980—; cons. estimator, Bklyn., 1968—. Author: Load Shedding brochure (Significant Achievement award Corps of Engrs., 1987,88), 1982. Mem. legis. adv. com. N.Y. State Senator, 21st Dist., Albany, 1979; mem. Republican Nat. Com., Washington; supporter St. Anselmi Catholic Ch., Bklyn. Recipient Superior Performance award Corps of Engrs., 1967, 76, Significant Achievement award Corps of Engrs., 1984, 85, Outstanding Leadership award Corps of Engrs., 1987. Mem. Soc. Naval Architects and Marine Engrs., Am. Mil. Engrs., AIEE, N.Y. Acad. Scis. Clubs: Crescent Hill, Athletic. Avocations: ship and airplane models. Office: Dept Army Corps Engrs NY Dist 26 Federal Pla New York NY 10278

DONCKERWOLCKE, EDMOND CESAR, textile executive, consultant; b. Brussels, Belgium, July 10, 1924; s. Leonce and Bertha (Demyttenaere) D.; Atheneum Bachelor, 1942; m. Elsa Billen, Oct. 10, 1944; children—Susan, Solange, Eddy, Hedwige, Jaques, Rose, David, Frank, Serge. Mgr., Cotolana, Brussels, 1944-52; free-lance rep. Belgian textile industries, 1952-57; pres. SACOTIL, Geneva, Switzerland, 1957-77; counselor, adv. Belgian textile firms, 1977-81; cons., 1981—. Adv., Chinese art studies, 1970—; adminstr. Ars Asiatica, Flanders/Belgium, 1980—. Served with Belgian Resistance, 1942-44. Decorated Medal of Resistance, Medal of War. Research in Chinese art, Wei and Tang period, 1980—. Address: 66 Dr Van Bockstaelestraat, 9218 Ledeberg Belgium

DONEFELD, MICHAEL SIMON, insurance company executive; b. Blkyn., Nov. 1, 1933; s. Morris and Ruth (Fishbein) D.; m. Sheila E. Gordon, June 19, 1954; children: Beth, Mindy. BA in Econs., Bklyn. Coll., 1962. CLU, chartered fin. counselor, life ins. counselor. From mail clk. to asst. v.p. Bankers Security, N.Y.C. and Washington, 1951-68; dir. pension adminstrn. Aetna Variable Annuity Life Ins. Co., Falls Church, Va., 1969-71; v.p. pension adminstrn. Aetna Variable Annuity Life Ins. Co., Falls Church, 1971-74; asst. v.p. ops. devel. Aetna Life & Casualty Ins. Co., Hartford, Conn., 1974-76; v.p. group ops. Maccabees Mut. Life Ins. Co., Southfield, Mich., 1976—; sr. v.p. pension adminstrn. Pension Portfolio Advisors (affiliate Maccabees), 1989—. Mem. Am. Mgmt. Assn., Am. Soc. CLU's, Am. Soc. Chartered Fin. Cons., Group Underwriters Assn. Am., Life Office Mgmt. Assn. (past pres.), Mikes of Am. Club, B'nai B'rith. Jewish. Home: 2236 Kiev Ct West Bloomfield MI 48033 Office: Maccabees Mut Life Ins Co 25800 Northwestern Hwy Southfield MI 48075

DONEHUE, JOHN DOUGLAS, newspaper executive; b. Cramerton, N.C., July 5, 1928; s. John Sidney and Annie (Shepherd) D.; m. Mary Phelps, Jan. 9, 1952 (dec. 1964); children: Teresa Jean, Marilyn Phelps; m. Sylvia Louise McKenzie, Feb. 11, 1966 (dec. Nov. 1971); children: Hayden Shepherd, John Douglas; m. Virginia Kirkland, June 28, 1975; children: Anne Mikell, Robertson Carr. Student Am. Press Inst., Columbia U., 1965, 71-73; D. of Humane Letters (hon.), Bapt. Coll., 1985. Sports writer Charleston, S.C. News and Courier, 1947, copy editor, 1956, state editor, 1959-62, city editor, 1962-68, mng. editor, 1968-71, promotion dir., 1971—, v.p. for corp. pub. relations, 1975—, compiler News and Courier Style Book, 1969; sports editor Orangeburg (S.C.) Times and Dem., 1948-50; polit. reporter Montgomery (Ala.) Advertiser, 1954-55; faculty advisor Bapt. Coll. at Charleston Student Newspaper; spl. adviser comdt. 7th USCG dist. for establishment dist.-wide pub. info. program, 1960-61; journalism lectr. Bapt. Coll., Charleston Coll.; sec. 1st bd. founders, 1969. Guest commentator Nat. Pub. Radio. Chmn. adv. bd. Salvation Army; chmn. regional adv. council S.C. Dept. Youth Services; chmn. United Way Planning Bd.; bd. dirs. S.C. Tricentennial Parade Com., 1972; pres. Palmetto Safety Council; Lay reader, vestryman, sr. warden Episc. Ch. Served with S.C. N.G., 1948-50, USAF, 1950-54, USMCR, 1955-56, USAR, 1956-59, USCGR, 1959-66, USNR, 1966-75. Recipient Freedoms Found. award, 1969, S.C. Family of Yr. award, Am. Advt. Fedn. Silver Medal award, 1987. Vets. Adminstrn. citation for Meritorious Service, 1971. Mem. John Ancrum Soc. of Soc. Prevention Cruelty to Animals, Carolina Art Assn., YMCA, Internat. Newspaper Promotion Assn., S.C. Press Assn. (pres. 1985), Air Force Assn. (dir. Charleston council), Navy League (v.p. Charleston council), Charleston Trident C. of C. (pres. 1983), Toastmasters Internat. (charter mem. Okinawa club), Okinawa Soc. Clubs: Downtown Athletic, Toastmasters Internat. (charter mem. Okinawa club). Lodge: Rotary (Charleston) (pres. 1974-75). Home: 66 Bull St Charleston SC 29401 Office: The News & Courier 134 Columbus St PO Box 758 Charleston SC 29401

DONELSON, ANGIE FIELDS CANTRELL MERRITT, real estate executive; b. Hermitage, Tenn., Dec. 2, 1914; d. Dempsey Weaver and Nora (Johnson) Cantrell; student public and pvt. schs., Hermitage, Nashville; m. Gilbert Stroud Merritt, Dec. 15, 1934 (dec.); 1 son, Gilbert Stroud; m. 2d, John Donelson, Jr., VII, Apr. 23, 1966 (dec.); step-children—John, Agnes Donelson Williams (dec.), William Stockley. Pres., So. Woodenware Co., Nashville, 1955-61, So. Properties, Co., Inc., Hermitage, 1961—. Chmn. comml. flower exhibits Tenn. State Fair, 1951; committeewoman and v.p. Davidson County Agrl. Soil and Conservation Community Com., 1959-60; bd. mem. Nashville Symphony Assn., 1961-64, regional council mem., 1977-79; chmn. bd. Nashville Presbyn. Neighborhood Settlement House; elder Presbyn. Ch., 1989—; founding bd. mem. Davidson County Cancer Soc.; bd. mem. Nashville Vis. Nurse Service; dist. chmn., speakers bur. Am. Red Cross. Proclaimed First Lady Donelson-Hermitage Community, 1986. Mem. Vanderbilt U. Aid, Peabody Coll. Aid, Tenn. Hist. Soc., Descs. of Ft. Nashboro Pioneers (bd. dirs. 1984-87), English Speaking Union. Clubs: Ladies Hermitage Assn. (dir. 1949-89), DAR, (chpt. regent 1941), Lebanon Rd. Garden Club (pres. 1947), Horticulture Soc. Davidson County (v.p. 1949). Clubs: Ravenwood Country, Centennial, Belle Meade. Contbr. to books and mags. on history of Tenn. Home: Stone Hall Stones River Rd Hermitage TN 37076 Office: Lebanon Rd Hermitage TN 37076

DONER, GARY WILLIAM, tire company financial executive; b. Louisville, Nov. 3, 1951; s. Charles and Billie (Miller) D.; m. Cynthia Ann Herman, July 7, 1973; 1 child, Laura. BS, Wright State U., 1974. CPA, Ohio. Tax analyst NCR Corp., Dayton, Ohio, 1975-80; tax mgr. Dayco Corp., Dayton, 1980-85; tax dir. Cooper Tire & Rubber Co., Findlay, Ohio, 1985—; part-time instr. Owens Coll., Toledo, 1985-86, acctg. adv. com., 1985—; operating com. mem. Ohio Pub. Expenditures Council. Mem. Am. Inst. CPA's, Ohio Soc. CPA's, Tax Execs. Inst., Ohio Bar Assn. (assoc.). Roman Catholic. Home: 710 Briarwood Circle Perrysburg OH 43551 Office: Cooper Tire and Rubber Co Lima and Western Aves Findlay OH 45840

DONHOWE, PETER ARTHUR, editor; b. Columbus, Nebr., Feb. 5, 1938; s. Joseph Oliver and Nada Vira (Graham) D.; m. Gail Ramsay, Feb. 3, 1962 (div. Sept. 1965); m. Marcia Kay Farrell, Aug. 1, 1979 (div. Feb. 1989); children: Joseph Farrell, Helen Nada. Student, Princeton U., 1975-76; BA in Am. Civilization, U. Iowa, 1962, postgrad., 1962-63. Editor Iowa Defender, Iowa City, 1961-63; reporter So. Illinoisan, Carbondale, Ill., 1963; reporter St. Louis Post-Dispatch, 1964-71, editorial writer, 1971-85; bus. and econs. editor U. Ill., Urbana, 1985—; exec. bd. Newspaper Guild Local 47, St. Louis, 1970-72; founding editor St. Louis Journalism Rev., 1972—; visitor program European Communities, Belgium, Eng., Fed. Republic Germany, France, 1983. Contbr. numerous articles to mags., newspapers. Discussion leader Great Decisions Series, St. Louis, 1969, 83-84; exec. com. Euclid Montessori Sch., St. Louis, 1983. Served with USN, 1956-58. Recipient Sloan fellowship in Econs. Princeton U., 1975-76, Outstanding Service award Coalition for the Environment, St. Louis, 1985, Appreciation award St. Louis Journalism Rev., 1985. Mem. Princeton Club (St. Louis and Chgo.). Home: 1909 Harding Dr Urbana IL 61801 Office: U Ill News Bur 807 S Wright St Champaign IL 61820

DONNAHOE, ALAN STANLEY, newspaper executive; b. Asheville, N.C., Aug. 27, 1916; s. Paul Albert and Kate (Stanley) D.; m. Elsie Pitts, 1938; children—Kate Stanley Donnahoe Vaughan. Student pub. schs. Bar: Va., N.C. Dir. research Richmond (Va.) C. of C., 1936-46, asst. exec. mgr., 1946-50; exec. sec. Richmond Inter-Club Council, 1938-41, Va. Soc. Pub. Accountants, Richmond, 1946-50; dir. research Richmond Newspapers, Inc., 1950-55, v.p., 1956-59, exec. v.p., asst. pub., 1959-65, pres., dir., 1966—; pres., chief exec. officer, dir. Media Gen., Inc., 1969-81, vice chmn., chief exec. officer, dir., 1982-84, vice chmn., 1984—; dir. Security Fed. Savs. & Loan Assn. (and subs.'s) ; mem. bus. adv. com. U.S. Bur. Labor Stats., 1948-49, U.S. Bur. Census, 1948-49; lectr. stats. U. Richmond, 1948-49; mem. Tax Study Commn., 1963-64, Va. Met. Area Study Commn., 1966-67; mem. fiscal study com. Va. Adv. Legis. Council, 1956-58; mem. adv. com. to sec. edn. State of Va., 1973; mem. listed co. adv. com. Am. Stock Exchange, 1975-85. Former mem. bd. dirs. Richmond Meml. Hosp.; bd. dirs. Nat. Center for Resource Recovery, Inc., Washington, Richmond Area Community Council, 1972, Citizens Study Council, 1973; bd. govs. United Givers Fund, 1960-63, 66-69; pres. Collegiate Schs., 1967-68; bd. dirs., past pres. Richmond Eye Hosp., RPI Found., Va. Commonwealth U., Richmond; mem. Nat. Commn. on Taxes and IRS, 1979—; chmn. Bus. Adv. Commn. on White Collar Crime, 1980—. Served from pvt. to 1st lt., C.E. AUS, 1943-46, ETO; as 1st lt. Gen. Staff U.S. Army, 1950-52. Recipient Good Govt. award Richmond First Club, 1967; Distinguished Service award Richmond Urban League, 1969. Mem. Am. Statis. Assn., Am. Newspaper Pubs. Assn. (newsprint com. 1976—), Am. Mktg. Assn. (pres. Va. chpt. 1954-55), C. of C. U.S. (communications com. 1970-75, chmn. postal service panel 1976-80), Richmond C. of C. (pres. 1968), Beta Gamma Sigma. Presbyterian. Clubs: Commonwealth (Richmond) (dir. 1972), Country of Va. (Richmond). Home: 8912 Alendale Rd Richmond VA 23229 Office: Media Gen Inc 333 E Grace St Richmond VA 23219

DONNELLY, BARBARA SCHETTLER, medical technologist; b. Sweetwater, Tenn., Dec. 2, 1933; d. Clarence G. and Irene Elizabeth (Brown) Schettler; A.A., Tenn. Wesleyan Coll., 1952; B.S., U. Tenn., 1954; cert. med. tech., Erlanger Hosp. Sch. Med. Tech., 1954; postgrad. So. Meth. U., 1980-81; children—Linda Ann, Richard Michael. Med. technologist Erlanger Hosp., Chattanooga, 1953-57, St. Luke's Episcopal Hosp., Tex. Med. Center, Houston, 1957-58, 1962; engring. research and devel. SCI Systems Inc., Huntsville, Ala., 1974-76; cons. hematology systems Abbott Labs., Dallas, 1976-77, hematology specialist, Dallas, Irving, Tex., 1977-81, tech. specialist microbiology systems, Irving, 1981-83, coordinator tech. service clin. chemistry systems, 1983-84, coordinator customer tng. clin. chemistry systems, 1984-87, supr. clin. chemistry tech. services, 1987-88, clin. chemistry customer support ctr., 1988—. Mem. Am. Soc. Clin. Pathologists (cert. med. technologist), Am. Soc. Microbiology, Nat. Assn. Female Execs., U. Tenn. Alumni Assn., Chi Omega. Contbr. articles on cytology to profl. jours. Republican. Methodist. Home: 204 Greenbriar Ln Bedford TX 76021 Office: 1921 Hurd St Irving TX 75061

DONNELLY, JOSEPH LENNON, utility company executive; b. Scranton, Pa., Mar. 17, 1929; s. Joseph L. and Irene (Dougher) D.; m. Lynn Haakonsen, Aug. 4, 1974; children: David Charles, Joseph Lennon III, Haakon Thomas. B.S., U. Scranton, 1950; J.D., U. Pa., 1953. Bar: Pa. 1954. Dep. atty. gen. Commonwealth Pa., 1955-58; with Pa. Power & Light Co., Allentown, 1958-79, v.p. fin., 1975-79; sr. exec. v.p., chief fin. officer Gulf States Utilities Co., Beaumont, Tex., 1979—, also dir. Pres. bd. trustee Allentown State Hosp., 1968-69; chmn. Lehigh County Mental Health, Pa. Mental Retardation Bd., 1968-71. Mem. ABA, Fin. Execs. Inst., Edison Electric Inst., Pa. Bar Assn. Democrat. Roman Catholic. Club: Beaumont Country. Office: Gulf States Utilities Co 350 Pine Beaumont TX 77701

DONNET, JEAN BAPTISTE, physical chemist, educator, scientific consultant; b. Pontgibaud, France, Sept. 28, 1923; s. Antoine and Marie (Berouhard) D.; PhD in Chem. Engring., U. Strasbourg (France), 1953; m. Suzanne Rittiman, Dec. 21, 1968; children by previous marriage: Anne-Michele, Pierre-Antoine, Marie-Christine. With Centre National de Recherche Scientifique, 1946-53, successively stagiaire, attaché, chargé de recherche; prof. dep. dir. U. Haute-Alsace, Mulhouse, France, 1958-73, dir., 1973-77, prof., pres. U. Haute-Alsace, 1977—, fundator, head Rsch. Ctr. of Physico-Chemistry of Solid Surfaces, 1967-86. Contbr. articles to profl. jours. Maj. French Air Force, 1977. Decorated officer de la Legion d'Honneur et de l'Ordre du Mérite, commdr. Acad. Palmes; recipient Gold medal Société pour l'Encouragement de l'Industrie Nationale, 1976; Silver medal French Assn. Advancement of Sci., 1979; George Skakel Meml. award Am. Carbon Soc., 1981, Karl Harris medal Deutsche Kautschuk. Gessels, 1985, George Colwin medal Plastic award Rubber Inst., Eng., 1988. Fellow Plastic and Rubber Inst. (London indsl. bd.), Royal Soc. Chemistry; mem. AAAS, Am. Chem. Soc. (Rubber div., George Stafford Whitby award 1989), Société Française de Chimie Physique, Societe Chimique de France, Soc. Plastic Engrs., French Assn. Rubber and Plastic Engrs. Club: Rotary. Author: Elastomers, 1958; Les Noirs de Carbone, 1965; Carbon Black 1976; Carbon Fiber, 1984, Active Carbon, 1988. Office: 24 ave President Kennedy, Mulhouse France

DONOGHUE, WILLIAM THOMAS, antiques dealer, gemologist; b. Houston, Nov. 13, 1932; s. Gerald Thomas and Louise (Huggins) D.; m. Christa Neidhardt, Apr. 6, 1957; children—Charlotte Luisa, Hilary. B.A. in Econs., U. Va., 1954. Ptnr., Christy Donoghue Antiques, Inc., Bad Nauheim, W. Ger., 1957-61, Victoria, Tex., 1961-69, pres., Victoria, 1969—. Bd. dirs. Victorial Regional Mus. Assn., 1970-80. Served to 1st lt. U.S. Army, 1954-57; ETO. Mem. Gemological Inst. Am., U. Va. Alumni Assn. Avocations: ranching, hunting. Home and Office: Christy Donoghue Antiques Inc 2424 N Navarro St Victoria TX 77901

DONOHO, BETTY BRITTAIN, electric company executive; b. Hendersonville, N.C., Oct. 12, 1935; d. Daniel Wade and Leila (Allison) Brittain; m. Tom J. Donoho, Apr. 6, 1959; children: Daniel, Susan E. Student, U. N.C., 1965-86. V.p., dir. fin. dept. Asheville Electric Co. Inc., N.C., 1962—; owner, mgr. Warehouse Beauty Ctr., Asheville, 1981—. Chmn. pub. relations com. A.C. Reynolds Mid. Sch., Asheville, PTA, 1978, pres., 1979, sec. adv. bd., 1980-81; active Jerry Silverman Scholarship Com., 1986-87; bd. dirs. Buncombe Alternatives, 1988—. Mem. Nat. Assn. Female Execs., Sub-Contractors Am. Democrat. Baptist. Home: 124 Gashes Creek Rd Asheville NC 28805 Office: Asheville Electric Co Inc 950 Fairview Rd Asheville NC 28813

DONOHO, BURNETT WILLINGHAM, retail executive; b. Paducah, Ky., July 22, 1939; s. Glen B. and Estelle (Willingham) D.; m. Jane P. Kirkpatrick, Aug. 25, 1962; children—Ann, Burnett W., Kirk. B.A., Vanderbilt U., 1961; M.A., U. Ky., 1964. With Maas Bros., Tampa, Fla., 1964-74; sr. v.p. personnel Joske's, Dallas, 1975; pres. Gimbels, Milw., 1975-84; pres. Marshall Field's, Chgo., 1984—; dir. First Bank, Milw. Bd. dirs. Chgo. Conv. and Tourism Bur., 1985—, Chgo. Crime Commn., 1984; adv. bd. dirs. DePaul U., Chgo., 1984. Mem. Vanderbilt U. Alumni Assn. (bd. dirs. 1987—). Republican. Presbyterian. Office: Marshall Field & Co 111 N State St Chicago IL 60690

DONOHOE, JEROME FRANCIS, lawyer; b. Yankton, S.D., Mar. 17, 1939; s. Francis A. and Ruth (Moore) D.; m. Elaine Joyce Bush, Jan. 27, 1968; 1 child, Nicole Elaine. BA, St. John's U., 1961; JD cum laude, U. Minn., 1964. Bar: Ill. 1964, S.D. 1964. Atty. Atchison, Topeka & Santa Fe Ry. Co., Chgo., 1967-73, gen. atty., 1973-78; gen. counsel corp. affairs Santa Fe Industries Inc., Chgo., 1978-84; v.p. law Santa Fe Industries, Inc., Chgo., 1984—, Santa Fe So. Pacific Corp., Chgo., 1984—. Mem. corp. council Interlochen (Mich.) Ctr. for Arts, 1987—; mem. ann. planning com. Ray Garrett Jr. Corp. and Securities Law Inst.; Northwestern U. Assocs. Capt. JAGC, U.S. Army, 1964-67. Fellow Ill. Bar Found.; mem. ABA, Am. Corp. Counsel Assn., Northwestern Univ. Assocs., Northwestern U. Corp. Counsel Ctr. (adv. bd.). Clubs: Chgo., Chgo. Athletic Assn.; Mich. Shores (Wilmette, Ill.). Office: Santa Fe So Pacific Corp 224 S Michigan Ave Chicago IL 60604

DONOHUE, ANDREW JOHN, lawyer, securities executive; b. Roslyn, N.Y., Aug. 22, 1950; s. Thomas Aloysius and Ellen Kathryn (McDermott) D.; m. Patricia Ann Cowloy, Nov. 1971; children: Andrew Jr., Kerry, Erin. BA, Hofstra U., 1972; JD, NYU, 1975. Bar: N.Y. 1976, N.J. 1988. Sec., gen. counsel 1st Investors Consolidated Corp. and Subs., N.Y.C., 1976—; sec. 1st Investors Group Funds, N.Y.C., 1979—, pres., bd. dirs., 1984—; sec., bd. dirs. 1st Investors Life Ins. Co., N.Y.C., 1984—. Office: 1st Investors Corp 120 Wall St New York NY 10005

DONOHUE, BRIAN CHRISTOPHER, lawyer; b. Newark, May 3, 1947; s. Edgar A. and Mary (Donlon) D.; m. Linda J. Sahlberg, May 28,1972; children: Molly Kathleen, Sean Patrick, Megan Elizabeth. BA, Fordham Coll., 1969; JD, Northrup U., 1977; MBA, George Washington U., 1972. Bar: Calif., U.S. Ct. Appeals (9th cir.). Officer data processing U.S. Army Fin. Info., Washington, 1970-72; legal asst. Legis. Counsel Office, Sacramento, Calif., 1973-75; systems analyst Sperry Univac, Los Angeles, 1975-79; chief computer contracts County of Los Angeles, 1979-82; prin. Donohue & Donohue, Torrance, Calif., 1982-86; v.p. Bank of Am., Concord, Calif., 1986—; instr. Golden Gate U., Walnut Creek, Calif, 1988—; dir. seminar Data Tech. Inst., Clifton, N.J., 1985-87; speaker Healthcare 86, Las Vegas, 1986, Nat. Conv. Liability Computers, 1986. Author: How to Buy an Office Computer, 1983, Software Licensing, 1988; columnist Software in Health Care, 1984-86. Asst. scout master Cub Scouts Am., Concord, 1988; dir. St. Patrick's Parade, Redondo Beach, Calif., 1983-86; coach Am. Youth Soccer Orgn., Cath. Youth Orgn. Track, Concord, 1986—. Mem. San Francisco Bar (computers sect.), Computer Law Assn., Rotary (Rotarian Yr. 1983). Roman Catholic. Home: 745 Daffodil Way Concord CA 94518 Office: Bank Am PO Box 37000 Dept #3411 San Francisco CA 94137

DONOHUE, CARROLL JOHN, lawyer; b. St. Louis, June 24, 1917; s. Thomas M. and Florence (Klefisch) D.; m. Juanita Maire, Jan. 4, 1943 (div. July 1973); children: Patricia Carol Donohue Stevens, Christine Ann Donohue Smith, Deborah Lee Donohue Wilucki; m. Barbara Lounsbury, Dec. 1978. A.B., Washington U., 1939, LL.B. magna cum laude, 1939. Bar: Mo. 1939. Assoc. Hay & Flanagan, St. Louis, 1939-42; asso. Salkey & Jones, 1946-49; partner Husch, Eppenberger, Donohue, Cornfeld & Jenkins, St. Louis, 1949—. Author articles in field. Campaign chmn. ARC, St. Louis County, 1950; mem. adv. com. Child Welfare, St. Louis, 1952-55; exec. com. Slum Clearance, 1949, bond issue com., 1955; bond issue com. St. Louis County Bond Issue, screening and supervisory coms., 1955-61, county citizen's com. for better law enforcement, 1953-56, chmn. com. on immigration policy, 1954-56, Mayor, Olivette, Mo., 1953-56; chmn. Bd. Election Commrs., St. Louis County, 1960-65; chmn. com. Non-Partisan Ct. Plan; vice-chmn. bd. Regional Commerce and Growth Assn.; bd. dirs. Downtown St. Louis, Inc., Civic Entrepreneurs Orgn.; bd. dirs. Gateway Mayors Emeritus Inc. Lt. USNR, 1942-45. Decorated Bronze Star medal, Navy and M.C. medal. Mem. Mo. Bar Assn. (past mem. bd. govs., chmn. annual meeting, editor jour. 1940-41), ABA, St. Louis Bar Assn. (past pres., v.p., treas.), Order of Coif, Omicron Delta Kappa, Sigma Phi Epsilon, Delta Theta Phi. Club: Mo. Athletic. Address: 100 N Broadway Saint Louis MO 63102

DONOHUE, DELAINE R., information company executive; b. Red Oak, Iowa, Mar. 1, 1931; s. Donald Russell and Margaret W. (Bond) D.; m. Dorothy Dahlstrom, May 5, 1957; children: Deborah M. Saul, Rebecca L. BA, U. Nebr., 1962. Nat. mgr. systems improvement Dun & Bradstreet Inc., N.Y.C., 1966-68; regional service mgr. Dun & Bradstreet Inc., Los Angeles, 1968-70; gen. serivce mgr. Dun & Bradstreet Inc., N.Y.C., 1970-72; v.p. nat. bus. info. ctr. Dun & Bradstreet Inc., Berkley Heights, N.J., 1972-79; v.p. ops., info. resources Dun & Bradstreet Inc., Allentown, Pa., 1979-83, sr. v.p., 1984—. Served to staff sgt. USAF, 1951-54. Home: 2773 Evergreen Circle Emmaus PA 18049 Office: Dun and Bradstreet Box 178 1 Imperial Way Allentown PA 18195

DONOHUE, JOHN WILLIAM, JR., insurance company executive; b. El Paso, Tex., Feb. 3, 1935; s. John W. and Marie R. Donohue; BS in Geology, U. Tex., El Paso, 1957; m. M. Elaine Abbott, Sept. 14, 1957; 1 dau., Lori Elaine. Agt., Aetna Life Ins. Co., El Paso, 1962-63, supr., 1963-66; life ptnr. Rogers & Belding Ins. Co., El Paso, 1966-77; pres. John W. Donohue, Jr. Assocs., Inc., ins. and investment sales cons. firm, El Paso, 1977—; adv. bd. Tex. Commerce Bank-West (formerly West El Paso Nat. Bank); participating ptnr. Exec. Life Ins. Co. Ariz. Founder, 1st chmn. Leadership El Paso, 1977-79; pres. El Paso Mental Health Assn., 1966-67; founder, chmn. bd. Casa Blanca Halfway House for mentally ill, El Paso, 1966-67; regional v.p. Boys Clubs Am.; bd. dirs. Tex. Leaders Roundtable, also 2d v.p., Upper Rio Grande Pvt. Industry Council. Served to 1st lt. U.S. Army, 1957-58. Life mem. Million Dollar Round Table. Mem. U. Tex. El Paso Alumni Assn. (pres. 1967-68), Tex. Assn. Life Underwriters (pres. 1971-72), El Paso Assn. Life Underwriters (pres. 1966-67, Man of Yr. 1975), Assn. Advanced Life Underwriters, Upper Rio Grande Pvt. Industry Council (bd. dirs.), El Paso C. of C. (bd. dirs.). Republican. Roman Catholic. Home: 1815 E Robinson St El Paso TX 79902 Office: John W Donohue Jr Assocs Inc 5845 Onix Ste 200 El Paso TX 79912

DONOHUE, MICHAEL EDWARD, coal company executive; b. St. Louis, June 4, 1951; s. James Thomas and Bertha Lois (Suggs) D. BS cum laude, U. Tenn., Martin, 1974. Mem. staff, sr. auditor Arthur Andersen & Co., Memphis, 1974-77; audit mgr. Arthur Andersen & Co., St. Louis, 1979-81, Jack Frost & Co., Little Rock, 1977-78; asst. controller Costain Coal, Inc. (formerly Indsl. Fuels Corp.), Troy, Mich., 1981, controller, 1981—, v.p., 1984—; pres., bd. dirs. Indsl. Fuels Equipment Co., Troy, 1984—, Indsl. Fuels Leasing Co., Troy, 1984—; v.p., sec. Wolverine Coal, Chapperal Coal, Empire Coal, Prater Creek Processing, Red Cedar Mining, 1984—. Pres. Bloomfield Concord Condominium Assn., Bloomfield Hills, Mich., 1988. Home: 389 Concord Pl Bloomfield Hills MI 48013 Office: Costain Coal Inc 3221 W Big Beaver Suite 304 Troy MI 48084

DONOVAN, JAMES ROBERT, business equipment company executive; b. Wichita, Kans., Apr. 11, 1932; s. Karl Genevay and Louise (Silcott) D.; A.B., Harvard U., 1954, M.B.A., 1956; m. Ottilie Schreiber, July 2, 1955; children—Amy Louise, Robert Silcott; m. Margaret Jones Esty, Oct. 31, 1981. Mgr. sales adminstrn., market research Hickok, Inc., Rochester, N.Y., 1956-59, regional sales mgr., 1959-62, asst. nat. sales mgr., 1963-65; group program mgr. Xerox Corp., Stamford, Conn., 1965-68, mktg. mgr. spl. products, 1968-70, mgr. copier products, 1970-72, dir. corp. pricing and competitive activity, 1972-78, dir. corp. mktg. strategy and planning, 1978-83; sr. v.p. corp. mktg. McDonnell Douglas Automation Co., St. Louis, 1983-84; v.p. mktg., planning Info. Systems Group, McDonnell Douglas Corp., St. Louis, 1984-87; pres., Bus. Adv. Services, Inc., Chatham, Mass., 1987— . Vice pres. Family Service, Rochester, 1971-72; dir. Family and Children's Services, Stamford, 1972-79; dir. Rochester Sales Execs. Club, 1966-71; mem. mktg. adv. bd. Columbia U. Bus. Sch., 1978-86; v.p. United Way of New Canaan, 1982-83; bd. dirs. Family Service Am., 1986—. Mem. Harvard Alumni Assn. (dir. 1978-83), Harvard Bus. Sch. Alumni Assn. (exec. council 1982-85). Clubs: Harvard (pres. Rochester 1971-72, pres. Fairfield County 1976-78, pres. St. Louis 1986-87), Harvard Bus. Sch. (pres. Rochester 1972, chmn. Westchester/Fairfield 1973-74); Old Warson Country (St. Louis); Woodway Country (Darien, Conn.).

DONOVAN, JOHN JOSEPH, JR., real estate broker and developer; b. Oakland, Calif., Mar. 10, 1916; s. John Joseph and May Ella (Coogan) D.; Ph.B., Santa Clara U., 1938; postgrad. Stanford U., 1938-40, Harvard U., 1942; m. Margaret Mary Abel, June 7, 1941; children—John Joseph III, Mary Margaret Donovan Szarnicki, Patricia Anne Donovan Jelley, Eileen Marie, Marian Gertrude Corrigan, George Edwin, Michael Sean. Sales mgr. Universal Window Co., Berkeley, Calif., 1940-41, v.p., 1946-49, pres., chmn. bd., 1949-66; real estate broker and developer, 1966—. Mem. aluminum window mfrs. adv. com. NPA, 1951-52; chmn. pace setters com., commerce and industry div. Alameda County United Crusade, 1961. Mem. Republican small businessmen's com., Alameda County, Calif., 1946. Bd. dirs. Providence Hosp., 1970-80, also Found., 1980-82; bd. dirs. Apostleship of the Sea Center, 1968-85, Hanna Boy's Center, Sonoma County, 1976-79; mem. Oakland Mayor's Internat. Welcoming Center, 1972-77; trustee, treas. Serra Internat. Found., 1980-87, pres., 1981-82; mem. Serra Bicentennial Commn., 1983-86; mem. membership enrollment maj. div. San Francisco Bay Area council Boy Scouts Am., 1984—; mem. bd. Jesuit Sch. Theology, Berkeley, 1982-85, Grad. Theol. Union, Berkeley, 1982-85. Served from ensign to lt. Supply Corps, USNR, 1940-46; in U.S.S. General Ballou; capt. Res. Named knight St. Gregory the Gt., Pope John XXIII, 1962 (pres. Oakland diocese 1970—); Knights of Malta, (decorated Cross of Comdr. Merit, 1978, Cross of Comdr. of Merit with swords Order of Malta, Rome, 1981; named grand officer of merit, Order of Malta with swords, 1983, Knight Grace and Devotion, Order of Malta, 1987, Knight of Obedience, Order of Malta, 1988); invested and decorated Knight of Grace, Sacred Mil. Constantinian Order of St. George, 1988. Mem. Western Archtl. Metal Mfrs. Assn. San Francisco (dir. 1956-65, exec. com. 1958-65, pres. 1959-60), Aluminum Window Mfrs. Assn. N.Y.C. (dir. 1950-58, 1st v.p. 1955-56), Newcomen Soc. N.Am., Naval Order U.S., Navy Supply Corps Assn. San Francisco Bay Area (2d v.p. 1970—), Father Junipero Serra 250th Anniversary Assn. (v.p., sec.), Internat. Council Shopping Centers, AIM (pres.'s council), Naval Res. Assn., VFW. Roman Catholic. Clubs: Berkeley Serra (charter mem.); Comml., Commonwealth, Pacific-Union (San Francisco); Monterey Peninsula Country (Pebble Beach, Calif.); Claremont Country (Oakland, Calif., bd. dirs. 1988—); Army-Navy (Washington). Home: 2 Lincolnshire Dr Oakland CA 94618 Office: PO Box 11100 Oakland CA 94611

DONOVAN, THOMAS GARLAND, auditor; b. Blythe, Calif., Aug. 28, 1943; s. Joseph Michael and Hermina Kathleen (Durr) D.; m. Mary Lynn, Oct. 7, 1967; 1 child, Jennifer. BBA, Notre Dame U., 1961; MBA, UCLA, 1966. Sr. fin. staff specialist Hughes Aircraft Co., Culver City, Calif., 1974-81; auditor County of Sonoma, Santa Rosa, Calif., 1981-88; chief fin. officer, bd. dirs. Burbank Housing Devel. Corp., Santa Rosa, Calif., 1982-88; internal auditor City of Tarpon Springs, Fla., 1988—; bd. dirs. Willowside Mut. Water Co., Santa Rosa. Served with U.S. Army, 1967-69.

DONOVAN, THOMAS ROY, futures exchange executive; b. Chgo., Sept. 13, 1937. B.A. in Bus. and Econs., Ill. Inst. Tech., 1972, M.P.A., 1975. Adminstrv. asst. to mayor City of Chgo., 1969-79; v.p., sec. Chgo. Bd. of Trade, 1979-81, exec. v.p., sec., 1981-82, pres., chief exec. officer, 1982—. Bd. dirs. Ill. Leadership Coun. for Agrl. Edn.; chmn. agribusiness adv. com. The Chgo. High Sch. for Agrl. Sci. Mem. Nat. Futures Assn. (bd. dirs., fin. com.), Chgo. Assn. Commerce and Industry (bd. dirs., exec. com.), Comml. Club of Chgo. Office: Chgo Trade Bd 141 W Jackson Blvd Chicago IL 60604

DOODY, ALTON FREDERICK, marketing consultant; b. New Orleans, Oct. 18, 1934; s. Alton Frederick and Althea (Leitz) D.; m. Anne Elizabeth Goetz, June 13, 1956 (div. 1974); children: Alton Frederick III, Patricia Lynn, John Christopher, Elizabeth Anne. BA, Ohio Wesleyan U., 1956; MBA, Ohio State U., 1957, PhD, 1961. Asst. Prof. Mktg. Ohio State U., Columbus, 1961-63, assoc. prof., 1964-67, prof., 1968-72; founder, pres. Mgmt. Horizons, Columbus, 1968-75, Alton F. Doody Co., Columbus, 1976—, The Doody Group, Cleve., 1984—; dir. The Newell Co. Author: Marketing in America: Settlement to Civil War, 1962, Retailing Management, 1972, Reinventing the Wheels: Ford's Spectacular Comeback, 1988. Trustee Ohio Wesleyan U., Delaware, Ctr. Sci. and Industry, Columbus. Served to 1st lt. USAF, 1968-71. Mem. Am. Mktg. Assn. (pres. Columbus chpt. 1968, chpt. Mktg. Man of Yr. 1980), Beta Gamma Sigma. Republican. Episcopalian. Clubs: Columbus, Scioto Country (Columbus).

DOODY, BARBARA PETTETT, computer specialist; b. Cin., Sept. 18, 1938; d. Philip Wayne and Virginia Bird (Handley) P.; student Sinclair Coll., Tulane U.; 1 son, Daniel Frederick Reasor, Jr. Owner, mgr. Honeysuckle Pet Shop, Tipp City, Ohio, 1970-76; office mgr. Doody & Doody, C.P.A.s, New Orleans, 1976-77, computer ops. mgr., 1979—; office mgr. San Diego Yacht Club, 1977-79. Mem. DAR, UDC, Jamestown Soc., Magna Charta, So. Dames, Colonial Dames of 17th Century, Nat. Soc. Daughters of 1812, Daus. Am. Colonists, Dames Ct. Honor. Republican. Lutheran. Home: 16 Cypress Covington LA 70433 Office: 821 Gravier St 1160 Commerce Bldg New Orleans LA 70112

DOODY, LOUIS CLARENCE, JR., accountant; b. New Orleans, Feb. 5, 1940; s. Louis Clarence and Elsie Clair (Connors) D.; B.C.S., Tulane U., 1963; m. Barbara Virginia Pettett, Oct. 9, 1982; children by previous marriage—Dana Lori, Mary Lyn, Kathleen Louise. Accountant, Louis C. Doody, C.P.A., 1963-68, partner Doody and Doody, C.P.A.'s, 1969—. C.P.A., La., Tex., Miss. Mem. Am. Inst. C.P.A.'s, La. Soc. C.P.A.'s. Home: 16 Cypress Covington LA 70433 Office: 821 Gravier St 1160 Commerce Bldg New Orleans LA 70112

DOOLEY, DONALD EDWIN, retired banker; b. Newton, Kans., Feb. 19, 1915; s. I.E. and Loretta (English) D.; B.S. in Bus., U. Kans., 1936; postgrad, Northwestern U., 1936-41; m. Helen Gordon Dodds, Aug. 29, 1941; children—John Edwin, Mary Frances (Mrs. Lowell D. Larsen), Elizabeth Ann (Mrs. Richard F. Schmalz), Margaret Caryl. Acct., Western Electric Co., Chgo., 1936-38; underwriter Western dept. Hartford Fire Ins. Co., Chgo., 1938-39; systems designer and chief auditor Wis. Electric Power Co., Milw., 1939-49; chief auditor Weyerhaeuser Co., Tacoma, 1949-65, dir. gen. office and plantsite services, 1965-73, fin. dir. Indonesian subs., Jakarta, 1974-76; treas. Am. Fed. Savs. & Loan Assn., Tacoma, 1976-80, v.p. and treas., 1980-83; v.p. Am. Savs. Bank, Tacoma, 1983-84, ret., 1984. Served to 1st lt. AUS, 1942-46. Recipient Bradford Cadmus Meml. award, 1969. Mem. Inst. Internal Auditors (pres. 1963-64), Am. Mgmt. Assn. (gen. services planning Council 1971-74), Delta Sigma Pi. Republican. Presbyterian. Home: 8708 Zircon SW Tacoma WA 98498 also: 9644 W Rimrock Ave Peoria AZ 85345

DOOLEY, J. GORDON, food scientist; b. Nevada, Mo., Nov. 15, 1935; s. Howard Eugene and Wilma June (Vanderford) D.; B.S. with honors in Biology, Drury Coll., Springfield, Mo., 1958; postgrad. (NSF grantee) U. Mo., Rolla, 1961, (NSF grantee) Kirksville (Mo.) State Coll., 1959; M.S. in Biology (NSF grantee), Brown U., 1966; postgrad. bus. mgmt. Alexander Hamilton Inst., 1973-75, No. Ill. U., 1964. Tchr. sci. Morton West High Sch., Berwyn, Ill., 1963-64; dairy technologist Borden Co., Elgin, Ill., 1964-65; project leader Cheese Products Lab., Kraft Corp., Glenview, Ill., 1965-73; sr. food scientist Wallerstein Co. div. Travenol Labs., Inc., Morton Grove, Ill., 1973-77; mgr. food sci. GB Fermentation Industries, Inc., Des Plaines, Ill., 1977-79, mgr. product devel., 1979-82; group leader Food Ingredients div. Stauffer Chem. Co., Clawson, Mich., 1982-84; sr. research scientist Schreiber Foods, Inc., Green Bay, Wis., 1984-87, Ridgeview, LaCrosse, Wis., 1987—; sci. lectr. seminars, Mexico, 1975; assoc. mem. Ad Hoc Enzyme Tech. Com., 1978—; dairy research adv. bd. Utah State U.; del. in field. Recipient Spoke award Nevada (Mo.) Jr. C. of C., 1960. Speaker, reporter People to People Sanitarians del. to China, 1989. Mem. Am. Dairy Sci. Assn., Inst. Food Technologists, Am. Chem. Soc., Cousteau Soc., Am. Inst. Biol. Scis., Nat. Sci. Tchrs. Assn., Whey Products Inst., Beta Beta Beta, Phi Eta Sigma. Republican. Presbyterian. Clubs: Toastmasters Internat. (pres. Baxter Labs. club 1976-77); Brown U. (Chgo.). Patentee in food and enzyme tech. field; contbr. sci. articles to profl. jours. Home: 723 Pleasant Ct Onalaska WI 54602 Office: Ridgeview 2340 Enterprise Ave La Crosse WI 54602

DOOLEY, RICHARD FRANCIS, international trade executive; b. N.Y.C., June 19, 1948; s. Richard F. and Jeanette (Nelson) D.; m. Vanessa Jones, June 19, 1975; children: Heather, Starr, Laurne Seana, Erin. BA in Econ., SUNY, Oneonta, 1970. Trader Fehr Bros., INc., N.Y.C., 1975-77; mktg. mgr. Fehr Bros., INc., Saugerties, N.Y., 1977-82, v.p., 1982-87, dir., 1985—, pres., 1987—. Office: Fehr Bros Ind Inc 5101 Kings Hwy Saugerties NY 12477

DOOLEY, THOMAS HOWARD, insurance company executive; b. N.Y.C., Sept. 22, 1934; s. Lawrence James and Lauretta May (Mulford) D.; m. Antoinette Rose Russo, Oct. 6, 1956; children: Karen M., Lawrence P. B.B.A., Clarkson U., 1956; J.D., U. Conn., 1964. Bar: Conn. 1964, U.S. Supreme Ct. 1968. Second v.p. Conn. Life Ins. Co., Bloomfield, 1968-77, v.p., 1977-83; sr. v.p. CIGNA Corp., Phila., 1983-85, exec. v.p., 1985—; mem. Conn. Ho. of Reps., 1970-74; dep. mayor Town of Vernon, Conn., 1976-80. Served with U.S. Army, 1957-59. Recipient Disting. Alumni award Clarkson U., 1981. Mem. Rockville Exchange Club (pres. 1970-72), Ins. Assn. Conn. (dir.). Democrat. Roman Catholic. Office: Cigna Corp 900 Cottage Grove Rd Bloomfield CT 06002

DOOLEY, TIMOTHY MICHAEL, financial analyst; b. Hammond, Ind., Feb. 14, 1959; s. Vincent Aloysius and Barbara Jane (Barker) D. Student, Tulane U., 1977-80; BBA, Cleve. State U., 1985. Asst. mgr. Martins Corner, Inc., Rocky River, Ohio, 1980-84; auditor's asst. Am. Electric Power Service Corp., Columbus, Ohio, 1985-87, internal auditor, 1987—. Active Young Reps., Washington, 1985. Mem. Inst. Internal Auditors, Sigma Chi. Roman Catholic. Office: Am Electric Power Svc Corp 1 Riverside Pla Columbus OH 43215

DOOSKIN, HERBERT P., manufacturing company executive; b. N.Y.C., Mar. 17, 1941; s. Leo S. and Anna (Horn) D.; m. Ruth H. Dorenbush, Dec. 24, 1963; children: Darren Michael, Hillary Anne, Nicole Jill. BA, CCNY, 1962; MBA, CUNY, 1965. CPA, N.Y. Chmn., mem. exec. com., ptnr. Grant Thornton, N.Y.C., 1964-86; exec. v.p. Ply Gem Industries Inc., N.Y.C., 1986—. V.p. Temple Sholom, Cedar Grove, N.J., 1985-86; trustee Mountainside Hosp., Montclair, N.J., 1985—. Office: Ply Gem Industries Inc 919 3d Ave New York NY 10022

DORAN, CHARLES EDWARD, textile manufacturing executive; b. Hartford, Conn., Mar. 31, 1928; s. Charles Edward and Josephine Catherine (Maher) D.; m. Anne Marie McGovern, May 18, 1957; children—Charles Francis, John Francis, Pamela Anne. B.A., Hamilton Coll., 1951; M.A., Yale, 1952. Trainee Gen. Elec. Co., 1953-56, financial mgmt. positions, 1956-65; asst. treas. Collins & Aikman Corp., N.Y.C., 1965-71; treas. Collins & Aikman Corp., 1971-88; mem. adv. bd. Arkwright-Boston Ins. Co., 1981-87. Served with USNR, 1946-48. Mem. Financial Execs. Inst., Phi Beta Kappa, Chi Psi. Republican. Roman Catholic. Clubs: Yale, Union League (N.Y.C.). Home: 10 Hardscrabble Circle Armonk NY 10504

DORAN, JAMES FRANCIS, real estate executive; b. N.Y.C., Aug. 27, 1943; s. Francis Doran and Genevieve (Davey) Thompson; m. Kathleen Ann Fleming, Aug. 4, 1973; divorced. BS in Fgn. Service, Georgetown U., 1965; MBA, Fordham U., 1972; M in Corp. Real Estate, Inst. Corp. Real Estate, 1987. Mgr. Equitable Life Ins. Co., N.Y.C., 1969-72, dir. sales planning, 1972-75, mgr. profl. hiring, 1975, exec. asst., 1976-78; asst. v.p. Denver, 1978-83; v.p. N.Y.C., 1983—. Mem. planned giving com. N.Y. Foundling Hosp., 1988. Served as maj. USAF, 1965-69. Mem. Internat. Assn. Corp. Real Estate Execs. (pres. N.Y. chpt. 1985-86), Bldg. Owners and Mgrs. Assn., Georgetown U. Alumnus Assn. (counselor). Democrat. Roman Catholic. Office: Equitable Life Ins Co 135 W 50th St New York NY 10020

DOREMUS, JOHN, radio and television producer; b. Sapulpa, Okla., Aug. 3, 1933; s. John W. and Arie D.; B.A., U. Tulsa, 1954; children: David, Frederick, Deidre, Paul. Announcer, newscaster Sta. KOME, Tulsa, 1951-52, Sta. KRMG, Tulsa, 1952-53, Sta. KVOO, Tulsa, 1953-54, Sta. WIND, Chgo., 1957-59, NBC AM and TV, Chgo., 1959-65, Sta. WAIT AM, Chgo., 1965-71, Sta. WGN AM, Chgo., 1971-73; founder, pres. John Doremus Inc., Chgo., 1965—; lectr. Northwestern U. Chmn., Roycemore Prep. Sch., 1967-69; mem. adv. bd. Bedside Network, 1976—; chmn. Chgo. Cerebral Palsy Drive, 1963; mem. bd. Dialogue for Blind, 1977—. Served with USMCR, 1950-51, USAF, 1954-57. Recipient Distinguished Alumnus award U. Tulsa, 1973, Chgo. Outstanding Radio Personality award Acad. Radio Arts, 1967. Mem. Chgo. C. of C., Nat. Assn. Broadcasters, Air Force Assn. Episcopalian. Clubs: Tavern, Chgo. Unlimited, Executives (chmn.) Rotary, Variety (Chgo.). Office: 1801 John Hancock Ctr Chicago IL 60611

DOREMUS, JOHN C., JR., investment banker; b. Garden City, N.Y., Dec. 19, 1931; s. John Clinton and Marguerite Louise (Heaton) D.; m. Ann Amelia Hoffman, Oct. 29, 1955; children—Dawn Ann, Carrie Shaw, Megg. B.A., Colgate U., N.Y., 1954. With Smith Barney & Co. Inc. (now Smith Barney, Harris Upham & Co., Inc.), N.Y.C., 1957—; former sr. v.p. nat. sales Smith Barney & Co. Inc. (now Smith Barney, Harris Upham & Co., Inc.), then exec. v.p.; now vice chmn., also dir. Smith Barney & Co. Inc. (now Smith Barney, Harris Upham & Co., Inc.), N.Y.C.; dir. Smith Barney

& Co., N.Y.C. Served to capt. USAF, 1954-57. Clubs: Rumson Country (N.J.); Bond of N.Y. (N.Y.C.); Seabright Beach (N.J.); Seabrook Island (S.C.). Office: Smith Barney Harris Upham & Co Inc 1345 Ave of the Americas New York NY 10105

DORF, JEROME, clothing corporation executive; b. Chgo., Sept. 29, 1936; s. Alfred A. and Josephine (Ziemba) D.; m. Sandra K. Pristash, Nov. 23, 1957; children: James J., Juliane S. BS in Commerce, DePaul U., 1958. CPA, Ill. Auditor Hartmarx Corp., Chgo., 1962-70, div. officer, 1970-78, controller, 1978-80, v.p., controller, 1980-85, sr. v.p., 1985-87, sr. v.p., chief fin. officer, 1987—. Office: Hartmarx Corp 101 N Wacker Dr Chicago IL 60606

DORF, PHILIP, public relations company executive; b. N.Y.C., Mar. 5, 1921; s. Max and Minnie (Siegelbaum) D.; m. Nathalie S. Bernstein, Mar. 30, 1947; children: Robert L., Lewis R., Margaret Sue. BA, NYU, 1942. Reporter, writer, editor United Press Assn., N.Y.C., 1946-56; account exec. pub. rels. dept. N.W. Ayer & Son, Inc., N.Y.C., 1956-58; account supr. Tex. McCrary, Inc., N.Y.C., 1958-60; v.p. Rowland Co., Inc., 1960-63, sr. v.p., 1963-70; v.p. Harshe-Rotman & Druck, Inc. (pub. rels. firm), N.Y.C., 1970-71; sr. v.p. Harshe-Rotman & Druck, Inc. (pub. rels. firm), 1971-73, exec. v.p., 1973-79, pres. eastern region, 1979-80; exec. v.p. Robert Marston & Assos., Inc., N.Y.C., 1980-88; pres. Robert Marston Corp. Communications, Inc., 1989—. Capt. AUS, 1942-46. Decorated Silver Star, Bronze Star, Purple Heart. Mem. Pub. Rels. Soc. Am., Nat. Investor Rels. Inst., Overseas Press Club Am. Home: 500 E 77th St New York NY 10162 Office: Robert Marston Corp Communications Inc 485 Madison Ave New York NY 10022

DORF, RICHARD CARL, electrical engineering and management educator; b. N.Y.C., Dec. 27, 1933; s. William Carl and Marion (Fraser) D.; m. Joy H. MacDonald, June 15, 1957; children: Christine, Renée. BS, Clarkson U., 1955; MS, U. Colo., 1957; PhD, U.S. Naval Postgrad. Sch., 1961. Registered profl. engr., Calif. Instr. Clarkson U., Potsdam, N.Y., 1956-58; instr., asst. prof. U.S. Naval Postgrad. Sch., Monterey, Calif., 1958-63; prof., chmn. U. Santa Clara, Calif., 1963-69; v.p. Ohio U., Athens, 1969-72; dean and prof. elec. engring. U. Calif., Davis, 1972—; lectr. U. Edinburgh, Scotland, 1961-62; cons. Lawrence Livermore (Calif.) Nat. Lab., 1981—; chmn. Sacramento Valley Venture Capital Forum, 1985—. Author: The Mutual Fund Portfolio Planner, 1988, The New Mutual Fund Advisor, 1988, Electric Circuits, 1989, Modern Control Systems, 5th edit., 1989; editor: Ency. of Robotics, 1987. Bd. dirs. Sta. KVIE, PBS, Sacramento, 1976-79; ruling elder Davis Community Ch., 1973-76. With U.S. Army, 1956. Recipient Alumni award Clarkson U., 1979. Fellow IEEE; mem. Am. Soc. Engring. Edn. (sr., chmn. div. 1980—), University Club (bd. dirs. 1988—), Rotary (bd. dirs. 1978-80). Presbyterian. Office: U Calif Elec Engring Dept Davis CA 95616

DORFMAN, HENRY S., meat products company executive; b. 1922; married. With Sausage Mfg. Bus., 1944-49, Gen. Machines Co., 1949-50, Hudson Motor Car Co., 1950-51, B.M. Shindler Meats Co., 1951-52; chmn. bd., chief exec. officer Thorn Apple Valley, Inc., Southfield, Mich., 1952—, pres., from 1952, also bd. dirs. Office: Thorn Apple Valley Inc 18700 W Ten Mile Rd Southfield MI 48075 *

DORFMAN, KAREN KING, corporate consultant, lecturer; b. Indpls., Mar. 3, 1950; d. John and Margie King; BA, U. Tex., 1972; MA, Ind. U., 1976. Sales rep. John H. Harland Co., 1979-76, internal cons., 1986—; guest lectr. Ind. U.-Purdue U., 1977—. Mem. various clubs. Home: 5678 N Meridian Indianapolis IN 46208

DORFMAN, MARK, financial executive; b. N.Y.C., July 2, 1963; s. Alfred and Ceil (Lipton) Oberlander. BSBA, Boston U., 1985. CLU; chartered fin. cons. Account exec. Capital Analysts, Westbury, N.Y., 1985-88; fin. planner Oberlander Dorfman Inc., Valley Stream, N.Y., 1988—. Mem. Nat. Assn. Securities Dealers (reg. rep.). Jewish. Club: Pres.'s of Fidelity Mut. Life Ins. Co. Office: Oberlander Dorfman Inc 71 S Central Ave Valley Stream NY 11580

DORGAN, JOHN JOSEPH, JR., oil company executive; b. Providence, Sept. 1, 1923; s. John Joseph and Isabelle Regina (Carroll) D.; m. Cynthia Codrington, June 8, 1946; children: Carroll S., Elizabeth B., Peter M., John C. A.B., Harvard, 1944, M.B.A., 1948. Economist Continental Oil Co., 1948-52, asst. to pres., 1952-54, landman, 1954-56, dir. credit and ins., 1956-58, asst. treas., 1958-59, treas., 1958-64, coordinator plant foods, 1964-65, v.p., coordinator plant foods, 1965-68, v.p., gen. mgr. plant foods, 1968-69, v.p., gen. mgr. supply and transp., 1969-70; dir. supply and transp. Conoco Continental Oil Co., Europe/London, 1970-72; mng. dir. Raffinerie Belge de Petroles S.A., Belgium, 1972; v.p., treas. Occidental Petroleum Corp., 1972-75, exec. v.p. finance, 1975—; petroleum economist Petroleum Adminstrn. for Def., Washington, 1951-52; dir. Can. Occidental Petroleum, Industrias Oxy S.A. Served to lt. (j.g.) USNR, 1943-46. Mem. Am. Petroleum Inst. Clubs: Lansdowne (London); Harvard (N.Y.C.) (treas. 1968-70), Links (N.Y.C.); Regency (Los Angeles). Home: 260 N Glenroy Ave Los Angeles CA 90049 Office: Occidental Petroleum Corp 10889 Wilshire Blvd Los Angeles CA 90024 *

DORIGO, WERNER FRITZ, JR., infosystems specialist; b. Miami, Fla., Dec. 4, 1947; s. Werner Fritz and Edith Alwine (Doering) D.; m. Nellie Tamari, Sept. 19, 1969; children: Fritz, Eric. AS in Data Processing, Broward Community Coll., 1973; BAS in Computer Sci., Fla. Atlantic U., 1977. Computer operator III Fla. Atlantic U., Boca Raton, 1972-73, computer programmer II, 1973-76, computer operator III, 1977; EDP coordinator City of North Miami, Fla., 1977-78; systems analyst Real Estate Data, Inc., Miami, 1978-79; sr. computer systems designer Ryder Truck Rental div. Ryder System Inc., Miami, 1979-84; pres. Dorigo Info. Services, Pembroke Pines, Fla., 1984—; sec.-treas. Fla. Telstar, Miramar, Fla., 1987—. First v.p. parish com. St. Bartholomew Roman Cath. Ch., Miramar, 1985-87. Served with U.S. Army, 1965-69. Mem. Data Processing Mgmt. Assn., Assn. for Computing Machinery. Club. St. Bartholomew Men's (sec. 1980-86). Home and Office: 8404 NW 17th Ct Pembroke Pines FL 33024-3406

DORIO, MARTIN MATTHEW, manufacturing executive; b. Bklyn., Nov. 12, 1945; s. Martin M. and Josephine V. (Marsala) D.; m. Gayle M. Morris, June 16, 1968; children: Paul, Jay. BS, SUNY, Stony Brook, 1967; PhD, U. Mass., 1975. Rsch. chemist Diamond Shamrock Corp., Painesville, Ohio, 1975-76; group leader Diamond Shamrock Corp., Painesville, 1977-79; venture mgr. Gen. Electric Lighting Bus., Cleve., 1979-81, mfg. tech. mgr., 1981-87; dir. quality and productivity FMC Corp., Chgo., 1987—; mem. adv. com. Dept. Energy, Washington, 1977-79, Am. Productivity and Quality Ctr., Houston, 1988—; mem. adv. com. on quality Encyclopedia Britannica. Author: Multiple Electronspect, 1979, Electron Resonance Spect; contbr. articles to profl. jours; patentee in field. Coach Little League Ball, Mentor, Ohio, 1982-84; pres. Homeowners Assn., 1983-85. Capt. USAF, 1968-71. Mem. First Bd. Examiners (Nat. Quality award), Nat. Bur. Standards, Am. Soc. Quality Control (exec. com. 1984-85), Am. Mgmt. Assn., Assn. Mfg. Excellence. Home: 1907 Keats Ln Highland Park IL 60035-1641 Office: FMC Corp 200 E Randolph Dr Chicago IL 60601

DORIS, MICHAEL ANTHONY, corporate controller; b. Bklyn., Jan. 19, 1955; s. Michael Frances and Carmel (Perri) D.; m. Mary Ellen Romano, Oct. 11, 1979 (div. Oct. 4, 1983). BS in Acctg., Fairfield U., 1977. Auditor David Berdon & Co., N.Y.C., 1977-81; sr. auditor Touche Ross, N.Y.C., 1981-83; asst. controller Equitable Bag Co., Inc., N.Y.C., 1983-86, controller, 1986—. Mem. Am. Assn. CPA's; N.Y.C. Soc. CPA's. Office: Equitable Bag Co 45 S Van Dam St Long Island City NY 11101

DORLAND, DODGE OATWELL, investment banker; b. N.Y.C., Feb. 27, 1948; s. Joseph Warner and Marion (Dodge) D.; m. Bonita Gillette Zeese, Jan. 9, 1971. Diploma, Choate Sch., 1966; BA, Colgate U., 1970; MBA, NYU, 1975. With Mfrs. Hanover Trust Co., N.Y.C., 1970-77, asst. sec., 1974-77; with Bank of Montreal Trust Co., N.Y.C., 1977-86, v.p., 1979-86, v.p. communications unit, 1982-86, U.S. industry coordinator for communications, 1983-86; v.p. Shearson Lehman Bros., Inc., N.Y.C., 1986-88; v.p. Gen. Electric Capital Corp.; bd. dirs. So. Telecom, Inc., West Ga. Cable, Inc. Author: The Communications Industry: An Informational Overview, 1983; contbr. papers in field to profl. jours. Treas. Learning for Living Inst., N.Y.C., 1977-81; chmn. bd. dirs. 325 E. 72d St. Apts., N.Y.C., 1978-81; participant NYU Grad. Sch. Bus. Mgmt. Decision Lab., 1977-79, now bd. dirs.; mem. investment com. Assn. for Relief of Elderly Inc., 1984—. Mem. Nat. Cable TV Assn., Nat Assn. Broadcasters, Cellular Telecommunications Industry Assn., The Elfun Soc. N.Y., Drama League N.Y., Broadcast Fin. Mgmt. Assn., Telocator Network of Am., Internat. Platform Assn., Media and Entertainment Analysts Assn. N.Y., Am. Film Inst., Smithsonian Inst., Vets. Corp. Arty., SAR, Soc. Colonial Wars, Mil. Order Loyal Legion of U.S., Knickerbocker Greys Vets. Corp., Holland Soc. Republican. Episcopalian. Clubs: Yale (N.Y.C.); Meadow, Bathing Corp. (Southampton, N.Y.)., Toastmasters (v.p. Mfrs. Hanover chpt. 1975-78), 21. Home: 103 E 75th St New York NY 10021 Office: Gen Electric Capital Corp 535 Madison Ave Ste 2700 New York NY 10022

DORMAN, ALBERT A., consulting engineer, architect; b. Phila., Apr. 30, 1926; s. William and Edith (Kleiman) D.; m. Joan Bettie Heiten, July 29, 1950; children: Laura Jane, Kenneth Joseph, Richard Coleman. B.S., Newark Coll. Engring., 1945; M.S., U. So. Calif., 1962. Registered profl. engr., Calif., N.Y., Ill., Oreg., Ariz., Hawaii, Pa., Nev., La. registered architect, Calif., Oreg. City engr., mem. City Planning Commn., Lemoore, Calif., 1954-67, Corcoran, Calif., 1955-65; owner firm Albert A. Dorman, Hanford, Calif., 1954-66; v.p. Daniel, Mann, Johnson & Mendenhall, Los Angeles, 1967-73; dir. Daniel, Mann, Johnson & Mendenhall, 1970—, exec. v.p., chief operating officer, 1973-74, pres., chief operating officer, 1974-77, pres., chief exec. officer, 1977-84, chmn., chief exec. officer, 1984—; chmn. Holmes & Narver, Inc., Orange, Calif., 1984—, Williams Bros. Engring. Co., Tulsa, 1984—; chmn. chief exec. officer Frederic R. Harris, Inc., N.Y.C., 1988—; pres., chmn. bd. dirs. Hanford Savs. & Loan Assn., 1963-72; pres. Hanford Service Co., Inc.; bd. dirs. Perland Environ. Tech. Inc., Burlington, Mass. Contbr. articles to profl. jours. Chmn. Kings County chpt. ARC, 1955-60; pres. Community Concerts Assn., 1962-64; mem. dean's council Sch. Architecture and Urban Planning, UCLA; bd. councilors Sch. Urban and Regional Planning, U. So. Calif.; bd. trustees Harvey Mudd Coll.; mem. bd. overseers N.J. Inst. Tech., 1989—; commr. Oiland Gas div. Calif. Dept. Conservation, 1972-75; trustee City of Hope, J. David Gladstone Found., 1988.; vice chmn. Los Angeles County Earthquake Fact-Finding Commn., 1980. Served with AUS, 1945-47. Recipient Civil Engring. Alumnus award U. So. Calif., 1976, Commendation L.A. County Bd. Suprs., 1985, Edward F. Weston medal N.J. Inst. Tech., 1986, Commendation L.A. City Coun., 1988, Disting. Community Service award Pacific Southwest Region Real Estate, Devel. and Construction div. Anti-Defamation League, 1988. Fellow ASCE (Harland Bartholomew award 1976, Parcel-Sverdrup Civil Engring. Mgmt. award 1987, pres. Los Angeles sect. 1984-85), Inst. for Advancement of Engring. (Outstanding Engr. award 1980, George Washington award 1988), FAIA, Am. Cons. Engrs. Council; mem. Nat. Conf. Christians and Jews, Real Estate Constr. Industries (Humanitarian award 1986), Am. Pub. Works Assn., Cons. Engrs. Assn. Calif. (bd. dirs. 1982-88, pres. 1985-86), Am. Water Works Assn., Water Pollution Control Fedn., Calif. C. of C. (bd. dirs. 1986—), Los Angeles Area C. of C. (bd. dirs. 1983-88, exec. com. 1985-87, Achievement award Constrn. Industries com. 1988, Herb Nash Econ. Devel. award 1988), Tau Beta Pi, Chi Epsilon. Clubs: Commonwealth (San Francisco); California (Los Angeles); Metropolitan (Washington); Kiwanis (pres. 1962). Office: Daniel Mann Johnson & Mendenhall 3250 Wilshire Blvd Los Angeles CA 90010 also: 1 Park Pla Los Angeles CA 90010

DORMAN, REX LEE, forest products executive; b. Wendell, Idaho, Jan. 13, 1934; s. Lee Roy and Leona Rose (Dillie) D.; m. Marilyn Jane Frazier, May 6, 1956; children; Donald, Michael, Diane. AA, Boise Jr. Coll., 1954; BS in Acctg./Econs., U. Idaho, 1961; postgrad., Stanford U., 1975. CPA, Idaho. Acct. Low, Viehweg, Hill and Grow, Boise, Idaho, 1961-66; supr., internal auditor Boise Cascade Corp., 1966-69, mgr. internal audit, 1969-73, asst. controller, 1973-75, controller, 1975-84, v.p. planning and control, 1984-86, v.p. control and info. services, 1986—; bd. dirs. Boise Cascade Can., Ltd., Toronto, Ont. Mem. adv. bd. U. Idaho, Moscow, 1968—; treas. Boise Philharm. Assn., 1969-72, Boise Civic Opera, Inc., 1977-80; chmn. Associated Taxpayers Idaho, Boise, 1982. Lt. (j.g.) USN, 1954-58. Mem. AICPA (internal control com. 1978-79), Idaho Soc. CPA's (pres. 1976-77), Am. Paper Inst., Fin. Acctg. Standards Bd. (task force 1979-86, cert. internal auditor 1962—). Republican. Clubs: Arid (Boise), Crane Creek Country. Office: Boise Cascade Corp PO Box 50 Boise ID 83728

DORMAN, THOMAS PATRICK, marketing professional, consultant; b. LaPorte, Ind., June 24, 1950; s. James Thomas and Edith Helen (Harris) D.; m. Mary Elizabeth Lapp, Aug. 20, 1976; 1 child, Matthew James. Student, Ind. U., 1968-71. Freelance musician Los Angeles, 1971-76; mgr. sales adminstrn. Franciscan Dinnerware, Los Angeles, 1976-79; mgr. nat. field mktg. Internat. Gold Corp., N.Y.C., 1979-83; exec. dir. Gold Filled Assn., N.Y.C., 1983-85; dir. investor products Engelhard Corp, Iselin, N.J., 1985-87; dir. mktg. Krementz and Co., Newark, 1987—. Mem. 24 Karat Club So. Calif., Boston Jewelers Club, Providence Jewelers Club. Republican. Congregationalist. Office: Krementz and Co 375 McCartga Hwy Newark NJ 07114

DORMANN, HENRY O., magazine publisher; b. N.Y.C., Mar. 5, 1932; s. Henry Maroni and Ivara (Soberg) D.; m. Alice Andreasen, Apr. 7, 1958; children—Kaari, Kristi. Chmn. bd. Nat. Enquirer, 1971-72, chmn. exec. com., 1987—; chmn. Internat. Bd. Indsl. Advisors, 1964—; pres., editor-in-chief S.I.P.A. News Service, N.Y.C., 1966—; pres. U.S. Tech. Devel. Co., 1969-70; pres., editor-in-chief Holiday Mag.; pres. editor-in-chief Leaders Mag., N.Y.C.; Mem. adv. council Joint Legis. Com. on Met. and Regional Areas Study N.Y. State, 1969-72; chmn. N.Y. State Assembly Council on Econ. Devel., 1972—. Mem. assn. bd. Mcht. Marine Acad., 1969—; founder Library Presdl. Papers, Inst. for Study of Presidency; trustee Am. U., Washington. Served with USCG. Office: 59 E 54th St New York NY 10022

DORNBUSCH, ARTHUR A., II, lawyer; b. Peru, Ill., Nov. 8, 1943; s. Arthur A. Sr. and Genevieve C. (Knudtson) D.; divorced; children: Kimberly, Brendan, Courtney, Eric. BA, Yale U., 1966; LLB, U. Pa., 1969. Bar: N.Y. 1970, U.S. Ct. Appeals. (2d cir.) 1971, U.S. Dist. Ct. (so. and ea. dists.) N.Y. 1971. Assoc. Dewey, Ballantine, Bushby, Palmer & Wood, N.Y.C., 1969-72; asst. gen. counsel Boise Cascade Corp., N.Y.C., 1972-75; asst. gen counsel Teleprompter Corp., N.Y.C., 1975-76; asst. gen. counsel Englehard Industries div. Englehard Minerals and Chems. Corp., Edison, N.J., 1976-80, v.p., gen. counsel, 1980-84, v.p., gen. counsel, sec., 1984—. Mem. Pelham (N.Y.) Union Sch. Dist. Bd. Edn., 1979-82; treas. Pelham People United Community Health, 1987. Mem. ABA, N.Y. State Bar Assn., Assn. of Bar of City of N.Y., Am. Corp. Counsel Assn., Am. Intellectual Property Law Assn., Am. Soc. Corp. Secs., Machinery and Allied Products Inst. (law council). Office: Engelhard Corp Menlo Pk CN 40 33 Wood Ave S Edison NJ 08818

DORNBUSH, VICKY JEAN, medical billing systems executive; b. Willowick, Ohio, Aug. 12, 1951; d. Charles W. and Josephine H. (Palumbo) Rader; m. Eric D. Erickson, Oct. 22, 1972 (div. June 1974); m. Thomas Dornbush, Dec. 29, 1979 (div. 1987); 1 child, Dana. Student, Kent State U., 1969-72, San Jose State U., 1982-84. Accounts receivable clk. MV Nursery, Richmond, Calif., 1975-76; accounts receivable and computer supr. Ga. Pacific, Richmond, 1976-78; acct. Ga. Pacific, Tracy, Calif., 1978-79, Crown-Zellerbach, Anaheim, Calif., 1979-80; acct. Interstate Pharmacy Corp., San Jose, Calif., 1981-83, contr., 1983-85; gen. ptnr. Med. Billing Systems, San Jose, 1984—; seminar trainer Systems Plus, Mountain View, Calif., 1987—. Mem. San Jose Civic Light Opera, 1987—, San Jose Repertory Co., 1986—. Mem. Women in Bus. Republican. Methodist. Office: Med Billing Systems 255 W Julian St #403 San Jose CA 95110

DORNEMAN, ROBERT WAYNE, manufacturing engineer; b. Oaklawn, Ill., Nov. 13, 1949; s. Robert John and Julia (Vorchenia) D.; M. Katrina Holland, July 30, 1977; children: Tamara, Tiana. BA in Biol. Sci., Calif. State U., Fullerton, 1974. Mfg. engr. Gen. Telephone Co., Anaheim, Calif., 1974-77, Xerox/Century Data, Anaheim, 1977-80; advance mfg. engr. MSI Data, Costa Mesa, Calif., 1980-83; sr. mfg. engr. Parker Hannifin, Irvine, Calif., 1983-86; sr. advanced mfr. engr. Western Digital, Irvine, 1986-89, mgr. advanced mfg. engring., 1989—; specialist automated assembly of circuits; cons. Base 2, Fullerton, 1980; developer surface mount tech. for computer mfg. industry; set up computer assemble plants internat. Innovator in field; contbr. articles in 3M-Alert to profl. jours. Mem. Nat. Assn. Realtors (broker), N. Orange County Bd. Realtors (broker), Calif. Assn. Realtors, Internat. Platform Assn., Internat. Soc. Hybrid Mfg., Phillips Ranch Assn., Tau Kappa Epsilon. Republican. Home: 56 Meadow View Dr Phillips Ranch Pomona CA 91766 Office: Western Digital 2802 Kelvin St Irvine CA 92714

DORRANCE, GEORGE MORRIS, JR., banker; b. Phila., Dec. 28, 1922; s. George Morris and Emily (Fox) D.; m. Carter Rogers; children: Mary Irwin, George Morris III. AB, U. Pa., 1949, MBA, 1951. With Fed. Res. Bank, Phila., 1949-51; with Phila. Nat. Bank subs. Core States Fin. Corp., 1951-87, chmn., 1969-87; chmn. Core States Fin. Corp., 1986-88; bd. dirs. Penn Va. Corp., R.R. Donnelly & Sons Co., Provident Mut. Life Ins. Co., Phila., Rohm and Haas Corp., Joh. Berenberg, Gossler & Co., Hamburg, Germany. Trustee U. Pa. Office: CoreStates Fin Corp NE Corner Broad & Chestnut Sts PO Box 7618 Philadelphia PA 19107

DORRANCE, JOHN THOMPSON, JR., food processing executive; b. Cinnaminson, N.J., Feb. 7, 1919; s. John Thompson and Ethel (Mallinckrodt) D.; m. Diana R. Dripps, Apr. 26, 1979; children: John Thompson, III, Bennett, Mary Alice Malone; stepchildren: Keith Bassett, Langdon Mannion, Robert D. Dripps, III, Susan Stauffer. Grad., St. George's School, Newport, R.I., 1937; A.B., Princeton, 1941. With Campbell Soup Co., 1946—, asst. treas., 1950, asst. to pres., 1955, chmn. bd., 1962-84, chmn. exec. com., 1984—, also dir.; dir. Neiman Marcus Group, Morgan Guaranty Trust Co. of N.Y., J.P. Morgan & Co., Inc. Served as capt. U.S. Army, World War II. Mem. Soc. Cin. Republican. Clubs: Union (N.Y.C.); Philadelphia (Phila.), Rittenhouse (Phila.), Union League (Phila.), Racquet (Phila.); Gulph Mills (Pa.) Golf; Pine Valley (N.J.). Golf, Nat. Golf Links of Am. (Southampton, N.Y.). Home: Monk Rd Gladwyne PA 19035 Office: 230 S Broad St 9th Fl E Philadelphia PA 19102 also: Campbell Soup Co Campbell Pl Camden NJ 08101

DORRANCE, STANLEY DAVID, financial planner; b. Glendale, Calif., Aug. 8, 1949; s. Paul M. and Roselma (Dewey) D.; m. Kay A. Nolan, Apr. 10, 1976; children: Ryan, Erin, Caitlin. BS, U. Calif., Berkeley, 1972; MBA, Calif. State U., Fresno, 1978. With criminalist dept. of justice State of Calif., Fresno, 1972-82; fin. planner State Bond Sales Corp., Fresno, 1979-83, Associated Fin. Advisors, Ltd., Fresno, 1984—. Mem. Internat. Assn. for Fin. Planning (pres. Fresno chpt. 1985-86), Inst. Cert. Fin. Planners (pres. 1986-87), Registry Fin. Planning Practitioners. Republican. Methodist. Home: 969 E Portland Fresno CA 93710 Office: Associated Fin Advisors Ltd 5260 N Palm Ave Ste 130 Fresno CA 93704

DORSETT, BURT, investment company executive; b. Chgo. Nov. 8, 1930; s. Burton and Della (Reader) D.; m. Judith Martin, Dec. 14, 1952 (div.); children: Mark, Deborah, Jeffrey, Cindy (dec.); m. Trixie Landsberger, Mar. 1, 1981. BA, Dartmouth Coll., 1953; MBA, Harvard U., 1959. Indsl. engr. E.I. duPont de Nemours, Seaford, Del. 1953-57; cons. Booz-Allen & Hamilton, N.Y.C., 1959-62; v.p. U. Rochester, 1962-70; exec. v.p., trustee Coll. Retirement Equities Fund, N.Y.C., 1970-79; chmn., pres. Westinghouse Pension Investment Corp., N.Y.C., 1979-86, Dorsett-McCabe Capital Mgmt. Inc., 1987-89; mng. dir. Mental Mgmt. Group, Inc., 1989—; treas., bd. dirs. Rsch. Corp., N.Y.C., 1972—, Shearson Hammill Funds, N.Y.C., 1974—; bd. dirs. Simms Golbal Fund, 1986-88, Rsch. Corp. Techs., Inc., 1986—; mem. investment com. Am. Psychol. Assn., 1969—. Mem. budget com. Community Chest, Rochester, 1967-70; trustee Convalescent Hosp. for Children, Rochester, 1967-70, Hillside Children's Home, Rochester, 1968-70, Keuka Coll., N.Y., 1968-71; mem. com. Boys Club of N.Y.C. William J. Cook scholar, 1953. Clubs: Dartmouth, Harvard Bus. Sch., Univ., Doubles Internat. (N.Y.C.); WeeBurn Country (Darien, Conn.). Author: (with others) Epoxy Resins, Market Survey and Users Reference, 1959. Office: 825 3d Ave New York NY 10022

DORSEY, EDWARD FRANCIS, JR., utilities executive; b. Milw., Sept. 8, 1926; s. Edward Francis and Margaret (Marine) D.; m. Dolores Martha Zych, Sept. 16, 1950; children: Donna Dorsey Buscaglia, Debra, Denise Dorsey Eigner. BBA, Marquette U., 1951. Sales supr. Wis. Gas, Milw., 1956-58, mgr. Mayfair, 1958-68, sales promotion mgr., 1968-73, metro mktg. mgr., 1973-77, pub. info officer, 1977-78, adminstrv. coordinator, 1978—; dir. and treas. Research Clearing House, Milw., 1987-88. Pres. Wis. Blue Flame Council, 1979-80; chmn. United Fund, Milw., 1962. With USN, 1944-46, PTO, CBI. Mem. Wauwatosa C. of C. (dir. 1981-88), Mid-Am. Econ. Devel. Council, Wis. Econ. Devel. Assn., Tuckaway Country Club, Rotary (pres. Wauwatosa club 1967-68), Eagles Lodge. Republican. Roman Catholic. Home: 16855 Martha Dr Brookfield WI 53005 Office: Wisconsin Gas Co 626 E Wisconsin Ave Milwaukee WI 53202

DORSEY, JEREMIAH EDMUND, pharmaceutical company executive; b. Worcester, Mass., Oct. 15, 1944; s. Jeremiah Edmund and Mary Theresa Dorsey; A.B., Assumption Coll., Worcester, 1966; M.B.A., Fairleigh Dickinson U., 1978; m. Nadia S. Vidach, Dec. 6, 1970; children—Todd Edmund, Jaime Erin, Megan Elizabeth, Kelly Ann. With Johnson & Johnson, New Brunswick, N.J., 1970-88, nat. indsl. engring. mgr., 1975-76, supt. ops. and maintenance, from 1976, now dir. ops. and mem. mgmt. bd.; v.p. ops. and sales Johnson & Johnson Dental Products Co.; exec. v.p. The Karlin Group, Bridgeton, N.J.,1988, pres. Towle Housewares Co., Newburyport, Mass., 1988—; pres. J.E. Dorsey Co, Carvel Hall Corp, Crisfield, Md. Active N.J. Commn. for Discharge Up-grade, Appalachian Trail Conf.; mem. alumni bd. dirs. Assumption Coll.; mem. adv. com. U. P.R. Sch. of Pharmacy; mem. mil. acad. selection com. U.S. Senate; vice chmn. N.J. Vietnam Vets. Leadership Program; mem. Mercer County Pvt. Industry Council (N.J.), N.J. SR-92 Coalition. Served with U.S. Army, 1966-69; Vietnam. Decorated Bronze Star with 2 oak leaf clusters, Purple Heart with 4 oak leaf clusters, Army Commendation medal, Air medal with oak leaf cluster; Medal of Honor, Gallantry Cross (Vietnam); recipient Corp. Affirmative Action award, 1981. named Mgr. of Yr., Johnson & Johnson, 1974-75. Mem. Sierra Club, Spl. Forces Assn., Smithsonian Assocs., DAV, Soc. First Div., Tiger Karate Soc. (Black Belt), K.C., Johnson & Johnson Mgmt. Club, Delta Epsilon Sigma. Roman Catholic. Editor: Spl. Forces Assn. News. Home: 10 Eastern Dr Kendall Park NJ 08824 Office: Towle Housewares Co 260 Merrimack St Newburyport MA 01950

DORWARD, W. WILSON, financial executive; b. Lancaster, Pa., Sept. 3, 1948; s. Lewis Holmes and Charlotte Burnley (Wilson) D.; m. Karen Stauffer, Aug. 25, 1973; children: Eric Ramage, Megan Burnley. BS in Metallurgy, Lehigh U., 1970; JD, Dickinson Sch. Law, 1973; MBA with distinction, U. Penn., 1979. Bar: Pa., 1973. Atty. Flurher, Medill & Shelley, York, Pa., 1973, Contract Mgmt. div. USAF, Albuquerque, 1973-77; fin. analyst W.R. Grace & Co., Balt., 1979-81; dir. fin. Susquehanna Broadcasting Co., York, 1981—; bd. dirs. Shiloh Nurseries Inc., York, 1983—. Bd. dirs. Vis. Nurses Assn., Rape & Victim Assistance Ctr., 1988—, Transmission Networks Internat., 1988—. Served to capt. USAF, 1973-77. Nat. Sci. Found. grantee, 1969-70. Mem. Cen. Pa. Investment Mgrs. Assn., Sigma Nu. Republican. Presbyterian. Home: 269 Brookwood Dr S York PA 17403 Office: Susquehanna Broadcasting Co 140 E Market St York PA 17401

DOSHI, JITENDRA BHAGWANDAS, financial planner; b. Bombay, Feb. 28, 1946; came to U.S., 1971; s. Bhagwandas Shivlal and Jayaben B. (Jhguiandas) D.; m. Sharda Ranchhudbhai Patel, Aug. 15, 1974; children: Snehal, Taral. BS, U. Bombay, 1970; MS, St. Michael's Coll., 1973; MBA, Long Island (N.Y.) U., 1978. Cert. fin. planner. Chemist Pub. Service & Gas Co. N.J., Linden, 1973-78, La. State Lab., New Orleans, 1979-81; sales rep. Metropolitan, Beaumont, Tex., 1982; fin. planner MONY Fin. Service, Beaumont, 1982—. Mem. Inst. Cert. Fin. Planners, Beaumont Life Underwriters Assn. Hindu. Home: PO Box 615 Silsbee TX 77656

DOSLAND, WILLIAM BUEHLER, lawyer; b. Chgo., Nov. 10, 1927; s. Goodwin Leroy and Beatrice Florence (Buehler) D.; m. Donna Mae Mathisen, Sept. 15, 1956; children: David William, Susan Elizabeth. BA, Concordia Coll., 1949; JD, U. Minn., 1954. Bar: Minn. 1954, U.S. Ct. Appeals (8th cir.) 1978. Sr. ptnr. Dosland, Dosland, Nordhougen, Lillihaug & Johnson P.A., Moorhead, Minn., 1957—; gen. counsel, corp. sec. Am. Crystal Sugar Co., 1973—; sec. No. Grain Co., 1975, gen. counsel, 1975—; gen. counsel Am. Bank & Trust, 1969—, bd. dirs., 1976-86; regent U. Minn.,

1979-85. Mem. Minn. State Senate, 1959-73. Capt. USNR, 1945-46, 51-53. Recipient Alumni Achievement award, Concordia Coll., 1979. Mem. Minn. State Bar Assn., Clay County Bar Assn., Lions, Masons. Republican. Lutheran. Lodges: Masons, Lions. Home: 3122 Rivershore Dr Moorhead MN 56560 Office: Dosland Dosland & Norhougen 730 Ctr Ave PO Box 100 Moorhead MN 56560

DOSS, DONNA SUE, software engineer; b. Dearborn, Mich., June 18, 1961; d. Norman Eugene and Carolyn Ann (Weber) Caldwell; m. Robert James Doss, May 22, 1982. BS, Eastern Mich. U., 1984. Computer programmer Morgan Electric, Inc., Southfield, Mich., 1984-85; software engr. Automated Systems div. Volvo N.Am. Corp., Sterling Heights, Mich., 1985-88, sr. software engr. BT Systems Inc., Sterling Heights, 1988—. Mem. Nat. Assn. Female Execs. Inc., Golden Key, Phi Kappa Phi. Presbyterian. Avocations: tennis, reading, boating. Home: 7962 Harding Ave Taylor MI 48180 Office: BT Systems Inc 7000 Nineteen Mile Rd Sterling Heights MI 48078

DOSS, LAWRENCE PAUL, accounting firm executive; b. Cleve., June 16, 1927; s. Raymond Milton and Velma Lorraine (Kendall) D.; children: Paula, Lawrence, Lawry. Student, Ohio State U., 1947-49, Fenn Coll., 1949-51, Am. U., 1954; M.A. in Pub. Adminstrn., Nova U. With IRS, Detroit, 1949-70; dir. data ctr. IRS, 1967-70; coordinator decentralization program Detroit Pub. Schs., 1970-71; pres. Detroit Urban Coalition, New Detroit, Inc., 1971-77; ptnr. Coopers & Lybrand, 1978—. Pres. Inner City Bus. Improvement Forum, Detroit, 1967-71; treas. Fed. Exec. Bd., 1968-70; chmn. Mich. Neighborhood Edn. Authority, 1971-77; operating chmn. Mayor's Detroit Crime Task Force, 1976-78; co-chmn. Move Detroit Forward, 1978—; mem. exec. com. Sch. Desegregation Monitoring Commn., 1976-78; vice chmn. bd. dirs., exec. com. Martin Luther King Center for Social Change; bd. dirs. mem. exec. com. New Detroit Econ. Growth Corp.; treas. Congl. Black Caucus, D.C. Com. to Promote Washington; bd. dirs. Africare, Am. Natural Resources, Inc.; trustee Hudson-Webber Founds., United Found., Detroit; chmn. devel. commn. Black United Fund of Detroit.; mem. Mich. Commn. on Jobs and Econ. Devel.; pres. Coleman A. Young Found.; exec. vice chmn. D.C. Commn. on Crime and Justice, 1982-83; chmn. Juvenile Justice Adv. Group, Washington, 1985—. Served with USNR, 1945-46. Recipient Meritorious Achievement award William A. Jump Found., 1964, Meritorious Achievement award U.S. Treasury Dept., 1964, Presdl. citation, 1964, Nat. Corp. Urban Affairs award Nat. Urban Coalition, 1984, Spl. award Op. Get Down, 1986. Mem. Omega Psi Phi (Citizen of Yr. 1974). Home: 345 E Crescent Ln Detroit MI 48207-5002 Office: Coopers & Lybrand 400 Renaissance Ctr Detroit MI 48243

DOSSA, ALFRED CARL, leasing company executive, lawyer; b. Oakland, Calif., Oct. 6, 1938; s. Louis and Caroline N. (Marchiando) D.; m. Elizabeth Ann Zentmyer, Aug. 9, 1969; children: Andrea, Jennifer, Julia. AB, U. Calif., Berkeley, 1960; MA, Oxford U., 1962; JD, Harvard U., 1967; MBA, Pepperdine U., 1979. Bar: Calif. 1967. Assoc. Brobeck, Phleger & Harrison, San Francisco, 1967-69, Rea, Frasse et al, San Jose, Calif., 1969-72; group v.p. Itel Corp., San Francisco, 1972-80; v.p., sec., gen. counsel Brae Corp., San Francisco, 1980-86; pres. CIS Aircraft Mgmt. Corp., San Francisco, 1986—. Bd. dirs. San Mateo (Calif.) County Suicide Prevention Ctr., 1979-80, Hillsborough (Calif.) Schs. Found., 1982-85, San Mateo County Cath. Charities, 1987—, San Mateo County Food Bank, Burlingame, 1987—. 1st lt. U.S. Army, 1962-64. Democrat. Home: 103 Bella Vista Dr Hillsborough CA 94133 Office: CIS Aircraft Mgmt Corp 1160 Battery San Francisco CA 94133

DOSSEY, RICHARD L., accountant; b. Peoria, Ill., May 11, 1937; s. Arthur B. and Mary A. Dossey; m. Carol A. Pontius, Nov. 8, 1960 (div. 1981); children: Richard, Christine, Craig, Lynda; m. Judy D. Humphries, Nov. 24, 1981. BS, Bradley U., 1959. CPA. From audit staff to mgr. Arthur Young & Co., Chgo., 1959-67; asst. controller Sangamo Electric Co., Springfield, Ill., 1967-68; mgr. Peat, Marwick, Main & Co., Chgo., 1968-70; ptnr. Peat, Marwick, Main & Co., Indpls., 1970-74; mng. ptnr. Indpls. office Peat, Marwick, Main & Co., 1974-88, mng. ptnr. Cleve. office, 1988—. Bd. dirs. Multiple Sclerosis Soc., Indpls., 1983-85, Crossroads Rehab. Ctrs., Indpls., 1986-88. Mem. Am. Inst. CPA's, Ill. CPA Soc., Ind. CPA Soc., Ohio CPA Soc. Republican. Methodist. Clubs: Skyline, Economic (Indpls.) (bd. dirs. 1974—), Union club. Lodge: Kiwanis. Office: Peat Marwick Main & Co 1600 National City Ctr Cleveland OH 44114

DOTO, PAUL JEROME, accountant; b. Newark, July 22, 1917; s. Anthony and Edith Margaret (Mascellaro) D. BS, NYU, 1947. Registered mcpl. acct., N.J.; registered pub. sch. acct., N.J. Acct. John Hewitt Foundry Co., East Newark, N.J., 1941-43; acct. S.D. Leidesdorf & Co., N.Y.C., 1947-56; CPA Peat Marwick Mitchell & Co., N.Y.C., 1956-64; asst. controller Lincoln Ctr. for the Performing Arts Inc., N.Y.C. 1964-69; controller Seton Hall U., South Orange, N.J., 1969-74, Belart Products, Applied Coatings, Maddock, Inc., N.J., 1974-80, Internat. Trading Sales, Inc., Pan Atlantic Paper Co., N.Y.C., 1980; cons. Controller's Office, City N.Y., 1966. Bd. dirs. Parkway, Ltd., 1973-78. Served with AUS, 1943-46. Mem. Nat. Police Hall of Fame. Mem. N.Y. State Soc. CPA's (chmn. govtl. accounting com. 1963-64, chmn. internal control quest on aid of municipalities N.Y. State), Am. Inst. CPA's, Cath. Accts. Guild (bd. govs. 1961-64), N.J. Soc. CPA's, N.Y. State Soc. CPA's, Am. Accounting Assn., Fin. Execs. Inst., N.Y. Assn. Profs., Smithsonian Assocs. (charter), Am. Legion, Am. Mus. Natural Hist. N.Y.C. (assoc.) Address: PO Box 2508 Bloomfield NJ 07003

DOTSON, DONALD L., lawyer; b. Rutherford County, N.C., Oct. 8, 1938; s. Herman A. and Lottie E. (Hardin) D. A.B., U. N.C., 1960; J.D., Wake Forest U., 1968. Bar: N.C., Pa., D.C., U.S. Supreme Ct. Atty. NLRB, 1968-73, chmn., 1983-87; labor counsel Westinghouse Electric Corp., 1973-75; labor atty. Western Electric Co., 1975-76; chief labor counsel Wheeling-Pitts. Steel Corp., 1976-81; asst. sec. labor 1981-83; ptnr. Keck, Mahin & Cate, Washington, 1987—. Served with USN, 1960-65. Mem. ABA. Republican. Episcopalian.

DOTSON, KEITH MACK, business development executive; b. Fletcher, N.C., Sept. 3, 1938; s. Luther Windel and Eva (Whitaker) D.; m. Agnes Pauline Chavez, May 15, 1957; children: Greg, Steven, Matt. Asst. ops. mgr. Dalton Transfer and Storage Co., Albuquerque, 1960-61; pres., gen. mgr. Santa Fe Storage and Transfer Co., 1961-70; state planning officer State of N.Mex., Santa Fe, 1970-72, spl. asst. to gov., 1972-74; sr. tech. asst. coordinator Four Corners Regional Commn., Farmington, N.Mex., 1974-79; dep. dir. Four Corners Regional Commn., Albuquerque, 1979-81; exec. dir. Four Corners Council of Govs., Albuquerque, 1981-83; organizer N.Mex. Bus. Devel., Albuquerque, 1983-85, pres., chief executive officer, 1985—; chmn. organizing bd. Tri-County Bank Edgewood, N.Mex., 1987—. Bd. dirs. N.Mex. Bus. Innovation Ctr., Albuquerque, 1985—; bd. dirs.Keep N.Mex. Beautiful, Albuquerque, 1984-87; pres. Enchanted Land Cert. Devel. Corp., 1987—; pres. Santa Fe chpt. March of Dimes, 1972; state treas. N.Mex. Dems., Santa Fe, 1968, precinct ofcl., Santa Fe and Albuquerque, 1967—; sr. v.p. N.Mex. Jaycees, 1967; pres. Santa Fe Jaycees, 1964. Served with USAF, 1956-60. Named Outstanding Young Man Santa Fe Jaycees, 1966, 69; recipient Basil O'Connor Meml. award Nat. Found. March of Dimes, 1972, Cert. of Appreciation, Am. Revolution Bicentennial, 1976. Mem. N.Mex. Entrepreneurs Assn. Lodges: Elks, Eagles, Lions (Santa Fe) (treas. 1970-71). Home: PO Box 112 Cedar Crest NM 87008 Office: NMex Bus Devel Corp 6001 Marble NE Ste 6 Albuquerque NM 87110

DOTTERER, HERBERT TERENCE, retail food chain executive; b. Plainfield, N.J., Oct. 23, 1944; s. Walter J. and Iona J. (Page) D.; m. Ann Haser, July 12, 1968; children: Brian, Jill. BS in Acctg., Drake U., 1966; MBA, U. Iowa, 1968. CPA, Ill. Fin. analyst Jewel Cos., Inc., Chgo., 1968-69, office mgr., 1969-71, dir. adminstrv. services, 1971-73, dir. acctg., 1973-74, store mgr., 1974-76, mgr. store services, 1976-78; v.p., controller Liberal Market, Inc., Dayton, Ohio, 1978-80; div. controller Kroger Co., Indpls., 1980-82; asst. corp. controller Kroger Co., Cin., 1982-88; v.p., contr. Eagle Food Ctrs., Milan, Ill., 1988—. Bd. dirs. Comprehensive Community Child Care, Cin., 1982—. Mem. Am. Inst. CPA's, Fin. Execs. Inst. Home: 7197 Hamilton Hills Dr Cincinnati OH 45244 Office: Eagle Food Ctrs 6136 Lakeshore Cir Davenport IA 52807

DOUCE, PATRICE, business executive; b. Epernay, France, Mar. 2, 1942; came to U.S., 1985; s. Henri and Therese (Jacquemot) D.; m. Agnes Boucher, Jan. 6, 1978; children: Quentin, Florent. MBA, Ctr. HEC-ISA, Paris, 1965. Advisor Ministry of Fin., Algiers, Algeria, 1965-71; gen. mgr. Sodeyho Mid. East Corp., Ryadh, 1972-85; sr. v.p. Sodeyho Corp., Paris, 1985—; chief exec. officer Internat. Catering Co., Waltham, Mass., 1985—; also bd. dirs.Sodeyho Internat. Catering Co.; chmn. bd. dirs. Seilers Co., Waltham, FDI Corp., San Francisco. Office: 153 2d Ave Waltham MA 02254

DOUCETTE, DAVID ROBERT, computer systems company executive; b. Pitts., Feb. 2, 1946; s. Mary Alyce (Newland) D. B.S.E.E., Poly. Inst. Bklyn., 1968, M.S.E.E., 1970, Ph.D., 1974. Asst. prof. elec. engring. Poly. Inst. N.Y. (now Poly. U.), 1973-74; assoc. prof. computer sci., 1975-82, prof., 1982—; sr. staff specialist advanced planning Grumman Data Systems Corp., Bethpage, N.Y., 1979-80, program mgr., 1979-80, mgr. graphics systems, 1980-84, from asst. dir. to dir. interactive systems support, 1984-86, dir. interactive systems, 1986—. Active Friends of Long Island Heritage, Nassau County Hist. Soc., Garden City Hist. Soc. Mem. IEEE (past sect. chmn.), Assn. Computing Machinery (past chpt. chmn.), L.I. Forum for Tech. (dir.), AIAA (sect. dir.), Planetary Soc., Am. Space Found., Sigma Xi, Tau Beta Pi, Eta Kappa Nu. Club: University of L.I. (dir.), Long Island Early Fliers. Home: 146 Washington Ave Garden City NY 11530 Office: Grumman Data Systems Corp Bethpage NY 11714

DOUD, ARTHUR ALTMAN, economist, consultant; b. Lyndhurst, N.J., July 15, 1943; s. Clarence and Josephine Emily (Shepherd) D. BS in Econs., U. Pa., 1966; MA in Econs., Temple U., 1972. Rsch. asst. Wharton Econometric Forecasting Assocs., Phila., 1973-76; rsch. assoc. commodities group, assoc. economist Phila., 1978-79; mgr. Phila. Model Forecasting Svc., Phila., 1979-81, dir. R&D long term model svc., 1981-83, dir. R&D U.S. svcs., 1983-84, dir. R&D, real estate, housing and demographic cons., 1984-86; pvt. practice econ. cons. Phila., 1986—; instr. econs. Albright Coll., Reading, Pa., 1973; mem. adj. faculty fin. dept. Wharton U. Pa., 1983-84; cons. Moody's Investors Svc., N.Y.C., 1986—, The WEFA Group, Inc., Bala Cynwyd, Pa., 1988—. Contbr. numerous articles to profl. jours. Fellow, Temple U., 1969-71. Mem. Internat. Assn. Energy Economists. Office: PO Box 30212 Philadelphia PA 19103

DOUD, WILLIAM FRANCIS, health care executive; b. Rochester, N.Y., Mar. 8, 1935; s. Alfred John and Hilda Marie (Burns) D.; m. Sandra L. Woodruff, Dec. 26, 1964; children: Stephanie, William J. BS in Acctg., U. Rochester, 1962. Staff acct. Price Waterhouse Co., Rochester, N.Y., 1962-66; v.p., treas. Kayex Corp., Rochester, 1966-69, Vari-Care, Inc., Rochester, 1969—. Mem. Nat. Assn. Accts., Fin. Execs. Inst., Nat. Health Lawyers Assn. Office: Vari Care Inc 277 Alexander St 800 Med Arts Bldg Rochester NY 14607

DOUGHERTY, DONALD KENELM, public relations executive; b. N.Y.C., Apr. 19, 1935; s. John Augustus and Madeline Loretto (Smythe) D.; m. Stella Vivianne Baher, Mar. 2, 1975. B.A., Georgetown U., 1957. With pub. relations dept. IBM, N.Y.C., 1960-64, Pepsi Co., N.Y.C., 1964-66, ITT, N.Y.C., 1966-69; sr. acct. exec. Internat. Pub. Relations co., N.Y.C., 1974-81; v.p. corp. relations Hongkong and Shanghai Bank Corp., N.Y.C., 1981—. Contbr. articles to profl. jours. Exec. dir. Assn. of Voluntary Agys. on Narcotics Treatment, N.Y.C., 1972-74. Recipient Gold Key award Pub. Relations News, N.Y.C., 1972, 81. Mem. Pub. Relations Soc. Am., Nat. Assn. Bus. Economists, Hong Kong Assn. (treas. 1984—). Clubs: Canadian (N.Y.C.). Home: Chestnut Hill Rd Stone Ridge NY 12484 Office: Hong Kong & Shanghai Banking Corp 5 E 59th St New York NY 10022

DOUGHERTY, JAMES JOSEPH, education administrator; b. Wilmington, Del., Dec. 1, 1951; s. James J. Sr. and Anne Dorothy (Babiarz) D.; m. Karol Marie Marker; children: Matthew, Aaron, Elizabeth, David. BA in Psychology, U. Del., Newark, 1973; MS in Criminal Justice, U. New Haven, West Haven, Conn., 1976. Corrections officer Jackson County Jail, Kansas City, Mo., 1973-74; research asst. U. New Haven, West Haven, Conn., 1974-75; dir. indsl. services Goodwill Industries, Kansas City, Mo., 1975-77; workshop mgr. Kansas City Pub. Sch. Dist., 1977-79; assoc. dir. Mo. Council on Criminal Justice, Kansas City, 1979-80; exec. dir. De La Salle Edn. Ctr., Kansas City, 1980—. Mem. Mayor's Council on Youth Devel., Kansas City, 1982—; participant, grad. Kansas City Tomorrow, 1984-85; vice chmn. St. Francis Xavier Sch. Bd., 1986—; mem. Diocesan Inner-City Schs. Com., 1988. Mem. Greater Kansas City Council on Philanthropy, Agy. Execs. Assn. (bd. dirs. 1985-86). Roman Catholic. Home: 2 E 56th St Kansas City MO 64109 Office: De La Salle Edn Ctr 3740 Forest Kansas City MO 64109

DOUGHERTY, JAMES THOMAS, industrial company executive, lawyer; b. Chgo., Aug. 31, 1935; s. Edward Warren and Edna Margaret (Macadory) D.; m. Rosemary Saballus, Nov. 21, 1959; children: Janet, Michael, Scott. BS, DePaul U., 1957, JD, 1960. Bar: Ill. 1960. Assoc. Arnstein & Lehr, Chgo., 1960-65; asst. gen. counsel Maremont Corp., Chgo., 1965-69, Rockwell Internat. Corp., Pitts., 1969-71; gen. counsel NVF Co., Yorklyn, Del., 1971-76, Sharon Steel Corp., 1971-76; v.p., gen. counsel, sec. Allegheny Internat., Inc., Pitts., 1976—. Bd. dirs. Sharon Indsl. Devel. Authority, 1972-76, Shenango Valley Charitable Capital Fund, 1972-75. Mem. Ill. Bar Assn., Chgo. Bar Assn. Office: Allegheny Internat Inc 2 Oliver Pla Pittsburgh PA 15222

DOUGHERTY, JOHN CHRYSOSTOM, III, lawyer; b. Beeville, Tex., May 3, 1915; s. John Chrysostom and Mary V. (Henderson) D.; m. Mary Ireland Graves, Apr. 18, 1942 (dec. July 1977); children: Mary Ireland, John Chrysostom IV; m. Bea Ann Smith, June 1978 (div. 1981); m. Sarah B. Randle, 1981. BA, U. Tex., 1937; LLB, Harvard, 1940; diploma, Inter-Am. Acad. Internat. and Comparative Law, Havana, Cuba, 1948. Bar: Tex. 1940. Atty. Hewit & Dougherty, Beeville, 1940-41; ptnr. Graves & Dougherty, Austin, Tex., 1946-50, Graves, Dougherty & Greenhill, Austin, 1950-57, Graves, Dougherty & Gee, Austin, 1957-60, Graves, Dougherty, Gee & Hearon, Austin, 1961-66, Graves, Dougherty, Gee, Hearon, Moody & Garwood, Austin, 1966-73, Graves, Dougherty, Hearon, Moody & Garwood, Austin, 1973-79, Graves, Dougherty, Hearon & Moody, Austin, 1979—; spl. asst. atty. gen., 1949-50; Hon. French Consul, Austin, 1971-86; lectr. on tax, estate planning, probate code, community property problems; mem. Tex. Submerged Lands Adv. Com., 1963-72, Tex. Bus. and Commerce Code Adv. Com., 1964-66, Gov.'s Com. on Marine Resources, 1970-71, Gov.'s Planning Com. on Colorado River Basin Water Quality Mgmt. Study, 1972-73, Tex. Legis. Property Tax Com., 1973-75. Co-editor: Texas Appellate Practice, 1964, 2d edit., 1977; contbr. Bowe, Estate Planning and Taxation; Texas Lawyers Practice Guide, 1967, 71, How to Live and Die with Texas Probate, 1968, 5th edit., 1988, Texas Estate Administration, 1975, 78; mem. bd. editors: Appellate Procedure in Tex., 1964, 2d edit., 1982; contbr. articles to legal jours. Bd. dirs. Grenville Clark Fund at Dartmouth Coll., 1976—; past bd. dirs. Advanced Religious Study Found., Holy Cross Hosp., Sea Arama, Inc., Nat. Pollution Control Found., Austin Nat. Bank; trustee St. Stephen's Episcopal Sch., Austin, 1969-83, U. Tex. Law Sch. Found., 1974—. Served as capt. C.I.C. AUS, 1941-44, JAGC, 1944-46, now maj. Res. Decorated Medaille Française France, Medaille d'honneur en Argent des Affairs Etrangeres France, Chevalier, L'Ordre Nat. du Merite. Fellow Am. Bar Found., Tex. Bar Found., Am. Coll. Probate Counsel, Am. Coll. Tax Counsel, Tex. State Bar Coll.; mem. Am. Arbitration Assn. (mem. nat. panel arbitrators 1958—), Inter-Am. Bar Assn., ABA (mem. ho. dels. 1982—), Travis County Bar Assn. (pres.-elect 1978, pres. 1979-80), State Bar Tex. (chmn. sect. taxation 1965-66, pres.-elect 1978, pres. 1979-80, chmn. State Bar Coll. Bd. 1983-84), Am. Judicature Soc. (bd. dirs. 1986-88), Internat. Law Assn., Am. Fgn. Law Assn., Am. Law Inst., Am. Soc. Internat. Law (exec. council 1959-62), World Assn. Lawyers, Internat. Acad. Estate and Trust Law (exec. com. 1986—), Am. Assn. Internat. Council Jurists, Philos. Soc. Tex. (pres. 1989), Cum Laude Soc., Phi Beta Kappa, Phi Eta Sigma, Beta Theta Pi (bd. dirs. Tex. Beta Students Aid Fund 1947-85). Presbyterian. Lodge: Rotary. Home: 6 Green Lns Austin TX 78703 Office: 2300 NCNB Tower 515 Congress Austin TX 78701 also: PO Box 98 Austin TX 78767

DOUGHERTY, RUSSELL ELLIOTT, lawyer, retired air force officer, association executive; b. Glasgow, Ky., Nov. 15, 1920; s. Ewell Walter and Bess (House) D.; m. m Geralee Shaaber, Apr. 26, 1943 (dec. Jan. 1978); children: Diane Ellen, Mark Elliott, William Bryant; m. Barbara Brooks Lake, Sept. 1978. A.B., Western Ky. U., 1941; J.D., U. Louisville, 1948; grad., Nat. War Coll., 1960; LL.D., U. Akron, 1975, U. Nebr., 1976, U. Louisville, 1977; D.Sc., Westminster Coll., 1976, Embry-Riddle Aeronautical U., 1986. Bar: Ky. 1948. Also U.S. Supreme Ct.; commd. 2d. lt. USAAF, 1943; advanced through grades to gen. USAF, 1972; various staff and command assignments in Far East Air Forces, SAC, U.S. European Command, World War II; dir. European region Office of Sec. of Def., 1965-67; dep. chief of staff for plans and operations Hdqrs. USAF, 1970; comdr. 2d Air Force (Strategic Air Command), 1971; chief of staff Supreme Hdqrs. Allied Powers Europe, 1972-74; comdr.-in-chief Strategic Air Command and dir. U.S. Strategic Target Planning, 1974-77, ret., 1977; exec. dir. Air Force Assn., 1980-86; corp. atty. McGuire, Woods, Battle and Boothe, 1986—; bd. dirs. Enron Corp.; vice chmn. bd. trustees Aerospace Corp.; mem. Def. Sci. Bd.; planned Operation Powerflight Mission, 1957; U.S. planner Stanleyville (Republic Congo) Rescue Operation, 1964; trustee Inst. Def. Analysis. Bd. visitors Nat. Def. U.; bd. dirs. Atlantic Council of U.S., Falcon Found., Air Force Assn. Decorated D.S.M. USAF; (3), D.S.M. Dept. Def.; (2), Legion of Merit; (3), Bronze Star.; recipient Outstanding Alumnus award Western Ky. U., 1976, David Sarnoff award Armed Forces Communications and Electronics Assn., 1980, Gen. Thomas D. White Nat. Def. award U.S. Air Force Acad., 1983; named Man of Yr. Nat. Jewish Hosp., 1976, Man of Yr. Los Angeles Philanthropic Soc.d, 1976, Disting. Grad., Louisville Law Sch., 1984, Outstanding Alumnus Ky., Gov. and Ky. Advocates, 1987. Mem. Ky. Bar Assn., Va. Bar Assn., Omicron Delta Kappa, Phi Alpha Delta, Lambda Chi Alpha. Home: Forest Hills 2359 S Queen St Arlington VA 22202 Office: 8280 Greensboro Dr Ste 900 McLean VA 22102 also: Aerospace Corp 2350 E El Segundo Blvd El Segundo CA 90245

DOUGHERTY, VINCENT MICHAEL, realty company executive, consultant; b. Tulsa, Mar. 1, 1962; s. Gene Vincent and Dolores (Quisenberry) D.; m. Anne Russo. BBA, U. Okla., 1985. Mktg. rep. Heals Health Plan, Emeryville, Calif., 1985-87; property mgr. Landmark Realty, San Francisco, 1987—. Mem. Sigma Chi. Republican. Roman Catholic. Home: 1600 Lincoln Village Circle #2138 Larkspur CA 94939

DOUGHTY, LESLIE JOHN TREVALYN (TREVOR), insurance company executive; b. Wimbledon, Eng., Aug. 20, 1922; s. Reginald John and Ethel Marian (Burch) D.; came to U.S., 1966, naturalized, 1972; student U. London, 1941-42, 47-48, Royal Acad. Dramatic Art, 1942. CLU; m. Reine Claire Berger, Feb. 22, 1960 (dec. Oct. 1971); m. 2d, Frances Farwell, Mar. 23, 1974. Tech. mgr. Anglo S. African Devel. Assn., 1948-50; chief purchasing officer PWD-MECH, No. Rhodesian Govt., 1950-56; v.p. 1st Permanent Bldg. Soc., East Africa Ltd., 1956-66; mgr. Occidental Life Ins. Co., Burbank, Calif., 1967-73, asst. dir. advanced mktg. dept., 1973-78, dir. tech. adminstrn., 1978-85; chief exec. officer Frances Farwell Sources Ltd., 1985—; chief mktg. officer Wall Street Group, 1985—; pres. Safari Traders Ltd., Doughty and Assocs., Bus. Cons.; actor and scriptwriter. Maj. Brit. Army, 1942-47. Fellow Inc. Soc. Valuers and Auctioneers, Gt. Britain Inst. Estate Agts., Auctioneers and Valuers Rhodesia; mem. Inst. Valuers South Africa, Glendale-Burbank Life Underwriters Assn. (past pres.), Royal Soc. St. George (past pres.). Clubs: Mombasa Yacht; L.A. Athletic. Lodges: Masons, Rotary. Contbr. articles to profl. jours. Home: 740 S Ridgeley Dr Los Angeles CA 90036

DOUGLAS, JOHN BREED, III, lawyer; b. Albany, N.Y., Oct. 29, 1953; s. John B. Jr. and Elizabeth (Foster) D.; m. Victoria Rubakaba, Nov. 29, 1986; 1 child, Katherine Elizabeth. AB, Colgate U., 1975; JD, Harvard U., 1978. Bar: D.C. 1978, Mass. 1985, U.S. Ct. Appeals (D.C. cir.) 1979, U.S. Dist. Ct. D.C. 1979. Assoc. Covington & Burling, Washington, 1978-81; internat. atty. Xerox, Stamford, Conn., 1981-83; ops. atty. Xerox, Palo Alto, Calif., 1983-84; gen. counsel Shugart Corp. (subs. Xerox), Sunnyvale, Calif., 1983-84; internat. counsel Stanhome Inc., Westfield, Mass., 1984-86; v.p., gen. counsel Reebok Internat. Ltd., Canton, Mass., 1986—; adj. prof. law Western New Eng. Sch. Law, Springfield, Mass., 1985-86. Mem. ABA, Mass. Bar Assn., D.C. Bar Assn., Am. Corp. Counsel Assn., New. Eng. Corp. Counsel Assn. (dir. 1988—), Council Better Bus. Burs. (bd. dirs.), Phi Beta Kappa. Republican. Episcopalian. Office: Reebok Internat Ltd 150 Royall St Canton MA 02021

DOUGLAS, JOHN HOFFMANN, foundation executive; b. Jersey City, May 25, 1920; s. Paul Hazzard and Florence (Hoffmann) D.; m. Joan Walbridge Battey, Dec. 10, 1949 (dec. July 1976); children: Parker Hazzard, Jonathan Battey, Johanna Vail, Bernard Martin III. Student, Trinity Coll., Hartford, Conn., 1939-41. Asst. sales mgr. Bourjois, Inc., N.Y.C., 1946-51; product mgr. Am. Safety Razor Corp., Bklyn., 1951-53; market devel. mgr. Shulton, Inc., N.Y.C., 1953-55, European liaison mgr., 1960-61; co-founder, gen. mgr. Shulton, N.V., Leiden, The Netherlands, 1955-60, Holland House Cosmetics, N.V., Haarlem, The Netherlands, 1961-76; sec., counselor Service Corps. Retired Execs., Stamford and Norwalk, Conn., 1978-84; co-founder, pres. English Speaking Union br., Greenwich, Conn., bd. dirs., mem. exec. com., N.Y. Trustee, sec. Greenwich Hist. Soc., 1983-88. Served with USCG, 1941-46. Mem. Delta Kappa Epsilon. Republican. Episcopalian. Club: Field (Greenwich). Home: 8 Weathervane Ln Cos Cob CT 06807 Office: English Speaking Union Greenwich PO Box 11022 Greenwich CT 06831

DOUGLAS, KENNETH JAY, food company executive; b. Harbor Beach, Mich., Sept. 4, 1922; s. Harry Douglas and Xenia (Williamson) D.; m. Elizabeth Ann Schweizer, Aug. 17, 1946; children: Connie Ann, Andrew Jay. Student, U. Ill., 1940-41, 46-47; J.D., Chgo. Kent Coll. Law, 1950; grad., Advanced Mgmt. Program, Harvard, 1962. Bar: Ill. 1950, Ind. 1952. Spl. agt. FBI, 1950-54; dir. indsl. relations Dean Foods Co., Franklin Park, Ill., 1954-64, v.p. fin. and adminstrn., 1964-70, chmn. bd., chief exec. officer, 1970-87, chmn. bd., 1987-89, vice-chmn., 1989—; bd. dirs. Centel Corp., Am. Nat. Bank & Trust Co., Am. Nat. Corp., Milk Industry Found., Richardson Electronics, Ltd., Andrew Corp. Life trustee West Suburban Hosp., Oak Park, Ill.; bd. overseers Ill. Inst. Tech. Chgo.-Kent Coll. Law. Served with USNR, 1944-46. Republican. Clubs: Chicago, Economic, Executives, Commercial (Chgo.); Oak Park Country, River Forest Tennis (Ill.); Steamboat Springs Country (Colo.); Old Baldy (Wyo.). Office: Dean Foods Co 3600 N River Rd Franklin Park IL 60131

DOUGLAS, MARION JOAN, labor negotiator; b. Jersey City, May 29, 1940; d. Walter Stanley and Sophie Frances (Zysk) Binaski; children: Jane Dee, Alex Jay. BA, Mich. State U., 1962; MSW, Sacramento State Coll., 1971; MPA, Calif. State U.-Sacramento, 1981. Owner, mgr. Linkletter-Totten Dance Studios, Sacramento, 1962-68, Young World of Discovery, Sacramento, 1965-68; welfare worker Sacramento County, 1964-67, welfare supr., 1968-72, child welfare supr., 1972-75, sr. personnel analyst, 1976-78, personnel program mgr., 1978-81, labor relations rep., 1981—; cons. State Dept. Health, Sacramento, 1975-76; cons. in field. Author/editor: (newsletter) Thursday's Child, 1972-74. Presiding officer Community Resource Orgn., Fair Oaks, Calif., 1970-72; exec. bd. Foster Parent's Assn., Sacramento, 1972-75; organizer Foster Care Sch. Dist. liaison programs, 1973-75; active Am. Lung Assn., 1983-87; rep. Calif. Welfare Dirs. Assn., 1975-76; county staff advisor Joint Powers Authority, Sacramento, 1978-81; mem. Mgmt. Devel. Com., Sacramento, 1979-80; vol., auctioneer sta. KVIE Pub. TV, Sacramento, 1970-84, 88—; adv. bd. Job and Info. Resource Ctr., 1976-77; spl. adv. task force coordinator Sacramento Employment and Tng. Adv. Council, 1980-81; vol. leader Am. Lung Assn., Sacramento, 1983-86 Calif. Dept. Social Welfare ednl. stipend, 1967-68, County of Sacramento ednl. stipend, 1969-70. Recipient Achievement award Nat. Assn. Counties, 1981. Mem. Mgmt. Women's Forum, Indsl. Relations Assn. No. Calif., Indsl. Relations Research Assn., Nat. Assn. Female Execs., Mensa. Republican. Avocations: real estate, nutrition. Home: 7812 Palmyra Dr Fair Oaks CA 95628 Office: County of Sacramento Dept Personnel Mgmt 700 H St Sacramento CA 95814

DOUGLAS, PAUL WOLFF, natural resource company executive; b. Springfield, Mass., Sept. 12, 1926; s. Paul Howard and Dorothy (Wolff) D.; m. Colette Smith, Nov. 19, 1926; children: Philip LeBreton, Carolyn Jory, Christine Sanders Tansey, Paul Harding. A.B., Princeton U., 1948; student, Leeds (Eng.) U., 1948. Dir. internal finance sect. ECA Mission to France, 1948-52; with Freeport Minerals Co., 1952—, exec., v.p., dir., 1970-75, pres., chmn. exec. com., 1975—; pres., chief exec. officer Freeport-McMoran Inc., 1981-83; chmn., chief exec. officer Pittston Co., 1984—; bd. dirs. Phelps Dodge Corp., U.S. Trust Co., Philip Morris Inc., The France Fund, Inc.; chmn. Community Planning Bd., N.Y.C., 1967—, N.Y. Life Ins. Co. Served with USNR, 1944-46. Home: 25 Charlton St New York NY 10014 Office: Pittston Co 1 Pickwick Pla Box 8900 Greenwich CT 06836

DOUGLAS, SUSAN, data processing specialist, consultant; b. Chgo., Oct. 29, 1946; d. Lawrence and Phoebe Fern (Sibbald) D.; m. John D. Hauenstein, Dec. 21, 1972 (div. June 1975). BA, U. Iowa, 1972; postgrad., U. Wis., Whitewater, 1985. Project coordinator Westinghouse Learning Corp., Iowa City, Iowa, 1967-75; echocardiology technician Chgo. Osteo. Hosp., 1975-78; systems programer, analyst Household Fin. Corp., Prospect Heights, Ill., 1978-81; applications analyst Burdick Corp., Milton, Wis., 1981—; cons. Edgerton, Wis., 1984—. Mem. Data Processing Mgmt. Assn., System 38 User's Group. Episcopalian. Home and Office: 8203 Hwy 184 Edgerton WI 53534

DOUGLAS, WILLIAM ERNEST, government official; b. Charleston, S.C., Nov. 26, 1930; s. William Ernest and Helen A. (Fortune) D.; m. Nancy Anne Gibson, July 18, 1980. A.B., The Citadel, 1956; postgrad., U. S.C., 1956-59. Asst. dist. dir. Jackson dist. IRS, Miss., 1972-73, Atlanta dist. IRS, 1973-74; asst. regional commr. S.E. region IRS, Atlanta, 1974-78, dir. Regional Service Ctr., 1978-80; commr. Fin. Mgmt. Service, Washington, 1980—. Served with U.S. Army, 1948-52. Home: 215 James Thurber Ct Falls Church VA 22046 Office: 401 14th St SW Washington DC 20227

DOUGLASS, HARRY ROBERT, hospital and health care consultant, architect, educator; b. McCook, Nebr., Mar. 27, 1937; s. Harry William and Irma Ruth Douglass; divorced; 1 son, William Robert. B.Arch., U. Nebr., 1963; M.Arch. in Hosp. Planning, U. Minn., 1965; grad. owner, pres. mgmt. program Harvard U. Bus. Sch., 1983. Chmn., chief exec. officer Robert Douglass Assocs. Inc., Hosp. Cons., Houston, 1973-88, merged with Deloitte, Haskins & Sells, 1988, ptnr., 1988—, also bd. dirs.; assoc. prof. Rice U., Tex. Sch. Pub. Health, 1973-75; adj. prof. health care planning Rice U., 1975—. AIA-Am. Hosp. Assn. Joint fellow, 1964-66. Fellow Am. Assn. Hosp. Cons., Am. Inst. Architects; mem. Soc. Hosp. Planners, AIA (nat. com. on architecture for health), Am. Assn. Hosp. Planning (dir. 1975-80), Am. Mgmt. Assn., Houston C. of C. (health com.). Episcopalian. Contbr. articles to profl. jours.; rep. exec. bd. WHO, Managua, 1972; organizer, dir. internat. seminar in hosp. and health care Panamerican Health Orgn., U. San Martin, Buenos Aires, 1971; designer, planner of numerous archtl. projects; recipient numerous design awards, including Presdl. Silver medal for Charles River Project, Boston, 1984. Clubs: Houston, City. Home: 1905 Wroxton Houston TX 77005 Office: Douglass Group Deloitte Haskins & Sells 1200 Travis Houston TX 77002

DOUGLASS, ROBERT JOSEPH, JR., computer scientist; b. Moline, Ill., June 8, 1951; s. Robert Joseph and Hattie Jane (Holmes) D.; m. Barbara Walker Mahan, June 3, 1973 (div. Aug. 1981). BEE magna cum laude, Princeton U., 1973; MS in Computer Scis., U. Wis., 1974, PhD in Computer Scis., 1978. Postdoctoral researcher dept. physics and astronomy U. London, 1978; asst. prof. computer sci. U. Va., Charlottesville, 1978-81; assoc. group leader for research Los Alamos (N.Mex.) Nat. Lab., 1981-85, collaborating scientist, 1985-86; machine ingelligence unit head Martin Marietta, Denver, 1985, dep. program mgr. Autonomous Land Vehicle, 1987—; Mem. panel Computer Architecture Pres.'s Sci. adv. Nat. Acad. Sci., Washington, 1984. Editor: Characteristic of Parallel Algorthums, 1987—; assoc. editor Jour. Parallel and Distributed Processing, 1984—; contbr. articles to profl. jours. Mem. IEEE, Assn. Computing Machinery, AAAS. Office: Martin Marietta Mail Stop 4443 PO Box 1260 Denver CO 80201

DOUGLASS, ROBERT ROYAL, banker, lawyer; b. Binghamton, N.Y., Oct. 16, 1931; s. Robert R. and Frances (Behan) D.; m. Linda Ann Luria, June 2, 1962; children: Robert Royal, Alexandra Brooke, Andrew. B.A. with distinction, Dartmouth Coll., 1953; LL.B., Cornell U., 1959. Bar: N.Y. Asso. Hinman, Howard & Kattell, 1959-64; 1st asst. counsel to Gov. N.Y. State, Albany, 1964-65; counsel to gov. Gov. N.Y. State, 1965-70, sec. to gov., 1971-72; partner Milbank, Tweed, Hadley & McCloy, 1972-76; exec. v.p., gen. counsel Chase Manhattan Bank, N.Y.C., 1976-83; exec. v.p. Chase Manhattan Bank, 1983-85, vice chmn., 1985—; dir. Rockefeller Center, Inc., 1976-82; chmn. Nelson Rockefeller's Campaign for Republican Nomination for Pres., 1968; commr. Port Authority of N.Y. State and N.J., 1972-76; trustee N.Y.C. Public Library, 1972-86; bd. dirs., chmn. exec. com. Downtown-Lower Manhattan Assn., N.Y.C., 1973—; mem. vis. com. John F. Kennedy Sch. Govt., Harvard U., 1974-79; mem. N.Y. Landmarks Conservancy, 1977-80. Trustee Dartmouth Coll., 1983—, Mus. of Modern Art, 1989—. With M.C., U.S. Army, 1954-56. Recipient Wallace award Am.-Scottish Found., 1974. Mem. ABA, N.Y. State Bar Assn., Council Fgn. Relations. Roman Catholic. Clubs: Century Assn, World Trade Center, Round Hill, Harbor, Blind Brook. Office: Chase Manhattan Corp 1 Chase Manhattan Pla New York NY 10081

DOUMAS, GENA KATHLEEN, controller; b. Winston-Salem, N.C., Nov. 27, 1963; d. Nick Harold and Susan Ellen (Ledwith) D. AAS in Bus. Computers, Davidson County Community Coll., 1984. Computer programmer Precision Part Systems, Inc., Winston-Salem, 1984-85, contr., 1986—; computer operator Stroh Container, 1985-86; ptnr., office mgr. Artisan Prodns. Ltd., Winston-Salem, 1986—. Author numerous poems. Recipient Radio Young Am. award 1973. Republican. Greek Orthodox. Home: 3155 Stratford Rd Winston-Salem NC 27103 Office: Precision Part Systems Inc 3401 Indiana Ave Winston-Salem NC 27105

DOUMLELE, RUTH HAILEY, communications company executive, broadcast accounting consultant; b. Charlotte County, Va., Nov. 6, 1925; d. Clarrie Robert Hailey and Virginia Susan (Slaughter) Ferguson; m. John Antony Doumlele, May 8, 1943; children—John Antony, Suzanne Denise Doumlele Owen. Cert. in commerce, U. Richmond, 1968; B.A., Mary Baldwin Coll., 1982. Sta. acct. WLEE-Radio, Richmond, Va., 1965-67, bus. mgr., 1967-73; area bus. mgr. Nationwide Communications Inc., Richmond, 1973-75; corp. bus. mgr., Neighborhood Communications Corp., Inc., Richmond, 1978-86, asst. v.p., 1981-86; owner Broadcast Acctg. Cons., Midlothian, Va., 1986—; treas., dir. Guests of Honor, Ltd., Richmond, 1984—; sec., Inner Light, Inc., 1984—. Contbr. articles to profl. jours. Mem. editorial rev. bd. The Woman C.P.A., 1980—. Mem. Am. Soc. Women Accts. (chpt. pres. 1974-76), Broadcast Fin. Mgmt. Assn., Nat. League Am. Pen Women (br. pres. 1984-86), Am. Fedn. Astrologers, Va. Assn. Ameteur Athletic Union (records chmn. 1959-62), Women's Club of Powhatan. Episcopalian. Avocations: salt water fishing; Civil War history; travel; astrology. Home and Office: 2510 Chastain Ln Midlothian VA 23113

DOVALE, ANTONIO JOSEPH, JR., chemical engineer; b. Newark, Feb. 25, 1954; s. Antonio Joseph and Rose (Bevacqua) DoV. BS in Chem. Engring., N.J. Inst. Tech., 1975; m. Fern Louise Crandall, Oct. 17, 1981. Sr. process engr. M.W. Kellogg Co., Hackensack, N.J., 1975-84; mgr. FGD systems Wheelabrator Air Pollution Control, Pitts., 1984—. Registered profl. engr., N.J., Mass., Conn., Fla. Mem. Am. Inst. Chem. Engrs., Sigma Xi, Omega Chi Epsilon, Tau Beta Pi. Roman Catholic.

DOVE, EDWARD STELLWAGEN, III, finance company executive; b. Washington, Apr. 22, 1952; s. Edward Stellwagen Jr. and Imogene (Neuhauser) D.; m. Jody M. Dove, Feb. 1, 1976; children: Sarah Phillips, Edward Stellwagen IV. Student, U. Warwick, Coventry, Eng., 1973-74, Exetor Coll., Oxford, Eng., 1974; BA in Econs. and English Lit., Duke U., 1974. Cert. fin. planner. Tax cons. Tax Ctr., Washington, 1975; real estate agt. Shannon & Luchs, Washington, 1975-76; ins. agt. Home Life, Bethesda, Md., 1976-79; owner Edward S. Dove, III, Silver Spring, Md., 1979-82; registered rep. Fin. Network Investment Corp., Torrance, Calif., 1980—; pres. ESD Adv. Services, Inc., Silver Spring, 1982—; tchr. adult edn. various local instns., 1980-87. Class agt. St. Albans Sch., 1971—. Mem. Internat. Assn. Fin. Planning (v.p., officer Nat. Capital chpt. 1981—, lobbyist 1985—). Republican. Episcopalian. Office: ESD Adv Svcs Inc 8403 Colesville Rd Metro Pla 2 Ste 810 Silver Spring MD 20910

DOVE, ROBERT WALLACE, investment banker; b. London, Feb. 16, 1954; came to U.S., 1983; s. Alexander Wallace and Evelyn (Bowden) D.; m. Karla Jeanne Grazier, July 23, 1983. With Nat. Westminster Bank, London, 1970-78; assoc. County Bank, London, 1978-83; rep. County Bank, N.Y.C., 1983-85; v.p. UBS Securities, Inc., N.Y.C., 1985-88, mng. dir., 1988—. Office: UBS Securities Inc 299 Park Ave New York NY 10171

DOVE, WILLIAM EDWIN, banker; b. Pontiac, Mich., Feb. 24, 1937; s. William Edwin and Elsie (Beecroft) D.; m. Marcia Elizabeth Ward, Dec. 17, 1960; children: Elisabeth, Heather, Katherine, William E. BBA, U. Mich., 1959, MBA, 1960. Asst. v.p. Nat. Bank Detroit, 1961-68; exec. v.p. Mich. Nat. Corp., Bloomfield Hills, 1968-75, 77-84; sr. v.p. TCF Bank Savs., Mpls., 1985—, Mark Twain Bancshares Inc., St. Louis, 1976—; mem. Robert Morris Assocs. With USAR, 1960-66. Republican. Presbyterian. Home: 1349 Chatterton Ct Eagan MN 55123 Office: TCF Bank Savs 801 Marquette Ave Minneapolis MN 55402

DOVEY, BRIAN HUGH, health care products company executive, venture capitalist; b. Cleve., Nov. 12, 1941; s. Hugh Albert and Dorothy (Garde) D.; m. Elizabeth Barrett Hartzell, Aug. 17, 1963; children—Laurel, Kimberly, Christine. A.B., Colgate U., 1963; M.B.A., Harvard U., 1967. Sales mgr. N.Y. Telephone, N.Y.C., 1963-69; dir. planning Howmet Corp., N.Y.C., 1969-70; dir. ops. Howmedica, Inc., Cheshire, Conn., 1970-71; v.p. ops. Survival Tech., Bethesda, Md., 1971-75, pres., 1975-83; pres. surg. products div. Rorer Group Inc., Fort Washington, Pa., 1983-86, exec. v.p., 1985-86; pres. Rorer Group Inc., 1986-88; gen. ptnr. Domain Assocs., 1988—; dir. Health Industry Mfrs. Assn., Washington, Survival Tech., Bethesda, Sonomed Tech., Lake Success, N.Y.; bd. dirs. Greenwich Pharm. Inventor syringe assembly. Mem. parents' council James Madison U., Harrisonburg, Va., 1982—, vice chmn., 1985-86, chmn., 1986—; trustee Germantown Acad., Fort Washington, 1983—, v.p. 1987—; overseer U. Pa. Sch. Nursing, Phila., 1985—; bd. dirs. Huntington's Disease Soc., 1986—; chmn. 1988—, Greater Phila. Economic Devel. Council, 1987-88. Mem. Young Pres.'s Orgn. (exec. com. 1977—, treas. exec. com. 1985-86), Proprietary Assn. (bd. dirs. 1987-88). Club: Penllyn (Pa.). Office: Domain Assocs 1 Palmer Sq Princeton NJ 08542

DOW, JEAN LOUISE, school system business manager; b. Mattoon, Ill., Dec. 20, 1955; d. Paul Leroy and Maria (Brandlhofer) Smith; m. Chris Alan Pfeiffer, June 1, 1974 (div. Nov. 1979); 1 child, Lisa Marie; m. John W. Dow, Aug. 1, 1986. B.S. in Bus., Ea. Ill. U., 1977, M.B.A., 1980. Office mgr. ED Buxton & Assocs., Charleston, Ill., 1974-77; personnel mgr. Unibuilt Structures, Charleston, 1977-80; bus. mgr. Eastern Ill Area Spl. Edn., Mattoon, 1980—. Ill. Assn. Sch. Bus. Ofcls. (scholarship 1984, com. mem. 1984—), Assn. Sch. Bus. Ofcls., Ill. Adminstrs. Spl. Edn. Republican, Kappa Delta Pi. Baptist. Avocations: sewing; jogging; swimming; racquetball; tennis.

DOW, MARY ALEXIS, financial executive; b. South Amboy, N.J., Feb. 19, 1949; d. Alexander and Elizabeth Anne (Reilly) Pawlowski; m. Russell Alfred Dow, June 19, 1971. BS with honors, U. R.I., 1971. CPA, Oreg. Staff acct. Deloitte, Haskins & Sells, Boston, 1971-74; sr. acct. Price Waterhouse, Portland, Oreg., 1974-77, mgr., 1977-81, sr. mgr., 1981-84; chief fin. officer Copeland Lumber Yards Inc., Portland, 1984-86; ind. cons. in field, 1986—; bd. dirs. Longview Fibre Co.. Mem. council and fin. com. Oreg. Mus. Sci. and Industry; bd. dirs., exec. com., chair budget com. Oreg. Trails chpt. ARC; mem. budget rev. com. Multnomah County. Mem. Am. Inst. CPAs, Oreg. Soc. CPAs, Fin. Execs. Inst. Roman Catholic. Clubs: City (bd. govs.), University (Portland), Multnomah Athletic. Contbr. articles to profl. publs.

DOW, PETER ANTHONY, advertising agency executive; b. Detroit, Oct. 7, 1933; s. Douglas and Mary Louise (Murray) D.; m. Jane Ann Ottaway, Mar. 21, 1959; children—Jennifer Dow Murphy, Peter Kinnersley, Thomas Anthony. B.A., U. Mich., 1955. Account exec. Campbell-Ewald Co., Detroit, 1958-66, exec. v.p., 1979-83, pres., 1983—; account supr. Young & Rubicam, Detroit, 1966-68; advt. dir. Chrysler Corp., Detroit, 1968-77, dir. mktg., 1977-79; bd. dirs. Invetech Co., Detroit. Mem. exec. com., v.p., dir. United Found., Detroit; trustee Harper Grace Hosp., Detroit, Lawrenceville Sch., N.J.; bd. dirs. Boys and Girls Clubs, Detroit. Served to lt. (j.g.) USNR, 1955-58. Mem. Mich. Advt. Industry Alliance (past pres.). Republican. Presbyterian. Clubs: Detroit Athletic, Adcraft (past pres.), Recess (Detroit); Country of Detroit (Grosse Pointe, Mich.); The Old Club (harsen's Island, Mich.). Office: 30400 Van Dyke Warren MI 48093

DOW, WILLIAM CRAIG, health care industry executive; b. Adams, Mass., July 29, 1946; s. John Francis and Ernestine Else (Adams) D.; m. Susan Lane Zerfoss, Feb. 22, 1969; children: Kristen Marie, Michael Allen, Laura Beth. BS, U.S. Naval Acad., 1968; MBA, So. Ill. U., 1982. Commd. ensign USN, 1968, advanced through grades to lt., 1975; regional mgr. Am. Hosp. Supply, St. Louis, 1975-79; dir. sales Nice Pak, Mt. Vernon, N.Y., 1979-82; gen. mgr. Terumo Corp., Piscataway, N.J., 1982-84; v.p. Respiratory Care Inc. Arlington Heights, Ill., 1984-87; pres., chief exec. officer Griffith Micro Sci. Internat., Alsip, Ill., 1987—. Recipient hon. mention All Am. Football award, 1966, 67; named Jaycee of Month, 1976. Republican.

DOWD, KENNETH LOWELL, JR., financial executive; b. Chgo., Nov. 3, 1940; s. Kenneth Lowell and Rita Ann (Melanson) D.; m. Judith Helen Manley, Nov. 3, 1962; children—Sara, Elizabeth, Warren. B.A., Middlebury Coll., 1962. V.p., dist. head retail banking Chem. Bank, N.Y.C., 1975-77, v.p., deputy head human resources, 1977-79, sr. v.p. hdqtrs. rel., 1979-81, sr. v.p. staff, 1981-82, sr. v.p. adminstrn., 1982-84, sr. v.p., div. head, 1984-86, mng. dir., div. head, 1986-88; mng. dir., chief exec. officer Chem. Investment Group, N.Y.C., 1988—. Corp. solicitor United Way of Tri-State, N.Y.C., 1982-84. Republican. Clubs: Union League, Country (New Canaan). Office: Chem Investment Group 30 Rockefeller Pla 59th Fl New York NY 10112

DOWDELL, KEVIN CRAWFORD, management executive; b. Schenectady, N.Y., Oct. 7, 1961; s. Crawford B. and Doris M. (Bailey) D. BSE, Princeton U., 1983; MBA, Wharton U., 1985. Assoc. Strategic Planning Assocs., Washington, 1985-87, sr. assoc., 1988—. Home: 4201 Cathedral Ave Washington DC 20016 Office: Strategic Planning Assocs 2300 "N" St NW 8th Fl Washington DC 20037

DOWELL, RICHARD PATRICK, professional services executive, consultant; b. Washington, Apr. 21, 1934; s. Cassius McClellan and Mary Barbara (McHenry) D.; m. Eleanor Craddock Halley, Dec. 23, 1957 (div. Sept. 1973); children: Richard Patrick Jr., Robert Paul, Christopher Lee; m. Sandra Susan Humm, June 16, 1974; children: Ethan Leslie Smith, Allison Courtney Smith. BS, U.S. Mil. Acad., 1956; MA, Stanford U., 1961, postgrad., 1962; postgrad., The Am. U., 1971-80; grad., The Nat. War Coll., 1975. Commd. 2d lt. USAF, 1956, advanced through grades to lt. col., 1974, ret., 1976; mgr. The BDM Corp., Fairfax, Va., 1977-79; sr. analyst Analytic Services, Inc., Arlington, Va., 1979-81, div. mgr., 1981-84, v.p., 1984—. Contr. articles to profl. jours. Pres. Alexandria (Va.) Taxpayer's Alliance, 1983. Decorated Bronze star, Air medal with 13 oak leaf clusters, D.F.C. with one oak leaf cluster. Mem. Mil. Ops. Research Soc., Air Force Assn. Republican. Roman Catholic. Home: 414 Franklin St Alexandria VA 22314 Office: ANSER Inc 1215 Jefferson Davis Hwy Ste 800 Arlington VA 22202

DOWELL, ROBERT JAMES, manufacturing company executive; b. Dyersburg, Tenn., Feb. 2, 1942; s. Robert Marion and Virginia (Law) D. AS, Dyersburg State U., 1964. Asst. office mgr. Heckethorn Mfg. Co., Dyersburg, Tenn., 1969-74; office mgr. Heckethorn Mfg. Co., Dyersburg, 1974-84, mgr. office and acctg., 1984-85, asst. treas., 1986-87, staff, 1987—. With U.S. Army, 1964-66. Mem. Am. Def. Prepatness Assn., Exchange Club (sec. 1978-80), Moose. Republican. Mem. Ch. of Christ. Home: 1731 Dennis Dyersburg TN 38024 Office: Heckethorn Mfg Co 2005 Forrest St Dyersburg TN 38024

DOWHANIUK, RONALD EDWARD, real estate executive; b. Portland, Oreg., Apr. 21, 1964; s. Harry and Mary Ellen (Finley) D. BS, Oreg. State U., 1986. Sales rep. E & J Gallo Winery, Portland, 1986-87; pres. R.D. Devel., Portland, 1987—; comml. real estate developer, broker Grubb & Ellis Comml. Real Estate Services, Portland, 1988—. Vol. Loaves & Fishes, Portland, 1987—. Mem. Delta Upsilon Internat. (bd. dirs. 1988—), Delta Upsilon (pres. 1985). Republican. Home: 11622 SE 31st St Milwaukie OR 97222 Office: RD Devel 7032 SE 84th Portland OR 07266

DOWLER, RANDAL LEE, accountant, consultant; b. North Chaleroi, Pa., June 27, 1953; s. Edwin A. and Bernice Elizabeth (Popp) D. Student, U. Cin., 1971-72, Lorain County Community Coll., 1972-74, Baldwin Wallace Coll., 1974-77. CPA, Ohio. Sr. staff acct. Floyd L. Woolridge, CPA, Lorain, Ohio, 1973-78; co-owner Walter A. Glick, Jr., CPA, Lorain, 1978-83; mng. ptnr. Glick & Dowler, CPA's, Lorain, 1983—. Mem. AICPA, Ohio Soc. CPA's, Leadership Lorain County Alumni Assn. (bd. dirs. 1988—, pres. elect 1988), Greater Lorain C. of C. (chmn. bd. dirs. 1988—), Lorain Internat. Assn. (pres. 1984-85, treas. 1978-84, 1985—), Nat. Audobon, Trailbreakers Club, Elks. Democrat. Office: Glick & Dowler CPA 209 6th St Ste 20 Lorain OH 44052-1703

DOWLING, PATRICK HENRY, accountant, lawyer, financial analyst; b. N.Y.C., Aug. 25, 1954; s. Frederick Richard and Alma Lucille (Ahearn) D.; B.S. in Acctg., Fordham U., 1976; J.D., Pace U., 1985; m. Kathleen Lacey, June 5, 1982. Sr. auditor Price Waterhouse & Co., Stamford, Conn., 1976-80; mgr. strategic planning Continental Group, Inc., Stamford, 1980-84; mgr. fin. reporting RCA, N.Y.C., 1984-86; mgr. bus. devel. Gen. Electric Capital Corp., 1986—. C.P.A., Conn. Mem. Am. Inst. C.P.A.s, Conn. Soc. C.P.A.s, N.Y. State Soc. C.P.A.s, Beta Alpha Psi, Beta Gamma Sigma. Club: Noroton Bay Beach, Darien Boat, Noroton Manor Tennis Assn. Office: 260 Long Ridge Rd Stamford CT 06902

DOWNEN, DAVID EARL, investment banking executive; b. Rockport, Ind., Oct. 31, 1941; s. Earl Ford and Mary Angeline (Richards) D.; m. Sheila Sue Boyce, May 28, 1966; 1 child, Michael David. AB, Wabash Coll., 1962; MBA, U. Pa., 1964. Fin. analyst Duff & Phelps, Inc., Chgo., 1964-69; assoc. Bacon, Whipple & Co., Chgo., 1969-77, ptnr., 1977-82; 1st v.p. Bacon, Stifel, Nicolaus, Chgo., 1982-84; 1st v.p. corp. fin. Blunt, Ellis & Loewi, Inc., Chgo., 1984-85, exec. v.p., 1985—; bd dirs. Miller Bldg. Systems, Deerfield, Ill. Mem. Inst. Chartered Fin. Analysts (cert.), Univ. Club Chgo. Republican. Methodist. Home: 2744 Marcy Ave Evanston IL 60201 Office: Blunt Ellis & Loewi 333 W Wacker Dr Chicago IL 60606

DOWNEY, DEBORAH ANN, systems specialist; b. Xenia, Ohio, July 22, 1958; d. Nathan Vernon and Patricia Jaunita (Ward) D. Assoc. in Applied Sci., Sinclair Community Coll., 1981, student, 1986—. Jr. programmer, project mgr. Cole-Layer-Trumble Co., Dayton, Ohio, 1981-82; sr. programmer, analyst, project leader Systems Architects Inc., Dayton, 1982-84, Systems and Applied Sci. Corp. (now Atlantic Rsch. Corp. Profl. Svcs. Group), Dayton, 1984-87; systems programmer, analyst Profl. Svcs Group Atlantic Rsch. Corp., Fairborn, 1987—; analyst Unisys, Dayton, 1984-87; cons. computer software M&S Garage/Body Shop, Beavercreek, Ohio, 1986-87. Mem. Nat. Assn. for Female Execs., Am. Motorcyclist Assn., Sinclair Community Coll. Alumni Assn., Cherokee Nation Okla., Cherokee Nat. Hist. Soc. Democrat. Mem. United Ch. of Christ.

DOWNEY, JOHN HAROLD, publishing executive; b. Yonkers, N.Y., July 30, 1956; s. Joseph and Lydia (Lopetz) D.; m. Joanne Patricia Collins, Aug. 02, 1980; 1 child, Gregory John. BA, Manhattan Coll., 1978; postgrad., NYU, 1981-83. Dir. circulation Backpacker Mag., Bedford Hills, N.Y., 1978; tchr. English/history Ives Sch. Lincoln Hall, Lincolndale, N.Y., 1978-81; v.p. publishing and dir. Editorial Oceana Ednl. Communications, Dobbs Ferry, N.Y., 1981-88; pres. Flashback/Video, Inc., Dobbs Ferry, N.Y., 1987-88; graphic artist freelance, Wynter Graphics, Croton, N.Y., 1985—; software cons. freelance to small publishers, Croton, 1985—; dir. spl. needs div. Globe Book Co., Simon and Schuster Sch. Group, Englewood Cliffs, N.J., 1988—. Author: Safe and Sound Children's Safety Primer Oceana, 1988; mng. editor: online database directory, Software in Print, 1985, looseleaf set, USMI: Market Directory, 1985; project dir./editor books: The Aware Bears Childrens' Personal Safety Series, 1987. Eagle Scout Boy Scouts Am., Somers, N.Y., 1974. Mem. Nat. Eagle Scout Assn., Vietnam Vet. Am. Assn. (assoc. mem.), Am. Nat. Standards Inst. (assoc. mem.), Internat. Reading Assn., Coun. for Exceptional Children. Office: Globe Book Co 190 Sylvan Ave Englewood Cliffs NJ 07632 also: Fearon Edn 500 Harbor Blvd Belmont CA 94002

DOWNEY, RICHARD RALPH, lawyer, accountant, management consultant; b. Boston, Apr. 22, 1934; s. Paul Joseph and Evelyn Mae (Butler) D.; B.S., Northeastern U., 1958; M.B.A., Harvard U., 1962; J.D., Suffolk U., 1979; LL.M., Boston U., 1981; children—Richard Ralph, Janice M., Erin C., Timothy M. Mem. audit staff Price Waterhouse & Co., Boston, 1962-64; asso. Assos. for Internat. Research, Inc., Cambridge, Mass., 1964-68, v.p., 1968—, also dir.; admitted to Mass. bar, 1979, Fed. bar, 1980. Treas., 1580 House Condominium Trust, 1979-80. C.P.A., Mass., Mem. Am. Inst. C.P.A.'s, Mass. Soc. C.P.A.'s, Am. Bar Assn., Mass. Bar Assn., Boston Bar Assn. Clubs: Algonquin; Harvard (Boston, N.Y.C.). Home: 25 Washington Ave Cambridge MA 02140 Office: 1100 Massachusetts Ave Cambridge MA 02138

DOWNING, BRIAN THOMAS, business executive; b. Shalimar, Fla., Sept. 20, 1947; s. Robert James and Margaret Rita (O'Toole) D.; m. Carroll Ann Foote, Feb. 1, 1969; children: Christopher M., Kevin A. B.B.A., Ohio U., 1969; M.B.A., Fairleigh Dickinson U., 1981. Corp. banking officer Mellon Bank, N.A., Pitts., 1973-77; mgr. banking and investments Airco, Inc., Montvale, N.J., 1977-78, asst. treas., 1978-82; treas. The BOC Group, Inc. (formerly Airco, Inc.), Montvale, 1982-86; v.p., treas. Textron Inc., Providence, 1986—. Served to capt. U.S. Army, 1969-73, Vietnam. Mem. Fin. Execs. Inst., Nat. Assn. Corp. Treasurers, Beta Gamma Sigma, Phi Eta Sigma, Phi Kappa Phi. Office: Textron Inc 40 Westminster St Providence RI 02903

DOWNING, MICHAEL J(OHN), state official; b. Kennett, Mo., June 14, 1954; s. John V. and Ly Dell (Golden) D.; m. Donna Beth Waddell, Aug. 11, 1979; 1 child, Christopher. Bachelors degree, Ark. State U., 1977; Masters degree, U. Mo., 1985. Planning dir. Bootheel Regional Planning Commn., Malden, Mo., 1979-82; policy coordinator Mo. Dept. Econ. Devel., Jefferson City, Mo., 1982-86, fin. mgr., 1986—; bd. dirs. Rural Mo., Inc.; spl. cons. to Nat. Assn. State Devel. Agys., Washington, 1988. Author: Tech. Manual; contbr. articles to profl. jours. Chmn. City of Kennett Recreation Com., 1979-82; state rep., com. mem. Council State Community Affairs Agys., Washington, 1983-86; commr. Jefferson City Planning and Zoning Com., 1987—; deacon First Bapt. Ch., Jefferson City. Recipient Cert. of Spl. Merit U.S. Dept. HUD, 1986.d. Mem. Mo. Indsl. Devel. Council, Am. Planning Assn. Baptist. Office: Mo Dept Econ Devel Box 118 Jefferson City MO 65102

DOWNING, TERRENCE MICHAEL, financial planning company executive; b. Buffalo, Sept. 12, 1952; s. Leo Joseph and Patricia (Cunningham) D.; m. Marilyn Theresa Elliott, Nov. 27, 1981; children: John Elliott, Bridget Elliott. BS in Acctg., Canisius Coll., 1974. Tax acct. Price Waterhouse & Co., Buffalo, 1974-79; mgr. Paychex Inc., Rochester, N.Y., 1979-82; fin. planner Downing & Young Assocs., Buffalo, 1982—. Campaign treas. Williamsville Republican Com., 1987. Mem. Inst. Cert. Fin. Planners, Internat. Assn. for Fin. Planners (v.p. 1982-84). Roman Catholic. Office: 5725 Main St Williamsville NY 14221

DOWNS, ANTHONY, urban economist, real estate consultant; b. Evanston, Ill., Nov. 21, 1930; s. James Chesterfield and Florence Glassbrook (Finn) D.; m. Katherine Watson, Apr. 7, 1956; children: Katherine, Christine, Tony, Paul, Carol. B.A., Carleton Coll., 1952; M.A., Stanford U., 1956, Ph.D., 1956. With Real Estate Research Corp., Chgo., 1959-77; chmn. bd. Real Estate Research Corp., 1973-77; asst. prof. econs. and polit. sci. U. Chgo., 1959-62; econ. cons. Rand Corp., Santa Monica, Calif., 1963-65; sr. fellow Brookings Instn., Washington, 1977—; dir. Urban Inst., Manpower Demonstration Research Corp., 1975-80, Standard Shares.; Dir. NAACP Legal and Ednl. Def. Fund, Inc.; mem. Nat. Commn. on Urban Problems, 1967-68; mem. adv. bd. Inst. for Research on Poverty, 1970-78; dir. Rush-Presbyn. St. Luke's Med. Center, Chgo., 1970-77. Author: An Economic Theory of Democracy, 1957, Inside Bureaucracy, 1967, Urban Problems and Prospects, 1970, 2d edit., 1976, Opening Up the Suburbs, 1973, Federal Housing Subsidies, 1973, Racism in America, 1970, Neighborhoods and Urban Development, 1981, Rental Housing in the 1980s, 1983, The Revolution in Real Estate Finance, 1985; co-author: Urban Decline and the Future of the American Cities, 1982; co-editor: Do Housing Allowances Work, 1981, Energy Costs, Urban Development, and Housing, 1984. Served with USNR, 1956-59. Mem. Am. Econ. Assn., Phi Beta Kappa, Lambda Alpha. Democrat. Roman Catholic. Home: 8483 Portland Pl McLean VA 22102 Office: 1775 Massachusetts Ave NW Washington DC 20036

DOWNS, HARTLEY H., III, chemist; b. Ridgewood, N.J., Oct. 21, 1949; s. Hartley Harrison and Jennie Mae (Smith) D.; B.S., Grove City Coll., 1971; M.S., Indiana U. of Pa., 1973; Ph.D., W. Va. U., 1978; student U. Colo., 1976-78; m. Cindy Marie Millen, June 19, 1976; children—Kathryn Marie, Jennifer Anne, Susanna Jayne. Postdoctoral research assoc. chemistry dept. U. So. Calif., Los Angeles, 1977-78; staff chemist corp. research labs. Exxon Research and Engring. Co., Linden, N.J., 1978-81, Houston, 1981-83, Annandale, N.J., 1983-86; research scientist, surface chemistry group supr., Baker Performance Chemicals, Houston, 1986—. Recipient Stan Gillman award U. Colo., 1977, Union Carbide award W. Va. U., 1975, Sigma Xi award Indiana U. of Pa., 1973. Mem. Am. Chem. Soc., Soc. Petroleum Engrs., Sigma Xi, Phi Lambda Upsilon. Presbyterian. Contbr. articles to profl. jours.; patentee in field.

DOWTY, NAVI JAMES, financial planner; b. Sturgis, Mich., Apr. 4, 1945; s. Ivan S. and Mary J.D. BS in Chemistry, Western Mich. U., 1968. Cert. fin. planner, comml. investment mem., enrolled agt. Pres. Navi Dowty Advisors, Inc., Wausau, Wis., 1987—; registered prin. Assoc. Planners Securities Corp., Los Angeles, 1985—; pres. Capital Security Investments, Inc., Wausau, 1973—. Contbr. articles on fin. to periodicals. Mem. Inst. Cert. Fin. Planners (dir. N.E. Wis. 1987-88, cert.), Inst. Cert. Comml. Investments Mems. (cert.), Nat. Assn. Enrolled Agts. (cert.), Internat. Soc. Pre-retirement Counselors, Wausau Area Taxpayers League, Wausau C. of C. Office: Navi Dowty and Assocs Inc 2404 Stewart Sq Ste D Wausau WI 54401

DOYLE, ARTHUR JAMES, utility company executive; b. Boston, June 19, 1923; s. M. Joseph and Grace M. (McPhee) D.; m. Glenda M. Luehring, Oct. 14, 1950; children: Teresa, Kevin, Kelley, Conaught, Briana, Michael, Brian, Christopher. J.D., Boston Coll., 1949. Bar: Mo. 1949, Mass. 1949. Assoc. Johnson, Lucas, Graces & Fane, Kansas City, Mo., 1949-51, Spencer, Fane, Britt & Browne, Kansas City, 1951-57; ptnr. Spencer, Fane, Britt & Browne, 1957-73; v.p., gen. counsel Kansas City Power & Light Co., 1973-77, dir., 1976—, exec. v.p., 1977-78, pres., 1978-87, chief exec. officer, 1979-88, chmn. bd., 1979—; bd. dirs. Businessmens' Assurance Co. Am. Served to lt. (j.g.) USN, 1942-46. Mem. Mo. Bar Assn. (chmn. adminstrv. law sect. 1973-74, vice chmn. 1969-73), Fed. Power Bar Assn., Mo. C. of C. (dir. 1968-70). Roman Catholic. Clubs: Kansas City, Mission Hills.

DOYLE, FRANK S., electronics executive; b. Dublin, Ireland, Aug. 11, 1935; came to U.S., 1956; s. James and Anne (Kelly) D.; m. Caroline Werthmuller, Sept. 30, 1961; children: Stephen, Kenneth. BBA, Pace U., 1966. Sr. fin. analyst CBS, N.Y., 1960-66, Singer Co., 1966-69; controller Singer Co., St. Louis, 1969-71; sr. v.p. Electro Audio Dynamics div. KLH, Mass., 1971-77; v.p. fin. and adminstrn. Harman Internat., L.I., 1977-79; chief fin. officer Am. Thread, Stamford, Conn., 1979-84; v.p. fin., chief fin. officer The Superior Electric Co., Bristol, Conn., 1984-86, sr. v.p., chief fin. officer, 1986—; v.p. fin. The Am. Superior Electric Co. Ltd.; bd. dirs., mem. adv. bd. Superior Electric Nederland, B.V., Unitron, Inc. subs. Superior Electric Co., Electro-Kinesis subs. Superior Electric Co., Conn. Bank and Trust Co.; pres. bd. dirs. The Superior Electric Export Sales Co. Served with U.S. Army, 1958-60. Mem. Fin. Execs. Inst. (bd. dirs.), McAuley Ctr. (bd. dirs.). Roman Catholic. Home: 10 Rexinger Ln Avon CT 06001 Office: The Superior Electric Co 383 Middle St Bristol CT 06010

DOYLE, KENNETH JOHN, accountant; b. N.Y.C., May 11, 1941; s. John H. and Eileen M. (Gormley) D.; m. Beverly J. Grimm, Feb. 1, 1964; children: Kenneth, John. BS summa cum laude, Fordham U., 1963. CPA, N.Y., Conn., Colo. Staff acct. Price Waterhouse, Stamford, Conn., 1965-67, sr. acct., 1967-70, mgr., 1970-73; mgr. N.Y.C., 1973-75; ptnr. Stamford, 1975-80; ptnr., nat. dir. Acquisitions & Mergers, N.Y.C., 1980-84; ptnr., nat. dir. communications and mktg. N.Y.C., 1984-86; mng. ptnr. office Denver, 1986—. Bd. dirs. Denver PBS Sta., 1987—, Colo. Ballet, 1988—; mem. pub. affairs com. Denver Ctr. for Performing Arts, 1986—; mem. Darien (Conn.) Rep. Town Com., 1980-82. 1st lt. USAF, 1963-65. Mem. AICPA, Colo. Soc. of C.P.A.'s, Econ. Club, Glenmoor Club, Petroleum Club of Denver, Rotary. Roman Catholic. Office: Price Waterhouse 950 17th St Denver CO 80202-2872

DOYLE, LARRY MICHAEL, educator, consultant; b. Fulton, Mo., Dec. 19, 1942; s. Edward and Anne Doyle; m. Dorothy Doyle. BS in Edn., N.E. Mo. State U., 1964; MS in Edn., Miss. Coll., 1968; PhD, St. Louis U., 1979. Tchr. Van-Far Sch. Dist., Vandalia, Mo., 1964-68; counselor Orchard Farm Sch. Dist., St. Charles, Mo., 1968-70, dir. personnel, 1970-77; bus. mgr. Ft. Zumwalt Sch. Dist., O'Fallon, Mo., 1977-80, supt., 1980-84; prof. Webster U., St. Louis, 1985—; pres. Sanford Brown Bus. Coll., St. Louis, 1984-87, Career Designs, St. Charles, 1985—; supt. Wentzville (Mo.) Sch. Dist., 1987—; chmn. Edn. Employees Credit Union, St. Charles, 1981-84; bd. dirs. Boatmans Bank, O'Fallon. Author: Collective Bargaining in the Public Sector, 1979. Pres. St. Charles County chpt. Am. Heart Assn., 1982-85. Mem. Am. Assn. Sch. Adminstrs., Am. Mgmt. Soc., Assn. Sch. Bus. Adminstrs., Rotary, Kiwanis. Office: Wentzville R-IV Sch Dist One Campus Dr Wentzville MO 53385

DOYLE, LAWRENCE SAWYER, insurance company executive; b. Bridgeport, Conn., June 14, 1943. BS, U. Conn., 1965. Claims mgr. The Hartford Ins. Group, Stamford, Conn. and Sayreville, N.J., 1968-75; asst. regional claims mgr. The Hartford Ins. Group, N.Y.C., 1975-76; regional claims mgr. The Hartford Ins. Group, 1976-77, div. claims mgr., 1977-78; dir. claims-Europe The Hartford Ins. Group, Worthing, Eng., 1978-80; sec. and staff asst. to chmn. and pres. The Hartford (Conn.) Ins. Group, 1980-81, sec. adn dir. internat. property an casualty ops., 1981-82, v.p., 1982-87, sr. v.p., 1987—; sr. v.p. and dir. property and casualty ops. Hartford Accident and Indemnity Co., Hartford Casualty Ins. Co., Hartford Fire Ins. Co., Hartford Ins. Co. of Ala., Hartford Ins. Co. of Ill., Hartford Ins. Co. of Midwest, Hartford Ins. Co. of S.E., N.Y. Underwriters Ins. Co., Nutmeg Ins. Co., Twin City Fire Ins. Co.; bd. dirs. Cameron & Colby Co., Inc., London and Edinburgh Ins. Group Ltd., Transatlantische Group; chief exec. officer First State Ins. Co., New Eng. Ins. Co., New Eng.d Reinsurance Corp.; pres., chief exec. officer, bd. dirs. Hartford Fire Internat., Ltd; bd. dirs. and v.p. Abbey Internat. Corp. Mem. Internat. Ins. Coun. (bd. dirs. 1986—). Office: The Hartford Ins Group Hartford Pla Hartford CT 06115

DOYLE, MARGARET MCCAFFREY, employee benefits consultant; b. Plainfield, N.J., Dec. 3, 1961; d. Thomas Bernard and Joan Violet (Kelly) D. BA, Trinity Coll., 1983. Trust adminstr. 1st Nat. Bank of Cin., 1984-85; trust specialist Bank of Boston, 1985-86; cons., mgr. Coopers & Lybrand, Boston, 1986-88; cons., dir. employee benefits Deloitte, Haskins & Sells, Morristown, N.J., 1988—; cons., N.J. Vol. George Bush for Pres., 1980, Congressman George McEwen, Senator Paula Hawkins, 1981-82, puppeteer The Kids on The Block Program, Inc., N.Y. Cares, Securities and Exch. Commn., 1983. Mem. Jr. League. Republican. Roman Catholic. Office: Deloitte Haskins & Sells 111 Madison Ave PO Box 1939 Morristown NJ 07962-1939

DOYLE, MICHAEL ANTHONY, insurance executive; b. Mpls., May 6, 1948; s. Michael Gorman and Marion Frances (Armstrong) D.; m. Amy Carole Gourley, Aug. 8, 1987. BBA, Husson Coll., 1978. CLU; registered prin. Maine, 1985. Agy. supr. Phoenix Mut. Life Co., Portland, Maine, 1972-73; agy. mgr. Chapman & Drake Co., Bath, Maine, 1973-76; pres. Doyle Agys., Portland, 1976-79; regional v.p. A.L. Williams, Portland, 1979-84, sr. v.p., 1984-87, dir. nat. sales, sr. v.p., 1987—. Chmn. bd. dirs. United Way, Portland, 1978, Heart Fund, 1977; explorer troup coordinator Boy Scouts Am., 1985. Served with USAR, 1969-75. Republican. Office: 819 Forest Ave Portland ME 04103

DOYLE, PATRICK LEE, insurance company executive; b. Pitts., July 17, 1929; s. Lee Patrick and Anne Louise (Stattmiller) D.; m. Ann Marie Yuhasz, Apr. 26, 1952; children: Robert Christopher, Patrick Brian, David Alan. B.A., Ohio State U., 1951. C.P.C.U., Am. Inst. Property Casualty Underwriters C.L.U. Assoc. in Risk Mgmt., Ins. Inst. Am. Life reins. mgr. Nationwide Ins. Cos., Columbus, Ohio, 1965-70, asst. to pres., 1970-79, v.p., adminstrv. asst. to pres., 1980-81, v.p. human resources, 1981-82, v.p. Office Gen. Chmn., 1982—; instr. Ohio State U., Columbus, 1969-82, Franklin U., Columbus, 1973-82; mem. exam. com. C.P.C.U., Am. Inst. for Property and Liability Underwriters, Phila., 1980—; trustee Griffith Found. for Ins. Edn., Columbus, 1975—. Bd. dirs. Cath. Social Services, Columbus, 1981-87; trustee Kinder Key, 1973—. Mem. Ins. Inst. Am., Soc. CPCU (ednl. dir. 1965-72, Outstanding Educator award), Soc. CLU, Soc. Ins. Research (dir. 1976-79), Gamma Iota Sigma. Republican. Roman Catholic. Home: 1919 Birkdale Dr Columbus OH 43232 Office: Nationwide Mut Ins Co 1 Nationwide Pla Columbus OH 43216

DOYLE, WILLIAM JAY, II, business consultant; b. Cin., Nov. 7, 1928; s. William Jay and Blanche (Gross) D.; B.S., Miami U., Oxford, Ohio, 1949; postgrad. U. Cin., 1950-51, Xavier U., 1953-54, Case Western Res. U., 1959-60; m. Joan Lucas, July 23, 1949; children—David L., William Jay, III, Daniel L. Sales rep. Diebold, Inc., Cin., 1949-52, asst. br. mgr., 1953-57, asst. regional mgr., Cin., 1957-62, regional mgr., Cin., 1962-74; founder, pres., chief exec. officer Central Bus. Group div. Central Bus. Equipment Co., Cin., 1974-89, chmn., 1989—, dir. parent co. and divs.; mem. area contractor's council Spacesaver Corp., 1985-89; speaker on bus systems, security concepts. Mem. Armstrong Chapel, Methodist ch., Indian Hill, Ohio, adminstrv. bd, 1987-89. Mem. Bus. Systems and Security Mktg. Assn. (nat. dir. 1977-79, 81-83, nat. pres. 1981-83, 84-85), Nat. Assn. Accts. Republican. Clubs: Kenwood Country, Masons, Shriners. Contbr. articles to co. and trade publs.; developer new concepts in tng., cash and securities handling, mobile and mechanized storage and filing, and other areas of bus. systems. Home: 6250 S Clippinger Dr Cincinnati OH 45243 Office: 10839 Indeco Dr Cincinnati OH 45241

DOYLE, WILLIAM STOWELL, advertising executive; b. Lowell, Mich., Aug. 14, 1944; s. William Stowell and Eunice Jane (Gulde) D.; m. Permele Elliott Frischkorn, Jan. 7, 1978; children: William Elliott, Permele Crawford. AB, Duke U., 1966. Copywriter Wallace-Blakeslee, Grand Rapids, Mich., 1966-68; dir. mktg. Wolverine Worldwide, Rockford, Mich., 1971-73; v.p., dir. mktg. Chase Manhattan Bank, N.Y.C., also London and Hong Kong, 1973-76, 79-82; pres. William S. Doyle & Co., Inc., N.Y.C., 1982-83; founder, exec. v.p. Henderson Friedlich, Graf & Doyle, N.Y.C., 1983-85; founder, pres., chief exec. officer Doyle, Graf, Raj, 1985—. Contbr. articles to profl. jours. Dep. commr. Dept. Commerce, State of N.Y., Albany, 1976-79. Bd. dirs. Neighborhood Coalition for Shelter, N.Y.C.; assoc. bd. dirs. Julliard Sch., N.Y.C. Served with USAF, 1968-69; 1st lt., U.S. Army, 1969-71. Mem. Internat. Inst. Strategic Studies (London), World Tourism Orgn., Confrerie de Chevaliers du Tastevin. Presbyterian. Clubs: Brook, Racquet and Tennis. Office: Doyle Graf Raj Inc 375 Hudson St New York NY 10014

DOZA, LAWRENCE O., accountant, food company executive; b. Ste. Genevieve, Mo., June 6, 1938; m. Kenneth J. and Anna Mae D.; m. Lorraine M. Dickherber, July 9, 1960; children: Douglas, Jan, Dean. B.S. in Bus Adminstrn., U. Mo., 1962. Various positions to audit mgr. Price Waterhouse & Co., St. Louis, 1962-72; asst. gen. controller Borden Inc., Columbus, Ohio, 1972-74, gen. controller, 1974-77, v.p., gen. controller, 1977-85, sr. v.p., chief fin. officer, 1985—. Mem. Fin. Execs. Inst. Republican. Roman Catholic. Clubs: Brookside Country, Columbus Athletic, Capital. Home: 4265 Reedbury Ln Columbus OH 43220 Office: Borden Inc 277 Park Ave New York NY 10172

DOZIER, GLENN JOSEPH, bowling equipment company executive; b. Lexington, Ky., Apr. 7, 1950; s. Emmitt and Henrietta Elsie (Geisler) D.; m. Paula Jean Cook, June 3, 1974; children: Laura Jean, Diana Leigh. BS in Indsl. Engring. and Ops. Rsch., Va. Poly. Inst., 1972; MBA, U. Va., 1975. Mfg. engr. Tex. Instruments, Dallas, 1972-73; fin. analyst Dravo Corp., Pitts., 1975-76, mgr. corp. fin. analysis, 1976-79, dir. corp. devel., 1980-82, dir. corp. planning and devel., 1982-83; v.p. fin. Dravo Constructors, Inc., Pitts., 1983-87; chief fin. officer, treas., asst. sec. AMF Bowling Internat. Inc. and AMF Bowling, Inc., Richmond, Va., 1987—. Author: Economic Development Finance, 1986. Mem. Colonies Civic Assn. Mem. Nat. Assn. Accts., Bus. Planning Bd., Contrs. Coun., Phi Eta Sigma, Alpha Pi Mu, Phi Kappa Phi, Tau Beta Pi. Republican. Baptist. Club: Pitts. Press, Colonies Swim and Tennis Club (bd. dirs.). Office: AMF Bowling Inc 901 E St Richmond VA 23219

DOZIER, THOMAS AUGUSTUS, editor, writer; b. Athens, Ga., Jan. 3, 1915; s. Olin Arnold and Mildred (Carson) D.; m. Florence Elizabeth Peyton, Oct. 5, 1936; children: Michele, David Thomas, Peter Marquis. BA in Journalism, U. Ga., 1935. Asst. night city editor Atlanta Constn., Atlanta, 1935-36; telegraph editor Nashville Banner, 1936-37; corr. United Press Internat., Atlanta, 1937-38, Washington, 1938-41; chief press div. Nelson Rockefeller Office, Washington, 1941-44; corr. Time-Life, N.Y., London, Paris, Rome, Madrid, 1947—; intelligence analyst Office of Dep. Chief of Staff, Washington, 1944. Author: Dangerous Sea Creatures, 1975, Whales and Other Sea Mammals, 1975, Creatures of the Coral Reef, 1976; editor The Asia Mag., 1971-73; contbr. articles to mags. (Jose Marti prize, 1959). Sec. Lowndes County Dem. Exec. Com., Valdosta, Ga., 1976-80. Served with M.I. Corps, 1944-45. Democrat. Roman Catholic. Clubs: Biftad (sec. 1933-35), Savile (London), The Overseas Press (N.Y.C.). Home: 1204 Gornto Rd Valdosta GA 31602

DOZIER, WELDON GRADY, real estate development marketing company executive; b. Gainesville, Tex., Oct. 21, 1938; s. Weldon G. and Dorothy M. (Woods) D.; BA, Union U., 1962; postgrad. North Tex. State U.; m. Pamela Kay Kerns, Dec. 15, 1978. Mgr., Hybrid Computer Center sponsored by NASA, Denton, Tex., 1962-69; EDP mgr. Continental Ins. Cos., Atlanta, 1970-72; dist. systems mgr. 14 states for TRW Data Systems, Inc., 1973-75; pres. Property Mktg., Inc., Denison, Tex., 1976—; cons. in field. Mem. coalition on organ and tissue donor awareness Dallas/Ft. Worth Metroplex. Mem. Nat. Speakers Assn., Internat. Platform Assn., Am. Land Developers Assn., Lake Texoma Assn., Denison C. of C., Woodlawn Country Club (Sherman, Tex.), Rod and Gun Country Club (Denison), Toastmaster (sec., treas., v.p., pres.). Author: The Bell, 1982, False Echoes, 1983, No Sanctuary, 1985, A Thousand Faces, 1987. Republican. Baptist. Home and Office: PO Box 165179 Irving TX 75016

DRABINSKY, GARTH HOWARD, entertainment company executive; b. Toronto, Ont., Can., Oct. 27, 1948; s. Philip and Ethel (Waldman) D.; m. Pearl Kaplan, June 22, 1971; children: Alicia, Marc. LLB, U. Toronto, 1973. Pres., chief executive officer Cineplex Odeon Corp., Toronto, 1978, also chmn. bd. dirs.; bd. dirs. Mt. Sinai Hosp.; bd. govs. Baycrest Ctr. for Geriatric Care, 1988-89; mem. adv. bd. Ctr. for Rsch. in Neurodegenerative Diseases U. Toronto. Author: Motion Pictures and the Arts In Canada: The Business and the Law, 1976. Trustee Sundance Inst., Utah, Am. Mus. of the Moving Image, N.Y.; bd. govs. Nat. Theatre Sch. Can., Montreal, Que.; co-chmn. Can. Centre for Advanced Film Studies, Toronto; bd. dirs. Vancouver Film Festival, Toronto Film Festival, The Actors Studio, Inc., N.Y.C., Am. Cinematheque, L.A. Recipient Chetwynd award for Entrepreneurial Achievement Can. Film and TV Assn., 1986, Award for Mktg Excellence Am. Mktg. Assn., 1986, Lifetime Achievement award Can. Calif. C. of C., 1987, Outstanding Contribution to the Bus. of Filmaking in Can. award Air Canada, 1987, Vanier award, 1987, ShoWest award Nat. Assn. Theatre Owners, 1988; named Renaissance Man of Film Montreal World Film Festival, 1987; hon. fellow Ryerson Poly. Inst., 1987. Mem. Am. Film Inst. (trustee, second decade coun.), Acad. Motion Picture Arts and Scis. Office: Cineplex Odeon Corp, 1303 Yonge St, Toronto, ON Canada M4T 2Y9

DRAGON, WILLIAM, JR., footwear company executive; b. Lynn, Mass., Dec. 1, 1942; s. William and Anne (Stavru) D.; m. Suzanne Gail Behlmer, Feb. 24, 1968; children: Todd Christopher, Heather Anne, Paige Katherine. B.S. in Engring. Mgmt., Norwich U., Northfield, Vt., 1964; M.S. in Mgmt. Scis., Rensselaer Poly. Inst., Troy, N.Y., 1965. With mfg., sales and mktg. staff Gen. Electric Co., Mass. and Ky., 1967-73; dir. product planning and design Samsonite div. Beatrice Corp., Denver, 1973-75, dir. mktg. Samsonite div., 1975-78; v.p. mktg. and sales Buxton div. Beatrice Corp., Springfield, Mass., 1978-81; gen. mgr. Johnston & Murphy Div. Genesco Inc., Nashville, 1981-85, exec. v.p., pres. U.S. Footwear Group, 1985—, also dir. Bd. dirs. Nashville Youth Hockey League, 1983-85; vice-chmn. Nashville United Way, 1985; mem. men's adv. bd. Cumberland Valley council Girl Scouts U.S.A., 1985-86; mem. adminstrv. bd. Brentwood United Meth. Ch., 1986. Served to 1st lt. U.S. Army, 1965-67, Vietnam. Decorated Bronze Star medal. Recipient Superior Achievement Recognition award Genesco Inc., 1984. Methodist.

DRAGONE, CHARLES C., financial consultant; b. N.Y.C., Oct. 24, 1937; s. Charles C. and Maria Stella (Vasile) D.; m. Elaine I. Conforti, Sept. 6, 1958; children: Diane, Paul. Student, Manhattan Coll., 1955-57, CCNY, 1957-59, Bklyn. Coll., 1959-62. V.p., chief fin. officer, dir. K-Tron Internat., Inc., Scottsdale, Ariz. and Pitman, N.J., 1965-81; cons. K-Tron Internat., Inc., Pitman, 1987—; corp. fin. cons. Phoenix and Sarasota, Fla., 1981-85; ptnr. Fin. Assocs., Sarasota, 1986—, also bd. dirs.; bd. dirs., chief exec. officer Syntech Internat., Inc., Reno; cons. Biodynamics Inc., Houston, 1983—, Fla. Life Care, Inc., Sarasota, 1986—, K-Tron Internat., Inc., Pitman, N.J., 1987—. Mem. Nat. Assn. Accts., U.S. Power Squadron. Republican. Roman Catholic. Club: University (Sarasota). Home: 924 Blvd of the Arts Sarasota FL 34236 Office: Fin Assocs 1606 Main St Ste 700 Sarasota FL 34236

DRAGOUMIS, PAUL, electric utility company executive; b. N.Y.C., Sept. 19, 1934; s. Andrew and Theologie (Pavlou) D.; m. Maria William, Sept. 15, 1957; children—Ann Marie, Andrew Paul. BSEE, Poly. Inst. Bklyn., 1956; MS in Nuclear Engring., Internat. Sch. Nuclear Sci. and Engring., Argonne, Ill., 1959; MA in Philosophy, Georgetown U., 1986. Asst. v.p. Am. Electric Power Co., N.Y.C., 1956-70; gen. mgr. corp. exec. staff Allis Chalmers Corp., W. Allis, Wis., 1970-71; v.p. nuclear projects and fossil fuel supply group Potomac Electric Power Co., Washington, 1971-75, v.p. policy, 1976-78, sr. v.p., mem. exec. policy com., 1978—; dir. nuclear affairs FEA, Washington, 1975-76; exec. dir. Pres.'s Energy Resources Council, 1975-76; mem. mgmt. com. PJM Interconnection; chmn. bd. dirs. Mid Atlantic Area council; bd. dirs., chmn. compensation com. John Hanson Savs. Bank FSB. Chmn. U. Md. Community Concerts; trustee, v.p., mem. exec. com. Washington Opera, 1980—; trustee, mem. exec. com. Greater Washington Research Center, 1978—. Named U.S. Outstanding Young Elec. Engr. Eta Kappa Nu, 1964, Outstanding Young Man of Am. Jaycees, 1966; recipient award for meritorious service USFEA, 1976. Mem. IEEE, Washington Bd. Trade, Md.-D.C. Utilities Assn. (past pres.). Republican. Greek Orthodox. Clubs: City Tavern Assn. (Washington), University (Washington). Office: Potomac Electric Power Co 1900 Pennsylvania Ave NW Washington DC 20068

DRAKE, EDWARD CURTIS, sales executive; b. Shreveport, La., Oct. 16, 1948; s. Robert Lee and Genevieve (Wall) D.; m. Brenda Kay Lewis, Oct. 26, 1968 (div. 1980); children: Sheri Lynne, Edward Curtis; m. Paula Jean Stoppello, Apr. 22, 1987. AA, Kennesaw Coll., 1968. Mgr. sales dept. Rich's Dept. Store, Atlanta, 1966-72; salesman Parker Bros. Games, Atlanta, 1972-79; assoc. v.p. sales Hasbro Inc., Pawtucket, R.I., 1979-88; v.p. Hasbro Inc., Pawtucket, 1988—. Served with USMC, 1968-72. Democrat. Office: Hasbro Inc 200 Narragassett Park Dr Pawtucket RI 02962

DRAKE, KINGSLEY DIMITRI, professional service company executive; b. Seattle, July 21, 1937; s. James D. and Margaret (Chambreau) D.; m. Penny A. Drake, Mar. 18, 1961; children: Betsy, Holly, Cathy. BS, U. Wash., 1960. Registered profl. engr., Wash., Oreg., Alaska, Pa. Ga. Ohio. Technician Pitts. Testing Lab., Seattle, 1960-61; br. mgr. Pitts. Testing Lab., Eugene, Oreg., 1961-67; dist. mgr. Pitts. Testing Lab., Seattle, 1967-85; exec. v.p. Pitts. Testing Lab., Pitts., 1985-86, PTL Inspectorate, Pitts., 1986-87, Profl. Service Industries, Pitts., 1987—. Chmn. bd. dirs. N.E. YMCA, Seattle, 1982-84. Mem. ASTM, Am. Concrete Inst., Structural Engrs. Wash., Chartiers Club (Pitts.). Office: Profl Svc Industries 850 Poplar St Pittsburgh PA 15220

DRAKE, MICHAEL WAYNE, finance executive, communications broker; b. Creston, Iowa, Sept. 19, 1953; s. Harold Wayne and Elsie Marie (Pitkin) Roberts D.; m. Kristin Lee Perry, Aug. 20, 1976 (div. Feb. 1985); children: Justin, Matthew. BSBA, Iowa State U., 1977. CPA, Colo. Supervising sr. Peat, Marwick & Mitchell, Des Moines, 1977-81, Fox and Co., Denver, 1981-82; mgr. Peat, Marwick & Mitchell, Denver, 1982-83; treas. Cardiff Pub. Co., Englewood, Colo., 1983-85; contr. Cardiff Communications, Inc., Englewood, 1983-85; v.p. fin. Bus. Venture, Inc., Englewood, 1985-86, Capsule Systems, Inc., Englewood, 1985-86, Auto-Sense, Ltd., Englewood, 1985—; treas. Pat Thompson Co., Englewood, 1985—, communications broker, 1988—. Mem. AICPA, Colo. Soc. CPAs. Home: 7656 S Monaco Circle W Englewood CO 80112

DRAKE, RODMAN LELAND, management consultant; b. Terre Haute, Ind., Feb. 2, 1943; s. Leland Rodman and Helen Virginia (Frederick) D.; m. Lenir Leme-Lambert, Sept. 26, 1975; children: Stephan Rodman, Philip Lambert. BA, Yale U., 1965; MBA, Harvard U., 1969. Assoc. Cresap, McCormick & Paget, Inc., N.Y.C., 1969-70, Monterrey, Mexico, 1971-72, mng. ptnr., São Paulo, Brazil, 1972-77, v.p., bd. dirs., N.Y.C., 1977-81, mng. dir., chief exec. officer, 1981—; bd. dirs. Alliance Internat. Fund, Alliance Global Fund Inc., Towers, Perrin, Forster & Crosby, The Over the Counter Securities Fund, Hollywood Way Pictures Inc. Served with U.S. Army, 1965-67. Mem. Young Pres.'s Orgn. Episcopalian. Clubs: Pinehurst (N.C.) Golf; Yale (N.Y.C.) (sec. class of 1965, 1980-85); Waccabuc (N.Y.).

DRAKE, WILLIAM FRANK, JR., lawyer; b. St. Louis, Mar. 29, 1932; s. William Frank and Beatrice (Olmmstead) D.; m. Margaret Carkener Barnes, June 28, 1975; children by previous marriage: Stephen C., Peter O., Thomas W.; stepchildren: Stuart Barnes, Ashley Barnes. B.A., Principia Coll., 1954; LL.B., Yale U., 1957. Bar: Pa. 1958. Practice Phila., 1958-68, 84—; mem. firm Montgomery, McCracken, Walker & Rhoads, 1958-68, 87—, of counsel, 1984-87; sr. v.p., gen. counsel Alco Standard Corp., 1968-79, sr. v.p. adminstrn., 1979-83; chmn., chief exec. officer Alco Health Services Corp., 1983-84; vice chmn. Alco Standard Corp., 1984—, also bd. dirs. Trustee The Found. Architecture, Phila., Peoples Light & Theatre Co., Malvern, Pa.; mem. Tredyffrin Twp. Mcpl. Authority; mem. East Whiteland-Tredyffrin Joint Transp. Authority. Served with U.S. Army, 1957-58. Mem. ABA, Pa. Bar Assn., Phila. Bar Assn. Christian Scientist. Clubs: Union League (Phila.); Merion Cricket (Haverford, Pa.), First Troop, Phila. City Calvary. Office: 3 Parkway Philadelphia PA 19102 also: Alco Standard Corp PO Box 834 Valley Forge FL 19482-0834

DRAKEMAN, DONALD LEE, corporate executive, lawyer; b. Camden, N.J., Oct. 21, 1953; s. Fred J. and Jean (Faucett) D.; m. Lisa Natale Drakeman, Aug. 23, 1975; children: Cynthia, Amy. AB magna cum laude, Dartmouth Coll., 1975; JD, Columbia U., 1979; MA, Princeton U., 1984, PhD, 1988. Bar: N.J. 1979, U.S. Dist. Ct. N.J. 1979, N.Y. 1980, U.S. Supreme Ct. 1984. Assoc. Milbank, Tweed, Hadley & McCloy, N.Y.C., 1979-82; gen. counsel Essex Chem. Corp., Clifton, N.J., 1982—, v.p., 1987—; pres. Essex Med. Products, Clifton, 1988—; adj. prof. polit. sci. Montclair (N.J.) State Coll., 1984. Co-editor Church and State in American History, 1986; contbr. articles to profl. jours. Chmn. Montclair Bd. Adjustment, 1984. Harlan Fiske Stone scholar, Columbia U., 1976-79. Mem. ABA, Assn. of Bar of City of N.Y., Nat. Council Chs. (religious liberty com.), Am. Corp. Counsel Assn., Am. Soc. Legal History, AAAS, Am. Arbitration Assn. (arbitrator), Am. Acad. Religion. Home: 98 Magnolia Ln Princeton NJ 08540 Office: 1401 Broad St Clifton NJ 07015

DRAN, ROBERT JOSEPH, lawyer; b. Abington, Pa., Apr. 12, 1947; s. Joseph A. and Claire B. (Kowalski) D.; m. Sandra Ann Hyatt, Aug. 16, 1969; children: Arjay, Stacey, Elizabeth. AB, Stanford U., 1969; JD, MBA, Harvard U., 1973. Bar: Calif. 1973, U.S. Dist. Ct. (cen. dist.) Calif. 1973. Assoc. Adams, Duque & Hazeltine, Los Angeles, 1973-75; assoc. gen. counsel Envirotech Corp., Menlo Park, Calif., 1975-79; mgr. legal dept. Cooper Labs. Inc., Palo Alto, Calif., 1979-82, assoc. gen. counsel, 1982-85, v.p., 1983-85; v.p., gen. counsel The Cooper Cos., Inc., Palo Alto, 1985-88, v.p., sec., gen. counsel and chief adminstrv. officer, 1988—. Commr. Am. Youth Soccer Orgn., Redwood City, Calif., 1982-83; bd. dirs., team mgr. Little League and Babe Ruth League Baseball, Redwood City and San

Carlos, Calif., 1983—. Mem. Am. Corp. Counsel Assn., Peninsula Assn. Gen. Counsel. Republican. Roman Catholic. Office: Cooper Cos Inc 3145 Porter Dr Palo Alto CA 94304

DRANOW, JOHN THEODORE, professional association administrator; b. Passiac, N.J., Dec. 29, 1948; s. Nathan Dranow and Betty Jane (Coleman) McGregor; m. Louise Gluck, Jan. 1, 1977; 1 child, Noah. BA, Boston U., 1971; MA, U. Iowa, 1972, MFA, 1974. Instr. U. Iowa, Iowa City, 1973-74, U. Mo., Columbia, 1974-76, Radford (Va.) U., 1976-77; dir. summer writing program Goddard Coll., Plainfield, Vt., 1977-79; co-founder, v.p. New Eng. Culinary Inst., Montpelier, Vt., 1979—. Author: Life in the Middle of the Century, 1988 (Cin. poetry rev. prize 1988); contbr. short stories to various jours. Leader local troop Boy Scouts Am., Plainfield, 1984-87. Vt. Coun. on Arts grantee, 1977; Iowa teaching, writing fellow, 1973; recipient 1st prize in novel competition Va. Highlands Lit. Festival, 1977, 1st prize Boston U. Alumni Writer's Contest, 1983. Home: Box 1400 RD 2 Plainfield VT 05667

DRAUGHON, SCOTT WILSON, lawyer, financial planner, investment specialist; b. Muskogee, Okla., June 17, 1952; s. Arthur Eugene and Helen Carrie (Vanhooser) D. AA, Tulsa Jr. Coll., 1972; BA, Okla. State U., 1974; JD, U. Tulsa, 1977; postgrad., Oxford U., Eng., 1978, U. Okla, 1987—. Bar: Okla. 1979, U.S. Tax Ct. 1979, U.S. Dist. Ct. (no. dist.) Okla. 1980, U.S. Ct. Appeals (10th cir.) 1984, U.S. Supreme Ct. 1984. Sole practice Tulsa, 1979—; stockbroker Tenneco Fin. Services, Inc., 1983—; pvt. practice fin. planning Tulsa, 1984—; founder, exec. dir. The Fin. Hotline, Tulsa, 1984—; adj. faculty Tulsa Jr. Coll., 1986—; v.p. govtl. and pub. affairs Okla. Credit Union League, Inc., 1988—. Bd. dirs. Arts and Humanities Council, Tulsa, 1982-83, Meals on Wheels, Tulsa, 1985, Internat. Council of Tulsa, 1987—, Ea. Okla. Chpt. March of Dimes, 1989—; v.p. Family Action Ctr., Inc., Tulsa, 1984-85; adv. bd. Am. Indian Theatre Co., Tulsa, 1985, YWCA, Tulsa, 1985—, Okla. Tribal Assistance Program, 1985-87; chmn. pub. relations com., mem. exec. com. Tulsa Human Rights Commn., 1987—; mem. ad hoc task force for minority recruitment Leadership Tulsa, Inc., 1987—, resource devel. com., 1988—; mem. adv. com. Am. Indian Law Orgn., 1986—; candidate tribal counsel Cherokee Nation of Okla., 1987—; mem. adv. bd. Native Am. Communications and Career Devel., Inc.; mem. Nat. Youth Involvement Bd., 1988—; mem. Indian Affairs Commn., City of Tulsa, 1989—. Mem. ABA, Nat. Assn. Accts., Okla. Bar Assn. (lawyers helping lawyers com.), Tulsa County Bar Assn., Okla. Credit Union League (v.p. govt. and pub. affairs), Credit Union Nat. Assn. Found. (liason to credit union), Nat. Assn. Retired Credit Union People (league liason 1988—), Credit Union Nat. Assn., Tulsa Personnel Assn. (com. pub. relations 1988—), Nat. Youth Involvement Bd. (liason), Tulsa Press Club, Sigma Delta Chi, Phi Delta Phi. Republican. Methodist. Club: All-Am. Fitness (Tulsa). Lodges: Rotary, Masons, Shriners. Office: PO Box 702297 Tulsa OK 74170

DREBUS, RICHARD WILLIAM, pharmaceutical company executive; b. Oshkosh, Wis., Mar. 30, 1924; s. William and Frieda (Schmidt) D.; m. Hazel Redford, June 7, 1947; children—William R., John R., Kathryn L. BS, U. Wis., 1947, MS, 1949, PhD, 1952. Bus. trainee Marathon Paper Corp., Menasha, Wis., 1951-52; tng. mgr. Ansul Corp., Marinette, Wis., 1952-55; asst. to v.p. Ansul Corp., 1955-58, marketing mgr., 1958-60; dir. personnel devel. Mead Johnson & Co., Evansville, Ind., 1960-65; v.p. corporate planning Mead Johnson & Co., 1965-66, internat. pres., 1966-68; v.p. internat. div. Bristol-Myers Co. (merger Mead Johnson Internat. div. with Bristol-Myers Co. Internat. div.), N.Y.C., 1968-77, sr. v.p., 1977-78, v.p. parent co., 1978-85, sr. v.p. pharm. research and devel. div., 1985—. Bd. dirs. Wallingford Symphony, Jr. Achievement S.E. Conn., Meriden-Wallingford Mfrs. Assn., Meriden Silver Mus., Meriden-Wallingford United Way, chmn. fundraising drive, 1988-89; trustee Quinnipiac Coll. With inf. AUS, 1943-45. Decorated Combat Inf. Badge, Purple Heart, Bronze Star. Mem. Am. Psychol. Assn., N.Y. Acad. Scis., Wallingford C. of C. (bd. dirs.), Meriden C. of C. (bd. dirs.), U. Wis. Bascom Hill Soc., Phi Delta Kappa. Clubs: Oshkosh Country; Oshkosh Power Boat. Home: PO Box 867 Wallingford CT 06492 also: 3720 Pau Ko Tuk Oshkosh WI 54901 also: 705 Nathan Hale Blvd Naples FL 33941 Office: PO Box 5100 5 Research Pkwy Wallingford CT 06492-7660

DRECHSEL, EDWARD RUSSELL, JR., utility company executive; b. Webster, Mass., Dec. 29, 1927; s. Edward R. and Eva A. (Kullas) D.; m. Marcella Marie Japko, Dec. 26, 1950; children: E. Russell, Carl M. BSEE, Worcester Poly. Inst., 1949; MSEE, N.J. Inst. Tech., 1956; grad. pub. utilities exec. program, U. Mich.; intermittent coursework, Rutgers U. Registered profl. engr., N.J. Sales mgr. Jersey Cen. Power and Light Co., Lakewood, N.J., 1959-60, div. engr., 1960-64, dist. supt., 1969-84; supt. div. ops. Jersey Cen. Power and Light Co., Old Bridge, N.J., 1984-87, Lakewood, N.J., 1987—; ptnr. Cornucopia Enterprises, Wrightstown. Mem. Friends of the Gardens, Monmouth County, Bklyn. Botanic Gardens; bd. dirs. Tom's River (N.J.) C. of C., 1978-84; bd. dirs. N.J. Shade Tree Fedn., New Brunswick, 1982—; v.p. No. Hanover Twp. Bd. Edn., 1982-83, pres. 1985—; chmn. No. Hanover Shade Tree Commn., 1985—, Zoning Bd. of Adjustment, No. Hanover, 1985—; mem. Sayreville Indsl. Commn.; past chmn. Ocean County Traffic Safety Commn., Raritan Valley C. of C. Served to staff sgt. Signal Corps., U.S. Army, 1950-53. Mem. IEEE (sr.), Nat. Soc. Profl. Engrs., N.J. Soc. Profl. Engrs., Internat. Soc. Arborists, Internat. Soc. Arbiculture, Am. Forestry Assn., N.J. Fedn. Shade Tree Commns., Air Force Assn. (life), Nat. Rifle Assn. (life), Am. Legion, Pa. Horticulture Soc., N.J. Pesticide Assn., Raritan Valley Regional C. of C., Ocean County Employees Legis. Com., Burlington County Employees Legis. Com., Monmouth County Employees Legis. Com. Republican. Roman Catholic. Home: Box 67-2 RD 2 Larrison Rd Wrightstown NJ 08750 Office: Jersey Cen Power & Light Co 55 River Ave Lakewood NJ 08701

DREHER, CHRIS, financial executive; b. Glatz, Germany, Mar. 25, 1945; came to U.S., 1983; s. Hans and Hildegard (Kleinert) D.; m. Nancy Louise Kowert, Aug. 8, 1970; children: David, Daniel, Deborah, Jonathon. Diploma, U. Hamburg, Fed. Republic of Germany, 1969; MBA, U. Tex., 1971. Fin. analyst Lever Bros., Hamburg, 1971-75; strategic planner Lever Bros., London, 1975-78; v.p. fin. Lever Bros., Bremerhaven, Fed. Republic of Germany, 1978-83; v.p. controlling Paramont Group, Inc., N.Y.C., 1983-84; exec. v.p. Alphatype, Arlington Heights, Ill., 1984-87; pres. Iodent Co., Champaign, Ill., 1987—; dir. Klinge Corp., Champaign. Author (manual): Accounting References, 1973. Cub master Greenwich (Conn.) area Boy Scouts Am., 1983-84. Fulbright scholar, 1969. Mem. German Am. C. of C. (bd. dirs. 1985—). Home: 1003 W Park Champaign IL 61820 Office: Iodent Co 1817 S Neil St Ste B Champaign IL 61820

DREHER, DONALD DEAN, furniture manufacturing executive; b. Great Bend, Kans., Oct. 18, 1949; d. Elmer C. and Thelma M. (Baugardt) D.; m. Sheryl Rae Behrends, July 26, 1969; children: Jeff, Jennifer, Julie. AA in Bus., Santa Ana Coll., 1970; BS in Acctg., Calif. State U., Long Beach, 1973; postgrad., UCLA, 1974-75. Sr. cost acct. U.S. Filter Corp., Whittier, Calif., 1973-74, asst. controller, 1974-75; asst. controller U.S. Filter Corp., Irvine, Calif., 1975-77; mgr. corp. systems Filtrol Corp., L.A., 1977; corp. contr. DMI Furniture, Inc., Louisville, 1977-79, v.p. fin., 1980-86, pres., chief exec. officer, 1986—. Mem. Fin. Execx. Inst., Am. Furniture Hall Fame (exec. dir.). Republican. Roman Catholic. Home: 9007 Laughton Ln Louisville KY 40222 Office: DMI Furniture Inc 10400 Linn Station Rd Louisville KY 40223

DREISBACH, JOHN GUSTAVE, investment banker; b. Paterson, N.J., Apr. 24, 1939; s. Gustave John and Rose Catherine (Koehler) D.; BA, NYU, 1963, postgrad. U. N.Mex.; m. Janice Lynn Petitjean; 1 child, John Gustave Jr. With Shields & Co., Inc., 1965-68, Model, Roland & Co., Inc., N.Y.C., 1968-72, F. Eberstadt & Co., Inc., N.Y.C., 1972-74; v.p. Bessemer Trust Co., 1974-78; pres. Community Housing Capital, Inc., 1978-80; chmn., pres. John G. Dreisbach, Inc., Santa Fe, N.Mex., 1980—; JGD Housing Corp., 1982—; bd. dirs., pres. The Santa Fe Investment Conf., 1986—; assoc. KNME-TV; active U. N.Mex. Anderson Schs. Mgmt. Affiliate Program. Mem. Santa Fe Community Devel. Commn. Served with USAFR, 1964. Mem. Internat. Assn. for Fin. Planning, NYU Alumni Assn., Venture Capital Club N.Mex., N.Mex. First, NYU Alumni Assn., Mensa, Santa Fe C. of C. Republican. Episcopalian. Clubs: St. Bartholomew's Community, Essex, Hartford, Amigos del Alcalde. Office: 730 Camino Cabra Santa Fe NM 87501-1596

DRENNAN, JOSEPH PETER, lawyer; b. Albany, N.Y., Apr. 15, 1956; s. Richard Peter and Ann Marie (Conlon) D.; m. Adriana Sonia Miramontes, Sept. 26, 1987; 1 child, Patricia Solange. BA in Polit. Sci., U. Richmond, 1978; JD, Cath. U. of Am., Washington, 1981. Bar: D.C. 1981, U.S. Dist. Ct. D.C. 1983, U.S. Ct. Appeals (fed. cir.) 1983, Va. 1984, U.S. Ct. Appeals (D.C. cir.) 1984, U.S. Dist. Ct. (no. dist.) Va. 1987, U.S. Ct. Appeals (4th cir.) 1987, U.S. Dist. Ct. (no. dist.) Miss. 1988. Sole practice Washington, 1981—. Mem. ABA, Assn. Trial Lawyers Am., Bar Assn. D.C. Republican. Roman Catholic. Club: Univ. Washington. Home: 1425 S Eads St #1305 Arlington VA 22202-2847 Office: 1420 16th St NW Washington DC 20036-2218

DRESCHER, DAVID ROBERT, apparel company marketing executive; b. Meriden, Conn., May 9, 1937; s. W. Robert and Jean (White) D.; m. Maryruth Green, Oct. 16, 1965; children: Robert William, David Scott, Lori Ann. BA, U. Conn., 1959. Systems designer Systems Devel. Corp., Santa Monica, Calif., 1962-64; assoc. brand mgr. Procter & Gamble, Cin., 1964-68; dir. mktg. Clairol Co. subs. Bristol-Myers, N.Y.C., 1968-80; exec. v.p. mktg. Fruit of the Loom, Inc., Bowling Green, Ky., 1980—. Pres. bd. dirs. Jr. Achievement, Bowling Green, 1984-85. Capt. USAF, 1959-62. Mem. Assn. Nat. Advertisers (TV mgmt. com. 1986). Republican. Episcopalian. Home: 111 Bent Creek Ct Bowling Green KY 42101

DRESSER, RICHARD NEWELL, safety professional; b. Eureka, Calif., Dec. 12, 1944; s. Kenneth Richard and Christine (Hagberg) D.; m. Sylvia Louise Ebin, Aug. 22, 1976; 1 child, Donald Samuel. BS, U. Vt., 1972; MEd, Tex. A&M U., 1975. Cert. safety profl. Driver edn. instr. Plymouth Area High Sch., N.H., 1975-77; loss prevention rep. Liberty Mut. Ins. Co., Greensboro, N.C., 1977-78; sr. loss control rep. Md. Casualty Co. (Am. Gen. Fire and Casualty Co.), Little Rock, 1979-86; risk control cons. Crawford Risk Mgmt. Svcs., Schaumburg, Ill., 1986-87; sr. safety specialist Great Am. Ins. Co., Schaumburg, 1987-88; safety mgmt. cons. Argonaut Ins. Co., Chgo., 1989—. Contbr. articles to profl. newsletter. Co-compiler Suggested K-12 Safety Curriculum, 1974. Served with U.S. Army, 1968-70. Mem. Am. Soc. Safety Engrs. (profl. mem., sec. Ark. chpt. 1981-82, pres. Northeaster Ill. chpt. 1989—), Am. Driver and Traffic Safety Edn. Assn. Democrat. Avocations: running, swimming, bicycling, skiing, triathlon. Home: 1610 W Brown St Arlington Heights IL 60004 Office: Argonaut Ins Co 8750 W Bryn Mawr Ave Chicago IL 60631

DRESSLER, DAVID CHARLES, aerospace company executive; b. Cleve., June 21, 1928; s. Walter Carl and Beatrice (Albin) D.; m. Dorothea Walker, Dec. 22, 1950; children: David Charles, Bradley, Christopher. B.A., Yale U., 1950; grad., Advanced Mgmt. Program, Harvard Bus. Sch., 1973. With Armstrong Cork Co., 1950-51; with Martin Marietta Corp., 1953—, pres. Master Builders div., 1977-80, pres. Martin Marietta Chems. Co., 1979-81, corp. v.p., 1979-83, sr. corp. v.p., 1983—; pres. Master Builders Co. Ltd., Toronto, 1977-81, Martin Marietta Aluminum, 1982-85; chmn. bd. Internat. Light Metals, 1985—; pres. Martin Marietta Materials, Bethesda, Md., 1987—; chmn. bd. Martin Marietta Ordnance Systems, 1985-87;. Bd. dirs. Nat. Future Homemakers Am., Washington. Served to capt. USMCR, 1951-53. Mem. Phi Beta Kappa. Episcopalian. Clubs: Congressional (Washington), Harvard Bus. Sch. (Washington) (pres. 1983, chm. bd. 1984); The Country (Cleve.). Office: Martin Marietta Corp 6801 Rockledge Dr Bethesda MD 20817

DRESSLER, MICHAEL BARRY, financial executive; b. Providence, July 14, 1950; s. Maurice Milton and Gloria (Freidlander) D.; m. Fredda Ellen Samdperil, June 1, 1973; children: Maurice, Allison. BS, Bryant Coll., 1973. Treas. Colfax, Inc., Pawtucket, R.I.; pres. NEWMDA, Waltham, Mass., 1985-87; real estate agt. Cress & Co., 1988. Trustee Miriam Hosp., Providence, 1986—. Office: Colfax Inc 38 Colfax St Pawtucket RI 02860

DREW, ERNEST HAROLD, chemical company executive; b. Springfield, Mass., Apr. 15, 1937; s. Ernest L. and Marjorie E. (Canney) D.; 1 dau. by previous marriage: Karen; m. Mary T. Mayorga, Dec. 6, 1969; children: Linda, Leticia. B.S., U. Georgia, 1958, Ph.D., 1962; M.S., U. Ill., 1959. Sales mgr. resins Celanese Coatings Co., Louisville, 1971-74; v.p., gen. mgr. resins Celanese Specialty Co., Louisville, 1974-75; v.p. sales Celanese Chem. Co., N.Y.C.-Dallas, 1975-78; v.p. planning Dallas, 1979-81; dir. strategic planning Celanese Corp., N.Y.C., 1981-82; pres., chief exec. officer Celanese Can. Inc., Montreal, Que., 1982-84; pres. Celanese Fibers Ops., N.Y.C., 1984-85; group v.p. Celanese Corp., N.Y.C., 1985-87; pres. Hoechst Celanese Corp., Somerville, N.J., 1987—, chief operating officer, 1987, chief exec. officer, 1987—; dir. Celanese Can., Inc., Bank Montreal Mortgage Corp., 1983-84; mem. Can. adv. bd. Allendale Ins. Co., Montreal, 1983-84. Served to capt. USAF, 1962-65. Woodrow Wilson fellow, 1958. Mem. Soc. Chem. Industry (bd. dirs. Can. sect. 1983), Am. Chem. Soc., Chem. Inst. Can., Phi Beta Kappa. Club: Mt.-Royal (Montreal). Home: 124 Cummings Point Rd Stamford CT 06902 Office: Hoechst Celanese Corp Rte 202-206 N Somerville NY 08876 *

DREW, SHIRLEY DELORES, insurance company executive; b. Mobile, Ala., Mar. 13, 1932; d. Charles Edward and Gertrude Elizabeth (Hansen) Coleman; m. Lewis Gordon Drew, Aug. 28, 1959 (div. 1977); children: Curtis Wayne, Timothy Gordon. Student, Huffsteler Bus. Coll., 1949-50. With Am. Family Life Assurance Co., Mobile, 1970—, dist. mgr., 1981-85, sales assoc., 1985—. treas. Mobile chpt. Altrusa Internat., 1983; charter mem. Rep. Task Force, Washington, 1986, Statue of Liberty-Ellis Island Com., 1986. Mem. Nat. Assn. Life Underwriters, Nat. Assn. Female Execs., Am. Bus. Women's Assn. (pres. 1985-86, named Woman of Yr. 1985-86), Exec. Women's Froum. Baptist. Home: 4154 Stanford Rd Mobile AL 36618 Office: Am Family Life Assurance Co 750 Downtower Blvd Mobile AL 36609

DREW, THOMAS ARTHUR, banker; b. Milw., Aug. 29, 1945; s. Frank Emmons and Irene Louise (Wolleager) D.; m. Constance C. Deckert, Sept. 9, 1978; 1 child, Jack Emmons. BA, DePauw U., 1967; MBA, Dartmouth Coll., 1969. Assoc. Booz, Allen & Hamilton Inc., Chgo., 1969-76; sr. v.p., chief fin. officer First Savs. Assn. Wis., Milw., 1976-83, exec. v.p., 1983-85; v.p. Mortgage Guranty Ins. Corp., Milw., 1985—; pres. Tyme Corp., 1980-82. Bd. dirs. Milw. Children's Hosp., 1980—, United Performing Arts Fund, 1981-85. Mem. Fin. Execs. Inst. Clubs: Dairyman's Country, U. Milw. Home: 10054 N Range Line Rd Mequon WI 53092 Office: Mortgage Guaranty Ins Corp PO Box 488 Milwaukee WI 53201

DREW, WALTER HARLOW, paper manufacturing company executive; b. Chgo., Feb. 23, 1935; s. Ben Harlow and Marion Elizabeth (Heineman) D.; m. Gracia Ward McKenzie, June 27, 1959; children: Jeffrey, Martha. B.S., U. Wis.,, 1957. Sales and gen. mgmt. Kimberly-Clark Corp., Cleve., Neenah, 1959-76, v.p., gen. sales mgr., consumer products div., 1976-86; sr. v.p. Kimberly-Clark Corp., Neenah, Wis., 1980-85, Neenah, 1980-85; exec. v.p. Kimberly-Clark Corp., Neenah, Wis., 1985-88, pres. sales and logistics group, 1985-86, pres. adult care sector, 1986-88; pres., chief operating officer Menasha Corp., 1989—, also bd. dirs., 1989, pres., chief econ. officer, 1989—; dir. Twin Cities Savs. and Loan Assn., Novus Services Inc., Wis. Taxpayers Alliance. Trustee Novus Health Group; bd. dirs. Camp Manitowish YMCA, 1983-86; bd. visitors bus. sch. U. Wis., Madison, 1988-91. Lt. USNR, 1957-59. Republican. Episcopalian. Club: North Shore Golf (Menasha, Wis.) (pres. 1983-85). Office: Menasha Corp PO Box 367 Neenah WI 54956

DREXLER, MICHAEL DAVID, advertising agency executive; b. N.Y.C., Nov. 2, 1938; s. Benn and Evelyn (Goldfarb) D.; m. Nancy Karen Drexler, Apr. 5, 1981; children: Staci Ann, Denise Susan, Lauren Michele. BS, L.I. U., 1959. Media asst. Ogilvy and Mather Inc., N.Y.C., 1960-62, media planner, buyer, 1963-66, v.p. assoc. media dir., 1967-69, sr. v.p., media dir., 1970-74; exec. v.p., media dir. Doyle Dane Bernbach, N.Y.C., 1974-86, Bozell, Jacobs, Kenyon and Eckhardt, N.Y.C., 1986—; vice-chmn. Audit Bur. Circulation, Schaumburg, Ill., 1980-86. Author: (with others) Marketing in an Electronic Age, 1985; contbr. articles to profl. pubs. Mem. Am. Assn. of Advt. Agencies (media council), Media Dirs. Council (bd. dirs., pres. 1980-81), Advt. Research Found. (co-chmn. TV Audience Measurement Com. 1980-81), Internat. Radio and TV Soc. (bd. dirs. 1980-85), Audit Bur. of Circulations (vice chmn. 1982-86).

DREXLER, RICHARD ALLAN, manufacturing company executive; b. Chgo., May 14, 1947; s. Lloyd A. and Evelyn Violet (Kovaloff) D.; m. Dale Sue Hoffman, Sept. 4, 1971; children: Dan Lloyd, Jason Ian. B.S., Northwestern U., 1969, M.B.A., 1970. Staff v.p. Allied Products Corp., Chgo., 1973-75, sr. v.p. adminstrn., 1975-79, exec. v.p., chief fin. officer, adminstrv. officer, 1979-82, exec. v.p., chief operating officer, 1982, pres., chief operating officer, 1982-86, pres., chief exec. officer, 1986—. Office: Allied Products Corp 10 S Riverside Pla Ste 1600 Chicago IL 60606

DREY, MICHAEL WELSH, financial planner; b. Winona, Minn., Nov. 20, 1934; s. Kelly I. and Margaret (Welsh) D.; m. Marion D. Miller, June 18, 1965; 1 child, Scott. BSBA, U. North Dakota, 1956. Chartered life underwriter, cert. fin. planner. Buyer Boeing Airplane Co., Wichita, Kans., 1956-58; analyst Northwest Nat. Life, Mpls., 1958-64, salesman, 1964-82; salesman Integrated Resources, Denver, 1982-86, Travelers Equity Sales, Hartford, Conn., 1986—. Mem. Internat. Assn. of Fin. Planners, Inst. of Cert. Fin. Planners, Elks, Am. Soc. of CLU. Home: RR 1 Box 288 Fergus Falls MN 56537

DREYER, DOUGLAS CHARLES, securities and investment company executive, branch manager; b. Teaneck, N.J., Feb. 12, 1940; s. Charles August and Blanche (Poma) D.; m. Joyce Lynn Hampson, Apr. 25, 1980; children: Douglas C., Suzanne W.; stepchildren: Susan LaPorte, Sandra LaPorte, Jennifer LaPorte. BA in Econs., Gettysburg Coll.; grad. Securities Industry Inst., Wharton Sch., U. Pa., 1983-85. Dist. sales mgr. PPG Industries, Inc., Wilmington, Del., 1965-68; account exec. Dean Witter and Co., Phila., 1968-71; v.p., sales dir. Philo Smith and Co., Stamford, Conn., 1971-75; asst. mgr. instns. Moseley Hallgarten Estabrook & Weeden, Inc., New Haven, 1975-83; br. mgr. Moseley Securities Corp., New Haven, 1983-87; sr. v.p., br. mgr. Legg Mason Wood Walker, Inc., New Haven, 1987—, mem. pres's. council, 1987-88; mem. adv. bd. Housatonic Bank & Trust, Ansonia, Conn., 1976—. 1st lt. U.S. Army Security Agy., 1962-64. Recipient Moseley Council award, Moseley Hallgarten et al, 1983-86. Republican. Episcopalian. Clubs: New Haven Country, Quinnipiack (New Haven), Landmark (Stamford), New Haven Stockbrokers. Home: 20 Elderberry Ln Huntington CT 06484 Office: Legg Mason Wood Walker Inc 195 Church St New Haven CT 06510

DREYER, ROBERT HUGO, actuary; b. Mt. Kisco, N.Y., Nov. 18, 1937; s. Charles Hugo and Gertrude (Rauh) D.; m. Betty M. Hand, Jan. 2, 1982; children: Laura Lee, Lynda Jane, Diana M. Davis. BA, Drew U., 1959. Various positions Met. Life Ins. Co., N.Y.C., 1958-64; cons. actuary Milliman & Robertson Inc., Wayne, Pa., 1965-83; v.p., chief actuary Erie (Pa.) Family Life Ins. Co., 1983—. Fellow Soc. Actuaries; mem. Am. Acad. Actuaries (com. chmn. 1968—), Lake Shore Country Club (tournament chmn.), Kahkwa Country Club. Office: Erie Family Life Ins Co 100 Erie Insurance Pl Erie PA 16530

DRIFTMIER, RICHARD PRENTICE, architect, design firm executive; b. Anacortes, Wash., Dec. 18, 1948; s. Benjamin William Jr. and Mary Jo (Ramaker) D.; m. Karen Frances Richards Sept. 23, 1972; children: Kim Richards, Lee Richards. BA in Environ. Designs, U. Wash., 1971, BBA, 1972. Registered architect, Wash., Alaska, Oreg., Hawaii. Draftsman Tracey Brunstrom Co., Seattle, 1972-75; designer John Anderson Assocs., Bellevue, Wash., 1976-78; architect Cummings/Schlatter Architects, Kirkland, Wash., 1978-80, Ken Long Assocs., Seattle, 1980-81; prin. The Driftmier Architects P.S., Kirkland, 1981-85, pres., 1985—. Architect bank design InterWest Bank, Chelan, Wash., 1985 (Honor award). Bd. dirs. St. Lukes Luth. Ch., Bellevue, 1978-82; guest lectr. Bellevue Pub. Schs., Monroe Pub. Schs., Seattle Pub. Schs. Mem. AIA (assoc.), Constrn. Specifications Inst., Internat. Conf. Bldg. Officials, Nat. Council Archtl. Regulations Bd. (cert.), Delta Chi. Office: The Driftmier Architects PS 720 1/2 Market St Kirkland WA 98033

DRIGGS, GARY HARMON, financial executive; b. Phoenix, July 13, 1934; s. Douglas H. and Effie (Killian) D.; m. Kay Taylor, June 9, 1959; children: Rebecca Driggs-Campbell, Kimberly, Taylor, Benjamin. Student, Stanford U., 1952-54; BA, Brigham Young U., 1959; MBA, Ind. U., 1960, DBA, 1962. Economist Western Savs. and Loan Assn., Phoenix, 1962—, v.p., 1969-73, pres., chief exec. officer, 1973-88, vice chmn., 1988-89, cons., 1989—; faculty lectr. real estate dept. Ind. U. Grad. Sch. Bus., 1960-62, vis. lectr. urban econs., 1962-76; lectr. econs. Ariz. State U., 1963-67; pres. Ariz. Tomorrow, Inc., chmn. Visions of Future; div. dir. Nat. Council Savs. Instns.; mem. dean's adv. council Ind. U. Sch. Bus.; bd. dirs. Newell Cos., Weidner Communications Inc.; v.p. Valley Leadership; mem. corp. adv. bd. Karl Eller Ctr.; chmn. nat. task force Gov.'s Com. Nat. and Internat. Commerce; fin. chmn. Gov.'s Transportation Task Force; mem. Maricopa Ctrs. Commn. Author: How to Reduce Risk in Apartment Lending, 1966. Mem. exec. bd. Phoenix Community Alliance; bd. dirs. Phoenix Together; adv. bd. Morrison Inst. Pub. Policy, Ariz. Rep. Caucus; mem. Ariz. State U. Centennial Bus. Support Com., dean's council of 100 Ariz. State U. Coll. Bus.; bd. advisors, exec. com. U. Ariz.; chmn. Phoenix Streets Adv. Com., Gov.'s State Urban Lands Task Force; bd. dirs. Silent Witness Program; served ch. mission Mormon Ch., Finland. Named Outstanding Young Man of Yr., Ariz. Jr. C. of C., 1968, named Outstanding Young Man of Yr., Phoenix Jr. C. of C., 1968-69; recipient Disting. Citizen award U. Ariz. Alumni Assn., 1982, Disting. Citizen award Ind. U. Sch. Bus. Acad. Alumni Fellows, 1983. Mem. Nat. Assn. State Savs. and Loan Suprs. (future planning com.), Internat. Union Bldg. Socs. and Savs. Assns., U.S. League (legis. policy com., spl. task force on deficit reduction, com. econ. affairs, com. capital stock and holding cos., mem. home ownership task force), Savs. and Loan League Ariz. (past pres.), Phoenix 40, Assn. for Corp. Growth, Chief Execs. Orgn., World Bus. Council, Inc. (chief exec. officer), U.S. C. of C. (banking, monetary and fiscal affairs com.). Republican. Lodge: Rotary. Office: Western Savs & Loan Assn 6001 N 24th St Phoenix AZ 85016 *

DRIGGS, JOHN D., bank executive; b. 1927. AB, Stanford U., 1952, MBA, 1954. Former chmn. Western Savs. and Loan Assn., Phoenix. Office: Western Savs & Loan Assn 6001 N 24th St Phoenix AZ 85016

DRILLING, RICHARD LLOYD, flying school executive; b. Batavia, N.Y., Apr. 3, 1935; s. Henry Walter and Susan (George) D.; m. Elizabeth Ann Smith, Sept. 26, 1959; children: Teresa Marie, Gretchen Ann, Jeffrey Scott. Student flying schs., Orchard Park, N.Y., Batavia and various other locations. Lic. pvt. pilot, comml. pilot, flight instr., instrument flight instr. Owner, bus. mgr. Akron Airways, 1961-64; flight instr. Page Airways, Inc., Rochester, 1964-67, Buffalo Air Park, West Seneca, N.Y., 1964-67; mgr., chief pilot Cox Aviation, Akron, 1967-69; airport mgr., chief pilot Batavia Aviation, Inc., 1969-72; owner, operator, bus. mgr. Genesee Airways, Albion, 1972-81; pres. Gt. Lakes Aviation, Inc., Batavia, 1982-86; pres., bus. mgr. Genesee Airways, Inc., Batavia, 1981-88, Lantana, Fla., 1988—. Mem. Fla. Aero Club, Buffalo Aero Club, Rochester Pilots Assn., Knowlesville Flyers (pres. 1975), Genesee Pilots Assn. (bd. dirs.). Republican. Roman Catholic. Office: Genesee Airways Inc 2633 Lantana Rd Lantana FL 33462

DRISCOLL, JOHN PATRICK, electronics executive; b. Quincy, Mass., June 17, 1935; s. Cornelius J. and Eleanor (Corson) D.; m. Leila Belle McDaniel, June 16, 1960; children: Robert, Stephen, Kimberly. BBA, Boston Coll., 1956, MBA, 1963. Exec. mktg. and sales Sprague Elec. Co., North Adams, Mass., 1961-79; sr. v.p. mktg. and sales Murata Erie Inc, Smyrna, Ga., 1979—; also bd. dirs. Murata Erie Inc, Smyrna. Lt. USNR, 1956-59. Mem. Electronics Industry Assn. (gov. 1985—, chmn., bd. dirs., 1985—), Electronic Components Conf. (rep. 1986), Japan Am. Soc., Pinetree Country Club. Republican. Roman Catholic. Home: 1510 Waynesborough Ct Marietta GA 30002 Office: Murata Erie Inc 2200 Lake Park Dr Smyrna GA 30080

DRISCOLL, RICHARD DENNIS, banker; b. Boston, Apr. 17, 1931; s. Daniel Francis and Edith Frances (Barry) D.; B.A., Boston Coll., 1952; M.B.A., Harvard Grad. Sch. Bus. Adminstrn., 1954; m. Rose Mary Shea, July 28, 1962; children—Richard D., Jr., Timothy B., William M., Paul R., John S., Mary F., James E. With Bank of New England N.A. Boston, 1957—, mgr. credit dept., 1961-66, mgr. br. dept., 1966-71, mgr. retail div., 1971-78, sr. credit policy officer, mgr. comml. banking div., 1978-84, pres., dir., 1984-87, chmn., 1987—; vice chmn., dir. Bank of New Eng. Corp., 1988—; bd. dirs. N.E. Capital Corp., N.E. Comml. Fin. Corp., BancNew England Leasing Group. Dir., chmn. exec. com. Mass. Bus. Devel. Corp.,

1980—; trustee council Boston Univ. Med. Center, 1971—, Family Counseling and Guidance Center, 1975—, Morgan Meml. Goodwill Industries; chmn. Boston Housing Partnership, 1988—. Dir. Greater Boston YMCA, 1972—. Served to 1st lt., USMCR, 1954-57. Mem. Mass. Bankers Assn. (bd. dirs. 1988—). Home: 116 Laurel Rd Chestnut Hill MA 02167 Office: Bank New Eng 28 State St Boston MA 02109

DRIVER, C. STEPHEN, environmental consulting company executive; b. Chgo., Mar. 26, 1936; s. Arthur Stephen Driver and Carlisle (Osborne) Driscoll; m. Deborah Connell, Sept. 25, 1960; 1 child, Paul Stephen. BSME, U.S. Mcht. Marine Acad., Kings Point, N.Y., 1958; MBA, U. Pitts., 1965. Engr. Westinghouse Electric Co., Pitts., 1958-67; adminstr. Perkin-Elmer Corp., Norwalk, Conn., 1967-69; mgr. Heritage Village, Southbury, Conn., 1970-72; v.p. Pilgrims Harbor, Inc., Wallingford, Conn., 1972-75, Albertson Sharp Ewing, Inc., Norwalk, 1975-87, Lockwood Kessler & Bartlett, Inc., Norwalk, 1987-89; pres. Limewood Cons., 1989—; real estate broker, Conn., 1971—; U.S. marine engr., 1958-68. Mem., vice chmn. Redding (Conn.) Planning Commn., 1971-76; mem. Redding Wetland Com., 1976-78, Redding Rep. Town Com., 1975—, Fairfield (Conn.) 2000, 1986—; v.p. New Eng. Resource Conservation and Devel., 1984—; pres. Kings Mark Resource Conservation and Devel., 1974—. Served with USNR, 1954-62. Mem. Am. Inst. Cert. Planners. Republican. Home: 4 Tunxis Trail West Redding CT 06896 Office: Limewood Cons 4 Tunxis Trail West Redding CT 06896

DRIVER, JOE LUTHER, insurance executive, consultant; b. Rockwall, Tex., Sept. 29, 1946; s. Marshall Laguin and Alice Elizabeth (Patillo) D.; m. Sandi Leigh Hamrick, Dec. 17, 1983; 1 child, Candice Nicole. BBA, U. North Tex., 1971. Head staff Steak & Ale Restauants, Dallas, 1971-73; law instr. Garland (Tex.) Ind. Sch. Dist., 1972; mgr. Marshall Driver Ins., Garland, 1972-73; trainee State Farm Ins. Cos., Dallas, 1973-75, mem. regional advt. bd., 1978-82; owner, agt. Joe Driver Ins.-State Farm, Dallas, 1975—; mem. devel. bd. Tex. Commerce Bank, Garland, 1984-86. Pres. Christian Singles Unltd., Garland, 1979; bd. dirs. 1st United Meth. Ch., Garland, 1979-81, Garland Econ. and Devel. Authority, 1986, Garland Crimestoppers, 1985-88; mem. bd. mgmt. Garland YMCA, 1983-86; mem. long range planning com. City of Garland, 1986-88; campaign mgr. for Tex. State Rep. Anita Hill, Garland, 1988. Recipient Human Relations award Dale Carnegie Cos., 1978. Mem. Nat. Assn. Life Underwriters (nat. quality award 1978-83, 86-87), Dallas Assn. Life Underwriters, Garland C. of C. (bd. dirs. 1983-87, chmn. 1986, corp. council 1988—), Tex. Dist. Exchange Clubs (dist. dir. 1984, Outstanding Dist. Dir. award 1985, Pres.'s award 1986), Noon Exchange Club Garland (bd. dirs. 1982-86, pres. 1983, Outstanding Service award 1986-87), Leadership Garland Alumni Assn., U. North Tex. Alumni Assn., Lambda Chi Alpha (pres. 1971). Republican. Office: 201 S Glenbrook Garland TX 75040-6296

DROHAN, WILLIAM MICHAEL, professional association executive; b. Providence, R.I., Feb. 22, 1954; s. William Joseph and Helen Ann (Kazin) D.; m. Sally Riddick, Nov. 10, 1984; 1 child, Michael Lockhart. B.S., Bryant Coll., 1976; M.B.A., George Washington U., 1981. Research assoc. Mass. Energy Policy Office, Boston, 1975, Atty. Gen. of R.I., Providence, 1975-76; pub. info. specialist Consumer Product Safety Commn., Washington, 1976; legis. rep. Solar Energy Industry Assn., Washington, 1977; exec. dir. Nat. Assn. of State Credit Union Suprs., Arlington, Va., 1978—; exec. dir. Am. Council State Savings Suprs., Arlington, 1986; pres. Drohan Mgmt. Group, Arlington, 1984—. Author: (with others) Use of Solar Energy in Space Heating and Hot Water, 1976, The Association Business Plan: Tying It All Together, 1985. Editor: (with others) Report on Credit Unions Monthly Magazine, 1982—. Mem. Am. Soc. Assn. Execs. (com. mem. 1980—, cons., evaluator 1984-85, membership devel. com., 1984), Greater Washington Soc. of Assn. Execs. (com. mem. 1980—, chief exec. officer Roundtable Devel. 1984), Exchequer Club. Democrat. Roman Catholic. Avocations: skiing, fishing, golf. Home: 10906 Leeds Ct Great Falls VA 22066 Office: Drohan Mgmt Group 1600 Wilson Blvd Ste 905 Arlington VA 22209

DROLL, RONALD WILLIAM, manufacturing company executive; b. San Angelo, Tex., Mar. 25, 1950; s. Harvey W. and Sidona M. (Multer) D.; m. Kathy M., Aug. 9, 1969; children: Scott, Angela. BS in Agrl. Engring., Tex. A&M U., 1972. Registered profl. engr., Tex. Research assoc. Tex. A&M U., Weslaco, 1972-74; project engr. FMC Corp., Ripon, Calif., 1974-79; mgr. engring. Ethicon, San Angelo, Tex., 1979-82; plant engr. Ethicon, Albuquerque, 1983-87; prodn. supt. Ethicon, Cornelia, Ga., 1987—. Patentee stowable loader. Mem. Soc. Mfg. Engrs., Tau Beta Pi. Roman Catholic. Home: 90 Club Dr Gainesville GA 30506 Office: Ethicon Inc PO Box 70 Cornelia GA 30531

DROOZ, DANIEL BERNARD, trading company executive; b. Wilmington, Del., Mar. 27, 1945; s. Herbert E. and Florence (Zubres) D.; m. Angela Klenter, Jan. 31, 1977; 1 child, Andrei. BA, Antioch Coll., 1967; MA in Communications, U. Mich., 1969. Editor ABC News Radio, Washington; reporter Chgo. Sun Times, Jerusalem, CBC, Jerusalem, Time/Life, Jerusalem; correspondent Chgo. Sun Times/Daily News, Johannesburg, Republic of South Africa; chief executive officer Commerce Internat., Wilmington, Del., 1984—; cons. fgn. risk, Indpls., 1978-86. Author columns Balt. Evening Sun, 1978—; contbr. numerous investigative features to various mags. Recipient Nat. Newspaper award Canadian Press Assn., 1976. Mem. Overseas Press Club.

DROSDICK, JOHN GIRARD, oil company executive; b. Hazelton, Pa., Aug. 9, 1943; m. Gloria J. Shenosky, May 10, 1944; children: Scott E., Candice M., Courtney J., Brooke K. BSChemE, Villanova U., 1965; MSChemE, U. Mass., 1968. Crude oil coordinator Exxon USA, Houston, 1973-74, marine planning mgr., 1974-76, corp. analysis mgr., 1978-81; facilities devel. dept. head Exxon USA, Baton Rouge, 1976-78, refinery ops mgr., 1981-83; v.p. refining Tosco Corp., Santa Monica, Calif., 1983-85, sr. v.p. refining, 1985-86, exec. v.p., 1986-87, pres., chief ops. officer, 1987—, also bd. dirs. Mem. Nat. Petroleum Refiners Assn. (bd. dirs. 1985—), Am. Petroleum Refiners Assn. (bd. dirs. 1985-87). Roman Catholic. Club: Jonathan. Office: Tosco Corp 2401 Colorado Ave Box 2401 Santa Monica CA 90406 *

DROST, MARIANNE, lawyer; b. Waterbury, Conn., Feb. 21, 1950; d. Albin Joseph and Henrietta Jean (Kremski) D. BA, Conn. Coll., 1972; JD, U. Conn., 1975. Bar: Conn. 1975. Assoc. Ritter, Tapper & Totten, Hartford, Conn., 1975-77; sr. atty. GTE Service Corp., Stamford, Conn., 1977-84, Chesebrough-Pond's Inc., Greenwich, Conn., 1984-85; corp. sec. GTE Corp., Stamford, 1985—. Tutor. Literacy Vols., Stamford, 1988—; dir. Stamford Ctr. for Arts, 1985—, Lit. Vols. Am., 1988—. Mem. ABA, Am. Soc. Corp. Secs. (pres. Fairfield-Westchester chpt.), Westchester-Fairfield County Corp. Counsel Assn. Democrat. Roman Catholic. Office: GTE Corp 1 Stamford Forum Stamford CT 06904

DROULLARD, STEVEN MAURICE, jewelry company executive; b. Pampa, Tex., June 28, 1951; s. Maurice Erskin and Betty (Bonnett) D.; m. Alessia Passalacqua, Dec. 31, 1978. Grad. gemology, Gemological Inst Am., Santa Monica, Calif., 1985. Lic. broadcaster, 1972. Asst. to pres. Standard Coal Co., San Francisco, 1976-78; pres. Adamas Gem Services, Kailua-kona, Hawaii, 1978-82; v.p. Intergem, Inc., Denver, 1982-85, pres., 1985-87, also bd. dirs.; pres., chmn. bd. GMA Inc., 1988—; cons. Wells Communications, Boulder, Colo., 1984—; mem. bd. advisors Colo. Computing Mag., Boulder, 1985—; chmn. Exec. Jewelry Buyers Club, 1988—. Contbr. articles to mags.; also cons. The Great American Sapphire, 1985. Named Bus. Assoc. of Yr. Am. Bus. Women Assoc., 1981. Mem. Gemological Inst. Am. Alumni Assn. (charter, pres. Colo. chpt. 1987—), Accredited Gemologists Assn., Am. Gem Trade Assn., Gem Mcht. Assocs. (pres. 1986), Kailua-Kona C. of C. (v.p. 1981). Office: 210 University Blvd #770 Denver CO 80206

DROZD, LEON FRANK, JR., lawyer, energy company executive; b. Victoria, Tex., Sept. 11, 1948; s. Leon Frank and Dorothy Lucille (Smith) D.; BBA, Tex. A&M U., 1971; J.D., U. Denver, 1979. Bar: Colo., U.S. Dist. Ct. Colo. U.S. Dist. Ct. (no. dist.) Calif., U.S. Ct. Appeals (10th cir.). Legis. asst. U.S. Ho. of Reps., also Dem. Caucus, Washington, 1971-74, chief clk. com. on sci. and tech., 1974-75; asst. to dean for devel. Coll. Law, U. Denver, 1975-79; v.p. Braddock Publs., Inc., Washington, 1975-79; land and legal counsel Chevron Shale Oil Co.; land and legal counsel Chevron Resources Co., 1980-87, land and legal counsel ins. div., 1987—; atty. Chevron Real Estate Mgmt. Co., 1989—, Chevron Corp. Law Dept. 1987-89, corp. div., 1989—, Chevron Overseas Petroleum and White Nile Petroleum Co. Ltd. (Sudan), 1983, Chevron Real Estate Mgmt. Co., 1989— Colo. elector Anderson/Lucey Nat. Unity Campaign, 1980. Mem. ABA, Fed. Bar Assn., Am. Trial Lawyers Assn., Denver C. of C. (steering com. 1981-82). Clubs: Nat. Lawyers (Washington), Commonwealth of San Francisco. Home: 255 Red Rock Way #H-204 San Francisco CA 94131 Office: Chevron Corp Law Dept 225 Bush St San Francisco CA 94104

DROZDA, JOSEPH MICHAEL, cemetery-funeral home executive; b. Chgo., Aug. 3, 1943; s. Albert and Bozena J. (Milonski) D.; m. Cynthia Elizabeth Gartin, Aug. 21, 1971; children: Joseph M. Jr., Patricia B. BS, Ind. U., 1969. Sales rep. EBSCO Industries, Columbus, Ohio, 1969-70; pres. The Stewart Howe Alumni Service, West Lafayette, Ind., 1970-79, Drozda Burchell Advt., Lafayette (Ind.) and Indpls., 1974-79; chmn. fin. Dole For Pres. Com., Alexandria, Va., 1979; sales mgr. Gibraltar Mausoleum Corp., Ind., Minn., Pa., 1980-84; asst. v.p. sales Gibraltar Mausoleum Corp., Indpls., 1984—. Author, editor: Chi Omega 50 Years at Indiana, 1972, Hub City History, 1984; contbr. articles to profl. jours. Precinct committeeman Rep. Party, Lafayette, 1979; cons. Haig for Pres. Com., Alexandria, 1979; v.p. Downtown Bus. Ctr. Corp., Lafayette, 1979. Served to maj. U.S. Army, 1966-69, Vietnam. Mem. Pub. Relations Soc. Am., Kappa Sigma (Dist. Grand Master 1972-78). Presbyterian. Lodge: Rotary (pres. Republic, Pa. club 1983-84). Office: Gibraltar Mausoleum Corp 8435 Keystone Crossing Indianapolis IN 46240

DROZDA, KIMBERLY KAY, public relations executive; b. Bainbridge, Md., Apr. 26, 1956; d. Janet G. (Vernon) Hepner; m. Richard Allen Drozda, May 19, 1977; 1 child, Scott R. Student, Ohio State U., 1975-76; BA, Am. Inst. Banking, Chgo., 1980; postgrad, LaRoche Coll., Pitts., 1982-83; postgrad., Fairfield (Conn.) U., 1984-85. Owner, operator The Best Cellar Shoppe, Dover, Ohio, 1977-81; actress N.Y., Calif., 1972—; cons. pub. relations, advt. various corps., Conn., N.Y., N.J., Calif., 1984—; pres., chief exec. officer Silverscreen Prodns., Mansfield, Ohio, 1985—; cons., dir. Madison Comprehensive High Sch., Mansfield, Ohio, 1987-88; cons. Advt. Area Media, Los Angeles, 1985-88; dir. Software Interface Internat., Independence, Ohio, 1988—. Author: (news digest Class In Style, 1988, Receptionist/Secretary's Handbook, 1988; (newsletter) Computing of Public and Private Security, 1988. Chairperson Mansfield Symphony, 1986-87; buyer, trustee Mansfield Art Ctr., 1986-87; com. chair person Downtown Mchts. Assn., Dover, 1978-83, Downtown Growth Assn., 1978-83. Mem. Screen Talent Ltd. (Extrodinary Workmanship award 1987), Nat. Orgn. Women, Profl. Bus. women Assn. (com. chmn. 1978-81). Methodist. Mktg. (Columbus, Ohio) (pres. 1987-88), Advt. Unltd. (St. Louis) (chairperson 1988-89). Office: Silverscreen Prodns PO Box 3515 Mansfield OH 44907

DROZDECK, STEVEN RICHARD, brokerage executive; b. N.Y.C., Apr. 23, 1951; s. Frank S. and Jane (Dzingelewski) D. Student Poly. Inst. Bklyn., 1969-70; B.S. cum laude in Fin., N.Y. Inst. Tech., 1973. Cert. master practitioner, 1985, trainer of neuro linguistic programming, 1987. Pres., Unltd. Leadership Potential, S.I., N.Y., 1973-74; account exec. Merrill Lynch, Pierce, Fenner & Smith, Bklyn., 1974-78, S.I., 1978-80, sr. sales trainer, N.Y.C., 1980—, adminstrv. mgr. tng. sch., 1983—, asst. v.p., 1984—; affiliate Eastern Neuro Linguistic Programming Inst., 1984—, market and sales cons., 1986, mgr. of fin. cons. profl. devel., 1987, mem. devel. team The Art of Friendly Persuasion, 1984—. Co-author: Power Persuasion. Mem. Internat. Assn. Fin. Planners, Nat. Soc. Registered Reps. (charter), N.Y. Stockbrokers Club, N.Y. Stock Exchange Qualifications Com. for Gen. Securities Examination, 1987, Nat. Assn. Securities Dealers Qualifications Com., 1988. Home: 265 E Village Rd Holland PA 18966 Office: 800 Scudders Mill Rd Plainsboro NJ 08536

DROZDZIEL, MARION JOHN, aeronautical engineer; b. Dunkirk, N.Y., Dec. 21, 1924; s. Steven and Veronica (Wilk) D.; B.S. in Aero. Engring., Tri State U., 1947, B.S. in Mech. Engring., 1948; postgrad. Ohio State U., 1948, Nigara U., 1949-51, U. Buffalo, 1951-52; m. Rita L. Korwek, Aug. 30, 1952; 1 son, Eric A. Stress analyst Curtiss Wright Corp., Columbus, Ohio, 1948; project engr. weight analysis Bell Aerospace Textron, Buffalo, 1949-52, stress analyst, 1952-60, asst. supr. stress analysis, 1960-64, chief stress analysis propulsion, 1964-79, chief engr. stress and weights, 1979-84, staff scientist, 1984-85, cons. structures and fractures mechanics, 1985—. Served with AUS, 1944-47; PTO. Recipient cert. of achievement NASA-Apollo, 1972; cert. commendation U.K. NATO program, 1982. Mem. AIAA (Membership Chairman's award, 1988, 89), Soc. Reliability Engrs., U.S. Naval Inst., Am. Space Found., Nat. Conservancy, Nat. Audubon Soc., Am. Acad. Polit. and Social Sci., Acad. Polit. Sci., AAAS, Union of Concerned Scientists, Air Force Assn., Nat. Space Soc., Soc. Allied Weight Engrs., Planetary Soc., Am. Mgmt. Assns., Bibl. Archeology Soc., Archeol. Inst. Am., Cousteau Soc., Smithsonian Assocs., Buffalo Audubon Soc., Bell Mgmt. Club, Natural History Mus., Internat. Hypersonic Rsch. Inst., Quarter Century Club. Republican. Roman Catholic. Home: 152 Linwood Ave Tonawanda NY 14150 Office: 152 Linwood Ave Tonawanda NY 14150

DRUEN, WILLIAM SIDNEY, lawyer; b. Farmville, Va., May 5, 1942; s. William Gills and Minnie (Kessler) D.; m. Janet Elizabeth Ward, Dec. 21, 1969; children—Courtney Paige, William Sidney II. B.A., Hampden Sydney Coll., 1964; LL.B., U. Va., 1968. Bar: Va. 1968, Ohio 1970. Spl. counsel Govs. Office State of Va., Richmond, 1968-70; with legal dept. Nationwide Ins. Co., Columbus, Ohio, 1970-82, v.p., assoc. gen. counsel, 1982—; asst. sec. Employer Mutual Ins. Wausau, Wis., 1986—; ptnr. Wagner, Schmidt, McCutchan, Hank & Birkhimer, 1970-76, McCutchan, Schmidt, Birkhimer & Druen, 1976-85, McCutchan, Schmidt & Druen, 1986-88, McCutchan, Druen, Maynard, Rath and Dietrich, 1988—. Pres. bd. trustees German Village Found., 1983-86; bd. housing appeals City of Columbus, 1988—. Mem. Am. Land Title Assn., Ohio Bar Assn., Va. Bar Assn., Ohio Land Title Assn., Columbus Bar Assn. Republican. Home: 85 Deshler Ave Columbus OH 43206 Office: Nationwide Mut Ins Co 1 Nationwide Pla Columbus OH 43216

DRUKER, HENRY LEO, investment banker; b. Des Moines, Aug. 20, 1953; s. Boni B. Druker and Dorothy (Marks) Vogel. BA, Colo. Coll., 1975; MBA, JD, U. Pa., 1980. Bar: Pa. 1980. Assoc. Goldman Sachs & Co., N.Y.C., 1980-82; v.p. Investors in Industry, Boston, 1982-83; mng. dir. Rothschild & Co., N.Y.C., 1983-88; ptnr. Gordon Investment Corp., N.Y.C., 1989—. Com. mem. Save Children Found., N.Y.C., 1985—. Office: Gordon Investment Corp 767 Fifth Ave New York NY 10153

DRUMHELLER, GEORGE JESSE, motel and hotel chain owner; b. Walla Walla, Wash., Jan. 30, 1933; s. Allen and Ila Margaret (Croxdale) D.; student Wash. State U., 1951-52, Whittier Coll., 1955-58; m. Carla Rene Cunha, May 4, 1965 (div. 1985). Asst. mgr. Olympic Hotel, Seattle, 1959; jr. exec. Westin Hotels, Seattle, 1959-63; founder, pres. George Drumheller Properties, Inc., motel holding co., Pendleton, Oreg., 1963—; founder, chmn. bd. Dalles Tapadera, Inc., motel and hotel holding co., The Dalles, Oreg., 1964-77; founder, pres. Lewiston Tapadera, Inc. (Idaho), motel holding co., 1970-77; founder, pres. Yakima Tapadera, Inc. (Wash.), 1971-77; founding ptnr. Drumheller & Titcomb (Tapadera Motor Inn), Ontario, Oreg., 1972-84; merger with Tapadera motel holding cos. and George Drumheller Properties, Inc., 1978—, founder Tapadera Budget Inns, Kennewick and Walla Walla, Wash., 1981-85, also merged with George Drumheller Properties, Inc., 1986; engaged in farming, eastern Wash., 1958-80. With USCG, 1952-55. Mem. Am. Hotel and Motel Assn. (nat. dir. 1980-84, pres.'s exec. com. 1983-84), Oreg. Hotel Motel Assn. (dir. 1974-78), Wash. State Lodging Assn. (dir., v.p. 1976-84), Spokane Club, Walla Walla Country Club, Washington Athletic Club, J.D. Shea Club, LaJolla Beach and Tennis Club, Kona Kai Club, San Diego Club. Home: 3132 Morning Way La Jolla CA 92037 Office: George Drumheller Properties Inc PO Box 1234 Walla Walla WA 99362

DRUMMOND, CHESTER HENRY, food manufacturing company executive; b. Camden, N.J., Oct. 29, 1927; s. Chester Henry and Mary Lawrence (Gundlach) D.; m. Mary J. Burt, Jan. 22, 1956; children: H. Robin, David C. Student, U. Pa., 1953-55, Rutgers U., 1957-58. With Campbell Soup Co., Camden, N.J., 1948-60, asst. mgr. ins., 1960-69, mgr. ins., 1969—; bd. dirs. Triple S, Inc., Washington. Served with USCG, 1945-48. Recipient United Way Service award, 1978. Mem. Ins. Mgrs. Assn., Phila. (gen. chmn. 1981—), Risk and Ins. Mgmt. Soc. (pres. Delaware Valley chpt. 1962-63). Republican. Clubs: Niagara Fire Co. (Merchantville, N.J.) (treas. 1982—); Glasstown Antique Fire Brigade (Millville, N.J.). Office: Campbell Soup Co 3 Executive Campus Cherry Hill NJ 08002

DRUMMOND, GERARD KASPER, resource development company executive, lawyer; b. N.Y.C., Oct. 9, 1937; s. John Landells and Margaret Louise (Kasper) D.; m. Donna J. Mason, Sept. 14, 1957 (div. 1976); children: Alexander, Jane, Edmund; m. Sandra Hamilton, Aug. 31, 1985. B.S., Cornell U., 1959, LL.B. with distinction, 1963. Bar: Oreg. 1963. Assoc. Davies, Biggs, Strayer, Stoel & Boley, Portland, Oreg., 1963-64; assoc., ptnr. Rives, Bonyhadi, Drummond & Smith, Portland, 1964-77; pres. Nerco, Inc., Portland, 1977—, chmn. bd. dirs., 1987—; mem. corp. policy group PacifiCorp, 1979—, exec. v.p., 1987—; bd. dirs. Pacific Telecom. Pres. Tri-County Met. Transit Dist., Portland, 1974-86, bd. dirs., 1974-86; mem. Oreg.-Korea Econ. Coop. Com., Portland, 1981-85, Oreg. Investment Council, 1987—; trustee Reed Coll., 1982—; bd. dirs. Oreg. Contemporary Theatre, 1983-85, Oreg. Symphony, 1987—; community bd. dirs. Providence Hosp., 1986—. Served to 1st lt. USAR, 1959-67. Mem. ABA, Oreg. Bar Assn., Am. Mining Congress (bd. dirs. 1986—), Silver Inst. (bd. dirs. 1987—). Clubs: Arlington, Univ. Home: 28815 S Needy Rd Canby OR 97013 Office: Nerco Inc 111 SW Columbia St Ste 800 Portland OR 97201

DRUMMOND, MALCOLM MCALLISTER, electronics engineer; b. London, Eng., Sept. 22, 1937; came to U.S., 1966, naturalized, 1977; s. George James and Winifred Ethel (Jaye) D.; BS in Elec. Engring. with honors, City U., London, 1961; Registered profl. elec. engr. m. Linda Jerome Banning, May 25, 1968; 1 dau., Heather Lynn. Engr., Brit. Fgn. Office, Cheltenham, Eng., 1964-66; sr. engr. Gen. Dynamics Corp., Rochester, N.Y., 1966-70; tech. rep. Tymshare Inc., Rochester, 1970-72; project engr. Sybron Corp., Taylor Instrument Co., Rochester, 1972-85, Hampshire Instruments Corp. 1985—; dir. Care & Service Inc., 1982—, pres. 1986—. Christian Sci. minister for VA Hosp., 1974-80. Mem. IEEE (sr., chmn. Rochester sect. 1979—, past chmn. pension task force 1983-84, Region I PAC coordinator 1980-82, Area D chmn. 1982-85, ASIC seminar chmn. 1987—), Engrs. and Scientists Joint Com. on Pensions (vice chmn. 1983-84, IEEE rep. 1982-85), Mgmt. Soc. (past chmn.), Computer Soc. (past pres.), Instrument Soc. Am., Rochester Engring. Soc. (dir. 1979-83), Am. Mgmt. Assns., Inst. Elec. Engrs. (Gt. Brit.). Home: 60 Marberth Dr Henrietta NY 14467 Office: Hampshire Instruments Corp 10 Carlson Rd Rochester NY 14610

DRURY, JOHN E., waste management company executive; b. 1944; married. Owner, ptnr. Lakeville Sanitary Service, 1964-68; with Atlas Disposal Service, 1967-70; bought by Browning-Ferris Industries Inc., 1970; with Browning-Ferris Industries, Inc., Houston, 1970—, exec. v.p. waste systems div. and mem. mgmt. com., 1972-83, pres., chief operating officer, 1983—, also dir. Office: Browning-Ferris Industries Inc 14701 St Mary's Ln Houston TX 77079 *

DRURY, LEONARD LEROY, oil company executive; b. Gillespie, Ill., Nov. 5, 1928; s. Roy August and Regina Loretta (Finnegan) D.; m. Myra Lee Klunk, June 30, 1951; 1 child, Marilyn Jo Drury Chandler. BS in Indsl. Mgmt., St. Louis U., 1950; MBA in Mgmt., U. Houston, 1957. Mgr. systems program info. and computer services Shell Oil Co., N.Y.C., 1966-68; mgr. data processing info. and computer services Shell Oil Co., Menlo Park, Calif., 1968, mgr. acctg. info. and computer services, 1968-69; mgr. MTM bus. systems div. info. and computer services Shell Oil Co., N.Y.C. and Houston, 1969-71; mgr. planning info. and computer services Shell Oil Co., Houston, 1971-73, mgr. planning and tech. info. and computer services, 1973-75, asst. treas. fin., 1975-77, gen. mgr. info. and computer services, 1977-80; liaison Shell Ctr. London Shell Oil Co., 1980-81; gen. mgr. products fin. Shell Oil Co., Houston, 1981-83, v.p. purchasing and adminstrn. services, 1983-86, v.p. info. and computer services, 1986—. Mem. United Way, Houston, 1982—; bd. dirs. South Main Ctr. Assn., Houston, 1986—. Mem. Fin. Execs. Inst., Am. Petroleum Inst., West Houston Assn. (bd. dirs. 1984-88), Houston Bus. Council (pres. 1985-86), Sigma Iota Epsilon. Roman Catholic. Clubs: Lakeside Country, Petroleum (Houston). Home: 12414 Old Oaks Dr Houston TX 77024 Office: Shell Oil Co 900 Louisiana Houston TX 77252-2463

DRY, MICHAEL POWELL, investment company executive; b. Chgo., Dec. 5, 1943; s. Henry and Faye (Wizner) D.; B.S. in Econs., U. Wis.-Madison, 1965; m. Joan Eileen Zisook, June 24, 1965; children—Randal, Terrence. Registered rep. Freehling & Co., Chgo., 1965-72, gen. partner, 1972-86; spl. ltd. ptner. Cowen & Co., 1986—, br. mgr. Freehling div. Cowen & Co., 1986—. Contbg. editor Money Maker Mag., 1979-86. Allied mem. N.Y. Stock Exchange, 1972-86, Am. Stock Exchange, 1972-86; sr. registered options prin. Chgo. Bd. Options Exchange, 1973-86; assoc. person Commodity Futures Trading Commn.; mem. Chgo. Merc. Exchange, 1978-86, Internat. Monetary Market, 1978-86, Index and Option Market, 1982-86. Registered investment adviser SEC. Served with AUS, 1966-71. Mem. Nat. Assn. Securities Dealers (prin., exec. com. dist. 8 1983-86). Home: 2440 N Lakeview Ave Chicago IL 60614 Office: 190 S LaSalle St Chicago IL 60603

DRYDEN, ROBERT CHARLES, manufacturing company executive; b. Peoria, Ill., Jan. 17, 1936; s. Walter E. and Virginia Bell (Hammitt) D.; m. Judith Anne King, June 24, 1956; children: Jeffrey, John, James, Joel, Joanna. BEE, U. Ill., 1959; MBA, U. Chgo., 1977. Staff engr. Caterpillar Tractor Co., Peoria, 1960-64, gen. supr., 1964-66, supt., 1966-69, div. mgr., 1969-70; dept. head Caterpillar Tractor Co., San Leandro, Calif., 1970-72, plant mgr., 1972-75; plant mgr. Caterpillar Tractor Co., Aurora, Ill., 1976-79; mng. dir., pres. Caterpillar Belgium S.A., 1980-81; v.p. Caterpillar Inc., Peoria, 1982—; bd. dirs. Caterpillar World Trading Corp., Peoria, Caterpillar Indsl. Products, Caterpillar Logistics Svcs. Inc. Mem. adv. bd. YWCA, Peoria, 1987—; gov. Ill. Young Reps., 1965; bd. dirs. Jr. Achievement Bay Area, Oakland, Calif., 1973-75. Mem. Am. Mgmt. Assn. Republican. Presbyterian. Office: Caterpillar Inc 100 NE Adams St Peoria IL 61629-3495

DUAL, JOSEPH FREDERICK, JR., management consultant; b. Chgo., Apr. 10, 1942; s. Joseph Frederick Sr. and Dorthy Marie (Bowie) D.; m. Joyce Faye Metoyer, July 15, 1963 (div. July 1980); children: Leah B., Joseph F. III, Karen M. AABA, AA in Edn., No. Va. Community Coll., 1974; BBA, Am. U., 1981. Enlisted U.S. Navy, 1960, advanced through grades to chief warrent officer, ret., 1979; assoc. Booz, Allen & Hamilton Inc., Arlington, Va., 1981-85; pres. Dual & Assocs. Inc., Gaithersburg, Md., 1983—; chmn. bd. dirs. Dual & Assocs. Inc. Republican. Roman Catholic. Office: Dual & Assocs Inc 2101 Wilson Blvd Ste 600 Arlington VA 22201

DUARTE, RALPH MARTIN, data processing executive; b. Los Angeles, July 20, 1950; s. Ralph and Beatrice (DoRasario) D.; m. Linda Sue Conroy, Feb. 9, 1985; 1 child, Lauren McKenna. BBA, Loyola U., 1972; MBA, UCLA, 1975. Property mgr. McKay Devel., Beverly Hills, Calif., 1972-73; industry specialist IBM Corp., Los Angeles, 1975-80; pres. Response Mgmt., Inc., Laguna Hills, Calif., 1980—. Calif. Assn. Realtors fellow, 1974. Republican. Roman Catholic. Club: Orange County (Calif.) Fin. Office: Response Mgmt Inc 23221 S Pointe Dr Ste 102 Laguna Hills CA 92653

DUB, ANTHONY V., investment banker; b. N.Y.C., Nov. 7, 1949; s. Francis George and Nadine (Nunes) D. B.A., Princeton U., 1971. Assoc. The First Boston Corp., N.Y.C., 1971-76, v.p., 1977-81, mng. dir., 1982—. Clubs: Piping Rock (Locust Valley, N.Y.); Racquet & Tennis, The Links (N.Y.C.). Office: The First Boston Corp Park Ave Pla New York NY 10055

DU BAIN, MYRON, diversified industry executive; b. Cleve., June 3, 1923; s. Edward D. and Elaine (Byrne) Du B.; m. Alice Elaine Hilliker, Sept. 30, 1944; children—Cynthia Lynn, Donald Aldous. BA, U. Calif., Berkeley, 1946; grad. exec. program, Stanford U., 1967. Pres., chief exec. officer Fireman's Fund Ins. Cos., 1974-75, chmn., pres., chief exec. officer, 1975-81; chmn., pres., chief exec. officer Fireman's Fund Corp., 1981-82; Pres., chief exec. officer, dir. Amfac, Inc., San Francisco, 1983-85; chmn. SRI Internat., Menlo Park, Calif., 1985—; bd. dirs. Pacific Telesis, SRI Internat., Carter Hawley Hale Stores Inc., First Interstate Bancorp., Potlatch Corp., Transamerica Corp., Chronicle Broadcasting Co. Contbg. author: Property and Casualty Handbook, 1960, The Practical Lawyer, 1962. Bd. dirs. San

Francisco Opera; bd. dirs., past chmn. Invest-In-Am., Inc.; chmn. bd. dirs. James Irvine Found.; sr. mem. Conf. Bd. With USNR, 1943-46, 50-52. Mem. Bohemian Club (San Francisco), Pacific Union Club (San Francisco), Calif. Tennis Club (San Francisco), Links Club (N.Y.C.), Lagunitas Country Club. Republican. Office: SRI Internat 1 Bush St 11th Fl San Francisco CA 94104

DUBBS, ROBERT MORTON, lawyer, health services company executive; b. Cleve., Aug. 31, 1943; s. Ben and Florence Audrey Dubbs; m. Judith Singer, July 3, 1965; children: Lisa Jacqueline, Nicole Leigh. BS in Econs., U. Pa., 1965; JD, U. Mich., 1968, MBA, 1968. Bar: Pa. 1968. Atty. U.S. Steel Corp., Pitts., 1968-69; assoc. gen. counsel Systems Capital Corp., Phila., 1970; chief counsel, also other legal positions Sun Co., Inc., Radnor, Pa., 1971-84; gen. counsel, corp. sec. Universal Health Svcs., Inc., King of Prussia, Pa., 1984—, Universal Health Realty Income Trust, King of Prussia, 1984—. Mem. ABA, Pa. Bar. Assn., Phila. Bar Assn., Fedn. Am. Health Systems (bd. dirs.,v.p. 1987—). Home: 20 Levering Circle Bala Cynwyd PA 19004 Office: Universal Corp Ctr 367 S Gulph Rd King of Prussia PA 19406

DUBE, JOHN, retired lawyer; b. Montreal, Que., Can., July 14, 1899; came to U.S., 1926, naturalized, 1945; s. Joseph Edmond and Marie Louise (Quintal) D.; m. Liliane Hibbert, 1981; 1 son by previous marriage, John Edmund. B.L., B.S., Montreal U., 1920, B.C.L., 1923; licentiate in Civil Law, Paris U., 1924; postgrad., U. Oxford, 1925. Bar: Montreal 1925, N.Y. 1945, apptd. king's counsel 1941, now Queen's counsel 1952, U.S. Supreme Ct. 1960. Assoc. Coudert Bros., N.Y.C. and Paris office, 1926-32, Nice, France, 1933-40; practice N.Y.C., 1945-89; Past pres. Le Moulin Legumes Corp., Wilmington, Del.; past v.p. Bengue, Inc., Union City, N.J.; consul of Monaco, N.Y.C., 1949-52; now consul gen.; dep. permanent observer for Monaco at UN, 1956-71, permanent observer, 1971—. Past trustee Soc. Rehab. Facially Disfigured; co-founder and co-comdr. Anglo-Am. Ambulance Corps., Cannes, France, 1939-40. Decorated Comdr. Order of Grimaldi (Monaco). Mem. Union Interalliée (Paris), Assn. Bar City of N.Y., ABA, Internat. Bar Assn., Am. Fgn. Law Assn., Am. Soc. Internat. Law, Soc. Fgn. Consuls, Société de Legislation Comparee. Clubs: Rockefeller Ctr. Luncheon, Sky (assoc.). Home: 18 Royal Palm Way Apt 309 Boca Raton FL 33432

DUBÉ-KASTNER, CHERYL ANN, insurance analyst; b. Bklyn., Aug. 22, 1963; d. Arthur and Marion (Thomas) Dubé; m. George Anthony Kastner, June 28, 1986. AAS in Computer Applications, NYU, 1988. Asst. mgr. Fayva Shoes subs. Moorse Shoe Corp., Ridgewood, N.Y., 1981-82; sec. M. Castellvi Inc., N.Y.C., 1982-83; reinsurance technician Sentry Reinsurance, N.Y.C., 1983; info. specialist Kidder, Peabody & Co., N.Y.C., 1983-85; syndicate acct. Drexel Burnham Lambert, N.Y.C., 1985-86; sr. analyst Cameron & Colby Co., Inc., N.Y.C., 1986—. Asst. editor: (mag.) Hocus Pocus, 1980. Mem. Nat. Assn. Female Execs. Republican. Office: Cameron & Colby Co Inc 7 World Trade Ctr New York NY 10048

DUBERCHIN, BARRY ALLAN, electronics executive, data processing executive; b. Chgo., June 25, 1944; s. Jack and Vivienne Irma (Witz) D.; m. Gail Ann Weinstein, July 17, 1987; children: Steven Robert, Kadmiel Yakov Stampfer, Karen Joy. BS, Calif. State U., Long Beach, 1967; MBA, Loyola U., Chgo., 1972. Programmer U.S. Steel Corp., San Francisco and Chgo., 1967-70; sr. analyst Container Corp. of Am., Chgo., 1970-74; mgr. devel. Motorola, Inc., Schaumburg, Ill., 1974—. Vol. Schaumburg Teen Ctr.; vol. fundraiser Labor Day Com., Schaumburg; treas. YMCA Parent and Children Orgn., Schaumburg. Home: 704 E Thames Dr Schaumburg IL 60193 Office: Motorola Inc 1301 E Algonquin Rd Schaumburg IL 60196

DUBERG, JOHN EDWARD, aeronautical engineer, educator; b. N.Y.C., Nov. 30, 1917; s. Charles Augustus and Mary (Blake) D.; m. Mary Louise Andrews, June 11, 1943; children—Mary Jane, John Andrews. B.S. in Engring, Manhattan Coll., 1938; M.S., Va. Poly. Inst., 1940; Ph.D., U. Ill., 1948; grad., Fed. Exec. Inst., 1971. Engr. Cauldwell-Wingate Builders, N.Y.C., 1938-39; rsch. asst. U. Ill., 1940-43; rsch. engr. NASA, 1943-46; chief structures Langley Labs. NASA, Hampton, Va., 1948-56; mem. staff Langley Rsch. Ctr. NASA, 1959-79, assoc. dir. Langley Rsch. Ctr., 1968-79; rsch. engr. Standard Oil Co. Ind., 1946-48; with Ford Aeros., Glendale, Calif., 1956-57; mem. faculty U. Ill., 1957-59; rsch. prof. aeros. George Washington U., 1979—; dir. Joint Inst. Advanced Flight Scis., 1971-79; mem. materials adv. bd. Nat. Acad. Sci., 1950; mem. subcom. profl. and sci. manpower Dept. Labor, 1971; mem. indsl. adv. com. U. Va., 1978-80; pres.'s adv. coun. Christopher Newport Coll., 1973-76, vice chmn., 1976; dir. Newport News Savs. Bank. Contbr. articles to profl. jours., chpts. to books. Trustee United Way Va. Peninsula, 1963-82; chmn. Hampton Roads chpt. ARC, 1984-86. Fellow AIAA (DeFlorez award 1977), AAAS; mem. Va. Acad. Scis., N.Y. Acad. Scis., Am. Soc. Engring. Edn. (dir.), Engrs. Club Peninsula (pres. 1955), Soc. Engring. Scis. (dir.), James River Country Club, Rotary (pres. Newport News chpt. 1967-68). Episcopalian. Home: 4 Museum Dr Newport News VA 23601 Office: GWU/JIAFS NASA Langley Rsch Ctr M/S 269 Hampton VA 23665

DUBIN, HARRY NATHAN, management consultant, psychology educator; b. Phila., July 18, 1919; s. Samuel and Ida (Weiss) D.; m. Gertrude Brook, Sept. 19, 1947; children: Rina, Diane. BS in Edn., Temple U., 1948, MEd, 1951, EdD, 1961. Lic. psychologist. Prof. psychology Kean Coll., Union, N.J., 1961-88; pres. Ctr. Organizational and Personal Effectiveness, Inc., Elizabeth, N.J., 1967—. Author: (with others) C.O.P.I.N.G. Successfully, 1980, (with others) Collegefields: From Delinquency to Freedom, 1980 (Disting. Award for Excellence, Am. Assn. Colls. Tchr. Edn.); contbr. numerous articles to profl. jours. Sgt. U.S. Army, 1941-45, ETO. Fellow Am. Assn. Mental Deficiency, John Dewey Soc.; mem. Cert. Cons. Internat. (charter mem.), Am. Psychol. Assn., Am. Soc. Tng. and Devel. Home: 580 Sayre Dr Princeton NJ 08540 Office: COPE Inc 55 W Jersey St Elizabeth NJ 07202

DUBIN, JAMES MICHAEL, lawyer; b. N.Y.C., Aug. 20, 1946; s. Benjamin and Irene (Wasserman) D.; m. Susan Hope Schraub, Mar. 15, 1981; children: Alexander Philip, Elizabeth Joy. BA, U. Pa., 1968; JD, Columbia U., 1974. Bar: N.Y. 1975, D.C. 1984, U.S. Dist. Ct. (so. and ea. dist.) N.Y. 1975, U.S. Ct. Appeals (2d cir.) 1975. Assoc. Paul, Weiss, Rifkind, Wharton & Garrison, N.Y.C., 1974-82, ptnr. 1982—; FOJP Svc. Corp. Bd. editors Columbia Law Rev., 1973-74. Bd. dirs. YM-YWHA of Mid-Westchester, Scarsdale, N.Y., 1983-86, chmn. budget and fin. com., 1984-85; chmn. Cable Oversight Com., Harrison, N.Y., 1983-85; bd. edn. Jewish Community Ctr. of Harrison. With U.S. Army, 1969-71. Mem. ABA, Assn. of Bar of City of N.Y., Am. Arbitration Assn. (comml. panel arbitrators 1989—), Sunningdale Country Club (bd. govs. 1989—), Hemisphere Club, Phi Delta Phi. Office: Paul Weiss Rifkind Wharton & Garrison 1285 Ave of Americas New York NY 10019

DUBIN, MICHAEL, financial executive; b. Louisville, Sept. 20, 1943; s. Samuel Sanford and Lydia Roth (Symons) D.; m. Randi Louise Thulin, June 5, 1982; children: Krista Alexandra, Erika Ashley. BA, Yale U., 1966; DBA, Harvard U., 1973. Asst. mgr. Brown Bros. Harriman & Co., N.Y.C., 1973-74, dep. mgr., 1973-75, mgr., 1975-82; exec. v.p. GFTA Services Corp., N.Y.C., 1983-86, pres., chief exec. officer, 1987—; pres., chmn. bd. dirs. Sectrend, Inc., Chgo.; bd. dirs. Firecom, Inc., Queens; lectr. in field. Author: Foreign Acquisitions and the Growth of the Multinational Firm, 1981; contbr. articles to profl. jours. Treas. Sports Village, Sherbourne, Vt., 1987—. Carnegie Endowment fellow, 1972-73; Ctr. Internat. Affairs scholar, 1972. Mem. Chgo. Mercantile Exchange, Am. Econ. Assn., Orgn. Internat. Bus., St. Elmo Soc., Broad St. Club, Yale Club, East Hampton Yacht Club. Home: 200 E 71st St New York NY 10021 Office: GFTA Svcs Corp 375 Park Ave Ste 2601 New York NY 10152

DUBIN, STEVEN HUGH, financial analyst; b. Bklyn., N.Y., Sept. 22, 1948; s. Edward Paul and Florence A. (Newman) D.; 1 child, Elizabeth Brynne; m. Merrie Joy Leighton, Oct. 1, 1988. BA, Bucknell U., 1970; MS in Taxation, Bentley Coll., 1980. Assoc. Sutton & Towne, N.Y.C., 1971-74, Fidelity Fin. Corp., Wellesley, Mass., 1975-77; prin. Williams & Dubin Inc., Quincy, Mass., 1978—; cons. Capital Analysts of N.E. Inc., Quincy, 1978—; bd. dirs. Boston Post Prodn. Studio Inc. Contbr. articles to profl. jours. Nat. Merit scholar. Mem. Boston Estate Bus. Planning Council, N.J. SBA, South Shore Estate and Bus. Planning Council (pres. 1988—). Jewish. Club: Chief Exec. Officers Boston. Home: 195 Old County Rd Lincoln MA 01773 Office: Williams & Dubin Inc 1266 Furnace Brook Pkwy Quincy MA 02169

DUBOIS, PETER ARNOTT, health science facility executive; b. Oakland, Calif., Nov. 24, 1947; s. Clifford W. and Phyllis G. (Cady) D.; m. Joan FitzGerald, Aug. 14, 1976. BA with honors, Amherst Coll., 1968; JD, Harvard U., 1974. Ptnr. Arthur Bolton Assocs., Sacramento, Calif., 1969-76; exec. dir. Calif. Mental Health Assn., Sacramento, 1977-79; v.p. adminstrn. MDT Corp., Los Angeles, 1979-82; dep. asst. dir. Los Angeles County Dept. Mental Health, Los Angeles, 1982-86; chief exec. officer Med. Group of Children's Hosp., Los Angeles, 1986—. Bd. dirs. Children's Research Inst. of Calif., Sacramento, 1982-86. Mem. Health Care Fin. Mgmt., Am. Mgmt. Assn., Med. Group Mgmt. Assn., Med. Adminstrn. of Calif., Amherst Alumni Club. Clubs: Harvard. Office: Med Group Childrens Hosp 4661 Sunset Blvd Los Angeles CA 90027

DUBOIS, SANDRA KAYE, marketing executive; b. Kalamazoo, Mich., June 22, 1961; d. Carl Wilbur and Helen Nadene (Alders) Lang; m. Martin James DuBois, Apr. 13, 1985. BS, Western Mich. U., 1983; MS, U. Iowa, 1984. Tchr.'s aide Dept. Stats. and Actuarial Sci. U. Iowa, Iowa City, 1983-84; mkting. research analyst Consumers Power Co., Jackson, Mich., 1985—. Republican. Mem. United Pentecostal Ch. Office: Consumers Powers Co 212 W Michigan N-912N Jackson MI 49203

DUBOUX, DENNIS VINCENT, sales engineer; b. Columbus, Ohio, Aug. 6, 1956; s. Robert Frank and Betty Lucille (Butcher) DuB.; m. Patricia Jane Hulik, May 17, 1986. BA, Ohio No. U., 1978; MBA, Bowling Green State U., 1985. Assoc. market planning specialist Westinghouse, Lima, Ohio, 1978-79, asst. sales engr., 1979-81; sales engr. Chgo., 1981-85, Telemachanique, Inc., Arlington Heights, 1985-87, Siemens Energy and Automation, Schaumburg, Ill., 1987—. Mem. Park Ridge Hist. Soc., Art Inst. Chgo., Omicron Delta Epsilon. Republican. Methodist. Home: 1025 Prairie Ave Park Ridge IL 60068 Office: Siemens Energy and Automation 1111 Plaza Dr Schaumburg IL 60173

DUBROW, MARSHA ANN, high technology company executive, composer; b. Newark, Dec. 27, 1948; d. Leo and Rose (Haberman) Dubrow; m. Daniel Leon Chaykin, Jan. 17, 1970 (div. 1985); 1 child, Alexander; m. David Lorin Rosenberg, July 3, 1988; 1 step-child, Oliver. BA cum laude, U. Pa., 1970; MA, NYU, 1975; MFA, Princeton U., 1977, postgrad., 1977-78, 81-82; postgrad., Tufts U., 1987, Am. Women's Econ. Devel. Corp. Inst., 1987-88, Leadership Am., 1988. Prodn. coord. Children's TV Workshop, N.Y.C., 1970-73; instr. Princeton (N.J.) U., 1976-78; mgr. mktg. communications, ops., human resources AT&T/Techs., Inc., Morristown, N.J., 1978-80; dir. mktg. and ops. Acadia Communications, N.Y.C., 1980-83; dir. planning and mktg. Access Methods, Inc., N.Y.C., 1984-85; prin. Marsha Dubrow Assocs., East Rutherford, N.J., 1981—; pres., chief exec. officer Technolog, Inc., East Rutherford, N.J., 1985—. Mem. program com., life mem. bus. and profl. group Nat. Coun. Jewish Women, Essex County, N.J., 1983—; mem. The Gathering, Hole Theater, Montclair, 1987—. Recipient Theodore Presser award U. Pa., 1970; William C. Langley fellow NYU, 1974, Princeton U. fellow, 1976-78, Josephine de Karman fellow Aerojet-Gen. Corp., 1981. Mem. NAFE, Am. Women Entrepreneurs, Am. Mgmt. Assn., Leadership Am. Alumnae Assn. Home: 34 Marion Rd Upper Montclair NJ 07043 Office: Technolog 1 Maple St East Rutherford NJ 07073

DUBS, ROBIN MICHAEL, general contractor, property developer; b. Elgin, Ill., Aug. 28, 1961; s. Alexander and Catherine (Schneider) D.; m. Theresa Marie Shanley, June 11, 1983; children: Whitney Marie, Brady Michael. BS in Fin., Roosevelt U., 1986. Fin. analyst Allstate Ins. Co., Northbrook, Ill., 1979-84; pres. The Dubs Co., South Barrington, Ill., 1984—, Whitney Properties, South Barrington, 1988—; assoc. Country Wood Realty, South Barrington, 1988—. Office: 39 S Barrington Rd South Barrington IL 60010

DUBUC, ANDRÉ, utility company financial executive; b. Montreal, Que., Can., Sept. 30, 1945; s. John René and Madeleine (Anderson) D.; m. Lucie Beaudoin, July 18, 1970; children: Etienne, Julien. BS in Econs., U. Montreal, 1967; MA in Econs., U. Ottawa, 1975. Chartered fin. analyst. Analyst Bank of Can., Ottawa, Ont., 1969-74; securities officer Bank of Can., Ottawa, 1974-75; mgr. pension funds Hydro-Quebec, Montreal, 1975-82, treas., 1982-85, v.p. fin., treas., 1985—; treas. Hydro-Quebec Internat., 1979—; bd. dirs. Somarex Inc. Mem. Inst. Chartered Fin. Inst., Swiss-Can. C. of C. (v.p. 1987—), St. James Club (Montreal). Office: Hydro-Que, 75 Rene Levesque Blvd W, Montreal, PQ Canada H2Z 1A4

DUCEMAN, MARK EUGENE, food service executive; b. Shamokin, Pa., Oct. 23, 1960; s. John Albert and Margaret Mary (Deeben) D. AS in Mech. Engring., Pa. State U., 1980, BA in Urban Planning, 1983. Asst. planner, engr. Northumberland County Planning Dept., Sunbury, Pa., 1983; planner Pa. Dept. Tranps., Harrisburg, 1984-86; real estate cons. Shamokin Enterprises, Inc., Albany, N.Y., 1987; pres. Jambion Devels, Inc., Toronto, Ont., Can., 1988—; mgr., owner Ben & Jerry's Homemade Ice Cream Franchise, Toronto, 1988—. Mem. Am. Planning Assn., Wilderness Canoe Assn., Sierra Club. Democrat. Methodist. Home and Office: 225 Crestwood Rd, Thornhill, ON Canada L4J 1A8

DUCHOW, FRANK RONALD, insurance company executive; b. Sheboygan, Wis., Nov. 10, 1948; s. Frank Marvin Paul and Emilie (Weber) D.; m. Ann Wille Laiblin, June 25, 1977; 1 child, Emilie. BA in Polit. Sci., Lawrence U., 1973. Mgr. of pub. events Lawrence U., Appleton, Wis., 1973-76; head of news, sports info. Lawrence U., 1976-79; dir. of pub. rels. U. Dubuque, Iowa, 1979-84; sales, registered rep. N.Y. Life, Dubuque, 1984-89; owner Duchow Ins. and Fin. Svcs., Dubuque, 1989—. Author of numerous articles in field. Active United Way, 1980—, pub. rels. com. mem., Dubuque, 1980-88. Mem. Nat. Assn. Life Underwriters, Iowa Assn. Life Underwriters, Dubuque Assn. Life Underwriters (chmn. pub. rels. 1985—), Optimists (chmn. pub. rels. 1987—). Methodist. Home: 247 Clarke Dr Dubuque IA 52001 Office: Duchow Ins and Fin Svcs Inn Pla 3430 Dodge St Dubuque IA 52001

DUCKWORTH, W. JOSEPH, real estate developer; b. Phila., Nov. 14, 1948; s. Joseph Carr and Wanda (Roskowski) D.; children by previous marriage : Jason Mathew, Christopher Thomas; m. Loretta Grace Ciocco, Dec. 5, 1981; children: David Ginsberg, Sheara Ginsberg. BS, Carnegie Mellon U., 1970; MBA, U. Pa., 1972. Cost engr. Sun Oil Co., Phila., 1970-72; cons. Day & Zimmerman, Phila., 1972-76; asst. to pres. Toll Bros. Inc., Horsham, Pa., 1976-78; v.p. devel. Toll Bros. Inc., Horsham, 1978-82, exec. v.p./chief operating officer, 1982-85; pres./chief exec. officer Realen Homes (formerly Realty Engring. Homes), Berwyn, Pa., 1985—; bd. dirs. Am. S.W. Fin. Corp., Phoenix, Bucks-Montgomery Builders Assocs., Horsham, Robertson Bros., Bloomfield Hills, Mich., Phila. Found. Arch. Mem. Urban Land Inst., Young Pres. Orgn., Carnegie Mellon Phila. (pres. Alumni 1973, chmn. fund raising, 1974), Andrew Carnegie Soc. Republican. Office: Realen Homes 1235 Westlakes Dr #350 Box 1342 Berwyn PA 19312

DUCLOS, KEITH FRANCIS, academic program director; b. Springfield, Mass., May 22, 1959; s. Francis Richard and Judith Ann (Minie) D.; m. Barbara Jean VandenBerghe, Oct. 3, 1987. BSBA, Western New Eng. Coll., 1982; MBA, Cornell U., 1986. Asst. controller Belmont Laundry, Springfield, Mass., 1982-84; project mgr. space infared telescope facility Cornell U., Ithaca, N.Y., 1986—. Republican. Methodist. Office: Cornell U Space Infrared Telescope Facilty 224 Space Sci Bldg Ithaca NY 14853-6801

DUDDLES, CHARLES WELLER, food company executive; b. Cadillac, Mich., Mar. 31, 1940; s. Dwight Irving and Bertha (Taylor) D.; m. Judith Marie Robinson, June 23, 1962; children: Paul, Steven, Lisa. B.S., Ferris State U., 1961. C.P.A. Mich., Mo. Audit mgr. Price Waterhouse & Co., Battle Creek, Mich., 1961-72; mgr. gen. acctg. Ralston Purina Co., St. Louis, 1973-77, dir. spl. acctg. services, 1977-79; v.p., controller Foodmaker, Inc., San Diego, 1979-81, sr. v.p. fin. and adminstrn., chief fin. officer, 1981-87, sr. v.p., chief fin. officer, 1988, exec. v.p., chief fin. officer, chief adminstrv. officer, 1988—. Mem. Fin. Execs. Inst., Nat. Assn. Accts., Am. Inst. C.P.A.s. Republican. Presbyterian. Lodge: Rotary (San Diego). Home: 1942 Hidden Mesa Rd El Cajon CA 92019 Office: Foodmaker Inc 9330 Balboa Ave San Diego CA 92123

DUDEK, HENRY THOMAS, management consultant; b. Queens, N.Y., Dec. 29, 1929; s. Wojciech and Magdalena (Swiader) D.; m. Olga Waranitsky, June 14, 1953; children: Kathryn, Nancy, Linda, Andrew, Henryk. BBA, CCNY, 1955. Acctg. mgr. A.D.T. Co., N.Y.C., 1948-54; asst. controller Dancer Fitzgerald Sample, Inc., N.Y.C., 1955-60; chief fin. officer Wunderman Ricotta & Kline, Inc., N.Y.C., 1961-69, Van Brunt & Co., N.Y.C., 1970; controller, stockholder Compton Advt., Inc., N.Y.C., 1971; pres., chief exec. officer Henry T. Dudek & Assocs., Inc., Floral Park, N.Y., 1972—; frequent speaker on finance and advt. Mem. Advt. Agy. Fin. Mgmt. Assn. (bd. dirs.). Roman Catholic. Home: 90 Beech St Floral Park NY 11001 Office: PO Box 478 Floral Park NY 11002

DUDLEY, ALFRED EDWARD, corporate executive; b. Fremont, Ohio, Sept. 12, 1928; s. John Peter and Mary Elizabeth (Oaly) D.; m. Lois Delene Murphy, July 3, 1949; children: John Alan, Richard. BS, Bowling Green U., 1951. Gen. mgr. ops. Union Carbide Corp., N.Y.C., 1972-75, v.p., gen. mgr. home prodns., 1975-78; v.p. ops. Union Carbide Corp., Danbury, Conn., 1978-86; chmn., pres., chief exec. officer First Brands Corp., Danbury, 1986—, also bd. dirs. Mem. Silver Spring Club, Foxfire Club (Naples, Fla.). Republican. Roman Catholic. Office: 1st Brands Corp 83 Wooster Heights Rd Danbury CT 06813

DUDLEY, DENNIS WAYNE, manufacturing executive; b. Eldora, Iowa, Nov. 12, 1951; s. Wayne Carroll and Norma Jean (Johnson) D.; m. Julia Marie Brunken, May 27, 1978; children: Nicole, Ryan, Kristin. Student, Iowa State U., 1969-72. Area distbr. O's Gold Seed Co., Parkersburg, Iowa, 1972-81; exec. v.p. Top Air Mfg., Parkersburg, 1981—, also bd. dirs. Mem. Theta Xi. Republican. Lutheran. Home: 1101 Hwy 20 Parkersburg IA 50665 Office: Top Air Mfg Hwy 20 and Dudley Rd Parkersburg IA 50665

DUDLEY, GEORGE WILLIAM, JR., corporate executive; b. Mullins, S.C., Apr. 21, 1931; s. George William Dudley Sr. and Annie Grace (Bethea) D.; m. Katherine Clark Lewis, Aug. 7, 1957 (div. Nov. 1980); children: Skip, Kari, Leigh. BA in Econs., Presby. Coll., 1953; MA in Guidance and Counseling, U. Ala., 1962. Assoc. dir. Florence-Darlington Tech., Florence, S.C., 1963-66; dir. Horry-Georgetown Tech., Conway, S.C., 1966-74; assoc. exec. dir. S.C. State Bd. Tech. and Computer Edn., Columbia, 1974-76, interim exec. dir., 1976, exec. dir., 1976-86; cons. and dir. contract services Daniel Mgmt. Ctr. U. S.C., Columbia, 1987—; speaker confs. and seminars on tech. edn. and econs. devel., 1980-83. Contbr. articles to profl. jours. Served to 2d lt. U.S. Army, 1953-54. Named Boss of Yr. Midlands Am. Bus. Women's Assn., 1979, Tech. Educator of Yr., S.C. Tech. Edn. Assn., 1980; recipient Presl. Medallion, Horry-Georgetown Tech, 1984, A. Wade Martin award, 1986; Order of the Palmetto, 1986. Mem. Am. Indsl. Devel. Council, S.C. Indsl. Devel. Council (bd. dirs.), So. Indsl. Devel. Council, Nat. Council State Dirs. of Community and Jr. Colls., Nat. Assn Industry Edn. Cooperation (bd.dirs.), S.C. Pvt. Industry Council. Office: U SC Daniel Mgmt Ctr Unit D 600 Woodrow St Columbia SC 29205

DUDLEY, JAMES GATEWOOD, financial consultant; b. Augusta, Ga., Jan. 26, 1955; s. James Crawford and Freddie Lelia (Gammage) D.; m. Fran Easterlin, July 28, 1979. Assoc. in Bus. Adminstrn., Ga. Mil. Coll., 1975; BBA, Ga. Coll., 1978. Cert. fin. planner. Rep. IDS/Am. Express, Birmingham, Ala., 1981-83, Prudential Life Ins. Co., Birmingham, 1983-86; fin. cons. 1st Fin. Group, Birmingham, 1986—. Mem. Inst. Cert. Fin. Planners (treas. Ala. chpt. 1987-88), Internat. Assn. Fin. Planning (pres. Ala. chpt. 1984-85), Toastmasters Club, Civitan Club (bd. dirs. 1986-87). Office: 1st Fin Group Bank for Savs Bldg 16th Fl Birmingham AL 35203

DUDLEY, KENNETH EUGENE, manufacturing company executive; b. Bellville, Ohio, Nov. 26, 1937; s. Kenneth Olin and Ethel Elizabeth (Poorman) D.; m. Judith Ann Brown, Apr. 15, 1972; children: Camaron J. McCluggage, Kenneth Alan. Inventory control mgr. Gorman-Rupp Industries, Bellville, 1958-67; prodn. mgr. Gorman-Rupp Industries, 1967-69, mgr. data processing, 1969-74, cost mgr., 1974-78, contr., 1978-82; treas., chief fin. officer Gorman-Rupp Co., Mansfield, Ohio, 1983—. With USAF, 1962-63. Republican. Lutheran. Home: 1375 Rouyal Oak Dr Mansfield OH 44906 Office: Gorman-Rupp Co PO Box 1217 Mansfield OH 44901

DUDLEY, PERRY, JR., electronics executive; b. New Haven, June 5, 1928; s. Perry and Ella (Leach) D.; m. Judith Virginia Hall, Jan 4, 1958 (div. July 1980); children: Bruce Lawrence, Virginia Barbara. BSEE, Purdue U., 1952; MBA, U. Santa Clara, 1966. Sales engr. Reliance Electric Co., Cleve. and Los Angeles, 1952-60, GTE Sylvania, Burlingame, Calif., 1960-65; sr. applications engr. Varian Assocs., Palo Alto, Calif., 1965-68; product mgr. Ampex Corp., Redwood City, Calif., 1968-70; program mgr. Genesys Systems, Inc., 1972-73; indsl. real estate broker, salesman 1974-80; program mgr. Dalmo Victor Ops., Bell Airospace Div., Textron, 1980-85; mktg. and program mgr. Loral Data Systems, San Diego, 1986-88; instr. mktg. and mgmt. San Francisco State U., 1982. Pres. Young Rep. Club, Pasadena, Calif., 1959; precinct capt. Rep. Party, Menlo Park, Calif., 1961-72. Served with USN, 1946-48. Mem. Nat. Assn. of Mgmt., Assn. of Old Crows, Purdue Alumni Club (pres. 1959), Mensa, Phi Gamma Delta. Presbyterian. Home: 3120 Morning Way La Jolla CA 92037

DUENSING, JAMES ARLIN, financial consultant; b. Marysville, Kans., May 10, 1959; s. Arlin Henry and Marcine Ruth (Rogge) D.; m. Julie Lynn Aldridge, Sept. 6, 1986. BS in Fin., Kans. State U., 1981; postgrad., Bradley U., 1984-85. Orders analyst Caterpillar Am. Co., Peoria, Ill., 1981-82, fin. analyst treasury dept., 1982-83; sr. credit analyst Caterpillar Fin. Svc. Corp., Peoria, 1984; sr. fin. rep. N.Am. Comml. div. Caterpillar, Inc., Peoria, 1985-86; mgr. ter. sales Caterpillar Fin. Svcs. Corp., Atlanta, 1986-88; engine merchandising cons. Caterpillar Fin. Svcs. Corp., Peoria, 1988—. Advisor Jr. Achievement, Peoria, 1981-82. Republican. Presbyterian. Home: 6309 Heather Oak Dr Peoria IL 61615 Office: Caterpillar Fin Svcs Corp 100 NE Adams St Peoria IL 61615

DUERINCK, LOUIS T., railroad executive; b. Chgo., Aug. 1, 1929; s. Aloys L. and Thais E. (De Backer) D.; m. Patricia A. Bird, June 27, 1953; children: Louis M., Kathleen M., Kevin F., Mark V., Lynn P., Brian T., Paul S. Student, U. Notre Dame, 1947-48; JD, DePaul U., Chgo., 1952. Bar: Ill. 1952. Commerce atty. N.Y. Cen. R.R., Chgo., 1955-65; gen. atty. Nat. Ry. Labor Conf., Chgo., 1967-68; with C&NW Ry. Co., Chgo., 1965-67, 68—; sr. v.p. law and real estate C&NW Transp. Co., 1979-83, sr. v.p. traffic, 1983-88, sr. v.p., 1988—. Served with AUS, 1952-55. Mem. ABA, ICC Practitioners Assn., Ill. Bar Assn., Chgo. Ry. Club. Roman Catholic. Clubs: Glen Oak Country; Tower (Chgo.), Met. (Chgo.). Home: 718 Midwest Club Oak Brook IL 60521 Office: Chgo & Northwestern Transp Co 165 N Canal St Chicago IL 60606

DUES, JOHN JOSEPH, real estate executive; b. Greenville, Ohio, Jan. 22, 1948; s. Joseph John and Luella (Simon) D.; m. Janet Elizabeth Fanning, June 10, 1978; children: Elizabeth Marie, John Joseph, Christopher Todd. BBA, U. Notre Dame, 1970; MBA, U. Dayton, 1976. Indsl. appraisal Am. Appraisal Assocs., Dayton, Ohio, 1971-74; v.p. The Dues Cos., Dayton, 1974-76; dir. corp. real estate The Mead Corp., Dayton, 1976—; pres. M-T Properties, 1985—, Mead Realty Group, 1986—. Bd. dirs. Vis. Nurses Assn., Dayton, 1982, Met. YMCA Dayton, Downtown Dayton Assn. (vice-chmn.); mem. bd. advisors coll. bus. adminstrn. Wright State U. Mem. Indsl. Devel. Research Council (bd. dirs.), Am. Inst. Corp. Asset Mgmt. (bd. dirs.), Urban Land Inst., Indsl. Real Estate Mgrs. Council, Soc. Indsl. Realtors, Nat. Assn. Corp. Real Estate Execs. Roman Catholic. Lodge: Rotary. Home: 500 Stonehaven Kettering OH 45429 Office: The Mead Corp Courthouse Pla NE Dayton OH 45463

DUESENBERG, RICHARD WILLIAM, lawyer; b. St. Louis, Dec. 10, 1930; s. (John August) Hugo and Edna Marie (Warmann) D.; m. Phyllis Evelyn Buehner, Aug. 7, 1955; children: Karen, Daryl, Mark, David. BA, Valparaiso U., 1951, JD, 1953; LLM, Yale U., 1956. Bar: Mo. 1953. Prof. law NYU, N.Y.C., 1956-62, dir. law ctr. publs., 1960-62; sr. atty. Monsanto Co., St. Louis, 1963-70, asst. gen. counsel, asst. sec., 1975-77, sr. v.p., sec., gen. counsel, 1977—; dir. law Monsanto Textiles Co., St. Louis, 1971-75;

corp. sec. Fisher Controls Co., Marshalltown, Iowa, 1969-71, Olympia Industries, Spartanburg, S.C., 1974-75; vis. prof. law U. Mo., 1970-71; faculty Banking Sch. South, La. State U., 1967-83. Author: (with Lawrence P. King) Sales and Bulk Transfers Under the Uniform Commercial Code, 2 vols, 1966, rev., 1984, New York Law of Contracts, 3 vols, 1964, Missouri Forms and Practice Under the Uniform Commercial Code, 2 vols, 1966; editor: Ann. Survey of Am. Law, NYU, 1961-62; mem. bd. contbg. editors and advisors: Corp. Law Rev, 1977-86; contbr. articles to law revs., jours. Mem. lawyers adv. council NAM, Washington, 1980, Adminstrv. Conf. of U.S., 1980-86, legal adv. com. N.Y. Stock Exchange, 1983-87, corp. law dept. adv. council Practising Law Inst., 1982; bd. dirs. Bach Soc. St. Louis, 1965-86, pres. 1973-77; bd. dirs. Valparaiso U., 1977—, chmn. bd. visitors Law Sch. 1966—, Luth. Charities Assn., 1984-87, vice chmn. 1986-87; bd. dirs. Luth Med. Ctr., St. Louis, 1973-82, vice chmn., 1975-80; bd. dirs. The Nat. Jud. Coll., 1984—, St. Louis Symphony, 1988—, The Opera Theatre of St. Louis, 1988—. Served with U.S. Army, 1953-55. Named Disting. Alumnus Valparaiso U., 1976. Fellow Am. Bar Found.; mem. ABA (chmn. com. uniform comml. code 1976-79, council sect. corp., banking and bus. law 1979-83, sec. 1983-84, chmn. 1986-87), Mo. Bar Assn., Am. Law Inst., Mont Pelerin Soc., Nat. Jud. Coll. (bd. dirs. 1984—), Order of Coif, Bach Soc., Am. Soc. Corp. Sec. (bd. chmn. 1987-88), Assn. Gen. Coun., Am. Arbitration Assn., St. Louis Club. Office: Monsanto Co 800 N Lindbergh Blvd Saint Louis MO 63167

DUFF, JAMES GEORGE, automobile company executive; b. Pittsburg, Kans., Jan. 27, 1938; s. James George and Camilla (Vinardi) D.; m. Linda Louise Beeman, June 24, 1961 (div.); children: Michele, Mark, Melissa; m. Beverly L. Pool, Nov. 16, 1984. B.S. with distinction (Sunray Mid-Continent Scholar; Bankers Scholar), U. Kans., 1960, M.B.A., 1961. With Ford Motor Co., Dearborn, Mich., 1962—; various positions fin. staff Ford Motor Co., 1962-71; dir. product, profit, price, warranty Ford of Europe, 1972-74; controller Ford Div., 1974-76, controller car ops., 1976, controller car product devel., 1976-80; exec. v.p. Ford Motor Credit Co., 1980-88, bd. dirs.; pres. U.S. Leasing Internat. Inc., San Francisco, 1988—, also bd. dirs.; dir. U.S. Leasing Corp., U.S. Airlease, U.S. Lease Fin., USL Securities Corp., U.S. Fleet Leasing, U.S. Instrument Rentals, U.S. Rail Svcs., U.S. Portfolio Leasing, Airlease Mgmt. Svcs. Mem. adv. bd. Sch. Bus., U. Kans., 1980—; chmn. bus. devel. unit United Found., 1980-85, chmn. edn. and local govt. unit, 1986-88. Home: 7 Russian Hill Pl San Francisco CA 94133 Office: US Leasing Internat 733 Front St San Francisco CA 94111

DUFFY, THOMAS EDWARD, publisher; b. Rochester, Nov. 6, 1947; s. Neil Harris and Rosemary (Perfield) D.; m. Barbara Joanne Gabrielsen, Feb. 5, 1972; children: Thomas E., Daniel, Sherry. BA, Coll. of the Holy Cross, 1969. Advt. sales McGraw Hill Inc., Atlanta, 1974-76, Phila., 1976-80; advt. sales mgr. McGraw Hill Inc., N.Y.C., 1980-84; pub. Internat. Thomson Inc., N.Y.C., 1984-85, The Hearst Group, N.Y.C., 1985—. Home: 104 Lafayette Dr Washington Crossing PA 18977 Office: Hearst Profl Mags Diversion Mag 60 E 42d St New York NY 10165

DUFOUR, GREGORY ANDRE, banker; b. Old Town, Me., May 6, 1960; s. F. Philip and Barbara Ann (Barton) D.; m. Doreen Denice Gallant, May 22, 1982. BS, U. Me., 1982; MBA, North Tex. State U., 1984. Fin. planner Tex. Instruments, Dallas, 1984-85, cost planning analyst, 1985-86; lead cost analyst Tex. Instruments, Lewisville, Tex., 1986-87; credit analyst The Merrill Trust Co., Bangor, Me., 1987; asst. treas., credit analyst Merrill/Norstar Bank, Bangor, 1988; asst. v.p. acctg. Fleet Bank Maine, Portland, 1988—. Mem. Delta Upsilon. Republican. Roman Catholic. Office: Fleet Bank Maine 1155 Lisbon St Lewiston ME 04240

DUFRESNE, ARMAND FREDERICK, management and engineering consultant; b. Manila, Aug. 10, 1917; s. Ernest Faustine and Maude (McClellan) DuF.; m. Theo Rutledge Schaefer, Aug. 24, 1940 (dec. Oct. 1986); children: Lorna DuFresne Turnier, Peter, m. Lois Burrell Klosterman, Feb. 21, 1987. BS, Calif. Inst. Tech., 1938. Dir. quality control, chief product engr. Consol. Electrodynamics Corp., Pasadena, Calif., 1945-61; pres., dir. DUPACO, Inc., Arcadia, Calif., 1961-68; v.p., dir. ORMCO Corp., Glendora, Calif., 1966-68; mgmt., engring. cons., Duarte and Cambria, Calif., 1968—; dir., v.p., sec. Tavis Corp., Mariposa, Calif., 1968-79; dir. Denram Corp., Monrovia, Calif., 1968-70, interim pres., 1970; dir., chmn. bd. RCV Corp., El Monte, Calif., 1968-70; owner DUFCO, Cambria, 1971-82; pres. DUFCO Electronics, Inc., Cambria, Calif., 1982-86, chmn. bd. 1982—; pres. Freedom Designs, Inc., Northridge, Calif., 1982-86, chmn. bd. dirs., 1982—. Patentee in field. Bd. dirs. Arcadia Bus. Assn., 1965-69; bd. dirs. Cambria Community Services Dist., 1976, pres., 1977-80; mem., chmn. San Luis Obispo County Airport Land Use Commn., 1972-75. Served to capt. Signal Corps, AUS, 1942-45. Decorated Bronze Star. Mem. Instrument Soc. Am. (life), Arcadia (dir. 1965-69), Cambria (dir. 1974-75) C. of C., Tau Beta Pi. Home: 901 Iva Ct Cambria CA 93428

DUFRESNE, GUY GEORGES, paper company executive; b. Montreal, Que., Can., Oct. 28, 1941; s. Andre M. and Anita (Lacoste) D.; m. Lucie Pellerin; children—Johanne, Sylvie, Robert, Louise. B.A., U. Montreal, Que., Can., 1960, B.Sc.A. in Engring., 1964; M.S. in Engring., MIT, 1965; M.B.A., Harvard U., 1967. Project mgr. Consol.-Bathurst, Montreal, Que., Can., 1970-74; woodlands mgr. Domtar, Montreal, Que., Can., 1974-76; v.p. mktg. Consol. Bathurst, Montreal, Que., Can., 1976-82, sr. v.p. pulp and paper ops., 1982-85, sr. group v.p. North Am. pulp and paper, 1985-89; bd. dirs. Aliments Delisle Ltd., Quebec Forest Industries Assn. Chmn. bd. Montreal World Trade Ctr., 1985; mem. Commn. dela santé de la sécuritée dutravail. Mem. Can. Pulp and Paper Assn. (bd. dirs. 1983). Club: Drs. Club (St. Denis). Home: 172 Mere d'Youville, Boucherville, PQ Canada J4B 2V7 Office: Consol-Bathurst Inc, 800 Dorchester Blvd W, Montreal, PQ Canada H3B 1Y9

DUGAS, RAYMOND GEORGE, marketing executive; b. Webster, Mass., July 29, 1941; s. Adolphe Israel and Leokadya Mary (Panek) D.; m. Marquerite Anne Eckert, Oct. 4, 1969; children: Adam, Matthew, Michelle, Rachel. BA in Math., Clark U., 1968. Mktg. rep. IBM Corp., Boston, 1968-73, mgr. mktg., 1974-80, mgr. nat. accounts, 1980-83; mgr. ops., region Cullinet Software, Braintree, Mass., 1986-87; chmn, co-founder Market Builders Internat., Sudbury, Mass., 1988—. Lectr. St. Julia's Ch., Weston, 1987—; coach Weston Soccer League, 1980; mem. adv. com. Pope John XXXIII Sem., Weston, 1982-87; bd. dirs., treas. Weston Drama Workshop, 1986. Sgt. U.S. Army, 1963-69. Republican. Roman Catholic. Office: Market Builders Internat 121 Boston Post Rd Sudbury MA 01776

DUGGAN, KEVIN, data processor; b. St. Louis, Feb. 29, 1944; s. Leo Patrick and Jean Claire (McHenry) D.; BA, U. S.C., 1977, MA, Webster U., 1988; m. Lillian Carol Cook, Dec. 29, 1973. With S.C. Nat. Bank, Columbia, 1970-79, mgr. tech. support, 1978-79; dir. info. sci. tech., Midlands Tech. Coll., Columbia, 1979—; cons. electronic data processing. Mem. Richland County Friends of Library, Literacy Council S.C., chmn. fin. com., 1987—; chmn. stewardship com., 1982-86; mem. evangelism and membership coms., 1982-86; mem. council on ministries, 1982—; mem. exec. com., 1987—; mem. adminstrv. bd. Washington St. United Meth. Ch. Served with USMC, 1963-67. Decorated Bronze Star (3). Mem. Assn. Systems Mgr., IBM Users Group, Data Processing Mgmt. Assn., Palmetto Fencing Soc., Amateur Fencing League Am. Methodist. Lodge: Rotary. Office: PO Box 2408 Columbia SC 29202

DUGGAN, T(HOMAS) PATRICK, management consultant; b. Hartford, Conn., Mar. 17, 1946; s. Edward O. and Mildred B. (Balf) D.; A.B., Providence Coll., 1968; postgrad. in mgmt. Western New Eng. Coll., 1969-71; m. Marcia McCormack, Aug. 31, 1968 (div. 1978); children—Mary-Christina, T. Patrick; m. Ann Hailey, Sept. 21, 1985. Mgr., Travelers Mgmt. Services, Hartford, 1968-75; mgr. mgmt. cons. services Coopers & Lybrand, N.Y.C., 1975-79; prin., dir. ins. mgmt. cons. services Hay Assocs., N.Y.C., 1979-84; exec. v.p., nat. dir. bus. Strategy cons. group Alexander & Alexander Mgmt. Cons. Services, N.Y.C., 1984; pres. Duggan Cons. Assocs., Greenwich, Conn., 1984—. Served to 1st lt., inf. USAR, 1968-75. Mem. Human Resource Planning Soc., Am. Mgmt. Assn., Ins. Accounting and Statis. Assn. (session chmn. 1975-79). Clubs: Golf of Avon, Hartford (Conn.). Home: 5 September Ln Weston CT 06883

DUHL, STUART, lawyer; b. Chgo., Dec. 3, 1940; s. Samuel H. and Gertrude (Crodgen) D.; m. Elaine S. Distenfield, Feb. 5, 1967; children: Gregory M., Joshua D. BS, Northwestern U., 1962, JD, 1965; LLM, John Marshall U., 1968. Bar: Ill. 1965. Assoc. D'Ancona & Pflaum, Chgo., 1965-70; ptnr. Schwartz & Freeman, Chgo., 1970—; Mem. Ill. Bd. Law Examiners, Chgo., 1979—; bd. mgrs. Nat. Conf. Bar Examiners, Chgo., 1986—; dir. Sales Force Cos., Inc., Chgo. Editor: The Bar Examiners Handbook, 1980; contbr. articles to Jour. of Taxation. Recipient Haskins & Sells Found. award 1962. Mem. Chgo. Bar Assn., Ill. State Bar Assn., ABA, Chgo. Council Lawyers. Club: Briarwood Country (Deerfield). Office: Schwartz & Freeman 401 N Michigan Ave Ste 3400 Chicago IL 60611

DUKE, DAVID ALLEN, glass company executive; b. Salt Lake City, Nov. 26, 1935; s. Otto and Beatrice (Taylor) D.; m. Hanne Jensen, Sept. 9, 1955; children—Katherine, Michael, Deborah, John. B.S., U. Utah, Salt Lake City, 1957, M.S., 1959, Ph.D., 1962. Mgr. advanced materials research Corning (N.Y.) Glass Works, 1962-70, bus. mgr. auto ceramics, 1970-74, gen. mgr. indsl. products, 1974-75, v.p., gen. mgr. telecommunications, 1976-85, sr. v.p. research/devel. and engring., 1985-88, vice chmn. tech., 1988—, 1988—, also bd. dirs.; bd. dirs. Ciba Corning Diagnostics Corp., Medfield, Mass., Siecor Corp., Hickory, N.C., Dow Corning Corp., Samsung Corning, Corning Glass Works, Ariz. Astronomy; trustee Corning Glass Works Found. Contbr. articles to profl. publs. Patentee in field. Troop leader Boy Scouts Am., Elmira, N.Y., 1963-85. Mem. Am. Ceramic Soc. Republican. Mormon. Office: Corning Glass Works R & D Labs Sullivan Pk Corning NY 14831

DUKE, GAIL FRANCES, accountant; b. Nuremberg, Fed. Republic of Germany, Mar. 24, 1948; d. Walter O. and Helene B. (Postemsky) H.; m. Gary A. Duke, Aug. 27, 1967; children: Carrie L., Stacey Scott. Student, Stephen S. Austin State U., 1967-69, Lamar U., 1980-81. CPA, Tex. Staff acct. Spain, Ham & Co. P.C., Pasadena, Tex., 1973-81; staff acct. McGee, Wheeler & Co., Houston, 1981-85, tax supr., 1985-86, tax mgr., 1986—. Bd. dirs. Harris County Mcpl. Utility Dist. 119, Houston, 1984-88, re-elected, 1988—, pres., 1988—; chmn. Houston rels. chpt. IRS Com. Mem. AICPA's, Tex. Soc. CPA's (com. mem. Houston chpt., chmn. com. on rels. with IRS), Am. Woman's Soc. CPA's. Republican. Home: 6222 Elkwood Forest Houston TX 77088 Office: McGee Wheeler & Co 4321 Directors Row Ste 100 Houston TX 77092

DUKE, ROBIN CHANDLER TIPPETT, corporate professional; b. Balt., Oct. 13, 1923; d. Richard Edgar and Esther (Chandler) Tippett; m. Angier Biddle Duke, May 1962; children: Jeffrey R. Lynn, Letitice Lynn Valiunas, Angier Biddle Jr. Grad. high sch., Balt. Fashion editor N.Y. Jour. Am., N.Y.C., 1944-46; freelance writer N.Y.C., 1946-50; rep. Orvis Bros., N.Y.C., 1953-58; mem. pub. relations staff Pepsi Cola Co., Internat., N.Y.C., 1958-62; bd. dirs. Am. Home Products, N.Y.C., Rockwell Internat., Pitts., Internat. Flavors & Fragrances, N.Y.C., Dreyfus, N.Y.C., East River Savs. Bank, New Rochelle, N.Y. Contbg. editor Archtl. Digest, 1987—. Vice-chmn., bd. dirs. Inst. Internat. Edn., N.Y.C., 1975—; co-chmn. Population Crisis Com., Washington, 1972; bd. dirs. Alan Guttmacher Inst., N.Y.C., 1976, Guggenheim Mus., N.Y.C., 1980. Mem. Colony Club, River Club. Democrat. Home: 435 E 52d St New York NY 10022

DULA, G. ELISABETH, real estate executive; b. Radford, Va., Apr. 17, 1958; d. James Braxton Jr. and Vivian (Miller) D. MusB in Piano Performance, U. N.C., 1980; MBA, Wake Forest U., 1987. Asst. to property mgr. Synco Properties Inc., Charlotte, N.C., 1982-83; fin. analyst Synco Inc., Charlotte, N.C., 1984-85, asst. v.p. acquisitions, 1985-87; v.p. Synco Inc., Charlotte, 1987-88, sr. v.p., 1988—. Dir. Charlotte Share-a-Home. Named one of Outstanding Young Women of Am. Mem. N.C. Income Property Assn., Mortgage Bankers Assn., Aircraft Owners and Pilots Assn., Charlotte Symphony Women's Assn. (bd. dirs.), Good Friends, U. N.C.-Charlotte Alumni Assn. (life), YMCA. Republican. Presbyterian. Home: 1336 Queens Rd Charlotte NC 28207 Office: Synco Inc 112 S Tryon St Ste 900 Charlotte NC 28284

DULAUX, RUSSELL FREDERICK, lawyer; b. West New York, N.J., Dec. 30, 1918; s. Frederick and Theresa A. (Noble) L.; m. Ann deFriedberg, Aug. 22, 1962 (dec.); m. Eva DeLuca, Dec. 24, 1985. Student Pace Inst., 1938-40, Fordham U., 1946-48; LLB summa cum laude, N.Y. Law Sch., 1950; postgrad. Pace Coll., 1951, Columbia U., 1955. Bar: N.Y. 1951, U.S. Dist. (so. dist.) N.Y. 1951, U.S. Ct. Appeals (2d cir.) 1951, U.S. Ct. Claims 1952, U.S. Tax Ct. 1952, U.S. Dist. Ct. (ea. dist.) N.Y. 1953, U.S. Ct. Customs and Patent Appeals 1963, U.S. Ct. Mil. Appeals 1963, U.S. Supreme Ct. 1963. Mem. staff N.Y. State Dept. Law, Richmond County Investigations, 1951-54, N.Y. State Exec. Dept. Office of Commr. of Investigations, 1954-57; comptroller-counsel Odyssey Productions, Inc., 1957-59; ptnr. Ryan, Murray & Laux, N.Y.C., 1951-61, Ryan & Laux, N.Y.C., 1961; sole practice, N.Y.C., 1961—. Active Met. Opera Guild. Served with AUS, 1940-46; capt. JAG, vet. corps of arty., spl. agt. counter intelligence corps, SIC, State of N.Y., 1975—; now col. U.S. Army. Recipient Eloy Alfaro Grand Cross Republic of Panama. Mem. Bronx County Bar Assn. (recipient Townsend Wandell Gold medal), Nat. Acad. TV Arts & Scis., Internat. Platform Assn., VFW, Order of Lafayette, Sons of Union Vets. of Civil War, Soc. Am. Wars, The Nat. Sojourners, Heroes of '76, Navy League, St. Andrews Soc. N.Y., St. George Soc. N.Y., Soc. Friendly Sons of St. Patrick, English Speaking Union, Asia Soc., China Inst. Am., Army and Navy Union U.S.A., Am. Legion, Mid Manhattan C. of C., Reserve Officers Assn. of U.S. (col.), Delta Theta Phi. Presbyterian. Clubs: Lambs, Knights Hospitaller of St. John of Jerusalem, Grand St. Boys', Soldiers', Sailors' and Airmen's. Lodges: Order of Eastern Star, Masons (past comdr. N.Y. Masonic war vets.), Shriners, Knight of Malta. Office: 71 W 23d St Ste 1530 New York NY 10010

DULCHINOS, PETER, infosystems specialist; b. Chicopee Falls, Mass., Feb. 2, 1935; s. George and Angeline D.; BS in Elect. Engring., Mass. Inst. Tech., 1956, MS in Elect. Engring., 1957; MS in Engring. Mgmt., Northeastern U., 1965; JD, Suffolk Law Sch., 1984; m. Thalia Verros, Aug. 28, 1960; children—Matthew George, Paul Constantine, Gregory Peter. Bar: Mass. 1984, U.S. Dist. Ct. (Mass.) 1984, U.S. Ct. Appeals (1st cir.) 1985, U.S. Supreme Ct. 1988. With Sylvania Co., Waltham, Mass., 1957-61, Needham, Mass., 1963-66, Tech Ops, Burlington, Mass., 1961, RCA, Burlington, 1962-63; with Raytheon Co., Bedford, Mass., 1966—, computer ops. mgr. tactical software devel. facility Patriot Ground Computer System, 1977-86, proprietary data mgr., 1986—; lectr. Fitchburg State Coll., 1985—; corporator Cen. Savs. Bank, Lowell, Mass., 1980—; sec.-treas. U. Lowell Bldg. Authority, 1974-70. Mem. human studies subcom. Bedford VA Hosp., 1987—; pres., Chelmsford Rep. Club, 1964-70; chmn. Chelmsford Rep. Town Com., 1972-76; assoc. Town Counsel for Tyngsborough (Mass.), 1985-87; chmn. Chelmsford Bd. Health, 1972-87; mem. Nashoba Tech. High Sch. Com., 1970-71. 2d lt., Signal Corps, U.S. Army, 1957-58. Registered profl. engr., Mass., N.H. Mem. IEEE, Mass. Bar Assn., , Boston Patent Law Assn. Republican. Greek Orthodox. Home: 211 Wellman Ave North Chelmsford MA 01824 Office: Raytheon Co Hartwell Rd Bedford MA 01730

DULUDE, JAMES ANDRE, fabrics manufacturing company executive; b. Attleboro, Mass., Aug. 3, 1955; s. Robert Andre and Helen (Graff) D.; m. Debora Lyn Pelletier, Oct. 11, 1980; children: Christopher, Kimberley. BS in Mech. Engring., Southeastern Mass. U., 1978; postgrad. in bus. adminstrn., Bryant Coll., 1984. Cert. prodn. inventory mgr. Sci. programmer Pratt & Whitney Aircraft Co., East Hartford, Conn., 1978-79; electronic data systems engr. Fed. Products, Providence, 1979; mgr. info. systems Univis Frame Co., North Attleboro, Mass., 1979-86; dir. info. systems Quaker Fabric Corp., Fall River, Mass., 1986-88, dir. planning and scheduling, 1988—. Mem. Am. Prodn. and Inventory Control Soc., Elks. Home: 59 Haduk Dr North Attleboro MA 02760 Office: Quaker Fabric Corp 941 Grinnell St Fall River MA 02721

DULUDE, RICHARD, glass manufacturing company executive; b. Dunbarton, N.H., Apr. 20, 1933; s. Joseph Phillip and Anna (Lenz) D.; m. Jean Anne MacDonald, Sept. 11, 1954; children: Jeffrey, Jonathan, Joel. BME, Syracuse (N.Y.) U., 1954; postgrad., MIT, 1969. With Allis Chalmers Mfg. Co., Milw., 1954-55; with Corning (N.Y.) Glass Works, 1957—, v.p., gen. mgr. tech. products div., 1972-75, v.p., gen. mgr. European ops., 1975-78, pres. European div., 1978-80, dir. mktg. and bus. devel., 1980-83, pres. Telecommmunications and Elect. group, 1983-85, group pres., 1985—, chmn., chief exec. officer Corning Europe, 1987—, also bd. dirs.; bd. dirs. N.H. Land Mgmt., Inc., Corning Internat. Corp., Siecor Corp., Siemens Communications Systems, Inc.; chmn. bd. dirs. Siecor Corp.; mem. adv. council Sch. Engring. Clarkson U.; mem. engring. adv. bd. Syracuse U. Patentee combination space lighting, heating and ventilation fixture. Past bd. dirs. Corning YMCA.; Past bd. dirs. Better Vision Inst., N.Y.C., Am. Sch., Paris, Am. Hosp., Am. C. of C., Paris; trustee Syracuse U.; chmn. bd. trustees Clarkson U. Served to 1st lt. AUS, 1955-57. Mem. Optical Soc. Am., Illuminating Engring. Soc., Nat. Ski Patrol System (past bd. dirs.). Club: Travellers (Paris). Home: RD 2 Spencer Hill Corning NY 14830 Office: Corning Glass Works Houghton Pk Corning NY 14831

DUMAS-LAFERRIERE, SANDRA LEE, personnel executive, personnel consultant; b. Malone, N.Y., Mar. 27, 1957; d. Leonard James and Myrtle Lucille (Beverlin) Dumas. A.S., NYU-Canton, 1976; student Tunxis Community Coll., 1977-79; cert. profl. in human resources Personnel Accreditation Inst., 1988. Receptionist N.W. Enterprises, Malone, 1972; receptionist, sec. Wasley Products, Inc., Plainville, Conn., 1973, time study estimator, 1974-76; prodn. control clk., 1976-77, personnel asst., 1977-79, asst. personnel mgr., 1979-82, personnel mgr., 1982—; cons. Wasley Lighting, Essex, Conn., 1982—, Precision Molding, New Britain, Conn., 1985—. Bd. dirs. United Way of Plainville, 1985-88, campaign chairperson, 1987-88, bd. dirs. Wheeler Clinic, Inc., Plainville, 1984-88; trustee UAW Local 376 Union Welfare Fund, Hartford, Conn., 1984-88; crisis intervention counselor Help Line, Plainville, 1983-84; rape crisis counselor YWCA, New Britain, Conn., 1984-85; Strike Back Against Crime rep. Strike Back, New Haven, 1984—; cons. Jr. Achievement Project Bus., Plainville, 1986; advisor Coop. Work Experience, Bristol Eastern High Sch., 1982-85. Recipient Outstanding Young Woman award Jaycee Women, Bristol, Conn., 1984, Conn. Outstanding Young Citizens award WFSB Channel 3, Conn. Jaycees, 1985, Proclamation, Mayor City of Bristol, 1985. Mem. Nat. Assn. Female Execs., Am. Soc. Personnel Adminstrn., Internat. Found. Employee Benefit Plans, Nat. Safety Council, Mfrs. Hartford County, Conn. Bus. and Industry Assn. Democrat. Roman Catholic. Club: Jr Women's (co-chmn. health and safety 1977-78) (Bristol). Avocations: bowling; swimming. Office: Wasley Products Inc Plainville Indsl Park Plainville CT 06062

DUMESNIL, EUGENE FREDERICK, JR., sales executive; b. Richmond Hills, N.Y., May 21, 1924; s. Eugene Frederick Sr. and Dorothy Evelyn (Reithmiller) D.; m. Beverly Ann Jones, June 29, 1957; children: Laura Ann, Eugene F. III. BME, Pratt Inst., 1944. V.p. sales Red Devil Inc., Union, N.J., 1967-75; dir. mktg. Tiptop Industries div. Beatrice Foods, Jersey City, 1975-79; v.p. sales and mktg. Grant Hardware, West Nyack, N.Y., 1979—. Lt. (j.g.) USN, 1942-46, PTO. Home: 27 Emerson Rd Glen Rock NJ 07452 Office: Grant Hardware Co High St West Nyack NY 10994

DUMETT, CLEMENT WALLACE, JR., oil company executive; b. Tacoma, Dec. 30, 1927; s. Clement Wallace and Dilma (Arnold) D.; m. Carolyn Jane Coulthurst, Mar. 9, 1957; children: Daniel, Joanne, Patricia. B.Sc. in Petroleum Engring, Stanford U., 1951. With Union Oil Co. Calif., 1951-55; with Unocal Can. Ltd., 1955—, v.p. exploration, then v.p. prodn., 1967-75; pres. Unocal Can. Ltd., Calgary, Alta., Can., 1975—. Served with AUS, 1946-47. Mem. Canadian Petroleum Assn. (dir.), Petroleum Soc., Soc. Petroleum Engrs., Petroleum Club, Ranchmen's Club, Calgary Golf and Country Club. Anglican. Home: 443 Scarboro Ave SW, Calgary, AB Canada T3C 2H7 Office: Unocal Can Ltd, PO Box 999, Calgary, AB Canada T2P 2K6

DUNAIF, ALEXANDRA L., financial planner; b. N.Y.C., Apr. 11, 1957; d. Nancy Marie (Peters) D. BA, SUNY, Purchase, 1979. Cert. fin. planner Coll. Fin. Planning. Registered rep., br. mgr. Jonathan Alan & Co., White Plains, N.Y., 1985—; bd. dirs. Am. Warmblood Registry, Dobbs Ferry, N.Y.; dir. Cirriculum Com. 5% Solution, White Plaines, 1988—. Recipient Jr. Equitation Gold medal U.S. Equestrian Team, 1975, finals A.S.P.C.A. Maclay Nat. Equitation, 1974; chosen for Olympic Screening Trails U.S. Equestrian Team, 1976. Mem. Internat. Assn. Fin Plannes, Nat. Assn. Female Execs., Nat. Assn. Securities Dealers, Am. Arbitration Assn. Office: Johnathan Alan & Co 10 New King St White Plains NY 10604

DUNAWAY, DONALD LUCIUS, manufacturing company executive; b. Omaha, Mar. 8, 1937; s. Lucius L. and Dagmar R. (Cook) D.; m. Betty Jo Kipp, Aug. 21, 1957; children: Catherine Lynne, David Kipp. BS in Bus., U. Kans., 1959. Salesman Hallmark Cards Co., Kansas City, Mo., 1959-60; wholesale credit dept. Mobil Oil Co., Kansas City, 1960-63; staff asst., credit dept. A.O. Smith Corp., Milw., 1963-65, credit mgr., 1965-66, mgr. banking and credit, 1966-67, asst. treas., 1967-75; pres., treas. AgriStor Credit Corp., Milw., 1967-76; v.p., gen. mgr. A.O. Smith Harvestore Products, Inc., Arlington Heights, Ill., 1976; v.p. A.O. Smith Corp., Milw., 1977-83; pres. A.O. Smith Harvestore Products, Inc., Arlington Heights, 1977-83; sr. v.p. A.O. Smith Corp., Milw., 1983-86, exec. v.p., 1986—; bd. dirs. Kemper Mut. Funds, Chgo.; bd. dirs. AgriStor Credit Corp., Milw.; bd. dirs. A.O. Smith Harvestore Products, Inc., DeKalb, Ill. Bd. dirs. Metro Milw. YMCA, 1985—. Served with Kans. N.G., 1959. Clubs: University, Blue Mound Country (Milw.). Office: A O Smith Corp 11270 W Park Pl 1 Park Pla Milwaukee WI 53224

DUNCAN, ALAN E., mechanical engineer; b. Wooster, Ohio, May 31, 1951; s. Harry T. and Evelyn M. (Leyda) D.; m. Elizabeth F. Lawrence, Jan. 30, 1981. BSME, U. Akron, 1974; MSE, U. Mich., 1976. Profl. engr., Mich. Cooperative student NASA Lewis Research Ctr., Cleve., 1972-74; material devel. engr. Chrysler Corp., Detroit, 1974-77; devel. engr. Chevrolet Motor Div., Detroit, 1977-84; pres., owner Automotive Analytics, Inc., Troy, Mich., 1984—. Mem. Soc. Automotive Engrs., Am. Soc. Mech. Engrs., Engring. Soc. Detroit. Republican. Unitarian. Home and Office: 938 Portsmouth Troy MI 48084

DUNCAN, ANSLEY MCKINLEY, aerospace co. mgr.; b. Homer City, Pa., Jan. 25, 1932; s. William McKinley and Marion Melissa (Davis) D.; student U. Denver, 1955-57, Pa. State U., 1957-59. Engring. adminstr. RCA, Van Nuys, Calif., 1959-61; program evaluation coordinator N.Am. Aviation, Anaheim, Calif., 1961-66; mfg. supr., Rockwell Internat., Anaheim Calif., 1966-70, program adminstr., 1970-76, program controls mgr., 1976-81, plans/schedule advisor, 1981—. Served with USN, 1951-55. Home: 12600 Willowood Ave Garden Grove CA 92640 Office: 3370 Miraloma Ave Anaheim CA 92803

DUNCAN, CHARLES WILLIAM, JR., investor, former government official; b. Houston, Sept. 9, 1926; s. Charles William and Mary Lillian (House) D.; m. Thetis Anne Smith, June 10, 1957; children: Charles William III, Mary Anne. B.S. in Chem. Engring., Rice U., 1947; postgrad. mgmt., U. Tex., 1948-49. Roustabout, chem. engr. Humble Oil & Refining Co., 1947; with Duncan Foods Co., Houston, 1948-64; adminstrv. v.p. Duncan Foods Co., 1957-58, pres., chmn. adv. bd., 1958-64; pres. Coca-Cola Co. Food Div., Houston, 1964-67; chmn. Coca-Cola Europe, 1967-70; exec. v.p. Coca-Cola Co., Atlanta, 1970-71; pres. Coca-Cola Co., 1971-74; chmn. bd., dir. Rotan Mosle Fin. Corp., Houston, 1974-77; dep. sec. Dept. Def., Washington, 1977-79; sec. Dept. Energy, Washington, 1979-81; now chmn. bd. Duncan, Cook & Co.; bd. dirs. Coca-Cola Co., Am. Express, Tex. Eastern Corp., United Technologies Inc., Cameron Iron Works, Inc., Chem. Banking Corp., Tex. Commerce Bancshares Inc.; trustee Welch Found. Chmn. bd. trustees Rice U.; trustee Brookings Instn. Served with USAAF, 1944-46. Mem. Sigma Alpha Epsilon, Sigma Iota Epsilon, Council Fgn. Relations. Methodist. Clubs: Houston Country (Houston), River Oaks Country (Houston), Allegro (Houston). Home: 9 Briarwood Ct Houston TX 77019 Office: 700 Louisiana St 50th Fl Houston TX 77002

DUNCAN, JAMES DANIEL, paper distribution company executive; b. LaSalle, Ill., June 12, 1941; s. Lawrence James and Margaret Mary (Brehm) D.; m. Sandra Ruth Crowe, Nov. 10, 1963; children: Lawrence, Brian, Stephen. BA in Journalism, U. Notre Dame, Ind., 1963; MBA in Mgmt., Xavier U., Cin., 1978. With sales dept. Campbell Soup Co., Chgo. and Mich., 1963-66; with sales and sales mgmt. depts. Weyerhaeuser Co., Chgo. and Houston, 1966-70; with sales mgmt. dept. Boise Cascade, Chgo. and Marion, Ind., 1970-71; with sales mgmt. and mgmt. depts. Internat. Paper Co., Pitts., N.Y.C. and Cin., 1971-82; exec. v.p., chief operating officer WWF

Paper Corp., Phila., 1982-87, also bd. dirs.; pres. Grant Paper Co., Pennsauken, N.J., 1988—; mem. exec. com. Paper Distbn. Coun., N.Y., 1987—. Editor sales tng. manual, 1976. Mem. Nat. Paper Trade Assn. (printing paper com. 1986—). Republican. Roman Catholic. Home: 104 Union Mill Rd Mount Laurel NJ 08054 Office: Grant Paper Co 8501 River Rd Pennsauken PA 08110

DUNCAN, JOHN C., minerals company executive; b. N.Y.C., Sept. 29, 1920; s. John C. and Doris (Bullard) D.; m. Barbara Doyle, Dec. 12, 1942; children: Lynn Duncan Tarbox, Wendy, Craig, Gale Duncan Simmons. BA, Yale U., 1942. With W.R. Grace & Co., 1946-70, exec. v.p. charge Latin Am. ops., 1960-64, exec. v.p., dir. corp., 1964-70; sr. v.p. St. Joe Minerals Corp., 1971, pres., 1971-82, then chmn. bd., chief exec. officer; chmn. bd. dirs. Cyprus Minerals Co., 1985—, also bd. dirs.; bd. dirs. BF Goodrich Co., Westvaco Corp., Bank of N.Y., The France Fund Inc., Acción Internat.; bd. dirs., Ams. Soc. Coun. for Ams., Inter-Am. Found. Capt. F.A., AUS, 1942-46, CBI. Presbyterian. Clubs: Links, Yale (N.Y.C.); Round Hill (Greenwich).

DUNCAN, JOHN LAPSLEY, manufacturing company executive; b. Nashville, Dec. 16, 1933; s. Ruel Laverne and Lorene (Ellis) D.; m. Patricia Louise Cogburn, Aug. 27, 1955; children: Sharon Gayle, John Lapsley, Ruel Laverne, II, Thomas Ellis. B.S. in Mech. Engring., U. S.C., 1960. Sales mgr. So. die casting div. Arwood Corp., 1966-69; v.p. mfg. and engring., power tool div., then dir. corp. bus. analysis Singer Co., 1969-78; pres., chief operating officer Murray Mfg. Co., Brentwood, Tenn., 1978-82; pres. Motor Products div. Singer Co., Pickens, S.C., 1982-85; v.p. electro-mech. group Singer Co., 1985-87; pres., chief exec. officer Murray Ohio Mfg. Co., Brentwood, Tenn., 1987—. Served with AUS, 1953-56. Mem. Outdoor Power Equipment Inst., Power Tool Inst. (dir.). Republican. Mem. Christian Ch. (Disciples of Christ). Office: Murray Ohio Mfg Co 219 Franklin Rd PO Box 268 Brentwood TN 37027

DUNCAN, JOSEPH WAYMAN, business economist; b. Cambridge, Ohio, Dec. 2, 1936; s. George Wendall and Elizabeth (Fuller) D.; m. Janice Elaine Gouveia, Aug. 19, 1961; children: Jeffrey Wayman, James Wendall. B.S. in Mech. Engring, Case Inst. Tech., 1958; M.B.A., Harvard U., 1960; Ph.D., Ohio State U., 1970. Economist Battelle Meml. Inst., Columbus, Ohio, 1961-68; coordinator urban affairs Battelle Meml. Inst., 1969-73; dep. asst. sec. for econ. policy Dept. Commerce, Washington, 1968-69; dep. assoc. dir. Office Mgmt. and Budget, Washington, 1974-78; dir. Office Fed. Statis. Policy and Standards, Dept. Commerce, Washington, 1978-81; asst. adminstr. for statis. policy Office of Info. and Regulatory Affairs, Office of Mgmt. and Budget, Washington, 1981; corp. economist and chief statistician Dun & Bradstreet Corp., 1982—, corp. officer, 1986—; chmn. coordination bd. OAS Com. on Improvement of Nat. Statistics, 1975-79; U.S. rep., chmn. UN Statis. Commn., 1981—. Author books, also numerous articles in field. Mem. vis. com. econ. dept. U. Pa., 1985—. Fellow Am. Statis. Assn.; mem. Nat. Economists Club (pres. 1979, chmn. 1980), Internat. Statis. Inst., Nat. Assn. Bus. Economists, Internat. Assn. Ofcl. Statisticians (v.p. 1987—). Club: Forecasters of N.Y. (pres. 1986-87, editor Stats. Corner, 1986—). Home: 700 Jeffery St Boca Raton FL 33487 also: 161 W 61st St #8B New York NY 10023

DUNCAN, ROBERT CASE, investment advisor; b. Hollywood, Calif., May 21, 1958; s. John Robert and Eve Marie (Tedali) D. BA, Loyola Marymount U., 1980. Cert. fin. planner; registered investment advisor. Account exec. Fin. Planning Cons., Westlake Village, Calif., 1981; owner, fin. planner Duncan & Myers, Westlake Village, 1981-83; v.p., fin. planner Thomson McKinnon Securities, Woodland Hills, Calif., 1983-88; v.p., sales mgr. Prudential-Bache Securities, Woodland Hills, 1988—; tchr. Simi Valley, City of Burbank, City of Agoura, Learning Tree, Everywomens Village, Los Angeles County, Ventura County, 1984—; cons. Vidal Sassoon, Litton, Lockheed, City of Hope, Nat. Tax Advisors Assn. Host fin. talk show Sta. KGIL, KFWB, KCSN, 1984—. Tchr. Burbank Josyln Sr. Ctr., 1984—, Agoura Sr. Ctr., 1985—. Named Tchr. of Month, Learning Tree, 1987, 89. Mem. Internat. Assn. Fin. Planners, Inst. Cert. Fin. Planners, Calif. Assn. Cert. Fin. Planners, Calif. Assn. Ednl. Office Employees, Credit Union Mgrs. Assn., U.S. Coast Guard Aux. Republican. Office: Prudential-Bache Securities 21800 Burbank Blvd Woodland Hills CA 91367

DUNCAN, RUSSELL CUSHMAN, III, industrial distribution executive; b. Mpls., Nov. 7, 1947; s. Russell C. Duncan Jr. and Eva (Erickson) Duncan Johnson; m. Nancy Marie Althouse, Feb. 14, 1976; children: Russell C. IV, Andrew A. AA, Normandale Jr. Coll., 1973; student, U. Minn., 1974. Treas. Duncan Co., Mpls., 1974-80, v.p., 1980-84, pres., 1984-88; pres., founder Indsl. Market Info., Mpls., 1987—; bd. dirs. Midwest China Ctr., St. Paul, Mktg. Machine Tool Supply. Mem. Nat. Assn. Indsl. Distbn. (2nd v.p. 1987-88, bd. dirs. 1986-87), Indsl. Distbn. Assn. (v.p. 1988, pres. 1989—), Rotary. Republican. Office: Machine Tool Supply Inc 3150 Mike Collins Dr Eagan MN 55121 also: IMI 1313 5th St SE Minneapolis MN 55414

DUNCAN, WILLIAM MILLEN, banker; b. Toledo, Ohio, July 25, 1939; s. John and Elizabeth (Job) D.; m. Patricia Munson, Apr. 27, 1986; children: Elizabeth J., Howard P., William M. Jr., Korinne J. Munson. BA, Trinity Coll., 1962. Sr. v.p. Chem. Bank, N.Y.C., 1962-86; chmn. 1st Am. Bank N.Y., N.Y.C., 1986—, also bd. dirs.; bd. dirs. 1st Am. Data Services, Reston, Va. Clubs: Racquet and Tennis (N.Y.C.); Belle Haven (Greenwich, Conn.), Econ. (N.Y.). Home: 80 Fairfield Rd Greenwich CT 06830 Office: 1st Am Bank NY 350 Park Ave New York NY 10022

DUNFEY, ROBERT JOHN, JR., real estate development executive; b. Lowell, Mass., July 5, 1951; s. Robert John Sr. and Shirley (Corey) D.; m. Susan L. Lesperance, Aug. 14, 1982; children: Robert J. III, Jessica. BBA, U. N.H., 1974. Various mgmt. positions Dunfey Hotels, Hampton, N.H., 1973-82; corp. dir. Omni-Dunfey Hotels, Hampton, 1982-85; pres. Dunfey Properties, Portland, Maine, 1985—; chmn. Dunfey, Collins, Manning Hospitality Group, Boston, 1986—; bd. dirs. Coastal Bank, Portland, Smith Office Supply, Portland. Trustee Cheverus High Sch., Portland, 1985—; bd. dirs. Dunfey Family Found., Portsmouth, 1986—; mem. Maine Compensation Commn., 1986—; mem. parish council St. Christopher Ch., York, Maine, 1987—. Mem. Maine Real Estate Developers Assn. Democrat. Office: 130 Middle St Portland ME 04101

DUNFORD, MICHAEL S., marketing professional. BS, Stout State U.; MBA, U. Wis. Mktg. rep., systems div. RCA Corp.; mktg. product mgr., consumer products group The Pillsbury Co.; assoc., mgr. corp. recruiting, cons. Booz, Allen & Hamilton, Inc., Chgo.; with Lamalie Assocs., Chgo. Office: Lamalie Assocs 123 N Wacker Dr Chicago IL 60606

DUNFORD, ROBERT A., diversified business executive; b. Toronto, Ont., Can., June 7, 1931; s. Horatio Alfred and Ellen (Brown) D.; m. Sofie Pyzyna, May 26, 1956; children—Lisa Gay, Paul Robb. B.A., U. Toronto; grad. barrister and solicitor, Osgoode Hall Law Sch., Toronto. Pvt. practice lawyer Dunford & Martin, Toronto, 1960-63; Lawyer Eaton's of Can., Toronto, Ont., 1963-67; atty. Cyanamid of Can., Montreal, Que., 1967-70; v.p. Eaton Fin. Services Ltd., Toronto, 1970-77; exec. v.p., chief adminstrv. officer Brascan Ltd., Toronto, 1977—; dir., chmn. bd. Great Lakes Group, Inc., Toronto; bd. dirs. Brascade Resources, Inc., Brascan Ltd., Hemlo Gold Mines Inc., Union Enterprises Ltd., Norcen Energy Resources Ltd., Lonvest Corp.; chmn., bd. dirs. Great Lakes Power Ltd. Mem. Law Soc. Upper Can. Office: Brascan Ltd, Commerce Ct W Ste 4800, Toronto, ON Canada M5L 1B7

DUNGAN, RONALD SAMUEL, utility executive; b. Abington, Pa., Jan. 27, 1939; s. Samuel S. and Emma V. Dungan; BS in Acctg., Muhlenberg Coll., 1960; m. Donna Lee Taylor, May 19, 1962; children—Nancy, Mark, Jodi. Audit supr. Ernst & Whinney, C.P.A.s, Phila., 1960-66; controller United Sierra Co., Trenton, N.J., 1966-69; controller, chief fin. officer Scriptomatic, Inc., Phila., 1969-72; v.p. fin. and adminstrn. Air Shields, Inc., Hatboro, Pa., 1972-74; controller Gen. Waterworks Corp., Bryn Marw, Pa., 1974-81, v.p., treas., 1981-86, sr. v.p. corp. devel., 1987-88, exec. v.p. 1989—. Served with USAR, 1961. C.P.A., Pa. Mem. Am. Inst. C.P.A.s, Fin. Execs. Inst., Fin. Execs. Inst., Pa. Inst. C.P.A.s. Home: 1193 Strathmann Dr Southampton PA 18966 Office: 950 Haverford Rd Bryn Mawr PA 19010

DUNGAN, WILLIAM JOSEPH, JR., insurance broker, economics educator; b. New London, Conn., Mar. 19, 1956; s. William Joseph and Alpha (Combs) D.; m. Janet Dudek, May 28, 1983. BS in Biology, Old Dominion U., 1978, postgrad. in Econs., 1978-80; postgrad., U. Pa., 1984-85, Coll. for Fin. Planners, 1983-84; MS in Fin. Svcs., Am. Coll., 1988. CLU; chartered fin. cons. Rep. Prudential Ins. Co., Norfolk, Va., 1979-80; assoc. Russ Gills and Assocs., Virginia Beach, Va., 1980-88; instr. Tidewater Community Coll., Virginia Beach, Va., 1979—; mgr. life and fin. svcs. Henderson & Phillips Inc., Norfolk, Va., 1988—. Mem. Internat. Assn. Fin. Planning (pres. Hampton Roads chpt.), Nat. Assoc. Life Underwriters, Inst. Cert. Fin. Planners, Inst. Cert. Employee Benefits Specialists, Am. Soc. CLU's, Norfolk Assn. Life Underwriters (bd. dir.), Monarch Bus. Soc., Old Dominion Univ.'s Ins. and Fin. Svcs. Ctr., Million Dollar Round Table, Norfolk Virginia Beach Exec. Club. Republican. Home: 4201 Mercedes Ct Virginia Beach VA 23455 Office: Henderson & Phillips Inc 235 E Plume St Norfolk VA 23510

DUNHAM, DONALD HARRISON, insurance consultant; b. Davies County, Mo., Sept. 15, 1913; s. Emory H. and Zula (Crain) D.; A.A., Pomona Coll., 1935; LL.B., Nat. U., Washington, 1941, LL.M., 1942; J.D., George Washington U., 1968; m. Lillian Mae Ingram, Aug. 21, 1941; 1 dau., Carol-Lynn Shirley. Instr. ins., office mgmt. Nat. Inst. Tech., Washington, 1946-47, dist. mgr. group dept. Mass. Mut. Life Ins. Co., 1947-48; regional mgr. group dept. U.S. Life, N.Y.C., 1948-50; region and group dir. Eastern Seaboard, Minn. Mut. Life Ins. Co., 1950-51: dir. retirement, safety and ins. dept., also contbg. editor Rural Electrification mag. Nat. Rural Electric Coop. Assn., 1951-58; asst. v.p. Church Life Ins. Corp., 1958-59, adminstrv. v.p., 1959-64, v.p., mgr., 1964-72, dir., 1962-72, mem. exec. com., 1964-72; sec. Ch. Agy. Corp., Ch. Finance Corp., 1966-72; asst. v.p. govt. relations Ch. Pension Fund P.E. Ch., 1959-72; dep. asst. adminstr. Tex. State Bd. Ins., 1972-74; dep. asst. adminstr., ins. contract specialist Tex. Dept. Human Services, 1974-77, adminstr. contractual devel., compliance rev., purchased health services, 1977-84 , HMO specialist, 1975-84 ; ins. cons., Dunham Assocs., 1950—; ins. cons. Nat. Telephone Coop. Assn.; mem. Gov.'s Com. on Nat. Health Ins. and Com. on Aging, 1977-78. Chmn. adv. com. problems aging to Borough Council, 1959-72; vice chmn. planning bd. Borough of New Providence, 1966-72; chmn. New Providence Indsl. Devel. Com., 1970-72; mem. Md. Gov.'s Citizens Com. Traffic Safety, 1951-72, Pres.'s Conf. Traffic Safety, Indsl. Safety; nat. safety counsel Ins. Conf. of Coop. League U.S. Served with USNR, 1944-46. Mem. A.I.M. (fellow pres.'s council), Am. Legion (post comdr.), Minn. State Soc. (past pres.), V.F.W., D.A.V., Nat. Assn. Ins. Commrs. (Episcopal Ch. rep. 1958-72), Group Health Fedn. Am., Nat. Health Lawyers Assn., Group Health Assn. Am., Nat. Assn. HMO Regulators, U.S. Power Squadron (No. N.J. safety com.), Kappa Sigma Kappa, Sigma Delta Kappa, Delta Psi Omega (mem. bishop's com. 1959-72). Mason (32 deg.). Clubs: Kenwood Golf and Country (Chevy Chase, Md.); Lucaya Golf and Country (Freeport, Grand Bahamas); Craftsman. Home and Office: 409 Cherokee Dr Temple TX 76504

DUNHAM, JEFFREY ALAN, investment advisor; b. Loveland, Colo., Sept. 12, 1961; s. Richard L. and Delene Kay (Danielson) D. BS in Fin., Diego State U., 1983, MBA in Mgmt., 1989. Cert. fin. planner. Owner J.A.D. Properties, San Diego, 1977—; founding ptnr. McKewon & Timmins, San Diego, 1983-85, Dunham & Greer, Inc., San Diego, 1985—. Contbr. articles to profl. jours. Mem. maj. gifts com. YMCA, La Jolla, 1987-88; adv. bd. The Stanger Registerm Shrewsbury, N.J., 1987. Mem. Inst. Cert. Fin. Planners, Golden Eagle Club. Office: Dunham & Greer Inc 5075 Shoreham Pl #240 San Diego CA 92122

DUNHAM, MICHAEL PHILLIP, financial analyst; b. Talequah, Okla., Feb. 6, 1956; s. J.T. and Jo (Bennett) D.; m. Susan Guthrie, Feb. 21, 1984. BS, Okla. State U., 1978; MBA in Fin., Oklahoma City U., 1982. Cert. fin. planner; cert. estate and bus. analyst. Officer 1st Nat. Bank Oklahoma City, 1979-83; prin., cons. Mike Dunham and Assocs., Oklahoma City, 1983-88, pres., 1988—. Paul Harris fellow Rotary Internat. Found., 1987. Mem. Internat. Assn. Fin. Planning, Inst. Cert. Fin. Planners, Nat. Exec. Inst., Am. Soc. Pension Actuaries (assoc.). Republican. Episcopalian. Lodge: Rotary. Office: Mike Dunham & Assocs Inc 1140 NW 63d St Ste 402 Oklahoma City OK 73116

DUNHAM-CRAGG, MELISSA KAY, banker; b. Chgo., Aug. 19, 1956; d. C. James Dunham and Monica (Kozasa) Mori; m. Thomas Leslie Cragg, May 5, 1984; 1 child, Kathryn Hana. BA, Washington U., St. Louis, 1978, MBA, 1979. Analyst Comerica Bank, Detroit, 1979-81, lending officer, 1981-86, first v.p., group mgr., 1986-88, first v.p., 1988—. Episcopalian. Home: 774 Westchester Grosse Pointe MI 48230 Office: Comerica Bank 211 W Fort St Detroit MI 48275-1233

DUNKIN, ARTHUR HARVEY, corporate executive; b. N.Y.C., Mar. 21, 1945; s. William and June (Ehrenberg) D.; m. Rita L. Posovsky, Jan. 13, 1969; children: Joshua, Jared, Danielle. Bachelors in Econs., U. Pa., 1966; MBA, CUNY, 1968. Fin. analyst PepsiCo., Purchase, N.Y., 1969-74; sr. fin. analyst The Continental Group, Greenwich, Conn., 1974-76; div. controller The Continental Group, Savannah, Ga., 1977-84; controller Rowe Furniture Corp., Salem, Va., 1984-85, asst. sec., asst. treas., 1985-86, sec., treas., chief fin. officer, dir., 1986—. Chmn. United Jewish Appeal, 1988, solicitor, 1978-83; dir. and treas., Temple Emanuel, Roanoke, Va., 1988; youth basketball coach County League, Roanoke, 1986-87, Savannah, 1981-84; treas. Wilmington Park Homeowners Assn., Savannah, 1980-82;. Mem. Am. Soc. Corp. Secs. Home: 5117 Remington Rd SW Roanoke VA 24014 Office: Rowe Furniture Corp 239 Rowan St Salem VA 24153

DUNLAP, CHARLES LEE, oil and refining company executive; b. Milw., May 3, 1943; s. Charles Ewing and Helen Florence (Chelminiak) D.; m. Carol Elise Jones, Feb. 3, 1968; children: Kristin, Megan, Charles. AB with honors, Rockhurst Coll., 1965; LLB, St. Louis U., 1968. Bar: Wis. 1968, Mo. 1968. Assoc. corp. counsel Clark Oil & Refining Corp., Milw., 1969-75, corp. sec., sr. corp. counsel, 1975-79; v.p. crude oil supply and transp. Clark Oil & Refining Corp., Dallas, 1979-82; mgr. crude oil acquisition and sales Atlantic Richfield Co., Los Angeles, 1982-84, mgr. refining supply and crude oil trading, 1984-85; exec. v.p. Pacific Resources, Inc., Honolulu, 1985—, also bd. dirs. Regent Chaminade U., Honolulu, 1986—; trustee Hist. Hawaii Found., Honolulu, 1987, Palama Settlement, Honolulu, 1987, PRI Found., Honolulu, 1987; bd. dirs. Econ. Devel. Coun. Honolulu, 1987, Hawaii Food Bank, 1988—, Boys and Girls Club Honolulu, 1989—; mem. exec. coun. Aloha coun. Boy Scouts Am., 1988—. Thomas More fellow St. Louis U. Law Sch., 1965-68. Mem. Am. Petroleum Inst., Wis. Bar Assn., Mo. Bar Assn., Nat. Petroleum Refiners Assn. (bd. dirs. 1985—), Navy League, Wailae Country Club, Jonathan Club, Pacific Club, Plaza Club. Office: Pacific Resources Inc 733 Bishop St Honolulu HI 96813

DUNLAP, DANIEL GIRARD, apparel company executive; b. Norfolk, Va., Apr. 3, 1948; s. John Fesler and Mary Alice (Woodard) Dunlap; m. Judith Anne Martin, Nov. 28, 1970; children: Peter Girard, Jonathon Martin, Philip Daniel. BA, Houghton Coll., 1970. Sales rep. Cone Mills Mktg. Co., N.Y.C., 1972-78, merchandising rep., 1978-82; v.p. mktg. Burlington Corduroy div. Burlington Industries, N.Y.C., 1982-84; v.p. Assembly Systems Inc, San Antonio, 1984-85, pres., 1985-87, chief exe. officer, 1987—. Served to 1st lt. USAF, 1970-72. Republican. Presbyterian. Office: Assembly Systems Inc 7417 Reindeer Trail San Antonio TX 78238

DUNLAP, F. THOMAS, JR., electronics company executive, engineer, lawyer; b. Pitts., Feb. 7, 1951; s. Francis Thomas and Margaret (Hubert) D.; divorced; children—Bridgette, Katie. B.S.E.E., U. Cin., 1974; J.D., U. Santa Clara, Calif., 1979. Bar: Calif., 1979, U.S. Dist. Ct. (no. dist.) Calif. 1979. Mgr. engring. Intel Corp, Santa Clara, Calif., 1974-78, adminstr. tech. exchange, 1978-80, European counsel, 1980-81, sr. atty., 1981-83, gen. counsel, sec., 1983-87, v.p., gen. counsel, sec., 1987—. drafter, lobbyist Semiconductor Chip Protection Act, 1984. Republican. Roman Catholic. Home: 127 Westhill Dr Los Gatos CA 95030 Office: Intel Corp 3065 Bowers Ave Santa Clara CA 95030

DUNLAP, GEORGE WILLIAM, banker; b. Rock Hill, S.C., Sept. 7, 1912; s. Herbert M. and Mary Joe (Witherspoon) D.; m. Ann Myddleton, June 24, 1939; 1 child, Ann Sheperd Williams. BA, Presbyn. Coll., 1935. Asst. sec. treas. Victoria Cotton Mill, Rock Hill, 1935-42; pres. Canada Dry Bottling Co., Rock Hill, 1947-56; pres., gen. mgr. Home Fed. Savs. Bank, Rock Hill, 1956—; bd. dirs. Investors Title Ins. Co., Chapel Hill, N.C.; bd. dirs. S.C. League of Savs., Columbia, S.C.; trustee Winthrop Coll., Rock Hill, 1980—. Mem. Winthrop Coll. found. Served to maj. U.S. Army, 1942-46. Named Man of Yr., Am. Legion, 1985. Mem. U.S. C. of C. Presbyn. Lodge: Rotary (pres. 1949). Office: Home Fed Savs Bank 224 E Main Rock Hill SC 29730

DUNLAP, JAMES LAPHAM, petroleum company executive; b. Bakersfield, Calif., Aug. 20, 1937. B.S. in Petroleum Engring, U. Okla., 1961; M.B.A., Columbia U., 1963. V.p. Texaco, Inc., Harrison, 1980-82; vice chmn. Texaco, Ltd., London, 1982-83; exec. v.p. Texaco Can., Toronto, Ont., 1983, pres., chief exec. officer, 1984-86, also bd. dirs.; pres. Texaco USA, Houston, 1987—; sr. v.p. Texaco Inc., 1987—. Mem. Soc. Petroleum Engrs. Office: Texaco USA PO Box 52332 Houston TX 77052

DUNLEVY, RALPH DONALD, electric utility executive, electrical engineer; b. Henryville, Ind., Dec. 8, 1925; s. Harry Hartley and Ida Mae (Norris) D.; m. Alta Marie Howser, Oct. 24, 1947; children: Tamara Ann Dunlevy Green, Melinda Ann Dunlevy Martin. B.S.E.E., Purdue U., 1949; M.B.A., U. Louisville, 1959. Elec. engr. Oliver Iron Mining Co., Duluth, Minn., 1949-53; coordinating engr. Kelso-Burnett Electric Co., Buechel, Ky., 1953-53; with research dept. C.I.A., Washington, 1953; design engr. Western-Knapp Engring., Jeffersonville, Ind., 1953-54; plant engr. Ind.-Ky. Electric Corp., Madison, Ind., 1954-63; v.p. Ind.-Ky. Electric Corp., N.Y.C., 1967-83; exec. v.p. Ind.-Ky. Electric Corp., Columbus, Ohio, 1983—; asst. to pres. Ohio Valley Electric Corp., N.Y.C., 1963-67, v.p., 1967-83; exec. v.p. Ohio Valley Electric Corp., Columbus, 1983—. Co-author: report Options for Control of Emissions from Power Plant, 1973, Managing for Plant Availability, 1986. Tutor for disadvantaged children, Newark, N.J. Served as cpl. U.S. Army, 1944-46, ETO. Sr. mem. IEEE. Presbyterian. Club: Worthington Hills Country (Ohio). Home: 824 Singing Hills Ln Worthington OH 43085 Office: Ohio Valley Electric Corp 1 Riverside Pla Columbus OH 43215

DUNN, CHARLES WESLEY, JR., investment management executive; b. N.Y.C., July 11, 1931; s. Charles Wesley and Alice Louise (Hafner) D.; m. Olivia Endicott Hutchins, Dec. 5, 1959; children: Charles Wesley III, John Endicott. BA, Middlebury Coll., 1953. Exec. trainee Chase Manhattan Bank, N.Y.C., 1954-56; charter broker William H. Muller Shipping Co., N.Y.C., 1957-59, Naess Shipping Co., N.Y.C., 1959-60; with Kidder Peabody & Co., Inc., N.Y.C., 1960—, asst. v.p., 1967, v.p., 1968-87, sr. v.p., 1987—; bd. dirs. Webster Mgmt. Co., subs. Kidder Peabody & Co. Inc. Pres. Tokeneke Tax Dist., Darien, Conn., 1973-78, bd. dirs., 1978; bd. dirs. Tokeneke Assn., 1978-83, v.p., 1978-79, pres., 1981-83. Trustee North Country Sch., Lake Placid, N.Y., 1975-83, Country Club of Fairfield (Conn.), Racquet and Tennis, Downtown Assn. (N.Y.C.), Pequot Yacht (Southport, Conn.), Union Club N.Y.C. Republican. Episcopalian. Home: 580 Sasco Hill Rd Fairfield CT 06430 Office: Kidder Peabody Co 20 Exchange Pl New York NY 10005

DUNN, DAVID J., computer company executive, venture capital company executive; b. Bklyn., 1930. BS, U.S. Naval Acad., 1955; MBA, Harvard U., 1961. With G. H. Walker and Co., 1961-62, J.H. Whitney and Co., 1962-70; mng. ptnr. Idanta Ptnrs., Ft. Worth, 1971—; chmn. Prime Computer Inc., Natick, Mass., Iomega Corp., Roy, Utah. Capt. USMC, 1950-51, 55-59. Office: Prime Computer Inc Prime Pk M515-13 Natick MA 01760 also: Idanta Ptnrs 201 Main St Fort Worth TX 76102 *

DUNN, JOHN STEWART, manufacturing executive; b. Cleve., June 25, 1958; s. William Franklin and Margaret (Stewart) D.; m. Deborah Ann Hodge, July 19, 1980; 1 child, William Clifford. BBA, Coll. William & Mary, 1980. Payroll mgr. Modern Machine & Tool Co., Inc., Newport News, Va., 1980-82; v.p. fin. mgmt. Modern Machine & Tool Co., Inc., Newport News, 1982-85, v.p. fin. mgmt. personnel, 1985—; arbitrator Better Bus. Bur., Newport, 1984—. Vice chmn. James CIty County Rep. Com., 1983-84, Robert's Dist. chmn., 1987-88. v.p. Mem. Peninsula Personnel Assn. Episcopalian. Club: Lafayette Gun (York County, Va.). Lodge: Shriners (sr. deacon 1988—). Home: 124 William Claiborne Williamsburg VA 23185 Office: Modern Machine & Tool Co Inc 11844 Jefferson Ave Newport News VA 23606-2587

DUNN, JOSEPH MCELROY, manufacturing company executive; b. Toledo, Aug. 9, 1926; s. Robert C. and Myrtle (Bridgeman) D.; m. Martha Louise Nutt, Dec. 29, 1950; children: Christopher, Kathryn, Barbara, David. BBA, Ohio State U., 1949. Jr. acct. Arthur Young & Co., Toledo, 1949-50; ptnr. Bob Dunn Automobile, Seattle, 1950-58; v.p., then pres. Moline (Ill.) Corp., 1958-64; sales trainee to pres. PACCAR Inc., Bellevue, Wash., 1964—, also bd. dirs. Bd. dirs. Seattle First Nat. Bank, Seafirst Corp. Served with Q.M.C. USN, 1944-45, PTO. Mem. Western Hwy. Inst. (v.p. at large 1987-88). Republican. Presbyterian. Clubs: Seattle Golf; Desert Island Golf (Rancho Mirage, Calif.). Lodge: Masons. Home: 1556 77th Pl NE Bellevue WA 98004 Office: PACCAR Inc 777 106th Ave NE Bellevue WA 98004

DUNN, RICHARD JOSEPH, investment counselor; b. Chgo., Apr. 5, 1924; s. Richard Joseph and Margaret Mary (Jennett) D.; A.B., Yale U., 1948; LL.B., Harvard U., 1951; M.B.A., Stanford U., 1956; m. Marygrace Calhoun, Oct. 13, 1951; children—Richard, Marianne, Anthony, Gregory, Noelle. Admitted to Tex. bar, 1952; mem. firm Carrington, Gowen, Johnson & Walker, Dallas, 1951-54; investment counselor Scudder, Stevens & Clark, San Francisco, 1956-84, v.p., 1965-77, sr. v.p., 1977-84, gen. partner, 1974-84; ret., 1984. Mem. Democratic State Central Com., Calif., 1962; mem. San Francisco Dem. County Central Com., 1963-66; bd. dirs. Mercy High Sch., 1978-81. Served with AUS, 1943-46. Decorated Purple Heart. Mem. Knight of the Sovereign Mil. Hospitaller Order of St. John of Jerusalem of Rhodes and of Malta 1978— (Officer Cross of Merit, 1986, Chancellor 1987, bd. of dirs. 1987—), Knight of the Sacred Mil. Constantinian Order of St. George 1988—. Roman Catholic. Home: 530 Junipero Serra Blvd San Francisco CA 94127

DUNN, RONALD HOLLAND, engineer; b. Balt., Sept. 15, 1937; s. Delmas Joseph and Edna Grace (Holland) D.; m. Verona Lucille Lambert, Aug. 17, 1958; children: Ronald H., Jr. (dec.), David R., Brian W. Student U. S.C., 1956-58; BS in Engring., Johns Hopkins U., 1969. Field engr. Balt. & Ohio R.R., Balt., 1958-66; chief engr. yards, shops, trackwork DeLeuw, Cather & Co., Washington, 1966-73; mgr. engring. support Parsons-Brinckerhoff-Tudor-Bechtel, Atlanta, 1973-76; dir. railroad engring. Morrison-Knudsen Co., Inc., Boise, Idaho, 1976-78; v.p. Parsons Brinckerhoff-Centec, Inc., McLean, Va., 1978-83; v.p., area mgr., tech. dir. ry. engring., profl. assoc. Parsons Brinckerhoff Quade & Douglas, Inc., McLean and Pitts., 1983-84; dir. transp. engring. R.L. Banks & Assocs., Inc., Washington, 1984; pres. R.H. Dunn & Assocs., Inc., Fairfax, Va., 1984—; insp. ry. and rail transit facilities, Europe, 1980, 82, 84, China and Hong Kong, 1985; involved in engring. of 15 railroads and 16 rail transit systems throughout N. Am.; guest Japan Railway Civil Engring. Assn., 1972, French Nat. Railroads and Paris Transport Authority, 1988; mem. adv. com. track engrs. U.S. Dept. Transp., 1968-71. Chmn. Cub Scout Pack, Boy Scouts Am., 1972-73, committeeman, 1973-75, troop committeeman, 1979-85. Mem. Am. Mgmt. Assn., Am. Ry. Engring. Assn., ASCE, Am. Public Transit Assn., Soc. Am. Mil. Engrs., Roadmasters and Maintenance of Way Assn. of Am., Am. Ry. Bridge and Bldg. Assn., Constrn. Specifications Inst., Nat. Soc. Profl. Engrs., Transp. Research Bd., Soc. Profl. Mgmt. Cons., Can. Soc. Civil Engring., Can. Urban Transit Assn., Inst. Transp. Engrs., Ry. Tie Assn., Inst. of Rapid Transit, Phi Kappa Sigma. Methodist. Office: 10608 Orchard St Fairfax VA 22030

DUNN, STEVEN BURKE, manufacturing executive; b. Cedar Rapids, Iowa, Dec. 3, 1955; s. Theodore Winton and Helen Elaine (Healey) D.; m. Marilyn Ruth Gasser, May 23, 1986; children: Jordan, Jeffrey, Mollie. BS in Indsl. Engring., U. Iowa, 1978. Indsl. planner Rockwell Internat., Anaheim, Calif., 1979-80; various positions Unit Rig & Equipment Co., Tulsa, 1980-84;

mgr. engring. and prodn. Hawkeye Products, Inc., Corona, Calif., 1984; dist. sales mgr. Standard Havens, Inc., Kansas City, Mo., 1985-87; mfg. rep. Dunn Equipment Co., Aurora, Colo., 1987—. Cub scout leader Boy Scouts Am., Aurora, 1987—; coach Aurora YMCA, 1987—. Republican. Home and Office: Dunn Equipment Co 1808 E Harvard Dr Aurora CO 80014

DUNN, VIRGINIA ROSE (GINGER), securities brokerage executive; b. Gardner, Mass., June 30, 1940; d. Henry Roger and Vivian June (Rouleau) Denis; m. James Edward Dunn, Sept. 19, 1959 (div. Aug. 1984); children: Debra Lynn, James Edward Jr., Jennifer Gaye, Clayton Scott. Grad. high sch., Alexandria, Va. Sec. CIA, Langley, Va., 1958-62; exec. asst. LogEtronics, Inc., Springfield, Va., 1964-69; office mgr. Witherspoon & Lane, Arlington, Va., 1969-77; gen. mgr. Wagonwerks, College Park, Md., 1978-79; sec. Internat. Money Mgmt., Greenbelt, Md., 1979-84, office mgr., 1984-85, v.p. ops., 1985-86, exec. v.p., 1986—, also bd. dirs.; bd. dirs. Internat. Money Mgmt. Corp., Greenbelt, Summit Capital Group, Inc. Mem. Am. Mgmt. Assn., Internat. Assn. Fin. Planners, Nat. Assn. Female Execs. Republican. Office: Internat Money Mgmt 6301 Ivy Ln #514 Greenbelt MD 20770

DUNN, WARREN HOWARD, lawyer, brewery executive; b. Omaha, Sept. 25, 1934; s. John Ralph and Frances (Liddell) D.; m. Nancy Ann Nolan, July 2, 1955; children—Kathleen, Erin, Theresa, Maureen. B.S. in Bus. Adminstrn, Creighton U., Omaha, 1956, J.D., 1958. Bar: Nebr. 1958, Wis. 1967. Claims adjuster U.S. Fidelity & Guarantee Co., Omaha, 1958-59; spl. agt. FBI, 1959-66; with Miller Brewing Co., Milw., 1966—, v.p., gen. counsel, 1973-84, sr. v.p. adminstrn., 1984—. Mem. ABA, Wis. Bar Assn., Nebr. Bar Assn., Milw. Bar Assn. Office: Miller Brewing Co 3939 W Highland Blvd Milwaukee WI 53208

DUNN, WENDELL EARL, III, management consultant, business educator; b. Boca Raton, Fla., Aug. 20, 1945; s. Wendell Earl Jr. and Lillian (Daniels) D.; m. Kathleen Ann Riley, Mar. 29, 1981; 1 child, Elissa Brooks. BA, Johns Hopkins U., 1966; MBA, U. So. Calif., 1973; PhD, U. Mich., 1981. Asst. to dir. personnel Johns Hopkins U., Balt., 1967-68; pilot project mgr. Chlorine Tech. Ltd., Sydney, Australia, 1968-71; energy analyst Alex Brown & Sons, Balt., 1973-74; lectr. bus. adminstrn. U. Mich., Ann Arbor, 1977-80; asst. prof. bus. adminstrn. Coll. of William and Mary, Williamsburg, Va., 1980-81; prin. W.E. Dunn & Assocs., Phila., 1981—; lectr. mgmt. Wharton Sch. U. Pa., Phila., 1981-82, 84-88; adj. assoc. prof., 1989—, course head Entrepreneurship & New Ventures (grad.), 1986—, faculty Exec. MBA Program, 1988—; adj. assoc. prof. Columbia U., 1983-84; mem. planning com. U.S. Dept. Commerce Nat. Innovation Workshops, 1986, leader N.Y.C. workshops, 1987; spl. advisor Hopkins/Nanjing program Sch. Advanced Internat. Studies Johns Hopkins U., Washington, 1987—. Contbr. articles to profl. jours.; mem. editorial bd. Jour. of Bus. Venturing, 1987—. Active Luth. Student Found., Ann Arbor, 1978-80, trustee Internat. Peace Policy Rsch. Inst., 1989—; cons. Bus. Vols. for Arts, Phila., 1982-83; active Luth. Retirement Homes, Phila., 1983-84; hon. mem. adv. coun. Internat. Biog. Centre, Cambridge, Eng. Robert Rodkey Found. fellow, 1974-75. Mem. Acad. Mgmt., Strategic Mgmt. Soc., Internat. Platform Assn., Intellectual Property Owners, Am. Soc. Inventors (bd. dirs. 1984-87, nat. pres. 1985-86), Beta Gamma Sigma, Phi Kappa Phi. Republican. Clubs: Down Town (bd. govs. 1986—), Faculty of U. Pa., Great Oak Yacht. Avocations: sailing, gardening. Home: 443 Gladstone Ave Haddonfield NJ 08033 Office: W E Dunn & Assocs PO Box 2036 Haddonfield NJ 08033 other: U Pa Wharton Sch 428 Vance Hall Philadelphia PA 19104-6301

DUNN, WILLIAM DAVID, lawyer, writer; b. Tampa, Fla., July 2, 1933; s. Thomas Henry and Eleanor (Stephens) D. B.S. in Journalism, Fla. State U., 1953; J.D., U. Fla., 1958; postgrad. in French studies U. Paris, 1965-66, in art history Ecole du Louvre, Paris, 1966-67. Bar: N.Y. 1972, U.S. Dist. Ct. (so. and ea. dists.) N.Y. 1974. Night news editor Nippon Times, Tokyo, 1954-55; arts editor St. Petersburg Times, Fla., 1958-65; bur. chief MacNens News Agy., Paris, 1965-66; account exec. Foote, Cone & Belding, Paris, 1967-68; editorial dir. Advt. Trade Publs., N.Y.C., 1968-70; def. atty. Legal Aid Soc., N.Y.C., 1972—. Editor monthly mag. Art Direction, 1968-70, FotoTimes, 1970-71. Area coordinator Gt. Books Found., discussion groups, Fla., 1959-63; mem. coordinating council Great Decisions, fgn. policy discussion groups, St. Petersburg, Fla., 1961-64; bd. dirs. Fla. Arts Council, 1963-65, Performing Arts Alumni Theatre, N.Y.C., 1983—; mem. adv. bd. New Mus., N.Y.C., 1975—. Served with U.S. Army, 1953-55. Recipient Key to City, Mayor of St. Petersburg, 1965. Mem. N.Y. State Bar Assn., New York County Bar Assn., N.Y. State Defenders (bd. dirs. 1976—, amicus curiae com. 1983—, treas. 1985—), Gold Key, Alpha Tau Omega, Delta Sigma Pi. Democrat. Clubs: Union (Tokyo); American (Paris). Home: 77 W 85th St Apt 2-C New York NY 10024 also: 2118 Marjory Ave Tampa FL 33606 Office: Legal Aid Soc 80 Lafayette St New York NY 10013

DUNN, WILLIAM WARREN, corporation financial executive; b. Bellows Falls, Vt., Aug. 19, 1936; s. William Warren and Katharine (Hamilton) D.; m. Gloria D. Digiulian, July 11, 1965; children: Christine J., Alexander W. BA, Bowdoin Coll., 1959; MBA, NYU, 1963. CPA, N.Y. Mgr. internal audit Sinclair Oil Co., N.Y.C., 1967-69; mgr. internal cons. Schlumberger Ltd., N.Y.C. and Paris, 1969-73, controller N.Am., 1973-76, controller Wireline group, 1976-79, corp. controller, 1980-87; v.p. fin. Ft. Howard Corp., Green Bay, Wis., 1987—. Mem. Am. Inst. CPA's, N.Y. State Soc. CPA's, Nat. Assn. Accts., Fin. Execs. Inst. Club: Board Room (N.Y.C.). Home: 3045 Nicolet Dr Green Bay WI 54311

DUNNE, DANA PHILIP C., banker; b. N.Y.C., July 30, 1963; s. Philip M. and Diane (Cantine) D. BA, Wesleyan U., 1985. Asst. treas. Chase Manhattan Bank, N.Y.C., 1985—. Author: Financial Instability: An Empirical Analysis; editor-in-chief Wesleyan Economic Review. Mem. Meals for Homeless St. James' Ch., 1985—; mentor Underprivileged Youths in South Bronx, 1986. Named Disting. Internat. Young Leader Cambridge U. Am. Biog. Inst., Eng., 1987. Episcopalian. Club: N.Y. Athletic. Home: 750 Park Ave New York NY 10021

DUNNE, DIANE C., advertising executive; b. Milw.; d. Francis and Ruth Carolyn (Borman) Cantine; 1 child, Dana Philip. BS, Marquette U., 1970; MBA, NYU, 1985. Mgr. advt. NBC, N.Y.C., 1975-77; dir. funding CBS, N.Y.C., 1977-80; dir. advt. Bloomingdale's, N.Y.C., 1980—; dir. 750 Park Ave. Corp., N.Y.C., 1985—; dir. Women's Econ. Round Table, 1988—. Author: Guidelines to Advertising All News Radio, 1976. Author: Guidlines for Catalogue Copywriters, 1985; asst. editor Am. Cancer Soc., Gourmet Guide for Busy People by Famous People, 1985, The Internat. Directory of Disting. Leadership; contbr. articles to profl. jours. Mem. Am. Cancer Soc., N.Y.C., 1980—; chair St. James Ch. Feed the Homeless com., N.Y.C., 1984—; mem. pastoral and community ministry com. St. James Altar Guild. Mem. Fashion Group (co-chair regional com.), Women's Econ. Roundtable (bd. dirs. 1988), NYU Exec. MBA Assn. Episcopalian. Avocations: opera, jogging, skiing, squash. Home: 750 Park Ave New York NY 10021 Office: Bloomingdales 155 E 60th St New York NY 10022

DUNNEWALD, DAVID ALAN, public relations executive; b. Rock Springs, Wyo., May 10, 1960; s. John Bishop and Mary Francis (Day) D. BA in Econs. magna cum laude, Colo. Coll., 1982. Cert. pub. relations profl. Specialist econ. communications Adolph Coors Co., Golden, Colo., 1983-84; analyst pub. affairs research Adolph Coors Co., Golden, 1984-85, mgr. systems publ. and special programs, 1985—. Editor: For Living In Today's Economy, 1983— (recipient Bronze Quill 1984, 85). Mem. Nat. Assn. Bus. Economists, Pub. Relations Soc. Am., Internat. Assn. Bus. Communicators (v.p. fin. 1984-85), Golden Lions, Toastmasters (area gov. 1987-88, pres. 1987, ednl. v.p. 1986), Phi Beta Kappa. Libertarian. Clubs: Golden Lions, Toastmasters (area gov. 1987-88). Home: 335 Wright St #11-107 Lakewood CO 80228 Office: Adolph Coors Co Community Affairs Dept NH410 Golden CO 80401

DUNNIGAN, T. KEVIN, electrical and electronics manufacturing company executive; b. 1938; married. B.A. in Commerce, Loyola U., 1971. With Can. Elec. Distbg. Co., prior to 1962; with Thomas & Betts Co., Raritan, N.J., 1962—; div. pres. Thomas & Betts Co., 1974-78, corp. exec. v.p. electronics, 1978-80, pres., 1980—, chief operating officer, 1980-85, chief exec. officer, 1985—, also bd. dirs.; bd. dirs. Foster Wheeler Corp., Nat. Starch and Chem. Corp. Mem. Electronics Industry Assn. (bd. govs.). Office: Thomas & Betts Corp 1001 Frontier Rd Bridgewater NJ 08807

DUNNINGTON, WALTER GREY, JR., lawyer, food and tobacco company executive; b. N.Y.C., Feb. 5, 1927; s. Walter Grey and Allen (Gray) D.; m. Jacqueline Cochran, Apr. 26, 1958; m. Patricia MacPhee, Sept. 21, 1972; children: Walter Grey III, India M. BA, U. Va., 1948, LLB, 1950. Bar: N.Y. 1952. Assoc. Rathbone, Perry, Kelley & Drye, N.Y.C., 1950-54; ptnr. Dunnington, Bartholow & Miller, N.Y.C., 1954-75, sr. ptnr., 1976-81; sr. v.p., gen. counsel Standard Brands Inc., N.Y.C., 1981; exec. v.p., gen. counsel Nabisco Brands, Inc., East Hanover, N.J., 1981-87; sr. v.p., dep. gen. counsel RJR Nabisco, Inc., N.Y.C., 1987-88, counsel to pres., chief exec. officer, 1988—; bd. dirs. Brittania Industries, Ltd., Bombay, Nabisco Brands, Toronto, Ont., Canada. Bd. govs. N.Y. Hosp., N.Y.C.; trustee Algernon Sydney Sullivan Found., Morristown, N.J., Boys' Club N.Y., N.Y.C., Sprague Found., N.Y.C.; trustee emeritus Woodberry Forest Sch., Va. Served with USNR, 1945. Mem. ABA, Assn. Bar City N.Y., N.Y. State Bar Assn., Grocery Mfrs. Am. (legal steering com.). Episcopalian. Clubs: Brook (N.Y.C.) (v.p., sec., gov.); Racquet and Tennis (N.Y.C.); Nat. Golf Links Am. (Southampton, N.Y.) (v.p., dir.); Deepdale (L.I., N.Y.); Somerset Hills Country (Bernardsville, N.J.). Home: Roxiticus Rd PO Box 479 Gladstone NJ 07934 Office: RJR Nabisco Inc 100 DeForest Ave East Hanover NJ 07936

DUNN-RANKIN, DEREK, newspaper publishing executive; b. Hackensack, N.J., Oct. 7, 1927; s. Frederic and Helen (Schoonmaker) D.-R.; m. Betty Jean Fryar, Apr. 18, 1953; children: Peter, David, Jeff, Debbie, Mike. BA, Rollins Coll., 1952; student, Guilford Coll. Reporter St. Petersburg (Fla.) Times, 1950-51; city circulation mgr. Miami (Fla.) News, 1952-65; circulation mgr. Greensboro (N.C.) News, 1965-69; pres., gen. mgr. Virginian Pilot, 1969-77; pres., publisher Sun Coast Media Group, Venice, Fla., 1977—; pres. Fla. Newspaper Pubs., 1984. Office: Sun Coast Media Group 200 E Venice Ave Venice FL 34285-2230

DUNSIRE, P(ETER) KENNETH, insurance company executive; b. Spearhill, Man., Can., Mar. 1, 1932; came to U.S., 1969; s. Robert Anderson and Margaret (Kinnear) D.; m. Lily Martha Bell (div. Nov. 1971); children: Robert K., Barbara L. Dunsire Belanger; m. Stephanie Alice Mooradian. Student, U. B.C., Can., 1949-50, U. Alta., Can., 1955-56. V.p. Avco Fin. Services, Newport Beach, Calif., 1961-71; exec. v.p. Carte Blanche, Los Angeles, 1971-74, pres., 1974-78; chmn. Am. Benefit Plan Adminstrn., Los Angeles, 1978-80; exec. v.p. Paul Revere Life Ins. Co., Worcester, Mass., 1980-84; exec. v.p. Lincoln Nat. Life Ins. Co., Ft. Wayne, Ind., 1984-86, also bd. dirs.; exec. v.p. Lincoln Nat. Corp., Ft. Wayne, Ind., 1986—; bd. dirs. Security Conn. Life Ins. Co., Avon, First Penn Pacific Life Ins. Co., Chgo., Western Security Life Ins., Phoenix; chmn. Cannon Lincoln Ltd., London, 1984—. Bd. dirs. Sta. WFWA-TV, Ft. Wayne, 1985—, Auburn Cord Duesenberg Mus., Ind., 1986—, Ft. Wayne Civic Theater, Ft. Wayne, 1985-86. Republican. Home: 8140 Auburn Rd Fort Wayne IN 46825 Office: Lincoln Nat Corp 1300 S Clinton St Fort Wayne IN 46801

DUNTON, JAMES KEGEBEIN, investment management company executive; b. White Stone, Va., Jan. 18, 1938; s. Ammon Gresham and Carolyn (Kegebein) D.; m. Janet Jamison, Nov. 7, 1958 (div.); children: James Gresham, Robert Anson, Elizabeth Ann Gould; m. Nancy Hilton, Sept. 24, 1977; children: Katherine Hilton. BA, U. Va., 1959, MBA, 1962. Chartered fin. analyst. Fin. analyst Capital Rsch. Co., N.Y.C. and L.A., 1962-66; v.p. Capital Rsch. Co., L.A., 1966-69, exec. v.p., 1982—; v.p. Capital Guardian Trust Co., L.A., 1969-72, sr. v.p., 1972-82; sr. v.p. Capital Rsch. and Mgmt. Co., L.A., 1985—; exec. v.p. Am. Mut. Fund, L.A., 1986—. Bd. trustees U. Va. Darden Grad. Sch. Bus. Adminstrn., Charlottesville, 1987—. Mem. L.A. Soc. Fin. Analysts (pres. 1981-82, Outstanding Mem. award), Fin. Analysts Fedn. (vice chmn., dir. 1988—), Internat. Soc. Fin. Analysts (pres. 1988—), Inst. Chartered Fin. Analysts, University Club (pres. 1979-80), The Valley Hunt Club, Flintridge Riding Club. Republican. Episcopalian. Home: 680 Burleigh Dr Pasadena CA 91105 Office: Capital Rsch Co 333 S Hope St Los Angeles CA 90071

DUPLANT, MAX STEPHANIE, accountant; b. Port Arthur, Tex., June 10, 1956; d. Gerald and Pat (Sinclair) Oubre; m. John K. Duplant, May 14, 1977; children: Jason, Stephanie, Julien. BBA with honors, Lamar U., 1977. CPA, Tex. Staff acct. Bruce W. Jackson, CPA, Beaumont, Tex., 1978; ptnr. Charles E. Reed & Assocs. CPAs, Port Arthur, 1978—. Bd. dirs. Montessori Sch., Port Arthur, 1983-84. Mem. Am. Inst. CPA's, Tex. Soc. CPA's, Southeast Tex. Soc. CPA's (pres. 1987-88), Bus. and Profl. Womens Assn. (treas. 1987-88, Young Career Woman award 1986), Nat. Assn. Female Execs., Port Arthur C. of C. (membership com. 1986-87). Office: Charles E Reed & Assocs PC CPAs 3636 Professional Dr Port Arthur TX 77619

DUPPER, LARRY LIN, medical center administrator; b. Denver, Mar. 20, 1953; s. Calvin C. and Lorraine (Andres) D.; m. Pamela G. Knopp, June 26, 1977; children: Kalin, Michelle, Jeremy, Corina. BBA, Union Coll., Lincoln, Nebr., 1975. Controller Tillamook (Oreg.) County Gen. Hosp., 1975-79, Platte Valley Med. Ctr., Brighton, Colo., 1979-82; asst. adminstr. fin. Arkansas City (Kans.) Meml. Hosp., 1982-84; regional dir. fin. Hosp. Mgmt. Profls. Inc., Nashville, 1984-86; asst. adminstr. fin. Phelps County Regional Med. Ctr., Rolla, Mo., 1986—. Mem. Healthcare Fin. Mgmt. Assn. (bd. dirs., sec. "Show-Me" chpt. 1988—). Seventh-Day Adventist. Lodge: Lions. Office: Phelps County Regional Med Ctr 1000 W 10th St Rolla MO 65401

DUPUIS, VICTOR EDWARD, financial planning company executive; b. Arlington, Va., Jan. 27, 1960; s. Victor Lionel and Mary (Miles) D.; m. Faith Ann Bailey, May 21, 1983; children: Joy Elizabeth, Victor Miles. BS in Polit. Sci., Pa. State U., 1982; cert., Coll. for Fin. Planning, 1987. Assoc. Wienken and Assocs., State College, Pa., 1982—; rep. Mut. Benefit Cos., Newark, 1982—; cons. retirement seminar Commonwealth of Pa., 1986—; instr. continuing edn. Pa. State U., 1987—, Bloomsburg, Pa., 1988—. Mem. Nat. Assn. Life Underwriters (nat. quality award 1982, 88, nat. sales achievement award 1988), Centre County Assn., Life Underwriters (pres. 1986-87, chmn. polit. action com. 1987-88), Pa. Assn. Life Underwriters (regional v.p. 1988—). Democrat. Baptist. Lodge: Elks. Office: Wienken & Assocs 3939 S Atherton ST State College PA 16801

DUPUY, HOWARD MOORE, JR., lawyer; b. Portland, Oreg., Mar. 15, 1929; s. Howard Moore and Lola (Dunham) D.; m. Anne Irene Hanna, Aug. 26, 1950; children: Loanne Kay, Brent Moore. BA, U. Portland, 1951; postgrad., Willamette U., 1951; LLB, Lewis and Clark Coll., 1956. Bar: Oreg. 1956. Since practiced in Portland; assoc. Green, Richardson, Green & Griswold, 1956; ptnr. Morton & Dupuy, 1957-67, Black & Dupuy (and predecessor firm), 1968—. Mem. fin. com. Oreg. Rep. Cen. Com., 1962. Served with AUS, 1946-47. Mem. Am., Oreg., Multnomah County Bar Assns., Am. Arbitration Assn. (nat. panel arbitrators), World Trade Club, Oregon Trial Lawyers Assn., Am. Judicature Soc. Club: World Trade (Portland). Home: 16116 NE Stanton St Portland OR 97230 Office: Black & Dupuy 1515 SW Fifth Ave Ste 515 Portland OR 97201

DURAY-BITO, SIEGFRIED PETER, securities company executive; b. Cleve., Oct. 14, 1957; s. Joseph and Cecile (Duray) D-B.; m. Sara Lynn Williams, June 16, 1984; 1 child, Cassandra. Student, U. Colo., 1979, Met. State Coll., 1980. Stockbroker Rauscher, Pierce & Refsnes, Denver, 1982-84, Prudential Bache, Boulder, Colo., 1984-85; chief fin. officer Schneider Securities, Denver, 1985—; v.p., fin. Schneider Mgmt. Co., Denver, 1987—; arbitrator, N.Y. Stock Exchange. Editor: The Met. Newspaper, 1979. Treas., bd. dirs. Colo. Fedn. of Arts, 1987—. Served with U.S. Army, 1975-77. Mem. Nat. Assn. of Securities Dealers. Home: 5475 Manitou Rd Littleton CO 80123 Office: Schneider Securities 104 Broadway Denver CO 80203

DURBROW, BRIAN RICHARD, management consultant; b. Milw., Apr. 26, 1940; s. Robert James and Marianne Winifred (Pengelly) D.; A.A., U. Fla., 1961; B.B.A., U. Iowa, 1962; M.S., No. Ill. U., 1968; Ph.D., Ohio State U., 1971; diploma, Indsl. Coll. Armed Forces, 1972; m. Barbara Helen Mustine; children—Robert E., William D. Jr. accountant Buick-Oldsmobile-Pontiac div. Gen. Motors Corp., South Gate, Calif., 1962-64, sr. accountant Chevrolet div., Janesville, Wis., 1964-66; payroll supr. No. Ill. U., 1966-68; financial analyst Ohio State U., 1968-70; pres. B.R. Durbrow and Assocs., Cin., 1969-72; asst. prof. mgmt. Wright State U., Dayton, 1970-71; prof. financial mgmt. Air Force Inst. Tech., 1972-73; pres., chmn. bd. Barbrisons Mgmt. Systems, Inc., Cin., 1972—; pres. Mgmt. Research and Devel. Inst., Cin., 1976-80, merged with Barbrisons Mgmt. Systems, Inc., 1980, pres., 1980—; v.p. PMC Assos., Cin., 1976-78, Selindex, Inc., Tulsa, 1977-81, Effectiveness, Inc., Tampa, 1978-80; vis. prof. mgmt. U. Ala., 1975; asso. prof. mgmt. Xavier U., Cin., 1975-77; speaker Nat. Mgmt. Assn. Active Young Republicans, Calif., Wis., Ill.; vice chmn. Young Reps., Janesville, Wis., 1964, chmn., 1965-66, county treas., 1964, vice chmn., 1965, chmn., 1966, 1st dist. vice chmn., 1965-66, mem. city, county, dist. and state exec. bd., 1965-66, conv. del., 1965; sustaining mem. Rep. Nat. Com., 1983. Mem. Acad. Mgmt., Nat. Mgmt. Assn., Soc. Advancement Mgmt., Am. Soc. Tng. and Devel., Internat. Coun. for Small Bus. Mgmt. Devel., Nat. Small Bus. Assn., Assn. Mgmt. Consultants, Fla. Coun. of 100, Internat. Platform Assn., Nat. Assn. Convenience Stores (assoc.), Commerce Execs. Soc., Sigma Iota Epsilon, Beta Gamma Sigma, Delta Tau Delta, Delta Sigma Pi. Author: Inter-Firm Executive Mobility, 1971; Management Dynamics, 1974, Modern Research on Accident Proneness, 1981; editor various reference works; co-author Accutrac Questionnaries; developer Accutrac Evaluation Systems, Accutrac Risk Analysis, Accutrac Needs Analysis Systems. Contbr. articles to profl. jours. Office: 10451 Grand Oaks Cincinnati OH 45242 Other: 9403 Kenwood Rd A201 Cincinnati OH 45242

DURDEN, CHARLES DENNIS, manufacturing company executive; b. Atlanta, Jan. 13, 1930; s. Cecil and Helen (Adams) D.; m. Diana Widrig, Feb. 11, 1955; children: Thomas, Merideth, Sarah, Matthew. B.S., Ga. Inst. Tech., 1951; M.A., U. Wash., Seattle, 1953, Ph.D., 1955. Cons. Larry Smith and Co., Washington, 1955-59, 60-62; dep. gen. mgr. Charles Center Project, Balt., 1959-60; exec. dir. Downtown Devel. Com., Cin., 1962-67; operating v.p. Federated Dept. Stores, Cin., 1967-75; sr. v.p. and spl. asst. to chief exec. officer RJR Nabisco, Atlanta, 1975—; adj. assoc. prof. Yale U., 1961-67. Vice chmn. Ohio Commn. Local Govt. Service, 1972-73; mem. Ohio Energy Adv. Council, 1974-75; sec. N.C. Council Mgmt. and Devel., 1978-86; mem. N.C. Commn. on Edn. for Econ. Devel., 1983-84; mem. bd. visitors Emory U., 1988—. Recipient award of excellence Urban Land Inst., 1980. Episcopalian. Home: 3333 Cochise Dr NW Atlanta GA 30339-4322 Office: RJR Nabisco 300 Galleria 21st Fl Atlanta GA 30339

DURETTE, PHILIPPE LIONEL, organic chemist; b. Manchester, N.H., Aug. 17, 1944; s. Emile P. and Marie Anne (Martin) D.; m. Anne Louise Patrizio, June 1967; children: Caroline Anne, Suzanne Louise. BS, Marquette U., 1966; PhD, Ohio State U., 1971. Fellow dept. chemistry U. London, 1971-72, U. Hamburg, Fed. Republic Germany, 1972-73; sr. rsch. chemist Merck & Co., Rahway, N.J., 1974-79, rsch. fellow, 1979-89, sr. rsch. fellow, 1989—. Mem. editorial adv. bd. Jour. Carbohydrate Chemistry, 1982-87; contbr. articles to profl. publs.; patentee in field. Mem. Am. Chem. Soc., Chem. Soc., Sigma Xi, Phi Lambda Upsilon. Home: 187 Pine Way New Providence NJ 07974 Office: Merck & Co PO Box 2000 Rahway NJ 07065

DURGAPRASAD, NEMANI, physicist; b. Vijayawada, Andhra Pradesh, India, Oct. 11, 1934; s. Venkatramiah and Annapoornamma (Goda) D.; m. Meera Durgaprasad, Apr. 22, 1968; children, Srinivas, Sapna. MSc, Andhra U., India, 1954; PhD, U. Bombay, 1964. Rsch. asst. and fellow Tata Inst. Fundamental Rsch., Bombay, India, 1955-64; fellow Tata Inst. Fundamental Rsch., Bombay, 1964-78, reader, 1978-85, assoc. prof., 1985—; lectr. Atomic Energy Establishment Tng. Sch., Bombay, 1957-70; resident rsch. assoc. NASA Goddard Space Flight Ctr., Greenbelt, Md., 1964-67; project scientist Spacelab-3 Indian experiment NASA, 1977-85. Contbr. articles to profl. jours. Recipient Pub. Svc. Group Achievement award NASA, 1986. Mem. Am. Geophys. Union (life), Internat. Astron. Union. Office: Tata Inst Fundamental Rsch, Homi Bhabha Rd, Colaba Bombay 400 005, India

DURHAM, G. ROBERT, metal refining company executive; b. 1929. BS, Purdue U., 1951. With Phelps Dodge Corp., N.Y.C., 1967—, exec. v.p. Phelps Dodge Aluminum Products Corp. div., 1967-71, pres. Consolidated Aluminum div., 1971-77, chmn. Phelps Dodge Internat. Corp. div., 1977-80, corp. v.p., 1980-82, sr. v.p., 1982-84, pres., chief operating officer, from 1984, chief exec. officer, 1987—, now also chmn., bd. dirs. *

DURHAM, JAMES MICHAEL, financial services company executive; b. Streator, Ill., May 19, 1950; s. James Vincent and Mary Anna (Littlejohn) D.; m. Barbara Sue Harp, July 19, 1977; children: Jonathan, Jason. BA in Acctg., St. Ambrose Coll., 1972. From staff acct. to audit mgr. Ernst & Whinney, Chgo. and Hartford, Conn., 1972-83; fin. v.p. Monarch Capital Corp., Springfield, Mass., 1983—. Bd. dirs., mem. fin. com. Vis. Nurses of Greater Hartford, 1982; bd. dirs. Jr. Achievement of Western Mass., Springfield, 1984—. Mem. Am. Inst. CPA's, Am. Coun. Life Ins. (fin. prins. com. 1986-1987), Wampanoag Country Club (West Harford, pres. 1987-88). Roman Catholic. Club: Wampanoag Country (West Harford, Conn.) (pres. 1987-89). Home: 7 Tunxis Rd West Hartford CT 06107

DURHAM, JOHN ROBERT, auditor; b. Chgo., Oct. 11, 1945; s. Frank and Evelyn Helena (Hartelius) D.; m. Deanna Barabas, June 26, 1976. Student, U. Ill., 1963-64, Bradley U., 1964-67; BS, Northland Coll., 1969. CPA; cert. internal auditor. Sr. acct. Canteen Corp., Chgo., 1967-68; sr. auditor, sr. acct. Kraft, Northbrook, Ill., 1969-1975; analyst Esmark, Inc., Chgo., 1975; sr. auditor Norchem, Omaha, 1976-85; supervisory sr. auditor Enron Corp., Houston, 1986—; mgr. acctg. USI Chemicals, 1986—. Served to capt. USAF, 1964-66. Mem. Inst. Internal Auditors. Republican. Lutheran. Home: 11659 Symmes Creek Dr Loveland OH 45140 Office: Quantum Chem Corp 11500 Northlake Dr Cincinnati OH 45249

DURHAM, MICHAEL JONATHAN, transportation company executive; b. N.Y.C., Jan. 19, 1951; s. Walter Allen and Joyce D. (Packham) D.; m. Marilyn James Marr, May 19, 1984; 1 child, Michael Allen. BA in Econs., U. Rochester, 1973; MBA in Fin., Cornell U., 1977. Asst. v.p. Bank Julius Bar & Co., N.Y.C., 1978-79; sr. analyst fin. planning Am. Airlines, Ft. Worth, 1979-80, mgr. corp. fin., 1980-82, dir. corp. fin., 1982-84, asst. treas. corp. fin., 1984-85, v.p. corp. devel., 1985-87, v.p. fin. and planning, 1987-89, v.p., treas., 1989—. Recipient Wall Street Jour. award, 1977; grantee U.S. Pub. Health Svc., 1975-76. Republican. Episcopalian. Club: Las Colinas Sports (Dallas). Home: 3941 Purdue University Park TX 75225 Office: Am Airlines PO Box 619616 MD2D51 Dallas-Fort Worth Airport TX 75261-9616

DURICK, MICHAEL DENNIS, labor relations executive; b. Council Bluffs, Iowa, Mar. 11, 1942; s. Dewey Theodore and Lorene (Davison) D.; m. Martha Claire Ashmore, Aug. 24, 1962 (div.); children: Kyle, Judi, Janice; m. Diana Lynn Lowrance, Dec. 12, 1978. BBA, U. Iowa, 1967. Sales rep. The Dow Chem. Co., Cin., 1967-69; credit rep. The Dow Chem. Co., Midland, Mich., 1969-70; credit mgr. AMSPEC, Inc., Columbus, Ohio, 1970-72; dir. activities S.D. Bldg. Contractors Assn., San Diego, 1972-73, exec. v.p., 1973-78; pres. Profl. Labor Relations, La Mesa, Calif., 1978-88; adv. bd. Mesa Coll., San Diego, 1972-78. Contbr. articles to profl. pubs. Trustee Roofers Benefit Funds, San Diego, 1985—. With USN, 1960-64. Recipient Seldon Hale award Nat. Assn. Home Builders, 1974, 75, 76, 77; named Spike of Yr. Bldg. Industry Assn., San Diego, 1983. Mem. Indsl. Relations Research Assn. Republican. Presbyterian. Club: Sertoma (San Diego) (pres. 1972-73). Office: Profl Labor Rels Inc 8278 University Ave La Mesa CA 92041

DURKEE, EDWARD RUDI, investment manager; b. Rapid City, S.D., Nov. 7, 1944; s. Wallace Nicholas and Elizabeth Louise (Ziehm) D.; m. Margaret Walker, June 30, 1968 (div. May 1974); m. Leslie Woicekoski, May 1, 1980; children: Asa R., Cornelia. BA, Princeton U., 1966; MBA, Harvard U., 1968. Assoc. Morgan Stanley & Co., N.Y.C., 1968-71; mgr. corp. fin. Clark Dodge & Co., Boston, 1971-74; pres. Durkee & Co., Suffield, Conn., 1974-83; exec. v.p. White Resources Inc., Marion, Mass., 1983-84; mng. dir. Athena Mgmt. Co., Boston, 1984-89; pres. Glen Magna Investment Corp., Boston, 1989—. Contbr. articles to profl. jours. With U.S. Army, 1968-69. Mem. Harvard Club, Cap & Gown Club. Republican. Episcopalian. Office: Glen Magna Investment Corp PO Box 1517 Boston MA 02104

DURKES, RICHARD WARREN, investment banker; b. Evanston, Ill., Feb. 10, 1950; s. Richard Steel and Betty Ann (Wehn) D.; m. Clementina Virgin, Aug. 26, 1972; children: Frances Wehn, Harriet Steel. BA, U. Va., 1972. Trust officer No. Trust Co., Chgo., 1972-77; pres. 1st City Bancshares, Dixon, Ill., 1977-82; v.p. Chgo. Corp., 1982-85, sr. v.p., 1985—, also bd. dirs. Bd. dirs. Children's Meml. Hosp. Found., Chgo., 1988—, Chgo. maternity ctr. Prentice Woman's Hosp., Chgo., 1988—, banking rsch. ctr. Northwestern U. Mem. Onwetsia Club. (gov. Ill. chpt.), Racquet Club, Casino Club, Chgo. Club, Snkaty Head Golf Club., Pine Valley Country Club. Republican. Presbyterian. Home: 6 E Scott Ave Chicago IL 60610 Office: Chgo Corp 208 LaSalle St Chicago IL 60604

DURKIN, DIANE BARBARA, accountant; b. Plainfield, N.J., Jan. 11, 1960; d. Daniel Edward and Barbara Joan (Coons) Craney; m. Kevin Michael Durkin, Oct. 9, 1956; 1 child, Alyssa Joy. BS in Acctg., Rider Coll., 1981. Sr. acct. Delmed, Inc., New Brunswick, N.J., 1984-88; tchr. bus. acctg. Neptune (N.J.) Sr. High Sch., 1988—. Presbyterian. Home: 106 Bay Way Lanoka Harbor NJ 08734 Office: Neptune Sr High Sch Neptune Blvd Neptune NJ 08734

DURRETT, DEWEY BERT, real estate, ranching; b. Belington, W.Va., May 16, 1929; s. Dewey Lee and Bernice Cinthy (Simon) D.; m. Pauline Ann Stefanik, May 3, 1958; children: Bryan Price, Keith Simon, Craig Steven. BS, W.Va. U., 1951; MS, U. Mass., 1957; student, Air U., Maxwell AFB, Ala., 1964, 67; cert. nat. security mgmt., Indsl. Coll. Armed Services, 1968. Capt. Delta Airlines, Boston, 1957-85; owner, chief exec. officer Durrett Enterprises, Salem, N.H., 1967—. Mem. Credit Bur. of Greater Lawrence, Mass., 1978—. Served to lt. col. USAFR, 1951-79. Durrett Hall named after him Erickson Alumni Ctr. W.Va. U., 1986; recipient Am. Farmer Degree award Future Farmers Am., 1949. Mem. Air Force Assn., Res. Officers Assn., Airline Pilots Assn., Aircraft Owners and Pilots Assn., Salem Contractors Assn., Greater Lawrence Rental Assn., Found. N.Am. Wild Sheep, Nat. Rifle Assn., Exptl. Aircraft Assn., Am. Legion, Nat. Cattlemen's Assn., W.Va. Cattlemen's Assn., N.H. Aviation Assn., Alpha Gamma Rho (Outstanding Alumnus 1977), Sphinx, Alpha Zeta. Clubs: Internat. C-180-185 (Phoenix) (bd. dirs. 1985—); Cub (Mt. Pleasant, N.Y.); Marmon (Willoughby, Ohio). Home: 377 Main St Salem NH 03079 Office: Durrett Enterprises 373 Main St Salem NH 03079

DURRETT, GEORGE MANN, corporate executive; b. Balt., Oct. 11, 1917; m. Ethel M. Durrett; children: Douglass, Roger W., Gary W., Kyle D. Student, Balt. City Coll., Johns Hopkins U.; Comml. Artist, Md. Inst. Art, 1938. V.p. William G. Wetherall Inc., 1945-63; pres. Ea. Shore Steel Co. Inc., 1957-62, Wetherall Machine Sales Co., 1958-62; pres. Durrett-Sheppard Steel Co., Inc., Balt., 1966—, gen. ptnr., 1984—; v.p. S-D Realty Co., 1964—, D-S Pipe & Supply co. Inc., 1979-88, Grinding Svcs. Inc., 1983—, Durrett Galleries Ltd., 1983—; pres. Durrett-Sheppard Steel Co. Inc., Balt., 1983—, Ridgely Leasing, Inc., Balt., 1983—. Bd. govs. Wesley Theol. Sem.; trustee, mem. adminstrv. bd. and fin. commn. Towson United Meth. Ch. With U.S. Army, 1941-45. Mem. Am. Numis. Assn., Md. Wildlife Fedn., Steel Club Balt., Balt. Country Club, Universal Autograph Collection Club, Masons. Home: 123 St Thomas Ln Owings Mills MD 21117 Office: Durrett Sheppard Steel Co Inc 6800 E Baltimore St Baltimore MD 21224

DURRIE, J. MICHAEL, marketing executive; b. Oakland, Calif., Aug. 25, 1937; s. Charles H. D.; m. Belinda Stead, Aug. 5, 1960; children: Robin, Nicholas, Jennifer, Jessica. Student, Stanford U., 1955-60. With GMAC, Oakland and San Francisco, 1960-69; asst. mgr. GMAC, Rome, 1969-74; control br. mgr. GMAC, Sao Paulo, Brazil, 1974; regional fin. mgr. Australia and New Zealand GMAC, Melbourne, 1974-78, Brazil, 1978-80; treas. GMAC, 1980, dir. overseas and Can. borrowings, 1983, dir. plans, 1984-86, v.p. plans, 1986-87, v.p., mem. exec. com., group v.p. mktg., 1986-88; v.p. cen. U.S. ops. GMAC, Detroit, 1988-89; gen. dir. fleet and govt. sales GM, Detroit, 1989—. Office: GM 3044 W Grand Blvd Detroit MI 48202

DURSIN, HENRY LOUIS, opinion survey company executive; b. Woonsocket, R.I., May 3, 1921; s. Henry and Mary Regina (Butler) D.; m. Margaret Alice Smith, Apr. 20, 1943 (dec.); children: Henry Peter, Philomene Louise, Margaret Elizabeth , Stefanie Marie; m. Marie Ann Novosedlik, May 22, 1982. AB with honors, Brown U., 1942; MBA, Harvard U., 1948. Supr. corp. research Gen. Electric Co., N.Y.C., 1948-63; supr. corp. research Harper-Atlantic Sales Co., N.Y.C., also dir. research and promotion, 1963-67; dir. research ORC Caravan Surveys Co., Princeton, N.J., 1968-70, pres., 1970—; v.p. Opinion Research Corp., Princeton, 1970-74, sr. v.p., 1974—. Chmn. agy. com. United Fund No. Westchester, 1960-68, pres. 1967-68; v.p. Westchester County United Fund, co-chmn. agy. com. 1966-67. Served with USAAF, 1942-46. Mem. Am. Assn. Pub. Opinion Research. Roman Catholic. Club: Harvard (N.Y.C). Home: 42 Bear Brook Rd Princeton NJ 08540 Office: Opinion Rsch Corp Box 183 Princeton NJ 08540

DURVASULA, SRIRAMA SASTRI, lawyer; b. Vizag, India, Mar. 1, 1938; came to U.S., 1970; s. Reddi Pantulu and Varahalamma D.; m. Nagasundari, May 21, 1967; children—Padmaja, Suryaprakash. ISc, A.V.N. Coll., Vizag, 1954; BL, Andhra U., Vizag, 1957; LLM, George Washington U., 1971. Bar: D.C. 1974, Md. 1977, U.S. Supreme Ct. 1977. Advocate High Ct., Andhra Pradesh, India, 1958—; pvt. practice law, Silver Spring, Md., 1974—; mem. faculty law sch., George Washington U., Washington, 1972-75; assoc. gen. counsel Md. Nat. Capital Park and Planning Commn., Silver Spring, 1973—; legal counsel Embassy of India, Washington, 1975—, Permanent Mission of India to UN, N.Y.C., 1980-88; counsel Law Offices of Levan, Schimel, Richman and Belman, P.A., 1989—; panel mem. A.A.A. Internat.and Comml. Arbitration, 1974—. Contbr. articles to profl. publs. Pres. India Cultural Coordination Com., Washington, 1974-79. Mem. ABA, D.C. Bar Assn., Md. State Bar Assn. Democrat. Hindu. Lodge: Masons (worshipful master 1965-66). Home: 2707 Silverdale Dr Silver Spring MD 20906 Office: Woodmere I 9881 Broken Land Pkwy Ste 400 Columbia MD 21046

DUTILLO, CHRISTINE A., financial planner; b. La Grange, Ill., Oct. 16, 1957; d. Grey B. and JoAnn (Scherling) Culberson; married. BA in Psychology, Wheaton Coll., 1981. With sales dept. IBM, Chgo., 1979-81; mktg. rep. Pfizer Labs., Greenbay, Wis., 1981-83; fin. planner Ctr. Estate & Fin. Planning, Tampa, Fla., 1983-87; pres. Fin. Planning Solutions, Inc., Tampa, 1987—. Chmn. ednl. council Lake Wales C. of C., 1984-86. Mem. Internat. Assn. Fin. Planning (bd. dirs. Tampa Bay chpt.), Inst. Cert. Fin. Planners, Investment Co. Inst., Harbor Island Athletic Club. Office: Fin Planning Solutions Inc 2701 N Rocky Point Dr #800 Tampa FL 33607

DUTY, TONY EDGAR, lawyer, former judge; b. Golinda, Tex., May 14, 1928; s. Tony and Glennie Mae (Butler) D.; m. Kathleen Lou Lear; children—Valerie Ann, Barbara Diane, Dan Richard. Student, U. Colo., 1947-49; B.B.A., Baylor U., 1952, J.D., 1953. Bar: Tex. 1954, U.S. Dist. CT. (we. dist.) Tex. 1970, U.S. Ct. Appeals (5th cir.) 1978, U.S. Ct. Appeals (11th cir.) 1981, U.S. Supreme Ct. 1982, U.S. Dist. Ct. (no. dist.) Tex. 1983. Sole practice Waco, Tex., 1954-56, 64—; 1st asst. atty City of Waco, 1957-63; mcpl. judge City Woodway, Tex., 1963-80, City of Lacy-Lakeview, Tex., 1976-78, City of Beverly Hills, Tex., 1976-78, City of Waco, 1957-87, City of Bellmead, Tex., 1964-86; prof. bus. law, corps. and real estate Baylor U., 1976-78; ptnr. Indian Creek Estates; dir. Shannon Devel. Co., Telco Systems Inc., Sun Valley Water and Devel. Co., Inc., Hewitt Devel. Co. Author: The Coronado Expedition, 1540-1542, 1970, James Wilkinson: 1757-1825, 1971, Champ D'Asile, 1972, The Home Front: McLennan County in the Civil War, 1974; contbr. articles to hist. jours. Mem. Waco Plan Commn., 1966-69, Waco-McLennan County Library Commn., 1968-72, chmn., 1971-72; mem. Waco Fire and Police Civil Service Commn., 1975-81, chmn., 1980-81; mem. Waco Am. Revolution Bicentennial Commn., 1974-76; chmn. Waco Heritage '76, 1974-76; mem. McLennan County Hist. Survey Commn., 1970—; chmn. Ft. House Mus., Waco, 1968-72; bd. dirs. Waco Heritage Soc., 1960—. Served with USAF, 1946-49. Mem. State Bar Tex., Waco-McLennan County Bar Assn., Waco-McLennan County Def. Lawyers Assn. (v.p.), 5th Cir. Bar Assn., Delta Theta Phi. Democrat. Baptist. Lodges: Masons, K.P. Home: 613 Camp Dr Waco TX 76710 Office: 2317 Austin Ave Waco TX 76701

DUVA, DONNA MARIE, financial executive; b. Paterson, N.J., June 28, 1956; d. Alfred Dominick and Frances P. (D'Andrea) D. AAS, Bergen Community Coll., 1976; BS in Acctg., Ramapo Coll., 1985. Bookkeeper Passaic County Treas. Office, Paterson, 1973-77; acctg. tutor Bergen Community Coll., Paramus, N.J., 1974-76; full charge bookkeeper Weisz Supermarket, Inc., Clifton, N.J., 1977-79; acct. Beecham, Inc., Clifton, 1980-85; chief fin. officer, controller Al Duva Enterprises, Inc., Paterson, 1976—; chief fin. officer, acctg. mgr. Power Battery Corp., Paterson, 1986—; Author newspaper editorials Paterson Evening News, 1976. Mem. N.J. Soc. Notary Pubs., Ramapo Coll. Alumni Assn., Bergen Community Coll. Alumni Assn., Nat. Assn. Female Execs. Democrat. Roman Catholic. Home: 205 Vernon Ave Paterson NJ 07503 Office: Power Battery Co Inc 543-53 E 42d St Paterson NJ 07513

D'UVA, ROBERT CARMEN, insurance and real estate broker; b. Castelpetroso, Italy, Aug. 25, 1920; s. Gabriele and Bettina D'Uva; m. Josephine C. Del Riccio, Sept. 5, 1948; children: Robert Gary, Gary James, James Joseph. Student, Rutgers U., 1946-47, postgrad., 1950-51; BA in Acctg., Seton Hall U., 1949. Spl. rep. Manhattan Life Ins. Co. of N.Y., 1949—; real estate sales rep. David Cornheim Agy., Newark, 1950-51; pvt. practice ins. and real estate broker Newark, 1951—; ptnr. Romaine Realty Co., Newark, 1962-83; gen. agt. Md. Am. Gen. Ins. Cos.; pres. Diversified Variable Annuities, Inc., Newark, 1968—, Del-Gior Corp., Bloomfield, N.J., 1971—, Diversified Ins. Agy., Inc., Caldwell, N.J., 1973—. Bd. dirs. Newark Boys Club, pres. Broadway unit, 1967; pres. real estate bd. of Newark, Irvington and Hillside, N.J. Served as cpl. Q.M.C. AUS, 1942-46, PTO. Mem. Nat. Real Estate Brokers Assn., Nat. Security Dealers Assn., N.J. Real Estate Assn., Nat. Assn. Real Estate Bd., Life Underwriters Assn., Ind. Ins. Agts. Assn. Roman Catholic. Lodge: Lions (North Newark) (pres., dep. dist. gov. 1964). Home: 27 Howland Circle W Caldwell NJ 07006 Office: Diversified Variable Annuities Inc 316 Mount Prospect Ave Newark NJ 07104 also: Del-Gior Corp 115 Bloomfield Ave Caldwell NJ 07006 also: Diversified Ins Agy Inc 41 Bloomfield Ave Caldwell NJ 07006

DUVAL, BETTY ANN, financial publishing and news service executive; b. Springfield, Mo., May 13, 1921; d. William and Marie T. (Townsend) D. B.A. in Psychology, DePauw U., 1943. Mgr. tng. RCA, Camden, N.J., 1943-57; dir. personnel planning and devel., also other personnel positions Gen. Foods Co., White Plains, N.Y., 1957-80; v.p. staff devel. Dow Jones & Co. Inc., N.Y.C., 1980-86, sr. v.p., 1986—. Mem. greater consistory Ref. Ch., Bronxville, N.Y., 1973—. Club: Siwanoy Country (Bronxville, N.Y.).

DUVALL, DAVID GARLAND, real estate company executive, accountant; b. Franklin, N.C., Apr. 21, 1949; s. Fred Garland and Margaret Louise Murray D.; m. Margaret Ann Holbrook, June 20, 1971; children: David Christopher, Amanda Leigh. BSBA, Western Carolina U., 1971. CPA, S.C. Staff acct. J.W. Hunt and Co., Columbia, S.C., 1972-80; chief fin. officer Columbia Mgmt. Corp., Columbia, 1980-82, L.P. Cox Co., Sanford, N.C., 1983-86; chief fin. officer U.S. Capital Corp., Columbia, 1980-83, exec. v.p., 1986—. Mem. AICPA, S.C. Assn. CPA's, Alpha Kappa Psi. Home: 2116 O'Hara Ct Columbia SC 29204 Office: US Capital Corp 1400 Main St Columbia SC 29211

DUVALL, JACK, television executive, fund raiser, speechwriter; b. San Diego, July 10, 1946; s. John William and Margaret (Clark) DuV. AB cum laude, Colgate U., 1968. Mgmt. cons. Ohio Bell, Cleve., 1969; spl. agt. Air Force Office of Spl. Investigations, 1969-72; compliance officer Price Commn. U.S., Washington, 1972-73; chief industry compliance br. Cost Living Council, Exec. Office Pres. U.S., Washington, 1973-74; dir. pub. affairs Nat. Soybean Processors Assn., Hearing Industries Assn., Nat. Assn. Child Devel. Edn., and Food Protein Council, Washington, 1975-80; dir. corp. relations U. Chgo., 1980-85; v.p. program resources WETA TV/Radio, Arlington, Va., 1985-89; prin. Mars Hill, Alexandria, Va., 1989—; cons. Albert Einstein Peace Prize Found., Chgo, 1983-84; advisor-cons. Military Reform Inst., Washington, 1984—. Author (with others) Historical Working Papers of the Economic Stabilization Program, 1975; contbr. poems and articles to various publs. Speechwriter Sen. Adlai Stevenson Ill. gov. campaign, 1982; Ill. spokesman Sen. Gary Hart pres. campaign, 1983-84; mem. Nat. Dem. Platform Com., Washington, 1984, Social Services Adv. Bd., Alexandria, 1986-87, mem. bd. advisors Ctr. for A New Democracy, Washington, 1985-87; issues, speech advisor presdl. campaign Gov. Michael S. Dukakis, 1987-88. Served to capt. USAF, 1969-72. Mem. Phi Beta Kappa, Phi Alpha Theta. Home: PO Box 707 Alexandria VA 22314 Office: WETA TV Radio 3700 S Four Mile Run Arlington VA 22206

DUVAR, IVAN ERNEST HUNTER, telephone company executive; b. Charlottetown, P.E.I., Can., Mar. 30, 1939; s. Arthur and Helen D.; m. Margaret Rodd, May 19, 1962; children: Jeffrey, Alan, Carolyn. Engring. cert., Mt. Allison U., Sackville, N.B., Can., 1960; BEE, Tech. U. N.S., Halifax, Can., 1962; cert. in indsl. mgmt., St. Mary's U., Halifax, 1973. Transmission engr. Bell Can., Montreal, Que., Can., 1962-66; transmission engr. Maritime Tel. and Tel. Co., Ltd., Halifax, 1966-68, supr. bus. systems planning, 1968-69, bus. info. systems mgr., 1969-73, chief engr., 1973-75, v.p. planning, 1975-82, v.p. ops., 1982-84, v.p. mktg., 1984-85, pres., chief exec. officer, 1985—; chmn. Island Tel. Co., Ltd., Charlottetown; bd. dirs. Telecom Can., Ottawa, Ont., Halifax Life Ins., Co., Toronto, Ont., Ea. Tel. and Tel. N.J., Basking Ridge, Oxford (N.S.) Frozen Foods, Air Nova, Halifax Indsl. Commn. Bd govs. Tech. U. N.S., Halifax, Dalhousie U. Co., Halifax; past pres. Halifax Bd. of Trade. Mem. IEEE, Assn. Profl. Engrs. N.S. Clubs: Halifax, Saraguay, Royal N.S. Yacht (Halifax). Office: Maritime Tel & Tel Co Ltd, 1505 Barrington St, Halifax, NS Canada B3J 2W3

DUVEEN, HENRY JULES, securities company executive; b. Amsterdam, Netherlands, Mar. 12, 1935; came to U.S., 1956; s. Abraham Mozes and Henriette (Frank) D.; B.A., Inst. van Praag, Amsterdam, 1955; m. Peggy R. Berkelouw, Mar. 30, 1971; 1 dau., Linda H. Founder, Merril Lynch Pierce Fenner & Smith, Amsterdam, 1960-65; asso. Francis I. DuPont Corp., Amsterdam, 1965-68; sr. v.p. Laidlaw, Adams & Peck, Brussels, 1971-78; art gallery pres. Duveen Inc., Houston, 1979-83; internat. investment advisor to fgn. and domestic fin. instns. Churchill Securities Inc.; lectr. internat. investment/art investments, 1960—; with Dominick & Dominick, Brussel, Belgium, 1989—. Served with U.S. Army, Germany, 1956-58. Mem. Woodlands Living Arts Council (dir. 1978-80). Clubs: Woodlands Country, Rotary. Home: 193 Waversesteenweg, 1990 Hoeilaart Belgium

DUVICK, DONALD NELSON, plant breeder; b. Sandwich, Ill., Dec. 18, 1924; s. Nelson Daniel and Florence Henrietta (Appel) D.; m. Selma Elizabeth Nelson, Sept. 10, 1950; children: Daniel, Jonathan, Randa. B.S., U. Ill., 1948; Ph.D., Washington U., St. Louis, 1951. With Pioneer Hi-Bred Internat., Inc., Johnston, Iowa, 1951—; corn breeding coordinator Pioneer Hi-Bred Internat., Inc. (Eastern and So. div.), 1965-71, dir. corn breeding dept., 1971-75; dir. plant breeding div. Pioneer Hi-Bred Internat., Inc., 1975-85, v.p. research, 1985—, sr. v.p. research, 1986—, co. dir., 1982—; mem. Nat. Plant Genetics Resources Bd., USDA; lectr. in field. Assoc. editor: Plant Physiology jour., 1977-78; contbr. articles on genetics and plant breeding, developmental anatomy and cytology, cytoplasmic inheritance, quantititive genetics. Pres. Johnston Consol. Sch. Bd., 1965-67. Served with AUS, 1943-46. Pioneer Hi-Bred fellow U. London, 1968. Fellow AAAS, Crop Sci. Soc. Am., Am. Soc. Agronomy, Iowa Acad. Sci.; mem. Bot. Soc. Am., Genetics Soc. Am., Am. Soc. Plant Physiologists, N.Y. Acad. Scis., Am. Soc. Agromomy, Crop Sci. Soc. Am. (pres. 1986), Am. Seed Trade Assn., Council Agrl. Sci. and Tech. (bd. dirs.), Nat. Council Comml. Plant Breeders (pres. 1984-86), The Nature Conservancy (bd. dirs. Iowa chpt.). Democrat. Mem. United Ch. Christ. Home: 6837 NW Beaver Dr Johnston IA 50131 Office: Pioneer Hi-Bred Internat Inc 700 Capital Sq 400 Locust Des Moines IA 50309

DUWE, JAMES ARTHUR, real estate corporation officer; b. Chgo., Jan. 9, 1955; s. Charles L. and Lois Mae (Scharringhausen) D.; m. Carrie Kaye Browning; children: Sara, Stephen. BA in Acctg., U. Wash., 1978. CPA, Wash. Acct. Arthur Andersen & Co., Seattle, 1978-80; asst. controller NW Bldg. Corp., Seattle, 1980-82, controller, 1982-85, treas., controller, 1985-86, chief fin. officer, treas., 1985-8; chief fin. officer Tramell Crow Residential Co., Bellevue, Wash., 1988—; cons. Timberline Systems Inc., Portland, Oreg., 1985—. Panel mem. United Way King County, Seattle, 1981-86; fundraiser Providence Med. Found., Seattle, 1982-86. Mem. Nat. Assn. Real Estate Cos., Wash. Soc. CPA's. Republican. Presbyterian. Club: Harbor (Seattle). Office: Tramell Crow Residential Co 11400 SE 8th St Ste 235 Bellevue WA 98104

DWEK, CYRIL S., banker; b. Kobe, Japan, Nov. 9, 1936; s. Nessim S. and Alice (Stambouli) D.; children: Nevil, Alicia. B.S., Wharton Sch., U. Pa., 1958. With Trade Devel. Bank, Geneva, Switzerland, 1962-65; with Republic Nat. Bank of N.Y., 1966—, dir., 1967—, exec. v.p., 1973—, vice chmn., 1983—; dir. Republic N.Y. Corp., 1974—, vice chmn., 1983—; Bd. advisers Brazilian Inst. Bus. Programs, Pace U. Mem. Brazilian Am. C. of C. (dir.). Club: Racing Club de France (Paris). Office: Republic NY Corp 452 Fifth Ave New York NY 10018

DWIGHT, DONALD RATHBUN, newspaper publisher, corporate communications executive; b. Holyoke, Mass., Mar. 26, 1931; s. William and Dorothy Elizabeth (Rathbun) D.; m. Susan Newton Russell, Aug. 9, 1952 (div. Aug. 1982); children: Dorothy Campbell, Laura Newton, Eleanor Addison, Arthur Ryan, Stuart Russell.; m. Nancy John Sinnott, Dec. 18, 1982; children: Christopher Sinnott, Helen Rathbun. AB, Princeton U., 1953; DSc (hon.), U. Lowell, 1974. Reporter, asst. to pub. Holyoke (Mass.) Transcript-Telegram, 1955-63, assoc. pub., 1966-69; assoc. commr. Mass. Dept. Pub. Works, Boston, 1963-66; commr. adminstrn. Commonwealth Mass., Boston, 1969-70, lt. gov., 1971-75; assoc. pub., v.p. Mpls. Star and Tribune, 1975-76, pub., sr. v.p., 1976-81; pres., pub. Star & Tribune Newspapers, Mpls., 1981-82; exec. v.p., dir. Cowles Media Co., 1981-82; chmn. Newspapers of New Eng., Inc., 1982—; assoc. The Prospect Group, N.Y.C., 1983-88; chmn., mng. ptnr. Clark, Dwight & Assocs., Inc., 1988—; v.p. Wood River Capital Corp., 1984-88; dir. Pillsbury Co., Inc., Mpls., 1973-83; pres. Dwight Ptnrs. Inc., 1988—; exec. v.p. Entretech Inc., 1988—; trustee Eaton Vance Mutual Funds, Boston. Mem. Town Meeting, South Hadley, Mass., 1957-69; chmn. bd. Guthrie Theatre Found., 1978-81; bd. dirs. Mpls. Soc. Fine Arts, 1976-82; trustee Twin Cities Pub. TV, 1976-82; v.p., dir. Nat. Corp. Theatre Fund, 1985-88; dir. Joint Action in Community Svc., Washington, 1989—. 1st lt. USMCR, 1953-55. Mem. Am. Newspaper Pubs. Assn., Sigma Delta Chi. Republican. Episcopalian. Clubs: Minneapolis; Princeton, Knickerbocker (N.Y.C.); The Field Club (Greenwich). Home: 20 Martin Dale Greenwich CT 06830 Office: Clark Dwight & Assocs Inc 1445 E Putnam Ave Old Greenwich CT 06870

DWORAK, LINDA LARAE, personnel manager; b. Omaha, Apr. 2, 1947; d. Marshall Merle Clevenger and Rosemary (Riecks) Glaze. BA, U. Nebr., Omaha, 1970, MA, 1979. Employment supr. Nebr. Dept. Labor Job Service, Omaha, 1973-81; employment mgr. U. Nebr., Omaha, 1981-85; personnel mgr Utell Internat., Omaha, 1986—; bus. cons. Govt. Job Placement Agencies, Omaha, 1981—, Job Partnership Tng. Agy.; seminar facilitator employment-related workshops for college career fairs, Omaha, 1977—. Editor (newsletter) Employment Adv. Council for Handicapped, 1975-85; contbr. articles to profl. jours. Mem. Personnel Assn. of Midlands Legis. Com. (chmn. 1984-85), Omaha C. of C. (cons., mem. bus. panel 1987). Roman Catholic. Office: Utell Internat 10606 Burt Circle Omaha NE 68114

DWORKIN, DAVID LEE, retail executive; b. Cleve., Nov. 30, 1943; s. Oscar Charles and Rebecca (Singer) D.; m. Judith Sunderland, Dec. 28, 1965; children: Wendy Leigh, Kira Elizabeth. BA, Webster Coll., 1974. Exec. trainee Abraham & Strauss, 1967-69; successively asst. buyer, buyer, store mgr., div. merchandise mgr., div. v.p., Famous Barr, 1969-77; regional dir. stores, sr. v.p. and dir. stores, sr. v.p., gen. mdse. mgr., Saks Fifth Ave, 1977-83; exec. v.p. merchandising Marshall Field's. 1983-84; pres. Neiman-Marcus, 1984-87; pres., ceo Bonwit Teller, 1987—. Bd. dirs. Nat. Boys Clubs Am., Nat. Jewish Ctr. Immunology and Respiratory Medicine, Webster U., St. Louis. Office: Bonwit Teller 1120 Ave of the Americas New York NY 10036

DWYER, DARRELL JAMES, financial executive; b. Vermillion, S.D., Nov. 27, 1946; s. Michael Leroy and Faye Awilda (Hansen) D.; div. 1988; 1 child, Sean Patrick. BS, Mankato State U., 1977; MBA, U. Calif., Berkeley, 1978. CPA; Cert. Mgmt. Acct., Internal Auditor. Acct. Touche Ross & Co., Salem, Oreg., 1978-79; cons. Arthur, Persons Co., Salem, 1980-82; v.p. fin. Evergreen Internat. Airlines Inc, McMinnville, Oreg., 1982-87; chief fin. officer The Erickson Group Ltd., Medford, Oreg., 1987—. Calif. State scholar; recipient award of merit Evergreen Internat. Aviation, McMinnville, Oreg., 1984. Mem. Am. Inst. CPA's, Inst. Cert. Mgmt. Accts., Oreg. Soc. CPA's. Republican. Roman Catholic. Office: The Erickson Group Ltd 3100 Willow Springs Rd Central Point OR 97502

DWYER, DENNIS D., information technology manager; b. Oak Park, Ill., July 19, 1943; s. John J. and Jessie M. Dwyer; m. Carolyn R. Schultz, Apr. 29, 1967; children: David, Julianne. Various positions Harris Bank, Chgo., 1967-85, mgr. info. technology planning, 1983-86, v.p. info. technology planning and acquisition, 1986—; resolutions chmn. Cooperating Users of Burroughs Equipment, Detroit, 1978-82; cons. Unisys mainframe computers. Pres. Hunting Ridge Homeowners Assn., 1983-85, Palatine Plan Commn., 1984—. Recipient Tom Grier award for excellence in info. tech. Unisys Users Group, 1988. Home: 1032 Raven Ln Palatine IL 60067-6649 Office: Harris Bank PO Box 755 Chicago IL 60690-0755

DWYER, EDWARD JAMES, former company executive; b. South Norwalk, Conn., Sept. 21, 1906; s. John Augustus and Alura Ann (Waters) D.; B.A., St. Johns Coll., Annapolis, 1930; M.Mech. Engring., Johns Hopkins U., 1933; J.D., George Washington U., 1938; m. Elizabeth MacLachlan, Dec. 30, 1933; children—Nancy Elizabeth (Mrs. W. Roy Kolb), John Adam. Bar: D.C. 1938. With Gen. Electric Co., Schenectady, also Washington, 1933-41, patent atty., 1938-41; with ESB Inc. (formerly Electric Storage Battery Co.), Phila. 1941-77, pres., 1959-71, chmn. bd., 1971-77; dir. Quaker Chem. Co., Selas Corp. Am. Hon. trustee, Thomas Jefferson U., Phila., 1973—, Phila. Adv. Council Opportunities Industrialization Center, 1966-76; pres. United Fund Phila., 1969-71. Republican. Presbyn. Clubs: Union League of Phila. (pres. 1973, 74); Huntingdon Valley Country (Abington, Pa.). Home and Office: 3 Tally-Ho Ln Blue Bell PA 19422

DWYER, GERALD PAUL, JR., economics educator, consultant; b. Pittsfield, Mass., July 9, 1947; s. Gerald Paul and Mary Frances (Weir) D.; m. Katherine Marie Lepiane, Jan. 15, 1966; children: Tamara K., Gerald P. III, Angela M., Michael J.L., Terence F. BBA, U. Wash., 1969; MA in Econs., U. Tenn., 1973; PhD in Econs., U. Chgo., 1979. Economist Fed. Res. Bank, St. Louis, 1972-74, vis. scholar, 1987-89; economist Fed. Res. Bank, Chgo., 1976-77; asst. prof. Tex. Agrl. and Mech. U., College Station, 1977-81, Emory U., Atlanta, 1981-84; assoc. prof. U. Houston, 1984-89; prof. Clemson (S.C.) U., 1989—; sr. research assoc. Law and Econ. Ctr. Emory U., Atlanta, 1982-84; vis. scholar Fed. Res. Bank, Atlanta, 1982-84; cons. FTC, Washington, 1983-84, Arthur Bros., Corpus Christi, Tex., 1980-81, Amerigas, Houston, 1985, Western Container Corp., 1987. Contbr. articles to profl. jours. NSF trainee U. Tenn., 1970-72; Weaver fellow Intercollegiate Studies Inst., 1974-75, Earhart Found. fellow 1975-77. Mem. Am. Econ. Assn., Am. Stats. Assn., Econometric Soc., Econ. History Assn., We. Econ. Assn., So. Econ. Assn., Beta Gamma Sigma, Phi Kappa Phi. Avocation: computers.

DWYER, JAMES L., health science consultant; b. St. Paul, June 2, 1932; s. James A. and Helene P. (Gallagher) D.; m. Carol M. Dwyer, June 15, 1961; children: Sean C., Peter A., Katherine C., Cullen M. BS, MIT, 1954, MS, 1959. Process engr. Sun Oil Co., Marlus Hook, Pa., 1954-56; devel. engr. W.R. Grace Co., Cambridge, Mass., 1959-61; sr. v.p. Millipore Corp., Bedford, Mass., 1961-87; pres. Ventec, Inc., Marlborough, Mass., 1987—; dir. Anatel Corp., Boulder, Colo., Specrovision Corp., Chelmsford, Mass., Zymark Corp., Hopkinton, Mass. Author: Detection and Analysis of Contamination, 1966. Mem. AAAS (chmn. local sect. 1987). Republican. Office: Ventec Inc 33 Locke Dr Marlborough MA 01752

DYE, CARL MELVYN, educational association executive; b. Cedar Rapids, Iowa, Oct. 7, 1940; s. Floyd Carmen and Inger Marie (Johansen) D.; BA, Parsons Coll., 1962; MEd, No. Ill. U., 1967. Dir. admissions counselors Parsons Coll., Fairfield, Iowa, 1962-68; acad. dean Bryant and Stratton Coll., Milw., 1968-69; pres. Coll. of the South, Pascagoula, Miss., 1969-70; acad. dean Massey Jr. Coll., Atlanta, 1970-71; pres. Am. Schs. Assn., Chgo., 1967—; dir., founder The Job Group, 1982. Served with U.S. Army, 1963-64. Mem. Am. Cons. League, Phi Kappa Phi. Home: 2252 N Fremont St Chicago IL 60614

DYE, DAVID RAY, tax accountant; b. Hobart, Ind., Aug. 4, 1951; s. Clifford C. and Lola May (Garrett) D.; m. Claudia Ann Forrester, June 20, 1974; children: Jason Charles, Eric David, Heather Ann. BBA in Acctg., Valparaiso U. CPA, Va., Ill. From staff mem. to sr. mgr. Peat, Marwick, Mitchell, Chgo., 1973-81; dir. tax ops. Touche, Ross & Co., Richmond, Va., 1982-85; ptnr., prin. Womacke & Burke, Richmond, 1986-88; exec. v.p. Deaton Fin. Services, Inc., Richmond, 1988—. Mem. congl., nat. and life rep. orgns. and precinct coms. Hobart (Ind.) Rep. Party, 1978-83. Mem. AICPA's (mem. tax com., personal F.P. com.), Va. Soc. CPA's, Ind. Soc. CPA's, Ill. Soc. CPA's, Econ. Soc., The Wilderness Soc., U.S. Jaycees, Omicron Epsilon, Sigma Tau Gamma. Lodges: Optimists, Lions, Civitans, Bull and Bear. Home: 8009 Dulles Dr Richmond VA 23235 Office: Deaton Fin Svcs Inc 1213 Westover Hills Blvd Ste 208 Richmond VA 23225

DYE, ROBERT LLOYD, international marketing consultant; b. Kansas City, Mo., Apr. 21, 1952; s. Robert J. and Miami Lorraine (Courdin) C.; m. Susan Elizabeth Willer, June 12, 1982; children: Katherine, Jared. BS, Kans. State U., 1976. Project mgr. Owens-Corning Fiberglas Corp., Toledo, 1976-85; estimator-engr. Performance Contracting, Inc., Lenexa, Kans., 1985-87; project dir. Environ. Tech., Inc., Overland Park, Kans., 1987-89; owner Dye & Assocs, Mission, Kans., 1989—. Chmn. bd. Westwood Christian Ch., Kans., 1988. Mem. Constrn. Specifications Inst., Mensa. Republican. Lodge: Masons. Office: Dye & Assocs 4210 Shawnee Misson Pkwy Ste 100 Mission KS 66205

DYER, ALEXANDER PATRICK, industrial gas manufacturing company executive; b. Santa Rosa, Calif., Aug. 30, 1932; s. John Alexander and Amie Marie (Moore) D.; m. Shirley Aiken Shine, Dec. 11, 1954; children: David Patirck, Steven Scott (dec.). BS in Engring, U.S. Mil. Acad., 1954; MBA, Harvard U., 1959. Registered profl. engr., Pa. With Esso Corp., 1959-63, Air Products and Chems., Inc., 1963—; no. area mgr., then pres. indsl. gas div. Air Products and Chems., Inc., Allentown, Pa., 1966-78; corp. v.p. Air Products and Chems., Inc., 1969-78, group v.p. gases, 1978-87, exec. v.p., 1987—, also bd. dirs.; bd. dirs. Sta. WLVT-TV Channel 39, Bethlehem, 1988—. Bd. dirs. Annie S. Kemerer Mus., Bethlehem, 1988—; trustee St. Luke's Hosp., Bethlehem, 1988—, WLVT-TV Channel 39, Bethlehem, 1988—. With U.S. Army, 1954-57. Mem. Compressed Gas Assn. (chmn. 1982), Internat. Oxygen Mfrs. Assn. (pres. 1981, chmn. 1982), Saucon Country Club (Bethlehem) (bd. govs. 1988—). Republican. Presbyterian. Home: Apple Tree Ln RD 4 Bethlehem PA 18015 Office: Air Products & Chems Inc PO Box 538 Allentown PA 18105

DYER, DAVID PAUL, dental service company executive; b. Big Springs, Tex., June 9, 1956; s. Dean Paul Dyer and Barbara (Maureen) Hunter; m. Paula Bush, Mar. 10, 1984. BS in Acctg., U. Kans., 1978; JD, So. Meth. U., 1981. Bar: Mo. 1981. Assoc. Hoskins, King, McGannon, Hahn & Hurwitz, Kansas City, Mo., 1981-85; pres. Dyer Orthodontic Lab. Inc., Kansas City, 1985—. Mem. ABA, Mo. Bar Assn., Kansas City Bar Assn. Home: 1005 Arno Rd Kansas City MO 64113 Office: Dyer Orthodontic Lab Inc 2538 W Pennway Kansas City MO 64108

DYER, JAYE FLOYD, oil and gas company executive; b. Moore, Okla., Apr. 22, 1927; s. Jessie Floyd and Velma I. (Trimble) D.; m. Betty Faye Brown, Aug. 28, 1948; children: Michael J., Janet S., Karen B. Dyer Howells. BS in Geology, U. Okla., 1951. Exploration geologist Cities Service Oil Co., Oklahoma City, 1951-54; exploration mgr.—Rocky Mountain dist. Anderson Prichard Oil Corp., Denver, 1954-58; exploration mgr. Apache Corp., Mpls., 1958-67, exec. v.p., 1967-71; pres., chief exec. officer Dyco Petroleum Corp., Mpls., 1971-85, chmn., pres., chief exec. officer, 1985—; bd. dirs. Diversified Energies Inc., Mpls., Northwestern Nat. Life Ins. Co., Mpls., Minn. Vikings. Chmn. bd. Minn. Diversified Industries, St. Paul, 1986—, Dyco Found., Mpls., 1977—; trustee U. Minn. Found., St. Paul, 1985—; bd. dirs. Minn. Vikings Football Club, Vikings Children's Fund, Mpls., 1985—, Guthrie Theater, Mpls., 1983—, Children's Heart Fund, Mpls., 1981—, Minn. Project on Corp. Responsibility, Mpls., 1979—, Minn. Bus. Ptnrship., Mpls. Served with USN, 1945-46. Recipient Appreciation award U. Minn. Athletic Dept., Mpls., 1986; inducted Minn. Bus. Hall of Fame. Mem. Am. Assn. Petroleum Geologists, Ind. Petroleum Assn. Am. Clubs: Mpls. (bd. govs.); Wayzata Country (Minn.) (past chmn.); So. Hills Country (Tulsa); Wyndemere Country (Naples, Fla.). Office: Dyco Petroleum Corp 1100 Interchange Tower 600 South Hwy 169 Minneapolis MN 55426

DYER, KENNETH EDWIN, manufacturing company executive; b. Norristown, Pa., July 4, 1949; s. Kenneth Edwin and Geraldine M. (Stroup) D. Grad. high sch., Fairview Village, Pa. Electrician Rees, Weaver & Co. Inc., Collegeville, Pa., 1968-69, purchasing agt., 1970-71; inside salesman Pump Power & Air Inc., Collegeville, 1971-74, gen. mgr., 1974-79, v.p., 1979-82; pres. Dyer Assocs., Fairview Village, Pa., 1982—; v.p. Evansburg Hardware, Inc., 1980, Domor Assoc., 1980. Mem. Collegeville Jaycees (bd. dirs. 1973-74, 78-79, JCI senator 1972, Spoke award 1972, pres.'s round table 1972). Home: Box 283 Collegeville PA 19426 Office: Dyer Assocs 3008 Germantown Pike Fairview Village PA 19403

DYER, MARYLIN HULSEY, management consultant; b. Leadwood, Mo., Apr. 6, 1938; d. Carl E. and Alberta Marie (Jordan) Hulsey; children: Phillip Andrew, Christina Noel. BA in Sociology, Upland Coll., 1962; MS in Human Devel., So. Ill. U., 1967. Cert. mgmt. cons. Tchr. Riverside County (Calif.) Pub. Sch., 1971-72; faculty Lane Community Coll., Eugene, Oreg., 1972-73, James Madison U., Harrisonburg, Va., 1973-76, Towson State U., Balt., 1976-79; cons. Dyer Assocs., Balt., 1976-80, Maryland Cons. Group, Inc., Balt., 1981—; mem. faculty Ind. U., 1966-69. Bd. dirs. Jubilee Jobs, Balt., 1988. Mem. Inst. Mgmt. Cons. (chmn. profl. devel. com. 1988—), Phi Delta Kappa. Republican. Home: 14009 Blenheim Rd Phoenix MD 21131 Office: 30 E Padonia Rd Ste 505 Timonium MD 21093

DYER, WILLIAM WINFIELD, JR., investment management executive; b. Atlantic City, May 7, 1934; s. William Winfield and Mary Elizabeth (Dahlmer) D.; m. Joan Cameron, Mar. 10, 1956 (div. Mar. 1985); children: Susan, William III, Elizabeth, Johanna, Daniel, Cary, Joan. BA, Brown U., 1956. Registered rep. H.C. Wainwright and Co., Boston, 1956-60, br. mgr., 1960-63, securities analyst, 1963-76; officer Century Shares Trust, Boston, 1976-85; sr. v.p., bd. dirs. Mass. Fiduciary Advisors, Boston, 1979—; trustee, dir. research Century Shares Trust, 1977—. Contbr. articles to profl. jours. Fellow Fin. Analysts Fedn.; mem. Boston Security Analysts Soc., Boston Computer Soc. Home: One Seal Harbor Rd #116 Winthrop MA 02152 Office: Century Shares Trust One Liberty Sq Boston MA 02109

DYKAS, JAMES DONALD, meteorologist, service company executive; b. South Milwaukee, Wis., July 6, 1940; s. Felix Stanley and Mary Vaughan (White) D.; BA, U. Calif., Santa Barbara, 1975; m. Kimberly Rae Salopek, June 24, 1989; children from previous marriage: James David, Laurie Suzanne, Jennifer Dayle. Meteorologist, Oceanographic Services, Inc., Santa Barbara, 1967-75, mgr. meteorology, 1975-80; pres. Universal Marine, Houston, 1980—; v.p. meterology, dir. Universal Weather & Aviation, Inc., 1982—. Pres., Park Wilmoor Assn., Carpinteria, Calif., 1971-72; coach Youth Basketball, 1972-78. Served with USMC, 1958-67. Named Coach of Yr., Youth Basketball, 1975, 77. Mem. Omicron Delta Epsilon. Republican. Lutheran. Contbr. articles to profl. jours. Office: 8787 Tallyho Houston TX 77061

DYKEMA, HENRY L., holding company executive; b. Hammond, Ind., Sept. 19, 1939; s. Chester and Deda Dykema; m. Judith K. Kuiper, Mar. 2, 1963; children: Erik P., Kristin A. BS in Chem. Engring., U. Ill., 1962; MBA in Fin. and Econs., NYU, 1970. Group dir., fin. planning Pepsi Cola Co., Purchase, N.Y., 1975-76, controller, 1976-79; v.p. fin. Pepsi Cola Bottling Group, Purchase, 1979-80; asst. v.p. fin. Northwest Industries, Chgo., 1980-82, v.p. corp. devel., 1983-85; v.p. fin. Insilco Corp., Meriden, Conn., 1985—. Republican. Presbyterian. Home: 89 Hickok Rd New Canaan CT 06840 Office: Insilco Corp 1000 Research Pkwy Meriden CT 06450

DYKES, ARCHIE REECE, financial services executive; b. Rogersville, Tenn., Jan. 20, 1931; s. Claude Reed and Rose (Quillen) D.; m. Nancy Jane Haun, May 29, 1953; children: John Reece, Thomas Mack. BS cum laude, East Tenn. State U., 1952; MA, E. Tenn. State U., 1956; EdD, U. Tenn., 1959. Prin., Church Hill (Tenn.) High Sch., 1955-58; supt. Greeneville (Tenn.) Schs., 1959-62; prof. edn., dir. U. Tenn. Ctr. for Advanced Grad. Study in Edn., Memphis State U., 1962-66; chancellor U. Tenn. at Martin, 1967-71, at Knoxville, 1971-73; chancellor U. Kans., 1973-80; chmn., pres., chief exec. officer Security Benefit Group of Cos., Topeka, 1980-88; chmn. Capital City Holdings Inc., 1988—; chmn. Security Mgmt. Co., Inc.; bd. dirs. Security Benefit Life Ins. Co., Whitman Corp., Chgo., Boatmen's 1st Nat. Bank Kansas City, Mo., Bank IV, Topeka, Fleming Cos. Inc., Oklahoma City, Coleman Co., Wichita, Hussmann Corp., St. Louis, Manville Corp., Denver, Edn. Corp. Am. Author: School Board and Superintendent, 1965, Faculty Participation in Academic Decision Making, 1968. Vice chmn. Commn. on Operation U.S. Senate, 1975-76; mem. Nat. Adv. Coun. Edn. Professions Devel., 1975-76; mem. bd. regents State of Kans.; trustee Truman Library Inst., 1973-80, Menninger Found., 1982-88, Nelson Art Gallery, 1973-80, Dole Found.; chmn. bd. trustees U. Mid-Am., 1978-79; mem. adv. commn. U.S. Army Command. and Gen. Staff Coll., 1974-79, chmn., 1978-79; mem. consultative bd. regents U. Qatar, 1979-80; mem. Bd. Regents State of Kans., 1982—. Ford Found. fellow, 1957-59; Am. Council on Edn. postdoctoral fellow U. Ill., 1966-67; named Outstanding Alumnus, E. Tenn. State U., 1970. Mem. Tenn. Coll. Assn. (pres. 1969-70), Am. Coun. Life Ins. (dir. 1981-86), Nat. Assn. State Univs. and Land Grant Colls. (coun. pres. 1971-80), Newcomen Soc. N.Am., Kans. Assn. Commerce and Industry (dir. 1975-82), Phi Kappa Phi. Home: 506 Belgrave Pk Nashville TN 37215 Office: BNA Corp Ctr Bldg 100 Ste 400 Nashville TN 37217

DYKES, JOHN HENRY, JR., finance executive; b. Wichita, Kans., July 14, 1934; s. John Henry Sr. and Kathryn (Klotzbach) D.; m. Lucille Beard, May 29, 1958; children: John Henry III, Robert Douglas, Laura Kathryn. BS in Engring. Physics, U. Okla., 1956, BSEE, 1957; MBA with high distinction, Harvard U., 1959. Fin. analyst TRW, Inc., Los Angeles, 1959-62; gen. mgr. TRW, Inc., Mexico City, 1962-65; internat. mgr. TRW, Inc., Chgo., 1965-70; dir. acquisitions Stanray Corp., Chgo., 1970-72, group v.p., 1972-75; pres. SAFT Am., Inc., Valdosta, Ga., 1975-78; chief fin. officer Engraph Inc., Atlanta, 1978—; bd. dirs. RPR Enterprises, Inc., Atlanta. Mem. adv. bd. St. Mary's Hosp., Ogden, 1971-74. Named Exporter of Yr. World Trade Assn., 1972. Mem. Fin. Execs. Inst. (bd. dirs. mgmt. info. systems com. 1985—, trustee research found.). Republican. Episcopalian. Club: Ashford (Dunwoody, Ga.). Lodge: Rotary (sec., treas. 1981-82, bd. dirs. 1986—). Home: 7275 Twin Branch Rd Atlanta GA 30328 Office: Engraph Inc 2635 Century Pkwy NE Ste 900 Atlanta GA 30345

DYKES, WAYNE F., bank data proccesing executive; b. Kentwood, La., Nov. 7, 1950; s. Ivy and Lorelise (Bankston) D.; m. Jenny Domin, June 19, 1971; children: Dwayne, Crysty, Daisye. AS in Computer Sci., Southwest Miss. Jr. Coll., 1970. Computer programmer First Guaranty Bank, Hammond, La., 1970-73, programmer supr., 1975-78; data processing mgr. Washington Bank, Franklinton, La., 1973-75, First Computer Svcs., Ruston, La., 1978-81; programmer supr. Cen. Bank, Monroe, La., 1981-82; data processing mgr. Ruston (La.) State Bank, 1982-84, Baton Rouge Bank, 1984—. Democrat. Roman Catholic. Clubs: Sertoma, ACT (dir. 1984). Home: 9954 Kinglet Dr Baton Rouge LA 70809 Office: Baton Rouge Bank 617 N Blvd Baton Rouge LA 70821

DYKSTRA, DAVID CHARLES, accountant, management consultant, author, educator; b. Des Moines, July 10, 1941; s. Orville Linden and Ermina (Dunn) D.; BSChemE, U. Calif., Berkeley, 1963; MBA, Harvard U., 1966; m. Ello Paimre, Nov. 20, 1971; children—Suzanne, Karin, David S. Corp. contr. Recreation Environs., Newport Beach, Calif., 1970-71, Hydro Conduit Corp., Newport Beach., 1971-78; v.p. fin. and adminstrn. Tree-Sweet Products, Santa Ana, Calif., 1978-80; pres., owner Dykstra Cons., Irvine, Calif., 1980-88; pres. Easy Data Corp., 1981-88; pub. Easy Data Computer Comparisons, 1982—; prin. Touche Ross Internat., Irvine, Calif., 1988—; prof. mgmt. info. systems Nat. U., Irvine, 1984—; pub. Dykstra's Computer Digest, 1984-88; sr. mgr. Touche Ross Internat., Irvine, 1988—. Chmn. 40th Congl. Dist. Tax Reform Immediately, 1977-80; mem. nat. com. Rep. Com.; vice-chmn. Orange County Calif. Rep. Assembly, 1979-80; bd. dir. Corona Del Mar Rep. Assembly, 1980—, v.p., 1980-87, pres. 1987—. CPA, Calif. Mem. Am. Inst. CPA's, Am. Mgmt. Assn., Calif. Soc. CPA's, Data Processing Mgmt. Assn., Ind. Computer Cons. Assn., Internat. Platform Assn., Data Processing Mgmt. Assn., Orange County C. of C., Newport Beach C. of C., Harvard U. Bus. Sch. Assn. Orange County (bd. dir. 1984—, v.p 1984-86, 87—, pres. 1986-87), Harvard U. Bus. Sch. Assn. So. Calif. (bd. dirs. 1986-87), Town Hall. Clubs: John Wayne Tennis, Lido Sailing. Lodge: Rotary (bd. dir. 1984-86). Author: Manager's Guide to Business Computer Terms, 1981, Computers for Profit, 1983; contbr. articles to profl. jours. Home: 1724 Port Ashley Pl Newport Beach CA 92660 Office: 2201 Dupont Dr Irvine CA 92715

DYKSTRA, WILLIAM DWIGHT, business executive, consultant; b. Grand Rapids, Mich., June 15, 1927; s. John Albert and Irene (Stablekamp) D.; m. Ann McGuiness, Nov. 5, 1957 (dec. 1988); children: William Hugh, Mary Irene. AB, Hope Coll., 1949; MBA, Ind. U., 1950. Asst. mgr. Ply-Curves, Inc., 1950, originator magnesium metal furniture 1951; pres. mfg. co. Dwight Corp., 1952-56; pres. W.D. Dykstra Group, 1956—; ptnr. Dykstra Assos.; bd. dirs. Sheldon Co., Graphic Murals, Inc. Author: Management and the 4th Estate; New Profits for Management. George F. Baker Scholar selector; elder Dutch Reformed Ch. Recipient Outstanding Furniture Merit award, 1955, Vehicle Color Design award, 1967, P.I.A. Graphic award, 1971, Am. Advt. Fedn. award, 1971, 73, 76, Disting. Entrepreneur Alumnus award Ind. U., 1983. Mem. Am. Econs. Assn., Am. Inst. Graphic Arts (Packaging award 1965, 67), Acad. Polit. Sci., Engring. Soc. Detroit, Am. Mktg. Assn. (Mktg. Man of Yr. 1981), Engring. Soc. of Detroit, Soc. Packaging and Handling Engrs., Rotary, Phi Kappa Psi, Pi Kappa Delta. Republican. Clubs: Charlevoix Yacht (Mich.). Home: 1145 Edison St NW Grand Rapids MI 49505 Office: Old Tallmadge Grange Hall 0-1845 W Leonard Rd Grand Rapids MI 49504

DYM, FRAN G., public relations consultant; b. N.Y.C.; d. Aaron and Goldie (Lustig) D.; m. Henry V. Goldstein, Feb. 13, 1958 (div. Dec. 1972); children: Janet, Jonathan. BA, Hunter Coll., 1976; postgrad. NYU, 1976-78. Vice-pres. Kalmus Corp., N.Y.C., 1965-77, Keller Haver Advt., N.Y.C., 1978-79; sr. v.p. Daniel S. Roher, Inc., N.Y.C., 1979-83; pres. Dym/SR&A, Inc., N.Y.C., 1983—; cons. KLH R&D Corp., Canoga Park, Calif., 1979-82, Bang & Olufsen of Am., Mount Prospect, Ill., 1980—, dbx, Inc., Newton, Mass., 1979—, Studer Revox of Am., Inc., Nashville, 1982—, Sparkomatic Corp., Milford, Pa., 1983-88, Inter-Link Technology, Ltd., London, 1984—, Altec Lansing Consumer Products, Milford, 1986—, Finial Tech., Sunnyvale, Calif., 1986—, Lexicon Inc., Waltham, Mass., 1984-86, Audio Dynamics Corp., San Bruno, Calif., 1988—, Carillon Corp., San Bruno, 1988—. Contbr. articles to profl. jours. Mem. Audio Engring. Soc., Internat. Motor Press Assn., Am. Women's Econ. Devel. Corp. Office: Dym/SR&A 355 Lexington Ave New York NY 10017

DYSART, BENJAMIN CLAY, III, environmental engineer, educator, consultant; b. Columbia, Tenn., Feb. 12, 1940; s. Benjamin Clay and Kathryne Virginia (Thompson) D.; m. Virginia Carole Livesay, Sept. 3, 1960. BCE, Vanderbilt U., 1961, M.S. in San. Engring., 1964; Ph.D. in Civil Engring., Ga. Inst. Tech., 1969. Staff engr. Union Carbide Corp., 1961-62, 64-65; from asst. prof., assoc. prof. to prof. Clemson U., 1968—, McQueen Quattlebaum prof. engring., 1982-83, dir. S.C. Waters Resources Rsch. Inst., 1968-75, dir. water resources engring. grad. program, 1972-75; sci. advisor Office Sec. of Army, Washington, 1975-76; mem. EPA Sci. Adv. Bd., from 1983; sr. fellow The Conservation Found., 1985—; mem. adv. coun. Electric Power Rsch. Inst., 1989—, mem., chief of engrs. environ. adv. bd. U.S. Army Corps Engrs., 1988—; mem. Glacier Nat. Park Sci. Coun., Nat. Park Svc., 1988—; mem. S.C. Gov.'s Wetlands Forum, 1989—; sec. appointee Outer Continental Shelf Adv. Bd. and OCS Sci. Com. Dept. Interior, 1979-82; mem. S.C. Environ. Quality Control Adv. Com., from 1980, chmn., 1980-81; mem. Sci. Panel to Rev. Interagy. Rsch. on Impact of Oil Pollution NOAA, Dept. Commerce, 1980; mem. Nuclear Energy Ctr. Environ. Task Force Dept. Energy-So. States Energy Bd., 1978-81; mem. Nonpoint Source Pollutant Task Force EPA, 1979-80; mem. civil works adv. com. Office Sec. Army-Young Pres.'s Orgn., 1975-76; mem. S.C. Heritage Adv. Bd. S.C. Wildlife and Marine Resources Dept., 1974-76; cons. on environ. protection, water resources, siting, energy prodn. matters to industry and govt. agys., 1969—. Contbr. articles on math. modeling in water quality and environ. mgmt. to profl. jours.; author numerous profl. papers, reports. Trustee Rene Dubos Ctr. for Human Environs., 1985—, sec., mem. exec. com., 1988—; bd. visitors Kanuga Episcopal Conf. Ctr., 1988—. Recipient Tribute of Appreciation for Disting. Service EPA, 1981, 86, McQueen Quattlebaum Engring. Faculty Achievement award Clemson U., 1982, Order of Palmetto Gov. S.C., 1984, Hon. Mem. award Water Pollution Control Fedn., 1987. Mem. Nat. Wildlife Fedn. (bd. dirs. 1974—, v.p. 1978-83, pres., chmn. bd. 1983-85), Am. Geophys. Union, ASCE, Assn. Environ. Engring. Profs. (bd. dirs. 1978-83, pres., chmn. bd. 1981-82), S.C. Wildlife Fedn. (bd. dirs. from 1969, pres., chmn. bd. 1973-74, S.C. Wildlife Conservationist of Yr), Phi Kappa Phi, Tau Beta Pi, Sigma Xi, Chi Epsilon, Omega Rho, Sigma Nu. Episcopalian. Club: Cosmos (Washington). Home: 216 Holiday Ave E Clemson SC 29631 Office: Clemson U 401 Rhodes Research Ctr Clemson SC 29634-0919

DYSART, JOEL ALYN, management consultant; b. Chgo., Dec. 15, 1940; s. Harold Francis and Elise Charlotte (Dillenger) D.; m. Mari Anne Ryan, Aug. 24, 1963; children: Patricia, Joan, Robert. BSEE, Purdue U., 1962; MBA, Northwestern U., 1964. Plant controller Container Corp. Am., Chgo., 1964-70; regional controller Singer Co., N.Y.C., 1970-72; from cons. to v.p. Booz, Allen & Hamilton Inc., Chgo., 1972-81; chmn. The Bridge Orgn. Inc., Chgo., 1981—. Mem. editorial bd. Strategic Planning Mgmt., 1983—; contbr. articles to profl. jours. Mem. Planning Forum, Inst. Mgmt. Cons. Home: 1203 Ashland Ave Wilmette IL 60091 Office: The Bridge Orgn Inc 33 N Dearborn St Ste 500 Chicago IL 60602

DYSART, MITCHELL DAVID, data processing executive; b. Columbus, Jan. 27, 1956; s. John Mitchell and Lucy Anna (Zigler) D. BS, Ohio State U., 1978. Systems programmer Ohio State U., Columbus, 1979—; chmn. bd., chief exec. officer Am. Tech. Bus. Services, Columbus, 1985—; cons. Gov.'s Commn. on Agr., Columbus, 1984. Adult leader Boy Scouts Am., Columbus, 1978. Mem. Nat. Soc. Profl. Engrs., Aircraft Owners and Pilots Assn., Mensa. Democrat. Office: Am Tech Bus Svcs PO Box 21226 Columbus OH 43221-0226

DZIADUL, W. JOHN, commercial mortgage broker; b. Ipswich, Mass., Nov. 14, 1947. BS in Acctg., Northeastern U., Boston, 1970. V.p. Empire Savs. and Loan Assn., Buffalo, 1971-78, Citizens Bank, Providence, 1978-80; mortgage officer Boston Mut. Life Ins. Co., Canton, Mass., 1981-83; regional mgr., v.p. Lomas & Nettleton, Inc., Boston, 1983-87; pres. Andover (Mass.) Mortgage Corp., 1987—. Served with U.S. Army, 1970-71. Mem. Greater Lawrence Bd. Realtors, Investment Network Am. Office: Andover Mortgage Corp 2 Dundee Park Andover MA 01810

DZIEDZIAK, BRYAN JOHN, accountant; b. Medina, Ohio, Feb. 12, 1958; s. John Joseph and Marilyn Joan (Tomko) D.; m. Caryll Marie Batt, May 24, 1980; children: Matthew, Daniel, Zachary. BS in Acctg., Case Western Res. U., 1980, MBA, 1981. CPA. Tax mgr. Deloitte, Haskins & Sells, Cleve., 1981-86; tax mgr. Deloitte, Haskins & Sells, Phoenix, 1986-87, sr. tax mgr., 1987—. Mem. AICPA, Ohio Soc. CPAs, Ariz. Soc. CPAs, Real Estate Syndication and Securities Inst. (bd. govs.), Nat. Assn. Office Parks, Pub. Affairs Profls. Ariz., Phoenix C. of C. Republican. Roman Catholic. Home: 4216 W Paradise Dr Phoenix AZ 85029 Office: Deloitte Haskins & Sells 100 W Washington St Ste 1000 Phoenix AZ 85003

DZIURDZIK, THOMAS EDWARD, publishing company executive; b. Chgo., May 5, 1954; s. Anthony A. and Josephine (Andracki) D.; m. Mary Ann Jadowic, May 15, 1976; children: Mark Thomas, Emily Marie, William Joseph. BS in Acctg., De Paul U., 1976, MBA, 1986. CPA, Ill. Acct. Arthur Andersen & Co., Chgo., 1975-81; asst. controller Scott, Foresman & Co., Glenview, Ill., 1981-83, v.p., controller, 1983-88, v.p. fin., 1988—. Mem. Fin. Execs. Inst., Am. Inst. CPA's, Ill. Soc. CPA's, DePaul U.'s Ledger & Quill, Beta Alpha Psi, Delta Mu Delta, Beta Gamma Sigma. Office: Scott Foresman & Co 1900 E Lake Ave Glenview IL 60025

EAGAN, TIMOTHY DEMONG, real estate developer; b. Syracuse, N.Y., Feb. 22, 1953; s. Leo William and Doris Louise (Walker) E.; m. Susan Penelope Stewart, Sept. 5, 1987. BA in English with hons., U. Utah, 1976. Acctg. clk. Aries Dewitt (N.Y.) Assocs., 1978-79, mgr. mall, 1979-81; dir. computer ops. Eagan Ctrs., Dewitt, 1982, v.p. leasing, 1983-84; v.p. site devel. LWE Assocs., Dewitt, 1985—; dir. Chase Lincoln First Bank, Syracuse, 1987—. Bd. dirs. Syracuse Symphony Orch., 1987—. Mem. Internat. Coun. Shopping Ctrs., Onon Club, Golf and Country Club. Office: LWE Assocs Inc PO Box A Dewitt NY 13214

EAGLEBURGER, LAWRENCE SIDNEY, federal official, former ambassador; b. Milw., Aug. 1, 1930; s. Leon Sidney and Helen (Van Ornum) E.; m. Marlene Ann Heinemann, Apr. 23, 1966; 1 son by previous marriage, Lawrence Scott; children: Lawrence Andrew, Lawrence Jason. Student, Cen. State Coll., Stevens Point, Wis., 1948-50; B.S., U. Wis., 1952, M.S., 1957; LLD (hon.), U. S.C., 1985, George Washington U., 1986. Teaching asst. U. Wis., 1956-57; joined U.S. Fgn. Service, 1957; 3d sec. Tegucigalpa, Honduras, 1957-59; assigned State Dept., 1959-62, 65-66; 2d sec. Belgrade, Yugoslavia, 1962-65; mem. staff NSC, 1966-67; spl. asst. under sec. State Dept., 1967-69; exec. asst. to asst. to Pres. for nat. security affairs 1969; polit. adviser, counselor for polit. affairs U.S. Mission to NATO, Brussels, Belgium, 1969-71; dep. asst. sec. Dept. Def., 1971-73, dep. asst. to Pres. for nat. security ops., 1973; exec. asst. to sec. state 1973-75, dep. undersec. state for mgmt., exec. asst. to sec. state, 1975-77; ambassador to Yugoslavia Belgrade, 1977-81; asst. sec. for European affairs Dept. State, 1981-82, undersec. for polit. affairs, 1982-84, dep. sec. state, 1989—; pres. Kissinger Assocs., Inc., N.Y.C., 1984—; bd. dirs. ITT Corp., Josephson Internat., Inc.; trustee Mutual of N.Y. Vice chmn. 7th Dist. Young Republicans Wis., 1950-51; mem. Wis. Young Rep. Exec. Com., 1949-51. Served to 1st lt. AUS, 1952-54. Recipient Disting. Civilian Service medal Dept. Def., 1973; President's award for disting. fed. civilian service, 1977; Dept. State Disting. Honor award. Mem. Alpha Sigma Phi. Republican. Lutheran. Office: Dept of State Washington DC 20520

EAGLES, STUART ERNEST, business executive; b. Saint John, N.B., Can., July 29, 1929; s. Ernest Lyle and Evelyn Gertrude (Feltmate) E.; m. Margaret Anne Gulliver, Sept. 20, 1952; children: James Stuart, Patricia Anne, Mark Edward. B.Sc., Acadia U., 1949. Pres. Aegean Devel. Inc., Toronto, 1988—; dir. Microcel Composites Inc.; past trustee and dir. Internat. Coun. Shopping Ctrs.; past pres. and dir. Can. Inst. Pub. Real Estate Cos. Bd. dirs. Jr. Achievement Can.; bd. govs. Acadia Univ. Mem. Ont. C. of C. (bd. dirs.), National Club (past pres.), Canadian Club, Empire Club. Home: 24 Garfield Ave, Toronto, ON Canada M4T 1E7 Office: Aegean Devel Inc, 67 Yonge St Ste 600, Toronto, ON Canada M5E 1J8

EAKIN, DAVID MCCLELLAN, banker; b. Grove City, Pa., Mar. 15, 1950; s. John M. and Margaret Agnes (Kennedy) E.; m. Janice M. Woods, Aug. 26, 1972; children: Kate E., Steven T. BS, Indiana U. Pa., 1972; MBA, Gannon U., 1977. Banking officer NW Bank, Meadville, Pa., 1973-76, br. mgr., 1976; adminstrv. officer NW Bank, Oil City, Pa., 1977-78, fin. officer, 1978, asst. v.p. fin., 1979-80, controller, 1981; controller NW Pa. Corp., Oil City, Pa., 1982-83; v.p., treas. Mellon Bank, Oil City, Pa., 1984, sr. v.p., treas., 1984—. Mem. Nat. Assn. Accts., Pa. Bankers Assn. (mem. tax com. 1985-89), Meadville Area C. of C. (com. mem. 1975-76), Oil City C. of C. Republican. Club: Wanago Country (Oil City). Home: RD 4 Box 508 Hollis Rd Meadville PA 16335 Office: Mellon Bank 100 Seneca St Oil City PA 16301

EAKIN, THOMAS CAPPER, sports promotion executive; b. New Castle, Pa., Dec. 16, 1933; s. Frederick William and Beatrice (Capper) E.; m. Brenda Lee Andrews, Oct. 21, 1961; children: Thomas Andrews, Scott Frederick. B.A. in History, Denison U., 1956. Life ins. cons. Northwestern Mut. Life Ins. Co., Cleve., 1959-67; dist. mgr. Putman Pub. Co., Cleve., 1968-69; regional bus. mgr. Chilton Pub. Co., Cleve., 1969-70; dist. mgr. Hitchcock Pub. Co., Cleve., 1970-72; founder, pres. Golf Internat. 100 Club, Shaker Heights, Ohio, 1970—; founder, pres., dir. Cy Young Mus., 1975-80; pres. TCE Enterprises, Shaker Heights, Ohio, 1973—; founder, pres. Ohio Baseball Hall of Fame, 1976—, Ohio Baseball Hall of Fame Celebration, 1977-79, Ohio Baseball Hall of Fame and Mus., 1980—, Ohio Sports Hall of

Fame, 1985—, Ohio Assn. of Sports Halls of Fame, 1985—, Ohio Sports Council, 1985—, U.S. Assn. of Sports Halls of Fame, 1989—; founder, chmn. Ohio Baseball Hall of Fame Golf Invitational, 1980—, Ohio Baseball Hall of Fame media award, 1981, The Streetsboro Ohio Athletic Found., 1989—; bd. dirs. New Hope Records, Greater Toledo Sports Hall of Fame; trustee Newcomerstown Sports Corp., 1975-80; founder, nat. chmn. Cy Young Centennial, 1967; founder, nat. chmn. Cy Young Golf Invitational, 1967-79, (champion 1967, 1969-72, 1979); mem. adv. bd. Cleve. Indian Old Timers Com., 1966-67, Portage County Sports Hall of Fame (Ohio), 1983—, Sportsbeat, 1985—, 88—, Sch. Calendar Co. Inc., 1984; hon. dir. Tuscarawas County (Ohio) Old Timers Baseball Assn., 1972—, commendation, 1970; Ohio exec. sponsor chmn. World Golf Hall of Fame, Pinehurst, N.C., 1979—; founder, pres. Toledo Baseball Bluecoats, 1984—, Tuscarawas County Sports Hall of Fame, 1980—; mem. adv. bd. Damascus Steel Casting Co., 1987—, Avantage Sports Co., 1989—, Base Sports Co., 1989; founder, chmn. Ohio Baseball Hall of Fame Lifetime Achievement award, 1987—; mem. disting. citizens adv. bd. Am. Police Hall of Fame & Mus., 1987—. Feature story in Amateur Athletics World, 1982; mem. adv. bd. M&M Publs., 1987—. Fund drive rep Boy Scouts Am., Cleve., 1959-60, United Appeal, 1959-63, Heart Fund, 1963-64; assoc. Merrick Art Gallery, 1980; mem. Cleve. Council Corrections, 1971-73; mem. adv. bd. Cuyahoga Hills Boys Sch., Warrensville Heights, Ohio, 1971—, Camp Hope, Warrrensville Twp., 1973—, Fitness Evaluation Services, Inc., 1977-79, Interact Club of Twinsburg (Ohio), 1981—, The Old Time Ball Players Assn. of Wis., Greater Youngstown Old Timers Baseball Assn., Cleve. Sports Legends Found., 1988—, Madison (Ohio) Hist. Soc., 1988—; mem. research bd. advisors Am. Biog. Inst., 1986—; founder, bd. dirs. TRY (Target/Reach Youth), 1971—, Interact Club Shaker Heights, 1971—; mem. exec. com. Tuscarawas County Am. Revolution Bicentennial Comm., 1974-76; trustee Tuscarawas County Hist. Soc., 1978-81; bd. dirs. Shaker Hts. Youth Center, 1975, Tuscarawas Valley Tourist Assn., 1979-81, Buckeye Tourist Assn., 1979-80; mem. adv. bd. Ohio Racquetball Assn., 1981-82; trustee Nat. Jr. Tennis League, 1985-87; mem. adv. bd. Middlefield Hist. Soc., 1986—; hon. trustee Clinton (Ohio) Hist. Soc., 1987—; mem. adv. bd. Windsor (Ohio) Hist. Soc., 1987—; founder, chmn. Bath-Richfield Ohio Community Fund, Streetsboro (Ohio) Athletic Found., 1989—; mem. Ohio Hist. Soc., Lawrence County Hist. Soc., 1989—. Served with AUS, 1956-58. Recipient commendation award Cy Young Centennial Com., 1967, commendation award Tuscarawas County C. of C., 1967, commendation award Sporting News, 1968, commendation awards Gov. James A. Rhodes, Ohio, 1968, 75, 78, commendation award Gov. John J. Gilligan, Ohio, 1972, commendation award Newcomerstown (Ohio) C. of C., 1967, commendation award N.C. Senate, 1984, commendation award State of Pa. Senate, 1984, Disting. Service award, Hubbard, Ohio, 1986; Outstanding Contbn. to Baseball award baseball commr. William Eckert, 1967; Sport Service award Sport mag., 1969, Feature Cover Story Personality lete's World mag., 1982; Civic Service award Cuyahoga Hills Boys Sch., 1970; citation of merit La. Stadium and Expn. Dist., 1972, Presdl. commendations Nixon, Ford, Reagan; Disting. Service award Camp Hope, 1974; Founder's award Interact Club Shaker Heights, 1974; Gov.'s Award for community action State of Ohio, 1974; award of achievement Ohio Assn. Hist. Socs., 1975; named to Order of Long Leaf Pine, State of N.C., 1984; Chief Newawatowes award Newcomerstown C. of C., 1975; Proclamation award, Thomas C. Eakin Day City of Cleve., 1974, and in numerous Ohio cities 1984-86, Ohio First Record (only person to ever have a day in his honor proclaimed by one city or village in every county in Ohio); Thomas C. Eakin day, State of N.Mex., 1987; Outstanding Alumnus award Phi Delta Theta Alumni Club, Cleve., 1975; commendation states of La., N.C., Ohio Senate, House of Rep.; certificate of merit Tuscarawas County Am. Revolution Bicentennial Commn., 1976; Appreciation award Am. Revolution Bicentennial Adminstrn., 1977; Cert. of Merit State of La., 1978; Gov.'s Award State of Ohio, 1978; named Hon. Citizen City of New Orleans, 1978, City of Memphis, 1986, City of Little Rock, 1986, numerous Ohio cities; Founder's award TRY, Target/Reach Youth 1979; inducted into Chautauqua Sports Hall of Fame (N.Y.), 1983, hon. bd. dirs., 1982—; Sch. Calendar Co. Inc. Hall of Fame, 1987; Commissioners' award Trumbull County Ohio, 1985; honor resolution New Orleans City Council, 1984; Commendation, N.C. Senate, 1984, Pa. Senate, 1984; Gov.'s citation State of Md., 1987, Hon. West Virginian award Gov. W.Va., 1987; recipient various honors resolutions, tributes and commendations; named to hon. order Ky. Cols., 1986, Venerable Order Michael the Archangel, patron saint police, Am. Police Hall of Fame, 1989; recipient Can. Internat. Friendship award Premier of Ont., Can., 1985. Fellow Intercontinental Biog. Assn., Am. Biog. Inst.; mem. Tuscarawas County Hist. Soc. (trustee 1978-81), Shaker Hist. Soc. (trustee 1980-82), Internat. Platform Assn., English Speaking Union, Denison U. Cleve. Men's Club (v.p. 1964-65), Soc. for Am. Baseball Research, Ohio Hist. Soc., Lawrence County Hist. Soc., Phi Delta Theta (pres. Cleve. alumni club 1970, Appreciation award 1971, dir. 1971-75, exec. com. nat. Lou Gehrig award com. 1975—, trustee Ohio Iota chpt. 1979-82). Baptist (mem. bd. 1966-69). Clubs: Executive (Woodmere, Ohio); PGA Nat. Golf (Palm Beach Gardens, Fla.) (internat. mem.); Legend Lake Golf (Chardon, Ohio); Univ. Sch. Tennis (Shaker Heights), Beachwood Athletic. Lodge: Rotary (pres. Shaker Heights 1970-71, founder and chmn. club's internat. student exchange program U.S. and Can. 1965-70, Outstanding Young Rotarian award 1962, Significant Achievement award 1970-71, founder, chmn. Henry G. Duchscherer Meml. award com. 1971, trustee V. Blakeman Qua Scholarship Fund 1972-73, Wahoo dir. 1975-77). Address: 2729 Shelley Rd Shaker Heights OH 44122

EAMER, RICHARD KEITH, health care company executive, lawyer; b. Long Beach, Calif., Feb. 13, 1928; s. George Pierce and Lillian (Newell) E.; m. Eileen Laughlin, Sept. 1, 1951; children: Brian Keith, Erin Maureen. B.S. in Acctg., U. So. Calif., 1955, LL.B., 1959. Bar: Calif. 1960; C.P.A., Calif. Acct. L. H. Penney & Co. (C.P.A.s), 1956-59; asso. firm Ervin, Cohen & Jessup, Beverly Hills, Calif., 1959-63; partner firm Eamer, Bell and Bedrosian, Beverly Hills, 1963-69; chmn. bd., chief exec. officer Nat. Med. Enterprises, Inc., Los Angeles, 1969—; also dir. Nat. Med. Enterprises, Inc.; dir. Union Oil Co. Calif., Imperial Bank. Mem. Am. Bar Assn., Am. Inst. C.P.A.s, Calif. Bar Assn., Los Angeles County Bar Assn. Republican. Clubs: Bel Air Country, Bel Air Bay; California. Office: Nat Med Enterprises Inc 11620 Wilshire Blvd Los Angeles CA 90025 *

EAMES, EARL WARD, JR., association executive, management consultant; b. Morris, Minn., Oct. 22, 1923; s. Earl Ward and Camilla (Hendricks) E.; m. Anyes de Horst, June 26, 1954; children—Elizabeth Anne, Earl Ward III, Erik Michael, Christopher Paul. Student, U. Minn., 1941; BS, MIT, 1949. Vice pres., then pres., dir. Consultants Inc., Boston and Amsterdam, Netherlands, 1949-54; prodn. specialist Found. Productivity Research, Helsinki, Finland, 1955-57; pres. Gen. Mgmt. Assos., Boston, 1957-63; sr. assoc. Cresap, McCormick & Paget, N.Y.C., 1963-66; v.p. ops. Council Internat. Progress in Mgmt., N.Y.C., 1966; pres., chief exec. officer, dir. Council Internat. Progress in Mgmt., 1967-69; v.p., dir. Reed, Cuff & Becker, N.Y.C., 1970-73; sr. asso. Wilmer Wright Assos., 1973-78; vis. prof. and mgmt. consultancy adivesor UN Indsl. Devel. Orgn. World Bank, Nigeria, 1978-80; advisor on small-scale industry UN Indsl. Devel. Orgn. World Bank, various locations, 1980-86; mgr. area ctr. Save the Children Fedn., Mpls., 1987—; Royal Danish consul for New Eng., 1952-55; lectr. internat. econs. Fisher Coll., 1954-55, 60-63; Mem. Gov. Com. Refugees, 1961—; chmn. trustees Nat. Service Secretariat, 1966—; rep. Internat. Council for Sci. Mgmt. to ECOSOC, 1967—; mem. ednl. council Mass. Inst. Tech., 1974—; adj. prof. Augsburg Coll., 1986; lectr. Coll. of St. Thomas, 1988—. Author: Managerial Requirements 1966, Non-Woven Fabrics, 1970; Contbr. Training Managers: The International Guide, 1969, University Involvement in Industrial Development, 1979. Treas. New Eng. Opera Theatre, 1958-63; mem. com. Friends of N.Y. Philharmonic, 1967—; corporate mem. Vols. for Internat. Tech. Assistance, 1967—. Served with USNR, 1942-46. Mem. Acad. Mgmt., MIT Alumni Assn. Republican. Lutheran. Clubs: M.I.T. Alumni (Washington); Staff (U. Ife). Home: 2601 Sunset Blvd Minneapolis MN 55416 Office: Save the Children Fedn PO Box 16086 Minneapolis MN 55416

EARLE, ARTHUR PERCIVAL, textile executive; b. Montreal, Que., Can., Apr. 23, 1922; s. Arthur Percival and Bernadette (Gosselin) E.; m. Muriel Elizabeth Vining, June 1, 1946; children: Arthur Percival, Richard John, Janet Elizabeth. B.E.E., McGill U., Montreal, 1949; M.M.P., Harvard U., 1957. Registered profl. engr., Que., Ont. With Shawinigan Water & Power Co., 1949-63, asst. mgr. prodn. and plant, 1949-63; with Dominion Textile Inc., Montreal, 1963—, chief engr. then group v.p. subs., 1970-78, sr. v.p. ops. svcs., 1978-87, sr. v.p., 1978-88, cons. corp. affairs, 1988—; dir. Hubbard Dyers Ltd., Foresbec Inc., Avec Techs.; past pres. Lana Knit Ltd., Fireside Fabrics Ltd., Fiber-World Ltd., Elpee Yarns Ltd., Jaro Ltd., Esmond Mills Ltd.; past chmn. Penmans Ltd. Bd. dirs. Ecole de Technologie Superieure, U. Que., 1978-85, mem. exec. com., 1981-85; pres. Montreal Bd. Trade, 1980-81; chmn. bd., exec. com. Phoenix Found., 1985—; bd. dirs. Lakeshore Gen. Hosp., Pointe Claire, Que., v.p., 1988—; chmn. Les Mercuriades Bus. Awards, 1985; chmn. Le Counseil de L'Aeroport Internat. de Montreal, 1987—. Served with RCAF, 1941-45. Mem. IEEE (past sect. chmn.), Order Engrs. Que., Assn. Profl. Engrs. Ont., Engring. Inst. Can. (hon. treas. 1986-88, sr. v.p. 1988—), Am. Textile Managerial Engring. Soc., Que. C. of C. (pres. 1983-84, chmn. 1984-85), Montreal Internat. Airport Council (chmn. bd.). Conservative. Anglican. Clubs: Royal Montreal Golf, Montreal Amateur Athletic Assn, Thistle Curling (pres. 1974-75), Mt. Stephen. Office: Dominion Textile Inc, 1950 Sherbrooke St W, Montreal, PQ Canada H3H 1E7

EARLE, HARRY WOODWARD, printing company executive; b. Norwalk, Conn., June 17, 1924; s. Harry W. and Rose Lillian (Agnew) E.; m. Barbara Aymar, Dec. 14, 1944; children: David, Penrhyn, John, Gordon, Barbara. B.A., Williams Coll., 1946. Vice-pres. mktg. McCall Printing Co., McCall Corp., N.Y.C., 1946-66; group v.p. consumer products div. Arcata Nat. Corp., Menlo Park, Calif., 1966-74; v.p. W.A. Krueger Co., N.Y.C., 1979—; chmn. bd., pres., chief exec. officer Banta Corp., Menasha, Wis.; dir. Nash Engring. Co., Norwalk, Conn., Menasha Corp., Neenah, Wis., Fox Valley Corp., Appleton, Wis. Bd. selectman, Darien, Conn., 1949-62, chmn. bd. fin., 1962-66, mem. police commn., 1976-78. Served with USAAF, 1942-45. Decorated D.F.C., 3 air medals. Home: 1071 Brighton Dr Menasha WI 54952 Office: Banta Corp 100 Main St Menasha WI 54952

EARLEY, ANTHONY FRANCIS, JR., utilities company executive, lawyer; b. Jamaica, N.Y., July 29, 1949; s. Anthony Francis and Jean Ann (Draffen) E.; m. Sarah Margaret Belanger, Oct. 14, 1972; children: Michael Patrick, Anthony Matthew, Daniel Cartwright, Matthew Sean. BS in Physics, U. Notre Dame, 1971, MS in Engring., 1979, JD, 1979. Bar: Va. 1980, N.Y. 1985, U.S. Ct. Appeals (6th cir.). Assoc. Hunton & Williams, Richmond, Va., 1979-85, ptnr., 1985; gen. counsel L.I. Lighting Co., Hicksville, N.Y., 1985-89, exec. v.p., 1988-89, pres., chief oper. officer, 1989—. Contbr. articles to profl. jours. Bd. dirs., sec. United Way of Long Island, 1987—. Served to lt. USN, 1971-76. Mem. ABA, Nassau County Bar Assn., Assn. of Bar of City of N.Y. Roman Catholic. Office: LI Lighting Co 175 E Old Country Rd Hicksville NY 11801

EARLY, BERT HYLTON, lawyer, legal search consultant; b. Kimball, W.Va., July 17, 1922; s. Robert Terry and Sue Keister (Hylton) E.; m. Elizabeth Henry, June 24, 1950; children—Bert Hylton, Robert Christian, Mark Randolph, Philip Henry, Peter St. Clair. Student, Marshall U., 1940-42; A.B., Duke U., 1946; J.D., Harvard U., 1949. Bar: W.Va. 1949, Ill. 1963, Fla. 1981. Assoc. Fitzpatrick, Marshall, Huddleston & Bolen, Huntington, W.Va., 1949-57; asst. counsel Island Creek Coal Co., Huntington, W.Va., 1957-60, assoc. gen. counsel, 1960-62; dep. exec. dir. ABA, Chgo., 1962-64, exec. dir., 1964-81; sr. v.p. Wells Internat., Chgo., 1981-83, pres., 1983-85; pres. Bert H. Early Assocs. Inc., Chgo., 1985—; Instr., Marshall U., 1950-53; cons. and lectr. in field. Bd. dirs. Morris Meml. Hosp. Crippled Children, 1954-60, Huntington Pub. Library, 1951-60, W.Va. Tax Inst., 1961-62, Huntington Galleries, 1961-62; mem. W.Va. Jud. Council, 1960-62, Huntington City Council, 1961-62; bd. dirs. Community Renewal Soc., Chgo., 1965-76, United Charities Chgo., 1972-80, Am. Bar Endowment, 1983—, sec. 1987—, Hinsdale Hosp. Found., 1987—, Internat. Bar Assn. Found., 1987—; mem. vis. com. U. Chgo. Law Sch., 1975-78; trustee David and Elkins Coll., 1960-63. mem., Hinsdale Plan Commn., Ill., 1982-85. Served to 1st lt. AC, U.S. Army, 1943-45. Life Fellow Am. Bar Found., Ill. State Bar Found. (charter); mem. Am. Law Inst. (life), Internat. Bar Assn. (asst. sec. gen. 1967-82), ABA (Ho. of Dels. 1958-59, 84—, chmn. Young Lawyers div. 1957-58, Disting. Service award Young Lawyers div. 1983), Nat. Legal Aid and Defender Assn., Am. Jud. Soc. (bd. dirs. 1981-84), Fla. Bar, W.Va. State Bar, Chgo. Bar Assn. Presbyterian. Clubs: Harvard (N.Y.C.); Metropolitan (Washington); University, Economic (Chgo.); Hinsdale Golf (Ill.). Office: Bert Early Assocs 111 W Washington St Suite 1421 Chicago IL 60602-2708

EARLY, JACK GAVIN, JR., accountant, trust company administrator; b. Tuscaloosa, Ala., Oct. 28, 1953; s. Jack Gavin Sr. and Betty Jean (Harwell) E. BSBA in Acctg., Auburn U., 1977. CPA, Ala. Staff acct. W.C. Mann, CPA, Bessemer, Ala., 1977-79, Hancock, Askew & Co., CPA's, Savannah, Ga., 1979-80; mgr. pension dept. Mut. Benefit Life Ins. Co., Birmingham, Ala., 1980-89; v.p. E&C Cons., Inc., Birmingham, 1983-89; adminstr. trust dept. Trust Co. Bank of South Ga., Albany, 1989—. Mem. Delta Tau Delta (pres. Birmingham alumni chpt. 1984-88, v.p. house corp. 1984-85, pres. house corp. 1986-88). Republican. Lutheran. Home: 2502 Canterbury Ct K-8 Albany GA 31707-1606 Office: Trust Co Bank of South Ga Trust Dept PO Box 1247 Albany GA 31703

EARLY, MARGARET HENDERSON, management consultant; b. Greenwich, Conn., Jan. 3, 1952; d. Thomas Gerard and Virginia Maury (Flannery) Early. BA, Hollins Coll., 1973. Cert. mgmt. cons., compensation profl. Conf. coord. The Mark Resort, Vail, Colo., 1974-78; cons. The Wyatt Co., Wellesley Hills, Mass., 1978-82; mng. prin. Stephen Heartt & Assocs., Boston, 1982-87, The Johnson Cos., Boston, 1987—; bd. dirs. Seven Gates Farm Corp., West Tisbury, Mass. Treas., bd. dirs. Friends of the Mus. Printing, Boston, 1986—; trustee, treas. 10-14 Remington St. Condominium Trust, Cambridge, Mass., 1987—; bd. mgrs. City Club Corp., Boston, 1989—. Mem. Am. Compensation Assn., Am. Mgmt. Assn., City Club. Home: 10 Remington St Cambridge MA 02138 Office: The Johnson Cos 25 Kingston St Boston MA 02111

EARLY, PATRICK JOSEPH, oil and gas company executive; b. Lincoln, Nebr., Feb. 4, 1933; s. John Joseph and Irene Cecelia (McManus) E.; m. Evelyn Louise Wiese, Aug. 30, 1955; children: Timothy, Christopher, Pamela, Kathleen, William, Andrew. BS in Engring., Colo. Sch. Mines, 1955; grad. mgmt. tng. program, U. Western Ont., Can., 1971; grad. advanced mgmt. program, Harvard U., 1980. Various operating and engring. positions Amoco Prodn. Co., Wyo., Tex. and La., 1955-75; regional prodn. mgr. Amoco Prodn. Co., Denver, 1975-76; v.p. prodn. Amoco Prodn. Co., Chgo., 1976-81, sr. v.p. prodn., 1981-86, exec. v.p. U.S.A., 1986-87, pres., 1987—. Served with USAF, 1957. Mem. Am. Petroleum Inst. (past chmn. operating com. prodn. dept.), Soc. Petroleum Engrs., The Mid-Am. Club, Naperville Country Club, The Chgo. Club. Republican. Roman Catholic. Office: Amoco Prodn Co 200 E Randolph Dr Chicago IL 60601

EARLY, STEWART, corporate planning executive; b. Rockford, Ill., Aug. 14, 1944; s. John and Janet (Stewart) E., m. Patricia E. Toon, July 8, 1967, children: Malcolm, Robert. BS in Engring. Mechanics, Lehigh U., 1966; PhB in Mgmt. Studies, Oxford U., 1968, M in Philosophy, 1983. Sales mgr. nuclear fuel Westinghouse Electric, Pitts., 1970-73, project mgr. nuclear steam supply system, 1974-76, cons. corp. planning, 1977-80; dir. strategic systems Rockwell Internat., Pitts., 1981-83; mgr. strategic planning FMC Corp., Chgo., 1983-88; dir. strategy and bus. devel. automotive and indsl. electronics group Motorola Inc., 1988—; cons. Guild for the Blind, Pitts., 1979, Seton Hill Coll., Greensburg, Pa., 1982-83, vis. scholar, adj. faculty mem. Lake Forest (Ill.) Grad. Sch., 1986—. Mem. No. Am. Soc. for Corp. Planning (exec. com. nat. v.p. 1981-84), The Planning Forum, Chgo. (exec. com. pres. 1985-86). Presbyterian. Clubs: PAA (Pitts.), University (Chgo.). Home: 228 Myrtle St Winnetka IL 60093 Office: Motorola Inc 4000 Commercial Ave Northbrook IL 60062

EARMAN, LARRY JOSEPH, accountant; b. Richmond, Ind., Nov. 8, 1947; s. Stanley Joseph Earman and Doris (Craig) Schleiger; m. Linda Lu Provost, Sept. 21, 1968; children: Lisa Marie, Laura Catherine. BBA, Ohio State U., 1969. CPA, Ohio. Staff acct. Arthur Andersen & Co., Columbus, Ohio, 1969-75, mgr., 1975-78; pvt. practice acct. Columbus, 1978-79; ptnr. Ary & Earman, Columbus, 1979—; lectr. fin. Ohio Pvt. Residential Assn., Columbus, 1983—. Treas. Cen. Ohio Radio Reading Service, Columbus, 1975-78; bd. dirs. Hilliard (Ohio) City Sch. Dist., 1985—, pres., bd. edn., 1988—. Mem. Am. Inst. CPA's, Ohio Soc. CPA's. Home: 3355 Kingsway Dr Hilliard OH 43026 Office: Ary & Earman 2929 Kenny Rd Suite 280 Columbus OH 43221

EAST, ERNEST EARL, JR., lawyer; b. Vallejo, Calif., Oct. 17, 1942; s. Ernest Earl East Sr. and Evelyn E. (Pendergrass) Walworth. BA, U. Tulsa, 1965; JD, U. Ark., 1969. Bar: Ark. 1969, Tex. 1973, U.S. Supreme Ct. 1973. Atty. SEC, Washington, 1969-73; assoc. Ritchie, Ritchie & Crosland, Dallas, 1973-74; assoc. gen. counsel Boise (Idaho) Cascade Corp., 1974-80, Ga. Pacific Corp., Atlanta, 1980-84; assoc. gen. counsel, asst. sec. Del Webb Corp., Phoenix, 1984-85, v.p., sec., gen. counsel, 1985—. Pres. Idaho Human Rights Commn., Boise, 1976-80; bd. dirs. Ariz. Hist. Soc., Phoenix, 1987—. Mem. ABA, Am. Soc. Corp. Secs., Am. Corp. Counsel Assn., State Bar Tex., Pla. Club, Mansion Club. Clubs: Plaza, Mansion (Phoenix). Home: 6817 N 4th Pl Phoenix AZ 85012 Office: Del Webb Corp 2231 E Camelback Rd Phoenix AZ 85016

EAST, FRANK HOWARD, paper company executive; b. Muncie, Ind., Dec. 25, 1937; s. F. Harold and Esther (Hall) E.; m. Lynn A. Haskett, Apr. 15, 1988; children: Kim L., Kathy A. BS, Ball State U., 1960, MS, 1972. CPA, Ind.; cert. ind. auditor. Mgmt. cons. Ernst & Whinney, Indpls., 1960-65; contr., v.p. fin. Bell Fibre Products, Marion, Ind., 1965-78, exec. v.p., 1978-80, pres., 1980—; bd. dirs. Menominee (Mich.) Paper Co., Summit Bank, Marion, Bell Fibre, Marion. Mem. adv. com. Marion Coll., 1979—; pres. Marion Easter Pageant, 1981-85; treas., bd. dirs. Marion Gen. Hosp., 1978-83; bd. dirs. YMCA, Marion, 1978-80, Jr. Achievement, 1972—; mem. Marion Redevel. Com., 1978-80. Mem. AICPA, Ind. Inst. CPAs, Pres.'s Assn., Young Pres.'s Assn., Fin. Execs. Inst., Ind. State C. of C. (bd. dirs. 1980—). Republican. Methodist. Office: Bell Fibre Products Corp 3102 S Boots St Marion IN 46953

EAST, LAURA JEAN, accountant; b. New Orleans, Oct. 15, 1957; d. Clarence Marion Jr. and Dorothy Marie (Beckley) E. BBA, Loyola U. of South, 1979. CPA, La. Acct. Carimi, Morici, Ltd., CPA's, New Orleans, 1979-83, LaPorte, Sehrt, Romig & Hand, CPA's, New Orleans, 1983-85, Kernion T. Schafer, CPA, Metairie, La., 1985-86; controller, exec. v.p. Personal Health Care Found., Metairie, 1986-87; pvt. practice Metairie, 1987—. Mem. La. Soc. CPA's, Am. Inst. CPA's, AM. Soc. Women Accts., Am. Mktg. Assn., Carnival Krewe Club of Venus, Delta Sigma Pi. Republican. Roman Catholic. Office: PO Box 9395 Metairie LA 70005

EASTBURN, RICHARD A., consulting firm executive; b. West Chester, Pa., Jan. 16, 1934; s. Louis W. and Alma S. (Shellin) E.; BA, Shelton Coll., 1956; MST, N.Y. Theol. Sem., 1959; MEd, Temple U., 1970; MBA, Columbia U., 1979; m. Heidi Fritz, June 15, 1963; children: Karin J., R. Marc. Ordained to ministry Am. Baptist Conv., 1959; minister, Laurelton, N.J., 1959-61; dir adult programs Central YMCA, Phila., 1961-65; dir. Opportunities Industrialization Ctr., Phila., 1965-67; mgr. tng. and devel. Missile & Surface Radar div. RCA, Moorestown, N.J., 1967-68, mgr. mgmt. devel. govt. and comml. systems group, dir. mgmt. devel., 1969-71; group mgr. personnel for internat. field ops. Digital Equipment, Maynard, Mass., 1971-75; corp. dir. orgn. and productivity devel. Am. Standard, Inc., N.Y.C., 1975-79; corp. dir. mgmt. devel. edn. and staffing TRW, Inc., Cleve., 1979-85; pres. Retirement Community Concepts, 1981—, founder Laurel Lake Retirement Community, Hudson, Ohio, 1985; sr. v.p. Strategic Mgmt. Group of Phila., Chagrin Falls, Ohio, 1985—; producer, moderator Ask the Clergy, Sta. WIP, Phila., 1965-67; bd. dirs. Wellsboro (Ohio) Foundry. Bd. dirs. exec. program adv. bd. U. Ind.; bd. dirs. Burlington County (N.J.) Community Com., 1967-69. Recipient Disting. Community Service award Shelton Coll. Alumni, 1956; Dedicated Service award Phila. March of Progress, 1967. Mem. Am. Soc. Tng. and Devel. (dir., 1979-80), Orgn. Devel. Network., Ops. Mgmt. Assn., Soc. Mfg. Engrs., Am. Prodn. and Inventory Control Soc. Mem. United Ch. Christ. Clubs: Chagrin Valley Athletic, A & A Sportsman, Wembley. Home: 170 Pheasant Run Chagrin Falls OH 44022 Office: PO Box 224 Chagrin Falls OH 44022

EASTLAND, WOODS EUGENE, agricultural products executive; b. Greenwood, Miss., Jan. 7, 1945; s. James Oliver and Anne Elizabeth (Coleman) E.; m. Lynn Ganier Wood, Nov. 23, 1974; children: Susan Lane, James Bradford. BA, Vanderbilt U., 1967; JD, U. Miss., Oxford, 1970. Bar: Miss. 1970. Assoc. Brunini, Grantham, Grower & Hewes, Jackson, Miss., 1972-73; ptnr. Sunflower Enterprises, Doddsville, Miss., 1974-86; pres. Staple Cotton Coop. Assn., Greenwood, 1986—; bd. dirs. Delta Council, Stoneville, Miss., Nat. Cotton Council, Memphis. Dir. Delta area council Boy Scouts Am., Clarksdale, Miss., 1985-87; layreader Episcopal Diocese Miss., Jackson, 1980-87. Served to lt. USNR, 1970-72. Mem. Miss. State Bar Assn. Home: 1304 Bayou Dr Indianola MS 38751 Office: Staple Cotton Coop Assn 111 W Market St Greenwood MS 38930

EASTMAN, HAROLD S., manufacturing company executive; b. 1939. BA, U. Puget Sound, 1960; MBA, Stanford U., 1962. With Ford Motor Co., 1960-64, Pioneer Bus. Forms, 1964-65, Boise Cascade Corp., 1965-72, Wheelabrator-Frye Inc., 1972-83; sr. v.p. Signal Cos. Inc., 1983-86; mng. dir. ops. Henley Group Inc., La Jolla, Calif., 1986—; also pres., chief operating officer Fisher Scientific Group. Office: Fisher Sci Group Inc 11255 N Torrey Pines Rd La Jolla CA 92037 *

EASTMAN, JOHN RICHARD, retired manufacturing company executive; b. Ottawa, Ohio, Sept. 28, 1917; s. Herbert Parrett and Marie (Brown) E.; m. Hope Ruth, June 12, 1943; 1 child, Janet Ruth. B.A., Ohio State U., Columbus, 1939, LL.B., 1941. Bar: Ohio 1941. With firm Eastman, Stichter, Smith & Bergman, Toledo, 1941-42, 46-75; ptnr. Eastman, Stichter, Smith & Bergman, 1950-75; sr. v.p., gen. counsel Sheller-Globe Corp., Toledo, 1975-77; pres. Sheller-Globe Corp., 1977-82, vice chmn., 1982-86; lectr. Coll. Law, U. Toledo, 1954-55. Bd. dirs. United Way, 1978-82, 84-87. Served with USNR, 1942-46. Decorated Purple Heart. Mem. ABA., Ohio Bar Assn., Lucas County Bar Assn. (pres. 1960), Toledo Bar Assn. (exec. com. 1963-69), Am. Judicature Soc., Internat. Assn. Ins. Counsel, Am. Coll. Trial Lawyers, Toledo C. of C. (chmn. 1985-86). Methodist. Clubs: Exchange (Toledo), Toledo (Toledo), Toledo Country (Toledo), Belmont Country (Toledo). Lodge: Masons (Toledo). Home: 29607 Gleneagles Rd Perrysburg OH 43551

EASTON, RANDALL CRAIG, water conditioning company executive; b. Postville, Iowa, Aug. 31, 1955; s. William howard and Irene (Burke) E.; m. Dorothy Moon, Jan. 21, 1978; children: Dorothy H., Randall Craig Jr. BBA, U. Iowa, 1978; MA in Tax, U. Denver, 1984. CPA, Colo., Ill., Iowa. Acct. Deloitte, Haskins & Sells, Chgo., 1978-81, Denver, 1981-86; sr. v.p. Bank Western Savs. BAnk, Denver, 1986; v.p. Republic Fin. Corp., Denver, 1986-88; pres. U.S. Water Co., Denver, 1988—, also bd. dirs. Mem. AICPA, Colo. Soc. CPA's, Rotary Club. Republican. Roman Catholic. Home: 3693 S Ventura Way Aurora CO 80013 Office: US Water Co 10065 E Harvard Ave Ste 311 Denver CO 80231

EASTON, THOMAS WILLIAM, reporter; b. N.Y.C., May 23, 1958; s. William and Joan (Katz) E. AB, Brown U., 1980; MBA, Columbia U., 1986. Reporter Capital Cities Shore Line Newspapers, Guilford, Conn., 1981-83, The Bridgeport (Conn.) Post, 1984; chief N.Y. bur., fin. correspondent Baltimore Sun, N.Y.C., 1986—. Office: 50 Rockefeller Plaza Ste 1015 New York NY 10020

EASTON-HAFKENSCHIEL, CYNTHIA RUTH, architect; b. San Francisco, Mar. 27, 1949; d. Ellis Herbert and Mary Alice (Scott) Easton; m. Joseph Henry Hafkenschiel, Sept. 28, 1972; children: Erin Thomas, Alexander Scott. BA in Environ. Design, U. Calif., Berkeley, 1972; BArch with honors, U. Md., 1975. Lic. architect, Calif. Intern architecture Leo A. Daly, Washington, 1972-75, Living Systems, Inc., Winters, Calif., 1975, Alan Oshima, Sacramento, 1976-80; pvt. practice architecture Sacramento, 1980—; writer Calif. Architect's Lic. Exam, 1987-88. Recipient Spl. Achievement award Legal Services, Washington, 1986. Mem. AIA (bd. dirs. 1981-82), Soc. for Mktg. Profls. (bd. dirs. 1980-81), Constrn. Specifications Inst. (co-editor 1980-81). Lodge: Soroptimist. Office: 2122 J St Sacramento CA 95816

EASTWOOD, DANA ALAN, banker; b. Poughkeepsie, N.Y., June 1, 1947; s. Donald Edward and Edith Margaret (Davis) E.; m. Cynthia Carol Allen,

Jan. 1, 1984; children: Athena Yvonne, Ashlee Lyn, Alysa Bryhn. Diploma, Am. Inst. Banking, Washington, 1980; Diploma with highest honors, Paralegal Inst., Phoenix, 1983. Proprietor Eastwood Studio, Hyde Park, N.Y., 1965-70; credit rep. Bankers Trust of Hudson Valley, Poughkeepsie, 1970-73; installment loan supr. Poughkeepsie Savs. Bank, 1973-75, installment loan mgr., 1975-78, consumer loan officer, 1978-79, compliance officer, 1979-87, compliance officer, data security adminstr., 1987—; pres., chmn. bd. Consumer Credit Assn. of Mid-Hudson Valley, Poughkeepsie, 1973-75; 1st v.p. Consumer Credit Group of N.Y. State, N.Y.C., 1978-79; 1st v.p. Internat. Consumer Credit Assn., Dist. 2, N.Y. and N.J., 1978-79; mem. consumer credit com. Savs. Banks Assn. of N.Y. State, N.Y.C., 1982-85. Author: Gravity Park, 1978; editor The Right Banker, 1979-82; also numerous modern acrylic paintings. Mem. legis. adv. com. State Assemblyman Emeel S. Betros, Albany, N.Y., 1970-76; mem. consumer edn. adv. com. Dutchess County Cooperative Extension Assn., Millbrook, N.Y., 1975-77. Recipient Award for Outstanding Leadership Consumer Credit Assn. Mid-Hudson Valley, Poughkeepsie, 1974, John C. Corliss Meml. award, 1977, Dedicated Service award Consumer Credit Group N.Y. State, N.Y.C., 1979. Fellow Soc. Cert. Consumer Credit Execs.; mem. Mid-Hudson Compliance Assn. (founding), Internat. Platform Assn. Home: 7 Carriage House Ct Hyde Park NY 12538 Office: Poughkeepsie Savs Bank FSB 21 Market St PO Box 31 Poughkeepsie NY 12602-0031

EATON, EDGAR PHILIP, JR., manufacturing executive; b. Milw., Jan. 17, 1923; s. Edgar P. and Dorothy (Morgenthau) E.; BS in Mech. Engring., Mass. Inst. Tech., 1944; MS in Bus. Adminstrn., Boston U., 1948; m. Rita Beverly Shachat, June 7, 1945 (div.); children: Richard Michael, Randall Charles; m. Helen Yansura. Asst. plant engr. Gen. Dynamics Corp., Groton, Conn., 1944-45; sales engr., supr. Allis Chalmers Mfg. Co., Boston, 1945-49, sales mgr., asst. to pres., 1949-51; exec. v.p. Carbone Corp., Boonton, N.J., 1951-56, pres., 1957—, also dir.; pres. Carbone-Lorraine Industries Corp., 1974-89; chmn. bd. Advance Carbon Products, Inc., San Gabriel, Helecoflex Corp., Carbone Lorraine Corp., Montreal, Que., Can., Ferraz, Rockaway, N.J., Xetron Corp., Cedar Knolls, N.J., Carbone U.S.A. Corp., Carbone-Lorraine Industries, Boonton, N.J.; dir. N.J. Blue Shield and Blue Cross; cons. to mgmt. personnel. Active Urban League; chmn. United Fund, 1959-60, 60-61; chmn. Morris County Community Chest, 1959-60, 60-61, pres., 1963-64; chmn. Morris-Sussex Regional Health Facilities Planning Council, 1960-79; chmn. hosp. governing bds. Am. Hosp. Assn., 1968-69; bd. dirs. Morristown Mem. Hosp., Morris Mus., 1985—, Ctr. for Addictive Illness Corp.; pres. Winston Sch., 1979—. Served with AUS, 1942-43. Mem. Young Pres.'s Orgn. (chmn. 1963-64), ASME, IEEE, Am. R.R. Assn., Nat. Elec. Mfrs. Assn. (treas., dir.), Assn. Iron and Steel Engrs., Morristown Club, Rockaway River Golf Club. Author: The Marketing of Heavy Power Equipment, 1948. Home: 30 Colonial Dr Convent Station NJ 07961 Office: Carbone Lonaine Industries Corp 400 Myrtle Ave Boonton NJ 07005

EATON, KIM DIANE, lawyer; b. Pitts., Apr. 27, 1956; d. Joseph Magee and June Alberta (Dodge) E. BA in Journalism, Pa. State U., 1978; JD, U. Pitts., 1981. Bar: Pa. 1981, U.S. Dist. Ct. (we. dist.) Pa. 1981, U.S. Dist. Ct. (mid. dist.) Pa. 1986, U.S. Ct. Appeals (3d cir.) 1982. Assoc. Rose, Schmidt, Hasley & DiSalle, Pitts., 1981-88, ptnr., 1988—. Columnist Pitts. Post Gazette. Mem. Allegheny County Bar Assn. (bench bar com. 1984-88, bd. govs. 1982-84, family law div.), Pa. State Club, Presbyn. Club. Democrat. Home: 121 Pointview Rd Pittsburgh PA 15227 Office: Rose Schmidt Hasley & Disalle 900 Oliver Bldg Pittsburgh PA 15222

EATON, LEWIS SWIFT, savings and loan executive; b. San Francisco, Aug. 10, 1919; s. Edwin M. and Gertrude (Swift) E.; m. Virginia Stammer, Apr. 21, 1950; children: William L., Joan E., John W. B.A., Stanford U., 1942. With Guarantee Savs. & Loan Assn., Fresno, Calif., 1946—; v.p. Guarantee Savs. & Loan Assn., 1950-56, pres., 1956-84, also chmn. bd.; dir. Fed. Home Loan Bank, San Francisco, 1964-70, MGIC Investment Corp., Milw., Pacific Gas & Electric Corp.; bd. dirs. KMTF Pub. Broadcasting, Channel 18, Fresno. Pres. Fresno Zool. Soc., 1967-68; Mem. Fresno City Bd. Edn., 1958-66; pres., 1959-62; Chmn. bd. govs. Fresno Regional Found., 1972-79; bd. dirs. Sta. KMTF Pub. TV, 1987, Yosemite Nat. Insts., 1986—; trustee Fresno Community Hosp., 1965-81, vice chmn. Fresno State Coll. Found., 1969—, Jr. Achievement, 1951—, Calif. Mus. Found., 1970—; mem. adv. bd. Fresno State Coll., 1965-75; chmn. bd. dirs. Fresno Met. Mus., 1980-86; Chmn. Nat. Parks Adv. Bd. Western Region, 1972-79. Served to capt. 77th Inf. Div. AUS, 1942-46. Mem. Calif. Savs. and Loan League (pres. 1959-60), U.S. Savs. and Loan League (pres. 1970-71), Calif. C. of C. (dir. 1977—), C. of C. Fresno City and County (pres. 1967), Yosemite Natural History Assn. (dir. 1977-79), Stanford Alumni Assn. (pres. 1975-76), Yosemite Nat. Inst. (bd. dirs. 1987—), Beta Gamma Sigma, Lambda Alpha. Home: 4115 N Van Ness Blvd Fresno CA 93704 Office: Guarantee Fin Corp Calif Guarantee Savs Bldg 1177 Fulton Mall Fresno CA 93721

EATON, ROBERT EDWARD LEE, retired air force officer, public relations and management executive; b. Hattiesburg, Miss., Dec. 22, 1909; s. Malcolm Jasper and Sallie Lucinda (Huff) E.; student U. Miss., 1926-27, Mass. Inst. Tech., 1936-37, Command and Gen. Staff Sch., 1942; B.S., U.S. Mil. Acad., 1931; m. Jo Kathryn Rhein, Jan. 1, 1939; children—Robert Edward Lee, Sallie, Charles. Commd. 2d lt., inf. U.S. Army, 1931; trans. to Air Corps, 1933; promoted through grades to maj. gen., 1947; operations officer 5th Bomb Squadron, 1935; weather officer, 1937; comdg. officer 7th Air Base Group, 1941; regional control officer 2d Weather Region, 1941; chief weather central div. A.A.F. hdqrs., 1942; comdg. officer 451st Bomb Group, Zone of Interior and Italy, 1943-44; dep. dir. operations U.S. Strategic Air Forces, Europe, 1944-45; office asst. chief air staff personnel A.A.F. hdqrs., 1945; Office of Dir. Information, 1946; dep. dir. Office of Legislative Liaison, Office of Sec. Def., 1949; dir. Legislation and Liaison Office of Sec. Air Force, 1951-53; comdr. Sixth Allied Tactical Air Force, Izmir, Turkey, 1953-55; comdr. 10th Air Force, Selfridge AFB, Mich., 1955-59; asst. chief staff res. forces, hdqrs., 1959-62, ret.; pres. Eaton Assos., Inc., pub. relations and mgmt. consultants, Washington, 1962—. Decorated Silver Star with oak leaf cluster, Legion of Merit, D.F.C. with oak leaf cluster, Bronze Star medal, Air medal with four oak leaf clusters, D.S.M., Croix de Guerre (France). Mem. Miss. State Soc. of Washington, Am. Legion (nat. comdr. 1973-74), 40 and 8. Episcopalian. Mason. Clubs: Columbia Country, Army-Navy, Metropolitan, Burning Tree (Washington); Pine Valley Golf (Clementon, N.J.). Home: 4921 Essex Ave Chevy Chase MD 20815 Office: 1725 K St NW Suite 1111 Washington DC 20006

EBAUGH, FRANK WRIGHT, consulting industrial engineer, investments executive; b. New Orleans, July 31, 1901; s. John Lynn and Mary (Wright) E.; m. Elizabeth Brown, Feb. 22, 1930; 1 dau., Betty Jane (Mrs. Gordon B. McFarland, Jr.). B in Chem Engring., Tulane U., 1923. Engr., asso. mgmt. Tex. Co., 1923-34; partner retail firm, Jacksonville, Tex., 1934-54; mgr., partner Ebaugh & Brown Investments, Jacksonville, 1955-61; prin. Frank W. Ebaugh, Profl. Engr., Cons.; dir., mem. fin. com. Palestine Savs. & Loan Assn. (Tex.); dir. Superior Savs. Assn. Pres. Upper Neches River Mcpl. Water Authority; bd. dirs. Neches River Conservation Dist., 1966-71, Tex. Indsl. Devel. Council; vice chmn. Tex. Mapping Adv. Com.; sec. Texas Coordinating Water Com.; pres. Neches River Devel. Assn., 1966-69; panel chmn. Cherokee County (Tex.) War Price and Ration Bd., 3 years; mem. Library Bd., 1976-79. Mem. regional com. Girl Scouts Am. Named Man of Month East Tex. C. of C., 1953, Man of Yr., Lions Club, 1953; honored by resolution Tex. Senate, 1967, Appreciation plaque Jacksonville Library, 1969. Registered profl. engr., Tex. Mem. NSPE (life), Tex. Soc. Profl. Engrs. (life, chmn. water com.), East Tex. Soc. Profl. Engrs., E. Tex. C. of C., Am. Chem. Soc. (life), AAAS, Tex. Acad. Sci., Nat. Trust for Historic Preservation. Presbyn. (elder, trustee). Rotarian (Pub. Svc. award 1989). Clubs: Headliners (Austin); Country of Jacksonville (past pres.). Patentee Ebaugh Mixer. Home: 428 S Patton St Jacksonville TX 75766 Office: PO Box 1031 Jacksonville TX 75766

EBBOTT, RALPH DENISON, manufacturing company executive; b. Edgerton, Wis., Apr. 8, 1927; s. Elmer Thomas and Anne Louise (Moss) E.; m. Elizabeth Adams, July 23, 1950; children—Andrew Denison, Douglas Martin, Alison Ann, Kendrick Alan. B.B.A., U. Wis., 1948, M.B.A., 1949. C.P.A., Minn. Jr. acct. Arthur Andersen & Co., N.Y.C., 1949-51; sr. acct. Arthur Andersen & Co., Mpls., 1954-55; with Minn. Mining & Mfg. Co., St. Paul, 1955—; v.p. mgmt. info. Minn. Mining & Mfg. Co., 1974-77, v.p., treas., 1977—; dir. Eastern Heights State Bank. Served with USAF, 1951-53. Mem. Am. Inst. C.P.A.'s, Fin. Execs. Inst. Republican. Mem. United Ch. of Christ. Club: Jesters. Home: 409 Birchwood Ave White Bear Lake MN 55110 Office: Minn Mining & Mfg Co 220 3M Ctr Saint Paul MN 55144

EBBS, GEORGE HEBERLING, JR., management consulting company executive; b. Sewickley, Pa., Sept. 20, 1942; s. George Heberling and Mae Isabelle (Miller) E.; children: Stacey Kirsten, Cynthia Lynn. BS in Engring., Purdue U., 1964; MBA, U. Wash., 1966; PhD in Bus., Columbia U., 1970. Sr. engr. Boeing Co., Seattle, 1966; assoc. Booz Allen & Hamilton, N.Y.C., 1969-72, sr. v.p., 1974-86; v.p. Fry Cons., N.Y.C., 1973; pres. The Canaan Group, Greenwich, Conn., 1986—; adj. prof. Columbia U., N.Y.C., 1978-80; chmn. bd. Jet Profls., Inc., Fairfield, Conn., 1987—. Chmn. 1980 fund drive Columbia Sch. Bus., N.Y.C., 1980. Bronfman fellow, Columbia U., N.Y.C., 1967; Purdue Old Master. Mem. Met. Opera Club, Omicron Delta Kappa, Beta Gamma Sigma. Presbyterian. Clubs: Wings, Country (New Canaan). Home: 9 Glen Ct Greenwich CT 06830 Office: The Canaan Group Ltd 500 W Putnam Ave Greenwich CT 06830

EBEID, RUSSELL JOSEPH, glass manufacturing executive; b. Detroit, Feb. 9, 1940; s. Joseph Zahour and Theresa (Salamie) E.; m. Carolee M. Cram, Feb. 14, 1961; children: Kevin, Evon, Carrie, Scott. B.E.E., Gen. Motors Inst., 1963; M.S. in Indsl. Engring., Wayne State U., 1969. Registered profl. engr., Mich. Sr. mech. engr. Gen. Motors Corp., Detroit, 1968-70; maintenance supt. Guardian Industries Corp., Carleton, Mich., 1970-71, plant engr., 1971-73, prodn. mgr., 1973-78; plant mgr. Guardian Industries Corp., Kingsburg, Calif., 1978-81, group v.p., 1981-85, pres. glass div., dir., 1985-88; mng. dir. Luxguard S.A., Luxembourg, 1981-83; dir. Del Claux Cia S.A., Bilbao, Spain, Vidrierias De Llodio S.A., Llodio, Alava, Spain, Guardian Industries, Northville, Mich.; chmn. bd. Buchman Industries. Author: Instrumentation of Welding, 1963. Decorated knight Order of Merit Luxembourg; recipient Employee of Yr. for Corp. award Guardian Industries Corp., 1979. Roman Catholic. Office: Guardian Industries Corp 43043 W Nine Mile Rd Northville MI 48167

EBERIUS, KLAUS OTTO, machine tool executive; b. Koethen, Germany, Feb. 13, 1940; s. Otto and Gertrud (Marx) E.; came to U.S., 1972; engring. degree Akademie of Engring., Cologne, Germany, 1967; m. Amei Brauns, Apr. 17, 1964; children—Edda, Susanne. Asst. plant mgr. Anton Piller Kg., Osterode, Germany, 1967-68; mgr. tng. center VDF Corp., Hannover, Germany, 1968-72; tech. services mgr. Upton, Bradeen & James, Sterling Heights, Mich., 1972-73, mgr. metal cutting div., 1973-76; v.p., gen. mgr. Unitec Nat. Co., Broadview, Ill., 1976-79; pres., dir. Uni-Sig Corp., 1979-82; corp. v.p. Oerlikon Motch Corp., 1983-84, corp. exec. v.p., 1984-85, pres., chief exec. officer, dir., 1985-89, pres., chief exec. officer, 1989—; pres., dir. Cone Blanchard Holding Co., Windsor, Vt., 1989—; chief exec. officer, dir. Cone Blanchard Machine Co., Windsor, 1988—; pres., dir. Pittler Inc.; pres. chief exec. officer, dir. Motch Corp., Cleve., 1989—; instr. programming night sch., Hannover. Recipient award NC-Rsch., 1969. Mem. Soc. Mfg. Engrs. Home: 7545 Muirwood Ct Chagrin Falls OH 44022 Office: 1250 E 222d St Cleveland OH 44117

EBERL, PAUL GEORGE, marketing professional; b. N.Y.C., Nov. 15, 1960; s. James Thomas and Iris (Bashian) E. BA in Mktg. Mgmt., Marietta Coll., 1983. Mktg. rep. IBM, Cleve., 1984—. Republican. Roman Catholic. Home: 21253 Chardon Rd Apt 3 Euclid OH 44117

EBERLIN, JOANNA MORSON, programmer, analyst; b. Leland, Miss., Apr. 14, 1958; d. Andrew Alexander and Dorothy Rae (Brown) Morson; m. Dana Edwin Eberlin, May 23, 1980. B in tech., U. North Fla., 1985; BBA, U. Miss., 1980. Asst. acct. Baddau Inc., Memphis, 1979; customer service rep. Fine Jewelers Guild, Jacksonville, Fla., 1982-84, new accounts operator, 1984-85; coop. program analyst IRS, Jacksonville, 1985, programmer analyst, 1985-87, programmer/analyst in hardware/software Naval Regional Data Ctr., 1987; data designer USN, Jacksonville, 1987—. Mem. Phi Beta Phi, Delta Sigma. Republican. Baptist. Home: 917 Frost St E Jacksonville FL 32221

EBERLY, HARRY LANDIS, computer company executive; b. Lancaster, Pa., Nov. 1, 1924; s. Chester Landis and Nola Marie (Clark) E.; m. Marion Ruth Royer, May 26, 1951; children—Jenny Ellen Eberly Holmes, Susan Lynn Eberly Patrick. B.S. in Chem. Engring., Pa. State U., 1945. Mgr. purchasing RCA, Palm Beach Gardens, Fla., 1968-72; v.p. Telex Computer Products, Inc., Tulsa, 1972-76, sr. v.p., 1976-77; pres. Communication Products div. Telex Computer Products, Inc., Raleigh, N.C., 1977-83; exec. v.p. Telex Computer Products, Inc., Raleigh, 1983-88; mem. exec. com. Telex Computer Products, Inc., Tulsa, 1984-88, dir., 1982-84; exec. v.p. Memorex Telex Corp., 1988—. Mem. adv. bd. Meridith Coll., Raleigh, 1981, Duke Children's Telethon; mem. Wake Tech. Community Coll. Found., Raleigh, 1982; mem. N.C. State U. Engring. Found., Raleigh, 1984-87; vice chmn. Triangle East of N.C., 1986—; bd. dirs., 1988 campaign chmn. United Way of Wake County. Mem. IEEE (sr.), Greater Raleigh C. of C. (bd. dirs. 1979-87), Delta Gamma Delta. Democrat. Methodist. Home: 7003 N Ridge Dr Raleigh NC 27615 Office: Memorex Telex Corp 3261 Atlantic Ave Ste 110 Raleigh NC 27604

EBERLY, ROBERT EDWARD, oil and gas production company executive, banker; b. Greensboro, Pa., July 14, 1918; s. Orville Sebastian and Ruth Rhoda (Moore) E.; m. Elouise Ross Conn (Sept. 25, 1982); children—Robert Edward Jr., Paul O. B.A. in Chemistry, Pa. State U., 1939. Chemist Dept. Navy, 1940-45; pres., gen. mgr. Eberly Natural Gas Co., Uniontown, Pa., 1945-86; pres., treas. GNB Corp., Uniontown, Pa., 1969-77, chmn. bd., 1977-85; chmn. bd. Gallatin Nat. Bank, Uniontown, 1977—; bd. dirs. Pennbancorp, Titusville, Pa., Integra Fin. Corp.; chmn. bd. Eberly and Meade, Inc., 1986—, Oklahoma City, Chalk Hill Gas Inc., Greystone Resources Inc.; gen. mgr. Eberly Family Trust, 1983—; sec., treas. Eberly Found., 1963-88, pres. 1988—. Pres. bd. trustees Uniontown Hosp. Assn., 1968-70, trustee emeritus, 1978—; bd. dirs. Penn's Southwest Assn., 1980—, trustee, 1978—; bd. dirs., past pres. Uniontown Indsl. Fund, 1971, Fayette Heritage, Inc.; nat. chmn. alumni fund Pa. State U., 1972-74, mem. Found. Bd., mem. adv. bd. Fayette Campus Br., nat. treas. Campaign for Penn State, 1985—; past sec. Uniontown Planning and Zoning Commn; mem. Western Pa. Conservancy; past pres. United Fund, Laurel Rest Home, Inc., Uniontown; mem. County Home Nursing Commn.; bd. dirs. Laurel Highlands, Inc., 1987—; active Westmoreland/Fayette council Boy Scouts Am. Recipient Rockwell Recognition award, 1970, Disting. Alumnus award Pa. State U., 1972, Jerusalem City of Peace award Fayette County Israel Bond Com., 1985, Silver Beaver award Boy Scouts Am., 1987. Mem. Okla. Oil and Gas Assn., Okla. Ind. Petroleum Assn., Ohio Oil and Gas Assn., W.Va. Oil and Gas Assn., Pa. Oil and Gas Assn., Pa. Geol. Soc., Ind. Petroleum Assn., Greater Uniontown C. of C. (bd. dirs., past pres., named Man of Yr. 1968), Theta Chi, Izaac Walton League. Club: Uniontown Country (past v.p., bd. dirs.). Lodges: Rotary (past pres. Uniontown); Masons (past master, hon. 33 deg.). Office: Eberly and Meade Inc PO Box 2023 Uniontown PA 15401

EBERSOLE, GEORGE DAVID, manufacturing executive; b. Plattsmouth, Nebr., July 11, 1936; s. George Benjamin and Wilma (Shepard) N.; m. Beverly F. Sullivan, Nov. 28, 1957; children: Karen, Kent, Kyle. BSME, Milw. Sch. Engring., 1961; MSME, U. Wis., 1963; PhD, U. Tulsa, 1971. Registered profl. engr., Okla. Cons. engr. Madison, Wis., 1963; sr. group leader Phillips Petroleum, Bartlesville, Okla., 1963-73; asst. v.p. research and devel. Frito Lay Inc., Irving, Tex., 1973-74; gen. div. mgr. Hoover Universal, Ann Arbor, Mich., 1974-80; pres. Energy Absorption Systems subs. Quixote Corp. of Chgo., Sacramento, Calif., 1980—, Spincast Plastics subs. Quixote Corp. of Chgo., South Bend, Ind., 1980—; Contbr. articles to profl. jours.; patentee in field. Mem. ASME. Home: 7831 Forest Hill Ln Palos Heights IL 60463 Office: Energy Absorption Systems 1 E Wacker Dr Chicago IL 60601

EBERSOLE, J. GLENN, JR., public relations and marketing executive; b. Lancaster, Pa., Feb. 8, 1947; s. J. Glenn and Marie Christine (Stoner) E.; student Ohio No. U., 1965-67; BSCE, Pa. State U., 1970, M in Engring. Sci., 1973; m. Helen Walton, July 11, 1970. Rsch. technician Pa. State U., University Park, 1968-70; civil engring. intern Pa. Dept. Transp., Harrisburg, 1970-71, asst. dist. design liaison engr., 1971, head rsch. and spl. studies Bur. Traffic Engring., 1971-76; asst. chief engr.-traffic Pa. Turnpike Commn., Harrisburg, 1976-78; chief transp. engr. Huth Engrs., Inc., Lancaster, 1978-81; exec. engr. GSGSB, Clarks Summit, Pa., 1981-82; founder and chief exec. J.G. Ebersole Assocs., Lancaster, Pa., 1982—; founder, chief exec. The Renaissance Group TM, Lancaster, Pa., 1983—; part-time lectr. Pa. State U.; mem. pub. rels. com., edn. com. Associated Builders and Contractors. Contbr. articles to profl. jours. Ch. sch. tchr., lector, chmn. brochure com. Ch. of the Apostles, mem. ch. coun., ch. steering com. for long range planning, chmn. ch. brochure com., chmn. cable TV com., communications com., chmn. faith promise campaign; past chmn. Rapho Twp. Planning Commn.; mem. regional devel. coun. Pa. State U., active Penn State legis. liaison program; bd. dirs., mem. devel. com., bd. dirs. Actors Co. of Pa.; co-chmn., mem. devel. com. Gt. Gatsby Gala. Registered profl. engr., Pa., Vt., Md., Del., N.J. Mem. Am. Mktg. Assn. (dir., past Cen. Pa. chpt. pres.), ASCE, Inst. Transp. Engrs., NSPE, Associated Builders and Contractors, Inc. (pub. rels. com., edn. com.), Internat. Platform Assn., Am. Road and Transp. Builders Assn. (transp. safety adv. coun.), Lancaster C. of C. (govt. affairs com., chmn. golf com. 1985-87, long range transp. task force), Pa. Soc. Profl. Engrs., Am. Mgmt. Assn., Pa. Soc. Pa. Hwy. Info. Assn., Pa. State Alumni Assn. (regional devel. council), Phi Eta Sigma, Alpha Sigma Phi. Clubs: Penn State of Lancaster County (past pres., bd. dirs.), Hershey Country. Lodges: Shriners, Masons (past master Mount Joy, Pa. club). Home and Office: 1305 Wheatland Ave Lancaster PA 17603

EBLING, TIMOTHY ANDREW, controller; b. Phila., Apr. 2, 1958; s. Thomas A. and Catherine E. (Burke) E.; m. April Campione, June 9, 1979; children: Taylor Amanda, Brett Elizabeth. BSBA, Ohio No. U., 1980. CPA, N.J. Audit sr. Touche Ross & Co., Phila., 1980-83; asst. mgr. fin. acctg. Sands Hotel & Casino, Atlantic City, 1983-84, hotel controller, 1984-85, casino controller, 1985, asst. corp. controller, 1985-87, corp. controller, 1987—; bd. dirs. Health Care Plan N.J., Cherry Hill. Mem. Am. Inst. CPA's. Office: Sands Hotel and Casino Indiana Ave and Brighton Park Atlantic City NJ 08401

EBNER, CHRISTOPHER WOODS, advertising executive; b. N.Y.C., June 2, 1947; s. Robert Charles and Elizabeth (Woods) E.; m. Frances Cynthia Bainor, Dec. 10, 1983. BS in Mktg., Pa. State U., 1969. Asst. advt. mgr. RCA Records, N.Y.C., 1969-71; v.p., mgmt. supr. DKG Advt., N.Y.C., 1971-79; sr. v.p., mgmt. supr. Ketchum Advt., N.Y.C., 1979-82; assoc. Anspach Grossman Portugal, N.Y.C., 1983-84; v.p. mktg. Am. Health Products, Orangeburg, N.Y., 1984-86; sr. v.p., group account dir. McCann-Erickson, N.Y.C., 1986—; instr. Parsons Sch. for Design, N.Y.C., 1980-83. Lutheran. Club: N.Y.C. Athletic.

EBRIGHT, GEORGE WATSON, health care company executive; b. Chadds Ford, Pa., Mar. 27, 1938; s. George Grant and Letitia Myrtle (McKee) E.; m. Catherine Edna Sharp, Sept. 30, 1961; children—Bradford, Katherine. B.A., Franklin and Marshall Coll., 1960; M.B.A., U. Del., 1965. Salesman Atlantic Refining Co., Phila., 1960-61; various mgmt. positions Sun Olin, Claymont, Del., 1961-63, Smith Kline Beckman Corp., Phila., 1963—; pres., chief operating officer SmithKline Beckman Corp., Phila., until 1989. Served with U.S. Army, 1960-66. Clubs: Merion Golf, Merion Cricket (Ardmore, Pa.), Union League, Sunday Breakfast. Lodge: Masons. Office: Smith Kline Beckman Corp 1 Franklin Pla Philadelphia PA 19101 also: Cytogen Corp 201 College Rd E Princeton NJ 08540

ECCLES, SPENCER FOX, banker; b. Ogden, Utah, Aug. 24, 1934; s. Spencer Stoddard and Hope (Fox) E.; m. Cleone Emily Peterson, July 21, 1958; children: Clista Hope, Lisa Ellen, Katherine Ann, Spencer Peterson. B.S., U. Utah, 1956; M.A., Columbia U., 1959; degree in Bus. (hon.), So. Utah State Coll., 1982; LLB (hon.), Westminster Coll., Salt Lake City, 1986. Trainee First Nat. City Bank, N.Y.C., 1959-60; with First Security Bank of Utah, Salt Lake City, 1960-61, First Security Bank of Idaho, Boise, 1961-70; exec. v.p. First Security Corp. Salt Lake City, 1970-75, pres., 1975—, chief operating officer, 1980-82, chmn. bd. dirs., chief exec. officer, 1982—; dir. Union Pacific Corp., Amalgamated Sugar Co., Anderson Lumber Co., Zions Corp., Merc. Instn., Aubrey G. Lanston & Co., Inc.; mem. adv. council U. Utah Bus. Coll. Served to 1st lt. U.S. Army. Recipient Pres.'s Circle award Presdl. Commn., 1984, Minuteman award Utah N.G., 1988; Named Disting. Alumni U. Utah, 1988. Mem. Am. Bankers Assn., Assn. Bank Holding Cos., Assn. Res. City Bankers, Young Pres. Orgn. Clubs: Salt Lake Country, Alta, Arid. Office: 1st Security Corp 79 S Main St Salt Lake City UT 84111

ECKER, ALLAN BENJAMIN, communications executive, lawyer; b. N.Y.C., June 29, 1921; s. Samuel and Frances (Schuman) E.; m. Elizabeth Jane Rice, May 19, 1956; children—David Rice (dec.), Sarah Rice. BA, Harvard U., 1941, LLB, 1953. Bar: N.Y., D.C., U.S. Dist. Ct. So. N.Y. Sec., dir. Warner Communications Inc., 1962—; sr. v.p., gen. counsel Damson Oil Corp., 1984-88; ptnr. Parker & Duryee, 1988—. Mem. ABA, Assn. Bar of City of N.Y. Clubs: Coffee House, Harvard of N.Y. Home: 133 E 94th St New York NY 10128 Office: Parker & Duryee 529 Fifth Ave New York NY 10017

ECKER, DANIEL B., brokerage house executive; b. Kadoka, S.D, Sept. 9, 1953; s. Bruce Harkness and Mildred M. (Kocian) E.; m. Suzann E. Curry, Dec. 17, 1983; 1 child, Bailey. BS in Community Services, No. State Coll., 1975. Registered securities prin. Social worker S.D. Dept. of Social Services, Pine Ridge, 1976-83; registered rep. EN SOF Securities Corp., Rapid City, S.D., 1983-85; pres., gen. mgr. EN SOF Securities Corp., Rapid City, 1985-88; state mgr. S.D. Retirement System/Supplemental Retirement Plan, Pierre, 1989—; bd. dirs. Tri-Star Devel. Corp., Rapid City. Mem. S.D. Internat. Assn. Fin. Planning. Democrat. Presbyterian. Home: RR 1 Box 3730 Rapid City SD 57702 Office: EN SOF Securities Corp 1240 Jackson Blvd Rapid City SD 57702

ECKER, DONALD NESS, accountant; b. Gettysburg, Pa.; m. Dianne Haskell; children: Kristi, Scott. BSBA, Calif. State Poly. Inst., 1986. CPA, Calif. Mng. ptnr. Ernst & Whinney, Riverside, Calif., 1982—; chmn. physician rsch. project Ernst & Whinney, Riverside, 1985-87; bd. dirs. Security Pacific Nat. Bank Inland Empire. Pres., bd. dirs. Econ. Devel. Coun.; mem. Estate Planning Coun., Riverside County, 1978—; chmn. edn. com. Inland Empire Young Pres.'s Orgn., pres., 1987; bd. dirs. Riverside Area United Way, 1978-85, assoc. chmn., 1981, campaign chmn., 1982, v.p., 1983-84, pres., 1984-85; co-founder Riverside County 2% and 5% Club, chmn. bd. dirs. 1985-86; original organizer Keep Riverside Ahead, gen. campaign chmn.; mem. World Affairs Coun., Monday Morning Group, Riverside Athletic Bd., 1978-83, YMCA, 1980—; mem. Riverside Community Hosp. Found., 1982—, asst. campaign chmn. capital, 1986-87; mem. adv. bd. sch. bus. adminstrn. U. Calif., Riverside, Calif. State Poly. U., mem. U. Calif. at Riverside Athletic Booster Club, 1978-85, Casa Colina Hosp. Found., 1982; pres., bd. dirs. Econ. Devel. Coun., Riverside Downtown Assn., 1982, Riverside Visitor Conv. Bur., City Riverside Yr. 2000 Strategic Planning Com.; mem. chancellor's com. Calif. Mus. Photography, 1987; mem. Chancellor's Blue Ribbon Com.; coach Riverside Youth Sports, 1978-84; treas. Efficient Transp. for Riverside County, 1988—; chmn. task force Bus. Vols. for the Arts, 1988—. Named United Way Vol. of Yr. award, 1985, Chamber Vol. of Yr. award United Way, 1985, Vol. of Yr. award Greater Riverside C. of C., 1985, Citizen of Yr. City of Riverside. Mem. AICPA, Calif. Soc. CPA's (state bd. dirs., mem. quality control of audit reports com.), Citrus Belt Chpt. CPA's (bd. dirs. 1980-85, chmn. credit grantors com. 1980, 82, pres. 1985), Med. Group Mgmt. Assn., Am. Group Practice Assn., Greater Riverside C. of C. (pres.-elect 1985, pres. 1986), L.A. C. of C. (bd. dirs.), Raincross Club of Riverside (founder 1987—). Office: Ernst & Whinney 3750 University Ave Ste 600 PO Box 1270 Riverside CA 92502-1270

ECKERT, THOMAS GUENTER, investment banker; b. Schweinfurt, Fed. Republic Germany, Sept. 21, 1963; came to U.S., in 1985; s. Hans Georg and Erika (Gerlach) E. BSBA, Fla. Internat. U., 1987; postgrad., Vanderbilt U., 1988—. Asst. to v.p. fin. FAG Interamericana AG, Miami, Fla., 1985-87; tech. advisor investment banking Vereins-Und Westbank AG, Miami, 1987-88; asst. coll. of bus. Fla. Internat. U., Miami, 1987. With army Federal Rep. Germany, 1982-83. Vanderbilt Internat. fellow, 1988. Mem. Fin. Mgmt. Assn., Beta Gamma Sigma, fin. Assn. (Miami).

ECKHART, JAMES MC KINLEY, electronics executive; b. Monroe, La., Jan. 21, 1931; s. Eldon M. and Ora Belle (Gray) E.; m. Jo Ann Ivy (div.); children: James, Brian, Suzanne; m. A. Rae Olsen, June 21, 1980; 1 child, William Mc Kinley. BSME, U. Tex., 1959. Engineer, mfg. Tex. Instruments, Dallas, 1959-62; branch mgr. Tex. Instruments, Houston, 1968-77, asst. v.p. terminals and peripherals div., 1977-80; asst. v.p. Tex. Instruments, Nice, France, 1980-82; dir. mfg. Spacecraft Inc., Huntsville, Ala., 1962-66; sr. v.p. ops. Beta-Tec, Inc., Harriman, Tenn., 1966-68; pres., chief exec. officer Prentice Corp., Sunnyvale, Calif., 1982-83; sr. v.p. ops. Compaq Computer Corp., Houston, 1983—. Bd. dirs. Am. Heart Assn., NW Harris County, Tex. Served to 1st lt. USAF, 1950-55. Republican. Office: Compaq Computer Corp 20555 FM 149 Houston TX 77070

ECKMAN, JOHN WHILEY, business executive; b. Forest Hills, N.Y., July 20, 1919; s. Samuel Whiley and Anna (Wolffram) E.; children: Alison Elizabeth, Stephen Keyler. Student, Yale U., 1937-38; B.S., U. Pa., 1943, LL.D. (hon.), 1984; L.H.D. (hon.), Pa. Coll. Podiatric Medicine, 1979; LL.D. (hon.), Phila. Coll. Pharmacy and Sci., 1981. With mktg. Smith Kline & French Labs., Inc., Phila., 1947-52; v.p. Thomas Leeming & Co., Inc., N.Y.C., 1952-62; exec. v.p. Rorer Group Inc. and predecessors, Ft. Washington, Pa., 1962-70; pres. Rorer Group Inc. and predecessors, 1970-80, chmn., chief exec. officer, 1976-85, chmn., 1985-86; chmn. Fed. Res. Bank Phila., 1977-81; bd. dirs. Provident Mut. Life Ins. Co., chmn. corp. responsibility com., 1976—; bd. dirs. Hither Creek Boat Yard, Inc., U.S. Bioscience, Betz Labs. Inc.; chmn. audit com. Rittenhouse Trust Co., 1984—, also bd. dirs. Life trustee U. Pa., 1967—, vice chmn., 1982-86, chmn. bd. overseers Sch. Arts and Scis., 1982-86; bd. mgrs. Wistar Inst. Anatomy and Biology, 1968-84, pres., 1975-84; bd. dirs. Winterthur Corp. Council, 1984—, World Affairs Council, 1978-82, chmn.'s adv. com., 1982-88, Community Home Health Services Phila., 1979-81, Greater Phila. First Corp., 1982-86, Phila. Urban Coalition, 1973-83, Presbyn.-U. Pa. Med. Ctr., 1984—, Independence Hall Assn., 1982—; bd. dirs. Community Leadership Seminars, 1984—, Urban Affairs Partnership, 1976—, co-chmn., 1982-84; bd. dirs. Univ. City Sci. Center, 1974-83, Opera Co. of Phila., 1985—; trustee Phila. Area United Way, 1974—, gen. chmn., 1985 campaign. Lt. USNR, 1943-46. Recipient Alumni award of merit U. Pa., 1972, Valley Forge Trail award Boy Scouts Am., 1985, Phila. Caring award Community Home Health Svcs. Phila., 1986, Louis Braille award Associated Svcs. for Phila. Blind, 1987; named Industrialist of Yr., Soc. Indsl. Realtors, 1975. Fellow N.Y. Acad. Sci., Coll. of Physicians of Pa.; mem. Pharm. Advt. Club N.Y. (pres. 1959-60), Pharm. Mfrs. Assn. (dir. 1975-85, chmn. 1981-82), Pharm. Advt. Coun. (hon. life), Greater Phila. C. of C. (dir. 1972-83), Hist. Soc. Pa. (dir., pres. 1980-86), Nantucket Hist. Assn., Nantucket Land Coun., German Soc. Pa. (hon. life), Internat. House (devel. com., human resource com., 1988—), AAAS, Acad. Scis. at Phila., Pa. Soc., Wharton Sch. Alumni Assn (dir. 1966-70, pres. 1968-70), Phila. Com. on Fgn. Rels., S.R., St. Andrews Soc., Confrerie de la Chaine des Rotisseurs, Faculty Club U. Pa. Nantucket Yacht Club, Rittenhouse Club (Phila., v.p. 1988—), Union League (Phila.), Yale Club (N.Y.C.), Mask and Wig Club (hon.), Sigma Chi (Significant Sig award 1981), Beta Gamma Sigma. Republican. Presbyterian. Office: Rorer Group 500 Virginia Dr Fort Washington PA 19034

ECTON, DONNA R., service company executive; b. Kansas City, Mo., May 10, 1947; d. Allen Howard and Marguerite (Page) E.; m. Victor H. Maragni, June 16, 1986; children: Mark, Gregory. BA, Wellesley Coll., 1969; MBA, Harvard U., 1971. V.p., dist. head Chem. Bank, N.Y.C., 1972-79; v.p. Citibank, N.A., N.Y.C., 1979-81; pres. MBA Resources, Inc., N.Y.C., 1981-83; v.p. adminstrn., officer Campbell Soup Co., Camden, N.J., 1983-89; chmn. Triangle Mfg. Corp. subs. Campbell Soup Co., Raleigh, N.C., 1984-87; sr. v.p. Nutri/System, Inc., Willow Grove, Pa., 1989—; bd. dirs. Mellon Bank Corp., Pitts., Mellon Bank N.A., Pitts., Barnes Group, Inc., Bristol, Conn.; commencement speaker Pa. State U., 1987. Bd. overseers Harvard U., 1984—, vis. com. sch. bus. adminstrn., 1986—; mem. Council Fgn. Relations, N.Y.C., 1987—; trustee Inst. for Advancement of Health, 1988—; mem. bus. adv. coun. Carnegie-Mellon Grad. Sch. Indsl. Adminstrn., 1988—. Named One of 80 Women to Watch in the 80's, Ms. mag., 1980, One of All Time Top 10 of Last Decade, Glamour mag., 1984, One of 50 Women to Watch, Bus. Week mag., 1987; recipient Wellesley Alumnae Achievement award, 1987; Fred Shelson Fund fellow, 1971-72. Mem. Harvard Bus. Sch. Assn. (pres. exec. council 1983-84), N.Y.C. Harvard Bus. Sch. Club (pres. 1979-80), Wellesley Coll. Nat. Alumnae Assn. (bd. dirs., 1st v.p.), Catalyst (bd. advisors 1986—). Office: Nutri/System Inc 3901 Commerce Ave Willow Grove PA 19090

EDELMAN, DANIEL JOSEPH, public relations executive; b. N.Y.C., July 3, 1920; s. Selig and Selma (Pfeiffer) E.; m. Ruth Rozumoff, Sept. 3, 1953; children: Richard, Renee, John. Grad., Columbia U., 1940; postgrad., Columbia U., 1941. Reporter Poughkeepsie (N.Y.) newspapers, UPI, 1941-42; news writer CBS, 1946-47; staff mem. Edward Gottlieb & Assocs., 1947; pub. rels. dir. Toni Co., Chgo., 1948-52; founder Daniel J. Edelman, Inc., Chgo., 1952, also Dallas, Houston, L.A., N.Y.C., St. Louis, Washington, San Francisco, London, Frankfurt, Dublin, Hong Kong, Kuala Lumpur, Paris, Singapore, Sydney, Tokyo. Mem. parents coun. Phillips Exeter Acad., 1972; mem. communications com. Boy Scouts Am., Chgo.; chmn. vis. com. U. Chgo. Library, 1976; bd. dirs. Ill. Children's Home and Aid Soc.; chmn. sustaining fellows individual campaign Chgo. Art Inst., 1982; nat. bd. Lyric Opera Chgo.; vis. com. Northwestern U. Music Sch.; mem. Philanthropy Task Force/Chgo. United, 1988; mem. adv. bd. Citizenship Coun. Met. Chgo. Served with AUS, 1942-46, ETO. Recipient Disting. Alumnus award Columbia U., 1988. Mem. Pub. Rels. Soc. Am. (past chmn. counselor sect., 19 Silver Anvil awards), Publicity Club Chgo., Young Pres. Orgn. (chmn. Chgo. chpt. 1963), Chgo. Club, Standard Club, Harmonie Club, Mid-Am. Club, Phi Beta Kappa, Zeta Beta Tau. Jewish. Home: 1301 N Astor St Chicago IL 60610 Office: Edelman Pub Rels 211 E Ontario St Chicago IL 60611

EDELMAN, REVELL JUDITH, data processing executive; b. Bayonne, N.J., July 24, 1941; d. Charles and Belle (Laks) Motin; m. Martin Edelman, July 18, 1981; children: Laura Mantell, Deborah Mantell. BS in Psychology cum laude, CUNY, 1969. Systems analyst Univac div. Sperry Corp., N.Y.C., 1961-66; programmer, analyst J.C. Penney Co., N.Y.C., 1966-67; systems and programming cons. Automated Concepts, Inc., N.Y.C., 1968-72; ind. systems and programming cons. N.Y.C., 1972-76; mgr. systems and programming Citibank, NA, N.Y.C., 1976-83; v.p. data processing Columbia Savs. and Loan Assn., Fair Lawn, N.J., 1983—. Mem. Fin. Mgrs. Soc., Assn. Info. Mgrs., Mensa. Democrat. Jewish. Home: 3 Jockey Ln New City NY 10956 Office: Columbia Savs & Loan Assn 25-00 Broadway Fair Lawn NJ 07410

EDELMAN, SAMUEL IRVING, lawyer, financial executive; b. N.Y.C., Oct. 8, 1929; s. Mitchell and Lillian (Stein) E.; m. Minna Jane Moscovitz, Aug. 16, 1952; children—Meredith Ann, Michael James. B.S., L.I. U., 1951; J.D., Bklyn. Law Sch., 1958. Bar: N.Y. 1959, U.S. Dist. Ct. (so. dist.) N.Y. 1962. Staff auditor Freeman and Davis, N.Y.C., 1950-55; internal auditor Kleinerts, Inc., N.Y.C., 1955-57, asst. controller, 1957-60, controller, 1961-66, exec. v.p., treas., 1967-69; assoc. Speiser, Shumate, Geoghan, Krause and Rheingold, N.Y.C., 1969-72; sec., treas. Cen. Nat. Corp., N.Y.C., 1972-76; exec. v.p., dir. Refined Sugars, Inc., Yonkers, N.Y., 1976-86; dir., sec., treas. Tate and Lyle, Inc., Yonkers, N.Y., 1980-86; now with Edelman & Edelman, Riverdale, N.Y.; adj. lectr Bklyn. Coll., 1963-65; dir. Unitank, Inc., Phila., Medin Corp., Wallington, N.J., Am. Container Tech., Wallington, Evans Refrigerator Mfg. Co. Inc., Mt. Vernon, N.Y., Aviation Edn. Systems Inc., Farmingdale, N.Y. Mem. N.Y. State Emergency Fin. Control Bd., Yonkers, 1984—; trustee St. Josephs Hosp., Yonkers, 1980—, chmn. bd. trustees, 1987—; bd. dirs. Jewish Community Ctr., Yonkers, 1982—, United Way, Yonkers, 1980-81, Legal Awareness for Women, Scarsdale, N.Y., 1982—; commr. North Riverdale Little League, 1975-76; campaign chmn. Am. Cancer Soc., White Plains, N.Y., 1982-83. Served with USAF, 1952-54. Mem. ABA, N.Y.C. Bar Assn., Westchester County Bar Assn., Bronx County Bar Assn., Yonkers Lawyers Assn., Yonkers C. of C. (pres. 1979-80, bd. dirs., 1979—). Lodge: Masons. Office: Edelman & Edelman 4941 Arlington Ave Riverdale NY 10702

EDELMANN, JULIUS JOSEPH, food company executive; b. Bklyn., Dec. 19, 1935; s. Julius O. and Kunigunda (Burger) E.; m. Mary Lou Wenz, Jan. 10, 1959 (div. 1987); children: Elizabeth, William, Julius Jr.; m. Sheila Rugeri, Oct. 23, 1988. BS in Chem. Engring., Bklyn. Poly. Inst., 1957. With Standard Brands, Inc., Hoboken, N.J. and New Orleans, 1957-78; dir. mfg. Grocery Div. Standard Brands, Inc., N.Y.C., 1975-78; dir. mfg. engring. Standard Brands, Inc., Stamford, Conn., 1978; v.p. mfg. Planters Div. Nabisco Brands, Inc., Suffolk, Va., 1978-85; v.p. corp. purchasing Nabisco Brands, Inc., Parsippany, N.J., 1985-88; v.p. ops. Del Monte Foods, Coral Gables, Fla., 1988—. Trustee ASU Ctr. for Advanced Purchasing Studies, 1988—. Mem. Nat. Assn. Purchasing Mgmt. (bd. dirs. 1987—). Republican. Roman Catholic. Clubs: Harbor (Norfolk, Va.); Pennbrook Country (Basking Ridge, N.J.). Home: 5618 Riviera Dr Coral Gables FL 33146 Office: Del Monte Foods 2 Alhambra Pla Coral Gables FL 33134

EDELSON, IRA J., accountant; b. Chgo., Dec. 30, 1946; s. Alvin L. and Naomi (Samiatezky) E.; m. Starr Gramaila, Feb. 11, 1973; children: Jason Avrum, Megan Anne. BS, DePaul U., 1968. Spl. advisor to chmn. Chgo. Housing Authority, 1983; acting dir. revenue City of Chgo., 1984; ptnr.-in-charge bus. svcs. dept. Deloitte, Haskins & Sells, Chgo., 1979-87, ptnr.-in-charge corp. fin., 1987—; fin. and policy adv. to Mayor City of Chgo., 1984-85; former instr. Kellogg Sch. Mgmt. Northwestern U.; cons., speaker in field. Co-chmn. Chgo. Sports Stadium Commn., 1985. Mem. AICPA, Ill. Soc. CPAs (editor Newsjour.), Nat. Assn. Securities Profls., Nat. Assn. Realtors, Real Estate Securities and Syndication Inst. (regulatory and legis. com., nat. realty com.). Office: Deloitte Haskins & Sells 200 E Randolph Dr Chicago IL 60601-6401

EDEN, NANCY LESTER, accountant; b. Shawsville, Va., Oct. 1, 1949; d. John W. and Myrtle (Martin) Lester; m. James A. Eden Jr., Nov. 5, 1969; 1 child, Michelle Andrea. BS, Radford (Va.) Coll., 1974, MS, 1975. CPA, Va. Office mgr. James Eden M.D., Blacksburg, Va., 1971-77; jr. acct. Gordon H. Winbery, CPA, Blacksburg, 1987-88; pvt. practice Blacksburg, 1989—. Mem. AICPA, Va. Soc. CPA's, Am. Women's Soc. CPA's. Home: Rte 1 PO Box 162 Pembroke VA 24136 Office: PO Box 10715 Blacksburg VA 24062-0715

EDEN, RAYMOND LER, medical school administrator; b. Lee, Ill., July 19, 1925; s. S. Bennie and Hannah (Edwards) E.; B.S., No. Ill. U., 1950 with high honors; postgrad. Northwestern U., 1950, N.Y. U., 1955, U. Chgo., 1961, U. So. Calif., 1973; m. Ellen M. Mercer, Aug. 17, 1945; 1 son, Steven M. Exec. sec. Crippled Children's Center, Peoria, Ill., 1953-59; exec. dir. Crippled Children's Service, Milw., 1959-62, Ill. Heart Assn., Springfield, 1962-66, Calif. Heart Assn., San Francisco, 1966-69; adminstr. San Mateo (Calif.) Med. Clinic, 1969-70; exec. v.p. Am. Heart Assn., Los Angeles, 1970-86; assoc. dean adminstrn. UCLA Sch. Medicine, 1986—. Chmn. objectives com. Calif. Regional Med. Program, 1968-73; v.p. Comprehensive Health Planning Agy., 1973-75; bd. dirs. UCLA Unicamp, 1974-76, Comprehensive Health Planning Council of Los Angeles County, 1975-77; mem. adv. com. UCLA Profl. Designation program for Voluntary Agy. Execs., 1972-74; faculty Center for Non-Profit Mgmt., 1978-82; pres. Council on Vol. Health Agys., Los Angeles, 1976-79, Los Angeles CPR Consortium, 1979-81; mem. Cardiac Care com. State of Calif., 1980-83; treas., chmn. fin. com. Little Co. of Mary Hosp., Torrance, 1977-81; chmn. South Bay (Los Angeles) Com. for Pres. Ford, 1976; mem. Atty. Gen.'s Task Force on Solicitations, 1977; chmn. Younger for Gov. Com., South Bay, 1978; chmn. bd. trustees Neighborhood Ch., Palos Verdes Estates, Calif., 1975; mem. Claremont Grad. Sch. Exec. Program adv. council, 1979-82; mem. clean air com., Los Angeles Area C. of C., 1980-82. Served with U.S. Army, 1944-46. Decorated Purple Heart, Bronze Star. Soc. Heart Assn. Profl. Staff fellow, 1980-81, 82-83; Alpha Gamma Delta Fellow award, 1955. Mem. Soc. Heart Assn. Profl. Staff (pres. 1981-82), Nat. Assn. Social Workers, Acad. Cert. Social Workers, So. Calif. Assn. Execs., Los Angeles Area C. of C., Sigma Alpha Eta. Republican. Clubs: Rotary, California, Masons, Shriners. Home: 9961 Durant Dr Beverly Hills CA 90212 Office: UCLA Sch Medicine 12-138 CHS Los Angeles CA 90024

EDERSHEIM, MAURITS ERNST, investment banker; b. Amsterdam, May 22, 1918; came to U.S., 1939, naturalized, 1942; s. Samuel and Ella Edersheim-Levenbach E.; m. Claire Kantyff, May 6, 1963; children: Leo, Arthur, Steven, Terri, Ellen, Judith, Peggy. Student, Ecole de Scis. Politiques, Paris, 1937-38. Mem. firm Herzfeld & Stern, N.Y.C., 1939-42; owner Stern & Co., N.Y.C., 1945-50; with Drexel Burnham & Co., Inc. (now Drexel Burnham Lambert Group Inc.), N.Y.C., 1950—; dep. chmn. Drexel Burnham & Co., Inc. (now Drexel Burnham Lambert Group Inc.), 1950—; chmn. bd. Fenimore; dir. Bauque Internat. Luxembourg, Esfinco, FGH Credit Corp.; chmn. bd. Worldwide Spl. Fund, Worldwide Securities Fund; mem. adv. bd. Internat. Asset Mgmt. Corp. Served with OSS, 1942-45. Mem. Netherlands Am. Community Assocs. Inc. (v.p.). Clubs: Netherlands, Sunningdale Country, Harmonie. Home: 927 Fifth Ave New York NY 10021 Office: Drexel Burnham Lambert Inc 60 Broad St New York NY 10004

EDGAR, GILBERT HAMMOND, III, airline executive; b. Wilkes-Barre, Pa., Jan. 5, 1947; s. Gilbert Hammond Jr. and Alice (Taylor); divorced; children: Gilbert H. IV, Cynthia; m. Angelina Bogert, Nov. 17, 1975. AS in Applied Sci. and Tech., Thomas Edison State Coll., Trenton, N.J., 1987. Cert. comml. pilot. Instr., charter pilot Cherry Ridge Flying Service, Forty Fort, Pa., 1972-75; mktg. rep. SRC Inc., Pittston, Pa., 1975-79; asst. to pres., v.p. mktg. Pocono Airlines, Avoca, Pa., 1979-86; corp. dir. adminstrv. services Patrick Media Group, Inc., Scranton, Penn., 1986—. Served with USNR, 1965-67. Republican.

EDGAR, JAMES MACMILLAN, JR., management consultant; b. N.Y.C., Nov. 7, 1936; s. James Macmillan Edgar and Lilyan (McCann) E.; B. Chem. Engring., Cornell U., 1959, M.B.A. with distinction, 1960; m. Judith Frances Storey, June 28, 1958; children—Suzanne Lynn, James Macmillan, Gordon Stuart. New product rep. E.I. duPont Nemours, Wilmington, Del., 1960-63, mktg. services rep., 1963-64; with Touche Ross & Co., 1964-78, mgr., Detroit, 1966-68, partner, 1968-71, partner in charge, mgmt. services ops. for No. Calif. and Hawaii, San Francisco, 1971-78, partner Western regional mgmt. services, 1978; prin. Edgar, Dunn & Conover, Inc., San Francisco, 1978—; mem. San Francisco Mayor's Fin. Adv. Com., 1976—, mem. exec. com., 1978—, Blue Ribbon com. for Bus., 1987—; mem. Alumnae Resources adv. bd., 1986—, mem. San Francisco Planning and Urban Research Bd., 1986—; mem. alumni exec. council Johnson Grad. Sch. Mgmt. Cornell U., 1985—, Cornell Council, 1970-73. Recipient Award of Merit for outstanding pub. service City and County of San Francisco, 1978; Honor award for outstanding contbns. to profl. mgmt. Johnson Grad. Sch. Mgmt., Cornell U., 1978. CPA, cert. mgmt. cons. Mem. Assn. Corp. Growth (v.p. membership San Francisco chpt. 1979-81, v.p. programs 1981-82, pres. 1982-83, nat. bd. dirs. 1983-86), AICPA, Calif. Soc. CPAs, Am. Mktg. Assn., Inst. Mgmt. Cons. (regional v.p. 1973-80, dir. 1975-77, bd. v.p. 1977-80), Profl. Services Mgmt. Assn., San Francisco C. of C. (bd. dirs. 1987—, v.p. econ. affairs 1988-89, mem. exec. com. 1988-89), Found. New Main Library (chmn. 1988—), Tau Beta Pi. Clubs: Univ., Pacific Union, Commonwealth of San Francisco, Marin Rod and Gun. Patentee nonwoven fabrics. Home: 10 Buckeye Way Kentfield CA 94904 Office: Edgar Dunn & Conover Inc 847 Sansome St San Francisco CA 94111

EDGAR, WILLIAM HENRY, construction company executive; b. Washington, Apr. 23, 1942; s. James and Anne (White) E.; m. Lynn Vallentine, Oct. 14, 1961 (div. Dec. 1988); children: Elizabeth Anne, Kathlene Lea, William Henry IV, James Robert. BBA, U. Fla., 1969, MBA, 1980. Pres. W.H. Edgar & Son, Inc., Detroit, 1963—; also bd. dirs. W.H. Edgar & Son, Inc.; loan officer, asst. v.p. Citizens & So. Bank, Atlanta, 1970-73; regional mgr., v.p. The Gale Orgn., Sarasota, Fla., 1973-78; chmn., chief exec. officer Phoenix Pub. Co., Gainsville, Fla., 1980-85; comptroller, v.p. Parham Engring, Inc., Newberry, Fla., 1985—; gen. mgr., v.p. Fields controls Inc., Newberry, 1985—; bd. dirs. Lake Shore Sugar Co., Detroit. Sgt. U.S. Army, 1961-64. Mem. Pres. Coun. U. Fla., Gator Boosters U. Fla., Heritage Club, Field Club. Republican. Episcopalian. Home: 328-9 SW 62d Blvd Gainesville FL 32607 Office: WH Edgar & Son Inc PO Box 2819 Gainesville FL 32601

EDGE, DONALD JOSEPH, marketing executive; b. Owensboro, Ky., Oct. 11, 1955; s. Joseph Franklin and Effie Samantha (Preston) E.; m. Brenda Louise Whistle, June 18, 1976; children: Terri, Jamie, Dustin, Jeffrey, Todd, Corey, Casey. BS, Brescia Coll., 1976. Sci. tchr., coach Trinity High Sch., Whitesville, Ky., 1976-80; ter. sales rep. Bristol-Myers U.S. Pharm. and Nutritional Group, Evansville, Ind., 1980-81; hosp. sales rep. Bristol-Myers U.S. Pharm. and Nutritional Group, Evansville, 1981-82, regional mgr., 1982-83, dist. mgr., 1982-87; clin. mktg. specialist Genentech, Inc., Conway, Ark., 1988; div. mgr. Western Gt. Lakes Genentech, Inc., Toledo, 1988—. Mem. KC. Home and Office: 6719 Glenrose Maumee OH 43537

EDGE, JAMES LAFAYETTE, III, manufacturing executive; b. Asheville, N.C., Apr. 16, 1934; s. James Lafayette and Nell Louise (Funderburk) E.; A.B., Catawba Coll., 1956; postgrad. N.C. State U., 1965, Grad. Sch. Sales Mgmt. and Mktg., Syracuse U., 1979; postgrad. exec. program Columbia, 1974, Wharton Sch., U. Pa., 1977, 83-84; m. India Joan Weems, Oct. 30, 1965; children—Claudette, Tracy, Bartley, Michael, Philip. Sales supr. Atlantic Refining Co., Miami, Fla., 1956-63; salesman Ortho Diagnostics Inc., Raritan, N.J., 1963-67, mgr. export devel., 1967-70, mgr. export sales, 1970-73, dir. internat. mktg., 1973—; mem. dist. export council U.S. Dept. Commerce. Mem. The Asia Soc., U.S./Arab C. of C., Far East Am. Council, Am. Mgmt. Assn., Nat. Exec. Council (Washington), Sales and Mktg. Execs. Internat., Nat. Fgn. Trade Council, N.J. Dist. Export Council, Pharm. Mfrs. Assn., N.J. Assn. Realtors, Nat. Assn. Realtors, Internat. Platform Assn. Republican. Presbyterian. Home: Chapel View Dr Flemington NJ 08822 Office: Ortho Diagnostics Systems Inc Raritan NJ 08869

EDGECUMBE, CRAIG HAMILTON, lawyer; b. Los Angeles, July 7, 1943; s. Robert Hamilton and Phyllis Lorraine (Gunderson) E.; m. Jeanette Webster, June 20, 1969; children: Scott Hamilton, Brent Robert. Student, U. So. Calif., Los Angeles, 1962-64; BS in Fin., UCLA, 1967; JD, Loyola U., Los Angeles, 1972. Bar: Calif., 1972. Dep. dist. atty. Los Angeles County, Los Angeles, 1972-74; assoc. firm Barrett, Stearns, Collins, Gleason and Kinney, Torrance, Calif., 1974-79, ptnr., 1980-85; gen. counsel Real Property Resources, Inc., Torrance, Calif., 1985—; speaker, U. Shopping Ctrs., Dallas, 1974, 75, 76, Calif. Continuing Edn. of Bar, 1981, 84. Served with U.S. Army, 1967-69. Mem. Internat. Council Shopping Ctrs., Los Angeles County Bar Assn., Calif. State Bar Assn. Republican. Episcopalian. Home: 27537 Rainbow Ridge Rd Palos Verdes Peninsula CA 90274 Office: Real Property Resources Inc 21235 Hawthorne Blvd Suite 200 Torrance CA 90503

EDGERLY, WILLIAM SKELTON, banker; b. Lewiston, Maine, Feb. 18, 1927; s. Stuart and Florence (Skelton) E.; m. Lois Stiles, June 12, 1948; children: Leonard Stuart, Stephanie Lois. B.S. in Econs. and Engring., MIT, 1949; M.B.A., Harvard U., 1955. With Eastman Kodak Co., 1949-50; with Cabot Corp., Boston, 1952-75, treas., 1960-63, v.p., 1963-66, v.p., gen. mgr. Oxides div., 1967-68, fin. v.p., 1969-75, also dir.; chief exec. officer State St. Boston Corp., 1975—, pres., 1975, chmn. and pres., 1976-85, chmn., 1985—, also bd. dirs.; bd. dirs., past chmn. Boston Housing Ptnrship; trustee, vice chmn. Com. Econ. Devel.; bd. dirs. Fed. Reserve Bank of Boston, Depository Trust Co., N.Y.C., Arkwright-Boston Ins. Co., Nat. Alliance Bus. Bd. dirs. Jobs for Mass., former pres.; dir. Boston Pvt. Industry Council, former chmn.; bd. dirs. Mass. Bus. Roundtable, Inst. for Fgn. Policy Analysis; former mem. fed. adv. council Fed. Reserve Bd., Washington. Served with USNR, 1945-46, 50-52. Mem. MIT Alumni Assn. (pres. 1973-74), Harvard Bus. Sch. Assn., Boston Econ. Club. Clubs: Somerset, Cambridge Boat. Office: State St Boston Corp 225 Franklin St Boston MA 02110

EDGERTON, RICHARD, restaurant/hotel owner; b. Haverford, Pa., May 2, 1911; s. Charles and Ida (Bonner) E.; LL.D. (hon.), Berry Coll., Mt. Berry, Ga.; m. Marie Lytle Page, Oct. 24, 1936; children—Leila, Margaret, Carol. Pres./owner Lakeside Inn Properties, Inc., Mt. Dora, Fla., 1935—; co-owner 28 Burger King restaurants, Pa., 1967—; gen. mgr., pres. Buck Hill Falls (Pa.) Co., 1961-65 ; pres., chief exec. officer Eustis Sand Co., Mt. Dora, Fla., 1961—founding dir. Fla. Service Corp., Tampa; v.p., dir. 1st Nat. Bank, Mt. Dora. Mem. Gov.'s Little Cabinet, 1955-61. Trustee emeritus Berry Coll.; bd. dirs. Mt. Dora Community Trust Fund; mem. Lake County Fla. Indsl. Devel. Commn.; trustee emeritus Lake Sumter Community Coll. Served to lt. USNR, 1944-46; ETO. Mem. Am. (dir.), Fla. (hon., past pres.) hotel and motel assns., N.H. Hotel Assn. (past pres.), Newcomen Soc., Welcome Soc., Pa. Soc. Clubs: Miami; Mt. Dora Yacht, Mt. Dora Golf. Home: 3d and McDonald Sts Mount Dora FL 32757 Office: 234 W 3d Ave Mount Dora FL 32757

EDGIN, ELDON J., electronics executive; b. Ozark, Ark., May 18, 1936; s. Raymond F. and Ruby Alice (Chandler) E.; m. Janice Ruth Deaton, May 28, 1957; 1 child, Eldon J. Jr. BSME, U. Tex., 1965; MS, So. Meth. U., 1972. Mfg. engr. LTV Aerospace, Dallas, 1956-65; engr. mgr. Tex. Instruments, Dallas, 1965-78; v.p. NEC Am., Irving, Tex., 1978—. Mem. gov.'s Tex./Couhila Bi-Devel. Comm., curriculum com. U. Dallas. Republican. Methodist. Home: 14908 Woodbriar Dr Dallas TX 75248 Office: NEC Am 1555 Walnut Hill Ln Irving TX 75038

EDIGER, NICHOLAS MARTIN, energy resources company executive, consultant; b. Winnipeg, Man., Can., June 25, 1928; s. Nicholas and Anna (Hamm) E.; m. Elizabeth Durden Cattley, Sept. 18, 1973; 1 child, Julia Anne. BS in Geology, U. Man., 1950; postgrad., U. Pitts, 1959, U. Okla., 1966, U. Denver, 1971. Various exec. positions Gulf Oil Corp, 1950-68; gen. mgr. Gulf Minerals Can., Ltd., Toronto, 1968-73; v.p., chief oper. officer Gulf Minerals Can. Ltd., Toronto, 1973-74; pres., chief exec. officer Eldorado Nuclear Ltd., Ottawa, Can., 1974-88, EDI Assocs. Ltd., Toronto, 1988—; exec. dir. Sentinel Assocs. Ltd., Toronto, 1988—; founding mem. coun. Uranium Inst., London, 1975—; bd. dirs. Mining Assn. of Can., Ottawa, Can. Nuclear Assn., pres., 1978-79, Toronto. Exec. dir. Elmwood Sch., Ottawa, 1984-88. Mem. Am. Assn. Petroleum Geologists, World Energy Congress (Can. adv. com. 1986—), Rideau Club Ottawa (bd. dirs. 1987-88), Glencoe Club Calgary. Office: Sentinel Assocs Ltd, 7 King St E #1609, Toronto, ON Canada M5C 1A2

EDISON, BERNARD ALAN, retail apparel company executive; b. Atlanta, 1928; s. Irving and Beatrice (Chanin) E.; m. Marilyn S. Wewers, Apr. 26, 1975. B.A., Harvard U., 1949, M.B.A., 1951. With Edison Bros. Stores Inc., St. Louis, 1951—; asst. v.p. Edison Bros. Stores Inc., 1957-58, v.p. leased depts., 1958-67, v.p., asst. treas., 1967-68, pres., 1968-87, chmn. fin. com., 1987—, also dir.; bd. dirs. Gen. Am. Life Ins. Co., Mercantile Bank, N.A., Mercantile Bancorp, Anheuser-Busch Cos., Inc., Chief Auto Parts, Inc. Office: Edison Bros Stores Inc 501 N Broadway Saint Louis MO 63102

EDLY, ALAN JOHN, food company executive; b. N.Y.C., June 22, 1935; s. Alexander John and Grace Catherine (Hauss) E. AB magna cum laude, Holy Cross Coll., 1957; MBA, N.Y. U., 1963. C.P.A., N.Y. Staff acct. Arthur Andersen & Co., N.Y.C., 1957-65; controller Gibbs & Co., N.Y.C., 1966-68; mgr. corp. acctg. Am. Maize-Products Co., N.Y.C., 1968-71; controller Am. Maize-Products Co., 1971-74, fin. v.p., 1974—, also dir.; bd. dirs. Am. Fructose Corp. subs. Am. Maize Products Co. Served with AUS, 1957. Mem. Am. Inst. C.P.A.s, N.Y. State Soc. C.P.A.s. Home: 81-02 Courtland Ave Stamford CT 06902 Office: Am Fructose Corp 250 Harbor Dr Stamford CT 06904 also: Amer Maize Products Co 250 Harbor Dr Stamford CT 06904

EDMAN, JOHN RICHARD, automotive financial services executive; b. Brighton, Mich., Oct. 14, 1927; s. Martin Wagner and Elizabeth Statira (Jacobs) E.; m. Betty Jean Bailey, Aug. 12, 1951; children: Jill, Thomas, Jody, Tracy, Julie, John. B.B.A., U. Mich., 1950, M.B.A., 1951. Comptroller Terex div. Gen. Motors, 1966-69, comptroller Packard Electric div., 1969-71; comptroller Gen. Motors Can., 1971-72, AC Spark Plug div. Gen. Motors, 1972-74; asst. comptroller Gen. Motors Corp., 1974-75, treas., 1975-78, v.p. fin., 1978-86; chmn. Gen. Motors Acceptance Corp., Detroit, 1987—. Served with U.S. Army, 1946-47. Mem. Fin. Execs. Inst. Republican. Presbyterian. Clubs: Detroit Athletic; Presidents (U. Mich.); Bloomfield Hills (Mich.); Birmingham (Mich.) Athletic. Home: 5175 Winlane Bloomfield Hills MI 48013 Office: GMAC 3044 W Grand Blvd Detroit MI 48202

EDMONDS, SALLY, computer company executive; b. Whitehall, N.Y., Jan. 10, 1949; d. Virginia (Rawson) Gonyea; m. Anthony Sliwkowski (div. 1985); children: Anthony, Bret, Carrie. Student, Hartford (Conn.) Inst. Acctg., 1967-69. Bookkeeper Alloy Foundries, Naugatuck, Conn., 1969-72;

owner, mgr. Louise Shop, Woodburn, Conn., 1978-80; bookkeeper Keating Enterprises, West Hartford, Conn., 1983-84, Capitol Fishouse Restaurant, Hartford, 1984-85; sales assoc. Colonial Realty, West Hartford, 1985-86; office mgr. Nanny's, West Hartford, 1985-86; owner, mgr. Nothing But The Best Interior Decorating, Farmington, Conn., 1988—; prin. Edmonds & Assocs., Farmington, 1986—. Mem. Nat. Assn. Female Execs., Hartford Track Club. Episcopalian. Home and Office: 26 Briarwood Rd Farmington CT 06032

EDMONDSON, JAMES WILLIAM (JAY EDMONDSON), insurance company executive; b. Artesia, Calif., July 1, 1930; s. Edward Vernon and Doris LaVerna (Hoisington) E.; m. Susanne Martin, Sept. 5, 1953; children: Susan, John. B.A., U. Calif.-Berkeley, 1952. V.p. State Farm Ins. Cos., Bloomington, Ill., 1954—; bd. trustees Maryland Automobile Ins. Fund, 1987—. Chmn. Human Relations Com., Normal, Ill., 1975-76; bd. dirs. United Way, McLean County, Ill., 1981—, Blomington-Normal Symphony, 1977—. Recipient Hardy prize Ins. Inst. Am., 1960. Republican. Roman Catholic. Office: State Farm Ins Cos 1 State Farm Pla Bloomington IL 61710

EDMONDSON, JOHN RICHARD, lawyer, pharmaceutical manufacturing company executive; b. N.Y.C., Mar. 1, 1927; s. Richard Emil and Josephine (Schroeter) E.; m. Rozanne Hume, Oct. 30, 1954; children: Lisa M., Kate H., Timothy H., Nicholas D., Julia N. A.B., Georgetown U., 1950; LL.B., Columbia U., 1953. Bar: N.Y. 1953. Asso. atty. Winthrop, Stimson, Putnam & Roberts, N.Y.C., 1953-59; with Bristol-Myers Co., N.Y.C., 1959—; asst. sec. Bristol-Myers Co., 1960-69, sec., 1969—, v.p., 1974-80, gen. counsel, 1977—, sr. v.p., 1980—. Served with AUS, 1945-47. Mem. Assn. Bar City N.Y. Clubs: University, The Board Room (N.Y.C.); Lake Waramaug Country (New Preston, Conn.); Hon. Co. Edinburgh Golfers (Gullane, Scotland). Home: 60 E 96th St New York NY 10128 Office: Bristol-Myers Co 345 Park Ave New York NY 10154

EDMONSON, ROBERT RAYMOND, computer company executive; b. West Palm Beach, Fla., Feb. 1, 1948; s. John Ross and Arline Fae (Morrison) E. Student, U. Houston, 1975-76. Regional sales mgr. Parkline Inc., Winfield, W.Va., 1977-79; dist. mgr. Kirby Bldg. Systems Inc., Houston, 1979-82; v.p. sales and mktg. Todays Am. Builder Inc., Houston, 1982-84; v.p. regional devel. Mr. Build South Tex. Inc., Houston, 1984; v.p., co-founder PCR Internat., Coral Gables, Fla., 1984—; also bd. dirs. PCR Internat. Sgt. U.S. Army, 1969-71, Europe. Office: PCR Internat 800 Douglas Entrance N Tower Ste 355 Coral Gables FL 33134

EDSALL, HOWARD LINN, consulting executive; b. N.Y.C., Nov. 17, 1904; s. John Linn and Alise (Stoughton) E.; student pub. schs., pvt. tutoring; m. Florence S. Small, July 5, 1930 (dec. 1986); children: Florence Linn (Mrs. Robert James Whitehouse). Sea-going radio operator, marine div. RCA, 1920-25, advt. and sales promotion mgr. electron tube div., 1944-47; with Curtis-Martin Newspapers, Inc., 1926; mktg., sales promotion exec., plans writer R.E. Lovekin Corp., 1928-34, Bridge & King, 1934-35. E.F. Houghton Co., 1935-37; co-founder, dir. G.S. Rogers & Co., Chgo., 1937-40, Ajax Metal Co. & Affiliates, 1940-44; exec. cons. Rockport Press, The Reporter, Household Fin. Corp., 1948; v.p., dir. Craven & Hedrick, AM TV's The Big Story, 1949-52; exec. v.p. Fred Wittner Advt., N.Y.C., 1953-57; sec., dir. Plastomics Products Co., Inc., 1946; pres., founder AIMS, Inc. (counselors to profl. mgrs.), 1959; ptnr. Bonniview Lodge. Lake Penage, Whitfish, Ont., Can. Mem. Re-Employment Planning Assocs., 1966; charter mem. Presdl. Task Force, 1984; dir. spl. events UN Council, 1944-45. Mem. Am. Soc. Metals (bd. editors 1944-47), Jewelry Industry Council (advt. dir. 1951), Soc. Profl. Mgmt. Cons. (charter 1960, v.p., dir. 1967-69), Inst. Mgmt. Cons. (founder-mem.), Poets and Writers Directory of Am. Fiction Writers, N.J. Writers Directory, SAR. Clubs: U.S. Senatorial (preferred mem.), Pen and Pencil (Phila.); Morse Telegraph; Listentome (N.J.). Author: An Unexplored Musical Resource, 1944; Borrow & Prosper, 1946; Management Consultant and Reporter, 1968; The How You Can Borrow and Prosper Kit, 1972; co-author One To Ten Thousand Copies, 1963; cons. editorial bd. Jour. Mgmt. and Bus. Consulting, 1976; author: Song of Free Men, 1985 (awarded Presdl. commn. 1986), Society of Wireless Pioneers, 1986; contbr. fiction and articles to nat. U.S. and fgn. mags. Inventor Violute, 1939. Home: 39A N Mountain Ave Montclair NJ 07042

EDSON, HERBERT ROBBINS, hospital executive; b. Upper Darby, Pa., Dec. 26, 1931; s. Merritt Austin and Ethel Winifred (Robbins) E.; m. Rose Anne McGowan, July 25, 1970; children: Patricia Anne, David William, Merritt Austin III, Herbert Robbins, Jr. BA, Tufts U., 1955; MBA, U. Pa., 1972. Commd. 2d lt. USMC, 1955, advanced through grades to major, 1967, adminstr., mgr., supr. various orgns., 1955-72; controller III Marine Amphibious Force and 3d Marine Div. USMC, Camp Butler, Japan, 1972-73; dir. acctg. Marine Corps Supply Activity USMC, Phila., 1973-75; ret. USMC, 1975; cons. acctg. Ardmore, Pa., 1975-77; chief fin. officer Mercy Meml. Hosp. Corp., Monroe, Mich., 1977—, Mercy Meml. Hosp. Found., Monroe, 1986—. Co-pres. Custer Elem. Sch. Parent Tchr. Orgn., Monroe, 1985-87; v.p., trustee Christ Evang. Luth. Ch., Monroe, 1981-86; treas., chmn. Taylor Endowment Fund com. St. Paul's Evang. Luth. Ch., Ardmore, Pa., 1974-76, trustee, chmn. property com., 1976. Decorated Purple Heart, Navy Commendation medal, Combat Action ribbon. Mem. Nat. Assn. Accts., Am. Hosp. Assn., Healthcare Fin. Mgmt. Assn., U.S. Naval Inst. (life), Marine Corps Inst., First Marine Div. Assn. (life), Edson's Raiders Assn. (1st Marine Raider Bn., hon. life), The Ret. Officers Assn. (life), Nat. Rifle Assn. (life), Monroe County C. of C. (dir. 1982-84). Republican. Lutheran. Club: Marine's Meml. (San Francisco); Monroe Rod and Gun, Army and Navy (Washington). Home: 526 Scott St Monroe MI 48161 Office: Mercy Meml Hosp Corp 740 N Macomb St Monroe MI 48161

EDSON, MARY CHRISTINE, service executive, consultant; b. Kenmore, N.Y., Dec. 9, 1959; d. Werner Alvin and Marguerite (Prefontaine) E. BS in Hotel Mgmt., Cornell U., 1983; postgrad., Johns Hopkins U., 1986—. Asst. mgr. Bloomingdale's Restaurant, McLean, Va., 1983-84; cons. Pannell Kerr Forster, Washington, 1984; point-of-sale cons. Balt. Country Club, 1985; cons. Praxis Assocs., Balt., 1985—; point-of-sale cons. Marriott Corp., Bethesda, Md., 1986—. Active Balt. Council on Fgn. Affairs, 1985-86. Mem. Roundtable for Women in Food Service, Cornell Soc. Hotelmen, Int. Visitors Bur., Johns Hopkins Internat. Club. Home: 5353 Smooth Meadow Way #2 Columbia MD 21044 Office: Marriott Corp 1 Marriott Dr Bethesda MD 20058

EDSTROM, JOHN OLOF, educator, industrialist; b. Stockholm, May 11, 1926; s. Johan and Martha Torborg (Andersson) E.; dipl.ing., Royal Inst. Tech., 1950, tech.lic., 1953, dr.sci., 1958; m. Gunnel Kling, Nov. 24, 1950; 1 child, Ingeborg. Research asst. Royal Inst. Tech., Stockholm, 1950-53, prof. ferrous metallurgy, 1960—, prof. prodn. tech., 1977—; research asso. U. Minn., Mpls., 1954; research metallurgist Jernkontoret, Stockholm, 1955-57; head metall. research dept. Sandvik Co., Sandviken, Sweden, 1958-60, v.p. research and devel., 1960-65, exec. v.p., 1965-70; pres. Norrbotten Steelworks, Luleå, Sweden, 1970-76; chmn. Swedish Welding Commn., 1986—; chmn. U. Luleå, 1970-77; hon. profl. E. China Inst. Metallurgy, 1987—. Decorated comdr. Order of Vasa; recipient Bergs medal Royal Inst. Tech., 1973. Mem. Royal Swedish Acad. Engring. (dir. 1979-82), Inst. Metal Research (dir. 1970—), MEFOS (dir. 1970—), Swedish Inst. Prodn. Engring. Research (dir. 1977-80), AIME, Metal Soc., Iron and Steel Inst. Japan (hon.), Svenska Metallografforbundet, Verein Deutsche Eisenhuttenleute. Clubs: Rotary, Svenska Bergsmannaforeningen, Sankt Orjans Gille. Contbr. articles to profl. jours.; patentee in field; inventor. Home: 2E Orrspelsvagen, 18275 Stocksund Sweden Office: Royal Inst Tech, Dept Prodn Tech, 25 Drottning Kristinas vag, 10044 Stockholm Sweden

EDWARDS, ALBERTA ROON, public affairs executive; b. Landeshut, Germany, Oct. 9, 1926; d. Max H. Burger and Karin Roon; m. Roger Borgeson, 1951 (div. May 1956); m. Roger Edwards; children: Jeff, Julie, Chris. BA in Econs., Oberlin (Ohio) Coll., 1946. Asst. to treas. Savs. Bank Life Ins. Fund, 1946-48; market research analyst Dun & Bradstreet, 1948-49; market analyst Charles Pfizer & Co., 1949-52, mgr., fgn. market research, 1952-56; with Schering-Plough Corp., Kenilworth, N.J., 1956-72; dir. mktg. info. and analysis Schering Corp., Kenilworth, N.J., 1972-74, dir. mktg. adminstrv., 1974-80, staff v.p. planning and adminstrn., 1980-84, staff v.p. internat. pub. affairs, mktg. services, 1984-87, staff v.p. planning, pub. affairs, market devel., 1987-88; v.p. pub. affairs Schering-Plough Internat. Corp., Kenilworth, N.J., 1988—; mem. First Am. Mktg. Del. to USSR, 1960. Contbr. articles to profl. jours. Mem. Pharm. Mfrs. Assn., Am. Mktg. Assn. (v.p. 1973-75), Internat. Mktg. Fedn. (v.p. 1972-74), Internat. Pharm. Mktg. Research Group (pres.). Office: Schering-Plough Internat Inc 2000 Galloping Hill Rd Kenilworth NJ 07033

EDWARDS, ALVA EUGENE, business analyst; b. Ft. Morgan, Colo., Apr. 11, 1928; s. Alva William and Beth (Tanner) E.; m. Patricia Hatch, Mar. 14, 1948; children: James Robert, Ellen Jean Edwards Bishop. Grad. high sch., Cheyenne, Wyo. Mem. mgmt. staff Branen's Food Mkts., Cheyenne and Casper, Wyo., 1949-57, Piggly Wiggly Stores, Rapid City, S.D., 1957-59; real estate broker Edwards & Co., Lander, Wyo., 1959-65; pres., dir. NEDCO Uranium Co., Lander, 1965-72; appraiser, analyst Family Housing Mgmt. Account, Fin. Mgmt. Adv. Com., FHA, VA, Cheyenne, 1974-81; dir. Spearhead Energy, Casper, 1974-80; sr. ptnr. Wyoming Appraisers, Cheyenne, 1981—; sr. rev. appraiser various banks and savs. and loan cos., Wyo., 1984—; pres. Titanium Corp. Am., Cheyenne, 1985—; bd. dirs. Micro Display Systems, Hastings, Minn., Lyric Energy Inc., Amarillo, Tex., Wyrocks, Cheyenne, Advanced Monitoring Systems, Denver. Editor various SEC memorandums. Vice-chmn. Planning and Zoning commn., Lander, 1963-65. Fellow Am. Inst. Mgmt. (bd. dirs.); mem. C. of C. Cheyenne. Republican. Mormon. Lodge: Kiwanis. Home: 6215 Deer Ave Cheyenne WY 82009 Office: Wyo Appraisers Am Nat Bank Bldg Suite 400 Cheyenne WY 82001

EDWARDS, BENJAMIN HARRISON, high technology company executive; b. Nashville, June 30, 1953; s. Ben H. Jr. and Norma P. (Fields) E.; m. Alice Marie Sanders, Aug. 14, 1976; children: Dante, Renee. BS in Bus., Tenn. State U., 1975; MS in Mktg., Webster U., 1988. Store mgr. Kroger Co., Nashville, 1975-80; mktg. rep. IBM Corp., Tulsa, 1980-82; fin. cons. Merrill Lynch, Overland Park, Kans., 1982-83; account mgr. Software AG, Overland Park, 1983-85; gen. mgr. Blue Ventures Technologies, Kansas City, Mo., 1985—. Bd. dirs. Project Literacy U.S., Kansas City, Lift-Mo. Found., Jefferson City, 1988—. Mem. Am. Mktg. Assn., Kansas City Direct Mktg. Assn., Johnson County Exchange Club, Alpha Phi Alpha. Roman Catholic. Home: 9912 E 84th St Raytown MO 64138 Office: Blue Ventures Technologies 201 E Armour Blvd Kansas City MO 64111

EDWARDS, BLAKE ALAN, pharmacist; b. Benton, Ill., June 27, 1959; s. Beverly Dale and Bernice Loretta (Medley) E.; m. Geri Rene Leek, June 22, 1980; children: Robbie Lynn, Lauren Nicole. BS in Pharmacy, St. Louis Coll., 1983, postgrad., 1986—. Registered pharmacist, Ill. Asst. dir. pharmacy Hamilton Meml. Hosp., McLeansboro, Ill., 1983-85, dir. pharmacy, 1986—; chief pharmacist Lovins Pharmacies Inc., Carmi, Ill., 1985-86; cons. pharmacist Hamilton Meml. Nursing Ctr., McLeansboro, 1986—; regional coordinator Clin. Pharmacokinetics Lab., Buffalo, 1987—; cons. pharmacist Home Health Agy., McLeansboro, 1987—. Mem. Am. Soc. Hosp. Pharmacists, Kappa Psi (sec. 1981, vice regent 1982). Home: Rte 4 PO Box 276 McLeansboro IL 62859 Office: Hamilton Meml Hosp 611 S Marshall Ave McLeansboro IL 62859

EDWARDS, CARL NORMAND, management consultant; b. Norwood, Mass., Jan. 22, 1943; s. Wilfred Carl and Cecile Marie-Anne (Pepin) E.; m. Mary Louise Buyse, Jan. 22, 1982. Student Brdigewater State Coll.; MEd, Suffolk U., 1969; postgrad. Harvard U. Cons. dept. social relations Harvard, 1966-69, research fellow, 1969-71, lectr. social relations, 1971-72; cons. research psychologist Cambridge Computer Assocs., Mass., 1966—; assoc. clin. prof. psychiatry Tufts U. Sch. Medicine, 1971—, research social psychologist Tufts-New Eng. Med. Center, 1969—; dir. Four Oaks Research Inst., Norfolk, Mass., 1974—; sr. assoc. for policy planning and research Justice Resource Inst., 1971—; field faculty grad. program Goddard Coll., Plainfield, Vt., 1972-82; chmn. bd. dirs. MEDx Systems, Ltd., Dover, Mass., 1985—; chmn. bd. trustees Ctr. for Birth Defects Info. Services, Inc., Dover, 1984—; tchr. seminars; cons. to major corps., govt. agys. and pub. instns. in human dynamics and pub. policy; lectr., thesis adviser, program devel. cons. schs., colls., insts. Contbr. articles to profl. jours., monographs, revs. Mem. USNG, 1963-64. Mem. Am., Mass. psychol. Assns., Soc. for Psychol. Study Social Issues, Peace Research Soc., Nat. Pilots Assn., Nat. Trust for Hist. Preservation. Clubs: Harvard (Boston); Appalachian Mountain, Norfolk Hunt, Blue Ridge Hunt. Author: Drug Dependence: Social Regulation and Treatment Alternatives. Contbr. articles to profl. jours., monographs, revs. Home: Four Oaks Off Springdale PO Box 279 Dover MA 02030

EDWARDS, CONNIE LYNNE, accountant; b. El Dorado, Ark., Oct. 5, 1955; d. James Clifton and Catherine (Varnell) Griffith; m. Bruce Tully Edwards, June 7, 1974; children: Hayley Elisabeth, Heath Michael. BBA summa cum laude, So. Ark. U., 1987. Bookkeeper Electra Inc., El Dorado, 1973-88, Hudson Nursing Home, El Dorado, 1978-85, Cook, Liles & Garner, El Dorado, 1988; acct. William P. Cook, El Dorado, 1988, Gen. Dynamics Co., Camden, Ark., 1988, Ensco Inc., El Dorado, 1988—. Mem. Alpha Chi, Phi Theta Kappa, Phi Beta Lamda. Republican. Home: Rte 3 PO Box 173 El Dorado AR 71730 Office: Ensco Incics Co PO Box 1957 El Dorado AR 71731-1957

EDWARDS, DAWN ANN, product marketing professional; b. Valley Forge, Pa., Jan. 13, 1956; d. George Francis and Severina (Bacer) E. BS, Syracuse U., 1978, MS, 1979. Account mgmt., staff asst. Ted Bates Worldwide, Inc., N.Y.C., 1980-83; asst. account exec. Backer & Spielvogel, Inc., N.Y.C., 1983-85; asst. product mgr. Am. Home Products, N.Y.C., 1985-86; asst. product mgr. Carter-Wallace, Inc., N.Y.C., 1986-88, product mgr., 1988—. Mem. Syracuse U. Alumni Assn., Delta Gamma Alumnae. Home: 1 Nevada Pla Apt 9-H New York NY 10023 Office: Carter-Wallace Inc 767 Fifth Ave New York NY 10153

EDWARDS, DEL M(OUNT), business executive; b. Tyler, Tex., Apr. 12, 1953; s. Welby Clell and Davida (Mount) E.; m. Susan Alicia Pappas, 1984 (div. 1986). AA cum laude, Tyler Jr. Coll., 1974; BBA, Baylor U., 1976. Corp. coord. Dillard Dept. Stores, Inc., Ft. Worth, 1976-77; v.p. W.C. Supply Co., Tyler, 1977—; pres., owner Walker Auto Spring, Inc., Shreveport, La., 1978-88, Edwards & Assocs., Inc., 1984—; v.p. W.C. Square, Inc., 1976—; chmn. bd. dirs., chief exec. officer Pruitt Co. Inc., Houston, 1988— . Mem. planning com. Tyler Heritage Tour, 1982-83; Originator Designer Show-Case, Tyler, 1983; founder, chmn. Rose Garden Trust Fund, 1981-87; bd. dirs. Carnegie History Ctr., 1984-85 ; pres. Smith County Youth Found., 1986-87, bd. dirs., 1984—, East Tex. Baylor Club, 1986-87; chmn. Sr. Citizens Day ann. program, East Tex. Fair, 1979—, bd. dirs. 1984—; mem. exec. com., Bd. Assocs. East Tex. Bapt. U., Marshall, 1988—; trustee Timberline Bapt. Camp and Conf. Ctr., 1987—. Mem. Coun. Fleet Specialists, Tyler Area C. of C., Smith County Hist. Soc. (chmn. bd. govs. 1984-85, 87-88, pres. 1984-85), mem. Smith County Hist. Commn., 1984-85, Hist. Tyler, Inc., Tyler Jaycees (v.p. 1982-83, bd. dir. 1981-85), Nat. Trust for Hist. Preservation, SCV (treas. camp 124, 1979-83). Baptist. Clubs: Tyler Petroleum, Willow Brook Country (Tyler). Home: 3415 S Keaton Ave Tyler TX 75701 also: Mountwood Ranch Rte 17 Box 30 Tyler TX 75704 Office: WC Square Front at Bonner Tyler TX 75710

EDWARDS, ELEANOR CECILE, comptroller; b. N.Y.C., July 23, 1940; d. Clifford Thaddeus and Lillian Louise (Taitt) Butte; m. Warren Thaddeus Edwards, Dec. 17, 1961; children: Angelique, Kelby. BBA and Acctg. summa cum laude, Mercy Coll., 1982. Supr. billing Formulette Co., Inc., Long Island City, N.Y., 1960-62; keypunch operator Temporary Agys., N.Y.C., 1963-68; tng. instr. Setab Computer Inst., N.Y.C., 1968-70; asst. office mgr. Kendrick Sytems, Inc., Elmsford, N.Y., 1970-71; office mgr. LPJ Computer Corp., Millwood, N.Y., 1972-75; full charge bookkeeper Lockwood Manor Home for Adults, New Rochelle, N.Y., 1975-77; comptroller Margaret Chapman Sch., Hawthorne, N.Y., 1977—; dir. Bradhurst Ctr. Corp., Hawthorne, 1980-88; cons. acct. Very Spl. Arts N.Y., 1983—. Vol. Spl. Olympics, Westchester, N.Y., 1980—, Very Spl. Arts N.Y., 1982—. Mem. Nat. Assn. Accts., Nat. Notary Assn., Delta Mu Delta, Alpha Chi. Democrat. Office: Margaret Chapman Sch 5 Bradhurst Ave Hawthorne NY 10532

EDWARDS, GARY JON, concrete products company executive; b. Balt., June 23, 1954; s. Grady Henry and Marcelle L. (Kloek) E.; m. Nancy Ellen Armacost, Oct. 20, 1984. BBA, Madison Coll., 1976. With Koontz Concrete Products, Inc., New Windsor, Md., 1976—, owner, pres., 1978—; sec., treas. River Rock Paving, Inc., New Windsor, 1980-84. Mem. Nat. Fedn. Ind. Bus., Hanover C. of C., Carroll County C. of C. Democrat. Methodist. Home: 403A Malcolm Dr Westminster MD 21157 Office: Koontz Concrete Products Inc 933 Wakefield Valley Rd New Windsor MD 21776

EDWARDS, GEORGE W., JR., electric utilities executive; b. 1939; married. BS, U. Ark., 1961; postgrad., Harvard U. Commd. 2d lt. U.S. Army, 1961, advanced through grades to maj., resigned, 1969; from asst. v.p. to exec. v.p. Ga. Power Co., 1969-85; pres., chief exec. officer United Illuminating Co., New Haven, 1985-87, chmn., chief exec. officer, 1987—. Office: United Illuminating Co 80 Temple St New Haven CT 06506

EDWARDS, HARRY LAFOY, lawyer; b. Greenville, S.C., July 29, 1936; s. George Belton and Mary Olive (Jones) E.; m. Suzanne Copeland, June 16, 1956; 1 child, Margaret Peden. LLB, U. S.C., 1963, JD, 1970. Bar: S.C. 1963, U.S. dist. ct. S.C. 1975, U.S. Ct. Apls. (4th cir.) 1974. Assoc. Edwards and Edmunds, Greenville, 1963; v.p., sec., dir. Edwards Co., Inc., Greenville, 1963-65; atty. investment legal dept. Liberty Life Ins. Co., Greenville, 1965-67, asst. sec., asst. v.p., head investment legal dept., 1967-70; asst. sec. Liberty Corp., 1970-75; asst. v.p. Liberty Life Ins. Co., 1970-75; sec. Bent Tree Corp., CEL, Inc., 1970-75; sec., dir. Westchester Mall, Inc., 1970-75; asst. sect. Libco, Inc., Liberty Properties, Inc., 1970-75; sole practice, Greenville, 1975—. Com. mem. Hipp Fund Spl. Edn., Greenville County Sch. System; mem. Boyd C. Hipp II Scholarship Com. Wofford Coll., Spartanburg, S.C.; scholarship com. mem. Liberty Scholars, U. S.C., 1984, 86-88; editor U. S.C. law rev., 1963 . Served with USAFR, 1957-63. Mem. ABA, S.C. Bar Assn., Greenville County Bar Assn., Phi Delta Phi, Greenville Lawyers, Poinsett Club (Greenville). Baptist. Home: 106 Ridgeland Dr Greenville SC 29601 Office: PO Box 10350 Federal Sta Greenville SC 29603

EDWARDS, HOWARD MCKAY, mining company executive; b. Salt Lake City, Utah, Nov. 6, 1956; s. Howard Lee and Carolyn (Bagley) E.; m. Pamela Doris Hamilton, Oct. 24, 1986. BA in English, U. Utah, 1981. Pres. Compliance Engring. Co., Salt Lake City, 1979-84, Park City (Utah) Consol. Mines Co., 1984—. Chmn. Wasatch Trails Found., Salt Lake City, 1983—. Recipient Gov.'s Cup for 1st Pl. slalom State of Wyo., 1977. Club: Alta (Salt Lake City). Office: Park City Consol Mines 614 Main St PO Box 497 Park City UT 84060

EDWARDS, HUGH MORTIMER, insurance company executive; b. Clarendon, Jamaica, July 13, 1942; came to U.S., 1972; m. Mary Jane McAnuff, Apr. 29, 1967. Student, Jamaica Sch. Agriculture, 1962-65, Long Island U., 1979. CLU. Sale rep. Met. Life Ins. Co., N.Y.C., 1975-79, sales mgr., 1979-82, br. mgr., 1982—. Mem. Gen. Agts. and Mgrs. Conf. (bd. dirs.). Home: 105-40 Flatlands 1st St Brooklyn NY 11236 Office: Met Ins Co 1535 Rockaway Pkwy Brooklyn NY 11236

EDWARDS, JAMES D., accounting company executive; b. Cleveland, Tenn., Nov. 4, 1943; s. James D. and Elizabeth (Reynolds) E.; m. Sharon E. Bordelon, May 2, 1968; 1 child, David. BS in Acctg., Bob Jones U., 1964. CPA, Ga. From staff acct. to ptnr. Arthur Andersen & Co., Atlanta, 1964-78; mng. ptnr. Atlanta office Arthur Andersen & Co., 1979-87; mng. ptnr. N.Am. Arthur Andersen & Co., N.Y.C., 1987—. Bd. dirs., exec. com. Atlanta C. of C., 1982-85, Woodruff Arts Ctr., Atlanta, 1986-87; chmn. Cen. Atlanta Progress, 1986-87. Mem. Board Room (N.Y.C.),d The Stanwich Club (Greenwich, Ct.) Atlanta Country Club. Baptist. Office: Arthur Andersen & Co 1345 Ave of the Americas New York NY 10105

EDWARDS, JAMES DALLAS, III, plastics company executive; b. Harriman, Tenn., Aug. 9, 1937; s. James Dallas Jr. and Helen Louise (Milburn) E.; m. Louisa Diane Fultz, July 15, 1961. BBA, U. Tenn., 1959. Customer service supr. Aluminum Co. Am., Alcoa, Tenn., 1964-67; staff product planner Aluminum Co. Am., Pitts., 1967-70, traffic mgr., 1970-74; plant mgr. Soundesign Corp., Santa Claus, Ind., 1974-78; v.p., gen. mgr. Thermwood Corp., Dale, Ind., 1978-81; pres., chief exec. officer Spencer Plastic Products Corp., Dale, 1981—, also bd. dirs.; pres. Restaurant Group, Ltd., Dale; bd. dirs. Grand Restaurant Corp., Lexington, Ky. Chmn. bd. dirs. So. Ind. Rehab. Services, Boonville, 1977-82; bd. dirs. Southwest Ind. Pvt. Industry Coun., 1989—; mem. Santa Claus Indsl. Park Bd., Santa Claus, 1978—. Mem. Am. Prodn. and Inventory Control Soc. (bd. dirs. 1970-72), Soc. Plastics Engrs., Soc. Mfg. Engrs., Naval Res. Assn. (pres. 1967—), SBA (Ind. adv. coun. 1989—), Res. Officers Assn., Dale C. of C., Rolling Hills Country Club, Kiwanis, Elks. Presbyterian. Home: 188 Balthazar Dr Santa Claus IN 47579 Office: Spencer Plastics Corp Old Buffaloville Rd Dale IN 47523

EDWARDS, JAMES EDWIN, lawyer; b. Clarkesville, Ga., July 29, 1914; s. Gus Calloway and Mary Clara (McKinney) E.; m. Frances Lillian Stanley, Nov. 22, 1948; children—Robin Anne Edwards Ralston, James Christopher, Clare Edwards Schlosser. Student U. Tex. 1931-33; B.A., George Washington U., 1935, J.D. cum laude, 1946. Bar: Fla. 1938, D.C. 1981, Va 1987. Practice law, Cocoa, Fla., 1938-42; hearing and exam. officer USCG, 1943-45; div. asst. State Dept., Washington, 1945-50; practice law Ft. Lauderdale, Fla., 1951-55, 59-77; mem. firm Bell, Edwards, Coker, Carlon & Amsden, Ft. Lauderdale, 1956-59; sole practice, Coral Springs, Fla., 1977-81, 84-85; asst. city atty. Fort Lauderdale, 1961, 63-65; mem. firm. Edwards & Leary, Coral Springs, 1981-84; mem. panel Am. Arbitration Assn., 1984—; sole practice, Albemarle County, Va., 1987-88, Charlottesville, Va., 1988—. Commr., Coral Springs, 1970-76, mayor, 1972-74; mem. bd. suprs. Sunshine Water Mgmt. Dist., 1976-80; chmn. Ft. Lauderdale for Eisenhower, 1952; pres. Fla. Conservative Union, Broward County, 1976. Served to lt. USCGR, 1943-45, to lt. col. JAG, USAFR, 1950-68. Mem. SAR. Presbyterian. Club: English Speaking Union (Charlottesville). Lodge: Rotary. Author: Myths About Guns, 1978. Office: Commonwealth Ctr 300 Preston Ave Ste 312 Charlottesville VA 22901

EDWARDS, JEAN MARIE GRUNKLEE, mortgage broker, consultant; b. Chgo., May 3, 1952; d. Anthony Raymond and Mary (Guiliano) Laudadio; m. William Charles Grunklee, May 13, 1978 (div. 1987); children: Daniel Enoch, David Elijah, Jenny Mary Ruth, Joy Melissa. Student, U. So. Calif., 1970-71, U. N.D., 1972, U. Oxnard, 1985-88. Real estate investor Orange County, Calif., 1971—; loan officer Shenandoah Properties Mortgage Loan Svcs., Santa Ana, Calif., 1978-85; chmn. Newport Capital Funding, Inc., El Toro, Calif., 1985—; cons., 1987-88; owner, mgr. Shoreline Appraisal Svcs., El Toro, 1986—; chmn. J&R Escrow, El Toro, 1987—. Vol. Orange County Girl Scouts U.S., 1987-88, Calvary ,Chapel Costa Mesa, 1970—. Mem. Saddleback C. of C., Better Bus. Bur., Multiple Listing Bd., Rep. Women Am. Office: Newport Capital Funding Inc 22932 El Toro Rd Ste 1 El Toro CA 92630

EDWARDS, JOHN KENNETH, transportation executive; b. Erie, Pa., June 4, 1944; s. Harold Victor and Myrtle (Hackett) E.; m. Tomy Yolanda Carmona, May 27, 1972; children: Kelly, Alan. BA, Clermont McKenna Coll., 1966; postgrad., Stanford U., 1966-67; MA, Vanderbilt U., 1972. Vol. Peace Corps, Colombia, 1967-69, regional dir., 1969-70; mgr. corp. responsibility Cummins Engine Co., Columbus, Ind., 1972-75, mgr. bus. planning, 1974-77; dir. mktg. Cummins Engine Co., Mexico City, 1977-80, dir. ops., 1980-83; area dir. Latin Am. Cummins Engine Co., Miami, Fla., 1983-85; exec. dir. internat. mktg. Cummins Engine Co., Columbus, 1985-86; pres. Cummins Brasil, Sao Paulo, 1986—. Pres. PTA, Sao Paulo, 1987-88. Mem. Am. C. of C. (bd. dirs Sao Paulo chpt. 1986—). Home: Ave Martin Luther King 2000, Osasco, São Paulo 06030, Brazil Office: Cummins Brasil, CX Postal 13, Guarulhos, São Paulo 07270, Brazil

EDWARDS, MARK, banker; b. Chgo., Oct. 17, 1959; s. Theodore James and Mary Alice (Rivers) R.; m. Stacia Octavia Stewart, Sept. 26, 1981; children: Mark James, Joshua Charles. BA in Bus. Adminstrn., Loyola U., Chgo., 1981. Asst. mgr. County Seat Store, Evanston, Ill., 1981-83; credit adminstr. Am. Nat. Bank, Chgo., 1983-85; credit analyst D & K Fin./GE Credit Corp., Lincolnshire, Ill., 1985-88; credit officer Citicorp N.AM., Schaumburg, Ill., 1988—. Coach Country Club Hills Park Dist., 1988. Mem. Link Unltd. Alumni Assn. (past pres.). Roman Catholic. Home: 17800 Sarah Ln Country Club Hills IL 60477 Office: GE Credit Corp 1900 E Golf Rd Schaumburg IL 60388

EDWARDS, R. D., savings and loan executive; b. 1918; married. BA, U. Calif., 1941. With Glendale Fed. Savs. & Loan Assn., 1945—, sec., 1949-51, v.p., 1951-60, exec. v.p., 1960-65, pres., 1965-72, chief exec. officer, 1965-85, chmn., 1972-88, also dir.; also chmn., chief exec. officer, dir. Glenfed, Inc. (parent), dir., 1985—. Office: GLENFED Inc 700 N Brand Blvd Glendale CA 91209

EDWARDS, RAY CONWAY, engineering corporation executive; b. Belleville, Ont., Can., Sept. 1, 1913; s. Ernest Alfred and Augusta (Fee) E.; B.A., UCLA, 1935; m. Marjorie Baisch; children—David, Douglas, Ruth, Diane, Robert (dec.), Helen. Engr., Carrier Corp., Syracuse, N.Y., 1935-42; physicist Gen. Lab., U.S. Rubber Co., Passaic, N.J., 1942-46; acoustical cons., founder, chmn. bd., pres. Edwards Engring. Corp., Pompton Plains, N.J., 1947—; founder, chmn. bd. Spi-Rol-Fin Corp., 1954-58; mfr. air conditioning and refrigeration equipment, gas treatment and pollution control equipment for petroleum industry; patentee in field. Registered profl. engr. N.Y., N.J., Va., Pa. Mem. ASHRAE (life), Theta Delta Chi. Home: 396 Ski Trail Smoke Rise Butler NJ 07405 Office: 101 Alexander Ave Pompton Plains NJ 07444

EDWARDS, RICHARD CHARLES, financial analyst; b. Jacksonville, Fla., Feb. 7, 1948; s. Robert David and Jean Alice (Bauer) E.; m. Robin Mary Morse, Aug. 30, 1970; children: Michael, Jonathan. BSEE, Princeton U., 1969; MBA, Stanford U., 1976. Mktg. mgr. Hewlett Packard Co., Cupertino, Calif., 1976-83; spl. ltd. ptnr. Robertson, Stephens & Co., San Francisco, 1983—. Editor photography, Bric-a-Brac, 1968; author: Using Edit2, 1981. Bd. dirs. Oakland (Calif.)-Piedmont Jewish Community Ctr., 1983-87. Served to lt. USN, 1970-74. Recipient NSF award, 1964. Mem. IEEE, San Francisco Soc. Security Analysts. Club: Lakeview (Oakland). Home: 2661 Mountain Gate Way Oakland CA 94611 Office: Robertson Stephens & Co 1 Embarcadero Ctr Ste 3100 San Francisco CA 94111

EDWARDS, ROBERT JOHN, financial executive; b. Atlanta, July 28, 1951; s. John A. and Elenore Adele (Walters) E.; m. Jean Moore, Mar. 18, 1978; children: Claire Reneé, Mark Robert. BA in Econs. magna cum laude, Tufts U., 1973; MBA in Fin., UCLA, 1978. Dir. fin. 20th Century Fox Film, L.A., 1978-84; dir. corp. devel. Sitmar Cruises, L.A., 1984-85; v.p. fin. and planning Thorn EMI Screen Entertainment, L.A., 1985-86; sr. v.p. corp. devel. and planning Anthony Industries, L.A., 1986—; bd. dirs. Thorn EMI/HBO Video, N.Y.C., Thorn EMI Screen Entertainment, Inc., L.A. Office: Anthony Industries Inc 4900 S Eastern Ave Los Angeles CA 90040

EDWARDS, S. ALBERT, food company executive; b. Rockford, Ill., Dec. 4, 1946; s. Scharon Alfred and Kathryn Dorothy (Kuhls) E.; m. Roberta Paulette Schuldt, May 2, 1970 (div. 1982); children: Jamison, Robert; m. Janice Margaret Bahl, June 25, 1983. BS in Pharmacy, U. Ill., 1969; PharmD, U. Mich., 1971. Registered pharmacist, Ill., Calif. Pharmacy resident U. Mich. Med. Ctr., Ann Arbor, 1969-71; asst. prof. Tex. So. U., Houston, 1971-74, N.D. State U., Fargo, 1974-75, U. Minn., Mpls., 1975-80; med. reviewer FDA, Rockville, Md., 1980-83; dir. drug info. Howard U., Washington, 1983-84; rsch. scientist NIH, Bethesda, Md., 1984-86; asst. dir. clin. rsch. Nutra-Sweet Co., Deerfield, Ill., 1987—; mem. cons. faculty Inst. Clin. Toxicology, Houston, 1973-74; assoc. mem. med. staff Neuropsychiat. Inst., Fargo, 1975. Contbr. articles to profl. jours. Mem. adv. bd. Pharmacists Against Drug Abuse, Springhouse, Pa., 1984—. Mem. Am. Soc. Hosp. Pharmacists, Drug Info. Assn., Nat. Forensic Ctr. (disting. expert), Am. Med. Writers Assn., Masons, Shriners, Rho Chi. Office: Nutra-Sweet Co 1751 Lake Cook Rd Deerfield IL 60015

EDWARDS, SEBASTIAN, educator, economist; b. Santiago, Chile, Aug. 16, 1953; came to U.S., 1977; s. Hernan Edwards and Magdalena Figueroa; m. Alejandra Cox, Aug. 27, 1976; children: Magdalena, Benjamin, Victoria. Licenciado, Cath. U. Chile, 1975; MA, U. Chgo., 1978, PhD, 1981. Rsch. fellow Cath. U., Santiago, 1975-77; sr. economist Empresas BHC, Santiago, 1976-77; cons. World Bank, Washington, 1982—; assoc. Nat. Bur. Econ. Rsch., Cambridge, Mass., 1983—; prof. UCLA, 1981—; cons. World Bank, Washington, 1982—, IMF, 1984, 87, 88. Co-author: The Chilean Experiment, 1987; editor: Exchange Rates in LDC's, 1986, Econ. Adjustment and Exchange Rates in Developing Countries, 1986; co-editor Debt Adjustment and Recovery, 1989; author: Exchange Rate Misalignment, 1988, Real Exchange Rates, Devaluation and Adjustment, 1989; numerous articles. Mem. Am. Econ. Assn., Can. Econ. Assn. Office: UCLA Dept Econs 405 Hilgard Ave Los Angeles CA 90024

EDWARDS, THOMAS HENRY, JR., retired construction company executive; b. Montgomery, Ala., Feb. 16, 1918; s. Thomas Henry and Florence Virginia (Cameron) E.; m. Marilyn Rae Myers, Nov. 18, 1943; children: Thomas Henry III, Mary Lynn Edwards Angell. BS in Civil Engring., Auburn U., 1939; postgrad. U. Mich., 1940-41. Registered profl. engr., Ala.; registered land surveyor, Ala. San. engr. W.K. Kellogg Found., Battle Creek, Mich., 1939-40; estimator Algernon Blair Constrn. Co., Montgomery, 1946-47; engr. Tenn. Coal and Iron div. U.S. Steel Corp., Birmingham, Ala., 1947-53; project mgr. Sullivan, Long, Hagerty, Birmingham, 1953-73, v.p., 1973-83; ret., 1983. Served with U.S. Army, 1942-45. Mem. Sigma Nu. Republican. Methodist. Lodge: Lions. Home: 3628 Kingshill Rd Birmingham AL 35223

EDWARDS, THOMAS RAYMOND, brokerage company executive; b. Balt., Sept. 4, 1935; s. Robert Joseph and Anna Helen (Godesky) E.; m. Carol Ann Barton, Feb. 25, 1962; children: Thomas Raymond, Gregory Christopher, Erin Siobhan, Matthew Sean. BA in Mktg., San Jose State U., 1961, student, 1967-68; student, U. Ariz., 1964-65; MBA, Fresno State U., 1966. Buyer Topco Assocs. Inc., Phoenix, 1959-62; jr. broker J-B Distributing Co. Inc., Phoenix, 1962-64; sr. broker Allied Distbg. Co., Phoenix, 1968-74, Edwards Mktg. Inc., Yakima, Wash., 1974-75; pres., chief exec. officer Four Seasons Inc., Yakima, Wash., 1975—; advisor Calif. Lettuce Adv., Santa Maria, 1968; fin. advisor St. Pauls Parish Fin., Yakima, 1987—; cons. Gen. Mgmt. and Cons., Yakima, 1985—. Fund raiser St. Jude's Children's Hosp., 1969-71, Sundusters, 1977—, St. Elizabeth's Hosp. Found., 1985—, United Way, 1987. Mem. Produce Mktg. Assn., Rotary (fundraiser 1976-77, Paul Harris fellow). Republican. Roman Catholic. Home: 340 Linden Way Yakima WA 98902 Office: Four Seasons Inc 711 N First St Yakima WA 98901

EDWARDS, WILLIAM FOSTER, oil and gas company executive; b. N.Y.C., Mar. 9, 1946; s. William F. and Catherine (Eyring) E.; m. Kathleen Harrington, June 19, 1970; children: Rebecca, David, Jennifer, William. B.A. in Math, U. Utah, 1970; M.B.A., Northwestern U., 1972. C.P.A., Calif., Utah. Mem. staff Arthur Andersen & Co. (C.P.A.s), San Francisco, 1972-75; v.p., chief fin. officer Mountain Fuel Supply Co., Salt Lake City, 1975—. Mem. Am. Inst. C.P.A.s. Republican. Mormon. Home: 4093 Gary Rd Salt Lake City UT 84124 Office: 180th E 1st S Salt Lake City UT 84147

EDWARDS, WILLIAM HENRY, hotel executive; b. Muskegon, Mich., 1917; m. Peggy Nolan; children: William H. Jr., Bradley N. BA in Econs., U. Mich., 1939; LLD (hon.), Northwood Inst., 1982. Asst. mgr. Grand Hotel, Mackinac Island, Mich., 1937-39, William Penn Hotel, Pitts., 1939-42; sales mgr. Statler Hotel, Detroit, 1945-54; asst. gen. sales mgr. Hilton Hotels Corp., 1954-57; resident mgr. Statler Hilton Hotel, Detroit, 1957-61; sales mgr. Palmer House Co., Chgo., 1961-66, v.p., mgr., 1966-67, v.p., gen. mgr., 1967-68; v.p. supervising Chgo. div. (Palmer House and Conrad Hilton Hotel) Hilton Hotels Corp., 1968-70, sr. v.p., 1970-71, exec. v.p. ops., bd. dirs., exec. com., 1971-85, pres. Hilton Hotel div., 1978, vice chmn., 1985-88, mng. dir. Palmer House Co., 1971—, also dir., with bd. trustees, 1988—; pvt. sector rep. Travel & Tourism Govt. Affairs Policy Council; co-chmn. 1984 Olympics Hotel and Housing Adv. Commn.; charter mem. Calif. Tourism Corp., Calif. Tourism Commn.; co-chmn. Nat. Tourism Week; mem. travel and tourism adv. bd. U.S. Dept. Commerce. Past dir. Gt. Lakes Region Health and Edn. Found., Inc.; past bd. advisors Mercy Hosp. and Med. Ctr.; trustee, v.p. So. Calif. chpt. Nat. Multiple Sclerosis Soc.; former mem., trustee Ednl. Found. Am. Soc. Oral and Maxillofacial Surgeons. Served to lt. USNR, 1942-45, MTO. Recipient Silver Plate award Internat. Foodservice Mfrs. Assn., 1977, Gold Chain award Multi-Unit Food Service Operators, 1982, Am. Tourism award New Sch. Social Research, 1983; named Gallery of Distinction Northwood Inst., 1982, Hall of Leaders Conv. Liason Council, 1985, Hall of Leaders Travel Industry, Travel Leader of Yr. Nat. Tour Assn., 1986. Mem. Nat. Restaurant Assn. (past bd. dirs., now hon. trustee), Am. Hotel and Motel Assn. (cert., founder, past chmn. industry adv. council, energy task force, pres., chmn., 1986-87, past v.p. Hospitality, Lodging and Travel Research Found., Service award 1983), Nat. Inst. for Foodservice Industry (pres. 1977-79, hon., trustee, Diplomate award 1981), Travel Industry Assn. Am. (nat. chmn. 1982-84, bd. dirs., exec. com.), Internat. Soc. Hotel Assn. Execs. (Outstanding Leadership as chmn. industry adv. council, 1975), Internat. Hotel Sales Mgmt. Assn. (Hall of Fame award 1979), Calif. Roundtable, Theta Delta Chi. Lodge: Knight of Malta Am. (v.p. inter-continental region). Office: Hilton Hotels Corp 9336 Civic Center Dr Los Angeles CA 90010

EDWARDSON, JOHN ALBERT, JR., chemical company executive; b. Terre Haute, Ind., July 23, 1949; s. John Albert and Mildred Ruth (Anderson) E.; m. Catharine Orr, June 11, 1971; children: Laura, Anne, Shelley. BS in Indsl. Engring., Purdue U., 1971; MBA in Fin. and Internat. Bus., U. Chgo., 1972. Comml. banking officer First Bank—St. Paul, 1972-77; v.p., treas. Ferrell Cos. Inc., Kansas City, Mo., 1977-83, sr. v.p. fin. services group, 1983-85; exec. v.p. fin., chief fin. officer Northwest Airlines Inc. and NWA Inc., St. Paul, 1985-88; exec. v.p., chief fin. and adminstrv. officer Internat. Minerals and Chems. Corp., Northbrook, Ill., 1988—; bd. dirs. TGIFriday's Inc., Addison, Tex. Bd. Trustees Ravina Festival Assn., Highland Park, Ill. Methodist. Office: Internat Minerals & Chem Corp 2315 Sanders Rd Northbrook IL 60062

EDWIN, MARK CARY, insurance executive, consultant; b. Chgo., Mar. 8, 1956; s. Werner and Dagmar R. (Picard) E.; m. Cheryl Lynn Bess, Oct. 24, 1981. BS, Loyola U., Chgo., 1978; diploma, Life Underwriting Tng. Council, 1983. Ins. cons., pres. Mark C. Edwin and Assocs., Phoenix, 1980—. Mem. Million Dollar Round Table, Nat. Assn. Life Underwriters (Nat. Quality award 1985-88, Nat. Sales Achievement award 1985-88), Nat. Assn. Health Underwriters, Am. Council Ind. Life Underwriters (qualifying), Ariz. Assn. Life Underwriters, Ariz. Assn. Health Underwriters, Phoenix Assn. Health Underwriters, Greater Phoenix Assn. Life Underwriters, Loyola U. Alumni Assn. (Pres.' club), Ariz. C. of C., Scottsdale (Ariz.) C. of C., Mensa. Republican. Jewish. Lodges: Kiwanis, B'nai B'rith. Home: 7810 E Foxmore Ln Scottsdale AZ 85258-3427 Office: 7119 E Shea Blvd Suite 106-257 Scottsdale AZ 85254-6199

EFAW, CARY R., manufacturing company executive; b. Waynesburg, Pa., Dec. 26, 1949; s. William C. and Julia M. (Whitfield) E.; m. Kathleen E. Dunkle, July 21, 1973; children: Dawn, Heather, Nathan. BS in Acctg./Econs., Waynesburg Coll., 1975; MBA, Youngstown State U., 1988. Sr. acct. Ernst & Whinney, Pitts., 1975-79; staff acct. Equitable Resources, Pitts., 1979-81; sr. fin. analyst Joy Mfg. Co., Pitts., 1981-82; owner, cons. Efaw Enterprise, Pitts., 1982—; mgr. gen. acctg. Cooper Industries, Grove City, Pa., 1987—; bd. dirs., advisor 84 Electronics, Houston, Pa., 1980-87; cons. Hodor Assocs., Eighty-Four, Pa., 1979-85, Lindley Enterprise, Washington, Pa., 1981-85. Contbr. articles to profl. jours. Advisor, State Rep., Upper St. Clair, Pa., 1981-84; Sunday sch. tchr. Westminster Ch., Upper St. Clair, 1982-85; deacon Calvin Ch., Zelienople, Pa. Served with USMC, 1969-71. Named Competent Toastmaster, 1980. Mem. Assn. MBA Execs., Am. Legion, VFW, DAV (life), Nat. Assn. Accts. (assoc. dir. 1977-78), Alpha Kappa Psi. Presbyterian. Club: Steel Town Corvettes (treas. 1977-80). Lodge: Masons, Shriners. Home: 717 Hemlock Sq Zelienople PA 16063 Office: Efaw Enterprise PO Box 56 Houston PA 15342

EFFINGER, CHARLES HARVEY WILLIAMS, JR., banker; b. Balt., Dec. 28, 1935; s. Charles Harvey Williams and Ann E. E. BS, Loyola Coll., Balt., 1961; LLB, U. Balt., 1964; m. Frances Ward, Feb. 2, 1985; children—Brian Abbott, Peter Kirk. Adminstrv. asst. Merc. Safe Deposit & Trust Co., 1961-66; staff counsel, mortgage underwriter The Rouse Co./James W. Rouse & Co., Inc., Columbia, Md., 1966-73; mortgage officer, 2d v.p. The Equitable Trust Co., Balt., 1973-77, v.p. mortgage dept., 1977-82; v.p. mortgage dept. Wilmington Trust Co. (Del.), 1982-84; v.p. real estate dept. Union Nat. Bank of Pitts., 1984-86, sr. v.p., 1986-88, v.p. Dollar Bank, F.S.B., 1989—; instr. real estate fin. Towson (Md.) State U., 1979-82. Bd. dirs. Towson Recreation Coun., 1978-80; commr. Towson Recreation Baseball Program, 1977. With USMC, 1954-57. Named Disting. Grad., Balt. Jr. C. of C., 1972. Mem. Mortgage Bankers Assn. Am. (bus. devel. com.), Md. Mortgage Bankers Assn. (gov. 1982, pres. 1978-79), Am. Bankers Assn. Real Estate Fin. Sch. (adv. bd.), Pitts. Mortgage Bankers Assn., Robert Morris Assocs., Greater Balt. Bd. Realtors (comml. investment com. 1980-82), Washington Mortgage Bankers Assn. (bd. govs. 1979, 80), Nat. Assn. Indsl. and Office Parks. Republican. Episcopalian. Clubs: Univ., Whist (Wilmington); Chartiers Country (Pitts.). Office: 614 Euclid Ave Cleveland OH 44114

EFFREN, JOHN KENNETH, research and consulting firm executive, educator, researcher, consultant; b. Hackensack, N.J., Apr. 21, 1949; s. Mack and Evelyn (Taylor) E.; m. Alyce Brie Stein, Jan. 17, 1976 (div. Nov. 1981). B.S., Hobart and William Smith Colls., 1971; M.S., New Sch. for Social and Polit. Research, 1974; Ph.D., Hofstra U., Am. West U., 1982. Cons., researcher Manhattan Psychiat. Ctr., N.Y.C., 1974-75; staff psychologist Bergen Pines Hosp., Paramus, N.J., 1976-78; research psychologist Cornell-Northshore Univ. Hosp, Manhasset, N.Y., 1977-78; exec. dir. Biofeedback Inst. Fla., Ft. Lauderdale, 1979-80, Biofeedback Ctr. N.J., Middletown, 1980-81; pres., chmn. bd. Patient Referral Systems, N.Y.C., 1980—; pres. Profl. Practice Developers, N.Y.C., 1972—; adj. prof. Adelphi U., Garden City, N.Y., 1980—; spl. cons. AMA, ADA, APA, Washington, 1980—; nat. adviser weekly radio broadcasts Nat. Physicians Radio Network, Stamford, Conn., 1985—; lectr. in field. Author: A Psychobehavioral Approach to Marketing, 1985; author papers in practice mktg.; inventor computer-assisted neuropsychodiagnostic test device. Foster parent Internat. Foster Parents Plan, 1982—; active Students Against Drunk Driving, 1984—. Recipient various honors and citations, 1974—; subject of various publs. including N.Y. Times, 1982. Mem. Internat. Assn. Bus. Communicators, Assn. Media Psychology (charter), Am. Psychol. Assn., Eastern Psychol. Assn., Pub. Relations Soc. of Am. (accreditation 1987), Physicians for Social Responsibility. Office: Profl Practice Developers 1 Pennsylvania Pla Ste 100 New York NY 10119

EFRON, SAMUEL, lawyer; b. Lansford, Pa., May 6, 1915; s. Abraham and Rose (Kaduchin) E.; m. Hope Bachrach Newman, Apr. 5, 1941; children: Marc Fred, Eric Michael. B.A., Lehigh U., 1935; LL.B., Harvard U., 1938. Bar: Pa. 1938, D.C. 1949, N.Y. 1967. Atty. forms and regulations div., also registration div. SEC, 1939-40; Office Solicitor Dept. Labor, 1940-42; asst. chief real and personal property sect. Office Alien Property Custodian, 1942-43; chief debt claims sect., also asst. chief claims br. Office Alien Property, Dept. Justice, 1946-51; asst. gen. counsel internat. affairs Dept. Def., 1951-53, cons., 1953-54; partner firm Surrey, Karasik, Gould & Efron, Washington, 1954-61; exec. v.p. Parsons & Whittemore, Inc., N.Y.C., 1961-68; now partner Arent, Fox, Kintner, Plotkin & Kahn, Washington.; Mem. internat. relations vis. com. Lehigh U. Author: Creditors Claims Under the Trading with the Enemy Act, 1948, Foreign Taxes on United States Expenditures, 1954, Offshore Procurement and Industrial Mobilization, 1955, The Operation of Investment Incentive Laws with Emphasis on the U.S.A. and Mexico, 1977. Served to lt. USNR, 1943-46. Decorated Order of the Lion of Finland 1st class. Mem. Am., Fed., Inter-Am. bar assns., Am. Soc. Internat. Law, Assn. Bar City N.Y., Bar Assn. D.C., Phi Beta Kappa. Clubs: Army-Navy (Washington), Cosmos (Washington), Harvard, Internat. (Washington), Nat. Press (Washington), University (Washington), Fed. Bar (Washington); Harvard (N.Y.C.), Lehigh (N.Y.C., Washington), Lotos (N.Y.C.). Home: 3537 Ordway St NW Washington DC 20016 Office: 1050 Connecticut Ave NW Washington DC 20036

EGAN, CHARLES JOSEPH, JR., greeting card company executive, lawyer; b. Cambridge, Mass., Aug. 11, 1932; s. Charles Joseph and Alice Claire (Ball) E.; m. Mary Bowersox, Aug. 6, 1955 (div. Dec. 12, 1988); children: Timothy, Sean, Peter, James. AB, Harvard U., 1954; LLB, Columbia U., 1959. Bar: N.Y. 1960, Mo. 1973. Assoc. Donovan, Leisure, Newton & Irvine, N.Y.C., 1959-62; ptnr. Hall, McNicol, Marett & Hamilton, N.Y.C., 1962-68; v.p., gen. counsel Thomson & McKinnon Securities, N.Y.C., 1969-70, Hallmark Cards, Inc., Kansas City, Mo., 1972—; bd. dirs. Am. Multi Cinema, Inc., Kansas City, Mo. Trustee Notre Dame de Sion Sch., Kansas City, 1973-77, Pembroke Country Day Sch., Kansas City, 1976082; bd. dirs. Kansas City YMCA, 1976-80. Served to 1st lt. USMC, 1954-56. Mem. Mo. Bar Assn., Kansas City Lawyers Assn., Harvard Alumni Assn. (pres. 1989—),. Roman Catholic. Clubs: Harvard (N.Y.C.) (Boston) (Kansas City) (pres. 1985-87); Gipsy Trail (Carmel, N.Y.). Office: Hallmark Cards Inc 2501 McGee Trafficway Box 580 Kansas City MO 64108

EGE, HANS ALSNES, securities company executive; b. Haugesund, Norway, Jan. 31, 1924; came to U.S. 1953; naturalized, 1961; s. Sigvald Svendsen and Hilda Svendsen (Hansen) E.; m. Else Mathea Lindstrom, July 11, 1953; children: Elisabeth, Anne Christine. Bus. degree, Oslo Handelsgymnasium, 1946; student spl. bus. courses, City of London Coll., 1947; MBA, Drexel U., 1950. Analyst Alderson & Sessions, Mgmt. & Mktg. Cons., Phila., 1950-51; exec. asst. to U.S. ambassador to Norway Oslo, 1951-53; asst. to pres., asst. v.p. corp. sec. A.M. Kidder & Co., Inc., N.Y.C., 1953-64; stockbroker Reynolds Securities Inc., N.Y.C., 1964-65; mgr. Ridgewood (N.J.) Office, 1965-71; mgr. and resident officer 1971-77; resident v.p., mgr. Dean Witter Reynolds, Inc., Ridgewood, 1978-82, v.p. investments, 1983—; trustee, treasurer The Bay Found., N.Y.C., C. Michael Paul and Josephine Bay Paul Found., N.Y.C. Mem. Pres.'s club Drexel U. Served with Norwegian Underground, 1942-45. Decorated War Medal. Mem. Am. Scandinavian Found., Norwegian Am. C. of C., Tau Kappa Epsilon. Club: Joe Jefferson (pres. 1966-67) (Saddle River, N.J.), The Norwegian (N.Y.C.). Home: 877 Roslyn River Rd Ridgewood NJ 07450 Office: 1200 E Ridgewood Ave Ridgewood NJ 07450

EGEN, RICHARD BELL, diversified medical products and services company; b. Hastings, Nebr., July 28, 1938; s. Lothar Fredrick and Ruth Pauline (Ellis) E.; m. Donna Diane Lambert, Aug. 18, 1962; children: Richard Bell Jr., Donna Elizabeth. BS in Engring, Colo. Sch. Mines, 1960; MS, Yale U., 1965. Engr. Atlantic Refining, Dallas, 1960-62; Engr. Atlantic Richfield Co., 1963; cons. McKinsey & Co., Washington and Chgo., 1965-74; various mgmt. positions Baxter Travenol Labs., Inc., Deerfield, Ill., 1974—, dir. Can. ops., 1974-75, pres. med. products div., 1976-82, exec. v.p. Europe, 1982-83; pres. European div. Travenol Internat. Svcs., Inc., Deerfield, Ill., 1983-85, sr. v.p., 1985-88; pres., chief exec. officer Clintec Internat. Inc., Deerfield, Ill., 1988—. Bd. dirs. Lyric Opera of Chgo., 1987—. Served to lt. U.S. Army, 1961-62. Republican. Home: 1216 Chestnut Ave Wilmette IL 60091 Office: Clintec Internat Inc 1 Parkway N PO Box 784 Deerfield IL 60015

EGGAN, HUGH MELFORD, accountant; b. Velva, N.D., Feb. 24, 1930; s. Elmer M. and Esther (Guernsey) E.; B.A. magna cum laude, U. Wash., 1956; m. Dorothy L. Rowland, June 3, 1949; children—Kathleen Eggan Davis, Gary, Laurie Eggan Berry. Mem. staff Deloitte Haskins & Sells, Seattle, 1956-64, mem. staff, Washington, 1964-67, ptnr., 1967-68, with exec. office, N.Y.C., 1968-72, ptnr. in charge, Cleve., 1972-78, ptnr. in charge So. region, Atlanta, 1977-85, retired 1985. Former chmn. Pacific (Wash.) Town Planning Comm.; former officer Calvary Luth. Ch., Federal Way, Wash.; former bd. trustees Citizens League Cleve.; adminstrv. sec., council mem., pres. Emmanuel Luth. Ch., Washington; former bd. trustees Luth. Planning Council Met. Washington; treas., bd. dirs. D.C. Inst. Mental Hygiene, 3d St. Music Sch., N.Y.C.; former bd. dirs. Goodwill Industries, Atlanta. CPA, Wash., N.C. Mem. AICPA, Ga. Inst. CPA's, Phi Beta Kappa, Beta Alpha Psi. Clubs: Capital City, Atlanta City. (Atlanta), Pine Lake Country. Contbr. to Jour. Accountancy.

EGGERS, PAUL WALTER, lawyer; b. Seymour, Ind., Apr. 20, 1919; s. Ernest H. and Ottelia W. (Carre) E.; m. Frances Kramer, Dec. 29, 1946; 1 son, Steven Paul; m. Virginia McMillin, Feb. 23, 1974. BA, Valparaiso U., 1941; JD, U. Tex.-Austin, 1948. Bar: Tex. 1948. Pvt. practice law, Wichita Falls, Tex., 1948-52; ptnr. Eggers, Sherrill & Pace, Wichita Falls, 1952-69; gen. counsel U.S. Treasury Dept., Washington, 1969-70; pvt. practice law, Dallas, 1971-75; pres. Eggers & Wylie, P.C., Dallas, 1977-79, Eggers & Greene, P.C., Dallas, 1979—, Tower, Eggers and Greene, Cons., Inc., 1987—. Chmn. Wichita County Rep. Club; mem. Pres.'s Task Force Narcotics and Dangerous Drugs; Rep. candidate for gov. of Tex., 1968, 70; Treasury Dept. liaison with White House on Minority Affairs; trustee Episc. Ch. Bldg. Fund, 1972-84; sr. warden vestry St. Michael and All Angels Episc. Ch. of Dallas, 1983-85; dir. St. Michael and All Angels Found.; chancellor Episc. Diocese of Dallas, 1978—, pres. Corp., 1983—; pres. Texans' War on Drugs Found., 1987—. Maj. USAAF, World War II. Recipient Silver Anniversary All-Am. award Sports Illustrated, 1966, Layman of Yr. award Episc. Diocese of Dallas, 1968; Disting. Alumnus award Valparaiso U., 1978. Mem. ABA, Fed. Bar Assn., Am. Judicature Soc., Dallas Estate Planning Coun., Tex. Bar Assn., Vis. Nurse Assn. (bd. dirs. 1982—), Vis. Nurse Assn. Found. (bd. dirs. 1984—), Vis. Nurses Assn. Tex. (hon. life mem.), Dallas Bar Assn. Republican. Clubs: Brook Hollow Golf (Dallas); Met. (Washington), Capitol Hill (Washington). Office: 1999 Bryan St Ste 3220 Dallas TX 75201

EGGERT, ROBERT JOHN, SR., economist; b. Little Rock, Dec. 11, 1913; s. John and Eleanora (Fritz) Lapp; m. Elizabeth Bauer, Nov. 28, 1935; children: Robert John, Richard F., James E. BS, U. Ill., 1935, MS, 1936; candidate in philosophy, U. Minn., 1938; LHD (hon.), Ariz. State U., 1988. Research analyst Bur. Agrl. Econs., U.S. Dept. Agr., Urbana, Ill., 1935; prin. marketing specialist War Meat Bd., Chgo., 1943; research analyst U. Ill., 1935-36, U. Minn., 1936-38; asst. prof. econs. Kans. State Coll., 1938-41; asst. dir. marketing Am. Meat Inst., Chgo., 1941-43; economist, asso. dir. Am. Meat Inst., 1943-50; mgr. dept. marketing research Ford div. Ford Motor Co., Dearborn, Mich., 1951-53; mgr. program planning Ford div. Ford Motor Co., 1953-54, mgr. bus. research, 1954-57, mgr. marketing research marketing staff, 1957-61; mgr. marketing research Ford div. Ford Motor Co. (Ford div.), 1961-64, mgr. internat. marketing research marketing staff, 1964-65, mgr. overseas marketing research planning, 1965-66; mgr. marketing research Ford div. Ford Motor Co. (Lincoln-Mercury div.), 1966-67; dir. agribus. programs Mich. State U., 1967-68; staff v.p. econ. and marketing research RCA Corp., N.Y.C., 1968-76; pres., chief economist Eggert Econ. Enterprises, Inc., Sedona, Ariz., 1976—; lectr. marketing U. Chgo., 1947-49; adj. prof. bus. forecasting No. Ariz. U., 1976—; mem. econ. adv. bd. U.S. Dept. Commerce, 1969-71, mem. census adv. com., 1975-78; mem. panel econ. advisers Congl. Budget Office, 1975-76; interim dir. Econ. Outlook Ctr. Coll. Bus. Adminstrn. Ariz. State U., Tempe, 1985-86, cons., 1985—; mem. Econ. Estimates Commn. Ariz., 1979—. Contbr. articles to profl. lit.; editor: monthly Blue Chip Econ. Indicators, 1976—; exec. editor Ariz. Blue Chip, 1984—, Western Blue Chip Econ. Forecast, 1986—. Mem. Ariz. Econ. Estimates Commn., 1978—. Recipient Econ. Forecast award Chgo. chpt. Am. Statis. Assn., 1950, 60, 68; Seer of Yr. award Harvard Bus. Sch. Indsl. Econs., 1973. Mem. Council Internat. Marketing Research and Planning Dirs. (chmn. 1965-66), Am. Marketing Assn. (dir., v.p. 1949-50, pres. Chgo. chpt. 1947-48, v.p. marketing mgmt. div. 1972-73, nat. pres. 1974-75), Am. Statis. Assn. (chmn. bus. and econ. statistics sect. 1957—, pres. Chgo. chpt. 1948-49), Fed. Statistics Users Conf. (chmn. trustees 1960-61), Conf. Bus. Economists (chmn. 1973-74), Nat. Assn. Bus. Economists (council 1969-72), Ariz. Econ. Roundtable, Am. Econs. Assn., Phoenix Econ. Club (hon.), Am. Quarter Horse Assn. (dir. 1966-73), Alpha Zeta. Republican. Mem. Ch. of Red Rocks. Club: Poco Diablo Country. Office: Eggert Econ Enterprises Inc Sedonan-North Bldg Jordon Rd Ste B 450 PO Box 2243 Sedona AZ 86336

EGGLESTON, CHARLES HAGGETT, accountant, bank consultant; b. Bayshore, N.Y., Apr. 2, 1941; s. Oswald Derrick and Katherine Jennie (Haggett) E.; m. Janet Marie Barbieri, Sept. 8, 1973; children: Michael, Lisa. Student, Northwestern U., 1959-61; BA in Math. and Acctg., Kent State U., 1965; MBA in Fin., U. Mass., 1969. CPA, Mo. Staff acct. Rochester (N.Y.) Telephone Corp., 1964-67; asst. v.p. Security N.Y. State Corp., Rochester, 1969-73, First Empire State Corp., Buffalo, 1973-76; v.p. Centerre Bank, St. Louis, 1976-83; ptnr. Price Waterhouse, St. Louis, 1983—; mem. faculty Am. Inst. Banking, St. Louis, 1977-83, FDIC Sch. for Bank Examiners, Washington, 1979-85, Grad. Sch. Banking U. Wis., Madison, 1978—, Ill. Bankers Sch., Carbondale, 1979—. Contbr. articles to mags. and banking jours. Mem. Am. Inst. CPA's (ex-officio mem. banking com.), Beta Gamma Sigma, Phi Kappa Phi, Pi Mu Epsilon. Club: Mo. Athletic (St. Louis), Forest Hills Country. Office: Price Waterhouse One Boatmen's Plaza Saint Louis MO 63101

EGGLESTON, CLAUD HUNT, III, telecommunications executive; b. Buffalo, June 21, 1954; s. Claud Hunt Jr. and Arlene (Shank) E.; m. Ann Pendleton, Feb. 14, 1988; 1 child, Brett. BA, Union Coll., 1976; MS, Columbia U., 1979, MEd, 1979. Owner Checo Electronics, Schenectady, N.Y., 1974-78; bus. mgr. performing arts div. Smithsonian Inst., Washington, 1978-79; staff mgr. long lines AT&T, Washington, 1980-81; dist. mgr. strategy and product devel. Morristown, N.J., 1981-82; mgr. venture devel. consumer products Morristown, 1982-84, corp. mgr. bus. devel., 1984-85; gen. mgr. Asia Internat., Morristown, 1985-87; dir. ventures U.S. West Inc., Denver, 1987-88, dir. mergers and acquisitions, 1988—. Editor: Financing Independent Education, 1978. Recipient Young Entrepeneur award Schenectady C. of C., 1975; Klingenstein fellow Columbia U., 1977-78. Mem. Am. Mgmt. Assn., Met. Club (Denver). Home: 5429 E Mineral Circle Littleton CO 80122 Office: US West Inc 7800 E Orchard Rd Englewood CO 80111

EGGLESTON, DENNIS LEE, manufacturing company executive; b. Dayton, Aug. 9, 1941; s. Benjamin C. Eggleston and Beatrice R. (Seymour) Eggleston-Tibbetts; m. Dorothy J. Humphrey, Nov. 1, 1964 (div. 1973); children: Gregory, Jennifer; m. Gayle A. Johahneman, Nov. 1, 1975. Student, U. Ky., Lexington, 1959-60, No. Ky. U., 1977-82. Indsl. engr. Interlake, Inc., Newport, Ky., 1964-70, asst. to plant mgr., 1970-71, asst. div. supt., 1972-79, div. supt., 1980; plant indsl. engr. Interlake, Inc., Toledo, 1971-72; v.p. ops. Newport Steel Corp. (formerly Interlake, Inc.), 1981-87, pres., 1987—. Bd. dirs. YMCA, Covington, Ky., 1985—, United Appeal, Jr. Achievement. Mem. Iron and Steel Soc., Assn. Iron and Steel Engrs., Mgmt. Club (pres.). Republican. Presbyterian. Home: 122 W Lakeside Ave Lakeside Park KY 41072 Office: Newport Steel Corp 9th & Lowell Sts Newport KY 41072

EGGLESTON, RALPH G., JR., accountant; b. Elkhart, Ind., Dec. 26, 1946; s. Ralph and Gladys (McKinney) E.; m. Julia A. Connolly, Oct. 25, 1969; children: Patrick A., Brian P. BSBA, U. Mo., 1969. CPA, Ind. Staff acct. McGladrey, Hendrixson, South Bend, Ind., 1969-72; pvt. practice Ind., Ariz., 1972-87; asst. to v.p., treas. Skyline Corp., Elkhart, 1972-80; dir. acctg. PVB Inc./Taco Bell, Phoenix, 1984—; diamond/sapphire mgr. Forever Living Products, Tempe, Ariz., 1980—; owner Box-N-Mail, Mesa and Chandler, Ariz., 1986—; pres. Alpha Omega Acctg., Phoenix, 1988—. Active Big Bros./Big Sisters of Am., 1978-79. Fellow AICPA, Ind. Assn. CPAs. Republican. Baptist. Home: 5366 E Fairbrook Mesa AZ 85205 Office: Alpha Omega Acctg Inc 2901 W Indian School Phoenix AZ 85017

EGNER, VICTOR CARL, investment broker; b. Jamestown, N.D., Feb. 10, 1944; s. Carl Otto and Fern Henrietta (Barth) E.; B.A. in Psychology and Econs., Baylor U., Waco, Tex., 1967; m. Pamelle Augspurger, Sept. 27, 1968. With Sperry-Univac, Mpls., 1967-70, 71-78; mgr. computer software devel. div. Weismantal Assos., St. Paul, 1970-71; engaged in investing, 1978—; investment broker Dean Witter Reynolds, Las Vegas, Nev., 1981-86, v.p. investments Paine Webber. Served with Army N.G., 1967-73. Mem. Nat. Assn. Securities Dealers. Libertarian. Methodist. Club: Elks. Co-designer computer operating systems. Home: 5895 W Patrick Ln Las Vegas NV 89118 Office: 3800 Howard Hughes Pkwy Ste 1200 Las Vegas NV 89109

EGRY, ANNE MARIE, business educator; b. Blawnox, Pa., Apr. 10, 1938; d. Julius R. and Anna (Dolhi) E. B.S., U. Pitts., 1968, M.Ed., 1970, Ed.D., 1976. Sec., Blaw-Knox Co., Blawnox, Pa., 1956-68; bus. tcr. New Kensington Comml. Sch., Pa., 1968-69, Gateway High Sch., Monroeville, Pa., 1969-70; bus. tcr., curriculum specialist Pitts. Public Schs., 1970—. Tchr.'s aide Pitts. Civic Garden Ctr., 1985. Mem. Eastern Bus. Edn. Assn. (advt. chmn. 1979), Nat. Secs. Assn., Nat. Bus. Edn. Assn., Tri State Bus. Edn. Assn. (exhbns. chmn. 1974-84), Pa. Bus. Edn. Assn., Am. Edn. Research Assn., Internat. Word Processing Assn. (nat. task force on word processing 1979—; bd. dirs. 1980), Delta Pi Epsilon. Grantee Pa. State Dept. Edn., 1982, Allegheny Conf. Community Devel., 1983, 85. Democrat. Roman Catholic. Home: 108 Mattier Dr Pittsburgh PA 15238 Office: Brashear High Sch 590 Crane Ave Pittsburgh PA 15216

EHL, RONALD HARIS, manufacturing engineer; b. Santa Monica, Calif., July 21, 1933; s. Harris Lavictor and Irma Mary (Morton) E.; m. M. Shirley Sweeney, May 9, 1951 (dec. 1976), 1 child, Larry; m. Lonna C. Kaelin, Mar. 11, 1977; stepchildren: Scott, Amy. AA in Mech. Engring., El Camino Coll., 1966. Registered profl. engr., Calif. Tool maker, designer McDonnell-Douglas, Santa Monica, 1955-67; sr. toll engr. Boeing Aircraft, Evertt, Wash., 1967-70; value engr. Gen. Electric Corp., Cin., 1970-71; mfg. engr. Gen. Electric Corp., Louisville, 1971-76, advance quality engr., 1976-77, advance mfg. engr., 1977-80, program mgr. mfg., 1980-82; mgr., mfg. engring. Liebert Corp., Columbus, Ohio, 1982-88; mgr. mfg. engr. Emerson Computer Support, Santa Anna, Calif., 1988—; tech. cons. Hitachi, Japan, 1974, Emerson Computer Supt. Group, Calif., 1987—, Mexicali, Mex., 1988—. Chmn. bd. deacons Ind. Protestant Ch., Palms, Calif., 1957-60, dir. Christian edn., Hawthorne, Calif., 1965, 66, adult Christian dir., Bellevue, Wash., 1969. Mem. Soc. Mfg. Engrs., Del. Indsl. Coun. Republican. Home: 24852 Camberwell Laguna Hills CA 92653

EHLERS, LARRY LEE, engineer; b. Kansas City, Mo., Mar. 10, 1953; s. Rufus Arndt and Wanda Marie (Pickett) E.; m. Teresa Ann Gunter, Jan. 24, 1981; children: Megan Ann, Austin Lee. MS, Purdue U., 1976; BME, Gen. Motors Inst., 1977. Cert. plant engr.; lic. profl. engr., Kans. Environ. engr. Gen. Motors Corp., Kansas City, Kans., 1976-79; corp. plant engr. Bendix/King div. Allied-Signal, Inc., Olathe, Kans., 1979—. Mem. ASHRAE, Internat. Communications Assn. (voting), DBX Users Assn. (bd. dirs. 1985-88, pres. 1987-88), Assn. Energy Engrs., Am. Inst. Plant Engrs., MidAm. Telecommunications Assn., Midwestern Soc. Telephone Engrs., Internat. Teleconferencing Assn. Libertarian. Lutheran. Home: 11512 W 108th St Overland Park KS 66210 Office: Allied Signal Inc Bendix/King Div 400 N Rogers Rd Olathe KS 66062

EHLERS, MICHAEL GENE, lawyer, transportation company executive; b. Waterloo, Iowa, Sept. 7, 1951; s. Gene Merle and Dorothy JoAnn (Vint) E.; m. Marlena Kay Hammonds, June 2, 1984. BA, U. No. Iowa, 1973; JD, U. Iowa, 1977. Bar: Iowa 1977. Ops. mgr. Gen. Leaseways, Inc., Davenport, Iowa, 1977-78, v.p., gen. counsel, 1978-84; exec. v.p., gen. counsel Gen. Car and Leasing System, Inc., Davenport, 1984—. Mem. ABA. Clubs: Davenport, Crow Valley Golf (Davenport). Home: 6401 Utica Ridge Rd # 12 Davenport IA 52807 Office: Gen Car & Truck Leasing System Inc 450 W 76th St Davenport IA 52806

EHMANN, FRANK A., office products industry executive; b. Chgo., Dec. 23, 1933; s. Henry E. and Victoria (Hengler) E.; m. Mary C. Corcoran; children: Victoria, Jean, Nancy. BA, Northwestern U., 1955, MBA, 1971. With Am. Hosp. Supply Corp., Evanston, Ill., 1957-85, pres., 1971-73, corp. v.p., pres. dental and pharm. groups, 1973-74, corp. v.p., pres. hosp. group, 1974-78; exec. v.p., pres. hosp. and pharm. bus. Am. Hospital Supply Corp., Evanston, Ill., 1978-80; v.p. hosp. bus. Am. Hosp. Supply Corp., Evanston, Ill., 1980-85, also bd. dirs., 1983—; pres., chief operating officer Am. Hosp. Supply Corp., 1985; exec. v.p., co-chief operating officer Baxter-Travenol Labs., Inc., Deerfield, Ill., 1985-86, also corp. dir., 1985-86; pres., chief operating officer United Stationers, Inc., Des Plaines, Ill., 1987—; bd. dirs. St. Jude Med. Inc., St. Paul, Lyphomed Inc., Rosemont, Ill., Kinetic Systems Inc., San Antonio, SPX Corp. Bd. dirs. Glenwood (Ill.) Sch. for Boys, Highland Park (Ill.) Hosp. Served with USN, 1955-57. Clubs: Chgo., Commercial (Chgo.). Home: 864 Bryant Ave Winnetka IL 60093 Office: United Stationers Inc 2200 E Golf Rd Des Plaines IL 60016-1267

EHRAMJIAN, VARTKES HAGOP, manufacturing company financial executive; b. Nov. 2, 1932; came to U.S., 1959; s. Hagop and Naomi E.; m. Laura Lee Schmoker, June 9, 1962; children: James, Tamar, Alyce, Ricardo, Katie. BSBA, Ea. Mich. U., 1962; MBA, Ind. U., 1963. Sr. fin. analyst Ford Motor Co., 1963-68; mgr. internat. finance Cummins Engine Co., Columbus, Ind., 1968-70, regional mgr. S. Latin Am., Sao Paulo, Brazil, 1970-71, dir. Latin Am. ops., 1972, dir. internat. corp devel., 1972-75, asst. treas., internat., 1975-79; asst. treas. Bendix Corp., Southfield, Michg., 1979-83, Allied Signal Corp., Morristown, N.J., 1983-84; sr. v.p., chief fin. officer H.B. Fuller Co., St. Paul, 1984—; task force mem. U.S. C. of C., Washington; industry mem., coms. on Gen. Agreement on Tariffs and Trade (GATT) Dept. Commerce, Washington. Bd. dirs. H.B. Fuller Found., 1986—. Mem. Fin. Execs. Inst., Am. Mgmt. Assn. Club: Lafayette (Orono, Minn.). Office: H B Fuller Co 1200 W Country Rd E Arden Hills MN 55112

EHRLICH, GERALDINE ELIZABETH, food service management consultant; b. Phila., Nov. 28, 1939; d. Joseph Vincent and Agnes Barbara (Campbell) McKenna; m. S. Paul Ehrlich, Jr., June 20, 1959; children: Susan Patricia, Paula Jeanne, Jill Marie. BS, Drexel Inst. Tech., 1957—. Supervisory dietitian ARA Service Co., Phila. and San Francisco, 1959-65; dietary mgmt. cons. HEW, Washington, 1967-68; nutrition cons., hypertension research team U. Calif. Micronesia, 1970; regional sales dir. Marriott Corp., Bethesda, Md., 1976-78; dir. sales and profl. services Coll. and Health Care div. Macke Co., Cheverly, Md., 1978, gen. mgr., 1978-79; v.p. ops., div., 1979-80, pres. Health Care div., 1980-81; regional v.p. Custom Mgmt. Corp., Alexandria, Va., 1981-83, v.p. mktg., 1983-87; v.p. mktg. and health-care sales Morrison's Custom Mgmt., Mobile, Ala., 1987-88; internat. v.p. sales, ARA Services, Phila., 1988—; cons. mktg. The Green House, Tokyo, 1987—; chmn. bd. Mktg. Matrix, Falls Church, Va., 1984—. Mem. Health Systems Agy. No. Va., 1976-77; chmn. Health Care Adv. Bd. Fairfax County Va., 1973-77; vice chmn. Fairfax County Community Action Com., 1973-77; treas. Fairfax County Dem. Com., 1969-73; trustee Fairfax Hosp., 1973-77; bd. dirs. Tennis Patrons, Washington, 1984—. Mem. Internat. Women's Assn., Am. Mgmt. Assn., Nat. Assn. Female Execs., Roundtable for Women in Food Service, Soc. Mktg. Profls. Club: Internat. (Washington). Avocation: reading. Home: 6512 Lakeview Dr Falls Church VA 22041 Office: Morrison's Custom Mgmt 209 Madison St Ste 353 Alexandria VA 22314

EHRLICH, MEL, public relations executive; b. Phila., May 25, 1938; s. Charles and Elsie (Wax) E.; m. Eleanor Hilda Rosner, May 6, 1979. BA, U. Pa., 1958, MA, 1963; diploma, U. Oxford, Eng., 1962. Account exec. Zachary and Front, N.Y.C., 1981-82; account supr. Daniel J. Edelman Inc., N.Y.C., 1982-83, v.p., 1984-85, sr. v.p., 1985-86, exec. v.p., dep. gen. mgr., 1986-87; exec. v.p., unit mgr. med. communications Creamer Dickson Basford Inc., N.Y.C., 1987-88; exec. dir. Gross Townsend Frank Hoffman Inc., N.Y.C., 1989—; asst. adj. prof. Mgmt. Inst., NYU, 1988—; cons. in field. Mem. Pub. Rels. Soc. Am. (Silver Anvil awards 1986, 87), Am. Med. Writers Assn., Internat. Assn. Bus. Communicators. Democrat. Home: 30 Waterside Pla Apt 10F New York NY 10010 Office: Gross Townsend Frank Hoffman 114 Fifth Ave New York NY 10011

EHRLICH, MORTON, airline executive; b. N.Y.C., Dec. 1, 1934; s. Milton and Anne (Tannenbaum) E.; B.B.A. cum laude, City Coll. N.Y., 1960; Ph.D. in Economics (Ford Found. fellow), Brown U., 1965; m. Rosalind, Feb. 7, 1960; children—Bruce, Ellen, Wendy. Economist, Fed. Res. Bank of N.Y., 1965-67, Nat. Indsl. Conf. Bd., N.Y.C., 1967-68; v.p. Eastern Airlines, Miami, Fla., 1968-76, sr. v.p. planning, 1976-85; exec. v.p. Transworld Airlines, N.Y., 1985—, also bd. dirs.; bd. dirs. IBM World Trade Ams./Far East Corp. Trustee, U. Miami; bd. dirs. Nat. Bur. Econ. Research. Served with U.S. Army, 1953-56. Mem. Am. Econ. Assn., Nat. Assn. Bus. Economists, Econ. Soc. South Fla. (dir.), Downtown Econs. Club New York, U.S. C. of C. Author: Discretionary Income, 1967; A Weekly Index of Business Activity, 1967; U.S. Foreign Trade, 1968; Computer Application in the Allocation of Airline Resources, 1975; An Integrated System for Airline Planning and Management Information, 1977. Home: 7 High Point Circle Chappaqua NY 10514-2503 Office: TWA Inc 605 3rd Ave New York NY 10158

EHRNST, CRAIG FRANCIS, auditor; b. Flint, Mich., July 25, 1964; s. Harry Francis and Mary Grace (Christy) E. Student, U. Mich., Flint, 1982-84; BS in Bus., U. Mich., Ann Arbor, 1986; student, Oxford U., 1985. Dir. CFE Enterprises, Flint, 1980-86; controller, auditor Exxon Co. USA, Baytown, Tex., 1986—, sr. auditor, 1988-89; sr. fin. analyst, lead profit/loss coord. Exxon Co. USA, Houston, 1989—; cons. Chinquapin Sch., Highlands, Tex., 1987-88. Campaign staff coordinator United Way, Houston, 1987; safety team capt. Exxon Co. USA Team 2, Baytown, Tex., 1987-88; tutor Chinquapin Sch., 1987—; bd. dirs. Bus. Sch. Student Council, Ann Arbor, 1985-86, Mich. Student Assembly, Ann Arbor, 1986. Mem. Am. Mgmt. Assn., Global Blue Network Club (bd. dirs. Ann Arbor chpt. 1986—), Lakewood Yacht Club. Home: 6550 N Port Hwy Apt #414 Flint MI 48505-2353 Office: Exxon Co USA 800 Bell St Houston TX 77252-2180

EICHER, DAVID DICKINSON, computer company executive; b. Orange, Conn., Apr. 20, 1958; s. David Lee and Jean (Dickinson) E.; m. Janet McDermott, Nov. 15, 1980; children: Christopher, John. BA in Polit. Sci., Pa. State U., 1980; MBA in Mgmt. Info. Systems, Babson Coll., 1982. Analyst mgmt. info. systems Addressograph-Farrington, Inc., Randolph, Mass., 1982-84; mgr. bus. planning Prime Computer, Inc., Natick, Mass., 1984-86; sr. mgr. fin. planning Prime Computer, Inc., Natick, 1986—; Republican. Avocations: power boating, sports. Office: Prime Computer Inc 500 Old Connecticut Path Framington MA 01701

EICHLER, LOU KNOTT, small business owner; b. Duncan, Okla., Feb. 12, 1943; d. Lonnie Austin Knott and Lorine (Gibson) Porter; m. John Carlysle Eichler, Apr. 18, 1966; children: Don, David, Ken, Kathy, Debbie, Robbie, Judy, Jerry, Barbara, Reenie, Molly. Student, Famous Artists Sch., 1967-69; BS in Anthropology, Mid. Tenn. State U., 1982; postgrad., Okla. U., 1982-83, Oklahoma City U., 1987. Nurse's aide Lindley Hosp., Duncan, 1965; bus. mgr. Hilda Patterson's Sch. of Dance, Duncan, 1973; owner Jelke Signs, Duncan, 1983—; freelance comml. artist. Costume designer Lawton Civic Theatre, 1973; choreographer's aide Miss Charm Pageant, 1973. Republican. Episcopal. Office: Jelke Signs 506 W Elder Duncan OK 73533

EICHMAN, DALE BRUCE, certified financial planner, educator; b. L.A., Apr. 30, 1953; s. Paul Eugene and Daisy Mae (Boswell) E.; m. Claudia Jean Scheier, July 16, 1977; children: Christopher James, Nicholas Ryan, Brittany Sarah. Student, El Camino Coll., Torrance, Calif., 1971-73, Calif. State U., Long Beach, 1973-75; grad., Coll. for Fin. Planning, Denver, 1987. Certified Fin. Planner, 1987. Account exec. Kelley Clarke Co., South Pasadena, Calif., 1976-78; dist. agt. Prudential Ins. Co. Am., Torrance, 1978-80; dist. mgr. Fin. Network Investment Corp., Torrance, 1980—; instr. Loyola Marymount U., L.A., 1988—. Mem. Inst. Cert. Fin. Planners, Internat. Assn. for Fin. Planning, Torrance Jaycees (bd. dirs. 1984-85, treas. 1985). Republican. Office: Fin Network Investment Corp 970 W 190th St Ste 200 Torrance CA 90502

EICHORN, JOHN FREDERICK GERARD, JR., utility executive; b. Boston, Mar. 3, 1924; s. John Frederick Gerard and Hazel (Morris) E. B.S. in Mech. Engring, U. Maine, 1949; postgrad., Northeastern U., 1963-64. Registered profl. engr., Mass. With New Eng. Elec. System, various locations, 1949-71; v.p., regional exec. Mass. Electric div. New Eng. Electric System, North Andover, Mass., 1968-71; exec. v.p. Eastern Utilities Assos., Boston, 1971-72; pres., chief exec. officer Eastern Utilities Assos., 1972-85, chmn., chief exec. officer, 1985—, also trustee; dir. Montaup Electric Co., Somerset, Mass., 1971—, pres., 1972-85, chmn., 1986—; dir. EUA Service Corp., Boston, 1971—, pres., 1972-86, chmn., 1986—; dir. Blackstone Valley Electric Co., Lincoln, R.I., 1971—, chmn., 1975—; dir. Eastern Edison Co., Mass., 1971—, chmn., 1973—; dir. EUA Power Corp., Concord, N.H., 1986—, pres., 1986-87, chmn. 1987—; dir. EUA Cogenex Corp., Andover, Mass., 1987—, chmn., 1987—; dir. Yankee Atomic Power Co., Rowe, Mass., Conn. Yankee Atomic Power Co., Haddem Neck, Conn., Maine Yankee Atomic Power Co., Wiscasett, Vt. Yankee Nuclear Power Corp., Vernon. Served with AUS, 1942-45. Mem. Edison Electric Inst. (dir.), Electric Council New Eng. Club: Downtown (Boston). Office: Ea Utilities Assocs 1 Liberty Sq PO Box 2333 Boston MA 02107

EICHTEN, ROBERT WILLIAM, financial company executive; b. New Ulm, Minn., Feb. 24, 1957; s. Richard William and Lyla Mae (Kemske) E.; m. Sharon Lee Meis, May 21, 1983; children: Meredith Leigh, John Robert. BA, Coll. St. Thomas, St. Paul, 1979. CPA, Minn.; cert. fin. planner. Agt. IRS, Mpls., 1979-83; sr. tax. acct. McMichael & Assocs., Mpls., 1983-84; advanced fin. planning mgr. IDS Fin. Svcs., Mpls., 1984-85, mgr. fin. plannning design, 1985-87; mgr. new bus. devel. IDS Fin. Corp., Mpls., 1987—. Contbr. articles to profl. jours. Mem. AICPAs, Minn. Soc. CPAs (chmn. fin. planning com. 1987-88), Internat. Assn. for Fin. Planning, Inst. Cert. Fin. Planners. Office: IDS Fin Corp IDS Tower 10 Minneapolis MN 55440

EIGEL, ROBERT LOUIS, computer services company executive; b. St. Louis, Jan. 10, 1937; s. Edwin George and Catherine (Rohan) E.; m. Charlotte Ross, Aug. 31, 1968; children: Karen, Robert Jr., Deborah, William. BEE, St. Louis U., 1959; MS in Indsl. Engring., Ga. Inst. Tech., 1968. Program mgr. Cin. Electronics, 1982-84; v.p., gen. mgr. Dayton div. RJO Enterprises, Inc., Lanham, Md., 1984—. chmn. activities com. Alter High Sch. Edn. Commn., Kettering, Ohio, 1986—; mem. Rep. Bus. Com., Dayton, 1986. Served to col. USAF, 1959-82. Mem. Am. Legion, Am. Mgmt. Assn., Am. Inst. Aeronautics and Astronautics, Am. Def. Preparedness Assn., Inst. Indsl. Engrs. (sr.), Air Force Assn., Nat. Security Indsl. Assn. Roman Catholic. Home: 2111 Old Vienna Dr Dayton OH 45459 Office: RJO Enterprises Inc 101 Woodman Dr Dayton OH 45431

EIKREM, LYNWOOD OLAF, business executive; b. Lansing, Mich., June 11, 1919; s. Arthur Rudolph and Gatha (Zupp) E.; m. Margaret Rosemarie McDonough, July 13, 1946; children: Margaret, John, Marie, Jeanne. BS, Mich. State U., 1941; MS, MIT, 1948. Assoc. prof. chemistry La. Poly. Inst., 1946; tech. dir. Jarrell-Ash Co., Newtonville, Mass., 1949-53; project engr. Baird-Atomic, Cambridge, Mass., 1953-59; staff engr. Geophysics Corp. Am., Bedford, Mass., 1959-60; mgr. product devel. dept. David W. Mann Co. div. Geophysics Corp. Am., Lincoln, Mass., 1960-63, dir. mktg., Burlington, Mass., 1963-65; v.p. mktg. Applied Research Labs. subs. Bausch & Lomb Inc., Sunland, Calif., 1965-72; dir. mktg. Darling & Alsobrook, Los Angeles, 1972-75; prin. Darling, Paterson & Salzer, 1975-79; pres. Paterson & Co., 1979-81; chmn. Strategic Directions Internat., 1981—. Fellow Am. Inst. Chemists; mem. Optical Soc. Am., ASTM, N.Y. Acad. Scis., Sales and Mktg. Execs. Assn., VFW. Lodge: K.C. Home: 605 N Louise St #201 Glendale CA 91206 Office: Strategic Directions Internat 6242 Westchester Pkwy Suite 100 Los Angeles CA 90045

EINHORN, ERIC JOHN, advertising executive; b. Cape Town, South Africa, Dec. 27, 1948; came to U.S., 1980; s. Heinz Dieter and Elsabe Carmen (Kuys) E.; m. June Hume, Jan. 12, 1979; children: Ashley Frances, Nicholas Hume. BS with honors, U. Capetown. Trapeze artist European Circuses, Eng., France, Germany, Italy, Belgium, 1970-71; market research mgr. Metro Cash 'N Carry, South Africa, 1972-73; product mgr. Bristol Myers, South Africa, 1974-77; account supr. D'Arcy, McManus & Masius, South Africa, 1977-78; dir. client services Goodgoll, Said, Campbell, Ewald, South Africa, 1978-80; sr. v.p., mgmt. supr. Lowe Marschalk, N.Y.C., 1980-84, exec. v.p., 1984—. Episcopalian. Home: 19 Boulder Brook Rd Greenwich CT 06830 Office: Lowe Marschalk Inc 1345 Ave of the Americas New York NY 10105

EINHORN, STEPHEN EDWARD, merger and acquisition company executive, business consultant; b. Bklyn., June 25, 1943; s. Benjamin and Rosalind (Nuss) R.; m. Nancy Lore, May 22, 1965; children: David, Daniel. BA, Cornell U., 1964; postgrad., U. Pa., 1965-66; MS in Chem. Engring., Bklyn. Polytech. Inst., 1967. Lic. real estate broker, securities broker dealer. With Adelphi Industries, Carlstadt, N.J., 1964-74; gen. v.p. Adelphi Industries, Carlstadt, 1974-80; pres. Mertz, Einhorn & Assocs., Inc., Milw., 1980-87, Einhorn Assocs., Inc., Milw., 1987—; chmn. Creative Systems Engring., Inc., Janesville, 1988—; bd. dirs. Northern Labs., Inc., Manitowoc, Wis., 1986—; pres. Broker/Dealer, Inc., Milw., 1985—; speaker Nat. Paint and Coatings Assn., Chgo., 1988, Creative Svcs. Engring., 1988—. Author: If You Try to Please Everybody..., 1983, Employee Stock Option Plans, 1985; contbr. articles to prpfl. jours.; patentee on handling latex paint, 1978. Mem. Assn. for Corp. Growth in Wis., 1987—, Ind. Bus. Assn. of Wis., Madison, 1987—, chmn. privitization com. Mem. Cornell Club (pres. 1986—). Home: 8205 N River Rd River Hills WI 53217 Office: 2323 N Mayfair Rd Suite 490 Milwaukee WI 53226

EINIGER, ROGER W., brokerage house executive; b. N.Y.C., Nov. 18, 1947; s. Jack Herbert and Glory (Salinger) E.; m. Carol Blum, Dec. 21, 1969; 1 child, Joshua H. Office: Oppenheimer & Co Inc Oppenheimer Tower World Fin Ctr New York NY 10281

EISBERG, JAMES STEPHEN, corporate lawyer; b. N.Y.C., Dec. 5, 1938; s. Rand R. and Mona B. (Margolis) E.; m. Sarah Louise Lemire, Dec. 10, 1971; children: Andrew, Jean. BA, Bucknell U., 1960; LLB, Fordham U., 1965. Bar: N.Y. 1966. Assoc. Roth & Goodman, N.Y.C., 1966-69, Lans Feinberg & Cohen, N.Y.C., 1969-73; gen. counsel The Franklin Holding Corp., N.Y.C., 1974—. Home: 125 E 93d St New York NY 10128 Office: The Franklin Holding Corp 767 Fifth Ave New York NY 10153

EISELE, PATRICIA O'LEARY, shopping center executive; b. Kansas City, Mo., Aug. 31, 1935; d. George Sexton and Dorothy Madeline (Stubbs) O'Leary; student Sarachon Hooley Bus. Sch., 1954-55, Rockhurst Coll., 1982-83; cert. Internat. Council Shopping Centers Mktg. Inst., 1978; m. John G. Eisele, July 16, 1955; children: Kathleen, Janice, Melissa, Patricia, John. Mktg. dir. Ward Pkwy. Center, Kansas City, Mo., 1974-79, mgr., 1979-80; mktg. counselor John Knox Village, Lee's Summit, Mo., 1981-83; gen. mgr. Leavenworth (Kans.) Plaza Shopping Ctr., 1983—; bd. dirs. local merchant's assn., 1977-80. Bd. dirs. Arthritis Found., Kansas City, Mo., 1980-82; bd. dirs., sec. Mid-Winter Art Fair Assn., Kansas City, 1980-82; chairperson Leavenworth Conv. and Visitors Bur., 1987. Recipient award Heart Assn., 1979, 80, Easter Seal Soc., 1979, Muscular Dystrophy Assn., 1978, Ararat Shrine, 1980, Boy Scouts Am., 1979, 80, Athena award. Mem. Am. Bus. Women's Assn. (Named Bus. Woman of Yr. 1987), Leavenworth Area C. of C. (bd. dirs. 1986, 87, exec. com. 1986, 87), Women's C. of C., Chi Omega. Clubs: Altar Soc., Catholic Women's. Home: 2803 W 73d Terr Prairie Village KS 66208 Office: 3400 S 4th Trafficway Leavenworth KS 66048

EISELE, WILLIAM DAVID, insurance agency executive; b. Iron Mountain, Mich., July 31, 1927; s. David Christian and Muriel Elizabeth (Ockstadt) E.; B.S., U. Mich., 1950; m. Helen Jeanne Holmberg, Dec. 27, 1953; children—David, Meg. Ins. agt. Employers Mut. of Wausau, Milw., 1951, West Bend, Wis., 1952-53, Watertown, Wis., 1953-56, Orlando, Fla., 1957, Tampa, Fla., 1958; pres. William D. Eisele & Co., Clearwater, Fla., 1959—. Charter pres. Heritage Presbyn. Housing Project, 1971-72; town commr., Belleair Shore, Fla.; elder Presbyn. Ch. Recipient disting. alumni service award U. Mich., 1975. Mem. Fla. Assn. Ins. Agts., Clearwater-Largo-Dunedin Insurors (past pres.), U. Mich. Alumni Assn. (dir., v.p.). Clubs: Clearwater Rotary; U. Mich. (organizer, past pres. Pinellas County, Fla.). Office: 13080 S Belcher Rd Largo FL 34643

EISEN, HARVEY P., investment company executive; b. St. Louis, Aug. 18, 1942; s. Alex and Sarah (Cohen) E. BBA, U. Mo., 1964; MBA, St. Louis U., 1966. Research analyst Wertheim, N.Y.C., 1966-68; portfolio mgr. Shareholders Mgmt., Los Angeles, 1969-73; pres., portfolio mgr. Eisen Capital Mgmt., Los Angeles, 1974-83; pres., sr. investment officer Integrated Resources Asset Mgmt., N.Y.C., 1983—. Office: Integrated Resources Asset Mgmt 10 Union Sq E New York NY 10003

EISENBERG, DAVID HENRY, drug store executive; b. Washington, June 14, 1936; s. Sidney Bernard and Sylvia (Pressler) E.; m. Frances Heft, July 19, 1959; children: Richard Alan, Bonnie Jo. BS, U. Md., 1959. Chief operating officer Peoples Drug Stores, Inc., Alexandria, Va.; vice chmn. ASSC Chain Drug Store, N.Y. Vice chmn. Am. Friends Hebrew U., Jerusalem, 1985-87. Named Merchandiser of Yr. Chain Drug Store Rev., 1986; Chair in Pharmacy named in his honor Hebrew U., 1986. Mem. Nat. Assn. Chain Drug Stores (chmn. 1985). Republican. Jewish. Lodge: Masons. Office: Peoples Drug Stores Inc 6315 Bren Mar Dr Alexandria VA 22312

EISENBERG, LARRY H., academic administrator; b. Los Angeles, Feb. 29, 1952; s. Morris and Julia Miriam (Agronovitz) E.; m. Christine Marie Eidsor, May 30, 1974; 1 child, Eric Christopher. BS in Urban Studies, MIT, 1974; M in Pub. Affairs, LBJ Sch. Pub. Affairs, U. Tex., 1976. With Wis. Dept. of Adminstrn., Madison, 1976-88, dir. gen. services, 1983-85, dir. state purchasing, 1985-88; v.p. adminstrn. U. Wis. System, Madison, 1988—. Chmn., State Sr. Mgrs. Conf., Madison, 1986; mem. MIT Ednl. council, 1984—. Samuel Lunden grantee 1970; grad. fellow LBJ Sch. Pub. Affairs, 1974-75. Mem. Nat. Assn. State Gen. Service Officers, Nat. Assn. State Purchasing Ofcls. (research com. 1985-88). Jewish. Home: 33 Belmont Rd

Madison WI 53714 Office: U Wis System 1930 Monroe St Rm 703 Madison WI 53708

EISENBRAUN, DAL (IKE), insurance company executive; b. Tripp, S.D., June 29, 1935; s. Alvin H. and Bertha P. (Goldhammer) E.; m. Carol Van Ness, Apr. 1, 1956; children: Pamela K., Michael D. BS, S.D. State U., 1957, M.S., 1958. CLU, Chartered fin. cons. Coach Brookings (S.D.) High Sch., 1959-63; agt. State Farm Ins., Brookings, 1963-66; agy. tng. dir. State Farm Ins., Santa Ana, Calif., 1966-69; agy. mgr. State Farm Ins., San Bernadino, Calif., 1969-70; agy. dir. State Farm Ins., Costa Mesa, Calif., 1970-76; exec. asst. agy. State Farm Ins., Bloomington, Ill., 1976-79; dep. regional v.p. State Farm Ins., Marshall, Mich., 1979—. Bd. dirs. Calhoun County ARC. Served with U.S. Army, 1958-59. Mem. Nat. Assn. Life Underwriters, Gen. Agts. and Mgrs. Assn., Soc. CLU's Nat. Mgmt. Assn. (adv. bd.). Republican. Lutheran. Home: 131 Whisperwood Ln Battle Creek MI 49015 Office: 410 East Dr Marshall MI 49069

EISENMAN, DALE CARL, entrpreneur; b. Cleve., Mar. 22, 1949; m. Carol J. Eisenman; children: Dawn, Heather, Halle. AB, Kenyon Coll., 1971; JD, Cleve. State U., 1976. Bar: Ohio 1976. V.p., pilot Midwest Air Charter, Cleve., 1971-73; exec. v.p. Ross Corp., Cleve., 1973-74; corp. pilot M.J. Kelly Co., Cleve., 1973-74; aircraft salesman Midwest Aerostar, Elyria, Ohio, 1974-76; pvt. practice of law 1976-81; ind. business Cleve., 1976-82; pres. Zee Med. Service Inc., Columbus, Ohio, 1976—. Bd. dirs. Columbus ZooTrustees, 1986—. Office: Zee Med Svc Inc 4401 A Lyman Dr Hillard OH 43026

EISENSTADT, SAMUEL, investment company executive; b. N.Y.C., June 21, 1922; s. Abraham and Lena (Posner) E.; m. Edith Cohen, Nov. 8, 1947; children—Richard, Linda. B.B.A., CCNY, 1943. With Value Line Inc., N.Y.C., 1946—, sr. v.p., research chmn., dir., 1975—. Served with AUS, 1943-46, ETO. Mem. Am. Statis. Assn., N.Y. Soc. Security Analysts. Avocations: personal computers, painting. Home: 253-39 61st Ave Little Neck NY 11362 Office: Value Line Inc 711 3rd Ave New York NY 10017

EISENSTAT, ALBERT A., lawyer, corporate vice president; b. N.Y.C., July 20, 1930; m. Constance Kend; children: Michael, Melissa. BS in Econs., U. Pa., 1952; JD, NYU, 1960. Bar: N.Y. 1961. Co-founder United Data Ctrs., N.Y.C., 1967-74; v.p., gen. counsel Tymeshare, Cupertino, Calif., 1974-79; sr. v.p., gen. counsel Bradford Nat. Corp., N.Y.C., 1979-81, sr. v.p., 1981—; v.p., gen. counsel Apple Computer, Inc., Cupertino, 1981-85, also bd. dirs.; bd. dirs. Computer Task Group, Buffalo, Comml. Metals, Dallas. Served to lt. USAF, 1952-56, ETO. Office: Apple Computer Inc 20525 Mariana Ave Cupertino CA 95014

EISENZIMMER, BETTY WENNER, insurance agency executive; b. Twisp, Wash., July 25, 1939; d. Bren William and Julia Emogene (Salmon) Wenner; m. Erwin LeRoy Cook, June 19, 1955 (div. 1960); 1 child, Richard Jeffrey; m. Jerome Anthony Eisenzimmer, Feb. 18, 1966. Cert. in gen. ins. Ins. Inst. Am., 1981; cert. profl. ins. woman. Clk. typist MR Ins., Seattle, 1957-59; records clk. Assigned Risk Plan, Seattle, 1959-61; acct. asst. Robinson Jenner, Inc., Seattle, 1961-66; sec., acct. asst. Falkenberg & Co., Seattle, 1966-75, adminstrv. asst., 1975-77; ins. agt., corp. officer Service Ins. Inc., Seattle, 1975—; mem. adv. bd. Sch. Ins., Wash. State U. Coll. Bus., 1981—. Asst. editor Today's Ins. Woman, 1980-81. Exec. bd. Wash. chpt. Cystic Fibrosis Found., 1978-86, pres., 1983-85; mem. Wash. State Centennial Speakers' Bur., 1987—; mem. long range planning com. Cedar Cross United Meth. Ch., 1986-87, mem. worship com., 1988—. Recipient Disting. Service award Cystic Fibrosis Found., 1984; named Vol. of Yr., Wash. chpt. Cystic Fibrosis Found., 1980. Mem. Seattle C. of C., Ins. Women Puget Sound (pres. 1970-72, Ins. Woman of Yr. 1978, 81, Industry award 1984 Wash. State Communicate with confidence speakoff winner), Ins. Women's Assn. Seattle (chmn. 1992 conf., Ins. Woman of Yr. 1981), Nat. Assn. Ins. Women (nat. sec. 1976-77, regional dir. 1981-82, mem. exec. bd. 1976-77, 81-82, You Make the Difference award 1977, Regional IX Lace Speakoff winner 1983), Ind. Ins. Agts. and Brokers Wash. (edn. com. 1982-83), Ind. Ins. Agts. and Brokers King County (chmn. bylaws 1984-85), Profl. Ins. Agts. Wash. (edn. com. 1982-86, chmn. 1983-86), Wash. Ins. Council (mem. speakers bur. 1980—), Women's Bus. Exchange, Women's Profl. and Managerial Women's Network, Nat. Assn. Life Underwriters, Women Life Underwriters Conf. (nat. bd. dirs., region I dir. 1987-88), Acad. Producer Ins. Studies (fellow of acad.), Network of Exec. Women, Seattle Assn. Life Underwriters, Nat. Assn. Female Execs. Club: Toastmasters (pres. Wallingford chpt. 1986-87, ednl. v.p. 1987-88, dist. 2 area 5 gov. 1987-88, Gov.'s Honor Roll dist. 2 1987, NC div. Lt. Gov. 1988-89, dist. 2 area Gov. of Yr, 1988, able toastmaster silver 1988 and other awards and positions). Home: 8932 240th St SW Edmonds WA 98020 Office: Svc Ins Inc 332 Securities Bldg Seattle WA 98101

EISNER, JOEL WILLIAM, physician, health maintenance organization executive; b. Phila., Jan. 27, 1938; s. Jerome H. and Margaret (Hirsch) E.; m. Judith Asher, Mar. 31, 1968; children: Elana, Dina, Alyssa, Lauren. BA, U. Pa., 1959; MD, Albert Einstein Coll. Medicine, 1963. Diplomate Am. Bd. Internal Medicine, Am. Bd. Allergy and Clin. Immunology, Nat. Bd. Med. Examiners. Pres. PMA Med. Specialists, Phoenixville, Pa., 1969—; chmn. bd. Freedom Health Care, Inc., Wayne, Pa., 1969—; chief medicine Phoenixville Hosp., 1971—; clin. prof. medicine Temple U., Phila., 1986—. Contbr. articles to med. jours. Pres. B'nai Jacob Synagogue, Phoenixville, 1982-83. Maj. U.S. Army, 1967-69. Named Man of Yr., Jewish Nat. Fund, 1979. Fellow ACP, Am. Acad. Allergy and Immunology, Phila. Coll. Physicians; mem. AMA, Am. Soc. Internal Medicine, B'nai B'rith, Phi Beta Kappa. Office: Freedom Health Care Inc 150 Stratford Ave Wayne PA 19087

EISNER, MICHAEL DAMMANN, motion picture company executive; b. N.Y.C., Mar. 7, 1942; s. Lester and Margaret (Dammann) E.; m. Jane Breckenridge; children: Michael, Eric, Anders. BA, Denison U., 1964. Began career in programming dept. CBS; asst. to nat. programming dir. ABC, 1966-68, mgr. spls. and talent, dir. program devel.-East Coast, 1968-71, v.p. daytime programming, 1971-75, v.p. program planning and devel., 1975-76, sr. v.p. prime time prodn. and devel., 1976; pres., chief operating officer Paramount Pictures, 1976-84; chmn., chief exec. officer Walt Disney Co., Burbank, Calif., 1984—. Bd. dirs. Denison U., Calif. Inst. Arts, Am. Film Inst., Performing Arts Council Los Angeles Music Ctr. Office: Walt Disney Co 500 S Buena Vista St Burbank CA 91521

EISNER, ROBERT, economics educator; b. N.Y.C., Jan. 17, 1922; s. Harry and Mary (Goldberg) E.; m. Edith Avery Chelimer, June 30, 1946; children: Mary Eisner Eccles, Emily. B.S.S., CCNY, 1940; M.A., Columbia U., 1942; Ph.D., Johns Hopkins, 1951; postgrad., U. Paris, 1945-46. Economist, statistician U.S. Govt., 1941-42, 46-47; instr. to asst. prof. econs. U. Ill., 1950-52; from asst. prof. to prof. econs. Northwestern U., 1952—, William R. Kenan prof., 1974—, chmn. econs. dept., 1964-67, 74-76; also sr. research assoc. Nat. Bur. Econ. Research, 1969-78; econ. cons.; vis. disting. prof. SUNY-Binghamton, 1971; chmn. exec. com. Conf. Research in Income and Wealth, 1967-68; mem. Conf. Bd. Econ. Forum, 1974-80. Author: The Total Incomes Systems of Accounts, How Real is the Federal Deficit?, Factors in Business Investment; bd. editors Am. Econ. Review, 1966-68, Jour. Econ. Lit., 1983-88, Jour. Econ. Edn., 1981—, Rev. Income and Wealth, 1985—; assoc. editor: Rev. Econs. and Stats., 1973—; advisor bd. Jour. Econ. Perspectives, 1987—; contbr. articles to profl. jours. Mem. McGovern Econ. Adv. Group, 1971-72; trustee Roycemore Sch., Evanston, 1969-84. Served to capt. F.A., AUS, 1942-46. Guggenheim fellow, 1960; fellow Ctr. Advanced Study in Behavior Scis., 1968. Fellow Econometric Soc., Am. Acad. Arts and Scis.; mem. Am. Econ. Assn. (exec. com. 1971-73, v.p. 1977, pres. elect 1987, pres. 1988), Midwest Econ. Assn. (pres.-elect 1981-82, pres. 1982-83), Social Sci. Research Council (bd. dirs., exec. com. 1977-79), Phi Beta Kappa. Home: 800 Lincoln St Evanston IL 60201

EISSMANN, ROBERT FRED, manufacturing engineer; b. Bklyn., Jan. 17, 1924; s. Fred Arno and Katherine Elizabeth (Petersohn) E.; student Pratt Inst., 1942-43, 46; m. June I. Vreeland, Dec. 29, 1950; 1 son, Roy Norman. Wireman, Western Electric Co., Kearney, N.J., 1946-49; assembler Indsl. TV, Clifton, N.J., 1949-51; leadman Bogue Electric, Paterson, N.J., 1951-60, 65-68; wireman, engring. asst. Kearfott, Gen. Precion, West Paterson, N.J., 1960-65; assembler-wireman Henderson Industries, Fairfield, N.J., 1968-72; prodn. mgr. Mipco Inc., West Caldwell, N.J., 1972-80, plant mgr., Fairfield, N.J., 1980-84, product support mgr., 1984-85, value engr., 1985-86; advance product design engr., 1986-87, design engr. indsl., elec. products, Amerace Corp., 1987—; staff mem. Russellstoll div. Midland Ross Corp., Livingston, N.J., 1980-83. Mem. freight container standards com. Elec. Task Force. Served with Signal Corps, U.S. Army, 1943-46. Republican. Methodist. Office: 530 W Mt Pleasant Ave Livingston NJ 07039

EISSMANN, WALTER JAMES, weight loss franchise owner; b. Newark, N.J., Apr. 20, 1939; s. Walter Curt Eissmann and Alice Delice (Irving) Clark; m. Dorothea Ann Donaldson, June 1, 1963; children—Patricia Helene, Walter William. B.S. in Indsl. Engring., Rutgers U., 1962. Account mgr. Gen. Electric, Engelwood Cliffs, N.J., 1962-67; regional sales mgr. Tymshare, Engelwood Cliffs, 1968-71, Buffalo, N.Y., 1971-73, Washington, 1973-74, v.p. mktg. service div., Cupertino, Calif., 1974-79, div. v.p., Cupertino, 1980-84; sr. v.p. McDonnell Douglas Corp., Cupertino, 1984-86; gen. ptnr. Archer Assocs., 1985—; bd. dirs. NSF Corp., Nutri/System Franchisee Corp. Bd. dirs. Saratoga Little League, Calif., 1976-81, Saratoga Boosters, 1981-84; active Vienna Theatre Players, Va., 1973; mem. Church Men's Choir, Saratoga, 1980-82. Named to President's Club Tymshare, Golden Circle. Mem. Pi Tau Sigma. Republican. Office: Archer Assocs 1510 Arden Way Suite 300 Sacramento CA 95815

EISZNER, JAMES RICHARD, food products company executive; b. Chgo., Aug. 12, 1927; s. William Henry and Gertrude (Peifer) E.; m. Joyce Carolyn Holland, Oct. 14, 1950; children: James Richard, Timothy John. Student, Drake U., 1945; B.S., U. Ill., 1950; Ph.D., U. Chgo., 1952. Chemist Standard Oil Co. (Ind.), Whiting, 1952-54; market analyst Indoil Chem. Co., Chgo., 1954-57; dir. market devel. Amoco Chems. Co., Chgo., 1957-63; v.p. mktg. Ott Chem. Co., Muskegon, Mich., 1963-65; exec. v.p. Ott Chem. Co., 1965-66, pres., 1967-70; also dir.; sr. v.p. indsl. div. CPC Internat. Inc., Englewood Cliffs, N.J., 1970-71, pres., 1971-76, v.p. parent co., 1971-76, dir., 1975—, exec. v.p., chief adminstrv. officer, 1977-79, pres., 1979-88, chief operating officer, 1979-84, chief exec. officer, 1984—, chmn., 1987—; Bd. dirs. Grocery Mfrs. Am., Ams. Soc.; mem. Chgo. Bd. Trade, 1971-80. Bd. dirs. Muskegon Area Econ. Planning and Devel. Assn., 1967-70. Served with AUS, 1946-47. Mem. Comml. Devel. Assn., Corn Refiners Assn. (dir. 1971-83, chmn. bd. 1981-82). Republican. Presbyterian. Clubs: Econ. (N.Y.C.), Sky (N.Y.C.); Knickerbocker Country (Tenafly, N.J.). Office: CPC Internat Inc PO Box 8000 Englewood Cliffs NJ 07632

EITEN, GEOFFREY J(OEL), financial planner; b. Perth Amboy, N.J., Aug. 31, 1950; s. Joseph and Amy (Goldschmidt) E.; m. Diane Elizabeth Plank, May 16, 1987; 1 child, Elizabeth Rose. BBA, Babson Coll., 1972. Registered investment advisor; lic. life, accident and health underwriter, Mass. Rep. Buttonwood Securities, Boston, 1971-80, Spencer, Swain Co., Boston, 1980-85; pub., researcher Over-the-Counter Research Corp. (pub. OTC Growth Stock Watch newsletter), Brookline, Mass., 1977—; personal fin. planner IDS Am. Express, Boston, 1986—. Served with USNG, 1970-76. Mem. Internat. Assn. Fin. Planners. Office: OTC Rsch Corp 1864 Centre St #4 West Roxbury MA 02132

EKBERG, KENT F., information and communications executive, educator; b. Bklyn., Nov. 5, 1947; s. Arthur F. and June P. (Greco) E.; m. Theresa Ann Kelly (div. 1981). BA, Hofstra U., 1969; MA, NYU, 1971, postgrad., 1971-81, cert. in bus., 1981; advanced cert., NYU, N.Y.C., 1984. Grad. fellow, lectr. CUNY, 1972-78; vis. lectr. Stevens Inst., Hoboken, N.J., 1974-76; instr. Northeastern U., Boston, 1978-81; mktg. mgr. strategic planning, bus. devel. Sony Corp., Park Ridge, N.J., 1981-89; mgr. mktg. Grumman Corp., Woodbury, N.Y., 1989—; cons. Ford Found., Haverstraw, N.Y., 1974. Contbr. articles to profl. jours. Mem. Planning Forum, Internat. Soc. for Planning and Strategic Mgmt. Home: 28 Oak Rd New City NY 10956 Office: Grumman Corp 280 Crossways Park Dr Woodbury NY 11797

EKEDAHL, DAVID D., finance company executive; b. 1930. Vice chmn, dir. Gen. Electric Credit Auto Lease Co., Stamford, Conn.; formerly v.p. Gen. Electric Capital Corp., N.Y.C.; now sr. v.p. Gen. Electric Capital Corp. Office: GE Capital Corp 1600 Summer St Stamford CT 06905 *

EKERN, GEORGE PATRICK, lawyer; b. Mexico, Mo., June 12, 1931; s. Paul Chester and Sallie Mays (McCoy) E.; m. Anita Elizabeth Poynton, June 3, 1961; children—Stephen G., Nigel P., Adrienne E. BA, U. Mo., 1953, JD, 1958. Bar: Mo. 1958, N.Y. 1962. Assoc. Dewey, Ballantine, Bushby, Palmer & Wood, N.Y.C., 1960-68; asst. gen. atty. Cerro Corp., N.Y.C., 1968-71; asst. sec. Freeport Minerals Co., N.Y.C., 1971-75, assoc. gen. counsel, 1975-83; v.p. legal services Homequity, Inc., Wilton, Conn., 1984; sec., gen. counsel Handy & Harman, N.Y.C., 1984-87, v.p., sec. and gen. counsel, 1987—. Mem. Darien Bd. Edn., Conn., 1978-81. Fulbright scholar The Netherlands, 1955-56; fellow Rotary Internat., London, 1959-60. Mem. ABA, N.Y. State Bar Assn. (exec. com. corp. counsel sect. 1981—), Assn. of Bar of City of N.Y., Am. Soc. Corp. Secs., Phi Beta Kappa. Republican. Presbyterian. Office: Handy & Harman 850 3rd Ave New York NY 10022

EKLE, THOMAS CHARLES, manufacturing company executive; b. Austin, Minn., May 30, 1951; s. Charles Aden ND Carol (Mae) E.; m. Cheryl Diane DeBoer, Jan. 8, 1970 (div. Feb. 1985); children: Kristine, Ryan; m. Kathryn Jeanne Stanley, Oct. 19, 1985; 1 child, Lara. BA in Acctg., BA in Econs. magna cum laude, Luther Coll., 1973. CPA, Ill., Minn. Inexperienced auditor Arthur Andersen & Co., Chgo., 1973-74, experienced auditor, 1974-75, sr. auditor, 1975-76; mgr. corp. auditing Arthur Andersen & Co., Mpls., 1978-79, mgr. internal reporting, 1979-80; supr. corp. auditor Dayton Hudson Corp., Mpls., 1977-78; asst. controller AMI Industries, Colorado Springs, Colo., 1980-83, chief fin. officer, 1983—; corp. auditor Dayton Hudson Corp., Mpls., 1976-77. Mem. Am. Inst. CPA's, Omicron Delta Epsilon. Republican. Episcopalian. Office: AMI Industries Inc 3200 N Nevada Ave Colorado Springs CO 80907

EKROM, ROY H., electronic equipment company executive; b. 1929. AB, U. Wash., 1951. With Boeing Airplane Co., Seattle, 1952-59, AiResearch Mfg. Co. Ariz., Phoenix, 1959-81; v.p., mgr. Pneumatic Systems div. Garrett Corp., 1981-83; pres., chief exec. officer Ampex Corp., Redwood City, Calif., 1983-86, Garrett Corp., L.A., 1986-87; pres. Aircraft Equipment Co., Torrance, Calif., 1987—, Allied-Signal Aerospace Co., Morristown, N.J., 1987—. Office: Allied-Signal Aerospace Co 2525 W 190th St Torrance CA 90509

ELAM, ANDREW GREGORY, II, insurance company executive; b. Winchester, Va., Feb. 6, 1932; s. Andrew Gregory and Frances Clayton (Gold) E.; m. Rebecca Rhea Cole, Oct. 26, 1958; children: Andrew Gregory III, Philip Cole, Dawna Frances. AB, Presbyn. Coll., 1955. Adminstrv. asst. Citizen's and So. Nat. Bank, Columbia, S.C., 1955-56; nat. exec. dir. Pi Kappa Phi, Sumter, S.C., 1956-59; pres. Carolina Potato Co., Inc., West Columbia, S.C., 1959-61; mem. pub. relations staff Kendavis Industries Internat., Inc., Ft. Worth, 1961-63; dir. sales promotion Pioneer Am. Ins. Co., Ft. Worth, 1963-64, dir. pub. relations and sales promotion, 1964-66; asst. v.p., 1966-68, v.p., mem. exec. com., 1968-71, bd. dirs., 1970-71; v.p. pub. relations and sales promotion Gt. Am. Res. Ins. Co., 1972—, J. C. Penney Life Ins. Co., Dallas, 1972-82. Mem. pub. relations adv. council Am. Council of Life Ins., Washington, 1971—; mem. pub. relations com. Tex. Life Conv., 1970-82. Mem. public info. adv. com. Am. Cancer Soc., Tex. div., 1969-80, chmn., 1972-78, exec. com., bd. dirs., 1972-78; vice-chmn. pub. relations com. Tarrant County United Fund, 1967; campaign leader Community Pride Campaign Performing Arts, 1969; chmn. 50th Anniversary Million Dollar Fund Drive. Bd. dirs., treas., vice-chmn. Tarrant County unit Am. Cancer Soc., 1963-71, bd. dirs. Dallas County unit, 1972—, sec., 1977-78; bd. dirs. Ft. Worth Community Theatre, 1971-72, Baylor U. Med. Ctr. Found., Dallas, 1980—; mem. adv. bd. Sammons Cancer Ctr., Dallas, 1980—; deacon Presbyn. Ch., Dallas, 1966-68, ruling elder, 1969-71, 81-84; mem. adv. com. Dallas Conv. and Visitors Bur., 1987—; chmn. 50th Anniversary Million Dollar Fund Drive. Mem. Life Ins. Communicators Assn. (dir. communications workshop 1970-71, exec. com. 1973-74, chmn. So. Round Table 1972, chair ann. meeting arrangements com. 1986), Pub. Relations Soc. Am., Tex. Pub. Relations Assn. (bd. dirs. 1966), Indsl. Editors Ft. Worth (pres. 1968), Ft. Worth C. of C. (chmn. publ. com. 1970), Dallas Advt. League, Dallas Ins. Club, Meeting Planners Inst. (pres. Dallas chpt. 1980, internat. dir. 1981-83, 86-87, Dallas chpt. Planner of Yr. 1985-86, Internat. Planner of Yr. 1987), Dallas Conv. and Vis.s' Bur. (adv. com. 1987—), Soc. Preservation and Encouragement of Barbershop Quartet Singing in Am. (chpt. pres. 1978, 88—, Southwestern dist. Barbershopper of Yr. 1982, treas. Southwestern dist. 1983-85, exec. v.p. 1986-87, mem. internat. com. logopedics and services 1985—, pres. 1988—), Life Ins. Mktg. Research Assn. (mktg. and communications com. 1985, vice chmn. 1986-87). Presbyterian. Home: 7730 Chattington St Dallas TX 75248 Office: 2020 Live Oak Dallas TX 75221

EL-BATRAWI, RAMY YOUSSEF, business owner; b. Geneva, Switzerland, May 23, 1961; s. Youssef Abdle-Rahman and Sekina Hamed (Zakie) El-B.; m. Maisa El-Mougi, May 7, 1981 (div. Mar. 1984). Grad. high sch., Montreal, Que., Can. Body shop owner, Tampa, Fla., 1977-79; owner Multiple Goals, Tampa, 1979-83, Zayre Key Ctr., Tampa, 1983-84, Sunray Vans, Tampa, 1984—; owner, founder Home Soda Fountains of Am. and E.P. Corp., Tampa, 1986—; owner Nationwide Van Ctr., 1987—, Nationwide Life Ins., 1987—; real estate investor. Office: Sunray Vans 4121 W Hillsborough Ave Tampa FL 33614

ELBERRY, ZAINAB ABDELHALIEM, insurance company executive; b. Alexandria, Egypt, Sept. 30, 1948; came to U.S., 1973; d. Abelhaliem Elberry and Nazieha Ahmed (Ezzat) E.; m. Mohammed Nour Naciri, Aug. 7, 1975; 1 child by previous marriage, Nadeem A.S. BA, Ain Shams U., Cairo, 1971; MA, Am. U., Cairo, 1975. Cataloger Vanderbilt Joint U. Librs., Nashville, 1976-77; sales rep. Equitable Life Assurance Soc., 1977-80; with Met. Life Ins., Nashville, 1980—, account rep., 1981—, mgr., 1984; mem. adv. bd. Parkview Surgery Ctr., 1983-84. Chmn. Com. Nashville Internat. Cultural Heritage, 1983—, also bd. dirs.; chmn. Internat. Women Nashville Fair, 1977-78; bd. dirs. YWCA. Recipient Spl. Contbn. award U.S. Coun. Internat. Disabled Persons, 1981. Mem. Nat. Assn. Life Underwriters, Nat. Assn. Profl. Saleswomen (Recognition award 1986), Gen. Agy. Mgrs. Assn., Altrusa Club. Islam. Home: 1815 Wedgewood Ave Nashville TN 37212

ELBERSON, ELWOOD L., food company executive; b. Ft. Wayne, Ind., May 30, 1918; s. Carl L. and Selma (Strasser) E.; m. Jean D. Pressler, Apr. 28, 1938; children: Tom L., Terry S., Karen Elberson Tubbs, Carol Elberson Sutherland, Michael D., Mary J. Elberson Hetz. Student, Ind. U. Extension Sch., 1936-40. Mem. sales staff Kuhner Packing Co., Ft. Wayne, 1936-43; mem. gen. acctg. dept. Gen. Electric Co., Ft. Wayne, 1943-44; sec.-treas. Dinner Bell Foods Inc., Defiance, Ohio, 1944-60, exec. v.p., 1960-68, pres., 1968—, chief exec. officer, 1968—, also chmn., dir.; dir. Browns Baker, State Bank & Trust Co., Toledo Edison Co., Bettcher Industries. Councilman City of Defiance, 1954-56; trustee Defiance Coll.; pres. bd. dirs. United Fund; bd. dirs. Defiance Hosp.; chmn. bd. 4 County Tech. Sch., Ohio. Mem. Am. Meat Inst. (bd. dirs. 1964—), Defiance C. of C. (bd. dirs. 1956-59, pres. 1958). Office: Dinner Bell Foods W High St PO Drawer 388 Defiance OH 43512

ELBERSON, ROBERT EVANS, food industry executive; b. Winston-Salem, N.C., Nov. 9, 1928; children: Nancy Ann, Charles Evans II. Grad., Choate Sch., 1946; BS in Engring, Princeton U., 1950; MBA, Harvard U., 1952. Mgmt. trainee Hanes Hosiery Mills Co., Winston-Salem, 1954-56; office mgr. Hanes Hosiery Mills Co., 1956-62, sec., 1959-62, v.p. mfg., 1962-65, mem. exec. com., dir., 1963-65; v.p. planning Hanes Corp. Hanes Hosiery Mills Co. (merger Hanes Hosiery Mills Co. and P.H. Hanes Knitting Co.), 1965-68, pres. hosiery div., v.p. corp., 1968-72, pres., chief exec. officer, 1972-79, dir., 1972-79; dir. Sara Lee Corp. (formerly Consol. Foods Corp.), 1979—, exec. v.p., 1979-82, vice chmn., 1982-83, pres., chief operating officer, 1983-86, vice chmn., 1986—; bd. dirs. W.W. Grainger Co., Skokie, Ill., Chgo., Sonoco Products Co., Hartsville, S.C. Bd. visitors Babcock Grad. Sch. Mgmt., Wake Forest U., 1977-83; trustee Salem Acad. and Coll., Winston-Salem, 1980—, Mus. Sci. and Industry, Chgo., 1984—. Lt. USAF, 1952-54. Office: Sara Lee Corp 3 First National Pla Chicago IL 60602

ELBERT, CARLA M., financial executive; b. Phoenix, Jan. 18, 1958; d. Leo John and Lucille Dora (Lindvig) E. BBA, U. Washington, 1979. Various mgmt. positions PACCAR, Inc., Bellevue, Wash., 1979-80; fin. rep. PACCAR, Inc. Fin. Corp., Dallas, 1980-82, asst. regional mgr., 1982-84; cash mgr. PACCAR, Inc., Bellevue, 1984-87, mgr. treasury ops., 1987-88, dir. treasury ops., 1988—; chmn. PACCAR Employees Polit. Action Com., Seattle, 1985-87, PACCAR U.S. Savs. Bond Campaign, Seattle, 1988—. Mem. allocations bd. United Way King County, Seattle, 1986-87; chmn. Seattle Art Mus. Met. Guild, 1987—. Mem. Northwest Cash Mgmt. Assn. (v.p., treas. 1986), Western Pension Conf. Republican. Roman Catholic. Club: Seattle Athletic. Home: 150 Melrose Ave E #404 Seattle WA 98102 Office: PACCAR Inc 777 - 106th Ave NE Bellevue WA 98004

ELBERT, JOANNA, real estate executive; b. Chgo.; d. Joseph and Mary (Alesia) Germano; m. Phillip Myron Elbert (div. 1977); children—Kimberly, Scott, Keith, Lynn, Phillip. B.S. in Journalism, U. Ill., 1951. Personnel mgr. Adminstrv. Offices, Jewel-Osco Co., Inc., Melrose Park, Ill., 1962-67; personnel adminstr. Anocut Engring. Co., Chgo., 1967-69; pres. Joanna Elbert, Inc., real estate sales, Houston, 1978—. Active Houston Symphony League. Contbr. poetry to various quars. and anthologies including Indigo, Poetry Today, Invictus, Am. Poet, N.Am. Mentor, Driftwood East. Republican. Roman Catholic. Club: Multi-Million. Office: Joanna Elbert Inc 1880 Dairy Ashford Suite 112 Houston TX 77077

ELBING, STEVEN RAY, marketing executive; b. Lansing, Mich., June 8, 1954; s. Raymond Henry and Lillian (Borst) E.; m. Susan Irene Johnson; children: Dustin, Ryan, Jessica. BS, U. Wis., 1976. Med. rep. Pfizer Labs., N.Y.C., 1976-78; sales rep. Johnson Graphics, Dubuque, Iowa, 1978-81; sales and mktg. mgr. Castle-Pierce Printing Co., Oshkosh, Wis., 1981-85; v.p. mktg. RPM Internat., Inc., Oshkosh, 1985—; pres. Acme Press, Inc., Appleton, Wis., 1985—; v.p. Svc. LithoPrint, Inc., Appleton, 1985—. Mem. Sales and Mktg. Execs. (bd. dirs. 1985—). Republican. Lutheran. Home: 1172 Shady Spring Ct Neenah WI 54956 Office: Svc LithoPrint Inc 50 W Fernau Oshkosh WI 54902

ELBRICK, ALFRED JOHNSON, investment banker, managing director; b. Norfolk, Va., Nov. 12, 1938; s. Charles Burke and Elvira Lindsay (Johnson) E.; m. Fern Bendall, Nov. 17, 1967; children: Tristan, Sophie, Alexia, Xanthe. BA, Georgetown U., 1960. Mng. dir. Alex Brown & Sons, Balt., 1978-85; head internat. dept. Alex Brown & Sons, London, 1985—. Capt. USMC, 1960-63. Mem. Met. Club, Chevy Chase Club (Washington). Home: Ardleigh Pk, Colchester EC2, England Office: Alex Brown & Sons, 1 Founders Ct, London England also: 135 E Baltimore St Baltimore MD 21202

ELDER, KATHERINE KERNS, real estate development company executive; b. East Orange, N.J., June 12, 1943; d. Robert Delano and Katherine (Kerns) E.; married July 10, 1965 (div. July 1978). BA, Syracuse U., 1965. Pres. Katherine Napper Assocs., Albany, N.Y., 1968-73, retail mktg. cons., 1978-85; regional mktg. dir. Homart Devel. Co., Chgo., 1973-78; leasing agt. Kaplan Group, Boston, 1983-86; leasing dir. Kravco Co., Phila., 1986—. Home: 234 Goddard Blvd King of Prussia PA 19406

ELERS, KARL EMERSON, mining company executive; b. Chgo., Sept. 26, 1938; s. Karl Alexander and Harriet (Emerson) E.; m. Sandra Tanner, June 8, 1962; children: Karl Frederick, Louisa Lee. BS in Geol. Engring., U. Ariz., 1960, BS in Mining Engring., 1961, hon. degree in geol. engring., 1974; postgrad. program for mgmt. devel., Harvard U., 1969. Mining engr. Duval Corp., Carlsbad, N.Mex., 1962-68, resident mgr., 1970-74; resident mgr. Duval Corp., Orchard, Tex., 1968-70; mgr. devel. Duval Corp., Tucson, 1975-81, v.p. devel., prodn., 1982-84; sr. v.p. ops. Pennzoil Sulphur Co., Carlsbad, 1985; mng. dir. Western Ag-Minerals Co., Houston, 1985-87; exec. v.p. Battle Mountain Gold Co., Houston, 1987-88, pres., chief oper. officer, 1988—, also bd. dirs.; bd. dirs. Equity Preservation Corp., Vancouver, B.C., Can., Nexus Resources, Vancouver. Mem. AIME. Home: 9331 Oakford Ct Houston TX 77024 Office: Battle Mountain Gold 333 Clay 42d Fl Houston TX 77002

EL-HAGE, NABIL NAZIH, financial company executive; b. Zhgarta, Lebanon, Sept. 2, 1958; came to U.S., 1975; s. Nazih Khalil and Odette Toufic (Melhem) El-H. BEE, Yale U., 1980; MBA with high distinction, Harvard U., 1984. Registered profl. engr. Mgmt. cons. McKinsey & Co., N.Y. and Brussels, 1980-82; fin. instr. Harvard U., Boston, 1984-85; venture investor TA Assocs., Boston, 1985-88; pres. Westwood Fin. Inc., Boston, 1988—; exec. v.p. Westwood Group, Inc., Boston, 1988—; bd. dirs. Intelli-call, Inc., Dallas. Baker scholar Harvard U., 1984. Fellow Yale Sci. and Engring., Tau Beta Pi (treas. 1979-80). Mem. Maronite Christian Ch. Club: Yale of N.Y.C. Home: 153 North Ave Weston MA 02193 Office: Westwood Fin Inc 855 Boylston St Boston MA 02116

ELICKER, GORDON LEONARD, lawyer; b. Cleve., May 27, 1940. BA in Math., U. Mich., 1962, JD, 1965; postdoctoral, U. Aix-Marseille, Aix-En Provence, France, 1965-66. Bar: Mich. 1967, N.Y. 1968, U.S. Dist. Ct. (so. dist.) N.Y. 1973. Stagiaire EEC, Brussels, 1966-67; assoc. Shearman & Sterling, N.Y.C., 1967-77, ptnr., 1977—; speaker in field. Contbr. articles to profl. jours. Mem. legal com. U.S.-U.S.S.R. Trade and Econ. Council, N.Y.C., 1978—; chmn. legis. com. N.Y. Dist. Export Council, N.Y.C., 1980-86; mem. Dem. Town Com., New Canaan, 1985-87; mem. bd. edn., New Canaan, Conn. Fulbright scholar, 1965. Mem. ABA (middle east and Soviet law coms.), Internat. Bar Assn., Assn. of Bar of City of N.Y. Democrat. Office: Shearman & Sterling 599 Lexington Ave New York NY 10022

ELIEFF, LEWIS STEVEN, stockbroker; b. Sofia, Bulgaria, Aug. 2, 1929; s. Steven and Vera (Svetcoff) E.; B.B.A., U. Mich., 1953, M.B.A., 1954; m. Evanka Brown, May 25, 1958; children—Nancy Ann, Robert and Richard (twins). Statistician, tax acct. Gen. Motors Corp., Flint, Mich., 1954-60; stockbroker Roney & Co., Flint, 1960-73, ltd. ptnr., 1973-79, gen. ptnr., 1979—, writer weekly stock market column Grand Blanc (Mich.) News; tchr. stock market curriculum Flint Public Schs., 1960-68, Genesee County Community Coll., 1968-73, U. Mich. Extension and Grad. Study Center, Flint Campus. Mem. Grand Blanc Twp. Econ. Devel. Commn.; mem. regents-alumni scholarship com. U. Mich., 1977—. Served with AUS, 1954-56. Mem. U. Mich. Alumni Club and Assn. Clubs: Genesee Valley Rotary, University (Flint). Home: 6612 Kings Pointe Grand Blanc MI 48439 Office: 3487 S Linden Rd Flint MI 48507

ELION, HERBERT A., optoelectronics company executive, physicist; b. N.Y.C., Oct. 16, 1923; s. Robert and Bertha (Kahn) E.; B.S. in Mech. Engring., CCNY, 1945; M.S., Bklyn. Poly. Inst., 1949, grad. in physics, 1954; PhD (hon) Hamilton State U., 1973; postgrad. Cambridge U., Eng., U. Bordeaux, France, Pa. State U., Rutgers U., Northeastern U.; MA U. Calif. Santa Barbara, San Francisco & Davis, Calif. Registered profl. engr., Mass.; Pa., N.Y. Group leader RCA, Camden, N.J., 1957-59; pres. Elion Instruments, Inc., Burlington, N.J., 1959-64; assoc. dir. space sci. GCA Corp., Bedford, Mass., 1965-67; mng. dir. electro-optics Arthur D. Little Inc., Cambridge, Mass., 1967-79; pres., chief exec. officer Internat. Communications and Energy, Inc., Framingham, Mass., 1979—; pres. Aetna Telecommunications Cons., Centerville, Mass., 1981-85, also ptnr., Hartford, Conn.; pres., chief exec. officer Internat. Optical Telecommunications, Mill Valley, Calif., 1981—; co-founder Kristallchemie M & Elion GmbH, Meudt, Fed. Republic Germany, 1961-64; cons. on data communications Exec. Office of Pres., Washington, 1978-79; cons. Ministry Internat. Trade and Industry, Tokyo, 1975-88; chmn. internat. conf. European Electro-optics Conf., Heeze, The Netherlands, 1972-78; internat. lectr. in field. Author, editor 27 books, including 11 on lightwave info. networks. Several Japanese and internat. world records in geothermal energy devel. Contbr. articles to profl. jours. Patentee in field. Pres. Elion Found., Princeton, N.J., 1960-67; founder Rainbow's End Camp, Ashby, Mass., 1960; elder Unitarian Ch., Princeton, 1963-64. Served with USN, 1944-46. Decorated Chevalier du Tastevin (France); recipient Presdl. awards Arthur D. Little Inc. Fellow Am. Phys. Soc.; mem. IEEE ((life mem., sr.), Am. Phys. Soc., Optical Soc. Am., Soc. Photo Instrumentation Engrs., Sigma Xi, Epsilon Nu Gamma. Office: 18 E Blithedale Ave Ste 23 Mill Valley CA 94941 also: 900 Larkspur Landing Circle Ste 230 Larkspur CA 94934

ELISH, HERBERT, manufacturing company executive; b. Bklyn., 1933; married. Student, Williams Coll.; LLB, Harvard U., 1957. Formerly commr. sanitation City of New York; then v.p. Citibank; then exec. dir. Mcpl. Assistance Corp., N.Y.C.; then v.p. Internat. Paper Co., then sr. v.p. adminstrn.; then sr. v.p. Dreyfus Corp.; with Weirton Steel Corp., now chmn., pres., chief exec. officer, 1987—, also bd. dirs., 1987—. Office: Weirton Steel 400 Three Springs Dr Weirton WV 26062 *

ELISHA, WALTER Y., textile manufacturing company executive; b. 1932; married. Student, Wabash (Ind.) Coll., Harvard U. Sch. Bus. Vice chmn. bd., dir. Jewel Cos., 1965-80; chmn., chief exec. officer Springs Industries Inc., Ft. Mill, S.C., 1980—, also bd. dirs. Office: Springs Industries Inc 205 N White St PO Box 70 Fort Mill SC 29715 *

ELKAN, HAROLD STANLEY, sports arena executive, real estate company executive; b. St. Louis, Jan. 4, 1943; s. Siegfried and Mae (Ofstein) E.; m. Sharon Rehg (div. Apr. 1986); children: Bradley, Andrew. Student, Washington U., St. Louis, 1961-65, U. Pa., 1976. Engring. draftsman KSH, Inc., St. Louis, 1963-65; mfr.'s rep. Phelan-Tramelli, Inc., St. Louis, 1965-68; pres., founder Elkan Industries, Inc., St. Louis, 1967-68; prin. Elkan & Assocs., St. Louis, 1968-71, Sanford Rose Assn. St. Louis, Inc., 1973-75, Elkan Realty and Investment Co., St. Louis, 1973—; co-founder, pres. Am. Cinema Corp., Mo. Cinema Corp., Ill. Cinema Corp., St. Louis, 1969-71; dir. mktg. and real estate devel. Koplar Enterprises, Inc., St. Louis, 1971-73; pres. Brandy Properties, Inc., St. Louis, 1979—, Sports Arena, Inc., San Diego, 1983—; co-chmn. creditors com. Dunes Hotel and Country Club., Las Vegas. Inventor profl. bd., spl. drafting table, artist's easel. Active Child Abuse Prevention Soc., San Diego, Rancho Santa Fe Youth, Rep. Congl. Leadership, Rep. Senatorial Inner Circle. Mem. Profl. Soc. Performing Arts San Diego, Rancho Santa Fe Farms Golf Club. Republican. Jewish. Home: PO Box 1068 Rancho Santa Fe CA 92067 Office: Sports Arenas Inc 5230 Carroll Canyon Rd Suite 310 San Diego CA 92121

ELKIN, IRVIN, milk marketing cooperative executive. Pres., dir. Associated Milk Producers, Inc., San Antonio. Office: Associated Milk Producers Inc 6609 Blanco Rd PO Box 32287 San Antonio TX 78216 *

ELKINS, JAMES ANDERSON, JR., banker; b. Galveston, Tex., Mar. 24, 1919; s. James Anderson and Isabel (Mitchell) E.; m. Margaret Wiess, Nov. 24, 1945; children—Elise, James Anderson III, Leslie K. B.A., Princeton U., 1941. With First City Nat. Bank, Houston, 1941—, v.p., 1946-50, pres. then chmn. bd., 1950-82; dir. First City Bancorp., Houston, 1982—; bd. dirs. Freeport-McMoran Inc., New Orleans, 1970—, Am. Gen. Cos., Houston, 1973—. Bd. dirs. Houston Grand Opera; trustee Tex. Children's Hosp., Baylor U. Coll. Medicine, 1970—. Episcopalian. Office: 1st City Bancorp Tex Inc 1001 Fannin St Houston TX 77253 also: PO Box 2387 Houston TX 77001

ELKINS, LLOYD EDWIN, petroleum engineer, energy consultant; b. Golden, Colo., Apr. 1, 1912; s. Edwin and Beulah M. (Feltch) E.; m. Virginia L. Crosby, May 27, 1934; children: Marylou, Barbara Lee, Lloyd Edwin Jr. Degree in Petroleum Engring., Colo. Sch. Mines, 1934; PhD in Sci, U. Ozarks. With Amoco Prodn. Co., 1934-77, successively field engr., petroleum engr. Tulsa gen. office, sr. petroleum engr., petroleum engring. supr., asst. chief prodn. engr., chief prodn. eng, 1949-77; energy cons. 1977—. Contbr. articles to profl. jours. Named to Engring. Hall of Fame Okla. State U., 1961; recipient Distinguished Service medal Colo. Sch. Mines, 1961; named to Engring. Hall of Fame U. Tulsa. Mem. Am. Assn. Petroleum Geologists, Am. Petroleum Inst. (chmn. mid-continent dist. div. prodn. 1948-49, chmn. adv. com fundamental research on occurrence and recovery petroleum 1941), Am. Inst. Mining, Metall, and Petroleum Engrs. (hon., v.p. 1953-59, pres. 1962, Anthony F. Lucas gold medal 1966), Nat. Acad. Engring., Tulsa Geol. Soc., Australian Inst. Mining and Metallurgy (hon.). Methodist. Clubs: Engineers (Tulsa) (pres. 1950-51), Petroleum (Tulsa), Tulsa Country (Tulsa). Home and Office: 2806 E 27th St PO Box 4745 Tulsa OK 74114

ELKINS, RONALD FLAGG, JR., manufacturing executive; b. Springfield, Mo., May 5, 1936; s. Ronald Flagg and Ilaverne (Peck) E.; m. Dona Karen Kubias, Sept. 12, 1959; children: Lisa, John. BSBA, Drury Coll., 1961. Sales mgmt. trainee Internat. Harvester Co., Springfield, Mo., 1958-60; sales agt. Mass Mut. Ins. Co., Springfield, 1960-61; pres., chief exec. officer EDCO Microfilming, Inc., Springfield, 1961—; instr. SW Mo. State U., Springfield, 1979-82; arbitrator Better Bus. Bur., 1987—. Insp. Nat. Horse Show Regulatory Commn., Shelbyville, Tenn., 1979—. Mem. Assn. Image and Information, Springfield C. of C., U.S. C. of C. Republican. Presbyterian. Club: Rotary (Paul Harris fellow 1987). Home: Rte 2 Box 136-G Ozark MO 65721 Office: EDCO Microfilming Inc 1429 N Cedarbrook MPO Box 7010 Springfield MO 65801-7010

ELKINS, STEVEN PAUL, architect; b. Ephrata, Wash., Feb. 18, 1949; s. Hugh Kyle Elkins and Fern Irene (Vining) Johnson; m. Linda Louise Harris, Aug. 6, 1977; children: Andrea Rouleau, Michael Rouleau, Jennifer. BArch, Wash. State U., 1972. Registered architect, Wash., Oreg. Designer, draftsman Eng & Wright Architects, Vancouver, B.C., Can., 1972-73, Harthorne-Hagen-Gross, Inc., Seattle, 1973-75, Leo A. Daly Co., Seattle, 1975-77; architect Lawrence Campbell & Assocs., Kent, Wash., 1977-81; prin. Steven P. Elkins Architects, Inc., Seattle, 1981—. Mem. community adv. com. Auburn (Wash.) Gen. Hosp., 1985—, mem. planning and bldg. com. Campus Way Covenant Ch., Federal Way, Wash., 1985—. Recipient Award of Excellence Wash. Precast Concrete Industry Assn., 1985, 86, Appreciation award Vocat. Indsl. Clubs Am., Wash., 1985, 86., Superintendant of Pub. Instrn., Auburn Sch. Dist., 1987. Mem. AIA (corp.), Nat. Trust for Hist. Preservation. Democrat. Protestant. Club: Washington Athletic. Home: 1326 183d Ave NE Bellevue WA 98008 Office: 610 Market St #201 Kirkland WA 98033

ELLARD, TIMOTHY DANIEL, marketing research executive; b. Salem, Mass., Dec. 20, 1934; s. Daniel J. and Anna Mary (Byrne) E.; m. Mary Patricia Amend, July 11, 1959; children: Marcia Ann, Daniel Joseph, Michael Patrick. AB, Harvard Coll., 1956; MBA, U. Pa., 1958. In brand mgmt. Procter & Gamble Co., Cin., 1961-64; survey dir., rsch. dir., v.p., sr. v.p. Opinion Rsch. Corp., Princeton, N.J., 1964-82, sr. v.p., mgr., Opinion Rsch. Corp., San Francisco, 1982—. Cons. Bus. Vols. for Arts. 1st Lt. USAR, 1958-61. Mem. Am. Mktg. Assn., Am. Assn. Pub. Opinion Rsch., Travel and Tourism Rsch. Assn., Am. Statis. Assn. Avocations: music, gardening. Home: 139 Wildwood Ave Piedmont CA 94610 Office: Opinion Rsch Corp 4 Embarcadero Ctr San Francisco CA 94111

ELLBERGER, STANLEY, mortgage executive; b. N.Y.C., Feb. 9, 1943; children: Garrett, Risa. BSCE, Drexel U., 1965. Exec. v.p. Sterling Thompson Group, Middletown, N.J., 1972-79; pres. Equity Sharing Plan corp., Ocean, N.J., 1980-82, Manco Mortgage, Millburn, N.J., 1983-85, Sterling Nat. Mortgage, Clark, N.J., 1985—; pres. Sterling Nat. Realty Group, Middletown, N.J., 1979-83. Author: The Sucess Book for Real Estate. Jewish. Home: 388 Ocean Ave Long Branch NJ 07740 Office: Sterling Nat Mortgage 77 Brant Ave Clark NJ 07066

ELLERBROOK, NIEL COCHRAN, gas company executive; b. Rensselaer, Ind., Dec. 26, 1948; s. James Harry and Margaret (Cochran) E.; m. Susan Lynne Stamper, Mar. 8, 1969; children: Jennifer, Jeffrey, Jayma. BS, Ball State U., 1970. CPA, Ind. Staff acct. audit Arthur Andersen & Co., Indpls., 1970-72, audit sr., 1972-75, audit mgr., 1975-80; asst. to sr. v.p. adminstrn. and fin. Ind. Gas Co., Inc., Indpls., 1980-81, v.p. fin., 1981-84, v.p. fin., chief fin. officer, 1984-87, sr. v.p. adminstrn. and fin., chief fin. officer, 1987—. Bd. dirs. Ctr. Grove Little League, Greenwood, Ind., 1983-87; mem. ch. fin. com. local Meth. ch., 1988. Mem. AICPA, Ind. CPA Soc. (bd. dirs. Indpls. chpt., past pres. 1977-83, state bd. dirs. 1984-87), Fin. Execs. Inst., Ind. Fiscal Policy Inst. (bd. dirs. 1985—, vice chmn. 1988—), Ind. State C. of C. (taxation com. 1982—, chmn. 1987—), Ind. Gas Assn. (treas., asst. sec. 1988—). Office: Ind Gas Co Inc 1630 N Meridian St Indianapolis IN 46202

ELLERIN, STEPHEN, name development agency executive; b. Chgo.; s. Milton and Faye E.; m. Kathleen Ellerin. BA, U. Conn., 1967; postgrad., U. Md., 1968-71. Dir. Stephens Mktg. Group, Stamford, Conn., 1975-79; lectr. U. Md., Fed. Republic of Germany, 1979-81; prin. Stephen Ellerin Cons., Marin County, Calif., 1981-83; pres. Namesmith-the Name Devel. Agy., Stamford, 1984—; lectr. U. Conn., Stamford, 1984; cons. area firms. Author: How to Succeed in Business by Trying Like Hell, 1989, How to Succeed in College by Trying Like Hell, 1989. Mem. United Cancer Council; chmn., bd. dirs. Tower Sch. Inc., Stamford. Mem. DAV (commdr.'s 1987-88, 89). Office: Namesmith 46 Chesterfield Rd Stamford CT 06902

ELLERTON, JOHN JAMES, oil company executive; b. Sheffield, Eng., Sept. 15, 1944; came to U.S., 1977; s. George and Dorothy Mable (Derringer) E.; m. Jessie Pauline Dupuy, Feb. 19, 1972; children: Bret Stephen, David Michael, Stephanie Anne. BS with honors, U. Toronto, 1969. Geologist, geophysicist Texaco Explorations, Inc., Calgary, Alberta, 1969-73; regional mgr. Bennett Petroleum Corp., Calgary, 1974-77; pres. J. Ellerton Cons., Ltd., Calgary, 1974-77, J. Ellerton Cons., Inc., Tyler, Tex., Denver, 1977—; chmn., pres. Com-Tek Resources, Inc., Denver, 1980—; chmn. Elflex Geophys., Inc., Denver, 1985—. Pub. arbitrator Nat. Assn. Security Dealers, Inc., Denver, 1985—. Home: 7333 S Downing Circle Apt E Littleton CO 80122 Office: Com Tek Resources Inc 1624 Market St Ste 209 Denver CO 80202

ELLERY, DALE RAPHAEL, accountant; b. Alpena, Mich., Dec. 1, 1939; s. Raphael H. and Mary (Minton) E.; m. Marguerite Santarossa, Feb. 15, 1963; children: Lisa, Rick. BBA, U. Mich., 1963; MS in Taxation with highest honors, Walsh Coll., 1978. CPA, Mich. Acct. Ford Motor Co., Mich., 1961-65; tax supr. Touche Ross & Co., Mich., 1965-69; tax mgr. Am. Motors Corp., Mich., 1969-76; asst. treas. Volkswagen of Am., Mich., 1977—; bd. dirs. Penrickton Ctr., Taylor, Mich. Chmn. Internat. Bus. Forum, Detroit, 1984. Mem. Nat. Assn. Accts., Nat. Assn. of Fgn. Trade Zones (bd. dirs. 1982-83), Tax Execs. Inst. (treas. 1982), Detroit C. of C. (bd. dirs. 1987—), World Trade Club (pres. 1987, chmn. 1988). Home: 14721 Williamsburg Ct Riverview MI 48192 Office: Volkswagen of Am 888 W Big Beaver Rd Troy MI 48007

ELLETT, ALAN SIDNEY, real estate development company executive; b. Seven Kings, Essex, Eng., Jan. 6, 1930; s. Sidney Walter and May (Fowler) E.; m. Linda Jacqueline Cortell, 1985; children by previous marriage—Denise, Michelle, Wayne. B.Sc. in Bldg. Constrn., 1951, also M.B.A. Mng. dir. Gilbert Ash Structures, 1960-68; dir., gen. mgr. Lyon Group (real estate), 1968-70; mng. dir. (pres.) Gilbert Ash Ltd., 1970-72; dir. Bovis Ltd.; chief exec. Audley Properties Ltd. (Bovis Property Div.), 1972-74; chmn. bd. Forest City Dillon, Inc., 1974-88, pres., 1974—; exec. v.p., dir. Forest City Enterprises, Inc., Cleve., 1974-89; chmn. Forest City Rental Properties, 1982; chmn., pres. Forest City Comml. Constrn. Co., Inc., 1987-89; chief exec. officer, pres. Lehrer McGovern Bovis, Inc., N.Y.C., 1989—. Contbr. articles to profl. jours. Fellow Inst. Builders, Inst. Mktg., Inst. Dirs.; mem. Brit. Inst. Mgmt. Mem. Conservative Party. Mem. Church of England. (London). Home: Kingswood 18800 North Park Blvd Shaker Heights OH 44122 Office: Lehrer McGovern Bovis Inc 387 Park Ave S New York NY 10016

ELLIG, BRUCE ROBERT, personnel executive; b. Manitowoc, Wis., Oct. 15, 1936; s. Robert Louis and Lucille Marie (Westphal) E.; B.B.A., U. Wis., 1959, M.B.A., 1960; 1 son, Brett Robert. With Pfizer Inc., N.Y.C., 1960—, mgr. compensation and personnel research, 1968-70, corp. dir. compensation and benefits, 1970-78, v.p. compensation and benefits, 1978-83, v.p. employee relations, 1983-85, v.p. personnel, 1985—; speaker at workshops, seminars and confs.; assoc. adv. council Commerce Clearing House, mem. pfizer standing coms. Employee Compensation and Mgmt. Devel., Employee Stock Ownership, Retirement Plan, Retirement Plann Assets, Savs. and Investment. Mem. Mayor's Adv. Pay Commn., N.Y.C., 1977-78, chmn., 1980; mem. bus. sector staff Council on Wage and Price Stability, 1979-80; mem. Ctr. for Advanced Human Resource Studies Cornell U., Human Resource Roundtable, Presdl. Quadrennial Pay Commn., 1976, U.S. Civil Service Commn. Merit Pay Task Force, 1979; mem. adv. bd. Ky. Ednl. TV, 1987—. Mem. Am. Compensation Assn. (charter pres. Ea. region; publ. award 1980), Am. Soc. Personnel Adminstrs. (accredited sr. profl. human rsources, mem. human resources strategies and issues council), N.Y. Assn. Compensation Adminstrs. (charter pres.), NAM (indsl. rels.), Am. Mgmt. Assn. (human resource council; Wall of Fame 1983), N.Y. Personnel Mgmt. Assn. (past pres.; anniversary award of merit 1980), Bus. Roundtable (employee relations com.), Conf. Bd. Council Human Resources Research, N.Y. Indsl. Relations Assn., Pharm. Mfrs. Assn. (personnel sect.), Sr. Execs. Forum, U. So. Calif. Ctr. for Effective Orgs. (corp. adv. bd.), U. Wis. Bus. Sch. Alumni (bd. dirs.), Phi Beta Kappa, Phi Eta Sigma, Phi Kappa Phi, Delta Epsilon, Beta Gamma Sigma, Alpha Kappa Psi (scholarship). Republican. Roman Catholic. Author: Compensation and Benefits: Analytical Strategies, 1978; Executive Compensation: A Total Pay Perspective, 1982; Compensation and Benefits: Design and Analysis, 1985; contbg. author: Encyclopedia of Professional Management, 1978; Handbook of Business Administration, 1984; cons. editor Compensation & Benefits Rev.; editorial bd., personnel adv. bd. Jour. Compensation & Benefits; contbr. articles to profl. jours. Office: Pfizer Inc 235 E 42d St New York NY 10017

ELLIN, MARVIN, lawyer; b. Balt., Mar. 6, 1923; s. Morris and Goldie (Rosen) E.; m. Stella J. Granto, Aug. 2, 1948; children: Morris, Raymond, Elisa. LL.B., U. Balt., 1953. Bar: Md. 1953, U.S. Supreme Ct. 1978. Practice law Balt., 1953—; mem. firm Ellin & Baker, 1957—; specialist in med. malpractice law; cons. med./legal trial matters lectr. ACS, U. Md. Law Sch., U. Balt. Law Sch., Md. Bar Assn., Bar Assn. Balt. City. Writer; producer ct. dramatizations featured on various TV and radio stas., Balt. Fellow Internat. Acad. Trial Lawyers. Home: 13414 Longnecker Rd Glyndon MD 21071 Office: 1101 Saint Paul St Baltimore MD 21202

ELLINGER, ROBERT OSCAR, utilities executive; b. DuBois, Pa., Oct. 18, 1952; s. Robert Miles and Maxine Lorraine (Johnson) E.; m. Marie Jayne Zbieg, Sept. 23, 1972; children: Jason, Matthew, Jessica. AS in Bus. Adminstrn., Pa. State U., 1980. Apprentice electrician Naval Surface Weapons Ctr., Silver Spring, Md., 1971-75, electrician, 1975; advisor energy mgmt. United Electric Corp., DuBois, 1975-86; gen. mgr. Delaware (Ohio) Rural Electric Co-op, 1986—. Co-founder Nat. Tom Mix Festival, DuBois, 1980. Mem. Delaware Area C. of C. (bd. dirs. 1988—), Jaycees (pres. DuBois chpt. 1980, Jaycee of Yr. 1980). Democrat. Roman Catholic. Lodge: Kiwanis. Home: 40 Marvin Ln Delaware OH 43015 Office: Delaware Rural Electric Corp 26 N Union St Delaware OH 43015

ELLINGSEN, OLAV, mechanical equipment company executive; b. Byrne, Norway, Mar. 22, 1941; s. Brynjulf and Jenny (Ness) E.; m. Liv Sorebo, July 19, 1969; 1 child, Bjarte Sorebo. Degree in Mech. Engring., Stavanger Tech. High Sch., 1966. Jr. engr. Norsk Hydro A/S, Oslo, 1966-67; mgr. Per Hetland Maskinfabrikk A/S, Bryne, 1967-70, Hatten & Jota A/S, Trysil, Norway, 1970-73, Industrikontakt, O. Ellingsen & Co., Floro, Norway, 1973—; chmn. bd. dirs. Kirkenes Engring. A/S, Kirkenes, Ellingsen and Assocs. A/S, Floro.; founder, bd. dirs. Noride A/S, Floro, Consensus A/S, Bergen, Norway, Lifecare A/S, Oslo, Norway, Petroleum Reservoir Cons. A/S, Oslo, Forest A/S, Oslo, Norpigg A/S, Höyanger. Inventor thermodynamic cuttings cleaning, thermodynamic enhanced oil recovery, artificial pancreas, solar energy generator; patentee in field. Recipient diplomas Klerk, Bergen, 1986, Norwegian Inventors Assn., 1980. Mem. Norwegian Indsl. Fedn., Norwegian Inventors Assn., Norwegian Petroleum Soc. Conservative. Lutheran. Club: Florö Yacht (Floro) (chmn. 1986). Lodge: Odd Fellow. Home: Kleiva 20, 6900 Florö Norway Office: Ellingsen & Assocs A/S, Boks 133, 6901 Florö Norway

ELLIOT, DOUGLAS GENE, chemical engineer, engineering company executive, consultant; b. Medford, Oreg., June 3, 1941; s. Don Joseph and Eleanor Joan (Sheets) E.; m. Noma Warnken, July 16, 1966 (div. 1979); 1 child, Jennifer M.; m. Patricia Jean Nichols, Mar. 15, 1980; children: Steven V. Bates, Michael A. Castillo. BSChemE, Oreg. State U., 1964; MS, U. Houston, 1968, PhD, 1971. Reservoir/prodn. engr. Humble Oil & Refining Co., Beaumont, Tex., 1964-66; co-founder, v.p. and bd. dirs. S.W. Wire Rope, Inc., 1967-70; cons. Gas Processors Assn., Houston, 1971; process/project engr. Hudson Engring. Co., Houston, 1971-78; mgr. process engring. Davy-McKee Corp., Houston, 1978-83, v.p. oil and gas, 1983-85; pres. D. G. Elliot & Assocs. Inc., Houston, 1985-86; sr. v.p., gen. mgr. Internat. Process Svcs. Inc., Houston, 1986—, also bd. dirs.; adj. prof. Rice U., Houston, 1976-77; mem. indsl. adv. com. Okla. State U., Stillwater, 1979-83; mgmt. cons. Norsk Hydro Oil & Gas Div., Oslo, 1984—. Contbr. articles to profl. jours.; mem. editorial rev. bd. Energy Process mag., 1981—; pantentee in field. Mem. Tex. Energy Adv. Com., Austin, 1978; founding mem., bd. dirs. Tex. Solar Energy Soc., Austin, 1978; mem. Ctr. of Excellence R&D rev. panel Okla. Ctr. for Advancement of Sci. & Tech. Mem. Am. Inst. Chem. Engrs. (sec./treas. South Tex. sect. 1979, chmn. elect 1980, chmn. 1981, bd. dirs. fuels and petochem. div. 1982-85), Soc. Petroleum Engrs., Gas Processors Assn. (sec./treas. 1983), Sigma Zi. Home: 12114 Greenglade Houston TX 77099

ELLIOTT, A. WRIGHT, banker; b. New Orleans; s. Anson E. and Edna Jo (Wright) E.; m. Jane Rader; children—Michael, Stephen, David. B.A., Princeton U., 1957; M.A., La. State U., 1964. With Whitney Nat. Bank, New Orleans, 1961-62; exec. v.p. Nat. Assn. of Mfgrs., Washington, 1964-74; exec. v.p. The Chase Manhattan Bank, N.A., N.Y., 1974—. Pres., Bronxville (N.Y.) Sch. Bd. Edn., 1983; bd. mem. South St. Seaport Mus., N.Y., 1983; bd. dirs. Bus.-Industry Pol. Action Com., Manhattan Inst. for Policy Research, 1983—. Served to capt., USMC, 1958-62. Mem. Am. Bankers Assn. (govt. rels. bd.), Econ. Club N.Y. Republican. Club: Siwanoy Country (N.Y.). Office: Chase Manhattan Corp 1 Chase Manhattan Pla New York NY 10081

ELLIOTT, DANIEL ROBERT, JR., manufacturing company executive, lawyer; b. Cleve., Mar. 15, 1939; s. Daniel Robert and Elizabeth Marie (Spangler) E.; m. Carol Reaser, Sept. 1, 1961 (div.); children—Daniel Robert III, Timothy Reaser; m. Margaret Moorman Caldwell, Jan. 1, 1983; children: Margaret Caldwell, Peter Ryan. B.A., Wesleyan U., Middletown, Conn., 1957-61; J.D., U. Mich., 1964. Bar: N.Y. 1965, Ohio 1970. Assoc. firm Cravath, Swaine & Moore, N.Y.C., 1964-68; assoc. firm Jones, Day, Reavis & Pogue, Washington, 1969, assoc. Cleve. office, 1969-71, ptnr., 1971-76; v.p. law, gen. counsel, White Consol. Industries, Inc., Cleve., 1976-86, sr. v.p., gen. counsel, sec., 1986—. Chmn. adv. commn. to Office on Sch. Monitoring and Community Relations, Cleve., 1978-82; pres. Greater Cleve. Interch. Council, 1981-84, also trustee; trustee, founder Cleve. Tenants Orgn.; mem. United Way Services Del. Assembly, Cleve; bd. trustee Ctr. for Human Relations, Inst. Child Advocacy, Neighborhood Ctrs. Assn., Judson Retirement Community; Mem. ABA, Cleve. Bar Assn., Machinery and Allied Products Inst., Assn. Home Appliance Mfrs. (chmn. legal ops. adv. com.), Am. Soc. Corp. Secs. Democrat. Mem. Disciples of Christ Ch. Office: White Consol Industries Inc 11770 Berea Rd Cleveland OH 44111

ELLIOTT, EDWARD, investment executive, financial planner; b. Madison, Wis., Jan. 11, 1915; s. Edward C. and Elizabeth (Nowland) E.; m. Letitia Ord, Feb. 20, 1943 (div. Aug. 1955); children: Emily, Ord; m. Melita Uihlein, Jan. 1, 1958; 1 dau., Deborah. B.S. in Mech. Engring, Purdue U., 1936. Engr. Gen. Electric Co., Schenectady, 1936-37; engr. Pressed Steel Tank Co., Milw., 1937-38, N.Y.C., 1939-41; dist. sales mgr. Pressed Steel Tank Co., Cleve., 1946-48, N.Y.C., 1949-54; sales mgr. Pressed Steel Tank Co., Milw., 1954-58; v.p. sales Cambridge Co. div. Carrier Corp., Lowell, Mass., 1958-59; mgr. indsl. and med. sales Liquid Carbonic div. Gen. Dynamics Corp., Chgo., 1959-61; v.p. Haywood Pub. Co., Chgo., 1961-63; pres. Omnibus, Inc., Chgo., 1963-67; gen. sales mgr. Resistoflex Corp., Roseland, N.J., 1967-68; investment exec. Shearson, Hammill & Co., Inc., Chgo., 1968-74; v.p. McCormick & Co., Inc., 1974-75; now v.p. Paine Webber, Inc., Naples, Fla., 1975—. Served with USAAF, 1941-46. Decorated officer Order Brit. Empire; inducted Indiana Basketball Hall of Fame. Mem. ASME, Air Force Assn., Inst. Cert. Fin. Planners, Internat. Assn. Fin. Planning, Phi Delta Theta. Republican. Episcopalian. Clubs: Shore Acres Golf (Lake Bluff, Ill.); Onwentsia (Lake Forest, Ill.); Milwaukee Country , University (Milw.); Chenequa Country (Hartland, Wis.); Lake (Oconomowoc, Wis.); Army-Navy Country (Arlington, Va.); Lafayette (Ind.) Country; Coral Beach (Paget Bermuda); Royal Poinciana Golf, Hole-in-Wall Golf, Naples Yacht, Naples Athletic (Naples). Lodge: Rotary. Home: 1285 Gulf Shore Blvd N Naples FL 33940 Office: Paine Webber Inc 1400 Gulf Shore Blvd N Naples FL 33940

ELLIOTT, HOWARD, JR., gas distribution company executive; b. St. Louis, July 4, 1933; s. Howard and Ruth Ann (Thomas) E.; student Brown U., 1956; J.D., Washington U., 1962; m. Susan Jane Spoehrer, Sept. 2, 1961; children—Kathryn Spoehrer, Elizabeth Gray. Admitted to Mo. bar, 1962; assoc. firm Boyle, Priest, Elliott & Weakley, St. Louis, 1962-65, partner, 1965-67; commr. Mo. Pub. Service Commn., 1967-70; commr. U.S. Postal Rate Commn., 1970-73; assoc. gen. counsel Laclede Gas Co., St. Louis,

1973-77, v.p. adminstrn., 1977—. Mem. com. on electricity and nuclear energy Nat. Assn. Regulatory Utility Commrs., 1968-70, mem. exec. com., 1971-73. Charter mem. com. of 40 for Adoption of St. Louis and St. Louis County Jr. Coll. Dist., 1962. Served with U.S. Army, 1956-58. Mem. Am. Gas Assn., ABA, Mo. Bar, Fed. Bar Assn., Fed. Energy Bar Assn., Bar Assn. Met. St. Louis. Republican. Presbyterian. Clubs: Noonday, St. Louis Country, Chevy Chase, Mo. Athletic. Home: 46 Clermont Ln Saint Louis MO 63124 Office: LaClede Gas Co 720 Olive St Saint Louis MO 63101

ELLIOTT, JAMES WILLIAM, JR., manufacturing company executive; b. Mobile, Ala., Aug. 11, 1950; s. James William and Myrtle Jo (Loper) E.; m. Diana Marie Lancaster, Aug. 18, 1986; children: Peyton, Paj. BS in Metall. Engring., U. Ala., 1972. Prodn. engr. Savannah River plant E.I. DuPont Co., Aiken, S.C., 1973-74; quality engr. Ingalls Shipbuilding Co., Pascagoula, Miss., 1974-76; pres., gen. mgr. Galvanizers, Inc., Mobile, 1976-78; asst. mgr., metallurgist Doran Ala. Propeller Co., Mobile, 1978-82; mgr. Pascagoula ops. Bird Johnson Co. (formerly Mich. Wheel, Coolidge Propeller), 1982—; metall. cons. S&E Investment Co., Mobile, 1986—. Mem. Soc. Naval Architects and Marine Engrs., Propeller Club Pascagoula, Soc. Metal Internat. (sec. 1986-87, vice-chmn. 1987-88), Navy League Am., Jackson County C. of C. (mil. affairs com. 1985—, bd. dirs. 1988), Miss. Mfrs. Assn., Jackson County Indsl. Mgrs. Assn., Alpha Sigma Mu, Mystic Stripers Soc. Republican. Baptist. Home: PO Box 914 Spanish Fort AL 36527 Office: Bird Johnson Co PO Box 1528 Pascagoula MS 39567

ELLIOTT, K. CHARLES, trucking company executive; b. Burkburnett, Tex., May 31, 1924; s. Wilbur Allen and Zebie (Gray) E.; m. Marcene Simmons, Dec. 2, 1944; children—Linda Diane Osborn, Kenneth C. B.B.A., U. Tex.-Austin, 1945. Asst. traffic mgr. Armour & Co., Ft. Worth, 1946-57; v.p. Commercial Oil Transp., Ft. Worth, 1957-66; exec. v.p. Bray Lines Inc., Cushing, Okla., 1966-71; owner, pres. D & H Trucking, Tulsa, 1971-76; chmn., pres. Redwing Carriers, Inc., Tampa, Fla., 1976—. Mem. Nat. Tank Truck Carrier Inc. (dir. 1966—), Fla. Trucking Assn. (pres. 1985). Republican. Methodist. Club: Tower (Tampa). Lodges: Elks, Masons. Home: 5024 Chattam Ln Tampa FL 33624 Office: Redwing Carriers Inc PO Box 30063 Tampa FL 33630

ELLIOTT, MARK PRICE, forestry company executive; b. Florence, Ala., May 8, 1956; m. Margaret T. Burr, Feb. 14, 1986. BS in Forestry, Auburn U., 1978, M in Forest Econs., 1982. Asst. county agt. Ala. Coop. Extension Svc., Wetumpka, 1978-80; assoc. county agt. Ala. Coop. Extension Svc., Ashland, 1982-85; mktg. mgr. Internat. Forest Seed Co., Odenville, Ala., 1985-87; unit mgr. container seedling ops. Internat. Forest Seed Co., Odenville, 1987—. Contbr. articles to profl. publs. Named one of Outstanding Young Men in Am., Outstanding Ams., 1984; recipient Environ. award Auburn U. Mosley Found., 1982. Mem. Soc. Am. Foresters (sec.-treas. Ala. div. 1988), Forest Farmers Assn., Ala. Forestry Assn., Birmingham Sailing Club (bd. dirs. 1983-88). Office: Internat Forest Seed Co PO Box 290 Odenville AL 35120

ELLIOTT, MARTHA ALGEORGE, small business owner; b. Jersey City, July 1, 1957. BS, NYU, 1980. Mem. staff First Jersey Nat. Bank, Jersey City, 1975-76; supr. fgn. dept. Chase Manhattan Bank, N.Y.C., 1976-80; asst. v.p. Dean Witter Reynolds, N.Y.C., 1980-88; pres., chmn. bd. The Elliott Group, N.Y.C., 1988—. Treas. U.S. Senate Campaign, N.J., 1988; mentor Harlem YMCA, 1985; bd. dirs. United Way Greater N.Y.C., 1986. Mem. Women's Econ. Devel. Corp., Securities Industry Assn.

ELLIOTT, R. KEITH, specialty chemical company executive; b. Abbeville, S.C., Feb. 25, 1942; s. Bridwell Douglas and Sara (Broome) E.; m. Geraldine Louise Tobia, July 30, 1966; children: M. Lance, Chad L. B.S., U. S.C.-Columbia, 1964; M.B.A., U. S.C-Columbia, 1965. With E.I. duPont de Nemours, Wilmington, Del., 1965-69, Mine Safety Appliances Co., Pitts., 1969-74; asst. treas. The Carborundum Co. (acquired by Kennecott Corp., 1978), Niagra Falls, N.Y., 1975-77, treas., 1977-79; asst. treas. Kennecott Corp., Stamford, Conn., 1979-80, v.p., treas, 1980-81; v.p., treas. Engelhard Corp., Edison, N.J., 1981-85, v.p. fin., chief fin. officer, dir., 1985-88, sr. v.p., chief fin. officer, 1988—. Cons. City Mgmt. Adv. Bd., Niagra Falls, N.Y., 1976-79; bd. dirs. Centenary Coll., Hackettstown, N.J., 1986—; bd. trustees Elizabeth Gen. Med. Ctr., Elizabeth, N.J., 1985—. Served with AUS, 1966-72. Mem. Fin. Execs. Inst., Nat. Assn. Corp. Treas., Machinery and Allied Products Inst. (chmn. fin. coun.). Home: 18 Shrewsbury Dr Rumson NJ 07760 Office: Engelhard Corp Menlo Pk CN 40 Edison NJ 08818

ELLIOTT, RICHARD GENE, communications executive; b. Logan, Utah, Aug. 29, 1948; s. Charles Alonzo Elliott and Dorothy Jane (Roberts) Heaton; m. Annette Fraser, June 1, 1968; children: Marci, Marti, Richard Charles. BS, U. Utah, 1970. Bus. mgr. BRD Drug Ctrs., Tremonton, Utah, 1970-72; sales mgr. Sta. KTFI, Twin Falls, Idaho, 1972-73; account exec. Sta. KLAK, Denver, 1973-74; v.p., gen. mgr. Sta. KEXO, Grand Junction, Colo., 1974-82; group exec. Communications Investment Corp., Salt Lake City, 1982-84; owner, pres. Sunrise Media Group, Inc., Salt Lake City, 1984—. Pres. Colo. West Advt. Fedn., Grand Junction, 1979-80. Mem. Rotary. Republican. Mormon. Home: 11229 S Brandon Park Dr Sandy UT 84092 Office: Sunrise Media Group 9160 S 300 West Sandy UT 84070

ELLIOTT, R(OY) FRASER, lawyer, holding and management company executive; b. Ottawa, Ont., Can., Nov. 25, 1921. B.Comm., Queen's U., Kingston, Ont., Can., 1943; grad., Osgoode Hall Law Sch., 1946, Harvard U. Sch. Bus. Adminstrn., 1947. Bar: Ont. 1946, Que. 1948; created queen's counsel. Ptnr. Stikeman, Elliott, Toronto, Ont., Montreal; chmn. CAE Industries Ltd., Toronto, SPB Can. Inc.; dir. Montreal Shipping Inc., Can. Imperial Bank Commerce, New Providence Devel. Co. Ltd., Frank W. Horner Ltd., Lafarge Corp., Standard Broadcasting Corp.; lectr. company law McGill U., Montreal, 1951. Contbg. author, editor: Que. Corp. Manual, 1948-53; co-editor: Doing Business in Canada. Mem. Montreal Bar Assn., Can. Bar Assn., Law Soc. Upper Can. Office: CAE Industries Ltd, Commerce Ct W Suite 1400, Toronto, ON Canada M5J 2J1

ELLIS, ANTHONY THORNTON, venture capitalist; b. Eminence, Ky., Feb. 26, 1929; s. Anthony Thornton and Georgiana (Swinney) E.; m. Jane Canning, Nov. 10, 1956; children: Susan, Winnifred, David. B.S., U. Calif.-Berkeley, 1951; M.B.A., Harvard U., 1956; grad. exec. program, Stanford U., 1971; advanced profl. cert. in acctg., NYU Grad. Sch. Bus., 1974. Asst. cashier First Nat. City Bank, N.Y.C., 1958-60; asst. v.p. First Nat. City Bank, 1960-62, v.p., 1962-70; treas. Kennecott Copper Corp., N.Y.C., 1970-76; v.p. fin. Kennecott Copper Corp., 1976-78, v.p., treas., 1978-79; exec. v.p. Am. Security Bank N.Am., Washington, 1979-81; gen. ptnr. Pacific Venture Ptnrs., Menlo Park, Calif., 1982—. Trustee Pacific Crest Outward Bound Sch. Lt. (j.g.) USN, 1951-54. Mem. Lincoln Club No. Calif., Burlingame (Calif.) Country Club, Harvard Club N.Y.C., Met. Club Washington, Beta Theta Pi. Office: Pacific Venture Ptnrs 3000 Sand Hill Rd Bldg 4 Ste 175 Menlo Park CA 94025

ELLIS, BERNICE, financial planning company executive, investment advisor; b. Bklyn., July 14, 1934; d. Samuel and Clara (Schrier) H.; m. Seymour Scott Ellis, Feb. 7, 1954; children: Michele, Wayne. BA, Bklyn. Coll., 1956; MS, Queens Coll., 1970. Cert. fin. planner, N.Y. 1987, elem. educator, N.Y.C. Elementary tchr. L.I. Sch. Dists., Merrick, N.Y., 1956-60; tchr. reading N.Y.C. Bd. of Edn., Bklyn., 1972-73; coordinator Reading is Fundamental, Lawrence, N.Y., 1973-75; pres., founder N.Y. State Assn. for the Gifted and Talented, Valley Stream, N.Y., 1974-87; pres. Ellis Planning, Valley Stream, N.Y., 1984-87; cons. Nassau County Bd. Coop. Ednl. Services, Westbury, N.Y., 1973-74; adminstrv. intern region II U.S. Office Edn., 1977-78; adj. asst. prof. Nassau Community Coll., Garden City, N.Y., 1975—. Contbr. articles to profl. jours and fin. newsletters. Dem. Committeewoman, Nassau, N.Y., 1987; bd. dirs. Nat. Council Jewish Women Career Group, Nassau, 1987. Recipient Ednl. Professions Devel. Act fellow CUNY Inst. for Remediations Skills for Coll. Personnel, Queensborough Community Coll., 1970-73. Mem. Inst. for Cert. Fin. Planners, Internat. Assn. for Fin. Planners (legislative com. 1986-87 L.I. chpt.), N.Y. State Reading Assn., Adj. Faculty Assn. Nassau Community Coll., Sales Exec. Club of N.Y., L.I., N.Y. C. of C. Office: Ellis Planning Inc. 628 Golf Dr Valley Stream NY 11581

ELLIS, CHERYL BONINI, banker; b. Torrington, Conn., Oct. 17, 1951; d. Edward Paul and Eleanor Marie (Yucas) Bonini; m. Lawrence R. Ellis III, Oct. 27, 1973 (div. 1983). BS in Bus., Skidmore Coll., 1973; MBA, Syracuse U., 1981. Customer svc. rep. Bank of Auburn, N.Y., 1974-75; credit analyst Bank of Auburn, 1975-76, mgr. credit dept., 1977-81, dir. personnel, v.p. adminstrv. svcs., 1981-83; regional ops. officer Security Trust Co., Rochester, N.Y., 1984; asst. regional mgr. Norstar Bank, Rochester, 1985; regional mgr. Norstar Bank, 1986; v.p., regional mgr. Norstar Bank of Cen. N.Y., Syracuse, 1987-88, v.p. sales & svc. administr., 1989—. Bd. dirs. Cayugo Counseling Svcs., Auburn, 1982-87, YMCA, Auburn, 1976-82. Mem. Am. Inst. Banking (bd. dirs., Syracuse chpt.), Nat. Assn. Bank Women, Beta Gamma Sigma. Home: 23 East St Skanateles NY 13152 Office: Norstar Bank Cen NY 1 Clinton Sq Syracuse NY 13221

ELLIS, GEORGE EDWIN, JR., chemical engineer; b. Beaumont, Tex., Apr. 14, 1921; s. George Edwin and Julia (Ryan) E.; B.S. in Chem. Engring., U. Tex., 1948; M.S., U. So. Calif., 1958, M.B.A., 1965, M.S. in Mech. Engring., 1968, M.S. in Mgmt. Sci., 1971, Engr. in Indsl. and Systems Engring., 1979. Research chem. engr. Tex. Co., Port Arthur, Tex., 1948-51, Long Beach, Calif., Houston, 1952-53, Space and Information div. N.Am. Aviation Co., Downey, Calif., 1959-61, Magna Corp., Anaheim, Calif., 1961-62; chem. process engr. AiResearch Mfg. Co., Los Angeles, 1953-57, 57-59; chem. engr. Petroleum Combustion & Engring. Co., Santa Monica, Calif., 1957, Jacobs Engring. Co., Pasadena, Calif., 1957, Sesler & Assos., Los Angeles, 1959; research specialist Marquardt Corp., Van Nuys, Calif., 1962-67; sr. project engr. Conductron Corp., Northridge, 1967-68; information systems asst. Los Angeles Dept. Water and Power, 1969—. Instr. thermodynamics U. So. Calif., Los Angeles, 1957. Served with USAAF, 1943-45. Mem. Am. Chem. Soc., Am. Soc. for Metals, Am. Inst. Chem. Engrs., ASME, Am. Electroplaters Soc., Am. Inst. Indsl. Engrs., Am. Mktg. Assn., Ops. Research Soc. Am., Am. Prodn. and Inventory Control Soc., Am. Assn. Cost Engrs., Nat. Assn. Accts., Soc. Mfg. Engrs., Pi Tau Sigma, Phi Lambda Upsilon, Alpha Pi Mu. Home: 1344 W 20th St San Pedro CA 90731 Office: Dept Water & Power Los Angeles CA 90012

ELLIS, GEORGE HATHAWAY, utility company executive; b. Orono, Maine, Jan. 29, 1920; s. Milton Ellis and Carrie (Voadecia) White; m. Sylvia Poor, Aug. 18, 1946; children—Rebecca Anne, George Milton, Randall Poor, Deborah Josephine. BA, U. Maine, 1941, LLD, 1962; MA, Harvard U., 1948, PhD, 1950; LLD, Nasson Coll., Springvale, Maine, 1961, Bates Coll., Univ. Mass., 1968; DCS, Western NE Coll., 1968. Pres. Fed. Res. Bank Boston, 1961-68; pres., chief exec. officer Keystone Funds, Boston, 1968-74, Home Savs. Bank, Boston, 1975-85; chmn. bd. dirs. Ch. of Christ Pension Bds., N.Y.C., 1985—; chmn. bd. Cen. Maine Power Co., Augusta, 1983—. Editor, contbg. author: The Economic State of New England, 1954; contbr. articles to profl. jours. Trustee Econ. Edn. Coun. Mass.; mem. devel. coun. U. Maine, Orono, 1960-84; corp. mem. Univ. Hosp., Boston, 1978-84; bd. dirs. Greater Boston Community Devel., 1979-86. Maj., inf. U.S. Army, 1941-45, PTO. Nat. honoree Beta Gamma Sigma, U. Mass., 1968. Fellow Am. Acad. Arts and Scis.; mem. Phi Beta Kappa, Phi Kappa Phi. Congregationalist. Clubs: Comml. Mchts., Boston Econ. Home: 177 Benvenue St Wellesley MA 02181 Office: Cen Maine Power Co Edison Dr Augusta ME 04336

ELLIS, JOHN W., utility company executive; b. Seattle, Sept. 14, 1928; s. Floyd E. and Hazel (Reed) R.; m. Doris Stearns, Sept. 1, 1953; children: Thomas R., John, Barbara, Jim. B.S., U. Wash., 1952, J.D., 1953. Bar: Wash. State bar 1953. With firm Perkins, Coie, Stone, Olsen & Williams, Seattle, 1953-70; with Puget Sound Power & Light Co., Bellevue, Wash., 1970—, exec. v.p., 1973-76, pres., chief exec. officer, 1976-87, also dir., chmn., chief exec. officer, 1987—; dir., chmn. Seattle br. Fed. Res. Bank of San Francisco, 1982-88; mem. Wash. Gov's. Spl. Com. Energy Curtailment, 1973-74; chmn. Pacific N.W. Utilities Coordinating Com., 1976-82; bd. dirs. Wash. Mut. Savs. Bank, Seattle, SAFECO Corp., Electric Power Research Inst., 1984-89, Nat. Energy Found., 1985-87, FlowMole corp., Associated Electric & Gas ins. Svcs. Ltd. Pres. Bellevue Boys and Girls Club, 1969-71, Seattle/King County Econ. Devel. Council, 1984—; mem. exec. dirs. Seattle/King County Boys and Girls Club, 1972-75; bd. dirs. Overlake Hosp., Bellevue, 1974—, United Way King County, 1977—, Seattle Sci. Found., 1977—, Seattle Sailing Found., Evergreen Safety Council, 1981, Assn. Wash. Bus., 1980-81, Govs. Adv. Council on Econ. Devel., 1984—; chmn. bd. Wash. State Bus. Round Table, 1983; pres. United for Washington; adv. bd. Grad. Sch. Bus. Adminstrn. U. Wash., 1982—, Wash. State Econ. Ptnrship., 1984—; chmn. Seattle Regional Panel White Ho. Fellows, 1985—; trustee Seattle U., 1986—. Mem. ABA, Wash. Bar Assn., King County Bar Assn., Nat. Assn. Elec. Cos. (dir. 1977-79), Edison Electric Inst. (dir. 1978-80, exec. com. 1982, 2d vice chmn. 1987, 1st vice chmn. 1988), Assn. Edison Illuminating Cos. (exec. com. 1979-81), Seattle C. of C. (dir. 1980—, 1st vice chmn. 1987-88, chmn. 1988—), Phi Gamma Delta, Phi Delta Phi. Clubs: Rainier (Seattle) (sec. 1972, v.p. 1984, pres. 1985), Seattle Yacht (Seattle), Corinthian Yacht (Seattle); Meydenbauer Bay Yacht (Bellevue), Bellevue Athletic. Lodge: Rotary (Seattle). Home: 901 SE Shoreland Dr Bellevue WA 98004 Office: Puget Sound Power & Light Co PO Box 97034 OBC-15 Bellevue WA 98009-9734

ELLIS, LOREN BURRELL, paint company executive; b. Nampa, Idaho, Apr. 15, 1952; s. Abram Burrell and Marjorie Joyce (Draper) E.; m. Carmen Maria Loera; 1 child, Lorenna Lee. Student, N.W. Nazarene Coll., 1971-73, Boise State U., 1977-79. Store mgr. Caldwell (Idaho) Paint & Glass, 1979-80, State Paint & Glass, Boise, Idaho, 1980-82; pres. Ponderosa Paint Mfg., Inc. (formerly Mountain States Paint Mfg. Co.), Boise, 1982—; bd. dirs. Treasure Valley Bank, Fruitland, Idaho. Co-founder Paint Your Heart Out, community svc. event, Boise, 1984; mem. adv. bd. Boise Salvation Army, 1985—; mem. president's community adv. bd. N.W. Nazarene Coll., Nampa, 1986—. Recipient Community Svc. award City of Boise, 1985. Mem. Color Guild Assocs., Rotary. Republican. Nazarene. Office: Ponderosa Paint Mfg Inc 4631 Aeronca Box 5465 Boise ID 83705

ELLIS, ROBERT GRISWOLD, engineer; b. Kokomo, Ind., Dec. 28, 1908; s. Ernest Eli and Ethel (Griswold) E.; AB, Ind. U., 1934; m. Rachel O. Burckey, Oct. 27, 1984. Mem. staff Ind. U., Bloomington, 1930-34; researcher Blackett-Sample-Hummert Inc., Chgo., 1934, asst. mgr. merchandising, 1935-36; prodn. mgr. Harvey & Howe, Inc., Chgo., 1936-37; Chgo./Midwest dist. mgr. L.F. Grammes & Sons, Inc., Allentown, Pa., 1937-45; with Ellis & Co., Chgo. and Park Ridge, Ill., 1945—, pres., chief engr., 1948—, mng. dir., chief engr. Ellis Internat. Co., Chgo. and Park Ridge, Ill., 1965—, chief engr. Ellis Engring. Co., Park Ridge, 1969—. Chmn. Citizens Com. for Cleaner and More Beautiful Park Ridge, 1957-60; mem., treas. bd. trustees 1st United Methodist Ch., Park Ridge, 1974-77. Recipient Civic Achievement award City of Park Ridge, 1959. Mem. Soc. Automotive Engrs., Armed Forces Communications and Electronics Assn. (life), Ind. U. Alumni Assn. (life), Quartermaster Assn. (pres. Chgo. chpt. 1957-58), Ind. Acad. Sci., Am. Powder Metallurgy Inst., Ill. Acad. Sci., Mfrs. Agts. Assn. Gt. Britain and Ireland, Internat. Union Comml. Agts. and Brokers, Am. Logistics Assn., Am. Soc. Metals, Indiana Soc. of Chgo., Union League, Varsity Club (pres. Chgo. 1957), Ind. U. Alumni (pres. Chgo. 1956-57), Emeritus of Ind. U., Internat. Trade. Republican. Home: 643 Parkwood St Park Ridge IL 60068 Office: PO Box 344 306 Busse Hwy Park Ridge IL 60068-0344

ELLIS, SEAN WESLEY, state administrator; b. Hammond, La., Nov. 2, 1962; s. Norman George and Halla Jo (Francis) E. BSBA, U. So. Miss., 1983, MBA, 1985. Contract specialist Miss. Gov.'s Office Energy and Community Svcs., Jakcson, 1985—. Mem. Fin. Mgmt. Honor Soc., Rho Epsilon, Gamma Beta Phi, Omicron Delta Epsilon. Republican. Methodist. Home: Rte 1 Box 77 Terry MS 39170

ELLMANN, SHEILA FRENKEL, investment company executive; b. Detroit, June 8, 1931; d. Joseph and Rose (Neback) Frenkel; BA in English, U. Mich., 1953; m. William M. Ellmann, Nov. 1, 1953; children: Douglas Stanley, Carol Elizabeth, Robert Lawrence. Dir. Advance Glove Mfg. Co., Detroit, 1954-78; v.p. Frome Investment Co., Detroit, 1980—. Mem. U. Mich. Alumni Assn., Nat. Trust Hist. Preservation. Home: 28000 Weymouth St Farmington Hills MI 48018

ELLSWORTH, DUNCAN STEUART, JR., retired utility company executive; b. N.Y.C., Mar. 25, 1928; s. Duncan Steuart and Esther Bowes (Stevens) E.; m. Molly Tyler West, Nov. 27, 1951; children: Esther Ellsworth Miller, Duncan Steuart, III, William West. A.B., Harvard U., 1950. Cadet Elizabethtown Gas Co., Elizabeth, N.J., 1959, purchasing agent, 1959-65, adminstrv. v.p., 1965-73, sr. v.p., 1973-75, exec. v.p., 1975-80, pres., chief operating officer, 1980-84, pres., chief exec. officer, 1984-86, dir.; bd. dirs. Nat. Westminster Bank, N.J. Trustee Morristown Meml. Hosp., Stevens Inst. Tech., Adult Diagnostic & Treatment Ctr. Served to 2d lt. U.S. Army, 1950-53; Korea. Mem. N.J. Utilities Assn. (past dir.), N.J. Gas Assn. (past pres. 1976-77, exec. com.), Am. Gas Assn., Soc. Gas. Lighting. Republican. Episcopalian. Home: 61 Stevens Ln RD #1 Far Hills NJ 07931

ELLSWORTH, ROBERT FRED, business executive, former government official; b. Lawrence, Kans., June 11, 1926; s. W. Fred and Lucile (Rarig) E.; m. Vivian Esther Sies, Nov. 10, 1956; children: Robert William, Ann Elizabeth. B.S., U. Kans., 1945; J.D., U. Mich., 1949. Bar: D.C., Mass., Kans., U.S. Supreme Ct. bars. Mem. 87th to 89th Congresses from 2d and 3d Dist., Kans., 1961-67; asst. to Pres. of U.S., Washington, 1969; U.S. ambassador to NATO, 1969-71; gen. partner Lazard Freres & Co., N.Y.C., 1971-74; asst. sec. for internat. security affairs U.S. Dept. Def., Washington, 1974-75; dep. sec. Def. U.S. Dept. Def., 1975-77; pres. Robert Ellsworth & Co., Inc., Washington, 1977—; chmn. Howmet Corp., Greenwich, Conn., 1984—; trustee Corp. Property Investors; dir. Price Communications Corp., Andal Corp, Aerospace Corp. Lay reader Episcopal Ch. Served with USNR, 1944-46, 50-53. Recipient Presdl. Nat. Security medal, 1977. Mem. Council Fgn. Relations, Internat. Inst. Strategic Studies (vice chmn. council). Home: 24120 Old Hundred Rd Dickerson MD 20842 Office: 2001 L St NW Washington DC 20016

ELLWANGER, MIKE (CYRIL ALBERT), retired utility executive; b. Fond du Lac, Wis., June 26, 1925; s. Michael Andrew and Pearl Catherine (Markwardt) E.; m. Alyce Ann Grimme, Aug. 28, 1948; children: Michael, Stephanie, Timothy, Melinda, Julia. LLB, U. Iowa, 1952. Atty. Iowa Pub. Service Co., Sioux City, 1952-78, dir. employee relations, 1978-79, v.p. personnel, 1979-83, sr. v.p. staff services, 1983-84, sr. v.p. consumer services, 1984-86, sr. v.p. gas ops., 1986-87, sr. v.p., chief operating officer, 1987-88, sr. v.p., 1988, also bd. dirs., ret., 1988; bd. dirs. Siouxland Labor-Mgmt. Com., Sioux City, 1986—. Bd. dirs. Sioux City YMCA, Am. Cancer Soc., Sioux City, Marian Health Ctr., Sioux City. Served with USN, 1943-46, PTO. Mem. Jr. C. of C. (pres.). Republican. Roman Catholic. Lodge: Rotary.

ELLZEY, RANDAL EDMOND, accountant; b. Memphis, Jan. 19, 1958; s. T.E. and Betty (Caldwell) E. BBA in Acctg., U. Miss., 1980, M in Acctg., 1982. CPA, Tenn., Ark.; cert. fin. planner. Staff Price Waterhouse, Houston, 1982-83, Craig and Casey, CPA's, Houston, Miss., 1983-84; staff-in-charge Fouts and Morgan CPA's, Memphis, 1984-85; acct. L. Cotton Thomas and Co. CPA's, Little Rock, 1985-87; pvt. practice CPA, cert. fin. planner Memphis, 1987—. Mem. Soc. CPAs, Am. Inst. CPA's, Ark. Soc. CPA's. Republican. Methodist. Club: Exchange. Home: 74 Redthorn Cove Cordova TN 38018

ELMAN, HOWARD LAWRENCE, aeronautical engineer; b. N.Y.C., Dec. 18, 1938; s. Dave and Pauline (Reffe) E.; m. Joan Carter, Dec. 28, 1974 (div. 1985); children: David Lawrence, Elizabeth Nadine. SB, M.I.T., 1960; M in Aerospace Engring., U. Okla., 1962; postgrad. Rensselaer Poly. Inst., 1963-65. Registered profl. engr., Conn., Ohio, Tex., Calif. Research engr. United Aircraft Research Labs., East Hartford, Conn., 1963-68; sr. rotor dynamics engr. Sikorsky Aircraft, Stratford, Conn., 1968-70; sr. analytical engr. Pratt & Whitney Aircraft, East Hartford, 1970-71; research engr. Kaman Aerospace, Bloomfield, Conn., 1972-76; sr. mission equipment coordinator Hughes Helicopters, Culver City, Calif., 1977-80; sr. engr., sect. leader in ops. analysis Fairchild-Republic, Farmingdale, N.Y., 1980-85; sr. engr. Gould, Inc., 1985-86; prin. engr. in ops. analysis Grumman Corp., 1986—; cons. mus. and hist. socs. Contbg. author: The Changing World of the American Military, 1978; contbr. articles to various jours. Served to 1st lt. USAF, 1960-63, to col. Res., 1964—. Mem. Conn. Aero. Hist. Assn. (life; dir. 1968-76, v.p. research 1969-73, exec. v.p. 1973-76), Inst. Aero. Scis., AIAA, Am. Helicopter Soc., Nat. Soc. Profl. Engrs., Am. Aviation Hist. Soc., Soc. World War I Aero. Historians, Air Force Assn., U.S. Naval Inst. Home: 31 Old Post Rd Port Jefferson NY 11777

ELMER, MARY ELIZABETH, executive recruiter, consultant; b. Utica, N.Y., Dec. 23, 1954; d. Bernard Edward and Ruth Marion (York) E.; m. Peter Julian Baskin, July 28, 1984. B.A., Siena Coll., 1977. Mktg. rep. Hartford Ins., Albany, N.Y., 1977-80, Gt. Am., Syracuse, N.Y., 1981-82; v.p., sec. Personnel Assocs., Inc., Syracuse, 1982—. Mem. Nat. Assn. Female Execs. (network dir.), Am. Soc. Profl. and Exec. Women, Nat. Assn. Woman Bus. Owners (v.p. govt. affairs Greater Syracuse chpt.), Nat. Assn. Personnel Cons. (cert. personnel cons., regent 1986—, dist. dir. 1987—), Assn. Personnel Cons. of N.Y. State, Inc., Ind. Personnel Cons. Central N.Y., Internat. Platform Assn., Siena Alumni Assn., Nat. Mus. of Women in Arts (charter). Republican. Roman Catholic. Avocations: reading, collecting antiques, refinishing furniture. Office: Personnel Assocs Inc 731 James St Courtyard Entrance Syracuse NY 13203

ELMORE, EDWARD WHITEHEAD, lawyer; b. Lawrenceville, Va., July 15, 1938; s. Thomas Milton and Mary Norfleet (Whitehead) E.; m. Gail Harmon, Aug. 10, 1968; children: Mary Jennifer, Edward Whitehead Jr. B.A., U. Va.-Charlottesville, 1959, J.D., 1962. Bar: Va. 1962. Assoc. firm Hunton & Williams, Richmond, Va., 1965-69; staff atty. Ethyl Corp., Richmond, 1969-78, asst. gen. counsel, 1978-79, gen. counsel, 1979-80, gen. counsel., sec., 1980-83, v.p., gen. counsel, sec., 1983—. Served to capt. AUS, 1962-65. Decorated Army Commendation medal. Mem. ABA, Va. Bar Assn., Internat. Bar Assn., Va. State Bar, Am. Corp. Counsel Assn., Bar Assn. Richmond, Am. Soc. Corp. Secs., Raven Soc., Phi Beta Kappa. Home: 2901 W Brigstock Rd Midlothian VA 23113 Office: Ethyl Corp 330 S 4th St Richmond VA 23219

ELMORE, PARKER ELLIOTT, actuary; b. Pitts., Oct. 5, 1963; s. Dan Elliott and Judith Ann (Doyle) E. BA in Math., Cen. Conn. State U., 1986. Actuarial analyst Travelers Ins. Co., Hartford, Conn., 1987—. Mem. Nat. Soc. Pershing Rifles (pub. info. officer 1981-82). Republican. Home: 631 Talcottville Rd Apt #7PH Vernon CT 06066 Office: Travelers Ins Co 1 Tower Square 12NB Hartford CT 06183

ELMORE, PAUL VINCENT, medical products company representative; b. Macon, Ga., June 4, 1962; s. Jasper Gregory Jr. and Carolyn Margaret (Vasta) E.; m. Carol Anne Burnham, Apr. 25, 1987. BBA, U. Ga., 1984. Med. rep. Am. Home Products, Savannah, Ga., 1984-85; advanced med. rep. 3M Riker, Macon, 1985-89; clin. hosp. rep. Genentech, Inc., Macon, 1989—. Mem. The Mus. Arts and Sci. Recipient Cert. Appreciation Ga. Soc. Med. Assts., 1986. Mem. Med. Service Rep. Macon, Ducks Unltd., Ocmulgee Investment Club, Phi Delta Theta (sec. 1983-84). Republican. Roman Catholic. Club: Ga. Bulldog. Office: Genentech Inc 375 Hines Terr Macon GA 31204

ELMS, JAMES CORNELIUS, IV, retired aerospace and energy consultant; b. East Orange, N.J., May 16, 1916; s. James Cornelius and Iva Marguerite (Corwin) E.; m. Patricia Marguerite Pafford, Jan. 4, 1942; children: Christopher Michael, Suzanne, Francesca, Deborah. B.S. in Physics, Calif. Inst. Tech., 1948; M.A. in Physics, UCLA, 1950. Registered profl. engr., Calif. Stress analyst Consol. Aircraft Corp., San Diego, 1940-42; chief devel. engr. G.M. Giannini & Co., Pasadena, Calif., 1948-49; research assoc. in geophysics UCLA, 1949-50; mgr. dept. armament systems, div. autonetics N.Am. Aviation Co., Downey, Calif., 1950-57; asst. chief engr. Martin Co., Denver, 1957-59; exec. v.p. Crosley div. AVCO Corp., Cin., 1959-60; gen. ops. mgr. aeronutronic div. Ford Motor Co., Newport Beach, Calif., 1960-63; dep. dir. Manned Spacecraft Center NASA, Houston, 1963-64; dep. assoc. adminstr. for manned space flight NASA Hdqrs., Washington, 1965-66; dir. Electronics Research Ctr. NASA, Cambridge, Mass., 1966-70; cons. to adminstr. NASA as dep. dir. Space Shuttle Assessment Team NASA, Washington, 1975; corp. v.p., gen. mgr. div. space and info. systems Raytheon, Sudbury, Mass., 1964-65; dir. Trans. Systems Center, Dept. Transp., Cambridge, 1970-74; cons. to adminstr. ERDA, 1975-77; cons. to mgmt. of aerospace and energy cos. Newport Beach, 1975-81; advisor to adminstr. NASA, 1981-85; mem. space systems com. space adv. council NASA, 1970-77; advisor to dir., mem. adv. com. Strategic Def. Initiative Orgn., 1984-88. Patentee in instrumentation, computers, radars and mechanisms. Served to capt. USAAF, 1942-46. Recipient Spl. award NASA, 1964, Exceptional Service medal, 1969, Outstanding Leadership medal, 1970; Sec.'s award for meritorious service Dept. Transp., 1974. Fellow IEEE, AIAA; mem. Nat. Acad. Engring., Am. Phys. Soc., Air Force Assn., Assocs. of Calif. Inst. Tech. (life), Res. Officers Assn., Soaring Soc. Am., Aircraft Owners and Pilot's Assn., Explorers Club, Am. Legion. Episcopalian. Clubs: Balboa Yacht; Army and Navy; USMC Open Mess. Home and Office: 112 Kings Pl Newport Beach CA 92663

ELROD, ELIZABETH, sales professional; b. Irvine, Scotland, Oct. 15, 1958; came to U.S., 1966; d. Billy Franklin and Elizabeth A.F. (Henry) E.; m. Timothy Dwight Burgess, Sept. 3, 1977 (div. 1985). Student, Tri-County Tech. Inst., 1976-81. With customer svc. dept. Gardisette U.S.A., Anderson, S.C., 1979-80, asst. dir. mktg., 1980-85; area mgr. sales Gardisette U.S.A., Atlanta, 1986-87; rep. archtl. sales Graber Industries, Atlanta, 1986; regional mgr. sales Superior Drapery Co., Atlanta, 1987—. Co-chmn. United Way, Anderson, 1981-85; vol. March of Dimes, Anderson, 1986, Spl. Olympics, Atlanta, 1988. Mem. NAFE, Nat. Housekeepers Assn., Sporting Club Atlanta. Office: Superior Drapery Co 4 Executive Park #2403 Atlanta GA 30329

ELSAESSER, ROBERT JAMES, retired manufacturing executive; b. Canton, Ohio, June 25, 1926; s. Otto Louis and Rose Augusta (Hoera) E.; m. Norma Ruth Adams, June 25, 1934. BA, Denison U., 1949. With Janson Industries, Canton, Ohio, 1949; with Ins. Co. North Am., Cleve., 1950, The Hoover Co., Los Angeles, 1952-88; br. office mgr. The Hoover Co., San Francisco, 1952-53; dist. mgr. The Hoover Co., Fresno, Calif., 1954, Santa Clara, Calif., 1954-55, Sacramento, 1956-60; br. mgr. The Hoover Co., San Francisco, 1961-63, Kansas City, Mo., 1964-66; div. mgr. of div. 5000 The Hoover Co., Kansas City, 1967-68; mgr. distributor sales and spl. accounts The Hoover Co., North Canton, Ohio, 1969-71; v.p. export western region The Hoover Co., North Canton, 1972-74, sr. v.p., 1975-82; dir. Hoover Worldwide Corp., North Canton, 1981; exec. v.p., dir. The Hoover Co., North Canton, 1982-88, pres., 1988, ret., 1988; Pres. Hoover Mexicana S.A. de C.V., Hoover Indsl. y Comml. S.A.; bd. dirs. The Hoover Co. and Hoover Worldwide Corp.; bd. dirs. Soc. Bank of Ea. Ohio; bd. trustees Stark Devel.; chmn. Juver Indsl. S.A. de C.V. Mem. adv. bd. Leadership Canton; exec. adv. council Jr. Achievement. With USAAF, 1944-45. Mem. U.S. and Mex. C. of C. (bd. dirs., exec. com. 1983-88), Blue Coats, Brookside Country Club (bd. dirs. 1977, 79), Phi Delta Theta. Republican. Home: 2730 Brentwood Rd NW Canton OH 44708

ELSER, JOHN ROBERT, retired insurance company executive; b. Harrisburg, Pa., Sept. 4, 1912; s. Aaron Hackman and Edna (Cooper) E.; m. Mary Duncan Wirt, Sept. 21, 1940; children: Robert Cooper, Mary Duncan, Jo Anne. Student, U. Pa., 1935-38. Successively office mgr., asst. sec., corp. sec., pres., chief exec. officer Mchts. and Businessmen's Mut. Ins. Co., Harrisburg, 1937-1978, chmn. bd. dirs., 1970-85, now bd. dirs. Chmn. Mechanicsburg (Pa.) Sch. Dist. Authority, 1953; mem. Mechanicsburg Area Joint Sch. Bd., 1953-65, pres., 1960, sec. 1965-73; pres. Mechanicsburg Area Pub. Library Bd., 1976-78; chmn. bd. dirs. West Shore YMCA, Camp Hill, Pa., 1974-76, mem. bd. dirs. 1984—; bd. dirs. Area YMCA, Harrisburg, 1978-84, vice chmn., 1980-82. 1st lt. U.S. Army, 1944-47, PTO. Mem. Rotary.

ELSEY, GEORGE MCKEE, former association executive; b. Palo Alto, Calif., Feb. 5, 1918; s. Howard McKee and Ethel May (Daniels) E.; m. Sally Phelps Bradley, Dec. 15, 1951; children: Anne Bradley (Mrs. Roger Kranz), Howard McKee. A.B., Princeton U., 1939; A.M., Harvard U., 1940; L.H.D., Am. Internat. Coll., 1982. Mem. staff White House, 1947-53; with ARC, 1953-61, v.p., 1958-61; with various divs. Pullman Inc., 1961-65, asst. to chmn. and pres., 1966-70; pres. Am. Nat. Red Cross, 1970-82, pres. emeritus, cons. to chmn., 1983—; bd. dirs. Security Storage Co., Perpetual Am. Bank F.S.B. Pres. Meridian House Found., Washington, 1961-66, vice chmn., 1967-68, counselor, 1971—; mem. Nat. Archives Adv. Council, 1974-79, mem. com. on presdl. libraries, 1988—; trustee George C. Marshall Research Found., 1973-83, Brookings Instn., 1971-83, Harry S. Truman Library Inst., 1973—, Suburban Health Found., 1989—; trustee emeritus Nat. Trust Hist. Preservation, 1976—; fin. chmn. League Red Cross and Red Crescent Socs., Geneva, 1977-87. Served to comdr. USNR, 1941-47. Decorated Legion of Merit; Order Brit. Empire; medals from Red Cross socs. Finland, Korea, Greece, Netherlands, W. Ger., Can. and Magen David Adom (Israel); recipient Disting. Pub. Svc. medal Dept. Def., Internat. Humanitarian award Am. Red Mogen David for Israel, Henry Dunant medal Internat. Red Cross. Mem. Columbia Hist. Soc., AAAS, Nat. Geog. Soc. (trustee 1977—), White House Hist. Assn. (dir. 1979—), Phi Beta Kappa. Presbyterian (ruling elder). Clubs: Princeton (N.Y.); Metropolitan (Washington), City Tavern Assn. (Washington). Home: 5351 MacArthur Blvd NW Washington DC 20016 Office: 17th and D Sts NW Washington DC 20006

EL-SHISHINI, ALI SALEM, financial executive; b. Tanta, Egypt, May 11, 1939; came to U.S., 1963; s. M.A. and Tawheeda M. (El-Dakrorey) El-S.; m. Linda Judithe Boring, Feb. 3, 1968; children: Oliver William, Omar Salem. BS, Cairo U., 1960; MS, U. Tenn., 1968, PhD, 1971. CLU, chartered fin. cons. Teaching asst., physics dept. U. Tenn., Knoxville, 1968-71; postdoctoral rsch. assoc. U. Pa., Phila., 1971-74; fin. svcs. mktg. cons. Equitable Fin. Cos., N.Y.C. and Nashville, 1974—. Contbr. articles to profl. publs. Mem. Nat. Assn. Life Underwriters, Am. Soc. CLU and Chartered Fin. Cons., Internat. Assn. Fin. Planners, Estate Planning Council (Nashville chpt.). Episcopalian. Office: Equitable Fin Cos PO Box 50317 Nashville TN 37205

ELSHOLZ, DENNIS CLARENCE, civil engineer; b. Sandusky, Mich., July 19, 1944; s. Clarence Edward and Clara Marie (Colclough) E.; m. Mary Grace Uren, Dec. 21, 1968 (div. Aug. 1983); children: Kristina Marie, Daniel Dennis; m. Teresa Anne Hooper, June 16, 1984; 1 child, Scott Lynn. BS in Civil Engring., Mich. Tech. U., 1967. Registered profl. engr., Mich.; lic. residential builder, Mich. Civil engr. Mich. State Hwy. Dept., Flint, 1967-70; coordinator Darin & Armstrong, Inc., Flint, Detroit, 1970-74; dir. scheduling Smith, Hinchman & Brylls, Inc., Detroit, 1974-76; div. mgr. J.A. Fredman, Pontiac, Mich., 1976-81; project dir. Barton Malow Co., Detroit, 1981—. Sec. Brandon Sch. Bd., Ortonville, Mich., 1982, trustee, 1981, 83; mem. Brandon Sch. Bldg. Com., Ortonville, 1980-83, Gold Carpet Network Mich. Tech. U., Houghton, 1987—, Oakland County Parks Found., Pontiac, 1987—. Mem. Nat. Soc. Profl. Engrs. (Profl. Engrs. in Constrn. com.), Mich. Soc. Profl. Engrs., Royal Oak C. of C, Elf, Khorafeh Temple Circus Club, Lions (pres. 1977-88), Masons. Republican. Home: 111 Oak St Brighton MI 48116 Office: Barton Malow Co PO Box 725008 Berkley MI 48072-5008

ELTING, JOHN WINSTON, broadcast executive, consultant, actor; b. Chgo., Mar. 9, 1943; s. Winston and Marjorie (Horton) E.; m. Nancy A. Johnston, Sept. 17; children: Aleta, Melissa. Student, U. Va., 1961-63; BS, Columbia U., 1966. Assoc. Goldman, Sachs & Co., N.Y.C., 1967-71; v.p., mem. adv. com. Model, Roland & Co., N.Y.C., 1971-75; v.p., dir. Robert Fleming Inc., N.Y.C., 1975-79; pres., bd. dirs. Elting Enterprises Inc., N.Y.C., 1979—; exec. v.p. Shipboard Satellite Network Inc., N.Y.C., 1986—, also bd. dirs.; v.p. In-Touch Radio Network, N.Y.C., 1980—, also bd. dirs. Contbr. various articles to profl. jours. Pres. Elting Meml. Burying Ground Assn., Hist. Huegenot N.Y. Historical Soc., New Paltz, 1987. Lance cpl. USMC, 1961-67. Mem. Bond Club N.Y., Screen Actors Guild, AFTRA, Racquet and Tennis Club, Mashomack Club, Farmington Country Club. Office: Elting Enterprises Inc 515 Madison Ave New York NY 10022

ELY, JOSEPH BUELL, II, corporate executive; b. Boston, Nov. 5, 1938; s. Richard and Louise (Ludwick) E.; m. Barbara Kurzina, Aug. 5, 1967; children: Joseph Buell, III, Christina, Peter Douglas, Sarah Ann. BS, Boston U., 1965. Chief exec. officer Amoskeag Co., Boston, 1978—, chmn., 1987—, also bd. dirs.; chmn. Fieldcrest Cannon, Inc., Eden, N.C., 1982—, chief exec. officer, 1985—, also bd. dirs.; chmn. Bangor (Me.) & Aroostook R.R. Co., 1982—, also bd. dirs.; chmn., chief exec. officer Westville Homes Corp., Plaistow, N.H., 1974—, also bd. dirs. Trustee Boston U., 1987—. Recipient Collegium Disting. Alumni Coll. Liberal Arts award Boston U., 1981.

EMCH, ARNOLD FREDERICK, management consultant; b. Manhattan, Kans., Nov. 3, 1899; s. Arnold and Hilda (Walters) E.; m. Minna Libman, July 22, 1927 (dec. Sept. 1958); m. Eleanore Merckens, June 30, 1960; children: Arnold Devere, Frederick Bolebec. A.B., U. Ill., 1925, A.M., 1926; postgrad., U. Chgo., 1930; Ph.D., Harvard, 1934. Pres. Emch Constrn. Co., Wichita, Kans., 1920-22; regional dir. Tambly & Brown Co., Chgo., 1926-29; exec. dir. Chgo. Hosp. Council, 1936-39; assoc. dir. Am. Hosp. Assn., 1939-42, U. Chgo. Inst. for Hosp. Adminstrn., 1939-42; mgr. Booz, Allen & Hamilton, mgmt. consultants, Chgo., 1942-48; partner Booz, Allen & Hamilton, mgmt. consultants, 1948-60, ret.; cons. corp. 1960—, pvt. and personal mgmt. cons.; pres. North End Water Co., Colo., 1964-67; sec.-treas. North End Water Co., 1967-83; dir. mgmt. cons. Calif.-Time Petroleum Corp., 1967-70; pres. Glory Ranch Arabian Stables, 1966-85; sec.-treas. Eagle Rock Ranches, 1971-84. Author: Crowded Years, Uncommon Letters to a Son, Life, Love, and Logic; Contbr. articles to various jours. Trustee William Alanson White Psychiat. Found., Washington, 1945-46, v.p., 1947, pres., 1948-52; dir. Washington Sch. Psychiatry, 1946-56, Mental Health Soc. Greater Chgo., 1958-59, Council on Hosp. Planning and Resources Devel. State Colo., 1961-77. Served in AEF, 1918-19, France; comdr. USNR; mgmt. cons. to Navy Surg. Gen., 1942-45; hon. cons. Navy Surg. Gen., 1945—. Mem. Am. Philos. Assn., AAAS, Shakespearean Authorship Soc., English Cocker Spaniel Club Am., Chi Psi. Clubs: Harvard, University (Chgo.); Colo. Arabian Horse. Address: Glory Ranch Devil's Gulch Rd Estes Park CO 80517

EMERICK, DAVID WILLIAM, accountant; b. Pawhuska, Okla., Dec. 25, 1945; s. Earl Atherton and Madge Gwendolyn (Warner) E.; m. Sylvia Phipps, Au. 20, 1966 (div. Dec. 1985); children: Kimberly, Wendy. BS in Bus., Okla. State U., 1969. CPA, Tex. Bookkeeper Carl McCaslin Lumber, Hereford, Tex., 1976-81; acct. Brown, Graham & Co, Hereford, 1981—, dir., office mgr., 1983—. Bd. dirs. Rainbow Girls, Hereford, 1984-88, Camp Fire Girls, 1981-84. Served with USAFR, 1964-70. Mem. AICPA, Tex. Soc. CPA's (com. IRS rels.), Deaf Smith County C. of C. (bd. dirs. 1987—). Republican. Club: Hereford Country (pres. 1985-86). Lodge: Masons. Office: Brown Graham & Co 218 W Third Hereford TX 79045

EMERLING, CAROL FRANCES, consumer products company executive; b. Cleve., Sept. 13, 1930; d. Bernard and Florence A. Greenbaum; m. Norton Harvey Noll, Oct. 1, 1950 (dec. July 1951); m. Stanley Justin Emerling, May 2, 1953 (div. Aug. 1971); children—Keith S., Susan C.; m. Jerrold A. Fadem, Aug. 24, 1974 (div. Oct. 1978). Student, Vassar Coll., 1948-49, Case Western Res. U., 1949-50; LL.B. summa cum laude, Cleve. State U., 1955. Bar: Ohio 1955, U.S. Supreme Ct. 1971, Calif. 1975, N.Y. 1982. Instr. Cleve. Coll., 1956-59; from staff atty. to atty.-in-charge Legal Aid Defenders Office, Cleve., 1962-70; regional dir. FTC, Cleve., 1970-74, Los Angeles, 1974-78; sec. Am. Home Products Corp., N.Y.C., 1978—; adv. com. criminal rules Supreme Ct. Ohio, 1970-73; chmn. Cleve. Fed. Exec. Bd., 1973. Co-author: The Allergy Cookbook, 1969; Contbr. articles to legal jours. Founder Pepper Pike (Ohio) Civic League, 1959; sec. Pepper Pike Charter Commn., 1966. Recipient Claude E. Clarke award Legal Aid Soc., 1967; Disting. Service award FTC, 1972. Mem. ABA, Assn. Bar City of N.Y., State Bar of Calif. Republican. Office: Am Home Products 685 3d Ave New York NY 10017

EMERLING, EDWARD GEORGE, trading company executive, researcher; b. Meriden, Conn., May 4, 1924; s. Ignatius William Fochtmann and Anna Rose (Tyczkowska) E.; m. June Marie Paik, June 1, 1976. Student, Colby Coll., 1943; BBA, St. Bonaventure U., 1951; MA, Cath. U. of Am., 1954, PhD, 1970. Instr. econs. Cath. U. of Am., Washington, 1953-54, grad. asst., lectr. econs., 1954-57; asst. prof. econs. St. Bonaventure U., Allegany, N.Y., 1956-67, assoc. prof., 1967-70, prof. econs., 1970-85; chief exec. officer Far West Trade Group Inc., Honolulu, 1982-88, cons. domestic and internat. bus., 1988—; chmn. dept. econs. St. Bonaventure U., Allegany, 1959-74, prof. emeritus econs., 1986—. Served to 1st lt. USAAf, 1942-46. Mem. Am. Econ. Assn., Pi Gamma Mu. Roman Catholic. Home: 46-478 Haiku Plantations Dr Kaneohe HI 96744

EMERSON, ANDI (MRS. ANDI EMERSON WEEKS), sales and advertising executive; b. N.Y.C., Nov. 1, 1932; d. Willard Ingham and Ethel (Mole) E.; student Barnard Coll.; m. George G. Fawcett, Jr. (div.); children—Ann Emerson II, George Gifford III, Christopher Babcock; m. Kenneth E. Weeks (div.); 1 child, Electra Ingham. Successively v.p. Eugene Stevens, Inc., N.Y.C.; pres., dir. Emerson Mktg. Agy., Inc., N.Y.C., 1960—; pres., dir. Mail Order Operating Co. Ltd., N.Y.C. and London, 1976-88; pres., dir. Ingham Hall, Ltd., 1977-83; chmn. bd. Sonal World Mktg. Ltd., N.Y.C., and Delhi, India, 1983-87; elected N.Y. State Del. to White House Conf. on Small Bus., 1986; instr. NYU, 1960-65, 87—. Block chmn. fund raising ARC, Multiple Sclerosis, Nat. Found., Crippled Children, Found. for Blind, 1954-63; vol. worker Children's Ward, Meml. Hosp., 1964-66, Hosp. for Spl. Surgery, 1967; mem. adv. com. African Students League, 1965-67; bd. dirs. Violet Oakley Meml. Found., Phila., 1964-81. Inducted into Silver Apple Hall of Fame, 1985. Mem. Nat. Assn. Women Bus. Owners, Direct Mktg. Assn., Sales Promotion Execs., Advt. Club, Mktg. Execs. Club, Direct Mktg. Club of N.Y. (treas. 1960-61), Mail Order Profls. Group, Soc. Profl. Writers, Direct Mktg. Creative Guild (pres. 1975—). Founder, chmn. The John Caples Awards, 1977—. Home: 16 E 96th St New York NY 10128 Office: Emerson Mktg Agy Inc 44 E 29th St New York NY 10016

EMERSON, ANDREW CRAIG, insurance executive, lawyer; b. Ft. Wayne, Ind., Feb. 11, 1929; s. Kenton Craig and Lucille Katherine (Godfrey) E.; m. Marilyn Annette Kling, June 17, 1951; children—Daniel, Mark, John, Michael. B.S., Purdue U., 1951; LL.B., Ind. U., 1953, M.B.A., 1958. Bar: Ind. 1953. Atty. Indpls. Life Ins. Co., 1958-66, counsel, 1966-68, gen. counsel, 1968-72, v.p. gen. counsel, 1972—. V.p. Meridian Kessler Assn., Indpls., 1966, 74; elder Presbyn. Ch., Indpls., 1965-86. Served to capt. USAF, 1953-56. Mem. ABA, Assn. Ind. Life Ins. Cos. (sec., treas. 1971—), Ind. Life and Health Ins. Guaranty Assn. (sec. 1981-86, chmn. 1986—), Ind. State Bar Assn. (chmn. com. 1972-87, bd. mgrs. 1987—), Indpls. Bar Assn. (chmn. com. 1987—, bd. mgrs. 1987—), Indpls. Estate Plan Coun., Am. Coun. Life Ins. (com.), Health Ins. Assn. Am. (com.). Democrat. Presbyterian. Clubs: Literary, Sertoma (Indpls.). Home: 5671 Central St Indianapolis IN 46220 Office: Indpls Life Ins Co PO Box 1230 Indianapolis IN 46206

EMERSON, ANNE DEVEREUX, university official; b. Boston, Oct. 6, 1946; d. Kendall and Margaret (Drew) E.; m. Paul Burr, Sept. 6, 1969 (div. 1980); children: Josephine, Hannah. BA magna cum laude, Brown U., 1968; MA, Tufts U., 1969. Asst. to dir. Pathfinder Fund, Brookline, Mass., 1970-71; asst. to dir tech.adaptation project MIT, Cambridge, Mass., 1971-73; exec. asst. to v.p. adminstrn. Boston U., 1977-85, dir. adminstrn., program devel., 1985-88; exec. officer Ctr. for Internat. Affairs Harvard U., Cambridge, 1988—; cons. State Legis. Leaders Found., Boston, 1984-87. Panelist NEH, 1987; bd. dirs. Integrated Foster Care, Cambridge, 1985; trusee Winsor Sch., 1989—. Mem. Phi Beta Kappa. Home: 200 Pond St Boston MA 02130 Office: Harvard U Ctr for Internat Affairs 1737 Cambridge St Cambridge MA 02138

EMERSON, DONALD MCGEACHY, JR., appraisal company executive; b. Clearwater, Fla., Oct. 21, 1952; s. Donald McGeachy and Ann (Parker) E. B.S. in Bus. Adminstrn. and Real Estate, U. Fla., 1975, M.A. in Real Estate, 1976. Appraiser Don Emerson Appraisal Co., Gainesville, Fla., 1973-75, v.p., 1975-87, pres., 1987—; treas. Emerson Realty, Inc., 1977-86, pres. Emerson Realty, 1986—; owner, appraiser Don Emerson Appraisal Co., 1973—, pres.,1986—. Registered real estate broker, Fla. Mem. Gainesville Bd. Realtors, Nat. Assn. Realtors, Southeastern Interfraternity Conf. (program dir. 1975-76), U. Fla. Interfrat. Council (pres. 1974-75), Fla. Blue Key (treas. 1976-77), Fraternity Purchasing Assn. (chmn. bd. 1979-87), Am. Inst. Real Estate Appraisers, Soc. Real Estate Appraisers, Order of Omega (pres. U. Fla. chpt. 1975-76), Centurion Council (pres. 1981-82), Gainesville C. of C. (bd. dirs. 1985-87), Delta Tau Delta. Democrat. Roman Catholic. Home: PO Box 113 Gainesville FL 32602 Office: PO Box 882 Gainesville FL 32602

EMERSON, DUANE E., corporation executive; b. Shelby, Ohio, June 16, 1937; s. Earald Wesley and Thelma Waive (Randall) E.; m. Suzanne Elizabeth Bourgeois, June 20, 1959; children: Kathryn Lynn, Thomas Duane, Mary Ann, Michael Colligan. BS in Commerce, Ohio U., 1959. Staff acct., audit sr., then audit mgr. Price Waterhouse, N.Y.C. and Toledo, 1959-73; asst. corp. controller Ball Corp., Muncie, Ind., 1973-76; v.p. fin., dir., then mng. dir. Avery Laurence (S) Pte. Ltd. Ball Corp., Republic of Singapore, 1976-80; v.p. adminstrn. Ball Corp., Muncie, 1980-85, sr. v.p. adminstrn., 1985—; dir. Ball-InCon Glass Packaging Corp., Muncie; mem. exec. council Fgn. Diplomat's Midwest Trade Briefing Ctr. Policy panel, Indpls., 1987-88. Chmn. budget com. panel United Way Delaware County, 1984-86; bd. dirs. Muncie YMCA, 1988. Appointed to council Sagamores of the Wabash, 1987. Mem. Am. Inst. CPAs, Muncie-Delaware County C. of C. (mem. trade and devel.-sister city internat. com. 1988). Republican. Roman Catholic. Office: Ball Corp 345 S High St Muncie IN 47305-2326

EMERSON, FREDERICK GEORGE, service company executive; b. Quincy, Mass., Dec. 6, 1933; s. George Bliss and Mildred Louella (Hynes) E.; m. Marion Orr Stewart, June 10, 1961; children: Elizabeth Lynn, David George. B.A. with honors in Philosophy, U. Va., 1955, J.D., 1960. Sec., counsel Commonwealth Gas Corp., N.Y.C., 1960-67; asst. sec. The Greyhound Corp. (and subs. cos.), Phoenix, 1967-77, sec., 1977-88, v.p., sec., 1988—. Bd. dirs. Inst. Cultural Affairs Ariz., 1971—, Lupus Found. Phoenix, 1980—, Tchr. Venture, Inc., Friendly House, Inc., 1974-78, Crisis Nursery, 1988—. Served to 1st lt. Transp. Corps, U.S. Army, 1955-57. Mem. Am. Soc. Corp. Secs., Va. State Bar Assn. Office: Greyhound Fin Corp Greyhound Tower Phoenix AZ 85077

EMERSON, JAMES TIMOTHY, banker; b. St. Joseph, Mo., Apr. 17, 1952; s. James Kenneth and JoAnn (Orr) E.; m. Anita Louise Glickley, July 12, 1980 (div. 1988); 1 child, James Albert; m. Dorinda Lee Howell, Dec. 3, 1988. AA, Johnson County Community Coll., 1972; BS, Kans. State U., Manhattan, 1974. With Lenexa (Kans.) Bank & Trust Co., 1974-78, asst. v.p., auditor, 1978-80, v.p., comptroller, 1980-83; v.p., cashier First Nat. Bank Lenexa, 1983-84, first v.p., 1984; exec. v.p. Bank IV Lenexa, 1984—, also bd. dirs. Treas. Salvation Army, Lenexa, 1985; team leader Heart of Am. United Way, Kansas City, Mo., 1987. Mem. Bank Adminstrn. Inst. (dir.), Robert Morris Assocs., Overland Park (Kans.) C. of C. Republican. Roman Catholic. Lodge: Rotary. Office: Bank IV Lenexa NA 12345 W 95th St Lenexa KS 66215

EMERSON, WILLIAM STEVENSON, retired chemist, consultant, writer; b. Boston, Mar. 25, 1913; s. Natt Waldo and Marion (Stevenson) E.; m. Flora Millicent Carter, Dec. 12, 1958. A.B., Dartmouth Coll., 1934; Ph.D., MIT, 1937. DuPont fellow U. Ill., Urbana, 1937-38, instr. chemistry, 1938-41; research chemist Monsanto Co., Dayton, Ohio, 1941-44, research group leader, 1944-51, asst. dir. cen. research dept., 1951-54, asst. dir. gen. devel. dept. St. Louis, 1954-56; mgr. cen. research dept. Am. Potash & Chem. Corp., Whittier, Calif., 1956-60; sr. staff assoc. Arthur D. Little, Inc., Cambridge, Mass., 1960-72, ret., 1972. Author: Guide to the Chemical Industry, 1983. Contbr. numerous articles to profl. jours. Patentee in field. Mem. Am. Chem. Soc. (chmn. Dayton sect. 1952), Am. Ornithologists Union, Am. Birding Assn., Phi Beta Kappa, Sigma Xi, Phi Lambda Upsilon. Republican. Club: Chemists (N.Y.C.). Avocations: fly fishing; birding; golf; squash; reading; philately. Home: PO Box 030 Bristol Rd Damariscotta ME 04543

EMERY, EARL EUGENE, steel company executive; b. Youngstown, Ohio, Apr. 1, 1931; s. Earl Eugene and Florence (Machin) E.; m. Mary Therese Orton, June 4, 1955; children—Maria, Catherine, Erin, Kevin, Martin, Sheila, Noreen, Terrence, Earl Eugene III, Mary. Met.E., Youngstown State U. Cert. purchasing mgr. Buyer, Youngstown Sheet & Tube Co., Ohio, 1959-71, mgr. purchasing, 1971-75, gen. mgr. purchasing, 1975-78; dir. purchases CF&I Steel Corp., Pueblo, Colo., 1978-83, dir. purchases and traffic, 1983—. Mem. exec. com. Mahoning County Republican Com., Youngstown, 1973-76; bd. dirs. John Neuman Catholic Sch., Pueblo, 1981-85, Goodwill Industries, Pueblo, 1982—; v.p. United Way of Pueblo, 1982-86 . Purchasing Mgmt. Assn. So. Colo. (pres. 1982-83, dir. nat. affairs 1983-84, 87-89), Assn. Iron and Steel Engrs. (chpt. chmn. 1983-84, nat. bd. dirs. 1985-86), Am. Iron and Steel Inst. Lodges: Elks, K.C. Home: 7 Kingsbridge Pueblo CO 81001 Office: CF&I Steel Corp 225 Canal St PO Box 316 Pueblo CO 81002

EMERY, JAMES L., government official; b. Lakeville, N.Y., July 31, 1931; s. James B. and Ruth (Wamser) E.; m. Jill Houghton. B.B.A., U. Cin., 1953; Hon. Doctorate in Civil Law, Mercy Coll., Dobbs Ferry, N.Y., 1980. With Sheriff's Dept., Livingston County, N.Y., 1955-64; assemblyman N.Y. State Assembly, Albany, 1965-82, dep. majority leader, 1969-74, asst. minority leader, 1975-78, minority leader, 1979-82; adminstr. St. Lawrence Seaway Devel. Corp., Dept. of Transp., Washington, 1983—. Past chmn. Genesee council Boy Scouts Am., N.Y.; chmn. Livingston County Republican Com., N.Y., 1967-72; Republican candidate for lt. gov. N.Y., 1982. Served to col. USAFR, 1953-80. Decorated Legion of Merit, 1983, Meritorious Service medal, 1982. Mem. Am. Legion. Lodge: Rotary (past pres. Livonia, N.Y.). Home: 16 5th St NE Washington DC 20002 Office: St Lawrence Seaway Devel Corp US Dept Transp 400 7th St SW Rm 5424 Washington DC 20590

EMERY, JOHN CARLTON, insurance company executive; b. Omaha, July 30, 1938; s. Robert Jaynes and Nola Emery; m. Sharon Kay Burke; children: Courtney Ann, Robert James. BS, U. Nebr., 1961; MS, Kearney State Coll., 1965; LLB, Blackstone Coll. Law, 1970. Lic. securities dealer, stock broker; registered health underwriter, fin. planner; CLU. Tchr. various schs., 1965-70; producing gen. agt., agy. supr. Hartford Ins. Group, Nebr., Colo., Kans., Mo. and Okla., 1965-70; div. mgr. R.D. Marcotte & Assocs., Omaha, 1970-75, sales mgr., 1975-80, assoc. gen. agt., 1975-86, bd. dirs.; asst. v.p. Mut. United of Omaha, 1986-87; with Ameritas Fin. Svcs. (formerly Bankers Life Nebr. Fin. Svcs.), Omaha, 1987—; instr. Creighton U., Omaha. Active United Way Omaha, Christ the King Ch.; bd. dirs. Make-a-Wish Found., Duchesne Acad., Omaha, also trustee. Mem. Am. Mgmt. Assn. (instr.), Internat. Assn. Fin. Planning (instr. 1985), Omaha CLU Soc. (pres. 1986-87), Nebr. Health Ins. Assn. (pres. 1975-77), Omaha Assn. Life Underwriters (pres. 1984-85), Masons (32d degree), Shriners. Home: 9504 Capitol Ave Omaha NE 68114 Office: Ameritas Fin Svc 302 S 36 St #410 Omaha NE 68131

EMERY, JOHN COLVIN, JR., air freight company executive; b. Madison, Wis., July 14, 1924; s. John Colvin and Janet (Millar) E.; m. Frances Toomy, May 28, 1960; children: John Colvin III, Susan Farlow, Ann Louise, Michael William, Patricia Millar. Student, Dartmouth Coll., 1942-43. With United Airlines, 1944-45, Nat. Airlines, 1945-46; with Emery Air Freight Corp., Wilton, Conn., 1946—; v.p. sales Emery Air Freight Corp., 1956-62, exec. v.p., 1963-68, pres., 1968—, chief exec. officer, 1975-88, chmn. bd., 1979-88, chmn. exec. com., 1988—, also dir.; chmn. Bank of Darien, Conn.; dir. Gen. Housewares, Stamford, Conn., Pitney Bowes, Inc., Stamford. Served with A.C. USNR, 1943-44. Mem. Sales Execs. Club N.Y. (pres. 1967-69, dir. 1963—), Nat. Def. Transp. Assn. (life). Episcopalian (vestry). Clubs: Wee Burn Country (Darien, Conn.); Wings (N.Y.C.) (pres. 1980-81). Office: Emery Air Freight Corp Old Danbury Rd Wilton CT 06897

EMERY, ROBERT FIRESTONE, economist, educator; b. Kenton, Ohio, Jan. 18, 1927; s. Clayton Sprague and Sarah Webster (Firestone) E.; m. Phyllis Eileen Swanson, June 29, 1957; children: Ross David, Ann Elaine, Hope Roberta. BA, Oberlin (Ohio) Coll., 1951; MA, U. Mich., 1952, PhD, 1956. Fellow U. Mich., 1954-55; economist Fed. Res. Bd., Washington, 1955—; adj. prof. econs. Southestern U., Washington, 1960-88; chmn. dept. fin. adminstrn Southeastern U., Washington, 1963-65, dean sr. div., 1965-68, prof. emeritus, 1988. Author: The Financial Institutions of Southeast Asia, 1971, The Japanese Money Market, 1983. Mem. admstrv. bd. Chevy Chase (Md.) United Meth. Ch., 1978-80. Served as midshipman U.S. Mcht. Marine Cadet Corps, 1945-47. Horace H. Rackham Grad. fellow U. Mich., 1952-53; Fulbright Grad. Research student U. Rangoon, Burma, 1953-54. Mem. Am. Econ. Assn., Soc. Govt. Economists (treas. 1976-78), Internat. Economists' Club (pres. 1977—). Republican. Methodist. Home: 3421 Shepherd St Chevy Chase MD 20815

EMKEN, ROBERT ALLAN, diversified company executive; b. Portland, Oreg., June 13, 1929; s. Cecil Wheeler and Grace (Hill) E.; m. Constance

Cook, May 1, 1954; children: Judith, Janice, Robert A. BS, U. Md., 1951; MA, George Washington U., 1957. Staff acct. Stoy, Malone & Co., Washington, 1956-58; comptroller R.J. Reynolds Tobacco Co., Winston-Salem, N.C., 1958-70, R.J. Reynolds Industries, Winston-Salem, 1970-75; exec. v.p. Sea-Land Service subsidiary, Edison, N.J., 1975-79; v.p. fin. and adminstrn. R.J. Reynolds Tobacco Co., Winston-Salem, N.C., 1979-83, exec. v.p. fin. and adminstrn., 1983—; mem. Region Bd. Mgrs. Wachovia Bank Northwest. Trustee Winston-Salem Arts Coun., 1988. Served with USCGR, 1951-54. Recipient Corp. Leadership award Winston-Salem Urban League, 1988. Mem. AICPA, Fin. Execs. Inst., Nat. Assn. Accts. Home: 305 Banbury Rd Winston-Salem NC 27104 Office: R J Reynolds Tobacco Co Corp Hdqrs Bldg Box 2959 Winston-Salem NC 27102

EMLEN, WARREN METZ, electronics engineer; b. Elizabeth, N.J., Oct. 12, 1932; s. Andrew Arnberg and Dorothy Emma (Metz) E.; m. Carol Ringold Taylor, Sept. 28, 1958; children: Deborah Metz Baker, David Taylor, Anne Arnberg. BS in Forestry, U. Calif., Berkeley, 1955; BSEE, Pa. State U., 1963; MS in Systems Engring., U. So. Calif., 1973; MA in Pub. Adminstrn., U. N.Mex., 1980. Jr. forester U.S. Forest Service, Klamath, Calif., 1955-56; electronic engr. USAF, Griffiss AFB, N.Y., 1967-87; cons. forester, ptnr. L&E Environ. Cons., Rome, N.Y., 1965-87; Trustee DEDANE Trust, ANDOREM Trust; co-chmn. Industry Looks At Rome Air Devel. Ctr., Griffiss AFB, 1981; sec. Def. Intelligence Tech. Forum, Washington, 1981-86; automated data processing cons., 1987—. Contbr. numerous articles in field to profl. jours. Served to capt. USAF, 1956-67. Mem. IEEE (sr., chmn. engring mgmt. group Mohawk Valley sect. 1975-76), Am. Soc. for Pub. Adminstrn. Republican. Methodist. Home: 1509 Monte Largo Dr NE Albuquerque NM 87112

EMLET, HARRY ELSWORTH, JR., systems analysis company executive, researcher; b. New Oxford, Pa., Sept. 21, 1927; s. Harry Elsworth and Mary Jane (Myers) E.; m. Elinor Kathryn Stolee, Oct. 3, 1951; children—Mark David, Susan Jennifer Emlet Furst. Tech. degree Mercersburg Acad., 1945; A.B., Princeton U., 1952; postgrad. Luth. Theol. Sem., 1953-55. Systems reviewer Prudential Ins. Co., Trenton, N.J., 1955-56; engr. Martin Co., Balt., 1956-57; research analyst Melpar, Inc., Alexandria, Va., 1957-58; systems analyst Analytic Services, Inc., Alexandria, 1958-64, mgr., v.p., Falls Church, Va., 1965-84, dir., Arlington, Va., 1984—. Editor: Operations Research and National Health Policy Issues, 1977; Challenges and Prospects for Advanced Medical Systems, 1978; Systems Approach to Strokes and Heart Disease, 1980. Mem. editorial bd. Jour. Med. Systems, 1976-88. Served with U.S. Army, 1945-47. Mem. Am. Assn. for Med. Systems Informatics (bd. dirs., v.p. 1985-87), AAAS, AIAA, Ops. Research Soc. Am. (sect. chmn. 1976-77), Washington Ops. Research Mgmt. Sci. Council, Soc. for Advanced Med. Systems (bd. dirs., pres.), Symposium for Computer Applications in Med. Care (bd. dirs.), Alliance for Engring. Medicine and Biology (bd. dirs., treas.). Democrat. Lutheran. Club: Princeton. Avocations: skiing; tennis; music; reading. Office: ANSER Crystal Gateway 3 1215 Jefferson Davis Hwy Suite 800 Arlington VA 22202

EMMELUTH, BRUCE PALMER, investment banker; venture capitalist; b. Los Angeles, Nov. 30, 1940; s. William J. and Elizabeth L. (Palmer) E.; children: William J. II (dec.), Bruce Palmer Jr., Carrie E.; m. Canda F. Samuels, Mar. 29, 1987. Sr. investment analyst corp. fin. dept. Prudential Ins. Co. Am., Los Angeles, 1965-70; with Seidler, Amdec Securities, Inc., Los Angeles, 1970—, sr. v.p., mgr. corp. fin. dept., 1976—, bd. dirs., 1974—; pres., bd. dirs. SAS Captial Corp., Venture capital subs. Seidler Amdec Securities; bd. dirs. Denar Corp.; allied mem. N.Y. Stock Exchange, Inc. Past. bd. dirs. UCLA Grad. Sch. Mgmt. Served with Army NG, 1965-71. Mem. Assn. for Corp. Growth (pres. Los Angeles chpt. 1979-80), Beta Gamma Sigma. Republican. Presbyterian. Club: Jonathan. Home: 17146 Palisades Circle Pacific Palisades CA 90272 Office: Seidler Amdec Securities Inc 515 S Figueroa St Los Angeles CA 90071

EMMEN, DENNIS R., electric utility executive; b. Clara City, Minn., May 14, 1933; s. Ulfert and Grace (Caspers) E.; grad. U. Minn., 1960; m. Audrey Y. Gaasterland, Sept. 19, 1958; children—Kirk, Mark. With Deloitte, Haskins & Sells, C.P.A.s, 1960-64; with Otter Tail Power Co., Fergus Falls, Minn., 1964—, sr. acct., 1964-69, controller, 1970-75, v.p. fin., 1975-78, sr. v.p. fin., 1978—, also bd. dirs.; bd. dirs. Security State Bank. Trustee Lake Region Hosp., First Luth. Ch.; trustee Ch. Found.; active Jaycees. Served with Paratroopers USAF, 1951-55. C.P.A., Wis., Minn. Mem. Am. Inst. C.P.A.s, Minn. Soc. C.P.A.s. Clubs: Rotary (pres. 1975), Elks, Masons, Shrine. Office: Otter Tail Power Co 215 Cascade St S Fergus Falls MN 56537

EMMERICH, JOHN PATRICK, micro-computer company executive; b. N.Y.C., Feb. 15, 1940; s. Clifford L. and Anna V. E.; B.S., Fla. State U., 1970; M.B.A., Syracuse U., 1974. Vice pres., treas. Applied Devices Corp., Hauppage, N.Y., 1960-75; exec. v.p. Ontel Corp., Woodbury, N.Y., 1976-82; sr. v.p. Visual Tech. Inc., 1983—; bd. dirs. Ontel Corp., Lowell, Mass, Visual Tech. Internat. Inc., Lowell. V.p. N. Creek Property Owners Assn. (N.Y.), 1976. Recipient commendation U.S. Army, 1962, 64. Mem. U.S. Naval Inst., Am. Mgmt. Assn., Nat. Microfilm Assn., Am. Def. Preparedness Assn., Pres. Club, L.I. Assn. Bus. Commerce. Roman Catholic. Contbr. articles to profl. jours. Home: 89 Cox St Nashua NH 03060

EMMERICH, KAROL DENISE, retail company executive; b. St. Louis, Nov. 21, 1948; d. George Robert and Dorothy (May) Van Houten; m. Richard James, Oct. 18, 1969; 1 son, James Andrew. B.A., Northwestern U., 1969; M.B.A., Stanford U., 1971. Nat. div. account officer Bank of Am., San Francisco, 1971-72; fin. analyst Dayton Hudson Corp., Mpls., 1972-73; sr. fin. analyst Dayton Hudson Corp., 1973-74, mgr. short term financing, 1974-76, asst. treas., 1976-79, treas., 1979—, v.p., 1980—. Bd. dirs. CHART., Minn. Council Econ. Edn.; mem. corp. bd. Ministers Life. Mem. Nat. Assn. Corp. Treas.s, Stanford Bus. Sch. Assn., Minn. Women's Econ. Roundtable. Club: Minneapolis. Home: 7302 Claredon Dr Edina MN 55435 Office: Dayton-Hudson Corp 777 Nicollet Mall Minneapolis MN 55402

EMMERT, RICHARD EUGENE, professional association executive; b. Iowa City, Iowa, Feb. 23, 1929; s. Frank Thomas and Okie Leona (Seydel) E.; m. Marilyn Ruth Marner, June 19, 1949; children: Debra Sue, Andrea Gale Mazzuca, Lisa Alison. B.S., U. Iowa, 1951; M.S., U. Del., 1952, Ph.D., 1954. Supt. mfg. textile fiber dept. E.I. du Pont de Nemours & Co., Martinsville, 1965-67; asst. plant mgr. fiber dept. E.I. du Pont de Nemours & Co., Wilmington, Del., 1967-69, mgr. engring. tech. and materials, 1969-73, dir. research and devel. pigments dept., 1973-75, dir. instruments products photo products dept., 1975-77, dir. electronic products photo products dept., 1977-79, gen. mgr. textile fibers dept., 1979-80, v.p. planning dept., 1980-83, v.p. electronics dept., 1983-87; exec. dir. Am. Inst. Chem. Engrs., 1988—. Author: Absorption and Extraction, 1963; contbr. articles to profl. jours. Vice chmn. Stanton Sch. Bd., Del., 1961-64; chmn. adv. bd. Coll. Engring. U. Iowa, Iowa City, 1976-82; mem. adv. bd. Dept. Chem. Engring. U. Calif., Berkeley, 1979-87, chmn. 1982-83; co-chmn. adv. bd. Dept. Chem. Engring. U. Del., Newark, 1984-88; bd. dirs. Med. Ctr. Del., Wilmington, 1984—, Del. Found. for Physical Edn., Wilmington, 1981-87. Served with U.S. Army, 1954-56. Recipient Disting. Engring. Alumni award U. Del., 1985, Disting. Alumni award U. Iowa, 1988. Mem. Am. Inst. Chem. Engrs., Am. Chem. Soc., Nat. Acad. Engring., Del. Tennis Assn. (pres. 1979-80), Tau Beta Pi, Sigma Xi, Phi Eta Sigma. Republican. Home: 162 75th St Avalon NJ 08202 Office: Am Inst Chem Engrs 345 E 47th St New York NY 10017

EMMETT, WALTER CHARLES, broker; b. Lawrence, Mass., July 6, 1925; s. Walter Thornton and Agnes Owens Emmett; m. Laurel Stinett, Nov. 21, 1975; children Jeffrey, Nancy, Scott; stepchildren: Wayne S. Dammier, Victoria Blackburn. student Dartmouth Coll., 1942-43, 46-47; lic. real estate broker, Tex., Okla. Owner, pres. Emmett Bus. Brokers, Inc., Amarillo, Tex., 1978-85, 87—; The Emmett Group, 1987—; dealer, operator, pres. Emmett-Simm's Motor Co., Inc., Panhandle, Tex., 1985-86; bus. broker Boston and Chamblin Realtors, Inc. 1986-87; owner Your Graphics Are Showing, Amarillo, 1977-79; salesman Ada Realtors, Amarillo, 1976-78; salesman Stevenson Motor, 1969-74, Russell Buick, 1974-76; lectr. Amarillo Jr. Coll.; ptnr. S.W.O.R.D., small bus. seminar prodns.; pres. Bus. Appraisal Services div. Emmet Bus. Brokers, cons. sales tng. and mgmt. Past bd. dirs. Maverick Boys Club; past mem. adv. com. on comml. art, fine arts adv. council Amarillo Coll., comml. arts adv. com. Amarillo Coll.; lay reader St. Andrew's Episcopal Ch., Amarillo. Served with A.C., USN, 1943-46. Mem. Internat. Bus. Brokers Assn., Career Exchange Network, Am. Mktg. Assn. (Amarillo chpt.), Tex. Assn. Bus. Brokers, Amarillo C. of C. (past chmn. small bus. council). Episcopalian. Clubs: Amarillo, Downtown, Kiwanis (bd. dirs. 1979-80, 1st v.p., pres.-elect 1987-88, pres. 1988-89), Masons, Shriners. Home: 2611 Henning St Amarillo TX 79106-4923 Office: Tex Commerce Bank Bldg Suite 303 2201 Civic Circle Amarillo TX 79109

EMMONS, DAVID WAYNE, economist; b. Portland, Me., July 3, 1954; s. Robert Wayne and Edna (Low) E.; m. Carol-Ann Fudala, July 26, 1981. BA, Drake U., 1976; MA, U. Tex., 1978, Johns Hopkins U., 1980; PhD, Johns Hopkins U., 1985. Lectr. Goucher Coll., Towson, Md., 1980-82; vis. asst. prof. Va. Poly. Inst. & State U., Blacksburg, 1982-83, Wayne State U., Detroit, 1983-86; research economist AMA, Chgo., 1986—; cons. Ctr. for Health Policy Studies, Columbia, Md., 1986; reviewer NSF, 1985-87; referee So. Econ. Jour., 1984-87, Jour. Macroecons., Detroit, 1984-86. Contbr. articles to profl. jours.; editor book: Socioeconomic Characteristics of Medical Practice, 1986. Mem. SAR, Am. Statis. Assn., Soc. for Promotion of Econ. Theory, Econometric Soc., Am. Econ. Assn., Gen. Soc. Descendants of Mayflower, Art Inst. Chgo. Office: Ctr Health Policy Rsch AMA 535 N Dearborn Chicago IL 60610

EMMONS, RAYMOND ALLEN, banker; b. St. Johnsbury, Vt., June 19, 1950; s. Robert A. and Kathleen (Hubbard) E.; m. Kathryn Radzevich, June 20, 1970; children: Elaine, Craig. AA, Hartford State Tech. Coll., 1971; BS in Acctg., U. Hartford, 1976, MBA in Fin, 1979. CPA, N.C. Asst. v.p. budget and planning Colonial Bancorp, Waterbury, Conn., 1974-79; liability mgmt. analyst BarclaysAmericanCorp., East Hartford, Conn., 1979-81; asst. v.p., mgr. fin. planing and treasury ops. BarclaysAmericanCorp., Charlotte, N.C., 1981-85, v.p., treas., 1985-88; sr. v.p. treas., dir. corp. planning BarclaysAmericanCorp., Charlotte, 1988-89; exec. v.p., chief fin. officer Ga. Fed. Bank, Atlanta, 1989—. Bd. advisors N.C. Child Adv. Inst., Raliegh, N.C., 1986—, Council for Children, Charlotte, 1988—. Mem. N.C. Assn. CPAs, Nat. Assn. Accts. (bd. dirs. 1985-86). Republican. Roman Catholic. Office: Georgia Federal Bank 20 Marietta St Atlanta GA 30303

EMOND, LIONEL JOSEPH, management consulting firm executive; b. Winnipeg, Man., Can., May 31, 1932; s. Henri R. and Anastasia E.; m. Elizabeth Boelen, Sept. 9, 1957; children: Catherine, Pierre, Marise, Robert. B in Commerce, McGill U., 1953, MBA, 1957. Chartered acct., Can. Pvt. practice auditing, 1953-55; with Shell Oil Co. of Can., Montreal, 1955-58; mgr. fiscal dept. Can. Chem. & Cellulose Co., 1958-60; asst. corp. controller Kruger Pulp & Paper Co., 1960-62, controller, 1962-65; mgr. fin. Dominion Bridge Co., Montreal, 1965-68; asst. gen. mgr. Churchill Falls Project, 1968-70; sr. fin. cons. Acres Internat., 1970-71; v.p. fin. Can. Gen. Ins. Co., 1971-75; v.p., treas. United Coops. of Ont., Toronto, 1976-80; v.p. fin. services The S.N.C. Group, Montreal, 1980-83; ptnr. Guerra Emond Internat. Mgmt. Cons., 1983-86; pres., Emondial, Inc., 1986—; lectr. fin. Concordia U. Mem. editorial bd. Cost and Mgmt., 1965—; contbr. articles to profl. jours. Pres. Etobicoke Rate Payers Assn., 1978-80; mem. bd. mgmt. Etobicoke Olympium, 1977-80; mem. exec. com. Canadian Coop. Credit Soc., 1977-80. Recipient citation Canadian Coop. Credit Soc., 1980. Mem. Fin. Exec. Inst. (pres. 1986-87), Inst. Chartered Accts., Soc. Mgmt. Accts., Am. Assn. Cost Engrs., Montreal Amateur Athletic Assn., Les Artisanats Centre-Ville Montreal (pres. 1984—). Roman Catholic. Home and Office: 203 Outremont Ave, Outremont, PQ Canada H2V 3L9

EMORY, JOHN BROOKS, III, real estate developer; b. Birmingham, Ala., Nov. 23, 1942; s. Charles Horton and Edna deNyse (Gully) E.; m. Sandra Clair Holder, Mar. 11, 1967; children: Virginia deNyse, John Brooks IV, Catharine Holder. AA, Marion (Ala.) Mil. Inst., 1964; BS in Bus., U. So. Miss., 1967. Br. mgr. Jefferson Fed. Savs. and Loan, Birmingham, 1970-76; pres. Emory Realty, Inc., Birmingham, 1976—; mem. polit. action com. Nat. Assn. Ind. and Office Realtors. Mem. exec. com. Nat. Vets. Day, Birmingham, 1972—; chmn. diplomatic corps Birmingham C. of C., 1980; chmn. U.S. Congrl. POW/MIA award, Ala. Recipients, Birmingham, 1984; bd. dirs. Birmingham Regional Red Cross, 1975-80, Indsl. Water Bd., Birmingham, 1987—; mem. adv. bd. Jefferson County Family Ct., Birmingham, 1986—. Served as capt. U.S. Army, 1967-70, Vietnam. Mem. Birmingham Bd. Realtors (mem. polit. action com. 1984), Bus. Council Ala., Homewood C. of C. (exec. v.p., bd. dirs. 1972-74), Alpha Tau Omega. Episcopalian. Clubs: Mountain Brook Swim and Tennis (bd. dirs., house chmn.), Mountain Brook Exchange (pres., bd. dirs. 1977-78), The Club (Birmingham). Home: 2917 Montevallo Rd Birmingham AL 35223 Office: Emory Realty Inc 2102 A Cahaba Rd Birmingham AL 35223

EMPEY, MARTIN B., financial executive; b. St. George, Utah, Apr. 13, 1943; s. Martin Lynne and Leonora (Wilson) E.; m. Nancy Elizabeth Young, Jan. 21, 1967; children: David, Jill, Mark, Sara, Blake, Megan. AA, Dixie Jr. Coll., 1965; BS, Brigham Young U., 1968. Cert. fin. planner. Sr. analyst Hughes Airwest Co., San Mateo, Calif., 1968-74; v.p. St. George (Utah) Savs., 1974-78, Postal Credit Union, Salt Lake City, 1980-82; supr. membership services Utah State Employees Credit Union, Salt Lake City, 1978-80; v.p., sec., dir. Merrill Blake Inc., Salt Lake City, 1983-88; sec. Blake and Assocs., Salt Lake City, 1988—; pres. Blake and Assocs., Inc., Salt Lake City, 1987—, also bd. dirs. Mem. Salt Lake Estate Planning Council. Recipient Cert. Appreciation Utah Supplier Devel. Council, 1987. Mem. Internat. Assn. Fin. Planning, Inst. Cert. Fin. Planners (v.p. edn.), St. George C. of C. (rep. 1976-78). Republican. Mormon. Club: Exchange (St. George) (sec. 1971-72). Office: Blake and Assocs Inc 420 E South Temple Suite 303 Salt Lake City UT 84111

EMPLIT, RAYMOND HENRY, electrical engineer; b. Darby, Pa., May 2, 1948; s. Henry Raymond and Caroline Winifred (Parker) E.; m. Patricia Jean Jezl, Aug. 7, 1976; children—Eric, Susan. BS summa cum laude in Engring., U. Pa., 1978, MS in Engring., 1979. Engr., Custom Controls Co., Broomall, Pa., 1972-75, tech. dir., 1975-78, v.p., 1979-82; chief engr. Robertshaw Controls, Havertown, Pa., 1982-87; pres. Electronic Devel. Corp., Edgemont, Pa., 1987—. Patentee indsl. level instrumentation in U.S. and Can. Served with U.S. Army, 1968-71. Recipient Hugo Otto Wolf Meml. prize U. Pa., 1978. Mem. IEEE, U.S. Power Squadron, Eta Kappa Nu, Tau Beta Pi. Republican. Avocations: reading, wine, investing, real estate, boating. Home: 71 Sweetwater Rd Glen Mills PA 19342 Office: Electronic Devel Corp 5 Miller Rd Edgemont PA 19028

EMRICK, CHARLES ROBERT, JR., lawyer; b. Lakewood, Ohio, Dec. 19, 1929; s. Charles R. and Mildred (Hart) E.; m. Lizabeth Keating; children—Charles R. III, Caroline K. B.S., Ohio U., 1951, M.S., 1952; J.D., Cleve. State U., 1958. Bar: Ohio 1958. Ptnr. Calfee, Halter & Griswold, Cleve., 1965—; lectr. U. Services Bus. Ctr., John Carroll U., 1970—; dir. Best Sand Co., Gt. Lakes Lithograph, Clamco Corp., Hunter Mfg. Co., Ken-Mac Metals, S & H Industries, Somerset Techs., Inc., Wedron-Silica Sand Co. Former trustee, br. bd. chmn. YMCA; former officer, trustee Lake Erie Jr. Nature and Sci. Ctr.; former adj. prof. Baldwin Wallace U.; adv. mem. Hartzell Propeller, Lake Erie Elec. Co., Bil-Jac Dog Food Co.; lectr. Chartered Life Underwriters Assn.; former adj. lectr. Case Western Res. U.; trustee Rocky River Pub. Library; trustee, treas. Cleve. Area Devel. Fin. Corp.; trustee Fairview Gen. Hosp., prin. enterprise bd. Cleve. Zool. Soc., Lake Ridge Acad.; former mem. nat. policy adv. com. New Eng. Mut. Life Ins. Co.; mem. vis. com. Cleve. State Law Sch.; bd. dirs. N.E. chpt. Am. Cancer Soc. Mem. Nat. Assn. Corp. Dirs. (sec., bd. dirs.) Methodist. Clubs: Westwood Country (former sec., legal counsel), Union, Cleveland Yachting, The Clifton. Office: Calfee Halter & Griswold 1800 Society Bldg Cleveland OH 44114

EMRY, DEAN EDWIN, insurance executive; b. Stanley, Wis., Dec. 16, 1952; s. Leonard J. and Alvina E. (Monson) E.; m. Frances L. Dus, Dec. 14, 1969; children: Shannon D., Danielle L. Student, Wis. Teleconf. Extension, 1972. Lic. ins. agt., Wis. Regional sales mgr. Spencer Press, Sacramento, 1970-71; salesman Met. Edn., Chgo., 1971-72; ins. agt. Emry's Ins. Agy., Sheldon, Wis., 1971-76; owner Emry's Ins. Agy., Sheldon, 1976—. Town constable McKliney Twp., Taylor County, Wis., 1978-82, mem. side bd., 1982-84; mem. community devel. bd. Town of McKinley, 1984. Mem. Profl. Ins. Agts. Home and Office: W 15459 Spur Rd Sheldon WI 54766

ENBERG, HENRY WINFIELD, legal editor; b. Bethlehem, Pa., Oct. 4, 1940; s. Henry Winfield and Mildred Elizabeth (Jordan) E. B.S., U. Denver, 1962; LL.B., NYU, 1965. Bar: N.Y. 1967. Digester, Winthrop, Stimson, Putnam & Roberts, N.Y.C., 1965-69; sr. legal editor Practising Law Inst., N.Y.C., 1969—; bd. dirs. ZPPR Prodns., Inc. Contbr. articles. Republican. Episcopalian. Clubs: Wolfe Pack, Priory Scholars (N.Y.C.). Home: 250 W 27th St New York NY 10001 Office: Practising Law Inst 810 7th Ave New York NY 10019

END, WILLIAM THOMAS, marketing executive; b. Milw., Oct. 31, 1947; s. Jack Arthur and Cecil (O'Brien) E.; m. Nancy Kolb, June 10, 1969 (div. 1974); 1 child, Laura; m. Elyse Soucy, Feb. 23, 1980; children—Alison, David. B.A., Boston Coll., 1969; student, U. Vienna, Austria, 1967-68; M.B.A., Harvard U., 1971. Group product mgr. Gillette Toiletries, Boston, 1971-75; exec. v.p. L.L. Bean, Inc., Freeport, Maine, 1975—; dir. Hannaford Bros. Co., Portland, Maine, Ariel, Inc., Augusta, Maine. Corporator Maine Med. Ctr., Portland. Republican. Roman Catholic. Office: L L Bean Inc Casco St Freeport ME 04033

ENDER, JON TERRY, investment management executive, banker; b. Lincoln, Ill., Jan. 11, 1942; s. Edward and Vernie Ruth (Lindberg) E.; m. Linda Willard, June 15, 1968; children: Katherine L., Edward W. BA, Harvard U., 1968; MBA, U. Chgo., 1970. Chartered fin. analyst. Sr. v.p., dir. chief investment officer The Chgo. Corp., 1970—; bd. dirs. Deerfield (Ill.) State Bank, Chicorp Commodities, Inc., Chgo., CAPM, Inc., Chgo. Bd. dirs. McCormick Theol. Sem., Chgo, 1983—, Chgo. Commons Assn., 1976—; chmn. Winnetka Congl. Ch., 1986—; guarantor Goodman Theatre, Chgo, 1980—. Fellow Fin. Analysts Fedn.; mem. Inst. Chartered Fin. Analysts, Investment Analysts Soc. Chgo. (dir. 1987—). Clubs: University (Chgo.) (dir. found. 1978); Mich. Shores (Wilmette, Ill.); Harvard (dir. 1978—); The Attic; Bond (Chgo.). Office: The Chgo Corp 208 S LaSalle St Chicago IL 60604

ENDERS, GERALD L., limousine company executive; b. Lykens, Pa., Apr. 14, 1948; s. Arthur and Melba (Enders) Nagle; divorced; children: Lisa M., Jeff. Grad. high sch., Schuylkill Haven, Pa. Supt. Pipe Line Constrn. Co., Pa., N.J., 1968-78; pres. Lynn Exec. Coaches, Inc., Cressona, Pa., 1981—; pres., chief exec. officer Lynn Exec. Coaches, Inc., Cressona, 1984—; exec. v.p. mktg. Celebrity Conversions, Elkhart, Ind., 1984—; dist. sales mgr. Armbruster/Stageway Limousines, Ft. Smith, Ark., 1985—; v.p. Rickshaw Limousine Service, Inc., Cressona, 1986—; pres. Jerry's Camper Sales, Deer Lake, Pa., 1972-82, NE Sales & Mktg., School Haven, Pa., 1981—; exec. v.p. mktg. Citation Motorcoach, Elkhart, Ind., 1981-85, Celebrity Conversions, Elkhart, Ind., 1985—; dist. dales mgr. Armbruster Stageway, Ft. Smith, Ark., 1985—. Active Rep. Nat. Com., Washington. Recipient Pres.' award Rep. Nat. Com., 1985. Republican. Evangelical. Lodge: Rotary (pres. 1984, Diamond award 1985), Elks. Office: Lynn Exec Coaches Inc Rte 61 PO Box 115 Cressona PA 17929

ENDRIES, JOHN MICHAEL, utility executive; b. New Berlin, N.Y., Sept. 10, 1942; s. Norton Leo and Alice (Simons) E.; m. Anne Jones, Sept. 9, 1967; children—Carrie Anne, John Michael. B.B.A. in Acctg, U. Notre Dame, 1964. C.P.A., N.Y. Audit mgr. Price Waterhouse & Co. (CPA's), Syracuse, N.Y., 1964-73; asst. to v.p. fin., then v.p., controller Niagara Mohawk Power Corp., Syracuse, 1973-80, sr. v.p., 1980-87, exec. v.p., 1987-88, pres., 1988—, also bd. dirs.; bd. dirs. Niagara Mohawk Power Corp., Marine Midland Bank, Midstate div., Utilities Mutual Ins. Co., Hydra-Co Enterprises, Inc. bd. dirs. Child and Family Service, Sta. WCNY-TV/FM, Cornell Coop. Extension, Boy Scouts Am., United Way, Crouse-Irving Meml. Hosp. Found. Mem. Am. Inst. C.P.A.'s, Edison Electric Inst., Fin. Execs. Inst. (dir., past pres. Syracuse chpt.), N.Y. State Soc. C.P.A.'s. Home: 8518 Equestrian Ridge Manlius NY 13104 Office: Niagara Mohawk Power Corp 300 Erie Blvd W Syracuse NY 13202

ENDYKE, DEBRA JOAN, marketing professional; b. Manchester, N.H., July 24, 1955; d. Paul Ronald and Theresa Joan (Smith) Cote; m. Michael Thomas Pidgeon, May 15, 1976 (div. Aug. 1984); m. Thomas Allen Endyke, Sept. 21, 1985. BS in Computer Sci., N.H. Coll., 1984. Mktg. specialist Bedford (N.H.) Computer Corp., 1981-84; sales and mktg. dir. electronic services program First Software Corp., Lawrence, Mass., 1984-86; account exec. Genesys Software Systems, Inc., Lawrence, 1986-87; group sales mgr. N.E. data communications div. Panasonic Co., Secaucus, N.J., 1987-88; sr. account exec. Bus. Systems Sales Group Gen. DataComm, Inc., Middlebury, Conn., 1988-89; sr. cons. Hollis (N.H.) Info. Assocs., 1989—100; cons. data communications, ind., Derry, N.H., 1987—. Republican. Roman Catholic. Home: 77 Drew Rd Derry NH 03038 Office: Hollis Info Assocs 153 N Pepperell Rd Hollis MA 03049

ENG, ANNE CHIN, broadcast account executive; b. N.Y.C., Aug. 9, 1950; d. Fuen and Suit Fong (Mark) Eng; m. George Chin, June 28, 1978; 1 child, Lauren. A.A.S., Manhattan Community Coll., 1970; student Baruch Coll., 1972. Sales asst. AVCO Radio Sales, N.Y.C., 1972; asst., jr. media buyer R.D.R. Timebuying Services, N.Y.C., 1972-74; TV media buyer, planner Ogilvy & Mather Advt., N.Y.C., 1974-78; broadcast account exec. H.R. Television, N.Y.C., 1978-79, RKO TV Reps., N.Y.C., 1979-80, Petry TV, N.Y.C., 1980—. Avocations: Plate collecting; exercise; skiing. Office: Petry Television 3 E 54th St New York NY 10022

ENGBERS, WILLIAM EUGENE, venture capitalist; b. Evansville, Ind., Dec. 27, 1942; s. Eugene Philip and Kathryn Elizabeth (Casey) E.; m. Mary Alice Donald, Aug. 20, 1962; children: Alison Claire, Gretchen Suzanne. BBA in Acctg., Marshall U., 1964, postgrad.; postgrad., Seattle U. With Inco, Ltd., N.Y.C., Toronto, Seattle, 1964-80; v.p. Inco Venture Capital Mgmt., N.Y.C., 1981-83, Whitehead Assocs., Greenwich, Conn., 1983-87; mng. dir. Advanced Materials Ptnrs., Inc., New Canaan, Conn., 1988—; chmn. Plant Genetics, Inc., Davis, Calif., 1981—; dir. Nine High Tech. Cos. Republican. Roman Catholic. Home: 22 Indian Hill Rd Wilton CT 06897 Office: Wee Assocs 22 Indian Hill Rd Wilton CT 06897

ENGEBRETSEN, ARDEN BERNT, chemical company executive; b. San Francisco. BS in Polit. Sci., U. Utah, 1953, LLB, JD, 1955. Legis. asst., asst. atty. gen. Gov. George D. Clyde, Utah, 1958; legal advisor to plant mgr. Hercules Inc., Salt Lake City, 1959-68; with corp. hdqrs. law dept. Hercules Inc., Wilmington, Del., 1968-74, asst. treas., 1974-75, treas., 1975-86, v.p., chief fin. officer, 1977-87, vice chmn., chief fin. officer, 1987—, also bd. dirs. Bd. dirs. YMCA of Wilmington, chmn. fin. com. New Castle County YMCA. Mem. ABA, Del. Bar Assn., Utah Bar Assn., Fin. Execs. Inst. (chmn. com. corp. fin.), Fin. Exec. Research Found. (trustee). Office: Hercules Incorp 1313 N Market St Wilmington DE 19894

ENGEL, ROBERT GEHRELS, banker; b. Teaneck, N.J., Feb. 7, 1932; s. Daniel Currie and Margaret Mary (Sweeney) E.; m. Jane Virginia Coe, June 20, 1953; children: Jennifer Margaret, Robert Andrew, Elizabeth Hunter. AB, Cornell U., 1953; postgrad., Columbia U. Grad. Sch. Bus., 1957-59. Sales engr. Corning Glass Works, N.Y., 1953-55; asst. treas. Morgan Guaranty Trust Co. N.Y. (formerly Morgan Guaranty Bank), N.Y.C., 1957-61, asst. v.p., 1961-64, v.p., 1964-71, sr. v.p., 1971-78, exec. v.p., treas., 1979-86, group. exec., corp. fin., 1986-87, group exec., 1987—; group exec. J.P. Morgan & Co., Inc.; bd. dirs. Rockefeller Group, Inc., N.Y.C., Ogilvy Group, Ind., N.Y.C., Raychem Corp., Menlo Park, Calif., Ditchley Found., N.Y.C. Trustee Cornell U.; bd. dirs. N.Y. Hosp.-Cornell Med. Ctr., Teagle Found.; mem. Bergen County (N.J.) Rep. Com., HoHoKus (N.J.) Bd. Edn. Served with CIC AUS, 1955-57. Mem. Psi Upsilon. Republican. Episcopalian. Clubs: Union League, Laurel Valley Golf, Hackensack Golf, Meadow Brook, Mid Ocean. Office: J P Morgan & Co Inc 23 Wall St New York NY 10015

ENGEL, WALTER EDWARD, industrial search firm executive; b. Cleve., Oct. 4, 1943; s. Marvin Walter and Evelyn Josephine (Cartier) E.; BA (scholar), Case-Western Res. U., 1965; m. Sara Elizabeth Broyles, Apr. 8, 1967. Systems analyst Packard Electric div. GM, Warren, Ohio, 1966-68, prodn. control supt., 1968-73, mfg. supt., 1973-81; plant mgr. Sangamo div. Schlumberger Ltd., Clayton, Ga., 1981-85, pres.; F-O-R-T-U-N-E Personnel Cons. of the Tri-Cities, Inc., Johnson City, Tenn., 1985—; teaching asst. U. Ga., 1965-66. Mem. Am. Soc. Personnel Adminstrn., Am. Prodn. and Inventory Control Soc. Roman Catholic. Club: Sky Valley. Home: PO Box 157 Jonesborough TN 37659-0157 Office: F-O-R-T-U-N-E Personnel Cons 2700 S Roan St Exec Pk S Ste 206 Johnson City TN 37601-7587

ENGELHARDT, JOHN HUGO, lawyer, banker; b. Houston, Feb. 3, 1946; s. Hugo Tristram and Beulah Lillie (Karbach) E.; m. Jasmin Inge Nestler, Nov. 12, 1976; children: Angelique D, Sabrina N. BA, U. Tex., 1968; JD, St. Mary's U., San Antonio, 1973. Bar: Tex. 1973. Tchr. history Pearsall High Sch., Tex., 1968-69; examining atty. Comml. Title Co., San Antonio, 1975-78, San Antonio Title Co., 1978-82; sole practice, New Braunfels, Tex., 1973-75, 1982—; adv. dir. M Bank Brenham, Tex., 1983—. Mem. ABA, Coll. State Bar Tex., Pi Gamma Mu. Republican. Roman Catholic. Office: HC 3 Box 1 New Braunfels TX 78132

ENGELHARDT, LEROY A., paper company executive; b. Saginaw, Mich., Mar. 15, 1924; s. Herman J. and Alma (Engelhard) E.; m. Arlene L. Papineau, July 12, 1947; children—Richard C., Kay C., Douglas R. B.B.A., U. Mich., 1949, M.B.A., 1950. Plant, div. or subsidiary controller Chrysler Corp., 1950-60; mgmt. controls cons. Diehl K.G., Nuremberg, Germany, 1960-63; sec. Genesee Brewing Co., Rochester, N.Y., 1963-67; v.p. fin. Consol. Papers, Inc., Wisconsin Rapids, Wis., 1967—; also dir. Consol. Papers, Inc.; dir. Consol. Water Power Co., Mead Realty Corp. Bd. dirs. Consol. Civic Found.; dir. Riverview Hosp. Assn. Served with AUS, 1943-46. Home: 444 2 Mile Ave Wisconsin Rapids WI 54494 Office: Consol Papers Inc 231 1st Ave N PO Box 8050 Wisconsin Rapids WI 54495-8050

ENGELKING, ELLEN MELINDA, foundry pattern company executive, real estate broker; b. Columbus, Ind., May 12, 1942; d. Lowell Eugene and Marcella (Brane) E.; children: Melissa Claire Fairbanks John David Prohaska, Ellen Margaret Prohaska. Student Sullins Coll., 1961, Franklin Coll., 1961-62, Ind. U., 1963. Vice chmn., pres., chief exec. officer Engelking Patterns, Inc., Columbus, Ind., 1980—, dir., treas., chief exec. officer Engelking Properties, Inc., Columbus, 1980—; guest speaker bus. sch. Ind. U., Bloomington, 1985-86, Ball State U., Muncie, Ind., 1986. Campaign chmn. Am. Heart Assn., Bartholomew County, 1980-81; chmn. Mothers March of Dimes, Bartholomew County, 1967; sec. Bartholomew County Rep. Party, 1976-80; bd. dirs. Found. for Youth, 1975-78, Quinco Found., 1978-79; protocol hostess Pan Am. Games X, Indpls., 1987. Mem. Alumni Coun. Franklin Coll., U.S. C. of C., Ind. C. of C., Columbus Area C. of C. (bd. dirs. 1987—), Ind. Mfg. Assn., Am. Foundrymens Soc., Internat. Platform Assn., Acad. of Model Aeronautics, Alumni Coun. of Franklin Coll., Delta Delta Delta. Roman Catholic. Avocations: study and present adaptation of Shaker work ethic, remote-controlled aircrafts, literature, oil painting. Office: Engelking Patterns Inc PO Box 607 Columbus IN 47202

ENGELMAN, IRWIN, bank executive; b. N.Y.C., May 9, 1934; s. Max and Julia (Shaoul) E.; m. Rosalyn Ackerman, Nov. 24, 1956; children: Madeleine F., Marianne L. B.B.A., CCNY, 1955; J.D., Bklyn. Law Sch., 1961. Bar: N.Y. 1962; C.P.A., N.J. Sr. acct. Pub. Acctg., N.Y.C., 1959-62; controller Razdow Labs., Inc., Newark, 1962-65; bus. mgr. Becker & Becker Asso., Inc., N.Y.C., 1965-66; with Xerox Corp., Rochester, N.Y., 1966-78; corp. v.p. Xerox Corp., 1975-78; v.p., chief fin. officer, dir. Singer Co., Stamford, Conn., 1978-81; exec. v.p., chief fin. officer Gen. Foods Corp., White Plains, N.Y., 1981-87; exec. v.p. The Blackstone Group, N.Y.C., 1987-88; pres., chief operating officer Citytrust Bancorp, Bridgeport, Conn., 1988—; assoc. prof. Monroe Community Coll., 1967-68; dir. Alcide Corp., Citytrust Bancorp., LMH Fund Ltd. Bd. dirs. Citizens Tax League, 1971-78, Long Wharf Theatre, New Haven, Conn., U. Bridgeport, Norwalk (Conn.) Hosp. Served with U.S. Army, 1957-58. Fellow Am. Bar Assn., Am. Inst. C.P.A.s; mem. Acctg. Research Found., Fin. Execs. Inst., N.J. Soc. C.P.A.s. Clubs: Econ. of N.Y, University. Home: 12 Old Hill Rd Westport CT 06880 Office: Citytrust Bancorp 961 Main St Bridgeport CT 06601

ENGELS, LAWRENCE ARTHUR, metals company executive; b. Darlington, Wis., Sept. 26, 1933; s. Henry Morris and Nell Ellen (O'Connor) E.; m. Marilyn Rae Stellick, Sept. 6, 1958; children: Laurie, Michael, Thomas, Stephen. B.B.A., U. Wis., 1959; M.B.A., Northwestern U., 1970. Dist. credit mgr. U.S. Steel Corp., Chgo., 1959-69; asst. treas. Nat. Can Corp., Chgo., 1969-77; corp. treas. Comml. Metals Co., Dallas, 1977—; chief fin. officer and treas. Comml. Metals Co., 1979—; v.p., treas., chief fin. officer Comml. Metals Co., Dallas, 1981—. Served with USN, 1952-55. Fellow Nat. Inst. Credit; mem. Cash Mgmt. Practitioners Assn. (Chgo. sec. 1975), Chgo. Midwest Credit Mgmt. Assn. (dir. 1973-75), Chgo. Midwest Credit Service Corp. (dir. 1975), Fin. Execs. Inst., Nat. Assn. Corp. Treas. Office: Comml Metals Co 7800 Stemmons Frwy Dallas TX 75247

ENGEN, LEE EMERSON, savings and loan executive; b. Clark, S.D., Sept. 8, 1921; s. Harold O. and Esther V. (Heig) E.; m. Elizabeth M. Eaton, Oct. 29, 1943; children: Barry Lee, Rodney Kent, Timothy Ray. BS, S.D. State U., 1947; postgrad. Ind. U., 1961. Furrier, Norris Furs, Sioux Falls, S.D., 1947-50; with Home Fed. Savs. and Loan Assn., Sioux Falls, 1953-86, pres., 1970-86. Treas., Sioux Empire United Way, 1968-73, campaign chmn., 1976, pres., 1982-83; bd. dirs. Sioux Valley Hosp., 1972-81; pres. Family Practice Ctr., 1977-78; treas. Crippled Children Hosp. and Sch., 1975-83; pres., 1983-84; pres. Jr. Achievement, 1971-72; sec. Sioux Falls Community Hotel Corp., 1975-85 ; mem. Sioux Falls City Planning Commn., 1968-76; treas. Sioux Falls High Sch. Found., 1973—; chmn. Sioux Valley Hosp. Found., 1984-86, bd. dirs., 1984-87; pres. Nordland Fest, 1987-88, also bd. dirs. 1983—; bd. dirs. MinnIaKota coun. Gir; Scouts U.S. Served with AUS, 1943-46, U.S. Army, 1950-53. Decorated Bronze Star with 2 oak leaf clusters, Purple Heart; named Boss of Yr., Sioux Falls Jaycees, 1967, Bus. Citizen of Yr., Sioux Falls Area C. of C. and Sioux Falls Sales & Mktg. Execs, 1985, Boss of Yr., Am. Bus. Womens Assn., 1986; recipient Bronze Leadership award Jr. Achievement, 1978, Silver Leadership award, 1985, Disting. Service award Sioux Falls Cosmopolitan Club, 1981. Mem. Sioux Falls Area C. of C. (pres. 1973-74). Mem. United Ch. of Christ. Club: Minnehaha Country. Lodges: Masons, Shriners, Elks. Home: 3000 West 34th St #301 Sioux Falls SD 57105 Office: 360 Boyce Greeley Bldg Sioux Falls SD 57102

ENGLAND, CHESTER ROLLA, III, food products executive; b. Bellevue, Pa., Dec. 4, 1945; s. John Robert and Helen (Chalker) E.; m. Carol Andrews, July 15, 1967; children: Christopher Todd, Bethany Lynn. BA in Microbiology, Cornell U., 1967. Mgr. quality audits H.J. Heinz Co., Pitts., 1967-77; group mgr. concentrate quality assurance PepsiCo, Inc., Purchase, N.Y., 1985—; group mgr. quality assurance Burger King Corp. subs. PepsiCo, Inc., Miami, 1977-1985, group dir. quality assurance, 1985—. Active Nat. Conf. on Foods Protection. Mem. Inst. Food Technologists, Am. Pub. Health Assn., Internat. Assn. Milk, Food Environ. Sanitarians, Am. Soc. Quality Control (cert. quality engr.), Quality Assurance Officers Group of Nat. Restaurant Assn. (chmn. 1987-88). Republican. Baptist. Office: Burger King Corp Box 520783 GMF Miami FL 33152

ENGLAR, JOHN DAVID, textile company executive, lawyer; b. Baldwin, N.Y., Feb. 19, 1947; s. Jack Donald and Edith (Blackwell) E.; m. Linda Meter, May 10, 1986. BA magna cum laude, Duke U., 1969, JD, 1972. Bar: N.Y. 1973. Assoc. Davis Polk and Wardwell, N.Y.C. and Paris, 1972-78; corp. atty. Burlington Industries, Inc., Greensboro, N.C., 1978—, v.p., gen. counsel, sec., 1984—. Chmn. bd. trustees Central N.C. chpt. Nat. Multiple Sclerosis Soc., 1984-86; mem. bd. visitors Wake Forest U. Sch. Law. Mem. ABA, N.C. Bar Assn., Order of Coif, Phi Beta Kappa. Home: 215 Ridgeway Dr Greensboro NC 27403 Office: Burlington Industries Inc 3330 W Friendly Ave Greensboro NC 27410

ENGLE, DONALD EDWARD, retired railway executive, lawyer; b. St. Paul, Mar. 5, 1927; s. Merlin Edward and Edna May (Berger) E.; m. Nancy Ruth Frank, Mar. 18, 1950; children: David Edward, Daniel Thomas, Nancy Ann. B.A., Macalester Coll., St. Paul, 1948; J.D., U. Minn., 1952, B.S.L., 1950. Bar: Minn. 1952, Mo. 1972. Law clk., spl. atty. Atty. Gen.'s Office Minn., 1951-52; atty., asst. gen. solicitor, asst. gen. counsel G.N. Ry., St. Paul, 1953-70; asso. gen. counsel Burlington No., Inc., 1970-72; v.p., gen. counsel S.L.-S.F. Ry., St. Louis, 1972-80; v.p. law, sec. S.L.-S.F. Ry., 1979-80; v.p. law Burlington No., Inc., St. Paul, 1980-81; v.p. corp. law Burlington No. Ry., St. Paul, 1981-83, sr. v.p. law and govt. affairs, sec., 1983-86, also dir.; ptnr. Oppenheimer, Wolff & Donnelly, 1986—; continuing edn. lectr. U. Minn. Bd. dirs. YMCA, St. Paul, 1981-84; bd. dirs. ARC, 1981-84. Served with USNR, 1945-46. Mem. Am., Mo., Minn., Ramsey County, St. Louis bar assns., Phi Delta Phi. Republican. Lutheran. Clubs: St. Paul Athletic, North Oaks Golf, Minnesota (St. Paul); Bellerive Country (St. Louis);. Home: 9 West Bay Ln Saint Paul MN 55127 Office: Oppenheimer Wolff & Donnelly 1700 1st Bank Bldg Saint Paul MN 55101

ENGLE, RICHARD CARLYLE, utilities executive; b. Atlantic, Iowa, May 11, 1934; s. Leland Stanford and Mabel Irene (Tuttle) E.; m. Marilyn Joy Lewis, June 15, 1958; children: Rachel Engle Johnson, Rebecca Engle Spears, Ruth Ann, Naomi Lynn. BSEE, Iowa State U., 1957. Registered profl. engr., Iowa. Field engr. Westinghouse Electric Corp., Sioux City, Iowa, 1957-65; substation engr. Iowa Pub. Service Co., Sioux City, 1965-75, asst. chief engr., 1975-79, v.p. corp. planning, 1979-81, v.p. prodn., 1981-83, v.p. ops., 1983-84, sr. v.p. ops., 1984-86, sr. v.p. electric div., 1986-88, sr. v.p., chief operating officer, 1988—; sr. v.p. Midwest Energy Co., Sioux City, 1987—; bd. dirs. Norwest Bank Sioux City Nat. Assn., Iowa Pub. Service Co., Midwest Energy Co., Sioux City. Contbr. articles to profl. jours. Bd. dirs. Sioux City Concert Course Assn., pres. 1975-82; bd. dirs., chmn. St. Luke's Regional Med. Ctr., Sioux City, 1978—; bd. dirs. Sioux City Symphony Orch. Assn., 1980—; Siouxland Found., 1988—, Morningside Coll., 1988—. Mem. IEEE (sect. chmn. 1964), Am. Interprofl. Inst., Sinfonia Frat. (chpt. pres. 1956-57), Rotary. Republican. Methodist. Home: 3624 Juniper Ct Sioux City IA 51106 Office: Iowa Pub Svc Co 401 Douglas PO Box 778 Sioux City IA 51102

ENGLEHART, LAWRENCE FRANZ, technology executive; b. Cass City, Mich., Nov. 5, 1948; s. Lawrence Arthur and Elfriede Anna (Bess); m. Sabdra Ruth Ross, Aug. 18, 1979; 1 child, Erin Margaret. Student, Fla. Jr. Coll., 1968-69, Macomb County Community Coll., 1971-73, Kellogg Community Coll., 1980-83; cert. in electronics, USN Electronics Inst., 1968. Owner Warren, Mich., 1971-74; mgr. quality control Essex, Plainwell, Mich., 1974-75; test. engr. quality control ITT, Oak Park, Mich., 1975-77; systems engr. Technicron Instruments, Tarrytown, N.Y., 1977-83, sales mgr., 1983-88, sales mgr. nat. accounts, 1988—. Active Algonquin Lake Assn. 4th July Commn., Hastings, 1982-87, 87-88. With USN, 1967-70. Mem. Clin. Lab. Mgrs. Assn., Soc. Mfg. Engrs., Centurian Club, Elks (chaplain Hastings club 1982-83, activity chair 1988—), Masons, Order Eastern Star, Rotary. Office: Technicon Instruments 953 N Larch Ave Elmhurst IL 60126

ENGLEHAUPT, WILLIAM MYLES, III, human resources executive; b. Chgo., May 6, 1954; s. William Myles and Dorothy (Fuller) E.; m. Carol H. Kingsland, Nov. 20, 1982. BS, Grand Valley State Coll., 1976; MA in Instructional Tech., Mich. State U., 1978; cert. in adult edn., Nat. Coll. Edn., 1983. Adminstrv. asst. St. Mary's Hosp., Grand Rapids, Mich., 1975-77; audio-visual producer Mt. Prospect, Ill., 1978-80; staff trainer Luth. Gen. Hosp., Park Ridge, Ill., 1980-82, No. Trust Co., Chgo., 1983-85; instructional designer Arthur Andersen and Co., Chgo., 1982-83; sr. cons. Carlson/Nathanson Group Inc., Wilmette, Ill., 1985-88; mgr. mgmt. devel. Square D Co., Palatine, Ill., 1988—. Vol. cons. Bus. Vols. for Arts, Chgo., 1985—; vol. arbitrator Better Bus. Bur., Chgo., 1987—. Mem. Nat. Soc. Performance and Instrn. (pres. elect Chgo. chpt. 1989—), Am. Soc. Tng. and Devel., Soc. Tech. Communication. Office: Square D Co 1415 S Roselle Rd Palatine IL 60067

ENGLER, J. CURTIS, insurance company executive; b. St. Louis, July 25, 1947; s. J. Marion and Martha (Lyter) E.; m. Rosalie McRee Ewing, June 27, 1970; children: Rosalie Ewing, McRee Leschen. BS, St. Louis U., 1970. Account exec. trainee Marsh & McLennan, St. Louis, Mo., 1970-75; cons. Marsh & McLennan, N.Y.C., 1975-76; v.p. Marsh & McLennan, St. Louis, 1976-81; chmn., chief exec. officer Bayly, Martin & Fay of Mo., St. Louis, 1981-87, Engler, Hundhausen & Lockos Ins. Group, St. Louis, 1987—. Founder, Samuel Cupples House Found., St. Louis, 1973—; mem. St. Louis Assn. Retarded Citizens, 1973—; dir. Edgewood Children's Hosp. Mem. The Pine St. Club, St. Louis Country Club, Racquet Club. Republican. Presbyterian. Home: 24 Lorenzo Ln Saint Louis MO 63124 Office: EHL Ins Group 300 Hunter Ave Saint Louis MO 63124

ENGLER, W. JOSEPH, JR., lawyer; b. Fountain Springs, Pa., May 7, 1940; s. W. Joseph and Mary Rita (King) E.; m. Leslie Carroll, Aug. 8, 1964; children: W. Joseph III, Mary Margaret, Thomas Carroll. AB, LaSalle Coll.; JD, Boston Coll. Bar: Pa., U.S. Dist. Ct. Pa., U.S. Ct. Appeals (2d and 3d cirs.). Law clk. U.S. Dist. Ct., 1965-66; assoc. Duane, Morris & Heckscher, Phila., 1966-71; v.p., gen. counsel Rochester and Pitts. Coal Co., Indiana, Pa., 1971—. Bd. dirs. Indiana Area Sch. Dist., 1975—, pres., 1984—. Mem. ABA, Pa. Bar Assn., Nat. Coal Assn., Am. Mining Congress, Pa. Coal Assn. (chmn. lawyers com.), Am. Corp. Counsel Assn., Oakmont Country Club, Indiana Country Club. Office: Rochester & Pitts Coal Co 655 Church St Indiana PA 15701

ENGLISH, BENO LEE, JR., management consultant, retired army officer; b. Pensacola, Fla., Apr. 10, 1937; s. Beno Lee and Virginia (Jones) E.; m. Heather Adams Pok, Dec. 23, 1967; 1 child, Norman Pok. Student, Fla. A&M U., 1958; BS, U. San Francisco, 1978, MPA, 1980, EdD, 1983. Commd. 2d lt. U.S. Army, 1958, advanced through grade to lt. col., 1974, ret., 1979; ops. adminstr. Novato (Calif.) Unified Sch. Dist., 1980-81; dir. energy, bldgs., grounds and planning Oakland (Calif.) Unified Sch. Dist., 1981-85; exec. dir. Associated Students of U. Calif., Berkeley, 1986-88; pres., chief exec. officer English, Inc., Novato, 1988—. Del. citizen amb. program People Internat., Beijing, 1988. Decorated Legion of Merit, Bronze Star (2), Air medal, Nat. Def. Service medal, Vietnam Gallantry Cross with Bronze Star, Schutsenschur III Gold (Germany), Meritorious Svc. medal; numerous others. Mem. Assn. Energy Engrs., Assn. Sch. Bus. Ofcls., Calif. Sch. Bus. Ofcls., Commonwealth Club Calif., Coun. Ednl. Facility Planners, Assn. U.S. Army, Napa Valley Wine Libr. Assn., Porsche Club Am., Kappa Alpha Psi. Home: 11 Fredson Ct Novato CA 94947 Office: 399 Elmhurst St Hayward CA 94544

ENGLISH, JAMES FAIRFIELD, JR., college president; b. Putnam, Conn., Feb. 15, 1927; s. James Fairfield and Alice Bradford (Welles) E.; m. Isabelle Spotswood Cox, July 9, 1955; children: Alice, James Fairfield, Margaret, William. Grad., Loomis Sch., 1944; BA, Yale U., 1949; MA, Cambridge (Eng.) U., 1951; JD, U. Conn., 1956; HLD, Northeastern U., 1982; LLD, U. Hartford, 1971, St. Joseph Coll., West Hartford, Conn., 1982. With Conn. Bank & Trust Co., Hartford, 1951—; sr. v.p. Conn. Bank & Trust Co., 1961-63, exec. v.p., 1963-66, pres., 1966-70, chmn. bd., 1970-80; v.p. fin. and planning Trinity Coll., Hartford, 1977-81; pres. Trinity Coll., 1981—; bd. dirs. Bank New Eng. Corp., Cigna Corp., Conn. Natural Gas Co., Conn. Bank and Trust Co., N.A. Bd. dirs. Inst. of Living. Served with AUS, 1944-46. Mem. United Ch. of Christ. Home: 31 Potter Ct Noank CT 06340 Office: Trinity Coll 300 Summit St Hartford CT 06106

ENGLISH, JOHN DOUGLAS, manufacturing company executive, marketing consultant; b. Columbus, Ohio, Oct. 2, 1947; s. Donald Wellsley and Frances Elizabeth (Arant) E. BA, Hobart Coll., 1970; postgrad., U. Colo., 1982. Pres. EEI, Boulder, Colo., 1979-84, The Protector Corp., Boulder, 1984—; cons. Boulder County Justice Ctr., 1983. Author: How to Care for Your Personal Computer, 1984; contbr. articles to profl. jours. Mem. Boulder County NWEC, 1982-85; bd. dirs. MANA, Boulder, 1982-85, pres. 1986. Mem. Nat. Office Products Assn. (cons.), Assn. Computer Retailers (assoc.). Club: Colo. Mountan (Denver). Office: The Protector Corp 6681 Arapahoe Boulder CO 80303

ENGLISH, LAWRENCE WILLIAM, insurance company executive; b. Columbus, Ohio, Mar. 9, 1942; s. Kenneth Raemer and Constance Pauline (Cooper) E.; m. Arlene Floan, Aug. 3, 1968; 1 child, Jennifer Victoria. BS, Case Inst. Tech., Cleve., 1964. Office: Am Internat Group Inc 70 Pine St New York NY 10270

ENGLISH, SALLY ANN, computer executive; b. Portsmouth, N.H., May 2, 1946; d. Anthony Joseph and Sally May (Griskiewicz) Daniels; m. Robert Glenn English, Jan. 25, 1969; children: Kimberly, Melissa, Jill. BS, U. N.H., 1968, M, 1976. Med. technologist Deaconess Hosp., Boston, 1968-69; med. technologist Exeter (N.H.) Hosp., 1970-75, lab. mgr., 1975-80; asst. chief technologist data processing Emory Hosp., Atlanta, 1980-81; ednl. rep. HBO & Co., Atlanta, 1982-83, installation rep. of new tech., 1983-84, product specialist, 1984-85, mgr. clin. systems installation and support, 1985-86, nat. mgr. clin. services, 1986-87, nat. sales exec., 1987-89, div. sales exec., 1989—. Mem. NOW, Nat. Assn. Profl. Saleswomen, Nat. Assn. Female Execs. Republican. Roman Catholic.

ENGLISH, THOMAS JAMES, healthcare company executive; b. Dearborn, Mich., July 25, 1942; s. George Thomas and Christine Katherine (Coss) E.; m. Marcia Carroll Kirchner, Apr. 26, 1980. BSBA, Miami U., Oxford, Ohio, 1964; postgrad., Ohio State U., 1965, 78. Asst. buyer Fisher Body div. Gen. Motors Corp., Columbus, Ohio, 1964-67; buyer Diamond Power Splty. Corp., Lancaster, Ohio, 1967-68; asst. mgr. Nat. Life and Accident Ins. Co., Columbus, 1968-71; mgr. sales Drustar Unit Dose Systems, Inc., Grove City, Ohio, 1971-73; exec. v.p. Artromick Internat., Inc., Columbus, 1973—. Mem. Jefferson Twp. Civic Assn., Blacklick, Ohio. Mem. Am. Soc. Cons. Pharmacists, Am. Soc. Hosp. Pharmacists, Columbus Area C. of C. Republican. Home: 6200 Windrush Ln Blacklick OH 43004 Office: Artromick Internat Inc 4800 Hilton Corp Dr Columbus OH 43232

ENGLISH, WILLIAM DESHAY, lawyer; b. Piedmont, Calif., Dec. 25, 1924; s. Munro and Mabel (Michener) English; m. Nancy Ames, Apr. 7, 1956; children: Catherine, Barbara, Susan, Stephen. AB in Econs., U. Calif., Berkeley, 1948; JD, U. Calif., 1951. Bar: Calif. 1952, D.C. 1972. Trial atty, spl. asst. to atty. gen. U.S. Dept. Justice, Washington, 1953-55; sr. atty. AEC, Washington, 1955-62; legal advisor U.S. Mission to European Communities, Brussels, 1962-64; asst. gen. counsel internat. matters COMSAT, Washington, 1965-73, v.p., gen. counsel, dir., 1973-76; sr. v.p. legal and govtl. affairs Satellite Bus. Systems, McLean, Va., 1976-86; v.p., gen. counsel Satellite Transponder Leasing Corp. (IBM), McLean, 1986-87. With USAAF, 1943-45. Decorated air medal. Fellow Coun. on Econ. Regulation; mem. A IAA (com. legal aspects aeronautics and astronautics 1983—, chmn. allocation space launch risks subcom. 1987), Competitive Telecommunications Assn. (bd. dirs. 1985-86, exec. com. 1985-86), ABA, D.C. Bar Assn., Fed. Communications Bar Assn., State Bar Calif., Fgn. Policy Discussion Group, Metropolitan. Home: 7420 Exeter Rd Bethesda MD 20814 Office: 8280 Greensboro Dr Ste 605 McLean VA 22102

ENNIS, CHARLES ROE, manufacturing company executive, lawyer; b. Grand Junction, Colo., Nov. 7, 1932; s. Paul R. and Marjorie M. (DuCray) E.; m. Ann L. Price, Aug. 28, 1958; children: Matthew, Christopher, Jonathan, Eve. AB, Dartmouth Coll., 1954; LLB, Columbia U., 1957. Bar: N.Y. 1958, Calif. 1967, Ohio, 1973. Labor atty. Western Electric Co., 1957-59; trial atty. NLRB, 1959-60; atty. Gen. Foods Corp., 1960-66; with TRW Inc., 1966-83; atty. systems group Redondo Beach, Calif., 1966-70; gen. counsel energy products group Los Angeles, 1970-73; v.p. law Cleve., 1973-83; v.p., gen. counsel Pool Co.-Assoc. Oil Tools, London, 1983-85, v.p., gen. counsel internat. ops., 1985-86; v.p., sec., gen. counsel GenCorp Inc., Akron, Ohio, 1986—. Mem. ABA, Akron Bar Assn. Office: Gencorp Inc 175 Ghent Rd Fairlawn OH 44313

ENNIS, THOMAS MICHAEL, health foundation executive; b. Morgantown, W.Va., Mar. 7, 1931; s. Thomas Edson and Violet Ruth (Nugent) E.; m. Julia Marie Dorety, June 30, 1956; children—Thomas John, Robert Griswold (dec.). Student, W.Va. U., 1949-52; A.B., George Washington U., 1954; J.D., Georgetown U, 1960. Dir. ann. support program George Washington U., 1960-63; nat. dir. devel. Project HOPE, People to People Health Found., Inc., Washington, 1963-66; nat. exec. dir. Epilepsy Found. Am., Washington, 1966-74; exec. dir. Clinton, Eaton, Ingham Community Mental Health Bd., 1974-83; nat. exec. dir. Alzheimer's Disease and Related Disorders Assn., Inc., Chgo., 1983-86; exec. dir., pres. French Found. for Alzheimer Rsch., Los Angeles, 1986—; clin. inst. dept. community medicine and internat. health Georgetown U., 1967-74; adj. assoc. prof. dept. psychiatry Mich. State U., 1975-84; lectr. Univ. Ctr. for Internat. Rehab., 1977; cons. health and med. founds., related orgns.; cons. Am. Health Found., 1967-69, Reston, Va.-Georgetown U. Health Planning Project, 1967-70;. Contbr. articles on devel. disabilities, mental health and health care to profl. jours. Mem. adv. bd. Nat. Center for Law and Handicapped, 1971-74; advisor Nat. Reye's Syndrome Found.; mem. Internat. Bur. Epilepsy, Nat. Com. for Research in Neurol. Disorders, 1967-72; mem. nat. adv. bd. Developmental Disabilities/Tech. Assistance System, U. N.C., 1971-78, Handicapped Organized Women, Charlotte, N.C., 1984—; Nat. del. trustee, v.p. Nat. Capitol Area chpt., bd. dirs., exec. com. Nat. Kidney Found., 1969-74, Nat. trustee, 1970-74, pres., 1972—; bd. dirs. Nat. Assn. Pvt. Residential Facilities for Mentally Retarded, 1970-74; bd. dirs., mem. exec. com. Epilepsy Found. Am., 1977-84, Epilepsy Center Mich., 1974-83; nat. bd. dirs. Western Inst. on Epilepsy, 1969-72; bd. dirs., pres. Mich. Mid-South Health Systems Agy., 1975-78; sec. gen. Internat. Fedn. Alzheimer's Disease and Related Disorders, 1984-86. World Rehab. Fund fellow Norway, 1980. Mem. Nat. Rehab. Assn., Am. Pub. Health Assn., Nat. Epilepsy League (bd. dirs. 1977-78), Mich. Assn. Community Mental Health Bd. Dirs. (pres. 1977-79), AAAS, Phi Alpha Theta, Phi Kappa Psi.

ENOUEN, WILLIAM ALBERT, paper corporation executive; b. Columbus, Ohio, Nov. 7, 1928; s. John J. and Bertha (Thiry) E.; m. Joan Claire Batsche, June 20, 1953; children: William A., Robert, Kathryn, James, Patricia. B.S., U. Dayton, 1952; student advanced mgmt. program, Harvard, 1975. Various accounting positions Touche, Ross & Co., Dayton, Ohio, 1952-59; asst. to controller, asst. to group v.p. and fin. cons. affiliated cos. Mead Corp., Dayton, 1959-68; controller Mead Corp., 1969-72, v.p., controller, 1972-81, v.p. fin. resources and control, 1981-82, v.p. Pulp affiliates, 1982-86, sr. v.p., chief fin. officer, 1986—; v.p. Brunswick Pulp & Paper Co., 1968-69; chmn. bd. Northwood Forest Industries Ltd., 1969-86; dir. Northwood Forest Industries, Ltd., Mead Re Inc., Westbury Ins. Co., B.C. Forest Products Ltd., 1982-86, Morris Bean. Served with AUS, 1946-47. Mem. Ohio Soc. C.P.A.s (v.p. Dayton chpt. 1959-60). Home: 700 Murrell Dr Dayton OH 45429 Office: Mead World Hdqrs Courthouse Pla NE Dayton OH 45463

ENRICH, EDWARD FRANK, stock brokerage firm executive; b. N.Y.C., Mar. 17, 1930; s. Henry A. and Frances E.; B.F.A., Drake U., 1951; postgrad. Yale U., 1951-52; children—Julie, Jennifer. Acct. exec. Merrill Lynch Pierce Fenner & Smith, Hollywood, Calif, 1961-68, McDonnell & Co., Inc., Beverly Hills, Calif, 1968-69, J. Barth & Co., Beverly Hills, 1969-70, H. Hentz & Co., Beverly Hills, 1970-73; prin. Samuel B. Franklin & Co., Inc., Beverly Hills 1973-79; prin., br. mgr. C.L. McKinney & Co., Inc., Beverly Hills 1979—. Mem. Nat. Assn. Security Dealers.

ENRIGHT, STEPHANIE VESELICH, financial company executive; b. L.A., Mar. 24, 1929; d. Stephen P. and Violet (Guthrie) Veselich; m. Robert James Enright (dec. Sept. 1982); children: Craig James, Brent Stephen, Erin Suzanne, Kyle Stephen. BA, U. So. Calif., 1952, MS, 1975. Fin. and engring. cons. Orange County, Santa Ana, Calif., 1976-79; fin. cons. The Sim-Ehrflo Group, Newport Beach, Calif., 1979-81; pres. Enright Fin. Cons., Torrance, Calif., 1981—; fin. columnist Copley Newspapers, 1987—; adj. faculty mem., UCLA, U. So. Calif. Contbr. articles to profl. jours. Mem. Com. Assn. of the Peninsula, Palos Verdes, Calif., 1986; active Little Co. of Mary Hosp., Torrance. Mem. Internat. Assn. Fin. Planning (bd. dirs. and officer 1982-84, Planner of Month 1984), Inst. Cert. Fin. Planners, Nat. Assn. Women Bus. Owners, Nat. Assn. Fin. Edn., Registry of Profl. Planners, Torrance C. of C., Pan Asian Soc., Centurion Club, Trojan Club and League (bd. dirs. 1978-79). Republican. Roman Catholic. Office: Enright Fin Cons Union Bank Tower Ste 900 21515 Hawthorne Blvd Torrance CA 90503

ENSWEILER, RICHARD LAURENCE, insurance company executive; b. Milw., Dec. 1, 1940; s. Donald George and Nancy Ruth (Kulk) E.; m. Judith Ann Johnson, Dec. 14, 1973; children: Michael Eddon, Jeffrey David. BBA, Lakeland Coll., 1963. Mgmt. trainee State Cen. Credit Union, Milw., 1964-65; treas., mgr. Harley Davidson Credit Union, Milw., 1965-68; field rep. Mich. Credit Union League, Southfield, 1969-71; pres. Minn. Credit Union League, St. Paul, 1971-74; pres., chief exec. officer Ill. Credit Union League, Oak Brook, 1974-84; sr. v.p. Cuna Mut. Ins. Group, Madison, Wis., 1984—; Chmn., U.S. Cen. Credit Union, Overland Park, Kans., 1982-84. Pres. Cherrywood Homeowner's Assn., Wis., 1986—; trustee Lakeland Coll., 1988—; v.p., bd. trustee Madison Art Ctr., 1987—. Served to 1st lt. USNG, 1963-74. Mem. Inst. Cert. Credit Union Execs. Republican. Lodges: Rotary, Lions (v.p. 1980-84), Masons. Home: 3652 Seguoia Trail Verona WI 53593

ENTWISTLE, WILLIAM AUGUSTUS, III, financial planner; b. Warwick, R.I., Oct. 3, 1956; s. William Augustus Jr. and Mary Suzanne (Nassraway) E.; m. Carla Marie Bray, Nov. 14, 1981; 1 child, Matthew Bray. BS in Fin., U. R.I., 1979. Cert. fin. planner. Sales rep. Met. Life, Warwick, 1979-81; account exec. W.J. Burke & Assocs. Inc., Warwick, 1981-84; fin. planner Warwick, 1984-87; assoc. Profl. Planning Group, Westerly, R.I., 1987—; cons. Nat. Ctr. for Fin. Edn., San Diego, 1987—; mentor internship program U. R.I., Kingston, 1987—. Con. Jr. Achievement-Project Bus. Mem. Internat. Assn. Fin. Planning, Inst. Cert. Fin. Planners, Greater Providence C. of C. Office: Profl Planning Group 7 Grove Ave Westerly RI 02891

EPLEY, THOMAS KERFOOT, III, information specialist; b. Brownwood, Tex., Jan. 9, 1947; s. Thomas K. and Peggy (Orton) E.; m. Kathryn A. Brownlee, May 18, 1969 (div. Apr. 1981); m. Kathye Rae McCaffrey, Apr. 10, 1982. BS in Math., North Tex. State U., 1969. Computer operator Cen. Data Processing, Texas City, Tex., 1969-72; computer operator U. Tex. Med. Br., Galveston, 1972-74, computer programmer, 1974-76, mgr. computer ops., 1976-83, asst. dir. info. and communication svcs., 1983—. Mem. Texas City Club, Optimists. Republican. Presbyterian. Office: U Tex Med Br Computing Svcs Ctr Galveston TX 77550

EPP, MARY ELIZABETH, project manager; b. Buffalo, Aug. 7, 1941; d. John Conrad and Gertrude Marie (Murphy) Winkelman; m. Harry Francis Epp, Aug. 31, 1963. BA in Math., D'Youville Coll., 1963; MS in Math., Xavier U., 1974, MBA in Fin., 1981, MBA in Mktg., 1987. Systems analyst GE, Evendale, Ohio, 1965-71; techniques and ops. mgr. Palm Beach Co., Cin., 1972-73; hardware systems engr. Procter & Gamble, Cin., 1973-76; systems engr. CalComp Inc., Anaheim, Calif., 1980-84; software engr. SDRC Inc., Cin., 1984-86; advanced systems project mgr. SAMI/Burke Mktg., Cin., 1986-89; prin. engr. Info. Advantage, Inc., Cin., 1989—; cons. Shelley & Sands, Zanesville, Ohio, 1983-85. Contbr. articles to profl. jours. Mem. Fairfield Charter Rev. Commn., 1981-83. Mem. AAUW (br. treas. 1975-79, state women's chair 1979-80, state treas. 1980-82), Assn. Computing Machinery (treas. Cin. chpt. 1987-88, pres. 1988—), Nat. Computer Graphics Assn., NAFE, Nat. Fedn. Music (Ohio fedn. music parade chair 1979-81.). Republican. Roman Catholic. Clubs: Mercy Hosp. Aux. (treas. 1978-79), Musical Arts. Avocations: bridge, skiing, music, fishing, travel. Home: 4900 Pleasant Ave Fairfield OH 45014 Office: Info Advantage Inc 655 Eden Park Dr Ste 500 Cincinnati OH 45202

EPPERLY, LARRY ROBERT, manufacturing company executive; b. Glidden, Iowa, Mar. 25, 1947; s. Robert Dean and Grace Francis (Walkup) E.; m. Teresa Faye Dekker, Sept. 20, 1986. Student, Northwestern Coll., Orange City, Iowa, 1966-67; auto technician diploma, Universal Trade Sch., Omaha, 1968. Mechanic DeJong Motors, Orange City, Iowa, 1969; mgr. Ray's A&W's, Colorado Springs, Colo., 1969-72; machinist K-Products, Inc., Orange City, 1972-73; plant mgr. K-Products, Inc., Rock Rapids, Iowa, 1974-78, Sioux Center, Iowa, 1978-83, Hawarden, Iowa, 1983—. Chmn. Big Sioux River Days, 1986-87, Quad-States CarFest, 1984-87, Hawarden; local chmn. Ragbrai XIII-Registers Annual Great Bike Ride Across Iowa, sustaining mem. Boy Scouts Am., Hawarden. Recipient Cert. Appreciation Hawarden City Council, 1985, Achievement award ISCA, 1985. Mem. Hawarden C. of C. (dir. 1984-87, pres. 1986-87, named Citizen of Yr., 1985), Border Bandits Car Club (Iowa-S.D. pres. 1986-87), Siouxland Car Counsel (Iowa, S.D., Minn. dir. 1986-87). Home: 501 9th St Hawarden IA 51023

EPPERLY, WILLIAM ROBERT, energy company executive; b. Christiansburg, Va., Mar. 17, 1935; s. William Rangeley and Myrtle Claire (Vest) E.; m. Sarah Ann Owen, June 9, 1957; children: William Robert, Jennifer Ann, Thomas Guthrie. B.S., Va. Poly. Inst., 1956, M.S., 1958. With Exxon Research & Engring. Co., and parent co., 1957—; mgr. Baytown research and devel. div., Tex., 1973-76; mgr. project devel. and planning Baytown research and devel. div., Florham Park, N.J., 1976-77; gen. mgr. liquefaction Baytown research and devel. div., 1977-79, gen. mgr. synthetic fuels dept., 1980-83, sr. program mgr., 1983-84; gen. mgr. corp. research 1984—; mem. air pollution research adv. com. Coordinating Research Council, 1969-71; mem. fossil energy program adv. com. Oak Ridge Nat. Lab., 1978-81; mem. com. synthetic fuels safety NRC, 1982, mem. com. on coop. govt. industry research, 1983. Author publs. in field; patentee in synthetic fuels, automotive emissions/gasoline composition, iron ore reduction, fuel cells, separations others. Mem. Am. Inst. Chem. Engrs. (award for chem. engring. practice 1983), Am. Petroleum Inst., AAAS. Methodist. Home: 18 Gloucester Rd Summit NJ 07901 Office: Exxon Rsch & Engring Co Clinton Twp Rte 22E Annandale NJ 08801

EPPERSON, ERIC ROBERT, financial executive; b. Oregon City, Oreg., Dec. 10, 1949; s. Robert Max and Margaret Joan (Crawford) E.; B.S., Brigham Young U., 1973, M.Acctg., 1974; M.B.A., Golden Gate U., 1977, J.D., 1981; m. Lyla Gene Harris, Aug. 21, 1969; 1 dau., Marcie. Instr. acctg. Brigham Young U., Provo, Utah, 1973-74; supr. domestic taxation Bechtel Corp., San Francisco, 1974-78; supr. internat. taxation Bechtel Power Corp., San Francisco, 1978-80; mgr. internat. tax planning Del Monte Corp., San Francisco, 1980-82, mgr. internat. taxes, 1982-85; internat. tax specialist Touche Ross & Co., San Francisco, 1985-87; dir. internat. tax Coopers & Lybrand, Portland, 1987-89; exec. v.p., chief fin. officer Dawntreader Internat., Inc., Salt LAke City, 1989—. Eagle Scout, 1965; scoutmaster, Boy Scouts Am., Provo, 1971-73, troop committeeman, 1973-74, 83—; mem. IRS Vol. Income Tax Assistance Program, 1972-75; pres. Mut. Improvement Assn., Ch. Jesus Christ of Latter-day Saints, 1972-74, pres. Sunday sch., 1977-79, tchr., 1974-80, ward clk., 1980-83, bishopric, 1983-87; ; bd. dirs. Oreg. Art Inst. Film Ctr.; Hist. Preservation League of Oreg. Mem. Am. Acctg. Assn., Tax Assn. Am., World Affairs Council, Japan/Am. Soc., Internat. Tax Planning Assn., Internat. Fiscal Assn., U.S. Rowing Assn., Beta Alpha Psi. Republican. Clubs: Riverplace Athletic Club, Commonwealth, Masters of Accountancy Brigham Young U. Author: (with T. Gilbert) Interfacing of the Securities and Exchange Commission with the Accounting Profession: 1968 to 1973, 1974. Office: Dawntreader Internat Inc Salt Lake City UT

EPPERSON, VAUGHN ELMO, civil engineer; b. Provo, Utah, July 20, 1917; s. Lawrence Theophilus and Mary Loretta (Pritchett) E.; m. Margaret Ann Stewart Hewlett, Mar. 4, 1946; children: Margaret Ann (Mrs. Eric V.K. Hill), Vaughn Hewlett, David Hewlett, Katherine (Mrs. Franz S. Amussen), Lawrence Stewart. BS, U. Utah, 1953. With Pritchett Bros. Constrn. Co., Provo, 1949-50; road design engr. Utah State Road Commn., Salt Lake City, 1951-53, bridge design engr., 1953-54; design engr. Kennecott Copper Corp., Salt Lake City, 1954-60, office engr., 1960-62, sr. engr., 1962, assigned concentrator plant engr., 1969-73, assigned concentrator project engr., 1973-78; cons. engr. Vaughn Epperson Engring. Service, Salt Lake City, 1978-87; project engr. Newbery-State Inc., Salt Lake City, 1980, geneal. computerized research programs, 1983-88, ancestral file programs family history dept. Ch. Jesus Christ of Latter-Day Saints, 1989—. Scoutmaster Troop 190, Salt Lake City, 1949-51. Served to capt. AUS, 1941-45; maj. N.G., 1951; col. Utah State Guard, 1952-70. Decorated Army Commendation medal; recipient Service award Boy Scouts Am., 1949, Community Service award United Fund, 1961, Service award VA Hosp., Salt Lake City, 1977. Mem. ASCE, Am. Soc. Mil. Engrs., Sons of Utah Pioneers. Republican. Mormon. Home: 1537 E Laird Ave Salt Lake City UT 84105 Office: PO Box 8769 Salt Lake City UT 84108

EPPERSON, WALLACE WILKINS, JR., securities analyst; b. Richmond, Va., Feb. 16, 1948; s. Wallace Wilkins Sr. and Dorothy Sue (Kelley) E.; m. Kathryn Nelson, Dec. 29, 1969; children: Kelley Seay, Wallace W. III. BS in Fin., U. Va., 1970; MBA, Coll. William and Mary, 1971. Asst. v.p. Scott and Stringfellow, Richmond, 1971-76; sr. v.p. Wheat First Securities, Richmond, 1976—. Mem. Richmond Soc. Fin. Analysts, Internat. Home Furnishing Reps. Assn. (bd. dirs., ednl. com. 1984—), N.Y. Home Products Analysts Assn., Salisbury Country Club, So. Furniture Club, M and M Club Chgo. Republican. Methodist. Office: Wheat First Securities 707 E Main St Richmond VA 23219

EPPLEY, ROLAND RAYMOND, JR., financial services executive; b. Balt., Apr. 1, 1932; s. Roland and Verna (Garrettson) E.; m. LeVerne Pittman, June 20, 1953; children: Kimberly, Kent, Todd. B.A., Johns Hopkins U., 1952, M.A., 1953; D.C.S. (hon.), St. John's U., 1984. Pres., chief exec. officr Comm. Credit Computer, Balt., 1962-68; pres., chief exec. officer CIPC, Balt., 1968-77; vice chmn. Eastern States Monetary, Lake Success, N.Y., 1982—; pres., chief exec. officer, dir. Affiliated Financial, Wilmington, Del., 1983-85, Eastern States Bankcard, Lake Success, N.Y., 1971—; adj. prof. St. John's U., 1973—; dir. Eastern States Monetary. Chmn. bd. trustees Calgary Bapt. Ch., Balt., 1969-71; chmn. investment com. Community Ch., Manhasset, N.Y., 1983—; bd. advisers St. John's U., 1973—. Recipient Disting. Service award St. John's U., 1981, 84 Laucheimer grantee, 1952-53. Mem. Am. Bankers Assn., Data Processing Mgmt. Assn., Am. Mgmt. Assn. Pres. Assn., Electronic Funds Transfer Assn., Mensa, Phi Beta kappa, Omicron Delta Epsilon, Beta Gamma Sigma, Sigma Phi. Epsilon (citation). Republican. Mem. Reformed Ch. Am. Clubs: Madison Square Garden, Meadowbrook, Plandome Country (dir. 1977-86), Hillendale. Lodges: Masons, Shrine. Home: 77 Westgate Blvd Plandome NY 11030 Office: 4 Ohio Dr Lake Success NY 11042

EPPLEY, STEPHEN CLYDE, investment banker; b. Gauley Bridge, W.Va., Dec. 2, 1949; s. Harold Arthur and Frances (McIntyre) E.; 1 child from previous marriage, Benjamin; m. Paula Jean De Caporale, Jan. 17, 1987. BSFS, Georgetown U., 1971; MBA, Columbia U., 1972. Internat. tax acct. Cooper & Lybrand, N.Y.C., 1972-73; pres. Evi, Inc., N.Y.C., 1974-75; assoc. Bache Halsey Stuart, Inc., N.Y.C., 1977-83; mng. dir. Wertheim Schroder & Co., Inc., N.Y.C., 1983—. Home: 200 E 74th St New York NY 10021 Office: Wertheim Schroder & Co Inc 787 7th Ave New York NY 10019

EPSTEIN, DAVID LEE, investment banker; b. Black River Falls, Wis., Oct. 19, 1947; s. Lewis and Elisabeth (Lee) E.; m. Johneen Ann Roth, June 7, 1969; 1 child, Grant William. BBA, U. Wis., Madison, 1970, MBA, 1973. Cert. managerial accountant. Cost acct. Ray-O-Vac, Madison, 1968-70, regional credit mgr., 1970-72; asst. v.p. First Nat. Bank Chgo., 1974-78; pres. Mosser Lee Co., Millston, Wis., 1978-80; v.p., regional exec. Chase Comml. Corp., Chgo., 1980-83; prin. J.H. Chapman Group, Ltd., Rosemont, Ill., 1983—; lectr. in field; chmn. bd. dirs. Deli, Inc., Millston; pres., dir. David L. Epstein, Ltd., Chgo., Millston Investors, Ltd.; dir. Pencor, Inc., Chgo. Columnist, Restaurant Bus. Mag.; contbr. to profl. publs. Mem. Inst. Cert. Mgmt., Assn. Continuing Edn., Wis. Alumni Assn. Office: JH Chapman Group Ltd 9700 Higgins Rd Rosemont IL 60018

EPSTEIN, EDWARD JOSEPH, textile company executive; b. Newark, N.J., Apr. 18, 1920; s. Herman and Rose (Jennis) E.; children: Jonathan, Judith, Robert. Student, NYU, 1938; BS, Lowell U., 1941; MBA, Seton Hall U., 1970. Cert. pub. mgr. V.p. Nat. Rayon Dyeing Co., Inc., Newark, 1950-57, No. Yarn Mills, Newark, 1957-70; pres. Spacetronics Industries, Newark, 1970-81; dir. revenue and patent accounts State of N.J., 1981—. Patentee in field. Served with USN, 1942, lt. USNR, 1946. Mem. Leaders Textile Industry, Tau Epsilon Sigma. Jewish. Home: 8 Mitchell Ave Piscataway NJ 08854 Office: Station A Marlboro NJ 07746

EPSTEIN, HENRY DAVID, electronics company executive; b. Frankfurt, Germany, Apr. 5, 1927; came to U.S., 1940, naturalized, 1945; s. Julius S. and Lola C. (Heilbronner) E.; m. Henny Wenkart, Sept. 6, 1952; children: Jonathan, Heitzi, Ari. MS in Engring., Brown U., 1948; BA in Bus. Adminstrn., Harvard U., 1950. Mgr. devel. engring. Metal & Controls Corp., Attleboro, Mass., 1952-59; mgr. precision controls dept. Tex. Instruments, Attleboro, 1959-67; mgr. div. control products 1967-77, asst. v.p., 1969-77; sr. group v.p. Loral Corp., N.Y.C., 1977-85; pres. Ideonics, 1985-87; chmn., chief exec. officer Computer Communications Inc., Torrance, Calif., 1986—; chmn., pres., chief exec. officer Penril Corp., Potomac, Md., 1987—; dir. Monitor Labs. Patentee in elec. controls, automotive safety, pollution control. Served with Signal Corps U.S. Army, 1945-46. Fellow IEEE; mem. Friends of Harvard Hillel, Am. Electronic Assn., Sigma Xi, Tau Beta Pi. Home: 40 Central Pk South New York NY 10019

EPSTEIN, JEFFREY LAWRENCE, manufacturing executive; b. N.Y.C., Oct. 27, 1942; s. Oscar and Pauline (Nierenburg) E.; m. Wilma M. Geller, Oct. 27, 1968; 1 child, Jill Stacy. BS, U. Mo., 1964; MS, C.W. Post Coll., 1966. V.p. Intervale Paint & Wallpaper Co., Bronx, 1964-71; pres. Evergrip Corp., 1971-73; v.p. mktg. Am. Tack & Hardware Co., Monsey, N.Y., 1973-79; v.p. sales and mktg. Evans Rule Co. div. Masco Corp., Charleston, S.C., 1979-86; exec. v.p. Mech. Plastics Corp., Pleasantville, N.Y., 1986—; cons. Hardware & Wall Anchor Mfr., 1979—. With USNG, 1964-69. Mem. Hardware Mktg. Council, Sales and Mktg. Internat., Am. Mktg. Assn., Uptown Racquet Club. Office: Mech Plastics Corp Castleton St Pleasantville NY 10570

EPSTEIN, SIDNEY, engineer, architect; b. Chgo., 1923; m. Sondra Berman, Sept. 4, 1987; children from previous marriage: Donna Epstein Barrows, Laurie Epstein Lawton. B.S. in Civil Engring. with high honors, U. Ill., 1943. Chmn. bd., dir. A. Epstein & Sons Internat., Inc., Chgo.; dir. Amal. Trust & Savs. Bank; trustee Northwestern Mut. Life Ins. Co. Chmn. Chgo. Youth Centers; past chmn. bd. trustees Michael Reese Hosp. and Med. Center; bd. govs. U. Chgo. Hosps. and Clinics; bd. dirs. Lyric Opera Chgo.; trustee Orchestral Assn. Chgo.; mem. Ill. Arts Council. Mem. Polish-U.S. Econ. Council, Sigma Xi, Tau Beta Pi, Sigma Tau, Phi Kappa Phi, Phi Eta Sigma, Chi Epsilon. Club: Standard (Chgo.) (past pres.). Home: 1430 N Lake Shore Dr Chicago IL 60610 Office: 600 W Fulton St Chicago IL 60606

EPSTEIN, THOMAS, investment principal; b. Toronto, Ont., Can., Mar. 19, 1957; s. Alexander and Florence Ofelia (Camara) E.; m. Nancy L.F. Rix, July 6, 1980; children: Elizabeth E., Elllen C. BA, Princeton U., 1978. V.p. Bankers Trust Co., N.Y.C., 1980-85; ptnr. ZS Ptnrs., N.Y.C., 1986—; bd. dirs. HHL Fin. Svcs. Inc., Great Neck, N.Y., Colorado Prime Corp., Farmingdale, N.Y., Sun TV and Appliance, Inc., Columbus, Ohio, Gentry's Inc., Cin., Glasstech Inc., Toledo; pres. Stai Holdings Inc., Wilmington, Del., 1988—. Republican. Jewish. Clubs: Princeton of N.Y.C.; Ivy. Office: Zaleski Sherwood & Co Inc 1270 Sixth Ave New York NY 10020

EPSTEIN, WILLIAM HORACE, building products company executive; b. Chgo., June 25, 1943. BA, Grinnell Coll., 1965; MA, U. Sussex, Eng., 1967. Pres. Berkeley (Mo.) Lumber Co., 1974—, Berkeley Homes Inc., 1986—; pres. Windler Windows & Patio Doors, Inc., 1987—, Restero Corp., 1987—. Mem. Berkeley C. of C. (pres.1976). Office: Berkeley Lumber Co 8555 Wabash Ave Berkeley MO 63134

EPSTEIN, WILLIAM STUART, trust company executive; b. N.Y., Apr. 20, 1940; s. David and Helen Epstein; m. Joan Elaine Rose; children—Douglas, Mitchell. Student, Cornell U., NYU Bus. Sch. Exec. v.p. to mng. dir. Bankers Trust Co., N.Y.C., 1964-80, 83—; exec. v.p. Republic Nat. Bank, N.Y.C., 1980-83; bd. dirs. Wickes Lumber Co., Cinexus Corp. Can. Mem. Braziliam Am. C. of C. (dir. 1983—), Japan Soc. Office: Bankers Trust Co 280 Park Ave New York NY 10017

ERAZMUS, WALTER THOMAS, steel company executive; b. Passaic, N.J., Apr. 27, 1947; s. Walter Paul and Jane (Pirog) E.; m. Vicki Ann Muskat, Nov. 1, 1969; children: Keri Ann, Keith Thomas. BS in Acctg., Canisius Coll., 1969. Sr. acct. Price Waterhouse, Buffalo, 1969-73; controller Gibraltar Steel Corp., Buffalo, 1973-75, treas., 1975-77, v.p. fin., chief fin. officer, 1977—. Active Lou Gehrig Youth Baseball League. Mem. Fin. Execs. Inst., C. of C. Republican. Roman Catholic. Office: Gibraltar Steel Corp 635 S Park Ave Buffalo NY 14240

ERBERT, VIRGIL, inventor, developer, consultant; b. Ellis, Kans., Dec. 26, 1924; s. Adolph Francis and Anna (Schuster) E.; m. Mary Weber, Oct. 30, 1943; children: Constance, Sandra, Vickie, Gaylen. BS, Kans. State U., 1957; postgrad., U. N.Mex., 1958-61. Propr. Erbert Electric Machine, Hays, Kans., 1947-57, E.T. Enterprises, Tijeras, N.Mex., 1984—; staff mem. Sandia Nat. Labs., Albuquerque, 1957-69, 75-84; inventor engr. Rolamite, Inc., Albuquerque, 1969-72; project physicist Sound Devel., Ltd., Albuquerque, 1972-75; project leader Hughes Aircraft Co., Culver City, Calif., 1973-75. patentee solar concentrator elec. power system, optical memeory disk system, fiber optic coupling and sample devices, range tester with simulated optical target, method to resolve transducer ambiguity, tilt sensing dveice, motion scanning device, numerous others. With USNR, 1942-45, MTO; with U.S. Army, 1950-51, Korea. Mem. Am. Mensa Ltd., Internat. Brotherhood Magicians, Kappa Mu Epsilon. Republican. Roman Catholic. Home and Office: Box 89 Tijeras NM 87059

ERBURU, ROBERT F., newspaper publishing company executive; b. Ventura, Calif., Sept. 27, 1930. BA, U. So. Calif., 1952; LLB, Harvard U. Law Sch., 1955. Chmn. bd., chief exec. officer Times-Mirror Co., Los Angeles, also bd. dirs.; bd. dirs. Tejon Ranch Co.; bd. dirs., chmn. Fed. Res. Bank San Francisco. Trustee Huntington Library, Art Collections and Bot. Gardens, 1981—, Flora and William Hewlett Found., 1980—, Brookings Instn., 1983—, Tomas Rivera Ctr., 1985—, Carrie Estelle Doheny Found., Fletcher Jones Found., 1982—, Pfaffinger Found., 1974—, J. Paul Getty Trust; mem. exec. panel on future of welfare state Ford. Found., 1985—; bd. dirs., chmn. Times Mirror Found., 1962—; bd. dirs. Los Angeles Festival, 1985—, Ralph M. Parsons Found., 1985—; mem. Nat. Gallery of Art Trustees Council. Mem. Am. Newspaper Pubs. Assn. (treas., bd. dirs. 1980—), Council on Fgn. Relations (bd. dirs.), Bus. Roundtable, Bus. Council. Home: 1518 Blue Jay Way Los Angeles CA 90069 Office: Times Mirror Co Times Mirror Sq Los Angeles CA 90053

ERDMAN, SHARON ROSEMARY, creative production manager; b. Seattle, Aug. 16, 1962; d. Richard Neal and Betty Lorraine (Morrison) E. BA in Mktg., Seattle Pacific U., 1983. Buyer Yak Works, Seattle, 1983-84; asst. mgr. Sporting Edge, Seattle, 1984-85; purchasing mgr. Tanaka, Sporting Edge, Bothell, Wash., 1985-87; dir. prodn. Sporting Edge, Bothell, 1987—. Mem. Direct Mktg. Assn., Concerned Women Am., Purchasing Mgmt. Assn. Wash. Republican. Mem. Assemblies of God Ch. Home: 2148 N 120th Seattle WA 98133

ERDMANN, MARVIN ELMER, food company executive; b. Milw., July 1, 1930; s. Walter and Lenora E.; student public schs., Milw., m. Lois Jean Yellick, Apr. 14, 1951; children—Mark Karter, Scott Kevin, Kim Robin. With A&P Tea Co., Milw., 1944-60, dept. mgr., 1949-51, store mgr., 1953-60; store mgr. Paulus Foods, Cedarburg, Wis., 1960-63; with Super Valu Stores, Inc., 1963—, field supr., 1964-69, sales mgr., Mpls., 1969-74, retail ops. mgr., Mpls., 1974-77, pres. Bismarck (N.D.) div., 1977—; dir. Norwest Bank, Bismarck; lectr. bus. adminstrn. at high schs., colls. Chmn. fin. of expansion Good Shepherd Ch.; bd. regents U. Mary; pres. lay bd. St. Alexius Hosp.; bd. dirs., pres., mem. YMCA. Served with U.S. Army, 1951-53. Decorated Bronze Star, Am. Spirit medal. Mem. N.D. Food Retailers Assn. (legis. cons.), Greater N.D. Assn. (speaker), Bismarck C. of C. (pres., dir., mem. exec. com., mem. indsl. com.). Republican. Lutheran. Clubs: Apple Creek Country. Home: 1217 Crestview Ln Bismarck ND 58501 Office: 707 Airport Rd Bismarck ND 58502

EREDIA, ELAINE, university official; b. Long Beach, Calif., May 14, 1950; d. Delorez Ortega and Georgina (Padron) E.; m. Anthony M. Delgado, Jan. 29, 1980 (div. Dec. 1986). AA, Nat. U., 1985, BBA in Fin., 1988, MBA in Fin., 1988. Sr. account exec. Calif. First Bank, Huntington Beach, 1975-80; mktg. dir. Omni Bank, Denver, 1980-83; regional dir. student book store Nat. U., Irvine, Calif., 1983—. Mem. Am. Mgmt. Assn. (v.p. Irvine chpt. 1988—), Am. Women Bankers (sec. 1986-87), Am. Women in Bus. (v.p. 1985-86), Nat. Career Women's Assn. (v.p. Oceanside, Calif. 1987-88). Republican. Office: Nat Univ 8 Executive Circle Irvine CA 92714

ERENBURG, STEVEN ALAN, communications executive; b. Bklyn., Sept. 8, 1937; s. Harry and Sophie (Karp) E.; m. Mary Kabasakalian, Nov. 10, 1970; children: Aram Lee, Mariam Jennifer. BEE, Pratt Inst., 1957; MS in Systems Sci., Bklyn. Poly. Inst., 1970. Project engr. Kearfott Co., Wayne, N.J., 1957-66; program mgr. Kollsman Instrument Corp., Syosset, N.Y., 1966-70; editor Electronic Design mag., N.Y.C., 1970-71; mng. editor EDN mag., Boston, 1971-73; mgr. pub. relations AT&T Bell Labs., Murray Hill, N.J., 1973-77; dir. corp. relations ITT Corp., N.Y.C., 1977—; bd. dirs. Hybrid Data Systems, Inc., Rahway, N.J. Patentee Gyrocompass, 1965. Mem. Assn. for Computing Machinery, IEEE (sr., dir. external affairs com. 1974-79). Democrat. Home: 35 S Mountain Rd Millburn NJ 07041 Office: ITT Corp 320 Park Ave New York NY 10022

ERHART, CHARLES HUNTINGTON, JR., diversified company executive; b. N.Y.C., July 31, 1925; s. Charles Huntington and Katherine (Kent) E.; m. Sylvia Montgomery, June 24, 1948; children—Victoria, Margaret, David, Stephen, Julia. Grad., Groton Sch., 1944; B.A., Yale U., 1949. With W.R. Grace & Co., 1950—, asst. treas., 1955-63, v.p. charge adminstrv. controls, 1963-68, exec. v.p., chief fin. officer, mem. appropriations com., 1968-81, vice chmn., chief adminstrv. officer, 1981-86, chmn. exec. com., 1986—; bd. dir. Chemed Corp., Cin., Omnicare Inc., Nat. Med. Care, Taco Villa, Inc., Roto Rooter, Inc.; trustee Seamen's Corp., N.Y.C. Bd. dirs. Leake and Watts Childrens Home, N.Y.C., Evergreens Cemetery, N.Y.C.; trustee Groton Sch., Mass. Mem. Newcomen Soc., Beta Theta Pi. Clubs: Racquet and Tennis, Church, N.Y. Yacht (N.Y.C.); Northeast Harbor Fleet. Office: W R Grace & Co 1114 Ave of the Americas New York NY 10036

ERICH, JACK WILLIAM, real estate corporation executive; b. Cleve., Dec. 19, 1947; s. Edward John Jr. and Regina Elizabeth (Cuneo) E.; m. Pamela Edith Perry, July 20, 1967. BS in Bus. Adminstrn., U. Cen. Fla., 1981. CPA, Fla. Acct. Allan Electric Co., Inc., Orlando, Fla., 1973-81; acct., tax intern Colley, Trumbower & Howell CPA's, Orlando, Fla., 1981-82; acct., audit intern Wynn, Dexter & Sampey CPA's, Orlando, Fla., 1982-83; acct. Sunflooring, Inc., Orlando, Fla., 1983-85; controller Picerne Devel. Corp., Winter Park, Fla., 1985—. Mem. Fla. Inst. CPA's, Nat. Assn. of Accts. (contrller's council). Republican. Roman Catholic. Home: 1424 Swann Ave Orlando FL 32809-6074 Office: Picerne Devel Corp 1000 N Orlando Ave Suite A Winter Park FL 32789

ERICH PETER, E. PETER, metals company executive; b. N.Y.C., Oct. 13, 1939; s. Heinz Joseph and Hertha (Hess) B.; m. Mary-Ann Klein, Dec. 18, 1965; children: Erich Towne, Lance Joseph. BSChemE, Newark Coll. Engring., 1964. With Metz Metall. Corp., South Plainfield, N.J., 1964—, successively rsch. asst., mgr. chem. products, mgr. metall. products, mgr. electronics, mgr. electronic materials div., mgr. maintenance and plant mgr., v.p., exec. v.p., now v.p., div. mgr. metallurgy. Served with U.S. Army, 1958-61. Mem. Am. Inst. Chem. Engrs., Internat. Precious Metal Inst. (charter), Internat. Soc. Hybrid Microelectronics. Office: Metz Metall Corp 3900 S Clinton Ave South Plainfield NJ 07080

ERICKSON, DAVID BRUCE, software executive; b. Lawrence, Kans., Oct. 29, 1947; s. Clarence E. and Margaret E. (Holsinger) E.; m. Kristy A. Entwistle, June 30, 1973. BS in Math., MIT, 1969. Programmer Mass. Computer Assn. subs. Applied Data Rsch., Wakefield, Mass., 1971-75; software developer, mgr. Atex, Inc., Bedford, Mass., 1976-83; chmn. XyQuest, Inc., Billerica, Mass., 1983—. Mem. Tech. Exec. Roundtable (mem. bd. advisors 1985—), Assn. for Computing Machinery. Home: 237 Fiske ST Carlisle MA 01741 Office: XyQuest Inc 44 Manning Rd Billerica MA 01821

ERICKSON, GEORGE EVERETT, JR., lawyer; b. Ft. Scott, Kans., July 20, 1937; s. George Everett Sr. and Cora Kathleen (Hayden) E.; m. Carrol Ann Guthridge, Dec. 23, 1966; children: Ingrid Ann, Karin Ruth. BS, U.S. Naval Acad., 1959; JD, Washburn U., 1966. Bar: Kans. 1966, Okla. 1966, U.S. Dist. Ct. Kans. 1966, U.S. Ct. Appeals (10th cir.) 1967, U.S. Supreme Ct. 1972, U.S. Ct. Mil. Appeals 1982, D.C. 1985. Atty. Amerada-Hess Corp., Tulsa, 1966-69; ptnr. Cosgrove, Webb & Oman, Topeka, 1969-73; pvt. practice Topeka, 1973-82; ptnr. Erickson, Hall, Topeka, 1982—; prof. Washburn U. Law Sch., Topeka, 1973-74; atty. City of Auburn, Kans., 1976-82. Mem. Auburn-Washburn Rural Sch. Bd., Topeka, 1977-79. Lt. USN, 1959-63, comdr. JAGC, USNR, 1988—. Mem. ABA, Fed. Bar Assn., D.C. Bar Assn., Kans. Bar Assn., Judge Advocates Assn., Nat. Lawyers Club, Army and Navy Club, Shawnee Country Club, Lions. Republican. Office: Erickson & Hall 3320 Harrison Topeka KS 66611

ERICKSON, RICHARD LEE, company executive; b. Youngstown, Ohio, Jan. 3, 1938; s. Albin E. and Martha L. (Sandberg) E.; m. Jean A. Brickley, Sept. 10, 1960; children: Carolyn, Diane, David. AA, North Park Coll., 1957; BSEE, Northwestern U., 1959; MS in Engring. Adminstrn., Syracuse U., 1969. Devel. engr. Motorola Inc., Chgo., 1958-61; project engr., engring. mgr. Gen. Electric Co., Syracuse, N.Y., 1961-71; Presdl. exchange exec. U.S. Dept. Transp., Washington, 1971-72; mgr. strategic planning Gen. Electric

Co., Erie, Pa., 1972-78; v.p. products planning Purolator Inc., Piscathaway, N.J., 1978-79; dir. planning TRW Indsl. Products Group, Cleve., 1979-84; v.p. planning and devel. TRW Automotive Worldwide, Solon, Ohio, 1984-86; pres. Strategic Ptnrs., Inc., Shaker Heights, Ohio, 1987—; mng. prin., chmn. The Allegheny Mktg. Group, Sewickley, Pa., 1988—; dir. Albin E. Erickson Co., Youngstown, 1960-77. Sch. dir., Liverpool, N.Y., 1970-71; mem. Millcreek Twp. Planning Commn., Erie, 1975-78, chmn., 1978; mem. County Exec. Republican Com., Erie, 1973-75; ch. chmn. Redeemer Evang. Covenant Ch., Liverpool, 1969-71; chmn. Middle East Conf. Evang. Covenant Ch. Am., 1975-78; mem. World Missions Bd., 1973-78; deacon The Chapel, Beachwood, Ohio, 1982-84; dir. Greater Cleve. Habitat for Humanity, 1987—; vol. coordinator Prison Fellowship Northeastern Ohio, 1987—. Mem. IEEE, Pres.'s Execs. Exchange Assn., The Planning Forum (bd. dirs. Cleve. chpt. 1988—), Am. Mktg. Assn., Elfun Soc. (chpt. sec. 1974-75, vice chmn. 1975-76). Office: 21025 Byron Rd Shaker Heights OH 44122

ERICKSON, RICHARD THEODORE, retail company executive; b. St. Paul, Feb. 8, 1932; s. Louis Amil and Leona Ruth (Bergeron) E.; m. Pearl Margaret Desimone, June 12, 1954; children: Patricia, Michael, Richard, Shari. B.A. in Bus., U. Wash., 1954. With J.C. Penney Co., Inc., 1956—; from mgmt. trainee to regional personnel mgr. J.C. Penney Co., Inc., Buena Park, Calif.; successively dist. mgr. J.C. Penney Co., Inc., Buena Park; stores personnel mgr. J.C. Penney Co., Inc., N.Y.C., personnel mgr., v.p. personnel, 1981-82, sr. v.p. personnel, 1982—; dir. Unemployment Benefits Advisors, Washington, 1983—. Served to lt. (j.g.) USN, 1954-56, PTO. Mem. N.Y.C. C. of C. and Industry (chmn. social ins. com. 1983), C. of C. of U.S. (mem. labor and employee benefits com., health care council 1985-87). Home: 1804 Watermill Dr Plano TX 75075 Office: J C Penney Co Inc 14841 N Dallas Pkwy Dallas TX 75240-6760

ERICKSON, ROBERT DANIEL, management services company executive; b. Chgo., Aug. 22, 1943; s. Manfred Oliver and Martha Sylvia Florence (Strand) E.; m. Barbara Tillman; children: Matthew Todd, Daniel Mark, Joshua Adam. BA in Econs. and Bus., Wheaton Coll., 1965; MBA, Northwestern U., 1969. CPA, Ill. With The ServiceMaster Co. L.P., Downers Grove, Ill., 1966—, numerous positions including mgr. health care bus., div. controller, div. v.p., v.p., chief acctg. officer and controller, group pres. East Mgmt. services, sr. v.p., chief fin. officer and treas., sr. mgmt. advisor, 1985-87, chief fin. officer, gen. ptnr., exec. v.p., 1986—, also bd. dirs.; bd. dirs. S.M. Home Health Care Svcs. subs. Van Kampen Merritt Adv. Corp., Naperville, Ill., Health Providers Ins. Co., Chgo. Mem. adv. bd. dirs. Honey Rock Camp of Wheaton (Ill.) Coll.; mem. Alumni bd. dirs. Kellogg Grad. Sch. Mgmt. Northwestern U., Evanston, Ill.; trustee Moody Bible Inst., Chgo. Baptist. Office: Servicemaster Co LP 2300 Warrenville Rd Downers Grove IL 60515

ERICKSON, ROLAND AXEL, financial and management consultant; b. Worcester, Mass., Sept. 8, 1913; s. Axel and Anna (Erickson) E.; m. Roxie Erickson, Apr. 6, 1940; children: Brent, Lorna (Mrs. E. Long). A.B. summa cum laude, Clark U., 1935; A.M., Tufts U., 1937; LL.B., Susquehanna U., 1970. Instr. econs. Tufts U., 1935-37; economist Norton Co., 1937-41; v.p. Guaranty Bank & Trust Co., 1941-45, v.p., treas., dir., 1945-47, pres., 1947-64, hon. dir.; sr. v.p., dir. Gen. Foods Corp., 1964-66, exec. v.p., dir., 1966-70; fin. mgmt. cons. 1970—. Contbr. articles on corporate fin., money and banking, fiscal policy to profl. publs. Trustee emeritus Clark U.; past pres. Swedish Council Am., Worcester (Mass.) United Way. Decorated knight Royal Order Vasa 1st class, knight comdr. Royal Order North Star, Sweden). Mem. Newcomen Soc., Phi Beta Kappa. Conglist. Clubs: Mason (N.Y.C.) (32 deg.), Worcester (N.Y.C.), University (N.Y.C.), Worcester Country (Odin), Royal Poinciana (Naples, Fla.), Naples Yacht. Home: The Laurentians Apt 8C 1285 Gulf Shore Blvd N Naples FL 33940 Office: 1140 Mechanics Tower Worcester MA 01608

ERICKSON, STEPHEN EMORY, motivation marketing executive; b. Fargo, N.D., Sept. 26, 1945; s. George Leonard and Ida May (Hollands) E.; m. Martha Ann McLees; children: Stephanie, Barton, Christine Elizabeth. Student, U. Minn., 1963-65, Brown Inst., Mpls., 1965, U. Wis., Eau Claire, 1965-66. Announcer, sales person Sta. KWFM/KTCR-FM, Mpls., 1966-67; dir. mktg. Dahlberg Electronics, Inc., Golden Valley, Minn., 1967-73; pres. Ave. North Orgn., Hopkins, Minn., 1973-76; dir. regional mktg. Carlson Cos., Inc., Mpls., 1976-78; v.p. mktg. svcs. S & H Motivation, Inc., Hillside, Ill., 1978-88, sr. v.p. mktg., 1988—. Home: 836 Oakwood Dr Westmont IL 60559 Office: S&H Motivation Inc 5999 Butterfield Rd Hillside IL 60162

ERICSON, ROGER DELWIN, timber resource company executive; b. Moline, Ill, Dec. 21, 1934; s. Carl D. and Linnea E. (Challman) E.; m. Norma F. Brown, Aug. 1, 1957; children: Catherine Lynn, David. A.B., Stetson U., DeLand, Fla., 1958; J.D., Stetson U., 1958; M.B.A., U. Chgo., 1971. Bar: Fla. 1958, Ill. 1959, Ind. 1974. Atty. Brunswick Corp., Skokie, Ill., 1959-62; asst. sec., asst. gen. counsel Chemetron Corp., Chgo., 1962-73; asst. v.p. Inland Container Corp., Indpls., 1973-75, v.p., gen. counsel, sec., 1975-83; gen. counsel, sec. Temple-Inland Inc., 1983—; v.p., sec., bd. dirs. Inland-Rome Inc. (formerly Ga. Kraft Co.); v.p. Guaranty Fed. Savs. Bank, Dallas; bd. dirs. Inland Container Corp., Inland-Orange, Inc., Temple-Inland Forest Products, Inland Real Estate Investments, Inc. Trustee Chgo. Homes for Children, 1971-74; mem. alumni council U. Chgo., 1972-76; mem. Palatine Twp. Youth Commn., 1969-72; sect. chmn. Chgo. Heart Assn., 1972, 73; alumni bd. dirs. Stetson U. Mem. ABA, Chgo. Bar Assn., Ill. State Bar Assn., Ind. Bar Assn., Fla. Bar Assn., Indpls. Bar Assn. (chmn. corp. counsel sect., mem. profl. responsibility com. 1982), Am. Soc. Corp. Secs., Am. Paper Inst. (past mem. govt. affairs com.), Indpls. C. of C. (mem. govt. affairs com.), Omicron Delta Kappa, Phi Delta Phi. Clubs: Plum Grove (Chgo.) (pres. 1969); Crown Colony Country (Lufkin, Tex.). Home: 4 Cypress Point Lufkin TX 75901 Office: Temple-Inland Inc Drawer N Diboll TX 75941

ERIKSON, EVANS WILBUR, former industrial systems and components manufacturing company executive; b. Rockford, Ill., 1926; married. BS, U. Ill., 1950. Custom engr. IBM Corp., 1950-52; with Sundstrand Corp., Rockford, 1952-88, chief application engr. aviation div., 1959-60, chief engr., 1960-66, gen. mgr. aviation div., 1966-67, group v.p. aerospace, 1967-73, group v.p. advanced tech., 1973-77, pres., 1977-80, chmn., 1980-88, also chief exec. officer, bd. dirs., until 1988; dir. First of Am. Bank and Trust Co. of Rockford; mem. exec. com. Machinery and Allied Products Inst. Served with USN, 1944-46. Mem. Aerospace Industries Assn. (bd. govs.). Office: Sundstrand Corp 4949 Harrison Ave PO Box 7003 Rockford IL 61125 *

ERLANDSON, DONNA MAE, financial executive; b. Hecla, S.D., May 5, 1940; d. William Norman and Ellen Grace (Pearson) Colestock; m. John L. Erlandson, Jan. 18, 1958; children: Laura Lynn, John L., Peggy Ann. AA in Bus., Aroka-Ramsey Community Coll., 1980. Paying and receiving teller Security Pacific Nat. Bank, San Diego, 1969-75; teller class tchr. Grossmont (Calif.) Regional Occupational Program, 1972-73; head teller First Nat. Bank of Mpls., 1975-79, supr. proof transit, 1979-80; spur. item processing Cen. Savs. & Loan, San Diego, 1980-83; asst. v.p. mgr. item prosessing Cen. Savs. & Loan, 1983-86; asst. v.p. mgr. item prosessing Imperial Corp. Am., San Diego, 1986-88, v.p., mgr. item processing, 1988—. Active various youth orgns., San Diego, 1969-75. Mem. NCR Users Group, Super Micr Users Group, Encinitas C. of C. Republican. Lutheran. Office: Imperial Corp Am 8787 Complex Dr San Diego CA 92123

ERLANDSON, RAY SANFORD, SR., retired former business educator; b. Wausau, Wis., May 3, 1893; s. Paul and Torgine (Olson) E.; m. Margery McKillop, Aug. 22, 1919; children: Paul McKillop, Ray Sanford, William. A.B., U. Wis., 1918; M.A., George Washington U., 1921. Sch. adminstr. Chippewa Falls, Wis., 1913-16; asst. sec., bus. mgr. NEA, 1919-24; bus. mgr. Internat. Council Religious Edn., 1924-27; sales exec. John Rudin & Co., 1927-29, Grigsby Grunow Co., 1929-32, Zenith Radio Corp., 1932-35; v.p. Rudolph Wurlizer Co., 1935-45; v.p. San Antonio Music Co., 1945-50, pres., 1950-53; pres. Bledsoe Furniture Co., 1950-53; dir. 1st Fed. Savs. & Loan Assn., San Antonio, 1952-84; hon. life dir. 1st Fed. Savs. & Loan Assn., 1984—; chmn. dept. bus. adminstrn. Trinity U., 1953-64, prof. emeritus, 1980—. Pres., chief exec. officer Children's Fund, San Antonio, 1964-70; founder, pres. Am. Inst. Character Edn., 1970-74, chmn. bd., chief exec. officer, 1970-87, emeritus, 1985—, chmn., hon. dir. life, 1987—; bd. dirs. SW Research Center, 1954—; founder Am. Sch. of Air, 1929; pres. Am. Music War Council, 1942-44; chmn. nat. trade practice code com., music industry, 1944-53; Nat. vice chmn. ARC, 1959-60; past bd. dirs. San Antonio chpt., San Antonio Symphony Soc., Taxpayers League, Community Welfare Council; bd. dirs., exec. com. S.W. Research Inst., chmn. bd. of control, 1961-64. Served as lt. F.A. U.S. Army, World War I; cons. joint Army-Navy com. on welfare, recreation World War II. Named Father of Year San Antonio, 1951; Distinguished Alumnus award Wis. State U., 1969. Mem. NEA (life), San Antonio Chamber Music Soc. (pres. 1950-56), Research and Planning Council (pres. 1957), San Antonio Council Presidents (pres. 1951), Nat. Assn. Music Mchts. (pres. 1950-52, hon. life). Republican. Presbyterian. Clubs: Knife and Fork (pres. 1954), Breakfast (pres. 1953), San Antonio, Torch of San Antonio (co-founder, past pres.); Masons, Rotary (gov. dist. 584 internat. 1958-59, hon. life mem., pres. 1954, 50 Yr. award 1987), Kiwanis (hon. life). Home: 401 Shook Ave San Antonio TX 78212

ERLENBACH, GARY LEE, manufacturing company executive; b. Columbus, Ohio, June 26, 1945; s. Lester James and Leona Estella (Jay) E.; m. Karen Joanne Sumpter, Sept. 28, 1974; children: Kasie Janel, Kyle Patrick. BSEE, Case Inst. Tech., 1967; MBA, U. Chgo., 1982. Systems engr. IBM, Cleve., 1965-69; mgr. Arthur Andersen & Co., Cleve., 1969-76; mgr. systems Emhart Corp., Boston, 1976-78; dir. mgmt. info. systems Joslyn Mfg. & Supply Co., Chgo., 1978-80, Mark Controls Corp., Chgo., 1980-83; v.p. ops. Curtis Industries, Inc., Cleve., 1983—. Home: 32350 Meadowlark Way Cleveland OH 44124 Office: Curtis Industries Inc 34999 Curtis Blvd Eastlake OH 44094

EROSH, WILLIAM DANIEL, financial services company executive; b. N.Y.C., Feb. 8, 1956; s. Walter William and Dorothy Irene (Ricci) E.; m. Barbara Ann Puga, June 25, 1978; 1 child, Pamela. BS in Econs., Wagner Coll., 1978. CPA, N.Y. Staff acct. Henry F. Malarkey and Co., CPAs, N.Y.C., 1977-79; sr. acct. Perel Smolin and Co., CPAs, N.Y.C., 1979-81; tax supr. Deloitte Haskins and Sells, CPAs, N.Y.C., 1981-84; asst. v.p., dir. tax compliance 1st Boston Corp., N.Y.C., 1984-87; 1st v.p., controller, dir. taxes Security Capital Corp., N.Y.C., 1987—. Mem. Am. Inst. CPAs, N.Y. State Soc. CPAs. Democrat. Roman Catholic. Home: 3 Stone Ridge Rd Old Bridge NJ 08857 Office: Security Capital Corp 1290 Ave of Americas 27th Floor New York NY 10104

ERTEL, GARY ARTHUR, accountant; b. Racine, Wis., Feb. 16, 1954; s. Arthur and Jean Ann (Potterville) E.; m. Judith Marie Vasy, Aug. 9, 1975; children: James Arthur, Emily Marie. BSBA in Acctg. cum laude, Drake U., 1975; MBA, Marquette U., 1984. CPA, Wis. Mem. staff Arthur Andersen & Co., Milw., 1975-77; mgr. Jezzo, Deppisch & Co., Cedarburg, Wis., 1978; gen. acctg. mgr., budget control analyst, fin. analyst, asst. to the treas., asst. treas. Grede Foundries, Inc., Milw., 1978—. Mem. Amateur Radio Emergency Service, Milw., 1984—; bd. dirs. Grace Evang. Luth. Ch., Milw., 1984-87, stewardship com., 1980—. Mem. AICPA, Wis. Inst. CPAs (chmn. acctg. careers com. 1979-87, dir. southeastern chpt. 1988, chmn. long-range planning com. 1987—, sec.-treas. 1989—, Svc. award 1987), Nat. Cash Mgmt. Assn., Wis. Cash Mgmt. Assn. (program com. 1985-87, v.p. 1987, pres. 1988), Risk and Ins. Mgmt. Assn. Home: 780 Garvens Ave Brookfield WI 53005 Office: Grede Foundries Inc 9898 W Bluemound Rd Milwaukee WI 53226

ERVIN, THOMAS MARION, investment executive; b. Greer, S.C., Dec. 6, 1953; s. Theodore and Viola Merle (Henson) E.; m. Deborah Dearing Moore, Jan. 3, 1981; children: Lindsay Moore, John Theodore. BBA, The Citadel, S.C., 1975, MBA, 1987. Asst. v.p. Farm Credit Banks Columbia, Charleston, S.C., 1976-82; v.p.,, chief officer Charleston Capital Corp., 1982—, also bd. dirs.; v.p., chief officer Yaschik Devel. Co., Inc., Charleston, 1982—, also bd. dirs.; ptnr. TEG Assocs., Charleston, 1984—, TNR Assocs., Charleston, 1985—, GER Assocs., Charleston, 1986—; owner, pres. Bellfield Farm McClellanville, S.C., 1987—; pres. Ashley Mills, Inc., North Charleston, S.C., 1988—, also bd. dirs.; cons. in field. Served to capt. USAFR, 1975-82. Mem. Drayton Assn., Drayton Civic Assn., Citadel MBA's Assn., Friends of Drayton Hall, Citadel Alumni Football Assn., Coffin Creek Island Club, The Brigadier Club, Breakfast Exch. Club. Baptist. Home: 2880 Ashley River Rd Charleston SC 29414 Office: Charleston Capital Corp 111 Church St PO Box 328 Charleston SC 29402

ERWIN, DOUGLAS HOMER, financial planner; b. Portsmouth, Ohio, Sept. 28, 1954; s. Homer and Maxine LaVerne (Dunham) E.; m. Shirley Ann Studebaker, May 24, 1975; children: Matthew D., Melissa A., Nicole R., David M. Grad. high sch., Springfield, Ohio. Cert. fin. planner. Prodn. mgr. O.S. Kelly Co., Springfield, Ohio, 1971-83; pvt. practice Springfield, 1983; fin. planner Fin. Ctr. for Planning, Springfield, 1984—; registered rep. Integrated Resources Equity Corp., Springfield, 1984—. Mem. Internat. Assn. Fin. Planners, Internat. Bd. of Cert. Fin. Planners, Nat. Assn. Estate Planners. Lodge: Eagles. Office: Fin Ctr for Planning 501 W High St Springfield OH 45506

ESAKOV, JANICE H., finance executive, educator; b. Charlotte, N.C., Aug. 21, 1951; d. J.B. and Margie (Sanders) Housley; m. Michael D. Easkov, Jan. 10, 1987; 1 child, Leslie Meredith Dimsdale. Student, Western Carolina U., 1969-71; BBA, U. S.C., 1979, MBA, 1983. Adminstrv. asst. U. S.C., Spartanburg, 1979-83; internal auditor Cryovac div. W.R. Grace & Co., Spartanburg, 1983-84, mgr. credit, 1984—; instr. Spartanburg Meth. Coll., 1984—, mem. adv. bd., 1987—; instr. part time U. S.C., Spatanburg, 1979-83. Named One of Outstanding Young Woman Am., 1982. Home: 714 Lakewinds Blvd Inman SC 29349 Office: WR Grace & Co Cryovac div PO Box 464 Duncan SC 29334

ESBER, EDWARD MICHAEL, JR., software company executive; b. Cleve., June 22, 1952; s. Edward Michael and Joanne Helen (Saah) E.; m. Margaret Renfrow, July 19, 1980; children—Dianne Michelle, Paul Andrew. B.S. in Computer Engring., Case Western Res. U., Cleve., 1974; M.S.E.E., Syracuse U., N.Y., 1976; M.B.A., Harvard U., Cambridge, 1978. Assoc. engr. IBM, Poughkeepsie, N.Y., 1974-76; mktg.. mgr. Tex. Instruments, Lubbock, Tex., 1978-79; v.p. mktg. Visi Corp., San Jose, Calif., 1979-83; ptnr. Esber-Folk Assocs., Dallas, 1983-84; exec. v.p. mktg. and sales Ashton-Tate, Torrance, Calif., 1984, pres., chief operating officer, 1984, pres., chief exec. officer, 1984—, chmn., chief exec. officer, 1986—; bd. dirs. Guantum Inc., Pansophic Systems Inc., Mediagenic. Trustee Case Western Res. U. Mem. Am. Electronic Assn. Republican. Office: Ashton Tate 20101 Hamilton Ave Torrance CA 90502

ESCALANTE, JUDSON ROBERT, business consultant; b. Schenectady, Jan. 31, 1930; s. James S. and Katherine H. (Judson) E.; BA, Union Coll., 1953; m. Charlotte D. Carpenter, June 7, 1958; children: David J., Katherine Anne. Asst. estate planning officer, Nat. Commercial Bank, Albany, N.Y., 1955-65; founder, v.p., sec., dir. Fidelity Bank of Colonie, Latham, N.Y., 1966-69; area dir., Gen. Bus. Services, Latham, N.Y., 1969-81, Micro Bus. Services, 1981—; dir. Manufacturer's Hanover Trust Co. Capital Region, 1970-88; v.p. fin. Gad Cruise Lines, Inc., 1987-88; instr. in field. Bd. dirs., treas. Capital Artists Opera Co., 1970-74, 79; mem. fund dr. com. Union Coll., 1979-80; vestryman, treas. Episcopal Ch.; treas., chief fin. officer; Chatham Vis. Nurse Assn., 1983—; trustee Chatham Vis. Nurse Assn. Profit Trust, 1985—; auditor Chatham Conservation Found., 1985—. Served with U.S. Army, 1953-55. Mem. Tax Cons. Assn., Colonie C. of C. (treas., dir. 1972-76), Union Coll. Alumni Soc. (pres. 1971-73, Alumni Gold medal 1978), Dutch Settlers Soc. of Albany, Boston Computer Soc. Republican. Home: 400 Old Comers Rd Chatham MA 02633

ESCHEDOR, CHARLES NORMAN, small business owner, educator; b. Pemberville, Ohio, Feb. 7, 1938; s. Norman William and Lonnie Mae (Coe) E.; m. Anita Louise Coon, Aug. 1, 1959; children: David Charles, Sheri Lou. BE, Bowling Green State U., 1968, MEd, 1969, EdS, 1974. Acad. dean Marion (Ohio) Tech. Coll., 1969-76; realtor Moerkerke Realty, Scottsdale, Ariz., 1976-80; adminstr. The Lamson Coll., Phoenix, 1980-83; devel. dir. Success Motivation, Inc., Waco, Tex., 1983-84; edn. dir. Nat. Ed. Corp., Phoenix, 1984-85; owner, operator Sky Harbor Recume and Secretarial Service, Phoenix, 1985—; owner, cons. The Write Source, Phoenix, 1986—; instr. Ariz. Career Coll., Maricopa Community Coll. Mem. Assn. for Supervision and Curriculum Devel., Delta Pi Epsilon, Phi Beta Lambda (pres. 1966-67, Bowling Green). Republican.

ESCOBEDO, ERNEST, international sales and marketing consultant; b. Harlingen, Tex., Mar. 25, 1948; s. Gilberto and Ruth (Plata) E.; m. Helen Estella LaFontaine, May 8, 1971; children: Christina Rebecca, Ernest Mariano. BA, Bowling Green (Ohio) State U., 1971; M in Internat. Mgmt., Am. Grad. Sch. Internat. Mgmt., Glendale, Ariz., 1973. Mgr. sales Bethlehem Steel Co., Rio de Janeiro, 1973-78; mgr. internat. sales and mktg. Slaughter Industry, Inc. Div. Internat. Paper, Inc., Dallas, 1978-79; mgr. mktg. Latin Am. Acco Babcock Internat., Inc., Fairfield, Conn., 1979-82; asst. div. mgr. Am. Cyanamid's Formica Div., Mexico City, 1982-83; pres. Internat. Bus. Cons. Group, Houston, 1984—. Vol., promoter Pat Robertson for Pres., 1988—; del. rep. Republican Party pct., Houston, 1988—. Office: Internat Bus Cons Group 4930 Dacoma St Ste G Houston TX 77092

ESFANDIARY, MARY S., physical science executive; b. Passaic, N.J., June 27, 1929; d. Peter J. and Veronica R. (Kida) Nieradka; m. Mohsen S. Esfandiary; children: Homayoun Austin, Dara S. BS in Chemistry, St. John's U., 1951; postgrad., Polytechnic Inst. N.Y., 1955-56. Research chemist Picatinny Arsenal, Dover, N.J., 1951-56; supr. phys. sci. Bur. Mines, Washington, 1956-61; asst. to dir. research Nat. Iranian Oil Co., Tehran, 1961-64; lectr. U. Tehran and Aryamehr Inst. Tech., Tehran, 1961-64, 69-73; dir. internat. affairs Acad. of Scis., Tehran, 1977-79; chief geog. names br. Def. Mapping Agy., Washington, 1981-86, chief prodn. mgmt. office, 1986-87, chief support div., chief inventory mgmt. div., 1987—. Contbr. papers and articles to tech. jours., 1952-78. Pres. UN Delegations Women's Club, N.Y.C., 1967-69, v.p., program dir., 1964-67; pres. Diplomatic Corps Com. for Red Cross, Bangkok, Thailand, 1974-76; v.p., bd. dirs. Found. for Blind of Thailand, Bangkok, 1973-77. Recipient Badge of Honor for Social Service, Thailand, 1975, 1st Class medal Red Cross, Thailand, 1976. Mem. AAAS, Internat. Platform Assn., Mensa. Democrat. Methodist. Home: 4401 Sedgewick St NW Washington DC 20016 Office: Def Mapping Agy 6101 MacArthur Blvd Room 309 Washington DC 20315

ESH, DALIA REGINA, insurance educator, financial planner; b. Jerusalem, May 15, 1950; came to U.S., 1980; d. Jedidya Mizrahi and Orah (Debby) Mizrahi Malka; m. David Esh; children: Odelia, Roy. Cert. proficiency in English, Cambridge U., Eng., 1969; BA, Bar Ilan U., Tel Aviv, 1972, teaching cert., 1976; postgrad. U. Mo.-St. Louis, 1981-82, Washington U., St. Louis, 1983-84. CLU; chartered fin. cons. English tchr. Lady Davis Sch., Tel Aviv, 1973-80; Hebrew tchr. Epstein Acad., St. Louis, 1981-82; sales rep. Met. Ins. Co., St. Louis, 1982-85, mktg. specialist, instr., Tulsa, 1985-86, branch mgr., Carrollton, Dallas, Tex., 1986—. Originated universal life-term sales concept, 1985. Active Jewish Community Ctrs. Assn., St. Louis, 1984-85, Tulsa, 1986, Dallas, 1987—. Human resources mgmt. grantee Washington U., 1983; recipient Career Builders award Met. Ins. Co., 1982, Leader's Conf. award, 1984, Nat. Quality award, 1984, 85; named to Million Dollar Round Table, 1985. Mem. Nat. Assn. Life Underwriters, Internat. Assn. Fin. Planning, Nat. Assn. Female Execs. Jewish. Avocation: folk dancing, tennis. Office: Met Ins Co 3620 N Josey Ln Carrollton TX 75007

ESKENAZY, DAVID MICHAEL, controller; b. Seattle, Apr. 26, 1962; s. Samuel Albert Eskenazy and Charlotte Ann (Bitterman) Larsen; m. Lisa Louise Sarkies, Aug. 21, 1987. BS, U. Nev., 1984. CPA, Wash. Asst. acct. Peat, Marwick, Main & Co., Seattle, 1984-85, staff acct., 1985-86, sr. acct., 1986-87, supervising sr. acct., 1987; controller Parkside Bldg. Co., Seattle, 1987-88, R.C. Hedreen Co, Seattle, 1988—. Mem. Wash. State Soc. CPA's. Office: R C Hedreen Co PO Box C-9006 Seattle WA 98109

ESKRIDGE, JAMES ARTHUR, toy company executive; b. San Diego, Dec. 25, 1942; s. Arthur Walker and Evelyn Louise (Meyers) E.; m. Sharen Elaine Creamer, Mar. 14, 1962; children: Jennifer, Mark. BA, U. Calif., Riverside, 1968; MBA, Harvard U., 1975. Acct. Gen. Motors Corp., L.A., 1968-70; dir. treasury Gen. Motors Corp., N.Y.C., 1970-77; exec. asst. pres. Gen. Motors Corp., Detroit, 1977-82; v.p. control and administrn. Gen. Mills Non Foods, Mpls. and N.Y.C., 1982-86; exec. v.p. fin. and adminstrn. Cooper Communities, Inc., Bentonville, Ark., 1986-88; exec. v.p., chief fin. officer Mattel Inc., Hawthorne, Calif., 1989—. Pres. adv. bd. First Meth. Ch., Bentonville; bd. dirs. YMCA, Minnetonka, Minn., 1984; mem. N.W. Ark. Symphony Guild. Baker scholar Harvard U., 1975; Gen. Motors fellow, N.Y.C., 1973-75. Mem. Harvard Club, Palos Verdes Golf Club. Republican. Home: 1547 Via Coronel Palos Verdes Estates CA 90274 Office: Mattel Inc 5150 Rosecrans Ave Hawthorne CA 90250

ESPINOLA, TERRY RUSSELL, treasurer, controller; b. Killeen, Tex., May 9, 1957; s. Francis Anthony and Dorothy Jean (Russell) S.; m. Lee Ann Hyatt, June 16, 1977; 1 child, T. Russell. BBA in Acctg., U. Mary Hardin-Baylor, 1981. Lic. pilot. Acct., office mgrs. Cen. Forwarding, Killeen, Tex., 1975-81; acct. BFW Constrn., Temple, Tex., 1981-83; jr. tax acct. Greenstein Logan, Temple, 1983-84, sr. tax acct., 1984; controller, treas. Flanagan Constrn. Co., Temple, 1984—. Vice chmn. Am. Heart Assn., Temple, 1985; mem. City Bldg. Bd. Adjustments, Temple, 1984. Recipient Eagle Scout with Palm and Ad Altare Dei awards Boy Scouts Am. Mem. Air Craft Owners and Pilots Orgn., Jaycees (bd. dirs. Temple chpt. 1984, treas. 1984-86, sec. 1986-87, Jaycee of Month 1985, Outstanding Young Man of Am. 1985). Republican. Roman Catholic. Home: 712 Brazos Temple TX 76501 Office: Flanagan Constrn Co Inc 6415 S General Bruce Temple TX 76503

ESPOSITO, BONNIE LOU, marketing professional; b. Chgo., July 20, 1947; d. Ralph Edgar and Dorothy Mae (Groh) Myers; m. Frank Merle Esposito, Aug. 15, 1969 (div. Sept. 1985); children: Mario Henry, Elizabeth Ann. BA, George Williams Coll., 1969. Caseworker Little Bros. of the Poor, Chgo., 1969-72; dir. Little Bros.-Friends of the Elderly, Mpls., 1972-78; owner Espo Inc./Mario's Ristorante, Mpls., 1978-85; mktg. mgr. City of Mpls. Energy Office, 1981—; dir. mktg. and tng. The Energy Collaborative, 1987—; dir. tng. The Energy Collaborative, 1987—. Organizer Community Crime Prevention, Mpls., 1978-81. Mem. NAFE (bd. dirs. Monday Night Network 1988), Midwest Direct Mktg. Assn., Minn. Multi-Housing Assn., Nat. Apartment Assn. Office: City of Mpls Energy Office 330 City Hall Minneapolis MN 55415

ESPOSITO, MICHAEL PATRICK, JR., banker; b. Hackensack, N.J., Oct. 6, 1939; s. Michael Peter and Maria Carmela Esposito; m. Ellen Lyons, Sept. 2, 1962; children: Michael, John, James. B.B.A., Notre Dame U., 1961; M.B.A., N.Y.U., 1967. Supr. Chase Manhattan Bank, N.Y.C., 1965-66; acctg. officer Chase Manhattan Bank, 1967-68, 2d v.p., 1968-70, v.p., 1970-74, sr. v.p., 1975-83, exec. v.p., controller, 1983-86, exec. v.p., chief fin. officer, 1986—. Served with USMCR, 1961-63. Mem. Bank Adminstrn. Inst. (chmn. acctg. and fin. commn. 1981-83, chmn. bd. 1988-89), Nat. Assn. Accts., Fin. Execs. Inst. Republican. Roman Catholic. Office: Chase Manhattan Corp 1 Chase Manhattan Pla New York NY 10081

ESPY, WILLIAM WRIGHT, real estate company executive; b. Savannah, Ga., Mar. 7, 1947; s. Joseph Samuel and Marjorie Hastings (Riley) E.; grad. The Lawrenceville Sch., 1965; BA, U. N.C., 1969. With The Bank of N.Y., N.Y.C., 1969-72; v.p. Real Estate Concepts, Atlanta, 1972-74; pres. The Espy-Michaels Co., Atlanta, 1974-81; pres. The Espy Co., Atlanta, 1981-87, mng. dir., 1988—; bd. dirs. Stan West Mining Corp., Scottsdale, Ariz. Bd. dirs. Am. Diabetes Assn. Atlanta; div. chmn. stewardship campaign Cathedral of St. Philip, Atlanta; mem. Carolina Fund Com., U. N.C. Mem. Mortgage Bankers Assn. Am., Mortgage Bankers Assn. Ga. (chmn. spl. interest com. 1978-79, chmn. comml. loan com. 1979-80), Urban Land Inst., Lawrenceville Sch. Alumni Assn. (exec. com. 1971—, v.p. assn. 1974-80, chmn. trustee selectors com., chmn. ann. giving 1987-88). Episcopalian. Clubs: Capital City, Savannah Golf, U. Ga. Gridiron Soc. Home: 64 Paces West Dr Atlanta GA 30327 Office: 100 Northcreek Suite 150 3715 Northside Pkwy Atlanta GA 30327

ESREY, ELIZABETH GOVE GOODIER, chemist; b. West Chester, Pa., Mar. 25, 1964; d. Robert Egan and Mary Ellen (Winslow) Goodier; m. James David Esrey, Nov. 28, 1987. BA in Biology, Maryville Coll., 1986. Lab. tech. Franklin Co., Wilmington, Del., 1987, Stine/Haskell Rsch., DuPont, Newark, Del., 1987—; owner Beth's Breads, Media, Pa., 1987—.

Mem. Circle K. (pres. 1985-86). Republican. Episcopalian. Office: Stine Haskell Rsch Labs PO Box 50 Newark DE 19714

ESREY, WILLIAM TODD, telecommunications company executive; b. Phila., Jan. 17, 1940; s. Alexander J. and Dorothy (B.) E.; m. Julie L. Campbell, June 13, 1964; children: William Todd, John Campbell. BA, Denison U., Granville, Ohio, 1961; MBA, Harvard U., 1964. With Am. Tel & Tel. Co., also N.Y. Tel. Co., 1964-69; pres. Empire City Subway Ltd., N.Y.C., 1969-70; mng. dir. Dillon, Read & Co. Inc., N.Y.C., 1970-80; exec. v.p. corp. planning United Telecommunications, Inc., Westwood, Kans., 1980-81, exec. v.p., chief fin. officer, 1981-82, 84-85; pres., chief exec. officer United Telecommunications, Inc., 1985—; pres. United Telecom Communications, Inc., Kansas City, Mo., 1982-85; bd. dirs. The Equitable Life Assurance Soc. U.S., Panhandle Eastern Corp., Gen. Mills, Inc.; pres., chief exec. officer U.S. Sprint, 1987—. Bd. dirs. U. Kansas City, Greater Kansas City Community Found.; trustee Denison U., Midwest Rsch. Com. for Econ. Devel. Mem. Mission Hills Country Club, River Club, Links Club, Kans. City Country Club, Phi Beta Kappa. Home: 2624 Verona Rd Shawnee Mission KS 66208 Office: United Telecommunications Inc PO Box 11315 Kansas City MO 64112

ESSICK, THEODORE FOREST, textile printing executive; b. Johnson City, Tenn.; s. Edward Lowell and Dorothy (Thomas) E.; m. Sarah Ann Parker, June 27, 1981; 1 child, Lauren Elizabeth. BBA, East Tenn. State U., 1980; MBA, U. Tenn. Asst. v.p. Park Nat. Bank, Knoxville, Tenn., 1981-83; dir. fin. and adminstrn. Knoxville C. of C., 1983-84; v.p., sr. comml. lender Commerce Union Bank, Johnson City, 1984-87; treas., chief fin. officer Baldauf, Inc., Johnson City, 1987—; instr. East Tenn. State U., Johnson City, 1985—. Active Leadership 2000, Johnson City, 1986; div. chmn. Johnson City United Way, 1985; treas. Appalachian council Girl Scouts U.S., Johnson City, 1986—; bd. dirs. Johnson City Arts Council, 1984-86. Mem. Johnson City C. of C. (chmn. local com. 1985-87), Rotary (sgt.-at-arms 1985-87). Republican. Presbyterian. Home: 1110 Ridgecrest Rd Johnson City TN 37604 Office: Baldauf Inc 2230 Eddie Williams Rd Johnson City TN 37601

ESSLINGER, ANNA MAE LINTHICUM, realtor; b. Clifton, Tenn., May 29, 1912; d. Wallace Prather and Minnie P. (Bates) Linthicum; student Miss. State Coll. Women, La. State U.; m. William Francis Esslinger, Sept. 29, 1932; children—Ann Lynn (Mrs. James C. Wilcox), Susan Angie (Mrs. Heinz J. Selig). Founder, Esslinger-Wooten-Maxwell Inc., real estate, Coral Gables, Fla., 1968—. Pres. Coral Gables Bd. Realtors, 1975. Mem. Fla. (dir.) Assn. Realtors, Nat. Assn. Realtors, DAR, Assistance League of Eugene, Am. Contract Bridge League, Eugene Garden Club, Eugene Symphony Guild, Chi Omega. Christian Scientist. Home: 759 Fair Oaks Dr Eugene OR 97401 Office: 1360 S Dixie Hwy Coral Gables FL 33146

ESTEP, BARBARA MELTON, corporate training consultant; b. Waco, Tex., Dec. 12, 1949; d. Robert Gano Melton and Virginia (Thompson) Ryan; m. Daniel Quen Estep, Dec. 18, 1971. BS in Edn. in Polit. Sci., U. Tex., 1971; postgrad., U. Ga., 1978. Cert. tchr. secondary edn. Tchr. Jefferson (Ga.) City Schs., 1976-79, Morgan County High Sch., Madison, Ga., 1979-82; tng. coordinator Eaton Corp., Athens, Ga., 1982-85; coordinator tng. and edn. Lithonia Lighting, Conyers, Ga., 1985-87; tng. cons. Creative Mktg. Assn., Atlanta, 1986-87, Slattery Ednl. Concepts, Marietta, Ga., 1987-88; seminar specialist Fed. Home Loan Mortgage Corp., Dallas, 1988—. Assoc. mem. Ga. Council on Econs. Edn., Atlanta, 1979-82; meeting coordinator Athens Indsl. Mgmt. Group, 1982-85. Named Star Tchr. Morgan County Bd. Edn., 1981. Mem. NAFE, AAUW (sec., treas. 1980-82), Am. Soc. Tng. & Devel., Assn. Ga. Coun. Econs. Edn. (assoc.). Episcopalian. Clubs: Toastmasters (Conyers) (v.p. 1986-87); Lithonia Lighting Mgmt. (Conyers) (v.p. 1985-86). Office: Creative Mktg Assocs 4343 W Northwest Hwy Suite 897 Dallas TX 75220

ESTERVIG, HOWARD RAYMOND, engineer; b. Madison, Wis., Dec. 29, 1947; s. Raymond Knute and Hazel Ruth (Shultis) E.; m. Patricia Leslie Simmons, June 14, 1970; children: Andrew Howard, Amy Marie, Erin Elizabeth. BS, U. Wis., Platteville, 1970. Machinist RAJO Industries, Inc., Waterloo, Wis., 1974-76; v.p. Gordon Engring, Inc., Madison, 1976-86, pres., chief exec. officer, 1986—. With USAF, 1970-74, Vietnam. Mem. Soc. Mfg. Engrs. (sr.), Wis. Ind. Distbrs. Assn., Wis. Ind. Bus., Nat. Fedn. Ind. Bus. (guardian), Masons (master 1974-76), Royal Arch (high priest 1976-79). Home: 920 Daniel St Sun Prarie WI 53590 Office: Gordon Engring Inc 501 Tasman St Madison WI 53714

ESTES, CARL LEWIS, II, lawyer; b. Fort Worth, Tex., Feb. 9, 1936; s. Joe E. and Carroll E.; m. Gay Gooch, Aug. 29, 1959; children: Adrienne Virginia, Margaret Ellen. B.S., U. Tex., 1957, LL.B., 1960. Bar: Tex. 1960. Law clk. U.S. Supreme Ct., 1960-61; assoc. firm Vinson & Elkins, Houston, 1961-69; ptnr. Vinson & Elkins, 1970—. Bd. dirs. Houston Grand Opera Assn. Fellow Am Bar Found., Tex. Bar Found.; mem. Am. Law Inst., Am. Coll. Probate Counsel, ABA, Internat. Bar Assn., Tex. Bar Assn., Internat. Fiscal Assn. (v.p.), Internat. Acad. Estate and Trust Law. Clubs: Houston, Ramada, Houston Country, Allegro, Les Ambassadeurs (London), Marks (London). Home: 101 Broad Oaks Cir Houston TX 77056 Office: Vinson & Elkins 3300 First City Tower 1001 Fannin Houston TX 77002

ESTES, DONALD WAYNE, trucking company executive; b. Allen, Kans., Sept. 15, 1930; s. Frank Lester and Florence M. (Lewis) E.; m. Arlene Joyce Hahn, Aug. 10, 1957; children: Gayla Dawn, Julie Ann. BBA, Washburn U., 1958. With Ryder Truck Rental, Inc., Miami, Fla., 1964—, account mgr., 1964-65, dist. mgr., Little Rock, 1965-70, regional mgr., Milw., 1970-74, area v.p., 1974-79, sr. v.p., 1979-81, exec. v.p., 1981-82, exec. v.p. ops., 1982-83, pres., 1983—; bd. dirs. Profl. Truck Drivers Inst. Am., Inc.; pres. Catrala Assocs., 1969-71, others. Bd. dirs. Salvation Army, Jackie Robinson Found; trustee Fla. Meml. Coll., 1988—. Served with USN, 1950-54. Mem. Ark. Bus and Truck Assn. (v.p., dir. 1965-71), Truck Rental and Leasing Assn, (dir. 1983—). Democrat. Methodist. Office: Ryder Truck Rental Inc 3600 NW 82nd Ave Miami FL 33166

ESTES, GERALD WALTER, newspaper executive; b. Memphis, Apr. 21, 1928; s. Edward Leon and Grace Virginia (Knight) E.; m. Mary Charlene Owen, Nov. 7, 1953 (div. July 1975); children: Patricia Estes Tischler, Charles, Susan, Jacqueline; m. Bernice Pendleton O'Mery, Mar. 20, 1976 (div. Nov. 1984); m. Mary Owen Estes, Nov. 17, 1984. Student, Memphis State U., 1949-50. Research asst. Washington Star, 1954-56, asst. prodn. mgr., 1956-68; prodn. mgr. Richmond (Va.) Newspapers, 1968-69; v.p., gen. mgr. SE Media, Inc., Richmond, 1969-73; v.p. newspaper div. Media Gen., Inc., Richmond, 1974-77; sr. v.p. Media Gen., Inc., 1977—; dir. Computer Software Co. Served with USAF, 1946-49. Mem. Am. Newspaper Pubs. Assn., So. Newspaper Pubs. Assn., So. Prodn. Program (dir.), Va. Cable TV Assn. (dir.), Central Richmond Assn., Richmond C. of C. Republican. Methodist. Clubs: Bull and Bear, Willow Oaks Country. Home: 13636 Northwick Dr Richmond VA 23113 Office: Media Gen Inc 333 E Grace St Richmond VA 23219

ESTES, JACK CHARLES, oil company executive, researcher; b. Rogers, Ark., Apr. 7, 1935; s. Jack Russell and Merle Clara (White) E.; m. Sandra Jean Reeves, Nov. 10, 1961; children: Michael Lynn, David Russell, Cristi Yvonne. BSChemE, U. Tulsa, 1965. Computer engr. Remington Rand Univac, Ilion, N.Y., 1960; rsch. tech. Pan Am. Petroleum Corp., Tulsa, 1960-65, rsch. engr., 1965-76; rsch. supr. Amoco Prodn. Co., Tulsa, 1976—. Contbr. articles to profl. jours.; patentee in field. With USAF, 1955-59. Mem. ASME (standardization com. chmn. 1989-92), Am. Petroleum Inst. (vice chmn. com. 13 1987—), Am. Assn. for the Advancement of Sci., Soc. Petroleum Engrs. (tech. editor Jour. Petroleum Tech. 1977-78, svc. award 1985), Am. Chem. Soc. (svc. award 1984), Masons, Moose, Sigma Xi., N.E. Okla. Sq. Dancing Assn. (historian 1987, publicity dir. 1986, state del. 1988). Methodist. Home: 10930 S Richmond Ave Tulsa OK 74137-7111

ESTES, LYNDA SHERRYL, editor; b. Lafayette, Ind., Nov. 7, 1945; d. Robert Lee and Charlotte Mildred (Morrison) Morehouse; m. C. John Estes, Dec. 6, 1975; children: Amy Elizabeth, Michelle Lynn, John Michael. BA, Purdue U., 1971; postgrad., U. Rochester, 1983-85. Mktg. exec. Xerox Corp., Miami, 1972-75, Rochester, N.Y., 1975-78; mktg. exec. to dir. strategic planning to v.p. mktg. info. systems Bausch & Lomb Inc., Rochester, 1978-83; pres. Corp. Research, Rochester, 1983-87; sr. editor Modern Applications News Metal Working Mag., Nokomis, Fla., 1988—. Mem. Am. Bus. Womens Assn. Republican. Home: 825 Madrid Ave Venice FL 34285 Office: Modern Application News Metalworking 2504 N Tamiami Trail Nokomis FL 34275

ESTES, MOREAU PINCKNEY, IV, real estate executive; b. Nashville, Oct. 10, 1917; s. Moreau Pinckney III and Lillian (Cole) E.; m. Bertha Lewis, Jan. 14, 1941; children: Moreau Pinckney V, Robert Lewis, Victoria Susanne. BA, Vanderbilt U., 1937; LLB, Cumberland U., 1938. Sole practice law Nashville, 1938-41, bldg. contractor, 1940-43, 46-53; dir. Davidson County Farm Bur., Nashville, 1950-56; v.p. Davidson Farmers Coop., 1955-56; gen. mgr. Harpeth Valley (Tenn.) Utilities Dist., 1963-67; founder, pres. Hillsboro-Harpeth Corp., 1964—; founder, sec.-treas. Alpha Publishing Co., Brentwood, Tenn., 1986—, also bd. dirs.; founder, owner Realty Investment Co., Nashville, 1964—. Property adminstr. State of Tenn., 1964-67, atty. property div., 1962-64; asst. commr. Tenn. Dept. Conservation, 1975; del. State Dem. Conv., 1951; sec. Williamson County Dem. Primary Commn., 1967-69; mcpl. Nashville and Middle Tenn. Tennis Singles and Doubles champion, 1939, 40. 1st lt. Signal Corps U.S. Army, 1942-46, with Res., 1946-51. Mem. Nashville Home Bldrs. Assn. (pres. 1951), Tenn. Horsemens' Assn. (dir. 1964), Tenn. Hist. Soc., Tenn. Bar Assn., Nashville Bar Assn., Am. Judicature Soc., Biblical Archaeology Soc., Nat. Audubon Soc., Smithsonian Assocs., Vanderbilt U. Alumni Assn., Am. Legion, Wildwood Swimming and Tennis Club (founder, 1st chmn.), Delta Kappa Epsilon. Democrat. Methodist. Home: 6434 Panorama Dr Brentwood TN 37027 Office: 3813 Hillsboro Rd Ste 250 Nashville TN 37215 Also: 3685 Valencia Rd Jacksonville FL 32205

ESTRIN, THELMA AUSTERN, electrical engineer; b. N.Y.C., Feb. 21, 1924; d. I. Billy and Mary (Ginsburg) Austern; m. Gerald Estrin, Dec. 21, 1941; children: Margo, Judith, Deborah. BSEE, U. Wis., Madison, 1947, MSEE, 1948, PhD, 1951. Cert. clin. engr. Research engr. UCLA Brain Research Inst., 1960-70, dir. data processing, 1970-80; prof. UCLA Sch. Engring. and Applied Sci., 1980—; dir. div. electronics, computer and systems engring. NSF, Washington, 1982-84; asst. dean Sch. Engring. and Applied Sci. UCLA, 1984-88; dir. dept. engring. UCLA Extension, 1984-88; trustee Aerospace Corp., 1979-82; mem. biomed. tech. resources com. NIH, 1981-86; mem. U.S. Army Sci. Bd., 1982-83; mem. energy engring. bd. NRC, 1985—. Contbr. articles to tech. jours. Mem. Los Angeles Women in Bus. Recipient Disting. Contbn. to Engring. Edn. award NSPE, 1985, Achievement award Soc. Women Engrs. 1981, Disting. Service citation U. Wis., 1976. Fellow IEEE (bd. dirs. 1979-80, exec. v.p. 1982, recipient Centennial medal 1984, pres. Engring. in Medicine and Biology Soc. 1977), AAAS (chair Engring. sect. 1989). Jewish. Office: UCLA Sch Engring & Applied Sci Boelter Hall Rm 7620 Los Angeles CA 90024

ESWEIN, BRUCE JAMES, II, advertising agency executive; b. San Mateo, Calif., Oct. 26, 1951; s. Bruce James and Janet Gordon (Copeland) E.; m. Sarah Anne Shames, Feb. 7, 1981; children: Thomas Jonathan, Elizabeth Anne. Student, U. Wash., 1969-71; A.B., U. Calif.-Berkeley, 1973, M.B.A., 1977. Brand asst. Clorox Co., Oakland, Calif., 1977-79, coll. relations mgr., 1979-83; mgr. exec. recruitment and devel. BBDO Worldwide, N.Y.C., 1983-84, v.p., 1984-87, v.p. personnel adminstrn., 1987-88, v.p. human resources, mgr. worldwide tng. and devel., 1988—. Mem. Am. Soc. for Tng. and Devel., U. Calif. at Berkeley Bus. Sch. Alumni Assn. (bd. dirs. 1980-83), Phi Beta Kappa, Chi Psi (v.p. 1972-73, bd. dirs. 1979-82, trustee 1983-84, trustee emeritus 1984—). Republican. Episcopalian. Home: 62 Grand St Croton-on-Hudson NY 10520 Office: BBDO Worldwide 1285 Ave of the Americas New York NY 10019-6095

ETHERIDGE, JEFF DAVID, JR., bank executive; b. Fayetteville, N.C., Jan. 26, 1949; s. Jeff D. Sr. and Frances (Eakes) E.; m. Judith Rusk, June 10, 1972 (div. Apr. 1986); children: Brian Rusk, Brooke Leigh; m. Karen Best, Aug. 29, 1987; children: Hunter, Brian S. BBA, Campbell U., 1971; cert. exec. program, U. N.C., 1985. Asst. v.p. First Citizens Bank, Raleigh, N.C., 1971-78; v.p. United Carolina Bank, Whiteville, N.C., 1978-80, sr. v.p., 1980-85, exec. v.p., 1985—; exec. v.p. United Carolina Bancshares, Whiteville, N.C., 1986—; Speaker numerous profl. orgns. and convs.; instr. Am. Inst. Banking; instr. Mgmt. Devel., Inc., U. N.C., Chapel Hill; assoc. dean, bd. dirs. N.C. Sch. Banking, Chapel Hill, 1985-86, dean , 1987—. Mem. exec. com. Cape Fear Council Boy Scouts Am., 1988—. Mem. Robert Morris Assn. (chmn. Eastern Carolina chpt. 1986), Am. Bankers Assn., N.C. Bankers Assn., Whiteville C. of C. (bd. dirs. 1988-91). Democrat. Episcopalian. Club: Whiteville Country (v.p., treas. 1980—), Tower. Home: 302 Edgewood Circle Whiteville NC 28472 Office: United Carolina Bank PO Box 632 Whiteville NC 28472

ETHERINGTON, GEOFFREY, II, manufacturing executive; b. London, Dec. 21, 1928; s. Harold and Elesa Ruth (Ashton) E.; m. Ida Jane Caruso, 1952 (div. 1974); children: Geoffrey, Amy Ruth, Harold Willis; m. Kathleen Finneran, Oct. 8, 1975; children: Charles Emmett, Edward John. BS in Mech. Engring., Purdue U., 1950; MBA, Northwestern U., 1951; JD, Loyola U., Chgo., 1957; MD, Yale U., 1976; LHD, Quinnipiac Coll., 1982. V.p. Sparton Corp., Jackson, Mich., 1966-69, The Allen Group, Inc., Melville, N.Y., 1971-73; pres. G&O, Inc., New Haven, 1969-71, Etherington Industries, Inc., New Haven, 1973-86; intern St. Raphael's Hosp., New Haven, 1976; bd. dirs. The Hydraulic Co., Bridgeport, Conn., Condere Corp., Hamden, Conn. Served with U.S. Army, 1946-47, Korea. Office: Etherington Industries Inc PO Box 706 New Haven CT 06503

ETHERINGTON, ROGER BENNETT, banker; b. Bayonne, N.J., Nov. 18, 1923; s. Charles K. and Ethel (Bennett) E.; m. Barbara H. Dean, Nov. 22, 1946; children—Sandra, Kim Anne, Caryn, R. Barrie. Student, Con. Wesleyan U., Middletown, 1941-43, 47-48; A.B., Columbia U., 1950. With Am. Nat. Bank & Trust N.J., Morristown, N.J., 1950—; pres. Am. Nat. Bank & Trust N.J., 1969-76, chmn. bd., chmn. exec. com., 1976—; chmn. Horizon Bancorp., N.J.; dir., chmn. Horizon Trust Co. N.A., 1981—; also dir; dir. Care Dwellings, Inc.; bd. dirs. Spartan Oil Co. 1st v.p., trustee Fairleigh Dickinson U., Waterloo Found. for Arts, Mt. Hebron Cemetery Assn.; bd. dirs., chmn. bd. Greer-Woodycrest Children's Services; mem. bus. adv. bd. Community Coll. Morris. Served as officer AUS, 1943-46, 51-52, PTO. Recipient Peace medal, 1981. Mem. Morris County C. of C. (dir., past pres.), Nat. Alliance Bus. (bus. adv. bd.), Morgan Horse Club, N.J. Morgan Horse Assn. (pres. 1967). Congregationalist (trustee, treas. 1964-67). Clubs: Montclair Golf, Sky Top, Morristown; Nassau (Princeton, N.J.); Green Boundary (Aiken, S.C.). Home: 465 Park St Upper Montclair NJ 07043 Office: Horizon Bancorp 225 South St Morristown NJ 07960

ETHRIDGE, MELVIN DEAN, cotton association executive, economist; b. Spur, Tex., Aug. 30, 1945; s. Sidney Melvin and Sammie Jo (Houston) E.; m. Wanda Lanell Lafon, Nov. 18, 1967; children: Lisa Fern, Tiffany Lanell. BS, Tex. Tech U., 1967; MS, U. Calif., Berkeley, 1968, PhD, 1971. Asst. prof. U. Ga., Athens, 1971-75; asst. prof. Texas A&M U., Coll. Sta., 1975-77, assoc. prof., 1977-81; economist U.S. Agy. Internat. Devel., Montevideo, Uruguay, 1978-80; dir. Nat. Cotton Council, Memphis, 1981—; cons. Market Research Ctr., Coll. Sta., 1975-77, 80-81, U.S. Dept. Agr., Washington, 1985. Author: Economic Outlook for U.S. Cotton, 1986; editor Monthly Econ. Rev., 1981—; contbr. articles to profl jours. Giannini Found. Fellow, Bank Am., 1968; Clayton Fund scholar, Anderson-Clayton Co., 1966. Mem. Am. Agrl. Econs. Assn., So. Agrl. Econs. Assn., Nat. Assn. Bus. Economists, Council Agrl. Sci. Tech., Western Econ. Assn. Internat., Phi Kappa Phi, Gamma Sigma Delta. Republican. Office: Nat Cotton Coun PO Box 12285 Memphis TN 38182

ETLING, JOHN CHARLES, reinsurance company executive; b. Bklyn., Nov. 14, 1935; s. John and Josephine (Weisman) E.; m. Marilyn Gloria Silvestri, Apr. 26, 1958; 1 child, Jacquelyn Carla. B.A., Manhattan Coll., 1957. Property underwriter Atlantic Cos., N.Y.C., 1957-61; property underwriter Gen. Reinsurance Corp., Greenwich, Conn., 1961-70, v.p., 1970-76, sr. v.p., 1976-82, exec. v.p., 1982-83, pres., chief exec. officer, 1984—; also bd. dirs. Gen. Reinsurance Corp., Greenwich; vice chmn. Gen. Re Corp., 1987—; bd. dirs. Gen. Re Services, Gen. Star Mgmt. Corp., Herbert Clough, Inc. Mem. Ruffed Grouse Soc., Quail Unltd., Ducks Unltd. Republican. Roman Catholic. Clubs: Fairfield Fish and Game; Rolling Rock, Minn. Horse and Hunt, Sandanona.

ETTER, CONSTANCE LYNNE, librarian, auditor; b. Litchfield, Ill., July 20, 1943; d. John Orla and Adeline Mae (Arkabauer) E. BA, So. Ill. U., 1965; MLS, U. Ill., 1967. Serials cataloger St. Louis U. Libr., 1967-68; libr. Alton (Ill.) Meml. Hosp. Sch. Nursing, 1968-70; from tech. svcs. dir. to ref. cons. to gen. cons. Cumberland Trail Libr. System, Flora, Ill., 1971-76; cons. Kaskaskia Libr. System, Smithton, Ill., 1976-78; libr. Ill. State Auditor Gens. Office, Springfield, Ill., 1979—, freedom info. officer, 1985—, state auditor, 1986—. Vol. Kumler Neighborhood Ministries, Springfield, 1983—; mem. Women's Internat. League for Peace and Freedom, Springfield, 1984—; sec. Northwest Condominium Assn., Springfield, 1983-86, pres., 1986-87, bd. dirs. 1983—; charter mem. Art for Peace, Springfield, 1985—. Mem. ALA, Beta Phi Mu, Lamda Iot a Tau. Democrat. Presbyterian. Office: Ill State Office Auditor Gen 509 S 6th St Springfield IL 62701

ETTER, ROBERT MILLER, consumer products executive, chemist; b. Chambersburg, Pa., July 13, 1932; s. John Edgar and Grace Elizabeth (Miller) E.; m. Jeane E. Beard, June 15, 1957; children—Robert Douglas, Jeffrey Beard, Roberta Marie. AB, Gettysburg Coll., 1954; postgrad., Harvard U., 1975; PhD, Pa. State U., 1959. Rsch. scientist Am. Cyanamid, Bound Brook, N.J., 1958-63; with S.C. Johnson & Son, Inc., Racine, Wis., 1963—; dir. R & D Europe and Africa S.C. Johnson & Son, Inc., Eng. and Netherlands, 1972-78; dir. R & D worldwide indsl. products S.C. Johnson & Son, Inc., 1978-80, v.p. R & D worldwide indsl. products, 1980-82; v.p. corp. rsch. S.C. Johnson & Son, Inc., Racine, 1982, v.p. R & D U.S. Consumer Products, 1982-88, v.p. external affairs, R & D, 1988—. Mem. Am. Chem. Soc., AAAS, N.Y. Acad. Sci., Indsl. Research Inst., Chem. Specialties Mfrs. Assn. (dir. 1986—), Sigma Xi. Home: 3665 N Bay St Racine WI 53402 Office: SC Johnson & Son Inc 1525 Howe St Racine WI 53403

ETTRICK, MARCO ANTONIO, theoretical physicist; b. Panama City, Panama, July 17, 1945; came to U.S., 1963; s. Clemente Adolfo and Olga Rosa (Birmingham) E.; m. Adys Marie Hippolyte, Oct. 22, 1966 (div. Mar. 1977); children: Rudolphe Antoine, Marc Edouard. BS in Math., Poly. Tech. U., Bklyn., 1968; MS in Math., Poly. Tech. U., 1986, doctoral study. Programmer analyst Citibank, N.Y.C., 1969-71; lic. bacteriologist Lincoln Hosp., N.Y.C., 1975-76; lectr. in math. Queens (N.Y.) Coll., 1980-81, L.I. U., Bklyn., 1981-82, N.Y. Tech. Coll., Bklyn., 1982-84, Huston Community Coll., Bklyn., 1984—, Medgar Evers Coll., Bklyn., 1986—. Contbr. articles to sci. jours. Mem. AAAS, Am. Fedn. Scientists, Am. Phys. Soc., Math. Assn. Am., Pi Mu Epsilon. Roman Catholic. Home: 79 Sterling St Brooklyn NY 11225

EUGSTER, JACK WILSON, retail executive; b. Mound, Minn., Oct. 7, 1945; s. George and Helen M. (Kerr) E.; m. Camie M. Rust; children: Nicholas J., Wilson M. BA in Chemistry, Carleton Coll., 1967; MBA in Fin., Stanford U., 1969. Mgr. ops. and merchandising Target Stores Inc., Mpls., 1970-72; exec. v.p. The Gap Stores, San Bruno, Calif., 1972-80; chmn., pres., chief exec. officer The Musicland Group, Inc., Mpls., 1980—; bd. dirs. Midwest Energy, Inc., Sioux City, Iowa, Iowa Pub. Svc. Co., Sioux City, E&B Marine Inc. Chmn. campaign div. United Way Mpls., 1980—. Recipient Human Relations Music and Video Div. award Anti-Defamation League, N.Y.C., 1986. Mem. Nat. Assn. Recording Merchandisers (bd. dirs. 1981—, pres. 1985-86), Country Music Assn. (bd. dirs. 1985—, chmn. 1987-88), Wayzata Country Club. Home: 6300 Knoll Dr Edina MN 55436 Office: Musicland Group Inc 7500 Excelsior Blvd Minneapolis MN 55426

EURY, LYNN WADE, utility company executive; b. Polkton, N.C., Jan. 18, 1937; s. James L. and Zula Mae (Whitley) E.; m. Alice Faye Young, Sept. 27, 1959; children: Beth, Leigh, Faith. B.S. in E.E., N.C. State U., 1959. Registered profl. engr., N.C., S.C. With Carolina Power & Light Co., Raleigh, N.C., 1959—, v.p. systems planning and coordination, 1979-80, v.p. power supply, 1980, sr. v.p. power supply, 1980-83, sr. v.p. fossil generation and power transmission, 1983—, sr. v.p. ops support, 1986-89, exec. v.p. power supply, 1989—; mem. EEI Nuclear Power Exec. Adv. Com., Washington, 1982—; bd. dirs. Profl. Engrs. N.C. Ednl. Found., Inc., Raleigh; bd. dirs. N.C. Mathcounts, fin. chmn. 1987-88; v.p. Carolina Va. Nuclear Power Assn., Inc., Columbia, 1982—. Mem. bd. advisors U. N.C. Sch. Pub. Health, 1988—; chmn. fin. com. Hayes Barton Meth. Ch., 1983. Served with U.S. Army, 1960. Mem. IEEE, Profl. Engrs. N.C., N.C. Soc. Engrs., Am. Nuclear Soc., Eastern Carolinas sect. Am. Nuclear Soc., Health Physics Soc. Republican. Methodist. Club: Glen Forest Swim (pres. 1983).

EUSTICE, RUSSELL CLIFFORD, consulting company executive; b. Hackensack, N.J., July 11, 1919; s. Russell C. and Ethel (Hutchison) E.; B.A., Colgate U., 1941; M.B.A., Am. U., 1973; m. Veronica B. Dabrowski, Mar. 15, 1946; children—Russell Clifford, David A., Paul M. With Vick Chem. Corp., N.Y.C., 1941-42, 46-47; with Johnson & Johnson, 1947-61, div. sales mgr., 1954-61; nat. sales mgr. Park & Tilford div. Schenley Affiliates, N.Y.C., 1961-62; pres. Mid-Atlantic Assos., Inc., Prospect Harbor, Maine, 1962—; dir. Small Bus. Inst., Husson Coll., Bangor, Maine, 1979-88, ARR New England Region - S.C.O.R.E.; asst. prof. bus. adminstrn., 1979-88; part-time instr. mktg. The Am. U., Washington, 1970-74. Served to capt. AUS, 1942-46. Mem. Assn. Mil. Surgeons, Reserve Officers Assn., Assn. Mktg. Educators, SBA. Republican. Methodist. Home: Lighthouse Rd Prospect Harbor ME 04669

EUSTIS, ALBERT ANTHONY, lawyer, diversified industry corporate executive; b. Mahanoy City, Pa., Nov. 8, 1921; s. Anthony and Anna E.; m. Mary Hampton Stewart, Apr. 25, 1959; children: Thomas Stewart, David Anthony. B.S., Columbia U., 1948; LL.B., Harvard U., 1951. Bar: N.Y. 1952, U.S. Dist. Ct. (So. dist.) N.Y 1955. Atty. firm Kelley, Drye & Warren, N.Y.C., 1951-61; atty. W.R. Grace & Co., N.Y.C., 1961-66; asst. gen. counsel W.R. Grace & Co., 1966-76, v.p., gen. counsel, sec., 1976-78, sr. v.p., gen. counsel, sec., 1978-82, exec. v.p., gen. counsel, sec., 1982-87; of counsel Holland & Knight, Washington, 1987—; chmn. bd. trustees, spl. counsel Found. for President's Pvt. Sector Survey on Cost Control; adj. prof. law Fordham Law Sch. Served with AUS, 1942-46. Mem. ABA, Am. Arbitration Assn. (bd. dirs., comml. arbitration panel). Home: 23 Farmington Dr Charlottesville VA 22901 Office: W R Grace & Co 919 18th St NW Washington DC 20006

EUTENEUER, JOSEPH JOHN, finance executive; b. Chgo., Aug. 14, 1955; s. Joseph and Victoria (Kwapien) E.; m. Pamela Houston; 1 child, Jill Elizabeth. Student, Western Ill. U., 1973-76; BS, Ariz. State U., 1978. CPA, Ariz. Sr. acct. Touche Ross Co., Phoenix, 1978-81, Price Waterhouse, Phoenix, 1981-82; mgr., asst. dir., mng. cons. Neff & Co., Phoenix, 1982-84; pres., chief exec. officer La Canasta Mexican Foods, Phoenix, 1984-85; v.p., fin. Storer Communications, Inc., Houston, 1985-88; dir. corp. devel. Comcast Corp., Phila., 1988—. Mem. Am. Inst. CPA's, Broadcast Fin. Mgmt. Assn., Cable TV Adminstrn. and Mktg. Soc., Nat. Assn. Accts. (dir. membership), Inst. Mgmt. Cons. Home: 912 Cloverhill Rd Wynnewood PA 19096 Office: Comcast Corp 1414 S Penn Sq 34th Fl Philadelphia PA 19102-2480

EVANS, CRAIG, association executive; b. Klamath Falls, Oreg., Apr. 14, 1949; s. Joseph Fuller Evans and Toni Opel (Hooper) Johnson; m. Susan Jean Murphy, Dec. 27, 1980. BA in English, Calif. State U., San Jose, 1971. Reporter San Jose (Calif.) Mercury News, 1968-71; adventurer end-to-end through the Alps North Face, Berkeley, Calif., 1972-73; freelance writer Los Gatos, Calif., 1973-75; editor Backpacker Mag., N.Y.C., 1975-77; author William Morrow & Co., N.Y.C., 1977-81; exec. dir. Am. Hiking Soc., Washington, 1979-81; owner, chief exec. officer Syntax, Mktg. Communications, Falls Church, Va., 1981-84; assoc. exec. dir. Population-Environment Balance, Washington, 1984-86; pres. The WalkWays Ctr., Washington, 1986—; mountain tour leader Better Camping Mag., French & Swiss Alps, 1972-73; trails cons. U.S. Dept. of the Interior, Washington, 1979-81; lobbyist Am. Hiking Soc., Washington, 1979-81; U.S. Rep. European Rambler's Assn., 1977-84. Author: (book series) On Foot Through Europe, 1982, (pub. law) National Trails System Act Amendments of 1983; project editor: (book) Backpacking Equipment Buyer's Guide, 1977; creator, author (travel mag.) Tripping, 1973; contbr. articles to profl. jours. Treas. Am. Trails Network, Washington, 1988—; vol. March of Dimes, Washington, 1987. Recipient One Show Merit award The Art Dirs. Club, Inc., N.Y.C., The Copy Club of

N.Y., 1974. Mem. Am. Soc. of Assn. Execs., Natural Resources Coun. of Am., Author's Guild. Democrat. Club: Appalachian Mountain (Boston) (chair internat. com. 1983-84). Home: 404 Kentucky Ave SE Washington DC 20003-3009 Office: The WalkWays Ctr 1400 16th St NW #300 Washington DC 20036

EVANS, D. BRUCE, convention management executive; b. N.Y.C., July 18, 1935; s. Stewart Howard and Kathleen (Fenton) E.; m. Lucy Mae Woolard, Sept. 23, 1957 (div. 1970); children: Elizabeth Joan, Jeffrey Bruce, Donald Scott, Keith Howard, Susan Leigh; m. Patricia Ann Ruppert, Aug. 23, 1970; 1 child, Deborah Lynne. BA, U. N.C., 1959; MBA, Calif. Coast U., 1987. Staff assoc. Middletown (Ohio) C. of C., 1961-63; exec. v.p. Ironton (Ohio) C. of C., 1963-64; pres. United Congl. Appeal, Washington, 1964-67; elected magistrate Fairfax (Va.) County Ct., 1967-71; mng. dir. Bldg. Industries Assn. N.J., Edison, 1971-75; pres. Printing Industries Assn. N.Y., Buffalo, 1975-81; exec. dir. Calif. Rental Assn., Woodland, 1984-88; pres. Cert. Conv. Mgmt. Co., Davis, Calif., 1988—; mem. adv. bd. Desert Resorts Conv. Bur., Palm Desert, Calif., 1986—. Bd. dirs. Ams. Nat. Def., Washington, 1964-71, Nat. Council Dangerous Drugs, Washington, 1970-75; mem. Rep. Nat. Com., Washington, 1985—. Mem. Am. Soc. Assn. Execs., Nat. Assn. Expn. Mgrs., Meeting Planners Internat., Western STates Auto Theft Investigators, Calif. Auto Theft Commn. Presbyterian. Club: Stonegate Country (Davis). Home: 8171 Severn Dr Boca Raton FL 33433 also: PO Box 1482 Pompano Beach FL 33061

EVANS, DANIEL RAY, distributing company executive; b. Portsmouth, Va., Nov. 16, 1955; s. George Owen and Juanita (Bowen) E.; m. Susan Elaine Evans, Aug. 17, 1985; 1 child by previous marriage, Daniel Ray; 1 child by current marriage, Amanda Louise. Student, Kee Bus. Coll., 1974-75. V.p. Evans, Inc., Portsmouth, Va., 1975-84; assoc. P-G Assocs., Whittier, Calif., 1984-85; mgr. product devel. Gem Products, Garden Grove, Calif., 1985-87; chief exec. officer Long Item Devel., Augusta, Ga., 1987—, also bd. dirs.; bd. dirs. W.D. Armstrong, Inc., Willoughby, Ohio. Mem. Augusta Jaycees, Churchland Jaycees (v.p. 1981). Republican. Methodist. Office: Long Item Devel 1247 Reynolds St Augusta GA 30901

EVANS, DONALD LEROY, real estate company executive; b. Madison, Wis., Apr. 22, 1933; s. LeRoy E. and Pearl U. Evans. BS, U. Wis., 1959, MS, 1964. Staff appraiser Am. Appraisal Group, Milw., 1959-64; founder, pres. D.L. Evans, Inc., Madison, 1964—. Served as sgt. U.S. Army, 1953-55, Korea. Recipient appreciation award, U. Wis. Real Estate Alumni Assn., 1979. Mem. Am. Soc. Appraisers (sr.; pres. 1968; Appreciation award 1968), Am. Soc. Real Estate Counselors, Am. Inst. Real Estate Appraisers (pres. 1972; Appreciation award 1972), Madison Bd. Realtors (bd. dirs. 1974-76; Appreciation award 1976). Republican. Lutheran. Club: Madison. Lodge: Rotary. Office: D L Evans Co Inc 6409 Odana Rd Madison WI 53719

EVANS, EDWARD PARKER, publishing and information services company executive; b. Pitts., Jan. 31, 1942; s. Thomas Mellon and Elizabeth Parker (Kase) E. BA, Yale U., 1964; MBA, Harvard U., 1967. V.p. Evans & Co., Inc., N.Y.C. and Mo., 1975-82; chmn. bd. H.K. Porter Co., Inc., Pitts., 1976-82, Mo. Portland Cement Co., 1975-82, Fansteel, Inc., 1977-82, Evans Broadcasting Corp., Mo., 1968-82; chmn. bd., chief exec. officer Macmillan, Inc., N.Y.C., 1979-88, also bd. dirs.; owner Spring Hill Farm, Casanova, Va., 1969—; bd. dirs. Fasig-Tipton Co., Inc. Mem. Andover Devel. Bd. Served with Air N.G., 1965-71. Clubs: Duquesne (Pitts.); River, Harvard Bus. Sch. (N.Y.C.); Round Hill (Greenwich, Conn.); Rolling Rock (Ligonier, Pa.); Blind Brook (Purchase, N.Y.); Spouting Rock Beach Assn. (Newport, R.I.); Lyford Cay (Nassau, Bahamas). Office: 599 Lexington Ave Ste 3600 New York NY 10022

EVANS, GARY CURTIS, print production specialist; b. Pitts., June 27, 1959; s. Edward William and Mary Ann (Hogsett) E. BS in Bus. and Econs. with honors, Carnegie-Mellon U., 1981; MBA in Fin. and Mktg., U. Ill., Chgo., 1986. Mgmt. trainee Charles P. Young Co., Chgo., 1981-86; print prodn. specialist Blade Box Corp., Pitts., 1987—. Orch. leader Phila. Ch., Chgo., 1984, sec., 1985. Republican. Home: 912 Miami Ave Pittsburgh PA 15228

EVANS, GORDON HEYD, management counselor; b. N.Y.C., Apr. 10, 1930; s. Charles Hawes and Eleanor Goodwin (Brown) E. BA, Columbia U., 1953, MA, 1959. Trainee Hornblower & Weeks, N.Y.C., 1954-55; security analyst Baker, Weeks & Co., N.Y.C., 1955; econ. researcher Nat. Bur. Econ. Research, N.Y.C., 1955-56; cons. Gen. Electric Co., N.Y.C., 1957, 1959; asst. prof. polit. economy SUNY, New Paltz, 1966-73; researcher, counselor Am. Mgmt. Assn., N.Y.C., 1960-66, 78—. Contbr. articles to jours. Mem. Nat. Assn. Corp. Dirs., Pilgrims of the U.S., Soc. of the Cincinnati. Mem. Reformed Ch. in Am. Home: Madison Towers 22 E 38th St New York NY 10016 Office: Am Mgmt Assn 135 W 50th St New York NY 10020

EVANS, JACK WILLIAM, real estate executive, educator; b. Washington, Dec. 27, 1945; s. William Richard and Hazel Belle (Brumley) E.; m. Barbara Ann Bulliner, June 7, 1969; 1 child, Mark Andrew. BSME, George Washington U., 1969. Sales engr. Potomac Elec. Power Co., Washington, 1969-78; dir. engring. Oliver T. Carr Co., 1978-81; regional mgr. Cabot Cabot & Forbes, Washington and Boston, 1981—; lectr. George Washington U., 1976-77; instr. Inst. Real Estate Mgmt., 1984. Contbr. articles to Power Engineer mag., 1979. Mem. Bldg. Owners and Mgrs. Assn. (cert. real property adminstr.), Nat. Assn. Power Engrs. (instr. 1979-81, chief engr. 1980), Inst. Real Estate Mgmt. (cert. property mgr.). Democrat. Home: 2016 Lanier Dr Silver Spring MD 20910 Office: Cabot Cabot & Forbes 250 W Pratt St Baltimore MD 21201

EVANS, JAMES STANLEY, communications company executive; b. Joplin, Mo., Apr. 28, 1921; s. Seymour S. and Jeanette (Sloan) E.; m. Beatrice Ware, Oct. 27, 1951; children: James A., John M. B.S. in Engring., Purdue U.; postgrad., Harvard U. Bus. Sch., 1972. Group v.p. Mead Corp., Dayton, Ohio, 1946-73; v.p. Media Gen. Inc., Richmond, Va., 1973-77, sr. v.p. newsprint ops., 1977-80, exec. v.p. ops., 1980-82, chief operating officer, 1982-85, pres., 1982—, chief exec. officer, 1985—, also dir. Mem. adv. bd. William and Mary Coll., Williamsburg, Va.; mem. found. bd. Sci. Mus. Va., Richmond; bd. dirs. Eye & Ear Hosp., Richmond, Maymont Found.; bd. trustees Mary Baldwin Coll. Office: Media Gen Inc 333 E Grace St Richmond VA 23219 *

EVANS, JANE, fashion retailing executive; b. Hannibal, Mo., July 26, 1944; d. L. Terrell Evans and Katherine (Rosser) Pierce; m. George Sheer, June 17, 1970; 1 child, Jonathan. B.A., Vanderbilt U.; postgrad., L'Universite d'Aix Marseille. Pres. I. Miller, N.Y.C., 1970-73; v.p. internat. mktg. Genesco, N.Y.C., 1973-74; pres. Butterick Vogue Patterns, N.Y.C., 1974-77; v.p. adminstrn. and corp. devel. Fingerhut, Mpls., 1977-79; exec. v.p. fashion Gen. Mills, Inc., N.Y.C., 1979-84; pres., chief exec. officer Monet Jewelers, N.Y.C., 1984-87; gen. ptnr. Montgomery Consumer Fund, San Francisco, 1987-89; pres., chief econ. officer Inter Pacific Retail Group, San Francisco, 1989—; dir. Equitable Life Assurance Soc., Philip Morris, N.Y.C., Catalyst, N.Y.C. Bd. dirs. Open Hand, San Francisco. Recipient award Women's Equity Action League, 1982; Entrepreneurial Woman award Women Bus. Owners N.Y.C., 1982; named Corp. Am.'s Top Woman Exec., Savvy Mag., 1983, Fin. Woman of Yr., Fin. Women's Assn., 1986; named one of Ten Most Wanted Mgrs., Fortune Mag., 1986. Mem. Young Pres. Orgn. (com. of 200), Fashion Group N.Y., Women's Forum, Fashion Inst. Tech. (bd. dirs. 1980—). Home: 167 Saint Thomas Way Tiburon CA 94920 Office: Inter Pacific Retail Group 351 California St San Francisco CA 94104

EVANS, JOEL RAYMOND, marketing educator; b. N.Y.C., Sept. 17, 1948; s. Joseph and Betty Erna (Loonstein) E.; m. Linda Ruth Lieber, Dec. 19, 1970; children: Jennifer Faith, Stacey Beth. BA, Queens Coll., 1970; MBA, Bernard M. Baruch Coll., 1974; PhD, CUNY, 1975. MBA dir. Hofstra U., Hempstead, N.Y., 1975-77, asst. prof., 1975-79, assoc. prof., 1979-84, prof. mktg., 1984—, assoc. dean, 1981-82; chmn. Dept. Mktg. Hofstra U., Hempstead, N.Y., 1978-85; disting. prof. bus. Retail Mgmt. Inst., 1989—; cons. N.Y. Telephone, 1978, Pepsico, 1979, N.Y. State Dept. Edn., 1980, ARA/Slater Food Services, 1981-82. Co-author: Marketing, 3d. ed., 1987, Retail Management, 3rd ed., 1986, Principles of Marketing, 2d. ed., 1988, Readings in Marketing Management, 1984. Recipient Disting. Service award, Hofstra U., 1982, Hofstra U. Sch. Bus. Dean's award, 1979, 81; named One of Outstanding Young Men of Am., 1979. Mem. Am. Mktg. Assn., So. Mktg. Assn., Acad. Mktg. Sci., Product Devel. & Mgmt. Assn., Am. Collegiate Retailing Assn., Southwestern Mktg. Assn., Beta Gamma Sigma. Home: 14 Melrose Ln Commack NY 11725 Office: Hofstra U Mktg Dept 111 Phillips Hall Hempstead NY 11550

EVANS, JOHANNES SANAO, business executive; b. Tokyo, Mar. 10, 1927; s. Paul Yuzuru Kawai and Vicky Wichgraf-Evans; B.S. in Fgn. Service, Akademie Fuer Welthandel, Frankfurt/Main, Germany, 1954; B.S. in Bus. Adminstrn., Georgetown U., 1964; M.B.A., U. Rochester, 1970; m. Maria Johanna Langer, Mar. 10, 1947; children—Helga, Richard, Alphonse. Positions with internat. trade companies, Germany, 1948-61; jr. acct. Stanton, Minter & Bruner, Alexandria, Va., 1964; with Xerox Corp., various locations, 1964—, sr. policy planner, Stamford, Conn., 1972-77, mgr. corp. cost acctg. policy, 1977—. C.P.A., Conn. Mem. Nat. Assn. Accts., Am. Acctg. Assn., Pvt. Sector Council (U.S. Army Task Force), Am. Inst. C.P.A.'s, Conn. Soc. C.P.A.'s, Mensa. Republican. Home: 9 Fawn Rd Bethel CT 06801 Office: Xerox Corp Stamford CT 06904

EVANS, JOHN DERBY, telecommunications company executive; b. Detroit, June 3, 1944; s. Edward Steptoe and Florence (Allington) E.; m. Susan Blair Allan, Apr. 7, 1973 (div. Nov. 1986); children: John Derby, Courtenay Boyd. AB, U. Mich., 1966. Pres. Evans Communications Systems Inc., Charlottesville, Va., 1970-72; v.p., gen. mgr. Capitol Cablevision Corp., Charleston, W.Va., 1972-76; regional mgr. Am. TV & Communications Corp., Denver, 1974-76; exec. v.p., chief ops. officer Arlington (Va.) TeleCommunications Corp., 1976-83; pres. Arlington Cable Ptnrs. Ltd., 1983—, Suburban Cable Ptnrs., Brooklyn Pk., Minn., 1985—, Hauser Communications, N.Y.C., 1985—; pres. Evans Telecommunications Corp., Arlington, 1983—, Montgomery Cablevision (LP), Rockville, Md., 1986—; v.p. North Cen. Cable Comminicaions Co., Roseville, Minn., 1986—; telecommunications cons. to asst. sec. for planning and devel. Dept. HEW, Washington, 1976, N. Cen. Cable Communications Co., Roseville, Minn.; bd. dirs. Cable Satellite Pub. Affairs Network (C-SPAN), 1978—. Served to lt. USN, 1966-70. Mem. Nat. Cable TV Assn. (nat. chmn. awards com. 1981, bd. dirs. 1982—, pres.'s award 1979, Challenger award 1984, chmn. govt. rels. com. 1985-86), Va. Cable Assn. (bd. dirs. 1979—, v.p. 1982, pres. 1983-84), Soc. Motion Picture TV Engrs. Republican. Episcopalian. Clubs: Farmington Country, Boars Head Sports (Charlottesville); Old Dominion Boat (Alexandria, Va.); Wintergreen (Va.) Sports; Washington Golf and Country (Arlington). Home: 1530 N Key Blvd PH 1310 Arlington VA 22209 Office: 2707 Wilson Blvd Arlington VA 22201

EVANS, JOHN JOSEPH, management consultant; b. St. Louis, Mar. 1, 1940; s. Roy Joseph and Henrietta Frances (Schweizer) E.; B.A., Centenary Coll., 1962; postgrad. Syracuse U., 1969, U. Wis., 1971, Harvard Bus. Sch., 1971-73; M.B.A., Pepperdine U., 1972; m. Jennie Trees Nutt, Dec. 19, 1962 (div. 1983); children—Todd, Karlyn, Jane, Mark. Pres., chief exec. officer Evans Distributing Cos., La., 1962-72; pres. Evans & Co., 1968—; gen. mgr. Wire & Cable div. Agmet, Inc., 1976-77; mgr. Exxon Office Products, L.A., 1977-78; dir. tng. and devel., Mitchell Internat., San Diego, 1982-88, Sun Electric Corp, Crystal Lake, Ill., 1988—; adj. prof. Centenary Coll. Bd. dirs. ARC, Mental Health Assn.; trustee Grad. Sch. Sales Mgmt. and Mktg.; pres. La. Real Estate Investment Trust; pres. N. La. Mental Health Hosp. Bd. Recipient awards United Way, 1965-69, ITVA awards, 1987-88. Mem. Nat. Beer Wholesalers Assn. (adv. dir.), Sales and Mktg. Execs. of Shreveport (pres.), S.W. Sales and Mktg. Execs. Council (pres.), Young Pres. Orgn., Conf. Bd., Aspen Inst., Sales and Mktg. Execs. Internat., Am. Soc. Tng. and Devel., Am. Soc. Personnel Adminstrn., Syracuse U. Grad. Sch. Sales Mgmt. and Mktg. Alumni Assn. (pres. 1974-75, trustee 1975-79), Westlake Village C. of C. (v.p., dir. 1981-82), Personnel and Indsl. Relations Assn. (vice chmn., dir. 1982—), Harvard Club of San Diego. Home: 10952 Scripps Ranch Blvd 1A San Diego CA 92131

EVANS, JOHNNY GLENN, accountant, savings bank executive; b. Portsmouth, Va., Mar. 8, 1950; d. James Woodrow and Dorothy (Hedgepeth) E. BSBA in Acctg., East Carolina U., 1972. CPA, Va. Auditor Waller and Woodhouse, Norfolk, Va., 1972-80; audit mgr. Price Waterhouse, Norfolk, 1980-83; v.p., controller Virginia Beach (Va.) Fed. Savs. Bank, 1984—. Bd. dirs. Atlantic Coast Conservation Assn., 1989—. Named Boss of Yr. Am. Bus. Women's Assn., Virginia Beach, Va., 1985. Fellow Va. Soc. CPAs; mem. Am. Inst. CPAs, Fin. Mgrs. Soc., Nat. Assn. Accts. (chmn. audit com. 1986), Va. Soc. CPAs, Atlantic Coast Conservation Assn. (charter mem. 1989). Club: Tidewater Anglers (Norfolk, Va.) (treas. 1983-85, bd. dirs. 1981—, pres. 1989—). Home: 1543 E Ocean View Ave Norfolk VA 23503 Office: Va Beach Fed Savs Bank 210 25th St Virginia Beach VA 23451

EVANS, LARY LEWIS, electronics company executive; b. Charlevoix, Mich., June 26, 1939; s. Joseph Howard and Annie (Colden) E.; m. Martha Jane Farmer, Sept. 28, 1968; children: Kristi, Laura, Lance, Gary. BS in Mech. Engring., Gen. Motors Inst., 1962; MS in Mech. Engring., MIT, 1962, PhD in Mech. Engring., 1967. Asst. prof. mech. engring. U. Mich., Ann Arbor, 1967-72; automation cons. DEC, Maynard, Mass., 1972-73; mgr. mfg. engring. DEC, Westfield, Mass., 1973-77; mgr. ops. Xerox, Webster, N.Y., 1977-78; mgr. mfg. engr. Diablo-Xerox, Hayward, Calif., 1978-82; v.p. mfg. Tandem Computers, Cupertino, Calif., 1982-84; v.p., gen. mgr. Culler Sci., Santa Barbara, Calif., 1984-86; v.p. mfg. Sequent Computers, Beaverton, Oreg., 1986—. Republican. Home: 16880 SW Bull Mountain Rd Tigard OR 97224 Office: Sequent Computer Systems Inc 15450 SW Koll Pkwy Beaverton OR 97008

EVANS, LOIS LOGAN, investment banker, former government official; b. Boston, Dec. 1, 1937; d. Harlan deBaun and Barbara (Rollins) Logan; m. Thomas W. Evans, Dec. 22, 1956; children: Heather, Logan, Paige. Student, Vassar Coll., 1954-55; BA, Barnard Coll., 1957. Alt. chief del. UN Commn. on Status Women, N.Y.C., 1972-74; bd. dirs. U.S. Commn. to UNESCO, Washington, 1974-78; pres. Acquisition Specialists, Inc., N.Y.C., 1977-81, 83-88; exec. v.p. Campbell Shea Inc., N.Y.C., 1988—; asst. chief protocol U.S. State Dept., N.Y.C., 1981-83; chmn. bd. Fed. Home Bank, N.Y.C., 1986-88, mem., 1984-88; mem. adv. bd. U.S. Export-Import Bank, 1988—, Nat. Fin. Com.; mem. George Bush Nat. Fin. Com. Vice chair devel. council Williams Coll., N.Y., 1979-81; co-chair Reagan-Bush Campaign, N.Y., 1984; bd. dirs. Bklyn. Jr. League, 1968-72. Mem. Women's Forum, Econ. of N.Y. Club, Barnard Club, River Club. Republican. Episcopalian. Office: Campbell Shea Inc 595 Madison Ave Ste 900 New York NY 10022

EVANS, LOREN KENNETH, manufacturing company executive; b. Aurora, Ind., May 8, 1928; s. Fred W. and Wilma E. (Walser) E.; m. Margaret Ann Ingels; children: Michael, Elaine, Scott. BS, Ind. U., 1950. Various mfg. mgmt. positions Arvin Industries, Inc., Columbus, Ind., 1953-68, v.p., gen. mgr., 1968-73, div. pres., 1973-77, group v.p., 1977-84, exec. v.p., 1985-87, pres., chief operating officer, 1987—, also bd. dirs.; bd. dirs. Ind. Energy, Inc., Irwin Union Corp. Mem. dean's adv. council Ind. U. Sch. Bus., Bloomington, 1986. Served to 1st lt. U.S. Army, 1951-53. Decorated Bronze Star; named Alumni fellow Ind. U. Sch. Bus., 1986. Mem. Harrison Lake Country Club (Columbus), Mission Valley Country Club (Venice, Fla.). Republican. Methodist. Office: Arvin Industries Inc 1531 13th St Columbus IN 47201

EVANS, MICHAEL DEAN, financial planner; b. Carthage, Tex., Dec. 26, 1953; s. Charles Henry and Joy Jean (Jones) E.; m. Karen Ruth Hall, May 20, 1975; children: Shelly, David. BS in Econs. and Fin., La. Coll., 1976. Loan officer La. Savs. Assn., Alexandria, La., 1976-78; dist. mgr. Dixiecolor, Inc., Lafayette, La., 1978-80; fin. cons. A.G. Edwards & Sons, Inc., Holiday, Fla., 1980-88; account exec., cert. fin. planner Integrated Resources Equity Corp., Tarpon Springs, Fla., 1988—; instr. investments La. Coll. Continuing Edn. Program, Pineville, La., 1982-83; mem. First Provisional Support Bn. Chairborne Rangers, Clearwater, Fla., 1987—. Named One of Outstanding Young Men in Am., 1979, 87. Mem. Internat. Assn. Cert. Fin. Planners, Internat. Assn. Registered Fin. Planners, Tampa Bay Soc. Republican. Baptist. Club: La. Coll. Bus. Adminstrn. Soc. (Pineville) (pres. 1974-75). Office: Integrated Resources Equity Corp 905 E Lake St #120 Tarpon Springs FL 34689

EVANS, RICHARD LEE, investment company executive; b. Hammond, Ind., May 13, 1947; s. LeRoy Benjamin and Gladys Faye (Minas) E.; children: Scott, Craig. BS in Fin., Ind. U., 1969; MBA, Northwestern U., 1970. Pub., dir. research. Dow Theory Forecasts, Hammond, Ind., 1970—. Contbr. articles to profl. jours. and mags.; contbr. to radio and TV programs. Home: 2633 Hawthorne Ln Flossmoor IL 60422 Office: Dow Theory Forecasts 7412 Calumet Ave Hammond IN 46324

EVANS, ROBERT CURTIS, financial executive; b. Eugene, Oreg., July 24, 1940; s. Dale Blain and Helen Ranheh (Haugann) E.; m. Anise Wahab, Oct. 19, 1986; children: Katherine, Harris Denver. AB, Calif. State U., San Jose, 1966; AM, Washington U., 1970, PhD, 1977. Analyst Sverdrup 8 Parcel Inc., St. Louis, 1977-78; corp. economist Fru Con Corp., St. Louis, 1978-81; prof. fin. So. Ill. U., Edwardsville, 1981-88; pres. Evans Research Co., St. Louis, 1987—. Participant TV Program The People Speak, St. Louis, 1986. Petty Officer U.S. Navy, 1956-60. Ford Found. fellow, 1970, numerous other fellowships, 1968-72. Mem. Am. Fin. Assn., Fin. Mgmt. Assn. Republican. Presbyterian. Home: 3655 Botanical Ave Saint Louis MO 63110 Office: Evans Rsch Co 3655 Botanical Ave Saint Louis MO 63110

EVANS, ROBERT SHELDON, corporate executive; b. Pitts., 1944. BA in History, U. Pa., 1966; MBA in Fin., Columbia U., 1968. Vice pres. Evans & Co. Inc., 1971-74; v.p. internat. ops. Crane Co., N.Y.C., 1974-78, sr. v.p., 1978-79, exec. v.p., dir., 1979-84, chmn., chief exec. officer, 1984-85, also bd. dirs., chmn., chief exec. officer, pres., 1985—; chmn., chief exec. officer, bd. dirs. Medusa Corp.; bd. dirs. Aristech Chem. Corp., HBD Industries Inc. Mem. dean's adv. council Columbia Grad. Sch. Bus. Trustee Allan Stevenson Sch., Eaglebrook Sch. Office: Crane Co 757 3rd Ave New York NY 10017

EVANS, RODNEY EARL, educational adminstrator; b. Pontiac, Mich., May 15, 1939; s. Hubert Elgene and Lillian Beatrice (Wilcox) E.; m. Judith Karen Garvin; children: Mark, Scott, Cynthia. BA, Mich. State U., 1961, MBA, 1963, PhD, 1966. Prof. dept. bus. adminstrn. U. Okla., Norman, 1970—, assoc. dean. coll. bus. adminstrn., 1976—, dir. office bus. and indsl. coop., 1986—; chmn. bd. Southwestern Premier Foods, Inc., Norman; pres. Forod Svcs., Inc., Oklahoma City, 1979—, R.E. Evans & Assocs., Norman, 1971—. Contbr. articles to profl. jours.; co-author: Marketing Strategy and Managment, 1976. Capt. USAF, 1967-69. Mem. Am. Mktg. Assn. Office: Office Bus & Indsl Coop U Okla Norman OK 73019

EVANS, THOMAS CHIVES NEWTON, media research executive; b. Corpus Christi, Tex., Apr. 20, 1947; s. Lynn Augustus and Tena Vivian (Wimbish) E.; m. Sandra Louise McKee, Sept. 1, 1985; 1 child, Thomas Chives Newton II. BA, Austin Coll., 1969; MDiv, Harvard U., 1972, postgrad., 1973; MA, Syracuse U., 1981, PhD, 1986; postgrad., Columbia U., 1983-84. Teaching asst. Syracuse (N.Y.) U., 1976-77; research assoc. U. Nairobi, Kenya, 1977-79; editorial asst. African Studies Rev., Syracuse, 1979-80; research analyst NBC, N.Y.C., 1981-82, adminstr. research and sales devel., 1982-85, dir. research, 1985-86; dir. research Mut. Broadcasting System, N.Y.C., 1986, dir. research Westwood One Radio Network div., 1986-87; v.p. research Westwood One, Inc., N.Y.C., 1987—; mem. Ossining (N.Y.) Cable TV Adv. Com., 1987. Mem. Cen. Park Precinct Community Council, N.Y.C., 1981—; chmn. 20th Precinct Community Council, N.Y.C., 1984-85. Recipient cert. of appreciation Mayor Office, City of N.Y., 1985; named Eagle Scout, Boy Scouts Am., 1959; Syracuse U. Faculty Senate research grantee, 1975; Shell Found. Internat. fellow, 1978-79. Mem. Am. Stats. Assn., N.Y. Radio and TV Research Council, Radio Advt. Bur. (mem. GOALS com.), Advt. Research Found. (mem. radio steering com.), Austin Coll. Nat. Alumni Assn. (bd. dirs.). Democrat. Presbyterian. Home: 19 Ferris Pl Ossining NY 10562 Office: Westwood One Inc 1700 Broadway New York NY 10019

EVANS, THOMAS PASSMORE, business and product licensing consultant; b. West Grove, Pa., Aug. 19, 1921; s. John and Linda (Zeuner) E.; B.S. in E.E., Swarthmore Coll., 1942; M.Engring., Yale U., 1948; m. Lenore Jane Knuth, June 21, 1947; children—Paula S., Christina L., Bruce A., Carol L. Engr., Atomic Power div. Westinghouse Electric Corp., Pitts., 1948-51; dir. research and devel. AMF, Inc., N.Y.C., 1951-60; dir. research O.M. Scott & Sons. Co., Marysville, Ohio, 1960-62; v.p. research and devel. W.A. Sheaffer Pen Co., Ft. Madison, Iowa, 1962-67; dir. research Mich. Tech. U., Houghton, 1967-80; dir. research, mem. faculty Berry Coll., Mt. Berry, Ga., 1980-88; prof. bus. adminstrn., 1980-86. Author, patentee in field. Served to lt. USN, 1943-46. Registered profl. engr., Pa. Mem. Am. Forestry Assn., Am. Def. Preparedness Assn., Am. Phys. Soc., IEEE, Soc. Plastics Engrs., Am. Mgmt. Assn., Yale Sci. and Engring. Assn., Nat. Council Univ. Research Adminstrs., Licensing Execs. Soc., Air Force Assn., Am. Legion, AAAS, Art Inst. Chgo., Community Concert Assn., Ga. Friends of Humanities, High Mus. Art, Hunter Mus. Art, Japan-Am. Soc. Ga., Nat. Trust Hist. Preservation, Nat. Ret. Tchrs. Assn., Am. Assn. Ret. Persons, Yale Club of Ga., Rome Little Theatre, Rome Symphony, VFW, Rotary Club, Sigma Xi, Tau Beta Pi. Home: 25 Wellington Way SE Rome GA 30161 Office: Berry Coll Dept Rsch PO Box 97 Mount Berry GA 30149

EVANS, WALTER HOWARD, III, lawyer; b. Portland, Oreg., Feb. 8, 1941; s. Walter Howard Jr. and Sara Elizabeth (Holloway) E.; m. Rebecca Jane Berg, Aug. 9, 1982; 1 child, Alexandra Brooks. BS, U. Oreg., 1963; JD, Willamette (Oreg.) U., 1967. Bar: Oreg. 1967, D.C. 1977. Law clk. to chief justice Oreg. Supreme Ct., Salem, 1967-68; dep. exec. dir. Oreg. Jud. Council, Salem, 1968-69; legal counsel to U.S. Sen. Mark Hatfield 1969-78; of counsel Ragen, Tremaine, Krieger, Schmeer & Neill, Washington, 1978—. Republican. Presbyterian. Home: 4929 Glenbrook Rd NW Washington DC 20016 Office: Ragen Tremaine Krieger Schmeer & Neill 2300 M St NW Ste 800 Washington DC 20037-1434

EVANS, WILLIAM JOHN, aerospace company executive; b. Norwich, Conn., Mar. 4, 1924; s. Charles William and Teresa Marie (Marshall) E.; m. Elizabeth Ann Lemon, Nov. 15, 1947; children: William J. Jr., Betsy Evans Melton, Richard T, Joan. BS in Engring., U.S. Mil. Acad., 1947. Commd. 2d lt. USAF, 1946, advanced through grades to gen.; served worldwide including Korea, Vietna; ret. USAF, 1978; corp. v.p., dep. def. and space systems group United Techs. Corp., Hartford, Conn., 1978—; bd. dirs. Norwich Savs. Soc. Trustee Falcon Found. Decorated D.F.C. with two oak leaf clusters, D.S.M. with oak leaf cluster, Silver Star, Air medal with 21 oak leaf clusters. Mem. Air Force Assn. Roman Catholic. Office: United Techs Corp United Technologies Bldg Hartford CT 06101

EVANS, WINSTON KENNETH, electrical engineer; b. West Chester, Pa., Dec. 15, 1928; s. Luther Weltmer and Alma Gertrude (Lady) E.; m. Carol Gwynne Allen, June 30, 1961; children: Cecelia Ann, Richard Stephen. BS in Civil Engring., The Citadel, 1952; MSEE, Ga. Inst. Tech., 1967. Enlisted U.S. Army, 1952, advanced through ranks to col.; inspector gen. U.S. Army Support Element I, Da Nang, Viet Nam, 1972-73; dir. ground ops., fire support directorate Spl. Readiness Study Group, Fort Leavenworth, Kans., 1973-74; chief staff ops. com. U.S. Army Command and Gen. Staff Coll., Fort Leavenworth, Kans., 1974-76; commander, dir. U.S. Combat Surveillance and Target Acquisition Lab., Ft. Monmouth, N.J., 1976-79; ret. 1979; research staff System Planning Corp., Arlington, Va., 1979-82; sr. cons. ORI/CALCULON, Rockville, Md., 1982-88; pres. Colonial Pewter, Severna Park, Md., 1988—. Mem. Tau Beta Pi, Eta Kappa Nu. Home and Office: 329 Tunstall Ct Severna Park MD 21146

EVARTS, GEORGE WILLIAM, investment banker; b. Newburgh, N.Y., July 18, 1936; s. Morley Kellogg and Jennie Hall (Stone) E.; student Cornell U., Ithaca, N.Y., 1954-57; B.S. in Indsl. Mgmt., Carnegie-Mellon U., Pitts., 1959; m. Marylyn L. Sayle, Apr. 10, 1965; children—Daniel W., L. Paisley, Michael S. Plant location engr. The Austin Co., 1961-62; assoc. Case & Co., Inc. Mgmt. Cons.'s 1962-66; dir. corp. growth Youngstown Steel Door Co., Cleve., 1966-68; v.p. corp. fin. Disbro & Co., Inc., Cleve., 1968-71, Baker & Co., Inc., Cleve., 1971-74; pres. Evarts Capital, Inc., Beachwood, Ohio, 1975. Former trustee, pres. Orange Community Athletic Assn.; mem. Cleve. Orch. Chorus; mem. alumni council Phillips Exeter Acad., pres. Exeter Alumni Assn. Western Res.; bd. dirs. Cleve. State U. Devel. Found.; trustee Fairmount Presbyn. Ch. Served to 1st lt., C.E., AUS, 1960-61. Mem. Assn. for Corp. Growth, Internat. Arabian Horse Assn. Republican. Club:

Canterbury Golf. Office: Evart's Capital Inc Suite 640 Three Commerce Park Sq 23200 Chagrin Blvd Beachwood OH 44122

EVENSEN, ALF JOHN, computer engineer; b. Marquette, Mich., June 30, 1938; s. Alf and Alice (Edna) E.; m. Judith Lynne Biddle-Dellinger, Jun. 22, 1979. BS, U. Mich., 1959; MA, Wayne State U., 1966. System engr. Computer Scis. Internat., Apledoorn, The Netherlands, 1969; project engr. System Devel. Corp., Huntsville, Ala., 1970-81; system engr. electronics div. AVCO Corp., Huntsville, 1981-82; project mgr. Sci. Applications Internat. Corp., Huntsville, 1982-85; staff engr. Teledyne Brown Engring. Corp., Huntsville, 1985—. Served to lt. USNR, 1961-68. Mem. IEEE, NRA, Masons, Scottish Rite, Knights Templar, Royal Order of Scotland. Home: 137 El Dorado Dr Madison AL 35758 Office: Teledyne Brown Engring Cummings Research Park Huntsville AL 35807

EVERBACH, OTTO GEORGE, lawyer; b. New Albany, Ind., Aug. 27, 1938; s. Otto G. and Zelda Marie (Hilt) E.; m. Nancy Lee Stern, June 3, 1961; children: Tracy Ellen, Stephen George. B.S., U.S. Mil. Acad., 1960; LL.B., U. Va., 1966. Bar: Va. 1967, Ind. 1967, Calif. 1975, Mass. 1978. Counsel CIA, Langley, Va., 1966-67; corp. counsel Bristol-Meyers Co., Evansville, Ind., 1967-74, Alza Corp., Palo Alto, Calif., 1974-75; sec., gen. counsel Am. Optical Corp., Southbridge, Mass., 1976-81; assoc. gen. counsel Warner-Lambert Co., Morris Plains, N.J., 1981-83; v.p. Kimberly-Clark Corp., Neenah, Wis., 1984-86, sr. v.p., gen. counsel, 1986—. Served with U.S. Army, 1960-63. Mem. Am., Va., Ind., Calif. bar assns. Office: Kimberly-Clark Corp Box 619100 DFW Airport Sta Dallas TX 75261-9100

EVERETT, CARL NICHOLAS, management consulting executive; b. Ardmore, Okla., June 4, 1926; s. Elmer Edwards and Cecile (Jones) E.; B.S., Columbia U., 1948; M.B.A. with distinction, Harvard U., 1951; m. Susan Blessing Lindstrom, Oct., 1975; children by previous marriages—Carl N., Karen Lee, E. Anthony. With Benton and Bowles, N.Y.C., 1951-54, asso. account exec. Gen. Foods Corp., asst. account exec. Hellmanns and Best Foods Mayonnaise; with Campbell Mithun, Mpls., 1954-56, sr. account exec. Pillsbury Mills, account exec. Pillsbury Refrigerated Products; with McCann Erickson, N.Y.C., 1956-62, bottle sales account exec. Coca Cola Co., sr. account exec. Esso. Standard Oil, accounts supr. Westinghouse Electric Corp., account dir. Liggett and Myers Tobacco, mem. marketing plans bd. and marketing and advt. cons. Coca Cola Co.; sr. v.p., dir. Western region operations Barrington & Co., N.Y.C., 1962-64; founder, pres. Everett Assos., Inc., marketing and mgmt. consultants, N.Y.C., 1964-74; founder, pres. Everett Corp., Scottsdale, Ariz., 1974—; cons. Chrysler Corp., Pepsico Inc., Michelin Tire Corp., Gen. Electric Corp., Can. Dry Corp., Allied Van Lines, Continental Airlines; co-founder, dir. Precision Investment Co., Denver, 1977—; founder, mng. partner Wilmot Properties, Scottsdale, Ariz., 1979—. Chmn. bd. dirs. Phoenix Meml. Hosp. Primary Care; bd. dirs. Phoenix Meml. Health Resources, Inc.; bd. adjustment Town of Paradise Valley, Ariz.; chmn. Commn. on Salaries for Elective Officers; mem. Ariz. Cost Efficiency Commn. Served with USNR, 1944-46. Mem. Am. Mgmt. Assn., Sigma Alpha Epsilon. Unitarian. Clubs: Harvard Bus. Sch. (bd. dirs. Ariz.), Harvard (bd. dirs.), Safari Internat. (bd. dirs.), Campfire. Patentee in field. Home: 6722 N 60th St Paradise Valley AZ 85253 Office: 5685 N Scottsdale Rd Suite 100 Scottsdale AZ 85253

EVERETT, ELBERT KYLE, mktg. mgr.; b. Knoxville, Tenn., June 17, 1946; s. David Abraham and Lois (Hill) E.; student E. Tenn. U., 1965-67; m. Jane Harville, June 13, 1967; 1 dau., Evelyn Anne. Sales rep. Met. Life Ins. Co., Knoxville, 1968-70, Creative Displays, Knoxville, 1970-73; market mgr. central and No. Calif., Nat. Advt. div. 3M Co., Stockton from 1973, dist. mgr. western dist., Fresno, 1984; owner Jane Everett's Country Wholesale Furniture Mfg.; advt. cons. athletic dept. U. Pacific, Fresno State U.; lectr. outdoor advt. and mktg. San Joaquin Delta Coll., Fresno City Coll., Fresno State U. Mem. subcom. on tourism State of Nev.; cons. Stockton Civic Theater. Served with AUS, 1964. Recipient certificate of recognition U.S. Treasury Dept., 1977, 78, 82, 83; recognition award for best design Advt. Age, 1974, 83; 2 recognition awards Outdoor Advt. Assn. Am., 1973; certificate of appreciation United Way, 1978, 81, 82, 83. Mem. U. Pacific Athletic Found., Fresno State Found., Stockton C. of C., Fresno C. of C., Advt. Club Sacramento, Advt. Club Fresno, Internat. Platform Assn., Fresno State Athletic Found., Phi Sigma Kappa. Presbyterian. Home: 6432 N Benedict Ave Fresno CA 93711

EVERETT, JACK WILCOX, financial planner; b. Nyack, N.Y., Aug. 30, 1942; s. Jack W. and Mabel Claire (Jones) E.; m. Glennis A. Fraser, June 13, 1964 (dec. Oct. 1979); children: Sherri, Jack; m. Patricia P. Olmstead, Jan. 21, 1984. BS, US Naval Acad., 1964; MBA, Golden Gate U., 1970. Cert. fin. planner. Sales rep. Burroughs Corp., Sacramento, Calif., 1972-74; real estate broker Sacramento, 1974-80; account exec., tax mgr. TMI Equities Inc., Sacramento, 1976-80; pres. The Fin. and Tax Planning Ctr., Sacramento, 1980—; pres. Credit Union Fin. Services, 1982-87. Author, pub.: A. Fin. Planning Newsletter, 1980—, Bus. Planning Letter, 1985—, (book) Winning Money Psychology, 1989. Treas. Sacramento Seapower, 1980—; treas. Delta King Mus. Assocs., 1985—. Lt. U.S. Navy, 1964-72. Mem. Sacramento Brokerage and Loan Assn. (bd. dirs.), Hidden Valley Community Assn. (treas. 1987—), Internat. Assn. Fin. Planners (chpt. pres. 1984-85, chpt. service award 1987), Inst. Cert. Fin. PLanners (chpt. treas. 1984-85), Nat. Ctr. Fin. Edn., Navy League US (v.p., treas. 1980-85), No. Calif. Ofcls. Assn. (wrestling chmn. 1985-86). Republican. Home: 8125 Morningside Dr Looms CA 95850 Office: The Fin & Tax Planning Ctr 2277 Fair Oaks Blvd Ste 205 Sacramento CA 95825

EVERETT, JAMES LEGRAND, III, retired utility executive; b. Charlotte, N.C., July 24, 1926; s. James LeGrand and Charlotte (Keesler) E.; m. Marjorie Miriam Scherf, Sept. 3, 1947; children: James LeGrand IV, Christopher Glenn, John Keesler. B.S. in Mech. Engring, Pa. State U., 1948, M.S., 1949; M.S. in Indsl. Mgmt, MIT, 1959; LL.D. (hon.), Phila. Coll. Osteo. Medicine, 1983. Registered profl. engr., Pa. Instr. mech. engring. Pa. State U., 1948-50; instr. civil and mech. engring. Drexel Evening Coll., 1950-52; head fuel sect. Atomic Power Devel. Assos., 1953-55; with Phila. Electric Co., 1950-88, exec. v.p., 1968-71, pres., 1971-82, chmn., chief exec. officer, 1982-88, also bd. dirs., chmn. exec. com. parent cos.; dir. Phila. Nat. Bank, CoreStates Fin. Corp., Fidelity Mut. Life Ins. Co., Tasty Baking Co., Martin Marietta Corp. Mem. bd. trustees Drexel U.; trustee Com. for Econ. Devel.; mem. exec. bd. Phila. council Boy Scouts Am., Northeast Regional Bd. Served to ensign USNR, 1944-46. Sloan fellow, 1958-59; Recipient Outstanding Young Man of Year award Phila. Jr. C. of C., 1961; Ann. Engring. Tech. award Temple U., 1963; Disting. Alumnus award Pa. State U., 1971; George Washington medal, 1974; Humanitarian award Am. Jewish Com., 1976; PAL award Police Athletic League, 1978; Exemplar award for interracial cooperation Phila. NAACP, 1981; named Engr. of Year Delaware Valley, Pa., 1972; Delaware Valley Council Citizen of Yr., 1972; YMCA Outstanding Layman of Yr., 1975; Semper Fidelis award Marine Corps Scholarship Found., Am. Traditions award B'nai B'rith Internat., 1983, Silver Beaver award Boy Scouts Am., Phila. council, 1986, Brotherhood award Nat. Conf. Christians Jews, 1986, Disting. Citizen award Boy Scouts Am., Phila. council, 1987, Robert Morris award Valley Forge Council Boy Scouts Am., 1987; Medal of Merit from U.S. Treasury Dept., 1986; Industrialist of Yr. award Soc. Indsl. Realtors. Fellow ASME; mem. Am. Nuclear Soc., Franklin Inst., IEEE, Soc. Am. Mil. Engrs., Nat. Acad. Engring., Engrs. Club Phila., Nat. Soc. Profl. Engrs., Pa. Soc. Profl. Engrs. (Outstanding Engr. in Mgmt. award 1983), Tau Beta Pi, Pi Tau Sigma, Pi Mu Epsilon.

EVERETT, JAMES WILLIAM, JR., lawyer; b. Buffalo, Oct. 26, 1957; s. James William and Esther (Kratzer) E. BA in Polit. Sci., Coll. Wooster (Ohio), 1979; JD, SUNY, Buffalo, 1984; LLM in Banking Law with honor, Boston U., 1985. Bar: N.Y. 1985. Officer Emil A. Kratzer Co., Inc., Buffalo, 1980—; assoc. John C. Peters, P.C., Hartford, Conn., 1986-87; counsel N.Y. Assembly coms. on banking, corps., ins. and small bus., Albany, 1987-88; asst. counsel to the N.Y. Senate Majority on Banks, Commerce, and Real Property Tax Laws, 1988—; speechwriter for chair policy com. for nat. adv. counsel on women's edn. programs. Contbr. polit. commentaries Buffalo News. Active Erie County (N.Y.) Rep. Com., 1979—. Recipient Cummings-Rumbaugh prize Coll. of Wooster. Mem. ABA, N.Y. State Bar Assn., Erie County Bar Assn. Republican. Presbyterian. Home: 38 Exeter Rd Williamsville NY 14221 Office: Office Senate Majority Counsel Capitol 433 Albany NY 12247

EVERETT, MARY ELIZABETH, retirement home administrator; b. Okmulgee, Okla., June 3, 1929; d. Frederick Joseph and Harriet Lucille (Daratt) Elrick; m. Thomas Henry Everett, May 29, 1951; children: Deborah Maciolek, Thomas Stephen. BA, Salem Coll., 1951. Pres. Greater Balt. Med. Ctr. Aux., 1981-83, chmn. geriatrics; pres. Md. Assn. Hosp. Aux., Balt., 1984-86, seminar planner; pres. bd. mgrs. Wesley Home, Balt., 1986—, trustee; lectr. in field. Leader Girl Scouts U.S.A., Towson, Md.; trustee Towson Meth. Ch. Mem. Md. Assn. Hosp. Aux. (bd. dirs.). Republican. Clubs: Three Arts, Salem (Balt.) (bd. dirs.). Home: 4 Candlelight Ct Lutherville MD 21093 Office: Wesley Home 2211 W Rogers Ave Baltimore MD 21209

EVERETT, MICHAEL GRAYSON, investment analyst; b. Tuscumbia, Ala., Oct. 12, 1954; s. J. Grady and C. Jeanette (Johnson) E. BSBA, Auburn U., 1977. Registered investment rep. Acct. Mutual Savs. Life Ins. Co., Decatur, Ala., 1978-79; acct. Central Bank of the South, Birmingham, 1979-82, investment analyst, 1982—. Mem. Nat. Fedn. Mcpl. Analysts, So. Mcpl. Fin. Soc. Office: Cen Bank South 701 S 20th St Birmingham AL 35296

EVERILL, CHARLES HENRY, direct marketing executive, communications-media company executive; b. Beloit, Wis., Mar. 25, 1943; s. Royal B. and Alice M. (Grenawalt) E.; m. Martha Ann Brownell, June 26, 1965; children: Charles Henry, Sarah Elaine. BA cum laude, Harvard Coll., 1965, MBA with highest distinction, 1972. Corp. dir. mktg. Harte-Hanks Communications, Inc., San Antonio, 1972-74, pres. nat. newspaper group, 1976-80, sr. v.p. mktg., 1980-85; acting pres. Harte-Hanks Cable, San Antonio, 1981-82; pres. Harte-Hanks Dir. Mktg., San Antonio, 1982-88; co-founder, pres., chief exec. officer AmeriComm Direct Mktg., Inc., Denver, 1988—; pub. The Jour. News, Hamilton, Ohio, 1974-80. Founding mem. Hamilton Devel. Corp. Served to lt. USN, 1965-70. Baker scholar Harvard Grad. Sch. Bus. Adminstrn., 1972; named Outstanding Young Ohioan Ohio Jaycees, 1976, Outstanding Young Man Hamilton Jaycees, 1976. Mem. Am. Newspaper Pubs. Assn., Dir. Mktg. Assn., Third Class Mailers Assn. Nat. Assn. Advt. Pubs., Nat. Assn. Advt. Distbrs., San Antonio C. of c. (chmn. mktg.-communications com. 1981-83). Republican. Congregationalist. Home: 5765 Oak Creek Ln Littleton CO 80121 Office: AmeriComm Direct Mktg Inc 380 Quivas St Denver CO 80223

EVERINGHAM, LYLE J., grocery chain executive; b. Flint, Mich., May 5, 1926; s. Kenneth L. and Christine (Everingham) E.; m. Rlene Lajiness, Mar. 31, 1929; children: Nancy, Mark, Christine. Student, U. Toledo, 1956-63. With Kroger Co., 1946—; v.p. Kroger Co. (Dayton div.), Ohio, 1963-64; v.p. produce merchandising Kroger Co. (Dayton div.), Cin., 1964-65; v.p. Kroger Co. (Dayton div.), from 1966; chmn., chief exec. officer Kroger Co., Cin. Mem. Cin. Bus. Com. Served with cav. AUS, 1943-46. Roman Catholic. Clubs: Coldstream Country, Queen City, Comml. Office: Kroger Co 1014 Vine St Cincinnati OH 45202-1119 *

EVERS, BARBARA JO, bank executive, consultant; b. Portland, Oreg., Jan. 22, 1949; d. Marvin Allen and Dorothy Geneva (Berry) Emerson; Student Mills Coll., 1967-69; BS summa cum laude in Mgmt., Woodbury U., 1979; AA with honors in Real Estate, Fullerton Coll., 1980, cert. in Escrow, 1982; cert. Mortgage Banking, Cypress Coll., 1980, MBA Harvard U., 1986. Loan servicing analyst, loan adminstrn. supr. Coldwell Banker Mgmt. Corp., Los Angeles, 1976-78; mktg. services mgr., document control mgr., systems devel. mgr. Standard Precision, Inc., Santa Fe Springs, Calif., 1978-80; mgr. various corp. projects, systems and procedures Home Fed. Savs. & Loan Assn., San Diego, 1980-84; cons. real estate div. First Interstate Bank Calif., Los Angeles, 1985; v.p. First Nat. Bank Highland, N.Y., 1986-87, M & T Bank, Buffalo, 1987-88, First Ops. Resource, Inc., Swedesboro, N.J., 1988; career counselor; organizational systems cons. Mem. Ops. Research Soc. Am., Women in Mgmt., Nat. Assn. Female Execs., Am. Soc. Profl. Exec. Women, Project Mgmt. Inst., Inst. Mgmt. Scis., Soc. Tech. Communications, Alpha Gamma Sigma, Phi Gamma Kappa (Key award 1979). Home: 45 Knollwood Dr Cherry Hill NJ 08002 Office: Center Square & Beckett Rds Swedesboro NJ 08085

EVES, JEFFREY P., paper, plastic company executive; b. Omaha, Nov. 3, 1946; s. Wayne P. Eves and Laurette (Marcotte) Naylor; m. Adelaida Martin, Dec. 23, 1986. BS, U. Nebr., 1968; MA, U. Calif., Berkeley, 1969. Sales rep. Crown Zellerbach Corn, San Francisco, 1969-71; chief spokesman The U.S. Price Commn., Washington, 1971-73; spl. asst. to pres. White House, Washington, 1973-76; mgr. govt. affairs Potlatch Corp., San Francisco, 1976-79; dir. govt. affairs, internat trade Scott. Paper Co., Phila., 1979-86; v.p. Ft. Howard Corp., Green Bay, Wis., 1986—; bd. dirs. St. Vincent Hosp., Green Bay, CFC Alliance, Washington; vice chmn., dir. Foodservice & Packaging Inst., Washington, 1988—. Lt. USAR, 1968-74. Mem. Green Bay C. of C. (bd. dirs. 1987—). Republican. Roman Catholic. Home: 3083 Nicolet Dr Green Bay WI 54311 Office: Ft Howard Corp 1919 S Broadway Green Bay WI 54307

EWALD, ROBERT FREDERICK, insurance association executive; b. Newark, May 5, 1924; s. Frederick J. and Florence M. (Reiley) E.; B.S. cum laude in Bus. Adminstrn., with spl. honors in Econs., Rutgers U., 1948; m. Jeanine Martinez, Jan. 3, 1976; children—Robert, Steven; children by previous marriage—William F., John C., George E. Asst. corp. auditor Prudential Ins. Co., Newark, Houston, Chgo., 1948-61; audit mgr. N.Y. Life Ins. Co., N.Y.C., 1962-64; treas. Mass. Gen. Life Ins. Co., Boston, 1965-68; adminstrv. v.p., controller Res. Life Ins. Co., Dallas, 1969-70; pres. Nat. Ben Franklin Life, Chgo., 1971-77; trustee, pres. Rockford (Ill.) Blue Cross Plan; pres., dir. Life Ins. Assos., Inc.; trustee Communities Health Plan, Inc., North Communities Health Plan, Inc., 1979-82; exec. dir. Ill. Life and Health Ins. Guaranty Assn., Chgo., 1984—; exec. dir. Ill. HMO Guaranty Assn., Chgo., 1988—; dir. emeritus Blue Cross and Shield Ill. Served with U.S. Army, 1943-46. Fellow Life Mgmt. Inst.; mem. Fin. Execs. Inst., Am. Arbitration Assn., Adminstrv. Mgmt. Soc., Mensa. Home: 12 Wisner St Park Ridge IL 60068 Office: 5519 N Cumberland Ave Suite 1012 Chicago IL 60656

EWAN, JAMES, electronics company executive; b. Chendu, Szechuan, People's Republic of China, Jan. 9, 1949; (parents Am. citizens); s. Nelson and Lucy E.; m. Mary Helen Rodriguez, Mar. 14, 1987. BS, UCLA, 1971, MS, 1973, PhD, 1978. Chief engr. United Detector Tech., Santa Monica, Calif., 1968-73; mem. tech. staff Hughes Research Labs, Malibu, Calif., 1974-80; sect. mgr. Aerospace Corp., El Segundo, Calif., 1981-85; v.p./exec. dir. Teledyne Monolithic Microwave, Mountain View, Calif., 1985—. Contbr. articles to profl. jours. Hughes fellow, 1975. Mem. IEEE, UCLA Alumni Assn., Assn. of Old Crows. Office: Teledyne Monolitic Microwave 1274 Terra Bella Ave Mountain View CA 94043

EWERS, R. DARRELL, food products company executive; b. Fredricktown, Ohio, May 24, 1933; M. Sue Wagner. BA in Econs., Coll. of Wooster. With Procter and Gamble, Cin., 1955-79; group v.p. internat. Wm. Wrigley Jr. Co., Chgo., 1979-84, exec. v.p., 1984—, also bd. dirs. Office: Wm Wrigley Jr Co 410 N Michigan Ave Chicago IL 60611

EWING, JOHN KIRBY, real estate, oil and investment executive; b. Mercedes, Tex., Apr. 23, 1923; s. Emile Kelty and Edna Lillian (Olson) E.; m. Virginia Wilson, Oct. 2, 1970; children: Steven Calder, Charlotte Kelty, Robin Virginia, Holly Hammond. Student U.S. Naval Acad., 1941-42; BA, U. Tex., 1946. Staff asst. to gov. Tex., 1943-46; asst. purchasing agt. Estate of John H. Shary, Mission, Tex., 1946-47; mortgage banker David C. Bintliff & Co., Inc., Houston, 1947-52; self-employed bldg. contractor and residential subdiv. developer, Houston, 1952-54; ptnr. Curtis & Ewing Realtors, Houston, 1957—; sales cons. Wilson Mfg. Co., Inc., Wichita Falls, Tex., 1970-74, dir., 1973-77, v.p., 1974-75, pres., 1975-76; pres. Wichita Clutch Co., 1975-76; pres., dir. Mt. Royal Mining & Exploration Co., 1973—, Old Ont. Mining Co., 1973-77. Active local Boy Scouts Am., 1935—, chmn. Buffalo dist. Friends of Scouting, 1962, Western div. show chmn., 1977, bd. dirs. Sam Houston Area council, 1980—, chmn. div. B, 1980-82, v.p. fin., 1984-85, exec. com., 1984-87, nat. council rep. 1987—; active fund raising United Way, 1950-51, 55; election judge Harris County, 1958-64; sec. credentials com. Tex. Democratic Conv., 1952, mem. Harris County exec. com., 1958-65, del. convs., 1952-64; bd. dirs. Nat. Mental Health Assn. Houston, 1969-74, nat. pub. affairs com. 1970-74, pres., 1970-73; bd. dirs. Tex. Assn. Mental Health, 1970-74; chmn. NBC-ARC CPR Race for Life Project, 1981; bd. dirs. Greater Houston chpt. ARC, 1983—, chmn. safety services com., 1981-82, del. conv., 1982, spl. events chmn. Health Awareness Week (with Harris County Med. Soc., Shell Oil Co. and Sta. KTR-TV), 1982, mem. ofcl. bd. St. Luke's United Methodist Ch., Houston, 1966-68, 69-71, 72-74, 78-80, 82-84, 86—. Recipient Disting. Service award Nat. Assn. Mental Health, 1973, Silver Beaver award Boy Scouts Am., 1983. Mem. Houston Bd. Realtors, Nat. Assn. Real Estate Bds., Am. Foundrymen's Soc., Tex. Assn. Realtors, U.S. Naval Acad. Alumni Assn. (past chpt. pres., nat. trustee 1981-88, mem. fin. com. 1981—, nat. v.p. 1983-88), Nat. Rifle Assn. (life), Am. Legion, Nat. Eagle Scouts Assn. (life), Tex. Rifle Assn. (life), Bayou Rifles, Silver Spur, Kappa Alpha Order, Pi Sigma Alpha. Lodges: Kiwanis (bd. dirs. Houston 1967-69, pres. 1988-89, lt. gov. div. III Tex.-Okla. dist. 1984-85, chmn. host com. 71st internat. conv. 1986, dist. chmn. internat. affairs 1987, dist. chmn. fund raising 1988, trustee Kiwanis found. 1988—, dist. chmn. internat. affairs 1988-89), Masons. Home: 1508 Kirby Dr Houston TX 77019 Office: 707 San Jacinto Bldg 911 Walker Ave Houston TX 77002

EWING, RAYMOND PEYTON, educator, management consultant; b. Hannibal, Mo., July 31, 1925; s. Larama Angelo and Winona Fern (Adams) E.; m. Audrey Jane Schulze, May 7, 1949; 1 child, Jane Ann. AA, Hannibal La-Grange Coll., 1948; BA, William Jewell Coll., 1949; MA in Humanities, U. Chgo., 1950. Mktg. mgmt. trainee Montgomery-Wards, Chgo., 1951-52; sr. editor Commerce Clearing House, Chgo., 1952-60; corp. communications dir. Allstate Ins. Cos. & Allstate Enterprises, Northbrook, Ill., 1960-85, issues mgmt. dir., 1979-85, pres. Issues Mgmt. Cons. Group, 1985—; assoc. prof., dir. corp. pub. relations program Medill Sch. Journalism Northwestern U., Evanston, Ill., 1986—; pub. relations dir. Chicago Mag., 1966-67, book columnist, 1968-70; staff Book News Commentator, Sta. WRSV, Skokie, Ill., 1962-70. Author: Mark Twain's Steamboat Years, 1981, Managing the New Bottom Line, 1987; contbr. articles to mags. Mem. Winnetka (Ill.) Library Bd., 1969-70; pres. Skokie Valley United Crusade, 1964-65; bd. dirs. Suburban Community Chest Council, Onward Neighborhood House, Chgo.; mem. House Commerce Com., Pvt. Sector Foresight Task Force, 1982-83. Served with AUS, 1943-46, ETO. Mem. Pub. Relations Soc. of Am. (accredited; Silver Anvil awards for pub. affairs, 1970, 72, for fin. relations 1970, for bus. spl. events 1976, chmn. nat. pub. affairs sect. 1984), Publicity Club of Chgo. (v.p. 1967, bd. dirs. 1966-68; Golden Trumpet award for pub. affairs, 1969, 70, 72, 79, for fin. relations 1970), Insurers Public Relations Council (pres. 1980-81), Issues Mgmt. Assn. (founder, pres. 1981-83, chmn. 1983-84), Mensa, World Future Soc., U.S. C. of C. (trends and perspective coun.), U.S. Assn. for Club of Rome, Chgo. Poets and Writers Found. (pub. relations dir. 1966-67), Club: Union League (Chgo.). Author: Mark Twain's Steamboat Years, 1981, Managing the New Bottom Line, 1987; contbr. articles to mags. Office: Northwestern U Medill Sch Journalism Evanston IL 60208

EWING, ROBERT, lawyer; b. Little Rock, July 18, 1922; s. Esmond and Frances (Howell) E.; m. Elizabeth Smith, May 24, 1947; 1 child, Elizabeth Milbrey. B.A., Washington and Lee U., 1943; LL.B., Yale U., 1945. Bar: Conn. 1945. Assoc. Shipman & Goodwin, Hartford, Conn., 1945-50; partner Shipman & Goodwin, 1950—; asst. pros. atty. West Hartford, Conn., 1953-55; dir., asst. sec. H.W. Steane Co. Inc., Rocktide Inc.; dir., pres. Still Pasture Corp.; asst. sec. Linvar Marwin, Inc. Mem. U.S. Constitution Bicentennial Commn. of Conn., 1986—; incorporator Hartford Hosp., Mt. Sinai Hosp.; bd. dirs. Travelers Aid Soc. of Hartford, 1951-57, treas., 1954-57; bd. dirs. Greater Hartford chpt. ARC, 1974—, chmn., 1977-79, mem. blood services com., 1986—, chmn., 1989; bd. dirs. Family Service Soc., 1961-65, Conn. Pub. Expenditure Council, 1986—. Paul Harris fellow, 1988. Fellow Am. Bar Found. (spl. master U.S. Dist. Ct. Conn.); mem. ABA, Conn. Bar Assn. (chmn. fed. practice com. 1976-79, exec. com. corp. sect. 1981-85), Hartford County Bar Assn., Am. Law Inst., Conn. Hist. Soc. (trustee 1974—, v.p. 1982—, chmn. personnel com.), Newcomen Soc. N.Am. Congregationalist. (sr. deacon 1972-75). Clubs: Twentieth Century (pres. 1975-76), Hartford (counsel, ex officio bd. govs.), Mory's Assn, Dauntless, Rotary (pres. Hartford 1966-67, Paul Harris fellow 1988). Home: 28 Birch Rd West Hartford CT 06119 Office: 799 Main St Hartford CT 06103

EXE, DAVID ALLEN, electrical engineer; b. Brookings, S.D., Jan. 29, 1942; s. Oscar Melvin and Irene Marie (Mattis) E.; m. Lynn Rae Roberts; children: Doreen Lea, Raena Lynn. BSEE, S.D. State U., 1968; MBA, U. S.D., 1980; postgrad. Iowa State U., 1969-70, U. Idaho, 1978-80. Registered profl. engr., Idaho, Oreg., Minn., S.D., Wash., Wyo., Utah. Applications engr. Collins Radio, Cedar Rapids, Iowa, 1969-70; dist. engr. Bonneville Power Adminstrn., Idaho Falls, Idaho, 1970-77; instr. math U. S.D., Vermillion, 1977-78; chief exec. officer EXE Assocs., Idaho Falls, Idaho, 1978-83; agys. mgr. CPT Corp., Eden Prairie, Minn., 1983-85; owner, chief exec. officer Exe Inc., Eden Prairie, 1983—; chmn. bd. Applied Techs. Idaho, Idaho Falls, 1979—; chmn., chief exec. officer Azimuth Cons., Idaho Falls, 1979-81; v.p. D & B Constrn. Co., Idaho Falls, 1980-83. Mem. Eastern Idaho Council on Industry and Energy, 1979—. Served with USN, 1960-64. Mem. Am. Cons. Engrs., IEEE, Nat. Soc. Profl. Engrs., Nat. Contrcts Mgrs. Assn., IEEE Computer Soc., Mensa, Am. Legion. Lodges: Masons, Elks. Office: Exe Inc 8220 Commonwealth Dr Eden Prairie MN 55344

EXLEY, CHARLES ERROL, JR., manufacturing company executive; b. Detroit, Dec. 14, 1929; s. Charles Errol and Helen Margaret (Greenizen) E.; m. Sara Elizabeth Yates, Feb. 1, 1952; children: Sarah Helen, Evelyn Victoria, Thomas Yates. B.A., Wesleyan U., Middletown, Conn., 1952; M.B.A., Columbia U., 1954. With Burroughs Corp., Detroit, 1954-76; controller Burroughs Corp. (Todd div.), 1960-63, corp. controller, 1963-66, v.p., group exec. office products group, 1966-71, v.p. fin., 1971-73, exec. v.p. fin., 1973-76; pres. NCR Corp., Dayton, Ohio, 1976-88, chief exec. officer, 1983—, chmn. bd., 1984—, also dir., mem. exec. com. Clubs: Grosse Pointe (Grosse Pointe Farms, Mich.); Moraine Country (Dayton); Dayton Racquet; The Brook (N.Y.C.). Home: 3720 Ridgeleigh Rd Dayton OH 45429 Office: NCR Corp 1700 S Patterson Blvd Dayton OH 45479 *

EXLEY, MARK KING, health care executive; b. Bryn Mawr, Pa., June 4, 1953; s. Gordon Rudolphus and Mildred (King) E.; m. Jill Anne Michener, June 4, 1977; children: Darren Mark, Meredith Anne, Caryn Elizabeth. BBA, U. Notre Dame, 1975; MBA, U. Pa., 1977. Adminstrv. asst. Presbyn. U. Pa. Med. Ctr., Phila., 1976-79, asst. hosp. dir., 1979-83; exec. v.p. PMA Med. Specialists, Phoenixville, Pa., 1983—; Research asst. Informed Consent issues, 1977; corp. sec. Center Post Housing, Inc., Phila., 1978-79; vice chmn., bd. dirs. West Phila. Community Mental Health Consortium, Inc., 1979-83; officer, dir. Freedom Health Care, Inc., Wayne, Pa., 1985—; active Del. Valley Hosp. Edn. and Research Found. Pres. Lower Providence Jaycees, Eagleville, Pa., 1984; dir., chaplain Skip-Perk Jaycees, Collegeville, Pa., 1985. Named one of Outstanding Young Men Am., 1985. Mem. Am. Coll. Healthcare Execs., Med. Group Mgmt. Assn., Phoenixville C. of C. Republican. Roman Catholic. Home: 8 Dana Dr Collegeville PA 19426 Office: PMA Med Specialists 702 Main St Phoenixville PA 19460

EYER, DONALD E., financial planner; b. Mill Hall, Pa., Dec. 16, 1929; m. Sally Ann Doane, June 26, 1957; children: Pamela Gail, Mark Stephen, Michele Dawn. Student, U. Md., 1950-52. Mgr. F.W. Woolworth Co., Phila., 1957-58, 61-62, Morgantown, W.Va., 1958-61, Williamsport, Pa., 1962-63, Columbia, Pa., 1963-65; ins. salesman Mut. Benefit Life, Newark, 1965—; prin. Don Eyer Assoc., Harrisburg, Pa., 1979—; bd. dirs. 222 Dutch Lanes, Inc.; nat. assoc. Mut. Benefit Life, 1986-87, pres. Star Honor Guard, 1974-87. Bd. dirs. Lancaster-Lebanon (Pa.) area Boy Scouts Am., 1974-76; chmn. East Hempfield Twp. Baseball, Basketball Programs, Lancaster, 1971-76; chmn. Lancaster chpt. Nat. Multiple Sclerosis Soc., 1977-78, pres., 1981—. Served as sgt. U.S. Army, 1952-54 Korea. Named Man of Yr. Gen. Agts. and Mgrs. Assn. of Pa., Harrisburg, 1983, 86, 87. Mem. Million Dollar Round Table (life), Nat. Assn. Life Underwriters, Nat. Assn. Securities Dealers. Republican. Presbyterian. Club: East Hempfield Exchange (pres. 1978-79). Lodge: Kiwanis (trustee 1958, 61). Home: 2121 Lynn Ave Lancaster PA 17601 Office: Don Eyer Assoc 2090 Linglestown Rd Harrisburg PA 17110

EYLES, DAVID L., banker. Vice chmn., chmn. credit policy com. Mellon Bank Corp., Pitts.; vice chmn. Mellon Bank N.A., Pitts. Office: Mellon Bank Corp Mellon Bank Ctr Pittsburgh PA 15258 *

EYTON, JOHN TREVOR, lawyer, business executive; b. Quebec, Que., Can., July 12, 1934; s. John and Dorothy Isabel (dec.) E.; m. Barbara Jane Montgomery, Feb. 13, 1955; children: Adam Tudor, Christopher Montgomery, Deborah Jane, Susannah Margaret, Sarah Elizabeth. B.A., Victoria Coll., 1957; LL.B., U. Toronto, 1960. Bar: Ont. 1962, created queen's counsel. Read law Tory, Tory, DesLauriers & Binnington, Toronto, Ont., 1960-62, assoc., 1962-67, ptnr., 1967-79; pres., chief exec. officer Brascan Ltd., Toronto, 1979—, also bd. dirs.; chmn., chief exec. officer Brascade Resources Inc., also bd. dirs.; dep. chmn., dir. Royal Trustco Ltd., Toronto; pres., dir. Edper Enterprises Ltd.; vice chmn., bd. dirs. Norcen Energy Resources Ltd.; chmn. Westmin. Resources Ltd.; bd. dirs. Trizec Corp. Ltd., Gt. Lakes Group, Inc., Gen. Motors of Can. Ltd., Hees Internat. Bancorp. Inc., Astral Bellevue Pathe Inc., Carena-Bancorp, Inc., Noranda Forest, Inc., The Hume Group Ltd., M.A. Hanna Co., London Life Ins. Co., Noranda Inc., John Labatt Ltd., Scott Paper Co., Trilon Fin. Corp., T.C.C. Beverages Ltd., MacMillan Bloedel Ltd., Silcorp Ltd., Stadium Corp. of Ont. Ltd., Standard Broadcasting Corp. Ltd.; mem. Merrill Lynch Adv. Council. Chmn. Internat. Trade Adv. Com.; bd. dirs., vice chmn. Trillium Found.; patron Grenville Christian Coll.; gov. Olympic Trust Can.; chmn. bd. govs. U. Waterloo; mem. Toronto Ont. Olympic Coun.; chmn. Friends of Harbourfront. Decorated Order of Can., 1986. Mem. Upper Can. Law Soc., Can. Bar Assn., Bus. Council on Nat. Issues, Phi Delta Theta. Progressive Conservative. Mem. United Ch. of Can. Clubs: Univ., Toronto, Royal Can. Yacht, Empire, Caledon Ski, Caledon Riding and Hunt, Caledon Mountain Trout; Devil's Pulpit Golf Assn., Coral Beach and Tennis (Bermuda); Boca Raton (Fla.) Hotel & Beach, Royal Palm Yacht and Country (Boca Raton). Home: RR 2, Caledon, ON Canada L0N 1C0 Office: Brascan Ltd, Commerce Ct W PO Box 48, Toronto, ON Canada M5L 1B7

EZAGUI, ALAN MARK, financial executive; b. Bklyn., Apr. 4, 1955; s. Isaac and Elaine Ella (Geld) E.; m. Diana Lynn Hrabosky, May 15, 1982; children: Shannon, Brek. BS, U. S.C., 1978; M.H.C.A., George Washington U., 1981. Cert. fin. planner. Regional sales dir. Surgidev Corp., Mpls., 1981-84; fin. planner Fin. Service Group Inc., Vienna, Va., 1984-88; pres. Ezagui Ins. Agy., Inc. (subs. Ezagui Enterprises, Inc.), Sterling, Va., 1988—. Contbr. articles to profl. jours., newspapers. Bd. dirs. devel. com. Loudoun Meml. Hosp., Leesburg, Va., 1988; fund raiser, organizer choral dept. Broad Run High Sch., Ashburn, Va., 1988; treas. Small Bus. Assistance Ctr., Loudoun County Inc., Leesburg, 1987—. Mem. Internat. Assn. Fin. Planning, Inst. Cert. Fin. Planners, Loudoun County C. of C. (membership com. 1987—, bd. dirs.), No. Va. ICFP, Farmers and Mchts. Bank (adv. bd.). Lodge: Rotary. Home: 27 Biscayne Pl Sterling VA 22170 Office: Ezagui Enterprises Inc 14 Pidgeon Hill Dr Suite 130240 Sterling VA 22170

EZELL, KERRY MOORE, utility company executive; b. Sharon, Tenn., Aug. 17, 1935; s. Will Allen and Robbie (Moore) E.; m. Dorothy Laird, June 21, 1957; children: Krista, Darren. Student, U. Tenn., Martin, 1953-55; BBA, U. Miss., 1957, postgrad., 1958. CPA, Miss. Accountant Ford Motor Co., Memphis, 1957; pvt. practice acctg. Sharon, Tenn., 1958-59; accountant Greenetone Record Distbg. Co., Nashville, 1959-60; v.p., treas. Miss. Power Co., Gulfport, 1960-83, v.p. fin., 1983—; bd. dirs. Waterfurnice Internat. of Ft. Wayne, Ind., Electric City Mdse. Corp. of Gulfport, Miss. Mem. Miss. Econ. Council. Served with U.S. Army, 1957-58. Mem. Am. Inst. CPA's, Miss. Soc. CPA's, Southeastern Electric Exchange, Edison Electric Inst., Nat. Tax Assn., Fin. Mgmt. Assn., Southeastern Assn. Tax Reps. (chmn. 1976), Miss. Mfrs. Assn. Baptist. Club: Gulfport Yacht. Home: 40 Greenbriar Dr Gulfport MS 39507 Office: Miss Power Co 2992 W Beach Blvd Gulfport MS 39501

EZELL, RUTH ANNE, infosystems specialist; b. Owensboro, Ky., Feb. 23, 1947; d. Everett Lee and Nellie M. (Smith) Hall; m. Freeman Edward Ezell, Feb. 26, 1965; children: Kevin Wayne, Mark Todd. AS, Ky. Wesleyan U., 1984. With Gen. Electric, Owensboro, 1966; keypunch and computer operator Owensboro Bus. Coll., 1967-68; keypunch operator Owensboro Mcpl. Utilities, 1968-69; data entry operator Tex. Gas Transmission Corp., Owensboro, 1969-74, computer operator, 1974-78, jr. programmer, 1978-80, analyst, programmer, 1980-82, sr. analyst, programmer, 1982-88, staff analyst, 1988, supr. application programming, 1988—. Democrat. Baptist. Home: 2660 Russell Rd Utica KY 42376

FABER, CAROL ANTOINETTE, petroleum company executive; b. Terre Haute, Ind., Dec. 26, 1937; d. Fred Malooley and Regina Carolyn (Collins) Breiner; m. Daniel Keith Faber, Sept. 14, 1963; children: John Craig Lund, Jeffrey Scott Lund, Lisa Anne Lund. Student, Valencia Jr. Coll., Orlando, Fla., 1979-80, Seminole Jr. Coll., 1980. Dental asst. Dr. McCormick, Indpls., 1955-57; office mgr. for various dentists Orlando, 1961-70, pvt. practice in interior design, 1978-81; gen. office worker Aero Petroleum, Inc., Orlando, 1981-82; field supr. Aero Petroleum, Inc., Bowling Green, Ky., 1982-84; pres., founder Cheyenne Petroleum, Inc., Bowling Green, 1984—; bd. dirs. Corvette World Hdqrs., Bowling Green. Active Selective Service Bd., Orlando, 1983—. Mem. Ky. Ind. Petroleum Producers Assn. (exec. bd. 1986-87), Ky. Oil and Gas Assn., Nat. Assn. Female Execs., Bowling Green C. of C., Landmark Assn., Friends of Arts-Capital Arts Ctr., Phi Theta Kappa. Republican. Episcopalian. Office: Cheyenne Petroleum Inc 400 West Par Ave Orlando FL 32804 Office: Cheyenne Petroleum Inc 1712 Rollingwood Way Bowling Green KY 42101

FABIANO, VITO THOMAS, equipment company executive; b. Catanzaro, Calabria, Italy, May 8, 1954; came to U.S., 1963; s. Orlando and Maria Rosa (Esposito) F.; m. Rosary A. DiBenedetto, May 27, 1978; children: Vito Jr., Michael, Marissa, Victoria. BS cum laude, Fordham U., 1976; MBA, Iona Coll., 1981. CPA, N.U. Supervising sr. acct. Arthur Young and Co., N.Y.C., 1976-79; sr. internal auditor Wheeler Group, New Hartford, Conn., 1979-81, controller, 1981-82; controller Pitney Bowes Credit Corp., Norwalk, Conn., 1982-85, v.p. fin., 1985-87, v.p. comml. and indsl. fin., 1987-88; v.p. fin. Pitney Bowes Bus. Systems, Stamford, 1988—. Mem. Fin. Execs. Inst., Am. Inst. CPA's, N.Y. Soc. CPA's. Office: Pitney Bowes Bus Systems Elmcroft Stamford CT 06926-0700

FACEY, JOHN ABBOTT, insurance executive, actuary; b. Buffalo, Feb. 18, 1926; s. John A. and Elizabeth (Crowell) F.; m. Mary Murphy; children: John A. 3d, Jeffrey A., James W., Julianna C., Marlene K., Jerald P. BS, Holy Cross Coll., 1947; MA, Boston U., 1948. Instr. U. Conn., New London, 1948-50, U. Md., College Pk., 1950-52; actuarial asst. Conn. Gen. Life, Hartford, 1952-60; asst. actuary Nat. Life and Accident Ins. Co., Nashville, Tenn., 1960-65; sr. v.p. Security-Conn. Life, Avon, Conn., 1965-85; exec. v.p. Conn. Am. Life Ins. Co., North Haven, Conn., 1985—; bd. dirs. Lincoln Security Life N.Y., Brewster. Mem. Employee Benefits Bd., Nashville, 1963-65; coach Jr. League Baseball, West Hartford, Conn., 1965—. Served with USN, 1944-46. Fellow Soc. Actuaries; mem. Am. Acad. Actuaries, Am. Legion, S.E. Actuaries Club, KC. Republican. Roman Catholic. Home: 22 Willowbrook Rd West Hartford CT 06107 Office: Conn Am Life Ins Co 370 Bassett Rd North Haven CT 06473

FACEY, KARLYLE FRANK, financial executive, consultant; b. Hempstead, N.Y., Mar. 21, 1926; s. Karl Mark and Carolyn (Frank) F.; m. Mary Elizabeth Boehm, Sept. 24, 1949; children: Mark, Peter, Carol, David, Katherine. BS in Acctg., NYU, 1948, MBA in Corp. Fin., 1956. Various acctg. positions firms in N.Y. area, 1947-57; systems acct. Grumman Corp., Bethpage, N.Y., 1957-59; methods asst. Bristol-Myers Co., N.Y.C., 1959-66; div. controller Walworth Co., N.Y.C., 1966-68; corp. controller Darling Valve Co., Williamsport, Pa., 1968-71, AAMCO Industries, Bridgeport, Pa., 1972-73; mgr. fin. ops. Pullman Power Products, Williamsport, Pa.; controller Williamsport Mcpl. Water Authority, 1982-85; cons. controller RP's Machinery Sales Inc., Jersey Shore, Pa., 1985-86; chief fin. officer SUSCON Inc., Williamsport, 1986—. Served with USAF, 1944-45. Mem. Nat. Assn. Accts., Am. Legion (Lynbrook, N.Y. post comdr. 1962). Republican. Episcopalian. Home: 241 Selkirk Rd Williamsport PA 17701

FACKLER, WILLIAM MARION, banker; b. Canton, Ga., June 24, 1938; s. Newman Eidson and Mary Edna (Williams) F.; m. Judith Virginia Tomme, June 27, 1965; children: William Marcus, Michael Tomme. B.A., Emory U., 1960; M.B.A., Ga. State U., 1967; diploma, Stonier Grad. Sch. Banking, 1970. V.p. mktg. research, planning and product devel. First Nat. Bank Atlanta, 1960-75; sr. v.p., dir. mktg. AmSouth Bancorp., Birmingham, Ala., 1975-83; exec. v.p. mktg. Barnett Banks, Inc., Jacksonville, Fla., 1983—; bd. dirs. Barnett Banks Trust Co.; bd. dirs., exec. com. Plus System, Inc.; bd. visitors Presbyn. Coll., bd. trustees Fla. History Assocs. Inc.; mem. faculty Stonier Grad. Sch. Banking. Editorial rev. bd.: Jour. Retail Banking. Trustee, mem. exec. com. St. Johns Country Day Sch. With USAF, 1961. Mem. Am. Mktg. Assn. (Mktg. Person of Year, Birmingham chpt. 1980), Bank Mktg. Assn. (dir., exec. com.), Am. Inst. Banking (pres. Atlanta chpt.) Sales and Mktg. Execs., River Club, Timuquana Country Club. Methodist. Home: 3809 Timuquana Rd Jacksonville FL 32210 Office: Barnett Banks Inc 100 Laura St Box 40789 Jacksonville FL 32231

FACUSSÉ, ALBERT SHUCRY, lawyer; b. Tegucigalpa, Honduras, Feb. 10, 1921; s. Nicholas and Maria (Barjum) F.; m. May Bandak, Dec. 22, 1946 (dec.); children—Vivian Neuwirth, Denise Lentz. J.D. cum laude, Loyola U., New Orleans, 1943. Bar: La. 1957. Sole practice, New Orleans, 1957—; pub. speaker. Mem. La. State Bar Assn., ABA, Internat. Platform Assn. Democrat. Roman Catholic. Comment editor Loyola U. Law Rev., 1943. Home: 6731 Manchester St New Orleans LA 70126 Office: 234 Loyola Ave Suite 832 New Orleans LA 70112

FADEN, RICHARD, financial executive; b. Bklyn., Dec. 26, 1944; s. Isidore and Sonya (Bazanski) Rosenkrantz F.; m. Estelle Iris Sir (div. 1980); m. Deborah Kuschick, Mar. 16, 1980; children: Meryl Anne, Stephanie Ilene. AB, Hunter Coll., 1965; M of Health Care, Mt. Sinai Med. Sch., 1981. Dep. project dir. Med. and Health Research Assn. City N.Y., 1971-75; asst. adminstr. Meyer-Manhattan Psychiat. Ctr., Ward's Island, N.Y., 1975-76; v.p., gen. mgr. Original Reprodns., Inc., N.Y.C., 1976-79; adminstr. Ralph Ave. Med. Care Ctr., Bklyn., 1979-81; fin. adminstr. Young Adult Inst., N.Y.C., 1981—; cons. Signmasters Inc., Hoboken, N.J., 1987—; rep. task force on fin. reports N.Y. State Office Mental Retardation and Devel. Disabilities, Albany, 1986—. Served with U.S. Army, 1965-67. Democrat. Jewish. Office: Young Adult Inst 460 W 34th St New York NY 10001

FADNESS, DAVID REUBEN, data processing executive; b. Clarkfield, Minn., Mar. 2, 1952; s. Reuben Alexander and Hazel (Olson) F.; m. Genelle Ann Bethke, June 11, 1988. BA, Concordia Coll., 1974. Underwriter Nat. Family Ins. Co., St. Paul, Minn., 1974-76; data processing mgr. Nat. Family Ins. Co., St. Paul, 1976—, All Nation Ins. Co., St. Paul, 1985—; com. mem. Property and Casualty Systems Users Group, Sheboygan, Wis., 1986—. Mem. Data Processing Mgmt. Assn. Republican. Lutheran. Office: All Nation Family Ins Co 155 Aurora Ave Saint Paul MN 55103

FAFINSKI, ROBERT RICHARD, JR., lawyer; b. Dunkirk, N.Y., July 1, 1957; s. Robert Richard Sr. and Patricia Mary (Benedict) F.; m. Mary Ellen Cullinan, Oct. 2, 1982; 1 child, Robert Richard III. BA in Fin., St. Thomas Coll., St. Paul, Minn., 1979; JD, William Mitchell Coll. Law, 1983. Bar: Minn. 1983, U.S. Dist. Ct. Minn. 1983, U.S. Ct. Appeals (8th cir.) 1983. Law clerk ITT Life Ins. Corp., Mpls., 1980-82, Petersen Tews and Squires, St. Paul, 1982-83; ptnr. Meagher Geer Markham Anderson Adamson Flaskamp & Brennan, Mpls., 1983—. Bd. dirs. Westover (Minn.) Homeowners Assn., 1984-87; moderator Continuing Legal Edn. Seminar, 1986. Mem. Minn. Defense Lawyers Assn., Minn. Bus. Aircraft Assn. Roman Catholic. Office: Meagher Geer et al 4200 Multifoods Tower Minneapolis MN 55402

FAGAN, WILLIAM EDWARD, sales executive; b. Mineola, N.Y., Feb. 28, 1945; s. Frederick William and Ethel Dorothy (Oberg) F.; m. Sharon Ann Korht, Nov. 10, 1978; children: Kelly Marie, Justin McClean. BS in Agr. Bus., Rutgers U., 1967. Sales rep. BioQuest (Becton-Dickinson Co.), Cockeysville, Md., 1972-74; nat. field sales coordinator Roche Diagnostics (Hoffman-LaRoche), Nutley, N.J., 1974-77; v.p. Teer Fin. Systems, Santa Ana, Calif., 1977-78; sales rep. Nuclear Med. Labs., Dallas, 1978-80, Kallestadt Labs., Austin, Tex., 1980-82; regional sales mgr. Surgiden Corp., Mpls., 1982-85; v.p. sales Eye Tech., Inc., St. Paul, 1985—. Pres. Summit (R.I.) Free Library, 1986—; trustee Conventry (R.I.) Town Library, 1987—. Served to capt. USAF, 1967-72. Mem. Am. Mgmt. Assn. Home: 8 Old Summit Rd Greene RI 02827 Office: Eye Tech Inc 1983 Sloan Pl Saint Paul MN 55117

FAGERBERG, ROGER RICHARD, lawyer; b. Chgo., Dec. 11, 1935; s. Richard Emil and Evelyn (Thor) F.; m. Virginia Fuller Vaughan, June 20, 1959; children: Steven Roger, Susan Vaughan, James Thor, Laura Craft. B.S. in Bus. Adminstrn., Washington U., St. Louis, 1958, J.D., 1961, postgrad., 1961-62. Bar: Mo. 1961. Grad. teaching asst. Washington U., St. Louis, 1961-62; assoc. firm Rassieur, Long & Yawitz, St. Louis, 1962-64; ptnr. Rassieur, Long, Yawitz & Schneider and predecessor firms, St. Louis, 1965—. Mem. exec. com. Citizens' Adv. Council Pkwy. Sch. Dist., 1974—, pres.-elect, 1976-77, pres., 1977-78; bd. dirs. Parkway Residents Orgn., 1969—, v.p., 1970-73, pres., 1973—; scoutmaster Boy Scouts Am., 1979-83; Presbyn. elder, 1976—, pres. three local congs. 1968-70, 77-78, 83-84. Mem. ABA, Mo. Bar Assn., St. Louis Bar Assn., Christian Bus. Men's Com. (bd. dirs. 1975-78, 87—), Full Gospel Bus. Men's Fellowship, Order of Coif, Omicron Delta Kappa, Beta Gamma Sigma, Pi Sigma Alpha, Phi Eta Sigma, Phi Delta Phi, Kappa Sigma. Republican. Lodges: Kiwanis (past bd. dirs. 1988—), Masons, Shriners. Home: 13812 Clayton Rd Town and Country MO 63011 Office: Rassieur Long Yawitz & Schneider 1150 Boatmen's Tower Saint Louis MO 63102

FAGIN, DAVID KYLE, natural resource company executive; b. Dallas, Apr. 9, 1938; s. Kyle Marshall and Frances Margaret (Gaston) F.; m. Margaret Anne Hazlett, Jan. 22, 1959; children—David Kyle, Scott Edward. B.S. in Petroleum Engring, U. Okla., 1960; postgrad., Am. Inst. Banking, So. Meth. U. Grad. Sch. Bus. Adminstrn. Registered profl. engr., La., Okla., Tex. Trainee Magnolia Petroleum Co., 1955-56; jr. engr., engr., then partner W.C. Bednar (petroleum cons.), Dallas, 1958-65; petroleum engr. NCNB Tex. Bank (formerly First Nat. Bank Dallas), Dallas, 1965-68; v.p. Rosario Resources Corp., N.Y.C., 1968-75; pres. Alamo Petroleum Corp., 1968-75; exec. v.p. Rosario Resources Corp., N.Y.C., 1975-77; dir. Rosario Resources Corp., 1975-80, pres., 1977-82; v.p. AMAX Inc. (merged with Rosario Resources Corp. 1980), N.Y.C., 1980-82; chmn., dir., pres., chief exec. officer Fagin Exploration Co., Denver, 1982-86; pres., chief operating officer Homestate Mining Co., San Francisco, 1986—, also bd. dirs.; with several T. Rowe Price Mutual Funds, Balt., Homestake Gold Australia, Ltd., Adelaide. Mem. Soc. Petroleum Engrs., Soc. Mining Engrs., AIME (chmn. investment fund 1979-82). Clubs: Dallas Petroleum; Denver Petroleum; World Trade, Bankers Club (San Francisco). Office: 650 California St San Francisco CA 94108

FAHEY, CHARLES JOSEPH, auto compnay executive; b. Kingston, Pa., Apr. 23, 1937; s. Charles Joseph and Helena (Swartwood) F. BS in Elec. Engring., G.M.I., 1964. Supr. Chevrolet, Flint, Mich., 1964-68, gen. supr., 1968-70, layout supr., 1970-72, engring. supr., 1972-75, supt., 1975-84; project engr. Saturn Corp., Troy, Mich., 1985, mgr., 1985—. Home: 1300 Lafayette #606 Detroit MI 48207 Office: Saturn Corp 1400 Stephenson Troy MI 48007

FAHN, JAY, investment company executive, consultant, art dealer; b. Dallas, Aug. 19, 1949; s. Eli and Marion Fahn. BA, Williams Coll., 1971; PhB, MPhil. in Internat. Relations, Oxford (Eng.) U., 1975. Assoc. Citibank, N.A., N.Y.C. and Nairobi, Kenya, 1976; asst. v.p. Citibank, N.A., Seoul, Republic of Korea, 1981-83; mgr. Citibank, N.A., Ltd., Johannesburg, Republic of South Africa, 1977-79; resident v.p. Citibank Zambia, Ltd., Lusaka, 1979-81; v.p. Citicorp U.S.A., Chgo., 1983-85, Citicorp Investment Bank, Chgo., 1985—; chmn. Citicorp Corp. Contbns. Com., Chgo., 1985—; prin., pres. Fahn & Assocs., Ltd., Chgo., 1986—; prin., owner Orca Aart, Chgo., 1987—. Author: Chimbuko, 1986; contbr., editorial assoc.: Government by the People, 1971, Edward Kennedy and the Camelot Legacy, 1975. Mem. exec. com. Lincoln Park Zool. Soc., Chgo., 1984—; rep. career counseling Williams Coll. Alumni Assn., Chgo., 1985-87; nat. youth coordinator Nat. Humphrey for Pres. com., Washington, 1971-72. Recipient Oxford U. scholarship, 1973, 74. Mem. Williams Club, River Club, Adventurers. Home: 2650 N Lakeview #2908 Chicago IL 60614 Office: Citicorp 200 S Wacker Dr Chicago IL 60606

FAHRINGER, CATHERINE HEWSON, retired savings and loan association executive; b. Phila., Aug. 1, 1922; d. George Francis and Catherine Gertrude (Magee) Hewson; grad. diploma Inst. Fin. Edn., 1965; m. Edward F. Fahringer, July 8, 1961 (dec.); 1 child Francis George Beckett. With Centrust Savs. Bank (formerly Dade Savs. and Loan Assn.), Miami, 1958-85, v.p., 1967-74, sr. v.p., 1974-82, sec., 1975-79, head savs. personnel and mktg. div., 1979-83, exec. v.p. office of chmn., 1984, dir., 1984—, co-chmn. audit com. of bd. dirs.; referral assoc. Referral Network Inc., subs. Caldwell Banker; bd. dirs. Old Am. Ins. Co. Trustee United Way of Dade County (Fla.) 1980-87, chmn. audit com. 1982-84; trustee Pub. Health Trust, Dade County, 1974-84, sec. 1976, vice chmn., 1977-78, chmn. bd., 1978-81; hon. bd. govs. U. Miami, Soc. for Rsch. in Med. Edn.; trustee South Fla. Blood Svc., Miami, 1979-84, vice chmn., 1980, chmn., 1981-84; trustee Dade County Vocat. Found., 1977-81; trustee Fla. Internat. U. Found., 1976—, v.p. bd., 1978-81, pres., 1982-84; bd. dirs. Sta. WPBT-TV, 1984, chmn. budget and fin com., 1986, mem. exec. com. 1985-86, sec. 1987, vice chmn., mem. investment com. 1988—; bd. dirs., mem. nominating com. Girl Scout Coun. Tropical Fla., 1985—, chmn. 1988—, mem. long range planning com., 1986—; citizens oversight com. Dade County Pub. Sch. System, 1986—, chmn. 1988—; bd. dirs. New World Sch. of the Arts, 1987, chmn. devel. com., 1987—; mem. fin. commn., chmn. capital improvement fund com. Coral Gables Congrl. Ch.; mem. grievance com. 11th Jud. Cir. Fla. Bar, 1988—; Named Woman of Yr. in fin. Zonta Internat., 1975, amb. Air Def. Arty., U.S. Army Air Def. Command, 1970, Woman of Yr. in Sports, Links Club, 1986; recipient Trail Blazer award Women's Coun. of 100, 1977, Community Headliner award Women in Communication, 1983, Outstanding Citizen of Dade County award, 1984; hon. BA U. Hard Knocks Alderson-Broaddus Coll., 1987. Mem. U.S. League of Savs. Assn., Nat. League Savs. and Loan Assn., Fla. Savs. and Loan League, Dade Bus. and Profl. Women's Club (past pres., Woman of Yr. 1974), LWV, Inst. Fin. Edn. (life; nat. dir., past pres. Local Greater Miami chpt.), Savs. and Loan Mktg. Soc. South Fla. (past pres.), Savs. and Loan Personnel Soc. South Fla., Fla. Women's Alliance (bd. dirs. 1983—, pres. 1987—), Coral Gables Country Club (women's golf assn., treas. 1988—), Links Fla. Internat. U. Club (dir., v.p.), Greenway Women's Golf Assn., Balt. Women's Golf Assn., Golden Panther Club (bd. dirs. 1988—). Democrat. Contbr. articles to profl. jours. Office: Centrust Savs Bank 101 E Flagler St Miami FL 33131

FAILOR, WILLIAM NED, insurance company executive; b. Toledo, July 5, 1950; s. Harlan N. and Shirley J. (Forman) F.; m. Susan Carol Hart, July 12, 1975; 1 child, Brian Adam. BA, Miami U., Oxford, Ohio, 1972. Sales rep. Comml. Union Assurance Co., Detroit, 1972-76; sr. sales rep. CNA Ins. Cos., Detroit, 1976-78; adminstr. recruitment and tng. CNA Ins. Cos., Chgo., 1978-80; sales mgr. CNA Ins. Cos., Mpls., 1980-81, dir. tng. devel., 1984-87; br. mgr. CNA Ins. Cos., Columbus, Ohio, 1987-88; mktg. dir. Great Am. Ins. Cos., Cin., 1981-82; mgr. regional sales Zurich Ins. Cos., Chgo., 1982-83; v.p., mgr. risk mgmt. services Corroon & Black of Ohio, Inc., Columbus, 1988—; cons. Xerox Learning Systems Mgmt. Group, Stanford, Conn., 1985-86. Editor: Insurance Agency Automation, 1987. Mem. Muscular Dystrophy Assn., Chgo. and Columbus, 1983—; mem. polit. action com. CNA Citizens for Good Govt., Chgo., 1987; bd. dirs., treas. Green Trail Improvement Assn., Lisle, Ill., 1985-87. Recipient Miami U. scholarship, 1968. Mem. Ill. Ins. Commrs. (vice-chmn. select commn. on ins. licensing and testing practices 1984-86), Ind. Ins. Agts. Am., Ins. Inst. Am. (mem. nat. adv. com. on mgmt.), Inst. Property and Liability Underwriters, Masons, Shriners, Kiwanis (sr. v.p. 1977-78). Republican. Presbyterian. Office: Corroon & Black Ohio Inc 700 Ackerman Rd Columbus OH 43202

FAIN, JAY LINDSEY, brokerage house executive, consultant; b. Ft. Worth, July 16, 1950; s. James Joel Fain and Jeannine Yvonne (Routt) Ashner; m. Beth Jernigan, Oct. 18, 1968; children: Lisa, Jacob. BBA, U. Tex., 1974. Cert. fin. planner. Acct. exec. Dallas Coca-Cola Bottling Co., 1968-74; unit sales mgr. Procter & Gamble, Houston, 1974-80; assoc. v.p. Dean Witter Reynolds, Houston, 1981—; speaker in field; panelist hearing bd. N.Y. Stock Exchange, 1987—. Sr. warden St. Cuthbert Episcopalian Ch., Houston, 1983; den leader Cub Scouts. Mem. Inst. of Cert. Fin. Planners, Bear Creek Assistance Ministries, Hearthstone Country Club. Episcopalian. Home: 14910 Beechmoor Houston TX 77095 Office: Dean Witter Reynolds 3200 SW Freeway Suite 2100 Houston TX 77027

FAIRCHILD, BRUCE CHARLES, service executive; b. Ames, Iowa, Mar. 27, 1959; s. Mahlon Lowell and Shirley Jean (Natvig) Fairchild. BS, U. Mo., 1982. Asst. mgr. S&M Foods, Columbia, Mo., 1975-79; front office mgr. Brock Hotel Corp., Columbia, 1979-82; food and beverage dir. Brock Hotel Corp., Peoria, Ill., 1982-83, East Peoria, Ill., 1983-84; dir. hotel ops., gen. mgr. Albanese Devel. Corp., Alton, Ill., 1984—. Pres. Adams Pkwy. Bus. Assn., Alton, 1986-87; bd. dirs. Alton Mus. Hist. and Art, 1986—; Greater Alton Twin Rivers Growth Assn., 1986—, v.p., 1986— (Chmn.'s award 1987). Mem. Hotel Motel Assn. Ill. (bd. dirs. 1986—). Lutheran. Home: 4422 Delta Queen Godfrey IL 62035 Office: Holiday Inn Alton 3800 Homer Adams Pkwy Alton IL 62002

FAIRCHILD, JANIS ANN, accountant, county official; b. Leadville, Colo., May 22, 1948; d. Charles H. and Marjorie M. (Fudie) Schlaepfer; m. Dennis W. Parson, May 31, 1966 (div. Mar. 1970); children: Pamela Nygren, Susan; m. Benny L. Fairchild, May 11, 1973; 1 child, Shontay. AA, Colo. Mtn. Coll., 1979; BA, Loretto Heights Coll., Denver, 1982. Bookkeeper Leadville Med. Ctr., 1971-73, Ellis B. Webster, Leadville, 1973-82; pvt. practice Leadville, 1982—; treas. Lake County, Leadville, 1987—; music aide Lake County Sch. Dist., 1970—. Head Organist, Leadville Presbyn. Ch., 1971—; accompanist High County Chorale, 1984—, Crystal Comedy Co., 1985—; mem. Lake County Pension Com., 1987—, Lake County Rep. Com., 1986—. Mem. Internat. Assn. Cert. Fin. Planners. Home: 134 W 8th St PO Box 314 Leadville CO 80461 Office: Lake County 505 Harrison Ave PO Box 276 Leadville CO 80461

FAIRCHILD, JOSEPH VIRGIL, JR., accounting educator; b. New Orleans, Nov. 26, 1933; s. Joseph Virgil and Georgiana Malone (Bourgeois) F.; m. Judith Champagne, Aug. 12, 1961; children: Georgianna, Joseph, Benjamin. BS in Geology, La. State U., 1956, MBA, 1963, PhD, 1975. CPA, La. Geologist United Core, Inc., Houston, 1956-57; assoc. acct. Humble Oil & Refining Co., New Orleans, 1963-64; ptnr. L.A. Champagne & Co., Baton Rouge, 1964-69; pvt. practice acctg. Thibodaux, La., 1969—; asst. prof. acctg. Nicholls State U., Thibodaux, 1969-75, assoc. prof., 1975-76, prof., 1976-84, Disting. Prof. Acctg., 1984—, asst. dean Coll. Bus., 1985-86, dir. grad. bus. studies, 1982-85; research reviewer USAF Bus. Research Mgmt. Ctr., Wright-Patterson AFB, Ohio, 1974-84; cons. Def. Systems Mgmt. Coll., Ft. Belvoir, Va., 1980-81. Author: (with others) The Acquisition and Distribution of Commercial Products, 1980, 1985-86 and 1986-87 Income Tax Guides for State Legislators; contbr. articles to profl. jours. Mem. St. Genevieve Sch. Bd., Thibodaux, 1979-83, E.D. White Cath. High Sch. Bd., 1985-87, chmn. fin. com., 1985-87; lector St. Genevieve Ch., 1975—. Served to 1st lt. USAF, 1957-60, lt. col. Res. ret. Trueblood Prof. Touche-Ross Found., N.Y.C., 1987. Mem. Am. Inst. CPA's, Soc. La. CPA's (lectr. seminars), Am. Acctg. Assn., Nat. Assn. Accts. Roman Catholic. Lodge: Krewe Christopher. Home: 412 Plater Dr Thibodaux LA 70301 Office: Nicholls State U Dept Acctg Thibodaux LA 70310

FAIRLEIGH, MARLANE PAXSON, business consultant, educator; b. Three Rivers, Mich., Feb. 28, 1939; d. Ronald Edward and Evelyn May (Roth) Paxson; m. James Parkinson Fairleigh, June 25, 1960; children: William Paxson, Karen Evelyn. MusB, U. Mich., 1960; MBA, Jacksonville State U., 1986. Adj. faculty Providence Coll., 1976-80, R.I. Coll., Providence, 1978-80; grad. asst. news bur. and info. ctr. Jacksonville (Ala.) State U., 1983-84, grad. asst. Coll. Commerce, 1984-85, account exec. Small Bus. Devel. Ctr., 1985—; presenter various seminars. Chairperson Jacksonville State U. campus United Way Calhoun County, 1986-87. Mem. Anniston Area Mgmt. Assn. (sr. v.p. 1987-88). Home: 70 Fairway Dr Jacksonville AL 36265 Office: Jacksonville State U Small Bus Devel Ctr Merrill Hall Jacksonville AL 36265

FAIRMAN, JARRETT SYLVESTER, automotive retail company executive; b. Anderson, Ind., Feb. 22, 1939; s. Charles Lawton and Ruth (Rich) F.; m. Delores Rae Anderson, Nov. 13, 1960; children: Adele Suzanne, Jarrett Scott, Angela Christine. BS, Purdue U., 1961. Exec. trainee, div. mgr. Sears, Marion, Ind., 1963-67, mdse. mgr., asst. store mgr., Bloomington, Ind., 1967-69, asst. retail sales mgr. sporting goods, Chgo., 1969-71, territorial mdse. mgr. sporting goods, toys and bus. equipment, Dallas, 1971-78; regional v.p. retail ops. White's Home and Auto Stores, 1978-81; pres. Banner, Hendrik & Grant Co., Inc., Dallas, 1981-86; pres. Rapid Distbg. Co. (subs. Otasco), Tulsa, 1986-88; v.p. devel. Coast-to-Coast Home and Auto, Denver, 1988—. Served with U.S. Army, 1961-63. Republican. Lutheran. Home: 526 Carol Ct Richardson TX 75081 Office: Coast-to-Coast Home & Auto 501 S Cherry St Denver CO 81222

FAISON, DELORES, government accountant; b. Atlanta, Aug. 28, 1945; d. Harry and Ella Maud (Hunter) Campbell; 1 child, Harold Ernest Campbell. Student CUNY, Helene Fuld Sch. Nursing, N.Y.C., U. Ariz.; grad. with high honors, Pima Coll., 1984; postgrad., Columbia Pacific U., 1987—. In various positions U.S. Govt., N.Y.C., 1965-74; health unit coordinator Polyclinic Med. Ctr., Harrisburg, Pa., 1978-81, St. Joseph's Hosp., Tucson, 1981-86; acctg. technician Agrl. Research Service, Dept. Agr., Tucson, 1984—; v.p. Tucson Employees Benefit Assn., 1984-85. Recipient Woman On The Move award YWCA, Tucson, 1985. Mem. Nat. Assn. Health Unit Coordinators, Nat. Assn. Female Execs., Federally Employed Women, Fed. Women's Program (alt. rep.), Phi Theta Kappa. Democrat. Baptist. Club: Federally Employed Women (com. chairperson 1985—) (Tucson). Avocations: writing; singing; public speaking.

FAISON, EDMUND WINSTON, JR., software engineer; b. Ft. Belvoir, Va., June 19, 1953; s. Edmund W. Faison and Sally Ann (Tischbein) Rigopoulos; m. Marilena Cadinaro, Jan. 14, 1978; children: Giulia Marsha, Claudia Blanche. BS in Elec. Engring., Calif. State U., Fullerton, 1982. Hardware designer EDX, Inc., Santa Ana, Calif., 1977-79; programmer Lear Siegler, Inc., Anaheim, Calif., 1979-80; sr. programmer Boehringer Mannheim, Inc., Tustin, Calif., 1980-81; sr. microprocessor engr. Beckman Instruments, Inc., Fullerton, 1981-82; pres. Eurosoft, Venice, Italy, 1983-87; project leader Alessi, Inc., Irvine, Calif., 1987—. Mem. IEEE, Am. Assn. for Artificial Intelligence, Assn. for Computing Machinery, Fourth Interest Group. Republican. Presbyterian. Office: Alessi Inc 35 Parker St Irvine CA 92718

FAISON, EDMUND WINSTON JORDAN, business educator; b. Rocky Mount, N.C., Oct. 13, 1926; s. Nathan Marcus and Margery Lucille (Jordan) F.; m. Lois Harger Parker; children: Charles Parker, Dorothy Anne, Barbara Jeane, Edmund Jr., Diane, Carol. A.B. in Psychology, George Washington U., 1948, M.A., 1950, Ph.D., 1956. Rsch. asst. NRC, Washington, 1948-49; mgr. exptl. lab. Needham, Louis and Brorby, Chgo., 1955-56; account exec. Leo Burnett Co., 1957-58; v.p. Market Facts, Inc., Chgo., 1959; pres. Visual Rsch. Internat., Zurich, Switzerland, 1960-63; adviser AID, Dept. State. Latin Am., 1963-68; prof. bus. adminstrn. U. Hawaii, Honolulu, 1968-89; chmn. mktg. dept. U. Hawaii, 1975-82; chmn. bd. Scandata Hawaii, Inc., East-West Rsch. and Design, Inc.; vis. prof. London Grad. Sch. Bus. Studies, 1974-75. Author: Advertising: A Behavioral Approach for Managers, 1980; editorial bd. Jour. of Mktg, 1958-63; contbr. articles to profl. jours. With USN, 1944-46, USAF, 1950-54. Mem. Am. Psychol. Assn., Soc. Consumer Behavior, Am. Mktg. Assn. (pres. Honolulu chpt. 1973-74), Acad. Mktg. Sci., Acad. Mgmt., Am. Acad. Advt., Am. Assn. Public Opinion, Sales and Mktg. Execs. Internat., Advt. Rsch. Found., Japan-Am. Soc., Honolulu Advt. Fedn., Market Rsch. Soc. (U.K.), C. of C. of Hawaii, Japanese C. of C., Hawaii Visitors Bur., Small Bus. Assn. Hawaii, Honolulu Acad. Arts, All-Industry Packaging Assn. (chmn. 1961), European Packaging Fedn. (U.S. rep. 1961), World Packaging Orgn., Sigma Xi, Pi Sigma Epsilon, Pacific Club, Oahu Country Club, Kaneohe Yacht Club, Rotary. Home: 619 Paopua Loop Kailua HI 96734 Office: East West Rsch Inst 735 Bishop St Ste 235 Honolulu HI 96813 also: U Hawaii Honolulu HI 96822

FAJARDO, FREDERICK JOSEPH, international financial public relations executive; b. Oruro, Bolivia, Aug. 30, 1935; came to U.S., 1939; s. Eduardo and Lola (Urquidi) F.; m. Katherine Lynn Humphrey, Mar. 4, 1983. AA in Social Sci., Los Angeles City Coll., 1960; BA in Journalism, San Francisco State U., 1962. Journalist Woodland (Calif.) Daily Dem., 1963-65; mgr. news bur. ops. Litton Industries, Inc., Beverly Hills, Calif., 1965-73; dir. corp. communications Unionam, Inc., L.A., 1973-77; dir. investor relations Fluor Corp., Irvine, Calif., 1977-87; v.p. fin. pub. relations Gavin Anderson & Co., N.Y.C., 1987—; bd. dirs. Brit. Gas Fin., Inc., Wilimington, Del., Investments Co. S.Am., La Paz, Bolivia. With USMC, 1952-56. Mem. Nat. Investor Relations Inst. (bd. dirs. L.A. chpt. 1972-73), Pub. Relations Soc. Am. Roman Catholic. Home: 16 Forest Hill Rd West Norwalk CT 06850 Office: Gavin Anderson & Co 261 Madison Ave New York NY 10016

FAJARDO, TERESA ANA GUZMAN, transportation company executive; b. Boyaca, Colombia, Dec. 1, 1938; d. Elias Campo Novoa and Luisa Maria Uzcategui; m. Guillermo Alfredo Guzman, Aug. 23, 1958 (div. Oct. 1978); children: Jose, Cristina, Liliana, Rodrigo. BS in Bus. Adminstrn., Universidad Nacional, Bogota, Colombia, 1957. Ocean export mgr. Fla. Internat. Forwarding, Miami, 1969-74; pres., owner Olympic Internat. Freight Forwarders, Miami, 1974—. Republican. Roman Catholic. Home: 11550 SW 97th St Miami FL 33176 Office: Olympic Internat Freight Forwarders 7300 NW 56th St Miami FL 33166

FALCON, RAYMOND JESUS, JR., lawyer; b. N.Y.C., Nov. 17, 1953; s. Raymond J. and Lolin (Lopez) F.; m. Debra Mary Bomeisl, June 4, 1977; children: Victoria Marie, Mark Daniel. BA, Columbia U., 1975; JD, Yale U., 1978. Bar: N.Y. 1979, U.S. Dist. Ct. (so. and ea. dist.) N.Y. 1979, U.S. Ct. Appeals (D.C. and 2d cirs.) 1983, Fla. 1987, N.J. 1988, U.S. Dist. Ct. N.J. 1988. Assoc. Webster and Sheffield, N.Y.C., 1978-82; ptnr. Falcon and Hom, N.Y.C., 1982-85; sr. atty. Degussa Corp., Ridgefield Park, N.J., 1985-88, v.p., sec., gen. counsel, 1989—. Contbr. articles to profl. jours. Dem. candidate Town Justice, Town of Rye, N.Y., 1983; Dem. jud. del., Westchester, N.Y., 1984—. Mem. ABA, N.Y. State Bar Assn., Assn. of Bar of City of N.Y., Fed. Bar Council, Assn. Trial Lawyers Am. Clubs: Yale (N.Y.C.); Columbia Alumni of Westchester County (v.p., dir. 1983—). Home: 1 Halstead Ave Port Chester NY 10573 Office: Degussa Corp 65 Challenger Rd Ridgefield Park NJ 07660

FALCONE, MICHAEL ANTHONY, real estate executive; b. Syracuse, N.Y., Feb. 17, 1939; s. Joseph Alexander and Mary F.; m. Joyce Togias, Aug. 22, 1973; 1 child, Stephanie Marie. BA, U. Miami, 1962; MA, St. John's U., N.Y.C., 1967; PhD, Syracuse U., 1974. V.p. FMJ Devel. Corp., Syracuse, 1963-66; dir. personnel Onondaga Community Coll., Syracuse, 1967-68, asst. acad. dean, 1968-70, dir. continuing edn., 1970-73; owner AMF Assocs., Canastota, N.Y., 1981-86; dean grad. studies SUNY Coll. Tech., Utica, 1973-87; pres. The Northfield Corp., Canastota, 1987—; mediator, cons. N.Y. State Pub. Employment Rels. Bd., Albany, 1974-86. Contbr. articles to profl. jours. Mem. Town of Lenox Zoning Bd. Appeals, Canastota C. of C., Greater Syracuse C. of C. Recipient Outstanding Svc. to Sr. Citizens award County of Oneida, 1979. Republican. Roman Catholic. Office: The Northfield Corp PO Box 399 Canastota NY 13032

FALCONE, NOLA MADDOX, financial company executive; b. Augusta, Ga., July 8, 1939; d. Louia Vernon and Geneva Elizabeth (Fox) Maddox; m. Charles Anthony Falcone, Dec. 6, 1968; 1 child, Charles Maddox. B.A., Duke U., 1961; M.B.A., U. Pa., 1966. Security analyst, portfolio mgr. pension and personal trust dept. Chase Manhattan Bank, N.Y.C., 1961-63, 66-70; investment officer personal trust dept. Chase Manhattan Bank, 1968-70; portfolio mgr. Lieber & Co., 1974-75; br. mgr., registered rep. Lieber & Co., Arlington, Va., 1978-79; portfolio mgr. Lieber & Co., Harrison, N.Y., 1979-80; ptnr. Lieber & Co., 1981—; pres. Evergreen Total Return Fund, Inc., Lieber & Co., 1985—; dir. Saxon Woods Asset Mgmt. Corp., Harrison. Mem. fin. com. Jr. League, Scarsdale, N.Y., 1972-75; trustee 1st Bapt. Ch. of White Plains, N.Y., 1973-74; numerous additional vol. activities. Mem. Fin. Analysts Soc. Democrat.

FALEY, ROBERT LAWRENCE, instruments company executive; b. Bklyn., Oct. 13, 1927; s. Eric Lawrence and Anna (Makahon) F.; B.S. cum laude in Chemistry, St. Mary's U., San Antonio, 1956; postgrad. U. Del., 1958-59; m. Mary Virginia Mumme, May 12, 1950; children—Robert Wayne, Nancy Diane. Chemist, E.I. Dupont de Nemours & Co., Inc., Wilmington, Del., 1956-60; sales mgr. F&M Sci., Houston, 1960-62; pres. Faley Assos., Houston, 1962-65; sales mgr. Tech. Inc., Dayton, Ohio, 1965-70; biomed. mkt. mgr. Perkin-Elmer Co., Norwalk, Conn., 1967-69; mktg. dir. Cahn Instruments, Los Angeles, 1970-72; pres. Faley Internat., El Toro, Calif., 1972—. Internat. speaker in field; dir. Whatman Lab. Products Inc., 1981-82, Status Instrument Corp., 1985-87; tech. mktg. cons. Whatman Ltd., Abbott Labs., OCG Tech., Inc., Pacific Biochem., Baker Commodities, Bausch & Lomb Co., Motorola Inc., Whatman Inc., Filtration Scis. Corp., PMC Industries. Mem. adv. com. on Sci., tech., energy and water U.S. 43d Congl. Dist., 1985-87. Served to 1st lt. USAF, 1948-53. Charter mem. Aviation Hall Fame. Fellow Am. Inst. Chemists, AAAS; mem. ASTM, Am. Chem. Soc. (sr.), Instrument Soc. Am. (sr.), Inst. Environ. Scis. (sr.), Aircraft Owners and Pilots Assn., U.S. Power Squadrons, Delta Epsilon Sigma. Club: Masons. Contbr. articles on technique of gas chromatography to profl. jours. Home: 27850 Espinoza Mission Viejo CA 92692 Office: PO Box 669 El Toro CA 92630

FALK, ROBERT HARDY, lawyer; b. Houston, Dec. 27, 1948; s. Arnold Charles and Sara Holmes (Pierce) F.; m. Donna Kay Watts, Aug. 18, 1973 (separated); children: Dorian Danielle, Dillon Holmes. BS summa cum laude, U. Tex., 1971; BA cum laude, Austin Coll., 1972; JD, U. Tex., 1975. Bar: Tex. 1975, D.C. 1977, U.S. Dist. Ct. (so. dist. Tex.) 1975, U.S. Patent Office, U.S. Ct. Appeals (5th cir.) 1976, Ct. Customs and Patent Appeals 1976, N.C. 1979, U.S. Dist. Ct. (we. dist. N.C.) 1982, U.S. Dist Ct. (no. dist. Tex.) 1984, U.S. Ct. Appeals (fed. cir.) 1982, U.S. Ct. Appeals (5th cir.) 1983, U.S. Ct. Internat. Trade 1985, U.S. Dist. Ct. (no. dist.) Tex. 1987. Process engr. Exxon Co., USA, Baytown, Tex., 1971-72; atty. Pravel, Wilson & Gambrell, Houston, 1975-77; patent and trademark counsel Organon Inc. div. Akzona, Inc., Asheville, N.C., 1977-84; ptnr. Hubbard, Thurman, Turner & Tucker, Dallas, 1984—; pres. Robert Hardy Falk, P.C. Pres. Haw Creek Vol. Fire Dept., Asheville, 1980-84; deacon Cen. Christian Ch., Dallas, 1985—. Fellow U. Tex., 1972. Mem. ABA, Tex. Bar Assn., N.C. Bar Assn., D.C. Bar Assn., Am. Patent Law Assn., Am. Trial Lawyers Assn., Dallas Patent Law Assn., Dallas Bar Assn., Licensing Execs. Soc. Republican. Club: University (Dallas). Home: 6030 Glen Heather Dallas TX 75252 Office: Hubbard Thurman Turner Tucker 2100 One Galleria Tower Dallas TX 75240

FALK, SIGO, health care administrator; b. Pitts., Nov. 9, 1934; s. Leon and Katharine (Sonneborn) F.; m. Jean Davis, June 24, 1966; children: Andrew D.; Margaret M., Lawrence L. AB, Harvard U., 1957; MS, Carnegie-Mellon U., 1960. Market research analyst Harbison-Walker Refractories Co., Pitts., 1960-62; instr. econs. and fin. Carnegie-Mellon U., Pitts., 1961-66; v.p., treas. Volaircraft, Inc., Alliquippa, Pa., 1964-65; pres. Chatham Ctr., Inc., Pitts., 1966-75, Webster Hall Hotel, Inc., Pitts., 1976-78; v.p. First Seneca Bank, Pitts., 1979-80; assoc. dir. Health Systems Agy. Southwestern Pa., Pitts., 1979-80; pres., chief exec. officer Cranberry Emergency & Diagnostic Ctr., Mars, Pa., 1987—; bd. dirs. Nat. Intertroup, Inc., Pitts., Duquesne Light Co.; trustee McKee Income Realty Trus, Menlo Park, Calif. Trustee Chatham Coll., Pitts.; Maurice Falk Med. Fund, Pitts. Served with U.S. Army, 1957-63. Club: Harvard-Yale-Princeton (Pitts.); Harvard (N.Y.C.). Home: 540 Hamilton Rd Pittsburgh PA 15205 Office: Cranberry Emergency and Diagnostic Ctr 3315 Grant Bldg Pittsburgh PA 15219

FALKNER, GREGORY PAUL, business owner, automotive educator; b. Buffalo, Nov. 25, 1950; s. William David and Lorraine Catherine (Cole) F.; m. Anna Marie Stadler, July 1, 1972. AAS in Automotive Tech., Erie Community Coll., 1985. Owner, mgr. Greg's Texaco Svc., West Seneca, N.Y., 1969-70, 71-76, Buffalo, 1970-71; owner, mgr. Falkner's Auto Svc., Buffalo, 1976—; guest lectr. Erie Community Coll., Orchard Park, N.Y.; instr. various automotive seminars, Western N.Y. Active politics Town of West Seneca; vol. Variety Club Telethon for Children's Hosp., Batavia Sch. for Blind, therapeutic horseback riding for handicapped Rivendell Riding Sch. Mem. Better Bus. Bur. Western N.Y., United Garage and Gasoline Retailers Assn., West Seneca C. of C. (Outstanding Bus. of Yr. award 1987), Allied Sportsman Club Western N.Y. (bd. dirs. 1985—). Home: 97 Cove Creek Run West Seneca NY 14224 Office: Falkners Auto Svc 2671 Seneca St West Seneca NY 14224

FALKNER, PANDORA ILONA, retail executive; b. Bklyn., Sept. 29, 1958; d. Nicholas Thomas and Betty (Lesser) Mazzio; m. Michael Walter Falkner, June 15, 1980; children: Michael Walter, Douglas Alan. AA, Rockland Community Coll., 1980; BBA, Pace U., 1983. Jr. prog. dir. New City Bowl, N.Y., 1977-78; customer svc. mgr. Photo Promotion Assocs., Monsey, N.Y., 1978-80; retail mgr. Jekyll's Hyde is Leather, Nanvet, N.Y., 1980-82; fin. analyst Credit Alliance Corp., Orangeburg, N.Y., 1982-83; retail mgr. Pretty Posies, Inc., Hackensack, N.J., 1984-86, Huckleberry Finn, Inc., Nanuet, N.Y., 1986, Revere Copper & Brass, Inc. (name change to Corning Inc.), Central Valley, N.Y., 1986—. Asst. to dir. Rockland Co. Spl. Olympics, 1986—. Mem. NAFE. Office: Corning Inc Rte 32 Woodbury Common Central Valley NY 10917

FALL, JOHN ROBERT, management and computer consultant; b. Rockford, Ill., Sept. 21, 1943; s. Robert Duane and Ruth (Hart) F.; m. Carol Emily Delia, July 4, 1975; 1 child: Brian Alexander. AB, San Diego State U., 1965. Systems engr. IBM, San Diego, 1965-70; v.p. Computer Intelligence Corp., San Diego, 1970-71; dir. corp. devel. Userware Internat., Escondido, Calif., 1972-73; pres. J.R. Fall & Co., San Diego, 1974—. Author: Living With a Fast Idiot, 1980. Mem. Ind. Computer Cons. Assn. Office: 16776 Bernardo Center Dr #203 San Diego CA 92128

FALLA, ENRIQUE CRABB, chemical company executive; b. Havana, Cuba, July 15, 1939; came to U.S., 1960; s. Laureano S. and Daisy (Crabb) F.; m. Lucrecia S. Smith, Jan. 26, 1963; children—Ileana, Enrique. B.B.A., U. Miami, Fla., 1965, M.S. in Econs. and Fin., 1967. Fin. staff asst. Dow Chem. Co.-Latin Am. area, 1967, treasurer, 1967-69, area credit mgr., 1969-70; internat. fin. mgr. Dow Chem. Co., Midland, Mich., 1970-71; area treasurer Dow Chem. Co.-Latin Am. area, 1971-73; pres. Dow Chem. Co., Mexico City, 1973-75; dir. adminstrn. Dow Chem. Co.-Latin Am. area, 1975-78, dir. bus. devel., 1978-79, comml. v.p., 1979-80; pres. Dow Chem. Latin Am., Coral Gables, Fla., 1980-84; fin. v.p. Dow Chem. Co., Midland, 1984—, chief fin. officer, 1987—, also bd. dirs.; cons. and lectr. in field; pres. Dow Quimica Mexicana S.A., Mexico City, 1973, 75; bd. dirs. Dow Corning Corp., Dowell Schlumberger, Houston, Comerica Bank, Midland, 1984—; mem. supervisory bd. Bank Mendes Gans nv, Amsterdam, 1986—. Contbr. articles to profl. jours. Trustee Council to the Americas, N.Y.C., 1980-84; dir. Internat. Ctr. of Fla., Coral Gables, 1980-84, North-Am. Chilean C. of C., N.Y.C., 1979-84; sponsor Opportunities Industrialization Ctr. of Dade County; mem. Citizens Bd., U. Miami, 1981-84, 200 Club of Greater Miami, 1981-84, Pres.'s Club, Miami, 1981-83. Served to maj. U.S. Army, 1960-62; Bay of Pigs. Named Leading Fin. Officer in U.S., 1986; recipient FACE award, Miami, 1985. Mem. Fin. Execs. Inst. (Midland chpt.). Clubs: Midland Country; Key Biscayne Yacht. Office: Dow Chem Co 2030 Willard H Dow Ctr Midland MI 48674

FALLS, MARILYNLEE, financial planner, stockbroker; b. Toledo, Oct. 4, 1949; d. Henry and Norma Jean (Fleitz) Nowakowski; m. Douglas P. Falls, Aug. 21, 1970 (div. 1975). B in Gen. Studies, U. Mich., 1971. With Corp. Planning Assocs., N.Y.C., 1982; cons. ABC, N.Y.C., 1983; account exec. Moseley Securities Corp., N.Y.C., 1984-86; v.p. investments Prudential Bache Securities, N.Y.C., 1987—. Mem. Internat. Assn. Fin. Planners, Inst. Cert. Fin. Planners (cert. fin. planner), Jr. League of Bklyn. (treas. 1986-88). Home: 89 Dean St Brooklyn NY 11201 Office: Prudential Bache Securities One Liberty Pla New York NY 10006

FAMADAS, JOSÉ, educator, journalist, translator; b. Rio de Janeiro, Brazil, April 10, 1908; s. João Famadas and Francisca (Herrera) F.; B.S. and Lit., Colegio S. Vicente de Paulo and Colegio Pedro II; Curso Leon Say and Instituto Comercial; C.P.A., Dept. Bus. Edn., Ministry of Edn.; Sch. English Lang. and Lit.; extension and grad. courses U. Rio de Janeiro, U. Distrito Federal, U. Pa. field course, U. Brasil, Instituto de Psicologia, Ministry Edn.; A.M., U. Mich., 1942; postgrad. courses U. Wis., Columbia U., 1942-55; 1 son, Nelson. Staff, Banco do Brasil, 1928-62; translator-editor United Press, 1938; instr. Tech. Council on Economics and Finance, 1939-40, Instituto Watson de Organização do Trabalho, I.B.M., 1939-40; dir. Instituto Britannia, 1937-42; asso. prof Colegio Pedro II, 1939-44; instr. Am. Council Learned Socs., Inst. Brazilian Studies, U. Vt., 1942, U. Mich. English Lang. Inst., 1942; teacher extension Columbia U., 1943-44, instr. faculty philosophy, 1944-47; dir. bibliography, library and cultural archives Hispanic Inst., 1943-47; translator 20th Century Fox, 1950-56, U.S. Dept. State, 1951-53, USIA, 1953-78, Universal Internat., 1953-74, United Artists, 1956-83, Paramount Pictures, 1971-74, others; instr. CCNY extension div., 1947-58; editor in chief Brazilian edit. The Reader's Digest, 1947-50; press officer Brazilian Mission to UN, 1950-55; radio commentator and mem. weekly round table discussion programs on networks, 1944-54. Recipient Order of Merlin Excalibur, Internat. Brotherhood Magicians; Inst. Internat. Edn. and Rockefeller Found. fellow. Life mem. AAAS, Nat. Acad. Econs. and Polit. Sci., MLA, Associação Brasileira de Imprensa, Linguistic Soc. Am., Acad. Polit. Sci., Am. Assn. Tchrs. Spanish and Portuguese (past v.p. N.Y. chpt.), Am. Econ. Assn., Am. Topical Assn., Soc. Am. Magicians; emeritus mem. N.Y. Acad. Sci., Latin Am. Studies Assn., AAUP; mem. Soc. Lang. Specialists (former pres.), Nat. Geog. Soc., Nat. Travel Club, Am. Mus. Natural History, Smithsonian Instn., Magicians Guild Am., others. Contbr. Columbia Dictionary of Modern European Lit., Revista de Filología Hispánica, The Romanic Rev., New Century Cyclopedia of Names, others. Address: PO Box 752 Flushing NY 11352

FAMIGLIETTI, NANCY ZIMA, computer executive; b. Hartford, Conn., Nov. 10, 1956; d. Joseph John and Angeline (Morello) Zima; m. Arthur R. Famiglietti Jr., May 23, 1981. BA in Math., Computer Sci., Eastern Conn. State Coll., Willimantic, 1978. Sr. programmer analyst Hamilton Standard, Windsor Locks, Conn., 1978-82; system analyst Cigna Corp., Hartford, 1982-83, system designer, 1983-86, lead system designer, 1986-89; system adminstr. Aetna, Hartford, 1989—. Active Conn. Trolley Mus., East Windsor, Conn. Fire Mus., East Windsor, Bushnell Carousel Soc., Hartford, Sturbridge Village, Conn. Pub. TV., Hartford, Channel 57, Springfield, Mass. Mem. Nat. Honor Soc., Kappa Mu Epsion Math. Honor Soc. Home: 81 McGrath Rd South Windsor CT 06074

FANCHER, GEORGE H., JR., oil company executive, petroleum engineer; b. Austin, Tex., Apr. 30, 1939; s. George Homer and Mattie (Stanfield) F.; m. Mary Ann Rousos, May 24, 1958 (div. July 1963); children: Lisa Renee Blonkvist, George Homer III; m. Carolyn Jane Keithly, Nov. 27, 1976; children: Michael Ryan, Kelly Christine. Registered profl. engr., Tex. Petroleum engr. Chevron Oil Co., Denver, 1962-66, Ball Bros. Research, Boulder, Colo., 1966-67, King Resources Co., Denver, 1967-69; ptnr. Smith-Fancher, Denver, 1969-80; owner Fancher Oil Co., Denver, 1980—. Mem. Chancellor's Council U. Tex., 1982—, Rep. Party State Fin. Com., 1982-85; dir. InterMountain Polit. Action Com., 1983—; bd. trustees St. Anne's Episcopal Sch., 1986. Mem. Ind. Petroleum Assn. Am. (bd. dirs.), Ind. Petroleum Assn. Mountain States (bd. dirs.), Soc. Petroleum Engrs. Episcopalian. Clubs: Cherry Hills Country (Denver), Castle Pines Country (Castle Rock, Colo.). Office: Fancher Oil Company 1801 Broadway #720 Denver CO 80202

FANSHIER, CHESTER, manufacturing executive; b. Wilson County, Kans., Mar. 2, 1897; s. Thomas J. and Nora Bell (Maxwell) F.; m. Ina Muriel Goens, Apr. 12, 1918; 1 child, Norma Elaine (Mrs. Robert B. Rice). Registered profl. engr., Okla. Gen. mgr. Bart Products Co., 1932-39; pres., gen. mgr. Metal Goods Mfg. Co., Bartlesville, Okla., 1939-88. Patentee in field. Commr. from Tulsa Presbytery to 156th Gen. Assembly, Presbyn. Ch. U.S.A., 1944; pres. Sunday Eve. Fedn. chs., 1937-38. Recipient Wisdom award Honor, 1970, Gutenberg Bible award; named to Ring Order of Engrs. Mem. NSPE, Okla. Soc. Profl. Engrs. (charter Bartlesville chpt.), ASTM, ASME (life), Profl. Photographers Am., Nat. Rifle Assn. (life), Okla. Rifle Assn., Am. Def. Preparedness Assn. (life), Bartlesville C. of C., SAR. Presbyterian. Club: Engr. (bd. dirs. 1948-49, 54-55). Lodge: Rotary (pres. 1956-57, Paul Harris fellow). Home: Bartlesville, Okla. Died Oct. 16, 1988.

FANTA, DONALD CHARLES, investment banker; b. Cleve., July 12, 1928; s. Charles W. and Winifred A. (Egan) F.; m. Anne Presley, July 29, 1950; children: Patricia Anne, Thomas W., Margaret. Student, Miami U., Oxford, Ohio, 1946-50, LHD (hon.), 1987. Sales and merchandising Minn. Mining and Mfg., Detroit, 1950-60; br. office mgr. Ohio Co., Dayton, 1960-65; sales mgr. Ohio Co., Columbus, 1965-69, v.p., sales mgr., 1969-71, pres., chief exec. officer, bd. dirs., 1971—; chmn. bd. dirs. Cardinal Funds, Columbus; bd. dirs. Cardinal Fin. Mgmt. Corp., Columbus, Taylor Woodcraft, Inc., Malta, Ohio, Big Bear Stores Co., Columbus, Ins./Ohio Co. Agy., Columbus, Ohio Equities, Inc., Columbus. Mem. nat. and local adv. bd. Salvation Army, Verona, N.J. and Columbus, 1987—; active Northwest Ordinance and U.S. Constitution Bicentennial Commn., Columbus, 1986—; account exec. United Way Franklin County, Columbus; trustee Columbus Assn. for Performing Arts, 1983—, Ballet Metro., Columbus, 1980—; bd. dirs. Ohio C. of C., Columbus, past chmn. bd. dirs. With U.S. Army, 1950-52, Japan. Named Ohio Businessperson of Yr. Alpha Kappa Psi, 1985. Mem. Securities Industry Assn. (bd. dirs.), Nat. Assn. Securities Dealers, Investment Dealers Ohio (pres, trustee), Columbus Stock and Bond Club, Rotary Club (bd. dirs. 1988—), Columbus Club, Leatherlips Yacht Club. Office: Ohio Co 155 E Broad St Columbus OH 43215

FANUELE, MICHAEL ANTHONY, retired electrical engineer; b. Bronx, N.Y., Feb. 24, 1938; s. Joseph A.and R. Fanny (Rubino) F.; m. Joyce L. Cassidy, May 23, 1964; children: Gina M., Peter A. BEE, NYU, 1959; MSEE, Rutgers U., 1968. Electronics engr. U.S. Army Combat Surveillance & Target Acquisition Lab., Fort Monmouth, N.J., 1960-72, sr. electronics engr., 1972-80, project officer, 1980-81, dir. ISTA systems div., 1981-85; chief systems and signals analysis div. U.S. Army Electronic Warfare, Reconnaissance Surveillance and Target Acquisition Ctr., Fort Monmouth, N.J., 1985-88; cons. in field; chmn. dept. electromagnetic engring. U.S. Army Internal Tng. Program, Ft. Monmouth, 1968-78, advisor, 1978—; Army chmn. Tri-Service Radar Symposium Steering Group, Ft. Monmouth, 1973—; Army mem. Internat. Tech. Group, 1977-81, Internat. Radar panel, 1984—. Patentee in field; contbr. articles to profl. jours. Served to 2d lt. U.S. Army, 1959-60. Mem. IEEE (sr.), Assn. Old Crows. Roman Catholic. Lodge: KC (treas. Brickton, N.J. 1968-70). Home: 440 Colleen Ct Toms River NJ 08755

FANWICK, ERNEST, corporate lawyer; b. N.Y.C., Feb. 28, 1926; s. Jacob and Jeanette (Lossof) F.; m. Lee Nathan, Sept. 1, 1951; children: Lewis, Leslie, Eric. BS in Elec. Engring., Pa. State U., 1948; JD, Columbia U., 1951. Bar: N.Y. 1952, Conn. 1988, U.S. Patent Office 1952, U.S. Ct. Appeals (2d cir.) 1952, U.S. Supreme Ct. 1958, U.S. Ct. Appeals (fed. cir.) 1982. Sr. patent atty. ITT Fed. Telephone Labs., Nutley, N.J., 1951-55; div. counsel Avion div. ACF, Paramus, N.J., 1955-57; patent counsel Burndy Corp., Norwalk, Conn., 1957-65, dir. legal dept., 1965-75, gen. counsel, 1975-82, v.p., gen. counsel, sec., 1982-89; mem. faculty Practising Law Inst., N.Y.C., 1964—; lectr. Conf. Legal Execs., Pa., 1970, 72. Bd. dirs. Aid to Retarded, Stamford, Conn., 1982-87; active Am. Arbitration Assn. Served to lt. U.S. Army, 1943-47. Mem. ABA, Am. Patent Law Assn., Am. Soc. Corp. Secs., Conn. Patent Law Assn. (pres. 1966), N.Y. Patent, Trademark and Copyright Law Assn., Westchester-Fairfield Corp. Counsel Assn., Am. Intellectual Property Assn., Am. Arbitration Assn. (arbitrator). Lodges: Masons, Shakespear.

FARBER, HUGH ARTHUR, environmental and health issues consultant; b. Muskegon, Mich., Oct. 6, 1933; s. Simon P. and Nehushta F. (Genson) F.; m. Betty J. Johnson, Sept. 1954; children: Cheryl, Susan, Julia. BS, Mich. State U., 1956; PhD in Organic Chemistry, Northwestern U., 1960. Research chemist Dow Chem., USA, Midland, Mich., 1959-62, sr. research chemist, 1962-66, project leader, 1966-71, group leader, 1971-76, environ. mgr., 1985-86; owner Farber Assocs., Midland, 1986—. Holder 12 patents in field, 1959-76; contbr. numerous articles to profl. jours. Recipient Gold medal Am. Inst. of Chemists, 1956. Mem. AAAS, Am. Chem. Soc., Air Pollution Control Assn., Sigma XI, Midland Steel Headers. Home and Office: 2807 Highbrook Dr Midland MI 48640

FARGIS, PAUL MCKENNA, publishing consultant, book developer, editor; b. N.Y.C., Mar. 19, 1939; s. George Bertrand and Elizabeth Harlin (McKenna) F.; m. Elizabeth Hackett, Aug. 22, 1964; children: John Hackett, Alison Kathryn; m. Dawn Sangrey, Apr. 23, 1977; 1 child, Christopher Sangrey. Student, Cath. U. Am., 1958; B in Social Sci., Fairfield U., 1961; MA (Publs. Tuition scholar), N.Y. U., 1962. Editorial asst. Prentice-Hall, Inc., Englewood Cliffs, N.J., 1961-62; editor Hawthorn Books, Inc., N.Y.C., 1963-67; v.p., editorial dir. Hawthorn Books, Inc., 1967-71; v.p., editor-in-chief Thomas Y. Crowell Co. and Funk & Wagnalls divs. Dun-Donnelley

Pub. Corp., N.Y.C., 1971-77; editor-in-chief Apollo Books, N.Y.C., 1972-77; managing dir. Thomas Y. Crowell div. Harper and Row, N.Y.C., 1977-78; pub., editor-in-chief The Stonesong Press div. Grosset & Dunlap, Inc., N.Y.C., 1978-80; founder, pres. and pub. The Stonesong Press, Inc., 1980—; pub. cons., 1980—; founder, owner The Biblioswitch, Bedford Hills, N.Y., 1973—; mem. adv. bd. Grad. Sch. Corp. and Polit. Communication Fairfield U., 1969-81; pub. arbitrator Am. Arbitration Assn., 1982—. Author: The Consumer's Handbook, 1966, rev. edit., 1974, Company's Coming, 1965; Am. editor: Twentieth Century Ency. Catholicism, 1963-67; patentee in field. Exec. dir. Harrison (N.Y.) Town Recreation Commn., 1970-72; dir. Harrison Town Forum, 1969-73; former bd. dirs. U.S. Cath. Hist. Soc.; past trustee Unitarian Fellowship of No. Westchester; patentee in field. Mem. Am. Book Coun. (bd. dirs. 1987-88), Am. Book Producers Assn. (pres. 1986-87, bd. dir. Charitable Book program 1987-89). Unitarian. Office: 211 E 51st St New York NY 10022

FARGO, JOAN ELLEN, personnel agency executive; b. Toledo, Mar. 6, 1955; d. Thomas Robert Love and Betty Jane (Heineman) Love Britten; divorced; 1 child, Michelle Angela. Sales attendant Ryan Homes, Toledo, 1980-81; sales rep. Renhill, Perrysburg, Ohio, 1981-82; dir. ops. AIM Temporaries (formerly Employers Overload), Toledo, 1985—. Com. rep. Opera Guild Sapphire Ball, 1986—; chmn. spl. events Toledofest, Arts Commn. Greater Toledo, 1985; vol. March of Dimes, Am. Lung Assn., Run Against Cancer, other civic orgns. Mem. Toledo C.of C., Sylvania C. of C. (bd. dirs. 1985-86, sec. 1986, chmn. spl. events 1986—, Winterfest chmn. 1988, active several comms.), YWCA Toledo (Tribute to Women in Industry award 1987-88) Ohio Assn. Personnel Cons., Toledo Personnel Mgmt. Assn., Nat. Assn. Temp. Services (1st Pl. Community Events Service award 1986), Nat. Assn. Personnel Cons. Clubs: Maumee River Yacht, Toledo Yacht. Office: AIM Executive Inc 6605 Central Ave Toledo OH 43617

FARGO, JOHN GUITO, construction executive; b. Indpls., Dec. 24, 1915; s. Benjamin and Angela (Ferrarin) F.; m. Elizabeth Eizenhoefer, Oct. 20, 1956; 1 child, Benjamin Frederick. BBA, Butler U., 1966. Prin. Midwestern Terrazzo Co., Indpls., 1938-41, sr. ptnr., 1947-76, pres., 1976—. Served to maj. U.S. Army, 1941-46, PTO. Mem. Constrn. Specifications Ins., Nat. Terrazzo and Mosaic Assn. (pres. 1963-65), Constrn. League Indpls. (pres. 1965-67). Republican. Roman Catholic. Office: Midwestern Terrazzo Corp 2601 Sherman Dr Indianapolis IN 46220

FARHA, CLAY THOMAS, business executive; b. Wichita, Kans., Feb. 4, 1959; s. Philip F. and Gloria May (Eddie) F.; m. Jamie Louise Caruthers, June 20, 1987. BSBA, U. Kans., 1981. Research analyst B.C. Christopher Stock Broker, Wichita, 1980; credit analyst Banc Tex. White Rock, Dallas, 1982; gen. ptnr./mgr. B.D. Eddie Enterprises, Oklahoma City, 1983—. Mem. stage ctr. spl. projects com. Arts Council of Oklahoma City, 1988; bd. dirs. Greens Homeowners Assn.; adv. bd. Salvation Army, 1989—. Mem. Okla. City C. of C. Republican. Antioch Orthodox Ch. Clubs: Oklahoma City Golf and Country, Men's Dinner, Bachelors of Oklahoma City, Young Men's Dinner (exec. com. 1988—). Lodge: Rotary (bd. dirs. 1989—, newsletter editor Oklahoma City 1987-88). Office: BD Eddie Enterprises 1601 NW Expressway Suite 1010 Oklahoma City OK 73118

FARHA, WILLIAM FARAH, food company executive; b. Lebanon, Nov. 27, 1908; s. Farah Farris and Nahima (Salamy) F.; m. Victoria Barkett, Apr. 15, 1934; 1 child, William George. Grad., U.S. Indsl. Coll., 1948, Brookings Inst., 1968, Doctorate, Hamilton State U., 1973, Colo. State Christian Coll. With F & E Wholesale Grocery Co., 1929-64; mgr. River Bend Shopping Ctr., Wichita, William F. Farha and Son Enterprises, Wichita. Bd. dirs. NCCJ, Kans. Found. for Blind; trustee Met. Bd., YMCA, also internat. bd. World Service; founder Antiochian Greek Orthodox Dioceses of N.Am.; bd. advisers Salvation Army; internat. bd. YMCA World Service; pres. bd. trustees St. George Ch.; chmn. Wichita Leadership Prayer Breakfast; co-founder, past bd. govs. St. Jude Research Hosp., Memphis; past chmn. Wichita Police and Fireman Pension Plan; past trustee Wichita Symphony Soc.; past bd. dirs. Wichita C. of C., St. Joseph Research Hosp. Ctr.; past nat. bd. Inst. Logopedics; nat. adv. bd. Am. Security Council; mem. Nat. Bd. Small Bus., U.S. Congl. Adv. Bd.; charter mem. Pres. Reagan's Republican Presdl. Task Force; mem. Rep. Nat. Com.; invited to presdl. prayer breakfasts in Eisenhower, Kennedy, Johnson, Nixon and Ford adminstrns. named hon. Okla. col., 1956; mem. Pres. Reagan's Rep. Presdl. Task Force, Rep. Nat. Com. recipient Gold medal for outstanding service to orthodoxy Antiochian Patriarch Alexander of Damascus, 1952, Antonian Gold medal of merit Antiochian Orthodox Christian Archdiocese of N.Y. and N.Am., 1972, Brotherhood award NCCJ. Lodge: Rotary (Paul Harris fellow). Home: 8630 Shannon Way Wichita KS 67206 Office: 8100 E 22d St N Bldg 1700 Wichita KS 67226 also: 8889 Gateway W El Paso TX 79925

FARIAS, CHRISTOPHER LOUIS, marketing executive; b. Bombay; came to U.S., 1982; s. Gratian Marian and Philomena (Pais) F.; m. Maria F. Fernandes, May 16, 1982; children: Michael Joseph, Stephen Gratian. BA of Tech., Indian Inst. Tech., Bombay, 1974; MBA, Indian Inst. Mgmt., Ahmedabad, India, 1980. Prodn. engr. Larsen and Toubro Ltd., Bombay, 1974-78; info. cons. Farias Cons., Bombay, 1980-82; sales exec. Noll Air Power, Paoli, Pa., 1982-84; bus. systems cons. Control Data Corp., Phila., 1984—. Home: 2855 Dogwood Ln Broomall PA 19008 Office: Control Data Corp 1900 Market St Ste 501 Philadelphia PA 19103

FARICY, (JAMES) ROLAND, truck and equipment dealer; b. Florence, Colo., Aug. 5, 1926; s. James Matthew and Elsie Fern (Price) F.; student Abbey Coll., Canon City, Colo., 1944; m. Teresa Mae Abell, July 21, 1945; children—Jerome A., H. Brian, James R., Huberta V., Melvin L., J. Kevin, Teresa Mae. Automobile and truck dealer, 1946—; pres. Rol Faricy Motor Co., Pueblo, Colo., 1968-77, Faricy Truck & Equipment Co., Pueblo, 1978—; chmn. exec. com. Abell Truck & Equipment Co., Pueblo, 1969-77; trustee, sec.-treas. Colo. Automobile Dealers Ins. Trust; mem. nat. advt. adv. council Internat. Harvester Co. truck group; founding stockholder, dir. Pueblo Bancorp.; dir., mem. exec. com. Pueblo Bank & Trust, 1983—. Founding dir. Pueblo Devel. Found., 1963; mem. Pueblo County Dem. Cen. and Exec. Com., 1960-64, advt. and campaign chmn., 1962; trustee St. Mary Corwin Hosp., Pueblo, 1979—, chmn. planning com., 1981—, vice chmn./chmn. elect bd. trustees, 1983-86, chmn. bd. trustees, 1986—; bd. dirs. St. Joseph Hosp., Florence, Colo., 1979-81, 85—; chmn. bd. trustees Colo. Automobile Dealers Ins. Trust. Served with USAAF, 1944-46. Named Truck Dealer of Year, Columbia U. Grad. Sch. Bus./Am. Truck Dealers Assn., 1981. Mem. Am. Truck Dealers Assn. (legis. chmn. Colo. 1977-78), Am. Trucking Assn., Nat. Automobile Dealers Assn., Colo. Automobile Dealers Assn. (pres. 1965, chmn. truck com. 1981—), Colo. Motor Carriers Assn., Gen. Motors Truck Dealers Nat. Council (vice chmn., chmn. elect 1987), Gen. Motors Pres.'s Council. Roman Catholic. Club: Pueblo Golf and Country. Lodges: Elks, KC (4 degree). Home: 12 Silverweed Ct Pueblo CO 81001 Office: 4425 N Elizabeth St Pueblo CO 81008

FARINELLI, JEAN L., public relations firm executive; b. Phila., July 26, 1946; d. Albert J. and Edith M. (Falini) F. B.A., Am. U., Washington, 1968; M.A., Ohio State U., Columbus, 1969. Asst. pub. relations dir. Dow Jones & Co., Inc., N.Y.C., 1969-71; account exec. Carl Byoir & Assocs., Inc., N.Y.C., 1972-74, v.p., 1974-80, sr. v.p., 1980-82; pres. Tracy-Locke/BBDO Pub. Relations, Dallas, 1982-87; pres. Creamer Dickson Basford, Inc., N.Y.C., 1987-88, chmn., chief exec. officer, 1988—. Recipient PR CaseBook, PR Reporter, N.H., 1984; Silver Spur, Tex. Pub. Relations Assn., Dallas, 1985. Mem. Pub. Relations Soc. Am. (Silver Anvil award 1980, 81, 85, Excalibur award Houston chpt. 1985, chmn. 1986 Silver Anvil awards, chmn. 1987 honors and awards com., chmn. 1989 Spring Conf. Counselors Acad.), Internat. Assn. Bus. Communicators (Gold Quill award 1985), Women in Communications, Women Execs. in Pub. Relations, Nat. Investor Relations Inst. Clubs: Nat. Arts (N.Y.C.). Home: 333 E 56th St New York NY 10022 Office: Creamer Dickson Basford 1633 Broadway New York NY 10019

FARISH, JAMES MATTHEW, accountant; b. Monroe, Va., Dec. 18, 1946; s. Robert Franklin and Josephine Elizabeth (Dudley) F.; m. Martha Ann Sawyers, Aug. 11, 1972; 1 child, Robert Joseph. B.S., Va. Commonwealth U., 1975, M.B.A., 1978. Pres. Farish & Assocs., Richmond, Va., 1975—; v.p. Sovran Fin. Corp., 1987—; sec.-treas. Farish, Dixon, Dalton, Inc., 1987—. Pres. Bethlehem Little League, Richmond, 1976-80; treas. Lakeside Little League, Richmond, 1982-85, v.p., 1986-87. Mem. Va. Soc. Pub. Accts., Va. State Umpires Assn. (treas. 1986-88). Republican. Baptist. Lodge: Lions (treas. 1977-81, 85-88). Avocation: golf. Home: 9711 Needles Way Glen Allen VA 23060

FARLEY, EUGENE JOSEPH, accountant; b. N.Y.C., Jan. 3, 1950; s. John Joseph and Rita Sara (Johnston) F.; m. Rosaleen Therese Scully, Jan. 10, 1981; children: Sarah, Laura, Patrick. BBA in Acctg., Siena Coll., 1977; MBA in Fin., Russell Sage Coll., 1985. CPA, N.Y. Cost acct. Callanan Industries, S. Bethlehem, N.Y., 1972-75; tax auditor N.Y. State Dept. Taxation and Fin., Albany, 1977-83, EDP auditor, 1983-85, assoc. acct., 1985—. Fund raiser Siena Coll. Alumni Fund; vol. Albany's Tri-Centennial Com., 1986. Mem. AICPA, N.Y. State Soc. CPAs, EDP Auditor Assn. Hartford (Conn.), Assn. Govt. Accts. (fin. mgmt. standards com. 1988—). Democrat. Roman Catholic. Home: 9 Middlesex Dr Slingerlands NY 12159 Office: NY Dept Taxation & Fin State Office Campus Albany NY 12227

FARLEY, JAMES BERNARD, financial services company executive; b. Pitts., Nov. 1, 1930; s. James and Marie (Wallace) F.; m. Mary W. Williams, Feb. 14, 1951; children—James J., Michele M., Constance M., J. Scott. B.B.A., Duquesne U., 1953; M.B.A., Case Western Res. U., 1961. Indsl. engr. U.S. Steel Co., Pitts., 1952-60; supt. Newburgh & So. Shore Ry. Co., Cleve., 1960-63; v.p. Booz, Allen & Hamilton, N.Y.C., 1963-73, pres., chief exec. officer, 1973-76, chmn. bd., chief exec. officer, 1976-85, sr. chmn. bd., 1985-88; pres., chief op. officer, trustee MONY Fin. Services, N.Y.C., 1988-89, chmn., pres., chief exec. officer, trustee, 1989—; dir. Holiday Corp., Memphis, Ashland Oil Inc., Ky., Conf. Bd., N.Y.C.; trustee Com. for Econ. Devel., N.Y.C. Clubs: Links, Sky (N.Y.C.); Gulf Stream Golf (Delray Beach, Fla.); Baltusrol Golf (Springfield, N.J.) (bd. govs. 1978-84). Office: MONY Fin Svcs 1740 Broadway New York NY 10019

FARLEY, JOHN MICHAEL, steel company executive; b. Bklyn., July 10, 1930; s. John F. and Lucile J. Farley; m. Dorothy O. Stacy, Nov. 29, 1959; children: Anne L., Joan E., John O. B.C.E. magna cum laude, Syracuse U., 1952; M.S., U. Ill., 1954. Registered prof. engr., Ohio, Pa. Mem. engring. staff Jones & Laughlin Steel Corp., Pitts., 1957-72, v.p. research and engring., 1972-75, v.p. raw materials, 1975-77; pres. raw materials div. Jones & Laughlin Steel Corp., 1977-82, v.p. raw materials, purchasing, traffic, 1982-85; pres., chief exec. officer Olga Coal Co., McDowell County, W.Va., 1979-86; v.p. research, engring. and traffic LTV Steel Co., 1985—. Served with USN, 1954-57. Mem. Am. Iron and Steel Inst., AIME, Iron and Steel Soc., Assn. Iron and Steel Engrs., Sigma Xi, Tau Beta Pi. Clubs: Duquesne (Pitts.); Union (Cleve.).

FARLEY, JOSEPH MCCONNELL, electric utility executive, lawyer; b. Birmingham, Ala., Oct. 6, 1927; s. John G. and Lynne (McConnell) F.; m. Sheila Shirley, Oct. 1, 1958 (dec. July 1978); children: Joseph McConnell, Thomas Gager, Mary Lynne. Student, Birmingham-So. Coll., 1944-45; B.S. in Mech. Engring., Princeton U., 1948; student, Grad. Sch. Commerce and Bus. Adminstrn., U. Ala., 1948-49; LL.B., Harvard, 1952; L.H.D., Judson Coll., 1974; LL.D. (hon.), U. Ala.-Birmingham, 1983. Bar: Ala. 1952. Assoc. Martin, Turner, Blakey & Bouldin, Birmingham, 1952-57; ptnr. successor firm Martin, Balch, Bingham & Hawthorne, 1957-65; exec. v.p., dir. Ala. Power Co., 1965-69, pres., dir., 1969-89; v.p. So. Electric Generating Co., 1970-74, pres., 1974-89, also dir.; exec. v.p. nuclear The Southern Co., Birmingham, 1989—; bd. dirs. AmSouth Bank, N.A., Am South Bancorp., Southern Co. Svcs. Inc., Torchmark Corp., Bus. Council Ala., So. Investment Group, Inc. Mem. exec. bd. Southeastern Electric Reliability Council, chmn., 1974-76; mem. Jefferson County Republican Exec. Com., 1953-65; counsel, mem. Ala. Rep. Com., 1962-65; permanent chmn. Ala. Rep. Conv., 1962; alternate del. Rep. Nat. Conv., 1956; bd. dirs. Edison Electric Inst., 1976-79; bd. dirs. Southeastern Electric Exchange, pres., 1984; bd. dirs. Kidney Found. Ala., Ala. Bus. Hall of Fame, All-Am. Bowl, Birmingham Area YMCA (hon. dir.), Operation New Birmingham, Warrior-Tombigbee Devel. Assn., Jefferson County Community Chest; chmn. bd. trustees So. Research Inst.; trustee Thomas Alva Edison Found., Tuskegee U., Ala. Symphony Assn.; trustee Children's Hosp. Birmingham, pres. bd. trustees 1983-85; mem. Pres.'s Cabinet U. Ala.-Tuscaloosa; mem. Pres.'s Council U. Ala.-Birmingham; bd. visitors U. Ala. Sch. Commerce; mem. bus. adv. council Sch. Bus., U. Ala., Birmingham. Served with USNR, 1948; now lt. ret. Mem. Ala. Bar Assn., Birmingham Bar Assns., NAM (bd. dirs.), U.S. Council for Energy Awareness (bd. dirs.), Am. Nuclear Energy Coun. (chmn. bd. dirs.), Newcomen Soc. N.Am., Phi Beta Kappa, Kappa Alpha, Tau Beta Pi, Beta Gamma Sigma (hon.). Episcopalian. Clubs: Birmingham Country, Relay House, Downtown (gov.), Shoal Creek, The Club, Mountain Brook (gov.); Princeton of N.Y. Lodge: Rotary. Home: 3333 Dell Rd Birmingham AL 35223 Office: The So Company PO Box 1295 Birmingham AL 35201

FARLEY, PEGGY ANN, finance company executive; b. Phila., Mar. 12, 1947; d. Harry E. and Ruth (Lloyd) F.; m. W. Reid McIntyre, Dec. 31, 1985. AB, Barnard Coll., 1970; MA with high honors, Columbia U., 1972. Admissions officer Barnard Coll., N.Y.C., 1973-76; adminstr. Citibank NA, Athens, Greece, 1976-77; cons. Organization Resources Counselors, N.Y.C., 1977-78; sr. assoc. Morgan Stanley and Co., Inc., N.Y.C., 1978-84; sr. v.p., chief operating officer AMAS Securities, Inc., N.Y.C., 1984—, also bd. dirs.; bd. dirs. AMAS Group, London. Author: The Place Of The Yankee And Euro Bond Markets In A Financing Program For The People's Republic of China, 1982. Mem. Asia Soc., China Inst., Columbia U. Seminar on China-U.S. Bus. Republican. Presbyterian. Club: Metropolitan (N.Y.C.). Home: 515 E 72d St Apt F5 New York NY 10021 Office: AMAS Securities Inc 520 Madison Ave New York NY 10022

FARLEY, RUSSELL CLIFFORD, business development and financial executive; b. Eugene, Oreg., May 8, 1957; s. Russell William and Myrtle Ellene F.; m. Cathy Joanne Jones, Sept. 4,1981; children: Andrew Russell, Bryan Michael. BBA, Oral Roberts U., 1979; postgrad., Portland State U., 1979-80. CPA, Oreg. Staff acct. Davis Dunn & Co., Portland, Oreg., 1979-80; interim mgr. Arthur Anderson & Co., Portland, 1980-85; supr. fin. reporting Nerco, Inc., Portland, 1985-86; pres. Tri-Con, Inc., Portland, 1986—, CDS, Inc., Portland, 1988; chief fin. officer Williams Controls, Inc., Portland, 1989—; cons. Plaid Pantries, Inc., Portland, 1986-87. Bd. dirs. Youth for Christ, Portland, 1987; active Jr. Achievement, Portland, 1984-85. Mem. Planning Forum (bd. dirs. Portland chpt. 1986--), Oreg. State Soc. CPA's (v.p. legis. policy com. 1987-88), Am. Inst. CPA's. Republican. Office: Williams Controls Inc 14100 SW 72nd Ave Portland OR 97224

FARLEY, TERRENCE MICHAEL, banker; b. N.Y.C., Mar. 6, 1930; s. Terrence M. and Mary A. (Dundon) F.; m. Audrey E. Churchill, June 8, 1952; children: Elizabeth C., Peter, Matthew. B.B.A., Coll. City N.Y., 1955. With Brown Brothers Harriman & Co., N.Y.C., 1951—; ptnr. Brown Brothers Harriman & Co., 1972-83, mng. ptnr., 1983—; bd. trustees Atlantic Mut. Ins. Co.; bd. dirs. Centennial Ins. Co., Atlantic Reinsurance Co. Clubs: University, Links, India House (N.Y.C.); Echo Lake Country (Westfield, N.J.); Wianno (Osterville, Mass.). Home: 309 Hillside Ave Westfield NJ 07090 Office: Brown Bros Harriman & Co 59 Wall St New York NY 10005

FARLEY, THOMAS T., lawyer; b. Pueblo, Colo., Nov. 10, 1934; s. John Baron and Mary (Tancred) F.; m. Kathleen Maybelle Murphy, May 14, 1960; children: John, Michael, Kelly, Anne. BS, U. Santa Clara, 1956; LLB, U. Colo., 1959. Bar: Colo. 1959, U.S. Dist. Ct. Colo. 1959, U.S. Ct. Appeals (10th cir.) 1988. Dep. dist. atty. City of Pueblo, 1960-62; pvt. practice Pueblo, 1963-69; assoc. Phelps, Fonda & Hays, Pueblo, 1970-75, Petersen & Fonda, P.C., Pueblo, 1975—; bd. dirs. Pub. Svc. Co. Colo., Denver, United Bank Pueblo, United Bank Sunset. Minority leader Colo. Ho. of Reps., 1967-75; chmn. Colo. Wildlife Commn., 1975-79, Colo. Bd. Agr., 1979-87; bd. regents Santa Clara U., 1987—; bd. dirs. Sangre de Christo Arts and Conf. Ctr., Pueblo, 1988—; commr. Colo. State Fair. Recipient Disting. Service award U. So. Colo., 1987. Mem. ABA, Colo. Bar Assn., Mile High Kennel Club (bd. dirs. 1979—), Rotary. Democrat. Roman Catholic. Office: Petersen & Fonda PC 650 Thatcher Bldg Pueblo CO 81003

FARLEY, WILLIAM F., corporation executive; b. Pawtucket, R.I., Oct. 10, 1942. AB, Bowdoin Coll., 1964; JD, Boston Coll., 1969; postgrad., NYU Grad. Sch. Bus., 1969-72. Bar: Mass. 1969. Sales mgr. Crowell Collier and MacMillan, 1966; dir. mergers and acquisitions NL Industries, N.Y.C.; head corp. fin. dept. Chgo. office Lehman Bros., Inc., 1973-78; chmn., owner Farley Industries, Chgo., 1976—; owner Doehler Jarvis Products, So. Fastening Systems, Magnus Tool & Engring. Co., Fruit of the Loom, Acme Boot Co.; co-owner, dir. Chgo. White Sox Baseball Club. Bd. dirs. U.S.-USSR Trade and Econ. Council, Lyric Opera, Chgo., Goodman Theatre; trustee Bowdoin Coll.; mem. Ill. Gov.'s Sci. and High Tech. Commn.; presdl. aide Boston Coll. Mem. Mass. Bar Assn., ABA, Young Pres.'s Orgn., Am. Bus. Conf., Mid-Am. Com., Council on Fgn. Relations, Ill. Ambassadors (chmn.), Urban League (bus. adv. council). Clubs: Saddle and Cycle, Chicago. Office: Farley Industries Sears Tower Ste 6300 233 S Wacker Dr Chicago IL 60606

FARLOW, MICHAEL WILLIAM, financial executive; b. Richmond, Ind., Mar. 9, 1957; m. Judith Anne Beard, Oct. 2, 1981; children: Erin Elizabeth, Lindsay Meredith, Emily Mychal. BS in Acctg., Ball State U., 1980; MBA, U. Ill., 1989. Staff accountant Peat, marwick, Mitchell & Co., Decatur, Ill., 1980-81; sr. accountant Peat, Marwick, Mitchell & Co., Decatur, Ill., 1981-82; controller Heartland Fed. Savs. & Loan (formerly Mattoon Fed Savs. & Loan), Mattoon, Ill., 1982-84; v.p., chief fin. officer Heartland Fed. Savs. & Loan (formerly Mattoon Fed Savs. & Loan), Mattoon, 1984—; mem. Adv. Bd. Fed. Home Loan Bank of Chgo., 1987—. Chmn. Am. Cancer Soc., Mattoon, 1985-87; treas. bd. dirs. Cen. East Alcohol and Drug Council, Charleston, Ill., 1983-87. Mem. U.S. League Savs. and Loans, Fin. Mgr.'s Soc. Home: RR 2 Box 145 Charleston IL 61920 Office: Heartland Fed Savs & Loan 1520 Charleston Ave Mattoon IL 61938

FARNHAM, DAVID ALEXANDER, lawyer, banker; b. Washington, Sept. 7, 1946; s. Waller and Leslie (Thompson) F. B.A., Yale U., 1969; J.D., Columbia U., 1975. Bar: Md. 1977, Va. 1981, U.S. Dist. Ct. Md. 1979, U.S. Dist. Ct. (we. dist.) Va. 1981, U.S. Ct. Appeals (4th cir.) 1981. Asst. counsel Bankers Trust Co., N.Y.C., 1975-76; assoc. Weinberg & Green, Balt., 1976-80; legal compliance officer Dominion Bankshares Corp., Roanoke, Va., 1980-82, v.p., corp. counsel, 1983—. Author: (with Earl E. McGuire, Jr.) A Banker's Guide to IRAs, 1982. With U.S. Army, 1969-72. Mem. ABA, Md. Bar Assn., Va. State Bar, Roanoke City Bar Assn. Episcopalian. Club: Yale (N.Y.C.); Jefferson (Roanoke). Home: PO Box 8682 Roanoke VA 24014 Office: Dominion Bankshares Corp 213 S Jefferson St Roanoke VA 24011

FARNSWORTH, DAVID L., manufacturing company executive; b. McPherson, Kans., Aug. 31, 1937; s. Wayne E. and Dorothy (Mosing) F.; m. Patricia Ann Fanning, Sept. 14, 1963; children: Laura, Andrew, Katherine. BSBA, Emporia State Coll., 1959; MBA, Harvard U., 1970. Enlisted USN, 1959, advanced through grades to comdr., resigned, 1979; exec. v.p. adminstrn. Chief Industries, Grand Island, Nebr., 1979-81; pres. Sealrite Windows, Inc., Lincoln, Nebr., 1981-85; exec. v.p. mfg. ops. Indal Ltd., Weston, Ont., Can., 1986—; also bd. dirs. Indal Ltd. Mem. Can. Mfrs. Assn. (bd. dirs. Toronto chpt. 1988). Office: Indal Ltd, 4000 Weston Rd, Weston, ON Canada M9L 2W8

FARNSWORTH, JEFFREY EARL, paper products company executive; b. Allegan, Mich., Dec. 12, 1959; s. James Stanley and Marilyn Joan (Porter) F.; m. Tracy Jean Eastman, May 14, 1988. BS in Pulp and Paper Engring., Western Mich. U., 1983; postgrad., Memphis State U., 1988—. Process engr. Boise Cascade Corp., DeRidder, La., 1983-85, prodn. engr., 1985-86, prodn. supr., 1986-87; prodn. supr. Kimberly Clark Corp., Memphis, 1987-88, prodn. team leader, 1988—. Mem. TAPPI, Phi Eta Sigma. Republican. Methodist. Home: 7774 Grouse Hollow Cove Cordova TN 38118 Office: Kimberly Clark Corp 400 Mahannah Ave Memphis TN 38107

FARNSWORTH, PHILIP RICHESON, lawyer, broadcasting and publishing executive; b. New Orleans, Dec. 30, 1941; s. Philip R. and Jane (Taylor) F. BA, Washington and Lee U., 1964; JD, Tulane U., 1967; LLM, NYU, 1968. Bar: La. 1967, D.C. 1972, N.Y. 1980. Assoc. Phelps, Dunbar, Marks, Claverie & Sims, New Orleans, 1968-69; atty. Securities and Exchange Commn., Washington, 1969-77; asst. sec. ABC, Inc., N.Y.C., 1977-86; asst. sec. Capital Cities/ABC, Inc., N.Y.C., 1986-88, sec., 1988—. Served with USCGR, 1963-69. Mem. Am. Soc. Corp. Secs., Stockholder Relations Soc. N.Y., ABA, Univ. Club. Republican. Episcopalian. Office: Capital Cities/ABC Inc 77 W 66th St New York NY 10023

FAROLE, GEORGE P., country club executive; b. Yonkers, N.Y., May 25, 1955; s. George and Veronica (Davenport) F.; m. Kathleen M. Villa, Jan. 20, 1974; 1 child, Michael Anthony. B in Bus., Pace U., 1978; grad., Am. Inst. Banking, 1979; student in ins. banking, LaSalle Acad., Chgo., 1979-82. Asst. br. mgr., officer in charge of loans Marine Midland Bank, N.Y.C., 1973-82; acct. Stouffer's Inn of Westchester, Harrison, N.Y., 1982-84; banquet officer Holiday Inn, Elmsford, N.Y., 1984-85; gen. mgr., officer in charge Williow Ridge Country Club, Harrison, 1985—. Mem. Met. Club. Mgrs. Assn., Club Mgrs. Assn. Am., Internat. Restaurant Assn., Met. Golf Assn., U.S. Golf Assn. Republican. Methodist. Club: Hilltop Swimming and Tennis (Yonkers) (cons. 1987—). Home: 148 Truman Ave Yonkers NY 10703-1022 Office: Willow Ridge Country Club North St Harrison NY 10528

FARQUHAR, GERALD BLAKE, chemical company executive; b. Washington, Aug. 8, 1949; s. Frank B. and Mary Susan (Cardwell) F. BA in Econs., Xavier U., 1972. Sales rep. Shannon & Lucks Real Estate Co., Clinton, Md., 1973-74, Bogley Real Estate, Bethesda, Md., 1974-75; mng. dir. Dunn & Ross Assocs., LaPlata, Md., 1975-76; ter. sales rep. Shell Oil Co., Columbia, Md., 1977-83; sr. instr. Shell Oil Co., Atlanta, 1984—; pres., chief exec. officer Atlantex Chems., Qualitex of Atlanta subs. Atlantex Corp., Atlanta, 1987—; also bd. dirs. Fikes Hunt Chem. Co., Atlanta; mng. dir. Atlanta and Nashville Group, 1988—; pres., chief exec. officer Hazwaste Inc., Hazwaste Transport & Trading Ltd., and Hazwaste Chem. Bank, Ltd. subs. Atlanta and Nashville Investment Group. Republican. Home: 1723 Jody Dr Marietta GA 30066 Office: Fikes Hunt Chem Co 1800 Water Pl Ste 280 Atlanta GA 30339

FARQUHAR, KAREN LEE, business forms company executive, consultant; b. Warwick, N.Y., May 27, 1958; d. Wesley Thomas and Margaret Anne (Storms) Kervatt; m. David W. Farquhar, July 17, 1982; 1 child, Lauren Nichole. Assoc. Sci., Roger Williams Coll., 1978, B.S. cum laude, 1980. Office mgr. Price-Rite Printing Co., Dover, N.J., summer 1975-76; cons. SBA, Bristol, R.I., 1978-80; account exec. P.M. Press Inc., Dallas, 1980—, sales trainer, 1984-85; v.p. KDF Bus. Forms Inc., Dallas, Tex., 1984—. Printer, Tex. Aux. Charity Auction Orgn., Dallas, 1985, Crescent Gala, Dallas, 1986. Recipient various awards Clampitt Paper Co., Dallas, 1982, P.M. Press Inc., 1983-86, 87, Mead Paper Co., 1985. Mem. Printing Industry in Am., Internat. Assn. Bus. Communicators, Nat. Bus. Forms Assn. Republican. Baptist. Avocations: piano; aerobics. Home: 429 Dillard Ln Coppell TX 75019

FARQUHAR, RICHARD ALLEN, broadcast engineer; b. Delaware, Ohio, Feb. 8, 1939; s. Kenneth Charles and Doris Irene (Marston) F.; m. Nancy Jean Tomlinson, Feb. 6, 1960; children: Monica Lee, Kenneth Richard. Student, Ohio State U., 1966-67. Cert. profl. broadcast engr., Soc. Motion Engrs. Enlisted USN, 1956, resigned, 1966; engr. Sta. WOSU-TV, Ohio State U., Columbus, 1966-67; engring. supr. Sta. WBNS-TV, Columbus, 1967-82; v.p. engring. SOS Prodns., Inc., Columbus, 1982—; engring. mgr. Video Indiana WTHR-TV, Indpls., 1984; corp. v.p. TPC Communications Inc., Pitts., 1984; Active nat. cert. com. Soc. Broadcast Engrs., 1984—. Recipient Emmy award for best achievement in videotape editing, 1973. Mem. Soc. Broadcast Engrs. (sec./treas. Columbus chpt. 1980-82, v.p. Indpls. chpt. 1984, nat. cert. com. 1984—, nat. sec. 1987-88), Soc. Motion Pictures and TV Engrs. (active), IEEE (sr.), Internat. Teleprodn. Soc. (engring. com.). Republican. Home: 4620 Timothy Ln Canal Winchester OH 43110 Office: SOS Prodns Inc 753 Harmon Ave Columbus OH 43223

FARR, NORMAN NELSON, oil company executive; b. N.Y.C., Oct. 30, 1928; s. Louis Elie and Leonore Sandra (Jaffee) F.; m. Akiko Yokoyama, Nov. 20, 1984. BS in Chemistry cum laude, Columbia U., 1951; postgrad., NYU, 1961-64. Asst. chief chemist Lucius Pitkin Inc., N.Y.C., 1951-53; sr. petroleum engr. Creole Petroleum (Exxon), Venezuela, 1953-61; planning mgr. Mobil Latin Am., N.Y.C., 1961-66; mktg. planning mgr. Mobil Internat., N.Y.C., 1966-69; plans and programs mgr. Mobil Mediterranean and Mobil South, Paris and N.Y.C., 1969-73; exec. v.p. Mobil Sekiyu K.K., Tokyo, 1973-76; chmn., pres. Mobil Oil Philippines/Micronesia, Manila, 1976-79; v.p. far east Mobil South Inc., N.Y.C., 1979-83; pres. Mobil Land Devel. Corp., N.Y.C., 1983-87; v.p. Mobil Oil Corp., Fairfax, Va., 1987—. Bd. dirs. Reston, Va., 1985-87. With USN, 1946-48. Mem. Urban Land Inst. (assoc.). Jewish. Office: Mobil Oil Corp 3225 Gallows Rd Rm FP-020 Fairfax VA 22037

FARRALL, ROBERT ARTHUR, electronics company executive; b. Evanston, Ill., July 2, 1932; s. Arthur William and Luella (Buck) F.; B.S. in Physics, Mich. State U., 1954; m. Nancy Mary Georgi, Dec. 22, 1955; children—John Robert, George William. Mgr. photometric engring. Gen. Electric Co., Lynn, Mass., 1954-63; exec. v.p. Clairex Corp., Mt. Vernon, N.Y., 1963-69, pres., 1969—; dir. Clairex Electronics of PR, N-Con Systems Corp. Bd. dirs. Mt. Vernon United Fund; trustee Mystic Seaport Mus. Served with AUS, 1954-56. Mem. Am. Phys. Soc., Soc. Photog. Scientists and Engrs., Rye Hist. Soc. (pres. 1981-82), Sigma Pi Sigma, Delta Upsilon. Club: Am. Yacht (Rye, N.Y.). Patentee photoconductive cell circuits. Home: 69 Hewlett Ave Rye NY 10580 Office: 560 S 3d Ave Mount Vernon NY 10550

FARRAR, DONALD KEITH, financial executive; b. Indio, Calif., May 18, 1938; s. Keith and Sarah S. (Turner) F.; m. Jo Ann Puttler, Dec. 16, 1961; children: Daniel K., Donald S., Douglas S., Kimberly. BSBA, U. So. Calif., 1960; MBA, Harvard U., 1965. With planning div. Paul Revere Life Ins. Co., Worcester, Mass., 1965, budget supr., 1966, asst. to pres., 1967, asst. sec., 1968-73, v.p. investment, 1969-73; v.p. planning Avco Corp., Greenwich, Conn., 1973-74, sr. v.p., chief acct. officer, 1975-77, exec. v.p., 1978-81, pres., 1981-85, also bd. dirs.; sr. exec. v.p., pres. Avco Ops. Textron Inc., Providence, R.I., 1985—, sr. exec. v.p. ops.; also bd. dirs. Textron Inc., Providence, RI. Mem. fin. com. Hahnemann Hosp., Worcester, 1969-73. Served with USNR, 1960-63. Home: 8 Bagy Wrinkle Cove Warren RI 02885 Office: Textron Inc 40 Westminster St Providence RI 02903

FARRAR, JAMES PAUL, electronics company official; b. Albuquerque, May 29, 1937; s. Clyde William and Lina Mae (Hudson) F.; m. Marilyn Austa Johnson, June 21, 1958; children: Paul Frederick, Jamie Austa, Kimberly Sue. BSEE, U. N.Mex., 1960; MBA, Pepperdine U., 1981; postgrad. in bus. adminstrn., Nova U., 1988—. Design engr. E.G. & G., Inc., Las Vegas, 1960-63; design, test engr. Govt. Electronics Group Motorola, Inc., Scottsdale, Ariz., 1963-66; quality assurance ops. mgr. Govt. Electronics Group, Scottsdale, Ariz., 1984—; engring. mgr. Collins Radio Co., Dallas, 1966-68; NIH spl. research fellow U. Tex. Med. Sch., 1968-70; program mgr. TRW Colo. Elecronics Co., Colorado Springs, 1970-74; automatic test equipment program mgr. Ford Aerospace & Communications Co., Colorado Spirngs, 1974-76, system integration mgr., Palo Alto, Calif., 1976-79; dir. prodn. support GenRad, Ind., Phoenix, 1979-84; mem. adj. facuty dept. fin., mgmt. and quantatative methods U. Phoenix, 1981—; bus. cons., Phoenix, 1983—. Mem. MAricopa County Tech. Adv. Council, 1982-84. With U.S. Army, 1955-63. Mem. Am. Electronics Assn., Acad. Mgmt. Republican. Roman Catholic. Home: 3634 E Cathedral Rock Dr Phoenix AZ 85044 Office: 8201 E McDowell Rd Scottsdale AZ 85252

FARRAR, MARCIA GERTRUDE, municipal center foundation executive; b. Phila., Nov. 1, 1941; d. Leon L. and Sylvia (Silcoff) Rhinehart; m. Wayne H. Farrar, Dec. 26, 1959; children: Crystal L., David A. BA, U. Mass., 1979. Program dir. People Bridge Action, Athol, Mass., 1976-79; exec. dir. Piedmont Neighborhood Ctr., Worcester, Mass., 1979-82; alumni dir. Cen. New Eng. Coll., Worcester, 1982-83; exec. dir. Martin Luther King Ctr., Newport, R.I., 1983—. V.p. Office for Children, Gardner, Mass., 1977-79; chairperson Worcester Neighborhood Assn., 1977-79; vice chairperson Worcester Tchr. Corps, 1977-79; mem. This is Worcester task force, 1977-79; pres. Newport County Coun. Community Svcs., 1985—; mem. food shelter bd. State of R.I., mem. Gov.'s Commn. on Handicapped; active Dem. gubernatorial campaign, Newport, 1985—. Recipient Excellence award United Way, 1987, Outstanding Svc. award Newport County Coun. Community Svcs., 1988. Methodist. Home: 45 Malbone Rd Newport RI 02840 Office: Martin Luther King Ctr 20 W Broadway Newport RI 02840

FARRAR, PAULINE ELIZABETH, accountant, real estate broker; b. Madison, Wis., July 2, 1928; d. William Charles and Mary Anna (Killalley) Selmer; m. James Walter Byers, Aug. 15, 1950 (dec. June 1972); children: Marvin Lee, Marjorie Sue; m. Robert Bascom Farrar, Apr. 14, 1974; stepchildren: Katrinka Jo Farrar Sandahl, Jon Randle Farrar. Student, U. Wis., 1946-49, U. Houston, 1956-57. Acct. Sterling Hogan, Houston, 1951-54, Lester Prokop, Houston, 1959-64, Holland Mortgage Co., Houston, 1964-68, Jetero Bldg Corp., Houston, 1968-71; real estate assoc. Mills Paulea Realtors, Houston, 1976-80, ERA, Nelson & Assocs., Missouri City, Tex., 1980-81; owner, broker Property-Wise Realty, Sugar Land, Tex., 1981—; tax assesor, collector Sequoia Utility Dist., Houston, 1969-71. Leader Girl Scouts U.S.A., Houston, 1962-72; organizer, coordinator ladies program Stafford (Tex.) Ch. of Christ, 1978-81. Mem. Tex. Assn. Realtors (bd. dirs. 1986-87, v.p. 1986-87), Cert. Real Estate Brokers (v.p. Tex. chpt., sec.-treas. 1988-89), Ft. Bend County Bd. Realtors (pres. 1987—), Women's Council of Realtors (founding chmn. Ft. Bend/SW Houston chpt. 1986, pres. 1988), Nat. Realtors Inst. (cert. residential specialist, cert. real estate broker, grad. realtors inst., Leadership Tng. Grad.), Women's Coun. Realtors. Office: Property-Wise Realty 6730 Hwy 6 Sugar Land TX 77478

FARRELL, DAVID COAKLEY, department store executive; b. Chgo., June 14, 1933; s. Daniel A. and Anne D. (O'Malley) F.; m. Betty J. Ross, July 9, 1955; children: Mark, Lisa, David. B.A., Antioch Coll., Yellow Springs, Ohio, 1956. Asst. buyer, buyer, br. store gen. mgr., mdse. mgr. Kaufmann's, Pitts., 1956-66, v.p., gen. mdse. mgr., 1966-69, pres., 1969-74; v.p. May Dept. Stores Co., St. Louis, 1969-75, dir., 1974—, chief operating officer, 1975-79, pres., 1975-85, chief exec. officer, 1979—, chmn., 1985—; dir. 1st Nat. Bank, St. Louis. Bd. dirs. St. Louis Symphony Soc., St. Louis Area council Boy Scouts Am., Arts and Edn. Fund Greater St. Louis; trustee Com. for Econ. Devel., St. Louis Children's Hosp., Washington U., St. Louis; active Salvation Army; mem. Bus. Com. for Arts, Civic Progress. Mem. Nat. Retail Mchts. Assn. (dir.). Roman Catholic. Clubs: University (N.Y.C.); Duquesne (Pitts.); Bogey (St. Louis), Mo. Athletic (St. Louis), Noonday (St. Louis), St. Louis (St. Louis), St. Louis Country (St. Louis). Office: The May Dept Stores Co 611 Olive St Saint Louis MO 63101 *

FARRELL, EDGAR HENRY, lawyer, building components manufacturing executive; b. N.Y.C., Aug. 31, 1924; s. Edgar Henry and Lillian Sarah (Lancaster) F.; student Tex. A&M U., 1943, Stanford U., 1943-45, George Washington U. Law Sch., 1948-49; J.D., U. Md., 1950; postgrad., Harvard U. Bus. Sch., 1965; m. Mary Louise Whelan, May 3, 1952; children—Brooke Larkin Cragan, Elizabeth Lancaster, Kimberley Hopkins. Exec. sales asst. A.C. Gilbert Co., N.Y.C., 1950; asst. legal counsel U.S. Senate Crime Com., 1951; zone mgr. Life Mag., N.Y.C., 1951-52; account exec. Time Mag., N.Y.C., 1952-55, Phila., 1955-59, Detroit, 1959-62, nat. automotive sales mgr., Detroit, 1962-64, div. sales mgr., 1964-68, world automotive products sales mgr., 1968; regional mgr. communications/research Machines, Inc., Mich., Ohio, 1968; central advt. dir. Petersen Pub. Co., Detroit, 1969; chief exec., officer Internat. Concrete Bldg. Group, London, 1974-79; asst. to pres. Dillon Co., Akron, Ohio, 1979-80; pres. and chief exec. officer Bldg. Components Group, Akron, 1980—; pres. Motorhome Holidays Internat., U.S. Motorhome Corp., pres. BEK Press, Camp Am., Inc.; housing cons. Saudi Arabia, Nigeria, Sri Lanka. Publicity chmn. Youth for Eisenhower Com., N.Y.C., 1952; trustee Baldwin Library, Birmingham, Mich., 1962-65. Served to lt. U.S. Army, 1945-46; PTO. Recipient Low Cost Housing award Ministry of Housing, Sri Lanka, 1979. Mem. Am. Mktg. Assn., Nat. Assn. Home Builders, Phi Delta Theta, Gamma Eta Gamma, Phi Alpha Sigma. Republican. Episcopalian. Author: Computer Center Construction, 1984. Home and Office: 1 Woodbury Hill Woodbury CT 06798

FARRELL, JOSEPH CHRISTOPHER, mining company executive; b. Boston, Sept. 27, 1935; s. Joseph C. and Ellen G. (Luttrell) F.; m. Barbara Grace Mullaney, Sept. 27, 1958; children—Christopher, Michael, John. BSEE, Northeastern U., 1958; MBA, Harvard U., 1963. Lic. pvt. pilot. Asst. treas. Freeport Indonesia, N.Y.C., 1968-72; treas. Queensland Nickel, Townsville, Australia, 1972-75; v.p. Freeport Minerals, N.Y.C., 1975-78; pres. Freeport Gold, Elko, Nev., 1978-84; exec. v.p., dir. Pittston Co., Greenwich, Conn., 1984—; bd. dirs. The Pittston Co., Greenwhich, Brink's Inc., Darien, Conn., Burlington Air Express, Irvine, Calif., Brink's Home Security, chmn., 1987—. Mem. Nev. Commn. on Mining and Natural Resources, 1982-84. Lt. comdr. USN, 1958-68. Mem. Am. Inst. Mining Engrs., Nev. Mining Assn. (v.p. 1980-84), Am. Mining Congress (western gov. 1982-84), Nat. Coal Council, World Coal Inst. (bd. dirs.). Clubs: Harvard (N.Y.C.); Burning Tree (Greenwich). Lodge: Rotary. Office: Pittston Co 1 Pickwick Pla Greenwich CT 06830

FARRELL, JUNE MARTINICK, public relations executive; b. New Brunswick, N.J., June 30, 1940; d. Ivan and Mary (Tomkovich) M.; B.S. in Journalism, Ohio U., 1962; M.S. in Public Relations, Am. U., Washington, 1977; m. Duncan G. Farrell, July 31, 1971. Public relations asst. Corning Glass Works, N.Y.C., 1963-65; assoc. beauty editor Good Housekeeping mag., N.Y.C., 1966; public relations specialist Gt. Am. Ins. Co., N.Y.C., 1967-68; assoc. editor Ea. Airlines, N.Y.C., 1968-82, regional public relations mgr., Washington, 1976-82; public relations dir. Nat. Captioning Inst., Falls Church, Va., 1982-83; dir. pub. rels. programs Marriott Corp., 1984—; staff cons. Office of Public Liaison, White House, 1981-82. Creator, condr. spl. career awareness program for inner city youth, Washington, 1979-80; mem. public relations com. Jr. Achievement, 1979; motivational counselor for youth Nat. Alliance of Businessmen, 1979; bd. dirs. Am. Travel Mktg. Services; trustee Nat. Hosp. Orthopedics and Rehab., 1984—. Mem. Soc. Am. Travel Writers (mem. pub. relations com.), Am. Soc. Travel Agts., Travel Industry Assn. Am. (nat. conf. planning com., pub. relations com.), Women in Communication, Phi Mu. Republican. Clubs: Zonta, Internat. Aviation. Home: 6630 Lybrook Ct Bethesda MD 20817 Office: Marriot Hotels/Resorts One Marriott Dr Washington DC 20058

FARRELL, THOMAS JOSEPH, insurance company executive; b. Butte, Mont., June 10, 1926; s. Bartholomew J. and Lavina H. (Collins) F.; m. Evelyn Irene Southam, July 29, 1951; children: Brien J., Susan M., Leslie A., Jerome T. Student U. San Francisco, 1949. CLU. Ptnr. Affiliated-Gen. Ins. Adjusters, Santa Rosa, Calif., 1949-54; agt. Lincoln Nat. Life Ins. Co., Santa Rosa, 1954-57, supr., 1957-59, gen. agt., 1959-74; pres. Thomas J. Farrell & Assos., 1974-76, 7 Flags Ins. Mktg. Corp., 1976-81, Farrell-Dranginis & Assocs., 1981—; pres., bd. dirs. Lincoln Nat. Bank, Santa Rosa, San Rafael. Pres. Redwood Empire Estate Planning Council, 1981-82, Sonoma County Council for Retarded Children, 1956—, City Santa Rosa Traffic and Parking Commn., 1963; del. Calif. State Conf. Small Bus., 1980; mem. Santa Rosa City Schs. Compensatory Edn. Adv. Bd.; bd. dirs. Santa Rosa City Schs. Consumer Edn. Adv. Bd.; pres., nat. dir. United Cerebral Palsy Assn., 1954-55; nat. coordinator C. of C.-Rotary Symposia on Employment of People with Disabilities, 1985—; v.p. Vigil Light, Inc.; chmn. bd. dirs. Nat. Barrier Awareness for People with Disabilities Found.;ound., Inc.; mem. Pres.'s Com. on Mental Retardation, 1982-86; chmn. Santa Rosa Community Relations Com., 1973-76; pres. Sonoma County Young Reps., 1953; past bd. dirs. Sonoma County Fair and Expn., Inc.; bd. dirs. Sonoma County Family Service Agy., Eldridge Found., North Bay Regional Ctr. for Developmentally Disabled; trustee Sonoma State Hosp. for Mentally Retarded. Recipient cert. Nat. Assn. Retarded Children, 1962, Region 9 U.S. HHS Community Service award, 1985, Sonoma County Vendor's Human Service award, 1986, Individual Achievement award Community Affirmative Action Forum of Sonoma County, 1986. Mem. Nat. Assn. Life Underwriters, Redwood Empire Assn. CLU's (pres. 1974—), Japanese-Am. Citizens League, Jaycees (Outstanding Young Man of Year 1961, v.p. 1955), Santa Rosa C. of C. (bd. dirs. 1974-75), Calif. PTA (hon. life). Lodge: Rotary. Home: 963 Wyoming Dr Santa Rosa CA 95405 Office: Farrell Dranginis & Assoc 1160 N Dutton Ave Suite 160 Santa Rosa CA 95401

FARRELL, WILLIAM EDGAR, sales executive, infosystems specialist; b. Jeanette, Pa., Mar. 13, 1937; s. Arthur Richard and Lelia (Ryder) F.; m. Sara Lynnette Swing, Aug. 20, 1960; children: Wendy J., Tracy L., Rebecca J. BS in Edn., Pa. State U., 1959. Location mgr. IBM Corp., Dover, Del., 1969-72; corp. lobbyist IBM Corp., Washington, 1972-74, planning cons., 1974-78, nat. mktg. mgr., 1978-80, exec. asst., 1980-81; account exec. IBM Corp., Denver, 1981-87, policy exec., 1987—; chief fin. officer Wide Horizon, Inc., Denver, 1987—; pres. Exec. Mgmt. Cons., 1987—. Founding mem. River Falls Community Assn., Potomac, Md., 1975; first reader First Ch. of Christ Scientist Chevy Chase, Md., 1976-80. Recipient Outstanding Contbn. award IBM Corp., 1968. Republican. Home: 6063 S Beeler St Englewood CO 80111 Office: IBM Corp 4700 S Syracuse Pkwy Denver CO 80237

FARRELL, WILLIAM MARSHALL, manufacturing executive; b. St. Louis, Apr. 29, 1943; s. William M. and Charleen (Power) F.; m. Nancy Weems, June 26, 1976; children: Mary Allison, Michael Patrick. BS in Metall. Engring., U. Mo., Rolla, 1965; MS in Mgmt., MIT, 1970. Nuclear fuel specialist to project mgr. Naval Nuclear Fuel div. Babcock & Wilcox, Lynchburg, Va., 1966-76; on spl. assignment Babcock Brown Boveri, Mannheim, Fed. Rep. Germany, 1976-78; prodn. svcs. mgr. to plant mgr. Fossil Power Generation div. Babcock & Wilcox, Canton, Ohio and West Point, Miss., 1978-82; mgr. contracts to mgr. naval nuclear components Fossil Power Generation div. Babcock & Wilcox, Barberton, Ohio, 1982-86; gen. mgr. ERI div. Babcock & Wilcox, Indpls., 1987-88; gen. mgr. Nuclear Equipment div. Babcock & Wilcox, Barberton, Ohio, 1988-89, v.p., gen. mgr., 1989—. Mem. Am. Def. Preparedness Assn., Navy League. Roman Catholic. Office: Babcock & Wilcox Nuclear Equipment Div 91 Stirling Ave Barberton OH 44718

FARRIES, JOHN KEITH, petroleum engineering company executive; b. Cardston, Alta., Can., July 9, 1930; s. John Mathew and Gladys Helen (Adams); B.S. in Petroleum Engring., U. Okla., 1955; postgrad. Banff Sch. of Advanced Mgmt., 1963; m. Donna Margaret Lloyd, Dec. 30, 1960; children—Gregory, Bradley, Kent. Engr., dist. engr., joint interest supt. Pan Am. Petroleum Corp., Calgary, Edmonton, Tulsa, Drayton Valley, 1955-65; pres. Tamarack Petroleums Ltd., Calgary, Alta., 1965-70, Canadian Well Services & Tank Co. Ltd., Calgary, 1968-70, Farries Engring. Ltd., 1970—, Wave Internat. Engring., Inc., Israel, 1975-88, Westridge Petroleum Corp, 1985—, Muskeg Oilfield Services, 1987—; v.p. Bobby Burns Petroleum Ltd., 1983-88; dir. Westgrowth Petroleums. Mem. AIME, Canadian Inst. Mining and Metallurgy (dir. petroleum soc. 1966-68), Assn. Profl. Engrs. of Alta., B.C. and Sask., Canadian Assn. of Drilling Engrs. (pres. 1977-78). Clubs: Calgary Petroleum, Willow Park Golf and Country. Past pub. chmn. Jour. Canadian Petroleum Tech. Home: 10819 Willowglen Pl, Calgary, AB Canada T2J 1R8

FARRIMOND, GEORGE FRANCIS, JR., business educator; b. Peerless, Utah, Sept. 23, 1932; s. George Francis Sr. and Ruth (Howard) F.; m. Polly Ann Fowler, Mar. 21, 1988; children: George Kenneth, Ronald Kay, Carrie Frances, Holly Jean. BS, U. Utah, 1955; MBA, U. Mo., 1968; postgrad., Portland State U., 1979—. Cert. profl. contracts mgr. Enlisted USAF, 1955, advanced through grades to lt. col., 1971; master navigator USAF, various locations, 1955-71; flight commdr. 360th tactical elec. war squadron USAF, Saigon, Socialist Republic of Vietnam, 1971-72; chief procurement ops. USAF, Wright-Patterson AFB, Ohio, 1972-73, chief pricing ops. div., 1973-76; retired USAF, 1976; asst. prof. bus. So. Oreg. State Coll., Ashland, 1976-82, assoc. prof., 1982—; cons. small bus., Jackson County, Oreg., 1976-88; cons. Japanese mgmt., Jackson County, 1981-88. Author: (computer program) Spanish Verb Conjugation, 1980, (workbook) Pricing Techniques, 1983. Chmn. Wright-Patterson AFB div United Fund, 1973-76; little league coach various teams, Ark. and Mo., 1963-71; Sunday Sch. tchr. Ch. of Latter-day Saints, various states. Decorated Disting. Flying Cross, 5 Air medals; Minuteman Ednl. scholar Air Force Inst. Tech., 1964, Education with Industry scholar Air Force Inst. Tech., 1970. Mem. Am. Prodn. and Inventory Control Soc. (v.p. edn. com. 1982-84), Cascade Systems Soc., Air Force Soc., Soc. Japanese Studies, Beta Gamma Sigma. Republican. Home: PO Box 805 Ashland OR 97520-0027 Office: So Oreg State Coll Sch Bus 1250 Siskiyou Blvd Ashland OR 97520

FARRINGTON, JERRY S., utility holding company executive; b. Burkburnett, Tex., 1934. B.B.A., North Tex. State U., 1955, M.B.A., 1958. With Tex. Electric Service Co., 1957-60; v.p. Tex. Utilities Co. (parent co.), Dallas, 1970-76; pres. Dallas Power & Light Co., 1976-83, Tex. Utilities Co. (parent co.), Dallas, 1983—; chmn., chief exec. officer Tex. Utilities Co., Dallas, 1987—; also chmn., pres., chief exec. officer Tex. Utilities Fuel Co., Dallas. Office: Tex Utilities Co 2001 Bryan Tower Dallas TX 75201 *

FARRINGTON, WILLIAM BENFORD, investment analyst; b. N.Y.C., Mar. 10, 1921; s. Harold Phillips and Edith C. (Aitken) F.; B.C.E., Cornell U., 1947, M.S., 1949; Ph.D., Mass. Inst. Tech., 1953; m. Frances A. Garratt, 1949 (div. 1955); children: William Benford, Phyllis Ashley, Timothy Colfax; m. Gertrude E. Eby, Jan. 3, 1979. Radio engr. Naval Research Labs., 1942-43; dir. Read Standard Corp., 1948-55; plant engr. Hope's Windows, Inc., 1950-51; instr. geology, geophysics U. Mass., 1953-54; research geophysicist Humble Oil & Refining Co., 1954-56; lectr. U. Houston, 1955-56; sr. investment analyst Continental Research Corp., N.Y.C., 1956-61; pres., dir. Farrington Engring. Corp., 1958-67; partner Farrington & Light Assos., Laguna Beach, Calif., 1967-82, Farrington Assocs., 1982—; v.p. Empire Resources Corp., 1961-62; asst. v.p. Empire Trust Co., 1962-64; dir. Commonwealth Gas Corp., N.Y.C.; sci. dir. Select Com. on Govt. Research, U.S. Ho. of Reps., 1964-65; lectr. U. Calif. at Los Angeles, 1968-72; sr. cons. Trident Engring. Assos., Annapolis, Md., 1965—; corporate asso. Technology Assos. So. Calif., 1971—. Chmn. crusade Am. Cancer Soc., Jamestown, N.Y., 1951. Chartered fin. analyst; registered geologist, Calif. Fellow AAAS, Fin. Analysts Fedn.; mem. Am. Assn. Petroleum Geologists, Am. Inst. Aeros. and Aeronautics, Geol. Soc. Am., Los Angeles Soc. Fin. Analysts, Sigma Xi. Episcolalian. Author articles in field. Home: 1565 Skyline Dr Laguna Beach CA 92651

FARRIOR, J. REX, JR., lawyer; b. Tampa, Fla., June 5, 1927; s. J. Rex and Lera Spotswood (Finley) F.; m. Mary Lee Nunnally, May 30, 1958; children—J. Rex III, Preston Lee, Hugh Nunnally, Robert Pendleton. Student Auburn U., 1945-46; B.S. in Bus. Adminstrn., U. Fla., 1949, J.D., 1951. Bar: Fla. 1951. Assoc. Shackleford, Farrior, Stallings & Evans, P.A. and predecessors, Tampa, Fla., 1951-55, ptnr., 1955—, sr. ptnr., past pres., also bd. dirs.; permanent guest lectr. U. Fla., Coll. Engring.; lectr. U. Fla., Stetson U.; mem. Fed. Jud. Nominating Comm., 1980—. Pres. Pres. Round Table of Tampa, 1965. Served with USNR, World War II. Named to Hall of Fame, U. Fla., 1951. Fellow Am. Coll. Probate Counsel, Fellows of ABA; mem. ABA (ho. of dels. 1976-81), Fla. Bar (pres. Fla. young lawyers sect. 1958, pres. 1975-76, Most Outstanding Local Bar Pres. 1977), Hillsborough County Bar Assn. (pres. 1966), Acad. Fla. Trial Lawyers, Am. Judicature Soc., Inter-Am. Bar Assn., Am. Counsel Assn. (pres. 1983-84), Assn. Trial Lawyers Am., Greater Tampa C. of C. (bd. govs.), Phi Delta Phi, Kappa Alpha Alumni Assn. (pres. 1957). Episcopalian. Clubs: Rotary, Sertoma (founder club 1952, pres. club 1964) Tampa), Masons, Shriners. Office: PO Box 3324 Tampa FL 33601

FARRIS, JOHN LEO, financial planner; b. Gastonia, N.C., June 4, 1947; s. John Leo and Lillian (Moses) F.; m. Julia Eskridge Farris, Sept. 22, 1979; 1 child, John. BA, Belmont Abbey, Belmont, N.C., 1968; MA, Appalachian State U., 1970; cert., Coll. Fin. Planning, Denver, 1982. Purchasing officer Edgecombe Gen. Hosp., Tarboro, N.C., 1975-79; fin. planner E.F. Hutton & Co., Charlotte, N.C., 1980-84; fin. planner, nat. portfolio mgr. Paine Weber, Inc., Charlotte, 1984—; investment advisor Cedars Investment Corp., Charlotte, 1987—; asst. prof. U. N.C., Chapel Hill, 1976. 1st lt. U.S. Army, 1971-75. Mem. Inst. Cert. Fin. Planners, Tarboro Martial Arts Assn. (founder), Shriners, KC. Roman Catholic. Home: 1621 Nottingham Dr Gastonia NC 28054 Office: Paine Webber Inc One NCNB Pla Ste 3400 Charlotte NC 28280

FARRIS, LOUIS ANTHONY, JR., banker; b. Palestine, Tex., Feb. 20, 1936; s. Louis Anthony and Fredericka M. F.; BS, So. Methodist U., 1958; children—Louis Anthony, Angela. Ptnr. Murchison Bros., Dallas, 1974—, pres. Empire Fin. Corp., 1987—; bd. dir. Calco Corp.Mem. So. Methodist U. Mustang Club (bd. dir.), Hella Temple Club, Masons. Episcopalian. Home: 5 Kelvingate Ct Dallas TX 75225 Office: Empire Fin Corp 8215 W Cheater Dallas TX 75225

FARRIS, MARC, entrepreneur, real estate developer; b. Stillwater, Okla., Nov. 19, 1947; s. Gus and Barbara (Rains) F.; m. Beryl Bergquist, Apr. 3, 1971; children: Kristin, Ariana. BS, U.S. Naval Acad., 1970; MBA in Fin., Ga. State U., 1978. Cert. real estate broker, Ga. Commd. ensign USN, 1970; advanced through grades to comdr. USNR, 1974—; pres. Farris Co., Atlanta, 1985—; chmn. bd. dirs. Law Offices, Ltd., Atlanta; bd. dirs. MBF, Ltd., Atlanta, B & V Inc., Atlanta; pres. LOL Offices Incubator Space for Bus. Pres. U.S. Naval Alumni Assn. Ga., Atlanta, 1983, High Mus. Decorative Arts Acquistions Trust, Atlanta, 1985-86; bd. dirs. Nexus Arts Ctr.; mem. High Mus. Friends Arts, Atlanta, 1982-86, YMCA, Atlanta, 1984-88. Served to cmdr. USNR, 1966—. Mem. Naval Res. Assn. (pres. Atlanta chpt. 1987-88, Navy Ball award 1982), Indsl. Devel. Research Found. (bd. dirs., profl. award 1981), Navy League (bd. dirs. nat. chpt.). Club: Druid Hills Golf (Atlanta). Office: Farris Co 55 Marietta St Suite 1401 Atlanta GA 30303

FARRIS, TRUEMAN EARL, JR., retired newspaper editor; b. Sedalia, Mo., June 2, 1926; s. Trueman Earl and Lillian Marie (Greenstreet) F.; m. Dorothy Jean Bielmeier, Jan. 21, 1956; children—Christine, James. Ph.B. in Journalism, Marquette U., Milw., 1948; postgrad., U. Wis.-Milw., 1984—. Reporter Milw. Sentinel, 1945-62, asst. city editor, 1962-75, city editor, 1975-79, mng. editor, 1977-89; juror Pulitzer Prizes, 1985-86; mem. adv. panel Coll. of Communications, Journalism and Performing Arts Marquette U. Author series of stories: Japan, 1980. Served with U.S. Army, 1955. Recipient By-Line award Marquette U., 1987. Mem. AP Mng. Editors Assn. (dir. 1980-87, editor annual reports 1979-85), Milw. Soc. Profl. Journalists (pres. 1982-83), Milw. Press Club (pres. 1968, several reporting awards, editorial writing award, 1957), Civil War Round Table, Mil. Order Loyal Legion of U.S. Methodist. Club: Civil War Round Table. Home: 7012 W Oklahoma Ave Milwaukee WI 53219 Office: Milwaukee Sentinel 918 N 4th St PO Box 371 Milwaukee WI 53201

FARROW, WILLIAM MCKNIGHT, investment banking and securities trading executive; b. Chgo., Feb. 23, 1955; s. William McKnight and Ruth (Haven) F.; m. Sandra High, Feb. 7, 1981; 1 child, Ashley Marie. BA, Augustana Coll., Rock Island, 1977; MBA in Mgmt., Northwestern U., 1979. Mgmt. fellow Northwestern Meml. Hosp., Chgo., 1978; cons. Arthur Anderson & Co., Chgo., 1979-83; mgr. bus. dev. G.D. Searle & Co., Skokie, Ill., 1983-85; dir. strategy and bus. devel. Dart & Kraft Inc., Northbrook, Ill., 1985-86; v.p., head mktg./head instl. and regional distbn. First Nat. Bank Chgo., 1986-89, First Chgo. Capital Markets Inc., 1989—; chmn. bd. dirs., instr. LEAD Inc.; bd. dirs. Ancilla Hosp. Systems Inc., Kellogg Bus. Sch.; cons. Inst. of Health Issues Mgmt., Northwestern U., various bus. Chgo. area. Home: 9007 Ewing Evanston IL 60203 Office: First Nat Bank Chgo 1 First Nat Plaza Chicago IL 60670

FARRUKH, MARWAN OMAR, construction company executive; b. Beirut, July 25, 1946; s. Omar Abdullah and Amneh Amin (Hilmi) F.; m. Kamar Nazih Baalbaki, June 1, 1978; children: Ghina, Mohammad. BS in Structural Engring., Ain Shams U., Cairo, 1970; MS in Structural Engring., U. Calif., Berkeley, 1978. Pvt. practice in structural engring. Beirut, 1971-72; bridge engr. W.S. Atkins & Ptnrs., Epsom, Surrey, Eng., 1972-74; structural engr. Khatib & Alami, Beirut, 1974-75; engr.-in-charge Sogex Contracting & Trading, Muscat, Beruit, Oman, Lebanon, 1975-77; sect. leader Sogex Services, Ltd., London, 1978-79, 1980-81; sect. leader Envirogenics System Co., Los Angeles, 1979-80; dep. project mgr., mgr. engring. and procuring Pegel Arabia, Dammam, Saudi Arabia, 1981-89, project mgr., 1989—. Mem. Am. Concrete Inst., Pre-stressed Concrete Inst., Post-tensioning Inst., Concrete Reinforcing Steel Inst., Internat. Assn. Bridge and Structural Engring. Office: Pegel Arabia, PO Box 2364, Dammam 31451, Saudi Arabia

FARWELL, LLOYD S., hotel executive; b. Concord, N.H., Aug. 15, 1922; s. Albert Stanley and Jennie B. (Colpitts) F.; m. Grace E. Murphy, Oct. 15, 1948; children: Wayne L., Keith Allan. BS, U. N.H. Cert. hotel adminstr. Mgr. sales Buffalo Statler, 1951-54; exec. asst. mgr. Hartford (Conn.) Hilton, 1954-60; gen. mgr. Atlanta Hilton Inn, 1960-64, Milw. Hilton, 1964-65; sr. v.p. Hilton Inns Inc., Chgo. and Beverly Hills, Calif., 1965-80; exec. v.p. Hilton Inns Inc., Beverly Hills, 1984—; sr. v.p. Hilton Hotels Corp., Beverly Hills, 1980-88. 1st lt. USAAF, 1942-45, ETO. Decorated Air medal with 3 oak leaf clusters, 3 Battle Stars, 1945. Mem. Internat. Franchise Assn. (bd. dirs., pres. 1984), Am. Hotel and Motel Assn. (chmn. polit. action com.

1983-88), Tavern Club, Camarillo (Calif.) Country Club, Kiwanis, Lions. Office: Hilton Inns Inc 9336 Civic Center Dr Beverly Hills CA 90210

FASCIANI, JOHN GUY, banker; b. N.Y.C., May 19, 1955; s. Guy James and Doris Rita (Stevens) F. BBA in Fin., CUNY, 1977; MBA in Acctg., Fordham U., 1980. Staff acct. Dun & Bradstreet, Inc., N.Y.C., 1978-83; acctg. supr. Am. Savs. Bank, N.Y.C., 1983-84; audit officer Bank Hapoalim B.M., N.Y.C., 1984-88; sr. audit officer Can. Imperial Bank of Commerce, N.Y.C., 1988—. Staff sgt. with USMCR, 1977—. Home: 118 11 84th Ave Kew Gardens NY 11415 Office: Canadian Imperial Bank Commerce 425 Lexington Ave New York NY 10020

FASHBAUGH, HOWARD DILTS, JR., lawyer; b. Monroe, Mich., Jan. 31, 1922; s. Howard Dilts and Ninetta Esther (Greening) F.; m. Joyce Dallas MacCurdy, Dec. 25, 1946; children—James Howard, Linda Carol, Patricia Lee. B.S.E., U. Mich., 1947, M.S.E. in Chem. Engring., 1948, M.B.A. with high distinction, 1960; J.D. cum laude, Wake Forest U., 1972; M.Law and Taxation, Coll. William and Mary, 1983. Bar: Va. 1973, Mich. 1975. Mgr. engring. and mfg. Dow Corning Corp., Midland, Mich., 1952-70; assoc. Williams, Worrell, Kelly & Greer, Norfolk, Va., 1972-76, ptnr., 1976-77; corp. counsel Va. Chems. Inc., Portsmouth, Va., 1977-83; ptnr. Williams, Worrell, Kelly & Greer, Norfolk, 1983-85, sole practice, Chesapeake, 1985—; gen. counsel CEP, Inc., 1985-87, pres., treas. and gen. counsel, 1987—. Elder Presbyn. Ch., 1966—; chmn. adv. bd. Salvation Army, Midland, Mich., 1967-69, mem. adv. bd., Portsmouth, 1975—. Served to lt. USNR, 1943-46, 50-52. Decorated Bronze Star medal. Mem. ABA, Va. Bar Assn., Norfolk-Portsmouth Bar Assn., Beta Gamma Sigma. Club: Kiwanis (pres. Portsmouth 1977-78). Home and Office: 4121 Stephanie Boyd Dr Chesapeake VA 23321

FASSOULIS, SATIRIS GALAHAD, communications company executive; b. Syracuse, Aug. 19, 1922; s. Peter George and Anastasia P. (Limpert) F. B.A., Syracuse U., 1945. Vice pres. Commerce Internat. Corp., N.Y.C., 1945-48; pres. Commerce Internat. Corp., 1949-75; chmn. Global Communications Co., N.Y.C., 1976—, Global Def. Products Inc., N.Y.C., 1976—; dir Comml. Exports (Overseas) Ltd., U.K., CIC Internat. Ltd., N.Y.C. Mem. U.S. Congl. Adv. Bd.; bd. dirs. Better Life Enterprises for the Blind, Inc.; mem. Rep. Presdl. Task Force. Served to 1st lt., USAAF, 1941-45. Decorated Purple Heart, Air medal with 3 oak leaf clusters. Mem. N.Y. C. of C., Am. Def. Preparedness Assn., Navy League U.S., Armed Forces Communications and Electronics Assn., U.S. Naval Inst., Air Force Assn., Assn. of U.S. Army, Internat. Platform Assn. Republican. Episcopalian. Clubs: N.Y. Athletic, Order of Ahepa. Home: 20 Waterside Pla New York NY 10010 Office: 10 Waterside Pla New York NY 10010

FASTHUBER-GRANDE, TRAUDY, financial planning company executive; b. Wels, Austria, July 26, 1950; came to U.S., 1974; d. Franz X. and Friederike (Enzlmuller) Fasthuber; m. John J. Grande, Mar. 27, 1987. Student, U. Vienna, 1973-74; BA, Rutgers U., 1976. CFP; registered investment advisor. Program dir. Alt's Gymnastics, inc., Shrewsbury, N.J., 1974-80; v.p. Tangible Resource Group, Inc., Red Bank, N.J., 1980-81, Grande Fin. Svcs., Inc., Ocean, N.J., 1987—; sr. fin. planner Raymond James & Assocs., Inc., Naples, Fla., 1982-85; registered prin. Investment Mgmt. & Rsch., Inc., Ocean, 1985—; hostess TV program Wall St.-Main St., Naples, 1983-84; guest speaker Am. Heart Assn., Fla., 1984-85; lectr. various women's investment seminars, N.J., 1986—. Mem. Inst. Cert. Fin. Planners. Office: Grande Fin Svcs Inc 1001 Deal Rd Ocean NJ 07712

FASY, WILLIAM IGNATIUS JOHN, controller; b. Phila., May 8, 1960; s. John Robert and Joan Marie (Cattie) F. BS, Drexel U., 1983, MS, 1987. CPA, Pa., N.J. Internal auditor, acct. Resorts Internat. Hotel Inc., Atlantic City, 1979-84; auditor U. Pa., Phila., 1984-85; contr., sales person Fasy Real Estate, Phila., 1984-86; asst. casino contr. Resorts Internat. Hotel Inc., Atlantic city, 1986—; instr. fin. and acctg. Stockton State Coll., 1987. Named one of Outstanding Young Men of Am., 1987. Mem. AICPA, Pa. Inst. CPA's, Atlantic City Casino Hotel Accts. Assn., Alpha Pi Lambda. Republican. Roman Catholic. Home: 509 Broad St Northfield NJ 08225 Office: Resorts Internat Hotel Inc N Carolina Ave and Boardwalk Atlantic City NJ 08401

FATE, MARTIN EUGENE, JR., utility company executive; b. Tulsa, Jan. 9, 1933; s. Martin Eugene and Frances Mae (Harp) F.; m. Ruth Ann Johnson, Aug. 28, 1954; children: Gary Martin, Steven Lewis, Mary Ann. B.E.E., Okla. State U., 1955; grad. Advanced Mgmt. Program, Harvard U., 1981. With Public Service Co. of Okla., Tulsa, 1955—; v.p. power Public Service Co. of Okla., 1973-76, exec. v.p., 1976-82, pres., chief exec. officer, 1982—; dir. Central & South West Services, Inc., First Nat. Bank & Trust Co., Tulsa, Ash Creek Mining Co., Energy Fuels Devel. Corp. Trustee Okla. Osteo. Hosp., U. Tulsa, Phillips Grad. Sem. Served to capt. USAF, 1955-57. Mem. Phi Kappa Phi, Eta Kappa Nu, Tau Beta Pi. Mem. Christian Ch. Club: Tulsa Summit. Office: Pub Svc Co Okla 212 E 6th PO Box 201 Tulsa OK 74102

FAUBEL, NANCY CAROLINE, business executive; b. Rochester, N.Y., July 10, 1958; d. Robert S. and Elisabeth (Torrey) F. BS, Alfred U., 1979; MBA, U. Rochester, 1983. Cert. flight instr., comml. pilot; lic. real estate agt.; notary pub. Engr. I, Babcock & Wilcox, Augusta, Ga., 1979-80, sales engr., Phila., 1980-82; v.p. Precision Equipment Services, Rochester, 1983-86; pres. Valley Aviation, Eastern W.Va. Regional Airport, 1986—; pres., owner Baron's Restaurant, Eastern W.Va. Regional Airport, 1986—. Del., 19th Ward Community Assn., Rochester, 1986; capt. CAP, 1985—. Mem. Nat. Assn. Female Execs., Rochester Pilots Assn., Rochester Real Estate Bd., Martinsburg-Berkeley C. of C. (aviation com.). Republican. Lodge: Kiwanis (bd. dirs. S. Berkeley, W.Va.). Avocations: flying, carpentry, art. Home: Rt 4 Box 431-C Martinsburg WV 25401 Office: Valley Aviation W Va Regional Airport Martinsburg WV 25401

FAUBEL, ROGER CHARLES, finance company executive; b. Passaic, N.J., Mar. 6, 1943; m. Niki Ann Marks, May 30, 1984; 1 child, Jared C. BSBA, Rutgers U., 1967. Cert. fin. planner. Chief acct. Grand Rx div. Grand Union Co., Elmwood Park, N.J., 1961-70; treas./controller Daylin, Inc., Union, N.J., 1970-74; treas. Consol. Wharehouses Co., Inc., Youngstown, Ohio, 1974-82; pres. Message Makers, Inc., Youngstown, 1982-83; investment advisor Paine Webber, Inc., Youngstown, 1983-84; pres. Dow Fin. Services, Youngstown, 1984—. Contbr. articles to local newspapers. Lodge: Rotary. Office: Dow Fin Svcs 1255 Boardman Canfield Rd Suite 200 Youngstown OH 44512

FAUBION, JERRY TOLBERT, fiber and chemical company executive, management consultant; b. Pidcoke, Tex., June 9, 1917; s. Roy Arthur and Lillie (Pendleton) F.; BS in Engring. Adminstrn., Tex. A&M U., 1940; m. Rena Louise Derouen, July 20, 1940; 1 child, Roy Michael. Salesman, McEvoy Corp., Houston, 1940-42; mech. engr., chem. engr., prodn. engr. Tex. div. Dow Chem. Co., Freeport, Tex., 1942-43, supt. prodn. control, 1943-55, mgr. prodn. coordination, 1955-57, mgr. planning and distbn., 1957-63; mgr. organic chems. product adminstrn. Dow Chem. Co., Midland, Mich., 1963-64, mgr. packaging dept., 1964-66; pres., dir. Dow Badische Co., Williamsburg, Va., 1966-75, Faubion Enterprises, Inc., Williamsburg, 1976—; bd. dirs. Virchem S.A./N.V., Brussels, 1978-82, United Va. Bankshares, Inc. (now Crestar Fin. Corp.), Richmond, 1973-88, Chesapeake Corp., Richmond, 1976-88, Crestar Bank, 1973-88, Am. Filtrona Corp., Richmond, 1983-88; v.p., bd. dirs. Shell Bank Woods Corp.; lectr. Coll. William and Mary. Mem. Brazosport (Tex.) Ind. Sch. Bd., 1952-57, pres., 1955-57; mem. Freeport City Coun., 1950-51; trustee Freeport Community Hosp., 1960-61; bd. dirs. Williamsburg Community Hosp., 1970-81, 1984—, chmn., 1988—; elder Presbyn. Ch. Registered profl. engr., Tex. Republican. Home: PO Box BT Williamsburg VA 23187 Office: 309A McLaws Circle Williamsburg VA 23185

FAULDERS, C. THOMAS, III, communications company executive; b. Pensacola, Fla., Sept. 2, 1949; s. C. Thomas Faulders Jr. and Bobbe (Peck) F.; m. Dana H. Faulders, Apr. 7, 1972; children: Kristen Lee, Laura Elizabeth. BA in Econs., U. Va., 1971; MBA in Fin., U. Pa., 1981. Strategic analyst Satellite Bus. Systems, McLean, Va., 1981, mgr. fin. svcs., 1981-82, dir. fin. planning, 1982-83, treas., 1983-85; v.p. MCI Communications Corp., Washington, 1985—; acting pres., Dick Herriman Ford, Vienna, Va., 1982. Pres. Summerwood Civic Assn., McLean, Va., 1984-86. Lt. USN, 1971-79. Episcopalian. Office: MCI Communications Corp 1133 19th St NW Washington DC 20036 also: 400 Perimeter Circle Terr Atlanta GA 30346

FAULKNER, DEXTER HAROLD, magazine publishing executive, editor; b. Grand Island, Nebr., Sept. 10, 1937; s. Jack L. and Wanetta May (Howland) F.; student U. Calif.-Fresno, 1956-58, Ambassador Coll., 1958-60; m. Shirley Ann Hume, Jan. 11, 1959; children—Nathan Timothy, Matthew Benjamin. Exec. editor Plain Truth Mag; editor Good News mag., Youth/89 mag. and Worldwide News-Tabloid internat. div. Ambassador Coll., Sydney, Australia, 1960-66, news research asst. dir. Ambassador Coll. Editorial, Pasadena, Calif., 1966-71, regional editor Plain Truth mag., Washington, 1971-75, asst. mng. editor, Pasadena, 1975-78, mng. editor, 1980-82, exec. editor, 1982—, mng. editor Good News mag., Worldwide News-Tabloid, 1978-85, editor, 1986—; mng. editor Youth/89 mag., 1981-85, editor, 1986—; instr. mass communications Ambassador Coll., 1980—; columnist Just One More Thing . . ., By the Way, Just Between Friends. Mem. Inst. Journalists (London), Profl. Photographers Am. Inc., Bur. Freelance Photographers (London), Nat. Press Club, World Affairs Council (Los Angeles), Internat. Assn. Bus. Communicators, Nat. Press Photographers Assn., Am. Mgmt. Assn., Sigma Delta Chi. Mem. Worldwide Ch. God; minister Worldwide Ch. God, 1988—. Contbr. articles, photos on internat. relations, social issues to Plain Truth mag., Good News mag., Worldwide News Publs. Club: Commonwealth of Calif. Home: 7859 Wentworth St Sunland CA 91040 Office: Plain Truth Mag 300 W Green St Pasadena CA 91129

FAULKNER, EDWIN JEROME, insurance company executive; b. Lincoln, Nebr., July 5, 1911; s. Edwin Jerome and Leah (Meyer) F.; m. Jean Rathburn, Sept. 27, 1933. B.A., U. Nebr., 1932; M.B.A., U. Pa., 1934. With Woodmen Accident & Life Co., Lincoln, 1934—; successively claim auditor, v.p. Woodmen Accident & Life Co., 1934-38, pres., dir., 1938-77, chmn. bd., chief exec. officer, 1977-83, hon. chmn., exec. counsel, 1983—; pres., dir. Comml. Mut. Surety Co., 1938—; dir. Lincoln Telecommunications Inc., Universal Surety Co., Inland Ins. Co.; past dir. 1st Nat. Bank & Trust Co., Lincoln; chmn. Health Ins. Council, 1959-60; mem. adv. council on social security HEW, 1974-75. Author: Accident and Health Insurance, 1940, Health Insurance, 1960; Editor: Man's Quest for Security, 1966. Chmn. Lincoln-Lancaster County Plan Commn., 1948-67; mem. medicare adv. com. Dept. Def., 1957-70; Neb. Republican State Finance chmn., 1968-73; Chmn., trustee Bryan Meml. Hosp.; trustee Doane Coll., 1961-70, Lincoln Found., Am. Coll. Life Underwriters, Cooper Found., Newcomen Soc. N.Am.; chmn. bd. trustees U. Nebr. Found.; bd. dirs. Nebraskans for Pub. TV., Bus. Industry Polit. Action Com., Washington. Served from 2d lt. to lt. col. USAAF, 1942-45. Decorated Legion of Merit; recipient Disting. Service award U. Nebr., 1957; Harold R. Gordon Meml. award Internat. Assn. Health Ins. Underwriters, 1955, Ins. Man of Year award Ins. Field, 1958; Dist. Service award Nebr. Council on Econ. Edn., 1986, Exec. of Yr. award Am. Coll. Hosp. Adminstrs., 1971; Nebr. Builders award, 1979; Disting. Service award Lincoln Kiwanis Club, 1980. Mem. Health Ins. Assn. Am. (1st pres. 1956), Am. Legion, Am. Life Conv. (exec. com. 1961-70, pres. 1966-67), Ins. Econs. Soc. (chmn. 1971-73), Nebr. Hist. Soc. (pres. 1982-84), Ins. Fedn. Nebr. (pres.), Phi Beta Kappa, Phi Kappa Psi, Alpha Kappa Psi (hon.). Republican. Presbyn. Lodges: Masons, Elks. Home: 4100 South St Lincoln NE 68506 Office: 1526 K St Lincoln NE 68508

FAULKNER, JUANITA SMITH, realtor; b. Houston, June 13, 1935; d. Alvin Blalock and Vera Gertrude (Carr) Smith; m. Corbitt D. Phillips, Feb. 5, 1955 (div. 1960); children: Constance Marie Phillips Walston, Deborah Jean Phillips Bass; m. William L. Faulkner, Mar. 18, 1961; 1 child, John William. Student, Harris County Community Coll., 1973, 78, U. Houston, 1974. Realtor, broker various orgns., Houston, 1972—; franchise owner Century 21, Houston, 1981—. Troup leader, N. Houston song dir. Campfire Girls, Houston, 1966-70; vol. Govt. Food Bank. Mem. Nat. Bd. Realtors, Tex. Bd. Realtors, Houston Bd. Realtors, Soc. Real Estate Appraisers, Order of Eastern Star. Home and Office: 13649 Reeveston Rd Houston TX 77039

FAULKNER, SEWELL FORD, realtor; b. Keene, N.H., Sept. 25, 1924; s. John Charles and Hazel Helen (Ford) F.; A.B., Harvard, 1949; M.B.A., 1951; m. June Dayton Finn, Jan. 10, 1951 (div.); children—Patricia Anne, Bradford William, Sandra Ford, Jonathan Dayton, Winthrop Sewell; m. 2d, Constance Mae Durvin, Mar. 15, 1969 (div.); children—Sarah Elizabeth, Elizabeth Jane. Product mgr. Congoleum Nairn, Inc., Kearny, N.J., 1951-55; salesman, broker, chmn., pres. Jack White Co. real estate, Anchorage, 1956-86 ; dir. Life Ins. Co. Alaska. Mem. Anchorage City Council, 1962-65, Greater Anchorage Area Borough Assembly, 1964-65, Anchorage Area Charter Commn., 1969-70. Pres., Alaska World Affairs Council, 1967-68; treas. Alyeska Property Owners, Inc., 1973-75, pres., 1977-78; pres. Downtown Anchorage Assn., 1974-75; mem. Girdwood Bd. Suprs. Served with USAAF, 1943-45. Mem. Anchorage Area C. of C. (dir. 1973-74), Urban Land Inst., Bldg. Owners and Mgrs. Assn., Nat. Inst. Real Estate Brokers. Clubs: Alaska Notch, Anchorage Petroleum. Office: Jack White Co 3201 C St Anchorage AK 99503

FAULSTICH, ALBERT JOSEPH, banking consultant; b. New Orleans, May 28, 1910; s. Albert and Mary (Balser) F.; m. Anna Emily Collignon, June 30, 1940; children: Albert Joseph, Richard Charles. BS in Acctg. and Econs, Columbus U., Washington, 1938, M.S. in Acctg. and Finance, 1948. With Treasury Dept., 1939-64, asst. to personnel dir., 1939-42, dir. positions evaluation and job analysis, 1942-43, indsl. relations specialist, 1943-45, dir. salary adminstrn., coordinator performance evaluation, also chmn. com. union relations, adminstr. policy and standards of govt. early-age retirement of spl. intelligence agts. from various depts., 1946-60, dir. Office Security, 1961, spl asst. to sec., 1961-64, asst. to comptroller currency, directed issuance and redemption of Fed. Reserve currency, 1962-64, coordinator fed. banking, 1964; dir. FDIC, 1965-66, dep. adminstr. nat. banks, 1965-74, asst. dir., 1973-74; treas., mem. Fed. Personnel Council, 1941; acting dir. personnel mgmt., wage bd. chmn., Treasury Dept., (intermittently) 1953-60; mem. rev. bd., spl. com. on liquidations, loans and purchases assets, FDIC, 1966-74; cons. Fin. Gen. Bankshares, Inc., 1974-76, for banks and govt., 1976—; dir. Am. Nat. Bank of Md., 1975-77. Chmn. comptroller currency orgn. for nation-wide campaign for Kennedy Library Fund, 1964. Served to lt. USNR, 1943-46. Recipient Naval Commendation medal, commendation Treasury Dept., 1962, 3 citations, 1972, Meritorious Service award, 1973, Disting. Service award, 1974, Albert Gallatin award, Am. Flag award, Equal Opportunity award, 1974. Democrat. Roman Catholic. Home and Office: 3004 N Ridge Rd Ellicott City MD 21043

FAUST, C. EDWIN, credit reporting company executive; b. Chgo., Jan. 22, 1937; s. Edwin C. Faust and Catherine (Stratton) Faust Klaffke; m. Sandra K. Replogle, Mar. 9, 1962; 3 children. BS in Mgmt. and Adminstrn., Ind. U., 1972. Cetr. credit bur. exec. Field rep., supr. Equifax Services, South Bend, Ind., 1962-72; supr. Equifax Services, Saginaw, Mich., 1972-73; asst. mgr. Equifax Services, Toledo, 1973-74; regional ops. mgr. Dataflo Systems/Equifax, Springfield, Ill., 1974-79; regional v.p. Systemedics/Equifax, Garden Grove, Calif., 1979-84; regional mgr. CBI/Equifax-N.J., Shrewsbury, 1984-86, CBI/Equifax-South Fla., North Miami Beach, 1986—; bd. dirs. Consumer Credit Counseling Service, Miami. Served with U.S. Army, 1956-59. Named Ky. Col. Commonwealth of Ky., 1977. Mem. Assoc. Credit Burs. Fla., Internat. Credit Assn., Greater Miami Credit Assn. (bd. dirs. 1986—, v.p.), Soc. Cert. Consumer Credit Execs. Office: CBI/Equifax Inc PO Box 609060 North Miami Beach FL 33160

FAUST, THOMAS JAMES, transporation and finance executive, business consultant; b. San Francisco; s. Thomas J. Faust; m. Ann Sparkman, Jan. 3, 1985. B.S. in Marine Transp., Tex. A&M U., 1969; M.B.A., Stanford U., 1973. Cons. Marine Transport Lines, N.Y.C., 1973-75; dir. planning Dillingham, Honolulu, 1976-77; pres. Faustug Group Inc., San Francisco, 1978—; gen. ptnr. Tractug, San Francisco, 1980—; dir., v.p. Bay Area Employment Devel., Napa, Calif., 1980—. Served with USN, 1969-82; Vietnam. Mem. Stanford Bus. Sch. Alumni, Engineers Club San Francisco. Home: 60 Collins St San Francisco CA 94118 Office: Faustug Group Inc Pier 15 The Embarcadero San Francisco CA 94111

FAVORITA, JOHN VINCENT, JR., industrial executive; b. N.Y.C., June 20, 1935; s. John Vincent Sr. and Rose Mary (White) F.; divorced; children: Carol Lynn, Claudine Marie, David Brian. BS in Indsl. Mgmt., U. Ky., 1959; MBA in Indsl. Mgmt., U. Bridgeport, 1965. Mgr. internat. purchasing Ingersoll Rand Co., The Hauge, Holland, 1969-73; dir. materials Joy Mfg. Co., Pitts., 1973-77; dir. materials, supplies Simplex Mgmt. Svcs., London, 1978; dir. purchasing Cooper Industries, Inc., Dallas, 1979-80; mgr. corp. purchasing Cooper Industries, Inc., Houston, 1981-82, Grove City, Pa., 1983; v.p. sourcing Tex. First Intercontinental Trading Co., Dallas, 1983-84; dir. purchasing Komatsu Dresser Industries Co., Peoria, Ill., 1985—. With USAFR, 1959-64. Mem. Nat. Assn. Purchasing Mgmt., Machinery and Allied Products Isnt. (mem. purchasing coun. 1981-83). Home: 3619 N Sandia Dr Peoria IL 61604 Office: Komatsu Dresser Co PO Box 240 Peoria IL 61650

FAVROT, HENRI MORTIMER, JR., architect, real estate developer; b. New Orleans, Apr. 23, 1930; s. Henri Mortimer and Helen Rebecca (Parkhurst) F.; m. Kathleen Loker Gibbons, Sept. 16, 1956; children: James P., Kathleen Favrot VanHorn, T. Semmes, Caroline. BArch, Tulane U., 1953; MArch, Harvard U., 1957. Lic. architect, La., Miss. Architect Favrot, Reed, Mathes & Bergman, New Orleans, 1955-56, Curtis & Davis, New Orleans, 1957-58; ptnr. Favrot & Grimball, New Orleans, 1958-62; pvt. practice architecture New Orleans, 1962-64; ptnr. Mathes, Bergman, Favrot & Assocs., New Orleans, 1964-69, Favrot & Shane, Metairie, La., 1969—; chmn. La. Architecture Selection Bd., Baton Rouge, 1976. Prin. works include: Parktowne Townhouses, 1971 (Design Honor award La. Architects Assn.), Favrot & Shane Office Bldg., 1982 (Design Honor award New Orleans chpt. AIA). Chmn. City Planning Commn., New Orleans, 1976, 77; commr. La. Housing Commn., Baton Rouge, 1985-86; bd. mem. Met. Area Com., New Orleans, 1985—; v.p. New Orleans Mus. Art, 1986-87; bd. adminstrs. Tulane U., 1986—. Recipient Outstanding Alumnus award Tulane U. Sch. Architecture, 1985. Mem. AIA (pres. New Orleans chpt. 1982-83), La. Architects Assn. (pres. 1984-85), New Orleans Apt. Assn. (pres. 1980-81), Constrn. Specifications Inst., Homebuilders Assn. Greater New Orleans. Democrat. Roman Catholic. Clubs: So. Yacht, New Orleans Tennis, Boston, La. Home: 1400 State St New Orleans LA 70118 Office: Favrot & Shane AIA Architects 3925 N Service Rd W Metairie LA 70002

FAWCETT, HOWARD HOY, chemical health and safety consultant; b. McKeesport, Pa., May 31, 1916; s. Harry Garfield and Ada (Deetz) F.; m. Ruth Allen Bogan, Apr. 7, 1942; children: Ralph Willard, Harry Allen. BS in Indsl. Chemistry, U. Md., 1940; postgrad. U. Del., 1945-47. Registered profl. engr., Calif. Research chemist Manhattan project E.I. DuPont de Nemours & Co., Inc., Chgo., Hanford, Wash., 1944-45, research and devel. chemist organic chemistry div., Deepwater, N.J., 1945-48; cons. engr. Gen. Electric Co., Schenectady, N.Y., 1948-64; tech. sec. com. on hazardous materials Nat. Acad. Scis.-NRC, Washington, 1964-75; staff scientist, project mgr. Tracor Jitco, Inc., Rockville, Md., 1975-78; sr. chem. engr. Equitable Environ. Health, 1978—; pres., sr. engr. Fawcett Consultations, Inc., 1981—; mem. adv. com. study on socio-behavioral preparations for, responses to and recovery from chem. disasters NSF, 1977—; adj. prof. Fed. Emergency Mgmt. Agency Acad., 1983—; cons. to industry and govt. agys. Author Am.-Can. supplement Hazards in Chemical Lab., 1983, Hazardous and Toxic Materials, Safe Handling and Disposal, 1984, 2d edit., 1988; co-editor: Safety and Accident Prevention in Chemical Operations, 2d edit., 1982; mem. editorial adv. bd. Jour. Safety Research, 1968—, Transp. Planning and Tech., 1972—; N. Am. regional editor Jour. Hazardous Materials, 1975—; also book chpt. Chief radiol. sect. Schenectady County CD, 1953-63; bd. dirs. Safety sect. Schenectady C. of C., 1957-64; tech. advisor Emergency Response Team, Montgomery County, Md., 1988—. Recipient Disting. Service to Safety citation Nat. Safety Council, 1966, Cameron award, 1962, 69. Fellow Am. Chem. Soc. (sec. com. chem. safety, chmn. council com. on chem. safety 1974-77, chmn. div. chem. health and safety 1977-79, councilor 1980-82, archivist, 1984—, author audio course on hazards of materials 1977). Fellow Am. Inst. Chemists; mem. ASTM (membership sec. 1972—, sub-chmn. D-34 com.), Am. Inst. Chem. Engrs. (com. on occupational health and safety 1977—, editor newsletter 1988-89), Internat. Platform Assn. Am. Indsl. Hygiene Assn. (dir. Balt.-Washington chpt. 1975-77), Alpha Chi Sigma. Home and Office: PO Box 9444 12920 Matey Rd Wheaton MD 20906-4053

FAWCETT, NOVICE GAIL, university administrator; b. Gambier, Ohio, Mar. 29, 1909; s. John Henry and Mary Allie (Lampson) F.; m. Maude E. Yarman, June 17, 1931 (dec. Sept. 1948); children: Mary Joan (dec.), Jane Elizabeth Fawcett-Hoover; m. Marjorie Elizabeth Keener, Aug. 19, 1949. BS magna cum laude, Kenyon Coll., 1931, LLD (hon.), 1952; MA, Ohio State U., 1937, postgrad., 1943-47, LLD (hon.), 1972; LLD (hon.), Kent State U., 1956, Miami U., Wittenberg U., Ohio, 1957, Heidelberg Coll., U. Cin., 1960, Millikin U., 1962, Cen. State Coll., 1964, Ind. State U., 1974; LittD (hon.), U. Akron, 1958; D.P.S. (hon.), Ohio Wesleyan U., 1959, Rio Grande Coll., 1964; HHD (hon.), U. Ams., Mex., 1967; D Pedagogy (hon.), Morris Harvey Coll., 1970. Tchr. Gambier High Sch., 1931-34, supt. schs., 1934-38; supt. schs. Defiance, Ohio, 1938-43, Bexley, Ohio, 1943-48; 1st asst. supt. schs. Akron, Ohio, 1948-49; supt. schs. Columbus, Ohio, 1949-56; pres. Ohio State U., Columbus, 1956-72, pres. emeritus ednl. cons., 1972—; acting commr. higher edn. State of Ind., 1973-74; co-founder Ohio Eminent Scholars Program; chmn. Ohio Commrs., Edn. Commn. States, 1975-82, mem. steering com., 1977-82; incorporator Gov.'s Council Cost Control, 1975-77, ednl. cons., 1977—; sr. cons. Ohio Bd. Regents, 1979-88; cons. Lilly Endowment, 1974-75; dir. emeritus Buckeye Fin. Corp.; trustee Nationwide Investing Found., Nationwide Separate Account Trust, Nationwide Tax Free Fund; chmn. adv. com. study home econs. Carnegie Corp., 1965-67; bd. dirs. Ohio State Life Ins. Co. Trustee, v.p. AAA Traffic Safety Found., 1983-85; past mem. bd. visitors Air U., Montgomery, Ala.; past trustee Air Force Mus. Found.; past mem. steering com. Devel. Com. Greater Columbus; past mem. bd. govs. Internat. Ins. Seminars, Inc., active Ohio Easter Seal Campaign; treas. Bipartisan Commn. to pass Issue I, Coal Research, 1985. Recipient Brotherhood Man of Yr. award Temple Israel, 1960, Pres. Gold medal Assn. U.S. Army, 1966, Wisdom award of honor Widsom Hall of Fame, 1970, Outstanding Citizen award Bldg. Industry Assn. Cen. Ohio, 1971, certs. of appreciation Columbus Pub. Schs., 1972, Disting. Service award Edn. Commn. of States, 1982, AAA Found. Traffic Safety, 1985, award Ohio State U. Women's Day Alumni Com., 1984. Mem. Assn. Am. Univs. (chmn. membership com. 1968-70), Am. Council Edn. (1st vice chmn. 1969-70), Nat. Assn. State Univs. and Land-Grant Colls. (chmn. adv. com. on econs. 1965-67), Argonne Univs. Assn. (trustee 1967-69), Internat. Assn. Univs., Inter-Univ. Council Ohio (past. chmn.), Am. Assn. Sch. Adminstrs. (Disting. Service award 1975), Ohio Coll. Assn. (pres. 1966-67, exec. com. 1967-68), Newcomen Soc., Columbus Area C. of C. (past dir., Columbus award 1971), Ohio Dental Soc. (hon.), Varsity "O" Assn. (hon. life), Phi Beta Kappa. Clubs: Scioto Country, Ohio State U. Faculty, University (hon.). Lodges: Masons, Rotary. Home: 3995 The Old Poste Rd Columbus OH 43026 Office: Fawcett Ctr 2400 Olentangy River Rd Columbus OH 43210

FAWCETT, SHERWOOD LUTHER, research laboratory executive; b. Youngstown, Ohio, Dec. 25, 1919; s. Luther T. and Clara (Sherwood) F.; m. Martha L. Simcox, Feb. 28, 1953; children: Paul, Judith, Tom. BS, Ohio State U., 1941; MS, Case Inst. Tech., 1948, PhD, 1950; hon. degrees, Ohio State U., Gonzaga U., Whitman Coll., Otterbein Coll., Detroit Inst. Tech., Ohio Dominican Coll. Registered profl. engr., Ohio. Mem. staff Columbus Labs. Battelle Meml. Inst., 1950-64, mgr. physics dept., 1959-64; dir. Pacific Northwest Labs., Richland, Wash., 1964-67; exec. v.p. Battelle Meml. Inst., Columbus, Ohio, 1967-68; pres., chief exec. officer Battelle Meml. Inst., 1968-80, chmn., chief exec. officer, 1981-84, chmn. bd. trustees, 1969—; bd. dirs. Columbia Gas Systems, Inc. Served with the USNR, 1941-46. Decorated Bronze Star; recipient Washington award Western Soc. Engrs., 1989. Mem. Am. Phys. Soc., Am. Nuclear Soc., Nat. Soc. Profl. Engrs., Am. Inst. Metall. Engrs., Sigma Xi, Delta Chi, Sigma Pi Sigma, Tau Beta Pi. Home and Office: 2820 Margate Rd Columbus OH 43221 also: Battelle Meml Inst 505 King Ave Columbus OH 43201

FAY, CHARLES FREDERICK, investment banker; b. Hammond, Ind., May 23, 1939; s. Gordon C. and Elma (Stage) F.; m. Edith Anne Edling, Aug. 25, 1962; children—Julie Anne, Zachary Edling. B.S., Drexel U., 1962; M.B.A., Washington U., St. Louis, 1968. Mgr., Gen. Refractories Co., Phila., 1962-67; corporate v.p. investment banking div. A.G. Edwards, Inc., St. Louis, 1968—. Pres., Full Gospel Businessmen's Fellowship Internat.,

Clayton, Mo., 1978—. Home: 12120 Belle Meade Rd Des Peres MO 63131 Office: A G Edwards Inc One N Jefferson Ave Saint Louis MO 63103

FAY, GARY L., management executive; b. Lansing, Mich., Dec. 2, 1942; m. Nancy, Dec. 2, 1967; children: Patrick, Jonathan. BS, Mich. State U., 1965, MBA, 1967. CPA, Ohio; Cert. Mgmt. Acct. Ops. researcher Cooper Tire & Rubber Co., Findlay, Ohio, 1970-75; mgr. fin. planning Cooper Tire & Rubber Co., Findlay, 1975—. Mem. Ohio Soc. CPA's, Planning Forum (Toledo Chpt. pres. 1986-88). Office: Cooper Tire & Rubber Co Western & Lima Ave Findlay OH 45840

FAY, ROBERT WOODS, financial executive; b. Phila., Dec. 11, 1946; s. Wayne Xalpha and June Elizabeth (Balliet) F.; m. Holly Howell, May 11, 1974; children—Wayne H., Randall C. B.A., Duke U., 1968; B.S., Villanova U., 1974; M.B.A., Drexel U., 1977. Systems engr. IBM Corp., Phila., 1968-72; mgr. cash systems and ops. Certain-Teed Corp., Valley Forge, Pa., 1972-78; div. controller Harris Corp., Melbourne, Fla., 1978-85, treas., 1985-87, v.p., treas, 1988—; mem. so. adv. council Arkwright Mut. Ins. Co., Atlanta, 1985—. Bd. dirs United Way Brevard County, Melbourne, 1985—; alumni recruiter Duke U. Served with U.S. Army, 1969-75. Mem. Machinery and Allied Products Inst., Fin. Execs. Inst. Office: Harris Corp 1025 W NASA Blvd Melbourne FL 32919

FAYORSEY, CLARENCE BAWA, industrial and commercial executive, cattle rancher, crop farmer; b. Ada, Ghana, Jan. 5, 1922; s. Tei and Salome Akuyo (Agbenyega) F.; m. Regina Akorkor Aggudey, Jan. 1, 1950; children—Vida, Clara, Ian, Bernard, Joyce, Archibald Harold, Angela, Cyril, Mavis. Student in commerce and industry Leeds U. Chmn., founder Combined Supplies Ltd., Ghana, 1960-62; chmn. found. soc. and bd. govs. Ada Secondary Coll., 1961-72; chmn., mng. dir. Central Logging and Sawmill Ltd., Ghana, 1973-81, City Food Supply Ghana Ltd., Accra; chmn. bd. dirs. Ghana Merchants Co. Ltd., 1984—; vice chmn. Consiltative Council to Govt. Ghana, 1983-85 ; chmn., founder Tongu Basin Agrl. Complex Ltd., Accra, Ghana, 1976—; promoter, founder Ada Rural Bank, Kasseh, Ghana. Fellow Fedn. Merchant Houses. Presbyterian. Named Best Adjudged Farmer of Yr., 1986. Avocations: golf; swimming. Home: PO Box 2801, Accra Ghana

FAZIO, PETER VICTOR, JR., lawyer; b. Chgo., Jan. 22, 1940; s. Peter Victor and Marie Rose (LaMantia) F.; m. Patti Ann Campbell, Jan. 3, 1966; children—Patti-Marie, Catherine, Peter. AB, Holy Cross Coll., Worcester, Mass., 1961; JD, U. Mich., 1964. Bar: Ill. 1964, U.S. Dist. Ct. (no. dist.) Ill. 1965, U.S. Ct. Appeals (7th cir.) 1972, U.S. Supreme Ct. 1977, U.S. Ct. Appeals (D.C. cir.) 1981. Assoc. Schiff, Hardin & Waite, Chgo., 1964-70, ptnr., 1970-82, 84—; exec. v.p. Internat. Capital Equipment, Chgo., 1982-83, also dir., 1982-85, sec., 1982-87; bd. dir. Planmetrics Inc., Chgo., 1984—, Chgo. Lawyers Commn. for Civil Rights Under Law, 1976-82, co-chmn., 1978-80; bd. dir. Seton Health Corp. No. Ill., Chgo 1987—, vice chmn., 1989—. Trustee Barat Coll., Lake Forest, Ill., 1977-82; mem. exec. adv. bd. St. Joseph's Hosp., Chgo., 1984-89, chmn., 1986-89, Pres.'s Coun., 1989—. Mem. ABA, Ill. State Bar Assn., Chgo. Bar Assn., Am. Soc. Corp. Secs. Clubs: Saddle & Cycle (sec. 1983-86), Tavern, Met. (Chgo.). Office: Schiff Hardin & Waite 233 S Wacker Dr 7200 Sears Tower Chicago IL 60606

FEAGLES, ROBERT WEST, insurance company executive; b. Ft. Wayne, Ind., July 23, 1920; s. Ralph L. and Mary Anna (West) F.; m. Anita Marie MacRae, Sept. 15, 1951; children: Wendy Lee, Cuyler MacRae, Priscilla Jane, Patrick Emerson. B.S., Ga. Inst. Tech., 1943, Am. Grad. Sch. of Internat. Mgmt., 1951; cert. of banking, Rutgers U. Grad. Sch. Banking, 1958. Sr. v.p. Citibank, N.A., N.Y.C., 1951-76, Travelers Ins. Co., Hartford, Conn., 1976-86; chmn., chief exec. officer Travelers Asset Mgmt. Internat. Corp., N.Y.C., 1979-87; vice chmn., chief exec. offcier The Conn. Ins. Co., Farmington, 1988—. Bd. fellows Am. Grad. Sch. Internat. Mgmt., Glendale, Ariz., 1973—; mem. adv. council Internat. Exec. Service Corps. Council, N.Y.C., 1970—; chmn. Hartford Area Manpower Planning Council, 1978-79, Hartford Area Pvt. Industry Council, 1979-83, State job Tng. Coordinating Council, Hartford, 1983-88. Served to capt. U.S. Army, 1943-47. Recipient Jonas Mayer award Am. Grad. Sch. Internat. Mgmt., 1978. Mem. Personnel Round Table (emeritus), University Club, Royal Automobile Club (London), Hartford Golf Club, Fishers Island (N.Y.) Club, Hartford Club. Republican. Presbyterian. Home: 182 Fern St West Hartford CT 06119 Office: Conn Ins Co 270 Farmington Ave Ste 204 Farmington CT 06038

FEATHERMAN, BERNARD, steel company executive; b. Phila., May 3, 1929; s. Jacob H. and Eva (Feldman) F.; m. Sandra Green, May 29, 1958; children—Andrew C., John James. B.S., Temple U., 1951, postgrad. Grad. Bus. Sch., 1951-52, Law Sch., 1952-54; postgrad. Wharton Sch., U. Pa., 1965-66. Pres. Bernard Franklin Co., Phila., 1958—, Western Steel Co., Phila., 1961—; chmn. bd. Western Metal Bed Co., Phila., 1978—, JBM Equipment Group, Inc., Phila., 1987—; chmn. bd. dirs. Automated Techs., Phila., 1988—; dir. Pa. Steel and Aluminum Corp., Huntingdon Valley, Pa.; chmn. bd. JBM Equipment Group, Phila. 1986—; bd. dirs. Material Handling Inst., Pitts., 1978-79. Contbr. articles to profl. jours. Inventor electronics locking locker. Mem. exec. bd. Southeast chpt. Nat. Found. March of Dimes, 1969-82, vice chmn., 1978-80; pres. Phila. Assn. for Retarded Citizens, 1975-77, trustee, 1983—; chmn. Mayor's Adv. Com. on Mental Health-Mental Retardation, Phila., 1979—; mem. tax policy and budget rev. com. City of Phila.; mem. bd. Costar, Inc., 1989—; co-chmn. Mayor's Small Bus. Adv. Com., Phila., 1979—; del. White House Conf. on Small Bus., 1980, Pa. del., vice chmn., 1986; chmn. small bus. council Democratic Nat. Com., 1982-84; fin. chmn. Pa. Democratic Orgn., 1985-86; mem. adv. bd. Coll. Liberal Arts and Scis., Temple U., 1982—, West Chester (Pa.) State U. Bus. Sch., 1986-87, Frankford Hosp., 1983—; chmn. 3d Congl. Small Bus. Council, Phila., 1984-88; bd. dirs. Phila. Citywide Devel. Corp., 1984—; bd. dir. Phila. Loan Fund, Inc., 1987-88. Recipient award of appreciation Small Bus. Council, Dem. Nat. Com., 1983; Gold medal of Honor Adult Trainees Found., Phila., 1976; citation White House Conf. on Small Bus., 1980. Mem. Assn. of Steel Distbrs. (nat. pres. 1975-76, 86-87, named Steel Distbr. of Yr. 1976), Shelving Mfrs. Assn. (nat. chmn. 1977-78), Pa. Soc. Lodge: B'nai B'rith (pres. 1980-82, Nat. Youth Services award Quaker City lodge 1985), Hunting Park West Bus. Assn. (pres. 1986—), Assn. Steel Distbrs. (nat. pres. 1975-76, 86-87). Home: 2100 Spruce St Philadelphia PA 19103

FEAZELL, THOMAS LEE, lawyer, oil company executive; b. Mount Hope, W.Va., Feb. 25, 1937; s. Thomas Lee and Drema Lyal (Walker) F.; m. Virginia Scott, Feb. 3, 1961; children—Ann Lindsay, Thomas Lee, Robert Kent. Student, W.Va. U., 1954-56; B.B.A., Marshall U., 1959; LL.B., Washington and Lee U., 1962. Bar: W.Va. 1962, Ky. 1965. Atty. Ashland Oil, Inc., Ky., 1965-74, sr. atty., 1975-76, gen. atty., 1976-78, asst. gen. counsel, 1978-79, assoc. gen. counsel, 1979-80, v.p., 1980, gen. counsel, 1981—; gen. counsel Ashland Coal, Inc., Huntington, W.Va., 1981—; adminstrv. v.p. Ashland Oil, Inc., 1988—; bd. dirs. Ashland Coal, Inc. Bd. dirs. Marshall U. Found., Inc., Huntington, W.Va., 1984—. Mem. ABA, W.Va. Bar Assn., Ky. Bar Assn., Maritime Bar Assn., Assn. Trial Lawyers Am. Democrat. Presbyterian. Club: Bellefonte Country. Office: Ashland Oil Inc PO Box 391 Ashland KY 41114

FECHER, CONRAD CHRISTOPHER, computer software company executive; b. N.Y.C., July 9, 1946; s. Konrad and Mary Elizabeth (Husek) F.; m. Billie Tate, June 10, 1972. BS, Elizabethtown (Pa.) Coll., 1978. With Electronic Data Systems, various locations, 1971-83; regional mgr. Electronic Data Systems, Dallas, 1983-84; mgr. vendor contracts Electronic Data Systems, Detroit, 1984-85; v.p. info. services Ducommun, Inc., Los Angeles, 1985-87; pres., chief exec. officer Integrated Info. Systems, San Diego, 1987—. Served to capt. U.S. Army, 1966-71, Vietnam. Decorated Bronze Star, 16 Air medals. Mem. AM/FM Internat., Urban Regional Info. Systems Assn. Republican. Roman Catholic. Office: Integrated Info Systems 450 B St Suite 1200 San Diego CA 92101

FEDCHAK, GREGORY GEORGE, columnist, publisher; b. Waverly, N.Y., Dec. 17, 1956; s. Philip and Jeane Veronica (Arnts) F.; m. M. Elaine Robinson, Aug. 11, 1979. BA, St. Lawrence U., 1979. Procurement specialist Dept. Energy, Washington, 1979; Korean lang. trainee Dept. Def., Washington, 1980-81, Korean linguist, 1981-83; columnist Park Newspapers of St. Lawrence, Inc., Ogdensburg, N.Y., 1983—; pub. Night Tree Press, Boonville, N.Y., 1985—; freelance writer, Boonville, 1983—; lectr. writing and publishing, Boonville, 1986—. Author: Yammering Away, 1985; editor, pub.: The Way to Heron Mountain, 1986, Lost River, 1988. Asst. vol. historian St. Lawrence County, Canton, N.Y., 1978; mem. St. Lawrence County Hist. Assn., Canton, 1978—. Recipient 1st place award N.Y. Press Assn., 1986. Mem. Phi Beta Kappa. Democrat. Roman Catholic. Home and Office: Rd #2 Box 140-G The Gorge Rd Rt 46 Boonville NY 13309

FEDER, SAUL E., lawyer; b. Bklyn., Oct. 8, 1943; s. Joseph Robert and Toby Feder; m. Marcia Carrie Weinblatt, Feb. 25, 1968; children: Howard Avram, Tamar Miriam, Michael Elon, David Ben-Zion Aaron. BS, NYU, 1965; JD, Bklyn. Law Sch., 1968. Bar: N.Y. 1969, U.S. Ct. Claims 1970, U.S. Customs Ct. 1972, U.S. Ct. Customs & Patent Appeals 1974, U.S. Ct. Appeals (2nd cir.) 1969, U.S. Supreme Ct. 1972. Mng. lawyer Queens Legal Services, Jamaica, N.Y., 1970-71; ptnr. Previte-Glasser-Feder & Farber, Jackson Heights, N.Y., 1972-73, Hein-Waters-Klein & Feder, Far Rockaway, N.Y., 1973-78, Regosin-Edwards-Stone & Feder, N.Y.C., 1979—; spl. investigator Bur. Election Frauds, Atty. Gen.'s Office, N.Y.C., 1976-77, spl. dep. atty. gen., 1969-70; arbitrator, consumer counsel small claims div. Civil Ct. City of N.Y., 1974—. Pres. Young Israel Briarwood, Queens, N.Y., 1978; chmn. polit. affairs com. Young Israel Staten Island, 1985—; rep. candidate State of N.Y. Assembly, Queens, 1976; chmn. Stat Pac Polit. Action Com., Young Israel Staten Island Pub. Affairs Com. Mem. N.Y. Bar Assn., Queens County Bar Assn. Nassau County Bar Assn., Am. Judges Assn., N.Y. Trial Lawyers Assn., Internat. Acad. Law & Sci., Am. Jud. Soc., Soc. Med. Jurisprudence, Am. Arbitration Assn. Republican. Home: 259 Ardmore Ave Staten Island NY 10314 Office: Regosin Edwards Stone & Feder 225 Broadway New York NY 10007

FEDERMANN, FRANKLIN HOWARD, educational association administrator, accountant; b. N.Y.C., Nov. 8, 1939; s. Alfred B. and Rose F. (Grabinsky) F.; m. Rochelle L. Seidner, June 15, 1963; children: Barbara, Daniel, Joshua. BS, Bklyn. Coll., 1966; MS, L.I. U., 1971. CPA, N.Y. Mem. staff Eisner & Lubin, N.Y.C., 1966-69; sr. auditor Associated Univs., Inc., Upton, N.Y., 1969-70, chief internal auditor, 1970—. With USCG, 1957-66. Mem. Nat. Assn. Accts., Am. Acctg. Assn., Am. Inst. CPA's, Inst. Internal Auditors, N.Y. State Soc. CPA's (mem. tax div., faculty). Home: 20 Hawkins Path Coram NY 11727 Office: Associated Univs Inc Bldg 134A Upton NY 11973

FEDEWA, LAWRENCE JOHN, computer software company executive, consultant; b. Lansing, Mich., Oct. 31, 1937; s. Norman Anthony and Agnes G. (Murphy) F.; m. Theresa Kathryn Goeser, Aug. 18, 1962; children: Kirsten Ann, Eric Christian, Lawrence John Jr. BA, Sacred Heart Sem., Detroit, 1959; postgrad., Mich. State U., 1960-61; PhD, Marquette U., 1969. Cert. high sch. tchr. Mem. editorial staff Denver Cath. Register, 1962-63; assoc. prof. St. Norbert Coll., De Pere, Wis., 1966-71; v.p., dean Park Coll., Kansas City, Mo., 1971-74; provost Park Coll./Crown Ctr., Kansas City, Mo., 1974-76; dir. internat. projects Control Data Corp., Washington, 1976-79; pres. Fedewa and Assocs., Washington, 1979-81; v.p., sec., bd. dirs. Cordatum Inc., Bethesda, Md., 1981—; exec. dir. Ednl. Computer Svc. NEA, Washington, 1983-86. Pub. Yellow Book of Computer Products for Education, 1983-86; author, pub. Guide to the Software Assessment Procedure, 1983-87; author: Do Computers Help Teachers Teach?, 1987. Mem. research and devel. com. Met. Washington YMCA, 1986—. Roman Catholic. Office: Cordatum Inc 7923 Jones Branch Dr McLean VA 22102

FEDIGAN, JOHN JOSEPH, banker; b. Rochester, N.Y., Mar. 31, 1924; s. William James Fedigan and Kathryn (Granville) Mulrooney; m. Josephine Battaglia, June 14, 1947; children: William Joseph, Barbara Fedigan Marsden, John James. BA, Assumption Coll., U. Western Ont., 1948; postgrad. U. Rochester, 1948-59, Rutgers U., 1963-66. With trust dept. Lincoln Rochester Trust Co., 1948-52, adminstrv. asst. to trust officer, 1952-60, asst. sec., trust ops. officer, 1960-61; trust officer First Western Bank & Trust Co., Los Angeles, San Francisco, 1961-62; trust officer Irving Trust Co., N.Y.C., 1962-65; asst. sec., treas. Bessemer Trust co., Newark, 1962-65, treas., 1965-67, v.p., 1967-69, exec. v.p., 1969-73, pres., 1973-75, also dir.; chmn. Fiduciary Investment Co. N.J., Roseland, 1975—, Security Nat. Bank & Trust Co. N.J., Roseland, 1976—; chmn. Bus. Realty of Ariz., Inc., Scottsdale, 1978—; dir. Okonite Co., Ramsey, N.J. Bd. dirs. W. Paul Stillman Sch. Bus. Seton Hall U., South Orange, N.J., Heart Research Inst. St. Michael's Hosp., Newark. Served with U.S. Army, 1943-46. Clubs: Hackensack Golf (Oradell, N.J.); N.Y. Athletic; Gainey Ranch Golf, Orange Tree Golf (Scottsdale, Ariz.); Essex Fells Country (N.J.). Office: Security Nat Bank & Trust Co of NJ 101 Eisenhower Pkwy Roseland NJ 07068

FEDJE, EARL WESLEY, insurance company executive; b. Mitchelle, S.D., July 31, 1928; s. Roy Anderson and Norma Catherine (Iverson) F.; m. Joan Beverly Russell, Oct. 15, 1955; children: Kirsten Louise, Jon Christian, Ingrid Julia. AB, Willamette U., 1946; STB, Boston U., 1954; ThM, Princeton U., 1968. Ordained to ministry Meth. Ch., 1954. Commd. lt. (j.g.) USN, 1957, advanced through grades to comdr., 1977; squadron chaplain Destroyer Squadron 5, Pacific Ocean, 1957-59; regimental chaplain Naval Tng. Ctr., Great Lakes, Ill., 1959-60; chapel coordinator Naval Tng. Ctr., Great Lakes, 1961-63; sr. chaplain U.S.S. Cascade, 1961-63; sr. Protestant chaplain Naval Sta., Washington, 1963-65; sr. chaplain McAir Sta., Iwakuni, Japan, 1965-67; project officer Naval forces Vietnam, 1968-70; spl. project officer, sr. chaplain Naval Sta., Roosevelt Rds., P.R., 1970-73; tng. officer Human Resource Mgmt. Ctr., 1973-75; regimental chaplain USMC, Kaneohe, Hawaii, 1975-77; ret. USN, 1977; pastor Rose City Pk. Meth. Ch., Portland, Oreg., 1954-57; agt. Investors Equity Life Ins. Co., Honolulu, 1978-80, div. mgr., 1980-82; pres. Planning Svcs.-Hawaii, Inc., Honolulu, 1982—. Mem. Oahu Traffic Safety Council, Honolulu, 1985—. Decorated Legion of Merit with Combat V, Cross of Gallantry. Fellow Internat. Oceanographic Inst; mem. Honolulu Assn. Health Underwriters,(charter), Nat. Assn. Health Underwriters, Nat. Assn. Life Underwriters, Am. Soc. CLU, Chartered Fin. Cons. (bd. dirs., chmn. edn. com. 1987—), Nat. Def. Transp. Assn. (bd. dirs.), Internat. Naval Sailing Assn., Beta Theta Pi, Masons. Office: Planning Svcs Hawaii Inc 737 Bishop St Ste 2120 Honolulu HI 96813

FEDORCHAK, TIMOTHY HILL, facility planning and program consulting executive; b. Lodi, Calif., Jan. 15, 1958; s. John and Betty Francis (Daugherty) F. Student, San Joaquin Delta Coll., 1976-77, U. Utah, 1977-78; BS in Urban Planning, Calif. State Poly. U., 1981. Pub. works technician City of Lodi, Calif., 1979-80, planner, 1980-81; assoc. Steinmann, Grayson, Smylie, L.A., 1981-87; dir. Steinmann, Grayson, Smylie, Sacremento, 1987—; project mgr., cons. Facilities Master Plan, Maricopa County, Ariz., 1982, Corp. Yard Relocation Plan, Scottsdale, Ariz., 1983, Marin County Civic Ctr. Master Plan, San Rafael, Calif., 1984, San Joaquin Human Svcs. Facility Program, Stockton, Calif., 1985-86. Pres. Lodi History Hunters, 1972; univ. rep. Calif. State Poly. Univ., 1980-81. Mem. Am. Planning Assn. (charter), Am. Pub. Works Assn., Calif. State Poly. U. Planning Alumni Assn. (treas. 1986-88), Phi Eta Sigma. Democrat. Home: 1525 3d St Sacramento CA 95814 Office: Steinman Grayson Smylie 428 J St Ste 300 Sacramento CA 95814

FEELEY, HENRY JOSEPH (HANK), JR., advertising agency executive; b. Cambridge, Mass., July 9, 1940; s. Henry Joseph and Florence Patricia (O'Connor) F.; m. Mary Diane Dudenhoefer, May 14, 1966; children: Kathleen Anne, Mary Patricia, Henry Joseph III, James Brian. B.A., Coll. Holy Cross, 1963; grad., Inst. Advanced Advt. Studies, Northwestern U., 1966; P.M.D., Harvard Bus. Sch., 1976. With Leo Burnett Co., Inc.,, Chgo., 1965—, v.p., 1973-76, sr. v.p., 1976-82, exec. v.p., 1982—, vice chmn. bd. dirs., 1985-86; chmn., chief exec. officer Leo Burnett Internat., 1986—. Bd. dirs. Allendale Sch., Chgo., Am. Ireland Fund; mem. Irish Fellowship Chgo., 1982—. Served to lt. USN, 1963-65. Republican. Roman Catholic. Club: Tavern, Chgo. Ad, Queen City, Plaza (Chgo.). Home: 1080 Pelham Rd Winnetka IL 60093 Office: Leo Burnett Co Inc 35 W Wacker Dr Chicago IL 60601

FEENEY, CARLA JEAN NEWTON, software development executive; b. Chattanooga, Dec. 13, 1955; d. Francis Augustus and Cynthia (Catron) N. BBA, U. Tenn., 1977. Sr. systems analyst First Tenn. Bank, Memphis, 1978-82; pvt. practice cons. Memphis, 1982-85; v.p., product mgr. Sterling Software, Memphis, 1985-87; software cons. Software Devel. Svcs., Memphis, 1987—. Mem. NAFE, Memphis Brooks Mus. System. Republican. Home and Office: 8107 Kerry Dr Cordova TN 38018

FEENEY, FRANK MICHAEL, lighting company executive; b. Kansas City, Mo., Sept. 2, 1928; s. Frank M. and Matilda Feeney; m. Rita Ann O'Leary, Jan. 15, 1949; children: Susan, Michael, Kathleen. Student pub. schs. Sales mgr. S.W. Porcelain Steel, Tulsa, 1955-62; v.p. mktg. Wide Lite Corp., Houston, 1963-68, exec. v.p., 1968-70; pres., chief exec. officer Sterner Lighting System, Winsted, Minn., 1971—. Office: Sterner Lighting Systems 351 Lewis Ave Winsted MN 55395

FEES, JAMES RICHARD, investment banker, corporation executive; b. Fairbury, Nebr., Sept. 21, 1931; s. Robert Anthony and Mildred Pauline (Holtz) F.; children: Christina Marie, Eric (dec.). B.A., U. Notre Dame, 1957; diploma Arabic, Georgetown U., 1959; diploma French, Alliance Francaise, Paris, 1965. Diplomat, Dept. State, Washington, Arab countries, Switzerland, 1960-80; chief exec. officer Tradeco Ltd., Geneva, 1980—; bd. dirs. Tradeco Ltd., Geneva, Nasseau, 1980—, LaCellulose des Ardennes, 1988—; chmn. Luxembourg Fin. Group, 1982—. Mem. Rep. Senatorial Inner Circle, Washington, 1981—, founder Rep. Presdl. Group, 1982—, internat. chmn. Reps. Abroad, 1987-89, internal chmn. Ams. Abroad for Bush-Quayle, 1988; bd. dirs. Reps. Abroad, 1989—. Served with AUS, 1953-55. Mem. Swiss-Am. C. of C., Am. C. of C. in Egypt, Am. C. of C. in Belgium. Roman Catholic. Clubs: American (Brussels, Geneva); St. James (London), Geneva, Brussels. Office: Tradeco Internat SA, Avenue Louise 433, 1050 Brussels Belgium also: Fargo Investment Corp, Blvd E Jacqmain, 180, 1210 Brussels Belgium

FEFFER, PAUL EVAN, publishing company executive; b. N.Y.C., June 27, 1921; s. Joseph A. and Eve (Max) F.; m. Juliette Fein, July 30, 1964; children: Paula, Hilary, Joseph, Alison, Emily, Nicholas. Student, Cornell U. Sch. Medicine, 1940-42, USCG Acad., 1944; postgrad., NYU, 1963-64. V.p. H.M. Snyder & Co., N.Y.C., 1946-55; founder, pres. Feffer & Simons, Inc. subs. Doubleday & Co., N.Y.C., 1955-86, chmn., 1986—; chmn. Baker & Taylor Co. div. W.R. Grace & Co., N.Y.C., 1986-88; Fleetbooks Ltd., Zurich Feffer and Simons, B.V., Holland; dir. Victory Pub., London,, Vakil's Feffer & Simons, Inc., India, Feffer and Simons, Australia, Feffer and Simons, Tokyo; mem. govt. adv. com. Am. Book PUb. Council, 1983—. Chmn. adv. com. USIA, 1982-88. Served to lt. (j.g.) USCGR, 1942-46. Mem. Assn. Am. Pubs. (dir. 1982-83, chmn. internat. div. 1982-83). Home: 60 Sutton Pl New York NY 10022 Office: 100 Park Ave New York NY 10017

FEIBEL, FREDERICK ARTHUR, financial consultant; b. Chgo., Oct. 27, 1942; s. Fred and Emma Feibel; B.S.E.E., Purdue U., 1964; M.B.A., Northwestern U., 1970; m. Marlene Ruth Edwards, Aug. 7, 1965; 1 son, Frederick Curtis. Project engr. Johnson Controls Corp., Milw., 1964-69; sr. mgmt. cons. Arthur Andersen & Co., Chgo., 1970-76; rep. pension fund evaluation A.G. Becker Securities Co., Chgo. 1976-77; spl. agt. Northwestern Mut. Life Ins. Co., Milw., 1977-82; pres. F.A. Feibel Fin. Assocs., Northbrook, Ill., 1982—. Chmn., Village of Northbrook Bicentennial Commn., 1975-76; v.p., Northbrook Civic Found., 1977, pres., 1978, also bd. dirs.; pres. Northbrook Hist. Soc., 1977, also bd. dirs.; deacon Northfield Community Ch. Recipient disting. service award State of Ill., 1976; Northbrook Rotary Man of Yr. award, 1978-79; Civic Service award Northbrook B'nai B'rith, 1981-82; Disting. Service award Northbrook Civic Found., 1983, Vol. Initiative of Pvt. Sector Recognition award, Northbrook C. of C. and Industry, 1985, Vol. Appreciation award Northbrook Park Dist., 1987; C.L.U. Mem. Nat. Assn. Life Underwriters, Internat. Assn. Fin. Planning, Eta Kappa Nu, Tau Beta Pi. Home: 1342 Hillside Rd Northbrook IL 60062 Office: FA Feibel Fin Assocs 1310 Shermer Rd Northbrook IL 60062

FEICHTEL, CARL JOSEPH, banker; b. Allentown, Pa., Oct. 1, 1931; s. Charles J. and Laura E. (Eby) F.; m. Julia Ann Green, Jan. 29, 1955; children: Denise Feichtel VonFunk, Carl Joseph Jr., Joseph, Jean Marie Feichtel Upton. Cert. achievement, Pa. State U., 1955, Bucknell U., 1960, Sch. Consumer Banking, U. Va., 1964, Nat. Comml. Lending Sch., U. Okla., 1971, Grad. Sch. Bus., Columbia U. Cert. comml. lender. With Mchts. Bank, Allentown, 1949—; sr. v.p. Mchts. Bank, 1973, exec. v.p. loan div., 1973-74, pres., 1974-87, chief exec. officer, 1976—; now also chmn., dir; chmn., chief exec. officer, dir. Mchts. N.A., Allentown, Pa., 1974—; bd. dirs. Mack Trucks Receivables Corp., Indsl. Devel. Corp., Allentown, WLVT-TV, Bethlehem, Pa., Park and Shop, Inc., Allentown, Lehigh Valley Partnership, Allentown; bd. dirs., vice chmn. Fidelcor, Inc.; past instr. Am. Inst. Banking. Past bd. dirs. Lehigh County Indsl. Devel. Corp., Sacred Heart Hosp.; past bd. dirs., v.p. Assoc. Credit Bur. Services, Inc.; trustee Allentown Coll. St. Francis De Sales, Ctr. Valley, Pa.; chmn. fin. and budget com. Allentown Coll. St. Francis De Sales; mem. Lehigh County Authority, coun. Moravian Coll., Bethlehem, bd. assocs. Muhlenberg Coll., Allentown, Lehigh County Overall Econ. Devel. Program, Allentown, fin. com. Diocese Allentown, task force on affordable housing Lehigh Valley Confedn. Homeless, Allentown, Ptnrs. for Pride, Allentown, Downtown Improvement Dist., Allentown; bd. dirs. Lehigh Valley Ptnrship. Served with AUS, 1952-54. Recipient De Sales medal Allentown Coll. St. Francis De Sales, 1981, Disting. Citizen award Sales & Mktg. Execs. of Allentown/Bethlehem, 1986. Mem. Pa. Soc., Robert Morris Assos., Allentown-Lehigh County C. of C. (dir., treas.). Republican. Roman Catholic. Clubs: Lehigh Country, Saucon Valley Country (Bethlehem), Pa. Soc. (Phila.). Office: Mchts Bank 702 Hamilton Mall Allentown PA 18101

FEICK, STUART ELLSWORTH, investment consultant; b. East Orange, N.J., Aug. 15, 1931; s. Edward Thomas and Mildred Alma (Gould) F. BS in Chemistry, Rutgers U., 1953. Research scientist U.S. Rubber Co., Wayne, N.J., 1956-59; securities analyst R.W. Pressprich & Co., N.Y.C., 1959-62; gen. ptnr. research, investment policy com., sales Baker, Weeks & Co., N.Y.C., 1962-69; pvt. practice investment advising Palm Beach, Fla., 1969—; equity cons. Stephens, Inc., Little Rock. With U.S. Army, 1953-55. Mem. Palm Beach Polo and Country Club, Madison Square Garden Club, Union Club, Everglades Club, Bath and Tennis. Republican. Home and Office: PO Box 749 Palm Beach FL 33480

FEIGENBAUM, ARMAND VALLIN, systems engineer, systems equipment executive; b. N.Y.C., Apr. 6, 1920; s. S. Frederick and Hilda (Vallin) F. B.S., Union Coll., 1942; M.S., Mass. Inst. Tech., 1948, Ph.D., 1951. Engr. test program Gen. Electric Co., Schenectady, 1942-45; factory tng. course Gen. Electric Co., 1945-47, sales engr., 1947-48; supr. tng. mfg. personnel Gen. Electric Co., Lynn, Mass., 1948-50; asst. to gen. mgr. aircraft gas turbine div. Gen. Electric Co., Cin., 1950-52; mgr. aircraft nuclear propulsion dept. Gen. Electric Co., N.Y.C., 1952; co. mgr. quality control Gen. Electric Co., 1956, company-wide mgr. mfg. operations and quality control, 1958-68; pres., chief exec. officer Gen. Systems Co., Inc., Pittsfield, Mass., 1968—; mem. bd. overseers Malcolm Baldridge Nat. Quality Program, Washington D.C.; pres. Internat. Acad. for Quality, 1966-79, chmn. bd. dirs., 1979—; trustee, mem. bd. investment Berkshire County Savs. Bank; adv. group U.S. Army, 1966—; lectr. Mass. Inst. Tech., U. Cin., Union Coll., U. Pa. Author: Quality Control-Principles and Practice, 1951, Total Quality Control-Engineering and Management, 1961, Management Programming, 1980, The Organization Process, 1980, Total Quality Control, 3d edit., 1983; contbr. articles to profl. jours. Chmn. inst. adminstrn., mgmt. council Union Coll., 1963—. Recipient Founders medal, 1977, Medaille Georges Borel by Republic of France, 1988. Fellow Am. Soc. Quality control (pres. 1961-63, chmn. bd. 1963-64, Edwards medal 1966, Lancaster medal 1982, honorary mem. 1986), AAAS (hon.); mem. Nat. Security Indsl. Assn. (nat. award merit 1965), ASME (life), Nat. Soc. Profl. Engrs., IEEE (life), Inst. Math. Statistics, Acad. Polit. and Social Scis., Am. Econ. Assn., Soc. for Advancement Mgmt., Indsl. Relations Research Soc., Council for Internat. Progress in Mgmt. (chmn. bd. 1968-70). Home: 123 Ann Dr Pittsfield MA 01201 Office: Berkshire Common South St Pittsfield MA 01201

FEIGENBAUM, MARK, treasurer; b. Boston, Sept. 12, 1958; s. Maurice and Dorothy (Lampert) F.; m. Gail Rath, Feb. 22, 1986; children: James, Max. BA in Econs., Tufts U., 1980; MBA, Boston U., 1987. Fgn. exchange broker Mabon Nugent Godsell, N.Y.C., 1980-82; exec. v.p., treas. Finelle

Cosmetics, N.Y.C., 1982—. Republican. Jewish. Office: Finelle Industries 137 Marston St Lawrence MA 01842

FEIGIN, BARBARA SOMMER, advertising executive; b. Berlin, Germany, Nov. 16, 1937; came to U.S., 1940, naturalized, 1949; d. Eric Daniel and Charlotte Martha (Demmer) Sommer; m. James Feigin, Sept. 17, 1961; children: Michael, Peter, Daniel. BA in Polit. Sci., Whitman Coll., 1959; cert. of Bus. Adminstrn., Harvard-Radcliffe Program Bus. Adminstrn., 1960. Mktg. rsch. asst. Richardson-Vick Co., Wilton, Conn., 1960-61; market rsch. analyst SCM Corp., N.Y.C., 1961-62; group rsch. supr. Benton & Bowles, Inc., N.Y.C., 1963-67; assoc. rsch. dir. Marplan Rsch. Co., N.Y.C., 1968-69; exec. v.p. strategic svcs. Grey Advt. Inc., N.Y.C., 1969—, mem. agy. policy council; bd. dirs. VF Corp. Contbr. articles to profl. jours. Vice-chmn., bd. overseers Whitman Coll. Recipient Women Achievers award YWCA, 1987. Mem. Advt. Rsch. Found. (bd. dirs. 1987), Am. Assn. Advt. Agys. (rsch. com.), Market Rsch. Coun., Agy. Rsch. Dirs. Coun., Communications Rsch. Coun. Home: 535 E 86th St New York NY 10028 Office: Grey Advt Inc 777 3rd Ave New York NY 10017

FEILER, JANE ABESHOUSE, small business owner; b. Balt., Oct. 24, 1936; d. Benjamin Samuel and Carolyn K. Abehouse; m. Edwin J. Feiler Jr., June 15, 1958; children: Andrew Benjamin, Bruce Stephen, Cari Aleen. BS in Art Edn., Painting and Design, U. Mich., 1958; postgrad., Armstrong State Coll., 1960-74; postgrad. in arts adminstrn., Harvard U., 1977; MBA, Emory U., 1980. Lic. residential contractor. Tchr. pub. schs. Savannah, Ga., 1958-70; dir. edn. Telfair Acad. Arts and Sci., Savannah, 1970-74, acting dir., 1975-76; contractor, v.p. mktg. Metro Developers, Inc., Savannah, 1970-89, cons., 1976-80; with Computer Bus., Atlanta, 1980-84; pres., co-founder CELSA Learning Systems Co., Savannah, 1985—; instr. Coastal Ga. Ctr. for Continuing Edn., Savannah, 1980—; cons. and lectr. in field. Bd. dirs. Savannah Sci. Mus., 1985—; bd. dirs. Royce Ctr. for Learning Disabilities, 1985—; participant Leadership Savannah, 1976-77, program dir., 1978-79, 81-82, chmn., 1982-84; judge local and regional art exhbns.; mem. bd. visitors Emory U.; mem. exec. com. State of Ga. Semi-quincentenary Commn., Savannah State Coll. Pres.'s Commn.; sec. Ga. Pub. TV Adv. Council; visual arts panel chmn. Ga. Council for Arts and Humanities; mem. Chatham County Jury Commn., City of Savannah Semi-quincentenary Com.; vice chmn. Chatham County Community Services Adv. Bd., Savannah Arts Commn.; chmn. edn. com. Mayor's Council. Named Outstanding Woman of Excellence, Oglethorpe Bus. and Profl. Women, 1986. Mem. Am. Soc. Tng. and Devel., Savannah Women Bus. Owners, Commerce Club for Women Execs., Savannah Women's Network, Beta Gamma Sigma, Tau Sigma Delta. Democrat. Office: Learning Systems Co 120 Habersham St Savannah GA 31401

FEIN, BERNARD, investments executive; b. N.Y.C., Jan. 15, 1908; s. Samuel and Anna (Fine) F.; m. Elaine Schneir, Dec. 26, 1948; children—Kathy Joyce, Lawrence Seth, Susan, Adam, David. LL.B., St. Lawrence U., 1929. Bar: N.Y. 1931. Practiced law N.Y.C., 1931-41; pres., chmn. bd. United Indsl. Corp., N.Y.C; dir. AAI Corp., Balt. Home: 80 Garden Rd Scarsdale NY 10583 Office: United Indsl Corp 18 E 48th St New York NY 10017

FEINBERG, FRANK NOEL, advertising agency executive; b. Chgo., Dec. 25, 1950; s. Frank Henry and Henrietta (Drolshagen) F.; B.A., U. Chgo., 1973. Asst. analyst Leo Burnett Co., Inc., Chgo., 1973-74, analyst, 1974-75, asso. research supr., 1976-77, research supr., 1978, assoc. research dir., 1979; assoc. research dir. Young & Rubicam, N.Y.C., 1979—, v.p., 1980—, mgr. new product planning, 1982—, mktg. mgr., 1984-86, strategic planning mgr., 1986—. Mem. Assn. Consumer Research, Phi Beta Kappa. Office: Young & Rubicam 285 Madison Ave New York NY 10017

FEINBERG, ROBERT S., plastics manufacturing company executive, marketing consultant; b. Newark, May 14, 1934; s. Clarence Jacob and Sabina (Zorn) F.; BA in English, BS in Chemistry, Trinity Coll., Hartford, Conn., 1955; MBA in Mktg., Fairleigh Dickinson U., 1966; advt. diploma Assn. Indsl. Advt., 1967, advt. diploma N.Y. Inst. Advt., 1967; Pres., Trebor Assocs. and Trebor Plastics Co., Teaneck, N.J., 1961—; mktg. cons. computer software Zettler Softwear Co., Burroughs Corp.; sr. council Yankelovich, Skelly and White, Inc.; cons. Greenwich Assocs.; co-chmn., ptnr. Edgeroy Co., Inc., Ridgefield and Palisades Park, N.J., 1973—; co-chmn., ptnr. LeMont Sales Co., Teaneck, 1973—; cons. plastic formulations W.R. Grace, Endicott Johnson, Brown Shoe Co., U.S. Shoe Co., Ciba, Uniroyal. Mem. Soc. Plastics Engrs. (sr.), Sporting Goods Mfrs. Assn., Sell Overseas Am., U.S. Profl. Tennis Assn., Bergen County Tennis League (v.p.). Club: Ahdeek Tennis. Author: Olympia Shoe Co., 1966; co-inventor Edgeroy Ball Press; Polymer patentee in field. Home: 81 Edgemont Pl Teaneck NJ 07666

FEINMAN, SHELDON, sales company executive; b. N.Y.C., Sept. 27, 1926; s. Morris D. Feinman and Sally (Trainer) Wolk; m. Beverly Rosenzweig, May 29, 1958; children: Andrew, Joshua. BBA, Baruch Coll./CUNY, 1962; MBA, NYU, 1965; postgrad. in export ops., World Trade Inst., 1986. Asst. sales mgr. Claridge Food Co., Flushing, N.Y., 1964-67; pres. Shelbe Sales Co., Bklyn., 1968-79; sales and mktg. mgr. Can-Am Organic Foods Inc., Bklyn., 1979-82; lectr. in mktg. N.Y.C. Tech. Coll., Bklyn., 1982—; cons. Small Bus. Devel. Ctr., Bklyn., 1986—. Editor: Export Marketing, 1982; contbr. articles to profl. jours. Served with U.S. Army, 1950-52. Mem. Am. Mktg. Assn., Bklyn. C. of C. (internat. trade com. 1982—). Home: 81 Ocean Pkwy Brooklyn NY 11218 Office: NYC Tech Coll Dept Bus 300 Jay St Brooklyn NY 11201

FEINSTEIN, JERALD LEE, engineering consulting company executive; b. St. Louis, June 22, 1943; s. Seymour S. and Lenore A. (Miller) F.; m. Dorothy Ellen Squire, Aug. 21, 1966; children: Andrew Morrison, Matthew Duane, Jennifer Squire. BS in Physics, Okla. U., 1965; MS in Engring. Sci., N.J. Inst. Tech., 1970. Sci. advisor Dept. of Def., Washington, 1966-75; v.p. DOT Systems, Inc., Vienna, Va., 1975-77; sr. research engr. Stanford Research Inst., Washington, 1977-79; ops. research analyst U.S. EPA, Washington, 1979-84; sr. assoc. Booz Allen and Hamilton, Bethesda, Md., 1984-86; v.p., ptnr. ICF/ Phase Linear Inc., Washington, 1986—; Organized, chaired internat. conf. on Expert System applications in Bus. and Fin., 1987. Mem. editorial bd. Internat. Jour. Knowledge Engring., 1988—, Expert Systems. Jour., 1988—; contbr. articles on mil. research and devel., artificial intelligence and cybernetics to profl. publs. Bd. dirs. Capitol Area Bur. Rehab., Washington, 1976-81, Soc. for Prevention Narcotics, Alcohol and Other Drugs of Abuse, Vienna, 1977-78, McLean (Va.) Soccer Assn., 1978-79; dep. dir., Bowie Coll. Inst. for Advanced Research, 1986—. Recipient Research Assistantship NSF, Brookhaven Nat. Labs., 1964, Appreciation award Army Intelligence, 1975, Outstanding Research award Dept. Def., 1968. Mem. IEEE (chmn. 1971-73), Am. Assn. Artficial Intelligence, Armed Forces Communications Electronics Assn., Mensa, Washington Ops. Research Council. Home: 6826 Dean Dr McLean VA 22101 Office: ICF/ Phase Linear Systems Inc 9300 Lee Hwy Fairfax VA 22031

FEIT, RICHARD ALVIN, finance executive; b. N.Y.C., May 11, 1941; s. Herbert Balfour and Sylvia (Kaufman) F.; m. Carole Ann Goldberg, July 5, 1965; children: David Evan, Steven Kenneth. BS in Chem. Engring., U. Pitts., 1963. V.p. Blyth Eastman Dillon Co., N.Y.C., 1975-80; sr. v.p. Dean Witter Reynolds Co., N.Y.C., 1980-86; mng. ptnr. Cohen Feit and Co., N.Y.C., 1986—. Chmn. S. Nassau United Jewish Appeal Fedn. Cabinet, L.I., N.Y., 1984—; mem. assoc. bd. S. Nassau Communities Hosp., Oceanside, N.Y., 1983—. Mem. Investment Assn. N.Y., L.I. Anti-Defamation League (regional bd. dirs. 1983—). Clubs: Middle Bay Country (Oceanside), Downtown Athletic (N.Y.). Office: Cohen Feit & Co 39 Broadway New York NY 10006

FEITH, KATHY LYNN, financial planner, investment consultant; b. Saginaw, Mich., Oct. 19, 1956; d. Donald Walter and Norma Lorraine (Lamont) Gary; m. David Albert Feith, Apr. 10, 1982; children: Michael, Christopher, Nicole. Cert., Lee Vo Tech, Ft. Myers, Fla., 1974, Edison Community Coll., 1973-75; student, U. So. Fla., 1975, Forsyth Tech. Inst., 1983-84; cert., Coll. for Fin. Planning, Denver, 1987. Sec. corp., bus. adminstr. Gary Corp., Ft. Myers, 1974-79; inside sales rep. Beacon Electronics, Johnson City, Tenn., 1980-82; bus. mgr. Dr. Ken Kulp, Winston-Salem, N.C., 1982-84; treas., sec. corp., bus mgr. Wilson (N.C.) Dermatology Clinic P A, 1984-87; fin. and bus. cons. Dr. Karen E. Burke, N.Y.C., 1985—; head of planning div., fin. planner Consol. Plannning, Inc., Wilson, 1986—. Columnist for Triangle East Business Paper. Lectr. at ednl. seminars to pub. and civic orgns; treas.-elect exec. bd. local Am. Cancer Soc., 1988-89; mem. Jr. Women's Club, 1988—; mem. Arts Council, Wilson, 1986—. Mem. Inst. Cert. Fin. Planners, Internat. Assn. Fin. Planning, Med. Group Mgrs.N.C., C. of C. Personnel Assn. Republican. Presbyterian. Home: 2411 Surry Rd Wilson NC 27893 Office: Consol Planning Inc 2500 W Nash St Wilson NC 27893

FEITIS, MARJORIE CAROLINE, translation service company executive; b. Bellingham, Wash.; d. Clarence and Margaret (Chambers) Still; m. Peter Feitis. BA, U. Wash., 1962; MA, Ohio State U., 1964; postgrad., Institut d'Etudes Politiques, Paris, 1967-68. Owner, chief exec. officer SCITRAN (Scientific Translation Service) Co., Santa Barbara, Calif., 1972—. Transl. numerous publs. from over 8 different langs. Active Santa Barbara Environ. Resources Council; mem. Santa Barbara Land Use Bd.; bd. dirs. Montecito (Calif.) Assn. Named del. to U.S.-China Joint Session on Industry, Trade and Econ. Devel., Beijing, 1988; named one of 40 Outstanding Women in Govt. Procurement SBA, 1981. Mem. Am. Translators Assn., AAUW, Nat. Womens' Edn. Fund, LWV. Club: Four Seasons Hotel (bd. dirs.). Office: SCITRAN Co 1482 E Valley Rd Santa Barbara CA 93108

FEJES, ALAN GLEN, fluid power company executive; b. Wooster, Ohio, Mar. 14, 1947; s. Julius and Bessie Rose (Walentek) F.; m. Debra Lee Hoover, Nov. 16, 1984. Grad. high sch., Staunton, Va. Asst. to pres. Crown Steel Products Co., Orrville, Ohio, 1966-69; pres. Flo-Tork, Inc., Orrville, 1970—, also bd. dirs. Grand commodore Assn. Ohio Commodores, Columbus; bd. dirs. Boy's Village Found., Smithville, Ohio, Ohio Trade Council, Columbus, Palm River Country Club (naples, Fla.), Juli-Fe View Country Club (pres. 1982—), Cleve. Athletic Club, Cascade Club. Mem. Palm River Country Club (Naples, Fla.), Juli-Fe View Country Club (Orrville, pres. 1982—), Cleve. Athletic Club, Cascade Club. Home: 1115 W High St Orrville OH 44667-1437 Office: Flo-Tork Inc 1701 N Main St Orrville OH 44667

FELBER, RONALD JEFFREY, manufacturing company executive; b. Newark, Apr. 25, 1946; s. Herman P. Felber and Anita (Putman) Lerman; m. Brenda Leigh Barber, Mar. 18, 1978. BA in English, Rutgers U., 1968; MBA, Portland State U., Oreg., 1984. Editor Simon & Schuster Inc., N.Y.C., 1969-70, U. Mass., Amherst, 1970-71; foreman Adams Industries, Westminster, Colo., 1971-73; supr. prodn. New Horizons Inc., Farmington, Mich., 1973-74; gen. mgr. Mid-Mich. Industries Inc., Mt. Pleasant, 1974-79; supt. plant Sealy Mattress Co. Inc., Portland, Oreg., 1979-80; mgr. materials Hearth Craft Inc., Portland, 1980-84; pres. Felber & Assocs., Portland, 1984-87; gen. mgr. Amcoat Inc./Pacific Coatings Inc., Portland, 1987—; cons. Tektronix Inc., 1984-86, Columbia Contech Inc., 1987. Author: (computer manuals) PLUS, 1985, XTAPS, 1985, PCAFS, 1986; editor symposium proceedings Project Mgmt. Inst., 1987. Mem. bus. and labor com. Portland City Club, 1986—; chair subcom. on Drugs in the Workplace, 1988—. Recipient Cons. award SBA, Portland, 1984. Mem. Perfect Roundtable, Portland C. of C. Democrat. Home: 5032 NE Simpson St Portland OR 97218 Office: Amcoat Inc/Pacific Coatings Inc 8400 SE 26th Pl Portland OR 97202

FELD, JOSEPH, construction executive; b. N.Y.C., June 25, 1919; s. Morris David and Gussie (London) F.; student CCNY, 1946-47; m. Doris Rabinor, Apr. 10, 1948; 1 dau., Elaine Susan. Builder housing, apt. projects, L.I., N.Y.C., N.J., 1948-54; pres. Kohl and Feld, Inc., builder housing devels., Rockland County, N.Y., 1955-57; pres. Feld Constrn. Corp., New City, N.Y., 1957—, Birchland Constrn. Corp., 1957-70, Ramapo Towers, Inc., 1963-83; dir. Rockland County Citizen Pub. Corp., 1959-60; vice chmn. People's Nat. Bank Rockland County, Monsey, N.Y., 1974-85. Mem. Clarkstown Bldg. Code Com., 1959; mem. indsl. devel. adv. com. Rockland County Bd. Suprs., 1969-71; chmn. housing adv. council Rockland County Legislature, 1976—; chmn. Housing Task Force, 1979-80; mem., past v.p. New City Jewish Ctr.; past pres. Men's Club; mem. Rockland County council Jewish War Vets., past comdr. New City post. Served to staff sgt. AUS, 1941-45. Mem. Rockland County Assn., Inc. (former dir.), Rockland County Home Builders Assn. (past pres., dir., chmn. rental housing com.), Nat. (past dir.; mem. rental housing com.), N.Y. State (past dir., mem. rental housing com.) assns. home builders, Rockland County Apt. Owners Assn. (pres., dir. 1971—), Rockland County Bd. Realtors, N.Y. State Assn. Realtors (past dir.), Nat. Inst. Real Estate Brokers, New City C. of C. Clubs: Masons, Lions (local pres. 1959-60; zone chmn. 1961-62), B'nai B'rith. Home: 9 Woodland Rd New City NY 10956 also: 3821 Environ Blvd Lauderhill FL 33319 Office: 20 S Main St New City NY 10956

FELD, NATHAN ARTHUR, real estate developer; b. Poland, Feb. 12, 1920; s. Harry Solomon and Helen (Bleemer) F.; BA, U. Calif.-Berkeley, 1947; postgrad. U. Geneva, 1947-49; m. Lillian Guttman, June 4, 1965; 1 child, Janet. With Lehman Assocs., Newark, 1953-60, Louis Schlesinger Co., Newark, 1960-62; real estate sales agt. Kennilworth Assocs., N.Y.C., 1962-65; real estate developer Feld & Feld, East Orange, N.J., 1965-72; owner, chief operating officer Feld & Co., West Paterson, N.J., 1972—. With AUS, 1943-46, PTO, MTO. Mem. N.J. State C. of C., Paterson C. of C., Clifton-Passaic C. of C., Passaic Valley C. of C., Commerce and Industry Assn. No. N.J., 10th Mountain Div. Assn., Indsl. Real Estate Brokers Assn., Nat. Assn. Corp. Real Estate Execs., Bldg. Owners and Mgrs. Assn., U. Calif. Alumni Assn. Jewish. Home: One Tower Dr West Paterson NJ 07424 Office: 5 Garret Mountain Pla West Paterson NJ 07424

FELDBERG, SUMNER LEE, retail company executive; b. Boston, June 19, 1924; s. Morris and Anna (Marnoy) F.; married; children: Michael S., Ellen R.; stepchildren: Mollye S., Beth, James. B.A., Harvard, 1947, M.B.A., 1949. With New Eng. Trading Corp., 1949-56; treas. Zayre Corp., 1956-73, sr. v.p., 1965-68, exec. v.p., 1969-73, chmn. bd., 1973-87, chmn. exec. com., 1987—, also dir.; trustee Mass. Mut. Corp. Investors, Mass. Mut. Participation Investors. Trustee Beth Israel Hosp., Combined Jewish Philanthropies of Greater Boston. Served to 1st lt. USAAF, 1943-46. Address: Zayre Corp PO Box 910 Framingham MA 01701

FELDER, RAOUL LIONEL, lawyer; b. N.Y.C., May 13, 1934; s. Morris and Millie (Goldstein) F.; m. Myrna, May 26, 1963; children—Rachel, James. B.A., NYU, 1955, J.D., 1959; postgrad. U. Bern (Switzerland), 1955-56. Bar: N.Y., 1959, U.S. Dist. Ct. (so. and ea. dists.) N.Y., 1962, U.S. Ct. Appeals (2d cir.), 1962, U.S. Supreme Ct., 1970. Sole practice, N.Y.C., 1959-61, 1964—; asst. U.S. atty., N.Y.C., 1961-64; mem. faculty, Practicing Law Inst., 1979, Marymount Coll., 1982-89, Ethical Culture Sch., 1981, 82. Fellow Internat. Acad. Matrimonial Lawyers; mem. Assn. Bar City N.Y. (spl. com. matrimonial law 1975-77), ABA (judge nat. finals client counseling competition), N.Y. State Bar Assn., N.Y. State Dist. Attys. Assn., N.Y. State Trial Lawyers Assn. (past chmn. matrimonial law 1974-75), Nat. Criminal Def. Lawyers Assn., N.Y. State Soc. Med. Jurisprudence, Am. Judicature Soc., Am. Acad. Matrimonial Lawyers, Am. Arbitration Assn., Nat. Council on Family Relations, N.Y. Women's Bar Assn. Author: Divorce, The Way Things Are, Not the Way Things Should Be, 1971; Lawyers Practical Handbook to the New Divorce Law, 1981; contbr. articles on law to profl. jours; columnist for Fame mag., 1988-89. Home: 985 Fifth Ave New York NY 10021 Office: 437 Madison Ave New York NY 10022

FELDMAN, ALLAN ROY, marketing executive; b. Chgo., June 2, 1945; s. Michael and Sophie (Grossman) F.; m. Micki McCabe, Sept. 21, 1984. BS, Roosevelt U., 1968; postgrad., U. Louvain, Belgium, 1969-71; MBA, U. Chgo. Asst. to dir. gen. Rank-Xerox, S.A., Brussels, Belgium, 1969-71; dir. new bus. ventures graphic systems group Rockwell Internat. Corp., Chgo., 1971-73, dir. mktg., consumer ops., 1973-75, gen. mgr. microwave oven div., 1975-78; group v.p. Chromalloy Am. Corp., N.Y.C., 1978-80; mng. ptnr. Mktg. Trademark Cons., N.Y.C., 1980-85; pres. Leveraged Mktg. Corp. Am., N.Y.C., 1986—; bd. dirs. Alimansky Venture Group, Inc., N.Y.C., ITC Integrated Systems, Inc., N.Y.C., Growthtech Corp., N.Y.C., Indsl. Computer Corp., Farmington, Conn.; guest lectr. Columbia U., 1987. Contbr. articles to profl. jours. Bd. dirs. Riverside Fund, N.Y.C., 1987. Office: Leveraged Mktg Corp 200 West 57th St New York NY 10019

FELDMAN, BEN, life insurance agent; b. N.Y.C., Sept. 7, 1912; s. Isaac and Bertha (Dardick) F.; m. Freda Zaremberg, 1939 (dec. 1974); children: Marvin H., A. Richard; m. Ethel Blumenfeld Helfant, Feb. 5, 1976. CLU. Debit agt. Equitable Life Ins. Co., Washington, 1939-42; life ins. agt. N.Y. Life Ins. Co., N.Y.C., 1942—; chmn. emeritus, adv. bd. dirs. N.Y. Life Ins. Co. Author: Creative Selling for the Seventies, The Feldman Method, 1974, 79, 89, Creative Selling for the 1990's, 1989, various tapes and cassettes on fin. and estate planning. Named Man of Yr. East Liverpool Ohio C. of C., 1983. Fellow Nat. Assn. Life Underwriters (John Newton Russel Meml. award 1984), Advanced Assn. Life Underwriters, Youngstown Assn. Life Underwriters (named to Hall of Fame), Am. Coll.; mem. Million Dollar Round Table (life). Jewish. Office: Fremar Corp Feldman Agy 16569 St Clair Ave PO Box 30 East Liverpool OH 43920

FELDMAN, CHARLES L., manufacturing executive; b. Yonkers, N.Y., Dec. 18, 1935; s. Samuel and Edith (Friedman); children: Arnold, Daniel, Amy, Nerissa. BS in Mech. Engring., MIT, 1958, MS in Mech. Engring., 1960, ScDin Mech. Engring., 1962. Registered profl. engr., Mass. Research asst. Brookhaven Nat. Labs., Cambridge, Mass., 1956; engr. E.G.&G., Cambridge, 1956-59; dir. research Joseph Kaye & Co., Cambridge, 1963-65; prof. mech. engring. Worcester (Mass.) Poly. Inst., 1965-75; sr. v.p. Electronics for Medicine, Pleasantville, N.Y., 1971-79; assoc. gen. mgr. med. div. Honeywell, Pleasantville, 1979-81; pres. CardioData Corp., Northboro, Mass., 1971—; cons. Autonetics, Downey, Calif., 1956-59, Mass. Gen. Hosp., Boston, 1966-71; research assoc. Harvard U. Med. Sch., Cambridge, Mass., 1966-71; prof. Mass. U. Med. Sch., Worcester, 1981—. Contbr. articles to profl. jours. patentee in field. Fellow Am. Coll. Cardiology (assoc.); mem. Assn. for Advancement of Med. Instrumentation. Office: CardioData Corp 71 Lyman St Northborough MA 01532

FELDMAN, JEROME IRA, lawyer, patent development executive; b. N.Y.C., July 17, 1928; s. George and Tanya (Rubenstein) F.; m. Terry Jean Harmon, Oct. 23, 1964; children: Rebecca Page, Michael Dana, Kyra Joelle, Sarah Allison. B.A., Ind. U., 1949; LL.B., NYU, 1951, J.D., 1951. Bar: N.Y. 1951. Partner Feldman & Pollak, N.Y.C., 1953-60; pres., chief exec. officer Nat. Patent Devel. Corp., N.Y.C., 1960—; also dir. Nat. Patent Devel. Corp.; dir. Interferon Scis. Inc.; corp. advisor to provost U. Va. Trustee Bard Coll., New Eng. Colls. Fund, Cornell U. Research Found. Mem. N.Y. Bar Assn. Jewish. Office: Nat Patent Devel Corp 9 W 57th St Ste 4170 New York NY 10019

FELDMAN, LEON DAVID, metal products executive; b. Freehold, N.J., July 14, 1929; s. William and Ethel (Taxman) F.; m. Sydell Walker, Sept. 16, 1956; children: Steven, Carol, Diane, Edward. BBA, CCNY, 1951; MBA, NYU, 1972. Acct. ABC Vending Corp., N.Y.C., 1951-53; credit mgr. Broadway Maintenance Corp., Long Island City, N.Y., 1953-57; controller New Power Wire & Electric Corp., N.Y.C., 1957-61; controller P & F Industries Inc., Farmingdale, N.Y., 1962-67, v.p. fin., 1967-81, exec. v.p., 1981—, also bd. dirs. Mem. Fin. Execs. Inst. (bd. dirs. 1968-70).

FELDMAN, MARK DAVID, tax and financial advisor; b. Bridgeport, Conn., Aug. 22, 1962; s. Allan J. and Barbara (Klein) F. BS, Ariz. State U., 1984. CPA, Ariz. Leadership facilitator Ariz. State U., Tempe, 1983-84; treas.-sec. Total Services, Inc., Phoenix, 1982-84; tax mgr. Arthur Andersen & Co., Phoenix, 1984—, mem. fin. planning team and life ins. products team, 1984—. Vol. Fiesta Bowl, Phoenix, 1985—; com. chmn. Make-A-Wish, Phoenix, 1985—. Mem. Am. Inst. CPA's, Ariz. Soc. CPA's, Internat. Assn. Fin. Planners. Republican. Jewish. Home: 1720 E Thunderbird #2092 Phoenix AZ 85022 Office: Arthur Andersen & Co Two N Central #1000 Phoenix AZ 85004

FELDSCHUH, JOSEPH, physician, business executive; b. Vienna, Austria, June 10, 1935; came to U.S., 1938; s. Carl and Celia (Wildman) F.; m. Roxanne Cohen, Nov. 22, 1962; children: Jonathan, Stephen, Michael. BA, Columbia Coll., 1957; MD, N.Y. U., 1961. Diplomate Am. Bd. Internal Medicine, Am. Bd. Cardiovascular Diseases. Intern Montefiore Hosp. and Med. Ctr., N.Y.C., 1961-62, resident, 1962-65, mem. staff, 1966—; asst. prof. medicine N.Y. Med. Coll., 1966-78, asst. prof. pathology, 1969-83, assoc. prof. medicine, 1978-83; pres. Sci. Med. Systems, N.Y.C., 1969-74, Daxor Corp., N.Y.C., 1974—; clin. asst. prof. Cornell U., 1981-88, 1988—; cons. Cardio-Metabolic Lab. Met. Hosp., 1983—. Cons. editor Am. Jour. Medicine, 1983—; contbr. articles to profl. jours. Columbia U. fellow Bellevue Hosp., 1965-66; grantee Ortho Research Found. , 1972, Birnbaum Found., 1983; Regents scholar, 1957; recipient Am. Assn. Lab. Suprs. award, 1973. Fellow Am. Coll. Physicians, Am. Coll. Cardiology, N.Y. Heart Assn.; mem. AMA, Am. Fertility Soc., Pan-Am. Med. Assn., N.Y. State Med. Soc., N.Y. Cardiological Soc., N.Y. Acad. Scis., Bronx County Med. Soc. Office: Daxor Corp 645 Madison Ave New York NY 10022

FELDSTEIN, LISA ZOLA, art dealer, consultant; b. Santa Monica, Calif., Dec. 9, 1958; d. Donald James and Dorothy Naomi (Kahn) Zola; m. Alan H. Feldstein, Oct. 19, 1980; 1 child, Sasha Leigh. BA in History, UCLA, 1980; MBA, Pepperdine U., 1986. Theater, community svc. mgr. L.A. Trade-Tech. Coll., 1980; corp. art dir. Louis Newman Galleries, Beverly Hills, Calif., 1980-84; dir., v.p. Toluca Lake Galleries, Burbank, Calif., 1984-86; owner Zola Fine Art, L.A., 1986—; speaker, panelist Art Expo N.Y. and Art Expo Dallas, N.Y.C., 1983; project art cons. Litton Industries, Beverly Hills, 1984-86, Union Bank, Los Angeles, 1986—, Bateman Eichler, Hill Richards, 1988—. Contbr. articles to mag. Canvasser Dem. Party, L.A., 1972; mem. Campaign for Econ. Democracy, L.A., 1986—. Carnation Found. scholar, 1985, 86. Mem. Amnesty Internat., NAFE, Century City Rotary, Alpha Epsilon Phi. Democrat. Jewish. Office: 8730 W Third St Los Angeles CA 90048

FELDSTEIN, MARTIN STUART, economist, educator; b. N.Y.C., Nov. 25, 1939; s. Meyer and Esther (Gevarter) F.; m. Kathleen Foley, June 19, 1965; children—Margaret, Janet. A.B. summa cum laude, Harvard U., 1961; M.A., Oxford U., 1964, D.Phil., 1967; D.Laws (hon.), Rochester U., 1984, Marquette U., 1985, Bentley Coll., 1988. Research fellow Nuffield Coll., Oxford U., 1964-65, ofcl. fellow, 1965-67, lectr. pub. fin., 1965-67; asst. prof. econs. Harvard U., 1967-68, assoc. prof., 1968-69, prof., 1969—; George F. Baker prof. Harvard U., 1984—; pres. Nat. Bur. Econ. Research, 1977-82, 84—; chmn. Council Econ. Advisers, 1982-84; dir. TRW, Am. Internat. Group, Great Western Fin.; mem. internat. adv. council Morgan Guaranty Bank; trustee Met-Vest Funds. Fellow Am. Acad. Arts and Scis., Econometric Soc. (council 1977-82), Nat. Assn. Bus. Economists; mem. Am. Econ. Assn. (John Bates Clark medal 1977, mem. exec. com. 1980-82, v.p. 1988), Inst. Medicine Nat. Acad. Scis., Council on Fgn. Relations, Trilateral Commn. (exec. com. 1987—), Phi Beta Kappa. Home: 147 Clifton St Belmont MA 02178 Office: Nat Bur Econ Rsch Inc 1050 Massachusetts Ave Cambridge MA 02138

FELICITA, JAMES THOMAS, aerospace company executive; b. Syracuse, N.Y., May 21, 1947; s. Anthony Nicholas and Ada (Beech) F.; AB, Cornell U., 1969; postgrad. Harvard U., 1969, U. So. Calif., 1970, UCLA, 1975-77. Contracting officer U.S. Naval Regional Contracting Office, Long Beach, Calif., 1974-80; sr. contract negotiator space and communications group Hughes Aircraft Co., El Segundo, Calif., 1980-81, head NASA contracts, 1981-84, mgr. maj. program contracts, 1984—. Recipient cost savs. commendation Pres. Gerald R. Ford, 1976. Mem. Cape Canaveral Missile Space Range Pioneer, Nat. Contract Mgmt. Assn., Cornell Alumni Assn. So. Calif., Planetary Soc. Republican. Club: Nat. Space, Hughes Mgmt. Home: 8541 Kelso Dr Huntington Beach CA 92646 Office: 909 N Sepulveda Blvd Los Angeles CA 90245

FELINSKI, WILLIAM WALTER, regional engineering coordinator; b. Phila., June 19, 1953; s. William Jr. and Elizabeth Miriam (Hare) F.; m. Christina R. Bleistine, Sept. 30, 1989. BA, La Salle U., 1976. Registered chemist. Patent rsch. chemist ARSYNCO, Inc., Carlstadt, N.J., 1976-78; chem. engr. Indsl. Risk Insurers, Hartford, Conn., 1978-81; cons. Alexander & Alexander, Inc., N.Y.C., 1981-83; sr. cons. Alexander & Alexander, Inc., Phila., 1983-85; regional cons. HSB I&I Co., Phila., 1985-86; regional mgr. HSB I&I Co., Atlanta, 1986-87; sr. corp. cons. HSB I&I Co., Hartford, Conn., 1987-89; regional coord. HSB I&I Co., Phila., 1989—. Patentee in field. Leader Boy Scouts Am., Valley Forge, Pa., 1985-86. Mem. Am. Chem. Soc., Soc. Fire Protection Engrs., Nat. Fire Protection Assn., Am.

Mgmt. Assn., La Salle U. Alumni Assn. Republican. Roman Catholic. Home: 7206 Valley Ave Philadelphia PA 19128 Office: Hartford Steam Boiler Inspection & Ins Co 610 Freedom Bus Center Dr #300 King of Prussia PA 19406

FELIX, ELAINE SAWTELLE, retail executive; b. Richmond, Va., June 24, 1958; d. Curtis Rucker and Dorothy (Daniels) Sawtelle; m. Brian David Felix, July 30, 1983. AA in Retailing, Va. Intermont Coll., Bristol, 1981, BA in Merchandising, 1981. With Kings Dominion, Doswell, Va., 1977-80, Miller & Rhoads, Richmond, 1980-81; store mgr. Life Uniform & Shoe Shop, Richmond, 1981, Bethesda, Md., 1981-82; store mgr. The Children's Pl., Gaithersburg, Md., 1982-83, Miami, Fla., 1983-84, Williamsburg, Va., 1984-85; dist. ops. dir. The Children's Pl., Richmond, 1985—. Leader Girl Scouts Am., Fredericksburg, Va., 1976. Lions Club scholar. Mem. Nat. Assn. Female Execs., Alpha Chi. Republican. Methodist. Home: 1406 Plum Grove Dr Mechanicsville VA 23111 Office: The Children's Place Regency Sq Richmond VA 23229

FELIX, JOHN HENRY, investments executive; b. Honolulu, June 14, 1930; s. Henry and Melinda (Pacheco) F.; m. Patricia Berry; children: Laura Haroskiewicz, Linda Diciro, Jayne Mordell, John Morgan, Annette Sherry. student Chaminade Coll., 1947, AB summa cum laude, San Mateo Coll., 1950; postgrad., U. Calif., San Francisco, 1950-52; Harvard 1971; BS, MS, Calif. Western U.; PhD, Walden U., 1975. Asst. to pres. AFL-CIO Unity House, 1955-57; exec. v.p. Hotel Oper. Co. of Hawaii, 1957-60; v.p. Music Polynesia, Inc.; asst. to Gov. of Hawaii, 1960-62; pres. LaRonde Restaurants, Inc., 1962-84, Hotel Assocs., Inc.; consul to Portugal, 1974—; vice consul to Spain, 1980—; dir., mem. exec. com., chmn. personnel com. Hawaii Nat. Bank; pres., chmn. exec. com. Hawaiian Meml. Park. Chmn. ARC, 1961-63, 72; del. League Red Cross Socs.; chmn. Gov.'s Jobs for Vets. Task Force, 1971-76, Honolulu Redevel. Agy., 1971, 72, Honolulu City & County Planning Com., 1959; chmn. Bd. Water Supply, 1973-75; chmn. Honolulu City County Bd. Parks Recreation; mem. City and County Honolulu Police Commn., 1979, chmn., 1984; pres. bd. Hawaii Public Radio, 1979; bd. govs. ARC, also chmn. Pacific div.; chmn. nat. council of vols. March of Dimes Birth Defects Found., chmn. ops. West, nat. trustee; mem. internat. com. Boy Scouts Am, council Commr. Pacific area; chmn. Rep. Nat. Hispanic Assembly, Hawaii, 1987; chmn. redevel. com. Castle Meml. Ctr.; U.S. del. South Pacific Commn., 1985; spl. asst. to pres. League of ARC, Red Crescent Soc., 1985. Served with AUS, 1952-54. Recipient Distinguished Service award Sales and Marketing Execs. Hawaii, 1968, Harriman award disting. vol. service ARC, 1975, Henri Duhant award, 1983, Silver Beaver award Aloha Council Boy Scouts Am., 1983, Disting. Eagle award, 1983; named Young Man of Yr., Hawaii Jr. C. of C., 1959, Salesman of Yr., Sales and Mktg. Execs. of Honolulu, 1981, others. Mem. Young Pres.'s Orgn., Hawaii Restaurant Assn. (pres. 1967), Air Force Assn. (pres. Hawaii), C. of C. of Hawaii (life), Nat. Eagle Scout Assn. (life, vice chmn. Hawaii chpt.), CAP-U.S. Air Force Aux. (comdr. Hawaii Wing 1980), Arts Club of Washington, Oahn Country Club, Pacific Club, Plaza Club, Rotary. Home: 700 Bishop St #1012 Honolulu HI 96813 Office: Borthwick Meml Svcs 700 Bishop St Ste 1012 Honolulu HI 96813

FELIX, RICHARD JAMES, engineering executive, consultant; b. Sacramento, Apr. 21, 1944; s. Joseph James and Faye Lola (Thornburg) F.; m. Nancy Tucker Thompson, 1970 (div. 1972). Cert., Electronics Tech. A Sch., Treasure Island, Calif., 1963; student, Am. River Coll., 1968-72, Calif. State U., 1972-74. Ptnr. ADRA, Sacramento, 1971-73, Doggie Domes, Sacramento, 1971-72, Fong and Co., Sacramento, 1976-79; project dir. Dynascan Project, Sacramento, 1976-88; dir. research Omni Gen. Corp., Sacramento, 1988—; ptnr. Am. Omnigraph, Sacramento, 1985—; instr. Calif. State U., Sacramento, 1973-74; cons. KDM Design, 1985—. Creator documentary film American River College Rat Decathlon, 1974; editor publicity manual, 1978; inventor omnigraph, 1967, Multiplex Video Display System, 1976, Multiplex Video Display System II, 1984. Vol. Leukemia Soc., Sacramento, 1984; artist Camellia City Ctr., Sacramento, 1983. Served with USN, 1962-66. Mem. Sacramento chpt. Mental Health Assn. (bd. dirs. 1980, Clifford Beers award 1983), Mensa. Republican. Episcopalian. Club: New Horizons (Sacramento) (editor 1977-79).

FELKER, ALEX D., communications executive; b. Fukuoka, Japan, Oct. 5, 1949; s. Alex and Phyllis Sally (Tobias) F.; m. Vonnie Rae Malek; children: Andrew Malek, Michelle Malek. BSEE, Va. Poly. and State U., 1972; MSEE, George Washington U., 1987. Elec. engr. for office exec. dir. FCC, Washington, 1972-73, elect. engr. comman carrier bur., 1973-74, policy analyst office plans and policy, 1979-86, dep. chief policy and rules div. mass media bur., 1986-87, chief, 1987—, asst. to chmn., 1987; radio sta. inspector field ops. Bur. FCC, Long Beach, Calif., 1974-76; specialist FCC, Norfolk, Va., 1976-79. Contbr. papers in field. Mem. Am. Radio Club, Relay League. Office: FCC Mass Media Bur 1919 M St NW Washington DC 20554

FELKER, DAVID R., manufacturing company executive; b. Torrance, Calif., Sept. 4, 1957; s. Roy Leon and Colleen Mae (Rowland) F.; m. Joanne Stephanie Feigin, Jan. 23, 1982 (div.); 1 child, Megan Kimberly. BS in Econs., UCLA, 1978. Store mgr. Stereo Plus, Los Angeles, 1977-79; gen. mgr. Bel-Aire Audio, Los Angeles, 1976-77, 79-80; nat. mktg. mgr. Leland Energy Corp., Los Angeles, 1980-83; pres. chief exec. officer Bi-Pro Industries, Inc., El Segundo, Calif., 1983—; mktg. cons., sales trainer for varied customers David Felker and Assoc., 1981—. Patentee trapping method for insects. Mem. Calif. Scholarship Fedn. (life), Mensa, Torrance C. of C. (Appreciation award). Republican. Roman Catholic. Club: Collie (v.p. 1985-86). Office: Bi-Pro Industries Inc 212 N Eucalyptus Blvd El Segundo CA 90245

FELKER, JAMES M., business executive; b. St. Louis, July 15, 1939; s. Henry W. and Margaret (King) F. B.A., Stanford U., 1960; M.B.A., U. of Ams., Mexico City, 1966. Pres. Perkins Engines Ltd., Peterborough, Eng., 1980-83; pres. tractor div. Massey Ferguson Ltd., Toronto, Ont., Can., 1983-86; sr. v.p. Varity Corp., Toronto, 1987-88; chmn. Simon U.S. Holdings Inc., Cin., 1989—. Mem. Inst. Mech. Engrs. (companion). Office: 6601 Pleasant St Cincinnati OH 45227

FELL, DONALD G., educational association administrator; b. Terre Haute, Ind., Nov. 4, 1945; s. Russell E. and Geraldine (Spears) F.; m. Judith A. Fell, July 15, 1967; children: Lara C., Barrett T. BA, Ind. State U., 1967, MS, 1968; postgrad., Ill. State U. Instr. econs. Ill. Valley Community Coll., Oglesby, 1968-75, chmn. dept. bus., 1975-78; pres. Ohio Council Econ. Edn., Columbus, 1978-84, Fla. Council Econ. Edn., Tampa, 1984—; adj. prof. Ohio State U., Columbus, 1978-84, U. South Fla., Tampa, 1984—. Author: Stock Market Game Manual, 1988. Co-chmn. Ill. Valley United Way, La Salle, 1977, chmn. 1978; chmn. adv. com. U. So. Fla. Econ. Dept., Tampa, 1986-87. Recipient Disting. Service award Pinellas County Schs., 1988, Citation Merit Joint Council Econ. Edn., 1982, Leadership award State Awards Program, 1987; named Outstanding Young Man Am. Nat. Jaycees, 1977. Mem. Nat. Assn. Econ. Edn. (chmn. devel. com. 1986—), Nat. Soc. Fund Raising Edn., Assn. Pvt. Enterprise Econs., Econ. Club Fla., Nat. Assn. Bus. Economists, Econ. Club Tampa Bay (pres. 1988). Republican. Methodist. Office: Fla Coun Econ Edn 1211 N Westshore Blvd Suite 300 Tampa FL 33607

FELL, JOSEPH D. (JOE), retail executive; b. Evanston, Ill., May 4, 1940; s. Abraham L. and Eleanor (Biruenstein) F.; m. Mary Loughran, Mar. 10, 1963 (div. 1978); children: Karyn, Sam; m. Karen Webster, Sept. 13, 1981. BS, Carnegie Mellon Inst. Tech., 1962. Mgmt. trainee W.F. Hall Printing Co., Chgo., 1962-64, rep. sales, 1964-66; rep. sales Lloyd Hollister, Inc., Wilmette, Ill., 1966-68; controller The Fell Co., Winnetka, Ill., 1968—. Pres. Winnetka C. of C., 1973-75; mem. planning commn. Village of Winnetka, 1975-81, trustee council, 1987—; trustee North Suburban Mass Transit Dist., Des Plaines, Ill., 1981-87; bd. dirs. Winnetka Community Theatre, 1978-81. Served with Ill. A.N.G., 1963-69. Mem. Menswear Retailers Am. (chmn. fin. and ops. group Washington chpt. 1976-78). Jewish. Office: The Fell Co 511 Lincoln Ave Winnetka IL 60093

FELLERMAN, LINDEN JAN, financial services executive; b. N.Y.C., Apr. 9, 1956; s. Myer P. and Rina (Nahmias) F.; m. Luann Schwartz, Apr. 9, 1978; children: Shannon, Nicole. BA in Econs., UCLA, 1977; MBA, Pepperdine U., 1980. With Telecredit, Inc., Los Angeles, 1975-81; v.p. sales Telecredit, Inc., Tampa, Fla., 1981-82, v.p. mgmt. info. services, 1982-85; pres. Telecredit Corp. Ga., Atlanta, 1985-86, Telecredit Service Corp., Tampa, 1986—. Mem. Payment Systems Edn. Assn. (dir. 1986—). Republican. Home: 14103 Riverstone Dr Tampa FL 33624 Office: Telecredit Svc Corp 5301 W Idlewild St Tampa FL 33634

FELLERS, RHONDA GAY, lawyer; b. Gainesville, Tex., July 20, 1955; d. James Norman and Gaytha Ann (Sanders) F.; m. Bruce C. Hinton, Oct. 15, 1981 (div. Oct. 1985). BA, U. Tex., 1977, JD, 1980; LLM in Taxation, U. Denver, 1987. Bar: Tex. 1981, Colo. 1981, U.S. Dist. Ct. (no. dist.) Tex. 1982, U.S. Dist. Ct. Colo. 1985, U.S. Tax Ct. 1985, U.S. Ct. Appeals (5th cir.) 1986. Assoc. Walters & Assocs., Lubbock, Tex., 1981-83; gen. counsel Security Nat. Bank, Lubbock, 1983; assoc. Melvin Coffee & Assocs., P.C., Denver, 1984-85, 87—; sole practice Lubbock, 1983-87. Mem. ABA, State Bar Tex., Colo. Bar Assn., Denver Bar Assn., Colo. Women's Bar Assn. Office: 2121 S Oneida Suite 336 Denver CO 80224

FELSEN, KARL EDWIN, state official; b. Hornell, N.Y., July 29, 1948; s. Irwin and Nell Marie F.; m. Carol Ann Terko, June 17, 1978; children: Kristen Elizabeth, Alexander Karl. BA, Santa Clara U., 1969; MA, SUNY, Albany, 1972, PhD, 1975. Dir. speaker's corr. unit N.Y. State Assembly, Albany, 1976-81; media specialist N.Y. State Council on Children and Families, Albany, 1981-82; dir. pub. relations N.Y. State Dept. Civil Service, Albany, 1982-84; dir. pub. info. N.Y. State Dept. Taxation and Fin., Albany, 1984—; participant U.S. Internat. Communications Agy., 1980.t. Classical music columnist Troy (N.Y.) Times Record, 1976-79; mem. editorial rev. bd. Managing N.Y. State, 1984—; contbr. articles to various publs. and mags. Advisor on govtl. affairs Council Orgns. Serving the Deaf, Albany, 1978-81; judge Martin Luther King Jr. Ann. Arts and Scis. Competition, Albany, 1985-88. Recipient Poetry award Writers' Digest, 1970, N.Y. State Mgmt./Confidential Spl. Achievement award, 1986. Mem. Nat. Assn. Govtl. Communicators, Alpha Sigma Nu. Home: 26 Pinewood Rd Guilderland NY 12084 Office: NY State Dept Taxation & Fin Bldg 9 State Office Campus Albany NY 12227

FELTER, JOHN KENNETH, lawyer; b. Monmouth, N.J., May 9, 1950; s. Joseph Harold and Rosanne (Bautz) F. BA magna cum laude, MA in Econs., Boston Coll., 1972; JD cum laude, Harvard U., 1975. Bar: Mass. 1975, U.S. Dist. Ct. Mass. 1976, U.S. Ct. Appeals (1st cir.) 1977, U.S. Supreme Ct. 1982. Assoc. Goodwin, Procter & Hoar, Boston, 1975-83, ptnr., 1983—; spl. asst. atty. gen. Commonwealth of Mass., 1982-84; spl. counsel Town of Plymouth, Mass., 1983—, Town of Salisbury, Mass., 1983-85, Town of Edgartown, Mass., 1985—; active devel. com. Greater Boston Legal Services, 1982—, bd. dirs. 1980—; mem. faculty Mass. Continuing Legal Edn., Inc., Boston, 1984—, Am. Law Inst.-ABA Com. Continuing Edn., 1986—; instr. trial adv. program Harvard Law Sch., 1981—; judge moot ct. competition Harvard Law Sch., 1978—. Mem. adv. com. The Boston Plan for Excellence in Pub. Schs.; VIP panelist Easter Seals Telethon, Boston, 1978-79. Mem. ABA (litigation sect., gen. practice sect., personal rights litigation com.), Mass. Bar Assn., Boston Bar Assn. (bd. dirs. law firm resources project 1985—, coll. and univ. law com. 1986—), Am. Arbitration Assn. (comml. arbitrator 1985—), Greater Boston C. of C. (edn. com., health care com.). Office: Goodwin Procter & Hoar Exchange Pl Boston MA 02109

FELTON, GUY PAIGE, III, employment advisor; b. Spartanburg, S.C., May 21, 1937; s. Guy Paige II and Winnie Nell (Thomas) F. BS in Edn, SUNY, Oneonta, 1961. Cert. tchr., N.Y., Nev. Tchr. Brewster Cen. Schs., N.Y., 1967-71, Washoe County Sch. Dist., Reno, 1971-73, Lander County Pub. Schs., Battle Mountain, 1977-83; ptnr. Little Press, Reno, 1973-77; chief exec. officer Guy P. Felton & Assocs., Reno, 1983-86, Resume Cons. Internat., Reno, 1986—. Pub., (cons. book) Sonic Booms vs. The American Way, 1987; author, publisher guide. Lander County chmn. Concerned Rural Nevadans, 1982-83; founding adv. Community Student Council, Reno, 1987-88.

FELTS, JOHN PATE, chief financial officer; b. Richmond, Va., Oct. 12, 1951; s. Ashton Meridith and Louise (Taylor) F. BS in Acctg., U. Richmond, 1974; MBA, William and Mary Coll., 1978. CPA, Va., Md., D.C. Auditor Peak & Drescher, CPA's, Franklin, Va., 1974-76; tax specialist Peat, Marwick, Mitchell & Co., Washington, 1978-79; mng. ptnr. Simmermacher & Felts, CPA's, Washington, 1979-81; chief fin. officer Gray and Co. Pub. Communication, Washington, 1981-86; regional fin. officer Hill & Knowlton, Inc., Washington, 1986-87; chief fin. officer Gray and Co. II, Washington, 1987—. Mem. Am. Inst. CPA's, D.C. Inst. CPA's. Home: 1023 Potomac St NW Washington DC 20007 Office: Gray & Co II 3255 Grace St NW Washington DC 20007

FEMMINELLA, CHARLES J., JR., real estate appraiser; b. Bklyn., Aug. 10, 1938; s. Charles J. and Rose (Lanza) F.; m. Mary Ann DeCaro, Sept. 11, 1965; children: Cindy L., Christy J. BS, Fairleigh Dickinson U., 1966. Pres. Cert. Valuations, Inc., Randolph, N.J., 1986—; pres. Randolph Hills Realty, Inc.; expert witness real estate affairs. Author: Real Property Appraisal, 1974 (Presdl. Citation 1978). Pres. Randolph Rep. Club, 1980, Pla. 447 Condominium Assn., 1986—, also bd. dirs. Cpl. USMC, 1958-61. Mem. Soc. Profl. Assessors, Randolph C. of C. (v.p., dir. 1972). Lodge: Kiwanis, KC. Office: Cert Valuations 447 Rt 10 St 6 Randolph NJ 07869

FENDRICK, ALAN BURTON, advertising executive; b. Bronx, N.Y., Mar. 22, 1933; s. Louis and Esther (Silberberg) F.; m. Beverly R. Schoenfeld, June 12, 1960; children—Sarah Lin, Lisa Augusta. A.B. with honors in Econs, Columbia, 1954; M.B.A., Harvard U., 1958. Asst. sales mgr. splty. div. Hankins Container Co., 1958-60; mgr. bus. adminstrn., operations and engring. NBC, 1960-67; with Grey Advt. Inc., 1967—, exec. v.p., sec., treas., 1972—. Trustee Woodlands High Sch. Scholarship Fund, Greenburgh, N.Y., pres., 1977-78; trustee Jewish Child Care Assn. N.Y., 1985—; mem. Greenville Community Theater, sch. bd. Mt. Pleasant Cottage Sch., 1985—. Served with AUS, 1954-56. Mem. Am. Assn. Advt. Agys. (chmn. com. on fiscal control 1979-81), Advt. Agy. Financial Mgmt. Group (chmn. exec. com. 1980-82, pres. 1982-84), Harvard Bus. Sch. Club N.Y., Fin. Execs. Inst., Otis Woodlands Club Inc. (bd. dirs. 1985—, treas. 1984-88). Jewish (trustee temple). Home: 30 Canterbury Rd White Plains NY 10607 Office: Grey Advt Inc 777 3rd Ave New York NY 10017

FENICHEL, SAUL MICHAEL, lawyer; b. Lakewood, N.J., Nov. 10, 1952; s. Lester J. and Rachel (Tilis) F.; m. Isabel Strauss, May 23, 1982; children: Jessica, Matthew. BS in Econs., U. Pa., 1974; JD, Rutgers U., 1977. Bar: N.J. 1977. U.S. Dist. Ct. N.J. 1977. Mem. tax staff Coopers & Lybrand, Newark, 1977-80; mgr. nat. tax svcs. group Coopers & Lybrand, Washington, 1980-82; tax mgr. Coopers & Lybrand, Newark, 1982-86, tax ptnr., 1986-87; ptnr. tax svcs. Coopers & Lybrand, Princeton, N.J., 1987—. Contbr. numerous articles to profl. jours. Mem. ABA, Am. Inst. CPAs, N.J. Soc. CPAs. Office: Coopers & Lybrand 136-300 Main st Princeton Forrest Village NJ 98540

FENN, ORMON WILLIAM, JR., furniture company executive; b. Tyler, Tex., Mar. 13, 1927; s. Ormon William and Madonna (Muphree) F.; m. Lucille Adrianne Kelley; children: Andrea Lee, Miles Linton, Kelly Sue, Michael Thomas. Student U. Minn., 1945, Okla. U., 1945, Imperial U., 1946; BS Yale U., 1949. Asst. dist. mgr. Armsrong Cork Co., Lancaster, Pa., 1949-59, asst. gen. sales mgr., 1959-70; vice pres., gen. sales mgr. Thomasville (N.C.) Furniture Industries, Inc., 1970-74, sr. v.p., gen. sales mgr., 1974-77; exec. v.p. sales and mktg. Stanley Furniture Co. Mead Corp., Stanleytown, Va., 1977-78, pres., 1978-79; pres. chief exec. officer Stanley Furniture Co., 1979-82; pres., chief operating officer LADD Furniture Co., High Point, N.C., 1982—, dir., 1982—; past chmn. bd. govs. Western Mdse. Mart, San Francisco; past chmn. market adv. bd. High Point So. Furniture Market Center; bd. dirs, v.p. Internat. Home Furnishings Mktg. Assn.; bd. dirs./exec. com. Home Furnishing Coun.; bd. dirs. Am. Furniture Mfrs. Hall of Fame; bd. dirs. 1st Fed. Carolinas, High Point, N.C. Served to 1st lt. U.S. Army, 1944-52, PTO. Episcopalian. Avocations: golf, hunting, physical fitness. Home: 510 Emerywood Dr High Point NC 27262-2812 Office: LADD Furniture Inc 1 Plaza Ctr Box HP3 High Point NC 27261

FENNEBRESQUE, KIM SAMUEL, investment banker; b. N.Y.C., Mar. 20, 1950; s. John Drouet and Frances Jane (Campbell) F.; m. Deborah Anne Johnson, Sept. 8, 1979; children: Quincy Campbell, John Drouet II. AB, Trinity Coll., 1972; JD, Vanderbilt U., 1975. Bar: Conn. 1975, N.Y. 1977. Assoc. Day, Berry & Howard, Hartford, Conn., 1975-76, Simpson, Thacher & Bartlett, N.Y.C., 1976-77; assoc. The First Boston Corp., N.Y.C., 1977-81, v.p., 1981-85, mng. dir., 1985—. Mem. Piping Rock Club. Racquet and Tennis Club, Links Club, St. Anthony Hall Lodge. Republican.

FENNO, JAMES ROBERT, pharmacist, medical facility administrator; b. Milw., Aug. 10, 1943; s. Robert Ray and Loraine Emma Hazel (Hardtke) F.; m. Jane Helen Stenerson, Oct. 15, 1966; children: James Andrew, Lauri Jane. BS in Pharmacy, U. Wis., 1966. Registered pharmacist, Wis. Intern, staff mem. Peters Pharmacy, Milw., 1965-68; staff pharmacist Appleton (Wis.) Meml. Hosp., 1968-73; clin. cons. Pharm. Svcs., Appleton, 1973-74, pharmacist, 1976-77; resident, clin. specialist U. Wis. Med. Ctr., Madison, 1974-76; dir. pharmacy and clin. pharmacy svcs. St. Joseph's Hosp., Chippewa Falls, Wis., 1977—; owner, mgr. Pharm Consulting Svcs., Chippewa Falls, 1980—; pub. health officer City of Chippewa Falls, 1986—; reviewer U.S. Pharmacopeial Conv., Rockville, Md., 1986—. Bd. dirs. Chippewa County United Way, 1979-82, Chippewa Falls chpt. Am. Cancer Soc., 1980-83; cons. Parents Against Chem. Abuse, Chippewa County, 1983—. Recipient Chippewa/Eau Claire Leadership award WEAU Broadcasting Co., 1982, Pharmacy Leadership award Nat. Assn. Retail Druggists, 1983, Pharmacy Achievement award Merck Sharp & Dohme Labs., 1986. Mem. Wis. Pharm. Assn. (pres. 1983-84, Mortar & Pestle award, 1986, A.H. Robins Bowl of Hygeia award, 1988), Chippewa Valley Pharm. Assn. (pres. 1980-81), U. Wis. Pharmacy Alumni Assn. (pres. 1987-88), Am. Pharm. Assn. (del. 1983-85), Am. Inst. History of Pharmacy (author, photographer slide show 1976). Home: 815 Dwight St Chippewa Falls WI 54729 Office: St Joseph's Hosp 2661 County Trunk I Chippewa Falls WI 54729

FENSTER, HARVEY, energy company executive; b. N.Y.C., Mar. 4, 1941; s. Sidney and Frances F.; m. Edy Lou Fenster; children: Craig Michael, Daniel Scott, Wendy Ann, Robert Douglas. BS in Acctg., Hunter Coll., 1963. CPA, N.Y. Ptnr. A. Sheiffer & Co., N.Y.C., 1970-84; exec. v.p. Pyro Energy Corp., Evansville, Ind., 1984—; pres. S&F Oil & Gas Mgmt. Co., Westbury, N.Y., 1981—; bd. dirs. Uranium Resources, Inc., Dallas, AL Land and Minerals Corp., Birmingham, Ala. Vice chmn. Mcpl. Youth Guidance Council, Roseland, N.J., 1974-75; bd. dirs. Bd. Edn., Roseland, 1976-79, v.p., 1978-79; chmn. Boy Scouts Am., Roseland, 1979-81, Cub Scouts, Roseland, 1979-81; v.p. Jewish Community Ctr., 1987-88. Fellow N.J. Soc. CPA's; mem. AICPA, N.Y. State CPA's, Ind. Soc. CPA's. Republican. Office: Pyro Energy Corp 653 S Hebron Ave Evansville IN 47715

FENSTER, MARVIN, lawyer, department store executive; b. Bklyn., Jan. 19, 1918; s. Isaac and Anna (Greenman) F.; m. Louise Rapoport, Nov. 13, 1953; children: Julie, Mark. AB, Cornell U., 1938; LLB, Columbia U., 1941. Bar: N.Y. 1942. Assoc. Lauterstein, Spiller, Bergerman & Dannett, N.Y.C., 1941-42, 46-48; atty., asst. gen. atty. R.H. Macy & Co., Inc., N.Y.C., 1948-60, sr. v.p., gen. counsel, sec., 1960-84, sr. v.p. spl. counsel, sec., 1984-87, dir., sr. v.p., spl. counsel, sec., 1987—; pres., dir. Macy's Bank, 1981—; sr. v.p., sec. Macy Credit Corp., N.Y.C., 1961-86, pres., dir., chief exec. officer, 1986—. Served to 1st lt. U.S. Army, 1943-46. Mem. Assn. of Bar, City of New York (corp. law depts. post-admission legal edn., council jud. adminstrn. 1983), Am. Coll. Real Estate Lawyers, Harmonie Club, Beach Point Club, Phi Epsilon Pi. Jewish. Office: R H Macy & Co Inc 151 W 34th St New York NY 10001

FENWICK, AVRIL HANNING, financial planner; b. Detroit, Apr. 22, 1947; d. George Milton and Marilyn May (Moore) Hanning; m. Richard William Fenwick Jr., Mar. 7, 1970. BBA, U. Mich., 1969. Cert. fin. planner. Field asst. Market Opinion Rsch., Detroit, 1969-70; sales coordinator Roper Corp., Kankakee, Ill., 1970-72; budget analyst Benrus Corp., Ridgefield, Conn., 1972-74; rsch. analyst Fed. Correctional Inst., Danbury, Conn., 1978-80; prin. Avril H. Fenwick, CFP, Danbury, 1985—. Mem. task force council Danbury Conservation Commn., 1982-84; vol., bd. dirs. Girl Scouts Coun. S.W. Conn., Wilton, 1978—, Women's Ctr. of Greater Danbury, 1982—; commr. Danbury Youth Commn., 1982-84. Mem. Inst. Cert. Fin. Planners (soc. pres. 1987-88), Internat. Assn. for Fin. Planning (chpt. bd. 1986-88), Women for Profl. and Personal Devel. (founding mem., sec. 1987-88). Republican. Home and Office: 5 Heritage Dr Danbury CT 06811

FENYVES, ALARICH GEORGE, banker; b. Fürth, Fed. Republic Germany, Jan. 5, 1945; s. Alexander and Babette (Eckert) F.; m. Wendy Lindner, Apr. 16, 1977; children: Arabella, Julia, Alexander. JD, U. Graz, Austria, 1969; postgrad., NYU, 1969-70. V.p. Creditanstalt-Bankverein, Vienna, Austria, 1972-79, dep. gen. mgr., 1982-85, gen. mgr., 1986—; sr. v.p. European Am. Bancorp, N.Y.C., 1979-82; dir. European Am. Bank, N.Y.C., Allgemeine Warentreuhand AG, Vienna. Mem. Overseas Bankers Club London. Office: Creditanstalt Bankverein, Schottengasse 6, 1010 Vienna Austria

FENZA, WILLIAM JOSEPH, JR., financial company executive; b. Ridley Park, Pa., May 21, 1929; s. William Joseph and Leona (Lane) F.; m. Myra Ann Wolf, Dec. 14, 1968; children—David, Christine, Jennifer, Richard. A.B., Johns Hopkins U., 1951; LL.B., U. Pa., 1956. Bar: Pa. bar. Law clk. firm Joseph E. Pappano, Chester, Pa., 1956-57; claims office mgr. State Farm Ins. Co., Dover, Del., 1957-59; partner firm Bernstein, Corcoran, Mueller & Fenza, Upper Darby, Pa., 1960-62; with Chrysler First Inc. (formerly Finance Am. Corp.), Allentown, Pa., 1962—; sr. v.p., gen. counsel. Chrysler First Inc. (formerly Finance Am. Corp.). Served with AUS, 1951-53. Mem. Am., Pa., Lehigh County bar assns. Home: 2830 Old S Pike Ave Allentown PA 18103 Office: Chrysler 1st Inc 1105 Hamilton St Allentown PA 18101

FERBER, NORMAN ALAN, retail executive; b. N.Y.C., Aug. 25, 1948; m. Rosine Ferber; children: Robert, Lauren, Richard. Student, L.I. U. Buyer, mdse. mgr. Atherton Industries, N.Y.C., 1976-79; v.p., mdse. mgr. Raxton Corp., N.Y.C., 1979-82; v.p. Fashion World, N.Y.C., 1982; v.p merchandising, mktg. and distbn. Ross Stores Inc., Newark, Calif., 1982-87, pres., chief operating officer, 1987-88, pres., chief exec. officer, 1988—. Home: 1455 Edgewood Dr Palo Alto CA 94301 Office: Ross Stores Inc 8333 Central Ave PO Box 728 Newark CA 94560

FERCHAT, ROBERT ARTHUR, telecommunications company executive; b. Toronto, Ont., Can., Nov. 17, 1934; s. Edmond Francis Louise and Winnifred Curwen (Coulter) F.; C.A., U. Toronto, 1962; m. Gwenyth Shirley Gibson; children—Craig, Donna. Formerly with Ford Motor Co. of Can.; with No. Telecom Ltd., Mississauga, Ont., from 1977, former exec. v.p., pres., 1984—, also dir.; Bell-No. Research. C.P.A. Mem. Fin. Execs. Inst., Conf. Bd. (council fin. execs.). Club: Credit Valley Golf and Country. Office: No Telecom Can Ltd, 2920 Matheson Blvd E, Mississauga, ON Canada L4W 4M7

FEREBEE, JOHN SPENCER, JR., corporate executive; b. Washington, Mar. 8, 1947; s. John Spencer Sr. and Louise (Barnes) F.; BS in Indsl. Engring., Lehigh U., 1969; MBA, Duke U., 1972; m. Nancy Stein, Oct. 11, 1969; children: John Spencer, III, Rachel Stein, Matthew Louis. Indsl. engr. RCA, Palm Beach Gardens, Fla., 1969-70; sr. cons. Price Waterhouse, Washington, 1972-75, mgr., 1975-78, sr. mgr., 1978-82; asst. adminstr. Social and Rehab. Svc., HEW, Washington, 1976-77; dir. internal audit dept. Marriott Corp., Washington, 1982-83, dir. mgmt. cons. dept., 1984-85, asst. corp. contr., 1985-86, v.p. corp. acct. and mgmt. cons., 1986; v.p. fin. Big Boy Restaurant System, Washington, 1987-88; v.p., chief fin. officer Marriott Family restaurants, Inc., 1988— . Mem. Duke U. Bus. Sch. Alumni Assn. (pres. 1980-82), Duke U. Gen. Alumni Assn. (bd. dir. 1981-83). Club: Congl. Country (Bethesda, Md.). Home: 125 Eagles Mere Great Falls VA 22066 Office: One Marriott Dr Washington DC 20058

FERENBACH, COLIN CAMPBELL, investment executive; b. Wilkes-Barre, Pa., Jan. 2, 1934; s. Gregory and Romayne (Schooley) F.; m. Hannah Thomas, June 23, 1956 (div. 1979); children: Elizabeth, Gregory, Peter; m.

Victoria Simons, Mar. 18, 1980. BA, Yale U., 1955. V.p. Goldman, Sachs & Co., N.Y.C., 1957-76; mng. dir. Kleinwort Benson McCowan, N.Y.C., 1977-80, McCowan Assocs., N.Y.C., 1980-83, Haven Capital Mgmt., N.Y.C., 1983—. Pres. Jacob Riis Settlement, Queens, N.Y., 1977-87; vestryman Holy Trinity Ch., N.Y.C., 1970-75. Capt. USAF, 1955-57. Mem. Union Club, N.Y. Yacht Club. Democrat. Episcopalian. Home: Plain Dealing Farm Royal Oak MD 21662 Office: Haven Capital Mgmt 605 Third Ave New York NY 10158

FERENCE, THOMAS WILLIAM, publishing executive; b. Cleve., Dec. 27, 1959; s. Lawrence William and Jennie Nancy (Verdino) F. BA, Kent State U., 1983. Account exec. Great Empire Broadcasting Co., Denver, 1983-84, Media-Com, Inc., Akron, Ohio, 1984-85; nat. account exec. Channing L. Bete Pub. Co., South Deerfield, Mass., 1985—. Mem. Internat. Assn. Bus. Communicators. Roman Catholic. Home: 143 Kimrose Ln Broadview Heights OH 44147

FERENSOWICZ, MICHAEL JAY, real estate company executive; b. Detroit, July 19, 1952; s. Anthony John and Margaret Mary (Denny) F.; m. Maria Von Der Ahe, Sept. 11, 1982; children: Claire, Rachel. BA, Harvard U., 1975; MBA, Northeastern U., 1983. Adminstrv. asst. Boston Mayor's Office Community Devel., 1975-78; fin. intern Fin. Group/Northeastern U., Boston, 1981-82; project dir./gen. ptnr. Real Property Resources, Inc., Torrance, Calif., 1983-88; ptnr. F.T. Von Der Ahe Co., Newport Beach, Calif., 1988—. Walker-Beale Fund scholar Harvard U., 1971-72, Edwin S. George Fund scholar, 1973-74. Roman Catholic. Club: Harvard So. Calif. Home: 559 S Helberta Ave Redondo Beach CA 90277 Office: F T Von Der Ahe Co 3151 Airway Ave Ste L-1 Costa Mesa CA 92626

FERGUSON, DOUGLAS HARPER, banker; b. Charleston, W.Va., Dec. 23, 1946; s. William H. and Virginia (Trowbridge) F.; m. Janet Caraker, Dec. 17, 1988; children: Heather, Joshua, Molly. BA in Econs., Marietta Coll., 1969; MBA, U. Conn., 1979. Asst. v.p. comml. dept. State Nat. Bank, Bridgeport, Conn., 1969-79; v.p. comml. dept. Mattatuck Bank & Trust Co., Waterbury, Conn., 1979-84; v.p. real estate dept. The Bank Mart, Bridgeport, Conn., 1984—. Office: The Bank Mart 948 Main St Bridgeport CT 06601

FERGUSON, HENRY, international management educator; b. Schenectady, May 31, 1927; s. Charles Vaughan and Harriet Esther (Rankin) F.; m. Joan Alice Metzger, July 18, 1953; children: Jean Rankin Gerbini, Cynthia Harriet Waldman, Henry Closson, Margaret Susan Ferguson Corrigan. A.B., Union Coll., 1950; A.M., Harvard U., 1954, Ph.D., 1958. With Conn. Gen. Life Ins. Co., Hartford, 1950-53; lectr., asst. prof., asso. prof. history, chmn. Non-Western studies com. Union Coll., Schenectady, 1957-69; dir. Ednl. Resources Ctr. N.Y. State Dept. Edn., 1967-69, dir. Ctr. for Internat. Programs, 1979-85; spl. lectr. Trinity Coll., Hartford, 1969-72; pres., dir. InterCulture Assocs., Inc., Thompson, Conn., 1969-79; pres. Henry Ferguson Internat., Inc., 1985—; faculty specialist SUNY, Albany, 1985-88; co-prin. Presentations by Experts, 1987—. Author: (with Joan M. Ferguson) Village Life Study Kit Guide and Village Life Study Kit, 1970, Changing Africa, a Guide, 1973, Manual for Multicultural and Ethnic Studies, 1977, (with N. Abramowitz) Opportunities for Interprofessional Collaboration, 1980, Manual for Multicultural Education, 1987, Tomorrow's Global Executive, 1988, Corporate Leadership in a Global Age, 1989; editor: Handbook on Human Rights and Citizenship, 1981, Community Resource Manual on Human Rights and Citizenship, 1981, Ferguson Fortnightly, 1979, Cross Cultural Currents, 1980, Global Business Observer, 1989—. Trustee Freedom Forum, Schenectady, 1963-66; citizen del. White House Conf. on Library and Info. Services, 1979; pres. Internat. Center of Capital Region, 1981-82, pres. world trade council, 1988-89; mem. adv. bd. Sagamore Seminar in Internat. Bus. Served with USN, 1945-46. Sr. fellow Oriental studies Columbia U., 1960-61; N.Y. State Bd. Regents sr. fellow in Non-Western studies, 1965-66; Fulbright research grantee Osmania U., India, 1961; Fulbright sr. research grantee, 1966-67. Mem. Soc. Intercultural Edn., Tng. and Research, Nat. Speakers Assn., Conn. Book Pubs. Assn., Am. Soc. Assn. Execs. (assoc.). Episcopalian. Club: Fort Orange (Albany). Lodge: Rotary. Home: Chestnut Hill N Albany NY 12211 Office: PO Box 11031 Albany NY 12211

FERGUSON, JAMES PETER, distilling company executive; b. Landis, Sask., Can., Aug. 12, 1937; s. James and Gertrude (Schmit) F.; m. Patricia Woodruff, Aug. 27, 1960; children—James, Carolyn. Chartered Acct., McGill U., 1971. Mgr. Clarkson Gordon, Montreal, Que., Can., 1965-73; lectr. McGill U., Montreal, Que., Can., 1970-72; controller CI Power Ltd., Montreal, Que., Can., 1973-74; mgr. taxation Hiram Walker-Gooderham & Worts Ltd., Windsor, Ont., Can., 1974-79, treas., v.p., chief fin. officer, 1979-82, sr. v.p., treas., chief fin. officer, 1982-87, 1986-88; exec. v.p., corp. devel. dir. Hiram Walker-Allied Vintners, 1988—, also bd. dirs.; bd. dirs. Suntory-Allied Lyons Ltd., Tokyo, Pedro Domeco S.A., Spain, Corby Distilleries Ltd., Montreal; dir. adv. bd. Allendale Mut. Ins., Toronto. Chmn. Met. Gen. Hosp., Windsor, Ont., 1979-80. Served to capt. Can. Air Force, 1956-65. Mem. Inst. Chartered Accts., Order Chartered Accts. Que. Club: Essex Golf, Renaissance. Home: 5965 Riverside Dr E, Windsor, ON Canada N8S 1B5 Office: Hiram Walker-Gooderham et al, Walkerville Box 2518, 2072 Riverside Dr E, Windsor, ON Canada N8Y 4S5

FERGUSON, LEONARD PRICE (BEAR), advertising executive, consultant; b. Bryan, Tex., Mar. 23, 1951; s. Thomas Morgan and Grace Evelyn (Barnett) F.; m. Kathleen Ann Winter, Feb. 15, 1986. BBA, Tex. A&M U., 1973; MS in Communications, U. Ill., 1975. Field supr. Agri-Systems Tex., Inc., Bryan, Tex., 1966-69; mgr., sales rep. Wang Labs., Inc., Beaumont and Houston, Tex., 1973-75; account exec. Leo Burnett Advt., Inc., Chgo., 1976-79, Clinton E. Frank Advt., Chgo., 1979-80; v.p., supr. account group Ogilvy & Mather Advt., Inc., Houston, 1980-84; co-founder, mgr. sales ops. Nat. Recycling Corp., Houston, 1984-85; v.p., supr. accounts, sr. v.p. Eisaman, Johns & Laws Advt., Houston, 1985—; pres. Pathfinder Cons., Houston, 1980—. Inventor glass crusher, recycling system. Chmn. Houstonians on Watch Program, Braeburn Glen and Houston, Tex., 1982-84. Grantee U. Ill., 1969, 73, Sam Houston U., 1970. Mem. Advt. Agy. Assn. Am. (affiliate), Direct Mail Mktg. Assn. Am. (affiliate), Advt. Research Found. (affiliate). Methodist. Home: 14011 Wickersham Ln Houston TX 77077 Office: Eisaman Johns & Laws 2121 Sage Suite 200 Houston TX 77056

FERGUSON, ROBERT R., JR., banker; b. Savannah, Ga., Dec. 31, 1923; s. Robert R. and Frances (McDonald) F.; m. Betty Jane King, Nov. 26, 1949; children: Robert R. III, James P. B.A., Lehigh U., 1947; M.B.A., U. Pa., 1949; LL.D., Seton Hall U., 1981; L.H.D. hon., Caldwell Coll., 1983. Trainee Fed. Res. Bank, Phila., 1947-49; v.p. Fed. Trust Co., Newark, 1949-58; pres., chief exec. officer First Nat. State Bank (known as First Fidelity Bank since 1984), Newark, 1958-88, First Nat. State Bancorp. (known as First Fidelity Bancorp. since 1984), Newark, 1969—; chmn. bd. First Fidelity Bancorp, Newark, 1989—; dir. Pub. Service Electric & Gas Co., 1980—. Episcopalian. Office: 1st Fidelity Bancorp 550 Broad St Newark NJ 07192

FERGUSON, RONALD EUGENE, reinsurance company executive; b. Chgo., Jan. 16, 1942; s. William Eugene and Elizabeth (Hahnneman) F.; m. Carol Jean Chapp, Dec. 27, 1964; children: Brian, Kristin. BA, Blackburn Coll., 1963; MA, U. Mich., 1965. Statistician Lumbermans Mut. Casualty Co., Long Grove, Ill., 1965-69; actuary Gen. Reins. Corp., Greenwich, Conn., 1969-70, asst. v.p, 1972-74, v.p., 1974-77, sr. v.p., 1977-82, exec. v.p., 1982, dir., 1983, chmn., 1985—; v.p., group exec. Gen. Re Corp., Stamford, 1981, pres., chief operating officer, 1983-87, chmn., pres., chief exec. officer, 1987—; bd. dirs. Finevest Food Svcs., Inc., Gen. Signal Corp., Colgate-Palmolive Co.; trustee Underwriters Labs. Inc. Contbr. articles to profl. jours. Served with USPHS, 1966-68. Fellow Casualty Actuarial Soc. (bd. dirs. 1978-81); mem. Am. Acad. Actuaries (dir. 1981—). Congregationalist. Clubs: Patterson. Office: Gen Re Corp 695 E Main St PO Box 10350 Stamford CT 06904

FERGUSON, SYBIL, franchise business executive; b. Barnwell, Alta., Can., Feb. 7, 1934; came to U.S., 1938, naturalized, 1976; d. Alva John and Xarissa (Merkley) Clarke; m. Roger N. Ferguson, July 10, 1952; children: Debra Kay, Michael David, Wade Clarke, Lois Christine, Julie Xarissa. Ed. pub. schs. Founder, pres. Diet Ctr. Inc., Rexburg, Idaho, 1970—; bd. dirs. Am. Health Cos. Inc., Diet Ctr. Counselor Tng., Diet Ctr. Shipping and Receiving Co., Diet Ctr. Print Shop, Audio Visual Studio, Sybils, Inc., Ferguson & Assocs., Golden Eagle Ranches. Author: The Diet Center Program, Lose Weight Fast and Keep It Off Forever, 1983, Diet Center Cookbook. Charter mem. women's aux. Madison Meml. Hosp., Rexburg; founding sponsor Children's Miracle Network Telethon; bd. advisors Exchange, Working Mother's Network; mem. nat. adv. council Brigham Young U., adv. bd. Ricks Coll., Boise State U.; mem. Rexburg Civic Assn. Recipient Bus. Leader of Yr. award Ricks Coll., 1980; named Great Figure of Franchising, 1987, to Community Leaders Am., one of Top 60 Women Entrepreneurs, Saavy mag., Idaho Bus. Leader of Yr., 1988, Woman of Distinction Birmingham So. Coll. Gala 9, 1989. Mem. Internat. Franchise Assn., Am. Entrepreneur Assn., Rexburg C. of C. (program dir. 1976), Com. of 200 (founder). Mem. LDS Ch. Lodge: Soroptimists (v.p. Rexburg chpt. 1975, award 1979). Office: Diet Center Inc 220 S 2d St W Rexburg ID 83440

FERGUSON, WILLIAM EMMETT, retired securities broker; b. Quincy, Mass., Dec. 21, 1902; s. Patrick J. and Margaret (O'Brien) F.; m. Loretta Mahon, July 6, 1935. Ed. high sch. With Thomson, McKinnon Securities Inc. (formerly Thomson & McKinnon, Inc.), N.Y.C., 1919—; gen. partner Thomson, McKinnon Securities Inc. (formerly Thomson & McKinnon, Inc.), 1948; former pres., chmn. bd., chief exec. officer, dir., now hon. chmn. bd. Formerly mem. bd. govs., vice chmn. exec. com. Midwest Stock Exchange, Chgo. Mem. Chgo., Kansas City bds. trade. Clubs: Union League (Chgo.); N.Y. Athletic (N.Y.C.). Office: Thomson McKinnon Securities Inc 630 5th Ave Rm 3070 New York NY 10005

FERGUSON, WILLIAM JOSEPH, automotive executive; b. Balt., Apr. 15, 1928; s. William Joseph and Nora (Hopkins) F.; m. Shirley Elizabeth Ferrin, Oct. 20, 1949; children: William J. Jr., Carles Ann., Mark A., Michael S. BSBA, Loyola Coll., Balt., 1949; cert. in Strategic Bus. Planning, MIT, 1985. Acct. Fisher Body div. Gen. Motors Corp., Balt., 1949-60; divisional auditor Fisher Body div. Gen. Motors Corp., Warren, Mich., 1961-64; asst. comptroller Fisher Body div. Gen. Motors Corp., Flint, Mich., 1965-68; resident comptroller assembly div. Gen. Motors Corp., Van Nuys, Calif., 1969-72, St. Louis, 1973-81; dir. fin., internal control and bus. planning Buick, Oldsmobile, Cadillac Group Gen Motors Corp., Wentzville, Mo., 1982-86; dir. fin., material control, bus. planning Buick, Oldsmobile, Cadillac Group Gen Motors Corp., 1987—. v.p. Pvt. Industry Council, St. Charles, Mo., 1988; chmn. United Way Tri-County bd., St. Charles, 1988; exec. com. St. Louis Metro area, 1988; mem. corp. assembly Blue Cross/Blue Shield, St. Louis, 1988. Mem. Am. Assn. Indsl. Mgmt. Republican. Roman Catholic. Home: 13665 Mason Oaks Ln Saint Louis MO 63131 Office: GMC Wentzville Assembly Ctr 1500 E Rte A Wentzville MO 63385

FERINO, CHRISTOPHER KENNETH, computer information scientist; b. Chgo., May 25, 1961; s. Natale Ferino and Carol Marie (Anderson) Huckeby; m. Anita Louise Vanderhoof, Oct. 19, 1985. Cons. Lachman Assn., Inc., Westmont, Ill., 1979-80; AS/RS operator W.W. Grainger, Niles, Ill., 1980-82; mem. computer staff Paddock Publs., Arlington Heights, Ill., 1982-84; data processing coord. Power Systems, Schaumburg, Ill., 1984-85; tech. specialist Follett Software Co., Crystal Lake, Ill., 1985-87; tech. service dir. Follett Software Co., Crystal Lake, 1987-88; tech. editor MacGuide mag., 1988—; conf. faculty Boston Macworld Expn., 1988, San Francisoc MacWorld Expn., 1988, 89. Mem. Boston Computer Soc. Home: PO Box 280571 Lakewood CO 80228

FERLAND, E. JAMES, electric utility executive; b. Boston, Mar. 19, 1942; s. Ernest James and Muriel (Cassell) F.; m. Eileen Kay Patridge, Mar. 9, 1964; children: E. James, Elizabeth Denise. BS in Mech. Engring., U. Maine, 1964; MBA, U. New Haven, 1979; postgrad. in program mgmt. devel., Harvard U. Grad. Sch. Bus. Adminstrn. Electric utility engr. HELCO, New London, Conn., 1964-67; supt. nuclear ops. NNECO, Waterford, Conn., 1967-78; dir. rate regulation N.E. Utilities, Berlin, Conn., 1978-80, pres., chief operating officer, 1983-86; pres., chief operating officer N.E. Utilities, Conn., Mass., 1986; exec. v.p., chief fin. officer NUSCO, Berlin, 1980-83; pres. Pub. Service Electric & Gas Co. (subs. Pub. Service Enterprise Group, Inc.), Newark, 1986, chmn., pres., chief executive officer, 1986—; chmn., pres., chief exec. officer Pub. Service Enterprise Group, Inc., Newark, 1986—; also bd. dirs. all Pub. Service Enterprise Group subs.; bd. dirs. Conn. Yankee Co., Vt. Yankee Co., Maine Yankee Co., Hartford Steam Boiler Inspection and Ins. Co., 1986—. Office: Pub Svc Electric & Gas Co 80 Park Pla Newark NJ 07101 *

FERLIS, NICHOLAS WILLIAM, investment executive; b. Kankakee, Ill., Sept. 17, 1947; s. William Nicholas and Magdeline Gail (Bogordos) F.; m. Sally Phillippi, Sept. 18, 1982. BBA, Loyola U., Chgo., 1970; MBA, Northwestern U., 1972. CPA, Ill.; registered investment advisors Registry Fin. Planning Practitioners; registered securities broker dealer; cert. fin. planner. Internal auditor Consol. Packaging Co., Chgo., 1968-70; sr. staff acct. Arthur Andersen & Co., Chgo., 1970-74; group controller Apeco Corp., Evanston, Ill., 1974-75; v.p. Splty. Fin. Services, Glenview, Ill., 1975-79; pres. Ferlis & Assocs., Des Plaines, Ill., 1979-82, Equity Advisors, Inc., Northfield, Ill., 1982-87, Ferlis Fin. Svcs., Inc., Northbrook, 1987—. Chmn. adv. com. Healing the Children. Mem. Am. Mgmt. Assn. (pres. club 1979—), Internat. Assn. Fin. Planners (nat. rev. com. 1983—), Inst. Cert. Fin. Planners, AICPA (accredited personal fin. specialist), Ill. Soc. CPAs, N.Am. Assn. Securities Dealers . Republican. Greek Orthodox. Office: Ferlis Fin Svcs Inc 630 Dundee Rd Northbrook IL 60062

FERMAN, IRVING, lawyer, educator; b. N.Y.C., July 4, 1919; s. Joseph and Sadie (Stein) F.; m. Bertha Paglin, June 12, 1946; children—James Paglin, Susan Paglin. B.S., N.Y.U., 1941; J.D., Harvard, 1948. Bar: La. 1948, D.C. 1974. Partner Provensal, Faris & Ferman, New Orleans, 1948-52; dir. Am. Civil Liberties Union, Washington, 1952-59, Am. Civil Liberties Clearing House, 1952-54; exec. vice chmn. Pres.'s Com. Govt. Contracts, 1959-60; v.p. Internat. Latex Corp., 1960-66; pres. Piedmont Theaters Corp., 1966-69; adj. asso. prof. mgmt. N.Y.U. Grad. Sch. Bus., 1964-68; adj. prof. law Howard U., 1968-69, prof. law, 1969-86, prof. emeritus, 1986—; dir. Project for Legal Policy, 1976—; vis. prof. law Am. U., 1971-72; mem. Am. Com. Cultural Freedom, 1954—; mem. Com. of Arts and Scis. for Eisenhower, 1956; mem. citizens adv. com. U.S. Commn. on Govt. Security, 1957; chmn. Police Complaint Review Bd., 1965-73; mem. Dept. HEW Reviewing Authority, 1969-79; chmn. Interdisco Ltd., London, 1986—; bd. dirs. Control Fluidics, Inc., Greenwich, Conn. Contbr. to books and revs. Mem. bd. dirs. New Orleans Acad. Art, 1948-51. Served from cadet to 1st lt. USAAF, 1942-46. Mem. Am., La., D.C., New Orleans bar assns. Jewish. Clubs: International (Washington); Army-Navy Country (Arlington, Va.); Harvard (N.Y.C.), Caterpillar (N.Y.C.). Home: 3818 Huntington St NW Washington DC 20015 also: Rt 1 Sullivan Harbor ME 04689 Office: 2935 Upton St NW Washington DC 20015

FERNANDES, GARY JOE, electronic data processing company executive; b. San Angelo, Tex., Aug. 10, 1943; s. Arthur and Mattie Lee (Williams) F.; m. Sandra Faye Lyday, June 6, 1964; children: Jennifer Logan, Jeremy Tildon, James Caleb. BA in Econs., Baylor U., 1965. Systems engr. Electronic Data Systems Corp., Dallas, 1969-70, project mgr., 1970-71, account mgr., 1971-72, br. mgr., 1972-74, mktg. rep., 1974-76; dir. industry mktg. Electronic Data Systems Fed. Corp., Bethesda, Md., 1976-77, v.p. mktg., 1977-78; pres. Electronic Data Systems Govt. Services, Bethesda, Md., 1978-84, Electronic Data Systems World, London, 1984-87; sr. v.p. internat., communications and comml. groups Electronic Data Systems Corp, Dallas, 1987—. Served to 1st lt. U.S. Army, 1966-69. Mem. Armed Forces Communications and Electronics Assn. (bd. dirs. 1982—). Office: Electronic Data Systems Corp 7171 Forest Ln A730 Dallas TX 75230

FERNANDEZ, MIGUEL ANGEL, energy conservation and process executive, consultant; b. Habana, Cuba, Oct. 30, 1939; came to U.S., 1957; s. Miguel Angel and Olga Eulalia (Rodriguez) F.; m. Barbara Frances LeGette, Jan. 7, 1967; children: Michael Anthony, Mark Angel, Stephen Hartley. B in Chem. Engring., Ga. Tech., 1962, MS in Chem. Engring., 1963, doctoral work in engring., 1965. Engr. E.I. DuPont, Richmond, Va., 1965-66; devel. group leader Phillips Fibers Corp., Greenville, S.C., 1966-80; mgr. energy and process engring. J P Stevens & Co., Greenville, S.C., 1980-83; mgr. industry and energy program S.C. Energy Research & Devel. Ctr., Clemson, S.C., 1983-85; cons. M.A. Fernandez & Assocs., Greenville, 1985—; cons. S.C. Energy Office, Columbia, 1985—. Patentee in field. V.p. parents Tchrs. Student Assn. Eastside High Sch., Greenville, S.C., 1987—. Mem. Am. Inst. Chem. Engrs. Baptist. Home: 3 Foxcroft Rd Greenville SC 29615 Office: M A Fernandez & Assoc PO Box 25788 Greenville SC 29616

FERNANDEZ, NINO JOSEPH, manufacturing company executive; b. Bklyn., June 17, 1941; s. Saturnino and Anna (Santeramo) F.; divorced; children: Nino Harold, Karla Leigh. BBA, Adelphi U., 1967; MBA, Pace U., 1971. Sr. analyst Am. Airlines, N.Y.C., 1967-70; asst. dir. investor relations GTE Corp., Stamford, Conn., 1970-73; v.p. investor relations Gen. Signal Corp., Stamford, 1974—. Served with USMCR, 1958-63. Mem. Nat. Investor Relations Inst. (bd. dirs.), Nat. Assn. Investment Club, Fin. Communications Soc., Landmark Club, Landmark Athletic Club. Republican. Roman Catholic. Home: 1 Strawberry Hill Ave Stamford CT 06902 Office: Gen Signal Corp Box 10010 High Ridge Pk Stamford CT 06904

FERNANDEZ, RICHARD MURRAY, retail executive; b. Baton Rouge, Sept. 14, 1954; s. Florau Joachim and Betty Abigail (Richard) F. Student, La. State U., 1972-75. Supr. Mid-South div. Southland Corp., Baton Rouge, 1974-81, zone security supr., 1981-83; security mgr. Chief Auto Parts Southland Corp., Cerritos, Calif., 1983-84; loss prevention mgr. South Cen. div. Southland Corp., Houston, 1984-87, Colo. div. Southland Corp., Englewood, 1987—; part-time officer Baton Rouge City Police Dept., 1981-83; with U.S. Justice Dept., 1983. Recipient Ann. Crime Prevention award Houston C. of C., 2d place award Nat. Assn. Town Watch, 1987. Mem. Am. Soc. Indsl. Security (cert. protection profl.), Inst. for Fin. Crime Prevention, Internat. Narcotic Enforcement Officers Assn., Internat. Soc. Crime Prevention Practitioners, Nat. Assn. Chiefs Police. Republican. Roman Catholic. Office: Southland Corp 7167 S Alton Way Englewood CO 80112

FERNANDEZ, TELESFORO, JR., clothing industry executive; b. San Juan, P.R., Nov. 25, 1942; s. Telesforo and Luisa (Martinez) F.; B.S. in Econs., U. Pa., 1965; m. Awilda A. Rodriguez, Nov. 23, 1967; children—Telesforo, Andres Alexis, Cristina Alexandra. Vice pres., treas. La Esquina Famosa, San Juan, 1965-68, v.p., treas., 1969-77, pres., 1977-86; pres. Telesforo Fernandez Martinez Enterprises, Inc., 1984—; account exec. Young & Rubicam P.R., Inc., San Juan, 1968-69; dir., v.p., treas., prin. Telesforo Fernandez & Hermano, Inc.; dir. Caribbean Bus. Mem. Menswear Retailers Am., P.R. C. of C., Sales and Mktg. Assn. San Juan (mgmt. award 1972), Young Pres.'s Orgn., AFDA Frat. Republican. Roman Catholic. Club: N.Y. Athletic. Office: GPO Box G 2624 San Juan PR 00936

FERNANDEZ-GUZMAN, CARLOS RAMON, banker; b. Havana, Cuba, May 14, 1956; s. Carlos J. Fernandez and Myriam R. (Guzman) Valle; m. Maria Elena Valdes, July 31, 1976; children: Natalie Michele, Carlos Eduardo, Melissa Elena. AA, Miami-Dade Community Coll., 1975; student, Fla. Internat. U., 1976-78; cert. Grad. Sch. Banking, La. State U., 1984. Sr. account exec. S.E. Banking Corp., Miami, 1974-79; sr. v.p. Consol. Bank N.A., Hialeah, Fla., 1979—; bd. dirs. Hispanic Heritage, Inc., Miami, Miami Capital Devel., Inc., Miami Citywide Devel., Inc. Co-chmn. fund raising United Way of Dade County, Miami, 1984; bd. dirs. Hialeah-Miami Springs C. of C., 1984, Performing Arts for Community and Edn., Miami. Recipient award for Excellence in New Club Bldg., Kiwanis Internat., 1979. Fellow Leadership Miami, Internat. Ctr. (investment com. 1981-83); mem. Fla. Bankers Assn. (mktg. com. 1983—), Greater Miami C. of C. (trustee). Republican. Roman Catholic. Lodge: Kiwanis (sec., treas. 1978-80). Office: Consol Bank NA 900 W 49th St Hialeah FL 33012

FERNSTROM, MEREDITH MITCHUM, financial services company executive, public responsibility professional; b. Rutherfordton, N.C., July 26, 1946; d. Lee Wallace and Ellie (Saine) Mitchum. B.S., U. N.C.-Greensboro, 1968; M.S., U. Md., 1972. Tchr. home econs. Prince Georges County pub. schs., Md., 1968-72; assoc. dir. market research H.J. Kaufman Advt., Washington, 1972-74; dir. consumer edn. Washington Consumer Affairs Office, 1974-76; dir. consumer affairs U.S. Dept. Commerce, Washington, 1976-80; v.p. consumer affairs Am. Express Co., N.Y.C., 1980-82, sr. v.p.-pub. responsibility, 1982—; former mem. consumer adv. council Fed. Res. System, Washington; bd. dirs. Nat. Consumers League, Washington, 1982—, N.Y. Met. Better Bus. Bur., N.Y.C., 1983—, Internat. Credit Assn., 1984—. Mem. policy bd. Jour. Retail Banking; contbr. articles to profl. jours. Bd. dirs. Womens' Forum N.Y., 1987—, Inst. for the Future; mem. bd. overseers Malcolm Baldridge Nat. Quality Award; commr. Nat. Commn. Working Women, 1987—. Recipient Consumer Edn. award Nat. Found. Consumer Credit Fedn., 1981, Disting. Woman award Northwood Inst., 1985, Matrix award N.Y. Women in Communications, Inc., 1986. Mem. Soc. Consumer Affairs Profls. (pres. 1985), Advt. Women N.Y. (Advt. Woman of Yr. award 1987), Fin. Women's Assn., Women's Econ. Roundtable, Am. Home Econs. Assn. Office: Am Express Co Am Express Tower World Fin Ctr New York NY 10285-4725

FERRAIOLI, ARMANDO, biomedical company executive; b. Foggia, Italy, Mar. 19, 1949; s. Alfonso and Luisa (Taurino) F.; Dr.Ing., U. Naples, 1973; M.Sc. in Bioengring., U. Strathclyde, 1974; Ph.D., U. Southampton, 1981; m. Maria T. Kindjarsky-D'Amato, Aug. 30, 1976; children—Solange A.P., Naike M.L., Anika M.V. Registered profl. engr., Salerno, Italy; chartered engr., Gt. Britain. Regional mgr. Gambro Soxil SpA, Bari, Naples, Italy, 1982-84; founder, gen. dir., A.G.A. Biomedica S.r.l., Cava dei Tirreni, 1985—; cons. Studio di Ingegneria Medica, Cava del Tirreni, 1984—; biomed. researcher, designer hosp. structures, Italy, internat. Brit. Council grantee, 1974-78. Mem. Instn. Elec. Engrs. Gt. Britain, IEEE, Associazione Elettrotecnica Italiana, Biol. Engring. Soc. Gt. Britain, Association for the Advancement of Med. Instrumentation, Biomed. Engring. Soc., Associazione Italiana di Ingegneria Medica e Biologica, Centro Nazionale Edilizia e Tecnica Ospedaliera. Mem. adv. bd. Italian biomed. jours.; contbr. over 30 articles on biomed. engring. to profl. jours.; book review editor for various jours. Home: Via A de Gasperi 5, 84013 Cava dei Tirreni Italy Office: Corso Italia n 232, 84013 Cava dei Tirreni Italy

FERRANTE, CAROL FRANCES, government administrator, real estate company executive; b. Cambria Hts., N.Y., Dec. 29, 1947; d. Dan and Nancy (Quenqua) F. AA, Nassau Community Coll., 1968; BA, BS, SUNY, Oswego, 1970; cert. in fin. planning, Adelphi U., 1980. Community coordinator Nassau County Youth Bd., Mineola, N.Y., 1974-77; dir. planning N.Y. Office Employment and Planning, Hempstead, N.Y., 1977-83; dir. employment Nassau County Dept. Social Services, Mineola, N.Y., 1983—; v.p. First Am. Realty Corp., Hammond, Ind., 1987—; cons. Meadowbrook Travel Co., East Meadow, N.Y., 1983—; co-sponsor Bus. Govt. Confs. Commiteewoman Bellmore (N.Y.) Rep. Club, 1987—; cons. adult edn. Nassau Tech. Ctr., mem. edn. com., 1987—. Recipient Mgmt. Tng. award Cornell U., 1978, Employment for Welfare Recipients award Nat. Assn. Counties, Washington, 1984. Mem. Leadership Tng. Inst., Kiwanis (v.p. Garden City club). Home: 2032 Russell St Bellmore NY 11710

FERRANTE, JEFFREY ANTHONY, financial consultant; b. Providence, Sept. 22, 1959; s. Frank F. and Rachel B. (Porreca) F.; m. Eugenia Corey, July 28, 1984. BS, Bryant Coll., 1981; MBA, U. Miami, 1985. CPA, Mass., Fla. Staff acct. Price Waterhouse, Miami, Fla., 1981-82; portfolio mgr. John Alden Life Ins., Miami, 1982-85; cons. Andover, Mass., 1985-86; fin. cons. Merrill Lynch, Burlington, Mass., 1986—. Republican. Roman Catholic. Office: Merrill Lynch 7 New England Exec Park Burlington MA 01803

FERRARA, ARTHUR VINCENT, insurance company executive; b. N.Y.C., Aug. 12, 1930; s. Thomas Joseph and Camille Virginia (Crescenzi) F.; m. Isabel D. Flynn, Dec. 26, 1953; children: Thomas G., Margaret Mary, James X. B.S., Holy Cross Coll., 1952. Group sales rep. Conn. Gen. Life Ins. Co., N.Y.C., 1955-56; group sales rep. Guardian Life Ins. Co. of Am., N.Y.C., 1957-60, agy. v.p., 1972-77, sr. v.p., 1977-80, exec. v.p., 1981-84, pres., 1985-88, pres., chief exec. officer, 1988—; v.p. sales Guardian Ins. & Annuity Co., 1972-78, pres., 1985—, dir., 1972—; dir. Guardian Investor Services Corp., 1981; trustee Guardian Life Welfare Trust. Served to 1st lt. U.S Army, 1952-55. Mem. Am. Soc. C.L.U.s, Nat. Life Underwriters Assn., N.Y. Life Suprs. Assn., N.Y. Life Underwriters Assn., Am. Soc. Pension Actuaries, Golden Key Soc. of C.L.U.s, Life Ins. Coun. N.Y. (bd. dirs.), Am. Coun.

Life Ins. (com. field relations). Home: 43 Brendon Hill Rd Scarsdale NY 10583 Office: Guardian Life Ins Co 201 Park Ave S New York NY 10003

FERRARA, DONALD FRANK, marketing executive; b. N.Y.C., Jan. 2, 1938; s. Frank and Catherine (Titolo) F.; m. Elizabeth Ann Willis, May 5, 1962; children: Kathleen Mary, Lynn Elizabeth, Jane Catherine. BS in Fin., Bucknell U., 1959. With Equitable Life Assurance Soc., N.Y.C., 1960—, investment dept. exec., 1963-70; dir. real estate Gen. Foods Corp., White Plains, N.Y., 1970-74; real estate exec. Chase Manhatten Corp., N.Y.C., 1974-83, investment mktg. exec., 1983—. Contbr. articles to profl. jours. 1st lt. U.S. Army, 1960-61. Mem. Assn. Investment Mgmt. Sales Execs., Nat. Assn. State Treas. Home: 36 Berkshire Rd Rockville Centre NY 11570 Office: Chase Investors Mgmt Corp 1211 Ave of the Americas New York NY 10036

FERRARI, JUAN, venture capitalist, real estate developer; b. Madrid, Oct. 19, 1950; s. Angel and María Teresa (Herrero) F. BA, Nuestra, Señora Del Pilar Sch., Madrid, 1967; MBA, Harvard U., 1978; licenciado, U. Complutesse, Madrid, 1979. Account officer Citibank N.A., Madrid, 1979-81; engagement mgr. McKinsey and Co., Madrid and Milan, 1981-85; ptnr. Asfin S.A., Madrid, 1985-86; chief exec. officer Forescal S.A., Madrid, 1986—. Served to sgt. arty. Spanish Army, 1984-85. Clubs: Harvard (Spain); Real Puera Hierro (Madrid); Real Tennis (Oriedo). Office: Nuñez De Balboa 81, 28006 Madrid Spain

FERRARO, JOHN FRANCIS, business executive, financier; b. N.Y.C., Jan. 3, 1934; s. John Anthony and Angelina Ferraro; B.S.I.E. with honors and distinction, N.Y. U., 1962; m. Linda Diane Zimmerman, Apr. 26, 1985; 1 stepson, Kenneth; children from previous marriage: Elizabeth Ann, John Robert, Laura Marie, Rosemary. With United Techs. Corp., Windsor Locks, Conn. 1962-66, sr. project engr., 1962-64, chief research and devel. promotion, 1964-66; founding ptnr. P.M.C. Corp., 1966-78; chmn. bd., chief exec. officer Thermodynetics, Inc.; pres. Spectrum Inc., 1966—, also dir.; sec., dir. Advanced Energy Concepts Inc.; dir. Turbotec Products, Inc., Xtec Corp. Chmn. Congl. Com. for Appointees to U.S. Air Force Acad., 1980; commr. Devel. Agy., Enfield, Conn., 1981; trustee Suffield (Conn.) Acad., 1980—, chair budget and fin. com., 1987—; trustee Birth right (Conn.); mem. exec. com. Holy Family Retreat League, 1984—. Served to 1st lt. USAF, 1954-58. Decorated Meritorious Service medal. Mem. Psi Upsilon. Club: Suffield Country. Contbr. numerous articles on bus., fin. and stock market to fin. publs., 1966-81; contbg. editor: Handbook of Wealth Management, 1977. Office: 651 Day Hill Rd Windsor CT 06095

FERRARO, ROXANNE, communications executive; b. Buffalo, Apr. 22, 1958; d. Ferdinando and Rosemary (Arena) F. Student, Erie Community Coll., U. Buffalo, Dale Carnegie Inst., 1988—. Sales coordinator Western Union, Buffalo, 1983-85; sales coordinator NYNEX Mobile Communications Co., Buffalo, 1984-86, mgr. adminstrv. office, 1987—; exec. sec. to v.p. MCI Southeast Hdqrs., Atlanta, 1986-87. Mem. Buffalo C. of C., Cheektowaga C. of C. Office: NYNEX Mobile Communications Co 2410 Walden Ave Buffalo NY 14225

FERRE, ANTONIO LUIS, newspaper publisher; b. Ponce, P.R., Feb. 6, 1934; s. Luis A. and Lorenza (Ramirez de Arellano) F.; A.B. magna cum laude, Amherst Coll., 1955; M.B.A., Harvard U., 1957; Inst. for Sr. Mgmt. and Govt. Execs., Dartmouth Coll., 1978; m. Luisa Rangel, Feb. 23, 1963; children: Maria Luisa, Antonio Luis, Luis Alberto, Maria Eugenia, Maria Lorenza. Vice chmn. Puerto Rican Cement Co. and Banco de Ponce,; dir Met. Life Ins. Co., Am. Newspaper Pubs. Assn., ; pres., pub. El Nuevo Dia., 1988—. Author: (essays) Un Alto en el Camino; Pan, Paz y Palabra. Pres., P.R. Council on Higher Edn., 1966-68, Gov.'s Adv. Council, 1968-72; mem. Gov.'s Labor Adv. Council, 1975; bd. dirs., Colegio Puertorriqueño de Niñas; pres. Com. for Econ. Devel. P.R. Served with U.S. Army, 1958. Recipient Presdl. citation, 1976; named one of Puerto Rico's Top Ten Businessmen by bus. newspaper Caribbean Bus., 1986, 87. Mem. P.R. Mfrs. Assn. (pres. 1965-66), Am. Mgmt. Assn., Inc. (pres.'s assn. 1963—), P.R. C. of C., Phi Beta Kappa. Roman Catholic. Clubs: Dorado Beach and Golf; Caribe Hilton Swimming and Tennis; Bankers of P.R.; Ponce Yacht; Club Deportivo de Ponce. Home: Guaynabo PR 00657 Office: GPO Box 4487 San Juan PR 00936

FERREIRA, GAIL VERONICA, banker; b. Medford, Mass., Apr. 3, 1952; d. V. Robert and Harriet Stella (Tashjian) Gagosian; m. Frank A. Ferreira Jr., May 27, 1978; 1 child, Carolyn Elizabeth. BA, Boston Coll., 1974, MBA, 1979. Bus. analyst Robert W. Weaver, Jr. & Assocs., Boston, 1975-77; cons. Arthur D. Little, Inc., Cambridge, Mass., 1977-83; sr. fin. planner Nat. Med. Care, Waltham, Mass., 1983-84; sr. cons. Peat Marwick Main, Boston, 1984-87; v.p. corp. planning The Coop. Bank of Concord, Acton, Mass., 1987—; bd. dirs. V.R. Gagosian Co., Inc., Arlington, Mass., 1986—; adj. asst. prof. fin. Bentley Coll. Grad. Sch., Waltham, Mass., 1982-83. Author (with others): Acquisition and Corporate Development, 1981. Corporator Arlington (Mass.) Boys and Girls Club, 1985; vol. Am. Heart Assn., Needham, Mass., 1985-88. Mem. Am. Mgmt. Assn, The Planning Forum, Alpha Kappa Delta, Lexington Golf Club. Republican. Office: The Cooperative Bank of Concord 125 Nagog Park Acton MA 01720

FERREIRA, JO ANN JEANETTE CHANOUX, housewares manufacturing company executive; b. Melrose Park, Ill., Dec. 3, 1943; d. John W. and June B. Chanoux; B.S., Purdue U., 1965, M.S. (NSF fellow), 1969; m. G. Dodge Ferreira, Apr. 21, 1979. With systems devel. research IBM, San Jose, Calif., 1965-67; asst. dir. mgmt. info. systems edn. Union Carbide Corp., N.Y.C., 1969; mgmt. cons. Touche Ross & Co., N.Y.C., 1970-72, Peat Marwick Mitchell, N.Y.C., 1974-75; dir. corp. devel. strategy cons. A.T. Kearney-Mgmt. Cons., Chgo., 1975-83; dir. Computer Devel. Center, United Airlines, 1983-88; pres. WSG Designs Inc., Northbrook, Ill., 1988—; lectr. Purdue U., 1969, 73-74; guest lectr. Northwestern U., 1981. Mem. Assn. for Corp. Growth (mergers and acquisitions profls.), Inst. Mgmt. Cons. (cert. mgmt. cons.), Am. Arbitration Assn. Phi Kappa Phi. Contbr. articles to profl. publs.; speaker various groups. Home: 1277 Forest Ave Highland Park IL 60035 Office: WSG Designs Inc 425 Huehl Rd #8 Northbrook IL 60062

FERREIRA, JOSE, JR., personal care products company executive; b. Naugatuck, Conn., Apr. 21, 1956; s. Jose Sr. and Rose (Soares) F.; m. Nancy Possiel, Aug. 10, 1980; children: Matthew Charles, Justin Paul. BS in Acctg., Cen. Conn. U., 1978; MBA in Fin., Fordham U., 1982. Accountant Marcade Group, N.J., 1978-79, mgr. acctg., 1979-80; product cost analyst Avon Products Inc., N.Y.C., 1980, planning analyst, 1980-81, sr. planning analyst, 1981-82, mgr. planning Latin Am., 1982-83, group mgr. fin. Latin Am., 1983-84, dir. fin. Latin Am., 1984-86, controller internat. div., 1986-88, v.p. fin. and operations, 1988—; mem. Internat. Exec. Com., N.Y.C., Council of Amercas, N.Y.C., Japan Soc. , N.UY.C. Mem. Convent Sta. Neighborhood Assn., N.J., 1984—, Chimney Hill Owners Assn., Inc., Vt., 1988—. Republican. Roman Catholic. Office: Avon Products Inc 9 W 57th St New York NY 10019

FERRELL, DONALD FORREST, newspaper editor and publisher; b. Oklahoma City, Jan. 6, 1929; s. Forrest Shae and Theresa (Cooper) F.; m. Sally May Bourne, Aug. 29, 1953; children: Susan Jane, Cynthia Jean Ashwood. BS in Journalism, Okla. State U., 1953. Reporter Daily Oklahoman, Oklahoma City, 1952-53; mng. editor Henryetta (Okla.) Daily FreeLance, 1953-54; asst. personnel dir. Okla. Pub. Co., Oklahoma City, 1954-62; editor, pub. The Lincoln County News, Chandler, Okla., 1962-88; legis. asst. U.S. Senate, Washington, 1980-81; pres. Suburban Associated Newspapers, Inc., Oklahoma City, 1984-86; bd. dirs. Union Nat. Bank, Chandler. Mem. Okla. State Senate, 1966-74; trustee, sec. Okla. Newspaper Found., 1986—; chmn. transition com. for Gov. Henry Bellmon, Okla., 1986-87; appointed Adjutant Gen. of Okla., 1987, promoted to Maj. Gen. Named to the Okla. Journalism Hall of Fame, 1985. Mem. Okla. Press Assn. (pres. 1984-85), Okla. State C. of C. (bd. dirs. 1981-87). Republican. Presbyterian. Club: Tulsa Press. Lodge: Lions. Home: 101 W Indian Trail Chandler OK 74834 Office: Okla Mil Dept 3501 Military Circle NE Oklahoma City OK 73111

FERRER, EDWIN, architect; b. N.Y.C., Dec. 2, 1928; s. Juan and Rosaura (Lopez) F.; m. Nadene Joan Reinders, Oct. 13, 1961 (div.); 1 child, Andrea; m. Barbara Sue Gibson, May 29, 1979. BS, U. Houston, 1957, BArch, 1958. Designer-project architect firm Rustay Martin & Vale, Houston, 1962-69; project architect Neuhaus & Taylor, Houston, 1969-71, Wyatt C. Hedrick, Houston, 1971-72, Koetter Tharp Cowell & Bartlett, Houston, 1973-76; design supr. C.E. Lummus Co., Houston, 1976-78; prin. Edwin Ferrer AIA, 1978—; instr. residential design and residential constrn. Houston Community Coll. Works include schs., comml., residential, chs. Served with AUS, 1946-48. Mem. AIA (hist. resources com. Houston chpt., mem. residential architecture com. Houston), Tex. Soc. Architects. Home: 10738 Hazen Rd Houston TX 77072 Office: 7887 Katy Freeway Ste 110 Houston TX 77024

FERRER, RAFAEL GREGORY, communications executive, accountant; b. Seattle, Aug. 16, 1955; s. Rafael George and Barbara (Gould) F. BS in Mktg. and Acctg., Wash. State U., 1978. CPA, Wash. Staff acct. Benson & McLaughlin, Seattle, 1981-84; asst. contr. Northland Communications Corp., Seattle, 1984-87; asst. treas. Northland Communications Corp., 1987, v.p., 1988—. Named Eagle Scout Boy Scouts Am. Mem. Am. Inst. CPA's. Republican. Congregationalist. Home: 3520 27th Pl Seattle WA 98199 Office: Northland Communications Corp 1201 3rd Ave # 3600 Seattle WA 98101

FERRIS, BARTON PURDY, JR., investment banker; b. N.Y.C., June 5, 1940; s. Barton Purdy and Evelyn (Van Dyk) F.; m. Susan Sheldon Moore, Apr. 17, 1965; children: Juliana, Jeffrey, Nathaniel. B.A., Princeton U., 1962; M.B.A., Columbia U., 1966. Actuarial trainee Equitable Life Assurance, N.Y.C., 1963-64; spl. asst. to dir. Office Fgn. Direct Investments, U.S. Dept. Commerce, Washington, 1970; v.p. Morgan Stanley & Co. Inc., N.Y.C., 1966-77; mng. dir. Morgan Stanley Can. Ltd., Montreal, Que., 1975-77; sr. v.p. E.F. Hutton & Co. Inc., N.Y.C., 1977-83, James D. Wolfensohn Inc., N.Y.C., 1983; mng. dir. investment banking Advest, Inc., Hartford, Conn., 1983—; also dir. Advest, Inc.; dir. Moore Investment Co., St. Clair, Mich. Mem. Twilight Park Assn., Haines Falls, N.Y. Served with U.S. Army, 1963-64. Mem. Sigma Xi. Clubs: Princeton (N.Y.C.), Union (N.Y.C.); University (Hartford). Home: 149 Main St Farmington CT 06032 Office: Advest Inc 1 Commercial Pla Hartford CT 06103

FERRIS, MICHAEL J(AMES), chemical company executive; b. Great Falls, Mont., Oct. 20, 1944; s. James Rolland and Ellen Marie (Stack) F.; m. Donna Marie Chalmers, Mar. 17, 1968; children: Brad Michael, Ryan Thomas. BS ChemE, Mont. State U., 1968; MBA, Wichita State U., 1971; advanced mgmt. program, Harvard U., 1982. CPA, Kans. Tech. service rep. Chems. div. Vulcan Materials Co., Wichita, Kans., 1968-70, controller, 1974-76, plant mgr., 1976-78, v.p. mfg., 1978-86, exec. v.p., 1986-87, pres., 1987—; auditor Arthur Young & Co., Wichita, 1971-72, cons., 1972-74; bd. dirs. Chlorine Inst., N.Y.C., vice chmn., 1989—; bd. dirs. Halogenated Solvents Indsl. Alliance, Washington, treas. 1986-88, chmn. 1989—. Bd. dirs. Boy Scouts Am., 1989—. Mem. Am. Inst. Chem. Engrs., AICPAs, Nat. Mgmt. Assn., Beta Gamma Sigma.

FERRIS, ROGER PATRICK, architect; b. Buffalo, Jan. 3, 1952; s. Herbert Parkhill and Dolores (Murphy) F.; m. Jessie Greenway, Sept. 18, 1982. BA in Econs., La Salle Coll., 1974; postgrad., U. Pa., 1974-75, Columbia U., 1976-77. Registered architect, Conn. Architect, Christ-Janer & Assocs., New Canaan, Conn., 1974-76; pres. Landworks Assocs., Southport, Conn., 1976-79; pres. Ferris Architects, P.C., Southport, Conn., 1979—. Mem. Conn. Soc. Architects (Award of Merit), AIA (cert., New England Regional Award of Excellence in Architecture), Nat. Council Archl. Registration Bds. (cert.), Nat. Trust for Historic Preservation, Conn. Trust for Historic Preservation. Republican. Club: Lyford Cay (Nassau, Bahamas). Avocations: racing sports cars, tennis, swimming. Office: Ferris Architects PC 2507 Post Rd Southport CT 06490

FERRITER, MAURICE JOSEPH, lawyer; b. Holyoke, Mass., Aug. 14, 1930; s. John J. and Aldea (Brouilette) F.; m. Margaret M. Hennigan, June 19, 1954; children: Maurice J., John J., Mary M., Joseph P. AA, Holyoke Jr. Coll., 1952, BA, U. Mass., 1979; JD, Western New Eng. Law Sch., Springfield, Mass., 1957. Bar: Mass. 1957, U.S. Dist. Ct. Mass. 1960, U.S. Supreme Ct. 1967, U.S. Ct. Appeals (1st cir.) 1980. Pres. Begley, Ferriter, Lavelle & Welch, P.C., Holyoke, Mass., 1957—; chmn. bd. dirs. Ferriter, Scobbo, Sikora, Caruso & Rodophele, P.C., Boston; gen. counsel emeritus Mass. Mcpl. Wholesale Electric Co.; bd. dirs. Heritage-NIS Bank. Pres. Holyoke Heritage Park R.R.; dir. Providence Hosp., ARC. With U.S. Army, 1948-51. Recipient Outstanding Servant of Pub. award Springfield TV Sta. WWLP Channel 22, 1976; Spl. Service award Mcpl. Electric Assn. Mass. 1981; award of merit Bur. Exceptional Children, 1979. Mem. ABA, Mass. Bar Assn., Hampden County Bar Assn., Holyoke Bar Assn., Assn. Trial Lawyers Am., Mass. Acad. Trial Lawyers, Am. Judicature Soc. (MBA fee arbitration com.), Holyoke C. of C. (past pres., appreciation award 1975). Home: 31 Longfellow Rd Holyoke MA 01040 Office: Ferriter Scobbo Sikora et al 1 Milk St Boston MA 02109 Office: Begley Ferriter Lavelle & Welch 1 Court Pla Holyoke MA 01040

FERY, JOHN BRUCE, forest products company executive; b. Bellingham, Wash., Feb. 16, 1930; s. Carl Salvatore and Margaret Emily (Hauck) F.; m. Delores Lorraine Carlo, Aug. 22, 1953; children: John Brent, Bruce Todd, Michael Nicholas. BA, U. Wash., 1953; MBA, Stanford U., 1955; D of Nat. Resources (hon.), Gonzaga U., 1982, D of Law (hon.), 1982; D of Nat. Resources (hon.), U. Idaho, 1983. Asst. to pres. Western Kraft Corp., 1955-56; prodn. mgr. 1956-57; with Boise Cascade Corp., Idaho, 1957—, pres., chief exec. officer, 1972-78, chmn. bd., chief exec. officer, 1978—; bd. dirs. Albertsons, Inc., Hewlett-Packard Co., The Moore Fin. Group, Inc., Nat. Park Found., Union Pacific Corp.; grad. mem. Bus. Coun.; sr. mem. Conf. Bd. Mem. adv. coun. sch. bus. Stanford U. With USN, 1950-51. Named Most Outstanding Chief Exec. Officer Fin. World, 1977, 78, 79, 80. Mem. Am. Paper Inst. (bd. dirs., past chmn., mem. exec. com.), Bus. Roundtable (policy com.). Clubs: Arid, Hillcrest Country, Link's, Arlington. Office: Boise Cascade Corp 1 Jefferson Sq Boise ID 83728

FESKOE, GAFFNEY JON, investment banker; b. N.Y.C., Feb. 21, 1949; s. George Jon and Mary Margaret (Gaffney) F.; children: Gregory, Alexandra, Julia, Elizabeth. BS, Boston Coll., 1971; MBA, Fordham U., 1976. With Mfrs. Hanover Trust, N.Y.C., 1971-75; asst. treas. European-Am. Bank, N.Y.C., 1975-77; asst. v.p. Citibank, N.A., N.Y.C., 1977-80; asst treas. U.S. Filter Corp., N.Y.C., 1980-82; v.p. Bank of N.Y., N.Y.C., 1982-84; cons. Arthur D. Little, Inc., N.Y.C., 1986—; exec. v.p. Madison One Group, N.Y.C., 1988—. Trustee Yale Library Assocs., 1983—; commr. Cable TV & Communications Commn., 1985-87. Roman Catholic. Clubs: Union, Apawamis (Rye, N.Y.). Home: 30 Sedgewick Ave Darien CT 06820 Office: Madison One Group Inc 331 Madison Ave New York NY 10017

FETRIDGE, WILLIAM HARRISON, publishing company executive; b. Chgo., Aug. 2, 1906; s. Matthew and Clara (Hall) F.; m. Bonnie Jean Clark, June 27, 1941; children: Blakely (Mrs. Harvey H. Bundy III), Clark Worthington. B.S., Northwestern U., 1929; LL.D., Central Mich. U., 1954. Asst. to dean Northwestern U., 1929-30; editor Trade Periodical Co., 1930-31, Chgo. Tribune, 1931-34, H. W. Kastor & Son, 1934-35, Roche, Williams & Cleary, Inc., 1935-42; mng. editor Republican mag., 1939-42; asst. to pres. Popular Mechanics mag., 1945-46, v.p., 1946, exec. v.p., 1953-59; v.p. Diamond T Motor Truck Co., Chgo., 1959-61; exec. v.p. Diamond T div. White Motor Co., 1961-65; pres. Dartnell Corp., Chgo., 1965-77, chmn. bd., 1977—; dir. Bank of Ravenswood, Chgo. Author: With Warm Regards, 1976; editor: The Navy Reader, 1943, The Second Navy Reader, 1944, American Political Almanac, 1950, The Republican Precinct Workers Manual, 1968. Trustee Greater North Michigan Ave. Assn., 1949-58; chmn. Ill. Tollway Dedication com., 1958; pres. United Republican Fund of Ill., 1968-73, 79-80; fin. chmn. Ill. Rep. Party, 1968-73; alt. del.-at-large Rep. Nat. Conv., 1956, del.-at-large, 1968, hon. del.-at-large, 1972; mem. Rep. Nat. Finance Com.; chmn. Midwest Vols. Nixon, 1960, Rep. Forum, 1958-60, Nixon Recount Com.; trustee Jacques Holinger Meml. Assn., Am. Humanics Found.; mem. nat. exec. bd., nat. v.p. Boy Scouts Am., 1958-76, chmn. nat. adv. bd., 1976-77; vice chmn. World Scout Found., Geneva, 1977-88; trustee Lake Forest Coll., 1969-77; pres. U.S. Found. for Internat. Scouting, 1971-79, hon. chmn., 1979—; past pres. trustees Latin Sch. Chgo.; chmn. bd. dirs. Johnston Scout Mus., North Brunswick, N.J.; elected lauriate Lincoln Acad. of Ill., 1985. Served as lt. comdr. USNR, 1942-45. Decorated chevalier Grand Priory of Malta, chevalier Order St. John of Jerusalem; recipient Abraham Lincoln award United Republican Fund, 1980; Silver Antelope, Silver Beaver, Silver Buffalo Boy Scouts Am., 1956, Bronze Wolf award World Scout Conf., 1973, Distinguished Eagle award, 1976. Fellow Baden-Powell; mem. Olave Baden-Powel Soc., Navy League U.S. (past regional pres.), Ill. C. of C., Ill. St. Andrew Soc. (Disting. Citizen award 1980), Newcomen Soc., Soc. Midland Authors, Beta Theta Pi. Clubs: The Casino, Chicago, Union League, Saddle and Cycle, Racquet (Chgo.); Capitol Hill (Washington); Chikaming Country (Lakeside, Mich.). Lodge: Rotary. Office: 4660 Ravenswood Ave Chicago IL 60640

FETTEROLF, CHARLES FREDERICK, aluminum company executive; b. Franklin, Pa., July 18, 1928; s. Harry B. and Beryl (Linsey) F.; m. Frances Spang, Apr. 11, 1953; children: Regan J., Scott F. BS in Chemistry, Grove City Coll., 1952. Sales trainee Alcoa Aluminum Co., Pitts., 1952, chemist, gen. salesman, 1953; chemist, gen. salesman Alcoa Aluminum Co., Louisville, 1959; chemist, gen. salesman Alcoa Aluminum Co., San Francisco, 1961, industry asst. flexible packaging, 1965, div. sales mgr., 1965-69; asst. dist. sales mgr. Alcoa Aluminum Co., Los Angeles, 1969; dist. sales mgr. Alcoa Aluminum Co., Phila., 1971, industry mgr. def., 1974, gen. mgr. mktg., 1975, gen. mgr. ops., 1977, v.p., 1977, v.p. Alcoa smelting process project, 1979, v.p. ops., 1979, v.p. sci. and tech., 1981, exec. v.p. mill products, 1981, pres., 1983—, chief operating officer, 1985—, also bd. dirs.; bd. dirs. Mellon Nat. Bank, N.Am., Union Carbide Corp., Allegheny Ludlum, Aluminum Co. Am. Bd. dirs. Grove City Coll., Pitts. Ballet Theatre, WQED Pub. Broadcasting; trustee Shadyside Hosp., U. Pitts.; mem. adv. bd. Coalition for Addictive Disease of S.W. Pa., 1982—. With USN, 1946-48. Recipient Alumni Achievementaward Grove City Coll., 1978. Clubs: Duquesne, Laurel Valley, Internat, Allegheny Country. Office: Aluminum Co Am 1501 Alcoa Bldg Pittsburgh PA 15219

FETTERS, NORMAN CRAIG, II, banker; b. Pitts., Aug. 27, 1942; s. Karl Leroy and Hazel (Lower) F.; m. Linda Wood, Aug. 14, 1965; children—Eric Craig, Kevin Edward, Brian Allan. A.B., Westminster Coll., 1964; M.B.A., U. Pitts., 1965. Various positions to v.p. Security Pacific Nat. Bank, Los Angeles, 1965-66, 69-74, v.p., 1974-82; sr. v.p. Rainier Nat. Bank (named changed to Security Pacific Bank 1989), Seattle, 1982—. Treas. troop 647 Boy Scouts Am., Mercer Island, Wash. Served to lt. U.S. Army, 1966-69. Mem. Robert Morris Assocs., Lions. Presbyterian. Office: Security Pacific Bank Wash PO Box 3966 T20-4 1301 Fifth Ave Seattle WA 98124

FEUERHERD, VICTOR EDMOND, management consultant; b. Mineola, N.Y., Apr. 23, 1925; s. Victor Edmond and Margaret L. (O'Donnell) F.; B.S., Fordham U., 1950; Advanced Mgmt. Program, Harvard U., 1977; m. Lillian C. Dolan, June 3, 1950; children—Victor, Elizabeth, Peter, David, Stephen (dec.), Joseph, Mary (dec.), Matthew. Sr. accountant Arthur Andersen & Co., N.Y.C., 1950-54; asst. to pres. Research Inst. Am., N.Y.C., 1954-61; gen. mgr. S.D. Corp., Sioux Falls, 1961-62; v.p. investments Small Bus. Investment Co., N.Y.C., 1962-64; dir. bus. analysis Schering-Plough Corp., Bloomfield, N.J., 1967-68; dir. spl. projects SCM Corp., N.Y.C., 1964-67, staff v.p. corporate devel., 1968-70, v.p. fin. planning, 1970-73, corp. v.p. planning and acquisitions, 1973-86; pvt. practice mgmt. cons., 1986—. Treas., bd. dirs. Friends of Handicapped. Served with inf., AUS, 1943-46; ETO. C.P.A., N.Y. Roman Catholic. Home: 26 Princeton St Garden City NY 11530

FEUERSTEIN, HERBERT, food company executive; b. Vienna, Austria, Dec. 22, 1927; came to U.S., 1947, naturalized, 1953; s. David and Eva (Seif) F.; m. Regina Katz, June 10, 1956; children: Robert Allen, Lisa Ann. Student, Gymnasium, Berne, Switzerland, 1942-47; postgrad., CUNY, 1948-50. With Mondial Co., Inc., N.Y.C., 1948-60, sr. ptnr., 1960-64; founder, pres. Rema Foods Inc., N.Y.C., 1964-80; v.p., gen. mgr. imports Universal Foods Corp., Carlstadt, N.J., 1980-85; v.p., gen. mgr. commodities Universal Foods Corp., Teaneck, N.J., 1985-88; pres. Rema Foods, Inc., Teaneck, 1988—; chmn. bd. On-Line Data Software, Pearl River, N.Y., 1986—. Pres. Jewish Community Ctr. of Ft. Lee, N.J., 1980-82; chmn. bd. Israeli Bond Orgn., Ft. Lee, 1982—. Jewish. Office: Rema Foods Glenpointe Ctr E Teaneck NJ 07666

FEULNER, EDWIN JOHN, JR., research foundation executive; b. Chgo., Aug. 12, 1941; s. Edwin John and Helen J. (Franzen) F.; m. Linda C. Leventhal, Mar. 8, 1969; children: Edwin John III, Emily V. BS, Regis Coll., 1963; MBA, U. Pa., 1964; PhD, U. Edinburgh, 1981; hon. degrees, Nichols Coll., 1981; hon. degree, Universidad Francisco Marroquin, Guatemala City, 1982, Hanyang U., Seoul, Korea, 1982, Bellevue Coll., Nebr., 1987. Richard Weaver fellow London Sch. Econs., 1965; pub. affairs fellow Hoover Instn., 1965-67; confidential asst. to sec. def. Melvin Laird, 1969-70; adminstrv. asst. to U.S. Congressman Philip M. Crane, 1970-74; exec. dir. Rep. Study Com., Ho. of Reps. 1974-77; pres. Heritage Found., Washington, 1977—; chmn. Inst. European Def. and Strategic Studies, 1977—; Chmn. U.S. Adv. Com. Pub. Diplomacy, USIA, 1982—; vice chmn. bd. dirs. Credit Internat. Bank; mem. sci. commn. Ctr. Applied Econ. Rsch., Rome; ; nat. adv. bd. Ctr. for Edn. and Rsch. in Free Enterprise, Tex. A&M U.; disting. fellow Mobilization Concepts, Devel. Ctr. Nat. Def. U.; mem. Pres. Commn. on White House Fellows, 1981-83, Carlucci Commn. on Fgn. Assistance, 1983; pub. del. UN 2d Spl. Session on Disarmament, 1982; White House cons. domestic policy, 1987. Author: Congress and the New International Economic Order, 1976, Looking Back, 1981, Conservatives Stalk the House, 1983; contbr. articles to profl. jours., chpts. to books. Trustee Lehrman Inst., Rockford Inst., 1981-87, Roe Found., Am. Coun. on Germany, Sarah Scaife Found.; chmn. bd. Intercollegiate Studies Inst.; bd. govs., mem. exec. com. Coun. Nat. Policy, Found. Francisco Marroquin; mem. Citizens for Am., chmn. Citizens for Am. Edn. Found.; mem. disting. adv. com. Sch. Communication Am. U.; mem. coun. acad. advisors Bryce Harlow Found. Recipient Disting. Alumni award Regis Coll., 1985, Dept. of Navy Superior Pub. Svc. award, Presdl. Citizens medal, 1989; named Free Enterprise Man of Yr. Tex. A&M U., 1985. Mem. Am. Econs. Assn., Am. Polit. Sci. Assn., Internat. Inst. Strategic Studies, U.S. Strategic Inst., Phila. Soc. (treas. 1964-79, pres. 1982-83), Mont Pelerin Soc. (treas.), Alpha Kappa Psi. Republican. Roman Catholic. Clubs: Belle Haven Country (Alexandria, Va.); Union League (N.Y.C.); Univ., Met. (Washington); Reform (London), Knights of Malta.

FEWELL, JEANNIE LOUISE, public administration consultant; b. York, S.C., Feb. 17, 1948; d. Joseph E. and Verna (Faris) F.; m. Richard L. Bowers, Dec. 29, 1984. BA in History, Winthrop Coll., 1969, MA in History, 1971; M in Pub. Adminstrn., U. S.C., 1974. Instr. dept. history Winthrop Coll., Rock Hill, S.C., 1971-74; regional planner Catawba Regional Planning, Rock Hill, 1974-75; dir. community devel. City of Anderson, S.C., 1975-77, City of Charleston, S.C., 1977-81; field dir. Nat. League Cities, Washington, 1981-82; dir. RAS, Inc., Washington, 1982-83; v.p. CMS, Inc., Washington, 1983-84; assoc. v.p., cons. Reynolds, Smith & Hills, Jacksonville, Fla., 1984—; cons. S.C. Main St. Program, Columbia, 1987—; v.p., bd. dirs. Carolina's Council Housing, N.C. and S.C., 1975-81. Contbr. articles to housing publs. Mem. Am. Soc. Pub. Adminstrs. (bd. dirs. S.C. chpt. 1980), Housing Advocates (bd. dirs. 1988). Democrat. Presbyterian. Home: 3007 Branchwood Ln Jacksonville FL 32256 Office: Reynolds Smith & Hills 6777 Southpoint Dr South Jacksonville FL 32216

FEYEREISEN, EDWARD CHARLES, education educator, company executive; b. Hudson, Wis., Aug. 8, 1941; s. Albert James and Mayree Elizabeth (Singleton) F.; m. Roberta Ann Knapp, Oct. 3, 1964; children: Joseph, Mark, Matthew. BS, Coll. St. Thomas, St. Paul, 1964; MNS, U. So. Dakota, 1970; MS in Edn., Chgo. State U., 1972; postgrad., No. Ariz. U., 1977—. Sci. tchr. St. Bernard's High Sch., St. Paul, 1964-67; sci. tchr. Sch. Dist. 228, Midlothian, Ill., 1967-73, counselor, 1973-86; pres., presenter Edu-Care, Sedona, Ariz., 1986—; tng. cons. Dale Carnegie Systems, Phoenix, 1986—; cons., motivator several No. Ariz. companies, 1987—. Patentee Kick-Sled, 1983, Snow Scooter, 1983, Ice Glider, 1983, Star-Reacher, 1988. Pres. Estados Homeowners Assn., 1987. Mem. Carnegians. Roman Catholic. Office: Edu-Care PO Box 20275 Village Oak Creek AZ 86341

FIALA, DAVID MARCUS, lawyer; b. Cleve., Aug. 1, 1946; s. Frank J. and Anna Mae (Phillips) F.; m. Maryanne E. McGowan, Jan. 4, 1969 (div. Mar. 1986); 1 child, D. Michael; m. Lyn McDonald Jones, May 31, 1986. BBA, U. Cin., 1969; JD, Chase Coll., No. Ky. State U., 1974. Bar: Ohio 1974, U.S.

Dist. Ct. (so. dist.) Ohio 1974, U.S. Tax Ct. 1974. Assoc. Benesch, Friedlander, Coplan and Aronoff, Cin., 1974-78, ptnr., 1979—; lectr. Southwestern Ohio Tax Inst., 1978-79, 88 ; bd. dirs. Elkhorn Collieries, Cin. Trustee, sec. Sta. WCET-TV, Cin., 1983-87, auction chmn., 1979, chmn. 1987—; trustee Jr. Achievement Greater Cin., 1979—, Mental Health Svcs. West, 1974-83, Contemporary Dance theatre, 1974-80. Mem. ABA, Ohio State Bar Assn., Cin. Bar Assn. (lectr. estate planning inst. 1989), Am. Culinary Fedn. Cin. (trustee 1985—). Office: Benesch Friedlander Coplan & Aronoff 1900 Carew Tower Cincinnati OH 45202

FIALKOW, STEVEN, accountant; b. Bklyn., July 24, 1943; s. Irving and Ida (Berglass) F.; BBA, City U. N.Y., 1965; MBA, 1970; m. Arlene Michele Klein, Oct. 19, 1963 (div. Oct. 1985); children: Cheri Ann, Laura Beth; m. Frances Theresa Miller, Apr. 15, 1986. Profl. staff Price Waterhouse & Co., N.Y.C., 1965-69; asst. treas., controller Anglo Am. Corp., N.Y.C., 1969-72; treas., controller Video Playbacks, Inc., N.Y.C., 1972-75; adminstrv. mgr. Kenneth Leventhal & Co., N.Y.C., 1975-77; instr. N.Y. Inst. Tech., N.Y.C., 1975-79; ptnr. Herzig, Blumenfeld & Fialkow, CPAs, N.Y.C., 1979-81; assoc. dir. nat. acctg. and audit profl. edn. Touche Ross & Co., N.Y.C., 1981-83; mng. ptnr. Steven Fialkow & Co., CPAs, Coram, N.Y., El Paso, Tex., 1983—; cons. Banis Securities Corps. N.Y. Dir. outreach program YMCA, L.I., N.Y. CPA, N.Y. Mem. AI CPAs, N.Y. State Soc. CPAs, Mensa, Masons. Republican. Home: 368 Woodland Ct Coram NY 11727 Office: Fialkow Bldg 976 Skyline Dr Coram NY 11727 also: 4800 N Stanton Suite 48 El Paso TX 79902

FIBIGER, JOHN ANDREW, life insurance company executive; b. Copenhagen, Apr. 27, 1932; came to U.S., 1934, naturalized, 1953; s. Borge Rottboll and Ruth Elizabeth (Wadmond) F.; m. Barbara Mae Stuart, June 22, 1956; children: Karen Ruth McCarthy, Katherine Louise. B.A., U. Minn., 1953, M.A., 1954; postgrad., U. Wis. With Lincoln Nat. Life Ins. Co., Ft. Wayne, Ind., 1956-57; with Bankers Life Ins. Co. Nebr., Lincoln, 1959-73; sr. v.p. group Bankers Life Ins. Co. Nebr., 1972-73; with New Eng. Mut. Life Ins. Co., Boston, 1973—; vice chmn., pres., chief operating officer New Eng. Mut. Life Ins. Co., 1981—; bd. dirs. Bay Bank Middlesex; trustee Babson Coll.; past pres. Am. Acad. Actuaries. Chmn. Museum Sci., Boston, 1980—; trustee New Eng. Med. Ctr., Mass. Taxpayers Found., Menninger Found., Shelburne Mus.; bd. dirs. Boston Classical Orch. Served with AUS, 1957-59. Fellow Soc. Actuaries; mem. Life Office Mgmt. Assn. (bd. dirs.), Boston Actuaries Club, Internat. Actuarial Assn. (council), Nat. Acad. Social Ins. (founding mem.), Merchants Club (Boston). Office: New Eng Mut Life Ins Co 501 Boylston St Boston MA 02116

FICKINGER, WAYNE JOSEPH, advertising executive; b. Belleville, Ill., June 23, 1926; s. Joseph and Grace (Belton) F.; m. Joan Mary Foley, June 16, 1951; children: Michael, Joan, Jan, Ellen, Steven. B.A., U. Ill., 1949; M.S., Northwestern U., 1950. Overnight editor United Press, Chgo., 1950-51; spl. project writer Sears-Roebuck & Co., Chgo., 1951-53; account exec. Calkins & Holden Advt. Agy., Chgo., 1953-56; account supr. Foote, Cone & Belding Advt. Agy., Chgo., N.Y.C., 1956-63; sr. v.p. J. Walter Thompson Co., Chgo., 1963-72; exec. v.p., dir. U.S. Western div. J. Walter Thompson Co., 1972-75, pres. N.Am. div., 1975-78; pres., chief operating officer J. Walter Thompson Co. Worldwide, 1978-79; pres. JWT Group, Inc., 1979-82, trustee retirement fund, dir., mem. exec. com., 1980-82; mng. dir. Spencer Stuart & Assocs., 1982-83; vice chmn., dir. Bozell, Jacobs, Kenyon & Eckhardt Inc., Chgo., 1984-89; pres. Mid-Am. Com., Chgo., 1989—; dir. Monroe Communications Corp., Evalucom, Frankel & Co., Alford-Ver Schave, Inc., Sullivan and Proobst, Inc. Fund raising cons. Nat. Mental Health Assn., 1970; communications counselor Cook County (Ill.) Republican Orgn., 1970; bd. dirs. Off-the-Street Club, Chgo., 1974-77, Mundelein Coll., 1985—, United Cerebral Palsy, 1986, Chgo. Conv. and Tourist Bur., 1986—; chmn. Chgo. funding Statue of Liberty, 1986, March of Dimes, 1987, Chgo. Tourism Coun., 1988—. Served with USNR, 1943-46. Recipient Five-Year Meritorious Service award A.R.C., 1963, Service award Mental Health Assn., 1970. Mem. Am. Assn. Advt. Agys., Council on Fgn. Relations (Chgo. com.), Sigma Delta Chi, Alpha Delta Sigma. Clubs: Exmoor Country (Highland Park, Ill.); N.Y. Athletic; Mid-Am. (Chgo.), Internat. (Chgo.). Office: Mid-Am Com 150 N Michigan Ave Chicago IL 60601

FICKLING, WILLIAM ARTHUR, JR., health care administrator; b. Macon, Ga., July 23, 1932; s. William Arthur and Claudia Darden (Foster) F.; m. Neva Jane Langley, Dec. 30, 1954; children: William Arthur III, Jane Dru, Julia Claudia, Roy Hampton. BS cum laude, Auburn U., 1954. Exec. v.p. Fickling & Walker, Inc., Macon, 1954-74; chmn. bd. dirs., chief exec. officer Charter Med. Corp., Macon, 1969-85, pres., chmn. bd. dirs., 1985—; bd. dirs. Ga. Power Co., Riverside Ford, Southlake Ford. Trustee Wesleyan Coll., Macon. Mem. Macon Bd. Realtors, Kappa Alpha, Delta Sigma Phi, Phi Kappa Phi. Methodist. Home: 4918 Wesleyan Woods Dr Macon GA 31210 Office: Charter Med Corp 577 Mulberry St Macon GA 31298

FIDDICK, PAUL WILLIAM, broadcasting company executive; b. St. Joseph, Mo., Nov. 20, 1949; s. Lowell Duane and Betty Jean (Manring) F.; m. Julie Hanna Lorms, July 31, 1983; children: Lea Elizabeth, Hanna Manring. BJ cum laude, U. Mo., 1971. Account exec. Sta. KCMO-KFMU, Kansas City, Mo., 1971-72; account exec. Sta. WEZW, Milw., 1972-74, dir. sales mktg., 1974-76, v.p., gen. mgr., 1976-81; sr. v.p. Multimedia Broadcasting Co., Milw., 1981; pres. Multimedia Radio, Cin., 1982-86, Radio Group, Heritage Communications, Inc., Des Moines, 1986-87, Radio Group, Heritage Media Corp., Dallas, 1987—; dir. Radio Advt. Bur., N.Y.C., 1983—, mem. exec. com., 1989—, chmn. rsch. com., 1985-88, chmn. Mng. Sales Conf., 1989; instr. Radio Sales U., 1987-88; mem. acad. staff U. Wis., Milw., 1978-81. Producer (indsl. film) Marketing of Radio, 1975; contbg. author: American Radio, 10th anniversary edit. Mem. Comprehensive Planning Task Force, Shorewood, Wis. Recipient Up and Coming Radio Exec. of Yr. award Radio Only mag., 1983; named to Hon. Order Ky. Cols. Office: Heritage Media Corp 13355 Noel Rd Ste 1500 One Galleria Tower Dallas TX 75240

FIEDEROWICZ, WALTER MICHAEL, lawyer; b. Hartford, Conn., Aug. 23, 1946; s. Michael and Sylvia Christine (Ramunno) F.; m. Gerry Prattson, June 1, 1968; children: Michael, Catherine. B.A., Yale U., 1968; J.D. (DuPont fellow), U. Va., 1971. Bar: Conn. 1971, U.S. Supreme Ct. 1977. Mem. firm Cummings & Lockwood, Stamford, Conn., 1971-76, ptnr. firm, 1979-88, of counsel, 1989—; pres. Covenant Mut. Ins. Co., Hartford, 1985—; White House fellow U.S. Dept. Justice, Washington, 1976-77; spl. asst. to Atty. Gen., Dept. Justice, Washington, 1976-77; assoc. dep. Atty. Gen., 1977-79. Mem. editorial bd.: Va. Law Review, 1969-71. Bd. dirs. Conn. Prison Assn., VITAM Found.; mem. grad. council Loomis-Chaffee Sch. Bd. Mem. ABA, Conn. Bar Assn., Order of the Coif. Roman Catholic. Home: 100 Westerly Terr Hartford CT 06105 Office: Covenant Mut Ins Co 241 Main St Hartford CT 06103

FIELD, MARSHALL, business executive; b. Charlottesville, Va., May 13, 1941; s. Marshall IV and Joanne (Bass) F.; m. Joan Best Connelly, Sept. 5, 1964 (div. 1969); 1 son, Marshall; m. Jamee Beckwith Jacobs, Aug. 19, 1972; children: Jamee Christine, Stephanie Caroline, Abigail Beckwith. B.A., Harvard U., 1963. With N.Y. Herald Tribune, 1964-65; pub. Chgo. Sun-Times, 1969-80, Chgo. Daily News, 1969-78; dir. Field Enterprises, Inc., Chgo., 1965-84, dir., mem. exec. com. Field Enterprises, Inc., 1965-84, chmn. bd., 1972-84; chmn. bd. The Field Corp., 1984—; chmn. bd. Cabot, Cabot & Forbes, 1984-85, chmn. exec. com., 1985-89, sr. dir., chief exec. officer, 1989—; pub. World Book-Childcraft Internat. Inc., 1973-78, dir., 1965-80; bd. dirs. First Chgo. Corp., First Nat. Bank Chgo. Mem. Chgo. Council Fgn. Relations; pres., trustee Art Inst. Chgo.; vice chmn., trustee, Field Mus. Natural History, Rush-Presbyn.-St. Luke's Med. Ctr.; trustee Mus. Sci. and Industry; bd. dirs. First Nat. Bank Chgo., 1970-85, Chgo. Tourism Council, Field Found. of Ill., McGraw Wildlife Found., Restoration Atlantic Salmon In Am., Inc., Trout Unltd., Lincoln Park Zool. Soc., hon. bd. dirs. Open Lands Project (CorLands); mem. univ. resources Harvard Coll.; mem. adv. bd. Brookfield Zoo. Mem. Nature Conservancy, River Club, Econs. Club, Chicago Club, Mid.-Am. Comml. Club, Econ. Club, Harvard Club, Racquet Club, Tavern Club, Hundred Club of Cook County, Onwentsia Club, Somerset Club, Jupiter Island Club. Econ. Club. Office: Field Corp 333 W Wacker Dr Chicago IL 60606

FIELD, PAUL L., cable television executive; b. Bklyn., Dec. 13, 1925; s. Paul and Hortense Josephine (Kraeger) F.; m. Irene LaVonne Parsons, Feb. 26, 1956; children: Christiane P., Alicia P. BA, Colgate U., 1947. Assoc. producer Remington Rand, N.Y.C., 1950-52; dir., producer Sound Masters Inc., N.Y.C., 1952-55; TV producer N.W. Ayer Agy., N.Y.C., 1955-60, Benton & Bowles Agy., N.Y.C., 1960-61; freelance writer, dir. N.Y.C., 1962-74; assoc. LaRue Media Brokers, N.Y.C., 1974-75; pres. Field Assocs., Bronxville, N.Y., 1975-77, Greenefield Communications Brokerage, Bronxville, 1977-79; chief exec. officer Essex Communications Corp., Greenwich, Conn., 1979-88, also chmn. bd. dirs; officer, dir. Mid-South Cable TV, 1988—; chmn. Bronxville CATV Com., 1980-83. Author: Who's on Second?, 1964; scriptwriter It's Our Choice, 1971 (Gold Camera award), Waste Not, 1972 (Gold Camera award). Mem. recreation council, Bronxville, 1983-85; co-chmn. Platform Tennis Com., Broxville, 1987-88; vol. Community Fund, Bronxville. 2d lt. USAAF, 1943-46. Mem. CATV Adminstrn. and Mktg. Assn., CATV Pub. Affairs Assn., Nat. Acad. Cable Programming, Dirs. Guild Am. Republican. Clubs: Bronxville Field (pres. 1979-81); N.Y. Athletic (N.Y.C.). Home: 503 River West Greenwich CT 06831 Office: Essex Communications Corp 235 Glenville Rd Greenwich CT 06831

FIELD, ROBERT BUNTEN, JR., lawyer; b. San Francisco, Feb. 8, 1943; s. Robert Bunten and Jean (Pierce) F.; m. Elizabeth Hoopes. Oct. 2, 1971; children: Robert Bunten III, Charles S., Victoria E. AB, Dartmouth Coll., 1964; JD, Boston U., 1970. Bar: N.H. 1970. Ptnr. Hamblett & Kerrigan, P.A., Nashua, N.H., 1970-80, Sheehan, Phinney, Bass & Green, P.A., Manchester and Portsmouth, N.H., 1980—; bd. dirs. Bank of N.H., Manchester, 1980—, New Eng. Trade Adjustment Assistance Corp., Boston. Trustee Children's Mus. of Portsmouth. Served to lt j.g. USNR, 1964-68, Vietnam. Mem. N.H. Bar Assn., Rockingham County Bar Assn., Warwick Club, Cuttyhunk (Mass.) Yacht Club (bd. govs., treas.), Nashua Country Club (bd. govs. 1978-80), Rotary. Republican. Congregationalist. Office: Sheehan Phinney Bass & Green PA 1 Harbour Pl Ste 325 Portsmouth NH 03801

FIELD, THOMAS CLARK, paint equipment and related products company executive; b. Minn., Feb. 14, 1942; s. Cyrus and Helen (Bowen) F.; m. Mary Bittle; children: Brian, Amanda. BA, Hamiline U., 1964; JD, U. Minn., 1967; MBA, U. Chgo., 1973. Gen. counsel Graco, Inc., Mpls., 1968-70, gen. mgr. finishing div., dir. corp. devel., 1970-75, v.p. corp. devel. and mktg., 1975-78, v.p. internat., 1978-84; pres. The DeVilbiss Co., Toledo, 1984—; bd. dirs. Toledo Trust Co. Mng. trustee Toledo Hosp., 1986—; co-chmn. Toledo United Way, 1985-87; steering com. Grace Community Ctr., Toledo, 1986; bd. trustees Sta. WGTE-TV. Mem. Am. Mgmt. Assn. Republican. Clubs: Toledo, Inverness (Toledo). Office: DeVilbiss Co 300 Phillips Ave PO Box 913 Toledo OH 43692

FIELD, THOMAS WALTER, JR., drugstore chain executive; b. Alhambra, Calif., Nov. 2, 1933; s. Thomas Walter and Pietje (Slagveld) F.; m. Ruth Inez Oxley, Apr. 10, 1959; children: Julie, Sherry, Cynthia, Thomas Walter, III, James. Student, Stanford U., 1951-53. V.p. retail ops. Alpha Beta Co., La Habra, Calif., 1972-73, sr. v.p., 1973-75, exec. v.p., 1975-76, pres., chief exec. officer, 1976-81; pres. Am. Stores Co., 1981-85; pres., chief exec. officer McKesson Corp., San Francisco, 1986—, also chmn. bd. Bd. dirs. La Habra Boys' Club. Mem. Calif. Retailers Assn. (dir.), Automobile Club So. Calif. (adv. bd.). Republican. Office: McKesson Corp 1 Post St San Francisco CA 94104 *

FIELDER, CHARLES ROBERT, business executive; b. Lubbock, Tex., Mar. 9, 1943; s. Clarence Daniel and Ola Marie (Sewell) F.; m. Mary Ruth Wills, May 31, 1964; 1 child, Sara Elizabeth. B.B.A., Tex. Tech. U., 1965, M.S. in Acctg., 1972. C.P.A., Tex. Staff acct. Peat, Marwick, Mitchell & Co., Dallas, 1965-66, Arthur Andersen & Co., Dallas, 1968-69; treasury acct. Halliburton Co., Dallas, 1969-71, treasury supr., 1971-72, asst. treas., 1972-78, treas., 1978—. Mem. Fin. Execs. Inst., Am. Inst. C.P.A.s, Tex. Soc. C.P.A.s, Phi Eta Sigma, Beta Alpha Psi, Beta Gamma Sigma, Phi Kappa Phi. Republican. Mem. Churches of Christ. Club: Tower. Office: Halliburton Co 3600 Lincoln Pla 500 N Akard St Dallas TX 75201

FIELDS, CURTIS GREY, public utility executive; b. Goldsboro, N.C., Oct. 23, 1933; s. C.F. and Ethel B. Fields; m. Apr. 5, 1953; children: Curtis Grey, Dwayne L. BS in Math. and Physics, East Carolina U., 1955; postgrad. U. N.C., 1957, U. Richmond, 1959. Mktg. and dist. comml. mgr. Carolina Tel. & Tel. Co., Tarboro, N.C., 1955-65, gen. directory mgr., 1965-69, div. comml. mgr., 1969-72; div. comml. mgr. United Telephone Co., Ohio, Mansfield, 1971-72, gen. comml. mgr., 1972-74, v.p. adminstrn., 1974-79, pres., chmn. bd. dirs., 1979-87; exec. v.p. United Telecommunications, Inc., 1987—; mem. Utilities Exec. Steering Com., Columbus, Ohio; bd. dirs. Toledo Trust Corp, Inc., Mansfield, United Telephone of Fla., 1987—, United Telephone Co. Ohio, 1979—, Carolina Tel. & Tel., 1987—, North Supply Co., 1987—, Trustee, bd. dirs., mem. exec. com. Richland Econ. Devel. Corp., Mansfield, 1981-87; trustee Mansfield Gen. Hosp., 1985-87, Richland County Found., 1985-86; head Richland County Pacesetter, 1986. Mem. Ohio Telephone Assn. (bd. dirs. 1979-87, exec. com. 1980-81), Mansfield C. of C. (bd. dirs. 1979-87), U.S. Telephone Assn. (bd. dirs. 1987—). Episcopalian. Office: United Telecommunications Inc 2330 Shawnee Mission Pkwy PO Box 11315 Kansas City MO 64112

FIELDS, DAVID STEPHEN, manufacturing executive; b. Hamilton, Ohio, July 21, 1941; s. Simon and Emma (Morgan) F.; m. Sylvia Neiswonger, Sept. 1, 1962; children: Gregory, Michael, Christie. BA, Anderson U., 1964; MBA, Ball State U., 1974. CPA, Ohio, Tex. Staff acct. Deloitte, Haskins & Sells, Dayton, Ohio, 1964-68; mgr. acctg. Consol. Thermoplastics, Chatham, N.J., 1968-69; mgr. cost acctg. and profit planning Consol. Thermoplastics, Odessa, Tex., 1969-70; controller Bell Fibre Products Corp., Marion, Ind., 1970-76; controller Gen. Portland Inc., Dallas, 1976-83, v.p., fin., 1983-88; exec. v.p. Profl. Service Industries Inc., Irving, Tex., 1988—; bd. dirs. Systech Corp., Dayton. Mem. Fin. Execs. Inst., Am. Inst. CPA's, Portland Cement Ass. Fin. Execs. (steering com.). Republican. Clubs: Gleneagles Country, Aerobics Activities Ctr. Home: 16209 Dalmalley Ln Dallas TX 74248 Office: Profl Svc Industries Inc 9901 E Valley Ranch Pkwy Ste 3000 Lockbox 35 Irving TX 75063

FIELDS, HARRY, retail executive; b. Cologne, Fed. Republic Germany, Mar. 29, 1924; came to U.S., 1947; s. Isidore and Gisela (Haber) F.; m. Barbara S. Shapiro, May 20, 1950. Grad. in chem. engring., U. Amsterdam, Holland, 1947. With Internat. Flavors and Fragrances Inc., N.Y.C., 1948—, currently pres., also bd. dirs. Trustee Ctr. for Preventative Psychiatry, White Plains, 1979. Republican. Jewish. Club: Harmonie (N.Y.C.). Office: Internat Flavors & Fragrance Inc 521 W 57th St New York NY 10019

FIELDS, JOYCE M., financial executive; b. Indpls., July 24, 1947; d. Martin Douglas and Edith (Gold) Garfield; m. Ronald L. Nelson, Oct. 7, 1984; 1 child, Jessica Fields. BBA, U. Mich., 1969; cert. exec. program, Stanford U, 1981. Portfolio analyst Merrill Lynch, N.Y.C., 1969-70; securities analyst Shearson, Hammill, N.Y.C., 1971-72; asst. to treas. Knapp King Size Corp., Brockton, Mass., 1973-75; cash adminstr. Times Mirror Co., L.A., 1975-79, cash and banking mgr., 1979-80, asst. treas., 1980-86, treas., 1986-88; treas. Times Mirror Co., N.Y.C., 1988—. Treas. Times Mirror Found., L.A., 1982-88, Pfaffinger Found., L.A., 1982-88; bd. dirs. L.A. Times Credit Union, 1983-88; mem. L.A. Pension Group, 1984—; mem. corp. allocations com. L.A. United Way, 1987-88. Mem. Fin. Execs. Inst. Home: 14 Dogwood Ln Rye NY 10580 Office: The Times Mirror Co 780 Third Ave New York NY 10017

FIELDS, KENNETH HARVEY, investment executive; b. Jersey City, May 19, 1942; s. Emanuel and Priscilla (Wagner) F.; m. Sheila May Fields, June 20, 1965; children: James Wagner, Susan Wagner. BS, Fordham U., 1964; MBA, Harvard U., 1966. Contract negotiator U.S. AEC, N.Y.C., 1966-68; rsch. analyst Lehman Bros., N.Y.C., 1968-70; mng. dir. Wertheim Schroder & Co., Inc., N.Y.C., 1970-88; pres., founder Klingenstein, Fields & Co., L.P., N.Y.C., 1989—. Office: Klingenstein Fields & Co 787 Seventh Ave New York NY 10019

FIENE, DOUGLAS WILLIAM, structural engineer; b. St. Charles, Ill., Dec. 11, 1953; s. Charles R. and Elaine L. (Bauler) F.; m. Janet L. Wrenn, Dec. 27, 1975; children: Elayna M., Owen Douglas, Kira Jaye. BS in Civil Engring., U. Ill., 1976. Registered profl. and structural engr., Ill. Constrn. engr. Mustang Corp., Naperville, Ill., 1977-80; design engr. Charles Pease Assocs., Des Plaines, Ill., 1980-82; project engr. Pavia-Marting Co., Roselle, Ill., 1983—, dir. structural engring., 1984—; prin. Douglas W. Fiene Assocs. Ltd., Glen Ellyn, Ill., 1982—. Mem. Am. Soc. Civil Engrs., Am. Inst. Steel Constrn., Am. Concrete Inst., Prestressed Concrete Inst.

FIERMAN, GERALD SHEA, electrical distribution company executive; b. Wilkes-Barre, Pa., Dec. 14, 1924; s. Abe and Mary (Jacobs) F.; A.B. in Liberal Arts, Pa. State U. 1948; m. Bernice Perloff, June 12, 1949; children: Robert Alan, Lawrence David, Daniel Jon. Pres. Shea Realty Corp., Wilkes-Barre, 1959—, Barre Realty Corp., Wilkes-Barre, 1955—, Chase Wholesale Elec. Supply, Stroudsburg, Pa. 1960—, Tomberg Elec. Supply Co., Wilkes-Barre 1954—, ANESCO, Kingston, Pa. 1949—; v.p. L&R Elec. Supply Co., Scranton, Pa., Effco Inc., Scranton. Chmn. United Jewish Campaign, Wilkes-Barre, 1963; pres. Jewish Fed. of Wyoming Valley (Pa.), 1971-74. Served with 82d Airborne Div., AUS, 1942-46. Decorated Purple Heart. Mem. Temple Israel of Wilkes-Barre. Clubs: Westmoreland of Wilkes-Barre, Jockey of Miami, Valley Tennis, Mason, Keystone Consistory. Home: 76 James St Kingston PA 18704 Office: 517 Pierce St Kingston PA 18704

FIETSAM, ROBERT CHARLES, accountant; b. Belleville, Ill., Oct. 18, 1927; s. Celsus J. and Viola (Ehret) F.; BS, U. Ill., 1955; m. Miriam Runkwitz, Apr. 12, 1952; children—Robert C., Guy P., Nancy A., Lisa R. CPA, Mo., Ill. Claims adjuster Ely & Walker Dry Goods, St. Louis, 1947-48; acct. Price Waterhouse & Co., 1949-54; staff acct. J.W. Boyle & Co., East St. Louis, 1955-59; owner R.C. Fietsam, CPA's, Belleville, Ill., 1959-68; mng. ptnr. R.C. Fietsam & Co. CPA's, 1969—. Mem. Belle-Scott Com., 1979—; bd. dirs., pres. Belleville Center, Inc., 1980-81; mem. adv. bd. Masterworks Chorale, 1984—; bd. dirs. Meml. Found., Inc., 1986—, Bellville Hosp. Golf Classic, mem., 1983—. Pres. United Ch. of Christ., St Paul, 1972-73. With USAF, 1951-53. Mem. Ill. CPA Soc. (pres. south chpt. 1972-73, Mr. South Chpt. award 1976, bd. dirs. 1979-81, sr. v.p. 1987-88, pres. 1988-89, Pub. Svc. award 1983), Mo. Soc. CPA's, Am. Inst. CPA's (coun. 1981—), U. Ill. Greater Belleville Illini Club (past pres.), Belleville C. of C. (pres. 1973-74), Belleville Jr. C. of C. (life, Key Man award 1959-60, Outstanding Citizen award 1976), Lambda Chi Alpha Alumnae Assn., St. Clair Country Club. Optimists (Belleville Chpt. pres. 1979-80, Disting. Pres. award 1979-80, Optimist of Yr. Belleville, 1977, Ill. Dist. 1980, Elks, Moose. Home: 23 Persimmon Ridge Dr Belleville IL 62223 Office: 325 W Main Belleville IL 62220

FIFE, WILLIAM FRANKLIN, drug company executive; b. Buffalo, W.Va., Nov. 6, 1921; s. Alfred Charles and Grace (Pitchford) F.; children—Scott Franklin, Susan Elizabeth, Cindy Francine. A.B., Berea Coll., 1949; M.S., U. Wis., 1950. Operating mgr. McKesson & Robbins, Chgo. and Kansas City, Mo., 1950-56, Cleve. Wholesale Drug Co., 1956-58; with Owens, Minor & Bodeker, Inc., 1958—; sr. v.p., sec. Owens, Minor & Bodeker, Inc. (now Owens & Minor, Inc.), Richmond, Va., 1981-87, exec. v.p., chief operating officer, 1987—; also dir. Owens & Minor, Inc. Served with C.E. U.S. Army, 1942-46. Mem. Nat. Wholesale Drug Assn. Democrat. Club: Rotary. Home: 507 S Gaskins Rd Richmond VA 23233 Office: Owens & Minor Inc 2727 Enterprise Pkwy Richmond VA 23229

FIFER, STEPHEN LAMAR, manufacturing company official; b. Fresno, Calif., Nov. 11, 1947; s. Karson Kirkland and Alma Christina (Mose) F.; student Calif. State U., Fresno, 1965-67, 71-74, A.B. in Internat. Econs., A.B. in Diplomatic History, 1974, M.Internat. Mgmt. in Internat. Econs. and Fin., Am. Grad. Sch. Internat. Mgmr., 1975; m. Mary Lorraine Joy, June 15, 1974. Export mgr. Reliance Crane and Rigging, Phoenix and Mexico City, Mex., 1975; staff Caterpillar Tractor Co., Peoria, Ill., 1976, staff Caterpillar Overseas S.A., Geneva, Switzerland, 1977, sales rep. Cat Overseas, Rome, Italy, 1978-80; sr. mktg. cons. Caterpillar Overseas S.A., Geneva, 1980-81, commodity mktg. support mgr., 1982-84; dist. mktg. mgr. Caterpillar Far East, Kuala Lumpur, Malaysia, 1984-89, regional mktg. mgr., Hong Kong, 1989—; SBA cons., 1976. Conservator World Wildlife Found. Served with USN, 1967-71. Recipient award of merit SBA, 1976. Mem. Am. Econs. Assn., M.B.A. Assn. Contbr. papers, reports in field to publs. Office: Caterpillar Far East Ltd, GPO 3069, Hong Kong Hong Kong

FIGGE, F. J., II, bank executive. Now chmn. credit policy NCNB Nat Bank N.C. Office: NCNB Corp 1 NCNB Pla Charlotte NC 28255 *

FIGGE, FREDERICK H., JR., publishing executive; b. Chgo., Apr. 8, 1934; s. Frederick H. and Theodora M. (Hosto) F.; m. Beverly J. Menz, June 20, 1956; children: Dora, Ann, Jane, Fred C. B.S., U. Ill., 1956. CPA, Ill. With Arthur Young & Co. (C.P.A.s), Chgo., 1958-64; controller Ency. Brit., Inc., Chgo., 1964-74, v.p., treas., 1974-85, sr. vp., 1985-86, exec. v.p., 1986—. Treas. Direct Selling Edul. Found., bd. dirs.; bd. dirs. Coll. Commerce, U. Ill., Plymouth Pl. Retirement Home, La Grange, Ill. Served with USNR, 1956-58. Mem. Beta Theta Pi, Beta Gamma Sigma. Democrat. Congregationalist. Clubs: LaGrange Country; Chgo. Athletic. Home: 221 S Blackstone St LaGrange IL 60525 Office: Ency Brit Inc 310 S Michigan Ave Chicago IL 60604

FIGGIE, HARRY E., JR., corporate executive; b. 1923; married; 3 children. B.S., Case Inst. Tech., 1947, M.S. in Indsl. Engring, 1951; M.B.A., Harvard U., 1949; LL.B., Cleve. Marshall Law Sch., 1953. Formerly with Western Automatic Screw Machine Co., Parker-Hannifin Corp. and, Booz, Allen & Hamilton; group v.p. indsl. products A. O. Smith Corp., 1962-64; with Figgie Internat. (formerly A-T-O Inc.), 1964—, chmn. bd., chief exec. officer, 1960—; also dir.; chmn. Clark Reliance Corp. Mem. World Bus. Council. Office: Figgie Internat Inc 1000 Virginia Center Pkwy Richmond VA 23295

FIGGINS, DAVID FORRESTER, construction company executive; b. Belfast, No. Ireland, Mar. 21, 1929; came to U.S., 1957, naturalized, 1966; s. David Peter and Irene Evelyn (Boomer) F.; m. Margaret McConnell, July 28, 1954; children: Margaret Lynne, David Peter, Michael Robert, Barbara Ann. B.S.C. in Civil Engring, Queen's U., Belfast, 1953. Field supt. Farrans Ltd., Belfast, 1952-54; gen. field supt. T.O. Lazarides & Assos., Toronto, Ont., Can., 1954-56; partner T.O. Lazarides & Assos., 1956-57; with Mellon-Stuart Co., Pitts., 1957-88; v.p. Mellon-Stuart Co., 1963-72, exec. v.p., 1972-78, sr. exec. v.p., 1978-80, pres., 1981-86, chmn. bd., 1986-88; pres. Figgins Constrn. Group, Inc., Pitts., 1989—; bd. dirs. Bell Fed. Savs. & Loan Assn., Liberty Mut. Ins. Co., Boston. V.p. Enterprise and Edn. Found., Pitts., 1977-83, bd. dirs., 1984-88; bd. dirs. Pa. Bus. Roundtable, 1987-89; mem. Fla. Council of 100, 1982-89; trustee Carlow Coll., Pitts., 1982—, Penn's S.W. Assn., 1985-89; chmn. adv. bd. Salvation Army, Pitts., 1978-80, mem. nat. adv. council, 1980-88; trustee Sewickley Acad., Sewickley, Pa., 1978-82; bd. dirs. Pitts. Symphony Soc., 1982-89, Am. Ireland Fund., 1987—, Pitts. Opera, 1982-85; chmn. bd. dirs. River City Brass Band, 1982—; trustee Civic Light Opera Assn., 1983-89; chmn. Three Rivers Rowing Assn., 1987—. Mem. Ont. Soc. Profl. Engrs., NSPE, Pa. Soc. Profl. Engrs. Republican. Episcopalian. Clubs: Duquesne, Oakmont Country, Fellows, Queen's U. Belfast Number 533, Rotary (dist. gov. 1979-80). Office: Figgins Constrn Group Inc Six PPG Pl Ste 850 Pittsburgh PA 15222

FIGNAR, R(OSEMARY) CASEY, management consultant; b. Pottsville, Pa., July 6, 1945; d. Joseph Edward and Marie (Burns) Casey; m. Eugene Michael Fignar, June 15, 1968. BS in Home Econs. Edn., Coll. Misericordia, Dallas, Pa., 1967; postgrad., U. Puget Sound, Robert Morris Coll. Tchr. in Home Econs. Pitts. Bd. Edn., 1968-70; dietician Kaufmann's Dept. Store, Pitts., 1971-73; mgr. consumer and pub. affairs Beecham Products, Pitts., 1974-79; mgr. consumer affairs Pepsi-Cola Bottling Group, Purchase, N.Y., 1979-81; pvt. practice in human resources mktg. cons. Old Greenwich, Conn., 1982-88; mgmt. cons. Marigold Assocs. Inc. div. Marigold Enterprises Inc., Greenwich, Conn., 1988—; arbitrator Better Bus. Bur. Mem. exec. bd. United Way, Greenwich, Conn. Mem. Women in Mgmt. (bd. dirs.), Am. Soc. Tng. and Devel., Issues Mgmt. Assn., Orgn. Devel. Network, Nat. Assn. Corp. and Profl. Recruiters. Home: 21 West End Ave Old Greenwich CT 06870 Office: Marigold Assocs Inc 32 Field Point Rd Greenwich CT 06830

FIGUEROA, HOWARD GEORGE, business machine corporation executive; b. Mineola, N.Y., Apr. 28, 1930; s. Roy Noel and Ida (Beach) F.; m. Marie Binner; children: Janice, Bruce, David. BA, Lehigh U., 1952. With IBM Corp., Puchase, N.Y., 1952—, now v.p. comml. and industry relations. Bd. dirs. Family Service Am., Milw., White Plains (N.Y.) Hosp. Med. Ctr. Served to 1st lt. U.S. Army, 1952-54. Mem. Computer and Bus. Equipment Mfrs. Assn. (chmn. bd. dirs. 1987-88). Republican. Episcopalian. Office: IBM Corp 2000 Purchase St Purchase NY 10577

FIGUEROA, LUIS, technology administrator, researcher; b. Havana, Cuba, Aug. 14, 1951; s. Luis and Julietta (Alea) F.; m. Tina Josephine Nessi, June 24, 1978. BS, U. Calif., Berekeley, 1973, MS, 1976, PhD, 1978. Mem. tech. staff Hughes Rsch. Labs., Malibu, Calif., 1978-81; asst. prof. elec. engring. N.C. State U., Raleigh, 1981-82; dir. opto-electronics tech. TRW-Electro-Optics Rsch. Ctr., Redondo Beach, Calif., 1982-85; assoc. prof. elec. engring. U. Fla., Gainesville, 1985-87; mgr. photonics tech. lab. Boeing High Tech. Ctr., Seattle, 1987—; cons. Rsch. Triangle (N.C.) Inst., 1981-82, TRW, Redondo Beach, 1985-87; co-chmn. U. Fla. Conf. on III-V compounds, Gainesville, 1987. Co-author: High Power Laser Diodes and Applications, 1988; editor Microwave and Optical Letters Jour., 1987—; contbr. articles to profl. jours., chpts. to books. Recipient Fla. Regents scholarship, 1969, Excellence award U.S. Govt.; NSF grantee. Mem. IEEE, Soc. Photo-Optical Instrumentation Engrs. (chmn. laser diode tech. and applications conf. 1988-89, author tech. proceedings 1988). Office: Boeing High Tech Ctr PO Box 24969 Seattle WA 98124-6269

FIKE, EDWARD LAKE, newspaper editor; b. Delmar, Md., Mar. 31, 1920; s. Claudius Edwin and Rosa Lake (Pegram) F.; m. Rosa Amanda Drake, Apr. 1, 1952; children: Rosa, Evelyn, Amy, Melinda. BA, Duke U., 1941; postgrad., U. Cin., 1941-42. Editor, co-pub. Nelsonville (Ohio) Tribune, 1945-48; dir. bur. pub. info. Duke U., Durham, N.C., 1948-52; mem. U.S. del. N. Atlantic Council, Paris, 1952-53; assoc. editor Rocky Mount (N.C.) Evening Telegram, 1953-57; editor, pub. Fike Newspapers, Lewistown and Glendive, Mont.; also Fike Newspapers, Wilmington and Tujunja, Calif., 1957-68; assoc. editor Richmond (Va.) News Leader, 1968-70; dir. news and editorial analysis Copley Newspapers, 1970-77; editor editorial pages San Diego Union, 1977—; lectr. journalism San Diego State U., San Diego Evening Coll. Mem. Pres.' Adv. Coun. San Diego State U., 1988—; bd. dirs. San Diego Salvation Army, San Diego United Way, El Cajon (Calif.) Boys Club, Armed Services YMCA. Served to lt. USNR, 1942-45. Recipient George Washington award Freedoms Found., 1969-71, 73, 78, Editorial Writing awards N.C. Press Assn., 1954-55, Va. Press Assn., 1969, Calif. Newspaper Pubs. Assn., 1969, 80. Mem. The Scholia Club of San Diego. Republican. Methodist. Home: 12244 Fuerte Dr El Cajon CA 92020 Office: San Diego Union 350 Camino de la Reina San Diego CA 92108

FILCOFF, RICHARD CRAIG, electronics manufacturing executive; b. Granite City, Ill., Nov. 8, 1951; s. Boris and Lorraine (Prusak) F.; m. Christine Lynn Ehlen, Sept. 21, 1974; children: Jennifer R., David M., Eric C. BSEE, Washington U., St. Louis, 1973, MSEE, 1979. Mgr. tech. svcs. Artronix Inc., St. Louis, 1973-76; mgr. mfg. Affinitec, St. Louis, 1976-79; v.p. ops. Micro-Term Inc., St. Louis, 1979-84; pres. Focus Electronics Inc., St. Louis, 1985—. Home: 14730 Mill Spring Dr Chesterfield MO 63017 Office: Focus Electronics Inc 1243 Hanley Industrial Ct Saint Louis MO 63144

FILES, MARK WILLARD, oil company executive; b. Bartlesville, Okla., Dec. 5, 1941; s. Francis Marion and Alice Wade (Webb) F.; m. Elizabeth Kay Maltby; children—Patrick, Jennifer Leigh. B.B.A., U. Okla., 1963, M.A., 1964. C.P.A., Okla., La. From asst. acct. to ptnr. Peat, Marwick, Mitchell & Co., Tulsa, 1964-80; exec. v.p. Graham Resources, Inc., Covington, La., 1980—. Exxon Corp. Grad. fellow U. Okla., 1964. Mem. Am. Inst. C.P.A.s, Okla. Soc. C.P.A.s (chmn. ethics com. 1975-76), La. Soc. C.P.A.s, Am. Petroleum Inst., Phi Eta Sigma, Beta Gamma Sigma, Pi Kappa Alpha. Republican. Episcopalian. Clubs: Beau Chene Golf and Racquet (Mandeville, La.). Home: 712 N Beau Chene Dr Mandeville LA 70448 Office: Graham Resources Inc 109 Northpark Blvd Covington LA 70433

FILIATRAULT, EDWARD JOHN, JR., utility company executive; b. Grand Forks, N.D., July 27, 1938; m. Penelope Smeby, Aug. 16, 1959; children: Kimberly, John. BCE, U. N.D., 1960; MBA, No. Ill. U., 1968, U. Chgo., 1978. Registered profl. engr., Ill. Various mgmt. positions No. Ill. Gas Co., Aurora, 1960-72, v.p., 1972-81, exec. v.p., 1981—; trustee Inst. Gas Tech., Chgo., 1981—; assoc. Northwestern U., 1984-88. Chmn. United Way Suburban Chgo., Hillside, Ill., 1976-78; vice-chmn. United Way Crusade of Mercy, Chgo., 1976-78, chief crusader, 1974-88. Urban Fellow of Chgo., 1969-70. Mem. Internat. Gas Union, Am. Gas Assn., So. Gas Assn., Midwest Gas Assn. (bd. dirs. 1982-89, chmn. 1987-88), Ill. State C. of C. (chmn. 1986-87). Republican. Lutheran. Clubs: Metropolitan (Chgo.). Office: No Ill Gas Co PO Box 190 Aurora IL 60507

FILIPPS, FRANK PETER, insurance company executive; b. N.Y.C., June 29, 1947; s. John G. and Angela (Fusco) Filipps; m. Patricia Maria DeVito, Apr. 8, 1967; children: Todd Peter, Mark Peter. B.A., Rutgers U., 1969; M.B.A., NYU, 1972. Asst. treas. Chase Manhattan, N.Y.C., 1969-73, 2d v.p., 1974-75; v.p. investments Am. Life Ins. Co., Wilmington, Del., 1975-77, Am. Internat. Underwriters, N.Y.C., 1978-81; treas. Am. Internat. Group Inc., N.Y.C., 1981—; dir. Latonia Investment Co., Geneva, Switzerland. Office: Am Internat Group Inc 70 Pine St New York NY 10270

FILLET, MITCHELL HARRIS, financial services executive; b. N.Y.C., Feb. 28, 1948; s. Robert Earl and Barbara Dee (Auerbach) F.; m. Jamie A. Driggs, Oct. 28, 1988. BA in Philosophy and Religion, Boston U., 1970; MBA in Fin., NYU, 1978. Trainee Dillon, Read & Co., N.Y.C., 1971-72; salesman Stone & Webster Securities Corp., N.Y.C., 1972-74; asst. v.p. First Boston Corp., N.Y.C., 1974-76; v.p. Bear, Stearns & Co., N.Y.C., 1976-79; exec. v.p., chief fin. officer Auerbach Bath Robe Corp., N.Y.C., 1979-81; v.p. corp. svcs. Merrill Lynch, N.Y.C., 1981—; adj. prof. fin. Martino Grad. Sch. Bus. Fordham U., N.Y.C., 1981—; lectr. in acctg. NYU, 1980-81. Mem. Citizens for Am., Washington, 1984-86, The Jefferson Circle, Washington, 1985, U.S. Senatorial Bus. Adv. Bd., 1988—; spl. adminstrv. asst. City Planning Commn., City of N.Y., 1969. Mem. Am. Biog. Rsch. Inst. (dep. gov.), Boston U. Alumni Assn., Alumni Assn. Grad. Sch. Bus. NYU. Republican. Club: Union League (N.Y.C.). Home: 155 W 68th St New York NY 10023 Office: Merrill Lynch 1185 6th Ave New York NY 10036

FILLET, ROBERT E., investment banker, research psychologist; b. N.Y.C., Nov. 29, 1921; s. Maxwell Edward and Fan (Palley) F.; m. Barbara Auerbach (div. 1969); children: Mitchell H, Andrea Sara. MetD, 1976; BBA cum laude, Nat. U., San Diego, 1978; MA, U. Humanistic Study, 1979, PhD, 1981; ThD in Metaphysics, Fathers of St. Thomas, Imperial Beach, Calif., 1981; student, Columbia U., NYU. Fin. and mgmt. cons. numerous orgns. and govts., N.J., Ill., N.Y.C., Haiti, Republic of Korea, Pakistan, 1948—; pres., founder U.S. China C. of C., Washington, 1972-79; also cons. U.S. Congress and Senate regarding China's comml. and econ. relations., Washington, 1972-76; pres. Fillet Capital Corp., Los Angeles, 1976—; instr. San Diego State U.; prof. U. Humanistic Studies; bd. dirs. Fillet Livestock Corp., Middleton, Idaho, Alverca Aerotek Internat., Lisbon, Portugal; joint venture ptnr. Nat. Housing Ptnrs.; chmn. bd. dirs. Am. Renewal Co.; asst. chmn. Heartland Energy Corp.; chmn. bd. dirs. Insulock Mfg. Corp. So. Calif.; real estate developer. Mem. acad. adv. bd. Nat. U., San Diego; com. mem. Tarrytown chpt. Boy Scouts Am. Decorated D.F.C., Air medal, Purple Heart; recipient Silver Star award Am. Legion. Mem. Mental Health Assn. (chmn. speakers bur. San Diego chpt.), Am. Mgmt. Inst. Home: 23 Northampton Ct Newport Beach CA 92660 Office: 24 Balboa Coves Newport Beach CA 92663

FILLET, TONI DEE, investment banker; b. N.Y.C., Apr. 17, 1957. BA, Am. U., 1979; Masters, London Film Sch., 1981. Corp. activity planner Smith Barney, N.Y.C., 1987—. Mem. Apr. in Paris Ball, 1987—, Michael Dukakis Dem. Campaign, N.Y.C., 1986-88, Mem. Dem. Bus. Coun., 1987-88; bd. dirs. Friends of Lenox Hill Hosp., 1981-88. Mem. Meeting Planners Assn. Home: 160 W 71st St New York NY 10023 Office: Smith Barney Harris Upham & Co Inc 1345 Avenue of the Americas New York NY 10105

FILLEY, RICHARD DAVID, writer, industrial engineer; b. Columbus, Ohio, July 28, 1955; s. Laurence Duane and Bette Elaine (Riley) F.; m. Phyllis Jane Carlton, July 14, 1979; children: Derek James, Dena Michelle, Denise Hélène BS in Indsl. Engring., U. Wash.-Seattle, 1978. Indsl. analyst, The Boeing Co., Seattle, 1978; indsl. engr. Garrett/AiResearch Mfg. Co., Phoenix, 1979-80; facilities engr. Sperry Flight Systems, Phoenix, 1980-81; people and technologies editor Indsl. Engring. Mag., Norcross, Ga., 1981-85; dir. tech. transfer programs CIM Systems Research Ctr., Ariz. State Univ., Tempe, 1985—; speaker bus. and profl. confs. Author: (with Drui, Hairfield and Johnson) Industrial Engineering in the Boeing Company, 1978, (mag. series) Communicate With Graphics, 1981-82; contbr. numerous articles to profl. jours. Founder, pres. AiResearch Employees Aluminum Can Recycling Program, Phoenix, 1979-81; founder ASU Indsl. Fellows program, 1986—; active Valley Leadership. Mem. Inst. Indsl. Engrs. (newsletter editor Cen. Ariz. chpt. 1980-81, pub. 1986-87, v.p. Atlanta chpt. 1983-85), Soc. Mfg. Engrs., Marc Ctr. (bd. dirs. 1988—, Marc award 1980), The Consortium U.S. Research Programs for Mex., Sigma Delta Chi. Republican. Presbyterian. Clubs: Seattle Mountaineers, Am. Alpine, Swiss Alpine. Avocations: mountain climbing, reading, skiing, travel. Home: 2445 W Pecos Ave Mesa AZ 85202 Office: Ariz State U Coll Engring Tempe AZ 85287

FILLION, RUTH ELLEN, small business owner; b. Melrose, Mass., Sept. 12, 1957; d. Robert Stevens and Helen Virginia (Wright) Bowser; m. Eric Henry Fillion, July 25, 1981. AS in Bus. Adminstrn., Johnson & Wales Coll., 1977. Sales mgr. Neptune-Bensen, Inc., West Warwick, R.I., 1981-87; pres., owner Fillion Assocs., Inc., Barrington, R.I., 1987—; speaker YMCA Coop.'s, New Eng. area, 1981—. Home: 1 Salisbury Rd Barrington RI 02806

FILOSA, GARY FAIRMONT RANDOLPH DE VIANA, II, private investor; b. Wilder, Vt., Feb. 22, 1931; s. Gary F.R. de Marco de Viana and Rosaline M. (Falzarano) Filosa; divorced; children: Marc Christian Bazire de Villadon, III, Gary Fairmont Randolph de Viana, III. Grad., Mt. Hermon Sch., 1950; PhB, U. Chgo., 1954; BA, U. Americas, Mex., 1967; MA, Calif. Western U., 1968; PhD, U.S. Internat. U., 1970. Sports reporter Claremont Daily Eagle, Rutland Herald, Vt. Informer, 1947-52; pub. The Chicagoan, 1952-54; account exec., editor house publs. Robertson, Buckley & Gotsch, Inc., Chgo., 1953-54; account exec. Fuller, Smith & Ross, Inc., N.Y.C., 1955; editor Apparel Arts mag. (now Gentlemen's Quar.), Esquire, Inc., N.Y.C., 1955-56; pres., chmn. bd. Teenarama Records, Inc., N.Y.C., 1956-62; pres., chmn. bd. Filosa Publs. Internat., N.Y.C., 1956-61, Los Angeles, 1974-83, Palm Beach, Fla., 1983-88; pres. Montclair Sch., 1958-60, Pacific Registry, Inc., Los Angeles, 1959-61, Banana Chip Corp. Am., N.Y.C., 1964-67; producer Desilu Studios, Inc., Hollywood, 1960-61; exec. asst. to Benjamin A. Javits, 1961-62; dean adminstrn. Postgrad. Ctr. for Mental Health, N.Y.C., 1962-64; chmn. bd., pres. Producciones Mexicanes Internationales (S.A.), Mexico City, 1957-68; chmn. bd., pres. Filosa Films Internat., Beverly Hills, 1962-83, Palm Beach, Fla., 1984—; pres. Casa Filosa Corp., Palm Beach, Fla., 1982-87; dir. tng. Community Savings, North Palm Beach, Fla., 1983-87; chmn. bd., pres. Cinematografica Americana Internationale (S.A.), Mexico City, 1964-74; pub. Teenage, Rustic Rhythm, Teen Life, Talent, Rock & Roll Roundup, Celebrities, Stardust, Personalities, Campus monthly mags., N.Y.C., 1955-61; v.p. acad. affairs World Acad., San Francisco, 1967-68; asst. to provost Calif. Western U., San Diego, 1968-69; assoc. prof. philosophy Art Coll., San Francisco, 1969-70; v.p. acad. affairs, dean of faculty Internat. Inst., Phoenix, 1968-73; chmn. bd., pres. Universite Universelle, 1970-73; bd. dirs., v.p. acad. affairs, dean Summer Sch., Internat. Community Coll., Los Angeles, 1970-72; chmn. bd., pres. Social Directory Calif., 1967-75, Am. Assn. Social Registries, Los Angeles, 1970-76; pres. Social Directory U.S., N.Y.C., 1974-76; chmn. bd. Internat. Assn. Social Registers, Paris, 1974—; surfing coach U. Calif. at Irvine, 1975-77; instr. history Coastline Community Coll., Fountain Valley, Calif., 1976-77; v.p. Xerox-Systemic, 1979-80; pres., chief exec. officer Internat. Surfing League, Palm Beach, 1987—; pres., chief exec. officer Filosa Harrop Internat., Phoenix, 1987-89. Editor: Sci. Digest, 1961-62. Author: (stage play) Let Me Call Ethel, 1955, Technology Enters 21st Century, 1966, musical Feather Light, 1966, No Public Funds for Nonpublic Schools, 1968, Creative Function of the College President, 1969, The Surfers Almanac, 1977, Payne of Florida (TV series), 1985, The Filosa Newsletter, 1986—, Conversations With America (TV series), 1989—. Contbr. numerous articles to mags., and profl. jours. and encys. including Sci. Digest, World Book Ency., Ency. of Sports. Trustee Univ. of the Ams., 1986—; candidate for Los Angeles City Council, 1959; chmn. Educators for Reelection of Ivy Baker Priest, 1970; mem. So. Calif. Com. for Olympic Games, 1977-84. Served with AUS, 1954-55. Recipient DAR Citizenship award, 1959; Silver Conquistador award Am. Assn. Social Registers, 1970; Ambassador's Cup U. Ams., 1967; resolution Calif. Legislature, 1977; Duke Kahanamoku Classic surfing trophy, 1977; gold pendant Japan Surfing Assn., 1978. Mem. Am. Surfing Assn. (founder, pres. 1960—), Internat. Surfing Com. (founder, pres. 1960—), U.S. Surfing Com. (founder, pres. 1960—), Am. Walking Soc. (founder, pres. 1980—), Internat. Walking Soc. (founder, pres. 1987—), Am. Assn. UN, Authors League, Alumni Assn. U. Americas (pres. 1967-70), Sierra Club, NAACP, NCAA (bd. dels. 1977-82), AAU (gov. 1978-82), Sigma Omicron Lambda (founder, pres. 1965—). Democrat. Episcopalian. Clubs: Embajadores (U. of Americas,.); Palm Beach Surf (Fla); Coral Reef Soc. (Palm Beach). Home: PO Box 3432 Palm Beach FL 33480 also: PO Box 1315 Beverly Hills CA 90213

FINBERG, ALAN ROBERT, lawyer, communications company executive; b. Bklyn., July 2, 1927; s. Chester F. and Anne B. (Gorfinkle) F.; m. Barbara J. Denning, June 21, 1953. B.A., Yale U., 1950; J.D., Harvard U., 1953. Bar: N.Y. 1954, D.C. 1974, U.S. Supreme Ct. 1974. Assoc. firm Cravath, Swaine & Moore, N.Y.C., 1953-61; ptnr. Stein, Kripke & Rosen, N.Y.C., 1961-64; asst. gen. counsel Gen. Dynamics Corp., N.Y.C., 1964-71; gen. counsel Washington Post Co., Washington and N.Y.C., 1971-88, v.p., sec., 1971—; dir. Newsweek, Inc., Daily Herald Co. Trustee Bard Coll.; mem. exec. com. Helsinki Watch; sec., bd. dirs. Hudson Valley Festival of the Arts, Inc., The Coffee House. With USNR, 1945-46. Mem. Am. Bar Assn., Assn. Bar City N.Y., Helsinki Watch (mem. exec. com.), Am. Arbitration Assn. (arbitration panel), Am. Soc. Corporate Secs., Phi Beta Kappa. Democrat. Clubs: Board Room (N.Y.C.), Coffee House (N.Y.C.). Home: 165 E 72d St New York NY 10021 Office: Washington Post Co 444 Madison Ave New York NY 10022

FINCH, DAVID S., banker; b. Des Moines, Dec. 9, 1941; s. Lindley and Fannie (Hook) F.; m. Veta K. Finch, May 9, 1980; children—David L., Michael S. Student, U. Iowa, 1960-61, Iowa State U., 1965; M.B.A., U. Chgo., 1967. Comml. trainee, credit analyst Harris Trust and Savs. Bank, Chgo., 1967-68, comml. banking rep. personnel div., 1968, mng. coll. recruitment personnel div., 1968-70, comml. banking officer banking dept., 1970-71, asst. v.p., sect. mgr. corp. fin. service, 1973, v.p., div. adminstr. personnel, 1973-78, sr. v.p., group exec. personal trust group, 1978-80, sr. v.p., group exec, instl. trust adminstrn., 1980-81, exec. v.p. trust dept., 1981-86, exec. v.p. investment dept., 1986-89, exec. v.p. pub. and employee rels. dept., 1989—; chief fin. officer Internat. Farm Systems, 1971-73; chmn. bd. Harris Trust Co. of Ariz., Scottsdale, 1981-86; bd. dirs. Derivative Markets Mgmt., Inc., Harris Futures Corp, Harris Brokerage Services, Inc., Harris Bank Hindsdale. Bd. trustees Roosevelt U., 1988—; bd. dirs. Midwest Securities Trust Co., 1985-88. Mem. Corp. Fiduciaries Assn. Ill. (sec.-treas. 1985-88). Clubs: St. Charles Country (Ill.); Monroe (Chgo.). Office: Harris Trust & Savs Bank 111 W Monroe St Chicago IL 60603

FINCH, HAROLD BERTRAM, JR., wholesale grocery company executive; b. Grand Forks, N.D., Oct. 13, 1927; s. Harold Bertram and Ruth M. F.; m. Catherine E. Cole, Sept. 6, 1950; children: Mark, James, Sarah, Martha, David. BBA, U. Minn., 1952, BChemE, 1952. Div. mgr. Archer-Daniels-Midland Co., Mpls., 1960-66; dir. long-range planning, then v.p. sales and ops. Nash Finch Co., Mpls., 1966-78, pres., 1978-85, chief exec. officer, 1982—, chmn., 1985—. Bd. dirs. Jr. Achievement Mpls., 1977-84, Mpls. YMCA, 1965-80; bd. trustees Westminster Presbyn. Ch., 1985—. Served with U.S. Maritime Service, 1945-47. Mem. Nat. Assn. Wholesale Grocers Am. (bd. govs.), Food Mktg. Inst. Presbyterian. Office: Nash Finch Co 3381 Gorham Ave Saint Louis Park MN 55426

FINCH, WALTER GOSS GILCRIST, lawyer, engineer, accountant; b. Balt., Jan. 25, 1918; s. Walter G. and Lena May (Koontz) F.; m. Mary Adele Roberts, June 25, 1943; children—Vida Marilena McCarty, Lillian Bonnie Murakoshi, Robin Lee, Ruth Mae; m. Patricia Anne Reed, Feb. 22, 1976. B.Engring., The Johns Hopkins U., 1940, M. Engring., 1950; LLB, Temple U., 1949, M.B.A., 1950, J.D., 1969; LL.M., George Washington U., 1949; grad., Command and Gen. Staff Coll., 1953, Nat. War Coll., 1965, Indsl. Coll. Armed Forces, 1965. Bar: Md. 1947, D.C. 1951, U.S. Supreme Ct. 1951; registered profl. engr. D.C.; CPA, Md. Asst. patent counsel Office of Sponsored Research, The Johns Hopkins U., Balt., 1951-57, patent counsel, 1957-73; sole practice patent, trademark, copyright and taxation law Balt., 1957—. Co-author: The Romance of Invention of the Eastern and Western Worlds; also numerous publs. on patents. Pres. Md. Crime Investigating Commn., 1963-66, gen. counsel, 1963-75; mem. World Peace Through Law Ctr., 1964—; mem. adv. council Catonsville Community Coll., 1959-76, sec.-treas., 1962-64, pres., 1967-68; mem. exec. bd. Balt. Area council Boy Scouts Am., 1965—; del. Md. Constl. Conv., 1967-68; Dem. candidate for U.S. Senate, 1968, 70, 74, 76, for U.S. Congress, 1956, 66, for atty. gen. Md., 1978. Served with AUS, 1941-46, ETO; col. Res. ret. 1973. Decorated Bronze Star. Recipient Silver Beaver award Boy Scouts Am., 1969. Mem. Bar Assn. Balt. City, Md. Bar Assn., Fed. Bar Assn. (bd. dirs. Balt. chpt. 1971-80), Inter-Am. Bar Assn., ABA, Internat. Bar Assn., Am. Patent Law Assn., Internat. Patent and Trademark Assn., Nat. Soc. Profl. Engrs., Md. Soc. Profl. Engrs., Md. Acad. Scis., ASME, Soc. Am. Mil. Engrs., Res. Officers Assn. (pres. Patapsco chpt. 1956-57), Balt. Assn. Commerce, Catonsville Community Assn., Md. Hist. Soc., English Speaking Union. Democrat. Presbyterian. Clubs: Johns Hopkins Faculty and Alumni, Merchants of Balt., Nat. Lawyers, Rolling Rd. Golf, Army and Navy (Washington). Lodges: Masons (K.T., Shriner), Scottish Rite. Office: 1501-1503 Fidelity Bldg Baltimore MD 21201

FINCHELL, A. RICHARD, financial marketing executive; b. N.Y.C., Jan. 18, 1927; s. Joseph H. and Henrietta (Fritz) F.; B.S. in Social Scis., CCNY, 1947; Doctorat-es-Lettres, U. Paris, 1951; m. Margherita Iskra, Dec. 21, 1971; 1 dau., Mayra Molne-Finchell. Pres., Greater Miami Savs. Center (Fla.), 1954-68, North Am. Fund Mgmt. Corp., London, 1959—, North Am. Group, London, 1961—, Noram Secured Income N.V., Amsterdam, Netherlands, 1970—, North Am. Mgmt. Corp., London, 1977—, North Am. Assets Trust Ltd., London, 1977—; mng. dir. Noramtrust, London, 1976—; chmn. dir. North Am. Fin. Markets Ltd., London, 1969—. Served with U.S. Army, 1945-46. Nichiren Shoshu Buddhist. Office: 15 Bedford Row, London WC1R 4BX, England

FINDLAY, HAPPY IRENE, marketing professional; b. Saskatchewan, Can., Apr. 23, 1942; came to U.S., 1964; d. Louis S. and Katherine A. (Leib) G.; divorced; 1 child, Robert. BSBA, Oklahoma City U., 1986. Dept. sec. Bapt. Med. Ctr., Oklahoma City, 1968-73; sales sec. Oscar Mayer & Co., Oklahoma City, 1973-86; exec. coord. TVC Mktg., Oklahoma City, 1986—. Sec. Zonta Bus. Women's Group., Oklahoma City, 1986. Mem. Jaycees Jaynes Okla. (pres. 1971, v.p. 1972, state treas. 1973). Home: 6401 N Nicklas Oklahoma City OK 73132

FINDLAY, STEVEN, oil company executive; b. Okinawa, Japan, Nov. 6, 1954; came to U.S., 1963; s. Delbert Ronald and Yoshi (Nakasone) F.; m. Sandra McEachran, June 1, 1974; children: Matthew, Nathan, Gabriel. BS, U. Mich., 1977; MPH, U. Tenn., 1979. Indsl. hygienist Tenn. Dept. Labor, Knoxville, Tenn., 1979-80, Union Carbide, Oak Ridge, Tenn., 1980-82, Union Oil Co. of Calif., Parachute, Colo., 1982-87; mgr. loss prevention Unocal, Schaumburg, Ill., 1987—. Mem. Am. Indsl. Hygiene Assn. Episcopalian. Home: 730 N Vista Algonquin IL 60102 Office: Unocal 1345 N Meacham Rd Schaumburg IL 60196

FINDLEY, MARY LOU MCBROOM, manufacturing company executive; b. Chgo., Aug. 31, 1945; d. John Kellett and Mary Jane (Kahlert) McB.; m. Leroy James Burlingame, Oct. 1, 1983; 1 child, Thomas Scott Findley; m. John William Findley, Aug. 17, 1968 (div. Dec. 1982). Mus. B., Lawrence U., 1967; postgrad. Marquette U., 1974-76. Programmer, analyst Gen. Systems Co., Kalamazoo, 1969-71, Marine 1st Nat. Bank, Racine, Wis., 1971-72; with Twin Disc, Inc., Racine, 1972—, supr. systems and procedures, 1978-79, mgr. bus. systems, 1979—. Bd. dirs. Racine Council Alcohol and Other Drug Abuse, 1982-88, also pres.; cons. Jr. Achievement, 1984. Mem. Am. Prodn. and Inventory Control Soc., Soc. Info. Mgmt. Republican. Presbyterian. Avocations: music, identifying birds and wild flowers. Home: 143 Robin Hill Dr Racine WI 53406 Office: Twin Disc Inc 1328 Racine St Racine WI 53403

FINE, BARRY KENNETH, manufacturing company executive; b. N.Y.C., May 15, 1938; s. Harry Harold and Ann (Elkind) F.; m. Rho Joy Stengel, Sept. 3, 1965; children: Scott Jefferson, Jill Ashley. BS, SUNY Empire State Coll., 1986; student, Touro Coll., 1986—. Jr. civil engr. N.Y.C. Transit Authority, 1957-58; pres. Active Industries (formerl Active Steel Drum Co.), L.I., N.Y., 1985—; founder, pres. Glass Tint Svcs., Inc., L.I., N.Y., 1985—. Patentee in field. Zone chmn. L.I. City Bus. Devel. Corp., 1988; project bus. cons. Queens Jr. Achievement, Queens, N.Y., 1984-88. With USAR, 1957-63. Mem. ABA (student mem.), NABADA-The Assn. of Container Reconditioners (chmn. legis. and regulatory com.). Republican. Jewish. Club: U.S. Power Squadrons (N.Y.C.). Lodges: Massons, B'nai Brith. Office: Active Industries Inc 52-30 Van Dam Str Long Island City NY 11101

FINE, BOB, real estate developer, lawyer; b. Mpls., Mar. 29, 1949; s. Ralph I. and Beverlee (Rockler) F.; m. Sylvia Latarus, June 20, 1971; children: Jacob, Andy Ellyn, Joe. BA, U. Minn., 1970; JD, Washington U., 1973. Bar: U.S. Dist. Ct. Minn. 1974, Minn. 1974, U.S. Supreme Ct. 1980. Sole practice Mpls., 1974-79; real estate developer, ptnr. Fine Assocs., Mpls., 1979—; referee Hennepin County Conciliation Ct., Mpls., 1977—. Commr. Mpls. Commn. Civil Rights, 1981—; Mpls. Zoning Bd. Adminstrs., 1984-86. Democrat. Jewish. Office: Fine Assocs 1916 IDS Ctr Minneapolis MN 55402

FINE, DAVID JEFFREY, hospital executive, consultant, lecturer; b. Flushing, N.Y., Oct. 10, 1950; s. Arnold and Phyllis Fine; m. Susan Gory, Dec. 29, 1985; 1 child, Jeffrey Jacob. BA, Tufts U., 1972; MHA, U. Minn., 1974. Asst. to dir. U. Calif. Hosp., San Francisco, 1974-76, asst. dir., 1976-78; sr. assoc. dir. U. Nebr. Hosp. and Clinic, Omaha, 1978-83; adminstr. W.Va. Univ. Hosp., Morgantown, 1983-84; pres. W.Va. Univ. Hosps., Inc., Morgantown, 1984-87; pres., chief operating officer Health Net, Charleston, W.Va, 1985-87; vice provost for health affairs, chief exec. officer U. Cin. Health System, 1987—; prof. pharmacy U. Cin., 1987—; cons. Merck, Sharp & Dohme, West Point, Pa., 1983—, Eli Lilly & Co., Indpls., 1984, DuPont Critical Care, Chgo., Johnson and Johnson, 1988—; bd. dirs., exec. com. Univ. Hosp. Consortium, Atlanta, 1983—. Mem. editorial bd. Hospital Formulary, 1982-87; contbr. jour. articles, book chpts. and films. Trustee Monongalia Arts Council, 1984-86, Cin. Chamber Orch., 1987—. Recipient James A. Hamilton prize, U. Minn., 1974; W. K. Kellog fellow. Fellow Am. Coll. Hosp. Adminstrs. (Robert S. Hudgens Young Adminstr. of Yr. award 1985), Royal Soc. Medicine, Royal Coll. Medicine; mem. Am. Hosp. Assn. (mem. regional policy bd., mem. ho. of dels., mem. governing council sect. on met. hosps.), Omicron Delta Epsilon. Jewish. Club: Cin. Bankers. Lodge: Rotary.

FINE, EDWARD, manufacturing executive; b. Bklyn., Nov. 21, 1942; s. Milton and Beatrice Dorothy (Rosenberg) F.; m. Ingrid Lantsch, Aug. 12, 1964; children: Stuart, Heidi Sandra. BS in Acctg., NYU, 1964. CPA, N.Y. Jr. acct. Westheimer, Fine, Berger & Co., CPA's, N.Y.C., 1963-65; sr. acct. Coopers & Lybrand, N.Y.C., 1965-67; auditor mgmt. Pfizer Inc., N.Y.C., 1968; mgr. corp. acctg. Reliance Group Inc., N.Y.C., 1969-70; controller, chief fin. officer Intercapital Planning Corp., N.Y.C., 1970-72; pres., chief exec. officer Dyna-Lease Corp., N.Y.C., 1972-78, Newtron Pharms. Inc., Bohemia, N.Y., 1979-85; pres., chmn. chief exec. officer Biopharmaceutics Inc., Bellport, N.Y., 1985—, Integrated Generics Inc., Bellport, 1987—. Mem. Nat. Assn. Pharm. Mfrs. (bd. dirs. 1983-88). Office: Biopharmaceutics Inc 990 Station Rd Bellport NY 11713

FINE, HOWARD ALAN, service executive, consultant; b. N.Y.C., Dec. 21, 1941; s. William and Shirley (German) F.; m. Ingvelde Rathkamp, Dec. 20, 1970. BS, NYU, 1961, MBA, 1964. Internat. sales mgr. Pfaff, A.G., Fed. Republic of West Germany, 1964-67; regional sales dir. Brit. Transport Hotels, London, Eng., 1967-70; dir. internat. mktg. Sonesta Internat. Hotels,

N.Y.C., 1970-71; dir. Pacific mktg. Trusthouse Forte Hotels, Los Angeles, 1971-74; dir. Atlantic area and Latin Am. mktg. Trusthouse Forte Hotels, N.Y.C, 1974-75, v.p. sales and mktg., 1975-78, exec. v.p., 1978-81; pres. Norwegian Am. Cruise Line, N.Y.C, 1981-83; pres., chief exec. officer Costa Cruise Line, Miami, Fla., 1983-87; vice chmn. Tourism Devel. Internat., Miami, 1987—; bd. dirs. Bahamas Devel. Found., Nassau, Traveling Times, Los Angeles. Contbr. articles to profl. jours. Mem. mayors adv. bd. City of Los Angeles, 1972-74; mem. senatorial commn. Rep. Senatorial Inner Circle, Washington, 1986—; bd. dirs. Calif. Dept. Agr. Wine Bd., 1974-75, Ptnrs. for Liveable Places, Washington, 1978-83, NYU Ctr. for Study of Foodservice, 1978-83, Fla. Crime Prevention Commn., 1984—, Boys Town of Italy, 1986—. Served to capt. USAR, 1961-66. Named Hon. Order Ky. Cols., 1986; named Man of Yr. Am. Jaycees, 1983, Man of Yr. Internat. Hotel Industry, 1980; recipient Disting. Marker of Yr. Sales and Mktg. Mgmt. Mag., 1979, Christopher Columbus award Nat. Columbus Day Com., 1986, Spirit of Life Humanitarian award City of Hope, 1987; numerous hotel and travel industry awards and citations from fgn. govts., 1972-87. Fellow Inst. Cert. Travel Agts.; mem. Young Pres.'s Orgn. (chmn. 1978—), Hotelier of the World Com. (bd. dirs. 1978—), Italian C. of C. (bd. dirs. 1975—), Brit. C. of C. (bd. dirs. 1975—), Norwegian C. of C. (bd. dirs. 1975—), South African C. of C. (bd. dirs. 1975—), Greater Ft. Lauderdale C. of C. (bd. of govs. 1986—), NYU Alumni Fedn., Sigma Alpha Mu. Clubs: NYU (N.Y.C.); 110 Tower (bd. dirs. 1987—), Harbor Beach (Ft. Lauderdale) (bd. dirs. 1987—). Office: Tourism Devel Internat PO Box 112940 Miami FL 33111

FINE, J(AMES) ALLEN, insurance company executive; b. Albemarle, N.C., May 2, 1934; s. Samuel Lee and Ocie (Loflin) F.; student Pfeiffer Coll., 1957-58; BS, U. N.C., 1961, MBA, 1965; m. Marie Nan Morris, Sept. 1, 1957; children: James A(llen), William Morris. Sr. accountant Haskins & Sells, CPA's Charlotte, N.C., 1961-62, Watson, Penry, & Morgan, Asheboro, N.C., 1962-64; instr. U. N.C., Chapel Hill, 1964-65; asst. prof. Pfeiffer Coll., Misenheimer, N.C., 1965-66; treas., v.p. adminstrn. Nat. Lab. for Higher Edn. (formerly Regional Edn. Lab. Carolinas and Va.), Durham, N.C., 1966-72; organizer, chief exec. officer, treas., dir. Investors Title Ins. Co., Inc., Chapel Hill, 1972—; chief exec. officer, treas., dir. Investors Title Ins. Co., Inc., Columbia, S.C., 1973—; pres., dir. Investors Title Co., Inc., Chapel Hill, 1976—; developer Carolina Forest Subdiv., Chapel Hill, 1970-78, Springhill Forest subdiv., Chapel Hill, 1977-80, Stoneycreek subdiv., 1978—; lectr. accounting U. N.C., Chapel Hill, 1967-70. Area officer ann. alumni giving U. N.C., Chapel Hill, 1968-69, 71-73, 75—. Served with USN, 1953-57. Recipient Haskins & Sells Found. award for excellence in accounting, 1961; N.C. Assn. CPA's award for most outstanding accounting student U. N.C., 1961. Mem. Am. Inst. CPA's, N.C. Assn. CPA's, Am. Accounting Assn., Am. Land Title Assn. (research com. 1983, membership com. 1984-85, exec. com. underwriters sect. 1986, recruitment, retention subcom., 1985—), Nat. Assn. Ins. Commrs. (liaison com. 1987—), CEDAR Bus. Mgrs. (chmn. nat. exec. com. 1971), Nat. Assn. Ins. Commrs. (liaison com. 1987—), Phi Beta Kappa, Beta Gamma Sigma (treas. 1961). Home: 112 Carolina Forest Chapel Hill NC 27514 Office: Investors Title Bldg Chapel Hill NC 27514

FINE, JAY LAURENCE, manufacturer's representative; b. Boston, Nov. 28, 1935; s. Murray Robert and Jeanette (Bluestone) F.; m. pauline Goldstein, June 10, 1957; children: Sidney G., Norman F., Elizabeth Amy. BBA, U. Mass., 1957. V.p. sales Sidney Goldstein Corp., Walpole, Mass., 1958—; trustee SIGOCO, Walpole. Mem. Am. Soc. Plumbing Engrs. Home: 18A Rainbow Pond Dr Walpole MA 02081 Office: Sidney Goldstein Corp 3 Industrial Rd Walpole MA 02081

FINE, KENNETH RICHARD, computer software consultant; b. Boston, Sept. 14, 1956; s. Henry Selwyn and Shirley Miriam (Lipof) F. AB, Syracuse U., 1978; MBA, Tulane U., 1984. Acct. exec. Arnold & Co., Boston, 1979; ter. rep. Addison-Wesley Pub., Reading, Mass., 1980; underwriter Gray and Co., Metairie, La., 1982-83; pres. Decision Analysis, New Orleans, 1984-85; software cons. Compumark, Inc., New Orleans, 1985-86; pres. Computer Info., Inc., New Orleans, 1986—, Software Wizardry, Inc., New Orleans, 1986-87; project leader Lewton Technologies Inc., Boston, 1987-88; software cons. Computer Enterprise, Inc., Newton, Mass., 1988—; software cons. Canal Street Assocs., New Orleans, 1981—, computer analyst Citta Enterprises, Inc., New Orleans, 1981. Sports corr. Needham (Mass.) Times, 1971-74. Staff worker campaign Jimmy Carter for Pres., Syracuse, 1976, McGovern for Pres., Needham, 1972. Democrat. Jewish.

FINE, STANLEY SIDNEY, pharmaceuticals and chemicals executive; b. N.Y.C., Sept. 26, 1927; s. Morris and Sophie (Brajer) F.; m. Eleanore D. Baker, July 21, 1955 (dec. 1972); children: Lauren Allison, Stephen Sidney (dec.); m. Astrid E. Merget, June 8, 1984 (div. Apr. 1987). Student, NYU, 1944-45; B.S., U.S. Naval Acad., 1949; postgrad., Coll. William and Mary, 1955-56, U. Va., 1956-57; MBA, Am. U., 1959; postgrad., Harvard U., 1963-65. Commd. ensign U.S. Navy, 1948, advanced through grades to rear adm., 1972; comdg. officer U.S.S. Hawk, 1954-56, Polaris Program, 1956-59, U.S.S. Lowe, 1961-63; comdr. Escort Div. 33, 1963; comdg. officer U.S.S. Ingraham, 1965-67; br. head Navy Material Command, Washington, 1967-68; exec. asst., naval aide to asst. sec. Navy 1968-70; study dir. Center for Naval Analysis Navy Dept., Washington, 1970; dep. dir. Navy Program Info. Center, 1970-71; br. head OPNAV, 1971; spl. asst. to dir. Navy Program Planning, Washington, 1971-72; dep. chief Programs and Fin. Mgmt.; comptroller Naval Ship Systems Command, Washington, 1972-73; dir. fiscal mgmt. div. Office Chief Naval Ops., Washington, 1973-78; dir. budget and reports Navy Dept., 1975-78; ret. 1978; sr. v.p. United-Guardian, Inc., Hauppauge, N.Y., 1979—; also bd. dirs. United-Guardian, Inc.; chmn., pres. Grant Enterprise Ltd., N.Y.C.; chmn., treas. Superior Constrn. Systems Inc., Va.; sec.-treas., bd. dirs. 1st United Corp., Jackson, Miss.; v.p., bd. dirs. New Energy Leasing Corp., McLean, Va.; bd. dirs. Redhead Brass, Shreve, Ohio, Pennate Corp., N.Y.C., Met. Bank N.A., Washington; cons. Arthur Andersen & Co., GAO. Co-author: The Federal Budget: Cost Based in the 1980's, 1979; contbr. articles to profl. jours. Mem. Presdl. transition team Dept. Commerce, 1980-81; bd. dirs. Found. for Election Law Edn., Alexandria, Va., Bronx High Sch. of Sci. Found., N.Y.C.; mem. fiscal affairs com. Montgomery County Council, 1987-88; mem. Com. for Nat. Security, 1987—. Decorated D.S.M., Navy Commendation medal, Legion of Merit with gold star; recipient Outstanding Mgmt. Analyst award Am. Soc. Mil. Comptrollers, 1971. Mem. Naval Inst., World Affairs Council D.C., Naval Acad. Alumni Assn., Am. Assn. Budget and Program Analysis, Montgomery County Fiscal Affairs Com., Harvard U. Bus. Sch. Alumni Assn., Am. Soc. Pub. Adminstrn.. Democrat. Jewish. Office: United-Guardian Inc 230 Marcus Blvd Hauppauge NY 11788

FINEBAUM, MURRAY L., securities executive; b. N.Y.C., Jan. 8, 1942; s. Hyman and Alice (Israel) F.; m. Harriet Glickman, Dec. 24, 1964; children: Bruce Gary, Elizabeth. BA, CUNY, 1962; JD, NYU, 1965. Bar: N.Y. 1965, Calif. 1973. Trial atty. SEC, N.Y.C., 1967-69; sr. compliance rep. Am. Stock Exchange, N.Y.C., 1969-71; exec. v.p. Cantor, Fitzgerald & Co., Inc., Beverly Hills, Calif., 1971-86; pres. Instinet Corp., N.Y.C., 1986-88, Mitchum, Jones & Templeton, Inc., L.A., 1988—; cons. Instinet/Reuters, N.Y.C., 1988—. Contbr. articles to profl. jours. and mags.; contbg. editor: Trust & Estates Mag. Mem. Nat. Assn. Securities Dealers (vice chmn. 1986-87, chmn. bus. conduct com. 1985-86, gov. 1984-87, chmn. capital & margin com. 1985-87, chmn. dist. bus. conduct com. 1982-83, bd. govs.). Office: Mitchum Jones & Templeton Inc 800 W 6th St Ste 500 Los Angeles CA 90017

FINEGOLD, RONALD, computer services executive; b. Bklyn., Nov. 17, 1942; s. Herman Hearsch and Ethel (Kanner) F.; B.S., City Coll. N.Y., 1963; m. Ellen Carole Sehr, Mar. 22, 1964; children—Sherry Dawn, Edward Jon. Supr. programming Celanese Chem. Co., N.Y.C., 1962-66; v.p. marketing Automation Scis., Inc., N.Y.C., 1966-69; pres. Computer Horizons Corp., N.Y.C., 1969-82, chmn. bd., 1977-82, dir., 1969-82; chmn. bd. Stamford Assos., Inc., N.Y.C., 1969-75; pres., dir. Rizons Brokerage, Inc., 1970-71, chmn. bd., dir., 1972-75; chmn. bd. Custom Terminals Corp., 1976-82; pres. Skylane Air Travel Corp., 1977—; chmn. bd., dir. Starlex Systems & Services, Inc., 1983—. Mem. Data Processing Mgmt. Assn., Am. Mgmt. Assn., Young Pres.'s Orgn., Aircraft Owners and Pilots Assn., Tau Epsilon Phi. Home: 154 Valley Forge Pl Orangeburg NY 10962 Office: 50 Chestnut Ridge Rd Montvale NJ 07645

FINER, MICHAEL SCOTT, accountant; b. Boston, Dec. 17, 1964; s. Philip Finer and Lorna Leslie (Milich) Kerner. BS, Babson Coll., 1987. Mng. assoc. MSE Realty Co., Mansfield, Mass., 1981-85; sr. assoc. ERA/VIP Real Estate, Inc., Sharon, Mass., 1985-87; tax acct. Arthur Andersen & Co., Boston, 1987—; chmn. bd. dirs. Finer Industries, Sharon. 2d lt. USAR, 1983—. Mem. Assn. of the U.S. Army (assoc.), Reserve Officers' Assn., Mansfield Jaycees, Zeta Beta Tau. Jewish. Home: PO Box 411 Sharon MA 02067 Office: Arthur Andersen & Co 1 International Pl Boston MA 02110

FINESILVER, JAY MARK, lawyer; b. Denver, June 10, 1955; s. Sherman G. and Annette (Warren) F.; m. Debra K. Wilcox, Apr. 6, 1979; children: Justin, Lauren. BA, Washington U., St. Louis, 1977; JD, U. Denver, 1980. Bar: Colo. 1981, U.S. Dist. Ct. Colo. 1980, U.S. Ct. Appeals (7th and 10th cirs.) 1981. Law clk. to presiding justice U.S. Ct. Appeals (7th cir.), Chgo., 1980-81; assoc. Rothgerber, Appel & Powers, Denver, 1981-85, Elrod, Katz, Preeo & Look, Denver, 1985-86; pvt. practice Jay M. Finesilver P.C., Denver, 1986—; instr. Denver Paralegal Inst., 1987-88. Author: Colorado Foreclosure and Bankruptcy, 1988; contbr. articles to profl. jours. Pres. Denver Citizenship Day Com., 1983-86, Mayfair Neighbors, Inc., Denver, 1984-87. Named Outstanding Neighbor Mayfair Neighbors Inc., 1988. Mem. ABA, Mortgage Bankers Assn. Am., Colo. Bar Assn., Denver Bar Assn., Colo. Mortgage Bankers Assn., Washingto U. Alunmi Assn. (Colo. chmn. 1982-87). Office: 717 17th St Ste 2300 Denver CO 80202

FINGER, DIAMON LEE, mining company executive; b. Lakeland, Fla., Aug. 14, 1927; s. Diamon L. and Elsie Marie (Reynolds) F.; m. Mafrie Louise Higgins, May 5, 1946; children: Ronald, Robert, Susan, Richard. Student, Fla. So. Coll., 1960. Gen. mgr. Theiss Peabody Mitsui, Australia, 1967-73; v.p., gen. mgr. Fla. Crushed Stone, Brooksville, Fla., 1973-74; dir. mine ops. Morrison-Knudsen Co., Inc., Boise, Idaho, 1974-77, gen. mgr. region/div., 1977-79, v.p. ops., mining, 1979-82, v.p. mine devel., ops., 1982-83, group v.p. mining, 1983-85, sr. v.p. mining, 1985—; pres. Kanawha Mining Co., Cannelton, W.Va., Atascosa Mining Co., Jourdanton, Tex., Blue Ridge Mining Co., Luttrell, Tenn., Navasota Mining Co., Carlos, Tex., Limecrest Mining Co., Newton, N.J.; bd. dirs. Westmoreland Resources, Billings, Mont. Mem. Am. Inst. Mining Engrs. Office: Morrison-Knudsen Co Inc 720 Park Blvd Boise ID 83712

FINGER, JOHN HOLDEN, lawyer; b. Oakland, Calif., June 29, 1913; s. Clyde P. and Jennie (Miller) F.; m. Dorothy C. Riley, Dec. 30, 1950; children: Catherine, John Jr., David, Carol. A.B., U. Calif., 1933. Bar: Calif. 1937. Pvt. practice of law San Francisco, 1937-42; chief mil. commn. sect. Far East Hdqrs. War Dept., Tokyo, 1946-47; mem. firm Hoberg Finger Brown Cox & Molligan, San Francisco, 1947—; trustee Pacific Sch. Religion, bd. chmn., 1969-78; bd. dirs. Calif. Maritime Acad., San Francisco Legal Aid Soc., 1955-70; bd. visitors Judge Adv. Gen. Sch., Charlottesville, Va., 1964-76, Stanford U. Law Sch., 1969-71. Pres. Laymen's Fellowship, No. Calif. Conf. Congl. Chs., 1951-53, moderator, 1954-55. Served to maj. JAGC AUS, 1942-46; col. Res. ret.; comdg. officer 5th Judge Adv. Gen. Detachment, 1962-64; U.S. Army Judiciary, 1967-68. Decorated Legion of Merit. Fellow Am. Bar Found., Am. Coll. Trial Lawyers; mem. Am. Judicature Soc., Am. Bar Assn. (ho. of dels. 1970-78, council jud. adminstrn. div. 1972-77, standing com. assn. communications), Bar Assn. San Francisco (dir. 1960-62, recipient John A. Sutro award for legal excellence 1980), Judge Adv. Assn. (dir. 1957—, pres. 1964-65), Lawyers Club San Francisco (pres. 1953, dir. 1950—), State Bar Calif. (bd. govs. 1965-68, pres. 1967-68), Sierra Club (exec. com. legal def. fund), Phi Alpha Delta, Sigma Phi Epsilon, Alpha Kappa Phi. Home: 12675 Skyline Blvd Oakland CA 94619 Office: Hoberg Finger et al 703 Market St San Francisco CA 94103

FINGLASS, RONALD N., banker; b. Balt., Apr. 2, 1948; s. Sidney and Dolly (Winograd) F.; m. Jean Lowy; children: Julie, Mara. BS, Lehigh U., 1970; MBA, U. Mich. V.p. Am. Fed. Savs. Bank, Rockville, Md., 1983—. Republican. Home: 7427 1st League Columbia MD 21046 Office: Am Fed Savs Bank 1700 Rockville Pike Rockville MD 20852

FINGON, ROBERT JAMES, school systems administrator; b. New Haven, Conn., Nov. 8, 1949; s. John J. and Helen (McDermott) F.; m. Joan Carroll, Apr. 22, 1977; children: Shallon, Collin. BS in Sociology, Northeastern U., 1973; MS in Computer Sci., U. New Haven, 1977. Computer programmer Sperry Remington, Bridgeport, Conn., 1976-77; data processing mgr. Rockingham Hosp., Bellowsfalls, Vt., 1977-78; programmer analyst Vt. Marble Co., Proctor, 1978-83; bus. mgr. Rutland (Vt.) Pub. Schs., 1983—. Mem. Assn. Sch. Bus. Ofcls. (research com., data processing com. 1986—), Vt. Assn. Sch. Bus. Ofcls. Home: Post Rd Rutland VT 05701 Office: Rutland Pub Schs 6 Church St Rutland VT 05701

FINK, AARON HERMAN, box manufacturing executive; b. Union City, N.J., Apr. 1, 1916; s. Jacob and Tessie (Dubow) F.; m. Roslyn Lamb, Dec. 6, 1942; children: Elliot, Illene. AB, Johns Hopkins U., 1938; PhD in Bus. Adminstrn. (hon.), Hamilton State U., 1977, World U., 1982, Marquis Guiseppe Scichules Univ., 1985. Treas., Associated Mills, 1938-45; now dir.; v.p., gen. mgr. Essex Paper Box Mfg. Co., Newark, 1945-48, pres., 1948—; pres. Internat. Gift Box Co., 1948—; U.S. del. Conf. Mfrs., Paris, 1954, Spl. Econ. Mission to Italy, 1954. Mem. N.J. Paper Box Mfg. Assn. (trustee), N.J. Box Craft Bur. (pres.), Am. Soc. Quality Control, TAPPI, NAM, Am. Mgmt. Assn. (pres.'s assoc.), AIM (fellow pres.'s council, adv. bd.), Nat. Soc. Bus. Budgeting, Confrerie de la Chaine des Rotisseurs, Am. Material Handling Soc., Am. Forestry Assn., Am. Soc. Advancement Mgmt., Nat. Paper Box Assn. (dir., assoc. chmn. met. div., chmn. plant ops. and manpower), AIAA, Am. Geophys. Union, Am. Ordnance Assn., N.Y. Acad. Scis., Nat. Space Inst., Fedn. Aeronautique Internat, Seaview C. of C. Assn. N.J. Clubs: Princeton, World Trade, Johns Hopkins (N.Y.C.); Crestmont Country (gov.) (Great Oak); Newark Athletic, Downtown (Newark); Broken Sound Golf, Boca Raton, Fla.; Le Mirador Country (Lake Geneva, Switzerland); Seaview Country. Home: 20 Crestwood Dr Maplewood NJ 07040 Office: 281 Astor St Newark NJ 07114

FINK, CHARLES AUGUSTIN, behavioral systems scientist; b. McAllen, Tex., Jan. 1, 1929; s. Charles Adolph and Mary Nellie (Bonneau) F.; A.A., Pan-Am. U., 1948; B.S., Marquette U., 1950; postgrad. No. Va. Community Coll., 1973, George Mason U., 1974; M.A., Cath. U. Am., 1979; m. Ann Heslen, June 1, 1955 (dec. June 1981); children; Patricia A., Marianne E., Richard G., Gerard A. Journalist, UP and Ft. Worth Star-Telegram, 1950-52; commd. 2d lt. U.S. Army, 1952, advanced through grades to lt. col., 1966, various positions telecommunications, 1952-56, teaching, 1956-58, exec. project mgmt., 1958-62, def. analysis and research, 1962-65, fgn. mil. relations, 1965-67, def. telecommunications exec., 1967-69, chief planning, budget and program control office Def. Satellite Communications Program, Def. Communications Agy., 1969-72, ret. 1972; pvt. practice cons. managerial behavior Falls Church, Va., 1972-77; pub. (jour.) Circle, 1988—; pres. Behavioral Systems Sci. Orgn. and predecessor, Falls Church, 1978—; leader family group dynamics, 1958-67. Adv. bd. Holy Redeemer Roman Cath. Ch., Bangkok, Thailand, St. Philip's Ch., Falls Church, Va., 1971-73. Decorated Army Commendation medals, Joint Services Commendation medal; named to Fink Hall of Fame, 1982; recipient Behavior Modeling award Internat. Congress Applied Systems Research and Cybernetics, 1980. Mem. Internat. Soc. Gen. Systems Research, Am. Soc. Cybernetics, Internat. Assn. Cybernetics, Internat. Network for Social Network Analysis, Assn. U.S. Army, Ret. Officers Assn., Finks Internat. (v.p. 1981—). Club: K.C. Developer hierarchial theory of human behavior, 1967—, uses in behavioral, social and biol. sci. and their applications, 1972—, behavioral causal modeling research methodology, 1974—, computer-aided behavior systems coaching for persons and orgns., 1982—; adv. for copyrighting computer graphics displays and multi-media communications in scis.; pub. Circle newsletter. Home: 3305 Brandy Ct Falls Church VA 22042 Office: PO Box 2051 Falls Church VA 22042

FINK, H. BERNERD, corporate professional; b. Topeka, Oct. 30, 1909; s. Homer Bernerd and Mattie (McNair) F.; m. Jane Mills, Sept. 14, 1935 (dec. 1953); children: Marcia Fink Anderson, Elizabeth Fink Farnsworth; m. Ruth Garvey, Mar. 31, 1955; children: Bruce G. Cochener, Diana C. Broze, Caroline C. Bolene. B.A., U. Kans., 1931. With Cen. Nat. Bank, Topeka, 1931-37; ptnr. Fink Bros. Gen. Ins., Topeka, 1937-42; mgr. Updegraff Buick, Topeka, 1945-51; ptnr. Midwest Livestock Co., 1951-55; corp. exec. CGF Industries, Inc., Topeka, 1955-89, chmn. bd. dirs., 1989—; dir. Continental Life Ins., Boise, Idaho, Bank IV of Topeka. Chmn., bd. dirs. Greater Univ. Fund of Kans., 1962-63; pres. City of Topeka United Fund, 1972; v.p. ARC, Topeka, 1951-52; mem. adv. bd. Sch. of Bus., U. Kans., Lawrence, 1970—. Served to lt. comdr. USN, 1942-46. Mem. Topeka C. of C. (v.p. 1964). Republican. Congregationalist. Clubs: Topeka Country; Alexandria Country (Minn.); Paradise Valley (Scottsdale, Ariz.). Home: 800 Bank IV Towers Topeka KS 66603 Office: CGF Industries Inc 800 Bank IV Tower Topeka KS 66603

FINK, LESTER HAROLD, engineering company executive, educator; b. Phila., May 3, 1925; s. Harold D. and Edna B. (Hopkins) F.; m. R. Naomi Veit, Dec. 10, 1955; children—Lois Hope, Carol Anne. BSEE, U. Pa., 1950, MSEE, 1961. Supr. engr. research div. Phila. Electric Co., 1950-74; asst. dir. Electric Energy Systems div. Dept. Interior, Washington, 1974-75, ERDA, 1975-77, Dept. Energy, 1977-79; pres. Systems Engring. for Power, Inc., Vienna, Va., 1979-83; chmn. Carlsen & Fink Assocs., Inc., 1983—; adj. prof. Drexel U., 1961-74, U. Md., 1979-80. Served with U.S. Army, 1943-46. Recipient Meritorious Service award U.S. Dept. Energy, 1979. Fellow IEEE, Instrument Soc. Am.; mem. Conf. Internationale de Grande Reseaux Electrique, Sigma Tau, Eta Kappa Nu, Tau Beta Pi. Presbyterian. Patentee underground power transmission and automatic generation control; contbg. author: Large Scale Systems, 1982; Power System Analysis and Planning, 1983; contbr. chpt. to electronics engring. handbook, 1982. Home: 11304 Full Cry Ct Oakton VA 22124 Office: Carlsen & Fink Assocs Inc 11244 Waples Mill Rd Suite D-2 Fairfax VA 22030

FINKEL, JOEL ROBERTS, anticounterfeiting specialist; b. Chgo., Mar. 10, 1937; s. Max Jay and Dorothy (Roberts) F.; m. Ila Joy Gutter, June 14, 1959; children: Howard Sanford, Leslie Allyn. Student Ill. Inst. Tech., 1954-56; BS in Chemistry, Roosevelt U., 1958; postgrad., Purdue U., 1958-60. Rsch. chemist Beckman Instruments, Fullerton, Calif., 1960-62; rsch. engr. Aerojet Gen., Azusa, Calif., 1962-66; sr. scientist Melpar, Inc., Falls Church, Va., 1966-69; environ. engr. Grumman Aerospace, Bethpage, N.Y., 1969-70; owner J. R. Finkel & Assocs., Oxon Hill, Md., 1969-71; tech. mgr. GTE Labs., Inc., Waltham, Mass., 1970-83; sr. systems engr., mgr. bus. devel., info. security systems dept. Xerox Spl. Info. Systems, Pasadena, Calif., 1983-86; pres. S-P-I Tech, Inc., Calabasas, Calif., 1986—, mgr. program Eaton Consol. Controls Inc., DVAD, El Segundo, Calif., 1988—; co-chmn. tech. task force Internat. Anticounterfeiting Coalition, 1984-85; also patents cons., 1984-85. Commr. Wayland, Little League, Mass., 1973-75; CPR instr., trainer, Wayland, 1977-83. Mem. ASTM (security com., counterfeiting subcom., access control subcom 1986—), N.Y. Acad. Scis., Sigma Xi. Home: 5800-53 N Owensmouth Ave Woodland Hills CA 91367 Office: PO Box 9232 Calabasas CA 91302

FINKEL, RICHARD PAUL, accountant; b. Waterbury, Conn., Mar. 28, 1951; s. Nathan and Martha (Shultz) F.; m. Ronnie Kershenbaum, Mar. 16, 1974; children: Matthew Nathan, Jessica Lauren. BS cum laude, U. Conn., 1973, MBA, 1977. CPA, Conn. Territory sales mgr. Burroughs Corp., East Hartford, Conn., 1973-76; sr. acct. Arthur Anderson & Co., Hartford, Conn., 1977-80; prin. Bobrow & Bobrow CPAs, West Hartford, Conn., 1980-83, Schnidman, Barron, Finkel & Yanaros PC, Hartford, 1983-88; founder The Finkel Co., Inc., Avon, Conn., 1988—. Pres. Avon United Way, Conn., 1983. Mem. AICPA, Conn. Soc. CPAs (com. mem.). Jewish. Home: 12 Elaine Dr Simsbury CT 06070 Office: The Finkel Co Inc 30 Tower Ln Avon CT 06001

FINKELDAY, JOHN PAUL, software company executive; b. Pleasantville, N.J., Nov. 20, 1943; s. Charles John Henry and Viola Sybilla (Eastlack) F.; student Glassboro State Coll., 1961-63, Rider Coll., 1965; m. Karen Lynn Mattoon, Nov. 16, 1963; 1 son, John Paul. With McGraw Hill Publ. Co., Hightstown, N.J., 1963-65; asst. controller Exel Wood Products Co., Inc., Lakewood, N.J., 1965-66, office mgr., 1966-82, mgr. data processing, 1970-78, v.p., dir. data processing, 1978-83, v.p. mgmt. info. services, 1983-86, v.p. adminstrn., 1983-84, v.p.Amici Systems, Inc., Brick, N.J., 1986—; mem. Del. Valley Computer Users Group. Third v.p. exec. com. Adm. Farragut Acad. Parents Assn., 1980-81. Mem. Am. Mgmt. Assn., Common, U.S. Golf Assn. (assoc.). Club: Moose. Home: PO Box 194 Greenville NC 27835-0194 Office: Amici Systems Inc 228 Brick Blvd Brick Town NJ 08723

FINKELMAN, JAY MATTHEW, personnel, financial services executive; b. N.Y.C., Nov. 3, 1945; s. Milton and Florence (Sokolov) F.; m. Carin Lesley Wong, June 29, 1985. BA, CUNY, 1966, MBA, 1968; PhD, NYU, 1970. Lic. psychologist, N.Y., Calif.; diplomate Am. Bd. Profl. Psychology, Am. Bd. Forensic Psychology. Prof. industrial psychology Baruch Coll. CUNY, 1967-79, mem. bus. doctoral faculty, 1974-79, dean, 1976-79; exec. v.p. Lenox, Inc., N.Y.C., 1980; mgr. Sta. KTVU-TV, San Francisco, 1981-84; pres. TV Mktg. Co., Seattle, 1984-85; v.p. mktg. Walt Disney Co., Burbank, Calif., 1985-87; exec. v.p. United Pers. Systems, L.A., 1988—; bd. dirs. Oakland Regency Hotel; mgmt. cons. BFS Assocs., N.Y.C., 1967-80. Editor: The Role Human Factors in Computers, 1977; contbr. to profl. publs. Bd. dirs. New Oakland (Calif.) Com., 1982; speaker in field. Mem. Am. Bd. Forensic Psychology, Am. Bd. Profl. Psychology, Beta Gamma Sigma, Delta Sigma Rho, Psi Chi, Tau Kappa Alpha. Home: 1735 Crisler Way Los Angeles CA 90069 Office: United Personnel Systems 555 Pointe Dr Ste 300 Brea CA 92621

FINKELSTEIN, EDWARD S., department store executive; b. New Rochelle, N.Y., Mar. 30, 1925; s. Maurice and Eva (Levine) F.; m. Myra Schuss, Aug. 13, 1950; children: Mitchell, Daniel, Robert. B.A., Harvard U., 1946, M.B.A., 1948; DCS (hon.), N.Y.U., 1988. Successively trainee, buyer mdse. adminstr. Macy's, N.Y.C., 1948-62; sr. v.p., dir. merchandising Macy's, N.J., 1962-67, exec. v.p., merchandising and sales promotion, 1967-69; pres. Macy's, Calif., 1969-74; pres., chmn., chief exec. officer Macy's, New York, 1974-80; chmn., chief exec. officer R.H. Macy & Co. Inc., 1980—; dir. R.H. Macy, Inc., 1971—; dir. Chase Manhatten Bank., Chase Manhattan Corp., Time Inc. Mem. nat. adv. council Cystic Fibrosis, 1975-80; trustee Cystic Fibrosis Found., 1977-80, hon. trustee, 1980—; bd. dirs. adv. bd. Harvard Bus. Sch., 1983—. Served with USN, 1943-46. Mem. Harvard Club. Jewish. Office: R H Macy & Co Inc 151 W 34th St New York NY 10001

FINKELSTEIN, JACK, JR., biomedical company executive; b. Houston, Mar. 3, 1952; s. Jack Finkelstein and Carol Sue (Nathan) F.; m. Linda Marie Parisi, June 11, 1978; 1 child, Laura Parisi. BBA, U. Tex., 1975. Pres. Brookstone Properties, Houston, 1978-82; v.p. Alpha I Biomedicals, Washington, 1982-84, pres., chief exec. officer, 1984—, also bd. dirs.; pres., chief exec. officer Viral Techs. Inc., 1986—, also bd. dirs.; bd. dirs. Finkelstein Found., Houston. Office: Alpha I Biomedicals Inc 777 14th St NW Suite 410 Washington DC 20005

FINKELSTEIN, MARK JON, service executive; b. Middletown, Conn., Jan. 24, 1947; s. Sidney and Hulda Louise (Holter) F; m. Donna Lee Groth, Aug. 6, 1978; children: Adam David, Matthew Aaron, Amanda Louise. BA, L.I. U., 1970, MA, 1977; adminstr. Adminstr. New Lakeview Convalescent Home, Cheshire, Conn., 1973-83; v.p. Regional Mgmt. Resources, Inc., Woburn, Mass., 1983-86, Greenery Rehab. Group, Inc., Cambridge, Mass., 1985-86; pres. Health and Rehab. Properties Trust, Cambridge, Mass., 1986—. Contbr. articles to profl. jours. Active Dem. Town Com., Portland, Conn., 1973—, chmn. bd. fin. 1980-84. Mem. Fellow Am. Coll. Health Care Adminstrs. (gov. at large 1984-86, pres. 1986—, Disting. Adminstr. Conn. chpt. 1981). Jewish. Lodge: Elks. Office: HRPT Advisors Inc 6 Joelle Dr Portland CT 06480

FINKLEA, ROBERT WEIR, III, public relations executive; b. Dallas, Mar. 30, 1944; s. Robert W. Jr. and Jeanne Elizabeth (Leaming) F.; m. Susan Baker, June 28, 1978 (div. Nov. 1979). BA, U. North Tex., 1972. Sr. reporter Dallas Morning News, 1964-74; regional corr. The N.Y. Times, 1968-76, Business Week mag., 1975-76; assoc. editor D Mag., Dallas, 1975-76; pres. The Cons. Group, Dallas, 1976-80; asst. mgr. pub. relations Diamond Shamrock Corp., Dallas, 1980-81; gen. mgr. Bozell and Jacobs Pub. Relations, Dallas, 1981-82; prin. Robert Finklea & Assocs., Dallas, 1982; ptnr. Kirk & Finklea Communications, Richardson, Tex., 1983-84; exec. v.p., mng. dir. Manning, Selvage & Lee Southwest, Dallas, 1984-87; chmn., chief exec. officer Worldmark Group, Inc., 1987—; advisor U. North Tex. Sch. Journalism, Denton, 1980—; mem. corp. sect. Internat. Latex Products, Inc.,

1988; pres. Worldmark Communications, 1988; ptnr. Internat. Mktg. Asst., Worldmark Aviation, Worldmark Leisure, Ltd., Internat. Med. Source, Worldmark Energy; dir. Am. Genetic Engring., Dallas, 1986—; dir., sec. Internat. Med. Resources, Dallas, 1987—. Counselor Positive Parents of Dallas, 1981—; bd. dirs. Leukemia Soc. Dallas, 1972-78. Sgt. USAFR, 1966-79. Mem. Tex. Pub. Relations Assn., Internat. Traders Assn., Press Club of Dallas (v.p. 1975-76), Kiwanis (pres. East Dallas club 1975-76). Office: Highland Pk Nat Bank 4514 Cole Ave Ste 600 Dallas TX 75205

FINLAY, ROBERT DEREK, food company executive; b. U.K., May 16, 1932; s. William Templeton and Phyllis F.; m. Una Ann Grant, June 30, 1956; children: Fiona, Rory, James. B.A. with honors in Law and Econs, Cambridge (Eng.) U., 1955, M.A., 1959. With Mobil Oil Co. Ltd., U.K., 1955-61; assoc. McKinsey & Co., Inc., 1961-67, prin., 1967-71, dir., 1971-79; mng. dir. H.J. Heinz Co. Ltd., U.K., 1979-81; sr. v.p. corp. devel. world hdqrs. H.J. Heinz Co., Pitts., 1981—; Bd. dirs. U.S. China Bus. Council. Mem. London com. Scottish Council Devel. and Industry, 1979—; trustee Mercy Hosp., Pitts. Served to capt. Gordon Highlanders, 1950-61; bd. dirs. Pitts. Pub. Theatre. Mem. Inst. Mktg., Inst. Mgmt. Cons. Clubs: Highland Brigade, Leander, Duquesne, Allegheny, Annabel's. Office: H J Heinz Co 600 Grant St Pittsburgh PA 15219

FINLAYSON, ANDREW PAUL, electronics company executive; b. Inverness, Scotland, July 26, 1947; came to U.S., 1982; s. Joseph Duthac and Jean (Gentle) F.; m. Sandra Carol Ulyett, 1971; children: James Dominic, Alasdair Duthac. Degree in Bus., Hatfield Poly., Eng., 1974; Diploma in Mktg., Oxford U., Eng., 1979. Area mgr. Rediffusion Co., Eng., 1975-82; gen. mgr. Redi Vision, Boston, 1982-84; v.p. Rediffusion Simulation Co., Dallas, 1984-85; pres. Diamond Acceptance Corp., Boston, 1986—. Lt. Royal Air Force, Eng., 1967-72. Mem. British Inst. Mgmt., Royal Air Force Club. Office: Diamond Acceptance Corp 612 Grove St Framingham MA 01701

FINLEY, GEORGE ALVIN, III, retail executive; b. Aurora, Ill., Apr. 25, 1938; s. George Alvin, II, and Sally Ann (Lord) F.; m. Sue Sellors, June 20, 1962; children: Valerie, George Alvin IV. BBA, So. Meth. U., 1962; postgrad. Coll. Grad. Program, Ford Motor Co., 1963. Rep. for Europe, Finco Internat., 1959-61; trainee Ford Motor Co., Dearborn, Mich., 1962-63; v.p. mktg. Internat. Motor Cars, Oakland, Calif., 1963-64, Sequoia Lincoln lease mgr., 1965; regional mgr. Behlen Mfg. Co., Dallas, 1965-67; pres. C C Hardware Inc., Corpus Christi, Tex., 1967—; guest instr. Sch. Bus., So. Meth. U.; dir. Charter Savs. and Loan. Pres. Nueces River Authority, 1976—; bd. dirs. Coastal Bend Alcoholic Rehab. Cntr. Inc., Tex., 1973—, pres., 1976-77. Mem. Nat. Wholesale Hardware Assn., Nat. Assn. Wholesalers, Am. Supply Assn., Wholesale Distbrs. Assn., Nat. Impact Industries Inc. (chmn. bd. Sandwich, Ill., Tex., past v.p. wholesale hardware assns.), Nat. Retail Hardware Assn., So. Hardware Assn., Phi Delta Theta. Democrat. Unitarian. Club: Rotary Internat. Asst. in design, engring., production, mktg. Apollo Automobile, 1963-64. Home: 3360 Ocean Dr Corpus Christi TX 78411 Office: 210 McBride Ln PO Box 9153 Corpus Christi TX 78469-9153

FINLEY, JACK DWIGHT, investments and consultation executive; b. Lawrence County, Ind., Aug. 7, 1927; s. Paul and Esther Irene (Keithley) F.; m. Beverly Janice Burpee, June 11, 1949; children: Janice Blair Finley Vance, Jennifer Brooke Finley Nichols, Jena Blake. BS, U.S. Mil. Acad., 1949; MS in Elec. Engring., U. Ill., 1953. Commd. 2d lt. U.S. Air Force, 1949, advanced through grades to capt., 1955, resigned, 1956; mem. tech. staff Ramo-Wooldridge Corp., L.A., 1956-60; v.p. R&D Data Corp., Dayton, Ohio, 1960-68; v.p., tech. dir., chmn. bd. dirs., founder EIKONIX Corp., Bedford, Mass., 1968-86, cons. investments, dir. svcs., 1986—; cons. R-W, L.A., 1960-61; vis. lectr. Rochester Inst. Tech. (N.Y.), 1966-68. Contbr. articles to profl. jours; patentee in field. Trustee Westbrook Coll., Portland, Maine, 1987—, vice chmn. bd., 1988—. Fellow Soc. Photo Optical Instrumentation Engrs.; mem. Missile Range and Space Pioneers (life charter mem.), IEEE (sr.), AIAA, Am. Soc. Photogrammetry, Soc. Photog. Scientists and Engrs., U. Ill. Alumni Assn., Assn. Grads. U.S. Mil. Acad., Eta Kappa Nu, Nashawtuc Country Club, Wyndemere Country Club, Lions. Home and Office: 338 Edgemere Way N Naples FL 33999 also: 30 Washington Dr Acton MA 01720

FINLEY, LEWIS MERREN, financial planner; b. Reubens, Idaho, Nov. 29, 1929; s. John Emory and Charlotte (Priest) F.; student public schs., Spokane; m. Virginia Ruth Spousta, Feb. 23, 1957; children—Ellen Annette, Charlotte Louise. With Household Finance Co., Portland, Oreg. and Seattle, 1953-56; with Doug Gerow Fin., Portland, 1956-61; pres. Family Fin. Planners Inc., Portland, 1961—; assoc. broker Peoples Choice Realty, Inc., Milwaukie, Oreg., 1977-82; Lewis M. Finley, Real Estate Broker, Inc., 1982—. Standing trustee Chpt. 13, Fed. Bankruptcy Ct., Dist. of Oreg., 1979-80. Served with U.S. Army, 1951-53. Mem. Oreg. Assn. Credit Counselors (past pres.), Northwest Assn. Credit Counselors (past treas.), Am. Assn. Credit Counselors (v.p. 1982—), Authors Guild. Republican. Methodist. Clubs: Masons (past master), Shriners. Author: The Complete Guide to Getting Yourself Out of Debt, 1975. Home: 3015 SE Riviere Dr Milwaukie OR 97267 Office: 2154 NE Broadway Suite 120 Portland OR 97232

FINN, DAVID, public relations company executive, artist; b. N.Y.C., Aug. 30, 1921; s. Jonathan and Sadie (Borgenicht) F.; m. Laura Zeisler, Oct. 20, 1945; children: Kathy, Dena, Peter, Amy. BS, CCNY, 1943. Co-founder Ruder & Finn, Inc., N.Y.C., 1948, pres., 1956-68, chmn. bd., chief exec. officer, 1968—, also bd. dirs.; adj. assoc. prof. NYU. One-man show New Sch. for Social Research, N.Y.C.; exhibited in group shows at Nat. Acad., Washington, Met. Mus. Art, N.Y.C., Boston Mus. Art, L'Orangerie, Paris, Andrew Crispo Gallery, N.Y.C., Westchester County Ctr., others; author: Public Relations and Management, 1956, The Corporate Oligarch, 1969; photographer: (books) Embrace of Life, 1969, As the Eye Moves, 1970, Donatello: Prophet of Modern Vision, 1973, Henry Moore Sculpture and Environment, 1976, Michelangelo's Three Pietas, 1975, Oceanic Images, 1978, The Florence Baptistry Doors, 1980, Sculpture at Storm King, 1980, Busch-Reisinger Museum, 1980, Canova, Giambologna, Donatello, Cellini, David by the Hand of Michelangelo, In the Mountains of Japan; contbr. articles and chpts. to profl. jours. and art publs. Mem. adv. bd. Council for Study Mankind; mem. adv. council advanced mgmt. programs Internat. Bus. Inst., Baruch Coll., N.Y.C.; bd. visitors CCNY; bd. dirs. New Hope Found., Ctr. for Research in Bus. and Social Policy, Victor Gruen Ctr. for Environ. Planning, Inst. Advanced Studies in Humanities, MacDowell Colony, Inst. for Future, Artists for Environment Found., Internat. Ctr. Photography, Am. Coll. Switzerland, Jewish Theol. Sem. Am.; bd. overseers Parsons Sch. Design, N.Y.C. Served to 1st lt. A.C. AUS, 1944. Mem. Am. Fedn. Arts, Am. Inst. Graphic Arts (past dir.), Internat. Pub. Relations Assn., Kappa Tau Alpha (hon.). Office: Ruder Finn Inc 301 E 57th St New York NY 10022

FINN, PETER, public relations executive; b. N.Y.C., Mar. 31, 1954; s. David and Laura (Zeisler) F.; m. Sarah Duncan; children: Noah J., Emily M. BA, Brown U., 1976; MA, Columbia U., 1977. Researcher Research & Forecasts Inc., N.Y.C., 1977-79, dir. ops., 1979-81, chmn., 1981-84; chmn. fin. com. Ruder-Finn, Inc. (formerly Ruder, Finn & Rotman, Inc.), N.Y.C., 1984—, chief fin. officer, 1985—, exec. v.p., 1986-87, chmn. exec. com., 1988—. Office: Ruder-Finn Inc 301 E 57th St New York NY 10022

FINNAN, JOHN O'NEILL, banker; b. Richmond, Ind., Sept. 2, 1953; s. Robert James and Florence I. (O'Neill) F.; m. Elaine Dawn Beier, Aug. 16, 1980; 1 child, Stephanie Louise. BA, Miami U., Oxford, Ohio, 1975; MBA, Ball State U., 1978; grad. degree in banking, Rutgers U., 1986. Pres. Star Bank, Covington, Ky. Chmn. No. Ky. United Way Campaign, 1982, Community Chest Bd., 1985; pres. YMCA No. Ky., 1985. Mem. N. Ky. C. of C. (chmn. elect 1988, chmn. govtl. affairs com. 1988). Republican. Roman Catholic. Home: 80 Sunnymeade Fort Mitchell KY 41017 Office: Star Bank 6th and Madison Covington KY 41011

FINNEGAN, LAURENCE PATRICK, JR., manufacturing company executive; b. Phila., June 26, 1937; s. Laurence P. and Anne T. (Breslin) F.; m. Geraldine J. Rookstool, May 1, 1960; children: Laurence, James, Regina, William, Joseph, Patricia. BS in Acctg., St. Joseph's U., Phila., 1961. Treas., controller Fischer & Porter Co., Warminster, Pa., 1962-70; sr. v.p. fin., chief fin. officer Fischer & Porter Co., Warminster, 1986—; div. controller Internat. Telephone and Telegraph, Phila., 1970-74; exec. v.p. Narco Sci., Inc., Ft. Washington, Pa., 1974-83; mgmt. cons. Finnegan and Assocs., Ambler, Pa., 1983-85; pres., chief exec. officer HMH Design Group, Ltd., Warminster, Pa., 1985-86; bd. dirs. Xcel Corp., Pasadena, Calif. Mem. Fin. Execs. Inst. Roman Catholic. Office: Fischer & Porter Co 271/B1 125 E County Line Rd Warminster PA 18974

FINNEGAN, NEAL FRANCIS, banker; b. Boston, Mar. 28, 1938; s. Neal Francis and Mary Theresa (McNeil) F.; m. Rosemarie A. Eldracher; children: Theresa, Lynn, Neal, Wayne. B.S., Northeastern U., 1961; M.B.A., Babson Coll., 1969. With Shawmut Bank of Boston, 1961-80, sr. v.p. OIC comml. banking, 1977-80; pres., chief exec. officer Worcester Bancorp Inc., Mass., 1980-82; chmn., chief exec. officer Worcester County Nat. Bank, 1980-82; sr. exec. v.p. Shawmut Corp., Boston, 1982-83, vice-chmn., 1983-86, dir., 1982-86; exec. v.p. Shawmut Bank of Boston, N.A., 1983-86; chief operating officer, dir. Bowery Savs. Bank, N.Y.C., 1986-88; exec. v.p. Bankers Trust Co., N.Y.C., 1988—. Trustee St. Vincent's Hosp., Worcester, 1980—, Emmanuel Coll., Boston, 1984—, United Neighborhood Houses, N.Y.C., 1988—; trustee Northeastern U. Office: Bankers Trust Co 280 Park Ave New York NY 10017

FINNEGAN, P. KERRY, insurance company executive; b. Oak Park, Ill., Apr. 2, 1959; s. Patrick Kenneth and Evelyn (Miller) F.; m. Dawn Marie Krahn, June 21, 1980; children: Sean Gregory, Ryan Christian. BA in Communications Studies, No. Ill. U., 1981. Svc. supr. Met. Life Ins. Co., Chgo., 1982; group rep. Met. Life Ins. Co., 1982-85, acct. exec., 1985-86, regional dir., 1986—. Mem. Health Ins. Assn. Am., Mid-Am. Club (Chgo.). Roman Catholic. Home: 1799 Whitt Ct Wheaton IL 60187 Office: Met Life Ins Co 200 E Randolph Dr Chicago IL 60601

FINNEGAN, SARA ANNE, publisher; b. Balt., Aug. 1, 1939; d. Lawrence Winfield and Rosina Elva (Huber) F.; m. Isaac C. Lycett, Jr., Aug. 31, 1974. B.A., Sweet Briar Coll., 1961; M.L.A., Johns Hopkins U., 1965; exec. program, U. Va. Grad. Sch. Bus., 1977. Tchr., chmn. history dept. Hannah More Acad., Reisterstown, Md., 1961-65; redactor Williams & Wilkins Co., Balt., 1965-66; asst. head redactory Williams & Wilkins Co., 1966-71, editor book div., 1971-75, assoc. editor-in-chief, 1975-77, v.p., editor-in-chief, 1977-81, pres. book div., 1981-88, group pres., 1988—; editor Kalends, 1973-78, 89—; exec. sponsor jour. Histochemistry and Cytochemistry, 1973-77. Trustee St. Timothy's Sch., Stevenson, Md., 1974-83, sec. bd., 1974-81; adv. bd. Balt. Ind. Schs. Scholarship Fund, 1977-81; adv. council grad. study Coll. Notre Dame of Md., 1983; overseer Sweet Briar Coll., 1987—, dir., 1988—. Mem. Assn. Am. Pubs. (exec. council profl. and scholarly pub. div. 1984-85), Intern. Sci., Tech. and Med. Pubs. Assn. (group exec. 1986—, chmn.-elect 1988—). Republican. Lutheran. Office: Williams & Wilkins Co 428 E Preston St Baltimore MD 21202

FINNERTY, JOHN DUDLEY, investment banker, financial educator; b. Glen Ridge, N.J., Apr. 23, 1949; s. John Patrick and Patricia (Conover) F.; m. Christine Watt, Dec. 29, 1973 (div. Jan. 1987); m. Louise Hoppe, May 21, 1988. AB, Williams Coll., 1967-71; BA, U. Cambridge (Eng.), 1971-73, MA, 1977; PhD, Naval Postgrad. Sch., 1977. Adj. prof. Naval Postgrad. Sch., Monterey, Calif., 1973-77; sr. assoc. Morgan Stanley and Co. Inc., N.Y.C., 1977-82; v.p. Lazard Frères and Co., N.Y.C., 1982-86; exec. v.p., chief fin. officer Coll. Savs. Bank, Princeton, N.J., 1986-89, also bd. dirs.; cons. McFarland Co., N.Y.C., 1989—; prof. Fordham U., N.Y.C., 1987—, prof., 1989—. Author: Bond Refunding Analysis, 1984, Corporate Financial Analysis, 1986, Financial Manager's Guide, 1988; assoc. editor Jour. of Corp. Fin., 1987—, Fin. Mgmt., 1982—; patentee Restructuring Debt Obligations, 1987, Funding a Future Liability of Uncertain Cost, 1988. Active in fund-raising for Williams Coll. Served to lt. USNR, 1973-77. Recipient Marshall Commn. Scholarship, London, 1971. Mem. Fin. Mgmt. Assn. (bd. dirs. 1984-86), Am. Fin. Assn., Western Fin. Assn. Republican. Roman Catholic. Club: Williams (N.Y.C.). Home: 506 2d Ave Spring Lake NJ 07762 Office: McFarland Co 30 Rockefeller Plaza New York NY 10020

FINNIGAN, JOSEPH TOWNSEND, public relations executive; b. Springfield, Ill., Aug. 26, 1944; s. Joseph Thomas and Mary Frances (McCarthy) F.; m. Kathleen Burke, July 2, 1966; children: Matthew, Brendan, Patrick. A.B., Marquette U., 1966. With Fleishman-Hillard, 1972—, v.p., 1975-77, partner, 1975—; exec. v.p. Fleishman-Hillard, St. Louis, 1977—. Bd. dirs. St. Louis Better Bus. Found., St. Louis Symphony Soc. Mem. Pub. Rels. Soc. Am., Sigma Delta Chi. Roman Catholic. Clubs: Sunset Country, Island Bay Yacht, St. Louis Press, Mo. Athletic. Home: 12415 Ballas Trails Dr Des Peres MO 63122

FINO, MARIE GEORGETTE KECK, real estate broker; b. Greenville, Pa., Jan. 30, 1923; d. Harvey I. and Winifred L. (Fuller) Keck; m. Alex F. Fino, Sept. 27, 1947; children: Timothy A., Jeffrey J. Cert. real estate, Pa. State U., 1980; grad., Realtors Inst., Harrisburg, Pa., 1981. Registered nurse, Pa.; lic. real estate broker. Broker, owner 305 Realty, Warren, Pa., 1983—; instr. Pa. State U., 1985—; treas. Warren County Bd. Realtors, 1981-84, v.p., 1984-86, pres., 1988—. Patentee fuel storage vent. Active Warren Hosp. Auxiliary, 1979—, Northwestern Pa. Regional Planning Commn. 1985—, exec. com. 1988—; bd. dirs. Warren County Devel. Assn. Named Woman of Yr. in Bus. and Industry county of Warren, 1986. Mem. Nat. Assn. Realtors, Pa. Assn. Realtors (bd. dirs. 1984-88, vice chmn. comml.-indsl. com. 1986-87), Soc. Indsl. Realtors, Internat. Orgn. Real Estate Appraisers, Internat. Orgn. Corp. Real Estate Execs., Warren County C. of C. Republican. Roman Catholic. Clubs: Philomel (bd. dirs. 1976), Warren Womens' (bd. dirs. 1978-80), Conewango Valley (Warren). Lodge: Zonta. Office: 305 Realty 305 Market St Warren PA 16365

FINOCCHIARO, ALFONSO GIOVANNI, international banking executive; b. Catania, Italy, Aug. 20, 1932; came to U.S., 1960; s. Giovanni and Giuseppina (Cavalieri) F.; m. Diana Louise Cavagnolo, May 14, 1960; children: John Paul, Carol Anne. D in Polit. Sci., U. Catania, 1958; MBA in Internat. Fin., Pace U., 1967. V.p. Chem. Bank, N.Y.C., 1966-77; pres., gen. mgr. Conn. Bank Internat., N.Y.C., 1977-78; exec. v.p., regional dir. Banco Portugues do Atlantico, N.Y.C., 1978—. Comdr., Order Infante D. Henrique, Republic Portugal. Fellow Internat. Mgmt. and Devel. Inst. (Leadership award); mem. Portugal-U.S. C. of C. (bd. dirs., past pres.), Am. Portuguese Soc. (bd. dirs. 1979—), Luso-Am. Bus. Council, Global Econ. Action Inst., Internat. Mgmt. and Devel. Inst., Pace U. Lubin Grad. Sch. Bus. Alumni Assn. (bd. dirs.). Republican. Roman Catholic. Lodge: Rotary. Office: Banco Portugues do Atlantico 2 Wall St New York NY 10005

FIONDELLA, ROBERT WILLIAM, insurance company executive; b. Bristol, Conn., May 19, 1942; s. Sisto William and Theresa (Nestico) F.; m. Carolyn Brozinski; children: Robert, Jeffrey. A.B., Providence Coll., 1964; J.D., U. Conn. Sch. Law, 1968. Computer programmer-analyst Travelers Ins. Co., Hartford, Conn., 1965; atty. Danaher, Lewis, Tamoney, Hartford, Conn., 1968-69; atty. law dept. Phoenix Mut. Ins. Co., Hartford, Conn., 1969-72, asst. counsel, officer, 1972-74, assoc. counsel, 1974-75, investment counsel, 1975-77, 2d v.p., counsel, 1977, v.p., gen. counsel, 1977-81, sr. v.p.-gen. counsel, 1981-83, exec. v.p. ind. line, 1983-87, pres., 1987—, also bd. dirs.; trustee Advest Group, Inc., Hartford, 1984—; trustee, bd. dirs. Bristol Savs. Bank, Conn., 1983—. Coach Edgewood Little League, Bristol, Conn., 1984-85; mem. Bristol City Council, 1969-71, Urban Renewal Commn., Bristol, 1971-76; chmn. Bristol Retirement Bd., 1978-83; bd. dirs. Urban Legaue of Greater Hartford, 1986—. Mem. Conn. Bar Assn. Democrat. Roman Catholic. Home: 36 Saw Mill Rd Bristol CT 06010 Office: Phoenix Mut Life Ins Co 1 American Row Hartford CT 06115

FIORAVANTI, NANCY ELEANOR, banker; b. Gloucester, Mass., Apr. 10, 1935; d. Richard Joseph and Evelyn Grace (Souza) Fioravanti; grad. high sch. Various positions and depts. Bank of New Eng.-North Shore (formerly Cape Ann Bank and Trust Co., successor to Gloucester Safe Deposit & Trust Co.), Gloucester, 1953—, with trust dept., 1959-86, asst. trust officer, 1970-84, trust officer, 1984-86; trust officer Cape Ann Savs. Bank, 1986—. Treas. art adv. com. Gloucester Lyceum and Sawyer Free Library. Mem. Nat. Assn. Bank Women, Bus. and Profl. Women's Club. Home: PO Box 1638 Gloucester MA 01930 Office: 109 Main St Gloucester MA 01930

FIORE, JAMES LOUIS, JR., public accountant, educator, lecturer, public speaker; b. Jersey City, Oct. 7, 1935; s. James Louis and Rose (Perrotta) F.; m. Alberta W. Pope, July 21, 1957; children: Carolyn Leigh, James Louis, Toni Lynn. BS in Acctg., Seton Hall U., 1957; MBA in Acctg. and Statis., Western Colo. U., 1978; PhD, Calif. Western U., 1979. Lic. acct. Pa., N.J.; accredited Accreditation Council for Accountancy, Wash. Field auditor, State of N.J. Trenton, N.J., 1959-60; supr. internal auditing Ronson Corp., Woodbridge, N.J., 1960-64; supr. gen. acctg. Electronic Assocs., West Long Branch, N.J., 1964-65; pvt. practice acctg., 1965—; pres. Bucks County Research Inst. Inc., 1972-79; mem. adj. faculty Allentown Coll. of St. Francis De Sales, Center Valley, Pa., 1979-81, Pa. Coll. Straight Chiropractic, 1986—. Author: (with others) Shareholder Loans, The National Public Accountant, 1988, Non-Absorption of Nitrofurazone from the Urethra in Men, 1976, Comparative Bioavailability of Doxycycline, 1974; contbr. articles to profl. jours. Bd. dirs. Brick Twp. (N.J.) Scholarship Found., 1963-67; mem. adv. council Inst. for Accts., Pa. State U.; trustee Pa. Coll. Straight Chiropractic, 1986—; founder, treas. Cath. Acad. of Sci. in U.S.A., Washington; bd. dirs. Neighborhood Devel. Council, Annapolis, Md. Served to 2d lt. U.S. Army, 1957. Named Jaycee of Year, 1962; recipient Legion of Honor, Chapel of Four Chaplains, 1979. Mem. Pa. Soc. Public Accts., Nat. Soc. Public Accts., Calif. Western U. Alumni Assn., Amateur Artists Assn. Am., Western Colo. U. Alumni Assn., Seton Hall U. Alumni Assn. (Crest and Century Clubs). Roman Catholic. Lodges: K.C., Rosicrucians (traditional martinist order). Home: 265 Thompson Mill Rd Upper Makefield Twp Newtown PA 18940

FIPPINGER, GRACE J., telecommunications company executive; b. N.Y.C., Nov. 24, 1927; d. Fred Herman and Johanna Rose (Tesio) F. B.A., St. Lawrence U., 1948; LL.D. (hon.), Marymount Manhattan Coll., 1980; D.Comml. Sci. (hon.), Molloy Coll., 1982. Dist. mgr. N.Y. Telephone Co., South Nassau, 1957-65; div. mgr. N.Y. Telephone Co., 1965-71; gen. comml. mgr. N.Y. Telephone Co., Queens, 1971—, Bklyn., 1973—; v.p., sec., treas. N.Y. Telephone Co., 1974-84; v.p., treas., sec. NYNEX Corp., N.Y.C., 1984—; mem. Manhattan East adv. bd. Mfrs. Hanover Trust Co.; bd. dirs. Conn. Mut. Life Ins., Gulf & Western Industries, Inc., Apple Bank for Savs., Bear Stearns Co., Pfizer, Inc. Former mem. State Manpower Adv. Council; former mem. Gov.'s Econ. Devel. Adv. Council; past bd. dirs. Consumer Credit Counseling Service Greater N.Y., 1972—; hon. bd. dirs. Am. Cancer Soc., 1974—, YMCA Greater N.Y., 1975—; former dir. A.R.C., L.I., Nassau County Health and Welfare Council; trustee Citizens Budget Commn., 1974—; former dir. exec. bd. Nassau County Fedn. Republican Women. Named Woman of Year, Bus. and Profl. Women Nassau County, 1969, Woman of Achievement, Flatbush Bus. and Profl. Women's Assn., 1974, Woman of Year, Soroptimist Club Nassau County; hon. mem. Soroptimist Club Central Nassau, 1974; recipient John Peter Zenger award Nassau County Press Assn., 1975, Outstanding Bus. Women of 1977 award Marymount Manhattan Coll., 1978; honoree Catalyst Inc., 1977, Women's Equity Action League, 1978, Republican Women in Bus. and Industry, Cath. Med. Ctr. Bklyn./Queens, 1983, Girl Scouts, 1984, Clark Garden, Long Island, 1985. Mem. Am. Mgmt. Assn. (former trustee and mem. exec. com.), Nat. Assn. Corp. Treas., Fin. Execs. Inst., Am. Soc. Corp. Secs., Am. Soc. Corp. Treas. Inc., Fin. Womens Assn. N.Y., N.Y. Chamber Commerce and Industry (chmn. mems. council 1977-79), L.I. Assn., Ladies Profl. Golf Assn. (hon.). Clubs: St. Lawrence of L.I. (N.Y.C.), Columbus, Board Room (N.Y.C.). Office: Nynex Corp 335 Madison Ave New York NY 10017

FIREMAN, PAUL, clothing company executive; b. Cambridge, Mass., Feb. 14, 1944. Student, Boston U. Formerly v.p. sales, treas. BC Recreational Industries, Canton, Mass.; pres. Reebok Internat. Ltd., Canton, 1979-86, chmn., chief exec. officer, 1986—. Office: Reebok Internat Ltd 150 Royal St Canton MA 02021 *

FIRST, THOMAS F., JR., hospital executive; b. 1938; married. BA, Vanderbilt U.; MD, Washington U. With Hosp. Corp. of Am., Nashville, 1968—, chmn., chief exec. officer, 1985—, also bd. dirs. With USAF, 1966-68. Office: Hosp Corp Am 1 Park Pla Nashville TN 37202 *

FIRST, WESLEY, publishing company executive; b. Erie, Pa., Feb. 18, 1920; s. Orson John and Pearle (Unger) F.; m. Margaret Elizabeth Whittlesey, Apr. 3, 1943 (div. June 1967); children: Karen Lee, Michael; m. Dianne Jones, Dec. 1975 (div. Sept. 1981); m. Suzanne Lavenas, Jan. 9, 1982. Student, U. Mich., 1937-40; B.S., Columbia U., 1958; M.A., New Sch. for Social Research, 1963. Reporter Erie Dispatch, 1943-47, asst. city editor, 1947-48, asst. to editor, 1948-50; with N.Y. World-Telegram and Sun, N.Y.C., 1950-63; successively copyreader, night news editor N.Y. World-Telegram and Sun, 1950-57, asst. mng. editor, 1957-60, mng. editor, 1960-63; prof. journalism Ohio State U., 1963-65; dir. univ. relations Columbia, N.Y.C., 1965-67; asst. to pres. Sarah Lawrence Coll., 1967-68, Juilliard School, N.Y.C., 1968-69; editor Travel Weekly, 1969-76; editor-in-chief Psychology Today, 1976-77; Staff v.p. editorial Ziff-Davis Pub. Co., 1977-82, cons., 1982—; guest lectr. newspaper design and makeup Fordham U.; instr. journalism Finch Coll., N.Y.C.; Rep. to newspaper design and makeup seminar Am. Press Inst., 1957. Editor: Columbia Remembered, University on the Heights. Served with USAAF, 1944-46. Woodrow Wilson Fellow, 1959. Mem. U. Mich., Columbia U. alumni assns., Phi Beta Kappa, Kappa Tau Alpha, Sigma Delta Chi. Clubs: Overseas Press, Silurians. Home: 305 E 86th St Apt 20-R W New York NY 10028

FISCHBACH, CHARLES PETER, railway executive consultant, lawyer, arbitrator; b. N.Y.C., Apr. 3, 1939; s. Howard C. and Pauline Lillian (Wasserman) F.; BS, U. Wis., 1960, J.D., 1967; MA, Rutgers U., 1962; m. Paula Rae Steinhorn, July 15, 1973. Bar: Wis. 1967, U.S. Supreme Ct. 1974. Pvt. practice, Madison, Wis., 1967-68; labor relations rsch.analyst and cons., N.Y.C., 1968-70; asst. to exec. officer labor relations and personnel N.Y.C. Transit Authority, N.Y.C., 1970; labor relations rsch. analyst, N.Y.C., 1970-72; exec. dir. Classified Mcpl. Employees Assn. Balt. City, 1972-74; labor relations cons./arbitrator, Balt., 1974-77; dir. labor relations, chief labor relations officer Chgo., Rock Island and Pacific R.R. Co., 1977-81, dir. personnel and employee relations, Chgo., 1981-84; dir. adminstrn. and human resources Chgo. Pacific Corp., 1984-85; labor arbitrator, 1985—; v.p. Rock Island Improvement Co., 1984-85; dir. Peoria and Bureau Valley R.R. Co.; lectr. Am. Mgmt. Assn., Am. Arbitration Assn. Collective Bargaining Inst. Mem. pub. sector labor relations conf. bd. U. Md., 1973-77, Ill. Econ. Bd., 1988—; mem. landlord-tenant law study commn., State of Md., 1976-77. Recipient Am. Jurisprudence prize in corp. law Joint Pubs. of Annotated Reports System, 1966; cert. for encouragement of vol. dispute settlement procedures Am. Arbitration Assn., 1981-84; named hon. fellow Harry S. Truman Library Inst., 1976, Mem. Nat. Hist. Soc., ABA, State Bar Wis., Am. Arbitration Assn. (labor panel arbitrators), Fed. Mediation and Conciliation Svc. Roster of Arbitrators, Nat. Mediation Bd. Register of Arbitrators, Ill. Pub. Employee Arbitration Mediation Panel, Indsl. Relations Rsch. Assn., Soc. Profls.in Dispute Resolution, Ill. Bd. Edn. Panel of Hearing Officers, Social Security Admistrn./Am. Fedn. Govt. Employees Arbitration Panel, Am. Found. Automation and Employment, Wis. Alumni Assn., Rutgers Alumni Fedn., Statue of Liberty-Ellis Island Found. (charter). Contbr. articles on labor relations and arbitration to profl. jours. Avocations: collecting commemorative coin series and first day medallic covers, reading, art.

FISCHER, ALVIN EUGENE, JR., marketing executive; b. Glendale, Calif., July 31, 1942; s. Alvin Eugene Sr. and Roberta Maxine (Barker) F.; m. Michel Jane Gorham, Dec. 20, 1960 (div. Oct. 1982); children: Theresa Michele, Todd Alan, Alvin Eugene III; m. Laurie Ann Simpson, Aug. 22, 1986. Student, Orange Coast Coll., 1960-70, UCLA, 1967, U. Calif., Irvine, 1970. Supt. constrn. K.W. Koll Builders, Costa Mesa, Calif., 1960-65; gen. sales mgr. Mills Inc., Santa Ana, Calif., 1965-70; gen. mgr. Royal Interiors Inc., Santa Ana, 1970-72; v.p. nat. ops. Larwin Home Ctr., Beverly Hills, Calif., 1972-74; broker Village Real Estate, Huntington Beach, Calif., 1975-78; v.p. sales Phillips Floor Covering, Santa Ana, 1978-81; gen. sales mgr. G.A.F./Tarkett/Star Distbn., Commerce, Calif., 1981-83, LD Brinkman, Ontario, Calif., 1984-85; v.p. sales and mktg. LaSalle-Deitch Co., Tustin, Calif., 1983-84; sales mgr. western region Nat. Floor Products Inc., Florence, Ala., 1986—; panelist Western Floor Convering Assn., 1979. Mgr. pubs. Newport Theatrical Arts, Newport Beach, Calif., 1983; mem. South Coast Community Ch., Irvine, Calif. Mem. So. Calif. Floor Covering Club,

Newport Sail Club. Office: Nat Floor Products Inc PO Box 354 Florence AL 35631

FISCHER, BRIAN DAVID, financial executive; b. Somerville, N.J., Nov. 19, 1960; s. Richard Eric and Joan Mary (Shepard) F.; m. Sandra Kolios, July 22, 1984. BBA, Pace U., 1982. CLU; chartered fin. cons. Dist. mgr. First Investors, Tampa, Fla., 1982-84; v.p. Econ. Concepts, Inc., Clinton, N.J., 1984—; tchr. Hunterdon Adult Edn., Flemington, N.J., 1986—; instr. Fairleigh Dickinson U. Mem. Tri-County Estate Planning Coun.; trustee Ctr. for Ednl. Advancement, Flemington, 1986—. Mem. Internat. Assn. Fin. Planning, Inst. Cert. Fin. Planners (cert.), Flemington C. of C. (mem. com. 1987—). Home: 837 Clawson Ave Neshanic Station NJ 08853 Office: Econ Concepts Inc Hwy 31 S Box 5276 Clinton NJ 08809

FISCHER, KENNETH ROBERT, auctioneer; b. St. Louis, Sept. 15, 1942; s. Irwin and Henrietta (Burbell) F.; m. Marjory B. Tureen, Nov. 21, 1965 (div. Jan. 1980); m. Barbara Jo Carter, Apr. 3, 1982; children: Julie Ross, Daniel Blair, Carrie Elizabeth. Pres. Diversified Metals div. Diversified Industries, Inc., St. Louis, 1964-78, sr. v.p., 1980-82; pres. City Recycling Corp., St. Louis, 1979-80; exec. v.p. Nat.Indsl. Services, Inc., St. Louis, 1982-84; pres. Bus. Network Group, St. Louis, 1984—; cons. Ross-Dove Co., Inc., Foster City, Calif., 1987—, Rabin Bros., Inc., San Francisco, 1987—. Diversified Industries, Inc., St. Louis, 1978-79, 87—. Bd. dirs. Anti-Drug Abuse Edn. Fund, St. Louis, 1976—; chmn. phys. fitness com. Jewish Community Ctr., St. Louis, 1988; chmn. Sr. Olympics, St. Louis. Served with Air NG, 1966-68. Mem. Am. Auctioneering Assn., Jewish Community Ctrs. Assn. (bd. dirs.). Republican. Jewish. Club: Copper. Home: 7 Highgate Rd Saint Louis MO 63132 Office: Bus Network Corp 501 N Lindbergh Blvd Ste 100 Saint Louis MO 63141

FISCHER, LELAND CARROLL (LEE), mortgage banker; b. Austin, Tex., Jan. 19, 1949; s. Robert C. and Louise (Mitchell) F.; m. Carol N. Neder, Dec. 10, 1977; children: Steven, Meredith. BS in Social Sci., Southwest Tex. State U., 1971, MBA, 1977. Mgr. distbn. Cummins Engine Co., Columbus, Ind., 1977-80; materials mgr. Datapoint Inc., Waco, Tex., 1980-81; v.p., gen. mgr. McDonald Automotive Co., Waco, Tex., 1981-83; agt. Kelly Realtors, Waco, Tex., 1983-84; v.p. 1st Fin. Corp., Waco, Tex., 1984—. Author: Base Stats, 1987, 88. Mem. Woodway (Tex.) Planning and Zoning Commn., 1985—; mem. corp. campaign United Way, Waco, 1985-87; bd. dirs. Palmer Drug Abuse, Waco, 1986. Mem. Mortgage Banking Assn., Nat. Manufactured Housing Fin. Assn. (bd. dirs. 1986-87), Rotary. Home: 203 Trailview Waco TX 76712 Office: First Fin Corp 800 Washington St Waco TX 76703

FISCHER, MARTIN ALAN, lawyer, state government commissioner; b. N.Y.C., Jan. 8, 1937; s. Paul and Frances (Hollander) F.; m. Susan Glatzer, Nov. 20, 1960; children: Nancy, Elizabeth, Michael. BA, Clark U., 1958; LLB, Bklyn Law Sch., 1964; postgrad., NYU. Bar: N.Y. 1964, U.S. Dist. Ct. (so. and ea. dists.) N.Y. 1965, U.S. Ct. Appeals (2d cir.) 1965. Assoc. Otterbourg, Steindler, Houston & Rosen, N.Y.C., 1964-67; assoc. gen. counsel, asst. sec. Warner Communications, Inc., N.Y.C., 1967-77; past pres., dir. Kinney System, Inc., N.Y.C.; of counsel Warshaw, Burstein, Cohen, Schlesinger & Kuh, N.Y.C.; chmn. bd. commrs. State Ins. Fund, N.Y.C., 1977—; bd. dirs. Winston Resources, Inc., The Berkshire Bank, N.Y.C. Mem. Assn. for Better N.Y.; trustee Temple Beth El, Cedarhurst, N.Y. Mem. ABA, N.Y. Bar Assn., Bklyn. Bar Assn. Office: Warshaw Burstein Cohen Schlesinger & Kuh 555 Fifth Ave New York NY 10017

FISCHER, STEPHEN HEIBERG, securities executive, financial consultant; b. Mankato, Minn., June 10, 1943; s. Walter B. and Augusta S. (Heiberg) F. B.S., Mankato State U., 1965. C.P.A., Minn. Mem. audit, tax staff Touche Ross & Co., Mpls., 1965-68; exec. v.p., sec., treas. McCauley Enterprises, Mpls., 1968-72, Reuss Thiss & Co., Mpls., 1973-76; mng. ptnr. Fischer Johnson Zuelke & Co., Mpls., 1976-81; pres. IRI Securities, Mpls., 1981-86, also v.p., sec., treas. IRI Stock Fund, Mpls., 1981-86, dir. 1981— ; dir., v.p., sec., treas. Midas Gold Shares & Bullion, Inc., 1985-86; dir., 1985—, sec. treas. IRI Asset Mgmt., Mpls., 1981-86; dir., pres. Bankers Systems Brokerage Services, Inc., exec. v.p., Granit Family of Six Mutual Funds, 1986—; dir. Fischer Johnson, Zuelke, Anderson Mktg., Eklof Dock & Pattern, Twin City Hose, Inc., AMFM Inc. Mem. AICPA, Minn. Soc. CPA's (fin. institutions com.), Minn. Securities Ops. Assn. (bd. dirs. 1969-72), Minn. Securities Dealers Assn., U. Minn. Goalline Club (pres., dir. treas. Mpls. chpt.). Republican. Roman Catholic. Home: 3950 Enchanted Ln Mound MN 55364 Office: Bankers Systems Brokerage Svcs PO Box 283 Saint Cloud MN 56302

FISCHER, SUSAN LOIS, financial services company executive; b. N.Y.C., Mar. 18, 1947; d. Julius and Bertha (Sviridow) Kulman; m. Robert J. Fischer, July 11, 1976. BS in Edn., NYU, 1969, MA in Edn., 1971; MBA in Fin., L.I. U., Dobbs Ferry, N.Y., 1984. Cert. tchr., N.Y. Tchr. N.Y.C. Bd. Edn., 1969-84; fin. analyst Integrated Resources Equipment Group, Inc., N.Y.C., 1984-85, asst. v.p., 1985-87; v.p. Integrated Resources Capital Markets Group, Inc., N.Y.C., 1987-88, Integrated Resources Equipment Group, Inc., N.Y.C., 1989—. Mem. LWV; bd. dirs. Walden Wood Homeowners Assn., 1986-88. Home: 144 Ogden Ave Dobbs Ferry NY 10522 Office: Integrated Resources Inc 733 3d Ave New York NY 10017

FISCHER, ZOE ANN, real estate and property marketing company executive, real estate consultant; b. Los Angeles, Aug. 26, 1939; d. George and Marguerite (Carrasco) Routsos; m. Douglas Clare Fischer, Aug. 6, 1960 (div. 1970); children—Brent Sean Cecil, Tahlia Georgienne Marguerite Bianca. B.F.A. in Design, UCLA, 1964. Pres. Zoe Antiques, Beverly Hills, Calif., 1973—; v.p. Harleigh Sandler Real Estate Corp. (now Merrill Lynch), 1980-81; exec. v.p. Coast to Coast Real Estate & Land Devel. Corp., Century City, Calif., 1981-83; pres. New Market Devel., Inc., Beverly Hills, 1983—; dir. mktg. Mirabella, Los Angeles, 1983, Autumn Pointe, Los Angeles, 1983-84, Desert Hills, Antelope Valley, Calif., 1984-85; cons. Lowe Corp., Los Angeles, 1985. Designer album cover for Clare Fischer Orch. (Grammy award nomination 1962). Soprano Roger Wagner Choir, UCLA, 1963-64. Mem. UCLA Alumni Assn. Democrat. Roman Catholic. Avocations: skiing, designing jewelry, interior design, antique collecting, photography.

FISCHMAN, MYRNA LEAH, accountant, educator; b. N.Y.C.; d. Isidore and Sally (Goldstein) F. BS, Coll. City N.Y., 1960, MS, 1964; PhD, NYU 1976. Asst. to controller Sam Goody, Inc., N.Y.C.; tchr. accounting Central Comml. High Sch., N.Y.C., 1960-63, William Cullen Bryant High Sch., Queens, N.Y., 1963-66, vocat. adviser, 1963-66; instr. acctg. Borough of Manhattan Community Coll., N.Y.C., 1966-69; self employed acct., N.Y.C., 1960—; chief acct. investigator rackets, Office Queens Dist. Atty., 1969-70, community relations coordinator, 1970-71; adj. prof. L.I. U., 1970-79, prof. acctg. taxation and law, 1979—, coordinator grad. capstone courses, 1982—, dir. Sch. Professional Accountancy Bklyn. campus, 1984—; dir. Faculty Acctg. Taxation and Law Bklyn. campus, 1986—. Editor Ea. Bus. Educators Jour., 1988. Research cons. pre-tech. program Bd. Edn., City N.Y.; acct.-adviser Inst. for Advancement of Criminal Justice; acct.-cons. Coalition Devel. Corp., Interracial Council for Bus. Opportunities; treas. Breakfree Inc., Lower East Side Prep. Sch.; mem. edn. task force Am. Jewish Com., 1972—; mem. steering com., youth div. N.Y. Dem. County Com., 1967-68, del. to Nat. Conv., Young Dems. Am., 1967, rep. assigned to women's activities com., 1967; mem. Chancellor Com. Against Discrimination in Edn., 1976—; chmn. supervisory com. Fed. Credit Union #1532, N.Y.C., 1983—; mem. legis. adv. bd. N.Y. State Assemblyman Denis Butler, 1979—; chmn. consumer council Astoria Med. Center, 1980—; mem. subcom. on bus. edn. to the econ. devel. and mktg. com. Bklyn. C. of C., 1984—. Recipient award for meritorious service Community Service Soc., 1969; C.P.A., N.Y. Mem. Jewish Guild for Blind, Jewish Braille Inst., Friends Am. Ballet Theatre, Friends Met. Mus. Art, Community Welfare Com., Assn. Govt. Accts. (bd. dirs. N.Y. chpt. 1984—, dir. research and manuscripts 1985—), Am. Acctg. Assn., Nat., Eastern (co-chmn. ann. meeting 1967) bus. edn. assns., Nat., Eastern (chmn. ann. meeting, 1968) bus. tchrs. assns., Internat. Soc. Bus. Edn., Grad. Students Orgn. NYU (treas. 1971-73, v.p. 1973-74), Nat. Assn. Accts. (dir. N.Y. chpt. 1983—), Assn. Govt. Accts. (dir. N.Y. chpt. 1983—), NEA, AAUP, Doctorate Assn. N.Y. Educators (v.p. 1975—), Am. Assn. Jr. Colls., Young Alumni Assn. ; chmn. supervisory com. Fed. Credit Union #1532, N.Y.C., 1983—; Coll. (mem. council), Emanu-El League Congregation Emanu-El, N.Y. (chmn. community services com. 1967-68), Nat. Assn. Accts. (bd. dirs. N.Y. chpt. 1985—, dir. profl. devel. 1986-87, dir. pub. relations 1987-88), Tax Inst. L.I. U. (dir. Bklyn. chpt. 1984—), Delta Pi Epsilon (treas. 1976). Jewish. Democrat. Club: Women's City (N.Y.C.). Developed new bus. machine course and curriculum Borough Manhattan Bus. Community Coll. Office: LI U Zeckendorf Campus Brooklyn NY 11201

FISCHMAR, RICHARD MAYER, controller, consultant; b. N.Y.C., Apr. 11, 1938; s. John B. and Sylvia (Moosnick) F.; m. Sandra P. Fensin, July 3, 1967; children: Brian, Laura. BS, U. Ill., 1959, MA, 1962. CPA, Ill. Sr. auditor L.K.H.&H., Chgo., 1962-66; controller Lake States Engr., Park Ridge, Ill., 1966-68, New Communities Enterprises, Park Forest South, Ill., 1968-70; dep. dir. Ill. Drug Abuse Program, Chgo., 1970-71; dir. internal audit Ill. Dept. Labor, Chgo., 1971-73; controller Ill. Dept. Employment Security, Chgo., 1973-78, D.L. Pattis Real Estate, Lincolnwood, Ill., 1978-86, Goodman Realty Group, Inc., Chgo., 1986—. Author: (booklet) Bibliography of Management Services, 1972; contbr. articles to profl. jours. Mem. Ill. Soc. CPA's (real estate com., mgmt. adv. services and constrn. com.). Office: Goodman Group Inc 6160 N Cicero Chicago IL 60646

FISH, LAWRENCE EDWIN, investment banker; b. Bklyn., Mar. 14, 1944; s. Robert Harold and Norma Lucille (Jost) F.; m. Sandra Ruth Allen, June 11, 1966 (div.); children: Peter Allen, Laurie Kristin; m. Therese Michelle Long, June 4, 1983. BS, U.S. Naval Acad., 1966; MBA, Dartmouth Coll., 1977. Sales engr. Am. Can. Co., Union, N.J., 1970-71; sr. account exec. I.E.S. Mgmt. Group, Irvington, N.J., 1971-72; portfolio mgr. R.I. Hosp. Trust Nat. Bank, Providence, 1972-74; fin. cons. Trend Assocs. Inc., Burlington, Mass., 1974-75; mng. dir. Smith Barney, Harris Upham, Dallas, 1977—; assoc. bd. dirs. Edwin L. Cox So. Meth. U., Dallas, 1985—. Lt. cdr. USNR, 1966-76. Mem. Navy League U.S., Dartmouth Club Dallas (exec. bd.), Am. Legion, U.S. Naval Acad. Alumni Assn., Dallas Symphony Orch. Guild. Republican. Episcopalian. Office: Smith Barney Harris Upham & Co Inc 200 Crescent Ct Dallas TX 75201 Also: Smith Barney Harris Upham & Co Inc 1345 Ave of the Americas New York NY 10105

FISH, LAWRENCE KINGSBAKER, banker; b. Chgo., Oct. 9, 1944; s. Alvin Kingsbaker and Beatrice (Brown) F.; m. Atsuko Toko, June 29, 1980; children: Leah Okajima, Edward Takezo, Emily Takako. B.A., Drake U., Des Moines, Iowa, 1966; M.B.A., Harvard Bus. Sch., Cambridge, 1968. U.S. aid officer U.S. Agy. Internat. Capital Devel, 1970-72; internal officer Bank of Boston, Brazil, 1972, dir. internat. ops., 1972-74, asst. v.p., gen. mgr., 1974-75, v.p., dep. gen. mgr., 1975, v.p., 1975; v.p., gen. mgr. Bank of Boston, Tokyo, 1978-79, 1st v.p., 1979-80; 1st v.p., head Pacific Asia div./Bank of Boston, Hong Kong, 1980-81, sr. v.p., 1981-82, exec. v.p., 1982-83; exec. v.p, head of trust function Asia div./Bank of Boston, Boston, 1983-84, exec. v.p, head of New England Group, 1984-88; pres., chief operating officer Columbia Savs. & Loan Assn., Beverly Hills, Calif., 1988—; bd. dirs. Mastercard Internat. Mem. exec. com. Children's Museum, Boston, 1984-85; pres. Boston/Kyoto Sister City Found., 1984-85; bd. dirs. Japan Soc. of Boston, 1984-85, Inst. Contemporary Art of Boston; mem. exec. bd. USAID Pvt. Enterprise, Washington, 1984-88; overseer New Eng. Conservatory Music. Woodrow Wilson Found. fellow, 1984. Club: Longwood (Brookline, Mass.). Office: Columbia Savs & Loan Assn 8840 Wilshire Blvd Beverly Hills CA 90211

FISH, PAUL MATHEW, lawyer; b. N.Y.C., Sept. 27, 1947; s. Louis and Shirley (Aaronowitz) F.; m. Patrice Ellen Schooley, Nov. 27, 1976. BA, Drake U., 1969; JD, Harvard U., 1972. Bar: N. Mex. 1972, U.S. Dist. Ct. N.Mex. 1972, U.S. Ct. Appeals (10th cir.) 1972. Assoc. Cotter, Atkinson, Campbell, Kelsey & Hanna, Albuquerque, 1972-74; ptnr. Modrall, Sperling, Roehl, Harris & Sisk, P.A., Albuquerque, 1974—; chmn. Chpt. 11 Local Rules Com., Albuquerque, 1981, bankruptcy law sect. N.Mex. State Bar, Albuquerque, 1983. Mem. ABA, N.Mex. Bar Assn., Albuquerque Bar Assn. Avocation: raising wine grapes. Home: Tunnel Springs Rd Box 7 Placitas NM 87043 Office: Modrall Law Firm PO Box 2168 Albuquerque NM 87103

FISH, PAUL WARING, lawyer; b. Ligonier, Pa., Apr. 12, 1933; s. Edmund R. and Catherine (McGuiggan) F.; m. Jacquelyn A. Shea, Sept. 19, 1959; children: Charles M., Edmund J., Catherine G., John H., Jacquelyn A. B.S. in Elec. Engring, Cath. U. Am., 1959, M.E.E., 1961; LL.B., George Washington U., 1965. Bar: D.C. 1965, N.Y. 1966, Mich. 1967, Wis. 1976, Ill. 1983. Patent agt., atty. Xerox Corp., Rochester, N.Y., 1965-66; patent atty., asst. dir. patent div. Burroughs Corp., Detroit, 1969; dir. patents Burroughs Corp., to 1976; asst. gen. counsel Jos. Schlitz Brewing Co., Milw., 1976-79; v.p., gen. counsel., sec. Jos. Schlitz Brewing Co., 1979-83; v.p., gen. counsel. Comdisco, Inc., Rosemont, IL, 1983-86, sr. v.p., gen. counsel, 1986—. Sec. North Shore Republican Club; bd. regents Cath. U. Am., 1985—. Served with USN, 1951-55. Mem. ABA, Am. Assn. Corp. Counsel, Am. Patent Law Assn., U.S. Trademark Assn., Ill. Bar Assn. Roman Catholic. Home: 130 Pine Tree Ln Riverwoods IL 60015 Office: Comdisco Inc 6400 Shafer Ct Rosemont IL 60018

FISHE, GERALD RAYMOND AYLMER, engineering firm owner; b. Farnham Royal, Eng., Feb. 22, 1926; s. Daniel Hamilton and Dorothy Vida (Norton) F.; m. Patricia Ann Roach, Aug. 18, 1949; children: Martha Vida Bindshedler, Raymond Patrick Hamilton, G. Keith Hamilton. BS in Mech. Engring., Duke U., 1949. Registered profl. engr., Ala., Fla., Ga., Ill., Iowa, Mo., Tenn., W.Va. Project engr. E.I. DuPont de Nemours & Co., Martinsville, Va., 1952-58; univ. archtl. staff engr. So. Ill. U., Carbondale, 1958-63; sec. Adair Brady & Fishe, Inc., Lake Worth, Fla., 1965-66; chief engr. Gamble Pownall & Gilroy, Ft. Lauderdale, Fla., 1963-65; cons. forensic engr. Ft. Lauderdale, 1966—; pres. Fishe & Kleeman, Inc., Ft. Lauderdale, 1974—, Fidelity Inspection and Service Co., Ft. Lauderdale, 1983—, Farletot Found., Inc., Ft. Lauderdale, 1985—. Patentee in field. Served with U.S.Army, 1944-45. Diplomate ASCAP, Nat. Acad. Forensic Engrs.; fellow Am. Acad. Forensic Scis. (chmn. engring. sect. 1988-89); mem Constrn. Specification Inst., Nat. Fire Protection Assn., ASHRAE. Republican. Epicopalian. Home: 2031 SW 36 Ave Fort Lauderdale FL 33312 Office: GRA Fishe Cons Engr 601 S Andrews Ave Fort Lauderdale FL 33301

FISHER, ALLAN CAMPBELL, railway executive; b. Westerly, R.I., Aug. 9, 1943; s. Arthur Chester and Norma Jean (Campbell) F.; m. Ellen Tryon Roop, June 14, 1969; children: Bradford Booth, Katherine Thayer. BA in Econs., St. Lawrence U., 1965; MS in Transp., Northwestern U., 1970. Research economist Gen. Motors Research Labs., Warren, Mich., 1969; mgmt. trainee Penn Central, 1970, asst. trainmaster, Chgo., 1970-71, trainmaster, Toledo, 1971-72, terminal trainmaster, Elkhart, Ind., 1972, trainmaster, Cleve., 1972-74, asst. terminal supt., Cleve., 1974, terminal supt., Balt., 1974-75, asst. div. supt. Chesapeake div., Balt., 1975-76, terminal supt. Conrail, Conway, Pa., 1976, div. supt. N.J. div., Elizabethport, 1977, Lehigh div., Bethlehem, Pa., 1978, regional supt. ops. improvement Central region, Pitts., 1978-80, dir. budget control, 1980-82, regional supt. indsl. engring. So. region, Indpls., 1982-83, system dir. operating rules, Phila., 1983—. Served with U.S. Army, 1966-67, Vietnam. Decorated Bronze Star medal; Urban Transp. fellow, 1969. Mem. Internat. Assn. Oper. Officers, Am. Inst. Indsl. Engrs. (sr.), Assn. Am. R.R.'s (operating rules com., chmn. transport spent nuclear fuel com.), Operating Rules Assn., Mayflower Descendents (life), Sigma Chi (life). Unitarian-Universalist. Club: Phila. Boys Choir and Men's Chorale (bd. dirs., Man of Yr. 1987). Lodge: Masons. Home: 215 Poplar Ave Wayne PA 19087 Office: 6 Penn Ctr Room 310 Philadelphia PA 19103-2959

FISHER, ANDREW LAWRENCE, record company executive; b. Bronx, June 7, 1952; s. Sidney Milton and Gertrude (Schwartz) F.; m. Paticia Clare Meaney, Mar. 29, 1975; children: David James, Leigh Rachel. Student, Am. U., Washington, 1969-71; BS, Bklyn. Coll., 1975. Salesman Brown Shoe Co., St. Louis, 1974-76; mgr. Revelations Shoe Corp., N.Y.C., 1976-87; dir. inventory control GRP Records Inc., N.Y.C., 1988—. Mem. Parkway PTA, E.Meadow, N.Y., 1987—; vol. E.Meadow Soccer, 1988, E.Meadow Little League, 1988. Mem. Two/Ten Orgn. Unitarian Universalist.

FISHER, CHARLES THOMAS, III, banker; b. Detroit, Nov. 22, 1929; s. Charles Thomas, Jr. and Elizabeth Jane (Briggs) F.; m. Margaret Elizabeth Keegin, June 18, 1952; children: Margaret Elizabeth (Mrs. F. Macy Jones), Curtis William, Charles Thomas IV (dec.), Lawrence Peter II, Mary Florence. A.B. in Econs, Georgetown U., 1951; M.B.A., Harvard U., 1953. C.P.A., Mich. With Touche, Ross, Bailey & Smart, Detroit, 1953-58; asst. v.p. Nat. Bank Detroit, 1958-61, v.p., 1961-66, sr. v.p., 1966-69, exec. v.p., 1969-72, pres., chief adminstrv. officer, 1972-82, chmn., pres., chief exec. officer, 1982—, also dir.; pres., dir. NBD Bancorp, Inc., 1973-82, chmn., pres., chief exec. officer, 1982—; dir. Internat. Bank of Detroit, Nat. Intergroup, Inc., Gen. Motors Corp., Am. Airlines. Civilian aide to sec. army for State of Mich., 1974-77; Chmn. Mackinac Bridge Authority.; chmn. Detroit Renaissance, Inc., United Found. of Detroit. Named Detroit Young Man of Year Detroit Jr. Bd. Commerce, 1961. Mem. Assn. Res. City Bankers, Am. Inst. C.P.A.s, Mich. Assn. C.P.A.s. Clubs: Bloomfield Hills (Mich.) Country; Country of Detroit (Grosse Pointe), Grosse Pointe; Detroit Athletic (Detroit), Detroit (Detroit), Yondotega (Detroit); Links (N.Y.C.); Metropolitan (Washington). Office: NBD Bancorp Inc 611 Woodward Ave Detroit MI 48226

FISHER, DAVID ANDREW, investment banker, lawyer; b. Nashville, Apr. 21, 1948; s. John Clark and Iris Anell (Pierce) F.; m. Sarah Ellen Maleady, Sept. 16, 1979; 1 child, John Clark III. BA, Davidson Coll., 1970; JD, Vanderbilt U., 1973; MBA, Harvard U., 1980. Bar: Tex. 1973, Calif. 1975. Atty. NBC-TV, Burbank, Calif., 1975; atty., prodn. exec. Elliott Kastner Orgn., Hollywood, Calif., 1976-77; dir. bus. affairs Columbia Pictures, Burbank, 1977-78; pres. Veritas Corp., Nashville, 1980-87; group v.p. Y Entertainment; gen. counsel Communications Equity Assocs., Tampa, Fla., 1988—; cons. entertainment bus., prodn., 1980-87. Dir., screenwriter: Liar's Moon, 1981 (Gold award), Toy Soldiers, 1984; producer various commls., home videos and TV motion pictures including Bat-21 with Gene Hackman, Danny Glover, 1988. Served to capt. USAR, 1966-77. Mem. Writers Guild Am., Omicron Delta Kappa (assoc. editor 1973 Vanderbilt Law Rev. 1973), Mensa, Harvard Club. Methodist. Office: Communications Equity Assocs PO Box 22558 Tampa FL 33622

FISHER, DENISE, biologist; b. Norwood, Pa., July 12, 1961; d. Joseph Francis and Diane Marie F. BS in Biology, Kutztown (Pa.) U., 1983. Cell biologist Caldwell Co. contracted to DuPont Co., Wilmington, Del., 1983-85; quality control biologist Barry Co. contracted to DuPont Co., Wilmington, 1985-87; regulatory affairs and compliance specialist Triad Techs. Inc., New Castle, Del., 1987-88; dir. regulatory affairs C&V Svcs. Inc., Newark, Del., 1988-89. Mem. NAFE, AAAS, Inst. Environ. Scis., Parenteral Drug Assn. Democrat.

FISHER, DENISE DANCHES, public relations executive, marketing consultant; b. Miami Beach, Fla., June 6, 1951; d. Aaron Abraham and Alexandra (Erkman) Danches; m. Raymond L. Fisher, May 14, 1977 (div. Feb. 1987); children: Nicholas Patrick, Katharine Alexandra. AA, Miami Dade Coll., 1975; BA in Communcations, U. Miami, 1977. Asst. continuity dir. WSVN-Channel 7, Miami, 1972-73; trade practice cons. Better Bus. Bur., Miami, 1973-74; asst. sales promotion dir. John Donnelly & Sons, Miami, 1974-75; mktg. dir. Dadeland Mall, Miami, 1978-83; advt. dir. Galleria Novita, Miami, 1983-84; freelance cons. Miami, 1984—; community relations dir. Am. Lung Assn., Miami, 1986—. Tchr. Confraternity of Christian Doctrine St. Joseph's Ch., 1988. Recipient Addy awards, 1978, 80, Communications Excellence award Congress Lung Assn., 1989. Mem. Pub. Relations Soc. Am., Advt. Fedn. Republican. Office: Am Lung Assn 830 Brickell Pl Miami FL 33131

FISHER, DONNE FRANCIS, telecommunications executive; b. Three Forks, Mont., May 24, 1938; s. Francis George and Dolreta (Chryst) F.; m. Sue Lynch Fisher, Sept. 10, 1960; children: William Kevin, Blake Francis, Scott Michael, Steven John. BS, Mont. State U., 1962. CPA, Alaska, Mont. Chief fin. officer, sr. v.p., treas. Tele-Communications Inc., Denver, also bd. dirs. Served with U.S. Army, 1956-58. Democrat. Roman Catholic. Home: 9513 Pinyon Trail Littleton CO 80124 Office: Tele-Communications Inc 4643 S Ulster St Denver CO 80237

FISHER, GEORGE MYLES CORDELL, electronics equipment company executive, mathematician, engineer; b. Anna, Ill., Nov. 30, 1940; s. Ralph Myles and Catherine (Herbert) F.; m. Patricia Ann Wallace, June 18, 1965; children: Jennifer, Barcy, William. BS in Engring., U. Ill., 1962; MS in Engring., Brown U., 1964, PhD in Applied Maths., 1964-66. Mem. tech. staff Bell Telephone Labs., Murray Hill, N.J., 1965-67; supr. Bell Telephone Labs., Holmdel, N.J., 1967-71; dept. head Bell Telephone Labs., Indpls., 1971-76; dir. mfg. systems. Motorola Inc., Schaumberg, Ill., 1976-77; asst. dir. mobile ops. Motorola Inc., Ft. Worth, Tex., 1977-78; v.p. portable ops. Motorola Inc., Ft. Lauderdale, Fla., 1978-81, v.p. paging div., 1981-84; asst. gen. mgr. communications sector Motorola Inc., Schaumberg, 1984-86, sr. exec. v.p., 1986-88, pres., chief exec. officer, 1988—. Contbr. articles on continuum physics; 3 patents in optical wave guides and digital communications. Trustee Brown U.; bd. dirs. U. Ill. Found., Nat. Merit Scholarship Bd., Chgo., 1986—. Mem. IEEE. Office: Motorola Inc 1303 E Algonquin Rd Schaumburg IL 60196

FISHER, HENRY, investment banker; b. Pitts., Feb. 17, 1936; s. Henry Clayton and Dorothea T. (Smith) F.; B.A., U. Pitts., 1960; student Wharton Sch. Investment Banking, 1967, 68; m. Ann Yeager, Aug. 6, 1960; children—Andrew Clayton, William Bradford. Gen. partner Singer Deane & Scribner, Pitts., 1961-69; exec. v.p. Chaplin McGuiness & Co., Inc., Pitts., 1969-73; pres., mng. dir. Commonwealth Securities and Investments, Inc., Pitts., 1974—; gen. ptnr. Investment Bldg., Pitts., 1982-84; ptnr. Perrymont Bldg., 1980-85; mem. N.Y. Stock Exchange, 1972-74. With USMC, 1954-56. Mem. Pitts. Securities Assn., Nat. Assn. Mcpl. Analysts, Pitts. Mcpl. Analysts Soc., Pa. Boroughs Assn., Pa. League of Cities, Pa. Twp. Assn., Pa. Mcpl. Authorities Assn., Internat. Bridge, Tunnel and Turnpike Assn., Pitts. Builders Exchange, Pitts. Bond Club, Sierra Club (founder Pitts. chpt.), Am. Youth Hostels, Inc. (past nat. v.p.), Pa. Soc. of N.Y. Clubs: Duquesne, Pitts., Allegheny, Rivers. Office: 1317 Investment Bldg Pittsburgh PA 15222

FISHER, HERBERT, retail executive; b. N.Y.C., Nov. 14, 1921; s. Arthur and May (Schnitzer) F.; m. Florence Temkin, Nov. 17, 1951; children: Meredith, Judith, Lesley. Student, CCNY, 1940-42. Co-owner A. Fisher & Sons, N.Y.C., 1945-50; owner Franklyn Shops, 1950-59, Royal Factory Outlet, Pittsfield, Mass., 1959-60; with Jamesway Corp., Secaucus, N.J., 1960—, chmn. bd., 1962—. Exec. adv. Coll. Bus. Adminstrn., Fairleigh Dickinson U., Madison, N.J., 1982—. With USAAF, 1942-45. Mem. Nat. Mass Retailing Inst. (chmn. 1973-75, chmn. polit. action com. 1980-88). Home: 994 Wildwood Rd Oradell NJ 07649 Office: Jamesway Corp 40 Hartz Way Secaucus NJ 07094

FISHER, JAMES T., small business owner; b. Mansfield, Ohio, May 20, 1956; s. Donald E. and Mary L. (Treece) F.; m. Risa Weinberger, June 16, 1979; 1 child, Robert Ward. BS in Engring. Sci., Vanderbilt U., 1978; MBA, So. Methodist U., 1983. Engr. Tex. Instruments, Dallas, 1980-82; fin. officer MCorp, Dallas, 1983-87; pres. Fisher Ventures, Inc., Dallas, 1986—. Pres. Vanderbilt U. Coll. Reps., Nashville, 1976; mem. Dallas County Young Reps., Dallas, 1983-88. Naval flight officer USN, 1978-80. Methodist. Club: Rush Creek Yacht (Dallas). Office: Fisher Ventures Inc 8923 Vista View Dr Dallas TX 75243

FISHER, JAMES W., JR., chemical company executive; b. Asheville, N.C., Aug. 14, 1942; s. James W. and Virginia (Gustafson) F.; m. Hannelore Enke, Aug. 15, 1966; children: Julia, Heidi, Michael, Elke. BA cum laude, Princeton U., 1964; MBA, Harvard U., 1966. With GM, Detroit, 1970-73, Ford Motor Co., Detroit, 1973-80; dir. compensation and benefits Air Products and Chems., Inc., Allentown, Pa., 1980-87, dir. orgn. planning and human resources devel., 1987—; bd. dirs. Airprochem Inc. Bd. dirs. Good Shepherd Rehab. Wrkshop and Vocat. Svcs. Mem. Nat. Assn. Corp. Dirs. (chair com. compensation orgn. and mgmt. succession 1984—), Assn. Mgmt. of Orgn. Design (bd. dirs). Capt. USAF, 1966-70. Home: Rte 2 Box 424 Emmaus PA 18049 Office: Air Products & Chems Inc 7201 Hamilton Blvd Allentown PA 18195

FISHER, JOHN EDWIN, insurance company executive; b. Portsmouth, Ohio, Oct. 26, 1929; s. Charles Hall and Bess (Swearingin) F.; m. Eloise Lyon, Apr. 25, 1949. Student, U. Colo., 1947-48, Ohio U., 1948-49, Franklin U., Columbus, Ohio, 1950-51. With Nationwide Mut. Ins. Co., Columbus, 1951—, v.p., office gen. chmn., 1970-72, pres., gen. mgr., dir., 1972-81, gen. chmn., chief exec. officer, 1981—, also dir.; gen. chmn., chief exec. officer, dir. Nationwide Gen. Ins. Co., Nationwide Mut. Fire Ins. Co.,

Nationwide Property & Casualty Ins. Co., Nationwide Life Ins. Co., Nationwide Variable Life Ins. Co.; dir. Neckura Versicherungs A.G., Oberursel, Germany, 1976—; gen. chmn., dir. Employers Ins. of Wausau, 1985—, Farmland Ins. Cos., 1985—; trustee Ohio Cener Co. Chmn. bd. Nationwide Found., 1981—; trustee Children's Hosp., pres., 1984-87. Mem. Chartered Property and Casualty Underwriters Assn., Chartered Life Underwriters Soc., Assn. Ohio Life Ins. Cos. (past pres.), Ohio Ins. Inst. (pres. 1975-77), Nat. Assn. Ind. Insurers, Am. Risk and Ins. Assn., Griffith Ins. Found. (chmn. 1981), Property-Casualty Ins. Council (chmn. 1981-82), Property and Liability Underwriters, Ins. Inst. Am., Am. Inst. Property-Liability Insurers (chmn. 1985—), Am. Inst. Property and Liability Underwriters, Ins. Inst. Am., Internat. Coop. Ins. Fedn. (chmn. 1984—), Am. Coun. Life Ins. (chmn.-elect 1988-89), Columbus C. of C. (chmn. 1981-82). Office: Nationwide Mut Ins Co 1 Nationwide Pla Columbus OH 43216 also: Employers Ins of Wausau 2000 Westwood Dr Wausau WI 54401

FISHER, JOHN MORRIS, association official, educator; b. Fairhaven, Ohio, Apr. 20, 1922; s. Marion Hays and Bessie (Morris) F.; AB, Miami U., Oxford, Ohio, 1947; postgrad. Bklyn. Law Sch., 1950-51, Northwestern U., 1954-55; LLD (hon.), Nasson Coll., 1972; m. Thelma Ison, Feb. 2, 1947; children: Steven Roger, Linda Lucille. With Belden Mfg. Co., Richmond, Ind., 1941; spl. agt. FBI, 1947-53; exec. trainee Sears Roebuck & Co., Chgo., 1953, exec. staff asst. to v.p. personnel and employee relations, 1953-57, chmn. security com., 1957-61; operating dir. Am. Security Council, 1956-57, pres., chief exec. officer, 1957—; pres. Am. Research Found., 1961—; pres., chief exec. officer Am. Security Council Found., 1962—; pres. Communications Corp. Am., 1972-80, chmn., 1980—; pres. Am. Coalition Patriotic Socs., 1978—; adminstrv. chmn. Coalition for Peace Through Strength, 1978—; dir. Center for Internat. Security Studies, 1977-83; organizer, pres. Fidelifax, Inc., 1956-57; chmn. merc. div. Nat. Safety Council, 1959-60, 1st vice chmn. trades and services sect., 1961-62. Chmn. Chgo. Retail Safety Conf., 1959-60; spl. adviser Ill. Supt. Pub. Instrn., 1963-64; cons. to Gov. Fla.; cons. to chmn. com. cold war edn. Nat. Gov.'s Conf., 1962-65, Ill. CD Adv. Council, 1965-68; pres. Am. Council World Freedom, 1971-72; mem. exec. com. Nat. Captive Nations Com., 1968—. Bd. visitors Freedoms Found., 1964-65; bd. dirs. Am. Fgn. Policy Inst., 1976-84, Security and Intelligence Fund, 1976-84, James Monroe Library, 1977-85; pres. Culpepper Meml. Hosp. Found., 1984-86; exec. chmn. U.S. Congl. Adv. Bd., 1982—; adminstrv. chmn. Coalition for Peace Through Strength, 1978—. Served to 1st lt. USAAF, 1943-45. Decorated Air medal with clusters; recipient 10th Anniversary medal and scroll Assembly Captive European Nations, Order Lafayette Freedom award, 1973, Disting. Service award Chapel of 4 Chaplains, 1979, others. Mem. Am. Soc. Indsl. Security (dir. 1959-62), Phi Kappa Tau. Republican. Presbyterian. Clubs: Army Navy (Washington); Kingsmill Country (Williamsburg, Va.); Nat. Dem. ; Capitol Hill. Home: 201 Roger Webster Kingsmill Williamsburg VA 23185 Office: Am Security Coun Found Boston VA 22713

FISHER, JOHN PHILIP, printing and publishing company executive; b. Knowlton, Que., Canada, June 9, 1927; s. Philip Sydney and Margaret (Southam) F.; m. Jean V. MacKay, 1978; 6 children: Amanda, Elizabeth, Julia, Robert, Adam, Simon. B.E., McGill U., 1951. With Dominion Engring. Works, Montreal, 1951-75, mgr. mktg. pulp and paper, 1971-7, sr. v.p., Fraser Inc., Edmundston, N.B., 1975, exec. v.p. 1975-76, pres. from 1976, chmn., chief exec. officer from 1982; pres., chief exec. officer Southam Inc., 1985—; Bd. dirs. Southam Newspaper Group, Southam Printing Ltd., Southam Bus. Info. and Communications Group, Coles Book Stores Ltd., Dittler Bros. Inc., Torstar Corp. Gov. McGill U., Montreal, Que. Office: Southam Inc, 150 Bloor St W, Toronto, ON Canada M5S 2Y8

FISHER, JON HERBERT, chemical company executive; b. Wheeling, W. Va., May 14, 1947; s. Herbert Austin and Mary Melissa (Lewis) F.; m. Sarah May Lewis, Dec. 3, 1966; children: Jon Jeffrey, Matthew Austin. Student Ohio U., 1965-67; MBA, Case Western Res. U., 1982. With Harshaw Chem. Co., Cleve., 1970-83, mgr., 1976-80, bus. mgr., 1980-81, dir., 1981-83; with Harshaw Filtrol, Cleve., 1983-88, v.p., 1983-85, v.p., gen. mgr., 1985-88; v.p., bus. dir. Engelhard Corp., , Edison, N.J., 1988—; dir. Harshaw Chem. BV, DeMeern, Holland, Harshaw Murata, Kobe, Japan, Harshaw Juarez, Mexico City, Harshaw Chem. Ltd., Daventry, Eng. Asst. scoutmaster Boy Scouts Am., Geneva, Ohio, 1971—; mem. United Way Regional Com., Greater Cleve. Growth Assn., Intrasci. Research Found., Republican Nat. Com. Recipient Honorable Order Ky. Col. Mem. Dry Color Mfrs. Assn. (bd. dirs., 1st v.p., pres.), Chem. Market Research Assn., Cleve. Com. on Fgn. Relations, Case Western Reserve U. Alumni Assn., Browns Backers Assn. Club: Madison Country. Avocations: golf, 18th century antiques, photography, traveling. Office: Engelhard Corp Pigments & Additives Div Menlo Park CN 28 Edison NJ 08818

FISHER, MARSHALL DWIGHT, retired realtor; b. Davenport, Iowa, Aug. 27, 1925; s. Harvey Marshall and Marie (Gude) F.; divorced; children: Jesse, Cynthia, Heidi. BA, U. Colo., 1950. V.p., nat. sales mgr. Pen Pal, Inc., Chgo., 1952-57; owner Fisher Real Estate Co., 1961-68; v.p., dir. sales and mktg. C.J. Seibert, Inc., 1969-71; co-founder, exec. v.p., bd. dirs. Century 21 Real Estate Corp., Irvine, Calif., 1971-77; owner Fisher Idea Systems, Inc., Honolulu and Irvine, 1977—. Originator IDEAFISHER. 2d lt. USAAF, 1943-45. Home: 6650 Hawaii Kai Dr Ste 212 Honolulu HI 96825 also: Balboa Bay Club 1221 West Coast Hwy Newport Beach CA 92663 Office: Fisher Idea Systems Inc 18881 Von Karman Ave Irvine CA 92715

FISHER, MARY MAURINE, federal agency official; b. Schenectady, N.Y., July 19, 1929; d. Maurice Lee and Beatrice Mae (Harris) Prescott; m. Eugene T. Fisher, Apr. 16, 1948 (dec. 1982); children: Gene Thomas, William Lee. BA, Strayer Coll., 1952; postgrad., U. Va., 1966-89. Credit mgr. Gen. Electric Credit Corp., Washington, 1950-70; with SBA, Washington, 1970—; mem. Pres.'s adv. com. on small and minority bus., 1979-85, on Native Am. affairs, 1979-80, on reservation devel., 1978-79, on Native Am. econ. devel., 1977-78. Mem. Fairfax (Va.) Little League, 1956-74, Fairfax Indsl. Devel. Authority, 1985—; treas. Warren Woods-Joyce Heights Civic Assn., Fairfax, 1958—; chmn. Friends of Fairfax City, 1982—. Mem. Nat. Contract Mgmt. Assn. Democrat. Methodist. Home: 4203 LaMarre Dr Fairfax VA 22030

FISHER, MICHAEL BRUCE, lawyer, corporate executive; b. Montgomery, Ala., Jan. 2, 1945; s. Philip and Rita (Joss) F.; m. Noreen Rene Zidel, June 25, 1967; children—Anne Elizabeth, Alex Nicholas. B.A., U. Minn., 1967; J.D., U. Calif.-Berkeley, 1970. Bar: N.Y. 1971, Minn. 1972, U.S. Dist. Ct. Minn. 1972. Assoc. Rosenman, Colin, et al, N.Y.C., 1970-71, Mullin, Swirnoff & Weinberg, P.A., Mpls., 1972-73; staff atty. Fingerhut Corp., Mpls., 1974, assoc. gen. counsel, 1975-80, gen. counsel, 1980-83, v.p., gen. counsel, sec., 1983—; dir. Mchts. Research Council, Chgo., 1976-80. Exec. com., dir. Big Sisters Mpls., Inc., 1976-83, Big Bros./Big Sisters Mpls., Inc., 1984—; v.p., bd. dirs. Herzl Camp Assn., Inc., Mpls., 1975—; vol. Minn. Pub. TV, St. Paul, 1980—, gen. auction chmn., 1988-89. Mem. Minn. Bar Assn., ABA, Am. Corp. Counsel Assn. Minn., Minn. Retail Mchts. Assn. (trustee 1983—, exec. com. 1988—), Direct Mktg. Assn. (govt. affairs com. 1980—), 3d Class Mail Assn. (sec., bd. dirs. 1981-86, exec. vice chmn. 1987—, chmn. bd. dirs. 1988—), Parcel Shippers Assn. (v.p., bd. dirs. 1980-86, pres. 1987, chmn. bd. dirs. 1988—),Calhoun Beach Club (Mpls.). Jewish. Office: Fingerhut Cos Inc 4400 Baker Rd Minnetonka MN 55343

FISHER, RICHARD B., investment banker; b. Phila., July 21, 1936; s. Ernest W. and Doris Virginia (Rans) F.; m. Emily Hargroves, Sept. 7, 1957; children: R. Britton, Catherine Curtis, Alexander Dylan. A.B., Princeton U., 1957; M.B.A., Harvard U., 1962. Mng. dir. Morgan Stanley & Co., Inc., N.Y.C., 1970—, pres., 1984—. Trustee Princeton U., Carnegie Corp. of N.Y., Urban Inst., Historic Hudson Valley; bd. dirs. Ministers and Missionaries Benefit Bd. of Am. Baptist Chs. Club: Links, Nat. Golf Links, Blind Brook, Rockaway Hunting. Office: Morgan Stanley Group Inc 1251 Ave of the Americas New York NY 10020

FISHER, THOMAS GEORGE, lawyer, media company executive; b. Debrecen, Hungary, Oct. 2, 1931; came to U.S., 1951; s. Eugene J. and Viola Elizabeth (Rittersporn) F.; m. Rita Knisley, Feb. 14, 1960; children: Thomas G. Jr., Katherine E. Vaaler. B.S., Am. U., 1957, J.D., 1959; postgrad., Harvard U., 1956. Bar: D.C. 1959, Iowa 1977; lic. real estate broker, Iowa. Atty and legal asst. FCC, Washington, 1959-61, 65-66; pvt. law practice Washington, 1961-65, 66-69; asst. counsel Meredith Corp., N.Y.C., 1969-72; assoc. gen. counsel Meredith Corp., Des Moines, 1972-76, gen. counsel, 1976-80, v.p. gen. counsel, 1980—, corp. sec., 1988—. Contbr. articles to profl. jours. Bd. dirs. Des Moines Met. Opera Co., Indianola, 1979—; bd. dirs. Civic Music Assn., Des Moines, 1982; chmn. legis. com. Greater Des Moines C. of C., 1976-77; bd. dirs. Legal Aid Soc. Polk County, 1986—. With U.S. Army, 1952-54. Mem. Iowa State Bar Assn. (chmn. corp. counsel subcom. 1979-82), ABA, Fed. Communications Bar Assn., Polk County Bar Assn., Am. Corporate Counsel Assn., Com. Fgn. Rels. (Des Moines chpt.), Wakonda Country Club, Embassy Club (Des Moines). Office: Meredith Corp 1716 Locust St Des Moines IA 50336

FISHER, THOMAS LEGATE, II, home building company executive; b. Boston, Feb. 17, 1919; s. Thomas Knight and Margaret Burns (Vose) F.; m. Alice Lamar Mathews, Aug. 1, 1942; children: Margaret V., Mary M., Thomas Legate III. BS, U.S. Mil. Acad., 1941; MA, U. Pa., 1950; postgrad., Columbia U., 1952, MIT, 1966. Lic. realtor, N.H. Commd. officer USAF, 1937, advanced through grades to col.; with Office Joint Chiefs of Staff Def. Def., Washington, 1959-61; chief liaison team to RAF, Air Ministry, London, 1961-63; dir. collection Hdqrs. USAF Europe, 1963-65; asst. to asst. sec. def. Washington, 1966-67; ret. 1967; dir. strategic studies Browne & Shaw div. Bolt Beranek & Newman, Inc., Cambridge, Mass., 1968-70; rsch. assoc. Fletcher Sch. Law and Diplomacy, Tufts U., Medford, Mass., 1970-78; pres. Cross Country Interests, Inc., Ashland, N.H., 1981-86; sr. ptnr. Cross Country Interests Assocs., Ashland, 1986—; chmn. bd. CCI Homes, Inc., Ashland, 1986—. Contbr. articles to profl. jours.; author, editor numerous rsch. studies. Bd. dirs. World Affairs Coun., Boston, 1976-78, Wolfcreek Wilderness Sch., Blairsville, Ga., 1970-76. Mem. Nat. Assn. Home Builders, N.H. Assn. Realtors, UN Assn. U.S.A. (bd. dirs. 1980—), Overseas Press Club (Manila), Harvard Club (Boston). Republican. Episcopalian. Office: CCI Homes Inc Box 819 West St Ashland NH 03217

FISHER, WENDY ASTLEY-BELL, marketing executive; b. London, Jan. 23, 1944; came to U.S., 1947; d. Leonard Astley and Rita (Duis) Astley-Bell; m. Richard Van Mell, Mar. 21, 1970 (div. May 1980); m. Lester Emil Fisher, Jan. 23, 1981. Student, Hood Coll., 1961-63, U. Alta., Can., summer 1963; BA honors, Northwestern U., 1965; postgrad., U. Chgo., 1965-66. Lab. technician Northwestern U. Med. Sch., Chgo., 1966-67; designer Okamoto/London Studio, Chgo., 1967-71, Communications Internat., Chgo., 1971-72; freelance artist K&S Photographics, Chgo., 1972-76; dir. spl. projects Lincoln Park Zool. Soc., Chgo., 1976-81; mem. pub. rels. staff Field Enterprises, Chgo., 1981; pres., creative dir. Mailworks, Inc., Chgo., 1981—; speaker in field. Co-author: The First Hundred Years, 1975; contbr. articles to profl. jours. Bd. dirs. Jr. League Chgo., 1965-74, Vis. Nurse Assn. Chgo, 1978-82; mem. women's bd. dirs. Lincoln Park Zool. Soc., 1981-84. Recipient Gold Cert. Chgo. Savs. and Loan Assn., 1973, Award of Merit Splty. Advt. Assn., 1979; named Outstanding Women Entrepreneur Chgo. chpt. Women in Communications, 1983. Mem. Nat. Soc. Fundraising Execs. (bd. dirs. Chgo. chpt. 1982-88, Pres.'s award 1987, cert. in fundraising), Chgo. Assn. Direct Mktg. (bd. dirs. 1982-87, bd. dirs. edn. found. 1985-87), Assn. Direct Response Fundraising Counsel, Women's Direct Response Group, Direct Mktg. Assn. (Leadership award 1978), Am. Assn. Mus., Am. Assn. Zool. Parks and Aquariums, Econ. Club Chgo. Office: Mailworks Inc 230 N Michigan Ave Chicago IL 60601

FISHMAN, ALAN H., banker; b. 1946; married. B.A., Brown U., 1968; M.A. in Econs, Columbia U., 1968. With Chem. Bank, N.Y.C., 1969—; v.p. Chem. Bank, 1974-76, sr. v.p., 1976-79, sr. v.p. fin., 1979-81, exec. v.p. fin., 1981-83, sr. exec. v.p., 1983—; exec. v.p., chief fin. officer Chem. N.Y. Corp., 1981-83, sr. exec. v.p., 1983—. Office: Chem Bank 277 Park Ave New York NY 10172

FISHMAN, MARK BRIAN, computer scientist, educator; b. Phila., May 17, 1951; s. Morton Louis and Hilda (Kaplan) F.; m. Alice Faber, Feb. 20, 1977 (div. 1986). AB summa cum laude, Temple U., 1974; postgrad. Northwestern U., 1974-76; MA, U. Tex., 1980. Bilingual tchr. Wilmette Pub. Schs., 1974; research assoc., programmer, asst. instr. U. Tex., Austin, 1976-80; instr. computer and info. scis. U. Fla., Gainesville, 1980-85; asst. prof. computer sci. Eckerd Coll., St. Petersburg, Fla., 1985—, dept. coordinator, 1988—; instrnl. cons. to IBM, 1980—; cons. artificial intelligence, Battelle Corp., 1987-89, USN Naval Tng. Systems Ctr., 1987—, Advanced Techs., Inc., 1988—. Editor: Proceedings of the First Florida Artificial Intelligence Research Symposium, 1988, Proceedings of the Second Florida Artificial Intelligence Research Symposium, 1989; steering com. First Internat. Conf. Human and Machine Cognition; contbr. articles to profl. jours. U. Tex. univ. fellow, 1978-80; F.C. Austin scholar, 1975; Nat. Def. Fgn. Lang. fellow, 1974. Mem. Assn. Computing Machinery (Tchr. of Yr. award U. Fla. 1984), IEEE Computer Soc., Am. Assn. Artificial Intelligence, Assn. Computational Linguistics, Fla. Artificial Intelligence Research Soc. (proceedings chair 1988—, sec. 1988-89, v.p. 1989), Am. Soc. Engring. Edn. (faculty research fellow summer 1986), Phi Beta Kappa, Phi Kappa Phi, Upsilon Pi Epsilon. Home: 6166 Lynn Lake Dr S Saint Petersburg FL 33712 Office: Eckerd Coll Computer Sci Dept Saint Petersburg FL 33733

FISHMAN, WILLIAM SAMUEL, business executive; b. Clinton, Ind., Jan. 26, 1916; s. Max and Fannie (Dumes) F.; student Sch. Internship Polit. Sci., Washington, 1934-35; BA with highest honors in Polit. Sci., U. Ill., 1936; postgrad. U. Chgo., 1936-37; DBus. Adminstrn., Bryant Coll., 1968; LLD, Lincoln Meml. U., 1969; m. Clara K. Silvian, June 28, 1936 (dec.); children: Alan F., Fred B., David J.; m. Selma Demchick Ellis, May 9, 1982; stepchildren: Joshua Ellis, Jill Ellis Feninger. Exec. v.p. Automatic Mdsg. Co., Inc., Chgo., 1942-56, pres. 1956-59; sr. v.p. ARA Services, Inc., Phila., 1959-63, exec. v.p., 1963-64, pres., 1964-77, chief exec. officer, 1975-83, chmn. bd., 1977-84; dir. VS Services, Ltd., Can., Fidelity Bank. Phila., Fidelcor, Phila. Past pres. Jewish Publ. Soc. Am.; fellow Brandeis U.; trustee Com. for Econ. Devel. Mem. Nat. Restaurant Assn., Nat. Automatic Merchandising Assn. (dir., exec. com. pres. 1958-59), Standard Club (Chgo.), Palm Beach (Fla.) Country Club, Locust, Philmont Country, Union League (Phila.), Phi Beta Kappa, Phi Kappa Phi, Delta Sigma Rho. Jewish (past pres. synagogue). Address: 411 Haywood Rd Merion PA 19066

FISZEL, GEOFFREY LYNN, real estate executive; b. N.Y.C., Aug. 9, 1942; s. John Henry and Rebecca (Wexman) F.; B.S. in Mgmt. and Ops. Research, N.Y. U., 1974; M.S. in Acctg. and Tax (Seminar award), U. Hartford, 1976; grad. scholar program econs. of fin. Trinity Coll., 1980; m. Barbara Ann Foohey, Jan. 30, 1970; children—Sharon Lynn, Morgan Bernard, Austin Tyler, Alexander William. Cost acct. O'Malley Cos., Phoenix, 1974; regional acct., asst. regional controller Sanitas Service Corp., Hartford, Conn., 1974-75; asst. to corp. controller Bristol Brass Corp. (Conn.), 1975-76; asst. controller Security Ins. Co. of Hartford, 1976-80; controller Chase Enterprises, Inc., 1980-81, v.p., controller, 1981, sr. v.p., controller, 1985, sr. v.p. corp. and real estate devel., mergers and acquisitions, 1988—; founder Assoc. Fin. Services, 1981; tax and fin. cons. U. Conn.; cons. to minority small bus.; lectr. various tax insts. and seminars. Served with USMC, 1959-63. Mem. Center for Study of Profl. Accounting., Real Estate Securities and Syndication Inst., Fin. Execs. Inst.; bd. govs. U. Hartford Tax Inst. Author: various real estate, tax and acctg. articles. Office: 1 Commercial Pla Hartford CT 06103

FITCH, MARY KILLEEN, human resources specialist; b. Carroll, Iowa, July 15, 1949; d. Michael Francis and Mildred (Pauley) Killeen; m. David Paul Fitch, July 3, 1971. BS, Iowa State U., 1971, MS, 1975; postgrad. U. Minn., 1982—. Personnel adminstr. Control Data Corp., Roseville, Minn., 1976-77; sr. compensation analyst/employee relations rep. Honeywell, Inc., Mpls., 1977-80; human resource mgr./compensation and benefits mgr. No. Telecom, Inc., Minnetonka, Minn., 1980-82; adj. instr., teaching asst. Lakewood Community Coll./U. Minn., Mpls., 1982-84; compensation cons. Gen. Mills, Wayzata, Minn., 1984-85; mgr. compensation Northwestern Nat. Life Ins., Mpls., 1985-87; prin. compensation specialist Comml. Bldgs. Group, Honeywell, Inc., Mpls., 1987; corp. mgr. compensation Nat. Car Rental Systems, Inc., Mpls., 1989—; cons. exec. compensation Honeywell Inc., Mpls., 1984; cons. human resources Les Kraus & Assocs., Edina, Minn., 1984; pres. Personnel Mgmt. Services of Twin Cities, St. Paul, 1983—. Author: (with Paul Muchinsky) Organization Behavior and Human Performance, 1975; (with John Fossum) Personnel Psychology, 1985. Chmn., bd. dirs. Kathadin, United Way Agy., Mpls., 1985—; curriculum com. U. Minn., 1983-84. George Catt Iowa State U. scholar, 1970. Mem. Indsl. Relations Research Assn., AAUW, Am. Psychol. Assn., Acad. Mgmt., Am. Compensation Assn., Psi Chi, Phi Kappa Phi. Avocations: dressage, karate. Home: 1188 90th St E Inver Grove Heights MN 55075 Office: Nat Car Rental Systems Inc 7700 France Ave S Minneapolis MN 55435

FITCH, STONA JAMES, corporate executive; b. Wetumka, Okla., Oct. 20, 1931; s. Stona Lee and Lessie Opal (Tims) F.; m. Barbara Lou Jager, Aug. 26, 1976; children: Valerie, Stona, Michael, Susan, Melissa. B.A., U. Okla., Norman, 1955. Personnel mgr. Procter & Gamble, Cin., 1963-67; plant mgr. Procter & Gamble, Augusta, Ga., 1968-69, Kansas City, Kans., 1969-72; mgr. mfg. Paper Products div. Procter & Gamble, Cin., 1979-83; mgr. indsl. relations Procter & Gamble, Cin., 1983, v.p. mfg., 1984—. Chmn. Vocat Edn. Adv. Council. Cin., 1983-85; steering com. Leadership Cin., 1984-85; mem. Cin. Bus. Com. Edn. Task Force, 1984—; chmn. bd. dirs., past pres. Children's Family House. Served with U.S. Army, 1950-52; Korea. Democrat. Episcopalian. Clubs: Indian Hill, Camargo Racquet, Queen City (Cin.). Office: Procter & Gamble Co 1 Procter & Gamble Pla Cincinnati OH 45202

FITCHETT, DELBERT ARTHUR, economist; b. Merced, Calif., Nov. 6, 1936; s. Arthur Leroy and Birdella Phyllis (Westcott) F.; BA magna cum laude, Pomona Coll., 1958; MA, Yale U., 1959; PhD, U. Calif., Berkeley, 1963; m. Carmen Gloria de la Flor, Oct. 22, 1962; children: Kirsten, Karen, Mercedes, Francesca. Economist, Rand Corp., Santa Monica, Calif., 1964-66; vis. econs. prof. Rockefeller Found. Program, Chile, 1966-69; research assoc. Resources for Future/Ford Found., Buenos Aires, Argentina, Washington, 1969-72; econ. adv. USAID/Panama, 1972-74; with Internat. Bank for Reconstrn. and Devel., Washington, 1974—, sr. economist Econ. Devel. Inst., 1988—; lectr. U.S. Internat. Communications Agy., Panama, 1980. Served to lt., Fin. Corps, U.S. Army, 1962-64. Fulbright grantee, Peru, 1961-62. Mem. Am. Econ. Assn., Internat. Geophys. Union, Nat. Economists Club, Latin Am. Studies Assn. Club: Kenwood Golf and Country. Home: 5800 Plainview Rd Bethesda MD 20817 Office: 1818 H St NW Washington DC 20433

FITES, DONALD VESTER, tractor company executive; b. Tippecanoe, Ind., Jan. 20, 1934; s. Rex E. and Mary Irene (Sackville) F.; m. Sylvia Dempsey, June 25, 1960; children: Linda Marie. B.S. in Civil Engring., Valparaiso U., 1956; M.S., M.I.T, 1971. With Caterpillar Overseas S.A., Peoria, Ill., 1956-66; dir. internat. customer div. Caterpillar Overseas S.A., Geneva, 1966-67; asst. mgr. market devel. Caterpillar Tractor Co., Peoria, 1967-70; dir. Caterpillar Mitsubishi Ltd., Tokyo, 1971-75; dir. engine capacity expansion program Caterpillar Tractor Co., Peoria, 1975-76, mgr. products control dept., 1976-79; pres. Caterpillar Brasil S.A., 1979-81; v.p. products Caterpillar Tractor Co., Peoria, 1981-85, exec. v.p., 1985—, also bd. dirs.; bd. dirs. Farm and Indsl. Equipment Inst., First Nat. Bank of Peoria. Trustee Farm Found., 1985—, Meth. Med. Ctr., 1985—, Knox Coll., 1986—; mem. adv. bd. Salvation Army, 1985—, adminstrv. bd. First United Meth. Ch., 1986—; bd. dirs. Keep Am. Beautiful. Mem. Agrl. Roundtable (chmn. 1985-87), SAE. Republican. Clubs: Mt. Hawley Country, Creve Coeur. Home: 7614 N Edgewild Dr Peoria IL 61614 Office: Caterpillar Inc 100 NE Adams St Peoria IL 61629 *

FITT, MICHAEL GEORGE, reinsurance company executive; b. Whitstable, Kent, Eng., May 16, 1931; came to U.S., 1976; s. Walter H. and Dorothy A. (Young) F.; m. Doreen Elizabeth Leitch, Oct. 1, 1955; children: Colin, Anne, Ian. Student, Brit. schs. Jr. clk. Can. Underwriters Assn., 1953; with Royal Exchange Assurance Ltd., 1953-69; br. mgr. Royal Exchange Assurance Ltd., Montreal, Que., Can.; with Employers Reins. Corp., 1969—; exec. v.p. Employers Reins. Corp., Overland Park, Kans., 1977-79; vice chmn. bd. Employers Reins. Corp., 1979-81, chmn. bd., 1981—, also dir., pres., chief exec. officer, 1983—; chmn. bd. dirs. First Excess and Reins. Corp., Overland Park, Bates Turner, Inc., Employers Reins. Ltd., London, Nordisk Reins. Co., Copenhagen; bd. dirs. Boatmen's First Nat. Bank Kansas City, Mo., Boatmen's Bancshares, St. Louis, Gen. Electric Capital Corp., Stamford, Conn., Gen. Electric Fin. Services, Inc., Stamford, Kansas City So. Industries, Inc. Served with Brit. Navy, 1948-53. Fellow Ins. Inst. Can.; mem. Mission Hills Country Club (Kansas City). Episcopalian. Clubs: Kansas City, Mission Hills Country.

FITTERON, JOHN JOSEPH, petroleum products company executive; b. Norwalk, Conn., Sept. 25, 1941; s. Joseph A. and Olivia F.; m. Leola Kellogg, Sept. 9, 1967; children: Derek, Deanne. B.S., U. Conn., 1967. C.P.A., Conn. Mgr. Arthur Andersen & Co., N.Y.C. and Stamford, Conn., 1967-75; controller Beker Industries Corp., Greenwich, Conn., 1975-76; v.p., controller Beker Industries Corp., 1976-78, sr. v.p. fin., treas., 1979-86, dir., 1984-86; sr. v.p., chief fin. officer Getty Petroleum Corp., Jericho, N.Y., 1986—. Served with USAF, 1959-63. Mem. Am. Inst. C.P.A.s, Conn. Soc. C.P.A.s (Scholastic award 1967), Fin. Execs. Inst. Office: Getty Petroleum Corp 125 Jericho Turnpike Jericho NY 11753

FITTS, C. AUSTIN, stater agency administrator; b. Phila., Dec. 24, 1950; d. William Thomas Jr. and Barbara Kinsey (Willits) F. AA, Bennett Coll., 1970; student, Chinese U., Hong Kong, 1971; BA, U. Pa., 1974, MBA, 1978. With Dillon, Read & Co., Inc., N.Y.C., 1978-89, sr. v.p., 1984-86, mng. dir., 1986-89; asst. sec. of housing and fed. housing commr. HUD, Washington, 1989—. Mem. bd. overseers Sch. Arts & Scis., adv. bd. U. Pa., Phila., 1986—; mem. N.Y. Rep. Sate Fin. Com., N.Y.C. Food Bank, 1987-89; bd. trustees Bank St. Coll. Edn., 1988-89. Recipient award Women's Bond Club N.Y., 1986. Mem. Pub. Securities Assn. (exec. com. mcpl. securities div. 1986-89), Bond Club of N.Y., Inc., Econ. Club of N.Y. Office: US Dept HUD 451 7th St SW Washington DC 20410

FITTS, MARTIN RUSSELL, economic development executive; b. Toledo, Dec. 24, 1954; s. Harry Russell and Imogene (Donegan) F.; m. Victoria Ann McGinnis, Sept. 26, 1981; 1 child, Brian. BA, U. Toledo, 1976, M in Pub. Adminstrn., 1978. Teaching asst. U. Toledo, 1976-78; planner Toledo-Lucas County Planning Unit, 1978-79; dir. pub. affairs Toledo Area C. of C., 1979-86; exec. v.p. Lima-Allen County Econ. Devel. Council, Ohio, 1986—. Mem. adv. bd. Toledo Pub. Schs. Career Edn., 1980-84; v.p. bd. dirs. Crossroads Crisis Ctr., Lima, Ohio, 1987; bd. dirs. Neighborhood Improvement Found. Toledo Inc., 1980-84. Mem. Ohio Devel. Assn., Rotary, Lost Creek Country Club. Democrat. Roman Catholic. Home: 2630 Snowberry Ln Lima OH 45806 Office: Lima-Allen County Econ Devel Coun 147 N Main St Lima OH 45806

FITZALAN-HOWARD, BENNETT-THOMAS HENRY ROBERT, investor, public administration and policy analyst, political theorist; b. Geneva, Oct. 10, 1955; came to U.S., 1966; s. Samih S. Azzam and Alice Audeh (Argyle-Campbel) F-H. AA, Jr. Coll. Albany, N.Y., 1973; BA, Union Coll., 1973; MS, Rutgers U., 1980; MA, Russell Sage Coll., 1987. Cert. fin. analyst, broker. Adminstrv. analyst Todd Logistics, Inc., N.J. and Saudi Arabia, 1980; owner, cons. Fitz Co., Internat., Albany, 1981—. Author: Expropriation Predictability and Politics, 1979, The Politics of the U.S. Budget, 1987, The Courts in a Democratic System, 1987, White House-Wall Street: The October 87 Crash and the Post Reagan Presidency, 1987, The Politics of Deficits, 1988; contbg. author: Toward a Global Government, 1972; composer chamber music and instrumentals. Active local ARC, RP Found. Served with U.S. Army, 1973-77, Fed. Republic Germany. Mem. Acad. Polit. Sci. (life), Am. Philatelic Soc. (life), Am. Psychol. Assn., Am. Vietnam Vets. Assn., Audubon Soc., Am. Numismatic Assn. (life), Fin. Analysts Fedn. (at large), Fin. Execs. Inst. (at large), Nat. Assn. Securities Dealers (at large), N.Y. Mercantile Exchange, Am. Enterprise Inst., Brookings Inst., Am. Legion, SAR, Am. Soc. Internat. Law, Am. Bach Found., AAAS, Am. Soc. Info. Sci., Am. Conservative Union. Club: Steuben (Albany); Nat. Press, Equestrian. Office: Fitz Co Internat PO Box 1744 Albany NY 12201

FITZGERALD, EDITH JACKSON, real estate and farming executive; b. Lumberton, N.C., May 6, 1932; d. Corbett and Blanche (Wilkins) Jackson; m. James Thomas Fitzgerald, June 24, 1972; children—S. Dianne Pridgen, Candi Swinson, Angela Fitzgerald Hanno. Student in Econs., N.C. State U., 1973, postgrad., 1979. Adminstr., N.C. Cancer Inst., Lumberton, 1960-70; instr. Army Edn. Ctr., Fort Bragg, N.C., 1970-78; pres. Shamrock Farms, Hope Mills, N.C., 1985—, Shamrock Isle Estate, Ltd., Raeford, N.C.,

1985—, also founder; bd. dirs. Fayetteville Tech. Inst. Founder Shamrock Scholarship, Fayetteville Tech. Coll. Recipient Disting. Leadership award for Outstanding Service to the Field of Econs., U.S. VA recognition award, Vita award. Mem. Am. Biog. Inst. (bd. govs., dep. gov.), Am. Soc. Notaries (charter life). Democrat. Baptist. Avocations: reading, outdoor sports. Office: Shamrock Isle Estate LTD Route 2 Box 177 Raeford NC 28376

FITZGERALD, EDMUND BACON, electronics industry executive; b. Milw., Feb. 5, 1926; s. Edmund and Elizabeth (Bacon) F.; m. Elisabeth McKee Christensen, Sept. 6, 1947; children: Karen, Kathleen, Edmund Greer, Rogers Christensen. BSEE, U. Mich., 1946. With Cutler-Hammer, Inc., Milw., 1946-78, v.p. in charge engring., 1959-61, adminstrv. v.p., 1961-63, pres., 1964-69, chmn., chief exec. officer, 1969-78; vice chmn. Eaton Corp., Cleve., 1978-79; mng. dir. Hampshire Assocs., Milw., 1979-80; pres., dir. No. Telecom Inc., Nashville, 1980-82, chmn., 1985—; chmn. bd. dirs. No. Telecom Ltd., Mississauga, Ont., Can., 1985—, chief exec. officer, 1985-89, also bd. dirs.; bd. dirs. No. Telecom Ltd., 1984—, Bell Can. Enterprises Inc. Former chmn., bd. dirs. Milw. Brewers Baseball Club, Inc.; former chmn. Com. for Econ. Devel.; mem. Pres.'s Nat. Security Telecommunications Adv. Com. Served to capt. USMCR, 1943-46, 51-52. Named Man of Yr., Milw. Jr. C. of C., 1956. Mem. Nat. Elec. Mfrs. Assn. (pres. 1968), Milw. Brewers Baseball Club Inc. (past chmn. com.). Office: No Telecom Inc 127 Woodmont Blvd Nashville TN 37205 also: No Telecom Ltd, 3 Robert Speck Pkwy, Mississauga, ON Canada L4Z 2G5

FITZ-GERALD, F. GREGORY, financial services company executive; b. Wichita, Kans., June 8, 1941; s. John F. and Lexie (Beverlin) Fitz-G.; children: J. Keith, Kerry L., Lori G. B.S. in Econs., U. Pa., 1963. With Merrill Lynch & Co., Inc., N.Y.C., from 1969, exec. v.p., chief fin. officer, 1978; now exec. v.p. corp. services Comml. Credit Co., Balt.; mem. adv. council Dept. Fin. Skidmore Coll., 1986. Episcopalian. Office: Comml Credit Co 300 St Paul Pl Baltimore MD 21202

FITZGERALD, GERALD FRANCIS, banker; b. Chgo., July 6, 1925; s. John J. and Olivia (Trader) F.; m. Marjorie Webb Gosselin, Sept. 10, 1949; children: Gerald Francis Jr., James Gosselin, Thomas Gosselin, Julie Ann Fitzgerald Schauer, Peter Gosselin. BS in Commerce, Northwestern U., 1949. Salesman Premier Printing Co., 1949-53; founder, ptnr. Fitzgerald & Cooke (now Hill and Knowlton, Inc. div. J. Walter Thompson), 1953-60, v.p., 1960-64; chmn. Lake Villa Trust & Savs. Bank, 1961—, Palatine Nat. Bank, 1961—, Suburban Nat. Bank of Palatine, Suburban Bank of Hoffman-Schaumburg, Suburban Bank of Cary-Grove, Suburban Bank of Rolling Meadows, Suburban Bank of Barrington, Suburban Bank of Bartlett, 1964—; chmn., pres. Suburban Bancorp, Inc., Palatine, 1982—; cons. Am. Del. to NATO CCMS, Brussels, 1976; chmn. Suburban Computer Corp., Palatine; former dir. World Book, Inc.; lectr. in banking field. Contbr. articles to profl. jours. Bd. dirs., past pres. Inverness Assn., former mem. Govs. Adv. coun. of Ill.; past mem. bd. dirs. Ill. Racing Bd.; mem. Chgo. coun. of Fgn. Rels.; cons. Portsmouth, R.I. Abbey Sch., 1978-80; pres. assoc., Newberry Libr.; mem. John Evans Club, Northwestern U. Sgt. U.S. Army, 1944-46, ETO. Mem. Ill. Thoroughbred Owners and Breeders Found., Nat. Assn. of State Racing Commrs., Newcomers Soc., Max McGraws Wildlife Found., Delta Upsilon, Chgo. Athletic Assn., Inverness Golf Club, Dairymen's Country Club, Bankers Club, Meadow Club (bd. govs.), Post and Paddock Club (bd. dirs.), Safari Internat. Club, Thoroughbred Club of Am., Caxton Club. Home: 19 Creekside Ln Barrington Hills IL 60010 Office: Suburban Bancorp Inc 50 N Brockway Palatine IL 60067

FITZGERALD, JOHN CHARLES, JR., investment banker; b. Sacramento, May 23, 1941; s. John Charles and Geraldine Edith (McNabb) F.; BS, Calif. State U. at Sacramento, 1964; MBA, Cornell U., 1966; m. Mildred Ann Kilpatrick, June 26, 1965; children—Geraldine Kathrine, Erec John. Dir. corp. planning Bekins Co., L.A., 1966-73; mgr. corp. planning Ridder Publs., Inc., L.A., 1973-75; chief fin. officer City of Inglewood (Calif.), 1975-77; treas./contr. Inglewood Redevel. Agy., 1975-77, Inglewood Housing Authority, 1975-77; v.p. mcpl. fin. White, Weld & Co., Inc., L.A., 1977-78; v.p. pub. fin. Paine Webber Jackson & Curtis, L.A., 1978-79; v.p. and mgr. for Western region, mcpl. fin. dept. Merrill Lynch Capital Markets, L.A., 1979-82, mng. dir. Western region, mcpl. fin. dept., 1982-86; mng. dir. Seidler-Fitzgerald Pub. Fin., L.A., 1986—; sr. v.p. Seidler Amdec Securities, Inc., L.A., 1986—, also bd. dirs., mem. exec. com.; instr. fin./adminstrn. El Camino Coll., Torrance, Calif., 1977—; bd. dirs., mem. exec. com. Seidler Amdle Securities Inc. Chmn. bd. dirs., exec. com., treas., chmn. fund raising com. L.A. chpt. Am. Heart Assn., 1977—; bd. dirs. Daniel Freeman Hosps. Inc., Corondelet Health Care Corp., Freeman Health Ventures, Inglewood; alumni coun. mem. Johnson Grad. Sch. of Mgmt. Cornell U. Mem. Fin. Execs. Inst., Mcpl. Fin. Officers Assn., Calif. Soc. Mcpl. Fin. Officers, League Calif. Cities, So. Calif. Corp. Planners Assn. (past pres.), L.A. Bond, Beta Gamma Sigma. Republican. Clubs: Jonathan, The Calif., Palos Verdes Country, Rancho Verdes Racquet. Lodge: Rotary.

FITZGERALD, KEVIN PETER, corporate finance executive; b. Roslyn, N.Y., Aug. 28, 1956; s. Eugene John and Veronica (Luscombe) F.; m. Ivona K. Zok, Aug. 11, 1984. BSEE, Carnegie-Mellon U., 1978; MBA in Fin., Fordham U., 1983. Engring. cons. Gen. Dynamics, Los Angeles, 1978-79; sr. cons. Sperry Systems Corp., Great Neck, N.Y., 1979-82; mgr. mergers and acquisitions group Deloitte Haskins & Sells, N.Y.C., 1982-87; mng. dir. Jennison & Fitzgerald, Inc., Purchase, N.Y., 1987—. Mem. Southampton (N.Y.) Hosp. Benefits Assn., 1982-84, Children's Aid Soc., 1986-87. Home: 4 Charlotte Pl Hartsdale NY 10530 Office: Jennison & Fitzgerald Inc 3010 Westchester Ave Purchase NY 10577

FITZGERALD, MICHAEL ANTHONY, insurance company executive; b. Boston, Mar. 18, 1944; s. John George and Margaret (McAllister) F.; m. Jeanne Zembiski, June 2, 1973; children: Sean Patrick, Laura Margaret. BA, Boston Coll., 1971; postgrad., Boston U., 1974-75. Underwriter Aetna Ins., Boston, 1964-68; v.p., chmn. nat. utility com. Alexander & Alexander, Boston, 1968-84; v.p., dep. regional mgr. utility com. Jardine Emett and Chandler, Boston, 1984—. Served with USCG, 1964-70. Democrat. Roman Catholic. Club: Andover (Mass.) Country. Home: 8 Worthen Pl Andover MA 01810

FITZGERALD, WALTER EARL, chemical company executive; b. Buffalo, N.Y., Dec. 20, 1932; s. Walter Earl Sr. and Mazie (Moritz) F.; m. Evelyn Carroll Everitt, Feb. 25, 1956; children: Walter E. III, Shawn E. BS in Chem. Engring., Lafayette Coll., 1954; postgrad., Command & Gen. Staff Coll., 1977. Various engring. and mgmt. positions Hooker Chem. & Plastics Corp., Niagara Falls, N.Y., 1954-55, 57-64, dept. head, 1965-67; asst. prodn. supt., fine chems. Hooker Chem. & Plastics Corp., Niagara Falls, 1968-70; prodn. supt. Niagara Works, Niagara Falls, 1971-72; mfg. mgr. Durez Plastics Div., Niagara Falls, 1972-73; prodn. mgr. Speciality Chem. Div., Niagara Falls, 1974-75, cpr. mgr. of energy, 1975-76; v.p., corp. officer Diamond Crystal Salt Co., St. Clair, Mich., 1977-86, exec. v.p., 1986-88; pres. Sol-Aire Salt & Chem. Co., Lake Point, Utah, 1987—; v.p. prodn. Internat. Salt Co., Clarks Cummit, Pa., 1988—; pres. Diamond Energy Co., St. Clair, 1983-88; chmn. bd. D.C. Transport Co., St. Clair, 1986—, Diamond Terminals, Port Newark, N.Y., 1986—. Councilman City of St. Clair, 1986-88; pres. St. Clair County United Way, Port Huron, Mich., 1986. Mem. Otsi Keta Yacht Club (vice commodore 1988-89). Republican. Home: PO Box 215 113 Upland Terr Clarks Summit PA 18411 Office: Internat Salt Co Abington Exec Park Morgan Hwy Clarks Summit PA 18411

FITZGERALD, WALTER GEORGE, marketing executive; b. N.Y.C., Aug. 5, 1936; s. George Harold and Florence Mary (Rank) F.; m. Gwen Ann, Aug. 27, 1957 (div. May 1984); children: Pamela, Drew. BS, NYU, 1963. Mktg. research analyst Ted Bates & Co., N.Y.C., 1956-59; sr. consumer analyst Lennen and Newell, Inc., N.Y.C., 1959-63; mgr. mktg. research Nestle Co., White Plains, N.Y., 1963-67; mktg. dir. Y&S Candies div. Hershey (Pa.) Foods, 1967-79; gen. mgr. Ward Candies Fund Raising div. Terson, Inc., Chgo., 1979-82; v.p. mktg. John Middleton, Inc., King of Prussia, Pa., 1982; cons. Boyer Bros., Altoona, Pa., 1982. Contbr. numerous articles to profl. jours., 1967-79; patentee in field, 1986. Fellow Am. Mktg. Assn.; mem. Am. Mgmt. Assn. Republican. Uniterian. Office: John Middleton Inc Church and Hillside Rds King of Prussia PA 19406

FITZGERALD, WILLIAM T., manufacturing company executive; b. Akron, Ohio, Sept. 1, 1926. Br. sales supr. Cooper Tire & Rubber Co., Findlay, Ohio, 1953-59, west coast sales mgr., 1959-61, sales mgr. Cooper brand, 1961-66, asst. v.p. sales, 1966-68, v.p. mktg., 1968-71, pres. tire div., 1971—, exec. v.p., 1982—, also bd. dirs.; bd. dirs. Greater Ohio Corp., Findlay, Ohio. Exec. com., bd. dirs. Community Devel. Found., Findlay, 1984—; pres. Put-Han-Sen Area Council Boy Scouts, Findlay, 1977-79. Served in USN, 1944-46. Mem. Am. Mgmt. Assn. Roman Catholic. Clubs: Findlay Country, Palmetto Pine Country. Office: Cooper Tire & Rubber Co Lima & Western Aves Findlay OH 45840

FITZPATRICK, FRANCIS JAMES, lawyer; b. N.Y.C., Apr. 29, 1916; s. Francis James and Susan Clemens (Tompkins) FitzP.; m. Ethel Marie Peters, Mar. 2, 1956. A.B., Duke U., 1938; postgrad. Harvard U. Grad. Sch. Bus. Adminstrn., 1939-40; J.D., Cornell U., 1947. Bar: Iowa 1951, N.J. 1954. Exec. trainee U.S. Fidelity & Guaranty Co., N.Y., 1940-41; counsellor, Western Electric Co., Kearny, N.J., 1942-45; practice, Orange, N.J., 1954—. Served with M.C., U.S. Army, 1941-42. Mem. ABA, N.J. State Bar Assn., Essex County Bar Assn., Am. Judicature Soc., Cornell Law Student Assn. (sec.-treas.), Cornell U. Law Assn., Duke U. Met. Alumni Assn., Delta Theta Phi (pres.), Am. Legion (former judge adv. Orange), Sigma Alpha Epsilon. Home: 5 Ledgewood Court Warren Township NJ 07060 Office: 308 Main St Orange NJ 07050

FITZPATRICK, HAROLD FRANCIS, lawyer; b. Jersey City, Oct. 16, 1947; s. Harold G. and Anne Marie Fitzpatrick; m. Joanne M. Merry, Sept. 22, 1973; children: Elizabeth, Kevin, Matthew, Christopher. AB, Boston Coll., 1969; MBA, NYU, 1971; JD, Harvard U., 1974. Bar: N.J. 1974, U.S. Dist. Ct. N.J. 1974, U.S. Ct. Internat. Trade, 1986. Securities analyst Chase Manhattan Bank, N.Y.C., 1970-71, Brown Bros., Harriman & Co., N.Y.C., 1971; staff asst. U.S. Senate, Washington, 1972; law clk. to assoc. justice N.J. Supreme Ct., Trenton, 1974-75; assoc. Cleary, Gottlieb, Steen & Hamilton, N.Y.C., 1975-78; sr. ptnr. Waters, McPeherson, McNeill & Fitzpatrick, Secaucus and Bayonne, N.J., 1978—; gen. counsel Housing Authority City of Bayonne, 1976—, Dry Color Mfrs. Assn., Alexandria, Va., 1978—, N.J. Assn. Housing & Redevel. Authorities, Bayonne, 1979—, Housing Authority Town of Secaucus, N.J., 1980-88, Rahway Geriatrics Ctr. Inc., N.J., 1981—, Housing Authority City of Englewood, N.J., 1985—, Housing Authority City of Rahway, N.J., 1986—, Edgewater Mcpl. Utilities Authority, 1986—. Mem. ABA, N.J. Ban Assn., Hudson County Bar Assn. (trustee 1984-87, officer 1987—), Nat. Assn. Bond Lawyers, Nat. Health Lawyers Assn., Am Soc. Assn. Execs. (legal sect.), Beta Gamma Sigma. Office: Waters McPherson McNeill Fitzpatrick PA 400 Plaza Dr Secaucus NJ 07094

FITZPATRICK, JOHN HENRY, corporate finance executive; b. Chgo., Nov. 1, 1956; s. John Michael and Bernice Hilma (Lambke) F.; m. Susan Gail Beaman, June 15, 1985; children: Sarah, Elizabeth. BBA, Loyola U., Chgo., 1979. CPA; chartered fin. analyst. Fin. analyst Kemper Corp., Long Grove, Ill., 1978-79, dir. investor rels., 1979-86, v.p. fin., 1986—. Named James S. Kemper Found. scholar, 1974-78. Mem. Nat. Investor Rels. Inst. (treas. 1980-81), Investment Analyst Soc. Chgo., Ill. Soc. CPAs. Republican. Roman Catholic. Home: 603 S Summit Barrington IL 60010 Office: Kemper Corp Kemper Ctr B4 Long Grove IL 60049

FITZPATRICK, JOHN MALCOLM, manufacturing executive; b. N.Y.C., Jan. 12, 1924; s. James M. and Laura B. (Stevenson) F.; m. Patricia Roche, June 9, 1945; children—Kathleen, James, Michael, Barbara, Robert, Brian. BS, U.S. Mil. Acad., 1945. Commd. 2nd lt. U.S. Air Force, 1945, advanced through grades to capt., resigned, 1953; chief test pilot Gen. Dynamics Corp., San Diego, 1953-62, mgr., Houston, 1962-67, dir. aerospace systems, Washington, 1967-75; v.p. govt. relations Figgie Internat., Inc., Washington, 1975—. Fellow Soc. Exptl. Test Pilots, AIAA (assoc.); mem. Balloon Fedn. Am. Republican. Roman Catholic. Home: 1811 Briar Ridge Ct McLean VA 22101 Office: Figgie Internat Inc 1735 Jefferson Davis Hwy Arlington VA 22202

FITZPATRICK, PETER BRYAN, lawyer; b. New Orleans, June 30, 1945; s. William H. and Frances (Westfeldt) F.; m. Anne L. Wallace, Aug. 24, 1968; children: Bryan W.W., Lydia W.C. BA, Princeton U., 1968; MA, Stanford U., 1969; JD, U. Va., 1973; postgrad. St. Antony's Coll. Oxford Univ., 1976. Bar: Va. 1974, N.Y. 1977, D.C. 1978. Assoc. Winthrop, Stimson, Putnam & Roberts, N.Y.C., 1976-80; asst. counsel Newsweek Inc., N.Y.C., 1980-83; counsel Hunton & Williams, Norfolk, Va., 1983—. Contbr. articles to profl. jours. Trustee St. Antony's Coll. Trust, Pembroke Coll. Found., Oxford, 1986; bd. advisors Va. Ctr. World Trade, Norfolk, 1984; pres. World Affairs Council Greater Hampton Rds., Norfolk, 1986. Mem. ABA, D.C. Bar Assn., Va. Bar Assn., Assn. Bar City N.Y. (com. human rights). Avocations: tennis, hiking, squash, reading, history. Office: Hunton & Williams 101 St Paul's Blvd Ste 1301 Norfolk VA 23510

FITZPATRICK, SUSAN G. BEAMAN, management consultant; b. Oct. 15, 1954; d. Ralph P. and Gloria D. (Nelmark) Beaman; m. John H. Fitzpatrick, June 15, 1985; children: Sarah, Elizabeth. B.S., registered O.T., U. Ill., 1976. Supr. outpatient services Rehab. Inst. of Chgo., 1976-79; br. mgr. Kemper Group, Chgo., 1979-80, div. mgr. Midwest, 1980-81, asst. dir. Natlsco Rehab. Mgmt., Inc., 1981-82, v.p., 1983-85; mgmt. cons. Coopers & Lybrand, Chgo., 1985-86; v.p., gen. mgr. Bensinger, DuPont & Assoc, 1986-88; mng. ptnr. Fitzpatrick Enterprises, 1988—; lectr. in field. Contbr. articles to profl. jours. Mem. Nat. Occupational Therapy Assn. Republican. Home: 603 S Summit Barrington IL 60010

FITZPATRICK, WILLARD EDMUND, insurance company executive; b. Milw., Oct. 26, 1924; s. Christopher Edward and Catherine Alice (Mee) F.; m. Jeanne Keller, Feb. 5, 1955; children—Gerald, John, Michael. B.A., U. Wis., 1952, J.D., 1952. Bar: Wis. bar 1952. Claims atty. Am. Family Ins. Co., Madison, Wis., 1952-55; claims mgr. Bolivar Ins. Co., Bogotá, Colombia, 1955-57; exec. v.p. Universal Ins. Co., Bogotá, 1957-60; with Nationwide Ins. Cos., Columbus, Ohio, 1960—, asst. to pres., 1965-72; v.p. sec., asst. to gen. chmn. 1965-72, 1972—; mem. Internat. Coop. Ins. Devel. Bur. Served with AUS, 1943-46. Mem. Wis. Bar Assn., Soc. C.P.C.U.'s, Soc. C.L.U.'s, Am. Soc. Corp. Secs. Republican. Roman Catholic. Club: Univ. (Columbus). Home: 4169 Rowanne Rd Columbus OH 43214 Office: Nationwide Mut Ins Co 1 Nationwide Pla Columbus OH 43216

FITZPATRICK, WILLIAM JOSEPH, lawyer, corporate executive; b. N.Y.C., June 30, 1941; s. William J. and Alice Marie (Mahon) F.; m. Maureen L. Brown, Nov. 26, 1983; children: Christen Marie, Lauren Catharine. BA, St. Bonaventure U., 1963; LLB, Columbia U., 1968. Bar: N.Y. 1969, Calif. 1973. Assoc. Gilbert, Segall & Young, N.Y.C., 1968-72; exec. v.p., gen. counsel, sec. Ticor, L.A., 1972-86, CalFed, Inc., L.A., 1987-89; dep. chmn., chief exec. officer Anglo Am. Ins. Co. Ltd., London, 1989—; pub. counsel, L.A., 1983-84. Bd. dirs. L.A. Boys Club, 1982-83. Mem. ABA, Am. Soc. for Corp. Secs., L.A. County Bar Assn. Home: 50 Jubilee Pl, London SW3 3TQ, England Office: Anglo Am Ins Co Ltd, 85 Gracechurch St, London EC3V 0AA, England

FITZSIMMONS, J(OSEPH) HEATH, insurance company executive; b. Wilkes Barre, Pa., Nov. 23, 1942; s. Francis Patrick and Regina (Hayes) F.; m. Sophie S. Fitzsimmons, Sept. 8, 1962; children—Gregory J., Raymond H., Douglas P. B.B.A., Iona Coll., 1965; postgrad., Cornell U., 1979. C.P.A., N.Y. Sr. acct. Deloitte, Haskins & Sells, N.Y.C., 1965-71; jr. officer Aetna Life & Casualty Co., Hartford, Conn., 1971-75, asst. v.p. investor relations, 1975-77, asst. v.p. corp. planning, 1977-81, asst. v.p. corp. comptroller, 1981-82, v.p. corp. controllers, 1982-83, v.p., corp. controller, 1983—; dir. Community Acctg. Aid & Services, Inc., Hartford, Morton Smith Inc., Providence; assoc. dir. Conn. Econ. Devel. Corp., Hartford; mem. exec. com. Conn. Pub. Expenditure Council Inc. Pres. Squadron Line Sch., PTA, 1974-75; mem. budget rev. com. United Way Greater Hartford, 1975-76, acctg. adv. council U. Conn., Fin. Acctg. Standards Bd., Fin. Ins. Adv. Group. With U.S. Army, 1961. Mem. Am. Inst. CPAs (ins. cos. com. 1982-85), Fin. Acctg. Standards Bd., Fin. Instrument Adv. Group, Soc. Ins. Accts., Am. Council Life Ins. (fin. reporting com. 1984—), Am. Ins. Assn. (fin. reporting com. 1984—), N.Y. State Soc. CPAs, Conn. Soc. CPAs (bd. govs. 1981-84). Office: Aetna Casualty & Surety Co 151 Farmington Ave Hartford CT 06156

FITZSIMMONS, ROBERT JAMES, finance company executive; b. Detroit, Dec. 10, 1940; s. Nicholas P. and Emma J. (Kearns) F.; m. Rosemarie Balestriere, Nov. 23, 1974. BS, Marquette U., 1962. Bond analyst Continental Ill. Bank, Chgo., 1964-66; credit mgr. Union Carbide Corp., Chgo., 1966-68; asst. treas. Greyhound Fin. Corp., Chgo., 1968-72; treas. Greyhound Fin. Corp., Phoenix, 1972-80, v.p., treas., 1980—; bd. dirs. Comml. State Bank, Phoenix, 1987. With U.S. Army, 1962-64. Recipient scholarship Evans Scholars Found., Golf, Ill., 1958. Roman Catholic. Office: Greyhound Fin Corp Greyhound Tower Phoenix AZ 85077

FITZSIMONDS, ROGER LEON, bank holding company executive; b. Milw., May 21, 1938; s. Stephen Henry and Wilhelmine Josephine (Rhine) F.; m. Leona I. Schwegler, July 11, 1958; children: Susan Fitzsimonds Hedrick, Stephen. BBA in Fin., U. Wis.-Milw., 1960, MBA in Fin., 1971. Mgmt. trainee 1st Wis. Nat. Bank, Milw., 1964-66, 1st level officer, 1966-69, exec. v.p. retail banking and real estate fin., 1978-84, exec. v.p. comml. fin. group, 1984-86, pres., 1986-87; pres. 1st Wis. Corp., 1987-88, 1st Wis. Bank Green Bay, 1970-73, 1st Wis. Mortgage Corp., 1974-89; pres. Firstar Corp., Milw., 1989—, also bd. dirs.; bd. dirs. 1st Wis. Nat. Bank, Miw., 1st Wis. Trust Co., Marinette Marine Corp. Bd. dirs. Milw. Boys and Girls Club, Milw., 1984—, Elmore Found., Milw., 1986—, Competitive Wis., Inc.; vice chmn., bd. dirs. Columbia Hosp., Milw., 1986—; mem. Greater Milw. Com., Gov. Tommy Thompson's Bus. Roundatble, Gov. Tommy Thompson's Council on Econ. Issues.; mem. adv. council Sch. Bus. U. Wis.; trustee The Nature Conservancy; past pres., dir. exec. com. U. Wis., Milw., Milw. Found., Milw. Boys and Girls Club; Served to capt. U.S. Army, 1960-64. Recipient Alumni of Yr. award U. Wis.-Milw., 1983. Mem. Wis. Assn. Mfrs. and Commerce (vice chmn., bd. dirs. 1988—), Assn. Rec. City Bankers, Am. Bankers Assn. (com. mem. 1987—). Republican. Lutheran. Club: Milwaukee (bd. dirs., trustee), Milw. Country. Home: 9155 N Upper River Rd Milwaukee WI 53217 Office: 1st Wis Corp 777 E Wisconsin Ave Milwaukee WI 53202

FITZSIMONS, SHARON RUSSELL, logistics and customer service executive; b. Toronto, Ont., Can., June 25, 1945; d. Leslie Alfred and Winifred Marjorie (Williston) Russell; m. John Henry Fitzsimons, Jan. 4, 1969; children: Luke Edward, Michael Russell. BA, U. So. Calif., 1968; MA, Calif. State U., 1971; MS in Bus. Adminstrn., U. Calif., Irvine, 1978. Mgr. research William Pereira Assocs., Newport Beach, Calif., 1970-71; asst. mgr. interior design Concept Environment Inc. subs. Ford Motor Co., Orange County, Calif., 1971-72; v.p. Urban Interface Group, Orange County, 1972-74; cons. in field, 1975-76; mgr. strategic planning Mission Viejo Co., Orange County, 1976-80; mgr. fin. Philip Morris Internat., N.Y.C., 1980-82, asst. treas., 1982-84, logistics exec., Melbourne, Australia, 1984-86, dir. U.S. export logistics and customer service, N.Y.C., 1987—. Office: c/o Philip Morris Internat 120 Park Ave New York NY 10017

FJELDGAARD, KJELD, oil company executive; b. Dronninglund, Denmark, Nov. 4, 1946; s. Gunnar and Elly (Nielsen) F.; m. Kirsten Larsen, Oct. 30, 1971; children: Kristian, Kristopher, Kjeld Alexander. BS in Mech. Engring., Aalborg U. Ctr., Denmark, 1971; New Frontiers of Mgmt., Columbia U., 1986. Petroleum engr. Gulf Oil, Denmark, 1972-75, Chevron Research, Los Angeles, 1975; sr. petroleum engr. Shell, Brunei, Indonesia, 1979-81; sr. petroleum engr. Maersk Oil & Gas, Copenhagen, 1976-79, ops. mgr., 1981-84, v.p., 1984-85, sr. v.p., 1985-86, prodn. dir., 1987—; chmn. North Sea Operators Com., Copenhagen, 1985—. Contbr. to profl. publs. Mem. Soc. Petroleum Engrs. Office: Maersk Oil & Gas, Esplanaden 50, 1263 Copenhagen Denmark

FLACH, WERNER, publisher; b. Hof/Saale, Bavaria, Germany, Feb. 2, 1935; s. Karl and Gertrud (Kuenzel) F.; m. Dorette Ebert, Sept. 13, 1958 (div. Jan. 1970); 1 child, Thomas. Pres. Werner Flach, Internat. Sci. Booksellers, Frankfurt, Fed. Republic Germany, 1957—, IDD Verlag Für Internat. Dokumentation Werner Flach KG, Frankfurt, 1973—, Verlag Für Humanistische Psychologie Werner Flach KG, Frankfurt, 1978—. Editor Jour. Sensus Kommunikation; contbr. articles to profl. jours. Mem. Börsenverein Deutschen Buchhandels. Office: Internat Sci Booksellers, Heddernheimer Landstr 78 a, 6000 Frankfurt M 50 Hessen Federal Republic of Germany

FLAHARTY, ROBERT RICHARD, management consultant, executive; b. Redding, Calif., Apr. 29, 1948; s. Richard Kenneth and Shirley Ann (Speece) Dimich; m. Cora Rebecca Marufo, Mar. 17, 1979; 1 child, Elena Ann. BS, U. Calif., Berkeley, 1970; MS, U. Calif., Los Angeles, 1971; postgrad., U. So. Calif., 1975-76. Cert. mgmt. cons. Systems analyst Pacific Stock Exchange, Los Angeles, 1972-73; mgmt. info. systems mgr. Jacobs Engring. Group, Pasadena, Calif., 1973-74; assoc. prof. Los Angeles Community Coll., 1974-78; mgr. Mgmt. Design Assocs., Bellevue, Wash., 1978-83; dir. Mgmt. Design Assocs., Denver, 1983-86; pres. Mgmt. Design Assoc., Denver, 1986—; adv. dir. Travel King, Boulder, Colo., 1985—; bd. dirs. Corus, Inc., Denver; instr. Am. Inst. CPA's, Columbus, Ohio, 1985—. Developer seminars on mgmt., info. tech. in bus. and mgmt. of an acctg. practice. Served to capt. U.S. Army, 1971-72. Mem. Inst. Mgmt. Cons. Home: 7926 E Windcrest Row Parker CO 80134 Office: Mgmt Design Assocs 4600 S Ulster St Ste 530 Denver CO 80237

FLAHERTY, DAVID THOMAS, JR., lawyer; b. Boston, June 17, 1953; S. David Thomas Sr. and Nancy Ann (Hamill) F.; m. Margaret Lynn Hoyle, Oct. 2, 1986; 1 child, Alexandra Lynn. BS in Math., German, U. N.C., 1974, JD, 1978. Bar: Mass. 1979, N.C. 1979, U.S. Dist. Ct. (we. dist.) N.C. 1979, U.S. Dist. Ct. (mid. dist.) N.C. 1981, U.S. Ct. Appeals (4th cir.) 1981, U.S. Tax Ct. 1982, U.S. Supreme Ct., 1987. Assoc. Wilson & Palmer, Lenoir, N.C., 1979-80, Ted West P.A., Lenoir, 1980-82; ptnr. Robbins, Flaherty & Lackey, Lenoir, 1982-85, Robbins & Flaherty, Lenoir, 1985-88, Delk, Flaherty, Swanson and Hartshorn, P.A., Lenoir, 1988—; mem. N.C. Ho. Reps. 46th Dist. Mem. exec. com. Caldwell County Reps., Lenoir, 1985-86, 88—. Mem. N.C. Bar Assn., Assn. Trial Lawyer Am., N.C. Acad. Trial Lawyers, 25th Judicial Dist. Bar Assn., Reps. Men's Club, Young Reps., Blue Key. Methodist. Home: 228 Pennton Ave SW Lenoir NC 28645 Office: Delk Flaherty Swanson and Hartshorn PA One Lenoir Sq Lenoir NC 28645

FLAHERTY, JOHN JOSEPH, quality assurance company executive; b. Chgo., July 24, 1932; s. Patrick J. and Mary B. F.; BEE, U. Ill., 1959; m. Norrine Grow, Nov. 20, 1954; children: John, Bridgette, George, Eileen, Daniel, Mary, Michael, Amy. Design engr. Admiral Corp., Chgo., 1959-60; project engr. Magnaflux Corp., Chgo., 1960-79, v.p., mgr. research and engring., 1979-84, v.p., mgr. mktg. and sales, 1984-86; v.p., gen. mgr. electronic products, 1986-88; pres. Flare Tech., Chgo., 1988—. Served with AUS, 1951-53. Mem. Am. Soc. Non-Destructive Testing, IEEE, Am. Soc. Metals (tech. bd. dirs.). Roman Catholic. Numerous patents, publs. on nondestructive testing, including med. ultrasonic; laser scanning. Home: 671 Grosvener Ln Elk Grove Village IL 60007 Office: 6140 W Higgins Rd Chicago IL 60640

FLAKE, JOHN J., real estate executive; b. Little Rock, Jan. 31, 1947; s. Leon and Margerite (Simpson) F.; m. Karen Elizabeth Goodhart, June 27, 1970; children: Jessica, Rebecca. AB, U. Ill., 1970; MBA in Corp. Fin., Babson Coll., 1972. Mgr. credit dept. Comml. Nat. Bank, Little Rock, 1972-73; realtor Barnes, Quinn, Flake & Anderson, Little Rock, 1973-79; chmn., pres. Flake & Co. Inc., Little Rock, 1979—; bd. dirs. 1st Comml. Bank, Little Rock, 1986—, Ark. Power & Light Co., Little Rock, 1987—, United Broadcasting Co., 1985-88, Little Rock Airport Commn., 1987—. Pres. Ark. Symphony Orchestra Soc., Little Rock, 1984-85, Downtown Partnership, Little Rock, 1987-88. Recipient of Roger W. Babson scholar, Babson Coll., Babson Park, Mass., 1972; award Big Bros. Found., Little Rock, 1976. Mem. Greater Little Rock C. of C. (chmn. 1987-88), Ark. Real Estate Assn., Nat. Assn. Realtors. Democrat. Roman Catholic. Office: Flake & Co Inc 425 W Capitol Ste 300 Little Rock AR 72201

FLAM, ERIC, engineer; b. Vienna, Austria, Feb. 14, 1935; came to U.S., 1938; s. Abraham Selig and Anna (Aptowitzer) F.; m. Loretta Irene Raab, May 12, 1963; children: Brenda Raymonde, Edward Ira. BS in Chem. Engring., CCNY, 1956; MS, So. Meth. U., 1961; PhD, NYU, 1968. Registered profl. engr., N.Y. Engr. propulsion LTV Industries, Dallas, 1958-60; materials scientist Tex. Instruments, Inc., Dallas, 1960-62; project engr. Singer

Corp., Little Falls, N.J., 1962-63; research fellow NYU, N.Y.C., 1963-67; research scientist Johnson & Johnson, New Brunswick, N.J., 1967-74; group leader Johnson & Johnson, New Brunswick, 1974-76, sr. group leader, 1976-80; mgr. research, devel., quality assurance C.R. Bard, Inc., Murray Hill, N.J., 1980-84; pres. NTL Assocs., Inc., E. Brunswick, N.J., 1985—; adv. com. N.Y. Acad. Scis., 1974-78; research advisor Breast Examination Bras, East Brunswick, 1975-83; adj. asst. prof. U. Medicine and Dentistry of N.J.-Robert Wood Johnson Med. Sch., Piscataway, 1977—; com. mem. Internat. Standards Orgn., Washington, 1981-84. Patentee in field. Bd. dirs. Raritan Valley Young Men-Young Women Hebrew Assn., Highland Park, N.J., 1978-83. Recipient fellowship NIH, 1963, Founders Day award NYU, 1969. Mem. Internat. Assn. Enterostomal Therapists, Am. Mktg. Assn., Am. Urol. Assn. Allied, NYU Bus. Forum, Tau Beta Pi. Home: 29 Ainsworth Ave East Brunswick NJ 08816 Office: NTL Assocs Inc 29 Ainsworth Ave East Brunswick NJ 08816

FLAM, MARVIN ARNOLD, architect, real estate consultant; b. N.Y.C., May 2, 1934; s. Simon and Minnie (Friedman) F.; m. Evelyn Pearl Schwartz, June 12, 1955; children: Lawrence Scott, Paul Howard, Stacey Barbara. BArch, U. Mich., 1957. Registered architect, N.Y., N.J., Conn., Mass., Mich., Ill., Ind., S.C., Fla., N.C. Draftsman Parsons, Brinckerhoff, Quade, Douglas, N.Y.C., 1957-60, Fellgraf, Ballou, Daly, Ridgefield Park, N.J., 1960-61; prin. Marvin A. Flam, Architect, Pearl River, N.Y., 1961-73, Ridgewood, N.J., 1973-77, Clearwater, Fla., 1986—; v.p. H.B.E. Corp., St. Louis, 1977-83; exec. v.p. Brant Constrn. Mgmt., Griffith, Ind., 1984-86; chmn. Archtl. Rev. Bd., Orangetown, N.Y., 1965-70; cons. I.D. Assocs., Inc., N.Y.C., 1968—; pres. Madecom Group, Clearwater, 1986—. Mem. Hist. Rev. Bd., Orangetown, 1965-70. Mem. AIA, Am. Soc. Hosp. Engrs., Nat. Fire Protection Assn., So. Standard Bldg. Code, Fla. Assn. AIA. Home: 2742 Sea Pine Circle Clearwater FL 34621 Office: The Madecom Group Inc 3023 Eastland Blvd Clearwater FL 34621

FLAMM, DONALD, radio broadcaster, writer, real estate, investments, theatrical producer; b. Pitts., Dec. 11, 1899; s. Louis and Elizabeth (Jason) F.; ed. pub. schs. N.Y., extension courses N.Y. U.; m. Elayne Knee, Dec. 9, 1979. Pub. mags. and books, 1921-30; owner, operator radio sta. WMCA, N.Y., 1925-41, WPCH, N.Y., 1927-32; pres. and operator Intercity Network, 1927-41; co-owner WPAT, Paterson, N.J., 1942-48; former owner, operator Sta. WMMM-AM, WDJF-FM, Westport, Conn., 1959-87; now engaged in theatre, real estate and social welfare activities; theatrical producer, N.Y.C., London, Eng.; pres. Flamm Realty Corp., N.Y.; dir. Oscar Lewestein Plays, Ltd., London, 1959-76. Former mem. N.Y. exec. com. Anti-Defamation League, mem. N.Y. regional bd., hon. life mem. nat. commn.; past chmn. N.J. Civil War Centennial Commn.; charter founder Eleanor Roosevelt Inst. Cancer Research, Denver; bd. dirs., v.p. Hebrew Free Loan Soc. N.Y.; past pres., trustee Mt. Neboh Temple, N.Y.C.; trustee, former officer Manfred Sakel Inst. Served as spl. liaison officer OWI, World War II; formulated plans for Am. Broadcasting Sta. in Eng. and Voice of Am. Mem. Royal TV Soc. (London), Internat. Radio and TV Soc. U.S.A., Drama Desk, United Hunts Racing Assn., Pa. Soc. Clubs: Rockefeller Ctr., Cath.Actors Guild, Friars, Dutch Treat, Alpine Country; Le Club (N.Y.C.); Annabel's, White Elephant (London). Contbr. articles on theatre, radio and TV to trade publs. in U.S. and Eng. Office: 25 Central Pk W New York NY 10023

FLAMSON, RICHARD JOSEPH, III, banker; b. Los Angeles, Feb. 2, 1929; s. Richard J. and Mildred (Jones) F.; m. Arden Black, Oct. 5, 1951; children: Richard Joseph IV, Scott Arthur, Michael Jon, Leslie Arden. B.A., Claremont Men's Coll., 1951; cert. Pacific Coast Banking Sch., U. Wash., 1962. With Security Pacific Nat. Bank, Los Angeles, 1955—, v.p., 1962-69, sr. v.p., 1969-70, exec. v.p. corp. banking dept., 1970-73, vice-chmn., 1973-78, pres., chief exec. officer, 1978-81, chmn., chief exec. officer, 1981—, dir., 1981-85; also dir. Security Pacific Corp., Los Angeles; vice-chmn. Security Pacific Corp., 1973-78, pres., 1978-81, chief exec. officer, 1978—, chmn., 1981—; bd. dirs. Northrop Corp., Kaufman and Broad, GTE Calif. Inc. Trustee Claremont Men's Coll. 1st lt. AUS, 1951-53. Mem. Res. City Bankers, Robert Morris Assocs., Town Hall, Stock Exchange Club. Clubs: Caif. Los Angeles Country; Balboa Bay (Newport Beach, Calif.), Balboa Yacht (Newport Beach, Calif.). Office: Security Pacific Corp 333 S Hope St Los Angeles CA 90071 *

FLANAGAN, EUGENE JOHN THOMAS, lawyer; b. N.Y.C., Mar. 27, 1923; s. Thomas F. and Louise V. (Verhoff) F.; m. Lucette A. Stumberg, Sept. 7, 1951; children: Claire (Mrs. David Duhaime), Janet (Mrs. Emory Morsberger), Anne (Mrs. Paul Kawas), Thomas, Gail. B.S., Yale U., 1946; J.D., Harvard U., 1948; M.B.A., NYU, 1957, LL.M., 1960. Bar: N.Y. 1949. Assoc., partner Bartels & Hartung (and predecessor firms), N.Y.C., 1949-56, Conboy, Hewitt, O'Brien & Boardman (now Hunton & Williams), N.Y.C., 1958-70; asst. sec. The Best Foods, Inc., N.Y.C., 1956-58; assoc. gen. counsel Philip Morris Cos. Inc., N.Y.C., 1970-88; sec. Philip Morris Cos. Inc., 1971-88, v.p., 1978-88; counsel Hunton & Williams, N.Y.C., 1988—; adj. prof. law NYU Sch. Law, 1960-80. Chmn. New Rochelle Youth Bur., 1966; mem. New Rochelle Bd. Appeals on Zoning, 1971-74; bd. dirs. NYU Alumni Fedn.; trustee NYU, 1984—, Town Hall Found. Inc. 1988—; legal adv. com. to N.Y. Stock Exchange Bd. Dirs., 1986—. Served with AUS, 1943-46. Recipient NYU Alumni Meritorious Service award, 1973. Mem. Am. Soc. Corp. Secs. (chmn., chief exec. officer 1982-83), Am. Law Inst., ABA, Internat. Bar Assn., N.Y. State Bar Assn., Assn. of Bar of City of N.Y., NYU Grad. Bus. Sch. Alumni Assn. (pres. 1963-65). Clubs: Harbour Ridge Country (Stuart, Fla.); Westchester Country (Rye, N.Y.) (gov.); N.Y. Univ. (pres. 1979-81), Harvard (N.Y.C.); Winged Foot Golf (Mamaroneck, N.Y.). Home: Biltmore Ave Rye NY 10580 also: 2005 Laurel Oak Ln Palm City FL 34990 Office: Hunton & Williams 100 Park Ave New York NY 10017

FLANAGAN, JAMES JOSEPH, III, gas company financial executive; b. Lowell, Mass., Feb. 16, 1950; s. James Joseph Jr. and Rose Rita (Fennell) F.; m. Deborah Newman, May 26, 1984; 1 child, Kendra Newman. BSBA in Fin., Northeastern U., 1976. Fin. assoc. GTE Corp., Stamford, Conn., 1976-78; rate analyst Gen. Telephone Co. Pa., Erie, 1978-79; fin. analyst Bay State Gas Co., Canton, Mass., 1980-81, asst. treas., 1981-83, treas., 1983-89, treas., corp. sec., 1989—. Mem. Fin. Execs. Inst., New Eng. Gas Assn., Nat. Investor Relations Inst., Am. Gas Assn. Republican. Home: 96 Potter Pond Lexington MA 02173 Office: Bay State Gas Co 120 Royall St Canton MA 02021

FLANAGAN, JOSEPH PATRICK, advertising executive; b. Chgo., Jan. 6, 1938; s. Charles Larkin and Helen Mary (Sullivan) F.; m. Charlotte Mary Stepan, Sept 9, 1961; children: Charlotte Ahern, Joseph P. Jr., Michael S., Larkin S., Brian A. BA, Mich. State U., 1959; MBA, U. Chgo., 1961. Dist. mgr. sales Time mag., Pitts. and Chgo., 1961-69; gen. mgr. Ctr. Advanced Research in Design, Chgo., 1969-75; v.p., dir. client services BBDO, Chgo., 1975-77; sr. v.p. Impact subs. Foote, Cone & Belding Communications Co., Chgo., 1977-85, pres., 1985—; corp. dir. sales promotion Foote, Cone & Belding Communications Co., Chgo., 1987—, also bd. dirs.; pres. Council on Sales Promotion Agys., 1986—. Mem. governing bd. Chgo. Symphony Orch., 1974-80; v.p. Lyric Opera Guild, Chgo., 1974. Roman Catholic. Club: Exmoor Country (Highland Park, Ill.). Home: 136 Chestnut St Winnetka IL 60093 Office: Impact FCB Ctr 101 E Erie Chicago IL 60611

FLANAGAN, JUDITH ANN, entertainment specialist; b. Lubbock, Tex., Apr. 28, 1950; d. James Joseph and Jean (Breckenridge) F. BS in Edn., Memphis State U., 1972. Area/parade supr. Walt Disney World, Orlando, Fla., 1972-81; parade dir. Gatlinburg (Tenn.) C. of C., 1981-85; entertainment prodn. mgr. The 1982 World's Fair, Knoxville, 1982; cons. Judy Flanagan Prodns./Spl. Events, Gatlinburg, 1982—, Miss U.S.A. Pageant, Knoxville, 1983; prodn. coordinator Nashville Network, 1983; account exec. Park Vista Hotel, Gatlinburg, 1986-87; prodn. mgr. The 1984 World's Fair Parades/Spl. Events, New Orleans, Neil Sedakarock video, Spandau Ballet rock video, Days of Our Lives daytime soap opera; dir. sales The River Ter. Resort, Gatlinburg, 1985-86; with planning and devel. Universal Studios, Fla., Universal City, Calif. Mem. Memphis State U. Acad. Donor Fund. Named One of Outstanding Young Women Am., 1981; recipient Gatlinburg Homecoming award, 1986. Mem. Fla. Hospitality Industry Assn. (assoc.), Memphis State U. Alumni Assn. Roman Catholic. Home: 511 E Magnolia St Kissimmee FL 32743

FLANAGAN, STEPHEN ROGER, investment banker; b. Flushing, N.Y., Feb. 18, 1956; s. Thomas V. and Joan (Elder) F.; m. Diane Michelle Digangi, Aug. 3, 1984; children: Nicholas, Thomas. BA in Econs., Assumption Coll., 1978. Mgmt. trainee letters credit Mfrs. Hanover Trust Co., N.Y.C., 1979-83, fgn. exchange dealer, 1984—; mem. Forex USA, Inc. Mem. Rep. Nat. Com., Washington, 1987, Am. Security Council, Washington, 1987. Home: 84 Oriole Way Westbury NY 11590 Office: Mfrs Hanover Trust Co 270 Park Ave New York NY 10017

FLANAGAN, WILLIAM STANLEY, banker, lawyer; b. Tulsa, Aug. 1, 1947; s. William Stanley and Ilene Florence (Greenlee) F.; m. Katherine Ann Loewen, Aug. 9, 1968; 1 child, William Stanley III. BBA, Western State Coll., 1969; JD, U. Tulsa, 1971. Bar: Okla. 1972. Vice pres. Am. Exchange Bank, Collinsville, Okla., 1972-75, exec. v.p., 1975—; assoc. Marsh Law Firm, Tulsa, 1972—, Armstrong Law Firm, —, 1972—. Mem. Community Bankers Assn. (pres. 1985-87, bd. dirs. 1987—), Ind. Bankers Assn. Am. (bd. dirs. 1988—), ABA, Okla. Bar Assn., Tulsa County Bar Assn., Internat. Profl. Rodeo Assn. Democrat. Methodist. Office: Am Exch Bank 111 N 11th St Collinsville OK 74021

FLANAGIN, MICHELE DIANE, marketing specialist; b. Aurora, Ill., Nov. 8, 1959; d. Lloyd Densmore and Hildegarde M. (Rehe) F. BA, Northwestern U., 1981, MM, 1986. Sales rep. Canon Inc., Chgo., 1981-82; mktg. rep. Internat. Imaging, Chgo., 1982-83, mktg. specialist, 1983-87; mktg. mgr. U. Chgo. Dept. Med., 1987—. Mem. Am. Hosp. Assn., Beta Gamma Sigma.

FLANDERS, CAROL ANN, accountant; b. Noblesville, Ind., Jan. 6, 1963; d. Jim and Jeanne F. BS in Acctg. summa cum laude, Ball State U., 1984. CPA, Ind. Supr. acct. Blue & Co., CPA's, Indpls., 1984—. Mem. AICPA, Ind. CPA Soc., NAFE, Blue Key, Alpha Lambda Delta, Beta Gamma Sigma. Republican. Baptist. Office: Blue & Co CPAs 9100 Keystone Crossing Indianapolis IN 46280

FLANDERS, DONALD HARGIS, manufacturing company executive; b. Memphis, Apr. 26, 1924; s. Henry Jackson and Mae (Hargis) F.; m. Phala Kathryn Davis, Dec. 15, 1946; children: Donald Hargis, Dudley Kennedy, Phala Kathyrn. Student, Tex. Christian U., 1943; BBA, Baylor U., 1947. Dir. cost acctg., purchasing agt. McCoy-Couch Furniture Mfg. Co., Benton, Ark., 1947-50, Garrison Furniture Co., Ft. Smith, Ark., 1950-54; pres., founder Flanders Mfg. Co., Ft. Smith, 1954-70, Flanders Industries, Inc., Ft. Smith, 1970—; chmn. bd. Lloyd/Flanders Industries, Menominee, Mich.; dir. 1st Nat. Bank, Ft. Smith, Arkla, Inc., Shreveport, La. Chmn. exec. com. Ft. Smith Freight Bur., 1960-61; chmn. furniture bd. govs. Dallas Mkt. Ctr., 1968; exec. com. Ark. Council on Econ. Edn., 1964-67; mem. Ark. Small Bus. Adv. Council, 1966-68; chmn. Ft. Smith United Fund drive, 1962; dist. chmn. Boy Scouts Am., Ft. SMith, 1960-62, pres. Westark Area council 1963-65, regional exec. com., 1964-72, vice chmn. region 5, 1967-69, chmn. region 5, 1969-72, nat. exec. bd., 1969-77; Com. of 100, 1965—; exec. dir. Ark. Indsl. Devel. Commn., 1981-83; trustee, vice chmn. Sparks Regional Med. Ctr., Hendrix Coll., Westark Coll. Found., North Ark. Conf. Meth. Ch. Served from apprentice seaman to lt. (s.g.) USNR, 1943-46. Recipient Silver Antelope, Silver Beaver, Silver Buffalo, Disting. Eagle Scout awards Boy Scouts Am., Free Enterprise award, 1964; named Industrialist of Yr. Ft. Smith Realtors Bd., 1965. Mem. SW Furniture Mfg. Assn. (pres. 1963), Ft. Smith C. of C. (dir. 1961-63, 73—), Ark. Wood Products Assn. (dir. 1965-68), Delta Sigma Pi. Methodist. Clubs: Masons (33d deg.), Shriners, KT. Home: 20 Berry Hill Rd Fort Smith AR 72903 Office: 1901 Wheeler Ave PO Box 1788 Fort Smith AR 72902-1788

FLANDERS, DWIGHT PRESCOTT, economist; b. Rockford, Ill., Mar. 14, 1909; s. Daniel Bailey and Lulu Iona (Nichol) F.; m. Mildred Margaret Hutchison, Aug. 27, 1939 (dec. Dec. 1978); children—James Prescott, Thomas Addison. BA, U. Ill., 1931, MA, 1937; teaching cert., Beloit (Wis.) Coll., 1934; PhD in Econs., Yale U., 1939. With McLeish, Baxter & Flanders (realtors), Rockford, 1931-33; instr. U.S. history and sci. in secondary schs. Rockford, 1934-36; asst. prof. econs. Coll. Liberal Arts and Scis.; also statistics Maxwell Grad. Sch., Syracuse (N.Y.) U., 1939-42; acad. staff econs. dept. social sci. U.S. Mil. Acad., West Point, N.Y., 1942-46; mem. faculty U. Ill., Urbana, 1946—; prof. econs. U. Ill., 1953-77; prof. emeritus dept. econs. Coll. Commerce and Bus. Adminstrn., 1977—; prof. emeritus dept. family and consumer econs. Coll. Agr., 1980—; chmn. masters research seminar, 1947-74, cons. in field; ptnr. McLeish and Flanders, 1978—. Author: Science and Social Science, 2d edit, 1962, Status of Military Personnel as Voters, 1942, Collection Rural Real Property Taxes in Illinois, 1938; co-author: Contemporary Foreign Governments, 1946, The Conceptual Framework for a Science of Marketing, 1964; contbr. numerous articles to profl. jours. Pres. Three Lakes (Wis.) Waterfront Homeowners Assn., 1969-71, dir., 1971-75, ofcl. bd., 1975-84. Served to lt. col. AUS, 1942-46. Univ. fellow U. Ill., 1936-37; Univ. fellow Yale U., 1937-39; recipient Bronze tablet U. Ill., 1931, Excellence in Teaching award, 1977. Mem. Am., Midwest econs. assns., Royal Econ. Soc., Econometric Soc., Phi Beta Kappa, Beta Gamma Sigma (chpt. pres. 1959-61), Phi Kappa Phi, Alpha Kappa Psi. Methodist (ofcl. bd.). Club: Yale (Chgo.). Home: 719 S Foley Ave Champaign IL 61820

FLANIGAN, ROBERT DANIEL, JR., educational finance official; b. Lithonia, Ga., Apr. 14, 1949; s. Robert Daniel and Maggie (Mabry) F.; BA, Clark Coll., 1970; MBA, Emory U., 1982; m. Anne Butler, Dec. 12, 1970. Auditor, Arthur Andersen & Co., Atlanta, 1969-70; comptroller Spelman Coll., Atlanta, 1970-75, bus. mgr., 1975-81, exec. dir. bus. and fin. affairs, 1981-82, v.p. bus. and fin. affairs, 1982—; fin. cons. NIH, U.S. Dept. Edn. Bd. dirs. Arts Festival Atlanta, Atlanta Internat. Sch.; bd. dirs., mem. fin. com. N.W. Ga. council Girl Scouts U.S.A. Mem. Nat. Assn. Accts., Nat. Assn. Coll. Aux. Svcs., Nat. Assn. Coll. and Univ. Bus. Officers, So. Assn. Coll. and Univ. Bus. Officers (fin. cons.), Am. Mgmt. Assn., IUU Black Men of Atlanta, Inc., Alpha Phi Omega. Democrat. Methodist. Office: 350 Spelman Ln Atlanta GA 30314

FLANNERY, JOSEPH PATRICK, manufacturing company executive; b. Lowell, Mass., Mar. 20, 1932; s. Joseph Patrick and Mary Agnes Egan F.; m. Margaret Barrows, June 1957; children: Mary Ann, Diane, Joseph, James, David, Elizabeth. BS in Chemistry, Lowell Tech. Inst., 1953; MBA, Harvard U., 1955; PhD, U. Lowell, Mass., 1981. Pres. Uniroyal Chem. Co., Naugatuck, Conn., 1975-77; exec. v.p. Uniroyal, Inc., Middlebury, Conn., 1977, pres., 1977—, chief exec. officer, 1980—; chmn. bd. Uniroyal, Inc., 1982—; chmn., pres., chief exec. officer Uniroyal Holding, Inc., Waterbury, Conn., 1986—; ptnr. Clayton & Dubilier Inc.; bd. dirs. Newmont Mining Corp., K Mart Corp., Ingersoll-Rand Co., Amstar Corp., O.M. Scott & Sons, Irish Am. Partnership. Mem. Am. Chem. Soc. Roman Catholic. Clubs: Country of Waterbury (Conn.); Vesper Country (Lowell); Oyster Harbors (Osterville, Mass.). Lodge: Knights of Malta. Office: Uniroyal Holding Inc 455 Chase Pkwy Waterbury CT 06708-3392

FLANSBURGH, EARL ROBERT, architect; b. Ithaca, N.Y., Apr. 28, 1931; s. Earl Alvah and Elizabeth (Evans) F.; m. Louise Hospital, Aug. 27, 1955; children: Earl Schuyler, John Conant. B.Arch., Cornell U., 1954; M.Arch., MIT, 1957; S.C.M.P., Harvard U. Sch. Bus., 1982. Job capt., designer The Architects Collaborative, Cambridge, Mass., 1958-62; partner Freeman, Flansburgh & Assos., Cambridge, 1961-63; prin. Earl R. Flansburgh & Assocs., Inc., Cambridge, 1963-69; pres., dir. design Earl R. Flansburgh & Assocs., Inc., 1969—; bd. dirs. Däka, Inc.; exec. v.p. Environment Systems Internat., Inc.; vis. prof. archtl. design Mass. Inst. Tech., 1965-66; instr. art Wellesley Coll., 1962-65, lectr. art, 1965-69; cons. Arthur D. Little, Inc., Cambridge, 1964—. Archtl. works include Weston (Mass.) High Sch. Addition, 1965-67, Cornell U. Campus Store, 1967-70, Cumnock Hall, Harvard U. Bus. Sch, 1973-75, Acton (Mass.) Elementary schs, 1966-68, 69-71, Wilton (Conn.) High Sch, 1968-71, 14 Story St. Bldg, 1970, Boston Design Ctr., 1985-86, Glenwood Sch., Dallas, 1985-88; exhibited works Light Machine I, IBM Gallery, N.Y.C., 1958, Light Machine II, Carpenter Center, Harvard, 1965, 5 Cambridge Architects, Wellesley Coll., 1969, Work of Earl R. Flansburgh and Assos, Wellesley Coll., 1969, New Architecture in New Eng, DeCordova Mus., 1974-75, Residential Architecture, Mead Art Gallery, Amherst Coll., 1976, works represented in, 50 Ville del Nostro Tempo, 1970, Nuove Ville, New Villas, 1970, Vacation Houses, 1970, Vacation Houses, 2d edit., 1977, Interior Design, 1970, Drawings by American Architects, 1973, Interior Spaces Designed by Architects, 1974, New Architecture in New England, 1974, Great Houses, 1976, Architecture Boston, 1976, Presentation Drawings by American Architects, 1977, Architecture, 1970-1980, A Decade of Change, 1980, Old and New Architecture, A Design Relationship, 1980, 25 Years of Record Houses, 1981; Author: (with others) Techniques of Successful Practice, 1975. Chmn. architecture com. Boston Arts Festival, 1964; chmn. Downtown Boston Design Adv. Com.; Bd. dirs. Cambridge Center Adult Edn.; chmn. bldgs. and properties com., 1976, 78-87; mem. exec. com., academic affairs com., bd. trustees Cornell U., 1972—; class sec. SCMP VII. Served to 1st lt. USAF, 1954-56. Recipient design awards Progressive Architecture, design awards Record Houses, design awards AIA, design awards City of Boston, design awards Mass. Masonry Inst., spl. design citations Am. Assn. Sch. Adminstrs., spl. 1st prize Buffalo-Western N.Y. chpt. AIA Competition., Walter Taylor award Am. Assn. Sch. Adminstrs., 1986; Fulbright research grantee Bldg. Research Sta., Eng., 1957-58. Fellow AIA; mem. Royal Inst. Brit. Architects, Boston Soc. Architects (chmn. program com. 1969-71, commr. pub. affairs 1971-73, commr. design 1973-74, dir. 1971-74, pres. 1980-81), Boston Found. Architecture (treas. 1984—), Cornell U. Council, Quill and Dagger Soc. (bd. trustees 1972—), Tau Beta Pi. Home: 225 Old County Rd Lincoln MA 01773 Office: 77 N Washington St Boston MA 02114

FLATEAU-GOODING, ADELE MARIE, public relations executive; b. Bklyn., Apr. 14, 1951; d. Sidney Joseph and Jeanne Marie (Hill) Flateau; m. Desmond Cornelius Gooding, Apr. 21, 1984; children: Desmond Toussaint, Jamil Grafton. BA in English, Bklyn. Coll., 1984. Copy editor, writer Harbor Press, N.Y.C., 1972-81; admissions coordinator Sch. Medicine NYU, N.Y.C., 1981-83; asst. editor Inst. Retail Mgmt. NYU, 1983-84; account exec. Hill and Knowlton, Inc., N.Y.C., 1984-87; asst. dir. communications Office Pub. Affairs N.Y.C. Health and Hosps. Corp., 1987-88, spl. asst. to v.p. pub. affairs, 1988—; assoc. editor Time Capsule Mag., N.Y.C., 1982-85; adj. instr. Bklyn. Coll.-CUNY, 1985-86. Bd. dirs., sec. 745 Owners Corp., Bklyn., 1987—; bd. dirs. Bedford-Stuyvesant Youth Devel. Ctr.-N.Y. State Div. Youth, Bklyn., 1988—. Mem. NAFE, Black Rep. Assn. N.Y., Vanguard Ind. Dem. Assn. Roman Catholic. Office: NYC Health & Hosps Corp 125 Worth St Room 502 New York NY 10013

FLATO, WILLIAM ROEDER, JR., petroleum chemical company executive; b. Corpus Christi, Tex., Apr. 20, 1945; s. William Roeder and Juanita Flato; m. Beatrice Pesl, Aug. 22, 1974; 1 child, Amanda Leigh. BBA, U. Houston, 1967. CPA, Tex. Acct. Hughes Tool Co., Houston, 1966-67; acct. Milchem, Inc., Houston, 1967-72, accounting mgr., 1972-73, asst. controller, 1973, corp. controller, 1973-78; v.p. fin., sec., treas. Baker Performance Chems. Inc. (formerly Magna Corp.), Houston, 1978-82, exec. v.p. fin. and planning, sec.-treas., 1982—. Active Country Village Civic Assn.; state chmn. Young Ams. for Freedom, 1964; precinct chmn. Harris County Rep. Exec. Com., 1966-67. Served with U.S. Army, 1968-69. Decorated Army Commendation medal. Mem. Am. Inst. CPA's, Tex. Soc. CPA's, Fin. Execs. Inst., Mensa. Presbyterian. Home: 11931 Drexel Hill Dr Houston TX 77077 Office: PO Box 27714 3920 Essex Ln Houston TX 77227-7714

FLATT, DENISE TANNER, retail executive; b. Grand Haven, Mich., Dec. 15, 1964; d. Wayne and Mary Lou (Buttke) Tanner; m. H. Curtis Flatt III, July 3, 1987. BSBA, David Lipscomb Coll., 1987. Sec. David Lipscomb Coll., Nashville, 1983-84, Nashville C. of C., 1984-85; sales assoc. Dillard's Dept. Store, Nashville, 1985-87, dept. mgr., 1987-88, area sales mgr., 1988—; researcher Nat. Study Accrediting Instns., Nashville, 1987. Com. head United Way, Nashville, 1986; counselor Nashville Crisis Ctr., 1987, Reelfoot Youth Camp, Samburg, Tenn., 1983-85; tchr. Nashville Assn. Adult Literacy, 1988. Recipient Semper Fidelis award USMC, 1986, Murray J. Martin award David Lipscomb Coll., 1987, Collegiate All-Am. award U.S. Achievement Acad., 1987. Mem. Nat. Mktg. Assn. (treas. 1987-88), Am. Mgmt. Assn., Sigma Alpha Iota Alumni Assn. (sec. 1987-88, Leadership award 1988), Delta Sigma (sec. 1986-87), Alpha Chi. Democrat. Mem. Ch. of Christ.

FLECK, GORDON PIERCE, accounting firm principal; b. Oak Park, Ill., Aug. 21, 1931; s. Peter Pierce and Esther (Anderson) F.; m. Yvonne Chaberski, May 25, 1968; 1 child, Jennifer. BA, Eastern Ky. U., 1953, MA, 1954; postgrad., Northwestern U., Chgo., 1964-68. Physcial edn. instr., coach Eastern Ky. U., Richmond, 1963-64; band dir. Carrollton (Ky.) High Sch., 1956-60; ptnr. Robertson, Behling and Fleck, Chgo., 1960-62; owner G.P. Fleck and Assoc., Chgo., 1962—. Mem. Chgo. Businessmens Symphony, 1960-72; judge Pan-Am. Games, Chgo., 1960. Served with U.S. Army, 1954-56. Mem. Nat. Assn. Pub. Accts. Home: 294 Maplewood Riverside IL 60546 Office: GP Fleck & Assocs 7804 W 26th St North Riverside IL 60546

FLECK, ROBERT WILSON, financial executive; b. Harvey, Ill., Feb. 11, 1944; s. Robert Arthur Fleck and Gertrude Helen (Hewstone) Hedrix; m. Elizabeth Jean Plue, Mar. 27, 1971; 1 child, Shelley Anne. AA, Fullerton Jr. Coll., 1964; BS, San Jose State U., 1967. CLU, chartered fin. cons. Brokerage cons. Cigna Fin. Services, San Francisco, 1970-72, sr. brokerage cons., 1972-76, acct. mgr. brokerage, 1976-81; pres. Fin. Adv. Services, Palo Alto, Calif., 1981—; pres. De Anza Holding Corp., Sunnyvale, Calif., 1987—, also bd. dirs.; chmn. bd. dirs. De Anza Bank, Sunnyvale, 1987—; bd. dirs. Fin. Adv. Services, Palo Alto ; mem. Fin. Profl. Adv. Panel, Calif., 1984-85; speaker in field. Scholar Assn. Research and Enlightenment, 1966; recipient Nat. Quality award Nat. Assn. Life Underwriters, 1968. Mem. Internat. Assn. Registered Fin. Planners, Internat. Assn. Cert. Fin. Planners, Am. Bankers' Assn., Am. Soc. Chartered Life Underwriters, Internat. Assn. Fin. Planners. Lodge: Elks. Office: Fin Adv Svcs 2600 El Camino Real Suite 500 Palo Alto CA 94306

FLEEGAL, TIM LEE, computer company executive; b. Harrisburg, Pa., July 28, 1945; s. Leo West and Hilda L. (Coleman) F.; m. Cheryl Lynn Brown, June 26, 1978; 1 child, Ginger Lee. BA, Lehigh U., 1967. Owner/operator F-Penn-L Personnel, Harrisburg, Pa., 1967-73; forms sales rep. Profl. Bus. Services, Harrisburg, 1973-74; with Olivetti Corp. Am., Harrisburg, 1974-76; cons. in data processing Harrisburg, 1976-77; data processing mgr. Speed Mail Services, Harrisburg, 1977-78; with R.T. Becker Assocs., Reading, Pa., 1978; asst. data processing mgr. Stabler Cos., Harrisburg, 1978-83; computer support exec. Growing Concerns Computer Support, Harrisburg, 1981—; cons. Community Gen. Osteopathic Hosp., Harrisburg, 1986—. Contbr. articles to profl. jours. Initiator City Island Youth Cleanup, Harrisburg, 1974; instr. Dauphin County Children & Youth, Harrisburg, 1986-87. Mem. Cen. Pa. IBM Users Group. Republican. Lutheran. Club: Harrisburg Camera (instr. 1986-87). Lodge: Sertoma (v.p. sponsorship 1987-88). Home: RD 1 Box 312A Halifax PA 17032 Office: Growing Concerns Computer Co 13 N Progress Ave Harrisburg PA 17109

FLEETWOOD, MARY ANNIS, education association executive; b. Winfield, Ala., July 31, 1931; d. George A. and Martha Ann (Perry) Sullivan; m. Lewis N. Fleetwood, Aug. 19, 1950; children: Juanita, Dexter Lewis, Melanie Louise. Student, HCC Community Coll., 1973-80. Gen. office staff Able Rose Mercentile Co., Birmingham, Ala., 1949-51; with auditing dept. Bank for Savs. & Trusts, Birmingham, Ala., 1951; account receivables clk. I.W. Phillips, Tampa, Fla., 1972-77; account clk. Sch. Bd. Hill County, Tampa, Fla., 1980, office mgr., 1981—. V.p. PTA, 1961-62; pres. Woman's Missionary Union, Birmingham, 1963-64. Mem. Nat. Inst. Govt. Purchasing (cert. profl. buyer). Baptist. Home: 601 W Sylvan Dr Brandon FL 33511 Office: Sch Bd Hillsborough County 901 E Kennedy Tampa FL 33601

FLEISCHER, CARL AUGUST, legal educator, consultant; b. Oslo, Aug. 26, 1936; s. Carl Johan and Marie (Mathiesen) F.; grad. Vestheim High Sch., Oslo, 1954; legal exam. laudabilis, U. Oslo, 1960, LL.D., 1964; m. Eva Sylvia Funder, Sept. 15, 1967. First sec. legal div. Ministry Fgn. Affairs, 1960-61; spl. cons. internat. law, 1962—; lectr. law U. Oslo Faculty Law, 1961-69, prof., 1969—; adviser in internat. law Ministry Fgn. Affairs, 1986—; lectr., cons., mem. dels. internat. confs. Mem. Internat. Council Environ. Law, Norwegian Petroleum Soc., Norwegian Soc. Int. Law. Author: Jurisdiction on Fisheries, 1963; International Law, 5th edit., 1984; Constitutional Limitations, 1969; The Law on Building and Regulation of Property, 4th edit., 1983; Commentary to the Act of Expropriation and Compensation, 1974: The Economic Zone, 1976; The Law of Expropriation, 1978; Expropriation

Procedure, 1980; Application and Interpretation of Judgements, 1981; Petroleum Law, 1983; La pêche (the fisheries), 1985; co-author: Traitée du Nouveau Droit de la Mer, 1985; Compensation to Fisheries for Offshore Devel. report, 1986, The New Regime of Maritime Fisheries, 1989; also articles, reports. Home: 13 Thomas Heftyes, Oslo 2, Norway Office: 7 Juni Pl, Oslo 1, Norway

FLEISCHMAN, EDWARD HIRSH, lawyer; b. Cambridge, Mass., June 25, 1932; s. Louis Isaac and Jean (Grossman) F.; m. Joan Barbara Walden, Dec. 27, 1953; children: Charles, Janet. BA, Harvard U.; LLB, Columbia U., 1959. Bar: N.Y. 1959, U.S. Supreme Ct. 1980. Assoc. Gaston Snow Beekman & Bogue (formerly Beekman & Bogue), N.Y.C., 1959-67, ptnr., 1968-86; commr. SEC, Washington, 1986—; adj. prof. NYU Law Sch. Contbr. articles to profl. jours. Served with U.S. Army, 1952-55. Mem. ABA (chmn. subcom. model simplified indenture 1980-83, chmn. adminstrv. law com. securities, commodities, and exchanges 1981-84, chmn. subcom. broker-dealer matters 1973-78, chmn. subcom. rule 144 1970-72, chmn. com. devels. in bus. financing 1987—), Internat. Bar Assn., Am. Law Inst., Am. Coll. Investment Counsel, Am. Soc. Corp. Secs., Internat. Law Assn. Republican. Jewish. Home: 10 Glen Blvd Glen Rock NJ 07452 also: 1200 23d St NW Washington DC 20037 Office: SEC 450 5th St NW Washington DC 20549

FLEISHER, GARY MITCHELL, employment and franchising industry consulting executive; b. Bklyn., July 10, 1941; s. Irving and Ceil F.; student Ogelthorpe U., 1959, U. Miami, 1960-61; m. Grace M. Reynolds; children—Nina, Gwen Megan. Gemologist, diamond broker, N.Y.C., 1962-67; nat. ops. mgr. Staff Builders, Inc., N.Y.C., 1967-70; v.p., gen. mgr. Career Tempforce, East Meadow, N.Y., 1970-76; exec. v.p. Uniforce Temporary Services, New Hyde Park, N.Y., 1976-83; pres. G.M. Fleisher & Assocs., Inc., 1984—, pres., dir. GMF Mgmt. Group., 1984—; guest speaker profl. groups and orgns. Mem. Am. Mgmt. Assn., Adminstrv. Mgmt. Soc., Am. Soc. Personnel Adminstrn., Internat. Franchise Assn., Internat. Platform Assn. Republican. Unitarian. Lodge: Masons. Office: 70 Charles Lindbergh Blvd Uniondale NY 11553

FLEISHER, JERRILYN, financial consultant; b. Phila., May 7, 1952; d. Earl D. and Bette (Romisher) F.; m. Steven M. Bierman, May 28, 1978; 1 child, Emily Larissa. B.A., Dickinson Coll., 1973; M.B.A., Wharton Sch., U. Pa., 1975. Promotion analyst Gillette Co., Boston, 1975-77; product mgr. Chesebrough Ponds Co., Greenwich, Conn., 1977-80, Loreal Co., N.Y.C., 1980-81; account exec. Futterman Orgn., N.Y.C., 1981-83; fin. cons. Shearson Lehman Bros., Greenwich, 1983—. Mem. Internat. Platform Assn., Phi Beta Kappa. Home: 12 Martin Dale N Greenwich CT 06830 Office: Shearson Lehman Bros 2 Greenwich Pla Greenwich CT 06830

FLEMING, ANTHONY CALDWELL, accountant; b. Louisville, July 18, 1939; s. Anthony and Addie (Caldwell) F. BBA, Loyola U., New Orleans, 1960, JD, 1963. Bar: La. 1963, CPA, La. Estate tax atty. IRS, New Orleans, 1963-71; tax law specialist IRS, Washington, 1971-73, valuation specialist, 1973-75; appellate conferee IRS, Dallas, 1975-76; supervisory atty. IRS, Nashville, 1976-80; sr. regional analyst IRS, Atlanta, 1980-81; sr. appeals officer U.S. Treasury, Jacksonville, Fla., 1981-83; acct. Gus W. Schram Jr. Ltd., Lake Charles, La., 1985-88; pres. Standard Valuation Svcs., Inc., Lake Charles, La., 1989—. Co-comment editor Loyola Law Rev., 1963. Mem. AICPA, La. Bar Assn., La. Soc. CPAs, Nat. Assn. Blind Lawyers, Nat. Assn. Retired Fed. Employees, Inst. Bus. Appraisers, Am. Fedn. of the Blind, La. Fedn. Blind, La. Coun. of Blind, Am. Coun. Blind, Nat. Right to Life, Am. United for Life, Blue Key, Beta Alpa Psi, Beta Gamma Sigma, Alpha Delta Gamma. Democrat. Roman Catholic. Lodge: KC (4th degree; various positions). Office: Standard Valuation Svc Inc 1409 Kirkman Lake Charles LA 70601

FLEMING, DOUGLAS RILEY, journalist, publisher, public affairs consultant; b. Fairmont, W.Va., Jan. 25, 1922; s. Douglas Riley and Sarilda Artemes (Short) F.; m. Irene Stachowicz, Oct. 28, 1944 (dec. 1979). B.S., Georgetown U., 1953. Commd. ensign U.S. Navy, 1944, advanced through ranks to comdr.; naval aviator; chief protocol NATO, Naples, 1962-67, ret. 1967; with Francis I. DuPont & Co., Investment Banking, Rome, 1968-70; exec. editor, gen. mgr. Daily American, Rome, 1970-75; pres. Stampa Generale, S.R.L., Pubs., Naples, Italy, 1975—; mng. dir. Italo-Am. Assn., Naples; dir. Am. Studies Ctr., Naples, 1975-80; pres. Gen. Press Services, Washington, 1979—; dir. Va. Winery Coop., Inc., Culpeper, 1985—; proprietor, operator Campicello Vineyards, Madison, Va., 1982—. Active Nat. Trust Hist. Preservation, Smithsonian Assocs., Assn. Naval Aviation. Mem. Associazione Della Stampa Estera in Italia, The Cogswell Soc., Georgetown U. Alumni Assn. (pres. Italy 1972-80), Am. C. of C. in Italy, Retired Officers Assn., Navy League of U.S., Nat. Press Club, Vinifera Wine Growers Assn., Jeffersonian Wine Grape Growers Soc., Va. Vineyards Assn. Clubs: Naval and Mil., Steering Wheel, Royal Aero (London); Circolo Canottieri (Naples); N.Y. Athletic; Dist. Yacht (Washington). Home: 515 S Fairfax St Alexandria VA 22314 also: Campicello Box 589 Madison VA 22727

FLEMING, MAC ARTHUR, labor union administrator; b. Walnut Grove, Miss., Sept. 22, 1945; s. Austin J. and Dorothy (Downey) F.; m. Phyllis Jean Tatro, May 18, 1984. AA, Jones County Jr. Coll., Laurel, Miss., 1967; student, So. Colo. State Coll., Pueblo, 1967-68; student in trade union program, Harvard U., 1979. System organizer Atchison, Topeka & Santa Fe System Fedn., Pueblo, 1972; asst. gen. chmn. Atchison, Topeka & Santa Fe System Fedn., San Bernardino, Calif., 1972-73; asst. chmn., sec.-treas. Atchison, Topeka & Santa Fe System Fedn., Newton, Kans., 1974-75, vice chmn., 1975-80, gen. chmn., 1980-86; grand lodge sec.-treas. Brotherhood Maintenance Ways Employees, Detroit, 1986—. Democrat. Baptist. Home: 3072 Newport Ct Troy MI 48084 Office: Brotherhood Maintenance Way Employees 12050 Woodward Ave Detroit MI 48203-3596

FLEMING, RICHARD CARL DUNNE, city planner; b. Balt., July 20, 1945; s. Winter M. and Ethel (Murphy) F. B.S. in Polit. Sci., Loyola U., Balt., 1967; M.B.A. (Carnegie-Mellon fellow), U. Pa., 1971, M. City Planning (H.B. Erhardt Found. fellow), 1971. Asst. devel. dir. Rouse Co., Columbia, Md., 1967-69; dir. planning Phipps Land Co., Inc., Atlanta, 1971-72; v.p. Cen. Atlanta Progress, Inc., 1972-76; sr. adviser to Pres.-elect Carter, 1976-77; gen. dep. asst. sec. for community planning and devel. Dept. Housing and Community Devel., Washington, 1977-80; pres., chief exec. officer Downtown Denver, Inc., 1980-86, Denver Partnership, Inc., 1980-86, Denver Civic Ventures, Inc., 1980-86, Greater Denver C. of C., 1987—, Greater Denver Corp., 1987—. Bd. dirs. Downtown Devel. Found., Inst. Urban and Pub. Policy, U. Colo.; bd. dirs. Historic Paramount Found., Sta. KCFR Pub. Radio; mem. Community Coll. Denver Adv. Bd. Mem. Urban Land Inst. (dir.), Internat. Downtown Execs. Assn. (past chmn. bd. dirs.), Common Cause. Democrat. Office: Greater Denver C of C 1301 Welton St Denver CO 80204

FLEMING, RICHARD H., finance executive; b. Milw., July 22, 1947; s. David M. and Mildred (Codere) F.; m. Diana Loane, Mar. 21, 1970; children: Douglas Codere, Petria Anne. BA, U. Pacific, 1969; MBA, Dartmouth, 1971. Fin. analyst Graco, Inc., Mpls., 1971-72, mgr. banking and fgn. exchange, 1972-73; fin. analyst Masonite Corp., Chgo., 1973-74, mgr. capital investment, 1974-77, asst. treas., 1977-82, treas., 1982-84, v.p. fin., chief fin. officer, 1985—. Bd. dirs. Family Care Services Met. Chgo., 1977—, pres. 1983-86; bd. dirs. Child Welfare League Am., Washington, 1987—. Home: 311 N Garfield Hinsdale IL 60521 Office: Masonite Corp 1 S Wacker Dr Chicago IL 60606

FLEMING, RICHARD LELAND, executive search consultant; b. Jackson, Mich., Apr. 25, 1929; s. Leland Addis and Mary (Thompson) F.; m. Anne Rowland, Aug. 20, 1950; children: Kathy, Jim, Julie. BS in Mktg., Ind. U., 1950, MBA, 1951. Personnel services dir. Armstrong Cork Co., Pitts., 1951-53; personnel dir. Vernco Corp., Columbus, Ind., 1953-55; dir. internat. personnel Cummins Engine Co., Columbus, 1957-66, corp. personnel dir., 1966-68; pres. Fleming Assocs., Columbus, 1968-82, Sarasota, Fla., 1982—; mem. dean's adv. council Ind. U. Sch. Bus., 1985—; mem. adv. council Ind. U. Exec. Devel., 1976-81; mem. Ind. State Personnel Bd., 1971-81; mem. exec. council Ind. U. Sch. Bus., 1963-66. Mem. Columbus City Council, 1964-72. Lt. USNR, 1955-57. Mem. Assn. Exec. Search Cons. (bd. dirs.), Harbour Oaks Assn. (pres.), Longboat Key Club, Beta Gamma Sigma. Republican. Methodist. Office: Fleming Assocs 240 N Washington Blvd Ste 322 Sarasota FL 34236

FLEMING, ROBERT WILLIAM, medical administrator; b. Toronto, Ont., Can., Mar. 12, 1928; came to U.S., 1945, naturalized, 1950; s. William Ivan and Mary M. (Findlay) F.; m. Janis Jensen, Aug. 23, 1949; children—Victoria, William, John, Tom. B.B.A., U. Minn., 1949. Mgmt. trainee Firestone Co., Mpls., 1949; head. ins. and coll. Mayo Clinic, Rochester, Minn., 1950-58; adminstrv. asst. Mayo Clinic, 1958-72, chmn. div. adminstrv. services, 1972-82, chmn. dept. adminstrn., 1982—, v.p., 1985—; bd. trustees Mayo Found., 1974—. Bd. dirs. Amateur Hockey Assn. U.S., Colorado Springs, Colo., 1963—, v.p., 1972-81; chmn. U.S. Olympic Ice Hockey Com., Colorado Springs, 1969-81; bd. dirs. InterStudy, Mpls., 1962-86. Mem. Med. Group Mgmt. Assn. (pres. 1985-86), Rochester C. of C. (bd. dirs. 1983—). Home: 600 SW 4th St #606 Rochester MN 55902 Office: Mayo Clinic 200 1st St SW Rochester MN 55905

FLEMING, RUSSELL, JR., utility company executive, lawyer; b. New Brunswick, N.J., Aug. 20, 1938; s. Russell and Margaret Olga (Kebly) F.; m. Cheryl Hall; children: Eileen, Russell III. AB, Rutgers U., 1960; JD, Columbia U., 1963. Bar: N.J. 1964. Ptnr. firm Sailer and Holzapfel, Elizabeth, N.J., 1965-73, Sailer and Fleming, Elizabeth, N.J., 1965-73; v.p., gen. counsel Elizabethtown Gas Co., 1973-80, exec. v.p., gen. counsel, 1980-85; gen. counsel, pres. svc. div. NUI Corp., Bridgewater, N.J., 1986—; gen. atty. Elizabethtown Water Co., 1973-80; v.p., gen. counsel NUI Corp., 1975-85; exec. com. Associated Gas Distbrs., 1979-85; counsel boroughs of, Milltown and Middlesex, 1969, 73. Pres. Milltown Bd. Edn., 1968-69; sec. Middlesex County Charter Study Commn., 1973; bd. dirs., br. pres. YMCA, Raritan Valley, N.J., 1971-73; trustee St. Peter's Med. Ctr., New Brunswick, 1982-83. Served to capt. USAR, 1963-65. Named Outstanding Young Man of Yr. Jaycees, 1968. Mem. ABA, N.J. Bar Assn. (chmn. public utility law sect. 1975), Fed. Energy Bar Assn., Am. Gas Assn. (legal sect., mng. com. 1978-86, chmn. fed. regulatory affairs 1984-86), Assoc. Gas Distbrs. (exec. com. 1979-86). Roman Catholic. Home: 2633 Far View Dr Mountainside NJ 07092 Office: NUI Corp 1011 Route 22 PO Box 6060 Bridgewater NJ 08807

FLEMING, SAMUEL CROZIER, JR., management consultant; b. Phila., Sept. 30, 1940; s. Samuel Crozier Sr. and Josephine Coverdale (Plowman) F.; m. Nancy Elizabeth McAdam, Sept. 7, 1963; children: David McAdam, Timothy Crozier. BChemE, Cornell U., 1963; MBA, Harvard U., 1967. Mgmt. cons. Arthur D. Little, Inc., Cambridge, Mass., 1967—, v.p., 1977-83, sr. v.p., 1983—; pres., chief exec. officer ADL Impact Svcs., Cambridge, 1976-79; pres., chief exec. officer Arthur D. Little Decision Resources, Cambridge, 1979-83, chmn. bd. dirs., 1983—; mem. Cornell Chem. Engring. Adv. Council, Ithaca, N.Y., 1986—; trustee Standish Ayer & Wood Investment Trust, Boston, 1986—; bd. dirs. Mastery Edn. Corp., Watertown, Mass., Arthur D. Little Internat., Cambridge; chmn. bd. dirs. Opinion Rsch. Corp., Princeton, N.J., Arthur D. Little Enterprises, Cambridge. Vestryman Trinity Ch., Boston, 1980-84; chmn. bd. dirs. New England Bapt. Health Care Corp., 1985—, New England Bapt. Hosp., Boston, 1985—. Served with U.S. Army, 1963-65. Mem. Soc. Chem. Industry, Country Club, Harvard Club, Lake Sunapee Yacht Club. Episcopalian. Home: 61 Meadowbrook Rd Weston MA 02193 Office: Arthur D Little Inc 25 Acorn Park Cambridge MA 02140

FLEMING, WILLIAM SLOAN, energy, environmental and technology company executive; b. Long Beach, Calif., Aug. 13, 1937; s. William Sloan and Helen Jean (Disler) F.; m. Jacquline M. Carrio, Mar. 9, 1960; children—Katherine A., Kimberly A.; BSME Calif. Maritime Acad., 1958; MBA, Syracuse U., 1970. Mech. engr. Carrier Corp., Syracuse, N.Y., 1967-70; regional sales mgr. Rheem Mfg., Atlanta, 1970-71; market devel. supr. Owens Corning Fiberglas, Toledo, 1971-73, pres. W.S. Fleming & Assos., Inc., Syracuse, 1975-86, chief exec. officer, chmn. bd., 1986—. chmn. bd. Assn. Intelligent System Tech., Inc., Syracuse; pres. Enerlog Systems, Inc., Syracuse, 1985—. Served with USN, 1958-67. Mem. ASHRAE (chmn. tech. com. solar energy utilization 1984-86, chmn. tech. com. system energy utilization 1981-83, chmn. ad hoc com. energy standard 1983-84, nat. program com. 1985-86), Assn. Energy Engrs. (charter), DAV, Am. Legion, Ret. Officers Assn., University Club (Syracuse). Roman Catholic. Contbr. articles to profl. jours.; author energy simulation computer program (SEE), 1975-80. Recipient Energy award Cen. N.Y., 1981. Avocations: skiing, boating, homework. Home: 3 Owagena Terr Cazenovia NY 13035 Office: Fleming Group 6308 Fly Rd East Syracuse NY 13057

FLENNIKEN, CECIL STEPHENSON, forest products company executive; b. Chickasaw, Ala., Aug. 11, 1925; s. Warren S. and Pearle M. (Stephenson) F.; m. Alyce Quince Parrish, June 15, 1948; 1 son, Bruce Phillips. BME, Ga. Inst. Tech., 1949. With Internat. Paper Co., 1949-69; mgr. pulp and paper mill Internat. Paper Co., Pine Bluff, Ark. and Bastrop, La., 1965-69; with Can. Pacific Forest Products Ltd. (formerly CIP Inc. and Canadian Internat. Paper Co.), Montreal, Que., 1969—, v.p., 1970, exec. v.p., 1971, chmn., pres., chief exec. officer, 1972—, also bd. dirs.; bd. dirs. Toronto-Dominion Bank,NBIP Forest Products Inc., Pulp and Paper Rsch. Inst. Can., Dominion Cellulose Ltd., Facelle Co., Ltd., Toronto. Served with USN, 1943-45. Mem. Canadian Pulp and Paper Assn. (exec. bd.), Paper Industry Mgmt. Assn. (trustee emeritus), TAPPI, Can. Mfrs. Assn. (adv. bd.). Clubs: Mt. Royal, Le Club St. Denis. Home: 1321 Sherbrooke St W E-50, Montreal, PQ Canada H3G 1J4 Office: Can Pacific Forest Products Ltd, 1155 Metcalfe St Ste 1400, Montreal, PQ Canada H3B 2X1

FLETCHER, CATHY ANN, auditor; b. Barnesville, Ga., Aug. 23, 1949; d. John James and Dorothy Lee (Banks) Fletcher; 1 child, Lisa Faye. Student, Ohio State U., 1969-70; AS, Mass. Bay Community Coll., 1982; BS, Northeastern U., Boston, 1984. Mail clk. Fed. Reserve Bank, Boston, 1971-72; office mgr. Breckenridge Sportswear, Boston, 1973-74; asst. dir. Whittier Street Health Ctr., Boston, 1974-81; sec. to dir. Northeastern U., 1981-84; auditor Def. Contract Audit Agy., Burlington, Mass., 1984—; sec., bd. dirs. Boston Tenant Policy Council, 1977-79. Author: Softball Team Book, 1975. V.p., bd. dirs. Bromley Health Tenant Mgmt. Corp., Jamaica Plain, Mass., 1976—; mem. fund-raising com. Com. to Elect Jessie Jackson Pres., Boston, 1984; apptd. fed. women program coordinator State of Mass., 1988. Mem. AAUW, Nat. Assn. Female Execs., Profl. Council, Hawkettes Social (pres.), Nat. Tenants Orgn., NAACP, Sigma Epsilon Rho. Club: Hawkettes Social (pres., mem. profl. council). Lodge: Elks. Avocations: reading, swimming, cooking, walking, travel. Office: Def Contract Audit Agy 2 Wayside Rd Burlington MA 01803

FLETCHER, DENISE KOEN, communications industry financial consultant; b. Istanbul, Turkey, Aug. 31, 1948; came to U.S., 1967, naturalized, 1976; d. Moris and Kety (Barkey) Koen; m. Robert B. Fletcher, Nov. 11, 1969; children—David, Kate. A.B. (Coll. scholar), Wellesley Coll., 1969; M.City Planning, Harvard U., 1972. Analyst Ea. div. Getty Oil Co., N.Y.C., 1972-73; sr. analyst Ea. div. Getty Oil Co., 1973-74, cash mgmt. and bldg. supr., 1974-76; cash mgmt. and bldg. supr. Getty Oil Co. (Eastern), 1976; asst. treas. N.Y. Times Co., N.Y.C., 1976-80; treas. N.Y. Times Co., 1980-88; pres. Flethcer Assocs. Inc., Larchmont, N.Y., 1988—. Bd. dirs. Overseas Edn. Fund Internat.; mem. budget com. City of Larchmont, N.Y., 1981; chmn zoning bd. of appeals, selection com. City of Mamaroneck, 1985-87; mem. Alumni exec. Council Harvard U. Sch. Govt., 1982-87; bd. dirs. YWCA N.Y. Mellon scholar, 1970. Mem. Fin. Execs. Inst., Fin. Women's Assn., Treasurers Club N.Y., Phi Beta Kappa. Club: Harvard (N.Y.C.).

FLETCHER, DONALD JOSEPH, airport manager; b. Piqua, Ohio, Dec. 9, 1944; s. Joseph Nevin and Florence Helen (Darr) F.; m. Juanita Mary Jones, Oct. 7, 1977; children: David Jonathan, Kelly Lynn. BBA, U. Toledo, 1970, MA in Polit. Sci., 1972. Dir. adminstrn. Toledo-Lucas Co. Port Authority, 1971-73, airport mgr., 1973-75, dir. aviation, 1975-86; airport mgr. Dept. Aviation City of Houston, 1986—. With USAF, 1963-67. Mem. Airport Ops. Council Internat. (bd. dirs. 1985-86), Ohio Airport Mgrs. Assn. (v.p. 1984-86), Am. Soc. Pub. Adminstrn. (pres. Toledo chpt. 1977, bd. dirs. Houston chpt. 1987), Pearland/Hobby Area C. of C. (bd. dirs. 1988-89), Am. Assn. Airport Execs. (del. 1979-80, mem. safety com. 1986-88), Am. Legion, KC (grand knight 1975-76). Republican. Roman Catholic. Office: City of Houston William P Hobby Airport 7800 Airport Blvd Houston TX 77061

FLETCHER, HAROLD L., investment firm executive; b. Lakeland, Fla., Oct. 31, 1954; s. Robert L. Fletcher and June N. (Harlow) Kiely. BS cum laude, Vanderbilt U., 1975; JD cum laude, Samford U., 1978. Bar: Tenn. 1978, Okla. 1981; cert. fin. planner. Tax atty. Glankler, Brown, Memphis, 1978-80, Bogatin, Lawson & Chiapella Attys., Memphis, 1980-81; self employed tax and securities atty. 1981-82; v.p. investments Dean-Witter Reynolds, Inc., Memphis, 1982—; asst. instr. Memphis State U., 1986—. Pres. Memphis Tax Watch Group, memphis, 1986. Mem. Okla Bar Assn., Racquet Club. Republican. Presbyterian. Office: Dean Witter Reynolds Inc 6410 Poplar Ave Ste 600 Memphis TN 38119

FLETCHER, JAMES ANDREW, infosystems specialist; b. Tulsa, May 8, 1945; s. Howard Bruce I and Edna Katherine (Jones) F.; m. Karen Kite, Oct. 14, 1967; children: Howard Bruce II, Jamie Katherine, Lancelot Lansing. BS in Aeronautics and Astronautics, MIT, 1967; MBA with highest distinction, Harvard U., 1972; MS in Mech. Engring. cum laude, Fairleigh Dickinson U., 1973. Rep. mktg. pub. sector office IBM Corp., Boston, 1972-73; adminstr. fin. program data processing product group White Plains, N.Y., 1974-75, Poughkeepsie, N.Y., 1975-76; contr. lab. Boulder, Colo., 1976-78; contr. Tucson, 1978-79; mgr. fin. program Armonk, N.Y., 1979-81; mgr. planning consolidation info. systems and communications group White Plains, 1981-83, mgr. fin. analysis IPD div., 1983; dir. plans and controls system printing bus. unit Boulder, 1983-85; dir. pricing Burroughs Corp., Detroit, 1985-87; v.p. pricing Unisys Corp., Blue Bell, Pa., 1987-89, v.p. fin. and communications line of bus. div. mktg., 1989—. Co-author: Friends Face the World, 1987; co-editor: A Quaker Speaks from the Black Experience, 1978. Mem. gen. staff Friends Com. for Nat. Legis., Washington, 1979—; active Am. Friends Service Com., 1979—, bd. dirs., 1979-85. White House fellow, 1973-74. Mem. White House Fellows Assn., NAACP, Black Exec. Exchange Program, Urban League. Democrat. Mem. Soc. of Friends. Office: UNISYS Corp Township Line and Walton Rd Blue Bell PA 19002

FLETCHER, JAMES CHIPMAN, government official; b. Millburn, N.J., June 5, 1919; s. Harvey and Lorena (Chipman) F.; m. Fay Lee, Nov. 2, 1946; children: Virginia Lee, Mary Susan, James Stephen, Barbara Jo. A.B., Columbia U., 1940; Ph.D., Calif. Inst. Tech., 1948; D.Sc. (hon.), U. Utah, 1971, Brigham Young U., 1977; LL.D., Lehigh U., 1978. Research physicist bur. ordnance Dept. Navy, 1940-41; spl. research assoc. Cruft Lab., Harvard U., 1941-42; instr. Princeton U., 1942-45; teaching fellow Calif. Inst. Tech., 1945-48; instr. UCLA, 1948-50; dir. theory and analysis lab. Hughes Aircraft Co., 1948-54; assoc. dir. guided missile lab., dir. electronics guided missile research div., later in space tech. labs. Ramo-Wooldridge Corp., 1954-58; pres., founder Space Electronics Corp., 1958; pres. Space-Gen. Corp. (merger between Space Electronics Corp. and Aerojet-Gen. Corp.), 1960; chmn. bd. Space-Gen. Corp., 1961-64; pres. U. Utah, 1964-71; adminstr. NASA, Washington, 1971-77; Whiteford prof. U. Pitts., 1977-84, disting. pub. service prof. engring. and tech., 1984-86; cons. engr. McLean, Va., 1977-86; adminstr. NASA, Washington, DC, 1986—; mem. subcom. on stability and control NACA, 1950-54; asst. sec. USAF, 1961-64, to ACDA, 1962-63, Aerojet-Gen. and Space-Gen. Corps., 1964-71; cons., then mem. Pres.'s Sci. Adv. Com., 1958-70; chmn. com. rev. Minuteman Command and Control System, 1961; mem. Air Force Sci. Adv. Bd., 1962-67; chmn. physics panel rev. com. NIH, 1962-64; mem. strategic weapons panel, 1959-61, mil. aircraft panel, 1964-67, chmn. naval warfare panel, 1967-73; mem. Pres.'s Nat. Crime Commn., 1966; mem. tech. assessment adv. council Office of Tech. Assessment,1978-86, mem. def. sci bd., 1982-86; chmn. safety adv. bd. Three Mile Island No. 2, 1981-86; governing bd. NRC, 1978-82; trustee Nat. Space Soc., 1977-86; bd. dirs. Astrotech Internat. 1984-86, Fairchild Industries, 1985-86, Amoco Corp., 1977-86, Burroughs Corp. 1977-86, COMARCO, Inc., 1979-86; internat. adv. bd. Pan Am. Airways, 1977-86. Author classified papers, sci. papers, chpts. in books; bd. editors, Addison-Wesley Pub. Co., 1958-64. Trustee Rockefeller Found., 1978-85, Theodore von Karman Meml. Found.; mem. governing bd. Univ. Corp. on Atmospheric Research, 1982-86, Argonne Nat. Lab., 1984-86; bd. regents Nat. Library Medicine, 1971; bd. visitors Def. Intelligence Sch., 1970-71; nat. adv. bd. Gas Research Inst., 1984-86. Recipient Disting. Service medal NASA; Exceptional Civilian Service award USAF; Dept. Energy award, 1982; John Jay award Columbia U. Fellow IEEE, Am. Acad. Arts and Sci., AIAA (hon.), Am. Astronautical Soc.; mem. Am. Phys. Soc., Nat. Acad. Engring. (governing council 1978-84), Sigma Xi. Club: Cosmos. Home: 7721 Falstaff Rd McLean VA 22102

FLETCHER, KIM, savings and loan executive; b. Los Angeles, 1927; married. Grad., Stanford U., 1950. Chmn. bd., chief exec. officer Home Fed. Savs. & Loan Assn., San Diego. Office: Home Fed Savs & Loan Assn 625 Broadway San Diego CA 92101

FLETCHER, MARY LEE, business executive; b. Farnborough, Eng.; d. Dugald Angus and Mary Lee (Thurman) F.; B.A., Pembroke Coll., Brown U., 1951. Ops. officer C.I.A., Washington, 1951-53; exec. trainee Gimbels, N.Y.C., 1953-54; head researcher Ed Byron TV Prodns., N.Y.C., 1954; copywriter Benton & Bowles, Inc., N.Y.C., 1955-63; creative dir. Alberto-Culver Co., Melrose Park, Ill., 1964-66; v.p. advt. and publicity Christian Dior Perfumes, N.Y.C., 1967-71; v.p. Christian Dior-N.Y., N.Y.C., 1972-78, exec. v.p., dir., 1978-85; cons. Fletcher & Co., N.Y.C., 1985—. Home: 12 Beekman Pl New York NY 10022 Office: 885 3d Ave New York NY 10022-4082

FLETCHER, PAUL LOUIE, businessman; b. Phila., Apr. 18, 1930; s. James Louie and Pearl (Lawson) F.; diploma mech. and archtl. drawing, McKee Vocat. Trade Sch., S.I., N.Y., 1958; m. Ying-Lun, Apr. 18, 1968; children—James, Raymond, Pearl, Dana, Paul Louie, England. With United Trading & Fletcher Inc., N.Y.C., 1950—, exec. v.p., 1950—, sec., 1950—; salesman Prosperity Laundry Machine Co., 1950-69; exec. v.p., sec. Canbeth Realty Corp., 1950—. Chmn., Chinatown div. March of Dimes, N.Y.C., 1960-64, Mei Wah Day Care Center, N.Y.C., 1977-80, Mei Wah Chinese Sch., 1977-80; pres. Soo Yuen Benevolent Assn., 1977-78; pres., chmn. Chinese Meth. Community Center, N.Y.C., 1977-80. Served with USAF, 1947-50. Recipient numerous community and service awards; Disting. Service award Council of Chs., City of N.Y.; knighted Order of St. Georges, 1986, received the Deputy Comdr. honours. Club: Lions (pres. Chinatown chpt., N.Y.C., 1975-76, charter pres. N.Y.C. Chinese Ams. 1978-80, dist. cabinet sec.-treas. 1980-81, dist. gov. 1982-83; numerous awards 1972—, council chmn. 1982-84, Internat. Pres.'s award 1982-84, 86-87). Home: 77 Lynhurst Ave Staten Island NY 10305 Office: 162 Canal St New York NY 10013

FLETCHER, ROSE MARIE, mortgage banker, consultant; b. Oakland, Calif., Dec. 8, 1940; d. Martin George Maher and Gertrude Elizabeth (Noe) Maher McCarthy; m. Jamie Franklin Fletcher, Aug. 1, 1960; children: Roberta JoAnne, Rebecca Louise, Jamie Suzanne. Student San Jose State U., 1958-60, West Valley Coll., 1972-76. Lic. real estate broker, Calif. Formerly br. mgr. Sutro Mortgage Co., San Jose, Calif., 3 yrs.; sr. v.p. Unified Mortgage Co., Cupertino, Calif., 1981-85; owner, pres., cons. Processing Place, San Jose, 1985—; dir. ops. Mortgage Loans Am., Campbell, Calif., 1986—; First Corp. Mortgage Co., 1988—; cons., lectr., trainer in lending field. Mem. Calif. Assn. Residential Lenders (1st v.p. 1985, pres. 1986), Assn. Profl. Mortgage Women (regional gov. 1980-81, Woman of Yr. 1979). Democrat. Roman Catholic. Avocations: water skiing; swimming; dancing. Home: 3704 Heppner Ln San Jose CA 95136 Office: First Corp Mortgage 2105 S Bascom Ave Campbell CA 95008

FLETCHER, WILLIAM ERIC, business executive; b. Los Angeles, Apr. 4, 1935; s. William Henry and Bernice Ruth Adele (Westberg) F.; student Calif. Inst. Tech., 1952-54; grad. smaller co. mgmt. program Harvard Bus. Sch., 1982; m. Judith Berne Sanders, Sept. 25, 1976; children from previous marriage—Marie, Katherine. Tech. dir. Telcomp Services, Bolt Beranek and Newman, Inc., Cambridge, Mass., 1960-68; pres. Modicon Corp., Bedford, Mass., 1968-71; dir. software devel. Delphi Communications Corp., Marina Del Rey, Calif., 1972; pres., dir. Termiflex Corp., Merrimack, N.H., 1973—; bd. dirs. Kimball Phsics Inc., Wilton, N.H. Chmn. N.H. del. to White House Conf. on Small Bus., 1980, 86; dir. Smaller Bus. Assn. New Eng., 1979—, chmn., 1985-86 . Served with USAF, 1954-60. Mem. Am. Electronics Assn. (nat. bd. dirs., chmn. New Eng. coun. 1988—), Aircraft

Owners and Pilots Assn. Republican. Club: Internat. Aerobatic. Home: 4 Blackfoot Dr Nashua NH 03063-1306 Office: 316 Daniel Webster Hwy Merrimack NH 03054

FLICK, FREDERICK EDWARD, trade association executive; b. Lynnwood, Calif., July 17, 1947; s. Edward and Helen Arline (beery) F.; m. Elizabeth Ann Twigg, Dec. 27, 1981. BA in Econs., Calif. State U., Los Angeles, 1969; MA in Econs., U. Minn., 1972; PhD in Econs., Washington U., St. Louis, 1981. Research economist U.S. Dept. Housing and Urban Devel., Washington, 1976-82; dir. econ. analysis Nat. Assn. Realtors, Washington, 1982-87, v.p. forecasting and policy analysis, 1987—; study dir. The Demand for Housing and Home Financing into the 21st Century, 1987, Real Estate in the U.S. Economy, 1988. Contbr. articles to profl. jours. Named Earhart fellow, 1976. Mem. Omicron Delta Epsilon. Home: 5537 N 18th Rd Arlington VA 22205 Office: Nat Assn Realtors 777 14th St Washington DC 20005

FLICK, WARREN EDMOND, retail executive; b. New Orleans, Dec. 11, 1943; s. Warren E. Sr. and Lucille (Ash) F.; m. Donna Lynn Brasiel, Oct. 19, 1963; children: Kelly, Warren, Aaryn. Student, La. State U., 1961-65. Various merchandising positions Sears Roebuck and Co., Chgo., 1966-78, div. mdse. mgr., 1978-80, v.p. mdse., 1988—; exec. v.p. Harper Industries, N.Y.C., 1980-84; v.p. mdse. Montgomery Ward, N.Y.C., 1984-87; exec. v.p. Randa Corp., N.Y.C., 1987-88. Republican. Roman Catholic. Home: 3314 N Lake Shore Dr #11A Chicago IL 60656 Office: Sears Roebuck & Co Sears Tower D/700-4 Chicago IL 60684

FLIEDER, JOHN JOSEPH, insurance executive, marketing professional; b. Bremerton, Wash., Aug. 15, 1936; s. Louis and Bertha Amelia (Hersley) F.; m. Barbara Ann Bartlett, Sept. 14, 1956; children: Jerald Louis, Susan Jeannine, Julie Diane, Karen Jo Michelle. Student, U. Wash., 1953-55; AB in Mktg., San Jose State U., 1957; cert. in advanced advt., Northwestern U., 1972; MS in Mktg. Communications, Roosevelt U., 1978. Budget analyst State of Calif., Sacramento, 1958-60; agt. Equitable Life Assurance Soc., Sacramento, 1960-61; co-owner Ames, Flieder & Schnetz, Sacramento, 1961-62; with Allstate Ins. Co., Sacramento, 1962-66; asst. advt. dir. Allstate Ins. Co., Northbrook, Ill., 1971-75; v.p. product acctg. and agt. support Allstate Ins. Co., Northbrook, 1987—. Exec. com., bd. dirs. Boys and Girls Clubs Chgo., 1972—. Capt. U.S. Army, 1957-63, with Res. 1963—. Mem. Direct Mktg. Edn. Found. (dir. 1977—), Assn. Nat. Advertisers, Direct Mktg. Assn. (Direct Mktg. Ins. Exec. award 1989), Chgo. Assn. Direct Mktg. (Direct Marketer of Yr. 1986). Republican. Office: Allstate Ins Co Allstate Pla B10 Northbrook IL 60062

FLINKSTROM, HENRY ALLAN, sales executive; b. Ashby, Mass., Feb. 19, 1933; s. William Elias and Selma Catherine (Aho) F.; m. Marian June Linnus, May 14, 1950; children: Leonard A., Eric A., Carl E. Grad. high sch., Ashby, 1951; diploma in constrn., Fitchburg (Mass.) High, 1953. Ind. carpenter Fitchburg, 1950-54; salesman Webber Lumber, Fitchburg, 1954-64; v.p. Morgan-Price Constrn., Ashburnham, Mass., 1964-66; contractor, sales mgr. Webber Lumber, Fitchburg, 1966-80; sales rep. Sawyer Lumber, Worcester, Mass., 1981-82, Webber Lumber (merger Sawyer Lumber and Webber Lumber), Worcester and Fitchburg, 1982—; home designer HAF Design, Fitchburg; dealer Sun Room Co., Leola, Pa., real estate broker Flinkstoms. Designer of over 2000 homes built in New Eng. area. Charter mem. Rep. Presdl. Task Force, Rep. Nat. Com., 1984—, Mass. Chiefs of Police Assoc., Fitchburg Art Mus. Mem. Profl. Fin. Assocs. (registered assoc.), Am. Plywood Assn. Club: Finnish-Am., Club of Saima-Fitchburg, U.S. Senatorial. Lodge: Masons. Home: HAF Design 19 Ashburnham State Rd Fitchburg MA 01420

FLINN, DAVID LYNNFIELD, financial consultant; b. Atlanta, Aug. 6, 1943; s. William Adams and Caroline Elizabeth (Blackshear) F.; m. Lucy Van Devere, July 5, 1969; children: Raymur Elizabeth, Marion Orme. BA, Ga. State U., 1967. With Citizens & So. Nat. Bank, Atlanta and Miami, Fla., 1967-70; asst. to pres. Panelfab Internat. Corp., Miami, 1970-72; v.p. Citibank, Miami, 1972-76; ind. fin. cons. Miami, 1976—; cons. various fgn. corps, 1981—; bd. dirs. Aljoma Lumber, Inc., Medley, Fla., Continental Trust Mortgage Corp., Miami. Bd. dirs. former pres. La Gorce Island Assn., 1974—; bd. dirs. Children's Home Soc., Miami, 1980-83. Mem. N.W. Dade County C. of C. (trustee, bd. dirs. 1986—), Miami Com. on Fgn. Relations. Republican. Episcopalian. Clubs: Bath (bd. dirs. 1986-88), La Gorce Country (Miami Beach, Fla.); Miami. Home and Office: 6675 Windsor Ln Miami Beach FL 33141

FLINN, MICHAEL DE VLAMING, investment banker, state legislator; b. Durham, N.C., June 15, 1941; s. Lawrence and Marion (de Vlaming) F.; B.A. magna cum laude, Yale U., 1962; J.D., Harvard U., 1965; m. Elizabeth Jamison Folk, Aug. 3, 1962 (div. Mar. 1985); children—William III, Michael de Vlaming, T. Rex, Randall E. Bar: Conn. 1968. Ltd. partner Ingalls & Snyder, 1970—; mem. Conn. Ho. of Reps. from 149th Dist., 1983-86 . Rep., Town Meeting, Greenwich, Conn., 1970-82; mem. Conn. Republican Fin. Com., 1972; mem. Greenwich Rep. Fin. Com., 1977-80; mem. Greenwich Rep. Town Com., 1980-85 , exec. com., 1982-84; trustee Green-Wood Cemetery, 1983—. Pres., bd. dirs. Greenwich Boys Club Assn.; pres., bd. dirs. Round Hill Assn., 1972-81. Served as capt. U.S. Army, 1966-68. Mem. Am., Conn., Greenwich bar assns., Hotchkiss Alumni Assn. (gov. 1979-83), Yale Alumni Assn. of Greenwich (gov. 1982-85). Clubs: Down Town Assn., Links, Burning Tree. Home: PO Box 1309 Greenwich CT 06830 Office: Ingalls & Snyder 61 Broadway New York NY 10006

FLINN, THOMAS HANCE, investment banking, financial consultant; b. Hutto, Tex., Jan. 30, 1922; s. Thomas Hance and Margaret (Bowden) F.; m. Georgeann Atwood, May 26, 1948; children: Mary Kathleen, Michael Hance, Mark Thomas. Grad. cert. Stonier Grad. Sch. Banking, 1961; BBA, U. Tex., 1949. Securities salesman various firms, San Antonio, 1949-54; v.p. M.E. Allison & Co., San Antonio, 1955-56; asst. v.p. Groos Nat. Bank, San Antonio, 1956-59; pvt. practice investment counsel, San Antonio, 1959-60; investment counsel Scudder, Stevens & Clark, Dallas, 1960-63; v.p. investments United Va. Bankshares Inc., Richmond, 1964-73, sr. v.p., corp. treas., 1973-82, ret., 1983, bd. dirs. various subs.; interim pres., chief exec. officer, bd. dirs. Fidelity Bank NA, San Antonio, 1984-85; lectr. in field. Vice-chmn. Chesterfield County (Va.) Rep. party, 1966. Served with USAAF, 1942-46, PTO. Mem. Delta Sigma Pi. Presbyterian. Clubs: Lakeway Yacht and Country. Lodges: Masons (32 deg.), Shriners. Home and Office: 206 Timpanagos Dr Austin TX 78734

FLINT, MARK ADDISON, financial executive; b. Burbank, Calif., July 2, 1946; s. Fred and Virginia (Gramlich) F.; m. Susan Barrett, Aug. 26, 1972. B.S. in Bus., SUNY, Buffalo, 1973, B.A. in Econs., 1974; M.B.A. in Fin., SUNY-Buffalo-1974, 1976. Sr. fin. analyst Peter J. Schmitt Co., Inc., Buffalo, 1979; mgr. fin. planning Peter J. Schmitt Co., Inc., 1980-81, dir. corp. planning, 1981-83, corp. treas, 1983-84, v.p. fin., 1984-85, corp. v.p. fin., chief fin. officer, 1986—. Served with USMC, 1966-68, Viet Nam. Mem. C. of C. Home: 432 N Forest Rd Williamsville NY 14221 Office: Peter J Schmitt Co Inc PO Box 2 Buffalo NY 14240

FLITCRAFT, RICHARD KIRBY, II, former chemical company executive; b. Woodstown, N.J., Sept. 5, 1920; s. H. Milton and Edna (Crispin) F.; m. Bertha LeSturgeon Hitchner, Nov. 14, 1942; children: Alyce, Anne, Elizabeth, Richard. BS, Rutgers U., 1942; MS, Washington U., 1948. With Monsanto Co., St. Louis, 1942—; dir. inorganic rsch. Monsanto Co., 1960-65, dir. mgmt. info. and systems dept., 1965-67, asst. to pres., 1967-68, group mgr. electronics enterprises, 1968-69, gen. mgr. electronic products div., 1969-71; v.p. Monsanto Rsch. Corp., 1971-75; dir. Mound Lab., 1971-75, v.p. ops., 1975-76; pres. Monsanto Resh. Corp., Dayton, 1976-82, ret., 1982; bd. dirs. Soc. Bank N.A., Medam. Health Systems Corp. Chmn., bd. dirs. United Way, Dayton; bd. dirs. City-Wide Devel. Corp.; past chmn. bd. trustees Miami Valley Hosp.; bd. dirs. Pvt. Industry Coun. Mem. AAAS, Am. Chem. Soc., Am. Inst. Chem. Engrs., Am. Inst. Chemists, Am. Mgmt. Assn., N.Y. Acad. Scis., Ohio Acad. Scis. (exec. com.), Dayton C. of C. (past bd. dirs., chmn.), Sigma Xi. Presbyterian. Clubs: Engrs., Moraine Country, Dayton Racquet.

FLOCH, MORTON HUGH, pharmaceutical company executive; b. N.Y.C., May 19, 1934; s. Sol F. and Ruth I. (Greenberg) F.; m. Constance Anne Marino, July 8, 1960; children: Pamela Joan Floch Awad, Mark Steven. BS, Alfred U., 1955; MBA, NYU, 1962. Br. v.p. World Book-Childcraft Internat., Chgo., 1969-82; v.p. mktg. Internat. Med. Ctrs., Miami, Fla., 1983-86, Comprehensive Am. Care, Miami, 1986; pres. HSN Pharms., Tampa, Fla., 1986-87; chief exec. officer The Prescription People, Miami, 1988—; also bd. dirs. The Prescription People; cons. Health Care Adv. Svc., Miami, 1986—. Mem. Am. Mktg. Assn., Am. Mgmt. Assn. Home: 3775 NE 209 Terrace North Miami Beach FL 33180 Office: The Prescription People Inc 4714 NW 165 St Miami FL 33014

FLOERCHINGER, THOMAS ALLEN, computer company executive; b. St. Louis, Aug. 28, 1945; s. Lawrence Louis and Ester (Shubert) F.; m. Diane Mary Pekarek (div. 1981); m. Susan Jane Moody, Nov. 26, 1982; children: Christian, Amy. BS, St. Louis U., 1967, MBA, 1970. V.p., chief operating officer Advent Corp., Boston, 1980-82; v.p. Harman Internat. Industries Inc., Washington, 1982-85; chief fin. officer, v.p., sec. Entre Computer Ctrs. Inc. Office: Entre Computer Ctrs Inc 1430 Spring Hill Rd McLean VA 22102

FLOM, EDWARD LEONARD, steel company executive; b. Tampa, Fla., Dec. 10, 1929; s. Samuel Louis and Julia (Mittle) F.; m. Beverly Boyett, Mar. 31, 1956; children—Edward Louis, Mark Robert, Julia Ruth. B.C.E., Cornell U., 1952. With Fla. Steel Corp., Tampa, 1954—; v.p. sales Fla. Steel Corp., 1957-64, pres., dir., 1964—; dir. NCNB Nat. Bank Fla., Teco Energy Inc. Bd. dirs. mem. exec. com. United Fund Tampa; advisory com. St. Joseph's Hosp., Tampa; bd. dirs. Family Service Assn. Tampa, Jewish Welfare Fedn. Tampa; exec. com. Com. of 100, Tampa. Served with C.E. AUS, 1952-54. Mem. Am. Iron and Steel Inst. (dir.), Young Pres.'s Orgn., Fla. Engring. Soc. Jewish (bd. dirs. temple). Clubs: Rotary (Tampa) (bd. dirs.); University, Palma Ceia Golf and Country, Tampa Yacht, Gasparilla Krewe. Home: 4936 Saint Croix Dr Tampa FL 33629 Office: Fla Steel Corp 1715 Cleveland St PO Box 23328 Tampa FL 33630

FLOOD, CHARLES F., JR., solid waste service company executive; b. Mt. Vernon, N.Y., Feb. 20, 1946; s. Charles F. and Janet Ann (Byrne) F.; m. Polly Ann Mishoe, Dec. 31, 1966; children—Kimberley Ann, Christopher Michael. B.Ed., U. Miami, 1968. Asst. to pres. SCA Services, Inc., Boston, 1976-77, dist. mgr., Ft. Worth, 1977-80, regional mgr. Tex. region, 1980-82, v.p., So. div. mgr., 1982-84; sr. v.p., gen. mgr. GSX Solid Waste Services Inc., 1984-86; pres. U.S. ops. Laidlaw Waste Systems, 1986-87; founder, pres. The Flood Group, Inc., 1988—. Mem. North Richland Hill (Tex.) Charter Com., 1980. Roman Catholic. Lodge: Ft. Worth Lions. Home: 1364 Lakeview Dr Southlake TX 76092 Office: Flood Group Inc PO Box 1198 Keller TX 76248

FLOOD, RANDOLPH GENE, government affairs business consultant; b. Huntingdon, Pa., Mar. 12, 1950; s. Donald Curtis and Janet (Crouse) F.; m. Judith Tucker, May 10, 1986; children: Jefferson Frederick. BS, Shepherd Coll., 1973. Mem. profl. staff com. on environment and pub. works Senate, Washington, 1973-79, legis. advisor to Sen. Harry F. Byrd Jr., 1979-83; pres. Randolph G. Flood & Assocs., Washington, 1983—; faculty, tchr. George Washington U., Washington, 1988; rep. to UN, N.Y.C., Jaycees Internat., Washington, 1983-85. Mem. steering com. Dem. Leadership Coun. Network. Named Outstanding Program Mgr. U.S. Jaycees, 1982, Outstanding Fed. Employee Va. Jaycees, 1982; recipient Outstanding Rep. award Jaycees Internat., 1983. Mem. Shipbuilders Counc. Am. (chmn. govt. affairs com. 1988—), U.S. Naval Inst., Propeller Club, U.S. Navy League. Democrat. Office: 422 1st St SE Washington DC 20003

FLORENCE, JERRY DEWAYNE, sales and marketing executive; b. Wichita, Kans., Oct. 6, 1948; s. Alise Lee and Rosa Lee (Washington) F.; m. Winifred Tarizona Watson, May 4, 1974; 1 child, Michael Brigham. BS in Chemistry, Wichita State U., 1971; cert. in exec. mgmt., Pa. State U., 1987. Cert. in mgmt. devel. Product devel. chemist Gen. Electric Silicones, Waterford, N.Y., 1974-75, tech. mktg. specialist, 1975-76; sales dept. specialist Gen. Electric Silicones, Cleve., 1976-78, mgr. coating program, 1979, mgr. tech. mktg., 1979-83, mgr. sealants mktg., 1983-84, mgr. market planning, 1984; mgr. bus. planning Packard Electric div. Gen Motors Corp., Warren, Ohio, 1984-87, mgr. sales, mktg. and bus. planning, 1987—. Inventor silicone additive to polyolefins. Trustee Trumbull County YMCA, Warren, 1985—, Western Reserve Girl Scouts USA, Akron, Ohio, 1985—, ARC, Trumbull county, Warren, 1988—; mem. allocation com. United Way, 1987—. Home: 1310 Berkshire Stow OH 44224 Office: GMC Packard Electric Div PO Box 431 Warren OH 44486

FLORES, FRANK FAUSTO, graphics and communications company executive; b. N.Y.C., Sept. 18, 1930; s. Frank E. and Marie (Navarro) F.; m. Elizabeth L. Weekes, Oct. 2, 1948; children—Donald, Stephen, Allen. Sales mgr. Marsden Offset Printing Co., Inc., N.Y.C., 1955-59, treas., 1959—; pres. Marsden Reprodns., Inc., N.Y.C., 1962—; bd. dirs. Nat. Minority Bus. Council, Cath. Interracial Council; bd. dirs. N.Y.-N.J. Minority Purchasing Council, chmn. vendor input com.; mem. Manhattan adv. council Salvation Army, Affirmative Action Adv. Bd. N.Y. State Dept. Transp. Com., City Coll. Sch. Edn. adv. bd., Hispanic Bus. adv. bd. for N.Y.C.; bd. dirs. Regional Plan Assn. (dir. exec. com.), Amistad MESBIC, Puerto Rican Family Inst., League of United Latin Am. Citizens Found., Private Industry Council, Alliance N.Y.C. Bus., Sch. and Bus. Alliance for N.Y.C., Shield Inst. for Retarded Children, 1986, United Way of Tri-State, 1988—, N.Y.C. Partnership, 1988—; trustee Blueprinting Union Health & Wealth Fund Local 966 Pension Fund. Named Hispanic Businessman of Yr., League United Latin Am. Citizens, 1981, N.Y. Minority Businessman of Yr., Nat. Minority Bus. Council, 1981, Employer of Yr., Goodwill Industries, 1982, 83, 84, Employer of Yr., Nat. Mental Health Assn. and Pres.'s Com. on Employment of Handicapped, 1983, Supplier of Yr. Nat. Minority Supplier Devel. Council Inc., 1986, Hispanic Businessman of Yr. Wall St. Chpt. of Image, 1986, Albany Hispanic Coalition, 1986; recipient Small Bus. award N.Y. Chamber Commerce and Industry, 1983, Minority Purchasing Council, Inc. award in grateful appreciation for outstanding contributions,1988, Crystal Shield award Salvation Army of Greater N.Y. Mem. Nat. Hispanic Bus. Group (founder, v. chmn. 1984—), Soc. Tech. Communication (past chmn.), Internat. Reprographics Assn., Nat. Assn. Photo Lithographers, Blue Printers Assn. N.Y., IMAGE (chmn. adv. bd. Wall St. chpt.), N.Y. State Hispanic C. of C. (Hispanic businessman of yr. 1985), Latino Commn. for United Way, P.R. Family Inst., Nat. Rifle Assn. Home: 40 Rockwood Ln Greenwich CT 06830 Office: 30 E 33d St New York NY 10016

FLORES, ORLANDO, accountant; b. San Antonio, Oct. 2, 1946; s. Joseph M. and Edelmira (Chapa) F.; m. Patsy Marks, Feb. 25, 1967; children: Orlando Jr., James J. AA, San Antonio Coll., 1972; BS, Our Lady of Lake U., 1976, MBA, 1986. CPA, Tex. Employed by USAF, 1966-75; auditor Def. Contract Audit Agy., San Antonio, 1975-83, supr. auditor, 1983-87; br. mgr. Def. Contract Audit Agy., Austin, Tex., 1988—; instr. St. Philips Coll., San Antonio, 1977-82, Our Lady of Lake U., 1980-87, Webster U., Ft. Sam Houston, 1987. Bd. dirs. St. Anthony Day Care Ctr., 1987. Mem. Am. Inst. CPAs, Tex. Soc. CPAs. Roman Catholic. Office: Def Contract Audit Agy PO Box 19349 Austin TX 78760

FLORES, SUZANNE, bookeeper, real estate company executive; b. Rosebud, Tex., May 31, 1931; d. Florentino Garza Villarreal and Maria Ynes (Cordova) Villarreal; m. Jesus Flores, May 27, 1950; children: Cynthia Anne, Denise Kaye. Cert., Cameron Bus. Coll., 1951, Real Estate Coll., 1976. Spl. interpreter adminstrn. and research Scott and White Health Clinic, Temple, Tex., 1949-60; acctg. clk. II Tex. Instruments, Dallas, 1961-68; owner, bookkeeper Flores Bookkeeping Services, Dallas, 1968—; acctg. clk. SW Med. Sch., Dallas, 1974-78; v.p., realtor Encore Real Estate, Inc., Dallas, 1984—; v.p., cons. Transplastic, Inc., Dallas, 1985—, D. Browne Creations, Inc., Dallas, 1985—; cons. Lancaster Investment Co. Mem. Mex. Am. Bus. and Profl. Women (founder, treas. 1972-74), Dallas Hispanic C. of C. (bd. dirs. 1981). Republican. Methodist. Home: 4124 Saranac Dr Dallas TX 75220 Office: Flores Bookkeeping Svcs 6300 N Central Expresssway Suite 105 Dallas TX 75206

FLORESCUE, BARRY WILLIAM, business executive; b. N.J., Dec. 5, 1943; s. Harold and Gertrude F.; m. Renate Schlessinger, May 13, 1979; children: Gretchen, Geremy, Bryan. B.B.A. in Acctg, U. Rochester, N.Y., 1966; M.B.A., NYU, 1970. C.P.A., N.Y. Acct., then sr. acct. Peat, Marwick, Mitchell & Co., N.Y.C., 1966-70; investment exec., securities analyst Scharson Hammill, N.Y.C., 1969-70; v.p. fin., controller Seronsonic Labs., N.Y.C., 1970-71; v.p. fin., dir. Threshold Tech. Inc., Delran, N.J., 1971-74; ptnr. Sharon Gardens Meml. Park, Ft. Lauderdale, Fla., 1974-80; lt. ptnr. Sharon Gardens Meml. Park, 1980—; pres., chmn. bd. Jesson, Inc., Delray Beach, Fla., 1974—; pres. Horn & Hardart Co., Inc., N.Y.C., 1977-82, chmn. bd., 1982-85, chmn. bd., pres., 1985—; dir. Color Systems Tech., Inc., Los Angeles, Am. Homestead Inc., Mt. Laurel, N.J. Bd. overseers food service dept. NYU; trustee U. Rochester Grad. Sch. Bus. Recipient U. Rochester award acctg. excellence Haskins & Sells Found., 1965. Mem. Am. Inst. C.P.A.s, Nat. Restaurant Assn., Am. Bus. Conf., N.Y. State Soc. C.P.A.s, Am. Bus. Conf. Office: Horn & Hardart Co 101 Convention Center Dr Las Vegas NV 89109 *

FLORESTANO, DANA JOSEPH, architect; b. Indpls., May 2, 1945; s. Herbert Joseph and Myrtle Mae (Futch) F.; m. Peggy Joy Larsen, June 6, 1969. BArch, U. Notre Dame, 1968. Designer, draftsman Kennedy, Brown & Trueblood, architects, Indpls., 1965-69, Evans Woolen Assn., architects, Indpls., 1966; designer, project capt. James Assos., architects and engrs., Indpls., 1969-71; architect, v.p. comml. projects Multi-Planners Inc., architects and engrs., 1972-73; pvt. practice architecture, Indpls., 1973—; pres. Florestano Corp., constrn. mgmt., Indpls., 1973—; co-founder, pres. Solargenics Natural Energy Corp., Indpls., 1975—; pres. Star Archery Corp., Indpls., 1989—; prof. archtl. and constrn. tech. Ind. U.-Purdue U. at Indpls.; instr. in field. Tech. adviser hist. architecture Indpls. Model Cities program, 1969-70; mem. Hist. Landmarks Found. Ind., 1970-72; chmn. Com. to Save Union Sta., 1970-71, founder, pres. Union Sta. Found. Inc., Indpls., 1971—. Dep. commr. and tournament dir. archery Pan-Am. Games, Indpls., 1987. Recipient 2d design award Marble Inst. Am., 1967, 1st design award 19th Ann. Progressive Architecture Design awards, 1972; Design award for excellence in devel. Marriott Inn, Indpls., Met. Devel. Commn.-Office of Mayor, 1977; 1st place award design competition for Visitor's Info. Ctr., Cave Run, Lake, Ky., 1978; 2d design award 1st Ann. Qualified Remodeler, Nat. Competition for Best Rehab. Existing Structures in Am., 1979. Mem. U. Notre Dame Alumni Assn., Notre Dame Club Indpls., AIA (nat. com. historic resources 1974—, commn. on community svcs., Speakers Bur. Indpls. chpt. 1976—), Ind. Soc. Architects (chmn. historic architecture com. 1970—), Ind. Archery Assn. (founder, pres. 1985—, Overall Male State Champion 1987), No. Archery Assn. (bd. dirs., pres. 1987—), Constrn. Specifications Inst., Constrn. Mgrs. Assn. Ind. (incorporator, dir. 1976—), World Archery Ctr. Home: 5697 N Broadway St Indianapolis IN 46220 Office: Dana Florestano AIA 6214 N Carrollton Ave Indianapolis IN 46220

FLORIO, DOMINIC ANTHONY, management executive; b. N.Y.C., Feb. 26, 1946; s. Michael Joseph and Maria Elena (Bonfiglio) F. BS, Iona Coll., 1972, MBA, 1974. Qualitative analyst N.Y.C. Human Resources Adminstrn., 1973-74; dir. ops. Conn. Med. Inst., New Haven, 1974-75; exec. dir. Richmond County Profl. Rev. Orgn., N.Y.C., 1975-76; bus. mgr., v.p. Citibank, N.A., N.Y.C., 1976-86; pres. Hickory Brewster Internat., Inc., Phila. and N.Y.C., 1986—. Pres. Thomas Paine Heights Assn., New Rochelle, N.Y., 1984-86. With U.S. Army, 1966-68. Republican. Roman Catholic. Home: 172 Valley stream cir Wayne PA 19087 Office: Hickory BrewsterInternat Inc 97 Broadview Ave New Rochelle NY 10804 Office: Hickory Brewster Inc 656 E Swedesford Rd Bldg 5 Wayne PA 19087 Office: Hickory Brewster Internat Inc 34 Trinity Pl New York NY 10801

FLORJANCIC, FREDERICK JOSEPH, JR., financial executive; b. Canonsburg, Pa., Jan. 29, 1947; s. Frederick J. and Olga L. (Delost) F.; m. Barbara J. Edmonds, Aug. 24, 1968; children: Frederick J., Nicole. BS, Ind. U., 1968, MBA, 1970. V.p., div. mgr. Continental Ill. Nat. Bank, Chgo., 1970-84; v.p., treas. McGraw Edison, Rolling Meadows, Ill., 1984-85; v.p. fin., treas. Brunswick Corp., Skokie, Ill., 1985-89; div. gen. mgr. Brunswick div. Muskegon, Mich., 1989—. Served to capt. USAR, 1970-76. Mem. Nat. Assn. Corp. Treas. (bd. dirs. 1985—). Clubs: Fin. Officers; University (Chgo.); Cress Creek Country (Naperville, Ill.). Office: Brunswick Corp 1 Brunswick Pla Skokie IL 60077

FLORY, ROBERT MIKESELL, computer systems analyst, personnel management specialist; b. Bridgewater, Va., Feb. 21, 1912; s. John Samuel and Vinnie (Mikesell) F.; m. Thelma Thomas, Sept. 14, 1942; 1 child, Pamela. B.A., Bridgewater Coll., 1932; M.A., U. Va., 1938; postgrad. U. Chgo., 1946-51. Job/methods analyst United Air Lines, Chgo., 1945-47; job analyst Julian Baer, Chgo., 1948; asst. to v.p. Fairbanks, Morse, Chgo., 1949-60; mgmt. cons. Yarger & Assocs., Falls Church, Va., 1961; computer systems analyst, various fed. agys., Washington, 1962-82; tchr. Roosevelt U., Chgo., 1956-61; seminar leader U. Chgo., 1960-61; cons. Va. Gov.'s Commn. for Reorgn. State Govt., 1961. Served to lt. comdr. USN, 1942-45, PTO. Mem. Inst. Mgmt. Scis. Home: 5501 Seminary Rd Apt 1204-S Falls Church VA 22041

FLOWER, WALTER CHEW, III, investment counselor; b. New Orleans, Mar. 3, 1939; s. Walter Chew II and Anne Elisa (Lusk) F.; B.A. in Econs., Tulane U., 1960; M.B.A. in Fin., Harvard U., 1964; m. Ella Smith Montgomery, Dec. 21, 1966; children—Anne Stuart, Lindsey Montgomery. Cons. AID, State Dept., 1964-65; fin. analyst Delta Capital Corp., New Orleans, 1965-66; v.p., mng. partner Loomis Sayles & Co. Inc., New Orleans, 1967-78; pres. Walter C. Flower & Co., Investment Counsel, New Orleans, 1978—; dir. Lusk Shipping Co. Inc.; dir., chmn. exec. com. So. Vital Records Inc.; dir. Starmount Cos. Bd. dirs. Preservation Resource Center, 1975-81; bd. dirs., chmn. HFSM Archtl. Revolving Fund, 1976—, Longue Vue Found., 1983—; vestryman, mem. parish council Trinity Ch., 1978—; dir., fin. adv. Jr. League New Orleans, 1978-82; fin. adv. Hermann Grima House, 1978—, Beauregard House, 1979—. Served with USNR, 1960-62. Mem. Phi Beta Kappa. Clubs: Boston, Pickwick, New Orleans Lawn Tennis, So. Yacht (New Orleans), Stratford, Lakeshore. Office: 408 Magazine Cor Poydras New Orleans LA 70130

FLOWERS, JAMES ARTHUR, sales executive; b. Louisville, June 5, 1938; s. Arthur Edward and Margaret Mary (Thompson) F.; m. Judy Lee Rogers, Feb. 14, 1981; children: Perry, Kelly, Letitia, Duane, Jeremy, Adam. Student, U. Louisville, 1956-58, U. Cin., 1981, Lamar U., 1982-83. Sales engr. Carrier Air Conditioning, Indpls., 1974-76; mgr. sales Carrier Air Conditioning, Detroit, 1976-80; sales engr. Carrier Air Conditioning, Beaumont, Tex., 1981-86; mgr. gen. sales Andrew's Distbg. Co., Chattanooga, 1986—. Mem. ASHRAE. Office: Andrews Distbg Co 3000 S Hickory Chattanooga TN 37407

FLOWERS, WILLIAM HOWARD, JR., food company executive; b. Thomasville, Ga., Nov. 14, 1913; s. William Howard and Flewellyn Evans (Strong) F.; m. Fontaine Maury Tice, June 22, 1936; children: Fontaine, Maury (Mrs. Joseph V. Shields Jr.), Daphne (Mrs. C. Martin Wood III), Taliaferro (Mrs. Robert P. Crozer). B.A. in Bus. Adminstrn, Washington and Lee U., 1933. With Flowers Baking Co. div. Flowers Industries, Inc., Thomasville, Ga., 1933-68, pres., chief operating officer, 1937-65, chmn., chief operating officer, 1966-68; chmn., chief exec. officer Flowers Industries, Inc., Thomasville, 1974-76, chmn., 1976-81, chmn. exec. com., 1981—, chmn. emeritus, 1984—. Chmn. Southeastern Legal Found., Atlanta, 1983-87, emeritus, 1987—; dir. The Prayer Book Soc., 1984-87, Thomas County Bi-Centennial/Sesqui-Centennial Commn.; mem. spl. adv. com. on pub. opinion U.S. Dept. State, 1970-72; mem. Thomas County Sch. Bd., 1953-58, Madeira Sch. Corp., Greenway, Va., 1960-68, Ga. Senate, 1964-68; city commr., Thomasville, 1941; pres. Thomasville YMCA, 1949-52; trustee John D. Archbold Meml. Hosp., 1953-71, Thomasville; pres. William Howard Flowers Jr. Found. Named Man of Year Thomas County C. of C., 1964. Mem. N.A.M. (dir. 1962-66), Young Presidents' Orgn., Chief Execs. Orgn., Ducks Unltd. (nat. trustee 1967—), Omicron Delta Kappa. Episcopalian. Clubs: Rotarian, Lyford Cay (Nassau); Wildcat Cliffs Country (Highlands, N.C.); Ga-Fl Field Trial; Glen Arven Country (Thomasville); Farmington Country (Charlottesville, Va.). Address: Flowers Industries Inc PO Box 1338 US Highway 19 Thomasville GA 31792

FLOYD, AARON BERNARD, defense systems executive; b. Opelika, Ala., June 15, 1938; s. Julius James and Annie Pearl (Miles) F.; m. LaVon Sciota Scott, Aug. 18, 1958; children: Angela Ann, Candace Scott, Cecelia LaVon. BS in Biol. Sci., Ball State U., 1960; MA in Mgmt., U. Nebr., 1974;

grad. sr. def. mgrs. course, Harvard U., 1984. Commd. 2d lt. USAF, 1960, advanced through grades to col., ret., 1984; def. mgr. intelligence sect. USAF, U.S., Republic of China, Eng., Thailand, 1960-82; officer Def. Intelligence Agy., 1982-84; sr. staff scientist Sci. Applications Internat. Corp., McLean, Va., 1984-87; pres., chief exec. officer Aaron B. Floyd Assocs., Inc., Springfield, Va., 1987—; cons. Booz, Allen & Hamilton, Inc., Crystal City, Va., 1988—, Sci. Applications Internat. Corp., 1987—; adj. faculty mem. Howard U., Washington, 1988—. Bd. dirs. Nat. Urban League, 1980-82. Recipient essay awards Freedoms Found., 1964, 65. Mem. Nat. Mil. Intelligence Agy., Am. Mgmt. Assn., Tuskegee Airmen, Inc. (nat. v.p. 1979-81). Methodist. Home and Office: 7933 St George Ct Springfield VA 22153

FLOYD, JAMES ESTON, JR., accountant; b. Homestead, Fla., Feb. 12, 1957; s. James Eston and Cynthia (Weaver) F.; m. Jill Diane Lanier, Feb. 23, 1974; children: James Eston III, Jason Lee. BA, U. South Fla., 1978. Cost. acct. Am. Shipbuilding Co., Tampa, Fla., 1978-79, Speedling Mgmt. Services, Sun City, Fla., 1980; chief acct. Fed. Constrn. Co., St. Petersburg, Fla., 1981-82; controller C. Randolph Wedding & Assocs., St. Petersburg, 1982-83, Risser Oil Corp., Pinellas Pk., Fla., 1983—; bd. dirs. Service World Internat., Clearwater, Fla. Treas. troop 88 Boy Scouts Am., Tampa, 1987. Mem. Nat. Assn. Accts. Office: Risser Oil Corp 5001 Park Blvd Pinellas Park FL 34665

FLOYD, JOHN TAYLOR, electronics executive; b. Quincy, Mass., Jan. 17, 1942; s. John Taylor and Virginia Marie (Watts) F.; m. Denise Angela Dufault, Oct. 4, 1969; children: Jennifer, Aimee. BA, Northeastern U., 1965; MBA in Fin., Boston Coll., 1972. Product group controller Tex. Instruments, Attleboro, Mass., 1972-75; asst. to v.p. fin. Waters Assocs., Milford, Mass., 1975-76; group fin. mgr. Digital Equipment Corp., Maynard, Mass., 1976-82; v.p. mfg. Computer Devices, Burlington, Mass., 1982-83; dir. fin. and adminstrn. Wang Labs., Lowell, Mass., 1984-85; v.p. ops. Charleswater Products, West Newton, Mass., 1985—; dir. The Devon Group, Waltham, Mass., Marlborough (Mass.) Hosp., New Health Enterprises, Inc. Served to capt. U.S. Army, 1965-70, Vietnam. Mem. Fin. Execs. Inst., Am. Electronics Assn., Treas.' Club of Boston, Am. Legion. Republican. Home: 68 Longfellow Rd Sudbury MA 01776 Office: Charleswater Products Inc 93 Border St West Newton MA 02165

FLOYD-TENIYA, KATHLEEN, business services executive; b. Berwyn, Ill., June 23, 1953; d. David James and Phyllis L. (Lyons) Floyd; m. Robert Don Teniya, June 20, 1982; one child: James David. Cert. credit and fin. analyst, lic. realtor, Ill. Indsl. specialist Technicon Instrument Corp., Elmhurst, Ill., 1971-74, service contract adminstr., 1974-76; asst. to pres. Elmed, Inc., Addison, Ill., 1976-77; credit rep. mgr. Memorex Corp., Lombard, Ill., 1977-79; nat. sales rep. Midcontinent Adjustment Co., Glenview, Ill., 1979-83, asst. v.p. sales, 1983-86; pres., chief exec. officer, (Inteletek) Innovative Telemktg. Techniques Inc., Itasca, Ill., 1986—. Newspaper editor, publicity chmn. Dupage County chpt. Young Ams. for Freedom, 1969-70, pres.; mem. bd. edn. Trinity Luth. Sch., Lombard, Ill, 1989—. Mem. Nat. Assn. Female Execs., Am. Soc. Profl. and Exec. Women. Lutheran. Clubs: Lombard Women's Rep., Ill. Fedn. Rep. Women. Home: 263 Evergreen Ln Bloomingdale IL 60108 Office: (Inteletek) Innovative Telemktg Techniques Inc PO Box 0163 Itasca IL 60143

FLUD, VIRGINIA STAPLER, employment service executive; b. Newnan, Ga., Apr. 13, 1942; d. Vancie Lee and Martha (Cole) Stapler; m. Clifford W. Flud, Apr. 15, 1961; children: Cynthia Flud Thompson, Troy W. Grad. high sch., Newnan. Teller, bookkeeper First Nat. Bank, Newnan, 1960-72; asst. cashier Bank of Coweta, Ga., 1972-75; asst. vi.p. Bank of Coweta, 1975-76, v.p., 1976-87; v.p., chief exec. officer First Community Bank of Cherokee, Woodstock, Ga., 1987-88; pres. Interstaff, Inc., Woodstock, 1988—; sec., treas. First Community Corp., First Community Mortgage Corp.; security officer First Community Bank. Mem. Cherokee County Hist. Soc., Cherokee County Dem. Women's Orgn. Mem. Bank Adminstrn. Inst. (treas. West Ga. chpt., dir.), Cherokee County C. of C., Woodstock Prof. and Bus. Assn., Pilot Club (pres.). Democrat. Baptist. Home: 316 Waldan Circle Acworth GA 30101 Office: 575 Parkway Ste 204 Woodstock GA 30188

FLUNO, JERE DAVID, business executive; b. Wisconsin Rapids, Wis., June 3, 1941; s. Rexford Hollis and Irma Dell (Wells) F.; m. Anne Marie Derezinski, Aug. 10, 1963; children: Debra, Julie, Mary Beth, Brian. BBA, U. Wis., 1963. CPA, Ill. Audit supr. Grant Thornton, Chgo., 1963-69; controller W.W. Grainger, Inc., Skokie, Ill., 1969-74, v.p., controller, 1974-75, v.p. fin., 1975-81, sr. v.p., chief fin. officer, 1981-84, vice chmn., 1984—, dir., 1975—; v.p., asst. treas., dir. W.W. Grainger, Internat., Skokie, Ill., 1977—; v.p. , dir. Grainger FSC, Inc.; v.p., dir., asst. treas. Dayton Electric Mfg. Co., Chgo., 1981—; bd. dirs. Midwest Clearing Corp. Bd. govs. Midwest Stock Exchange, Chgo., 1989—; mem. Bascom Hill Soc. U. Wis., Madison, 1979—; trustee Glenkirk Found., Northbrook, Ill., 1981—; vice-chmn., bd. dirs. U. Wis. Found., 1985—. Mem. AICPA, Fin. Execs. Inst., Ill. CPA Soc., Econ. Club Chgo. (bd. dirs. 1979—), U. Wis. Alumni Assn. (bd. dirs.). Republican. Roman Catholic. Clubs: Knollwood (gov., Lake Forest, Ill.); U. Wis. (Chgo.); Island Country (Marco Island, Fla.). Office: W W Grainger Inc 5500 W Howard St Skokie IL 60077

FLYG, WILLIAM THEODORE, retail executive; b. Madison, Wis., Aug. 26, 1942; s. William Theodore Jr. and Margaret Marie (Johnson) F.; m. Kathleen Anne Burke, July 22, 1972; children: Kara April and Reagan Ashley. BA, U. Wash., 1964. With Richardson-Merrell Inc., N.Y.C., 1967-74; corp. controller Fisher Foods Inc., Cleve., 1974-80; operating v.p. fin. Service Mdse. Co. Inc., Nashville, 1980-85; chief fin. officer, v.p., treas. Big Bear Inc., Columbus, 1985—. Served to 1st lt. USMC, 1964-67, Vietnam. Republican. Presbyterian. Club: River Oaks Boat People (Brentwood, Tenn.). Home: 1037 Newark-Granville Rd Granville OH 43023 Office: Big Bear Inc 770 W Goodale Blvd Columbus OH 43212

FLYNN, ANNETTE THERESA, infosystems specialist; b. Miami, Fla., July 10, 1953; d. William Lowry and Ann Theresa (Karnafel) F. AA in Pre-Computer Systems, Miami-Dade Community Coll., 1973; BS in Computer Sci., Fla. Internat. U., 1975. Computer programer, analyst City of Miami Beach, Fla., 1975-79; project mgr. Burroughs Corp., Miami, Fla., 1979-84; sr. project mgr. Ericsson Info. Systems, Miami, 1984-87; sr. project adminstr. ISC Systems Corp., Miami, 1987-88. Mem. Phi Theta Kappa. Democrat. Roman Catholic. Home and Office: 7845 W Meridian St Miramar FL 33023

FLYNN, DONALD EDWARD, diversified investment company executive; b. Lincoln, Nebr., May 7, 1940; s. James Raphael and Marjorie L. (Rosenbaum) F.; m. Janice Marie Oberreuter, Aug. 25, 1962; children: Ann Marie, Michael Joseph, Patricia Ann. BA, U. Iowa, 1962; MBA, San Diego State U., 1970. Investment analyst San Diego Trust & Savs., 1969-70; portfolio mgr. Security Pacific Nat. Bank, Los Angeles, 1970-71; v.p. investments Life Investors Inc., Cedar Rapids, 1971-80; v.p. Moram. Capital Corp., Cedar Rapids, 1980-85; pres. Investam. Venture Group, Inc., Cedar Rapids, 1985-88; v.p. Aegon USA, Inc. (formerly Life Investors Inc.), Cedar Rapids, 1988—. Treas. Cedar Rapids United Way, 1978. Served to capt. USAF, 1962-68, Vietnam. Decorated Air medal. Mem. Iowa Soc. Fin. Analysts. Roman Catholic. Club: Cedar Rapids Country. Home: 3227 Parkview Ct SE Cedar Rapids IA 52403 Office: Aegon USA Inc 4333 Edgewood Rd NE Cedar Rapids IA 52499

FLYNN, ELIZABETH ANNE, advertising and public relations company executive; b. Washington, Aug. 21, 1951; d. John William and Elizabeth Goodwin (Mahoney) F. A.A., Montgomery Coll., Rockville, Md., 1972; B.S. in Journalism, U. Md., 1976; postgrad. San Diego State U., 1976. Writer, researcher, Sea World, Inc., San Diego, 1977-79; sr. writer Lane & Huff Advt., San Diego, 1979-80; account exec. Kaufman, Lansky, Baker Advt., San Diego, 1980-82; mng. dir. Excelsior Enterprises, Beverly Hills, Calif., 1983-84; sr. account exec. Berkhemer & Kline, Inc., Los Angeles, 1985; pres. Flynn Advt. & Pub. Relations, Los Angeles, 1985—; cons. Coca-Cola Bottling Co. Los Angeles, 1982-84. Bd. dirs. Friends of Reconstructive Surgery, Beverly Hills, 1983—. Recipient Cert. of Distinction, Art Direction Mag., 1982. Mem. Nat. Assn. Female Execs., Beverly Hills C. of C., Republican. Roman Catholic. Avocations: screenwriting; short stories; painting; horseback riding. Office: Flynn Advt & Pub Rels 1440 Reeves St Suite 104 Los Angeles CA 90035

FLYNN, JAMES LEONARD, financial executive; b. Cleve., Oct. 14, 1934; s. H. Leonard and K. Nadine (Yanney) F.; m. Shirley Ann Mix, July 8, 1967; children—Sharon, Douglas. A.B., Dartmouth Coll., 1956, M.B.A., 1957. Mgr. budgeting and acctg. Intertype div. Harris Corp., Bklyn., 1957-61, asst. mgr. material control, 1961-63; asst. controller Corning Glass Works, N.Y., 1964-66, asst. to treas., 1963-64, prodn. supt. Bradford plant, 1966-68, dir. corp. planning, 1968-72, gen. mgr. chem. systems dept., 1972-74, asst. treas. to treas., 1974-76, treas., 1976-81, v.p., treas., 1981-85, sr. v.p., treas., 1985-86, sr. v.p. fin., 1986—; dir. Harding Bros., Elmira, N.Y., 1984—, Dow Corning, Midland, Mich., 1982, MetPath Labs, Teterboro, N.J., 1982, Hazleton Labs., Herndon, Va., 1987—. Trustee Arnot Ogden Hosp., Elmira, 1983. Served with USAF, 1957. Gen. Elec. fellow, 1956-57. Mem. Dartmouth Coll. Alumni Assn. Republican. Methodist. Home: 12039 Churchill Pl Big Flats NY 14814 Office: Corning Glass Works Houghton Pk Corning NY 14831

FLYNN, JOHN WILLIAM, financial services executive; b. Fall River, Mass., June 16, 1939; s. George P. and Anna M. (Brown) F.; m. Joan M. Brissette, May 4, 1968; children: Kathleen, Nicole, Susan. BSBA, Providence Coll., 1961. CPA. Sr. acct. Ernst & Whinney, Providence, R.I., 1961-67; sr. acct., contr. Pearson-Grumman Yachts, Portsmouth, R.I., 1967-69; controller Fleet Info. Fleet/Norstar Fin. Group, Providence, 1969-72, controller, 1976-81; controller Fleet Nat. Bank, Providence, 1972-76; exec. v.p., chief fin. officer Fleet/Norstar Fin. Group, Providence, 1981—. Served with U.S. Army, 1962-64. Mem. Fin. Exec. Inst., Am. inst. CPA's, R.I. Soc. CPA's. Republican. Roman Catholic. Office: Fleet/Norstar Fin Group 50 Kennedy Pla Providence RI 02903

FLYNN, KAREN JEAN, financial planner; b. Miami Beach, Fla., Dec. 30, 1950; d. Patrick Joseph Flynn Jr. and Catherine (Puffer) Flynn Bohannan; m. Carl Payberg, June 14, 1969 (div. 1971); children: Holly anne, J. Bradley. AA, Miami Dade Community Coll., 1979; BBA in Fin., U. Miami, 1981. Cert. fin. planner. Fin. planner Cert. Fin. Svcs., Inc., Longwood, Fla., 1982-84, 1st Capital Planning, Longwood, 1984-86, Blackwell, Bloch, Meier & Nestor Fin. Group, Winter Park, Fla., 1986-87, Fin. Continuity, Inc., Longwood, 1987-88; fin. systems con. Computer Continuity Inc, Longwood, 1988—; instr. Rollins Coll., Winter Park, 1986-87, Stetson U., Deland, Fla. 1986-87, Valencia Community Coll., Orlando, 1985-86. Mem. Inst. Cert. Fin. Planners, Internat. Assn. Fin. Planning (pres. 1986-87), Phi Kappa Phi. Republican. Roman Catholic. Office: Computer Continuity Inc 450 Crown Oak Dr Longwood FL 32750

FLYNN, KIRTLAND, JR., accountant; b. Orange, N.J., Aug. 27, 1922; s. Kirtland and Jane Elizabeth (Miller) F.; m. Lucy Jane Andrews, June 11, 1948; children: Patricia Carson Flynn Moore, Gail Miller, James Kirtland. BA, Colgate U., 1943. Acctg. staff Celanese Corp., Newark, Houston and Charlotte, N.C., 1947-65; sec.-treas. Little Constrn. Co., Inc., Charlotte, 1965-66; mem. controller's staff J.P. Stevens & Co., Inc., Charlotte, 1966-81, mgr. info. services div., Charlotte and Greer, S.C., 1981-85; pvt. practice acctg., 1985—. Bd. dirs., treas. Charlotte Exchange Student Program, 1979-83; chmn. Tryon Fire Protection Dist. Bd. Commrs., 1986—; bd. dirs. Tryon Fine Arts Ctr., 1987—; bd. dirs., treas. Polk County Sheltered Workshop, 1987—. Served as 1st lt. USMCR, 1943-46. Decorated D.F.C., Air medals. Mem. Nat. Assn. Accts. (chpt. pres. 1966-67, nat. dir. 1971-73, pres. Carolinas Council 1973-74, nat. v.p. 1978-79), Stuart Cameron McLeod Soc. (bd. govs. 1979-81, treas. 1981-82, sec. 1982-83, v.p. 1983-85, pres. 1985-86), Tryon C. of C. (bd. dirs., treas. 1985—). Lodges: Masons, Shriners, K.T. Home: Sourwood Ridge PO Box 1138 Tryon NC 28782 Office: 307 N Trade St Tryon NC 28782

FLYNN, MICHAEL JAMES, farm, lawn, garden outdoor power equipment distributor; b. Atlanta, Dec. 11, 1920; s. Leo Gilbert and Iola (Brozitsky) F.; student Hemphill Diesel Sch., 1938-39; m. Dorothy C. Daria, Apr. 6, 1947; children—Michael G., Patricia Ann, Kevin Charles. With Amer-Ind Inc., N.Y.C., 1946-47; area sales rep. John Reiner & Co., L.I. City, N.Y., 1947-49; with Deere & Co., Moline, Ill., 1949-55; rep. in Africa, 1955-58, Australia, 1958-60; owner, pres. M.J. Flynn, Inc., East Syracuse, N.Y., 1962—. Mem. N.Y. State Farm Equipment Club, Internat. Platform Assn. Republican. Roman Catholic. Office: M J Flynn Inc 6408 Collamer Rd East Syracuse NY 13057-1032

FLYNN, RICHARD JAMES, lawyer; b. Omaha, Dec. 6, 1928; s. Richard T. and Eileen (Murphy) F.; m. Kay House Ebert, June 28, 1975; children: Richard McDonnell, William Thomas, Kathryn Eileen Merritt, James Daniel. Student, Cornell U., 1944-46; B.S., Nothwestern U., 1950; J.D., Northwestern U., 1953. Bar: D.C. 1953, Ill. 1954. Law clk. to Chief Justices Vinson and Warren, 1953-54; assoc. Sidley, Austin, Burgess & Smith, Chgo., 1954-63; ptnr. Sidley, Austin, Burgess & Smith, Washington, 1963-66, Sidley & Austin, 1967—. Contbr. articles to profl. jours. Mem. exec. com. Washington Lawyers Com. for Civil Rights Under Law. Served with USN, 1946-48. Fellow Am. Coll. Trial Lawyers, mem. ABA, Fed. Bar Assn., Fed. Energy Bar Assn., Assn. Transp. Practitioners, Nat. Lawyer Club, Chgo. Bar Assn., D.C. Bar Assn., Order of Coif, Phi Beta Kappa, Phi Delta Phi, Sigma Chi. Republican. Presbyterian. Clubs: Economic of Chgo, Legal, Kenwood Golf and Country; Metropolitan (Washington). Home: 2342 S Queen St Arlington VA 22202 Office: Sidley & Austin 1722 Eye St NW Washington DC 20006

FLYNN, ROBERT EMMETT, process controls equipment company executive; b. Montreal, Que., Can., Sept. 10, 1933; came to U.S., 1957; s. Emmett Joseph and Pauline Perrier (Lupien) F.; m. Irene P. Kantor, July 28, 1960; children: Donna, Darren, Diane. B.S. in Physics, Loyola Coll., Montreal, 1955; B.E. in Engring, McGill U., 1957; M.B.A., Rutgers U., 1962. V.p. Carborundum Co., Niagara Falls, N.Y., 1973-76, group v.p., 1976-79, sr. v.p. carborundum, 1979-81; exec. v.p. Fisher Controls Internat. Inc., St. Louis, 1981-82; pres., chief exec. officer Fisher Control Internat. Inc., St. Louis, 1982-85; chmn. bd., chief exec. officer Fisher Control Internat. Inc., 1985—; bd. dirs. Nutra Sweet Co. Trustee Foundry Edn. Found., Chgo., 1977-80; bd. dirs. United Way, Niagara Falls, 1972-81, campaign chmn., 1978; mem. pres.'s council St. Louis U., 1984—; bd. dirs., mem. exec. com., chmn. tech. task force St. Louis Regional Commerce and Growth Assn, 1985—; bus. devel. com. City of Clayton, Mo.; mem. adv. com. Fontbonne Coll., 1986—; mem. adv. bd. Gateway Mid-Am.; chmn. St. Louis Tech. Ctr., 1988—; mem. Nat. Council for Sch. Engring. and Applied Sci., Washington U., St. Louis, 1987—. Served with USMCR, 1958. Mem. St. Louis Club, Old Warson Country Club. Republican. Roman Catholic. Home: 2 Barclay Woods Saint Louis MO 63124 Office: Fisher Controls Internat Inc 8000 Maryland AVe Clayton MO 63105

FLYNN, ROBERT THOMAS, real estate executive; b. Ridgewood, N.J., Jan. 1, 1957; s. James F. and Margaret (Rowan) F. BBA, U. Notre Dame, 1979; MBA, U. Denver, 1986. CPA, Colo.; lic. real estate broker. Acct. to sr. acct. Deloitte, Haskins & Sells, Denver, 1979-82; controller Carma Developers Colo., Inc., Denver, 1982-85, gen. mgr., 1985-86; chief fin. officer Amerimar Realty Mgmt. Co.-Colo., Denver, 1986—; v.p. fin. Amerimar Realty Co. West, Denver, 1988—. Mem. Pro Denver, 1987-88; coach baseball Arapahoe Youth League, Englewood, Colo., 1981-82. Mem. Am. Inst. CPA's, Colo. Soc. CPA's. Republican. Roman Catholic. Club: Internat. Athletic (Denver). Home: 1591 S Roslyn St Denver CO 80231 Office: Amerimar Realty Co West 999 18th St Suite 300 Denver CO 80202

FLYNN, SHARON ANN (MRS. C. J. ROELL), marketing executive, educator; b. Kings Park, N.Y., Apr. 14, 1955; d. John Joseph and Mary Rose (Dwyer) F.; m. Carl J. Roell Jr., Oct. 12, 1986. Degree in Nursing Sci., Suffolk County Community Coll., 1976; R.N., NY State Psychiat. Sch. Nursing, 1977; student Barry Univ., 1987—. Psychiat. therapist Kings Park Psychiat. Ctr., N.Y., 1971-77, psychiat. registered nurse, 1977-79; acute hemodialysis nurse Boca Raton Community Hosp., Fla., 1981-83; home infusion therapy educator Am. Hosp. Supply Corp., S.E. Fla., 1983-84, mktg. territory mgr., 1984-85; mktg. devel. specialist home infusion therapy Hosp. Corp. Am., Ft. Lauderdale, Fla., 1985—, designer and mgr. Apnea Monitoring Service, 1986-88; adminstrv. dir. Diabetes Mgmt. Ctr. Health Trust, Inc., Plantation, Fla., 1988—; cons., advisor HomeCare Palm Beaches, Inc., Lake Worth, Fla., 1984—; instr. continuous ambulatory peritoneal dialysis Boca Raton Community Hosp., 1982, instr. diabetic edn., 1981. Mem. Aspartame Consumer Safety Network, chmn. med. com. on aspartame consumer safety, 1987. Mem. Nat. Assn. Female Execs., Discharge Planners Assn., Assn. Profl. Saleswomen, Internat. Platform Assn., Am. Legion Aux. Republican. Roman Catholic. Avocations: scuba diving, tennis. Office: 401 NW 42d Ave Plantation FL 33317

FLYNN, THOMAS JOSEPH, hospital management executive; b. Pitts., Dec. 28, 1936; children: Sean Patrick, Kelly Lynn; m. Donna Moore, Feb. 12, 1988. B.S., Mt. St. Mary's Coll., Emmitsburg, Md., 1958; LL.B., Duquesne U., Pitts., 1964. Bar: Pa. 1964, Ky. 1976. Atty. Westinghouse Electric Corp., Pitts., 1964-74; exec. v.p., gen. counsel Humana Inc., Louisville, 1974—. Mem. Am. Bar Assn., Am. Hosp. Assn., Ky. Bar Assn., Allegheny County Bar Assn. Roman Catholic. Clubs: Pendennis, Valhalla, Hunting Creek Country. Office: Humana Inc 500 W Main St Louisville KY 40201

FLYNN, THOMAS MICHAEL, banker, consultant; b. Carbondale, Pa., Nov. 13, 1939; s. Walter and Mary (Danchak) F.; m. Dorothy M. Matircho, June 29, 1963; children: Kelly, Kevin, Kerry. A in Acctg., Lackawanna Coll., 1965; BS in mgmt., Rider Coll., 1975; MBA in Fin., 1977. Credit supr. Am. Standard Corp., Piscataway, N.J., 1961-64; credit mgr. Schering Corp., Union, N.J., 1964-66; gen. credit mgr. Johnson & Johnson, Somerville, N.J., 1966-69; sr. v.p. Somerset Trust Co., Somerville, 1969-79; exec. v.p. T.M.S. Investment Corp., Springfield, N.J., 1980-83; pres., chief exec. officer Commerce Bancorp, Cherry Hill, N.J., 1983-85, Independence Bancorp, Ramsey, N.J., 1985—. Contbr. articles to profl. publs. Bd. govs. Good Samaritan Hosp., Suffern, N.Y.; com. mem. Am. Lung Assn. N.J., Hackensack, 1986—. With USN, 1957-61. Fellow Nat. Credit Inst.; mem. Nat. Assn. Credit (award), Am. Bankers Assn., N.J. Bankers Assn., Robert Morris Assn., Commerce and Industry Assn., N.J. Builders Assn. (assoc.). Republican. Roman Catholic. Office: Independence Bancorp 1100 Lake St Ramsey NJ 07446

FLYNN, WILLIAM JOSEPH, insurance executive; b. N.Y.C., Sept. 6, 1926; s. William and Anne (Connors) F.; m. Margaret M. Collins, Mar. 21, 1952; children: William, Maureen, James, Robert. MA in Econs., Fordham U., 1951. V.p. group ops. Equitable, N.Y.C., 1953-71; pres. Mut. Am., N.Y.C., 1971-72, pres., chief exec. officer, 1972-82, chmn. bd., chief exec. officer, 1982—; bd. dirs. Richmond Hill Savs. Bank, Floral Park, N.Y. Pres. bd. dirs. N.Y. Foundling Hosp., N.Y.; bd. dirs. U.S. Cath. Hist. Soc., S.I., N.Y., United Student Aid Funds, Indpls., Coll. Constrn. Loan Ins. Assn., Washington, Elie Wiesel Found. for Humanity, N.Y.C., Williamsburg Charter Found., Washington, United Student Aid Fund, N.Y.C., United Way Internat., Alexandria, Va; past chmn. adv. com. U.S. Holocaust Meml. Council, Bd. Life Ins. Council N.Y., St. Vincent's Svcs. Served with USAF, 1951-53, Korea. Recipient Disting. Community Service award Brandeis U. 1980, Ubi Cantas Deus Ibi award Cath. Charities 1983, Nat. Profl. Leadership award United Way Am. 1984, Brotherhood award NCCJ, 1984, Disting. Service award United Way Bergen County, 1985. Mem. Am. Council Life Ins. Clubs: University (N.Y.C.); Garden City (N.Y.) Country. Home: 69 2d St Garden City NY Office: Mutual of Am Life 666 Fifth Ave New York NY 10103

FOA, CONRAD MARIO, insurance brokerage executive; b. N.Y.C., Nov. 17, 1941; s. Mario and Marie (Costa) F.; m. Linda Rimanich, July 11, 1970; children: C. Justin, Barrett C. BS, U. Pa., 1962; MS, U. London, 1964. Pres., Foa & Son Corp., N.Y.C., 1967—; mem. adv. council City of N.Y. Office Bus. Devel. Served to capt. U.S. Army, 1964-66. Mem. Ins. Brokers Assn. N.Y. (pres.), Ins. Brokers Round Table, Young Pres.'s Orgn., Italy Am. C. of C. (chmn. external affairs), Execs. Assn. N.Y.(bd. dirs.). Home: 911 Park Ave New York NY 10021 Office: 18 Vesey St New York NY 10007

FOCKLER, HERBERT HILL, foundation executive; b. Summersville, W.Va., Feb. 18, 1922; s. William Okey and Annie Lee (Fitzwater) F.; m. Mary Hildegarde Ziegler, May 15, 1950; 1 child, Herbert. BA, W.Va. U., 1946, MA, 1947; cert., Oxford (Eng.) U., 1948, Harvard U., 1949. Adminstr. library Princeton (N.J.) U., 1952-54, Library of Congress, Washington, 1956-58; advisor White House Confs., Washington, 1959-60; exec. NIH, Bethesda, Md., 1961-69; chmn. Sci. and Tech. Coms., Washington, 1969-70; exec. dir. Sci. Founds., Washington, 1971-72; trustee, chmn. Am. Arts Internat. Found., Washington, pres., 1984—, also bd. dirs.; chmn., trustee World Tech. Found., Washington, 1988—; advisor NSF, 1975, White House Conf. on Bus., 1975, 78, Montgomery Coll., Rockville, Md., 1978, World Bank, 1986, Winston Churchill Found., 1988, various pub. sos., 1980—, various tech. industries, 1986—; mem. adv. council Coolfont Found., Berkeley Springs, W.Va., 1980-87; dir. Info. Svcs. Co., 1988—; mem. Presdl. Rsch. Group; assoc. Woodrow Wilson Internat. Ctr., 1988. Editor: Contemporary South, 1968, also conf. records and newsletters; author sci. research reports and bibliographies. Trustee Threshold Environ. Found., Washington, 1969-75; mem. pres.'s council Shenandoah Coll., Winchester, Va., 1982-87. Served as staff sgt. U.S. Army, 1941-45. Mem. Acad. Polit. Sci., Am. Polit. Sci. Assn., AAAS, Washington Acad. Sci., Fgn. Policy Inst., World Affairs Council, Policy Studies Orgn. Clubs: Harvard U., Princeton U., W.Va. (Washington). Home and Office: 10710 Lorain Ave Silver Spring MD 20901

FODIMAN, AARON ROSEN, restaurant chain executive; b. Stamford Conn., Oct. 10, 1937; s. Yale J. and Thelma F.; BS, Tulane U., 1958; LLB, N.Y. U., 1960, MBA, 1961; grad. L'Academie de Cuisine Canardier, Washington, 1977. Admitted to N.Y. bar, 1960, D.C. bar, 1961, Va. bar, 1965; FTC, Washington, 1961-65; practiced in Arlington, Va., 1965-78; pres. Fast Food Operators, Inc., N.Y.C., 1978-84; pres. Hampton Healthcare, 1984—, Tampa Bay Publs., 1986—; pub., editor Tampa Bay Mag.; bd. dirs. Tampa Players Inc., Washington Ballet, Manhattan Punch Line Theatre; pres. Dunedin Art Ctr.; chmn. Pinellas County Arts Council, Golda Mier Ctr.; community advisor Clearwater Dunedin Jr. League.; mem. adv. bd. Am. Film Inst.; chmn. Ford Presdl. Campaign, 1976; cons. spl. services U.S. Dept. State spl. envoy to Iran, Poland, Russia, Senegal, 1964-78; TV host local sports show, Dine Line, Tampa Bay Mag.; advisor Fed. Res. Bank Atlanta. Participant, Leadership Pinellas; participant, founder Leadership Tampa Bay, Nat. Conf. Christians and Jews. Recipient Miniature Palette award Miniature Art Soc. of Fla., 1987, Hyam Soloman Freedom award, 1974; chmn. A Taste of Pinellas. Recipient Order of Salvador medal Dali Mus., 1989. Mem. Pinellas County Restaurant Assn. (pres.), Fla. Restaurant Assn. (bd. dirs.), Internat. Legal Frat., Phi Delta Phi. Club: Barrister Inn (pres.) (Washington). Lodge: B'nai Brith (pres. Washington).

FOEHL, EDWARD ALBERT, chemical company executive; b. Phila., May 30, 1942; s. Edward A. and Geneva (Horner) F.; m. Katherine Broberg, Jan. 13, 1970. BS in Engring., U.S. Mil. Acad., 1965; MBA, George Washington U., 1971. Commd. 2nd lt. U.S. Army, 1965, advanced through grades to capt., 1967, resigned, 1970; fin. product planner Ford Motor Co., Dearborn, Mich., 1971-74; mgr. planning First Nat. Bank Chgo., 1974-76; dir. corp. fin. Mfrs. Hanover Trust Co., N.Y.C., 1977; dir. fin. planning Freightner Corp., Portland, Oreg., 1977-82; pres. Great Western Chem. Co., Portland, 1982—; bd. dirs. McCall Oil and Chem. Co.; guest lectr. Portland State U., 1979-86. Mem. exec. council Boy Scouts Am., Portland, 1986. Decorated Silver Star, Bronze Star, Vietnamese Cross of Gallantry. Mem. Planning Forum (past pres.), Fin. Execs. Inst., C. of C. (internat. trade com.), West Point Soc. of Oreg. (pres.). Republican. Methodist. Clubs: Multnomah Athletic (Portland), Royal Oaks Country (Vancouver, Wash.). Lodge: Rotary. Home: 2545 Scenic Dr SW Portland OR 97225 Office: McCall Oil & Chem Corp 808 15th Ave Portland OR 97205

FOEHL, JOHN MELVILLE, JR., banker; b. Waterbury, Conn., Feb. 21, 1956; s. John Melville and Audrey Mae (Stone) F.; m. Linda A. Scrivani, May 10, 1980; 1 child, Patrick John. BS, Union Coll., 1978; MBA, U. Hartford, 1984; postgrad., U. Wis., 1982-84. Asst. controller Am. Nat. Bank, Hamden, Conn., 1979-83; fin. planning officer The Banking Ctr., Waterbury, Conn., 1983-86; exec. v.p., chief operating officer Colony Savs. Bank, Wallingford, Conn., 1986—. Bd. dirs. Big Bros. Big Sisters, Wallingford, 1987—; mem. Pub. Bldg. Commn., Cheshire, Conn., 1987—, Rep. Town Com., Cheshire, 1988. Mem. Nat. Council Savs. Instns. (nat. com. 1986—), Savs. Bank Assn. Conn. (treas. group 1 1987-88), Community Bankers Assn. Conn. Republican. Club: Jaycees (Cheshire, Conn.). Home:

11 Colonial Ct Cheshire CT 06410 Office: Colony Savs Bank 909 N Colony Rd Wallingford CT 06492

FOERST, JOHN GEORGE, JR., counselling service executive; b. Queens, N.Y., June 8, 1927; s. John George and Mary Elizabeth (McGinn) F.; m. Marion Theresa Cassidy, June 27, 1953; children: Gerard M.; m. Kathryn J.A. BA, St. Johns U., Queens, N.Y., 1950. Regional rep. Nat. Found. for Infantile Paralysis, N.Y.C., 1950-52; campaign dir., v.p. Community Counselling Service, N.Y.C., 1952-59, v.p., asst. to pres., 1965-69, pres., 1969-87, chmn. 1987— ; pres. John G. Foerst, Inc., N.Y.C., 1959-65; dir. 59 Wall St. Fund, N.Y.C. Contbg. author: Complete Guide to Corporate Fund Raising, 1982. Bd. dirs. St. Francis Hosp., Roslyn, N.Y., 1972—, Nassau Ctr. for Disabled, Woodbury, N.Y., 1974-87, Human Resources Ctr., Albertson, N.Y., 1988—; chmn. Am. Assn. Fund Raising Counsel, N.Y.C., 1982; mem. Cardinal's Com. of Laity, Roman Catholic Archdiocese N.Y., 1984—. Mem. Am. Irish Cultural Inst., Nat. Council and Civil Bd. Dirs. Soc. Propagation of the Faith. Republican. Club: Union League. Lodge: Knights of Malta. Home: 77 Dover Rd Manhasset NY 11030 Office: Community Counseling Svc Co 350 Fifth Ave Suite 7210 New York NY 10118

FOGEL, IRVING MARTIN, consulting engineer; b. Gloucester, Mass., Apr. 15, 1929; s. Jacob and Ethel (David) F.; B.S., Ind. Inst. Tech., 1954, D.Eng. (hon.), 1982; children: Ethan, Ronit. Civil engr. Ill. Hwy. Dept., Peoria, 1954-55; field engr. Peter Kiewit Sons Co., East Gary, Ind., 1955, field engr., progress engr., cost engr., Ogdensburg, N.Y., 1955-56; supt. grading and paving Merritt, Chapman & Scott, Binghamton, N.Y., 1956; cost engr. Drake-Merritt, Goose Bay, Labrador, 1956-57; constrn. mgmt. engr. Mil. Estimating Corp., Madrid, Spain, also P.I., 1957-58; project mgr. Ministry of Def., State of Israel, 1958-59, Frederic R. Harris (Holland) N.V., The Hague, also Tehran, Iran, 1959-61; project mgr. Solel Boneh & Assocs., Addis Ababa, Ethiopia, 1961-63; asst. to tech. dir. Frederic R. Harris, Madrid, 1963-64; chief engr. McKee-Berger-Mansueto, Inc., N.Y.C., 1964-65, v.p. constrn. mgmt., 1965-69; pres. Fogel & Assocs., Inc., N.Y.C., also Detroit, Carmel (Calif.), Ft. Lauderdale (Fla.), 1969—; lectr. Registered profl. engr., 22 states, D.C., Israel. Fellow ASCE; mem. Am. Arbitration Assn., Am. Assn. Cost Engrs., Am. Inst. Constructors, Am. Mgmt. Assn., Constrn. Specifications Inst., Nat. Contract Mgmt. Assn., Nat. Soc. Profl. Engrs., N.Y. Bldg. Congress, Project Mgmt. Inst., Soc. Am. Mil. Engrs. Author guides and handbooks on constrn. bus., latest being: Planning, Financing, and Constructing Health Care Facilities, 1983. Contbr. articles to profl. jours. Home: 525 E 86th St New York NY 10028 Office: 373 Park Ave S New York NY 10016

FOGELSONGER, NED RAYMOND, insurance agency executive; b. Chambersburg, Pa., Jan. 24, 1947; s. Ned Martin Fogelsonger and Barbara Elizabeth (Stermer) Mummert; m. Cheryl Marie Hogle, Oct. 18, 1969; children: Lisa Marie, Bryan Andrew. BSBA, Shippensburg U., 1971. Agt. G. Leonard Fogelsonger Agy., Shippensburg, 1969-75, ptnr., 1975-82; bd. dirs. Orrstown (Pa.) Bank. Bd. dirs. Cumberland County unit Am. Cancer Soc., 1973—, Shippensburg U. Found., 1984—; pres. Shippensburg United Way, 1979, dir., 1977-82. Fellow Acad. Producer Ins. Studies, mem. Ind. Ins. Agts. Am., Ind. Ins. Agts. Pa. (bd. dirs., mem. edn. com. 1984—), Profl. Ins. Agts. Am., Life Underwriters Assn. (bd. dirs. 1973-75, Nat. Quality award 1975-76), Soc. Cert. Ins. Counselors, Aetna's Agts. Adv. Council (chmn. 1986-87), Shippensburg C. of C. (dir. 1979-81, past pres. 1981), Clowns Am. Internat., Shippensburg Fish and Game, NRA, Masons, Sons of the Am. Legion, Tall Cedars of Lebanon. Republican. Roman Catholic. Home: 264 Hostetter Ave Shippensburg PA 17257 Office: Fogelsonger Agy Inc 66 E King St Shippensburg PA 17257

FOGERTY, ARTHUR JOSEPH, farm supply cooperative company executive; b. Troy, N.Y., June 1, 1938; s. Arthur Anthony and Mary Catherine (Shanahan) F.; m. Mary Jane Grindrod, Aug. 17, 1963; children: Mark, Tara, Matthew. B.A., Siena Coll., 1960. Dist. dir. N.Y. State CD Commn., Albany, 1962-71; mgr. govt. relations Agway Inc., Syracuse, N.Y., 1971-73, sr. v.p. corp. relations, 1982—; bd. dirs. Curtice-Burns Food, Rochester, N.Y.; trustee, v.p. Am. Inst. Cooperation, Washington, 1982—, Agrl. Co-op. Devel. Internat., Washington, 1982—. Pres. Citizens Found, Syracuse, 1978-80; trustee Future Bus. Leaders Am., N.Y. State, 1979—; bd. dirs. Community Gen. Hosp., Syracuse, Literacy Vols. N.Y.C., 1980-83. Mem. Bus. Council N.Y. State, U.S. C. of C. (vice-chmn. agr. com.), Syracuse C. of C. (bd. dirs. 1982—), Fertilizer Inst., Nat. Council Farmer Coops. Roman Catholic. Home: 7459 Armstrong Rd Manlius NY 13104 Office: Agway Inc PO Box 4933 Syracuse NY 13221

FOHL, OTTO ANDREW, manufacturing company executive; b. Perth Amboy, N.J., Sept. 15, 1928; s. Andrew and Mary Elizabeth (Lucas) F.; B.S., Villanova (Pa.) U., 1952; postgrad. N.Y. U.; m. Helen W. Gillingham, Oct. 31, 1959; children: Michele, Eric, Kurt, Noelle. Dir. mktg. research O.S. Tyson & Co., N.Y.C., 1959-60; research group head Ted Bates & Co., N.Y.C., 1960-64; mgr. mktg. research ops. Chesebrough-Ponds Inc., N.Y.C., 1964-66; dir. market research household products div., chmn. consumer group market research com. Am. Cyanamid Co., Wayne, N.J., 1966-81, dir. bus. info. Shulton Inc. U.S.A. div., 1981-84, dir. bus. info. Shulton Internat. div. Served with USN, 1946-48. Mem. Am. Mktg. Assn. (chmn. mktg. intelligence com. 1971). Republican. Roman Catholic. Clubs: Lake Mohawk Country, Lake Mohawk Golf. Home: 21 Fairway Trail Sparta NJ 07871 Office: Shulton Group Am Cyanamid Co Clifton NJ 07015

FOK, THOMAS DSO YUN, civil engineer; b. Canton, China, July 1, 1921; came to U.S., 1947, naturalized, 1956; s D. H. and C. (Tse) F.; m. Maria M.L. Liang, Sept. 18, 1949. B.Eng., Nat. Tung-Chi U., Szechuan, China, 1945; M.S., U. Ill., 1948; M.B.A. Dr. Nadler Money Marketeer scholar, NYU, 1950; Ph.D., Carnegie-Mellon U., 1956. Registered profl. engr., N.Y., Pa., Ohio, Ill., Ky., W.Va., Ind., Md., Fla. Structural designer Lummus Co., N.Y.C., 1951-53; design engr. Richardson, Gordon & Assocs., cons. engrs., Pitts., 1956-58; assoc. prof. engring. Youngstown U., Ohio, 1958-67, dir. computing ctr., 1963-67; ptnr. Cernica, Fok & Assocs., cons. engrs., Youngstown, Ohio, 1958-64; prin. Thomas Fok & Assocs., cons. engrs., Youngstown, Ohio, 1964-65; ptnr. Mosure-Fok & Syrakis Co., Ltd., cons. Engrs., Youngstown, Ohio, 1965-76; cons. engr. to Mahoning County Engr. Ohio, 1960-65; pres. Computing Systems & Tech., Youngstown, Ohio, 1967-72; chmn. Thomas Fok and Assocs., Ltd., cons. engrs., Youngstown, Ohio, 1977—. Contbr. articles to profl. jours. Trustee Pub. Library of Youngstown and Mahoning County, 1973—; trustee Youngstown State U. Found, 1975—; trustee Youngstown State U., 1975-84, chmn., 1981-83. Recipient Walter E. and Caroline H. Watson Found. Disting. Prof.'s award Youngstown U., 1966, Outstanding Person award Mahoning Valley Tech. Socs. Council, 1987. Fellow ASCE; mem. Am. Concrete Inst., Internat. Assn. for Bridge and Structural Engring., Am. Soc. Engring. Edn., Nat. Soc. Profl. Engrs., AAAS, Soc. Am. Mil. Engrs., Ohio Acad. Sci., N.Y. Acad. Sci., Sigma Xi, Beta Gamma Sigma, Sigma Tau, Delta Pi Sigma. Lodge: Rotary. Home: 325 S Canfield-Niles Rd Youngstown OH 44515 Office: 3896 Mahoning Ave Youngstown OH 44515

FOLBERTH, WILLIAM MITCHELL, III, merchant banking executive; b. Garden City, N.Y., Apr. 12, 1944; s. William Mitchell Folberth Jr. and Jean (Schilling) Chockley; m. Elizabeth Holmes Rich, June 7, 1969; children: Liza McKenzie, William Mitchell IV. BS, Yale U., 1966; MBA, Columbia U., 1971; postgrad., Harvard U., 1988—. Cert. fin. planner. V.p. Hornblower & Weeks, N.Y.C., 1971-74, Dean Witter Reynolds, N.Y.C., 1975-79; 1st v.p. Smith Barney, N.Y.C., 1980-84; mng. ptnr. Kaufmann Folberth Capital Group, N.Y.C., 1985-87. Chmn. fin. com. Am. Found. for The Blind, N.Y.C., 1976—; mem. fin. com. Christ Ch., Bronxville, N.Y., 1987. Mem. Securities Industry Assn. (direct investment com.), Bronxville Field Club, Nantucket Yacht Club, Shenorock Shore Club, New Rochelle Rowing club, Powerton Assn. Home: 81 Tanglewylde Ave Bronxville NY 10708-3220 Office: The Metropolis Group 1775 Broadway Ste 2300 New York NY 10019-1903

FOLDEN, VIRGIL ALVIS, III, financial planning executive; b. Fredericksburg, Va., June 20, 1953; s. Virgil Alvis Jr. and Frances (DeShazo) F.; m. Barbara Ann Kimberlin, Feb. 20, 1982. BS in Mktg., Va. Poly. Inst., 1975. Cert. fin. planner. Bus. mgr. Thomas N. Laurence, MD, Fredericksburg, 1976-79; sales rep. Mass. Mut. Life Ins., Fredericksburg, 1979—, registered rep., 1983—; pres. Fredericksburg Fin. Services, 1982—. Editor newsletter: The Comunicator, 1986—. Bd. dirs. Fredericksburg Theatre Co., 1981—, YMCA, Fredericksburg, 1987—, treas., 1988-89; campaign mgr. United Way, Fredericksburg, 1983, 85; mem. Econ. Adv. Bd. Spotsylvania, Va., 1986—; coach Fredericksburg Parks and Recreation, 1977—; jr. warden Trinity Episcopal Ch., 1984-87. Served to capt. USAF, 1976. Mem. Inst. Cert. Fin. Planners (v.p. 1987-88, pres. 1988-89, southeastern regional liaison for edn., editor newsletter cen. Va. chpt. 1986-88), Estate Planning Council (bd. dirs. 1980—). Lodge: Kiwanis (treas. local club, 1985-87, pres. 1987-88). Home: PO Drawer 747 Fredericksburg VA 22404 Office: Fredericksburg Fin Svcs Inc 417 William St Fredericksburg VA 22401

FOLEY, DANIEL EDMUND, real estate develelopment executive; b. St. Paul, Mar. 1, 1926; s. Edward and Gerry (Fitzgarld) F.; student U. Minn., 1941-43; m. Paula Evans, Apr. 1, 1946. Chmn. bd. Realty Ptnrs. Ltd., Los Angeles; pres. Alpha Property Mgmt. Served with AUS, 1943-46.

FOLEY, EDWARD FRANCIS, financial executive, commercial lender; b. Asheville, N.C., Oct. 13, 1954; s. Edward F. and Marguerite (Guilka) F.; m. Janet Bouton, Oct. 23, 1976; children: Michael, David Ryan. Student, U. Notre Dame, 1972-74; BS, U. Md., 1976; postgrad., Loyola U., Balt., 1983-85. Notary public, Md. Credit mgr. Gen. Electric Capitol, Plainview, N.Y., 1976-85; ter. ops. mgr. Caterpillar, Columbia, Md., 1985—; dir. First Fin. Services, Columbia, 1985—. Office: Caterpillar 1000 Centruy Pla Columbia MD 21044

FOLEY, EUGENE ARTHUR, controller; b. San Jose, Calif., May 6, 1953; s. Eugene Frank and Shirley Ann (Merrill) F.; m. Kathleen Anne Welles, May 15, 1976; children: Eugene Welles, Patrick Michael, Brian Ross. BSBA, U. Hartford, 1976; MS in Taxation, Golden Gate U., 1979. CPA, Calif., Conn.; cert. mgmt. acct.; cert. info. systems auditor. Acct. J.K. Lasser et al, San Jose, 1976-79; internal auditor Carter Hawley Hale, Los Angeles. 1979-81; lectr., asst. prof. Calif. State U., Sacramento, 1979-84; owner, cons. E.A. Foley Accountancy, Sacramento, 1981-84; corp. audit mgr. Emhart Corp., Farmington, Conn., 1984-86; controller Powers Mfg. div. Emhart Corp., Elmira, N.Y., 1986. Sec., treas. and exec. dir. Elmira YMCA, 1986 and 1987; treas. Supreme Ct. Project, Calif., 1985-86; v.p. fin., 1987 and treas., 1988, Sullivan Trail Council Boy Scouts Am.; treas. Calif. Pub. Policy Found., 1987-88. Mem. Am. Inst. CPA's, Calif. Soc. CPA's, Inst. Internal Auditors (cert.), Inst. Mgmt. Accts., EDP Auditors Assn., Inst. Cost Analysts (cert.), Mensa, Am. Numismatic Assn., Am. First Day Cover Soc., Am. Topical Assn. (life), Am. Soc. Personnel Adminstrn., Data Processing Mgmt. Assn. Lodges: Masons, Scottish Rite. Home: 514 Underwood Ave Elmira NY 14905 Office: Powers Mfg Inc 1140 Sullivan St Elmira NY 14901

FOLEY, PATRICK JOSEPH, lawyer; b. N.Y.C., Oct. 2, 1930; s. John and Anne (Sheehan) F.; m. Ann Tubman; children: Maura, John. BA, Iona Coll., 1957; JD, N.Y. Law Sch., 1961. Bar: N.Y. 1961, U.S. Dist. Ct. (so., no., ea. and we. dists.) N.Y., U.S. Tax Ct., U.S. Ct. Customs, U.S. Ct. Claims, U.S. Ct. Appeals (2d cir.), U.S. Supreme Ct. Asst. underwriter Atlantic Mutual, N.Y.C., 1958-60; acct. exec. Hagedorn and Co., N.Y.C., 1960-62; with Am. Internat. Group, Inc. and subs. cos., N.Y.C., 1963—; now v.p., assoc. gen. counsel Am. Internat. Group, Inc., N.Y.C.; sr. v.p., gen. counsel all domestic brokerage cos. of Am. Internat. Group, Inc. Recipient Outstanding Young Ins. Man award, 1965. Mem. ABA (sect. corp. banking and bus. law), N.Y. State Bar Assn. (ins. law sect.), Westchester County Bar Assn., N.Y. State Trial Lawyers Assn., Am. Judges Assn., Ins. Fedn. of N.Y. (pres., bd. dirs.), Ins. Fedn. Pa., N.Y. Ins. Exchange (bd. dirs., chmn. security fund), N.Y. state Ins. Assn. (bd. dirs.), Council of Ins. Brokers of State of N.Y., Downtown Assn., India House, Gaelic Soc. N.Y. (pres.), Friendly Sons of St. PAtrick, Players Club, Landmark Club, N.Y. Athletic Club, Univ. Club Albany, Elks, K.C., Phi Delta Phi. Republican. Roman Catholic. Lodge: Knights of Malta. Office: Am Internat Group Inc 70 Pine St 22nd Fl New York NY 10270 *

FOLEY, ROBERT H., cement and concrete company executive; b. Driggs, Idaho, Aug. 25, 1930; s. Thomas Henry and Ronella (Jenson) F.; divorced; children: Stephen H., Janet R., Robert C., Kenneth I., J. Patrick; m. Barbara Joan Brack, June 18, 1988. B.S. in Chem. Engring., U. Idaho, 1953; M.B.A., Harvard U., 1958. Various positions Tex. Industries, Inc., Dallas, 1961-70, treas., 1970-73, sr. v.p., 1978-88; pres., owner Structural Tex., Inc., Dallas, 1988—. Home: 308 Tampico St Irving TX 75062 Office: Tex Industries Inc 8100 Carpenter Frwy Dallas TX 75247

FOLEY, WILLIAM PATRICK, title insurance company executive; b. Austin, Tex., Dec. 29, 1944; s. Robert F. ; m. Carol Ann Johnson, Nov. 15 1969; children: Lindsay, Robert P. III, Countney Diane, William P. III. BS, U.S. Mil. Acad., 1967; MBA, Seattle U., 1970; JD, U. Wash., 1974. Assoc. Streich, Lang, Weeks, Cardon & French P.A., Phoenix, 1974-76; ptnr., pres., dir. Foley, Clark & Nye P.A., Phoenix, 1976-84; pres. chief exec. officer Land Resources Corp., Scottsdale, Ariz., 1983-84; chmn. bd., pres., chief exec. officer Fidelity Nat. Title Ins., Irvine, Calif., 1981—, also bd. dirs.; chmn. bd., chief exec. officer, bd. dirs. Lake Mortgage Corp., No. Counties Title Ins. Co., Ramada Inn Old Town Mgmt., Inc., So. Title Ins. Co., Inc., Title Services, Inc., Western Am. Mortgage Corp., Western Pacific Property & Casualty Agy., Inc.; chmn. bd., bd. dirs., Fidelity Nat. Title Agy., Inc., Fidelity Nat. Agy. Maricopa County, Inc., Rocky Mountain Aviation Inc.; numerous other chairmanships and directorships in fin. industry. Office: Fidelity Nat Title Ins 2100 SE Main St Suite 400 Irvine CA 92714

FOLGER, LEE MERRITT, investment company executive; b. Washington, May 5, 1934; s. John Clifford and Mary Kathrine (Dulin) F.; m. Nancy McElroy, 1961 (div.); children: Neil, Peter, Nicholas; m. Juliet Campbell Birmingham, 1976. A.B., Harvard U., 1956. With Folger Nolan Fleming Douglas, Inc., Washington, 1959—; vice chmn. Folger Nolan Fleming Douglas, Inc., 1976-81, chmn., 1981—; v.p. Piedmont Mortgage Co., Washington, 1960-82; pres. Cumberland Trust Co., Knoxville, Tenn., 1962—; mng. partner H.L. Dulin Co., Knoxville, 1960—; dir. Washington Star Newspaper., Allbritton Communications. Chmn. D.C. chpt. ARC, 1971-77; bd. govs. Am. nat. ARC, 1976-82, vice chmn., 1978-82; bd. govs. St. Albans Sch., Washington, 1970-83, chmn., 1975-76; trustee, treas. Corcoran Gallery Art, Washington; vice chmn. United Way Nat. Capital area, 1975-78; mem. D.C. Arts Comm., 1972-75, Protestand Episcopal Cathedral Found., 1980—; v.p. Folger Fund, Washington, 1958—. Served to lt. j.g. USNR, 1956-58. Mem. Nat. Assn. Security Dealers (dist. com. 1971-74), vice chmn. (1973-74). Clubs: Brook (N.Y.C.), Downtown Assn. (N.Y.C.); Chevy Chase (Md.); Metropolitan (Washington), Federal City (Washington); Essex County (Boston). Home: 80 Kalorama Circle NW Washington DC 20008 Office: 725 15th St NW Washington DC 20005

FOLK, SHARON LYNN, printing company executive; b. Bellefontaine, Ohio, June 13, 1945; d. Emerson Dewey and Berdena Isabelle (Brown) F.; A.A. in Liberal Arts, Sacred Heart Coll., 1965, L.H.D. (hon.), 1985; A.B. in Econs. and Bus. Adminstrn., Belmont Abbey Coll., 1968. Exec. v.p. Nat. Bus. Forms, Inc., Greeneville, Tenn., 1968-73; sec., treas. Nat. Forms Co., Inc., Gastonia, N.C., 1969-73, chairperson, bd. dirs., pres., 1973—, SF Enterprises, Inc., Greeneville, 1987—, Andrew Johnson Golf Club, Inc., Greeneville, 1987—; mem. bus. adv. com. Bus. Ptnrs., Inc., Washington, 1987—; bd. dirs. Andrew Johnson Bank, Greeneville, chairperson employee relations com., Internat. Bus. Forms Industries, Arlington, Va., 1978-83. Mem. fin. com. YMCA, Greeneville, 1977-78, bd. dirs., 1977-80; bd. dirs. United Way, 1980-85, Greeneville, Takoma Hosp. Found., Greeneville, 1987—; mem. presdl. steering com. U.S. Senator Howard Baker, 1979-80; mem. Republican Presdl. Task Force, 1981—; life mem. Rep. Nat. Com., 1981—; mem. Rep. Senatorial Inner Circle, Washington, 1984—; vice-chmn. parish council Notre Dame Cath. Ch., Greeneville, 1984-85, chmn., 1985-87; founding mem. Com. 200, Chgo., 1981—, vice chmn., membership chmn. Southeast region, 1983-84, bd. dirs. 1984-85, v.p., bd. dirs., 1985-86; mem. bd. advisors Belmont Abbey Coll., 1984—, trustee, 1986-89; trustee Sacred Heart Coll., Belmont, N.C., 1985—; 2d lt. CAP, 1984—; maj. Civilian Guard, Middleboro, Ky., 1986—; oblate Order of St. Benedict, Our Lady Help of Christians Abbey, Belmont, 1967—. 1st lt. Search and Rescue Pilot Civil Air Patrol, Aux. USAF, Maxwell Air Force Base, Ala., 1984—. Mem. Nat. Bus. Forms Assn., Forms Mfrs. Credit Interchange, Am. Mgmt. Assn., Tenn. Bus. Roundtable (bd. dirs. 1986), Belmont Abbey Alumni Coll. Assn. (bd. dirs. 1986—), U.S. Tennis Assn. (life), Airplane Owners and Pilots Assn. Avocations: tennis, airplane pilot, photography, golf, reading, music. Home: 1131 Hixon Ave Greeneville TN 37743 Office: Nat Bus Forms Co Inc 100 Pennsylvania Ave Greeneville TN 37743

FOLKERT, DAVID FLOYD, steel supply corporation executive, lawyer; b. Holland, Mich., Jan. 14, 1948; s. Floyd J. and Janet (Sneller) F.; m. Carol Ruth Rycenga, June 12, 1970; children—Lucinda Lea, Todd David. B.A., Hope Coll., 1970; J.D., Valparaiso U., 1973. Bar: Mich. 1973. Ptnr. Marietti, Mullally, Grimm, & Folkert, Muskegon, Mich., 1978-79; gen. counsel Westran Corp., 1979-81, sec., 1981-85, v.p., 1983-85, pres. Harbor Steel and Supply Corp., 1985—; Rycenga Homes, Inc., Spring Lake, Mich. Trustee Westran Found., 1983-85; sec. Internat. Aid., Inc., 1980—. Mem. Mich. Bar Assn., Muskegon County Bar Assn. Republican. Home: 16139 Harbor View Dr Spring Lake MI 49456 Office: Harbor Steel & Supply Corp 1115 E Broadway Muskegon MI 49444

FOLLANSBEE, NANCY DAMON, investment management executive; b. Rochester, N.Y., Dec. 1, 1958; d. Winthrop Damon and Carolyn (Allen) Follansbee. B.A., William Smith Coll., 1980. Corp. sec., mgr. mktg. services Grace Capital Inc., N.Y.C., 1980-84; corp. sec. Dirs. Capital Inc., N.Y.C., 1982-84, Dirs. Mgmt. Corp., N.Y.C., 1983-84; mktg. rep. Gardner and Preston Moss, Inc., Boston, 1985-89, v.p., 1989—; guest lectr. Am. Mgmt. Assn., N.Y.C., 1983. Tutor Vol. Services for Children, N.Y.C., 1982-84; corr. Prison Action Group, Rochester, 1980. Mem. Jr. League Boston, Assn. Investment Mgmt. Sales Exec., Internat. Found. Employee Benefit Plans. Republican. Presbyterian. Home: 9A Oak Square Ave Boston MA 02135 Office: Gardner & Preston Moss Inc One Winthrop Sq Boston MA 02110

FOLLICK, EDWIN DUANE, chiropractor, law educator, educational administrator; b. Glendale, Calif., Feb. 4, 1935; s. Edwin Fulfford and Esther Agnes (Catherwood) F.; m. Marilyn K. Sherk, Mar. 24, 1986. BA Calif. State U., Los Angeles, 1956, MA, 1961; MA Pepperdine U., 1957, MPA, 1977; PhD, ThD St. Andrews Theol. Coll., Sem. of the Free Protestant Episcopal Ch., London, 1958; MS in Libr. Sci., U. So. Calif., 1963, MEd in Instructional Materials, 1964, AdvMEd in Edn. Adminstrn., 1969; Calif. Coll. Law, 1965; LLB Blackstone Law Sch., 1966, JD, 1967; DC Cleve. Chiropractic Coll., Los Angeles, 1972; PhD, Academia Theatina, Pescara, 1978. Tchr., library adminstr. Los Angeles City Schs., 1957-68; law librarian Glendale U. Coll. Law, 1968-69; coll. librarian Cleveland Chiropractic Coll., Los Angeles, 1969-74, dir. edn. and admissions, 1974-84, prof. jurisprudence, 1975—, dean student affairs, 1976—, chaplain, 1985—; assoc. prof. Newport U., 1982—; extern prof. St. Andrews Theol. Coll., London, 1961; dir. West Valley Chiropractic Health Ctr., 1972—. Contbr. articles to profl. jours. Served as chaplain's asst. U.S. Army, 1958-60. Decorated Cavaliere Internat. Order legion of Honor of Immacolata (Italy); knight of Malta, Sovereign Order of St. John of Jerusalem; chevalier Ordre Militaire et Hospitalier de St. Lazare de Jerusalem, numerous others. Mem. ALA, NEA, Am. Assn. Sch. Librarians, Los Angeles Sch. Library Assn., Calif. Media and Library Educators Assn., Assn. Coll and Research Librarians, Am. Assn. Law Librarians, Am. Chiropractic Assn., Internat. Chiropractors Assn., Nat. Geog. Soc., Internat. Platform Assn., Phi Delta Kappa, Sigma Chi Psi, Delta Tau Alpha. Democrat. Episcopalian. Home: 6435 Jumilla Ave Woodland Hills CA 91367 Office: 590 N Vermont Ave Los Angeles CA 90004 also: 7022 Owensmouth Ave Canoga Park CA 91303

FOLSOM, HENRY RICHARD, federal agency administrator; b. Wilmington, Del., July 19, 1913; s. Henry Richard and Elizabeth (Stoots) F.; m. Grace Broadway, Feb. 4, 1937. BSME, U. Del., 1936. Registered profl. engr., Del. With engring. staff DuPont Co., Wilmington, 1938-73; cons. Water Resources Agy., New Castle County, Del., 1980-81; adj. prof. U. Del., Newark, 1980-81, 81-82; commr. Postal Rate Commn., Washington, 1982—. Councilman City of Newark, 1961-66; councilman New Castle County, 1967-72, coun. pres., 1973-80, county exec., 1976. Recipient Merit award U. Del., 1981, Good Govt. award Com. of 39, New Castle County, 1981, Recognition award Com. of 100, New Castle County, 1980; named Outstanding Adminstr. Del. Assn. Pub. Adminstrs., 1980. Republican. Methodist. Home: 1900 S Eads St #1228 Arlington VA 22202-3023 Office: Postal Rate Commn 1333 H St NW Ste 300 Washington DC 20268-0001

FOMON, ROBERT M., investment banker; b. Chgo., 1925. Grad., U. So. Calif., 1947. Pres., chief exec. officer E.F. Hutton & Co. Inc., N.Y.C., 1970-77, chmn. bd., 1977-1987; pres., chief exec. officer Robert M. Fomon and Co., N.Y.C., 1987—; bd. dirs. PS Group, Inc. Mem. adv. bd. UCLA Med. Sch., U. So. Calif. Bus. Sch.; trustee Thayer Sch., Dartmouth, Gov.'s Com. on Scholastic Achievement. Office: Robert M Fomon & Co Inc 350 Park Ave New York NY 10022

FONG, HIRAM L., former U.S. senator; b. Honolulu, Oct. 1, 1907; s. Lum Fong and Chai Ha Lum; m. Ellyn Lo; children—Hiram, Rodney, Merie-Ellen Fong Mitchell and Marvin-Allan (twins). A.B. with honors, U. Hawaii, 1930, LL.D., 1953; J.D., Harvard U., 1935; LL.D., Tufts U., 1960, Lafayette Coll., 1960, Lynchburg Coll., 1970, Lincoln U., 1971, U. Guam, 1974, St. John's U., 1975, Calif. Western Sch. Law, 1976, Tung Wu (Soochow) U., Taiwan, 1978, China Acad., Taiwan, 1978; L.H.D., L.I. U., 1968. With supply dept. Pearl Harbor Navy Yard, 1924-27; chief clk. Suburban Water System, 1930-32; dep. atty. City and County of Honolulu, 1935-38; founder, partner law firm Fong, Miho, Choy & Robinson, until 1959; founder, chmn. bd. Finance Factors, Grand Pacific Life Ins. Co., Finance Investment Co., Market City, Ltd., Fin. Enterprises Ltd.; chmn. bd. Hwy. Constrn. Co., Ltd.; pres. Ocean View Cemetery, Ltd.; owner, operator farm; dir. numerous firms, Honolulu; hon. cons. China Airlines. Mem. Hawaii Legislature, 1938-54, speaker, 1948-54; mem. U.S. Senate, 1959-77, Post Office and Civil Service Com., Judiciary Com., Appropriations Com., Spl. Com. on Aging; U.S. del. 150th Anniversary Argentine Independence, Buenos Aires, 1960, 55th Interparliamentary Union (World) Conf., 1966, Ditchley Found. Conf., 1967, U.S.-Can. Inter-Parliamentary Union Conf., 1961, 65, 67, 68, Mex.-U.S. Inter-Parliamentary Conf., 1968, World Interparliamentary Union, Tokyo, 1974; mem. Commn. on Revision Fed. Ct. Appellate System, 1975—; Active in civic and service orgns.; v.p. Territorial Constl. Conv., 1950; del. Rep. Nat. Conv., 1952, 56, 60, 64, 68, 72; founder, chmn. bd. Fin. Factors Found.; bd. visitors U.S. Mil. Acad., 1971—, U.S. Naval Acad., 1974—. Served from 1st lt. to maj. USAAF, 1942-44; ret. col. USAF Res. Recipient award NCCJ, 1960; Meritorious Service citation Nat. Assn. Ret. Civil Employees, 1963; Horatio Alger award, 1970; citation for outstanding service Japanese Am. Citizens League, 1970; award Am. Acad. Achievement, 1971; award outstanding service Orgn. Chinese Ams., 1973; award Nat. Soc. Daus. Founders and Patriots Am., 1974; certificate Pacific Asian World, 1974; decorated Order of Brilliant Star with Grand Cordon Republic of China; Order of Diplomatic Service Merit; Gwanghwan Medal Republic of Korea). Mem. Am. Legion, VFW, Phi Beta Kappa. Congregationalist. Home: 1102 Alewa Dr Honolulu HI 96817

FONTAINE, BURT CASPAR MARIA, multi-national company executive; b. Amsterdam, Netherlands, July 15, 1928; s. Franciscus and Lamberta (Kannegieter) F.; came to U.S., 1960; student St. Ignatius Coll., Amsterdam, St. Canisius Coll., Djakarta, Indonesia, 1950-51; grad., Station for Maalderij en Bakkerij, Wageningen, The Netherlands, 1948; m. Elly van der Heijden, Aug. 4, 1958; children: Marc, Patrick (dec.), Christina, Thomas. Officer mgr. Borneo Sumatra Trading Co., Sumatra, Indonesia, 1951-57, div. supr., The Hague, Netherlands, 1957-60, with N.Y.C. office, 1960-61; first asst. to gen. purchase and sales mgr. Ocean Marine Ins., Tuteur and Co., Inc., N.Y.C., 1961-65; import mgr. E. Miltenberg, Inc., N.Y.C., 1965—, mgr. sporting goods and hardward div., 1966—, asst. treas., 1967-68; asst. v.p. fin. Brasil/FCIA/Africa Worldwide, N.Y.C., 1968; with Philipp Bros. div. Engelhard Minerals and Chems., N.Y.C., 1968—, v.p., 1979-81, v.p. Philipp Bros. Inc. Subs. Phibro-Salomon Bros., 1981—, dir. trade financing, v.p., Philipp Bros. div. Salomon Bros., 1986-87; v.p. M.G. Trade Fin. Corp. subs. Metallgesellschaft Corp., N.Y.; cons. traders, banks. Past mem. steering com. parish council Roman Cath. Ch. Served as platoon comdr., commando Royal Dutch Air Force, 1948-51. Decorated Medal Order and Peace. Mem. Am. Mgmt. Assn. Home: 1439 E 15th St Brooklyn NY 11230-6601 Office: Metallgesellschaft Corp Trade Fin Corp 520 Madison Ave New York NY 10022-4213

FONTAINE, DENIS LOUIS, automobile parts executive, lawyer; b. Rumford, Maine, June 19, 1940; s. Herman and Marie (Guarniaeri) F.; m.

Glenda Ann Childers, Jan. 19, 1980; children: Gregory, Christopher, Julie. BS, Fla. So. Coll., 1962; JD, Stetson U., 1965; Owner Pres. Mgmt. Grad., Harvard U., 1988. Bar: Fla., U.S. Ct. Appeals (10th cir.). Pub. defender Stetson U., St. Petersburg, Fla., 1964-65; ptnr. Troiano & Roberts, Attys., Lakeland, Fla., 1965-75; prosecutor City of Lakeland, 1971-72, mcpl. judge, 1972-74; sr. ptnr. Fontaine & Comparetto, P.A., Lakeland, 1976—; pres. Discount Auto Parts, Inc., 1975—; atty. Imperial Bank Lakeland, 1966-72, Polk City, Fla., 1966-74, City of Mulberry, Fla., 1972-85; speaker law econs., Lakeland, 1970-80; bd. dirs. Sun Bank of Polk County. Chmn. campaign U.S. congressman, Polk County, 1974; pres., bd. dirs. Lakeland Family YMCA, 1979-87, chmn. fund drive, 1982-83; chmn. durg rehab. program Turnaround, Inc. Lakeland, 1987; organizer new ct. system City of Lakeland, 1972. Capt. U.S. Army, 1967-68. Decorated four oak leaf clusters; named one of Outstanding Young Men in Am., Boss of Yr., U.S. Jaycees 1975. Mem. ABA, Fla. Bar Assn., Lakeland Bar Assn., Am. Arbitration Assn., Lakeland C. of C. (leadership com. 1987), Am. Parts Accessory Assn., Pier Point Homeowners Assn. (pres. 1986-87), Windmill Sailing Class Assn. (pres., v.p., bd. dirs. 1975). Office: Discount Auto Parts Inc 4900 S Frontage Rd Lakeland FL 33801

FONTAINE, EDWARD PAUL, mining company executive; b. Hagerstown, Md., Jan. 5, 1936; s. Athanas Paul and Arline (McGrath) F.; m. Jane Kasten, June 13, 1959; children: Michele, Catherine, Lynne, Paul. BBA, U. Mich., 1958, MBA, 1959. Various positions Chase Manhattan Bank, N.Y.C., 1959-61, Mobil Oil Co., N.Y.C., 1962-71; treas. Newmont Mining Corp., N.Y.C., 1972-79, v.p., treas., 1978-79, v.p. fin., 1979-85, group v.p., chief financial officer, 1985-86, sr. v.p., chief financial officer, 1986—, also bd. dirs.; adv. panel Biotech. Investments Inc., London; bd. dirs. Peabody Holding Co. Inc., St. Louis, Newmont Gold Co., Carlin, Nev. Mem. Metropolitan Club, Mid-Ocean Club, Ridgewood Country Club. Roman Catholic. Home: 211 Heights Rd Ridgewood NJ 07450 Office: Newmont Mining Corp 230 Park Ave 32d Fl New York NY 10169

FONTENOT, JUDY DAVIS, entrepreneur; b. Bradenton, Fla., May 4, 1945; d. Glen Randolph and Louise (Duffey) Davis; m. J. Roger Fontenot; children—Kristina Louise, Virginia Dianne, Georgia Glen. B.A., Brenau Coll., 1967. Owner Norrell Temporary Service, Orlando, Fla., 1973—. Dalindy Personnel, Orlando, 1980—; exec. v.p. Currier Davis Pub., Orlando, 1984—. Mem. Fla. Exec. Women. Republican. Baptist. Office: Norrell Svcs 2445 Lee Rd Winter Park FL 32789

FOOS, RAYMOND ANTHONY, metallurgical company executive; b. Bowling Green, Ohio, Sept. 30, 1928; s. Clarence Herman and Clara Agnes (Neiling) F.; m. Rita Catherine Corcoran, July 11, 1953; children: Catherine, Thomas, Elisa, David, Karen, Stephanie, Michele, Renee, Brian, Andrea, Kevin. BS, Xavier U., Cin., 1946-50; MS, Xavier U., 1950-51; PhD, Iowa State U., Ames, 1954. Group leader Union Carbide Corp., Niagra Falls, N.Y., 1954-57; supr. reserach and devel. Nat. Distillers, Cin., 1957-60; mgr. ore extraction dept. The Brush Beryllium Co., Elmore, Ohio, 1960-65, mgr. metal oxide div., 1965-69; dir. corp. research and devel. The Brush Beryllium Co., Cleve., 1969-70, v.p. research and devel., 1970-72, v.p. proudct devel. and research, 1972-74; sr. v.p. Brush Wellman Inc. (formerly The Brush Beryllium Co.), Cleve., 1974-76, sr. v.p. friction and crystal products, 1976-79; sr. v.p. Beryllium Products Group, Cleve., 1979-86; pres. beryllium products group Brush Wellman Inc. (formerly The Brush Beryllium Co.), Cleve., 1984—, exec. v.p., pres., 1986-87, pres., chief operating officer, 1988—, pres., chief exec. officer, 1988—, chmn., pres., chief exec. officer, 1989—, also bd. dirs.; bd. dirs. Am. Colloid Co., Arlington Heights. patented over 20 U.S. patents in field. Mem. AIME, Am. Chem. Soc. Roman Catholic. Home: 30972 Pinehurst Dr Westlake OH 44145 Office: Brush Wellman Inc 1200 Hanna Bldg Cleveland OH 44115

FOOTE, PAUL SHELDON, business educator, seminar leader, consultant; b. Lansing, Mich., May 22, 1946; s. Harlon Sheldon and Frances Norene (Rotter) F.; B.B.A., U. Mich., 1967; M.B.A. (Loomis-Sayles fellow), Harvard U., 1971; advanced profl. cert. NYU, 1975; Ph.D., Mich. State U., 1983; m. Badri Seddigheh Hosseinian, Oct. 25, 1968; children—David, Sheila. Br. mgr., divl. mgr. Citibank, N.Y.C., Bombay, India and Beirut, Lebanon, 1972-74; mgr. planning and devel. Singer Co., Africa/Middle East, 1974-75; instr. U. Mich., Flint, 1978-79; lectr. acctg. Mich. State U., East Lansing, 1977; asst. prof. U. Windsor (Ont., Can.), 1979-81; assoc. prof. Saginaw Valley State Coll., University Ctr., Mich., 1981-82; asst. prof. Oakland U., Rochester, Mich., 1982-83; asst. prof. NYU, 1983-87; assoc. prof. Pepperdine U., Malibu, Calif., 1987—; founder, pres. The Computer Coop., Inc., 1981-82. Served to lt. AUS, 1968-69. Haskins and Sells Doctoral Consortium fellow, 1977. Mem. Am. Accounting Assn., Internat. Assn. Bus. Forecasting (bd. dirs.), Nat. Speakers Assn., EDP Auditors Assn., Internat. Inst. Forecasters, Strategic Mgmt. Soc.

FOOTLIK, IRVING M., consulting engineer; b. Chgo., Feb. 7, 1918; s. Louis and Rose (Elman) F.; m. Sylvia Gollay, Mar. 10, 1940; children: Janice Bernice, Robert Barry. BS, Ill. Inst. of Tech., 1939. Registered profl. engr. Engr. U.S. Air Corp., Dayton, Ohio, 1939; chief of perishable tool sect. U.S. Army Ordinance, Chgo., 1941-45; asst. to v.p. Ekco Products Co., Chgo., 1946-48; plant mgr. Galter Products, Chgo., 1948-50; pres. Footlik & Assocs., Evanston, Ill., 1950-87; also chmn. Footlik & Assocs., Evanston, 1987—; bd. dirs. Bozzuto's, Inc., Cheshire, Conn., Amalgamated Bank, Chgo. Contbr. articles to profl. jours. Mem. Skokie Traffic Commn., Skokie, Ill., 1971-74, citizens adv. group Winnetka Planning Commn., Winnetka, Ill., 1977; pres. Kaplan Jewish Community Ctr., Skokie, 1981-83; pres. Engrs. for Ort., N.Y.C., 1985—. Recipient Am. Material Handling Soc. honors award, Internat. Materials Mgmt. Soc. Ten Yr. Presdl. award; named Man of Yr. Am. Orgn. Rehab. through Tng. Fedn., 1989. Mem. NSPE, ASME (sec. 1968), Soc. Profl. Engrs., Assn. Profl. Engrs. in Pvt. Practice, Assn. Profl. Material Handling Cons. (founder 1958—). Home: 1548 Tower Rd Winnetka IL 60093 Office: Footlik & Assocs 1548 Tower Rd Winnetka IL 60093

FORBES, EDWARD COYLE, diversified company executive; b. Bangalore, India, Sept. 5, 1915; s. Sherman Guy and Bertha (Coyle) F.; m. Anne Fromm Forbes, June 28, 1980; children: Christina, Lucien, Alexandra, Sherman Guy, Edward, Alvaro. Grad., Phillips Exeter Acad., 1934; B.S. in Elec. Engring, Auburn U., 1938; M.S. in Aero. Engring, Air Force Aero. Inst., 1945. Registered profl. engr. N.J., Ohio. With Gen. Electric Co., 1939-41, Internat. Gen. Electric Co., Paris, 1946-51; pres. Gen. Electric Portugal, 1951-55; gen. mgr. Gen. Electric Argentina, 1955-60; v.p. corporate planning Worthington Corp., Harrison, N.J., 1960-64; v.p., group exec. Worthington Corp., 1964-67, chmn., chief exec. officer, 1971-74; pres., chmn. Alco Products, Inc., 1967-69; v.p., group exec. Studebaker-Worthington, Inc., 1967-74; chmn., dir. MLW-Worthington, Ltd., Can., 1967-74; pres. E.D.E.A., Inc., 1974—; pres., vice chmn. Liberia Mining Co., Ltd., 1974-78; pres., chief exec. officer Am. Ship Bldg. Co., Tampa, Fla., 1978-83, vice chmn., 1983—; mem. exec. com. Engring. Coun. Auburn U.; lectr. on mgmt. to profl. assns. U.S., Argentina; bd. dirs., founder Argentine Inst. for Devel. Execs., 1953-64; bd. dirs., treas. Centro de Estudios Sobre Libertad, Argentina, 1957-63. Trustee Eaglebrook Sch., Deerfield, Mass., 1945-61; bd. dirs. Newport Music Festival, 1986—; dir. Newport Art Mus. Maj. USAAF, 1941-46. Mem. ASME, Acad. Polit. Sci., Masters of Foxhounds Assn. Am., So. Srs. Golf Assn., N.Y. Yacht Club, Two Rivers Hounds Club (past master), Shinnicock Hills Golf and Country Club, Clambake Club, American Men's Club (Lisbon, past pres.), Clambare Club (Newport, R.I.), Eta Kappa Nu, Kappa Alpha. Home: PO Box 3789 Newport RI 02840 Office: EDEA Inc 1151 Aquidneck Ave Middletown RI 02840 also: Am Ship Bldg Co 2502 Rocky Point Rd Tampa FL 33607

FORBES, FRED WILLIAM, architect; b. East Liverpool, Ohio, Aug. 21, 1936; s. Kenneth S. and Phylis C. Forbes; B.S. in Architecture, U. Cin., 1960, postgrad.; m. Carolyn Lee Eleyet, Dec. 27, 1969; children—Tallerie Bliss, Kendall Robert. Material research engr. USAF Materials Lab., 1960-61, structural research engr. Flight Accessories Lab., 1961-63, tech. area mgr. Aero Propulsion Lab., 1964-67; prin. Fred W. Forbes, Architect, Xenia, Ohio, 1966-68; br. chief U.S. Air Force Aero Propulsion Lab., Wright Patterson AFB, Ohio, 1967-72, pres. Forbes and Huie, Xenia, 1968-73; pres. Forbes, Huie & Assos., Inc., Xenia, 1973-76; pres. Fred W. Forbes & Assos., Inc., Xenia, 1976—; instr. U. Dayton, 1963-64. Past pres. Xenia Area Living Arts Council. Recipient Exceptional Civilian Service award U.S. Air Force, 1966; Archtl. Award of Excellence for Moraine Civic Center, Masonry Inst., 1976, Archtl. Award of Merit for Xenia br. of 3d Nat. Bank, 1981 Excellence in Masonry, Spl. award for renovation Dayton Area Red Cross Bldg., 1982; Dayton City Beautiful award for Martin Electric Co., 1977; award of merit Greene County Mental Health Facility 1983. Fellow Brit. Interplanetary Soc.; mem. Greene County Profl. Engrs. Soc. (past pres.), Am. Astron. Soc. (past nat. dir.), AIA, Ohio Soc. Profl. Engrs. (Young Engrs. award 1970), Nat. Soc. Profl. Engrs. (top 5 Outstanding Young Engr. award 1972), Nat. Asbestos Contractors Assn. (assoc.), Xenia Area C. of C. (v.p. econ. devel. 1985-86, pres. 1986-87), Elks (trustee 1988-89), Theta Chi. Republican. Methodist. Contbr. articles to profl. jours.; patentee in field. Office: 158 E Main St Xenia OH 45385

FORBES, JOHN EDWARD, financial consultant; b. Chgo., Sept. 18, 1925; s. Harry Charles and Jeanette Anne (Field) F.; m. Dorsey Connors, Aug. 10, 1961. Student, Rensselaer Poly. Inst., 1943-44, Franklin and Marshall Coll., Lancaster, Pa., 1943; BA, Monmouth coll., 1949; postgrad., Northwestern U., 1949-50. Account exec. and commodity mgr. Merrill Lynch, Pierce, Fenner and Smith, Inc., Chgo., 1949-61; pres. San Jose Cigarette Co., Calif., 1958-68; account exec. Hornblower & Weeks, Hemphill, Noyes, Inc., Chgo., 1961-71, assoc. resident mgr., 1971-75, v.p., resident mgr., 1975-78; corp. v.p. Loeb, Rhoades, Hornblower & Co., Chgo., 1981—, Shearson Lehman Bros., Chgo., 1961—; pres. 227 E. Delaware Corp, Chgo., 1980-86; bd. dirs. Trend Industries, Chgo. Served with USN, 1943-46, PTO. Clubs: Econ., Chgo. Bond, Hundred Club of Cook County, Tavern (pres. 1981-82), Saddle and Cycle (bd. dirs. 1983-86). Lodge: Soc. St. Andrew. Home: 227 E Delaware Pl Chicago IL 60611 Office: Shearson Lehman Hutton Inc 10 S Wacker Dr Ste 2800 Chicago IL 60606

FORBES, MALCOLM STEVENSON, publisher, author, former state senator; b. N.Y.C., Aug. 19, 1919; s. Bertie Charles and Adelaide (Stevenson) F.; m. Roberta Remsen Laidlaw, Sept. 21, 1946 (div. 1985); children: Malcolm Stevenson Jr., Robert Laidlaw, Christopher Charles, Timothy Carter, Moira Hamilton Forbes Mumma. Grad. cum laude, Lawrenceville Acad., 1937; AB, Princeton U., 1941; LHD (hon.), Nasson Coll., 1966; LLD (hon.), Okla. Christian Coll., 1973; LittD (hon.), Milliken U., 1974, Ball State U., 1980; DFA (hon.), Franklin Pierce Coll., 1975; DSc of Bus. Adminstrn. (hon.), Bryant Coll., 1976; D of Journalism (hon.), Babson Coll., 1977, Central New Eng. Coll., 1981; LLD (hon.), Am. Grad. Sch. Internat. Mgmt., 1977, Pace U., 1979, Potomac Sch. Law, 1979, Kean Coll. N.J., 1981, Westminster Coll., 1981, Seton Hill Coll., 1981, U. Vt., 1982, U. No. Colo., 1983, E. Tex. State U., 1984, Lehigh U., 1984, Webster U., 1984, Wittenberg U., 1985; D of Econ. Journalism (hon.), Lakeland Coll., 1980; HHD (hon.), Hofstra U., 1981, Ohio U., 1981, Southwestern at Memphis, 1983; DBA (hon.), Bloomfield Coll., 1982, Husson Coll., 1983; LHD (hon.), Lincoln Coll., 1983, U. Denver, 1983, Hillsdale Coll., 1984, Johns Hopkins U., 1984, Pratt Inst., 1985, St. Peter's Coll., 1986, Hampden-Sydney Coll., 1986; LittD (hon.), Miami U., 1983, Franklin and Marshall Coll., 1984, Rider Coll., 1986; DCS (hon.), St. Bonaventure, 1986; LLD (hon.), U. Aberdeen, 1986, Lewis and Clark Coll., 1986; Degree in Internat. Entrepreneurship (hon.), Armand Hammer United World Coll. of Am. West; DCS (hon.), Suffolk U., 1987; LHD (hon.), Carnegie-Mellon U., 1987, Centenary Coll., 1987; LLD (hon.), U. Mo., 1987; D of Bus. Adminstrn., Johnson & Wales Coll., 1987; LLD (hon.), Southwestern Adventist Coll., 1987, Spring Garden Coll., 1987; LHD (hon.), U. Tampa, 1988, Loyola Coll., 1988, Wilkes Coll., 1988; LLD (hon.), Syracuse U., 1988, Trenton Coll., 1988; D of Pub. Svc. and Bus. Leadership, Adams State Coll., 1988. Owner, pub. Fairfield Times (weekly), Lancaster, Ohio, 1941; est. Lancaster Tribune (weekly), 1942; assoc. pub. Forbes Mag. Bus., N.Y.C., 1946-54, pub., editor-in-chief, 1957—; v.p. Forbes Inc., N.Y.C., 1947-64, pres., 1964-80, chmn., chief exec. officer, 1980—; chmn. bd. 60 Fifth Ave. Corp.; pres. Forbes Trinchera Inc.; chmn. Fiji Forbes; founder, pres., pub. Nations Heritage (bi-monthly), 1948-49; chmn. bd. Sangre de Cristo Ranches Inc.; 1st person to fly coast-to-coast in U.S. in hot air balloon; set 6 world records in hot air ballooning, 1973; founded the world's 1st balloon mus., Chateau de Balleroy in Normandy, France, 1973; made 1st free flight of hot air balloon over Beijing, also 1st motorcycle tour of People's Rep. of China, 1982. Author: Fact and Comment, 1974, The Sayings of Chairman Malcolm, 1978; Around the World on Hot Air and Two Wheels, 1985; The Further Sayings of Malcolm Forbes, 1986, They Went That-a-way, 1988. Campaign chmn. ARC, Somerset Hills, N.J., 1949; mem. Borough Council Bernardsville, N.J., state senator, 1952-58, Republican candidate for gov., N.J., 1957, N.J. del.-at-large Rep. Nat. Conv., 1960; bd. dirs., Naval War Coll., 1975-77; trustee St. Mark's Sch., 1976-80, Princeton U., 1982, charter trustee, 1986—; bd. dirs. Coast Guard Acad. Found.; chmn. N.J. Rhodes Scholarship Com., 1976, 78, 79; mem. Princeton Art Council, 1973-79. Served with inf. AUS, 1942-45. Decorated Bronze Star, Purple Heart, Order of Merit France, Order of Ouissam Alaoyite (Morocco), President's Medal of Achievement (Pakistan); assoc. officer Order of St. John; recipient Freedoms Found. Medal, 1949; named Young Man of Year N.J. Jr. C. of C., 1951; recipient Aeronauts trophy, Harmon award, 1975; named hon. paramount chief Nimba tribe, Liberia, Philanthropist of Yr. Greater N.Y. chpt. Nat. Soc. Fund Raising Execs., 1986, Grand Dad of Yr. Old Grand Dad Club, 1986; recipient Eaton Corp. award Internat. Platform Assn., 1979, Disting. Achievement award in Periodical Journalism U. So. Calif. Joulism Alumni Assn., 1979; Image award for bus. and industry Men's Fashion Assn. Am., 1979; Bus. Leadership award Columbia U. Sch. Bus., 1980; Man of Conscience award Appeal of Conscience Found., 1980; Franklin award for disting. service Printing Industries Met. N.Y., 1981; Sacred Cat award Milw. Press Club, 1981; award for entrepreneurial excellence Yale U. Mgmt. Sch., 1982; Superstar of Yr. award Police Athletic League, 1982; Manstyle award Gentlemen's Quar., 1983; Community Service award Greenwich Village C. of C., 1983; Communicator of Yr. award Bus. Profl. Advt. Assn., 1983; Communicator of Yr. award 33d Ann. Enterprise award, award Council for Econ. Edn., 1983, Pub. of Yr. award Mag. Pubs. Assn., 1983; Medal of Honor Culinary Inst. of Am., 1983; Henry Johnson Fisher award, 1984; Free Enterprise award Ins. Fedn. N.Y., 1984; Mr. N.Y.'s Finest Championship award Patrolmen's Benevolent Assn., 1984; Person of Yr. award French-Am. C. of C. in U.S., 1985; Ann. Citation of Merit, Salvation Army Assn., 1985; inducted into Aviation Hall of Fame of N.J., 1985; Am. Eagle award Invest in Am. Nat. Council, 1986, Hands in Applause award Sales Execs. Club of N.Y., 1986; recipient Diplome Montgolfier Fedn. Aeronautique for outstanding contrib. to devel. ballooning, 1986; named Philanthropist of Yr. Greater N.Y. chpt. Nat. Soc. Fund Raising Execs., 1986, Assoc. Comdr. Brother of the Most Venerable Order Hosp. St. John of Jerusalem, 1986; Honored by the Govs. Com. on Scholastic Achievement, 1986; Salmagundi Honor award and the Richard M. Cyert Medal for Profl. Excellence Carnegie-Mellon U., 1987; Motorcyclist of Yr. award Motorcyclist Mag., 1987; Internat. Motorcyclist of Yr. award Internat. World of Motorcycles, 1988; inducted into Hall of Fame of N.Y. Fin. Writers Assn., 1988; promoted to the rank of officer by the French Gov. Legion of Honor, 1988; apptd. Knight Grand Cross of the Most Noble Order of the Crown of Thailand, 1988. Mem. St. Andrew's Soc., 84th Inf. Div. Assn., Def. Orientation Conf. Assn., N.J. Hist. Soc., Nat. Aero. Assn. (dir., exec. v.p.), Internat. Balloonists Assn., Balloon Fedn. Am. (dir. 1974-76), Aircraft Owners and Pilots Assn., Lighter than Air Soc., Brit. Balloon and Airship Club, Internat. Soc. Balloonpost Specialists, Newcomen Soc., Confrerie des Chevaliers du Tastevin, Pilgrims of U.S., Asian Inst. Technology (trustee 1988). Episcopalian (vestryman). Clubs: Princeton, Essex Fox Hound, New York Racquet and Tennis, New York Yacht, Links, Explorers. Office: Forbes Inc 60 Fifth Ave New York NY 10011

FORD, ALLEN HUNTINGTON, former oil company executive; b. Cleve., July 29, 1928; s. David K. and Elizabeth (Brooks) F.; m. Constance Towson, Feb. 19, 1954; children—Hope Murphy, Sarah Whitener, James T. B.A., Yale U., 1950; M.S., Case Inst. Tech., 1964. With Pickands Mather & Co., Cleve., 1953-69; v.p. fin. Pickands Mather & Co., 1967-69; treas. Diamond Shamrock Corp., Cleve., 1969; v.p. fin. Diamond Shamrock Corp., 1969-75, exec. v.p., 1976-80; sr. v.p. Standard Oil Co., Ohio, 1981-86; mem. adv. bd. The Transaction Group, Cleve.; bd. dirs. AmeriTrust Corp., Parker Hannifin Corp., Elwell-Parker Electric Co.; trustee First Union Real Estate Investments. Chmn. bd. trustees Case Western Res. U.; trustee Western Res. Hist. Soc., Cleve., Martha Holden Jennings Found., Mus. Arts Assn., Cleve. Orch., Univ. Hosps. Served with AUS, 1950-52. Home: 50 Mill Hollow Dr Chagrin Falls OH 44022 Office: 1666 Hanna Bldg Cleveland OH 44115

FORD, ASHLEY LLOYD, consumer products company executive, lawyer; b. Cin., Mar. 10, 1939; s. Starr MacLeod and Mary Lloyd (Mills) F.; m. Barbara Hill, Apr. 23, 1965; children—Christopher Ashley, Elizabeth Hill. A.B., Princeton U., 1960; J.D., Yale U., 1963. Bar: Ohio 1963. Assoc., Dinsmore & Shohl, Cin., 1965-69; counsel Procter & Gamble Co., Cin., 1969-71, div. counsel, 1971—, sec., 1979—. Shareholder, Cin. Mus. Assn.; trustee Cin. Hist. Soc. Served as lt. USNR, 1966-72. Mem. ABA, Ohio Bar Assn., Cin. Bar Assn., Am. Soc. Secs., Order of Coif, Phi Beta Kappa. Episcopalian. Clubs: Cin. Country, Athletic, University (Cin.). Office: Procter & Gamble Co 1 Procter & Gamble Pla Cincinnati OH 45202

FORD, GILBERT (GIB), sporting goods company executive; b. Tulia, Tex., Sept. 14, 1931; s. Rufus Perry and Emma Jo (Butler) F.; m. Jane Denise Girrior, Aug. 31, 1972; children: Sarah, Jason. BBA, U. Tex., 1954. Mktg. adminstr. Phillips Petroleum Col, Bartlesville, Okla., 1957-59, bus. mgr., 1959-61; sales and promotion rep. Converse Inc., Saratoga, Calif., 1961-66; asst. gen. mgr. sporting goods Converse Inc., Melrose Park, Ill., 1966-69; nat. sales mgr. Converse Inc., Malden, Mass., 1969-72; v.p. sales Converse Inc., North Reading, Mass., 1972-81, v.p. mktg. and sales, 1981-85, exec. v.p., 1985-86, pres., 1986—. 1st lt. USAF, 1955-57. Mem. Sporting Goods Mfrs. Assn. (bd. dirs. 1977-85, chmn. industry show com. 1977-83, chmn. bd. 1983-85), Nat. Sporting Goods Assn. (Hall of Fame com.), World Fedn. Sporting Goods Mfrs., Athletic Inst. (bd. dirs.), Salem (Mass.) Country Club. Republican. Office: Converse Inc 1 Fordham Rd North Reading MA 01864

FORD, JAMES STEPHEN, real estate appraiser; b. McAllen, Tex., Apr. 15, 1943; s. James Scott and Helen (Survillo) F.; m. Betty Sue McIntosh, July 1, 1965; children: John Russell, James Scott II. AS, BS, Embry Riddle Aero. U., 1974; MBA, U. Tex., San Antonio, 1983. Ins. agt., builder Ford Cos., McAllen, 1965-68; flight instr. Enterprise (Ala.) Flying Svc., 1968-71; air traffic control specialist U.S. Civil Svc., Cairns AAF, 1971-78; real estate appraiser Love & Dugger, Real Estate Appraisers, San Antonio, 1978-83, mng. ptnr., 1983-85; pres. Ford Realty Counselors & Appraisers, San Antonio, 1985—; speaker Caribbean Real Estate Congress, Barbados, Brit. West Indies, 1986; adj. faculty Embry-Riddle Aeronautical U. Col. Alamo Wing Confederate Air Force, San Antonio, 1986. Served with U.S. Army, 1963-65. Radio/TV scholar U. Tex., 1959. Mem. Internat. Real Estate Inst. (sr., chpt. pres. 1984-85), Nat. Assn. of Real Estate Appraisers (sr.), Urban Land Inst., Internat. Right of Way Assn. (chmn. valuation com. chpt. 39), Tex. Pilot's Assn. (bd. dirs. San Antonio chpt. 1987—), Northside C. of C. (speakers bur. 1987—), Greater San Antonio C. of C. Office: Ford Realty Counselors & Appraisers 105 Biltmore Dr Ste 102 San Antonio TX 78213

FORD, JOE THOMAS, telephone company executive, former state senator; b. Conway, Ark., June 24, 1937; s. Arch W. and Ruby (Watson) F.; m. Jo Ellen Wilbourn, Aug. 9, 1959; children: Alison, Scott. BS, U. Ark., 1959. With Allied Telephone Co., Little Rock, 1959-83, v.p.-treas., 1963-77, pres., 1977-83; pres. ALLTEL Corp., 1983-87; pres., chief exec. officer ALLTEL Corp., 1987—; mem. Ark. Senate, 1967-82; dir. Comml. Nat. Bank, 1970-85, Little Rock, Security Savs. and Loan Assn., Conway. Trustee Baptist Med. Center, Little Rock; former mem. bd. dirs. Little Rock Boys Club. Recipient Disting. Alumni cert. U. Ark., 1987. Mem. Greater Little Rock C. of C. (dir.). Baptist. Home: 2100 Country Club Ln Little Rock AR 72207 Office: Alltel Corp PO Box 2177 Little Rock AR 72203

FORD, JOHN CHARLES, communications executive; b. Washington, Oct. 8, 1942; s. Edgar Martin and Mary (Crowley) F. BA, U. Md., 1964, postgrad., 1964-65; MA, NYU, 1966; postgrad. N.Y. Inst. Finance, 1967-68, New Sch. for Social Research, 1969, Crowell-Collier Inst., 1969, Friesen-Kaye Inst., 1971, Sterling Inst., 1975, U. Wis., 1977, Colgate-Darden Sch. Bus., U. Va., 1978, Harvard U., 1982. TV prodn. asst. USIA, Washington, 1963-65; instr. U. Md., 1965; acct. exec. Ruder & Finn Inc., N.Y.C., 1965-66; asst. to exec. v.p., mgr. ednl. services Am. Stock Exchange, N.Y.C., 1966-70; mgr. communications and audio visual tng. Merrill Lynch, Pierce, Fenner & Smith Inc., N.Y.C., 1970-74; dir. edn. and tng. CBS Inc., 1974-77, dir. employee devel. and edn., 1977-79; pres. Travel U., v.p. Travel Network Corp. subs. ABC, N.Y.C., 1979-81; dir. human resources Home Box Office, Inc., 1981-84; communications cons., pres. John C. Ford Assocs., 1984—; mem. faculty N.Y. Inst. Fin., 1971-73, Katherine Gibbs Sch., 1972-74. Bd. dirs., treas. Archeus Found.; trustee U. Md. Found., 1984—; mem. U. Md. Pres.'s Club, bd. dirs., 1984—; chmn. Carnegie Hall concert U. Md. Piano Festival; bd. dirs. Care, Inc., One-to-One; bd. overseers Emerson Coll., Boston, 1978—; mem. bd. advisors corp. and cable communications program Manhattan Community Coll., CUNY; mem. devel. council Neumann Coll., Aston, Pa.; bd. dirs., v.p. 15 W 81st St. Tenants Corp., 1978-80, pres., 1979; mem. Council of West Side Coops., 20th Precinct Community Council, N.Y. Police Dept.; guest speaker Iowa Assn. for Life Long Learning. Mem. Nat. Acad. TV Arts and Scis. (bd. govs., trustee 1969—, sec. 1971—, trustee 1973—), Am. Soc. Tng. and Devel. (award 1978), Fin. Industry Tng. Assn. (pres. 1969-71), AAUP, Speech Communications Assn., Eastern Communication Assn. (area chmn. 1975), N.Y. State Communication Assn. (speaker), West 70th St. Assn., Fedn. West Side Block Assns., W. 82d St. Block Assn., Internat. Radio & TV Soc., Nat. Soc. Programmed Instrn., Nat. Audio-Visual Assn., Wall Street Tng. Dirs.'s Assn., Presidents Assn. of Am. Mgmt. Assns. (seminar leader), U. Md. Alumni Assn. Greater N.Y. (dir. 1966—), N.Y. Personnel Mgrs. Assns., Organizational Devel. Network, Group for Strategic Organizational Effectiveness, N.Y. Human Resource Planners, Internat. Platform Assn., Omicron Delta Kappa, Phi Delta Theta. Home: 15 W 81st St New York NY 10024 Office: 485 Fifth Ave Suite 1042 New York NY 10017

FORD, JOHN STEPHEN, treasurer; b. Clinton, Mass., Apr. 27, 1957; s. James Joseph and Rita (Hart) F.; m. Mary Andrejczyk, Apr. 15, 1978; children: Michelle, Amanda, William. BS, Lowell U., 1979. CPA, Mass.; notary pub., Mass. Staff acct. Main, Hurdman, Cranston, CPA's, Worcester, Mass., 1979; sr. acct. William S. Reagan & Co. CPA's, Fitchburg, Mass., 1979-82; treas. Peterborough Oil Co., Inc., Leominster, Mass., 1982—; cons. in field. Treas. Dem. Town Com., Lancaster, Mass., 1982—; v.p. Lancaster Softball Assn., 1982. Fellow Mass. Soc. CPA's; mem. Am. Inst. CPA's (mem. personal fin. planning div., tax div.), Internat. Platform Assn. Roman Catholic. Office: Peterborough Oil Co 665 N Main PO Box 787 Leominster MA 01453

FORD, JUDITH ANN, retired natural gas distribution company executive; b. Martinsville, Ind., May 11, 1935; d. Glenn Leyburn and Dorotha Mae (Parks) Tudor; m. Walter L. Ford, July 25, 1954 (dec. 1962); children—John Corbin, Christi Sue. Student, Wichita State U., 1953-55; student, U. Nev.-Las Vegas. Legal sec. Southwest Gas Corp., Las Vegas, 1963-69, adminstrn. sec., 1968-79, asst. corp. sec., 1969-72, corp. sec., 1972-82, v.p., 1977-82, sr. v.p., 1982-88, also bd. dirs., dir. 7 subs. Trustee Nev. Sch. Arts, Las Vegas, 1979—, chmn. bd. dirs., 1985-86; trustee Disciples Sem. Found., Claremont Sch. Theology, Calif., 1985—; mem. Ariz. Acad., Ariz. Town Halls, 1986—. Mem. Am. Soc. Corp. Secs., Greater Las Vegas C. of C. (bd. dirs. 1979-85), Pacific Coast Gas Assn. (bd. dirs. 1984-88), Ariz. Bus. Women Owners (exec. com. 1985-88). Democrat. Mem. Christian Ch. (Disciples of Christ). Office: SW Gas Corp PO Box 98510 Las Vegas NV 89193-8510

FORD, M. JANE, city official; b. Mineola, N.Y., Nov. 17, 1945; d. John Frank and Maria Olga (DiGeronimo) Fradel; m. William E. Ford, July 29, 1967; 1 child, Amanda J. Student, U. Pitts., 1963-67; BS, U. Mass., 1971; MBA, U. Nebr., 1980. Technician Cooley Dickinsen Hosp., Northampton, Mass., 1967-68; head clin. chemistry U. Health Svcs., Amherst, Mass., 1968-71; caseworker Madison County, Norfolk, Nebr., 1971-72; mental health educator N.E. Mental Health Clinic, Norfolk, 1972-73; state mental health educator State of Nebr., Lincoln, 1973-74; project rev. coord. S.E. Nebr. Health Planning Coun., Lincoln, 1974-75; acting dir. S.E. Nebr. Health Planning Coun., 1975-76; exec. dir. S.E. Nebr. Health Systems Agy., Lincoln, 1976-81; health dir. City of Lincoln, 1981—. Mem. steering com. Ctr. for Disease Control Assesment Program for Excellence Pub. Health Project, Atlanta, 1987—; mem. state adv. com. Cancer Project State of Nebr., Lincoln, 1988—; bd. dirs. Lincoln Med. Ctr. Assn., 1985—, ARC, Lincoln chpt. Recipient Recognition award HEW, 1978. Mem. Nat. Assn. County Helath Ofcls. (bd. dirs. 1986—), Am. Pub. Health Assn., Nat. Environ. Health Assn., Soc. Pub. Health Edn., Nebr. Pub. Health Assn. (bd. dirs. 1983-85), Nebr. Environ. Health Assn. (bd. dirs. 1984-86), Altrusa Club (sec. 1985). Republican. Mem. United Ch. of Christ. Home: 7630 Myrtle St Lincoln NE 68506 Office: Lincoln-Lancaster Health Dept 2200 Saint Mary's Ave Lincoln NE 68500

FORD, THOMAS JEFFERS, industrial developer; b. Charleston, S.C., Sept. 9, 1930; s. Rufus and Mildred (Jeffers) F.; AB, Wofford Coll., 1952; postgrad. U. N.C., 1956-58, 59-61, U. Okla., 1965-67; m. Barbara Jean Jackson, Dec. 28, 1954; children: Thomas Jeffers, Edward Rufus. Asst. mgr. Albany (Ga.) C. of C., 1956; mgr. Rock Hill (S.C.) C. of C., 1957-58; dir. trade devel. Greenville (S.C.) C. of C., 1959-60, dir. bus. and indsl. relations, 1961; exec. dir. Marlboro County Devel. Bd., Bennettsville, S.C., 1962-65, Lakeland (Fla.) Indsl. Bd., 1966-67; dir. Chesterfield-Marlboro Tech. Edn. Center, Cheraw, S.C., 1968-72; dir. area devel. dept. 6th Congl. Dist. S.C., Florence, 1973-74; dir. bus. devel. Eskridge & Long Constrn. Corp., Sanford, N.C., 1975; chief exec. officer Greater Orangeburg (S.C.) C. of C.; chief exec. officer Orangeburg County Devel. Commn., 1976-79, exec. dir., 1979—. Served with USN, 1952-53. Cert. indsl. developer. Fellow Am. Econ. Devel. Council (past mem. internat. certified indsl. devel. bd.; regent ednl. programs); mem. S.C. Indsl. Developers Assn. (founder, past pres.), So. Indsl. Devel. Council (past dir.), Blue Key, SAR, Sigma Alpha Epsilon. Methodist. Lodge: Rotary (past club pres.). Home: 2978 Lakeside Dr NE Orangeburg SC 29115 Office: PO Box 1303 Orangeburg SC 29116

FORD, WILLIAM CLAY, automotive company executive; b. Detroit, Mar. 14, 1925; s. Edsel Bryant and Eleanor (Clay) F.; m. Martha Firestone, June 21, 1947; children: Martha, Sheila, William Clay, Elizabeth. B.S., Yale U., 1949. Sales and advt. staff Ford Motor Co., 1949; indsl. relations, labor negotiations with UAW, 1949; quality control mgr. gas turbine engines Lincoln-Mercury Div., Dearborn, Mich., 1951, mgr. spl. product ops., 1952, v.p., 1953, gen. mgr. Continental Div., 1954, group v.p. Lincoln and Continental Divs, 1955, v.p. product design, 1956-80; dir. 1948—, chmn. exec. com., 1978—, vice chmn. bd., 1980-89; chmn. fin. com. Ford Motor Co., 1987—; pres., owner Detroit Lions Profl. Football Club. Chmn. Edison Inst.; trustee Eisenhower Med. Center, Thomas A. Edison Found.; bd. dirs. Nat. Tennis Hall of Fame, Boys Clubs Am. Mem. Soc. Automotive Engrs. (asso.), Automobile Old Timers, Econ. Club Detroit (dir.), Masons, K.T., Phelps Assn., Psi Upsilon. Office: Ford Motor Co Design Ctr PO Box 6012 Dearborn MI 48123 other: Detroit Lions 1200 Featherstone Rd PO Box 4200 Pontiac MI 48057

FORD, WILLIAM FRANCIS, bank holding company executive; b. Albany, N.Y., Mar. 11, 1925; s. Patrick J. and Ellen M. F.; m. Marcia J. Whalen, Jan. 7, 1956; children: William Francis, Michael P., Timothy K., Daniel J., Cathleen A. B.A. in Acctg. with honors, St. Michaels Coll., 1950. V.p. Equitable Credit Corp., Albany, 1950-60, Am. Fin. Systems Inc., Silver Spring, Md., 1960-65, Gen. Electric Credit Corp., Stamford, Conn., 1965-74; chmn., chief exec. officer Security Pacific Fin. Corp., San Diego, 1974-81; exec. v.p., adminstr. specialized fin. services group Security Pacific Corp., Los Angeles, 1981-84; vice chmn. Security Pacific Corp., 1984—. Served with USN, 1943-46. Mem. Am. Fin. Services Assn. (chmn., dir. exec. com.). Club: Stone Ridge Country.

FORDICE, DANIEL KIRKWOOD, JR., construction company executive; b. Memphis, Tenn., Feb. 10, 1934; s. Daniel Kirkwood and Clara Aileen (Augustine) F.; m. Patricia Louise Owens, Aug. 13, 1955; children: Angela Leigh Fordice Roselle, Daniel K. III, Hunter L., James Owens. BSCE, Purdue U., 1956, MS in Indsl. Mgmt., 1957. Registered profl. engr., Miss., La. Engr. Exxon, Baton Rouge, 1956-62; ptnr. Fordice Constrn. Co., Delta, La., 1962-76, pres., chief exec. officer, 1976—; bd. dirs. Mchts. Nat. Bank, Vicksburg, Miss. Sec. Miss. Rep. Party, Jackson, 1981-88; vice-chmn. Vicksburg-Tallulah Dist. Airport Bd.; chmn. Econ. Devel. Found., Vicksburg, 1984. Served to col. C.E., USAR. Named One of Outstanding Young Men of Am., U.S. Jaycees, 1969, Vol. Laureate in Indsl. Devel., Gov. of Miss., 1985. Fellow ASCE (pres. Vicksburg br. 1982); mem. NSPE, Am. Inst. Contstructors, Cons. Constructors Council Am., Soc. Am. Mil. Engrs., Assoc. Gen. Contractors Am. (v.p. 1988, nat. life dir., pres. Miss. Valley flood control br. 1970), Tau Beta Pi, Chi Epsilon. Republican. Methodist. Club: Rivertown (Vicksburg). Home: 1457 Parkside Dr Vicksburg MS 39180 Office: Fordice Constrn Co 1 Mississippi River Delta LA 71233

FORDYCE, EDWARD WINFIELD, JR., lawyer; b. St. Louis, Sept. 23, 1941; s. Edward Winfield and Jane (Nol) F.; m. Nancy Cairns Abbott, June 13, 1964; children: Edward Winfield III, Douglas A., Russell S. A.B. cum laude, Harvard Coll., 1963; LL.B., U. Va. Law Sch., 1966. Bar: Pa. 1966, Mo. 1968. Assoc. firm Dechert, Price & Rhoads, Phila., 1966-67; atty. Monsanto Co., St. Louis, 1967-70; asst. to pres. New Eng. Mut. Life Ins. Co., Boston, 1970-71; assoc., partner Fordyce and Mayne, St. Louis, 1971-75; corp. counsel Nat. Gypsum Co., Dallas, 1975-76, sr. dir. counsel, 1976-77, asst. gen. counsel, 1977-79, v.p., gen. counsel, 1979-88; of counsel Ray, Trotti, Hemphill & Finrock, Dallas, 1988—. Chmn. trustees Parish Day Sch., 1980-81. Mem. ABA, Dallas Bar Assn., Bent Tree Country Club. Republican. Episcopalian. Home: 13228 Hughes Ln Dallas TX 75240 Office: 1401 Elm St Ste 1800 Dallas TX 75202

FOREMAN, EDWIN FRANCIS, broker; b. Syracuse, N.Y., July 24, 1931; s. Herve Joseph and Ruth Margaret F.; m. Colleen Frances Tapp, July 7, 1962; children—Lisa C., Eric E. BAE in Econs. and Fgn. Trade, U. Fla., 1957; postgrad. in real estate Fla. Internat. U., 1974-75. Owner, prin. Edwin F. Foreman, Mortgage Broker, Hollywood, Fla., 1974—; with Consol. Energy Corp., Hollywood, 1977—, pres., chmn. bd., 1977—; v.p. Ea. State Securities, Inc., 1977—; owner, prin. Edwin F. Foreman, Real Estate Broker, 1978—; pres., chmn. One-Fore-Devel., Inc., 1985, Three-Fore-Devel., Inc., 1985, L&E Communications Inc., 1985; chmn., chief exec. officer Universal Traction, Hollywood, 1988—; gen. ptnr. Four-Fore Devel. Ltd., Five-Fore-Devel. Ltd., Six-Fore Devel., Ltd., 1987—. Econ. cons. Michael I. Warde de Colombia Ltd.; guest lectr. econs. Xavier U., Bogota, Colombia. Served with USAF, 1950-53. R.J. Reynolds fellow U. N.C., 1961. Mem. Hollywood C. of C., Ft. Lauderdale World Trade Council. Democrat. Unitarian. Clubs: Jockey, Grove Isle (Miami), Fisher Island. Avocations: camping, fishing, music, photography, travel. Office: PO Box 7570 Hollywood FL 33081-1570

FORET, MICKEY PHILLIP, air transportation company executive; b. McComb, Miss., Oct. 23, 1945; s. Fadias Phillip and Christine (Brown) F.; m. Mary Ann Tramonte, Aug. 12, 1966; 1 child, Keri. BS in Fin., La. State U., 1971, MBA in Fin., 1971. Dir. credit/interim dir. internal audit Tex. (Houston) Internat. Airlines, 1975-77, dir. cash mgmt., 1977-78, asst. treas., 1978-81, v.p. fin. svcs., 1981-82; v.p., treas. Continental Airlines, L.A., 1982-84, v.p., chief fin. officer, 1984-86, also bd. dirs.; sr. v.p. fin. and internat. Eastern Airlines, Miami, Fla., 1987-88, v.p., chief fin. officer, 1986—, also bd. dirs.; sr. v.p. Tex. (Houston) Air Corp., 1988—; exec. v.p. fin. and planning Continental Airlines, Houston, 1988—; hmn. bd. dirs. Chelsea Catering Co., Houston. Pres. Clear Wood Improvement Assn., Houston, 1975-78; coach Friendswood (Tex.) Girls Softball Team, 1981. Served with USAF, 1968-69, Vietnam. Mem. Phi Kappa Phi, Beta Gamma Sigma. Republican. Baptist. Home: PO Box 97 0229 Miami FL 33197 Office: Ea Airlines Miami Internat Airport Miami FL 33148

FORGUES, JORGE RAUL, accountant, tax consultant; b. Buenos Aires, July 22, 1955; came to U.S., 1975; s. Jorge Luis and Dora (Gual) F.; m. Maria Thomae, Aug. 7, 1976; children: Nicholas, Sebastian, Christina. BS in Acctg., George Mason U., 1983, MBA in Fin., 1984. CPA, Va. Adminstrv. officer OAS, Washington, 1976-79, acct., 1979-82; retail controller Peoples Drug Stores, Inc., Alexandria, Va., 1984-86; controller Best Programs, Inc., Arlington, Va., 1987—; tax preparer, Springfield, Va., 1979—. Treas. Educo, Springfield, 1987-88. Bus. honor soc. and Washington chpt. Soc. Logistics Engrs. scholar George Mason U., 1983. Mem. Am. Inst. CPA's, Nat. Assn. Accts., Assn. Internat. Music Friends (treas. 1986). Republican. Roman Catholic. Home: 6612 Burlington Pl Springfield VA 22152 Office: Best Programs Inc 2700 S Quincy St Ste 270 Arlington VA 22206

FORMAN, DAVID C., pharmaceutical company executive; b. 1936; married. BA, Ohio State U., 1958, Hebrew Union Coll., 1960. Cons. employee benefits 1960-70; regional dir. mktg. Intercontinental Mktg. Corp., 1970-72; v.p., corp. dir. personnel Lane Drug Co., 1972-76; asst. v.p. People's Drug Stores Inc., Alexandria, Va., 1976-77; v.p. human resources, then v.p., now exec. v.p. People's Drug Stores Inc., Alexandria, 1977—, also bd. dirs. Office: Peoples Drug Stores Inc 6315 Bren Mar Dr Alexandria VA 22312 *

FORMAN, PAULA, advertising agency executive. Market rsch. trainee BBDO; sr. v.p., mgmt. supr. Wells, Rich, Greene; now exec. v.p., exec. mgmt. dir. Saatchi & Saatchi DFS Inc., N.Y.C. Office: Saatchi & Saatchi DFS Inc 375 Hudson St New York NY 10014 *

FORMAN, WILLIAM JOEL, accountant; b. Phila., Nov. 5, 1946; s. Herbert Bernard and Jean Doris (Reingold) F.; m. Elaine Bernstein, Sept. 12, 1971; children: Steven, Jason, Michelle. AA, Pierce Jr. Coll., 1967; BA, Phila. Coll. Textiles and Scis., 1974. Lic. pub. acct., Pa. Account clk. City of Phila., 1967, account technician, 1967-75, acct. I, 1975—; pvt. practice acctg. Phila., 1975—. Named Outstanding Alumni, Ken-crest NE Parents Assn., 1984. Mem. Nat. Soc. Pub. Accts., Pa. Soc. Pub. Accts., Phila. Assn. Retarded Citizens, Spl. People in Northeast., Chapel Four Chaplains. Jewish. Home and Office: 2720 Taunton St Philadelphia PA 19152

FORMANEK, PETER RAEMIN, auto parts company executive; b. 1943. BA, U. N.C., 1966; MBA, Harvard U., 1968. Adminstrv. asst. to pres., asst. prof. bus. adminstrn. LeMoyne-Owen Coll., Tenn.; exec. v.p. Super Drugs, 1969-72, pres. 1972; with Malone & Hyde, Inc., Memphis, 1968—, asst. to pres., 1968-73, v.p. drugs and rack svc., 1973-79, group v.p. retailing 1979-81, exec. v.p. specialty retailing 1981-86, pres. Auto Zone Inc., 1986—. Office: AutoZone Inc PO Box 2198 Memphis TN 38101

FORNOFF, FRANK, JR., retired chemistry educator; b. Mt. Carmel, Ill., Mar. 29, 1914; s. Frank and Ada (Arnold) F.; A.B., U. Ill., 1936; M.S., Ohio State U., 1937, Ph.D. (Proctor & Gamble fellow), 1939. Asst. prof. Lehigh U., Bethlehem, Pa., 1942-44; chem. engr. Western Electric Co., N.Y.C., 1944-45; asst. prof. chemistry Lehigh U., 1945-47, asso. prof., 1947-53; asso. prof. Kans. State U., Manhattan, 1953-56; lectr. Rutgers U., New Brunswick, N.J., 1956-84; sr. examiner Ednl. Testing Service, Princeton, N.J., 1956, group head, 1956-83. Active Boy Scouts Am., Princeton, 1957—. NRC fellow U. Calif., Berkeley, 1939-40. Mem. Am. Chem. Soc. (chmn. local sect. assn. publs. 1960-70), AAAS, Am. Soc. Engring. Edn., Nat. Sci. Tchrs. Assn., Nat. Council Measurements in Edn., N.J. Acad. Sci. Methodist. Contbr. articles to profl. jours.; editor AP Chemistry newsletter, 1976—. Home: 338 Franklin St Princeton NJ 08540 Office: Ednl Testing Svc Princeton NJ 08541

FORREST, HERBERT EMERSON, lawyer; b. N.Y.C., Sept. 20, 1923; s. Jacob K. and Rose (Fried) F.; m. Marilyn Lefsky, Jan. 12, 1952; children: Glenn Clifford, Andrew Matthew. B.A. with distinction, George Washington U., 1948; J.D. with highest honors, 1952; student, CCNY, 1941, Ohio U., 1943-44. Bar: Va. 1952, D.C. 1952, U.S. Supreme Ct. 1956, Md. 1959. Plate printer Bur. Engraving and Printing, Washington, 1942-43, 1946-52; law clk. to chief judge Bolitha J. Laws U.S. Dist. Ct., Washington, 1952-55; practice in Washington, 1952—; mem. firm Welch & Morgan, 1955-65; mem. firm Steptoe & Johnson, 1965-85, of counsel, 1986-87; trial atty. Fed. Programs Br. Civil div. U.S. Dept. Justice, Washington, 1987—; chmn. adv. bd. D.C. Criminal Justice Act, 1971-74; sec. com. admissions and grievances U.S. Ct. Appeals, D.C., 1973-79; mem. Title-1 audit hearing bd. U.S. Office Edn. HEW, 1976-79; mem. edn. appeals bd. U.S. Dept. Edn., 1979-82; mem. Lawyer's Support Com. for Visitors Service Center, 1975-87. Contbr. articles to legal jours.; advisory bd.: Duke Law Jour, 1969-75. Pres. Whittier Woods PTA, 1970-71. Served with F.A., Signal Corps U.S. Army, 1943-46. Recipient Walsh award in Irish history, 1952, Goddard award in commerce, 1952. Fellow Am. Bar Found.; mem. George Washington Law Assn., Am. Judicature Soc., ABA (council 1972-75, 1981-84, budget officer 1985-88, vice chmn. task force on sect. devel. 1987—, chmn. com. on agy. rule making 1968-72, 1976-81, chmn. membership com. 1984-85, editor ann. reports 1973-88, adminstrv. law sect., mem. communications com. public utilities law sect., vice chmn. industry regulation com. 1985-86, chmn. communications subcom. 1983-85 antitrust law sect., internat. law sect., sec. judicial adminstrn., sect. sci. and tech., communications forum), Va. State Bar Assn., Fed. Bar Assn. (chmn. jud. rev. com. 1981-85, vice chmn. adminstrv. law sect. 1985-87), Fed. Communications Bar Assn. (del. to ABA Ho. Dels. 1979-81, exec. com. 1967-71, 76-84, v.p. 1981-82, pres. 1982-83, chmn. telecommunications com. 1983-87), D.C. Bar Assn. (past sec., exec. com.), NAM, Nat. Assn. Bar Pres., Washington Council Lawyers, Legal Aid and Pub. Defender Assn., Am. Arbitration Assn. (comml. panel 1976-87), D.C. Unified Bar (bd. govs. 1976-79, chmn. com. on employment discrimination complaint service 1973-79, chmn. task force on services to public 1974-78, chmn. com. on appointment counsel in criminal cases 1978-88, co-chmn. com. on participation govt. employees in pro bono activities 1977-79), Broadcast Pioneers, Order of Coif, Phi Beta Kappa, Pi Gamma Mu., Artus, Phi Eta Sigma, Phi Delta Phi. Democrat. Lodge: B'nai Brith. Home: 8706 Bellwood Rd Bethesda MD 20817 Office: US Dept Justice 10th & Pennsylvania Ave NW Room 3342 Main Bldg Washington DC 20530

FORREST, JAMES EMERY, corporate executive; b. Mar. 19, 1949. BS, Mich. State U., 1971; MBA, Harvard U., 1975. Electronic engr. Harry Diamond Labs., Washington, 1971-73; various adminstrv. positions Gould, Inc., Cleve., 1975-81, v.p., gen. mgr., 1981-83, pres. RSD, 1983-86; v.p. strategic planning Gould, Inc., Rolling Meadows, Ill., 1986—. Mem. IEEE, Am. Electronics Assn., Am. Mktg. Assn., Am. Mgmt. Assn., Eta Kappa Nu, Tau Beta Pi.

FORREST, RICHARD ALAN, mining company executive, geologist; b. N.Y.C., Feb. 9, 1948; s. Richard D. and Ann A. Forrest; children: Elaina J., Christina R. BA in Geology, Colo. Coll., 1969; MS in Geology, Mont. Coll. of Mineral Sci. and Tech., 1971. Cert. profl. geologist; lic. geologist, Alaska; registered geologist, Calif., Ariz. Sr. exploration geologist Sunshine Mining Co., Kellogg, Idaho, 1971-77; sr. geologist Amoco Minerals Co., Englewood, Colo., 1977-80; v.p. exploration and ops. Tex. Gen. Minerals Corp., Golden, Colo., 1980-82; sr. v.p. Consol. Mining Resources, Inc., Golden, Colo., 1982-84; sr. v.p. exploration adminstrn., corp. sec. Horizon Gold Shares, Inc., Evergreen, Colo., 1984—, also bd. dirs.; bd. dirs. Autosure, Inc., Evergreen, Sunrise Gold Corp., Evergreen. Mem. AIME, Soc. Econ. Geologists, Colo. Mining Assn. Republican. Home: Box 3453 Evergreen CO 80439 Office: Horizon Gold Shares Inc 1536 Cole Blvd Suite 140 Golden CO 80401

FORRESTER, DOUGLAS ROBERT, state pension director; b. Glendale, Calif., Jan. 24, 1953; s. Robert Walter and Lucille (Cotton) F.; m. Andrea Lee Howard, Aug. 2, 1975; children: Alexander, Ryan, Briana. AB in Philosophy and Govt., Harvard U., 1975; MDiv, Princeton Seminary, 1983. Dir. research N.J. State Assembly, Trenton, 1978-82; asst. state treas. State of N.J., Trenton, 1982-83, dir. pensions, 1984—; sr. lectr. U. Pa. Fels Ctr. of Govt., 1987—. Mem. town council Twp. of West Windsor, N.J., 1979-83, planning bd., 1980-82, environ. commn., 1980-82, mayor 1981-82. Office: Div Pensions 20 W Front St CN 295 Trenton NJ 08625

FORRESTER, WILLIAM DONALD, public relations executive; b. Port Chester, N.Y., Dec. 20, 1931; s. John J. and Catherine (McDonald) F.; BS, Columbia U., 1955; m. Margaret A. Ward, Feb. 2, 1952. V.p. George Peabody & Assocs., N.Y.C., 1957-64; dir. public relations project Am. Export Isbrandtsen Lines, N.Y.C., 1964-65; account supr. Cunningham & Walsh, N.Y.C., 1965-67; gen. mgr. PR Communications, Clifton, N.J., 1967-69; v.p. Burson-Marsteller, N.Y.C., 1969-74; v.p. adminstrn. and communications U.S.-USSR Trade and Econ. Council, N.Y.C./Washington/Moscow, 1974—, apptd. acting pres. 1988—. Served with USMC, 1950-52. Mem. Public Relations Soc. Am. Contbr. articles to bus. jours. Home: Overhill Road RD 2 Town of Cortlandt Peekskill NY 10566 Office: 805 Third Ave New York NY 10022

FORROW, BRIAN DEREK, lawyer, corporation executive; b. N.Y.C., Feb. 6, 1927; s. Frederick George and Doris (Williams) F.; m. Eleanor Reid, Mar. 8, 1952; children—Lisa Coggins, Brian Lachlan, Catherine Frances, Derek Skylstead. A.B., Princeton, 1947; J.D., Harvard, 1950. Bar: N.Y. 1950, Conn. 1967. From assoc. to ptnr. Cahill, Gordon, Sonnett, Reindel & Ohl (and predecessors), 1950-68; v.p., gen. counsel Allied Chem. Corp., 1968—, dir., 1969-85; sr. v.p., gen. counsel Allied-Signal Inc., 1985—; bd. dirs. Union Tex. Petroleum. Contbr. articles to profl. publs. Vestryman, former senior warden, former dicoesan rep., Episcopal Ch. Served to 1st lt. USAF, 1951-53. Mem. ABA, Am. Law Inst., Internat. Bar Assn., Conn. Bar Assn., N.Y. State Bar Assn., Bar Assn. City N.Y. (chmn. com. corp. law depts.), Am. Arbitration Assn. (bd. dirs. 1987—), Southwestern Legal Found. (vice chmn. bd. dirs.), Westchester Fairfield Corp. Counsel Assn. (bd. dirs. 1986—), Am. Corp. Counsel Assn. (bd. dirs. 1987—), Assn. Corp. Counsel N.J. (former pres.). Republican. Episcopalian. Home: 704 Lake Ave Greenwich CT 06830 Office: Allied-Signal Inc PO Box 3000 R Morristown NJ 07960

FORSGREN, JOHN H., JR., entertainment executive; b. Cleve., Aug. 31, 1946; s. John H. and Jeanne Marie (Sullivan) F. B.A., Georgetown U., 1967; M.B.A., Columbia U., 1969; M.S., U. Geneva, Switzerland, 1972. With Alcan, 1969-75; dir. internat. fin. Sperry Corp., N.Y.C., 1977-80, staff v.p., 1980-83, treas., 1983-86; v.p., treas. The Walt Disney Co., Burbank, 1986—. Trustee Georgetown U. Library, Washington, 1983. Republican. Roman Catholic. Clubs: N.Y. Athletic; Essex Yacht (Conn.); Cercle de l'Union Internalliee (Paris); Metropolitan (N.Y.C.). Home: Box 4041 Lyme CT 06371 Office: Walt Disney Co 500 S Buena Vista St Burbank CA 91521

FORSTE, NORMAN LEE, management consultant; b. Carthage, Mo., Aug. 18, 1935; s. John Edward and Lula Mae (Martin) F.; m. Catherine Jean Culver, July 20, 1958; children: Patricia, Diana, John II, Karl. AA, Am. River coll., 1961; BA, Calif. State U., 1964, MA, 1971; MBA, Golden Gate U., 1973; PhD in Higher Edn., U. Wash., 1984. Adminstrv. analyst State of Calif., Sacramento, 1962-64, sr. data processing systems analyst, 1966-67, supr. info. systems devel., 1967-68; sr. adminstrv. analyst County of Sacramento (Calif.), 1964-66, dir. systems and data processing dept., 1968-74; dir. adminstrv. data processing div. U. Wash., Seattle, 1974-76; mgr. mgmt. adv. services Deloitte Haskins & Sells, 1976-81, dir. mgmt. adv. services, 1981-85; pvt. practice mgmt. cons., Carmichael, Calif., 1985—; instr. mgmt. scis. program U. Calif. at Davis, 1968; professorial lectr. mgmt. info. systems Golden Gate U., Sacramento, 1971-74, 79—; instr. info. systems Calif. State U.-Sacramento, 1982-83; instr. systems analysis and introduction to data processing Am. River Coll., Sacramento, 1968-71. Mem. curriculum adv. com. for data processing Am. River Coll., Sacramento, 1969-74, mem. com. to evaluate vocational and tech. edn. program for accreditation, 1972-73. Served with USAF, 1954-57, 62, maj. USAFR, Ret. Mem. Am. Soc. Pub. Adminstrn. (dir. 1969-71, 84-85), Data Processing Mgmt. Assn. (chpt. pres. 1968-69), Methods and Procedure Assn. (pres. 1969), Calif. Assn. County Data Processors (1st v.p. 1973-74), Air Force Res. Officers Assn. (chpt. v.p. 1971-74, 79-82), Air Force Calif. Dept. Res. Officers Assn. (jr. v.p. 1971). Home and Office: 5401 Valhalla Dr Carmichael CA 95608

FORSTER, HOMER W., financial planner; b. Memphis, Apr. 2, 1944; s. Homer Miller and Marbel (Webb) F.; m. Ydia A. Placer, Dec. 4, 1970 (div. 1981); children: Ydia, Pedro, Sean, Kevin; m. Karen F. Jackson, Nov. 30, 1982; children: Christopher, Michael, Kristi. BA in Psychology, Fla. Atlantic U., 1978; cert. in advanced portfolio mgmt. and estate planning. Cert. fin. planner; registered fin. planning practitioner. Sales rep. New Eng. Life Ins. Co., Miami, Fla., 1968-69; agy. mgr. Mut. N.Y., Miami, 1969-70; fin. planner PFP Corp., Miami, 1970-74; fin. planner Forster & Assocs., Sarasota, Fla., 1974-77, Ft. Lauderdale, Fla., 1977-81, Huntington, W.Va., 1981-87, Atlanta, 1987—; dir. investment div. Century 21 So. Fla., Inc., Miami, 1979. Contbr. to profl. publs.; winner Nat. Fin. Planning Case Study Competition, 1989. Mem. Rep. exec. com. Sarasota and Broward, Fla., 1974-76, 78-79; pres. Tri-State Area council Boy Scouts Am., Huntington, 1985-87; named hon. Ky. Col., 1983. Mem. Inst. Cert. Fin. Planners, Internat. Assn. Fin. Planning (pres. W.Va. chpt. 1985-88, chmn. S.E. regional coun. 1988), Planned Giving Council Ga., Estate Planning Council Huntington, Masons, Shriners. Episcopalian. Office: Forster & Assocs Inc 1950 Spectrum Circle Ste A395 Marietta GA 30067

FORSTER, PETER H., utility company executive; b. Berlin, Germany, May 28, 1942; s. Jerome and Margaret Hanson; m. Susan E. Forster. B.S., U. Wis., 1964; postgrad., Bklyn. Law Sch., Columbia U., 1972. Engr. trainee Wis. Electric Power Co., 1960-64; head regional planning Am. Electric Power Service Corp., 1964-73; atty. Dayton Power & Light Co., Ohio, from 1973, v.p. adminstrn., treas., 1977, v.p. fin. and adminstrn., 1977-78, v.p. energy resources, 1978-79, exec. v.p., 1980-81, exec. v.p., chief operating officer, 1981-82, pres., chief operating officer, 1982-84, pres., chief exec. officer, 1984-88, chmn., pres., chief exec. officer, 1988—; bd. dirs. Bank One, Dayton, Ohio. Bd. dirs. Amcast, Comair, F.M. Tait Found.; trustee Med Am. Health Systems. Mem. Am. Bar Assn., Ohio Bar Assn., Dayton Bar Assn. Club: Dayton Engrs. Office: DPL Inc Courthouse Pla SW PO Box 1247 Dayton OH 45401

FORSTER, VIRGINIA (LUCIE), corporate professional; b. Beverly, Mass., Feb. 20, 1953; d. Walter H. and Lucie Jacques F. AS in Bus. Mgmt., AA in Liberal Arts, Bunker Hill Community Coll., Boston, 1985. Gen. mgr. Hdqrs. Cos., Boston, 1984-87; corp. project mgr., facilities planner Internat. Data Group, Framingham, Mass., 1987—. Vol. Beverly Hosp., 1969-72, Big Sisters Am., 1983; pres. Fenway Rider's Com., 1978. Mem. Am. Mgmt. Assn., Am. Airlines Kiwi Club. Home: 115 W Squantum St #407 North Quincy MA 02171 Office: Internat Data Group 5 Speen St Framingham MA 01701

FORT, JOHN FRANKLIN, III, fire protection/flow control systems, electrical and electronic components/packaging manufacturing company executive; b. N.Y.C., Oct. 12, 1941; s. John Franklin and Florence (Baumrucker) F.; m. Nancy Barnett, Feb. 18, 1967; children: John Franklin, Alexandra S., Tucker H., Elizabeth B. BS, Princeton U., 1963; MS, MIT, 1966. V.p., gen. mgr. Simplex Wire & Cable Co., Newington, N.H., 1970-74, pres., 1974-79; v.p. ops. Tyco Labs., Inc., Exeter, N.H., 1979-82, sr. v.p. ops., 1982, pres., chmn. bd., chief exec. officer, 1983—. Trustee Berwick Acad. Recipient Corp. Leadership award MIT, 1984. Office: Tyco Labs Inc 1 Tyco Pk Exeter NH 03833

FORTE, VINCENT JOSEPH, JR., electrical engineer; b. Albany, N.Y., Apr. 4, 1956; s. Vincent Joseph and Michelina (Rizzo) F.; m. Barbara Ann Franke, Apr. 26, 1980. BS in Elec. Power Engring., Rensselaer Polytech. Inst., 1978, MS in Elec. Power Engring., 1979. Registered profl. engr., N.Y. Engr. N.Y. State Electric & Gas Corp., Binghampton, 1979-81, staff engr., 1981; asst. engr. Niagara Mohawk Power Corp., Albany, N.Y., 1981-83, assoc. engr., 1983-86, engr., 1986, lead engr., 1986—. Mem. Eta Kappa Nu. Roman Catholic. Office: Niagara Mohawk Power Corp 1125 Broadway Albany NY 12204

FORTENBAUGH, SAMUEL BYROD, III, lawyer; b. Phila., Nov. 6, 1933; s. Samuel Byrod and Katherine Francisca (Wall) F.; m. Patricia Lee Dooley, June 7, 1975; children: Samuel Byrod IV, Cristina Carlson, Katherine Dooley, Francesca Cowden. BA, Williams Coll., 1955; LLB, Harvard U., 1960. Bar: N.Y. 1961, U.S. Dist. Ct. (so. dist.) N.Y. 1961. Assoc. Kelley, Drye & Warren, N.Y.C., 1960-69, ptnr., 1970-79; ptnr. Morgan, Lewis & Bockius, N.Y.C., 1980—; bd. dirs. Western Pub. Group, Inc., N.Y.C., Baldwin Tech. Co., Inc., Stamford, Conn.; bd. dirs., sec. Goodman Equipment Corp., Chgo., Furgueson Capital Mgmt. Inc., N.Y.C.; chmn. bd. dirs., sec., Knight Textile Corp., Wall Industries, Inc.; gen. ptnr. Palmetto Restoration Assocs., Columbia, S.C., 1981—; trustee Patroni Scholastici, New Brunswick, N.J., 1978—, sec. 1985—. Contbr. articles to profl. jours. Mem. ABA, Assn. of the Bar of City of N.Y. (mem. Young Lawyers com. 1962-65, corp. law com. 1976-79, com. on securities regulation 1982-85, chmn. issue an distbn. of securities 1984-85), Phi Beta Kappa. Clubs: Racquet & Tennis, University (N.Y.C.); Bay Head (N.J.) Yacht. Office: Morgan Lewis & Bockius 101 Park Ave New York NY 10178

FORTH, KEVIN BERNARD, beverage distributing executive; b. Adams, Mass., Dec. 4, 1949; s. Michael Charles and Catherine Cecilia (McAndrews) F.; m. Alice Jane Farnum, Sept. 14, 1974; children: Melissa, Brian. AB, Holy Cross Coll., 1971; MBA, NYU, 1973. Div. rep. Anheuser-Busch, Inc., Boston, 1973-74, dist. sales mgr., L.A., 1974-76, asst. to dir. mktg. staff, St. Louis, 1976-77; v.p. Straub Distbg. Co., Ltd., Orange, Calif., 1977-81, pres., 1981—, chmn., chief exec. officer, 1986—, also bd. dirs.; bd. dirs. Anaheim visitors and Conv. Bur., 1989—, Olympia Brewing Co. Wholesaler Forum. Commr. Orange County Sheriff's Adv. Coun., 1988—; mem. adv. bd. Rancho Santiago Community Coll. Dist. 1978-83; bd. dirs. Children's Hosp. of Orange County, 1980-84, St. Joseph's Hosp. Found., Orange County Sports Hall of Fame, 1982—; exec. com., bd. dirs. Nat. Coun. on Alcoholism, 1980-84; mem. pres.' coun. Holy Cross Coll., 1987—; mem. Orange County Trauma Soc.; pres. Calif. State Fullerton Titan Athletic Found., 1983-85, bd. dir. 1983-85, v.p. Freedom Bowl 1984-85, pres., 1986, chmn., 1986-87, Anaheim Vis. & Conv. Bur., 1989—; mem. Rep. Silver Circle; bd. dirs. Orangewood Children's Home, 1988; mem. Calif. Rep. State Cen. Com. Benjamin Levy fellow, 1971-73. Mem. Nat. Beer Wholesalers Assn. (bd. dirs., asst. sec. 1989—), Calif. Beer and Wine Wholesalers Assn. (bd. dirs., exec. com., pres. 1985, asst. sec. 1980—), Industry Environ. Coun., Holy Cross Alumni Assn., NYU Alumni Assn., Nat. Assn. Stock Car Auto Racing, Small Bus. Inst., Sports Car Club Am. (Ariz. state champion 1982), Beta Gamma Sigma. Roman Catholic. Club: Lincoln, Holy Cross (Southern Calif.). Home: 4333 Mahagony Circle Yorba Linda CA 92686 Office: Straub Distbg Co Ltd 410 W Grove Ave Orange CA 92667

FORTINBERRY, GLEN W., advertising executive; b. Monticello, Miss., Nov. 22, 1927; s. Charles Lane and Elizabeth (Magee) F.; m. Mildred Bell, Sept. 29, 1951; children—Glen, Charles, Richard. Student, Cornell U., 1945-46; B.S. in Bus. Adminstrn., Northwestern U., 1949. Account exec. Ruthrauff & Ryan, Inc., 1952-57; asst. to pres. Maxon, Inc., Detroit, 1957-60; v.p. Maxon, Inc., 1963-65; also dir.; v.p. D'Arcy Advt. Co., Houston, 1960-63; with J. Walter Thompson Co., N.Y.C., 1965-80; vice chmn. J. Walter Thompson Co., 1977-80; pres., chief operating officer Ross Roy, Inc., Detroit, 1980-81; pres., chief exec. officer Ross Roy, Inc., 1981-83, chmn. bd., pres., 1983—. Bd. dirs. Detroit Symphony Orch., United Found., Detroit Inst.. Arts. Served with A.C. U.S. Navy, 1945-46. Recipient Chgo. Tribune award, 1949. Mem. Am. Assn. Advt. Agys. (bd. dirs., vice chmn.), Am. Advt. Fedn. (bd. dirs., chmn. 1985-86), U.S. Council of Internat. C. of C. (former exec. com.), Nat. Council for Children and TV, Council Better Bus. Burs. (bd. dirs.). Clubs: Detroit, Detroit Athletic, Economic (bd. dirs.); Wentworth Golf (London); Bloomfield Hills (Mich.) Country; Yale (N.Y.C.).

FORTNEY, DONALD EUGENE, marketing executive; b. Champaign, Ill., Jan. 24, 1947; s. James Pickering and Helen (Maier) F.; m. Nancy Joan Duffy, July 11, 1970; children: James Daniel, Donald Eric. BS, Regis Coll., 1969. Sales agt. Fidelity Union Life Ins. Co., Chgo., 1971—; gen. agt. Don Fortney and Assocs., Milw., 1972—; pres., dir. sales U.S. Mktg. Corp., Milw., 1979—, also bd. dirs.; sr. officer ins. div. Continental Bank, Milw., 1984-86; cons. 1st Interstate Bank Wis., Milw., 1987-89; bd. dirs. Ins. Systems Inc., Milw., Duvall Ins. Services Inc., Milw. Coach basketball St. Eugene's Sch., Fox Pt., Wis., 1985—. Served with U.S. Army, 1970. Mem. Nat. Assn. Life Underwriters, Wis. Bankers Assn. Republican. Roman Catholic. Office: US Mktg Corp PO Box 11699 Milwaukee WI 53211

FORTUNE, ROBERT RUSSELL, business executive; b. Collingswood, N.J., Nov. 22, 1916; s. Colin C. and Minnie M. (Brown) F.; m. Christine E. Dent, Nov. 10, 1956. B.S. in Econs., U. Pa., 1940. C.P.A., Pa. With Haskins & Sells (C.P.A.s), 1940-42, 46-48; with Pa. Power & Light Co., Allentown, 1948-84; v.p. fin. Pa. Power & Light Co., 1966-75, exec. v.p. fin., dir., 1975-84; chmn., chief exec. officer Associated Electric and Gas Ins. Services Ltd., 1984—, Dirs. and Officers Liability Ins., Ltd., 1985—; dir. Ind. Sq. Income Securities, Inc., Temp. Investment Fund, Inc., Chestnut St. Exchange Fund, Prudential-Bache Utility Fund, Inc., Municipal Fund for Temporary Investment, Trust for Short-Term Fed. Securities, Chestnut St. Cash Fund, Portfolios for Diversified Investment, Prudential-Bache Income Vertible Plus Fund ; mem. tech. adv. com. fin. FPC, 1974-75. Treas. Allentown Sch. Dist. Authority, 1963-85, Lehigh-Northampton Airport Authority, 1985—. Served in USN, 1942-46. Mem. Fin. Execs. Inst., Am., Pa. insts. C.P.A.s. Republican. Club: Lehigh Country. Home: 2920 Ritter Ln Allentown PA 18104 Office: Harborside Fin Ctr 700 Plaza Two Jersey City NJ 07311-3994

FOSBACK, NORMAN GEORGE, stock market econometrician, researcher; b. Astoria, Oreg., July 15, 1947; s. Oscar George and Lucy (Hoagland) F.; m. Myrna Liebowitz, June 13, 1982. B.S., Portland State U., 1969. Pres., research dir. Inst. Econometric Research, Ft. Lauderdale, Fla., 1971—. Author: Stock Market Logic, 1976; fin. newsletter editor: Market Logic, 1975—, New Issues, 1978—, The Insiders, 1980—, Income and Safety, 1981—, Mut. Fund Forecaster, 1985—. Mem. Am. Econ. Assn., Am. Statis. Assn., Econometric Soc., Ops. Research Soc. Am., Common Cause, ACLU. Home: 2600 NE 30th Ave Fort Lauderdale FL 33306 Office: Inst for Econometric Rsch 3471 N Federal Hwy Fort Lauderdale FL 33306

FOSCO, ANGELO, labor union executive. Pres. Laborer's Internat. Union N.Am. Office: Laborers Internat Union N Am 905 16th St NW Washington DC 20006

FOSHER, DONALD H., advertising company executive, inventor; b. St. Louis Mo., Jan. 6, 1935; s. Hobart L. and Alby U. (Andrews) F.; m. Charlotte B. Reich, Oct. 6, 1956 (div. Dec. 1976); 1 child, Carey B.; Janet L. Leiber, Dec. 31, 1977. BS, in Bus. Adminstrn., Washington U., St. Louis Mo., 1956. Copywriter Gen. Am., St. Louis, Mo., 1956-59; art dir. Artcraft, St. Louis, 1959-67; creative dir. Frank Block Assocs., St. Louis, 1967-69; account exec. Vangard/Wells, Rich, Green, St. Louis, 1969-74; ptnr., v.p. Vinyard & Lee, St. Louis, 1974-77; sr. v.p., creative dir. Hughes Advt., St. Louis, 1977—; pres., owner Don Fosher, Inc., St. Louis, 1974—; co-owner Stiches, and Sew On and Sew Forth, 1988, BrandBank div. Don Fosher Inc., 1986—. Author: Art for Secondary Education, 1962. Contbr. articles on cuisine to popular mags. Patentee sports, medicine, mech. design. Advisor, St. Louis County Spl. Sch. Dist., 1966-76; bd. dirs. Vocat. Schs., St. Louis, 1969-88; campaign designer St. Louis Better Bus. Bur., 1975, St. Louis Arts & Edn. Fund, 1984. Recipient Art Dir. of Yr. award Soc. Communications Arts, 1967; Venice Biennial, Internat. Congress Designers, 1966, Package Design award Am. Fishing Tackle Mfrs. Assn., 1981, numerous Creative awards Art Directors, 1959-1988. Mem. Internat. Congress Designers, Soc. Communications Arts (pres. 1966-67), Direct Mail Mktg. Assn., SAR. Mem. Christian Ch. Club: Glen Echo Country. Avocations: inventing, cooking, collecting primative art. Home: 7266 Creveling Dr University City MO 63130 Office: Hughes Advt Inc 130 S Bemiston Clayton MO 63105

FOSMIRE, FRED RANDALL, forest products company executive; b. Mission, Tex., June 23, 1926; s. Frank David and Marjorie Pauline (Davis) F.; m. Barbara Helen Schunk, Oct. 24, 1953; children: Helen, David, Lee, Emily. BA, U. Tex., 1948, MA, 1949, PhD, 1952. Cert. Am. Bd. Examiners in Profl. Psychology. Instr. to asst. prof. psychology U. Mont., Missoula, 1950-54; postdoctoral fellow U. Pa., Phila., 1954-56; clin. psychologist VA Hosp., Sheridan, Wyo., 1956-58; assoc. to full prof. U. Oreg., Eugene, 1958-81; v.p. Weyerhaeuser Co., Tacoma, 1981-83, sr. v.p., 1983—. Dir. Seattle Symphony, 1986-88, Forest History Soc., 1988—, St. Joseph Hosp., Tacoma, 1989—; mem. Can.-Am. Com., 1987—. With USN, 1944-46, PTO. Republican. Home: 505 S Marine Hills Way Federal Way WA 98003 Office: Weyerhaeuser Co Tacoma WA 98477

FOSSE, E(RWIN) RAY, insurance company executive; b. Marion, Ill., Dec. 3, 1918; s. Erwin Adam and Bessie (Gulledge) F.; m. Lloyd Elisabeth Alexander, Dec. 12, 1941; children: David Ray, Janet D. B.S., U. Ill., 1940, postgrad., 1948-51. Cert. tchr., Ill., Ind. Tchr. city schs. Boonville, Ind., 1940-41, Greenfield, Ill., 1945-52; mgr. farm and crop. ins. dept. CNA Ins., Chgo., 1952-67; mgr., exec. sec. Crop-Hail Ins. Actuarial Assn., Chgo., 1968-83; bd. dirs. Fed. Crop Ins. Corp., Washington, 1981-86, mgr., 1986-87, ret., 1987; mem. food and agr. com. U.S. C. of C., 1979-80. Author: (with others) Reinsurance, 1980. Served to lt. col. USAAF, 1941-45. Republican. Club: Union League of Chgo. Lodges: Masons; Lions; Kiwanis. Address: PO Box 99 Goreville IL 62939

FOSTER, ARTHUR LOUIS, bank executive; b. N.Y.C., July 29, 1947; s. Walter Horton and Ann Josephine (Chanese) F.; m. Joan Roberta McCormac, June 27, 1971; children: Arthur Louis, James Walter. BSBA, Bradley U., 1969; MBA, Monmouth Coll., 1980. Platform officer Sheridan Village State Bank, Peoria, Ill., 1967-68; acct. Stephen F. Radics, CPA & Co., Patterson, N.J., summers 1966, 67, 68; sr. v.p. Collective Fed. Savs. Bank, Egg Harbor, N.J., 1972—; guest lectr. Monmouth State Coll., West Long Branch, N.J., 1981-84, Stockton (N.J.) State Coll. Mayor, committeeman Egg Harbor Twp., 1983-85; mem. sch. bd., 1978-79, 80-82, planning bd., 1985; vol. fireman, treas. Bargaintown (N.J.) Vol. Fire Co., N.J., 1977—; pres. Rep. Club, 1978-86; mem. Egg Harbor Twp. Rep. County Com., 1986—, chmn., 1987—. Mem. Atlantic County Savs. League (pres. 1987-88). Roman Catholic. Home: RD 2 Box 209C Delaware Ave Bargaintown NJ 08232 Office: Collective Fed Savs Bank 158 Philadelphia Ave Egg Harbor NJ 08215

FOSTER, CAR M., educational facility executive, consultant; b. Harodsburg, Ky., Dec. 5, 1925; s. Mark D. and Mattie (Roberts) F.; m. Jewell Lovett, m. Sept. 14, 1946; children: Sharon, Carolyn, Mark. BS, U. Ky., 1949; MS, Ind. U., 1957; PhD, Purdue U., 1965. Lic. psychologist, Ky. Tchr. Ind. pub. schs., 1949-57, prin., 1957-64; instr. Purdue U., Lafayette, Ind., 1964-65; prof. U. Ky., Louisville, 1965-69; asst. supt. Louisville pub. schs., 1969-72; prin. Jefferson County Schs., Louisville, 1972-86; pres. The Learning Connection, Inc., Louisville, 1986—; mem. Ind. Gov.'s Sci. Com.; book reviewer, lectr. and cons. in field. Creator 4 ednl. films; contbr. articles to profl. jours. Mem. Student-Parent Advocacy Resource Ctr., Jefferson County; chmn. T.J. Unitarian Ch. Served with USN, 1944-46. Named Ind. Tchr. of Yr.; grantee in field. Mem. Think Tanks (co-chmn.). Home and Office: 4938 Brownsboro Rd Louisville KY 40222

FOSTER, CATHERINE RIERSON, metal components manufacturing company executive; b. Balt., Mar. 14, 1935; d. William Harman and Ella Fredericka (Magsamen) Rierson; m. Morgan Lawrence Foster, Nov. 17, 1957; children: Diana Kay, Susan Ann, Morgan Lawrence, Heather Lynne. Student Balt. City Coll., 1955, Johns Hopkins U., 1956-57, Glendale Coll., 1962-63. Sec., Martin Co., Balt., 1956-57, adminstrv. sec., 1957-58; v.p., corp. sec. Fostermation, Inc., Meadville, Pa., 1971—, also dir.; mem. adv. com. Vocat./Tech. Sch., Meadville, 1982-86. Pres. La Crescents, La Crescenta, Calif., 1962; active City Hosp. Aux., Meadville, 1969-86; active Republican Women's Workshop, Glendale, Calif., 1966-68, Com. to Elect Ronald Reagan, Glendale, 1967; bd. dirs. YWCA, Meadville, 1988—, also chmn. fin. com., 1988—. Mem. Nat. Assn. Female Execs., Daus. Am. Revolution. Lutheran. Lodge: Order Eastern Star. Avocations: genealogy, history, bridge. Home: 1121 Lakemont Dr Meadville PA 16335 Office: Fostermation Inc 200 Valleyview Dr Meadville PA 16335

FOSTER, DAVID MICHAEL, trust company executive; b. Mpls., June 23, 1960; s. Douglas W. and Lillie A.M. (Junge) F.; m. Jenny L. Mathison, Oct. 5, 1985. BS in Bus., U. Minn., 1982; MBA, Northwestern U., 1987. Corp. trust adminstr. First Trust Co., Inc., Mpls., 1982-86; with comml. banking dept. No. Trust Co., Chgo., 1987—; corp. fiduciaries First Trust Co., Inc., Mpls., 1984-86. Advisor Jr. Achievement, Edina, Minn., 1983-86; team leader Metro-Paint-a-thon, Mpls., 1985, St. Paul, 1986; bd. dirs. YMCA (vol. of yr. 1984-85), North Mpls., 1984-85. Recipient U.S. Congl. award, 1984-85. Office: Northern Trust Co 50 S LaSalle St Chicago IL 60675

FOSTER, EDSON L., retired mining and manufacturing company executive, consultant; b. Kearny, N.J., Jan. 22, 1927; s. Edson L. and Mary Raye (Jarome) F.; m. Jean C. Slater, June 16, 1951; children—Jill, Lori, Todd, Jody, Cary. B.B.A. cum laude, Pace Coll., 1953. Pub. accountant Pogson & Peloubet, N.Y.C., 1951-57; asst. to controller Stanadyne, Inc., Chgo., 1957-61; asst. comptroller Tex. Gulf Sulphur Co., N.Y.C., 1961-67; v.p., comptroller Anaconda Co., N.Y.C., 1967-77; v.p., comptr. Phelps Dodge Industries, Inc., N.Y.C., 1977-79; v.p., comptr. Phelps Dodge Corp., N.Y.C., 1979-87, sr. v.p., chief fin. officer, 1987-89, ret., 1989; cons. Brielle, N.J., 1989—; Mem. Bd. Fin. Wilton, Conn., 1967-72, chmn. bd., 1972. Mem. Fin. Execs. Inst., Nat. Assn. Accts., AICPA, N.J. Soc. CPAs, Am. Mining Congress.

FOSTER, JAMES HENRY, advertising/public relations executive; b. Kansas City, Mo., May 14, 1933; s. Wendell F. and Lillian M. (East) F.; B.A., Drake U., 1955, postgrad., 1957. Reporter, editor Des Moines (Iowa) Register, 1951-61; pub. relations and advt. exec. J. Walter Thompson Co., N.Y.C., 1961-73, 79—, v.p., 1970-73, sr. v.p., gen. mgr. Brouillard Communications div., 1979-81, exec. v.p., gen. mgr. Brouillard Communications div., 1981-84, pres., 1985—; v.p. pub. affairs Western Union Corp., Upper Saddle River, 1973-79; bd. dirs. J. Walter Thompson Co. Trustee, mem. exec. com. Rensselaerville Inst. (N.Y.), 1968—; bd. dirs. Edmund Niles Huyck Preserve, Rensselaerville, 1982—; adv. bd. Am. U. Sch. Communications, Washington, 1986—; chmn. advt. com. United Way Tri-State, N.Y.C., 1987—. Mem. Nat. Investor Relations Inst. Presbyterian. Clubs: Economic of N.Y., Union League. Office: Brouillard Communications 420 Lexington Ave New York NY 10017

FOSTER, JAMES ROBERT, financial executive; b. Hammond, Ind., Dec. 10, 1945; s. Robert William and Mary Myrtle (Gammell) F.; m. Mary Graham Ponder. AB, Cornell U., 1967; MBA, U. Chgo., 1971. Vice pres. Chase Manhattan Bank, N.Y.C., 1971-82; v.p., treas. Fuqua Industries Inc., Atlanta, 1982—. Mem. Fin. Execs. Inst. Home: 3403 W Paces Ferry Ct Atlanta GA 30327 Office: Fuqua Industries Inc 4900 Ga-Pacific Ctr Atlanta GA 30303

FOSTER, JOE B., oil company executive; b. Arp, Tex., July 25, 1934; s. William R. and Ruth D. (Knox) F.; m. Mary Alice Warren, Feb. 1, 1958; children: Warren, Ken, Jennifer. BS in Petroleum Engring., Tex. A&M U., 1957, BBA, 1957. Jr. petroleum engr. Tenneco Oil Co., Oklahoma City, 1957-59; petroleum engr. Tenneco Oil Co., Lafayette, La., 1959-62; dist. engr. Tenneco Oil Co., 1962-66; adminstrv. asst. to exec. com. Tenneco Oil Co., Houston, 1966-68, chief econ. planning and analysis, 1968-70, mgr. exploration, 1970-72, v.p., 1972-74, sr. v.p., 1974-76, exec. v.p., 1976-78, pres. Tenneco Oil Exploration and Prodn., 1978-81; exec. v.p. Tenneco, Inc., Houston, 1981-89; chmn. Newfield Exploration Co., Houston, 1989—. Bd. dirs. Houston Area Research Ctr., Met. YMCA, Houston Mus. Natural Sci. Served to 2d lt. U.S. Army, 1958. Mem. Soc. Petroleum Engrs. of AIME, Am. Petroleum Inst. (bd. dirs.), Houston Club, Petroleum Club, Heritage Club, Met. Racquet Club. Methodist. Office: Newfield Exploration Co 1100 Milam Bldg Ste 2711 Houston TX 77002

FOSTER, JOHN MCNEELY, computer company executive; b. Denver, Mar. 7, 1949; s. Wallin G. and Marilyn Hope (Coxhead) F.; m. Bonnie McCune, Aug. 23, 1970 (div. 1978); m. Sharon Kay Sheffield, May 8, 1982; children: Katherine McNeely, Matthew Thomas. BA in Econs., Colo. Coll., 1971. CPA, Tex. Treas. Meis and Co., Inc., Colorado Springs, Colo., 1971-73; sr. audit mgr. Price Waterhouse Co., Houston, 1973-81; v.p. fin. Krusen Energy Co., Houston, 1981-83; v.p., treas. Compaq Computer Corp., Houston, 1983—; adv. dir. Protection Mut. Ins. Co. Inc., Chgo., 1985—; bd. dirs. Dominion Energy and Minerals Co., Houston, 1985—. Mem. Am. Inst. CPA's, Fin. Execs. Inst., Phi Beta Kappa. Republican. Episcopalian. Office: Compaq Computer Corp 20555 FM 149 Houston TX 77070

FOSTER, KENNETH BREDIN, JR., marketing executive; b. Pitts., Nov. 15, 1925; s. Kenneth Bredin Sr. and Leona Lorraine (Dale) F.; m. Jean Ann Bendig, Nov. 23, 1946 (dec. Apr. 1978); children: Thomas, Jill Ann, Amy Lynn, Beth Ann; m. Margo Dieterich, Mar. 29, 1980; stepchildren: George, Debbie. BEE, U. Wis., 1946. Trainee sales Westinghouse Elec. Corp., Pitts., 1946-47; engr. inside sales Westinghouse Elec. Corp., Cin., 1947-48; engr. sales Westinghouse Elec. Corp., Pitts., 1949-54; engr. sales Elliott Co., Pitts., 1954-58, asst. mgr. dist., 1958-59; v.p., engr. sales Foster-McClinton Inc., Pitts., 1959-71, pres., engr. sales, 1971—. Served to lt. U.S. Navy, 1943-46. Mem. Assn. Iron and Steel Engrs., Engring. Soc. Western Pa., Mfgrs. Agts. Nat. Assn., Nat. Elec. Mgrs. Rep. Assn. (pres. western Pa. chpt. 1984-86, bd. dirs.). Republican. Presbyterian. Clubs: Valley Brook Country (McMurray). Office: Foster-McClinton Inc 110 Fort Couch Rd Pittsburgh PA 15241

FOSTER, LESTER ANDERSON, JR., steel company executive; b. Granite Quarry, N.C., Apr. 4, 1929; s. Lester Anderson and Annie Lee (Swink) F.; student Elon Coll., 1947-50; B.S., N.C. State U., 1952; m. Patricia White, July 9, 1955; children—Leslie Ann, Caroline Suzann, Lester Anderson, Samuel Timothy. With Bethlehem Steel Corp., Sparrows Point, Md., 1952—, engr., 1956-57, mech. foreman, 1957-59, asst. gen. foreman, 1959-61, asst. master mechanic, 1961-67, master mechanic, 1967—. Pres. PTA, Sparrows Point, 1963-65; mem. exec. bd. nominating com. Balt. County Sch. Bd., 1964-65; dist. field service chmn. Boy Scouts Am., Balt., 1972-78, bicentennial show program chmn., 1976, dist. commr., 1979-83, dist. chmn., 1983—; pres. 7th Dist. Republican Club, 1969-72; mem. Md. Rep. State Central Com., 1980. Served with U.S. Army, 1952-54. Recipient Silver Beaver award Boy Scouts Am., 1975, award of Merit, 1984. Mem. Am. Inst. Iron and Steel Engrs., Soc. Mfg. Engrs., Am. Mgmt. Assn., Soc. Advancement Mgmt., Nat. Football Found. and Hall of Fame, SAR (Silver Good Citizenship medal). Republican. Lutheran. Clubs: Sparrows Point Country, Sparrows Point Engrs. Clubs: Masons, Shriners, K.T. (Grand Comdr.). Home: 3006 Dunmore Rd Dundalk MD 21222 Office: Bethlehem Steel Corp Steelmaking Mech Sparrows Point MD 21219

FOSTER, MARILYN FRIEDA, construction company executive; b. Chattanooga, Mar. 22, 1948; d. Roy E. and Rosemary (Ward) F.; m. James R. Foster, Mar. 22, 1969; 1 child, Robert L. Grad., Clara Carpenter Sch. Practical Nursing, Chattanooga, 1967; BS, U. Tenn., 1982, MS, 1987. Lic. practica nurse, Tenn. Staff nurse Hutcheson Med. Ctr., Ft. Oglethorpe, Ga., 1967-69, Women's Hosp., Chattanooga, 1970-72, Diagnostic Hosp., Chattanooga, 1975-77, N.W. Ga. Mental Health Clinic, Ft. Oglethorpe, 1977-78; sec.-treas. Foster Constrn., Inc., Chattanooga, 1979—. Mem. Nat. Criminal Justice Assn., Chattanooga C. of C. Baptist. Office: Foster Constrn Inc 2009 Calhoun Ave Chattanooga TN 37373

FOSTER, MARK EDWARD, lawyer, consultant, international lobbyist; b. Detroit, May 12, 1948; s. Herbert Edward and Joyce Mary (Campbell) F.; m. Miyoko Katabami, Apr. 20, 1974; children—Lorissa Chieko. B.A., Alma Coll., 1970; M.A., U. Calif.-Berkeley, 1973, Japanese lang. cert., 1982, J.D., 1981. Bar: Calif. 1981. Grantee, Rockefeller Found., Geneva and Tokyo, 1973-74; law clk. U.S. Dist. Ct., San Francisco, 1980-81; atty. Hetland & Hansen, Berkeley, Calif., 1981-82; cons. Foster Assocs. Internat., 1982—; atty. Braun Moriya Hoashi, Tokyo, 1982-84; ptnr. Lindsay, Hart, Neil & Weigler, Portland, 1985-88; mng. ptnr. Law Offices Mark E. Foster, Portland, 1988—. Spl. Counsel U.S. Embassy, Tokyo, 1983-85; Japan Counsel U.S. Electronic Industries Assn., 1985-86; lectr., cons. on internat. tech. standards, tech. transfer, product compliance, engring. to Internat. Standards Orgn., U.S. Dept. Commerce; mem. tech. standards com. Japanese Ministry of Posts and Telecommunications, 1984-86, tech. standards com. Ministry of Internat. Trade and Industry, 1984-86. Author articles, books in internat. law and tech. Mem. ABA, Internat. Bar Assn., State Bar Calif., Am. C. of C. in Japan, World Trade (Tokyo, Portland, Oreg.), World Affairs Council. Presbyterian. Office: ABS Bldg 2-4-16, 3-F, Kudan Minami Tokyo 102, Japan also: One World Trade Ctr 121 SW Salmon Portland OR 97204

FOSTER, MICHAEL EDWARD, communications executive; b. Rochester, N.Y., Feb. 10, 1949; s. Edward Wells and Virginia (Bowes) F.; m. Jan Chapman, Aug. 17, 1974; 1 child, Christy. BBA, St. Edward's U., Austin, Tex., 1971; MBA, De Paul U., 1978. Sales rep. Corning (N.Y.) Glass Works, 1974-75; mgr. sales Sargent Welch Sci., Skokie, Ill., 1975-78; sr. v.p. sales and mktg. AGS&R Communications, Chgo., 1978—. V.p. Elmhurst (Ill.) Jaycees, 1981-83. Mem. Assn. Multi-Images, Internat. Assn. Bus. Communicators, Meeting Planner Internat., Am. Soc. Tng. and Devel., Maywood (Ill.) Sportsmans Club, Elks. Office: AGS&R Communications 314 W Superior St Chicago IL 60610

FOSTER, R. MICHAEL, financial executive; b. Toronto, Ont., Can., Jan. 13, 1946; s. Walter Richard and Sybil H. (Robinson), F.; m. Elizabeth Anne Aykroyd, Dec. 2, 1967; children: James, Barbara, Kenneth. BA, U. Toronto, 19(7; grad. chartered acct., York U., 1974. Auditor Coopers and Lybrand, Toronto, 1970-76; controller Russelsteel Ltd., Toronto, 1976-79; gen. mgr. York Steel Ltd., Toronto, 1979-82; corp. controller PPG Industries Can., Toronto, 1982-84; v.p. fin. Dominion Stores Ltd., Toronto, 1984-86; exec. v.p., chief fin. officer Core-Mark Internat. Inc., Vancouver, B.C., Can., 1986—. Bd. dirs. Providence Villa and Hosp. Toronto, 1984-86. Served to capt. Can. Armed Forces, 1967-70. Mem. Can. Inst. Chartered Accts., Ont. Inst. Chartered Accts. Roman Catholic. Office: Core-Mark Distbrs Inc 1800 N Vine St Hollywood CA 90028 *

FOSTER, THOMAS ELMORE, bank executive; b. Hope, Ark., Nov. 6, 1941; s. Autrey Ernest and Betty Jane Foster; m. Charlotte Ann Nave, Mar. 25, 1972; children: Carrie Elizabeth, Christopher Thomas. BBA, So. Meth. U., 1963, MBA, 1967. Asst. cashier First RepublicBank of Dallas, 1968-70, asst. v.p., 1970-71, v.p., 1971-75, sr. v.p., 1975-81, exec. v.p., 1981—. Office: 1st RepublicBank Corp PO Box 660020 Dallas TX 75266

FOSTER, WALTER HERBERT, JR., real estate company executive; b. Belmont, Mass., Nov. 2, 1919; s. Walter Herbert and Gertrude (Sullivan) F.; m. Hazel Campbell, Aug. 7, 1942 (div. July 1981); children: Katherine D., Walter H. III. Stephen C., Banton T.; m . Nedra Ann Thompson, July 3, 1981; 1 child, Timothy John. Student, Harvard U., 1937-38; BS, U. Maine, 1947; grad. in real estate, Tri-State Inst., 1968-70. Cert. appraiser and real estate broker. Owner, mgr. Foster Bros., Lyndeborough, N.H., 1947-56; ter. sales mgr. Beacon Milling Co., Oakland, Maine, 1956-64; v.p. Sherwood & Foster, Inc., Old Town, Maine, 1964-67; sales rep. Bangor (Maine) Real Estate, 1967-73; chief appraiser James W. Sewall Co., Old Town, 1970-73; mgr. J.F. Singleton Co., Bangor, 1973-80; pres. Coldwell Banker Am. Heritage, Bangor, 1980—; dean Tri-State Inst., 1981; mem. Maine Real Estate Commn., 1987. Mem. Rep. Nat. Com., Washington, 1980, Assessment Bd. Appeals, Old Town, Maine. Served to capt. USAF, 1941-46. Mem. Nat. Assn. Realtors (bd. dirs. 1980-81), Maine Assn. Realtors (bd. dirs. 1976-80, pres. 1980; Realtor of Yr. 1976 and 1984), Maine Real Estate Commn., Bangor Bd. Realtors (bd. dirs. 1973-74, pres. 1976; Realtor of Yr. 1984), Nat. Assn. Rev. Appraisers, Am. Assn. Cert. Appraisers, Res. Officers Assn., Soc. Real Estate Appraisers (assoc.). Episcopalian. Clubs: Tarratine (Bangor); Harvard (Maine). Lodge: Rotary. Home: Mistover Dole Hill Rd RFD 2 Box 692 East Holden ME 04429 Office: Coldwell Banker Am Heritage 510 Broadway Bangor ME 04401

FOUDREE, CHARLES M., accountant, corporate executive; b. Macon, Mo., June 29, 1944; s. L. Winifred and Lois H. (Malone) F.; m. Colleen Patton, Aug. 9, 1964; children: Mark, Melanie. BS in Acctg., Northeast Mo. State U., 1966. CPA, Kans., Mo. Acct. Peat Marwick Mitchell & Co., Kansas City, Mo., 1966-72; from controller to chief fin. officer and exec. v.p. Harmon Industries, Inc., Blue Springs, Mo., 1972—, also sec., treas. amd bd. dirs.; bd. dirs. Mark Twain Independence (Mo.) Bank, Vale-Harmon Enterprises, Ltd., Dorval, Quebec, Can., Electro Pneumatic Corp., Inc., Riverside, Calif., Modern Industries, Inc., Louisville, Harmon Electronics, Inc., Grain Valley, Mo., Phoenix Data Inc., Phoenix, Consol. Asset Mgmt. Corp. Inc., Blue Springs, Cedrite Technologies Inc., Kansas City, Kans. Dir., chmn. adminstrv. bd. Christ United Meth. Ch., Independence. Mem. AICPA, Nat. Assn. Accts., Mo. Soc. CPAs, Fin. Execs. Inst. (pres., bd. dirs. Kansas City chpt., 1989-90), Nat. Assn. Corp. Secs., Independence C. of C., Jaycees (pres. 1973, internat. senator), Blue Key, Sigma Tau Gamma. Republican. Home: 4124 Pembroke Ln Lee's Summit MO 64064 Office: Harmon Industries Inc PO Box 1570 1900 Corporate Ctr Blue Springs MO 64015

FOUGHT, SHERYL KRISTINE, environmental scientist, engineer; b. Washington, Mo., Oct. 17, 1949; d. James Paul and Alice Marie (Kasper) McSpadden; m. Randy Bruce Stucki, Nov. 23, 1968 (div. 1973); children: Randy Bruce, Sherylynne Sue; m. Larry Donald Fought, July 31, 1980 (div. 1982); 1 child, Erin Marie. BS, N.Mex. State U., 1976, postgrad., 1977-79. Tchr. N.Mex. State U., Las Cruces, 1977-78; hydrologist U.S. Dept. Interior, Las Cruces, 1978-81; environ. scientist U.S. EPA, Dallas, 1981-84; hazardous waste inspector Ariz. Dept. Health Svc., Phoenix, 1984-85; environ. engr., technician Yuma Proving Ground U.S. Army, 1985-87, chief phys. scientist environment div. Yuma Proving Gound, 1987-88, chief hazardous waste mgmt br. Aberdeen Proving Ground, 1988—. Co-author: The Ghost Town Marcia, 1975, tng. manuals. With USMC, 1968-69. Recipient 2 Quality awards U.S. Army, 1986, Army Materiel Command, 1986. Mem. NAFE, Nat. Environ. Tng. Assn., Federally Employed Women, Fed. Women Engrs. and Scientists, The Wildlife Soc., Air Pollution Control Assn., Dept. Def. Excellent Installations. Democrat. Home: PO Box 228 Gunpowder Br Aberdeen MD 21010-0228 Office: US Army Aberdeen Proving Ground STEAP-SA-DSHE-E Aberdeen MD 21001

FOUNDS, HENRY W., diagnostics company executive, microbiologist; b. Mar. 6, 1942; s. Henry W. and Elaine V. (Smargis) F.; m. Ferne A. Brunner, Nov. 7, 1971; children: Steven, Jennifer, Jeffrey, Sarah. BS in Biology, Villanova U., 1964; MS in Biology, U. Notre Dame, 1968; PhD in Microbiology, Rutgers U., 1981. Tchr. chemistry Bayley Ellard High Sch., Madison,

N.J, 1964-68; assoc. prof. microbiology Morris County Coll., Randolph Twp., N.J, 1968-83; mgr. cell growth Ventrex Labs., Inc., Portland, Maine, 1983-84, dir. rsch. and devel., 1984-86, v.p. rsch. and devel., 1986-87, 1987—; cons. microbiologist Personal Diagnostics, Whippany, N.J., 1981-83. Mem. Am. Soc. Microbiology, Am. Assn. Clin. Chemistry. Office: Ventrex Labs Inc 217 Read St PO Box 9731 Portland ME 04104-5031

FOUNTAIN, ROBERT ALLEN, transportation executive; b. Toledo, Nov. 19, 1947; s. Ellis Allen Fountain and Florence Delores (Hay) Stump; m. Mary Ann Buckmaster, Mar. 7, 1975; children: Donna, Meredith. AS, State Tech. Inst., 1987; BS summa cum laude, Tusculum Coll., 1989. Quality controller Burroughs Corp. (UNISYS), Holland, Ohio, 1969-73, field service rep., 1973-78, internat. traffic analyst and specialist, 1978-81; gen. traffic mgr. Buckman Labs., Inc., Memphis, 1981-85, mgr. transp. and credit adminstrn., 1985—. Author computer programs. With USN, 1967-69. Recipient Cert. honor Internat. Trade Mart, 1983; named Hon. Harbor Master of Port of New Orleans Bd. Commrs. of Port of New Orleans, 1983. Mem. State Tech. Inst. Alumni Assn. (v.p. 1988-89), Delta Nu Alpha, Phi Theta Kappa (v.p. 1986-87). Republican. Home: 4144 Catalpa Hill Bartlett TN 38135 Office: Buckman Labs Inc 1256 N McLean Blvd Memphis TN 38108

FOUST, STEPHEN LEWIS, financial analyst; b. Bellefonte, Pa., Oct. 26, 1950; s. Warren Leroy and Mildred Melissa (Swatsworth) F.; m. Carolyn Faye Barr, June 13, 1969; children: Michelle Charlene, Heather Nichole. BS, Pa. State U., 1972. Cert. fin. planner. Agt. Coll. Life Ins. Co., Indpls., 1981-82; fin. planner Wienken and Assocs., State College, Pa., 1982-87; fin. planner, ednl. trainer Profl. Planning Cons., State College, 1987—; pres. Charitable Planning, Inc., Boalsburg, Pa., 1987—. Mem. Status of Liberty Ellis Island Found., N.Y.C., 1984-85, Citizens Choice, Washington, 1982-85; mem. adminstrv. bd. Fairbrook United Meth. Ch., Pennsylvania Furnace, Pa., 1984—. Served with U.S. Army, 1972-75. Mem. Nat. Assn. Life Underwriters (Nat. Quality award 1985—), Inst. Cert. Fin. Planners, Internat. Bd. Standards and Practices for Cert. Fin. Planners, Pa. Assn. Life Underwriters, Centre County Assn. Life Underwriters, Cen. Pa. Soc. Inst. Cert. Fin. Planners (sec. bd. dirs. 1988), Pa. State U. Alumni Assn. Republican. Methodist. Lodge: Moose, Elks. Office: Profl Planning Cons 315 S Atherton St PO Box 590 State College PA 16801

FOUTS, JAMES FREMONT, mining company executive; b. Port Arthur, Tex., June 3, 1918; s. Horace Arthur and Willie E. (Edwards) F.; m. Elizabeth Hanna Browne, June 19, 1948; children: Elizabeth, Donovan, Alan, James. B Chem Engring., Tex. A&M U., 1940. Div. supt. Baroid div. N.L. Industries, U.S. Rocky Mountain area and Can., 1948-60; pres. Riley-Utah Co., Salt Lake City, 1960-67, Fremont Corp., Monroe, La., 1967—, Auric Metals Corp., Salt Lake City, 1972—; bd. dirs. La Fonda Hotel, Santa Fe, N.Mex., High Plains Natural Gas Co., Canadian, Tex. Hon. asst. sec. of State of La. Served to lt. col. arty U.S. Army, 1942-46. Mem. Wyo. Geol. Assn. (v.p. 1958), Rocky Mountain Oil & Gas Assn. (bd. dirs. 1959), Res. Officers Assn. Wyo. (pres. 1948), Am. Assn. Petroleum Geologists, Internat. Geol. Assn., Mont. Geol. Assn., Ind. Petroleum Producers Assn. Republican. Episcopalian. Club: Univ. Lodge: Elks. Home: 4002 Bon Aire Dr Monroe LA 71203 Office: Fremont Corp PO Box 7070 Monroe LA 71211 also: Auric Metals Corp 2220 Wilson Ave Salt Lake City UT 84108

FOUTZ, SHIRLEY LAUDIG, newpaper executive; b. Indpls., Mar. 8, 1934; d. Wayne Raymond Laudig and Maxine (Greenlee) Hopper; m. William Carlyle Foutz, Aug. 17, 1956; children: William C., Jr., Laura Elizabeth, Craig Weston. BA magna cum laude, Lynchburg (Va.) Coll., 1956; MEd, Va. Commonwealth U., 1974, PhD, 1987. Tchr. Lynchburg Pub. Schs., 1956-57, Chesterfield County Schs., Chesterfield, Va., 1957-58; newspaper in edn. coordinator Richmond (Va.) Newspapers, 1974-80, dir. edn. services, 1980—; cons. U. Ky., Lexington, 1977-84; adj. faculty Longwood Coll., Farmville, Va., 1979-88; presenter Lifelong Learning Research Conf. U. Md., 1988, Adult Edn. Research Conf.U. Calgary, 1988. Co-author: Aliteracu: People Who Can Read But Won't, 1984. Soloist St. Paul's Episcopal Ch.; music dir. Bon Air (Va.) Christian Ch., 1966-80,; adult sponsor youth fellowship, 1972-80; bd. dirs. Literacy Volunteers in Va. Inst., 1985—, Metro-Richmond Literacy Council, 1988—. Mem. Am. Soc. Trainers and Developers, Am. Soc. for Curriculum Devel., Am. Newspapers Pubs. Assn. (nat. inst. edn. com.), So. Newspaper Pubs. Assn. (literacy com.), Nat. Inst. Edn. (session leader), Va. Councils for Social Studies, Va. State Reading Assn., Phi Delta Kappa. Home: Rural Rt #1 Box 227 Columbia VA 23038 Office: Richmond Newspapers Inc PO Box C 32333 Richmond VA 23293

FOWBLE, WILLIAM FRANKLIN, manufacturing company executive; b. Huntington, W.Va., May 29, 1938; s. Okey Clyde and Madge Evola F.; m. Ann Marie Lindal (div. 1986); 1 child, William; m. Arlene Marie Grudak, June 21, 1986; children: Karen, Diane, Linda Jones. BS in Physics, Purdue U., 1960, MS in Indsl. Mgmt., 1961; MS in Mgmt., MIT, 1981. Various tech. assignments Eastman Kodak Co., Rochester, N.Y., 1961-74; asst. supt. film emulsion coating div. Eastman Kodak Co., Rochester, 1975; supt. sensitizing Eastman Kodak Co., Windsor, Colo., 1978; dir. bus. products and photog. planning Eastman Kodak Co., Rochester, 1982, dir. copy products and mfg. equipment, 1983, dir. magnetic products and photog. div., 1984, v.p., dir. planning and photog. div., 1984; group v.p., gen. mgr. Eastman Kodak Diversified Techs., Rochester, 1985; sr. v.p., gen. mgr. mfg. Eastman Kodak Co., Rochester, 1986—, sr. v.p., gen. mgr. mfg., distribution and field support, 1988—; Bd. dirs. Nat. Assn. Mfrs., Washington; bd. dirs. Eastman Savs. and Loan, Rochester. Office: Eastman Kodak Co 343 State St Rochester NY 14650

FOWLER, AUSTINE BROWN, educational association administrator, professor; b. Washington, Apr. 6, 1936; d. Amos Cummings Brown and Marian (Woody) Stephens; m. Milton Otis Fowler Sr., June 18, 1959; 1 child, Milton Otis Jr. BS, D.C. Tchrs. Coll., 1960; Ma in Edn., George Washington U., 1969, EdS, 1972. Sales clk. Crosby's Shoe Store, Washington, 1957-60; tchr. Washington D.C. Pub. Schs., 1960-70, dir. head start, 1970-77, dir. health services, 1978-79, edn. supr., 1985—; edn. specialist U.S. Dept. HHS, Washington, 1979-80; social sci. research analyst U.S. Dept. HHS, 1980-82; mgmt. analyst Nat. Archives, Capitol Heights, Md., 1983-85; trainer nat. head start Program, Washington, Md. and Pa., 1970-77; guest lectr. MAT program Trinity Coll., Washington, 1975-80; mem. 19th St. Bapt. Lab. Sch. Bd., Washington, 1987—, Dept. Labor Day Care Bd., Washington, 1985-87; adj. prof. U. D.C., 1976—. Mem. exec. com. Nat. Capitol Area chpt. March of Dimes-Birth Defects Found., also vice chair exec. com., 1985-87, Birth Defects Found., 1987—, chmn. exec. com. 1987—; bd. dirs. D.C. Assn. Retarded Citizens, 1982-84; trustee St. Paul Bapt. Ch., D.C., 1984—; bus. mgr. LeDroit Park Reunion Com., Washington, 1983-85, chairperson 1985—. Fellow NSF, Rockefeller Found. Mem. Nat. Assn. for Edn. of Young Children, Assn. for Curriculum Devel., Washington Assn. for Edn. of Young Children (mem.-at-large), Delta Sigma Theta, Phi Delta Kappa, Phi Lambda Theta, Phi Delta Kappa. Democrat. Baptist. Club: Circle #1 Missionary Soc. Home: 4530 Fort Totten Dr NE #412 Washington DC 20011

FOWLER, BRADLEY ALLISON, investment company executive; b. Austin, Tex., Jan. 11, 1935; s. Marion and Marion (Penn) F.; B.A., U. Tex., Austin, 1957, LL.B., 1958; m. Sally Pope, May 28, 1960; children—Elizabeth, Brad, Edward, Eleanor. Admitted to Tex. bar, 1958; pvt. practice law, Austin, 1958-61; with Merrill Lynch, Austin, 1962-76; v.p. Rotan Mosle, Austin, 1976-79; pres. Fin. Services Austin, Inc. and subs. FSA Capital Mgmt., Inc., FSA Properties, FSA Valuations Inc., 1979—; dir. Nova/Graphics Internat. Corp., Tex. Gas Transport Co., Inc., Biomed. Research Group, Inc. Mem. State Bar Tex., Phi Gamma Delta. Office: Fin Svcs-Austin Inc 301 W 6th St Austin TX 78701

FOWLER, GEORGE SELTON, JR., architect; b. Chgo., Jan. 20, 1920; s. George Selton and Mabel Helena (Overton) F.; m. Yvonne Fern Grammer, Nov. 25, 1945; 1 child, Kim Ellyn. Cert. Hamilton Coll., 1944; B.S., Ill. Inst. Tech., 1949, postgrad. 1968; cert. Elec. Assn. Ill., 1976. Registered architect, Ill., Ohio. Co-founder, pres. The Modern Arts Press, Chgo., 1946; instr. archtl. and related engring. subjects Am. Sch. and Tech. Soc., Chgo., 1948-65; urban planner Chgo. Land Clearance Comm., 1949-50; liaison architect Chgo. Housing Authority, 1950-68, chief design-tech. div., 1968-80, dir. dept. engring., 1980-84; prin. George S. Fowler, Architect, Chgo., 1984—; treas., bd. dirs. Chgo. Housing Authority Credit Union, 1963-65; architect, planner and cons. Interconco., 1965-66; cons. in field. Author: (text book study guide) Reinforced Concrete Design, 1959. Patentee. Mem. Mayor's Adv. Commn. to Revise the Bldg. Code, 1986—; founder, pres. EFCO, Chgo., 1988—. Served with C.E., U.S. Army, 1942-46. Recipient Citation for Residential Devel., Mayor Richard J. Daley, Chgo., 1960, Black Achievers of Industry Recognition award YMCA, Chgo., 1977; Kappa Alpha Psi grantee, 1936. Mem. Architects in Industry, Nat. Assn. Housing and Redevelopment Officials, Inventors Council of Chgo. Avocations: classic cars; classical music; jazz. Home and Office: 8209 S Rhodes Ave Chicago IL 60619

FOWLER, JAMES EDWARD, oil company executive, lawyer; b. Boise, Idaho, Dec. 8, 1931; s. Jim and Beulah (Cazer) F.; m. Carolyn Elizabeth Jacobus, Aug. 16, 1958; children: Barbara Ann, Thomas Edward. AB summa cum laude, Princeton U., 1953; LLB, Yale U., 1959. Bar: N.Y. 1960. Assoc. Debevoise, Plimpton, Lyons & Gates, N.Y.C., 1959-68; corp. counsel Mobil Oil Corp., N.Y.C., 1968-69; gen. counsel Mobil East Inc., N.Y.C., 1969-72; asst. gen. counsel internat. div. Mobil Oil Corp., N.Y.C., 1972-74, gen. counsel internat. div., 1974-77, assoc. gen. counsel corp., 1977-83, gen. counsel mktg. and refinery div., 1983-86, gen. counsel, 1986—. Mem. bd. editors Yale Law Jour., 1958-59. Mem. Chappaqua (N.Y.) Sch. Dist. Bd. Edn., 1970-73, pres., 1972-73; trustee Am. Farm Sch., Thessalonike, Greece, 1980—; chmn. Chappaqua Orchestral Assn., 1981-82. Served with AUS, 1953-56. Mem. ABA, N.Y. State Bar Assn., Internat. Bar Assn., Assn. of Bar of City of N.Y., Am. Soc. Internat. Law, Yale Law Sch. Assn. N.Y.C. (pres. 1972-73), Phi Delta Phi. Office: Mobil Corp 150 E 42nd St New York NY 10017-5666 *

FOWLER, JOHN DOUGLAS, mining company executive; b. Toronto, Ont., Can., Apr. 5, 1931; s. Joseph and Elizabeth (Douglas) F.; m. Bette Gray, Sept. 8, 1956; children: Scott, Gray, Heather Ann. BS in Metallurgical Engring., Queen's U., Kingston, Ont., 1955. Cert. engr. Devel. engr. Cominco Ltd., Montreal and Toronto, Can., 1955-57; sales engr. Pennsalt Chems. Can. Ltd., Oakville, Ont., Can., 1957, Sask. Cement Co. Ltd., Saskatoon, 1958-60; sales and devel. engr. Inland Cement Industries Ltd., Edmonton, Alta., 1960; mgr. mktg. services Inland Cement Industries Ltd., Edmonton, 1961-62; with Lake Ont. Cement Ltd., Toronto, 1962-72, pres., chief exec. officer, 1972-85, vice chmn., 1985; pres., chief oper. officer Denison Mines Ltd., Toronto, 1985—, also bd. dirs.; bd. dirs. Denison Mines, Ltd., Lawson Mardon Group, Zemex Corp., Reiss Lime Co.; bd. dirs. Quintette Coal, Ltd., vice-chmn., chief exec. officer, 1988—. Home: 22 Edenbridge Dr, Islington, ON Canada M9A 3E9 Office: Denison Mines Ltd, Royal Bank Pla #3900 Box 40, Toronto, ON Canada M5J 2K2

FOWLER, ROBERT ARCHIBALD, infosystems company executive; b. Lewistown, Pa., May 29, 1931; s. Harry K. Fowler and Margaret (Elder) Mann; m. Gail Brewer; children: R. Wendell, Ann, Allen. BS in Econs., Franklin and Marshall Coll., 1953; MBA, Cornell U., 1958. Auditor Gen. Motors Corp., Rochester, N.Y., 1953-54; exec. trainee Mfr.'s Hanover Bank, N.Y.C., 1958-60; credit rep. Cen. Trust Corp., Rochester, 1960-61; mktg. exec. Voplex Corp., Rochester, 1961-70; chmn. 5 W Info. Services, Rochester, 1970—; treas. Clover Investment Group, Rochester, 1960—. Author: Careerism, 1970, Buyerism, 1971, Creative Winemaking, 1973; contbr. articles to profl. jours. Served with U.S. Army, 1954-56. Mem. Am. Legion. Republican. Presbyterian. Club: Penfield Golf. Office: 5W Info Svcs Inc 1475 Winton Rd N Rochester NY 14609

FOWLER, ROBERT GLEN, exploration company executive; b. Mart, Tex., Apr. 29, 1930; s. J.H. and Elizabeth F.; m. Bonita Faye Conner, Mar. 22, 1955; children: Becky Ann, Robert Glen. B.S. in Petroleum Engring, Okla. U., 1958; grad., Advanced Mgmt. Program, Harvard U., 1975. With Enserch Exploration, Inc. (and predecessor), 1958—; v.p., then exec. v.p. Enserch Exploration, Inc. (and predecessor), Dallas, 1972-78; pres., chief operating officer Enserch Exploration, Inc. (and predecessor), 1978—, also dir. Mem. Am. Petroleum Inst., Ind. Petroleum Assn. Am., Am. Petroleum Landmen's Assn., Permian Basin Natural Gas Men's Assn., Soc. Petroleum Engrs., Dallas Petroleum Landmen's Assn., Houston Natural Gas Men's Assn., Harvard Advanced Mgmt. Assn. Baptist. Club: Dallas Petroleum. Office: Enserch Exploration Ptnrs Ltd 1817 Wood St Dallas TX 75201

FOWLER, WALTON BERRY, real estate developer; b. Tulsa, Dec. 4, 1946; s. Walton Rector Fowler and Martha Jean (Berry) Oliver; m. Deborah Martz, Oct. 1, 1972 (div. Feb. 1985); 1 child, Cullen Brian; m. Anne Sadler, Sept. 23, 1985; 1 child, Nicole Anne. BA, Chapman Coll., 1972; teaching cert., Calif. State U., Fullerton, 1973. Mgr. Al Mayton Prodns., Universal City, Calif., 1968-72; dept. chmn., tchr. Anaheim (Calif.) High Sch. Dist., 1973-78; founder, chmn. Sylvan Learning Corp., Montgomery, Ala., 1979-88; pres. Krypton Corp., Mercer Island, Wash., 1986—; v.p., treas. Vincent, Hanna, Fowler Investments, Bellevue, Wash., 1987—; dept. chmn., tchr. Anaheim (Calif.) High Sch. Dist., 1968-72; bd. dirs. The Wilcox Group, Mercer Island; lectr. Nat. Honor Soc. Mem. Com. for Tchr. Tng. Chapman Coll., Orange, Calif., 1973, planning com. Boy Scouts Am., Mercer Island. Mem. NEA, Internat. Franchise Assn., Venture Founders Assn. Republican. Office: Krypton Corp PO Box 154 Mercer Island WA 98040

FOWLER, WILLIAM DIX, construction company executive; b. Glendale, Calif., Jan. 29, 1940; s. H. Dix and Bertha Grace (Graveling) F.; m. Sheila Antonia Sandstrom, Feb. 7, 1964; children—Kurtis Walter Dix, Kara Antonia Grace, Kevin William Victor, Keir Andrew Bexar. B.B.A., Tex. Christian U., 1964, M.P.A., 1967. C.P.A., Alaska, Tex. Sr. v.p., mgr. J.L. Cox & Son, Inc., Kansas City, Mo., 1973-74; project adminstrn. mgr. Perini Arctic Assn., Delta Junction, Alaska, 1974-77; Alaska div. mgr. Majestic Wiley Contractor, Fairbanks, Alaska, 1974-77; v.p., treas. Frank Moolin & Assocs., Anchorage, 1977-78; sr. v.p., gen. mgr. Alaska Internat. Constrn. Inc., Fairbanks, 1978-80; pres. Alaska Internat. Constrn. Inc., 1980-85, FANCO Engring. & Constrn.Inc., 1986—, Southeast Pipeline Contractors, Inc., Ariz. and Alaska, 1987-88. U. Alaska Found. fellow. Mem. Am. Inst. CPA's, Alaska Soc. CPA's, Tex. Soc. CPA's, Associated Gen. Contractors (bd. dirs. Fairbanks 1984-86), Beta Alpha Psi. Republican. Episcopalian. Lodge: Rotary. Home: PO Box 82010 Fairbanks AK 99708 Office: FANCO Engring & Constrn Inc PO Box 60288 Fairbanks AK 99706

FOX, BERNARD MICHAEL, utilities company executive, electrical engineer; b. N.Y.C., July 16, 1942; s. Bernard Edward and Anna Theresa (Mazziotti) F.; m. Marilyn Ann Millar, Aug. 31, 1964; children—Christine, Jennifer, Douglas. B.S.E.E., Manhattan Coll., N.Y.C., 1963; M.S.E.E., Rensselaer Polytech. Inst., Troy, N.Y., 1964; mgmt. devel. program, Harvard Bus. Sch., Boston, 1979. Registered profl. engr., Mass., Conn. Planning engr. N.E. Utilities, Hartford, Conn., 1966-73, engr. nuclear ops., 1973-76, nuclear project mgr., 1976-79, systems dir. engring. mgmt. services, 1979-81, v.p., gen. mgr. gas bus., 1981-83, sr. v.p., chief fin. officer, 1983-86, exec. v.p., chief fin. and adminstrv. officer, 1986-87, pres., chief operating and fin. officer, 1987—; also trustee N.E. Utilities; bd. dirs. Conn. Yankee Atomic Power Co., Vt. Yankee, Maine Yankee, Yankee Atomic Cos., Conn. Nat. Bank, GroupAm. Chmn. Hartford corp. adv. com. Conn. Spl. Olympics; bd. dirs. Inst. of Living. Named Young Engr. of Yr., Hartford County Profl. Engrs., 1977. Mem. IEEE (sr.), Am. Leadership Forum. Republican. Roman Catholic. Home: 29 Saint Andrews Dr Avon CT 06001 Office: NE Utilities PO Box 270 Hartford CT 06141 also: Connecticut Light & Power Co Selden St Berlin CT 06037

FOX, CARYN, financial analyst, accountant; b. Chgo., Jan. 16, 1964; d. Rudolph and Alma (Chiappori) F. BS, Ill. State U., 1986. Counselor Fin. Fed. Savs. Bank, Olympia Fields, Ill., 1986; acct. Shand, Morahan & Co., Evanston, Ill., 1987-88, fin. analyst, 1988-89, info. analyst, systems cons., 1989—. Mem. NAFE. Home: 7403 N Ridge Blvd #1-G Chicago IL 60645 Office: Shand Morahan & Co Shand Morahan Pla Evanston IL 60201

FOX, DAVID WAYNE, banker; b. Aurora, Ill., Aug. 29, 1931; s. Wayne Stauffer and Helen Katherine (Lynch) F.; m. Mary Ann Evans, Sept. 22, 1956; children: Susan E., David Wayne, Katherine A., Thomas E. BS in Fin., U. Notre Dame, 1953; MBA, U. Chgo., 1958. With No. Trust Co., Chgo., 1955—, sr. v.p., 1974-78; exec. v.p. No. Trust Corp. and Co., Chgo., 1978-81, vice chmn., dir., 1981-87, pres., chief operating officer, 1987—, also bd. dirs.; bd. dirs. USG Corp., Chgo. Chmn. bd. govs. Hinsdale Community House, Ill., 1983; trustee Adler Planetarium, Chgo., 1983—, Northwestern Meml. Hosp., Chgo., 1983—, DePaul U., 1988—, Chgo. Symphony Orcxh., 1988—; mem. bus. adv. council U. Notre Dame, Ind., 1981-87, DePaul U., Chgo., 1982—, Kellogg Grad. Sch. Bus. Northwestern U., Evanston, 1988—; bd. dirs. United Way Chgo., 1988—. Mem. Assn. Res. City Bankers, Robert Morris Assocs., Marine Corps Res. Officers Assn. Republican. Roman Catholic. Clubs: Chicago, University, Commonwealth, Economic, Commercial, Mid-Day (Chgo), Hinsdale (Ill.) Golf. Office: No Trust Co 50 S LaSalle St Chicago IL 60675

FOX, EDWARD A., association executive; b. N.Y.C., July 17, 1936; s. Herman and Ruth F.; divorced; children: Brian, Laura, Jacqueline. A.B., Cornell U., 1958; M.B.A., NYU, 1963. Pres., chief exec. officer Student Loan Mktg. Assn., Washington, 1973—; bd. dirs. Perpetual Savs. Bank, F.S.B. Past trustee Talladega Coll.; past pres. D.C. chpt. ARC; bd. dirs., past pres. Washington Performing Arts Soc.; past pres. bd. dirs. Washington Ballet; vice chmn., bd. dirs. Reading is Fundamental; mem. bd. overseers GBA NYU; mem. adv. bd. Nat. Ctr. Fin. Services; bd. visitors Sch. Fgn. Svc. Georgetown U.; bd. dirs. Fed. City Coun. Office: Student Loan Mktg Assn 1050 Thomas Jefferson St NW Washington DC 20007

FOX, JEANNINE ELISE, financial company executive; b. West Point, Ga., Apr. 10, 1946; d. Robert Ashley and Kathleen (Betts) F.; m. Michael O. Sutton, June 9, 1968 (div. July 1984); children: Kristen Elise, Amanda Ashley. BS, U. Ala., 1968; MBA, U. Houston, 1981. CPA, Tex. Survery statistician USPHS, Washington, 1969-73; fin. plan specialist Assocs. in Fin. Planning, Houston, 1981; dir. client planning ops. Houston Asset Mgmt. Co., 1981-83; pres. Fox Fin. Advisors, Inc., Houston, 1983—. Treas. Addicks Elem. Sch. PTO, Houston, 1982; sec. Alliance for Better Human Relations, Houston, 1988. Mem. Internat. Assn. Fin. Planning (treas. 1981-83, v.p. 1984), Inst. Cert. Fin. Planers. Methodist. Office: Fox Fin Advisors Inc 777 N Eldridge Pkwy Ste 150 Houston TX 77079

FOX, JOHN MICHAEL, business director, consultant; b. Esher, U.K., Dec. 26, 1912; came to U.S., 1913; s. James and Grace Elizabeth (Blott) F.; m. Floy Binkley George, Mar. 16, 1938; children: Byron M., Susan S., John Stephen. B.A., Colgate U., 1934; D.Com. Sci. (hon.), Webber Coll., 1983. Br. mgr. IBM, Worcester, Mass., 1934-43, dir. Armonk, N.Y., 1968-83; v.p. Nat. Research Corp., Boston, 1943-45; pres., chief exec. officer Minute Maid Corp., Orlando, Fla., 1945-60; pres., chmn., chief exec. officer United Fruit Co., Boston, 1960-70, Hood, H.P., Boston, 1970-77; bd. dirs., Harvey Group, Gt. Neck, N.Y., 1980—, Ferranti, London, 1987—, pres. Natural Pak Produce, Inc., Closter, N.J., 1986—. Republican. Episcopalian.

FOX, JOSEPH CARTER, pulp and paper manufacturing company executive; b. Petersburg, Va., Sept. 8, 1939; s. William Tarrant and Virginia (Newell) F.; m. Carol Spaulding Fox, June 16, 1962; children: Carol Faulkner, Lucy Carter, Baylor Tarrant. B.S., Washington and Lee U., 1961; M.B.A., U. Va., 1963. With Chesapeake Corp., West Point, Va., 1963—, controller, 1969-71, controller, asst. treas., 1971-74, v.p. corp. planning and devel., asst. treas., 1974-79, sr. v.p., asst. treas., 1979-80, pres., chief exec. officer, 1980—, dir. affiliate cos.; dir. Robertshaw Controls Co., Crestar Fin. Corp.; trustee N.C. State Pulp and Paper Found. Chmn. ann. fund Washington and Lee U., 1973-75; mem., bd. dirs. YMCA, Richmond, 1988—. Mem. Am. Paper Inst. (bd. dirs. 1985—), U. Va. Alumni (bd. dirs. 1982—), Nat. Council for Air and Stream Improvement (bd. govs. 1986—). Episcopalian. Clubs: West Point Country (past pres.), Commonwealth. Home: 1449 Floyd Ave Richmond VA 23220 Office: Chesapeake Corp 1021 E Cary St Richmond VA 23218 *

FOX, JOSEPH MARLIN, bank executive, insurance executive; b. Longford, Kans., July 23, 1915; s. Hurley Wellington and Eva Kathryn (Marty) F.; m. Mildred Maxine Randall, Aug. 25, 1946; children—Lynette, Jonathan. B.A., U. Colo., 1937. With Fowler (Colo.) State Bank, 1937—, v.p., cashier, dir., 1945-54, pres., dir., 1955—, chmn. bd., 1986—; co-owner Fox Agy., Fowler. Treas. bd. edn. Sch. Dist. 26 Otero County, Colo., 1945—; treas. Local Rodeo Assn.; active Ark. Valley Fair Assn., Colo. Arkansas Valley, Inc.; regional chmn. for banks Colo. 4-H Club Found., 1964; mem. 16th Jud. Dist. Nominating Commn. for Judges, 1967; dist. chmn. Rocky Mountain council Boy Scouts Am. Served with U.S. Army, 1941-44. Mem. Am. Bankers Assn., Colo. Bankers Assn. (mem. 50 Year Club), Ind. Bankers Am., Bank Adminstrn. Inst., Ark. Valley Clearing House Assn. (pres.), Am. Legion (local service officer). Democrat. Methodist. Clubs: Pueblo (Colo.) Country, Lions. Home: 3308 Rd KK 75/100 Fowler CO 81039 Office: Fowler State Bank 201 Main St Fowler CO 81039

FOX, MICHAEL GERARD, comptroller; b. Olean, N.Y., Nov. 1, 1954; s. Francis John and Jacqueline Mary (Shortell) F.; m. Suzanne M. Finley, July, 19, 1975; children: Cristin Marie, Catherine Ann. BS in Acctg., Coll. Steubenville, 1976. Chief acct. aviation Resorts Internat. Inc., North Miami Beach, Fla., 1980-81; comptroller Devcon Internat. Corp., Deerfield Beach, Fla., 1981—, chief fin. officer, 1982—. Mem. Constrn. Fin. Mgmt. Assn., Nat. Assn. Accts. Republican. Roman Catholic. Office: Devcon Internat 1350 E Newport Center Dr Deerfield Beach FL 33443

FOX, MICHAEL JOE, manufacturing company executive, accountant; b. Danville, Ill., Aug. 7, 1945; s. Donald R. and Lillian (Parrett) F.; m. Janet K. Turnpaugh, July 2, 1965; children: Mitzi, Richard, Susan. Degree in Acctg., Ind. State U., 1967. CPA, Ind., Ill.; cert. fin. planner. Pres. Kesler & Co., Ltd., CPAs, Danville, Ill., 1967-87; pvt. practice acctg. Williamsport, Ind., 1987—; chief fin. officer Cronkhite Industries, Inc., Westville, Ill., 1987—. Mem. Am. Inst. CPA's, Ind. Assn. CPA's, Ill. CPA Soc., Inst. Cert. Fin. Planners. Republican. Lodge: Elks. Home: Rt 2 Box 161 Danville IL 61832 Office: PO Box 67 Williamsport IN 47993

FOX, ROBERT AUGUST, food company executive; b. Norristown, Pa., Apr. 24, 1937; s. August Emil and Elizabeth Martha (Deimling) F.; m. Linda Lee Carnesale, Sept. 19, 1964; children: Lee Elizabeth, Christina Carolyn. B.A. with high honors, Colgate U., 1959; M.B.A. cum laude, Harvard U., 1964. Unit sales mgr. Procter & Gamble Co., 1959-62; gen. sales mgr. T.J. Lipton Co., 1964-69; v.p. mktg. Can. Dry Corp., 1969-72; pres., chief exec. officer, dir. Can. Dry Internat., 1972-75; exec. v.p., dir. Hunt-Wesson Foods, Inc., 1975-78; pres., chief exec. officer, dir. R.J. Reynolds Tobacco Internat. S.A., 1978-80; chmn., chief exec. officer, dir. Del Monte Corp., San Francisco, 1980-85; vice chmn. Nabisco Brands, Inc., East Hanover, N.J., 1986-87; pres. Continental Can Co., Inc., Norwalk, Conn., 1988—; bd. dirs. New Perspective Fund, Growth Fund Am., Income Fund Am., Am. Balanced Fund, Indsl. Indemnity Co., Quantum Corp., Clarke Hooper PLC; trustee Euro-Pacific Growth Fund. Trustee Colgate U. Mem. San Francisco C. of C. (dir.), Colgate U. Alumni Assn. (dir., pres. 1984). Office: Continental Can Co Inc PO Box 5410 Norwalk CT 06856

FOX, THOMAS JOHN, accountant; b. Paterson, N.J., June 17, 1960; s. William Paul and Patricia Dorothy (Frazer) F.; m. Lynn Marie Karen Montemarano, June 2, 1984. BBA in Acctg., Montclair State Coll., 1982; MBA in Fin., Rutgers U., 1988. Acctg. reviewer Prudential Ins. Co., Roselane, N.J., 1982-84, asst. acctg. analyst, 1984-85; asst. tax acct. Prudential Ins. Co., Newark, 1985-86, tax analyst, 1986-88, mgr. tax, 1988—. Roman Catholic. Office: Prudential Ins Co 745 Broad St Newark NJ 07101

FOX, VIRGINIA GAINES, public broadcasting executive; b. Campbellsville, Ky., Apr. 30, 1939; d. Harold Durrett and Kathryn (Arnold) Gaines; m. Victor Fox, Dec. 27, 1963. B.A. in Edn., Morehead State U., 1961; M.S.L.S., U. Ky., 1969. Cert. tchr., librarian, Ky. Tchr. Franklin County Schs., Frankfort, Ky., 1961-62, Mason County Schs., Maysville, Ky., 1962-63, Whiteland Elem. Sch., Ind., 1963-64; tchr., librarian Fayette County Schs., Lexington, Ky., 1964-68; utilization specialist Ky. Ednl. TV, Lexington, 1968-69, asst. dir. edn. for evaluation, 1969-70, exec. asst. to exec. dir., 1970-71, dir. edn., 1971-74, dir. edn. and programming, 1974-75, dep. exec. dir., 1974-80; pres., chief exec. officer So. Ednl. Communications Assn., Columbia, S.C., 1980—; mem. nat. adv. com. Children's TV Workshop, N.Y.C., 1979—, Teleconnect Database Mktg. Co., Cedar Rapids, Iowa, informal sci. edn. panel NSF, Washington, 1986—; dir. Editorial Integrity Project, Columbia, 1984—. Exec. producer TV programs: Just One Day, 1979 (Eudora Welty award 1980), Vectoria, 1978 (Corp. for Pub. Broadcasting award 1979), GED. Named Woman of Yr. in Edn., Lexington Bus. and Profl. Women's Club, 1971-72. Mem. Am. Soc. Assn. Execs., Nat. Assn. Ednl. Broadcasters, ALA, Assn. for Ednl. Communications and Tech. (Edgar Dale award region V 1975), Wildlife Action. Episcopalian. Avocations: reading; golf; piano; running. Home: PO Box 5416 Columbia SC 29250 Office: So Ednl Communications PO Box 5008 Columbia SC 29250

FOX, WILLIAM EARLE, banker; b. Shamokin, Pa., July 24, 1950; s. James Edward and Charlotte Noreen (Haley) F.; m. Sandra Jean Farrow, Aug. 20, 1977 (div. 1986); children: Evelyn, Christopher. BSBA, Bloomsburg U., 1972. Trust officer Guarantee Trust Co., Shamokin, 1972-77; corp. trust officer No. Cen. Bank, Williamsport, Pa., 1977-81, asst. v.p., 1981-84, v.p., 1984—; bd. dirs. Mellon Fin. Services Users Group, Pitts., 1986—. Mem. Inst. Cert. Fin. Planners (treas. cen. Pa. chpt. 1986—). Republican. Presbyterian. Lodges: Kiwanis, Masons. Home: 1440 Washington Blvd Williamsport PA 17701 Office: No Central Bank 102 W 4th St Williamsport PA 17701

FOXEN, GENE LOUIS, insurance executive; b. Chgo., Mar. 28, 1936; adopted son Henry and Mary Foxen; student public schs.; m. Diane E. Young, 1986; children from previous marriage: Dan, Kathleen, Michael, Patricia, James, Karen, Ellen. With New Eng. Life Ins. Co., 1957—, assoc. gen. agt., 1970-73, gen. agt., Chgo., 1973—. Cubmaster DuPage council Boy Scouts Am., 1963; Midwest regional dir. Adoptees Liberty Movement Assn. Served with USMC, 1954-57. Recipient life membership award Gen. Agents and Mgrs. Conf.; named as life mem. Hall of Fame, New Eng. Life Ins. Co., 1972, life mem. Million Dollar Round Table. C.L.U. Mem. Nat. Assn. Life Underwriters, Execs. Club Chgo., Gen. Agents and Mgrs. Assn., Am. Soc. C.L.U.'s (pres. Chgo. chpt. 1977-78, v.p. Midwest region 1981-82), Chgo. Estate Planning Council (pres. 1981-82), Am. Soc. Life Underwriters. Republican. Roman Catholic. Club: Metropolitan. Home: 2247 Hidden Creek Ct Lisle IL 60532 Office: Foxen Fin 120 S Riverside Pla Chicago IL 60606

FOXHOVEN, SISTER CHARLITA, nun, religious organization administrator; b. Earling, Iowa, Sept. 26, 1931; d. Henry M. and Frances M. (Kaufman) F. BA in Mgmt., Alverno Coll., 1976; MBA, Northwestern U., 1985. Bookkeeper, acct. John W. Stang Corp., Omaha, 1950-56; acct. Sch. Sisters of St. Francis, Milw., 1958-69, treas. internat., 1980—. Bd. dirs. St. Francis Svc. Found., Milw., Alverno Coll., Milw., 1969-77, St. Mary's Hill Hosp., Milw., 1969-87. Mem. Nat. Assn. Religious Treasurers (presenter nat. conv. 1980, 86), Regional Assn. Religious Treasurers, U.S. Cath. Conf. (acctg. practices com. 1985, 86). Office: Sch Sisters St Francis 1501 S Layton Blvd Milwaukee WI 53215

FOXHOVEN, MICHAEL JOHN, retail/wholesale company executive, retail merchant; b. Sterling, Colo., Mar. 2, 1949; s. Mark John and Mary Kathryn (Hagerty) F.; m. Catherine Marie Carricaburu, Feb. 16, 1980; children—Patrick Michael, Rachel Marie. Student U. Colo., 1967-70, U. San Francisco, 1971-72, postgrad. Columbia Pacific U., 1987—. Comml. sales mgr. Goodyear Tire & Rubber Co., Denver, 1978-80, area sales mgr., 1980-81, store mgr., 1981-83, wholesale mgr., 1983-84, appeared in TV commls., 1972; v.p. Foxhovens, Inc., Sterling, 1984—; cons. Foxhoven Bros., Inc., Sterling, 1984—; participant dealer mgmt. seminar, Akron, Ohio, 1973, 85. Mem. mgmt. adv. com. Northeastern Jr. Coll., Sterling, 1976-78; sec. Highland Park Sanitation Dist., Sterling, 1984—. Mem. Logan County C. of C. Republican. Roman Catholic. Club: Sterling Country. Lodges: Elks, Kiwanis. Home: 107 Highland Ave Sterling CO 80751 Office: Foxhovens Inc 1100 W Main St Sterling CO 80751

FOY, RICHARD DANIEL, human resources executive; b. N.Y.C., Nov. 17, 1929; s. Peter Joseph and Virginia Maria (McKeon) F.; m. Mary Ellen Morley, Dec. 10, 1970; children: Peter Joseph III, Bridget Morley. BA in Math., Marist Coll., 1950, LLD (hon.), 1979; MS in Math., St. John's U., 1954; PhD in Math., NYU, 1962; LLD (hon.), Iona Coll., 1961. Tchr. Archbishop Molloy H.S., Queens, N.Y., 1950-57, Cardinal Hayes H.S., Bronx, N.Y., 1957-58; pres. Marist Coll., Poughkeepsie, N.Y., 1958-79; sr. v.p. for fin. and adminstrn., treas. Boyden Internat., Inc., N.Y.C., 1979—; Bd. dirs. Dutchess Bank & Trust, Poughkeepsie; freelance cons. for small computer systems, Poughkeepsie, 1977-81. Pres. United Way of Dutchess County, N.Y., 1972; bd. dirs. Mid-Hudson Civic Ctr., Poughkeepsie, 1975-79. Chair endowed in name Marist Coll., 1981; named Person of Yr., B'nai B'rith, 1975. Mem. Poughkeepsie Area C. of C. (pres. 1974), Am. Math. Soc., Math. Assn. Am. Roman Catholic. Home: 717 Washington Ave Chappaqua NY 10514 Office: Boyden Internat Inc 260 Madison Ave New York NY 10016

FOY, ROBERT WILLARD, moving and storage company executive; b. San Francisco, Sept. 18, 1936; m. Barbara B. Barron, Oct. 21, 1967; children: Matthew S., Peter A. BS with honors in Bus. and Indsl. Mgmt., San Jose State U., 1959. Mgmt. trainee, purchasing agt. Continental Group Inc. (formerly Continental Can Co.), Stockton, Calif., 1962-64; with Pacific Storage Co., Stockton, 1964—, pres., 1977—, also bd. dirs.; bd. dirs. Calif. Water Svc. Co., San Jose; bd. dirs., corp. sec. Wagner Corp., Reid Travel Assocs.; mem. agt. adv. coun. Bekins Van Lines Co. Mem. selection com. Military Acad. 14th Congl. Dist., 1979, vol. adv. com. State Calif. Atty. Gen. Office, San Joaquin County Grand Jury; chmn. presdl. task force U. Pacific, Nat. Moving and Storage Assn.; bd. dirs. Boy's Club, San Joaquin County (Calif.) Better Bus. Bur., San Joaquin County Mental Health Assn.; chmn. Stockton parole adv. com. State Calif.; active local and state chpts. United Way, St. John's Episcopal Ch., Stockton; pres. San Joaquin Employer's Coun.; chmn. bd. commrs. Stockton Port Dist.; chmn. bd. trustees St. Joseph's Med. Ctr.; co-chmn. Make Brighter Tomorrows campaign A Safe Place for Battered Women. Capt. USAR. Recipient Conservative of Yr. award Norman D. Shumway-Lincoln Club Cen. Calif., 1987, Disting. Alumnus award Sch. Bus. San Jose State U., 1981. Mem. Cen. Valley Purchasing Agts. Assn. (chmn.), Nat. Def. Transp. Assn., Am. Soc. Pub. Adminstrn. (mem. com. on rels. bus., industry), Calif. Moving and Storage Assn. (pres., sec.-treas., v.p.), Nat. Moving and Storage Assn. (chmn. bd. dirs.), Greater Stockton C. of C. (bd. dirs., pres.), West Lane Tennis Club, Yosemite Club (bd. dirs.), Pioneer Mus. and Haggin Gallery Mus. Club (pres.), San Jose State U. Alumni Assn., San Jose State U. Quarterback Club. Republican. Address: 933 W Monterey Ave Stockton CA 95204 Office: Bekins-Pacific Storage Co PO Box 334 Stockton CA 95201

FOZZATI, ALDO, automobile manufacturing company executive; b. Italy, Mar. 10, 1950; s. Danilo and Piera (Bretto) F.; m. Ana Maria Ruiz, June 7, 1977; children: Giacomo, Hugo, Daniel. PhD in Aero. Engring., Poly. U. of Turin, Italy, 1975. Registered profl. engr., Europe, U.S. and Can. Project mgr. Fiat Aerospace, Turin, 1975-78; U.S. rep. Fiat Corp., N.Y.C. and Detroit, 1978-82; ind. internat. bus. cons. Los Angeles, Paris and N.Y.C., 1982-84; program dir. Gen. Motors Corp., Detroit, 1984-87; dir. new bus. devel. Gen. Motors Europe, Zurich, Switzerland, 1987—. Mem. Soc. Automotive Engrs., Am. Security Council. Republican. Roman Catholic. Home: 250 Marlboro Bloomfield Hills MI 48013 Office: Gen Motors Corp 3044 W Grand Blvd Detroit MI 48126

FRACCHIA, CHARLES ANTHONY, financial advisor, teacher; b. San Francisco, Aug. 10, 1937; s. Charles Bartholomew and Josephine (Giacosa) F; m. Ann Escobosa, Feb. 10, 1962 (div. 1971); children: Laura E., Carla A., Charles A. Jr., Francesca S.; m. Elizabeth Ann Feaster, Aug. 15, 1987. AB in History, U. San Francisco, 1960, postgrad., 1959-61; MLS, U. Calif., Berkeley, 1976; MA in History, San Francisco State U., 1979; MA in Theology, Grad. Theol. Union, Berkeley, 1981. Stockbroker J. Barth & Co., San Francisco, 1961-65; v.p. mktg. Brennan Fin. Group, San Francisco, 1965-70; gen. mgr., analyst Walker's Manual div. Hambrecht & Quist, San Francisco, 1971-73; fin. advisor Planned Investments Inc., 1981—; instr. San Francisco Community Coll., 1980—. Author: Converted Into Houses, 1976, So This is Where You Work, 1980, Second Spring, 1980, Living Together Alone, 1979, How to Be Single Creatively, 1979. Trustee Calif. Hist. Soc., San Francisco, 1966-76; mem. San Francisco Hist. Landmarks Adv. Bd., San Francisco, 1968-72; pres. San Francisco Hist. Soc., 1988—. Democrat. Roman Catholic. Home: 1653 Baker St San Francisco CA 94115 Office: Planned Investments Inc PO Box 569 San Francisco CA 94010

FRAGNER, BERWYN N., strategic planning executive; b. Uniontown, Pa., Aug. 5, 1927; s. Rudolph and Rose (Lebowitz) F.; B.A. with distinction, U. Del., 1950; M.A., Harvard U., 1952; m. Marcia Ruth Salkind, June 11, 1950; children—Robin Beth, Matthew Charles, Lisa Rachel. Vice pres. Royer & Roger, Inc., N.Y.C., 1952-62; dir. Western div. Goodway Printing Co., Los Angeles, 1962; v.p., dir. indsl. relations TRW Def. and Space Systems Group, Redondo Beach, Calif., 1963-77, v.p. human relations TRW Systems and Energy, Redondo Beach, 1977-81, TRW Electronics and Def., 1981-87; v.p. strategic bus. devel. TRW Space and Def., 1988—; mem. adv. bd. 1st Women's Bank of Calif. Chmn. Los Angeles City Pvt. Industry Council, 1979-81; mem. Calif. Ednl. Mgmt. and Evaluation Commn., 1974-82; chmn. bd. trustees Calif. Acad. Decathalon, 1980-81; mem. bus. execs. adv. com. So. Calif. Research Council, 1979—; USAR mem. Res. Forces Policy Bd., 1981-84; mem.-at-large U.S. Army Res. Forces Policies Com., 1979-82. Bd. dirs. Ind. Coll. So. Calif., 1982-86; bd. govs. U. So. Calif. Sch. Pharmacy, 1982—; chmn. Los Angeles County Pvt. Industry Council, 1983-88. Served with AUS, 1944-47. Decorated Meritorious Service medal with 2 oak leaf clusters, Legion of Merit, D.S.M.; recipient Presdl. citation, 1981; Calif. Medal of Merit. Mem. Assn. U.S. Army, Res. Officers Assn., Internat. Assn. Applied Social Scientists (cert.). Clubs: Army and Navy (Washington); Los Angeles Athletic. Contbr. to New World of Managing Human Resources, 1979. Office: One Space Park E2 11092 Redondo Beach CA 90278

FRALEY, JOHN L., transportation company executive; b. 1920; married. Asst. supt. Rhyne Houser Mfg. Co., 1939-40; sec., treas., gen. mgr., dir. Bucknit Processing Co., 1945; with Carolina Freight Corp., Cherryville, N.C., 1949—, asst. gen. sales mgr., 1951-53, exec. v.p., 1953-70, pres., 1970-76, chief exec. officer, 1976-84, vice chmn., 1976-87, chmn., 1987—. Office: Carolina Freight Corp NC Hwy 150 E PO Box 697 Cherryville NC 28021 also: Carolina Freight Corp PO Box 545 Cherryville NC 28021 *

FRAME, CLARENCE GEORGE, oil and gas refining company executive, former banker; b. Dakota County, Minn., July 26, 1918; s. George and Helen (Hunter) F. AB, U. Minn., 1941; JD, Harvard U., 1947. Bar: Minn. 1947. With First Nat. Bank, St. Paul, 1947-80, asst. cashier, 1953-54, cashier, 1954-57, v.p., cashier, 1957-59, v.p., 1959-61, sr. v.p., 1961-68, exec. v.p., 1968-72, pres., 1972-80; vice-chmn. First Bank System, Inc., Mpls., 1980-83; chmn. bd. dirs., chief exec. officer Tosco Corp., St. Paul and Santa Monica, Calif., 1986—; bd. dirs. Northland Co., Mpls., Opus U.S. Corp., Mpls., Morison Asset Allocation Fund, Mpls., Chgo. Milw. Corp., Chgo., Courier Dispatch Group, Atlanta, Independence One Mutual Funds, Farmington Hills, Mich., TG Friday's Inc., Dallas, Mutual Funds advised by Voyageur Fund Mgrs., Mpls. Trustee Breck Sch., Mpls. Lt. comdr. USNR, 1942-46, to comdr. 1951-53. Mem. Somerset Country Club (St. Paul Club), Mpls. Club. Office: Tosco Corp W-875 First Bank Bldg 332 Minnesota St Saint Paul MN 55101

FRAMPTON, EDMUND GREGORIE, tax administrator; b. Charleston, S.C., Dec. 13, 1944; s. Edmund Gregorie and Geraldine (MacNeal) F.; m. Macy Harris, June 9, 1970; children: Emdund, Harris. BS, Clemson U., 1970. Field appraiser S.C. Tax Commn., Columbia, 1970-73, tax appraiser, 1973-74, asst. exec. dir., 1974-75, asst. dir., 1975-82, exec. dir., 1982—. Scoutmaster Boy Scouts Am., Columbia, 1979-82, asst. scoutmaster, 1986—; agy. head United Way, Columbia, 1982—. Mem. N.Am. Gasoline Tax (pres. 1982), Fedn. Tax Adminstrs., South Eastern Tax Adminstrs. (bd. dirs. 1983-87). Club: Numerical Soc. (Clemson, S.C.). Home: 1572 Shady Ln Columbia SC 29206

FRAMSON, JOEL, accountant; b. Bridgeport, Conn., Oct. 19, 1947; s. Seymour and Beulah (Mellitz) F.; m. Joanne Mendelsohn, May 9, 1982; children: Jessica, Celia, Ian. BS, U. Bridgeport, 1970; MA in Bus. Taxation, U. So. Calif., L.A., 1982. CPA, Calif. Co-owner Phillips & Robinson, L.A., 1978-81, Oppenheimer, Appel, Dixon & Co., CPAs, L.A., 1982-84, Charles, Blank, Framson & Zimmer, Encino, Calif., 1984—. Mem. Assn. Calif. Accts., Fin. Planners, L.A. Soc. Personal Fin. Planners (chmn. fin. planning com. 1988—), Jaycees (pres. 1977), Ojai Club. Office: Charles Blank Framson & Zimmer 15910 Ventura Blvd #800 Encino CA 91436

FRANCE, JOSEPH DAVID, securities analyst; b. Smithville, Mo., July 24, 1953; s. Raymond Hughes France and Bonnie Lee (Cavin) Vinzant; m. Judith Ann Tehel, May 29, 1976; 1 child, Lucille Terrell. BS in Pharmacy, U. Kans., 1977, MBA, 1980. Registered pharmacist; chartered fin. analyst. Staff pharmacist U. Kans. Med. Ctr., Kansas City, 1977-80; securities analyst First Nat. Bank Chgo., 1980-82; securities analyst Smith Barney, Harris Upham & Co., Inc., N.Y.C., 1982-86, mng. dir., 1986—. Mem. Am. Soc. Hosp. Pharmacists, Healthcare Fin. Mgmt. Assn., N.Y. Soc. Securities Analysts, Fin. Analysts Fedn., Inst. Chartered Fin. Analysts. Democrat. Roman Catholic. Office: Smith Barney Harris Upham & Co 1345 Ave of the Americas New York NY 10105

FRANCIOSA, JOSEPH ANTHONY, pharmaceutical company executive; b. Easton, Pa., Apr. 24, 1936; s. Joseph and Letitia Beatrice (Cascioli) F.; m. Antonietta Battistoni, Feb. 8, 1964 (div. 1972); m. Barbara Ann Neilan, Aug. 3, 1973; 1 son, Christopher David. B.A., U. Pa., 1958; M.D., U. Rome, 1963. Diplomate Am. Bd. Internal Medicine; lic. in Pa., Md., Ark. Intern USPHS Hosp., S.I., N.Y., 1964-65; resident Washington Hosp. Ctr., 1967-69; cardiology fellow VA Hosp.-Georgetown U., Washington, 1969-71; chief ICU, VA Hosp., Washington, 1971-73; asst. prof. medicine Georgetown U. Med. Sch., , 1971-73, assoc. dir. cardiovascular tng. program, 1973-74; dir. CCU VA Hosp., Mpls., 1974-76; asst. prof. medicine U. Minn., Mpls., 1977-79; chief cardiology VA Hosp., Phila., 1979-82; assoc. prof. U. Pa., Phila., 1979-82, adj. prof., 1987—; clin. prof. medicine Mt. Sinai Med. Sch., N.Y.C., 1987—; dir. cardiology div. U. Ark., Little Rock, 1982-86, prof., 1982-86; dir. cardio-renal drugs ICI Americas Inc., Wilmington, Del., 1986-88; v.p. rsch. & devel. Zambon Corp., East Rutherford, N.J., 1988—. Contbr. numerous articles to med. jours. Mem. med. research com. Am. Heart Assn., Mpls., 1976-79, Phila., 1981-82. Served to lt. comdr. USPHS, 1965-67. VA grantee, 1974-84; U. Ark. grantee, 1982-83. Fellow ACP, Am. Coll. Cardiology, Am. Coll. Chest Physicians (chmn. hypertension com. 1981-83, gov. Ark. 1984-86), Am. Heart Assn. (circulation council 1978—, council high blood pressure research 1982—, clin. cardiology council 1984); mem. Am. Soc. Clin. Pharmacology and Therapeutics (vice chmn. cardiopulmonary com. 1981—, Assn. Univ. Cardiologists. Avocations: computers, gardening, physical fitness. Office: Zambon Corp 1 Meadowlands Pla East Rutherford NJ 07073

FRANCIS, ALBERT JOHN, II, finance executive, accountant; b. Brownsville, Pa., Aug. 21, 1954; s. Albert John and Elizabeth Ann (Giles) F.; m. Nancy Jane Simmons, Mar. 7, 1981; 1 child, Albert John III. AA, Brevard Community Coll., Cocoa, Fla., 1974; BSBA, U. Cen. Fla., 1977; cert. fin., Tex. Tech U., 1985. CPA, Fla. Staff acct. Dobson, Bjerning, Merritt Island, Fla., 1978, staff auditor, 1978-79, audit supr., 1980-81, acctg. service mgr., 1981-82; dir. fin. and adminstrn. Canaveral Port Authority, Cape Canaveral, Fla., 1982—; v.p. Cape Florist, Inc., Cape Canaveral, 1977—. Treas. Harbor Oaks Condo Assn., Cape Canaveral, 1985-87. Mem. Am. Inst. CPA's, Fla. Inst. CPA's, Nat. Assn. Accts., Govt. Fin. Officers Assn., Cocoa Beach (Fla.) C. of C. Republican. Roman Catholic. Lodge: Rotary (pres. Cocoa Beach club 1985-86, dist. rep. 1986-87). Office: Canaveral Port Authority PO Box 267 Cape Canaveral FL 32920

FRANCIS, EID NAYEF, restaurant executive; b. Zagreen, Lebanon, Dec. 25, 1930; s. Nayef Louis and Zahra Mary (Germanos) F.; ed. high sch.; m. Paulette Marie Saumure, June 25, 1960; children—Daniel, Linda, Robert, Michael. Asst. supr. C&AT Co., Persian Gulf, 1948-54; various positions Cameo Restaurant, Can., 1955-62, asst. chef, 1962; exec. chef, dir. ops. Windsor Steak House, Zanesville, Ohio, 1962-66; asst. mgr., gen. mgr., dist. mgr. Marriott Corp., Washington, 1966-73; pres., gen. mgr. Francis Enterprises Inc., Cambridge, Ohio, 1973—, pres., chief exec. officer, Francis Fine Foods, 1983, chmn. bd. Jays Food Corp., 1984. Mem. Internat. Food Service Execs., Ohio Restaurant Assn. Roman Catholic. Clubs: K.C., Land O Lake, Kiwanis. Democrat. Address: Francis Enterprises Inc PO Box 638 Cambridge OH 43725

FRANCIS, ELAINE PAGANO, investment banker; b. Phila., Mar. 9, 1957; d. Jochaim Bernard and Rosemarie (Mascino) P.; m. Raymond A. Francis, III, Sept. 29, 1984. BA, Temple U., 1979; MBA, Drexel U., 1984. Fin. analyst Butcher & Singer, Phila., 1979-81; fin. appraiser Marshall & Stevens, Phila., 1981-84; sr. corp. fin. officer Mellon Bank, Phila., 1984-86; assoc. Howard, Lawson & Co., Phila., 1986—. Study chmn. econ. subcom. Phila. Past, Present and Future, 1981; active United Way, Phila., 1986. Mem. NAFE, Nat. Employee Stock Ownership Plan Assn., Phila. Fin. Assn., World Affairs Council Phila., Nat. Hon. Econ. Soc. Republican. Roman Catholic. Office: Howard Lawson & Co Two Penn Center Pla Ste 410 Philadelphia PA 19102

FRANCIS, JAMES DELBERT, oil company executive; b. Orange, N.J., Jan. 8, 1947; s. Delbert Matthew and Margaret Janet (Thornley) F.; children: Elizabeth M., John A., David S., Virginia A., Grace A.; m. Shirley Ann Waters. B.S. in Commerce, U. Va., 1970; J.D., U. Fla., 1973. Bar: Fla. 1973. Ptnr. Smith and Hulsey, Jacksonville, Fla., 1973-82; exec. v.p. Charter Oil Co., Jacksonville, 1982-83; pres. Charter Oil Co., 1983-86; chmn., chief exec. officer Ray Distbg. Co. of Jacksonville, Inc., 1987—. Bd. dirs., chmn. Children's Home Soc., Jacksonville, 1976—; elder St. Johns Presbyterian Ch., 1985—. Mem. ABA, Fla. Bar, Jacksonville Bar Assn. Republican. Clubs: Fla. Yacht; River (Jacksonville). Home: 4250 Ortega Forest Dr Jacksonville FL 32210 Office: Ray Distbg Co PO Box 43250 Jacksonville FL 32203

FRANCIS, MARY FRANCES VAN DYKE, business executive, editor; b. Sedalia, Mo., Nov. 17, 1925; d. Frank B. and Mary Irene (Sims) Van Dyke; student Central Mo. State Coll.; m. Harold E. Francis, Apr. 23, 1944 (div. 1980); children—David Eugene, Lois Irene (Mrs. Ed Jackson), Roland Wayne, Eric Brian. Tchr. grade sch. Pettis County, Mo., 1943-44; timekeeper Montgomery Ward & Co., Kansas City, Mo., 1944-45; instr. new operators Southwestern Bell Telephone Co., Independence, Mo., 1945-47; real estate salesman Russell Realtors, Independence, 1958-66; owner Mary Francis, Realtor, Independence, 1967—; exec. sec., editor Eastern Jackson County Bd. Realtors, 1962-68; exec. asst., pub. relations dir., editor Kansas City Realtor, 1968-71; marketing asst. South Central region Chgo. Title Ins. Co., Kansas City, 1971-75; pres. Maranco, Inc., real estate, 1975—; v.p. Raintree Lake Realty, 1980-83 . Cub Scout den mother council Boy Scouts Am. Recipient Outstanding Service award Eastern Jackson County Bd. Realtors, 1964, Salesmanship award, 1965, CPW Real Estate Exchange award, Expo, 1983. Mem. Nat. Assn. Real Estate Bds. (charter pres. Greater Kansas City chpt., gov., pres. Mo. Women's Council), Mo. Real Estate Assn. (mem. Speakers Bur.). Club: Soroptimist (past pres., Independence). Contbr. articles to realty publs. Address: PO Box 1158 Independence MO 64051

FRANCIS, RICHARD HERMAN, transportation executive; b. Allentown, Pa., Apr. 23, 1932; s. Willard F. and Lucy M. (Rupp) F.; m. Gislina Jonsdottir, June 18, 1957; children—Lynn, Lori. BS, Lehigh U., 1954; postgrad. in advanced mgmt., Harvard U., 1982. Ins. mgr. Westinghouse Airbrake (merged with Am. Standard), Pitts., 1960-65, asst. treas., 1965-68, treas., 1968-73; v.p., treas. Am. Standard Inc. (subs. Pan Am. World Airways), N.Y.C., 1973-83, v.p., chief fin. officer, 1983-85, sr. v.p., chief fin. officer, 1985—; dir. Allendale Mut. Ins., Johnston, R.I. Project mgr. army task force Pres.'s Pvt. Sector on Cost Containment, Washington, 1982. Served with U.S. Army, 1954-56. Fellow Fin. Exec. Inst., Machinery and Allied Products Inst. (fin. council II). Republican. Congregationalist. Clubs: Union League, Economic (N.Y.C.); Short Hills (N.J.). Office: Pan Am World Airways Pan Am Bldg New York NY 10017 also: Pan Am World Airways Pan Am Bldg New York NY 10017

FRANCISCO, WAYNE M(ARKLAND), automotive executive; b. Cin., June 14, 1943; s. George Lewis and Helen M. (Markland) F.; student Ohio State U., 1962-63; BS in Mktg. and Acctg., U. Cin., 1967; m. Susan Francisco; children: Diana Lynn, W. Michael. Unit sales mgr. Procter & Gamble, Cin., 1967-69; mktg. mgr. Nat. Mktg. Inc., Cin., 1969-70; pres. Retail Petroleum Marketers, Inc., Cin., 1970-72, chmn. bd., chief exec. officer, Phoenix, 1972-85; chmn. bd., chief exec. officer DMC Industries, Inc., 1985-88; pres., chief exec. officer Cassia Petroleum Corp., Vancouver, B.C., Can., 1980-84; bd. dirs. P.F.K. Enterprises, F.I.C. Inc., Internat. Investment and Fin. Enterprises, Inc., Alpha Realty, Inc. Mem. Phoenix Bd. Appeals, 1978-80; v.p. Cuervanaca Homeowners Assn., 1982, pres., 1983-86. Recipient Image Maker award Shell Oil Co., 1979; Top Performer award Phoenix dist. Shell Oil Co., 1979, 80. Mem. Petroleum Retailers Ariz. (pres. 1977-79), Nat. Congress Petroleum Retailers (adv. bd.), Nat. Inst. Automotive Service Excellence (cert.), Culver Legion (life), Studebaker Drivers Club (zone coord. Pacific S.W. 1983, 84, 85, 86; nat. v.p. 1986-89; Grand Canyon chpt. pres. 1986), Avanti Owners Assn. (nat. bd. dirs. 1975-88, internat. pres. 1986-90). Republican. Lodge: Optimists (bd. dirs. Paradise Valley club 1984, sec.-treas. 1984). Office: 21824 N 19th Ave Phoenix AZ 85027

FRANCK, WILLIAM FRANCIS, textile company executive; b. Fayetteville, N.C., July 29, 1917; s. William Francis and Martha Elizabeth (Lawhon) F.; m. Carolyn Ann Pannill, Nov. 29, 1941; children—Martha (Mrs. Overman Rollins), William Francis III, Carolyn Ann (Mrs. Alex Gordon), John M. B.A., Duke, 1939. Salesman Belk Leggett Co., Durham, N.C., 1935-40; cost clk. DuPont Co., Martinsville, Va., 1940-43; personnel mgr. Pannill Knitting Co., Martinsville, 1946-50; v.p. gen. mgr. Sale Knitting Co., Martinsville, 1950-53; chmn., chief exec. officer Tultex Corp., Martinsville, 1953-88, chmn. emeritus, 1989—; bd. dirs. Piedmont Bank Group, Inc.;. Bd. mem. Martinsville YMCA, 1969-78; fund chmn. Meml. Hosp. drive, 1966-67, bd. mem., 1963—; mem. Martinsville Sch. Bd., 1956-61, Blue Ridge Airport Authority, 1962—. Served to 1st lt. Q.M.C. AUS, 1943-46, ETO. Mem. Martinsville C. of C. (1st pres. 1959-61). Presbyterian (elder 1954-76). Clubs: Kiwanis, Chatmoss Country. Office: Tultex Corp Box 5191 Martinsville VA 24115

FRANCO, ANTHONY M., public relations executive; b. Detroit, July 7, 1933; s. John Richard and Evelyn Louise F.; m. Melissa R. Rohde, Aug. 27, 1983; children: Catherine, Suzanne, Anne, Anthony, Patricia, Michael, David, Meredith, Sam. Student, U.S. Naval Acad., 1955-57; BS, Wayne State U., 1958. Dir. pul. rels. Dawson-Murray Advt., Detroit, 1958-60, Fred M. Randall Co., Detroit, 1960-62, Denman & Baker Advt., Detroit, 1962-64; chmn. Anthony M. Franco, Inc., Detroit, 1964—. Past Trustee Marygrove Coll., Detroit; trustee U. Detroit; corp. bd. dirs. Boys Clubs Met. Detroit, 1972-87; pres. Met. Detroit coun. Boy Scouts Am., 1985; chmn. Channel 56. With U.S. Army, 1953-55. Mem. Internat. Pub. Relations Group of Cos. (v.p., dir.), Pub. Rels. Soc. Am. (pres. 1986, dir. Detroit chpt., pres. 1974, chmn. east cen. dist.,), Mich. C. of C., Greater Detroit C. of C. (vice-chmn. exec. com.), U.S. Naval Acad. Alumni Assn. Roman Catholic. Clubs: Detroit Athletic, Press, Bloomfield Hills Country, Detroit, Renaissance; Wilderness Country (Naples, Fla.); Detroit. Home: 345 Woodridge Bloomfield Hills MI 48013 Office: Anthony M Franco Inc 400 Renaissance Ctr Ste 600 Detroit MI 48243

FRANCO, JOHN ALBERT, insurance holding company executive; b. N.Y.C., Apr. 1, 1942; s. Dominick and Theresa (DiBlasi) F.; m. Mary Elizabeth Drake, May 27, 1967; children: John Albert, Susan, Margaret, Carol. AB, Columbia U., 1963; LLB, NYU, 1967. Bar: N.Y. 1967. Tax atty. Westvaco Corp., N.Y.C., 1970-74, asst. compt., 1974-79, 1979; exec. v.p., chief fin. officer Capital Holding Corp., Louisville, 1979-84, agy. group pres., 1984-87, vice- chmn., pres. accumulation and investment group, 1987—. Trustee Bellarmine Coll., Louisville, 1985—; bd. dirs. Cystic Fibrosis Found., Louisville, 1985—. With U.S. Army, 1967-69, Vietnam. Decorated Bronze Star. Mem. Louisville C. of C. (bd. dirs. 1987—). Office: Capital Holding Corp 680 4th Ave PO Box 32830 Louisville KY 40232

FRANCO, PHILIP JOSEPH, financial coordinator; b. Emerson, N.J., Oct. 13, 1922; s. Joseph Philip and Marion (Onorato) F.; m. Katherine M. Callas, Oct. 18, 1947; 1 child, Peter Steven. BS, Seton Hall U., 1949. Asst. dir. pub. relations Community Chest, Newark, 1949-57; pub. relations dir. United Fund, Trenton, N.J., 1957-72; registered rep. First Investors Corp., Newark, 1954—, asst. v.p., 1974-78; resident v.p. First Investors Corp., Iselin, N.J., 1978-84, sr. resident v.p., 1985—. Served with U.S. Army, 1943-46. Named Man of Yr., First Investors Corp., 1978; numerous other honors and awards, 1980—. Republican. Roman Catholic. Home: 99 Riverbend Dr North Brunswick NJ 08902

FRANCOEUR, LEOPOLD, engineering company executive; b. St. Anne de Bellevue, Que., Can., Oct. 29, 1927. B. Commerce, McGill U., Montreal, Can.; C.A., Inst. Chartered Accts., Que. Chartered acct., Can. Comptroller div. Hawker Siddeley Can., Inc., Montreal, 1965-78; corp. comptroller Hawker Siddeley Can., Inc., Toronto, 1978-81, v.p. fin., 1981—; dir. Hawker Siddeley Can. Inc., Toronto, Racair, Toronto, CGTX Inc., Montreal, Dosco Overseas Engring. Ltd., Tuxford, Eng., CanCar Inc., Atlanta, Kockums CanCar Corp., Atlanta. Mem. Ordre des Comptables Agrees du Quebec, Inst. Chartered Accts. Ont. Home: 3179 Cedar Tree Crescent, Mississauga, ON Canada L4Y 3G3 Office: Hawker Siddeley Can Inc, 3 Robert Speck Pkwy, Ste 700, Mississauga, ON Canada L4Z 2G5

FRANCOIS, PIERRE ANTONE, mechanical engineer; b. Roanoke, Ill., Sept. 1, 1933; s. Pierre Martin and Lena (Gerino) F.; m. Jane Ann Trimble, Sept. 8, 1956; children: Ann, Diane, Paul. BSME, Purdue U., 1957. Registered profl. engr., Ind. Project engr. Revco, Inc., Deerfield, Mich., 1957-59, Chrysler Corp., Dayton, Ohio, 1959-62; with Union Carbide Corp., Indpls., 1962—, mgr. nat. prodn., 1984-88, mgr. mfg. strategy, 1988—. Patentee in field. Served to capt. U.S. Army, 1957-58. Republican. Presbyterian. Home: 225 Royal Oak Ct Zionsville IN 46077 Office: Union Carbide Corp 1500 Polco St Indianapolis IN 46224

FRANCOIS, WILLIAM ARMAND, packaging company executive, lawyer; b. Chgo., May 31, 1942; s. George Albert and Evelyn Marie (Smith) F.; m. Barbara Ann Sala, Aug. 21, 1965; children—Nicole Suzanne, Robert William. B.A., DePaul U., 1964, J.D., 1967. Bar: Ill. bar 1967. Sole practice Lyons, Ill., 1967-68; with Am. Nat. Can Co., Chgo., 1970—, sec., 1974—, v.p., 1978—, assoc. gen. counsel, 1987, v.p., dep. gen. counsel, sec., 1988—. Served to capt. U.S. Army, 1968-70. Mem. ABA, Ill. Bar Assn., Chgo. Bar Assn., Am. Soc. Corporate Secs. Home: 326 Earls Ct Deerfield IL 60015 Office: Am Nat Can Co 8770 W Bryn Mawr Ave Chicago IL 60631

FRANK, ANTHONY MELCHIOR, federal official, former financial executive; b. Berlin, Germany, May 21, 1931; came to U.S., 1937, naturalized, 1943; s. Lothar and Elisabeth (Roth) F.; m. Gay Palmer, Oct. 16, 1954; children: Tracy, Randall. B.A., Dartmouth Coll., 1953, M.B.A., 1954; postgrad. in finance, U. Vienna, 1956. Asst. to pres., bond portfolio mgr. Glendale (Calif.) Fed. Savs. Assn., 1958-61; v.p., treas. Far West Fin. Corp., Los Angeles, 1962; adminstrv. v.p., v.p. savs. First Charter Fin. Corp., Beverly Hills, Calif., 1962-66; pres. State Mut. Savs. and Loan Assn., Los Angeles, 1966-68, Titan Group, Inc., N.Y.C. and Los Angeles, 1968-70, INA Properties, Inc., 1970-71; pres. Citizens Savs. & Loan, San Francisco, 1971-73, vice chmn., chief exec. officer, 1973-74; chmn. bd., pres., chief exec. officer FN Fin. Corp., 1974—; Postmaster General US Postal Service, 1988—; also pres., vice chmn., industry dir. Fed. Home Loan Bank San Francisco, 1972-77; trustee, treas. Blue Shield of Calif., 1976—; dir. Allianz Ins. Co. Am., Fed. Home Loan Bank of San Francisco. Chmn., dir. Calif. Housing Fin. Agy., Sacramento, 1978—; trustee Am. Conservatory Theater; chmn. bd. visitors Sch. Architecture and Planning UCLA, 1971—; bd. overseers Tuck Sch.; del. Calif. Democratic Conv., 1968. Served with AUS, 1954-56. Mem. Chief Execs. Orgn., World Bus. Forum, Dartmouth Club No. Calif., University Club (Los Angeles), Bohemian Club. Office: US Postal Svc Office of Postmaster Gen 475 L'Enfant Pla W SW Washington DC 20260 •

FRANK, BRUCE HOWARD, management consultant; b. N.Y.C., May 15, 1937; s. Sylvan Walter Frank and Annette Dorothy (Lieberman) Frank Shapiro; B.S. in Math., N.Y. U., 1957; M.B.A., Boston U., 1961; m. Geraldine Faith Zalvan, Dec. 24, 1959; children—Laurence Edward, Andrew David, Lisa Joy. With Raytheon Co., Newton, Mass., 1957-61; mgr. project planning and control Sylvania Electronic Systems, Waltham, Mass., 1961-67; mgr. adminstrn. Wakefern Food Corp., Elizabeth, N.J., 1967-69; dir. project mgmt. and computer services S.J. & H., Mgmt. Cons., N.Y.C., 1969-71; v.p. info. services Programming Methods div. GTE, N.Y.C., 1971-75; founder, pres. A.L.L. Assos., Cons. to Mgmt., North Brunswick, N.J., 1975—; instr. Northeastern U., Rutgers U. Mem. North Brunswick Bicentennial Commn., 1975-76. Mem. Assn. Systems Mgmt., Project Mgmt. Inst. Contbr. articles to profl. jours. Home and Office: 1585 McKinley Ave North Brunswick NJ 08902

FRANK, CAROLINE KACHURA, tax manager, consultant; b. Queens, N.Y., June 24, 1943; d. John and Anne (Predko) Kachura; m. Richard F. Frank, Feb. 20, 1965; children: Richard, John. BS in Biology, Adelphi U., 1965, MA in Edn., 1972; postgrad., N.Y. Inst. Tech., 1985-86, L.I. U., 1986—. Tchr. chemistry St. Anthony's High Sch., Kings Park, N.Y., 1979; tax preparer H&R Block Inc., Commack, N.Y., 1981-84; mgr. bus. services H&R Block Inc., East Northport, N.Y., 1986-87; gen. mgr. Home World, Huntington, N.Y., 1984-85; tax acct. David Vermut CPA, PC, Jericho, N.Y., 1986-87, tax mgr., 1987-88; pres., chmn. bd. dirs. K.C. Frank and Assoc. Inc., Huntington, 1988—; dir. pub. rels., radio and TV seminars H&R Block, 1984-85 (pub. relations award 1984, 85); bd. dirs. RSF Visual Fantasies Corp. Mem. Am. Inst. CPA's (jr. mem.), Nat. Notary Assn. Republican. Roman Catholic. Home: 203 Little Plains Rd Huntington NY 11743

FRANK, CHARLES RAPHAEL, JR., investment banker; b. Pitts., May 15, 1937; s. Charles Raphael and Lucille (Briscoe) M.; m. Susan Patricia Backman, Mar. 9, 1963 (div. June 1976); children: Elizabeth Grace, Stephen Raphael; m. Eleanor Sebastian, July 19, 1976; children: Paul Sebastian, Philip Sebastian. BS in Math., Rensselaer Poly. Inst., 1959; MA in Econs., Princeton U., 1961, PhD in Econs., 1963. Sr. rsch. fellow East African Inst. Social Rsch. Makerere U. Coll., Kampala, Uganda, 1963-65; asst. prof. econs. Yale U., New Haven, 1965-67; assoc. prof. econs. and internat. affairs Princeton (N.J.) U., 1967-70, prof., 1970-74; assoc. dir. rsch. program econ. devel. Woodrow Wilson Sch., 1967-70, dir., 1970-74; sr. fellow Brookings Inst., 1972-74; mem. policy planning staff U.S. Dept. State, 1974-77, dep. asst. sec. state for econ. and social affairs, 1977-78; v.p. Salomon Bros. Inc., 1978-87; pres. Frank & Co. Inc., 1987-88; sr. v.p., mgr. energy project fin. GE Capital Corp., Stamford, Conn., 1988—; ops. rsch. analyst U.S. Steel, summers 1960, 61; cons. Govt. Uganda, 1964, UN Econ. Commn. for Asia and Far East, 1969, IBRD, 1969-72, Korea Devel. Inst., 1973-74, Mathematica, 1967-68, Nat. Conf. Bd., 1969-70, Nat. Bur. Econ. Rsch., 1970-75, Brookings Instn., 1969; mem. rsch. adv. com. AID, 1971-75, cons., Washington, 1966-68, Korea, 1971-73. Author: Production Theory and Indivisible Commodities, 1969, The Sugar Industry in East Africa, 1965, (with Brian Van Arkadie) Economic Accounting and Development Planning, 2d edit., 1969, Debt and the Terms of Aid, 1970, Statistics and Econometrics, 1971, American Jobs and Trade with the Developing Countries, 1973, Foreign Exchange Regimes and Economic Development, The Case of South Korea, 1975, Foreign Trade and Domestic Adjustment, 1976, Income Distribution and Economic Growth in the Less Developed Countries, 1977. Mem. adv. council Ctr. Internat. Affairs Princeton U. Mem. Council Fgn. Relations. also: 531 Main St New York NY 10044 Office: GE Capital Corp 1600 Summer St Stamford CT 06905

FRANK, DAVID ABRAHAM, finance executive; b. Bklyn., Nov. 9, 1947; s. Sam and Sylvia (Schonwetter) F.; m. Carolyn Anne Frank, Aug. 21, 1981; children: Jessica, Amy. BS, MIT, 1969; JD, Harvard U., 1973; MBA, Boston U., 1977. Tchr. Albany (N.Y.) Pub. Schs., 1969-70; cons. Mitre Corp., Bedford, Mass., 1973-74; counsel Honeywell, Waltham, Mass., 1974-76; planning analyst Primerica Corp., Greenwich, Mass., 1977; various titles Primerica Corp., Greenwich, 1978-84, sr. v.p., treas., 1985—; adv. bd. Nederland branch Algemene Bank, N.Y.C., 1987—; bd. dirs. Am. Capital Mgmt. and Research, Houston, Primerica Found., Greenwich. Mem. Soc. Internat. Treas. Office: Primerica Corp American Ln Greenwich CT 06830

FRANK, ROBERT ALLEN, advertising executive; b. Albany, N.Y., Sept. 26, 1932; s. Edward and Marian (Kostelanetz) F.; m. Cynthia Tull, Aug., 1984; children: David, Chelsea, Alison. B.A., Colby Coll., 1954; M.B.A., Amos Tuck Sch. Bus. Adminstrn., Dartmouth Coll., 1958. Cost control adminstr. ABC-TV, N.Y.C., 1958-59, corp. auditor CBS, Inc., N.Y.C., 1959-60, TV sales service account exec., 1961, account exec. radio network sales, 1962-69; exec. v.p., co-founder SFM Media Corp., N.Y.C., 1969—, pres. Media Service div., 1981. Radio-TV cons. Nat. Kidney Fund., 1974. Active radio TV for various polit. campaigns including Robert Kennedy for Senator, 1964, Richard Nixon for Pres., 1972, Ford for Pres., 1976, Bush for Pres., 1980, Reagan for Pres., 1980, Du Pont for Pres., 1988; mem. Leadership Council Nat Rep. Congl. Com., Rep. Nat. Com., 1980—, Pres.' Club, 1984—, Rep. Nat. Senatorial Com. Inner Circle, 1985—, Citizens for Rep. Pres. Com., 1984—; trustee Nat. Child Labor Com., Myasthenia Gravis Found., 1984—; Served to capt. USAF, 1954-56. Mem. Internat. Radio-TV Soc., Amos Tuck Alumni Assn. N.Y. (pres. 1976-77, dir. 1979—), Internat. Platform Assn., Pi Gamma Mu. Club: Dartmouth (N.Y.C.). Home: 35 Lounsbury Rd Ridgefield CT 06877 Office: SFM Media Corp 1180 Ave of Americas New York NY 10036

FRANK, ROBERT ALLEN, real estate securities analyst; b. Watertown, N.Y., Feb. 24, 1950; s. Robert Francis and Vera (Parinello) F.; m. Lucille Marie Prinzivalli, June 21, 1975; children: Laura, Stephen. BA, SUNY, Buffalo, 1972; MBA, U. Balt., 1975. Mgr. Merritt Savs. and Loan Assn., Balt., 1973-75; sr. analyst Alex Brown & Sons, Inc., Balt., 1975—. Mem. Real Estate Analyst Group (pres. 1987), Nat. Assn. Reits (gov. 1984-87), Balt. Securities Soc. Republican. Office: Alex Brown & Sons 135 E Baltimore St Baltimore MD 21204

FRANK, RONALD EDWARD, marketing educator; b. Chgo., Sept. 15, 1933; s. Raymond and Ethel (Lundquist) F.; m. Iris Donner, June 18, 1958; children: Linda, Lauren, Kimberly. B.S. in Bus. Adminstrn, Northwestern U., 1955, M.B.A., 1957; Ph.D., U. Chgo., 1960. Instr. bus. statistics Northwestern U., Evanston, Ill., 1956-57; asst. prof. bus. adminstrn. Harvard U., Boston, 1960-63, Stanford U., 1963-65; assoc. prof. mktg. Wharton Sch., U. Pa., 1965-68, prof., 1968-84, chmn. dept. mktg., 1971-74, vice dean, dir. research and Ph.D. programs, 1974-76, assoc. dean, 1981-83; dean, prof. mktg. Krannert Grad. Sch. Mgmt., Purdue U., 1984—; bd. dirs. Lafayette Life Ins. Co., The MAC Group, Home Hosp. Lafayette, Ind.; cons. to industry; mem. strategic issues com. Am. Assembly Collegiate Schs. of Bus., 1988—. Author: (with Massy and Kuehn) Quantitative Techniques in Marketing Analysis, 1962, (with Matthews, Buzzell and Levitt) Marketing: an Introductory Analysis, 1964, (with William Massy) Computer Programs for the Analysis of Consumer Panel Data, 1964, An Econometric Approach to a Marketing Decision Model, 1971, (with Paul Green) Manager's Guide to Marketing Research, 1967, Quantative Methods in Marketing, 1967, (with Massy and Lodahl) Purchasing Behavior and Personal Attributes, 1968, (with Massy and Wind) Market Segmentation, 1972, (with Marshall Greenberg) Audience Segmentation Analysis for Public Television Program Development, Evaluation and Promotion, 1976, The Public's Use of Television, 1980, Audiences for Public Television, 1982. Bd. dirs., fin. com. Home Hosp. of Lafayette, 1985—. Recipient pub. TV research grants John and Mary R. Markle Found., 1975-82. Mem. Am. Mktg. Assn. (dir. 1968-70, v.p. mktg. edn. 1972-73), Inst. Mgmt. Sci., Assn. Consumer Research, Am. Assn. Pub. Opinion Research. Home: 144 Creighton Rd West Lafayette IN 47906 Office: Purdue U Grad Sch Mgmt West Lafayette IN 47907

FRANK, RONALD WILLIAM, corporate finance lawyer, financier; b. Greensburg, Pa., Mar. 11, 1947; s. William John and Louise (Mautino) F.; m. Marsha Ann Kolesar, Aug. 30, 1969. BS in Chem. Engring., Carnegie-Mellon U., 1969; JD, Duke U., 1972. Bar: Pa. 1972. Ptnr. Buchanan Ingersoll Profl. Corp., Pitts., 1972—, also bd. dirs.; gen. ptnr. TD Energy Assocs., Pitts., 1983—; v.p., bd. dirs. Capital Opportunities, Pitts.; bd. dirs. Benshaw, Inc., Pitts., Buchanan Ingersoll (Europa) Gmbtt, Frankfurt, Fed. Republic Germany, 1987—. Contbr. articles to profl. jours. Chmn. Nat. Fund Raising Com., Carnegie- Mellon U., Pitts. 1983-88; mem. exec. com. Andrew Carnegie Soc., Pitts., 1983-89; mem. bd. visitors sch. law Duke U., Durham, N.C. Mem. ABA, Pa. Bar Assn. (coun., corp. sec. 1982-85), Allegheny County Bar Assn., Am. Immigration Lawyers Assn. Democrat. Presbyterian. Clubs: Duquesne, Shannopin Country (Pitts.). Home: 1660 Sturbridge Dr Sewickley PA 15143 office: Buchanan Ingersoll Profl Corp 5700 USX Tower Pittsburgh PA 15219

FRANK, RUBY MERINDA, employment agency executive; b. McClusky, N.D., June 28, 1920; d. John J. and Olise (Stromme) Hanson; m. Robert G. Frank, Jan. 14, 1944 (dec. 1973); children: Gary Frank, Craig. student Coll. Mankato, Minn., Aurora (Ill.) U., Aurora Coll. Exec. sec., office mgr. Nat. Container Corp., Chgo., 1943-50; owner, pres. Frank's Employment, Inc., St. Charles, Ill., 1957—; bd. dirs. St. Charles Savs. & Loan Assn.; corp. sec. Sta. WFXW-FM, Geneva, 1988—; chmn. Baker Hotel, 1989—; sec. bd. trustees Delnor Hosp., St. Charles, 1959-78, chmn. bd., 1985—. vocat. adviser Waubonsee Coll.; bd. dirs. Aurora U. Active mem. Women's aux.; vice chmn. Kane County (Ill.) Republican Com., 1968-77; pres. Women's Rep. Club, 1969-77; local bd. Am. Cancer Soc.; adv. council Dellora A. Norris Cultural Arts Center; bd. govs. Luth. Social Service Baker Hotel (sec. 1987, vice chmn. 1988); bd. dirs. St. Charles Hist. Soc., 1989; chmn. bd. Delnor Hosp., Baker Hotel, 1989; co-vice chmn. Delnor Community Health System; mem. exec. bd. Aurora Found., 1989—. Recipient Exec. of Yr. award Fox Valley PSI; Charlemagne award for community service, 1982; bd. dirs. Aurora Found. Mem. St. Charles C. of C. (pres., bd. dirs. 1976-82, ambassador), Kane-DuPage Personnel Assn. (v.p. 1971—), Nat., Ill. employment assns., Ill. Assn. Personnel Cons. (dir.), Women in Mgmt. Lutheran. Clubs: St. Charles Country; Execs. of Chgo., St. Charles Ambs. Club. Contbr. weekly broadcast Sta. WGSB, 1970-80, WFXW weekly interview program. Home: 534 Longmeadow Circle Saint Charles IL 60174 Office: Arcada Theater Bldg 12 S 1st Ave Saint Charles IL 60174

FRANK, STANLEY DONALD, publishing company executive; b. N.Y.C., June 30, 1932; s. Arthur and Jessie (Schwartz) F.; m. Sheila Rose, Dec, 25, 1958; children: Bradley Scott, Tracy Lynne. BS, CCNY, 1953, MS, 1956; EdD, Columbia U., 1961. Counselor N.Y.C. Pub. Schs., 1955-61; dir. pupil personnel services San Diego County Dept. Edn., 1959-61; Dir. mktg. Sci. Research Assocs. subsidiary IBM, Chgo., 1961-68; v.p. mktg. and ops. Sci. Research Assocs. subsidiary IBM, 1968-73; pres. Holt, Rinehart & Winston, Inc. subsidiary CBS, N.Y.C., 1974-77, CBS Ednl. Pub. Div., 1975-78; exec. v.p., chief operating officer CBS Pub. Group, 1978-80, pres., 1980-84; pres. Britannica Learning Corp., Chgo., 1985—; chmn. bd. dirs. Am. Learning Corp., 1985—; bd. dirs. Childcraft Ednl. Corp., Designware, Inc. Mem. Bd. Edn. Dist. 67, Niles, Ill., 1972-73; mem. council Rockefeller U. Served with AUS, 1953-55. Andrew Wellington Cordier fellow Columbia U. Sch. Internat. Affairs. Mem. Am. Psychol. Assn., Phi Delta Kappa.

FRANK, STEPHEN EDWARD, financial executive; b. Schnectady, Dec. 18, 1941; s. Edward J. Frank; m. Nancy K. Wilson, Jan. 8, 1966; children—Kerry M., Derek S. B.A. in Econs., Dartmouth Coll., 1965; M.B.A., U. Mich., 1972; A.M.P., Harvard U., 1982. With U.S. Steel Corp., Pitts., 1966-84, GTE Corp., 1984-88; exec. v.p., chief fin. officer TRW Inc., Cleve., 1988—. Office: TRW Inc 1900 Richmond Rd Cleveland OH 44124

FRANK, VINCENT ANTONIO, lawyer, medical facility executive; b. Rochester, N.Y., Sept. 27, 1952; s. Vincent Pasquale and Angela (Palma) F.; m. Jill Kathryn Linehan, Oct. 22, 1977; children: Kathryn Maura, Patrick Vincenzo. BA, U. Rochester, 1974; JD, Northwestern U., 1977. Bar: Pa. 1977, N.Y. 1979, Ill. 1980, Calif. 1982, U.S. Dist. Ct. (we. dist.) Pa. 1977, U.S. Dist. Ct. (we. dist.) N.Y. 1979, U.S. Dist. Ct. (no. dist.) Ill. 1980, U.S. Dist. Ct. (so. dist.) Calif. 1982. Atty. U.S. Steel Corp., Pitts., 1977-78; assoc. Harter, Secrest & Emery, Rochester, N.Y., 1978-79; ptnr. Johnson & Colmar, Chgo., 1979-81; v.p. Molecular Biosytems, Inc., San Diego, 1981-83, exec. v.p., 1983-85, pres., 1985—; bd. dirs. Assn. Corp. Growth, San Diego. Pres. bd. dirs. Beach Area Commn. Health Ctr., San Diego, 1983-88. Mem. ABA, Calif. Bar Assn., San Diego Bar Assn. Republican. Roman Catholic. Home: 10967 Riesling Dr San Diego CA 92131 Office: Molecular Biosystems Inc 10030 Barnes Canyon Rd San Diego CA 92126

FRANK, WILLIAM FIELDING, computer systems design executive, consultant; b. N.Y.C., Oct. 27, 1944; s. Karl Frederick and Margaret Ruth (Denisson) F.; m. Linda Carol Hainfield, Dec. 20, 1965 (div. 1972); children: Aaron, Tobin. BA, Middlebury Coll., 1966; MA, U. Chgo., 1969; PhD, U. Pa., 1976. Assoc. prof. Oreg. State U., Corvallis, 1969-79; mem. tech. staff Bell Labs., Whipping, N.J., 1979-81; pres. Integrated Info. Systems Assocs., Warren, Vt., 1982—; vis. scholar MIT, Cambridge, 1981-85; cons. Citibank, 1982—, Digital Equipment Corp., 1987—, AT&T, 1984, N.Y. Times, 1985, State of Calif., 1986—. Contbr. articles to profl. jours. Research grantee NSF, 1971, 77, NEH, 1976, 81. Mem. Assn. for Computing Machinery, Computer Soc. IEEE. Republican. Congregationalist. Home: Lincoln Gap Rd Box 146 Warren VT 05674 Office: Integrated Info Systems Assocs Box 1045 Peck Slip Sta New York NY 10072

FRANK, WILLIAM H., food products company executive; b. Chgo., Jan. 8, 1943; s. Joseph J. and Ann H. Frank; BS, U. Ill., 1964; MBA, DePaul U., Chgo., 1968; m. Joyce Ann Vondra, Aug. 28, 1966; children: Steven, Jill, Jaime. Dir. fin. services, then controller consumer products Internat. Paper Co., N.Y.C., 1972-78; v.p., controller AM Internat. Co., Los Angeles, 1978-79; v.p., controller then sr. v.p. fin. and planning United Brands Co., N.Y.C., 1979-84; sr. v.p. chief fin. officer, bd. dirs. Inspiration Resources Corp., N.Y.C., 1985; sr. v.p., chief fin. officer Castle & Cooke, Inc. (Dole Food Co.), Los Angeles, 1986—. Mem. Am. Inst. CPA's, Calif. Soc. CPA's, Ill. Soc. CPA's, Fin. Execs. Inst., N.Y. State Soc. CPA's. Office: Castle & Cooke Inc 10900 Wilshire Blvd Los Angeles CA 90024

FRANK, WILLIAM NELSON, financial marketing executive; b. Cin., June 3, 1953; s. Nelson A. and Marion A. (Kirbert) F. Student, Capital U., 1971-74; BS in Edn., Bowling Green State U., 1975; JD, U. Toledo, 1978; postgrad., U. Cin., 1980-82. Bar: Ohio, 1978; CPA, Ohio; cert. tchr., Ohio. Asst. city prosecutor City of Columbus, Ohio, 1978-80; asst. pub. defender Hamilton (Ohio) County, 1981-84; sole practice William N. Frank, Columbus, 1978-85; regional fin. mktg. mgr. A.L. Williams, Columbus, 1984—; auditor Phillip Willeke, Inc., Columbus, 1985-87; securities rep. First Am. Nat. Securities, Columbus, 1985—. Mem. Hamilton County Rep. Club, Cin., 1981—. Named to Hon. Order Ky. Cols. Commonwealth of Ky., 1978, One of Outstanding Young Men in Am., 1987. Mem. ABA, Cin. Bar Assn., Ohio Soc. CPA's, Delta Tau Upsilon, Phi Alpha Delta Law Fraternity. Republican. Mem. Ch. of Christ. Lodges: Masons (32 degree), Shriners, Order of DeMolay (Chevalier degree 1972). Home: 277 Mohawk Ave Westerville OH 43081 Office: 6089 Frantz Rd Ste 102 Dublin OH 43017

FRANKE, ARNOLD GENE, business management educator, arbitrator; b. Mount Olive, Ill., Nov. 3, 1932; s. Bernard and Hannah (Scheiter) F.; m. Roseanne Moruskey, June 19, 1954; children: Cara Lyn, Lisa Kay, Jenny Jo, Susan Jean. BS, Eastern Ill. U., 1955; MS, Purdue U., 1960; PhD, Sussex Coll., England, 1968. Cert. arbitrator. Analyst Shell Oil Co., Wood River, Ill., 1960-65; assoc. prof. bus. mgmt. So. Ill. U., Edwardsville, 1965-67, asst. v.p., 1968-77, dir. small bus. devel. ctr., 1984—; mem. small bus. investment com., Ill. S. Conf., Springfield, 1980—; rep. White House Small Bus. Conf., Washington, 1985-86. Pres. Ill. Ctr. for Autism, Fairview Hts., Ill., 1976-78; local chmn. United Way, 1984—; facilitator Spirit of St. Louis. Served to lt. USN, 1955-60. Mem. Am. Arbitration Assn. (arbitrator), Fed. Mediation and Conciliation Service (arbitrator), Atlantic Econ. Assn., Acad. of Mgmt. (assoc.), Am. Legion. Club: Sunset Hill Country (Edwardsville). Lodge: Moose. Home: 730 Saint Louis St Edwardsville IL 62025 Office: Southwestern Ill Small Bus Devel Ctr Box 1107 SIUE Edwardsville IL 62026

FRANKE, BRENT DOUGLAS, real estate executive; b. Milw., Feb. 13, 1949; s. Herbert Carl and Margaret A. (Custer) F.; m. Barbara Ellen Doerner, Mar 12, 1977 (div. Apr. 1983); m. Patricia Ann Bode, Dec. 7, 1985. Assoc. Equitable/Stefaniak Realty, Brookfield, Wis., 1985-89; agt. Nat. Guardian Life, Menomonee Falls, Wis., 1987-88; account exec. Elmbrook Fin., Brookfield, Wis., 1987-88; assoc. Prudential Life Ins. Co., 1989—; owner Poplar Creek Enterprises Inc., Hartland, Wis., 1989—, Poplar Creek Ltd., Hartland, 1989—. Served with USNR, 1970-76. Mem. Grad. Realtors Inst. Home: 2995 Nassau Dr Brookfield WI 53005 Office: Poplar Creek Enterprises 555 Industrial Dr Ste 1 Hartland WI 53029-2323

FRANKE, RICHARD JAMES, investment banker; b. Springfield, Ill., June 23, 1931; s. William George and Frances Marie (Brennan) F. BA, Yale U., 1953; MBA, Harvard U., 1957. With John Nuveen & Co., Chgo., 1957—, v.p., 1965-69, exec. v.p., 1969-74, chief adminstrv. officer, 1970-74, pres., chief exec. officer, 1974—, chmn., 1988—, also dir., 1969—; successor trustee Yale Corp., 1987—. Mem. investment com. Yale U.; mem. Yale Devel. Bd.; successor trustee, Yale Corp., 1987—; chmn. Ill. Humanities Council; vice chmn., trustee Chgo. Symphony Orch.; trustee U. Chgo.; bd. dirs. Lyric Opera Chgo., Chgo. Pub. Library Found. 1st lt. U.S. Army, 1953-55. Mem. Securities Industry Assn., Bond Club Chgo., Mid.-Am., The Attic, Carlton Club, Glenview (Ill.) Club, Garden of the Gods (Colorado Springs), Chgo. Club, Chi Phi. Office: John Nuveen & Co Inc 333 W Wacker Dr Chicago IL 60606

FRANKE, WILLIAM AUGUSTUS, corporate executive; b. Bryan, Tex., Apr. 15, 1937; s. Louis John and Frances (Hanna) F.; m. Carolyn D. Walker, July 16, 1977; children: Catherine Anne, Paige Estelle, Brian Hanna, David Parker, Rebecca Ann Walker. BA, Stanford U., 1959, LLB, 1961. Bar: Wash. 1961. Assoc. MacGillivray, Jones, Clark & Schiffner, Spokane, 1962-67, ptnr., 1967-70; v.p., sec., corp. counsel S.W. Forest Industries, Phoenix, 1970-72, sr. v.p., sec., 1972-73, exec. v.p., asst. chief exec. officer, 1973-75, pres., 1975—, chief oper. officer, 1977-78, chief exec. officer, 1978; chmn. bd. dirs. S.W. Forest Industries (merged with Stone Container Corp.), Phoenix, 1986—; pres., owner WAFCO Capital, Inc., Scottsdale, Ariz., 1987—; prin. Sterling Prodn. Co.; bd. dirs. Phelps Dodge Corp.; chmn. exec. com. Circle K Corp., Valley Nat. Bank. Mem. dean's council Stanford U. Law Sch., Ariz. State U. Sch. Bus. Served to capt. U.S. Army, 1961-62. Mem. ABA, Wash. Bar Assn., Spokane County Bar Assn., Young Pres.'s Orgn. Episcopalian. Clubs: Stanford, Paradise Valley Country, Phoenix Country, Mansion (Phoenix); Plaza. Home: 7701 N Saguaro Dr Paradise Valley AZ 85253 Office: 7373 N Scottsdale Rd Ste D-102 Scottsdale AZ 85253

FRANKEL, DARLEEN HILL, marketing executive; b. Elba, Ala., Dec. 3, 1953; d. Joseph Raymond and Dorothe Ann (Harper) H.; m. Bennett Edmond Frankel, Dec. 8, 1970 (div. Nov. 1974); 1 child, Alyssia. BA, U. So. Fla., Tampa. Cert. tchr. Fla. Corp. credit mgr. Progressive Lighting Corp., Tampa, Fla., 1978-81; mktg. coordinator Polk County Sch. System, Bartow, Fla., 1982-85; adminstrv. dir. Nat. Alliance Bus., Atlanta, 1985-86; project mgr. Heartland Pvt. Industry Council, Lakeland, Fla., 1986-87; S.E. program mgr. Henkels & McCoy, Inc., Blue Bell, Pa., 1987—. Mem. Suncoast Area Tchrs. Tng. Assn., Mid-Fla. Personnel Assn., Fla. State Burglar and Fire Alarm Assn., Ga. State Burglar and Fire Alarm Assn., Ala. State Burglar and Fire Alarm Assn., La. State Burglar and Fire Alarm Assn., Fla. State Cable TV Assn., Ga. State Cable TV Assn., Fla. State Telephone Assn., Ala. State Telephone Assn., Miss. State Telephone Assn., S.C. State Telephone Assn., Ga. State Telephone Assn., La. State Telephone Assn. Democrat. Baptist. Club: Tasters Guild. Home: 1920 E Edgewood Dr N10 Lakeland FL 33803 Office: Henkels & McCoy Inc 9416 E Buffalo Ave Tampa FL 33622

FRANKEL, ISRAEL, computer systems company executive; b. Chgo., Apr. 1, 1952; s. Nathan and Fern (Perlman) F.; m. Randi Jo Markowitz, Feb. 14, 1974 (div. Apr. 1976); m. Deborah Susan Koepke, Jan. 29, 1977; 1 child, Dov. BA, Northeastern Ill. U., Chgo., 1979; B of Jewish Studies, Spertus Coll., Chgo., 1981; postgrad., U. Chgo., 1982-84. Rep. sales Frankel Leather Co., Chgo., 1976-77; pres. Bus. Solutions, Inc., Evanston, Ill., 1977—. Assoc. editor: Shoe Service mag., 1984-86. Served with USMC, 1973-76. Mem. Interex. Jewish.

FRANKEL, MARTIN RICHARD, statistician, educator, consultant; b. Washington, June 16, 1943; s. Lester R. and Vera B. Frankel; m. Jean L. Kaiser, Mar. 24, 1970; children: Jennifer, Margaux. AB, U. N.C., 1965; MA, U. Mich., 1967, PhD, 1971. Asst. prof. stats. U. Chgo., 1971-73, assoc. prof., 1974-76; prof. stats. and computer info. systems Baruch Coll., CUNY, 1977—; tech. dir. Nat. Opinion Research Center, U. Chgo., 1972—; chnm. Quality Research Council, Advtg. Research Found., 1988—; cons. statis. methods and quality control, 1965—; mem. panel on occupational and health stats., com. on nat. stats. Nat. Rsch. Coun., NAS, 1985-87. Author: Inference from Survey Samples: An Empirical Investigation, 1971; (co-author) SEPP: Sampling Error Program Package, 1972, Total Survey Error: Applications to Improve Health Surveys, 1979; also articles; mem. editorial bd. Pub. Opinion Quar., Ency. Statis. Scis., Sociol. Research and Methods. Fellow Am. Statis. Assn. (chmn. census adv. com. 1981, chmn. sect. survey research methods 1975-76, editorial bd. jour.), Royal Statis. Soc., Internat. Statis. Inst.; mem. Am. Assn. Pub. Opinion Research (chmn. standards com.), Market Rsch. Coun. Home: 14 Patricia Ln Cos Cob CT 06807 Office: 17 Lexington Ave New York NY 10010

FRANKEL, STANLEY ARTHUR, public relations executive; b. Dayton, Ohio, Dec. 8, 1918; s. Mandel and Olive (Margolis) F.; m. Irene Baskin, Feb. 20, 1946; children—Stephen, Thomas, Nancy. B.S. with high honors, Northwestern U., 1940; student, Columbia U., 1940, U. Chgo., 1946-49.

Reporter Chgo. News Bur., 1940; publicist CBS, 1941; asst. to pres. Esquire and Coronet mags., N.Y.C., 1946-56; pres. Esquire Club, 1956-58; with McCall Corp., N.Y.C., 1958-61; asst. to pres. and pub. McCall Corp., 1958-61, v.p., 1959-61; v.p., dir. corporate devel. Ogden Corp., 1961—, cons., 1988—; cons. Manning, Selvage & Lee Pub. Relations Corp., N.Y.C., 1961—; dir. Michaelis Prodns., Inc., Rockwood Corp., Careful Office Service Inc., Western Calif. Canners Corp., Internat. Terminal Operating Co., Inc., Ogden Am. Corp.; adj. prof. Baruch Coll., CUNY, 1974—, Pace U., 1983—; bd. dirs. Baruch Coll. Ctr. of Mgmt., 1986—; bd. visitors PhD Program Baruch Coll., 1986—; guest lectr. N.Y. U., 1974; mem. Pres.'s Adv. Council on Peace Corps, 1965, Pres.'s Adv. Council on Youth Opportunity.; Mem. chancellor's panel State U. N.Y., 1970—; mem. N.Y. State Task Force on Higher Edn., 1974—; bd. mem., exec. com. Nat. Council Crime and Delinquency; bd. mem., vice chmn. Nat. Businessmen's Council; bd. dirs., officer Scarsdale Adult Sch. Author: History of 37th Division, 1947; contbr. articles to popular mags. Exec. bd. Writers for Stevenson, 1952, 56, for Kennedy, 1960, McGovern for Pres., 1972; pub. relations dir. Stevenson-for-Pres., 1956; chmn. Writers for Senator Humphrey Vice-Presdl. campaign, 1964; exec. bd. Businessmen for Humphrey-Muskie, 1968; chmn. N.Y. Writers for Humphrey-Muskie, 1968; mem. nat. exec. com. McGovern for Pres., 1972; vice chmn. N.Y. State McGovern for Pres. Com., 1972; bd. overseers Rutgers U., 1977—; chancellor's external relations com. City U. N.Y., 1977—; bd. dirs., v.p., mem. exec. com. YMCA of Greater N.Y.; founder Public Relations Bd., Inc., N.Y. and Chgo., Bedford Stuyvesant Project (T.R.Y.); mem. Vice President's Task Force on Youth Unemployment, 1979—. Served to maj. AUS, 1940-46. Decorated 2 Presdl. Citations, 3 Bronze Stars; recipient Peabody award for TV Series Adlai Stevenson Reports, 1961-63; Northwestern U. Alumni Merit award, 1964. Mem. Am. Mgmt. Assn. (chmn. pub. relations course 1971), Phi Beta Kappa, Phi Beta Kappa Assocs. (pres., trustee), Phi Beta Kappa Assn., Scarsdale-Westchester (pres. 1980—). Clubs: Northwestern U. of N.Y. (pres. 1964); Overseas Press (N.Y.C.); Scarsdale (N.Y.) Town (bd. govs.), Sunningdale; County. Home: 109 Brewster Rd Scarsdale NY 10583 Office: Ogden Corp 2 Pennsylvania Pla New York NY 10121

FRANKENHEIM, SAMUEL, lawyer; b. N.Y.C., Dec. 20, 1932; s. Samuel and Mary Emma (Ward) F.; m. Nina Barbara Mennerich, Sept. 2, 1960; children—Robert Mennerich, John Frederick. BA, Cornell U., 1954, LLB, 1959. Bar: N.Y. 1959, Mass. 1976. Law clk. N.Y. Ct. Appeals, 1959-61; assoc. Shearman & Sterling, attys., N.Y.C., 1961-68, ptnr., 1968-69; sr. v.p., dir. Damon Corp., Needham Heights, Mass., 1969-78; sr. v.p., gen. counsel mem. Office of Chmn. Gen. Cinema Corp., Chestnut Hill, Mass., 1979—; bd. dirs. The Neiman-Marcus Group Inc., Chestnut Hill, Mass. Trustee Newton-Wellesley Hosp., Newton, Mass., 1973-85, pres., 1980-82; bd. govs. Newell Health Corp., 1983—; overseer Wang Ctr. for Performing Arts, Boston, 1985-87, trustee, 1987—; trustee First Night, Inc., 1988. 1st lt. USAF, 1955-57. Mem. Assn. of Bar of City of N.Y., ABA, N.Y. State Bar Assn., Boston Bar Assn., Am. Corp. Counsel Assn., Am. Soc. Corp. Secs. Club: India House (N.Y.C.). Home: 115 Shornecliffe Rd Newton MA 02158 Office: Gen Cinema Corp 27 Boylston St Chestnut Hill MA 02167

FRANKFURT, STEPHEN O., advertising agency executive; b. Dec. 17, 1931. Grad., NYU; D of Fine Arts, Pratt Inst. Joined Young & Rubicam, 1955, art and copy supr., 1957, v.p., dir. spl. projects, 1960, sr. v.p., co-creative dir. of agy., 1964, creative dir., 1967-74, pres., from 1968; with Kenyon & Eckhardt (now Bozell, Jacobs, Kenyon & Eckhardt), N.Y.C., 1974—, now vice chmn., creative dir., until 1988. Former trustee Children's Theatre Workshop, Pratt Inst.; trustee Am. Film Inst., 1964-70, The Art Ctr.; mem. creative rev. com. Media-Advt. Partnership for Drug-Free Am. Recipient gold medal N.Y. Art Dirs. Club, 1958-59, 61-63, Spl. Gold medalfor outstanding TV advt., 1961, TV award Venice Film Festival, 1964, Achievement award N.Y. Arts Dirs. Club, 1968; named to Art. Dir. Hall of Fame, 1983. Office: Bozell Jacobs Kenyon & Eckhardt Inc 40 W 23rd St New York NY 10010 *

FRANKHOUSER, HOMER SHELDON, JR., engineering and construction company executive; b. Reading, Pa., Sept. 6, 1927; s. Homer Sheldon Sr. and Helen May (Geisewite) F.; m. Betty Carpenter, Sept. 2, 1972; children: Karl, Lorelei, Kurt, Michelle, Brandt. BCE, Lehigh U., 1952. Engr., then supt. Dravo Corp., Pitts., 1954-69; v.p. Dravo Ocean Structures, New Orleans, 1969-72; sr. project mgr. Brown & Root Inc., Houston, 1972-74, v.p., 1977-85; v.p. Brown & Root (U.K.) Ltd., London, 1974-77, dep. chmn., 1980—; sr. v.p. Brown & Root Internat. Inc., Houston, 1985—; bd. dirs. Highland Fabricators, Nigg Bay, Scotland, NPC Marine Contractors A.S., Oslo, Norway, Brown & Root Vickers Ltd., London; chmn. bd. Brown & Root Norge A.S., Oslo. Mem. Brown & Root Polit. Action Com., Houston. 1st lt. U.S. Army, 1952-54, Korea. Mem. ASCE, Inst. of Dirs. (London), Masons. Republican. Home: 32 Harley House, Marylebone Rd, London NW1 5HF, England Office: Brown & Root Inc PO Box 3 Houston TX 77001 Also: Brown & Root Internat Inc 4100 Clinton Dr Houston TX 77020

FRANKLAND, G. THOMAS, accountant, finance company executive; b. Evansville, Ind., Jan. 17, 1947; s. George Edward and Betty Ann (Singleton) F.; m. Candace Renee Canady, Nov. 23, 1974; children: Valerie Renee, Paige Nicole. BSBA, U. Fla., 1970. CPA. With Price Waterhouse Co., 1970—, Tampa, Fla., 1970-76, 79-86, N.Y.C., 1976-79; mng. dir. Price Waterhouse Co., Jacksonville, Fla., 1986—; chmn. steering com. U. Fla. Fisher Sch. Accountancy, 1982-88. Participant Leadership Fla., 1988. Mem. AICPA, Fla. Inst. CPAs, Jacksonville C. of C. (treas., exec. com., bd. govs. 1988). Office: Price Waterhouse 2500 Independent Sq Jacksonville FL 32202

FRANKLIN, BARBARA HACKMAN, management consultant, corporate director, educator; b. Lancaster, Pa., Mar. 19, 1940; d. Arthur A. and Mayme M. (Haller) Hackman; m. Wallace Barnes, Nov. 29, 1986. BA with distinction, Pa. State U., 1962; MBA, Harvard U., 1964; DS. (hon.), Bryant Coll., 1973. Mgr. environ. analysis Singer Co., N.Y.C., 1964-68; asst. v.p. Citibank, N.Y.C., 1969-71; mem. White House staff, Washington, 1971-73; commr., vice chmn. U.S. Consumer Product Safety Commn., Washington, 1973-79; sr. fellow, dir. govt. and bus. program Wharton Sch., U. Pa., Phila. and Washington, 1979—; pres., chief exec. officer Franklin Assocs., Washington, 1984—; adviser to comptroller gen. U.S., 1984—; bd. dirs. Aetna Life and Casualty Co., Dow Chem. Co., Westinghouse Electric Corp., Black & Decker Corp., Automatic Data Processing, Inc., Nordstrom, Inc. Trustee, Pa. State U.; mem. Pres.'s Adv. Com. Trade Negotiations, 1982-86; bd. visitors Def. Systems Mgmt. Coll.; services policy adv. Com. of U.S. Trade Representatives. Recipient Disting. Alumni award Pa. State U., 1972, Catalyst Award for Corp. Leadership, 1981, Excellence in Mgmt. award Simmons Coll., 1981, ann. award Am. Assn. Poison Control Ctrs., 1979, cert. appreciation, Am. Acad. Pediatrics, 1978, Award for Corp. Social Responsibility, CUNY, 1988. Fellow Nat. Assn. Corp. Dirs.; mem. Am. Inst. CPA's (bd. dirs.), Women's Forum Washington, Nat. Women's Econ. Alliance Found. (bd. govs., Dir.'s Choice award 1987), Nat. Women's Forum. Republican. Lutheran. Club: F Street (Washington); Econ. of N.Y. Contbr. articles to publs. Avocations: exercise, skiing, sailing. Office: U Pa Wharton Sch Bus 115 Vance Hall Philadelphia PA 19104

FRANKLIN, BENJAMIN DAVID, financial executive; b. Champaign, Ill., Sept. 8, 1957; s. Lewis Leonard and Dorothy Marie (Hegenbart) F.; m. Charlotte Kay Knott, Oct. 30, 1976; children: Benjamin David, Jonathan Lewis, Timothy Andrew, Joshua Paul. AS in Bus. Adminstrn., Parkland Jr. Coll., 1981; BS with high honors in Fin., U. Ill., 1989. Cert. fin. planner. Estate tax planner Franklin Agy., Tuscola, Ill., 1976-79; owner, fin. planner Franklin Fin. Svcs., Urbana, Ill., 1979-82, Lincoln Fin. Planning, Urbana, 1983-87; fin. planner Lincoln Tax Shelter and Fin. Planning, Prescott, Ariz., 1983; dir. fin., planning Ins. Risk Mgrs. Ltd., Savoy, Ill., 1987—. Mem. Internat. Assn. Fin. Planning, Inst. Cert. Fin. Planners. Republican. Office: Ins Risk Mgrs Ltd 1803 Woodfield Dr Savoy IL 61874

FRANKLIN, H. ALLEN, electric company executive; b. 1945. BEE, U. Ala., 1966. Various engring. positions Southern Co., Birmingham, Ala., 1970-79; exec. v.p. Southern Co., Birmingham, 1983—; asst. to exec. v.p. Ala. Power, 1979-81, sr. v.p., 1981-83. Office: So Co Svcs Inc 800 Shades Creek Pkwy Birmingham AL 35209

FRANKLIN, LARRY DANIEL, communications company executive; b. Commerce, Tex., July 16, 1942; s. John Asia and Annie Mae (Castle) F.; m. Charlotte Anne Walker, Aug. 18, 1962; children: Kelly Leigh, Kristi Lynn. BBA, East Tex. State U., 1965; MBA, Tex. Tech. U., 1966. Mem. audit staff Arthur Andersen Co., Dallas, 1966-67; controller, treas. Paris Milling Co., Tex., 1967-69; mem. audit staff Price Waterhouse Co., Dallas, 1969-71; asst. corp. dir. acctg. Harte-Hanks Communications Inc., San Antonio, 1971, corp. dir. fin. services, 1971-72, chief fin. officer, treas., 1972-74, v.p. fin., treas., 1974-75, v.p. fin., sec.-treas., 1975-78, sr. v.p., pres. newspaper ops., 1978-80, exec. v.p., now also chief operating officer, 1980—, dir.; dir. Interfirst Bank, San Antonio. Mem. mass communication adv. com. Tex. Tech U., Lubbock; mem. mass communications adv. com. St. Thomas Episcopal Ch., San Antonio; mem. adv. council Sch. Bus. Incarnate Word Coll.; mem. program ops. com. United Way; past mem. graphic arts adv. com. Rochester Inst. Tech.; bd. dirs. East Tex. State U. Found., Commerce. Mem. Am. Inst. C.P.A.s, Fin. Execs. Inst. (founding dir., past pres. South Tex. chpt.), Am. Newspaper Pubs. Assn. (newsprint com.), So. Newspaper Pubs. Assn. (bd. dirs.), Am. Press Inst. (bd. dirs.), Tex. Daily Newspaper Assn. Office: Harte-Hanks Communications Inc Merc Bank Bldg PO Box 269 San Antonio TX 78291 *

FRANKLIN, WILLIAM P., computer programmer; b. Oct. 8, 1953; s.Billy Wayne Franklina dn Kikue (Hanaoka) Johnston. Student, West Tex. State U., 1972-74; AS, Lakeland Coll., 1986. Data processing mgr. Customized Service Co., Inc., Amarillo, Tex., 1979-81; dist. acct. Browning Ferris, Inc., Amarillo, 1981-84; sr. programmer Fedders Air Conditioning USA Inc., Effingham, Ill., 1986—. Del. Tex. Rep. Conv., 1972. Episcopalian. Home: RR #2 Box 415-A Mattoon IL 61938 Office: Fedders Air Conditioning USA 415 Wabash Effingham IL 62401

FRANKLIN, WILLIAM WARREN, utility executive; b. Chgo., May 17, 1915; s. Howard B. and Natalie (Purdy) F.; m. Mary Ellen Gerard, Jan. 6, 1940; children: Barbara I. Franklin Biraski, Patricia E., Richard G. BEng, U. Calif., Berkeley, 1939. Dist. mgr. So. Calif. Water Co., Big Bear Lake, 1940-41; div. mgr. So. Calif. Water Co., Claremont, 1946-50, v.p. ops., 1950-60, pres., 1960-70, chmn. bd., 1970—. Lt. col. Signal Corps, AUS, 1944-45. Office: So Calif Water Co 3625 W 6th St Los Angeles CA 90020

FRANKOVIC, THOMAS LOUIS, small business owner, consultant; b. Pitts., June 21, 1935; s. Frank and Ann (Stampahar) F.; m. Patricia Robinson, July 16, 1960; children: Kathleen, Michelle, Kelley, Eric. BS, Duquesne U., 1957. Analyst U.S. Steel, Pitts., 1959-60; v.p. Md. Va. Milk, Balt., 1960-64; sr. v.p. Carling Nat. Breweries, Balt., 1964-78; chief operating officer The Tobacco Inst., Washington, 1978-81; owner, chief operating officer Azar Nut Co., El Paso, Tex., 1981-83; v.p. St. Joseph Hosp., Balt., 1984-88; pres., owner Mktg. Specialists, Balt., 1983—; cons. Better Bus. Bur., Balt., 1983—, York (Pa.) Imaging Ctr., 1985—, Loyola Coll. Balt., 1986-87; instr. Am. U., Washington, 1978-81. Pres. Ariz Super Corp., Phoenix, 1970-72, Ariz. Assn. Industries, Phoenix, 1972-73; active Towson Devel. Corp. Served to ist lt. U.S. Army, 1957-59. Mem. Advt. Club Balt. Home: 110 West St Towson MD 21204 Home: One Wyndam Ct Lutherville MD 21093

FRANTZ, JACK THOMAS, advertising executive; b. Indpls., Dec. 27, 1939; s. John Richard and Edna Louise (Bennett) F.; m. Georgene Mary Meyers, Aug. 18, 1962; 1 child, John Bennett. B.S. in Mktg, Ind. U., 1961. Media buyer Ted Bates & Co., N.Y.C., 1962-65; account exec. Papert, Koenig, Lois Inc., N.Y.C., 1965-69; account exec. Grey Advt. Inc., N.Y.C., 1969, account supr., 1969-72; sr. v.p. account mgmt. Grey Advt., Inc., 1979-83, exec. v.p., 1983—. Served with USAR, 1962. Recipient numerous advt. awards. Office: Grey Advt Inc 777 3rd Ave New York NY 10017

FRANTZEN, HENRY ARTHUR, investment company executive; b. Orange, N.J., Nov. 28, 1942; s. Henry and Natalie (Johnson) F.; m. Julie Louise Haverty, Aug. 14, 1965; children—John Blair, Jill Marie, Eric Patrick. Student, Hamline U., 1960-62; B.S.B.A., U. N.D., 1964. Sr. securities analyst Chem. Bank, 1968-71; adminstrv. asst. Coll. Retirement Equities Fund, 1971, asst. investment officer, 1972, investment officer, 1973, asst. v.p., 1974-76, 2d v.p., 1976, v.p., investment mgr., mem. investment com., 1976; sr. v.p., investment mgr. Tchrs. Ins. and Annuity of Am., N.Y.C., 1980-87, Coll. Retirement Equities Fund, N.Y.C., 1980-87; dir. SBC Portfolio Mgmt. Internat. Inc., Amsterdam, 1987—; chmn., chief investment officer Yamaichi Capital Mgmt. Corp., 1988—; chmn., pres. Yamaichi Funds Inc., 1988—; dir. Swiss Bank Corp., Internat. Portfolio Mgmt., Inc., CREF B.V., Amsterdam, SBC Internat. Portfolio Mgmt., Inc., N.Y.C. Served to lt. USNR, 1964-68. Fellow Fin. Analysts Fedn.; mem. N.Y. Soc. Security Analysts, Electro-Sci. Analysts Group, Computer Ind. Analysts Group, Sigma Nu, Alpha Kappa Psi. Republican. Episcopalian. Lodge: Lions. Home: 2 Fireside Dr Colts Neck NJ 07722 Office: 2 World Trade Ctr Ste 9828 New York NY 10048 *

FRANTZVE, JERRI LYN, industrial psychologist, management consultant; b. Huntington Beach, Calif., Sept. 9, 1942; d. Rolland and Marjorie Cleone (Ferrin) Weiland; m. Kenneth Wayne Himsel, Oct. 22, 1965 (div. Feb. 1975); 1 child, Deborrah Marie. Student, Purdue U., 1964-68; BA in Psychology and History, Marian Coll., 1969; MS in Organizational Psychology, George Williams Coll., 1976; PhD in Indsl. and Organizational Psychology, U. Ga., 1979. Case worker Marion County Welfare Dept., Indpls., 1970-71; mkgt. research analyst Quaker Oats Co., Barrington, Ill., 1971-75; mgmt. cons. J.L. Frantzve & Assocs., Marlboro, Mass., 1978—; asst. prof. sch. of mgmt. SUNY, Binghamton, N.Y., 1979-83; personnel research advisor Conoco, Inc., Ponca City, 1983-84; personnel research coordinator Conoco, Inc./DuPont, Ponca City, 1984; personnel research and acad. affairs coordinator Conoco, Inc., Ponca City, 1984-86, welfare benefits dir., 1986-88; cons. psychologist Allen Assocs., Northboro, Mass., 1988—; instrn. cons. USAF, Rome, N.Y., 1979-83; dir. Israel Oversears Research Program, Ginozar, Israel, 1982, Japanese Overseas Research Program, Tokyo, 1983. Author: Behaving in Organizations: Tales from the Trenches, 1983, Guide to Behavior in Organizations, 1983; contbr. articles to profl. jours. Bd. dirs. Broome County Alcoholism Clinic, Binghamton, N.Y., 1980-83, bd. dirs. Broome County Mental Health Clinic, Binghamton, 1981-83; del. Dem. Caucus, Okla., 1985. Mem. Am. Psychol. Assn. (com. on women in psychology 1986-88), Acad. of Mgmt. (placement dir. 1982), Am. Soc. for Personnel Adminstrn., Soc. for Personality and Social Psychology, Assn. for Women in Psychology, AAUW, Delta Sigma Pi. Home: 34-10 Briarwood Ln Marlborough MA 01752 Office: Allen Assocs Inc 82 W Main St Northborough MA 01532

FRANZ, DANIEL THOMAS, financial planner; b. Dayton, Ohio, Jan. 30, 1949; s. Albin Benedict and Monica Elizabeth (Moeller) F.; m. Sally Ann Stickley, Oct. 11, 1968; children: Amanda Marie, Stephanie Ann. BS, Bapt. Coll., 1971, postgrad., 1975; postgrad., S.C. State U., 1974. Cert. fin. aid adminstr., fin. planner. Coach, admissions officer Bapt. Coll., Charleston, S.C., 1971-72, dir. fin. aid, 1972-76; pvt. practice fin. planning Greenville, Ohio, 1977—; cons. S.C. Bapt. Conv., Columbia, 1974-76, U.S. Office Edn., Atlanta, 1974-76, Corning Glass Works, Greenville, 1984—, Franklin-Monroe High Sch., Pitsburg, Ohio, 1985—, United Telephone Co., Bellefontaine, Ohio, 1986—. Bd. dirs. Darke County Supts. Roundtable, Greenville, 1983—, Darke County Widows Assn., Greenville, 1984-86; mem., chmn. bd. dirs. S.C. Com. Higher Edn., Columbia, 1974-76, Darke County Mental Health Clinic, Greenville, 1984—; chmn. bd. dirs. Transfiguration Cath. Ch., West Milton, Ohio, 1978-82. Mem. Inst. Cert. Fin. Planners, Internat. Assn. Fin. Planners, Nat. Assn. Life Underwriters, Miami Valley Assn. Life Underwriters, S.C. Assn. Student Fin. Aid Adminstrs. (bd. dirs. 1971—), Darke County C. of C. (bd. dirs. 1986—). Republican. Roman Catholic. Lodge: Lions. Office: Fin Achievement Svcs 5140 Childrens Home Rd PO Box 177 Greenville OH 45331

FRANZ, DONALD EUGENE, JR., merchant banker; b. Mineral Wells, Tex., Oct. 12, 1944; s. Donald E. and Ruth M. (Eichelman) F.; m. Caroline Jones, Dec. 1, 1973. BA, Villanova U., 1966; MBA, Columbia U., 1969. Cert. N.Y. Stock Exchange supervisory analyst. Investment analyst Middendorf, Colgate & Co., N.Y.C., 1969-73, U.S. Trust Co., N.Y.C., 1969, G.H. Walker & Co., N.Y.C., 1973; dir. research Shelby Cullom Davis & Co., N.Y.C., 1973-74; asst. v.p. Smith Barney Harris Upham & Co. Inc., N.Y.C., 1974-76, v.p., 1977, 1st v.p., 1978-82, 83-84; sr. v.p., mng. dir. Smith Barney Harris Upham & Co. Inc., 1985-87; cons. Gulf United Corp., Jacksonville, Fla., 1982-83, Avemco Corp., Frederick, Md., 1987; mng. dir. Fin. Security Advisers, Inc., 1987—; pres. Gold Coast Air Taxi, Inc., 1981—; mem. internat. adv. bd. Am. Acad. Overseas Studies, 1986—; bd. dirs. Fin. Securities Fund. Pres. Com. of 100, Rutland, Vt., 1981—. Named to Investor All Star Team, Instl. Investor Mag., 1978-86. Fellow Assn. Ins. and Fin. Analysts (mem. exec. com. 1982). Republican. Roman Catholic. Clubs: N.Y. Athletic, Doubles Internat., Le Club, Knickerbocker (N.Y.C.); Coral Beach & Tennis (Paget, Bermuda); Maryland. Home: Limespring Farm 5530 E Glen Arm Rd Glen Arm MD 21057 also: Windermere Island, Eleutera Bahamas also: 235 W 56th St New York NY 10019 Office: 405 Park Ave Suite 1102 New York NY 10022

FRANZ, G. ANDREW, pharmaceutical company executive; b. Dennison, Ohio, Sept. 11, 1952; s. Eugene Joseph and Ethel Josephine (Lokie) F.; m. Rosemary L. Franz (div. June 1985). BA in Comprehensive Sci., Walsh Coll., 1974. Dir. lab. Bowman Pharms. Co., Canton, Ohio, 1974-76, prodn. coordinator, 1976-80, dir. quality assurance, 1980-82, plant mgr., 1982-84; v.p. JMI-Canton Pharms. Inc., Canton, 1984—. Mem. Network 730. Home: 915 Hillcrest Ave SW North Canton OH 44720 Office: JMI Pharms Inc 119 Schroyer Ave SW Canton OH 44702

FRANZ, LYDIA MILLICENT TRUC, real estate executive; b. Chgo., Jan. 11, 1924; d. Walter and Lydia (Kralovec) Truc; Mus.B., Ill. Wesleyan U., 1944; Mus.M., Northwestern U., 1949; m. Robert Franz, Aug. 27, 1952 (dec. Aug. 1983). Tchr. music pub. schs., Muskegon, Mich., 1947-48; mktg. research analyst Grant Advt. Agy., Chgo., 1949; mktg. research asst. Buchen Co., Chgo., 1949-52; asst. to dir. mktg. research Sherman Marquette Advt. Co., Chgo., 1952; asst. to pres., dir. media and research Andover Advt. Agy., 1952-55; salesman Boehmer & Hedlund, realty, Barrington, Ill., 1960-63; pres. Century-21-Country Squire, Inc., Barrington, 1963-87, sr. v.p. Koenig & Strey, Realtors, Barrington, 1987—; dir. Clyde Fed. Savs. & Loan Assn., 1984—. Recipient Disting. Alumni award Ill. Wesleyan U., 1988. Mem. adv. com. Office of Real Estate Research, U. Ill., Champaign. Served with WAC, 1944-46. Mem. Women in Real Estate (pres. 1966-67), Barrington Bd. Realtors (pres. 1968-69), Ill. Assn. Realtors (dir. 1972-75, 81—, gov. Realtor's Inst. of Ill. 1972-78, exec. com. 1977—, pres. 1984, Realtor of Yr. 1988), Nat. Assn. Realtors (dir. 1982—), Realtors Nat. Mktg. Inst. (bd. govs. 1979, regional gov. 1980), Barrington C. of C. (pres. 1974, dir. 1972-75, 84—, Merit award 1985), Barrington Bus. and Profl. Women's Club, Mensa, Sigma Alpha Iota. Republican. Home: 408 E Hillside Ave Barrington IL 60010 Office: 209 Park Ave Barrington IL 60010

FRANZEN, PETER, banker, business economist; b. Ludwigslust, Mecklenburg, Germany, Apr. 2, 1943; s. Peter and Johanna (Koeth) F.; m. Renate Reintke, July 23, 1968; children: Jutta, Axel. Sparkassen-Betriebswirt (hon.), Sparkassenschule, Cologne, Fed. Republic Germany, 1970. Banker, bank mgr. Commerzbank A.G., Remscheid, Fed. Republic Germany, 1960-63, Deutsche Bank A.G., Remscheid, 1965, Stadtsparkasse Hueckeswagen, Fed. Republic Germany, 1965-69, Kreissparkasse, Cologne, 1969-81; pres. Franzen & Winkler Gmbh, Cologne, 1981-84, Franzen Vermoegensverwaltung Gmbh, Hueckeswagen, Fed. Republic Germany, 1984—; pres. Classic Ventures, Inc., San Mateo, Calif., 1982—, Bavarian Tech., Inc., Montclair, N.J., 1985-89, Baba Enterprises, Inc., Montclair, 1986-89; chmn. W.I.N.E., Inc., Montclair, 1986-88, Covasorb, Inc., Montclair, 1986—; dir. Steiner Optics Internat., Inc., Nutley, N.J., 1989—. Home: Gardelenberg 21, D-5609 Hueckeswagen Federal Republic of Germany Office: Steiner Optics Internat Inc 536 Kingsland St Nutley NJ 07110

FRANZKOWSKI, RAINER, association executive; b. Berlin, Apr. 8, 1935; s. Karl and Johanna (Robbert) R.; m. Hanna Maria Doring, Jan. 11, 1963; children—Johannes, Cornelia. Diplom-Ingenieur, Tech. U. Berlin, 1966. Factory engring. mgr. electron tube div. AEG-Telefunken, Berlin, 1966-70, Ulm, Fed. Republic Germany, 1970-79; factory engring. mgr. Videocolor GMBH, color picture tube prodn., Ulm, 1979-80; edn. and tng. mgr. German Soc. Quality, Frankfurt, 1980—; lectr. quality tech., 1977—; chmn. com. statis. methods European Orgn. for Quality Control, 1983—; mem. tech. com. statis. methods Internat. Orgn. Standardization and Deutsches Instituta Normung, 1980—. Mem. Deutsche Physikalische Gesellschaft, Verein Deutscher Ingenieure, Deutsche Statistische Gesellschaft, European Orgn. Quality Control, Deutsche Gesellschaft Qualitat, Am. Soc. Quality Control, Am. Statis. Assn. Home: 18 An Der Eiskaut, D 6390 Usingen Federal Republic Germany Office: 95 Kurhessenstrasse, D-6000 Frankfurt-Main Federal Republic of Germany

FRARY, ELIZABETH LOEITA, retired banker; b. Tunbridge, Vt., July 24, 1926; d. Lesle E. Maxfield and Marguriete B. (Dodge) Richardson; m. Adrian W. Frary Jr., July 24, 1944; children: Ann Marie, Richard A., David L., Walter J. Grad. high sch., South Royalton, Vt. Teller First Twin State Bank, White River Junction, Vt., 1965-67, clk., 1977-80, officer, 1980-85, mgr., officer, 1985-88. Mem. Emblem Club, Snowmobile Club, Odd Fellows (mem. Rebekahs). Republican. Congregationalist. Home: RFD #2 Box 84 South Royalton VT 05068

FRARY, RICHARD SPENCER, international consulting company executive; b. Greybull, Wyo., Jan. 29, 1924; s. Frederick Spencer and Margaret Lee Ellen (Chalfant) F.; m. Eros Hunsaker, July 19, 1946; children: Richard Jr., Lorraine, John, James. BSEE, U. Colo., 1949; postgrad., N.Mex. A&M U., 1954-55, So. Meth. U., 1956-57. Mgr. engring. RCA, Cherry Hill, N.J., 1952-62; v.p. Ultronic Systems Corp., Pennsauken, N.J., 1962-67; v.p. govt. systems Sperry Univac, various locations, 1967-80; v.p. research and engring. A.B. Dick Co., Niles, Ill., 1980-83; with Arthur D. Little Inc., Washington, 1983—. Served with USMC, 1943-45, 50-51. Mem. IEEE, Assn. Computing Machinery, Am. Fedn. Info. Processing Societies, Am. Soc. for Info. Sci. Republican. Mormon. Home: 3038 Meeting St Falls Church VA 22044 Office: Arthur D Little Inc 955 L'Enfant Plaza SW Suite 4200 Washington DC 20024

FRASER, DAVID CHARLES, investment banker; b. Phila., Aug. 2, 1942; s. Charles Walter and Althea Mary (Mathis) F.; m. Carole Ann Geren, June 16, 1962; children—Mark Samuel, Steven David, Tanya, Adam Scott, Luke Wesley. B.A., Taylor U., 1965. Pres. Am. Intertel Corp., Mt. Holly, N.J., 1969-74, Figure World, Inc., Moorestown, N.J., 1978-80; corp. fin. dir. Herzog, Heine, Geduld, Inc., N.Y.C., 1982-84; sr. v.p. Lord Securities Corp., N.Y.C., 1984—, dir. 28 fin. cos. managed by Lord Securities, pres., chief exec. officer Lord Capital Corp.; fin. and mgmt. cons. Mem. Taylor U. Alumni Assn. (pres. 1972-74). Republican. Baptist. Avocations: tennis; music. Home: 32 Partridge Way Colts Neck NJ 07722 Office: Lord Securities Corp 45 Broadway New York NY 10006

FRASER, JACK MALCOLM, diversified business executive; b. London, May 20, 1933; s. Joseph Percival and Anna Maud (Taylor) F.; m. Patricia Ann Kingston Garraway, Dec. 22, 1956; children—Noel Alistair Kingston, Melissa Jane Kingston. B.A. with honours, London U., 1954. Mng. dir. Crane Ltd., London, 1970-85; exec. v.p. Crane Co., N.Y.C., 1985—. Served as 2d lt. Royal Arty., 1954-56. Mem. Ch. of England. Office: Crane Co 757 3rd Ave New York NY 10017 *

FRASER, JOHN FOSTER, management company executive; b. Saskatoon, Sask., Sept. 19, 1930; s. John Black and Florence May (Foster) F.; m. Valerie Georgina Ryder, June 21, 1952; children: John Foster Jr., Lisa Ann. B.Commerce, U. Sask., 1952. Pres. Empire Freightways Ltd., Saskatoon, Sask., 1953-62, Empire Oil Ltd., Saskatoon, 1960-62, Hanford Drewitt Ltd., Winnipeg, 1962-68, Norcom Homes Ltd., Mississauga, Ont., 1969-78; pres., chief exec. officer Fed. Industries Ltd., Winnipeg, 1978—, also bd. dirs.; bd. dirs. Air Canada, Bank of Montreal, Investors Group, Inc., Inter-City Gas Corp., Thomson Newspapers, Can. Devel. Investment Corp.; vice chmn. bd. dirs. Bus. Council Nat. Issues; chmn. bd. White Pass and Yukon Corp., Ltd. Chmn. bd. Council for Bus. and Arts in Can.; bd. dirs., founding chmn. Assocs. Faculty of Mgmt. Studies U. Man.; past pres. Man. Theatre Centre; past bd. govs. St. John's Ravenscourt Sch., Winnipeg; mem. cultural rev. policy com. Province of Man., 1979. Recipient Peter D. Curry award U. Man., 1984, Outstanding Bus. Achievement award as Citizen of Yr. Man. C. of C., 1984. Mem. Am. Mgmt. Assn. (pres.'s assn.). Progressive Conservative. Presbyterian. Clubs: Manitoba, Royal Lake of the Woods Yacht, York, Toronto. Home: 900-237 Wellington Crescent,

Winnipeg, MB Canada R3M 0A1 Office: Fed Industries Ltd, 1 Lombard Pl, Winnipeg, MB Canada R3B OX3

FRASER, KENNETH WILLIAM, JR., textile company executive; b. N.Y.C., Oct. 28, 1937; s. Kenneth William and Emma Kathryn (Ruch) F.; m. Susan Towne Mattison, June 20, 1959; children: John William, Elisabeth Grenell, Charles Angus, Andrea Mary. BME, Cornell U., 1960; MBA in Acctg., NYU, 1968. Sales engr. Ingersoll-Rand, Inc., Boston, 1960-63; asst. treas. John P. Maguire & Co., Inc., N.Y.C., 1963-67; treas. John P. Maguire & Co., Inc., 1967-70; fin. v.p., treas. Fieldcrest Cannon, Inc., Eden, N.C., 1970-77, sr. v.p. fin., 1977—; bd. dirs. Gate City Fed. Savs. and Loan, Greensboro, N.C. Treas. Eden YMCA, 1973-74, pres., 1975; treas. Morehead Meml. Hosp., Eden, 1971-75, v.p., 1978-79, pres., 1980, trustee. Mem. Fin. Execs. Inst. (pres. 1976). Methodist. Club: Union League (N.Y.C.). Lodge: Rotary. Office: Fieldcrest Cannon Inc 326 E Stadium Dr Eden NC 27288

FRAWLEY, ROBERT DONALD, lawyer; b. Newark, Sept. 15, 1947; s. William John and Grace (Moreau) F.; m. Martha S. Van Liere, Aug. 7, 1976; children: Meghan Martha, William Garrett. BA, Lehigh U., 1969; JD, Georgetown U., 1973. Bar: Va. 1973, N.J. 1983. Assoc. William D. Stokes, Arlington, Va., 1973-74; staff atty. Pharm. Mfrs. Assn., Washington, 1974-78; sr. atty. Beecham, Inc., Clifton, N.J., 1978-81; gen. atty. Carter, Wallace, Inc., Cranbury, N.J., 1981-83; v.p., gen. counsel Biosearch Med. Products, Inc., Somerville, N.J., 1983-85; ptnr. Stark & Stark P.C., Princeton, N.J., 1985—; sec. HHydromer, Inc., Whitehouse, N.J., 1985—; bd. dirs., asst. sec. Digital Solutions, Inc., East Brunswick, N.J., 1987—; bd. dirs., sec. HiTc Superconco, Inc., Lambertville, N.J., 1987—. Co-author: (jour.) Bankrupt Firms Can Be Attractive Acquisitions, 1989, Restrictive Employment Covenants in New Jersey, 1989; contbr. articles to profl. publs. Bd. dirs. Jr. Achievement, Mercer County, N.J., 1989—. Eckley B. Coxe scholar Lehigh U., 1965-69. Mem. ABA, N.J. Bar Assn., Am. Soc. Corp. Secs., Food & Drug Law Inst., Mid Atlantic Venture Capital Assn., Pi Sigma Alpha. Republican. Club: Nassau (Princeton). Office: Stark & Stark PC 993 Lenox Dr CN5315 Princeton NJ 08540

FRAY, LIONEL LOUIS, management consultant; b. Paris, Jan. 17, 1935; came to U.S., 1942; s. Maurice and Esther Fray; m. Joanne Caroline Liberman, June 30, 1963; children: Sharon June, Elizabeth Ann. BS, MIT, 1957, MS, 1958; MBA, Harvard U., 1962. Co-founder U.S. Sonics, Inc., Cambridge, Mass., 1957-58; with Mitre Corp., Bedford, Mass., 1958-60, Mgmt. Systems Corp., 1962-64; v.p. Harbridge House, Boston, 1964-73, TBS Capital Corp., Lexington, Mass., 1973-86, Temple, Barker & Sloane, Lexington, Mass., 1973-86; pres. Lionel L. Fray Assocs., Inc., Lexington, Mass., 1986—. Author: Handbook of Strategic Management, 1985; contbr. articles to profl. jours. Mem. Planning Forum, Inst. Mgmt. Cons. Club: Harvard. Home: 2361-A Massachusetts Ave Lexington MA 02173 Office: 1620 Massachusetts Ave Lexington MA 02173

FRAZEE, ELIZABETH LYNN, company official; b. Princeton, N.J., Sept. 12, 1957; d. John Harold and Constance Jean (Clinton) F.; m. Olaf Paleos (div.). BSBA, Drexel U., 1984. Statis. asst. A.J. Wood Rsch. Co., Phila., 1980; rsch. tech. Response Analysis Corp., Princeton, 1981, rsch. asst., 1981-82, sr. rsch. asst., 1982-83, rsch. assoc., 1983-84; project dir. Matrix, Inc., Princeton, 1984-85, sr. account mgr., 1985—. Mem. Assn. Pub. Opinion Rsch. (treas. Cen. N.J. chpt.), Nature Conservancy, Nat. Wildlife Fedn. Home: 56 Abernethy Dr Trenton NJ 08618 Office: Matrix Inc 3490 US Rt 1 Bldg 11 Princeton NJ 08540

FRAZER, MICHAEL ONEN, lawyer; b. Battle Creek, Mich., Mar. 14, 1938; s. David H. Jr. and Alice (Onen) F.; m. Floice Ellis, Apr. 5, 1962; children—Sarah, Jonathan, Christopher, Susan. B.A., Williams Coll., 1961; J.D., U. Mich., 1964. Bar: Mich. 1964. Sole practice, Battle Creek, Mich., 1966—; dir. Southeastern Mich. Gas Enterprises, Inc. Bd. dirs. Battle Creek Civic Art Ctr., 1983—. Mem. Mich. Bar Assn., Calhoun County Bar Assn. Republican. Episcopalian. Club: Athelstan. Office: 705 Mich Nat Bank Bldg Battle Creek MI 49017

FRAZER, ROBERT E., utility company executive; b. 1928. BS, Cen. Mich. U., 1950. Acct. Consumer Power Co., 1950-52; audit mgr. Anderson Authur & Co., 1952-61; v.p. fin. Duke Power Co., 1961-75; with Dayton (Ohio) Power & Light Co., 1975—, pres., 1976-82, chief operating officer, 1978-82, chief exec. officer, 1982-84, formerly chmn. bd. dirs. Office: Dayton Power & Light Co PO Box 1247 Dayton OH 45401 *

FRAZIER, ALAN D., biotechnology research executive; b. Seattle, Aug. 26, 1951; s. L. Thomas and E. Kendall (Warner) F.; m. Mary Devins, May 1, 1982. BA in Econs., U. Wash., 1975. Controller Pacific Trailways, Bend, Oreg., 1973-75; acct. Arthur Young and Co., Seattle, 1975-78, prin., 1980-83; ptnr. Alan Frazier and Co., Seattle, 1978-80; treas. Immunex Corp., Seattle, 1983-84, v.p. fin., chief fin. officer, 1984-88, exec. v.p., 1988—. Mem. Fin. Exec. Inst. (bd. dirs. Seattle chpt. 1986—), Indsl. Biotech. Assn. (chmn. ins. com. 1988—), Am. Inst. CPA's, Wash. State Soc. CPA's. Republican. Roman Catholic. Clubs: Wash. Athletic, Mercer Island Country (Seattle). Office: Immunex Corp 51 University St Seattle WA 98101

FRAZIER, DOUGLAS BYRON, health care consultant; b. Danville, Va., Jan. 18, 1957; s. Calvin Luther and Frances Ann (Benbow) F.; m. Linda Camille Kane, Apr. 25, 1981. BS in Fin. with honors, U. Fla., 1979. Ops. analyst Whittaker Gen. Med., Miami, Fla., 1980, div. mgr., 1980-85; health care cons. Abbott Labs., Chgo., 1985-86, sr. health care cons., 1986—. Mem. Abbott Labs. Better Govt. Fund. Republican. Office: Abbott Labs Dept 99D Bldg AP6C Abbott Park IL 60064

FRAZIER, J(OHN) PHILLIP, manufacturing company executive; b. Beech Grove, Ind., Mar. 2, 1939; s. Stanley C. and Dorothy E. Frazier; m. Carole Gilbert, Aug. 15, 1964; children: Gregory and Bradley (twins), Natalie. BS, Butler U., 1965; MBA, Harvard U., 1969. Acct. Wolf & Co., Indpls., 1962-65; acct. Cummins Engine Co., Inc., Columbus, Ind., 1965-73, controller, 1970-73; pres., chief exec. officer Hyster Co., Portland, Oreg., 1973—, also bd. dirs.; bd. dirs. Guy F. Atkinson Co. Calif. Bd. dirs. United Way-Columbia Willamette. Served with USAR, 1957-61. Mem. Harvard U. Bus. Sch. Assn. (past pres., chmn. Oreg. chpt), Portland Golf Club, Arlington Club. Republican. Presbyterian. Home: 722 NW Albemarle Terr Portland OR 97210 Office: Hyster Co PO Box 2902 2701 NW Vaughn Ste 900 Portland OR 97210

FRAZIER, OWSLEY B., beverage company executive; b. 1935; married. BS, U. Louisville, 1959, JD, MBA. With Brown-Forman Corp., Louisville, 1955—, v.p., sec., 1968-71, corp. sr. v.p., sec., 1971-83, vice-chmn., 1983—, also bd. dirs.; chmn., chief exec. officer Bettners Inc. Office: Brown-Forman Inc 850 Dixie Hwy Louisville KY 40210 *

FRAZIER, WALTER RONALD, real estate investment company executive; b. Dallas, Mar. 3, 1939; s. Walter and Gracie Neydene (Bowers) F.; m. Bertina Jan Simpson, May 10, 1963; children—Ronald Blake, Stephen Bertram. B.S. in Civil Engring., Tex. A&M U., 1962, B.S. in Archtl. Constrn., 1962. Tech. dir. Marble Inst., Washington, 1965-68; dir. mktg. Yeonas Co., Vienna, Va., 1969-72; pres. McCarthy Co., Anaheim, Calif., 1972-76, The Frazier Group, Annandale, Va., 1977-79; chmn. Equity Programs Investment Corp., Falls Church, Va., 1980-85; pres., dir. Community Constrn. Co., Falls Church, 1982-85; pres. Palestrina Corp., Falls Church, 1986-89, Sycamore Homes, Inc., 1989—; bd. dirs. Annandale Jaycees, 1967-69, Annandale Nat. Little League, 1983-85. Served to 1st lt. U.S. Army, 1963-65. Named to Outstanding Young Men Am., U.S. Jaycees, 1973. Republican. Methodist. Avocations: golf; boating. Home: 4203 Elizabeth Ln Annandale VA 22003 Office: Sycamore Homes Inc 3302 Old Bridge Rd Woodbridge VA 22192

FRECH, ROBERT ADOLPH, banker; b. Chgo., July 24, 1924; s. Robert L.D. and Adolphina (Umbricht) F.; Anna Mae Behrens, June 25, 1949; children: Roger W., William R. BS in Mgmt. with honors, U. Ill., 1949. Mgr. charge accounts Marshall Field & Co., Chgo., 1949-80; chmn. bd. Carpentersville (Ill.) Savs. Bank, 1980-83, First Comml. Bank of Rolling Meadows, Ill., 1983—; pres. Marshall Field & Co. Employee's Credit Union, 1963-64; v.p., bd. dirs. McIntosh Ltd. , Crystal Lake, Ill., 1986; bd. dirs. McIntosh Ltd.-Leisure, Crystal Lake, Ill., 1986; bd. dirs. Plum Grove Ltd., Woodstock, Ill. Bd. govs. Northwest Community Health Services Found., Arlington Heights, Ill., past bd. dirs. Lutheran Gen. Hosp. Men's Assn., Park Ridge, Ill., Dir. 1973-76; mem. Econ. Devel. Commn. Rolling Meadows, Ill. Mem. Ill. Bankers Assn. (chmn., bank dirs. commn. 1987), Midwest Assn. of Credit Unions (past mem. exec. com., past bd. dirs.), Rolling Meadows C. of C. (bd. dirs. 1983-88), Econ. Devel. Council of Chgo., Kappa Delta Rho. Clubs: Chgo. Farmers (bd. dirs. 1981-83); Turnberry Country (Lakewood, Ill.). Home: 1479 Shire Circle Inverness IL 60067 Office: First Comml Bank 2801 Algonquin Rd Rolling Meadows IL 60008

FRECON, ALAIN JEAN-CHRISTIAN, lawyer; b. Casablanca, Morocco, Jan. 27, 1946; came to U.S. 1974; Diploma, Centre Notarial de Formation et D'information Professionnelle and Faculté de Droit-Paris II, 1969; Lic. en Droit, Faculté de Droit-Paris II, 1974; LLM in Internat. Bus., Stanford U., 1976; JD, William Mitchell Coll. Law, 1982. Bar: France 1968, Minn. 1982. Assoc. Ader, Rochelois & Roy, Paris, 1969-74; of counsel Jones, Bell, Simpson, & Abbott, L.A., 1976-81; assoc. Dorsey and Whitney, Mpls., 1981-85; ptnr., chmn. internat. bus. practice Popham, Haik, Schnobrich & Kaufman Ltd., 1985—; seminar promoter and guest speaker on internat. bus. Author: (handbooks) Negotiation of International Contracts, 1984, Legal Issue of Doing Business in India, 1985, Practical Issues of Doing Business in the United States, 1986, Legal Issues of Doing Business in France, 1986, Practical Considerations in Going International, 1988. Reader Nat. Assn. Blind, Paris, 1973; internat. press rels. com. Valery Giscard D'Estaing campaign, Paris, 1974; vol. Stanford, Calif. Legal Aid Soc., 1975; chmn. Minn. French Festival, Mpls., 1985-86; appointed to bd. dirs. Minn. Export Fin. Authority by Gov. Perpich, 1987—; decreed Conseiller du Commerce Exterieur to French Govt., 1988. Mem. ABA, Internat. Bar Assn., Fed. Bar Assn., Minn. Bar Assn., Hennepin Bar Assn., Am. Arbitration Assn., French Am. C. of C. (bd. dirs. 1984—, pres. 1987—), Mpls. Club, Rotary. Office: Popham Haik Schnobrich & Kaufman Ltd 3300 Piper Jaffray Tower Minneapolis MN 55402

FREDERICK, CYNDIE LOUISE, banker; b. McAllen, Tex., Mar. 14, 1961; d. John Robert and Doris Ann (Nauer) Bacak; m. David Charles Frederick, July 24, 1981; children: Ryan David, Brandon Robert. Student, Austin Community Coll., 1985. Service mgr. H.E. Butt Grocery, Austin, Tex., 1977-82; br. mgr. Tex. Fed. Savs., Austin, 1982-83, human resources specialist, 1983-85; br. mgr. Bright Banc Savs. Assn., Austin, 1985-86, retail banking officer, 1986-87, asst. v.p., 1988—. Vol. March of Dimes, Austin, 1983—, United Way, 1985, Tex. Spl. Olympics, 1988, Make-A-Wish Found., 1988—; mem. Texans Civil Justice, 1987—. Mem. Nat. Assn. Female Execs., Eanes Bus. & Profl. Assn., Inst. Fin. Edn. (bd. dirs.), Austin Bd. of Realtors (affiliate), Cedar Park (Tex.) C. of C. Republican. Roman Catholic. Home: 10134 Canal Dr Whitmore Lake MI 48189 Office: Bright Banc Savs Assn 13928 Research Blvd Austin TX 78750

FREDERICK, FRANK, investment banker; b. Salt Lake City, May 31, 1932; s. Simon and Suzanne (Seller) F.; m. Mary C. Tanner, Oct. 15, 1988; children by previous marriage: Jenny Ann, Laura Kim. BA, Yale U., 1954; MBA, Stanford U., 1958. Securities analyst Smith Barney & Co., N.Y.C., 1958-69; ptnr. Lehman Bros., N.Y.C., 1969-84; mng. dir. Shearson Lehman Hutton, N.Y.C., 1984—; bd. dirs. Telerate, Inc., N.Y.C., Molecular Design, Ltd., San Leandro, Calif., R.P. Scherer, Troy, Mich., Automated Call Processing, San Francisco. Chmn. bd. Nat. Genetics Found. With U.S. Army, 1954-56. Mem. N.Y. Soc. Security Analysts. Republican. Jewish. Home: 1070 Park Ave New York NY 10128 Office: Shearson Lehman Hutton Am Express Tower New York NY 10285-0017

FREDERICK, GEORGE FRANCIS, manufacturing executive; b. Cleve., Jan. 24, 1937; s. George Henry and Margaret Mary (Gibson) F.; m. Mary Jane Masielli, Oct. 20, 1956; children: Denise Marie, George Charles, Donna Marie, Karl Stephen. Assoc. in Machine Design, Cleve. Engring. Inst., 1957; BS, SUNY, Albany, 1977. Cert. mfg. engr. Supr. mfg. engring. Sq. D Co., Cleve., 1956-66; supr. standards engring. TRW, Cleve., 1966-69; mgr. engring. Rossgear div. TRW, Ind. and Tenn., 1969-80; ops. mgr. Control Concepts div. TRW, Newton, Pa., 1980-82; gen. mgr. Falcon Products, Greeneville, Tenn., 1982-84; v.p. ops. Lockley Mfg. Co., Inc., New Castle, Pa., 1984—. Mem. exec. bd. New Castle Area Labor Mgmt. Com., 1987-88; dist. chmn. Boy Scouts Am., Greeneville, 1982-83, 1987-88; bd. dirs. United Way, 1981. Mem. Inst. Indsl. Engrs. (sr. mem. exec. bd. 1972-74). Republican. Roman Catholic. Club: Lawrence. Lodges: KC, Lions (exec. bd. local chpt.). Home: 22 W Oakwood Way New Castle PA 16105 Office: Lockley Mfg Co Inc 310 Grove St New Castle PA 16103

FREDERICK, NANCY LORELLE, real estate broker; b. Cleve., Apr. 1, 1942; d. William Houston Ackerman and Margaret Jorder (Ainslie) Post; m. Nicholas Frederick, June 26, 1965; children: Jacqueline, Barbara, Nicholas. BS in Elem. Edn., Taylor U., 1964; postgrad., Glassboro State U. Lic. real estate salesperson, N.J., real estate broker. Tchr. Kingstone Elem. Sch., Cherry Hill, N.J., 1964-68; real estate salesperson Sterling Assocs., Somerdale, N.J., 1974-75, Bob Pritchett & Co., Cherry Hill, 1975-79; office mgr. Bob Pritchett & Co., Merchantville, N.J., 1980-81, Cherry Hill, 1981-82; sales rep., broker Fox & Lazo Realtors, Cherry Hill, 1982—; mem. social planning com., fellow Camden County Bd. Realtors, Cherry Hill, 1974—; site mgr. Home Equity Relocation Co., Danbury, Conn., 1983—. Bldg. rep. Cherry Hill Edn. Assn., 1965-68; vol. officer Camden County Probation Dept., 1970-72; tchr. Sunday sch. Bethel Bapt. Ch., Cherry Hill, 1967-77; sec. bd. trustees Ocean Colony Condominium, Ocean City, N.J., 1988—; chmn. memberships Home and Sch. Assn., Cherry Hill, 1983; fellow mem. Rep. Woman's Club Cherry Hill, 1981—; mem. Barclay Farm Civic Assn., Cherry Hill. Fellow N.J. Assn. Realtors (Million Dollar Sales award 1984, 85, 86, 87, 88), Barclay Farm Swim Club. Home: 188 Pearlcroft Rd Cherry Hill NJ 08034 Office: Fox & Lazo Realtors 100 Barclay Pavilion Cherry Hill NJ 08034

FREDERICK, SAMUEL ADAMS, lawyer; b. N.Y.C., Mar. 17, 1946; s. Robert George and Mary Elizabeth (Adams) F.; m. Elizabeth Lothrop Moore, June 18, 1977; children: Alyssa Adams, Julia Moore, Charles Payson. BA, Yale U., 1968; JD, U. Pa., 1974; grad., Northeastern U. Mgmt. Devel. Program, 1987. Bar: N.Y. 1975, U.S. Dist. Ct. (so. and ea. dists.) N.Y. 1975, U.S. Ct. Appeals (2d cir.) 1975, Mass. 1983. Assoc. Wickes, Riddell, Bloomer, Jacobi & McGuire, N.Y.C., 1974-77, Milbank, Tweed, Hadley & McCloy, N.Y.C., 1977-78, Brown & Wood, N.Y.C., 1978-81; counsel Eastern Gas and Fuel Assocs., Boston, 1982-87; sr. corp. counsel Lotus Devel. Corp., Cambridge, Mass., 1988—; asst. sec. Eastern Associated Real Estate Corp., Boston, 1984-87, Eastern Energy Systems Corp., Boston, 1984-87; v.p., bd. dirs. U.S. Mut. Liability Ins. Co., Boston, 1984-87; mem. panel on mgrs. legal function M.I.T. Sloan Sch., 1988—. Author: Papering Procedures Manual for the Superior Court Division of the U.S. Attorney's Office for the District of Columbia, 1970. Served to lt. (j.g.) USNR, 1968-70. Mem. ABA, N.Y. State Bar Assn., Mass. Bar Assn. (preventive law com., high technology com. 1988—), Am. Corp. Counsel Assn., New Eng. Corp. Counsel Assn., Assocs. Club (pres., bd. dirs. 1985-86). Home: 35 Locust Ave Lexington MA 02173 Office: Lotus Devel Corp 55 Cambridge Pkwy Cambridge MA 02142

FREDERICKS, WARD ARTHUR, technology executive; b. Tarrytown, N.Y., Dec. 24, 1939; s. Arthur George and Evelyn (Smith) F.; BS cum laude, Mich. State U., 1962, MBA, 1963; m. Patricia A. Sexton, June 12, 1960; children: Corrine E., Lorrine L., Ward A. Assoc. dir. Technics Group, Grand Rapids, Mich., 1964-68; gen. mgr. logistics systems Massey-Ferguson Inc., Toronto, 1968-69, v.p. mgmt. services, comptroller, 1969-73, sr. v.p. fin., dir. fin. Americas, 1975—; comptroller Massey-Ferguson Ltd., Toronto, Ont., Can., 1973-75; cons. W.B. Saunders & Co., Washington, 1962—; sr. v.p. mktg. Massey/Ferguson, Inc., 1975-80, also sr. v.p., gen. mgr. Tractor div., 1978-80; v.p. ops., Rockwell Internat., Pitts., 1980-84; v.p. Fed. MOG., 1983-84; pres. MIXTEC Corp., 1984—, also dir., chmn.; dir. Badger Northland Inc., Tech-Mark Group Inc., SPECTRA Tech., Inc., MIXTEC Corp., Compu-Kore Ltd., Unicorn Corp., Harry Ferguson Inc., M.F. Credit Corp., M.F. Credit Co. Can. Ltd. Bd. dirs., mem. exec. com. Des Moines Symphony, 1975-79; exec. com. Conejo Symphony, pres. 1988-90; mem. exec. com. Alliance for Arts.; mem. Constn. Bicentennial Com., 1987-88, v.p. Com. Leaders Club, 1988, pres., 1989, Gov.'s Task Force on Tech., Am. Transp. Assn. fellow, 1962-63; Ramlose fellow, 1962-63. Mem. Am. Mktg. Assn., Nat. Council Phys. Distbn. Mgmt. (exec. com. 1974), IEEE, Soc. Automotive Engrs., U.S. Strategic Inst., Tech. Execs. Forum, Toronto Bd. Trade, Westlake Village C. of C. (chmn.), Old Crows, Assn. for Advanced Tech. Edn., Community Leaders Club, Pres.'s Club Mich. State U., Rotary, Beta Gamma Sigma. Author: (with Edward W. Smykay) Physical Distribution Management, 1974, Management Vision, 1988; contbr. articles to profl. jours. Office: 32123 Lindero Canyon Rd Westlake Village CA 91361 also: 625 I St Washington DC 20001

FREDERICKS, WESLEY CHARLES, JR., businessman, lawyer; b. N.Y.C., Mar. 31, 1948; s. Wesley Charles and Dionysia W. (Bitsanis) F.; m. Jeanne Maria Judson, May 19, 1973; children: Carolyn Anne, Wesley C. III. BA Johns Hopkins U., 1970; JD, Columbia U., 1973. Bar: N.Y. 1974, Conn. 1976, U.S. Supreme Ct. 1979. Assoc. Shearman & Sterling, N.Y.C., 1973-76, 76-83, Cummings & Lockwood, Stamford, Conn., 1976; dir. Automobile Importers Am., Inc., Washington, 1983-87, British Performance Car Imports, Inc., Norwood, N.J., 1982-86, Carbodies N. Am., Inc., Dover, Del., 1983-84; chmn. bd. Lotus Performance Cars, L.P., Norwood, 1983-86, chief exec. officer, 1986-87; group exec. cons. Group Lotus PLC, 1987—. Honors judge Columbia U. Law Sch. Stone Moot Ct. Honors Program, 1980—; mem. Johns Hopkins U. Alumni Schs. Com.; trustee Wilton Hist. Soc., 1986—. Served with USMC, 1968-69. Mem. Blue Key Soc., Sigma Phi Epsilon. Republican. Congregationalist. Clubs: India House (N.Y.C.); Steering Wheel (London), Sandanona, Campfire Am. (N.Y.); Weston Gun (Conn.). Home: 221 Benedict Hill Rd New Canaan CT 06840 Office: Lotus Cars USA 530 Walnut St Norwood NJ 07648

FREDSTON, ARTHUR H., lawyer; b. Chgo., July 25, 1929; s. Leo and Jeanette Fredston; m. Elinor A. Abramson, June 14, 1951; children: Dale Carol, Susan Terri, Jill Ann. BBA, U. Mich., 1949; LLB, Yale U., 1954. Bar: N.Y. 1954. Assoc. Winthrop, Stimson, Putnam & Roberts, N.Y.C., 1954-62, ptnr., 1962—; bd. dirs. Sabreliner Corp., St. Louis. Lt. (j.g.) USNR, 1951-53. Home: 3 Cedar Island Larchmont NY 10009 Office: Winthrop Stimson Putnam & Roberts 1 Battery Pk Pla New York NY 10004

FREEBERG, DON, healthcare executive; b. 1924. Student, U. Minn., 1948. With Summit Health Ltd., L.A., 1961—, now chmn.; pres., chief exec. officer Sierra Land & Livestock Inc., Glendale, Calif., also bd. dirs. Office: Summit Health Ltd 1800 Ave of the Stars Los Angeles CA 90067 *

FREED, KARL FRANCIS, marketing executive; b. Gladwin, Mich., Dec. 13, 1944; s. Robert C. and Anita C. (Haas) F.; m. Susan L. Machinski, Oct. 28, 1978; 1 child, Bretton James. BS, Mich. State U., 1968; MA, Western Mich. U., 1975. Planner Tri County RPC, Lansing, Mich., 1967-68, Kalamazoo (Mich.) County, 1968-71; sr. planner Gove Assocs., Kalamazoo, 1971-73, dir. planning, 1973-75, v.p. planning, 1975-80, v.p. planning and mktg., 1980-84, v.p. planning and mktg., treas., 1984—. Mem. Am. Planning Assn., Beacon Club. Office: Gove Assoc Inc 1601 Portage St Kalamazoo MI 49001

FREED, SUSAN GORDON, financial planning executive; b. Newport News, Va., Dec. 29, 1954; d. Julian and Gertrude (Silverman) Gordon; m. Charles L. Freed, June 9, 1985. BA cum laude, Tulane U., 1976; cert., Coll. for Fin. Planning, Denver, 1984. Fin. planner McLean (Va.) Fin. Group, 1983-84, Lander & Assocs. Inc., Washington, 1984-87; pres., chief exec. officer Susan Gordon Freed, CFP, Washington, 1987—; lectr. Mt. Vernon Coll., 1986—. Contbr. articles to fin. and tax planning to profl. jours. Active United Jewish Appeal, Washington, 1984—; v.p. Burleigh Citizens Assn., Washington, 1987—. Mem. Internat. Assn. for Fin. Planning (asst. dir. membership 1987), Inst. for Cert. Fin. Planners. Democrat. Office: 1110 Vermont Ave NW Ste 400 Washington DC 20005

FREEDMAN, BARRY MARTIN, financial executive; b. Lynn, Mass., Oct. 26, 1941; s. Kenneth and Ruth (Kramer) F.; m. Phyllis Ross, June 12, 1965; children: Marc, Jeffrey, Andrew. BSBA, Babson Coll., 1964. Cert. fin. planner. Fin. planner IDS Fin. Services, Peabody, Mass., 1968-88; pres. Freedman Fin. Assocs., Peabody, 1988—; corporator Warren Five Cents Savs. Bank, Peabody, 1985-87. Mem. Internat. Assn. Fin. Planning (pres. Greater Boston chpt. 1987—), Boston Soc. Inst. Cert. Fin. Planners (bd. dirs. 1985—), Inst. Cert. Fin. Planners (adj. faculty 1985-88), Babson Coll. Alumni Assn. (bd. dirs. 1984-86), Peabody C. of C. (bd. dirs. 1980—). Office: 5 Essex Green Dr Ste 22 Peabody MA 01960

FREEDMAN, ELLIOTT SAMUEL, management consultant; b. Bklyn., Jan. 5, 1918; s. Harry Hillel and Harriet (Cohen) F.; m. Eleanore Schwartz, Apr. 6, 1941; children: Susan Alice, Beryl Fillis. Student, St. John's U., 1940. Sales rep. Page & Shaw Chocolate Co. Inc., Cambridge, Mass., 1950-57; exec. v.p. Page & Shaw Sales Corp., New Hyde Park, N.Y., 1957-59; founder, pres., chmn. bd. Butane Products Corp., Baldwin, N.Y., 1959-83; pres. E & S Freedman Assocs. Inc., Lake Worth, Fla., 1959—; founding mem. bd. dirs. mem. exec. com. Gateway State Bank, S.I., N.Y. With USAAF, 1941-45. Mem. Old Westbury Golf and County Club, Fountain Golf and Country Club. Democrat. Jewish.

FREEDMAN, MARSHALL KEVIN, communications company manager; b. Denver, May 23, 1962; s. Al M. and Betty Eva (Chaitman) F. Cert. in communications tech., Emily Griffith Sch., Denver; AS in Electronic Tech., Denver Auraria Community Coll.; lic. gen. radiotelephone, FCC, 1982. Mobile tel. communications trainee Communication Svc. Co., Englewood, Colo., 1982; installer, bench technician, asst. mgr. Contact Communications, Lakewood, Colo., 1983-84; owner, gen. mgr. Comm. Enterprises, Inc., Denver, 1985—; advisor Mobile Tel. Communications Tech. Cons., 1985. Adminstr. charity loan fund Chai-Gemach Fund, Denver, 1985. Mem. Assn. Communications Tech. (sr.). Office: Comm Enterprises Inc 60 Federal Blvd Denver CO 80219

FREEDMAN, RICHARD S., trust company executive, investment advisor; b. Brookline, Mass., May 12, 1942; s. David and Celia D. Freedman; m. Iris M. Wolf, June 1964 (div. Jan 1968); 1 child, Ross S. BBA, U. Ariz., 1964; postgrad., U. Miami, 1967. Exec. v.p. Am. Birthright Trust, Palm Beach, Fla., 1972-81; pres. Paragon Systems Inc., Palm Beach, 1981—; v.p. Bank of Boston of Fla., Palm Beach, 1985-87; pres. Paragon Leasing Corp., Palm Beach, 1985—; v.p. First Am. Bank and Trust, Palm Beach, 1987—. Mem. Nat. Options and Futures Soc., Econ. Soc. South Fla., East Coast Estate Planning Council, Internat. Assn. Fin. Planners, Estate and Trust Roundtable. Home: PO Box 3223 Palm Beach FL 33480 Office: First Am Bank & Trust 140 N County Rd Palm Beach FL 33480

FREEDMAN, SUZANNE KOSLAP, human resources executive, consultant; b. Yonkers, N.Y., Aug. 29, 1955; d. John Joseph and Mildred (Bliss) Koslap; m. Douglas Freedman, Apr. 14, 1985 (div. June 1988); m. Michael Pilnick, Feb. 19, 1989. BA in English, Tufts U., 1976; MA in Human Resource Mgmt., New Sch. for Social Rsch., N.Y.C., 1988. Sec. Am. Can Co., Greenwich, Conn., 1977-78, coll. relations asst., 1978-79, employment asst., 1979-81, coord. human resource planning, 1981; tng. specialist Reader's Digest Assn., Pleasantville, N.Y., 1981-86, sr. tng. specialist, 1986, mgr. corp. tng., 1986-87, assoc. dir. human resources, 1987—; vol. trainer Inroads Intern Program, Stamford, Conn., 1986-87. Instr. CPR Greenwich Hosp., 1981-83; troop leader Girl Scouts U.S., Hastings-on-Hudson, N.Y., 1980-84. Mem. Am. Soc. Tng. and Devel., Orgn. for Positive Employee Rels. Home: 3 Foster Pl Pleasantville NY 10570 Office: Readers Digest Assn Pleasantville NY 10570

FREELAND, FLORA ELLEN, radio station executive, accountant; b. Fayetteville, Tenn., Aug. 10, 1930; d. Albert Hargis and Amy Flora (Meeks) Elmore; m. Michael Rudolph Freeland, Nov. 30, 1948; children: Michael Rudolph Jr., Patricia Sharon Freeland Poe, Steven Allen, Douglas Lee, David Elmore. BA in Bus. Adminstrn. magna cum laude, Bethel Coll., 1962; MS in Speech and Communication, Murray State U., 1973. CPA, Tenn. Receptionist, bookkeeper Sta. WEKR, Fayetteville, 1948-51, gen. mgr., 1981—; office mgr. Sta. WHDM, McKenzie, Tenn., 1953-56; treas. Sta. WFWL, Camden, Tenn., 1956-77; mgr. Sta. WKTA-FM, McKenzie, 1963-74; tchr. Steelville (Ill.) High Sch., 1967-68, Motlow Community Coll., Tullahoma, Tenn., 1983-84; ptnr. Freeland & Freeland CPA's, McKenzie, 1981-

84. Mem. CLEAN, Fayetteville, 1987—. Mem. Christian Bus. and Profl. Women (treas. 1986—), Toastmasters Club (First pl. area speech award 1988). Home: Rt 9 Box 53 Fayetteville TN 37334 Office: Sta WEKR PO Box M 311 Old Boonshill Rd Fayetteville TN 37334

FREELAND, WILLIAM THOMAS, engineering company executive, civil engineer; b. Greenwood, S.C., Apr. 11, 1944; s. James nd Hattie (White) F.; m. Carolyn Zachary, Aug. 13, 1966; children: Thomas, Zac, Corey. BSCE, Clemson U., 1966. Sr. v.p. bus. devel. CRS Sirrine Inc., Greenville, S.C., 1966—. Capt. U.S. Army, 1967-70. Home: 43 Club Forest Ln Greenville SC 29605 Office: CRS Sirrine Inc 216 S Pleasantburg Dr Greenville SC 29606

FREEMAN, CASSANDRA LEE, legal secretary; b. New Kensington, Pa., Mar. 4, 1950; d. John Wesley Wilkins and Ellestine (Harvey) Hayes; divorced; children: Tuwanda Lee, Kevin Richard. AS in Bus. Mgmt. cum laude, No. Va. Community Coll., 1984; BBA high honors, Strayer Coll., 1986. Secretary Pittsburgh Paint & Glass Industries, Pitts., 1969-73; adminstrv. asst., officer Georgetown Hosp., Washington, 1973-80; legal sec. Fried, Frank, Harris, Shriver & Jacobson, Washington, 1980-88, evening/weekend coordinator, 1988—; adj. instr. bus. dept. Strayer Coll., Washington, 1988—. Vol. sec. Hammond Jr. High Sch., Alexandria, Va., 1983-85. Recipient Appreciation award sports program Georgetown Hosp., 1976, Exemplary Service award Honor Club Strayer Coll., 1986. Fellow Nat. Assn. Legal Secs., Soc. Advancement Mgmt., Am. Soc. Notaries, Mid-Atlantic Notary Assn. (edn. com.), NVCC Alumni Assn,, Strayer Coll. Alumni Assn. Office: F Frank H Shriver & Jacobson 1001 Pennsylvania Ave NW Suite #800 Washington DC 20004-2505

FREEMAN, CHARLES ROBERT, chemical engineer; b. St. Paul, Dec. 15, 1931; s. Charles Lyle and Bernice (Louella Hart) F.; m. Jacqueline Schafer, 1953 (div. 1961); children: Robert, Timothy, Patrick; m. Diana Ruth Smith (div. 1979); children: Douglas, Brian; m. Irene Pruzan, 1988. BA in Chemistry, St. John's U., Collegeville, Minn., 1953. Chemist 3M Co., St. Paul, 1956-66, research supr., 1966-69, devel. supr., 1970-74, research specialist, 1974-84; prin. chem. engr. UNISYS, Roseville, Minn., 1984—. Patentee rubber tape, film adhesive, pressure sensitive tape, plated wire memory, high strength adhesives. Served with U.S. Army, 1953-56. Mem. UNIVAC Computer Club St. Paul (librarian 1984-87). Home: 1042 Fairmount Ave Saint Paul MN 55105 Office: UNISYS 2276 Highcrest Rd Roseville MN 55113

FREEMAN, DAVID, chemical company excutive; b. Gateshead, Durham, Eng., Apr. 14, 1944; came to U.S., 1981; s. Sidney and Mary (Ross) F.; m. Sylvia Bailey, Mar. 16, 1968; children: Mark David, Michael Christopher. Chartered acct. Co. sec. Huwood-Ellis Ltd., Gateshead, 1966-68; controller Amoco Fabrics Europe, London, 1968-73; gen. mgr. Propytex, Ltd., Hartlepool, Eng., 1973-74; fin. dir. Loctite Ltd. div. Loctite Corp., London, 1974-79; v.p. fin. Loctite S.A.R.L. div. Loctite Corp., Paris, 1979-81; v.p. fin. internat. Loctite Corp., Newington, Conn., 1981-83, chief fin. officer, 1983-85, pres. N. Am., from 1985, now sr. v.p. fin.; bd. dirs. Loctite Can., Permatex Venezuala, Loctite (U.K.) Ltd., Kean Leisure Ltd.; dir. adhesives and sealants Coun. Edn. Found. Bd. dirs. Jr. Achievement, Hartford, Conn., 1987. Fellow Inst. Chartered Accts. Eng. and Wales. Roman Catholic. Office: Loctite Corp Hartford Sq N 10 Columbus Blvd Hartford CT 06106 *

FREEMAN, DONALD WILFORD, real estate developer, Arabian horse breeder; b. Brooksville, Fla., Sept. 25, 1929; s. Fred Maxwell and Dovie (Keef) F.; B.S., U. Ala., 1953, LL.B., 1953; LL.M., N.Y. U., 1957; m. Ruby Jane Lewis, Feb. 25, 1956; children—Clifton Lewis, Susan Anne. Acct., Ernst & Ernst, Atlanta, 1953-55; tax atty. Office Chief Counsel, U.S. Treasury Dept., N.Y.C., 1955-57, West Point Mfg. Co. (Ga.), 1957-58; asst. treas. Ryder System, Inc., Miami, Fla., 1958-61; v.p., dir. Henderson's Portion Pak, Inc., 1961-63; pres. Biscayne Capital Corp., Miami, Fla., 1964-66; sr. asso. Lazard Freres & Co., N.Y.C., 1967-69; pres. James A. Ryder Corp., Miami, 1969-78; owner Kiyara Arabians, 1978—. Served with AUS, 1946-48; PTO. C.P.A., Ga. Mem. Fla. Inst. C.P.A.s, Phi Kappa Sigma, Beta Gamma Sigma. Episcopalian. Home: Rte 1 PO Box 239 AA Reddick FL 32686

FREEMAN, G. P. M., food company executive; b. Calgary, Alta., Can., Feb. 24, 1946; s. Arthur Patrick and Madelene Florence (Austin) F.; m. Susan Lyn Needam; children: Ashley, Michael. BSc, Mich. Tech. U., 1969. Product mgr. H.D. Heinz, Toronto, Can., 1971-72; product mgr. Quaker Oats Co., Peterborough, Ont., Can., 1972-73, group product mgr., 1973-75; plant mgr. Quaker Oats Co., Trenton, Ont., 1975-77; gen. mgr. Quaker Oats Co., Seo Paulo, Brazil, 1977-79; exec. v.p. Skol Breweries, Rio de Jeniero, Brazil, 1979-80; v.p., gen. mgr. Labatt Breweries B.C., Vancouver, Can., 1980-83; exec. v.p. Labatt Breweries B.C., Toronto, 1983-85; chmn., chief exec. officer Ault Foods Ltd., Toronto, 1985—. Trustee Humben Coll., Toronto, 1985—. Mem. Nat. Dairy Council (bd. dirs., exec. com. 1986—), Ice Cream Inst. (bd. dirs. 1986—). Office: Ault Foods Ltd, 405 The West Mall, Toronto, ON Canada M8C 5J1 *

FREEMAN, HARRY LOUIS, financial services company executive; b. Omaha, Mar. 1, 1932; s. Joseph H. and Celia (Rivonne) F.; m. Lucile Carpenter, Dec. 26, 1965; children: Bennett, Lansing, Rachel, Alexandra. A.B., U. Mich., 1953; J.D., Harvard U., 1956. Bar: Nebr. 1956, Calif. 1957, U.S. Supreme Ct. 1967, D.C. 1968. Clk. U.S. Ct. Appeals, 9th Circuit, 1956-57; mem. firm Janin, Morgan, Brenner & Freeman, San Francisco, 1957-66; dir. Ins. div. AID, Dept. State, Washington, 1966-69; v.p. corp. planning OPIC, Washington, 1969-71; v.p. fin. OPIC, 1974-75; mgr. comml. projects, mgr. project fin. group Bechtel Corp., San Francisco, 1972-74; v.p. Am. Express Co., Washington, 1975-77; sr. v.p. Am. Express Co., N.Y.C., 1977-79; sr. v.p., office of chmn. Am. Express Co., 1979-83, exec. v.p., 1984—; adj. prof. internat. law U. Calif., Berkeley, 1974, Georgetown U., 1975-76; prin. Ctr. for Excellence in Govt.; trustee U.S. Council for Internat. Bus. Contbr. articles to profl. jours. Trustee World Affairs Council No. Calif., 1960-66; bd. dirs. Calif. Clinic for Psychotherapy, San Francisco, 1964-66, Fund for Multinat. Edn., 1984—, Travelers Aid Soc., Travelers Aid Washington Trustee Com. Econ. Devel., 1983—; active Council on Fgn. Relations. Recipient Disting. Service award AID, 1969, Disting. Service award OPIC, 1971. Mem. ABA, Calif. Bar Assn., Nebr. Bar Assn., Washington Bar Assn., Council on Fgn. Relations. Democrat. Jewish. Clubs: Internat. (Washington); Harvard (N.Y.C.); Stock Exchange (San Francisco). Home: 4708 Dorset Ave Chevy Chase MD 20815 Office: Am Express Co Am Express Tower World Fin Ctr New York NY 10004

FREEMAN, JOE BAILEY, corporation executive; b. Dallas, Apr. 18, 1937; s. Joe Bailey and Beulah Gertrude (Caraway) F.; m. Teresa Adams, Apr. 1, 1984; children: Jon, James, Lisa. B.B.A., North Tex. State U., 1958; M.B.A., So. Meth. U., 1968. C.P.A., Tex. With Collins Radio Co., Richardson, Tex., 1959-67; sr. fin. analyst Tex. Instruments Co., Dallas, 1967-68; v.p., controller automotive group Maremont Corp., Chgo., 1968-73, v.p., controller corp., 1973-76, sr. v.p., chief fin. officer, 1976-80; sr. v.p., chief fin. officer, dir. Cronys Industries, 1980-81; sr. v.p., chief fin. officer Am. Internat. Inc., Chgo., 1981-82, pres., chief exec., chmn. bd., 1982-84; founder, chmn. Freeman Assocs. Inc., 1984—; pres., chief exec. officer Gardinier, Inc., 1985; chmn. chief exec. officer, pres. Kendavis Holding Co., 1987—. Served with AUS, 1958-59, 61-62. Home: 4424 Glen Oaks Dr Flower Mound TX 75028 Office: Kendavis Holding Co 106 W 6th St Fort Worth TX 76102

FREEMAN, JOHN YELVERTON, investment banker; b. Atlanta, Nov. 1, 1950; s. Neill Willis and M. Helen F. BS in Commerce, U. Va., 1972, MBA, 1978. CPA, Va. With Coopers & Lybrand, Washington, 1972-76; v.p., mergers and acquisitions dept. Citicorp Investment Bank, N.Y.C., 1978-86; head mergers and acquisitions group, dir. Tucker, Anthony & R.L. Day, Inc., N.Y.C., 1986-88; pres. J.Y. Freeman & Co., N.Y.C., 1989—. Office: JY Freeman & Co 400 Madison Ave Ste 1600 New York NY 10271

FREEMAN, MILTON VICTOR, lawyer; b. N.Y.C., Nov. 16, 1911; s. Samuel and Celia (Gelfand) F.; m. Phyllis Young, Dec. 19, 1937; children: Nancy Lois (Mrs. Gans), Daniel Martin, Andrew Samuel, Amy Martha (Mrs. Malone). A.B., Coll. City N.Y., 1931; LL.B., Columbia U., 1934. Bar: N.Y. 1934, D.C. 1946, U.S. Supreme Ct. 1943. With gen. counsel's office SEC, 1934-42, asst. solicitor, 1942-46; staff securities div. FTC, 1934; with firm Arnold & Porter and predecessor firms, Washington, 1946—; adj. prof. Yale U., 1947, Georgetown U. Law Sch., 1952; vis. scholar various univs., 1978-79; mem. adv. bd. Bur. Nat. Affairs, Securities Regulation and Law Report, Washington, Nat. Law Jour., N.Y., Internat. Fin. Law Rev., London. Contbr. articles to profl. jours.; bd. editors Columbia Law Rev., 1933-34 (Ordronaux prize 1934). Mem. exec. com. Securities Regulation Inst., U. Calif., San Diego; bd. visitors U. San Diego Law Sch. Mem. ABA (chmn. subcom. on SEC practice and enforcement 1972-83, exec. com. fed. regulation of securities com. 1983—, ad hoc com. on corp. governance project, ad hoc com. on insider trading), Fed. Bar Assn., D.C. Bar Assn., Internat. Law Inst. (hon. chmn. 1977—, trustee 1955—). Club: International (Washington). Home: 3405 Woolsey Dr Chevy Chase MD 20815 Office: 1200 New Hampshire Ave NW Washington DC 20036

FREEMAN, NEIL, accounting and computer consulting firm executive; b. Reading, Pa., Dec. 27, 1948; s. Leroy Harold and Audrey Todd (Dornhecker) F.; m. Janice Lum, Nov. 20, 1981. BS, Albright Coll., 1979; MS, Kennedy-Western U., 1987, PhD, 1988. Cert. systems profl.; cert. data processing specialist. Acct. Jack W. Long & Co., Mt. Penn, Pa., 1977-78; comptroller G.P.C., Inc., Bowmansville, Pa., 1978-79; owner Neil Freeman Cons., Bowmansville, 1980-81; program mgr., systems cons. Application Systems, Honolulu, 1981-82; instr. Chaminade U., Honolulu, 1983—; owner Neil Freeman Cons., Kaneohe, Hawaii, 1982—. Author: (computer software) NFC Property Management, 1984, NFC Mailing List, 1984; (book) Learning Dibol, 1984. Served with USN, 1966-68, Vietnam. Mem. Nat. Assn. Accts., Am. Inst. Cert. Computer Profs., Data Processing Mgmt. Assn., Assn. Systems Mgmt. Office: 45-449 Hoene Pl Kaneohe HI 96744

FREEMAN, PAUL RANDOLPH, controller; b. Columbus, Ohio, Apr. 4, 1957; s. Jack Taylor and Edith Irene (Marlow) F.; m. Cheryl Lynn Rose Kisela, Mar. 1, 1986; children: Melissa Ann, Jason Paul. AA, Lakeland Community Coll., 1979; BBA, Garfield Sr. Coll., Painesville, Ohio, 1980. CPA, Ohio. Staff acct. mannheimer, Seitz & Co., Beachwood, Ohio, 1980-81; acct. Leaseway Fleet Mgmt. Co., Beechwood, 1981-83; fin. analyst Harris Wholesale Co., Solon, Ohio, 1983-84; acting gen. mgr. Harris Wholesale Co., Randolph, Mass., 1984; mgr. spl. projects Harris Wholesale Co., Miami, Fla., 1984-85; asst. supr., fin. acctg. Harris Wholesale Co., Solon, 1985-86, cash mgr., 1986-87; asst. controller Internat. Thomson Indsl. Press., Inc., Solon, 1987; controller Internat. Thomson Communications, Inc., Solon, 1987—. Republican. Methodist. Home: 1710 Glenwood Dr Twinsburg OH 44087 Office: Internat Thomson Communicaitons Inc 6521 Davis Indsl Pkwy Solon OH 44139

FREEMAN, PETER SUNDERLIN, textile executive; b. Bklyn., Apr. 23, 1944; s. Graydon Lavern and Ruth Crosby (Sunderlin) F.; m. Linda Raissa Blanco, Sept. 23, 1972. BS, Cornell U., 1966; MBA in Fin., Syracuse U., 1969; cert. acctg., NYU, 1979. CPA, Colo. New bus. devel. and product mgr. CBS Pub. Group, N.Y.C., 1970-73; sr. fin. analyst W.R. Grace Retail and Textiles, N.Y.C., 1973-75; dir. fin. analysis and reporting Grace Textiles, N.Y.C., 1975-79, div. controller, 1979-81; v.p. fin. Toyobo subs. Rosewood Fabrics, N.Y.C., 1981-85; v.p. fin. and adminstrn. Vitreous Internat. Trading Co., Inc., Great Neck, N.Y., 1985-86; corp. controller Liberty Fabrics, Inc., N.Y.C., 1986—. Served with U.S. Army, 1968-70, Vietnam. Mem. AICPA, Colo. Soc. CPA's, Cornell U. Lambda Alumni (pres. 1987—, bd. dirs. 1982—). Presbyterian. Home: 280 1st Ave #5B New York NY 10009 Office: Liberty Fabrics Inc 295 Fifth Ave New York NY 10016

FREEMAN, RICHARD DEAN, service executive; b. Rushville, Ind., Nov. 27, 1928; s. Verne Crawford and Mary Phyllis (Dean) F.; m. Mary Jane Barkman, Aug. 21, 1950; children: Debra Dean, Phyllis Lynn, Richard Paul, Tom Crawford. BS in Aero. Engring., Purdue U., 1950, BS in Naval Sci. and Tactics, 1950, MS in Indsl. Mgmt., 1954. Supr. indsl. engring. Gen. Motors Corp., Warren, Ohio, 1954-58; prodn. mgr. Ramo Wooldridge div. TRW Corp., Denver, 1958-62; mgr. missile programs Hughes Aircraft Co., Los Angeles, 1962-68; v.p. E-Systems Inc., Dallas, 1968-72, Rockwell Internat. Co., Los Angeles, 1972-74; pres. Internat. Pacific Co., Newport Beach, Calif., 1974—; sr. lectr. West Coast U., Los Angeles, 1974-78; sec. Proteus Corp., Newport Beach, 1978-80; chmn. Tech. Assocs. Corp., Newport Beach, 1984-85, Equicenters, Irvine, 1988. Author: Economation Approaches, 1958, Equator, 1984 (also film); prod. documentary film Zeros of the Pacific, 1979. Cubmaster, scoutmaster, dist. chmn. Boy Scouts Am., various locations, 1966-76. Served to capt. USMC, 1946-58, Korea. Named Man of Yr., Sigma Alpha Tau, West Lafayette, Ind., 1971; recipient Disting. Engring. Alumnus award Purdue U., 1973. Mem. Am. Inst. Indsl. Engrs., Purdue Alumni Assn., Nat. Eagle Scout Assn., Kappa Sigma. Republican. Lodge: Masons (consistory 32 degree v.p.). Home: 3910 Topside Ln Corona Del Mar CA 92625 Office: Internat Pacific Co 240 Newport Center Dr Newport Beach CA 92660

FREEMAN, ROBERT MALLORY, banker; b. Richmond, Va., 1941. Grad., U. Va., 1963, Stonier Grad. Sch. Banking. With Wachovia Bank & Trust Co., Raleigh, NC, 1963-71; pres., chief exec. officer Signet Banking Corp., Richmond, 1980—, also bd. dirs.; chmn. adv. bd. U. Va. McIntire Sch. Commerce; bd. dirs. Va. Indsl. Devel. Corp. Trustee, past chmn. United Way Greater Richmond; mem. adv. bd. Robert E. Lee council Boy Scouts Am. Mem. Va. Bankers Assn. (pres. 1986-87), Assn. Res. City Bankers, Assn. Bank Holding Cos., Young Pres.'s Orgn., Richmond Met. C. of C. (bd. dirs.), Bull and Bear Commonwealth Club, Country Club of Va., Sigma Phi Epsilon (trustee nat. housing com.). Office: Signet Banking Corp PO Box 25970 Richmond VA 23260

FREEMAN, ROBERT MARK, financial executive; b. Cambridge, Mass., June 12, 1942; m. Margo Harmon, Sept. 6, 1969; children: Carie, Clayton, Edward. B.A., Dartmouth Coll, 1964; postgrad., Columbia U., 1965-68. Risk arbitrageur Goldman & Sachs, N.Y.C., 1970—, ptnr.; bd. dirs. Flexi-Van Corp., N.Y.C. Trustee N.Y. Coll. Osteopathic Medicine, 1982—. Office: Goldman Sachs & Co 85 Broad St New York NY 10004 *

FREEMAN, RUSSELL ADAMS, banker; b. Albany, N.Y., July 22, 1932; s. Russell Marvin and Edith (Adams) F.; m. Elizabeth Frances McHale, June 30, 1956; children: Lynn, James. B.A., Amherst Coll., 1954; J.D., Albany (N.Y.) Law Sch., 1957; LL.M., U. So. Calif., 1966. Bar: N.Y. 1957, Calif. 1960. Practiced in Albany, 1957-59; with Security Pacific Nat. Bank, Los Angeles, 1959—; v.p. Security Pacific Nat. Bank, 1968-72, counsel, 1968-74, head legal dept., 1968-74, sr. v.p., 1972-81, exec. v.p., 1981-87, gen. counsel, 1984-87; gen. counsel Security Pacific Corp., 1973—, exec. v.p., 1981—; bd. govs. Fin. Lawyers Conf., 1972-74; faculty Pacific Coast Banking Sch., 1980-81; lectr. in field, 1965—. Contbr. articles to profl. publns. Trustee Flintridge Prep. Sch., La Canada, Calif., 1978-80. Mem. ABA, Am. Bankers Assn. (mem. govt. relations com. 1981-84, del. to Leadership Conf. 1984-86), Assn. Banking Holding Cos., Calif. Bankers Assn. (dir., chmn. govt. relations group 1979-81, 86-88, dir. and chmn. fed. govt. relations 1985-86), Calif. Bankers Clearing House Assn. (chmn. public policy adv. com. 1980-81, 88-89), Calif. State Bar, Los Angeles County Bar Assn. (past chmn. comml. law and bankruptcy sect.), Constl. Rights Found. (bd. dirs. 1986—). Office: Security Pacific Corp 333 S Hope St 54th Fl Los Angeles CA 90071

FREEMAN, SAMUEL RALPH, business executive, lawyer; b. N.Y.C., Sept. 2, 1929; s. Benjamin S. and Ethel S. (Salit) F.; m. Joyce Siegel, Dec. 21, 1958; children: Laura, Susan, Carol. LL.B., Bklyn. Law Sch., 1951. Bar: N.Y. 1951, Colo. 1954. Asst. atty. gen. Colo., 1955-58; ptnr. Van Cise, Freeman, Tooley & McClearn, Denver, 1959-72; v.p., gen. counsel Rio Grande Industries, Inc., Denver, 1973-89, Denver Rio Grande Western RR Co., Denver, 1973-89; assoc. Concord Assocs., Denver, 1989—; bd. dirs. Belcaro Bank, Denver, Ramtron Internat., Greenwood Holdings; vice chmn. Stolar Inc.; mem. urban transp. adv. com. U.S. Dept. Transp., 1969-74; ind. sec. adv. com. on energy U.S. Dept. Commerce, 1986—; mem. exec. com. Interstate Oil Compact, 1976-86, 1st vice chmn., 1985; chmn. Colo. Oil and Gas Conservation Commn., 1974-85; judge adv. Colo. N.G., 1954-63. Mem. ABA, Colo. Bar Assn., Denver Bar Assn., Am. Corp. Counsel Assn. (bd. dirs. Colo. chpt. 1984—). Jewish. Office: Concord Assocs Three Pk Cen #900 1515 Arapahoe Denver CO 80202

FREEMAN, SHELLEY, financial services marketing executive, freelance editor and writer; b. Greensburg, Pa., Oct. 8, 1958; d. Martin Freeman and Felice (Oxman) Salsburg. Student, Muhlenberg Coll., 1976-80; BA in English, Wilkes Coll., 1982; postgrad., U. Pa., 1982-83. Publicity asst. Harper & Row, N.Y.C., 1983-84; mktg. assoc. E.F. Hutton & Co., N.Y.C., 1984-85, asst. v.p., 1985-87; v.p. Shearson Lehman Hutton, N.Y.C., 1988—. Mem. Internat. Assn. for fin. Planning, Nat. Assn. Female Execs. Democrat. Jewish. Office: Shearson Lehman Hutton 26 Broadway Rm 1211 New York NY 10004

FREEMAN, WILLIAM DAVID, marketing professional, consultant; b. Stoneham, Mass., Sept. 27, 1951; s. Miles W. and Merilyn (Bucklin) F.; m. Linda J. Marino, Oct. 12, 1974; children: Amanda Lynne, Michael William, Bradford William. AS, Midwestern State U., 1972; BA, U. Mass., 1977; MBA, Anna Maria Coll., 1983. Dir. radiology systems Middlesex County Hosp., Waltham, Mass., 1977-79; dir. imaging systems Richmond (Va.) Meml. Hosp., 1979-81; administr., dir. radiology Carney Hosp., Boston, 1981-83; cons. mktg. Meditech Inc., Westwood, Mass., 1983-85; sr. sales rep. Baxter Healthcare Corp., Deerfield, Ill., 1985—; cons. Techsystems Inc., Atlanta, 1988—; chmn. adv. com. Sch. Radiation Scis., 1980. Editor: Mayflower Official State Newsletter, 1979. Served to sgt. USAF, 1971-75. Recipient Top Delta Svcs. Salesperson award, 1988, Pres.'s Circle award, 1988. Mem. Am. Registry Radiologic Technologists (cert.). Republican. Roman Catholic. Office: Baxter Healthcare Corp 600 Memorial Dr Cambridge MA 02138

FREER, JAMES LEWIS, accounting company executive; b. Ephrata, Washington, Feb. 13, 1948; s. Ross V. and Margaret (Andrews) F.; m. Becky A. Peterson, Aug. 9, 1969; children: McKenzie S., K.C. BSBA, Cen. Wash. U., 1970; postgrad., Wash. State U., 1966-67. CPA, Wash., Calif. Audit ptnr. Ernst & Whinney, Seattle, 1971-86; ptnr., dir. human resources Ernst & Whinney, Los Angeles, 1986—; bd. visitors Sch. Bus. Cen. Wash. U., Ellenburg, 1985—; bd. dirs, exec. com. Wash. Council on Internat. Trade, Seattle, 1984-86, Wash. State China Relation Council, Seattle, 1984-86. Adv. bd. Seattle Pub. Schs., Seattle, 1985; trustee Wash. State U. Acctg. Devel. Fund, Pullman, 1985—; pres., bd. dirs. Big Brother, King County, Wash., 1986. With USNG, 1970-76. Recipient Leadership Tomorrow award Seattle C. of C., 1985, Making a Difference award, Sta. KING-TV, 1985. Mem. Am. Inst. CPA's, Wash. Soc. CPA's., Calif. Soc. CPA's, Rotary Club. Roman Catholic. Office: Ernst & Whinney 515 S Flower St Ste 2700 Los Angeles CA 90071

FREESE, ROBERT GERARD, financial executive; b. N.Y.C., Oct. 6, 1929; s. Sylvester V. and Helen (Haverty) F.; m. Joan Anne Walsh, Sept. 6, 1952; children—Bernadette Freese Pavlis, Maryellen, John M. BBA, Manhattan Coll., 1951; MBA, NYU, 1953. Internal auditor Texaco, Inc., N.Y.C., 1951-56; various fin. mgmt. positions Grumman Corp., Bethpage, N.Y., 1956-72, treas., 1972—, v.p., 1974-80, sr. v.p. fin., 1980-86, vice chmn. fin., 1986—, also bd. dirs.; regional dir. The Bank of N.Y.; trustee Roslyn Savs. Bank. Served as cpl. U.S. Army, 1953-55. Office: Grumman Corp 1111 Stewart Ave Bethpage NY 11714

FREIBERGER, WALTER FREDERICK, mathematics educator, actuarial science consultant, educator; b. Vienna, Austria, Feb. 20, 1924; came to U.S., 1955, naturalized, 1962; s. Felix and Irene (Tagany) F.; m. Christine Mildred Holmberg, Oct. 6, 1956; children: Christopher Allan, Andrew James, Nils H. B.A., U. Melbourne, 1947, M.A., 1949; Ph.D., U. Cambridge, Eng., 1953. Rsch. officer Aero. Rsch. Lab. Australian Dept. Supply, 1947-49, sr. sci. rsch. officer, 1953-55; tutor U. Melbourne, 1947-49, 53-55; asst. prof. div. applied math. Brown U., 1956-58, assoc. prof., 1958-64, prof., 1964—, dir. Computing Center, 1963-69, dir. Ctr. for Computer and Info. Scis., 1969-76, chmn. div. applied math., 1976-82, chmn. grad. com., 1985-88, assoc. chmn. div. applied math., 1988—, chmn. univ. com. on statis. sci., 1989—; lectr., cons. program in applied actuarial sci., Bryant Coll., 1986—; mem. fellowship selection panel NSF, Fulbright fellowship selection panel. Author: (with U. Grenander) A Short Course in Computational Probability and Statistics, 1971; Editor: The International Dictionary of Applied Mathematics, 1960, (with others) Applications of Digital Computers, 1963, Advances in Computers, Volume 10, 1970, Statistical Computer Performance Evaluation, 1972; Mng. editor: Quarterly of Applied Mathematics, 1965—; Contbr. numerous articles to profl. jours. Served with Australian Army, 1943-45. Fulbright fellow, 1955-56; Guggenheim fellow, 1962-63; NSF Office Naval Research grantee in field. Mem. Am. Math. Soc. (asso. editor Math. Reviews 1957-62), Soc. for Indsl. and Applied Math., Am. Statis. Assn., Inst. Math. Stats., Assn. Computing Machinery. Republican. Episcopalian. Club: Univ. (Providence). Home: 24 Alumni Ave Providence RI 02906 Office: 182 George St Providence RI 02912

FREIHERR VON KLEYDORFF, LUDWIG OTTO ALEXANDER, consulting company executive; b. Munich, Fed. Republic Germany, May 17, 1926, came to U.S., 1949, naturalized, 1955; s. Eberhardt and Angelica (Heye) F.; m. Carolina Mazzocca, Apr. 1, 1952 (div. 1973); children: Anita A. Roger, Alexander E., Axel J., Andrew; m. Ursula E. Kurth. Student U. Munich, 1946-48, U. Zurich, Switzerland, 1948-49; BS in Advt., Babson Coll., 1952. Asst. to pres. internat. div. Richardson-Vick, N.Y.C., 1952-58; mktg. exec. L.W. Froehlich Advt., N.Y.C., 1958-59; exec. dir. Il Paradiso S.A., Lamone, Switzerland, 1960-84, Paradiso Gmbh, Munich, 1958—; pres. Paradiso Inc., Wilton, Conn., 1958—; lectr. in field; assoc. dir. Union Trust Co., Norwalk, Conn. Contbr. articles to profl. jours. Trustee U. Bridgeport, Conn., 1978, internat. fellow; trustee Norwalk Hosp., 1981; vice chmn. Joint Conf. Com.; chmn. Cost Containment Com.; mem. Exec. Com. Recipient citations U.S. Dept. Commerce, 1964, Internat. Trade citations, 1964, Silver medal Advt. Assn. Am., 1958. Mem. Council Internat. Fellows, Internat. Assn. Univ. Presidents, Nat. Fgn. Trade Council, Am. Foreign Policy Assn., Am. Mfrs. Assn., Greater Norwalk C. of C., U.S. C. of C. Republican. Lutheran. Avocations: gardening, photography, traveling, literature, history. Office: Paradiso Inc PO Box 797 Wilton CT 06897

FREIMARK, JEFFREY PHILIP, retail supermarket executive; b. Bklyn., Mar. 11, 1955; s. Benjamin and Fay (Lefton) F.; m. Hollis Joan Hauser, Aug. 27, 1978; children: Samara, Brandon. BS, U. So. Fla., 1976; MBA, NYU, 1980, JD, 1984. CPA, N.J., Fla.; bar: N.J. 1985. Sr. staff acct. Abraham and Straus, Bklyn., 1976-78; internal audit dir. Stern's Dept. Store, Paramus, N.J., 1978-79; dir. acctg. Kings Super Markets, West Caldwell, N.J., 1979-82, controller, 1982-83, controller, sec., 1983-84, v.p. fin., 1985-86; sr. v.p. fin. and adminstrn., chief fin. officer, treas. Pueblo Internat. Inc., Pompano Beach, Fla., 1986—. Vol. dir. NYU Grad. Sch. Bus. Mgmt. Decision Lab., 1980-81. Mem. ABA, N.J. Bar Assn., Am. Inst. CPA's, Fla. Soc. CPA's, N.J. Soc. CPA's, Assn. MBA Execs., Fin. Execs. Inst. Republican. Jewish. Home: 3015 Andrews Pl Boca Raton FL 33434 Office: Pueblo Internat Inc 1300 NW 22nd St Pompano Beach FL 33069

FREIMUTH, JOSEPH MICHAEL, accounting company executive; b. Sebring, Fla., Feb. 21, 1944; s. Frank Frederick and Freda L. (Miller) F.; m. Catherine Ann Elliott, Dec. 26, 1981; children: Joseph Frank, Mark Elliott. BSBA, Creighton U., 1966; JD, Georgetown U., 1969. Bar: Nebr. 1969, Colo. 1969, U.S. Tax Ct. 1969; CPA, Colo., Nebr., D.C., Md. Tax profl., ptnr. Touche Ross, Omaha, 1973-83; nat. dir. tax ops. Touche Ross, Washington, 1983—; treas. Tytran, Inc., 1988—. Editor Tax Adviser mag., 1985—. Treas. Douglas County Rep. Com., Omaha, 1980-83; bd. dirs. Swanson Ctr. for Nutrition, Omaha, 1983—, Nebr. Soc. Washington, 1988—. Served with U.S. Army, 1969-70. Recipient Alumni Merit award Creighton U., 1986. Mem. AICPA, ABA, Va. Soc. CPA's, Nebr. Soc. CPA's, Internat. Club, Tower Club (McLean, Va.), Tyran Transp. Assn., Fairfax C. of C. Home: 6510 W Langley Ln McLean VA 22101 Office: Touche Ross & Co 8201 Greensboro Dr McLean VA 22102

FREIMUTH, STANLEY G., investment advisor, portfolio manager; b. Vancouver, Wash., June 8, 1948; s. Glenn and Lorraine (Benson) F.; m. Cynthia Sherwood, Mar. 20, 1970; children: Alicia, Andrea. BA in Econs., U. Wash., 1970; cert., Coll. Fin. Planning, 1982. Cert. fin. planner. Various staff positions Merrill Lynch, Seattle, 1969-70, v.p., account exec., 1971-80; br. mgr. Foster & Marshall (name changed to Shearson Lehman Hutton), Bellevue, Wash., 1980-84; first v.p./fin. cons. Shearson Lehman Hutton, Bellevue, 1984-89; sr. v.p., dir. Regan Mackenzie, Inc., Seattle, 1989—. Contbr. articles to Bellevue Jour. Am. Newspaper, 1987-88. Mem. , past pres., bd. dirs. Big Bros. of King County, Seattle, 1971—; chmn. Planning Com., Hunts Point, Wash., 1987—. Mem. Registry Fin. Planners, Internat. Assn. Fin. Planners, Chartered FIn. Analysts. Clubs: Seattle Yacht, Columbia Tower, N.W. Forum (Seattle); Bellevue Athletic. Home: 3432 Hunts Point Rd Bellevue WA 98004 Office: Regan Mackenzie 999 3d Ave Ste 4300 Seattle WA 98104

FREITAS, ANTOINETTE JUNI, insurance company executive; b. Kansas City, Mo., Feb. 14, 1944; d. Anthony P. and Mariam L. Freitas; BA, Calif. State U.-Long Beach, 1966; MA, U. So. Calif., 1974; m. Stephen R. Krajcar, July 4, 1980. Chartered life underwriter, chartered fin. cons. Counselor, U. So. Calif., 1967-70, assoc. dir. fin. aid, 1970-75; sales agt. Equitable Life Assurance Co., 1975-79, dist. mgr., San Francisco, 1979-84; pres. Group Mktg. Services, Inc., field dir. Northwestern Mut. Life, San Francisco, 1984-86; pres. Freitas-Krajcar and Assocs., 1986—; mktg. mgr. Home Life, H.L. Fin. Group, San Jose, Calif., 1986—; registered rep. W.S. Griffith Co., securities. Recipient various sales and mgmt. awards; mem. Million Dollar Round Table. Mem. Nat. Assn. Life Underwriters, AAUW, U. So. Calif. Alumni Assn., Women Life Underwriters Conf. Republican. Episcopalian. Author: A Study in Changing Youth Values, 1974. Office: HL Fin Group N 1st St Pla Suite 360 San Jose CA 95131

FREIZER, LOUIS A., radio news producer; b. N.Y.C., Oct. 10, 1931; s. Morris and Celia (Lassersohn) F.; m. Michèle Suzanne Orban, July 6, 1968; children: Sabine, Eric. BS, U. Wis., 1953; postgrad., U. Heidelberg, Fed. Republic Germany, 1956; MA, Columbia U., 1964, postgrad., 1966—. Corr. UPI, Madison, Wis., 1953-54; desk asst. CBS News, N.Y.C., 1956-59, newswriter, 1959-60; newswriter Sta. WCBS, N.Y.C., 1960-62, news editor, 1963-68, sr. news producer, 1968-73, sr. exec. news producer, 1973—; adj. prof. communications Fordham U.; lectr., cons. journalism and internat. relations. Producer: (pub. affairs series) Let's Find Out, 1966, International Briefing series, 1968-72. Served to 1st lt. U.S. Army, 1954-56; capt. USAR. Recipient Am. Legion medal; Radio Journalism award AMA, Radio Journalism award Nat. Headliners Club, Radio Journalism Nat. award for Outstanding Newscast UPI, 1st place award for Best Regularly Scheduled Local News Program N.Y. State AP Broadcasters Assn., spl. mention for Best One Day News Effort N.Y. State AP Broadcasters Assn.; fellow CBS News Found. Mem. Am. Polit. Sci. Assn., Acad. Polit. Sci., Am. Acad. Polit. and Social Scis., Radio-TV News Dirs. Assn., Broadcast Pioneers, Sigma Delta Chi. Home: 1619 3d Ave New York NY 10128 Office: Sta WCBS 51 W 52d St New York NY 10019

FRELINGHUYSEN, JOSEPH SHERMAN, JR., banker; b. Morristown, N.J., Aug. 10, 1941; s. Joseph Sherman and Emily (Lawrence) F.; m. Sylvia Margaret Stiassni, July 13, 1963; children: John, Joy, Nicholas. BA, Princeton U., 1963; postgrad., Rutgers U., Newark, 1966-70. V.p. family bus. Somerville, N.J., 1966-68; mng. dir. investment banking dept. The First Boston Corp., N.Y.C., 1969-88. Pres. Bernards Area Scholarship Com., Bernardsville, N.J., 1983-88. 1st. Lt. USMC, 1963-66, Vietnam. Mem. River Club. Republican.

FRENCH, ARTHUR LEEMAN, JR., process control and instrumentation company executive; b. Beaumont, Tex., May 16, 1940; s. Arthur Leeman and Roberta Floy (Smith) F.; m. Susan Dianne Winston, Aug. 29, 1959; children: Laura, Arthur L. B.S. in Mech. Engring., Tex A&M U., 1963; B.S. in Bus. Adminstrn., Tex. A&M U., 1963. Process industry mgr. Fisher Controls Co., Marshalltown, Iowa, 1973-76, gen. sales mgr., 1976-77, v.p. instrumentation, 1977-79, v.p. tech. and devel., 1979-80; exec. v.p. Fisher Controls Internat., Inc., Clayton, Mo., 1980-82; exec. v.p. and chief operating officer Fisher Controls Co., Clayton, Mo., 1982-85, pres., chief operating officer, 1985—; trustee Tex. A&M Research Found., College Station, 1980—. Bd. dirs. Iowa Valley Community Coll. Dist., Marshalltown, 1975-79; county campaign dir. Charles Grassley 3d dist. U.S. Congl. Campaign, Marshall County, Iowa, 1974. Served to capt. U.S. Army, 1963-66. Mem. Instrument Soc. Am., Sci. Apparatus Makers Assn. (dir. process measurement and control div. 1975-78). Republican. Presbyterian. Home: 13 Muirfield Ln Saint Louis MO 63141 Office: Fisher Controls Internat Inc 8000 Maryland Ave Clayton MO 63105

FRENCH, CLARENCE LEVI, JR., retired shipbuilding company executive; b. New Haven, Oct. 13, 1925; s. Clarence L. Sr. and Eleanor (Curry) F.; m. Jean Sprague, June 29, 1946; children: Craig Thomas, Brian Keith, Alan Scott. B.S. in Naval Sci., Tufts U., 1945, B.S. in Mech. Engring., 1947. Registered profl. engr., Calif. Foundry engr. Bethlehem Steel Corp., 1947-56; staff engr., asst. supt. Kaiser Steel Corp., 1956-64; supervisory engr. Bechtel Corp., 1964-67; with Nat. Steel & Shipbldg. Co., San Diego, 1967-86; exec. v.p., gen. mgr. Nat. Steel & Shipbldg. Co., to 1977, pres., chief operating officer, 1977-84, chmn., chief exec. officer, 1984-86; mem. maritime transp. rsch. bd. NRC. Bd. dirs. United Way, San Diego, YMCA, San Diego; past chmn., bd. dirs. Pres. Roundtable; chmn. emeritus bd. trustees Webb Inst. Lt. USN, 1943-53. Fellow Soc. Naval Architects and Marine Engrs. (hon., past pres.), Shipbuilders Council Am. (past chmn. exec. com.), ASTM, Am. Bur. Shipping; mem. Am. Soc. Naval Engrs., U.S. Naval Inst., Navy League U.S., Propeller Club U.S.

FRENCH, HAROLD S., food company executive; b. Bklyn., Oct. 2, 1921; s. Morris and Fay (Kaufman) F.; m. Claire E. Weingart, Oct. 3, 1943 (dec. Mar. 1983); children: Madelaine Diane, Janet Gail; m. Gloria Rosario, June 2, 1984. BA, L.I. U., 1942; postgrad., NYU, 1950, Columbia U., 1960. Asst. buyer R.H. Macy Co., N.Y.C., 1949-52; group mgr. Abraham & Straus Co., Hempstead, N.Y., 1952-54; mdse. mgr. Popular Club Plan, Passaic, N.J., 1954-60, Nat. Silver Co., N.Y.C., 1964-69; mktg. dir. Waverly Products Co., Phila., 1970-74; pres. Pet Food Industries, Inc., N.Y.C., 1974—, Harold French & Co., Inc., N.Y.C., 1974—; chmn. Rosario Homes, Inc., P.R.; pres. King Agro-Indsl. Corp., 1986, King Agro-Shellfish (Nigeria) Ltd., 1988—, King Agro-Cattle Ranching (Nigeria) Ltd., 1988—. Patentee in field. Served with M.I., U.S. Army, 1943-45. Decorated Bronze Star. Home: 60 E 8th St New York NY 10003 Office: 432 Park Ave S New York NY 10016

FRENCH, HENRY PIERSON, JR., historian, educator; b. Rochester, N.Y., Nov. 21, 1934; s. Henry Pierson and Genevieve Lynn (Johnson) F.; AB, U. Del., 1960; MA, U. Rochester, 1961, MA in Edn., 1962, EdD, 1968; m. Beverly Anne Bauernschmidt, Aug. 22, 1959; children—Henry Pierson III, Donna Lynn (dec.), William Dean, Susan Gayle, John Douglas. Tchr. Pittsford (N.Y.) Cen. High Sch., 1962-66; field service asso. U. Rochester, N.Y., 1962-66, asso. lectr., 1967-68, vis. asst. prof. Coll. Edn. and E. Asian Ctr., 1968-69; adj. asst. prof. history SUNY-Monroe Community Coll., 1964-67, asst. prof. history, 1967-70, assoc. prof., 1970-74, prof., 1974—, chmn. dept. history and polit. sci., 1979-85, chmn. tenure, promotion com., sabbatical leave, 1986; asst. prof. edn. U. Rochester, 1969-70, assoc. prof., 1970-72, lectr. East Asian studies East Asian Ctr., 1972-74, sr. lectr., 1974—; vis. prof. history, 1988-89; prof. Canisius Coll., summers 1968, 69, 71, 73, 89, Dunlop Tire Corp. Japan Inst. faculty, 1989; Rochester Inst. Tech., 1969-70, spring 1977, SUNY, Brockport, summer 1971; adj. mentor State U. N.Y.-Empire State Coll., 1976; dir. polit. insts. Robert A. Taft Inst. for Govt., 1962-65; co-dir., adminstr. NDEA insts., 1965-69; bd. dirs. Rochester Assn. UN, 1972-83, 85—, chmn. policy com., 1972-74, v.p., 1975-77, pres., 1977-78, chmn. bd., 1978-79, chmn. nominating com., 1983-84; panelist 10th conf. Internat. Assn. Historians of Asia, Singapore, 1986. Vestryman St. Thomas Episcopal Ch., Rochester, 1965-68; vestryman Christ Episc. Ch., Pittsford, 1976-79, jr. warden, 1979-80, sr. warden, 1980-81, chmn. rector selection com., 1982; del. to diocesan Conv., 1989—; mem. commn. on Ordained Ministry, Episcopal Diocese of Rochester (N.Y.), 1988; trustee Friends of Rochester Pub. Library, 1983—, v.p., 1986-88, pres., 1988—; chmn., presenter Rochester Literary Award to James Baldwin, 1986. Served with AUS, 1955-57. Ctr. for Internat. Programs and Comparative Studies grantee, 1970. Mem. Assn. Asian Studies, Am. Acad. Polit. and Social Scis., Chinese Lang. Tchrs. Assn., AAUP, Torch Clubs Internat. (dir. Rochester chpt. 1973-76, v.p. 1973-74, pres. 1974-75), Rochester Com. on Fgn. Relations, Delta Tau Delta. Episcopalian. Club: University (dir. 1973-76, 87-90, v.p. 1975-76, sec. 1988—, chmn. nominating com. for bd. dirs. 1977) (Rochester). Moderator, permanent panelist Fgn. Policy Assn. and Rochester Assn. for UN Great Decisions-1973, 77, 78 series Channel 21 Ednl. TV, Rochester; cons., panelist Great Decisions TV series, 1982, 84; moderator, host Disciplines Within the Social Sciences series, 1968. Contbr. articles to profl. jours. Home: 78 Smith Rd Pittsford NY 14534 Office: U Rochester Asian Studies Faculty Ctr for Spl Degree Programs Rochester NY 14627 also: SUNY-Monroe Community Coll Rochester NY 14623

FRENCH, JAMES WILLIAM, oil company executive; b. Guthrie Center, Iowa, Aug. 3, 1935; s. Dean William and Emma Lynette (Carmichael) F.; m. Sharon Kay Biggs; children: Jennifer, Jeffrey. BS in Indsl. Adminstrn., Iowa State U., 1957; MBA in Acctg., Denver U., 1963. Exec. Arthur Anderson & Co., Denver, 1958-59, Coastal Corp., Houston, 1959—. Capt. arty. U.S. Army. Mem. Am. Inst. CPA's., Westside Racquet Club, Houston City Club, Corinthian Point Yacht and Racquet Club. Office: Coastal Holding Corp 9 Greenway Pla E Houston TX 77046

FRENCH, JOHN, III, lawyer; b. Boston, July 12, 1932; s. John and Rhoda (Walker) F.; m. Leslie Ten Eyck, Jan. 11, 1957 (div. 1961) children: John B., Lawrence C.; m. Ann Hubbell, Jan. 9, 1965 (div. 1983); children: Daniel J., Susanna H.; m. Marina Kellen, Nov. 21, 1987. BA, Dartmouth Coll., 1955; JD, Harvard U., 1958. Bar: N.Y. 1959. Assoc. Milbank, Tweed, Hadley & McCloy, N.Y.C., 1961-68, Satterlee & Stephens, N.Y.C., 1968-73; asst. gen. counsel Continental Group, Inc., Stamford, Conn., 1973-81; v.p., gen. counsel, sec. Peabody Internat. Corp., Stamford, Conn., 1981-82; ptnr. Appleton, Rice & Perrin, N.Y.C., 1982-84, Beveridge and Diamond, N.Y.C., 1985—; lectr. Practising Law Inst., 1979-83, Am. Law Inst., 1978; bd. dirs. Resorts Mgmt., Inc., U.S Tel. Inc., N.Y.C. Contbr. articles to profl. jours. Trustee Hudson River Found., 1982—, YM-YWCA Camping Services of Greater N.Y., Inc., 1983—; bd. dirs. Third St. Music Sch. Settlement House, Inc., N.Y.C., Internat. House, Inc., N.Y.C., Young Concert Artists, Inc., 1980—; mem. Westchester County Planning Bd., 1974-85; mem. N.Y. State Environ. Bd., 1976-88. Served to capt. JAGC, USAF, 1958-61. Mem. ABA, N.Y. State Bar Assn. (lectr.), Assn. Bar City N.Y. (lectr.), Environ. Law Inst., Am. Soc. Corp. Secs. Republican. Clubs: River, Harvard, Knickerbocker (N.Y.C), Century. Home: 33 E 70th St New York NY 10021 Office: Beveridge & Diamond 101 Park Ave Suite 1202 New York NY 10178

FRENCH, LEW DANIEL, III, chemical engineer; b. Houston, Dec. 9, 1960; S. Lew Daniel Jr. and Frances Anne (Edwards) F.; m. Alyssa Rubin, Aug. 2, 1987. BS in Chem. Engring., Rensselaer Poly. Inst., 1983; MBA, U. Houston, Clear Lake, 1986. Tech. sales rep. Stauffer Chem. Co., Houston, 1984-85, process engr., 1985-87; assoc. cons. ICF Kaiser Engrs., Washington, 1987-88; lead chem. engr. ICF Kaiser Engrs., Fairfax, Va., 1988—. Mem. Am. Inst. Chem. Engrs., Rensselaer Poly. Inst. Alumni (v.p. 1983-88), Theta Chi, Rensselaer Club Houston (pres. 1984-86), Rensselaer Club Washington (v.p. 1987-88, pres. 1988-89). Office: ICF Kaiser Engrs 9300 Lee Hwy Fairfax VA 22031-1207

FRENCH, LINDA JEAN, lawyer; b. Newark, N.Y., Nov. 12, 1947; d. Allyn B. and Willa E. (Cronk) Wrench; m. William J. French, Aug. 27, 1966; children: Mark W., David A. BA summa cum laude, William Jewell Coll., 1969; JD with distinction, U. Mo., 1978. Bar: Mo. 1978, U.S. Dist. Ct. (we. and ea. dists.) Mo. 1978, U.S. Ct. Appeals (8th and 10th cirs.) 1978, U.S. Ct. Appeals (D.C. cir.) 1979. Assoc. Blackwell Sanders Matheny Weary & Lombardi, Kansas City, Mo., 1978-82, ptnr., 1983-84; gen. counsel, sec. Payless Cashways Inc., Kansas City, 1984-86, v.p., gen. counsel/sec., 1986—; bd. dirs. Legal Aid Western Mo.; vis. instr. grad. program Webster Coll., Kansas City, 1979. Pres. Town and Country Homes Assn., Shawnee Mission, Kans., 1987, v.p., 1985-86; mem. Kansas City Task Force on Drug Abuse, 1986-87; chmn. William Jewell Coll. Commn. on Adult and Student Recruitment, Liberty, Mo., 1984—, Alumni bd. govs. and exec. com., 1987-88, Kansas City Tomorrow, 1988-89; mem., bd. dirs. Legal Aid of Western Mo., 1989—; bd. dirs. Greater Kansas City Jr. Achievement, 1985-86, Kansas City Tomorrow Leadership Program, 1988-89. Named one of Outstanding Young Women in Am., 1974, one of Top 100 Women in Corp. Am. Bus. Month, 1989. Mem. ABA (com. on labor and employment law, com. on bus., banking and corps.), Mo. Bar Assn., Kansas City Met. Bar Assn. (vice chmn. corp. house counsel com. 1986, chmn. corp. house counsel com. 1987; lectr. continuing legal edn. program), Kansas City Assn. Women Lawyers, Am. Corp. Counsel Assn., Am. Soc. Corp. Secs., U. Mo. Kansas City Alumni Assn., William Jewell Coll. Alumni Assn. (bd. govs. 1984—, bd. govs. exec. com. 1987-88, Kansas City Club (mem. pers. com. 1987—), Cen. Exch. Club (personnel com. Kansas City chpt. 1987—). Presbyterian. Clubs: Kansas City, Cen. Exchange (Kansas City) (mem. personnel com. Office: Payless Cashways Inc 2300 Main St PO Box 419466 Kansas City MO 64141-0466

FRENCH, MARGO ANN, financial planner; b. Morehead City, N.C., Jan. 9, 1948; d. Robert Arthur and Dolores (Holtman) F.; m. Edwin A. Vogt, May 29, 1971 (div. Sept. 1975). Student, St. Petersburg Jr. Coll., Clearwater, Fla., 1975; BA, U. South Fla., 1984; postgrad., U. Tampa, 1985-87. Cert. fin. planner; registered respiratory therapist. Rsch. technician Merrell Nat. Labs., Cin., 1966-73; respiratory therapist Tampa (Fla.) Gen. Hosp., 1975-86; fin. planner IDS/Am. Express, Tampa, 1986-89; adj. clin. instr. St. Petersburg Jr. Coll., 1978-79. Mem. Phi Theta Kappa.

FRENCH, MARK DENNIS, business lobby and association executive; b. Istanbul, Turkey, Aug. 12, 1954; s. Harry George and Dorothy G. (Meister) F.; m. Carol Lynn Klipple, Aug. 28, 1982; children: Kathleen Michelle, Brian David. BA, Loyola U., Los Angeles, 1976; MBA, Loyola Marymount U., 1979. Asst. nat. bank examiner U.S. Dept. Treasury, Los Angeles, 1976-78; asst. v.p. City Nat. Corp., Beverly Hills, 1978-79; nat. account mgr. U.S. C. of C., Dallas, 1979-82; dir. devel. U.S. C. of C., Washington, 1982-87; v.p. corp. relations Am. Trucking Assn., Alexandria, Va., 1987—; mem. bus. adv. council Ind. U. Pres. Westmoreland Hills Citizens Assn., Bethesda, 1985. Mem. Am. Soc. Assn. Execs., Am. Trucking Assn. (v.p. corp. relations). Republican. Roman Catholic. Club: Brookhaven Country (Dallas). Home: 8017 Greentree Rd Bethesda MD 20817 Office: Am Trucking Assn Inc 2200 Mill Rd Alexandria VA 22314

FRENCH, PHILIP FRANKS, agricultural cooperative corporate executive; b. Albion, Ind., June 16, 1932; s. Charles E. and Helene Alwilda (Franks) F.; m. Jo Ann Pyle, Nov. 21, 1951 (dec. July 1979); children: Douglas G., Randall B., Deborah A., French Farmer, Rebecca L. Meidema; m. Kathleen Louise DeBaun, Mar. 22, 1980. B.S. in Commerce, Internat. Bus. Coll., 1952. Asst. mgr. Clay County Farm Bur. Coop., Brazil, Ind., 1957-62; gen. mgr. Allen County Farm Bur. Coop., New Haven, Ind., 1962-66; mgr. mem. services Ind. Farm Bur. Coop., Indpls., 1966-70, asst. exec. v.p., 1970-80, pres., 1980—; mem. exec. com. CF Industries, Long Gorve, Ill., 1975—; observer on bd. A.C. Toepfer, Internat., Hamburg, W. Ger., 1980—. Mem. U.S. Nat. Alcohol Fuels Commn., Washington, 1980-81; bd. dirs. Ind. Inst. Agr. Food and Nutrition, Grad. Inst. Cooperative Leadership, U. Mo. Mem. Nat. Council of Farmer Coops. (dir.). Republican. Methodist. Club: Columbia (Indpls.). Office: Ind Farm Bur Coop Assn 120 E Market St Indianapolis IN 46204

FRENZER, PETER FREDERICK, insurance company executive; b. Omaha, Aug. 19, 1934; s. William J. and Ruth E. (Berliner) F.; m. Mary Virginia Yates, June 1, 1957; children: Peter, Michelle M., Christopher P., Jennifer S., Paula B. B.S. summa cum laude, Creighton U., 1956; student, Creighton U. Coll. Law, 1956-57; LL.B. cum laude, William Mitchell Coll. Law, 1961; LLD (hon.), Otterbein Coll., 1988. C.P.A., Nebr. Investment analyst, cost acct. Prudential Ins. Co., Mpls., 1957-62; v.p. securities, 2d v.p., analyst United Benefit Life Ins. Co., Omaha, 1962-74; v.p. investments Heritage Securities Inc., Columbus, Ohio, 1974-81; v.p. securities investment Nationwide Ins. Cos., Columbus, 1977-81, exec. v.p. investments, 1981—. Trustee Otterbein Coll., Westerville, Ohio, 1983—. Served to capt. U.S. Army, 1957. Mem. ABA, Nebr. Bar Assn., Minn. Bar Assn., Fin. Analysts Fedn. Roman Catholic. Office: Nationwide Mut Ins Co 1 Nationwide Pla Columbus OH 43216

FRESE, EDWARD SCHEER, JR., information systems executive, consultant; b. N.Y.C., Oct. 17, 1944; s. Edward Scheer and Sylvana (Cerutti) F.; stepson Mary Margaret (Richardson) F.; m. Christine Ann Robinson, Oct. 27, 1979; 1 child, Edward Robinson. AB in Latin, Hamilton Coll., 1966; postgrad., NYU, 1970-72. Programmer trainee Mfr.'s Hanover Trust Co., N.Y.C., 1969-70, systems analyst, 1970-75, officer, 1975-81; project mgr. Macmillan, Inc., N.Y.C., 1981-84, dir. fin. systems, 1984—. Episcopalian. Clubs: Point O' Woods, University (N.Y.C.). Home: 7 W 14th St Apt 7G New York NY 10011 Office: Macmillan Inc 866 Third Ave New York NY 10022

FREUND, RICHARD L., communications company executive, consultant, lawyer; b. N.Y.C., Jan. 30, 1921; s. Sidney J. and Cora (Strasser) F.; m. Esta Neiman, Apr. 16, 1950; children: Alice, Robert, Charles. BA, NYU, 1941; LLB, Columbia U., 1944. Bar: N.Y. 1944, U.S. Dist. Ct. (so. dist.) N.Y. 1944. Assoc. Lauterstein, Spiller, Bergerman & Dannett, N.Y.C., 1943-46; labor adminstr. Publix Shirt Corp., N.Y.C., 1946-47; atty. R.H. Macy & Co. Inc., N.Y.C., 1947-54; labor atty. NBC, N.Y.C., 1954-57; dir. labor relations ABC-Paramount Theatres Inc., N.Y.C., 1957-60; v.p. labor relations ABC, N.Y.C., 1960-72, corp. v.p. labor relations, 1972-86; corp. v.p. labor relations Capital Cities/ABC Inc., N.Y.C., 1986-87, cons., 1987—; co-chmn. bd. trustee Am. Fedn. Musicians Pension Fund, N.Y.C., 1967-87; trustee AFTRA Health and Retirement Fund, N.Y.C., 1964-87, Nat. Assn. Broadcast Employees and Technicians Pension Fund, N.Y.C., 1964-87. Contbg. author: Susbidiary Rights and Residuals, 1968. Mem. Phi Beta Kappa. Jewish. Home and Office: 90 Gerard Ave W Malverne NY 11565

FREUND, WILLIAM CURT, economist; b. Nuremberg, Germany, Sept. 4, 1926; came to U.S., 1937, naturalized, 1942; s. Hugo and Paula (Gruenstein) F.; m. Judith Irmgard Steinberger, Aug. 14, 1951; children: Hugo, Nancy, Sandra. B.B.A., CCNY, 1949; M.S., Columbia U., 1950, Ph.D., 1954. Economist Prudential Ins. Co. Am., 1950-59; asso. prof. fin. N.Y. U. Grad. Sch. Bus. Adminstrn., 1959-62; exec. dir., chief economist Prudential Ins. Co. Am., 1963-67; sr. v.p., chief economist N.Y. Stock Exchange, 1968-85; prof. econs. Pace U. Grad. Sch. Bus., 1972—, N.Y. Stock Exchange prof. econs. and internat. bus., chmn. dept., 1985—; mem. econ. policy council to Gov. of N.J., 1989—. Author: Investment Fundamentals, 5th edit, 1981, (with E. Epstein) People and Productivity, 1984; also articles. Named Disting. Alumnus Coll. City N.Y., 1974. Mem. Am. Econ. Assn., Met. Econ. Assn., Am. Finance Assn., Am. Statis. Assn., Nat. Assn. Bus. Economists. Office: Pace Univ Pace Plaza New York NY 10038

FREVERT, DOUGLAS JAMES, financial consultant; b. Englewood, N.J., Dec. 11, 1952; s. James Wilmot and Jean Sunderlin F.; m. Vada Sue Dyle, Sept. 10, 1983. BS in Bus. Adminstrn., U. Fla., 1981. Cert. fin. planner. Air traffic controller USN, Rota, Spain, 1972-77; securities broker Lincoln Investment Planning, Phila., 1981-83; fin. planner Cert. Fin. Services, Orlando, Fla., 1983-85; fin. cons. Thomson McKinnon Securities, Inc., North Palm Beach, Fla., 1985—. Mem. Nat. Rep. Com., Washington, 1979—. Named Mgmt. Devel. Project of Yr. U.S. Jaycees, 1986-87. Mem. Internat. Assn. Fin. Planning (edn. v.p. 1988-89), Inst. Cert. Fin. Planners, Internat. Bd. Standards and Practices Cert. Fin. Planners, Palm Beach-Martin County Estate Planning Council. Club: North Palm Beach-Palm Beach Gardens Jaycees (fin. mgmt. v.p. 1988-89). Home: 4424 Althea Way Palm Beach Gardens FL 33410 Office: Thomson McKinnon Securities Inc 713 US Hwy 1 North Palm Beach FL 33408

FREVERT, JAMES WILMOT, financial planner; b. Richland Twp., Iowa, Dec. 19, 1922; s. Wesley Clarence and Grace Lotta (Maw) F.; m. Jean Emily Sunderlin, Feb. 12, 1949; children—Douglas James, Thomas Jeffrey, Kimberly Ann. B.S. in Gen. Engrg., MIT, 1948. Prodn. mgr. Air Reduction Chem. Co., Calvert City, Ky., 1955-61; plant mgr. Air Products & Chems., West Palm Beach, Fla., 1961-62; pres. Young World HWD, Ft. Lauderdale, Fla., 1962-66; v.p. Shareholders Mgmt. Co., Los Angeles, 1966-73; v.p. cert. fin. planner Thomson McKinnon Securities, Inc., North Palm Beach, Fla., 1973—. Founder, past pres. MIT Club Palm Beach County, dir., 1976—, ednl. council mem., 1977-81. Served to 1st lt. USAF, 1943-46. Mem. Internat. Assn. Fin. Planning (dir. Gold Coast chpt. 1968-87), Inst. Cert. Fin. Planners (cert. 1975, registry fin. planners 1983—). Republican. Presbyterian. Club: Palm Beach Pundits. Home: 883 Country Club Dr North Palm Beach FL 33408 Office: Thomson McKinnon 713 US Hwy 1 North Palm Beach FL 33408

FREWIN, WILLIAM ARTHUR, JR., cable television executive; b. Queens, N.Y., Oct. 5, 1942; s. William Arthur and Rita Grace (Amorese) F.; BBA, Pace U., 1966; m. Lillian Veronica Burns, Feb. 15, 1969; children: William Patrick, Lynda Marie. Mgmt. trainee Chase Manhattan Bank, N.Y.C., 1960-65; pub. accountant Peat, Marwick, Mitchell & Co., 1966-69; asst. corporate controller, subs. controller Athlone Industries, Inc., 1969-70; controller, asst. to chmn. bd. Harvey's Stores, Inc., N.Y.C., 1970-71; controller; chief fin. officer Yankelovich, Skelly & White, Inc. subs. Reliance Group, Inc., N.Y.C., 1971-77; controller Cablevision Co., Woodbury, N.Y., 1977—. Active Syosset Civic Assn., 1975—. Served with AUS, 1966-67. CPA, N.Y. Mem. Nat. Assn. Accountants (dir. socio-econ. program 1973—), Am. Inst. CPA's, N.Y. State Soc. CPA's (retail accounting com. 1971—, community affairs com. 1974—, cooperation with bankers com. 1973, 80, 81, 82, commerce and industry com. 1979-82, chmn. com. 1982-83, exec. bd. 1983, 84, treas. 1985-86), Tax Inst. C.W. Post Coll., Am. Mgmt. Assn. Office: One Media Crossways Woodbury NY 11797

FREY, DALE FRANKLIN, manufacturing company executive; b. Lancaster, Pa., Aug. 14, 1932; s. Franklin W. and Mary A. (Strickler) F.; m. Betty Ann Heistand, Aug. 22, 1953; children—Scott, Philip, Kyle, Susan. B.S. in Econs., Franklin and Marshall Coll., 1954; M.B.A., NYU, 1957. With Gen. Elec. Co., Fairfield, Conn., 1957—, mgr. group fin. ops., 1975-77, internat. and Can. group staff exec., internat. sector, 1977-80, v.p., treas., 1980-84; v.p. corp. investments, treas. Gen. Elec. Co., Stamford, 1984—; chmn. bd., pres. Gen. Elec. Investment Corp., Stamford, 1984—; bd. dirs. Gen. Elec. Capital Corp., Stamford, Arkwright Ins. Co., Waltham, Mass., Health-tex, Inc., 1987, Wyndham Foods, Westmark Systems, Inc. Served to capt. USAF, 1955-57. Mem. Fin. Execs. Inst. (chmn. com. corp. fin. 1983-85). Clubs: Aspetuck Valley Country (Weston, Conn.), Landmark (Stamford). Office: Gen Elec Investment Corp 3003 Summer St PO Box 7900 Stamford CT 06904 also: Gen Electric Co 3135 Easton Turnpike Fairfield CT 06431

FREY, DONALD NELSON, engineer, educator, manufacturing company executive; b. St. Louis, Mar. 13, 1923; s. Muir Luken and Margaret Bryden (Nelson) F.; m. Mary Elizabeth Glynn, June 30, 1971; children by previous marriage: Donald Nelson, Judith Kingsley, Margaret Bente, Catherine, Christopher, Elizabeth. Student, Mich. State Coll., 1940-42; BS, U. Mich., 1947, MS, 1949, PhD, 1950, DS (hon.), 1965; DS, U. Mo., Rolla, 1966. Instr. metall. engring. U. Mich., 1949-50, asst. prof. chem. and metall. engring., 1950-51; research engr. Babcock & Wilcox Tube Co., Beaver Falls, Pa., 1951; various research positions Ford Motor Co. (Ford div.), 1951-57, various engring. positions, 1958-61, product planning mgr., 1961-62, asst. gen. mgr., 1962-65, gen. mgr., 1965-68, co. v.p., 1965-67, v.p. for product devel., 1967-68; pres. Gen. Cable Corp., N.Y.C., 1968-71; pres. Bell & Howell Co., Chgo., 1973-81, chmn., chief exec. officer, 1971-88, also bd. dirs.; prof. of indsl. engring. and mgmt. sci. Northwestern U., Evanston, Ill., 1988—; bd. dirs. Clark Equipment Co., Cin. Milicron, Spring Industries, Andrew Corp., Spring Industries, Andrew Corp. Co-chmn. Gov.'s Commn. of Sci. and Industry, Ill., 1988—. Served with AUS, 1943-46. Named Young Engr. of Yr., Engring. Soc. Detroit, 1953, Outstanding Alumni, U. Mich. Coll. Engring., 1957, Outstanding Young Man of Yr., Detroit Jr. Bd. Commerce, 1958. Mem. Am. Inst. Mining Metall. and Petroleum Engrs. (chmn. Detroit chpt. 1954, chmn., editor Nat Symposium on Sheet Steels 1956), Am. Soc. Metals, Nat. Acad. Engring. (mem. council 1972), ASME, Soc. Automotive Engrs. (vice chmn. Detroit 1958, Russell Springer award 1956), Detroit Engring. Soc. (bd. dirs. 1962-65), Nat. Acad. Engrs., Elec. Mfrs. Club, Council on Fgn. Relations, Chgo. Club, Saddle and Cycle Club, Tavern Club, Sigma Xi, Phi Kappa Phi, Tau Beta Pi, Phi Delta Theta. Home: 3470 Lake Shore Dr Chicago IL 60657 Office: Northwestern U Tech Inst 2145 Sheridan Rd Evanston IL 60208

FREY, HERMAN S., publishing company executive; b. Murfreesboro, Tenn., Apr. 19, 1920; s. Saleem McCool and Minnie May (Felts) F.; m. Daisy Rook Corlew, Apr. 3, 1946; 1 child, Pamela Anne. Cert. commerce, U. Va., 1958; cert., Internat. Ct. Justice, The Netherlands, 1959; BA, Am. U., 1964; MBA, George Washington U., 1965; cert. constl. history, Oxford U., 1974, cert. fgn. and imperial policy, 1975. Commd. navigator USN, 1937-61; advanced through grades to lt. comdr., 1955; with navigation dept. USS Quincy, 1937-41, navigator USS Sagamore, 1941-42, asst. navigator USS Iowa, 1942-44, with Naval Schs., Norfolk, Va., N.Y.C., Miami, 1944-

45, navigation and gunnery officer USS Zuni, 1945-46, exec. officer USS Chickasaw, 1946-47, comdg. officer, 1947-48; instr. Naval Sch., Boston, 1948-51; comdg. officer USS Sisken, 1951-52; comdr. mine div., task unit, 1952-54; exec. officer USS McClellan, 1954-55; officer detailer Bur. Naval Personnel, Washington, 1955-58; advisor, liaison Am. Embassy, The Netherlands, 1958-61; stock broker Auchincloss, Parker & Redpath, Arlington, Va., 1966-67; asst. prof. Georgetown U., Washington, 1967, U. Va., Charlottesville, 1967-69; freelance journalist Europe, U.S., 1972-76; pres. Frey Enterprises, 1976—; faculty U. Md., College Park, 1978; mem. bd. govs. Am. Sch. of Hague, Netherlands, 1959-61; cons. State of Tenn., 1969-70. Author: Jefferson Davis, 1977. Ran for U.S. Senate, Tenn., 1970, 72; bd. govs. Meth. Ch., Arlington, 1962-64; mem. U.S. Hist. Soc., Nat. Trust for Hist. Preservation; research bd. advisors Am. Biog. Inst., Inc. Mem. Am. Bus. Men's Assn., The Hague, 1958-61. Mem. World Inst. Achievement, Soc. Advancement Mgmt. (pres. 1964), AAUP, Internat. Platform Assn., U.S. Naval Inst. (life), Tenn. Hist. Soc., Tenn. Sheriff's Assn., Ret. Officers Assn. (life), Nat. Assn. Uniformed Services (life), Am. Legion, VFW (life), Navy League of U.S., Vets. Assn. of USS Iowa, Phi Alpha Theta. Democrat. Club: Mil. Dist. Officer's (Washington). Avocations: history, literature, collecting rare books, travel, amateur cooking. Office: Frey Enterprises 2120 Crestmoor Rd Nashville TN 37215

FREY, MARC LUTHER, small business owner; b. Norfolk, Nebr., Mar. 18, 1931; s. Immanuel Paul and Elizabeth (Janz) F.; m. Neva Luella Kattke, Sept. 15, 1956; children: Marc B., Lindsay, Miriam. BSBA, Denver U., 1955. Pres. Frey's Hallmark, San Antonio, 1982—; bd. dirs. Ch. Mut. Ins., Merrill, Wis.; instr. U. Tex., San Antonio, 1982-83. With USAF, 1951-53. Mem. Sales and Mktg. Execs. (pres. 1979, Fred Klemp award 1982). Republican. Lutheran. Home: 1402 Tayton Ln San Antonio TX 78231 Office: 4729 Shavano Oak San Antonio TX 78249

FREY, ROBERT IMBRIE, lawyer; b. Washington, July 28, 1943; s. Donald S. and Janet (Imbrie) F.; m. Peggy Lynne LaBuda, Dec. 18, 1965; children: Robert Imbrie Jr., James Christopher. BA, Colo. State U., 1965; JD, Duke U., 1968. Bar: Ohio 1968, Mich. 1988. Assoc. Arter & Hadden, Cleve., 1968-71; atty. TRW Inc., Cleve., 1972-83; sr. counsel Whirlpool Corp., Benton Harbor, Mich., 1983-84, asst. gen. counsel, 1984-85, v.p., gen. counsel, 1985—, asst. sec., 1986. Mem. ABA, Mich. Bar Assn., Ohio Bar Assn., Cleve./Cuyahoga County Bar Assn., Berrien County Bar Assn. Club: Berrien Hills Country (Benton Harbor). Home: 3414 Valley View Dr Saint Joseph MI 49085 Office: Whirlpool Corp 2000 M-63 N Benton Harbor MI 49022

FREY, STUART MACKLIN, automobile manufacturing company executive; b. Peoria, Ill., Feb. 13, 1925; s. Muir Luken and Margaret Bryden (Nelson) F.; m. Lillian Maxine Paxton, 1951; children: Mellissa June, Muir Paxton. B.S. in Mech. Engring, U. Mich., 1949; S.M. in Indsl. Mgmt, Mass. Inst. Tech., 1961. With Budd Co., 1949-53; with Ford Motor Co., 1953—; chief car research engr. Ford Motor Co., Dearborn, Mich., 1974-75; chief vehicle engr. Ford Motor Co., 1975-80, v.p. car engring., 1980-83, v.p. car product devel., 1983-87, v.p. engring. and mfg. staff, 1987-88, v.p. tech. affairs, 1988—. Contbr. articles to profl. jours. Served as officer AUS, 1943-46, 51-52. Sloan fellow, 1960-61. Fellow Soc. Automotive Engrs., Engring. Soc. Detroit; mem. Am. Soc. Body Engrs., Tau Beta Pi, Pi Tau Sigma. Republican. Home: 3790 N Darlington St Birmingham MI 48010 Office: Ford Motor Co The American Rd Detroit MI 48121

FREYD, WILLIAM PATTINSON, fund raising executive, consultant; b. Chgo., Apr. 1, 1933; s. Paul Robert Freyd and Pauline Margaret (Pattinson) Gardiner; m. Diane Marie Carlson, May 19, 1984. B of Sci. and Foreign Svc., Georgetown U., 1960. Field rep. Georgetown U., Washington, 1965-67; campaign dir. Tamblyn and Brown, N.Y.C., 1967-70; dir. devel. St. George's Ch., N.Y.C., 1971; assoc. Browning Assocs., Newark, 1972-73; regional v.p. C.W. Shaver Co., N.Y.C., 1973-74; founder, chmn. IDC, Bloomfield, N.J., 1974—. Mem. Nat. Soc. Fund Raising Execs. (N.Y. chpt. pres. 1974-76, treas. 1980-81, cert. 1982), Am. Assn. Fund Raising Counsel (sec. 1984-86), N.Y. Yacht Club, Union League Club of N.Y., Essex Club, Masons, Nassau Club, Circumnavigators Club. Home: 96 S Terrace Short Hills NJ 07078 Office: IDC 1260 Broad St Bloomfield NJ 07003

FREYTAG, DONALD ASHE, management consultant; b. Chgo., Apr. 17, 1937; s. Elmer Walter and Mary Louise (Mayo) F.; m. Elizabeth Ritchie Robertson, Dec. 19, 1964; children: Donald C., Gavin K., Alexander M. BA, Yale U., 1959; MBA, Harvard U., 1963. Pres. Mgmts. West, LaJolla, Calif., 1963-65; mktg. asst. Norton Simon, Inc., Fullerton, Calif., 1965-67; product mgr. Warner-Lambert, Inc., Morristown, N.J., 1967-70; group mgr. mktg. and planning, dir. advt. Pepsi-Cola Co., Purchase, N.Y., 1970-72; from v.p. mktg. to exec. v.p. Beverage Mgmt., Inc., Columbus, Ohio, 1972-76, pres., 1976-79, vice-chmn., 1979-80; pres. Freytag Mgmt. Co., Columbus, 1980-82, 84—, G.D. Ritzy's, Inc., Columbus, 1982-84; bd. dirs. Guradian Electronics Co., InaComp Computer Ctrs., Quinn's Sleep Ctrs., Zee Med. Svcs., all in Columbus. Pres. Cen. Ohio Ctr. for Econ. Edn., 1978-80, 81-87; bd. dirs. Columbus Acad., 1982-84. Capt. U.S. Army, 1959-61. Mem. Nat. Assn. Corp. Dirs., HBS Club Columbus, Yale Cen. Ohio. Office: 7710 Olentangy River Rd Columbus OH 43235

FRICK, ROBERT HATHAWAY, lawyer; b. Cleve., June 28, 1924; s. Claude Oates and Urshal May (Hathaway) F.; m. Lenore R. Maurin, Aug. 16, 1947; children—Elaine D., Barbara A. Frick Bundick, Catherine L. Frick Cayer. BBA, U. Mich., 1948, JD, 1950; postgrad. Harvard Bus. Sch., 1965. Bar: Mich. 1951, Ill. 1951, Ohio 1952, N.Y. 1962, U.S. Supreme Ct. 1981. Atty., Amoco Corp. (formerly Standard Oil Co. Ind.), Chgo., 1950, 52-60, Paris, 1960-62, N.Y.C., 1962-68, Chgo., 1968-71, assoc. gen. counsel, Chgo., 1972-87; pvt. practice, Cleve., 1951-52. Served with USAAF, 1943-46. Mem. ABA, Am. Soc. Internat. Law, Ill. Bar Assn., Chgo. Bar Assn., Order of Coif, Westmoreland Country Club, Execs. Club, Mid Am. Club, Sigma Phi Epsilon. Republican. Home: 330 Cumnor Rd Kenilworth IL 60043

FRICKE, MARJORIE ONETA, tax consultant; b. Gainesville, Tex., Nov. 17, 1932; d. Herman Clay and Gladys Weatherman (Strange) Lewter; m. Fred H. Fricke, Jr., May 7, 1962; children: Merle, Darwin, Adeline. BA, BS, Tex. Woman's U., 1955; PhD, Tex. State Coll. for Women, 1978. Membership dir. pub. utilities commn. Rural Electric Assn., Gainesville, Dallas, Denton, Houston, 1946-76; owner, trustee Surety Corp., Dallas, 1958; financier, chmn. membership Fed. Power Commn. Lone Star Gas Industries, Washington, 1949—; ptnr. Christian Broadcasting Network, Inc. Richmond, Va., 1976—; pres., trainee Meth. Youth Seminar Clubwoman, Whitesboro, Tex., 1950—; financier, exec. adminstr. Found. for Christina Living, Pawling, N.Y., 1948—; trustee Confederated State Soc., 1976—. Counselor Camp Fire Girls Am.; leader Boy Scouts Am.; benefactress, binomailment Dept. Transp., Omaha, 1951—. Mem. Confederated State Soc. (trustee 1976—), Real Estate Land Owners (assoc.), Concerned Women for Am., Tex. Libraries Systems Svcs. Republican. Baptist. Home: 422 Dwights S Ave Dallas TX 75211-6240 Office: Real Estate Properties Tax Cons 614 Dwights S Ave Dallas TX 75211-6240

FRICKE, RICHARD IRVIN, insurance company executive; b. Buffalo, Mar. 25, 1922; s. Richard F. and Julia S. (Cooper) F.; m. Jeanne Hines, July 22, 1943 (dec.); children—Richard J., Diane L., Kathryn J. David R.; m. Ruth Byerly Tinker, March 26, 1967; children—Mark C., Michael A., Jodie P., John H. A.B., Cornell U., 1943, J.D. with distinction, 1947; grad., Advanced Mgmt. Program, Harvard U., 1965. Bar: N.Y. 1947, Mich. 1958, Vt. 1978. Assoc. atty. Kenefick, Cooke, Mitchell, Bass & Letchworth, Buffalo, 1947-52; asst. prof., then assoc. prof. law Cornell U. Law Sch., 1952-57; assoc. counsel Ford Motor Co., 1957-62; v.p. gen counsel Mut. Life Ins. Co. N.Y., 1962-67, sr. v.p., 1967-69, exec. v.p., 1969-72, chmn. bd., 1972-76; vice chmn. bd. Nat. Life Vt., 1976-77, pres., chief exec. officer, 1977-85, chmn. bd., chief exec. officer, 1985-87, chmn. exec. com., 1987—; interim pres., chief exec. officer Bank of Vt., 1987-89; bd. dirs. Sentinel Group Funds, Inc., Sentinal Cash Mgmt. Co., Monsanto Co., Green Mountain Power Corp., BankVermont; mem. speakers bur. Buffalo Council World Affairs, 1952; cons. N.Y. State Law Revision Commn., 1952-57; Mem. adv. council Cornell Law Sch., Cornell U. Council. Editor: Law quarterly, Cornell U., 1946 47. Trustee Vt. Law Sch., Champlain Coll. Served with field arty. AUS and USAAF, 1943-45. Fellow Am. Bar Found.; mem. Am., Vt., bar assns., Cornell Law Assn. (pres. 1965-67), Order of Coif, Am. Judicature Soc., Phi Kappa Phi, Phi Delta Phi. Clubs: University (N.Y.C.); Burlington Country, Ethan Allen, Longboat Key. Home: Overlake 26 545 S Prospect St Burlington VT 05401 Office: Nat Life Ins Co National Life Dr Montpelier VT 05604

FRICKE, WILLIAM ALLEN, physician, federal agency administrator; b. Oak Park, Ill., Sept. 16, 1949; s. Albert F. and Marie (Neitzert) F.; m. Susan Hyman, Mar. 11, 1984. AB, Washington U., St. Louis, 1971; MD, Washington U., 1979. Resident N.C. Meml. Hosp., Chapel Hill, N.C., 1979-83, fellow in coagulation, 1983-84; fellow in blood banking NIH, Bethesda, Md., 1984-86; fellow office biologics FDA, Bethesda, 1986-88, med. officer, 1988—. Mem. Am. Assn. Blood Banks, Council on Thrombsis, Internat. Soc. Thrombosis and Hemostasics. Office: FDA Office Biologics 8800 Rockville Pike Bethesda MD 20892

FRICKS, ERNEST EUGENE, marketing executive; b. Knoxville, Tenn., Jan. 16, 1948; s. Ernest E. Fricks and Barbara (Clark) Griffey; A.B., B.S.M.E., Rutgers U., 1970; M.S., Pa. State U., 1974; m. Dorothy Stanton; children—Natalie, Karen. Lead engr. Pub. Service Elec. & Gas Co., Newark, 1972-76, Stone & Webster Engring. Corp., Cherry Hill, N.J., 1976-78, mgr. lic., 1978-79, bus. devel., 1979-85, mgr. govt. mktg., 1985—; cons. Office Sec. of Navy, 1975. Served to lt. col. USAFR, 1970—. Decorated Air Force Commendation medal, Meritorious Service medal; named Outstanding Res. Augmentee Officer, Mil. Airlift Command, 1977. Fellow Royal Philatelic Soc. (London); mem. ASME, Royal Aero. Soc. U.K., Air Force Assn., Soc. Am. Mil. Engrs., Am. Philatelic Soc. (v.p. 1977-80), Rutgers Alumni Assn. (exec. council, Loyal Son award 1982), Rutgers Alumni Fedn. (treas. 1985-86, univ. sen. 1986-88), Rutgers Engring. Soc. (pres. 1976-77). Democrat. Baptist. Club: Collectors (N.Y.C.). Lodge: Masons. Author: The Thermodynamic Effect in Developed Cavitation in Freon 113, 1974. Office: PO Box 5200 Cherry Hill NJ 08034

FRIDHOLM, GEORGE H., management consultant; b. Blue Island, Ill., Oct. 24, 1921; s. Oscar and Anna (Bolin) F.; B.E.E., Purdue U., 1949; m. Sheila Mary Malley, May 11, 1957; children—Gregory, Christian, John, Rachel. Test engr. Gen. Electric Co., Phila. also Ft. Wayne, Ind., 1949-50, design engr., 1950-53, mem. advanced product planning team, Lynn, Mass., 1953-54, design engr., Ft. Wayne, 1954-55, design engr., Schenectady, 1955-57, fin. specialist, 1957-59, mfg. engr., 1959-60, mem. corp. staff value cons., 1960-62, value program mgr. value programs for industry, Schenectady, 1962-68; pres. George Fridholm Assocs., Cons. Value Mgmt. Systems, Burnt Hills, N.Y., 1968—; leader, facilitator Creative Problem-Solving Inst., Buffalo. Vice-chmn. Ballston (N.Y.) Zoning Bd. Appeals, 1969-82; troop com. chmn. Schenectady County council Boy Scouts Am., 1970-80. Served with USAAF, 1941-45. Decorated Bronze Star medal. Cert. mgmt. cons., value specialist. Fellow Paul Harris; mem. Internat. Platform Assn., Soc. Mfg. Engrs. (sr. mem.), Inst. Mgmt. Cons., IEEE, Soc. Am. Value Engrs., Assn. Mgmt. Cons., Eta Kappa Nu. Republican. Lutheran. Club: Burnt Hills-Ballston Lake. Lodge: Rotary. Home: One Fridholm Dr Burnt Hills NY 12027 Office: PO Box 88 Burnt Hills NY 12027

FRIDHOLM, ROGER THEODORE, beverage company executive; b. Blue Island, Ill., Mar. 18, 1941; s. Theodore William and Bernice (Ver Hulst) F.; m. Bonnie Sylvester, Feb. 23, 1963 (div. Feb. 1981) children: Michael, Hilary, Holly; m. Henrietta Barlow, Apr. 16, 1983. BA, U. Wis., 1963; MBA with distinction, U. Mich., 1964. Account mgr. Benton & Bowles Advt., N.Y.C., 1964-69; cons. McKinsey and Co., N.Y.C., 1969-75; div. v.p. Heublein, Inc., Farmington, Conn., 1975-78; pres. Stroh Brewery Co., Detroit, 1978—, also bd. dirs.; bd. dirs. Comerica, Inc., Detroit, MCN Corp, Dana Corp. Mem. vis. com. U. Mich. Grad. Sch. Bus., Ann Arbor, 1983—; bd. dirs. Detroit Symphony Orch., 1984—; trustee Henry Ford Health Corp., Detroit, 1987—. Clubs: Detroit Athletic (bd. dirs. 1985-88); Yondotega (Detroit); Country of Detroit (Grosse Pointe, Mich.). Office: Stroh Brewery Co 100 River Pl Detroit MI 48207 *

FRIED, BURTON THEODORE, lawyer; b. N.Y.C., Feb. 26, 1940; s. Meyer S. and Minnie (Grossberg) F.; m. Gail K. Morgenstern, July 25, 1964; children: Marsha, Howard, Shari. B.S., NYU, 1961; LL.B., Bklyn. Law Sch., 1964. Bar: N.Y. 1964, U.S. Dist. Ct. (ea. and so. dists.) N.Y. 1971. Assoc. atty. H. Bermack, N.Y.C., 1964-66, I. Towbis, N.Y.C., 1966-68; gen. counsel Medispas, Inc., N.Y.C., 1968-72; real estate counsel Michael Industries, Inc., N.Y.C., 1972-74, exec. v.p., gen. counsel and sec., 1974-86; exec. v.p., gen. counsel and sec. The LVI Group, Inc., N.Y.C., 1982-85; vice chmn., gen. counsel, dir. The LVI Group, Inc., 1985—; pres. LVI Environmental Services Group Inc., 1987—. Vice chmn. sch. bd. Forest Hills Jewish Ctr. Religious Sch., N.Y., 1983-84, chmn. sch. bd., 1984-85, trustee, 1985-88. Lodge: K.P. (Chancellor comdr. 1972-73). Office: LVI Group Inc 345 Hudson St New York NY 10014

FRIED, EDWARD STUART, construction company executive; b. Bridgeport, Conn., Nov. 27, 1946; s. Max Fried and Alice (Freedman) Powers; m. Leslie Jane Morris, May 1, 1971; children: Joshua Justin, Jordan. BA, Franklin Pierce Coll., 1969. Draftsman Higgins Fire Protection, Manhassett, N.Y., 1971-73; v.p. Lejac Metal Specialists, Wesbury, N.Y., 1973-78; pres. Luke F. Sweeny Inc., Danbury, Conn., 1978—; treas. Brookfield (Conn.) Bank, 1986—, also bd. dirs.; pres. Edwards & Edwards Devel., Brookfield, 1988—; trustee Detahr Inc., Brookfield, 1984-87, bd. dirs., J.E. Stuart Inc. V.p., bd. dirs. Family and Children's Aid, Danbury, 1985—. Served with U.S. Army, 1969-75. Democrat. Jewish. Club: Rolling Hills Country (Wilton, Conn.). Office: Luke F Sweeney Inc 15 Bates Pl Danbury CT 06810

FRIED, JEFFREY MICHAEL, health care administrator; b. Kansas City, Mo., Apr. 9, 1953; s. Harvey J. and SuEllen (Weissman) F.; m. Rosalyn Sue Matz. Student, Drake U., 1971-73; BGS, U. Kans., 1975; MHA, Washington U., St. Louis, 1979. Adminstrv. asst. Research Med. Ctr., Kansas City, Mo., 1979-80; asst. to pres. Research Health Services, Kansas City, 1980-81; asst. v.p. Sinai Hosp. Balt., 1981-83, Lancaster (Pa.) Gen. Hosp., 1983-85; v.p., chief operating officer Lancaster (Pa.) Gen. Services Corp., 1985-86, pres., 1986-88; sr. v.p. Lancaster Gen. Hosp., 1989—; pres., bd. dirs. Lancaster Med. Equipment, Barge Ganse Vena Care; sec., bd. dirs. Preferred Health Care, Lancaster; bd. dirs. Lancaster Diagnostic Imaging, Inc.; v.p., bd. dirs. Welsh Mountain Med. and Dental Ctr., Lancaster; mng. ptnr. Rohrerstown Imaging Assocs., Lancaster, 1986—; part-time mem. faculty dept. health adminstrn. and devel. Pa. State U., 1988—, Coll. St. Franics, 1988—. Contbr articles to profl. jours. Mem. Leadership Lancaster, 1987-88; pres., bd. dirs. Lancaster Chapter Nat. Commn. for Prevention of Child Abuse, 1986—; treas., bd. dirs. Lancaster Jewish Fedn., 1986—. Fellow Am. Coll. Healthcare Execs.; mem. Cen. Pa. Health Care Adminstrs. Jewish. Home: 2524 Golden Dr East Petersburg PA 17520 Office: Lancaster Gen Services Corp 607 N Duke St Lancaster PA 17602

FRIED, JOHN H., chemist; b. Leipzig, Fed. Republic Germany, Oct. 7, 1929; s. Abraham and Frieda F.; m. Heléne Gellen, June 29, 1955; children: David, Linda, Deborah. AB, Cornell U., 1951, PhD, 1955. Steroid chemist, research assoc. Merck and Co., Rahway, N.J., 1956-64; with Syntex Research, Palo Alto, Calif., 1964—, dir. inst. organic chemistry, 1967-74, exec. v.p., 1974-76, pres., 1976—; sr. v.p. Syntex Corp., 1981-86, vice chmn., 1986—. Mem. Am. Chem. Soc. Office: Syntex Rsch 3401 Hillview Ave Palo Alto CA 94304

FRIED, WALTER JAY, lawyer; b. N.Y.C., May 27, 1904; s. Joseph and Flora V. (Shamberg) F.; m. Louise E. Goldman, June 8, 1934; 1 son, Michael W.; m. Brita Digby-Brown, July 8, 1948. B.A. magna cum laude, Harvard, 1924; LL.B., Columbia U., 1928. Bar: N.Y. 1929, D.C. 1966. Practiced in N.Y.C., 1929—; former mem. firm, now counsel Fried, Frank, Harris, Shriver & Jacobson; mem. faculty Bklyn. Law Sch., 1931-39; dir. Salant Corp. Chmn. bd. dirs. Am. Chess Found.; hon. trustee Guild Hall, East Hampton, N.Y., chmn., 1974-78; trustee Southampton Hosp. Served to maj. AUS, 1942-45. Decorated Legion of Merit. Mem. Assn. Harvard Chemists, Phi Beta Kappa. Clubs: Maidstone (East Hampton), Harvard (N.Y.C.), Manhattan Chess (N.Y.C.) (hon. dir.). Home: 14 E 75th St New York NY 10021 also: Lily Pond Ln East Hampton NY 11937 Office: 1 New York Plaza New York NY 10004

FRIEDERICH, JAN, retail grocery executive; b. 1944; married. Grad., U. Hamburg, 1968. With Bund deutscher Konsumjenossenjchoften, 1968-71, Coop Rhein-Main, 1972-76, DHG Leibbrand OHG, 1976-79; with Furr's Inc., Lubbock, Tex., 1979—, past pres., now chief exec. officer. Office: Furr's Inc 1708 Ave G Lubbock TX 79408 *

FRIEDERICHS, NORMAN PAUL, lawyer; b. Ft. Dodge, Iowa, Sept. 13, 1936; s. Norman Paul and Dorothy Mae (Vinsant) F.; m. Marjorie Darlene Farrand, Aug. 23, 1959; children: Laurie Lynne, Norman Paul, Stacie Lynne. AA, Ft. Dodge Community Coll., 1956; BA, Wartburg Coll., 1959, JD, U. Iowa, 1966. Bar: Iowa 1966, Mich. 1968, Minn. 1974, U.S. Ct. Appeals (7th, 8th and fed. cirs.) 1978. Tchr. chemistry Janesville Sch. Dist., Iowa, 1960-63; mem. Woodhams, Blanchaud & Flynn, Kalamazoo, 1966-68; atty. PPG Industries, Pitts., 1968-69, Gen. Mills, Inc., Mpls., 1969-76; mem. Merchant, Gould, Smith, Edell, Welter & Schmidt, Mpls., 1976—; bd. dirs. Saturn Systems Inc., Kendrick Johnson and Assocs., Inc., JB2 Inc. Editor: (booklet) Report of Economic Survey, 1983. Mem. Minn. Rep. Cen. Com.; chmn. St. Louis Park Sch. Dist., Minn., 1973; mem. Suburban Hennepin Vocat.-Tech. Bd., 1980-84, chmn. 1982-84. Mem. Eden Prairie C. of C. (bd. dirs. 1979-88, pres. 1989), Am. Patent Law Assn. (com. chmn. 1980-84), Minn. Patent Law Assn. (chmn. small bus. com.), ABA, Optimist (pres. 1971-72, lt. gov. 1976-77), Masons. Baptist. Home: 6421 Kurtz Ln Eden Prairie MN 55344 Office: Merchant Gould Smith Edell Welter & Scmidt PA 3100 Northwest Ctr Minneapolis MN 55402

FRIEDHEIM, JERRY WARDEN, newspaper association and foundation executive; b. Joplin, Mo., Oct. 7, 1934; s. Volmer Havens and Billie Alice (Warden) F.; m. Shirley Margarette Beavers, Oct. 17, 1956; children: Daniel Volmer, Cynthia Diane, Thomas Eric. BJ, U. Mo., 1956, AM, 1962. Reporter, editor, editorial writer Neosho (Mo.) Daily News, Joplin (Mo.) Globe, Columbia Missourian, 1956-61; instr. journalism U. Mo., Columbia, 1961-62; aide to Congressman Durward Hall from Mo., Washington, 1962-63; legis. asst., pres. sec., exec. asst. to U.S. Senator John Tower from Tex., Washington, 1963-69; dep. asst. Sec. Def. for Pub. Affairs, U.S. Dept. Def., Washington, 1969-72; asst. Sec. Def. for Pub. Affairs, Washington, 1973-74; v.p. pub. and govt. affairs AMTRAK, 1974-75; exec. v.p., gen. mgr. Am. Newspaper Pubs. Assn. and ANPA Found., Washington, 1975-87, pres., 1987—; pub. presstime mag., 1980—; bd. dir. World Press Freedom Com., chmn. Nat. Press Found.; vice-chmn. Washington Journalism Ctr. Author: Where are the Voters, 1968. Capt. AUS, 1956-58. Congl. fellow Am. Polit. Sci. Assn.; recipient Disting. Svc. medal Dept. Def., 1972, 74. Mem. Am. Soc. Assn Execs, (former bd. dir.), Soc. Profl. Journalist, Nat. Press Found. (chmn.), Washington Journalism Ctr. (vice chmn), Nat. Pres. Club, Georgetown Club, Met. Club, City Club, Tower Club, Hidden Creek Club. Home: 11070 Thrush Ridge Rd Reston VA 22091 Office: Am Newspaper Pubs Assn 11600 Sunrise Valley Dr Reston VA 22091 also: Am Newspaper Publishers Assn The Newspaper Center Box 17407 Dulles Internat Airport Washington DC 20041

FRIEDLAND, EDWARD A., lawyer; b. N.Y.C., June 17, 1956; s. Stuart and Rhoda (Stocknoff) F.; m. Lisa Turgell, Mar. 27, 1982; children: Adam, Peter. BA magna cum laude, Williams Coll., 1978; JD, Georgetown U., 1981. Bar: N.Y. 1982. Assoc. Kronish, Lieb, Weiner & Hellman, N.Y.C., 1981-83; asst. gen. counsel, asst. sec. MacMillan Inc., N.Y.C., 1983-88, assoc. gen. counsel, asst. sec., 1988—. Mem. Phi Beta Kappa.

FRIEDLAND, RICHARD STEWART, electronics company executive; b. Pittsfield, Mass., Nov. 27, 1950; s. Armand and Frieda (Sugarman) F.; m. Shelley Mador, Aug. 29, 1971; children: Jason Michael, Nikki Gayle. BS in Acctg., Ohio State U., 1972; MBA in Fin., Seton Hall U., 1985. CPA, N.Y., N.J. Auditor Price Waterhouse & Co., Morristown, N.J., 1972-78; mgr. acctg. policies Gen. Instrument Corp., Clifton, N.J., 1978-79, mgr. fin. reporting, 1979-81, dir. fin. reporting, 1981-83, dir. fin. analysis, 1983-85, dir. treasury ops., 1985-86; v.p., treas. Gen. Instrument Corp., Lyndhurst, N.J., 1987-88, v.p., contr., 1988—. Treas., trustee Rehab. Ctr. for Handicapped Children and Adults, Morris Plains, N.J., 1977-86. Mem. N.Y. Soc. CPA's, N.J. Soc. CPA's, Nat. Corp. Treas. Assn. Jewish. Office: Gen Instrument Corp 767 Fifth Ave New York NY 10153

FRIEDLAND, SEYMOUR, economist, educator; b. N.Y.C., Oct. 8, 1928; s. David and Eva (Klausner) F.; B.S., Boston U., 1950, M.B.A., 1951; Ph.D., Harvard U., 1956; m. Eleanor Swartzfeld, May 15, 1980; children from a previous marriage—Randall R., Andrew B., Sharyn C. Instr. Middlebury (Vt.) Coll., 1951, Harvard U., Cambridge, Mass., 1952-53, M.I.T., Cambridge, Mass., 1954-55, Boston U., 1955-58, Rutgers U., New Brunswick, N.J., 1958-60, Claremont (Calif.) Grad. Sch., 1960-67; prof. fin. and econs. York U., Toronto, Ont., Can., 1967—; vis. prof. N.Y.U., 1966; cons. in field; dir. Koffler Stores, 1971-78, Fed. Trust Co., 1970-80; mem. Time Can.'s Bd. Economists, 1972-76; commentator radio, TV. Ford fellow, 1969-73; Gulf Research fellow, 1964. Mem. Am. Fin. Assn., Am. Econs. Assn. Jewish. Clubs: Empire, Can. of Toronto, Salamagundi (N.Y.C.). Contbr. articles on fin. to profl. jours.; mem. editorial bd. Fin. Times Can., 1979-89. Home: 423 Ave Rd, Toronto, ON Canada M4V 2H8 Office: 920 Yonge St, Suite 500, Toronto, ON Canada M4W 3C7

FRIEDLANDER, WILLIAM ALFRED, financial analyst; b. Cin., Sept. 27, 1932; s. Alfred J. and Jane (Klee) Steinfirst; m. Susan Steinharter, April 3, 1955; children: David, Lynne F. Jenco, Ellen. BA, Amherst Coll., 1954; student, Harvard U., 1956-57. Chartered fin. analyst. Investment counselor Bartlett & Co., Cin., 1957—, gen. ptnr., 1960-87, chmn., chief exec. officer, 1968—; bd. dirs. Cin. Bell, Inc., Union Cen. Life Ins. Co., Clopay Corp., 1980-85. Bd. dirs. Jewish Hosp., Cin., 1967-80, chmn. 1977-80; bd. dirs. Greater Cin. Found., 1981—, chmn., 1985-87; trustee Cin. Symphony Orch., 1985—. Served with U.S. Army, 1954-56. Mem. Cin. Soc. Fin. Analysts, Cin. C. of C. (bd. dirs. 1989—). Club: Commercial (Queen City). Home: 440 Whitman Ct Cincinnati OH 45202 Office: Bartlett & Co 36 E 4th St Cincinnati OH 45202

FRIEDLEY, DAVID P., electronics manufacturing company executive; b. 1939; married. BSEE, Cornell U., 1962. With Genrad Inc., 1962-74, Tektronix Inc., Beaverton, Oreg., 1974—; mktg. mgr. Tektronix Inc., 1974-78, bus. unit mgr., 1978, exec. v.p., gen. mgr. Grass Valley group, 1978-83, v.p., gen. mgr. communications, then v.p., mgr. communications group, 1983-88, pres., chief exec. officer, dir., 1988—; bd. dirs. MIT Ctr. Advanced TV Studies. With U.S. Army, 1963-65. Office: Tektronix Inc PO Box 500 Delivery Sta 50 409 Beaverton OR 97077 *

FRIEDMAN, ARTHUR MORTON, sales company executive; b. Yonkers, N.Y., Sept. 30, 1931; s. Isadore O. and Regina (Hertz) F.; B.S. in Mgmt., N.Y. U., 1960. Asst. dir. quality control J. P. Stevens & Co., Inc., N.Y.C., 1955-65; sales mgr. Cheraw Dyeing & Fin. Co., Cheraw, S.C., 1965; chief exec. officer, pres., chief stockholder Marcamy Sales Corp., 1965—; pres. Fall River Dyeing & Finishing Corp., 1982—, Robison River Dyeing & Printing Corp., 1984—. Served with U.S. Army, 1952-54. Mem. N.Y. Credit Men's Assn. Lodge: B'nai B'rith.

FRIEDMAN, BARRY LEE, investment banker; b. Memphis, Apr. 26, 1950; s. Sidney Joe and Zelda Rose (Person) F. BS in Mktg., U. Mo., Columbia, 1971. Terr. mgr. Dow Chem. Co., Dallas, 1973-75; dist. sales mgr. Stephens Industries, Inc., Dallas, 1975-77; pres. 1st Continental Leasing Corp., Dallas, 1977-82; chmn. First Continental Fin. Corp., Dallas, 1982—; lectr. and cons. in field. Named Ambassador of Good Will, State of Tex., 1979; named one of Constrn. Men of Yr. 1986. Mem. Am. Assn. Equipment Lessors, Dallas C. of C., Am. Pub. Works Assn., U. Mo. Alumni Assn. (bd. dirs. Dallas chpt.), Hotchkiss Alumni Assn., Ky. Cols. Republican. Jewish. Home: 14105 Rocksprings Ct Dallas TX 75240 Office: 8080 N Central Expwy Suite 850 Dallas TX 75206

FRIEDMAN, BENJAMIN MORTON, economics educator; b. Louisville, Aug. 5, 1944; s. Norbert and Eva (Lipsky) F.; m. Barbara Allan Cook, Dec. 17, 1972; children: John Norton, Jeffrey Allan. AB summa cum laude, Harvard U., 1966, AM, 1969, PhD, 1971; MSc King's Coll., Cambridge U., 1970. Economist Morgan Stanley & Co., N.Y.C., 1971-72; asst. prof. econs. Harvard U., Cambridge, Mass., 1972-76, assoc. prof., 1976-80, prof., 1980—; dir. fin. markets and monetary econs. Nat. Bur. Econ. Research, Cambridge,

1977—; dir. Pvt. Export Funding Corp., N.Y.C.; trustee Coll. Retirement Equities Fund, N.Y.C., 1981—. Author: Economic Stabilization Policy, 1975, Monetary Policy in the United States, 1981, Day of Reckoning, 1988; editor: New Challenges to the Role of Profits, 1978, The Changing Roles of Debt and Equity in Financing U.S. Capital Formation, 1982, Corporate Capital Structures in the United States, 1985, Financing Corporate Capital Formation, 1986; assoc. editor: Jour. Monetary Econs., 1977—. Marshall scholar Cambridge U., 1966-68; Soc. Fellows jr. fellow Harvard U., 1968-71. Mem. Council Fgn. Relations, Brookings Panel Econ. Activity, Am. Econ. Assn., Am. Fin. Assn. Club: Harvard (N.Y.C.). Home: 74 Sparks St Cambridge MA 02138 Office: Harvard U 127 Littauer Ctr Cambridge MA 02138

FRIEDMAN, BRIAN KEITH, lawyer; b. St. Louis, July 24, 1956; s. Mel Al and Sonya Lee (Powell) F. BS, U. Kans., 1978; JD, Washington U., 1981. Bar: Mo., 1982, U.S. Dist. Ct. (we. dist.) Mo., 1982. Gen. mgr., assoc. gemologist Barry Hyatt Jeweler Inc., St. Louis, 1975-81; sole practice law and bus. cons. St. Louis, 1982-83; v.p., gen. counsel Sun Devel. Co., St. Louis, 1984—; v.p., gen. counsel, cons. Allen E. Fishman and Co., St. Louis, 1984—; gen. counsel, asst. sec. Tipton Ctrs. Inc., St. Louis, 1984—; gen. ptnr. Bernadette Ctr. Assocs., St. Louis, Mo., 1985—; gen. counsel, dir. real estate Silo Inc., Phila., 1987—; lectr. in field; dir. staff fin. and deal structuring Direct Communication Services Inc., St. Louis, 1984—. Editor: How to Finance Your Bus.; writer, developer (computer source) Matching Businesses. Bd. dirs. Life Skills Found., St. Louis. Mem. ABA, Mo. Bar Assn., Met. St. Louis Bar Assn., Am. Soc. Fin. Counselors (bd. dirs. 1984-86). Republican. Club: Meadowbrook Country. Office: Silo Inc 6900 Lindbergh Blvd Philadelphia PA 19142

FRIEDMAN, BRIAN PAUL, investment banker; b. Paterson, N.J., Nov. 2, 1955; s. Sam and Rae (Simowitz) F.; m. Barbara J. Shulman, Aug. 16, 1981. BS, U. Pa., 1976, MS, 1977; JD, Columbia U., 1980. Bar: N.Y., N.J.; CPA, N.Y. Assoc. Wachtell, Lipton, Rosen & Katz, N.Y.C., 1980-84; sr. mng. dir. Furman Selz Mager Dietz & Birney Inc., N.Y.C., 1984—; bd. dirs. Coast Distbn. System, San Jose, Calif., Furman Selz Holding Corp., N.Y.C. Office: Furman Selz Mager Dietz & Birney 230 Park Ave New York NY 10169

FRIEDMAN, FRANCES, public relations firm executive; b. N.Y.C., Apr. 8, 1928; d. Aaron and Bertha (Itzkowitz) Fallick; m. Clifford Jerome Friedman, June 17, 1950; children—Kenneth Lee, Jeffrey Bennett. B.B.A., CCNY, 1948. Dir. pub. relations Melia Internat., Madrid, N.Y.C., 1971-73; sr. v.p. Lobsenz-Stevens, N.Y.C., 1973-75; exec. v.p. Howard Rubenstein Assocs., N.Y.C., 1975-83; pres., prin. Frances Friedman Assocs., N.Y.C., 1983-84; pres., chmn. bd. dirs. GCI Group Inc., N.Y.C., 1984—. Bd. dirs. ACRMD-Retarded Children, N.Y.C., 1983-85, City Coll. Fund, N.Y.C., 1970-79; mem. adv. bd. League for Parent Edn., N.Y.C., 1961-65; editor South Shore Democratic newletter, North Bellmore, N.Y., 1958-61, press sec. N.Y. State Assembly candidate, 1965, N.Y. State Congl. candidate, 1968; officer Manhasset Dem. Club, N.Y., 1965-69; mem. adv. com. N.Y.C. Council candidate, 1985. Mem. Pub. Relations Soc. Am., Women in Communications (Matrix award for pub. relations 1989), The Counselors Acad., Pride and Alarm, City Club N.Y. Democrat. Jewish. Home: 860 Fifth Ave New York NY 10021 Office: GCI Group Inc 777 Third Ave New York NY 10017

FRIEDMAN, FRANK BENNETT, oil company executive, lawyer; b. Newark, May 1, 1940; s. Martin and Gertrude (Tow) F.; m. Esta Kossack, June 2, 1962; children—Amy, Emily. A.B., Columbia U., 1962, J.D., 1965. Bar: D.C., Pa., Colo., Calif. Atty., FCC, Washington, 1965-67, Dept. Justice, Washington, 1967-70; counsel Atlantic Richfield Co., Phila., 1970-71, Denver, 1971-73, Los Angeles, 1973-78; dir. environ. health and safety ARCO Chem. Co., Phila., 1978-79, mgr. external affairs occupation and environ. protection, Los Angeles, 1979-81; v.p. health, environ. and safety Occidental Petroleum Corp., Los Angeles, 1981—. Mem. exec. com., bd. dirs. Environ. Law Inst., 1979—. Mem. ABA (natural resources sect. chmn. air quality commn. 1975-78, council nat. resource sect. 1978-81, co-chmn. nat. conf. on hazardous wastes, superfund and toxic substances), Am. Law Inst., Nat. Environ. Devel. Assn. (bd. dirs. 1984—). Office: Occidental Petroleum Corp 10089 Wilshire Blvd Los Angeles CA 90024

FRIEDMAN, JOEL STEPHEN, manufacturing company executive; b. N.Y.C., Oct. 12, 1937; s. Jacob and Sophie Helen (Fisher) F.; m. Marjorie Linda Resnek, Aug. 15, 1963; children: Andrew, David, Karen. BS in Mech. Engring., Rensselaer Poly. Inst., 1957; MBA, Harvard U., 1963. With mfg. tng. program Gen. Electric Co., 1957, 59-61; distbr. sales mgr. Sola Electric Co., Elk Grove Village, Ill., 1963-66; mktg. mgr. Beede Elec. Instrument Co., Penacook, N.H., 1966-72; pres. Guardian Light Co. div. Gen. Signal, Chgo., 1972-75, O-Z-Gedney Co. div. Gen. Signal, Terryville, Conn., 1975-83; pres., group exec. Mixing Equipment Co. div. Gen. Signal, Rochester, N.Y., 1984-87; sr. v.p. ops. Gen. Signal, Stamford, Conn., 1987—. Served with U.S. Army, 1957-59. Office: Gen Signal Corp High Ridge Pk PO Box 10010 Stamford CT 06904

FRIEDMAN, JONATHAN ROY, sales executive; b. N.Y.C., Feb. 20, 1957; s. James Lionel and Irma (Lesser) F.; m. Brenda Mendoza, July 26, 1987. BA, Yale U., 1979; MBA, Harvard U., 1984. Securities analyst Value Line, Inc., N.Y.C., 1980-82; account rep. Unisys, San Jose, Calif., 1984-87, sr. account rep., 1988-89; mgr. program mktg. Unisys, Blue Bell, Pa., 1989—. Fellow Am. Prodn. and Inventory Control Soc. (cert., bd. dirs. Santa Clara Vleley chpt., v.p. communications), Phi Beta Kappa. Democrat. Home: 4070 Thompson Rd Lafayette Hill PA 19444

FRIEDMAN, MICHAEL STEVEN, lawyer; b. White Plains, N.Y., June 2, 1953; s. Martin Stanley and Myrna (Schacht) F.; m. Jo-Anne Marie Damron, Aug. 17, 1975; children: Mark Samuel, Aaron David. AB, Clark U., 1975; JD, Rutgers U., 1978. Bar: Pa. 1978, N.J. 1978, Va. 1979, U.S. Ct. Appeals (4th cir.) 1979, D.C. 1981, U.S. Supreme Ct. 1986. Atty. Office of Gen. Cousel USAF, Pentagon, 1978-81, CACI, Inc., Arlington, Va., 1981-83; v.p., dir. legal div. CACI Internat., Inc., Arlington, 1983—; dir. Maritime Applied Physics Corp., Washington, Assn.'s Mgmt., Inc., Burke, Va. Served to capt. USAF, 1975-81. Mem. ABA, Pa. Bar Assn., Am. Corp. Counsel Assn., Washington Met. Area Corp. Counsel Assn., Community Assn. Mgmt. (bd. dirs.). Home: 15400 Meherrin Ct Centreville VA 22020 Office: CACI Internat Inc 1700 N Moore St Arlington VA 22209

FRIEDMAN, MILTON, economist, educator emeritus, author; b. Bklyn., July 31, 1912; s. Jeno Saul and Sarah Ethel (Landau) F.; m. Rose Director, June 25, 1938; children: Janet, David. AB, Rutgers U., 1932, LLD, 1968; AM, U. Chgo., 1933; PhD, Columbia U., 1946; LLD, St. Paul's (Rikkyo) U., 1963; LLD (hon.), Kalamazoo Coll., 1968, Lehigh U., 1969, Loyola U., 1971, U. N.H., 1975, Harvard U., 1979, Brigham Young U., 1980, Dartmouth Coll., 1980, Gonzaga U., 1981; DSc (hon.), Rochester U., 1971; LHD (hon.), Rockford Coll., 1969, Roosevelt U., 1975, Hebrew Union Coll., Los Angeles, 1981; LittD (hon.), Bethany Coll., 1971; PhD (hon.), Hebrew U., Jerusalem, 1977; DCS (hon.), Francisco Marroquín U., Guatemala, 1978. Assoc. economist Nat. Resources Com., Washington, 1935-37; mem. research staff Nat. Bur. Econ. Research, N.Y.C., 1937-45, 1948-81; vis. prof. econs. U. Wis., Madison, 1940-41; prin. economist, tax research div. U.S. Treasury Dept., Washington, 1941-43; assoc. dir. research, statis. research group, War Research div. Columbia U., N.Y.C., 1943-45; assoc. prof. econs. and statistics U. Minn., Mpls., 1945-46; assoc. prof. econs. U. Chgo., 1946-48, prof. econs., 1948-62, Paul Snowden Russell disting. service prof. econs., 1962-82, prof. emeritus, 1983—; Fulbright lectr. Cambridge U., 1953-54; vis. Wesley Clair Mitchell research prof. econs. Columbia U., N.Y.C., 1964-65; fellow Ctr. for Advanced Study in Behavioral Sci., 1957-58; sr. research fellow Stanford U., 1977—; mem. Pres.'s Commn. All-Vol. Army, 1969-70, Pres.'s Commn. on White House Fellows, 1971-74, Pres.'s Econ. Policy Adv. Bd., 1981-88; vis. scholar Fed. Res. Bank, San Francisco, 1977. Author: (with Carl Shoup and Ruth P. Mack) Taxing to Prevent Inflation, 1943, (with Simon S. Kuznets) Income from Independent Professional Practice, 1946, (with Harold A. Freeman, Frederic Mosteller, W. Allen Wallis) Sampling Inspection, 1948, Essays in Positive Economics, 1953, A Theory of the Consumption Function, 1957, A Program for Monetary Stability, 1960, Price Theory: A Provisional Text, 1962, (with Rose D. Friedman) Capitalism and Freedom, 1962, (with R.D. Friedman) Free To Choose, 1980, Tyranny of the Status Quo, 1984, (with Anna J. Schwartz) A Monetary History of the United States, 1867-1960, 1963, (with Schwartz) Monetary Statistics of the United States, 1970, (with Schwartz) Monetary Trends in the U.S. and the United Kingdom, 1982, Inflation: Causes and Consequences, 1963, (with Robert Roosa) The Balance of Payments: Free vs. Fixed Exchange Rates, 1967, Dollars and Deficits, 1968, The Optimum Quantity of Money and Other Essays, 1969, (with Walter W. Heller) Monetary vs. Fiscal Policy, 1969, A Theoretical Framework for Monetary Analysis, 1972, (with Wilbur J. Cohen) Social Security, 1972, An Economist's Protest, 1972, There's No Such Thing As A Free Lunch, 1975, Price Theory, 1976, (with Robert J. Gordon et al.) Milton Friedman's Monetary Framework, 1974, Tax Limitation, Inflation and the Role of Government, 1978, Bright Promises, Dismal Performance, 1983; editor: Studies in the Quantity Theory of Money, 1956; bd. editors Am. Econ. Rev, 1951-53, Econometrica, 1957-69; adv. bd. Jour. Money, Credit and Banking, 1968—; columnist Newsweek mag, 1966-84, contbg. editor, 1971-84; contbr. articles to profl. jours. Recipient Nobel prize in econs., 1976, Pvt. Enterprise Exemplar medal Freedoms Found., 1978, Grand Cordon of the Sacred Treasure Japanese Govt., 1986, Presdl. medal of Freedom, 1988, Nat. medal of Sci., 1988; named Chicagoan of Yr. Chgo. Press Club, 1972, Educator of Yr. Chgo. United Jewish Fund, 1973. Fellow Inst. Math. Stats., Am. Statis. Assn., Econometric Soc.; mem. Nat. Acad. Scis., Am. Econ. Assn. (mem. exec. com. 1955-57, pres. 1967; John Bates Clark medal 1951), Am. Enterprise Inst. (adv. bd. 1956-79), Western Econ. Assn. (pres. 1984-85), Royal Economic Soc., Am. Philos. Soc., Mont Pelerin Soc. (bd. dirs. 1958-61, pres. 1970-72). Club: Quadrangle. Office: Stanford U Hoover Instn Stanford CA 94305-6010

FRIEDMAN, NEIL STUART, insurance company executive; b. N.Y.C., Sept. 20, 1934; s. Aaron T. Friedman and Tillie (Levinthall) Shaffer; m. Constance Wecker, Nov. 17, 1957; children: Alan, Rena. BS in Acctg., NYU, 1957. Cert. fin. planner. Asst. to pres. Imperial 400 Co., Englewood Cliffs, N.J., 1962-64; pres. Neil S. Friedman, Inc., N.Y.C., 1964-70, Meyers Friedman Agy., N.Y.C., 1970-79, Accu-Plan Cos., Rockville Ctr., N.Y., 1979—. Served with U.S. Army, 1952-54. Mem. Million Dollar Round Table, Gen. Agent Mgrs. Assn., Nat. Assn. Ind. Life Brokerages, Am. Soc. Pension Actuaries, Nassau Assn. Life Underwriters. Jewish. Lodge: Masons. Office: Accu-Plan Cos 53 N Park Ave Rockville Centre NY 11570

FRIEDMAN, ROBERT ALAN, investment banking executive; b. Albany, N.Y., Apr. 21, 1941; s. Louis F. and Evelyn (Hershkowitz) F.; m. Linda S. Shulman, Dec. 20, 1964; children: David, Lori. B.E.E., CCNY, 1962, M.B.A., 1967. C.P.A., N.Y. Mgmt. cons. Coopers & Lybrand, N.Y.C., 1965-68; fin. analyst Goldman, Sachs & Co., N.Y.C., 1968-77, v.p., controller, 1977-80, ptnr., 1980—; mem. mgmt. com., 1984—; trustee Instl. Liquid Assets, Instl. Tax Exempt Assets, Chgo., Asset. Mgmt. Portfolios, Chgo., Exempt Assets Portfolios, Instl. Diversified Assets, Instl. Income Fund., Instl. Securitized Assets; bd. dirs. Depository Trust Co. Bd. dirs. Greater N.Y. Coun. Boy Scouts Am.; overseer Colby Coll. Served with U.S. Army, 1962-63. Mem. Pub. Securities Assn., Am. Inst. C.P.A.s, N.Y. State Soc. C.P.A.s, Securities Industry Assn., Fin. Execs. Inst. Clubs: Broad Street, Brae Burn Country, City Athletic, India House. Office: Goldman Sachs & Co 85 Broad St New York NY 10004

FRIEDMAN, ROBERT MICHAEL, lawyer; b. Memphis, June 19, 1950; s. Harold Samuel and Margaret (Siegel) F.; m. Elaine Freda Burson, Dec. 21, 1975; children: Daniel Justin, Jonathan Aaron. B.S., U. Tenn., 1973, J.D., 1975; postgrad., Exeter U., Eng., 1974, Nat. Coll. Trial Advocacy, 1985. Bar: Tenn. 1976, U.S. Dist. Ct. (we. dist.) Tenn. 1977, U.S. Dist Ct. (no. dist.) Miss. 1979, U.S. Ct. Appeals (5th cir.) 1979, U.S. Supreme Ct. 1983, U.S. Dist. Ct. (so. dist.) Tex. 1986, U.S. Ct. Appeals (6th cir.) 1986. Assoc., Cassell & Fink, Memphis, 1976-78; pres., sr. ptnr. Friedman & Sissman, P.C., Memphis, 1978—; corp. legal/litigation counsel, dir. Tenn. Interpreting Service for Deaf, Memphis, 1981—, Mid-South Hospitality Mgmt. Ctr., Inc., Memphis, 1984—; legal counsel Moss Hotel Co., Inc., 1986—, Helena Hotel Co., 1986—, Charlestown Hotel Co., 1986—, Jackson Hotel Co., 1986—, Murfreesboro Hotel Co., 1986—, Santee Hotel Co., 1986—, Kingsport Hotel Co., 1986—, Raleigh Hotel Assocs., Ltd., 1986, Ozark Regional Eye Ctr., 1986—, Brookfield Mortgage Co., Inc., 1987—, Mt. Pleasant Hotel Co., 1987—, Hattiesburg Hotel Assocs. Ltd., 1987—, Wright and Assocs. Constrn. Co. Inc., 1987—; legal counsel, pres. Biloxi Hotel Co., Inc., 1986—; litigation counsel Independence Fed. Bank Batesville (Ark.), 1987—. Mem. staff, contbr. Tenn. Law Rev., 1974-75, recipient cert., 1975. Bd. dirs. Project 1st Offenders, Shelby County, Tenn., 1976-78; bd. dirs., legal counsel Memphis Community Ctr. for Deaf & Hearing Impaired, 1980-81; bd. dirs. Eagle Scout Day, Chickasaw council Boy Scouts Am., 1978—. Served with USCG, 1971-72. Recipient Outstanding Service award and Key Alpha Phi Omega, 1972, Am. Jurisprudence award Lawyers Co-op. Pubg. Co. and Bancroft-Whitney Co., 1973-74, Chancellor's Honor award George C. Taylor Sch. Law, U. Tenn., 1975; A.S. Graves Meml. scholar, 1974-75. Mem. ABA, Assn. Trial Lawyers Am., Bar Assn. Tenn., Tenn. Trial Lawyers Assn., Nat. Assn. Criminal Def. Lawyers, Memphis and Shelby County Bar Assn., Fed. Bar Assn., Nat. Criminal Justice Assn. (charter 1984—). Alpha Phi Omega, Delta Theta Phi. Democrat. Jewish. Home: 3303 Spencer Dr Memphis TN 38115 Office: Friedman & Sissman P C 100 N Main St Suite 3010 Memphis TN 38103 also: 1052 Brookfield Memphis TN 38119

FRIEDMAN, STEPHEN J., investment company executive. AB magna cum laude, Princeton U., 1959; LLB magna cum laude, Harvard U., 1962. Law clk. to justice William J. Brennan Jr., U.S. Supreme Ct., 1963-64; spl. asst. to maritime adminstr. Maritime Adminstrn., Dept. Commerce, 1964-65; assoc. Debevoise & Plimpton, N.Y.C., 1965-70, ptnr., 1970-77, 81-86; lectr. in law Columbia U., N.Y.C., 1974-77, 82-85; formerly exec. v.p., gen. counsel, mem. mgmt. com. E.F. Hutton Group Inc., N.Y.C., from 1986—; now exec. v.p., gen. counsel Equitable Life Assurance Soc. U.S., N.Y.C.; bd. dirs. Chgo. Bd. Options Exchange, Overseas Devel. Council; chmn. ann. inst. on securities regulation Practicing Law Inst.; mem. legal adv. com. N.Y. Stock Exchange; dep. asst. sec. for capital markets policy Dept. Treasury, 1977-79; commr. SEC., 1980-81. Office: Equitable Life Assurance Soc US 787 7th Ave New York NY 10017 *

FRIEDMAN, SUE TYLER, technical publications executive; b. Nürnberg, Fed. Republic Germany, Feb. 28, 1925; came to U.S., 1938; d. William and Ann (Federlein) Tyler (Theilheimer); m. Gerald Manfred Friedman, June 27, 1948; children: Judith Fay Friedman Rosen, Sharon Mira Friedman Azaria, Devora Paula Friedman Zweibach, Eva Jane Friedman Scholle, Wendy Tamar Friedman Spanier. R.N., Beth Israel Sch. Nursing, 1941-43. Exec. dir. Ventures and Publs. of Gerald M. Friedman, 1964—; owner Tyler Publications, Watervliet and Troy, N.Y., 1978-86; treas. Northeastern Sci. Found., Inc., Troy, 1979—; treas. Gerry Exploration, Inc., Troy, N.Y., 1982—; office mgr. Rensselaer Ctr. Applied Geology, Troy, 1983—. Pres. Pioneer Women/Na'amat, Tulsa, 1961-64, treas., Jerusalem, Israel, 1964, pres., Albany, N.Y., 1968-70; bd. dirs. Temple Beth-El, 1965—, dir. Hebrew Sch., 1965-80. Sue Tyler Friedman medal for distinction in history of geology created in her honor, Geol. Soc. London, 1988. Jewish. Avocation: world travel. Home: 32 24th St Troy NY 12180 Office: Rensselaer Ctr Applied Geology 15 3d St Box 746 Troy NY 12181

FRIEDRICHS, NIELS GEORG, b. Luebeck, West Germany, Dec. 22, 1929; s. Peter H. and Gertrud (Hahn) F.; came to U.S., 1958; ed. Katharineum, Luebeck, 1949; m. Ilona Grund, Dec. 18, 1957; children—Kirsten, Dirk. Printer, Flint, Mich., 1959-61; salesman Lufthansa Airlines, Chgo., 1961-63; mng. dir. German Am. C. of C., Chgo., 1963—; lectr. in field. Recipient Order of Merit (Fed. Republic Germany), 1978, Officer's Cross of Fed. Republic Germany, 1988. Mem. Internat. Trade Club of Chgo., Chgo. Assn. Commerce and Industry, Assn. German Fgn. Chamber Mgrs. (Bonn, Germany), Chgo. Fgn. Trade Commn. Group. Lutheran. Clubs: Chgo. Athletic Assn., Execs. Office: 104 S Michigan Ave Ste 600 Chicago IL 60603-5978

FRIELING, GERALD HARVEY, JR., specialty steel company executive; b. Kansas City, Mo., Apr. 29, 1930; s. Gerald Harvey and Mary Ann (Coons) F.; m. Joan Lee Bigham, June 14, 1952; children: John, Robert, Nancy. B.S. in Mech. Engring, U. Kans., 1951. Application engr. Westinghouse Elec. Corp., Pitts., 1951-53; mfg. mgr. Madison-Faessler Tool Co., Moberly, Mo., 1956-60; gen. mgr. wire and tubing Tex. Instruments Inc., Attleboro, Mass., 1960-69; v.p. Air Products & Chems. Co., Allentown, Pa., 1969-79; pres., chief exec. officer, chmn. bd. dirs. Nat.-Standard Co., Niles, Mich., 1979—; bd. dirs. Old Kent Bank & Trust Co.-S.W., Niles, CTS, Protection Mut. Ins. Co.; adv. bd. Liberty Mut. Ins. Co., Tokheim; instr. Brown U., 1965-68. Author; patentee in field. Served to lt. USNR, 1953-56, Korea. Recipient Wire Assn. medal, 1966, Disting. Engring. Service award U. Kans., 1986. Republican. Presbyterian. Clubs: Union League (Chgo.); Point O' Woods, Signal Point Country, Pickwick, Summit. Office: Nat-Standard Co Corp R & D 1618 Terminal Rd Niles MI 49120

FRIEND, ROBERT NATHAN, financial counselor, economist; b. Chgo., Feb. 2, 1930; s. Karl D. and Marion (Wollenberger) F.; AB, Grinnell Coll., 1951; MS, Ill. Inst. Tech., 1953; m. Lee Baer, Aug. 12, 1979; children: Karen, Alan. With K. Friend & Co., Chgo., 1953—, v.p., early 1960's, 1st v.p., 1964—, dir. merger activities with Standard Oil Co. (Ind.), trustee employees' benefit trust, 1958—; pres. Twelve Nine Corp., active Friend Finl. Services. Admissions cons. Grinnell Coll., Ill. Inst. Tech., 1968-70; Alumni career counselor Ill. Inst. Tech.; bd. dirs. Nat. Anorexia Nervosa & Associated Disorders Assn. Fellow Am. Finance Assn., So. Finance Assn., Southwestern Fin. Assn., Acad. Internat. Bus., Am. Acad. Polit. and Social Sci., Am. Assn. Individual Investors (dir.), Vintage Soc., Renaissance Soc., Sarah Siddons Soc., Art Inst. Chgo. (life), Newcomen Soc. N.Am., Chgo. Council Fgn. Relations, Am. Econ. Assn., Acad. Polit. Sci., Phi Kappa Phi. Clubs: Carlton, Yale. Home: 1300 Lake Shore Dr Chicago IL 60610 Office: 222 W Adams St Chicago IL 60606

FRIEND, TONY, software company executive; b. Sydney, New South Wales, Australia, Jan. 31, 1945; came to U.S., 1983; s. Ronald Frederick and Joan Friend; m. Ilona Friend, Nov. 30, 1968 (div. 1980); m. Dianne Friend, Sept. 15, 1983. B in Engring., U. Sydney, 1966. Cons. Kinhill Pty. Ltd., Melbourne, Australia, 1967-78; from rep. to sales mgr. IBM Australia Pty. Ltd., Sydney, 1978-79; account exec. Itel Pty. Ltd., Sydney, 1979; br. mgr. Prime Computer Pty. Ltd., Sydney, 1979-81; mng. dir. Mostem Pty. Ltd., Sydney, 1981-83; br. mgr. Prime Computer, Inc., San Francisco, 1984-86; pres. Solid Logic, Inc., Corte Madera, Calif., 1986—. Office: Solid Logic Inc 5725 Paradise Dr Suite 200 Corte Madera CA 94925

FRIEND, WILLIAM KAGAY, lawyer; b. Columbus, Ohio, June 19, 1946; s. Wendell Kagay and Evelyn (Steele) F.; m. Linda Vance, Aug. 24, 1969; 1 child, Elizabeth Anne. B.B.A., Ohio U., 1968; J.D., Ohio State U., 1972. Bar: Ohio 1972, Mass. 1989. Staff atty. SCOA Industries, Inc., Canton, Mass., 1972-75, asst. corp. counsel, 1975-79, sr. counsel, asst. sec., 1979-80, sr. counsel, sec., 1980-81, corp. counsel, sec., 1981-85, v.p., sec., corp. counsel, 1985-86; v.p., sec., corp. counsel Hills Dept. Stores, Inc. and Hills Stores Co., Canton, 1986—; corp. counsel, pres. SCOA Credit Union, Columbus, 1973-80. Mem. exec. bd. Central Ohio Council Boy Scouts Am., 1983, 84, 85; mem. exec. bd., sec. Central Ohio council Camp Fire, Inc., 1984, 85. Mem. ABA, Ohio State Bar Assn., Mass. Bar Assn., Am. Corp. Counsel Assn. (v.p., sec. cen. Ohio chpt. 1984-85), Am. Soc. Corp. Secs., Columbus Athletic Club, Phi Delta Phi, Phi Delta Theta. Home: 704 Main St Hingham MA 02043 Office: Hills Dept Stores Inc 15 Dan Rd Canton MA 02021

FRIERSON, DANIEL K., textile company executive; b. 1942; married. BA, U. Va., 1964, MBA, 1966. With Ti Caro Inc., 1963—, now chmn., chief exec. officer; with Dixie Yarns Inc., Chattanooga, 1973—, v.p. Candlewick div., 1975-77, exec. v.p., then pres. Candlewick div., 1977-79, chmn., chief exec. officer, dir., 1979—. Office: Dixie Yarns Inc 1100 Watkins St PO Box 751 Chattanooga TN 37401 *

FRIES, ARTHUR LAWRENCE, insurance broker; b. Bklyn., Aug. 21, 1937; s. Jack Edwin and Sophia (Kabat) F.; m. Cindy Ann Blum, Mar. 27, 1960; children: Stacey Jill, Todd Steven. AB, Nichols Coll., 1956; BS, Syracuse U., 1958. Registered health underwriter. Various positions ins. sales and adminstrn. various firms, N.Y.C., 1962-72; life and health ins. agt. Washington Nat. Ins. Co., Los Angeles, 1973-85; pvt. practice, N.Y.C., Los Angeles and Northridge, Calif., 1962-72, Northridge, 1982—; blood chmn. Washington Nat. Ins. Co., 1976-79; speaker, lectr., expert witness on individual disability income ins. Contbr. articles to profl. jours. Chmn. memberships Vista Del Mar Men's Assn. for Orphaned Children, 1975; active Guardians Jewish Home for the Aged. Recipient Nat. Sales Achievement award Los Angeles Gen. Agts. and Mgrs. Assn., 1965-88, Health Ins. Quality award, 1965-88, Agt. of Yr. award, 1976, 78, 88, Nat. Quality award, 1980-88. Mem. Nat. Assn. Life Underwriters (million dollar round table, blood chmn. 1976-79), Nat. Assn. Health Underwriters (leading producers round table), Calif. Assn. Life Underwriters, Calif. Assn. Health Underwriters, Los Angeles Assn. Health Underwriters (conf. speaker, speakers chmn. 1983-84, program chmn. 1984, bd. dirs., membership chmn. 1987-88), Am. Council Ind. Life Underwriters, Abraham Lincoln High Sch. Alumni Assn. (bd. dirs.), Am. Diabetic Assn., Friars Club (Beverly Hills, Calif.), Northridge Tennis Club. Democrat. Home and Office: 11512 Porter Valley Dr Northridge CA 91326

FRIES, GILBERT BRADLEY, financial executive; b. Hollywood, Calif., Jan. 14, 1956; s. Gilbert Lee and Marnie (Hans) F.; m. Heidi L. Clark, Oct. 19, 1985. Student, Pierce Community Coll., LA, U. So. Calif., Calif. Luth. Coll. With IATSE Local 720, Las Vegas, Nev., 1975-78, B.C. Engring., Santa Monica, Calif., 1978-82; svc. advisor Ogner Porsche/Audi, 1983-85; stock broker Crowell Weedon, Long Beach, Calif., 1986-87; with Integrated Resources Equity Corp., Newport Beach, Calif., 1987—; fin. advisor Concord Asstes, Long Beach, Calif., 1986; stockbroker Crowell, Weedon & Co., Long Beach, 1986-87. Mem. Newport Harbor C. of C., Huntington Beach C. of C., Internat. Assn. Fin. Planners (bd. dirs. 1988—). Home: 19712 Shorecliff Ln Huntington Beach CA 92648 Office: Integrated Resources Equity Corp 4590 MacArthur Blvd Ste 550 Newport Beach CA 92660

FRIES, MALCOLM GRAHAM, financial planner; b. Charleroi, Pa., Feb. 6, 1934; s. Thomas Malcolm and Dorothy (Graham) F.; m. Mary Rachael Drake, May 28, 1981; children by previous marriage: Robert Malcolm, William Graham, Bradley Fuller. BA, Allegheny Coll., 1956; MA, Cen. Mich. U., 1976. Cert. fin. planner. Commd. officer USAF, 1956, advanced through grades to lt. col., 1975; assigned to Hdqrs. 7th Air Force, Saigon, Vietnam, 1971-72, SAC, Omaha, 1972-75, Pentagon, Washington, 1975-77; ret. 1977; br. mgr. Am. Fin. Cons., Silver Spring, Md., 1977-83; pres. Malcolm G. Fries & Assocs. Inc., Newport News, Va., 1983—; talk show host. Sta. WNIS, 1984—; instr. continuing edn. Coll. William and Mary, 1985—; mem. adv. coun. Hibbard Brown & Co. Inc., Greenbelt, Md., 1987—; bd. dirs. Planners Devel. Corp., Atlanta. Bd. dirs. Jr. Achievement, Hampton, Va., 1986—; chmn. Recruiting for Project Bus., Hampton Roads, Va., 1987-88. Mem. Internat. Assn. Fin. Planning (pres. 1981-83), Inst. Cert. Fin. Planners, Registry Fin. Planning Practitioners, Kiwanis. Republican. Methodist. Office: 749 Thimble Shoals Blvd Newport News VA 23606

FRIESE, GEORGE RALPH, retail executive; b. Chgo., Feb. 15, 1936; s. George R. and Marie D. (Pilz) F.; m. Patricia J. Brown, Aug. 24, 1957; children: Christine Carol, Kurt Michael. BA, Monmouth Coll., 1956; JD, Chgo. Kent Coll. Law, 1960. Bar: Ill. 1961, U.S. Dist. Ct. Ill. (no. dist.) 1961, U.S. Supreme Ct. 1965. Asst. gen. counsel, v.p. Banner Mut. Ins. Cos., Chgo., 1959-63; ptnr. Madsen & Friese, Park Ridge, Ill., 1963-68; corp. counsel, sec. SCOA Industries, Inc., Columbus, Ohio, 1968-71, v.p. legal, sec., 1971-81, pres., 1981-85; vice chmn., dir. Hills Dept. Stores Inc., Canton, Mass., 1985—. Bd. dirs. Columbus Symphony Orch., Greater Columbus Arts Council, New Eng. Red Cross; trustee Opera Co. of Boston, 1988—, New Eng. Red Cross, 1988—, Boy Scouts Am., Columbus, 1981-86. Mem. ABA, Ill. Bar Assn., Tau Kappa Epsilon, Phi Delta Phi. Unitarian. Clubs: Athletic (Columbus); Lotos (N.Y.). Home: 300 Boylston Apt 709 Boston MA 02116 Office: Hills Dept Stores Inc 15 Dan Rd Canton MA 02021

FRIESECKE, RAYMOND FRANCIS, management consultant; b. N.Y.C., Mar. 12, 1937; s. Bernhard P. K. and Josephine (De Tomi) F.; BS in Chemistry, Boston Coll., 1959; MS in Civil Engring., MIT, 1961. Product specialist Dewey & Almy Chem. div. W. R. Grace & Co., Inc., Cambridge, Mass., 1963-66; market planning specialist USM Corp., Boston, 1966-71; mgmt. cons., Boston, 1971-74; dir. planning and devel. Schweitzer div. Kimberly-Clark Corp., Lee, Mass., 1974-78; v.p. corp. planning Butler Automatic, Inc., Canton, Mass., 1978-80; pres. Butler-Europe Inc., Greenwich, Conn. and Munich, Fed. Republic Germany, 1980; v.p. mktg. and planning Butler Greenwich Inc., 1980-81; pres. Strategic Mgmt. Assocs., San

Rafael, Calif., 1981—; corp. clk., v.p. Bldg. Research & Devel., Inc., Cambridge, 1966-68. State chmn. Citizens for Fair Taxation, 1972-73; state co-chmn. Mass. Young Reps., 1967-69; chmn. Ward 7 Rep. Com., Cambridge, 1968-70; vice chmn. Cambridge Rep. City Com., 1966-68; vice-chmn. Kentfield Rehab. Hosp. Found., 1986-88, chmn., 1988—; Rep. candidate Mass. Ho. of Reps., 1964, 66; pres. Marin Rep. Council, 1986—; chmn. Calif. Acad., 1986-88; sec. Navy League Marin Council, 1984—. Served to 1st lt. U.S. Army, 1961-63. Mem. Am. Chem. Soc., World Affairs Coun., The Planning Forum , Am. Mktg. Assn., The World Affairs Coun., Am. Rifle Assn. Author: Management by Relative Product Quality; contbr. articles to profl. jours. Home and Office: 141 Convent Ct San Rafael CA 94901

FRIESEN, WES MARK, real estate agent, accountant; b. Mpls., Dec. 18, 1957; s. Malvern and Patricia (Kiger) F.; m. Debra Hopper, Sept. 21, 1979; children: Amy, Alyssa. BSBA, Grove Fox Coll., 1980; MBA, U. Portland, 1982; PhD, Columbia Pacific U., 1985. Cert. mgmt. acct. Acct. Portland (Oreg.) Gen. Elec., 1980-83, sr. bus. analyst, 1983-85; budget coordinator Portland Gen. Corp., 1985—; realtor Oreg. Realty, Portland, 1986—; instr. City U., Tigurd, Oreg., 1984—; cons. Small Bus. Inst. Program, 1979-80. Bd. dirs. Milwaukie (Oreg.) Bapt. Ch., 1988; fundraiser Boy Scouts Am., Portland, 1981; activist Oreg. Citizens Alliance, Portland, 1986—. Mem. Inst. Mgmt. Acctg., Nat. Assn. Accts., Nat. Mgmt. Assn. (v.p. 1983-84), N.W. Elec. Light and Power Assn., Elks, Mu Epsilon. Republican. Home: 14034 SE Portland View Portland OR 97236 Office: Portland Gen Corp 121 SW Salmon Portland OR 97204

FRIGO, JAMES PETER PAUL, industrial hardware company executive; b. Iron Mountain, Mich., Jan. 11, 1942; s. Louis and Giustina (Carollo) F.; m. Patricia Mary Nellen, June 21, 1969; children: Christine, Catherine, P.J., Pamela, Steven, Sandy. BBA, U. Miami, 1966. Sales rep. Great Dane Trailers, Miami, 1966-67, Foster Inc., Miami, 1968, Lawson Products Inc., Miami, 1968—; pres. James Frigo Inc., Miami, 1972—. Republican. Roman Catholic. Home: 7420 SW 175th St MIami FL 33157 Office: James Frigo Inc 7420 SW 175th St Miami FL 33157

FRIGON, HENRY FREDERICK, diversified company executive; b. Bridgeport, Conn., Nov. 16, 1934; s. Henry Xavier and Veronica Anne (Beloin) F.; m. Anne Marie McCarthy, Sept. 20, 1965; children: Megan, Michele, Henry, Scott, Mark, Stephanie. B.S.C.E., Tufts U., 1957; post-grad., U. Pa., 1958-59; M.B.A., NYU, 1962. With Gen. Foods Corp., 1960-68, various fin. and mktg. positions, 1960-66; chief fin. officer, internat. ops. Gen. Foods Corp., White Plains, N.Y., 1966-68; v.p. fin., sec., treas. Gen. Housewares Corp., N.Y.C., 1968-70; pres. Gen. Housewares Corp. (Giftware Group), Stamford, Conn., 1970-74; also dir. parent co.; group v.p. Masco Corp., Taylor, Mich., 1974-81; exec. v.p., chief fin. and adminstrv. officer Batus Inc., Louisville, 1981-83, pres., 1983-85, pres., chief operating officer, 1985, pres., chief exec. officer, 1985—; bd. dirs. Batus, Inc., B.A.T. Capital Corp. (apptd. main bd., London, 1988) , Appleton Papers Inc., Marshall Field & Co., Saks Fifth Ave., First Ky. Nat. Corp., First Nat. Bank Louisville, Joint Council Econ. Edn. Bd. dirs. Ky Econ. Devel. Corp.; adv. coun. Coll. Bus. Adminstrn. U. Notre Dame. Served with USNR, 1957-65. Mem. Conf. Bd., The Brookings Inst., World Bus. Council, Bretton Woods Com. Home: 4810 Upper River Rd Louisville KY 40222 Office: Batus Inc 2000 Citizens Pla Louisville KY 40202

FRISBEE, DON CALVIN, retired utilities executive; b. San Francisco, Dec. 13, 1923; s. Ira Nobles and Helen (Sheets) F.; m. Emilie Ford, Feb. 5, 1947; children: Ann, Robert, Peter, Dean. BA, Pomona Coll., 1947; MBA, Harvard U., 1949. Sr. investment analyst, asst. cashier investment analysis dept. 1st Interstate Bank Oreg., N.A., Portland, 1949-52, now dir.; with PacifiCorp, Portland, 1953—, treas., 1958-60, then v.p., exec. v.p., pres., 1966-73, ret., 1989, chmn., 1989—; bd. dirs. First Interstate Bancorp, Weyerhaeuser Co., Standard Ins. Co., Portland., Precision Castparts Corp., Portland, First Interstate Bank of Oreg., Portland, Pacificorp Fin. Svcs. Trustee Reed Coll., Com. for Econ. Devel., Safari Game Search Found.; chmn. assn. coun. YMCA; pres., bd. dirs. Oreg. Community Found., Oreg. Bus. Coun., Oreg. Wildlife Heritage Found., Oreg. Indep. Coll. Found.; cabinet mem. Columbia Pacific Coun. Boy Scouts Am. 1st lt. AUS, 1943-46. Mem. Japan-Western U.S. Assn. (exec. coun.). Clubs: Arlington, University, Multnomah Athletic. Office: PacifiCorp 825 NE Multnomah Lloyd Tower Ste 1055 Portland OR 97232

FRISCH, FRED I., real estate executive; b. Indpls., Oct. 19, 1935; s. Leon and Blanka (Frankovitz) F.; m. Rochelle L. Fein, Sept. 15, 1957; children: Caryn, Susan, Daniel. BBA, U. Miami, Fla., 1957. Lic. real estate broker. Pres. Frisch & Assocs., Indpls., 1976—; pres. Prime Property Investment Group; bd. dirs. Hooverwood Homes, Indpls.; bd. dirs. comml. and indsl. div. Met. Indpls. Bd. Realtors, pres. 1984. Served with USAF, 1960-64. Mem. Real Estate Securities and Syndication Inst. Republican. Jewish. Club: Indpls. Men's (pres. 1966-68). Office: 10333 N Meridian Indianapolis IN 46290

FRISCH, JOHN HENRY, financial executive; b. Joliet, Ill., Mar. 3, 1932; s. Henry P. and Helen W. (Riley) F.; m. Karen M. Blitz, Nov. 22, 1956; children: Penni J. Frisch Dalton, Gary J., Wendi J., Kristi K. BS, Lewis U., 1954. Div. controller Fairchild Industries, Manhattan Beach, Calif., 1956-64; dir. fin. planning Planning Rsch. Corp., L.A., 1965-74; corp. controller, treas. Holmes & Narver, Inc., Orange, Calif., 1974-80; controller Bethlehem Steel Corp., L.A., 1980-81; v.p., corp. controller Becket Group/Welton Becket Assocs., Santa Monica, Calif., 1981-84; corp. controller Modern Alloys, Inc., Stanton, Calif., 1985-86; v.p. fin. and adminstrn. E&L Tech. subs. Ebasco, Long Beach, Calif., 1986—; prin., cons. FGM Assoc., Manhattan Beach, 1984-85. Chmn. Manhattan Beach Planning Commn., 1972-74. Lt. (j.g.) USN, 1954-56. Mem. Nat. Assn. Accts. (bd. dirs. 1965-67), Manhattan Beach Badminton Club (pres. 1965-67), Elks. Republican. Roman Catholic. Home: 920 John St Manhattan Beach CA 90266 Office: E&L Tech 4001 Via Oro Long Beach CA 90810

FRISCH, ROBERT STEVEN, consumer products executive; b. Lynn, Mass., May 22, 1956; s. Louis Bertram and Bernice (Labovitz) F. BA, Tufts U., 1978; M of Pub. and Pvt. Mgmt., Yale U., 1983. Legis. aide Mass. Legislature, Boston, 1978-81; cons. Boston Consulting Group, L.A., 1983-86; dir. planning Dial Corp., Phoenix, 1986-87; pres. Bucilla Co., Secaucus, N.J., 1987—. Mem. Yale Club (N.Y.C.), Blue Sky Club (New Haven). Jewish. Office: Bucilla Co 150 Meadowland Pkwy Secaucus NJ 07094

FRISCHENMEYER, MICHAEL LEO, sales executive; b. Ottawa, Kans., Feb. 8, 1951; s. Edwin Francis and Patricia Louise (Scheibmeir) F.; m. Helen N. Bright, May 19, 1974; children: Lindsay Patrice, David Edward. BA in Chemistry, U. Mo., 1973, MBA in Mtkg., 1975. Mktg. asst. Mallinckrodt Inc., St. Louis, 1975, asst. product mgr., 1975-77; mgr. tech. services Standard Havens, Inc., Kansas City, Mo., 1977-79; nat. sales mgr. Standard Havens, Inc., Kansas City, 1979-83; sales engr. Nat. Filter Media Corp., St. Louis, 1983; div. sales mgr. Nat. Filter Media Corp., Memphis, 1983-85, Hamden, Conn., 1986—; nat. sales mgr. Nat. Filter Media Corp., Memphis, 1985-86, Salt Lake City, 1988—. Recipient 5 Star Major Advancement award Pollution Engring. mag. 1978, 79. Mem. Air Pollution Control Assn. Jewish. Home: 8244 Set Point Circle Sandy UT 84093 Office: Nat Filter Media Corp 691 N 400 St Salt Lake City UT 84103

FRISCHKORN, DAVID EPHRAIM KEASBEY, JR., investment banker; b. Huntington, W.Va., Apr. 11, 1951; s. David Ephraim Keasbey Frischkorn and Permele Elliott (Francis) Booth; m. Anne Cochran, May 9, 1981. BA magna cum laude, Tufts U., 1973; MBA, Columbia U., 1976. Corp. fin. assoc. Rotan Mosle, Houston, 1976-77, asst. v.p., 1977-79, v.p., 1979-82, sr. v.p., 1982-85; v.p. Kidder, Peabody & Co., Houston, 1985-87, Frischkorn & Co. Investment Bankers, Houston, 1988—; bd. dirs. Meacham, Inc., Charleston, W.Va. Bd. dirs. Houston Child Guidance Ctr., 1981—, pres. bd. dirs. 1984-86; trustee The Hill Sch., Pottstown, Pa., 1978-80. Republican. Presbyterian. Clubs: Racquet & Tennis, N.Y. Athletic, Doubles (N.Y.C.); Houston Country, Coronado (Houston); Argyle (San Antonio); Mill Reef (Antiqua, W.I.). Office: Frischkorn & Co 1100 Milam Suite 3480 Houston TX 77002

FRISCHMUTH, ROBERT ALFRED, landscape planner, filmmaker; b. N.Y.C., Dec. 15, 1940; s. Alfred P. and Emma (Glas) F.; student SUNY, Albany, 1958-60; BBA, Pace U., 1973; m. Marlis Lowenhagen, July 15, 1967 (div. 1979); children: Bettina, Malissa. Statis. analyst N.Y. Central System, N.Y.C., 1961-68; landscape planner Rosedale Nurseries, Hawthorne, N.Y., 1969—; founder RAF Prodns., 1980—; producer films: Gardening: A Brief History, 1979, Tree Transplant, 1980, Florida, 1981, Best of the West, 1982; Kenya Safari, 1983; Of Temples and Tombs, 1984; exhibitor of films, Paramount Ctr., 1987—. Bd. dirs. Paramount Ctr. for the Arts, 1981-87, pres. 1983-85. WU.S. Army, 1963-65. Cert. nurseryman, N.Y. State. Mem. Am. Film Inst., Info. Film Producers Am. Lutheran. Home: 31 Ogden Ave Peekskill NY 10566 Office: Rosedale Nurseries 51 Saw Mill River Rd Hawthorne NY 10532

FRISK, JACK EUGENE, recreational vehicle manufacturing company executive; b. Nampa, Idaho, Jan. 22, 1942; s. Steinert Paul and Evelyn Mildred (Letner) F.; m. Sharon Rose Caviness, Aug. 3, 1959; 1 dau., Toni. With Ideal of Idaho, Inc., Caldwell, purchasing mgr., 1969-75, gen. mgr., sec.-treas., 1975-82; sales mgr. Traveleze Industries div. Thor Industries, Sun Valley, Calif., 1982-88; owner, pres. Crossroads Industry div. Cross Enterprises Inc., Mesa, Ariz., 1988—. Mem. Recreational Vehicle Industry Assn., Mesa C. of C. Episcopalian. Home: 1430 N Parsell Circle Mesa AZ 85203 Office: 644 W McKellips Rd Mesa AZ 85201

FRISTEDT, HANS, manufacturing company executive; b. 1943. Exec. v.p. Esselte Bus. Systems Inc., Garden City, N.Y., 1984-86, pres., chief exec. officer, 1986—. Office: Esselte Bus Systems Inc 71 Clinton Rd Garden City NY 11530 *

FRITSCH, THOMAS JOSEPH, federal agency administrator; b. Buffalo, Jan. 15, 1947; s. Thomas John and Rita Ann (Haley) F.; m. Barbara Ann Balcer, Nov. 1, 1970 (div. July 1979); m. Joann Theresa Toll, Aug. 31, 1980. BSBA, Canisius Coll., 1970; MBA, U. Chgo., 1984. Labor relations examiner Penn Cent. Inc., Cleve., 1970-71; bus. agt. Civil Svc. Employees Assn., AFL-CIO, Albany, N.Y., 1971-73; dist. dir. employee and labor relations U.S. Postal Svc., N.J., Md., 1973-79; exec. instr. U.S. Postal Svc., Washington, 1980-81; regional dir. employee and labor relations U.S. Postal Svc., Chgo., 1981-85; asst. postmaster gen. labor relations U.S. Postal Svc., Washington, 1985-88, asst. postmaster gen. delivery svcs., 1988—; cons. Metzler Assocs., Milburn, N.J., 1975-77. With U.S Army Res., 1968-74. Mem. Am. Arbitration Assn., Indsl. Relations Research Assn., Nat. Pub. Employer Labor Relations Assn., Fed. Soc. Labor Relations Profls., Univ. Chgo. Exec. Club. Home: 217 S Fayette St Alexandria VA 22314-3519 Office: US Postal Svc 475 L'Enfant Pla SW Washington DC 20260

FRITZ, TERRENCE LEE, investment banker, strategic consultant; b. Ft. Dodge, Iowa, Mar. 10, 1943; s. George and Julia Evelyn (Katnik) F.; children: Erich, Kevin, Tanya. BS in Indsl. Engring., Iowa State U., 1967. Registered profl. engr., Colo. Mfg. system analyst Martin-Marietta, Denver, 1967-68; system fin. analyst N.Am. Philips, Denver, 1968-69; mgmt. cons. Denver, 1970-74; exec. dir. Met. Transit Authority-Iowa Dept. Transp., Des Moines, 1974-78; sr. v.p. mktg., strategic planning Holiday Inns, Trailways, Dallas, 1978-80; pres. Strategic Actions, Dallas, 1984—. Bd. dirs. Dallas, Ft. Worth Adv. Bd., 1980-84; cons. Dallas, Ft. Worth Transp. Authority, 1980; bd. mem. Govs. Com. on Tech., Austin, 1982-83. Mem. Dallas C. of C. (pres., chief exec. officer 1980-84). Clubs: Tower, Univ. Home: 9347 Briarhurst Dr Dallas TX 75243 Office: Strategic Actions First Interstate Bank Tower Ste 800 Dallas TX 75201

FRITZ, THOMAS VINCENT, accountant, lawyer; b. Pitts., July 6, 1934; s. Zeno and Mary M. (Briley) F.; m. Barbara L. Jacob, Jan. 31, 1959; children: William T., James Z., Juliann W. BBA in Acctg., U. Pitts., 1960; JD, Duquesne U., 1964; LLM, NYU, 1966; cert. Advanced Mgmt. Program, Harvard U., 1975. Bar: Pa. 1964; C.P.A. With Arthur Young & Co., 1960—, ptnr., 1970—, vice chmn., mng. ptnr., 1977—, mem. mgmt. com., 1977—. Active Century Club, Duquesne U.; mem. exec. com. Grad. Sch. of Bus. U. Pitts.; bd. dirs. Evermay Civic; mem. adv. bd. Pvt. Sector Council; chmn. bd. Alliance for Free Enterprise. Served with U.S. Army, 1955-57. Mem. ABA, Am. Inst. C.P.A.s, D.C. Inst. C.P.A.s, Va. Soc. C.P.A.s, Pa. Inst. C.P.A.s. Clubs: Duquesne, Rolling Rock, Capitol Hill, Edgewood Country; Metropolitan (Washington), TPC Avenel. Home: 6303 Long Meadow Rd McLean VA 22101 Office: Arthur Young & Co 3000 K St NW Washington DC 20007

FROCK, EDMOND BURNELL, banker, youth home official; b. Hanover, Pa., Nov. 26, 1910; s. Edmond A. and Vivian (Huff) F.; m. Rebecca Black, Apr. 24, 1936; children: Edmond Burnell Jr., J. Daniel, Judith A., James W. (dec.). BA, Catawba Coll., 1933, LLD (hon.), 1986. Mdse. mgr. Atlantic & Pacific Tea Co., Hanover, Pa., 1933-45; pres. Hanover Wire Cloth, 1945-81; v.p. CCX, Inc. (formerly Continental Copper & Steel Industries, Inc.), N.Y.C., 1948-74, exec. v.p., 1974-81; ret. 1981; chmn. bd. Bank of Hanover & Trust Co., 1963-89, pres., 1970-77; past pres., dir. Downtown Hanover Inc.; past pres. Wire Weavers Assn., Indsl. Wire Cloth Inst., Hanover Pub. Library; pres., chief exec. officer Hanover Bancorp., Inc., 1983-88. Pres., mem. fin. com. Hoffman Homes for Youth, 1987—; vice-chmn. Christian Bus. Men Com.; past pres. Emmanuel U. Ch. Consistory; past pres. Hanover Dist. Sch. Bd.; bd. dirs. Hanover Gen. Hosp.; emeritus trustee Catawba Coll., Hanover YMCA.; chmn. adv. com. York County Earn It Ct. Program; mem. York chpt. S.C.O.R.E.; pres., trustee Hoffman Home for Youth, Hart Ctr., Gettysburg, Pa. Named Disting. Pennsylvanian Phila. C. of C., 1982. Mem. Hanover Area Indsl. Mgmt. Club (founder), Mfrs. Assn. York (past pres. dir.), Hanover Area C. of C. (past pres.), Indsl. Mgmt. Club York County (past pres.), Christian Businessmens Club Hanover, Christian Businessmens Club U.S.A. Club: Pine Valley Golf. Lodges: Masons, Shriners. Home and Office: 7 Oak St Hanover PA 17331 Office: Hanover Bancorp Inc 33 Carlyle St Hanover PA 17331

FROEHLICH, DEAN ALAN, financial executive; b. Twin Falls, Idaho, Feb. 28, 1950; s. Joseph Jacob and Dorothea (Cook) F.; m. L. Shannon Freeman, July 17, 1976; children: Ryan Dean, Clint James. BBA, Idaho State U., 1972; MBA, Boise State U., 1984. Staff auditor Legis. Auditor's Office, Boise, Idaho, 1972-76; mng. auditor Legis. Auditor's Office, Boise, 1976-78; bus. mgr. Idaho Sch. Deaf and Blind, Gooding, Idaho, 1978-85; budget officer Lewis Clark State Coll., Lewiston, Idaho, 1985-87; fin. v.p. Lewis Clark State Coll., Lewiston, 1987—; bd. dirs., treas. Ednl. and Assistance Found., Lewis Clark State Coll., 1987—. Mem. Lewis Clark State Coll. Alumni Assn. (treas. 1987—), Western Assn. Coll. Univ. Bus. Officers. Home: 3416 Selway Dr Lewiston ID 83501 Office: Lewis Clark State Coll 8th Ave and 6th St Lewiston ID 83501

FROELICH, FREDERICK KARL, financial consultant; b. Oceanside, N.Y., Aug. 10, 1946; s. Frank Joseph and Lillian May (Foster) F.; m. Linda Ann Avallone, Nov. 12,1949; children: Frederick Karl Jr., Daniel, Andrea. Cert. in fin. planning, Adelphi U., 1985. Researcher Met. Transp. Authority, N.Y.C., 1967-70; acct. County of Nassau, Mineola, N.Y., 1979-82, retirement counselor, 1982-87; pvt. practice fin. cons. Hempstead, N.Y., 1985—. Deacon, fin. sec. Luth. Ch. of Epiphany, Hempstead, 1982-87; bd. dirs. Nassau County Police Dept. Fed. Credit Union, Mineola, 1984-88; dir., sec. Police Relief Assn. Nassau County, Mineola, 1984-88. Served as sgt. U.S. Army, 1964-67, Korea. Mem. Inst. Cert. Fin. Planners (v.p. programs and edn., bd. dirs. L.I. chpt. 1986-87), Internat. Assn. Fin. Planning, Am. Mgmt. Assn., Inst. Continuing Edn. (co-founder, v.p.), Registry Fin. Planning Practitioners. Home and Office: 247 Belmont Pkwy Hempstead NY 11550

FROHLINGER, BARRY MICHAEL, bank consultant; b. Amityville, N.Y., Oct. 26, 1954; s. William and Debra (Kantrowitz) F. BA, SUNY, Stonybrook, 1976; MS in Mgmt, Purdue U., 1978; Advanced Profl. Cert., NYU, 1981. Asst. v.p. Bank of Am., N.Y.C., 1978-82; v.p. Tex. Commerce Bank, N.Y.C., 1982-84; dir. Omega Cons., San Francisco, 1984—; pres. BMF Assocs., Sharon, Conn., 1985—. Pres. N.W. Corner Polit. Action Com., Sharon, 1985-86. Mem. NYU Alumni Assn. Republican. Jewish. Club: Big Apple Triathlon (N.Y.C.). Home and Office: Main St Falls Village CT 06031

FROHNHOEFER, FRANCIS WILLIAM, economist, accountant, educator; b. Bklyn., Dec. 30, 1939; s. Francis Jacob and Elizabeth Lucille (Kent) F.; AA, St. Joseph's Coll., 1959; AB, Cath. U. Am., 1963; MA, U. Pa., 1965, MBA, 1978; CPA, Miss. Asst. prof. Tougaloo (Miss.) Coll., 1966-68; nat. rep. Woodrow Wilson Nat. Fellowship Found., Princeton, N.J., 1968-69; asst. prof. Millsaps Coll., Jackson, Miss., 1972-79; asst. prof. econs. and bus. Cath. U. Am., Washington, 1979-85, assoc. prof. acctg., Howard U., Washington, 1986—; Woodrow Wilson fellow, 1963-64. Mem. Am. Econ. Assn., Am. Acctg. Assn., Am. Fin. Assn., AICPA, Miss. Soc. CPAs, D.C. Inst. CPAs, Inst. Mgmt. Acctg. (cert. in mgmt. acctg.), Miss. Soc. of Washington, Phi Beta Kappa. Roman Catholic. Home: 801 N Pitt St Alexandria VA 22314 Office: Howard U Washington DC 20059

FROHRING, PAUL ROBERT, former business executive; b. Cleve.; s. William E. and Martha L. (Bliss) F.; m. Maxine A. Prince, Mar. 7, 1941; children: Martha Louise, Paula Christine. Student, Ohio State U., 1921-22; B.S. in Chem. Engring, Case Inst. Tech., 1926. With research labs. S.M.A. Corp. (formerly Lab. Products Co.), 1926-34, v.p., 1942-44; pres. Eff Labs., Inc., 1940-61; gen. mgr. Gen. Biochems., Inc., Chagrin Falls, Ohio, 1940-61, Emdee Labs., 1942-44; pres. Life Products, Inc., 1942-45; dir. Cleve. Machine Controls, Inc., Irvin & Co., Shaker Heights, Ohio, Alco Standard, Inc., Phila., Newbury Industries, Inc., Ohio, Horsburg & Scott, Cleve.; mem. pharm. mfrs. adv. com. WPB, 1942; del. Pres.'s Conf. Indsl. Safety, 1954. Trustee, hon. chmn. Cleve. Health Edn. Mus.; trustee Hiram (Ohio) Coll., John Cabot Coll., Rome, Italy, Fla. Zool. Soc.; overseer Case Western Res. U.; mem. corp. Planned Parenthood, Cleve.; bd. dirs. Mercy Hosp. Found., Miami. Recipient Gold medal award for achievement Case Alumni Assn. Fellow Garfield Soc., N.Y. Acad. Scis.; mem. Ohio Acad. Sci., Am. Chem. Soc., Am. Dairy Sci. Assn., Am. Oil Chemist Soc., AAAS, Navy League (life), Newcomen Soc., Ohio Soc. (N.Y.), Alpha Chi Sigma. Clubs: Chagrin Valley Hunt (Gates Mills, Ohio); Union (Cleve.); Key Biscayne Yacht (Key Biscayne, Fla.); Commodore Club of Key Biscayne (dir.). Home and Office: Box 428 Chagrin Falls OH 44022

FROMM, ERWIN FREDERICK, insurance company executive; b. Kalamazoo, Oct. 24, 1933; s. Erwin Carl and Charlotte Elizabeth (Wilson) F.; student U. Mich., 1951-52, Flint Jr. Coll., 1952-53; B.A., Kalamazoo Coll., 1959; postgrad. Ill. State U., 1970-72. Underwriter, State Farm Ins., 1959-72; cons. Met. Property & Liability Ins. Co., Warwick, R.I., 1972-73, dir. underwriting and policyholders services, 1973, asst. v.p., 1973-74, v.p., 1974—; sr. v.p. Royal Ins. Co., Charlotte, N.C., 1979—; past chmn. All Industry Ins. Com. for Arson Control; chmn. bd. dirs. Nat. Council on Compensation Ins.; chmn. Comml. Lines Com. Ins. Svc. Office; bd. dirs. Workers Compensation Research Inst.; mem. adv. com. underwriting program Ins. Inst. Am. Mem. adv. council Bus. Sch., U. R.I; bd. dirs. Charlotte Symphony, N.C. Ins. Edn. Served to 1st lt. U.S. Army, 1953-56. CPCU, CLU. Mem. CPCU Assn. (N.C. chpt.), English Speaking Union. Clubs: Masons, Shriners. Home: 3601 Sharon Rd Charlotte NC 28211 Office: 9300 Arrowpoint Blvd Charlotte NC 28217

FROMM, JOSEPH L., financial consultant; b. Detroit, May 22, 1930; s. Charles and Elizabeth F.; A.B. cum laude, Princeton U., 1953; M.B.A., Harvard U., 1958; m. Beverly C. Booth, June 18, 1960; children—Charles, Laurence, Kenneth, Lisa, Brian. Research asst. Harvard Bus. Sch., 1959; asst. to pres. Gen. Electronic Labs., Cambridge, Mass., 1960-62; with Chrysler Corp., Highland Park, Mich., 1963-68; treas. Marantette & Co., Detroit, 1969; asst. treas. Am. Motors Corp., Southfield, Mich., 1970-87; pres. Fiduciary Advisors, Inc., Grosse Pointe, Mich., 1988—; dir. pension asset mgmt. Eastern Airlines, Miami, Fla., 1988—; instr. U. Detroit Evening Div., 1964-65. Councilman, City of Grosse Pointe Farms, 1973-86, mayor, 1986—; trustee Bon Secours Hosp., Grosse Pointe, 1975—. Served with AUS, 1954-56. Mem. Sentinel Pension Inst., Midwest Pension Conf. Republican. Roman Catholic. Club: Grosse Pointe Indoor Tennis, Country of Detroit. Office: Eastern Airlines Miami Internat Airport Miami FL 33148 Also: Fiduciary Advisors Inc 316 Belanger Grosse Pointe Farms MI 48236

FROMMER, HENRY, financial executive; b. N.Y.C., July 30, 1943; s. Barney and Eleanor Jeanette (Peller) F.; B.S. in Econs., U. Pa., 1964; M.B.A., Columbia U., 1966; J.D. magna cum laude, Bklyn. Law Sch., 1976; m. Barbara Gay Hymson, Feb. 3, 1980; children—David P., Katharine B. Fin. analyst N.Y. Central System, N.Y.C., 1964; asst. sec. Irving Trust Co., N.Y.C., 1968-71; asst. cashier Franklin Nat. Bank, N.Y.C., 1971-72; exec. v.p., sr. credit officer Comml. Funding, Inc., N.Y.C., 1972-85; pres., chief exec. officer Charter Fin. Inc., N.Y.C., 1985—. Served with U.S. Army, 1966-68. Decorated Army Commendation medal. Mem. Am. Bar Assn., N.Y. State Bar Assn. Clubs: Columbia Golf and Country (Claverack, N.Y.); Princeton (N.Y.C.). Home: PO Box 532 Claverack NY 12513 Office: One Rockefeller Pla New York NY 10020

FROSCH, ROBERT ALAN, physicist, automobile manufacturing executive; b. N.Y.C., May 22, 1928; s. Herman Louis and Rose (Bernfeld) F.; m. Jessica Rachael Denerstein, Dec. 22, 1957; children: Elizabeth Ann, Margery Ellen. A.B., Columbia U., 1947, A.M., 1949, Ph.D., 1952; D. Engring (hon.), U. Miami, 1982, Mich. Technol. U., 1983. Scientist Hudson Labs. Columbia U., 1951-53, asst. dir. theoretical div., 1953-54, asso. dir., 1954-56, dir., 1956-63; dir. nuclear test detection Advanced Research Projects Agy., Office Sec. Def., 1963-65; dep. dir. Advanced Research Projects Agy., 1965-66; asst. sec. navy for research and devel. Washington, 1966-73; asst. exec. dir. UN Environment Programme, 1973-75; asso. dir. for applied oceanography Woods Hole (Mass.) Oceanographic Instn., 1975-77; adminstr. NASA, Washington, 1977-81; pres. Am. Assn. Engring. Socs., N.Y.C., 1981-82; v. p. in charge Research Labs. Gen. Motors Corp., Warren, Mich., 1982—; chmn. U.S. del. to Intergovtl. Oceanographic Commn. meetings UNESCO, Paris, 1967, 70. Research and publs. numerous sci. and tech. articles. Recipient Arthur S. Flemming award, 1966, NASA Disting. Service award, 1981. Fellow AAAS, AIAA, Acoustical Soc. Am., Am. Astronautical Soc. (John F. Kennedy astronautics award 1981), IEEE; mem. Am. Geophys. Union, Seismol. Soc. Am., Soc. Exploration Geophysicists (Spl. Commendation award 1981), Marine Tech. Soc., Nat. Acad. Engring., Am. Phys. Soc., Soc. Naval Architects and Marine Engrs., Soc. Automotive Engrs., Engring. Soc. Detroit. Office: Gen Motors Rsch Labs Warren MI 48090-9055 also: GM Gen Motors Bldg Detroit MI 48202

FROST, A. CORWIN, architect, consultant; b. Bronxville, N.Y., Nov. 18, 1934; s. Frederick George Jr. and Gwendolyn Belle (Corwin) F.; m. Rosalie Randolph Halsey, Sept. 26, 1959; children: Frederick Halsey, Anne Randolph. AB, Princeton U., 1956; BS, R.I. Sch. Design, 1959. Registered architect, N.Y., other states. Designer, draftsman Harrison & Abramovitz, N.Y.C., 1959-60; project architect Frederick G. Frost Jr. and Assocs., N.Y.C., 1960-63, assoc., 1963-68; ptnr. Frost Assocs., N.Y.C., 1968-78; assoc. dir. archtl. and engring. services CBS Inc., N.Y.C., 1978-80, dir. planning and design, 1980-86, dir. facilities engring., 1986-88; prin. Frost Assocs. Cons., Bronxville, N.Y., 1988—. Trustee Council for Arts in Westchester, White Plains, N.Y., 1972-81, pres. 1974-75; mem. Bronxville Adult Sch., 1982-88; mem. Bronxville Planning Commn., 1977-80. Mem. AIA (exec. com. N.Y. chpt 1974-76, ethics com. 1978-80, corp. architects com. 1980-82, fin. com. 1981-87). Clubs: Princeton (N.Y.C.); Bronxville Field. Home: 11 Sunset Ave Bronxville NY 10708 Office: Frost Assocs Cons 11 Sunset Ave Bronxville NY 10708

FROST, CARL E., consulting electrical engineer; b. Bellingham, Wash., May 22, 1949; s. Climuth Eugene and Irene Elizabeth (Hall) F.; m. Georgia Christene Goltsos, June 28, 1981; 1 child, Constantine Edward. BS in Engring. Physics with honors, Oreg. State U., 1972; MSEE, Northeastern U., 1984. Field mech. engr. Bechtel Power Corp., Richland, Wash. and Midland, Mich., 1972-77; design engring. contractor Tech. Aid Corp., Boston, 1977-79; cons. engr. Frost Tech. Services, Somerville, Mass., 1979-84, S. Natick, Mass., 1984—; exec. dir. Dobkins/Cordell, Los Angeles, 1979-87; contract engr. Stone & Webster Engring., Boston, 1977-79, Bergen-Patterson Pipesupport, Hempstead, N.Y., 1978; cons. engr. Teledyne Engring. Services, Waltham, Mass., 1979-81, Cygna Energy Services, Boston, 1980-81, Robert L. Cloud & Assocs., Cotuit, Mass., 1981-83, Westinghouse Electric Corp., Pitts., 1982, Bechtel Power Corp., Avila Beach, Calif., 1983, MIT Lincoln Lab., Lexington, Mass., 1984—. Mem. IEEE. Baptist. Lodge: Elks. Home: 20 Dover Rd South Natick MA 01760 Office: MIT Lincoln Lab 244 Wood St Lexington MA 02173

FROST, JAMES LYON, financial planner; b. Hartford, Conn., May 10, 1953; s. Edwin Laverne and Marjorie (Wright) F.; m. Laurey Lou Picher, June 15, 1974 (div. 1987); m. Maaret Karina Valkama, July 31, 1987. BS in Econs, and Fin., U. Pa., 1975; MS in Mgmt. and Fin., MIT, 1980. Cert. fin. planner. Fin. analyst Exxon Corp., N.Y.C., 1975-78, Exxon Enterprises, Inc., N.Y.C., 1979-80; planning assoc. Morgan Stanley and Co., N.Y.C., 1980-82; v.p. Assocs. Fin. Planning, Inc., Burlington, Vt., 1983-86; br. mgr., prin. Investment Mgmt. and Research, Inc., Jupiter, Fla., 1983—; pres. Frost Fin. Services Inc., Jupiter, Fla., 1986—, J.L. frost and Co., Inc., Jupiter, Fla., 1986—. Exec. advisor Jr. Achievement of N.Y., 1975-78 (recipient Service to Youth award, 1978); dept. solicitation coordinator N.Y. United Way, 1977; solicitor United Way of Greater Burlington, 1985. Mem. Inst. Cert. Fin. Planners, Internat. Assn. Fin. Planners, Jupiter/Tequesta C. of C. Republican. Club: MIT of Palm Beach County. Home: 825 W Center St 21 B Jupiter FL 33458 Office: JL Frost & Co 900 E Indiantown Rd Suite 309 Jupiter FL 33477

FROST, JOHN ELLIOTT, minerals company executive; b. Winchester, Mass., May 20, 1924; s. Elliott Putnam and Hazel Lavera (Carley) F.; m. Carolyn Catlin, July 12, 1945 (div. 1969); children: John Crocker, Jeffrey Putnam, Teresa Baird, Virginia Nicholl; m. Martha Hicks, June 6, 1969 (div. 1984); m. Catherine Kearns, July 27, 1985. BS, Stanford U., 1949, MS, 1950, PhD, 1965. Geologist Asarco, Salt Lake City, 1951-54; chief geologist, surface mines supt. Philippine Iron Mines Inc., Larap, Camarines Norte, 1954-60; chief geologist Duval Corp. (Pennzoil Corp.), Tucson, 1961-67; minerals exploration mgr. Exxon Corp., Houston, 1967-71; minerals mgr. Esso Eastern Inc. div., 1971-80; sr. v.p. Exxon Minerals Co. div., Houston, 1980-86; pres., Frost Minerals Internat., 1986—; bd. dirs., United Engring. Trustees, N.Y.C., 1982—, chmn. real estate com., 1986-89, v.p. 1989—. Mem. adv. bd. Sch. Earth Scis., Stanford (Calif.) U., 1983-85; pres. SEG Found., 1984. Served to 1st lt. USAAF, 1943-45; PTO. Fellow Geol. Soc. Am.; mem. Soc. Econ. Geologists (pres. elect 1988, pres. 1989, councilor 1982-84, program com., nominating com. chmn. 1982), AIME (chmn. edn. com. Soc. Mining Engrs. 1971; Charles F. Rand medal 1984, Disting. Mem. award 1984), Australian Inst. Mining and Metallurgy, Sigma Xi. Republican. Congregationalist. Clubs: Mining (N.Y.C.); Mining of Southwest (Tucson). Home and Office: 602 Sandy Port Houston TX 77079

FROST, ROBERT, financial consulting firm executive; b. N.Y.C., Nov. 4, 1939; s. Arnold and Fae (Feingold) F.; m. Lois Rifkind, Aug. 7, 1960; children—Alan, Karen. A.B., U. Pa., Phila., 1960; postgrad., NYU Grad. Sch. Bus., 1963-65. Reporter New York Times, N.Y.C., 1963-65; asst. fin. editor Bus. Week, N.Y.C., 1965-69; exec. v.p. Booke & Co., N.Y.C., 1969-74; pres. ECOM Cons. Inc., N.Y.C., 1974—. Served to lt (j.g.) USN, 1960-63. Democrat. Jewish. Home: 53 Ward Dr New Rochelle NY 10804 Office: ECOM Cons Inc 1140 Ave of the Americas New York NY 10036

FROST, RUSSELL, III, real estate executive; b. N.Y.C., Mar. 24, 1921; s. Russell II and Mary (Burnell) F.; m. Patricia Grace Lauber, Apr. 11, 1981. BA, Yale U., 1943. V.p. Howe Furniture Corp., Norwalk, Conn., 1950-86; ptnr. Frost-Graham-Overlock, Norwalk, 1986—; dir. Merchants Bank and Trust Co., Norwalk, 1966—, Reincorp Internat. Inc., Boston, 1984—, Community Hotel-Motel Corp, Norwalk, 1952-86. Chmn. Norwalk Hosp., 1983-84, Norwalk Devel. Agy, 1959—, Yankee Heritage Tourism Dist., 1985—. Served to sgt. U.S. Army, 1943-45, ETO. Republican. Episcopal. Clubs: Yale (N.Y.C.), Shore and Country (Norwalk), Roxbury (Bantam, Conn.). Home: 130 Good Hill Rd Weston CT 06883 Office: Frost-Graham-Overlock 520 West Ave Norwalk CT 06850

FROST, THOMAS CLAYBORNE, banker; b. San Antonio, Oct. 29, 1927; s. Thomas Clayborne and Ilse (Herff) F.; m. Patricia Holden, June 9, 1951; children: Thomas Clayborne III, William, Donald, Patrick. B.S. in Commerce summa cum laude, Washington and Lee U., Lexington, Va., 1950; LL.D., Austin Coll. With Frost Nat. Bank, San Antonio, 1950—; pres. Frost Nat. Bank, 1962-71, chmn. bd., 1971-81, 85; chmn. bd. Cullen/Frost Bankers, Inc., 1973—; adv. dir. Elsinore Cattle Co.; dir. Fed. Reserve Bank Dallas, Cullen/Frost Bank of Dallas N.A., La Quinta Motor Inns, Inc., Southwestern Bell Telephone Co., Tesoro Petroleum Corp., Cullen Center Bank & Trust, Houston, Frost Nat. Bank San Antonio; past dir. San Antonio br. Fed. Res. Bank; past mem. fed. adv. council Fed. Res. System; past 1st chmn. regional adv. com. to comptroller of currency. Trustee Tex. Research and Tech. Found., San Antonio Med. Found., S.W. Research Inst., McNay Art Inst., Austin Coll.; hon. Trustee S.W. Tex. Meth. Hosp.; Trustee emeritus Washington and Lee U.; Trustee Morrison Trusts; past exec. chmn., bd. trustees Tex. Mil. Inst.; past chmn. Tex. Ind. Coll. Fund; mem. devel. bd. U. Tex. Health Sci. Center; bd. dirs. San Antonio Econ. Devel. Found. Served with AUS, 1946-47. Named Outstanding Young Man San Antonio Jr. C. of C., 1961; Mr. South Tex. Laredo (Tex.) George Washington Birthday Celebration Assn., 1974; First Outstanding Alumnus Tex. Mil. Inst., 1974; San Antonio Man of Year Exchange Club, 1974, Brotherhood award Nat. Conf. Christians and Jews, 1980, Inst. Juman Relations award Am. Jewish Com., 1981, W.T. Bondurant Sr. Disting. Humanitarian award San Antonio Acad., 1983, People of Vision award Tex. Soc. to Prevent Blindness, 1985. Mem. Tex. Bankers Assn. (past pres.), San Antonio Clearing House Assn. (past pres.), Tex. Assn. Bank Holding Co. (past dir.), Assn. Res. City Bankers (pres. 1977), Philos. Soc. Tex., Tex. Cavaliers, Sons Republic of Tex. (hon.), Order of Alamo, Phi Beta Kappa, Beta Gamma Sigma, Alpha Kappa Psi, Phi Eta Sigma, Sigma Chi. Clubs: San Antonio Country, San Antonio German, Plaza, Argyle. Home: 234 Rosemary St San Antonio TX 78209 Office: Cullen/Frost Bankers Inc PO Box 1600 San Antonio TX 78296

FROTTEN, ROBERT PAUL, financial executive; b. Yarmouth, N.S., Can., July 30, 1947; s. Joseph Paul and Marceline Anne (Doucette) F.; m. Anne Marie Muise, Aug. 23, 1969; children: Kristina, Yvette. BBA, Salem (Mass.) State Coll., 1970. Staff acct. Hendrie's Inc., Southborough, Mass., 1970-75, office mgr., 1975-80, asst. contr., 1980-85, corp. contr., 1986—. Pres. Easton Youth Soccer League, Mass., 1984-85, Easton Field Authority, 1986-87. Mem. Nat. Assn. Accts., Am. Mgmt. Assn., KC. Home: 82 rockland St N Easton MA 02356 Office: Hendries Inc PO Box 1 Southborough MA 01772

FROWEN, STEPHEN FRANCIS, economist, educator; b. Remscheid, Germany, May 22, 1923; arrived in Eng., 1949; naturalized, 1956; s. Adolf and Anne (Bauer) Frowein; m. Irina Minskers, Mar. 21, 1949; children: Michael Bernard James, Tatiana Mary Anne Frowen Hosburn. Student, U. Cologne, Fed. Republic of Germany, 1943-44, U. Würzburg, Fed. Republic of Germany, 1944-45, U. Bonn, Fed. Republic of Germany, 1945-48; Diplom-Volkswirt, U. Bonn, 1948. Asst. editor Bankers' Mag., London, 1954-55, editor, 1956-60; econ. advisor Indsl. and Comml. Fin. Corp. Ltd., London, 1959-60; research officer Nat. Inst. Econ. and Social Research, London, 1960-62; lectr. Thames Poly., London, 1962-63, sr. lectr., 1963-67; sr. lectr. in monetary econs. U. Surrey, Eng., 1967-87; prof. econs. U. Frankfurt, Fed. Republic Germany, 1987; Bundesbank prof. monetary econs. Free Univ. Berlin, 1987—. Author: (with H.C. Hillmann) Economic Issues, 1957, (with others) Monetary Policy and Economic Activity in West Germany, 1977; editor: A Framework of International Banking, 1979, Controlling Industrial Economies, 1983, Business, Time and Thought: Selected Papers by G.L.S. Shackle, 1988, Unknowledge and Choice in Economics, 1989; translator: Value, Capital and Rent (Knut Wicksell), 1954, The Role of the Economist as Official Adviser (W.A. Jöhr and H.W. Singer), 1955; co-editor: Enzyklopädisches Lexikon für das Geld-, Bank- und Börsenwesen, 2 vols., 1957; editor Woolwich Econ. Papers, 1963-67; Surrey Papers in Econs, 1987, Essays in Honor of Stephen Frowen, Contemporary Issues in Money and Banking, 1988; contbr. articles to leading profl. jours.

FRUEH, JOHN CURT, financial executive; b. Grand Rapids, Mich., June 23, 1934; s. Martin and Hilda F.; m. Gretchen Bahr, Dec. 27, 1956; children: Curt David, Carol Linda. BA, Kalamazoo Coll., 1956; MBA, U. Mich., 1958. Asst. controller Monsanto Co., St. Louis, 1969-74; v.p. fin., chief fin. officer Globe Union Inc., Milw., 1974-79; exec. v.p. Centex Corp., Dallas, 1979-81; sr. v.p. fin., chief fin. officer Wheeling Pitts. Steel Co., Pitts., 1981-84; exec. v.p. fin. and adminstrn. L.B. Foster Co., Pitts., 1984-86; pres. Aegis Group, Inc., Pitts., 1987—; bd. dirs. Ziegler Co., West Bend, Wis. Served to 1st lt. U.S. Army, 1958-62. Mem. Fin. Exec. Inst. Presbyterian. Clubs: Duquesne, Pitts. Field. Home: 106 Rockwood Dr Pittsburgh PA 15238 Office: 2210 William Pitt Way Ste 156 Pittsburgh PA 15238

FRUEHLING, DONALD LAVERNE, publishing company executive; b. Ft. Madison, Iowa, May 29, 1931; s. Jesse William and Elma Melissa (Fowler) F.; m. Ann Stacy; children—Gregg, Jeff, Melissa; m. Rosemary Theresa Leoni Shanus, July 25, 1969. BA, No. Iowa U., 1957; LLD (hon.), Rider Coll., 1982. With McGraw-Hill, Inc., N.Y.C., 1958—; pres. McGraw-Hill Book and Broadcast Cos. subs. McGraw-Hill, Inc., N.Y.C., 1970-74, exec. v.p., 1974-79; pres. McGraw-Hill Internat. Book Co. subs. McGraw-Hill, Inc., N.Y.C., 1979-82, McGraw-Hill Book Co. subs. McGraw-Hill, Inc., N.Y.C., 1982-84; exec. v.p. pub. ops. McGraw-Hill, Inc., N.Y.C., 1985-88; pres., bd. dirs. Maxwell Pergamon Pub. Group, Greenwich, Conn., 1988—; bd. dirs. Macmillan Inc., group v.p. edn. pub.; mem. Fowler-McCracken Commn. Policy Com. on Edn., Washington, 1984—. Master sgt. U.S. Army, 1948-53, Korea. Recipient Alumni Achievement award U. No. Iowa, 1974. Mem. Am. Assn. Pubs. (bd. dirs. 1985-87, vice chmn.), Am. Soc. Tng. and Devel. (bd. govs. 1984—), Am. Assn. Higher Edn. (bd. dirs. 1985), Moss Creek Club (Hilton Head, S.C.). Office: Macmillan Pub 866 3rd Ave New York NY 10022

FRUITMAN, FREDERICK HOWARD, investment banker; b. Toronto, Ont., Can., Oct. 8, 1950; s. Herbert Lance and Libby (Kamin) F.; m. Marlin Sue Potash, Nov. 21, 1981; children: Laura, Hilary. SB, MIT, 1972; BA, Oxford (Eng.) U., 1974, MA, 1981; LLB, U. Toronto, 1976; MBA, Harvard U., 1981. Assoc. Davies, Ward & Beck, Toronto, 1976-77, Merrill Lynch White Weld Capital Markets Group, N.Y.C., 1978-79; cons. Bain & Co., Boston, 1981-82; v.p. Investors in Industry Corp., Boston, 1982-84; assoc. E.M. Warburg, Pincus & Co. Inc., N.Y.C., 1984-86; sr. v.p. The Stuart James Co. Inc., N.Y.C., 1986—. Mem. Law Soc. Upper Can., Can. Soc. of N.Y. Club: Harvard (N.Y.C.), Can. Soc. N.Y.C. Home: 1133 Park Ave New York NY 10128 Office: The Stuart James Co Inc 805 Third Ave New York NY 10022

FRUMKES, HERBERT M., discount stock broker; b. N.Y.C., Aug. 27, 1926; s. John Grover and Mildred (Sheckel) F.; B.S., U. Ill., 1949; m. Mildred Steinberg, (Patti Marlowe), Dec. 18, 1952; children—Jonni Robin, Cindy, Wendy. Sr. partner H.M. Frumkes & Co., N.Y.C., 1957-65; exec. v.p. TPO Inc., 1965-70; pres. Tradex Brokerage Service Inc., N.Y.C., 1979—; mem. N.Y. Stock Exchange, 1958—. Served with USN, 1943-46, 50-52. Home: 425 E 58th St New York NY 10022 Office: Tradex Brokerage Svc 20 Vesey St New York NY 10007

FRUNGILLO, NICHOLAS ANTHONY, JR., accountant; b. Newark, N.J., Sept. 8, 1960; s. Nicholas Anthony and Marie Theresa (Russo) F.; m. Mary Margaret LaMonica, May 11, 1985. BA, Rutgers U., 1982. Staff acct. Besser, Colner, Herbst C. Lustbader CPA's, West Orange, N.J., 1981-82, Magla Products Inc, Irvington, N.J., 1982-83; asst. v.p. United Counties Trust Co., Cranford, N.J., 1983—. Mem. Bankers Adminstrn. Inst. Republican. Roman Catholic. Home: 401 Pine Ave Garwood NJ 07027 Office: United Counties Trust Co 4 Commerce Dr Cranford NY 07016

FRY, DIANE LYNN, insurance company executive; b. Greenville, Pa., Sept. 13, 1962; d. Gordon A. and Roberta V. (Roberts) F. BS in Fin., Penn. State U., 1984. Finance, ins. mgr. John Rugala Ins. Agy., Andover, Ohio, 1985—. Republican. Methodist. Office: John Rugala Ins Agy 6209 E Main St Andover PA 44003

FRY, HARRY WELLMAN, tool company executive; b. Bozeman, Mont., Mar. 22, 1932; s. William Everett and Naida Olive (Wellman) F.; m. Keige Allaire Mosby, Sept. 11, 1954; children: Ronald S., Valerie N. Student, U. Mont., 1953; BS in Indsl. Engring., Mont. State U., 1955. Engr. phys. distbn. Dow Chem. Co., Midland, Mich., 1955-62; div. mgr. distbn. and traffic Dow Chem. Co., Cleve., 1962-65; mgr. distbn. ctr. Mattel Toy Co., Holmdel, N.J., 1965; dir. phys. distbn. Snap-On Tools Corp., Ottawa, Ill., 1966-70; dir. phys. distbn. and info. services Snap-On Tools Corp., Kenosha, Wis., 1970-73, v.p. phys. distbn. and info. services, 1973-79, v.p. adminstrn., 1980-81, sr. v.p. adminstrn., 1981—, also bd. dirs.; bd. dirs. 1st Fin. Assn., Inc., Kenosha, 1st Nat. Bank, Kenosha; bd. bus. advisors U. Wis., Parkside. Pres., v.p., bd. dirs. United Way Kenosha, 1973-80; chmn. exec. com., bd. dirs. Pvt. Industry Council Southeastern Wis., Kenosha, 1983—; pres., chmn. exec. com., bd. dirs. Kenosha Area Devel. Corp., 1987— (mem. County Blue Ribbon com., county wide assessment, County Task Force Econ. Devel.); mem. south Port Lakeshore Devel. Com. Club: Kenosha Country (bd. dirs. 1984-86), "306" Club. Lodges: Rotary (bd. dirs. Kenosha club 1975), Elks. Office: Snap-On Tools Corp 2801 80th St Kenosha WI 53140

FRY, JAMES C., textile company executive; b. 1930; married. BS, Ga. Inst. Tech., 1951, 55. Cons. Kurt Salmon Assocs., 1965-67; exec. v.p. Am. Yarn Spinners Assn., 1968-72; with Ti-Caro Inc., 1972—, v.p., 1973-74, exec. v.p., 1974-81, exec. v.p., chief operating officer, 1981-84, chmn., pres., chief exec. officer, 1984-87, pres., chief operating officer, dir., 1987—; with Dixie Yarns Inc., Chattanooga, 1972—; pres., chief operating officer, dir. Dixie Yarns Inc., 1987—. Office: Dixie Yarns Inc 1100 Watkins St Chattanooga TN 37401 *

FRY, MARY ANN (DEE), collection and litigation professional; b. Chgo., Aug. 27, 1948; d. Arthur George and Eileen Blanche (McNamara) Stegmaier; divorced; children: Terri L. Bowen, Steven L. Bowen, Scott R. Student, Roosevelt U., 1985—. Asst. equity dept. Continental Credit Corp., Barrington, Ill., 1974-75, asst. nat. leasing mgr., 1976-77; credit and collection supr. Am. Internat. Leasing Corp., Schaumburg, Ill., 1977-79, adminstr. litigated accounts, 1980-84, dir. litigation, 1984-86; collection rep. Dekalb Equipment Leasing Corp., Geneva, Ill., 1986-87, collection and litigation mgr., 1987—. Roman Catholic. Office: Dekalb Equipment Leasing Co 1 W State St PO Box 385 Geneva IL 60134

FRY, MAXWELL JOHN, economist, educator; b. Maidenhead, U.K., Feb. 12, 1944; came to U.S., 1974; s. Thomas Maxwell and Jeanne Mary (Kislingbury) F.; m. Celia Gordon, June 17, 1972; children—Benjamin, Zoe, Jeremy, Caroline. BS, London Sch. Econs., 1965; MA, UCLA, 1966; PhD, London Sch. Econs., 1970. Lectr. Morley Coll., 1966-67; lectr. Middle East Tech. U., Ankara, Turkey, 1967-69; lectr. fin. econs. City U. London, 1969-74; prof. econs. U. Hawaii, Honolulu, 1974-81; vis. prof. Bogazici U., Istanbul, 1977-79, UCLA, 1981-85; prof. econs. U. Calif.-Irvine, 1981—, chmn. dept., 1983-85; advisor minister fin., Kabul, Afghanistan, 1972-73, Gov. Cen. Bank Nepal, 1974-77, Gov. Cen. Bank Portugal, 1976-79, Minister State Econ. Enterprises, Turkey, 1978-79, Gov. Cen. Bank Bangladesh, 1984-86; cons. to internat. agys., central banks, AID; vis. fellow Brasenose Coll., Oxford U., Eng., 1986. Author: Finance and Development Planning in Turkey, 1972, The Afghan Economy, 1974, Money and Banking in Turkey, 1979, American Money and Banking, 1984, Improving Domestic Resource Mobilization through Financial Development, 1985, Money, Interest and Banking in Economic Development, 1988; contbr. articles to profl. jours.; research on monetary policy, domestic resource moblzn., fgn. debt, balance of payments in developing countries; editorial bd. Economia, Savings and Devel., 1981—. Fulbright scholar 1965, UCI Rsch. fellow, 1982; recipient Brit. Social Sci. Rsch. council award, 1971, NSF Rsch. award, 1975, 84, Rsch. Revolving Fund award U. Hawaii, 1975. Home: 3085 Nestall Rd Laguna Beach CA 92651 Office: U Calif Dept Econs Irvine CA 92717

FRY, THOMAS RICHARD, computer company executive; b. Wilkes-Barre, Pa., Oct. 28, 1948; s. Robert Winthrop and Rita Ann (Davison) F.; m. Karen Sue Holder, Dec. 21, 1971; children: Jennifer, Thomas, Matthew. BBA in Acctg., U. Cin., 1971. CPA, Tex. Asst. controller The Kanter Corp., Forest Park, Ohio, 1968-71; pres. Charleston (S.C.) Data Ctr., 1971-73; acctg. ops. mgr. Electronic Data Systems Corp., Dallas, 1974-79; br. mgr. CompuServe, Inc., Dallas, 1979-83; v.p. sales Execucom Systems Corp., Austin, Tex., 1983-88; pres., chief exec. officer Telecalc, Inc., Bellevue, Wash., 1988—, also bd. dirs. With U.S. Army, 1971-77. Mem. Tex. Soc. CPAs. Roman Catholic. Office: Telecalc Inc 4122 128th Ave SE Bellevue WA 98006

FRYE, CLAYTON WESLEY, JR., financial executive; b. Los Angeles, May 18, 1930; s. Clayton Wesley Sr. and Mary Virginia (Briggs) F.; AB, Stanford U., 1953, MBA, 1959; m. Dorothy Dee Rumsfeld, Jan. 14, 1957; children—Carolyn Ann Halloran, Marilyn Diane. Pres., Sutter Hill Devel. Co., Palo Alto, Calif., 1962-69; gen. ptnr. Johnson & Frye Investment Co., San Antonio, 1970-73; sr. assoc. Laurance S. Rockefeller, N.Y.C., 1973—; bd. dir. Calif. Pacific Comml. Corp. (Palo Alto), Col. Williamsburg Hotel Properties, Inc., Rockefeller & Co., Inc., N.Y.C., Times Mirror Co., L.A., Tejon Ranch Co., L.A., Woodstock Resort Corp. (Vt.); Ptnr. Embarcadero Ctr., Ltd., San Francisco. Trustee Hist. Hudson Valley, Tarrytown, N.Y.; bd. trustees Jackson Hole Preserve, Inc., Woodstock Found. With USNR, 1948-49. Mem. Urban Land Inst. Republican. Clubs: Knickerbocker, Univ. (N.Y.C.); Field (New Canaan, Ct.); Calif. (Los Angeles). Home: 834 Fifth Ave New York NY 10021-7047 Office: 30 Rockefeller Pla Rm 5600 New York NY 10112

FRYE, JUDITH ELEEN MINOR, editor; b. Seattle; d. George Edward and Eleen G. (Hartelius) Minor; student U. Cal. at Los Angeles, evenings 1947-48, U. So. Calif., 1948-53; m. Vernon Lester Frye, Apr. 1, 1954. Accountant, office mgr. Colony Wholesale Liquor, Culver City, Calif., 1947-48; credit mgr. Western Distbg. Co., Culver City, 1948-53; partner in restaurants, Palm Springs, Los Angeles, 1948, partner in date ranch, La Quinta, Calif., 1949-53; partner, owner Imperial Printing, Huntington Beach, Calif., 1955—; editor New Era Laundry and Cleaning Lines, Huntington Beach, 1962—; registered lobbyist, Calif., 1975-84. Mem. Laundry and Cleaning Allied Trades Assn., Laundry and Dry Cleaning Suppliers Assn., Calif. Coin-op Assn. (exec. dir. 1975-84), Cooperation award 1971, Dedicated Service award 1976), Nat. Automatic Laundry and Cleaning Council (Leadership award 1972), Women in Laundry/Drycleaning (past pres.; Outstanding Service award 1977), Printing Industries Assn., Master Printers Am., Nat. Assn. Printers and Lithographers, Huntington Beach C. of C. Office: 22031 Bushard St Huntington Beach CA 92646

FRYE, ROLAND MUSHAT, JR., lawyer; b. Princeton, N.J., Feb. 8, 1950; s. Roland Mushat and Jean (Steiner) F.; m. Susan Marie Pettey, Jan. 23, 1988. AB cum laude, Princeton U., 1972; JD with specialization in Internat. Legal Affairs, Cornell U., 1975. Bar: Pa. 1975, D.C. 1978. Assoc. White and Williams, Phila., 1975-77; litigation atty. U.S. Dept. Energy, Washington, 1977-79, asst. solicitor, 1979-80; presiding officer Fed. Energy Regulatory Commn., Washington, 1980-83, chief presiding officer, 1983-85, supervisory atty., 1985-88, sr. atty., 1988—; mediator Ctr. for Community Justice, D.C. Superior Ct., 1983-85. Editor Cornell Law Rev., 1974-75; contbr. articles to profl. jours. Mem. schs. com. Princeton U., Washington and Phila., 1978—; arbitrator Better Bus. Bur. Greater Washington, 1981—. Capt. U.S. Army, 1972-80. Recipient Outstanding Young Man Am. award U.S. Jaycees, 1979. Mem. ABA, Fed. Energy Bar Assn., D.C. Bar Assn. (fee arbitration panel 1981—, com. on alt. dispute resolution 1984—), Sidwell Friends Sch. Alumni Assn. (exec. com. 1985-89, v.p. 1987-89, pres. exec. com. 1989—), Soc. Cin., St. Andrews Soc. Democrat. Presbyterian. Home: 218 N Columbus St Alexandria VA 22314 Office: Fed Energy Regulatory Commn 825 N Capital St NE Washington DC 20426

FRYER, APPLETON, publisher, sales executive, lecturer; b. Buffalo, Feb. 25, 1927; s. Livingston and Catherine (Appleton) F.; AB cum laude, Princeton U., 1950; m. Angeline Dudley Kenefick, May 16, 1953; children: Appleton, Daniel Kenefick, Robert Livingston, Catherine Appleton. Head interpreter Hewitt-Robins, Inc., Buffalo, 1950-51; advt. dept. Buffalo Evening News, 1953-55; field rep. Ketchum, MacLeod & Grove, Inc., advt., 1955-56; pres. Duo-Fast of Western N.Y., Inc., Buffalo, 1956-84; pub. Buffalo Bus. Jour., 1984-86; hon. consul gen. of Japan, Buffalo, 1979—. Dep. sheriff, Erie County, N.Y., 1954-68; adv. bd. Children's Hosp. of Buffalo; mem. Community Welfare Council Buffalo and Erie County; co-chmn. Corp. Div. Episc. Charities, 1988; mem. bd. Erie County Sesquicentennial Commn., 1970-71; co-chmn. Erie Bicentennial Commn., 1974-76; adviser City Buffalo Environ. Mgmt. Commn., 1973-75; trustee Theodore Roosevelt Inaugural Nat. Historic Site Found., 1969-87; bd. dirs. Zool. Soc. Buffalo, 1972-78, Buffalo Fine Arts Acad., Albright-Knox Art Gallery, 1973-76; chmn. Buffalo-Kanazawa Sister Cities Com., 1978-79; pres. Arboretum of Met. Buffalo, 1977-78; bd. dirs. Maud Gordon Holmes Arboretum, 1974-88, pres., 1976-78; mem. Buffalo Landmark and Preservation Bd., 1978-87, Erie County Preservation Adv. Bd., 1978-82; mem. council Charles Burchfield Center, 1974—; mem. council Central Erie deanery Diocese Western N.Y., 1970; mem. Erie County Sesquicentennial Commn., 1970-71; mem. com. Young Life on Niagara Frontier, 1971-72; chmn. planning com. Venture in Mission, 1979, mem. campaign exec. com., 1979-80; chmn. N.Y. State sect. ann. giving Princeton U., 1979—, chmn. Western N.Y. annual giving regional com., 1978-79, mem. nat. ann. giving com.; mem. adv. bd. Erie County Cultural Resources, 1986—, Concerned Ecumenical Ministry (West Side), 1986—; chmn. devel. com. Crane Cutting Ctr., 1987—. Served with USNR, 1945-46, to 1st lt. AUS, 1951-52. Mem. Niagara Frontier Indsl. Distbrs. Assn., Buffalo Area C. of C. (Buffalo Beautiful Com. 1975—), Am. Assn. Museums (trustee 1978-81), SR (pres. Buffalo Assn. 1966-73), Soc. Mayflower Descs. (regent Buffalo colony 1961-65), Soc. Colonial Wars, Holland Soc. of N.Y. (pres. Niagara Frontier br. 1969-79), Buffalo and Erie County Hist. Soc. (bd. mgrs. 1969—, v.p. 1977-82, pres. 1982-84), Buffalo Soc. Natural Scis., Landmark Soc. Niagara Frontier, Outstanding award 1979 (pres. 1969-73), Old Ft. Niagara Assn. (dir. 1980—), Order. Colonial Lords of Manors, Princeton Alumni Assn. (chmn. schs. com. Western N.Y. area 1974-77). Episcopalian (warden, licensed lay reader). Clubs: Masons, Rotary of Buffalo (internat. service com. 1978—, bd. dirs. 1983-86); Princeton (N.Y.C.); Princeton of Western N.Y. (pres. 1960), Saturn (vice dean 1963, 86) (Buffalo); Nassau, University Cottage (Princeton, N.J.); Porcupine (gov. 1969-73) (Nassau). Home: 85 Windsor Ave Buffalo NY 14209

FTHENAKIS, EMANUEL JOHN, electronics and space exploration systems manufacturing company executive; b. Greece, Jan. 30, 1928; came to U.S., 1952, naturalized, 1956; s. John and Evanthia (Magoulakis) E.; m. Hermione Jane Coates, 1972; children: John, Basil. Diploma mech. and elec. engring., Tech. U. Athens, 1951; MS in Elec. Engring., Columbia U., 1954; postgrad., U. Pa., 1961-62. Mem. tech. staff Bell Tel. Labs., 1952-57; dir. engring. missile and space div. G.E., Phila., 1957-61; v.p., gen. mgr. space and re-entry div. Philco-Ford Co., Palo Alto, Calif., 1961-69; pres. ITT Aerospace Co., L.A., 1969-70, Am. Satellite Corp., Germantown, Md., 1971-85; v.p. Fairchild Industries, Germantown, 1971-80, sr. v.p., 1980-84, exec. v.p., 1984; pres., chief exec. officer Fairchild Industries, Chantilly, Va., 1985-86, chmn., chief exec. officer, 1986—; adj. prof. U. Md. 1981-84; mem. Pres.'s Nat. Security Telecommunications Adv. Coun., 1982—. Author: A Manual of Satellite Communications, 1984; patentee in field. mem. bd. visitors Coll. Engring., U. Md., 1980—; bd. dirs. Challenger Ctr. for Space Sci. and Edn., 1988—. Named Man of Yr., Electronic & Aerospace Systems Conf., 1982. Fellow IEEE; mem. AIAA (assoc.), City Club of Washington, The George Town Club. Greek Orthodox. Office: Fairchild Industries Inc 300 W Service Rd Box 10803 Chantilly VA 22021

FUCCI, JOSEPH LEONARD, architectural services company executive; b. Mt. Vernon, N.Y., Jan. 31, 1950; s. Joseph Vito and Roselyn (Pecoraro) F.; m. Adrianne Darway, Aug. 7, 1977. AA, Bronx Community Coll., 1971; BA in English Lit., Herbert H. Lehman Coll., 1972; MLS, Columbia U., 1974; BArch, Pratt Inst., 1985. Head serials dept. Sarah Lawrence Coll. Library, Bronxville, N.Y., 1974-76; head circulation dept., Westchester Med. Ctr. Library, N.Y. Med. Coll., Valhalla, N.Y., 1976-77; head periodicals dept. Orange County Community Coll. Library, Middletown, N.Y., 1977-82; owner Archtl. Editing, Graphics & Info. Services, Middletown, 1982—; mem. curriculum com. Orange County Community Coll., 1978-81, mem. acad. affairs bd., 1978-81. Editor: Architecture: Classified Bibliography, 1980, 3d. rev. ed., 1982. Regents scholar, N.Y. State, 1968-72, Myra E. Sayer Meml. scholar in English, CUNY, 1970; recipient commencement scholarship awards in French, English, CUNY, 1971, cert. of merit in archtl. tech., SUNY, 1982. Mem. AIA Mid-Hudson chpt. Roman Catholic. Home & Office: 38 Roosevelt Ave Middletown NY 10940

FUCHS, JEROME HERBERT, management consultant; b. N.Y.C., Jan. 7, 1922; s. Berthold and Fannie (Neuschotz) F.; m. Eleanor May DeRoo, May 26, 1945; children—Jerome S. Taylor, Susan Fuchs Decker, Sandra Fuchs Lombino. B.S. cum laude, Syracuse U., 1950, M.B.A., 1951. Systems and methods analyst Carrier Corp., 1951-52; supr. systems and methods Lukens Steel, Coatesville, Pa., 1952-54; mgr. systems and methods PennWalt Co., Phila., 1955-57, mgr. systems and methods and office svcs. Amax, Inc.,

Greenwich, Conn., 1958-60; exec. asst. to pres. Rockbestos Wire & Cable Co., 1960-61; v.p. mfg. United Aircraft Products, Dayton, Ohio, 1970-71; exec. v.p. Bus. Supplies Corp. Am., N.Y.C., 1972; sr. ptnr. Fuchs Assocs., Massapequa, N.Y., 1960—; bd. dirs. Del Electronics Corp., Extended Techs., indsl. research asst., Syracuse (N.Y.) U., 1949-51; lectr. Syracuse U., 1950-52, John Hopkins U., Balt., 1953-54, Drexel Inst., Phila., 1955-57, Queens Coll., N.Y.C., 1963-65, SUNY, Stony Brook, 1987—; adj. prof. Hofstra U., 1988—; bd. dirs. Del. Electronics Corp., Extended Technologies, Inc. Author: Making the Most of Management Consulting Services, 1975; Managment Consultants in Action, 1975; Computerized Cost Control Systems, 1976; Computerized Inventory Control Systems, 1977; Administering the Quality Control Function, 1979, The Prentice-Hall Illustrated Handbook of Advanced Manufacturing Methods, 1988. Served as 2nd lt. AC, U.S. Army, 1943-46. Mem. Soc. Profl. Mgmt. Cons. (charter, pres. 1977-79), Inst. Mgmt. Cons. (cert., founding mem.). Home and Office: 30 Cabot Rd W Massapequa NY 11758

FUELLHART, DAVID CLARK, broadcasting executive; b. Pitts., Oct. 16, 1938; s. William Clarke and Katherine Modiset (Marsh) F.; m. Patricia Ann O'Reilley, Sept. 9, 1961 (div.); children: David Clark, Elizabeth Ann; m. Judith Sandra MacFarland, Oct. 31, 1969 (div.); 1 child, Mathew Scott; m. Stephanie Ann Cunningham, Feb. 1, 1985. BS, Ithaca Coll., 1963. Staff announcer Stas. WNAE-WRRN, Warren, Pa., 1958-59; disc jockey, sportscaster Sta. WTKO, Ithaca, N.Y., 1960-61; program dir. N.E. Radio Network, Ithaca, 1961-62; account exec. Cogan Advt., Ithaca, 1962-63; exec. producer Sun Dial Films, Washington, 1967-68; regional sales mgr. Stas. WPIK-WXRA, Alexandria, Va., 1968-70; gen. mgr. Sta. WPST, Trenton, N.J., 1970-74, Sta. WPOC, Balt., 1974—; group mgr. Nationwide Communications Inc, 1985—; instr. sales and mktg. Broadcast Inst. Md., 1979-81; Mem. adv. bd. ABC Radio Direction Network Affiliates, past chmn., 1983-88; chmn. client adv. bd. Eastman Radio, Inc., 1986-87, Arbitron Radio Adv. Council, 1984, 1988—; mem. adv. council ABC Radio Networks Affiliate, 1988—, ABC Radio Network, 1988—. Past mem. public relations subcom. Johns Hopkins Children's Center; past bd. dirs. Am. Lung Assn., Trenton, N.J.; past chmn. broadcast skills bank Balt. Urban League; trustee Md. Econ. Edn. Commn. Served with USN, 1963-67. Decorated Armed Forces Expeditionary medal, 1965; recipient ann. award Aviation Adv. Council N.J., 1972-73, citation and Merit award Mayor of Balt., 1982, Silver award Mayor of Balt., 1984. Mem. Broadcast Pioneers, Md., D.C., Del. Broadcasters Assn. (past pres.), Advt. Assn. Balt. (past pres. two terms), Radio Execs. Balt. (v.p. 1987-88, past pres. two terms), Balt. Broadcasters Coalition (past pres.), Greater Trenton Execs. Assn. (past v.p.), Am. Bowling Congress, Am. Broadcasting Co. Radio Network (adv. coun. 1988—). Presbyterian. Club: Hunt Valley Golf (Balt.). Office: Sta WPOC-FM 711 W 40th St Baltimore MD 21211

FUERSICH, JANET THERESA, compensation consultant, corporate executive; b. N.Y.C., Oct. 13, 1945; d. James and Theresa (Attisani) Buono. BA, Queens Coll., 1970; MA, CUNY, 1976; MBA, Fordham U., 1984. Tchr. U.S. Govt., V.I., 1970-75; assoc. dir. Exec. Compensation Svcs., N.Y.C., 1975-80; ptnr. Coopers & Lybrand, N.Y.C., 1980—. Office: Coopers & Lybrand 1251 Ave of the Americas New York NY 10020

FUGATE, IVAN DEE, banker, lawyer; b. Blackwell, Okla., Dec. 9, 1928; s. Hugh D. and Iva (Holmes) F.; m. Lois Unita Rossow, June 3, 1966; children: Vickie Michelle, Roberta Jeanne, Douglas B., Thomas P. AB, Pittsburg (Kans.) State U., 1949; LLB, U. Denver, 1952, JD, 1970. Bar: Colo. 1952. Exec. sec., mgr. Jr. C. of C. of Denver, 1950-52; also sec. Colo. Jr. C. of C.; individual practice law Denver, 1954—; chmn. bd., pres. Green Mountain Bank, Lakewood, Colo., 1975-82, Western Nat. Bank of Denver; pres., chmn. exec. com. North Valley State Bank, Thornton, Colo.; chmn. bd. Ind. State Bank of Colo., 1978—; bd. dirs. Kit Carson State Bank, Colo.; sec. First Nat. Bank, Burlington, Colo.; owner, farms, ranches, Kans., Colo.; instr. U. Denver Coll. Law, 1955-60; mem. Colo. Treas.'s. Com. Investment State Funds, 1975—. Treas. to Rep. Assos., Colo., 1959-61, trustee, 1959-64. 1st lt. AUS, 1952-54. Mem. ABA, Colo. Bar Assn., Denver Bar Assn. (trustee 1962-65), Colo. Bankers Assn. (bd. dirs.), Ind. Bankers Colo. (founder, chmn. bd. 1973—), Ind. Bankers Assn. Am. (pres. 1978, adminstrv. com., exec. coun. 1976—, bd. dirs. fed. legis. com., chmn. spl. tax com., instr. One Bank Holding Co. seminars 1976—), Denver Law Club, Phi Alpha Delta. Methodist. Clubs: Petroleum (Denver), Denver Athletic (Denver), Lakewood Country. Home: 12015 W 26th Ave Lakewood CO 80215 also: 6580 N 78th Pl Scottsdale AZ 85253 Office: 5350 South DTC Pkwy Bldg 52 Englewood CO 80111

FUGER, SIMON JAMES, manufacturing executive; b. Melbourne, Victoria, Australia, Nov. 6, 1952; came to U.S., 1975; s. James Charles and June Louise (Green) F.; m. Rebecca Lynn Bowers, Mar. 1, 1975 (div. Dec. 1981); m. Eileen Ann Dubiel, Dec. 17, 1985. BA, U. Western Australia, Perth, 1974. Account exec. Shearson Hayden Stone, Houston, 1976-77, White Weld and Co., Houston, 1978, Kidder Peabody and Co., Inc., Houston, 1978-80; exec. v.p., treas.-sec. Cardiac Control Systems, Palm Coast, Fla., 1980-88, pres., 1988—, also bd. dirs. Club: Hobie Fleet 80 (treas. 1987—) (Daytona Beach, Fla.). Office: Cardiac Control Systems 3 Commerce Blvd Palm Coast FL 32037

FUGIEL, FRANK PAUL, insurance company executive; b. Chgo., Aug. 23, 1950; s. Richard A. and Sally (McKinney) F.; m. Nancy Campbell, Sept. 15, 1973; children: Michele, Rachelle. Student, SUNY, Albany. CLU. Individual underwriter Prudential Ins. Co., Merrillville, Ind., 1971-80, group claims mgr., 1980-82, underwriting mgr., 1982-84; group claims officer Employers Health Ins. Co., Green Bay, Wis., 1984-86, underwriting officer, 1986-88, managed care officer, 1988; 2d v.p. individual health ins. Washington Nat. Ins. Co., 1988—. Councilman Hobart, Ind. C. of C., 1981. Served as sgt. USMC, 1970-76. Fellow Life Office Mgmt. Inst., Acad. Life Underwriting; mem. Internat. Claims Assn. (assoc. life and health claims), Nat. Assn. Security Dealers (registered rep.), Life Underwriting Edn. Com., Inst. Home Office Underwriters. Home: 24 Washington Ct Mundelein IL 60060 Office: Washington Nat Ins Co 1620 Chicago Ave Evanston IL 60201

FUHRMAN, HOWARD D., finance executive; b. Bklyn., Sept. 4, 1944; s. Saul and Bertha (Friedheim) F.; m. Laura Ann Marer, Mar. 19, 1967; children: Gregory, Scott, Karen. BSBA, UCLA, 1966; MBA, Calif. State U., Long Beach, 1972. Audit mgr. Kenneth Leventhal & Co., Los Angeles, 1969-79; v.p., controller Lesny Devel. Co., Beverly Hills, Calif., 1979-82; v.p. fin. Heritage Group, Santa Monica, Calif., 1982-85, Janss Corp., Los Angeles, 1985-89; prin. HF Real Estate Group, 1989—. Pres. Ladera Heights Civic Assn., Los Angeles, 1977, editor newsletter, 1980—; v.p. Pacific Coast Adv. Bd. to Pacific Coast Region BBYO, Los Angeles, 1987; youth chmn. Beverly Hills B'nai Brith, 1986—; youth advisor John Fitzgerald Kennedy, Aleph Zadik Aleph, Los Angeles, 1985—. Served with U.S. Army, 1967-69. Mem. Am. inst. CPA's, Calif. Soc. CPA's, Internat. Assn. Fin. Planners. Office: HF Real Estate Group 9920 S La Cienega Ste 700 Inglewood CA 90301

FUHRMAN, ROBERT ALEXANDER, aerospace company executive; b. Detroit, Feb. 23, 1925; s. Alexander A. and Elva (Brown) F. B.S., U. Mich., 1945; M.S., U. Md., 1952; postgrad., U. Calif., San Diego, 1958; Exec. Mgmt. Program, Stanford Bus. Sch., 1964. Project engr. Naval Air Test Center, Patuxent River, Md., 1946-53; chief tech. engring. Ryan Aero. Co., San Diego, 1953-58; mgr. Polaris 1958-64, chief engr. MSD, 1964-66; v.p., asst. gen. mgr. missile systems div. Lockheed Missiles & Space Co., Sunnyvale, Calif., 1966-68; v.p., gen. mgr. Lockheed Missiles & Space Co., 1969, v.p., 1973-76, pres., 1976-83, chmn., 1979—; v.p. Lockheed Corp., Burbank, Calif., 1969-76; group pres. Missiles, Space & Electronics System Lockheed Corp., 1983-85; pres., chief operating officer Lockheed Corp., Calabasas, Calif., 1986-88; vice chmn. bd., chief operating officer Lockheed Corp., 1988—; also dir., pres. Lockheed Ga. Co., Marietta, 1970-71; pres. Lockheed Calif. Co., Burbank, 1971-73; bd. dirs. Bank of the West, Charles Stark Draper Lab, Inc.; mem. FBM Steering Task Group, 1966-70. Mem. adv. coun. Sch. Engring., Stanford U.; mem. adv. bd. Coll. Engring., U. Mich., 1981—. Ensign USNR, 1944-46. Recipient Silver Knight award Nat. Mgmt. Assn., 1969, John J. Montgomery award, 1964; award Soc. Mfg. Engrs., 1973; Disting. Citizen award Boy Scouts Am., 1983; Donald C. Burnham award Soc. Mfg. Engrs., 1983; Recipient Eminent Engr. award Tau Beta Pi, 1983. Fellow AIAA (hon., dir.-at-large, Von Karman 1978), Soc. Mfg. Engrs.; mem. Nat. Acad. Engring., Am. Astron. Soc. (sr.), Nat. Aero. Assn., Ga. C. of C. (dir.), Am. Def. Preparedness Assn. (dir., exec. com.), Navy League U.S. (life), Air Force Assn., Assn. U.S. Army, Soc. Am. Value Engrs. (hon.), Santa Clara County Mfrs. Group (past chmn.), Beta Gamma Sigma. Clubs: Los Altos Country (Calif.),Burning Tree (Bethesda, Md.), N. Ranch Country (Westlake Village). Office: Lockheed Corp 4500 Park Granada Blvd Calabasas CA 91399 *

FUHRMANN, CHARLES J., II, banker; b. Seattle, Feb. 21, 1945; s. Carl I. and Darlene (Reynolds) F.; m. Eugenie A. Livanos, June 24, 1967 (div. 1982); children Katharine Reynolds, Alexandra Livanos; m. Martha M. Harris, Oct. 17, 1987. AB summa cum laude, Harvard Coll., 1967, MBA with honors, 1969. Sr. v.p. White Weld & Co., Inc., N.Y.C., 1969-78; mng. dir. Merrill Lynch Capital Markets, N.Y.C., 1978—. Vestry, St. James' Episcopal Ch., N.Y.C., 1979-84, treas. 1981-84. Clubs: River (N.Y.C.); Delphic (Cambridge, Mass.). Home: One W 64th St New York NY 10023-6739 Office: Merrill Lynch Capital Markets Merrill Lynch World Hdqrs N Tower-World Fin Ctr New York NY 10281-1327

FUJIWARA, NOBUO, trading company executive; b. Ichikawa, Japan, Feb. 1, 1933; s. Noboyuki Fujiwara and Yoshiko Yomo; m. Ikuko Sekine, July 21, 1977; children: Seiichiro, Eijiro. Law degree, U. Tokyo, 1955; diploma in econs., U. Cordoba, 1959; advanced mgmt. program, Harvard U., 1977. With Mitsui & Co. Ltd., Tokyo, 1956-58; & Mitsui Argentina S.A., Buenos Aires, 1958-61; asst. gen. mgr., transp. machinery Mitsui & Co. (U.S.A.) Inc., N.Y.C., 1966-71; sec. bd. dirs. Mitsui & Co. Ltd., Tokyo, 1971-72, gen. mgr. ship div., 1972-82; pres. Mitsui de Mexico S.A., Mexico City, 1982-85; sr. v.p., chief operating officer Mitsui & Co. (U.S.A.) Inc., N.Y.C., 1985—. Del., Yacht Club Argentina, Buenos Aires, 1961—. Clubs: Sky (N.Y.C.); Bonnie Briar Country (Larchmont, N.Y.). Office: Mitsui & Co USA Inc 200 Park Ave New York NY 10166

FUKAE, KENSUKE, information systems company executive, consultant; b. Kanazawa, Japan, May 13, 1926; came to U.S., 1955; s. Hajime and Hashiko (Inoyue) F.; B.S., Tokai Sci. Coll. (Japan), 1947; M.A., U. Tokyo, 1954; m. Roswitha Frey, Dec. 28, 1957; children—Kenneth A., Amy C., Mark T. Reporter internat. news Hokkaido Shinbun, Tokyo, 1952-55; U.S. rep. Minolta Camera Co. Ltd., Osaka, Japan, 1955-60; v.p. Minolta Corp., Ramsey, N.J., 1955-82; pres. Info./Communication Inc., Allendale, N.J., 1982; pres., chief exec. officer Kentek Info. Systems, Inc. Allendale, 1982—; cons. mktg. and product devel. and planning. Mem. Nat. Microfilm Assn., Optical Soc. Am., Soc. Photo-Optical Instrumentation Engrs. Shinto religion. Home: 1 Fessler Dr Monsey NY 10952 Office: 6 Pearl Ct Allendale NJ 07401

FUKAZAWA, YOJI, manufacturing executive; b. Yokohama, Japan, Sept. 6, 1933; came to U.S., 1979; s. Sakae and Yoshiko (Toyota) F.; m. Miharu Nagakubo, Mar. 8, 1959; 1 child, Taro. Diploma in Law, Keio U., Tokyo, 1959. Assoc. dir. Mitsubishi Corp., Tokyo, 1986; sr. v.p., bd. dirs. Mitsubishi Internat. Corp., N.Y.C., 1986—; chmn., chief exec. officer MC Minerals Corp., N.Y.C., 1988—. Office: MC Minerals Corp 767 3rd Ave New York NY 10017 Also: Mitsubishi Internat Corp 520 Madison Ave New York NY 10022

FUKUI, HATSUAKI, electrical engineer; b. Yokohama, Japan, Dec. 14, 1927; came to U.S., 1962, naturalized, 1973; s. Ushinosuke and Yoshi (Saito) F.; m. Atsuko Inamoto, Apr. 1, 1954 (dec. 1973); children: Mayumi, Naoki; m. Kiku Kato, Dec. 12, 1975. Diploma, Miyakojima Tech. Coll. (now Osaka City U.), 1949; D.Eng., Osaka U., 1961. Research assoc. Osaka City U., 1949-54; engr. Shimada Phys. and Chem. Indsl. Co., Tokyo, 1954-55; sr. engr. to supr. Sony Corp. semi-condr. div., Tokyo, 1955-61; mgr. engring. div. Sony Corp., 1961-62; mem. tech. staff Bell Telephone Labs., Murray Hill, N.J., 1962-69, supr., 1969-73; v.p. Sony Corp. Am., N.Y.C., 1973; asst. to chmn. Sony Corp., Tokyo, 1973; staff mem. Bell Labs., Murray Hill, N.J., 1973-81; supr. Bell Labs., 1981-83, AT&T Bell Labs., 1984—; lectr. Tokyo Met. U. (part-time), 1962. Author: Esaki Diodes, 1963, Solid-State FM Receivers, 1968; contbr. to: Semiconductors Handbook, 1963, GaAs FET Principles and Technologies, 1982; editor: Low-Noise Microwave Transistors and Amplifiers, 1981; contbr. articles to profl. jours.; patentee in field. Fellow IEEE (standardization com. 1976-82, editorial bd. IEEE Transactions on Microwave Theory and Techniques 1980—, com. on U.S. competitiveness 1988—, Microwave prize 1980); mem. Inst. Electronics, Info. and Communication Engrs. Japan (Inada award 1959), IEEE Communications Soc., IEEE Electron Devices Soc., IEEE Lasers and Electro-Optics Soc., IEEE Microwave Theory and Techniques Soc., com. on U.S. Competiveness, Japan Soc. Applied Physics, Inst. TV Engrs. Japan (tech. com. 1973-75), Gakushi-Kai, Internat. House Japan. Home: 53 Drum Hill Dr Summit NJ 07901 Office: AT&T Bell Labs 600 Mountain Ave Murray Hill NJ 07974

FUKUNAGA, GEORGE JOJI, corporate executive; b. Waialua, Oahu, Hawaii, Apr. 13, 1924; s. Peter H. and Ruth (Hamamura) F.; BA, U. Hawaii, 1948; cert. Advanced Mgmt. Program Harvard U./U. Hawaii, 1955; HHD (hon.) U. Hawaii, 1984; m. Alice M. Tagawa, Aug. 5, 1950; 1 son, Mark H. Adminstrv. asst., dir. Svc. Motor Co., Ltd. (named changed to Servco Pacific Inc. 1969), Honolulu, 1948-52, v.p., 1952-60, pres., 1960-81; chmn., 1981—, also chmn. and bd. dirs. 15 subs. and affiliates, Svc. Fin., Ltd. (name now Servco Fin. Corp.), Servco Svcs. Corp., Am. Ins. Agy. Inc., Servco Ins. Agy. Inc., Servco Securities Corp., Servco Investment Corp., Servco Calif. Inc., Servco Japan, Inc., Servco Fgn. Sales Corp. (Guam), Hawaiiana Advt. Agy., Pacific Internat. Co. Inc. (Guam), Pacific Fin. Corp. (Guam), Pacific Motors Corp. (Guam), Pacific Internat. Marianas Inc., (Saipan), Pacific Marshalls Inc., (Majuro); dir. Am. Fin. Svcs. Hawaii Inc., Am. Trust Co. of Hawaii Inc., Island Ins. Co. Ltd., Hawaiian Pacific Resorts, Inc. Bd. govs. Iolani Sch.; mem. Japan-Hawaii Econ. Coun.; trustee Fukunaga Scholarship Found., Servco Found., Contemporary Arts Ctr., Oceanic Inst., U.S. Army Mus.; bd. govs. Pub. Schs. Found., East-West Ctr. Found., Hawaii Pacific Coll., Hawaiin Japanese Cultural Ctr. Found. 2d lt. AUS, 1945-47, to 1st lt., 1950-52. Mem. C. of C. Hawaii (v.p. 1970, 83-84, bd. dirs. 1970-75, 82-84), Honolulu Japanese (pres. 1969, bd. dir. 1963—) C. of C., Bus. Roundtable Hawaii (bd. dirs.), Hawaii Econ. Study Club (pres. 1962), U.S.-Japan Soc. (dir. 1983—, v.p. 1986—), Plaza Club (bd. dirs.), Club 200, Deputies Club, Oahu Country Club, Rotary. Methodist. Office: Servco Pacific Inc 900 Fort Street Mall Honolulu HI 96813

FUKUSHIMA, BARBARA NAOMI, accountant; b. Honolulu, Apr. 5, 1948; d. Harry Kazuo and Misayo (Kawasaki) Murakoshi; B.A. with high honors, U. Hawaii, 1970; postgrad. Oreg. State U., 1971, 73, U. Oreg., 1972; m. Dennis Hiroshi Fukushima, Mar. 23, 1974; 1 son, Dennis Hiroshi Jr. Intern, Coopers & Lybrand, Honolulu, 1974; auditor Haskins & Sells, Kahului, Hawaii, 1974-77; pres. Book Doors, Inc., Pukalani, 1977—; pres. Barbara N. Fukushima C.P.A., Inc., Wailuku. 1979—; sec. treas. Target Pest Control, Inc., Wailuku, 1979—; internal auditor, acct. Maui Land & Pineapple Co., Inc., Kahului, 1977-80; auditor Hyatt Regency Maui, Kaanapali, 1980-81; ptnr. D & B Internat., Pukalani, 1980—; instr. Maui Community Coll., Kahului, 1982-85; fin. cons. Merrill Lynch, Pierce, Fenner & Smith, Inc., 1986—. Recipient Phi Beta Kappa Book award, 1969. Mem. Am. Inst. C.P.A.s, Hawaii Soc. C.P.A.s, Nat. Assn. Accts., Hawaii Assn. Public Accts., Bus. and Profl. Women's Club. Tenrikyo. Home: 200 Aliiolani St Pukalani HI 96768 Office: 270 Hookahi St Suite 210 Wailuku HI 96793

FULBRIGHT, MAQUESTIA J., accountant, consultant; b. Paris, Tex., Jan. 7, 1955; s. C.B. and Ruby Lee (Cofield) F.; divorced; children: Eric, Deric. AS, Paris Jr. Coll., 1976; BBA, U. Tex., Arlington, 1979. CPA, Tex. Sr. acct. Arthur Young & Co., Dallas, 1979-84; prin., cons. M.J. Fulbright CPA, Dallas, 1984—. Youth dir. 4th Ave. Ch. of Christ, Dallas, 1983—; bd. dirs. The Chance Ctr., Dallas, 1988. Named Outstanding Young Man Am., 1989. Mem. Am. Inst. CPA's, Tex. Soc. CPA's, Dallas Soc. CPA's, Dallas C. of C., U.S. C. of C. Office: 2651 N Harwood St Ste 220 Dallas TX 75201

FULCHER, CAROLYN JEAN, real estate executive; b. New Bern, N.C., Dec. 4, 1956; d. Murray Thomas and Jean Kathryn (Stephenson) F. BS in Early Childhood Edn., U. N.C., 1979. Lic. real estate sales agt., S.C. Real estate sales agt. Dunes Mktg. Group, Daytona Beach, Fla., 1981-82, Hilton Head Island, S.C., 1982-84; real estate sales agt. Russel E. Brown & Assocs., Hilton Head Island, 1984-89; with Brown, Everett & Assocs., Hilton Head Island, 1989—. Baptist. Office: Brown Everett & Assocs Harbor Town Yacht Club 149 Lighthouse Rd Hilton Head Island SC 29928

FULGENZI, BENJAMIN, data processing company owner, consultant, marketing professional; b. Arkansas City, Kans., Oct. 27, 1925; s. Benjamin and Daisy June (Logan) F.; m. Betty Jean Ehman, Sept. 24, 1943 (dec. Nov. 1982); children: Sheila Ann, Benjamin III; m. Susan Anne Power, May 29, 1985. Student, Okla. A&M Coll., 1946-47, U. Miami, 1947-51. Internat. lic. coordinator ACF Industries, Houston, 1961-64; mgr. export sales Comml. Filters Div. Carborundum Co., Lebanon, Ind., 1964-71; v.p., chief exec. officer Systems Mfg. Corp., Indpls., 1972-76, also bd. dirs.; v.p., chief exec. officer SMC Pneumatics, Inc., Indpls., 1977-86, also bd. dirs.; pres. B. Fulgenzi & Co., Inc., Indpls., 1972—; pres., chief exec. officer Software Job Shop, Inc., Shield Electronics Inc. Served with USN, 1941-46, PTO. Mem. Adminstrv. Mgmt. Assn., Data Processing Mgmt. Assn., Fluid Power Soc., Sales Exec. Internat., World Trade Club Ind., Ind. C. of C., Internat. Wang Users Group, Am. Legion. Republican. Home: 8461 Westport Ln Indianapolis IN 46234 Office: B Fulgenzi & Co Inc 7457 W 10th St Indianapolis IN 46214-2517

FULGHUM, BRICE ELWIN, consultant.; b. Fredonia, Kans., Aug. 27, 1919; s. Byron Harmon and Myrtle (Broderick) F.; student U. Kansas City, San Francisco State Coll.; 1 child by previous marriage, Linda Lee Fulghum McDonald. Asst. to sales mgr. Gas Service Co., Kansas City, Mo., 1939-41, sales mgr. Ace Auto Rental & Sales Co., Kansas City, 1945-48; asst. mgr. Owl Drug Co., San Francisco, 1948-50; mgr. Pacific Mut. Life Ins. Co., 1950-61; v.p. Gordon H. Edwards Co., 1960-63; v.p. Federated Life Ins. Co. Calif., 1963-66; gen. mgr. Los Angeles Fulghum agy. Pacific Mut. Life Ins. Co., 1966-71; v.p. Hendrie Bonding & Ins. Corp., Huntington Beach, Calif., 1976-77; chmn. bd. PGA Ins. Services, Inc., Torrance, Calif., 1976—; cons. Am. Health Profiles, Inc., Nashville; sr. fin. cons. Shearson Hayden Stone Inc., Newport Beach, Calif., 1977-79; cons. Penn Gen. Agys., Los Angeles and Employee Benefit Cons.'s, Santa Ana, Calif., 1979-80; cons. Assn. Calif. State U. Profs., 1959—, Profl. Sponsoring Fund, 1979—. Chmn. Cancer drive; active Community Chest, Am. Heart Assn., founder Opera Pacific. Served with Q.M.C., U.S. Army, 1941-43. C.L.U. Mem. Am. Soc. C.L.U.s (Golden Key Soc.), Leading Life Ins. Producers No. Calif. (life mem., pres. 1955), San Francisco Peninsula (charter), Los Angeles-San Fernando Valley (life) estate planning councils, Orange County Life Underwriters Assn. Republican. Clubs: Commonwealth, Town Hall of So. Calif. (charter mem. charitable giving council, Orange County), El Niguel Country. Mem. editorial advisory bd. Western Underwriter. Columnist Orange Coast mag.; contbr. articles to ins. publs. Home: 125 Belinda Circle Anaheim CA 92801 Office: PO Box 4608 Anaheim CA 92803-4608

FULK, LANCE MONROE, financial services executive; b. Vandalia, Ill., Dec. 14, 1964; s. Carroll Everett and Mary Karleen (Burnett) F. AS, Lake Land Coll., Mattoon, Ill., 1985; BS, Ea. Ill. U., 1987. Dist. mgr. A.L. Williams, Vandalia, 1984-87, First Am. Nat. Securities, Inc., Vandalia, 1986-87; prin. Lance M. Fulk Investments & Ins., Brownstown, Ill., 1987—. Committeman blood drive Vandalia Rotary, 1988—, funnel cake chmn., 1988; prog. committeeman YMCA, Vandalia, 1988—, bd. dirs. 1988—; bd. dirs. Fayette County chpt. Am. Cancer Soc., 1989. Mem. Rotary (treas. Vandalia club 1988-89, sec. 1989—). Republican. Home: PO Box 182 Brownstown IL 62418 Office: Rt 40 E Brownstown IL 62418

FULKS, WILLIAM BERTON, communications company executive; b. Salina, Okla., Feb. 10, 1932; s. Glover Francis and Mamie (Pilcher) F.; m. Ada Louise Webb, Sept. 9, 1950; children: Michael, Susan, Lisa. BS, Ariz. State U., 1958, MA, 1962. Mgr. Mountain Bell, Denver, 1966-71, dist. mgr., 1976-83; portfolio mgr. AT&T, N.Y.C., 1971-76; gen. mgr. Farmers Telephone Co., Pleasant View, Colo., 1983—; pres., chief exec. officer Intercell Corp., Cortez, Colo., 1983—. Bd. dirs. Anasazi Econ. Devel. Assn., Cortez, 1985. Mem. Better Bus. Bur. (bd. dirs. 1986—), Colo. Ind. Telephone Assn. (pres. 1987-88, bd. dirs. 1984-88). Office: Intercell Corp 26077 N US Hwy 666 Pleasant View CO 81331

FULLER, GILBERT AMOS, manufacturing company executive; b. Salt Lake City, Jan. 23, 1941; s. Noel A. and Matilda T. F.; m. Lynda Merle Caldwell, June 27, 1967; children: Brittany, Brandon, Scott, Cambrey. B.S., U. Utah, 1966, M.B.A., 1967. Sr. auditor Coopers Lybrand, Salt Lake City, 1969-70; controller Boyles Bros. Drilling Co., Salt Lake City, 1970-72; asst. treas. Christensen, Inc., Salt Lake City, 1972-74, treas., 1974-78, asst. v.p. fin., 1978-80, v.p. fin., treas., 1980-84; v.p., treas. Norton Company, Worcester, Mass., 1984—; bd. dirs. Winder Dairy Inc., Salt Lake City. Mem. AICPA, Utah Assn. CPAs, Nat. Assn. Corp. Treas. Republican. Mormon. Office: Norton Co 120 Front St Worcester MA 01608-1446

FULLER, HARRY LAURANCE, oil company executive; b. Moline, Ill., Nov. 8, 1938; s. Marlin and Mary Helen (Ilsley) F.; m. Nancy Lawrence, Dec. 27, 1961; children: Kathleen, Laura, Randall. B.S. in Chem. Engring., Cornell U., 1961; J.D., DePaul U., 1965. Bar: Ill. 1965. With Standard Oil Co. (and affiliates), 1961—, sales mgr., 1972-74, gen. mgr. supply, 1974-77; exec. v.p. Standard Oil Co. (Amoco Oil Co. div.), Chgo., 1977-78; pres. Amoco Oil Co., Chgo., 1978-81; exec. v.p. Standard Oil Co. of Ind. (now Amoco Corp.), Chgo., 1981-83, pres., 1983—; bd. dirs. Chase Manhattan Corp., Chase Manhattan Bank N.A., Am. Petroleum Inst. Bd. dirs. Chgo. Rehab. Inst.; trustee Northwestern U., Orchestral Assn. ; bd. dirs. central area com. Chgo. United. Mem. Ill. Bar Assn. Republican. Presbyterian. Clubs: Mid-Am, Chgo. Golf, Chicago. Office: Amoco Corp 200 E Randolph Dr Chicago IL 60601 *

FULLER, MARILYN JOAN, compensation professional; b. Attleboro, Mass., June 5, 1942; d. Henry Jr. and Gladys Marie (Therrien) Polednik; m. Richard Fuller (div. 1974); children: Tammy R., Michael H., James R., Timothy M. BBA, Bryant Coll., Smithfield, R.I., 1984; MBA, Lesley Coll., 1987. Group staffing adminstr. Texas Instruments, Inc., Attleboro, 1977-78, div. pers. rep., 1978-83, mgr. group EEOC, 1983-85, mgr. group domestic compensation, 1985—; compensation cons. Human Resource Profls., Attleboro, Plainville, Ma. 1986—; instr. R.I. Coll., Providence, 1986—. Bd. dirs. New Hope program for battered woman, Attleboro, 1987—; chairpersonShepherd's Pantry for Homeless, No. Attleboro, 1987—. Mem. NAFE, Attleboro Pers. Assn. (v.p. 1987—), Mass. Compensation Assn. (bd. dirs. 1986—). Democrat. Episcopalian. Office: Texas Instruments Inc 34 Forest St MS 12-3 Attleboro MA 02703

FULLER, MARK ADIN, JR., forest products company executive; b. Cin., Jan. 1, 1933; s. Mark Adin and Ellen Dudley (Webb) F.; m. Julia Dula Van Patten, June 9, 1956; children: Mark Adin, Ellen McClain, Mallory McKnight. B.A., Princeton U., 1954. With Champion Internat. Corp., Stamford, Conn., 1957—; v.p. sales Champion Internat. Corp., 1971-79, v.p., gen. mgr., 1979—, exec. v.p., 1980—. Mem. fin. com. Graphic Arts Tech. Found, Pitts.; trustee Xavier U., New Orleans; bd. dirs. New Canaan (Conn.) Nature Ctr. Served with USN, 1954-57. Mem. Am. Paper Inst. Clubs: Princeton (N.Y.C.); Muirfield Village Golf, Woodway Country; Country of Fla. (Golf). Office: Champion Internat Corp 1 Champion Pla Stamford CT 06921

FULLER, ROBERT L(EANDER), lawyer; b. N.Y.C., Sept. 8, 1943; s. Robert Leander and Elsie Virginia Fuller; m. Barbara Braverman, Dec. 5, 1973. BS cum laude, SUNY, Stony Brook, 1971; MBA, Columbia U., 1972; JD, Cath. U., Washington, 1977; M. Laws in Taxation, Georgetown U., 1981. Bar: Md. 1977, D.C. 1978. Acct. Ernst & Whinney, N.Y.C., 1972-74; controller Warner-Jenkinson East Inc., N.Y.C., 1974-75, Atomic Indsl. Forum, Inc., N.Y.C., Washington, 1975-76; tax analyst So. Rwy. Co., Washington, 1976-78; asst. tax counsel CACI, Inc., Arlington, Va., 1978-84; tax counsel, mgr. VSE Corp., Alexandria, Va., 1984-87, dir. taxes Newmont Mining Corp., N.Y.C., 1987-88, CIBA Corning Diagnostics Corp., Medfield, Mass., 1988—. Served with USN, 1961-67. CPA, N.Y., D.C. Mem. ABA (tax sect.), Tax Execs. Inst. (chpt. dir. and officer 1983-87), Am. Inst. CPA's, Mayflower Descendants, SAR, Sigma Pi Sigma. Home: 151 Grove St Wellesley MA 02181-7001 Office: CIBA Corning Diagnostics Corp 63 North St Medfield MA 02052

FULLER, SHARON S., insurance agent; b. Hagerstown, Md., Sept. 6, 1946; d. Gerald Browning and Lillian Dorathy (Lane) Smith. Student schs. Hagerstown. Cert. ins. agt., Fla.; lic. ins. rep., mgr. With Washington Adventist Hosp., Takoma Park, Md., 1968-79; word processing coordinator Fla. Hosp., Orlando, 1979-84; info. systems adminstr. Broad & Cassel, Miami,

Fla., 1984-85; ins. agt., Orlando, 1985—; owner, gen. mgr. Fuller Agy., 1987—. Contbr. articles to profl. publ. Active Competency Evaluation Com. Orange County Pub. Schs., Orlando, 1984-85. Mem. Assn. Info. Systems Profls. (v.p. 1985). Seventh-day Adventist. Avocations: reading; travel. Home: 8712 Gopher Ln Orlando FL 32829 Office: Fuller Agy PO Box 720356 Orlando FL 32822

FULLER, STEPHEN HERBERT, publishing company executive; b. Columbus, Ohio, Feb. 4, 1920; s. Josiah Allen and Mary Ellen (Quinn) F.; m. Frances Mulhearn, Jun 23, 1951; children: Teofilo M., Rogelio M., Mark B., Joseph B. BA, Ohio U., 1941, PhD, 1977; grad. Indusl. Adminstr., Harvard U., 1941-43, MBA, 1947, D in Bus. Adminstrn., 1958; PhD, Ateneo de Manila, Philippines, 1964, De LaSalle Coll., Manila, 1971, Lawrence Inst. Tech., 1978. From instr. to assoc. prof. in bus. adminstrn. Harvard U., Boston, 1947-61, prof. in bus. adminstrn., 1961-71, assoc. dean. for external affairs, 1964-69; Chua Tiampo prof. in bus. adminstrn. Harvard U., Cambridge, Mass., 1982-85; pres. Asian Inst. Mgmt., Manila, 1969-71; v.p. personnel adminstrn. and devel. staff Gen. Motors Corp., Detroit, 1971-82; chmn., chief exec. officer World Book Inc., Chgo., 1985—; instr. in econs. and labor relations Ohio U., Athens, 1977; bd. dirs. Midway Airlines, Chgo. Author: (with others) Problems in Labor Relations, 1950, 3d edit. 1964. Served to capt. AUS, 1943-46. Recipient Presl. Medal Merit, Republic Philippines, 1971. Mem. Internat. Acad. Mgmt., Nat. Mgmt. Assn., Philippine Am. Soc., Phi Beta Kappa, Phi Eta Sigma, Omicron Delta Kappa, Beta Gamma Sigma, Delta Tau Delta. Republican. Roman Catholic. Clubs: Bald Peak Colony (Melvin, N.H.); Chicago; Harvard (N.Y.C.). Office: World Book Inc 510 Merchandise Mart Pla Chicago IL 60654

FULLER, THOMAS RALPH, manufacturing company executive; b. Cedar Rapids, Iowa, 1927; married. BBA, U. Wis., 1949. With Thomas Industries Inc., 1950—, v.p. sales residential lighting div., then corp. exec. v.p., 1958-72, pres., 1972—, chief exec. officer, 1979—, chmn. exec. com., 1987—, also bd. dirs.; dir. 1st Ky. Nat. Corp., Associated Industries of Ky. Mem. Nat. Assn. Manufacturers (bd. dirs.). Office: Thomas Industries Inc 4360 Brownsboro Rd PO Box 35120 Louisville KY 40232

FULLER, WAYNE MAURICE, transportation safety systems company executive; b. Sanford, Maine, May 25, 1946; s. Robert Warren and Claire (Chevalier) F.; m. Pamela Jean Ann Martell, Nov. 4, 1967; children: Christine, Bobbi-Jo, Patrice. Grad., Am. Inst. Hypnotherapy, 1985. Chief exec. officer Transp. Safety Systems, Anaheim, Calif., 1979—; cons. in field. Patentee in field. Pres. The Fuller Co. With USN, 1963-70, Vietnam. Mem. Calif. Coun. Hypnotherapy, Nat. Coun. Hynotherapy. Home: 723 Riverside St Portland ME 04101 Office: Transp Safety Systems 295 Forest Ave Ste 177 Westbrook ME 04101

FULLER-ROGERS, BRENDA SUE, infosystems specialist, accountant; b. Ponca City, Okla., Dec. 27, 1955; d. Jennings Bryan Fuller and E. Dene (Brewer) Fredricks; m. Lowell Edwin Rogers, Nov. 30, 1974. BBA, Okla. State U., 1982, postgrad., 1985—. CPA, Okla. V.p. Dene's Stork Shop, Inc., Ponca City, 1980—; staff acctg. systems analyst Conoco, Inc., Ponca City, 1983—. Mem. Okla. Soc. CPA's (by-laws com. 1985—, sec., treas. Kay chpt. 1985-86, v.p. 1987—, liaison with ednl. instns. com. 1988—), Phi Kappa Phi, Beta Alpha Psi. Democrat. Baptist. Home: 403 Lora Ave Ponca City OK 74601 Office: Conoco Inc 1000 S Pine PO Box 1267 Ponca City OK 74603

FULLMER, STEVEN MARK, banker; b. San Francisco, Mar. 15, 1956; s. Thomas Patrick and Patricia Ann (Carroll-Boyd) F. BA in Chemistry, Willamette U., 1978, BA in Biology, 1978; postgrad., Ariz. State U., 1988—. Sr. engr., project leader Honeywell Large Computer Products, Phoenix, 1981-86; analyst First Interstate Bank Ariz., Phoenix, 1987—; cons. J.A. Boyd & Assoc., San Francisco, 1985—, ImaginInc. Consulting, Phoenix, 1985—, Resources Internat., Scottsdale, 1986. Contbr. articles to profl. jours. Mem. exec. bd. Theodore Roosevelt council, Boy Scouts Am., scoutmaster, 1983—; founder, lt. comdr. Maricopa County Sheriff's Adj. Posse, 1982-86. Named Eagle Scout Boy Scouts Am., Phoenix, 1974; Recipient Order of Merit Boy Scouts Am., 1988. Mem. Data Processing Mgmt. Assn., Am. Inst. for Certification Computer Profls. (cert. data processor 1985), Mensa, Phi Lambda Upsilon, Phi Eta Sigma, Kappa Sigma (v.p. 1973-74), Alpha Chi Sigma. Republican. Roman Catholic. Lodge: KC (membership dir. 1988). Office: First Interstate Bank Ariz 114 W Adams Phoenix AZ 85003

FULTON, DONALD WILLIAM, JR., bank holding company executive; b. Norfolk, Va., Oct. 22, 1946; s. Donald William and Virginia (Thompson) F.; m. Daniela D. Harlow; children—Jason Andrews, Jonathan Belote. BS, U. Va., 1968; cert. Va.-Md. Sch. Bank Mgmt., 1974, Stonier Grad. Sch. Banking, 1979. Asst. v.p., mgr., Nat. Bank & Trust Co., Lovingston, Va., 1973-79, asst. v.p., Charlottesville, Va., 1971-73, fin. planning officer, 1979-81, sr. fin. planning officer, 1981-82; investor rels. officer Jefferson Bankshares, Inc., Charlottesville, 1982-83, v.p. investor rels., 1983—; instr. Am. Inst. Banking, Charlottesville, 1970-71, 81-83. Treas. Soccer Orgn. Charlottesville-Albemarle, 1987—; bd. dirs. Piedmont Area Heart Assn., Lynchburg, Va., 1974-77. Mem. Securities Assn. Va., Va. Bankers Assn. (pres. group iv 1975), Richmond Soc. Fin. Analysts, Nelson Jaycees (pres. 1975-76). Episcopalian. Office: Jefferson Bankshares Inc 123 E Main St Charlottesville VA 22901

FULTON, GLEN STEVEN, small business executive; b. Phila., Dec. 12, 1956; s. James Lee and Amelia Catherine (Martino) F.; m. Helen Ann Brown, Apr. 20, 1979 (div. 1987); chidren: Sarah Jean, Ryan Brown. BS in Sec. Edn., East Stroudsburg U., 1979. Cert. tchr., Pa. Tchr. Avon-Grove Sch. Dist., Pa., 1979-80, East Penn Sch. Dist., Emmaus, Pa., 1980-83; prin. Crawford Tours Allentown (Pa.), Inc., 1982-88, Curriculum Travel of Am., Inc., Allentown, 1988—; cons. in field. Home: 1100 Barnside Rd Allentown PA 18103 Office: Curriculum Travel Am Inc 5194 Hamilton Blvd Allentown PA 18106

FULTON, JOE KIRK, JR., banker, investor; b. Lubbock, Tex., Sept. 12, 1957; s. Joe Kirk Sr. and Mary Alice (Braselton) F. Student, Tex. Tech U., 1976-79. Profl. motorcycle racer 1970-76; diesel mechanic R.H. Fulton, Inc., Lubbock, Tex., 1970-76; specialist Pantera Specialist Inc., Calif., 1976-78; v.p. Quein Sabe Investments dept. Plains Nat. Bank, Lubbock, 1979-88, bd. dirs.; pilot Profl. Airshows, 1979—; with Kirk Fulton Gen. Contractor, Inc., 1988—, Paige & Fulton Construction, 1988—; field rep. Robbe Model Sport, 1988—. Recipient numerious aerobatic flying awards. Mem. Internat. Council Airshows, Nat. Aerobatics Assn., Profl. Banker's Assn., Internat. Aerobatic Club, (v.p. 1986—), Exptl. Aircraft Assn., Fedn. Aero. Internat., Am. Model Aeros. Republican. Clubs: Experimental Aircraft Assoc., Oshkosh, Wisc., Am. Model Aeronautics. Office: Quein Sabe Investments 1601 W Loop 289 Lubbock TX 79416

FULTON, NORMAN ROBERT, home entertainment company executive; b. Los Angeles, Dec. 16, 1935; s. Robert John and Fritzi Marie (Wacker) F.; A.A., Santa Monica Coll., 1958; B.S., U. So. Calif., 1960; m. Nancy Butler, July 6, 1966; children—Robert B., Patricia M. Asst. v.p. Raphael Glass Co., Los Angeles, 1960-65; credit adminstr. Zellerbach Paper Co., Los Angeles, 1966-68; gen. credit mgr. Carrier Transicold Co., Montebello, Calif., 1968-70, Virco Mfg. Co., Los Angeles, 1970-72, Superscope, Inc., Chatsworth, Calif., 1972-79; asst. v.p. credit and adminstrn. Inkel Corp., Carson, Calif., 1980-82; corp. credit mgr. Gen. Consumer Electronics, Santa Monica, Calif., 1982-83; br. credit mgr. Sharp Electronics Corp., Carson, Calif., 1983—. Served with AUS, 1955-57. Fellow Nat. Inst. Credit; mem. Credit Mgrs. So. Calif., Nat. Notary Assn. Home: 31820 Cottontail Ln Malibu CA 90265

FULTON, PAUL, food products company executive, manufacturing company executive; b. 1934; married. BS, Univ. N.C., 1957. V.p. mktg. svcs. Hanes Corp., 1959-81; v.p., gen. mgr. L'eggs Products, 1969-72, pres., 1972-76; exec. v.p. Hanes Corp., 1976-81; with Sara Lee Corp., 1981—, sr. v.p., 1986—, then sr. v.p., group exec., then exec. v.p., to 1988, pres., 1988—. With USN, 1957-59. Office: Sara Lee Corp 3 First National Pla Chicago IL 60602 *

FULTON, RICHARD F., JR., stockbroker, investment advisor; b. Beaver Falls, Pa., July 31, 1954; s. Richard F. and Betty June (Wilcox) F.; m. Jill Klein, July 29, 1977; children: Richard F. III, William. BSBA, Frostburg State U., 1977. Cert. fin. planner. Fin. advisor Merrill Lynch and Shearson Lehman Bros., Pitts., 1978-84; pres. Fulton Fin. Group, Pitts., 1984—, Wendwest Corp., Beaver, Pa., 1986—; chmn., chief exec. officer Am. Restaurants Corp., Ventura, Calif., 1987—. Republican. Presbyterian. Home: 6108 Kentucky Ave Pittsburgh PA 15206 Office: Fulton Fin Group 312 Blvd of the Allies Pittsburgh PA 15222

FULTON, ROBERT HAWLING, transportation company executive; b. Leesburg, Va., Mar. 16, 1952; s. Arthur Hawling and Dorothy Ellen (Henry) F.; m. Martha Ann Goode, Aug. 5, 1972; 1 child, Andrew Hawling. Student, Wake Forest U., 1970-73. V.p. Arthur H. Fulton, Inc., Stephens City, Va., 1973-83; pres. Ram Trans, Inc., Wheatridge, Colo., 1983—. Mem. Denver Transp. Club. Republican. Lutheran. Office: Ram Trans Inc 11049 W 44 Ave 201 Wheat Ridge CO 80033

FULTON, SUSAN BREAKEFIELD, financial advisor; b. Boston, Dec. 10, 1939; d. Durward Ellsworth and Anna Belle (Owens) Breakefield; m. Richard Alsina Fulton, Apr. 13, 1971. BA, Wilson Coll., 1961. Cert. fin. planner; registered investment advisor. Pres. Fulton-Lauroesch & Assocs., Bethesda, Md., 1984—. Episcopalian. Home: 3813 Garrison St NW Washington DC 20016 Office: Fulton-Lauroesch & Assocs 7201 Wisconsin Ave #310 Bethesda MD 20814

FULTON-BEREAL, ARLENE R., construction and maintenance company executive; b. Phila., Nov. 6, 1946; d. Moses and Ruth Fulton. Student Entrepreneurial Devel. Tng. Ctr., Phila., 1970, Antioch U., 1978-80, Temple U., 1977-78. Cert. gen. contractor, Phila., Pa. Mentor supr. pub. relations Juvenile Justice, Phila., 1975-77; Southeast Pa. dir. Project J.O.E.Y., Commonwealth of Pa. Dept. Children & Youth, Phila., 1978-80; chief exec. officer, pres. Bereal Constrn. and Maintenance Co., Inc., Phila., 1980—; mem. Pa. Dept. Transp. Cert. Appeals Bd., 1986—; apptd. Mayor's Small Bus. Adv. Council, 1987. Author alternative to prison youth program, 1977. Bd. dirs. Pa. Dem. Inst., Phila., 1985; pres. C.H. Mason Found., chmn. youth dept. Chs. of God in Christ, Ea. Jurisdiction of Pa., Phila., 1988—. Recipient Humanitarian award Chapel of Four Chaplains, 1978. Mem. Nat. Assn. Minority Contractors, Coalition Minority Contractors (bd. dirs. 1983—), Nat. Assn. Negro Bus. and Profl. Women, Am. Women's Heritage Soc. (bd. dirs., chairwoman constrn.), Nat. Polit. Congress Black Women (bd. dirs., officer 1985), Nat. Assn. Women in Constrn. (legis. awareness chmn. 1983-84). Democrat. Mem. Pentecostal Ch. Avocations: reading, music, creative writing. Office: Bereal Constrn and Maintenance Co Inc 401 N Broad St Ste 240 Philadelphia PA 19108

FUNK, RICHARD, financial executive; b. Forest Hills, N.Y., Nov. 25, 1957; s. Ernest and Emily (Riesenburger) F. BS with hon. and distinction, Cornell U., 1979, MBA, 1982. CPA, N.Y.; cert. fin. planner. Tax acct. Arthur Young & Co., N.Y.C., 1982-84, Peat, Marwick, Mitchell & Co., N.Y.C., 1984-87; asst. v.p. tax dept. U.S. Trust Co. of N.Y., N.Y.C., 1987—. Mem. Am. Inst. CPA's, N.Y. State Soc. CPA's, Inst. Cert. Fin. Planners. Office: US Trust Co NY 45 Wall St New York NY 10005

FUQUA, JOHN BROOKS, consumer products and services company executive; b. Prince Edward County, Va., June 26, 1918; s. J.B. Elam and Ruth F.; m. Dorothy Chapman, Feb. 10, 1945; 1 son, John Rex. Ed. pub. schs., Virginia; LL.D. (hon.), Hampden-Sydney Coll., 1972, Duke U., 1973, Oglethorpe U., 1986; L.H.D. (hon.), Fla. Meml. Coll., 1982, Queens Coll., 1987. Chmn., chief exec. officer Fuqua Industries, Inc., Atlanta, 1965—. mem. Augusta Aviation Commn., 1945-67; past mem., fin. chmn. Augusta Hosp. Authority; past mem. Ga. Sci. and Tech. Commn.; mem. Ga. Ho. of Reps., 1957-64, chmn. House Banking Com., 1959-62; mem. Ga. Senate, 1963-64, chmn. Senate Banking and Fin. Com., 1963-64; chmn. Democratic Party and Exec. Com. Ga., 1962-66; bd. visitors Emory U., 1970-76; former mem. adv. council Ga. State U.; former trustee Ga. State U. Found.; trustee Duke U., 1974, Hampden-Sydney Coll., 1976—mem. bd. dirs. Horatio Alger Assn. Disting. Americans; donor $5.5 million to build the Dorothy Chapman Fuqua Conservatory, Atlanta Bot. Gardens, 1989. Named Broadcaster-Citizen of Yr., Ga. Assn. Broadcasters, 1963, Broadcast Pioneer of Yr., 1979; Boss of Yr., Augusta Jr. C. of C., 1960; recipient Disting. Entrepreneurship award U. Pa. Wharton Grad. Sch. Bus., 1984; Horatio Alger award, 1984; Duke U. Fuqua Sch. Bus. named in his honor, 1980; Award of Merit for Disting. Entrepreneurship, U. Pa. Wharton Entrepreneurial Center, 1985, Outstanding Business Leader award, Northwood Inst., 1986; Mktg. Statesman award Sales and Mktg. Execs.-Internat, 1986, Bus. Statesman award Harvard Bus. Sch., 1987, Exceptional Service to Community award Christian Council Met. Atlanta, 1987, Highest Effort award Sigma Alpha Epsilon, 1987. Mem. Atlanta C. of C. (past dir.), World Bus. Council, Chief Exec. Orgn., Conf. Bd., Bus.-Higher Edn. Forum. Home: 3574 Tuxedo Rd NW Atlanta GA 30305 Office: Fuqua Industries Inc 4900 Ga-Pacific Ctr Atlanta GA 30303

FURBAY, WALTER M., economist; b. Cardington, Ohio, May 27, 1920; s. Walter R. and Leta (Young) F.; B.S., Ohio State U., 1941; M.S., 1956, Ph.D., 1960; m. Margie V. Beckwith, June 18, 1941 (dec.); children—Rebecca Lee, Virginia Dale; m. Camelia G. Tuthill Apr. 3, 1980. Vocat. agr. tchr. Ohio schs., 1941-44, high sch. tchr., 1946-52; sales Bankers Life Ins. Co., Des Moines, 1952-54; vocat. agr. tchr. Ohio high schs., 1954-56; econ. researcher Ohio Agrl. Expt. Sta., 1957-60; agrl. economist Campbell Soup Co., 1960-63, U.S. Dept. Agr., Farmer Coop. Service, 1964-68; head bus. and econs. dept. King's Coll., 1968-81, Shelton Coll., Cape May, N.J., 1981-87; mem. Madagascar Survey Team, 1966. Served to lt. USNR, 1944-46. Mem. Am. Mktg. Assn., Am. Econ. Conv., Gamma Sigma Delta. Mem. Soc. of Friends. Lodges: Lions, Kiwanis. Home and Office: PO Box 4727 RD 2 US 42 E Cardington OH 43315 also: 224 South Winds Dr Sarasota FL 34231

FUREY, JAMES JOSEPH, executive consultant; b. Pitts., Feb. 13, 1938; s. James Joseph and Kathleen (Adams) F.; B.B.A., LaSalle Coll., 1970; m. Andree Chalumeau, Dec. 2, 1958; children—Arleen, James, Renee, Philippe. Indsl. engr. Standard Pressed Steel Co., Jenkintonn, Pa., 1959-69; plant supt. Henry Troemner, Inc., Phila., 1969-70; cons. Booz, Allen & Hamilton, Inc., N.Y.C., 1970-72, asso., 1972-74, asso., Dallas, 1974-77, prin., 1977-79; v.p. mfg. Purolator Inc., Rahway, N.J., 1979-80; pres., chief operating officer Purolator Technologies Inc., Newbury Park, Calif., 1980; pres. James Furey & Assos., Inc., Mgmt. Cons., Dallas, 1980-85; exec. v.p. CMI Corp., Oklahoma City, 1985—. Served with USAF, 1955-59. Mem. Am. Mgmt. Assn. Republican. Roman Catholic. Home: 2800 Quail Ridge Carrollton TX 75006 also: 4804 Sky Tail Ridge Yukon OK 73099

FURLAUD, RICHARD MORTIMER, pharmaceutical company executive; b. N.Y.C., Apr. 15, 1923; s. Maxime Hubert and Eleanor (Mortimer) F.; children: Richard Mortimer, Eleanor Jay, Elizabeth Tamsin; m. Isabel Phelps Furlaud. Student, Institut Sillig, Villars, Switzerland; AB, Princeton U., 1944; LLB, Harvard U., 1947. Bar: N.Y. 1949. Assoc. Root, Ballantine, Harlan, Bushby & Palmer, 1947-51; with legal dept. Olin Mathieson Chem. Corp., 1955-56, asst. to exec. v.p. for finance, 1956-57, asst. pres., 1957-59, v.p., 1959-64, gen. counsel, 1957-60, gen. mgr., v.p. internat. div., 1960-64, exec. v.p., 1964-66; now dir.; pres., dir. E. R. Squibb & Sons, Inc., 1966-68; pres., chief exec., dir. Squibb Beech-Nut, Inc. (renamed Squibb Corp. 1971), Princeton, N.J., 1968-74; chmn., chief exec., dir. Squibb Beech-Nut, Inc. (renamed Squibb Corp. 1971), Princeton, 1974—; bd. dirs. Mut. Benefit Life Ins. Co., Am. Express Co., Shearson Lehman Bros. Holdings, Inc. Mem. profl. staff Ho. of Reps. Com. Ways and Means, 1954; trustee Rockefeller U.; bd. mgrs. Meml. Sloan-Kettering Cancer Ctr. 1st lt., JAGC U.S. Army, 1951-53. Mem. Assn. Bar City N.Y., Pharm. Mfrs. Assn. (dir. 1965-89), Coun. on Fgn. Rels., Links Club, River Club. Home: 644 Pretty Brook Rd Princeton NJ 08540 Office: Squibb Corp PO Box 4000 Princeton NJ 08543-4000

FURLONG, CHARLES RICHARD, broadcasting executive; b. Glen Ridge, N.J., Mar. 12, 1950; s. Robert Gordon and Mary Frances (Johnson) F.; m. Silvia Maria Martinez, Jan. 12, 1949; children: Lisa Davis, Emily Cochran, Audrey Frances. Cert., St. Andrews (Scotland) U., 1972; AB in English, Fordham Coll., 1973; postgrad., Columbia U., 1976—. Promotion coordinator ABC-TV Network, N.Y.C., 1973-76, copywriter, 1976-78, sr. copywriter, 1978-79; editor Info. Services Group W, Westinghouse Broadcasting Co., N.Y.C., 1979-82, mgr. Info Services Group W, 1982-83, dir. Editorial Services Group W, 1983-84, dir. Communications Group W Radio, 1984-87, dir. Corp. Communications, Communications Group W Radio and Westinghouse Broadcasting Co., 1987—; speechwriter Washington Cable Club, 1987, Radio Bur. Can., 1987. Exec. producer: (radio documentary) The Dream Forever, 1987 (Gold medal Internat. Radio Festival N.Y.). Liasion Martin Luther King, Jr. Fed. Holiday Commn., Washington, 1986; bd. dirs. ARC, Montclair, N.J., 1979. Mem. Internat. Radio and TV Soc. (mem. steering com. industry faculty conf.), Radio Advt. Bur. Pub. Relations (mem. adv. bd.). Republican. Roman Catholic. Office: Westinghouse Broadcasting Co 888 7th Ave New York NY 10016

FURLONG, EDWARD V., JR., paper company executive; b. Phila., Feb. 15, 1937; s. Edward V. and Joy (Sadler) F.; m. Rosemary Cerne, Apr. 1968; children: Tracy L., Edward V. III. BA, Princeton U., 1959; MBA, Harvard U., 1963. Sucessively asst. to pres., treas., exec. v.p. WWF Paper Corp., Bala Cynwyd, Pa., 1963-72, pres., 1972—. Served to lt. j.g. USN, 1959-61. Mem. Inst. Dirs. London, Merion Cricket Club, Union League Club, The Ivy Club, Little Egg Harbor Yacht Club. Republican. Methodist. Home: 318 Julip Run Saint Davids PA 19087 Office: WWF Paper Corp 2 Bala Pla Bala-Cynwyd PA 19004

FURLOW, MACK VERNON, JR., general contracting and commercial real estate development company executive; b. Summit, Miss., Aug. 20, 1931; s. Mack Vernon and Trudie Dena (Ratcliff) F.; m. Barbara Elaine Rolfs, Mar. 20, 1954 (div. Dec. 1985); children—David Wayne, Kevin Rolfs. B.S., La. State U., 1953; grad., advanced mgmt. program Harvard, 1968. Financial and systems analyst Humble Oil & Refining Co., Baton Rouge, 1957-61; asst. controller Skyland Internat. Corp., Chattanooga, 1961-65; v.p., corp. controller Blount, Inc., Montgomery, Ala., 1965-71; pres. Pipeco Steel Co., Inc., Wilmington, Del., 1971-73; v.p. fin., treas. Huber, Hunt & Nichols, Inc., Indpls., 1973—; dir. Huber, Hunt & Nichols, Inc., 1977—; Asst. treas. 54th Advanced Mgmt. Program class Harvard Bus. Sch., 1968—. Served to 1st lt. AUS, 1953-57. Mem. La. State U. Alumni Assn. (mem. adv. com. Montgomery chpt. 1967-71), Nat. Assn. Accts., Fin. Execs. Inst. Republican. Lutheran. Home: 7322 Lions Head Dr Indianapolis IN 46260 Office: Huber Hunt & Nichols Inc 2450 S Tibbs Ave Indianapolis IN 46241

FURMAN, ANTHONY MICHAEL, public relations executive; b. Los Angeles, Nov. 5, 1934; s. LeRoy S. and Geraldine P. F.; B.A., Bethany (W.Va.) Coll., 1957; postgrad. Columbia U. 1957-58; m. Betty Gayle Morgan, Nov. 1, 1970; 1 son, Michael Jason. Asst. account exec. Jules Beitler, Pub. Relations, Newark, 1958; account exec. Barber & Baar Pub. Relations Corp., N.Y.C., 1959-60; account exec., media dir. Sydney S. Baron & Co., Inc., N.Y.C., 1961-66; pres. Anthony M. Furman, Inc., N.Y.C., 1966-81; v.p., mng. dir. sports devel. div. Hill & Knowlton, Inc., 1981-85; pres., Dorf and Stanton Sports Mktg., 1985-86, pres., Anthony M. Furman, Inc., N.Y.C., 1986—. adj. prof., L.I. U., 1986—; bd. dirs. FKP Assos., Lake Placid, N.Y.; v.p., sec. Woman's Profl. Ski Championships, Inc. Recipient Outstanding Alumnus award Bethany Coll., 1987. Served with M.C., U.S. Army, 1957-58. Mem. Pub. Relations Soc. Am. Democrat. Jewish. Exec. producer film: Floating Free, 1977 (1978 Acad. award nominee). Office: 250 W 57th St Ste 1515 New York NY 10107

FURMAN, DAVID, retail grocery executive; b. 1918; married. With Morris Furman Produce Co., 1938-59; now chmn. Farm Fresh Inc., Norfolk, Va. Office: Farm Fresh Inc 1151 Azalea Garden Rd Norfolk VA 23502 *

FURMAN, HARRY SUTTON, lumber distribution company executive; b. Boston, Feb. 10, 1947; s. John Rockwell and Mary Hale (Sutton) F.; m. Karen Louise Malsnee, May 30, 1970; children—Kyle Eric, Nicholas Andrew, Kelley Elizabeth. B.A. in Govt., Cornell U., 1969. Unit mgr. Procter & Gamble, 1969-72; salesman Furman Lumber, Inc., Portland, Oreg., 1972-77; sales mgr. Furman Lumber, Inc., Boston, 1977-82, pres., chief operating officer, 1982—; dir. Waferboard Corp., Timmins, Ont., Can., Highland Am. Corp., East Providence, R.I.; columnist Nat. Home Ctr. News, 1978-88. mem. coun. Cornell U., chmn. New Eng. fundraising. Mem. Am. Plywood Assn. (chmn. adv. bd. 1980—), Am. Lumber Standards Com. (alt.). Methodist. Clubs: (Sudbury, Mass.); Cornell (Boston).

FURMAN, JOHN ROCKWELL, wholesale lumber company executive; b. Wellsville, N.Y., June 25, 1917; s. Harry Brennan and Helen (Rockwell) F.; m. Mary Hale Sutton, Aug. 2, 1941; children: John Rockwell III, Margery, Harry S. BA in Econs., Cornell U., 1939. New Eng. mgr. Dant and Russell, Inc., Portland, Oreg., 1948-56; founder, pres., chief exec. officer Furman Lumber, Inc., Boston, 1956—; bd. dirs. Boston 5-Cent Savs. Bank. Trustee Northeast Growth Fund, Boston, 1980—, Tilton (N.H.) Sch., 1963—. Lt. Comdr. USNR, 1941-46. Mem. N.Am. Wholesale Lumber Assn. (bd. dirs. 1967-75), Fed. Club, Comml. Club. Office: Furman Lumber Inc 360 Newbury St Boston MA 02115 also: Furman Lumber Inc 108 Massachusetts Ave Boston MA 02115

FURMAN, ROY LANCE, investment banker; b. N.Y.C., Apr. 19, 1939; s. Joseph M. and Frances L. (Kurlander) F.; m. Frieda Anne Bueler, Nov. 7, 1965; children: Jill Tracy, Stephanie Gail. A.B., Bklyn. Coll., 1960; LL.B., Harvard U., 1963. Atty. Western Electric Co., N.Y.C., 1964-67; v.p. Continental Tel. Supply Co., N.Y.C., 1967-68; pres., sec., dir. Seiden & de Cuevas, Inc., N.Y.C., 1968-73; pres., chief exec. officer, dir. Furman Selz Mager Dietz & Birney Inc., N.Y.C., 1973—; past chmn. splty. firms adv. com. N.Y. Stock Exchange; bd. dirs. Westfield Internat., Excelsior Fund, Apollo Pictures. Treas. Assocs. Mt. Sinai Hosp.; trustee Bklyn. Coll. Found.; treas., bd. dirs. N.Y.C. Opera; pres. Film Soc. Lincoln Ctr.; mem. dean's adv. coun. Harvard Law Sch.; nat. chmn. Harvard Law Sch. Fund. Mem. N.Y. Soc. Securities Analysts, Securities Industry Assn. N.Y. (bd. dirs.). Office: Furman Selz Mager Dietz & Birney Inc 230 Park Ave New York NY 10169

FURR, QUINT EUGENE, advertising executive; b. Concord, N.C., Sept. 21, 1921; s. Walter Luther and Mary (Barnhardt) F.; m. Helen Wilson, Dec. 30, 1961; children: Tiffany Grantham, Quentin, Robert; stepchildren: Pamela Erickson, Erik Erickson. Grad. Belmont Abbey Coll., BA, U. N.C., Chapel Hill, 1943, postgrad. Law Sch., 1946-47. Promotion rep. Sears, Roebuck & Co., Atlanta and Greensboro, N.C., 1947-49; nat. advt. and sales promotion mgr. Western Auto Supply Co., Kansas City, Mo., 1949-61; regional mgr. J.F. Pritchard Co., Charlotte, N.C., 1961-63; gen. mgr. Hogan Rose Advt., High Point, N.C., 1963-65; regional mgr. Top Value Enterprises, Washington, 1965-67; v.p. corp. mktg. Textilease Corp., Beltsville, Md., 1967-85; v.p. sales and mktg. Am. Directory Service Agy., Bethesda, Md., 1985—. Served as lt. USNR, World War II, Korea. Recipient Mktg. award Textile Leasing Industry, 1970-74. Mem. Sales and Mktg. Execs. Internat., Inst. Indsl. Laundries (past chmn. mktg. com.), Am. Legion, VFW, Pi Kappa Alpha. Roman Catholic. Club: AD (Washington). Lodges: Moose, Elks. Home: 9232 Three Oaks Dr Silver Spring MD 20901 Office: 4719 Hampden Ln Bethesda MD 20814

FURRER, JOHN RUDOLF, business executive; b. Milw., Dec. 2, 1927; s. Rudolph and Leona (Peters) F.; m. Annie Louise Waldo, Apr. 24, 1954; children: Blake Waldo, Kimberly Louise. B.A., Harvard U., 1949. Spl. rep. ACF Industries, Madrid, 1949-51; asst. supr. Thermo nuclear Devel. and Test-Los Alamos, Eniwetok Atoll, 1952-53; dir. product devel. ACF Industries, N.Y.C., 1954-59; dir. machinery, systems group, central engring. labs. FMC Corp., San Jose, Calif., 1959-68; gen. mgr. engineered systems div. FMC Corp., San Jose, 1968-70; v.p. in charge planning dept., central engring. labs. an engineered systems div. FMC Corp., Chgo., 1970-71, v.p. material handling group, 1971-77, v.p. corp. devel., 1977-88, sr. v.p., 1988—; bd. dirs. Centocor, Cimflex Teknowledge Corp. Patentee in field. Trustee Ravinia Festival, 1986—. Served with USN, 1945-46. Mem. ASME, Council of Planning Execs. (chmn. conference bd. 1986-87). Clubs: Harvard (N.Y.C. and Chgo.); Glen View Country (Golf, Ill.); Economic,, Mid-America, Chgo. Yacht Club. Home: 1242 N Lake Shore Dr Chicago IL 60610 Office: FMC Corp 200 E Randolph St Chicago IL 60601

FURSE, JAMES ROBERT, communications industry executive; b. Saskatoon, Sask., Can., Nov. 6, 1939; m. Shirley M. Haus; children: Graham, Joanna. B of Commerce, U. Sask. Chartered acct., Can. Ptnr. Clarkson,

Gordon, Calgary and Toronto, Can., 1964-85; v.p. fin., chief fin. officer Maclean Hunter Ltd., Toronto, 1985—. Office: Maclean Hunter Ltd, 777 Bay St, Toronto, ON Canada M5W 1A7

FURSTMAN, SHIRLEY ELSIE DADDOW, advertising executive; b. Butler, N.J., Jan. 26, 1930; d. Richard and Eva M. (Kitchell) Daddow; grad. high sch.; m. Russell A. Bailey, Oct. 1, 1950 (div. Oct. 1967); m. 2d, William B. Furstman, Dec. 24, 1977. Asst. corporate sec. Hydrospace Tech., West Caldwell, N.J., 1960-62; sec. to pres. R.J. Dick Co., Totowa, N.J., 1962-63, Microlab, Livingston, N.J., 1963; asst. corporate sec. Astrosystems Internat., West Caldwell, N.J., 1963-65; corporate sec. Internat. Controls Corp., Fairfield, N.J., 1965-73; sec. to pres. Global Financial Co., Nassau, Bahamas, 1974-75; office mgr. Internat. Barter, Nassau, 1975-76; sec. to pres., corp. sec. Haas Chem. Co., Taylor, Pa., 1976-77; asst. to pres., pub. Am. Home mag., N.Y.C., 1977-78; office mgr. Gilbert, Whitney & Johns, Inc., Whippany, N.J., 1979—. Home: 11A Foxwood Morris Plains NJ 07950

FURTH, ALAN COWAN, corporate director, lawyer; b. Oakland, Calif., Sept. 16, 1922; s. Victor L. and Valance (Cowan) F.; m. Virginia Robinson, Aug. 18, 1946; children: Andrew Robinson, Alison Anne. A.B., U. Calif., Berkeley, 1944, LL.B., 1949; grad., Advanced Mgmt. Program, Harvard U., 1959. Bar: Calif., U.S. Supreme Ct. With So. Pacific Co., San Franciso, 1950-87, gen. counsel, from 1963, v.p., 1966, exec. v.p. law, 1976-79, pres., 1979-87, also dir. and mem. exec. com.; bd. dirs. Indsl. Indemnity Co., Bank of Calif., Am. Home Shield Corp., Flecto Corp., Oreg. Steel Mills. Trustee Merritt Hosp., Oakland, Calif.; trustee Pacific Legal Found. Capt. USMCR, 1944-46, 51-52. Mem. Calif. State Bar Assn. Clubs: Bohemian (San Francisco), Pacific-Union (San Francisco), San Francisco Golf (San Francisco). Home: 244 Lakeside Dr Oakland CA 94612 Office: So Pacific Co 1 Market Pla Stewart St Tower San Francisco CA 94105

FURUMOTO, HORACE WATARU, medical products company executive; b. Honolulu, Dec. 13, 1931; s. Kitaru and Shuzuko (Okita) F.; m. Laurel Waishnor, June 10, 1959; children: Robin, Jill. BS, Calif. Inst. Tech., 1955; PhD, Ohio State U., 1963. Mem. staff research and devel. div. Avco, Wilmington, Mass., 1963-66; asst. br. chief NASA, Cambridge, Mass., 1966-70; mem. staff U.S. Dept. Transp., Cambridge, Mass., 1970-72; dep. dir. Avco Everett (Mass.) Research Lab., 1972-77; pres. Candela Laser Corp., Wayland, Mass., 1977—, also chmn. bd. dirs.; vis. lectr. Harvard U. Med. Sch., Cambridge, 1984—. Contbr. articles to profl. jours.; patentee in field. Served to 1st lt. USAF, 1955-57. Fellow Am. Soc. Laser Medicine and Surgery; mem. IEEE, Am. Phys. Soc., Laser Inst. Am., Optical Soc. Am. Democrat. Home: 14 Woodridge Rd Wellesley MA 02181 Office: Candela Laser Corp 530 Boston Post Rd Wayland MA 01778

FUSCO, ANDREW G., lawyer; b. Punxsitawney, Pa., Jan. 11, 1948; s. Albert G. and Virginia N. (Whitesell) F.; m. Deborah K. Lucas; children: Matthew, Geoffrey, David. BS in Bus. Adminstrn. and Fin., W.Va. U., 1970, JD, 1973. Bar: W.Va. 1973, U.S. Supreme Ct. 1977, U.S. Ct. Appeals (4th cir.) 1974, U.S. Ct. Appeals (Fed. cir.) 1985. Sole practice, Morgantown, W.Va., 1973-85; ptnr. Fusco & Newbraugh, Morgantown, 1985—; pros. atty. Monongalia County, W.Va., 1977-81; instr. Coll. Bus. and Econs., W.Va. U., 1975-76; dir. Pitts. Environ. Systems Inc., 1983—. Author: Antitrust Law (West Virginia Practice Handbook), 1989; editor, contbg. author: Twenty Feet From Glory (John R. Goodwin), 1970, Business Law (John R. Goodwin), 1972, Beyond Baker Street (Michael Harrison), 1976. Bd. dirs. W.Va. Career Colls., 1971-76; mem. profl. adv. bd. Childbirth and Parent Edn. Assn., Rape and Domestic Violence Info. Ctr.; mem. W.Va. Sec. State's Tribunal on Election Reform, 1977-81; chmn. Monongalia County Drug Edn. Task Force, 1978-80. Mem. ABA, Monongalia County Bar Assn., W.Va. Bar, Assn. Trial Lawyers Am., W.Va. Trial Lawyers Assn., Internat. Platform Assn., Baker St. Irregulars of N.Y., Sherlock Holmes Soc. of London, W.Va. Dist. Attys. Assn., Nat. Dist. Attys. Assn., Sons of Italy, W.Va. Law Sch. Assn., Monongalia Arts Ctr. (pres., treas., trustee). Recipient Am. Jurisprudence award Bancroft-Whitney Publ. Co. 1971; named Outstanding Young Man of 1979, Morgantown, 1979. Democrat. Roman Catholic. Home: 20 Harewood Morgantown WV 26505 Office: 220 Pleasant St Morgantown WV 26505

FUSCO, ANTHONY SALVATORE, controller; b. N.Y.C., Mar. 13, 1954; s. Joseph Anthony and Angela Loretta (Ciniglio) F.; m. Anna Maria Oliveri, June 30, 1984; children: Joseph Carl, Carl Anthony. BBA, Pace U., 1977, postgrad. CPA, N.J., N.Y. Staff acct. M. Sternlieb & Co., Hackensack, N.J., 1977-81; sr. acct. Oppenheim Appel Dixon & Co., N.Y.C., 1982-84; mgr. Oppenheim Appel Dison & Co., N.Y.C., 1985-86; controller Jones, Lang, Wootton & Co., N.Y.C., 1984-85, Competrol Real Estate Ltd., N.Y.C., 1986—. Mem. Am. Inst. CPA's, N.Y. State Soc. CPA's. Home: 58-34 82d St Middle Village Queens NY 11373 Office: Competrol Real Estate Ltd 505 Park Ave New York NY 10022

FUSSELL, RONALD MOI, spacecraft avionic systems educator; b. Lakeland, Fla., Jan. 12, 1956; s. Moi Monroe and Ima Jean (Thomas) F.; m. Mella Sue Knowles, May 29, 1974 (div. 1989); children: Scott Monroe, Dayna Michelle. AS in Radar Tech., Community Coll. Air Force, Maxwell Air Force Base, 1981; student, Brevard Community Coll., 1984—. Diesel mechanic Refrigerated Transport, Inc., Dundee, Fla., 1975-76; pvt. investigation Research Reports, Inc., Tampa, Fla., 1978-79; avionics technician McDonnell Douglas Services, Inc., Dhahran, Saudi Arabia, 1982-83; quality control analyst avionics div. McDonnell Douglas Services, Inc., Taif, Saudi Arabia, 1983-84; program support tng. specialist avionics McDonnell Douglas Space Systems Co., Kennedy Space Ctr., Fla., 1984—; pres. Advanced Human Techs., Inc., Titusville, Fla., 1988—. Mem. Fla. Farm Bur. Served with USAF, 1976-82. Mem. Nat. Mgmt. Assn., McDonnell Douglas Mgmt. Assn., Port St. John Jaycees (v.p. community devel.). Democrat. Baptist. Home: 5120 Patricia St Cocoa FL 32927 Office: McDonnell Douglas Space Systems Co PO Box 21233 Kennedy Space Center FL 32815

FUTRELL, JONAS RICHARD, JR., banker; b. Hertford, N.C., Mar. 6, 1931; s. J. Richard and Alice Futrell; m. Billie Bateman, June 15, 1957; 1 child, Mary. BA in Polit. Sci., U. N.C.; postgrad., La. State U. Past sr. v.p. NCNB, Raleigh; pres., dir., mem. exec. com. Planters Nat. Bank and Trust Co., Rocky Mount, N.C., The Planters Corp., Rocky Mount. Bd. dirs., mem. exec. com. Tarboro Arts Commn.; bd. dirs. Downtown Renaissance, Inc.; trustee N.C. Cen. U., Durham; mem. bd. visitors N.C. Wesleyan Coll.; past mem. N.C. Edn. Assistance Authority; mem. Nash County Indsl. Devel. Commn.; past chmn. Craven County Indusl. Devel. Authority, New Bern, N.C.; bd. dirs. N.C. Citizens for Bus. and Industry; mem. East Carolina Univ. Found., Inc.; past vice chmn. Downtown Revitalization Com., Durham; mem. bd. assocs. Meredith Coll., adv. bd. N.C. Child Advocacy Inst. Mem. N.C. Bankers Assn. (bd. dirs.), Rocky Mount Area C. of C. (past pres., past mem. bd. dirs.). Office: Planters Nat Bank & Trust Co 131 N Church St Rocky Mount NC 27804

FUTRELL, ROBERT FRANK, historian, consultant; b. Waterford, Miss., Dec. 15, 1917; s. James Chester and Sarah Olivia (Brooks) F.; m. Marie Elizabeth Grimes, Oct. 8, 1944 (dec. 1978); m. Jo Ann McGowan Ellis, Dec. 15, 1980. BA with distinction, U. Miss., 1938, MA, 1939; PhD in History, Vanderbilt U., 1950. Spl. cons. U.S. War Dept., Washington, 1946; historian USAF Hist. Office, Washington, 1946-49; assoc. prof. mil. history Air U., Maxwell AFB, Ala., 1950-51, prof., 1951-71, sr. historian, 1971-74, prof. emeritus mil. history, 1974—; professorial lectr. George Washington U., 1963-68; guest lectr. Air U. Squadron Officer Sch., Air Command and Staff Coll., Air War Coll., Air Force Acad., Army War Coll., Militärgeschichtliches Forschungsamt, German Fed. Republic, 1951—; participant Militärgeschichtliches Forschungsamt, Freiburg, German Fed. Republic, 1988; vis. prof. mil. history Airpower Research Inst., Ctr. for Aerospace Doctrine Research and Edn., Air U., 1982-85, hist. advisor to USAF project Corona Harvest, 1969-74; cons. East Aviation Services & Tech., Inc., Chantilly, Va. Author: Ideas, Concepts, Doctrine: A History of Basic Thinking in the United States Air Force, 1907-1964, 1971, rev. edit., 1907-84, 2 vols., 1989, The United States Air Force in Korea, 1950-1953, 1961, rev. edit., 1983, The United States Air Force in Southeast Asia: The Advisory Years to 1965, 1981, (with Wesley Frank Craven, James L. Cate) The Army Air Force in World War II, 1948-1958; contbr. chpts. to hist. books, articles to scholarly publs. Served to capt. USAAF, 1941-45, lt. col. Res., ret. Recipient Meritorious Civilian Service award USAF, 1970, Exceptional Civilian Service decoration Sec. of USAF, 1973. Mem. Ala. Hist. Assn., SAR (pres. Montgomery County chpt. 1971-74), So. Hist. Assn., Air Force Hist. Found. (mem. editorial advisors 1969-81, trustee 1985—), Inst. Mil. Affairs, Montgomery Capital City Club, Phi Eta Sigma, Pi Kappa Pi. Methodist. Address: 908 Lynwood Dr Montgomery AL 36111

GAALOVA, BARBARA KANZLER, banker; b. Hampton, Va., Mar. 24, 1953; d. Robert Joseph and Jeanne Margaret (Boublis) Kanzler; m. Alexander Jozef Gaal, May 9, 1981; 1 child, Tatiana Alexandra. Student, Boston U., 1971-73, U. Bridgeport, 1985—. Customer relations rep. Union Trust Co., Norwalk, Conn., 1973-76, mktg. mgr., 1980-84, mgr. sales and tng., 1984-87, asst. treas., compliance mgr., 1987—; sales coordinator Carlan, Inc., Stamford, Conn., 1976-80; founding mem., dir., sec. Bank Compliance Assn. Conn., 1989—. Active Friends of Animals, Norwalk, 1984—, People for the Ethical Treatment of Animals, Washington, 1984—. Mem. Nat. Assn. Bank Women, Bank Compliance Assn. Conn. (founder, sec., dir. 1989—), Alliance Francaise of Greenwich. Office: Union Trust Co 5 Research Dr Shelton CT 06484

GABERMAN, HARRY, lawyer, economic analyst; b. Springfield, Mass., May 6, 1913; s. Nathan and Elizabeth (Binder) G.; m. Ingeborg Luise Gruda, Sept. 24, 1953; children—Claudia Natalie Gaberman Razzook, Victor Lucius. J.D. George Washington U., 1941; LL.M., Catholic U. Am., 1954. Bar: D.C. 1942. Atty.-investigator, atty.-advisor U.S. Mil. Govt. and U.S. High Commn. for Germany, Berlin, Frankfurt, Bonn, 1945-53, also indsl. specialist, bus. economist, legal and intercorp. relations analyst, asst. chief industry control sect.; asst. legal advisor and attache Am. embassy, Rome, 1953; sole practice, Washington, 1953-55; intelligence analyst Army Transp. Intelligence Agy., Gravelly Point, Va., 1955-56; supervisory atty.-advisor, atty.-advisor Air Force Systems Command, Andrews AFB, Md., 1956-75; asst. to U.S. mem. Four-power liquidation of German War Potential Com., Berlin, 1946; chief deconcentration br. U.S. High Commn., Frankfurt, 1949; acting dep. U.S. mem. law com. Allied Kommandatura, Berlin, 1951; U.S. mem. 3-power Film Reorgn. Com., Bonn, 1949-50. Contbr. articles to profl. jours. Recipient Profl. Achievement award George Washington U. Law Alumni, 1983. Mem. Fed. Bar Assn. (chmn. govt. contracts council 1970-75, 78-79, dep. chmn. sect. internat. law, editor internat. law sect. newsletter, numerous Disting. Service awards), D.C. Bar Assn. (chmn. govt. contracts com. 1964-66), Diplomatic and Consular Officers Ret. Avocations: walking; swimming; reading. Address: 5117 Overlook Park Annandale VA 22003

GABLE, CARL IRWIN, auto parts manufacturing company executive; b. Charleston, S.C., Aug. 7, 1939; s. Carl Irwin and Charlotte Belle (Kersey) G.; m. Sarah Alice Bogle, June 6, 1964; children: Ashley Grinnell, Carl Irwin III, James Kersey. BA, Harvard U., 1961; JD, Harvard, 1964. Bar: Ga. 1964, D.C. 1976. Assoc. Kilpatrick and Cody, Atlanta, 1964-70, ptnr., 1970-84; pres. Interface Inc., Atlanta, 1984-85; vice chmn. Intermet Corp., Atlanta, 1985—, also bd. dirs.; bd. dirs. Interface, Inc. Contbr. articles on internat. law to profl. jours.; inventor interlocking modular carpet. Bd. dirs. Japan-Am. Soc. Ga., 1983—, Atlanta Council for Internat. Visitors, Inc., 1987—, Atlanta Civic Opera Assn, Inc., 1980—; founder Atlanta Opera Endowment, Inc., 1986—. Fellow Am. Coll. Investment Counsel; mem. ABA., Atlanta Bar Assn., Internat. Bar Assn., Capital City Club, Atlanta Lawyers Club. Office: Intermet Corp 2859 Paces Ferry Rd Ste 1600 Atlanta GA 30339

GABLE, JOANIE CAROLE, financial management executive; b. Birmingham, Ala., Jan. 29, 1954; d. John Daniel and Marjorie (Payne) Lindsey; m. Philip E. Gable, June 9, 1974 (div. 1989); children: Cassie, Wesley, Jamie. BS in Acctg., U. Ala., 1976. Pharm. acct. Jefferson Health Found., Birmingham, 1975-77; contr. Pyramid Mining, Birmingham, 1977-79, Heavy Duty Parts, Inc., Birmingham, 1979-81; acctg. cons. Birmingham, 1981-84; dir. planning Drummond Coal Co., Jasper, Ala., 1984-86; v.p. fin., contr. AC3 Computer Ctrs., Birmingham, 1986—; cons. Birmingham Area C. of C., 1979-84. Choir mem. Shades Mt. Bapt. Ch., Birmingham. Mem. Nat. Assn. Accts., The Planning Forum (pres. 1987-88), Fin. Execs. Inst., NAFE, Rotary. Home: 2109 Partridge Berry Rd Birmingham AL 35244

GABLE, ROBERT ELLEDY, real estate investment company executive; b. N.Y.C., Feb. 20, 1934; s. Gilbert E. and Paulina (Stearns) G.; m. Emily Brinton Thompson, July 5, 1958; children—James, Elizabeth, John. B.S., Stanford U., 1956. John. With The Stearns Co. Ltd. (formerly Stearns Coal & Lumber Co. Inc.), Lexington, Ky., 1958—, asst. to pres., 1958-60, sec., 1960-70, treas., 1961-62, v.p., 1962-70, chmn. bd., 1970—, pres., 1975-78, also dir.; former chmn. bd., dir. Ky. & Tenn. Ry., Lexington; former chmn. bd. Lumber King Inc., Lexington; former dir., mem. audit com. Kuhn's-Big K Stores Corp., Nashville, 1979-81; dir. emeritus Blue Cross and Blue Shield Ky.; former dir. Bank of McCreary County. Commr. Ky. Dept. Parks, 1967-70; mem. pub. lands com. Interstate Oil Compact Commn., 1968-70; mem. adv. com. Ky. Ednl. TV, 1971-75; former mem. Breaks Interstate Park Commn.; past pres., past dir. McCreary County Indsl. Devel. Corp.; former trustee Stearns Recreational Assn., Inc.; mem. S.E. regional adv. com. Nat. Park Service, 1973-78, sec., 1977-78; former bd. dirs. Ky. Mountain Laurel Festival Assn., v.p., 1974-75; mem. McCreary County Air Bd., 1967-81; mem. adv. bd. U. Ky. for Somerset Community Coll., 1965-73. Republican candidate for U.S. Senate from Ky., 1972; Ky. co-chmn. Finance Com. for Re-election of Pres., 1972; mem. Rep. Nat. Com., 1986—, Rep. Nat. Finance Com., 1971-76; Rep. state finance chmn., 1973-75, 86; mem. Ky. Rep. Central Com., 1974—; state chmn. Rep. Party Ky., 1986—; Rep. nominee for gov. Ky., 1975; trustee George Peabody Coll. for Tchrs., Nashville, 1970-79, mem. exec. com., 1976-79, chmn. bd., 1979; former trustee Capital Day Sch., Frankfort, Ky.; bd. dirs., past chmn., past pres., founder Ky. Council on Econ. Edn., Inc.; bd. dirs. Joint Council Econ. Edn., N.Y.C., 1982—; trustee Ky. State U. Found., 1979-82; trustee Vanderbilt U., Nashville, 1979—, former mem. budget com.; past mem. bd. dirs. Ky. Better Roads Council, Inc., vice chmn., 1976-79; former mem. missions bd. Episcopal Diocese of Lexington; bd. dirs. Lexington Conv. and Tourist Bur., 1982-85, Ky. Opera Assn., 1982—, Rehab. Found., Inc., Louisville, 1982-84, Headley-Whitney Mus., Lexington, 1985—; founding bd. Lexington Fund for the Arts, 1984-86. Served to lt. (j.g.) USNR, 1956-58. Named Ky. Col., Mr. Coal of Ky., 1970. Former mem. Ky. Coal Assn. (dir. 1972—, exec. com. 1974-78, sec. 1979-86), Ky. C. of C. (regional v.p., 1971-72, 76-80, exec. com. 1971-72, 76-80, dir. 1971-80, fin. com. 1978-79), Lexington C. of C. (dir. 1982, 84-87), Urban Land Inst., Tau Beta Pi, Alpha Kappa Lambda (past chpt. pres.). Clubs: Frankfort (Ky.) Country; Keeneland, Lafayette, Bluegrass Auto (dir.) (Lexington); Pendennis, River Valley (Louisville); Capitol Hill (Washington). Home: 1715 Stonehaven Dr Frankfort KY 40601 Office: The Stearns Co 410 W Vine St Lexington KY 40507

GABOR, FRANK, insurance company executive; b. Budapest, Hungary, Apr. 15, 1918; s. William and Lyvia (Nauer) G.; came to U.S., 1921, naturalized, 1928; student Boston U., 1936; m. Selma M. Cluck, Aug. 18, 1940; children—Jeffrey Alan, Ronald Steven, Cynthia B. Gabor Cushman. Pres. Gabor & Co., Inc., Miami, Fla., 1946-83, Anglo-Am. Agrl. Underwriters, Inc., Havana, Cuba, 1950-52; pres. Variable Income Planning Co., Miami, 1965—; chmn. Gabor Agy., Inc., 1983—; pres. Gabor Mgmt. Services, Inc., 1983—; pres Gabor Reins. Mgmt. Corp., Miami, 1976—; v.p., dir. Wilson Nat. Life Ins. Co., Lake City, Fla., 1957-73; dir., mem. exec. com. Stanwood Corp., Charlotte, N.C., 1975—; pres. Bent Tree Farm, Inc., Ocala, Fla., 1972—; dir. Bio-Med. Scis., Inc., 1972-74, Am. Reliance Group, Inc., N.J., 1979—. Served with USNR, 1944-46. Mem. Internat. (dir. 1964-68), Fla. (pres. 1960-66) Assns. Health Underwriters. Mason (Shriner). Home: 600 Biltmore Way Coral Gables FL 33134 Office: 1320 S Dixie Hwy Coral Gables FL 33146

GABORIAULT, ANDREW LOUIS, oil company executive, corporate lawyer; b. Cleve., May 19, 1923; s. Aloysis Lawrence and Agnes (Rauwolf) G.; m. Elise Wills, Aug. 15, 1951; children: Diane, Peter. BS in Chem. Engring., Cath. U. Am., 1945; postgrad, Johns Hopkins U., 1944-46; JD, NYU, 1954; postgrad. in Bus. Adminstrn., Harvard U., 1967. Bar: N.Y. 1955, U.S. Supreme Ct. 1977. Research assoc. Am. Petroleum Inst., Washington, 1945-46; chem. engr. Mobil Oil Corp., Paulsboro, N.J., 1946-49; patent agt. Mobil Oil Corp., N.Y.C., 1950-55, patent atty., 1955-68, gen. patent counsel, 1968-74, gen. counsel N.Am. div., 1974-75, gen. counsel mktg. and refining div., 1975-83, assoc. gen. counsel, 1983-86, v.p., 1986—; pres. Mobil Found., N.Y.C., 1987—; bd. dirs. Montgomery Ward & Co. Inc., Chgo., 1986—. Served with U.S. Army, 1949-50. Mem. ABA, Assn. Bar City N.Y. Club: Lake (Wilton, Conn.)(pres. 1983-84). Office: Mobil Oil Corp 150 E 42nd St New York NY 10017

GABRIA, JOANNE BAKAITIS, information processing systems equipment company executive; b. Washington, Pa., Jan. 16, 1945; d. Vincent William and Mary Jo (Cario) Bakaitis. BA in English, U. Dayton, 1965, MA in Mktg. Communications, 1973, MBA, 1979. Advt. writer Dancer-Fitzgerald-Sample, Dayton, Ohio, 1969-72; advt. coordinator Monarch Marking Systems, Dayton, 1972-73; product tech. editor Frigidaire div. GM, Dayton, 1973-77; dir. tech. communications Mead Tech. Lab., Dayton, 1977-79; publs. mgr. NCR Corp., Dayton, 1979-81, internat. product mgr., 1981-86, mgr. internat. market analysis, 1986-87, mgr. Internat. Market Research, 1987—. bd. dirs. Contact-Dayton, 1984-85. Author: Microwave Cooking in 3 Speeds, 1976, Communications Standards, 1978, Retail Operations, 1982; editor: Ivy Jour., 1980-82. Chair numerous coms. St. Leonard Community, Centerville, Ohio, 1978-88; telephone vol. Contact-Dayton Crisis Intervention, 1982-86; big sister Big Bros./Big Sisters, Dayton, 1985-86; bd. dirs. Miami Valley chtp. Nat. Kidney Found. of Ohio, 1987—; mem. Ohio Patient adv. com. Tri-State Renal Network, Inc., 1989—. Recipient Disting. Achievement award Contact-Dayton, 1985, Outstanding Service award Miami Valley chpt. Nat. Kidney Found. of Ohio, 1988. Mem. Dayton Soc. Natural History, Marianist Affiliates (co-chmn. 1981-86). Democrat. Roman Catholic. Avocations: gardening, nature, classical music. Home: 7807 Graceland St Dayton OH 45459 Office: NCR Corp World Hdqrs-2 1700 S Patterson Blvd Dayton OH 45479

GABRIEL, ETHEL MARY, entertainment executive; b. Milmont Park, Pa., Nov. 16, 1921; d. Karoly and Margaret (Horvath) De Nagy; m. Gustav Gabriel, Aug. 10, 1958 (dec. July 1973). Student, Temple U., 1939-40, Columbia U., 1945, 48. Leader dance band En and Her Men, Pa., 1934-39; trombonist Phila. Women's Symphony Orch., 1939-40; co-owner, tchr. Nagy Ceramic and Liberal Arts Sch., N.Y.C., 1948-52; artist and repertoire producer RCA Records, N.Y.C., 1957-80, dir. east coast artist and repertoire dept., 1980-82, dir. dept. talent mgmt. contemporary music, v.p. artist and repertoire, 1982-84; pres. Global Entertainment and Cultural Ctrs., N.Y.C., 1984—; pres. Dunhill Music Co., Weaver Music Co., Hillshire Music Co., Tribune Music Co., Miss Music Pub. Co. Producer over 2500 albums for RCA, 1957-84, numerous artists including Chet Atkins, Teresa Brewer, Arthur Murray, The Insects, King Curtis, The Legendary Performer series, RCA Pure Gold economy line, Camden Records, Bluebird Complete series, Living series (Living Strings, Living Voices, etc.), (other albums) Perry Como Sings Merry Christmas Music (Gold Record award), Roger Whittaker-The Last Farewell and Other Hits (Gold Record award), The Best of Roger Whittaker (Gold Record award), Turned On Swing by Larry Elgart (Gold Record award), The Tommy Dorsey/Frank Sinatra Sessions Vols. 1, 2, 3 (Grammy award 1983); co-producer: (album) Beautiful Isle of Somewhere by Jake Hess (Grammy award), (songs) Wish Me a Rainbow by the Living Voices (Grammy nomination 1967), Angel in the Morning by the Living Voices (Grammy nomination 1969). Mem. Nat. Acad. Rec. Arts and Scis. (bd. govs. 1983-87). Office: Global Entertainment 272 W 19th St New York NY 10011

GABRIEL, MARK ALAN, publishing executive; b. N.Y.C., Jan. 26, 1954; s. John Arthur and Laura (Oakes) G.; m. Melissa Ann Cafiero, Aug. 28, 1982; children: Paula Mare Gabriel, Lana Ilyse. BA in Soc. Sci., Fordham U., 1976. Reporter Paramus (N.J.) Post, 1975-76; asst. bur. chief Patterson (N.J.) News, 1976-77; mng. editor Ski Bus., N.Y.C., 1977-78, Ski Racing Mag., Poultney, Vt., 1978-82; pres., pub. Sports Ink Mags., Inc., Fair Haven, Vt., 1982—; Pres. SIM Cons., Poultney, 1982—, Vt. Investment Realty Co., Fair Haven, 1985—, Disc Sports, Inc., Fair Haven, 1985—. Editor: Sailboard News Blue Book, 1984, 85; editor, designer (newspaper) Ski Show Daily, 1981; editor, creator (mag.) Sailboard News, 1982; creator Water Sports Bus., 1988. Recipient award Excellence in Journalism Mistral Sailboards, 1985. Mem. U.S. Ski Writers Assn., U.S. Boating Writers Assn. Jewish. Office: Box 159 2 S Park Pl Fair Haven VT 05743

GABRIEL, MARY ANNE, marketing professional; b. Chgo., May 4, 1950; d. Roy Arthur and Helen (Bocieck) Wallace. AA, Harper Jr. Coll., Palatine, Ill., 1970. Programmer analyst A.C. Nielsen, Northbrook, Ill., 1971-75; application specialist banking Weiland Computer Group, Oakbrook, Ill., 1975-80; systems mgr. Deutsche Credit Corp., Deerfield, Ill., 1980-85; v.p. systems Heller Fin., Chgo., 1985-87, v.p. mktg. and planning, 1987—; cons. in field. Mem. Structured Techniques Assn. (bd. dirs., founder 1980-85). Office: Heller Fin 200 N LaSalle St Chicago IL 60601

GACONIS, STANLEY LAWRENCE, electrical engineer; b. Chgo., Oct. 5, 1950; s. Stanley and Sophie (Wistart) G.; m. Annamarie Marek, Apr. 26, 1980; 1 child, Michael James. BEE, Ill. Inst. Tech., 1972. With Commonwealth Edison Co., various locations in Ill., 1973-80; prin. engr. fossil div. Commonwealth Edison Co., Chgo., 1980-83; tech. staff Commonwealth Edison Co., Waukegan, Ill., 1983-85, sr. engr. nuclear sta., 1985-87; lead engr. prodn. services nuclear div. Commonwealth Edison Co., Chgo., 1987—. Mem. IEEE. Republican. Roman Catholic. Office: Commonwealth Edison Co Box 767 35 FNW Chicago IL 60690

GAD, LANCE STEWART, investment advisor; b. Peekskill, N.Y., Dec. 11, 1945; s. Martin Harold and Claire (Entner) G.; m. Janiece Lee Feiden, Feb. 14, 1987. BA cum laude, SUNY, Stony Brook, 1967; JD, Cornell U., 1970, MBA, 1971; LLM in Taxation, NYU Law Sch., 1975. Assoc. Spear & Hill, N.Y.C., 1971-72, Wien, Malkin & Bettex, N.Y.C., 1972-74; mgr. Wheelabrator-Frye, N.Y.C., 1974-75, Citicorp, N.Y.C., 1975-86; mgr. Citibank N.A., N.Y.C., 1975-77, asst. v.p., 1977-79, v.p., 1979-86; v.p., gen. counsel and sec. Citicorp Services, Inc., N.Y.C., 1980-85; v.p. Citicorp Investment Bank, N.Y.C., 1985-86; investment advisor WR Family Assocs., N.Y.C., 1986—, Am. Securities Corp., N.Y.C., 1986—; pres., treas., dir. The Lance and Janiece Gad Found., Inc., 1987—. Mem. ABA, N.Y. State Bar Assn., Assn. of Bar of City of N.Y., Met. Tax Lawyers' Assn., Cornell Law Assn., Johnson Sch. Mgmt. Alumni Assn. Home: 6 Peter Cooper Rd New York NY 10010 also: 14 N Hollow Dr East Hampton NY 11937 Office: WR Family Assocs 122 E 42d St 24th Floor New York NY 10168 also: Am Securities Corp 80 Pine St New York NY 10005

GADSBY, ROBIN EDWARD, chemical company executive; b. St. Leonards on the Sea, Eng., Mar. 22, 1939; came to U.S., 1977; s. John Ernest and Emily Louisa (Burt) G.; m. Olwyn Diane Bowen, Aug. 5, 1961 (div. 1981); children: Tricia Clare, Tracey Carolyn; m. Margaret Alice Fuessel, Dec. 29, 1983. MA in Natural Scis., Cambridge U., Eng., 1960, MA in Chem. Engring., 1961; MBA, U. Chgo., 1982. Chartered engr., U.K. Chem. engr. ICI Billingham (Eng.) div., 1961-62, corp. planner, 1962-65; plant mgr. ICI PLC Agrl. div., Heysham, Eng., 1965-67; chem. engring. mgr. ICI PLC Agrl. div., Billingham, 1967-70, process tech. mgr., 1970-76, research group mgr., 1976-77; pres. Katalco Corp., Oak Brook, Ill., 1978-83; gen. mgr. Rubicon Chems. Inc., Wilmington, Del., 1984-86; pres. Polyurethanes Group, Div. ICI Americas, Inc., Wilmington, 1986—; bd. dirs. Rubicon, Inc., Geismar, La., Planned Solutions, Inc., LaGrange, Ill.; officer ICI Americas, Inc., Wilmington, 1986—. Dir. alumni bd. U. Chgo. Grad. Sch. Bus., 1985—. Mem. Am. Inst. Chem. Engrs., U.K. Inst. Chem. Engrs. (editorial bd. 1976-77), Soc. Plastics Industry (bd. dirs. 1988), Beta Gamma Sigma (Ill. chpt. 1982—). Club: Concord Country (Pa.). Home: 455 Fox Meadow Ln West Chester PA 19382 Office: ICI Ams Inc Concord Pike & New Murphy Wilmington DE 19897

GAERTNER, THOMAS GERARD, financial planner; b. Stuttgart, Fed. Republic Germany, Sept. 20, 1955; came to U.S., 1957; s. Howard Henry and Grace Mary (McNulty) G.; child from previous marriage, Michelle Lynn. BA, Cardinal Stritch Coll., 1977, MEd, 1980; student, Coll. Fin. Planning, 1984. Assoc. Harris Assocs. Fin. Group, Milw., 1980—. Named Agt. of Yr. Milw. Gen. Agts. and Mgrs. Assn., 1984. Mem. Inst. Cert. Fin. Planners, Nat. Assn. for Life Underwriters, Cardinal Stritch Coll. Alumni Assn. Avocation: camping, whitewater rafting, hunting. Office: Harris Assocs Fin Group 2401 N Mayfair Rd Ste 100 Milwaukee WI 53226

GAFF, BRIAN MICHAEL, electrical engineer; b. Boston, Mar. 14, 1962; s. Gilbert Gerard and Josephine Claire (Franklin) G. BSEE magna cum laude,

U. Mich., 1983, MSEE, 1984. Engr. GTE Communications Products Corp., Westborough, Mass., 1984; mem. tech. staff Draper Lab., Cambridge, Mass., 1984-88; engring. specialist GPT Stromberg-Carlson, Lake Mary, Fla., 1989—; founder, prin. Solid-State Cons., Swampscott, Mass./Orlando, Fla., 1983—. Mem. IEEE, NSPE, Am. Phys. Soc., Am. Mgmt. Assn., Semiconductor Equipment and Materials Internat., Am. Vacuum Soc., Fla. Engring. Soc., Mensa. Republican. Roman Catholic. Home: 931 State Rd Ste 232 Altamonte Springs FL 32714-7045 Office: GPT Stromberg-Carlson Corp Reflections Rsch and Engring Ctr 400 Rinehart Rd Lake Mary FL 32746-2598

GAFFEY, THOMAS MICHAEL, JR., consumer products executive; b. Elmira, N.Y., Mar. 1, 1934; s. Thomas Michael and Alice (Faul) G.; m. Constance R. Watkins, May 23, 1964. B.S. in Acctg., Syracuse (N.Y.) U., 1956. C.P.A., N.Y. Auditor, cons. Lybrand Ross Bros. & Montgomery (C.P.A.s), N.Y.C., 1956, 58-64; with Liggett Group Inc., 1964-83, asst. controller, then controller, 1969-76; treas. Liggett Group Inc., Durham, N.C. and Montvale, N.J., 1976-80; v.p., treas. Liggett Group Inc., 1980-82, sr. vp., chief fin. officer, dir., 1982-83; with GrandMet USA, Inc. (formerly Liggett Group Inc.), 1983—, sr. v.p., chief fin. officer, dir., 1983-86, exec. v.p., 1987—; dir. Durham City bd. N.C. Nat. Bank, 1972-76; mem. adv. bd. Arkwright-Boston Ins. Co. Mem. N.Y. County Republican Com., 1965-67. Served with U.S. Army, 1956-58. Mem. Am. Inst. C.P.A.s, Fin. Execs. Inst. (pres. N.C. chpt. 1977-78, chmn. admissions com. 1983-85), N.Y. State Soc. C.P.A.s. Roman Catholic. Clubs: Ridgewood (N.J.) Country; Union League (N.Y.C.); Pine Tree Golf (Boynton Beach, Fla.). Home: 15 Deerhill Dr Ho-Ho-Kus NJ 07423 also: 2701 S Ocean Blvd Highland Branch FL 33487 Office: Grandmet USA Inc 100 Paragon Dr Montvale NJ 07645

GAFFIGAN, MICHAEL A., banker; b. Springfield, Ill., Jan. 21, 1936; s. Joseph Patrick and Cecilia (Gardiner) G.; m. Marcia Mitchell, May 17, 1958; children: Catherine, Pamela, Michael A. II, Richard M., Joseph P., James C. BS, Georgetown U.; MBA, NYU. Asst. treas. Chase Manhattan Bank, N.Y.C., 1957-65; exec. v.p. Central Nat. Bank, Chgo., 1965-76; pres., chief exec. officer, dir. Merc. Nat. Bank of Ind., Hammond, 1976—; Lake Comml. Corp., Hammond, Merc. Bancorp, Inc., Hammond, Alverno Hammond Health Corp. Chmn. exec. com. St. Margaret Hosp., Hammond, 1985-88, chmn. Citizens Adv. Bd. 1985—; chmn. exec. com. Purdue U. Calumet, Hammond, 1984—, chmn. Chancellor's adv. council, 1984—; chmn. N.W. Ind. Forum Inc., Merrillville, 1987—; mem. Diocesan Fin. Council, Merrillville, 1987—; mem. Labor-Mgmt. Council N.W. Ind., Hammond, 1984—; mem. Mayor's Adv. Council, Hammond, 1984—. Mem. Am. Bankers Assn., Ind. Bankers Assn., Economic Club, University Club, Bankers Club., Woodmar Country Club, Sand Creek Country Club. Roman Catholic. Office: Merc Nat Bank Ind 5243 Hohman Ave Hammond IN 46325

GAFFNEY, THOMAS FRANCIS, investment company executive; b. Rockford, Ill., Aug. 29, 1945; s. Francis William and Catherine Zeta (Haeberle) G.; m. Donna Lee Gottfried, Apr. 17, 1971; 1 child, Cory. BA, Brown U., 1967; MBA, U. Chgo., 1969. CPA, Ill. Fin. cons. Duff and Phelps, Inc., Chgo., 1969-70; dir. adminstrn. Masury-Columbia Co. subs. Alberto-Culver Co., Melrose Park, Ill., 1970-75; exec. v.p., dir. Guardian Industries Corp., Northville, Mich., 1975-87, 1988—; chmn. bd. Oxford Investment Group, Bloomfield Hills, Mich., 1988—; mem. adv. bd. Allendale Mut. Ins. Co., Providence, R.I., 1983—, Liberty Mut. Ins. Cos., Boston, 1985—; bd. dirs. Continental Inc., Detroit, Cen. Life Assurance Co., Des Moines, Theodore Bargman Co., Coldwater, Mich., Forest City Industries Inc., Rockford, Yale Rubber Mfg. Co. Recipient Chevalier de L'Orde Grand Ducal de le Couronne de Chene Grand Duchy Luxembourg, 1983. Mem. AICPA. Home: 4279 Echo Rd Bloomfield Hills MI 48013 Office: Oxford Investment Group 2000 N Woodward Ave Ste 130 Bloomfield Hills MI 48013

GAGAIN, EDWARD FRANCIS, JR., insurance company executive; b. Waterbury, Conn., Aug. 27, 1947; s. Edward Francis and Alice Mae (Greaturex) G.; m. Janet Lynn Bailey, Mar. 14, 1969 (div. 1975); children: Edward Francis III, Scott Bailey; m. Brenda Jo Browning, Aug. 17, 1984. BA in Bus. Adminstrn., Huron Coll., 1970. Successively claim rep., sr. claim rep., claim supr., claim supt. Aetna Life and Casualty, Washington, 1971-86; v.p. First So. Ins. Co., Tampa, Fla., 1986, sr. v.p., 1987—. Pres. Greenwich Green Homeowners Assn., Nokesville, Va., 1976. Mem. Southeastern Claim Execs. Assn., Fla. Claim Mgrs. Assn., Tampa Claim Mgrs. Council. Roman Catholic. Home: 129 Harbor Woods Circle Safety Harbor FL 34695 Office: First So Ins Co 201 E Kennedy Blvd Tampa FL 33602

GAGE, GEORGE H(ENRY), high technology company executive, retired; b. Rochester, N.Y., Oct. 1, 1924; s. George Henry and Ethel (Morley) G.; m. Frances Irvine, Dec. 21, 1946; children—Betsey Gage La Breche, James George, Nancy Gage Mandeville. B.S.E.E., Rensselaer Poly. Inst., 1948. Application engr. Gen. Electric Co., Owensboro, Ky., 1948-56, comml. engr., Syracuse, N.Y., 1957-58; mgr. product planning CBS Electronics, Danvers, Mass., 1959-61; dir. planning EG&G, Inc., Bedford, Mass., 1962-75, v.p., Wellesley, Mass., 1975-83, sr. v.p., 1983-86; dir. Adams Russell Co., Inc., Waltham, Mass.; gov. Newell Health Corp., Newton-Wellesley Hosp., 1979-87. Contbg. author: Industrial Electronics Handbook, 1957; Implementation of Strategic Planning, 1982. Served to staff sgt. U.S. Army, 1943-46, PTO. Mem. Sigma Xi (assoc.), Tau Beta Pi, Eta Kappa Nu. Avocations: computer simulations; reading; walking. Home: 23 Fiddlers Green Lansing NY 14882

GAGNÉ, PAUL ERNEST, paper and pulp company financial executive; b. Hearst, Ont., Can., Sept. 17, 1946; m. Shari Mayer, Aug. 26, 1951; 1 child, Sara-Anne. B in Commerce, U. Ottawa, Ont., Can., 1972; Cert., Ont. Inst. Chartered Accts., 1974; MBA, Queen's U., Kingston, Ont. Can., 1975. Pub. acct. Normandin and Séguin, 1972-74, 75-76; various positions CIP Inc., Montreal, Que., Can., 1976-79, asst. to comptroller, 1979-80, chief internal auditor, 1981-82, treas., 1983-84, v.p. fin., 1984-86, v.p. fin., acctg. and logistics, 1986-88; v.p. fin. Dominion Cellulose Ltd., Toronto, Ont., Can., 1980-81; v.p. fin., accounting and logistics Can. Pacific Forest Products Ltd., Montreal, 1988—; bd. dirs. Mayo Forest Products Ltd., NBIP Forest Products Inc. Office: Can Pacific Forest Products, Ltd 1155 Metcalfe St 14th Fl, Montreal, PQ Canada H3B 2X1

GAGNE, RUSSELL CARL, financial executive; b. Biddeford, Maine, Feb. 28, 1960; s. Bertrand R. and Constance P. (Dubois) G.; m. SUsan J. Faucher, June 11, 1983; 1 child, Christopher C. BS in Mgmt. Adv. Svcs., N.H. Coll., 1982. CPA, Maine. Acct. Coopers & Lybrand, Portland, Maine, 1982-85; dir. br. fin. ops. Coca-Cola Co. No. New Eng., South Portland, Maine, 1985; v.p., chief fin. officer Porteous, Mitchell & Braun Co., Portland, 1985—; bd. dirs. Credit Counselling Ctrs. Maine, Portland, 1987—. V.p. sch. bd. St. Joseph's Sch., Biddeford, 1986—. Mem. Maine Soc. CPA's. Office: Porteous Mitchell & Braun Co 522 Congress St Portland ME 04101

GAHAGAN, LARRY WESLEY, oil company executive; b. Bastrop, La., Oct. 3, 1946; s. Raymond and Larraine G.; m. Sandra Louise Schooley, July 2, 1976. BBA in Econ., U. Houston, 1972; MBA in Fin., Pepperdine U., 1980. Ops. programmer Pennzoil, Houston, 1970-72; ops. mgr. Fannin Bank, Houston, 1972-73; systems group mgr. Occidental Petroleum Corp., Los Angeles, 1973-77; mgr. internal auditing R.J. Reynolds Co., Winston-Salem, N.C., 1977-79, mgr. mgmt. info. systems, 1979-83; mgr. policy and planning Standard Oil Co., Cleve., 1983—; bd. dirs. APCO Internat. Inc., Houston, Apco Trinidad and Tobago. Author: Organizational Startegies for E&P Company's, 1980. Served as sgt. U.S. Army, 1966-70, Vietnam. Club: Houston Yacht (LaPort, Tex.). Home: 8335 Prairie Wind Ln Houston TX 77040 Office: Standard Oil Co 5151 San Felipe Houston TX 77210

GAIBER, LAWRENCE JAY, financial company executive; b. Chgo., Mar. 20, 1960; s. Sy Bertrym and Mildred (Dickler) G. BS in Econ., U. Pa., 1982. Mgmt. intern Eisai Co. Ltd, Tokyo, 1980; dept. mgr. Anglo Am. Corp., Johannesburg, Republic of South Africa, 1982-84; pres. Sandton Fin. Group, L.A., 1984—; pres. Swellendam Fin. Group, Studio City, Calif., 1984—, also bd. dirs.; bd. dirs. Lawrand Ltd, Satellite Telecommunication, Inst. Cellular Nutritional Immunology, Introlagater, Gaiber, Introlagater, L.A. Greetings; chmn. Mechanics Express Inc. Contbr. articles to profl. jours and mags. Mem. South Africa Found., Johannesburg, 1984—, Town Hall Calif., 1986; bd. dirs. Brentwood Arts Coun.; vice chmn. western region 1986 Pres.' dinner Rep. Nat. Com., Washington. Recipient Most Active Vol. award S. African Inst. Internat. Affairs, 1983; honoree for contbns. to aspiring entrepreneurial women Mayor Tom Bradley's Office and Nat. Network of Hispanic Women, L.A., 1986. Mem. L.A. Venture Assn., L.A. C. of C., L.A. Jr. C. of C., Van Nuys C. of C., L.A. County Rep. Lincoln Club, L.A. County Young Reps., Brentwood Rep. Club (Pres. 1984—). Clubs: Wharton Bus. Sch., Calif. Yacht.

GAILEY, CHARLES FRANKLIN, JR., maritime consultant; b. Eads, Colo., Apr. 2, 1926; s. Charles Franklin and Mary Francis (Cranston) G.; m. Dorothy J. Swarens, Jan. 29, 1950; children: Dan Michael, Pamela Eileen, Cheryl Francine. Commd. USCG, 1943-74; commanding officer afloat USCG, Juneau, Alaska, 1966-68; dir. aux. USCG, Long Beach, Calif., 1968-71; chief mil. plans section USCG, Washington, 1972-74; owner Gailey & Gailey Partnership, Oak Harbor, Wash., 1975—; dir. Real Estate Partnership, Oak Harbor, 1975—; cons. Maritime Environ. Cons., Ridgefield, Wash., 1976—. Chmn. allocation panel United Way, Oak Harbor, 1985—; vol. IRS-Vita Program, Oak Harbor, 1985-88. Mem. Retired Officers Assn., Am. Legion. Republican. Office: PO Box 664 Oak Harbor WA 98277

GAILIUS, GILBERT KEISTUTIS, manufacturing company executive; b. Boston, June 21, 1931; s. Joseph B. and Mary K. G.; B.S. in Bus. Adminstrn., Suffolk U., 1958; M.B.A., Boston Coll., 1962; m. Lillian P. Romanskis, Sept. 6, 1954; children—Gregory, Laura, Louise, Gilbert, Linda, Gary. Plant controller, staff asst. corp. controller Continental Group, N.Y.C., 1954-66; v.p. fin. Foster Grant Co., Inc., Leominster, Mass., 1966-77, Midland Glass Co., Cliffwood, N.J., 1977-78, Am. Biltrite Inc., Wellesley Hills, Mass., 1978—, also bd. dirs. Served with U.S. Army, 1952-54. Mem. Fin. Execs. Inst. Home: 616 Hayward Mill Rd Concord MA 01742 Office: Am Biltrite Inc 57 River St Wellesley Hills MA 02181

GAILLARD, GEORGE SIDAY, III, architect; b. Miami, Fla., Apr. 24, 1941; s. George Siday and Sarah Margaret (Crawford) G.; m. Charlalee Bailey, 1965 (div. 1969); m. Sylvia Gayle Bridgewater, July 18, 1977; 1 child, Barron Matthew. B.S., Ga. Inst. Tech., 1965; postgrad., Ga. State U. Registered architect Ga., Fla. Sole propr. Fox Magnanimus, Atlanta, Ga., 1971-78, Gaillard & Assocs., Atlanta, 1978-81, 83—; mgr. design dept. Deca Inc., Miami, 1982. Sculpture exhibited in group shows at Piedmont Arts Festival, 1971, 73. Cubmaster Cub Scouts Am., Stone Mountain, Ga., 1988—. With USMCR, 1962. Mem. AIA (chmn. liason com. So. Coll. Tech. for Atlanta chpt.), High Mus. Art Atlanta, Huguenot Soc. S.C. Avocations: reading; camping; sailing; photography.

GAINES, LEONARD M., economic and demographic researcher; b. Bklyn., May 19, 1956; s. Jules and Babette (Lowenfeld) G.; m. Nancy M. Labitt, Oct. 9, 1988. BS, Rensselaer Poly. Inst., 1978, MS in Urban and Environ. Studies, 1980; MBA, SUNY, Albany, 1985. Statistician trainee N.Y. State Dept. Labor, Albany, 1981; program research specialist N.Y. State Econ Devel. (name formerly N.Y. State Dept. Commerce), Albany, 1981—; adj. prof. Empire State Coll., Saratoga Springs, N.Y., 1985—. Author: Course Guide for Advanced Quantatative Methods in Management, 1988, Tabulations from the Current Population Survey for New York State, 1986, 88. Regional asst. research dir. Soc. for Creative Anachronism, 1987—; CPR-First Aid instr. ARC, Troy, N.Y., 1986—. Mem. Am. Statistical Assn. Democrat. Jewish. Home: 2103 Sausse Ave 1A Troy NY 12180 Office: NY State Dept Econ Devel One Commerce Pla Albany NY 12245

GAINES, LUDWELL EBERSOLE, financial executive; b. Charleston, W.Va., Apr. 21, 1927; s. Ludwell Ebersole and Betty (Chilton) G.; m. Sheila Kellogg, Nov. 24, 1956; children: L. Ebersole, Leith Mitchell, Kellogg Chilton, Audrey Noyes. A.B., Princeton U., 1951. Tribunal clk. Am. Arbitration Assn., N.Y.C., 1951-53; sales mgmt. exec. Plax Corp.-Monsanto Chem. Corp., West Hartford, Conn., 1953-60; sales mgmt. exec., asst. to pres. Continental Can Co., Chgo. and N.Y.C., 1960-65; mktg. mgr. Nationwide Paper div. U.S. Plywood Champion, 1965-67; exec. v.p., dir. Diversa-Graphics, Inc., Chgo., 1969-72; exec. v.p. Overseas Pvt. Investment Corp., Washington, 1981—. Chmn. bd. trustees Ketchum-Sun Valley Community Schs., Sun Valley, Idaho, 1974-77; vice chmn. Idaho Park Found., Sun Valley, 1974-81; Idaho State fin. chmn. George Bush for Pres., mem. nat. central com., Republican chmn., Blaine County, Idaho. Served with USN, 1945-46, PTO. Clubs: Cypress Point (Pebble Beach, Calif.), Princeton (N.Y.C.), Links (N.Y.C.); Chevy Chase (Md.), Press (Washington), Rolling Rock. Home: 4369 Westover Pl NW Washington DC 20016 Office: Overseas Pvt Investment Corp 1615 M St NW Washington DC 20527

GAINES, WILLIAM MAXWELL, publishing executive; b. N.Y.C., Mar. 1, 1922; s. Max C. and Jessie K. (Postlethwaite) G.; m. Hazel Grieb, Oct. 21, 1944 (div. Feb. 9, 1948); m. Nancy Siegel, Nov. 17, 1955 (div. Mar. 1, 1971); children: Cathy, Wendy, Chris; m. Anne Griffiths, Feb. 21, 1987. Student, Poly. Inst. Bklyn., 1939-42; B.S. in Edn. N.Y. U., 1948. Pres. E. C. Publs. Inc. (pub. MAD Mag.), N.Y.C., 1948—. Served with AUS, 1942-46. Mem. Wine and Food Soc., Phi Alpha. Office: 485 Madison Ave New York NY 10022

GAITHER, JOHN FRANCIS, accountant; b. Louisville, Oct. 26, 1918; s. Thomas R. and Marice F. Gaither; m. Marjilee Schaeffer, Nov. 26, 1942; children: John Francis, James M. BCS, U. Notre Dame, 1941; postgrad. U. Louisville. CPA, Ind. Controller Evansville (Ind.) div. Whirlpool Corp., 1946-54; assoc. prof. fin. U. Evansville, part-time 1946-56; sr. ptnr. Gaither, Koewler, Rohlfer & Luckett, CPA's, 1954—; city controller, dep. mayor City of Evansville, 1972-76. Contbr. articles to profl. jours. Past pres. Buffalo Trace coun. Boy Scouts Am.; past co-chmn. Summa Fund drive U. Notre Dame; adv. com. Ind. Vocat. Rehab.; past mem. fin. com. Roman Cath. Diocese Evansville; past trustee Brescia Coll., Owensboro, Ky.; mem. regional community adv. coun. Ind. U. Med. Sch.; chmn. community adv. coun. Evansville Ctr. Med. Edn.; past chmn. Ind. Select Com. Ednl. Fin., chmn. Ind. Utility and Energy Regulation Adv. Commn.; past chmn. Ind. Health Facilities Fin. Authority; mem. Ind. Transp. Coordinating Bd.; past Gov.'s rep. Ind. Hosp. Rate Rev. Commn.; past officer local YMCA, Cancer Soc., Sierra Club. Served as officer USNR, 1941-46. Recipient various awards Boy Scouts Am. Mem. AICPA, Ind. Assn. CPA's, Ill. Assn. CPA's, Ky. Assn. CPA's, Evansville Assn. CPA's, Nat. Assn. Accts. (past pres. Evansville), Ind. Assn. Cities and Towns Controllers Assn. (past pres.), Ind. Soc. Chgo. (v.p.), SAR, Evansville C. of C., Evansville Country Club Country (past pres.), Kennel Club, Petroleum Club, Columbia Club, Union League Club. Republican. Home: 730 Colony Rd Evansville IN 47714 Office: 111 Main St Evansville IN 47708

GAITHER, LAURENCE GREGORY, investment broker; b. Los Angeles, Nov. 17, 1945; s. Laurence Finly and Mary Ann (Anatasia) G.; m. Linda Norine Martin, May 20, 1966; children: Lorie Michelle, Amy Noel, Sunny Dawn. BA, Northeastern U., Tahlequah, Okla., 1972, MEd, 1973; EdD, Kans. U., 1984. Psychologist Hill City (Kans.) Sch. Dist., 1973-75, East Cen. Kans. Coop. in Edn., Baldwin City, Kans., 1975-78; supt. Interlocal 614 Sch. Dist., Baldwin City, Kans., 1978-84; investment broker Edward D. Jones & Co., Van Buren, Ark., 1984-88, Muskogee, Okla., 1988—; pres. Kans. Assn. Psychologists, 1976-77; regional bd. dirs. Nat. Assn. Psychologists, 1974-77; chmn. legis. com. United Sch. Adminstrs. Kans., 1980-83. Author: Implementation of an Inter-related Educational Program, 1983, Service Delivery System in Rural Districts, 1983, Behavior Modification for Classroom, 1983. Chmn. Indsl. Devel. Com., Van Buren. With USAF, 1966-69, S.E. Asia. Mem. Nat. Assn. Security Dealers, C. of C. (pres. Van Buren chpt. 1984, Exceptional Accomplishment award 1987, bd. dirs. Muskogee chpt.), Rotary (bd. dirs.). Republican. Baptist. Office: Edward D Jones & Co 9 S 7th St Van Buren AR 72956

GAJKOWSKI, JOHN JOSEPH, financial planner; b. North Riverside, Ill., Nov. 25, 1954; s. Edwin J. and Eleanor (Sedivy) G.; m. Cathleen Mary Muldoon, Feb. 16, 1985; children: Lauren Cathleen, Michelle Ann. Student, Triton Coll., 1972-74, U. Ill., 1974-75; BS, Ill. State U., 1977. Cert. fin. planner; registered fin. planner. Paralegal Clausen, Miller, Gorman, Caffrey and Witous, Chgo., 1978; sales engr. Valenite Metals, Burr Ridge, Ill., 1979-80; account exec. GTE Sylvania, Elk Grove, Ill., 1980-84; fin. planner IDS/Am. Express, Oak Brook, Ill., 1984-87; v.p. fin. planning Money Mgrs., Ltd., Oak Brood, 1987—. Contbg. editor Sun/Life News, LaGrange, Ill., 1984—, Suburban Life, Berwyn, Ill., 1984—. Recipient Mercury award IDS Am. Express, Oak Brook, Ill., 1984. Mem. Internat. Assn. Fin. Planning, Inst. Cert. Fin. Planners, Internat. Assn. Registered Fin. Planners. Home: 87 Bassford LaGrange IL 60525 Office: Money Mgrs Ltd 1301 W 22d Oak Brook IL 60521

GALANE, IRMA ADELE BERESTON, electronic engineer; b. Balt., Aug. 23, 1921; d. Dr. Arthur and Sarah (Hillman) Bereston; B.A., Goucher Coll., 1940; postgrad. Johns Hopkins, 1940-42, Mass. Inst. Tech., 1943, George Washington U., 1945, 65, 73, 77, 79, U. Md., 1958, Army Mgmt. Sch., 1964; 1 dau., Suzanne Felice Galane Duvall. Physicist, Naval Ordnance Lab., 1942-43; electronic engr. Navy Bur. Ships, 1943-49, Army Office Chief Signal Officer, 1949-51, Navy Bur. Aeros., 1951-56, Air Research and Devel. Command, USAF, 1956-57, FCC, 1957-60, NASA, 1960-62; supervisory electronic engr. USCG Hdqrs., 1962-64; sci. specialist engring. scis. Library of Congress, 1964-65; project engr. Advanced Aerial Fire Support System, Army Materiel Command, 1965-66; engr. Naval Air Systems Command, 1966-71; electronic engr. Spectrum Mgmt. Task Force, FCC, 1971-76, sr. research engr. FCC, 1976—; Judge nat. capitol awards for engrs. and architects, 1975. Registered profl. engr., D.C. Mem. IEEE (sr.), Am. Inst. Aeros. and Astronautics, Nat. Soc. Profl. Engrs. (chmn. publs. com. 1959-60, co-chmn. civil def. com. 1965, spl. asst. to pres. 1965), Soc. Women Engrs. (sr. mem.; nat. membership chmn. 1952, nat. dir. 1953, mem. nat. scholarship com. 1958), Armed Forces Communications and Electronics Assn., Fedn. Profl. Assn., Am. Ordnance Assn., Johns Hopkins Alumni Assn., AAAS, U.S. Naval Inst., Marine Tech. Soc., Internat. Platform Assn., Smithsonian Inst. (assoc.), Mensa. Editor: The Met. Washington Profl. Engr., 1958-60. Home: 4201 Cathedral Ave NW Washington DC 20016

GALATIANOS, GUS A., computer scientist, information systems consultant, educator; b. Hermoupolis, Siros, Greece, Jan. 18, 1947; came to U.S., 1973.; s. A. Constantine and Despina Athanassios (Stefanou) G.; m. Katerina E. Saridis, Sept. 29, 1974; children: Athanassios, Deborah. BSEE, N.Y. Inst. Tech., 1974; MSEE, Columbia U., 1977; MS in Computer Sci., Stevens Inst. Tech., 1977; PhD in Computer Sci., Poly. U., N.Y.C., 1986. Mgr. ops. Solomos Bus. Machines, Athens, Greece, 1970-73; computer cons. Univ. Computer Ctrs., N.Y.C., 1973-77; tech. dir. Computer Dynamics Corp., N.Y.C., 1977-79; assoc. prof., chmn. dept. computer sci. SUNY, Old Westbury, N.Y., 1979—; computer cons. Keane Inc., N.Y.C., 1980-81, Ins. Services Office, N.Y.C., 1981-82, Computer Corp. Am., N.Y.C., 1983-84; mgr. fin. systems Singer/Electronic Systems Div., Little Falls, N.J., 1984-87; pres. Advanced Computer Cons. Internat., N.Y.C., 1988—. Author: Principles of Software Engineering, 1986, Principles of Database Systems, 1986. Mem. Statue of Liberty Found. Inc., N.Y.C., 1984—, Nat. Fedn. Blind, Balt., 1988, Rep. Presdl. Task Force, Washington, 1984—, Greater Whitestone Taxpayers Civic Assn., N.Y.C., 1984—. Served with Greek Air Force, 1965-67. Mem. IEEE, AAAS, Assn. Computing Machinery, N.Y. Acad. Scis., Am. Mgmt. Assn., Am. Assn. Artificial Intelligence, Am. Cons. League, Fin. Mgmt. Club. Republican. Greek Orthodox. Club: Hellenic Univ. (N.Y.C.). Home: 17-24 Parsons Blvd Whitestone NY 11357 Office: SUNY Dept Computer Sci Old Westbury NY 11568

GALBRAITH, JAMES RONALD, hotel executive; b. Crystal Falls, Mich., Mar. 18, 1936; s. Edwin and Lillian (Robichaud) G.; m. Mary Elizabeth Redington, June 23, 1962; children—Richard Lee, Timothy Scott, John Redington. BA, Calif. State U., Los Angeles, 1960. Reporter, news editor Ind. Star-News, Pasadena, Calif., 1955-60; adminstrv. asst. U.S. Congress, Washington, 1960-62; U.S. Supreme Ct. broadcaster NBC-Three Star Extra, Washington, 1962-64; mng. editor Washington World Mag., Washington, 1962-64; asst. dir. pub. relations Nat. Republican Congl. Com, Washington, 1964-69; dir. pub. relations Republican Gov.'s Assn., Washington, 1969-71, exec. dir., 1971-75; v.p. Ticor, Los Angeles, 1976-81; sr. v.p. Hilton Hotels Corp., Beverly Hills, Calif., 1981—; dep. Calif. Roundtable, San Francisco, 1976—; co-chmn. edn. council Constl. Rights Found., Los Angeles, 1978-81; cons. Nat. Acad. Pub. Adminstrn., U.S. Presdl. Mgmt. Panel, Washington, 1979-80. Co-founder, mem. The Cogswell Soc., Washington, 1973—; mem. Los Angeles Pub. Affairs Officers Assn., 1977—, chmn., 1984; trustee Calif. Hist. Soc., San Francisco, 1979-86; mem. adv. bd. Calif. Mus. Sci. and Industry, Los Angeles, 1979-80; trustee Edmund G. "Pat" Brown Inst. Govt. Affairs, Beverly Hills, Calif., 1984—; mem. Statue of Liberty-Ellis Island Centennial Commn., 1985—. Recipient Outstanding Toastmaster of Yr. award, Capitol Hill Toastmasters, 1969. Mem. Nat. Press Club. Republican. Roman Catholic. Club: Capitol Hill (Washington). Office: Hilton Hotels Corp 9336 Santa Monica Blvd Beverly Hills CA 90210

GALBREATH, LIZANNE, real estate developer; b. Columbus, Ohio, Sept. 28, 1957; d. Daniel Mauck and Elizabeth (Lind) G.; m. John Frederic Megrue Jr., June 28, 1986. BA, Dartmouth Coll., 1979; MBA, U. Pa., 1984. Officer's asst. Chem. Bank, N.Y.C., 1979-82; mng. dir. The Galbreath Co., N.Y.C., 1984—. Mem. jr. com. Mus. of Natural History, N.Y.C., 1986-88; mem. resource coun. Girls Club Am., N.Y.C., 1987-88; bd. dirs. U. Pa. Coun. of Women, Phila., 1987—. Mem. Urban Land Inst. (vice-chmn. coun. 1987)., River Club. Office: The Galbreath Co 150 E 42d St Ste 800 New York NY 10017

GALE, JOHN, banker; b. Workington, Cumbria, Eng., Aug. 23, 1929; came to U.S., 1982; s. Frank Pearson and Elizabeth (Rudkin) G.; m. Joan Gale; children—Stephen Nicholas, Susan Elizabeth. With Nat. Westminster Bank PLC, 1945—; sr. exec. v.p., chief adminstrv. officer, dir. Nat. Westminster Bank U.S.A., N.Y.C., 1982—. Mem. Guild of Freemen, London, 1977, Farriers Livery Co., London, 1978. Served with Brit. Royal Air Force, 1947-49. Mem. Inst. Bankers London, N.Y. State Bankers Assn. (dir. 1984—), Assn. Res. City Bankers. Conservative. Presbyterian. Club: Ridgewood Country. Office: Nat Westminster Bank USA 175 Water St New York NY 10038 *

GALE, MELVIN HAROLD, sales finance and bank service organization executive; b. N.Y.C., Jan. 23, 1931; s. Solomon and Etta G.; student Pace U., 1949-51; m. Saundra Greenstein, Nov. 21, 1951; children—Marsha F., Mitchell A.; m. 2d, Leona Block, Sept. 13, 1981. Br. mgr. Tilo Co., constrn., 1954-59; v.p. Coastal Constrn. Co., Inc., Franklin Sq., N.Y., 1959-63, pres., 1963-65; pres. Dartmouth Plan, Inc., Carle Place, N.Y., 1965-74, chmn. bd., 1974—; consumer loan cons. to various banks; arbiter N.Y. Better Bus. Bur. Mem. N.Y. State Joint Legis. Com. on Higher Edn., 1970-74; bd. dirs. Am. Cancer Soc.; bd. govs. Human Resources; active Am. Heart Assn. Served with USMCR, 1952-54. Mem. Nat. Remodelers Assn. (pres. N.Y. chpt.), Nat. Home Improvement Council, Sales Execs. Club, L.I. Bankers Assn., L.I. Assn. for Commerce and Industry. Clubs: Mended Hearts, Sky Island, Masons. Office: 1301 Franklin Ave Garden City NY 11530

GALE, NEIL JAN, finance company executive, consultant; b. Chgo., Jan. 12, 1960; s. Jack and Adele (Field) G. AA, Wright Coll., 1980. Mgr. Gen. Fin. Co., Chgo., 1980-84; mktg. mgr. Midland Fin. Co., Chgo., 1984-85; mktg. dir. Diamond Mortgage Corp., Chgo., 1985-86; sr. fin. analyst McKay Mazda-Nissan, Evanston, Ill., 1987-88; pres., chief exec. officer Nat. Consumer Credit Cons., Chgo., 1988—. First aid chmn. Walk with Israel, 1977. Recipient Bus. in Urban Environment Chgo. Bd. Edn. and Ill. Bell, Chgo., 1978, Outstanding Achievement Chgo. Pub. Library, 1979. Mem. Auto Credit (hon.), Friendship Circle Club (treas. 1976-78). Home: 2836 W Arthur Ave Chicago IL 60645

GALE, THOMAS CHARLES, automotive design executive; b. Flint, Mich., June 18, 1943; s. Woodrow and Elizabeth Marie (Taliaferro) Payne; m. Charlene Gale, Sept. 17, 1966; children—Jeffrey, Timothy. B.A., Mich. State U., East Lansing, 1966, M.A., 1967; M.B.A., Mich. State U., Troy, 1978. Grad. asst. Mich. State U., East Lansing, 1966-67; body engr. Chrysler Corp., Design, Highland Park, Mich., 1967-71, designer, stylist, 1971-76; sr. analyst Chrysler Corp., Planning, Highland Park, Mich., 1976-77; mgr.-dir. Chrysler Corp., Design, Highland Park, Mich., 1977-85, v.p.-design, 1985—. Patentee. Mem. Engring. Soc. Detroit, Industrial Designers Soc. Am., Beta Gamma Sigma, Phi Kappa Phi. Office: Product Design Office PO Box 637 Detroit MI 48288

GALEA, JOHN HENRY, retired lawyer; b. Albany, N.Y., Jan. 18, 1924; s. John Fortune and Virginia (Sterling) G.; m. Helen Flynn Conway, Aug. 14, 1948; children: Michelle Galea Jeter, Mark C., Mary Ellen, Monica,

Madeleine. AB cum laude, Holy Cross Coll., 1947; LLB, Harvard U., 1951. Bar: Ohio 1952, Ky. 1953, Va. 1959. Assoc. Grossman Schlesinger & Carter, Cleve., 1951-53; with Reynolds Metals Co., Richmond, Va., 1953-89; asst. gen. counsel Reynolds Metals Co., Richmond, 1964-72, gen. atty., 1972-76, v.p., gen. counsel, 1976-85, sr. v.p., gen. counsel, 1985-89. With USAAF, 1943-45, ETO. Decorated D.F.C., Air medal with three oak leaf clusters. Mem. ABA, Assn. Gen. Counsel, Va. Bar Assn., Richmond Bar Assn., Am. Corp. Counsel Assn., Harvard Club of Va., Hermitage Country Club. Republican. Roman Catholic.

GALECKE, ROBERT MICHAEL, financial company executive; b. Stevens Point, Wis., Sept. 18, 1942; s. Michael B. and Julia (Cieslewicz) G.; m. Jackie Derocher, Apr. 19, 1979; children: Beth, Tricia, Amy. BS, U. Wis., Stevens Point, 1964; postgrad., U. Wis., 1976. Nat. bank examiner U.S. Comptroller of Currency, Milw., 1965-71; exec. v.p. 1st Bank Milw., 1971-84; pres., chief oper. officer Amrecorp Realty, Dallas, 1984-86; exec. v.p., treas. Southmark Corp., Dallas, 1986—; pres. Naco Fin. Corp., Dallas, 1987—. Mem. Am. Bankers Assn. (mem. exec. com. 1982-84). Republican. Roman Catholic. Office: Southmark Corp 1601 LBJ Fwy Suite 800 Dallas TX 75234

GALEF, ANDREW GEOFFREY, investment and management corporations executive; b. Yonkers, N.Y., Nov. 3, 1932; s. Gabriel and Anne (Fruchter) G.; m. Suzanne Jane Cohen, June 26, 1954 (div. Feb. 1963); children: Stephanie Anne Galef Streeter, Marjorie Lynn Galef England, Michael Lewis; m. Billie Ruth Medlin, Nov. 7, 1964 (div. May 1988); children: Phyllis Anne Galef Bulmer, Catherine Marie; m. Bronya Kester, Dec. 18, 1988. B.A., Amherst Coll., 1954; M.B.A., Harvard U., 1958. Vice pres. Kamkap, Inc., N.Y.C., 1958-60; pres. Kemline Calif., San Jose, 1960-61, Zeigler Harris Corp., San Fernando, Calif., 1961-63; v.p. Fullview Industries, Glendale, Calif., 1963-65; cons. Mordy & Co., Los Angeles, 1965-68; prin. Grisanti & Galef, Inc., Los Angeles, 1968-84; pres. Spectrum Group, Inc., Los Angeles, 1978—; chmn., chief exec. officer MagneTek, Inc., Los Angeles, 1984—; chmn. bd. dirs. Midland Color, Inc. (formerly Roberts & Porter, Inc.), Chgo., Exide Corp., Horsham, Pa., Warnaco Inc., Los Angeles, Grantree Corp., Portland, Petco, Inc., San Diego; bd. dirs. Post Group, Inc., Hollywood, Calif. Mem. nat. adv. bd. Childhelp, USA, Woodland Hills, Calif., 1984—; bd. dirs. Pacific Homes, Encino, Calif. Served to capt. USAF, 1956-58. Office: Spectrum Group Inc 11111 Santa Monica Blvd Los Angeles CA 90025

GALIARDO, JOHN WILLIAM, lawyer; b. Elizabeth, N.J., Dec. 28, 1933; s. Joseph A. and Genevieve A. (Luxich) G.; m. Joan A. DeTurk, Aug. 26, 1961; children: Richard C., Christopher D., Elizabeth A. BS, U. Md., 1956; LLB, Columbia U., 1962. Bar: N.Y. 1962. Assoc. Dewey, Ballantine, Bushby, Palmer & Wood, N.Y.C., 1962-71; asst. gen. counsel E.R. Squibb & Sons, Inc., Princeton, N.J., 1971-77; v.p., gen. counsel Becton Dickinson and Co., Franklin Lakes, N.J., 1977—. Treas. Charter Commn. Scotch Plains, N.J., 1970-71; mem. Joint Consol. Com. Princeton, N.J., 1973-76; mem. legal adv. council Atlantic Legal Found., N.Y.C., 1986—; trustee Ind. Coll. Fund of N.J., Summit, 1986—. Served with AUS, 1956-58. Mem. Am. Bar Assn., N.Y. State Bar Assn., Assn. of Bar of City of N.Y. Home: 56 Crooked Tree Ln Princeton NJ 08540 Office: Becton Dickinson & Co 1 Becton Dr Franklin Lakes NJ 07417

GALIE, LOUIS MICHAEL, electronics company executive; b. Phila., Aug. 10, 1945; s. Adam Michael and Phyllis Anne (Bowers) G.; m. Elizabeth D. Viviano, June 23, 1969 (div. June 1980); 1 child, Kathryn Louise; m. Charlene Mary Gates, Aug. 27, 1983 (div. 1988). BS, U. Chgo., 1967, MS, 1968. Prin. researcher System Devel. Corp., Santa Monica, Calif., 1975-80; dir. devel. Burroughs Corp., Danbury, Conn., 1980-82; dir. engring. Timex Corp., Waterbury, Conn., 1982-86, v.p. research and devel., 1986—. Author: Means for Database Search, 1980, Electronic Spelling Correction, 1981; patentee in field. Warden Trinity Episcopal Ch., Newtown, Conn., 1985—. Served to comdr. USN, 1969-75. Mem. IEEE, Soc. for the History of Tech. Republican. Home: 141 Brushy Hill Rd Newtown CT 06470 Office: Timex Corp Waterbury CT 06720

GALIMORE, MICHAEL OLIVER, marketing communications company executive; b. Bloomington, Ind., June 15, 1947; s. Howard Fenwick and Donna (Patterson) G.; m. Kathryn Carol Kaser, Nov. 30, 1975; 1 child, Jonathan Michael. Student, Ind. U., 1966-68; B.A., Ambassador Coll., Pasadena, Calif., 1972. Art dir. White Arts, 1976-79; advt. mgr. Cook, Inc., Bloomington, 1979-80, graphics dir., 1980—; writer, graphics cons. Wyldefyre Communications, 1987—. Graphic artist The Plain Truth mag., 1972. Recipient Recognition award for graphic arts excellence Consol. Papers, Inc., 1983. Mem. Ch. of God Seventh Day. Club: Ambassador Spokesman. Home: Rte 1 Box 752 Spencer IN 47460 Office: Cook Inc 925 S Curry Pike Bloomington IN 47401 also: Wyldefyre Communications PO Box 271 Bloomington IN 47402

GALL, LAWRENCE HOWARD, lawyer, consultant; b. Leesville, S.C., Dec. 17, 1917; s. John J. and Bertha (Smyer) G.; m. Winifred Belle Nelson, Dec. 18, 1948; children: Sally Patricia, Linda, Constance. A.B., U. S.C., 1939, LL.B., 1941. Bar: S.C. 1941, D.C. 1948, U.S. Supreme Ct. 1952, Tex. 1966. Mem. legal dept. E.I. duPont de Nemours & Co., Inc.; asst. to gen. counsel Remington Arms Co., Bridgeport, Conn., 1941-43; assoc., then ptnr. Disney & Gall, Washington, 1946-52; research dir., gen. counsel Ind. Natural Gas Assn. Am., Washington, 1952-61, exec. dir., 1961-65; v.p., gen. counsel Transcontinental Gas Pipe Line Corp., 1965-74; v.p., gen. atty. Transco Energy Co., 1974-80, v.p. govtl. affairs, 1980-83, legal cons., 1983—. Houston Met. dir. Nat. Alliance Businessmen, 1971; bd. dirs. Tex. Mfrs. Assn., 1971-73, Tex. Research League, 1975-83. Served to lt. (s.g.) USNR, 1943-46. Mem. Am. Fed. Energy, Tex., Houston Bar Assns. Home: 643 Shartle Circle Houston TX 77024

GALLAGHER, ANNE PORTER, business executive; b. Coral Gables, Fla., Mar. 16, 1950; d. William Moring and Anne (Jewett) Porter; m. Matthew Philip Gallagher, Jr., July 31, 1976; children: Jacqueline Anne, Kevin Sharkey. BA in Edn., Stetson U., 1972. Tchr. elem. schs., Atlanta, 1972-74; sales rep. Xerox Corp., Atlanta, 1974-76, Fed. Systems, Rosslyn, Va., 1976-81; sales rep. No. Telecom Inc. Fed. Systems, Vienna, Va., 1981-84, account exec., 1984-85, sales dir., 1985-87, mktg. dir., 1987—. Mem. Nat. Assn. Female Execs., Pi Beta Phi. Episcopalian. Avocations: skiing, aerobics, needlepoint. Home: 4052 Seminary Rd Alexandria VA 22304 Office: No Telecom Fed Systems Inc 8614 Westwood Center Dr Vienna VA 22180

GALLAGHER, BERNARD PATRICK, editor, publisher; b. N.Y.C., Feb. 25, 1910; s. Bernard A. and Mary Helen (Fitzsimmons) G.; m. Harriet Denning, Oct. 17, 1942; 1 dau., Jill. Student, Columbia U., 1928-29, Akron U., 1941-44. Single-copy sales mgr. Crowell Pub. Co., 1932-34; sales mgr. charge sales tng. Stenotype Co., Inc., Chgo., 1934-39; pres. Stenotype Co. Ohio, Inc., Cleve., 1939-45, World Wide Publs. Inc., 1945-83, Gallagher Communications, Inc., 1974—; editor-in-chief pub. The Gallagher Report, 1952—, The Gallagher Presidents' Report, 1965—, Gallagher Med. Report, 1983—; pres. Gallagher Found., 1978—. Served with AUS, 1944-45. Mem. Southampton Assocs. Clubs: Canadian, Met. Office: The Gallagher Report Inc 230 Park Ave New York NY 10017

GALLAGHER, GERALD RAPHAEL, venture capitalist; b. Easton, Pa., Mar. 17, 1941; s. Gerald R. and Marjorie A. G.; m. Ellen Anne Mullane, Aug. 8, 1964; children: Ann Patrice, Gerald Patrick, Megan Ann. B.S. in Aero. Engring., Princeton U., 1963; M.B.A. (Exec. Club Chgo. fellow 1969), U. Chgo., 1969. Dir. strategic planning Metro-Goldwyn-Mayer, N.Y.C., 1969; v.p. Donaldson, Lufkin & Jenrette, N.Y.C., 1969-77; v.p. planning and control, then sr. v.p. planning and control Dayton Hudson Corp., Mpls., 1977-79; exec. v.p., chief adminstrv. officer subs. Mervyn's, Hayward, Calif.; then vice chmn., chief adminstrv. officer 1979-85, vice chmn., chief adminstrv. office parent co., 1985-87, also dir.; gen. ptnr. Oak Investments Ptnrs., Mpls., 1987—. Bd. regents St. John's U., Collegeville, Minn., 1978-87; mem. council for U. Chgo. Grad. Sch. Bus.; bd. dirs. Minn. Orch., Fairview Hosp. and Healthcare Services. Served with USN, 1963-67. Mem. N.Y. Soc. Security Analysts, Beta Gamma Sigma. Roman Catholic. Clubs: Princeton (N.Y.C.); Minneapolis; Interlachen Country. Office: Oak Investment Ptnrs 4550 Norwest Ctr 90 S 7th St Minneapolis MN 55402 *

GALLAGHER, JOSEPH A., banker; b. 1928; married. B.S., LaSalle Coll., 1950. With Indsl. Valley Bank & Trust Co., Phila., 1958—, pres., 1972-79, chmn., chief exec. officer, from 1979, dir.; chmn., dir. Fidelcor, Inc., Rosemont, Pa. Served to maj. USMC. Office: Fidelcor Inc Broad & Walnut Sts Philadelphia PA 19109 *

GALLAGHER, PHILIP MICHAEL, financial planner; b. Pitts., Aug. 14, 1940; s. Hugh P and Ann (Cannon) G.; Kathleen Graaff, Mar. 3, 1979; children: Meghan, Hugh. BA, St. Vincent Coll., Latrobe, Pa., 1962; STL, Gregorian U., Rome, 1966, postgrad., 1986; MEd, U. Pitts., 1972. Ordained priest Roman Cath. Ch., 1965; cert. fin. planner, 1983. Priest Roman Cath. Ch., 1966-78, laicized, 1978; fin. planner Allegheny Fin. Group, Pitts., 1978—; bd. dirs. Allegheny Fin. Group, Ltd., Pitts., Allegheny Investments, Ltd.. Contbr. articles to profl. jours. Chmn., bd. dirs. Pitts. Pastoral Inst., 1985—. Mem. Inst. Cert. Fin. Planners, Internat. Assn. Fin. Planners. Democrat. Home: 8171 Post Rd Pittsburgh PA 15101 Office: Allegheny Fin Group 3000 McKnight E Dr Pittsburgh PA 15237

GALLAGHER, RICHARD REYNOLDS, management consultant; b. Elizabeth, N.J., Feb. 22, 1931; s. Irving James and Mary K. (Keimig) G.; m. Dale Ruth Siam, July 13, 1967; children: Timothy Richard, Amy Ruth. BBS, Georgetown U., 1953; MBA, Seton Hall U., 1958; PhD (hon.), Tutor Coll., 1979, NYU; DBA (hon.), Ind. No. U. Prof. Rutgers U., Newark, 1967-70; bus. cons. Mgmt. Svcs., Inc., Greenville, S.C., 1970-80; prof. Bob Jones U., Greenville, 1970-74, Anderson (S.C.) Coll., 1974-80, Ocean County Coll., Toms River, 1982-87; pres. Tutor Coll. Svcs., Inc., Toms River, 1970—; exec. dir. Cons. in Am., Toms River, 1985—; small bus. cons. in field; advisor Am. Biographical Inst., Cambridge, Eng., 1987—, White House, SBA, Washington, 1974-88. Author: Small Business Made Simple, Bookkeeping Made Simple, 1986; asst. editor: Ocean County Bus. Today, 1988—, Western Views, 1988—. Mem. Cons. in Am. (v.p. 1985—), Univ. Profs. for Acad. Order (exec. bd. 1984—, 2nd v.p. 1982—, 1st v.p. 1989—). Home and Office: 107 France St Toms River NJ 08753

GALLAGHER, ROBERT MELVIN, publishing executive; b. Charlotte, N.C., Sept. 4, 1950; s. Edward Felix Jr. and Iva Lea (Graybeal) G.; m. Jacquelyn Emily Summey, Aug. 17, 1973; children: Sean, Kelly, Conor, Kevin, Brian. BA in Econs. and bus., Belmont Abbey Coll., 1972; JD, Samford U., 1975; LLM, Georgetown U., 1981. Asst. v.p., gen. counsel Goodwill, Inc., Gastonia, N.C., 1975-79, pres., chief exec. officer, 1984—; ptnr. Albright, Horowitz & Gallagher, Gastonia, 1980-84; pres. Goodwill Mgmt. Svcs., Gastonia, 1984—. Mem. Christian Legal Soc., 1976—; bd. dirs. Mary Dore Sch., Belmont, N.C., 1977-79, Gaston County Heart Assn., 1977-78, trustee, 1988—; mem. parish council St. Michael's Cath. Ch., 1978-79; mem. bd. advisors Belmont Abbey Coll., 1983—, mem. fin. com., 1985-87, trustee, 1988—. Mem. ABA, N.C. Bar Assn., Gaston County Bar Assn., Pi Gamma Mu. Republican. Roman Catholic. Office: Goodwill Inc 1520 S York Rd PO Box 269 Gastonia NC 28052

GALLAGHER, WILLIAM JOSEPH, equipment company executive; b. Beacon, N.Y., June 26, 1937; s. William J. and Helen A. (Robillard) G.; m. Patricia Lynn Hutchings, Aug. 5, 1961; children: Jennifer Anne Gallagher Herereg, Joan, Jeanne, Jane, William Jr. BS in Chem. Engring., U. Ill., 1961; postgrad., Purdue U., 1971-72. Registered profl. engr., Ill., Ind. Tech. services engr. Universal Oil Products Co., Des Plaines, Ill., 1961-66; process engr. Continental Oil Co., Lake Charles, La., 1966-68; plant mgr. Continental Oil Co., Hammond, Ind., 1968-72; v.p., gen. mgr. Browning Ferris Inc., Lemont, Ill., 1972-74; mfg. supt. Caterpillar, Inc., Mossville, Ill., 1974-79; purchasing mgr. Caterpillar, Inc., Peoria, Ill., 1979. Patentee neutralization apparatus. Republican. Roman Catholic. Office: Caterpillar Inc 100 NE Adams St Peoria IL 61629

GALLANT, WADE MILLER, JR., lawyer; b. Raleigh, N.C., Jan. 12, 1930; s. Wade Miller and Sallie Wesley (Jones) G.; m. Sandra Kirkham, Sept. 15, 1979. BA summa cum laude, Wake Forest U., 1952, JD cum laude, 1955. Bar: N.C. 1955. Since practiced in Winston-Salem, N.C.; ptnr. Womble, Carlyle, Sandridge & Rice, 1963—; bd. dirs. EuroCaribe Bank & Trust Co. Ltd., Brenner Cos., Inc., Piece Goods Shops Corp., Trinity Am. Corp.; lectr. continuing edn. N.C. Bar Found., 1966—. Contbr. articles to legal publs. Pres. Forsyth County Legal Aid Soc., 1963-67; assoc. Family and Child Service Agy., Winston-Salem, 1962-65, Winston-Salem Symphony Assn., 1965-66, Forsyth Mental Health Assn., 1972-73, N.C. Mental Health Assn., 1974-75; dir.-at-large Nat. Mental Health Assn., 1978-84, v.p., 1981-82; bd. dirs., exec. com. Blumenthal Jewish Home for the Aged Inc. Fellow Am. Bar Found. (life); mem. Internat. Bar Assn., N.C. Bar Assn., Forsyth County Bar Assn., Am. Counsel Assn. (hon.), Am. Law Inst., Old Town Club, Twin City Club, Piedmont Club, Bald Head Island (N.C.) Club, Phi Beta Kappa, Omicron Delta Kappa, Phi Delta Phi. Democrat. Episcopalian. Home: 2534 Warwick Rd Winston-Salem NC 27104 Office: Womble Carlyle Sandridge & Rice 2400 Wachovia Bldg Winston-Salem NC 27101

GALLARY, PETER HAYDEN, management consultant company executive; b. Waterbury, Conn., July 23, 1945; s. Edward Thomas and Mary (McGovern) G.; m. Patricia Anne Kattman, June 5, 1971; children: Hayden, Kyle. BS in Math., Fairfield U., 1967; MBA, Boston Coll., 1970. Project mgr. Hooker Chem., Grand Island, N.Y., 1969-82; ptnr. Touche, Ross & Co., Detroit, 1972-80, Coopers & Lybrand, Boston, 1980—; program chmn. Planning Exec. Inst., Boston, 1984-85. Mem. Planning Forum, Boston C. of C. (exec. club 1982—), Brae Burn Country Club, Dennis (Mass.) Yacht Club. Office: Coopers & Lybrand 1 Internat Pl Boston MA 02110

GALLAS, DANIEL O., oil pipeline company executive. BS, U. Okla., 1954. With Atlantic Richfield Co., 1954—; sr. v.p. ops. Arco Pipe Line Co., Independence, Kans., 1985-86, pres., 19876, also bd. dirs. Served to 1st lt. AUS. Office: ARCO Pipe Line Co 200 Arco Bldg Independence KS 67301

GALLELA, FRANCIS ANTHONY, forensic economist, business consultant; b. Harrisburg, Pa., Aug. 11, 1943; s. Michael Samuel and Pauline Elizebeth (Buela) G. BA in Econs., St. Francis Coll., Loretta, Pa., 1965; MBA in Fin., W.Va. U., 1967. Economist U.S. Dept. Commerce, Anchorage, 1972-74; bus. cons. Coopers & Lybrand, CPAs, Anchorage, 1974-80, Leonard Lane Assocs., Anchorage, 1980-81; owner, mgr., economist Francis Gallela & Assocs., Anchorage, 1981—; lectr. U. Alaska, Anchorage, 1973-74; dir. Minority Bus. Devel. Ctr., Anchorage, 1983-88. Author: Theory of Fund Accounting, 1979. Charter pres. N.W. Community Coun., Anchorage, 1977. Capt. USAF, 1967-72; lt. col. Alaska Air N.G., 1972—. Republican. Roman Catholic. Home and Office: 2440 Tagalak Dr Anchorage AK 99504

GALLERANO, ANDREW JOHN, retail company executive; b. Houston, Dec. 2, 1941; s. Andrew H. and Victoria J. (LaNasa) G.; m. Evelyn Cornelius, June 6, 1964; children: Kelly Lynn, Wendy Michelle. B.A., U. Tex., Austin, 1964; J.D., S. Tex. Coll. Law, 1968. Bar: Tex. 1968, U.S. Supreme Ct. 1973. Asst. atty. gen. State of Tex., 1968-71; regional atty. Montgomery Ward & Co., 1971-72; v.p. Foley's, div. Federated Dept. Stores Inc., 1972-79; v.p., gen. counsel, sec. Nat. Convenience Stores Inc., Houston, 1979—; adj. prof. S. Tex. Coll. Law, 1973-75. Pres. S. Tex. Hosp. Fin. Agy., 1979—; mem. devel. bd. U. Tex. Health Sci. Center, Houston, 1978—; mem. adv. council Tex. Hosp., 1984-85; bd. dirs. YMCA, 1973-86, Assn. Community TV, 1974-80. Served with USNR, 1959-65. Mem. Am. Soc. Corp. Secs., Tex. Bar Assn. (grievance com.), Houston Bar Assn., U. Tex. Ex-Students Assn., Houston Retail Mchts. Assn. (bd. dirs. 1973—, pres. 1976-78), Tax Research Assn. (bd. dirs. 1975—). Clubs: Houston; Headliner's (Austin). Home: 13515 St Mary's Ln Houston TX 77079 Office: Nat Convenience Stores Inc 100 Waugh Dr Houston TX 77007

GALLIGAN, JOHN DONALD, chemist; b. Washington, Oct. 9, 1932; s. Joseph Donald and Mary Theresa (Flaherty) G.; m. Audrey Field, Dec. 27, 1958; children: Martin, Dorothy, Monica, Thomas, Charles. B.S., Georgetown U., 1952, Manhattan Coll., 1955; postgrad., Emory U., 1956. Sr. chemist Harris Research Labs., Washington, 1957-61; project chemist Gillette Safety Razor Co., Boston, 1962-65; v.p. Gillette Research Inst., Rockville, Md., 1966-72; v.p. research and devel. Gillette Co., 1973-83; corp. group dir., v.p. research and devel. Gillette Co., Boston, 1983—. Patentee in field. Sec. D.C. Welfare Council, 1970-72; bd. dirs. Confrat. Christian Doctrine, 1962-64, 71-73. Mem. Soc. Cosmetic Chemists, Am. Chem. Soc., AAAS, Sakonnet Tacht Club, Pi Alpha. Office: The Gillette Co Boston Rsch & Devel Prudential Tower Bldg Boston MA 02199

GALLIGAN, THOMAS JOSEPH, III, retail footwear company executive; b. Syracuse, N.Y., Nov. 9, 1944; s. Thomas J. Jr. and Lauretta (Durkin) G.; m. Ann Costello, June 3, 1972; children: Kathleen, Gregory, William, Elizabeth. BS in Biology, Boston Coll., 1966; MBA in Fin., Harvard U., 1971. CPA, N.Y. Acct. Arthur Young & Co., N.Y.C., 1971-76; dir. corp. acctg. PepsiCo Inc., Purchase, N.Y., 1976-78, asst. controller, 1978-79; v.p., chief fin. officer PepsiCola Bottling Group, Purchase, N.Y., 1979-81, PepsiCo Internat., Purchase, 1981-84; sr. v.p., treas., chief fin. officer Morse Shoe Inc., Canton, Mass., 1984—, also bd. dirs. Served to 1st lt. U.S. Army, 1966-69, Vietnam. Mem. Treasurers' Club Boston, Fin. Execs. Inst., Am. Mgmt. Assn. (fin. council). Clubs: Harvard, Commercial (Boston). Office: Morse Shoe Inc 555 Turnpike St Canton MA 02021

GALLIHER, KEITH EDWIN, JR., lawyer; b. Fond du Lac, Wis., July 29, 1947; s. Keith Edwin and Dolores Mae (Hazen) G.; m. Linda Lee Dessauer, May 18, 1985; children: Patrick, Christy Lyn. B.S, U. Nev. at Las Vegas, 1970; J.D., Ariz. State U., 1974. Bar: Nev. 1974, U.S. Dist. Ct. Nev. 1974, U.S. Ct. Appeals (9th cir.) 1976. Assoc. Lionel, Sawyer & Collins., Las Vegas, 1974-75; atty. Clark County Pub. Defender, Las Vegas, 1975-76; sr. ptnr. Mills, Galliher, Lukens, Gibson, Schwartzer & Shinehouse, Las Vegas, 1976-80, Galliher & Tratos, Las Vegas, 1980-83; pres., sr. ptnr. Keith E. Galliher, Jr., Chartered, Las Vegas, 1983—; instr. hotel law U. Nev.-Las Vegas, 1980; alt. mcpl. judge City Las Vegas, 1983—. Author: Supplement to Comparison Analysis of ABA Criminal Justice Standards to Nevada Law, 1976. State del. Democratic Party, 1976; bd. govs. March of Dimes, Las Vegas, 1978. Mem. Nat. Assn. Trial Lawyers, Nev. Trial Lawyers Assn., ABA, Nev. Bar Assn., Clark County Bar Assn., State Bar Nev. (mem. fee dispute com. 1983), Comml. Law League Am., Real Estate Securities and Syndication Inst., Nat. Coll. Criminal Def. Lawyers and Pub. Defenders. Lutheran. Home: 6855 Stone Dr Las Vegas NV 89110 Office: 1850 E Sahara Ave Suite 100 Las Vegas NV 89104

GALLINARO, NICHOLAS FRANCIS, business executive; b. Somerville, Mass., Feb. 25, 1930; s. Joseph Michael and Mary Marie (Valerio) G.; B.A., Boston Coll., 1952, M.B.A., 1964; B.S. in Mech. Engring., Notre Dame U., 1953; m. Inez Hanken, July 27, 1957; children—Michael J., James J., Stephen P., Robert N. With Clark Equipment Corp, Battle Creek & Benton Harbor, Mich., 1951-53; v.p., Harnischfeger Internat, Corp., Milw., Wis., 1953-63; v.p., dir. McLaughlin Equipment Corp., N.Y.C., 1963-71; v.p., dir. Prudential Internat. Corp., N.Y.C., 1971-72; pres. GAR Internat. Corp., GAR Equipment Corp., South Plainfield, N.J., 1972—; chmn. bd. CIMAT S.r.l., Milan Italy. Trustee, Christian Brothers Acad. Served with USMC, 1949-51. Mem. Soc. Am. Mil. Engrs., N.Y. World Trade Assn., Pan Am. Soc., Am. Mining Congress, Associated Equipment Distbrs. Republican. Roman Catholic. Clubs: K.C., Navesink Country. Home: 31 Esshire Dr Middletown NJ 07748 Office: 3005 Hadley Rd S Plainfield NJ 07080

GALLIPO, JAMES JOSEPH, treasurer; b. Rutland, Vt., Apr. 26, 1946; s. Francis W. Gallipo; m. Lynne N. Noble; children: Jay Michael, Courtney Lynne. BS, U. Vt., 1968. CPA, Vt., R.I. Staff acct. 1968-69, 71-72, Joseph Saunders, CPA, Manchester, Vt., 1972-73; treas. John A. Russell Corp., Rutland, Vt., 1973—. Auditor Town of Wallingford, Vt., 1974-79. Served to capt. U.S. Army, 1969-71, ETO. Mem. Rotary (pres., treas. 1980-82). Office: John A Russell Corp 117 Strongs Ave Rutland VT 05701

GALLMAN, CLARENCE HUNTER, textile executive; b. Rock Hill, S.C., Jan. 3, 1922; s. Clarence Calhoun and Hattie (Wood) G.; m. Beatrice Byers; children: Martha Gallman Alewine, Thomas Clarence. BS in Textile Engring., Clemson U., 1943. Various positions with J.P. Stevens, Greenville, S.C. and N.Y.C., 1943-80; sr. v.p. corp. mfg. M. Lowenstein Corp., N.Y.C., 1980-87; group v.p. domestics mfg. Springs Industries, Ft. Mill, S.C., 1987-88, ret., 1988; pres. C. Hunter Gallman Mgmt. Svcs., Greer, S.C., 1988—; bd. dirs. Textile Hall, Greenville. Mem. J.E. Sirrine Textile Found., Greenville. Served to capt. U.S. Army. Recipient Exec. of Yr. award Assn. Textile Indsl. Engrs., 1982, Chapman award So. Textile Assn., 1985. Mem. S.C. Textile Mfg. Assn. (pres. 1985-86, textile leader of yr. award 1984), Nat. Air Craft Owners & Pilots Assn. Baptist. Clubs: Greenville Gun, Beechcraft Aero. Lodges: Rotary, Masons, Elks. Office: C Hunter Gallman Mgmt Svcs 125 E Poinsett St PO Box 929 Greer SC 29652

GALLO, VINCENT JOHN, financial planner; b. N.Y.C., Aug. 13, 1943; s. Nicholas and Catherine (Vitiello) G.; m. Blanche Marie Poplin, Apr. 15, 1972; children: Steven, Mark. BA, U. Dayton, 1965. Registered fin. planner; CLU; Chartered Fin. Cons. Mgr. methods engring. Daniel Internat. Corp., Greenville, S.C., 1971-75; exec. v.p. Am. Ind. Elec. Contractors Assn., Arlington, Tex., 1975-77; pres. Vincent J. Gallo & Assocs., Inc., Winston-Salem, N.C., 1977—; adj. instr. Am. Coll., Bryn Mawr, Pa., 1984-86; dir. advanced mktg. Snavely Fin. Group, Winston-Salem, 1985—. Served to capt. USAF, 1966-71. Mem. Am. Soc. CLU's and Chartered Fin. Consultants (continuing edn. chmn. 1984), Million Dollar Roundtable Investment Advisor, Internat. Assn. Fin. Planners, Nat. Assn. Securities Dealers, Mensa. Home: 8800 Harwich Ct Clemmons NC 27012 Office: Vincent J Gallo & Assocs Inc Drawer 2499 Winston-Salem NC 27102

GALLOGLY, BARRY ANDREW, banker, lawyer; b. Bklyn., Dec. 14, 1952; s. Andrew Frances and Bridget Veronica (McConville) G. BA, Baruch Coll., 1975; JD, Bklyn. Law Sch., 1980. Bar: N.Y., 1981; U.S. Dist. Ct. (ea. dist.) 1981. V.p. Mfrs. Hanover trust, N.Y.C., 1979-83, Tullet and Tokyo Ltd., N.Y.C., 1983-84; first v.p., treas. N.Y. br. Bank Leu, Ltd., N.Y.C., 1984—. Mem. ABA, N.Y. State Bar Assn., Bklyn. Bar Assn., Inst. Fgn. Bankers. Democrat. Roman Catholic. Office: Bank Leu Ltd 65 E 55th St New York NY 10022

GALLOGLY, JAMES JOHN, healthcare executive, financier; b. N.Y.C., May 24, 1948; m. Janice Trupiano, July 29, 1966; children: Lori, James, Mike. BBA, Manhattan Coll., 1969. Cost acct. Johnson & Johnson Co., New Brunswick, N.J., 1970-74, mktg. controller, 1974-77; plant controller Johnson & Johnson Co., Athens, Ga., 1977-79; group controller Johnson & Johnson Co., Solon, Ohio, 1979-81; v.p. fin. and mgmt. info. systems Richards Med. Co., Memphis, 1981-83, pres., microsurgery div., 1984-88; pres., chief exec. officer Resound Corp., Palo Alto, Calif., 1988—. Served with USAR, 1970-75. Mem. Health Industry Mfg. Assn. Home: 1930 Idyllwild Ave Redwood City CA 94061 Office: Resound Corp 1075 Lassen Dr Menlo Park CA 94025

GALLOWAY, DAVID ALEXANDER, publishing company executive; b. Toronto, Ont., Can., Nov. 1, 1943; s. Robert and Dorothy Elizabeth (Kennedy) G.; m. Judy K. Clarkson, June 10, 1966; children: Andrew, Stephanie. BA, U. Toronto, 1966; MBA, Harvard U., 1968. Mktg. profl. Gen. Foods Corp., Toronto, 1968-71; ptnr. Can. Consulting Group, Toronto, 1971-80; v.p. corp. devel. Torstar Corp., Toronto, 1980-81, exec. v.p., 1981-82; pres. Harlequin Enterprises, Ltd., Toronto, 1983-84, chief exec. officer, 1984; pres. Torstar Book Pub. and Direct Mktg. Div., Toronto, 1985—; also chmn. bd. dirs. Torstar Corp., Toronto; Bd. dirs. TV Ont. Clubs: Badminton & Racquet; Caledon; Toronto. Home: 20 Chestnut Park Rd, Toronto, ON Canada M4W 1W6 Office: Torstar Corp, 1 Yonge St, Toronto, ON Canada M5E 1P9 also: Silhouette Books 300 E 42nd St New York NY 10017 other: Harlequin Enterprises Ltd, 225 Duncan Mill Rd, Don Mills, ON Canada M3B 3K9

GALLOWAY, HARVEY SCOTT, JR., insurance company executive; b. Middletown, Ohio, Jan. 30, 1934; s. Harvey Scott and Clara (Sherman) G.; m. Virginia Lee Williams, June 13, 1953; children: Jill, Julie, Scott. BA, Olivet Coll., 1955; postgrad., Drake U., 1955-57. With Southland Life Ins. Co., Dallas, 1957-69, asst. v.p., assoc. actuary, 1957-69; group actuary Nationwide Ins. Co., Columbus, Ohio, 1969-71; actuary Nat. Svcs. Inc., Columbus, 1971-72; v.p. Nationwide Corp., Columbus, 1972-81; v.p. chief actuary Nationwide Life and Nationwide Corp., Columbus, 1981-83, sr. v.p., chief actuary, 1983—; sr. v.p., chief life actuary Farmland Life Ins. Co., Dem Moines, 1982—; bd. dirs. PEBSCO; pres., bd. dir. Nat. Health Care Corp., Columbus, 1989—; bd. dirs., Health Matrix Corp., Nat. Premium & Benefit

Svcs. Corp., 1983—; sr. v.p., chief actuary Nationwide Mut. Fire Ins. Co., Nationwide Gen. Ins. Co., Nationwide Property & Casualty Ins. Co., 1989—. Served with USAR, 1958. Fellow Soc. Actuaries (chmn. credit ins. com. 1979-83); mem. Am. Acad. Actuaries, Tri-State Actuarial Club, S.W. Actuaries Club (sec. 1968-69), U.S. Power Squadron, Columbus Actuarial Club. Office: Nationwide Ins Co One Nationwide Pla Columbus OH 43216

GALLUPS, VIVIAN LYLAY BESS, federal agency administrator; b. Vicksburg, Miss., Jan. 14, 1954; d. Vann Foster and Lylay Vivian (Stanley) Bess; m. Ordice Alton Gallups, Jr., July 12, 1975. BA, Birmingham So. Coll., 1975, MA in Mgmt., 1985; MA in Edn., U. Ala., Birmingham, 1975. Counselor Columbia (S.C.) Coll., 1975-76; case mgr. S.C. Dept. Social Services, Lexington, 1976; benefit authorizer, payment determination specialist then recovery reviewer Social Security Adminstrn., Birmingham, 1977-85; contract adminstr. U.S. Dept. Def., Birmingham, 1985—. Hospice vol. Bapt. Med. Ctr.-Montclair, Birmingham, 1982; trustee, treas. Resurrection House, Birmingham, 1984-85; vol. counselor Cathedral Ch. of Advent, Birmingham, 1987. Mem. Nat. Contract Mgmt. Assn. (chpt. sec. 1987), Nat. Cathedral Assn., Ala. Zool. Soc. Episcopalian. Home: 566 12th Ct PO Box 126 Pleasant Grove AL 35127-0126 Office: US Dept Def Def Logistics Agy 2121 8th Ave N Suite 104 Birmingham AL 35203

GALSON, STEVEN PAUL, consulting company executive; b. Wilkes-Barre, Pa., Dec. 17, 1928; s. Harry S. and Julia (Letukas) G.; BA in Math. and Psychology, NYU, 1951; m. Paula Fisher, Feb. 15, 1947; children: Julianna, Linda Ann. Statis. analyst Nat. Bur. Casualty Underwriters, N.Y.C., 1951-57; supr. statis. ops. Ins. Rating Bd., N.Y.C., 1957-63; mgr. EDP, Ins. Data Processing Center, N.Y.C., 1963-72; v.p. EDP services Ins. Svcs. Office, N.Y.C., 1972-79; v.p. EDP svcs. Group Health Inc., N.Y.C., 1979-85; pres. Cameo Research Ltd., 1986-88, chmn. bd., 1988—; pres. Comprehensive Bldg. Inspection Svcs., 1986—. Mem. Nat. Rep. Com. Served with USMC, 1946-48. Decorated 2 Purple Hearts, Navy Cross; named to Aviation Hall of Fame. Mem. N.Y. Acad. Scis., GUIDE. Roman Catholic. Home: 10746 Stonebridge Blvd Boca Raton FL 33498 Office: CBIS 2440 SE Federal Hwy Regency Sq Ste L Stuart FL 33994

GALUP, LUIS NEMESIO, medical laboratory executive, pathologist; b. Lima, Peru, Oct. 19, 1936; came to U.S., 1963; s. Luis Enrique and Ines (Fernandez Concha) G.; m. Sara Canales, Dec. 28, 1963 (div. Dec. 1982); children: Luis Enrique, Cecilia; m. Leslie Topping, Mar. 25, 1983; children: Mark Alexander, Evan Elyse. Student, U. Buenos Aires, 1954-56; MD, U. Nat. Mayor San Marcos, 1963. Pathologist South Bend Med. Found., Inc., Ind., 1967—, med. dir., 1976—, pres., 1981—; clin. assoc. prof. pathology Ind. U. Sch. Medicine, 1980—; adj. assoc. profl. microbiology dept., U. Notre Dame, South Bend, 1980—. Served to maj., M.C., U.S. Army, 1969-71. Mem. AMA, Am. Soc. Clin. Pathology, Coll. Am. Pathology, Ind. State Med. Assn., Ind. Assn. Pathologists. Office: South Bend Med Found Inc 530 N Lafayette Blvd South Bend IN 46601-1098

GALVIN, MADELINE SHEILA, lawyer; b. N.Y.C., Jan. 31, 1948; d. Rod Sheil and Madeline (Twiss) G. BA cum laude with highest honors, Russell Sage Coll., 1970; JD, Albany Law Sch., 1973. Bar: N.Y. 1974, U.S. Dist. Ct. (no. dist.) N.Y. 1974, U.S. Supreme Ct. 1978; cert. parliamentarian, lic. real estate broker. Atty. N.Y. State Dept. Law, Albany, 1973-74; sr. atty. Dormitory Authority State of N.Y., Elsmere, 1974-78; sole practice, Delmar, N.Y., 1974—. Bd. dirs., mem. endowment com., mem. exec. bd. YMCA, Albany, 1980-86; bd. dirs. Mercy House, 1980-83, v.p., 1981-82; mem. fin. com. Ronald McDonald House, 1981-83; mem. alumni bd. Doane Stuart Sch., 1988—; mem. Bethlehem Zoning Bd. Appeals; Rep. committeeman 15th dist. Town of Bethlehem, vice chmn. land use mgmt. adv. com., 1989—. Kellas scholar, 1967-70. Mem. AAUW (recognition cert. Albany br., pres. 1983-84), Nat. Assn. Parliamentarians, ABA, N.Y. State Bar Assn. (numerous coms.), Albany County Bar Assn., N.Y. State Trial Lawyers Assn., Albany Claims Assn., Women's Bar Assn., Albany Law Sch. Alumni Assn., N.Y. Geneal. and Biog. Soc., Strafford Hist. Soc., Russell Sage Coll. Alumni Assn. (pres. 1983-87, pres. bd. dirs., 1987-88), Albany Inst. History and Art, DAR (regent 1980-82, bd. dirs.), Bethlehem C. of C., Capital Dist. Trial Lawyers Assn., Bus. and Profl. Women Assn., Athenian Honor Soc., Russell Sage Coll. Alumni Assn. (pres. 1983-87, bd. dirs. 1987—, past pres.), NYU Club, Zonta (Albany), Union U. Outing Club, Doane Stuart Sch. Alumni Assn. (bd. dirs. 1988—), Phi Alpha Theta. Roman Catholic. Office: 217 Delaware Ave Delmar NY 12054

GALVIN, ROBERT W., electronics executive; b. Marshfield, Wis., Oct. 9, 1922. Student, U. Notre Dame, U. Chgo.; LL.D. (hon.), Quincy Coll., St. Ambrose Coll., DePaul U., Ariz. State U. With Motorola, Inc., Chgo., 1940—, exec. v.p., 1948-56, pres., from 1956, chmn. bd., 1964—, chief exec. officer, 1964-86, also dir. Former mem. Pres.'s Commn. on Internat. Trade and Investment.; chmn. industry policy adv. com. to U.S. Trade Rep.; mem. Pres.'s Pvt. Sector Survey; chmn. Pres.'s Adv. Council on Pvt. Sector Initiatives; chmn. Ill. Inst. Tech., U. Notre Dame; bd. dirs. Jr. Achievement Chgo. Served with Signal Corps, AUS, World War II. Named Decision Maker of Yr. Chgo. Assn. Commerce and Industry-Am. Statis. Assn., 1973; Sword of Loyola award Loyola U., Chgo.; Washington award Western Soc. Engrs., 1984. Mem. Electronic Industries Assn. (pres. 1966, dir., Medal of Honor 1970, Golden Omega award 1981). Office: Motorola Inc 1303 E Algonquin Rd Schaumburg IL 60196 *

GAMACHE, RICHARD DONALD, business development executive; b. Fall River, Mass., Aug. 30, 1935; s. Armand Wilfred and Imelda (Gagnon) G.; m. Kathleen Florence Smith, Nov. 22, 1958; children: Mariette, Nanette, Lisette. BS, St. Peter's Coll., 1958. Account exec. Harold Shore Assocs., N.Y.C., 1965-67; v.p. Van Dyck Corp., Southport, Conn., 1967-69; pres. Shippan Corp., Stamford, Conn., 1969; pres. INNOTECH. Corp., Trumbull, Conn., 1969—, chmn., 1985—. Contbg. author Handbook for Creative and Innovative Managers, 1988, New Directions in Creative and Innovative Management, 1988; contbr. numerous articles to profl. jours. Mem. Creative Edn. Found. Served to 1st lt. U.S. Army, 1959-60. Mem. World Future Soc. Home: 3200 Park Ave Bridgeport CT 06604 Office: INNOTECH Corp 2285 Reservoir Ave Trumbull CT 06611

GAMARCI, JORGE LUIS, international banker; b. Concordia, Argentina, Nov. 14, 1944; came to U.S., 1970; s. Geronimo Luis and Sara Obdulia (Roza) G. m. Elisea Beatriz von Reihs, Aug. 6, 1969; children: Juliet, George Lee. B in Acctg., Escuela Superior de Comercio, Santa Fe, Argentina, 1960; diploma, Am. Inst. Banking, 1971; diploma in Banking, Rutgers U., 1975; grad. Program Mgmt. Devel., Harvard U., 1979. V.p., mgr. Lloyds Bank Internat. Ltd., Chgo., 1977-78; sr. v.p., mgr. Lloyds Bank Internat. Ltd., N.Y.C., 1979-82; sr. v.p., internat. treas. Bank Montreal, N.Y.C., 1982-83; exec. v.p., dep. gen.mgr. Lloyds Bank PLC, N.Y.C., 1983-86, exec. v.p., gen. mgr., 1986—; chmn., chief exec. officer Lloyds govt. Securities Corp., N.Y.C., 1987—; bd. dirs. subs. Lloyds Bank Group, USA, Eng., other countries. Mem. Greenwich County Club, Greenwich Skating Club. Roman Catholic. Office: Lloyds Bank PLC 199 Water St New York NY 10038

GAMBEE, ROBERT RANKIN, investment banker; b. N.Y.C., Aug. 26, 1942; s. A. Sumner and Eleanor Elizabeth (Brown) G. Grad. Phillips Exeter Acad.; AB, Princeton U., 1964; MBA, Harvard U., 1966. Assoc. corp. fin. White, Weld & Co., N.Y.C., 1966-71, v.p., 1971-73; v.p. Schroder Capital Corp. affiliate J. Henry Schroder Wagg-London, N.Y.C., 1973-78; v.p. Atlantic Capital Corp. affiliate Deutsche Bank, Frankfurt and Dusseldorf, Germany, 1978-84; 1st v.p. Deutsche Bank Capital Corp., 1985—. Trustee Dwight-Englewood Sch. 1978-85; v.p. Apollo, Atlas, Hercules, Hermes, Mercury, Olympus, Orion, Pegasus, Taurus, Titan and Zeus Instl. Investments, Inc.; v.p., sec., treas. The Germany Fund, Inc. Author, photographer: Nantucket Island, 1973, rev. edit., 1974, 81, paper edit., 1978, 87, color edits., 1986, 88, Manhattan Seascape: Waterside Views Around New York, 1975, Exeter Impressions (intro. by Nathaniel Benchley), 1980, Princeton in Color (intro. by Robert F. Goheen), 1987, paper edit., 1988, A Wall Street Christmas, 1989. Mem. Princeton Alumni Assn. Nantucket (gov.). Republican. Presbyterian. Clubs: Nantucket Yacht; University, Princeton (gov.), City Midday, Downtown Athletic (N.Y.C.); Englewood. Home: 1230 Park Ave New York NY 10028 Office: Deutsche Bank Capital Corp 52d St New York NY 10019

GAMBILL, MALCOLM W., metal products company executive; married. B.S., Yale U. With Harsco Corp., 1955—, v.p. Heckett div., 1967-69, div. v.p. internat. ops., 1969-73, div. sr. v.p. ops., 1973-85, div. pres., 1975—, corp. exec. v.p., 1984-85, corp. pres., chief exec. officer, 1987—, also dir. Served to 1st lt. USMC. Office: Harsco Corp PO Box 8888 Camp Hill PA 17011 *

GAMBILL, TED RONALD, insurance company executive; b. Sullivan, Ind., May 17, 1948; s. Wendell L. and Mary L. (Dietz) G.; m. Rosemary Lloyd, June 6, 1971; children: Jill Michelle, Lindsey Suzanne. BSE, Ind. State U., 1970; MBA, Ind. U., Indpls., 1979. Personnel specialist Meridian Ins., Indpls., 1971-74, mgr. compensation adminstrn., 1974-76, mgr. manpower planning. and devel., 1976-79, mgr. underwriting staff svcs., 1979-80, mgr. personal lines underwriting and auto project team, 1980-81, dir. underwriting, 1981-84, v.p., 1983-86, dir. sales, 1984-86, exec. v.p. adminstrv. ops., 1986-88, exec. v.p. ins. ops., 1988—; acting mgr. Meridian Security Ins. Co., Indpls., 1979-80. Contbr. articles to pubs. in field. Sr. lay leader Carmel United Meth. Ch., 1983—, mission interpretation trip to Africa, So. Ind. Meth. Conf., 1984; active Cen. Ind. United Drive, 1988; v.p., Village of Mt. Carmel Homeowners Assn., 1981, pres. 1982-84). Hamilton County Mens' Doubles Tennis Champion, 1984, Hamilton County League's Mixed Doubles Champion, 1977. Mem. Indpls. Ams., Indpls. C. of C. (membership drive, co-chmn. local issues com. 1989, United Way 1988). Home: 1501 Brookmill Ct Carmel IN 46032 Office: Meridian Ins Co 2955 N Meridan St Indianapolis IN 46206

GAMBINO, S(ALVATORE) RAYMOND, medical laboratory executive, educator; b. N.Y.C., Oct. 13, 1926; s. Salvatore Benedict and Rose (Ragona) G.; m. Madeline Russo, Apr. 5, 1953; children: Catherine Rose Garroni, Stephen Raymond. BS, Antioch Coll., 1948; MD, U. Rochester, 1952. Diplomate Am. Bd. Pathology. Labs. dir. Englewood (N.J.) Hosp., 1961-68; prof. pathology Columbia U., N.Y.C., 1968-82; dir. chemistry labs. Presbyn. Hosp., N.Y.C., 1968-77; labs. dir. St. Luke's-Roosevelt Hosp., 1978-82; chief med. officer, exec. v.p. MetPath, Inc., Teterboro, N.J., 1983—, also bd. dirs.; adj. prof. pathology Columbia U., N.Y.C., 1983—; bd. dirs. Hazelton, Vienna, Va., 1987—, Ciba Corning Diagnostics, Medfield, Mass., 1988—; mem. Corning (N.Y.) Mgmt. Group, Corning, 1984—. Co-author: Beyond Normality, 1975; editor: (newsletter) Lab Report for Physicians, 1979—. Mem. Englewood Cliffs (N.J.) Sch. Bd., 1966-69. Served with U.S. Navy, 1945-46. Mem. Am. Soc. Clin. Pathologists (editor check sample program 1968—), Alpha Omega Alpha. Roman Catholic. Office: MetPath Inc One Malcolm Ave Teterboro NJ 07608

GAMBLE, JOHN LEE, industrial engineer, production executive; b. Van Wert, Ohio, Nov. 30, 1958; s. Max Leroy Gamble and Mary Lou (Ringwald) Butler; m. Beth Ellen Keber, June 22, 1984; 1 child, Philip John. BS in Indsl. Tech., Ohio U., 1981; postgrad., Pfeiffer Coll., 1981—. Indsl. engr. Aeroquip Corp., Van Wert, 1981-84, sr. indsl. engr., 1984-86; prod. engring. mgr. Aeroquip Corp., Noorwood, N.C., 1986-87, prodn. mgr., 1987—. Mem. Van West City Council, 1986. Republican. Roman Catholic. Lodge: Sertoma (bd. dirs. 1982-86). Home: 25293 Stony Mountain Rd Albemarle NC 28001 Office: Aeroquip Corp Rte 3 PO Box 50H Norwood NC 28128

GAMBLE, THEODORE ROBERT, JR., investment banker; b. St. Louis, Sept. 18, 1953; s. Theodore Robert and Rispah Adele (Dowse) G.; m. Susan Lee Stupin, Mar. 3, 1984. AB, Princeton U., 1975; MArch, Harvard U., 1977, MBA, 1979. Assoc. Morgan Stanley & Co., Inc., N.Y.C., 1979-84, v.p., 1984-86, prin., 1986-87; pres. The Prescott Group, Inc., N.Y.C., 1987—. Bd. dirs., exec. v.p. greater N.Y. councils Boy Scouts Am.; trustee N.Y. Hist. Soc.; co-chmn. adv. com. real estate devel. grad. sch. design Harvard U.; visiting com., bus. com. Met. Mus. Art. Mem. Urban Land Inst., Real Estate Bd. N.Y., Internat. Council Shopping Ctrs., Young Mortgage Bankers Assn. Republican. Episcopalian. Clubs: River, Racquet & Tennis, University, Knickerbocker, The Links, Doubles, Harvard, Princeton (bd. govs., exec. com., treas.) (N.Y.C.); Harvard (Boston); City Club of Miami. Home: 860 United Nations Pla New York NY 10017 Office: The Prescott Group Inc 767 Fifth Ave New York NY 10153

GAMET, DONALD MAX, appliance company executive; b. Mapleton, Kans., Feb. 21, 1916; s. Carl Adolph and Pearl May (McClanahan) G.; m. L. Pauline Fleming, Apr. 14, 1938 (dec. Dec. 1981); children: Merilyn Kay Gamet Paris, Carleton Lenoir, Kathy Lynn Gamet Stephenson; m. Marilyn Lang, Jan. 15, 1983. BBA, Ft. Hays State Coll., 1938; MBA, U. Kans., 1939, JD, 1942. CPA, Mo. Staff acct. Arthur Andersen & Co., Kansas City, Mo., 1942-46, mgr., 1946-54, ptnr., 1954-78, mng. ptnr. Kansas City office, 1956-70; vice chmn. tax practices Arthur Andersen & Co., Chgo., 1970-77, sr. ptnr., 1977-78; cons. Kansas City, 1978-84; v.p.-treas. Chgo. Pacific Corp., 1984-85, exec. v.p. fin., 1985-87, spl. cons. to chief exec. officer, 1987—; bd. dirs. Am. Carriers Inc., Overland Park, Kans. Pres., chmn. bd. dirs. Heart Am. United Funds, Met. Kansas City, 1967-68, chmn. spl. reorgn. study com., 1980-84; mem. adv. bd. Salvation Army Kansas City, 1982-84; mem. personnel com. Village United Presbyn. Ch., 1982-84; pres., bd. dirs. Estate Planning Council Kans., 1962-63, Minority Supplier's Devel. Council Kansas City, 1983-84; bd. dirs., mem. exec. com., treas. Civic Council Kansas City, 1967-70; bd. dirs., chmn. long range planning com. Geriatic Resources Corp. Kansas City, 1982-84; bd. dirs. Metro Kansas City C. of C., 1962-70, pres., 1969-70; bd. dirs. Kansas City Indsl. Found., 1968-70, Jr. Achievement Kansas City, 1960-65. Named Boss of Yr., Met. Kansas City Jaycees, 1962; recipient Alumni Achievement award Ft. Hays State Coll., 1969. Mem. Am. Inst. CPA's. Republican. Clubs: Kansas City (bd. dirs.); University (Chgo.). Home: 8721 Catalina Dr Prairie Village KS 66207 Office: Chgo Pacific Corp 200 S Michigan Ave Chicago IL 60604

GAMEY, RONALD KENNETH, transportation executive; b. Victoria, B.C., Canada, Aug. 6, 1945; s. Kenneth J. and Helga I. (Franzen) G.; m. Nancye J. Walker; 1 child, Tyler. BA in Math. with honors, U. Victoria, 1967; MBA in Fin. and Transp., U. B.C., 1969. With Canadian Pacific Ltd., 1969—; research analyst Canadian Pacific, Montreal, 1969-71; ops. analyst Canadian Pacific Rail, Vancouver, 1971-73, mgr. analysis and planning projects, 1973-74; dir. spl. projects office chmn. and pres. Canadian Pacific Ltd., Montreal, 1974-75; mgr. mktg. planning and econ. analysis Canadian Pacific Bermuda, 1975-76, gen. mgr., 1976-79, v.p., 1983-85, also bd. dirs.; mng. dir. ship mgmt. services div. Canadian Pacific Steamships Ltd., London, 1979-84; pres., chief exec. officer Canadian Pacific Bulkship Services Ltd., London, 1984-85; group v.p. Canadian Pacific Ltd., Calgary, 1985-88; exec. v.p. Canadian Pacific Ltd., Toronto, 1988—; bd. dirs. Arion Ins. Co. Ltd., CNCP Telecommunications, Can. Maritime Agys. Ltd., Canadian Pacific Express and Transport, Canadian Pacific Hotels, CanPac Internat. Freight Services Inc., Laidlaw Transp. Ltd., Marathon Realty Co. Ltd., Telecommunications Terminal Systems, Soo Line Corp., The Standard Steamship Owners' Protection and Indemnity Assoc. (Bermuda) Ltd., The Standard Steamship Owners' Mut. War Risk Assoc., The Brittania Steamship Ins. Assoc. Ltd.; mem. C.D. Howe Inst. Clubs: Bow Valley (Calgary); Montreal Racquet; L'Hotel Recreation (Toronto). Home: 86 Glen Rd, Toronto, ON Canada M4W 2V6 Office: 123 Front St W Ste 800, Toronto, ON Canada M5J 2M8 also: Can Pacific Ltd, PO Box 6042 Sta A, Montreal, PQ Canada H3C 3E4

GAMMELL, GLORIA RUFFNER, sales executive; b. St. Louis, June 19, 1948; d. Robert Nelson and Antonia Ruffner; m. Doyle M. Gammell, Dec. 11, 1973. AA in Art, Harbor Coll., Harbor City, Calif., 1969; BA in Sociology, Calif. State U., Long Beach, 1971. Cert. fin. planner. Bus. analyst Dun & Bradstreet Inc., Los Angeles, 1971-81; rep. sales Van Nuys, Calif., 1981-86; v.p., sec. bd. dirs. Gammell Industries, Paramount, Calif., 1986—. Mem. Anne Banning Assistance League, Hollywood, Calif., 1981-82; counselor YWCA, San Pedro, Calif., 1983-84; fundraiser YMCA, San Pedro, 1984-85; mem. womens adv. com. Calif. State Assembly, 1984-86. Recipient Best in the West Presdl. Citation, 1981-86. Home: 991 Channel St San Pedro CA 90731

GAMMIE, ANTHONY PETRIE, pulp and paper manufacturing company executive; b. London, Dec. 17, 1934; married. With Bowater U.K., from 1955, mgr., 1970-75, chmn. bd., mng. dir., from 1975; with Bowater, Inc., Darien, Conn., 1978—, now chmn., pres., chief exec. officer, dir. Office: Bowater Inc 1 Parklands Dr Box 4012 Darien CT 06820

GAMMILL, DARRYL CURTIS, business executive; b. Milw., Jan. 20, 1950; s. Lawrence H. and Eunice G. (Birkett) G.; BS, U. Colo., 1973; m. Maureen Mulcahy, Sept. 16, 1972; children: Rebecca, Bridgett, Maureen, Bryann. Lic. Gen. Prin., Fin. Prin., Registered Options Prin., Sr. Compliance Officer, Registered Rep., SEC, registerd investment advisor, broker dealer, SEC. Stockbroker, Douglas, Stanat, Inc., Denver, 1974; dir. research Pittman Co., Denver, 1975; option specialist B.J. Leonard & Co., Denver, 1976; v.p. research, corp. fin. Neidiger, Tucker Bruner, Denver, 1977; chmn., pres., chief exec. officer G.S. Omni Corp., 1979-82; chmn., chief exec. officer Gammill and Co., 1981—; mng. broker GSI Ltd., 1988—; mng. ptnr. G.S. Oil, G.S. Leasing; dir. Valudyne, Inc., 1973-79; pres. Chalton Investment Services; chmn., pres. Fusion Mgmt. Corp., 1981-83; chmn. Applied Fusion Research & Tech. Corp., 1982, Pres. Research Mgmt., 1984; gen. partner Fusion Ltd. Trustee Gammill Found.; pres. Platinium Club Inc., 1985—; founder AudioOptics. Founder Nicholas R. Massano Ednl. Scholarship, 1985; co-founder Opera Colo. Mem. Fin. Analysts Fedn., Nat. Assn. Security Dealers, Denver Soc. Security Analysts, IEEE, Am. Nuclear Soc., Nat. Energy Assn. (nat. chmn.), U.S. Ski Assn. Clubs: Optimists, Elks. Contbr. articles to profl. jours. Home: 28 Red Fox Ln Littleton CO 80127

GAMMILL, LEE MORGAN, JR., insurance company executive; b. N.Y.C., Mar. 25, 1934; s. Lee Morgan and Blanche (Reeves) G.; m. Jane Houchin, Apr. 2, 1960; children: Christopher Morgan, Sarah Louise. BA, Dartmouth Coll., 1956. CLU. Mgmt. trainee N.Y. Life Ins. Co., San Francisco, 1957-58, field underwriter, 1958-60, sales mgr., 1960-64, gen. mgr., 1965-71, regional supt., 1971-75, gen. mgr., 1975-86, sr. v.p., 1986—; pres. N.Y. Life and Annuity Corp., N.Y.C., 1987; bd. dirs. N.Y. Life Securities Corp., N.Y.C., N.Y. Life Equity Corp., N.Y.C., N.Y. Life Realty Corp., N.Y.C. Chmn. Town Recreational Adv. Bd., Ross., Calif., 1977; trustee Ross Sch. Dist., 1978-84. Mem. Gen. Agts. and Mgrs. Assn. (pres. San Francisco chpt. 1985), Nat. Assn. Life Underwriters, CLU Assn. Republican. Presbyterian. Clubs: Mill Valley Tennis (pres. 1972-73); Lagunitas Country (Ross); Pacific Union (San Francisco). Office: NY Life Ins Co 51 Madison Ave New York NY 10010

GAMMON, MATTIE JEAN, comptroller; b. Los Angeles, Aug. 11, 1924; d. Roy E. and Mary Lucille (Slack) Gould; m. Robert R. Gammon, Dec. 18, 1948; children: Mark R., Greg B. BS, U. Calif., Berkeley. Comptroller Nat. Council Juvenile and Family Ct. Judges, Inc., Reno, 1971—; bd. dirs. Fallon Mobile Homes, Inc., Reno, 1972—, Internation Inst. Youth, Inc., Mt. Vernon, Ind., 1984—. Mem. AAUW, Calif. Alumni, Alpha Xi Delta. Clubs: Croesus, Inc. Home: 1455 Vulgamore Pl Reno NV 89509

GAMORAN, ABRAHAM CARMI, management consultant, real estate broker; b. Cin., Mar. 15, 1926; s. Emanuel and Mamie (Goldsmith) G.; m. Ruth Kump, Apr. 14, 1973; children: Shirley, Mary, Samuel, Benjamin, Joseph. BBA, U. Cin., 1948; MBA, NYU, 1950. CPA, N.Y.; lic. real estate broker, N.Y., Ohio. Mem. staff Harris, Kerr Forster & Co., N.Y.C., 1949-52, supr. mgmt. services div., 1962-67; mgmt. cons. Burke, Landsberg & Gerber, Balt., 1953-54; v.p. Helmsley-Spear, Inc., N.Y.C., 1969-81; v.p. Helmsley-Spear, Inc., Cleve., 1981—; lectr. Cornell U., Mich. State U., Okla. State U., Am. Hotel and Motel Assn., others; vis. prof. U. Nev., Las Vegas, Coll. Hotel Adminstrn., 1985-87. Author articles in field, also real estate rev. portfolios. Recipient medal Wall St. Jour., 1948; Benjamin Franklin award, 1982. Mem. Am. Inst. CPA's, Am. Soc. Real Estate Counselors, Am. Soc. Appraisers (sr.), N.Y. State Soc. CPA's, Ohio Realtors Assn., Nat. Assn. Corp. Real Estate Execs., Cleve. Area Bd. Realtors. Democrat. Jewish. Home: 100 Brookmont Rd Akron OH 44313 Office: 1310 Terminal Tower Cleveland OH 44113

GAMPER, ALBERT R., JR., insurance executive; b. 1942; married. BA, Rutgers U.; PMD, Harvard U. With Mfrs. Hanover Trust Co., 1962—, v.p., 1971-80, sr. v.p., 1980-83, exec. v.p., 1983—, chmn. CIT group, 1987—; sector exec.v.p. Mfrs. Hanover Corp., 1985—. Office: Mfrs Hanover Corp 270 Park Ave New York NY 10017 *

GAMRON, W. ANTHONY, finance executive; b. Seymour, Ind., Nov. 15, 1948; s. William Alva and Odetta (Nicosin) G.; m. Lynn Marie LaShorne, July 31, 1976; children: Anthony, Benjamin, Kimberly. BS, Ind. State U., 1971; MBA, Ind. U., 1977. Sales rep. Pfizer, Inc., N.Y.C., 1971-75; various fin. positions Chrysler Corp., Detroit, 1977-79, Kimberly-Clark Corp., Neenah, Wis., 1980-84; asst. treas. Kimberly-Clark Corp., Dallas, 1984-86, v.p., treas., 1986—. Mem. adv. bd. dirs. Irving (Tex.) AID, 1988—. Mem. Fin. Execs. Inst. Republican. Methodist. Home: 104 Carnoustie Dr Trophy Club TX 76262 Office: Kimberly-Clark Corp 545 E Carpenter Frwy Irving TX 76062

GAMROTH, ARTHUR PAUL, small business owner; b. Independence, Wis., Jan. 1, 1930; s. George Dominic and Frances Kathleen (Sylla) G.; m. Arline Hellen Leipski, Feb. 14, 1953; children: Shawne, Bradley Paul, Todd Arthur, Timothy Curtis, Gary Mac. Diploma, Milw. Area Tech. Ctr., 1950. Mechanic Bonded Heating, Elm Grove, Wis., 1949-55; real estate salesman Anchor Realty, Waukesha, Wis., 1959-70; v.p. Ablenc, Inc., Waukesha, Wis., 1967—; pres. Energy Mgmt. of Wis., Waukesha, 1977—; cons. E.M.O.W., Waukesha, 1977—. Patentee biomass burner. Lobbyist RDF, Wis., 1987—. With U.S. Army, 1950-52, Korea. Recipient Spl. Recognition award U. Wis., 1986. Mem. Am. Contract Bridge League, Waukesha Bridge Club Am. Republican. Lodge: Eagles.

GANATRA, TANSUKH VALLABHDAS, telephone company executive; b. Masindi, Uganda, Sept. 5, 1943; came to U.S., 1969; s. Vallabhdas M. and Kanchanbala (Karia) G.; m. Sarla Vanmalidas Sodha, June 24, 1967; 1 child, Rajesh T. BEE, U. Nairobi, Kenya, 1968. Student engr. Rochester (N.Y.) Telephone Co., 1969-72, sr. engr., 1972-79; project engr. Rotelcom Bus. Systems, Rochester, 1979-81; asst. gen. mgr. Rotelcom Cons., Rochester, 1981-82, engring. mgr., 1982-85, dir. network engring., 1985-86; v.p. ACC Long Distance Corp., Rochester, 1987-89, pres., chief operating officer, 1989—. Mem. Inst. Elec. Engrs. Eng., Rochester Engring. Soc., India Assn. Rochester. Hindu. Home: 150 Greystone Ln Rochester NY 14618 Office: ACC Corp 39 State St Rochester NY 14614

GANGI, RAYNA MARIE, telecommunications company executive, estate financial planner; b. Jamestown, N.Y., Mar. 20, 1950; d. Alfred C. and Ruby (Ball) G. BA in Am. Studies, Communications, SUNY, Buffalo, 1979. Computer engr. IBM Corp., Buffalo, 1971-76; computer specialist SUNY, Buffalo, 1976-83; site engr. Timeplex, Inc., N.J., 1984-85; v.p. data communications Clarity Research, Inc., Buffalo, 1985-88; fin. planner IDS Fin. Svcs., Inc./AMEX, Buffalo, 1986—; cons. Women's Studies Coll., SUNY-Buffalo, 1971-80, ASK-WOMEN, Buffalo, 1987—; pres. Housestory, Inc., Buffalo, 1983—. Editor: Women in Work Force, 1920-85; contbr. articles to profl. jours. Pres. Main-Jewett Tenants Assn., 1982, Auburn Block Assn., Buffalo, 1986. Served as lance cpl. USMC, 1968-71. Mem. Internat. Assn. Computer Cons., Internat. Assn. Fin. Planning, Nat. Assn. Female Execs., SUNY-Buffalo Alumni Assn. (senator profl. staff com. 1985-87), Zonta, AAUW, Phi Beta Kappa. Democrat. Office: GANGI Fin Svcs Inc 568 Auburn Ave Buffalo NY 14222

GANGLOFF, JOHN JOSEPH, manufacturing company executive; b. Pensacola, Fla., Apr. 17, 1942; s. Joseph Arthur and Dora Jewell Gangloff; m. Linda Faye Tate, Nov. 26, 1965; children—Lara Ann, Kelly, Suzanne. Student, U. Tulsa, 1962, Pensacola Jr. Coll., Fla., 1962-63; BS in Fin. and Acctg., Fla. State U., 1965. Acct., internal auditor Gulf Power Co., Pensacola, Fla., 1965-67; with fin. mgmt. program Gen. Electric Co., Pittsfield, Mass., 1967-68; mgr. cost. acctg. R.J. Reynolds Foods, Winston-Salem, N.C., 1968-73, R.J. Reynolds Sea-Land, 1973-75; corp. budget mgr. R.J. Reynolds Industries, 1975-77, dir. bus. planning, 1979-81; asst. comptroller R.J. Reynolds Tobacco Co., Winston-Salem, N.C., 1981-83, comptroller, 1983-84, v.p. fin., chief fin. officer, 1984-87, chief fin. officer, sr. v.p., 1987—; tchr. acctg. for small bus. Pensacola Jr. Coll., 1965. Active United Way, Arts Council; fund raiser YMCA; bd. dirs. Salvation Army Boys Club. Served with USMCR, 1962-65, USNR, 1965-71. Mem. Fla. State U. Coll. Bus. Alumnia Bd., Fin. Execs. Inst., Nat. Assn. Accts., Delta Sigma Pi. Democrat. Roman Catholic. Clubs: Westwood Tennis, Forsyth Country. Home: 1200 Wilmar Place Ct Winston-Salem NC 27104 Office: R J Reynolds Tobacco USA PO Box 2959 Winston-Salem NC 27102

GANLEY, JAMES FRANCIS, banker; b. Bklyn., Dec. 21, 1935; s. John Joseph and Mae (Hannon) G.; m. Geraldine Curtin, May 11, 1963; children: Sheila, James P. B.S. in Econs, NYU. With Irving Trust Co., N.Y.C., 1956—; asst. v.p., then v.p., mgr. record services Irving Trust Co., 1969-75, sr. v.p., div. mgr., 1975-80, exec. v.p. banking ops. group, 1980-84, sr. exec. v.p. operational activities, 1984—; former dir. Depository Trust Co., N.Y.C.; mem. steering com. N.Y. Clearing House. Office: Irving Trust Co 1 Wall St New York NY 10005

GANN, GREGG, real estate executive; b. Los Angeles, July 6, 1948; s. John and Iris (Allen) G. BA, Calif. State U., Los Angeles, 1977; JD, Loyola Law Sch., Los Angeles, 1980. Bar: Calif., 1980; lic. real estate broker, Calif. V.p. Grubb & Ellis Co., Los Angeles, 1981-84, 85-87; mng. ptnr. Westside Comml. Brokerage Co., Los Angeles, 1984-85; pres. API Investment Properties, Inc., Los Angeles, 1987—. Served with USAF, 1967-69. Mem. Calif. Bar Assn. Roman Catholic. Office: API Investment Properties Inc 12233 W Olympic Blvd Los Angeles CA 90064

GANNES, STUART HARRISON, editor, writer; b. Detroit, May 18, 1949; s. Lawrence D. and Marion D. Gannes; m. Catherine Gregory, Oct. 1, 1977; children: Elizabeth, Dorothy, Nina. BA, U. Mich., 1971; MEd, Harvard U., 1972. Assoc. editor Change Mag., New Rochelle, N.Y., 1972-73; writer Fairchild Publ., N.Y.C., 1973-74; writer, editor Time Inc., N.Y.C., 1974-82; editor Time Teletext, N.Y.C., Va., 1982-83; writer Discover mag., N.Y.C., 1984; assoc. editor Fortune mag., N.Y.C., 1984—. John S. Knight Journalism Fellow, Stanford U., 1988-89. Home: 12 Elston Rd Montclair NJ 07043 Office: Fortune Mag Time Life Bldg Room 1653 1271 Ave of the Americas New York NY 10020

GANO, CLIFTON WAYNE, JR., risk management executive; b. Washington, Aug. 12, 1941; s. Clifton Wayne and Frankie Loreen (Counts) G.; m. Ellen Waterbury, Aug. 1962 (div. 1968); children: Susan L. Gano Brattland, Ann Jennifer; m. Mary Lou Campbell, Apr. 23, 1970; children: Wanda D., Timothy W., Clifton W. III. AB in Physics, Grinnell Coll., 1963; MBA, U. Iowa, 1967. Tchr., coach Newton (Iowa) Community Sch. Dist., 1963-65; mgr. contract and program mgmt. Aviation Div., Sunstrand Corp., Rockford, Ill., 1967-74, credit mgr., 1974-76, ins. mgr., 1976-81; dir. risk mgmt. IC Industries Inc., Chgo., 1981-87; asst. v.p. risk mgmt. Whitman Corp. (formerly IC Industries Inc.), Chgo., 1988; pres. IC Industries Ins. Co. Ltd., Hamilton, Bermuda, 1984—; v.p. ins. and loss control ConAgra, Inc., Omaha, 1988—; bd. dirs. Exel Ltd., Cayman Islands. Contbr. articles to profl. jours. Leader Rockford coun. Boy Scouts Am., 1979-80, Lincolnshire coun., 1981-82. Mem. Risk Mgmt. Coun., Machinery and Allied Products Inst., Risk and Ins. Mgmt. Soc. (bd. dirs. 1987-88), R.R. Ins. Mgmt. Assn. Republican. Congregationalist. Home: 21935 Stanford Circle Elkhorn NE 68022 Office: ConAgra Inc Omaha NE 68102

GANS, DENNIS JOSEPH, construction manager; b. Yokohama, Japan, Sept. 7, 1949; came to U.S., 1951; s. Harry Leo and Hope Lorene (Everett) G.; m. Carolyn Johnson O'Grady, 1986. BS in Bldg. Constrn., Tex. A&M U., 1971. Project mgr. Denver Comml. Builders, 1972-73, 78-79, 86-87; quality control engr. Martin Zachry Constrn., Kwajalein, Marshall Islands, 1975-76; co-owner B.G.S.Y. Enterprises, Denver, 1975; project mgr. State of Colo., 1977-78, 79-80; co-owner Denver Skatewear, 1978-80; mgr. scheduling Morrison Knudsen Co., Zaire, 1980-82; constrn. engr. Bechtel Internat., Jubail, Saudi Arabia, 1982; constrn. mgr. Village at Breckenridge (Colo.) Resort, 1984-86. Mem. Tex. A&M U. Assn. Former Students. Republican. Clubs: Front Range Ada Working Group, Rocky Mountain Triumph (Denver), Colo. Mountain. Home and Office: 3640 S Hillcrest Dr Denver CO 80237

GANS, SAMUEL MYER, temporary employment service executive; b. Phila., June 10, 1925; s. Arthur and Goldie (Goldhirsh) G.; grad. in acctg. Peirce Jr. Coll., 1946-49; m. Ada S. Zuckerman, Aug. 1, 1948; children: Gary M., Jeffrey R. Public acct., 1949-55; sales exec., 1955-58; franchise owner, pres., chief exec. officer Manpower, Inc. Delaware Valley, Pennsauken, N.J., 1958-86; owner Micrographic Services Inc., Pennsauken, 1986-72; with Allstate Services Inc., County Maintenance Corp., Affiliated Personnel Service; owner Antique & Classic Cars Storage Garage Inc., Voorhees, N.J. ; franchise cons.; instr. motivation courses. v.p., exec. bd. United Fund Camden County; v.p., bd. dirs. So. N.J. Devel. Council, ARC Camden County, Nat. Conf. of Christian and Jews; bd. mgrs. Am. Cancer Soc. Camden County; active Boy Scouts Am., Employer Legis. Com., Camden County Bicentennial Com., Score and Ace programs, Camden, YMCA, Allied Jewish Appeal, World Affairs Council; mem. N.J. Gov.'s Mgmt. Commn., 1971; trustee Camden County Heart Assn., Camden County Mental Health Assn.; exec. bd., founder Big Bros. Assn. Camden County; public relations com. U.S. Savs. Bonds, Camden and Trenton. Served with USNR, 1943-46. Mem. Nat. Assn. Temp. Services (chpt. relations com. 1973), Nat. Soc. Public Accts., Camden County C. of C., S. Jersey Public Relations Assn. (pres. 1967), S. Jersey Mfg. Assn. (exec. bd., treas.), S. Jersey Personnel Assn. (treas.), Cherry Hill C. of C. (bd. dirs., v.p.), Better Bus. Bur. Camden County, Adminstrv. Mgmt. Soc., N.J. Assn. Temp. Services (pres. 1970-72, bd. dirs.), South Jersey Purchasing Agts. Assn., Assn. of Manpower Franchise Owners, Jewish War Veterans; Jewish (exec. bd. dirs. congregation). Club: Dolphin Beach Condo. Lodges: Masons, Lions (pres. Camden 1972-73, Lion of Year 1977), Shriners, B'Nai B'Rith, Home: 4 N Derby Ave Ventnor NJ 08406 Office: 3801 Marlton Pike Pennsauken NJ 08105

GANT, DONALD ROSS, investment banker; b. Long Branch, N.J., Oct. 5, 1928; s. Raymond LeRoy and Evelyn (Ross) G.; m. Jane Harriet Taylor, Sept. 12, 1953; children: Laura R., Christopher T., Sarah R., Alison A. B.S., U. Pa., 1952; M.B.A., Harvard U., 1954. Assoc. Goldman, Sachs & Co., N.Y.C., 1954-64, ptnr., 1965—; bd. dirs. Diebold, Inc., Canton, Ohio, Liquid Air Corp., San Francisco, Stride Rite Corp., Cambridge, Mass. Mem. exec. council Harvard Grad. Sch. Bus. Adminstrn., Cambridge, Mass., 1981-84. Served with U.S. Army, 1946-48. Republican. Presbyterian. Home: Young's Rd New Vernon NJ 07976 Office: Goldman Sachs & Co 85 Broad St New York NY 10004

GANT, JOHN WILLIAM, JR., lawyer; b. Scottsboro, Ala., Nov. 2, 1955; s. John William and Virginia (White) G.; m. Schuyler Ann Joyner, Nov. 15, 1986. BS in Commerce and Bus. Administrn., U. Ala., 1977, JD, 1980; LLM in Taxation, NYU, 1981. Bar: Ala. 1980. Assoc. Lange, Simpson, Robinson & Somerville, Birmingham, Ala., 1980-85, ptnr., 1986—; bd. dirs., sec. Baggett Transp. Co., Birmingham, Hwy. Equipment Co., Inc., Birmingham. Hugo Black scholar U. Ala., 1979. Mem. ABA, Fed. Bar Assn., Estate Planning Council, Ala. Bar Assn., Birmingham Bar Assn., Birmingham Tax Club. Republican. Presbyterian. Office: Lange Simpson Robinson & Somerville 1700 First Ala Bank Bldg Birmingham AL 35203

GANTMAN, GERALDINE ANN, marketing executive, consultant; b. N.Y.C., Jan. 14, 1945; d. Robert Marquette and Mary (Terrazzi) Rhynus; m. David Joseph Gantman, Aug. 21, 1964 (div. 1981). BA in History, CUNY, 1965. Project dir. Audits & Surveys, Inc., N.Y.C., 1966-68; sr. v.p. CCI, Inc., N.Y.C., 1968-80; v.p., account supr. N.W. Ayer, Inc., N.Y.C., 1980-83; exec. v.p. Tel. Mktg. Resources, Inc., N.Y.C., 1983-88; sr. ptnr. Oetting & Co., Inc., N.Y.C., 1983—. Mem. Direct Mktg. Assn. (chmn. tel. mktg. coun. 1987-89). Office: Oetting & Co Inc 1995 Broadway New York NY 10023

GANTT, DEAN, retail food company executive; b. 1936. BE, East Tex. State U., 1959. With Safeway Stores Inc., 1957—, now v.p. retail div. Office: Safeway Stores Inc 201 4th St Oakland CA 94660 *

GANTZ, WILBUR HENRY, III, health care company executive; b. York, Pa., Dec. 5, 1937; s. Wilbur Henry and Flora Shaw (Kashner) G.; m. Linda Theis, Mar. 22, 1962; children: Matthew John, Leslie Shaw, Caroline Ruhl. AB, Princeton U., 1959; MBA, Harvard U., 1964. With Aetna Life Ins. Co., Hartford, Conn., 1959-62, 64-66; asst. to pres. Baxter Internat., Inc., Deerfield, Ill., 1967-69; asst. gen. mgr. Baxter Internat., Inc., Mexico City, 1967-69; v.p. Europe Baxter Internat., Inc., Brussels, 1969-75; pres. Internat. div. Baxter Internat., Inc., Deerfield, Ill., 1976-79; group v.p. Baxter Internat., Inc., Deerfield, 1979, exec. v.p., 1979-83, chief operating officer, 1983-87, pres., 1987—; dir. Harris Bankcorp, Harris Trust and Savs. Bank, W.W. Grainger, Inc., Zenith Electronics Corp. Trustee Nat. Coll. Edn., Chgo. Council on Fgn. Relations, Episcopal Charities; dir. Evanston Hosp. Corp. Clubs: Chicago, Commonwealth, Economic, Commercial (Chgo.); Sunset Ridge Country; Indian Hill Country. Office: Baxter Travenol Labs Inc 1 Baxter Pkwy Deerfield IL 60015

GANTZER, MARY LOU, research chemist; b. Mpls., Oct. 3, 1950; d. Richard John and Mary Jane (Copistrant) G. B Chemistry, U. Minn., 1972, MS, 1976; PhD in Chemistry, U. Va., 1980. Instr., postdoctoral fellow dept. chemistry U. Va., Charlottesville, 1980-81; rsch. scientist diagnostics div. Miles, Inc., Elkhart, Ind., 1981-84, sr. rsch. scientist, 1984-86, staff scientist, 1986-87, supr. R & D, 1987—; mem. Women in Mgmt. del. to People's Republic China, 1988. Contbr. articles to chemistry jours.; patentee in field. Fellow Am. Inst. Chemists; mem. Am. Chem. Soc. (sec. Chgo. sect. 1985—), Am. Assn. Clin. Chemistry (chmn. Chgo. sect. 1988, Chmn.'s award 1988), N.Y. Acad. Scis., Iowa Sigma Pi. Roman Catholic. Home: 25723 Kiser Ct Elkhart IN 46514 Office: Miles Inc Diagnostics Div PO Box 70 (BB04A) Elkhart IN 46515

GARAJALDE, FERNANDO ALBERTO, computer systems analyst; b. N.Y.C., July 8, 1953; s. Wenceslao and Haydee (Sosa) Garajalde. Student, Fordham U., 1971-74, Hudson County Community Coll., Jersey City, N.J., 1981-83, Wake Tech. Coll., Raleigh, N.C., 1985-86. From mailhandler to maintenance mechanic U.S. Postal Service, N.J., 1973-84; info. systems coordinator Nat. Info. Systems Devel. Ctr., Raleigh, N.C., 1984-86, computer programmer, 1986-88; computer systems analyst Data Base Mgmt Div. USPS Hdqrs., Washington, 1988-89, project mgr., 1989—. Mem. Am. Mensa Ltd., Ea. N.C. Mensa (mem-at-large 1984-86, parliamentarian 1986-88, coord. spl. interest group, 1989—). Democrat. Roman Catholic. Office: US Postal Svc Data Base Mgmt Div 475 L'Enfant Pla SW Room 2670 Washington DC 20260

GARBACZ, GERALD GEORGE, chemical products company executive; b. San Francisco, Oct. 12, 1936; s. George and Violette (Derbeck) G.; m. Jane E. Snyder, July 1, 1961; children: Geoffrey, Gregory. Student, Dartmouth Coll., 1954-55, M.B.A., 1965; B.S., U.S. Naval Acad., 1959; postgrad., U.S. Naval War Coll., 1978. Asst. to v.p. corp. planning Cummins Engine Co., Columbus, Ind., 1965-66; exec. dir. fin. planning and analysis Cummins Engine Co., 1967; asst. to sec. defense (White House fellow) 1968-69; dir. corp. planning Boise Cascade Corp., Idaho, 1970-72; v.p. finance, treas. Phillips Industries, Dayton, Ohio, 1972-74; ops. asst. W.R. Grace & Co., N.Y.C., 1974-75; v.p. W.R. Grace & Co., 1975-80, pres. Baker & Taylor div., 1980-83, sr. v.p., 1983-86, exec. v.p., 1986—, also dir.; instr. Ind. U., 1967-68, UCLA, 1972-74; cons. Dept. Def., 1969-70; bd. dirs. Handy & Harman Corp. Chmn. Idaho steering com. Common Cause, 1972; bd. overseers Amos Tuck Sch. Bus. Adminstrn., Dartmouth, 1970-76; mem. regional selection panel Pres.'s Commn. on White House fellows, 1971, 72, 79-81, 84-86. Served to maj. USMCR, 1959-82. Mem. U.S. Naval Acad. Alumni Assn. Presbyterian (elder 1967-69, 71-72, 78-81). Club: Dartmouth (N.Y.). Office: W R Grace & Co 1114 Ave of the Americas New York NY 10036

GARBACZ, R(ON) RAND, diversified industries executive; b. Summit, N.J., Nov. 20, 1938; s. George and Violette (Derbeck) G.; children: David Jodok, Christina Brewster. BS with highest honors, Norwich U., 1961; MBA in Fin., Amos Tuck Sch., Dartmouth Coll., 1963. With Cummins Engine Co., Columbus, Ind., 1965-70, asst. corp. controller, 1966-67, dir. product planning, 1968, dir. corp. planning, 1969, pres. K2 Corp., subs., Seattle, 1969-70; asst. to chief exec. officer, dir. corp. planning Gould Inc., Chgo., 1971, dep. to chief operating officer, 1972, v.p., gen. mgr. Sonotone Corp., subs., Elmsford, N.Y., 1973; v.p. corp. planning Pullman Inc., Chgo., 1974-77; dep. chief strategic officer, dir. corp. planning FMC Corp., Chgo., 1978-83, dep. gen. mgr. defense systems group, 1983-84; vice chmn., mng. dir. Callard and Madden Assocs., Chgo. 1985—; corp. v.p., chief strategic officer ADP, 1987—; mng. dir. Reorganized Securities Group Seidler Amdec Securities; instr. econs. and fin. Ind. U., 1968-70; strategic lectr. Amos Tuck Sch., Dartmouth Coll. Served to capt. CIC/CIA, U.S. Army, 1963-65. Republican. Presbyterian (deacon). Clubs: Saddle and Cycle, Racquet, Chgo. Yacht, Econ. of Chgo.; Coral Beach and Tennis (Bermuda).). Home: 1120 N Lake Shore Dr Chicago IL 60611 also: 2227 Empire Grade Santa Cruz CA 95060

GARBAN, STEVE ALEXANDER, academic administrator, treasurer; b. Grindstone, Pa., Sept. 28, 1937; s. Andrew Stephen and Anna (Mizenko) G.; m. Penny A Garban, May 7, 1960; children: Donna Elizabeth, Andrew William, Douglas Stephen. BBA in Acctg., Pa. State U., 1959, cert. in teaching, 1961. Sales corr. Am. Steel and Wire Corp., Cleve., 1959-61; asst. bus. mgr. athletics Pa. State U., 1961-66, coord. acctg. dept., 1966-68, dep. contr., 1968-71, contr., 1971-73, acting budget officer, 1978, contr., staff asst. to sr. v.p. for fin., ops. treas., 1973-81, v.p., contr., 1981-82, sr. v.p. fin. ops., 1982-84, sr. v.p. fin., ops. treas., 1984—; mem. bd. trustees, treas. Pa. Rsch. Corp.; bd. dirs., treas. Corp. for Penn State; pres., chief exec. officer, bd. dirs. Nittany Title Corp.; mem. Econ. Devel. Corp.; mem. bus. adv. bd. Zero Stage Capital of Pa.; mem. regional adv. bd. Arkwright Mfrs. Mut. Ins. Co.; bd. dirs. Met. Life Ins. Co., Met. Series Fund, Met. Variable Accounts. Pres. Park Forest Jr. High PTA, 1976-77; mem. bd. trustees Centre Community Hosp., 1981-82. Mem. Coll. Football Assn. (bd. dirs., sec., treas. 1987-88), Nat. Assn. Coll. and Univ. Bus. Officers (rep.), Pa. State U. Coll. Bus. Adminstrn. Alumni Assn. (bd. dirs. 1966-75, 80-82). Republican. Roman Catholic. Office: Pa State U 208 Old Main University PA 16802

GARBARINO, DR. JOSEPH WILLIAM, economics and business educator; b. Medina, N.Y., Dec. 7, 1919; s. Joseph Francis and Savina M. (Volpone) G.; m. Mary Jane Godward, Sept. 18, 1948; children: Ann, Joan, Susan, Ellen. B.A., Duquesne U., 1942; M.A., Harvard U., 1947, Ph.D., 1949. Faculty U. Calif., Berkeley, 1949—; prof. U. Calif., 1960-88, dir. Inst. Bus. and Econ. Research, 1962-88, prof. emeritus, 1988—; vis. lectr. Cornell U., 19S9-60, UCLA, 1949, SUNY, Buffalo, 1972; Fulbright lectr. U. Glasgow, Scotland, 1969; vis. scholar U. Warwick; mem. staff Brookings Instn., 1959-60; vis. lectr. U. Minn., 1978; labor arbitrator. Author: Health Plans and Collective Bargaining, 1960, Wage Policy and Long Term Contracts, 1962, Faculty Bargaining: Change and Conflict, 1975, Faculty Bargaining in Unions in Transition. Served with U.S. Army, 1942-45, 51-53. Decorated Bronze Star. Mem. Indsl. Relations Research Assn. Democrat. Roman Catholic. Home: 7708 Ricardo Ct El Cerrito CA 94530

GARBER, ALAN JOHN, transportation executive; b. Dayton, Ohio, Aug. 18, 1962; s. Paul Jr. and Carolena Delores (Giambrone) G. BBA, U. Cin., 1986; postgrad., U. Dayton, 1988—. Ops. mgr. Yellow Freight System, Columbus, Ohio, 1986-87; mktg. rep. Churchill Truck Lines, Chillicothe, Mo., 1987—. Active Young Reps., Cin., 1984-86. Recipient Falcon award Kettering, Ohio Sch. Bd., 1981. Mem. Miami Valley Traffic Club, Upper Valley Traffic Club, Am. Mktg. Assn., U. Cin. Alumni Assn., Delta Sigma Pi. Roman Catholic. Home: 3608 Braddock St Kettering OH 45420 Office: Churchill Truck Lines 1756 Stanley Ave Dayton OH 45401

GARBER, HARRY DOUGLAS, life insurance executive; b. Detroit, June 28, 1928; s. John Tennant and Mary Helen (Canfield) G.; B.A., Yale U., 1950; m. Joy Ruth Buckley, June 29, 1957; children: Deborah MacKelcan, Juliet, John Tennant, Buckley. With Equitable Life Assurance Soc. U.S., 1950—, v.p., actuary, 1971-74, sr. v.p. and actuary, 1974-76, exec. v.p., 1976-84, vice chmn., 1984—; bd. dirs. Genesco, Inc., EVLICO, AWED. Served with USNR, 1952-54. Fellow Soc. Actuaries (dir. bd. Govs.); mem. Am. Acad. Actuaries, Sigma Xi. Democrat. Mem. United Ch. Christ. Home: 76 Mulberry Ave Garden City NY 11530 Office: Equitable Life Assurance Soc US 787 7th Ave Ste 4805 New York NY 10019

GARBER, JANICE MCGUIRE, bank executive; b. Banner Elk, N.C., Dec. 19, 1946; m. Joseph R. Garber. BA in Phys. Anthropology, Hunter Coll., 1980. Various positions Citibank, N.A., N.Y.C., 1968-72, asst. mgr. corp. tax dept., 1973-77; relationship mgr., v.p. Citibank, N.A. (North Am. Banking Group), N.Y.C., 1977-84; treasury mgr. Citicorp Savs., Oakland, Calif., 1984—. Office: Citicorp Savs 180 Grand Ave Oakland CA 94604

GARBER, SAMUEL BAUGH, lawyer, retail company executive; b. Chgo., Aug. 16, 1934; s. Morris and Yetta (Cohen) G.; children: Debra Lee, Diane Lori. JD, U. Ill., 1958; MBA, U. Chgo., 1968. Bar: Ill., 1958; pntr. Brown, Dashow and Langluttig, Chgo., 1960-62; corp. counsel Walgreen Co., 1962-69; v.p., gen. counsel, exec. asst. to the pres. Carlyle & Co., 1969-73; dir. legal affairs Stop & Shop Co., Inc., 1973-74; gen. counsel Goldblatt Bros., Inc., 1974-76; v.p., sec., gen. counsel Evans, Inc., 1976—; prof. mgmt. DePaul U., 1975—. With U.S. Army, 1958-60. Mem. ABA, Nat. Retail Mchts. Assn., Ill. Retail Mchts. Assn., Carlton Club, East Bank Club. Home: 320 Oakdale Chicago IL 60657 Office: Evans Inc 36 S State St Chicago IL 60603

GARBERDING, LARRY GILBERT, utilities executive; b. Albert City, Iowa, Oct. 29, 1938; s. Gilbert D. and Lavern Marie (Specketer) G.; m. Elizabeth Ann Hankens, Aug. 20, 1961; children: Scott Richard, Kathryn Ann, Michael John. BS, Iowa State U., 1960. CPA, Nebr. Ptnr. Arthur Andersen & Co., Chgo., 1960-71; chief fin. officer Kans.-Nebr. Natural Gas Co., Inc., Hastings, Nebr., 1971-81; chief fin. officer Tenn. Gas Transmission, Houston, 1981-83, exec. v.p., 1983-87; pres. Tenn. Gas Mktg., Houston, 1987-88, NICOR Inc., Naperville, Ill., 1988—. With U.S. Army, 1961. Mem. AICPA. Republican. Lutheran. Office: NICOR Inc 1700 W Ferry Rd Box 200 Naperville IL 60566-0200

GARBIS, ANDREW NICHOLAS, shipping company executive; b. June 26, 1936; s. Nicholas A. and Mary V.G.; m. Dana Field Blauvelt, Apr. 9, 1960; children: Paul Andrew, Elizabeth Anne. BA, CUNY, 1964. Fin. exec. Transoceanic Marine Co., N.Y.C., 1956-65; v.p. Hudson Waterways Corp., N.Y.C., 1965-74; fin. exec. Seatrain Lines Inc., N.Y.C., 1974; corp. officer Cove Shipping Inc., N.Y.C., 1975—; v.p. Cove Shipping Inc., Mobile, Ala. Vice chmn. Lincoln Park Twp. (N.J.) Planning Bd., 1969-70; chmn. Citizens' Planning Com., Montville, N.J., 1973-75, fin. adv. bd. Montville, 1976-80; mem. Morris County Bd. Pub. Transp., 1976-78; treas., chmn. Major Polit. Club Orgn., Lincpln Park, 1965-70. With U.S. Army, 1959-61. Mem. Assn. Water Transp. Ofcls., Mobile C. of C., Propeller Club (Mobile). Office: Cove Shipping Inc 200 Virginia St Mobile AL 36603-2018

GARCIA, ED, financial services company executive; b. Vega Bjoa, P.R., May 25, 1936; came to U.S., 1955; s. Edmundo and Virginia (Pumarejo) G.; m. Evelyn Garcia, Mar. 6, 1976; children: Abdias, Edvelyn, Victor, Enrigue, Madelyn; stepchildren: Julio, Everling. Grad., Spanish Am. Inst., N.Y.C., 1960. Pres. Abdias Enterprises, San Juan, P.R., 1962-78; chmn. Cellar 2 Dome Enterprises, Winter Springs, Fla., 1978-84; v.p. Edsteam A.L. Williams, Altamonte Springs, Fla., 1984—; TV talk show host Sta. WCIU-TV, Chgo., Sta. KEMO-TV, San Francisco. Republican. Pentecostal. Office: Edsteam Al Williams 710 E Altamonte Dr #104 Altamonte Springs FL 32701

GARCIA, FERNANDO SALCEDO, financial consultant; b. Manila, July 3, 1960; Came to U.S., 1970; s. Dionicio Castillo and Nenita Baquir (Salcedo) G.; m. Agnes Gaitanis, Feb. 14, 1988. BBA, Loyola U., Chgo., 1983. Cert. fin. planner, real estate agt., Ill. Dept. mgr. Carson Pirie Scott and Co., Chgo., 1983-84; computer operator Comml. Nat. Bank, Chgo., 1984-85; fin. planner IDS Fin. Services, Des Plaines, Ill., 1985-86, Southmark Fin. Services, Northbrook, Ill., 1986-87; rep. Lowry Fin. Svcs., North Palm Beach, Fla., 1986-87; fin. cons. Merrill, Lynch, Pierce, Fenner & Smith, Chgo., 1987—; prin., owner Integrated Realty and Investment Corp., Chgo., 1988—; prin. Integrated Realty and Investment Corp., Chgo.; fin. cons. Merrill Lynch, Pierce, Fenner & Smith, Inc., Chgo., 1987—. Recipient Mercury award IDS Fin. Services, Inc., 1986. Mem. Internat. Assn. Fin. Planning, Inst. Cert. Fin. Planners, Nat. Futures Assn., Nat. Assn. Securities Dealers (series 3, 7, 8, 24, 27, and 63), Ill. Dept. Ins. (producer), Nat. Assn. Life Underwriters, Notaries Assn. Ill., Theta Xi (athletic coordinator 1979-80). Republican. Roman Catholic. Clubs: Kapwa (Chgo.) (pres. 1980-82), Investment (Chgo.) (pres. 1985—). Home: 2721 W Winnemac Chicago IL 60625-0640 Office: Merrill Lynch Pierce Fenner and Smith Inc One South Wacker Dr Mezzenine Level Chicago IL 60606

GARCIA, HECTOR THOMAS, accountant; b. San Juan Bautista, Calif., Oct. 28, 1926; s. Tomás Jose Garcia y Espinosa and Aurelia María Esparza y Terrazas; m. Leah Adele Mumm, Nov. 3, 1951; children: Thomas R., Carolyn A., Daniel C., Susan L. BS, U. Calif.-Berkeley, 1950; MBA, Santa Clara U., 1966; MS, Golden Gate U., San Francisco, 1978. Cost acct. Bethlehem Steel Corp., South San Francisco, 1951-54; supr. cost acctg. Western Gear Corp., Belmont, Calif., 1954-56; supr. microwave cost acctg. Varian Assos., Palo Alto, Calif., 1956-62; sr. budget analyst Lockheed Missiles & Space Co., Sunnyvale, Calif., 1962-66; supr. auditing Calif. Dept. Finance, Sacramento, 1966-70; chief acct. San Jose State U., 1971-72; prin. acct., Office of Pres., U. Calif., Berkeley, 1972-80; dir. Internal audit U. Calif., Davis, 1980—. Tech. sgt. inf., U.S. Army, 1944-46; PTO, ETO. CPA, Calif. Mem. Am. Inst. CPA's, Calif. Soc. CPA's, Inst. Internal Auditors (cert.). Home: 630 Cleveland St Davis CA 95616 Office: U Calif Internal Audit Office Orchard Park Dr Davis CA 95616

GARCIA, LIAN FATIMA, footwear company official; b. Havana, Cuba, June 23, 1962; came to U.S., 1967; d. Aurelio Ramon Garcia and Amelia Venancia (Garcia) Alvarez; m. Alejandro Chamizo, Apr. 16, 1988. BS in Apparel Mgmt., Fla. Internat. U., 1984. Exec. sec. Cushman & Wakefield, Miami, Fla., 1980-82; mgr. Soél Shoes (Simon and Garcia), Miami, 1982-84; sales mgr. Aurelio Garcia Imports, Miami, 1984—. Republican. Roman Catholic. Office: Aurelio Garcia Imports 7401 NW 8th St Ste L Miami FL 33126

GARCIA, LORETTA JEAN, lawyer; b. Denver, Mar. 3, 1955; d. Leo Segundo and Maria Cruz (Martinez) G. BA with distinction, U. Colo., 1979; MS in Internat. Affairs, Georgetown U., 1984, JD, 1984. Bar: Pa. 1984, D.C. 1985, U.S. Ct. Appeals (D.C. cir.) 1985. Atty. FCC, Washington, 1984-88; assoc. LeBoeuf Lamb Leiby & MacRae, Washington, 1988—. Mem. Women's Bar Assn. (chmn. membership com. D.C. 1986-88, communications law forum 1988—), Fed. Communications Bar Assn., Hispanic Bar Assn. Democrat. Office: 1333 New Hampshire Ave NW Washington DC 20036

GARCIA, MICHAEL STEPHEN, marketing professional; b. Oakland, Calif., May 27, 1951; s. Elpidio Pete and Arline (Tolleson) G.; m. Janice Mull, Nov. 28, 1980; children: Stephen Ross, Kelli Ann. BS in Bus., Calif. Poly. State U., 1973; MBA, U. Nebr., 1980. Purchasing agt. Burns Vet. Supply, Oakland, 1974-76; budget, systems mgr. Burns-Biotec Labs., Oakland, 1976-77; asst. controller Burns-Biotec Labs. div. Schering Corp., Omaha, 1977-79; product mgr. Schering Animal Health, Omaha, 1979-81; mktg. dir. Paragon Optical, Inc., Mesa, Ariz., 1982-85, Farnam Cos., Phoenix, 1985-88; pres. Advanced Consumer Products, Mesa, Ariz., 1988—. Campaign worker various congl. candidates, 1982—. Recipient Readex Advt. Effectiveness award Nat. Hog Farmer, 1979, Addy award Phoenix Advt. Club, 1984. Mem. Am. Mgmt. Assn. Republican. Roman Catholic. Home: 2118 S El Marino Mesa AZ 85202 Office: Advanced Consumer Products 225 E Chilton Dr Ste 15 Chandler AZ 85225

GARCIA, STACY LYNN, small business owner; b. Tecumseh, Mich., May 6, 1957; d. Phillip Frederick and Geraldean (Bickford) Belleville; m. Michael Orlando Garcia, June 16, 1979; children: Grant Michael, Sarah Marie. BS, Calif. State U., Long Beach, 1980. Owner Garcia Cabinetmakers, Huntington Beach, Calif., 1978—. Mem. Nat. Kitchen and Bath Assn., Am. Soc. Interior Designers (pres. Long Beach chpt. 1978-79), Pi Beta Phi. Republican. Home: 473 Schooner Way Seal Beach CA 90740 Office: Garcia Cabinetmakers 5770 Research Dr Huntington Beach CA 92649

GARCIA-GRANADOS, SERGIO EDUARDO, brokerage house executive; b. Mexico, June 11, 1942 (citizen of Guatemala); s. Jorge and Miriam Garcia-Granados; Licenciado en Ciencias Juridicas y Sociales with honors (scholar 1960-66), U. San Carlos, 1966; postgrad. U. Paris, Inst. Scis. Politiques, Paris, 1966-68; m. Elizabeth Bentley, Apr. 3, 1973; children: Tatiana, Sybil. Admitted to bar, 1966; research assoc. The Hague Acad. Internat. Law, 1969, Internat. Bur. Fiscal Documentation, Amsterdam, 1969-70; partner law firm Saravia y Muñoz, Guatemala City, 1970-77; v.p. sales mgr. Merrill Lynch Capital Market Internat., N.Y.C., 1982-88, v.p. resident mgr. internat. div. Shearson Lehman Hutton, N.Y., 1988—; lectr. tax problems in Central Am. Common Market, U. San Carlos, bus. orgns., U. Landivar; dir. Rawmat

Corp., Tucasa S.A., Maprigna S.A.; bd. adminstrn. Gebira Investment Corp., 1977-81; Bd. dirs. Patronato de Bellas Artes, 1977-84, Guatemala Nat. Theatre Directorate, 1979-80. Mem. Colegio de Abogados, Internat. Bar Assn., Internat. Fiscal Assn. (gen. council 1972--84), Am. Soc. Internat. Law. Contbr. articles to profl. jours. Organizer, 1st editor loose-leaf corporate taxation in Latin Am., 1970. Address: 11 Larchmont Ave Larchmont NY 10538

GARDE, JOSEPH L., wholesale distribution company executive; b. 1929; married. With Garde Drug Co., Phila., 1950-60; with Spectro Industries, Inc., Jenkintown, Pa., 1968—, now chmn., pres. Office: Spectro Industries Inc Jenkintown Pla Jenkintown PA 19046 •

GARDILL, JOSEPH CONRAD, transportation executive; b. Balt., Jan. 24, 1959; s. George Conrad and Mary Rose (O'Donnell) G.; m. Mary Quinn, June 21, 1986. BSBA, Towson State U., 1981; MS in Fin., Loyola Coll., Balt., 1984. Assoc. staff acct./investment mgr. Alexander & Alexander, Inc., Towson, Md., 1981-82; computer salesperson The Graymar Co., Balt., 1983, Profit Programming, Inc., Balt., 1983-84; treasury analyst Emons Industries, Inc., York, Pa., 1984-86; mgr. treasury ops. Emons Industries, Inc., York, 1986-87, dir. spl. projects, 1987-88; asst. treas. Emons Holdings, Inc., York, 1988—. Bd. dirs. Knollwood Donnybrook Community Assn., Towson, Md., 1987. Mem. Am. Mgmt. Assn., Assn. MBA Execs. Republican. Roman Catholic. Office: Emons Holdings Inc 96 S George St York PA 17401

GARDINER, DONALD KENT, professional association administrator; b. Rochester, N.H., Dec. 17, 1939; s. Everett Earl and Lucile (Brownell) G.; m. Diane Elizabeth Olesen; children: Wendy Biggerstaff, Pamela, Jeffrey, Christopher. BS in Econs. and Bus. Adminstrn., Russell Sage Coll., 1963. Cert. assn. exec. Exec. asst. N.Y., N.J., Conn. Profl. Ins. Agts. Assns., Glenmont, N.Y., 1964-69, assoc. exec. dir., 1969-71, exec. dir., 1971-84; exec. v.p. Nat. Assn. Profl. Ins. Agts., Alexandria, Va., 1984—; sec. PIA Services, Inc., Alexandria, Va., 1984—; cons. in field, Glenmont, 1968-84. Served to sgt. USAR. Mem. Am. Soc. Assn. Execs. (chmn. task force edn., 1986, recipient 14 mgmt. awards, 1968-87). Republican. Baptist. Office: Profl Ins Agts 400 N Washington St Alexandria VA 22314

GARDINER, GEORGE R., diversified corporation executive; b. Toronto, Ont., Can., 1917. Ed., U. Toronto, 1939; ed., Harvard U. Grad. Sch. Bus., 1941. Chmn. Scott's Hospitality, Inc., Toronto, Gardiner Group Capital Ltd., Toronto; chmn. bd. dirs. Green Line Investor Services Inc., Toronto, Commonwealth Hospitality Ltd., Toronto, Gardiner Oil and Gas Ltd., Calgary, Can., Commonwealth Holiday Inns, Garbell Holdings Ltd. Trustee Toronto Gen. Hosp., Royal Ontario Mus., Toronto; trustee, v.p. Ontario Jockey Club, Toronto; chmn. bd. dirs. George R. Gardiner Mus. Ceramic Art., Toronto. Office: Gardiner Group Stockbrokers, World Trust Tower Ste 2402, Box 530 Toronto, ON Canada M5H 2S8

GARDINO, VINCENT ANTHONY, broadcasting executive; b. N.Y.C., Sept. 19, 1953; s. Anthony John and Carmelina Mary (Boglia) G. BA magna cum laude in History, St. Francis Coll. V.p. N.Y. sales mgr., dir. spl. programming and sales Metro Radio Sales, N.Y.C., 1976-79; acct. exec. WABC Radio, N.Y.C., 1979-81; dir. ABC Radio Network, N.Y.C., 1981-85, ABC Direction and Entertainment Radio Networks, 1981-85; pres., chief ops. officer Selcom Radio, N.Y.C., 1985—; gen. sales mgr. Sta. WOR-AM, N.Y.C., 1985—. Mem. Internat. Radio and TV Soc., Mus. Broadcasting, St. Francis Coll. Alumni Assn. (bd. dirs.). Roman Catholic. Avocations: tennis, jogging, racquetball, hist. autograph collecting. Office: WOR Radio 1440 Broadway New York NY 10018

GARDIS, GILDA J., quality analyst; b. Jersey City, Jan. 16, 1944; d. William Patrick and Gilda Esther (Weber) Cornett; m. David Richard Gardis, Oct. 8, 1966 (div. 1981). Student, Oceanside-Carlsbad Jr. Coll., Santa Monica City Coll. Prin. typist clk. UCLA, 1966-69, adminstrv. asst., 1969-73, acctg. asst., 1973-75, mgmt. services officer, UCLA, 1975-79; mgmt. services officer U. Calif., San Diego, La Jolla, 1979-85; quality analyst Teledyne Kinetics, Solana Beach, Calif., 1986—; part-time sales rep. Mervyn's, Oceanside, Calif., 1986—. Active Oceanside High Sch. Booster Club, 1980-83. Recipient Tiffany award Manpower, Inc., Carlsbad, Calif., 1985. Mem. Am. Mgmt. Assn. (assoc.), Nat. Assn. Female Execs., Network Exec. Women, Am. Soc. Profl. and Exec. Women, Teledyne Kinetics Recreation Assn. (sec. 1987, chairperson 1988). Roman Catholic. Avocations: tennis, bicycling, art, bowling. Home: 3559 Guava Way Oceanside CA 92054 Office: Teledyne Kinetics 410 S Cedros Solana Beach CA 92075 also: PO Box 1401 Oceanside CA 92054

GARDNER, DAVID EDWARD, baking company executive; b. Portsmouth, Ohio, Dec. 5, 1923; s. David Edward and Mary Petrea (Gableman) G.; m. Marie Emma Nickles, Oct. 17, 1948; children: David Alfred, Ernest Edward, Philip Gableman, Mary Emma. Student, U. Mich., 1941-43, U. Ill., 1944, Shrivenham (Am.) U., Eng., 1945; BA, Ohio Wesleyan U., 1948; grad., Am. Inst. Baking, 1962. With Alfred Nickles Bakery, Inc., Navarre, Ohio, 1948—, sec., 1956—, v.p. adminstrn., 1967-80, pres., 1980—, also bd. dirs.; bd. dirs. W.E. Long Ind. Bakers Coop., Chgo. Mem. Blue Cross Community Resource Bd., 1976-82; bd. dirs. Massillon (Ohio) Community Hosp., 1978-82. Served with USAAF, Signal Corps. U.S. Army, 1943-46. Mem. Am. Soc. Bakery Engrs., Am. Inst. Baking Alumni Assn., Phi Kappa Psi, Omicron Delta Kappa, Pi Delta Epsilon, Pi Sigma Alpha. Republican. Mem. United CH. of Christ. Home: 557 Park Navarre OH 44662 Office: 26 Main St Navarre OH 44662

GARDNER, DAVID JOHN, communications executive, recording engineer; b. Binghamton, N.Y., Jan. 8, 1953; s. Daniel Sparrow and Anne Mae (Worthing) G.; m. Wendy Ellen Churnside, Dec. 24, 1974 (div. Apr. 1978); m. Denise Lynn Browne, Apr. 5, 1980; 1 child, Deborah Anne. Assocs., Broome Community Coll., Binghamton, 1973; BA, Hofstra U., 1975. Prodn. control analyst IBM, Systems Mfg. Div., Endicott, N.Y., 1971-73; rec. engr. Eye-Full Films, San Francisco, 1972-78; gen. mgr. J.K. Theater Corp., Binghamton, 1975-77; rec. engr. The Image Works, Binghamton, 1977-80; audio/video engr. Sta. WBNG, Binghamton, 1977-78; media technician Nat. Sci. Found., Washington, 1978-79; tech. ops. RCA Americom Services, Inc., Princeton, N.J., 1980-84, supr. ops., 1984-86; mgr. network ops. ctr. Gen. Electric Americom, Inc., Princeton, 1986—; owner, pres., rec. engr. Ind. Sound, Binghamton, 1963—; bd. dirs. New Orleans Rec. Co., 1980—, Street Rhythm Prodns., Bklyn., 1980—. Mem. Soc. Broadcast Engrs., Soc. Motion Picture and TV Engrs. Episcopalian. Lodge: Order of DeMolay. Home: 11 Janice Dr Sussex NJ 07461 Office: Gen Electric Americom Inc 100 Edsall Dr Sussex NJ 07461

GARDNER, DAVID PIERPONT, university president; b. Berkeley, Calif., Mar. 24, 1933; s. Reed S. and Margaret (Pierpont) G.; m. Elizabeth Fuhriman, June 27, 1958; children: Karen, Shari, Lisa, Marci. BS, Brigham Young U., 1955, DH (hon.), 1981; MA, U. Calif., Berkeley, 1959, PhD, 1966; DLitt (hon.), U. Utah, 1983; LLD (hon.), U. of the Pacific, 1983, U. Nev., Las Vegas, 1984, Westminster Coll., 1987; HHD (hon.), Utah State U., 1987; Docteur Honoris Causa, de l' Universite de Bordeaux, 1988. Dir. Calif. Alumni Found., U. Calif. at Berkeley, 1962-64; asst. to the chancellor, asst. prof. higher edn. U. Calif. at Santa Barbara, 1964-67, asst. chancellor, asst. prof. higher edn., 1967-69, vice chancellor, exec. asst., assoc. prof. higher edn., 1969-70; v.p. U.,Calif. System, Berkeley, 1971-73, pres., 1983—; prof. higher edn. U. Calif., Berkeley, 1983—; pres., prof. higher edn. U. Utah, Salt Lake City, 1973-83, pres. emeritus, 1985; vis. fellow Clare Hall, Cambridge U., 1979, assoc., 1979—. Author: The California Oath Controversy, 1967; mem. editorial bd. Higher Edn. Quarterly; contbr. articles to profl. jours. Bd. dirs. First Security Corp., Fluor Corp., George S. and Dolores Dore Eccles Found., The Nature Conservancy, Calif. C. of C., Calif. Econ. Devel. Corp.; trustee Tanner Lectures on Human Values; chmn. Southwestern Dist. Rhodes Scholarship Selection Com.; mem. Hong Kong U. Sci. and Tech. Coun. Decorated Legion d'Honneur (France), 1985; recipient Benjamin P. Cheney medal East Wash. U., 1984, James Bryant Conant award Edn. Commn. of the States, 1985, Calif. Sch. Bds. Rsch. Found. Hall of Fame award, 1988; 40th Anniversary Disting. Fellow, Fulbright Found., 1987. Fellow Am. Acad. Arts and Scis.; mem. Nat. Assn. State Univs. and Land Grant Colls., Nat. Acad. Pub. Adminstrn., Assn. Am. Univs., Higher Edn. Forum (mem. exec. com. bus.), Phi Beta Kappa (hon.), Phi Kappa Phi (hon.). Home: 70 Rincon Rd Kensington CA 94707 Office: U Calif Office of Pres 300 Lakeside Dr Oakland CA 94612-3550

GARDNER, DORSEY ROBERTSON, finance company executive; b. Montclair, N.J., Sept. 19, 1942; s. Alexander Hoffman and Louise Josephine (Cartwright) G.; m. Lucy Mapes Kramer, June 10, 1967; children: Nina-Marie, Andre, Stephanie, William. BA, Yale U., 1965; MBA, Harvard U., 1967. Chartered fin. analyst. V.p. Fidelity Mgmt. & Rsch. Co., Boston, 1970-80; pres. Kelso Mgmt. Co., Boston, 1980—; bd. dirs. Ports-of-Call, Denver, Deltak, Mpls., Quaker Fabrics; chmn. bd. GRI Corp., Chgo. Mem. Union Club (Boston), Harvard, Boston Racquet Club. Republican. Episcopalian. Home: 49 Pinckney St Boston MA 02114 Office: Kelso Mgmt Co 27 State St Boston MA 02109

GARDNER, JAMES RICHARD, pharmaceutical company executive; b. Wellsville, N.Y., Nov. 18, 1944; s. James Myers and Adelaide (Stockman) G.; m. Linda Marie Cuomo, Oct. 14, 1967; children: Alexandra K., Mindy M. BS in Engring., U.S. Mil. Acad., 1966; M in Pub. Adminstrn., Princeton U., 1968, PhD, 1977; MBA, Long Island U., 1977. Commd. U.S. Army, 1966, advanced through grades to maj., resigned, 1977; staff asst. Office of U.S. Atty. Gen., 1973; asst. prof. U.S. Mil. Acad., West Point, N.Y., 1974-77; dir. agrl. planning Pfizer, Inc., N.Y.C., 1977-81, dir. corp. strategic planning, 1981—; v.p. Pfizer Found., N.Y.C., 1985—; faculty U.S. Army Command and Gen. Staff Coll., 1986—, U.S. Army War Coll., 1989; adv. council Ctr. of Internat. Studies, Princeton U., 1987—; polit. mil. affairs Dept. Army, 1988—. Author: (with others) American National Security, 1981, Business Competitor Intelligence, 1984; editor: Handbook of Strategic Planning, 1986; contbr. articles to profl. jours. Strategic planning com. United Way of Tri-State, N.Y.C., 1984-87; dir. adminstrn. Pfizer Inc. United Way Campaign, N.Y.C., 1985-87; dir. Greater N.Y. Councils Boy Scouts Am, 1988—. Col. USAR, 1977—. Decorated three Bronze Stars, Air Medal, Rep. Vietnam Gallantry Cross with Silver Star; recipient George Washington medal The Freedoms Found., Valley Forge, Pa., 1970. Mem. Planning Forum (pres. N.Y.C. chpt. 1985-86), N. Am. Soc. Corp. Planning (nat. v.p. 1984-85), West Point Soc. N.Y. (bd. dirs. 1984—, v.p. 1986-88, pres. 1988—), Phi Kappa Phi. Republican. Roman Catholic. Home: 250 Mamaroneck Rd Scarsdale NY 10583 Office: Pfizer Inc 235 E 42nd St New York NY 10017

GARDNER, JEWELLE BAKER, business executive, interior designer; b. Ayden, N.C., May 23, 1925; d. Roland Ray and Helen Wingate (Jackson) Cannon; m. Paul Thomas Baker, July 25, 1956 (dec. 1963); children:Paula Jewelle Baker Bryan, Paul Thomas; 1 stepchild, Blanche Baker Miller; m. Fred Calvin Gardner, Apr. 19, 1969 (dec. May 1983); 1 stepchild, Angela Gardner Jones. Student Woods Bus. Sch., New Bern, N.C., 1942-45; BA, Am. Sch. Design, N.Y.C., 1948; BFA, U. N.C., Greensboro, 1950. Dept. head Navy Supply, Cherry Point, N.C., 1941-45; ptnr. Cannons Paint & Wallpaper Co., Ayden, 1945-70; exec. v.p. Baker Furniture Co., Kinston, N.C., 1950-63; operator Cannon Farms, Ayden, 1956—; pres., treas. Baker Furniture Co., Kinston, 1963-69; with consumer program Drexel Co., 1965-66; owner Jewelle Baker Cons., Kinston, 1969—; v.p. Gardner Homes, Elizabeth City, N.C., 1972-81; bus. cons. Gardner Constrn. Co., Kinston, 1975-81; bus. cons. Lenoir Plumbing & Heating Co., Kinston, 1975-81; chief exec. officer Gardner Homes, Elizabeth City, 1982—; chmn. bd., chief exec. officer Lenoir Plumbing & Heating Co., 1982—, Gardner Constrn. Co., 1982—; cons. Carolina Power & Light, 1963-65, N.C. Solar Energy Assn., 1977-79, Nutritional Therapy, Durham, 1979-81; lectr., 1950-63; del. U.S.-China Joint Session on Industry, Trade, and Econ. Devel., Beijing, 1988. Mem. Devel. Auth. of Neuse River Council of Govts., 1984-85. Columnist, Ayden Dispatch and Greenville News Leader, 1940-56; producer Performer Baker's Commls., 1960-69. Mem. C. of C. Kinston (bd. dirs., v.p., chmn. retail mchts. div.), So. Retail Furniture Assn., Nat. Retail Furniture Assn., N.C. Mchts. Assn., N.C. Farm Assn., Assoc. Gen. Contractors Am., Community Council for the Arts, Internat. Platform Assn., N.C. Zool. Assn., N.C. Art Soc., Kinston Country Club, Coral Bay Club, Pineknoll Golf and Country Club, Sea Water Marina Club. Democrat. Mem. Ch. Disciples of Christ. Home: 1708 Elizabeth Dr Kinston NC 28501 Office: Gardner Constrn Co PO Drawer 1278 Kinston NC 28501

GARDNER, MARY JOSEPHINE, corporate executive; b. Lebanon, Pa., Sept. 10, 1943; d. John Edward and Gertrude Marie (Scanlon) G.; m. W. Stephen Lupack, Dec. 28, 1963 (div. Jan. 1974); children: Susan, Joyce. BA magna cum laude, Fordham U., 1971; MA, Columbia U., 1983. Tchr. Cardinal Spellman High Sch., N.Y.C., 1971-77; tng. specialist Prudential Ins. Co., Newark, 1977-79; mgr. mgmt. devel. Am. Express Co., N.Y.C., 1979-82; 2d v.p. Chase Manhattan Bank, N.Y.C., 1982-84; pres. mgmt. cons. firm Gardner Enterprises, N.Y.C., 1984—. Mem. Water Quality Com., Culver Lake, N.J., 1985—; vol. instr. Am. Womens Econ. Devel., 1984—. Named one of Outstanding Young Women of Am., 1978, 79. Mem. Nat. Speakers Assn., Nat. Soc. Performance and Instrn., Bus. and Profl. Womens Assn. (3d v.p. 1988), Alpha Sigma Lambda. Democrat. Home and Office: 215 W 88th St New York NY 10024

GARDNER, NANCY HAZARD, small business owner; b. Washington, Feb. 17, 1949; d. Everette Browning and Vera Catherine (Rushworth) G. BS, U. Md., 1972. Trainer Equitable Trust Bank, Balt., 1970-74; program analyst U. Md., College Park, 1974-77; adminstr. Nat. Acad. Scis., Washington, 1977-80; office mgr. Ctr. for Population Options, Washington, 1980-81; compt. Carltech Assocs., Inc., Columbia, Md., 1981-83; fin. dir. Helschien Health Ctr., Columbia, 1983-84; pres. Sensitive Systems, Inc., Balt., 1982—; chmn. bd. dirs. Sensitive Systems, Inc., Balti. Mem. NAFE. Office: Sensitive Systems Inc 2914 O'Donnell St Baltimore MD 21224

GARDNER, RICHARD HARTWELL, oil company executive; b. Cambridge, Mass., Oct. 9, 1934; s. Richard Hosmer and Marjorie Georgine (Pierce) G.; m. Helen Carolyn McIntyre, Oct. 11, 1957; children—Pamela, Hartwell. A.B., Colgate U., 1956; M.B.A., Harvard U., 1961. Treas. Mobil Latin Am. Inc., N.Y.C., 1964-66; asst. treas. internat. div. Mobil Internat., 1966-68; treas. Mobil Europe Inc., London, 1968-70; treas. N. Am. div., N.Y.C., 1970-72, dep. treas., 1972-73; corp. treas. Mobil Oil Corp., 1974—; treas. Mobil Corp., 1976—. Trustee Am. Sch. London, 1968-70, Danbury Hosp. Served to 1st lt. USAF, 1956-59. Mem. Am. Petroleum Inst., Fin. Execs. Inst. (chmn. 1986-87). Democrat. Office: Mobil Corp 150 E 42nd St New York NY 10017

GARDNER, RICHARD KEVIN, lawyer; b. Chico, Calif., May 5, 1961; s. Richard Dalbert and Nancy Noel (Long) G.; m. Kathleen Ann Anderson, Mar. 16, 1985. BS, U. Utah, 1983; student, U. San Diego Inst. Comparative Law, London, 1987; JD, Calif.-Western U., 1987. Bar: Calif. 1987, U.S. Dist. Ct. (so. dist.) Calif. 1987. Fin. forecaster Tollman Hundley Corp., N.Y.C., 1984-85; treas. Gardners, Inc., Lake Tahoe, Nev., 1985-86; legal asst. Home Fed. Savs. & Loan, San Diego, 1987-88; v.p. ops. and acquisition Mallard Devel., Bellevue, Wash., 1988—. Mem. ABA, Calif. Bar Assn. (div. corp. and banking, div. property, probate and trust), Sigma Alpha Epsilon. Republican. Episcopalian. Office: 1111 118th Ave SE Ste 1 Bellevue WA 98005

GARDNER, ROBERT JACK, electric utility executive; b. Dowagiac, Mich., Nov. 13, 1928; s. Dick B. and Genette (Pixley) G.; m. Susan Crecraft, June 13, 1953; children—Robert, Joseph, James, Susan. B.S.M.E., U. Mich., 1950, LL.B., 1953; grad. advanced mgmt. program, Harvard U., 1975. Bar: Fla. Various positions Fla. Power & Light Co., Juno Beach, 1954-72, v.p. strategic planning, 1973-81, sr. v.p., 1981-87; ret. Fla. Power & Light Co., 1988; pres. Telesat Cablevision, Inc. subs. FPL Group, Inc., 1985-87, FPL Energy Services Inc. subs. FPL Group, Inc., 1985-87; v.p. FPL Group, Inc., 1986—; bd. dirs. Colonial Penn Group Inc., Praxis Group Inc., ESI Energy Services Inc., Telesat Cablevision Inc. subs. FPL Group Inc. Congregationalist. Club: Biscayne Bay Yacht. Office: 4401 University Dr Coral Gables FL 33146

GARDNER, RONALD BRUCE, gas company executive; b. Cherokee, Okla., Aug. 16, 1944; s. Donald Bruce and Barbara Gardner; m. Candalyn Combs, Sept. 28, 1969; children: Rebekah Beth, Geoffrey Bruce, Stephanie Jill, Laura Christine. BS in Econs., West Tex. State U., 1967. Mktg. rep. IBM, Houston, 1968-71; asst. supt. mgmt. info. State of Ill., Springfield, 1971-73; mgmt. cons. Touche Ross & Co., Chgo. and Houston, 1973-80; pres. Colo. Interstate Gas Co., Colorado Springs, Colo., from 1980; now exec. v.p. So. Natural Gas Co., Birmingham, Ala. Chmn., trustee Meml. Hosp., Colorado Springs, 1981—; bd. dirs. 1st Nat. Bank Colorado Springs, 1985—, Colo. Assn. Commerce and Industry, 1984—. Republican. Home: 2434 Mountain Vista Birmingham AL 35243-2855 Office: So Natural Gas Co 1st Nat-So Natural Bldg Birmingham AL 35203 •

GARDNER, SHIRLEY MAE, software company executive; b. Chgo., Mar. 7, 1932; d. Ross Edward and Viola (Schwartz) Blake; m. William Rex Gardner, June 9, 1973. AA in Bus. Adminstrn., North Park Coll., 1952; BS in Bus. Adminstrn., U. Ill., Chgo., 1954. Print prodn. coordinator Poole Bros., Chgo., 1954-60; graphic arts coordinator Combined Ins. Co., Chgo., 1960-65; asst. print shop supr. Standard Rate & Data Service, Skokie, Ill., 1965-70; supr. art, typesetting Schiele Graphics, Chgo., 1970-73; print prodn. operator Regensteiner Corp., Chgo., 1973-75; purchasing agt. Morongo Unified Sch. Dist., Twenty-Nine Palms, Calif., 1975-78, Soc. for Visual Edn. div. Singer Inc., Chgo., 1980-84; dir. purchasing Mindscape, Inc., Northbrook, Ill., 1984—; founder, owner Eagle Bindery Inc., Lincolnwood, Ill., 1988—. Chmn. bd. dirs. United Cerebral Palsy, Lincolnwood, Ill. Mem. Printing Industry of Ill., Nat. Assn. Female Execs., VFW Aux., Phi Pi Omega. Roman Catholic. Home: 8924 Robin Dr Des Plaines IL 60016 Office: Mindscape Inc 3444 Dundee Rd Northbrook IL 60662

GARDNER, TRUDI YORK, lawyer, insurance company executive; b. Portland, Oreg., Mar. 19, 1947; d. Harry and Martha (Gevurtz) York; m. Alan Joel Gardner, Dec. 19, 1971; children: Jordan Casey, Andrew Ryan. BA, UCLA, 1969; MS, Portland State U., 1971; postgrad. N.Y. Law Sch., 1975-76; JD Lewis and Clark Law Sch., 1977. Bar: Washington 1978, U.S. Dist. Ct. (we. dist.) Wash. 1979; cert. tchr. Calif., Oreg. Law clk. U.S. Atty.'s Office (so. dist.) N.Y.C., 1976, to law firm, Portland, Oreg., 1977; fin. relations specialist Puget Sound Power & Light Co., Bellevue, Wash., 1978-79; asst. atty. gen. Dept. Labor and Industries, State of Wash., Seattle, 1979-80; sole practice, Bellevue, 1980-81; regional atty. for Mont., Idaho, Wash., Oreg, Utah and Wyo., Ins. Corp. of Am., Houston, 1981-84, regional v.p., 1984-87; curriculum cons. Portland (Oreg.) Pub. Schs., 1972. Assoc. editor: Multnomah Lawyer, Multnomah County Bar Assn., Portland, 1973. Contbr. articles, cover stories to Sunday supplement of The Oregonian, radio scripts for Am. Heritage Assn. to Sta. KWJJ; contbr. short stories to mags. Mem. King County United Way Conf. Panel for Developmentally Disabled, Seattle, 1978-79. Mem. Wash. State Bar Assn. (pub. relations com. 1978-81), Seattle-King County Bar Assn., Portland City Club, Seattle Mcpl. League, Pi Sigma Alpha, Pi Lambda Theta. Clubs: Women's Univ.; Bellevue Athletic. Home and Office: 5182 S Ironton Way Englewood CO 80111

GARDNER, WARREN JOSEPH, JR., insurance executive; b. Pitts., Sept. 21, 1951; s. Warren Joseph and Elsie Clair (Da'Rin) G.; BS in Mgmt., Pa. State U., 1975, postgrad. civil engring., Mountain State U., 1976; m. Nancy Jean Antolovich (div. 1981). Mgr., Windy Hill Farms, Mayport, Pa., 1975-76; trainee counselor Fidelity Union Life Ins. Co., Dallas, 1976; supr. Bankers Life Ins. Co. Nebr., Pitts., 1977-78; gen. mgr. Andrew J. Bell, Inc., Pitts., 1978-79; account exec. spl. accounts, mgmt. tng. Sentry Ins., A Mut. Co. (SIAMCO), Pitts., 1979-82; v.p. AIS, Inc., Pitts., 1982-88; pres. C.H. Penn Cons., Inc., Monroeville, Pa., 1982—; pres. Adv. Group Mgmt. Inc., 1985-88; cons., Heritage Agy. Inc., Monroeville, 1988—; ptnr. Adv. Risk Inc., Pitts., 1987; treas. Accuvest, Inc., Pitts.; tchr. in field; cons. insurance and employee benefits Volkswagen of Am. New Stanton, Pa., 1980-83; ptnr. Salt-Lick Devel. Co., 1988—, Seven Springs Water Resources, 1988—. Committeeman, Allegheny (Pa.) County Republican Com., 1978-80; mem. exec. com. Pitts. Symphony Orch., 1988—. Murrysville (Pa.) Women's Club scholar, 1969; Pa. State U. scholar, 1973-75; NIH fellow, 1975; named Sentry rep. of distinction, 1980, 82; nominated for 1986 register of Men and Women under 40 Who are Changing the Nat., Esquire Mag. Mem. Nat. Assn. Life Underwriters, Ind. Ins. Agts. Assn., Am. Mgmt. Assn., Lions (dir. Monroeville), Seneca Trail Club, Fox Chapel Yacht Club (charter), Monroeville Racquet Club, Sentry Vice President's, Triangle. Home: 3646 School Rd Murrysville PA 15668 Office: 1 Monroeville Ctr Ste 150 Monroeville PA 15146

GARDNER, WILLIAM ALBERT, JR., pathologist, medical foundation executive; b. Sumter, S.C., Aug. 2, 1939; s. William A. and Betty Lee (Kennedy) G.; m. Kathryn Ann Medlin, June 30, 1960; children: Mary Elizabeth, Kathryn Lee, William Dylan. B.S., Wofford Coll., 1960; M.S. in Anatomy, Med. Coll. S.C., 1963, M.D., 1965. Diplomate: Am. Bd. Pathology. Intern Johns Hopkins Hosp., Balt., 1965-66, asst. resident, 1966-67, fellow in pathology, 1965-67; asst. resident Duke U., Durham, N.C., 1967-68, chief resident, 1968-69, instr. pathology, 1968-69; chief lab. service VA Hosp., Charleston, S.C., 1969; asst. prof. pathology Med. U. S.C., 1969-72, assoc. prof., 1972-76; prof. pathology Vanderbilt U., Nashville, 1976-81, vice chmn. dept. pathology; chief lab. service VA Hosp., Nashville, 1976-81; prof., chmn. dept. pathology U. South Ala., Mobile, 1981—, pres. health svcs. found., 1988—. Contbr. articles on oncology, urology, parasitology and pathology to profl. jours. Recipient Outstanding Teaching award Med. U. S.C., 1975, Disting. Alumnus award Med. U. S.C., 1988. Fellow Am. Soc. Clin. Pathologists, Coll. Am. Pathologists (del. for govtl. pathology); mem. Internat. Acad. Pathology (U.S. and Can. Acad. Pathology Council), Acad. Clin. Lab. Physicians and Scientists, AMA, Ala. Med. Assn., Assn. Pathology Chairmen (mem. council), Alpha Omega Alpha. Methodist. Home: 1565 Fearnway Mobile AL 36604 Office: U South Ala 2451 Fillingim St Mobile AL 36617

GAREY, DONALD LEE, pipeline and oil executive; b. Ft. Worth, Sept. 9, 1931; s. Leo James and Jessie (McNatt) G.; B.S. in Geol. Engring., Tex. A. and M. U., 1953; m. Elizabeth Patricia Martin, Aug. 1, 1953; children—Deborah Anne, Elizabeth Laird. Reservoir geologist Gulf Oil Corp., 1953-54, sr. geologist, 1956-65; v.p., mng. dir. Indsl. Devel. Corp. Lea County, Hobbs, N.Mex., 1965-72, dir., 1972-86, pres., 1978-86; v.p., dir. Minerals, Inc., Hobbs, 1966-72, pres., dir., 1972-86, chief exec. officer, 1978-82; mng. dir. Hobbs Indsl. Found. Corp., 1965-72, dir., 1965-76; v.p. Llano, Inc., 1972-74, exec. v.p., chief operating officer, 1974-75, pres., 1975-86, chief exec. officer, 1978-82, also dir.; pres., chief exec. officer, Pollution Control, Inc., 1969-81; pres. NMESCO Fuels, Inc., 1982-86; chmn., pres., chief exec. officer Estacado Inc., 1986—; pres. Llano Co2, Inc., 1984-86; cons. geologist, geol. engr., Hobbs, 1965-72. Chmn., Hobbs Manpower Devel. Tng. Adv. Com., 1965-72; mem. Hobbs Adv. Com. for Mental Health, 1965-67; chmn. N.Mex. Mapping Adv. Com., 1968-69; mem. Hobbs adv. bd. Salvation Army, 1967-78, chmn., 1970-72; mem. exec. bd. Conquistador council Boy Scouts Am., Hobbs, 1965-75; vice chmn. N.Mex. Gov.'s Com. for Econ. Devel., 1968-70; bd. regents Coll. Southwest, 1982-85. Served to capt. USAF, 1954-56. Registered profl. engr., Tex. Mem. Am. Inst. Profl. Geologists, Am. Assn. Petroleum Geologists, AIME, N.Mex., Roswell geol. socs., N.Mex. Amigos. Club: Rotary. Home: 315 E Alto Dr Hobbs NM 88240 Office: Broadmoor Bldg PO Box 5587 Hobbs NM 88241

GARFIELD, LESLIE JEROME, real estate executive; b. N.Y.C., Mar. 23, 1932; s. Jack and Anne (Weinert) G.; m. Johanna Rosengarten, Sept. 28, 1960; children: Clare Louisa, Jed Herbert, Cory Alexander. BA, U. Wis., Madison, 1953; MA, Harvard U., 1956; MBA, Columbia U., 1958. V.p. Pease & Elliman, Inc., N.Y.C., 1965-68, William A. White & Sons, Inc., N.Y.C., 1968-78; pres. Leslie J. Garfield & Co., Inc., N.Y.C., 1978—. Chmn. bd. N.Y. Youth Symphony, 1986, pres. bd., 1975-86; bd. dirs. Carnegie Hill Neighbors, N.Y.C., 1985-88; mem. com. on prints and illustrated books Mus. Modern Art. Cpl. U.S. Army, 1954-55. Mem. Real Estate Bd. N.Y. (chmn. sales brokers com. 1985-86), The Drawing Soc. (bd. dirs.). Clubs: Century Assn., Nat. Arts, Harvard, Grolier. Office: 654 Madison Ave New York NY 10021

GARFINKEL, HARMON MARK, specialty chemicals company executive; b. Bklyn., May 20, 1933; s. Samuel and Elsie (Schwartz) G.; m. Lorraine Plawsky, Mar. 4, 1956; children—Elyse, Michelle. B.A., Bklyn. Coll., 1957; Ph.D., Iowa State U., 1960; postgrad. program for mgmt. devel., Harvard U. Bus. Sch., 1973. Dir. bio-organic tech. Corning Glass Works, N.Y., 1973-74, dir. applied chemistry and biology, 1974-75, dir. biomed. and chem. tech., 1975-78, dir. research, 1978-85; v.p. research and devel. Engelhard Corp., Edison, N.J., 1985—; bd. dirs. Nippon/Engelhard, Englehard/Kali-Chemie; instr. math. Elmira Coll., 1964. Patents and publs. in field. Mem. Am. Chem. Soc., Am. Phys. Soc., Am. Inst. Chemists, Am. Ceramics Soc.

Republican. Jewish. Home: 1584 Mountain Top Rd Bridgewater NJ 08807 Office: Engelhard Corp R & D Labs Menlo Park CN 28 Edison NJ 08818

GARIPPA, JOAN, management consultant; b. N.Y.C., Jan. 21, 1945; d. John and Victoria (Rotteveel) Welch; m. Thomas Garippa, May 17, 1969. BBA, Bernard M. Baruch Coll., 1983. Tchr. N.Y.C. Bd. Edn., 1984-85; mgmt. analyst N.Y.C., 1985-89; pres. JG Enterprises, Little Neck, N.Y., 1989—. mem. exec. bd. Little Neck Community Assn., 1974-83, Queens (N.Y.) Borough Pres.'s Transit Adv. Bd., 1983—; pres., exec. dir. youth programs Little Neck-Douglaston Community Coun. Inc., 1978-82; mem., co-chair transp. com. Community Planning Bd., Bayside, N.Y., 1980—; v.p. Little Neck Pines Assn., 1988—; candidate community sch. bd. #26, N.Y.C. coun. 16th dist., 1981. Recipient Citizenship award Little Neck-Douglaston Meml. Day Parade Com., 1982. Mem. Networking Exec. Women Queens/Western Nassau, Nat. Assn. Female Execs., Am. Soc. Profl. and Exec. Women, Nat. Mgmt. Honor Soc., Rep. Club 25 Assembly Dist. Republican. Roman Catholic. Home: 41 31 248th St Little Neck NY 11363

GARLAND, CHARLES STEDMAN, JR., investment banker; b. N.Y.C., Sept. 17, 1927; s. Charles and Aurelia (Stoner) G.; B.A., Yale U., 1949; m. Joan B. Cardwell, Sept. 17, 1954; children—Margaret, Elizabeth, Charles. With Merrill Lynch, Pierce, Fenner & Smith, N.Y.C., 1950-52, Louisville, 1952-54, Alex Brown & Sons, Balt., 1954—, ptnr., 1964—. Pres., Balt. Opera Co., 1979—; trustee Chesapeake Bay Found., 1980—. Served in USN, 1945-46. Republican. Episcopalian. Clubs: Elkridge, Maryland, Merchants (Balt.); Yale, Ausable (N.Y.C.). Office: Alex Brown & Sons Inc 15 Devon Hill Rd Baltimore MD 21210

GARLAND, DIANE MARY, financial planner; b. Winchester, Mass., Mar. 16, 1947; d. George Martin and Jane Elaine (Farrar) Radulski; m. James Warren Garland. Student, U. Mass., 1965-67, U. N.H., 1972-74; cert., Coll. Fin. Planning, 1984. Cert. fin. planner. Lab. technician Nashua (N.H.) Meml. Hosp., 1972-78; pres. Tech Support, Merrimack, N.H., 1978-79; fin. planner IDS, Nashua, 1979-85; staff planner Peek Fin. Svcs., Windham, N.H., 1985-87; dir. fin. svcs., fin. cons. Palmer Fin. Group, Merrimack, N.H., 1988—; adj. faculty Coll. Fin. Planning, Denver. Author: (video) The House, 1982. Mem. Internat. Assn. Fin. Planning (pres. 1987-88), Assn. Employee Benefits. Democrat. Roman Catholic. Home: 46 Wilson Hill Rd Merrimack NH 03054 Office: Palmer FG 402 Amherst St Nashua NH 03054

GARLOUGH, WILLIAM GLENN, marketing executive; b. Syracuse, N.Y., Mar. 27, 1924; s. Henry James and Gladys (Killam) G.; m. Charlotte M. Tanzer, June 15, 1947; children: Jennifer, William, Robert. BEE, Clarkson U., 1949. With Knowlton Bros., Watertown, N.Y., 1949-67, mgr. mfg. services, 1966-67; v.p. planning, equipment systems div. Vare Corp., Englewood Cliffs, N.J., 1967-69; mgr. mktg. Valley Mould div. Microdot Inc., Hubbard, Ohio, 1969-70; dir. corp. devel. Microdot Inc., Greenwich, Conn., 1970-73, v.p. corp. devel., 1973-76, v.p. adminstrn., 1976-77, v.p. corp. devel., 1977-78; v.p. corp. devel. Am. Bldg. Maintenance Industries, San Francisco, 1979-83; pres. The Change Agts., Inc., Walnut Creek, Calif., 1983—; bd. dirs. Gourmet To Go Inc.; mem. citizens adv. com. to Watertown Bd. Edn., 1957. Bd. dirs. Watertown Community Chest, 1958-61; ruling elder Presbyn. ch. Served with USMCR, 1942-46. Mem. Am. Mgmt. Assn., Bldg. Service Contractors Assn., Internat. Sanitary Supply Assn., Mensa, Am. Mktg. Assn., TAPPI, Assn. Corp. Growth (pres. San Francisco chpt. 1984-85, v.p. chpts. west 1985-88), Lincoln League (pres. 1958), Am. Contract Bridge League (life master), Clarkson Alumni Assn. (Watertown sect. pres. 1955), Tau Beta Pi. Clubs: Olympic; No. N.Y. Contract (pres. 1959), No. N.Y. Transp. Home: 2557 Via Verde Walnut Creek CA 94598 Office: The Change Agts Inc 1990 N California Blvd Walnut Creek CA 94596

GARNER, CHESTER ALEXANDER, agriculturist, consultant; b. Lebanon, Ind., Sept. 25, 1897; s. Abner Anderson and Effie Almyra (Alexander) G.; m. Frances Johanna Schotthoeffer, Sept. 21, 1923 (dec.); children: Edmund Gale, Joan Lenore. Diploma in violin, Music Conservatory, Indpls., 1916; BSA, Purdue U., 1921; MS, Iowa State U., 1924; postgrad., U. Ill., 1925-26, U. So. Calif., 1928. Mgr. muck soil exploration stas. U.S. Dept. Agr., Washington and N.Y., 1922-25; prof. olericulture U. Ill., Champaign, 1925-26; fed. and state plant quarantine guardian L.A., 1926-29; involved with domestic and fgn. commerce El Centro, Fullerton, L.A., Calif., 1928-33; contractor-cons. agrl. industries U.S. and abroad, 1933-40; agronomist engr. U.S. Dept. Def., L.A., Ariz., Porto Rico, 1940-43; civilian chief to Adm. Ingram Region 6, Bahia, Brazil, 1943; coordinator Inter-American Affairs, Brazil, 1944; contractor-cons. Biol. Controls, Stamd. Oil, Colombia, L.A., Ventura, 1944-73; dir.-entomogist Rotenone Chemical Co., L.A., 1930-40; chmn. Inst. Tropical Rsch. Harvard U., Barro, Colo., Panama, 1939-40; raw products explorer Am. Colombian Corp., Lands O'Loba, Colombia 1940; exec. cons. Canengco Ltd. Engrs., Montreal, Can., 1955-56; mgr. Muck Soil Exptl. Sta., Williamson, N.Y., South Bend, Ind. Author: Aborigines' Medicinal Plants (Pioneer and Indian Sourcebook),1974-75, Biomedica! Manual: Emollients from Plants, 1975-77. Contbr. articles to profl. jours. Patentee in field. Sponsor fgn. grad. student exchange program, L.A., 1973-74; explorerfor antitumor plants Nat. Cancer Inst., Ind., Fiji, Australia and West Indies, 1977-86, Colo., Mojave Desert, West Indies; musical vol. Motion Picture Country House, Calabasas, Calif., 1986-88, Beverly Hosp., Canoga Park, Calif., 1980—; ch. organist. With U.S. Army, 1917-18. Named Grad. scholar Purdue U., 1921-22, Outstanding Vol. Beverly Enterprises, Canoga Park; recipient Distinguished Svc. to Fgn. Com. award L.A. C. of C., 1942, Motion Picture TV Fund award as Music Therapist. Mem. Earthwatch, World Wildlife Fund, Smithsonian Inst. (assoc.), Platinum Club, Biomedical Found. (pres., chief exec. officer 1977—), Humana Hosp. Srs. (Woodland Hills chpt.), Motion Picture Guild Arts and Crafts, Alpha Gamma Rho (Delta chpt.). Mem. Ecumenical Ch. Home: Lynn Ranch 1007 Camino Magenta Thousand Oaks CA 91360 Office: Harmony Found PO Box 1746 Thousand Oaks CA 91360

GARNER, DAN REED, accounting firm executive; b. Victoria, Tex., Nov. 21, 1944; s. Carl and Louise (Alexander) G.; Greer Thompson, Aug. 25, 1964; children: W. Reed, Alex A. B in Bus. Adminstrn., U. Tex., 1966. CPA, Tex. Auditor Arthur Young & Co. CPA's, Dallas, 1966-78; internat. ptnr. Arthur Young & Co. CPA's, Frankfurt, Fed. Republic Germany, 1978-81; office dir. entrepreneurial services Arthur Young & Co. CPA's, Dallas, 1981-85; nat. dir. entrepreneurial services Arthur Young & Co. CPA's, Dallas and N.Y.C., 1985—. Author: Arthur Young Guide to Financing for Growth, 1986. Mem. Dallas Venture Capital Forum (founder, bd. dirs. 1983—), SW Venture Capital Conf. (founder), Small Bus. Council, U.S. C. of C., Am. Inst. CPA's, Am. Electronic Assn. Republican. Methodist. Office: Arthur Young & Co 2121 San Jacinto St Ste 500 Dallas TX 75201

GARNER, LINDA NANELLA, investment banker; b. Little Rock, Ark., Dec. 3, 1946; d. Bennie Gordon and Helen Cleo (Derryberry) G. BA, U. Ark., 1975; MPA, U. Ark., Fayetteville, 1979. Supr. Ark. Merit System, Little Rock, 1975-77; dir. research and coms. Ark. Legis. Council, Little Rock, 1977-80; dir. legislation and budgets Ark. Gov.'s Office, Little Rock, 1980-82; commr. ins. Ark. Dept. Ins., Little Rock, 1983-85; corp. fin. assoc. Stephens, Inc., Little Rock, 1985—. Named Outstanding Citizen State of Ark., gov. of Ark., 1982. Office: Stephens Inc 114 E Capitol St Little Rock AR 72201

GARNES, RAMONA APRIL, newspaper editor; b. Bklyn., Dec. 3, 1951; d. Raymond and Joyce (Roberts) G. BA, CUNY, 1978. Sub-editor N.Y. Post, N.Y.C., 1978—. Mem. Am. Soc. Female Execs., N.Y. Fin. Writers Assn., NAACP. Democrat. Office: NY Post 210 South St 4th Fl Bus News New York NY 10002

GARNETT, STANLEY IREDALE, II, utility company executive, lawyer; b. Petersburg, Va., Aug. 11, 1943; s. Stanley Arthur and Edith (Keirstead) G.; m. Carol Witt, June 24, 1967; children—Matthew S.A., Andrew F.W. B.A., Colby Coll., 1965; M.B.A., Wharton Sch., U. Pa., 1967; J.D., NYU, 1973. Bar: N.Y. 1974. Sr. fin. analyst Standard Oil Co. of N.J., N.Y.C., 1967-70; assoc. Milbank, Tweed, Hadley & McCloy, N.Y.C., 1973-81; v.p.-legal and regulatory Allegheny Power System, Inc., N.Y.C., 1981—; chmn. oper. com. Living Lakes, Inc. Joseph P. Wharton scholar, 1965-67. Mem. ABA, N.Y. State Bar Assn., Republican. Episcopalian. Home: 39 Briarcliff Rd Mountain Lakes NJ 07046 Office: Allegheny Power System Inc 320 Park Ave New York NY 10022

GAROFALO, DENISE ANNE, librarian, automation consultant; b. Norwich, N.Y., July 26, 1959; d. John Andrew and Irene Anne (Boucher) Listovitch; m. James Anthony Garofalo, Aug. 29, 1987. BA, SUNY, Albany, 1980, MLS, 1982. Librarian Pawtucket (R.I.) Pub. Library, 1982-85; head tech. services and automated systems Warwick (R.I.) Pub. Library, 1985-87; automation cons. N.H. State Library, Concord, 1987—. Reviewer Library Jour., 1983—. Mem. ALA, NAFE, Nat. Trust for Hist. Preservation, New Eng. Library Assn., N.H. Library Assn. Democrat. Roman Catholic. Office: GMILCS Manchester City Libr 405 Pine St Manchester NH 03104

GARON, GERALD STEPHEN, financial planning executive; b. Portland, Maine, Dec. 16, 1942; s. Harry J. and Shirley F. (Frank) G.; m. Susan Alpert, Nov. 25, 1973; children: Cynthia, Kenneth, Michael, Joshua. AB, Colby Coll., 1965; MBA, Boston U., 1967. Cert. fin. planner. Security analyst State Mut. Life Ins. Co., Worcester, Mass., 1967-70; pres. Midway Motel, Wells, Maine, 1971-83, Taxbridge Fin. Group, Cambridge, Mass., 1986—; v.p. Tax Man, Inc., Cambridge, Mass., 1971—, also bd. dirs. Trustee Lookout Resort Condos, Ogunquit, Maine, 1986—. Mem. Intenat. Assn. Fin. Planning, Inst. Cert. Fin. Planners. Jewish. Home: 5 Old Ridge Rd Canton MA 02021 Office: Taxbridge Fin Group 678 Massachusetts Ave Cambridge MA 02139

GARPOW, JAMES EDWARD, financial executive; b. Detroit, July 30, 1944; s. Roy Joseph and Jeanne Beechner (Brader) G.; B.B.A., U. Mich., 1968; m. Elizabeth Marie Conte, Aug. 30, 1969; children—Barbara Jean, Susan Marie. Audit mgr. Ernst & Whinney, Detroit, 1966-73; mgr. corp. acctg. Fed. Mogul Corp., Detroit, 1973-79; corp. controller LOF Plastics, Inc., Detroit, 1979-80; treas. chief fin. officer KMS Industries, Inc., Ann Arbor, Mich., 1980-83; corp. controller Simpson Industries, Inc., Birmingham, Mich., 1983—; audit mgr. Ernst & Whinney. C.P.A., Mich. Mem. Am. Inst. C.P.A.s, Nat. Assn. Accts., Mich. Assn. C.P.A.s, Fin. Execs. Inst., Beta Alpha Psi, Alpha Kappa Psi. Office: Simpson Industries Inc 32100 Telegraph Rd Suite 120 Birmingham MI 48010

GARR, CARL ROBERT, manufacturing company executive; b. Olean, N.Y., Apr. 4, 1927; s. Frederick H.J. and Mary Magdalene (Zimmerman) G.; m. Arlene Crawford, Dec. 20, 1947; children: Christine Garr Weber, Anne H., Elizabeth Garr Reese. B.S. in Physics, Kent State U., 1950; M.S. in Physics, Case Inst. Tech., 1953, Ph.D. in Metall. Engring, 1957. Supr. engring. Bettis plant Westinghouse Co., 1956-58; supt. tech. services, nuclear fuel ops. Olin Mathieson Chem. Corp., 1958-62; dir. engring. and research Albuquerque div. ACF Industries Inc., N.Y.C., 1962-68, v.p. research and devel., 1968-70; v.p. ACF Industries, Inc., N.Y.C., 1976-82; pres., chief exec. officer Polymer Corp. subs. ACF Industries, Inc., Reading, Pa., 1970-76, 1984-86, chmn., 1987—; pres., chief exec. officer Empire Steel Castings, Inc., Reading, 1982-84; v.p. Chesebrough-Pond's Inc., 1984-86; chief exec. officer, chmn. bd. Bank of Pa., Reading, 1988—; vice-chmn. Dauphin Deposit Corp., 1988—; dir. Dauphin Dep., Harrisburg, Pa., Carpenter Tech. Corp., Washington Aluminum Co., Balt. Served with USN, 1944-46. Mem. Am. Soc. Metals, Sigma Xi. Club: Berkshire Country (Reading). Home: 1175 Reading Blvd Wyomissing PA 19610 Office: PO Box 15210 Reading PA 19612

GARREAU, BRUCE J., savings and loan executive, accountant. BS in Pub. Accountancy, SUNY, Albany, 1972. CPA, N.Y., Conn. From sr. mgr., sr. computer specialist Peat Marwick Main & Co., Albany, 1974-83; auditor NE Savs., Hartford, Conn., 1983-87, sr. v.p., contr., 1987-88, exec. v.p., contr., 1988—. Office: NE Savs Northeast Pla at State House Sq Hartford CT 06102

GARRETT, JOSEPH PATRICK, pension fund and real estate executive; b. Mesa, Ariz., Sept. 14, 1955; s. Joe Maurice and Norma Jean (Crowder) G.; m. Debra Brooks, June 7, 1980; children: Joseph Blake, Brooke Norell. BS in Fin. and Real Estate, Ariz. State U., Tempe, 1977. Asst. to pres. Ariz. State Senate, Phoenix, 1975-77; real estate trust officer Valley Nat. Bank of Ariz., Phoenix, 1977-80; real estate acquisitions officer The Travelers, Dallas, 1980-81; ptnr. Randy Heady Co., Dallas, 1981-83; pres., chmn. bd. Garrett Realty Advisors, Dallas, 1980—. Mem. Urban Land Inst., Pension Real Estate Assn., Internat. Found. Employee Benefit Plans, Nat. Conf. Pub. Employee Retirement System, Nat. Council Tchrs. Retirement, Am. Real Estate and Urban Econs. Assn., Indsl. Devel. Research Council, Police, Fire and Pub. Safety, Assn. Investment Mgmt. Sales Execs., Investment Co. Inst., Nat. Assn. State Retirement Adminstrs., State Assn. County Retirement Adminstrs., Calif. Assn. Pub. Retirement Systems, Chgo. Athletic Assn. Republican. Clubs: Bent Tree Country, The Tower. Office: Garrett Realty Advisors 1509 Main St Suite 1105 Dallas TX 75201

GARRETT, JOY LEE, personnel director; b. Kansas City, Mo., Dec. 4, 1927; d. James Edward and Sadie Blanche (Hagood) O'Neil; m. Joe P. Rieck, Dec. 16, 1950 (div. Jan. 1968); children: Deborah A. Boswell Christenson, Carole S. Rieck Hope, Teri J. Rieck Mc Guigan, Christie L. Rieck Bryant; m. Orval W. Garrett. Student, Cowley Community Coll., 1969-77. Dir. billing dept. Gordon & Platt, Inc., Winfield, Kans., 1961-69; adminstrv. asst. Arkansas City (Kans.) Meml. Hosp., 1969-81, pers. mgr., 1981—; sec. adv. bd. Arkansas City Meml. Hosp., 1970-81, sec. bd. trustees, 1981-84. Mem. Am. Bus. Women's Assn. (pres. 1976-77, Woman of Yr. 1977), Arkansas City C. of C. (Leadership Ark City Tng. Class 1986), Kans. Hosp. Pers. Mgmt. Assn. (bd. dirs. dist. 4 1987-88), Soroptimists (asst. treas. 1986-87, del. 1988—, Disting. Achievement in Svc. award 1987).

GARRETT, KRISTINE REED, real estate executive; b. Titusville, Pa., Sept. 8, 1958; d. David Andrew and Virginia Anne (Rogers) Reed; m. Jonathan Miles Garrett, Nov. 21, 1987. BA in History, Allegheny Coll., 1982. Loan processor, closer Sun State Savs. & Loan Assn., Phoenix, 1983-84, loan officer, 1984-85, asst. v.p., asst. mgr., 1985-87, v.p., dept. mgr., 1987—. Mem. allocations panel Valley of the Sun United Way, Phoenix, 1987—; mem. Sun State Polit. Action Com., 1987—; mem. Valley Partnership, Phoenix, 1987—. Mem. Women in Comml. Real Estate, Assn. Profl. Mortgage Women, Young Mortgage Bankers Assn. Republican. Presbyterian. Office: Sun State Savs & Loan Assn 4250 E Camelback Rd #200 K Phoenix AZ 85018

GARRETT, ROBERT DEAN, insurance company executive; b. Fairfield, Ill., Apr. 13, 1933; m. Peggy Jean Spence, Dec. 8, 1955; children: Daniel Bryant, Evelyn, Brenda, Ronald. BA, Ea. Ill. U., 1988. With U.S. Post Office, Chgo., 1954-60, Gen. Telephone Co., So. Ill., 1960-67; agt. MFA Ins. Co., Mt. Carmel, Ill., 1967-70; with Fed. Kemper Ins. Co., Decatur, Ill., 1970—, v.p. adminstrn., 1977-86, v.p. adminstrn., sec., 1986—. Bd. commrs. Decatur Housing Authority, 1987—; bd. dirs. Jr. Achievement, Decatur, 1978-81, Council of Community Services, Decatur, 1978-83, pres., 1983-84; bd. dirs. Decatur Boys Club, 1979-84, pres., 1981-83; facilitator, writer long-range community strategic plan Decatur Advantage, 1987-88; bd. dirs. United Way Decatur and Macon Counties, 1985-88; trustee Richland Community Coll., 1985—; sec. bd. trustees Richland Community Coll., 1988—. Served with USAF, 1950-54. Recipient Cert. in Gen. Ins., Ins. Inst. Am., 1975. Mem. Pvt. Industry Council (chmn. 1983-84), C. of C. Office: 2001 E Mound Rd Decatur IL 62526

GARRETTO, LEONARD ANTHONY, JR., insurance company executive; b. N.Y.C., Apr. 13, 1925; s. Leonard and Evenia (Egidio) G.; BEE, Manhattan Coll., 1951; m. Theresa Cennamo, Aug. 6, 1949; children: Deborah, Mark, Michael, Paula, David. Engr., Gen. Precision Lab. Inc., Pleasantville, N.Y., 1951-53, project adminstr., 1953-55, project mgr., 1955-58, subcontracts mgr., 1958-59; adminstrv. engr. Sperry Systems Mgmt. div. Sperry Rand Corp., Great Neck, N.Y., 1959-61, mgmt. services adminstr., 1961-63, mgmt. services mgr., 1963-65, fin. planning mgr., 1965-66, planning mgr., 1966-68, dir. adminstrn., 1968; agt. First Investors Corp., N.Y.C., 1966-69, dist. mgr., 1969-70; gen. mgr. David Gracer Co., N.Y.C., 1970-72; v.p. regional sales Somerset Capital Corp., N.Y.C., 1972-75; regional dir. Wis. Nat. Life Ins. Co., Oshkosh, 1975-77, regional sales v.p., Englewood Cliffs, N.J., 1977-84, sr. regional sales v.p., 1984-86, area sales v.p., Stroudsburg, Pa., 1986—. With U.S. Army, 1943-45, ETO. Mem. Am. Soc. Nataries, Nat. Assn. Life Underwriters. Democrat. Roman Catholic. Office: Wis Nat Life Ins Co 804 Sarah St Ste 107 Stroudsburg PA 18360

GARRISH, THEODORE JOHN, lawyer; b. Detroit, Jan. 6, 1943; s. Theodore and Adella Beatrice (Kimball) G.; m. Joy Ann Ziegler, Aug. 4, 1967 (div. 1979); children: Theodore John, Amelia Sutter. A.B., U. Mich., 1964; J.D. cum laude, Wayne State U., 1968. Bar: Mich. 1969, D.C. 1972. Trial atty. U.S. Dept. Justice, Washington, 1969-72; pub. opinion analyst Com. for Reelection of Pres., Washington, 1972; chief advt. substantiation FTC, Washington, 1973-74; asst. spl. counsel to Pres. Washington, 1974; asst. to sec. U.S. Dept. Interior, Washington, 1976, legis. counsel, 1981-82; gen. counsel Consumer Product Safety Commn., Washington, 1976-78; ptnr. Deane, Snowdon, Shutler, Garrish & Gherardi, Washington, 1978-81; gen. counsel Dept. Energy, Washington, 1983-85, asst. sec., 1985-89; fed. inspector Alaska Natural Gas Transp. System, 1986-89; Wash. counsel The Flanagan Group, 1989—; pres. Brewery Mgmt. Co., 1989—, Kent Island Investment Co., 1989—; mng. ptnr. Wild Goose Brewery, 1989—; mem. U.S. Adminstrv. Conf., Washington, 1976-78, 83-85, Pres.'s Commn. on Catastrophic Nuclear Accidents, 1988—. Del. Mich. Republican Conv., 1966; asst. to group dir. Presdl. Inaugural Com., 1973, dep. exec. dir., 1981; mem. adv. com. on human concerns Rep. Nat. Com., 1979. Mem. Fed. Bar Assn., Mich. Bar Assn., D.C. Bar Assn., Alpha Delta Phi. Congregationalist. Club: Peninsular Soc. (Ann Arbor, Mich.). Home: 603 Canal Ln Annapolis MD 21401 Office: 11 Canal Ctr Ste 250 Alexandria VA 22314

GARRISON, GARY, life insurance services executive; b. Springfield, Mass., Oct. 20, 1934; s. Nathan Smith and Doris Izella (Powers) G.; m. Barbara Dowd, July 5, 1979; children: Steven Alan, Patricia Lynn, Susan Elaine Garrison Goodhue. BA in Bus. Adminstrn., Roger Williams Coll., Providence, 1975. CLU; accredited pub. relations profl. Asst. news dir. WHYN Radio and TV, Springfield, Mass., 1956-63; dir. corp. communications Mass. Mut. Life Ins. Co., Springfield, 1963-79; asst. v.p. sales promotion Sun Ins. Services, Inc., Atlanta, 1979-83; v.p. corp. services John Alden Life Ins. Co., Miami, Fla., 1983—. Contbr. articles on meeting planning to profl. jours. Mem. Life Communicators Assn., Meeting Planners Internat., Ins. Conf. Planners Assn., Pub. Relations Soc. Am. Home: 1821 SW 52nd Ave Plantation FL 33317 Office: John Alden Life Ins Co PO Box 020270 Miami FL 33102-0270

GARRISON, JAMES ROBERT, horse registry executive; b. Coshocton, Ohio, Feb. 2, 1951; s. Robert Grady and Ruby Elizabeth (Covington) G.; m. Katherine Marie Otis, Mar. 29, 1969 (div. June 1972); 1 child, Jennifer Marie; m. Kathleen Marie Stanfill, Dec. 16, 1975; children: Sarah Elizabeth, Molly Kathleen, Aaron James. BA, Met. State U., 1980. Mgr. store King Soopers, Denver, 1968-78; dir. ops. Arabian Horse Registry, Westminster, Colo., 1979—. Mem. Rocky Mt. Energizers Toastmasters (pres. 1988—). Republican. Home: 4411 W 111th Ave Westminster CO 80030 Office: Arabian Horse Registry 12000 Zuni Westminster CO 80234

GARRISON, STEPHEN ALLAN, management consultant; b. Portsmouth, N.H., May 10, 1940; s. Malcolm E. and Dorothea (Brooks) G.; m. Catherine R. Duke, Dec. 9, 1962 (div. 1977); children: Daniel A., Charles R.; m. Frances Faye Parker, May 1, 1981. BS, U.S. Naval Acad., 1962; MBA in Fin., Harvard U., 1969. Commd. ensign USN, 1962, advanced through grades to lt., resigned, 1967; instl. analyst Underwood Neuhaus & Co., Houston, 1969-70; v.p. Vaughan, Nelson & Boston, Inc., Houston, 1970-73; sr. v.p. Heidrick & Struggles, Inc., Dallas, 1973-82; office mgr. Ward Howell Internat., Dallas, 1982-85, mem. office pres., 1985-86, mng. ptnr., 1986-88, chmn. bd., chief exec. officer, 1988—; bd. dirs. Buford TV Inc., Tyler, Tex.;. Mem. assoc. bd. So. Meth. U., Dallas, 1980—, Dallas Citizen's Coun. Mem. Dallas Partnership of Dallas C. of C. (bd. dirs. N. Tex. Commn.), Harvard U. Bus. Sch. Alumni Assn. (bd. dirs., sponsor 1976—). Episcopalian. Club: Dallas. Office: Ward Howell Internat Inc Thanksgiving Tower 1601 Elm St Ste 900 Dallas TX 75201 also: 99 Park Ave New York NY 10016

GARRISON, WALTER R., corporate executive; b. St. Louis, July 7, 1926; s. Walter Raymond and Esther Elizabeth (Kohlhepp) G.; m. Rose Faye Wilson, Aug. 10, 1946 (dec.); children; Bruce, Susan Garrison, Mark, Pamela Garrison Phelan, C. Jeffrey; m. Jayne Bacon, Apr. 15, 1973; stepchildren: James, Jack. B.S.A.E., U. Kans., 1948, M.S.A.E., 1950; DBA (hon.), Spring Garden Coll., 1986. Registered profl. engr., Pa., N.J., Fla., Ill. Structural engr. Boeing Airplane Co., Seattle, 1950-53, cons. engr., 1953-56; staff engr. CDI Corp. and predecessor Comprehensive Designers, Inc., Phila., 1956-58, v.p., 1958-61, pres., chmn. bd., 1961—; dir., chmn. bd. Modern Engring. Co., Detroit; dir. Mgmt. Recruiters Internat., Cleve., CDI Temporary Services, Phila., Stubbs Overbeck & Co., Houston, The M & T Co., King of Prussia, Pa.; mem. World Affaris Council, Phila., 1983—, World Bus. Council, 1985—;. Trustee, chmn. bd. Pa. Inst. Tech., Media, 1953—; mem. Upper Providence Twp. Environ. Adv. Council, 1977-82, Pa. Bd. Pvt. Schs., 1965-71; mem. adv. bd. Sol C. Snider Entrepreneurial Ctr. Wharton Sch., U. Pa., 1987—. Mem. ASME (industry adv. bd. 1987—), Phila. Pres. Orgn. (past chmn., bd. dirs.), Young Pres.' Orgn., World Bus. Council (pres. 1985—), World Affairs Council Pa., NSPE, Tau Beta Pi, Sigma Tau. Republican. Presbyterian. Club: Union League. Home: 238 Sycamore Mills Rd Rose Tree PA 19063 Office: CDI Corp 10 Penn Ctr Philadelphia PA 19103

GARRITY, PAUL GERARD, manufacturing and marketing executive; b. Concord, N.H., May 2, 1923; s. Frank Edward and Eileen Marie (Leahy) G.; m. Dorothy Shaw, May 27, 1950; children—Kevin Shaw, Paul Gerard, Sean Richards. B.S., Harvard U., 1946, M.B.A., 1948. With Swank, Attleboro, Mass., 1948-50, Schick, Lancaster, Pa., 1951-56, Bentley, N.Y.C., 1956-67; pres., chief exec. officer, dir. Garrity Industries, Madison, Conn., 1967—, Garrity Industries Ltd., Toronto, Ont., Can.; dir. State Nat. Bank, Bridgeport, Conn., Beacon Printing Ink, Boston. Served as lt. USNR, 1942-46, PTO, 1950-51, Korea. Mem. World Bus. Council. Roman Catholic. Clubs: Harvard of N.Y.C., Grad. of New Haven, Stamford Yacht, Harvard Varsity, Fox, Pieta, Hasty Pudding, Inst. of 1770. Home: 247 Ocean Dr West Stamford CT 06902

GARRUTO, JOHN ANTHONY, cosmetic research chemist; b. Johnson City, N.Y., June 18, 1952; s. Paul Anthony and Katherine Helen (DiMartino) G.; m. Denise Kitty Conlon, Feb. 19, 1971 (div. May 1978); 1 child, James Joseph; m. Anita Louise, May 12, 1979 (div. Sept. 1984); 1 child, Christopher Russell; m. Debra Lynn Brady (div. Dec. 1986); m. Michelle Bartok, Apr. 2, 1988. BS in Chemistry, SUNY, Binghamton, 1974; AAS in Bus. Adminstrn., Broome Coll., 1976. Research chemist Lander Co. Inc., Binghamton, 1974-77; research dir. Lander Co. Inc., St. Louis, 1977-79, Olde Worlde Products, High Point, N.C., 1979-81; v.p. research and devel. LaCosta Products Internat., Carlsbad, Calif., 1981—; cons. Trans-Atlantic Mktg., Binghamton, 1975-78. Mem. AAAS, Am. Chem. Soc., Soc. Cosmetic Chemists (newsletter editor 1980-81, publicity chmn. 1984—, edn. chmn. 1987), Fedn. Am. Scientists, Internat. Platform Assn., N.Y. Acad. Scis. Democrat. Roman Catholic. Home: PO Box 793 Carlsbad CA 92008 Office: La Costa Products 2251 Las Palmas Dr Carlsbad CA 92008

GARRY, FREDERICK WILTON, electrical manufacturing company executive; b. New Haven, July 12, 1921; s. Frederick Truman and Nellie Melvina (Flint) G.; m. Mary Elizabeth Griswold, June 28, 1948; children: Diana E., Kenneth G. BSME, Rose-Hulman Inst., 1951, DEng (hon.), 1968. Design engr. Gen. Electric Co., Evandale, Ohio, 1951-68, v.p. tech. div., 1968-74; v.p. engring. and mfg. Gen. Electric Co., Fairfield, Conn., 1980—; pres. Rohr Industries, San Diego, 1974-76, chmn., chief exec. officer, 1976-80; mem. adv. com. NSF, Washington, 1983-87. Inventor transit bus feature. Bd. mgrs. Rose-Hulman Inst., 1967—; trustee Clarkson U. Served to capt. USMCR, 1943-46. Recipient Wickenden award Am. Soc. Engring. Edn., 1987. Mem. Conn. Assn. Sci. and Engring., Soc. Automotive Engrs., Soc. Mfg. Engrs. (trustee found.), Nat. Soc. Profl. Engrs. (chmn. industry adv. com. 1982—), Air Force Assn., Nat. Acad. Engring., Aircraft Owners and Pilots Assn., Navy League, USAF Assn., Assn. U.S. Army, Am. Helicopter Soc. Club: Queen City Club, Capitol Hill Club. Home: 3200 Park Ave Bridgeport CT 06604 Office: GE 3135 Easton Turnpike Fairfield CT 06431

GARSIDE, MARLENE ELIZABETH, advertising executive; b. Newark, Dec. 1, 1933; d. Abraham and Shirley (Janow) Carnow; B.S. in Commerce and Fin., Bucknell U., 1955; m. Stanley Kramer, Aug. 7, 1955 (dec. 1967); children—Deborah Frances, Elizabeth Anne; m. Martin Lutman, Aug. 27, 1969 (dec. 1981); m. Michael J. Weinstein, Apr. 9, 1983 (dec. 1984); m. Normand Garside, Apr. 5, 1986. Asst. research dir. Modern Materials Handling Co., Boston, 1955-57; econ. analyst, project adminstr. United Research Co., Cambridge, Mass., 1957-58; free lance tech. writer, econ. analyst, 1958-66; asst. mgr. survey planning and market research IBM, White Plains, N.Y., 1967-69; mgr. research services McKinsey & Co., Cleve., 1969-72; former v.p., dir. Am. Custom Homes, former dir. Liberty Builders, Inc., Cleve.; owner, v.p., dir. Am. Custom Builders Inc., Cape Coral, Fla., 1978—; ptnr., dir. Star Realty Inc., Cape Coral, 1980—; account exec. Media Graphics, Inc., Naples, Fla., 1984; advt. mgr. Fox Electronics, Ft. Myers, Fla., 1984-86; v.p. Langdon Advt., Ft. Myers, 1987-88; asst. mgr. facility State of Fla. Dept. Health and Rehabilitative Services, Ft. Myers, 1988—. Mem. Econ. and Indsl. Devel. Task Force, City of Cape Coral, 1979. Mem. Nat. Assn. Homebuilders, Bldg. Industry Assn., Constrn. Industry Assn., Nat. Bd. Realtors. Home: 1482 Sautern Dr Fort Myers FL 33919 Office: State of Fla Dept Health Rehab Svcs 6719 Winkler Ave Fort Myers FL 33919

GARTENBERG, MICHAEL WILLIAM, civil engineer, city official; b. St. Louis, Sept. 18, 1959; s. William Ralph and Joyce (Korn) G.; m. Susan Cohen, Oct. 1, 1983; 1 child, Elizabeth Paige. BSCE, U. Mo., 1983; postgrad., Washington U., St. Louis, 1986—. Cert. engr. in tng. Constrn. insp. Mo. Hwy. and Transp. Dept., Kansas City and St. Louis, 1983-84; constrn. coord. Edison Bros. Stores Inc., St. Louis, 1984-85; city engr., dir. pub. works City of Crestwood, Mo., 1985—. Dir. transp. St. Louis Sr. Olympics, 1988-89. Mem. ASCE, Am. Pub. Works Assn., Nat. Soc. Profl. Engrs., Profl. Engrs. in Govt., Mo. Soc. Profl. Engrs. Jewish. Home: 11817 Spruce Haven Dr Saint Louis MO 63146 Office: City of Crestwood 1 Detjen Dr Crestwood MO 63126

GARTENBERG, SEYMOUR LEE, recording company executive; b. N.Y.C., May 27, 1931; s. Morris and Anna (Banner) G.; m. Anna Stassi, Feb. 18, 1956; children: Leslie, Karen, Mark. BBA cum laude, CCNY, 1952. Asst. controller Finlay Straus, Inc., N.Y.C., 1950-56; controller Tappin's Inc., Newark, 1956; exec. v.p. Columbia House div. CBS, N.Y.C., 1956-73; pres. CBS Toys Div., Cranbury, N.J., 1973-78; v.p. CBS/Columbia Group, N.Y.C., 1978—; sr. group v.p. CBS Records Group, 1979—; exec. v.p. CBS Records Inc., 1987—. V.p., bd. dirs. City Coll. Fund; treas., bd. dirs. T.J. Martell Found. Leukemia, Cancer and AIDS Research. Mem. Mill Island Civic Assn., Nat. Assn. Accts., Am. Mgmt. Assn., Recording Industry Assn. Am. Office: 51 W 52d St New York NY 10019

GARTNER, W. JOSEPH, business executive; b. Chgo., Apr. 8, 1928; s. Andrew W. and Edith M. (Frame) G.; B.A., Knox Coll., 1950; postgrad. Northwestern U., 1954-60; m. Lois Ellen McQueen, Aug. 7, 1954; children—Lisa Dianne, Bryan Wright, Andrew Scott. Creative writer Montgomery Ward & Co., Chgo., 1953-58; planning and research mgr. Lions Internat., 1958-62; creative account supr. E.F. McDonald Co., 1962-63; dir. response advt. mgr. Encyclopaedia Britannica, 1964-68; creative dir. V.J. Giesler Co., 1968-74; founder, chmn., chief exec. officer Gartner & Assocs., Inc., 1974—. Served as officer U.S. Army, 1951-53; Korea Mem. Nat. Soc. Fund Raising Execs. (dir. 1979-86), Assn. for Children with Learning Disabilities (nat. pres. 1971-72), Ill. Assn. for Children with Learning Disabilities (pres. 1968-70), Direct Mktg. Assn., Direct Mktg. Creative Guild, Chgo. Assn. Direct Mktg., S.P.E.B.Q.S.A. Barbershop Quartet Soc. Congregationalist. Club: Cliff Dwellers (Chgo.). Lodge: Lions (pres. 1961-62) (Glen Ellyn, Ill.). Home: 406 Hill Ave Glen Ellyn IL 60137 Office: Gartner & Assocs Inc 2 N Riverside Plaza Suite 2400 Chicago IL 60606

GARTON, STEPHEN, transit analyst; b. N.Y.C., Dec. 30, 1961; s. James and Helen (Yackery) G.; m. Anne Gatto, Oct. 11, 1986. AAS, CUNY, Bayside, 1982; BS, St. John's U., 1984. Sr. micrographics technician Eastern States, Lake Success, N.Y., 1984-86; tech. support aid N.Y.C. Transit Authority, 1986-88, assoc. transit mgmt. analyst, 1988—. Advisor legis. adv. com. N.Y. State Senate, Queens, N.Y., 1987, 88; steward Ch. of the Nazarene, Valley Stream, N.Y., 1986—. Home: 137-04 255th St Saint Rosedale NY 11422 Office: NYC Transit Authority 3961 Tenth Ave New York NY 10034

GARVER, FREDERICK MERRILL, industrial engineering executive; b. Indpls., Mar. 25, 1945; s. Clyde Louis and Elizabeth Kemp (Finch) G.; m. Ruth Sikkema, Nov. 8, 1969. BS, Western Mich. U., 1967; postgrad., Grand Valley State Coll., 1976-77; student, Western Mich. U., 1987—. Cert. mfg. engr. Methods analyst Boeing Co., Seattle, 1968-69; indsl. engr. Wolverine World Wide, Inc., Rockford, Mich., 1969-72; mgr. indsl. engring. Leigh Products Inc., Coopersville, Mich., 1972-77; dir. indsl. engring. Integrated Metal Techs., Spring Lake, Mich., 1977-79; mgr. mfg. engring. Haworth Inc., Holland, Mich., 1979-88, Hart & Cooley, Inc., Holland, 1988—; cons. Mich. Engring. Systems, Grand Rapids, 1984—. Mem. Inst. Indsl. Engrs. (sr.), Soc. Mfg. Engrs. (sr., ad hoc govt. relations com.), Chem. Coaters Assn., Assn. Bus. Advocating Tariff Equity, Assn. Finishing Processes, Jaycees (treas. Ithaca, Mich. chpt. 1971-72). Republican. Mem. Reformed Church of America. Home: 7039 Magnolia Dr Jenison MI 49428 Office: Hart & Cooley Inc 500 E 8th St Holland MI 49423

GARVIN, ROBERT EDWARD, marketing research professional; b. Harmony, Pa., Sept. 16, 1928; s. Delmont Milton and Ruth Rosetta (Stauffer) G.; m. Dolores Helen Toth, Mar. 30, 1951 (div. 1975); children: Mark Douglas, Valerie Lynn, Eric Bruce, Jeffrey Jay. BA, Muskingum Coll., 1950; postgrad., U. Fla., 1950-51. Statistician Koppers Co. Inc., Pitts., 1951-52, mktg. research analyst, 1952-61, internat. mktg. analyst, 1961-67, investment and growth planning analyst, 1967-68, sr. internat. mktg. analyst, 1968-81, chief economist, 1971-86, mgr. mktg. and econ. analysis, 1986-88, fin. planner, 1988—; bd. dirs. Econ. Club Pitts., 1986—; mem. panel Economists Roundtable, Fed. Res. Bank, Cleve. Pres. Harmonist Hist. and Meml. Assn., Harmony, 1967-69; chmn. Harmony Planning Commn., 1969-71; treas. ACLU, Pitts., 1970-74. Mem. Chem. Market Research Assn., Nat. Economists Club, Nat. Assn. Bus. Economists, Am. Waterworks Assn., Zelienople (Pa.) Mutual Investment Club (investment officer 1957-62, pres. 1962-65). Democrat. Home: HC3/Box 820 Bandera TX 78003 Office: Koppers Co Inc 436 Seventh Ave Pittsburgh PA 15219

GARVIN, THOMAS MICHAEL, food products company executive; b. Chgo., 1935; married. BSC, Loyola U., 1957, MBA, 1969. CPA, Ill. With Lybrand Ross Bros. & Montgomery, 1957-61; contr. Ekco Products Co., 1962-65; group contr. Am. Home Products Co., 1966-69; contr. Keebler Co., Elmhurst, Ill., 1969-70, v.p. fin. and treas., from 1970, then exec. v.p. ops., now pres., chief exec. officer, also bd. dirs. Office: Keebler Co 1 Hollow Tree Ln Elmhurst IL 60126

GARY, GAYLE HARRIET MARGARET, communications executive; b. N.Y.C., Dec. 23, 1920; d. Michael H. and Lilian E. (Robbins) Summers; m. Arthur John Gary, Oct. 28, 1943; 1 child, Sandra G. Student, U. Miami, 1939, NYU, 1940-43, Columbia U., 1944-45. Pres., owner Gayle Gary Assocs. Radio-TV Cons., N.Y.C., 1954—. Interviewer, producer radio program and news bur. Views and People in the News. Pres. Guild of St. Bartholomew Protestant Episcopal Ch., N.Y.C., 1954-56, convocation and diocesan officer, 1954—; mem. prize com. debutante ball N.Y. Infirmary, N.Y.C.; mem. Friends of Philharm. Com., N.Y.C., 1950—; mem. fund-raising com. Women United Hosp. Fund, N.Y.C., 1950; mem. nat. adv. com. Narconon, 1950—; mem. spl. events com. Eleanor Roosevelt Meml. Found., N.Y.C., 1958—; bd. dirs. spl. social svcs. NYU-Bellevue Med. Ctr.; mem. exec. com. Hope Cotillion, N.Y.C., 1958—; bd. dirs. Nat. Radio-TV Com. for Am. Observance Human Rights Week, 1955—; co-leader N.Y.C. Assembly Dist., 1960-70; bd. dirs., rec. sec. Churchwomen's League for Patriotic Svc. Mem. Pub. Rels. Soc. Am. (accredited), Internat. Radio and TV Execs. Soc., Nat. Inst. Social Scis., Religious Pub. Rels. Soc. Am., Am. Women in Radio and TV, Hort. Soc. N.Y., Hubbard Assn. Scientologists Internat., Sea Orgn., Navy League, English-Speaking Union, Women's Nat. Rep. Club (nat. chmn. pub. rels. coun.), Women's Chess Club N.Y. (exec. v.p. 1968—). Home and Office: 1212 5th Ave #13B New York NY 10029

GARY, JAMES FREDERICK, business executive; b. Chgo., Dec. 28, 1920; s. Rex Inglis and Mary Naomi (Roller) G.; m. Helen Elizabeth Gellert, Sept. 3, 1947; children: David Frederick, John William, James Scott, Mary Anne. BS, Haverford (Pa.) Coll., 1942. With Wash. Energy Co. and predecessors, Seattle, 1947-67; v.p. Wash. Energy Co., 1956-67; pres., chief exec. officer Pacific Resources Inc., Honolulu, 1967-79, chmn., chief exec. officer, 1979-84, chmn., 1985, chmn. emeritus, 1986—; bd. dirs. Bancorp. Hawaii, Inc., Bank of Hawaii, Castle & Cooke, Inc., Wash. Energy Co., Seattle, Wash. Nat. Gas Co., Airborne Freight Corp., Seattle, GDC, Inc., Chgo., Petroleum Industry Research Found., Inc., N.Y. Pres. Chief Seattle council Boy Scouts Am., 1966-67, Aloha council, 1973-74; mem. Nat. Council, 1964—, v.p. western region, 1978-85, pres., 1985—, also bd. dirs.; chmn. Aloha United Way, 1978, pres., 1979, chmn., pres., 1980; bd. regents U. Hawaii, 1981—; trustee Linfield Coll., McMinnville, Oreg.; bd. mgrs. Haverford Coll., 1983—; adv. bd. Kamehameha Schs., Honolulu; bd. dirs. Research Corp. of U. Hawaii, 1971-77, chmn., 1974-77; bd. dirs., officer and trustee Oahu Devel. Conf., Hawaii Employers Council, Hawaii Loa Coll., Friends of East-West Ctr., Honolulu Symphony Soc., East-West Ctr. Internat. Found.; chmn. The Hawaii Community Found., 1987—. Capt. AUS, 1942-46. Recipient Distinguished Eagle award Boy Scouts Am., 1972, Silver Beaver award, 1966, Silver Antelope award, 1976, Silver Buffalo award, 1988. Mem. Am. Gas Assn. (bd. dirs. 1970-74), Pacific Gas Assn. (pres. 1974; Basford trophy 1960), Nat. LP-Gas Assn. (bd. dirs. 1967-70), Am. Petroleum Inst., Inst. Gas Tech. (trustee 1975-86), Hawaii Econ. Council, Nat. Petroleum Council, Hawaii Dist. Export Council, Japan-Hawaii Econ. Council, U.S Nat. Com. for Pacific Econ. Cooperation, Pacific Basin Econ. Council (chmn. U.S. com. 1985-86), Japan-Am. Soc. Honolulu, Pacific Forum, Honolulu Commn. on Fgn. Relations, Hawaii C. of C. (chmn. 1979). Episcopalian. Clubs: Pacific Union (San Francisco); Oahu Country, Waialae Country, Outrigger Canoe, Pacific, Plaza (Honolulu); Seattle Tennis, Wash. Athletic (Seattle), Rainier. Office: 130 Merchant St Ste 1080 Honolulu HI 96813

GARY, KATHLEEN NOLAND, public relations executive; b. Long Beach, Calif.; d. Richard Lee and Grace Irene Noland; m. Richard N. Gary. BA, U. Wash., 1967. Assoc. editor Kaiser News, Kaiser Aluminum & Chem. Corp., Oakland, Calif., 1968-73; dir. communications Kaiser Engrs., Oakland, 1973-74; mgr. internal communications Kaiser Industries Corp., Oakland, 1975-77; dir. pub. relations and advt. Kaiser Steel Corp., Oakland, 1977-80, v.p. pub. affairs, 1979-80; corp. v.p. pub. affairs and communications Syntex Corp., Palo Alto, Calif., 1981—. Chmn. steering com. St. Mary's Coll. Exec. Seminar.; mem. Bay Area council steering com. Nat. Investor Relations Inst.; bd. dirs. U. Washington Devel. Fund. Mem. Pub. Relations Soc. Am., World Affairs Council, Calif. Mfrs. Assn., Pharm. Mfrs. Assn. (pub. affairs sect.), Silverado Country Club, Forum West Club. Author: (with Don Fabun) Dimensions of Change, 1971, Children of Change, 1970. Office: Syntex Corp 3401 Hillview Ave Palo Alto CA 94304

GARZARELLI, ELAINE MARIE, economist; b. Phila., Oct. 13, 1951; d. Ralph J. and Ida M. (Pierantozzi) G.; BS, Drexel U., 1973, MBA, 1977; doctoral candidate NYU, 1980. With A.G. Becker, N.Y.C., 1973-84, v.p., economist, 1975-84, mng. dir., 1984; exec. v.p. Shearson Lehman Bros., 1984—; lectr. in field. Named Businesswoman of Yr. Fortune Mag., 1987. Mem. Nat. Assn. Bus. Economists, Women's Fin. Assn., Am. Statis. Assn., Women's Bond Assn. Developer Sector Analysis, econometric model for predicting industry profits and stock price movements. Home: 280 Butler Rd Springfield PA 19064 Office: Shearson Lehman Hutton Inc World Fin Ctr Tower C New York NY 10285

GASCHEN, FRED, health care management specialist; b. Phila., June 14, 1959; s. Fredrick Sidney and Eleanor Marie (Berg) G. BS in Mgmt., U. R.I., 1971; MBA in Health Care, George Washington U., 1973. Commd. 2d lt. U.S. Army, 1971, advanced through grades to maj., 1985; v.p. support svcs. Northridge (Calif.) Med. Ctr., 1981—; chief oper. officer Meml. Health Techs., Long Beach, Calif., 1984—; chief exec. officer Diagnostic Imaging So. Calif., Sherman Oaks, 1986—. Mem. ACHE, DAV. Home: 23421 Balmoral Ln West Hills CA 91307 Office: Diagnostic Imaging So Calif 5170 Sepulveda Blvd Ste 250 Sherman Oaks CA 91403

GASICH, WELKO ELTON, consulting aerospace executive; b. Cupertino, Calif., Mar. 28, 1922; s. Elija J. and Catherine (Paviso) G.; m. Patricia Ann Gudgel, Dec. 28, 1973; 1 child, Mark David. A.B. cum laude in Mech. Engring. (Bacon scholar), Stanford U., 1943, M.S. in Mech. Engring., 1947, cert. in fin. and econs. (Sloan exec. fellow), 1967; Aero. Engr., Calif. Inst. Tech., 1948. Aerodynamicist Douglas Aircraft Co., 1943-44, supr. aeroelastics, 1947-51; chief aero design Rand Corp., 1951-53; chief preliminary design aircraft div. Northrop Corp., Los Angeles, 1953-56; dir. advanced systems Northrop Corp., 1956-61, v.p., asst. gen. mgr. tech., 1961-66, corp. v.p., gen. mgr. Northrop Ventura div., 1967-71, corp. v.p., gen. mgr. aircraft div., 1971-76, corp. v.p., group exec. aircraft group, 1976-79, sr. v.p. advanced projects, 1979-85, exec. v.p. programs, 1985-88, ret., 1988. Patentee in field. Chmn. adv. council Stanford Sch. Engring., 1981-83; past mem. adv. council Stanford Grad. Sch. Bus.; chmn. United Way, 1964; chmn. Scout-O-Rama, Los Angeles council Boy Scouts Am., 1964; chmn. explorer scout exec. com., 1963-64. Served to lt. USN, 1944-46. Fellow AIAA, Soc. Automotive Engrs.; mem. Nat. Acad. Engring., Navy League, Stanford Grad. Sch. Bus. Alumni Assn. (pres. 1971). Republican. Clubs: Wings, Conquistadores del Cielo, Bel Air Country. Office: 3517 Caribeth Dr Encino CA 91436

GASKILL, RICHARD HOWARD, banker; b. Rahway, N.J., Oct. 2, 1942; s. William Nivison and Anna Jane (Bentley) G.; m. Karen May Copple, Mar. 14, 1964; children: Richard, Daniel, Susan. BA, Rutgers U., 1969, MA in Banking, 1979. Asst. br. mgr. Marine Midland Bank, N.Y.C., 1969-72; asst. v.p. United Jersey Bank, Hazlet, N.J., 1972-74; sr. head liquidator Fed. Deposit Ins. Corp., Washington, 1974-83; liquidator-in-charge Hamilton Nat. Bank, Chattanooga, 1980; supervising liquidator Mut. Savs. Bank Industry, 1981-82; liquidator-in-charge Pan-Am. Bank, Union City, N.J., 1982-83, United Southern Bank, Nashville, 1983, First Nat. Bank Midland, Tex., 1983; sr. v.p. Apple Bank for Savs. Inc., N.Y.C., 1983—. Councilman City of Highlands, 1988—. With USN, 1961-65. Mem. Hudson High Sch. Boosters, Lions, Kiwanis. Home: 37 E Highland Ave Atlantic Highlands NJ 07716

GASKIN, MICHAEL ANTHONY, corporation executive; b. Detroit, Nov. 14, 1934; s. Mervyn Guy and Margaret (Brown) G.; m. Sara Lee McCormick, Aug. 24, 1957; children: Victoria, William, Catherine, James, Benjamin. BS in Engring., Yale U., 1957; MBA, U. Mich., 1959. With Taylor & Gaskin Inc., Detroit, 1959-88, chief exec. officer; regional sales mgr. Ransohoff Co., Hamilton, Ohio, 1988—; bd. dirs. Prab Robots, Kalamazoo, Mich.; sec. N.Am. Mfrs. Ins. Co. Ltd., Hamilton, Bermuda, 1978—. Trustee Madonna Coll., Livonia, Mich. Office: Taylor & Gaskin Inc 20200 Nine Mile Rd Saint Clair MI 48080-1791

GASMAN, LAWRENCE DAVID, telecommunications marketing consultant; b. London, Aug. 4, 1949; came to U.S., 1979; s. John Israel and Alice (Drizen) G.; m. Diane Cecilia Weber, Nov. 18, 1978. BSc with honors, Manchester (Eng.) U., 1970; MSc in Econs., London Sch. Econs., 1974; MBA, London Bus. Sch., 1978. Mng. dir. John Gasman & Bros., London, 1974-79; sr. cons. Planning Research & Systems, London, 1979; pres. Communications Industry Researchers, Washington, 1979—. Author: The Telecommunications Manager's Guide to Inside Wiring, 1987, Manager's Guide to the New Telecommunications Network, 1988; also numerous profl. articles. Mem. IEEE (assoc.). Office: Communications Industry Rsch PO Box 11079 Washington DC 20008

GASN, HARVEY VICTOR, banker; b. N.Y.C., Nov. 6, 1947; s. Paul Sidney and Evelyn (Zeller) G.; m. Beverly Rockow, Apr. 18, 1970; children: Jana Leigh, Marni Alyse. BS in Acctg., C.W. Post- L.I. U., 1973, MBA in Fin., 1975. Mgr. fin. and adminstrn. Burroughs Corp., N.Y.C., 1973-75; budget mgr. WCBS-TV, N.Y.C., 1975-76, mgr. bus. affairs, 1976-77; mgr. planning and analysis McGraw-Hill Broadcasting Co., N.Y.C., 1977-79; 2nd v.p. market analysis Chase Manhattan Bank, N.Y.C., 1979-87, v.p. research and planning, 1988—; dir. Mature Market Inst., Washington, 1987-88; cons. in field. Exec. com. mem. Citizens United for Responsible Edn.; trustee Commack (N.Y.) Bd. of Edn., 1988—. Served to sgt. USAF, 1967-71. Mem. Internat. Inst. Forecasters. Home: 47 Havemeyer Ln Commack NY 11725

GASPAR, GEORGE JACOB, petroleum analyst; b. June 19, 1936; s. George Joseph and Theresa (Pfaffl) G.; m. Anna Clair Sweeney, Jan. 21, 1961; children: Mary Beth, Megan, Anne, Sheila, George Jonathan. BBA, Marquette U., 1958. V.p., investment analyst Frederick and Co., Inc., Milw., 1960-75, 1st v.p., dir., petroleum analyst, 1976—. Author: The Gaspar Report Robert W. Barid and Co., Inc., 1975. Bd. dirs. Milw. Tennis Classic Found., 1976—, Performing Arts Ctr., Milw., 1985—; Dominican High Sch. Devel. Coun., 1988—. With C.E., U.S. Army, 1958-60. Mem. Fin. Analysts Fedn., Milw. Soc. Investment Analysts, Nat. Ocean Industries Assn., Soc. Petroleum Engrs., Milw. Athletic Club, Univ. Club, Town Club. Roman Catholic. Office: Robert W Baird & Co Inc 777 E Wisconsin Ave Milwaukee WI 53202

GASPER, RUTH EILEEN, real estate executive; b. Valparaiso, Ind., July 16, 1934; d. Reuben John and Effie (Wesner) Tenpas; m. Ralph L. Gasper, May 25, 1957. Student Purdue U., 1952-56; BA, Govs. State U., 1982. Analyst computer systems Leo Burnett Advt., Chgo., 1958-69; nat. adminstr. registrars Sports Car Club Am., Denver, 1977-79; pres. Ainslie, Inc., Chgo., 1982—; mem. North River Commn. Housing Com., Chgo., 1982-83, fin. com. Mayor's Task Force on Homelessness City of Chgo. Area coordinator Concerned Action Party, Lansing, Ill., 1977; chief race registrar Ind. Northwest Region Sports Car Club Am., 1969-80. Mem. Chgo. Property Owners Assn., Single Room Operators Assn. (treas.), Albany Park C. of C. Avocations: sports car racing, classical music.

GASPERONI, EMIL, SR., real estate developer; b. Hillsville, Pa., Nov. 13, 1926; s. Attico and Rose Mary (Sarnicola) G.; m. Ellen Jean Lias, May 28, 1955; children: Samuel Dale, Emil Attico, Jean Ellen. Diploma real estate U. Pitts., 1957. Owner, pres. Gasperoni Real Estate, New Castle, Pa., 1956-63, Ft. Lauderdale, Fla., 1965—; founder, chmn. bd. Fill-R-Up Auto Wash Systems Inc., Ft. Lauderdale, 1967-70; pres., owner Sweetwater Golf and Country, Orlando, Fla. Served with U.S. Army, 1945-46, ETO. Mem. Nat. Inst. Real Estate Brokers, Internat. Real Estate Fedn., Nat. Soc. Fee Appraisers, Fla. Assn. Mortgage Brokers. Club: Lake Toxaway (N.C.) Country Home: 1126 Brownshire Ct Longwood FL 32779 Office: 505 Wekiva Springs Rd Suite 800 Longwood FL 32779

GASS, CHARLES, retail company executive; b. N.Y.C., June 12, 1918; s. Benjamin and Sophie (Eberlin) G.; B.B.A., CCNY, 1940; m. Rosalyn Becker, June 23, 1945; children—Jeffrey, Marc. With Darling Stores Corp., 1946-62, asst. controller, 1956-62; controller Grayson Robinson Stores Corp., 1962-64; v.p. internal audit MMG Stores div. McCrory Corp., N.Y.C., 1966-71, v.p. McCrory Corp., 1971-87, sr. v.p. ops. S. Klein Dept. Stores div., 1972-74, sr. v.p. mgmt. services McCrory Stores div., 1974-77, exec. v.p. McCrory Stores div., 1978-87; v.p. J.J. Newberry Co., 1982-87; pres. K.N. Distbrs., Inc., 1972-74. Served with AUS, World War II; ETO. Decorated Silver Star, Bronze Star, Purple Heart, Combat Inf. badge, Presdl. citation. Mem. CCNY Alumni Assn. Home: 1105 Gulf of Mexico Dr Longboat Key FL 34228

GASSER, ROBERT CHARLES, rubber products company executive; b. Detroit, Mar. 30, 1936; s. Harold Hamlin and Eileen (Tanton) G.; m. Barbara Ann Folin, Nov. 30, 1957; children: Stephen, Sarah, David, Cynthia. BA, Mich. State U., 1957. Sales rep. Kelsey Hayes Co., Romulus, Mich., 1957-61; account rep. Manley, Bennett, McDonald & Co., Detroit, 1961-63; sales rep. United Metal Products, Detroit, 1963-64; sales rep. Teledyne Monarch Rubber Co., Detroit, 1964-77, mgr. auto sales, 1977-82; v.p. sales and mktg. Teledyne Monarch Rubber Co., Hartville, Ohio, 1982-83; v.p. sales and mktg. Indsl. Products Div. Cooper Tire & Rubber Co., Auburn, Ind., 1983-87, pres. Indsl. Products Div., 1987—; v.p. Cooper Tire & Rubber Co., Findlay, Ohio, 1987—. Mem. Rubber Mfrs. Assn. (vice chmn. div. molded and extruded products 1987—). Episcopal. Office: Cooper Indsl Products 725 W 11th St Auburn IN 46706

GASSERE, EUGENE ARTHUR, lawyer, business executive; b. Beaumont, Tex., Oct. 20, 1930; s. Victor Eugene and Althea June (Haight) G.; m. Mary Alice Engelhard, Aug. 4, 1956; children—Paul, John, Anne. B.S., U. Wis., 1952, J.D., 1956; postgrad., Oxford U., 1956-57. Bar: Wis. bar 1956. Asst. counsel Wurlitzer Co., Chgo., 1958-61, Campbell Soup Co., Camden, N.J., 1961-65; asst. to pres. Thilmany Pulp & Paper Co., Kaukauna, Wis., 1966-68; with Skyline Corp., Elkhart, Ind., 1968—; v.p., gen. counsel, asst. sec. Skyline Corp., 1973—. Pres., bd. dirs. Elkhart Urban League, 1972-73, Elkhart Symphony, 1975-76, Elkhart Concert Club, 1976-77. Served with U.S. Army, 1952-54. Mem. Am. Bar Assn., Wis. Bar Assn., Am. Soc. Corp. Secs., Phi Mu Alpha. Home: 420 Aspin Dr Elkhart IN 46514 Office: Skyline Corp 2520 Bypass Rd Elkhart IN 46515

GASSMAN, WILLIAM GROH, marketing professional; b. Balt., Dec. 18, 1926; s. Joseph and Helen (Roeder) G.; m. Mary Stoner, Dec. 29, 1951; children: William Jr., Robert, Andrea Anderson, Jane Gregg. BS in Chemistry, Franklin & Marshall Coll., Lancaster, Pa., 1947. Analytical chemist Hamilton Watch Co., Lancaster, 1947-53, prodn. engr., 1953-56, mgr. product planning, 1956-60, dir. sales, spl. markets, 1960-68, dir. mdsing., 1970-71; gen. mgr. Vantage product div., East Petersburg, Pa., 1968-70; sr. v.p., gen. mgr. Longines Symphonette, New Rochelle, N.Y., 1971-75; pres. Direct Action Mktg., Inc., Levittown, N.Y., 1975—; also bd. dirs. Direct Action Mktg., Inc. Served with USAF, 1945. Republican. Office: Direct Action Mktg INc 3601 Hempstead Turnpike Levittown NY 11756

GASTLER, HAROLD LEE, railroad executive; b. Wellsville, Mo., May 16, 1927; s. Leo J. and Thelma L. (Oliver) G.; m. Joyce D. Isman, Sept. 13, 1952; 1 son, Kim Leigh. B.S. in Engring., U. Mo., 1951; grad., Advanced Mgmt. Program, Harvard U., 1962. With Frisco R.R., 1951-66, v.p. staff, 1962-63, gen. mgr., 1963-66; pres. Toledo, Peoria & Western R.R., Peoria, Ill., 1966-67; v.p. ops. Chgo. & Northwestern R.R., Chgo., 1968-73; pres., chief operating officer Missouri-Kansas-Texas R.R. Co., Dallas, 1973—, also bd. dirs. Served to ensign USN, 1945-46. Democrat. Lutheran. Office: Mo-Kans-Tex RR Co Katy Bldg Dallas TX 75202

GASTON, HAROLD RAY, civil engineer; b. Madisonville, Ky., May 26, 1960; s. Earl R. and Margie Louise (Davis) G. BCE, U. Ky., 1982. Registered profl. engr., Ky., Ill. Sr. design engr. Cornette Engring. Svcs., Madisonville, 1982—; instr. Madisonville Community Coll., 1984. Mem. Chi Epsilon. Baptist. Home: 622 Murray St Madisonville KY 42431 Office: Cornette Engring Svcs 2850 N Main St Madisonville KY 42431

GASTON, HUGH PHILIP, marriage counselor, educator; b. St. Paul, Sept. 12, 1910; s. Hugh Philander and Gertrude (Heine) G.; B.A., U. Mich., 1937, M.A., 1941; postgrad. summers Northwestern U., 1938, Yale U., 1959; m. Charlotte E. Clarke, Oct. 1, 1945 (dec. 1960); children: Trudy E. Gaston Crippen, George Hugh. Counselor, U. Mich., Ann Arbor, 1936; tchr., counselor W. K. Kellogg Found., Battle Creek, Mich., 1937-41; tchr. spl. edn., Detroit, 1941; instr. airplane wing constrn. Briggs Mfrs. Co., Detroit, 1942; psychologist VA, 1946-51; sr. staff asso. Sci. Research Asso., Chgo., 1951-55; marriage counselor Circuit Ct., Ann Arbor, 1955-60; pvt. practice marriage counseling, Ann Arbor, 1955—; former chief Guidance Center, U. Mich. and Mich. State U.; lectr., Eastern Mich. U., Ypsilanti, 1964-67, asst. prof., 1967-81; mem. Study Group for Health Care of Elderly, China, USSR, 1983, Profl. Study Group on Family Affairs, USSR, 1986. Acting postmaster, Ann Arbor, 1960-61. Chmn. Wolverine Boys State, Am. Legion, 1957-86; chmn. com. on Christian marriage Presbyn. So. Mich., 1962-69; mem. exec. com., legis. agt., chmn. legis. com. Mich. Council Family Relations, 1972-74; bd. dirs. Internat. Parents Without Partners, 1968-69, 1st pres. Mich. chpt., 1961; bd. dirs. Ann Arbor Sr. Citizens, 1982-85, Washtenaw County Council Alcoholism, 1982-84. Served with U.S. Army, 1943-46. Decorated Purple Heart (2), Bronze Star; Medallion of Nice (France); named Citizen of Year, Am. Legion, 1968, Single Parent of Yr., 1978, Patriot of Yr. State of Mich., Mil. Order of Purple Heart, 1987-88. Mem. Am. Assn. Marriage Counselors, Circumnavigators Club, Am. Personnel and Guidance Assn., Nat. Vocat. Guidance Assn., D.A.V. (past comdr.), Am. Soc. Tng. Dirs., Mich. Indsl. Tng. Council (charter), SAR (past pres.), U. Mich. Band Alumni Assn. (pres. 1957-58), Mil. Order Purple Heart (nat. exec. com. 1977-82, 1st comdr. chpt.

459 Mich., state comdr. Mich. 1984-85, nat. historian 1981-85), Phi Delta Kappa (past pres. U. Mich.). Lodge: Rotary. Address: 513 4th St Ann Arbor MI 48103

GASTWIRTH, DONALD EDWARD, lawyer, music publishing company executive, literary agent; b. N.Y.C., Aug. 7, 1944; s. Paul and Tillie (Scheinert) G.; B.A., Yale U., 1966, J.D., 1974. Mem. advt. staff New Yorker mag., N.Y.C., 1967-68; v.p. Reader's Press, New Haven, 1968-74, dir., 1968-85; exec. v.p. Mainstream TV Studio, New Haven, 1974-77, dir., 1974-79; pres. Quasar Assocs., New Haven, 1979—; account exec. Bache Halsey Stuart Shields Inc., New Haven, 1977-79; partner firm Gastwirth, McMillan & Still, New Haven, 1981-84; pres. Don Gastwirth & Assocs. Literary Agy., 1984—; lectr. in field; advisor fund raising John Steinbeck Literacy Project, 1986—; gen. counsel Conn. Coalition Literacy, 1986-88. Trustee, Colony Found., 1975-79; v.p., gen. counsel, dir. Friends of New Haven Shubert Theatre, 1979-87; legal advisor to New Haven Uptown Council, 1985-87; mem. Conn. Vol. Lawyers Arts, 1987—; mem. benefit com. John Steinbeck Literary Project, 1986—, Folger Shakespeare Libr. Mem. Am. Mgmt. Assn., Assn. Trial Lawyers Am., ABA (forum com. on entertainment and sports industries), Conn. Bar Assn. (mem. exec. com. on intellectual property, lectr. copyright law), Internat. Platform Assn., Berzelius Soc. Democrat. Clubs: Yale (N.Y.C., and New Haven); Elizabethan (New Haven). Contbr. to Nat. Rev., Wall St. Jour., New Haven Register, The Nation. Office: 265 College St Suite 7-G New Haven CT 06510

GATES, CHARLES CASSIUS, rubber company executive; b. Morrison, Colo., May 27, 1921; s. Charles Cassius and Hazel LaDora (Rhoads) G.; m. June Scowcroft Swaner, Nov. 26, 1943; children: Diane, John Swaner. Student, MIT, 1939-41; BS, Stanford U., 1943; DEng (hon.), Mich. Tech. U., 1975, Colo. Sch. of Mines, 1985. With Copolymer Corp., Baton Rouge, 1943-46; with Gates Rubber Co., Denver, 1946—, v.p., 1951-58, exec. v.p., 1958-61, chmn. bd., 1961—, now also chief exec. officer; chmn. bd. The Gates Corp., Denver, 1982—, chief exec. officer, from 1982, also bd. dirs.; bd. dirs. Hamilton Bros. Petroleum Corp., Denver, Robinson Brick Co., Denver. Pres., trustee Gates Found.; trustee Denver Mus. Natural History, Calif. Inst. Tech., Pasadena. Recipient Community Leadership and Service award Nat. Jewish Hosp., 1974; Mgmt. Man of Year award Nat. Mgmt. Assn., 1965; named March of Dimes Citizen of the West, 1987. Mem. Conf. Bd. (dir.), Conquistadores del Cielo. Clubs: Denver Country, Cherry Hills Country, Denver, Outrigger Canoe, Waialae Country, Boone and Crockett, Club Ltd, Country Club of Colo, Roundup Riders of Rockies, Shikar-Safari Internat. (dir.), Augusta Nat. Golf, Castle Pines Golf. Office: Gates Corp 900 S Broadway Denver CO 80209

GATES, MILO SEDGWICK, construction company executive; b. Omaha, Apr. 25, 1923; s. Milo Talmage and Virginia (Offutt) G.; m. Anne Phleger, Oct. 14, 1950 (dec. Apr. 1987); children: Elena, Susan, Virginia, Mariquita Anne, Milo T.; m. Robin Templeton Quist, June 18, 1988. Student, Calif. Inst. Tech., 1943-44; B.S., Stanford U., 1944, M.B.A., 1948. With Swinerton & Walberg Co., San Francisco, 1955—, pres., 1976—, chmn., 1988—. Bd. dirs., trustee Children's Hosp. San Francisco; bd. trustees Grace Cathedral, San Francisco. Lt. (j.g.), USNR, 1944-46. Republican. Clubs: Pacific-Union, Bohemian (San Francisco). Home: 3757 Washington St San Francisco CA 94118 Office: Swinerton & Walberg Co 580 California St San Francisco CA 94104

GATES, RICHARD DANIEL, manufacturing company executive; b. Trenton, Mo., Mar. 27, 1942; s. Daniel G. and Effie Wright (Johnson) G.; m. Jean Gates, Jan. 26, 1966; 1 child, Daniel Wright. B.S., U. Mo., 1964; M.C.S., Rollins Coll., Winter Park, Fla., 1968; postgrad., Harvard U., 1976. Mgmt. assoc. Western Electric Co., N.Y.C., 1964-66; bus. mgmt. adminstr. Martin Marietta Aerospace Co., Orlando, Fla., 1966-68; chief indsl. engring. Martin Marietta Aerospace Co., 1968-69; fin. analyst Martin Marietta Co., N.Y.C., 1969-70; sr. acct. Martin Marietta Co., 1970-71; controller Dragon Cement Co., div. Martin Marietta Co., 1971-72, N.E. div. Martin Marietta Aggregates Co., 1972-73; asst. controller, then asst. treas. Rubbermaid, Inc., Wooster, Ohio, 1973-79; treas. Rubbermaid, Inc., 1979-80, v.p., treas., 1980—; pres. Rubbermaid Found., Wooster. Mem. Wooster City Fin. Task Force, All Am. City Com.; chmn. Wooster Growth Assn.; active local Cub Scouts.; adviser Art Center, chmn. maj. indsl. capital campaign Boy Scouts Camp; trustee, chmn. Wayne Ctr. Arts; mem. parents' com. St. Paul's Sch. Mem. Nat. Assn. Corporate Treas., Main St. Wooster Inc. (bd. trustees), Beta Gamma Sigma, Omicron Delta Kappa. Clubs: Harvard Bus. Sch, Wooster Country (bd. dirs.). Address: Rubbermaid Inc 1147 Akron Rd Wooster OH 44691

GATES, ROBERT MICHAEL, management executive; b. Waynesville, Mo., May 27, 1947; s. Robert Wheldon and Opal Leigh (Reid) G.; m. Julie Jean Stong, Dec. 6, 1986; 1 child, Tanner Michael. BS in Bus., NW Mo. U., 1972, MBA, 1973. City mgr. Am. Multi Cinema, Kansas City, Mo., 1973-76; div. ops. mgr. Am. Multi Cinema, Dallas, 1976-78, mgr. spl. projects, 1978-80; mgr. ops. Theatre Amusement, Los Angeles, 1981-84; exec. v.p., chief fin. officer Cointel Corp. (name changed to Geminex Indusitires, Inc.), Los Angeles, 1984—, also bd. dirs. Mem. Big Bros. Greater Los Angeles, 1983—, sec. 1987—. Served as sgt. USMC, 1969-71, Vietnam. Mem. NW Mo. U. Alumni Assn. (pres. 1986—). Office: Geminex Industries Inc 23801 Calabasas Rd Ste 1020 Calabasas CA 91302

GATES, STEPHEN FRYE, lawyer; b. Clearwater, Fla., May 20, 1946; s. Orris Allison and Olga Betty (Frye) G.; m. Laura Daignault, June 10, 1972. B.A. in Econs., Yale U., 1968; J.D., Harvard U., 1972, M.B.A., 1972. Bar: Fla. 1972, Mass. 1973, Ill. 1977, Colo. 1986. Assoc. Choate Hall & Stewart, Boston, 1973-77; atty. Amoco Corp., Chgo., 1977-82, gen. atty., 1982-86; regional atty. Amoco Production Co., Denver, 1987-88; asst. treas., Amoco Corp., Chgo., 1988—. bd. dirs. Corp. Officers and Dirs. Assurance, Ltd. Knox fellow, 1972-73. Mem. ABA, Chgo. Bar Assn. Clubs: Univ. (Chgo.); Yale (N.Y.C.). Office: Amoco Corp 200 E Randolph Dr Chicago IL 60601

GATES, WALTER EDWARD, rental company executive, business owner; b. Glens Falls, N.Y., Aug. 15, 1946; s. William B. and Dawn K. (Preston) G.; m. Toni A. Naren, June 26, 1945; children: Lindsey Erin, Ryan Walter. BS, SUNY, Albany, 1968; EdM, Boston U., 1972; MBA, Harvard U., 1974. Asst. mgr. Wilson Sporting Goods Inc., River Grove, Ill., 1974-76; mgr. Wilson Sporting Goods Inc., River Grove, 1976-79; dir. Pizza Hut Inc., Wichita, Kans., 1979; sr. dir. Pizza Hut Inc., Wichita, 1979-80, v.p., 1980-82, sr. v.p., 1982-85; exec. v.p. Rent-A-Ctr. Inc., Wichita, 1985-86, pres., chief operating officer, 1986-87, pres., chief exec. officer, chief operating officer, 1987—; pres., chief exec. officer Gates Enterprises, 1985—. Bd. dirs. Wichita Symphony, 1984-87, Wichita Children's Theater, 1984-87; active Wichita Music Theatre, 1987—, Boy Scouts of Am., 1989—. Mem. Wichita C. of C. Office: Rent-A-Ctr Inc 8200 E Rent-A-Center Dr Wichita KS 67226

GATEWOOD, DIANE RIDLEY, lawyer, stock exchange executive; b. St. Louis, June 20, 1951; d. Benjamin James and Vera Delores (Dickerson) R.; m. Lamerol Alexander, Sept. 1, 1979. AB, Washington U., 1973; JD, Northwestern U., 1975. Bar: Ill. 1982, U.S. Dist. Ct. (no. dist.) Ill. 1982, U.S. Ct. Appeals (7th cir.) 1982. Instr. YMCA Community Coll., Chgo., 1976-77; legal asst. Wilson, Smith & McCullin, St. Louis, 1977-78; securities analyst A.G. Edwards, St. Louis, 1978-87; new listings mgr. Am. Stock Exch., N.Y.C., 1987—; bd. dirs. KMT Vision Inc., St. Louis, 1986—. Treas. Equity Community Found., St. Louis, 1985-87; bd. dirs. KMT Vision, Inc., St. Louis, 1986—. Recipient Award of Merit City of East St. Louis, 1981, Cert. Appreciation U.S. Govt. Fed. Exec. Bd., 1982; named one of Outstanding Young Women Am., 1985. Mem. ABA, Ill. Bar Assn., Nat. Assn. Securities Profls., Met. Black Bar Assn., Black Filmmakers Found. Office: Am Stock Exch 86 Trinity Pl New York NY 10006

GATEWOOD, JUDITH ANNE, business manager; b. Wichita, Kans., May 28, 1944; d. Alec Hunter and Mary Louise (Grecian) Stratton; m. Charles Eugene Gatewood, Jan. 26, 1962; children: Lori Lynn Gatewood Murphy, Charles Hunter. Cert. bus. communication, Topeka High Sch., 1983, cert. micro-computer ops., 1986. Clk. typist State of Kans., Topeka, 1964; exec. sec. H.M. Goodman and Co., Topeka, 1965-71; payroll supr. Hwy. Oil, Inc., Topeka, 1971—; corp. sec., treas. Gatewood Roofing, Inc., Topeka, 1983—. Commr. Mayor's Commn. Status of Women, Topeka, 1987—; mem. adv. coun. Friends of Kaw Valley Girl Scouts U.S. Mem. Nat. Assn. Female Execs., Am. Bus. Women's Assn. (pres. Panache chpt. 1985-86, Echo chpt. 1984-85, sec., treas. Topeka area council, 1987-88, v.p. exec. chpt., 1988-89, Woman of Yr., 1984, Star in your Crown award, Nat. Hdqs., 1985, chmn. bull. receiving West Cen. Spring Conf., 1986), Every Woman's Resource Ctr., Am. Soc. Profl. and Exec. Women, Pi Tau Omega (Tau Kappa Nu chpt.). Democrat. Presbyterian. Club: Topeka Mustang. Lodge: Moose. Home: 3829 SE 23d St Terr Topeka KS 66605 Office: Highway Oil Inc Bank IV Tower 12th Fl Topeka KS 66603

GATEWOOD, LEONARD B., oil company executive; b. Lafayette, La., June 24, 1947; s. Leonard B. and Ruby (May) G.; m. Dana Laurel Frey, Sept. 13, 1969; children: Ashley Lynn, Laura Brooke. BS in Math., U. Miss., 1969; MA in Econs., Memphis State U., 1974; postgrad., Harvard Bus. Sch., 1983. Economist Nat. Cotton Council Am., Memphis, 1969-75; economist, cons. Pace Cons. and Engrs., Houston, 1976-78; corp. economist Tex. Eastern Corp., Houston, 1978-80; v.p. mktg. La Gloria Oil and Gas Co., Houston, 1981-84, v.p. mfg., 1984-86, pres., 1986—; trustee Exec. Ventures Group, Denver. Vol. United Way, Houston, 1986-88; vice chmn. Tex. Eastern Polit. Action Com., Houston, 1986-88; bd. dirs. Juvenile Diabetes Found. Fellow Am. Leadership Forum; mem. Houston Ctr. Club, Quail VAlley C.C. Episcopalian. Club: HBS (Houston). Home: 3258 Hunters Glen Missouri City TX 77459 Office: La Gloria Oil & Gas Co PO Box 2521 Houston TX 77459

GATHANY, VAN R., banker; b. Evanston, Ill., July 16, 1926; s. William Vandervoort and Isabel (Risser) G.; m. Hilda Lang Denworth, Oct. 13, 1951; children: Virginia Lynn (Mrs. Henry Page, Jr.), Douglas Vandervoort, Robin Elizabeth (Mrs. Kevin Shea). B.A., Swarthmore Coll., 1950; M.B.A., U. Chgo., 1953. Vice pres. No. Trust Bank, Chgo., 1963-67, sr. v.p., 1967-85, exec. v.p., 1985—; chmn. bd. No. Trust Co. Calif.; bd. dirs. No. Trust Co. Ariz., Top Star, Inc., First Nat. Bank of Lake Forest; pres. NorTrust Farm Mgmt., 1970-77; instr. Advanced Mgmt. Inst., Lake Forest (Ill.) Coll., 1965-82. Mem. adv. council U. Chgo. Grad. Sch. Bus.; mem. Lake Forest Elem. Sch. Bd., 1963-70; pres. Chgo. Home for Incurables; bd. dirs. Johnson R. Bowman Health Center, 1975-87; past chmn. bd. regents Nat. Trust Sch. at Northwestern U.; trustee Nat. Coll. Edn., Evanston, Otho Sprague Inst., Presbyn. Home. Served with AC USNR, 1944-46. Mem. Am. Bankers Assn. (chmn. trust div. 1984), Ill. Bankers Assn. (past pres. trust div.). Presbyterian (elder). Clubs: Lake Forest (past pres., dir.); University of Chgo.. Office: No Trust Co 50 S La Salle St Chicago IL 60675

GATI, WILLIAM EUGENE, architect, urban designer and planner. BS, CCNY, 1980, BArch, 1981; M in Urban Planning, Design, CUNY, 1983. Registered architect, N.Y. Freelance designer N.Y.C., 1978-83; designer Urban Living, Inc., N.Y.C., 1983-84, Robert L. Henry, Architect, N.Y.C., 1984-86; urban designer Glass & Assocs., N.Y.C., 1986-87; prin. architect William E. Gati, RA, AIA, N.Y.C., 1987—; prof. architecture, N.Y. Inst. Tech., N.Y.C., 1985—. Author: Solar Energy Techniques, 1979 (AIA Recognition award 1979), Frank L. Wright, 1981, Theory of Modern Architecture, 1981, Boston's Public Space, 1985. Campaigner New Yorkers for Koch, 1985-86. Mem. AIA (chmn. religious architecture com. N.Y.C. chpt.), Mcpl. Art Soc. (assoc.), Archtl. League (assoc.), CCNY Alumni Assn. (v.p. 1983—), Smithsonian Instn., N.Y. Arts Group, Christian Architects Fellowship. Home (temp): 115-25 84th Ave Kew Gardens NY 11418 Office: Designers & Planners 115-25 84th Ave Kew Gardens NY 11418

GATTING, CARLENE J., lawyer; b. Hartford, Conn., Apr. 12, 1955; d. Charles W. and Jean A. (Murkowicz) G. BS, U. Conn., 1977; JD, Rutgers U., 1983. Assoc. Skadden, Arps, Slate, Meagher & Flom, N.Y.C., 1987—. Mem. ABA. Office: Skadden Arps Slate Meagher & Flom 919 3d Ave New York NY 10022

GATTO, DOMINICK DAN, treasurer, accountant; b. Chgo., Oct. 27, 1920; s. George and Emily (Manuzzi) G.; m. Norma D. Gentile, Sept. 12, 1943; children: George, Robert, Patricia, Dominick, Jeannine, Vincent. Student, Herzl Jr. Coll., Chgo., 1940-42; cert. in acctg., LaSalle Extension U., 1961, Walton Sch. Commerce, 1968. CPA, Ill. Office mgr., controller Truck-Rail Terminals Inc., Chgo., 1942-60, Lasham Cartage Co. Inc., Chgo., 1960-70; controller Arrow Motor Transit, Chgo., 1970-73, Wesko Plating Inc., Chgo., 1973-76; pres. Gatto Industries Inc., Chgo., 1976-82, treas., chief fin. officer, 1982—. Mgr., commr. Villa Park (Ill.) Little League Baseball Team, 1973-75; treas., v.p. Villa Park Youth Football, 1975-78. Mem. Am. Electroplating Soc., Chgo. Metal Finishers Inst., U.S. C. of C., Ill. C. of C., Chgo. Assn. Commerce and Insustry, Ill. Mfrs. Assn. Republican. Office: Gatto Industries Inc 4620 W Roosevelt Rd Chicago IL 60650

GATZA, JAMES, academic administrator; b. Buffalo, Sept. 18, 1933; s. Edward Paul and Helen (Kocinski) G.; m. Marie Melanie Slominski, July 31, 1954 (div. 1982); children: Mark F., Edward K., Lee Ann, Mary Beth, Paul A.; m. Kathleen Marie Carroll, May 19, 1984. BS with highest dinstinction, SUNY, Buffalo, 1955, MBA, 1956; D in Bus. Administrn., Harvard U., 1965. Chmn. mgmt. dept. Villanova U., Phila., 1964-69; v.p. Am. Inst. Property and Liability Underwriters, Malvern, Pa., 1969—. Author: Decision Making in Administration, 1979, Computers in Insurance, 1980, Managing Automated Activities, 1988; editor: Essentials of Supervision, 1985, Supervisory Skills, 1985, Automation in Insurance, 1987. 1st lt. USAF, 1957-62. Recipient Lawrence D. Bell award, SUNY, Buffalo, 1953; Ford Found. fellow, 1962. Mem. Soc. CPCU, Acad. Mgmt., Eastern Acad. Mgmt. (treas. 1975-78), Soc. Ins. Trainers and Educators, Internat. Ins. Soc., Beta Gamma Sigma. Home: 745 Inverness Dr West Chester PA 19380 Office: Am Inst Property & Liability Underwriters 720 Providence Rd Malvern PA 19355

GAUBERT, RONALD JOSEPH, management consultant; b. Lafayette, Ind., Dec. 1, 1946; s. Harold E. and Cecile (Mouton) G.; m. Linda Bock; children: Ellen, Brad. BS, U. So. La., Lafayette, 1973. Controller Lafayette Drug Co., 1973-76; treas. Mar-Low Corp., Lafayette, 1976-78; pres. Ron J. Gaubert & Assoc., Lafayette, 1978—, Lanscor Devel. Corp., Lafayette, 1978—; chmn. Venture Capital Forum, Lafayette. Pres. adv. bd. Cathedral Carmel Parents Booster Assn., Lafayette, 1985-86, mem. sch. bd., 1985-86, pres. Parish Council, Holy Cross Ch. Served with U.S. Army, 1966-69. Mem. Lafayette C. of C. (bd. dirs.), La. Realtor's Assn. (Baton Rouge), Nat. Assn. of Realtors., Am. Assn. Petroleum Inds., La. Assn. Ind. Producers and Royalty Owners. Republican. Roman Catholic. Clubs: Petroleum, Lafayette Town House, Krewe of Townhouse, Krewe of Gabriel. Office: PO Box 53152 Lafayette LA 70505

GAUGHAN, JOHN ANTHONY, lawyer; b. Washington, Mar. 29, 1947; s. John Vincent and Marguerite (Portland) G.; m. Janelle Williams, Apr. 28, 1984. BS, U.S. Coast Guard Acad., 1970; JD, U. Md., 1977. Bar: D.C. 1978, U.S. Dist. Ct. D.C. 1978. Atty. Fed. Maritime Commn., Washington, 1980-81; officer congl. rels. U.S. Dept. Transp., Washington, 1981-84, dir. external affairs U.S. maritime adminstrn., 1984, dep. asst. sec., 1984-85, adminstr. U.S. maritime adminstrn., 1985-89, chief of staff, 1989—. Lt. comdr. USCG, 1970-79, comdr. USCGR. Mem. ABA, D.C. Bar Assn., Maritime Law Assn., Am. Legion (vice comdr. 1984—). Republican. Roman Catholic. Home: 5301 Roosevelt St Bethesda MD 20814 Office: US Dept Transp 400 7th St SW Washington DC 20590

GAUGHAN, THOMAS ROBERT, information systems executive; b. Shenandoah, Pa., Feb. 26, 1936; s. Thomas Robert and Mary Helen (Tomko) G.; m. Rosemary Elizabeth McDevitt, June 13, 1959; children: Mary Patricia, Thomas, Maureen, Dennis. BBA, Drexel U., 1958, MBA, 1962. Systems analyst, programmer Gen. Electric Co., Phila., 1958-61; asst. controller, mgr. systems Richardson Morrell, Inc., Phila., 1961-65; div. controller Textron Corp., New Brunswick, N.J., 1965-67; dir. systems svcs. Celanese Corp., Charlotte, N.C., 1967-76; v.p. info. systems Standard Brands, Inc., N.Y.C., 1976-82, Primerica Corp., Greenwich, Conn., 1982—; bd. dirs. Omicron, Monclair, N.J., Profit Originated Systems Planning, Dallas. Tech. adviser Second Harvest Food Banks, Chgo., 1984-87; bd. dirs. Conn. Food bank, New Haven, 1985-87; spl. project mgr. Southeast Conn. Industry Assn., Stamford, 1986-87; mem. Adv. Conf. Bd., N.Y.C., 1988. Capt. USAR, 1958-66. Recipient Tech.-Leadership award Omicron, 1987. Mem. Soc. Info. Mgmt., Am. Mgmt. Assn. (mem. adv. bd. info. systems div. 1987—). Republican. Roman Catholic. Home: 331 Hemlock Rd Fairfield CT 06430 Office: Primerica Corp American Ln Greenwich CT 06836

GAUL, GEORGE BRUBAKER, banker; b. Reading, Pa., Nov. 11, 1916; s. Charles Warren and Louise Elizabeth (Brubaker) G.; m. Emy Lou Worrilow, Apr. 11, 1942 (dec. 1978); children—Elizabeth B., Emmy Lou Gaul Prescott, Kimberly Gaul Morgan; m. Diane L. Bowers, 1986. B.S. in Commerce, U. Va., 1940. Chmn. Pa. Savs. Bank, Wyomissing, Pa., 1965-88, also dir.; pres. Arbee Corp., Wyomissing, Pa., 1975—. Dir. Thun Investment Co., Wyomissing, 1984-86; Arbee Corp., Wyomissing, Berks Products Corp., Reading, Pa., Harrington Hölsts div. Arbee Corp., Manheim. Trustee Penn Sq. Mut. Fund, Wyomissing. Served to lt. USNR, 1942-46. Republican. Methodist. Clubs: Berkshire Country (Reading); Hamilton (Lancaster, Pa.), Atlantis (Fla.) Golf Club. Home: 144 Reading Blvd Wyomissing PA 19610 Office: Arbee Corp 1015 Penn Ave Wyomissing PA 19610

GAULT, ROBERT ALLEN, manufacturing company executive; b. Ft. Wayne, Ind., Nov. 15, 1959; s. Robert Arnold and Thelma Grace (Conner) G.; m. Lisa Elaine Fox, Aug. 18, 1984; 1 child, Sarah Kendall. BS in Physics, Ga. Inst. Tech., 1982, MS with highest hons., 1986. Rsch. scientist I Ga. Inst. Tech., Atlanta, 1982-86; salesman Eminence (Ky.) Speaker Corp., 1986-87, v.p. mfg., 1987—. Mem. Audio Engring. Soc., Jaycees.

GAULT, STANLEY CARLETON, manufacturing company executive; b. Wooster, Ohio, Jan. 6, 1926; s. Clyde Carleton and Aseneth Briton (Stanley) G.; m. Flo Lucille Kurtz, June 11, 1949; children: Stephen, Christopher, Jennifer. BA, Coll. of Wooster, 1948. With GE (and subs.), 1948-79; v.p. and group exec. maj. appliance bus. group GE (and subs.), Louisville, 1970-77; v.p. and sector exec. consumer products and svcs. sector GE (and subs.), Fairfield, Conn., 1977; sr. v.p., sector exec. GE (Indsl. Products and Components sector), 1977-79; vice chmn. bd. Rubbermaid Inc., Wooster, Ohio, 1980; chmn. bd., chief exec. officer Rubbermaid Inc., 1980—; dir. Avon Products, Inc., Internat. Paper Co., PPG Industries, Inc., The Timken Co., Goodyear Tire & Rubber Co.; mem. Adv. Com. on U.S. Trade Policy and Negotiations, 1987. Trustee Coll. of Wooster, chmn. bd., 1987—. With USAAF, 1944-46. Mem. NAM (bd. dirs., chmn. bd. 1986-87). Republican. Methodist. Office: Rubbermaid Inc 1147 Akron Rd Wooster OH 44691

GAULTNEY, JOHN ORTON, life insurance agent, consultant; b. Pulaski, Tenn., Nov. 7, 1915; s. Bert Hood and Grace (Orton) G.; m. Elizabethine Mullette, Mar. 30, 1941; children: Elizabethine G. McClure, John Mullette, Walker Orton, Harlow Denny. Student, Am. Inst. Banking, 1936; diploma, Life Ins. Agy. Mgmt. Assn., 1948, Little Rock Jr. Coll., 1950; Mgmt. C.L.U. diploma, 1952; grad. sales mgmt. and mktg., Rutgers U., 1957. CLU. With N.Y. Life Ins. Co., 1935—; regional v.p. N.Y. Life Ins. Co., Atlanta, 1956-64; v.p. N.Y. Life Ins. Co., N.Y.C., 1964-67; v.p. in charge group sales N.Y. Life Ins. Co., 1967-68, v.p. mktg., 1969-80, agt., 1980—; life ins. cons. 1981—; v.p. N.Y. Life Variable Contracts Corp., 1969-80; hon. dir. Bank of Frankewing (Tenn.), 1984—. Elder Presbyn. Ch.; chmn. Downtown YMCA, Atlanta, 1963-65; mem. Bd. Zoning Appeals Bronxville, N.Y., 1970-80; active Nashville YMCA, 1981— ; mem. pub. relations com. Nat. Council YMCAs, 1965-80; mem. internat. world service com. YMCA, 1968-80; chmn. Vanderbilt YMCA, 1974-76, Bd. dirs., N.Y.C., 1966-76; Bd. dirs. Memphis YMCA, 1939-40, Little Rock YMCA, 1941-55, Atlanta YMCA, 1959-65, Greater N.Y. YMCA, 1975-80. Served to capt., inf. AUS, 1942-45, MTO. Decorated Silver Star, Bronze Star with 3 clusters, Purple Heart with 2 clusters.; recipient Devereux C. Josephs award N.Y. Life Ins. Co., 1954; named Ark. traveler, 1955; hon. citizen Tenn., 1956; Tenn. ambassador, 1981-87; Ky. col., 1963. Mem. Am., Tenn. socs. CLU's, Nat., Tenn. assns. life underwriters, Sales and Mktg. Execs. Internat., Am. Risk and Ins. Assn., Heritage Found., Carnton Assn. (bd. dirs. 1981—, pres. 1987-88), N.Y. So. Soc. (trustee 1965-80), Williamson County Hist. Soc. (pres. 1983-85), Giles County Hist. Soc., 361st Inf. Assn. World War II (pres. 1967-70), SAR (N.Y. state dir. 1970-80), St. Nicholas Soc. City N.Y., Soc. Colonial Wars, Descendants of Colonial Clergy, Tenn. Sons of Revolution, Assn. Preservation Tenn. Antiquities (trustee), Tenn. Soc. in N.Y. (pres. 1971-74, trustee 1980—), Newcomen Soc. in Am. Clubs: Capital City (Atlanta); Siwanoy (Bronxville, N.Y.); Md. Farms Racquet and Country (Brentwood, Tenn.); Nashville City. Lodges: Rotary, Masons, Shriners, Sojourners, Sovereign Military Order of the Temple of Jerusalem. Home: 6109 Johnson Chapel Rd Brentwood TN 37027 Office: One Nashville Pl Ste 1610 Nashville TN 37219

GAUT, NORMAN EUGENE, electronics firm executive; b. Gilman, Colo., Sept. 20, 1937; s. Marvin Joseph and Margaret Elmo (Carl) G.; m. Madeleine Suzanne Dupuy, Aug. 29, 1964; children: Christopher Carl, Eric Kerwin, Jeffrey Gareth. BA in Physics, UCLA, 1959; MS in Meteorology, M.I.T., 1964, PhD in Meteorology, 1967; grad. advanced mgmt. program, Harvard U., 1976. V.p. Environ. Research and Tech., Inc., Concord, Mass., 1968-77, pres., 1977-85; pres., chief exec. officer PictureTel Inc., Peabody, Mass., 1986—; bd. dirs. Nat. Mgmt. Systems, Inc., Remediation Techs., Inc. Served with USAF, 1959-62. NASA grantee, 1963-67. Mem. Am. Meteorol. Soc., Am. Geophys. Union, AAAS, Sigma Xi. Office: PictureTel Inc 1 Corporation Way Peabody MA 01960

GAUTHIER, CLARENCE JOSEPH, utility executive, retired; b. Houghton, Mich., Mar. 16, 1922; s. Clarence A. and Muriel V. (Beesley) G.; m. Grayce N. Wicall, July 25, 1941 (dec. 1988); children: Joseph H., Nancy M. B.S. in Mech. Engring, U. Ill., 1943; M.B.A., U. Chgo., 1960. Registered profl. engr., Ill. With Pub. Service Co. No. Ill., 1945-54; with No. Ill. Gas Co., 1954-86, v.p. finance, 1960-62, v.p. ops., 1962-64, exec. v.p., 1965-69, pres., 1969-76, chmn., 1971-86, chief exec. officer, 1971-81, dir., 1965-86; chmn., pres., chief exec. officer, dir. NICOR Inc., 1976-86, chief exec. officer, chmn. and dir. subs.; dir. GDC, Inc., Bank of Yorktown, Lombard, Ill., 1968-84, GATX Corp., Nalco Chem. Co., Sun Electric Corp., Chgo. and NorthWestern Transp. Co.; vice chmn., dir. AEGIS, Ltd., 1978-88; bd. dirs. Acme Steel Corp., CNW Corp., Cole Taylor Fin. Group. Contbr. articles to profl. jours. Trustee Council Energy Studies, 1977—; bd. dirs. Gas Research Inst., 1977-82; mem. Northwestern U. Assos., 1977-85; citizens bd. U. Chgo., 1972—; chmn. devel. campaign Good Samaritan Hosp., Downers Grove, Ill., 1974-77; trustee George Williams Coll., Downers Grove, 1968-77, Ill. Inst. Tech., 1976-86, IIT Research Inst., 1976-80; bd. dirs. Mid-Am. chpt. ARC, 1962-78; trustee Met. Crusade of Mercy, Chgo., 1965-77; mem. Ill. Savs. Bond Com., 1975-85, U. Ill. Presidents Council, 1978—, U. Ill. Adv. Council, 1981-86, U. Ill. Found.; bd. sponsors Evangel. Hosp. Assn., Oak Brook, Ill., 1977-85. Served to capt. C.E. AUS, World War II, PTO. Decorated Silver Star, Bronze Star with V; recipient Distinguished Alumnus award, 1971, Alumni Honor award U. Ill., 1974, Loyalty award, 1977. Mem. Internat. Gas Union (council 1970-75, chmn. Com. Gas Utilization 1970-73), Am. Gas Assn. (dir. 1970-76, chmn. bd. 1975, Disting. Service award 1976), Midwest Gas Assn. (dir. 1964-67), So. Gas Assn. (dir. 1966-69), Ind. Natural Gas Assn. Am. (dir. 1972-73), Inst. Gas Tech. (trustee 1964-70, 71-78, chmn. bd. trustees 1976-78), AAAS, Am. Finance Assn., U. Chgo. Grad. Sch. Bus. Alumni Assn. (pres. 1964-65), Ill. C. of C., Chgo. Council on Fgn. Relations (Chgo. com. 1974-86), Chgo. Assn. Commerce and Industry (dir. 1966-71, 73-79), ME-IE Alumni Assn. U. Ill. (pres. 1976-77, dir. 1973—), Sigma Pi, Pi Tau Sigma, Tau Beta Pi, Beta Gamma Sigma, Tau Nu Tau. Clubs: Commercial (Chgo.). Home: 15 Lochinvar Ln Oak Brook IL 60521 Office: 477 E Butterfield Rd Suite 206 Lombard IL 60148

GAUTHIER, THOMAS JOSEPH, accountant; b. Northbridge, Mass., Mar. 11, 1948; s. Leon Alfred and Beatrice Elizabeth (Christian) G.; m. Binnie Dubofsky, Sept. 2, 1973; children: Saul Leon, Suzanne Lynette. BBA, Nichols Coll., 1971; MBA, U. Conn., 1976. CPA, Va.; cert. internal auditor. Auditor U.S. Dept. Transp., Washington, 1971-80; audit supr. Wash. Pub. Power Supply System, Richland, 1980-82; mgr. internal audit and mgmt. cons. Cen. La. Electric Co., Pineville, 1982—. Bd. dirs. central La. chpt. ARC, Alexandria, 1985. Mem. Inst. Internal Auditors, Am. Inst. CPA's, Alpine Men's Golf Assn. Republican. Club: Toastmasters Internat. (pres. local chpt. 1983). Home: 8652 Ridgemont Dr Pineville LA 71360 Office: Cen Louisiana Electric Co 2030 Donahue Ferry Rd Pineville LA 71361-5000

GAVERT, ROY VERNER, JR., electric company executive; b. Turtle Creek, Pa., Dec. 16, 1933; s. Roy V. and Margaret (Christopher) G.; m. Rita Ann Jay, Nov. 12, 1955; children: Kathryn J., Judith Gavert Ragazzini. BS, Bucknell U., 1955; MBA, U. Detroit, 1963. Dist. sales mgr. indsl. group Westinghouse Elec. Corp., Detroit, 1965-67; mgr. industry and product planning indsl. group Westinghouse Elec. Corp., Pitts., 1967-69; gen. mgr. control products div. Westinghouse Elec. Corp., Beaver, Pa., 1969-71; v.p. corp. mktg. Industry Products Co. Westinghouse Elec. Corp., Pitts., 1971-74, v.p. mktg. Industry Products Co., 1974-79, exec. v.p. learning and leisure group, Pub. Systems Co., 1979-83, exec. v.p. mktg. and services, Industries and Internat. div., 1983—. Contbr. articles to profl. jours. Active United Way, Boy Scouts Am.; trustee Bucknell U., Lewisburg, Pa., 1986—; bd. dirs. Housing Opportunities, Inc., McKeesport, Pa., 1987—. Served to 1st lt. U.S. Army, 1955-57. Mem. Engrs. Soc. Western Pa. (past pres., bd. dirs.), Soc. Logistics Engrs., Conf. Bd. Republican. Clubs: Duquesne (Pitts.); Rivers; Oakmont Country (Pa.); Beaver Valley Country; Sky (N.Y.C.). Lodge: Masons. Office: Westinghouse Electric Corp 6 Gateway Ctr Westinghouse Bldg Pittsburgh PA 15222 *

GAVEY, JAMES E., real estate investment and construction company executive; b. Buffalo, June 6, 1942; s. George W. and Clara E. (Hanley) G.; m. Joan M. Moran, June 6, 1964; children: Philip W., Peter J., John P. BS, LeMoyne Coll., 1964; MBA, Columbia U., 1965. Acct. Peat, Marwick, Mitchell & Co., Buffalo, 1960-64; bus. cons. Arthur Andersen & Co., N.Y.C., 1965-73; pres. Gavey & Company, Inc., N.Y.C., 1973-87; founder, 1988—. Contbr. articles to profl. jours. Chmn. com. United Fund, Bronxville, N.Y., 1970—; commr. Tuckahoe (N.Y.) Housing Authority, 1974-76, chmn., 1976-81; capt. N.Y. ann. fund Fordham Prep. Sch., 1980-83. Recipient various achievement awards. Mem. Am. Inst. CPA's, N.Y. State Soc. CPA's, Fla. Soc. CPA's, Fla. Inst. CPA's, Nat. Assn. Rev. Appraisers, Internat. Inst. Valuers, Nat. Apt. Assn., Nat. Assn. Home Builders, Internat. Platform Assn., Newcomen Soc. N.Am. Republican. Roman Catholic. Clubs: Union League, Cooperstown Country. Home and Office: PO Box 2158 Marco Island FL 33969

GAVIAN, PETER WOOD, investment banker; b. Brewster, Mass., Dec. 8, 1932; s. Sarkis Peter and Ruth Millicent (Wood) G.; m. Natalie Greenough, Sept. 10, 1955 (div. 1966); children—Sarah, Deborah; m. Kathleen Byrne Covert, Aug. 30, 1975; 1 child, Margaret Elizabeth. B.A., Yale U., 1954; M.B.A., Harvard U., 1959. Chartered fin. analyst. Assoc. McKinsey & Co., N.Y.C., 1959-61; sec./treas. Greater Washington Investors, 1961-64, 70-71; v.p. fin. NUS Corp., Washington, 1965-66; asst. to group v.p. internat. Carborundum Co., Niagara Falls, N.Y., 1966-68; pvt. investment banking, Washington, 1968-70, 71-76; pres. Corp. Fin. of Washington, Inc., 1976—; pres. Welco Leasing, 1985—; expert witness in bus. valuation, 1980—; lectr. Am. U., Washington, 1978-80; trustee Calvert Group Funds, Bethesda, Md., 1980—. Contbr. articles to profl. jours. Served to lt. USN, 1954-57. Fellow Fin. Analysts Fedn. (conf. chmn. 1981), Washington Soc. Investment Analysts (pres. 1978-79). Club: Naval Acad. Sailing Squadron. Avocation: sailboat racing. Home: 3005 Franklin Rd Arlington VA 22201 Office: Corp Fin Washington Inc 1326 R St NW Washington DC 20009

GAVIN, T. EDWARD, investor; b. Jersey City, Aug. 20, 1922; s. Thomas P. and Josephine E. (Groves) G.; B.S., St. Peter's Coll., 1945; M.S., Stevens Inst. Tech., 1955; postgrad. N.Y. U., 1955-59; Ph.D. (hon.), 1980; m. Allene Helen Scheithauer, Aug. 18, 1951. Asst. sales mgr. B.T. Babbitt Co., N.Y.C., 1951-53; sales mgr. Gallawhau Chem. Co., N.Y.C., 1953-55; mktg. research account exec. Batten, Barton, Durstine & Osborn, N.Y.C., 1955-58; dir. research Lennen Newell Co., N.Y.C., 1958-61; dir. corp. research for devel. Am. Cyanamide Co., Wayne, N.J., 1958-63; mgr. comml. research and intelligence Cyanamide Internat., 1963-66; investor, real estate developer, farm operator, 1966-81. Mem. bd. regents St. Peter's Coll., pres. bd., 1980-81, trustee, 1982—; chief exec. officer World Trade Industries, 1985—; dir. ARDA, 1987—; active Mental Health Assn. Hudson County (N.J.). Mem. Am. Chem. Assn., Chem. Industry Assn., Chem. Market Research Assn., Assn. Governing Bds. Univs. and Colls., Nat. Time Sharing Assocs. Am. Land Devel. Assn., Nature Conservancy. Clubs: Hudson County University, Chemists, Towanda Hunt, Bergen Carteret, Ducks Unlimited, Nags Head Woods. Home: 201 St Pauls Ave Jersey City NJ 07306 also: SR 275 Kitty Hawk NC 27949

GAVIN, THOMAS JOSEPH, banker; b. Detroit, Dec. 16, 1953; s. Ralph J. and Eleanor Gavin; m. Elaine E. Milz, Apr. 7, 1954; children: Anne Marie, Timothy Joseph, Susan Elaine, David Joseph. BBA, Wayne State U., 1977. Mgr. pub. fin. 1st of Mich. Corp., Detroit, 1975-83; mgr. investment banking Van Kampen Merritt, Lisle, Ill., 1983—. Mem. Govt. Fin. Officers Assn., Mich. Mcpl. League. Office: Van Kampen Merritt 1001 Warrenville Rd Lisle IL 60532

GAVLICK, FRANCES MARJORIE, insurance agent; b. Mt. Vernon, N.Y., July 14, 1939; d. Wallace Ploss and Frances (Barker) Weise; m. George A. Pafumi (div. 1969); children: George Ross, Steven James. Student, SUNY-New Paltz, 1957; grad., Life Underwriters Tng. Coun., N.Y. Dep. town clk. Town of Lloyd, N.Y., 1965-71; customer svc. rep. Marshall and Sterling, Poughkeepsie, 1972-79; with sales Metro Ins. Co., N.Y., 1980-81; agt. Allstate Ins. Co., Pleasant Valley, N.Y., 1981-88; ind. ins. agt. Frances M. Gavlick Ins., Wappingers Falls, N.Y., 1988—. Mem. Nat. Assoc. Life Underwriters, Womens Life Underwriters. Home: 17 Gilmore Blvd S Wappingers Falls NY 12590 Office: Frances M Gavlick Ins 5 W Main St Wappingers Falls NY 12590

GAVLOCK, EUGENE HARLAN, retail drinking water equipment company executive; b. Rockford, Ill., Mar. 28, 1925; s. Paul G. and Melvina C. (Smith) G.; master barber degree Cedar Rapids Barber Coll., 1955; m. Margaret Berneice Andersen, Feb. 15, 1952; children—Gregory Douglas, Sheryl Lynn, Carol Jean, Sharon Kay, Peggy Ann, Karla Raye, Kary Kaye. Drummer, bandleader various nat. bands, Gene Harlan Orch., 1942-54; barber, Waterloo, Iowa, 1954-60; owner, mgr. Violet Ray Coin Laundry, Waterloo, 1960-65; pres. Locktow Products, Inc., Waterloo, 1965-70; auto. salesman Simpson Dodge, Waterloo, 1967-70; pres. Pure Water Assos., Waterloo, 1974-79, Pure Water Assos., Internat., Inc., Waterloo, 1979—; pres., founder Distillerland Discount Centers, Inc., Cedar Falls, Iowa, 1979—; pres. Midwest Distilled Water Bottlers, Inc., Inc., Cedar Falls, 1983—. Pres. Blackhawk Village Mchts. Assn., 1982—. Named Outstanding Sales Individual for Yr., Pure Water, Inc., 1979. Mem. Nat. Assn. Self-Employed, Nat. Fedn. Ind. Bus., Internat. Platform Assn., C. of C., Family Motor Coach Assn. Home: 132 Hampshire Rd Waterloo IA 50701 Office: 600 State St Cedar Falls IA 50613

GAW, DAVID JOSEPH, sales executive; b. Phila., June 26, 1952; s. Francis William and Helen Marie (Greenwood) G. BA in Psychology, Mansfield U., 1975; BS in Bus., Bloomburg U., 1986; ins. and real estate lic., Temple U., 1986. Owner Groucho's Restaurant, Montgomeryville, Pa., 1980-82; v.p. mktg. and sales W.R. Breen Inc., Toronto, Can., 1982-85; mid-Atlantic regional sales rep. Beatrice Corp., 1985—; owner Studio 900 Prodn., Landsdale, Pa., 1985—; bd. dirs. Montgomery Motors, Phila. Editor med. jour. Breenews, 1983-85. Mem. Smithsonian Instn., Washington, 1985—, Nat. Christian Choir, Washington, 1983—. Mem. Am. Mktg. Assn., Pa. Interscholastic Athletic Assn. (ofcl. 1971-76), Sigma Tau Gamma. Republican. Baptist. Home: 900 Breezewood Ln Lansdale PA 19446

GAY, ALICE FELTS, advertising company executive; b. Atlanta, Oct. 3, 1949; d. Thomas Gordon and Jane (Copas) F.; 1 child, Kimberly Creed. AB in Psychology, U. Ga., 1971, ABJ in Journalism, 1971, MEd in Mental Retardation, 1973; postgrad., Ga. State U. Coll. Law, 1988—. Tchr. spl. edn. Commerce (Ga.) City Schs., 1972-73; community relations specialist Ga. Retardation Ctr., Athens, 1978-80; dir. pub. relations St. Mary's Hosp., Athens, 1980-83; account exec. The Adsmith, Athens, 1983-86; co-owner advt. agy. And Assocs., Athens, 1986—; cons. pub. relations Athens Regional Library, 1986—. Author, dir. (videotape) The Spirit of Athens, 1984 (Grand award 1984); contbr. articles to mags and profl. jours. Crusade chmn. United Cerebral Palsy of Ga., Athens, 1976, Am. Cancer Soc., Athens, 1976, pub. edn. chmn., 1978, bd. dirs. 1978-85; mem. Leadership Athens, 1985; assoc. deacon First Bapt. Ch., Athens, 1988—; bd. dirs. Jr. League of Athens, 1986—; pres. Athens Jr. Woman's Club, 1978; pres.-elect. Jr. League Athens, 1988-89, pres., 1989—. Recipient Gold Archie award, Athens AdClub, 1983, 84; Award of Merit, So. Indsl. Devel. Council, 1984, Video Communications award, Atlanta Chpt. Internat. TV Assn., 1984; named one of Outstanding Young Women of Am., 1978, 79, 82, 84. Mem. Ga. Fedn. of Women's Clubs (chmn. state edn. dept. 1980-82, chmn. state edn. jr. conf. 1978-80), Delta Gamma. Baptist. Lodge: Order of the Eastern Star. Home and Office: 260 Skyline Pkwy Athens GA 30606

GAY, E(MIL) LAURENCE, lawyer; b. Bridgeport, Conn., Aug. 10, 1923; s. Emil D. and Helen L. (Mihalich) G.; m. Harriet A. Ripley, Aug. 2, 1952; children: Noel L., Peter C., Marguerite S., Georgette A. BS, Yale U., 1947; JD magna cum laude, Harvard U., 1949. Bar: N.Y. 1950, Conn. 1960, Calif. 1981, Hawaii 1988. Assoc. Root, Ballantine, Harlan, Bushby & Palmer, N.Y.C., 1949-51; mem. legal staff U.S. High Commr. for Germany, Bad Godesberg, 1951-52; law sec., presiding justice appellate div. 1st dept. N.Y. Supreme Ct., N.Y.C., 1953-54; assoc. Debevoise, Plimpton & McLean, N.Y.C., 1954-58; v.p., sec.-treas., gen. counsel Hewitt-Robins, Inc., Stamford, Conn., 1958-65; pres. Litton Gt. Lakes Corp., N.Y.C., 1965-67; sr. v.p. finance AMFAC, Inc., Honolulu, 1967-73; vice chmn. AMFAC, Inc., 1974-78; fin. cons. Burlingame, Calif., 1979-82; of counsel Pettit & Martin, San Francisco, 1982-88, Goodsill, Anderson, Quinn & Stifel, Honolulu, 1988—. Editor Harvard Law Rev., 1948-49. Pres. Honolulu Symphony Soc., 1974-78; trustee Loyola Marymount U., 1977-80, San Francisco Chamber Soloists, 1981-86; officer, dir. numerous arts and ednl. orgns. 2d lt. AUS, 1943-46. Mem. ABA, State Bar of Calif., State Bar of Hawaii, Plaza Club (Honolulu), Phi Beta Kappa. Republican. Roman Catholic. Home: 1159 Maunawili Rd Kailua HI 96734 Office: Goodsill Anderson Quinn & Stifel PO Box 3196 Honolulu HI 96801

GAY, MICHAEL HUBERT, lawyer; b. Honolulu, May 11, 1944; s. Hubert Henry and Betty Jane (Plaister) G.; m. Gloria Mildred Knox, Mar. 15, 1975. BS, UCLA, 1967; JD, U. Calif., 1974; LLM, NYU, 1975. Bar: Calif. 1974, U.S. Supreme Ct. 1979. Ptnr. Gay, Pfister & Gay, La Jolla, Calif., 1975-77; v.p., gen. counsel Dyna Industries Inc., Carlsbad, Calif., 1977-85; corp. counsel Fujitsu Systems of Am. Inc., San Diego, 1985—; bd. dirs. Interactive Inc., San Diego; adj. prof. bus. law San Diego State U., 1979-81. Mem. San Diego County Pub. Welfare Adv. Com., 1967-77; arbitrator San Diego Mcpl. & Superior Ct., 1980-85. Served to capt. U.S. Army, 1967-71, Vietnam. Mem. ABA, Am. Soc. Corp. Counsel, State Bar Calif., San Diego County Bar Assn., Assn. Former Intelligence Officers. Republican. Office: Fujitsu Systems of Am Inc 12670 High Bluff Dr San Diego CA 92130

GAYLORD, KAREN WHITACRE, financial executive; b. Stuttgart, Fed. Republic of Germany, Dec. 25, 1951; d. Eugene Maxwell and Marion Eileen (Jones) W.; m. John William Gaylord. BS in Acctg. cum laude, Pa. State U., 1973. CPA, CLU, chartered fin. cons., N.J. Auditor Peat, Marwick, Mitchell & Co., Trenton, N.J., 1973-75; chief mgmt. analyst N.J. Housing FIn. Agy., Mercerville, N.J., 1975-81; sales mgr., field underwriter Mut. of N.Y., North Brunswick, N.J., 1981-87; pres. P&R Fin. Svcs. and Tax Planning, East Windsor, N.J., 1984-87; sr. sales trainer Merrill Lynch Pierce, Fenner and Smith, Princeton, N.J., 1987—; instr. Middlesex County Coll., Edison, N.J., 1983. Mem. Am. Inst. CPA's, N.J. Soc. CPA's, NAFE., Am. Women's Soc. of CPA's. Home: 1 Witherspoon Ct East Windsor NJ 08520 Office: PO Box 9032 Princeton NJ 08543-9032

GBEWONYO, SYLVESTRE KWADZO, financial manager; b. Sekondi, Ghana, Mar. 16, 1942; s. James Constance Awovor and Dorothea Aku (Sedode) G.; m. Gifty Esi Ribeiro, June 28, 1969; children: Sylvestre Jerry, Hugh Fifi, Theophile Edem, Rene Dela. Degree in hosp. adminstrn., U. Ghana, Legon, 1967; MSc in Fin. Mgmt., U. Southampton, Eng., 1985. Hosp. adminstr. Ministry of Health, Accra, Ghana, 1967-70, Volta River Authority, Ghana, 1970-75; chief acct. motors div. UTC Ghana Ltd., Accra, 1975-79; chief acct., adminstrv. mgr. Jos Hansen & Soehne Ghana, Ltd., Accra, 1979-81; fin. mgr. World Vision Internat., Accra, 1981-87; regional fin. mgr. World Vision Internat., Western Africa, 1987—; lectr. acctg. Accra Poly., 1975-77, U. Ghana, 1986—; lectr. bus. fin. Inst. Profl. Studies, Accra, 1987—. Recipient Norman Griffiths prize Corp. Cert. Secs., London, 1967. Mem. Inst. Chartered Secs. and Adminstrs., Brit. Inst. Mgmt., Soc. Strategic and Long Range Planning. Lodge: Rotary. Home: 3 Bamboo St, Teshie/Nugua Estates, Accra Ghana Office: World Vision Internat, Pvt Mail Bag, Accra North Ghana

GEARHART, MARVIN, oil company executive; b. Erie, Kans., May 13, 1927; s. Charles Herman and Marjorie Catherine (Hudson) G.; m. Jan Olson, Feb. 14, 1947; children: Dee Ann Gearhart Stenberg, Dale Alan, Jill Sue Gearhart Johnston, Janice Kay Parys. B.S. in Mech. Engring., Kans. State U., 1949. Logging engr. Welex, 1949-53; chief field engr. Security Engr. div. Dresser, 1953-55; co-founder, chmn., pres. Gearhart Industries Inc., Ft. Worth, 1955-89; dir. Halliburton Logging Svcs., Ft. Worth, 1989—; dir. subs. Go Oil Well Services (now Gearhart Industries Inc.); dir. Justin Industries Inc., Ft. Worth; chmn. Rock Bit Industries, Inc., Ft. Worth. Contbr. tech. papers in field. Trustee Tex. Christian U., Ft. Worth, 1978—; bd. dirs. Am. Paralysis Assn., Dallas, 1979; div. chmn. United Way Campaign, Ft. Worth, 1979; dir. Tex. Assn. Taxpayers, 1979-81. Served with USAF, 1944-46. Recipient Ike Harrison award Tex. Christian U. Mgmt. Alumni Assn., 1979; named Hon. Alumnus Tex. Christian U. Mgmt. Alumni Assn., 1982, Bus. Exec. of Yr. Tex. Wesleyan Coll., Ft. Worth C. of C., 1982. Mem. Soc. Petroleum Engrs. (disting. lectr. 1981-82), Soc. Profl. Well Log Analysts (pres. Dallas-Ft. Worth chpt. 1969), Am. Petroleum Inst. Clubs: Nomads (bd. regents) (1971-72); Petroleum, Ft. Worth, Wildcatters (chmn. exec. com. 1983). Office: Rock Bit Industries Inc 7601 Will Rogers Blvd Fort Worth TX 76140

GEARING, WILLIAM ANDREW, food and lodging executive; b. Carmichaels, Pa., Apr. 23, 1945; s. John Francis and Louella Marie (Havlach) G.; m. Susan Ann Mosolovich, Jan. 11, 1969; 1 child, Amy Rebecca. BS, Pa. State U., 1968. Asst. mgr. Cleaves Food Service, Washington, 1968-70; food service dir. Servomation Corp., Balt., 1970-73; v.p. pricing and systems Marriott Corp., Washington, 1973—. Republican. Roman Catholic. Office: Marriott Corp Dept 95104 1 Marriott Dr Washington DC 20058

GEARY, DAVID LANNON, brewing company executive; b. Portland, Maine, Apr. 19, 1945; s. Jack Lannon and Joyce Evelyn (Goldman) G.; m. Karen Kay Kramer, Apr. 1, 1967; children: Kelly Jane, Matthew David. BS Eng. Lit., Purdue U., 1967, MBA, 1972. Mgr. mktg. Ross Labs, Columbus, Ohio, 1972-78; v.p. sales Daynomed Corp., Portland, 1978-82, pres., 1978-82; pres. D.L. Geary Brewing Co., Portland, 1983—. Mem. Assn. Brewers (bd. advs. 1987—). Office: DL Geary Brewing Co 38 Evergreen Dr Portland ME 04103

GEARY, DAVID LESLIE, communication executive, educator, military officer; b. Connellsville, Pa., Sept. 30, 1947; s. Harry and Edith Marie (Halterman) G.; BA, Otterbein Coll., 1969; MSJ, W.Va. U., 1971; postgrad. U. Denver, 1974-75; diploma Def. Info. Sch., 1971; exec. communications curriculum U. Okla., 1978; Def. Dept. Sr. Pub. Affairs Officers Course, 1984; Fgn. Svc. Inst., U.S. Dept. State, 1984; Nat. Def. U., 1986. Admissions counselor Otterbein Coll., 1968-69; instr. English, staff counselor Office of Student Ednl. Svcs., W.Va. U., Morgantown, 1969-71; dir. info. Luke AFB, Ariz., 1971-72; course dir. English and communications U.S. Air Force Acad., Colo., 1972-76; dir. pub. affairs Loring AFB, Maine, 1976-79, spl. asst. pub. affairs, Seymour Johnson AFB, N.C., 1980; dir. pub. affairs, USAF Engring. and Svcs. Center, Tyndall AFB, Fla., 1980-84, U.S. Air Forces, Korea, 1984-85; asst. prof. aerospace studies, asst. dept. chmn. U. Ala., 1985-88; nat. dir. community relations USAFR, 1988—; guest lectr. U. Maine, 1976-79, USAF Inst. Tech., 1981-82, Fla. State U., 1982-83, U. Md., 1984-85, U. So. Calif., 1984-85, Seoul (Korea) Nat. U., 1985. Decorated 3 Meritorious Service medals, 2 Air Force commendation medals, Air Force Achievement medal, Armed Forces Reserve medal, Humanitarian Svc. medal, Nat. Def. Svc. medal, various others; recipient Pres.'s Extraordinary Svc. award Otterbein Coll., 1969, Nat. Disting. Svc. medal Arnold Air Soc., 1986, George Washington Honor medal from Freedoms Found., 1988; named Outstanding Faculty Advisor, U. Ala. Student Govt. Assn., 1988; nominee U. Ala. Outstanding Commitment to Teaching award, 1987; Reader's Digest Found. grantee, 1970. Mem. Nat. Acad. TV Arts and Scis., Am. Assn. Pub. Opinion Research, Pub. Relations Soc. Am., Internat. Assn. Bus. Communicators. Republican. Episcopalian. Home: PO Box 250 Bolingbroke GA 31004 Office: USAFR Nat Community Rels Hdqrs Robins AFB GA 31098

GEARY, RICHARD, construction company executive; b. Portland, Oreg., Mar. 21, 1935; s. Arthur McCornack Geary and Martha Alice (Dorman) Smith; m. Patricia Leone Lehto, 1952 (div. Jan. 1972); children: Arthur Raymond, Elizabeth Diane Geary Parker; m. Janet Lee Hendrickson, March 10, 1972; 1 child, Suzanne Janet; stepchildren: Sarah Anne Geary Ottem, David Walter Garner. BSCE with great distinction, Stanford U., 1956, MSCE, 1957. Engr. Peter Kiewit Sons' Co., Vancouver, Wash., 1957-59, supt., 1959-64, area mgr., 1964-69; Northwest dist. mgr. Peter Kiewit & Sons, Vancouver, Wash., 1969-84, mgr. Pacific div., 1984—, also dir. Mem. Oreg.-Columbia Associated Gen. Contractors (bd. dirs. 1971—, pres., 1977), Phi Beta Kappa. Republican. Presbyterian. Office: Kiewit Pacific Co PO Box 1769 Vancouver WA 98668

GEARY, WILLIAM JOHN, computer company executive; b. Boston, Mar. 4, 1959; s. Michael Vincent and Dorothy Marie (Mancusi) G.; m. Kristi Lynn Jones, Aug. 28, 1982. BS in Acctg. and Fin., Boston Coll., 1980. CPA, Mass. Staff auditor Arthur Andersen & Co., Boston, 1980-82, audit supr., 1982-84; supr. fin. analysis Congoleum Corp., Portsmouth, N.H., 1984-85; contr., fin. officer Boston Envelope Co., Mansfield, Mass., 1985-87; v.p. fin. and adminstrn., treas. MathSoft, Inc., Cambridge, Mass., 1987—. Merit scholar Boston Coll., 1976. Mem. AICPA, Mass. Soc. CPA's (com. high tech.), Mass. Computer Software Coun., Boston Coll. Alumni Asssn. Republican. Roman Catholic. Home: 25 Atwood St Wellesley MA 02181 Office: MathSoft Inc One Kendall Sq Bldg 200 Cambridge MA 02139

GEBHARDT, GARY FREDERICK, management consultant; b. Cleve., Mar. 26, 1963; s. Alfred and Hildegard U. (Kuprat) G. BS in Acctg., U. Akron, 1985; MBA, Case Western Res. U., 1989. CPA, Ohio. Mgmt. cons. Price Waterhouse, Cleve., 1985—. Counselor Regional Council on Alcoholism, Cleve., 1979-82, Beech Brook Children's Home, Pepper Pike, Ohio, 1986-87; mem. Cleve. Ballet Council, 1988, Cleve. Waterfront Coalition. Mem. Nat. Assn. Accts., Toastmasters, Beta Alpha Psi (pres. Gamma Eta chpt. 1984-85), Omicron Delta Kappa. Republican. Baptist. Office: Price Waterhouse BP Am Bldg 200 Public Sq 27th Fl Cleveland OH 44114-2301

GECKLE, JEROME WILLIAM, business services company executive; b. Balt., June 16, 1929; s. George Francis and Rose Christina (Katzenberger) G.; m. Mary Margaret Trageser, June 9, 1951; children—Timothy James, Teresa Ann, Stephen Lawrence, Karen Joy. Student pvt. schs. Supr. Internat. Harvester Co., Balt., 1949-52; mgr. machine acctg. Lever Bros. Co., Balt., 1952-55; with PHH Corp., Balt., 1955—, pres., 1974—, chief exec. officer, 1979—, chmn., 1980—, also bd. dirs.; mem. The Conf. Bd.; bd. dirs. 1st Md. Bancorp., Balt. Gas & Elec., Crown Cen. Petroleum Corp. Trustee Villa Julie Coll., 1973—, Goucher Coll., 1981-84; mem. Greater Balt. Com., 1977, Md. Port Commn.; mem. bd. advisors USMC Hist. Found.; bd. dirs. MEGA, Inc., Econ. Devel. Coun. Greater Balt., 1979—, vice-chmn., bd. trustees Mt. St. Mary's Coll., 1988. With USMC, 1946-48, 50-51. Mem. Data Processing Mgmt. Assn., Conf. Bd. Democrat. Roman Catholic. Clubs: Balt. Country, Ctr. Office: PHH Corp 11333 McCormick Rd Hunt Valley MD 21031

GEDDIE, THOMAS EDWIN, small business owner; b. Athens, Tex., Oct. 7, 1930; s. Nolen Dawson and Fannie (Troublefield) G.; BS in Agr., Okla. State U., 1951; postgrad. Tex. A&M U., 1951; m. Minnie Maxine Smith, Feb. 18, 1968; children: Susan, Tommy, Sherry. Owner, operator Thomas E. Geddie Assocs., Athens, 1955—. Served with U.S. Army, 1952-54. Republican. Presbyterian. Mem. Masons (32 deg.), Shriners. Home: 901 Clifford St Athens TX 75751 Office: 314 Faulk St Athens TX 75751

GEENTIENS, GASTON PETRUS, JR., former construction management consultant company executive; b. Garfield, N.J., Apr. 6. 1935; s. Gaston Petrus and Margaret (Piros) G.; B.S. in Civil Engring., The Citadel, 1956; m. Barbara Ann Chamberlain, Oct. 14, 1960; children—Mercedes Frith, Faith Piros. Plant engr. Western Elec. Co., Inc., Kearny, N.J., 1956-58, owner's rep., N.Y.C., 1960-64; v.p. Gentyne Motors, Inc., Passaic, N.J., 1958-60; project engr. Ethyl Corp., Baton Rouge, La., 1964-65; mgr. Timothy McCarthy Constrn. Co., Atlanta, 1965; asst. to v.p. A.R. Abrams, Inc. and Columbia Engring., Inc., Atlanta, 1965-66; supr. engring. and constrn. Litton Industries, N.Y.C., 1966-71; pres. G.P. Geentiens Jr., Inc., Charleston, S.C., 1971-82; gen. partner Engineered Enterprises Co., Charleston, 1973-76; dir. Cayman Broadcasting Assos., Cayman Islands, B.W.I., 1977-82. Mem. Ramapo (N.Y.) Republican Com., 1961-64. Served to 1st lt. C.E., AUS, 1956-58. Registered profl. engr., 13 states. Mem. ASCE, S.C. Indsl. Developers Assn. Club: Charleston Yacht. Home: 1219 Pembroke Dr Charleston SC 29407

GEER, JOHN FARR, diversified company executive; b. N.Y.C., Oct. 15, 1930; s. William Montague and Edith Jaffray (Farr) G.; m. Carolyn Boston, June 25, 1954; children: Jennifer, Evelyn, John Farr. B.A., Princeton U., 1952; LL.B., Columbia U., 1957. Bar: N.Y. State 1957. Asso. firm Sullivan & Cromwell, N.Y.C., 1957-65, Whitman & Ransom (and predecessor firms), N.Y.C., 1965-67; partner Whitman & Ransom (and predecessor firms), 1967-73; v.p., gen. counsel, sec. Am. Standard Inc., N.Y.C., 1973—. Trustee Protestant Episcopal Soc. for Promoting Religion and Learning in State N.Y., 1960-82, treas., 1968-82; trustee Gen. Theol. Sem., 1980—, vice chmn. bd. trustee, 1986— ; mem. Corp. for Relief Widows and Children of P.E. Clergymen in State N.Y., 1960—, treas., 1967—. Served to 1st lt. F.A. AUS, 1952-54, Korea. Mem. Phi Delta Phi. Episcopalian. Club: Princeton (N.Y.C.). Home: 151 Central Park W New York NY 10023 Office: Am Standard Inc 40 W 40th St New York NY 10018 *

GEER, THOMAS LEE, lawyer; b. Johnstown, Pa., Sept. 26, 1951; s. Frank Densmore, III, and Lillian Louise (Vivoda) G. BA cum laude, Boston U., 1973; JD, U. Pitts., 1976; MLT., Georgetown U., 1978. Bar: Pa. 1978, U.S. dist. (ea. dist.) Mich. 1978, U.S. Tax Ct. 1978, Ohio 1982. Clk. NW Pa. Legal Services, Sharon, 1975; assoc. Silverstein & Mullins, Washington, 1976-78, Dykema, Gossett, Spencer, Goodnow & Trigg, Detroit, 1978-80, Keywell & Rosenfeld, Troy, Mich., 1980-81; ptnr. Carson, Vieweg, Geer & Smereck, Bloomfield Hills, Mich., 1981-82, Schwartz, Kelm, Warren & Rubenstein, Columbus, Ohio, 1982—; adj. prof. Walsh Coll., Troy, Mich., 1981, Franklin U., Columbus, 1983-86, Capital U., Columbus, 1986-87. Author: 274-2nd T.M. Casualty Losses, 1979; 298-2nd T.M. Private Foundation-Definition & Classification, 1982; 337-2nd T.M. Exempt Organizations, 1984; columnist The Tax Times, 1986-88; also articles. Mem. ABA (chmn. continuing legal edn. subcom. tax acctg. problems com. 1981-82), Ohio State Bar Assn., Columbus Bar Assn. (chmn. task force on provision of legal services to nonprofit entities 1982-84). Home: 8977 Saltcoats Ct Dublin OH 43017 Office: Schwartz Kelm Warren & Rubenstein 41 S High St Columbus OH 43215

GEFRIDES, L. TERRY, manufacturing company executive; b. Athens, Greece, Jan. 21, 1944; came to U.S., 1963, naturalized, 1967; s. George and Vanetta B. Gefrides; m. Ann Adams Moxley, July 1, 1965; children: Alec Paul, Nick George, Chris Charles. Student, Kans. State U., 1963-65; BBA in Mgmt. cum laude, N. Tex. State U., 1976-80, postgrad., 1980—. Designer Frigiking-Cummins Co., Dallas, 1966-68, prodn., inventory mgr., 1969-72; mgr. material Folsom Mfg. Co., Dallas, 1973-75; asst. dir. material Dallas Corp., 1976-81, dir. material, 1981-86; gen. mgr. Thermacore div. Dallas Corp., Williamsport, Pa., 1986—; pvt. practice mgmt. cons. Dallas, 1976—; owner Terra Mannequines, Carrollton, Tex., 1983-85; instr. N. Tex. State U., Denton, 1981-82. Mem. Am. Prodn. Inventory Control Soc., Nat. Assn. Purchase Mgrs. Republican. Methodist. Office: OHD Thermacore Inc 3200 Reach Rd PO Box 3555 Williamsport PA 17701

GEHL, EUGENE OTHMAR, power company executive; b. Kohler, Wis., Sept. 6, 1923; s. Math N. and Wilhelmina Mary (Gall) G.; m. Barbara Bendinger, June 25, 1949; children: Kathleen H., Sally J., Timothy E. BBA, U. Wis., 1949, JD, 1951. Bar: Wis. 1951. Assoc. Schubring, Ryan, Petersen & Sutherland, Madison, Wis., 1951-55; ptnr. Brynelson, Herrick, Gehl & Bucaida, Madison, 1955-85; exec. v.p., gen. counsel Wis. Power and Light Co., Madison, 1985—; instr. torts and trial advocacy U. Wis. Law Sch., 1956-73, guest lectr. pub. utilities law, environ. law, trial practice, 1973—, guest lectr. product safety and liability, 1987—. Co-author: (textbook) Thayer's Legal Control of the Press, 6th edit., 1950; contbr. articles to legal publs. Trustee U. Wis. Hosp., Madison, 1986—; commr. Madison Met. Sewerage Dist., 1986—; trustee Edgewood Coll., 1987—. Served to lt. USN,

1942-46. Fellow Am. Coll. Trial Lawyers, Am. Bar Found.; mem. ABA, State Bar Wis., Fed. Power Bar Assn., Internat. Assn. Ins. Attys., Am. Bd. Trial Advocates, Dane County Bar Assn., Seventh Cir. Fed. Bar Assn., Def. Research Inst., Edison Electric Inst. (legal com.), Am. Bd. Trial Advs., Order of Coif, Phi Eta Sigma. Clubs: Madison, Nakoma Country. Office: Wis Power & Light Co 222 W Washington Ave Madison WI 53703

GEHLING, JOHN ADAM, manufacturing company executive; b. Cambridge, Mass., July 23, 1920; s. Daniel C. and Hazel A. (Dyson) G.; m. Madelyn Virginia Brown, July 25, 1943; children: Nancy, Martha, Jack, Bill, Jim, Tim, Virginia, Jane. BSME magna cum laude, Tufts U., 1943; MBA, Harvard U., 1947. V.p. mfg. WCI Kelvinator, Grand Rapids, Mich., 1969-70; exec. v.p. WCI Greenville (Mich.) Prodns., 1970-72, pres., group v.p., 1972-83, corp. v.p., pres., 1983-86; group v.p., gen. mgr. WCI Refrigerator Div., Greenville, from 1986; now pres. Greenville (Mich.) Prodns. Co. Past mem. Sch. Bd., Cold Springs Harbor, N.Y., Planning Commn., South Russell, Ohio, City Council, South Russell. Served to lt. USN, 1943-46. Mem. Assn. Home Appliance Mfrs. (past chmn. refrigerator freezer exec. bd.). Club: Cascade Hills Country (Grand Rapids). Home: 7314 Cascade Rd Grand Rapids MI 49508 Office: Greenville Products Co 635 W Charles St Greenville MI 48838 *

GEHLMANN, TIMOTHY SHAWN, financial executive; b. Washington, Feb. 16, 1960; s. Donald Eugene and Barbara Ann (Elder) G. AA, Lorain County (Ohio) Community Coll., 1980; BBA in Acctg., Ohio U., 1982; postgrad., Cleve.-Marshall Coll. of Law, 1985, Golden Gate U., 1986. CPA, Calif., Ohio. Asst. mgr., tng. coordinator McDonald's Corp., Amherst, Ohio, 1978-80; acct. Gen. Motors Corp., Flint, Mich., 1981; audit and tax specialist Ernst & Whinney, Cleve., 1982-84; tax cons. Deloitte Haskins & Sells, Cleve., 1985, San Francisco, 1985-86; controller Lincoln Property Co., Foster City, Calif., 1986-88; ptnr. Source Fin., San Francisco, 1988—. Contbr. articles to company publs. Mem. judiciary candidate evaluation com. Citizens League of Greater Cleve., 1985, current affairs com. Commonwealth Club of Calif., San Francisco, 1985—. Mem. Am. Inst. CPA's, Ohio Soc. CPA's (Congl. Key Person, 1985—), Calif. Soc. CPA's, Real Estate Securities and Syndication Inst. (nat. budget com., regulatory-legis. com. 1986-88), Nat. Assn. Accts., EDP Auditors Assn. Club: City (Cleve.) (trustee 1984-85). Office: Source Fin 345 California St San Francisco CA 94104

GEHRING, DAVID AUSTIN, medical director, cardiologist; b. Bryn Mawr, Pa., Dec. 6, 1930; s. Harry Rittenhouse and Anne Gardiner (Bozarth) G.; m. Joan Helen Lotz, June 7, 1953 (div. Aug. 1982); children: David, Paul, Peter, Sue, Barbara, Eric; m. Victoria Marie Damiano, Sept. 2, 1982; children: Theresa, Judy Lynne, Michael Austin. BA magna cum laude, U. Pitts., 1952, MD, 1956. Diplomate Am. Bd. Internal Medicine. Commd. USN, 1956, advanced through grades to lt. comdr.; intern, then resident in internal medicine U.S. Naval Hosp. USN, Phila., 1956-60, mem. staff internal medicine U.S. Naval Hosp., 1960-61; chief internal medicine heart sta. U.S. Naval Hosp. USN, Annapolis, Md., 1961-63; resigned USN, 1963; cardiologist K.G.E. Med. Group, Woodbury, N.J., 1963-82; cardiologist, pres. Hobbs Cardiology, P.A., Hobbs, N.Mex., 1982-86; med. dir. Polk (Pa.) Ctr., 1986—; testing cardiologist Anthropometrics United Med. Group, Cherry Hill, N.J., 1974-82; clin. asst. prof. medicine Temple U. Hosp., Phila., 1975-82; adj. asst. prof. medicine Jefferson Meml. Coll., Phila., 1981-82; chief cardiac rehab. unit Lea Regional Hosp., Hobbs, 1982-86; chief med. services 829th Sta. Hosp. USAR, Lubbock, Tex., 1984-86; cons. cardiology Oil City, Pa., 1986—. Author: EKG Workbook, 1972, EKG Workbook I, 1978; contbr. articles to profl. jours. Project dir. 23 Greater Del. Valley Regional Med. Program, Pa., 1971-75; mem. ACLS Inst. and affiliated faculty Pa. Heart Assn., 1986—, bd. dirs. N.W. chpt., 1988—; bd. dirs. adv. com., chmn. personnel com. med. health, rehab., drugs and alcohol Venango County, Franklin, Pa., 1986—, pres., 1988—; lector St. Joseph Ch., Oil City, 1987—; active Pitts. Opera Soc. Lt. Col. USAR, 1983—. Recipient Outstanding Service award Am. Cancer Soc., N.J., 1967, Benjamin Berkowitz award N.J. Heart Assn., 1975, Nat. Def. Svc. medal, 1975, USAR Components Achievement medal, 1988, Army Svc. Ribbon, 1987, Letter of Commendation USAR, 1988, Pres.'s medal of Merit Rep. Task Force, 1984; Cert. of Appreciaton Sec. of State, N.Mex., 1982, Venango County Commr's., 1987, 88. Fellow Am. Coll. Cardiology, Am. Coll. Chest Physicians, Coll. Physicians Phila., Am. Coll. Clin. Pharmacology; mem. AMA, AM. Coll. Physicians (life, Recognition awards 1967-70), St. Jude Soc., Holy Name Soc., Assn. Miraculous Medal (promoter 1987—), Venango County Med. Soc. (pres. elect, 1989—), Franklin Club. Roman Catholic. Home: 7 Crestview Dr Oil City PA 16301-2009 Office: Polk Ctr PO Box 94 Polk PA 16342-0094

GEHRKE, ALLEN CHARLES, corporation executive; b. Milw., Sept. 29, 1934; s. Earl F. and Angeline (Pasdirtz) G.; m. Roberta K. Bohrer, July 23, 1955; children: Christine K., Lynda F., Mark A. With Midwest Contractors, Milw., 1952-60; designer Godfrey Co., Waukesha, Wis., 1960-68, constrn. mgr., 1968-70, dir. design and constrn., 1970-76, v.p. store devel., 1976-80, sr. v.p. corp. devel., 1980—. Served with USNR, 1951-59. Mem. Wis. Food Dealers Assn., Food Mktg. Inst. Republican. Roman Catholic. Clubs: Woodland Sportsmens (pres. 1970-73), Gt. Lakes Sport Fishermen, Milw. Yacht. Office: Godfrey Co 1200 W Sunset Dr Waukesha WI 53186

GEIER, HENRY GEORGE, financial executive; b. Jersey City, Dec. 16, 1940; s. George Edward and Helen Mary (Francone) G.; m. Patricia Ann O'Donnell, June 16, 1962; children—Kathleen, Henry George Jr., Frank, Sean, Kelly. B.S. in Acctg., St. Peter's Coll., Jersey City, 1962; M.B.A., Fordham U., 1973. C.P.A., N.J. Mgr. Deloitte, Haskins & Sells, N.Y.C., 1964-75; chief examiner Am. Stock Exchange, N.Y.C., 1975-77; v.p. Morgan Stanley & Co., Inc., N.Y.C., 1977-79; treas. First Boston, Inc., N.Y.C., 1979—. Council pres. Westwood Governing Body, N.J., 1979; chmn. Westwood Parking Authority, 1980-85; trustee Westwood Sr. Citizens Housing Authority, 1985. Served to 1st lt. U.S. Army, 1962-64, Korea. Mem. Fin. Execs. Inst., Securities Industry Assn. (bd. dirs. fin. mgmt. div. 1982-85), N.J. State Soc. C.P.A.s, Am. Inst. C.P.A.s. Republican. Roman Catholic. Office: 1st Boston Inc care 1st Boston Corp Park Avenue Pla New York NY 10055 *

GEIER, JAMES AYLWARD DEVELIN, manufacturing company executive; b. Cin., Dec. 29, 1925; s. Frederick V. and Amey (Develin) G.; children: Deborah Anne, James Develin, Aylward Whittier. Attended, Williams Coll., 1947-50. With Cin. Milacron Inc., 1951—, became v.p., 1964, dir., 1966, exec. v.p., 1969, pres., chief exec. officer, 1970, also chmn.; dir. Clark Equipment Co., USX Corp. Trustee Cin. Museum Natural History; mem. adv. bd. Cin. Council on World Affairs; mem. Kenton County Airport Bd.; trustee Children's Home of Cin., Rensselaer Poly. Inst., 1987—; bd. dirs. Cin. chpt. ARC.; adv. council Cin. Zoo. Served with USAAF, 1944-46. Mem. NMTBA (chmn. 1988—), Conf. Bd., Machinery and Allied Products Inst. (exec. com.), Mgmt. Execs. Soc. (exec. com.). Republican. Clubs: Commercial, Commonwealth, Queen City, Camargo. Home: 3018 Golden Ave Cincinnati OH 45226 Office: Cin Milacron Inc 4701 Marburg Ave Cincinnati OH 45209

GEIER, PHILIP HENRY, JR., advertising executive; b. Pontiac, Mich., Feb. 22, 1935; s. Philip Henry and Jane (Gillen) G.; m. Faith Power, children—Hope, Johanna Geier. B.A., Colgate U., 1957; M.S., Columbia U., 1958. With McCann-Erickson, Inc., Cleve., 1958-60, N.Y.C., 1960-68; chmn. McCann-Erickson Internat. U.K. Co., London, 1969-73; exec. v.p. McCann-Erickson Europe, 1973-75; vice chmn. internat. ops. McCann Worldwide, London, 1973-75; vice chmn. internat. Interpublic Group of Cos., Inc., N.Y.C., 1975-77; pres., chief operating officer Interpublic Group of Cos., Inc., 1977-80, chmn., chief exec. officer, 1980—, pres., 1985—; dir. EAC Industries, Inc. Bd. dirs. Sch. Am. Ballet; trustee N.Y. Foundling Hosp., Boy's Club N.Y., MU of DKE Found.; Dean's Adv. Council Columbia Bus. Sch.; pres.' council Marymount Manhattan Coll. Mem. Am. Assn. Advt. Agys. (com. agy. mgmt.), Advt. Council (vice chmn. fin. com.), Coalition Service Industries. Clubs: Doubles (N.Y.C.); River (N.Y.C.); Sloane (London); Hurlingham (London). Office: Interpub Group Cos Inc 1271 Ave of the Americas New York NY 10020 *

GEIGER, EDWARD R., telecommunications company executive; b. Allentown, Pa., Apr. 14, 1942; s. Donald R. and Katharine J. (Ealer) G.; m. Edri C. Pappenberger, June 19, 1965; children: Suzanne C., Heather R. BS in Acctg., Lehigh U., 1964, MBA, 1965. CPA, Alaska. Acct. Berg Schultz & Green, CPAs, Allentown, 1964-65, GE, Cleve., 1965-66; mgr. acctg. Pillsbury Co., Mpls., 1970-72; controller Fairbanks (Alaska) Mcpl. Utilities, 1972-76; v.p. fin. Alascom, Inc., Anchorage, 1976-82; v.p. adminstrn. Pacific Telecom, Inc., Vancouver, Wash., 1982-89, contr., 1989—; supr. Columbia Credit Union, Vancouver, 1987—. Bd. dirs. Clark Coll. Found., Vancouver, 1987—; mem. adv. bd. Wash. State U., Vancouver, 1987—. Served to lt. USN, 1966-70. Mem. AICPA, Alaska Soc. CPAs, Fin. Execs. Inst. (treas. 1988, v.p. 1989—), Vancouver C. of C. (bd. dirs. 1987—).

GEIGER, RICHARD LAWRENCE, entrepreneur; b. N.Y.C., Apr. 18, 1917; s. Jerome C. and Ruth (Alton) G.; BS, CCNY, 1935; Indsl. Engr., NYU, 1951; registered profl. engr., N.J.; m. Emmy L. Epstein, Feb. 2, 1946; children: Ellen Catherine, James Lawrence. Prodn. control mgr. Eagle Pencil Co., N.Y.C., 1947-50; indsl. rels. dir. Maidenform, Bayonne, N.J., 1950-51; contr. Am. Aluminum Co., Newark, 1951-55; gen. mgr. Telautograph Corp., N.Y.C., 1955-56; assoc. N.W. Levin & Co., N.Y.C., 1956-60; pres. de Vegh Internat. Corp., N.Y.C., 1960-64; fin. cons., N.Y.C., 1964-68; gen. ptnr. Geiger & Fialkov, N.Y.C., 1968-77; pres. Richard L. Geiger, Inc., Fin. Cons., 1981—; ptnr. Poly Ventures, Farmingdale, N.Y., 1987-88; vice chmn. bd. Microsemi Corp., Santa Ana, Calif.; bd. dirs. Standard Microsystems, Hauppage, N.Y., Geotel, Inc., Hauppauge, N.Y., Worldwide Computer Svcs., Inc., Wayne, N.J., San Jose, Calif., Laser Recording Systems, Inc., Sprata, N.J. Adviser J.M. Kaplan Fund, 1964-68, 82-86; advisor Grotech Ptnrs., Ltd., Balt., mem. adv. bd. Sch. Continuing Edn., NYU, 1985—. Capt. USNR., 1940-47. Named Disting. Alumnus N.Y. Poly. U. Mem. Tech. Socs. Coun. N.J. (past pres.), Am. Phys. Soc., Fin. Analysts Fedn., N.Y. Soc. Security Analysts, Army Navy Club (Washington), NYU Club, Alpha Pi Mu. Home: 10 Euclid Ave Summit NJ 07901

GEIN, ROBERT ALLEN, accountant; b. Bklyn., Jan. 18, 1945; s. Allen William and Virginia E. (Waters) G.; m. Nancy Ellen Aiello, Jan. 24, 1970; children: Patrick, Noreen. BS cum laude, L.I. U., 1969, MBA, 1971. CPA N.Y., N.J; registered securities dealer rep. Acct. Touche Ross & Co, N.Y.C., 1969-76, Gein, Connolly & Switaj, Holmdel, N.J., 1976-87; pres. Transaction Billing Resources Inc, Hazlet, N.J., 1985—; also bd. dirs. Transaction Billing Resources Inc, Hazlet; bd. dirs. Aldor Prodns. Butler, N.J., Transaction Billing Resources, Hazlet; cons. John Richard Assocs., Hazlet, 1984—. Mem. Am. Inst. CPA's, N.Y. Soc. CPA's, N.J. Soc. CPA's, Lions (local pres. 1974-76). Republican. Roman Catholic. Home: 108 Conover Ln Red Bank NJ 07701 Office: Transaction Billing Resources 24 Village Court Hazlet NJ 07730

GEISE, HARRY FREMONT, retired meteorologist; b. Oak Park, Ill., Jan. 8, 1920; student U. Chgo., 1938-39, Meterorol. Service Sch., Lakehurst, N.J., 1943-44; m. Juanita Calmer, 1974; children—Barry, Gary, Harry (triplets); children by previous marriage—Marian Frances, Gloria Tara. Pioneered in extending pvt. weather services in Chgo., 1937; chief meteorologist Kingsbury Ordnance, 1943; meteorologist radio sta. WLS, and Prairie Farmer Newspaper, 1941, 42, 46; asso. Dr. Irving P. Krick, meteorol. cons., 1947-49; Army Air Corps research, 1948-49, developed new temperature forecasting technique; condr. weather and travel shows WBKB-TV, Chgo., also radio sta. WOPA, Oak Park, 1950-51; developed radio and television shows, San Francisco and San Jose, Cal., 1954-55; dir. media div. Irving P. Krick Assos., 1955-59; produced, appeared on weather programs Columbia Pacific Radio and TV Networks, also weatherman KNXT, Hollywood, Calif., 1957-58; comml. weather service, 1962-80; instr. meteorology Santa Rosa Jr. Coll., 1964-66, Sonoma State Coll., 1967-68; weather dir. WCBS-TV, 1966-67, established weather center for CBS, N.Y., 1966-67. Research relationship between specified solar emission and major change in earth's weather patterns, tornado forecasting and long-range forecasting up to 4 years in advance. Meteorologist, Nat. Def. Exec. Res., 1968-74. Served with USMC, 1944-45. Recipient 1st Calif. Teaching Credential for Eminence in Meteorology, 1964. Mem. Royal Meterol. Soc. (life fgn. mem.). Author articles in field, contbr. to newspapers and mags. Contbr. long range forecasts. Mailing Address: 49975 Avenida Obregon La Quinta CA 92253 Home: 4585 Brighton Way Santa Maria CA 93455

GEISEL, MARTIN SIMON, dean of college, educator; b. Grand Rapids, Mich., Nov. 27, 1941; s. Bernard and Jeanette (Rozema) G.; m. Susan Amendola, Sept. 28, 1963 (div. 1974); children: Sandra L., Matthew B.; m. Kathy E. Bell, Jul. 25, 1987. BS in Mgmt. Sci., Case Inst. Tech., 1963; MBA in Bus. Econs., U. Chgo., 1965, PhD in Bus. Econs., 1970. Process engr. E.I. DuPont de Nemours, East Chicago, Ind., 1963-65; asst. then assoc. prof. Carnegie-Mellon U., Pitts., 1968-75; assoc. prof. grad. sch. mgmt. U. Rochester, N.Y., 1975-79, assoc. dean for acad. affairs, 1979-85; dean sch. mgmt. U. Tex. at Dallas, Richardson, 1985-87; dean, prof. Owen grad. sch. mgmt. Vanderbilt U., Nashville, 1987—. Contbr. articles to profl. jours. Bd. visitors Edwin L. Cox Sch. Bus. So. Meth. U., Dallas, 1988—; mem. migratory waterfowl stamp adv. com., State of N.Y., 1984-85; bd. dirs. Am. Assembly Collegiate Schs. Bus., St. Louis, 1987-88. Mem. Am. Statis. Assn., Econmetric Soc., Univ. Club. Home: 453 Beech Creek N Brentwood TN 37027 Office: Vanderbilt U Owen Grad Sch of Mgmt 401 21st Ave S Nashville TN 37203

GEISHECKER, JOHN ANDREW, JR., financial consultant; b. Boston, July 16, 1937; s. John Andrew and Dorothy (Whittemore) G.; A.B., Georgetown U., 1959; M.B.A., Northeastern U., 1966; m. Brenda Sullivan, Nov. 28, 1964; children—Kristin, John Andrew. With State Street Boston Corp. and subs., 1962-78, v.p. State Street Bank, 1962-78, exec. v.p. SSB Investments, Inc., 1970-78, v.p. fin. Rule Industries, Inc., 1978—, pres. KREW, Inc., 1978—; dir. Gelman Scis., Inc., Keltron Corp., Rule Industries, Hussey Seating Corp., EPC Labs. Inc.; chmn. bd. dirs. Phillips Screw Co.; lectr., Babson Coll., 1978—. Served with USCGR, 1959-62. Mem. Georgetown U. Alumni Assn. (bd. govs. 1972-78, pres. Boston chpt. 1969-76). Republican. Roman Catholic. Home: 1313 Great Plain Needham MA 02192 Office: Cape Ann Indsl Pk Gloucester MA 01930

GEISLER, NATHAN DAVID, stockbroker; b. Kokand, Russia, Jan. 22, 1946; s. Leon and Esther (Korn) G.; B.A., Ohio State U., 1968; J.D., U. Toledo, 1970; m. Susan D. Starsky, 1982; 1 child, Jonathan Starsky Geisler. Asst. v.p. Merrill Lynch Pierce Fenner & Smith, Toledo, 1973-88, v.p., 1988—. Served to capt. USAF, 1971-73; lt. col. Ohio Air N.G. Mem. Air Force Assn., Ohio Air N.G. Assn., Ohio State Alumni Assn., U. Toledo Alumni Assn., Toledo C. of C., Phi Alpha Delta. Home: 2600 Forestvale Rd Toledo OH 43615 Office: 300 Madison Ave Toledo OH 43604

GEIST, JERRY DOUGLAS, electric company executive; b. Raton, N.Mex., May 23, 1934; s. Jacob D. and Jessie Kathleen (Wadley) G.; m. Sharon Ludell Kaemper, June 12, 1956; children: Douglas, Bruce, Robert. Student, U. Mo., 1952-54; BEE, U. Colo., 1956. Registered profl. engr., N.Mex. With Pub. Service Co. N.Mex., Albuquerque, 1960—, v.p. engrng. and ops., 1970-71, v.p. corp. affairs, 1971-73, exec. v.p., 1973-76, pres., 1976-82, chmn., pres., 1982—, also bd. dirs., mem. exec. com.; bd. dirs. Ch2M Hill, Lectrosonics Inc., Venture Advisors Investment Funds, Aegis Ins. Services, Inc.; chmn. Utech Venture Capital Corp. Ltd.; mem. Pres.'s Export Council. Bd. dirs. Nat. Symphony, S.W. Community Health Services; chmn. adminstrv. bd. 1st United Meth. Ch.; co-chmn. N. Mex. Com. Nat. Holocaust Mus., Albuquerque, 1987; chmn. growth devel. com. Albuquerque Econ. Forum; chmn. U. N.Mex. Found. Lt. USN, 1952-59. Mem. Edison Electric Inst., Albuquerque C. of C. (pres. 1972-73), Bus. Roundtable, Four Hills Country Club, Albuquerque Country Club, Alubquerque Petroleum Club, Links, Tau Beta Pi, Sigma Tau, Eta Kappa Nu, Pi Mu Epsilon. Methodist. Office: Pub Svc Co N Mex Alvarado Sq Albuquerque NM 87158

GEITHNER, PAUL HERMAN, JR., banker; b. Phila., June 7, 1930; s. Paul Herman and Henriette Antonine (Schuck) G.; m. Irmgard Hagedorn, Sept. 6, 1956; children—Christina, Amy, Paul. B.A. cum laude, Amherst Coll., 1952; M.B.A. with distinction, U. Pa., 1957. Sec.-treas. Ellicott Machine Co., Balt., 1957-68; successively v.p., sr. v.p., exec. asst., chmn., First Va. Banks, Inc., Falls Church, 1968-85, pres., chief adminstrv. officer, 1985—, vice chmn., 1986—, also bd. dirs.; pres. First Va. Life Ins. Co., 1974—, bd. dirs.; bd. dirs. First. Va. Bank, Arlington Mortgage Co. Sec., bd. dirs. Fairfax (Va.) Symphony Orchestra, 1988—; bd. dirs. Va. Coll. Fund, 1987—; trustee Va. Banker Sch. Bank Mgmt., 1988—. Lt. USNR, 1952-55. Home: 5406 Colchester Meadow Ln Fairfax VA 22030 Office: 1st Va Banks Inc 6400 Arlington Blvd Falls Church VA 22046

GELATT, TIMOTHY ARTHUR, lawyer, educator; b. N.Y.C., Aug. 12, 1955; s. Roland Bernard and Esther Rachel (Frishkoff) G. BA, U. Pa., 1977; JD, Harvard U., 1981. Bar: D.C. 1981, N.Y. 1988. Assoc. Baker & McKenzie, Hong Kong, Beijing, 1981-84, Paul, Weiss, Rifkind, Wharton & Garrison, N.Y.C., 1984—; lectr. law Harvard U., Cambridge, Mass., 1986—, U. Paris, 1986; adj. prof. NYU Law Sch., 1988—. Author: Corporate and Individual Taxation in the People's Republic of China, 1986; contbr. articles on law of the People's Republic of China to profl. jours. Mem. Phi Beta Kappa. Club: Harvard (N.Y.C.). Office: Paul Weiss Rifkind Wharton & Garrison 1285 Ave of the Americas New York NY 10019

GELB, BRUCE S., pharmaceutical company executive; b. N.Y.C., Feb. 24, 1927; s. Lawrence M. and Joan Friedman (Hewett) G.; m. Lueza Denise Thirkield, June 6, 1953; children: John T., Joan H., Richard E., Mary C. B.A., Yale U., 1950; M.B.A., Harvard U., 1953. With Clairol Inc., 1950-51, from 1958, exec. v.p., 1961-65, pres., from 1965; brand mgr. Procter & Gamble, 1953-57; former pres. Charter Corp.; former exec. v.p. Bristol-Myers Co., N.Y.C., vice chmn., 1985—, also bd. dirs. Bd. dirs. Madison Sq. Boys Club; chmn. bd. trustees Choate Rosemary Hall Sch. Office: Bristol-Myers Co 345 Park Ave New York NY 10154 *

GELB, JOSEPH DONALD, lawyer; b. Wilkes-Barre, Pa., Dec. 13, 1923; s. Edward and Esther (Fierman) G.; student Pa. State Coll., 1943; B.S., U. Scranton, 1950; LL.B., George Washington U., 1952; m. Anne Mirman, July 3, 1955; children—Adam, Roger. Adjudicator, War Claims Commn., 1952-54; admitted to D.C. bar, 1954, Md. bar, 1963; practiced in Washington, Md., 1954—; partner Gelb & Pitsenberger, Washington, 1969-74; prin. Joseph D. Gelb Chartered, 1974-80, Gelb, Abelson & Siegel, P.C., 1980-82, Gelb & Siegel, P.C., 1982-85; prin. Joseph D. Gelb, Chartered, 1985-85; prin. Joseph D. Gelb, Chartered, 1985—. Served with USAAF, 1943-46. Mem. Am. Bar Assn., Md. Bar Assn., D.C. Bar, Assn. Trial Lawyers Am. Bar Assn. D.C., Assn. Plaintiff's Trial Attys. Clubs: Bethesda Country, Masons, B'nai B'rith. Home: 9620 Annlee Terr Bethesda MD 20817 also: 525 N Ocean Blvd Pompano Beach FL 33062 Office: 1120 Connecticut Ave NW Washington DC 20036

GELB, RICHARD LEE, pharmaceutical corporation executive; b. N.Y.C., June 8, 1924; s. Lawrence M. and Joan F. (Bove) G.; m. Phyllis L. Nason, May 5, 1951; children: Lawrence N., Lucy G., Jane E., James M. Student, Phillips Acad., 1938-41; B.A., Yale, 1945; M.B.A. with Distinction, Harvard U., 1950. Joined Clairol, Inc., N.Y.C., 1950; pres. Clairol, Inc., 1959-64; exec. v.p. Bristol-Myers Co., 1965-67, pres., 1967-76, chief exec. officer, 1972—, chmn. bd., 1976—; bd. dirs. N.Y. Times Co., N.Y. Life Ins. Co., Fed. Res. Bank N.Y. Chmn. Crime Control Planning Bd., State of N.Y.; mem., co-vice chmn. N.Y. City Police Found.; trustee Com. Econ. Devel., Silver Shield Found., N.Y. Racing Assn.; charter trustee Phillips Acad.; bd. dirs. Lincoln Ctr. for Performing Arts; vice chmn. bd. overseers and mgrs. Meml. Sloan-Kettering Cancer Ctr.; chmn. bd. mgrs. Sloan-Kettering Inst. for Cancer Research. Mem. Coun. on Fgn. Rels., Bus. Coun., Conf. Bd., Bus. Roundtable. Home: 1060 Fifth Ave New York NY 10128 Office: Bristol-Myers Co 345 Park Ave New York NY 10154

GELFAND, IVAN, investment advisor; b. Cleve., Mar. 29, 1927; s. Samuel and Sarah (Kruglin) G.; m. Suzanne Frank, Sept. 23, 1956; children: Dennis Scott, Andrew Steven. B.S., Miami U., Oxford, Ohio, 1950; postgrad., Case-Western Res. U., 1951; grad., Columbia U. Bank Mgmt. Program, 1968; certs., Am. Inst. Banking, 1952-57. Acct. Cen. Nat. Bank Cleve., 1950-53, v.p., mgr. bank and corp. investments, 1957-75; chief acct. Stars & Stripes newspaper, Darmstadt, Germany, 1953-55; account exec. Merrill, Lynch, Pierce, Fenner & Smith, Inc., Cleve., 1955-57; chmn., chief exec. officer Gelfand, Quinn & Assos., Inc., Cleve., 1975-83; v.p., mng. dir. Prudential-Bache Securities, Inc., 1983-85; pres. Lindow, Gelfand and Quinn, Inc., 1976-83; co-editor Gelfand-Quinn/Liquidity Portfolio Mgr. Newsletter, 1978-81, Gelfand-Quinn Analysis/Money Market Techniques, 1981-84; money market columnist Nat. Thrift News, 1976-78, guest money market columnist, 1982-85; pres. Ivan Gelfand & Assocs., Inc., 1985-88; sr. v.p. Prescott, Ball & Turben, Inc., 1986-88; v.p., dir. fixed income investments Roulston & Co., 1988—; instr. investments adult div. Cleve. Bd. Edn., 1956-58, Am. Inst. Banking, 1958-68; guest lectr., speaker nat. and local TV and radio stas.; lectr. in econs., fin. instn. portfolio mgmt., cash mgmt., 1972—. Mem. investment com. United Torch Cleve., 1972-74; study-rev. team capt. Lake Erie Regional Transp. Authority, 1973-77; trustee Mt. Sinai Med. Ctr., Cleve., 1983—, treas., 1986—, trustee Jewish Community Fedn., 1986, 89, Cleve. Coll. Jewish Studies, 1988—; mem. bond com. Jewish Community Fedn., Cleve., 1979—, mem. fin. com., 1981-85; mem. Cuyahoga County Republican Fin. Com., 1978-82; mem. exec. com. Cuyahoga County Rep. Orgn., 1982—. With AUS, 1945-47. Mem. Cleve. Soc. Security Analysts, Les Politiques, Masons, Commerce Club, Oakwood Club, Union Club, University Club, Cleve. Economist Club, Thursday Economist Club. Home: 2900 Alvord Pl Pepper Pike OH 44124 Office: 4000 Chester Ave Cleveland OH 44103

GELFAND, NEAL, oil company executive; b. Bronx, N.Y., Nov. 8, 1944; s. Daniel and Faye (Frank) G.; m. Jane Auerbach, Sept. 11, 1982. B.S., CCNY, 1965; M.S., Western Mich. U., 1967; Ph.D., U. Houston, 1972. Lic. Psychologist, Pa. Ptnr. Hay Assocs., N.Y.C., 1972-80; sr. v.p. human resources Amerada Hess Corp., N.Y.C., 1980—. Mem. Am. Psychol. Assn. Office: Amerada Hess Corp 1185 Ave of the Americas New York NY 10036

GELLER, ANDREW MICHAEL, architect, designer; b. Bklyn., Apr. 17, 1924; s. Joseph Boris and Olga (Gernsten) G.; m. Shirley-Del Marie Morris, Oct. 22, 1944; children: Gregory Brook, Jamie Gail. V.p., design dir. Raymond Loewy/William Smith, N.Y.C., 1946-73; prin. archtl. firm, Northport, N.Y., 1973-83; v.p. Creative Design Internat., Riverdale, N.Y., 1983—; Mem. architects in schs. program, Nat. Commn. for Arts, Baldwin, N.Y., 1980—, AIA Hdqrs. Nat. Exhibit, Washington and N.Y., 1988. Designs include Lord and Taylor, Bloomingdale's, A&S, Stewarts, Higbees, Burdines, Richs, Gimbels, R.H. Macy's, Iveys, Sibleys, Filenes Market Basket stores; exhibited in Brooklyn Mus., Mus. of Modern Art N.Y., Guild Hall Princeton U. Chmn. Northport Archtl. Rev. Bd., 1976-79. Served with C.E. U.S. Army, 1941-45, ETO. Recipient House of Yr. award Interiors mag., 1960, Better Homes and Gardens, 1966, Cooper Union Alumnus'45. Mem. Am. Audubon Soc. (Humane medal 1938), Am. Forestry Assn. Home: 123 Highland Ave Northport NY 11768

GELLER, DAVID ZVI, financial analyst; b. N.Y.C., Feb. 16, 1964; s. Nathaniel and Sandra (Spierer) G. BS in Fin., Touro Coll., N.Y.C., 1986; postgrad., Clark U., 1988—. Registered securities dealer. Fin. analyst E. Magnus Oppenheim & Co. Inc., N.Y.C., 1986—. Mem. Omicron Delta Epsilon. Republican. Jewish. Home: 144-45 Melbourne Ave Kew Gardens Hills NY 11367

GELLER, ROBERT JAMES, advertising agency executive; b. N.Y.C., May 5, 1937; s. Jerome and Pearl (Klein) G.; m. Lois Dee Fromkin, June 9, 1968; children: Richard Evan, Stephen Laurence. BS CCNY, 1958. Account exec. Furman, Feiner & Co., N.Y.C., 1958-62; media supr. Interpublic Group of Cos., N.Y.C., 1962-64; asst. media dir. Foote, Cone & Belding, N.Y.C., 1964-69; pres. Adforce Inc., N.Y.C., 1970—. Contbr. numerous articles to profl. jours. Mem. Assn. Nat. Advertisers (mem. mgmt. policy com. 1980—), Am. Advt. Fedn. (bd. dirs. 1988—), Advt. Club N.Y.C. Republican. Home: 155 E 76th St New York NY 10021 also: Ocean Rd Bridgehampton NY 11932 Office: Adforce Inc 235 E 42d St New York NY 10017

GELLERSTEDT, MARIE ADA, manufacturing company executive; b. Davenport, Iowa, Oct. 19, 1926; d. Charles Beecher and Marie Elizabeth (Pasvogel) Kaufmann; m. Keith Orval Gellerstedt, Mar. 16, 1957; children: Lori Beth Doroba, Keith Todd, Jon Erik, Cory Andrew. BBA, Augustana Coll., 1950. Gen. mgr., pres. Nixalite Co. Am., East Moline, Ill., 1957—. Life mem. Moline Sr. High Sch. PTA, also bd. dirs., 1973-76. Mem. Ill. Mfrs. Assn., Nat. Trade Show Exhibitors Assn., Internat. Exhibitors Assn., Nat. Pest Control Assn., Nat. Animal Damage Control Assn., Nat. Assn.

Women Bus. Owners, Nat. Assn. Ind. Bus., East Moline Bus. Assn., Constrn. Specifier Inst. Republican. Lutheran. Clubs: Moline-Rock Island, Zonta (bd. dirs. 1980-84). Lodges: Daus. of Mokanna Zal Caldron, Daus. of Nile.

GELLERT, GEORGE GEZA, food importing company executive; b. N.Y.C., Apr. 15, 1938; s. Imre and Martha (Tessler) G.; m. Barbara Rubin, July 21, 1963; children—Andrew, Amy, Thomas. B.S., Cornell U., 1960, M.B.A., 1962, LL.B., 1963. Bar: N.Y. State bar 1963. Atty. SEC, Washington, 1963-64; v.p., exec. v.p., pres. Atalanta Corp., N.Y.C., 1966—; chmn. bd. Atalanta Corp., 1978—; chmn. U.S.-Rumanian Econ. Council; bd. dirs. Am. Importers Meat Products Group;. Mem. Cornell U. Council. Served to 1st lt. Office Staff Judge AUS, 1964-66. Decorated Army Commendation medal. Mem. Am. Importers Assn. (dir., exec. com. meat product group), Am. Assn. Exporters and Importers (bd. dirs.), Young Pres.'s Orgn. Home: 625 Briarwood Ct Oradell NJ 07649 Office: Atalanta Corp Atalanta Pla Elizabeth NJ 07206

GELVEN, MICHAEL PAUL, retail company executive; b. Boston, June 4, 1946; s. Abraham and Sarah Rebecca (Glick) G.; student Boston State Coll., 1964-66, Northeastern U., 1969-71; cert. Southeastern Mass. U., 1978; m. Wendy Ellen Tanzer, Oct. 20, 1968; children—Marc Ian, Shana Lee. Mgr. trainee Contan Liquors, Inc., Somerville, Mass., 1967-68, mgr., 1968-73; mgr. Tanza Liquors, Inc., Somerville, 1973-74; pres., chief exec. officer Perry's Liquor Inc., North Dartmouth, Mass., 1974-82 ; pres. GTC Assos. Inc., North Easton, Mass., 1978-85; pres., chief operating officer MPG Mktg. Inc., 1985—; pres. DeRoy's Package Store, Chicopee, Mass., 1979-80; pres. Computer 'N Things, Inc., North Dartmouth, 1982-85 ; pres. Medi-Save Cos., North Dartmouth, 1987—; instr. Bristol Community Coll., 1979—. Served with Army N.G., 1966. Mem. Mass. Beverage Assn., Soc. Wine Educators, Les Amis DuVin, La Confrerie Saint-Etienne d'Alsace, Assn. Better Computer Dealers, Mensa. Democrat. Jewish (pres. temple 1978-80, dir. 1980-84, 87—). Lodges: Lions, Masons, KP, B'nai B'rith (pres. 1973-74). Home: 41 William Bradford Rd North Dartmouth MA 02747 Office: Box 9518 North Dartmouth MA 02747

GEN, MARTIN, corporate executive; b. Feb. 14, 1926; s. Max and Gussie (Bluestone) G., m. Sara Tobin; children: Gilda Paul, Sam Gen. Student, Syracuse U., 1946-50; BA, Pace U., 1950. V.p., treas. Merlin, Inc., North Bergen, N.J., 1950-73; pres. Washmasters, Inc., North Bergen, 1950-73; v.p., treas. Expert Investigation and Protective Industries, Inc., Kenilworth, N.J., 1974—; pres. InterGlobal Trading, Kenilworth, N.J.; exec. dir. EIP, Inc., Kenilworth, N.J., 1973-74. Bd. dirs. Jewish Nat. Fund, Teaneck, N.J., 1986—, YMHA, Union, N.J., 1970, Fedn. Union County, N.J., 1970, Jewish Ednl. Ctr., Elizabeth, N.J., 1960. Served with USN, 1943-46, ETO, PTO. Named Man of Yr., YMHA. Mem. Am. Soc. Indsl. Security, Club 100. Club: 100 (Teaneck). Home and Office: Box 195 Kenilworth NJ 07033

GENDRON, EDWARD CHARLES, steel company executive; b. Uxbridge, Mass., July 1, 1928; s. Charles L. and Grace E. (Wilmot) G.; m. May P. Gagnon, Sept. 6, 1948; children—Judy, Jay. Student, Coll. of Holy Cross, 1945-47; B.B.A., U. Detroit, 1959. Mgr. mktg. adminstrn. RCA, Needham, Mass., 1962-64; pres., treas. AcraMation, Inc., North Adams, Mass., 1964; plant controller Internat. Tel. & Tel. Corp., Clinton, Mass., 1965-66; divisional controller Internat. Tel. & Tel. Corp., Morton Grove, Ill., 1966; v.p. Crucible Steel Co., Pitts., 1967-68; pres. Crucible Steel Co. (Crucible Stainless Steel div.), 1968-69; pres. Midland Ross Corp., Cleve., from 1969, now vice-chmn., also bd. dirs. Home: 421 Darbys Run Bay Village OH 44140 Office: Midland-Ross Corp 20600 Chagrin Blvd Cleveland OH 44122 *

GENEREUX, ANN MARIE, accountant, government revenue agent; b. Woonsocket, R.I., Oct. 31, 1960; d. Richard Alfred and Lorraine Claire (Levasseur) G. BSBA, Bryant Coll., 1982, MBA, 1983, MST, 1989. Staff acct. N.E. Apparel Inc., Braintree, Mass., 1983-84; revenue agt. IRS, Marlboro, Mass., 1984-87, Boston, 1987—. Mem. NAFE, Am. Women's Soc. CPAs. Democrat. Office: IRS Quality Rev Staff PO Box 9096 JFK PO Boston MA 02203

GENETSKI, ROBERT JAMES, economist; b. N.Y.C., Dec. 26, 1942; s. Alex and Helen (Turbek) Genetski. B.S., Eastern Ill. U., 1964; M.A., NYU, 1968, Ph.D., 1972. Tchr. English St. Procopius Acad., Lisle, Ill., 1965-66; research analyst Nat. Econ. Research Assn., N.Y.C., 1967-68; lectr. econs. NYU, N.Y.C., 1969-70; econ. analyst Morgan Guaranty Trust Co., N.Y.C., 1969-71; sr. v.p., economist Harris Trust & Savs. Bank, Chgo., 1971-88; pres. Stotler Econs., Chgo., 1988—; lectr. in econs. NYU, 1969-70, U. Chgo., 1973; vis. prof. Wheaton Coll., Wheaton, Ill., 1986; mem. census adv. com. U.S. Dept. Commerce, 1983-86. Author: (with Beryl Sprinkel) Winning with Money, 1977, Taking the Voodoo out of Economics, 1986, 88. Chmn. ednl. com. Sch. Bd. Dist. 25, West Chicago, Ill., 1973-79. Mem. Am. Statis. Assn., Am. Econ. Assn. (fin. com. 1983—), Nat. Assn. Bus. Economists (editor Newsletter 1978), Western Econ. Assn., Am. Bankers Assn. (econ. adv. com. 1980-83), U.S. C. of C. (econ. adv. com. 1985—). Office: Stotler Econs 200 W Adams Ste 2400 Chicago IL 60606

GENGOR, VIRGINIA ANDERSON, financial planning executive, educator; b. Lyons, N.Y., May 2, 1927; d. Axel Jennings and Marie Margaret (Mack) Anderson; m. Peter Gengor, Mar. 2, 1952 (dec.); children: Peter Randall, Daniel Neal, Susan Leigh. AB, Wheaton Coll., 1949; MA, U. No. Colo., Greeley, 1975, 77. Chief hosp. intake service County of San Diego, 1966-77, chief Kearny Mesa Dist. Office, 1977-79, chief Dependent Children of Ct., 1979-81, chief child protection services, 1981-82; registered rep. Am. Pacific Securities, San Diego, 1982-85; assoc. Pollock & Assocs., San Diego, 1985-86; pres. Gengor Fin. Advisors, 1986—; cons. instr. Nat. Ctr. for Fin. Edn., San Diego, 1986—; instr. San Diego Community Coll., 1985—. Mem. allocations panel United Way, San Diego, 1976-79; chmn. com. Child Abuse Coordinating Council, San Diego, 1979-83; pres. Friends of Casa de la Esperanza, San Diego, 1980-85, bd. dirs., 1980—; 1st v.p. The Big Sister League, San Diego, 1985-86, pres., 1987—. Mem. Inst. Cert. Fin. Planners, Internat. Assn. Fin. Planning, Inland Soc. Tax Cons., AAUW (bd. dirs.), Nat. Assn. Securities Dealers (registered prin.), Nat. Ctr. Fin. Edn., Am. Bus. Women's Assn., Nat. Assn. Female Execs., Navy League, Freedoms Found. Valley Forge, Internat. Platform Assn. Presbyterian. Avocations: community service, travel, reading. Home: 6462 Spear St San Diego CA 92120 Office: Gengor Fin Advisors 4950 Waring Rd Suite 7 San Diego CA 92120

GENNETT, MARTHA REID SANDERS, advertising and marketing executive; b. Nashville, Aug. 16, 1952; d. Harvey Wade and Ellen Degraphenreid (Williams) S.; m. David C. Gennett, Mar. 12, 1988. BA, Tulane U., 1974; postgrad. in human devel., Peabody Vanderbilt U., 1983-84. V.p. promotions Sanders Mfg. Co., Nashville, 1974—. Contbr. articles to profl. jours. Bd. dirs. Women's Forum on Alcoholism, Nashville, 1983, Family and Children's Svc., Nashville, 1987. Mem. Specialty Advt. Assn. Internat. (bd. dirs. 1982-87, sr. vice chairwoman 1985, 1st chairwoman bd. 1986, Young Exec. of Yr. 1984), Nashville Advt. Fedn. (awards chairwoman 1983), Nashville C. of C. Presbyterian. Office: Sanders Mfg Co 1422 Lebanon Rd Nashville TN 37210

GENOVESE, THOMAS LEONARDO, lawyer; b. Flushing, N.Y., Feb. 28, 1936; s. Robert Pasquale Sisto and Jean Laura (Lundari) G.; m. Linda Luella Le Maire, Nov. 30, 1980; children: Torene Lucia, Andrea Lisa, Richard Michael. A.B., U. Va., 1957; J.D., Fordham U., 1960. Bar: N.Y. 1961. Atty. FAA, Jamaica, N.Y., 1961-65, NBC, N.Y.C., 1965-66, Grumman A/C Engring. Co., Bethpage, N.Y., 1966-70; gen. counsel Grumann Data Systems Co., Bethpage, N.Y., 1970-73; gen. counsel Grumman Corp., Bethpage, N.Y., 1979—, v.p., 1981—; dir. Paumanock Ins. Ltd., Hamilton, Bermuda; adj. prof. SUNY-Stony Brook, 1976-78; mem. civil case flow com. U.S. Dist. Ct. for Eastern Dist. N.Y. Contbr.: legal articles to Fordham Law Rev. Chmn. United Way Grumman corp., 1983. Mem. ABA, Am. Corp. Counsel Assn., N.Y. State Bus. Coun. (mem. gen. counsel's com.). Episcopalian. Office: Grumman Corp 1111 Stewart Ave Bethpage NY 11714

GENSERT, RICHARD MICHAEL, structural engineer, consultant; b. Cleve., Oct. 10, 1922; s. Lewis Michael and Coletta Louise (Waldeisen) G.; m. Ruth Bernice Hersko, May 30, 1980; children: Stuart, Clyde, Laurel, Christopher, Kurt. BS, Case Western Res. U., 1944; MS, Ohio State U., 1947. Designer, draftsman J. Gordan Turnbull, Cleve., 1947-48; designer, draftsman Jules Schwartz Assoc., Cleve., 1948-50; designer Dalton & Dalton, Cleve., 1950-52; cons. engr. R.M. Gensert Assocs., Cleve., 1952-80, Gensert Bretnall Assocs. Inc., Cleve., 1980—; pres. Cleve. Cons. Engrs. Assoc.; prof. Fenn Coll., Cleve., 1946-47, Case Western Res. U., Cleve., 1960-68; Andrew J. Mellon vis. prof., Pitts., 1968-79; mem. Nat. Archtl. Accreditation Bd., Washington, 1971-73; mem. Masonry Research Adv. Bd., Washington, 1979—; spl. advisor NSF, Washington, 1980—. Author: (with others) Building Design Handbook, 1960, Design of Prestressed Concrete Apartment Buildings, 1972, Problems with Masonry Structures ASTM; also articles in engring. and archtl. jours. Arbitrator, Am. Arbitration Bd., Cuyahoga County, Ohio, 1974-80. Served to lt. (j.g.) USN, 1944-46; PTO. Recipient Martin P. Korn award Prestressed Concrete Inst., 1975. Fellow Am. Concrete Inst. and ASCE (past chmn. masonry com. 1982-85, joint masonary com. 1985-88), ASTM (Alfred E. Lindau award 1982), Internat. Assn. Bridge and Structural Engrs. Home: PO Box 36 Point Chautaugua Dewittville NY 14728 Office: Gensert Bretnall Assocs Inc 718 The Arcade Cleveland OH 44114

GENTER, JOHN ROBERT, winery executive; b. Huntsville, Ala., Oct. 16, 1957; s. John C. and Madge (McDaniel) G.; m. Margaret F. MacNaughton, Sept. 5, 1981; children: John Thomas, Lois Katharine. BS in Mktg. and Bus., U. Ala., 1980. Sales rep. food div. Procter & Gamble, Cin. and Jacksonville (Fla.), 1980-81, dist. field rep., 1981; unit mgr. Procter & Gamble, Cin., Tampa (Fla.), 1982-84; div. trade devel. mgr, regional mgr. Frito-Lay, Inc., Dallas, Tampa, 1984-85; field mktg. mgr. vintage div. E&J Gallo Winery, Modesto (Calif.), Tampa, 1985, state mgr., 1986, div. mgr., 1986—; trainer Sales Mgmt. Tng. Sch. Procter & Gamble, Cin., 1982-83, Sales Devel. Program Frito-Lay, Dallas, 1984-85. Author: (with others) E&J Gallo Field Marketing Manual, 1986. Mem. St. John's Ch., Tampa, 1985—. Mem. Am. Mgmt. Assn., Speakers and Toastmasters Assn., U. Ala. Alumni Assn. (bd. dirs.), Soc. de Vinum Honoratus, Beta Gamma Sigma. Republican. Episcopalian. Home: 577 Luzon Ave Tampa FL 33606

GENTES, JULIE L., trust company executive; b. Paxton, Ill., Nov. 3, 1947; d. Donald L. and LaVera A. (Leenerman) G.; B.S. in Mktg., U. Ill., 1969. Programmer, No. Trust Co., Chgo., 1969-72, program, system analyst, 1972-74, project leader, div. mgr., 1974-78, systems officer, 1974-81, standards, acctg., planning officer, 1978-82 , bus. systems planning mgr., 82, 2d v.p., 1981-87, corp. info. services costing and billing cons., 1983—, v.p., 1987—. Contbg. author: Advances in Computer Programming Mangaement, 1980. Mem. Adler Planetarium. Mem. Am. Mgmt. Assn., U. Ill. Alumni Assn., Lincoln Park Zool. Soc., Ford County Hist. Soc., Felines, Inc., Chgo. Acad. Sci. Home: 3150 N Sheridan Rd Chicago IL 60657 Office: 125 S Wacker Dr Chicago Il 60675

GENTILE, ANTHONY, coal company executive; b. Aquila, Italy, Nov. 1, 1920; s. Gregorio and Antonietta (Duronio) G.; m. Nina Angela DiScipio, Mar. 4, 1943; children: Robert Henry, Anita Marie, Rita Ann, Thomas Gregory. Student Youngstown Coll., 1939-42; LHD (hon.), U. of Steubenville, 1977, DHL (hon.), 1988. Co-owner Pike Inn-Restaurant, Bloomingdale, Ohio, 1946-52; asst. to owner Huberta Coal Co., Steubenville, Ohio, 1952-55; gen. mgr. Half Moon Coal Co., Weirton, W.Va., 1955-57; gen. mgr. Ohio River Collieries Co., Columbus, 1957-59, pres., 1959—; pres. Lafferty Coal Mining Co., Eastern Ohio Coal Co., 1959—; v.p. Big Mountain Coals, Inc., Prenter, W.Va., 1962—, chmn. bd., 1962—; pres. Bither Mining Co. W.Va.; v.p. N & G Constrn., Bannock Land Co.; chmn., pres. Bannock Coal Co., Lafferty, Ohio, 1985-88, chmn., 1988—; chmn. bd. dirs. Mining and Reclamation Council Am., Washington; bd. dirs. Union Bank, Stuebenville. Mem. 1st Ohio Trade Commn. to Europe, 1965; mem. adv. bd. St. John Med. Ctr., Steubenville; mem. bd. trustees Coll. Steubenville, Ohio Valley Hosp., past chmn., Steubenville. Served to 1st lt AUS, 1942-45, capt. Res. ret. Decorated Purple Heart, Silver Star; recipient Citizen of Yr. award Wintersville C. of C., 1976, Conservation award for Ohio River Collieries from Gov. Ohio, 1977, Humanitarian award Jeffersonian Lodge, Jefferson County, Ohio, 1979. Mem. Am. Mining Congress (mem. adv. council coal div. 1965). Home: 4 Normandy Dr Wintersville OH 43952 Office: Ohio River Collieries Co Box 128 Bannock OH 43972

GENTILE, JACK VITO, corporate and commercial jet aircraft specialist, international trading company executive; b. Flushing, N.Y., Aug. 14, 1950; s. Vito and Angela (Tandoi) G.; grad. Manhattan Sch. Printing, 1970. Asst. prodn. mgr. Frank Orlandi Printers, N.Y.C., 1970-75; electronic technician Hobart Corp., Troy, Ohio, 1975-76; mgmt. position Reliance Electric Co., Cleve., 1976; pres., chief exec. officer Giacomo Internat. Trading Co., Bayside, N.Y., 1977—; pres. N.Y. Aviation, 1987-88; cons. to fgn. govts. on trading raw materials and aircraft. Served with U.S. Army, 1969-73. Mem. Smithsonian Assos. Roman Catholic. Club: Internat. Lions, U.S. Senatorial. Office: PO Box 438 LaGuardia Airport Flushing NY 11371

GENTIS, IAN ALFRED, manager information systems, industrial engineer; b. Somerset West, Republic of South Africa, Nov. 18, 1954; s. Alfred Gentis and Anna Catherina (Riddering) Dannert; m. Michele Marie McKinney, June 26, 1981; children: Francois, Phillip. BS in Indsl. and Systems Engring., U. So. Calif., 1980. Commd. USAF, 1980; indsl. and contingency engr. Vandenberg AFB, Calif. and Zweibrucken, Fed. Republic Germany, 1980-85; served to capt. USAF, resigned, 1985; cost analyst Schneider Nat. Inc., Green Bay, Wis., 1985-87; mgr. applications devel. Internat. Transport, Inc., Rochester, Minn., 1987—. Mem. IEEE (sr.). Republican. Presbyterian. Home: 1709 8 1/2 Ave SE Rochester MN 55904 Office: Internat Transport Inc 2450 S Marion Rd SE Rochester MN 55904

GENTRY, WILLIAM NORTON, safety consultant; b. Greenwood, Ark., May 29, 1908; s. William Fred and Lola (Caudle) G.; m. Margaret Sue Whaley, May 25, 1938 (dec.); children: Susan Margaret, William David. BS in Bus. Adminstrn., U. Ark., 1929; BA, U. Ark.-Little Rock, 1984. Wire chief SW Bell Telephone Co., Hope, Ark., 1932-34, constrn. foreman, 1935-40, exchange engr., 1940-42, 46-50, plant tng. supr., 1950-57, plant personnel and tng. supr., 1958-67, plant tng. and employment supr., 1967-73; safety cons. Little Rock Mcpl. Water Works, 1974-85; safety cons. Hiway Safety Corp., Ft. Smith, Ark., 1986-87. Div. leader Community Chest, Little Rock, 1949-52; pres., del. from Ark., Pres.'s Conf. on Occupational Safety, 1958; organizing pres. United Cerebral Palsy of Central Ark., 1959-60; chmn. Little Rock Safety Commn., 1970-71, mem., 1966-85, vol. instr., 1985—; registered instr. Nat. Safety Council's driver improvement program bd. dirs. Little Rock Central YMCA, 1972-74; worker, mem. organizing bd. Contact Inc., Crisis Prevention Center, Little Rock, 1968-76; mem. Gov.'s Com. on Employment of Handicapped, Ark., 1973-80; del. to Pres.'s Conf. on Employment of Handicapped, Washington, 1977; chmn. work area on evangelism First United Meth. Ch., Little Rock, 1980, lay speaker, 1980-82, del. internat. conf., London, 1981. Served with Signal Corps, U.S. Army 1942-46. Recipient W.H. Sadler trophy Community Chest of Little Rock, 1950-51, Service award United Cerebral Palsy of Ce..tral Ark., 1969, Safety award of commendation Ark. Dept. Labor, 1973; Cert. of Service First United Meth. Ch., Little Rock, 1983. Mem. Am. Soc. Safety Engrs. (charter mem. Ark. chpt., sec. 1974-80, vice chmn. 1959-60, gen. chmn. 1960-61, chmn. ann. safety inst. 1972-76), So. Safety Conf. (pres. 1968-69, exec. dir. 1969-72, dir. 1962-86), Reserve Officers Assn. (life), Telephone Pioneers Am. (life), The Order of Bookfellows (treas. 1987-88), Phi Alpha Theta. Democrat. Address: 1421 N University Apt N 108 Little Rock AR 72207-5226

GEOGHEGAN, PATRICIA, lawyer; b. Bayonne, N.J., Sept. 9, 1947; d. Frank and Rita (Mihok) G. BA, Mich. State U., 1969; MA, Yale U., 1972, JD, 1974; LLM, NYU, 1982. Bar: N.Y. 1975. Assoc. Cravath, Swaine & Moore, N.Y.C., 1974-82, ptnr., 1982—. Mem. ABA, N.Y. State Bar Assn., Assn. of Bar of City of N.Y. Office: Cravath Swaine & Moore 825 Eighth Ave New York NY 10019

GEORGAS, JOHN WILLIAM, beverage manufacturing company executive; b. Freeport, N.Y., Jan. 14, 1928; s. William and Helen J. (Laricos) G.; m. Tarsi Babis, Apr. 24, 1955; children—William John, Gregory Evan, Laura Michelle. B.B.A., Syracuse U.; M.B.A., Hofstra U. Mem. sales and mktg. staff Gen. Foods Corp., White Plains, N.Y., 1951-62; sr. v.p. J. Walter Thompson Co., Chgo., 1962-74; formerly sr. v.p. Coca-Cola Co., Atlanta, from 1974, now exec. v.p. Mem. Japan-Am. Soc. Ga., U.S. Nat. Commn. for Pacific Econ. Cooperation, U.S.-Asian Ctr. Tech. Exchange, U.S.-Korea Soc., Sch. Advanced Internat. Studies (bd. dirs.), Philippine Am. C. of C. Greek Orthodox. *

GEORGE, ARIAL WELLINGTON, III, financial manager; b. New London, Conn., Mar. 20, 1964; s. Arial Wellington Jr. and Tammy (Evans) G. BS, Skidmore Coll., 1986; postgrad., Tufts U., Boston, 1986. Exec. officer Schooner Tabor Boy, Marion, Mass., 1980-82; owner, pres. Constrn. Unltd. Co., Andover, Mass., 1982-86; mgr. Shawmut Bank N.Am., Lowell, Mass., 1986—. Mem. SCA Club, Saratoga (N.Y.) Club, Cape Ann Rifle Club. Home: 125 Dascomb Rd Andover MA 01810

GEORGE, DICK, pharmaceutical company executive. Pres. Sav-On Drugs Inc, Anaheim, Calif. Office: Sav-On-Drugs 1500 S Anaheim Blvd Anaheim CA 92805 *

GEORGE, ERNEST THORNTON, III, financial executive; b. Charleston, S.C., Dec. 29, 1950; s. Ernest Thornton and Betty (Long) T.; m. Frances Thomson, Sept. 30, 1977; children: Ernest Thornton IV, Andrew Neal, Katherine Frances. Student, U. Miss., 1970-71; BS in Mktg., Miss. State U., 1973. Cert. fin. planner; registered investment advisor. Field underwriter Mut. of N.Y., 1974—, Mfrs. Life Ins. Co., 1981—; rep. Integrated Resources Equity Corp., Starkville, Miss., 1981—; owner, prin. Ernie George & Assocs., Starkville, 1982—; founding mem. bd. dirs. First Bank of Starkville. Contbr. articles to profl. jours. Bd. dirs. Republican Party; past pres. Men of Ch., Presbyterian Ch., chmn. bd., elder, men's Sunday Sch. tchr. Mem. Advanced Assn. Life Underwriting, Nat. Assn. Life Underwriters, Nat. Assn. Securities Dealers, East Miss. Life Underwriters Assn. (program chmn.), Quarterback Club, Rotary (bd. dirs. Starkville chpt.), Sigma Chi, Pi Sigma Epsilon. Home: Rt 6 20 Valley Hills Starkville MS 39759 Office: Integrated Resources Equity Corp 102 S Jackson St PO Box 963 Starkville MS 39759

GEORGE, HARRY ALLAN, computer software executive; b. Chgo., July 5, 1948; s. Harry Allan and Marguerite Ethel (Savage) G.; m. Tirsa Margaret Scott, Apr. 9, 1988. BA, Bowdoin Coll., 1970. V.p. fin., co-founder, dir. Kurzweil Computer Products, Inc., Cambridge, Mass., 1973-80, Interleaf, Inc., Cambridge, 1981—; bd. dirs. Layered, Inc., Boston, Wisdom Simulations, Cambridge. Office: Interleaf Inc 10 Canal Park Cambridge MA 02141

GEORGE, JOHN ANTHONY, health corporation executive; b. New Kensington, Pa., July 11, 1948; s. Moses and Veronica (Raymond) G.; BS, Duquesne U., Pitts., 1970; MBA, U. Pitts., 1973; MS in Taxation, Robert Morris Coll., Pitts.; cert. fin. planner; m. Leah Diane Vota, Oct. 30, 1971; children: Jessica, Cara, John. Asst. adminstr. mental health and mental retardation program Western Psychiat. Inst. and Clinic, Pitts., 1971-72; asst. dir. Latrobe Area Hosp., Latrobe, Pa., 1973-76; asst. dir. Presbyn. Univ. Hosp., Pitts., 1976-80; owner, prin. George-Anstey Food Distributing Corp., Pitts., 1978-81; mgmt. cons. Arthur Young & Co., Pitts., 1980-82; exec. dir. Eastern Allegheny County Health Corp., 1982-85; pres. Alpha Health Network, 1985-88; exec. v.p. Intergroup Service Corp., 1988—; lectr. in field. Contbr. articles to profl. jours. Chmn. environ. adv. com., Forest Hills, Pa. Mem. Am. Coll. Health Care Execs., Am. Hosp. Assn., Healthcare Fin. Mgmt. Assn., IACFP, Pitts. Assn. Fin. Planners, Nat. Assn. Life Underwriters, AAPPO (adv. bd. dirs.), Inst. Cert. Fin. Planners. Roman Catholic. Home: 107 Cherry Valley Rd Pittsburgh PA 15221 Office: 201 Penn Center Blvd Suite 400 Pittsburgh PA 15235

GEORGE, NICHOLAS, investment planning executive; b. Seattle, July 11, 1952; s. Harry and Mary (Courounes) G.; m. Christine Mary Derezes, Sept. 10, 1983; 1 child, Harry Nicholas. BA in Polit. Sci. cum laude, Whitman Coll., 1974; MBA in Mktg. and Corp. Planning, U. Chgo., 1979; postgrad. in law, U. Puget Sound, 1986—. Lic. real estate broker. Fin. cons. Pacific Western Investment Co., Lynnwood, Wash., 1975-77; planning dir. Clinton Capital Ventures, Seattle, 1979-81; corp. planning mgr. Tacoma Boatbldg., 1981-83; pres. MegaProf Investors, Bellevue, Wash., 1983—; bd. dirs. Surgicorp, Lynnwood; free-lance coll. counselor, Seattle, 1980—. Author: Legitimacy in Government: Ideal, Goal, or Myth? 1974. Bd. auditor St. Demetrios Greek Orthodox Ch., Seattle, 1982-83; bd. dirs. Hellenic Golfers Assn., Seattle, 1981—. Mem. Phi Alpha Delta. Club: Wash. Athletic. Home: 2505 130th Ave SE Bellevue WA 98005 Office: MegaProf Investors 8422 NE 27th Pl Bellevue WA 98004

GEORGE, PATRICE FREEBURGER, textile executive, designer; b. Allentown, Pa., Sept. 25, 1948. BA in History of Art, U. Mich. Stylist Cohama Decorative Fabrics, N.Y.C., 1975-79; design cons. Patrice George Designs, N.Y.C., 1979—; expert UN Indsl. Orgn., Kingston, Jamaica, 1982-83; cons. in field.; mem. faculty Sch. Visual Arts, N.Y.C., 1984—. Contbr. articles to profl. jours. Mem. Graphic Artists Guild. Office: Patrice George Designs 110 Chambers New York NY 10007

GEORGE, ROBERT CURTIS, financial planning executive; b. Charleston, W.Va., Feb. 7, 1939; s. Olin Curtis and Camile Mary (Rinaldi) G.; m. Carol Rita Inverso, Apr. 8, 1961; 1 child, Robert Tyler. BA, U. Nebr., 1969; MBA, Hofstra U., 1977. Commd. 2d lt. U.S. Army, 1963, advanced through grades to lt. col., 1979, ret., 1983; investment broker Wheat 1st Securities Inc., Richmond, Va., 1984-88; v.p. fin. planning Fin. Corp. Va., Richmond, 1988—. Mem. Rep. com. Chesterfield County, 1983-86, Goochland County, 1988—. Fellow Internat. Assn. Cert. Fin Planners, Inst. Cert. Fin. Planners. Roman Catholic. Home: 345 Holly Lake Dr Manakin-Sabot VA 23103

GEORGE, WILLIAM DOUGLAS, JR., consumer products company executive; b. Chgo., Nov. 21, 1932; s. William D. and Kathryn (McWhinney) G.; m. Elinor A. Elsing, June 20, 1964; children: David W., Douglas E., Stephen J. B.A., Depauw U., 1954; M.B.A., Harvard U., 1959. With Gen. Mills, Mpls., 1959-70; dir. corp. devel. Brown Group, Inc., St. Louis, 1970-74, v.p., 1974-81; exec. v.p. S.C. Johnson & Son, Inc., Racine, Wis., 1981—. Bd. dirs. St. Luke's Meml. Hosp., Inc., Racine, 1988—. With U.S. Army, 1955-57. Office: S C Johnson & Son Inc 1525 Howe St Racine WI 53403

GEORGE, WILLIAM ICKES, manufacturing company executive; b. Bowling Green, Ohio, Oct. 6, 1931; s. Galen Gladstone and Lois (Ickes) G.; m. Shirley Schubert, Dec. 28, 1954; 4 children. B.S. in Mech. Engring., Cornell U., 1954; postgrad., Brown U. With Tex. Instruments, Inc., Dallas, 1960—; exec. v.p. Tex. Instruments, Inc., 1984—. *

GEORGE, WILLIAM WALLACE, manufacturing company executive; b. Muskegon, Mich., Sept. 14, 1942; s. Wallace Edwin and Kathryn Jean (Dinkeloo) G.; m. Ann Tonnlier Pilgram, Sept. 6, 1969; children: Jeffrey, Jonathan. BS in Indsl. Engring. with honors, Ga. Inst. Tech., 1964; MBA with high distinction, Harvard U., 1966. Asst. to asst. sec. Dept. Def., Washington, 1966-68; spl. civilian asst. to sec. Navy, Washington, 1968-69; with Litton Industries, 1969-78; dir. long-range planning Litton Industries, Cleve., 1969-70; v.p. Litton Industries, 1976—; with Litton Microwave Cooking Products, 1970-78; v.p. Litton Microwave Cooking Products, Mpls., 1970-71; exec. v.p. Litton Microwave Cooking Products, 1971-73, pres., 1973-78; v.p. corp. devel. Honeywell, Mpls., 1978-80, exec. v.p., 1983-87; pres. Honeywell Europe (S.A.), 1980-82, Indsl. Automation, 1987, Space and Aviation Systems, Mpls., 1988-89; pres., chief oper. officer Medtronic Inc., Mpls., 1989—; pres., Space and Aviation Systems, 1988—; bd. dirs. Valspar Corp. Bd. dirs. Minn. Symphony Orch., 1976-80, United Way, 1976-79, nat. chmn., Belgium, 1982-83; bd. dirs., pres., treas. Guthrie Theater, 1977-84; vice-chmn. United Theol. Sem., 1977-80, Abbott-Northwestern Hosp., 1984—; trustee MacCalaster Coll., 1987—. Recipient Meritorious Civilian Service Award Sec. Navy, 1969. Sigma Chi (Internat. Balfour award 1964); (trustee 1971-77). Episcopalian. Clubs: Minneapolis, Minikahda. Home: 2284 W Lake of Isles Blvd Minneapolis MN 55405 Office: Medtronic Inc 7000 Central Ave NE Minneapolis MN 55432

GEORGE-PERRY, SHARON JUANITA, management consultant; b. Modesto, Calif., Sept. 21, 1938; d. H. Edward and Beatrice C. (Wright) Melin; m. John L. George, Apr. 27, 1956 (div. 1974); children: Terri A., Tami L., Timothy J., Tobin E.; m. William E. Perry Jr., Apr. 19, 1980. BS in Edn. magna cum laude, Calif. State U., Hayward, 1965; MEd Guidance in

Counseling, Hardin-Simmons U., 1976; MBA in Mgmt., Golden Gate U., 1980. Cert. elem. edn., Calif., elem., secondary counseling, Tex. Tchr. elem. Hayward (Calif) Unified Sch. Dist., 1965-73; tchr. diagnostics, group therapist Tex. Youth Coun., Brownwood, 1974-75; assoc. dir. New Directions Psychiat. Half Way House, Abilene, Tex., 1975-77; exec. dir. Mental Health Assn., Abilene, 1977-78, San Francisco, 1979-84; assoc. ptnr. Perry Assoc. Mgmt. Cons., San Francisco, 1983—; exec. dir., cons. Vision of Am. At Peace, Berkeley, Calif., 1984, Oakes Children's Ctr., San Francisco, 1985—; mktg. dir. Mental Health Providers of Calif., 1987—; vis. lectr. McMurry Coll., Abilene, 1976-78; cons. Dyess AFB, Abilene, 1976-78, Abilene Youth Ctr., 1976-78; speaker in field, 1979—. Chair Commn. on Status of Women of Marin County, Calif., 1985—; mem. adv. com. Displaced Homemaker Project, Sacramento, 1985—; founder, Children's Mental Health Policy Bd., 1984—; pres. Artisans Gallery, Mill Valley, Calif., 1984—; mem. Children's Mental Health Policy Bd., 1984—. Grantee Fed. Dept. Justice, Brownwood, 1975, pvt. community founds., Calif., 1979-87. Mem. NAFE, Council of Calif. Mental Health Contractors, Am. Soc. Profl. Exec. Women. Avocations: travel, gourmet cooking, hiking, public speaking. Home: 317 Morning Sun Ave Mill Valley CA 94941 Office: 100 Shoreline Hwy Ste 2953 Mill Valley CA 94941

GEORGES, JOHN A., paper company executive; b. El Paso, Feb. 24, 1931; s. John A. and Opal (Biffle) G.; m. Zephera M. Givas, June 15, 1952; children: Mark, Andrew, Elizabeth. B.S., U. Ill., 1951; M.S. in Bus. Adminstrn, Drexel U., 1957. Exec. v.p. internat. and wood products and resources Internat. Paper Co., N.Y.C., 1979, vice chmn., 1980, pres., chief operating officer, 1981-85, chmn., chief exec. officer, 1985—, also dir.; bd. dirs. Warner Lambert Co., N.Y. Stock Exchange, Fed. Res. Bank N.Y. Dir. Bus. Council N.Y. State. Served with U.S. Army, 1953-55. Club: N.Y. Yacht. Office: Internat Paper Realty Corp 2 Manhattanville Rd Purchase NY 10577

GEORGES, RICHARD MARTIN, lawyer, educator; b. St. Louis, Nov. 17, 1947; s. Martin Mahlon Georges and Josephine (Cipolla) Rice. AB cum laude, Loyola U., New Orleans, 1969; JD cum laude, Stetson Coll. Law, 1972. Bar: 1972, U.S. Dist. Ct. (mid. dist.) Fla. 1973, U.S. Ct. Appeals (11th cir.) 1981, U.S. Supreme Ct. 1982. Ptnr. Kieffer & Georges, St. Petersburg, Fla., 1973-80, Kieffer, Georges & Rahter, St. Petersburg, 1980-85; sole practice St. Petersburg, 1985—; adj. prof. Fla. Inst. Tech., Melbourne, 1977-86, Stetson Coll. Law, 1985—; adj. prof. Eckerd Coll., St. Petersburg, 1986—. Contbg. author: Florida Law of Trusts, 1983. Arbitrator, United Steelworkers Union, Continental Can Co., 1975—; hearing examiner City of St. Petersburg, 1982—; mem. citizen's adv. com. Pinellas County Met. Planning Orgn., 1986-87; exec. committeeman Pinellas County Rep. Party, Clearwater, Fla., 1981-82. Served to 1st lt. U.S. Army, 1972. Recipient Rafael Steinhardt award Stetson Coll. Law, 1972, Clint Green award, 1972. Mem. ABA, Fla. Bar, St. Petersburg Bar Assn. (chmn. legal check-up course), Pinellas County Trial Lawyers Assn., Fla. Camera Club Council (pres. 1985), Phi Alpha Delta. Roman Catholic. Clubs: Feather Sound Country, Suncoast Camera (Clearwater) (v.p. 1982-84; pres. 1985). Office: 3656 First Ave N Saint Petersburg FL 33713

GEORGESCO, RICK VICTOR, printing company executive; b. Bucharest, Romania, Mar. 17, 1948; came to U.S., 1978; s. Paul D. and Maria C. (Bender) G. B.S., Poly. U., Bucharest, 1968. Overseas br. mgr. Metal Import Export, Bucharest, 1968-77; asst. mgr. Otto Botner GMBH, Duesseldorf, W. Ger., 1977-78; purchasing agt. Trico Industries, Torrance, Calif., 1978-86; exec. v.p. ops. Beverly Ctr. Printing Co., Los Angeles, 1986—. Mem. Purchasing Mgmt. Assn. (Los Angeles chpt.). Home: 1207 N Flores St #10 W Hollywood CA 90069 Office: 8104 W 3d St Los Angeles CA 90048

GEORGESCU, PETER ANDREW, advertising executive; b. Bucharest, Romania, Mar. 9, 1939; came to U.S., 1954, naturalized, 1954; s. V.C. Rica and Lygia (Bocu) G.; m. Barbara Anne Armstrong, Aug. 21, 1965; 1 son, Peter Andrew. A.B. cum laude, Princeton U., 1961; M.B.A., Stanford U., 1963. With Young & Rubicam, Inc., N.Y.C., 1963—; dir. mktg. Young & Rubicam, Inc., 1977-79; exec. v.p. Cen. Region Young & Rubicam, Inc., Chgo., dir., 1979-82; pres. Young & Rubicam Internat., N.Y.C., 1982-86, Young & Rubicam Advt., N.Y.C., 1986—; bd. dirs. Briggs & Stratton, Inc. Mem. Council on Fgn. Relations, Am. Assn. Advt. Agencies (bd. dirs.), Internat. Advt. Assn., Inc. (bd. dirs.). Clubs: Princeton, Links, River (N.Y.C.); Racquet, Casino (Chgo.); Marks, Brooks (London). Home: 901 Lexington Ave New York NY 10021 Office: Young & Rubicam Inc 285 Madison Ave New York NY 10017

GEORGHIOU, MICHAEL, construction and development executive; b. Cyprus, Nov. 14, 1932; s. George and Ourania (Haralambous) G.; m. Helen P. Modenos, Aug. 15, 1961; 1 child, Christina. BS in Acctg. and Fin., London U., 1952. Comptroller, treas. James W. Elwell & Co., Inc., N.Y.C., 1968-83; exec. v.p., treas. Theodore & Theodore Assocs., Inc., N.Y.C., 1984—; also bd. dirs. Theodore & Theodore Assocs., Inc.; bd. dirs. South Nassau Realty Inc., N.Y.C., 10 Fifth St. Corp., N.Y.C., Metro Restaurnat Suppliers, Inc., N.Y.C. Trustee St. Demetrios Greek Orthodox Ch., N.Y.C., 1969—; sec., v.p. Am. Cyprus Congress, N.Y.C., 1984—. Recipient Humanitarian award Greek Orthodox Archdiocese, 1975, Govt. of Cyprus, 1975. Home: 76-44 170th St Flushing NY 11366

GEORGIUS, JOHN R., bank executive; b. 1944. Grad., Ga. State U. With N.C. Banking Group, 1966-75, sr. v.p.; with 1st Union Nat. Bank, Charlotte, N.C., 1975—, now pres., also bd. dirs.; vice chmn., mem. corp. mgmt. com. First Union Corp. Office: 1st Union Corp 1 First Union Ctr Charlotte NC 28288

GERARD, W. GENE, finance company executive; b. 1933; married. Sr. v.p., treas., chief fin. officer I.T.T. Fin. Corp., St. Louis. Office: ITT Fin Corp 12555 Manchester Rd Saint Louis MO 63131 *

GERBER, DONALD WAYNE, real estate financier, consultant; b. Coaldale, Pa., Sept. 18, 1963. BS in Bus. and Indsl. Psychology, BS in Communications, U. Pitts., 1983. Project assoc. Gulf Oil Corp., Pitts., 1983; cons. WC Assocs., Souderton, Pa., 1984-85; dir. ops., regional mgr. MACI Inc., Port Charlotte, Fla., 1985-87; bus. devel. dir., asst. v.p. Northeastern Bank Pa., Northampton, 1987-88; pres. DWG Enterprises, Lansford, Pa., 1988—; chmn., chief exec. officer Handcrafted Homes Inc., E. Stroudsburg, Pa., 1988—. Mem. Lehigh Valley Bldg. Industries Assn., Lehigh-Northampton County Bd. Realtors, Internat. Assn. Bus. Communicators, Mortgage Bankers Assn., Soc. Tech. Communication. Republican. Home: PO Box 551 Lehighton PA 18235

GERBER, HARVEY FRANKLIN, JR., small bus. owner, lawyer; b. Plainfield, N.J., Apr. 18, 1948; s. Harvey F. and Elizabeth (Collins) G.; m. Wendy Ann Horgan, Sept. 15, 1977; children: Elizabeth Mansfield, Katherine Collins. BA, Yale U., 1970; JD, Fordham U., 1974. Bar: N.J. 1974, N.Y. 1975. Assoc. DeForest & Duer, N.Y.C., 1974-77; owner Gerber Builders, Inc., N.Y.C., 1977-82, Hoboken, N.J., 1982-87, Newtown, Conn., 1987—; lectr. NYU Real Estate Inst., 1978-82. Co-founder Corp. for a Better City, Hoboken, 1984. Mem. N.Y. Athletic Club, Rock Ridge Country Club. Republican. Presbyterian. Office: Gerber Builders Inc 30 Pecks Ln Newtown CT 06470

GERBER, HEINZ JOSEPH, computer automation company executive; b. Vienna, Austria, Apr. 17, 1924; came to U.S., 1940; s. Jacques and Bertha (Spielmann) G.; m. Sonia Kanciper, 1952; children—David Jacques, Melisa Tina. B.S. in Aero. Engring., Rensselaer Poly., 1943, Dr. Engring. (hon.), 1981. Engr. Hamilton Standard, Windsor Locks, Conn., 1947-51; pres. Gerber Sci. Instrument Co., South Windsor, Conn., 1948—, Gerber Sci. Inc., South Windsor, Conn.; chmn. bd. Gerber Garment Tech., Gerber Sci. Instrument Co., Gerber Sci. Products, Gerber Systems Tech. Inc.; dir. Boston Digital Corp., Milford, Mass. Gerber Sci. U.K. Ltd., Gerber Sci. Italy Srl; pres. Gerber Sci. Europe, Belgium. Holder 569 U.S. and fgn. patents issued and pending. Trustee Rensselaer Poly Inst., Hartford Grad. Ctr. Recipient Eli Whitney award Conn. Patent Law Assn., 1980, Holden medal The Clothing and Footwear Inst., 1983, Sci. and Tech. award ORT, 1988. Mem. Nat. Acad. Engring. (elected 1982), Conn. Acad. Sci. and Engring. (elected 1983). Home: 34 Highwood Rd West Hartford CT 06117 Office: Gerber Sci Inc 83 Gerber Rd W South Windsor CT 06074

GERBER, WILLIAM KENTON, financial executive; b. St. Louis, Feb. 20, 1954; s. Benjamin T. and Virginia B. (Kenton) G.; m. Pamela L. Macomber, Dec. 5, 1984. BS in Econs., U. Pa., 1975; MBA, Harvard U., 1979. CPA, Ill. Sr. mgmt. cons. Arthur Andersen & Co., Chgo., Boston, 1975-78; fin. mgr. Gould Inc., Jackson, Tenn. and St. Louis, 1979-81; controller Solar Turbines div. Caterpillar Tractor Co., San Diego, 1981-83; dir. fin. The Ltd., Inc., Columbus, Ohio, 1983-86, v.p., corp. controller, 1987—. Mem. Am. Inst. CPA's. Republican. Home: 5454 Eaglenest Dr Westerville OH 43081 Office: The Ltd Inc 2 Limited Pkwy Box 16000 Columbus OH 43216

GERDING, BENJAMIN F(RANKLIN), III, industrial consulting company executive; b. N.Y.C., Mar. 7, 1916; s. Benjamin Franklin and Hilda Margaret (Scott-Smith) G.; BSME, Ga. Inst. Tech., 1938; m. Elizabeth M. McKee, Mar. 24, 1940; children: Elizabeth Ann, Sarah Allen. Vice pres. ops., gen. mgr. Drexel Dynamics, Horsham, Pa., 1964-67; v.p. ops. Angstrohm Precision, Van Nuys, Calif., 1967-68; gen. mgr. resistor div. Sprague Electric, Nashua, N.H., 1969-70; v.p. engring, Robinson-Halpern, Plymouth Meeting, Pa., 1971-74; pres. Problem Solvers for Industry, Chalfont, Pa., 1974—; adj. prof. evening coll. Drexel U., 1946-67. Elder, Lenepe Valley Presbyn. Ch.; mem. New Britain Planning Com., 1958-67; co-founder Am. Bus. Club, Lansdale, Pa., 1966. Mem. Am. Assn. Indsl. Mgmt. (dir. mgmt. services), Inst. Mgmt. Cons. (cert. mgmt. cons.), Am. Arbitration Assn. (comml. panel 1983—), Bucks County C. of C., Phi Eta Sigma. Republican. Researcher on architecture and history; contbr. articles to profl., publs.; patentee. Office: PSI Box 193 Chalfont PA 18914

GEREMSKI, TERRENCE EUGENE, automotive parts manufacturing company executive; b. Toledo, July 18, 1947; s. Francis Chester and Helen Victoria (Mylek) G.; m. Cecelia Marie Osborn, July 20, 1968; children: Eric Francis, Sara Ann. BBA, U. Toledo, 1972; MBA, Ohio State U., 1983. CPA, Ill., Ohio. Sr. auditor Price Waterhouse, Chgo., 1973-75; tax mgr. Price Waterhouse, Toledo, 1976-79; internal audit mgr. Lasalles div. RH Macy, Toledo, 1975; mgr. corp. taxes Dayton (Ohio)-Walther Corp., 1979-82, asst. treas., 1982-84; treas. Dayton (Ohio) Walther Corp., 1984-87, v.p. fin., treas., chief fin. officer, sec., 1987—; spl. cons. to bd. dirs. Monitronix, Inc., Columbus, 1984-87; treas. Dayton-Walther Can. Ltd., Guelph, Ont., 1982-87, v.p. fin., 1987—; treas. Dayton-Walther Export Sales, Dayton, 1982-87, v.p., treas., 1987—, also bd. dirs.; v.p. fin. Walther Corp., Dayton, 1987—, also bd. dirs.; v.p. fin. Camden (Tenn.) Castings Ctr., 1987—, also bd. dirs.; v.p. fin. Dayton-Walther Ltd., Runcorn, Cheshire, Eng., 1987—, also bd. dirs.; bd. dirs. Min-Cer, Mexico City;. Treas. Toledo Opera Assn., 1977-79; trustee, bd. dirs. Dayton Opera Assn., 1979-81; chmn. Local Selective Service Bd. 133, Dayton, 1983—. Served with U.S. Army, 1966-69, Vietnam. Decorated Purple Heart. Mem. Am. Inst. CPA's, Ohio Soc. CPA's, Ill. CPA Soc., Tax Exec. Inst. (bd. dirs. Cin. chpt. 1985-87). Republican. Roman Catholic. Home: 5601 Rahn De Vue Pl Dayton OH 45459 Office: Dayton Walther Corp 2800 E River Rd PO Box 1022 Dayton OH 45439

GERHARD, HARRY E., JR., management and trade consultant; b. Phila., Aug. 7, 1925; s. Harry E. and Frances Jane (Edwards) G.; children: Susan Jillson, John, Barbara Thomas. Student Muhlenberg Coll., 1943-44; AB, George Washington U., 1968; MA, 1969. Commd. ensign U.S. Navy, 1943, advanced through grades to rear admiral, 1971; exptl. test pilot, 1955-57; ret., 1976; exec. v.p., chief operating officer Costa Line Cargo Services, Inc., N.Y.C., 1976-80; gen. mgr. Olayan Transp. Group, Dammam, Saudi Arabia, 1980-82; pres., owner Domestic & Overseas Countertrade & Cons. Services, Ltd., Pa., N.Y., Washington, 1983—; pres., Research and Locating Assocs., Ltd., 1986—; arbitrator Am. Arbitration Assn., Nat. Assn. Securities Dealers, N.Y. Stock Exchange, Soc. Maritime Arbitrators. Active Boy Scouts Am. Decorated Silver Star, D.F.C. (2), Meritorious Service medal (2), Air medals (16), Navy Commendation medals with combat V (2), Ground Combat Action Ribbon, Navy Unit Citation. Mem. Assn. Naval Aviation, Air Force Assn., Am. Def. Preparedness Assn., Navy League U.S., Nat. Aero. Assn., Ret. Officers Assn., Order of Daedalians, Tailhook Assn., Cousteau Soc., Four C's, Fleet Res. Assn., Maritime and Environ. Cons., Mil. Order World Wars, Nat. War Coll. Alumni Assn., Soc. Maritime Arbitrators, Soc. Marine Cons., U.S. Def. Com., Am. Security Council, Internat. Platform Assn., Greater Pitts. C. of C., Smaller Mfrs. Council. Republican. Lutheran. Clubs: Wings, N.Y. Yacht, Army Navy, London #1. Lodge: Masons, Shriners. Address: Gateway Towers 17N Pittsburgh PA 15222

GERHARDT, GLENN RODNEY, sales executive; b. Chgo., Aug. 3, 1923; s. Louis Arther and Myrtle (Wallander) G.; m. Ruth Jean Lorch, Oct. 18, 1923; chldren: Robert L., Thomas F., Kim. Student, Iowa State Coll., 1941-43; BBA, U. Wis., 1949. Salesman Eppler, Guerin and Turner Investments, Dallas, 1952, Holeproof Hosiery-Kayser-Roth, Dallas, 1952-56, Lillan Russell Originals, Mobile, Ala., 1956-58; sales mgr. Evenflo Products, Ravenna, Ohio, 1958-88, J. Myers Sales Co., Dallas, 1988—; pres. H.A. Investors, Dallas, 1952; pres. Rumhil Arabians, Inc., McKinney, Tex., 1963-85. Pres. Culleoka (Tex.) Water Supply Corp., 1980. Served with USAF, 1943-45, PTO, India. Mem. USCG Auxillary, U.S. Power Squadron, N.Tex. Arabian Horse Club (pres. 1965), Arabian Horse of Tex. (treas. 1964). Republican. Episcopalian. Home: 2308 San Gabriel Dr Plano TX 75074

GERHARDT, PAUL LOUIS, professional association executive; b. Chgo., Nov. 17, 1935; s. Ralph Mattis and Ruth (Erck) G.; B.S., U. Colo., 1958; m. Barbara Peterson, June 21, 1958; children—Katherine Lynn, John Michael. Stock control acct. Gen. Mills, Inc., 1961; internat. sales adminstr. Signode Steel Corp., 1962-65; gen. mgr. Nationwide Motorists Assn., 1965-66; exec. dir. Am. Acctg. Assn., Sarasota, Fla., 1966—; bd. dirs. Acctg. Careers Council, 1968-69. Bd. dirs. Park Manor Civic Assn., Chgo., 1964, Citizens Honest Elections Found., Chgo., 1964, Joint Civic Com. Elections, Chgo., 1962; v.p. Casey Key Protection Assn., 1988. Served with AUS, 1958-61. Mem. Am. Soc. Assn. Execs., Meeting Planners Internat., Fla. Soc. Assn. Execs. (dir., v.p., pres.-elect, pres.). Home: 3250 Casey Key Rd Nokomis FL 34275 Office: Am Acctg Assn 5717 Bessie Dr Sarasota FL 34233

GERKEN, WALTER BLAND, insurance company executive; b. N.Y.C., Aug. 14, 1922; s. Walter Adam and Virginia (Bl) G.; m. Darlene Stolt, Sept. 6, 1952; children: Walter C., Ellen M., Beth L., Daniel J., Andrew P., David A. BA, Wesleyan U., 1948; MPA, Maxwell Sch. Citizenship and Pub. Affairs, Syracuse, 1958. Supr. budget and adminstrv. analysis Wis., Madison, 1950-54; mgr. investments Northwestern Mut. Life Ins. Co., Milw., 1954-67; v.p. finance Pacific Mut. Life Ins. Co., L.A., 1967-69, exec. v.p., 1969-72, pres., 1972-75, chmn. bd., 1975-87; chmn. exec. com. Pacific Mut. Life Ins. Co., Los Angeles, 1987—, also dir.; bd. dirs. Whittaker Corp., Carter Hawley Hale Stores, So. Calif. Edison Co., Times Mirror Co. Bd., Mgmt. Compensation Group, DAC; mem. bd. overseers Rand/Ulla Ctr. for Study of Soviet Internat. Behavior. Bd. Dirs. Keck Found., James Irvine Found., Hoag Meml. Presbyn. Hosp.; chmn. bd. overseers U. Calif.-Irvine; trustee Occidental Coll., L.A., Wesleyan U., Middletown, Conn., United Way Am. Capt. USAAF, 1942-46. Decorated D.F.C., Air medal. Mem. Calif. Club, Dairymen's Country Club (Boulder Junction, Wis.), Met. Club (Washington), Balboa Bay Club (Newport Beach, Calif.), Automobile Club (So. Calif. chpt., bd. dir.), Calif. Roundtable, Pauma Valley Country Club, Calif. Stock Exch. Club (L.A.), Pacific Union Club (San Francisco). Office: Pacific Mut Life Ins Co 700 Newport Center Dr Newport Beach CA 92660

GERLOUGH, ROBERT TILLMAN, management consultant; b. New Brunswick, N.J., Dec. 7, 1930; s. Tillman Daniel and Mary Aloysia (Driscoll) G.; m. Catherine Margo Riegger, Aug. 15, 1959; children: Todd, Kate, Beth. AB, Cornell U., 1952, MBA, 1955. Cert. mgmt. cons. Systems analyst Johnson & Johnson, New Brunswick, 1955-57; assoc. William E. Hill and Co. subs. Dun and Bradstreet, N.Y.C., 1957-60, prin., 1960-66, v.p., 1966-75, chmn., 1975-79; pres. Robert Gerlough and Assocs., Ltd., N.Y.C., 1979—. Contbr. articles on strategic planning and market research to profl. jours. Trustee Mktg. Sci. Inst., Cambridge, Mass., 1976-79. Served to 1st lt. U.S. Army 1952-54, Germany. Mem. Inst. Mgmt. Consultants (founding), Planning Forum, Am. Mgmt. Assn., World Future Soc. Roman Catholic. Home: 215 Dune Ave Mantoloking NJ 08738 Office: Robert Gerlough & Assocs Ltd 500 E 83d St New York NY 10028

GERMAIN, GERALD, advertising executive; b. Bklyn., June 29, 1942; s. Harry and Rose (Raider) G.; m. Paula H. Feldman, Mar. 4, 1967; children: Victor Alan, Mitchell Bradley. BS in Acctg., Bklyn. Coll., 1963; JD, NYU, 1966. Various positions to sr. v.p., treas. Benton & Bowles, Inc., N.Y.C., 1967-78; exec. v.p., chief fin. officer Saatchi & Saatchi/Compton, Inc., N.Y.C., 1978-84; exec. v.p., chief fin. officer DDB Needham Worldwide, Inc., N.Y.C., 1984—, also bd. dirs. Mem. Am. Assn. Advt. Agys. (audit com. 1980-84, fiscal control com. 1988—), Advt. Research Found. (bd. dirs.), Advt. Agy. Fin. Mgmt. Group (chmn. N.Y.C.), KP. Home: 1959 Wilson Ave North Bellmore NY 11710 Office: DDB Needham Worldwide Inc 437 Madison Ave 11th Fl New York NY 10022

GERMANN, RICHARD P(AUL), chemist; b. Ithaca, N.Y., Apr. 3, 1918; s. Frank E.E. and Martha Mina Marie (Knechtel) G.; m. Malinda Jane Plietz, Dec. 11, 1942; 1 child, Cheranne Lee. Student (lab. asst.), U. N.Mex., summers 1938, 39; student (meteorology), Calif. Inst. Tech., 1939; BA, Colo. U., 1939, postgrad., 1940-41; student, Western Res. U. (Naval Rsch. fellow), 1941-43, Brown U., 1954. Chief analytical chemist Taylor Refining Co., Corpus Christi, 1943-44; rsch. devel. chemist Calco Chem. div. Am. Cyanamid Co., 1944-52; devel. chemist charge pilot plant Alrose Chem. Co. div. Geigy Chem. Corp., 1952-55; new product devel. chemist, rsch. div. W.R. Grace & Co., Clarksville, Md., 1955-60; chief chemist soap-cosmetic div. G.H. Packwood Mfg. Co., St. Louis, 1960-61; coord., promoter chem. product devel. Abbott Labs., North Chicago, Ill., 1961-71; internat. chem. cons. to mgmt. 1971-73; pres. Germann Internat. Ltd., 1973-82, Ramtek Internat. Ltd., 1973—; real estate broker, 1972—; cons. dept. chemistry Bowling Green (Ohio) State U., 1988. Author: Science's Ultimate Challenge—The Re-Evaluation of Ancient Occult Knowledge, Decomtamination of Plant Wastes-An Overview; patentee in U.S. and fgn. countries on sulfonamides, vitamins, detergent-softeners and biocides. Rep. Am. Inst. Chemists to Joint Com. on Employment Practices, 1969-72; vestryman St. Paul's Episc. Ch., Norwalk, Ohio, 1978-81, also chmn. adminstrn. and long-range planning commn., 1980-81; trustee Svcs. for the Aging, Inc., 1982—; chmn. nutritional coun. Ohio Dist. Five Area Agy. on Aging, 1983-84; sr. adv. Ohio Assn. Ctrs. for Sr. Citizens, Inc., 1982—; bd. dirs. Christie Lane Industries, 1981—, chmn., 1988—; mem. com. Huron County Disaster Svcs. Agy., 1987—. Fellow AAAS, Am. Inst. Chemists (chmn. com. employment rels. 1969-72), Chem. Soc. (London); mem. Am. Chem. Soc. (councilor 1971-73, chmn. membership com. chem. mktg. and econs. div. 1966-68, chmn. program com. 1968-69, del. at large for local sects. 1970-71, chmn. 1972-73, chmn. Chgo. program com. 1966-67, chmn. Chgo. endowment com. 1967-68, dir. Chgo. sect. 1968-72, chmn. awards com. 1972-73, sec. chem. mktg. and econs. group Chgo. sect. 1964-66, chmn. 1967-68), Internat. Sci. Found., Sci. Rsch. Soc. Am., Comml. Chem. Devel. Assn. (chmn. program com. Chgo. conv. 1966, mem. fin. com. 1966-67, ad hoc com. of Comml. Chem. Devel. Assn., Chem. Market Rsch. Assn. 1968-69, co-chmn. pub. rels. Denver conv. 1968, chmn. membership com. 1969-70, mem. directory com. 1967-68, employment com. 1969-70), Midwest Planning Assn., Nat. Security Indsl. Assn. (com. rep. ocean sci. tech. com., maintenance adv. com., tng. ad. com. 1962-70), Midwest Planning Assn., Am. Assn. Textile Chemists and Colorists, Am. Pharm. Assn., Midwest Chem. Mktg. Assn., Am. Pharm. Assn., N.Y. Acad. Scis., Internat. Platform Assn., Water Pollution Control Fedn., Lake County Bd. Realtors, World Future Soc., Midwest Planning Assn., Am. Fedn. Astrologers, Ancient Astronauts Soc., AARP (pres. Huron county Firelands chpt. 1986-88), Chemists Club, Torch Club, Toastmasters, Lions (sec. Allview, Md. 1956-a5), Kiwanis, Masons, (32nd degree), Knights Templar, Rotary, Sigma Xi, Alpha Chi Sigma (chmn. profl. activities com. 1968-70, pres. Chgo. chpt. 1968-70). Home and Office: 6 Vinewood Dr Norwalk OH 44857

GERRETSEN, REINDER WILLEM, petroleum and chemical engineering company executive; b. Groningen, The Netherlands, Jan. 24, 1925; s. Willem Jan and Jacobina Hillegonna (Speelman) G.; m. Annie Zuidema, Feb. 14, 1952; children: Robert, Marcel, Willem Justus. B MechE, Delft U., The Netherlands, 1950. Design engr. Conrad Stork, Haarlem, Netherlands, 1952-56; mgr. project controls Badger B.V., The Hague, Netherlands, 1956-68, dir. engring., 1968-75, dir. ops., 1975-83, v.p., gen. mgr., 1983-86; pres. The Badger Co. Inc., Cambridge, Mass., 1986—, also bd. dirs., 1986—. Served to 2d lt., tech. ordnance, Netherlands, 1950-52. Mem. Royal Inst. Engrs. Club: Algonquin (Boston). Office: Badger Co Inc One Broadway Cambridge MA 02142

GERRIE, ROBERT BRUCE, retired manufacturing company executive; b. Oak Park, Ill., Feb. 28, 1924; s. Archibald Munro and Frances Irene (O'Connor) G.; m. Janice M. Gamble, Sept. 1, 1949; children: Alison G. Lindsey, Nancy G. Bowen. B.S., Northwestern U., 1948, J.D., 1951. Bar: Ill. 1951. Assoc. McBride, Baker, Wienke & Schlosser, Chgo., 1951-57; partner McBride, Baker, Wienke & Schlosser, 1958-73; v.p. legal affairs, gen. counsel Morton Thiokol, Inc., Chgo., 1974-87; sec. Morton Thiokol, Inc., 1974-76, ret., 1987. Commr. Wilmette Park Dist., 1965-77, pres., 1967-71; pres. New Trier Citizens League, 1969-73; chmn. New Trier Twp. Com. on Youth, 1972-75. Served to 1st lt., inf. AUS, 1943-46. Mem. ABA, Law Club Chgo., Legal Club Chgo., Phi Delta Phi. Republican. Episcopalian. Clubs: Skokie Country (Glencoe, Ill.); Royal Poinciana (Naples, Fla.); Mid-America. Home: 630 Park Dr Kenilworth IL 60043

GERRINGER-BUSENBARK, ELIZABETH JACQUELINE, systems analyst, consultant; b. Edmund, Wis., Jan. 7, 1934; d. Clyde Elroy and Matilda Evangeline Knapp; student Madison Bus. Coll., 1952, San Francisco State Coll., 1953-54, Vivian Rich Sch. Fashion Design, 1955, Dale Carnegie Sch., 1956, Arthur Murray Dance Studio, 1956, Biscayne Acad. Music, 1957, Los Angeles City Coll., 1960-62, Santa Monica (Calif.) Jr. Coll., 1963; Hastings Coll. of Law, 1973, Wharton Sch., U. Pa., 1977, London Art Coll., 1979; Ph.D., 1979; attended Goethe Inst., 1985; m. Roe (Don David) Devon Gerringer-Busenbark, Sept. 30, 1968 (dec. Dec. 1972). Actress, Actors Workshop San Francisco, 1959, 65, Theatre of Arts Beverly Hills (Calif.), 1963, also radio; cons, and systems analyst for banks and pub. accounting agys.; artist, singer, songwriter, playwright, dress designer. Pres., tchr. Environ Improvement, Originals by Elizabeth, Dometrik's, JIT-MAP, San Francisco, 1973—; steering com. explorations in worship, ordained min. 1978. Author: Explorations in Worship, 1965, The Magic of Scents, 1967, New Highways, 1967; Happening - Impact-Mald, 1971; Seven Day Rainbow, 1972; Zachary's Adversaries, 1974; Fifteen from Wisconsin, 1977; Bart's White Elephant, 1978; Skid Row Minister, 1978; Points in Time, 1979; Special Appointment, A Clown in Town, 1979; Happenings, 1980, Votes from the Closet, 1984, Wait for Me, 1984, The Stairway, 1984, The River is a Rock, 1985, Happenings Revisted, 1986, Comparative Religion in the United States, 1986, Lumber in the Skies, 1986, The Fifth Season, 1987, Summer Thoughts, 1987, Toast Thoughts, 1988. Address: PO Box 1640 7th and Mission Sta San Francisco CA 94101

GERRISH, HOLLIS G., confectionery company executive; b. Berwick, Maine, June 23, 1907; s. Perley G. and Grace (Guptill) G.; A.B., Harvard U., 1930, postgrad. Bus. Sch., 1930-31; m. Catherine G. Ruggles, Sept. 10, 1946. With Squirrel Brand Co., mfg. confectioners, 1931—, pres., 1939-42, 46—. Bd. dirs. Middlesex-Cambridge (Mass.) Lung Assn., Cambridge YMCA, East End House, Cambridge Home for the Aged; trustee Lesley Coll., Cambridge; corp. mem. New Eng. Deaconess Hosp. Served as lt. comdr. USNR, 1942-46; capt. Res. Mem. Am. Soc. Candy Technologists, Cambridge Hist. Soc., Nat. Tax Assn., Mass. Audubon Soc. Episcopalian (trustee). Clubs: Harvard, Faculty, New England Confectioners, Norfolk Trout, Flycasters, Cambridge, Economy. Lodge: Rotary. Home: 207 Grove St Cambridge MA 02138 Office: 10-12 Boardman St Cambridge MA 02139

GERSCHBACHER, CORINE MARIE, computer and electronics manufacturing company executive; b. Whittier, Calif., Mar. 8, 1961; d. Frank Joseph Gerschbacher and Shirley Ann Stahl. BA in Mktg., Whittier Coll., 1983. Acctg. analyst Health Valley Foods, Montebello, Calif., 1982-84; mktg. coordinator Bland Contracting Co., Whittier, 1984-85; project mktg. specialist research and devel., Taxan Corp., City of Industry, Calif., 1985-87; microcomputer systems cons Creative Micro Systems Group, Whittier, 1985—, hi-tech industry analyst, 1987-89; dir. of corp. communications M&A div. Toyo Bus. Ptnrs., Inc., Torrance, Calif., 1989—; cons. computer systems, Whittier, 1985-87; lectr. Computer Trading Post, Civic Auditorium, Glendale, Calif., 1987—. Editorial corr., writer: The Computer Inputer mag., 1987—; contbg. writer: PC Mag.; contbg. editor: Computer Graphics

World mag., reader rev. bd., 1986-87; prodn. corr. nat. TV program: The Computer Show, 1986—; photo journalist, reporter: Computer PR Advisor. Recipient cert. of appreciation Pi Sigma Epsilon, 1986; Milo Hunt Merit scholar Whittier Coll., 1980-83. Mem. MBA Assn. (local activities dir. 1983-84), Calif. Scholarship Fedn. (life), Alpha Pi Delta. Home: 11611 Broadway Apt A Whittier CA 90601 Office: 1880 S Crenshaw Blvd Ste 106 Torrance CA 90501

GERSTEIN, HILDA KIRSCHBAUM, clothing company executive; b. 1911. With Petrie Stores Corp., Secaucus, N.J., 1932—, v.p., 1956-71, sr. v.p., 1971-72, pres., 1972-82, also vice chmn. bd. dirs., 1982—. Office: Petrie Stores Corp 70 Enterprise Ave Secaucus NJ 07094 *

GERSTEIN, IRVING R., jewelry company executive; b. 1942. With Zale Corp., 1962—; pres., chief exec. officer Zale Corp., Irving, Tex., 1986—. Office: Zale Corp 901 W Walnut Hill Ln Irving TX 75038 *

GERSTEIN, MEL, research and marketing executive; b. N.Y.C., Jan. 30, 1937; s. Frank and May (Brown) G.; B.B.A., Pace Coll., 1955; postgrad. Columbia, 1957; m. Gayle Gerstein; children—Teddy, Madeline, Amy. Vice pres. research and devel. fin. mktg. and packaging Thermwell Products Co., Inc., N.Y.C., 1957—, Lever Machine Corp., N.Y.C., 1958—; v.p., treas. Woodlowe Realty Corp., Paterson, N.J., Lever Mfg. Corp., Paterson, Thermwell Mfg. Corp., Filmco Industries Inc., Spiral Bagging Machine Corp., Mortite, Inc., Kankakee, Ill., Sealtite, Inc., Mt. Holly, N.J., Sullivan St. Playhouse, N.Y.C., N.J. Nets, Vandenberg Tulip Fields, Ltd., Fog Industries, Inc., Eden Orchards, Regent Tapeco, Boston, Kraver Screeen Co., Miami, Fla.; dir. Vogue Studios, Inc., Belleville, N.J., Royal Crown Bottling Co., Newark, Lever Mfg. Corp. Bd. dirs. Paterson Cultural Center; trustee, co-chmn. Barnert Meml. Hosp., Paterson. Exhibited art at Ahda Artzt Art Gallery, N.Y.C., Kiron Art Gallery, N.Y.C.; cartoonist; designer greeting cards. Trustee, Barnert Hosp. Center, Paterson J.C.C. on the Palisades, Tenafly, N.J.; bd. dirs. Daus. of Miriam Nursing Home, Clifton, N.J., Temple Sinai, Tenafly, Guild for Jewish Blind, N.Y.C., United Jewish Appeal, Hackensack, N.J. Mem. Am. Mgmt. Assn., N.J., Greater Paterson (dir.) chambers commerce. Developer houseware and hardware products. Home: Buckingham Dr Alpine NJ 07620 Office: 150 E 7th St Paterson NJ 07524

GERSTELL, A. FREDERICK, cement, aggregates, asphalt and concrete manufacturing company executive; b. 1938. Vice pres. mktg., dir. Alpha Portland Cement Co., 1960-75; v.p. Calif. Portland Cement Co., L.A., 1975-81, pres., chief operating officer, 1981-84; pres., chief operating officer CalMat Co., L.A., 1984-88, pres., chief exec. officer, chief operating officer, 1988—. Office: CalMat Co 3200 San Fernando Rd Los Angeles CA 90065

GERSTEN, HARRY ROBERT, real estate executive; b. Reno, Nev., Apr. 10, 1946; s. Milton and Mary (Uzekevich) G.; BS, San Diego State U., 1973; m. Cynthia Kathryn Greek, May 2, 1969; children: Andrew, Matthew, Christina. Lic. real estate broker, Calif. Property mgr. The Gersten Cos., Beverly Hills and San Diego, 1967-80; real estate officer Calif. First Bank-Trust Dept., San Diego, 1980—. Mem. Nat. Assn. Rev. Appraisers and Mortgage Underwriters (cert. rev. appraiser, registered mortgage underwriter), Inst. Real Estate Mgmt. of Nat. Assn. Realtors (cert. property mgr.), Mensa. Home: 893 Mesa Pl Chula Vista CA 92010 Office: 530 B St Ste 700 San Diego CA 92101

GERSTNER, LOUIS VINCENT, JR., financial services executive; b. N.Y.C., Mar. 1, 1942; s. Louis Vincent and Marjorie (Rutan) G.; m. Elizabeth Robins Link, Nov. 30, 1968; children—Louis, Elizabeth. B.A., Dartmouth Coll., 1963; M.B.A., Harvard U., 1965. Dir. McKinsey & Co., N.Y.C., 1965-78; exec. v.p. Am. Express Co., N.Y.C., 1978-81; vice chmn. bd. Am. Express Co., 1981-83, chmn. exec. com., 1983-85, pres., 1985—, also bd. dirs.; bd. dirs. Caterpillar Inc., Squibb Corp., The New York Times Co. Bd. mgrs. Meml. Sloan Kettering Hosp., 1978—; trustee Joint Council on Econ. Edn., 1975-87, chmn. 1983-85; bd. dirs. Greenwich Boys' Club Assn., Lincoln Ctr. for Performing Arts, Internat. Mgmt. Inst. Found., Geneva; mem. vis. com. Harvard U.; mem. Bus. Com. for Arts, Nat. Cancer Adv. Bd.; mem. bd. trustees Ctr. for Strategic and Internat. Studies, Inc., bd. dirs. Am-China Soc. Mem. Council Fgn. Relations. Office: Am Express Co Am Express Tower 200 Vesey St New York NY 10285-5120

GERSTNER, WILLIAM CARL, utility company executive; b. Detroit, June 3, 1924; s. William Carl and Mamie Marie (Schneider) G.; m. Anna Fredrikke Bertun, Mar. 17, 1945; children: Jan Steven, William Carl. Certs., Internat. Corr. Schs., 1949, 52, 56. Registered profl. engr., Ill. With Ill. Power Co., 1945—; mgr. energy supply Ill. Power Co., Decatur, 1971-72, v.p., 1972-76, exec. v.p., 1976—, dir. Mem. Galesburg (Ill.) Electric Commn., 1958-66; dir. Elec. Energy Inc., 1976—; bd. dirs. Galesburg Prairie council Boy Scouts Am., 1961-66. Served with USNR, 1942-45. Decorated Air medal. Mem. Edison Electric Inst. (chmn. air quality subcom. environment and energy com. 1973-75, mem. adv. com. environment and energy div. 1975—, chmn. PCB task force 1976—). Republican. Home: 535 N Country Club Rd Decatur IL 62521 Office: Ill Power Co 500 S 27th St Decatur IL 62525 *

GERVAIS, DARWIN, banker, insurance executive; b. St. Paul, June 23, 1921; s. Harry and MayAnna (Nadeau) G; m. Kathryn Jean Kearns, Apr. 18, 1949; children: Renard, Annette Gervais Bogusz. BS, Rockhurst Coll., 1948; MS, U. Kansas City, 1958. Pvt. practice insurance broker Kansas City, Mo., 1948-66; sr. v.p. Insurance Consultants Inc., St. Louis, 1966-74; chmn. Suncoast Insurors Inc., Sarasota, Fla., 1974—, Cen. Nat. Bank, Sarasota, 1985—. Mem. Kiwanis (gov. 1965). Roman Catholic. Home: 3809 Prairie Dunes Dr Sarasota FL 34238 Office: Suncoast Insurors Inc 1090 S Tamiami Tr Sarasota FL 34236

GERVAIS, PAUL NELSON, public relations executive, broadcast news director, evangelistic foundation administrator; b. Augusta, Maine, June 28, 1947; s. Adrien and Phyllis (Sullivan) G. B in Bible and Doctrine/Ministerial Studies, Berean Coll., 1975; M, U. Maine, 1987, cert. in Constl. Law, 1969; D, N.Am. Biblical Sem., Buffalo, 1987. Cert. behavioral analyst. Reporter No. New Eng. div. News dept. NBC Radio div., N.Y.C., 1966-70; dir. pub. relations Kennebec Valley Med. Ctr., Augusta, 1970-73, Penobscot Bay Med. Ctr., Rockport, Maine, 1973-74; pres., chmn. bd. dirs. Ministry of Miracles Evangelistic Assn., Maine, 1975—; news dir. Maine Broadcasting System, Augusta, 1966-70; advisor, assoc. dir. pub. relations state VA services, Maine, 1969-70; family counselor, Gracelawn Meml. Park, Auburn, Maine. Pioneered one of first radio and TV health edn. programs from which proceeded other nat. and internat. programs in field. Active Rep. Nat. com., Washington, 1987, Dole for Pres. Exploratory com., 1987—, also adv. com., 1987, steering com.; Campaign Am., 1987-88; mem. Presdl. Task Force, Washington, 1989, Rep. Senatorial Inner Circle, 1989—; exec. dir. Gracelawn Meml. Park, Auburn, Maine, 1988—. Recipient Vice-presdl. Citation Office of U.S. V.P. Hubert Humphrey, 1968, Malcolm T. MacEachern Citation Am. Health Congress, 1973; cert. in pub. relations Chgo. chpt. Am. Hosp. Assn. Mem. Publicity Club of Boston (disting. bell ringer award 1974). Baptist.

GERWICK-BRODEUR, MADELINE CAROL, marketing and sales professional; b. Kearney, Neb., Aug. 29, 1951; d. Vern Frank and Marian Leila (Bliss) Gerwick; m. David Louis Brodeur; 1 child, Maria Louise. Student, U. Wis., 1970-72, U. Louisville, 1974-75; BA in Econs. magna cum laude, U. N.H., 1979; postgrad., Internat. Trade Inst., Seattle. Indsl. sales rep. United Radio Supply Inc., Seattle, 1980-81; mfrs. rep. Ray Over Sales Inc., Seattle, 1981-82; sales engr. Tektronix, Inc., Kent, Wash., 1982-83; mktg. mgr. Zepher Industries, Inc., Burien, Wash., 1983-85, Microscan Systems Inc., Tukwila, Wash., 1986—; market devel. URS Electronics, Inc., Portland, 1986-88; sr. product specialist John Fluke Mfg. Co. Inc., 1989—; bd. dirs., sec. Starfish Enterprises Inc., Tacoma, 1984-87; com. chmn. Northcon, Seattle and Portland, 1984-86, 88; speaker to Wash. Women's Employment and Edn., Tacoma, 1983—. Recipient Jack E. Chase award for Outstanding Svc. and Contbn. Northern Founder's Orgn., 1988. Mem. Electronic Mfrs. Assn. (sec. 1982, sec.-treas. 1988, v.p. 1989—), Phi Kappa Phi. Office: John Fluke Mfg Co Inc PO Box C9090 MS 266D Everett WA 98206

GERWIN, RONALD PAUL, direct marketing consultant; b. Toledo, Sept. 16, 1933; s. Harry Adam and Delia Amelia (Suprise) G.; BBA, U. Toledo, 1955; postgrad. U. Pa., 1969; m. Shirley Ann Hart, Apr. 9, 1955; children—Scott Edward, Stuart Glenn. Editor, OMI Pub. Co., Toledo, 1955-56, 58-59; public relations mgr. Gladieux Corp., Toledo, 1959-63; pub. rels. dir. Linton's Food Svcs., Phila., 1963-65; copy supr., v.p. Mel Richman, Inc., Phila., 1965-70; program dir., v.p. philatelics, v.p. mktg. internat. The Franklin Mint, Franklin Ctr., Pa., 1970-78; v.p. philatelics and spl. projects Calhoun's Collectors Soc., Mpls., 1978-80, v.p. mktg., 1980-81; v.p. Mdse. Svcs. div. Am. Express, N.Y.C., 1981-85; pres. Gerwin Direct, Inc., Short Hills, N.J., 1985—; lectr. NYU Ctr. for Direct Mktg. Co-author Direct Marketing Handbook; contbg. editor Catalog Mktg. Active Channel 13 Pub. Broadcasting, Newark, N.Y.C., Cen. Park Conservatory, N.Y.C. With U.S. Army, 1956-58. Mem. Bklyn. Bridge Centennial Commn., Short Hills Assn., Friends of the N.Y. Pub. Libr., Met. Mus. Art, U. Toledo Alumni Assn., Nat. Assn. for the Self-Employed, Am. Topical Assn., World Future Soc., Direct Mktg. Assn. (chmn. mktg. coun.), Internat. Network of Ind. Direct Mktg. Agys. (U.S.A., Windsor, Eng. chpt.), Millburn-Short Hills C. of C., Sigma Alpha Epsilon. Republican. Lutheran. Home and Office: 26 Woodland Rd Short Hills NJ 07078

GESAR, ARAM, publisher, photographer, television producer; b. Geneva, Oct. 5, 1952; s. Mihran Gesar and Nadia (Bezaz) Sursock; m. Constance Louise Appel, June 26, 1981; 1 child, Alexandra Marie. Student, Geneva, until 1974, Sch. Visual Arts, N.Y.C., 1975. Freelance photographer and art dir. 1978—; studio mgr., photographer Pete Turner, Inc., N.Y.C., 1976-77; founder, pres. Gesar, Inc., 1985—, Pyramid Graphics & Pub., 1986—. Photographs appear in popular and profl. mags; one-man shows include Modernism Gallery, San Francisco, 1980, Nikon House, N.Y.C., 1983; group shows include Gallerie Canon, Geneva, 1979, Nikon Gallery Made in USA, Zurich, 1979, Mus. of City of N.Y., 1981, Neikrug Gallery, N.Y.C., 1984, N.Y. State Mus. Taking Liberty, Buffalo, Albany, N.Y.C., 1986; photographer Steven Speilberg's Close Encounters of the Third Kind, 1977, Sidney Lumet's Prince of the City, 1980, Peter Hyams' Outland, 1981. Recipient Merit award Art Dir's. Club, N.Y.C., 1984. Office: Pyramid Graphics & Pub 250 W 57th St Rm 1527 New York NY 10107

GESCHWINT, IRA, bank executive; b. N.Y.C., May 29, 1931; s. Sam and Ruth (Anker) G.; m. Zina Goldberg, May 29, 1955; children—Caryn, Jill. BBA, CUNY, 1964. Exec. v.p., chief exec. officer Chem. Bank N.J., N.A., Morristown, NJ, 1964—. Trustee St. Clares Riverside Hosp., Denville, N.J., Hospice, Morristown. W USN, 1951-55. Office: Chem Bank NJ NA 334 Madison Ave Morristown NJ 07960

GESTAL-GARCIA, JOSÉ ROGELIO, marketing executive; b. La Coruña, Spain, Nov. 20, 1951; came to U.S., 1967; s. José and Antonia (Garcia) Gestal. BA with honors, NYU, 1973; MA, Harvard U., 1974. CLU. Mgr. ops. div. Allstate Ins. Corp., White Plains, N.Y., 1974-76; asst. contr. Allstate Ins. Corp., Huntington, N.Y., 1976-78; dir. mktg. Met. Life Ins. Co., N.Y.C., 1978-88, asst. v.p. internat. fin. mgmt., 1988—. Pres. Spanish Cultural Circle, N.Y.C., 1988—; cons. U.S. Pres.'s Athletic Coun., 1988—. Home: 199 W 10th St New York NY 10014 Office: care Martina Schmid Met Life Ins Co 1 Madison Ave Area 22U New York NY 10010

GETTIER, GLENN HOWARD, life insurance company executive; b. Portsmouth, Va., 1942. Grad., U. Va., 1964. Exec. v.p., chief fin. officer Equitable Life Assurance Soc. U.S. Office: Equitable Fin Cos 787 7th Ave New York NY 10019

GETZ, GEORGE FULMER, JR., holding company executive; b. Chgo., Jan. 4, 1908; s. George Fulmer and Susan Daniel (Rankin) G.; m. Olive Cox Atwater, Jan. 17, 1933 (dec. Sept. 22, 1980); children: George Fulmer, III (dec.), Bert Atwater. Pres. Eureka Coal & Dock Co., 1935-45; chmn. bd., chief exec. officer Globe Corp.; chmn. bd. Getz Coal Co., 1939-48, pres., 1948-53; dir. Chgo. Nat. League Ball Club, 1940-72; mem. exec. com., dir. A.T. & S.F. Ry., 1955-80, Sante Fe Industries, Inc., 1968-80; dir. Upper Ave. Nat. Bank, Chgo., 1936-74, Chgo. Transit Authority, 1945-47. Mem. United Republican Fund Ill.; mem. citizens bd. U. Chgo., 1956-71; bd. dirs. Jr. Achievement Chgo., 1939—, v.p., 1947-49; v.p. Met. Jr. Achievement, 1942-44; mem. Pres.'s Commn. White House Fellowships, 1982, 83; bd. dirs. Getz Found., Ind. U. Found.; pres., dir. Arthur R. Metz Found.; hon. trustee Chgo. Zool. Soc.; past v.p. finance, treas. Nat. Safety Council; pres. Geneva Lake Water Safety Com., Inc., 1949-54, bd. dirs., 1949-69, hon. dir., 1969—; mem. Ill. Com. Crusade for Freedom, Inc., 1957, 58; pres., dir. Nat. Hist. Fire Found., Globe Found.; bd. dirs. Ariz. Zool. Soc., 1966-81, 84—; trustee Am. Grad. Sch. Internat. Mgmt., vice chmn. bd., 1976-78; mem. organizing com., mem. Chgo. Rotary Found., 1936-45; mem. Nat. Rep. Fin. Com., 1976—; trustee Grand Cen. Art Galleries, N.Y.C., 1982—(mem. emeritus); bd. dirs. Scottsdale Meml. Health Found., 1984—. Mem. Chgo. Assn. Commerce and Industry (com. mem. govtl. affairs council); emeritus mem. Phoenix 40. Episcopalian. Clubs: Chicago, Tavern, Chicago Yacht, Economic (Chgo.); Los Rancheros Visitadores (Santa Barbara, Calif.); Paradise Valley Country (Ariz.); Circumnavigators; Phoenix Symphony Assn. 400; Valley Field Riding and Polo (Ariz.); Balboa (Mazatlan, Mexico). Home: 80 Mountain Shadows W Scottsdale AZ 85253 Office: Globe Corp 3634 Civic Center Plaza Scottsdale AZ 85251 also: 16555 W Hwy 120 Libertyville IL 60048

GETZ, LOWELL VERNON, financial advisor; b Schenectady, Feb. 28, 1932; s. Leon and Harriet Esther (Friedman) G.; BS in Econs., U. Pa., 1953; MBA, Harvard U., 1955; m. Judith Ruth Schwartz, Oct. 14, 1956; children—Marshall, Andrew. Treas., R. Dixon Speas Assos., Inc., Manhasset, N.Y., 1969-72, Coverdale & Colpitts, Inc., N.Y.C., 1972-74; fin. mgr. Bovay Engrs., Inc., Houston, 1974-79; sec., treas. Rice Center, Houston, 1979-82; guest lectr. U. Houston, 1980-81, Harvard Grad. Sch. Design, 1985—; overseas instr. Hong Kong Mgmt. Assn., 1986—; cons. in fin. mgmt. to architects, engring. firms, 1980—; condr. seminars in field. Served as lt. USNR, 1955-58. Mem. Profl. Svcs. Mgmt. Assn. (pres. 1988, treas. 1981-82, bd. dirs. 1979-88, 86-88), Tex. Soc. CPA's (chmn. mgmt. adv. svcs. com. Houston chpt. 1982-83), Am. Inst. CPA's (mem. various mgmt. adv. svcs. subcoms. 1981-87), Fin. Execs. Inst., Assn. Corp. Growth. Author: Financial Management and Project Control for Consulting Engineers, 1983; Financial Management for the Design Professional, 1984, Business Management in the Smaller Design Firm, 1986, Managing Ownership Transition in Design Firms, 1987; contbr. articles to profl. publs. Home: 11701 Spriggs Way Houston TX 77024 Office: 3815 Richmond Ste 111 Houston TX 77027

GETZELMAN, JOHN CHAPELL, banker; b. Oak Park, Ill., Nov. 26, 1942; s. Benjamin and Nancy (Fedou) G.; m. Rita Ann Garvey, Nov. 4, 1963; children—John Chapell Jr., Anne Renee, David. B.A., U. Colo., 1965; M.B.A. in Internat. Econs., U. Denver, 1966. Exec. v.p. Security Pacific Nat. Bank, Los Angeles, 1971—; dir. The Bank of Canton, Hong Kong, Tricontinental Holdings, Melbourne, Australia, Marac Holdings Ltd., Auckland, New Zealand, Security Pacific Australia Ltd., Sydney. Mem. Internat. C. of C. Clubs: Rolling Hills Country (Calif.); Jonathan (Los Angeles). Office: Security Pacific Nat Bank PO Box 2097 Terminal Annex Los Angeles CA 90051 *

GEZURIAN, DOROTHY ELLEN, accounting executive; b. N.Y.C., May 7, 1956; d. John and Surpug Susan (Sarkisian) G. BBA in Acctg., Econs. summa cum laude, CUNY, 1976. Sr. auditor Ernst & Ernst, N.Y.C., 1977-79; spl. asst. to v.p. fin. Olivetti Corp., N.Y.C., 1977-79; mgr. corp., bus. planning Olivetti Corp., Tarrytown, N.Y., 1979-82; treas., chief fin. officer The Ctr. for Humanities, Inc., Mt. Kisco, N.Y., 1982-85; controller, chief fin. officer 235 Main St. Assocs., affiliated cos., White Plains, N.Y., 1985-87; v.p. fin. Mid-Atlantic Med. Services, Fort Lee, N.J., 1987—. Recipient N.Y. Soc. of CPA's award, 1976. Mem. Nat. Assn. Female Execs. Republican. Home: 10 Clearview Ave Danbury CT 06811

GHANI, ASHRAF MUHAMMAD, mechanical engineer, consultant; b. Wazirabad, Pakistan, Oct. 12, 1931; emigrated to Saudi Arabia, 1967; s. Abdul and Alam (Bibi) G.; m. Yasmeen Elahi, Nov. 15, 1964; children: Faiza, Saad, Farha. BS in Mech. Engring., Ind. Inst. Tech., 1962; MS in Mech. Engring., Columbia U., 1963; PhD in Mgmt., Franklin U., 1977. Tech. dir. Engring. Controls, Karachi, Pakistan, 1963-67; asst. prof. Riyadh U., Saudi Arabia, 1967-76; tech. expert Saudi Fund for Devel., Riyadh, 1976-86; cons. dir. Poly Engring. Co., Riyadh, 1979-87; chmn. Polyconsult, Riyadh, 1979—, Inter-Services Corp., Metuchen, N.J., 1982—, chmn. Vols. Orgn. for Tech. Assistance to Underdeveloped Countries, U.K., 1985—; convener Internat. Solidarity for Peace, U.K., 1986—; sec. Internat. Vols. for Human Relief, Vienna, 1986—. Author: Management of Complex Development Projects, 1979. Hon. sec. Pakistan Red Crescent Soc., Lahore, 1965. Recipient William Henry Caswell award Ind. Inst. Tech., 1961. Fellow Pakistan Assn. Mgmt. Cons. (Achievement award 1981); mem. Soc. Am. Mil. Engrs., mem. Brit. Inst. Mgmt. (assoc.), Soc. Internat. Devel., Internat. Journalists Assn. London, Am. Soc. for Tng. and Devel. Moslem. Club: Gymkhana (Lahore, Pakistan). Home: 11-H Gulberg Three, Lahore Pakistan

GHAZNAVI, JOHN JAHANGIR, investment company executive; b. Kashan, Iran, July 19, 1935; came to U.S. in, 1959; s. Ahmad Ghaznavi and Jamilleh (Saleh) G.; m. Sylvia Turner, Aug. 3, 1963; children: Ahmad L., Leila C. Student, Georgetown U., 1959, U. W. Va., 1963, Chgo. U., 1965. Pres. J&S, Inc., Indianola, Pa., 1973—, Apex Resources, Inc., Pitts., 1979—, R&A Devel., Pitts., 1979—; chmn., pres. Ghaznavi Investments, Inc., Indianola, 1979—; dir. Glenshaw (Pa.) Glass Co., Inc., 1987—, chmn. bd., 1988—; engr. W. Va. Adv. Planning Dept.; cons. G.C. Murphy Co., McKeesport, Pa. Active Rep. Nat. Com., Washington, 1980; bd. dirs. Capital Campaign Steering Com. Found. for Abraxas. Recipient Gold award, United Way. Mem. Nat. Rifle Assn. (life), Pitts. Athletic Assn., Allegheny Club, Duquesne Club. Home: 108 Riding Trail Ln Pittsburgh PA 15215 Office: Ghaznavi Investments Inc Rt 910 Indianola PA 15051

GHELARDI, RAYMOND EUSEBIUS, financial analyst, urban planner; b. Bloomsburg, Pa., July 26, 1951; m. Lourdes M. Frau, Apr. 30, 1984. B.S. in Community Devel., Pa. State U., 1973; M.C.P., (EPA fellow), Harvard U., 1975; M.B.A. (Merit scholar), Emory U., 1985. Planning asst. Centre Regional Planning Commn., State College, Pa., 1972; land use planner Conn. Dept. Environ. Protection, Hartford, Conn., 1974; assoc. planner Mass. Exec. Office Environ. Affairs, Boston, 1975-79; policy analyst Environ. Research & Tech., Inc., Concord, Mass., 1979-80, sr. analyst policy and planning, 1980-82; pres. R. Ghelardi, Inc., 1982; sr. planner, mgr. mergers and acquisitions group EG & G Inc., Waltham, Mass., 1982-83; cons. city planner in pvt. practice, 1983; fin. analyst Laventhol & Horwath, Phila., 1985, subs. Valuation Counselors, Inc., Princeton, N.J., 1986-88, v.p. corp. fin. group, Mellon Bank, Phila., 1988—; guest lectr. Harvard Grad. Sch. Design, Lowell (Mass.) Technol. Inst. Chmn. urban policy com. N.E. Sierra Club, 1978-79; mem. exec. com. Greater Boston Group, Sierra Club. Mem. Am. Inst. Cert. Planners (charter), Am. Planning Assn. (charter), Am. Mktg. Assn., Air Pollution Control Assn., Assn. for Corp. Growth. Home: 11 Theresa Dr Lawrenceville NJ 08648 Office: 3 Mellon Ctr Princeton NJ 19102

GHENT, PEER, management consultant; b. Washington, Sept. 13, 1939; s. Pierre Mowell Ghent and Helen V. (Mork) Dyer; m. Sonya Renate Schmid, Oct. 12, 1962 (div. 1975); children: Carol R. Ghent-Singley, Erika Lynn, Peer Jr. BCE, Cornell U., 1961; MBA, Harvard U., 1966. Registered civil engr. and land surveyor, La. Sr. ops. research analyst Office Sec. Def., Washington, 1966-69; pres. Plaskolite Inc., Columbus, Ohio, 1969-71; cons. U.S. Price Commn., Washington, 1971-72; dir. corp. devel. Buckeye Internat., Columbus, 1972-74; pres. Peterson Baby Products, North Hollywood, Calif., 1974-78; v.p., chief fin. officer Oakleaf Corp., Chatsworth, Calif., 1980-81; v.p. CMB Investment Counselors, Los Angeles, 1983-85, Stars to Go Inc., Los Angeles, 1986-88; prin. Peer Ghent & Assocs., Van Nuys, Calif., 1989—; lectr. Grad. Sch. Mgmt. UCLA, 1979-88. Author: (with others) Computer Graphics: A Revolution in Design, 1966. Served to capt. U.S. Army, 1961-63. Democrat. Episcopalian. Home: 13422 Oxnard St Van Nuys CA 91401-4041 Office: Peer Ghent & Assocs 13422 Oxnard St Van Nuys CA 91401-4041

GHERLEIN, GERALD LEE, diversified manufacturing company executive, lawyer; b. Warren, Ohio, Feb. 16, 1938; s. Jacob A. and Ruth (Matthews) G.; m. Joycelyn Hardin, June 18, 1960; children: David, Christy. Student, Ohio Wesleyan U., 1956-58; B.S. in Bus. Adminstrn, Ohio State U., 1960; J.D., U. Mich., 1963. Bar: Ohio 1963. Assoc. Taft Stettinius & Hollister, Cin., 1963-66; corp. atty. Eaton Corp., Cleve., 1966-68; European legal counsel Eaton Corp., Zug, Switzerland, 1968-71; asst. sec., asso. counsel Eaton Corp., Cleve., 1971-76; v.p., gen. counsel Eaton Corp., 1976—. Trustee Citizen's League Greater Cleve., 1971-81, v.p., 1977-79, pres., 1979-81; trustee Cleve. Ballet, 1983—, vice chmn., 1985-87. Mem. ABA, Greater Cleve. Bar Assn. (pres.-elect 1988, trustee), Ohio Bar Assn., Am. Soc. Corp. Secs. (pres. Ohio regional group 1977). Clubs: Union, Mayfield Country. Home: 3679 Greenwood Dr Pepper Pike OH 44124 Office: Eaton Corp 1111 Superior Ave NE Cleveland OH 44114

GHIRALDINI, JOAN, financial executive; b. Bklyn., Mar. 31, 1951; d. Robert and Anne (Centineo) G.; B.A., Smith Coll., 1972; M.B.A., U. Pa., 1975. Intern, N.Y.C. Econ. Devel. Adminstrn., 1971; econ. specialist Western Electric Co., N.Y.C., 1975-76; sr. fin. analyst Internat. Paper Co., N.Y.C., 1976-78, mgr. strategic planning, 1978-81; dir. fin. planning Executone Inc., Jericho, N.Y., 1981-82, dir. strategic bus. planning, 1982-83; dir. corporate analysis Equitable Life Assurance, N.Y.C., 1983-84; asst. v.p. First Boston Corp., N.Y.C., 1985—. Mem. Am. Fin. Assn., N.Am. Soc. for Corp. Planning, Fin. Women's Assn. N.Y. Clubs: Wharton Bus. Sch. (past v.p.), Smith Coll. N.Y. (bd. dirs.). Home: 155 E 38th St New York NY 10016 Office: First Boston Corp 5 World Trade Ctr New York NY 10048

GIACCO, ALEXANDER FORTUNATUS, diversified plastics company executive; b. St. John, Italy, Aug. 24, 1919; s. Salvatore J. and Maria Concetta (de Maria) G.; m. Edith Brown, Feb. 16, 1946; children: Alexander Fortunatus, Richard John, Mary P. Giacco Walsh, Elizabeth B. Giacco Brown, Marissa A. Giacco Rath. BSChemE, Va. Poly. Inst., 1942; postgrad. in mgmt., Harvard U., 1965; DBA (hon.), William Carey Coll., Hattiesburg, Miss., 1980; D.Bus. (hon.), Goldey Beacom Coll., 1984; LLD (hon.), Widener U., 1984; LHD (hon.), Mt. Saint Mary's Coll., 1988. With Hercules Inc., Wilmington, Del., 1942-87, gen. mgr. polymers dept., 1968-73, dir., 1970-87, gen. mgr. operating dept. (Hercules Europe), 1973, v.p. parent co., 1974-76, mem. exec. com., 1974-87, exec. v.p., 1976-77, pres., chief exec. officer, chmn. exec. com., 1977-87, chmn. bd., 1980-87; chmn. bd. HIMONT Inc., Wilmington, Del., 1983—, chief exec. officer, 1987—; vice chmn., chief exec. officer Montedison SpA, Milan, 1988—; bd. dirs. Montedison S.p.A., China Trust Bank; mem. U.S. Com. on New Initiatives in East-West Co-op., 1976—. Patentee in field. Trustee, bd. dirs., mem. exec. com. Med. Ctr. of Del., 1975-88, rector, 1984-87; trustee, bd. visitors Va. Poly. Inst. and State U., 1980-87; chmn. bd. dirs. Grand Opera House, Wilmington, 1980—; bd. dirs. WHYY, Inc., 1983-88. Decorated commendatore Order of Merit (Italy); recipient Disting. Achievement award Va. Poly. Inst. and State U., 1989; named One of Ten Outstanding Chief Exec. Officers Fin. World, 1980, 87, Best Chief Exec. Officer in Chem. Industry Fin. World, 1984, Outstanding Chief Exec. Officer in the Chem. Industry Wall Street Transcript, 1983, 84, 85, 87. Mem. Am. Assn. of the Sovereign Mil. Order of Malta, Soc. Plastics Industry, Soc. Chem. Industry, Soc. Automotive Engrs., Nat. Acad. Engrs., Am. Ordnance Assn. (past dep. chmn.), Del. Roundtable (chmn. econ. devel. com.). Clubs: Wilmington, Wilmington Country (bd. dirs.), Vicmead Hunt, Hercules Country, Rehoboth Beach Country, Rodney Sq. (bd. dirs.), Jonathan's Landing Country (Fla.). Lodge: Knights of Malta. Office: Himont Inc 2801 Centerville Rd PO Box 15439 Wilmington DE 19850-5439

GIACOLINI, EARL L., agricultural products company executive. Formerly vice-chmn. Sun Diamond Growers of Calif., Pleasanton, now chmn. Office: Sun-Diamond Growers Calif 1050 S Diamond St Stockton CA 95201 *

GIACOMAZZI, FRANK PAUL, retail grocery executive; b. Boston, May 12, 1931; s. Joseph M. and Jennie (Marino) G.; m. Viola Gentile, Sept. 4, 1950; 1 child, Deborah Shapiro. Student, Harvard U. Pres. Purity Supreme, Inc., Billerica, Mass., 1949—, chief exec. officer, from 1949, also bd. dirs. Bd. dirs. Boys and Girls Town Italy, Mass., 1980, Nazareth, Mass., 1984. Named Man of the Yr., Boys and Girls Town Italy, 1983. Mem. Grocery Mfrs. Reps. Assn. (bd. dirs. 1984). Roman Catholic. Club: Winchester Country. Office: Purity Supreme Inc 2 Billerica Pk North Billerica MA 01862 *

GIACONTIERE, RAYMOND JOSEPH, JR., accountant; b. New Orleans, Oct. 26, 1963; s. Raymond Joseph and Julie Ann (Keith) G. BBA, Loyola U., New Orleans, 1984. CPA, La. Staff acct. Price Waterhouse Co., New Orleans, 1985—. Mem. AICPA, La. Soc. CPAs. Democrat. Roman Catholic. Home: 1201 W Esplanade Ave Apt 1917 Kenner LA 70065 Office: Price Waterhouse Co 601 Poydras St Ste 2000 New Orleans LA 70130

GIAMARINARO, PETER CHARLES, controller; b. Bklyn., Oct. 20, 1950; s. John and Charlotte (Schreiber) G.; m. Patricia Reznicek, June 30, 1974; children: Adam Peter, Matthew Peter. BBA, Pace U., 1973; MBA, Temple U., 1983. CPA, Pa., N.J. Supr. cost acctg. Am. Can Co., Morrisville, Pa., 1974-79; acctg. mgr. field svc. QYX div. Exxon Enterprises, Lionville, Pa., 1979-81; mgr. accounts receivable, inventory control Exxon Office Systems Co., Florham Park, N.J., 1981-84; contr. Coserv div. Hattori Corp. Am., Mahwah, N.J., 1984—; instr. CPA rev. course Becker Sch., Paramus, N.J., 1986—. Staff sgt. USAF, 1973-74. Mem. Inst. Cert. Mgmt. Accts., AICPA, Nat. Assn. Accts. (v.p. profl. devel.), N.J. Soc. CPAs, Beta Gamma Sigma. Lutheran. Home: 200 Spencer Rd Basking Ridge NJ 07920 Office: Hattori Corp Coserv Div 1111 MacArthur Blvd Mahwah NJ 07430

GIAMBALVO, RICHARD J., director field operations; b. N.Y.C., Feb. 28, 1943; s. Joseph and Frances (Graziano) G.; m. Mary Ann Inzone, Feb. 27, 1965 (div. Nov. 1975); children: Joseph, Maria; m. Lisa P. Gelman, Apr. 4, 1976; children: Beth Ashley, Richard Jr. AAS, N.Y.C. Community Coll., 1962. Field engr. Burroughs Corp., N.Y.C., 1963-68; field engr., mgr. Nixdorf Computer Corp., N.Y.C., 1968-77; nat. mgr. field ops. ITT, N.Y.C., 1977-83; dir. field ops. InteCom, Inc., Rutherford, N.J., 1983—. Sgt. USMC, 1960-62. Recipient Patriotic Svc. award Dept. Treasury, 1981. Mem. Assn. Field Svc. Mgrs. (sec. 1984-85). Republican. Roman Catholic. Home: 240 Kent Rd Howell NJ 07731 Office: InteCom Inc 301 Rt 17 N Rutherford NJ 07070

GIAMBRONE, TIMOTHY PAUL, controller; b. Bklyn., Oct. 17, 1957; s. Rosario Joseph and Madeline (Ceruso) G. BS in Acctg., St. Francis Coll., 1979. CPA, N.Y., Tenn. Sr. acct. Deloitte, Haskins & Sells, N.Y.C., 1979-84; supervising auditor Phibro-Salomon Inc., N.Y.C., 1984-85; controller, ops. mgr. Nat. Pinkert Steel div. Nat. Material Ltd. Partnership, Nashville, 1985—. Sec., treas. Chardonnay Condominium Assn., Nashville, 1985—. Mem. Am. Inst. CPAs, N.Y. Soc. CPAs, Tenn. Soc. CPAs, Nashville Jaycees, Phi Rho Pi. Republican. Roman Catholic. Lodge: KC. Office: Nat Pinkert Steel 3731 Amy Lynn Dr Nashville TN 37218

GIAMMARINARO, PETER CHARLES, controller; b. Bklyn., Oct. 20, 1950; s. John and Charlotte (Schreiber) G.; m. Patricia Reznicek, June 30, 1974; children: Adam Peter, Matthew Peter. BBA, Pace U., 1973; MBA, Temple U., 1983. CPA, N.J. Cost acctg. supr. Am. Can Co., Morrisville, Pa., 1974-79; field svc. acctg. mgr. QYX div. Exxon Enterprises, Lionville, —, 1979-81; inventory control and accounts receivable mgr. Exxon Office Systems Co., Florham Park, N.J., 1981-84; contr. Coserv div. Hattori Corp. Am., Mahwah, N.J., 1984—; instr. CPA rev. course Becker Sch., Paramus, N.J. 1986—. Sgt. USAF, 1973-74. Mem. AICPA, N.J. Soc. CPA's, Inst. Cert. Mgmt. Accts., Nat. Assn. Accts. (dir. profl. devel.), Beta Gamma Sigma. Lutheran. Home: 200 Spencer Rd Basking Ridge NJ 07920 Office: Hattori Corp Conserv Div 1111 MacArthur Blvd Mahwah NJ 07430

GIANGIULIO, JOSEPH JOHN, financial planner; b. Norristown, Pa., Feb. 16, 1953; s. Joseph C. and Rosalie (Granese) G.; m. Margaret Ann McKenna, July 3, 1982. BS, Shippensburg State U., 1975. CPA, Tex. Sr. internal auditor Celanese Corp., N.Y.C., 1978-81, Otis Engring., Dallas, 1981-83; fin. planner Fin. Strategies Adv. Corp., Fin. Network Investment Corp., Dallas, 1983—; seminar leader successful money mgmt., Dallas, 1986—. Contbr. articles to various popular publs., including Money, USA Today, U.S. News & World Report. Mem. Inst. Cert. Fin. Planners, AICPA, Tex. Soc. CPAs, Dallas Estate Planning Coun., Greater Dallas C. of C., North Dallas C. of C. Office: Fin Network Investment Corp 5420 LBJ Freeway Dallas TX 75240

GIANINO, JOHN JOSEPH, insurance executive; b. Waltham, Mass., Aug. 3, 1935; s. Salvatore and Elizabeth Louise (Chapin) G.; m. Elaine Margaret Barry, Sept. 1, 1956; children—John J., Jr., Paul Barry. A.B. in Math., Providence Coll., 1957; exec. program in bus. Columbia U., 1978. Various actuarial positions John Hancock Mut. Life Ins. Co., Boston, 1957-72, 2d v.p., 1972-77, v.p., 1977—. Alumni chmn. St. John's Prep. Sch., Danvers, Mass., 1979-80. Fellow Acad. Actuaries, Soc. Actuaries; mem. Health Ins. Assn. Am. (forum chmn. 1980, mem. exec. council 1981-82), Home Office Life Underwriters Assn. Roman Catholic. Club: Boston Actuaries (pres. 1974-75). Home: 2 Westway Lynnfield MA 01940 Office: John Hancock Mut Life Ins Co PO Box 111 Boston MA 02117

GIANTURCO, MAURIZIO ANTONIO, beverage company executive; b. Potenza, Italy, Dec. 2, 1928; s. Giulio and Lisa G.; m. Rita Cacciapuoti, Oct. 7, 1954; children—Giulio Mark, Luca Francesco. Grad., U. Rome; Fulbright postdoctoral research fellow, U. Ill., 1952-53, sr. research asso., 1953-56. Asst. prof. chemistry U. Rome, 1951-52; research chemist Tenco div. Coca-Cola Co., 1956-61, head research sect., 1961-63; head tech. research and devel. sect. Coca-Cola Co., Atlanta, 1963-68; dir. corp. research and devel. Coca-Cola Co., 1968-73, asst. to v.p., 1973-75, asst. to sr. vp., 1975-76, v.p. for sci., 1976-81, sr. v.p. for sci., 1981—. Author: also articles. Interpretive Spectroscopy; The Chemistry and Physiology of Flavor. Donegani Research Found. fellow. Mem. N.Y. Acad. Scis., AAAS, Am. Chem. Soc., Chem. Soc. (London), Am. Inst. Chemists, Am. Inst. Food Technologists, Gamma Alpha. Roman Catholic. Clubs: Commerce, Capital City (Atlanta). Office: Coca-Cola Co 1 Coca-Cola Pla NW Atlanta GA 30313

GIANTURCO, PAOLA, advertising executive; b. Urbana, Ill., July 22, 1939; d. Cesare and Verna Bertha (Daily) Gianturco; m. David Sanderson Hill, Mar. 12, 1988; 1 child from previous marriage, Scott Sangster. BA, Stanford U., 1961; postgrad. U. So. Calif., 1971. Pub. relations dir. Joseph Magnin, San Francisco, 1961-67; pub. relations dir., account exec. Hall & Levine Advt. Agy., Los Angeles, 1968-73, v.p., account supr., 1973-76, sr. v.p., 1977-82; v.p. Dancer Fitzgerald Sample, 1982-87, v.p., mgmt. supr. Saatchi and Saatchi DFS, Inc., 1988—. Past bd. dirs. The Country Schs., Mem. Women in Communications, Stanford Profl. Women (past mem. bd. dirs.), Nat. Investers Relations Inst., Internat. Assn. Bus. Communicators, Bus. and Profl. Advt. Assn. Home: 30 Cecily Ln Mill Valley CA 94941 Office: Saatchi & Saatchi DFS Corp Communications Group 1010 Battery St PO Box 7166 San Francisco CA 94120

GIAQUINTO, PHILIP M., banker. Sr. v.p. Chase Manhattan Corp., N.Y.C., Chase Manhattan Bank N.Am., N.Y.C. Office: Chase Manhattan Corp 1 Chase Manhattan Pla New York NY 10081 *

GIARINI, ORIO, economist; b. Trieste, Italy, Jan. 31, 1936; s. Mario and Bianca (Contini) G.; Liceo Scientifico Oberdan, Trieste; postgrad. (Fulbright scholar), U. Tex., 1955-56; Ph.D. in Polit. Sci., U. Trieste; children: Sabine Anne, Francesca Therese. Mem. sales promotion staff Montecatini Co., Milan and Basle, 1959-62, Nitrex Co., Zurich, 1962-65; dir. indsl. econs. and services div. Battelle Inst., Geneva, 1965-73; European sec. gen. European Federalist Movement, Paris, 1962-69; sec. gen., adminstr. Internat. Assn. Ins. Econs. Research, 1973—; prof. service economics Univ. Inst. European Studies, Geneva, 1971—; founder, dir. ProductLife Rsch. Inst., Geneva, 1983—. Mem. Club of Rome, List Gesellschaft, Centre Europeen de la Culture, others. Clubs: Ocean Inst., Sailing, Tennis. Author: L'Europe et l'Espace, 1968; Les ressources de la mer et l'Europe, 1977; The Diminishing Returns of Technology, 1978; Dialogue on Wealth and Welfare, 1980; Cycles, Value and Employment, 1984, 86; The Limits to Certainty, 1989; editor: Rassegna Europea, 1959-63, Geneva Papers on Risk and Insurance, 1976—. Home and Office: 18 Chemin Rieu, CH-1208 Geneva Switzerland

GIBBONS, MRS. JOHN SHELDON (CELIA VICTORIA TOWNSEND), editor, publisher; b. Fargo, N.D.; d. Harry Alton and Helen (Haag) Townsend; student U. Minn., 1930-33; m. John Sheldon Gibbons, May 1, 1935; children—Mary Vee, John Townsend. Advt. mgr. Hotel Nicollet, Mpls., 1933-37; contbg. editor children's mags., 1935—; partner Youth Assos. Co., Mpls., 1942-65; pub. art dir. Mines and Escholier mags., 1954-65; founder Bull. Bd. Pictures, Inc., Mpls., 1954, pres., 1954—; founder Periodical Litho Art Co., Mpls., 1962, pres., 1962-65; artist Cath. Boy mag., 1938; chief photographer Cath. Miss mag., 1955. Mem. Women's aux. Mpls. Symphony Orch.; mem. Fort Lauderdale (Fla.) Art. Mus. Republican chairwoman Golden Valley, Minn., 1950; alternate del. Hennepin County Rep. Conv., 1962. Mem. Mpls. Inst. Arts, Internat. Inst., St. Paul Arts and Sci., Art Guild Boca Raton, Delta Zeta. Clubs: Woman's, Minikahda; Deerfield Beach Women's. Home: 1416 Alpine Pass Tyrol Hills Minneapolis MN 55416 Office: 1057 A-1-A Hillsboro Beach FL 33441

GIBBONS, PATRICK THOMAS, service company executive, entrepreneur; b. Louisville, Jan. 16, 1940; s. Harold J. and Ann M. (Culter) G.; divorced; children: Merideth A., Pamela S.; m. Judith L. Swofford, Dec. 21, 1982; children: Shelley D. Smith, Chad D. Smith, Patrick D. AB, Mo. U., 1862; MBA, Harvard U., 1969. Asst. to pres. ARA Services, Phila., 1971-74; sr. v.p., dir. La Quinta Motor Inns, San Antonio, 1974-80; chmn., chief exec. officer Texian Inns, San Antonio, 1980-85. Div. chmn. annual campaign United Way, San antonio, 1984-85; Capt., USAF, 1964-71. Mem. Harvard Club, Argyle Club. Office: Pace Svc Mmgt Co PO Box 101506 San Antonio TX 78201

GIBBONS, ROBERT PHILIP, management consultant; b. Bklyn., Nov. 5, 1933; s. Thomas S. and Jessie L. (McGrath) G.; B.S.M.E., Stevens Inst. Tech., 1955; M.S. in Indsl. Mgmt., Purdue U., 1959; m. Mary Jane M. Jamieson, June 12, 1965; children—Laura Ann, Robert John. Partner, Touche Ross Co., N.Y.C., 1959-74; v.p., gen. mgr. Carborundum Co., Niagara Falls, N.Y., 1975-78; ptnr. Main Hurdman, N.Y.C., 1978-84, Zolfo, Cooper & Co., 1984-86, ptnr. Gibbons, Quintero & Co., N.Y.C., 1986—; dir. Weldotron Corp. Contbr. sect. to Am. Mgmt. Assn. Management Handbook, 1970. With U.S. Army, 1956-58. Mem. Inst. Mgmt. Cons., Am. Prodn. and Inventory Control Soc. (cert.). Home: 46 Knoll Rd Tenafly NJ 07670 Office: 145 Fourth Ave New York NY 10003

GIBBS, JANICE RUTH, accountant; b. Hawkinsville, Ga., Dec. 29, 1957; d. Raymond E. Nutt and Ruth J. Owen; m. Elmer R. Gibbs, May 29, 1977 (div. 1987). ABA in Acctg., Middle Ga. Coll., 1977; BBA in Acctg., U. Ga., 1978. Computer terminal operator Pinehurst (Ga.) Equipment Co., 1973-75; bookkeeper Graphic Composition, Inc., Athens, Ga., 1979-80; cost acct. Cut Art Stone Co., Savannah, Ga., 1981-82; acct. auditor State Bank and Trust Co., Unadilla, Ga., 1982-88; gen. acct. mgr. Kellwood Co., Perry, Ga., 1988; acct. Sunbrite, Inc., Macon, Ga., 1988—. Vol. Ga. Acad. Blind, Macon, 1988—, Girl Scouts U.S., Macon, Ga., Med. Ctr. Cen. Ga., Macon, Big sister; mem. Vol. Macon, Macon Little Theatre, 1988—. Mem. Nat. Assn. Accts. (sec. 1988—), Middle Ga. Ski Club. Republican. Baptist. Clubs: Mid. Ga. Dive (Macon); Internat. City Scuba (Warner Robins, Ga.).

GIBBS, JOHN PATRICK, physician, educator; b. Tecumseh, Nebr., Mar. 17, 1948; s. Leonard Keith and Mary Myrtle (Murphy) G.; m. Elise Marie Buras, Aug. 30, 1973; 1 child, Caroline Michele. BS in Chem. Engring. with high distinction, U. Nebr., 1970; MD, U. Tex., Galveston, 1976. Diplomate Am. Bd. Preventive Medicine, Nat. Bd. Med. Examiners. Rsch. engr. Shell Oil Co. div. Shell Devel. Co., Houston, 1970-73; resident in internal medicine U. Okla. Health Ctr., Oklahoma City, 1976-77; contract emergency physician Houston, 1980—, Pasadena, Tex., 1981—; plant med. dir. Ethyl Corp., Pasadena, 1981-88, asst. corp. med. dir., 1988—; mem. steering com. environ. health sect. Tex. Chem. Council, Houston, 1985—; asst. prof. occupational medicine Sch. Pub. Health U. Tex., Houston, 1988—. Mem. planning com. community awareness and emergency response Chem. Mfrs. Assn., Harris County, Tex., 1987—. Lt. USMC, USNR, 1977-80. Fellow Am. Occupational Med. Assn. (sec.-treas. Tex. chpt. 1987); mem. AMA (Physician's Recognition award 1981), Tex. Med. Assn., Harris County Med. Assn., Am. Acad. Occupational Medicine. Home: 13047 Ferry Hill Houston TX 77015 Office: Ethyl Corp PO Box 472 Pasadena TX 77501

GIBBS, LAWRENCE B., federal agency administrator; b. Hutchinson, Kans., Aug. 31, 1938; married; 2 children. BA, Yale U., 1960; JD, U. Tex., 1963. Assoc. Branscomb, Gary, Thomasson & Hall, Corpus Christi, Tex., 1963-72; ptnr. Johnson & Swanson, Dallas, 1976-86; dep. chief counsel, acting. chief counsel IRS, Dept. Treasury, Washington, 1972-73, asst. commr., 1973-75, commr., 1986-89. Office: IRS 1111 Constitution Ave NW Washington DC 20224

GIBEON, LEONARD, management consultant; b. London, July 27, 1945; s. Isaac and Lily (Pentel) G.; m. Martha Russell, Jan. 3, 1971; 1 child, Peter. A levels, City of Westminster Coll., Eng., 1967; MA cum laude, Oxford U., 1972. Exec. asst., analyst Sandelson & Co., London, 1961-69; fin. planner Fidelity Fin. Corp., Wellesley, Mass., 1972-73; fin. analyst Ford Motor Co., Dearborn, Mich., 1973-75; controller Kripalu Ctr., Summit Station, Pa., 1975-77; sr. analyst strategic planning Campbell Soup Co., Camden, N.J., 1977-81, mgr. strategic planning, 1981-83; gen. ptnr. Estates Investment L.P., Oaks, Pa., 1983—; dir. strategic plan implementation Sperry Corp., Blue Bell, Pa., 1983-84, dir. bus. ventures, 1984-87; cons., ptnr. Day & Gibeon, Wallingford, Pa., 1987—; part-time lectr. in corp. fin. Wayne State U., Detroit, 1974-75; speaker internat. seafood conf. Future Challenge Seafood Industry, Vienna Austria, 1983. Home: PO Box 220 Sumneytown PA 18084 Office: Day & Gibeon Main St Sumneytown PA 18084

GIBLIN, PATRICK DAVID, banker; b. St. Louis, July 24, 1932; s. Patrick Joseph and Ann Jane (Gill) G.; children: Mary Clare, Christopher, Gregory. BBA, Manhattan Coll., 1954; MBA, St. John's U., Jamaica, N.Y., 1965. Staff auditor Peat, Marwick, Mitchell & Co., N.Y.C., 1956-59; chief plant acct. div. Am. Machine & Foundry, Bklyn., 1959-63; with CBS, N.Y.C., 1963-73; controller electronic video rec. div. CBS, 1968-73, dir. corp. acctg., 1967-68; vice chmn., chief fin. officer CRESTAR Fin. Corp., Richmond, 1973—. Served with U.S. Army, 1954-56. Mem. Delta Mu Delta. Roman Catholic. Home: 13 Dahlgren Rd Richmond VA 23233 Office: Crestar Fin Corp 919 E Main St PO Box 26665 Richmond VA 23261-6665

GIBNEY, FRANK BRAY, publisher, editor, writer, foundation executive; b. Scranton, Pa., Sept. 21, 1924; s. Joseph James and Edna May (Wetter) G.; m. Harriet Harvey, Dec. 10, 1948 (div. 1957); children: Alex, Margot; m. Harriet C. Suydam, Dec. 14, 1957 (div. 1971); children: Frank, James, Thomas; m. Hiroko Doi, Oct. 5, 1972; children: Elise, Josephine. BA, Yale U., 1945; DLitt (hon.), Kyung Hee U., Seoul, Korea, 1974. Corr., assoc. editor Time mag., N.Y.C., Tokyo and London, 1947-54; sr. editor Newsweek, N.Y.C., 1954-57; staff writer, editorial writer Life mag., N.Y.C., 1957-61; pub., pres. SHOW mag., N.Y.C., 1961-64; pres. Ency. Brit. (Japan), Tokyo, 1965-69; pres. TBS-Brit., Tokyo, 1969-75, vice chmn., 1976—; v.p. Ency. Brit., Inc., Chgo., 1975-79; vice chmn., bd. editors Ency. Brit., Chgo., 1978—; pres. Pacific Basin Inst., Santa Barbara, Calif., 1979; adj. prof. Far Eastern studies U. Calif., Santa Barbara, 1986—; bd. dirs. Hudson Reports Internat., Paris, 1981—; cons. Com. on Space and Aero Ho. of Reps., Washington, 1957-59; vice chmn. Japan-U.S. Friendship Commn., 1984—, U.S.-Japan Com. on Edn. and Cultural Interchange, 1984—. Author: Five Gentlemen of Japan, 1953, The Frozen Revolution, 1959, (with Peter Deriabin) The Secret World, 1960, The Operators, 1961, The Khrushchev Pattern, 1961, The Reluctant Space Farers, 1965, Japan: The Fragile Super-Power, 1975, Miracle by Design, 1983; editor: The Penkovskiy Papers, 1965; Presdl. speech writer, 1964. Served to lt. USNR, 1942-46. Decorated Order of the Rising Sun 3d Class Japan, Order of Sacred Treasure 2d Class Japan. Mem. Council on Fgn. Relations, Tokyo Fgn. Corr. Club, Am. C.of C. (Tokyo), Japan-Am. Soc., Japan Soc. Roman Catholic. Clubs: Century Assn., Yale (N.Y.C.); Tokyo; Tavern, The Arts (Chgo.). Home: 1901 E Las Tunas Rd Santa Barbara CA 93103

GIBNEY, JAY LEO, steel executive; b. Phila., Oct. 2, 1936; s. James Leo and Irene (Buckland) G.; m. Elizabeth Ann Blum, Sept. 6, 1958; children: Cheryl, Jeff, Chris, Beth. BS in Econs., Villanova U., 1958. V.p. ops. Gen. Mills, Inc., Toledo, 1970-72, Mt. Clemens, Mich., 1972-76; v.p. ops. Brassc-raft Mfg. Co., Detroit, 1976-80; pres. McNeil Akron (Ohio), Inc., 1980-86; pres., chief exec. officer Gulf States Steel, Inc., Gadsen, Ala., 1986—. Bd. dirs. Community Health Found., Gadsen, 1986—, United Way, Gadsen, 1987—, Ala. Bus. Counc., Montgomery, 1987—. Mem. Am. Iron and Steel Inst. (bd. dirs. 1988—), Gadsen C. of C. (bd. dirs. 1986—). Home: 116 Montcrest Gadsden AL 35904 Office: Gulf States Steel Inc 174 S 26th St Gadsden AL 35904-1935

GIBNEY, THERESE ANNE, banker; b. Fall River, Mass., Feb. 14, 1949; d. Louise Omer and Jeanne (Morneault) Chouinard; m. John Francis Gibney, Feb. 4, 1969 (div. 1980); 1 child, John Louis. BS, Southeastern Mass. U., 1985. Asst. cashier Bank of New Eng. Bristol Co., Fall River, 1982-84, asst. v.p., 1984-86; v.p. Bank of New Eng. N.Am., Fall River, 1986-87, sr. v.p., 1987—; bd. dir. Southeastern chpt. Bank Adminstrn. Inst. Bd. dirs. Community Health Care Svcs., Fall River, 1986—, Jr. Achievement, 1988—, Boy Scouts Am., 1988—. Mem. Nat. Assn. Bank Women. Office: Bank of New Eng NAm 55 N Main St Fall River MA 02720

GIBSON, BRETT JARRETT, telephone systems company executive; b. Terre Haute, Ind., Dec. 15, 1968; s. Garry Ray and Nikki Joy (Owens) G. Grad. high sch., Terre Haute. Owner, mgr. Mid-Am. Telephone Supply Co., Terre Haute, 1980—. Mem. Terre Haute N. Mktg. Edn. Assn. (pres. 1986-87). Baptist. Home: 4575 Wabash Ave Terre Haute IN 47803 Office: Mid Am Telephone Supply 1628 Wabash Ave Terre Haute IN 47807

GIBSON, CHARLES ERNEST, non-profit organization administrator; b. San Angelo, Tex., June 13, 1947; s. Rodney Jr. and Amalia (Goetz) G.; m. Margaret Elizabeth Friberg, July 17, 1976; children: Catherine Elizabeth, Jonathan Charles, Julianne Erin, Benjamin Galen. BA, Adams State Coll., 1969; postgrad., Fuller Sem., 1988—. Mgmt. trainee OEO, Washington, 1969-70; ptnr. Internat. Concessionaries, Washington, 1970-71; title search worker Duphorne Title Co., Aransas, Tex., 1971-72; purchasing agt. N.Mex. Boys Ranch, Boys Ranch, 1972-73, dir. devel., 1973-74, asst. supt., 1974-75, supt., 1975-85; exec. dir. N.Mex. Boys and Girl's Ranch, Boys Ranch, 1985—, Belen, 1985—; instr. fundraising workshops. Author, editor brochures, newsletters. Organizer La Mesa Community Sch., Belen, 1986, pres., 1986—. With USN, 1965-66. Mem. Southwestern Assn. Execs. Homes for Children (treas. 1985-87, pres. 1988-89), N.Mex. Christian Child Care Assn. (pres. 1980), Christian Ministries Mgmt. Assn. (bd. dirs. 1987—), Nat. Assn. Homes for Children, Rotary (pres. Belen chpt. 1985, N.Mex.-Tex. dist. rep. 1988, organizer Los Lunas chpt. 1987). Baptist. Home: 109 Avenida del Fuego Belen NM 07002 Office: NMex Boys Ranch Inc Boys Ranch NM 87002

GIBSON, CYRUS FRANK, management consultant; b. Columbia, S.C., Feb. 11, 1937; s. Cyrus Frank and Sammie Louise (Smith) G.; m. Joanne Patricia Fay, Feb. 16, 1966; children: Katherine Louise, Timothy Joseph, Philip Francis. BE, Yale U., 1960; MBA with distinction, Harvard U., 1965; PhD MIT 1969. Design engr. Standard Oil Co. Calif., San Francisco, 1960-61; tchr. Govt. of Ghana, 1961-63; assoc. Ford Found., Mex., 1965-67; assoc. prof. Bus. Sch. Harvard U., Boston, 1967-78; v.p. Index Systems, Inc., Cambridge, Mass., 1978-87; sr. v.p. Index Group, Inc., Cambridge, 1987—. Co-author: A Casebook for Management Information Systems, 1976, 2d edit., 1981, The Information Imperative. 1987; author: Managing Organizational Behavior, 1980.; contbr. articles to profl. publs. Named one of Top 10 Mgmt. Info. Svc. Cons., Info Week, 1988. Mem. Sigma Xi, Tau Beta Pi. Home: 92 Walden St Concord MA 01742 Office: Index Group Inc 5 Cambridge Ctr Cambridge MA 02142

GIBSON, GEORGE M., manufacturing company executive; b. 1934; married. BSc, U. Notre Dame, 1956. V.p., treas. Procter and Gamble Co., Cin. Lt. (j.g.) USN, 1956-60. Office: Procter & Gamble Co 1 Procter & Gamble Pla Cincinnati OH 45202 *

GIBSON, GEORGE THOMAS, telecommunications company executive; b. Muskogee, Okla., June 23, 1933; s. Jesse A. and Jessie L. (Merriman) G.; m. Dorothy Martin, Dec. 5, 1952; children: Tara Jo Gibson Myers, Philip Gregg. AA, Muskogee Jr. Coll., 1953; BA in Math. and Physics, U. Tulsa, 1955. Registered profl. engr., Okla. Staff engr. Southwestern Bell Telephone Co., Oklahoma City, 1955-58, asst. engr., 1958-60, sr. engr., 1960-61; transmission engr. Southwestern Bell Telephone Co., St. Louis, 1961-63; outside plant transmission and protection engr. Southwestern Bell Telephone Co., Little Rock, 1963-65; dist. plant supt. Southwestern Bell Telephone Co., Fort Smith, Ark., 1965-67; plant supr. Southwestern Bell Telephone Co., Little Rock, 1967-68; bldg. and equipment engr. Southwestern Bell Telephone Co., Houston, 1968-69; gen. network mgr. Southwestern Bell Telephone Co., Oklahoma City, 1969-89, asst. to pres., 1989—; adj. prof. engring. mgmt. U. Okla., Norman, 1984—. Co-author: This Is Wideband Data Service Today, 1963. Bd. advisors U. Okla., 1984—, U. Tulsa, 1986—, Okla. Christian Coll., Oklahoma City, 1986—. Mem. IEEE (sec. Region 5 1980), NSPE (nat. bd. dirs. 1977-79, Indsl. Profl. Devel. award 1976), Okla. Soc. Profl. Engrs. (pres. 1979-80, Indsl. Profl. Devel. award 1971, Outstanding Engring. Mgmt. award 1972), Okla. Engring. Found. (pres. 1980-86), Am. Soc. for Engring. Edn., Am. Soc. for Engring. Mgmt., Okla. State C. of C. (dir. edn. and bus. coalition 1989—), Engrs. Club Oklahoma City (various offices 1970—). Democrat. Presbyterian. Office: Southwestern Bell Telephone Co 800 N Harvey St Room 480 Oklahoma City OK 73102

GIBSON, HELENA CHRISTINE, financial executive; b. Great Falls, Mont., July 22, 1937; d. Albert Henry Birch and Edith Lillian (Kyhn) Barth; divorced; children: Forrest Christian, Sherwood Paul, Carolyn Diane. BS, Calif. State U., Sacramento, 1980. MS, MA, 1982. Cert. fin. planner; registered prin.; registered rep. Prin. Chris Gibson, Enrolled Agt., Sacramento, 1976-82; pres. Gibson's Fin. Planning and Investment Services Inc., Planned Investments Inc., Carmichael, Calif., 1982—; expert witness, securities. Vol. Boy Scouts Am., Sacramento and Roseville, Calif., 1969-76. Recipient Silver Bear award Boy Scouts Am., 1974. Mem. Inst. Cert. Fin. Planners, Internat. Assn. Fin. Planning (program chmn. 1988—), Comstock Club, Sacramento Met. C. of C. Office: Planned Investments Inc 5031 El Camino Ave Carmichael CA 95608

GIBSON, LESTER DALE, JR., accounting manager; b. Newcastle, Pa., Sept. 21, 1954; s. Lester Dale Sr. and Mary Elizabeth (Dickey) G.; m. Cynthia Janene, Sept. 20, 1975; 1 child, Kelli. BS in Acctg., Mgmt., U. Ariz., 1977. Tax acct. Whitehurst & Wood, CPA's, Tucson, 1978-79; acct. Evergreen Air Ctr., Marana, Ariz., 1979-80; contr. Chapman/Dyer Steel, Inc., Tucson, 1980-83, Pace Constrn., Inc., Tucson, 1983-86; mgr. acctg. and adminstrn. Del E. Webb Communities, Inc., Tucson, 1986—. Active Land Devel. Com., Tucson, 1987-88, Tucson Tomorrow, 1987-88. Mem. Nat. Assn. of Accts., Data Processing Mgmt. Assn., So. Ariz. Home Builders Assn., Assn. of Builders and Contractors, Ember Ridge Homeowners Assn. (pres. 1987-88, treas.), Sun City Vistoso Homeowners Assn. (treas. 1987-88). Republican. Baptist. Office: Del E Webb Communities Inc 1565 E Rancho Vistoso Blvd Tucson AZ 85737

GIBSON, LYNN ALLEN, research administrator; b. Corpus Christi, Tex., June 13, 1955; s. William Mack and Selma Lee (Harney) G.; m. Julia D. Allen. BA in English, Tex. A&M U., 1979; BBA in Fin., S.W. Tex. State U., 1984. Mgr. Lyndon B. Johnson Ctr. S.W. Tex. State U., San Marcos, 1978-80; administrv. ops. supr. U.S. Census Bur., Mequite, Tex., 1980; congrl. asst. U.S. Ho. Reps., Washington, 1980-83; dir. data svcs. Tex. Atty. Gen., Austin, 1983-85; dir. laser rsch. Baylor Rsch. Inst., Dallas, 1985-87, v.p. rsch. adminstrn., 1987—; mem. com. Internat. Info. Access '87, Dallas, 1986—; project mgr. Free Electron Laser, Dallas, 1985-86. Exec. editor: (jour.) Baylor Proceedings, 1986. Mem. Dallas Mus. Arts., 1985-86; fundraiser Hart for Pres., Austin, 1984; bd. dirs. Meml. Student Ctr. Enrichment Found., College Station, Tex., 1981-83; mem. Opportunity Dallas Leadership Program, 1988. Mem. Data Processing Mgmt. Assn., Optical Soc. Am., Nat. Health Lawyers Assn. Methodist. Office: Baylor Rsch Found 3500 Gaston Ave Dallas TX 75226

GIBSON, ROGER CASS, investment firm executive; b. Butler, Pa., Apr. 26, 1951; s. Don Bishop and Marianne A. (Newell) G.; children: Sarah Beddow, Adam Cass. BS in Math., Grove City (Pa.) Coll., 1973; MS in Indsl. Adminstrn., Carnegie Mellon U., 1981. Chartered fin. analyst, Pa.; cert. fin. planner, Pa. Claims rep. Social Security Adminstrn., Sharon, Pa., 1973-77; ops. supr. Social Security Adminstrn., Pitts., 1977-79; fin. advisor Allegheny Fin. Group, Ltd., Pitts., 1981-1986, prin., ptnr., 1985—, investment portfolio mgr., 1987—; investment portfolio mgr. Allegheny Investments, Ltd., Pitts., 1985—. Contbr. articles to The Financial Planning Mag. (Fin. Writer's

Award 1982). Tribe chief Indian Princesses, Pitts. YMCA, 1986—. Fellow Inst. Chartered Fin. Analysts; mem. Inst. Cert. Fin. Planners (nat. speaker, edn., regulatory coms., nat. bd. dirs. 1987—, dean residency program 1988), Internat. Assn. for Fin. Planning, Pitts. Assn. for Fin. Planning (sec., bd. dirs., 1984-87). Republican. Lutheran. Club: Shannopin Country (Pitts.). Home: 1304 Regency Dr Pittsburgh PA 15237 Office: Allegheny Fin Group Ltd 3000 McKnight E Dr Pittsburgh PA 15237

GIBSON, THOMAS JAMES, naval architect; b. Newark, Apr. 11, 1957; s. Thomas James and Frances Jane (Farley) G.; m. Sheila Buck, May 24, 1980; children: James Farley, Carolyn McCauley. BS in Naval Architecture, U.S. Naval Acad., 1979; M. Marine Affairs, U. R.I., 1989. Cmmd. ensign USN, 1979, advanced through grades to lt., 1983, resigned, 1985; sailing instr. USN, Annapolis, Md., 1979-80; missile officer USS Biddle, Norfolk, Va., 1980-82; exec. officer USS Affray, Newport, R.I., 1982-84; instr. Surface Warfare Officer Sch., Newport, 1984-85; naval architect Raytheon Co., Portsmouth, R.I., 1985-87, mgr. anti-submarine warfare program, 1988—. Active Newport Hist. Soc., 1986, Save the Bay, Providence, 1986, City Planning Bd., Newport, 1986, Aquidneck Island Planning Com., Newport, 1987. Mem. USN Inst., Soc. Naval Architects and Marine Engrs., U.S. Naval Acad. Alumni Assn. (v.p. Newport chpt. 1985—). Roman Catholic. Home: 31 Thames St Newport RI 02840 Office: Raytheon Co 1847 W Main Rd Portsmouth RI 02871

GIBSON, THOMAS JOSEPH, diversified holding company executive; b. Washington, Mar. 13, 1935; s. Henry Justus and Margaret Mary (Biggins) G.; m. Shirley Ann Claus, June 9, 1956; children: Patricia Lynne Gibson Dixon, Glenn Thomas. B.E.E., Rensselaer Poly. Inst., 1956; J.D., George Washington U., 1962. Bar: Colo. 1963. Electronics engr. FCC, Washington, 1958-59; elec. engring. assoc. Nugent S. Sharp Engrs., Washington, 1959-60; elec. design engr. Datronics Engrs., Inc., Bethesda, Md., 1960-61; mgr. Honeywell, Inc., Denver, 1961-65; dir. Gates Rubber Co., Denver, 1965-75, v.p., 1975-78, sr. v.p., 1978-82; exec. v.p. Gates Corp., Denver, 1982—; bd. dirs. Protection Mut. Ins. Co., Park Ridge, Ill. Pres. Orchard Hills Homeowners Assn., Englewood, Colo., 1970-72; bd. dirs. Denver Council for Pub. TV, 1986—. Served to lt. USNR, 1956-62. Mem. Colo. Assn. Commerce and Industry, Denver C. of C. Republican. Club: The Econ. of Denver (founding). Lodge: Rotary. Office: Gates Corp 900 S Broadway PO Box 5887 Denver CO 80217

GIBSON, THOMAS RICHARD, automobile import company executive; b. Sept. 2, 1942; s. Gilbert G. and Mary Ellen (Wilbraham) G.; m. Sophie Harned, Oct. 14, 1967; children: Matthew B., Katherine A., Caroline Q.; AB, DePauw U., 1964; MBA, Harvard U., 1967. Various sales mgmt. positions, Ford Motor Co., Dearborn, Mich., 1967-80; dir. mktg. ops., Chrysler Corp., Highland Pk., Mich., 1980-81, sr. v.p. sales and mktg., Subaru of Am., Cherry Hill, N.J., 1981-84, exec. v.p. ops., 1984-86, pres., chief operating officer, 1986—. Bd. dirs. Childrens Hosp. Phila., 1986—, Glassboro (N.J.) State Coll, 1985—. Served with USMC, 1964-65. Mem. DePauw U. Alumni Assn. (bd. dirs. 1987). Avocations: tennis, golf, paddle tennis. Office: Subaru Am Inc 2235 Rte 70 W Cherry Hill NJ 08002 *

GIBSON, WILLIAM EDWARD, banker; b. Farragut, Idaho, Apr. 11, 1944; s. William E. and Lucille E. (Dickehut) G.; m. Judith Ten Brock, July 19, 1980; children: William Edward, Christopher Daniel. AB, U. Chgo., 1964, MA, 1965, PhD, 1967. Chartered fin. analyst. Asst. prof. UCLA, 1967-70; sr. staff economist Pres.'s Council Econ. Advisers, Washington, 1971-74; v.p. Chase Manhattan Bank, N.Y.C., 1974-76; 1st v.p. Smith Barney, Harris Upham, N.Y.C., 1976-79; sr. v.p. McGraw-Hill, Inc., N.Y.C., 1979-81, Republic Bank Corp., Dallas, 1981-86; exec. v.p. Continental Ill. Nat. Bank and Trust Co., Chgo., 1986-88; chmn. bd., pres. Am. Fed. Bank, Dallas, 1988—; chmn. bd. dirs. First Fed. Savs. and Loan Assn., Rochester, N.Y., 1981—; vice chmn. bd. dirs. V'Soske Carpets, Inc., Vega Baja, P.R., First Fed. Savs. Bank, San Juan, P.R., Connie Lee Ins. Co., Coll. Constrn. Loan Ins. Assn., Washington; bd. dirs. Fed. Home Loan Bank Dallas. Author: Monetary Economics, 1972; contbr. articles to profl. jour. Trustee Howe Mil. Acad., (Ind.), 1983—; mem. Chgo. Met. Planning Council, Com. on Fgn. Affairs, Chgo. and Dallas; bd. dirs. Am. Diabetes Assn. Named Disting. Alumnus Howe Mil. Acad., 1983. Mem. Am. Econs. Assn., Am. Fin. Assn., Nat. Coun. Savs. Instns. (bd. dirs.). Methodist. Clubs: University (N.Y.C. and Dallas); Cosmos (Washington); Chgo.; Prestonwood Country (Dallas). Home: 303 Woodley Rd Winnetka IL 60093-3740 Office: Am Fed Bank 5080 Spectrum Dallas TX 75248

GIBSON, WILLIAM LEE, manufacturing company executive; b. Newark, Dec. 1, 1949; s. Joseph Wilton Gibson and Margaret (Reynolds) Gibson Leavens; stepson William Barry Leavens, Jr.; BA in Chemistry, Bucknell U., 1972, BS in Chem. Engring., 1972; postgrad. Harvard Bus. Sch., 1977; MBA NYU, 1987; m. Lorraine Wrightson Besch, July 10, 1982. With Bur. Solid Waste Mgmt., EPA, Cin., 1970-71; chemist Dow Chem. Co., Midland, Mich., 1972-75; mktg. cons. Westvaco, Charleston, S.C., 1976; sales rep. Diamond Shamrock Co., Cleve., 1977-79; market devel. specialist strategic planning and ventures operation, plastics bus. div. Gen. Electric Co., Pittsfield, Mass., 1979-81; mktg. programs mgr. Allied-Signal Corp., Morristown, N.J., 1981-86, mgr. tech. and bus. devel., 1986—. Trustee Hartford Family Found. Mem. Soc. Plastic Engrs., Harvard Bus. Sch. Club N.Y., Mensa, Kappa Sigma (pres. Alpha Phi chpt.). Club: Toastmasters (exec. officer). Home: 8 Lone Oak Rd Basking Ridge NJ 07920 Office: PO Box 2332 R Morristown NJ 07960

GIDDES, KENNETH B., JR., finance company executive; b. Plainfield, N.J., July 23, 1937; s. Kenneth B. and Helen (Frederixon) G.; m. Barbara Garrett, Aug. 17, 1963; children: Wendy, Gregg. BA, Western Md. U., 1959; MBA, L.I. U., 1971. Sales mgr. Exxon, L.I., N.Y., 1959-68; sr. sales mgr. Weyerhauser, N.Y.C., 1968-71; v.p. Greyhound Fin. Corp., Atlanta, 1971—; speaker A.A. Equipment Leasors. With U.S. Army, 1960. Mem. Dunwoody Country Club. Office: Greyhound Fin Corp 6400 Powers Ferry Rd Atlanta GA 30339

GIDDINGS, CLIFFORD FREDERICK, corporate executive; b. East Dorset, Vt., May 28, 1936; s. Frederick Daniel and Natalie (Abbott) G. BA, U. Vt., 1958; MA, U. Wis., 1961; postgrad., Sorbonne U., Paris, 1958, U. Chgo., 1963-65. French master Lake Forest (Ill.) Acad., 1961-63; asst. head reference dept. The Newberry Library, Chgo., 1964-68, assoc. head reference dept., 1972-74; dir. library services Scott, Foresman and Co., Glenview, Ill., 1968-71; asst. mgr. Albert E. Barrett, Inc., Trenton, N.J., 1975-80, exec. v.p., 1980—. Fulbright scholar U.S. Dept. State, Grenoble, France, 1958-59. Mem. Associated Gen. Contractors of N.J., N.J. Asphalt Pavement Assn., Nat. Asphalt Pavement Assn., Utility and Transp. Contractors Assn. N.J. Episcopalian. Home: 66 Line Rd Hamilton Square NJ 08690 Office: Albert E Barrett Inc 2485 E State St Trenton NJ 08619

GIDEL, ROBERT HUGH, real estate advisor; b. Ft. Dodge, Iowa, Sept. 19, 1951; s. Wayne D. and Mary A. (Ziegler) G.; m. Linda Carol Lombardo, Oct. 23, 1976; children: Jill, Allison, Robert. BSBA, U. Fla., 1973. Comml. loan officer Century Bank, St. Petersburg, Fla., 1975-77; asst. v.p. N.Y. Life, Washington, 1977-81; exec. v.p. Heller Real Estate Fin. Co., Chgo., 1981-86; mng. dirs. Alex Brown Realty Advisors, Balt., 1986—; dir. Alex Brown Real Estate Group, Balt. Contbr. articles to profl. publs. Mem. Mortgage Bankers Assn. (sec. Washington chpt. 1985), Pension Real Estate Assn., Urban Land Inst., Center Club, L'Hirondelle Club. Republican. Roman Catholic. Clubs: Center (Balt.), Monroe (Chgo.). Home: 5109 Saint Albans Way Baltimore MD 21212 Office: Alex Brown Realty Advisors 2 North Charles St Baltimore MD 21201

GIDEON, KENNETH WAYNE, lawyer; b. Lubbock, Tex., July 25, 1946; s. Melton Jean and Mary B. (Lanham) G.; m. Carol Almack, June 2, 1968; children—Christopher Lynn, Kevin Almack, Timothy Charles, Emily Susan. B.A., Harvard U., 1968; J.D., Yale U., 1971. Bar: Tex. 1971, U.S. Tax Ct. 1971, U.S. Ct. Claims 1972, U.S. Supreme Ct. 1981, D.C. 1984. Ptnr., assoc. Fulbright & Jaworski, Houston, 1971-81, Washington, 1983-86; chief counsel IRS, Washington, 1981-83; ptnr. Fried, Frank, Harris, Shriver & Jacobson, Washington, 1986—. Mem. Spring Valley City Council, Tex., 1978-79. Served to capt. U.S. Army, 1971-72. Fellow Am. Coll. of Tax Counsel; mem. ABA (chmn. ct. procedure com. tax sect. 1979-81, chmn. govt. relations com. 1984-86, council 1987—). Office: Fried Frank Harris et al 1001 Pennsylvania Ave NW Ste 800 Washington DC 20004

GIDEON, RICHARD WALTER, broadcasting management consultant; b. Phila., Nov. 23, 1928; s. Walter Richard and Amelia Molly (Ebinger) G.; m. Yolanda Elena Josefe, Jan. 12, 1957; children—Richard E. and Michael J. (twins). BS in Econs., U. Pa., 1952. Statis. clk. Triangle Pubs. Inc., Phila., 1952-55, rsch. mgr., 1955-62; asst. dir. media rsch. Young & Rubicam, N.Y.C., 1962-63; with John Blair & Co., N.Y.C., 1963-75, dir. rsch., 1967-75, v.p., 1969-75, dir. sales strategy, 1973-75; pres. Dick Gideon Enterprises, Medford, N.J., 1975—; prin. Gideon and Altman Rsch. Inc., Medford, 1984-87, Verus Info. Corp., Cherry Hill, N.J., 1985—. Editor: Statistical Trends In Broadcasting, 1970-77. Dist. leader Westchester County Republican Com., 1974-76; mem. adv. com. to N.Y. Assemblyman Gordon Burrows, 1974-76. With USMC, 1946-48. Mem. Sigma Phi Epsilon. Home and Office: 29 Huntington Circle Dr Medford NJ 08055

GIDWANI, BAHAR NARAIN, securities analyst; b. Columbus, Ohio, Apr. 16, 1955; s. Narain Sahijram Gidwani and Joanna (Withrow) Dobson. BAin Physics, Astronomy magma cum laude, Amherst Coll., 1976; MBA with distintion, Harvard U., 1981. CFA. Rep. Burroughs Corp., Boston and Hong Kong, 1976-79; cons. McKinsey & Co., N.Y.C., 1981-83; analyst Kidder, Peabody Inc., N.Y.C., 1983—; v.p. Kidder Peabody. Mem. Fin. Analysts Fedn., Software Analysts Splinters Group, SME, N.Y. Soc. Securities Analysts, Software Pubs. Assn., ADAPSO. Club: Harvard (N.Y.C.). Office: Kidder-Peabody & Co Inc 10 Hanover Sq New York NY 10005

GIDWITZ, GERALD, cosmetics company executive; b. Memphis, 1906; married; 5 children. BA, U. Chgo., 1927. Chmn. bd., chmn. exec. com. Helene Curtis Industries, Inc., Chgo. Trustee Roosevelt U., Auditorium Theatre Council; bd. dirs. Chgo. Crime Commn. Mem. Ill. Mfg. Assn. (past bd. dirs.). Office: Helene Curtis Industries Inc 325 N Wells St Chicago IL 60610

GIDWITZ, RONALD J., personal care products company executive; b. Chgo., 1945. Grad., Brown U., 1967. With Helene Curtis Industries, Inc., Chgo., 1968—, pres., 1979—, chief exec. officer, 1985—, also bd. dirs.; bd. dirs. Continental Materials Corp. Bd. dirs. Field Mus. Nat. History, Lyric Opera Chgo.; chmn. Econ. Devel. Commn. City of Chgo.; mem. exec. bd. library council Northwestern U.; mem. nat. bd. dirs., trustee Boys Club Am.; trustee Lincoln Acad. Ill.; Rep. committeeman 43d Ward Chgo. Mem. Chgo. Assn. Commerce and Industry (bd. dirs.), Chgo. Council Fgn. Relations. Office: Helene Curtis Industries Inc 325 N Wells St Chicago IL 60610

GIERER, VINCENT A., JR., tobacco company executive; b. N.Y.C., Oct. 21, 1947; s. Vincent A. Sr. and Isabel (McEwen) G.; m. Josephine Lindenmayer; children: Gregory, Vincent, Beth. BBA, Iona Coll., 1969. CPA, N.Y. Audit supr. Ernst & Whinney, White Plains, N.Y., 1971-77; dir. fin. reporting U.S. Tobacco Inc., Greenwich, Conn., 1978-83, controller, 1983-86, sr. v.p., chief fin. officer, 1986-88, exec. v.p., chief fin. officer, 1988—, also bd. dirs. Mem. Wilton (Conn.) Newcomers; mgr. Little League, Wilton. Served with U.S. Army, 1969-71, Vietnam. Mem. Am. Inst. CPA's, Am. Mgmt. Assn., Fin. Execs. Inst. Roman Catholic. Office: UST Inc 100 W Putnam Ave Greenwich CT 06830

GIERING, RICHARD HERBERT, information systems executive; b. Emmaus, Pa., Nov. 27, 1929; s. Harold Augustus and Marguerite (Bruder) G.; BS in Engring. and Math., U. Ariz., 1962; m. Carol Alice Scott, Aug. 16, 1959; children: Richard Herbert, Scott K. Enlisted U.S. Army, 1947, commd. 2d lt., 1963, advanced through grades to capt., 1965; sect. chief data processing Def. Intelligence Agy., Washington, 1965-67; ret., 1967; with Data Corp. (name changed to Mead Tech. Labs. 1968), Dayton, Ohio, 1967-77, v.p. tech. ops., 1970-71, dir. info. systems, 1971-77; pres., chief exec. officer DG Assos., Inc., 1974—; pres. Infotex Assos., 1977-86, mgr. Product Systems, Commerce Clearing House, Inc., 1986—; instr. data processing U. Ariz., Tucson, 1962-63. Mem. Assn. Computing Machinery, Am. Soc. Info. Scis. Inventor Data/Cen. (used to establish electronic newspaper libraries). Home: 906 Red Top Dr Libertyville IL 60048 Office: 4025 Peterson Chicago IL 60648

GIERTZ, ROBERT WILLIAM, manufacturing consultant; b. Clifton, Ill., Mar. 24, 1925; s. William Chris and Emma Louise (Meyer) G.; m. Vera Rosalie Herrmann, Nov. 30, 1946; children: Deborah Giertz Staack, Nancy Giertz Natvig, Norman, James, Julie Giertz Elias. BS, U. Ill., 1950; postgrad. MIT, 1964. Registered profl. engr., Ill. Mech. engr. John Deere Waterloo Tractor Works of Deere & Co., Waterloo, Iowa, 1950-64, chief engr., 1964-67, gen. mgr., 1967-74, dir. mfg., Moline, Ill., 1974-86; pres. Giertz Enterprises, Ltd., Bettendorf, Iowa, 1986—. Mem. Dist. Jud. Nominating Commn., 1969-75; mem. Waterloo Indsl. Devel. Assn., 1968-75; past mem. United Services of Black Hawk County. Trustee Schoitz Meml. Hosp., 1968-74, Mt. Mercy Coll., Cedar Rapids, Iowa, 1979-82; bd. govs. Iowa Coll. Found., vice chmn., 1976, chmn., 1977; bd. govs. U. No. Iowa Found., pres. 1973-75; past bd. dirs. Waterloo Civic Found.; bd. dirs. Quad City World Affairs Council, pres., 1980-81. Served with USAF, 1946-47. Mem. Soc. Automotive Engrs., Am. Soc. Agrl. Engrs., Inst. Mgmt. Cons., U. Ill. Alumni Assn. (bd. dirs. 1987—). Republican. Lutheran. Clubs: Crow Valley Golf, Symposium. Home and Office: 2410 Eagle Circle Bettendorf IA 52722

GIESE, ROBERT JOSEPH, corporate executive; b. N.Y.C., June 16, 1934; s. Emil Joseph and Noreen (Black) G.; m. Dolores J. Moran, Nov. 19, 1960; 1 child, Lara. Student, Bklyn. Coll., 1952-57, NYU, 1968-69. Archtl. draftsman Ebasco Services, Inc., N.Y.C., 1952-53, adminstrv. asst. to supt. design, 1953-56, engring. coordinator on pulp and paper projects, 1956-57, adminstrv. asst. to engring. mgr., 1957-60, mgr. advt. and publicity, 1960-73, mgr. corp. communications, 1973-78, dir. mktg. and corp. communications, 1973-78, 1978-80, dir. govtl. relations, 1980-85; pres., chmn. bd. CDI cons. Developers Energy Systems Corp., Franklinville, N.J., 1985—; spl. investigator N.Y. Atty. Gen.'s Office, N.Y.C., 1959-61; bd. dirs. Britten Plastics Inc., Am. Guarantee and Credit Corp.; chmn. bd. dirs. Developers Energy Systems Corp. Caribbean Inc., P.R. Elected judicial del. City of N.Y., 1960; liaison officer Dep. Mayor's Office of Econ. Devel. of N.Y.C. Served with USNR, 1951-59. Mem. Advt. Club, N.Y. Alumni Assn., N.Y. Chamber Commerce and Industry, U.S. C. of C. Roman Catholic. Clubs: World Trade Ctr., Forsgate. Home: 314 Pinebrook Rd Englishtown NJ 07726 Office: 452 Coles Mill Rd Franklinville NJ 08322 also: 117 Eleanor Roosevelt Blvd Hato Rey PR 00918

GIESEN, HERMAN MILLS, consulting engineering manager; b. San Antonio, Sept. 22, 1928; s. Herman Iglehart and Emeline Barbara (Frey) G.; student Tex. A&M U., 1946-47; B.S. in Engring., U.S. Naval Acad., 1951; M.S. in Elec. Engring., USAF Inst. Tech., 1960; M.S. in Ops. Mgmt., U. So. Calif., 1966; m. Linda B. Williams, Aug. 9, 1979; 1 son, Jonathan Williams; children by previous marriage—John Herman, David Douglas, Amy Lynn. Commd. 2d lt. USAF, 1951, advanced through grades to maj., 1966; served as aircraft maintenance mgr., 1954-56, flight instr., 1957-59, research and devel. program officer, 1960-63, aircraft, flight commdr., 1963-64, elec. engr.-analyst, 1964-66, resigned, 1966, now col. Res., ret.; exec. adviser in program control McDonnell-Douglas Corp., Huntington Beach, Calif., 1966-68; sr. bus. planner E-Systems, Inc., Greenville, Tex., 1968-71; pres. Giesen & Assos., Inc., indsl. mgmt. engring. cons., Dallas, 1971-72, 78—; plant engr. Dixie Metals of Tex., Dallas, 1972-73; plant engr. Murph Metals Div., R.S.R. Corp., Dallas, 1973-74, ops. maintenance/engring. mgr., 1974-76; mfg. mgr. Ferguson Industries, Dallas, 1976-78; self-employed cons. design engr., 1978-84; dir. engring. services AID Cons. Engrs., Inc., Dallas, 1985—. Decorated Air medal, USAF Commendation medal, Air Force Meritorious Service medal; registered profl. engr., Tex.; cert. flight instr., advanced instrument ground aircraft instr. FAA. Mem. NSPE, Tex. Soc. Profl. Engrs. Contbr. articles to profl. jours. Home: 3636 Shenandoah Dallas TX 75205

GIFFIN, KENNETH NEAL, utility executive; b. Martinsville, Ind., Feb. 23, 1944; s. Kenneth Carlyle and Alice Jane (Stokesberry) G.; m. Marjorie Gates, May 17, 1975; children: Brian, Robert, Christopher, Matthew. BS, Ind. U., 1966. Asst. to bd. chmn. Indpls. Water Co., 1972-83, v.p. corp. affairs, 1983—; v.p., bd. dirs. Utility Data Corp., Indpls., Waterway Holdings Inc., Indpls. City councilman, Indpls., 1972-76, 84—; asst. to Congressman William Bray, Ind., 1965-70; nat. dir., treas. Am. Legion Endowment Fund Corp., 1984—. With USNG, 1966-72. Mem. Am. Water Works Assn. (chmn. state govt. relations com.), Columbia Club, Country Club Indpls., Masons. Republican. Methodist. Office: Indianapolis Water Co 1220 Waterway Blvd Indianapolis IN 46206

GIFFORD, CHARLES KILVERT, banker; b. Providence, Nov. 8, 1942; s. Clarence H. and Priscilla (Kilvert) G.; m. Anne Dewing, Oct. 3, 1964; children—Ramsay, Charles, John, Jessica. B.A., Princeton U., 1964. Trainee Chase Manhattan Bank, N.Y.C., 1964-66; pres. Bank of Boston, 1967—; bd. dirs. Mass. Mut. Life Ins. Co. Trustee New Eng. Aquarium, Boston, 1982, Pingree Sch., Hamilton, Mass., 1982, Sydney Farber Cancer Ctr., Boston, 1982; bd. dirs. Boston Children's Hosp. Office: Bank of Boston 100 Federal St Boston MA 02110

GIFFORD, NELSON SAGE, manufacturing company executive; b. Newton, Mass., May 3, 1930; s. Gordon Babcock and Hariette Rose (Dooley) G.; m. Elizabeth B. Brow, Nov. 12, 1955; children: Susan Helen, Ian Christopher, Diane Brow. AB, Tufts Coll., 1952. With Dennison Mfg. Co., Framingham, Mass., 1954—, mem. acctg. staff, 1954-63, controller, 1964-65, gen. mgr., 1965-67, v.p., 1967-72; pres. Dennison Mfg. Co., Framingham, 1972-86, chmn., 1986—; bd. dirs. Reed & Barton, John Hancock Mut. Life Ins. Co., Boston, Boston Edison Co., Bank of Boston, M/A Com, Burlington, Mass. Bd. dirs. New Eng. Colls. Fund; trustee Newton Wellesley Hosp., Mass. Gen. Hosp.; past chmn. Wellesley Personnel Bd.; trustee Woods Hole Oceanographic Inst., Mass.; chmn. bd. trustees Tufts U. Lt. comdr. USNR, 1952-60. Mem. Silvanus Packard Soc., Mass. Bus. Roundtable (bd. dirs., vice-chmn.), Associated Industries Mass. (bd. dirs.), Kittansett Club, Brae Burn Country Club. Home: 14 Windsor Rd Wellesley MA 02181 Office: Dennison Mfg Co 275 Wyman St Waltham MA 02254

GIGGEY, JAMES WALKER, chemical company executive; b. Somerville, Mass., Apr. 16, 1931; s. Willard Oscar and Gladys Margaret (Craig) G.; m. Constance Guilfoyle, July 13, 1957; children: Michael James, Shawna, Maureen, Matthew, Brennan, Paul Patrick. BS in Chemistry, Northeastern U., 1954. Product mgr. electrochemicals dept. E. I. du Pont Nemours & Co., Wilmington, Del., 1966-69, dist. mgr. electrochemicals dept., 1969-70, mktg. mgr. electrochemicals dept., 1970-73, venture mgr. plastics dept., 1973-74, div. mgr. photo products dept., 1974-77, div. dir. polymer products dept., 1977-81, dir. departmental plans polymer products dept., 1981-82, v.p. polymer products, 1982-87, v.p. corp. plans dept., 1987—. Pres., bd. dirs. Gerar Place Condominiums, Rehoboth, Del., 1980-84; vice chmn., bd. trustees Goldey Beacom Coll., Wilmington, 1986—. Mem. Soc. of Plastics Industry (exec. com., fin. com. 1983-85). Office: E I Du Pont de Nemours & Co 1007 Market St Wilmington DE 19898

GIGLIO, PETER M., JR., sales executive; b. Tampa, Fla., July 31, 1944; s. Peter L. and Rose M. G.; B.S., Fla. State U., 1963; m. Elisabeth Fink, Sept. 25, 1975. Sales rep. Gen. Foods Corp., Montgomery, Ala., 1968-70; account mgr., Miami, 1970-72; dist. mgr. Anderson Clayton Foods, Miami, 1972-73; regional sales mgr. H. P. Hood, Inc., Dunedin, Fla., 1974-75, dir. sales dairy product div., 1988—; pres. Nat. Food Brokers, Tampa, 1975-77, regional sales dir. foodservice div., 1977-88. Pres. Gulf Gardens Condominium Assn., 1986—; mayor Valrico, Fla. 1987. Recipient Golden Fellowship award, 1983; named Nat. Salesman of Yr. H.P. Hood, Inc., 1984, 87. Mem. Valrico Commerce Assn. (pres. 1985). Office: H P Hood Inc 427 San Christopher Dr Dunedin FL 33528

GIGNOUX, DOMINIQUE M. P., data processing executive; b. Grenoble, France; came to U.S., 1955; d. Maurice Irene and Marie Gabrielle (Garel) G.; m. Alexandra Dencks, Aug. 13, 1956 (div. 1969); children: Alexandra, Suzanne; m. Monique Tonnard, Nov. 28, 1976; 1 child, Christopher. BSc, U. Paris, 1951; AM, Harvard U., 1953. Clubs: Met. (Washington); Harvard U. (N.Y.C.). Office: Data Measurement Corp PO Box 490 Gaithersburg MD 20884

GILBANE, THOMAS F., JR., building company executive; b. Providence, June 7, 1947; s. Thomas F. and Jean A. (Murphy) G.; m. Mary O'Donnell, June 9, 1973; children—Thomas F., Daniel, Martha, Michael. B.S.B.A., Babson Coll., 1970; M.S., MIT, 1975; postgrad. in advanced mgmt., Harvard Bus. Sch., 1984. Various positions Gilbane Bldg. Co., Providence, 1964-76; v.p. Gilbane Bldg. Co., Cleve., 1976-83; exec. v.p. Gilbane Bldg. Co., Providence, 1983—; bd. dirs. Fleet Nat. Banks, Providence. Alumni dir., mem. corp. Babson Coll., Wellesley, Mass., 1974-76; bd. dirs. Boy Scouts Am., Cleve., 1981-83, Providence, 1985—; trustee Greater Cleve. Roundtable, 1983-85; R.I. Assn. for Blind, Providence, 1985—; bd. dirs. United Way-Southeastern New Eng., Providence, 1985—, campaign chmn. 1986; trustee City of Hope, 1984—, Catholic Charities. Served to 2d lt R.I. N.G., 1970-76. Recipient Spirit of Life award City of Hope, 1984. Mem. Sigma Chi, Phi Kappa Si. Roman Catholic. Clubs: Union (Cleve.); Firestone Country (Akron, Ohio); Agawan Hunt (East Providence, R.I.); Point Judith Country (Narragansett, R.I.), Hope. Lodge: Knights of Malta. Summer Address: 155 Dunes Ct Narragansett RI 02882 Office: Gilbane Bldg Co 7 Jackson Walkway Providence RI 02940

GILBERT, FREDERICK SPOFFORD, JR., executive manager; b. Orange, N.J., Mar. 29, 1939; s. Frederick Spofford and Annis Burnham (Stearns) G.; m. Margaret Andrus Moon, Sept. 6, 1961; children: Malcolm Andrus, Frederick Christopher, Douglas Hamlin. BA in History, Williams Coll., 1961; postgrad., NYU, 1962-66, Harvard U., 1966-70. Mgmt. trainee Citibank, N.Y.C., 1961, asst. mgr., 1965, asst. v.p., 1969, v.p., 1972-88, div. exec., 1988—; pres. Citicorp Bus., Inc., N.Y.C., 1977-82; exec. v.p. Citicorp Indsl. Credit, Inc., Harrison, N.Y., 1980-88; speaker numerous seminars and confs. Contbr. articles to profl. jours. Mem. rep. Darien Town Meeting, 1971-75; treas. Darien YMCA Indian Guides, 1972-74; trustee New Canaan Country Sch., 1979-82. With AUS, 1961-66. Recipient Disting. Community Svc. award Brandeis U., 1985, Nat. Humanitarian award Nat. Jewish Ctr. Immunology and Respiratory Medicine, 1987. Mem. Nat. Comml. Fin. Assn. (bd. dirs. 1977-88, exec. com. 1979-86, v.p. 1980-84, pres. 1985, chmn. 1986), Credit Fin. Mgmt. Alumni Assn., Kappa Alpha. Republican. Presbyterian. Clubs: University (N.Y.C.), Wee Burn Country (Darien). Home: 46 Ridge Acres Darien CT 06820-2614 Office: Citibank NA 153 E 53rd St New York NY 10043

GILBERT, GERALD FREDERICK, JR., diversified industry executive; b. Reading, Pa., Apr. 28, 1926; s. Gerald Frederick and Florence Adella (Anderson) G.; m. Shirley Louise Douty, June 14, 1952; children—Heidi Jo, Gretchen Louise. B.S., Lehigh U., 1950. With Atlas Mineral Products Co., Mertztown, Pa., 1950-62; asst. sec. Harsco Co., Camp Hill, Pa., 1962-72, sec., 1972—, sr. v.p., 1978—. Served to 1st lt. AUS, 1944-46. Mem. Internat. Brotherhood Magicians. Republican. Methodist. Home: 27 Meadow Dr Green Lane Farms Camp Hill PA 17011 Office: Harsco Corp PO Box 8888 Camp Hill PA 17011

GILBERT, JACQUELINE ANN, pharmeceutical sales executive; b. Park Forest, Ill., Oct. 17, 1954; d. Rubin and Jean (Serlin) G. BS in Physical Therapy, U. Ill. Med. Ctr., Chgo., 1976; MBA, Nat. U., 1988. Lic. physical therapist. Staff physical therapist Tradewinds Rehab., Gary, Ind., 1976-78; itinerant physical therapist Wash. Elem. Sch.Dist., Phoenix, 1978-80; profl. sales rep. Parke-Davis Co., Las Vegas, Nev., 1980—; Speaker program devel. Wash. Elem. Sch. Dist., 1978. Del. Dem. Party-County/ Las Vegas, 1988. Mem. Ariz. Physical Therapist Assn. (speaker 1980), Southern Nev. Pharmeceutical Reps. Assn. (pres. 1984-87) NAFE. Democrat. Jewish.

GILBERT, RAY WILSON, JR., controller, corporate secretary; b. West Point, Ga., July 31, 1951; s. Ray Wilson Sr. and Mildred (Lumpkin) G.; m. Joan Elizabeth Gilmore, June 5, 1971; children: Ray Wilson III, Jennifer Joan. BS in Acctg., Auburn U., 1974, MBA, 1977. Acct. gen. ledger West Pt. Pepperell, Inc., West Pt., Ga., 1974-77; acct. consolidation West Pt. Pepperell, Inc., Fairfax, Ala., 1977-78; plant controller West Point (Ga.) Pepperell, Inc., Fairfax, Ga., 1978-82; acctg. mgr. Interface Flooring Systems, Inc., Lagrange, Ga., 1982-85; corp. sec., contr. Mesa Industries, Inc., Opelika, Ala., 1985—. Mem. Nat. Assn. Accts. (officer Lake West Point chpt. 1984—). Methodist. Home: 1908 1st St Lanett AL 36863 Office: Mesa Industries Inc 2507 S Uniroyal Rd Opelika AL 36801

GILBERT, ROBERT B., heating and air conditioning manufacturing company executive. BS, Purdue U., 1948. With Rheem Mfg. Co., N.Y.C., 1948—, sales trainee, 1948, product mgr., 1955-69, v.p. mktg., environ. products group, 1969-73, v.p., gen. mgr., 1973-78, pres. air conditioning div., 1978-85, corp. pres., chief exec. officer, 1985—. Served with USN, 1943-45. Office: Rheem Mfg Co 350 Park Ave New York NY 10022

GILBERT, RUSSELL JAMES, electronics executive; b. Flushing, N.Y., Sept. 18, 1952; s. James William and Veronica Gilbert; B.S. in Mgmt., St. John's U., 1974; postgrad in bus. C.W. Post Coll., 1976; J.D., Western State U., 1980. Planning analyst Grumman Aerospace Corp., Bethpage, N.Y., 1974-76; with electronics div. Gen. Dynamics Co., San Diego, 1976—, sr. systems analyst, 1980-83 , sr. project mgr., 1983-86; mem. Automated Data Collection working group with Gen. Dynamics Corp., 1983-85; mgmt. systems specialist Info. Resource Mgmt., 1985—; project mgr. MRP Material Cost Mgmt. Project, 1988-89; engring. cons. for small high tech. cos. Cert. on Ramis II. Recipient Outstanding Acheiver award Info. Resource Mgmt. Dept. Mem. Nat. Mgmt. Assn.(1st v.p. gen. dynamics electronics div. 1986-87), Lions (dir. 1982-83, Internat. award 1981), San Diego Mission Bay Boat and Ski Club (bd. dirs. 1986-87, 1st vice commodore 1987-88). Author: Manufacturing and Material Control Systems for an Integrated Environment, 1977; Planning Management Information System, 1981; Parts Labor History; Automated Data Collection System Utilizing Bar Code High Technology. Home: 8864 La Camesa San Diego CA 92129 Office: Gen Dynamics Electronics Div 5011 Kearny Villa Rd PO Box 85039 Mail Zone 8232-C San Diego CA 92138

GILBERTI, COSMO A., III, bailbondsman, mortgage company executive; b. Waltham, Mass., Mar. 1, 1942; s. Cosmo and Mary E. (DeMarco) G.; m. Therese M. Tardif, June 21, 1970 (dec. 1982); children: Jayson, Alyssa J., Anthony J.; m. Diane C. St. Pierre, Aug. 14, 1983. Cert., Mass. Inst. Ins., 1968. Lic. in ins. and real estate, Mass. With Gilberti's Meat Market, Boston, 1961-64; founder, owner Aldo's Pizza and Sub Shop, Waltham, 1964-67; pres., bailbondsman Gilberti Bail Bonds, Waltham, 1968—; pres. Bedford Mortgage Corp., Waltham, 1985—. With U.S. Army, 1960-61. Mem. Elks. Roman Catholic. Home: 6 Landmark Rd Westford MA 01886 Office: 914 Main St Waltham MA 01886

GILBERTSON, OSWALD IRVING, marketing executive; b. Bklyn., Mar. 23, 1927; s. Olaf and Ingeborg (Aase) Gabrielsen; m. Magnhild Hompland, Sept. 11, 1954; children: Jan Ivar, Eric Olaf. Electrotechnician, Sorlandets Tekniske Skole, Norway, 1947; BSEE, Stockholms Tekniska Institut, Stockholm, Sweden, 1956. Planning engr. test equipment design and devel. Western Electric Co., Inc., Kearny, N.J., 1957-61, planning engr. new prodn., 1963-67, engring. supr. test equipment, 1963-67, engring. supr. submarine repeaters and equalizers, 1967-69; engring. mgr. communication cables ITT Corp., Oslo, Norway, 1969-71, mktg. mgr. for ITT's Norwegian co., Standard Telefon og Kabelfabrik A/S (STK), 1971-87, STK Factory rep., 1987—; div. mgr. Eswa Heating Systems, Inc., 1980-87, pres., 1987—. Hon. Norwegian consul, 1981—. Served with AUS, 1948-52. Registered profl. engr., Vt. Mem. IEEE, Norwegian Soc. Profl. Engrs., Soc. Norwegian Am. Engrs., Sons of Norway. Patentee in field. Home: 6240 Brynwood Ct San Diego CA 92120 Office: Eswa Heating Systems Inc STK Cables Royal Norwegian Consulate 4380 Viewridge Ave Ste D San Diego CA 92123-1620

GILBREATH, FREIDA CAROL, data processing executive; b. Huntsville, Ala., Oct. 26, 1949; d. Murray and Edna Merle (Smith) Dixon; m. Robert Keith Gilbreath, May 4, 1969; children: Scott McKinley, Emily Luanne. Student, N.E. Jr. Coll., Rainsville, Ala., 1967-69. Cashier Dunnavant's Dept. Store, Huntsville, 1968-69; sec. Pensacola (Fla.) Mill Supply Co., 1970-71; bookkeeper Arkay Trucking Co., Guntersville, Ala., 1971-72, Creswell Indsl. Supply, Guntersville, 1972; computer operator Guntersville Hosp., 1972-77, Housing Devel. Co., Huntsville, 1977-79; data systems coord. Bapt. Med. Ctr., Fort Payne, Ala., 1979-84, Centre, Ala., 1982-84; programmer-analyst Bapt. Med. Ctr., Birmingham, Ala., 1984—. Mem. Data Processing Mgmt. Assn., NAFE. Methodist. Office: Bapt Med Ctr 3201 4th Ave S Birmingham AL 35222

GILBRECH, DONNA HARPER, management consultant, real estate executive; b. Chicago, Ariz., Nov. 2, 1943; d. Vito J. and Eileen (Kennelly) T.; m. Earl P. Gilbrech; children: Jeanne Marie, Melissa Leigh. Pres. Valley Income Properties, Phoenix, 1979-83, Am. Investors, Phoenix, 1983—. Mem. Am. Achievement Found. (bd. dirs.), Nat. Speaker's Assn. Club: Toastmasters. Office: Am Investors 1236 E Northern Phoenix AZ 85020

GILBRIDE, JOHN THOMAS, JR., manufacturing executive; b. Bklyn., Mar. 9, 1945; s. John Thomas and Rosemary (Shelare) G.; m. Victoria N. Caragol, Aug. 26, 1967; children—John Thomas III, Michael J., Elizabeth Shelare, Matthew T. BS in Indsl. Engring. cum laude, Lehigh U., 1968, BSBA cum laude, 1968. Registered profl. engr., Wash. Ship supt. Todd Pacific Shipyards, Seattle, 1969-70, asst. gen. supt., 1970-71, gen. supt., 1972-75, asst. gen. mgr. prodn., 1975-79, v.p., gen. mgr., 1979-86, pres., chief ops. officer, Jersey City, 1986-89; dir. ops. support Boeing Helicopters, Phila., 1989—. Mem. Western Shipbuilders Assn. (pres., bd. dirs. 1983-85), Soc. Naval Architects and Marine Engrs., Am. Soc. Naval Engrs., Greater Seattle C. of C. (trustee 1985), Nat. Propeller Club U.S., Wash. Athletic Club (dir. 1984). Roman Catholic. Home: 3 E Spring Oak Circle Media PA Office: Boeing Helicopters PO Box 16858 MS P30-46 Philadelphia PA 19142-0858 also: Todd Shipyards Corp 11025 W Massachusetts Seattle WA 98134

GILBRIDGE, JOHN THOMAS, JR., shipyard executive; b. Bklyn., Mar. 9, 1945; s. John Thomas and Rosemary (Shelare) G.; m. Victoria Caragol, Aug. 26, 1967; children: John Thomas III, Michael James, Elizabeth Shelare, Matthew Todd. BSBA in Acctg., Lehigh U., 1968, BS in Indsl. Engring., 1968. Registered profl. engr., Wash. With Todd Shipyards Corp., Seattle, 1968—, v.p., asst. gen. mgr., 1977-79, v.p., gen. mgr., 1979-86; pres., chief ops. officer Todd Shipyards Corp., Jersey City, 1986-89, dir. ops. support, 1989—, also bd. dirs. Mem. Am. Soc. Naval Engrs., Western Shipbldg. Assn. (pres., bd. dirs. 1983-85), Seattle C. of C. (trustee 1983-86), Navy League (life, pres., bd. dirs. 1984-86, Nat. Scroll Honor award), Wash. Athletic Club (Seattle, bd. dirs. 1983-86). Roman Catholic. Home: 108 Rotary Dr Summit NJ 07901 Office: Todd Shipyards Corp One Evertrust Pla Jersey City NJ 07302

GILCHRIST, WILLIAM RISQUE, JR., economist; b. Lexington, Ky., July 16, 1944; s. William Risque and Susan (McLemore) G.; B.B.A., U. Miami, 1966, M.B.A., 1970; postgrad. Northwestern U., 1973—; m. Peggy Linder Gardner, Mar. 20, 1968; children—William Risque, Shannon Linder, Heather Susan. Asso. dir. conf. services div. continuing edn. U. Miami, Coral Gables, Fla., 1966-71; asst. dir. edn. and tng. Mortgage Bankers Assn. Am., Washington, 1971-73; pres. Ventura Fin. Corp., Fort Lauderdale, Fla., 1973-76; pres. Gilchrist and Assos., Pompano Beach., Fla., London, and Santiago, Chile, 1976—; pres. Intervault, Inc., Ft. Lauderdale and Basel, Switzerland, Orlando, Houston; cons. in field. Recipient Cert. of Achievement, Savs. and Loan Execs. Seminar, 1971. Mem. Broward County (Fla.) C. of C., NAB, Econ. Soc. South Fla., Mortgage Bankers Assn., Nat. Assn. Pvt. Security Vaults (pres. 1986—)., Senatorial Inner Circle. Republican. Episcopalian. Clubs: Kiwanis. Marina Bay, Mutiny. Author: International Monetary Systems—Alternatives, 1969; Eurodollar Outlook-OPEC and the LDC's, 1978. Home: 1341 SE 9th Ave Pompano Beach FL 33060

GILDEHAUS, THOMAS ARTHUR, manufacturing company executive; b. Little Rock, Sept. 29, 1940; s. Arthur Frederick and Susanna (Packham) G.; m. Barbara Lee Quimby, Oct. 29, 1960; children: Elizabeth, Thomas Arthur, Jr., Charles, Christopher, Allen. B.A. in History, Yale U., 1963; M.B.A. with distinction, Harvard U., 1970. With Citibank, N.Y.C. and P.R., 1963-70; v.p. Temple, Barker & Sloane, Inc., Lexington, Mass., 1970-80; sr. v.p. Deere & Co., Moline, Ill., 1980-82; exec. v.p. Deere & Co., 1982—, also dir.; bd. dir. Davenport Bank and Trust Co., Iowa. Trustee Nat. 4-H Coun., 1983—. Office: Deere & Co John Deere Rd Moline IL 61265

GILES, CHARLES DAN, data processing executive; b. Nacogdoches, Tex., Nov. 2, 1929; s. Dorris David and Vida (Gray) G.; m. Mildred Butte, June 27, 1953; children: Mark Dan, Walter Crew. BS, Austin U., 1951, MEd, 1953. Tchr. math. Kilgore (Tex.) Pub. Schs., 1951-55; programmer Texaco, Houston, 1955-58; mgr. programming Tex. Instruments, Dallas, 1958-62; mgr. system eng. Data Processing Dept. IBM, Ft. Worth, 1962-65; mgr. field system ctr. Data Processing Dept. IBM, Dallas, 1965-70, br. mgr. SW region, 1970-73, mgr. mktg. support SW region, 1974-80; mgr. info. systems edn. CHQ Div. IBM, Irving, Tex., 1980-86; dir. info. and office systems edn. CHQ Div. IBM, Irving, 1986—; mem. adv. bd. U. N.Tex., Denton, Tex., J. Connally Tech., Waco, Tes., com. recruiting of women and minorites sci. career State of Tex., Austin. Office: IBM 1212 Corporate Dr Irving TX 75038

GILES, CLARENCE ALFRED, communications company executive; b. Lake Charles, La., June 12, 1946; s. Leroy William Sr. and June (Murphy) G.; m. Cathy Susan Anderson, July 5, 1967; 1 child, Brandon Hall. BS, Miss. Coll., 1974, JD, 1981. Bar: Miss. 1981, U.S. Dist. Ct. Miss. 1981. With S. Cen. Bell Telephone Co., Jackson, Miss., 1967-71; data systems specialist S. Cen. Bell Telephone Co., Jackson, 1971-78, systems mgr., 1978-83; systems mgr. AT&T Info. Systems, Jackson, 1983-84; location mgr. AT&T Info. Systems, Mobile, Ala., 1984—; owner, chief exec. officer Bus. Communications Distbrs. of Ga., Altanta, Bus. Communications Distbrs. of La., New Orleans, Bus. Communications Distbrs., Inc., Mobile, Ala.; chmn. bd. dirs. Bus. Communications Distbrs. Ga. and La. Mem. Nat. Assn. Telecommunications Dealers (chmn. bd. dirs. 1986—), Miss. Bar Assn., ABA Mobile Area C. of C. Republican. Presbyterian. Office: Bus Communications Distbrs PO Box 9581 Mobile AL 36691

GILES, HOMER WAYNE, lawyer; b. Noble, Ohio, Nov. 9, 1919; s. Edwin Jay and Nola Blanche (Tillison) G.; m. Marcia Ellen Hurt, Oct. 3, 1987; children: Jay, Janice, Keith, Tim, Gregory. A.B., Adelbert Coll., 1940; LL.B., Western Res. Law Sch., 1943, LL.M., 1959. Bar: Ohio bar 1943. Mem. firm Davis & Young, Cleve., 1942-43, William I. Moon, Port Clinton, Ohio, 1946-48; pres. Strabley Baking Co., Cleve., 1948-53; v.p. French Baking Co., Cleve., 1953-55; law clk. 8th Dist Ct. Appeals, Cleve., 1955-58; ptnr. Kuth & Giles, Cleve., 1958-68, Walter, Haverfield, Buescher & Chockley, Cleve., 1968—; pres. Clinton Franklin Realty Co., Cleve., 1958—, Concepts Devel., Inc., 1980—; sec. Holiday Designs, Inc., Sebring, Ohio, 1964—; trustee Teamster Local 52 Health and Welfare Fund, 1950-53; mem. Bakers Negotiating Exec. Com., 1951-53. Contbr. articles to profl. publs.; editor: Banks Baldwin Ohio Legal Forms, 1962. Troop com. chmn. Skyline council Boy Scouts Am., 1961-63; adviser Am. Security Council; trustee Hiram House Camp, Florence Crittenton Home, 1965; chmn. bd. trustees Am. Econ. Found., N.Y.C., 1973-80, chmn. exec. com., 1973-80. Served with AUS, 1943-46, ETO. Mem. Am. Bar Assn., World Law Assn. (founding), Am. Arbitration Assn. (nat. panel), Com. on Econ. Reform and Edn. (life), Inst. Money and Inflation, Speakers Bur. Cleve. Sch. Levy, Citizens League, Pacific Inst., Phila. Soc., Aircraft Owners and Pilots Assn., Cleve. Hist. Soc., Mus. Modern Art, Met. Mus., Mercantile Library, Delta Tau Delta, Delta Theta Phi. Club: The City. Unitarian. Clubs: Cleve. Skating, Cleve. Econ., Harvard Bus., The City. Home: 2588 S Green Rd University Heights OH 44122 Office: Am Econ Found 1215 Terminal Tower Cleveland OH 44113

GILES, JEAN HALL, corporate exececutive; b. Dallas, Mar. 30, 1908; d. C. D. and Ida (McIntyre) Overton; m. Alonzo Russell Hall, II, Jan. 23, 1923 (dec.); children—Marjorie (Mrs. Kenneth C. Hodges, Jr.), Alonzo Russell III; m. 2d, Harry E. Giles, Apr. 24, 1928 (div. 1937); 1 dau., Janice Ruth; 1 adopted dau., Marjean Giles. Capt., comdg. officer S.W. Los Angeles Women's Ambulance and Def. Corps., 1941-43; maj., nat. exec. officer Women's Ambulance and Def. Corps, 1944-45; capt., dir. field ops. Communications Corps of the U.S. Nat. Staff, 1951-52; dir. Recipe of the Month Club. Active Children's Hosp. Benefit, 1946; coordinator War Chest Motor Corps, 1943-44; dir. Los Angeles Area War Chest Vol. Corps and Motor Corps, 1945-46; realtor Los Angeles Real Estate Exchange, 1948—, now ret.; also partner Tech. Contractors, Los Angeles. Bd. dirs. Tchr. Remembrance Day Found. Inc. Mem. Los Angeles C. of C. (women's div.), A.I.M., Los Angeles Art Assn., Hist. Soc. So. Calif., Opera Guild So. Calif., Assistance League So. Calif., Needlework Guild Am. (sect. pres. Los Angeles), First Century Families Calif., Internat. Platform Assn. Clubs: Athletic; Town Hall, The Garden (Los Angles); Pacific Coast. Home: P O Box 01-443 Long Beach CA 90801

GILES, JIM, advertising company executive; b. Borger, Tex., Dec. 5, 1942; s. Johnnie Archie and Mary Ellie (Nugent) G.; m. Sherry Knight, Apr. 1967 (div. 1974); children: Michael, Michelle; m. Carol Ruth Brumley, May 29, 1980; children: Tracy, Courtney. Student, BMI, Longview, Tex., 1963-64, U. South Fla., 1965-66. Mem. sales staff Diversy Chem. Co., Chgo., 1969-72; sales mgr. West Chem. Prodn. Co., L.I., N.Y., 1972-75, Sun Star, Garland, Tex., 1975-76; pres. Gwenco, Inc., Longview, 1976-84; gen. mgr. Tri-Cities Asphalt Co., Longview, 1984-85; v.p. Exec. Hotel Publs., Garland, 1985-86; pres. Selig, Inc. doing bus. as Leisure Host, Creative Concepts, Nat. Fin. Svcs. and AM/PM Answering Service, Longview, 1986—. Active Leadership Longview; bd. dirs., past pres. Longview Jr. Achievement, 1981—; del. Harrison County Dem. Party, 1988; candidate for sch. bd. Hallsville, Tex., 1988. With U.S. Army, 1961-64. Mem. Longview C. of C. (bd. dirs. 1980-84), Kiwanis (bd. dirs. 1980-84). Baptist. Office: Selig Inc 510 E Loop 281 Longview TX 75601

GILL, DANIEL E., optical manufacturing company executive; b. Ziegler, Ill., June 24, 1936; s. Herron E. Gill; m. Dorothy Ann McBride, May 28, 1960. BS in Fin., Northwestern U., 1958. With Abbott Labs., Chgo., 1965-78, corp. v.p., pres. hosp. products div., 1976-78; group v.p. Soflens Products div. Bausch & Lomb, Rochester, N.Y., 1978-80, pres., chief operating officer, 1980-81; pres., chief exec. officer Bausch & Lomb, Rochester, 1981-82, pres., 1982-86, chmn., 1982—, chief exec. officer, 1986—, also bd. dirs. Office: Bausch & Lomb Inc 1 Lincoln First Sq Box 54 Rochester NY 14601 *

GILL, PETER LAWRENCE, electronics company executive; b. Morristown, N.J., Apr. 23, 1942; s. Samuel James and Mildred Evelyn (Lawrence) G.; m. Joyce Gail Varro, Jan. 8, 1966; children: Timothy Dillon, James Lawrence. BS in Biology, Moravian Coll., 1963. Plant bacteriologist Success Chem. Co., Bklyn., N.Y., 1964-65; supr. production E.R. Squibb Inc., New Brunswick, N.J., 1966-71; supt. plant Avery Label, div. Avery Prodns., New Brunswick, N.J., 1971-76; plant mgr. Normandie Press Inc., L.I., N.Y., 1976-80; dir. product devel. Checkpoint Systems Inc., Thorofare, N.J., 1980-83, v.p. product assurance, 1983-85, v.p. tech., 1985—. Co-patentee article surveillance tags. Vestryman St.James Episcopal Ch., Hackettstown, N.J., 1981-83. Served to ensign USNR, 1965-66. Republican. Episcopalian. Lodge: Lions. Office: Checkpoint Systems Inc 550 Grove Rd Thorofare NJ 08086

GILLEN, FLORENCE, computer software company executive; b. N.Y.C., Dec. 3, 1956. Student, U. Rochester, N.Y., 1974-76. Mgr. product support div. Informatics/Decision Strategy, N.Y.C., 1976-81; pres. Source of Future Tech. Inc, N.Y.C., 1981—. Office: Source Future Tech Inc 137 Varick St New York NY 10013

GILLEN, JAMES ROBERT, insurance company executive; b. N.Y.C., Nov. 14, 1937; s. James Matthew and Katharine Isabel (Fritz) G.; m. Rita Marie Wahleithner, June 15, 1963; children: Jennifer Elaine, Nancy Louise, Paula Anne. A.B. magna cum laude, Harvard U., 1959, LL.B. cum laude, 1965. Bar: N.Y. 1966, N.J. 1975. Assoc. firm White & Case, N.Y.C., 1965-72; v.p., assoc. gen. counsel Prudential Ins. Co. Am., Newark, 1972-77, sr. v.p., assoc. gen. counsel, 1977-80, sr. v.p. pub. affairs, 1980-84, sr. v.p., gen. counsel, 1984—; mem. legal adv. com. New York Stock Exchange, 1986—. Trustee United Way Essex and West Hudson Counties, 1981—, pres., 1986-88; mem. Mendham Twp. (N.J.) Bd. Edn., 1981-82; trustee Mendham Twp. Library, 1979-82. Served to lt. (j.g.) USN, 1959-62. Mem. ABA, N.J. Bar Assn., Assn. Life Ins. Counsel. Club: Essex (Newark). Home: 12 Hamilton Dr Morristown NJ 07960 Office: Prudential Ins Co Am Prudential Plaza 23 Pla Newark NJ 07101

GILLENS, CLARA B(ELLE), management consultant, construction executive, consultant; b. Orangeburg, S.C., May 5, 1954; d. Saul and Annie Mae (Lee) G.; m. Eurgle Leroy Ruan Sr., Feb. 23, 1973 (div. Feb. 1982); children: Eurgle Leroy Jr., Katrice LaVerne. Student, Hofstra U., 1971-73, SUNY, Westbury, 1982-83, Adelphi U., 1983—. With spl. svcs. European Am. Bank, Mineola, N.Y., 1978-82; ops. mgr. Accurate Enterprises, N.Y.C., 1982-85; pres., chief exec. officer G&M Bus. Assocs., Hempstead, N.Y., 1984—; lectr. Hempstead Pub. Schs., 1985-87, N.Y. state chpt. NOW, N.Y.C., 1984-86, Hempstead Town Minority Bus. Coun., 1985—. Chairperson L.I. Equal Opportunity Coun., Hempstead, 1980—; exec. dir. L.I. Affirmative Action Program, Hempstead, 1986-87. Recipient Cert. Appreciation Family Service Assn., 1983, Vol. Service award L.I. Women's Equal Opportunity, 1985, Citation, Town of Hempstead, 1988. Mem. Am. Mgmt. Assn., Assn. Minority Enterprises. Republican. Methodist. Office: G&M Bus Assocs 250 Fulton Ave Ste 507 Hempstead NY 11550

GILLENWATER, CHAD MICHIE, management consultant; b. Elkins, W.Va., Dec. 30, 1947; s. Joseph Barron and Jean (Michie) G.; m. Mary Elizabeth Gillenwater, Dec. 18, 1971 (div. 1974); m. Mary Ellen Gillenwater, Jan. 29, 1983; children: Heather, Chad Michie Jr., Lyndsey. BS, U. Md., 1973; MBA, George Washington U., 1982. CPA, Md. Pres. Oak Mar Constrn. Co., Inc., College Park, Md., 1978-82; chief fin. officer Dylarabia Co. Ltd., Riyadh, Saudi Arabia, 1982-84, Md. Sound Industries, Inc., Balt., 1984—; sr. account facilitator Orgn. Mgmt. Co., Balt., 1986—. Contbr. articles to entertainment and fin. publs. Vice chmn. Pvt. Industry Coun. Prince Georges County, 1980; mem. Howard County Republican Com. Mem. AICPA, Md. Assn. CPA's (cooperation with fin. instns. com.), Assoc. Builders and Contractors (bd. dirs. 1980), Assn. for Corp. Growth, Masons, Lions (v.p. 1988, pres.-elect 1989). Presbyterian. Office: Md Sound Industries Inc 4900 Wetheredsville Rd Baltimore MD 21207

GILLER, NORMAN MYER, bank executive; b. Jacksonville, Fla., Feb. 14, 1918; s. Morris and Esther (Seltzer) G.; m. Frances Schwartz, June 30, 1946; children: Ira D., Anita Giller Grossman, Brian. Student, Ga. Inst. Tech., 1943-44; BArch, U. Fla., 1945; postgrad. in banking, Bankers Adminstrn. Inst., 1965-66. Chmn. bd. Norman M. Giller and Assocs., Miami Beach, Fla., 1945—; chmn. bd., pres. Interam. Nat. Bank, Miami Beach, 1964-68; vice chmn. Jefferson Bancorp, Miami Beach, 1968—; pres., vice chmn. Jefferson Nat. Bank, Sunny Isles, Fla., 1968—; bd. dirs. Jefferson Nat. Bank, Miami Beach, Jefferson Nat. Bank of Palm Beach, Boca Raton, Fla., Jefferson Bank of Broward, Hollywood, Fla.; cons. U.S. Dept. State, Washington, 1961-70, Govts. Panama, Nicaragua, Brazil, Colombia, El Salvador, 1961-70. Author: An Adventure in Architecture, 1977, A Century in America, 1986; contbr. articles on architecture to profl. jours. Chmn. Miami Beach Housing Authority, 1970, Fla. State Bd. Architecture, Tallahassee, 1979, Design Rev. Bd. City of Miami Beach, 1985; pres. So. Fla. council Boy Scouts Am., 1961-63, Concerned Citizens of NE Dade County, Miami Beach, 1970; sec. Nat. Council Archtl. Registration Bd., SE Atlanta, 1981; mem. Sunny Isles Tak Force, Fla., 1982. Served to lt. (j.g.) USNR, 1942-46. Named Man of Yr., Gold Coast C. of C., 1973; bridge named in his honor, Fla. Legis., Miami Beach, 1983. Fellow AIA (pres. South Fla. chpt. 1945—, Silver medal 1979); mem. Fla. Assn. Architecture (bd. dirs. 1945—, Community Service award 1982), Am. Bankers Assn., Fla. Bankers Assn. (mem. com. 1965—), Fla. Bankers Holding Co. Assn., Miami Beach C. of C. (pres. 1970—). Democrat. Jewish. Lodges: Masons, Shriners. Office: Jefferson Bancorp Inc 301 Arthur Godfrey Rd Miami Beach FL 33140

GILLES, KENNETH ALBERT, governmental administrator, biochemist; b. Mpls., Mar. 6, 1922; s. Albert Peter and Alma Ruby (Stodghill) G.; m. Beverly Elaine Barrows, July 1, 1944; children—Jeffrey Alan, Diane Elaine. B.S., U. Minn., 1944, Ph.D., 1952. Research engr. Pillsbury Co., Mpls., Minn., 1946-49; research fellow, instr. U. Minn., St. Paul, 1949-52; project leader Gen. Mills, Inc., Mpls., 1952-61; prof., chmn. cereal chemistry dept. N.D. State U., 1961-69; v.p. agr. N.D. State U., Fargo, 1969-81; adminstr. Fed. Grain Inspection Service USDA, Washington, 1981-86; asst. sec., dir. Commodity Credit Corp. USDA, Washington, DC, 1986—; chmn. Great Plains Agrl. Council, Lincoln, Nebr., 1972-73; guest lectr. Royal Australian Chem. Inst., Canberra, 1970. Editor-in-chief Cereal Chemistry, 1961-68; also articles and monographs. Chmn. City Planning Commn., Roseville, Minn., 1955-60, Park Bd., Roseville, 1960-61; bd. dirs. Fargo Indsl. Devel. Corp., 1977-81. Served to lt. (j.g.) USNR, 1943-46; PTO. Named Man of the Yr., Roseville C. of C., 1961. Fellow AAAS; mem. Am. Assn. Cereal Chemists (pres. 1971-72, bd. dirs. 1969-73, chmn. bd. Geddes award 1976), Am. Chem. Soc. (program com.), Inst. Food Techs., Assn. Operative Millers, N.D. Stockmen's Assn. (hon. life mem.), N.D. Wheat Producers Assn. (hon. Kernel 1981), Sigma Xi, Alpha Zeta. Republican. Episcopalian. Lodges: Lions, Masons, Shriners. Office: Dept Agr Mktg & Inspection Svcs 14th & Independence Ave SW Washington DC 20250

GILLESPIE, ALEXANDER JOSEPH, JR., lawyer; b. N.Y.C., Sept. 2, 1923; s. Alexander Joseph and Catharine (Allen) G.; m. Elizabeth Margaret Roth, Dec. 4, 1944; children: Robert Daniel, James Edward, William Gerard, Patricia Elise, Anne Marie. A.B. magna cum laude, Dartmouth Coll., 1943; J.D., Fordham U., 1957. Credit mgr. cosmetic div. Vick Chem. Co., 1946-50; dist. sales mgr. Avco Mfg. Co., 1950-54; assoc. atty. Breed Abbot & Morgan, 1957-60; asst. gen. counsel ASARCO Inc. (formerly Am. Smelting & Refining Co.), N.Y.C., 1960-68; sec. ASARCO Inc. (formerly Am. Smelting & Refining Co.), 1968-69, sec., gen. counsel, 1969-86, v.p., 1972-77, sr. v.p., sec., gen. counsel, 1977-84, gen. counsel, 1984-86, vice chmn., dir., 1986-89; of counsel Breed, Abbott & Morgan, N.Y.C., 1989—; arbitrator Nat. Assn. Security Dealers, Am. Arbitration Assn. Mem. adv. bd. Southwest Legal Found., Parker Sch. Internat. Law Columbia U.; bd. dirs. Silver Hill Found. Served to lt. (j.g.) USNR, 1943-46, PTO. Mem. ABA, N.Y. State Bar Assn., Assn. Bar City N.Y., Conn. Bar Assn., N.Y. County Lawyers Assn., Americas Soc., Assn. Gen. Counsel, N.Y. Chamber Commerce and Industry, Peruvian Am. Assn., Phi Beta Kappa, Delta Upsilon, Gamma Eta Gamma. Episcopalian. Clubs: Wall St. (gov. 1984—), Dartmouth Coll., World Trade (N.Y.C.); Stanwich (Greenwich, Conn.). Home: 30 Will Merry Ln Greenwich CT 06831 Office: Asarco Inc 180 Maiden Ln New York NY 10038

GILLESPIE, EDWARD MALCOLM, hospital administrator; b. Mpls., Oct. 19, 1935; s. Harold Livingston and Alice May (Thompson) G.; children: Karin, Timothy, Kenneth. B.S., U. Minn., 1957, M.P.A., 1959, M.H.A., 1962. Engaged in refugee adminstrn. Linz, Austria, 1958-60; asst. adminstr. Lutheran Med. Center, Denver, 1962-66; asst. gen. sec. Methodist Bd. Health and Welfare Ministries, Evanston, Ill., 1966-69; adminstr. Meth. Hosp., Rochester, Minn., 1969-74, Univ. Hosp., Augusta, Ga., 1974—; bd. dirs. Augusta Area Mental Health, Augusta Speech and Hearing Center, St. John's Towers, CSRA Blood Assurance; chmn. hosp. div. certification council Meth. Health and Welfare. Bd. dirs. local United Way, Boy Scouts Am. Fellow Am. Coll. Hosp. Adminstrs.; mem. Am., Ga. hosp. assns. Methodist. Club: Augusta Rotary (dir.). Home: 1413 Waters Edge Augusta GA 30909 Office: U Hosp 1350 Walton Way Augusta GA 30910

GILLESPIE, HARRY ROBINSON, management consultant; b. Oak Park, Ill., May 24, 1922; s. Harry Robinson and Margaret Louise (Weisskirchen) G.; m. Shirley Hodek, June 21, 1944; children: Anne Louise, Andrew Scott, Douglas Robinson. BSME, Ill. Inst. Tech., 1944; student exec. program, U. Chgo., 1954-55; postgrad., Claremont Coll., 1960; MBA, Pepperdine U., 1975; D Bus. Adminstrn., U.S. Internat. U., 1980. Registered profl. engr., Ill. Engr., engring. mgr. then div. mgr. Cinch Mfg. Corp., Chgo., 1947-58; div. mgr. Edcliff Instruments, Inc., Monrovia, Calif., 1958-62; pres., gen. mgr. Robinson Components Co., Temple City, Calif., 1962-70; gen. mgr. Los Angeles div. Virco Mfg. Co., 1970-75; v.p. adminstrn. B.P. John Co., Santa Ana, Calif., 1975-76; pres., gen. mgr. Hancock Mfg. Co. subs. Samsonite Corp., San Diego, 1977-81; cons. gen. mgmt. and telecommunications Mgmt. Analysis Co., San Diego, 1981—; adj. prof. Mgmt. Nat. U., San Diego, 1981—. Author: Advanced Mathematics and an Introduction to Calculus, 1947; co-author Telecommunications Challenges for the Electric Utility Industry, 1987; contbr. chpt. The Seven Phases of Strategic Planning, 1986; contbr. articles to profl. jours. Served with USN, 1945-47. Mem. IEEE, Acad. Mgmt., Stategic Mgmt. Soc. Republican. Presbyterian. Home: 7960 Via Capri La Jolla CA 92037 Office: Mgmt Analysis Co 12671 High Bluff Dr San Diego CA 92130

GILLESPIE, J. MARTIN, sales and distribution company executive; b. Detroit, Sept. 27, 1949; s. John Martin and Shirley Ann (Rees) G.; BBA, Xavier U., 1971; MBA, U. Mich., 1973; m. Jeannette Downes, Sept. 27, 1975; children: Heather, Tara. Account exec. Foote Cone & Belding, Chgo., 1973-76; account supr., 1976-77; mktg. mgr. Hansen Corp., Walled Lake,

Mich., 1977-80, gen. mgr., 1980-82; chmn., chief exec. officer Hansen Mktg. Services, Inc., Walled Lake, 1982—. Recipient Merit award Nat. Alliance Businessmen, 1973. Mem. Assn. MBA Execs., Am. Mgmt. Assn., Nat. Acad. TV Arts and Scis., Nat. Assn. Credit Mgmt., Nat. Bldg. Materials Distbn. Assn., Alpha Kappa Psi. Home: 3792 W Pemberton Bloomfield Hills MI 48013 Office: Hansen Mktg Svcs Inc 1000 Decker Rd PO Box 638 Walled Lake MI 48088

GILLESPIE, JOE DANIEL, real estate investor; b. Longview, Wash., June 21, 1947; s. Emmett Harold and Louise Joan (Sparks) G.; m. Gail Elizabeth Bordon,. Nov. 29, 1968; 1 child, Joe Daniel. BS, U. Wash., 1969. Lic. real estate broker, Wash. Mgr. dist. sales Crowell Collier & McMillan Inc., Portland, Oreg., 1969-72; sr. sales cons. Coldwell Banker Comml. Real Estate, Portland and Seattle, 1972-81; v.p., dir. mktg. Coldwell Banker Comml. Real Estate, Houston, 1981-83; acquisitions officer, ltd. gen. ptnr. Hall Fin. Group, Dallas, 1983-84; v.p., dir. acquisitions Am. Residential Properties, Houston, 1984-86; v.p., dir. acquisitions, ptnr. Drever Ptnrs., Houston, 1987—. Mem. Rotary Club. Office: Drever Ptnrs 4801 Woodway St 300E Houston TX 77056

GILLESPIE, JOHN FAGAN, mining executive; b. Cleve., Aug. 16, 1936; s. James Patrick and Mary Isabelle (Fagan) G.; student John Carroll U., 1955-58, U. Tulsa, 1970-71; m. Dorothy May LaForest, July 6, 1962; 1 son, Kelly Joseph. With Great Lakes Dredge and Dock Co., Cleve., 1955-63, project supt., 1962-63; owner, operator Tri-Angle Bldg. and Wrecking Co., Bay City, Mich., 1963-65; with Martin Marietta Corp., 1965-71; with Aetna Portland Cement Co., Bay City, 1965-69, prodn. supt., 1968-69; maintenance supt. Dewey Rocky Mountain Cement Co., Tulsa, 1969-71; plant mgr. Kellstone Inc., Kelley's Island, Ohio, 1971-73; plant mgr. Lyon Sand and Gravel Co., Wixom, Mich., 1973-75; area mgr. J. P. Burroughs & Son, Inc., Aggregate div. subs. Blount, Inc., Montgomery, Ala., 1975, asst. to pres., 1975-76, mgr. ops., 1976-78, gen. mgr., 1978-81; pres., chief exec. officer, chmn. bd. Tilcon N.Y. Inc., Haverstraw, N.Y., 1981—; pres., chief exec. officer Tilcon Quarries New York Inc., 1981—. Vice-chmn. Mich. Mineral Resources Assn., 1977-81; mem. Small Bus. Conf., State of Mich., 1977-81. Bd. visitors Helen Hayes Hosp., 1985—; mem. corp. adv. council Columbia Presbyn. Hosp.; bd. dirs. Rockland Community Coll., 1985—, Rockland Econ. Devel. Corp., NYACK Hosp. Found., 1985—. Mem. Detroit Engring. Soc., Am. Mgmt. Assn., Pvt. Industry Council (bd. dirs. 1985—), Mich. Mineral Resources Assn. (past vice-chmn.), Nat. Sand and Gravel Assn., Nat. Crushed Stone Assn. (chmn. flugas com.), Mich. Sand and Gravel Producers Assn. (chief negotiation, sec.-treas.). Republican. Roman Catholic. Home: 11 Wildwood Rd Katonah NY 10536 Office: PO Box 362 Haverstraw NY 10927

GILLESPIE, JOSEPH RAYMOND, bank executive, lawyer; b. Louisville, May 17, 1950; s. Joseph E. and Anna L. (Portman) G.; m. Gloria G. Sanders, Dec. 13, 1979; 1 child, Scott. BA, U. Louisville, 1975, JD, 1981. Bar: Ky. 1981. Dept. mgr. K Mart Stores, Louisville, 1970-72; area supr. Ayrway Dept. Stores, Louisville, 1972-73; zoning officer Jefferson County Govt., Louisville, 1973-75; dir. Southwest Govt. Ctr., Louisville, 1975-78; regional dir. Office of the Gov., Frankfort, Ky., 1978-79; stockbroker, account exec. Blackburn-Sanford Securities, Louisville, 1980-81; employee benefits officer Stock Yards Bank and Trust Co., Louisville, 1981—; sole practice law Louisville, 1981—; bd. dirs. Lab. Physicians Inc. (sec. 1984—). Active Grass Roots Dem. Club, Louisville, 1973-78; mem. Louisville Employee Benefits Council. Mem. Ky. Bar Assn., Louisville Bar Assn., Louisville Estate Planning Forum. Presbyterian. Club: Lakeside Swim (louisville). Home: 2228 Saratoga Dr Louisville KY 40205 Office: Stock Yards Bank & Trust Co 1040 E Main St Louisville KY 40206

GILLESPIE, ROBERT WAYNE, banker; b. Cleve., Mar. 26, 1944; s. Robert Walton and Eleanore (Parsons) G.; m. Ann. L. Wible, June 17, 1967; children: Laura, Gwen. B.A., Ohio Wesleyan U., 1966; M.B.A., Case Western Res. U., 1968; postgrad., Harvard U., 1979. Credit analyst Soc. Nat. Bank, Cleve., 1968-70, v.p., 1970-76, sr. v.p., 1976-79; exec. v.p. Soc. Nat Bank, Cleve., 1979-81; vice-chmn., chief operating officer Soc. Nat. Bank, Cleve., 1981-83, pres., chief operating officer, 1983-85, chief exec. officer, 1985—, pres., 1987—, chmn., 1988—; chmn. North Coast Devel. Corp. Trustee Case Western Res. U., Ohio Wesleyan U., Univ. Hosps. of Cleve., Greater Cleve. Roundtable, Cleve. Tomorrow. Office: Soc Corp 800 Superior Ave Cleveland OH 44114

GILLET, ANDRE, food products executive; b. Paris, 1926. Grad., U. Paris, 1944. With Internat. Multifoods Corp., 1951—, div. v.p., gen. mgr. internat. div., 1968-79, exec. v.p. internat. div., 1979-83, pres., chief operating officer, 1983-84, pres., chief exec. officer, 1984-85, chmn., chief exec. officer, 1985—. Office: Internat Multifoods Corp Box 2942 Minneapolis MN 55402 *

GILLET, RONALD ALLEN, energy company executive; b. Louisville, Dec. 21, 1941; s. Elmer William and Kathryn Alice (kouts) G.; m. Merry Sue Haeber, Oct. 4, 1968. BA, U. Tex., 1967; MBA, Tex. A&I U., 1974. Programmer thru asst. v.p. Coastal Corp., Houston, 1967-85; v.p. ANR Pipeline, Detroit, 1986—; bd. dirs. Rolling Fork Utility Dist., 1982. Mem. exec. bd. Attic Theater, Detroit, 1988. Served with U.S. Army, 1962-65. Mem. Am. Gas Assn., So. Gas Assn., Soc. for Info. Mgmt., Data Processing Mgmt. Assn. (chpt. pres 1985), Mensa. Republican. Clubs: Grosse Pointe (Mich.) Newcomers; Detroit Athletic; Rolling Fork (bd. dirs. 1984) (Houston). Home: 1000 Three Mile Dr Grosse Pointe Park MI 48230 Office: ANR Pipeline 500 Renaissance Ctr Detroit MI 48243

GILLETT, VICTOR WILLIAM, JR., title insurance company executive; b. El Paso, Tex., Feb. 4, 1932; s. Victor William and Alice Cecelia (Kemper) G.; BBA, Tex. A&M U., 1953; m. Anita Johanne Dexter, Mar. 1, 1975; children: Victor William, III, Blake Andrew. V.p., dist. mgr. Stewart Title Guaranty Co., Corpus Christi, Tex., 1955-61; pres., chief exec. officer Stewart Title & Trust Co., Phoenix, 1961-77, dir., 1965-77; sr. v.p., nat. mktg. dir. Stewart Title Guaranty Co., Houston, 1977—, dir., 1981—; sr. v.p. Stewart Title Guaranty Co., Irvine, Calif., 1988—; dir. Stewart Info. Svcs. Corp. Bd. dirs. Ariz. Heart Assn., 1970-73; bd. dirs., sec. Phoenix Civic Improvement Corp., 1974-76; mem. Newport Harbor Art Mus. With AUS, 1953-54. Mem. Am. Land Title Assn. (gov. 1969-71), Nat. Assn. Corp. Real Estate Execs., Mortgage Bankers Assn. Am., Nat. Assn. Indsl. and Office Parks, Internat. Council Shopping Ctrs., Assn. U.S. Army (pres., dir. 1968), Navy League, Former Students Assn. Tex. A&M U., Aggie Club (Tex. A&M U.). Episcopalian. Home and Office: 10 Harbor Crest Irvine CA 92714

GILLETTE, HALBERT SCRANTON, publisher; b. Chgo., June 29, 1922; s. Edward Scranton and Claribel (Thornton) G.; B.S., M.I.T., 1944; m. Mary Livingston, Feb. 12, 1949 (dec. Jan. 1962); children—Anne Livingston, Susan L.; m. Karla Ann McCall, June 8, 1963; children—James McCall, Halbert G., Edward S. II. Space buyer Andrews Agy., 1946-48; advt. mgr. Good Roads Mach. Co., Minerva, Ohio, 1948; exec. v.p. Gillette Pub. Co., Chgo., 1949-72, Scranton Pub. Co., Chgo., 1972-77, Ins. News, Inc., Phoenix; pres. Scranton Gillette Communications, Inc., 1977—; chmn. bd., pres. Doctor's Tax Letter, Inc., Publisher's Paper Co., Inc., Ednl. Screen Inc., Diapason, Inc., Piano Trade Mag., Florist and Nursery Exchange, 1972-77; chmn. bd. Occidental Life Ins. Co. N.C., 1973-74, McMillen Co., Jacksonville, Fla., 1974-77; dir. Occidental Fire & Casualty Co., Denver. Mem. Lake Forest City Council. Served to ensign USNR, World War II. Mem. Phi Gamma Delta. Club: Onwentsia (Lake Forest, Ill.). Home: 255 Foster Pl Lake Forest IL 60045 Office: 380 NW Hwy Des Plaines IL 60016

GILLEY, JAMES RAY, real estate/financial services executive; b. Surry County, N.C., Apr. 25, 1934; s. William Hassel and Delsie May (Brinkley) G.; m. Sylvia Ray Messick, Mar. 28, 1954; children: William Michael, Elizabeth Dale, Nita Ann. B.A., Wake Forest U., 1957, M.B.A., 1972. Pres. 7-11 Food Store N.C., Inc., Winston-Salem, 1959-61; pres. Stop & Shop of N.C., Winston-Salem, 1957-66, Gilley Leasing Co., Winston-Salem, 1966-69, Convenient Systems, Inc., Winston-Salem, 1969-73; exec. v.p., chief fin. officer The Washington Group, Inc., Winston-Salem, 1973-75; pres. The Washington Group, Inc., 1975-77; chmn. bd., pres., chief exec. officer Hungry Bull Assocs., Spartanburg, S.C., 1978-80; pres. Southmark Communities, Inc., 1981—; v.p. Southmark Corp., 1981—, exec. v.p., 1984—; dir. Integon Corp., Northwestern Bank, Salem Carpet Co., Piedmont Fed. Savs. and Loan Assn., all Winston-Salem. Mem. Mayors Com. Recreation Parks, Forsyth County, N.C.; chmn. bd. dirs. Better Bus. Bur., Winston-Salem, 1974-76; trustee Wake Forest U., 1974-78, Gardner Webb Coll., 1969-73; bd. visitors Babcock Sch. Mgmt., Wake Forest U., 1973—. Recipient Disting. Alumni Service citation Wake Forest U., 1974. Mem. Winston-Salem C. of C., Fin. Execs. Inst., Newcomen Soc. Baptist (deacon). Clubs: Forsyth Country (Winston-Salem), Twin City (Winston-Salem). Office: Southmark Corp 1601 LBJ Frwy Dallas TX 75234 *

GILLHAM, ROBERT, bank executive; b. N.Y.C., Aug. 21, 1938; s. Robert Marty and Elizabeth (Enright) G.; m. Carol Searing, Apr. 12, 1969; children: Robert C., Timothy N. B.A., Harvard U., 1962; postgrad., NYU Grad. Sch. Bus. Adminstrn., 1967-68. With Chem. Bank, N.Y.C., 1966—, asst. sec., 1969-72, asst. v.p., 1972-74, v.p., 1974-82, sr. v.p., from 1982, now mng. dir. Served with U.S. Army, 1962-65. Democrat. Unitarian. Home: 4 Glen Blvd Glen Rock NJ 07452 Office: Chem Bank 277 Park Ave New York NY 10172

GILLIAM, JAMES H., JR., corporation lawyer; b. Balt., Apr. 21, 1945; m. Randilyn Woodruff; children: Alexis Randilyn, Leslie Brooke. BA in English, Morgan State U., 1967; JD, Columbia U., 1970. Bar: Del., N.Y. Assoc. Paul, Weiss, Rifkind, Wharton & Garrison, N.Y.C., 1970-73, Richards, Layton & Finger, Wilmington, Del., 1973-76; cabinet sec. Dept. Community Affairs and Econ. Devel., State of Del., 1977-79; v.p. legal Beneficial Corp., 1979-81, sr. v.p. legal 1982-85, sr. v.p., 1986-89, gen. counsel, 1986—, sec., 1987—, exec. v.p., 1989—, also mem. exec. com. bd. dirs. Beneficial Corp.; chmn. bd. dirs. Beneficial Nat. Bank; bd. dirs. Beneficial Real Estate Joint Ventures, Inc., Bell Atlantic Corp. Trustee, bd. dirs. Med. Ctr. Del.; trustee Howard Hughes Med. Inst., Adv. Ctr. to Del. region NCCJ. Active Del. Roundtable, Inc., Nat. Guardsmen, Inc.; chmn. Del. campaign United Negro Coll. Fund, 1987; former chmn. bd. Del. C. of C.; chmn. bd. trustees Goldey Beacom Coll.; mem. bd. overseers Widener U. Sch. Law Mem. ABA, NBA, Del. Bar Assn., Univ. Club, Whist Club, Rodney Square Club (bd. govs.), Brandywine Country Club, Monday Club, Sigma Pi Phi, Kappa Alpha Psi. Avocations: tennis, jogging, water sports. Home: 109 Weldin Park Dr Wilmington DE 19803 Office: Beneficial Corp PO Box 911 Wilmington DE 19899

GILLICE, SONDRA JUPIN (MRS. GARDNER RUSSELL BROWN), personnel executive; b. Urbana, Ill.; d. Earl Cranston and Laura Lorraine (Rose) Jupin; BS, Lindenwood Coll., 1958; MBA, Loyola Coll., 1982; m. Gardner Russell Brown, Jan. 12, 1980; 1 son, Thomas Alan Gillice. Div. tng. supr. Liberty Mut. Ins. Co., Chgo., N.Y.C., 1958-68; personnel officer N.Y. Citibank, 1968-70, 1st Nat. Bank of Chgo., 1970-72; mgr. human resources Potomac Electric Power Co., Washington, 1973-81; dir. personnel U.S. Synthetic Fuels Corp., Washington, 1981-86, v.p. human resources, Guest Services, Inc., 1987—. Mem. industry adv. bd. Behrend Coll., Pa. State U. Mem. Edison Electric Inst. (chmn. tng. and mgmt. devel. com.), AAUW (pres. Falls Church br. 1976-78), Washington Nat. Restaurant Assn., Am. Soc. Personnel Adminstrs., Washington Personnel Assn., Greater Met. Washington Bd. Trade, Soroptimists (pres. Washington chpt. 1979-80), DAR, Army Navy Country, Soc. Magna Charta Dames, Edgartown Yacht Club, Country Club of Culpeper, Inc. Republican.

GILLIGAN, MARTIN EDWARD, JR., manufacturing executive; b. Ventura, Calif., Mar. 26, 1938; s. Martin Edward Sr. and Emilia P. (Franek) G.; m. Paula S. Wilms, June 13, 1959 (div. 1966); children: Martin Edward III, Letitia Lynn; m. Darylann Bracken, Feb. 22, 1969; 1 child, Laura Lynn. BS in Mech. Engring., Loyola U., L.A., 1961, JD, 1965. Rsch. engr., contract adminstr. Precision Producers div. Western Gear Corp., Lynwood, Calif., 1959-63, mgr. contracts, adminstrn. Precision Products div., 1967-73; supr. systems and procedures, exec. asst. space div. Rockwell Internat., Downey, Calif., 1963-67; v.p. sales and adminstrn. Precision Structures div. Automation Industries, Inc., Abilene, Tex., 1973-77; v.p., gen. mgr. Moore Internat., Memphis, 1977-79; v.p. ops. York (Pa.) Shipley, Inc., 1979-86; sr. v.p. mktg. Donlee Technologies, Inc., York, 1986—; bd. dirs. Control Techtronics, Inc., Harrisburg, Pa., Small Enterprise Devel. Corp., York; lectr. Pa. State U., 1987—; mem. adv. bd. Ben Franklin Partnership Program, 1981—, CYBER Ctr. Small Bus. Incubator, York, 1982—. Founding dir. York County Labor-Mgmt. Council, 1985-87. Mem. Soc. Mfg. Engrs., Licensing Execs. Soc., Nat. Contract Mgmt. Assn., Am. Boiler Mfrs. Assn., Mfrs. Agts. Nat. Assn., York Area C. of C. (bd. dirs. 1985-88). Republican. Roman Catholic. Home: 2250 Boddington Pl York PA 17402 Office: Donlee Technologies Inc 693 N Hills Rd York PA 17402

GILLIS, CHRISTINE DIEST-LORGION, financial planner, stockbroker; b. San Francisco; d. Evert Jan and Christine Helen (Radcliffe) Diest-Lorgion; B.S., U. Calif., Berkeley; M.S., U. So. Calif.; children—Barbara Gillis Pieper, Suzanne Gillis Seymour (twins). Cert. fin. planner. Account exec. Winslow, Cohu & Stetson, N.Y.C., 1962-63, Paine Webber, N.Y.C., 1964-65; sr. investment exec. Shearson Hammill, Beverly Hills, Calif., 1966-72; cert. fin. planner, asst. v.p. EF Hutton, 1972-87; 2nd v.p. Shearson Lehman Hutton, Glendale, Calif., 1988; v.p. investments Dean Witter Reynolds, Glendale, 1988—. Cert. fin. planner. Mem. Inst. Cert. Fin. Planners, Town Hall of Calif. (life, corp. sec. 1974-75, dir., gov. 1976-80), Women Stockbrokers Assn. (founding pres. N.Y.C. 1963), Women of Wall Street West (pres. 1979-84), Navy League (life; dir.), Assistance League Pasadena, AAUW (life; trustee ednl. found.), Bus. and Profl. Women, U. Calif.-Berkeley Alumni Assn. (life), Town and Gown (life), Rotary (charter), DESCAMSO, Sunrise Club, Phi Chi Theta (life). Episcopalian. Home: 959 Regent Park Dr La Canada Flintridge CA 91011 Office: 801 N Brand Blvd Ste 908 Glendale CA 91209

GILLIS, MARVIN BOB, investor, consultant; b. Treutlen County, Ga., Apr. 5, 1920; s. Bob Lee and Pearl (Gillis) G.; m. Helen Reed, Dec. 23, 1946; children: Margaret Susan, Marvin Reed, Kenneth Robert. B.S.A., U. Ga., 1940; Ph.D., Cornell U., 1947. Research asso. Cornell U., 1947-51; research chemist Internat. Minerals and Chem. Corp., from 1947, asst. dir. research, 1956-57, dir. research, 1957-64, dir. animal health and nutrition, 1964-66, div. v.p., 1966-70, corp. v.p., 1970-72, sr. v.p., 1972-82; pres., dir. IMC Chems. Group, Inc., 1976-78; pres. Animal Products Group, 1978-82, cons. to exec. office, 1982-86; pres. Micro-Pacific Ltd., Glenview, Ill., 1982—; sec. Agrl. Research Inst., Nat. Acad. Scis.-NRC, 1958-59, v.p., 1960-62, 66-67, pres., 1962-63, 68-69, mem. agrl. bd., 1962-67; bd. dirs. Animal Health Inst., 1966-69. Author numerous papers in field; patentee in field. Served to 1st lt. USAAF, 1942-45. Decorated D.F.C. with oak leaf cluster, Air medal with 3 oak leaf clusters. Mem. Am. Chem. Soc., Blue Key, Sigma Xi, Gamma Alpha, Alpha Zeta, Phi Kappa Phi, North Shore Country Club, Sea Island Club, St. Simons Island (Ga.). Baptist. Office: Micro-Pacific Ltd 2116 Larkdale Dr Glenview IL 60025

GILLIS, NELSON SCOTT, financial executive; b. Pitts., May 6, 1953; s. Nelson Williams and Elinor (Miller) G.; m. Vickie Sue Hall, Nov. 22, 1980; children: Michael David, Matthew Daniel. Nathan Alexander. BS in Acctg., Fla. State U., 1975; postgrad. AEA Exec. Inst., Stanford, 1984. CPA, Ga. Audit sr., Price Waterhouse & Co., Atlanta, 1975-78; sr. acct. Siemens Energy and Automation, Inc., 1978-80; div. controller, Portland, Oreg., 1980-83; v.p. fin. Integrated Circuits Inc., Redmond, Wash., 1983-85; dir. Controls Evaluation and Audit Kaufman & Broad, Inc., Atlanta, 1985— . Mem. fin. officers com. Life Insurers Conf.; mem. fin. compliance com. Sun Life Group Am., Inc. Spl. rep. World Radio Missionary Fellowship; mem. stewardship com., treas., deacon, Sunday sch. tchr. Briarwood Bapt. Ch. Fellow Life Mgmt. Inst.; mem. Am. Inst. CPAs, Inst. Internal Auditors, Ins. Internal Audit Group, Life Office Mgmt. Assn. (fin. controls and reports com.), Ga. Soc. CPAs (mem. ins. adv. com.), Atlanta Fellow Life Mgmt. Inst. Soc., Fla. State Alumni Assn., Beta Gamma Sigma, Lambda Chi Alpha. Republican. Office: Kaufman & Broad Inc care Sun Life Group 260 Peachtree St NW Atlanta GA 30303

GILLMAR, STANLEY FRANK, lawyer; b. Honolulu, Aug. 17, 1935; s. Stanley Eric and Ruth (Scudder) G.; m. Constance Joan Sedgwick; children: Sara Tamsin, Amy Katherine. AB cum laude with high honors, Brown U., 1957; LLB, Harvard U., 1963. Bar: Calif. 1963. Ptnr. Graham & James, San Francisco, 1970—. Co-author: How To Be An Importer and Pay For Your World Travels, 1979; co-pub.: Travelers Guide to Importing, 1980. Sec. Calif. Council Internat. Trade, 1973—; mem. Mayor San Francisco Adv. Council Econ. Devel., 1976-82; mem. Title IX Loan Bd., 1982—, sec. 1986—. Served with USNR, 1957-60. Mem. ABA, Calif. State Bar, Bar Assn. San Francisco. Clubs: Bankers (San Francisco); Villa Taverna, Inverness Yacht. Office: Graham & James Ste 300 Alcoa Bldg 1 Maritime Pla San Francisco CA 94111

GILLMOR, JOHN EDWARD, lawyer; b. Phila., Oct. 26, 1937; s. John Edward and Louise Ann (Porter) G.; m. Allis Dale Brannon, Aug. 17, 1968; children: Sarah, Abigail, Susan, Eleanor, John, Matthew. B.A., Swarthmore Coll., 1959; LL.B., U. Pa., 1962. Bar: N.Y. 1963, Tenn. 1972, Pa. 1980, D.C. 1962. Asso. Dewey Ballantine Bushby Palmer & Wood, 1962-63, 66-71; v.p., corp. counsel Hosp. Affiliates Internat., Nashville, 1971-78; sr. v.p., gen. counsel Hosp. Affiliates Internat., 1978-79; staff v.p., asst. gen. counsel INA Corp., Phila., 1980; sr. v.p., gen. counsel INA Health Care Group, 1981; partner Gillmor, Mills & Gillmor, 1981-83; dir., exec. v.p. Health Am. Corp., 1983-86; ptnr. Gillmor, Anderson & Gillmor, 1986—. Served with USMC, 1963-66. Mem. Am. Bar Assn., Bar Assn. City N.Y. Republican. Clubs: World Trade (N.Y.C.). Home: 1700 Graybar Ln Nashville TN 37215 Office: 3322 W End Ave Ste 414 Nashville TN 37203

GILMAN, JOHN RICHARD, JR., marketing professional; b. Malden, Mass., July 6, 1925; s. John Richard and Philomene (Gradie) G.; A.B., Harvard, 1945; postgrad. Georgetown U., 1945-46; M.S.W., NYU, 1983; m. Julia Streeter, Feb. 6, 1960; children—Derek, Susan. Cert., N.Y., R.I. Dir. publicity John H. Breck, Inc., Springfield, Mass., 1949-53, asst. advt. mgr., 1950-53, dir. new products, 1955-56, tech. dir., 1956-63; dir. new products Acco Labs., Am. Cyanamid Co., Wayne, N.J., 1963; treas., exec. v.p. August Sauter of Am., Inc., N.Y.C., 1964, pres., 1965-79, also chief exec. officer; pres. John R. Gilman Inc., N.Y.C., 1980—; dir. Slee Internat., Inc., N.Y.C., Finex Mining Co., Reno; asso., Fisher Cons. Internat. Inc. N.Y.C., 1980—, assoc. C.M. Oppenheim & Co. Inc. N.Y.C., 1981-86; cons. Right Assocs., Inc., Providence, 1986—. Trustee, Sculpture Center, N.Y.C., 1977—, mem. exhibition com., 1980-82, v.p., 1983-86. Augustus St. Gaudens Meml., Cornish, N.H., 1982; budget com. Town of Tiverton (R.I.), 1977-79. Served with USNR, 1943-46. Mem. Soc. Cosmetic Chemists, N.Y. Acad. Scis., Am. Pharm. Assn., Am. Orthopsychiatric Assn., Soc. Photog. Scientists and Engrs., Profl. Photographers Am., Art Students League. Clubs: Chemists; Harvard, Nat. Arts (N.Y.C.). Film maker: Water, 1950; Dear Nancy, 1953; co-pub. Arcadia Press, N.Y.C., 1979—. Home: 395 Punkateest Neck Rd Tiverton RI 02878 Office: 1 Richmond Sq Providence RI 02906

GILMAN, KENNETH B., retail executive. Formerly v.p., corp. contr. The Limited Inc., Columbus, Ohio, now exec. v.p., chief fin. officer. Office: Ltd Inc 2 Limited Pkwy Columbus OH 43230 *

GILMAN, S.I., automotive executive; b. Ft. Monroe, Va., Apr. 17, 1938. AB, Boston U., 1962; MS, Carnegie-Mellon U., 1964. Exec. dir. info. systems Ford Motor Co., Dearborn, Mich., 1964—. Office: Ford Motor Co The American Rd Dearborn MI 48120

GILMARTIN, RAYMOND V., health care products company executive; b. Washington, Mar. 6, 1941; m. Gladys Higham; 3 children. BS in Elect. Engring., Union Coll., 1963; MBA, Harvard U., 1968. Sr. cons. Arthur D. Little Inc., 1968-76; v.p. corp. planning Becton Dickinson & Co., Paramus, N.J., 1976-79, pres. Becton Dickinson div., 1979-87, group pres., 1982-83, sr. v.p., 1983-86, exec. v.p., 1986-87; pres. Becton Dickinson & Co., Franklin Lakes, N.J., 1987—, chief exec. officer, 1989—, also bd. dirs. Trustee Valley Hosp., Ridgewood, N.J.; exec. bd., v.p. Bergen council Boy Scouts Am., N.J., Respiratory Health Assn., Paramus, N.J.; bd. dirs. United Way Bergen County, N.J. Mem. Health Industry Mfrs. Assn. (bd. dirs.). Office: Becton Dickinson & Co 1 Becton Dr Franklin Lakes NJ 07417

GILMORE, GERARD GREGORY, marketing executive; b. St. Louis, Feb. 28, 1936; s. George Joseph and Getrude Marion (Dillon) G.; m. Mary Cecilia Hyland, June 20, 1964; children: John Gregory, Stephen Joseph, Anne Maureen, Brian Francis. BArch, BS in Archtl. Scis., Washington U., 1960. Prin. Hellmuth, Obata & Kassabaum, Inc., St. Louis, 1963-84, sr. v.p., 1986—; pres. Gilmore, Malcic & Cannon, Inc., St. Louis, 1984-85. Chmn. Archdiocesan Art Commn., St. Louis, 1984-85. Served to 1st lt. (j.g.) USNR, 1960-63. Mem. AIA (assoc.), Profl. Services Mgmt. Assn., Urban Land Inst., Soc. Archtl. Historians, Soc. Am. Mil Engrs. Roman Catholic. Clubs: Mo. Athletic (St. Louis); Army and Navy (Washington). Home: 12 Clif-Side Dr Glendale MO 63122 Office: Hellmuth Obata & Kassabaum Inc 1831 Chestnut St Saint Louis MO 63103

GILMORE, JOHN THOMAS, college dean; b. Alamosa, Colo., July 24, 1945; s. William Cammon and Lenora Martha (Steffens) G.; m. Patrice Diane Lester, Sept. 29, 1970; children: Jeffrey, Mark, Erin. BA, Adams State Coll., 1967, MA, 1968; PhD, Colo. State U., 1976. Asst. v.p. 1st Nat. Bank, Alamosa, 1970-73; econ. devel. specialist So. Colo. Econ. Devel. Dist., Alamosa, 1973-76; asst. prof. Sch. Bus. Adams State Coll., Alamosa, 1976-78, dean, 1978—; bd. dirs. San Luis Valley Fed. Savs. & Loan, Alamosa. Contbr. articles to profl. jours. Chmn. bd. dirs. San Luis Valley Ctr. for Handicapped, 1971-77; mem. Alamosa Devel. Corp., 1973-76, Six County Area Regional Devel. Commn., 1982-84; chmn. fin. com. Ch. of Sacred Heart, Alamosa, 19756. Mem. Midwest Finance Assn., Alamosa C. of C. (bd. dirs. 1981-84), Small Bus. Devel. Ctr. Network. Democrat. Home: 3666 S 105th St Alamosa CO 81101 Office: Adams State Coll Sch Bus Alamosa CO 81102

GILMORE, ROBERT CURRIE, railroad company executive; b. Vancouver, B.C., Can., Aug. 22, 1926; s. Robert H. and Isabel M. (Currie) G.; m. Shelagh M. Rowlette, Mar. 9, 1957; children: Katherine, Claudia, Robin, Jennifer. B. Comm., U. B.C., 1954. With Can. Pacific Rail, 1961—; asst. to gen. mgr. and mgr. mktg. Can. Pacific Rail, Montreal, Que., Can., 1961-66, systems mgr. market planning, 1966-70; regional mgr. mktg. and sales Can. Pacific Rail, Toronto, Ont., Can., 1970-71, gen. mgr. mktg. and sales, 1972-74; asst. v.p. mktg. and sales Can. Pacific Rail, Montreal, Que., Can., 1974-75, 77, v.p. mktg. and sales, 1977-84; exec. v.p. Can. Pacific Rail, 1984-86; pres., chief operating officer Soo Line Railroad Co., from 1986; dir. Aroostook River R.R. Co., Can. Pacific Steamships Ltd., CanPac Terminals Ltd., Houlton Br. R.R. Co., Incan Ships Ltd., Incan Superior Ltd., Internat. R.R. Co. of Maine, Soo Line R.R. Co., Thunder Bay Terminals Ltd.; apptd to coal industry adv. bd. Internat. Energy Agy., Paris, 1980. Mem. Nat. Freight Transp. Assn., Montreal Bd. Trade. Clubs: Whitlock Golf (Hudson, Que.); Can. Ry. Traffic of Montreal. Home: 630 Main Rd, Hudson Heights, PQ Canada J0P 1J0 Office: Soo Line RR Co 800 Soo Line Bldg Box 530 Minneapolis MN 55440 *

GILMORE, TIMOTHY JONATHAN, executive recruiter; b. Orange, Calif., June 24, 1949; s. James and Margaret (Swanson) G.; m. Blanche Jean Panter, Sept. 3, 1984; children: Erin, Sean and Brian (twins). BA, St. Mary's Coll., Moraga, Calif., 1971. Adminstrv. asst. Gov. Ronald Reagan, Sacramento, Calif., 1971-73; salesman Penn Mutual, Anaheim, Calif., 1973-76; asst. devel. dir. St. Mary's Coll., Moraga, 1976-81; devel. dir. St. Alphonsus Hosp., Boise, Idaho, 1981-83; adminstr. Blaine County Hosp., Hailey, Idaho, 1983-86; exec. dir. Poudre Hosp. Found., Ft. Collins, Colo., 1986-87; nat. recruiting dir. Power Securities Corp., Denver, 1987-89; pres. Gilmore and Assocs., Ft. Collins, 1989—. Republican. Roman Catholic. Lodge: Kiwanis (pres. Moraga club 1980-81, sec. Boise club 1982-83). Home: 2914 Bassick St Fort Collins CO 80526 Office: Gilmore and Assocs 3307 S College Ste 201 Fort Collins CO 80525

GILMOUR, ALLAN DANA, automotive company executive; b. Burke, Vt., June 17, 1934; s. Albert Davis and Marjorie Bessie (Fyler) G. AB cum laude, Harvard U., 1956; MBA, U. Mich., 1959. Fin. analyst, sect. supr., dept. mgr., asst. to exec. v.p. Ford Motor Co., Dearborn, Mich., 1960-72; exec. v.p. adminstrn. Ford Motor Credit Co., Dearborn, 1972-73; exec. v.p. adminstrn. and spl. financing ops. Ford Motor Credit Co., 1973-75, pres., 1975-77; exec. dir. Ford Motor Co., 1977-79, v.p., contr., 1979-84, v.p. external and personnel affairs, 1984-85, exec. v.p., chief fin. officer, dir., 1986-87, exec. v.p. international automotive operatives, 1987-89, exec. v.p. corp. staffs, 1989—, also bd. dirs., exec. v.p. corp. staff, 1989—. Mem. vis. com. grad. sch. bus. adminstrn. U. Mich.; trustee U. Detroit, Henry Ford Health Care Corp. Mem. Phi Kappa Phi, Beta Gamma Sigma. Clubs: Fairlane (Dearborn); Econ. (Detroit). Home: 36 Blair Ln Dearborn MI 48120 Office: Ford Motor Co The American Rd Dearborn MI 48121

GILRAIN, RONALD FRANCIS LAWRENCE, tool manufacturing company executive; b. Elizabeth, N.J., Mar. 7, 1927; s. Francis Lawrence and Mary W. (Judge) G.; m. Alice Carol Reed, Jan. 3, 1950; children: Leigh, Wendy, David, Kevin, Mark. BS in Chemistry, Seton Hall U., 1949; MBA, Rutgers U., 1953. Advt. mgr. Merck & Co. Inc., Rahway, N.J., 1949-60; mktg. mgr. Stanley Tools, New Britain, Conn., 1960-63, sales mktg. mgr., 1963-69, sales & mktg. dir., Europe, 1969-72, pres., gen. mgr. Stanley Magic Door, Farmington, Conn., 1972-80; v.p. pub. affairs The Stanley Works, Avon, Conn., 1980—; Bd. dirs. Central Conn. State U. Found., 1984, New Britain Found. Giving, 1984, United Communities Services, New Britain, 1984, New Britain Mcpl. Action Council. Served with USN, 1944-46. Do It Yourself Research Inst. (treas. 1981—, exec. com.), Machinery and Allied Products Inst., New Britain C. of C. Republican. Congregationalist. Office: The Stanley Works 1000 Stanley Dr New Britain CT 06050

GILSON, ARNOLD LESLIE, engineering company executive; b. Perrysburg, Ohio, Apr. 10, 1931; s. Leslie Clair and Velma Lillian (Hennen) G.; B.S. in Mech. Engring., U. Toledo, 1962; m. Phyllis Mary Seiling, Sept. 15, 1951 (dec. May 1982); children—David, Jeffrey, Luann, Suzanne. Engr., Miller, Tillman & Zamis engrs., Toledo, 1962-67, regional mgr., Phoenix br., 1967-69; owner, mgr. A B S Tech. Services, Phoenix, 1969—. Served with U.S. Army, 1952; Korea. Decorated Bronze Star. Mem. Nat. Mil. Intelligence Assn. Republican. Roman Catholic. Commd. extraordinary minister, 1975. Patentee in several fields. Home: 8226 E Meadowbrook Ave Scottsdale AZ 85251 Office: PO Box 2440 Scottsdale AZ 85252

GIMMESTAD, NANCY CORINNE, financial consultant; b. Dawson, Minn., Jan. 13, 1932; d. Bernard Arthur and Agnes (Omtvedt) G. BA, St. Olaf Coll., 1954; MA, Middlebury Coll., 1965; PhD, U. Mich., 1972. Cert. fin. planner. Tchr. English Pelican Rapids (Minn.) High Sch., 1954-56, Northfield (Minn.) High Sch., 1956-58, Glendora (Calif.) High Sch., 1958-60, Edina (Minn.) High Sch., 1971-75; asst. prof. English U. Wis., Madison, 1971-75; adminstrv. aide Mpls. City Counc., 1978-84; fin. planner IDS Fin. Svcs., Inc., St. Paul, 1984-88; owner Gimmestad Fin. Svcs., Mpls., 1988—. Co-author: instructional program Poetry Unfolding, 1975. Mem. Inst. Cert. Fin. Planners, Internat. Assn. Fin. Planning. Republican. Lutheran. Home and Office: 2645 Humbolt Ave S Minneapolis MN 55408

GINADER, GEORGE HALL, business executive; b. Buffalo, Apr. 5, 1933; s. George Edward and Meredith (Hall) G. B.A., Allegheny Coll., 1955; M.S. in Library Sci, Drexel U., 1964. Asst. Buyer Lord & Taylor, N.Y.C., 1957-59; job analyst Ins. Co. N.Am., Phila., 1959-60; asst. buyer John Wanamaker, Phila., 61960-61; acting curator Automobile Reference Collection, Free Library Phila., 1961-63; librarian N.Y. C. of C., N.Y.C., 1964-66; chief librarian N.Y. Stock Exchange, N.Y.C., 1966-67; exec. dir. Spl. Libraries Assn., N.Y.C., 1967-70; chmn. bus. and fin. div. Spl. Libraries Assn., 1974-75, pres., 1981-82; mgr. research library Morgan Stanley & Co., N.Y.C., 1970-79; cons. to spl. libraries and info. centers 1979-82; dir. ops. Internat. Creative Mgmt., N.Y.C., 1982-86; pres. Info/Tech Planning Service, Inc., Cranbury, N.J., 1986—. Mem. N.Y. Geneal. and Biog. Soc., Internat. Platform Assn., Am. Records Mgmt. Assn. (treas. N.Y. chpt. 1975-76), Adminstrv. Mgmt. Soc., Nat. Microfilm Assn., Nat. Trust for Historic Preservation, N.Y. C. of C., S.A.R., Phi Delta Theta (asst. sec. chpt. 1967-68, pres. N.Y. alumni club 1970—). Republican. Episcopalian. Home and Office: 45 S Main St Cranbury NJ 08512

GINDY, BENJAMIN LEE, insurance company executive; b. Detroit, July 23, 1929; s. Roy E. and Anne M. Gindy; B.S., U. Fla., 1951; m. Judith Youngerman, Dec. 20, 1953; children—Deborah, Daniel, David. Field rep. Penn Mut. Ins. Co., 1957-59; brokerage mgr. Mass. Indemnity Co., Miami, Fla., 1959-68; gen. agt. Guardian Life Ins. Co. Am., Miami, 1968—; pres. Internat. Risk Cons., Inc.; mktg. dir., Party Magic, Inc.; instr. Life Underwriter Tng. Council, C.L.U. diploma course U. Miami; past columnist Miami Rev.; guest speaker in field. Recipient Nat. Health Ins. award Guardian Life Ins. Co. Am., 1977, 83. C.L.U. Mem. Am. Soc. C.L.U.'s (past pres. Miami chpt., named Man of the Yr., 1987), S. Fla. Inter-Profl. Council (past pres.), Gen. Agts. and Mgrs. Assn. (past pres.), Miami Assn. Life Underwriters (past pres., Man of Yr. 1972). Home: 1018 Aduana Ave Coral Gables FL 33146 Office: Gindy Agy/Guardian Life 7615 SW 62d Ave South Miami FL 33143

GINGERELLA, DAVID ANTHONY, accountant; b. Westerly, R.I., Feb. 22, 1956; s. Louis W. and A. Madilynne (Capalbo) G.; m. Lisa Anne Boisclair, Nov. 17, 1979; children: Ashley E., David T. BS in Acctg., Roger Williams Coll., 1978; MBA in Bus., Rensselaer Poly. Inst., 1985. Asst. controller Ostby and Barton, Warwick, R.I., 1979-81; corp. acct. Spiriol Internat., Danielson, Conn., 1981-84; acctg. supr. Harris Graphics, Pawcutuck, Conn., 1984-86; group mgr. Analysis & Tech., Inc., North Stonington, Conn., 1986—; chmn. Westerly Fin. Bd., 1986—. Asst. campaign chmn. Westerly Rep. Com., 1986; coordinator DiPrete for Gov., 1986, 88, Dole for Pres., 1988. Mem. Nat. Assn. Accts., Nat. Corp. Cash Mgmt. Assn., Hilltop Club (trustee 1982—), Elks. Republican. Roman Catholic. Home: Rock Ridge Rd Westerly RI 02891 Office: Analysis & Tech Inc RR 2 Technology Park North Stonington CT 06359

GINGERY, JAMES MONTGOMERY, real estate developer; b. Washington, Mar. 11, 1958; s. Donald Edward and Mary Helen (Robbins) G. BBA, Am. U., Washington, 1980. Comml. real estate broker Cushman & Wakefield, Washington, 1981-84; comml., indsl. developer Gingery Devel. Group, Rockville, Md., 1984—. Mem. Nat. Assn. Office and Indsl. Parks, Montgomery County Hist. Soc. Republican. Office: Gingery Devel Group 1001 Rockville Pike Suite 503 Rockville MD 20850

GINGOLD, DENNIS MARC, lawyer; b. Plainfield, N.J., June 23, 1949; s. Michael Richard and Sally (Weiss) G.; m. Anne Carol Pearson, Sept. 4, 1970; children: Stacy Michele, Samantha Anne. BA, Rollins Coll., 1971; JD, Seton Hall U., 1974; LLM in Internat. Legal Studies, NYU, 1975; postgrad. in Econs., SUNY, Buffalo, 1975-76; postgrad. Joint Program, Princeton U. Bar: N.J. 1974, U.S. Dist. Ct. N.J. 1974, Colo. 1981, U.S. Dist. Ct. Colo. 1981, U.S. Ct. Appeals (10th cir.) 1984, U.S. Supreme Ct. 1985, D.C. 1989. Atty.-advisor U.S. Comptroller Currency, Washington, 1976-79; regional counsel 12th Nat. Bank Region U.S. Comptroller Currency, Denver, 1979-80; ptnr. Gorsuch, Kirgis, Campbell, Walker & Grover, Denver, 1980-82, Kirkland & Ellis, Denver and Washington, 1982-85; lead banking ptnr. Squire, Sanders & Dempsey, Washington, 1985-88; ptnr. Foley, Hoag and Eliot, Washington, 1988—; adj. prof. law U. Denver, 1981-82. Sr. mem. Seton Hall U. Law Rev. Named one of the Top 20 Banking Lawyers in U.S. Nat. Law Jour., 1983; Reginald Heber Smith fellow, 1975-76. Mem. D.C. Bar Assn., Colo. Bar Assn., N.J. Bar Assn., Denver Bar Assn., Banking Law Inst. (adv. council 1983-86). Democrat. Jewish. Clubs: Denver Athletic; Bethesda (Md.) Country. Home: 8712 Crider Brook Way Potomac MD 20854 Office: Foley Hoag & Eliot 1615 L St NW Ste 950 Washington DC 20036

GINGRICH, HAROLD, insurance executive. V.p. Farmers Group Inc., L.A. Office: Farmers Ins Exch PO Box 2478 Terminal Annex Los Angeles CA 90051 *

GINGRICH, JOHN DANIEL, financial statement analyst; b. Galveston, Tex., Nov. 12, 1944; s. Wendell Daniel and Dorothy Caroline (McCusker) G.; children: Christopher, Michael, Megan. BBA, U. Houston, 1967. Supr. Tex. Commerce Bank, Houston, 1970-74; acct. Gelephone Credit Union, Houston, 1974-77; mgr. gen. acct. Maloney Co., Houston, 1977-79; supr., gen. acct. Tapco Internat., Houston, 1979-86; cost acct. Oerlikon Welding, Houston, 1986-87; fin. statement analyst Hi/Lo Auto Supply, Houston, 1988—; treas. Maloney Credit Union, Houston, 1978-79. Coach Tex. Youth Soccer Assn., 1980-84. Served with U.S. Army, 1967-69. Mem. Nat. Assn. Accts. Home: 9220 Nathaniel #841 Houston TX 77075 Office: 8601 Tavenor Houston TX 77075

GINN, JOHN CHARLES, newspaper publisher, communications company executive; b. Longview, Tex., Jan. 1, 1937; s. Paul S. and Bernice Louise (Coomer) G.; m. Diane Kelly, Jan. 2, 1976; children—John Paul, Mark Charles, William Stanfield. B.J., U. Mo., 1959; M.B.A., Harvard U., 1972. From reporter, to copy editor, to chief copy desk Charlotte (N.C.) Observer, 1959-62; editor Kingsport (Tenn.) Times-News, 1962-63; city editor Charlotte News, 1963-69; mgr. advt., pub. relations Celanese Corp., 1969-70; dir. corp. devel. Des Moines Register & Tribune, 1972-73; editor, pub. Jackson (Tenn.) Sun, 1973-74; v.p. Harte-Hanks Communications, Inc., 1978—, pres. S.E. region, 1977-86; pres., pub. Anderson Ind.-Mail, 1974—; dir. Anderson Nat. Bank; dir., mem. exec. com. Anderson Meml. Hosp.; mem. Pulitzer Prize jury, 1977-79; adj. prof. Northwestern U., 1985-87; frequent lectr., chmn. S.E. region adv. com. Am. Press Inst. Chmn. Anderson County Civic Ctr. Authority, 1985—, Anderson Cancer Treatment Ctr. Fund Drive; pres. Anderson Area C. of C., 1977, 85, Anderson YMCA, 1975-76; mem. adv. council Anderson Coll., 1985; v.p., vice chmn. So. Newspaper Pubs. Assn. Found.; bd. dirs. U. Ga. Red and Black; mem. pres.'s adv. council Winthrop Coll., 1985; chmn. bd. dirs. Columbia Missourian. Served with USAFR, 1959-61. R.H. Macy Retail fellow Harvard U., 1972; recipient award for best editorial of year Tenn. Press Assn., 1964, 73,74. Mem. Am. Newspaper Pubs. Assn., Am. Soc. Newspaper Editors, So. Newspaper Pubs. Assn. (dir.), S.C. Press Assn. (exec. com.), Sigma Delta Chi. Home: 2835 Old Williamston Rd Anderson SC 29621 Office: Anderson Independent-Mail 1000 Williamston Rd Anderson SC 29621

GINN, ROBERT MARTIN, retired utility company executive; b. Detroit, Jan. 13, 1924; s. Lloyd T. and Edna S. (Martin) G.; m. Barbara R. Force, 1948; children: Anne, Martha, Thomas. B.S. in Elec. Engring., U. Mich., 1948, M.S. in Elec. Engring., 1948. With Cleve. Electric Illuminating Co., 1948-89, controller, 1959-62, v.p. gen. services, 1963-70, exec. v.p., 1970-77, pres., 1977-83, chief exec. officer, 1979-88, chmn., 1983-89; chmn., chief exec. officer Centerior Energy Corp., Toledo Edison Co., 1986-88; dir. Soc. Corp., Soc. Nat. Bank Cleve., Ferro Corp. Mem. Shaker Heights Bd. Edn., (Ohio), 1968-75, pres., 1973-74; pres. Welfare Fedn. Cleve., 1968-69; chmn. Cleve. Commn. on Higher Edn., 1983-86; trustee John Carroll U., Martha Holden Jennings Found., 1983—; chmn. Cleve. Opera, 1986—. Served with USAAF, 1943-46. Office: Centerior Energy Corp PO Box 5000 Cleveland OH 44101

GINN, SAM L., telephone company executive; b. St. Clair, Ala., Apr. 3, 1937; s. James Harold and Myra Ruby (Smith) G.; m. Meriann Lanford Vance, Feb. 2, 1963; children: Matthew, Michael, Samantha. B.S., Auburn U., 1959; postgrad., Stanford U. Grad. Sch. Bus., 1968. Various positions AT&T, 1960-78; with Pacific Telephone & Telegraph Co., 1978—; exec. v.p. network Pacific Telephone & Telegraph Co., San Francisco, 1979-81, exec. v.p. services, 1981-82, exec. v.p. network services, 1982, exec. v.p., strategic planning and adminstrn., 1983, vice chmn. bd., strategic planning and adminstrn., 1983-84; vice chmn. bd., group v.p. PacTel Cos. Pacific Telesis Group, San Francisco, 1984-86, vice chmn. bd., pres., chief exec. officer PacTel Corp., 1986, pres., chief operating officer, 1987-88, chmn., chief exec. officer, 1988—; mem. adv. bd. Sloan program Stanford U. Grad. Sch. Bus., 1978-85; bd. dir. 1st Interstate Bank. Trustee Mills Coll., 1982—. Served to capt. U.S. Army, 1959-60. Sloan fellow, 1968. Republican. Clubs: Blackhawk Country (Danville, Calif.); World Trade, Pacific-Union; Rams Hill Country (Borrego Springs, Calif.), Bankers. Office: Pacific Telesis Group 130 Kearny St San Francisco CA 94108

GINNOW, ARNOLD OWEN, publishing company executive, lawyer; b. July 10, 1924; s. Arnold O. and Amelia (Breitling) G.; m. Mary Ann Pierson, Aug. 29, 1948; children: Stephanie Bergsma, Amy. Ph.B., U. N.D., 1949, J.D., 1949. Bar: N.D. 1949. Editor, West Pub. Co., St. Paul, 1949-50, asst. editorial counsel, 1960-64, mng. editor, 1964-70, editor-in-chief, 1970—, v.p., 1978—. Pres. St. Paul Council Arts and Scis.; pres. bd. Guthrie Theatre, Mpls. Served to lt. (j.g.) USN, 1942-46. Mem. ABA, Am. Judicature Soc. Club: Minn. (St. Paul). Office: West Pub Co PO Box 64526 Saint Paul MN 55164

GINSBERG, EMILY SUZANNE, high technology executive; b. Horseheads, N.Y., Sept. 26, 1935; d. John and Anna (Nosko) Boor; m. David Lawrence Ginsberg, Dec. 30, 1969; children: Daniel, Laura. BA in Econs. and Math., Elmira Coll., 1956; MS in Computer Sci., Poly. U. N.Y., 1981. Sr. job analyst N.Y. Life Ins., N.Y.C., 1956-64, personnel researcher, 1977-78; mgr. commissions Mgmt. Assistance, Inc., N.Y.C., 1965-67, br. adminstrn. mgr., 1967-68; exec. asst. to pres. Programming Techniques, Inc., N.Y.C., 1968-69; teaching asst. Poly. U., White Plains, N.Y., 1980-81; mgr. verification systems Fingermatrix, Inc., North White Plains, N.Y., 1981-84, v.p., 1984—. co-inventor fingerprint verification method, 1986. Mem. Am. Soc. Indsl. Security, Assn. Computing Machinery, NOW, Phi Beta Kappa. Clubs: The Town, Old Scarsdale Assn. (N.Y.). Home: 18 Autenrieth Rd Scarsdale NY 10583 Office: Fingermatrix Inc 30 Virginia Rd North White Plains NY 10603

GINSBERG, ERNEST, lawyer, banker; b. Syracuse, N.Y., Feb. 14, 1931; s. Morris Henry and Mildred Florence (Slive) G.; m. Harriet Gay Scharf, Dec. 20, 1959; children: Alan Justin, Robert Daniel. B.A., Syracuse U., 1953, J.D., 1955; LL.M., Georgetown U., 1963. Bar: N.Y. 1955, U.S. Supreme Ct. 1964. Sole practice Syracuse, 1957-61; mem. staff, office chief counsel IRS, Washington, 1961-63; tax counsel Comptroller of Currency, Washington, 1964-65, assoc. chief counsel, 1965-68; v.p. legal affairs, sec. Republic Nat. Bank, N.Y.C., 1968-74, sr. v.p. legal affairs, sec., 1975-86, exec. v.p., gen. counsel, sec., 1984-86, vice chmn. bd., gen. counsel, 1986—, also bd. dirs.; sr. v.p., sec. legal affairs Republic New York Corp., N.Y.C., 1975-84, exec. v.p., gen. counsel, sec., 1984-86, vice chmn. bd., gen. counsel, 1986—, also bd. dirs.; bd. dirs. Republic New York Corp., The Williamsburgh Savs. Bank, N.Y.C., SafraBank, Miami, Fla., SafraBank II N.A., Pompano Beach, Fla., SafraBank Calif., L.A. Served with AUS, 1955-57. Mem. ABA, N.Y. State Bar Assn., Phi Sigma Delta, Phi Delta Phi. Office: Republic NY Corp 452 Fifth Ave New York NY 10018

GINSBURG, CHARLES DAVID, lawyer; b. N.Y.C., Apr. 20, 1912; s. Nathan and Rae (Lewis) G.; m. Marianne Laïs; children by previous marriage: Jonathan, Susan, Mark. A.B., W.Va. U., 1932; LL.B., Harvard U., 1935. Atty. for public utilities div. and office of gen. counsel SEC, 1935-39; law sec. to Justice William O. Douglas, 1939; asst. to commr. SEC, 1939-40; legal adviser Price Stblzn. Div., Nat. Def. Adv. Com., 1940-41; gen. counsel Office Price Adminstrn. and Civilian Supply, 1941-42, OPA, 1942-43; pvt. practice law Washington, 1946—; partner firm Ginsburg, Feldman & Bress; adminstrv. asst. to Senator M.M. Neely, W.Va., 1950; adj. prof. internat. law Georgetown U. (Grad. Sch. Law), 1959-67; Dep. commr. U.S. del. Austrian Treaty Commn., Vienna, 1947; adviser U.S. del. Council Fgn. Ministers, London, 1947; Mem. Presdl. Emergency Bd. 166 (Airlines), 1966; mem. Pres.'s Commn. on Postal Orgn., 1967; chmn. Presdl. Emergency Bd. 169 (Railroads), 1969; exec. dir. Nat. Adv. Commn. Civil Disorders, 1967. Author: The Future of German Reparations; Contbr. to legal jours. Bd. mem., chmn. exec. com. Nat. Symphony Orch. Assn., 1960-69; bd. govs. Weizmann Inst., 1965 (hon. fellow 1972); mem. vis. com. Harvard-Mass. Inst. Tech. Joint Center on Urban Studies, 1969; trustee St. John's Coll., 1969-75, chmn. bd., 1974-76; overseers com. Kennedy Sch. Govt. Harvard, 1971—; mem. council Nat. Harvard Law Sch. Assn., 1972—, gen. counsel Dem. Nat. Com., 1968-70. Served from pvt. to capt. AUS, 1943-46; dep. dir. econs. div. Office Mil. Govt., 1945-46, Germany. Decorated Bronze Star medal, Legion of Merit; recipient Presdl. Certificate of Merit. Mem. Am. Law Inst., Council on Fgn. Relations, Phi Beta Kappa. Democrat. Clubs: Metropolitan, Federal City, Army and Navy. Home: 619 S Lee St Alexandria VA 22314 Office: 1250 Connecticut Ave NW Washington DC 20036

GINSBURGH, ROBERT NEVILLE, financial consultant, retired air force officer; b. Ft. Sill, Okla., Nov. 19, 1923; s. A. Robert and Elsie (Pinney) G.; m. Nancy Brand, Dec. 28, 1948 (div. Feb. 1958); children: Robert Brand, Charles Lee; m. Gail H. Whitehead Winslow, Apr. 4, 1959; children: Carolyn, Anne; stepchildren: Alan F. Winslow III, William C. Winslow. Grad., Phillips Acad., Andover, 1940; B.S., U.S. Mil. Acad., 1944; M.P.A., Harvard, 1947, M.A., 1948; Ph.D., 1949; postgrad., Field Arty. Sch., 1944, Air Tactical Sch., 1950, Air Command and Staff Coll., 1953, Indsl. Coll., 1960, Air War Coll., 1961, Nat. War Coll., 1963. Commd. 2d lt. F.A., 1944; advanced through grades to maj. gen USAF, 1971; asst. prof. social scis. U.S. Mil. Acad., 1948-51; with Air Force Legis. Liaison, 1951-55, Allied Air Forces So. Europe, Naples, 1955-58, Air Proving Ground Center, 1958; pub. affairs Dept. Def., 1959; asst. exec. air force chief of staff 1959-62; research fellow Council Fgn. Relations, 1963-64; with Policy Planning Council, State Dept., 1964-66; staff group Office of Chmn. JCS; sr. staff mem. Nat. Security Council, 1966-69; comdr. Aerospace Studies Inst., Air U., Maxwell AFB, Ala., 1969-71; chief Air Force History, 1971-72; dir. Air Force Info., 1972-74; dep. dir. joint staff Orgn. Joint Chiefs Staff, 1974-75; editor in chief Strategic Rev., 1975-76, Neville Assos., 1977—; dir. Sterling Drilling & Prodn., Inc.; bd. dirs. Air Force Hist. Found. Author: US Military Strategy in the Sixties, 1965, US Military Strategy in the Seventies, 1970, The Nixon Doctrine and Military Strategy, 1971; editor: Principles of Insurance, 1949-50; contbr. to Economics of National Security, 1950, also articles in profl. jours. Bd. regents Coll. for Fin. Planning. Decorated D.S.M., Silver Star, Legion of Merit with oak leaf cluster, Purple Heart Joint Services, Purple Heart Air Force, Army commendation medals. Mem. Council on Fgn. Relations. Clubs: Kenwood; Internat. (Washington); Rehoboth Bay Sailing Assn.; Naples Bath and Tennis. Home: 5319 Oakland Rd Chevy Chase MD 20815

GINSKY, MARVIN H., corporate executive, lawyer; b. N.Y.C., Aug. 2, 1930; married. LL.B., NYU, 1955. Bar: N.Y. 1955, Conn. 1989. Atty. Paramount Pictures, N.Y.C., 1955-60; assoc. Mervin Rosenman, N.Y.C., 1960-61; asst. gen. counsel Champion Internat. Corp., Stamford, Conn., 1961-65, sec., 1965-67, assoc. counsel, 1967-69, gen. counsel, 1969-73, v.p., gen. counsel, 1973-81, sr. v.p., gen. counsel, 1981—. Mem. ABA. Office: Champion Internat Corp 1 Champion Pla Stamford CT 06921

GINTEL, ROBERT MORRIS, investment advisor; b. Bklyn., Mar. 31, 1928; s. Oliver and Frieda Gintel; BA, Columbia U., 1949; MBA, Harvard U., 1951; m. Barbara Lois Ray, June 16, 1951; children—Debra Lynn, Jay Ronald, Bruce Edward. Security analyst Thompson & Rittmaster, N.Y.C., 1954-57; partner Cady Roberts & Co., 1957-62; v.p., ptnr. Andresen & Co., 1962-69; sr. ptnr. Gintel & Co., Greenwich, Conn., 1969—, chmn. bd., chief exec. officer Gintel Equity Mgmt., Inc., 1971—; chmn. bd. Gintel Fund, 1981—, Gintel ERISA Fund, 1982—, Gintel Capital Appreciation Fund, 1986—; condr. seminars on investment mgmt.; radio and TV guest Wall Street Week; former dir. Superscope, Mpls. Moline Co., Interway. Mem. Rep. Senatorial Trust, 1979—, Rep. Eagles, 1980, 84; trustee Jeane J. Kirkpatrick Forum for Pub. Leadership and Pub. Policy, 1986-87, Poly. Prep. Country Day Sch., 1987—; bd. dirs. N.Am. Friends of Israel Oceanographic and Limnological Rsch. Inst. 1st lt., USAF, 1951-53. Office: Gintel Equity Mgmt Inc Greenwich Office Park 6 Greenwich CT 06830

GINYARD, MARTIN CECIL, real estate executive, consultant; b. Phila., Aug. 19, 1952; s. Joseph and Cecelia (Jackson) G. BA, Temple U., 1975, postgrad., 1976-78. Acct. mgr. Burroughs corp., Phila., 1979-83; acct. exec. Wang Labs., Mt. Laurel, N.J., 1983-86; mktg. specialist Xerox Corp., Phila., 1986—; pres. Acccutax Income Tax Svc., Phila., 1983—; pres., chief exec. officer MCG Mgmt. Inc., Phila., 1987—. Conbtr. articles to newspaper. Cons. Secondary Edn. Vocation Career Assn. Youth Career Assn. 1979. Home: 12305 Treetop Dr #42 Silver Spring MD 20904 Office: Xerox Corp 4340 East West Hwy Bethesda MD 20814

GIOCONDI, GINO V., automotive company executive; b. 1931; married. BSBA, Duquesne U., 1956; MBA, Mich. State U., 1979. With Chrysler Motors Corp., Detroit, 1963—, mgr. sales, 1976-77, mgr. sales planning and analysis, 1977-78, mgr. mktg. info. svc., 1978-79, exec. asst. to exec. v.p., 1979-80, dir. parts sales and svc., 1980-85, v.p. svc. and parts ops., 1985—. Office: Chrysler Motors Corp 26311 Lawrence Ave Center Line MI 48288 *

GIONFRIDDO, JAMES GREGORY, accounting firm executive; b. Miami, Fla., July 18, 1954; s. Joseph Santo and Florence (Murasso) G.; m. Krystal Pollard (div. 1978); m. Lillian Ann VanDenburgh, Apr. 19, 1979. BA in Acctg., St. Thomas U., Miami, 1976. Tech. support mgr. ADP, Atlanta, 1976-79; v.p ops. Computer Resources, Greenville, S.C., 1979-80, Profl. Computer Services, Atlanta, 1980-81; ptnr. Coopers & Lybrand, Atlanta, 1981—. Mem. Assn. Prodn. and Inventory Control, Internat. Customer Service Assn., Nat. Assn. Accts. Home: 3641 Frey Lake Rd Kennesaw GA 30144

GIORDANO, ERNEST, fashion designer; b. Naples, Italy, Dec. 23, 1926; came to U.S., 1954; s. Gaetano and Lucia (Boniello) G.; m. Guidith Gialanella, July 19, 1953; children: Luciana, Michael. B. in Elem. Edn., Salerno (Italy) Coll., 1948; MFA, Naples Coll., 1951. Asst. clothing designer U.S. Industries, Scranton, Pa., 1954-55; clothing designer, quality controller U.S. Industries, Scranton, 1955-74; head designer, mgr. Vermont Clothing, Scranton, Pa., 1974—; pres., chief exec. officer Fashion Internat., Inc., Scranton, Ertodami Enterprises, Inc., Scranton. With Italian Army, 1948-50. Mem. Italian Sport Soc., N.J. Internat. Clothing Designers (pres. 1982-83, 87-88). Home: 1223 Ash St Scranton PA 18510

GIORDANO, JOSEPH, JR., financial planner, investment consulting firm executive; b. Detroit, July 28, 1953; s. Joseph and Josephine Marie (Dellicolli) G.; m. Margaret Ann Ball, Apr. 20, 1985. BS in Fin., Bus. Econs., Wayne State U., 1977. Cert. fin. planner, 1986. Sr. cost analyst Nat. Bank Detroit, 1978-81; registered rep. IDS Fin. Services Inc., Mpls., 1981-83, dist. mgr., 1983-86; pres. Joseph James Fin. Services Inc., Rochester Hills, Mich., 1986—, Investors Fin. Adv. Inc., Rochester Hills, 1986—; instr. Macomb Community Coll., Warren, Mich., 1988; cons. various clients, 1981—; host Making Sense of your Money, Sta. WEXL-Radio. Mem. Inst. Cert. Fin. Planners, Nat. Assn. Security Dealers. Lodge: Elks. Office: Joseph James Fin Svcs Inc 705 Barclay Circle Suite 125 Rochester Hills MI 48063

GIORDANO, NICHOLAS ANTHONY, stock exchange executive; b. Phila., Mar. 7, 1943; s. Nicola and Aida (Gioiso) G.; m. Joanne M. Pizzuto, Oct. 21, 1967; children: Jeannine, Colette and Nicholas (triplets). B.S., LaSalle Coll., 1965. C.P.A., Pa. Mem. staff Price Waterhouse & Co., Phila., 1965-68; with various brokerage cos. Phila., 1968-71; controller stock exchange and stock clearing corp PBW (later Phila.) Stock Exchange, Inc., 1971-72, v.p. ops., 1972-75, sr. v.p., 1975-76, exec. v.p., 1976-81, pres., 1981—, also dir.; chmn. bd. Stock Clearing Corp. Phila., Phila. Depository Trust Co., Fin. Automation Corp. Phila.; dir. Options Clearing Corp. Trustee LaSalle U.; bd. dirs. Urban Affairs Partnership, Nat. Italian Am. Found., Met. Phila. Family of YMCA's, Greater Phila. Econ. Devel. Coalition. Served with Pa. Air N.G., 1965-70. Clubs: Union League of Phila. Home: 1755 Governors Way Blue Bell PA 19422 Office: Phila Stock Exch Inc 1900 Market St Philadelphia PA 19103

GIORDANO, SALVATORE, JR., air conditioner manufacturing company executive; b. N.Y.C., Aug. 28, 1938; s. Salvatore and Carmela G.; m. Anne Giordano; children: Salvatore III, John, Anthony, Michael, Robert. BS, L.I. U., 1963. Asst. to exec. v.p. Fedders Corp., Peapack, N.J., 1960-64, mgr. mktg., 1964-65, v.p. dir. mktg., 1965—, exec. v.p., 1967-86, pres., chief oper. officer, 1976-86, vice chmn., chief exec. officer, 1988—, also bd. dirs.; vice-chmn. NYCOR, Inc., Peapack, 1987—, chief exec. officer, 1988—. Office: Fedders Corp 158 Hwy 206 Box 265 Peapack NJ 07977 also: NYCOR Inc 158 Hwy 206 PO Box 502 Peapack NJ 07977

GIORDANO, SALVATORE SCOTT, computer company executive, consultant; b. Morristown, N.J., Nov. 22, 1954; s. Salvatore and Rose (Tronco) G.; m. Jewel Ann Adele Nicony, Nov. 19, 1983. BA, NYU, 1975; MBA, Fairleigh Dickinson U., 1981. With sales dept. Burroughs Corp., Bloomfield, N.J., 1979-81, Sperry Corp., Parsippany, N.J., 1981-86; with mktg. dept. Data Gen. Corp., N.Y.C., 1986—. Mem. Am. Soc. Mag. Photographers. Home: 55 Renselaer Rd Essex Fells NJ 07021 Office: Data Gen. Corp 757 3d Ave New York NY 10017

GIOVENCO, JOHN V., hotel corporation executive; b. 1936. BS in Commerce, Loyola U., 1958. With Harris Kerr Forster & Co., 1957-71; v.p. fin. Hilton Hotels Corp., 1972-74, sr. v.p., treas., 1974-80, exec. v.p., 1980—; pres. Hilton Nev. Corp., 1987—, also bd. dirs. Office: Hilton Hotels Corp Las Vegas Hilton Rd 3000 Paradise Las Vegas NV 89101

GIOVETTI, ALFRED CHARLES, accountant, consultant, lecturer; b. Alexandria, Va., Sept. 24, 1948; s. Alfred and Alice Jean (McKee) G.; m. Christine Kraft Chandler, Mar. 19, 1977; children—Allison, Catherine, Amanda, Michael. B.A., LaSalle U., 1970, postgrad., 1985; Ph.M., George Washington U., 1979. Cert. fed. taxation Accreditation Council Accountancy. Sr. acct., sr. ptnr. Giovetti and Giovetti, Pub. Accts., Balt., 1968—; owner Computer Wizards, Catonsville, Md., 1983—; mem. credit faculty Catonsville Community Coll., 1987—; food and drug officer FDA, Rockville, Md., 1971-72, Washington, 1972-77; research coordinator dept. medicine U. Md., Balt., 1977-81; supervisory research officer VA Hosp., Balt., 1977-81; mem. mgmt. bd., dir. research and devel., tng. coordinator, quality control supr. Md. Med. Lab., Inc., Balt., 1981; sr. ptnr. World Divers Co., 1962-77, Eagles Internat., 1977-85; instr. and research asst. George Mason Coll., U. Va., Fairfax, 1970-71; supr., sr. ptnr. Am., Eastern, World Aquatics Cos., 1966-77; cons. and project mgr. Hazleton Labs., Vienna, Va., 1972; cons. in counselling Randolph-Macon Women's Coll., Lynchburg, Va., 1975-76; cons. in research mgmt. Royal Iranian Govt., Tehran, 1978; dir. various small cos.; lectr. George Mason U., Catonsville Community Coll., U. Md. and various profl. orgns. Author research papers and abstracts Mem. editorial Com. Free State Acct. jour. Active polit. campaigns; mem. Republican Nat. Com. Presdl. scholar, LaSalle Coll., 1966. Mem. Nat. Soc. Pub. Accts. (mem. by-laws com., IRS liaison com.), Nat. Assn. Enrolled Agts. (mem. inaugural class Nat. Tax Practice Inst. 1986—), Md. Soc. Accts., Mensa. Roman Catholic. Home and Office: Giovetti and Giovetti 1615 Frederick Rd Catonsville MD 21212

GIRARDI, LAURENCE LEONARD, graphic designer; b. Sewickley, Pa., Sept. 23, 1953; s. Leonard and Annabella Helen (Yurcak) G.; m. Carol Lyn Hernandez, Aug. 1985. A.A., Los Angeles Pierce Coll., 1975. Art dir. Wine World Mag., Van Nuys, Calif., 1975-76, La Rose Graphics, Van Nuys, 1976-77; pres., chief exec. officer Girardi Design, Canoga Park, Calif., 1977-78, Grafica, Woodland Hills, Calif., 1978—; design cons. Fiberworks, Center for Textile Arts, Berkeley, Calif., 1981—. advisor Graphic Communications Program-L.A. Pierce Coll. 1975-79. Bd. dirs. Monte Nido Valley Property Owners Assn., 1987 (corresponding sec.). Recipient Community Recognition award Los Angeles Pierce Coll., 1980. Mem. Nat. Fedn. Ind. Bus., Graphic Artists Guild, Alpha Gamma Sigma. Republican. Roman Catholic. Office: Grafica 7529 Remmet Ave Canoga Park CA 91303

GIRDNER, ALWIN JAMES, credit union executive; b. Albuquerque, Oct. 10, 1923; s. Glen Clark and Marie Ellen (Holcomb) G.; B.S. in Bus. Adminstrn., U. Ariz., 1948, M.A., 1950; m. Marjorie Jo Wilson, Sept. 1, 1946; children—Allen James, Sharon Lynn, Kennan Eugene, Mari Jo. Sales adminstrn. RCA Victor, Camden, N.J., 1952-53; asst. purchasing Temco Aircraft Co., Dallas, 1954-58; asst. dir. edn, Tex. Credit Union League, 1958-61; asst. mng. dir. N.Mex. Credit Union League, 1961-64, mng. dir., 1964-73; treas. N.Mex. Central Credit Union, 1963-73; pres. NMCUL Service Corp., 1971-73; pres. Tenn. Credit Union League, 1973—, TCUL Service Corp., 1973—; chmn. Tenn. Central Credit Union, 1978-79; lectr. in field. Chmn. Credit Union Legislative Action Council, 1972-73; mem. liaison com., chmn. fin. Middle Tenn. State U., 1985—. Mem. Internat. Assn. Mng. Dirs. (sec.), Credit Union Nat. Assn. Internat. (Founders Club award 1962, world extension com. 1967—), Am. Soc. Assn. Execs., Internat. Platform Assn. Republican. Methodist. Author: Navaho-U.S. Relations, 1950; Chapter Leader's Handbook, 1959; Credit Union Informational Manual, 1960. Home: 7829 Parkshore Circle Chattanooga TN 37343 Office: PO Box 21550 1317 Hickory Valley Rd Chattanooga TN 37421

GIRLINGHOUSE, LYNN MARIE, business owner; b. Honolulu, June 30, 1954; d. Francis Eugene and Carol Ann (Maurer) Hill; m. David Girlinghouse (div. Aug. 1987); 1 child, Christine Penny. BA in Acctg., U. Md. Commodities broker E.F. Hutton, Stuart, Fla., 1980-85; owner, tchr. LMG Investor Svc., Stuart, 1985—. Mem. Treasure Coast Ins. Women, Jensen Beach C. of C. (bd. dirs. 1986—). Republican. Office: Hartman Tilton Ins Agy 815 Colorado Ave Ste 101 Stuart FL 34997

GIROVICH, MARK JACOB, mechanical engineer; b. Kharkov, Ukraine, U.S.S.R., June 23, 1934; came to U.S., 1978; s. Jacob Mark and Talla Abraham (Gindina) G.; m. Galina Michael Voroina, Nov. 14, 1958; 1 child, Irene. MS in Mech. Engring., Poly. Inst. Kharkov, 1957; BS in Physics, State U. Kharkov, 1965; Phd in Mech. Engring., Poly. Inst. Moscow, 1974. Registered profl. engr., Md. Mech. engr. Diesel Mfg. Plant, Kharkov, 1957-59, head. design bur., 1959-61, mgr. dept. automation of mfg. processes, 1961-78; R&D engr. Koppers Co., Balt., 1978-80; chief mech. engr. Koppers Co. div. Enelco, Balt., 1980-81; mgr. enginrg. Enelco Waste Disposal Group, Balt., 1981-86, mgr. spl. incineration systems, 1986-89; mgr. project devel. & thermal processing Bio-Gro Systems, Annapolis, Md., 1989—. Contbr. articles to profl. jours.; inventor in field. Bd. dirs. Associated Jewish Charity and Welfare Fund, Placement and Guidence Bur., Balt., 1979-86; v.p. Jewish Union of Russian Immigrants, Balt., 1978-85. Mem. ASME. Home: 13 Suntop Ct Unit 302 Baltimore MD 21209

GIRVIN, RICHARD ALLEN, film executive; b. Chgo., Feb. 10, 1926; s. Harry J. and Esther (Easter) G.; Mus.B., Chgo. Music Coll., 1950, Mus.M., 1954; D.F.A., Ga. Tchrs. Coll., 1954; m. Sharon Hillertz, June 9, 1968; children—Gregory, Kimberly, Scott. Instr. in music Bob Jones U., 1950-52; tchr. music Chgo. Public High Schs., 1954-56; dir. radio and TV, NBC, Chgo., 1956-57; asst. prodn. dir. Coronet Instructional Films, Chgo., 1957-62; producer, editor Gilbert Altschul Prodns., Chgo., 1962-64; free-lance producer, writer, Chgo. and Hollywood, Calif., 1964-65; instr. Columbia Coll., 1970-81; author (screenplays) Wine of Morning, 1957 (Cannes Film Festival award 1957), Point of Law, 1986, (book) To See the Stars, 1982, Death Penalty, Burrow, 1988; v.p. Zenith Cinema Service (now div. Dick Girvin Prodns.), Chgo., 1965-73, owner, 1973—, pres. Dick Girvin Prodns. Inc., Chgo., 1967—, owner numerous subs. including Timbrewood Prodn. Music, Timbrewood Pub., Sharilda Pub., Zenith Camera, Typing Unltd., Phase 5 Prodns., db Studios. Served to lt. USAAF, 1943-45. Recipient Indsl. Arts award, 1964, 74, Cine Golden Eagle award USIA, 1964, 67, Atlanta Silver award, 1971, Freedom's Found. award, 1961. Fellow Brit. Internat. Audio Soc.; mem. Audio Engring. Soc., Nat. Assn. TV Arts and Scis., Nat. Assn. Rec. Arts and Scis., Soc. Motion Picture Technicians and Engrs., Aircraft Owners and Pilots Assn., Internat. Brotherhood Magicians. Composer: The Seventh Psalm, 1953; composer film scores: Macbeth, 1951, Pound of Flesh, 1952; composer music for Wild Kingdom TV show, 1973-86, also composer indsl. and ednl. film scores, film library program music scores.

GITHENS, ANNE GENERES, financial consultant; b. New Orleans, Jan. 7, 1939; d. Allen Hart and Grace (Kerkhoff) Generes; m. John P. Fields, Aug. 19, 1961 (div. 1971); children: John A. Fields, Timothy G. Fields; m. Sherwood Githens III, May 22, 1976. BA, U. Southwestern La., 1960; MA, U. Md., 1964; MBA, U. New Orleans, 1977. English instr. U. Md., College Park and Balt., 1963-73, U. New Orleans, 1973-78; fin. planner F. Javier Banos and Co., New Orleans, 1978-80; fin. cons. Shearson, Lehman Hutton, New Orleans, 1980—; instr. fin. planning U. New Orleans, 1978—. Mem. Inst. Cert. Fin. Planners, Women' Profl. Council, Profl. Fin. Planners Greater New Orleans (pres. 1983, 85), Common Cause, ACLU, La. Com. for Fiscal Reform. Club: Friends of Music (New Orleans). Office: Shearson Lehman Hutton 909 Poydras St Ste 1600 New Orleans LA 70112

GITLOW, ABRAHAM LEO, retired university dean; b. N.Y.C., Oct. 10, 1918; s. Samuel and Esther (Boolhack) G.; m. Beatrice Alpert, Dec. 12, 1940; children: Allan Michael, Howard Seth. BA, U. Pa., 1939; MA, Columbia U., 1940, PhD, 1947. Substitute instr. Bklyn. Coll., 1946-47; instr. NYU, N.Y.C., 1947-50, asst. prof., 1950-54, assoc. prof., 1954-59, prof. econs., 1959-89, prof. emeritus, 1989—; acting dean NYU Coll. Bus. and Pub. Adminstrn., 1965-66, dean, 1966-85, dean emeritus, 1989—; bd. dirs. Bank Leumi Trust Co. N.Y.; pres. bd. edn. Ramapo (N.J.) Cen. Sch. Dist. 2, 1963-66; pres., sec. Samuel and Esther Gitlow Found., N.Y.C. Author: Economics, 1962, Labor and Manpower Economics, 1971; co-editor: General Economics: A Book of Readings, 1963; contbr. articles to profl. jours. Served to 1st lt. USAAF, 1943-46, PTO. Recipient Univ. medal Luigi Bocconi U., 1983. Mem. Am. Arbitration Assn. (mem. nat. panel 1948—), Am. Econ. Assn., Royal Econ. Soc., Indsl. Relations Research Assn. Home: 9 Island Ave Miami Beach FL 33139 Office: NYU Stern Sch Bus Washington Sq New York NY 10003

GITNER, GERALD L., aviation executive; b. Boston, Apr. 10, 1945; s. Samuel and Sylvia (Berkovitz) G.; m. Deanne Gebell, June 24, 1968; children: Daniel Mark, Seth Michael. BA cum laude, Boston U., 1966. Staff v.p. TransWorld Airlines, N.Y.C., 1972-74; sr. v.p. mktg. and planning Tex. Internat. Airlines, Houston, 1974-80; pres., founder People Express Airlines, Newark, 1980-82; chmn. Pan Am. World Services Inc., N.Y.C., 1982-85, exec. v.p., chief fin. officer, 1983-85; vice chmn. Pan Am. World Airways, N.Y.C., 1982-85, Pan Am Corp., 1984-85; pres. Tex. Air Corp., Houston, 1985-86; chief exec. officer, pres. ATASCO USA, Inc., aircraft trading firm, N.Y.C., 1986—; bd. dirs. Plymouth Lamston Corp., Presdl. Airways Inc., Tribeca Holdings Inc. Trustee, mem. exec. com. Boston U., 1984—. Named to Collegium of Disting. Alumni, Boston U., 1982. Mem. Young Pres.'s Orgn. (Disting. Alumni award 1984), Phi Alpha Theta. Clubs: Sky; Wings (N.Y.C.)(bd. govs. 1989—). Office: ATASCO USA Inc 551 Fifth Ave Suite 509 New York NY 10176

GITTLEMAN, MORRIS, consulting metallurgist; b. Zhidkovitz, Minsk, Russia, Nov. 2, 1912; came to U.S., 1920, naturalized; s. Louis and Ida (Gorodietsky) G.; B.S. cum laude, Bklyn. Coll., 1934; postgrad. Manhattan Coll., 1941, Pratt Inst., 1943, Bklyn. Poly. Inst., 1946-47; m. Clara Konefsky, Apr. 7, 1937; children—Arthur Paul, Michael Jay. Metall. engr. N.Y. Naval Shipyard, 1942-47; chief metallurgist, chemist Pacific Cast Iron Pipe & Fitting Co., South Gate, Calif., 1948-54, tech. mgr., 1954-57, tech. and prodn. mgr., 1957-58; cons. Valley Brass, Inc., El Monte Calif., 1958-61, Vulcan Foundry, Ltd., Haifa, Israel, 1958-65, Anaheim Foundry Co. (Calif.), 1958-63, Hollywood Alloy Casting Co. (Calif.), 1960-70, Spartan Casting Co., El Monte, 1961-62; Overton Foundry, South Gate, Calif., 1962-70, cons., gen. mgr., 1970-71; cons. Familian Pipe & Supply Co., Van Nuys, Calif., 1962-72, Comml. Enameling Co., Los Angeles, 1963-68, Universal Cast Iron Mfg. Co., South Gate, 1965-71; pres. MG Coupling Co., 1972-79; instr. physics Los Angeles Harbor Coll., 1958-59; instr. chemistry Western States Coll. Engring., Inglewood, Calif., 1961-68. Registered profl. engr., Calif. Mem. Am. Foundrymen's Soc., Am. Foundrymen's Soc. So. Calif. (dir. 1955-57), AAAS, Am. Soc. Metals, N.Y. Acad. Scis., Internat. Solar Energy Soc. (Am. sect.). Contbr. to tech. jours.; inventor MG coupling, patents worldwide. Home: 17635 San Diego Circle Fountain Valley CA 92708 Office: 17044 Montanero St Carson CA 90746

GITTLIN, A. SAM, industrialist, banker; b. Newark, Nov. 21, 1914; s. Benjamin and Ethel (Bernstein) G.; m. Fay Lerner, Sept. 18, 1938; children: Carol Franklin, Regina (Mrs. Peter Gross), Bruce David, Steven Robert. B.C.S., Rutgers U., 1938. Ptnr. Gittlin Bag Co. (name now changed to Gittlin Cos. Inc.), Livingston, N.J., No. Miami, Fla., N.Y.C., 1935-40, v.p., dir. Gittlin Bag Co., 1954—, chmn. bd., 1963—; v.p., dir. Abbey Record Mfg. Co., Newark, 1958-60; chmn., treas. Packaging Products & Design Co. (now PPD Corp.), Newark and Glendale, Calif., 1959-71, chmn. exec. com., treas., 1972—; chmn. Pines Shirt & Pajama Co., N.Y.C., 1960-85, Pottsville Shirt & Pajama Co. (Pa.), 1960—, Barrington Industries, N.Y.C., 1963-72, First Peninsula Calif. Corp., N.Y.C., 1964-68, Peninsula Savs. and Loan, San Francisco and San Mateo, Calif., 1964-68, Wall-co Imperial, Miami, Fla., 1965-87, Levin & Hecht, Inc., N.Y.C., 1966-72, Wallco of San Juan (P.R.), Brunswick Shirt Co., N.Y.C., 1966-72, Fleetline Industries, Garland, N.C., 1966-72, All State Auto Leasing & Rental Corp., Beverly Hills, Calif., 1968-72, Packaging Ltd., Newark, 1970-76, Kans. Plastics, Inc., Garden City, 1970-76, Bob Cushman Distbrs., Inc. (now Wallpapers Inc.), Phoenix, 1972-87, Wallpaper Supermarkets, Phoenix, 1976-80, Wallco Internat. Inc., Miami, 1976, Overwrap Equipment Corp., Fairfield, 1978-86, GCI Ala. Inc., Birmingham, 1981—; chmn. Wallpapers Inc., Oakland, Calif., 1982-86, Portland, Oreg., Honolulu, Denver, Los Angeles and Phoenix, 1982-86; pres. Covington Funding Co., N.Y.C., 1963—; vice chmn. bd. Peninsula Savs. and Loan Assn., San Mateo and San Francisco, 1964-67, chmn., 1967-68; chmn. bd., treas. Bob Cushman Painting & Decorating Co. (now Wallco West), Phoenix, 1972-86; treas., dir. Flex Pak Industries, Inc., Atlanta, 1973-76, Ploy Plax Films, Inc., Santa Ana, Calif., 1973-76; sec., chmn. exec. com. Zins Wallcoverings, Newark; ptnr. Benjamin Co., N.Y.C., Laurel Assocs. (Md.), Seaboard Realty Assocs., Miami, 1980—, GHG Realty Assocs., N.Y.C., 1980, Parkway Assocs., Miami, 1987—; ptnr., investors cons. Mission Pack, Inc., Los Angeles; vice chmn., dir., chmn. exec. com. Falmouth Supply, Ltd., Montreal, Que., Can., Ascher Trading Corp., Newark, Aptex, Inc., Newark; dir., fin. cos. Ramada Inns, Phoenix; bd. dirs., fin. cons. Ramada Inns Realty Equities Corp. N.Y., N.Y.C.; bd. dirs. Harris Paint & Wall Covering Super Marts, Miami, Morgan Hill Mfg. Co., Reading, Pa. Chmn. N.C. com. B'nai B'rith, 1940; treas. N.C. Fedn. B'nai B'rith Lodges, 1941-43, v.p., 1943-44, pres., 1944-47; mem. com. to rev. dept. banking and ins. N.J. Commn. on Efficiency and Economy in State Govt., 1967—; trustee Benjamin Gittlin Charity Found., Newark, BAMA Master Retirement Program, Hillel Found. at Rutgers U., Temple Emanuel, Miami; bd. visitors Franklin & Marshall U., Allentown, Pa; founders bd. Miami Gardens Home Aged. Jewish (pres., trustee B'nai Abraham, Livingston N.J., trustee Temple Emanuel, Miami, 1987—). Clubs: Greenbrook Country (Caldwell, N.J.), Turnberry Yacht and Golf (Turnberry Isle, Fla.), Westview Country (Miami, Fla.). Lodge: B'nai B'rith. Home: 59 Glenview Rd South Orange NJ 07079 also: 2875 NE 191st St North Miami Beach FL 33180 Office: 21 Penn Plaza New York NY 10001 also: 801 Biscayne Blvd Suite 400 North Miami Beach FL 33180

GIUFFRIDA, BARBARA ANN, mathematics and computer science educator; b. Bryn Mawr, Pa., June 23, 1952; d. Ulderino Anthony and Jean Mary (DiFelice) Sulpizio; m. Alfred Carmen Giuffrida, Dec. 27, 1980. BA in Math. Edn., Shippensburg (Pa.) U., 1974; MA in Guidance Edn., Villanova (Pa.) U., 1977, MS in Library Sci., 1989. Cert. secondary tchr., Pa., guidance specialist, libr. sci. specialist. Secondary tchr. math. and computer sci. Upper Merion Area Sch. Dist., King of Prussia, Pa., 1974—, computer coord., 1985—, tchr. computer applications and programming, 1980—, basketball coach, 1974-76, hockey and lacrosse coach, 1974-80, class sponsor, 1984—; instr. SAT, computer and word processing Upper Merion Adult Evening Sch., 1978-87. Mem. Nat. Coun. Tchrs. Math., Upper Merion Area Edn. Assn. (sec. 1976, grievance chmn. 1977, v.p. 1988, pres.-elect 1988, pres. 1989—), Phila. Area Computer Soc., Phi Kappa Phi, Delta Kappa Gamma (v.p. 1988-90), Delta Zeta (sec. 1978-80, v.p. 1986-88). Home: 251 Brownlie Rd King of Prussia PA 19406 Office: Upper Merion Area High Sch Crossfield Rd King of Prussia PA 19406

GIUGGIO, JOHN PETER, newspaper executive; b. Boston, July 5, 1930; s. John Peter and Theresa H. (Gagliard) G.; m. Barbara Savage, May 9, 1953; children: Barbara, John, Patricia, Stephen. B.S. in Bus. Adminstrn, Boston Coll., 1951. With Boston Globe Newspaper, 1945—, pres., 1978—; pres., chief oper. officer Affiliated Publs., dir. Trustee Boston Coll. High Sch., Carney Hosp., Emmanuel Coll.; bd. dirs. North Conway (Mass.) Inst. Mem. Boston Coll. Alumni Assn. (pres. 1981-82), Boston C. of C. (dir.), Boston Better Bus. Bur. (assoc. chmn.). Club: Univ. (Boston) (pres.). Home: 46 Jerusalem Rd Cohasset MA 02025 Office: Affiliated Pubs 135 Morrissey Blvd Boston MA 02107 *

GIULIANO, JAMES ANTHONY, financial executive; b. Rochester, N.Y., Sept. 4, 1941; s. Thomas and Madeline (Cenname) G.; m. Carol Polito, June 29, 1963; children: James Thomas, David Anthony. BBA, St. John Fisher Coll., 1963. Mgr. fin. Gen. Dynamics Corp., Rochester, 1964-70; v.p. fin. Gen. Dynamics Corp., Orlando, Fla., 1970-82, Plessey, Inc., Orlando, 1982-83, United Technologies Bldg. Systems, Framington, Conn., 1983-85; controller United Technologies Hamilton Standard, Windsor Locks, Conn., 1985-86; v.p. fin., adminstrn. United Technologies Control Systems, Farmington, 1986—. Roman Catholic. Office: United Technologies Control Systems 4 Farm Springs Farmington CT 06034

GIULIANO, ROBERT PAUL, pharmacist; b. N.Y.C., Mar. 7, 1943; s. Salvatore Anthony and Marie Rita (LoScalzo) G.; BS in Pharmacy, Fordham U., 1965; MS in Hosp. Pharmacy Adminstrn., L.I. U., 1970; m. Maja Hreljanovic, July 2, 1966; children—Christopher Robert, Kenneth Paul. Clin. pharmacist Columbia-Presbyterian Med. Center, N.Y.C., 1965-70; dir. pharmacy dept. St. Barnabas Hosp., N.Y.C., 1970-71; dir. dept. pharm. scis. Misericordia Hosp. Med. Center, N.Y.C., 1971-78, adminstrv. dir. materiel mgmt., 1978-79, asst. adminstr. Misericordia Hosp. Med. Center, 1979-81; pres. Apotheke Assos. Ltd., N.Y.C., 1980-81; pres., dir., chief exec. officer U.S. Home Health Care Corp. and Steri-Pharm subs., 1981—; affiliated instr. St. John's U., 1971-81; pharmacy cons.; home health care cons. Am. Cancer Soc., 1988—, Robert Wood Johnson Found., 1985; mem. clin. pharmacy adv. bd., 1971-81; mem. exec. com., Bronx Emergency Med. Services Council, 1975-80, chmn. tng. com., 1975-79, chmn. council, 1979-80; sr. emergency med. technician instr./coordinator N.Y. State Dept. Health, Bur. Emergency Med. Services, 1975-81; speaker's bur., CPR instr. Am. Heart Assn., 1975-81; CPR instr. Westchester Heart Assn., 1977-80; speaker's bur. Misericorida Hosp. Med. Center, Westchester County Soc. Hosp. Pharmacists. Asst. Cub Scout master, Eastchester, N.Y., 1976-78; coach youth baseball T.Y.A., Eastchester, 1975-83. Certified Am. Bd. Diplomates in Pharmacy, Nat. Registry Emergency Med. Technicians. Mem. Am. Pharm. Assn., Italian Pharm. Assn., Am. Soc. Hosp. Pharmacists, N.Y. State Council Hosp. Pharmacists, Nat. Assn. Sr. Emergency Med. Technician Instrs., Nat. Assn. Emergency Med. Technicians (founding), Am. Soc. Parenteral-Enteral Nutrition, League IV Therapists, Nat. IV Therapy Assn., Fordham U. Pharmacy Alumni Assn. (dir. 1982—). Republican. Roman Catholic. Club: N.Y. Athletic. Editor Misericorida Hosp. Pharmacy Newsletter, 1971-78. Home: 157 Oakland Ave Eastchester NY 10707 Office: US Home Health Care Corp 670 White Plains Rd Scarsdale NY 10583

GIVAN, B. E., aircraft company executive. Formerly v.p., treas. The Boeing Co., Seattle, now v.p. fin. ops. Office: Boeing Co 7755 E Marginal Way S Seattle WA 98108 *

GIVANT, PHILIP JOACHIM, mathematics professor, real estate investment executive; b. Mannheim, Fed. Republic of Germany, Dec. 5, 1935; s. Paul and Irmy (Dinse) G.; m. Kathleen Joan Porter, Sept. 3, 1960; children: Philip Paul, Julie Kathleen, Laura Grace. BA in Math., San Francisco State U., 1957, MA in Math., 1960. Prof. math. San Francisco State U., 1958-60, Am. River Coll., Sacramento, 1960—; pres. Grove Enterprises, Sacramento, 1961—; pres. Am. River Coll. Acad. Senate, Sacramento, 1966-69; v.p. Acad. Senate for Calif. Community Colls., 1974-77; mem. State Chancellor's Acad. Calendar Com., Sacramento, 1977-79. Founder, producer Annual Sacramento Blues Music Festival, 1976—; producer Sta. KVMR weekly Blues music program, 1978—, music festivals Folsom Prison, 1979-81, Vacaville Prison, 1985. Pres. Sacramento Blues Festival, Inc., 1985—; mem. Lake Tahoe Keys Homeowners Assn., 1983—, Sea Ranch Homeowners Assn., 1977—. Recipient Spl. Service Commendation, Acad. Senate Calif. Community Colls., 1977, Spl. Human Rights award Human Rights-Fair Housing Commn., Sacramento, 1985, W.C. Handy award for Blues Promoter of Yr. Nat. Blues Found., Memphis, 1987. Mem. Faculty Assn. Calif. Community Colls., Am. Soc. Psychical Research, Nat. Blues Found. (adv. com., W.C. Handy Blues Promoter of Yr. 1987). Home and Office: 3809 Garfield Ave Carmichael CA 95608

GIVENS, DAVID W., banker; b. Gary, Ind., Mar. 18, 1932; s. James M. Givens; m. Betty J. Davis, July 3, 1955; children: Kathryn D., David W. Jr. AB, Wabash Coll., 1956; JD, Ind. U., 1960. Ptnr. Krieg, DeVault, Alexander & Capehart, Indpls., 1960-74; v.p., gen. counsel Ind. Nat. Bank, Indpls., 1974-76, sr. v.p., gen. counsel, 1976-79, exec. v.p., 1979—; vice chmn. Ind. Nat. Corp., Indpls., 1979-85; pres. Ind. Nat. Corp. (name now INB Fin. Corp.), Indpls., 1985—; bd. dirs. VISA/U.S.A. Pres. 500 Festival Assocs., 1982; mem. devel. council Ind. U. Sch. Law; vice chmn. adv. council Corner Prairie Settlement, chmn. capital devel com. 1986; bd. dirs., mem. exec. com. Indpls. Holiday Com., Inc.; bd. dirs., mem. tour service and fin. coms. Hist. Landmarks Found. Ind.; chmn. corp. fund drive Ind. Sports Corp.; chmn. corp. sect. Indpls. Symphony Orch. Fund Drive, 1986; bd. dirs., asst. treas., exec. com., human services com. Greater Indpls. Progress Com.; trustee Krannert Charitable Trust; trustee, mem. exec. com. Wabash Coll.; exec. com., sec. bd. dirs., chmn. safety and security com. Commn. for Downtown, Inc.; mem. program com. Community Service Council; mem. Coalition for Human Svcs. Planning City of Indpls. Served to sgt. U.S. Army, 1953-54. Mem. ABA, Ind. Bar Assn., Indpls. Bar Assn., Indpls. Bar Found., Ind. Legal Found. Inc. (bd. dirs.), Assn. Bank Holding Cos., Assn. Res. City Bankers, Govtl. Affairs Soc. Ind., State Ind. Bd. Law Examiners, Bank Capital Markets Assn. (com. competitive securities markets), Am. Bankers Assn. Office: Ind Nat Corp 1 Indiana Sq #501 Indianapolis IN 46266

GIZINSKI, GERARD HOWARD, industrial company executive; b. Balt., Jan. 22, 1944; s. Howard J. and Sylvia V. (Jablonsky) G.; m. Angela Irene Piccione, Aug. 25, 1973. BS, Johns Hopkins U., 1965; MS, MIT, 1967; MBA, U. Pa., 1971. Sr. intelligence analyst CIA, Vienna, Va., 1967-70; bus. planning analyst Combustion Engring., Stamford, Conn., 1972-74, sr. econ. analyst, 1977-78, mgr. econ. analysis, 1978-81, dir. mktg., 1981-84, dir. planning, 1984-85, dir. bus. devel., 1985-86; sr. fin. analyst Ashland Oil Co., Ky., 1974-75, sr. econ. analyst, 1975-77; pres. Market Dynamics Cons., Inc., 1986—. Pub. The Sophisticated Traveler's Pocket Guide to Airport Facilities and Ground Services, 1987. Mem. Am. Inst. Chem. Engrs., Assn. MBA Execs., Sigma Xi. Roman Catholic. Avocations: sports cars, swimming, hiking, travel. Home: 61 Hawthorne Ln Wilton CT 06897 Office: Market Dynamics Cons Inc Town Green PO Box 130 Wilton CT 06897

GLACEL, BARBARA PATE, management consultant; b. Balt., Sept. 15, 1948; d. Jason Thomas Pate and Sarah Virginia (Forwood) Wetter; m. Robert Allan Glacel, Dec. 21, 1969; children: Jennifer Warren, Sarah Allane, Ashley Virginia. AB, Coll. William and Mary, 1970; MA, U. Okla., 1973, PhD, 1978. Tchr. Harford County (Md.) Schs., 1970-71; tchr. Dept. Def. Schs., W.Ger., 1971-73; ednl. counselor U.S. Army, W.Ger., 1973-74; lectr. U. Md., W.Ger., 1973-74; adj. prof. Suffolk U., Boston, 1975-77, C.W. Post Ctr., L.I. U., John Jay Coll. Criminal Justice, N.Y.C., 1979-80, St. Thomas Aquinas Coll., N.Y.C., 1981; acad. adviser Central Mich. U. 1981-82; adj. prof. St. Mary's Coll., Leavenworth, Kans., 1981, Anchorage Community Coll., 1982; asst. prof. U. Alaska-Anchorage, 1983-85; ptnr. Pracel Prints, Williamsburg, Va., 1981-85; sr. mgmt. tng. specialist Arco Alaska, Inc., 1984-85; mgmt. cons. Barbara Glacel & Assocs., Anchorage, 1980-86, Washington, 1986-88; gen. mgr. mgmt. programs Hay Systems, Inc., Washington, 1986-88; founder and prin. Pace Cons. Group, Burke, Va., 1988—; 2d v.p. Chesapeake Broadcasting Corp. Md.; guest lectr. U.S. Mil. Acad. Chmn. 172d Inf. Brigade Family Council; mem. U.S. Army Sci. Bd., 1986—. Recipient Comdr.'s award for pub. service U.S. Dept. Army, 1984. AAUW grantee, 1977-78. Mem. Am. Soc. Tng. and Devel. (bd. dirs. Anchorage chpt.), Am. Psychol. Assn., Am. Soc. Pub. Adminstrn., Am. Polit. Sci. Assn. Pi Sigma Alpha. Author: Regional Transit Authorities, 1983; (with others) 1000 Army Families, 1983. Home: 5617 Tilia Ct Burke VA 22015 Office: Pace Cons Group 8996 Burke Lake Rd Ste 305 Burke VA 22015

GLADSTONE, RICHARD BENNETT, publishing company executive; b. Orwell, N.Y., June 29, 1924; s. Irving Rea and Dorothy Bennett (Shufelt) G.; m. Kathleen L. Dandy, June 12, 1953; children: Sarah Martin, Margaret Ellen, Emily Bennett, William Dandy. A.B., Harvard U., 1948. With Houghton Mifflin Co., Boston, 1948—, editorial dir., 1973, v.p., dir. ednl. div., 1973-74, sr. v.p., 1974—, sr. v.p., dir. publishing, 1975-80, exec. v.p., publisher, 1981-86, vice chmn., 1986—, also bd. dirs. Mem. adv. com. Ctr. for the Book, Library of Congress; bd. dirs. Sch. Vols. of Boston; former dir. Book Industry Study Group. Served with AUS, 1943-46. Mem. Am. Ednl. Pubs. Inst. (past dir.), Assn. Am. Pubs. (dir.). Clubs: St. Botolph; Union (Boston). Office: Houghton Mifflin Co 1 Beacon St Boston MA 02108

GLADSTONE, WILLIAM, literary agent; b. N.Y.C., Dec. 12, 1949; s. Milton H. and Selma (Lowitz) G.; m. Cynthia J. Sands, May 1, 1983; children: Tara Rose, Cyrus Jay. BA, Yale U., 1972; MA, Harvard U., 1977. Researcher Alan Landsberg Prodns., Hollywood, Calif., 1973; tchr. Phillips-Andover Acad., Andover, Mass., 1974-75; editor Arco Pub., N.Y.C., 1977-80; sr. editor Harcourt Brace Jovanovich, San Diego, Calif., 1980-81; pres. Waterside Pub. Inc., Del Mar, Calif., 1982—; literary agt. Del Mar. Author: Test Your Own Mental Health, 1978. Bd. dirs. Mingei Children's Mus., La Jolla, Calif., 1983-84. Office: Waterside Pub Inc 832 Camino del Mar Ste 2 Del Mar CA 92014

GLADSTONE, WILLIAM LOUIS, accountant; b. Bklyn., May 23, 1931; s. Archie C. and Bernice T. (Turk) G.; m. Mildred R. Rosenberg, June 21, 1953; children: Susan, Douglas. B.S., Lehigh U., 1951; LL.B., Bklyn. Law Sch., 1955; grad., Harvard U. Advanced Mgmt. Program, 1970. Bar: N.Y. 1956; C.P.A., N.Y., other states. Staff acct. Arthur Young & Co., N.Y.C., from 1951, ptnr., 1963, mng. ptnr., 1981-88, chmn., 1985—; lect. acctg. Columbia U., N.Y.C., 1960-63. Contbr. articles to profl. jours. Mem. vis. com. Coll. Bus. and Econs. Lehigh U., 1984—; mem. Corp. Congress N.Y. Pub. Libr., 1987—, conf. bd., 1987—, trustee com. for econ. devel., 1988—. Served to lt. USAF, 1952-53. Mem. Am. Inst. C.P.A.s, N.Y. State Soc. C.P.A.s, Lehigh Alumni Assn. (award 1976), Bklyn. Law Sch. Alumni

Assn., Beta Gamma Sigma (dir. table 1982—), Board Room (bd. govs. 1983—), Fin. Acctg. Found. (trustee 1988—). Home: 5 Knollwood Dr Larchmont NY 10538 Office: Arthur Young & Co 277 Park Ave 23rd Fl New York NY 10172

GLANTZ, PAUL ARTHUR, insurance company executive, realtor; b. Highland Park, Mich., July 17, 1957; s. Jack R. and Gladys (Glusac) G.; m. Mary K. Wallis, June 1, 1985. BBA, Wayne State U., 1980; MS in Tax, Walsh Coll., 1984. CPA, Mich. Comml. loan analyst Comerica Bank, Detroit, 1981-82; tax sr. Ernst & Whinney, Detroit, 1982-84; risk mgr. Pulte Home Corp., Bloomfield Hills, Mich., 1984-86; pres. 1st Line Ins. Services subs. Pulte Home Corp., Bloomfield Hills, 1987—; realtor assoc. Century 21 Today Realtors, Detroit, 1977—. Wayne State U. merit scholar, 1975-80. Mem. Am. Inst. CPA's, Mich. Assn. CPA's. Office: Pulte Home Corp 33 Bloomfield Hills Pkwy Suite 200 Bloomfield Hills MI 48013

GLANZMAN, STEVEN BLAISE, controller; b. Amityville, N.Y., Apr. 15, 1955; s. Samuel Joseph and Barbara Irene (Grimm) G.; m. Wanda Gail Mauney, Jan. 17, 1981; 1 child, Kimberly Alison. BBA, U. S.C., 1979. CPA, Mass., D.C., Va. Mgr. Melville Corp., Worcester, Mass., 1973-76; sr. acct. NRA, Washington, 1979-81; dir. acctg. Am. Alliance for Health, Reston, Va., 1981-85; controller Nat. Assn. Attys. Gen., Washington, 1985—. Mem. Am. Soc. Assn. Execs., Greater Washington Soc. Assn. Execs. (budget com. 1986—). Republican. Roman Catholic. Home: PO Box 3422 Reston VA 22090 Office: Nat Assn Attys Gen 444 N Capitol St NW Washington DC 20001

GLASBERG, PAULA DRILLMAN, advertising executive; b. Dusseldorf, Germany, Nov. 22, 1939; came to U.S., 1940, naturalized, 1942; d. Solomon and Regina (Rubin) Drillman; m. H. Mark Glasberg, June 19, 1960; children: Scot Bradley, Hilary Jennifer. B.A., Bklyn. Coll., 1957; M.A., New Sch. Social Research, 1959, Ph.D., 1962. Research asst. McCann Erickson, N.Y.C., 1962-64; v.p. Marplan, Inc., N.Y.C., 1964-70, Tinker/Pritchard Wood, Inc., N.Y.C., 1970-72; exec. v.p., chmn. exec. com. Rosenfeld, Sirowitz & Lawson, Inc., N.Y.C., 1972-78; exec. v.p., chmn. exec. com., dir. Marschalk Co. div. Interpublic Group of Cos., N.Y.C., 1978-1982; exec. v.p., dir., dir. strategic planning McCann-Erickson World Wide, Inc., 1983—; bd. dirs. Stern Coll. for Women; sponsor mem. Yeshiva U. Women's Orgn., 1985—. Mem. Am. Assn. Advt. Agys., Am. Mktg. Assn., Advt. Research Found., AAAS, Am. Psychol. Assn., Internat. Platform Assn.; fellow N.Y. Acad. Scis., N.Y. Assn. Psychologists, 1975—. Home: 14 E 73rd St New York NY 10021 Office: 750 3rd Ave New York NY 10017

GLASER, ALVIN, manufacturing company executive; b. New Bedford, Mass., Jan. 8, 1932; s. Morris and Jennie (Brody) G.; student public schs., New Bedford; m. Rosalyn S.F. Clasky, Jan. 20, 1963; children—Iris, Linda, Marjorie, Jeffrey. Mgr., Morris Glaser Glass Co., New Bedford, 1949—; treas. Glaser Inc., 1964—, pres. Glaser Glass Corp., 1985—; corporator New Bedford Five Cents Savs. Bank. Mem. Dartmouth (Mass.) Youth Commn. Mem. Nat. Glass Assn., New Bedford C. of C. Lodges: Masons, Order Eastern Star, Shriners, B'nai B'rith, Moose. Home: 2 Ann Ave North Dartmouth MA 02747 Office: 1265 Purchase St New Bedford MA 02740

GLASER, DOUGLAS EDWARD, automotive executive; b. Cin., Sept. 24, 1951; s. Frank Maxmillion and Mary Louise (Sheehan) G.; m. Mary Kristina Friedhoff, June 12, 1976 (div.); 1 child, Douglas Edward Jr.; m. Susan Lynn Kroner, Nov. 14, 1987. BS in Acctg., Thomas More Coll., 1973. Office mgr. Ridgeview Lincoln, Covington, Ky., 1972-74, bus. mgr., 1974-77; office mgr. John Nolan div. Ford, Inc., Cin., 1977-78; sec.-treas. Kesselring div. Ford, Inc., Batavia, Ohio, 1978-84, gen. mgr., 1984—. Bd. dirs. Clermont County Youth, Batavia, 1984-85, Clermont County Hosp. Services, Batavia, 1983-84. Mem. Batavia Jaycees (charter pres. 1983-84), Ohio Gun Collectors, Colt Collectors Assn. Republican. Roman Catholic. Lodge: Lions. Home: 8619 Forest Rd Cincinnati OH 45255 Office: Kesselring Ford Inc 610 W Main St Batavia OH 45103

GLASER, GLENN EDWARD, distillery supervisor; b. New Albany, Ind., Dec. 24, 1952; s. Edward Elmer and Marion Joan (Bickett) G.; m. Beverly Ann Davis, Oct. 26, 1974; children: Paul Andrew, Julie Marie. BSBA, Ind. U., New Albany, 1976; MBA, U. Louisville, 1977. Supr. Phillip Morris USA, Louisville, 1976; distillery supr. Brown-Forman, Inc., Louisville, 1981—. Home: 405 E Riverside Dr Jeffersonville IN 47130

GLASER, LOUIS FREDERICK, retail pharmacy executive; b. Clayton, Mo., Jan. 9, 1933; s. Morris and Edith (Katcher) G.; m. Ada Lee Hughes, July 16, 1967; children—Amy Sara, Robin Lee. Student, Rollins Coll., 1951-52; B.S., Washington U., St. Louis, 1957. With Medicare Pharmacies div. Glaser Drug Co., St. Louis, exec. v.p. Medicare-Glaser Corp., St. Louis, 1957—; dir. Landmark North County Bank & Trust Co. Trustee, St. Louis Coll. Pharmacy, Mary Inst. Sch.; pres. St. Louis Benefit Polo Inc. Served with USMC, 1952-55. Mem. Nat. Assn. Chain Drug Stores, St. Louis Down Town, Inc. Republican. Jewish. Clubs: St. Louis, Racquet Ladue.

GLASGALL, FRANKLIN, restaurant executive, real estate broker; b. Newark, Nov. 23, 1932; s. Adolf and Esther (Buchacher) G.; m. Natalie Benjamin, Dec. 27, 1959 (div. June 1979); children: Ellen Sue, Lori Beth; m. Anita Lands, May 20, 1984. BS in Bus. Adminstrn., Ohio State U., 1954; postgrad., NYU, 1956-57. V.p. Sanndrel, Inc., N.Y.C., 1971-74; real estate broker Franklin-Glasgall, Rocky Hill, N.J., 1968—; asst. dir. real estate Restaurant Assocs., N.Y.C., 1968-71, v.p. real estate, 1974—; bd. dirs. Rawson Food Service, Rocky Hill, N.J. Mem. Trump Tower Merchants Assn. (v.p., bd. dirs. 1985—), Internat. Council Shopping Ctrs., Nat. Assn. Corp. Real Estate Execs. (pres. Restaurant div. 1984—), Real Estate Bd. N.Y. Home: 165 West 66th St New York NY 10023 Office: Restaurant Assocs Industries Inc 1155 Ave of Americas New York NY 10036

GLASGOW, LAWRENCE ERVIN, corporate lawyer; b. Beaumont, Tex., Aug. 3, 1957; s. Larry Ervin Glasgow and Ruth Ann (Cummings) Wofford. BBA, U. Tex., 1979; JD, So. Meth. U., Dallas, 1983; MBA, U. Tex., Tyler, 1985. Bar: Tex., 1984. Assoc. Winstead, McGuire, Sechrest & Minick, Dallas, 1983-85; asst. gen. counsel Zale Corp., Dallas, 1985-87; corp. atty. J.C. Penney Co. Inc., Dallas, 1988—; pres. Conlegium Tempietto, Dallas, 1984—, also bd. dirs.; gen. counsel Cystic Fibrosis Beach Ball, Dallas, 1987—. Author: Chapter 4 Foreclosure of Stock of Texas Foreclosure Manual, 1984; sr. editor So. Meth. U. Law Rev., 1982-83. Mem. The 500 Inc., Dallas, 1982-86, Dallas County Community Coll. Adv. Council, 1987, March of Dimes Fundraiser, Dallas, 1987. Named one of Oustanding Young Men Am., Jaycees, Dallas, 1983, 84; Easterwood scholar So. Meth. U., 1983. Mem. ABA, State Bar Tex., Dallas Bar Assn. (mem. corp. council 1986—), Dallas Assn. Young Lawyers, Tex. Exes Assn., Metroplex Gen. Counsel Assn., Phi Delta Phi. Republican. Home: 4147 Dunhaven Dallas TX 75220 Office: JC Penney Co Inc 14841 N Dallas Pkwy Dallas TX 75240

GLASIER, CHARLES HENRY, corporation executive; b. N.Y.C., Feb. 5, 1912; s. Charles H. and Anna (Lockyer) G.; m. Ellen M. O'Leary; children: Evelyn, David. Grad., Harvard U., 1949. Pres. indsl. gas div., Air Reduction, Inc., N.Y.C., 1964-66; exec. v.p. Big Three Industries, Inc., Houston, 1966-78, bd. dirs., 1972—. Home: 59ll Masters Dr Houston TX 77069 Office: Big Three Industries Inc 3535 W 12th St Houston TX 77008

GLASS, ANDREW JAMES, editor in chief; b. Warsaw, Poland, Nov. 30, 1935; came to U.S., 1941, naturalized, 1948; s. Martin Allan and Wanda (Mosewicka) G.; m. Eleanor Attianese Sorrentino, June 3, 1962; 1 child, Samuel Sorrentino. BA, Yale U., 1957. Fin. reporter N.Y. Herald Tribune, 1959-62, chief congl. corr., 1963-66; mem. nat. staff Washington Post, 1966-68; exec. asst. to U.S. Senator Charles Percy, Washington, 1968-70; sr. editor Nat. Jour., Washington, 1970-74; Washington corr. Cox Newspapers, 1974-77, chief Washington bur. 1977—; syndicated columnist N.Y. Times News Service, 1980—. Co-author: A Guide to the 1972 Elections, 1972. Chmn. Corr. Com. Refugee Relief, 1975-78. With U.S. Army, 1958; mem. Res., 1958-64. Mem. Gridiron Club. Office: Cox Newspapers Washington Bur 2000 Pennsylvania Ave NW Suite 10000 Washington DC 20006

GLASS, BOBBY LEE, financial planning executive; b. Pasadena, Tex., Feb. 7, 1943; s. James Monroe and Emma Ester (Forehand) G.; m. Marion Ann Yost, Sept. 16, 1967; children: Stephanie Lynn, Janice Rene, Amy Ann. BS in Marine Engring., US. Mcht. Marine Acad., 1965; MS in Fin. Svcs., The Am. Coll., Bryn Mawr, Pa., 1985; cert., Coll. for Fin. Planning, 1983. CLU, cert fin. planner; chartered fin. cons. Rep. Investors Diversified Svcs., Inc., Mpls., 1970-73, FMR Securities, Inc., Churchton, Md., 1973-83; prin. Investment Planning Svcs., Inc., Fairfax, Va., 1983-85; v.p., dir. Investment Planning Adv. Svcs., Inc., Fairfax, 1985—; registered rep. Investment Mgmt. and Rsch., Inc., St. Petersburg, Fla. 1983—. Mem. Am. Coll. Life Underwriters, Am. Assn. Practicing Fin. Planners, Internat. Assn., Inst. Cert. Fin. Planners. Office: IPS Fin Ctr 3600 Chain Bridge Rd Fairfax VA 22030

GLASS, DAVID D., department store company executive; b. Liberty, Mo., 1935; married. Gen. mgr. Crank Drug Co., 1957-67; v.p. Consumers Markets Inc., 1967-76; exec. v.p. fin. Wal-Mart Stores Inc., Bentonville, Ark., to 1976, vice chmn., chief fin. officer, 1976-84, pres., 1984—, chief operating officer, 1984-88, chief exec. officer, 1988—, also bd. dirs. Office: Wal-Mart Stores Inc 702 SW 8th St Bentonville AR 72716 *

GLASS, ERNEST WILSON, JR., financial planner; b. Lumberton, N.C., Sept. 27, 1949; s. Ernest W. and Marjorie (Magruder) G. BS, Wake Forest U., 1971; MS, U. Oreg., 1973. Cert. fin. planner. Tchr., coach Eugene (Oreg.) Sch. Dist., 1974-76; swim coach River Rd. Swim club, Eugene, 1972-76; aquatics dir. Mt. Park Recreations Ctr., Lake Oswego, Oreg., 1976-79; swim coach East Ridge Country Club, Shreveport, La., 1979-81; registered rep. Waddell & Reed, Shreveport, 1981-84, dist. mgr., 1984-87, div. mgr., 1987—; instr. Bossier Parish Community Coll., Bossier City, La., 1983—. Mem. Internat. Assn. Fin. Planning, Inst. Cert. Fin. Planner. Republican. Baptist. Office: Waddell & Reed 2620 Centenary St Ste 235 Shreveport LA 71104

GLASS, JOHN SHELDON, manufacturing executive; b. Glens Falls, N.Y., Mar. 10, 1936; s. John Wilbur and Josephine Emily (Sheldon) G.; m. Sharon Brackett, June 20, 1987; children by previous marriage: John S., Sarah S. AB, Union Coll., Schenectady, 1958; MS, MIT, 1960. Asst. sec. No. Nigeria Ministry of Econ. Planning, Kaduna, 1960-62; with Polaroid Corp., Cambridge, Mass., 1962-68; mktg. mgr. Millipore Corp., Bedford, Mass., 1968-76; dir. investor relations Millipore Corp., Bedford, 1976-85, gen. mgr., 1985—; bd. dirs., exec. com. Protein Databases, Inc.; mem. adv. bd. A Plus Inc. Pres., regional gov. Sloan Club MIT, Cambridge, Mass., 1980—, mem. Carroll Wilson award com., 1985-86. Recipient Frank Bailey prize, Union Coll., 1958; Eliphalet Nott scholar, 1958; MIT fellow in Africa, 1960-62. Mem. Nat. Investor Relations Inst. (dir. 1978-83), Phi Beta Kappa, Kappa Sigma. Club: Kaduna. Home: 48 Main St Boxford MA 01921 Office: Millipore Corp 80 Ashby Rd Bedford MA 01730

GLASS, MICHAEL STUART, II, real estate development executive; b. Lancaster, Pa., Apr. 20, 1963; s. Michael Stuart and Laralee (Boyd) G.; m. Lynne Lacey, Aug. 15, 1987. BA, St. Lawrence U., 1985. Assoc. dir. devel. Boyd/Wilson Devel., Lancaster, 1985-87; dir. sales and mktg. Boyd/Wilson Inns, Lancaster, 1987-88, v.p., 1988—. Republican. Office: Boyd/Wilson 600 Olde Hickory Rd Lancaster PA 17601

GLASS, MILTON LOUIS, manufacturing company executive; b. Burlington, Vt., Mar. 7, 1929; s. Joseph and Mary Lena (Smith) G.; m. Renee Peritz, Feb. 5, 1950; children: Jill Sharlene, Mikel Lewis. Grad., Bentley Coll., 1948; BBA with high honors, Northeastern U., 1954, MBA, 1956; postgrad. in program for mgmt. devel., Harvard U., 1962. With Gillette Co., Boston, 1952—; now v.p. fin. Gillette Co.; vice chmn. Blue Shield Mass., Inc., 1968—. Chmn. Sch. Com., Mashpee, Mass., 1970-76; copres. Jaw Joints Found.; officer Exec. Res. Corps, U.S. Govt.; chmn. Internat. Bus. Ctr. of New Eng.; chmn. New Eng. Health Rsch. Inst.; trustee A.D. Little Mgmt. Edn. Inst.; chmn. investment com. Hillel Founds. of Greater Boston; bd. dirs. Boston Opera Assn.;bd. dirs., treas. United Way of Massachusetts Bay; trustee Am. Rep. Theater. With AUS, 1948-51. Named Am.'s Best chief fin. officer cosmetics industry, Instl. Investor, 1986. Fellow B'nai B'rith Anti-Defamation League; mem. Nat. Assn. Corp. Treas.' (bd. dirs.), Harvard Alumni Assn., Bentley Alumni Assn., Northeastern Alumni Assn., Sigma Epsilon Rho, boston Treasurers Club, Univ. Club. Home: 790 Boylston St Boston MA 02199 Office: Gillette Co Prudential Tower Bldg Boston MA 02199

GLASSCO, JAMES RUSSELL, JR., financial executive; b. Webster Groves, Mo., Jan. 17, 1925; s. James Russell and Leta Marie (Heim) G.; m. Elizabeth Eleanor Brainard, Feb. 12, 1955; children—Elizabeth Buell, James Morgan, Benjamin Bristow, William Shoemaker. B.A., Trinity Coll., 1950; postgrad. U. Houston, 1954-55, Amherst Coll., 1966. Trainee, Draper Corp., Hopedale, Mass., 1950-53; cost acct. Anderson Clayton, Houston, 1953-56; asst. cashier/loan officer Nat. Bank Commerce, Houston, 1956-60; asst. cashier Bond investments, Aetna Life & Casualty Ins. Co., Hartford, Conn., 1960-68, asst. v.p., cashier, 1968-70, asst. v.p. fin., 1970-71, dir. bond investment, 1971-73; treas. U.S. Postal Service, Washington, 1973—. Served with USNR, 1943-46. Episcopalian. Club: University, Hartford Golf. Avocation: squash. Home: 1024 Pine Hill Rd McLean VA 22101-2233 Office: US Postal Svc 475 L'Enfant Pla Washington DC 20260-5130

GLASSER, JAMES J., leasing company executive; b. Chgo., June 5, 1934; s. Daniel D. and Sylvia G.; m. Louise D. Rosenthal, Apr. 19, 1964; children: Mary, Emily, Daniel. A.B., Yale U., 1955; J.D., Harvard U., 1958. Bar: Ill. 1958. Asst. states atty. Cook County, Ill., 1958-61; mem. exec. staff GATX Corp., Chgo., 1961-69; pres. GATX Corp., 1974—, chmn. bd., chief exec. officer, 1978—, also dir.; gen. mgr. Infilco Products Co., 1969-70; v.p. GATX Leasing Corp., San Francisco, 1970-71, pres., 1971-74; dir. Harris Bankcorp, Inc., Harris Trust & Savs. Bank, Mut. Trust Life Ins. Co., Oak Brook, Ill., B.F. Goodrich Co., Stone Container Corp. Bd. dirs. Northwestern Meml. Hosp., Chgo., Michael Reese Hosp. and Med. Center.; trustee Chgo. Zool. Soc. Mem. Econ. Club Chgo., Chi Psi. Clubs: Casino (Chgo.), Chicago (Chgo.), Racquet (Chgo.), Tavern (Chgo.), Commercial (Chgo.); Onwentsia (Lake Forest, Ill.), Winter (Lake Forest, Ill.); Lake Shore Country (Glencoe, Ill.). Home: 644 E Spruce Ave Lake Forest IL 60045 Office: GATX Corp 120 S Riverside Pla Chicago IL 60606

GLASSGOW, WILLIS ALLEN, banker; b. Omaha, Nov. 24, 1934; s. Willis A. and Hansetta (McHugh) G.; m. Judith A. Gureno, Dec. 26, 1962; children: Matthew, Lisa, Mark, John. BBA, Coe Coll., 1960; postgrad., SSE Imede, Lausanne, Switzerland, 1980. Asst. v.p. Morris Plan Co. Iowa, Cedar Rapids, 1963-67; v.p., cashier Bank of Lisle, Ill., 1967-71; pres. Bank of Rolling Meadows, Ill., 1971-75, Palatine (Ill.) Nat. Bank, 1975-88; chmn. Suburban Nat. Bank of Aurora, Ill., 1987—, Suburban Nat. Bank of Lake County, Lincolnshire, Ill., 1988—; vice-chmn. Suburban Nat. Bank of Palatine, 1988—; bd. dirs. Suburban Bancorp, Inc., Palatine, N.E. Ill. M.R.I., N.W. Suburban Golden Corridor. Mem. Woodridge Indsl. Devel. Commn., 1970; sch. bd. St. Joan of Arc, Lisle, Ill., mem. fin. com. Our Lady of the Wayside, Arlington Heights, Ill., 1972-75; chmn. Rolling Meadows (ill.) Crusade of Mercy, 1972; bd. dirs. Palatine Bus. Devel. Commn., 1984-87; pres. Rolling Meadows C. of C., 1973, 74. With USN, 1954-58. Mem. Palatine C. of C. (bd. dirs. 1975-79). Republican. Roman Catholic. Office: Suburban Bancorp Inc 50 N Brockway Palatine IL 60067

GLASSMAN, GERALD SEYMOUR, metal finishing company executive; b. Hartford, Conn., July 6, 1932; s. Abram and Lena (Rulnick) G.; B.S., U. Vt., 1954; m. Edwina Wellins, Dec. 1, 1963; children—Cynthia Anne, Barbara Diane, Richard Philip. Exec., Bland Co., Hartford, Conn., 1954-63, Coleco Industries, Hartford, 1963-75; pres. Stanley Plating Co., Forestville, Conn., 1977-82; chmn. CBR Industries, Plainville, Conn., 1977-82; pres. Plainville Electro Plating Co., 1975—, Plainville West doing bus. as Marro Plating, 1986—, Internat. Metal Finishing, Inc., 1986—; mem. regional adv. bd. Bank of Boston Ct., Plainville, 1979—. Pres. Tunxis Community Coll. Found., 1978—; trustee Wheeler Clinic, 1979—, Plainville YMCA, 1980—; mem. Assocs. U. Hartford; active Simsbury (Conn.) Little League. Mem. Nat. Assn. Metal Finishers, Conn. Assn. Metal Finishers (v.p.), Metal Finishers Assn. Conn. (pres.), NAM, Am. Electroplaters Soc., Plainville C. of C. Jewish. Lodge: Masons. Home: 129 Westledge Rd West Simsbury CT 06092 Office: 21 Forestville Ave Plainville CT 06062

GLASSMEYER, JAMES MILTON, aerospace and electronics engineer; b. Cin., Mar. 31, 1928; s. Howard Jerome and Ethel Marie (Nieman) G.; m. Anita Mary Tschida, Apr. 21, 1979. Student U. Cin., 1947-49; BSEE with spl. honors, U. Colo., Boulder, 1958, MS in Aeronautics and Astronautics, MIT, 1960. Commd. 2d lt. U.S. Air Force, 1950, advanced through grades to lt. col., 1971; astron. engr. Air Force Space Systems Div. Hdqrs., Los Angeles, 1960-64, astronautical engr. and astronautics tech. intelligence analyst Air Force Rocket Propulsion Lab., Edwards AFB, Calif., 1967-73; ret., 1973; pvt. practice aerospace and electronics research and analysis, 1973—. Contbr. articles to jours. in field. Recipient Air Force Inst. Tech. scholarship, U. Colo., 1956-58, MIT, 1958-60, USAF Master Missileman badge, Air Force Rocket Propulsion Lab., 1970. Mem. AIAA, Air Force Assn., Planetary Soc., Ret. Officers Assn., Tau Beta Pi (1st grand prize Greater Interest in Govt. Nat. Essay Contest 1957), Eta Kappa Nu, Sigma Tau, Sigma Gamma Tau, Sigma Xi. Roman Catholic. Home: 5801 E N Wilshire Dr Tucson AZ 85711 Office: 5610-B E Glenn St Tucson AZ 85712

GLASSON, LINDA, hospital security and safety official, healthcare consultant; b. Nassawadox, Va., July 2, 1947; d. William Robert and Doris (Savage) G.; m. Charles William Lemon, Jr., Mar. 21, 1969 (div. 1973). Student Eastern Shore Br. U. Va., 1965-67, J. Sargent Reynolds Community Coll., 1976-80, Old Dominion U., 1981, Va. Wesleyan Coll., 1985. Cert. ambulance emergency med. technician. Clk.-typist G.L. Webster Co., Inc., Cheriton, Va., 1962-70; tchrs. aide Cape Charles High Sch., Va., 1970-72; dir. recreation and infirmary asst. United Meth. Children's Home, Richmond, Va., 1972-73; stockroom mgr. Flair Clothing Store, Richmond, 1973-74; with med. record dept. Richmond Meml. Hosp., 1974-75, asst. utilization rev. coord., 1975-80, hosp. police sgt., 1977-80; dir. safety and security Maryview Hosp., Portsmouth, Va., 1980—, chmn. hosp. safety com., 1980—, mem. disaster com., 1980—, chmn., 1986—. Contbg. author tng. manuals; contbr. articles to profl. publs. Instr. first aid and personal safety ARC, 1970-85, multimedia first aid instr., 1983-88, first aid chmn. bd. dirs. Henrico chpt., 1979-80, vol. emergency med. technician ambulance state fair annually 1974—. Mem. NAFE, Internat. Assn. Hosp. Security (sr., chmn. Region III 1985, v.p., sec. 1985-88, spl. agt. to bd. 1988-89), Am. Soc. Indsl. Security (mem. nat. standing com. healthcare security 1979-84, v.p. 1983-84). Baptist. Avocations: golf, softball, swimming, reading, classical music. Office: Maryview Hosp 3636 High St Portsmouth VA 23707

GLATFELTER, PHILIP HENRY, III, pulp and paper executive; b. Spring Grove, Pa., Mar. 17, 1916; s. Philip H. and Cassandra (McClellan) G.; m. Anne C. Manifold, Nov. 15, 1940; children: Patricia Anne Glatfelter McQuaid, Elizabeth M. Glatfelter Kegler. A.B., Brown U., 1938; L.H.D. (hon.), York Coll., 1977. With P.H. Glatfelter Co., Spring Grove, 1938—; pres. P.H. Glatfelter Co., 1954-80, chmn., 1980-88; staff asst. W.P.B., 1941-42. Bd. dirs. York Welfare Fedn., 1952-54; past trustee U. Maine Pulp and Paper Found. Served with USNR, 1942-46. Mem. Inst. Paper Chemistry (trustee 1976-83), Printing Paper Mfrs. Assn. (chmn. 1961-62), Am. Paper Inst. (past dir.), Am. Forest Inst. (dir.), Nat. Council Air and Stream Improvement (past dir.), Mfg. Assn. York (pres. 1954). Home: Hickory Hill Spring Grove PA 17362 Office: P H Glatfelter Co 228 S Main St Spring Grove PA 17362

GLATZER, ROBERT ANTHONY, marketing and sales executive; b. N.Y.C., May 19, 1932; s. Harold and Glenna (Beaber) G.; m. Paula Rosenfeld, Dec. 20, 1964; m. Mary Ann Murphy, Dec. 31, 1977; children: Gabriela, Jessica, Nicholas. BA, Haverford Coll., 1954. Br. store dept. mgr. Bloomingdale's, N.Y.C., 1954-56; media buyer Ben Sackheim Advt., N.Y.C., 1956-59; producer TV commls. Ogilvy, Benson & Mather Advt., N.Y.C., 1959-62; dir. broadcast prodn. Carl Ally Advt., N.Y.C., 1962-63; owner Chronicle Prodns., N.Y.C., 1963-73; dir. Folklife Festival, Smithsonian Inst., Washington, 1973, Expo 74 Corp., Spokane, Wash., 1973-74; pres. Robert Glatzer Assocs., Spokane, 1974—; ptnr. Delany/Glatzer Advt., Spokane, 1979-84; dir. sales/mktg. Pinnacle Prodns., Spokane; adj. faculty Ea. Wash. U., 1987—. Bd. dirs. Riverfront Arts Festival, 1977-78; bd. dirs. Comprehensive Health Planning Council, 1975-78, Spokane Quality of Life Council, 1976-82, Allied Arts of Spokane, 1976-80, Art Alliance Wash. State, 1977-81, Spokane chpt. ACLU, 1979-83, Wash. State Folklife Council, 1983—; commr. Spokane Arts, 1987—; mem. Spokane Community Devel. Bd., 1988—; mem. Shorelines Update Commn., 1988—. Recipient CINE Golden Eagle award (2). Mem. Dirs. Guild Am. Democrat. Jewish. Author: The New Advertising, 1970; co-scenarist Scorpio and other TV prodns. Office: W 905 Riverside Ave Spokane WA 99201

GLAUBER, MICHAEL A., manufacturing company executive; b. East St. Louis, Ill., Mar. 10, 1943; s. Wilfred B. and Mary E. (Wakefield) G.; m. Mary Louise Barry, Aug. 29, 1964; children: Christine L., Marcella A. BA in Acctg., St. Mary's U., San Antonio, 1965. CPA, Tex. Bus. mgr. Main Lincoln Mercury, San Antonio, 1964-66; staff acct. Alexander Grant & Co., Dallas, 1966-69; controller Leggett & Platt, Carthage, Mo., 1969-76, treas., 1976-78, v.p. fin., treas., 1978—. Mem. Am. Inst. CPAs. Republican. Roman Catholic. Office: Leggett & Platt 1 Leggett Rd Carthage MO 64836

GLAUBINGER, LAWRENCE DAVID, manufacturing company executive, consultant; b. Newark, Nov. 26, 1925; s. Samuel I. and Pauline (Sandler) G.; B.S. with honors, Ind. U., 1949; M.B.A., Columbia U., 1977; m. Lucienne Lefebvre, Nov. 11, 1967. Adminstrv. asst. to pres. Ronson Inc., Newark, 1949-51; mdse. mgr. United Mchts., N.Y.C., 1951-65; v.p. Marietta Silk Mills (Pa.), 1965-66; pres., chief exec. officer Channel Textile Co. Inc., Bradford, Vt., 1966-75; chmn. bd., chief exec. officer Stern & Stern Industries, Inc., N.Y.C., 1977—, also dir. & pres. Lawrence Econ. Cons. Inc., Hallandale, Fla., 1977—; dir. Leucadia Nat. Corp., Marisa Christina, Inc., House of Ronnie, Inc., Transp. Capital Corp., Gordon's Deep Discount. Chmn. ann. funds campaigns Columbia U. Sch. Bus., 1980-82. Served with USCGR, 1943-46. Mem. Hoosier Hundred, Ind. U. Dean's Assos., Columbia U. Bus. Assos., Campaign for Columbia (co-chmn. bus. sch.), Am. Arbitration Assn., Beta Gamma Sigma. Republican. Jewish. Clubs: Princeton (N.Y.); Green Brook Country. Home: 437 Golden Isle Dr Hallandale FL 33009 Office: Stern & Stern Industries Inc 708 3rd Ave New York NY 10017

GLAVIN, WILLIAM FRANCIS, business machines company executive; b. Albany, N.Y., Mar. 29, 1932; s. John G.; m. Cecily McClatchy, Sept. 24, 1955; children: Joanne, William F., Patricia, Christine, Thomas, Cecily, Richard. B.A., Coll. of Holy Cross, Worcester, Mass., 1953; M.B.A., U. Pa., 1955. Numerous exec. positions including dir. markets requirement planning IBM Corp., 1955-68; v.p. ops. Service Bur. Corp. subs. IBM, 1968-70; exec. v.p. Xerox Data Systems div. Xerox Corp., Stamford, Conn., 1970, group v.p., pres. div., 1970-72, group v.p., pres. Bus. Devel. Group div., 1972-74; mng. dir., chief operating officer Rank Xerox Ltd. subs. Xerox Corp., London, 1974-80; exec. v.p., chief staff officer Xerox Corp., Stamford, 1980-82, exec. v.p. reprographics and ops., 1982-85, pres. bus. equipment groups, 1983-85, vice chmn., 1985—; also dir., mem. exec. com., corp. mgmt. com., corp. operating com. Xerox Corp.; pres. Babson Coll., Babson Park, Mass., 1989—; dir., mem. corp. office with primary responsibility for reprographics and systems groups, research and relationsship with Fuji Xerox Co., Ltd.; dir. Rank Xerox Ltd., State Street Bank Boston, Gould, Inc., Chgo., Norton Co., Xerox Found. Trustee, mem. president's council Coll. of Holy Cross; bd. overseers Wharton Sch., U. Pa., also mem. exec. council Wharton Grad. Sch., mem. U.S. Cerebral Palsy Assn. (exec. com.), Cath. Charities U.S.A. (exec. cabinet), adv. bd. Wharton Ctr. for Internat. Mgmt. Studies, Joseph H. Lauder Inst. Mgmt. and Internat. Studies; nat. chmn. Xerox United Way. Mem. Computer and Bus. Equipment Mfrs. Assn. (bd. dirs.). Office: Xerox Corp PO Box 1600 Stamford CT 06904

GLAZE, ROBERT HOWE, real estate executive; b. St. Joseph, Mo., Nov. 9, 1952; s. Andrew S. and Elizabeth H. Glaze. BA, Westminster Coll., 1975; MBA, So. Meth. U., 1976. Credit analyst credit dept. Boatmen's Nat. Bank, St. Louis, 1976-78; comml. banking rep. credit tng. program First Nat. Bank, Chgo., 1978-79, comml. banking officer retailing cos. div. U.S. Banking dept., 1979-82, asst. v.p. retailing cos. div., 1983-85; investment mgr. acquisitions and sales dept. The Prudential Realty Group, Chgo., 1985—. Mem. Art Inst. Chgo., Chgo. Archtl. Found.; bd. assocs. Chgo. Child Care Soc., 1980-85; jr. bd. Lawrence Hall Sch. for Boys, 1980-88; assoc. Bd. of Mental Health Assn., Greater Chgo., aux. mem.; mem. Met. Bd. Youth Guidance, Chgo., 1986—; mem. Black and White Ball com. Mental Health Assn. Chgo., 1986—. Mem. English Speaking Union (bd.), Westminster Coll.

Alumni Coun., Univ. Club. Home: 2500 N Lakeview Ave #503 Chicago IL 60614 Office: Prudential Realty Group Prudential Pla Ste 3300 Chicago IL 60601

GLAZER, IRA L., financial executive; b. N.Y.C., May 8, 1951; s. Soloman and Ruth Pearl (Laub) G.; m. Joan Anita Horowitz, Dec. 14, 1974; children: Joshua, Justin. BBA, Pace U., 1975; car. Mgr. dividends Chase Manhattan Bank, N.Y.C., 1975-77, credit trainee, 1977-78, asst. treas., 1978-79, 2d v.p., 1979-81, v.p., team leader, 1981-82, v.p., div. exec., 1982-83; asst. v.p. fin. Maidenform Inc., N.Y.C., 1983-86, treas., 1986-88, treas., v.p. fin., 1988—. Served to sgt. N.Y.N.G. Republican. Jewish. Office: Maidenform Inc 90 Park Ave New York NY 10016

GLAZER, MARK JONATHAN, lawyer, labor arbitrator; b. Detroit, Jan. 3, 1949; s. B. Benedict and Ada (Spieyle) G.; m. Marilyn Elizabeth Ruby; 1 child, Catherine. BA, U. Mich., 1970, JD, 1973. Bar: Calif. 1973, Mich. 1974. Pvt. practice Birmingham, Mich., 1976-80; labor arbitrator Birmingham, 1980—. Contbr. articles to profl. jours. Legal advisor Handicapped Children North Oakland County, Waterford, Mich., 1982. Fellow Nat. Acad. Arbitrators; mem. Indsl. Rels. Rsch. Assn., Soc. Profls. and Dispute Resolution, Mich. Bar Assn., Calif. Bar Assn. Office: 3705 W Maple Birmingham MI 48010

GLEACHER, ERIC JAY, banker; b. N.Y.C., Apr. 27, 1940; s. Joseph and Marjorie (Carr) G.; m. Susan Gleacher (div. Oct. 1978); children: John, Sarah, James, Jay; m. Anne Gilchrist, Dec. 7, 1978. BA, Northwestern U., Evanston, Ill., 1962; MBA, U. Chgo., 1967. Mng. dir. Lehman Bros., N.Y.C., 1968-83, Morgan Stanley & Co. Inc., N.Y.C., 1983—. Lt. USMC, 1963-66. Office: Morgan Stanley & Co Inc 1251 Ave of Americas New York NY 10020

GLEADELL, RICHARD EUGENE, JR., medical products executive; b. Dayton, Ohio, Oct. 4, 1950; s. Richard Eugene Sr. and Wanda Maxine (Woolley) G.; m. Marilyn Sue Baker, Feb. 26, 1984. BBA, Ohio State U., 1973; MBA, U. Denver, 1982. Mgr. computer systems and prodn./inventory control Marquest Med. Products, Inc., Englewood, Colo., 1982-83, 84—; dir. mgmt. info. systems Monolithic Systems, Denver, 1983-84. Mem. Handgun Control, Washington, 1981. Mem. Am. Prodn. and Inventory Control Soc. Office: Marquest Med Products 11039 E Lansing Circle Englewood CO 80112

GLEASON, GREGORY LYNN, accountant, consultant; b. Chgo., July 27, 1950; s. Leslie Willard and Christine (Barnett) G.; m. Kristine Sue Rector, July 27, 1974; children: Amanda Claire, Laura Elizabeth. BA, Hanover Coll., 1972; MBA, U. Chgo., 1984. CPA, Minn. With Arthur Andersen & Co., Chgo., 1974-86; ptnr. Arthur Andersen & Co., Mpls., 1986—. Exec. v.p. Internat. Visitors Ctr. Chgo., 1982-86, bd. dirs., 1984-86; bd. dirs. Cathedral Counseling Ctr., 1986, Council for Young Professionals, 1984-86; pres., bd. dirs., treas. Landmarks Preservation Council Ill., 1979-86; mem. com. on fgn. affairs Chgo. Council Fgn. Relations, 1982-86; vestry mem., jr. warden Ch. of Our Saviour, 1976-82; mem. community council Jr. League Chgo., Inc., 1982-86; bd. dirs., v.p. Chgo. Jr. Assn. Commerce and Industry, 1976-78; bd. dirs. The Wells Bd., The Cathedral Ch. St. Mark, 1988—; bd. dirs., mem. fin. com. Minn. Opera, St. Paul, 1987—; bd. dirs., treas., mem. devel. com. N.W. Ballet, Mpls., 1987—. Mem. Am. Inst. CPAs, Minn. CPA Soc., Econ. Club Chgo., Tower Club, Mpls. Athletic Club, Union League Club. Office: Arthur Andersen & Co 45 S 75th St Minneapolis MN 55402

GLEASON, GREGORY WILLIAMS, bank executive; b. Charlottesville, Va., Sept. 10, 1951; s. Hope Woods and Dorothy Elizabeth (Williams) G.; m. Jerrilynn Carracher, Apr. 20, 1985. BBA, U. Miami, Coral Gables, Fla., 1975. Asst. v.p. Atlantic Fed. Savs. and Loan, Ft. Lauderdale, Fla., 1978-84; v.p. mortgage banking div. Va. First Savs. Bank, Richmond, 1984—; Bd. dirs. Inst. Fin. Edn., Richmond, 1984—; course instr. Inst. Fin. Edn.-John Tyler Community Coll., Richmond, 1986—. Bd. dirs. Miami chpt. Am. Cancer Soc., 1981-84 (pres. jr. bd. dirs. 1981-82), Richmond chpt. Am. Lung Assn., 1984-86. Recipient Outstanding Achievement award Am. Cancer Soc., 1982, 83; named one of Outstanding Young Men of Am. U.S. Jaycees, 1985. Mem. Richmond Mortgage Bankers, Richmond Bd. Realtors, Va. Real Estate Bur. (lic. 1977). Republican. Methodist. Clubs: Downtown (Richmond), Farmington Country (Charlottesville). Office: Va 1st Savs Bank Franklin at Adams St Petersburg VA 23804

GLEASON, JOHN FRANCIS, paint and chemical coatings company executive; b. N.Y.C., Sept. 13, 1928; s. John Francis Sr. and Viola (Huber) G.; m. Nancy Dee Buermann, Jan. 25, 1955; children: Leslie, Donald, Hilary, Jared, Sean, Chad. B in Mech. Engring., U. Va., 1954. V.p., gen. mgr. automotive, indsl., and marine Coatings and Specialties Co. div. Celanese Corp., Louisville, 1972-73, v.p. profit ctr. mgr. trade sales, 1973-75, v.p., gen. mgr. coatings group, 1975-76; group v.p. Grow Group, Inc., N.Y.C., 1976-77, exec. v.p., 1977—, also bd. dirs. Served with USAF, 1951-53. Mem. Nat. Paint and Coatings Assn. (trade sales com. 1977-81, mem. steering com., mem., dir. budget and fin. coms. 1981-83, dir. exec. com. 1983-84). Club: Board Room (N.Y.C.). Office: Grow Group Inc 200 Park Ave New York NY 10166

GLEASON, LEONARD GEORGE, savings and loan executive, lawyer; b. Jersey City, Mar. 30, 1954; s. Leonard Richard and Evelyn Frances (Johnson) G.; m. Deborah Ann D'Amore, July 6, 1985. BS in Acctg., St. Peter's Coll., Jersey City, 1976; JD, Seton Hall U., 1981. Bar: N.J. 1983. Sr. tax acct. Arthur Andersen & Co., Newark, 1975-78; tax assoc. Sills, Beck, Cummis, Zuckerman, P.A., Newark, 1980-82; v.p. corp. tax Carteret Savs. Bank, F.A., Morristown, N.J., 1983-87; v.p. tax Beneficial Corp., Peapack, N.J., 1987-88; asst. v.p. tax Berkeley Fed. Savs. & Loan, Millburn, N.J., 1988—. Mem. ABA (taxation sect.), N.J. State Bar Assn. (taxation sect.), Nat. Council Savs. Instns. (taxation com.). Home: 33 Hansen Dr Edison NJ 08820-1677 Office: Berkeley Fed Savs & Loan 21 Bleeker St Millburn NJ 07041

GLEAVES, JAMES LESLIE, investment company executive; b. Dallas, Jan. 5, 1952; s. R.L. and Ethel (Treadway) G. BBA, U. Tex., 1974, MBA, 1977. Investment analyst Equitable Life Assurance Soc. U.S., N.Y.C., 1977-84; from asst. v.p. to v.p. Am. Gen. Cor., Houston, 1984—. Mem. Fin. Analysts Fedn., Houston Soc. Fin. Analysts, U. Tex. Club. Methodist. Office: Am Gen Corp 2929 Allen Pkwy Houston TX 77019

GLEIJESES, MARIO, grain company executive; b. Rome, Feb. 27, 1955; came to U.S., 1985; s. Luigi Gleijeses and Rosalba Catanoso. Student, U. Naples, 1977. Chartering mgr. Itex subs. Italgrani, Zurich, 1977-82; asst. to pres. Italgrani Spa, Naples, Itlay, 1982-85; exec. v.p., bd. dirs. Italgrani USA Inc. and Italgrani Elevator Co., St. Louis, 1985—; v.p., bd. dirs. New Eng. Milling Co., Ayer, Mass., 1987—; bd. dirs. Green Bay Elevator Co., Burlington, Iowa; v.p., bd. dirs. Mayco Export, Inc., Mpls., 1988—; pres., bd.dirs. McLean Elevator Co., Benedict, N.D., 1989—. Home: 200 S Brentwood Blvd Saint Louis MO 63105 Office: Italgrani USA 7900 Van Buren Saint Louis MO 63111

GLENN, ALBERT H., aerospace company executive. Formerly pres., U.S. ops. Gulfstream Aerospace Corp., Travis Field, Ga.; now vice-chmn. Gulfstream Aerospace Corp., Savannah, Ga. *

GLENN, DEBORAH ANNE, retail executive; b. Portsmouth, Va., Apr. 19, 1955; d. Gerald Henri Joseph and Cecelia Marie (Brown) Racicot; m. Robert Michael Glenn, Oct. 8, 1983; 1 child, Michelle Zavier. AA, Lab. Inst. of Tech., N.Y.C., 1976. Distbr., planner Korvettes, N.Y.C., 1976, asst. buyer, 1977, assoc. buyer, 1977-78, buyer, 1978-80; buyer Abraham & Straus, N.Y.C., 1980-82, Montgomery Ward, N.Y.C., 1982-85; v.p. merchandising and design L.B.J. Sales/Pappagallo Hosiery, N.Y.C., 1986-89; exec. v.p. Sock Connection, Ft. Lee, N.J., 1987-89; v.p. merchandising and sales Highpoint Industries, N.Y.C., 1989—. Office: Highpoint Industries 1350 Broadway New York NY 10016

GLENN, ROBERT BRIAN, financial executive; b. Lewiston, Maine, Feb. 2, 1957; s. Gardner Henry and Natalie Fay (Porter) G.; m. Catherine Annette Liggett, Apr. 19, 1980; children: Brian, Scott, Allen. BS, Brigham Young U., 1981; postgrad., U. Hartford, 1985. Cert. fin. planner. Chartered fin. analyst Hamilton Gregg & Co., Falls Village, Conn., 1981-84; fin. counselor S. T. Sadlak & Co., Hartford, Conn., 1984-86, Lakeshore Fin. Advisors, Dallas, 1986-87, Cigna Individual Fin. Services Co., Irving, Tex., 1987—; adviser Dallas County Small Bus. Devel. Ctr., 1987—; instr. Brookhaven Community Coll., Farmers Branch, Tex., 1987—. Author workbook: Write Your Own Financial Plan, 1987; contbr. articles to profl. jours. Mem. 500 Inc., Dallas, 1987—. Fellow Fin. Analysts Fedn.; mem. Registry Fin. Planning, Toastmasters, Dallas C. of C. (mem. small bus. com. 1987). Lodge: Kiwanis. Office: Cigna Individual Fin Svcs 600 E Las Colinas Blvd #1400 Irving TX 75039

GLENN, ROY JOHNSON, manufactured housing executive; b. Birmingham, Ala., Dec. 23, 1920; s. Willis and Maggie (Johnson) G.; student acctg. Massey Bus. Coll., 1938-39; student engring. Auburn U., 1941-42; m. Sammie Lee Spradling, Feb. 14, 1941; children: Ellen Glenn Andersen, Jerry Alan. Mold loftsman, Higgins Industries, New Orleans, 1943-44; ptnr. Glenn Constrn. Co., Birmingham, Ala., 1946-50; profl. golfer, 1950-57; pres. Crab Orchard Golf Club, Inc., Carterville, Ill., 1958-63; sec., treas. Cavaness-Glenn-Storme, Inc., Carterville, 1964-75; pres. Glenn & Co., Inc., Carterville, 1963-76; sec. Component Building Systems, Inc., Carbondale, Ill., 1976—; ptnr. Roydon & Assocs., Carbondale, 1982—; owner Crest Builders Assocs., 1977-86, Design Cons., 1983—; cons. various golf and country clubs; designer golf courses and bldgs. Bd. trustees John A. Logan Coll., 1968-70; mem. govs. task force on Future of Rural Ill., 1986. Served with USN, 1944-46. Republican. Baptist. Home and Office: Rte 2 Carbondale IL 62901

GLENN, STEVEN CLAUDE, financial executive; b. N.Y.C., Jan. 26, 1947; s. Jack and Lillian (Dankner) Goloshin; m. Penelope Wertz, Aug. 9, 1969 (div. 1982); m. Kathy Mathews, May 23, 1985; children: Darren, Chad Mathews, Ryan, Tara Mathews, Roscoe Goloshin. BA, U. Miami, Fla., 1970; postgrad., Am. Coll., 1976, 82, 87, 88. Cert. CLU, chartered fin. cons. Agt. Occidental Life Ins. Co., Miami, 1970-75; assoc. gen. agt. Conn. Mut. Life Ins. Co., Miami, 1975-78; agy. mgr. Bankers Life Ins. Co., Jacksonville, Fla., 1978-81; regional v.p. Cigna Corp., Jacksonville, 1981-85; v.p. Lincoln Planning Group, Inc., Jacksonville, 1985-88; pres. Steven C. Glenn, CLU, ChFC, Orange Park, Fla., 1989—. Contbr. to books: Your Money and Your Life, 1979, ABC's of Investing Your Retirement Funds, 1980; contbr. articles to profl. jours. Bd. dirs. Jacksonville Gen. Agts. and Mgrs. Assn., 1981-84. Mem. Internat. Assn. Fin. Planning, Jacksonville Soc. CLUs and Chartered Fin. Cons. Home: 3061 Hwy 17 South Orange Park FL 32073 Office: 1857 Wells Rd Orange Park FL 32073

GLENN, THOMAS LEWIS, JR., insurance agency executive; b. Margate, N.J., Oct. 8, 1934; s. Thomas Lewis and Serena (Wheeler) G.; m. Anne-Marie Mohn, June 11, 1960; children: Kerri M., Thomas Lewis III. BA, Colgate U., 1957. With Glenn Ins., Absecon, N.J., 1957—, pres., 1966—, chmn., 1984—; bd. dirs. Midlantic Nat. Bank, Neptune, N.J.; dir. South Jersey Industries. With USNG, 1957-63. Mem. Union League of Phila. Office: Glenn Ins Inc 500 E Absecon Blvd Absecon NJ 08201

GLENN, THOMAS MICHAEL, pharmaceutical company executive; b. Detroit, July 20, 1940; s. Spencer S. and Mary C. (Snell) G.; m. Patricia Ann Ross, Aug. 25, 1962; children: Thomas M. Jr., Timothy P., Christine D. AB, Rockhurst Coll., 1962; MS, U. Mo., Kansas City, 1965, PhD, 1968. Assoc. prof. pharmacology N.D. State U., Fargo, 1966-68, Fla. A&M U., Tallahassee, 1968-69; postdoctoral fellow dept. pharmacology U. Va., 1969-71; assoc. prof. dept. pharmacology U. Pa., 1971-73; prof., chmn. dept. pharmacology U. South Ala., 1973-82, co-dir. clin. pharmacology research unit, 1981-82; exec. dir. biology research, pharmaceuticals div. Ciba-Geigy Corp., 1982-84, sr. v.p., dir. research pharm. div., 1984-88; v.p. pharmacological scis. Genentech Inc., South San Francisco, 1988—; vis. assoc. prof. pharmacology U. Miss., Oxford, 1969; mem. cardiovascular and renal ad hoc study sect. NIH, 1978-80, exptl. cardiovascular diseases study sect., 1980-81; mem. Emergency Med. Tng. Adv. Bd., 1979-82; mem. adv. panel cardiovascular drugs U.S. Pharmamcopeial Conv., 1980—; mem. med. staff USA Med. Ctr., 1982; corp. rep. Indsl. Research Inst., 1985-88; cons. Merck, Sharpe and Dohme, 1971-73, Johnson & Johnson Baby Products, Inc., 1981-82. Cons. editor Circulatory Shock, assoc. editor, 1974-80; mem. editorial bd. Internat. Jour. Tissue Reactions, Internat. Jour. Immunotherapy, Drug Devel. Research; manuscript referee Circulation Research, Life Sci., Jour. Pharmacology and Exptl. Therapeutics, Jour. Cardiovascular Pharmacology; contbr. numerous articles to profl. jours. Coach/mgr. Little League Baseball, 1974-78; advisor med. post 410 Boy Scouts Am., 1975-79; mem. Archdiocesan Bd. Cath. Edn., 1979-82, pres.; mem. exec. leadership team Cath. Engaged Encounter, Archdiocese Mobile, 1980-82; trustee N.Y. Hall Sci., 1985-88. NIH fellow, 1965-66, Nat. Heart and Lung Inst. fellow, 1969-71; recipient Alumni Achievement award U. Mo.-Kansas City, 1985. Mem. Am. Soc. Clin. Pharmacology and Therapeutics, Am. Soc. Pharmacology and Exptl. Therapeutics, Am. Physiol. Soc., Indsl. Research Inst., Am. Mgmt. Assn. (research and devel. council 1985—), N.Y. Acad. Sci., Am. Heart Assn. (reserch com. Ala. affiliate 1975-78, chmn. com. for youth 1979-82, bd. dirs. 1980-83, pres. Mobile County div. 1978-79, nominating com. 1980-81, bd. dirs. Northwest N.J. chpt. 1983-85), AAAS, Am. Coll. Clin. Pharmacology, Am. Chem. Soc. (medicinal chemistry div.), Soc. Explt. Biology and Medicine, Pharm. Mfrs. Assn. (chmn. research and devel. steering com. 1985—), Shock Soc. (councillor 1978-80, publs. com. 1980-81), Microcirculatory Soc., Am. Soc. Exptl. Pharmacology, Am. Soc. Experimental Pharm. Therapy, Am. Soc. Clin. Pharmacology, Rho Chi, Sigma Xi. Republican. Roman Catholic. Home: 116 Mesa Verde Way San Carlos CA 94070 Office: Genentech Inc 460 Point San Bruno Blvd South San Francisco CA 94080

GLENNEY, LYNN HARREN, service executive; b. Marshalltown, Iowa, Feb. 8, 1934; s. Paul McClean and Edith Banff (Harren) G.; student Iowa State Coll., 1951-53; BS with honors, UCLA, 1960, MBA, 1961; m. Fumie Morimoto, Mar. 24, 1958; children: Paul Masaya, Kathleen Mizuho. Asst. to v.p. sales Flying Tiger Lines, Inc., Burbank, Calif., 1960-62; market analyst Douglas Aircraft Co., Inc., Santa Monica, Calif., 1962-64; sr. assoc. Planning Rsch. Corp., L.A., 1964-69; dir. corp. planning Lear Siegler, Inc., Santa Monica, 1969-87; bus. unit v.p. APEX Tech., Inc., Camarillo, Calif., 1988—; expositor planning and strategy Instituto de Aministración Científica de las Empresas, Republic of Mex., 1981; tech. expert on planning Asian Productivity Orgn., Tokyo, 1979. Chmn. priorities com. Western Region, United Way, 1974-78, 80-81, chmn. planning coun., 1982-84, bd. dirs. Western region, 1982—; bd. dirs. Westside Ind. Svcs. for Elderly, 1981—; mem. West L.A. Coll. Found., 1984—; mem. Ad hoc com. on productivity City of L.A., 1984-85; mem. strategic process com., United Way, 1985—; chmn. adv. coun. Western Region Asian Am. Program, 1988—, pres. 1988, mem. 1983—. With USMC, 1954-58. Recipient Outstanding Vol. Service award United Way, 1976. Mem. N.Am. Soc. Corp. Planning, Inc. (v.p. 1981-83), The Planning Forum, So. Calif. Corp. Planners Assn. (pres. 1976-77), Assn. Asian Studies, Marine Corps Assn., Internat. Affiliation Planning Socs. (v.p. 1977-80), Acacia. Republican. Presbyterian. Home: 428 Gretna Green Way Los Angeles CA 90049 Office: APEX Tech Inc 1317 Del Norte Rd Camarillo CA 93010

GLENNON, ROBERT EUGENE, lawyer; b. Decatur, Ill., Apr. 23, 1948; s. Robert and Martha (Chapman) G.; m. Helen G. Blechman, Aug. 14, 1983; 1 child, Michael Robert. BS, U. Ill., 1971; JD, U. Fla., 1974, LLM in Taxation, 1975. Bar: Fla. 1974, U.S. Tax Ct. 1975, D.C. 1976, U.S. Supreme Ct. 1977. Instr. law U. Fla., Gainesville, 1975-76; assoc. Williams & Jensen, P.C., Washington, 1976-80, ptnr., 1980—. Mem. Pres.'s coun., U. Fla., bd. advisors grad. program in taxation. Capt. USAR, 1971-79. Mem. ABA. Home: 3 Washington Circle NW Apt 806 Washington DC 20037 Office: Williams & Jensen PC 1101 Connecticut Ave NW Washington DC 20036

GLICK, ALLAN H., business executive; b. N.Y.C., Nov. 15, 1938; s. Henry Bernard and Rose (Brensilver) G.; m. Marilyn Edythe Rubin, Aug. 21, 1960; children: Madeleine, Cherise. A.B., Dartmouth Coll., 1960, M.B.A., 1961. C.P.A., N.Y. Acct. S.D. Leidersdorf & Co., N.Y.C., 1961-66, Henry Brout & Co., N.Y.C., 1966-68; gen. ptnr. First Manhattan Co., N.Y.C., 1968—. Mem. Am. Inst. C.P.A.s, N.Y. Soc. C.P.A.s, Fin. Analyst Fedn. Club: Dartmouth (pres. 1973-76). Office: First Manhattan Co 437 Madison Ave New York NY 10022

GLICK, DEBORAH KELLY, accountant; b. Waterbury, Conn., Sept. 9, 1953; d. John Francis and Jeanne Doris (Weaving) Kelly; m. William Martin Glick Jr., June 30, 1973 (div. Oct. 1977); children: Kimberly, William III. BS, Post Coll., Waterbury, 1982. CPA, Conn. Staff acct. DeAngelis Lombardi & Kelly CPA's, Waterbury, 1981-82, John J. Baldelli, CPA, Naugatuck, Conn., 1982-84; ptnr. Baldelli Glick & Co. CPA's, Naugatuck, 1984—. Mem. Am. Inst. CPA's, Conn. Soc. CPA's, Nat. Soc. Pub. Accts., Nat. Soc. Exec. Females. Democrat. Roman Catholic. Office: Cornerstone Profl Park PO Box 1129 Woodbury CT 06798-1129

GLICK, IRWIN I., hotel and hospitality industry consultant; b. Cleve., Mar. 11, 1935; s. Phil E. and Lillian R. (Rosenberg) G.; m. Jill R. Robinson, Sept. 19, 1959; children: Lisa, Jeri. BS in Commerce, Ohio U., 1957. Cost acct. TRW, Inc., Cleve., 1959-62; controller Robert Silverman, Inc., Cleve., 1962-67; v.p. fin. Associated Motor Inns, Cleve., 1967-76; mgr. Laventhol & Horwath, Cleve., 1976-79; ptnr. Laventhol & Horwath, Miami, Fla., 1979—. Author: Economic Feasibility, 1981. Treas. Greater Miami Visitors and Conv. Bur., 1984-86. Lt. U.S. Army, 1957-59. Mem. Hospitality Accts. (bd. dirs. 1980-82), Am. Hotel Assn., Nat. Restaurant Assn., Miami Beach C. of C. (trustee), Fla. Hotel Assn., South Fla. Hospitality Accts., Ohio Restaurant Assn., Ohio U. Alumni Assn. Jewish. Office: Laventhol & Horwath 2 Alhambra Pla Coral Gables FL 33134

GLINES, ALAN CLAIR EDWIN, space systems manager, consultant; b. Independence, Kans., Jan. 1, 1943; s. Lewis Clair and Mary Ellen (Patty) G. B.S. in Elec. Engring., U. Kans., 1966 M.S. in Systems Mgmt., U. So. Calif., 1983. With NASA Johnson Space Ctr., Houston, 1966-79, asst. flight dir. mission control Apollo-Soyuz test project, Gemini, Apollo and Skylab programs, astronaut rep. Space Shuttle mfg., approach and landing test, Palmdale, Calif., 1976-79; sub-project mgr. payload integration TRW Space and Tech. Group, Redondo Beach, Calif., 1979-84, subproject mgr. space shuttle payload integration orbital maneuvering vehicle and gamma ray obs. projects, 1984-85 ; subproject mgr. Space Station Ops., 1985-88; part-time prof. U. So. Calif. Grad. Sch. in Systems Mgmt., 1986-88; instr. space shuttle/sta. integration and ops. TRW After Hours Program, 1984-88; manned space flight engring. and ops. contract mgr. to European Space Agy. on Columbus and Hermes programs, 1988—. Recipient Presdl. Medal of Freedom for contbns. to NASA Apollo 13, NASA spl. award Shuttle ALT, 1978, NASA achievement award, 1975, NASA Skylab Flight Crew award, 1975, NASA Apollo achievement award, 1969. Mem. Nat. Space Council. Republican. Home: Am Schwimmbad 30, D-6104 Jugenheim Federal Republic of Germany Office: ESA/ESOC, Robert Bosch Strasse 5, D6100 Darmstadt Federal Republic of Germany

GLINSKY, SIMON, management consultant; b. Atlanta, Sept. 29, 1962; s. Salomon and Rebeca (Teichberg) G. Student, U. Edinburgh, Scotland, 1983; BS in Econs. and Fin. magna cum laude, U. Pa., 1984. Rsch. asst. Busch Ctr. for Social Sci., Phila., 1982; bus. planning intern IBM Corp., Atlanta, 1983; rsch. coord. fin. dept. Wharton Sch. U. Pa., Phila., 1983-84; bus. analyst McKinsey & Co., Inc., Atlanta, 1984-87; asst. product mgr. Radius, Inc., San Jose, Calif., 1988—. Long range planning com. Woodruff Arts Ctr., Atlanta, 1986-87, Alliance Theatre, Atlanta, 1985-86. Benjamin Franklin scholar U. Pa., 1981-84; named one of Outstanding Young Men Am., 1986. Mem. U. Pa. Philomathean Soc. (vice-chmn. 175th anniversary com., endowment fund drive 1984—, moderator 1984), Amnesty Internat., Wharton Alumni Club of Bay Area, Wilson Ctr. (Washington), Commonwealth Club (San Francisco). Jewish. Office: Radius Inc 1710 Fortune Dr San Jose CA 95131

GLOBIG, DAVID PHILLIP, college business manager and treasurer; b. Flint, Mich., June 13, 1951; s. Roland Phillip and Eleanor M. (Critchlow) G.; m. Jane E. Ragain, July 5, 1975; children: David, Shannon, Karen, John. BA, Cedarville Coll., 1973; MBA, U. Akron, 1978. CPA, Iowa. Credit trainee, asst. internal auditor Dayton Corp., Mpls., 1973-75; acct., acting bus. mgr. Cuyahoga Valley Christian Acad., Cuyahoga Falls, Ohio, 1975-78; bus. mgr. Timberlake Christian Schs., Lynchburg, Va., 1978-84; bus. mgr., treas. Faith Bapt. Bible Coll. and Sem., Ankeny, Iowa, 1984—; freelance fin. cons., Ankeny, 1976—. Bd. dirs. Ankeny YMCA, 1987—; mem. Ankeny People Educating People Comm., 1986—. Mem. Am. Inst. CPAs, Assn. Bus. Administrs. Christian Colls. (liaison com for ins., 1985—). Republican. Baptist. Office: Faith Bapt Bible Coll & Sem 1900 NW 4th St Ankeny IA 50021

GLOGOWSKI, PATRICIA CAROL, real estate company executive; b. Rahway, N.J., Dec. 22, 1942; d. Bernard Anthony and Helen (Sisco) Duff; m. John Peter Glogowski, Dec. 2, 1961 (div. Feb. 1976); children: John J., Michael D. Student, Drake's Bus. Coll., 1962, Kean Coll., 1975. Lic. broker, N.J. Freelance real estate saleswoman/broker Kenilworth, N.J., 1971-77; owner, mgr., broker Happy Homes Realty, Kenilworth, 1977-83; broker, Union county dir. Berg Realtors, Clark, N.J., 1983-85; comml. and investment mgr. Berg Realtors/ First Metro Comml., Roselle Park, N.J., 1985-86; owner, mgr., broker Glowgowski Realty, Inc., Roselle Park, 1986—. Active Boy Scouts Am., 1975-78. Recipient Realtor of Yr. award, 1983, Real Estate award of Merit Suburban News, 1986. Mem. N.J. Assn. Realtors (polit. action com. 1986-88, Made Am. Better award 1980, 83, Pres.'s Excellence award 1987), Greater Eastern Union County Bd. Realtors (1st v.p. 1985-86, pres. 1986-87, congl. coord. 1987-88, Outstanding Leadership award 1980). Club: Plainfield Ski (sec. 1983-84). Home: 29 Tisbury Ct Scotch Plains NJ 07076 Office: 342 E Westfield Ave Roselle Park NJ 07204

GLOOR, CHRISTOPHER BARTA, corporate professional; b. San Diego, May 6, 1949; s. Fred Gloor and Clarice Barta; m. Agathe Maria Gobertina Winter , Nov. 28, 1987. Student, U. Calif., San Diego, 1969-71. Ptnr. Middlearth, San Diego, 1969-72; pres. Middlearth Internat. Inc., San Diego, 1972—, Middlearth Internat. Inc. dba Corp. Svcs. Internat., San Diego, 1985—, Australia House, San Diego, 1988—; bd. dirs. Antak Proprietary Ltd., Queensland, Australia, 1983—; ptnr. Australia Day, 1986; bd. dir. Australia House, San Diego, 1987—. Mem. Inventors Assn. Australia, Australian-Am. C. of C. Republican. Office: Corp Svcs Internat 4009 S Hempstead Circle San Diego CA 92116

GLORIE, FRANCIS ETIENNE, electronics executive; b. Calais, Pas-de-Calais, France, May 2, 1950; came to U.S., 1973; s. Francis Raymond and Madeleine (Duffy) G.; m. Catherine Louise Brothers, Aug. 5, 1983; children: Simone Adrienne, Danielle Francoise. BBA, Ecole Superieure de Commerce, France, 1973; MBA, U. Mich., 1975. Sr. cons. 1st of Ann Arbor, Mich., 1975-77; v.p. Midwest Microwave, Inc., Ann Arbor, 1977-80; chief operating officer Jodon, Inc., Ann Arbor, 1980-83; sr. v.p., chief fin. officer, founder Irwin Magnetic Systems, Inc., Ann Arbor, 1983—. Office: Irwin Magnetic Systems Inc 2101 Commonwealth Blvd Ann Arbor MI 48105

GLOTH, ALEC ROBERT, retail grocery executive; b. Spokane, Wash., Mar. 26, 1927; s. Erich Carl and Ella L. (Felsch) G.; m. Catharine E. Seabloom, May 26, 1954; children: A. Stephen, Rebecca J. Parlet. Grad., Stanford exec. program Boise State U., 1975. With Albertson's, 1951—; v.p. mktg. Albertson's, Boise, Idaho, 1972-74, v.p. store planning, 1974-76, dist. mgr., 1976-77; v.p., div. mgr. Albertson's, Spokane, Wash., 1977-79; sr. v.p., regional mgr. Albertson's, Boise, 1979-81, sr. v.p. store planning, 1981—. Active Boy Scouts Am., Eagle Scout; bd. dirs. Discovery Ctr. Idaho. With U.S. Army, 1954-56. Mem. Am. Mgmt. Assn., Food Mktg. Inst. Republican. Methodist. Clubs: Exchange, Hillcrest Country, Spokane. Lodge: Elks. Home: 1193 Kingfisher Boise ID 83709 Office: Albertson's Inc 250 Parkcenter Blvd Boise ID 83726

GLOVER, CHARLES E., newspaper publishing company executive; b. 1925; married. Mem. staff Dayton Newspapers, 1949-76; pres. Cox Enterprises Inc., Atlanta, 1977-87; now editor-in-chief Cox Newspapers, Atlanta. Office: Cox Newspapers PO Box 105720 Atlanta GA 30348

GLOVER, RICHARD M., manufacturing company executive. married. BSME, U. Ariz., 1963. With Procter and Gamble Co., 1963—, now v.p. Office: Procter & Gamble Co 1 Procter & Gamble Pla Cincinnati OH 45202 *

GLOYD, LAWRENCE EUGENE, diversified manufacturing company executive; b. Milan, Ind., Nov. 5, 1932; s. Oran C. and Ruth (Baylor) G.; m. Delma Lear, Sept. 10, 1955; children—Sheryl, Julia, Susan. B.A., Hanover Coll., 1954. Salesman Shapleigh Hdwe., St. Louis, 1956-60, W. Bingham Co., Cleve., 1960-61; salesman Amerock Corp., Rockford, Ill., 1961-68, regional sales mgr., 1968-69, dir. consumer products mktg., 1969-71, dir. merchandising, 1971-72, dir. mktg. and sales, 1972-73, v.p. mktg. and sales, 1973-81, exec. v.p., 1981-82, pres., gen. mgr., 1982-86; v.p. Hardware Products Group, Anchor Hocking Corp., Lancaster, Ohio, 1983-86; pres., chief operating officer CLARCOR, Rockford, Ill., 1986-88, pres., chief exec. officer, 1988—, also bd. dirs.; bd. dirs. AMcore Fin. Inc., Rockford, Thomas Industries Inc., Louisville, Ky., Towle Mfg. Co., Newburyport, Mass.; mem. Middle West adv. bd. Liberty Mut. Ins. Co. Bd. dirs. Council of 100, Ill. Council on Econ. Edn.; trustee Rockford Coll., SwedishAmerican Corp. Served with AUS, 1954-56. Mem. Am. Hardware Mfrs. Assn. (bd. dirs.), Presidents Assn., Masons. Republican. Home: 4979 Crofton Dr Rockford IL 61111 Office: CLARCOR 2323 6th St PO Box 7007 Rockford IL 61125

GLUCK, HENRY, resort complex executive; b. Aurich, Germany, May 11, 1928; married. BS, U. Pa., 1950. Former pres., chief operating officer Monogram Industries, Inc.; chmn., pres., chief exec. officer Magnasync-Moviola, Inc.; chmn. Standun, Inc., 1978—; chief exec. officer Caesars World, Inc., 1982—, now also chmn., bd. dirs., 1982—; chmn. Caesars N.J. Inc., Atlantic City, 1983—. Served with U.S. Army, 1950-53. Office: Caesars World Inc 1801 Century Pk E Los Angeles CA 90067 *

GLUTH, ROBERT C., diversified holding company executive; b. 1924; married. BBA, U. Wis., 1949. With The Marmon Group Inc., Chgo., 1963—, now exec. v.p., also bd. dirs. Office: Marmon Group Inc 225 W Washington St Chicago IL 60606 *

GLUYS, CHARLES BYRON, marketing management consultant; b. Richmond, Ind., Apr. 16, 1928; s. J. Howard and Reba Anna (Macy) G.; m. Patricia Wheeler, July 25, 1953; children: Gary William, Robert Lee, Marcia Kay, James Duke. BS in Indsl. Econs., Purdue U., 1955. Sales mgr. Carlyle Constrn., Columbus, Ohio, 1958; asst. product mgr. Palmer-Donavin Mfg., Columbus, 1958-61; new product mgr. KCL Corp., Shelbyville, Ind., 1963-64; prin. Gluys & Assocs., Greenfield, Ind., 1964—. Asst. scoutmaster Boy Scouts Am., Greenfield, 1953-54, Columbus, 1958-60, organizer and chmn., Columbus, 1960-61. Served with USN, 1946-48. Mem. Am. Mktg. Assn. (bd. dirs. 1970-73), Inventor's Assn. Ind. (1st. v.p. 1986), Entrepreneur's Alliance, Assn. Indsl. Advertisers (treas. 1971-72). Club: Venture of Ind. Lodge: Masons. Office: PO Box 399 Greenfield IN 46140

GLYNN, JEANNETTE ESTELLE, corporate librarian; b. Savannah, Ga., Nov. 6, 1927; d. John and Estelle Lanier (Bowers) G. BA, U. Ga., 1948; M of Librarianship, Emory U., 1955. Reference libr. Atlanta Pub. Library, 1956-59; head Fulton County Dept., Atlanta Pub. Library, 1959-61; reference libr. Oakland (Calif.) Pub. Library, 1962-64; regional libr. Alameda County Libr., Hayward, Calif., 1964-67, head, bus. and govt. libr., 1968-71; county libr. Inyo County Library, Independence, Calif., 1971-76; head Vallejo (Calif.) region Solano County Library, 1976-79; head dept. rsch. Neighborhood Housing Am., Oakland, 1980-82; mgr. tech. library Bank Am., Concord, Calif., 1982—. Author: Who Knows Who, 1987. Mem. ALA, Spl. Library Assn., Am. Soc. Info. Sci. Democrat. Office: Bank Am 1755 Grant St Ste 3099 Concord CA 94520

GNEHM, MAX WILLI, financial consultant; b. Switzerland, July 15, 1943; s. Max Hans and Frieda Gnehm; m. Henrietta D. Schwarz, July 1, 1984; children: Alexandra Barbara, William Anthony. MBA, Swiss Sch. Bus., 1963; postgrad. Swiss Inst. Mktg. and Fgn. Trade Research. Asst. mgr. Maxwell Sci. Internat. Book Co., 1964-66; mgr. book and periodical div. Internat. Univ. Booksellers, N.Y.C., 1966-69; dir. Internat. div. Richard Abel Co., 1969-74; v.p. mktg. Blackwell of N.Am., Inc., Beaverton, Oreg., 1974-76, pres., 1976-79, also bd. dirs.; pres., chmn. bd. Swiss-Am. Investment Group Inc.; bd. dirs. Swiss Am. Data Net, Swiss Am. Data Exchange, Atlin Investment Group, Inc.; pres., bd. dirs. Transpacific Holding Group Ltd., Malcolm Smith, Inc, Concorde Pacific Exploration, Inc., Interpacific Printing, Inc., Hong Kong Fin. Group Ltd., Pacific Mining, Inc., 1987—; bd. dirs. Macedon Resources Ltd., Lore Corp. Author: New Reference Tools for Librarians, 1965. Mem. ALA, Pres.'s Assn. Home: Rte 2 Box 376 Forest Grove OR 97116 Office: TransPacific Holding Group Inc 10 Thomas Rd Irvine CA 92718

GNOSPELIUS, RICHARD ARTHUR, accounting firm executive; b. Boston, Oct. 29, 1939; s. Gunnar Arthur and Elsa (Mattson) G.; m. Suzanne D'Allessandro, Nov. 21, 1965; children: John A., James A., Sharon M. BS in Acctg., Bentley Coll., 1965. CPA. With Coopers & Lybrand, Boston, 1961-72; gen. practice ptnr. Coopers & Lybrand, N.Y.C., 1972-79, nat. dir. auditing, 1980-83; mng. ptnr. cen. region Coopers & Lybrand, Chgo., 1983-88; vice-chmn. S.W. region Coopers & Lybrand, Houston, 1988—. Chmn. profl. adv. bd. dept. acctg. U. Ill., Champaign/Urbana, 1985-87; chmn. bd. trustees Bentley Coll., Waltham, Mass., 1971—; mem. Lake Forest (Ill.) Caucus, 1984-88; bd. dirs. Lincoln Park Zool. Soc., Chgo., 1986-88, WNYC Found., N.Y.C., 1979-82, Lake Forest Symphony, 1984-88. 1st lt. USAR, 1964-68. Fellow Ill. Soc. CPAs, Mass. Soc. CPAs, N.Y. Soc. CPAs; mem. AICPA, Chgo. Club, Stanwich Club (Greenwich, Conn.), Swedish Am. Soc. (Chgo.), Houston Tennis & Raquet Club, Petroleum Club. Office: Coopers & Lybrand 1100 Louisiana Houston TX 77002

GOBAR, ALFRED JULIAN, economic consultant, educator; b. Lucerne Valley, Calif., July 12, 1932; s. Julian Smith and Hilda (Millbank) G.; B.A. in Econs., Whittier Coll., 1953, M.A. in History, 1955; postgrad. Claremont Grad. Sch., 1953-54; Ph.D. in Econs., U. So. Calif., 1963; m. Sally Ann Randall, June 17, 1957; children—Wendy Lee, Curtis Julian, Joseph Julian. Asst. pres. Microdot Inc., Pasadena, 1953-57; regional sales mgr. Sutorbilt Corp., Los Angeles, 1957-59; market research assoc. Beckman Instrument Inc., Fullerton, 1959-64; sr. marketing cons. Western Mgmt. Consultants Inc., Phoenix, Los Angeles, 1964-66; ptnr., prin., chmn. bd. Darley/Gobar Assocs., Inc., 1966-73; pres., chmn. bd. Alfred Gobar Assocs., Inc., Brea, Calif., 1973—; asst. prof. finance U. So. Calif., Los Angeles, 1963-64; assoc. prof. bus. Calif. State U.-Los Angeles, 1963-68, 70-79, assoc. prof. Calif. State U.-Fullerton, 1968-69; mktg., fin. adviser 1957—; pub. speaker seminars and convs. Contbr. articles to profl. publs. Home: 1100 W Valencia Mesa Dr Fullerton CA 92633 Office: 201 S Brea Blvd Brea CA 92621

GOCKEL, JOHN RAYMOND, construction executive; b. Ft. Madison, Iowa, June 12, 1947; s. Carl R. and Virginia Jeanne (Schultz) G.; children: Rose M., Christina Ann. BSCE, Iowa State U., 1970. Registered profl. engr., Mich., Minn. Cost estimator Barton Malow Co., Detroit, 1975-76, project mgr., 1976-82, project adminstr., 1982-83; project exec. Gilbane Building Co., Maplewood, Minn., 1983-84; constrn. mgr., dir. phys. plant Minn. Racetrack, Inc., Shakopee, 1984-85; v.p. Scottland, Inc., Shakopee, Minn., 1985-86, Knutson Constr. Co., Mpls., 1987-88, Encompass Inc., Bloomington, Minn., 1988—; project mgr. Mpls. Metrodome; constrn. mgr. Canterbury Downs, Mpls., cons. to various developers, contractors; lectr. various civic, profl., acad. groups, Minn. Arbitrator Am. Arbitration Assn., throughout Midwest, 1982. Recipient Honor award Cons. Engrs. Coun., Minn., 1985. Mem. Profl. Engrs. in Constrn. (v.p. 1983, pres. 1984, bd. dirs. 1985), Am. Concrete Inst., Minn. Soc. Profl. Engrs. (bd. dirs. 1985-86, Seven Wonders of Engring. award 1982, 85), Constrn. Specifications Inst., Constrn. Mgmt. Forum, Iowa State U. Alumni Assn., Tau Beta Pi. Republican. Roman Catholic. Home: 300 W 96th St #2L Bloomington MN 55420 Office: Encompass Inc 2850 Metro Dr Minneapolis MN 55425

GODBOLD, FRANCIS STANLEY, investment banker, real estate/oil and gas executive; b. Charleston, S.C., Mar. 4, 1943; s. Francis Stanley and Ula Leigh (Waddey) G.; m. Lelia Elizabeth Harman, Sept. 24, 1966; children: John A., Laura H. BS in Indsl. Engring. with honors, Ga. Inst. Tech., 1965; MBA, Harvard U., 1969. V.p. Raymond, James & Assocs., Inc., St. Petersburg, Fla., 1969-74, sr. v.p., 1974-78, exec. v.p., 1978—; vice chmn. bd. GeoVest Energy, Inc., 1981—; pres., bd. dirs. Raymond James Fin., Inc. 1986—. Leadership St. Petersburg, 1974-88; mem. Lakewood High Sch. Parent Action com., 1984-88, pres. 1987. Served to capt. AUS, 1965-67. Mem. Securities Industry Assn. (vice chmn. So. dist. 1980, chmn. 1987, treas. 1986), Tau Beta Pi, Phi Kappa Phi, Alpha Pi Mu, Phi Delta Theta. Republican. Methodist. Clubs: Harvard of West Coast Fla. (pres. 1971-74), Harvard Bus. Sch. (treas. 1984), Squires, University, Quarterback. Office: Raymond James & Assocs Inc 880 Carillon Pkwy Saint Petersburg FL 33716

GODCHAUX, FRANK AREA, III, food company executive; b. Nashville, Feb. 5, 1927; s. Frank Area, Jr. and Mary Lawrence (Ragland) G.; m. Agnes Kirkpatrick, May 23, 1953; children: Katherine Area, Mary Lawrence, Leslie Kirkpatrick, Frank Kirkpatrick. BBA, Vanderbilt U., 1949. Pres. Lastarmco Inc., Abbeville, La., 1964-78; chmn. bd. Lastarmco Inc., 1978—, Riviana Foods Inc., Houston, 1965—; chief exec. officer Riviana Foods Inc., 1980-84; v.p. Colgate-Palmolive Co., N.Y.C., 1976—; dir. New Orleans br. Fed. Res. Bank Atlanta, 1958-63, Acadian TV Corp., Lafayette., La., 1957-83, Chart House, Inc., Lafayette, First Nat. Bank Lafayette, Coastal Chem. Co. Inc., Abbeville, Diversifoods, Inc., Itasca, Ill., 1984-85; bd. dirs. First Commerce Corp., New Orleans, Pacific Ocean Enterprises, Inc., Solana Beach, Calif.,Sysco Corp.; mem. nat. rice adv. com. Dept. Agr., 1964-66, 71-73, 76. Mem. Evangeline area coun. Boy Scouts Am., dist. chmn., 1954-55; trustee Vanderbilt U., 1967—; mem. U. Southwestern La. Found., 1955—. With USNR, 1945-46. Mem. Vanderbilt Alumni Assn. (bd. dirs. 1959-63), Atlantic Salmon Fedn. (bd. dirs. 1987), Phi Delta Theta. Episcopalian. Clubs: Augusta Nat. Golf, Augusta Country, Abbeville Country (La.), City (Lafayette, La.), Mark's (London), The River (N.Y.C.), River Oaks Country (Houston), Belle Meade Country (Nashville). Home: 501 S Main Abbeville LA 70510 Office: Riviana Foods Inc 2777 Allen Pkwy Houston TX 77019

GODEC, MAKSIMILIJAN, engineering executive; b. Zagreb, Croatia, Yugoslavia, Aug. 17, 1937; s. Franjo and Olga (Zajec) G.; m. Caroline Majcenic, June 11, 1960; children: Gordan, Karin. BSE, Purdue U., 1975; MBA, Ind. U., 1979. Supt. Elektrolux, Zagreb, 1962-64; project engr. Delta AB, Malmo, Sweden, 1964-67; sales rep. Electrolux AB, Malmo, 1967-69; design engr. P.R. Mallory Co. Inc., Indpls., 1969-70; design engr. Von Duprin Inc., Indpls., 1970-71, supr. research and devel., 1971-73, dir. research and devel., 1973-75; engring. mgr. Ingersoll Rand Co., Athens, Pa., 1975-79, v.p. engring., 1979—; Indianapolis; bd. dirs. Chevap Shop Inc., Indpls. Patentee in field. With Yugoslavian Army, 1957-58. Mem. IEEE, Am. Mgmt Assn., ASTM, Am. Soc. Indsl. Security. Roman Catholic. Home: 202 Hayden St Sayre PA 18840 Office: Ingersoll Rand Co 101 N Main St Athens PA 18810

GODFREY, ROBERT R., financial services executive; b. Sweetwater, Tex., May 22, 1947; s. Ross R. and Lillian L. (Bradford) G.; B.B.A., Tex. Tech. U., 1969, postgrad. in bus. adminstrn., 1969-71; m. Diane M. Kalinowski, June 30, 1972. Underwriter, Aetna Life and Casualty Co., Lubbock, Tex. and Hartford, Conn., 1969-72; teaching fellow Tex. Tech. U., 1969-71, Central Conn. State Coll., 1972; asst. mgr. Gulf Ins. Group, Dallas, 1972-76; asst. v.p. Scor Reins. Co., Dallas, 1976-79; pres. Rollins Burdick Hunter Mgmt. Co., N.Y.C., 1979-81; founder, pres., dir. St. Regis Ins. Group/Drum Fin. Corp., 1981-85; exec. v.p. MBIA, Inc., 1985—. Bd. dirs. Fairfield & So. Corp., Mcpl. Bond Investors Assurance Corp., Union League Pension Com. With U.S. Army, 1970. Club: Union League (N.Y.C.). Also: MBIA/MISC 445 Hamilton Ave White Plains NY 10602

GODICK, NEIL BARNETT, accounting firm executive; b. Phila., Oct. 6, 1942; s. Samuel and Jeanette (Goldman) G.; children from previous marriage: Gene S., Marc S., Joshua B. BS in Econs. cum laude, Villanova U., 1964. CPA, Pa., N.Y., N.J. Prin. Deloitte, Haskins & Sells, Phila., N.Y., 1964-72; controller, treas. McGovern for Pres., Phila., 1972; mgr. Laventhol & Horwath, Phila., 1972-73; adminstrv. ptnr. Rudolph Palitz, Phila., 1973-80; pres. Godick and Co., Phila., 1980—; bd. dirs. James Longon T/A HQ Corp., Phila. Contbr. articles to profl. jours. and speaker to numerous profl. and industry seminars. Mem. adv. council U.S. Small Bus. Adminstrn., 1986; pres., bd. dirs. All-Star Forum and Philly Pops, liaison rep. admissions office Villanova U., 1973—; chmn. sub-com. continuing edn. Phila Controller's Com. for Quality Performance 1974—; bd. dirs., treas. Found. for Alternative Cancer Therapies 1982—; treas., Youth Devel Corp. 1975-78, Temple Beth Zion/Beth Israel, 1984-88; cubmaster Cub Scouts Am. 1976-78; bd. dirs. Police Athletic League 1979—; com. fin. advisor Save the Theatre, Inc., N.Y., 1982-84; mem. Villanova U. Devel. Found., 1984—; del. Conf. on Small BUs., 1985, tax reform proposal Mayor Goode's 100 Day Project, 1984. Mem. Am. Inst. CPA's, Pa. Inst. CPA's, N.Y. Soc. CPA's, N.J. Soc. CPA's, Nat. Assn. Accts., Nat. Assn. Corp. Dirs., Phila. C. of C. Democrat. Jewish. Club: Locust (Phila.). Home: 211 Spruce St Philadelphia PA 19106 Office: Godick & Co 421 Chestnut St Philadelphia PA 19106

GODINER, DONALD LEONARD, lawyer; b. Bronx, N.Y., Feb. 21, 1933; s. Israel and Edith (Rubenstein) G.; m. Caryl Mignon Nussbaum, Sept. 7, 1958; children: Clifford, Kenneth. AB, NYU, 1953; JD, Columbia U., 1956. Bar: N.Y. 1956, Mo. 1972. Gen. counsel Stromberg-Carlson, Rochester, N.Y., 1965-71; assoc. gen. counsel Gen. Dynamics Corp., St. Louis, 1971-73; v.p., gen. counsel Permaneer Corp., St. Louis, 1973-75; ptnr. Gallop, Johnson, Godiner, Morganstern & Crebs, St. Louis, 1975-80; v.p., gen. counsel Laclede Gas Co., St. Louis, 1980—. Editor Columbia U. Law Rev., 1955-56. Served with U.S. Army, 1956-58. Mem. ABA, N.Y. State Bar Assn., Met. St. Louis Bar Assn., Assn. of Bar of City of N.Y. Club: Noonday (St. Louis). Home: 157 Trails West Dr Chesterfield MO 63017 Office: Laclede Gas Co 720 Olive St Saint Louis MO 63101

GODWIN, JENNIE FLOYD, strategic marketing programs executive; b. Kinston, N.C., May 31, 1958; d. Henry B. and Rubie M. (Fore) Floyd; m. Billy R. Kerley, Aug. 12, 1978 (div. Jan. 1983); m. L. Mark Godwin, Aug. 24, 1985. BSBA, U. Ala., 1979; cert. in exec. mgmt., Birmingham-Southern U., 1987. Territory mgr. Burroughs Corp., Huntsville, Ala., 1979-81; account exec. So. Cen. Bell, Birmingham, Ala., 1981-82, AT&T-IS, Birmingham, 1983-84; asst. product mgr. Bell So. Svcs., Birmingham, 1984-85, market rsch. analyst, 1986-87; mgr., strategic market rsch. No. Telecom, Nashville, 1987-88, mgr. strategic analysis and rsch., 1988, dir. mktg. devel., 1988—. Vol. Salvation Army, Birmingham, 1984-87. Recipient Wall Street Jour. award. Mem. Fellowship Contemporary Christian Musicians. Baptist. Home: 1108 Blythe Ct E Nashville TN 37221 Office: No Telecom Inc 200 Athens Way Nashville TN 37228-1803

GODWIN, PAMELA JUNE, insurance company executive; b. Council Bluffs, Iowa, Mar. 29, 1949; d. Fred Norman and Carol Ethel (Hatfield) Humphrey; m. Wallace Gill Godwin, Dec. 20, 1970; 1 child, Christopher Humphrey. BA in French, Pa. State U., 1970; postgrad., West Chester (Pa.) State U., 1971-74. Tchr. various schs., Phila., 1971-74; various underwriting/tng. positions Colonial Penn Ins. Co., Phila., 1974-77, mgr., 1977-81, dir., 1981-84, v.p., 1984-86; v.p. Colonial Penn Group, Inc., Phila., 1986-87, sr. v.p., 1987-88; sr. v.p. strategic planning Nat. Liberty Corp., Valley Forge, Pa., 1988—. Bd. dirs. Wheels, Inc., JFK Vocat. Tech. Sch., Phila., 1984-85; mem. Westgate Hills Civic Assn., Havertown, Pa., 1974—. Mem. Ins. Soc. Phila. (bd. dirs.), The Forum of Exec. Women, Soc. Property and Casualty Underwriters (pres. Phila. chpt. 1987-88), Nat. Soc. CPCU, Phi Beta Kappa, Phi Sigma Iota. Democrat. Lutheran. Home: 219 Green Briar Ln Havertown PA 19083 Office: Nat Liberty Corp Valley Forge PA 19493

GODWIN, RALPH LEE, JR., real estate executive; b. Raleigh, N.C., July 20, 1954; s. Ralph Lee Sr. and Hilda Faye (Sellars) G. BS in Commerce, U. Va., 1976; MBA, Dartmouth Coll., 1982. Fgn. exchange trader N.C. Nat. Bank, Charlotte, 1976-78; mgr. N.Y. office 1st Nat. Bank Atlanta, N.Y.C., 1979-80; assoc. corp. fin. Goldman Sachs & Co., N.Y.C., 1982-84; assoc. Eastdil Realty, Inc., N.Y.C., 1984-88; dir. Jones Lang Wootton, U.S.A., N.Y.C., 1988—; pres. Centurion Devel. Corp., Wilmington, N.C., 1976—; officer Eastdil Equities, Inc., N.Y.C., 1984-86. Recipient Devel. cert. DARE Inc., Wilmington, 1984, 88. Mem. Real Estate Bd. N.Y., N.C. Soc. N.Y., U. Va. Alumni Assn., Dartmouth Coll. Alumni Assn., Omicron Delta Kappa. Republican. Episcopalian. Office: Jones Lang Wootton USA 101 E 52d St 20th Floor New York NY 10022

GOEBEL, CHILTON GODFREY, JR., public relations executive; b. Ridley Park, Pa., June 29, 1944; m. Maryanne Greto, Sept. 4, 1967; children: Chad, Cory. BA in English, Widener U., 1966. Pub. relations rep. DuPont Co., Wilmington, Del., 1969-78; v.p., acct. mgr. Aitkin Kynett, Phila., 1978-81; v.p., gen. mgr. McKinney Pub. Relations, Phila., 1981-83; ptnr. Goebel, Kirk & Pilato Pub. Relations, Inc., Phila., 1983—. With U.S. Army, 1966-69, Vietnam. Decorated Bronze Star. Mem. Pub. Relations Soc. Am. (accredidation membership com.), Counselors Acad. (adv. bd. applications devel. ctr., pres. assn.). Office: Goebel Kirk & Pilato Inc 1845 Walnut St Philadelphia PA 19103-7071

GOEBEL, JIL THERESE, electronics company executive; b. San Diego, Apr. 5, 1958; d. Robert Louis and Mary Kathryn (Beard) G.; m. Randel Ross Castleberry, Aug. 26, 1985. BBA, U. San Diego, 1980, MBA, 1982. Market researcher Phillips Ramsey Advt. and Pub. Rels., San Diego, 1980-81, Cen. Fed. Savs. & Loan, San Diego, 1981; supr. product promotion LSI Products div. TRW, San Diego, 1981-85; mgr. mktg. communications Honeywell Inc., Colorado Springs, Colo., 1985-86; co-founder, co-owner Origin Systems, Inc., Colorado Springs, 1986—; programs com. San Diego Electronics Network, 1984-85. Moderator East San Diego Presbyn. Ch., 1984-85; com. mem. Women's Opportunities Week, San Diego, 1981-83; sec. Marina Park Condominium Assn., San Diego, 1983. Mem. Am. Mktg. Assn. (pres. 1984-85), Bus. and Profl. Advt. Assn. (charter), Colorado Springs MARCOM Network, San Diego Electronics Network, San Diego Women's Opportunities Network (mem. com. 1984-85), Delta Epsilon Sigma, Kappa Gamma Pi, Alpha Kappa Psi (v.p. 1980-84). Republican. Avocations: reading, music, dance, hiking. Office: Origin Systems Inc 120B Plaza del Sol Terr Colorado Springs CO 80907

GOEDDE, ALAN GEORGE, financial company executive; b. Irvington, N.J., Feb. 27, 1948; s. Albert and Herta (Konrad) G.; m. Julie S. Withers, June 30, 1981. BS in Engring., Duke U., 1970, PhD in Econs., 1978. Economist U.S. Treasury, Washington, 1976-79, Export-Import Bank, Washington, 1979-81; mgr. Arthur Andersen & Co., Chgo., 1981-84; v.p. bus. planning 1st Nat. Bank Chgo., 1984-86; dir. strategic planning The NutraSweet Co., Chgo., 1986-87; pres., chief exec. officer Mentor Internat., Northbrook, Ill., 1987-88; cons. Coopers & Lybrand, Chgo., 1988—. Office: Coopers & Lybrand 203 N LaSalle St Chicago IL 60601

GOEHRING, EDWARD LEE, insurance company executive; b. Des Moines, Dec. 4, 1929; s. Adrian Willets and Wilda (Sears) G.;m. Mary Ann Jablonski, Nov. 24, 1951; children: Nancy Jean Montague, Robert Lawrence, Sally Kay. Student, Grandview Coll., 1948-49, Drake U., 1949-50. Furniture sales L. Ginsburg & Sons, Des Moines, 1950-59; agy. builder All Am. Life and Casualty Co., Chgo., 1959-69; pres., chief exec. officer Interstate Mktg. Assn., Inc., Des Moines, 1969-79; sr. v.p., nat. sales dir. Continental Western LIfe, Western Des Moines, Iowa, 1979-86; chief exec. officer LifeCo. Investment Group, Maitland, Fla., 1986—; pres., bd. dirs. Nat. Heritage Life Ins. Co., Maitland, Farmers and Ranchers Life Ins. Co., Oklahoma City; co-founder, pres., chief exec. officer Life Co. Investment Group Ins., Maitland; bd. dirs. Life Co. Mktg. Services Inc., Maitland. Recipient Nat. Mgmt. award Gen. Agts. and Mgrs. Assn., 1975, 76, 77, 78. Mem. Nat. Assn. Life Underwriters, Nat. Assn. Life Cos. Republican. Lutheran. Club: Antique Auto of Am. (sr. master judge 1988). Home: 33545 Lakeshore Dr Tavares FL 32779

GOELE, DHRUV (OSTARO), publisher, financial consultant; b. Delhi, India, May 25, 1937; came to U.S., 1973; s. Shri Shiam Lal and Smt. Luxmi Goel; m. Zoa D. Rued, Oct. 1965. Student, U. Delhi, 1959-61. Registered SEC. Editor, pub. Astronews, pres. Cardinal Star Corp., N.Y.C., 1976-80, pub. Ostaro's Market Newsletter, 1980—; Host Ostaro Show Manhattan Cable TV, N.Y.C., 1974—; pres., lectr. Internat. Devel. Improvement & Assistance Inc., N.Y.C, 1979—. Contbr. articles to Astronews. Mem. AFTRA, Nat. Acad. TV Arts Scis., Screen Actors Guild, Soc. for Investigation of Recurring Events. Lodge: Rosicrucians. Home: 402 E 74th St New York NY 10021

GOELKEL, GARY MORGAN, computer software designer; b. Dec. 2, 1953; s. Walter Leo William and Nancy (Rosenaur) G.; m. Kathleen Andrea Leder, Nov. 23, 1978; 1 child, Christopher. BA, Eckerd Coll., 1976. Sales supr. Pacific Mut. Life Ins. Co., St. Petersburg, Fla., 1976-78; dir. planned giving Eckerd Coll., St. Petersburg, 1978-80; exec. v.p. Power Control Products, Inc., Clearwater, Fla., 1980-81; pres. Profit Mgmt. Systems, Inc., St. Petersburg, 1981—. Bd. dirs. Alternative Human Svcs., St. Petersburg, 1988—. Mem. St. Pete Yacht Club. Home: 6911B 16th St NE Saint Petersburg FL 33702 Office: Profit Mgmt Systems Inc 9800 4th St N Saint Petersburg FL 33702

GOELTZ, RICHARD KARL, distilled spirits and wine company executive; b. Chgo., Sept. 11, 1942; s. Karl George and Adeline Caroline (Hoffeins) G. A.B., Brown U., 1964; M.B.A., Columbia U., 1966; student, London Sch. Econs., 1962-63. Financial analyst Office Treas. Exxon Corp., N.Y.C., 1966-70; asst. treas. Joseph E. Seagram & Sons, Inc., N.Y.C., 1970-73; exec. v.p. fin. Joseph E. Seagram & Sons, Inc., 1976—, also dir.; trustee 59 Wall Street Fund. Pres. Opera Orch. N.Y. Mem. Beta Gamma Sigma. Clubs: Sleepy Hollow Country, Metropolitan Opera, Racquet & Tennis. Home: 953 Fifth Ave New York NY 10021 Office: Seagram Co Ltd 375 Park Ave New York NY 10022

GOESSEL, WILLIAM W., heavy equipment manufacturing company executive; b. 1927; married. B.S., Carthage Coll., 1950. Exec. v.p. Beloit Corp., 1950-52; pres., chief operating officer Harnischfeger Corp., Milw., 1982-86, chief exec. officer, 1982—, chmn., 1986—. Office: Harnischfeger Corp PO Box 554 Milwaukee WI 53201 *

GOETZ, CARL, sales executive; b. N.Y.C., Dec. 14, 1943; s. Karl and Marie (Unger) G.; m. Jean A. Radlein, Jul. 21, 1966; children: Erika, Carla. BS, N.Y. State Maritime Coll., 1965; MBA, Bernard M. Bancock, 1970. Product, sales mgr. AMF Inc., N.Y.C., London, 1970-77; dir. internat. sales Rawlings Sporting Goods, St. Louis, 1977-81; mktg. mgr. Imperial Eastman, Chgo., 1981-83; dir. mktg. Crane Co., N.Y.C., 1984-86; v.p. sales and mktg. Cooper Instrument Corp., Middlefield, Conn., 1986—. Served to lt. USNR, 1965-72. Mem. ASHRAE, Internat. Svc. Agys., Nat. Assn. Svc. Merchandising, Gen. Mdse. Distributors Coun. Republican. Protestant. Club: Ridgewood Country, Danbury Ct. Lodge: Masons (master 1970). Home: 82 Ritch Dr Ridgefield CT 06877

GOETZ, CHARLES FREDERICK, strategic planner; b. N.Y.C., Mar. 4, 1956; s. Stanley Herbert and Renee Helen (Alberts) G.; m. Gail G. Goldberger, Aug. 4, 1979; children: Jeffrey Howard, Ariel Nichole. BS in Econs., Emory U., 1976, BA in History, 1977; MBA in Mktg., MPA in Mktg., U. Tex., Austin, 1979. V.p. Citicorp., Md., Colo., N.Y., 1979-83; mgr. Deloitte, Haskins & Sells, Atlanta, 1983-85; pres. Strategic Solutions Group, Inc., Atlanta, 1985—; bd. dirs. Seatech, Houston, Loverseas, Richmond, Va., Mindis Industrial, Atlanta. Contbr. articles to fin. publs. Recipient Spl. Svc. Award Nat. Assn. Sr. Living Industries, 1987. Mem. Nat. Assn. Profl. Cons., Atlnata C. of C. Office: Strategic Solutions Group Inc 100 Ashford Ctr N Suite 420 Atlanta GA 30338

GOETZMANN, HARRY EDWARD, JR., leasing company executive; b. Buffalo, June 10, 1937; s. Harry Edward and Ruth E. (Affolter) G.; m. Sylvia Ridgeway Ingraham, July 11, 1959; children: Craig, Daniel, Eric, Darlene, Harry III. BS in Mktg., Syracuse U., 1959. Data processing sales rep. IBM, 1963-66, sales mgr., 1966-67, asst. to dist. mgr., 1967; dir. mktg. Datamedia Corp., 1967-68; founder, pres., chmn. bd. dirs. CIS Corp., Syracuse, 1968—; bd. dirs. Am. Gen. Life Ins. Co. N.Y. Adv. com. Syracuse U. Sch. Mgmt.; adv. bd. Salvation Army; trustee Syracuse U., Hiawatha Boy Scout Council Am., 1987, Greater Syracuse Services Corp.; bd. dirs. Citizens Found., 1979-82, Metro. Devel. Assn., Syracuse Symphony., Crouse Irving Meml. Found. Lt. U.S. Army, 1959-62. Mem. Computer Dealers and Lessors Assn. (bd. dirs., past pres., chmn. bd. dirs.), Greater Syracuse C. of C. (bd. dirs., chmn. bd. dirs.), Century Club, St. Regis Yacht Club, Skaneateles Country Club, Phi Kappa Alpha. Republican. Office: Continental Info Systems Corp 1 CIS Pkwy Box 4785 Syracuse NY 13221-4785

GOFF, DOUGLAS ROBERT, commercial photographer, small business owner; b. South Bend, Ind., June 4, 1947; s. James William and Germaine Tresa (Richard) G. Student, Ohio U., 1965-67. Owner, pres. Quicksilver Photography, Inc., Columbus, Ohio, 1972—. With U.S. Army, 1968-70. Decorated Bronze Star. Mem. Am. Soc. Mag. Photographers (bd. dirs. 1987—), Vietnam Vets. Assn. (leadership program 1986). Roman Catholic. Office: Quicksilver Photographer Inc 66 W Whittier St Columbus OH 43206

GOFF, ROBERT EDWARD, health plan executive; b. Worcester, Mass., Nov. 19, 1952; s. Julius Lewis and Doris (Katz) G.; m. Jill P. Galber, Aug. 19, 1978 (dec. Aug. 1982); m. Jinny Sue Yaver, June 30, 1985; 1 child, Blake Adam. BBA with honors, Northeastern U., Boston, 1976; MBA with honors, Babson Coll., 1978; cert., Cornell U., 1981. Adminstrv. dir. Adirondack PSRD, Inc., Glens Falls, N.Y., 1977-80; v.p. No. Met. Hosp. Assn., Newburgh, N.Y., 1980-83, Good Samaritian Hosp., Suffern, N.Y., 1983-85; exec. dir., chief exec. dir. WellCare N.Y., Inc., Newburgh, 1985—; cons. in field. Bd. dirs. Hospice Care, Inc. Recipient Vigil Honor award Order Arrow, 1969, Eagle Scout award Boy Scouts Am., 1970. Mem. Hudson Valley Hosp. Exec. Assn. (pres., bd. dirs. 1982-85), Healthcare Fin. Mgmt. Assn., Am. Coll. Hosp. Adminstrs., Beta Gamma Soc. Home: Rd 1 Castle Point Rd Wappingers Falls NY 12590 Office: WellCare NY 300 Stony Brook Ct Newburgh NY 12550

GOFF, STANLEY NORMAN, furniture retailing and manufacturing company executive; b. Worcester, Mass., June 26, 1923; s. Joseph Edward and Fannie (Alperin) G.; m. Elaine Helen Krowech, June 27, 1946; children: Susan, Joni. BS, UCLA, 1947. CPA, Calif. Sr. ptnr. Goff, Lehmann, Stone & Wolff, CPA's, L.A., 1955-68; pres. chief exec. officer Datamation Corp., L.A., 1966-68; mgr. ptnr. Josam Investment Co., L.A., 1968—; corp. sec. RB Industries, Inc., L.A., 1972-83; chief exec. officer Sauflon Internat., L.A., 1975-78; chmn., chief exec. officer RB Furniture, Inc., L.A., 1984-87, exec. v.p. chief oper. officer, 1984—, also bd. dirs. Bd. govs. Cedars-Sinai Med. Ctr., Los Angeles, 1985—; active home furnishings div. United Jewish Fund, L.A., 1986—; mem. mentor program John Anderson Grad. Sch. Bus. of UCLA. With U.S. Army, 1942-44. Mem. Am. Inst. CPA's, Nat. Assn. Corp. Dirs., Hillcrest Country Club. Office: RB Industries Inc 1801 Century Park Los Angeles CA 90067

GOGAN, JAMES WILSON, corporate executive; b. Springhill, N.S., Can., May 19, 1938; m. Mary Maureen Richards, Oct. 26, 1963; children: James Richard, Mary Monique, John Paul, Suzanne Maureen. B in Commerce, Dalhousie U., Halifax, N.S., 1959. With H.R. Doane, Amherst, New Glasgow and Antigonish, N.S., Can., 1959-62; chief fin. officer Empire Group, Stellarton, N.S., Can., 1962-74; exec. v.p. Empire Group, Stellarton, N.S., 1975-85, pres., 1985—; chmn. Atlantic Shopping Centres Ltd., Sobey Leased Properties Ltd.; pres. Empire Co. Ltd., Island Realty Ltd., others; sec. Kepec Holdings Ltd., Topsail Rd. Shopping Centre Ltd., others; v.p. A.S.C. Investments Ltd., others; bd. dirs. Sobeys Stores Ltd., Barclays Bank Can., Hannaford Bros. Co., U.S.A. Sec., treas. United Appeal, New Glasgow; charter mem. YMCA/YWCA Pictou County; mem. St. John The Bapt. Roman Cath. Ch.; mem., bd. govs. St. Francis Xavier U. Mem. Lloyd's of London (underwriting), Fin. Execs. Inst. Can., Gyro Club, Abercrombie Golf and Country Club. Roman Catholic. Office: Empire Co Ltd, 115 King St, Stellarton, NS Canada B0K 1S0

GOGGIN, JOSEPH ROBERT, mortgage banking company executive; b. Chgo., Apr. 24, 1926; s. William Nobel and Loretta Ann (Davis) G.; m. Barbara Jean Laibach, Sept. 21, 1957; children: Tracy Jean Goggin Layton, Sandra Lynn Goggin Adams. With Mut. Trust Life Ins. Co., Chgo., 1947; exec. v.p. Mut. Trust Life Ins. Co., 1968-88, dir., 1970-88; dir. Enterprise Savs. Bank, Chgo., 1986—; pres., dir. Focus Fin. Group, Inc., 1988—; Bd. dir. Enterprise Savs. Bank, Chgo., 1986—. Served with USMCR, 1942-46. Mem. Investment Analysts Soc. Chgo., Financial Execs. Inst. Clubs: Chgo. (Chgo.), Met. (Chgo.). Home: 101 E 29th St LaGrange Park IL 60525 Office: 200 W Madison St Chicago IL 60606

GOGLIETTINO, JOHN CARMINE, insurance company executive; b. Danbury, Conn., Sept. 5, 1952; s. Nicholas and Josephine (Staffieri) G.; m. Deborah Ann Russo, Sept. 25, 1976. BA in History, Western Conn. State Coll., 1975. Sales rep. Met. Life Ins. Co., Danbury, 1978-81; account exec. Thomas A. Settle, Inc., Danbury, 1981-88, Hodge Ins. Agy., Danbury, 1988—. Editor: (newspaper) Yankee Doodler, 1983-84. Rec. sec. State of Conn. Bd. Vet. Medicine, Hartford, 1984—; candidate Danbury Dem. Town Com., 1986; active Italian Heritage Soc., mem. fin. com. Danbury Dem. Town Com., 1988—. Recipient Statesman award Conn. Jaycees, 1983; named one of Outstanding Young Men of Am., 1982. Mem. Life Underwriters Assn. (cert. 1982), Health Underwriters Assn., Danbury Ins. Men Orgn., Western Conn. State Coll. Alumni Assn. (activator memberships 1985-87), No. Fairfield County Bus. People Assn., Danbury Jaycees, Kiwanis (v.pl, pres. Danbury Club 1984-86), Elks, Americo Vespucci Club. Roman Catholic. Home: PO Box 2598 Danbury CT 06813 Office: Hodge Ins Agy 283 Main St Danbury CT 06810

GOHD, MARJEAN ANN, construction executive; b. Huron, S.D., Nov. 25, 1952; d. Dale Oliver and Virginia Elaine (Aasby) Trabing; m. Peter Casturao, Dec. 13, 1975 (div. June 1980); m. Jeffrey Gohd, May 19, 1984. AA, Daytona Beach Community Coll., 1977; BS, Fla. State U., 1980. Mgr., residential designer Bruno Galleries, New Orleans, 1980; constrn. expeditor Gibbons Pools, Jefferson, La., 1981; estimator, project mgr. B. F. Carvin Constrn. Co., Inc., St. Rose, La., 1981—; instr. adult edn. Delgado Community Coll., New Orleans, 1981. Mem. St. Rose Vol Fire Dept., 1983—. With U.S. Army, 19740-76. Mem. Profession Estimators Soc. (assoc.), NAFE. Democrat. Lutheran. Office: B F Carvin Constrn Inc 1166 River Rd PO Box 569 Saint Rose LA 70087

GOHDE, ROBERT PAUL, water treatment equipment company executive; b. Newark, Oct. 5, 1951; s. Walter L. Jr. and Patricia (Ritter) G.; BS, Montclair State Coll., 1979; m. Sandra J. Eshrich, May 5, 1974; children: Andrew Charles, Lauren Michelle. Sales rep. Pella Window Co., West Caldwell, N.J., 1970-73; tech. field rep. Eifler Electric, Union City, N.J., 1973-74; sales rep., then ter. mgr. Chesebrough-Ponds, Inc., Greenwich, Conn., 1974-75; sales rep. Dearborn Chem. Co., Whippany, N.J., 1975-76, distbr. accounts mgr., 1977; area mgr. Nalco Chem. Corp., Springfield, N.J., 1977-78; area mgr. Alken Murray Corp., N.Y.C., 1978-79, dist. mgr., 1979-81; dist. mgr. Betz Entec, Horsham, Pa., 1981-85, regional mgr., 1985-86; regional mgr. Polymetrics, Inc., San Jose, Calif., 1986-88, gen. mgr., 1988—; v.p. sales and mktg. S&W Waste, Inc., South Kearny, N.J.; water/environ. mgmt. cons. Roman Catholic. Home: 22 Lakeview Dr Morris Plains NJ 07950 Office: 115 Jacobus Ave South Kearny NJ 07932

GOHMANN, TIMOTHY, marketing research executive; b. Indpls., June 12, 1947; s. Charles Henry and Loretta (Scheer) G.; m. Trudy Joan Kuhnert, Oct. 7, 1983. AB, U. Notre Dame, 1969; MA, U. Va., 1972, PhD, 1973. Prin. Va. Rsch. Assoc. Ltd., Charlottesville, 1972-73; project dir. Burke Mktg. Rsch., Cin., 1973-74, account assoc., 1974-76, group tech. advisor, 1975-76; mgr. custom rsch. Coca-Cola Foods, Houston, 1976-77, mgr. internat. mktg. planning and rsch., 1977-78; mgr. bus. devel. for Cen. Europe Coca-Cola Foods, Essen, Fed. Republic Germany, 1978-79; mgr. brand devel. Coca-Cola Foods, Houston, 1979-81, mgr. strategy devel. and planning, 1981-82; dir. planning and mktg. rsch. Ponderosa Restaurants, Dayton, Ohio, 1983-85; dir. account services Wirthlin Group, McLean, Va., 1985-86, dir. advanced rsch. applications, 1986-87, v.p., 1987—. Cons. editor Jour. Mktg. Rsch., 1976-79. Mem. Ind. Soc. Washington, Friends Nat. Zoo, Notre Dame Club. Republican. Roman Catholic. Office: Wirthlin Group 1363 Beverly Rd McLean VA 22101

GOHO, THOMAS SMALLWOOD, business educator; b. Harrisburg, Pa., Aug. 7, 1942; s. William Smallwood and Mary Elizabeth (Nestler) G.; m. Joan Suzanne Matter, May 23, 1964 (dec. May 1975); m. Barbara Bouvet, Aug. 9, 1978; children: Mark, Karen, Susan. BS, Pa. State U., 1964, MBA, 1966; PhD, U. of N.C., Chapel Hill, 1970. Mgmt. trainee Mellon Bank, Pitts., 1964; prof. bus. N.Mex. State U., Las Cruces, N.Mex., 1970-76, Wake Forest U., Winston-Salem, N.C., 1976—; pres. Piedmont Fin. Planning, Winston-Salem, N.C., 1981—; cons. various firms, Southeastern U.S., 1980—. Co-author: Economics of the Solar Energy Industry, 1977; contbr. articles to profl. jours. Bd. dirs. Overland Express Inc., Little Rock, Ark., 1988—; Treas. Baptist Hosp. Credit Union, Winston-Salem, 1979-80, bd. dirs., 1980-82. Mem. AAAS (v.p. 1975-76); Am. Fin. Assn., Fin. Mgmt. Assn. Home: 3311 Kirklees Rd Winston-Salem NC 27104 Office: Piedmont Fin Planning Reynolds Sta PO Box 6206 Winston-Salem NC 27109

GOIZUETA, ROBERTO CRISPULO, food and beverage company executive; b. Havana, Cuba, Nov. 18, 1931; came to U.S., 1964; s. Crispulo D. and Aida (Cantera) G.; m. Olga T. Casteleiro, June 14, 1953; children: Roberto S., Olga M., Javier C. BS, BChemE, Yale U., 1953. Process engr. Indsl. Corp. Tropics, Havana, 1953-54; tech. dir. Coca-Cola Co., Havana, 1954-60; asst. to sr. v.p. Coca-Cola Co., Nassau, Bahamas, 1960-64; asst. to v.p. research and devel. Coca-Cola Co., Atlanta, 1964-66, v.p. engring., 1966-74, sr. v.p., 1974-75, exec. v.p., 1975-79, vice chmn., 1979-80, pres., chief operating officer, 1980-81, chmn. bd., chief exec. officer, 1981—, also bd. dirs.; dir., mem. exec. com. Coca-Cola Export Corp., from 1980; dir. SunTrust Banks, Inc., Ford Motor Co., Sonat Inc.; bd. govs. Japan Soc. Inc.; trustee Emory U., 1980—, The Am. Assembly, 1979—, Atlanta Arts Alliance, Atlanta Univ. Ctr., Boys Clubs Am. Bd. govs. Lauder Inst.; mem. Bus. Council. Mem. Bus. Council, Bus. Roundtable, Council on Fgn. Relations. Office: Coca-Cola Co PO Drawer 1734 Atlanta GA 30301 *

GOLASKI, WALTER MICHAEL, machinery company executive; b. Torrington, Conn., Aug. 12, 1913; s. Paul and Helen (Kulesza) Golaszewski; M.E., Drexel Inst., 1946, completing B.S. degree: D.Sc., Alliance Coll., 1968; m. Helen D. Ambrose, Sept. 5, 1942 (dec. Aug. 1968); 1 dau., Michelle; m. 2d, Alexandra Budna, Oct. 25, 1969; children—Alexandra Maria, John Paul, Edmund Walter. With The Torrington Co., 1928-45; ptnr. Bearing Products Co., Phila., design and manufacture spl. machinery, 1945-47, owner-mgr., 1947-63, pres., mgr., 1963—; pres., treas., Overbrook Knitting Corp., Phila., 1956—; pres. Golaski Labs., Inc., 1967—; former chmn. bd. Nowy Swiat newspaper; dir. 3d Fed. Savs. & Loan Assn. Nat. chmn. bd. trustees Kosciuszko Found. Ball, 1960, 76, co-chmn., 1980; chmn. bd. trustees Kosciuszko Found., 1973-82; mem. adv. bd. Holy Family Coll., 1958-76. Recipient medal Drexel Inst. Tech., 1953, alumni citation, 1961, George Washington medal, 1972; inducted into Wisdom Hall of Fame, 1970. Mem. AAAS, N.Y. Acad. Scis., Am. Soc. Artificial Internal Organs, Am. Ordnance Assn., Pa. Soc., Pa. Mfrs. Assn., Polish Intercollegiate Club (alumni pres.), Germantown Cricket, Sigma Delta. Contbr. papers to profl. jours.; patentee in field. Invented processes converting hosiery machinery to finer gauges, and for making neckties and sweaters, machinery for mfr. blood vessels. Home: 6452 Woodbine Ave Philadelphia PA 19151 Office: Golaski Labs Inc 4567 Wayne Ave Philadelphia PA 19144

GOLD, ALAN, computer industry executive; b. N.Y.C., June 7, 1944; s. Irving and Gwendoline (Levine) G.; m. Susan Eve Greenwald, Dec. 20, 1964; children: Alyson, Warren. BA, Hofstra U., 1966; MS in Adminstrn., George Washington U., 1969. Treas. Royal Cigar Co., Bklyn., 1964-66; credit reporter Dun & Bradstreet, N.Y.C., 1966-67; aide de camp U.S. Army, Washington, 1967-69; account exec. Merrill, Lynch, N.Y.C., 1969-75; prof. Hofstra U. Sch. of Bus., Hempstead, N.Y., 1969-72; cons. AG Co., Dix Hills, N.Y., 1975-80; pres., chief exec. officer Global Health Systems, Rockville, Md., 1981—. Office: Global Health Systems 1701 Research Rd Rockville MD 20850

GOLD, ALLEN ERIC, administrative analyst, training coordinator; b. Cleveland Heights, Ohio, Nov. 16, 1963; s. Richard Stevan Erika (Taubner) G. BA in Criminology and Criminal Justice, Ohio State U., 1986; MS in Judicial Adminstrn., U. Denver, 1987. Criminal investigator Pub. Defender Svc., Washington, 1984; legis. intern Ohio State Senate, Columbus, 1984; intern Franklin County Ct. of Common Pleas, Columbus, 1986; legal messenger Calfee, Halter & Griswold, Cleve., 1986-87; personnel adminstrn. intern U.S. Dist. Ct., Denver, 1986-87; systems analysis intern State Utah Adminstrv. Office of the Cts., Salt Lake City, 1987; adminstrv. analyst, tng. coord. U.S. Dist. Ct. (no. dist.) Ohio, Cleve., 1987—. Mem. Fed. Ct. Clks. Assn., Nat. Assn. for Ct. Mgmt., Am. Judicature Soc., Assn. of Legal Adminstrs., Zeta Beta Tau. Jewish. Office: US Dist Ct 201 Superior Ave Cleveland OH 44114

GOLD, HERBERT FRANK, insurance executive; b. Boston, Jan. 2, 1939; s. Harry and Sophie E. (Levine) G.; m. Paula Wagner, June 27, 1962 (div. 1982); children: Scott, Lesley; m. Judith Barron, May 5, 1984. BS, Boston U., 1961. CLU. Ins. agt. John Hancock Life Ins. Co., Danvers, Mass., 1961-63; supr. John Hancock Life Ins. Co., Wakefield, Mass., 1963-67; gen. agt. John Hancock Life Ins. Co., Brookline, Mass., 1967-80; sr. v.p. John Hancock Life Ins. Co., Boston, 1980-86, exec. v.p., 1987—; chmn. bd. dirs. Profesco Corp., 1981—, Commonwealth Bank-Norfolk, Brookline, 1973-82; bd. dirs. John Hancock Subs. Bd., Boston, The Internat. Profit Ctr. Bd., Boston, John Hancock Freedom Securities Corp., N.Y.C., John Hancock Variable Life Ins. Co., Boston, Maritime Life Assurance Co., Halifax, N.S.; mem. John Hancock Mgmt. Com. Bd. dirs. Fisher Hill Neighborhood Assn., Brookline; bd. dirs. Hebrew home for Aged, 1976. Mem. Boston Life Underwriters Assn. (bd. dirs. 1973-77), Gen. Agts. and Mgrs. Assn. (bd. dirs. 1978). Jewish. Home: 1501 Beacon St Apt 1905 Brookline MA 02146 Office: John Hancock Mut Life Ins Co PO Box 111 Boston MA 02117

GOLD, JEFFREY MARK, investment banker, financial adviser; b. Bronx, N.Y., Jan. 7, 1945; s. Samuel L. and Sylvia E. Gold; m. Lenore N., May 29, 1966; children: Brian, Steven, Samuel. B.B.A. in Acctg, Pace U., 1967. Sr. acct. Peat, Marwick, Main, N.Y.C., 1967-71; v.p., corp. controller Nat. Patent Devel. Corp., N.Y.C., 1971-78; exec. v.p. fin. and adminstrn., chief fin. officer Esquire, Inc., N.Y.C., 1978-84; exec. v.p. Simon & Schuster, N.Y.C., 1984; chmn., chief exec. officer Goldmark Industries Ltd., Goldmark Capital, Goldmark Ptnrs., Ltd., N.Y.C., 1984—; guest lectr. Columbia U. Grad. Sch. Bus.; chmn. The Automotive Group, Inc. Mem. Fin. Execs. Inst., Fairview Country Club. Home: 48 North Way Chappaqua NY 10514 Office: Goldmark 320 Park Ave New York NY 10022

GOLD, KENNETH HARRIS, lawyer; b. Boston, Oct. 15, 1942; s. Max and Selma (Harris) G.; divorced; children: Darren, Justin. BS, Babson Coll., 1963; JD, NYU, 1967, LLM, 1968. Bar: N.Y. 1967, Mich. 1972. Assoc. Parker Chapin Flattau, N.Y.C., 1969-72; ptnr. Smith Miro Hirsch & Brody, Detroit, 1972-81, Miro Miro & Weiner, Bloomfield Hills, Mich., 1981—. Mem. securities law adv. com. Mich. Corp. and Securities Bur., Lansing, 1979—. Mem. ABA (fed. regulation securities com., com. on commodities regulation, corp. banking and bus. law sect. sect.), Detroit Bar Assn. (securities law com.), N.Y. State Bar Assn., Mich. Bar Assn. (co-chmn. Blue Sky law subcom., mem. council bus. law sect.). Democrat. Jewish. Home: 1111 N Woodward Ave Apt B221 Birmingham MI 48009 Office: Miro Miro & Weiner PC 500 N Woodward Ste 200 PO Box 908 Bloomfield Hills MI 48303

GOLD, RICHARD N., management consultant; b. Chgo., May 27, 1945; s. Irving Louis and Victoria (Saltzman) G.; m. Renee Bonnie Rein, Nov. 3, 1968; children: Jedd Steven, Amanda Caryn. BSI, U. Wis., 1967; MBA with honors, Columbia U., 1971; MA with honors, NYU, 1971. Tchr., supr. Ocean-Hill Brownsville, N.Y.C. pub. schs., 1968-71; brand mgr. packaged soap and detergent div. Procter & Gamble Co., Cin., 1971-76; exec. v.p. Glendinning Assocs., Westport, Conn., 1976-81; pres. R.N. Gold & Co., 1981—. Producer, ptnr. Enterplan, N.Y.C., 1983-85; dir. mktg. Downtown Council, Cin., 1975-77. Mem. Pres. Assn., Am. Mgmt. Assn. Avocations: sports, theatre, collecting antique electronic musical devices. Office: RN Gold & Co 3 Indian Point Ln Westport CT 06880

GOLD, STANLEY P., chemical company executive, manufacturing company executive; b. 1942. AB, U. Calif., 1964; JD, U. So. Calif., 1967. Ptnr. Gary Tyre and Brown, 1967—, Shamrock Holdings Inc., 1985—; also chmn., chief exec. officer Enterra Corp., dir.; pres., chief exec. officer Shamrock Holdings. Office: Shamrock Holdings 4444 Lakeside Dr Burbank CA 91510 also: Enterra Corp PO Box 1535 Houston TX 77251 *

GOLDBERG, ARTHUR ABBA, lawyer, investment banker; b. Jersey City, Nov. 25, 1940; s. Jack Geddy and Ida (Steinberg) G.; A.B. with honors, Am. U., 1962; J.D., Cornell U., 1965; m. Jane Elizabeth Gottlieb, Aug. 10, 1968; children—Ari Matthew, Shoshana Eve, Benjamin Saul, Talia Akiva. Bar: N.J. 1965, Conn. 1966. Intern, staff mem. to senator, 1962; law clk. DeSevo & Cerutti, Jersey City, 1964; practiced in Jersey City, 1965—; asst. prof. law U. Conn. Sch. Law., 1965-67; cooperating atty. NAACP Legal Def. Fund, 1965—; adminstrv. asst. to congressman Ohio, 1966-75; dep. atty. gen. N.J., counsel Dept. Community Affairs and Housing Finance Agy., 1967-70; exec. v.p., dir., mgr. mcpl. fin. dept. Matthews & Wright, Inc., N.Y.C., 1970—; exec. v.p., dir. Landamatic Systems Corp., 1982-85, vice chmn., Matthews & Wright Realty, 1986—, Matthews & Wright Pacific, 1986—; pres. New Am. Fed. Credit Union, 1981-87; v.p. Alfus Corp., 1958-85, Basow Corp., 1965—; partner Shayna Enterprises, 1978-87, York Builders, Hudson Mgmt. Services; mng. partner Bank Bldg. Assos., Inst. Profl. and Exec. Devel.; vis. lectr. Rutgers U., 1971-80, Practising Law Inst. 1969-76; mem. exec. com. N.J. Commn. Discrimination in Housing, 1975-80; mem. urban adv. council Anti-Defamation League, 1965-72; spl. cons. exclusionary zoning Nat. Com. Discrimination in Housing, 1965-70; cons. scholarship edn. Def. Fund for Racial Equality, 1965-72; gen. counsel N.J. chpt. Mcpl. Fin. Officers Assn., N.J. chpt. Nat. Assn. Housing and Redevel. Ofcls., 1966-74, chmn. Com. for Absorption of Soviet Emigrees (CASE), 1974—; pres. CASE-UNA Community Devel. Corp., 1976; v.p. Opthamalic Mission Trust (India). Co-pres. New Synagogue, Jersey City, 1974-80; bd. dirs. Jersey City Hebrew Free Loan Assn., 1976-77; pres. Met. N.Y. Coordinating Com. for Resettlement of Soviet Jewry, 1978-80; treas. Hebrew Free Loan N.J., 1977-88, Hillel Acad., 1985—; dir. Jewish Community Ctr., 1987, United Jewish Appeal, 1984—; bd. dirs. South Bronx Community Housing Inc., 1977-81; adv. bd. Housing and Devel. Reporter, 1975—; chmn. Novy Americanitz, 1980-84; bd. dirs. Citizens Housing and Planning Council; pres. Case Mus. Russian Contemporary Art in Exile, 1980—, pres. Freedom Synagogue, 1982—; bd. dirs. Boys Club of Jersey City, 1975—; mem. Settlement House Fund; treas. Council Jewish Orgns., Jersey City, 1977. mem. bd. edn. Yeshiva of Hudson County, 1977-85; v.p. Found. for Detached Retinal Surgery, 1988—. Mem. Conn. Assn. Mcpl. Attys. (exec. com., editor newsletter 1965-68), Nat. Housing Conf., ABA, N.J. (chmn. com. housing and urban renewal), Conn., Hudson County bar assns., Am. Polit. Sci. Assn., Nat. Acad. Polit. and Social Sci., Nat. Leased Housing Assn. (nat. pres. 1972-74, chmn. emeritus 1975—), Public Securities Assn. (legis. com. 1978), Nat. Housing Rehab. Assn. (dir. 1982—, v.p. 1985), Omicron Delta Kappa, Pi Gamma Mu, Pi Sigma Alpha, Pi Delta Epsilon. Author: Financing Housing and Urban Development, 1975; Zoning and Land Use, 1972; adv. bd. Housing and Devel. Reporter; contbr. articles to law revs. Home: 83 Montgomery St Jersey City NJ 07302 Office: Matthews & Wright Inc 100 Broadway New York NY 10005

GOLDBERG, ARTHUR H., financial services company executive; b. N.Y.C., May 13, 1942; s. Irving and Pearl (Ruben) G.; m. Hedy S. Krauss; children: Jill Marla, Mia Joy. B.S., NYU, 1963, J.D., 1966. Atty. Javits & Javits, N.Y.C., 1966-69; exec. Integrated Resources, Inc., N.Y.C., 1969-73, pres., 1973-89, pres., chief exec. officer, 1989—; chmn. bd. Resources Life Ins. Co.; trustee RPS Realty Trust; bd. dirs. Providence Life Ins. Co., Guardsman Life Ins. Co., Integrated Resources Life Ins. Co., Capitol Life Ins. Co. Trustee Am. Friends Haifa U., Jerusalem Inst. Mgmt., Boston, Children's Med. Fund of N.Y., N.Y.C.; bd. dirs. Chamah Internat. Orgn. to Aid Soviet Jewry; bd. overseers NYU; charter mem. Dems. Exec. Com., N.Y.C. Named Man of Yr. Boys Town Jerusalem, 1982; recipient John Madden award NYU Alumni, 1986. Mem. N.Y. State Bar Assn., Young Presidents Orgn., Am. Bus. Conf. (trustee), Investment Partnership Assn. (chmn. bd. trustees), Order of Coif. Office: Integrated Resources Inc 666 3rd Ave New York NY 10017

GOLDBERG, DALE STEPHEN, accountant; b. Phila., Mar. 22, 1954; s. Morton and Betty Roslyn (Fox) G.; m. Cynthia Ann Golden, Sept. 5, 1982; 1 child, Rebecca. BS in Acctg., Delaware Valley Coll., 1975; MBA in Fin., Temple U., 1977. CPA, Pa. Acct. Alexander Grant & Co., Phila., 1978-80; tax mgr. Sears Industries, Inc., N.Y.C., 1980-82; v.p. fin., chief fin. officer Miss Erika, Inc., N.Y.C., 1982-85; founder, chief exec. officer Dale Svc., Inc., Phila., 1986—, also bd. dirs.; tax cons. various nat. and internat. cos. Contbr. articles to various publs., course materials for personal tax preparation, 1985. Jewish. Home: 1085 Squirell Rd Jenkintown PA 19046 Office: Dale Tax Svs Inc 6735 Castor Ave Philadelphia PA 19149

GOLDBERG, HARVEY, financial executive; b. Bklyn., Jan. 30, 1940; s. Joseph and Regina (Goldkrantz) G.; m. Joyce Baron, Nov. 22, 1962; children—Keith, Jodi. BS in Acctg., Bklyn. Coll., 1962; postgrad. CCNY, 1963. CPA, N.Y. Sr. acct. Schwartz, Zelin & Weiss CPA's, N.Y.C., 1962-66; mgr. fin. analysis Columbia Records div. CBS, Inc., N.Y.C., 1966-70; asst. controller Revlon, Inc., N.Y.C., 1970-71; treas. Central Textile, Inc., Jersey City, 1971-74; controller Marcade Group, Inc., Jersey City, 1974-81, v.p., controller, 1981-86; v.p., chief fin. officer Paul Marshall Products, Inc., subs. Marcade Group, Long Beach, Calif., 1982-86, sr. v.p. chief fin. officer, 1988—; v.p., chief fin. officer, Players Internat., Inc., Calabasas, Calif., 1986-88, sr. v.p., chief fin. officer, 1988—. County committeeman Monmouth County Dem. Com., N.J., 1979-80; chmn. adv. bd. High Point Ctr., Marlboro, N.J., 1978-82; mem. Marlboro Twp. Bd. Edn., 1980-82, v.p., 1981-82; bd. dirs. Family Consultation Ctr., Freehold, N.J. , 1982-83. Mem. AICPA, N.Y. State Soc. CPA's, Met. Retail Fin. Execs. Assn. Home: 19798 Greenbriar Dr Tarzana CA 91356 Office: Players Internat Inc 23901 Calabasas Rd Calabasas CA 91302

GOLDBERG, HARVEY JAY, radiological engineer; b. Providence, Apr. 10, 1941; s. William and Sylvia (Gittleman) G.; m. Jane K. Peterson, Feb. 4, 1981; 1 child, Jack. BS, U. R.I., 1963; MS, Kans. State U., 1966, PhD, 1975. Postdoctoral fellow U. Del., Newark, 1975-76; vis. asst. prof. Lincoln U., Oxford, Pa., 1976; research prof. Joint Ctr. Grad. Studies, Richland, Wash., 1977-78; radiol. engr. Rockwell Hunford Ops., Richland, 1978-87, Westinghouse Hanford Co., Richland, 1987—. Served with U.S. Army, 1966-68. Mem. Health Physics Soc., Am. Phys. Soc., Am. Assn. Physics Tchrs. Jewish. Home: 1872 Alder Richland WA 99352 Office: Westinghouse Hanford Co N1-31 PO Box 1970 Richland WA 99352

GOLDBERG, LEE WINICKI, furniture company executive; b. Laredo, Tex., Nov. 20, 1932; d. Frank and Goldie (Ostrowiak) Winicki; student San Diego State U., 1951-52; m. Frank M. Goldberg, Aug. 17, 1952; children—Susan Arlene, Edward Lewis, Anne Carri. With United Furniture Co., Inc., San Diego, 1953-83, corp. sec., dir., 1963-83, dir. environ. interiors, 1970-83; founder Drexel-Heritage store Edwards Interiors, subs. United Furniture, 1975; founding ptnr., v.p. FLJB Corp., 1976—, founding ptnr., sec. treas., Sea Fin., Inc., 1980, founding ptnr., First Nat. Bank San Diego, 1982. Den mother Boy Scouts Am., San Diego, 1965; vol. Am. Cancer Soc., San Diego, 1964-69; chmn. jr. matrons United Jewish Fedn., San Diego, 1958; del. So. Pacific Coast region Hadassah Conv., 1960, pres. Galilee group San Diego chpt., 1960-61; supporter Marc Chagall Nat. Mus., Nice, France, Smithsonian Instn., Los Angeles County Mus., La Jolla (Calif.) Mus. Contemporary Art, San Diego Mus. Art. Recipient Hadassah Service award San Diego chpt., 1958-59. Democrat. Jewish.

GOLDBERG, LEONARD, television and movie producer; b. N.Y.C., Jan. 24, 1934; s. William and Jean (Smith) G.; m. Wendy Howard, Nov. 26, 1972; 1 child, Amanda Erin. B.S. in Econs, U. Pa., 1955. With research dept. ABC, 1956; supr. spl. projects NBC-TV Research, 1957-61; charge daytime television programs, overall broadcasting coordinator Batten, Barton, Durstine & Osborne, 1961-63; mgr. program devel. ABC-TV, N.Y.C., 1963-64; dir. program devel., v.p. charge daytime programming ABC-TV, 1964-66, v.p. network programming, 1966-69; v.p. in charge of prodn. Screen Gems (name now Columbia Television), Los Angeles, 1969-72; co-owner, operator Spelling-Goldberg Prodns., Los Angeles, from 1972; owner, operator Leonard Goldberg Prodns. (now Leonard Goldberg Co.), form 1972, Mandy Films; now pres., chief operating officer Twentieth Century-Fox Film Corp., Beverly Hills, Calif. Creator form for TV Movies of the Week; producer (TV) The Rookies, Charlies Angels, Starsky & Hutch, Family (Emmy award), Hart to Hart, The Cavanaughs; producer (TV movies) Something about Amelia (Film Adv. Bd Excellence award, 1984, Emmy award, 1984, Humanitarian award NCCJ, 1987), Alex-The Life of a Child; producer (film) Baby Blue Marine, California Split, Bad News Bears in Breaking Training, Wargames, Space Camp, 1986. Bd. dirs. Cedars Sinai Hosp. Recipient Peabody award for Brian's Song, 1984. Mem. Producers Assn., Hollywood Acad. TV Arts and Scis., Hollywood Radio and TV Soc., Acad. Motion Picture Arts and Scis. Club: Malibu Racket. Office: 20th Century-Fox Film Corp Box 900 Beverly Hills CA 90213 *

GOLDBERG, LUELLA GROSS, corporate director; b. Mpls., Feb. 26, 1937; d. Louis and Beatrice (Rosenthal) Gross; m. Stanley M. Goldberg, June 23, 1958; children: Ellen Goldberg Luger, Fredric, Martha. BA, Wellesley Coll., 1958; postgrad. in philosophy, U. Minn., 1958-59. Dir. Northwestern Nat. Life Ins. Co., Mpls., 1976—, 1st Trust Co. St. Paul, 1978-85, TCF Banking and Savs., F.A., Mpls., 1986—, Piper Jaffray Investment Trust Co., Mpls., 1987—, Am. Govt. Income Fund Co., Mpls., 1988—. Pres. Minn. Orch. Women's Assn., Mpls., 1972-74; regent St.

John's U., Collegeville, Minn., 1974-83; sec. U. Minn. Found., Mpls., 1978—; chmn. Minn. Orch. Assn., Mpls., 1980-83; mem. bd. overseers Sch. Mgmt., U. Minn., Mpls., 1980—; chmn. bd. trustees Wellesley (Mass.) Coll., 1985—; bd. dirs. Mpls. chpt. United Way, 1978-88, Ind. Sector, Washington, 1984—. Recipient Community Service Leadership award Mpls. YWCA, 1982, Disting. Service award Minn. Orch. Assn., 1983. Mem. Women's Econ. Round Table, Minn. Women's Econ. Round Table, Phi Beta Kappa. Club: Cosmopolitan (N.Y.C.). Home: 7019 Tupa Dr Minneapolis MN 55435

GOLDBERG, MARC EVAN, biotechnology company executive; b. Boston, Mar. 14, 1957; s. Ray Allan and Thelma (Englander) G.; m. Pamela Francine Winer, June 11, 1983; children: Frederick Warren, Alyssa Rachel. AB, Harvard U., 1979, MBA, JD, 1983. Bar: Mass. 1985. Mgr. bus. devel. Genetics Inst., Inc., Cambridge, Mass., 1983-87; v.p. fin. and corp. devel., chief fin. officer, treas. Safer, Inc., Newton, Mass., 1987—; founding pres. Mass. Biotech., 1985-87, bd. dirs. Coun., Bioseeds Internat., Inc., Mpls., Neo Phyte, Inc., Can.; advisor Mass. Dept. Food and Agriculture. Pres's. Circle Beth Israel Hosp., 1985-88; trustee Harvard Yearbook Pubs., 1981—; mem. exec. adv. bd. Harvard Varsity Club 1982—; bd. dirs. Newton Centre (Mass.) Neighborhood Assn., 1987—; fin. com. Michael Dukakis for Pres., Inc., Boston, 1987-88. Mem. Mass. Bar Assn. Office: Safer Inc 189 Wells Ave Newton MA 02159

GOLDBERG, SAMUEL, holding company executive; b. Buffalo, Aug. 12, 1928; s. Benjamin Nathan and Norma (Mendelson) G.; m. Barbara Koonin, Feb. 3, 1952; children: Robert William, Thomas Richard, Margaret Ellen, Karen Susanne, Michael Edward. BA in Fgn. Studies, U. Va., 1951; postgrad., Georgetown U., 1951-52. Various operational and supervisory positions CIA, Washington and overseas, 1951-67; fgn. service officer Dept. State, Washington and Bonn, Fed. Republic Germany, 1967-70; legis. asst., chief staff U.S. Senator Charles Mathias, Washington, 1970-74; legis. dir. Fed. Energy Office, Washington, 1974; dep. asst. sec. of state Dept. State, Washington, 1974-77; chief of staff U.S. Senator John Heinz, Washington, 1977-79; v.p. Inco U.S., Inc., N.Y.C., 1979-84, pres., 1985—; bd. dirs. Bus. Council Internat. Understanding, N.Y.C. Commr. Nat. Strategic Materials and Minerals Program Adv. Com., Washington, 1984—; mem. Office of Tech. Assessment U.S. Congress, Washington, adv. panel 1985-87; bd. dirs. Ams. for Energy Independence, Washington, 1983—, Nat. Strategy Info. Ctr., 1988—. Served as cpl. U.S. Army, 1955-56. Mem. Fgn. Policy Assn. (gov., dir. 1980—), Council on Fgn. Relations, Am. Indonesian C. of C. (bd. dirs. 1981—), Scientists and Engrs. Secure Energy, Am. Soc. Metals Internat. Republican. Jewish. Home: 17 E 16th St New York NY 10003 Office: Inco US Inc 1 New York Pla New York NY 10004

GOLDBERG, STANLEY IRWIN, real estate executive; b. Newport News, Va., May 13, 1934; s. David and Sara (Levy) G.; m. Marilyn Levin, Nov. 22, 1963 (dec. Oct. 1970); 1 child, Andrew Garfield. Student, Coll. William and Mary, 1952-54, U. Va., 1954-55. Lic. real estate broker, Va. V.p. Bedding Supply Co., Inc., Newport News, 1956-59, exec. v.p., 1960-61, pres., 1962-70; gen. ptnr. Goldkress Investment Co., Newport News, 1970—, also bd. dirs.; pres. Mutual Realty Corp., Newport News, 1973—. Trustee Temple Sinai, Newport News. Served with USAF, 1957-58. Mem. Nat. Assn. Realtors, Va. Assn. Realtors, Newport News-Hampton Bd. Realtors. Lodge: Elks. Home: 19 Hopemont Dr Newport News VA 23606 Office: 11116 Jefferson Ave Newport News VA 23601

GOLDBERG, TED H., financial executive; b. Newark, Jan. 14, 1940; s. Barney and Gertrude (Moskowitz) G.; m. Ruth Higgins, Aug. 25, 1963 (div. 1969); m. Gloria Zepatos, July 11, 1969; children: Edward Scott, Todd Howard. BA, Jersey City State Coll., 1963. Tchr. Toms Rivers (N.J.) Schs., 1963-81; mgr. bookstore Ocean County Coll., Toms River, 1966-86; br. mgr. Integrated Resources Equity, Toms River, 1981-83; pres. Fed. Auto Advisors, Toms River, 1986—, Ted Goldberg & Assocs., Inc., Toms River, 1988—. Mgr. Toms River Little League, 1980-88. Mem. Nat. Assn. Securities Dealers, N.Y. Mets Dream Team Club. Office: Ted Goldberg & Assocs Inc 34 Main St Toms River NJ 08753

GOLDBERG, VICTOR JOEL, data processing company executive; b. Chgo., Oct. 19, 1933; s. Albert J. and Ruth R. (Rosenberg) G.; m. Harriet A. David, June 1, 1958; children—Susan A., Alan J. B.S., Northwestern U., 1955, M.B.A., 1956. With IBM Corp., Armonk, N.Y., 1959—; corp. dir. bus. plans IBM Corp., Armonk, 1977-78; v.p. communications IBM Corp., Armonk, N.Y., 1979-81; corp. v.p., pres. communication products div. IBM Corp., Armonk, 1981-83, pres. nat. distbn. div., 1983-86, v.p. asst. group exec. marketing, 1986-88, v.p. mgmt. systems and orgn., 1988—. Mem. Forum for World Affairs, 1988—; bd. govs. Westchester chpt. Am. Jewish Com., 1976—; mem. Inst. Internat. Edn., 1979—, mem. exec. com. 1984—, vice chmn., 1988; trustee Mental Health Assn. Westchester, 1984—. Served with U.S. Army, 1956-59. Mem. Beta Gamma Sigma. Office: IBM Corp Old Orchard Rd Armonk NY 10504

GOLDBERGER, ARTHUR STANLEY, economics educator; b. N.Y.C., Nov. 20, 1930; s. David M. and Martha (Greenwald) G.; m. Iefke Engelsman, Aug. 19, 1957; children: Nina Judith, Nicholas Bernard. B.S., N.Y.U., 1951; M.A., U. Mich., 1952, Ph.D., 1958. Acting asst. prof. econs. Stanford U., 1956-59; assoc. prof. econs. U. Wis., 1960- 63, prof., 1963-70, H.M. Groves prof., 1970-79, Vilas research prof., 1979—; vis. prof. Center Planning and Econ. Research, Athens, Greece, 1964-65; Keynes vis. prof. U. Essex, 1968- 69. Author: (with L.R. Klein) An Econometric Model of the United States, 1929-52, 1955, Impact Multipliers and Dynamic Properties, 1959, Econometric Theory, 1964, Topics in Regression Analysis, 1968, Functional Form and Utility, 1987; Editor: (with O.D. Duncan) Structural Equation Models in the Social Sciences, 1973, (with D.J. Aigner) Latent Variables in Socioeconomic Models, 1976; Assoc. editor: Jour. Econometrics, 1973-77; bd. editors: Am. Econ. Rev, 1964-66, Jour. Econ. Lit, 1975-77. Fulbright fellow Netherlands Sch. Econs., 1955-56, 59-60; vis. prof. U. Hawaii, 1969, 71; fellow Center for Advanced Study in Behavioral Scis., Stanford, 1976-77, 80-81; Guggenheim fellow Stanford U., 1972-73, 85. Fellow Am. Statis. Assn., Econometric Soc. (council 1975-80, 82-87), Am. Acad. Arts and Scis., AAAS; mem. Am. Econ. Assn. (Disting. fellow 1988), Nat. Acad. Scis. Home: 2828 Sylvan Ave Madison WI 53705 Office: U Wis Dept Econs Madison WI 53706

GOLDBERGER, MARVIN LEONARD, educator, administrator, physicist; b. Chgo., Oct. 22, 1922; s. Joseph and Mildred (Sedwitz) G.; m. Mildred Ginsburg, Nov. 25, 1945; children: Samuel M., Joel S. B.S., Carnegie Inst. Tech., 1943; Ph.D., U. Chgo., 1948. Research assoc. Radiation Lab., U. Calif., 1948-49; research assoc. Mass. Inst. Tech., 1949-50; asst.-assoc. prof. U. Chgo., 1950-55, prof., 1955-57; Higgins prof. physics Princeton U., 1957-77, chmn. dept., 1970-76, Joseph Henry prof. physics, 1977-78; pres. Calif. Inst. Tech., Pasadena, 1978-87; dir. Inst. Advanced Study, Princeton, N.J., 1987—; Mem. President's Sci. Adv. Com., 1965-69; Chmn. Fedn. Am. Scientists, 1971-73; dir. Gen. Motors Corp., Haskel, Inc.; bd. dirs. Associated Univs., Inc., Aspen Inst. Humanistic Studies. Bd. dirs. Norton Simon Mus., Sloan Found. Fellow Am. Phys. Soc., Am. Acad. Arts and Scis.; mem. Nat. Acad. Scis., Am. Philos. Soc., Council on Fgn. Relations. Club: Princeton (N.Y.C.).

GOLDBERGER, STEPHEN A., retail stores executive. s. Herbert H. and Phyllis (Finkelstein) G. Pres. Hills Stores Co. (formerly SCOA Industries, Inc.), Canton, Mass.; chmn. bd., chief exec. officer, pres. Hills Dept. Stores, Canton, Hills Stores Co., Canton. Office: Hills Dept Stores Inc 15 Dan Rd Canton MA 02021

GOLDBLATT, BARRY LANCE, manufacturing company executive; b. Palo Alto, Calif., July 29, 1945; s. Samuel and Joan Charlotte (Morton) G. BS, U. So. Calif., 1967, MBA, 1968. Supr. market rsch. for brands Procter & Gamble Co., Cin., 1968-71; mgr. market rsch. Personal Products Co. subs. Johnson & Johnson, 1971-74; asso. dir. consumer rsch. Johnson & Johnson Baby Products Co., Skillman, N.J., 1974-87; dir. market rsch. Johnson and Johnson Dental Care Co., New Brunswick, N.J., 1987—. Bd. dirs. New Brunswick Hot Line, 1973; vol. Urban Cons. Group, 1977—. Recipient Cert. of Recognition Nat. Symposium Hispanic Bus. and Economy, Chgo., 1981, Cert. of Appreciation U. So. Calif., L.A., 1981. Mem. U. So. Calif. MBA's, U. So. Calif. Commerce Assocs., Advt. Rsch. Found., Am. Mktg. Assn., Assn. MBA Execs., Am. Philatel. Soc., U. So. Calif. Assocs., U. So. Calif. Alumni Club, Skull and Dagger, Zeta Beta Tau. Republican. Club: U. So. Calif. Alumni of N.J. (pres.). Home: 20 Andrews Ln Princeton NJ 08540 Office: Johnson & Johnson 501 George St New Brunswick NJ 08903-2400

GOLDEN, BALFOUR HENRY, private investor; b. Bangor, Maine, Aug. 23, 1922; s. Samuel Henry and Helen (Rybier) G.; AB cum laude, Bowdoin Coll., 1944; postgrad. Columbia U., 1945-47; m. Emma Jane Krakauer, June 22, 1956; children: Peter Balfour, Betsy Jane, Robert Henry. Pres., Golden Food Svcs. Corp. of N.Y., 1951-70, of N.J., 1951-70, of Iowa, 1951-70, Golden Co. of Maine, 1952-70, Golden Base Svcs. Corp., 1952-70, Plaza Eats, Inc., 1958-70, Dubonnet Restaurant Corp., 1960-70; food svc. cons., 1970-74; pres. Guardian Food Svc. Corp., N.Y.C., 1974-85, Ropes Tremblay, Inc., 1986—. Mem. exec. bd. Ridgewood (N.J.)-Glen Council; program coord. Ridgewood chpt. Boy Scouts Am. With AUS, 1943-45. Mem. New Eng. Soc. in N.Y.C., N.Y. Restaurant Assn. (dir.), Williams Club, Phi Beta Kappa. Home: 325 Beechwood Rd Ridgewood NJ 07450

GOLDEN, JAMES ANDREW, leasing company executive; b. Barnstable, Mass., Dec. 6, 1946; s. Jackson J. and Irene G.; BS, Boston U., 1970. Service mgr. Colonial Car Lease Co., Inc., Plymouth, Mass., 1969-71, sales rep., 1971-73, sales mgr., 1973-74, v.p., 1974-75, pres., chief exec. officer, 1976-86. Mem. Jewish Big Brother Assn. Served with AUS, 1968-70. Mem. Car and Truck Rental and Leasing Assn. Mass. (pres. 1975-76, dir. 1974—), Nat. Car and Truck Rental and Leasing Assn. (dir. 1976-78, exec. com. 1977-78), Am. Auto Leasing Assn. (dir. 1980-85), Nat. Assn. Fleet Adminstrn., Am. Car Rental Assn. Home and Office: 140 Rangeley Rd Chestnut Hill MA 02167

GOLDEN, ROBERT CHARLES, brokerage executive; b. Bklyn., July 12, 1946; s. Charles Joseph and Audrey (Griffin) G.; B.S. in Acctg., Fordham U., 1968, M.B.A. in Fin., 1978. Vice-pres. internal audit Walston & Co., Inc., N.Y.C., 1969-73; v.p.-fin. Acan X-Ray Co., Inc., Detroit, 1973-76; Sr. v.p. Prudential Bache Securities, Inc., N.Y.C., 1976—. Bd. dirs. Cath. Guardian Soc., Bklyn. and Queens, N.Y., 1985—; trustee Xaviaran High Sch., Bklyn. Recipient citation Council of City of N.Y., Franciscan Heritage award Franciscan Sisters of the Poor at Plaza Hotel, 1987; named Educator of Yr. Assn. of Teachers of N.Y., 1986, Cath. Guardian Soc. Humanitarian of Yr. 1985; named to Diocesan Court of Honor Diocese of Bklyn. Mem. Securities Industry Assn., Mcpl. Fin. Officers Assn., Mcpl. Club Bklyn., Bayfort Assocs. (past pres.), St. Patrick Soc. of Bklyn., Emerald Assn. L.I., Fort Hamilton Hist. Soc., Acad. Magical Arts, The Friendly Sons St. Patrick City N.Y. Roman Catholic. Clubs: KC, Cathedral of Bklyn. (past pres.), Bay Ridge Mens, Fordham U. Pres., Brooklyn. Lodge: Ancient Order of Hibernians (div. 22). Home: 33 Columbia Ave Staten Island NY 10305-3739 Office: 199 Water St New York NY 10292

GOLDEN, TERENCE C., government official; b. Honesdale, Pa., Aug. 1, 1944; s. Leo J. and Alice (Matthews) G.; m. Kathleen Skopec, Apr. 6, 1968; children—Ryan Christopher, Matthew Bailey. B.S., U. Notre Dame, 1966; M.S., MIT, 1967; M.B.A., Harvard U., 1970. Mgr. Babcock Brown Boveri Reaktor GmBh, Mannheim, Fed. Republic Germany, 1971-73; pres. Palmas del Mar Co., P.R., 1973-76; mng. ptnr. Trammell Crow Residential Co., Dallas, 1976-84; asst. sec. adminstrn. Dept. Treasury, Washington, 1984-85; adminstr. GSA, Washington, 1985-88; chmn. Bailey Mgmt. Corp., Washington, 1989—. Office: Bailey Mgmt Corp 1155 15th St Ste 500 Washington DC 20005

GOLDENBERG, GEORGE, pharmaceutical company executive; b. N.Y.C., Mar. 12, 1929; s. Gersh and Rose (Kolpacci) G.; student Blkyn. Coll., 1946-47; B.S., Bklyn. Coll. Pharmacy of L.I. U., 1951; m. Arlene Sandra Yudell, May 22, 1955; children—Steven Alan, Heidi Michele Goldenberg Handelsman, Jeffrey Evan. Pharmacist, Dolcorts Pharmacy, N.Y.C., 1951-56; export mgr. Chem. Specialties Co., Inc., N.Y.C., 1956-58; sales mgr. Syntex Chem. Co., Inc., N.Y.C., 1958-60; asst. to pres. Syntex Labs., Inc., N.Y.C., 1960-61; gen. sales mgr. Panray-Parlam Corp., Englewood, N.J., 1961-63; v.p. Ormont Drug & Chem. Co., Inc., Englewood, 1963-64, exec. v.p., dir., 1964-66, pres., dir., 1966-81; sec., dir. Goldleaf Pharmacal Co., Inc., Englewood, N.J., 1966-81; pres., dir. Moleculon Biotech, Inc., 1982-87; pres., chief exec. officer, dir. Argus Pharmaceuticals Inc., The Woodlands, Tex., 1988—; bd. dirs. Fed. Pharmacal Co., Ft. Lauderdale, Fla., Bedford Acme Surg. Co., Inc., Bklyn., Lawton Labs., Inc., Englewood, Ormont Diagnostics Ltd., London. Trustee L.I. U., Bklyn. Coll. Pharmacy. Mem. Bklyn. Coll. Pharmacy Alumni Assn. (pres.), Fedn. Alumni Assns. L.I. U. (pres.), Am. Pharm. Assn., Englewood Jr. C. of C., Young Pres. Orgn., Am. Mgmt. Assn., Drug and Allied Trades Assn., Delta Sigma Theta. Club: B'nai B'rith. Home: 338 Charles River St Needham MA 02192 also: 3070 N 34th St Hollywood FL 33022 Office: 10600 Six Pines Dr The Woodlands TX 77380

GOLDFARB, ALAN KEITH, financial planning advisor; b. N.Y.C., Aug. 24, 1941; s. Walter I. and Adele S. (Lenke) G.; Terry L. Schweitzer, July 4, 1966; 1 child, Diana Lynn. BS in Indsl. Engrng., Fairleigh Dickinson U., 1966; MBA in Mgmt. Econs., N. Tex. State U., 1970; cert. Coll. for Fin. Planning, 1978. Cert. fin. planner. Admitted to Registry Practicing Fin. Planners. Dist. dir. Fin. Svc. Corp., Dallas, 1971-75; pres. Fin. Strategies Corp., Dallas, 1975-81; pres., chief exec. officer Fin. Strategies Group, Dallas, 1981—; program dir. fin. planning svcs. grad. sch. of mgmt. U. Dallas; adj. faculty Dallas County Community Coll. Dist.; mem. faculty Coll. Fin. planning. Former bd. dir., co-chmn. planned and deferred gifts com. Am. Heart Assn., Silver and Golden Heart Awards Tex. affiliate; bd. dirs., v.p. membership Temple Emanu-el Brotherhood; mem. investment, tax and, legal coms. Found. of Jewish Fedn. of Greater Dallas. Mem. Internat. Assn. Fin. Planning, (nat. dir., bd. dir., past pres. N. Tex. chpt.), Inst. Cert. Fin. Planners (dir., treas.), Am. Arbitration Assn. (fin. planning arbitration panel), Nat. Assn. Securities Dealers (bus. practice com.), North Dallas Fin. Forum (pres.). Columnist Dallas/Ft. Worth Bus., Dallas Morning News, Park Cities News. Office: Fin Strategies Group 5420 LBJ Frwy LB 54 Two Lincoln Centre Ste 1345 Dallas TX 75240

GOLDFARB, BERNARD SANFORD, lawyer; b. Cleve., Apr. 15, 1917; s. Harry and Esther (Lenson) G.; m. Barbara Brofman, Jan. 4, 1966; children—Meredith Stacey, Lauren Beth. A.B., Case Western Res. U., 1938, J.D., 1940. Bar: Ohio bar 1940. Since practiced in Cleve.; sr. partner firm Goldfarb & Reznick, 1967—; spl. counsel to atty. gen. Ohio, 1950, 71-74; mem. Ohio Commn. Uniform Traffic Rules, 1973—. Contbr. legal jours. Served with USAAF, 1942-45. Mem. Am., Ohio, Greater Cleve. bar assns. Home: 39 Pepper Creek Dr Pepper Pike OH 44124 Office: 1800 Illuminating Bldg Cleveland OH 44113

GOLDFARB, IRENE DALE, financial planner, consultant; b. Newark, N.J., Jan. 13, 1929; d. Philip and Lucie (Mintz) Dale; m. Samuel Goldfarb, Jan. 28, 1951; children: Ruth Koizim, David Alan, Sally Fay, Judith Valerie. BS in Chemistry, Rutgers U., 1950; MBA, U. Pa., 1979. Cert. fin. planner. Asst. to assoc. provost Princeton (N.J.) U., 1968-70, asst. to provost, 1970-72, computer programmer, 1972-74, mgr. personnel svcs., 1974-75, asst. dir. personnel, 1975-84; fin. planner, mgr. A.L. Herst Assocs., Inc., Princeton, 1984-86; cons. Princeton, 1986—, pvt. practice, 1986—. Mem. Internat. Assn. Fin. Planning (pres. 1988—, bd. dirs., founding officer Princeton/Western N.J. chpt., 1986—), Inst. Cert. Fin. Planners, Nat. Assn. Personal Fin. Advisors, Assoc. Alumnae Douglass Coll. (v.p. adminstrn. 1988—, chmn. annual fund 1982-84), Phi Beta Kappa. Home: 69 Balsam Ln Princeton NJ 08540 Office: 104 Carnegie Ctr Suite 210 Princeton NJ 08540

GOLDFARB, MURIEL BERNICE, marketing and advertising consultant; b. Bklyn., Mar. 29, 1920; d. Barnett Goldfarb and May (Steinberg) Goldfarb Oshman; B.A., U. Miami, Coral Gables, Fla., 1942; postgrad. CCNY, 1950. Advt. mgr. Majestic Specialities Co., N.Y.C., 1942-43; pub. info. asst. UNESCO, Paris, 1946-47; retail promotion mgr. Glamour Mag., 1955-61; advt. dir. Country Tweeds Co., N.Y.C., 1961-65; advt. dir. S. Augstein & Co., N.Y.C., 1966-72, Feature Ring Co., Inc., Gotham Ring Co., Inc., Fidco Inc., N.Y.C., 1972-79; dir. advt. and promotion Wasko Gold Products Corp., N.Y.C., 1979-81; advt. and mktg. cons., 1981—; advt. prodn. dir. N.E.I. Enterprises, Inc., 1984-85 . Served to lt. WAVES, 1943-46. Mem. Fashion Group N.Y. Inc., Women's Jewelry Assn. (corr. sec. 1983-85). Jewish.

GOLDFARB, ROBERT LAWRENCE, accountant; b. N.Y.C., May 10, 1951; s. Harold and Leonore (Goldenheim) G.; m. Linda Louise Trupiano, June 24, 1979. BBA, Pace U., 1973; MS, Adelphi U., 1975; MBA, Hofstra U., 1982. Cert. fin. planner; CPA, N.Y. Tax mgr. Price Waterhouse, N.Y.C., 1977-82; pvt. practice acctg. Great Neck, N.Y, 1982-85; ptnr. Gobstein, Weingarten & Goldfarb, Lake Success, N.Y., 1986—; permanent adj. prof. of acctg. and fin. planning Adelphi U., Garden City., N.Y. Contbr. articles to profl. jours. Mem. AICPAs, N.Y. State Soc. CPAs (mem. com. fin. planning), Nat. Conf. CPA Practioners (mem. edn. com.), Nat. Soc. Pub. Accts., Inst. Cert. Fin. Planners, Great Neck C. of C. (adminstrv. sec. 1985—), Lions, Masons.

GOLDFEDER, HOWARD, retired retail executive; b. N.Y.C., Apr. 28, 1926; s. Herman and Betty (Epstein) G.; m. Helen Wiggs; children: Carole, Joan. B.A., Tufts U., 1947. With Bloomingdale's, N.Y.C., 1947-67; exec. v.p. Famous-Barr, St. Louis, 1967-69; pres. May Co., Los Angeles, 1969-71; pres., then chmn. Bullock's, Los Angeles, 1971-77; with Federated Dept. Stores, Inc., Cin., 1977-88, pres., 1980-88, chief exec. officer, 1981—, chmn., 1982-88, also dir.; dir. J.P. Morgan and Morgan Guaranty Trust Co., Conn. Mut. Life Ins. Co. Recipient Nat. Brotherhood award NCCJ, 1981. Mem. Bus. Council, Cin. Inst. of Fine Arts (dir.). Clubs: Queen City (Cin.), Losantiville Country (Cin.). Office: 7 W 7th St Cincinnati OH 45202

GOLDFIELD, EMILY DAWSON, finance company executive, artist; b. Bklyn., May 31, 1947; d. Martin and Renee (Solow) Dawson; m. Stephen Gary Goldfield, June 17, 1973; children—Stacy Rose, Daniel James. B.S., U. Mich., 1969; M.Ed., Pa. State U., 1971; Ph.D., U. So. Calif., 1977. Chmn. bd. Provident Mut. Escrow, Encino, Calif., 1982—; exec. v.p. Hanover Investment Services, Encino, 1982—; v.p. Rancho Campo el Oro; dir. Hanover Funding, 1985—; dir. Real Estate Trustee Svcs., Encino, Bell Canyon Leasing. Author: The Value of Creative Dance, 1971; Development of Creative Dance, 1977. Minister Ch. of Scientology. U. Mich. scholar, 1969; Pa. State U. fellow, 1970, U. So. Calif. fellow, 1972. Mem. Calif. Ind. Mortgage Brokers Assn., Calif. Consumer Fin., Am. Technion Soc., Encino C. of C., San Fernando Valley Bd. Realtors , Calif. Escrow Assn., Nat. Assn. Realtors, Calif. Assn. Realtors, Visual Arts Assn., Am. Horse Show Assn., Paso Fino Horse Assn., Sierra Club, Bell Canyon Homeowners Assn. Club: Ferrari Owners. Office: Provident Mutual Escrow Suite 832 15760 Ventura Blvd Encino CA 91436

GOLDFUS, DONALD WAYNE, glass company executive; b. Mpls., Feb. 17, 1934; s. Alex Goldfus and Ruby Jane (Elliott) Bolander; m. Therese Marie Smuda, Aug. 22, 1959; children: Karen Goldfus O'Connor, Brian John. Student, U. Minn., 1956-59. Advt. mgr. Harmon Glass Co., Mpls., 1959-61, sales mgr., 1961-63, v.p. sales, 1963-67, pres., 1967-79; sr. v.p. Apogee Enterprises, Mpls., 1979-83, pres., 1983—, chief exec. officer, 1985—, chmn., 1988—; bd. dirs. Hypro Corp., Nat. Assn. OTC Cos. Editor Sporting Goods Jour., Mpls., 1958-59. Mem. adv. bd. Leukemia Research Fund, U. Minn., 1973—. Served with USAF, 1951-55. Named Glass Dealer of Yr. The Glass Digest, 1984; named to Pres. Club U. Minn., 1986. Mem. Nat. Glass Assn. (pres. 1983-84), Sales and Mktg. Exexs. of Mpls. (bd. dirs. 1967-71, Man of Yr., 1970, Bus. Exec. of Yr. 1986), Auto Glass Industry Com. (bd. dirs.). Club: Lafayette Country (Mpls.); Excelsior Bay Yacht (Minn.). Lodge: Masons. Office: Apogee Enterprises Inc 7900 Xerxes Ave S Bloomington MN 55431

GOLDHOFF, KENNETH LOUIS, financial executive; b. Cin., Feb. 23, 1961; s. Leon Louis and Rita May (Fogel) G.; m. Carrie Saeks, Dec. 22, 1985. BS in Fin., U. Ariz., 1983. Ins. sales rep., adminstrv. asst. Farmers Ins. Co.: The Ins. House, Tucson, 1980-82; life ins. sales rep. Penn Mutual Life Ins. Co., Tucson, 1982-83; life ins. sales rep., investment broker Irvin L. Schwartz & Assocs., Cin., 1983-84; investment broker R.H. Leshner & Co., Midwest Group, Cin., 1984-85, Gradison Fin. Services, Cin., 1985—. Mem. exec. com. United Jewish Appeal, Cin., 1987—. Mem. Inst. Cert. Fin. Planners. Republican. Home: 443 Warren Ave Cincinnati OH 45220 Office: Gradison Fin Svcs 580 Bldg Cincinnati OH 45202

GOLDING, BRAGE, former university president; b. Chgo., Apr. 28, 1920; s. Leon M. and Viola B. (Brage) G.; m. Hinda F. Wolf, Dec. 21, 1941; children: Brage, Susan, Julie. BS, Purdue U., 1941, PhD, 1948; LLD, Wright State U., 1975. Assoc. dir. research Lilly Varnish Co., Indpls.; also research assoc. Purdue U., 1948-57; vis. prof. engring. Purdue U., dir. research Lilly Varnish Co., 1957-59; head Sch. Chem. Engring. Purdue U., 1959-66; v.p. Ohio State U. and Miami U., 1966-67; pres. Wright State U., Dayton, Ohio, 1967-72, San Diego State U., 1972-77, Kent State U., 1977-82, Met. State Coll., Denver, 1984-85; acting pres. Western State Coll., Gunnison, Colo., 1985—; cons. Dept. Higher Edn., Pa. and N.J.; bd. dirs. Armco, Inc., Rogers Corp. Author: Polymers and Resins, 1959; Contbr. articles to profl. jours. Fellow AAAS; mem. Am. Chem. Soc., Phi Beta Kappa (hon.). Address: 17 Dorset Ln Bedminster NJ 07921

GOLDING, CHARLES WILLIAM, private investor, lawyer; b. Richmond, Va., Mar. 4, 1931; s. Harold Frederick and Lucile Winifred (Davis) G.; m. Katharine Rose Alexander, Sept. 5, 1955; children: William A., Davis, Peter. BS, Wake Forest U., 1951; LLB, Cornell U., 1956. Bar: Wash. 1956. Assoc., then ptnr. Riddell, Williams, Voorhees, Ivie & Bullitt, Seattle, 1956-63; pres., chief exec. officer, controller Pacific Marine Schwabacher, Seattle, 1964-77; pres., chief. exec. officer No. Comml. Co., Seattle, 1976-82; pvt. investor Seattle, 1982—. Author: What it Takes..., 1983. Mem. vis. com. U. Wash. Law Sch., Seattle; trustee Seattle Chamber Music Festival, Lakeside Sch., Seattle, Epiphany Day Sch., Seattle, Epiphany Episcopal Ch., YMCA, Seattle, Seattle Symphony Orch., Nat. Found., Seattle, Seattle Day Nursery. lt. j.g. USCG, 1952-54, Korea. Mem. ABA, Wash. State Bar Assn., Seattle-King County Bar Assn., Rainier Club, Univ. Club, Seattle Tennis Club. Home: 814 E Highland Dr Seattle WA 98102 Office: 1001 4th Ave Plaza Ste 3020 Seattle WA 98154

GOLDMAN, HERMAN N., real estate executive; b. Balt., Mar. 14, 1924; s. Phillip J. and Sarah (Rudman) G.; m. Violet Francis, Feb. 5, 1977; children: Barbara Clagett, Leslye Katz. Student, Balt. City Coll., 1941. Mdse. mgr. Isaac Hamburger & Sons, Balt., 1948-67; v.p., gen. mgr. Stevens Stores, New Orleans, 1968-70; pres. Shulman & Co., Norfolk, Va., 1971, Morville Stores, Phila., 1971-75; gen. mgr. Harry Rosen Stores, Toronto, 1975-77, Joe Feller Stores, Ottawa, Ont., Can., 1977-83; dir. real estate Jos. A. Bank Clothiers, Balt., 1983—. Contbr. articles to profl. jours. With U.S. Army, 1944-46. Mem. Boys Apparel Buyers Assn. (pres.), Internat. Conf. Shopping Ctrs.. Democrat. Jewish. Home: 1101 N Calvert St 1006 Baltimore MD 21202 Office: Jos A Bank Clothiers 25 Crossroads Dr Baltimore MD 21117

GOLDMAN, JAMIE LEE, insurance company executive; b. Boston, Oct. 6, 1957; d. Paul Richard and Sylvia Charlotte (Kravath) G. BS in Visual and Verbal Communication Arts, Emerson Coll., 1979; MA in Speech and Bus. Communications, U. Maine, Orono, 1981. Lic. ins. advisor Commonwealth of Mass., 1989. With inside sales and customer svc. depts. MCI Telecommunications, Boston, 1981; claims adjuster Liberty Mut. Ins. Co., Boston and Portland, Maine, 1982-83; claims mgr. N.E. region Browning Ferris Industries, Inc., Houston, 1983-84; claims supr. Fred S. James & Co., Boston, 1984-86; corp. ins. mgr. The Sheraton Corp., Boston, 1986-88; dir. ops. Tufts Assocs. Health Plan (Managedcomp), Waltham, Mass., 1989—. Mem. election and survey unit Dem. Nat. Conv., Augusta, Maine, 1980. Mem. Mass. Risk and Ins. Mgmt. Soc. (cert.). Jewish. Office: Tufts Assocs Health Plan Totten Pond Rd Waltham MA 02109

GOLDMAN, PATRICIA ANN, government official; b. Newton, N.J., Mar. 22, 1942; d. Jacob Joseph and Miriam Louise (Cassiday) G.; BA in Econs., Goucher Coll., 1964; m. Charles E. Goodell, July 1, 1978 (dec.). Rsch. asst. Joint Econ. Com. of Congress, 1964-65; legis. asst. ad hoc subcom. on war on poverty, edn. and labor com. U.S. Ho. of Reps., 1965-66; rsch. cons. U.S. C. of C., 1966, dir. manpower and poverty programs, 1967-71; legis. counsel Nat. League Cities, also U.S. Conf. of Mayors, 1971-72; exec. dir. The House Wednesday Group, U.S. Ho. of Reps., 1972-79; mem. Nat. Transp. Safety Bd., Washington, 1979-88, vice chmn., 1982-88; sr. v.p. US Air, Arlington, Va., 1988—; vis. prof. Woodrow Wilson Nat. Fellowship Program; lectr. Brookings Instn. Program for Sr. Govt. Execs. Trustee Goucher Coll.; bd. dirs. Found. Am. Communications; former treas. Nat. Women's Edn. Fund; former mem. adv. bd. Nat. Women's Polit. Caucus, also past chmn. Republican Women's Task Force; former chair governing bd. Ripon Soc. Fellow Kennedy Inst. Politics, Harvard U., 1978. Named Woman of Yr., Women's Transp. Seminar, 1982. Office: US Air Group 1911 Jefferson Davis Hwy Arlington VA 22202

GOLDMAN, ROBERT HURON, lawyer; b. Boston, Nov. 24, 1918; s. Frank and Rose (Sydeman) G.; m. Charlotte R. Rubens, July 5, 1945; children: Wendy Eve, Randolph Rubens. A.B., Harvard U., 1939, LL.B., 1943. Bar: N.Y. State 1945, Mass. 1951. Practiced in N.Y.C., 1945-50, Lowell, Mass., 1951—; law clk. Judge Learned Hand, U.S. Ct. Appeals, 1943-44; partner firm Goldman and Curtis (and predecessor firms), 1951—; columnist Lowell Sunday Sun Daily, 1954-78; v.p., asso. pub. Malden (Mass.) Evening News, 1969-86, Medford (Mass.) Daily Mercury, 1969-86, Melrose (Mass.) Evening News, 1969-86; mem. adv. bd. Baybank Middlesex., 1966-84; Radio commentator on internat. affairs, 1954-86. Author: A Newspaperman's Handbook of the Libel Law of Massachusetts, 1966, rev., 1974, The Law of Libel—Present and Future, 1969; Editor: Harvard Law Review, 1943. Chmn. Greater Lowell Civic Com., 1952-55, Lowell Hist. Soc., 1957-60, Lowell Devel. and Indsl. Commn., 1959-60; Del. Republican State Conv., 1960-62; Bd. dirs. Boston World Affairs Council, 1960-82. Named Citizen of Year Greater Lowell Civic Com., 1956. Mem. ABA (mem. nat. com. on consumer protection 1972-73, Sherman Act com. 1973—), Mass. Bar Assn. (chmn. bar-press com. 1973-76), Middlesex County Bar Assn., Lowell Bar Assn., Boston Bar Assn., Phi Beta Kappa. Club: Harvard (dir. Lowell 1968—). Home: 8 Rolling Ridge Rd Andover MA 01810 Office: 4th Fl 144 Merrimack St Lowell MA 01852

GOLDMAN, STEVEN JASON, lawyer, accountant; b. Boston, Nov. 11, 1947; s. Philip Charles and Selma Laura (Goldblatt) G. BSBA, Northeastern U., Boston, 1970, MBA, 1974; JD, New Eng. Sch. Law, 1987. Bar: R.I., 1987, U.S. Dist. Ct. R.I. 1988, U.S. Tax Ct. 1987; CPA, R.I. Staff auditor CPA firms, Boston and Providence, 1970-72; sr. accountant Peat, Marwick, Mitchell & Co., Providence, 1972-73; controller Warwick Fed. Savs. & Loan Assn. (R.I.), 1974, v.p., 1975-79, exec. v.p., 1980-82; pres. Fin. Adv. Svcs., Unltd., 1982-87; pvt. practice, Warwick, 1987—. Fellow AICPA; mem. ABA (taxation div.), R.I. Soc. CPAs, R.I. Bar Assn. (taxation com.), Turk's Head Club, Aircraft Owners and Pilots Assn., Edgewood Yacht Club. Jewish. Avocations: flying, sailing, tennis. Office: 1429 Warwick Ave Ste 12 Warwick RI 02888-5062

GOLDNER, SHELDON HERBERT, export-import company executive; b. Bklyn., Aug. 3, 1928; s. David and Esther (Maskowsky) G.; m. Lila Diane Silber, Aug. 14, 1954; children: Jonathan Shepard, Jeffrey Scott, Barbara Jill. B.S. in acctg., L.I. U., 1950. C.P.A., N.Y. Acct. S.H. Goldner & Co., N.Y.C., 1950-59; v.p. fin. Connell Rice & Sugar Co., Inc., Westfield, N.J., 1959—. Pres., trustee Temple Israel, Union, N.J. Served with U.S. Army, 1946-47, PTO. Mem. AICPAs, N.Y. State Soc. CPAs, Halloween Yacht Club (Stamford, Conn.), Royal Veere (The Netherlands) Yacht Club. Home: 999 Chimney Ridge Dr Mountainside NJ 07092 Office: Connell Rice & Sugar Co Inc 45 Cardinal Dr Westfield NJ 07092

GOLDRESS, JERRY E., diversified business executive. Chmn., chief exec. officer Best Products Co., Richmond, Va., 1988—; now chmn. Wherehouse Entertainment Inc., Torrance, Calif.; also chmn., chief exec. officer Cardis Corp., Buena Park, Calif. Office: Wherehouse Entertainment Inc 19701 Hamilton Ave Torrance CA 90502 also: Cardis Corp 9401 Wilshire Blvd Beverly Hills CA 90212 also: Best Products Co Inc 1400 Best Pla Richmond VA 23227 *

GOLDRING, NORMAN MAX, advertising executive; b. Chgo., June 22, 1937; s. Jack and Carolyn (Wolf) G.; m. Cynthia Lois Garland, Dec. 20, 1959; children: Jay Marshall, Diane. B.S. in Bus., Miami (Ohio) U., 1959; M.B.A., U. Chgo., 1963. Advt. account mgr. Edward H. Weiss & Co., Chgo., 1959-61; sr. v.p., dir. mktg. services Stern, Walters & Simmons, Inc., Chgo., 1961-68; chmn. Goldring & Co., Inc. (mktg. research), Chgo., 1968—; pres. CPM, Inc. (advt.), 1969—; instr. mktg. and advt. mgmt. Roosevelt U., 1965-68. Mem. editorial bd. Jour. Media Planning. Commr. Ridgeville Park Dist., Evanston, Ill., 1971-75; bd. dirs., v.p. Mus. Broadcast Communications, 1983—; pres. Ridgeville Park Dist., 1974-75. Mem. Am. Mktg. Assn. (speaker), Advt. Council Inc. (Midwest adv. bd. 1983—), Am. Mgmt. Assn. Home: 505 N Lake Shore Dr Chicago IL 60611 Office: CPM Inc 240 E Ontario St Chicago IL 60611

GOLDSBERRY, RICHARD EUGENE, mobile intensive care paramedic; b. Colorado Springs, Feb. 17, 1956; s. Eugene Theodore and Martha Blanche (Geiser) G. Cert. paramedics, U. Calif., San Diego, 1979. Cert. mobile intensive care paramedic. With Circle K Corp., El Centro, Calif., 1970-75, La Junta (Colo.) Med. Ctr., 1975-76, Pioneers Meml. Hosp., Brawley, Calif., 1976-77; emergency rm. technician Pioneers Meml. Hosp., Brawley, 1977-79; mobile intensive care paramedic Gold Cross Ambulance Co., El Centro, 1979—, mgr., 1984—; instr., cons. Imperial Valley Coll., 1984—; cons., advisor Imperial Valley Reg. Occupational Program, 1984. Rep. Emergency Med. Care Com., El Centro, Calif., 1987—. Mem. Calif. Rescue and Paramedic Assn., Cousteau Soc., Greenpeace USA, Sierra Club. Office: Gold Cross Ambulance Co 905 S Imperial Ave El Centro CA 92243

GOLDSCHEIDER, SIDNEY, lawyer; b. Balt., Mar. 27, 1920; s. Harry and Esther Goldscheider; m. Sylvia Glick, June 13, 1943; children: Judith, Alan, Eileen (dec.). JD summa cum laude, U. Balt., 1942. Bar: Md. 1942, U.S. Ct. Appeals (4th cir.) 1942. Pvt. practice law Balt., 1942—; with enforcement div. Office of Price Adminstrn., Balt., 1943-45; bd. dirs. Budget Rent-a-Car of N.Y.C. Mem. Balt. Mus. of Art, Save-a-Heart Found, Am. Jewish Congress, Shaarei Tfiloh Congregation, Shaarei Zion Congregation, Ohel Yaacov Congregation, Beth Tfiloh Brotherhood, Beth Jacob Brotherhood; bd. dirs. Beth Jacob Congregation, Balt., Safety First Club of Md.; bd. dirs. Md com. State of Israel Bonds; sec. One Slade Condominium Coun. of Co-owners, Balt.; co-chmn. Shaare Zedek Med. Ctr. in Jerusalem, com. mem. Israel Bonds Amb.'s Ball; mem. Met. Civic Assn. Honoree Beth Jacob Congregation, 1973, 86, State of Israel Bonds, 1976; recipient citations Gov. Md., 1982, 86, City of Balt., 1982; Sidney Goldscheider Day proclaimed by Baltimore County and by City of Balt., 1986, Disting. Svc. Resolution Md. Ho. of Dels., 1986. Mem. Balt. City Bar Assn., Md. State Bar Assn., Md. Trial Lawyers Assn., U. Balt. Alumni Assn., Balt. C. of C., Jewish Hist. Soc., Zionist Orgn. Am., Hebrew Orthodox Meml. Soc., Associated Jewish Charities and Welfare Fund (lawyer's div.), Israel Prime Minister's Club, Am. Philatelic Soc., Heuisler Honor Soc., Phi Delta Tau. Lodge: Schreter B'nai B'rith (Outstanding Citizen award 1982). Home: 1 Slade Ave Baltimore MD 21208 Office: 218 E Lexington St Baltimore MD 21202

GOLDSMITH, BRAM, banker; b. Chgo., Feb. 22, 1923; s. Max L. and Bertha (Gittelsohn) G.; m. Elaine Maltz; children: Bruce, Russell. Student, Herzl Jr. Coll., 1940, U. Ill., 1941-42. Asst. v.p. Pioneer-Atlas Liquor Co., Chgo., 1945-47; pres. Winston Lumber and Supply Co., East Chicago, Ind., 1947-50; v.p. Medal Distilled Products, Inc., Beverly Hills, Calif., 1950-75; pres. Buckeye Realty and Mgmt. Corp., Beverly Hills, 1952-75; exec. v.p. Buckeye Constrn. Co., Inc., Beverly Hills, 1952-75; chmn. bd., chief exec. officer City Nat. Corp., Beverly Hills, 1975—; dir. City Nat. Bank, Beverly Hills, 1964—, chmn. bd., chief exec. officer, 1975—; bd. dirs. Cedars/Sinai Med. Ctr.; past dir. Los Angeles br. San Francisco Fed. Res. Bank. Pres. Jewish Fedn. Council of Greater Los Angeles, 1969-70; nat. chmn. United Jewish Appeal, 1970-74; regional chmn. United Crusade, 1976; co-chmn. bd. dirs. NCCJ; chmn. Am. com. for Weizman Inst. Sci. Served with Signal Corps U.S. Army, 1942-45. Mem. Los Angeles Philharmonic Assn. (v.p., bd. dirs.). Jewish. Clubs: Hillcrest Country, Masons (Los Angeles), Balboa Bay. Office: City Nat Corp 400 N Roxbury Dr Beverly Hills CA 90210

GOLDSMITH, KATHLEEN MAWHINNEY, accountant; b. Bklyn., July 16, 1957; d. James R. and Carmela (Ditria) Mawhinney; m. Marc Bruce Goldsmith, Oct. 7, 1979; 1 child, James Ryan. BS, Alfred U., 1979; MBA, U. Conn., 1986. CPA, Conn. Acct., Price Waterhouse, Stamford, Conn., 1979-83; controller OCE Bus. Systems Inc., Stamford, 1983—. Adv., Jr. Achievement, 1980-81. Named Outstanding Young Women of Am. Mem. Am. Inst. CPAs, Conn. Soc. CPAs, Phi Kappa Phi, Delta Mu Delta. Home: 24 Lampost Dr West Redding CT 06896 Office: OCE Inc 1351 Washington Blvd Stamford CT 06902

GOLDSMITH, ROBERT HOLLOWAY, manufacturing company executive; b. Buffalo, May 15, 1930; s. Henry Stanhope and Frances Edmere (Shickluna) G.; m. Diane Cecilia Kramer, June 27, 1957 (div. Sept. 1981); children: Janeen, Daena, Maria, Lisa, Joseph; m. Catherine Helen Draper, Oct. 3, 1981; stepchildren: Deborah, Lori. BME, U. Buffalo, 1951; MBA, Xavier U., 1960. Engr. Allied Chem. and Dye Corp., Buffalo, 1951-54; successively engr., mgr., gen. mgr., v.p. and gen. mgr. aircraft engine projects, v.p. strategic planning, v.p. and gen. mgr. gas turbine div. GE, various, 1956-81; sr. v.p. aerospace and indsl. Pneumo Corp., Boston, 1981-82; cons. Robert H. Goldsmith Assocs., Gloucester, Mass., 1982-83; vice chmn., chief ops. officer Precision Forge Co., Oxnard, Calif., 1983-84; sr. v.p. ops. Rohr Industries, Inc., Chula Vista, Calif., 1984-88, sr. v.p. bus. ops., 1988—, also bd. dirs. Contbr. articles to profl. jours. Mem. pres.'s council San Diego State U., 1987—; bd. dirs. United Way, San Diego, Calif., 1987—. With U.S. Army, 1954-56. Republican. Roman Catholic. Office: Rohr Industries Inc Foot of H St PO Box 878 Chula Vista CA 92012

GOLDSPIEL, ARNOLD NELSON, internal auditor; b. N.Y.C., Aug. 4, 1949; s. Julius and Minna (Nelson) G. BA in Econ., Rutgers U., 1971. EDP auditor Chubb and Son, Inc., Short Hills, N.J., 1972-74; audit coordinator, tech. support Merrill Lynch and Co., N.Y.C., 1974-76; sr. EDP auditor Hoffman-LaRoche, Inc., Nutley, N.J., 1976-78; sr. EDP auditor then EDP audit assoc. Mut. Benefit Life Ins. Co., Newark, 1978-82, asst. comptroller corp. data security, 1982-85; sr. EDP auditor Bristol-Myers Co., N.Y.C., 1985—; Mem. Info. Mgmt. System com. IBM Share-Audit Project, 1980-81. Mem. citizens planning adv. com. Nutley Sch. Bd., 1978. Served to staff sgt. N.J. Air N.G., 1968-74. Mem. EDP Auditors Assn. (cert.), Inst. Internal Auditors, Am. Mgt. Assn.

GOLDSPIEL, STEVEN IRA, financial information executive; b. Bklyn., Sept. 22, 1946; s. Max Joseph and Anne (Dubroff) G.; children: Denise Sharon, Michael Edward. BBA, Monmouth Coll., 1967. Sales rep. Disclosure Inc., N.Y.C., 1972-74, eastern sales mgr., 1974-76; dir. mktg. Disclosure Inc, N.Y.C., 1976-78; v.p. mktg. and sales Disclosure Inc, Bethesda, Md., 1978-83; pres. Disclosure Inc, Bethesda, 1987—; exec. v.p. Disclosure Info. Group, Bethesda, 1983-87. Home: 2301 McCormick Rd Rockville MD 20850 Office: Disclosure Inc 5161 River Rd Bethesda MD 20816

GOLDSTEIN, BERNARD, investment banker; b. N.Y.C., Nov. 19, 1930; s. Jacob and Jean (Furman) G.; m. Patricia Ann Rediker; children: Mark Harris, Bruce Evan, Nancy Beth. BS, U. Pa., 1953; MS, Columbia U., 1963. Exec. v.p. Computech Inc., N.Y.C., 1958-65; dir. N.Y. dist. Control Data Corp., N.Y.C., 1965-67; pres. United Data Ctrs., Greenwich, Conn., 1967-74; sr. v.p. Tymshare Inc., Darien, Conn., 1974-78; chmn. Nat. CSS, Inc., Wilton, Conn., 1978-79; ptnr. Broadview Assocs., Ft. Lee, N.J., 1979—; past chmn. Adapso Co., Washington; chmn. bd. trustees Adapso Found., Washington; bd. dirs. Cycare Systems, Phoenix. Co-author: Information Technology: The Trillion Dollar Opportunity, 1986. Trustee Riverside Research Inst. Served as lt. (j.g.) USNR, 1954-58. Mem. Fairview Country Club (Greenwich), Harmonie Club (N.Y.C.). Jewish. Office: Broadview Assocs 2115 Linwood Ave Fort Lee NJ 07024

GOLDSTEIN, DIANA MARIE, corporate executive; b. Petalumia, Calif., July 10, 1959; d. Darrell Dean and Colleen Marie (Goyke) Kearns; m. W. David Goldstein, June 19, 1983. AAS in Data Processing, Mercer County Community Coll., 1986, cert. in real estate, 1987. Lic. real estate agt., N.J. Adminstrv. asst. U.S. Dept. Health and Human Services, Hyattsville, Md., 1978-80, adminstrv. asst., supr. word processing, 1982-83; bookkeeper Engineered Inspection System, Princeton Junction, N.J., 1983-85; sec.-treas. Engineered Inspection System, Robbinsville, N.J., 1986-88; v.p. AMBIC Bldg Inspection Cons, Inc., Robbinsville, 1988—. Mem. Nat. Assn. Realtors, N.J. Assn. Realtors, Phi Theta Kappa. Roman Catholic. Home: 23 Dunbar Dr Robbinsville NJ 08691 Office: AMBIC Bldg Inspection Cons Inc 23 Dunbar Dr Robbinsville NJ 08691

GOLDSTEIN, HOWARD BERNARD, investment banker, advertising and marketing executive, artist, photographer; b. Bronx, N.Y., Dec. 4, 1943; s. Maurice and Matilda Goldstein; B.F.A., Pratt Inst., 1970; m. Susan Nadine Goldberg, June 25, 1967; children—Jill Alecya, Brett Adam. Art dir. Fairfax Advt. div. Ogilvy & Mather, Inc., N.Y.C., 1968-72; creative dir. Hoffman Advt., N.Y.C., 1972-80, Miller, Addison, Steele, Inc., N.Y.C., 1980-82; pres. Gould Advt., Cliffside Park, N.J., 1969—; registered securities broker,1969, br. officer tax shelter coordinator E.F. Hutton & Co., Inc., 1983-85; registered security broker, sr. v.p., mem chmn.'s coun., dir.'s coun. Lehman Bros. Shearson Lehman Bros., Inc., 1985—. Vice pres., bd. dirs. Winston Tower 200, Condominium Assn.; Mem. Internat. Assn. Fin. Planning, Inst. Cert. Fin. Planners, Coll. Cert. Fin. Planners, Denver Grad. Police & Fire Acad. of Bergen County, N.J., June 12, 1986. Fin. officer N.J. State Police Office of Emergency Mgmt., Cliffside Park, 1986; spl. police officer Cliffside Park Police Dept., N.J. State Police Benevolent Assn., 1986—; mem. Graphic Artists Guild, 1976-80, Bronx Coutny Hist. Soc., 1968-71, Cliffside Park Baseball Assn., 1979—, coach, 1981, 83; sponsor Project High Frontier, U.S. Govt., 1986, sustaining mem. Rep. Nat. Com., 1981—; preferred mem. U.S. Senatorial Club, 1984—; Sachs art scholar, 1955; Exhibited Bronx Hist. Soc. photo show, N.Y.C., 1970; paintings at Soc. of Illustrators show, 1971-72; numerous other shows. Recipient medal for art service Youth Friends Assn., 1961, Ga. Pacific award, 1978. Mem. Tenafly Rifle and Pistol Club Inc., Nat. Rifle Assn. Jewish. Clubs: Fort Lee Racquetball. Lodge: Bnai Brith. Address: 200 Winston Dr Cliffside Park NJ 07010

GOLDSTEIN, IRVING, communications company executive; b. Catskill, N.Y., Mar. 27, 1938; s. Hyman and Leah (Koletsky) G.; m. Susan Wallack, Dec. 21, 1962; children: Elizabeth Jane, Jill Audrey. Student, U. Buffalo, 1955-57; B.A., Queens Coll., CUNY, 1960; J.D., N.Y. U., 1963. Bar: N.Y. 1964, D.C. 1967, U.S. Supreme Ct 1967. Gen. atty. internat. communications FCC, Washington, 1963-66; with Communications Satellite Corp., 1966—; gen. atty. office gen. counsel Communications Satellite Corp., Washington, 1966-71; dir. European office Communications Satellite Corp., Geneva, 1971-74; dir. internat. affairs Communications Satellite Corp., Washington, 1974-77; asst. gen. mgr. external relations and bus. devel., internat. communications Communications Satellite Corp., 1977-79, v.p. internat. ops., 1979-80, sr. v.p. internat. communications services, 1980-81; exec. v.p. Communications Satellite Corp., Washington, 1982-83, pres., dir., 1983-85; chmn., chief exec. officer, dir. Communications Satellite Corp., 1985—; pres., dir. Satellite Television Corp., Washington, 1981-82; bd. govs. Internat. Telecommunications Satellite Orgn., 1974-81, chmn., 1980-81; bd. dirs. Security Trust Co. Contbr. articles to profl. jours. Bd. dirs. Wolf Trap Found., 1984—; chmn. bd. trustees Queens Coll. (CUNY) Found., 1987—. Mem. D.C. Bar Assn., FCC Bar Assn. Clubs: International, City (Washington); Georgetown. Office: Communications Satellite Corp 950 L'Enfant Pla SW Washington DC 20024

GOLDSTEIN, JEFFREY, corporate professional; b. N.Y.C., Feb. 27, 1946; s. Abraham Allan and Jeanette (Hyman) G.; m. Pamela S., July 9, 1967; children: Eric S., Kenneth S. BS, Rensselaer Poly. Inst., 1967; MBA, Columbia U., 1969. CPA, N.Y., N.J. Auditor C & L, N.Y.C., 1967-75; tchr. Brentwood (N.Y.) Sch. System, 1968-72; dir. fin. Stelber Indsl., Medford, N.Y., 1975-76; v.p. fin. Venus Sci., Huntington, N.Y., 1977-79, Arkay Pkg. Corp., 1979-85; exec. v.p., treas. Kane Industries, Inc., Ridgefield Park, N.J., 1985—. Home: 11 Coventry Rd Livingston NJ 07039 Office: Kane Indsl Inc PO Box 300 Ridgefield Park NJ 07660

GOLDSTEIN, LIONEL ALVIN, financial planner, consultant; b. Bklyn., Oct. 19, 1932; s. Alexander and Ruth (Spitzer) G.; m. Judy Calk, May 19, 1973; children: Alex Nolan, Sharon Anne. Student, So. Meth. U., 1965; MS, U. Dallas, Irving, Tex., 1977; cert. fin. planner, Coll. Fin. Planning, 1983; PhD, Golden State U., 1986. CPA, Tex., La., Ark.; cert. fin. planner, cert. info. systems auditor. V.p. fin., treas. Arrow Industries, Inc, Carrollton, Tex., 1965-76; pres. Goldstein & Co., CPA, Dallas, 1976-87; prin., co-founder Quest Capital Mgmt., Inc., Dallas, 1987—; dir. MBA program fin. planning services U. Dallas Grad. Sch. Mgmt., 1988. Served with U.S. Army, 1951-53. Mem. Am. Inst. CPA's, Tex. Soc. CPA's. (com. chmn. Dallas chpt. 1978-80), La. Soc. CPA's., Nat. Assn. Accts. (internat. bd. standards and practices for cert. fin. planners, bd. examiners), Inst. Cert. Fin. Planners (pres. Dallas chpt. 1987-88, chmn. Dallas chpt. 1988-89), Internat. Assn. Fin. Planners, Dallas Estate Planning Council. Republican. Jewish. Home: 2861 Parkhaven Dr Plano TX 75075 Office: Quest Capital Mgmt Inc 8235 Douglas Ave Suite 600 Dallas TX 75225

GOLDSTEIN, LOUIS LAZARUS, state official; b. Prince Frederick, Md., Mar. 14, 1913; s. Goodman and Belle G. Goldstein; m. Hazel Horton, Nov. 22, 1947; children: Philip, Louisa, Margaret Senate. BS, Washington Coll., 1935, LLD (hon.), 1977; JD, U. Md., 1938; LLD (hon.), Morgan State U., 1973, Western Md. Coll., 1973, U. Balt., 1977; LHD (hon.), Towson State U., 1985. Mem. Md. Ho. of Dels., Annapolis, 1939-42; mem. Md. Senate, Annapolis, 1947-59, former majority floor leader, former pres. senate, 1951-59; comptroller State of Md., Annapolis, 1959—; chmn. Md. Retirement and Pension Systems, Balt., 1959—, Md. Bd. Revenue Estimates, Annapolis, 1959—; mem. Md. State Banking Commn., 1959—, Md. Hall of Records Commn., Annapolis, 1959—. Del. Dem. Nat. Convs.; chmn. bd. visitors, bd. govs. Washington Coll., Chestertown, Md., 1978—; bd. dirs. Balt. Symphony Orch., 1970—, Md. Hist. Soc., Balt., 1960—. 1st lt. USMC, 1942-46, PTO. Recipient Calvert prize for hist. preservation Md. Hist. Trust, 1978, Pres.'s Medal Mt. St. Mary's Coll., 1978, Fin. Leadership award Nat. Assn. Govt. Accts., 1986. Mem. Nat. Assn. State Auditors, Comptrollers and Treas. (pres. 1969), Md. Pub. Fin. Officers Assn., Govt. Fin. Officers U.S. and Can., ABA, Md. Bar Assn., D.C. Bar Assn., Sigma Delta Chi, Lions. Jewish. Home: Oakland Hall Prince Frederick MD 20678 Office: Office of Comptroller Goldstein Treasury Bldg PO Box 466 Annapolis MD 21404

GOLDSTEIN, MANFRED, consultant; b. Vienna, Austria, Jan. 30, 1927; came to U.S., 1939, naturalized, 1945; s. Isadore and Anna (Hahn) G.; m. Shirley Marie Lavine, Aug. 27, 1950; children—Cindy Marie, Lynn Alyse. Student Manhattan Trade Center, 1947; E.E., Capitol Radio Engring. Inst., 1963; student L.I. U., 1961, Indsl. Coll. Armed Forces, 1967-68. Sr. technician Bklyn. Radio, 1953-55, Budd Stanley, Inc., Long Island City, N.Y., 1955; lead engr. telephone equipment Precision Indsl. Design Newark, 1955-57; project engr., contract adminstr., sales mgr. Lieco, Inc., Syossett, N.Y. 1957-65, v.p., 1964-65; mgmt. and engring. cons., 1965—; pres. Positive Cons.'s Inc., Bellmore, N.Y., 1967-86, Lake Luzerne, N.Y., 1986—. Owner Lake Luzerne (N.Y.) Seaplane Base, 1969—; mem. small bus. adv. com. to Congressman Thomas J. Downey; mem. small bus. adv. council L.I. Assn. Commerce. Served with AUS, 1945-46. Fellow Nat. Contract Mgmt. Assn. (bd. dirs. L.I. chpt., v.p. 1983-85), IEEE (sr.); mem. Soc. Plastics Engrs., Am. Indsl. Preparedness Assn. (exec. bd. mgmt. div.), ABA (assoc.), Air Force Assn., Capitol Radio Engring. Inst. Alumni (sr.), Nat. Pilots Assn., Aircraft Owners and Pilots Assn., Internat. Platform Assn., Lake Luzerne C. of C. (chmn. indsl. devel. com.). Inventor torpedo fire control cable and connector for Polaris, high pressure seals for Polaris submarine antennae. Address: 1998 Bay Rd PO Box 430 Lake Luzerne NY 12846

GOLDSTEIN, MARK KINGSTON LEVIN, high technology executive, researcher; b. Burlington, Vt., Aug. 22, 1941; s. Harold Meyer Levin and Roberta (Butterfield) G.; m. Kyoko Matsubara, Mar. 8, 1985. B.S. in Chemistry, U. Vt., 1964, Ph.D., U. Miami-Coral Gables, 1971. Pres. IBR, Inc., Coral Gables, Fla., 1970-74; group leader Brookhaven Nat. Lab., Upton, N.Y., 1974-77; sr. researcher East-West Ctr., Honolulu, 1977-79; sr. tech. advisor JGC Corp., Tokyo, 1979-81; pres., chmn. bd. Quantum Group, Inc., La Jolla, Calif., 1981—; exec. dir. Magnatek, Inc., Brotas, Brazil, 1982—. Contbr. articles to profl. jours.; contbr. poetry to mag. NSF fellow, 1964, 65. Mem. Am. Chem. Soc., AAAS. Club: Hawaii Yacht (Honolulu). Patentee, inventor devices including gas safety valve. Home: 2500 Torrey Pines Rd Apt 805 La Jolla CA 92037 Office: Quantum Group Inc 11211 Sorrento Valley Rd San Diego CA 92121

GOLDSTEIN, MICHAEL, accounting and consulting firm executive; b. N.Y.C., Mar. 14, 1928; s. Arthur and Anna (Storch) G.; m. Elaine Vivien Dann, June 13, 1954; children: Susan F., Thomas M., Andrew C., Peter A. BA, NYU, 1948; MBA, CUNY, 1953. CPA, N.Y., Pa. Ptnr. Homer Merkur & Co., Hempstead, N.Y., 1956-70; ptnr. Laventhol and Horwath, N.Y.C., 1970-82, audit ptnr., 1970-72; regional dir. mgmt. adv. services Laventhol & Horwath, N.Y.C., 1972-75, asst. ptnr.-in-charge, 1975-77, adminstrv. ptnr., 1977-80, mng. ptnr., 1980-83; nat. mng. ptnr. profl. svcs. Laventhol & Horwath, Phila., 1983—; internat. liaison ptnr. Laventhol & Horwath, 1977—, mem. nat. coun., bd. dirs. 1980-86; mem. internat. council, bd. dirs., sec.-treas. Horwath & Horwath Internat., 1980—. Treas. Nat. Mus. Am. Jewish History, Phila., 1984—; nat. bd. trustees Boys Clubs Am., N.Y.C., 1985—; trustee Found. for Acctg. Edn., 1976-82, pres. 1981-82; bd. dirs. N.Y. State Bd. Accountancy, 1982-83. Named Acct. of Yr. Adelphi U., 1980; recipient Robert S. Pace Soc. award Pace U., 1981. Mem. AICPA (council 1976-84), N.Y. State Soc. CPA's (pres. 1980-81, pres. Nassau chpt. 1974-75), Locust Club, Knickerbocker Yacht Club. Republican. Jewish. Office: Laventhol & Horwath 1845 Walnut St 19th Fl Philadelphia PA 19103

GOLDSTEIN, MICHAEL, retail executive. Formerly exec. v.p., treas., chief fin. officer Toys R Us Inc., Rochelle Park, N.J., now exec. v.p. fin. and adminstrn. Office: Toys R Us Inc 395 W Passaic St Rochelle Park NJ 07662 *

GOLDSTEIN, MICHAEL STUART, systems executive; b. N.Y.C., Apr. 22, 1945; s. David and Anne (Klotz) G.; BA, UCLA, 1966; m. Penelope Donaldson, May 4, 1968; children: David John, Darren Stuart. Cert. data processor, computer programmer, computer profl. Promotions mgr. Transamerica Fin., Los Angeles, 1966-70; Western regional mgr. Trans Union Systems, Corp., L.A., Chgo., 1970-78; pres. Mutogo Data Corp., Santa Ana, Calif., 1978—; condr. seminars in field; cons. in field. Mem. Am. Mgmt. Assn., Data Processing Mgmt. Assn., Data Entry Mgmt. Assn. Office: 1801 Newport Circle Santa Ana CA 92705

GOLDSTEIN, MORRIS, international economist; b. N.Y.C., Oct. 13, 1944; s. Lewis and Belle (Hagler) G.; m. Margaret A. Aruck, July 26, 1970; children: Daniel, David, Lewis. AB, Rutgers U., 1966; PhD, NYU, 1971. Economist Internat. Monetary Fund, Washington, 1970-77, sr. economist, 1977-81, advisor, 1981-85, asst. dir., 1985-87, dep. dir., 1987—; mem. editorial bd. Internat. Monetary Fund, 1986—, IMF Staff Papers, 1986. Editor: Growth-Oriented Adjustment Programs, 1987; contbr. articles to profl. jours. Mem. Am. Econ. Assn. Avocations: fishing. Office: Internat Monetary Fund 19th & H St NW Washington DC 20431

GOLDSTEIN, RODNEY LOUIS, investment firm partner; b. Peoria, Ill., Jan. 16, 1952; s. Harry M. and Inette (Cohen) G.; m. Helen Keith Kiley, Jan. 27, 1979; 1 child, Henry Hall. AB cum laude, Princeton U., 1974; MBA, U. Pa., 1978. Assoc. Salomon Bros., Inc., N.Y.C., 1977; mgmt. cons. Booz, Allen & Hamilton, Inc., Chgo., 1978-81; gen. ptnr. Frontenac Co., Chgo., 1981—; bd. dirs. Am. Healthcorp. Inc., Nashville, Eastern Lobby Shops Ltd., Chgo., Consol. Stores Corp., Columbus, Ohio, Contemporary Books, Inc., Chgo., De Vry, Inc., Evanston, Ill. Trustee, Youth Guidance, Chgo., 1984—, Found. for Excellence in Teaching, Chgo., 1986—, Phillips Acad., Andover, Mass., 1986—, Michael Reese Hosp., Chgo., 1986-87; active Ill. Rep. Com. Clubs: Economic, Racquet, Saddle and Cycle (Chgo.); Lake Shore Country (Glencoe, Ill.). Office: Frontenac Co 208 S La Salle St Room 1900 Chicago IL 60604

GOLDSTEIN, SAMUEL R., oil company executive; b. N.Y.C., Apr. 2, 1918; s. Rubin and Rose (Gluck) G.; m. Gloria Elaine Mintz, June 16, 1945 (dec. Apr. 1975); children—Carol Jean Goldstein Jones, Richard Henry. B.A. in Sci., Bklyn. Coll., 1939. Salesman Liggett & Myers Tobacco Co., N.Y.C., 1939-42; instr. Civil Service, Belleville, Ill., 1942-43; ptnr. Standard Tool & Mfg. Co., St. Louis, 1946-48; salesman Apex Oil Co., St. Louis, 1948-61, chmn. bd., 1961—. Bd. dirs. St. Louis Assn. Retarded Citizens, 1981—, Arts and Edn. Council, St. Louis, 1982—, St. Louis Mcpl. Theatre, 1982—, Jewish Fedn. St. Louis, 1980—. Served with USAF, 1943-46. Office: Apex Oil Corp 8182 Maryland Ave Saint Louis MO 63105

GOLDSTEIN, STANLEY P., retail company executive; b. 1934; married. Grad., Wharton Sch., U. Pa., 1955. V.p. Mark Seven, Inc., 1955-61, Francis I. DuPont, 1961-63; exec. v.p. Consumer Value Stores, 1963-69; pres. CVS div. Melville Corp., Harrison, N.Y., 1969-71, corp. v.p., pres. CVS div., 1971-85, then corp. exec. v.p., 1985-87, pres., 1986—, chmn., chief exec.

officer, 1987—, also bd. dirs. Office: Melville Corp 3000 Westchester Ave Harrison NY 10528

GOLDWEITZ, SAUL, publishing company executive; b. N.Y.C., Aug. 9, 1920; s. Benjamin and Gussie (Dolin) G.; m. Harriet Carlton, 1943 (div. Apr. 1978); children—Mark, Jonathan, Elissa, Julie; m. Joan Sebel, May 23, 1980. B.S., CCNY, 1940; M.B.A., Harvard U., 1942. Editor modern materials handling Cahners Pub. Co., Boston, 1946-49; v.p., treas. Cahners Pub. Co., 1949-58, exec. v.p., 1958-65, pres., 1965—; pres., chief exec. officer Cahners Pub. Co., Newton, Mass., 1984—, chmn., 1985—; dir. Reed Holdings, Inc., Boston, Reed Pub., Ltd., London, Bus. Publs. Audit of Circulation, N.Y.C. Author (selection guide) The Palletizer; (manual) Materials Handling Manual; contbr. articles to profl. jours. Served to lt. USNR. Mem. Am. Bus. Press (past chmn. bd.). Republican. Jewish. Clubs: University (gov.), Temple Reyim (trustee). Home: 221 Beacon St Boston MA 02116 Office: Cahners Pub Co 275 Washington St Newton MA 02158

GOLDWYN, RALPH NORMAN, financial company executive; b. Chgo., Jan. 24, 1925; s. Herman and Rissie F. Goldwyn; B.S., UCLA, 1948; m. Joan J. Snyder, Dec. 25, 1954; children—Bob, Greg, Lisa. Partner, Arc Loan Co., Los Angeles, 1948-52; v.p. Arc Discount Co., Los Angeles, 1952-73; pres. Arc Investment Co., Los Angeles, 1952-73; partner First Factors, Los Angeles, 1960-78; pres. First Comml. Fin., Los Angeles, 1978—; dir. Roy J. Maier, Inc.; trustee UCLA Found. Served to lt. (j.g.) USN, 1943-46. Mem. World Affairs Council, UCLA Chancellor Assos., Anti-Defamation League. Jewish. Clubs: Town Hall of Calif. (life), Brentwood Country, Los Angeles. Office: First Comml Fin 4221 Wilshire Blvd Suite 470 Los Angeles CA 90210

GOLIN, ALVIN, public relations company executive; b. Chgo., June 19, 1929; s. Charles and Jeanette G.; m. June Kerns, Aug. 25, 1961; children: Barry, Karen, Ellen. B.J., Roosevelt U., 1950. Publicity rep. MGM Pictures, N.Y.C., 1951-54; chmn. Golin Harris Communications Inc., Chgo., 1975—; lectr. to numerous univs. Advisor Chgo. council Boy Scouts Am.; advisor Nat. Multiple Sclerosis Soc., U. Tenn. Mem. Pub. Relations Soc. Am., Publicity Club of Chgo. Office: Golin Harris Communications Inc 500 N Michigan Ave Chicago IL 60611 *

GOLUB, ALAN, clothing company executive; b. 1939. BS, Babson Inst., 1957. With Personal Sportswear Inc., Boston, 1961-65; with Leslie Fay Cos., N.Y.C., 1965—, pres., 1987—, also bd. dirs. Office: Leslie Fay Cos 1400 Broadway New York NY 10018 *

GOLUB, HARVEY, financial services company executive; b. N.Y.C., Apr. 16, 1939; s. Irving and Pearl (Fader) G.; m. Roberta Elizabeth Glunts, Aug. 16, 1980; 1 child, Joshua; children from previous marriage: Matthew, Amy, Jeremy. BS, NYU, 1961. Jr. ptnr. McKinsey & Co. Inc., N.Y.C., 1967-74, sr. ptnr., 1977-83; pres. Shulman Air Freight, N.Y.C., 1974-77; sr. officer Am. Express Co., N.Y.C., 1983-84; pres., chief exec. officer IDS Fin. Corp., Mpls., 1984—. Office: IDS Fin Corp 2900 IDS Tower 10 Minneapolis MN 55440

GOLUB, HOWARD VICTOR, lawyer; b. N.Y.C., Jan. 20, 1945; s. Irving W. and Mary Golub. AB cum laude, Hunter Coll., 1965; JD, Harvard U., 1968. Bar: N.Y. 1968, Mass. 1970, Calif. 1973, U.S. Dit. Ct. (no. dist.) 1972, U.S. Ct. Appeals, D. C. 1973, U.S. Ct. Appeals. (9th cir.) 1973, U.S. Supreme Ct. 1973. Asst. dist. atty. N.Y. Dist. Atty.'s Office, N.Y.C., 1968-69; atty. Pacific Gas and Electric Co., San Francisco, 1973-86, v.p., gen. counsel, 1987—. Active Calif. Hist. Soc., San Francisco, 1975—, San Francisco Soc. for Prevention of Cruelty to Animals, 1979—. Capt. JAGC, USNR, 1969-73. Mem. ABA, Edison Electric Inst. (legal and environ. adv. coms.), Am. Gas Assn. (legal sect. mng. com.), Harvard Club of San Francisco, San Francisco Bar Assn. (exec. com. corp. law sect.). Clubs: Harvard, City (San Francisco). Office: Pacific Gas & Electric Co 77 Beale St San Francisco CA 94106

GOLUB, LEWIS, supermarket company executive; b. 1931. BS, Mich. State U., 1953. With Golub Corp., 1953—, v.p., 1963-71, exec. v.p., 1971-72, pres., treas., 1972-82, chmn. bd., 1982—; also chief exec. officer, dir. Golub Corp., Schenectady. Served with U.S. Army. Office: Golub Corp 501 Duanesburg Rd Schenectady NY 12306

GOMENA, JOHN EDWARD, food products company executive; b. 1927; married. BS, U. R.I., 1951; postgrad., Carnegie-Mellon U., 1972. Indsl. engr. U.S. Rubber Co., 1951-52, Bostitch Inc., 1952-54; area mfg. and engring. mgr. Birds Eye div. Gen. Foods Corp., 1964-66; with Amfac Inc., 1966—; v.p. ops. Lamb-Weston, 1966-73, pres., 1973-80; vice chmn. Amfac Foods Group, 1980-81, chmn., 1981; now exec. v.p. Amfac Inc. Served with USNR, 1945-46. Mem. Am. Frozen Food Assn. (past chmn.), Frozen Foods Assn. (past v.p.). Office: Amfac Inc 81 Blue Ravine Rd Folsom CA 95630 also: Amfac Inc 44 Montgomery St San Francisco CA 94104 *

GOMES, NORMAN VINCENT, industrial engineer, business broker; b. New Bedford, Mass., Nov. 7, 1914; s. John Vincent and Georgianna (Sylvia) G.; grad. U.S. Army Command and Gen. Staff Coll., 1944; B.S. in Indsl. Engring. and Mgmt., Okla. State U., 1950; M.B.A. in Mgmt., Xavier U., 1955; m. Carolyn Moore, June 6, 1942 (dec. Apr. 1983). Asst. chief engr. Leschen div. H.K. Porter Co., St. Louis, 1950-52; staff mfg. cons. Gen. Electric Co., Cin., 1952-57; lectr. indsl. mgmt. U. Cin., 1955-56; vis. lectr. indsl. mgmt. Xavier U. Sch. Bus. Adminstrn., 1956-57; staff indsl. engr. Gen. Dynamics, Ft. Worth, 1957-60; chief ops. analysis Ryan Electronics, San Diego, 1960-64; sr. engr., jet propulsion lab. Calif. Inst. Tech., Pasadena, 1964-67, mem. tech. staff, 1967, mgr. mgmt. systems, 1967-71; industry rep. and cons. U.S. Commn. on Govt. Procurement, Washington, 1970-72; adminstrv. officer GSA, Washington, 1973-78, program dir., 1979; now engaged in bus. brokerage; vis. lectr. mgmt. San Antonio Coll., 1982-85. Active Beautify San Antonio Assn. Served as 2d lt. to maj. C.E., AUS, 1941-46; engring. adviser to War Manpower Bd., 1945. Decorated Army Commendation medal, Armed Svcs. Res. medal; recipient Apollo Achievement award, 1969; Outstanding Performance award GSA, 1974- 75, 76, 77, 79. Tex. Mem. Am. Inst. Indsl. Engrs. (nat. chmn. prodn. control research com., 1951-57; bd. dirs. Cin., Fort Worth, San Diego, Los Angeles, San Antonio chpts. 1954-84, pres. Cin. chpt. 1956-57, pres. Los Angeles 1970-71, nat. dir. community services 1969-73), Nat. Calif. socs. profl. engrs., Ret. Officers Assn. U.S. (chpt. pres. 1968-69, recipient Nat. Pres. certificate Merit 1969), Nat. Security Indsl. Assn. (mgmt. systems subcom. 1967-69), Vis. Nurse Assn. of San Antonio (mem. adv. coun. 1988—), Freedoms Found. at Valley Forge (v.p. edn. and youth leadership programs San Antonio chpt. 1987-89), Old Datmouth Hist. Soc., Equestrian Order of the Holy Sepulchre of Jerusalem (papal knight). Republican. Roman Catholic. Club: K.C. (4th deg.). Home: 2719 Knoll Tree San Antonio TX 78247 Office: 7330 San Pedro Ave Suite 376 San Antonio TX 78216

GOMEZ, FRANCISCO, auditor; b. N.Y.C., Aug. 1, 1948; s. Armando Gregorio and Maria Raquel (Perez) G. BS in Acctg., L.I. U., 1974, MBA in Fin., 1986. Cert. fraud examiner. Internal auditor B.F. Goodrich, Akron, Ohio, 1974-80; sr. internal auditor Mgmt. Assistance, Inc., N.Y.C., 1980-81; mgr. internal audit Comml. Alliance Corp., N.Y.C., 1981-82; asst. dir. internal audit Nat. Benefit Fund, N.Y.C., 1982—; cons. various small bus., N.Y., 1977-80. Vol. instr. English Internat. Ctr. N.Y., Inc., N.Y.C., 1983—; campaign vol. Sal Albanese, Bklyn. councilman, Bayridge, N.Y., 1982. With U.S. Army, 1968-70, Korea. Recipient Outstanding Svc. award Internat. Ctr. N.Y., N.Y.C., 1986. Mem. Inst. Internal Auditors, Internat. Found. Employee Benefit Plans, Appalachian Mountain Club, Met. Opera Guild, Inst. Fin. Crime Prevention. REpublican. Roman Catholic. Home: 9101 Shore Rd Apt 626 Brooklyn NY 11209

GOMEZ, MICHAEL JOSEPH, real estate executive; b. New Orleans, Dec. 30, 1964; s. Pedro Efrain Gomez and Olga Marina (Pineda) Weber;. Real estate cert., Austin (Tex.) Comm. Coll., 1985. Owner, pres. The Oil and Energy Co., Houston, 1980-82; asst. supt. Dinerstein Builders, Houston, 1982-86; asst. mgr. leasing Dinerstein Mgmt. Co., Houston, 1985-86; leasing, mktg. dir. LBI Mgmt. Co., Inc., Houston, 1986-87; asst. mgr. New Beginnings, Unltd., Houston, 1987—; leasing cons. United Tex. Real Estate Mgmt. Co., Inc., Houston, 1988—, W.K. Reid & Co., Inc., 1989—; notary pub., Tex., 1987. Recruiter Houston Apheresis Blood Ctr., Houston, 1986-87; mem. 700 Club ministry, Va. Beach, Va. 1980—; fin. ptnr. Success in Life Ministries, 1987-88; fin. ptnr. U. Tex. M.D. Anderson Cancer Ctr., 1988—. Mem. Am. Soc. Notaries. Republican. Baptist. Home and Office: 14230 Wunderlich Rd #203 Houston TX 77069-3458

GOMORY, RALPH EDWARD, mathematician, business machines manufacturing company and foundation executive; b. Brooklyn Heights, N.Y., May 7, 1929; s. Andrew L. and Marian (Schellenberg) G.; m. Laura Dumper, 1954 (div. 1968); children: Andrew C., Susan S., Stephen H. BA, Williams Coll., 1950, ScD (hon.), 1973; postgrad., Kings Coll., Cambridge U., Eng., 1950-51; PhD, Princeton U., 1954; LHD (hon.), Pace U., 1986; DSc (hon.), Poly. U., 1987, Syracuse U., 1989, Worcester Poly. U., 1989, Carnegie-Mellon U., 1989. Rsch. assoc. Princeton U., 1951-54, asst. prof. math., Higgins lectr., 1957-59; with IBM, Yorktown Heights, N.Y., 1959-86; dir. math. scis., rsch. div. IBM, Armonk, 1968-70, dir. rsch., 1970-86, v.p., 1973-84, sr. v.p., 1985-89, sr. v.p. for sci. and tech., 1986-89, also mem. corp. mgmt. bd., 1983-89, dir. Asia Pacific Group, 1982-88; pres. Alfred P. Sloan Found., N.Y.C., 1989—; Andrew D. White prof.-at-large Cornell U., 1970-76; bd. dir. Bank of N.Y., Nova Pharm. Corp., Washington Post Co.; mem. adv. coun. dept. math. Princeton, 1982-85, chmn., 1984-85; mem. adv. coun. Sch. Engring. Stanford U., 1978-85; chmn. vis. com. div. applied scis. Harvard U., 1987—; mem. White House sci. coun., Coun. on Fgn. Rels.; chmn. adv. com. to Pres. on High Temperature Superconductivity, 1987-88; mem. coun. on grad. sch. Yale U., 1988—; mem. vis. com. elec. engring. and comuter sci. MIT, 1988—; researcher in integer and linear programming, non-linear differential equations. Trustee Hampshire Coll., 1977-86, Princeton U., 1985-89, Alfred P. Sloan Found., 1988-89; mem. governing bd. Nat. Rsch. Coun., 1980-83. With USN, 1954-57. Recipient Lanchester prize Ops. Rsch. Soc. Am., 1964, Harry Goode Meml. award Am. Fedn. Info. Processing Socs., 1984, John Von Neumann Theory prize Ops. Rsch. Soc. Am. and Inst. Mgmt. Scis., 1984, IRI medal Indsl. Rsch. Inst., 1985, Engring. Leadership Recognition award IEEE, 1988, Nat. Medal of Sci., 1988; IBM fellow, 1964. Fellow Econometric Soc., Am. Acad. Arts and Scis.; mem. Nat. Acad. Scis. (coun. 1977-78, 80-83), Nat. Acad. Engring. (coun. 1986—), Am. Philos. Soc. (coun. 1986—). Home: 260 Douglas Rd Chappaqua NY 10514 Office: Alfred P Sloan Found 630 Fifth Ave New York NY 10111

GONG, MERY LEE, data processor; b. Cleve., June 14, 1931; d. Wing and Shee (Woo) Gong; B.S., Ohio State U., 1954. With Ohio State U. Instrn. and Research Computer Center, Columbus, 1954—, computer operator, 1954-56, programmer, cons., 1956-61, ops. supr., 1961-65, adminstrv. asst., 1965-72, asst. dir., 1972-80, assoc. dir., 1980—. Computer cons. Cole-Layer-Trumble Co.; instr. Ohio State U. continuing edn. Children's Hosp., Columbus, 1969. Mem. Ohio Commn. on Status of Women. Mem. Am. Mgmt. Assn., Assn. Computing Machinery, Data Processing Mgmt. Assn., Air Force Assn., Assn. Systems Mgmt., Ohio State U. Alumni Assn., Northwest Area Council for Human Relations, LWV, Upper Arlington Civic Assn., Columbus Area Civil Rights Council, Nat. Assn. Female Execs., Assn. Info. Systems Profls. Club: Quota (Columbus). Home: 1776 Ridgecliff Rd Columbus OH 43221 Office: 1971 Neil Ave Columbus OH 43210

GONGAWARE, DONALD FRANCIS, insurance company executive; b. L.A., Dec. 20, 1935; s. Walter Gongaware and Agnes Belle (Lane) Hanke; m. Patricia Ruth Kinsinger, Sept. 27, 1957; children: Douglas, Richard, Randall. AA, Am. River Coll., 1963; BA, Calif. State U., Sacramento, 1966. CLU. Various exec. positions in subs. Am. Gen. Corp., Houston, 1964-85; exec. v.p., chief ops. officer Conseco, Inc., Carmel, Ind., 1985—. With USAF, 1954-61. Mem. Soc. CLU. Office: Conseco Inc 11825 N Pennsylvania St Carmel IN 46032

GONSALVES, WILLIAM DANIEL, hydrographic company executive; b. New Bedford, Mass., Feb. 11, 1950; s. Albert M. and Arlene F. (Perry) G.; m. Donna Marie Sherman, June 28, 1974; children: Jennifer Lee, Jill Catherine, Jesse Albert. AS in Elec. and Mech. Engring. Tech., Bristol Community Coll., 1980. Aviation technician Killeen (Tex.) Air Service, 1973-74; electronics engr. Braincon Corp., Marion, Mass., 1974-75; project engr. Environ. Devices, Marion, 1975-83; mgr. engring. dept. Endeco, Inc., Marion, 1983-88, v.p. mfg., 1988—. Mem. Precinct One, North Dartmouth, Mass. Served with U.S. Army, 1970-73, Vietnam. Roman Catholic. Home: 1080 Hixville Rd North Dartmouth MA 02747 Office: Endeco Inc 13 Atlantis Dr Marion MA 02738

GONZALEZ, JOE MANUEL, lawyer; b. N.Y.C., Aug. 18, 1950; s. Reinaldo Fabregas and Mary Louise (Cermeno) G.; m. Ruia Jane Whiteside, Dec. 30, 1977; children—Matthew Ray, Jane Marie, Jeffrey Joseph. B.A., U. South Fla., 1972; J.D., Gonzaga U., 1980; LL.M. in Taxation, Georgetown U., 1981. Bar: Fla. 1981, U.S. Tax Ct. 1983, U.S. Dist. Ct. (mid. dist.) Fla. 1984, U.S. Ct. Appeals (11th cir.) 1984, U.S. Supreme Ct. 1985. Atty., Gonzaga U. Legal Services, Spokane, Wash., 1980; mng. ptnr. Cotterill, Gonzalez, Hayes & Grantham, Fla., 1981-88; Cotterill, Gonzales & Grantham, 1982-89; atty. Hispanic Def. League, Tampa, Fla., 1982-88. Assoc. editor Gonzaga Law Rev. Spl. Report: Pub. Sector Labor Law, 1980. Mem. Sheriff's Hispanic Adv. Council, Hillsborough County, Fla., 1982-89 , City of Tampa Hispanic Adv. Council, 1983-89; mem. Hisslborough County Planning commn., citizens adv. com., 1988—; pres. Tampa Hispanic Heritage, Inc., 1985-87; founder Carnavale En Tampa, Inc., 1986-87; master of ceremonies Gasparilla Sidewalk Art Festival, 1988; chief Hispanic adv. commn. for Tampa Police Dept., 1988. Mem. ABA, Hillsborough County Bar Assn., Assn. Trial Lawyers Am., Nat. Inst. for Trial Advocacy, Phi Delta Phi. Democrat. Presbyterian. Lodge: Rotary. Home: 1708 Richardson Pl Tampa FL 33606 Office: Cotterill Gonzalez & Grantham Northfork Profl Ctr 1519 N Dale Mabry Hwy Suite 100 Lutz FL 33549

GOO, ABRAHAM MEU SEN, aircraft company executive; b. Honolulu, May 21, 1925; s. Tai Chong and Lily En Wui (Dai) G.; m. Shin Quon Wong, June 12, 1950; children: Marilynn, Steven, Beverly Cardinal. BEE U. Ill., 1951; postgrad. MIT, 1975. With The Boeing Co., Seattle, 1951-73; B-1 avionics program mgr. Boeing Aerospace Co., Seattle, 1974-75, v.p., gen. mgr. aircraft armament div., 1975-77; v.p. mil. systems Boeing Mil. Airplane Co., Wichita, Kans., 1977-79, exec. v.p., 1979-84, pres., 1984-87; pres. Boeing Advanced Systems, Seattle, 1987—. With USAAF, 1946-47. Recipient Chinese-Am. Engrs. and Scientists of So. Calif. Achievement award Sci. and Engring., 1989. Mem. Nat. Aero. Assn., Army Aviation Assn. Am., Army Sci. Bd., Air Force Assn., Am. Def. Preparedness Assn., Armed Forces Communication and Electronics Assn., Army Sci. Bd. Home: 18909 SE 282d Ct Kent WA 98042 Office: Boeing Advanced Systems PO Box 3707 Seattle WA 98124-2207

GOOCH, J. GLENN, utility company executive; b. Port Talbot, Wales, July 4, 1922; came to U.S., 1929; s. John and Elizabeth Ann (Jones) G.; m. Bette J. Miller, Dec. 15, 1944; 1 son, Bradley D. B.S. in Commerce and Fin., Bucknell U., Wilkes-Barre, Pa., 1948; M.B.A., Wilkes Coll., 1973. Auditor Pa. Gas and Water Co., Wilkes-Barre, 1950-58, asst. controller, 1958-67, controller, 1967-71, v.p. fin., treas., 1971-78, pres., chief exec. officer, 1978-87, vice chmn. 1987—, also dir.; v.p., treas. Pa. Enterprises, Inc., Wilkes-Barre, 1974-78, pres., chief exec. officer, 1978-87, vice chmn. 1987—, also dir.; dir. First Ea. Bank, N.A. Wilkes-Barre. Trustee, treas. Marywood Coll., Scranton, Pa.; bd. dirs. United Way, Wilkes-Barre, 1978-84, Econ. Devel. Council, 1978—, Pa. Economy League, Wilkes-Barre, 1980—, Crime Clinic, Wilkes-Barre, 1980-88, com. for econ. growth, 1983—, Northeastern Pa. Bus. Council on Health Care, 1983-88; pres. St. David's Soc. Wyo. Valley, 1989—. Served with USAAF, 1942-45. Named Outstanding Jaycee of Yr., Wilkes-Barre Jr. C. of C., 1959. Mem. Am. Gas Assn., Pa. Gas Assn. (chmn. 1985-86, bd. dirs. 1978-88), Nat. Assn. Water Co. (bd. dirs. 1978-87), Pa. Soc. Am. Mgmt. Assn., Wilkes-Barre C. of C. (bd. dirs. 1978-84), Scranton C. of C. (bd. dirs. 1978-84). Republican. Clubs: Westmoreland (Wilkes-Barre); Irem Temple (Dallas, Pa.); Pa. Soc. Lodge: Kiwanis. Office: Pa Gas & Water Co 213 Joseph Dr Kingston PA 18704

GOOD, BARRY C., financial analyst; b. N.Y.C., Sept. 27, 1932; s. F. Campbell Good and Vinelia (Nolte) Hess; m. Martha L. Byorum, Mar. 10, 1978; children: Hillary H. Stone, Brian C., Ashley C. Student, Yale U., 1950-52. Fin. analyst Dean Witter and Co., N.Y.C., 1953-65; v.p., fin. analyst Laird Inc., N.Y.C., 1965-73; mng. dir., fin. analyst Morgan Stanley and Co., N.Y.C., 1973—. Mem. Oil Analysts Group N.Y. (pres. 1979-80), Nat. Assn. Petroleum Investment Analysts (bd. dirs. 1980-82), Union Club (gov. 1984—), Maidstone Club (East Hampton, N.Y.).

GOOD, ROY SHELDON, financial executive; b. Cleve., Dec. 13, 1924; s. Julius and Sally (Sharpe) G.; m. Wendy Rae Polasky, Sept. 12, 1982; children by previous marriage: Jeri Good Dansky, Michael. BBA, Western Res. U., 1948, MBA, 1951. CPA, Mich, Ohio. With tax dept. Touche, Ross & Co., Detroit, 1952-57, supr., 1957-59, mgr., 1959-61; adminstrv. asst. to controller Am. Motors Corp., Detroit, 1961-63, asst. controller, 1963-68; mgr. employee benefits fin. adminstrn. Chrysler Corp., Detroit, 1968-77, mgr. investment rev., 1977-78; mgr. investment rev. and spl. financing, 1978-80; v.p. Alexander & Alexander Consulting Group, Detroit, 1981—; lectr., author employee benefits and pension fund investment mgmt., 1970—; bd. dirs. Health Alliance Plan, 1982-86. Served with U.S. Army, 1943-46, ETO. Mem. Am. Inst. CPAs, Mich. Assn. CPAs, Midwest Pension Conf., Burmingham Athletic Club, Beta Alpha Psi. Democrat. Jewish. Home: 31462 Hunters Circle Farmington Hills MI 48018 Office: 700 Fisher Bldg Detroit MI 48202-3053

GOODALE, ROBERT SELDON, food retailing executive; b. Marshalltown, Iowa, Dec. 12, 1933; s. Ralph Selson and Clara Marie (Zuercher) G.; m. Donna Jane Nelson, Aug. 20, 1956 (div. July 1972); children: Rob Donald, Elizabeth Anne, Susan Marie; m. Janet Marie Nunn, Sept. 30, 1973; children: Rebecca Marie, Jennifer Mae, Amy Joyce. BS, Iowa State U., 1955; MBA, U. Kans., 1980. Mktg. mgr. Fairmont Foods Co., Omaha, 1968-70, nat. accounts mgr., 1970-71, sales mgr., 1971-72, mktg. mgr. snack div., 1972-76, sales mgr. dairy group, 1976-77; dir. of dairy Fleming Foods, Topeka, 1977-80; sr. v.p. Harris-Teeter Super Markets, Charlotte, N.C., 1980-82, exec. v.p., 1982-85, pres., chief exec. officer, 1985—, also bd. dirs.; bd. dirs. Harris-Teeter Properties, Charlotte. Pres. Florence Crittenton Services, Charlotte, 1985-87; chmn. Charlotte/Mecklenburg Pub. Broadcasting Authority, Charlotte, 1986-87; pres.-elect Charlotte Jr. Achivement, 1987; bd. mgrs. Charlotte YMCA, treas., 1985-87; chmn. Amethyst Found., Charlotte, 1987. Recipient Cardinal Key award Iowa State U., Ames, 1955, Circle of Excellence award Leadership Charlotte, 1984, Old Master award Purdue U., West Lafayette, Ind., 1985. Mem. Charlotte C. of C. (exec. com. 1987). Republican. Episcopalian. Office: Harris/Teeter Supermarkets Inc 7500 E Independence Blvd PO Box 33129 Charlotte NC 28212 *

GOODALL, JACKSON WALLACE, JR., restaurant company executive; b. San Diego, Oct. 29, 1938; s. Jackson Wallace and Evelyn Violet (Koski) G.; m. Mary Esther Buckley, June 22, 1958; children: Kathleen, Jeffery, Suzanne, Minette. BS, San Diego State U., 1960. With Foodmaker, Inc., San Diego, 1965-70, pres., 1970—, chief exec. officer, 1979—, chmn. bd., 1985—; founder, bd. dir. Grossmont Bank, La Mesa, Calif.; bd. dirs. Budget Rent A Car Corp. Bd. dirs. Faith Chapel, Greater San Diego Sports Assn., Mercy Hosp. Found.; trustee U. San Diego. Recipient Disting. Alumni of Yr. award San Diego State U., 1974, Golden Chain award, 1982, Silver Plate award Internat. Foodsvc. Mfg. Assn., 1985, Golden Chain Operator of Yr. award Multi Unit Food Svc. Operators, 1988. Mem. Am. Restaurant Assn., San Diego State U. Alumni Assn. (bd. dirs.). Republican. Club: Fairbanks Ranch Country (founder). Office: Foodmaker Inc 9330 Balboa San Diego CA 92123

GOODE, BRYAN COLLIER, JR., medical device company executive; b. Montgomery, Ala., Dec. 20, 1935; s. Bryan Collier Sr. and Katherine (McSwean) G.; m. Nancy Sandra Permenter, July 14, 1961; children: Nancy Melissa, Bryan Collier III, Sandra Allison. BS in Engring. Physics, Auburn U., 1958. Ops. mgr. Tech. Measurement Corp., Atlanta, 1959-66; mgr. Gen. Electric Co., St. Petersburg, Fla. and Milw., 1966-77; dir. research and devel. Concept, Inc., Clearwater, Fla., 1977-78; dir. ops. Applied Med. Research, Tampa, Fla., 1978-80, Vita-State Med. Services, St. Petersburg and Bellevue, Wash., 1980-83; pres. Eureka X-Ray Tube, Inc., Chgo., 1983—. Sch. bd mem. Pinellas County Bd. Pub. Instrn., Clearwater, 1972-74. Served to capt. USAR, 1958-66. Mem. Nat. Elec. Mfrs. Assn. (bd. dirs. diagnostic imaging and therapy systems div.). Republican. Presbyterian. Office: Eureka X Ray Tube Co 3250 N Kilpatrick Ave Chicago IL 60641

GOODE, CHARLES BARRINGTON, company director; b. Melbourne, Australia, Aug. 26, 1938; s. Charles Thomas and Jean Florence G.; m. Cornelia Baillieu; 1 stepchild, Robert; m. Cornelia Ladd, June 1, 1987. B in Commerce with honors, Melbourne U.; MBA, Columbia U. Assoc. Potter Ptnrs., Ltd., Melbourne, 1961-69; ptnr. Potter Ptnrs., Ltd., 1969-80, sr. ptnr., 1980-86; chmn. Potter Ptnrs. Group Ltd., Melbourne, 1986—; bd. dirs. Pacific Dunlop Ltd., Oliver J. Nilsen (Australia) Ltd., Hallmark Cards Australia Ltd., Woodside Petroleum Group, Legal and Gen. Assurance Holdings Ltd., Queensland Treasury Corp. Investment Bd. Chmn. Inst. Pub. Affairs, 1984—. Fellow Australian Soc. Accts., Securities Inst. Australia. Clubs: Australian (Melbourne), Royal Melbourne Golf. Home: 294 Walsh St, 3141 South Yarra, Victoria Australia Office: Potter Ptnrs Group Ltd, 325 Collins St, Melbourne 3000, Australia also: Potter Ptnrs Group Ltd Equitable Ctr 787 7th Ave New York NY 10022

GOODE, MICHAEL LANDERS, small business owner; b. Richmond, Va., June 4, 1947; s. Ralph Samuel and Margaret Demarilac (Landers) G.; m. Linda Irwin, June 20, 1970 (div. July 1983); m. Linda Baker, Nov. 30, 1985; children: Elizabeth, Cynthia. BSEE, USAF Acad., 1969; MS in Human Resources, U. Utah, 1977. Commd. 2d lt. USAF, 1969, advanced through grades to maj., resigned, 1980; sales rep. Landers PC Products, Pompano Beach, Fla., 1980-81; computer programmer Allison Crain, Sarasota, Fla., 1981-82; F-16 mktg. rep. Gen. Dynamics, Ft. Worth, 1982-84; regional sales mgr. Simuflite Tng. Internat., Dallas, 1984-87; pres., founder BYTE Mgmt., Inc., Ft. Worth, 1987—. Maj. USAFR, 1980—. Republican. Roman Catholic. Home: 7113 Stonehaven Ct Fort Worth TX 76179 Office: BYTE Mgmt Inc 4907 Blue Mound Rd Fort Worth TX 76106

GOODE, RICHARD HARRIS, investment banker; b. Chgo., Sept. 13, 1939; s. William Richard and Lois May (Harris) G.; S.B. in Chem. Engring. and Indsl. Mgmt., MIT, 1961, S.M. in Chem. Engring. and Indsl. Mgmt. (Pullman-Kellogg Inc. scholar), 1965; m. Eleanor Louise, June 26, 1965; 1 son, James Scott. Mgt. internat. sales Pullman-Kellogg Inc., N.Y.C., 1961-69; v.p., mgr. sales Davy Internat. Inc., N.Y.C., 1969-73; internat. sales mgr. Mitchell, Hutchins Inc., N.Y.C., 1973-75; v.p., mgr. internat. dept. Spencer Trask Inc., N.Y.C., 1975-77; sr. v.p.-mgr. internat. Sales dept. Lehman Bros. Kuhn Loeb Inc., N.Y.C., 1977-84; exec. v.p. internat div., Alex. Brown & Sons Inc., 1984-87; pres. Pacific Div. First Manhattan Co., 1987— . Mem. task force on energy crisis and alt. fuels FPC, 1970-73; admissions officer MIT Alumni Ednl. Council; mem. Vol. Urban Cons. Group, Harvard U.-MIT, N.Y.C. Mem. MIT Alumni Center. Home: 81 White Oak Ridge Rd Lincroft NJ 07738 Office: 437 Madison Ave New York NY 10022

GOODELL, JOSEPH EDWARD, manufacturing executive; b. El Paso, Tex., Aug. 18, 1937; s. Joseph Edward and Grace Louise (Beck) G.; m. Margaret Rives, Aug. 12, 1961 (div. June 1978); children: Marian, Margaret, Martha, Maryellen. BSME, MIT, 1959; MBA, Harvard U., 1961. Project engr. Bechtel Corp., San Francisco, 1961-65; mfg. engr. Chase Brass and Copper Co., Cleve., 1965-67; adminstrv. mgr. Montpelier, Ohio, 1967-69, Waterbury, Conn., 1969-71; v.p., gen. mgr. Montpelier, 1971-76; group v.p. Chase Brass and Copper Co., Cleve., 1976-79, Pangborn div. Carborundum, Hagerstown, Md., 1979-81; v.p. planning Standard Oil Ind. Products, Cleve., 1981-82, sr. v.p., 1982-85; pres., chief exec. officer Am. Brass Co., Buffalo, N.Y., 1985—; bd. dirs. Nitto Metals, Tokyo, 1974-79; TWI Porperties, El Paso, Tex., 1975—, Tech. Devel. Corp, Buffalo, Tech. Bldg. Corp., Boston. various positions Boy Scouts Am., Waterbury, Conn. Republican. Club: Country of Buffalo. Home: 152 Rivermist Dr Buffalo NY 14202 Office: Am Brass Co 70 Sayre St Buffalo NY 14207

GOODELL, ROBERT CHARLES, insurance company executive; b. Calicoon, N.Y., Dec. 28, 1954; s. Robert Sewall and Sallie Lou (Smith) G.; m. Theresa Majich, Aug. 15, 1975 (div. Sept. 1984); m. Suzanne Melissa Barker, Sept. 15, 1985; 1 child, Carolyn L. BA, U. So. Calif., 1975, MBA, 1980. Systems analyst Litton Guidance and Control, Woodland Hills, Calif., 1975-77; controller Fin. Indemnity Co., Los Angeles, 1977-79; treas. Great Cen. Ins. Co., Peoria, Ill., 1979-80; sr. mgr. Peat Marwick Main and Co., Los Angeles, 1980-83; v.p. Cal Fed., Inc., 1983-84; sr. v.p., chief fin. officer

Amwest Ins. Group, Inc., Woodland Hills, 1984—. Home: 23864 Berdon St Woodland Hills CA 91367 Office: Amwest Ins Group Inc 6320 Canoga Ave Suite 300 Woodland Hills CA 91367

GOODEN, BARBARA ANN, credit union executive; b. Waycross, Ga., July 14, 1946; d. James William and Juanita Christine (Davis) G. A.A. in Psychology, A.A. in Bus. Adminstrn., A.A. in Edn., Waycross Jr. Coll.; grad. Sch. Fin. Counseling, Fla. State U., 1986; student Cert. Credit Union Execs. Cert. consumer credit executive; lic. real estate salesman, Ga. With Eli Witt Co., Tampa, Fla., 1968-80, credit union rep., 1974-80; credit card coordinator 1st R.R. Community Fed. Credit Union F/K/A Waycross Seaboard System Fed. Credit Union, 1980-84, collection coordinator, 1984—; owner Craftmasters, 1987—. Contbr. articles on consumer credit to Waycross Jour. Herald, 1985. Women's rep. Southeast Area Employment and Tng. Council, Waycross, 1972-80. Mem. Waycross Credit Women (pres. 1984-85), Soc. Cert. Consumer Credit Execs., Ga. Soc. Credit Union Loan and Collection Coordinators (charter), League Credit Unions. Baptist. Club: Okefenokee Bus. and Profl. Women's (v.p. 1972-74). Avocations: reading, cake decorating, floral art, crafts, cooking. Home and Office: 513 Riverside Dr Waycross GA 31501 Office: 1st RR Community Fed Credit Union F/K/A Waycross Seaboard System PO Box 1256 Waycross GA 31502

GOODENOUGH, RICHARD WHITE, insurance agency executive; b. Waterbury, Conn., Feb. 16, 1931; s. Robert Delancey and Florence (Abajian) G.; children: Keith, Gwenneth, Darci. BA, Grove City Coll., 1954; MBA, Nat. U., San Diego, 1976. Pres. Goodenough Ins., Coronado, Calif., 1960—. Served as cpl. U.S. Army, 1954-56. Mem. Ind. Ins. Agts. and Brokers Assn. Lodge: Rotary. Home: 761 B Ave Coronado CA 92118 Office: Goodenough Ins Inc 817 Orange Ave PO Box 9001 Coronado CA 92118

GOODENOW, JOHN ELLIOTT, banker; b. Omaha, Mar. 19, 1935; s. Royal Lewis and Jeanette (Puthoff) G.; m. Karen Kolbe, June 28, 1961; children: Sara Jan Goodenow Blum, Stephen John. BA in Bus., Buena Vista Coll., 1958; Cert. in Bank Mgmt., U. Colo., 1972. Bank examiner FDIC, 1958-63; pres., chmn. bd. dirs. Wall Lake (Iowa) Savs. Bank, 1963; with Goodenow Bancorp., Spirit Lake, Iowa, 1988; bd. dirs. Pester Corp., Des Moines, Fairmont (Minn.) Nat. Bank, Corn Belt Telephone Co., Wall Lake, Everly (Iowa) State Bank, 1st Nat. Bank, Colfax, Iowa, Colfax Bancorp.; chmn. bd. dirs. First Nat. Bank, Jackson, Minn.; pres., bd. dirs. Goodenow Bancorp, Everly Bancorp; pres., chmn. bd. dirs. Fairmont BanCorp. Trustee Buena Vista Coll., Storm Lake, Iowa, 1978-80, Iowa Natural Heritage Found., Des Moines, 1987—. Served with U.S. Army, 1958-60. Mem. Young Pres. Orgn., Des Moines Club, Okoboji (Iowa) Yacht Club, Wahpeton Tennis Club. Home: Fairoaks Beach RR Box 5396 Spirit Lake IA 51360 Office: Goodenow Bancorp Spirit Lake IA 51360

GOODES, MELVIN RUSSELL, manufacturing company executive; b. Hamilton, Ont., Can., Apr. 11, 1935; s. Cedric Percy and Mary Melba (Lewis) G.; m. Arlene Marie Bourne, Feb. 23, 1963; children: Melanie, Michelle, David. B in Commerce, Queen's U., Kingston, Ont., Can., 1957; MBA, U. Chgo., 1960. Research assoc. Can. Econ. Research Assocs., Toronto, Ont., 1957-58; market planning coordinator Ford Motor Co. Can., Oakville, Ont., 1960-64; asst. to v.p. O'Keefe Breweries, Toronto, 1964-65; mgr. new product devel. Adams Brands div. Warner-Lambert Can., Scarborough, Ont., 1965-68; area mgr. Warner-Lambert Internat., Toronto, 1968-69; regional dir. confectionary ops. Warner-Lambert Europe, Brussels, 1969-70; pres. Warner-Lambert Mex., 1970-76; pres. Pan-Am. zone Warner-Lambert Internat., Morris Plains, N.J., 1976-77, pres. Pan-Am. and Asian zone, 1977-79; pres. consumer products div. Warner-Lambert Co., Morris Plains, N.J., 1979-81, sr. v.p., pres. consumer products group, 1981-83, exec. v.p., pres. U.S. ops., 1984-85, pres., chief operating officer, 1985—, also bd. dirs.; bd. dirs. Chem. Banking Corp., Chem. Bank, Unisys; mem. exec. adv. council Nat. Ctr. Ind. Retail Pharmacy, 1984-85. Bd. dirs. Coun. on Family Health, N.Y.C., 1981-86, Advt. Edn. Found., N.Y.C., 1989—; mem. fin. com. Joint Coun. on Econ. Edn., 1984—, trustee, mem. exec. com., 1986—; mem. adv. coun. Sch. of Bus., Queen's U., Kingston, Ont., Can., 1980-84; trustee Drew U., Madison, N.J., 1985-88, Queen's U. 1988—. Fellow Ford Found., 1958, Sears, Roebuck Found., 1959. Mem. Nat. Wholesale Druggists Assn. (assoc. adv. com.), Nat. Assn. Retail Druggists (exec. adv. coun. 1983-85), Pharm. Mfrs. Assn. (bd. dirs. 1989—), Proprietary Assn. (v.p. 1983-88, bd. dirs., mem. exec. com. 1981-88), Nat. Alliance Bus. (bd. dirs. 1984-86). Unitarian. Clubs: Plainfield Country (N.J.); Econ. (N.Y.C.). Office: Warner-Lambert Co 201 Tabor Rd Morris Plains NJ 07950

GOODGAME, RONALD EDWARD, lawyer, business executive; b. Los Angeles, Nov. 14, 1938; s. Robert Edward G. and Virginia Louise Braverman; children: Robert Edward, Randolph Colyear. B.A., U. So. Calif., 1961, LL.B., 1964. Bar: Calif. 1965. Atty. Carnation Co., Los Angeles, 1969-80, asst. gen. counsel, 1980-81, v.p., gen. counsel, 1981—; presentator Mng. the Corp. Law Dept., 1986;. Contbr. articles to legal jours. Mem. ABA, Calif. State Bar Assn., Los Angeles County Bar Assn., State Bar Calif. (past mem. exec. com. antitrust and trade regulation law sect.), Am. Corp. Counsel Assn. (bd. dirs.). Club: Los Angeles Country. Office: Carnation Co 5045 Wilshire Blvd Los Angeles CA 90036

GOODGER, JOHN VERNE, specialty materials company executive; b. Milton, Wis., Mar. 25, 1936; s. Harry E. and Elsie (Wachlin) G.; m. Priscilla Coriene Arnold, Oct. 18, 1958; children: Steven J., Karin Marie. Student, Whitewater State Coll., 1954-56; B.B.A., U. Wis., Milw., 1958; postgrad., Harvard U., 1979. C.P.A., Wis. Staff auditor Price, Waterhouse & Co., Milw., 1958-63; mgr. corp. data processing Bucyrus Erie Co., Milw., 1963-66; mgr. internal auditing Koehring Co., Milw., 1966-69, mgr. corp. accounting, 1969-71, asst. treas., 1971-74; treas. Ferro Corp., Cleve., 1974—; v.p. Ferro Corp., 1984—. With U.S. Army, 1959-62. Mem. AICPA, Fin. Execs. Inst. (bd. dirs. 1979-82, 85—), Ohio Inst. CPA's, Cleve. Treas. club (trustee 1983-85, v.p. 1983-84, pres. 1984-85), Nat. Investor Rels. Inst., Cleve. Growth Assn., Cleve. Playhouse Club, Cleve. Athletic Club. Republican. Presbyterian. Home: 2996 Falmouth Rd Shaker Heights OH 44122 Office: Ferro Corp 1000 Lakeside Ave Cleveland OH 44114

GOODGOLD, JAY SAMUEL, investment banking; b. N.Y.C., Nov. 23, 1954; s. Maurice and Sally Ann (Gottfried) G.; m. Diane Marjorie Shister, Sept. 8, 1984 (div. Oct. 1986). BA in Humanities, Johns Hopkins U., 1976; MBA, NYU, 1978. Compliance specialist U.S. Dept. Labor, N.Y.C., 1977-78; assoc. Goldman Sachs & Co., N.Y.C., 1978-79; assoc. Goldman Sachs & Co., St. Louis, 1979-82, v.p., 1982-88; v.p. Goldman Sachs & Co., Chgo., 1988—. Mem. Opera Theater of St. Louis, 1983—. Mem. Am. Technion Soc., Nat. Assn. Bus. Economists, Am. Jewish Hist. Soc. Democrat.

GOODIS, ALENE ROBIN, cable television executive; b. Miami, Fla., Nov. 1, 1954; d. Max and Elaine (Warner) G. AA in Liberal Arts, Miami Dade Jr. Coll., 1974; BS in Constrn. Mgmt., Fla. Internat. U., 1979; MBA, Nova U., 1981. Distbn. clk. U.S. Postal Service, Miami, 1974-77; engring. asst. State Dept. Transp., Miami, 1978; plant contract supr. So. Bell Telephone Co., Miami, 1979-82; constrn. adminstr. Gen. Telephone Co., Durham, N.C., 1982-83; supr. facility design So. New Eng. Telephone Co., New Haven, 1083-85; cable TV coordinator Broward County Bd. Commrs., Ft. Lauderdale, Fla., 1987—. Mem. Nat. League Cities, Nat. Cable TV Assn., Women in Cable, Fla. Bd. Realtors. Home: 14140 SW 84th St Apt H310 Miami FL 33183 Office: Broward County Bd Commrs Telecommunicaitons 115 S Andrews Ave Fort Lauderdale FL 33301

GOODKIN, LEWIS MICHAEL, real estate market analytical company executive; b. Passaic, N.J., Sept. 13, 1935; s. Robert Rubin and Lillian (Ellman) G.; A.B., Temple U., 1956; m. Joanne Myers, Jan. 1, 1980; children—Valarie, Sherrie, Andria. Pres., founder Goodkin Research Corp., Ft. Lauderdale, Fla., 1975—; bd. dirs. Barnett Bank So. Fla.; lectr. in field. Author: When Real Estate and Home Building Become Big Business, 1974; pub. Goodkin Real Estate Report; contbr. articles to profl. jours. Mem. adv. bd. U. Fla. Bus. Sch., Nova U. Served with U.S. Army, 1958-60, USAR, 1960-64. Mem. Inst. Resdl. Mktg., Urban Land Inst. (program vice chmn.), Real Estate Editors Assn., Coral Ridge Country Club. Office: Goodkin Rsch Corp 275 Commercial Blvd Lauderdale by the Sea FL 33308

GOODKIN, MICHAEL JON, investment company executive; b. N.Y.C., June 10, 1941; s. Harold and Rose (Mostkoff) G.; m. Helen Graham Fairbank, Oct. 1, 1971; children: Graham Laird, Nathalie Fairbank. B.A., Harvard U., 1963; postgrad., U. Chgo. Bus. Sch., 1964. Trainee Random House, N.Y.C., 1964-65; asst. dir. Simulmatics, N.Y.C., 1966-67; account exec. World Book Ency., Inc., Chgo., 1967-70; research dir. World Book Ency., Inc., 1970-73, v.p. mktg., 1973-76, v.p., gen. mgr. mail order div., 1976-78, pres., chief operating officer, 1978-86, chmn., chief exec. officer, pres., dir., 1983; exec. v.p. World Book Inc., 1978-84, pres., 1984-86, sr. v.p., 1979-80; exec. v.p., corp. dir. mktg., dir. World Book Internat. Inc., 1983-84; pres. World Book Life Ins. Co., 1983, Chgo. City Captial Group, 1989—; dep. dir. World Book Pty. Ltd. (Australia), 1983-86; prin. Chgo. City Capital Group, 1987—; chmn. Med. Holdings, Inc., 1987—. Bd. dirs. Chgo. Area Project; pres. aux. bd. Art Inst. Chgo., 1975-77, trustee, 1975—, also chmn. mktg. com., mem. 20th century com.; trustee Modern Poetry Assn., Latin Sch. Chgo., 1983—, chmn. ednl. policy com., sec. 1988, DMA Edn. Found., 1983—; mem. vis. com. visual arts U. Chgo. Served with Army N.G., 1963-69. Mem. Direct Mktg. Assn. (internat. council steering com. 1983, trustee Ednl. Found. 1983), Direct Selling Assn. (instl. com. 1982-86), Young Presidents' Orgn. Clubs: Racquet, Harvard (N.Y.C.); Harvard (Boston); Met.; Casino, Saddle and Cycle (Chgo.). Office: Chgo City Capital Group Sears Tower Ste 9300 Chicago IL 60606

GOODMAN, CHARLES SCHAFFNER, JR., food product executive; b. Phila., Nov. 15, 1949; s. Charles Schaffner Sr. and Dorothy Ruth (Irwin) G. BA, U. Pa., 1971. Warehouse and distb. mgr. Odyssey Records, Santa Cruz, Calif., 1974-75; mgr. Paradiso's, Santa Cruz, Calif., 1978-79; sales mgr. Mask Prodns., Chatsworth, Calif., 1980; regional sales mgr. Harmony Foods, Inc., Santa Cruz, 1981-85, nat. sales mgr., 1983-85, nat. sales mgr. foodsvc., 1985-88, v.p. foodsvc., 1988—; bd. dirs. Noema Software. Mem. No. Calif. Food Svc. Mktg. Assn., The Foodsters. Home: 4713 Soquel Creek Rd Soquel CA 95073 Mailing address: PO Box 5271 East Santa Cruz CA 95063 Office: Harmony Foods Inc PO Box 1191 Santa Cruz CA 95061

GOODMAN, EVELYN KITTENPLAN, banker; b. Richmond, Va., Dec. 24, 1924; d. Philip and Hannah (Harfeld) K.; m. Bernard Stuart Goodman, June 15, 1947; children: Debra Sue, John William. Grad., Rutgers U. Stonier Grad. Sch. Banking, 1973; B in Commerce, U. Richmond, 1981. Proof transit clk. Cen. Nat. Bank, Richmond, 1941-43, proof transit mgr., 1943-45, acctg. clk., 1945-51, collateral custodian, 1957-62, with trust dept. investments, 1963-65, with trust dept., acctg. control, 1966-68, ops. officer, mgr., wire transfer, 1968-76, with methods, procedures, 1976—, asst. v.p., 1978; pres. hon. mem. Richmond chpt. A.I.B., 1968-69, Commonwealth Group N.A.B.W., Richmond, 1970-71. Bd. dirs. Sauer's Garden Civic Assn., Richmond, 1981-83; v.p. Temple Beth-El, Richmond, 1986—; charter bd. dirs. Literacy Coun. Met. Richmond, 1982—, sec., 1987—. Mem. Am. Inst. Banking (hon., pres. Richmond chpt. 1968-69, Banker of Yr. 1975), Nat. Assn. Bank Women (pres. 1970-71). Jewish. Office: Cen Nat Bank 219 E Broad St Richmond VA 23219

GOODMAN, GEORGE JEROME WALDO (ADAM SMITH), author, editor, investment executive; b. St. Louis, Aug. 10, 1930; s. Alexander Mark and Viola (Cremer) G.; m. Sallie Cullen Brophy, Oct. 6, 1961; children: Alexander Mark, Susannah Blake. A.B. magna cum laude, Harvard U., 1952; A.B. Rhodes scholar, Oxford (Eng.) U., 1952-54. Reporter N.Y. Herald Tribune, 1952, Collier's mag., 1956, Barron's, 1957; contbg. editor, asso. editor Time and Fortune mags., 1958-60; portfolio mgr., v.p. Lincoln Fund, 1960-62; co-founder New York mag., 1967, contbg. editor, v.p., 1967-77; mem. editorial bd. N.Y. Times, 1977; exec. editor, then cons. Esquire, 1978-81; 1st editor, exec. v.p., bd. dirs. Instl. Investor, 1967-72; chmn. Continental Fidelity Group, 1980—, also dir.; exec. v.p., dir. Instl. Investor Systems, 1969-72; dir. USAIR, Inc., 1978—, Hyatt Hotels, 1977-81, Cambrex, Inc., Providentia Ltd., 1984-86, Westergaard Fund, 1983-84; occasional lectr. Harvard Bus. Sch., Princeton; occasional columnist Newsweek, 1973; commentator NBC News, 1974, PBS, 1981—; host, editor-in-chief Adam Smith's Money World, PBS, 1984—; editorial chmn. N.J. Monthly, 1976-79; adv. com. publs. U.S. Tennis Assn., 1978-83. Screenwriter, Los Angeles, 1962-65; Author: (novels) The Bubble Makers, 1955, A Time for Paris, 1957, Bascombe, The Fastest Hound Alive, 1958, A Killing in the Market, 1958, The Wheeler Dealers, 1959; under pseudonym Adam Smith: The Money Game, 1968, Supermoney, 1972, Powers of Mind, 1975, Paper Money, 1981, The Roaring 80's, 1988, also articles. Trustee Glassboro (N.J.) State Coll., 1967-71, co-chmn. presdl. selection com., 1968; trustee C.G. Jung Found., 1981-88; mem. adv. council econs. dept. Princeton U., 1970—, chmn., 1975—; rep. com. on shareholder responsibility Harvard U., 1971-74, mem. vis. com. psychology and social relations dept., 1974—, mem. vis. com. Middle East Inst.; mem. adv. council Sloan Fellowships, Princeton U., 1976-79; trustee The Urban Inst., 1986—, Found. for Child Devel., 1986-88. Served with AUS, 1954-56. Recipient G.M. Loeb award for distinguished achievement in writing about bus. and fin. U. Conn., 1969, Media award for econ. understanding for TV documentary The Forty-Five Billion Dollar Connection Amos Tuck Sch., Dartmouth Coll., 1978; nominated for Emmy award, 1985, 86, 87. Mem. Writers Guild Am. (West), Asso. Harvard Alumni (dir. 1972-75), Authors Guild (dir. 1975—). Clubs: Harvard (N.Y.C.), Century (N.Y.C.). Office: Adam Smith's Money World 45 W 45th St New York NY 10036

GOODMAN, JESS THOMPSON, manufacturing company executive, educator, retired naval officer; b. Joplin, Mo., Jan. 18, 1936; s. Walter Raymond and Opal Mae (Tanner) G.; A.B., U. Mo., 1959; postgrad. George Washington U., 1968; M.A., Naval Postgrad. Sch., 1975; postgrad. Naval War Coll., 1976; Ph.D. candidate U. Hawaii, 1979—; m. Yvonne Vasquez, May 27, 1972; 1 son, Walter Raymond II. Commd. ensign, U.S. Navy, 1959, advanced through grades to lt. comdr., 1967; flight trainee, 1962-63; patrol squadron tactical coordinator, 1963-66; anti-submarine warfare acad. and inflight tactics/weapons/avionics instr. Fleet Airborne Electronics Tng. Unit, Atlantic, 1966-69; aide, flag sec. to Comdr. Carrier Div. 7, 1969-70; patrol squadron, mission comdr. P3B Aircraft and exec. asst., head tng. and adminstrv. dept., 1970-73; ops. intelligence analyst and spl. projects officer Intelligence Center Pacific and comdr. in Chief Pacific, 1978; Cincpac rep. to Dept. Def., 1978; tchr. sci. Carl Junction (Mo.) Sch. Dist., 1979-80; prodn. supr., quality assurance mgr. Electronics div. Eagle-Picher Industries, 1980-82; quality control mgr., engr. electronics div. LaBarge Inc., Joplin, 1982—. Mem. World Affairs Forum of Hawaii, 1975-79, World Affairs Council of Pitts., 1978-82; nat. coordinator, founder Mensa Spl. Interest Group in Internat. Affairs, 1978-79. Decorated Navy Commendation Medal, Navy Achievement medals (2). Mem. Air Force Assn., Acad. Polit. Sci., AAAS, Am. Acad. Polit. and Social Sci., Am. Def. Preparedness Assn., Am. Entrepreneurs Assn., Am. Film Inst., Am. Legion, Am. Mgmt. Assn., Am. Mensa Ltd., Am. Mil. Inst., Am. Mus. Natural History, Am. Polit. Sci. Assn., Am. Prodn. and Inventory Control Soc., Am. Security Council Edn. Found., Am. Soc. Internat. Law, Am. Soc. for Quality Control (chmn. Joplin-Springfield chpt. 1985-86), Am. Univs. Field Staff, Asso. Nat. Archives, Arms Control Assn., Center for Study of Presidency, Common Cause, Fedn. Am. Scientists, Fgn. Policy Assn., Humanist Assn., Internat. Entrepreneurs Assn., Internat. Inst. for Strategic Studies, Internat. Platform Assn., Fgn. Policy Research Inst., Internat. Studies Assn., Joplin Boys Club, Mil. Order World Wars, Nat. Geog. Soc., Nat. Mil. Intelligence Assn., Nat. Rifle Assn., Overseas Devel. Council, Retired Officers Assn., Security and Intelligence Fund, Smithsonian Inst., Soc. Mfg. Engrs. (chmn. Ozark chpt. 1984-85), U. Mo. Alumni Assn. (life), U.S. Naval Inst., U.S. Strategic Inst., VFW, World Future Soc., Pi Kappa Alpha. Democrat. Methodist. Clubs: Masons, Shriners, Toastmasters, Kiwanis. Editor, pub.: The Mintas' Hoot, 1978. Home: 2725 Schifferdecker Joplin MO 64804 Office: 1505 Maiden Ln Joplin MO 64802

GOODMAN, JON PROOSLIN, academic program director, consultant; b. N.Y.C., Oct. 14, 1941; s. Milton Gregory Prooslin and Emma (Kirshner) Schwartz; children: Samantha, James Breakstone. BA, Finch Coll., 1962; MBA, U. Conn., 1976; PhD, U. Ga., 1980. Pub. relations rep. Columbia Pictures Corp., N.Y.C., 1962-64; publicist Dino De Laurentis Prodns., N.Y.C., 1964-65; booking agt. West Coast Buena Vista Distbn. Corp., N.Y.C., 1965-66; cons., prin. Jon Goodman Assocs., Stamford, Conn., 1969-77; instr. U. Ga., Athens, 1977-80; asst. prof. U. Houston, 1980-84, dir. small bus. devel. ctr., 1984—; vice chmn. bd. Houston Internat. Hosp., 1984—; gen. ptnr. Septentrion Ventures. Contbr. numerous articles to profl. jours. Mem. Commr.'s Commn. on Decentralization Houston Police Dept., 1981-83, econ. devel. subcom. Gov.'s Commn. on Sci. and Tech., Austin, Tex., 1986, Tex. Tech. Industry Legis. Task Force, 1988—, adv. bd., Tex. Trend in Biotech., 1987—; bd. dirs., Tex. Innovation Info. Network System; pres. Houston Bus. Devel. Found., 1985—; active Tex. Strategic Econ. Policy Comm., 1988—. Mem. Small Bus. Devel. Ctrs. (exec. com. 1985—), Nat. Assn. Corp. Dirs. (adv. bd. 1985—), Acad. Mgmt., Internat. Strategic Mgmt. Soc. Office: U Houston SBDC 401 Louisiana Ave Houston TX 77002

GOODMAN, KENNETH WAYNE, financial planner; b. Dallas, Mar. 26, 1946; s. Harold A. and Dora (Einhorn) G.; m. Diane Brustein, July 1, 1973; children: Matthew Todd, Dana Brittany. BBA, U. Tex., 1969. Cert. fin. planner. Fin. planner IDS Fin. Svcs., Dallas, 1969—. Mem. Lions (past pres.). Jewish. Home: 7101 Crooked Oak Dallas TX 75248 Office: IDS Fin Svcs 801 E Campbell Ste 330 Richardson TX 75081

GOODMAN, MICHAEL FREDERICK, advertising executive; b. Ringgold, Ga., Dec. 15, 1951; s. Frederick Doherty and Hilda Naomi (Benton) G.; m. Renee Elizabeth Penny, Mar. 24, 1980. BS in Mktg., Ventura (Calif.) Coll., 1973; postgrad., Chattanooga State U., 1976. V.p., gen. mgr. Comml. Advt. Corp., Chattanooga, 1971-73; pres. Michael Goodman & Assocs., Inc., Chattanooga, 1973-78; nat. sales mgr. Pennco Internat., Inc., Mansfield, Ohio, 1978-84; pres., chief exec. officer M. Goodman & Co., Inc., Chattanooga, 1984—; bd. dirs. Leisure Life Care, Inc.; pres. MG&A, Inc.; speaker in field. Mem. Tenn. Govt. Affairs Com., 1986—, Fed. Govt. Affairs Com., Chattanooga, 1987; publicity chmn. Chattanooga Bus.-to-Bus. Expo, 1987; chmn. Chattanooga Bus. Week, 1988. Mem. Am. Assn. Advt. Agys., Chattanooga Small Bus. Council. Republican. Presbyterian. Club: Optimist. Office: M Goodman & Co Inc 3720 Amnicola Hwy Suite 129 Chattanooga TN 37406

GOODMAN, PHILIP, computer company executive; b. LaCrosse, Wis., May 14, 1937; s. William and Lilian Goodman; B.A., Miami U., Oxford, Ohio, 1958; 1 son, Charles Daniel. Eastern regional mgr. Gen. Automation Co., Stamford, Conn., 1971-73; v.p. Digital Computer Controls Inc., Fairfield, N.J., 1973-77; v.p. Digi-Log Systems Inc., Horsham, Pa., 1977-79; v.p., dir. Control Transaction Corp., Fairfield, 1979-80; chmn. bd. Data Safe, Inc. (name changed to Fastcomm Data, Inc.), McLean, Va., 1981-85; dir. sales Internat. Robomation/Intelligence, Princeton, N.J., 1985-86, v.p., 1986—; dir. Transidyne Gen. Corp., Ann Arbor, Mich. Mem. Phi Beta Kappa. Home: 4F Brookline Ct Princeton NJ 08540 Office: Internat Robomation-Intelligence 100 Thanet Dr Princeton NJ 08540

GOODMAN, PHILLIP LANE, chemical company executive; b. Concord, N.C., Mar. 17, 1948; s. Adam Lamont and Louise (Turner) G.; m. Deborah Jean Wenger, June 30, 1971; 1 child, Carey Danielle. BS in Textile Chemistry, N.C. State U., 1970; MBA, U. N.C., 1986—. Lab. tech. Lin Corrier Corp., Landis, N.C., 1966-70; devel. chemist BASF Corp., Charlotte, N.C., 1970-72, tech. mgr., 1972-74, mktg., sales exec., 1974-79; mgr. sales Hydrolabs Corp., Patterson, N.J., 1979-82; mktg. dir. Boehme Filatex, Inc., Greensboro, N.C., 1982-86, v.p. mktg., 1986—; also dir. Contbr. articles to profl. jours. Fellow Textured Assn. Am., Am. Assn. Textile Technologists, Leather Chemists Am.; mem. Am. Assn. Textile Chemists and Colorists (social chmn. 1974—), MBA Assn., Sigma Tau Sigma, Theta Chi, Moose, Lions (person of yr., 1978). Republican. Lutheran. Home: 4704 Royalshire Dr Greensboro NC 27406

GOODMAN, SAM RICHARD, electronics company executive; b. N.Y.C., May 23, 1930; s. Morris and Virginia (Gross) G.; m. Beatrice Bettencourt, Sept. 15, 1957; children—Mark Stuart, Stephen Manuel, Christopher Bettencourt. BBA, CCNY, 1951; MBA, NYU, 1957, PhD, 1968. Chief acct. John C. Valentine Co., N.Y.C., 1957-60; mgr. budgets and analysis Gen. Foods. Corp., White Plains, N.Y., 1960-63; budget dir. Crowell Collier Pub. Co., N.Y.C., 1963-64; v.p., chief fin. officer Nestle Co., Inc., White Plains, 1964; chief fin. officer Aileen, Inc., N.Y.C., 1973-74, Ampex Corp., 1974-76; exec. v.p. fin. and adminstrn. Baker & Taylor Co. div. W.R. Grace Co., N.Y.C., 1976-79, Magnuson Computer Systems, Inc., San Jose, Calif., 1979-81; v.p., chief fin. officer Datamac Computer Systems, Sunnyvale, Calif., 1981—; pres. Nutritional Foods Inc., San Francisco, 1983-84; chmn., chief exec. officer CMX Corp., Santa Clara, Calif., 1984-88; dir., sr. v.p. Masstor Systems Corp., Santa Clara, 1988—; lectr. N.Y. U. Inst. Mgmt., 1965-67; asst. prof. mktg. Iona Coll. Grad. Sch. Bus. Adminstrn., 1967—; prof. Golden Gate U., 1974—; prof. finance and mktg. Pace U. Grad. Sch. Bus. Adminstrn., 1969—. Author: also articles. Controller's Handbook. Lt. (j.g.) USNR, 1951-55. Mem. Fin. Execs. Inst., Nat. Assn. Accts., Am. Statis. Assn., Am. Econs. Assn., Planning Execs. Inst., Am. Arbitration Assn. Home: 60 Shearer Dr Atherton CA 94025 Office: Masstor Systems 5200 Great America Pkwy Santa Clara CA 95050

GOODMAN, STUART F., brokerage house executive; b. Bklyn., July 3, 1943; s. Philip L. and Roselle G. (Fishman) G.; m. Susan Wiland, June 30, 1968; children: Jodie, Lynn. BS in Acctg., Bklyn. Coll., 1965. CPA, N.Y. Staff acct. Simonoff Peyser & Citrin, N.Y.C., 1965-69; asst. controller Cowan & Co., N.Y.C., 1969-70, controller, 1970-85, chief fin. officer, 1985—. Office: Cowen & Co Financial Sq New York NY 10005

GOODMAN, WILLIAM RICHARD, insurance adjusting company executive; b. Staunton, W.Va., Sept. 19, 1930; s. Harry and Ruth (Meyer) G.; m. Alice Helene Katzenstein, June 13, 1954; children: Harvey, Laurie, Barry. BS, U. Md., 1952; JD, U. Balt., 1955. Pub. ins. adjuster Goodman-Gable-Gould Co., Balt., 1952-73, v.p., 1973-85, pres., 1985—. Chmn. Balt. County Indsl. Devel. Commn., 1967-69; mem. Met. Transit Authority, Balt., 1969-71, bd. rev. Dept. Transp., Md., 1971-76, Md. Racing Commn., 1984. Mem. Nat. Assn. Pub. Ins. Adjusters (dir., v.p., pres., chmn. bd. dirs., Disting. Service award 1987). Democrat. Jewish. Home: 7811 Park Heights Ave Baltimore MD 21208 Office: Goodman Gable Gould Co 32 W Pennsylvania Baltimore MD 21204

GOODREAU, NELSON ARTHUR, brokerage house executive; b. Sanford, Fla., Jan. 30, 1961; s. Nelson A. and Evelyn (Caprioli) G. BA in Fin., U. South Fla., 1983, MBA, 1986. Broker, br. mgr. Olde Discount Stockbrokers, Tampa, Fla., 1986—. Republican. Roman Catholic. Home: PO Box 273212 Tampa FL 33688 Office: Olde Discount Stockbrokers 8910 N Dale Mabry Hwy 1 Tampa FL 33614

GOODRICH, MAURICE KEITH, business forms/systems and services company executive; b. New Haven, Jan. 14, 1935; s. Maurice Franklin and Ola Catherine (Keith) G.; m. Sara Jane Wooding, June 1, 1957; children: Scot, John, David, Elizabeth. BS in Indsl. Adminstrn., Yale U., 1956. Indsl. engring. trainee Kaiser Aluminum & Chem. Corp., Erie, Pa., 1956-57; standards engr. Foster Wheeler corp., Dansville, N.Y., 1958-59; indsl. engr. Moore Bus. Forms Inc., Elmira, N.Y., 1959-63; supt. of services Rutland, Vt., 1964-66; prodn. tng. supt. Niagara Falls, N.Y., 1967-68, staff engr., 1969-70; plant mgr. Elmira, N.Y., 1970-72; gen. prodn. mgr., ea. div. Niagara Falls, 1972-77; v.p., dir. info. services Glenview, Ill., 1978-79, v.p., dir. mfg., 1980-83; pres. U.S. Forms and Systems Div., 1983-85; exec. v.p., chief operating officer Moore Corp. Ltd., Toronto, Ont., Can., 1986, pres., chief exec. officer, 1987—. Chmn. adv. council Niagara U. Sch. Bus. Adminstrn., Buffalo, 1977; bd. dirs. Capabilities Inc., Elmira, 1972; past mem. alumni bd. Yale U.; past pres. Yale Club, Vt. Mem. Am. Inst. Indsl. Engrs., Am. Soc. Quality Control. Clubs: Forge, Meadow (Chgo.); National, Yale (Toronto). Office: Moore Corp Ltd Box 78, 1 1st Canadian Pl, Toronto, ON Canada M5X 1G5

GOODSON, JAMES BUTLER, bank holding company executive; b. Waco, Tex., Aug. 15, 1923; s. William Lloyd and Susie (Butler) G.; m. Molly Barnes, Mar. 20, 1949; children: Laurie, Liza, James Butler, Thomas Barnes. B.B.A., U. Tex., 1948. Analyst Rauscher, Pierce & Co., Dallas, 1948-52; with Southland Life Ins. Co., Dallas, 1952-85; pres., chief exec. officer Southland Life Ins. Co., 1969-80, chmn., chief exec. officer, 1980-85, also bd. dirs., mem. exec. com.; exec. v.p., dir. Southland Fin. Corp.; vice chmn. Texas Commerce Bancshares Inc, Houston, 1985—; dir. Sabine Corp., Tex. Commerce Bank, Dallas. Past pres., bd. dirs. Children's Devel. Ctr., Dallas, 1967; past mem. exec. com. Dallas Council Chs.; mem. Dallas Assembly, 1962, Cotton Bowl Council, after 1962; active United Fund, YMCA;

bd. dirs. Goodwill Industries Dallas, Hope Cottage, Dallas, Jr. Achievement Dallas. Served with AUS, World War II. Mem. Salesmanship Club Dallas (bd. dirs. 1965-66), Sigma Alpha Epsilon. Presbyterian (chmn. deacons 1961, elder 1962-65, deacon 1961). Office: Tex Commerce Bank Pla of the Americas Pearl at Bryan Dallas TX 75201 *

GOODSON, RICHARD CARLE, JR., chemist, hazardous waste management consultant; b. Toledo, June 22, 1945; s. Richard Carle Goodson Sr. and Norma (Buhler) Robinson; m. Deborah Ann Hart, Mar. 29, 1969 (div. Feb. 1978); 1 child, Geoffrey Carle; m. Thelma Agnes Matthews, Nov. 22, 1978. BS in Chemistry, Union Coll., 1967; MS in Inorganic Chemistry, U. Conn., 1970. Dist. engr. Drew Chem. Corp., Boonton, N.J., 1972-74; product supr. Drew Chem. Corp., Boonton, 1974-75, regional tech. supr., 1975-76; chief chemist, tech. dir. Environ. Waste Removal, Waterbury, Conn., 1976-79; gen. mgr., dir. tech. lab. Conn. Treatment Corp., Bristol, Conn., 1979-82; pres., owner Goodson Assocs., Avon, Conn., 1982—. Mem. Am. Chem. Soc. Republican. Home and Office: 51 Anvil Dr Avon CT 06001

GOODSPEED, SCOTT WINANS, hospital administration executive; b. Boston, Jan. 6, 1954; s. Robert Fall and Joanne (Way) G.; m. Mary Ellen McDonough, Sept. 25, 1976; children: Kathleen, Brendan. BS, Ithaca Coll., 1976; postgrad., Harvard U., 1977; MHA, U. Minn., 1980. Research asst. adminstrn. health services dept. Ithaca (N.Y.) Coll., 1974-75; statistician, br. mgr. Bur. Vital Records and Health Statistics, Concord, N.H., 1976-78; adminstrv. resident R.I. Hosp., Providence, 1979-80; planning assoc. Elliot Hosp., Manchester, N.H., 1980-82; dir. planning, systems and cost containment Elliot Hosp., Manchester, 1982-83, v.p. adminstrv. services, 1983-86, sr. v.p., chief operating officer, 1986—; instr. Rivier Coll., Nashua, N.H., 1982—; clin. faculty assoc. U. N.H., Durham, 1982—, U. N.C., Chapel Hill, 1982—; presenter in field. Contbr. articles on strategic and bus. planning and quality assurance to profl. jours. Mem. Task Force on Planning, N.H. Hosp. Assn., 1980-84; mem N.H. Gov.'s Com. on Long-Term Care, 1981; mem. Regional Emergency Med. Services Council, 1981-85; bd. dirs. Manchester Assn. Retarded Citizens, Inc., 1982-84; chmn. planning com. United Way Greater Manchester, 1983-86; mem. Manchester Mgmt. Rev., Inc., 1984-85; bd. dirs. United Way Greater Manchester, 1984—, chmn. venture grant com. , 1986-87, chmn. nominating com., 1988; bd. dirs. Cypress Med. Park Condominium Assn., 1985—; bd. dirs. Stat Care, 1985-88, chmn. bd., 1987-88; sec. N.H. Heart Council, 1986; mem. council community affairs N.H. Hosp. Assn., 1986—; Gov.'s appointee N.H. Job Tng. Coun., 1988—. Recipient James A. Hamilton award U. Minn., 1980, Vernon E. Weckwerth award, 1982; named one of Outstanding Young Men of Am., U.S. Jaycees, 1980. Mem. Am. Coll. Health Care Execs. (mem. regent's adv. coun. 1988—), Am. Assn. Hosp. Planning and Mktg., Am. Hosp. Assn., Soc. Hosp. Planning Am. Hosp. Assn., Freestanding Ambulatory Surgery Assn., Am. Mgmt. Assn., Greater Manchester C. of C. (Leadership Manchester program 1988, chmn. health and edn. div. membership div. 1989—), U. Minn. Alumni Assn. Lodge: Rotary. Home: 41 Wellesley Dr Bedford NH 03102 Office: Elliot Hosp 955 Auburn St Manchester NH 03103

GOODSTEIN, DAVID HENRY, electronic publishing consultant; b. N.Y.C., Sept. 14, 1948; s. Bernard Jack Goodstein and Phyllis (Freeman) Gustafson; m. Carol R. Furst, Feb. 26, 1969 (div. 1973); m. Ingrid Marie Aue, May 1, 1979; children: Julian, Justin, Gabrielle. Student, MIT, 1965. Pres. Matrix Assocs., Portland, Oreg., 1970-76; cons. IFRA, Darmstadt, Fed. Republic of Germany, 1976; mktg. specialist Arsy Com Corp., Amsterdam, The Netherlands, 1976-77; dir. sales and mktg. Xenotron Ltd., Diss, Norfolk, Eng., 1977-78; pres., chief exec. officer Interconsult, Inc., Arlington, Mass., 1978—. Jewish. Office: Intercons Inc 366 Massachusetts Ave Arlington MA 02174

GOODWICK, DAVID LEE, advertising agency executive; b. Beloit, Wis., Oct. 20, 1954; s. James Lee and Helen Maude (Alton) G.; m. Christie Wren Spencer, Apr. 18, 1981; children: Jesse David, Lindsey Leah. B.A. in Polit. Sci., U. Wis.-Whitewater, 1976, B.A. in Journalism, 1976. Intern J. Walter Thompson, Chgo., 1975; advt. mgr. LRP, Inc., Lake Geneva, Wis., 1976; mktg. services mgr. Mercury Marine, Fond du Lac, Wis., 1976-77; advt. mgr. Johnson Outboards, Waukegan, Ill., 1977-79; account mgr. Gen. Electric Co., Fairfield, Conn., 1979-82; pres. Goodwick Assocs., Inc., Newtown, Conn., 1982—; ptnr. Hist. Property Preservation Ltd., 1987—, Profl. Services Assocs., Inc., 1987—, GW Prodns., Newtown, 1985—, Paige and Goodwick Advt., Bronxville, N.Y., 1986—, Lakeside Advt., Fond du Lac, Wis., 1978-79; advisor Insight Assocs., Westport, Conn., 1984—. Pub. The Alternative, 1974-76. Press sec. to Gov. Patrick Lucey of Wis., Madison, 1974; co-producer Ox Ridge Charity Horse Show, Darien, Conn., 1984-86; chmn. communications com. United Way, Danbury, Conn., 1987-88. Recipient Matty award of Excellence, Ad Club of Fairfield County, 1980, Best Ad of Issue award Industry Week, 1981, readership awards various mags. Mem. Am. Entrepenurial Assn., Internat. Platform Assn. Republican. Avocations: musician; fishing. Home: 201 Hattertown Rd Newtown CT 06470 Office: Goodwick Assocs Inc 117 S Main St Newtown CT 06470

GOODWIN, JAMES BARTON, venture capitalist; b. Birmingham, Ala., Jan. 14, 1947; s. Andrew Jackson Goodwin and Charlotte (Head) Simmons; m. Elizabeth Fentress, Sept. 11, 1971; children: Carson, Eliot, James. BA, Washington & Lee U., 1969; MBA, Columbia U., 1974. V.p. Kidder Peabody & Co., N.Y.C., 1974-86; mng. dir. Bridge Capital Advisors, Teaneck, N.J., 1986—; bd. dirs. FlowMole Corp., Kent, Wash., Baker Fentress, Chgo., Serv-Tech Inc., Houston, Am. Powdered Metals, Conovan, N.C. Served to lt. USNR, 1969-72. Mem. Nat. Assn. Corp. Dirs. Republican. Episcopalian. Clubs: Union League (N.Y.C.), Tuxedo, Doubles. Home: 112 W 78th St New York NY 10024 Office: Bridge Capital Advisors Glenpointe Ctr W Teaneck NJ 07666

GOODWIN, PAUL RICHARD, transportation company executive; b. N.Y.C., Feb. 6, 1943; s. Paul Richard Fetyko and Ellen Mary Goodwin; m. Nina Presant, Oct. 10, 1965; children: Elizabeth, Ross. B.C.E., Cornell U., 1965; M.B.A., George Washington U., 1970. Mgmt. trainee Chessie System, Balt., 1965-66, in various mgmt. positions fin. dept., 1966-76; asst. to v.p. fin. Chessie System, Cleve., 1977-78, asst. v.p. fin., 1978-80, v.p. fin., 1980-81, sr. v.p. fin., 1982-85; sr. v.p. fin. and planning Chessie System, Balt., 1985-86, CSX Transp. Rail Transport Group, Jacksonville, Fla., 1986-87; sr. v.p. CSX Transp., Jacksonville, 1987—. Mem. Fin. Execs. Inst. Office: CSX Transp 500 Water St Jacksonville FL 32202

GOODWIN, PHILLIP HUGH, hospital administrator; b. Paragould, Ark., Sept. 10, 1940; s. Ray H. and Helen L. (Griffin) G.; m. Pamela J. Davis, June 24, 1962; children: Philip Grey, Julie Ann. BA in Bus. and Econs., Hendrix Coll., 1962; M in Hosp. Adminstrn., Washington U., St. Louis, 1968. Bus. mgr. Stuttgart (Ark.) Meml. Hosp., 1962-64; asst. adminstr. Union Meml. Hosp., El Dorado, Ark., 1964-67; adminstrv. asst. to assoc. adminstr. Hillcrest Med. Ctr., Tulsa, 1968-77, v.p., adminstr., chief operating officer, 1977-82; exec. v.p. Charleston (W.Va.) Area Med. Ctr., 1982-87, pres., chief exec. officer, 1987—; adj. faculty Wash. U., St. Louis, W.Va. U., Med. Coll. Va., W.Va. Coll. Grad. Studies; chmn. bd. dirs. Mid-Atlantic Clin. Engring., Alexandria, Va.; bd. dirs. Auther B. Hodges Nursing Home, Charleston; frequent speaker ednl., profl. and bus. assns. Co-author: Time Management for Hospital Administrators; contbr. articles to profl. publs. Bd. dirs. Kanawha Hospice, Inc., Charleston, 1987—, Vol. Mgmt. Assistance Program, Charleston, 1987—, Nat. Inst. Chem. Studies, Charleston, 1988-89; pres. Civitan Club, Tulsa, 1970. Fellow Am. Coll. Healthcare Execs.; mem. W.Va. Hosp. Assn. (pres. 1987, 88), Am. Hosp. Assn. (ho. of dels. 1988—), Vol. Hosps. Am. (bd. dirs. 1978-82), Charleston Rennaisance Soc., W.Va. C. of C., Charleston C. of C., Ducks Unltd., Berry Hill Country Club. Republican. Methodist. Office: Charleston Area Med Ctr PO Box 1547 Charleston WV 25326

GOODWIN, WILLIAM DEAN, oil company execuvtive; b. Independence, Kans., Aug. 3, 1937; s. William Brice and Rozella Delia (Lillibridge) G.; m. Jane Louise Varnum, Oct. 23, 1960 (div. 1973); children: Deborah Diane, Laura Louise; m. Linda Ann Booth, July 26, 1980; 1 child, William D. II. BS in Advt. and Bus., U. Kans., 1961. Editor Marshall County News, Marysville, Kans., 1961-63; dir. pub. relations U.S. Jaycees, Tulsa, 1963-67; account exec. Carl Byoir & Assocs., Chgo., 1967-68, Holder, Kennedy & Co., Nashville, 1968-70; press sec. U.S. Senator Bill Brock, Washington, 1970-74; exec. v.p. Nat. Energy Corp., Nashville, 1974-78, Tenn. Land & Exploration, Nashville, 1979-80; pres. Commerce Oil Co., Nashville, 1980-83; pvt. practice oil producer Crossville, Tenn., 1984—; treas. Tenn. Oil Producers Polit. Action Com., Nashville, 1983—. Editor-in-chief: Future mag., 1966-67; editor (mag.) Nat. Young Reps., 1971-72; (newsletter) The Oilpatch. Chmn. Davidson County Reps., Nashville, 1979; nominee Candidate for U.S. Congress 5th Dist. Tenn., 1978; cons. Nat. Rep. Senatorial Com., Washington, 1973; dir. publicity Com. to Reelect the Pres., 1972; vice chmn. Tenn. Commn. on Status of Women, 1979-80. Served with USN, 1956-57. Mem. Nat. Assn. Royalty Owners (life, bd. govs. 1986—), Tenn. Oil and Gas Assn. (exec. v.p. 1975-82; names Tenn. Oil Man of Yr., 1981), VFW. Methodist. Club: Lake Tansi (Crossville). Home: 109 S Oakley Crossville TN 38555 Office: Hwy 127 N Box 728 Crossville TN 38557

GOOGINS, ROBERT REVILLE, lawyer, insurance company executive; b. Cambridge, Mass., June 2, 1937; s. Robert Wendell and Patricia M. (Reville) G.; B.S., U. Conn., 1958, J.D., 1961; M.B.A., U. Hartford, 1970; m. Sonya Ann Forbes, June 21, 1958; children—Shawn W., Glen R. Bar: Conn. 1961. Atty. Conn. Mut. Life Ins. Co., Hartford, 1961-62, asst. counsel, 1964-67, assoc. counsel, 1967-70, counsel, 1970-72, counsel, sec., 1972-74, v.p., counsel, sec., 1974-75, v.p., gen. counsel, sec., 1975-77, sr. v.p., gen. counsel, 1977-80, exec. v.p., gen. counsel, 1980—, exec. v.p., 1982-89; ptnr. Hoberman & Pollock, P.C., 1989—; adj. prof. law U. Conn. Sch. Law; dir. Thermodynectics, Fin. Savs. Bank; dep. mayor Town of Glastonbury, Conn., 1976; majority leader Glastonbury Town Council, 1977. Served to capt. U.S. Army, 1962-64. Mem. ABA, Conn. Bar Assn., Assn. Life Ins. Counsel, Nat. Assn. Securities Dealers (gov.-at large 1976-79). Republican. Roman Catholic. Office: Hoberman & Pollack 1 State St Hartford CT 06103

GOOKIN, THOMAS ALLEN JAUDON, civil engineer; b. Tulsa, Aug. 5, 1951; s. William Scudder and Mildred (Hartman) G.; m. Leigh Anne Johnson, June 13, 1975 (div. Dec. 1977); m. Sandra Jean Andrews, July 23, 1983. BS with distinction, Ariz. State U., 1975. Registered profl. engr., Calif., Ariz., Nev. Civil engr., treas. W.S. Gookin & Assocs., Scottsdale, Ariz., 1968—. Chmn. Ariz. State Bd. Tech. Registration Engring. adv. com., 1984—. Mem. NSPE, Ariz. Soc. Profl. Engrs. (sec. Papago chpt. 1979-81, v.p. 1981-84, pres. 1984-85, named Young Engr. of Yr. 1979, Outstanding Engring. Project award 1988), Order Engr., Ariz. Congress on Surveying and Mapping, Am. Soc. Civil Engrs., Ariz. Water Works Assn., Tau Beta Pi, Delta Chi (Tempe chpt. treas. 1970-71, sec. 1970, v.p. 1971), Phi Kappa Delta (pres. 1971-73). Republican. Episcopalian. Home: 10760 E Becker Ln Scottsdale AZ 85259 Office: W S Gookin & Assocs 4203 N Brown Ave Scottsdale AZ 85251

GORALNICK, HAROLD MARK, credit union executive; b. Haverhill, Mass., Mar. 24, 1949; s. Howard Sidney and Ethel (Gross) G.; m. Janice Lee Feldman, Apr. 8, 1973; children: JAimie Beth, Jared Seth. BA, Bowdoin Coll., 1971; cert. in acctg., Bentley Coll., 1973; MBA, Northeastern U., 1980. Auditor Price Waterhouse, Boston, 1973-74; acct. H.J. Ferngold Co., Boston, 1974-75; asst. mgr. acctg. First Nat. Stores, Somerville, Mass., 1975-78; ops. mgr. Polaroid Employees Fed. Credit Union, Cambridge, Mass., 1978-80; dir. fin. and ops. Digital Employees Fed. Credit Union, Maynard, Mass., 1980—. Mem. Credit Union Exec. Soc., Custon Computer Applications Users Group (exec. com. Memphis), Temple Shalom Emeth Brotherhood, Anthroposophical Soc. Republican. Jewish. Office: Digital Credit Union 141 Parker St Maynard MA 01754

GORANS, GERALD ELMER, accountant; b. Benson, Minn., Sept. 17, 1922; s. George W. and Gladys (Schneider) G.; m. Mildred Louise Stallard, July 19, 1944; 1 child, Gretchen. BA, U. Wash., Seattle, 1947. CPA, Wash. With Touche, Ross & Co., CPAs and predecessor, Seattle, 1947-88; ptnr. Touche, Ross & Co., 1957-88, in charge Seattle office, 1962-82, mem. policy group, adminstrv. com., 1964-69, dir., 1974-83, sr. partner, 1979-88, chmn. mgmt. group, 1982-88, ret., 1988. V.p. budget and fin. Seattle Worlds Fair, 1962; chmn. budget and fin. com. Century 21 Ctr., Inc., 1963-64; mem. citizens adv. com. Seattle Lic. and Consumer Protection Com., 1965; head profl. div. United Way King County, Seattle, 1963-64, head advanced gifts div., 1965, exec. v.p., 1966, pres., 1967; trustee United Way Endowment Fund, 1984—; adv. bd. Seattle Salvation Army, 1965-80, treas., 1974-80; fin. com. Bellevue Christian Sch., 1970-77; citizens adv. bd. pub. affairs Sta. KIRO-TV, 1970-71; treas., bd. dirs., exec. com. Scandinavia Today in Seattle, 1981-83; treas., bd. dirs. Seattle Citizens Coun. Against Crime, 1972-80, pres., 1976, 77; bd. dirs. U. Wash Alumni Fund, 1967-71, chmn., 1971; trustee U. Wash. Pres.'s Club, 1980-83; bd. dirs., chmn. devel. com. N.W. Hosp. Found., 1977-83, trustee hosp., 1980—, treas. bd., 1981-84, vice-chmn. bd. hosp., 1984-89, chmn. bd. trustees, 1989—, chmn. fin. com., 1987—; chmn. fin. com. Com. for Balanced Regional Transp., 1981—; co-chmn. United Cerebal Palsy Seattle Telethon, 1986; chmn. fin. com. fund raising Mus. Flight, 1983-87; mem. assoc. bd. Pacific Scis. Ctr., Seattle, 1986—; active Japanese/Am. Conf. Mayors. Lt. (j.g.) USNR, 1943-45. Mem. Assoc. Am. Inst. CPA's (chmn. nat. def. com. 1969-75, mem. spl. investigation com. 1984-87), Nat. Office Mgmt. Assn. (past pres.), Wash. Soc. CPA's (Outstanding Pub. Svc. award 1988), Seattle C. of C. (chmn. taxation com. 1970-71, bd. dirs. 1971-74, 76-79, 80-81, 85—, mem. exec. com. 1980-83, v.p. 1981-84, 1st vice-chmn. 1983-84, chmn. 1984-85, vice-chmn. facilities fund drive, 1982-84), Nat. Def. Exec. Res., Nat. Club Assn. (bd. dirs. 1984—), Assn. Wash. Bus. (bd. dirs. 1983-86). Clubs: Seattle Golf, Wash. Athletic (pres. 1975-76), Rainier (treas. 1976-77), Lake. Home: 9013 NE 37th Pl Bellevue WA 98004 Office: Touche Ross & Co 1111 3rd Ave Seattle WA 98101

GORBIS, BORIS ZINOVJEVICH, lawyer; b. Odessa, USSR, Aug. 29, 1950; came to U.S., 1975; s. Zinoviy R. and Nelli (Goldenstein) G.; m. Eda Jacobashvili, Nov. 29, 1981. Student Odessa Inst. Tech., 1967-80; M.A., U. Odessa, 1972; J.D., U. Calif.-Berkeley, 1980. Bar: Calif. 1980, U.S. Dist. Ct. (cen. dist.) Calif. 1981. Vis. prof. Stanford U., 1976; assoc. Graham & James, Los Angeles, 1980-82; prin. Boris Z. Gorbis, Los Angeles and San Francisco, 1982—; gen. counsel Almanac-Panorama, Russian weekly, Los Angeles, 1980—. Contbr. articles to profl. jours. Bd. dirs. Am. Jewish Congress, San Francisco, 1977, Jewish Community Ctr., Los Angeles, 1982-84. Mem. ABA, Assn. Trial Lawyers Am., Calif. Trial Lawyers Assn., Boalt Hall Dean's Coun., Los Angeles Trial Lawyers Assn., Assn. Soviet Jewish Immigrants, New Times Club, Guardians Club (L.A.). Republican. Office: 8484 Wilshire Blvd Ste 660 Beverly Hills CA 90210

GORCZYCA, RICHARD MARIAN, manufacturer's representative company executive; b. Munstrel, Fed. Republic Germany: came to U.S., 1951, naturalized, 1968; s. Marian and Anna (Rajczonek) G.; m. Darlene Cowgill, July 22, 1972; children: Dawn, Kristina. Engring. aide Schaevitz Engring., Pennsauken, N.J., 1969-70, prodn. supr., 1970-73, regional sales mgr., 1973-78; pres. R.G. Assocs., Inc., Tolland, Conn., 1978—. Mem. parish council religious edn. com. St. Matthew Ch., Tolland, 1985-86. Mem. Instrument Soc. Am. (sr. pres. Conn. Valley sect. 1986-87), Inst. Environ. Scis., Electronic Reps. Assn., Mfg. Agts. Nat. Assn. Republican. Club: Toastmasters (Glastonbury, Conn.) (v.p. membership 1985-86). Lodge: K.C. Home: 33 Bennett Dr Tolland CT 06084 Office: RG Assocs Inc 33 Bennett Dr Tolland CT 06084

GORDON, ALAN LEONARD, real estate executive; b. Rockville Ctr, N.Y., Mar. 12, 1935; s. Manney and Sadie (Deutsch) G.; m. Marilyn S. Siegel, Oct. 27, 1956; children: Stuart I., Cindy M. BS in Econs., U. Pa., 1957. Auditor Touche Ross & Co., N.Y.C., 1957-63; treas. Keystone Bolt & Nut Co., N.Y.C., 1963-65; asst. treas. Diners Club, N.Y.C., 1965-73; treas., v.p. Loeb Ptnrs. Realty, N.Y.C., 1973—. Mem. Am. Inst. CPAs, N.Y. State Soc. CPAs. Office: Loeb Ptnrs 521 5th Ave New York NY 10175

GORDON, BARON JACK, stock broker; s. George M. and Rose (Salsbury) G.; midshipman U.S. Naval Acad., 1946; BS, Lynchburg Coll., 1953; m. Ellin Bachrach, Aug. 20, 1954; children—Jonathan Ross, Rose Patricia, Alison. Vice pres. Consol. Ins. Agy., Norfolk, 1948-55; asst. treas. Henry Montor Assos., Inc., N.Y.C., 1956; v.p., sec. Propp & Co., Inc., N.Y.C., 1957-58; ptr. Koerner, Gordon & Co., N.Y.C., 1959-62; sr. ptnr. Gordon, Kulman Perry, and predecessor firm, N.Y.C., 1962-71, pres., chmn. bd., 1971-74; pres., chmn. bd. Palison, Inc., mems. N.Y. Stock Exch., White Plains, N.Y., 1974—; chmn. bd. Rojon, Inc., real estate and investments, Williamsburg, Va., 1979—. Mem. Harrison (N.Y.) Archtl. Rev. Bd., 1970-72, Harrison Planning Bd., 1975-77; bd. dirs. Montefiore Hosp. Assn., YM-YWHA, Lafayette Ednl. Fund., Inc., 1986—; aide de-camp to gov. State of Va., 1989—. Lt. USNR, 1953-55. Mem. Folk Art soc. (bd. dirs. 1987—), U.S. Naval Acad. Alumni Assn. (life). Clubs: Stock Exch. Luncheon (N.Y.C.), Poinciana (Palm Beach, Fla.), Town Point (Norfolk, Va.), Kingsmill Golf (Williamsburg, Va.). Home: 113 Elizabeth Meriwether Williamsburg VA 23185 Office: Drawer JG Williamsburg VA 23187

GORDON, CHRISTOPHER JACQUES, broadcasting executive; b. N.Y.C., Feb. 13, 1955; s. Nicholas and Gladys (Sack) G. AB, U. Chgo., 1976. Reporter City News Bur., Chgo., 1973-75; account exec. Television, Radio Age Mag., N.Y.C., 1978-79; account exec. John Blair Television, Chgo., 1979-80, N.Y.C., 1980-83; mgr. sta. sales LBS Communications, N.Y.C., 1983-85, v.p., mgr. sta. sales, 1985; account exec. D.L. Taffner Ltd., N.Y.C., 1985-87; exec. v.p. Palladium TV Distbn. Inc., N.Y.C., 1987—. Mem. Phi Gamma Delta. Club: Univ. (N.Y.C.). Home: 6000 Independence Ave Bronx NY 10471 Office: Palladium TV Distbn Inc 444 Madison Ave New York NY 10022

GORDON, DANIEL PAUL, jewelry company executive; b. Houston, 1942; married. B.S., Wharton Sch. Bus., U. Pa., 1963. With Gordon Jewelry Corp., Houston, 1963—, v.p., 1969-77, sr. v.p. ops., from 1977, now pres., chief exec. officer, also dir. Office: Gordon Jewelry Corp 820 Fannin St Houston TX 77002 *

GORDON, DIANNA LYNN, savings and loan executive; b. Corpus Christi, Tex., Mar. 25, 1952; d. George David and Betty Kathleen (Smith) McFarlin; m. Randal Lamar Gordon, Apr. 10, 1976; children: Cherie Lynn, Randal Duane. Student, Del Mar Jr. Coll., Corpus Christi, 1971-72, U. Tex., 1973-75, St. Edwards U., Austin, Tex., 1981, Inst. Fin. Edn., 1975-81. With Franklin Savs. Assn., Austin, 1974—, div. head, sr. v.p. mortgage loan svcing., 1986, div. head., sr. v.p. collateral and collections, 1986—; cons. Project Bus., Jr. Achievement, Austin, 1982-84. Com. mem. budget and fin. Downtown Austin Ptnrs., 1986-88, govt. affairs com., 1988—. Mem. Fin. Mgrs. Soc. (pres. 1984-87). Republican. mem. Ch. of Christ. Office: Franklin Fed Bancorp 600 Congress Ave Ste 1400 Austin TX 78701

GORDON, GEORGE GARY, industrial psychologist, consulting firm executive; b. Jersey City, Apr. 18, 1935; s. Abe and Jean (Eskow) G.; m. Janet Sue Rosenblatt, Dec. 29, 1958; children: Cynthia Beth, Alexander Harris. BA, Rutgers U., 1957; MS, Purdue U., 1961, PhD, 1963. Lic. psychologist. Sr. research cons. Prudential Ins. Co., Newark, 1963-66; project dir. Ednl. Testing Services, Princeton, N.J., 1966-69; exec. v.p. Hay Mgmt. Cons., Phila., 1970-87; assoc. prof. Rutgers U., Newark, 1987—. Author: Managing Management Climate, 1979. Served to 1st lt. USAF, 1957-60. Mem. Am. Psychol. Assn., Acad Mgmt. Republican. Jewish. Office: Hay Mgmt Cons 229 S 18th St Rittenhouse Sq Philadelphia PA 19103

GORDON, HERBERT DAVID, advertising executive; b. Medford, Mass., Sept. 18, 1938; s. Roy Young and Anna Belle (Stanley) G.; m. Annemarie, Nov. 6, 1971; children—Michael, Christian, Stephen. B.A. in Econs., Tufts U., 1960; grad. A.M.P., Harvard U., 1985. Media dir. Frye Sills, Denver, 1969-71; media supr., assoc. media dir. Ketchum Advt., Pitts., 1971-72; media dir. Ketchum Advt., 1972-80, v.p., 1974-76, sr. v.p., 1976—, dir. media and ops., 1978-80, dir. media services, 1980—; exec. v.p. Ketchum Yellow Pages, Pitts., 1979-81; pres. Ketchum Yellow Pages, 1981—; exec. v.p. Ketchum Communications Inc., Pitts., also bd. dirs. Mem. McIntyre Area Civic Assn., Pitts., 1978-85; bd. dirs. Jr. Achievement of Southwestern Pa. 1st lt. USAF, 1960-65. Mem. Audit Bur. Circulations, Bus. Profl. Advt. Assn., Nat. Yellow Pages Agy. Assn., Nat. Yellow Pages Service Assn., Pitts. Advt. Club, Pitts. Advt. Racquet Assn. (pres. 1980). Republican. Episcopalian. Clubs: Duquesne, Edgeworth, Allegheny Athletic (Pitts.). Home: 309 Orchard Ln Sewickley PA 15143 Office: Ketchum Yellow Pages 6 PPG Pl Pittsburgh PA 15222 *

GORDON, HOWARD LYON, advertising and marketing executive; b. Chgo., Oct. 8, 1930; s. Milton Arthur and Betty Z. (Ginsburg) G.; BS, U. Ill., 1953; MS, Northwestern U., 1954, MBA, 1962; m. Lois Jean Kaufman, Aug. 21, 1955; children: Carolyn Ann, Leslie Meredith. Mktg. rsch. mgr. Marsteller Inc., advt., Chgo., 1960-68, v.p. mktg. services Marsteller Inc. and Burson Marsteller, Chgo., 1968-76; dir. client service Britt and Frerichs Inc., mktg. research and advt. cons., Chgo., 1977-78, sr. v.p., 1978—, prin., 1979—, ptnr., 1986—; lectr. advt. and mktg. Northwestern U., 1963—, vis. prof. Medill grad. studies in advt., 1981—; advt. prof. in residence No. Ill. U., DeKalb, 1974-76; lectr., seminar leader Am. Mgmt. Assn., 1965-72; bd. dirs. Bus. Advt. Resch. Coun., 1985—, chmn. life style rsch. com., 1985—; mem. alumni awards com. Medill Sch. Northwestern U., 1986, fund-raising com. Kellogg Grad. Sch. Northwestern U., 1986—. Contbr. articles to profl. publs. Regional chmn. Crusade of Mercy, Evanston, Ill., 1969; founding dir. Alumni Assn. Medill Sch., 1984—; adv. council athletic dept., Northwestern U., 1985—. With AUS, 1954-56. Recipient award Dept. Def., 1956, Alumni Award Northwestern U., 1989. Mem. Am. Mktg. Assn. (dir., v.p. mktg. mgmt.), Northwestern U. Faculty, Kellogg Alumni Assn. (program com.), Sigma Delta Chi. Contbr. articles to profl. publs. and mktg. texts. Office: 400 E Randolph St Chicago IL 60601

GORDON, JAMES C., jewelry company executive; b. 1946. BBA, U. Tex., 1969. With Gordon Jewelry Corp., 1961—, v.p., later sr. v.p., 1972-82, exec. v.p., 1982—, now also chief operating officer, also bd. dirs. Office: Gordon Jewelry Corp 820 Fannin St Houston TX 77002 *

GORDON, JOHN CHALMERS, pharmaceutical company executive; b. Mecklenburg, Va., Aug. 1, 1925; s. James Thomas and Agnes (Pomeroy) G.; m. Gertrude Elizabeth Hoyt; children: Camille Grabb, John Hoyt, Thomas David, Susan G. Shelton. BS in Bus. Adminstrn., U. Richmond, 1949. Cert. adminstrv. mgr. Various positions A.H. Robins Co. Inc., Richmond, Va., 1949-79, asst. v.p. adminstrv. services, 1979-84, v.p. adminstrv. services, 1984—. Past chmn. Va. State Adv. Council on Vocat. Edn., Blacksburg, 1976-77, adv. com. on vocat./tech. edn. Va. Commonwealth U., Richmond, 1985. Served with USN, 1944-46. Mem. Adminstrv. Mgmt. Soc. (pres. Richmond chpt. 1971-72, ambassador 1987), Office Automation Assn. Richmond (pres. 1974-75), Va. Telecommunications Assn. (pres. 1981-82), Engrs. Club. Presbyterian. Office: A H Robins Co Inc 1407 Cummings Dr Richmond VA 23261

GORDON, MELVIN SHELDON, consulting executive; b. N.Y.C., July 1, 1927; s. Abraham and Beatrice (Brecker) G.; m. Jane Read Fox, June 5, 1949 (div. Sept. 1968); m. Karen R. Kreidler, Mar. 21, 1971; children: Ellen A. Rosenkranz, Mark S. BA, U. Chgo., 1949. CLU, chartered fin. cons. Pres. Conestoga Vineyards, Birchrunville, Pa., 1957-74; ptnr. Corp. and Profl. Planning Assocs., Inc., Phila., 1960-70; pres. Corp. and Profl. Planning Assocs., Inc., West Chester, Pa., 1970—. Editor: Restaurant Guide to North America. Served with USMC, 1944-45. Mem. Million Dollar Round Table, Top of the Table, Internat. Forum, Assn. Advanced Life Underwriting, Chester County Life Underwriters, Am. Soc. CLU's, Internat. Wine and Food Soc. (N.Am. bd. of govs., pres. Phila. chpt. 1981-83), Lotos Club (N.Y.C.), Explorer's Club. Office: CAPP Assocs Inc 101 E Chestnut St PO Box 800 West Chester PA 19381

GORDON, NEIL ROGER, financial executive; b. Bronx, Jan. 17, 1948; s. Sherman S. and Miriam (Lerner) G.; m. Saralee Pepper, Oct. 16, 1980; children: Douglas, Rebecca. BS in Acctg., Pa. State U., 1969. CPA, N.Y. Staff acct. Deloitte Haskins & Sells, N.Y.C., 1969-77; controller Westbury Resources, Inc., N.Y.C., 1977-79; dir. fin. Empire of Carolina, Inc., N.Y.C., 1979-82; mgr. treasury services Centronics Data Computer Corp., Hudson, N.H., 1982-87; dir. treasury services Centronics Corp., Nashua, N.H., 1987; treas. Ekco Group, Inc., Nashua, 1987—. Chmn. Glen Rock (N.J.) Environ. and Ecology Commn., 1980; bd. dirs. Andover (Mass.) Soccer Assn., 1988. Served with USNR, 1970-72, Vietnam. Mem. Am. Inst. CPAs, Glen Rock Jaycees (pres. 1980). Office: Ekco Group Inc 98 Spit Book Rd Nashua NH 03062

GORDON, PAUL C(URTIS), electronics and communications service company executive; b. Balt., Apr. 8, 1927; s. Paul C. and Viola V. (Primrose) G.; m. Maureen Angela Cadogan, Apr. 23, 1955; children: Jeanne, Paul, Maureen, Thomas, Timothy. B.S. in Bus. Adminstrn. cum laude, U. Notre Dame, 1949; M.B.A., N.Y. U., 1955. Profl. basketball player for Balt. Bullets, 1949-50; spl. agt. FBI, 1950-57; with ITT Corp., 1957—; now chmn., pres. ITT Fed. Electric Corp., Paramus, N.J.; and corp. v.p. ITT. Bd. govs. Ramapo Coll. N.J. Served with USNR, 1945-46. Mem. Commerce and Industry Assn. N.J. (bd. dirs., past chmn.). Office: Fed Electric Corp 621 Industrial Ave Paramus NJ 07652

GORDON, PETER JOHN DOUGLAS, investment company executive, portfolio manager; b. Falkirk, Scotland, Nov. 3, 1946; came to U.S., 1954; s. Douglas and E. Mary (Durant) G.; m. Susan Wayne Powell, Dec.3, 1966 (dec. Sept. 1974); 1 child, Allison; m. Connie Jean Johnson, Nov. 8, 1975; 1 child, Ian. BA in Econs., U. Louisville, 1969; MBA, Loyola Coll., Balt., 1983. Trust officer Irwin Union Bank & Trust Co., Columbus, Ind., 1970-72, v.p. investments, 1973-77; registered rep. J.J.B. Hilliard and W.L. Lyons, Columbus, 1972-73; v.p., dir. T. Rowe Price Assocs., Balt., 1977—; pres., bd. dirs., chmn. adv. com. T. Rowe Price Tax-Free Funds; mem. Mcpl. Securities Rulemaking Bd., Washington, 1983-86. Mem. Fin. Analysts Fedn. Office: T Rowe Price Assocs Inc 100 E Pratt St Baltimore MD 21202

GORDON, RICHARD ANDREW, marketing analyst; b. Queens, N.Y., Aug. 1, 1955; s. Norman Lawrence and Pauline (Lemberg) G.; m. Pia Rochelle Gordon, May 31, 1981. PhD in Music History (hon.), Columbia U., 1981; BS in Mktg., SUNY, Old Westbury, 1987; postgrad., St. John's U., Jamaica, N.Y., 1988—. Pres. Marmette Records, Inc., 1977-82; mem. mktg. staff Entenmann's div. Gen. Foods Corp., Bay Shore, N.Y., 1987; mktg. analyst Synergy Gas Corp., Farmingdale, N.Y., 1988—. Composer Discombobulation Blues, 1978. Mem. Reb Mor Found. (pres. 1984—). Home: PO Box 5 Amityville NY 11701 Office: Synergy Gas Corp 175 Price Pkwy Farmingdale NY 11735

GORDON, RICHARD JOSEPH, gas distribution company executive; b. Waterloo, Iowa, June 6, 1933; s. William Cheyne and Zeta Margaret (Clark) G.; m. Nancy Lee Varrington, May 10, 1957 (dec. 1974); children—William Jeffrey, Scott Richard, Linda Lee; m. Linda Louise Kurtz, Oct. 26, 1974; children—Bryan Mathew, Jennifer Lynn. B.S. in Civil Engring., Rose-Hulman Inst., 1955. Registered profl. engr., Ohio. Jr. engr. Ohio Fuel Gas Co., Columbus, 1955-56; distbn. engr. Columbia Gas of Ohio, Elyria, 1957-59, Norwalk, 1959-61; local mgr. Columbia Gas of Ohio, Oberlin, 1961-62; div. mgr. Columbia Gas of Ohio, Mansfield, 1962-63, Alliance, 1967-71; Lake Erie dist. mgr. Columbia Gas of Ohio, Norwalk, 1971-78; v.p. engring. Columbia Gas Distbn. Cos., Columbus, 1978-82, sr. v.p., 1982-88; pres. Columbia Gas of Ky., Pa., Md., N.Y., Columbus, 1988—; div. mgr. Ohio Valley Gas Co., Steubenville, 1963-67; pres. Columbia Gas of Pa., Inc., 1989—, Columbia Gas of N.Y., Inc., 1989—, Columbia Gas of Md., Inc., 1989—, Columbia Gas of Ky., Inc., 1989—; dir. subs. cos. Served to capt. U.S. Army, 1955-62. Mem. Nat. Soc. Profl. Engrs., Ohio State Soc. Profl. Engrs., Franklin County Soc. Profl. Engrs. (trustee). Republican. Roman Catholic.

GORDON, RICHARD LEWIS, mineral economics educator; b. Portland, Maine, June 19, 1934; s. Benjamin M. and Sara I. Gordon; m. Nancy Ellen Helfand, June 8, 1958; children: David William, Benjamin Mark. A.B., Dartmouth Coll., 1956; Ph.D., MIT, 1960. Econ. analyst Union Carbide Corp., 1960-64; asst. economist First Nat. City Bank, N.Y.C., 1964; mem. faculty Pa. State U., State College, 1964—, prof. mineral econs., 1970—; Shell lectr. on energy econs. Surrey (Eng.) U., 1981. Author: The Evolution of Energy Policy in Western Europe, 1970, U.S. Coal and the Electric Power Industry, 1975, Coal in the U.S. Energy Market, 1978, An Economic Analysis of World Energy Problems, 1981, Reforming the Regulation of Electric Utilities, 1982, World Coal Economics, Policies and Prospects, 1987. Recipient Scholars medal The Pa. State U., 1989. Mem. AIME (chmn. council econs. 1973 Mineral Econs. award), Internat. Assn. Energy Economists, Am. Econ. Assn., Econometric Soc., Royal Econ. Soc., AAAS. Jewish. Home: 429 Kemmerer Rd State College PA 16801 Office: Pa State U 204 Walker Bldg University Park PA 16802

GORDON, ROBERT ALLEN, financial planner; b. Worcester, Mass., Oct. 17, 1955; s. Leo Eugene and Irene Dorothy (Broomhall) G.; m. Lanae Ann Dean, June 4, 1982; children: Nicholas Robert, Ashley Jolene. Student, Boston State Coll., 1974-76; BA in Econs., Framingham State Coll., 1979; cert. in fin. planning, Coll. for Fin. Planning, Denver, 1987. Realtor K&L Real Estate Inc., Springfield, Ill., 1979-83; fin. analyst bur. budget State of Ill., Springfield, 1979-81; pvt. practice fin. planning Bob Gordon & Assocs., Springfield, 1983—; lectr. Ventures Midwest Inc., Springfiel, 1983—; regional v.p. A.L. Williams, Duluth, Ga., 1983—. Mem. Inst. Cert. Fin. Planners, Am. Bus. Club (fund raiser), Internat. Assn. Fin. Planning. Office: 1414 S 5th Springfield IL 62703

GORDON, ROBERT DOUGLAS, holding company executive; b. Saskatoon, Sask., Can., Oct. 30, 1948; came to U.S., 1970; s. John Angus and Kathlyn (McManus(G.; m. Brenda Joy Mauretzen, July 30, 1982; children: Katherine, Colin. B in Commerce, U. Sask., 1970; MBA, U. Chgo., 1975, PhD (hon.). Lectr. U. Chgo., 1975-79; sr. study dir. Nat. Opinion Research, Chgo., 1983; cons. McKinsey and Co., Chgo., 1983-87; exec. v.p. First Bank System, Mpls., 1984—; chief fin. officer Lee Data Corp., Eden Prairie, Minn., 1987, pres., 1988—. Recipient spl. doctoral award Can. Council. Home: 912 Smithtown Terr Excelsior MN 55331 Office: Lee Data Corp 7075 Flying Cloud Dr Eden Prairie MN 55344

GORDON, RUTH, stockbroker, writer; b. Plain City, Ohio, June 30, 1941; d. Calvin McGowan and Cleetus Mae (Loveless) Tumlin; m. John Harold Elkinton, Dec. 10, 1970 (div. Jan. 1974); 1 child, Alyssa Susan; m. Anthony Glenn Arango, June 27, 1981. Student, U. So. Fla., 1974. Account exec. E.H. Russell & Co., Chgo., 1962-66; writer, actress N.Y.C., 1966-68; advt. mgr. Playboy Enterprises, Chgo., 1968-70; pres. The Gordon Agy., Tampa, Fla., 1971-72; v.p. corp. communications Medfield Corp., St. Petersburg, Fla., 1973-79; chmn., pres. Securities Discount Corp., Clearwater, Fla., 1979-81; br. office mgr. Fidelity Brokerage Services, Inc., Clearwater, Fla., 1981-82; investment officer Williams Securities Group, Inc., Tampa, 1982-86; syndicate mgr., registered prin. retail services Allen C. Ewing & Co., Tampa, 1986—. Recipient Best Annual Report for Individual Investor award Nat. Assn. Investment Clubs, 1977, Merit award Fin. World mag., 1977-78. Mem. Investment Assn. N.Y. Republican. Home: 4402 Beach Park Dr Tampa FL 33609 Office: Allen C Ewing & Co 600 N Florida Ave Tampa FL 33602

GORDON, STEVEN JOE, commercial general contractor; b. Winfield, Kans., Oct. 14, 1956; s. Gilbert Joe and Florence Lucille (Floyd) g.; m. Marcia Ellen Utt, June 2, 1984; 1 child, Molly. BS, Kans. State U., 1978. Sales mgr. Gordon's House of Cabinetry, Wichita, Kans., 1978-83; pres. Gordon Contruction Co., Wichita, 1983—. Active Sedgewick County Rep. Part, Wichita, 1988. Mem. Assn. of Homebuilders, Shriners, Masons, Alpa Kappa Lambda. Republican. Mem. Christian Ch. Home: 2457 Perry Ave Wichita KS 67204 Office: Gordon Constrn Co 1206 E 1st Ave Wichita KS 67214

GORDON, STUART PAUL, real estate developer, investment adviser, consultant, educator; b. Bronx, N.Y., Sept. 10, 1952; s. Irwin and Marilyn Gordon; m. Sandra Thomas, May 29, 1977; 1 child, Jessica Ryane. BA, Trenton (N.J.) State Coll., 1974; MA, U. Pacific, 1977; PhD, N.C. State U., 1981. Project mgr. Water Resources Inst. N.C. State U., Raleigh, 1979-81; cons. Nathaniel Hill & Assocs., Raleigh, 1981-82; pres., founder Gordon & Assocs., Raleigh, 1982—, Gordon Investment Realty, Inc., Raleigh, 1983—; instr. real estate N.C. State U., Raleigh, 1985—; bd. dirs. Brians Corp., Raleigh. U.S. Dept. Energy grantee, 1981. Mem. Nat. Assn. Securities Dealers, Raleigh Bd. Realtors, Comml. Listing Svc., Raleigh C. of C. Home and Office: Gordon Investment Realty Inc 6304 Lakeland Dr Raleigh NC 27612

GORDON, SYDNEY LEWIS HOWARD, banker, broker; b. Aldershot, Eng., Aug. 22, 1942; came to U.S., 1958, naturalized, 1968; s. Joseph Fenton and Vera Pamela (Garratt) G.; m. Melinda Ellen Miller, Nov. 17, 1985; children: Matthew, Danielle, Kelly, Jamie. BBA, Hofstra U., 1969. Sr. mktg. officer N.Y. Stock Exchange, 1969-73; dir. Depository Trust Co., N.Y.C., 1975-78; v.p. Chase Manhattan Bank, N.Y.C., 1978-83; v.p. Citibank, N.A., 1983-84; sr. v.p. Wall St. Clearing Co., N.Y.C., 1984-87; v.p. Citicorp, N.Y.C., 1987—; guest lectr. in field. Served with AUS, 1964-66, Vietnam. Mem. Am. Bankers Assn., Securities Industry Assn. Republican. Episcopalian. Clubs: Rockville Links, Conn. Golf Club. Home: 115 Woods End Rd Chappaqua NY 10514

GORE, DAVID CURTISS, software company executive; b. Conway, S.C., Dec. 4, 1964. BS, U. S.C., 1986. Co-owner, v.p. Gem-Clarke Co., Inc., Columbia, S.C., 1985—. Mem. Lambda Chi Alpha (treas. 1984-85). Republican. Baptist. Office: Gem-Clarke Co Inc PO Box 7304 Columbia SC 29202-7304

GOREN, WILLIAM HART, financial planning company executive; b. N.Y.C., Oct. 4, 1946; s. Shelley S. and Beulah (Schweitzer) G.; m. Barbara Kwit, May 20, 1973 (div. Mar. 1976); m. Anne Marie Diurno, June 6, 1976; children: Brent, Mariel. BS in Psychology, U. Pitts., 1968; MA in Secondary Edn., Adelphi U., 1971. cert. fin. planner, 1987; CLU; chartered fin. cons. Tchr. sci. N.Y.C. Bd. Edn., Bronx, 1968-71, dean 8th grade, 1972-74, asst. prin., 1974-77; life ins. agt. MONY Fin. Svcs., N.Y.C., 1977-82; fin. planner, investment counselor Goren & Goren Ltd., N.Y.C., 1982-85; pres., cons., fin. advisor New Age Fin. Svcs., N.Y.C., 1985—; stock broker, Atlanta, 1978—; mem. adv. council Nuveen Bond Funds, N.Y.C., 1986; salesman Annie Harper Realty, Mt. Kisco, N.Y., 1986—; instr. fin. planning, asst. dean N.Y. Ctr. for Fin. Studies, 1981—; instr. fin. planning Iona Coll., New Rochelle, N.Y.; moderator Life Underwriting Tng. Council. Soccer coach Yorktown (N.Y.) Community Athletic League. Mem. Nat. Assn. Life Underwriters, Nat. Assn. Health Underwriters, Internat. Assn. Fin. Planners, Million Dollar Round Table (speaker 1982), Westchester C. of C., Yorktown C. of C., B'nai B'rith. Jewish. Office: New Age Fin Svcs 22 Saw Mill River Rd Hawthorne NY 10532

GORGES, HEINZ AUGUST, research engineer; b. Stettin, Germany, July 22, 1913; came to U.S., 1959; s. Gustav and Marga (Benda) G.; m. Sapienza Teresa Coco, Sept. 2, 1957. ME, Tech. U. Dresden (Germany), 1938; PhD, Tech. U. Hannover (Germany), 1946. Registered profl. engr., D.C. Group leader LFA Aero Research Establishment, Braunschweig, Germany, 1940-45; with Royal Aircraft Establishment, Farnborough, Eng. 1946-49; prin. sci. officer Weapons Research Establishment, Adelaide, South Australia, 1949-59; sci. asst. George C. Marshall Space Flight Center, NASA, Huntsville, Ala., 1959-61; dir. advanced projects Cook Technol. Center, Morton Grove, Ill., 1961-62; sci. adviser Ill. Inst. Tech. Research Inst., Chgo., 1962-66; asst. v.p. environ. and phys. scis. Tracor, Inc., Austin, Tex., 1966—; v.p. Tracor-Jitco Inc. Rockville, Md., 1972-75; pres. Vineta Inc., Falls Church, Va., 1975—; prof. Redstone extension U. Ala., 1960. Fellow AIAA (assoc.); mem. ASME, Acoustical Soc. Am., N.Y. Acad. Scis. Club: Cosmos. Research super and hypersonics resources mgmt., environ. scis., system engring. and analysis. Address: 3705 Sleepy Hollow Rd Falls Church VA 22041

GORHAM, DAVID L., newspaper executive; b. Salt Lake City, Nov. 16, 1932; s. Roy B. and Leah Janet (Williams) G.; m. Carolyn J. Cartwright, Aug. 5, 1954; children—Joyce, James, Roger, Sarah, Stephen. B.S., U. Utah, 1955; M.B.A., U. Calif.-Berkeley, 1968. C.P.A., Calif. Staff Ernst & Ernst, Salt Lake City, Oakland, Calif., 1954-55, 59-63, 67-68; div. controller DeLaval Turbine, Inc., Oakland, 1963-67; treas. DeLaval Separator Co., N.Y.C., 1969-70; controller Gen. Signal Corp., N.Y.C., 1970-74; corp. controller N.Y. Times Co., N.Y.C., 1974-80, sr. v.p., chief fin. officer, 1980—. Mem. adv. com. Dean Bus. Sch. U. Calif.-Berkeley, 1984—. Served to capt. USAF, 1955-59. Mem. Am. Inst. C.P.A.s, Calif. Soc. C.P.A.s. Home: 481 W Saddle River Rd Upper Saddle River NJ 07458 Office: NY Times Co 229 W 43rd St New York NY 10036

GORHAM, LINDA JOANNE, financal planning company executive; b. Boston, June 25, 1951; d. Joseph Leo and Rose (Avila) G. AS, Northeastern U., 1975, BS, 1976; MBA, Babson Coll., 1978. Various positions Stop & Shop Co. Inc., Boston, 1974-83; sr. analyst Capital Fin. Planning, Needham, Mass., 1983-85; fin. cons. United Resources, Needham, 1985-86; mng. dir. Mingolelli Fin. Svcs., Framingham, Mass., 1986-88; v.p. Mingolelli & Assocs., Framingham, 1986-88; with Lyons Planning Group, Waltham, Mass., 1988—; adj. faculty Northeastern U., 1988—. Mem. Inst. Cert. Fin. Planners, Am. Soc. Profl. and Exec. Women, Nat. Assn. Female Execs., Babson Coll. Women Alumni in Bus., Babson Women Investors Club, Babson Mentor Program (chairwoman 1986—), Babson Women in Bus., Sigma Epsilon Rho. Office: Lyons Planning Group Ltd 51 Sawyer Rd Waltham MA 02154

GORING, PETER ALLAN ELLIOTT, real estate executive; b. Sudbury, Ont., Can., Jan. 3, 1943; s. Allan Elliott and H. Marie (Legrow) G.; m. Erica E. Pratt, Dec. 16, 1972; children: Simon, Sarah. B. Comm., Laurentian U., Sudbury, 1967. Staff acct. Clarkson Gordon & Co., Toronto, Ont., 1967-70; v.p. Canmort Cons. Ltd., Toronto, 1970-80, Wood Gundy Ltd., Toronto, 1978-80; v.p., treas. Bramalea Ltd., Toronto, 1980-85, sr. v.p. corp. fin. and treasury, 1985-86, exec. v.p. corp. fin. and treas., 1986-87, exec. v.p., treas., 1987—; bd. dirs. Bramalea Properties Ltd., Toronto, 1986—, Trilea Centres Inc., Toronto, 1986—. Bd. govs. Laurentian U., 1987; mem. rent review adv. com. to Govt. Ont., Toronto, 1986; bd. dirs. URBAN Devel. Inst. Ont., 1981-83, FAIR Rental Policy Orgn. Ont., 1985-87, dir., treas. Ont. New Home Warranty Program, 1987—. Mem. Urban Land Inst. (coun. 1986—), Fin. Execs. Inst., Inst. Chartered Accts. Ont., Ont. Club, Royal Can. Yacht Club, Toronto Hunt Club. Office: Bramalea Ltd, 1867 Yonge St, Toronto, ON Canada M4S 1Y5

GORMAN, BENJAMIN FRANK, wholesale executive; b. Lancaster, Pa., July 30, 1931; s. Benjamin Sterling and Dorothy Harriet (Musser) G. BS in Econs., Franklin and Marshall Coll., 1952. Acct. Paul S. Bertz & Co., Lancaster, 1952; asst. mgr. Gorman's Market, Lancaster, 1955-70; mgr., owner Gorman Distbrs., Lancaster, 1971-81; pres. Gorman Distbrs., Inc., Lancaster, 1982—. Served with U.S. Army, 1952-54, Korea, with Res. 1954—. Mem. Nat. Automatic Mdse. Assn., Pa. Automatic Mdse. Assn., Pa. Coin Laundry Assn., Nat. Automatic Cleaning Council, Assn. of the U.S. Army. Republican. Lutheran. Clubs: Olde Hickory Racquet (Lancaster); Artisans (Phila.). Home and Office: 351 N Mulberry St Lancaster PA 17603

GORMAN, JOHN EDWARD, management consultant; b. Aurora, Mo., Aug. 28, 1942; s. Edward Francis Jr. and Margaret Elizabeth (Moore) G.; m. Connie Ann Ausemus, Nov. 27, 1965; children: John E. Jr., Jennifer Lynn. BS in Engring., U.S. Naval Acad., 1964. Commd. ensign U.S. Navy, 1964; lt. U.S. Navy, San Diego and Honolulu; resigned U.S. Navy, 1969; mktg. rep. IBM, St. Louis, 1969-76; with mktg. support IBM, Palo Alto, Calif., 1976-78; mgr. mktg. IBM, Dallas, 1978-80, mgr. sales tng., 1980-82; dir. mgmt. cons. Coopers & Lybrand, Dallas, 1982-83, ptnr., cons., 1983—. Mem. Soc. Info. Mgmt., Royals Oaks Country Club (dir. 1988—), 2001 Club. Democrat. Roman Catholic. Office: Coopers & Lybrand 1999 Bryan St Ste 3000 Dallas TX 75201

GORMAN, JOSEPH TOLLE, corporate executive; b. Rising Sun, Ind., 1937; m. Bettyann Gorman. B.A., Kent State U., 1959; LL.B., Yale U., 1962. Assoc. Baker, Hostetler & Patterson, Cleve., 1962-67; with legal dept. TRW Inc., Cleve., 1968-69, asst. sec., 1969-70, sec., 1970-72, v.p. sr. counsel automotive worldwide ops., 1972-73, v.p., asst. gen. counsel, 1973-76, v.p., gen. counsel, 1976-80, acting head communications function, 1978, exec. v.p. indsl. and energy sector, 1980-84, exec. v.p., asst. pres., 1984-85, pres., chief operating officer, 1985—, mem. policy group, 1975—, chmn., chief exec. officer, 1988—, also bd. dirs.; bd. dirs. Soc. Corp., Soc. Nat. Bank Cleve., Standard Oil Co. Trustee Univ. Circle, Inc., Cleve. Play House, Cleve. Inst. Art, Leadership Cleve., United Way Services, Cleve. Council on World Affairs, Musical Arts Assn., Denison U.; past trustee Cleve. Fedn. Community Planning, Govtl. Research Inst.; past mem. exec. com. Ctr. of Pub. Resources Project on Dispute Resolution; bd. advisors Yale Law Sch. Urgent Issues Program. Mem. ABA, Assn. Gen. Counsel (emeritus), Ohio Bar Assn., Cleve. Bar Assn., Yale Law Sch. Assn. (exec. com.), Greater Cleve. Growth Assn. (trustee, exec. com.), U.S. C. of C. (past chmn. corp. governance and policy com.), Council on Fgn. Relations. Office: TRW Inc 1900 Richmond Rd Cleveland OH 44124 *

GORMAN, LAWRENCE JAMES, banker; b. Albany, N.Y., Mar. 22, 1948; s. Lawrence Edward and Olive Gertrude (MacDowell) G.; grad. Nat. Grad. Trust Sch., 1980; BS, Syracuse U., 1970; JD, Albany Law Sch. Union U., 1973; m. Barbara J. Pisarek, Aug. 4, 1973; children: Ryan Patrick, Michael Patrick. Admitted to N.Y. bar, 1976; assoc. Grasso, Rivizzigno & Woronov, Syracuse, 1973-76; asst. v.p. Trust and Investment div. Lincoln 1st Bank N.A., Syracuse, 1976-79; v.p. Trust and Investment div. Bank of N.Y., Syracuse, 1979-83; v.p. 1st Va. Banks, Inc., 1983-88; pres. L.J. Gorman & Assocs., Inc., 1988—; adj. prof. Onondaga County Community Coll.; faculty N.Y. State Bar, 1980-81. Dir. Our Town Fredericksburg, 1985—, pres., 1986-87; mem. investment com. Am. Cancer Soc. N.Y. State chpt., 1981-83; trustee N.Y.C. chpt. Leukemia Soc. Am., 1982-83. Mem. N.Y. State Bar Assn., Onondaga County Bar Assn. (chmn. bank liaison com. 1980-82), Fredericksburg Bar Assn., Estate Planning Council Fredericksburg (pres.). Clubs: Fredericksburg Country, Commonwealth (Fredericksburg). Lodge: Rotary. Home: 3 Russell Rd Fredericksburg VA 22405 Office: 505 Charlotte St Fredericksburg VA 22401

GORMÉZANO, KEITH STEPHEN, publisher; b. Madison, Wis., Nov. 22, 1955; s. Isadore and Miriam (Fox) G.; m. Emma Lee Rogers, Aug. 17, 1986. BGS U. Iowa, 1977; postgrad. in law U. Puget Sound, 1984-86. Pub. Le Beacon Presse, Seattle, 1980—; arbitrator Better Bus. Bur. Greater Seattle, 1987—, PSMLA, 1988-89, NASD, 1989—. Op. Improvement Found., 1980-81; pub. info. officer chmn. Iowa City Young Ams. for Freedom, 1979-81; vol. VISTA, 1982-83; dir. ACJS, Inc., 1981-82. Vice chmn. Resource Conservation Commn., Iowa City, 1979-80; bd. dirs. Seattle Mental Health Inst., 1981-83, Youth Advocates, Seattle, 1984, Atlantic St. Ctr., 1984; mem. City of Seattle Animal Control Commn., 1984-86, vice chmn., 1985-86, chmn. 1986; mem. Selective Svc. System, 1982—, vice chmn. civilan rev. bd. 742, 1985—. Mem. League United Latin Am. Citizens Amigos (chair 1984-86), U. Iowa Alumni Assn. (life). Republican. Jewish. Editor, M'godolim, 1980-81. Home: 7520 37th Ave NE #3FI Seattle WA 98115-8023 Office: PO Box 15945 Seattle WA 98115-0945

GORMLEY, DENNIS JAMES, manufacturing company executive; b. 1939. Grad., Rensselaer Poly. Inst., 1963. With Fed.-Mogul Corp., Southfield, Mich., 1963—, dir. corp. planning, 1978-79, group mgr. gen. products group, 1979-82, v.p., from 1980, exec. v.p., pres., chief operating officer, 1988—, dir., 1988—. Office: Fed-Mogul Corp PO Box 1966 Detroit MI 48235 also: Fed-Mogul Corp 26555 Northwestern Hwy Southfield MI 48034

GORMLY, WILLIAM MOWRY, financial consultant; b. Pitts., Mar. 15, 1941; s. Thomas Wilson and Lourene (Blaine) G.; m. Barbara Diesner, Aug. 21, 1965; children: Kirsten Eve, Kellie Blaine. BA in Econs., Dickinson Coll., Carlisle, Pa., 1963; postgrad. Northwestern U., 1967, DePaul U., 1968; grad. banking degree, Rutgers U., 1978. Regional mgr. Harris Bank, Chgo., 1967-69; corp. banking officer Wells Fargo Bank N.A., San Francisco, 1969-73; v.p. 4th Nat. Bank of Wichita, 1973-74, Union Nat. Bank of Pitts., 1974-79; v.p., sr. nat. accts. officer Ariz. Bank, Phoenix, 1979-82; pres. Cons. in Pub. Fin., Ltd., Scottsdale, Ariz., 1982—. Mem. Dickinson Coll. Alumni Council, 1975-80; bd. dirs. Ariz. Theatre Co., Phoenix, 1980-83; trustee Northland Pub. Library, Pitts., 1975-79. 1st lt. U.S. Army, 1963-65. Mem. Am. Hosp. Assn., Econ. Club Phoenix, Phi Delta Theta. Republican. Methodist. Office: Cons Pub Fin Ltd 23150 N Pima Rd Suite 1 Scottsdale AZ 85255

GORNTO, ALBERT BROOKS, JR., banker; b. Norfolk, Va., Aug. 23, 1929; s. Albert Brooks and Oretha (Brinn) G.; m. Barbara Joan Lassiter, Sept. 26, 1953; children: Neil Brooks, Suzanne Gornto Parr, Lynanne. BS in Bus. Adminstrn., Old Dominion U., 1956; diploma, Comml. Bankers Sch. U. Va., 1958, NABAC Sch. U. Wis., 1961, Stoner Grad. Sch. Banking Rutgers U., 1970. With Nat. Bank Commerce Norfolk, 1957-63, asst. cashier, 1958-61, cashier, 1961-63; founder Va. Nat. Bank, Norfolk, 1963, v.p., cashier, 1968-70, sr. v.p., cashier, 1970, corp. exec. officer, cashier, 1970-72, corp. exec. officer, 1972-80, exec. v.p., 1980—; founder Va. Nat. Bankshares Inc., Norfolk, 1972—, asst. sec., asst. treas., 1972-80; exec. v.p. Va. Nat. Bankshares Inc., 1980—; founder Va. Nat. Bldg. Corp., Norfolk, 1963—, sec., treas., 1963-80, v.p., 1980—, project mgr. hdqrs. bldg. and garage, 1963-68; founder Sovran Fin. Corp., Sovran Bank N.A., Norfolk, 1983, sr. exec. v.p., 1983, pres., 1988-89, pres., chief exec. officer, 1989—. Bd. dirs. Old Dominion U. Ednl. Found., Norfolk, 1964, Sentara Hosps., Norfolk, 1985, Chrysler Museum, Norfolk, 1983, Forward Hampton Rds., Norfolk, 1988, Med. Coll. Hampton Rds. Found., Norfolk, 1988; bd. dirs., trustee Sentara Health System, Norfolk, 1983. Named Disting. Alumni Old Dominion U., Norfolk, 1979, Outstanding Alumni Sch. Bus. Adminstrn. Old Dominion U., Norfolk, 1982. Mem. Assn. Bank Holding Cos., Assn. Reserve City Bankers, Va. Bankers Assn., Harbor Club (bd. dirs 1983—), Princess Anne Country Club, Town Point Club. Presbyterian. Office: Sovran Fin Corp 1 Commercial Pl Norfolk VA 23510

GORR, IVAN WILLIAM, rubber company executive; b. Toledo; s. Paul Robert and Edna Louise (Wandt) G.; m. Dorothy J. Brandt, June 21, 1951; children: Louise (Mrs. Gary Stephenson), Jean (Mrs. Donald Jones), Robert C., Amy S., Sally M. B.S. in Bus. Adminstrn., U. Toledo, 1951. C.P.A., Ohio. Prin. Arthur Young & Co., Toledo, Ohio, 1953-72; corp. controller Cooper Tire & Rubber Co., Findlay, Ohio, 1972-75, chief fin. officer, 1975-82, treas., 1976-77, exec. v.p., treas., 1977-82, pres., chief operating officer, 1982—; dir. First Ohio Bancshares Inc., Toledo, Cooper Tire & Rubber Co. Chmn., pres. Blanchard Valley Health Assn., Findlay, 1982-85, bd. dirs., 1974-88; chmn. bus. adv. council U. Toledo, 1986-88; advisor Findlay Area Arts Council. With U.S. Army, 1951-53, Korea. Mem. Nat. Assn. Accountants (pres. Northwestern Ohio chpt. 1977), Ohio Soc. C.P.A.'s (bd. dirs. 1972). Republican. Lutheran. Clubs: Rotary, Findlay Country. Home: 1705 Windsor Pl Findlay OH 45840 Office: Cooper Tire & Rubber Co Lima & Western Aves Findlay OH 45840

GORSKE, ROBERT HERMAN, lawyer, arbitrator; b. Milw., June 8, 1932; s. Herman Albert and Lorraine (McDermott) G.; m. Antoinette Dujick, Aug. 28, 1954; 1 child, Judith Mary (Mrs. Charles H. McMullen). Student, Milw. State Tchrs. Coll., 1949-50; B.A. cum laude, Marquette U., 1953, J.D. magna cum laude, 1955; LL.M. (W.W. Cook fellow), U. Mich., 1959; student, Hague Acad. Internat. Law, The Netherlands, 1981. Bar: Wis. bar 1955, D.C. bar 1968, U.S. Supreme Ct. bar 1970. Assoc. firm Quarles, Spence & Quarles, Milw., 1955-56; atty. Allis-Chalmers Mfg. Co., West Allis, Wis., 1956-62; instr. law U. Mich. Law Sch., Ann Arbor, 1958-59; lectr. law Marquette U. Law Sch., Milw., 1963; assoc. firm Quarles, Herriott & Clemons, Milw., 1962-64; atty. Wis. Electric Power Co., Milw., 1964-67, gen. counsel, 1967—, v.p., 1970-72, 76—; mem. firm Quarles & Brady, Milw., 1972-76; gen. counsel Wis. Energy Corp., Milw., 1981—. Contbr. articles to profl. jours.; Editor-in-chief: Marquette Law Rev, 1954-55. Bd. dirs. Guadalupe Children's Med. Dental Clinic, Inc., Milw., 1976-86; trustee Ronald McDonald House, Wauwatosa, Wis., 1987—. Mem. State Bar Wis., Am. Bar Assn., Edison Electric Inst. (vice chmn. legal com. 1975-77, chmn. 1977-79), Am. Arbitration Assn. (panelist comml. arbitrators 1985—), Ctr. for Pub. Resources (com. on alt. dispute resolution 1984—). Home: 12700 Stephen Pl Elm Grove WI 53122 Office: Wis Electric Power Co 231 W Michigan St Box 2046 Milwaukee WI 53201

GORSUCH, LEONARD FRANCIS, real estate developer; b. Lancaster, Ohio, Aug. 12, 1944; s. Frank L. Gorsuch and Mary M. Kurtz; married; children: Jennifer, Elizabeth, Alison. BS in Bus., Wittenburg U., Springfield, Ohio, 1966; postgrad., Ohio U., 1971. Salesman Gorsuch Inc. Real Estate, Lancaster, 1969-71; salesman Fairfield Homes, Inc., Lancaster, 1971-75, exec. v.p., 1975-79, pres., 1979—; chmn. bd. zoning appeals, Lancaster, 1981—. Bd. dirs. Jr. Achievement, YMCA; mem. Builder's Coun. Columbus, 1989, Columbus Builders Industry Assn. Served to 1st lt. U.S. Army, 1966-69, Vietnam. Mem. Lancaster Real Estate Bd. (pres. 1975-76), Lancaster Home Builders Assn. (pres. 1973-74), Lancaster C. of C. (pres. 1982, bd. dirs. 1975-82), Columbus Apt. Assn., VFW, Ohio Apt. Assn. (bd. dirs. 1989—). Republican. Presbyterian. Club: Lancaster Country (pres. 1983). Lodges: Rotary, Masons. Office: PO Box 190 Lancaster OH 43130

GORTER, JAMES POLK, investment banker; b. Balt., Dec. 10, 1929; s. T. Poultney and Swan (Deford) G.; m. Audrey Fentress; children: James Jr., David F., Mary H. A.B., Princeton U., 1951; postgrad., London Sch. Econ., 1951-52. Ptnr. Goldman, Sachs & Co., 1956-88, ltd. ptnr., 1989—; chmn. Baker, Fentress & Co., Chgo., 1989—. Vice chmn. Lake Forest Coll.; mem. adv. Northwestern U. Kellogg Sch. Mgmt. Served with USN, 1952-55. Clubs: Chicago Commonwealth, Chicago, Economic, Commercial; Metropolitan (Chgo.). Office: Baker Fentress & Co 200 W Madison St Ste 3510 Chicago IL 60606

GORUP, GREGORY JAMES, marketing executive; b. Kansas City, Kans., Mar. 27, 1948; s. Mike and Helen F. Gorup; m. Kathleen Susan Grogan, Apr. 12, 1986; 1 child, Michael Thomas. B.A. in Econs., St. Benedict Coll., 1970; M.B.A., U. Pa., 1972. Market analyst product planning and devel. dept. Citibank, N.Y.C., 1972-73, market planning officer corp. product mgmt. div., 1973-74, product mgr. securities services, 1974-75; v.p., dir. product devel. Irving Trust Co. N.Y.C., 1975-80, mgr. product mgmt. dept., 1980-81; v.p. mktg. Credit Suisse, U.S. area, 1981-84; sr. cons. Wesley, Brown and Bartle, N.Y.C., 1985-86; bank mktg. mgr. Digital Equipment Corp., N.Y.C., 1986-87; money mktg. mgr. Reuters N.Am., 1987-88; pres. Gorup Assocs., 1988—. Mem. fund-raising com. Big Bros. of N.Y., 1975—. Mem. Am. Mgmt. Assn., Ducks Unltd. Republican. Roman Catholic. Club: Wharton Bus. Sch., Princeton of N.Y. (N.Y.C.). Home: 47 Kingsbury Rd New Rochelle NY 10804 Office: Reuters Info Svcs 1700 Broadway New York NY 10019

GORVETT, ROBERT L., accountant; b. Chgo., May 13, 1940; s. Charles W. and Nina M. (Phillips) G.; m. Lou J. Luske, Aug. 19, 1961; children: Scott, Gayle. BSBA, U. Denver, 1962. CPA. Mng. ptnr. Price Waterhouse, Richmond, Va., 1973-82; mng. ptnr. Milw., 1982-88, Hartford, Conn., 1988—; mem. policy bd. N.Y.C., 1986—. Bd. dirs. Jr. Achievement Wis., Milw., 1982—, Milw. Ballet, 1983—, Milw. Symphony Orch., 1984—. Mem. Am. Inst. CPA's, Wis. Inst. CPA's. Republican. Congregationalist. Office: Price Waterhouse 1 Financial Pla Hartford CT 06103

GOSE, RICHARD VERNIE, lawyer; b. Hot Springs, S.D., Aug. 3, 1927; s. Vernie O. and Mame K. (Thompson) G.; BS, U. Wyo., 1950; MS in Engring., Northwestern U., 1955; LLB, George Washington U., 1967; JD, George Washington U., 1968; children—Beverly Marie, Donald Paul, Celeste Marlene. Bar: N.Mex. 1967, U.S. Supreme Ct. 1976, Wyo. 1979. Exec. asst. to U.S. Senator Hickey, Washington, 1960-62; mgr. E.G. & G., Inc., Washington, 1964-66; asst. atty. gen. State of N.Mex., Santa Fe, 1967-70; sole practice law, Santa Fe, 1967—; assoc. prof. engring. U. Wyo., 1957-60; owner, mgr. Gose & Assocs., Santa Fe, 1967-78; pvt. practice law, Casper, Wyo., 1978-83; co-chmn. Henry Jackson for Pres., M.Mex., 1976, Wyo. Johnson for Pres., 1960. With U.S. Army, 1950-52. Registered profl. engr., N.Mex., Wyo. Mem. 1st Jud. Dist. Bar Assn. (past pres.), N.Mex. Bar Assn., Wyo. Bar Assn., Phi Delta Theta, Pi Tau Sigma, Sigma Tau. Methodist. Lodge: Masons. Home and Office: PO Box 8301 Santa Fe NM 87504

GOSLINE, NORMAN ABBOT, real estate appraiser, consultant; b. Gardiner, Maine, Nov. 6, 1935; s. Arthur N. and Katherine R. (Wadsworth) G.; m. Shirlene Heath; children: Lee Demers, Jeffrey C., Mark A., Jolene Hoch Collins, Ellen M. Hoch, William K. Hoch Jr. BA, U. Maine, 1957. Realtor, Gardiner, 1959—; mem. faculty (part-time) U. Maine, Augusta, 1973-81; cons. in real estate to various agys. and firms in No. New Eng., 1965—. Past mem. Gardiner Planning Bd. Named Realtor of the Yr., Kennebec Valley Bd. Realtors, 1967. Mem. Am. Inst. of Real Estate Appraisers (pres. N.E. chpt. 1985), Soc. of Real Estate Appraisers (pres. Maine chpt. 1975-76, 81-82), Nat. Assn. Realtors (bd. dirs. 1967), Maine Assn. Realtors (pres. 1967) Am. Soc. Real Estate Counselors, Kennebec Valley Bd. Realtors (pres. 1963-64), Rotary (Paul Harris fellow), Shriner. Home: 87 West Hill Rd Gardiner ME 04345 Office: PO Box 247 Gardiner ME 04345

GOSNELL, F. LAURENCE, electronics company sales executive; b. Auburn, N.Y., July 5, 1925; s. Frank L. and (Helen) Evelyn (Conard) G.; BS in Engring. with highest honors, Princeton U., 1946; MBA, Harvard U. Grad. Sch. Bus. Adminstrn., 1954; m. Marilyn J. Zneimer, Oct. 11, 1952; children: James L., Elizabeth M., Peter W., Andrew C. Mgmt. analyst aircraft nuclear propulsion dept. Gen. Electric Co., Evendale, Ohio, 1954-56; sr. sales engr. Weston Instruments, Wellesley, Mass., 1956-60; v.p. sales and market devel. Wang Labs., Tewksbury, Mass., 1960-68; dir. mktg. Bolt, Beranek & Newman, Cambridge, Mass., 1968-69; regional mgr. Measurement Instruments, Inc., Wellesley, Mass., 1969-73; v.p. corp. devel. Tranti Systems, Inc., North Billerica, Mass., 1973—; staff instr. engring. and oceanology Naval Res. Officers Sch., Boston, 1956-66; dir. Auto Veyor, Inc., Boston, 1983—. Trustee, New Eng. Bapt. Hosp., Boston, 1969—, chmn. Sch. Nursing com., 1971—, devel. com., 1985-87; bd. govs. Vol. Trustees of Not-for-Profit Hosps., Washington, 1982—; bd. dirs. Christian Community Found., 1982—; vestryman Trinity Ch., Boston, 1964-70. lay reader St. Andrews Episcopal Ch., Wellesley, 1980—, vestryman, 1984-87; vice chmn. for West Suburban Boston, Princeton U. Alumni Schs. Com., 1975-85, chmn., 1985-87. Served to lt. comdr. USNR, 1943-46, 51-53. Mem. IEEE, Instrument Soc. Am. (sr.; pres. Boston sect. 1964-65), Diploma Nurses Assn., Harvard Bus. Sch. Assn. Boston, Princeton Assn. New Eng. (dir. 1980-87), Tau Beta Pi. Republican. Clubs: Nehoiden Golf; Princeton of New York; Wellesley Coll. Office: E K Shriver Ctr 200 Trapelo Rd Waltham MA 02254

GOSS, ARTHUR BURNETT, II, accountant; b. Bellevue, Ohio, Oct. 21, 1961; s. Herbert John Goss and Betty Mae (Chase) Tibboles; m. Shari Dorlene Lovins, Sept. 10, 1983. BSBA, Ohio State U., 1985. CPA, Ohio. Supervising sr. acct. Peat Marwick Main & Co., Columbus, Ohio, 1985—. Loaned exec. United Way Franklin County, Columbus, 1986, co-chmn. lead community svcs. com., 1987, 88. Mem. Ohio Soc. CPA's, Phi Eta Sigma, Beta Gamma Sigma. Republican. Roman Catholic. Office: Peat Marwick Main & Co Two Nationwide Pla Columbus OH 43215

GOSS, DANIEL FREDERICK, financial consultant; b. Haverhill, Mass., Dec. 27, 1932; s. Daniel T. and Edna A. (Currier) G.; B.S. cum laude, Johnson and Wales Coll., 1976; m. Donna S. Muirhead, Dec. 1973; children by previous marriage—Karleen, Laurel, Dana. Joined U.S. Air Force, 1951, advanced through grades to master sgt., 1968; with Hdqrs. USAF, Office of Surgeon Gen. for Staffing and Edn., 1965-68, ret., 1971; controller Pinal County Hosp., Florence, Ariz., 1971-72; sr. auditor Blue Cross Ariz., Phoenix, 1972-74, Blue Cross R.I., Providence, 1974-76; reimbursement specialist Meml. Hosp., Pawtucket, R.I., 1976; dir. adminstrn. and fin. Marlborough (Mass.)-Westborough Community Mental Health Center, 1977-80; bus. mgr. Solomon Mental Health Center, 1980-85; mem. fin. com. Danvers State Hosp., 1980-84. Decorated Air Force Commendation medal with 2 oak leaf clusters. Methodist. Clubs: Masons, K.P., Order Eastern Star. Home and Office: 240 Five Iron Dr Mulberry FL 33860

GOTKIN, MICHAEL STANLEY, lawyer; b. Washington, Aug. 15, 1942; s. Charles and Florence (Rosenberg) G.; A.A., Montgomery Community Coll., 1962; B.S., Columbia U., 1964; J.D., Vanderbilt U., 1967; m. Diana Rubin, Aug. 22, 1964; children—Lisa, Steven. Admitted to D.C. bar, 1968, Tenn. bar, 1973; trial atty. Bur. Restraint of Trade, FTC, Washington, 1967-70; atty. H.J. Heinz Co., Pitts., 1970-73; partner firm Moseley & Gotkin, Nashville, 1973; atty. K.F.C. Corp., Louisville, 1974-75; sr. v.p., gen. counsel Farley Candy Co., Skokie, Ill., 1975—, also dir.; pres. World Consolidated Industries Inc. Mem. ABA, Am. Corp. Counsel Assn. (v.p., bd. dirs. Chgo. chpt.), D.C. Bar Assn., Tenn. Bar Assn., Montgomery Community Coll. Assn. (past pres.), Skokie C. of C. (past pres., dir.), Columbia U. Alumni Assn., Candy Prodn. Club, Vanderbilt U. Alumni Assn. Club: Sportsman's Country (Northbrook, Ill.). Lodge: B'nai Brith. Office: 4820 Searle Pkwy Skokie IL 60077

GOTSHALL, JAN DOYLE, certified financial planner; b. Pa., Nov. 5, 1942; d. Edward Albert and Rose M. (Leahy) Doyle; m. Ralph M. Gotshall Jr., Dec. 24, 1963; children: Rosemarie, Annmarie, Elizabeth Marie. AA, Neuman Coll., 1979; postgrad., Am. Coll., Bryn Mawr, 1988—. Co-founder Radnor Planning Assocs., Devon, Pa., 1979-82; fin. cons. Exeter Fin. Svcs. Co., Devon, 1982-85; owner, pres. GM Fin. Planners, Devon, 1985—. Minority-majority insp. Del. County Electorate, Broomall, Pa., 1973-83; mem. fin. bd. St. Pius X Ch., Broomall, 1988. Mem. Inst. Cert. Fin. Planners (cert. Fin. Planner 1982, pres. 1986-87, chmn. 1987-89), Internat. Assn. Fin. Planners (v.p. 1980-88), Nat. Assn. Ins. Women (cert. Profl. Ins. Woman 1985, bd. dirs. local chpt. 1980-82), Del. County Estate Planning Coun. (exec. com. 1989-90). Republican. Home: 304 Rose Ln Broomall PA 19008 Office: GM Fin Planners 15 N Devon Blvd Box 675 Devon PA 19333

GOTSOPOULOS, BARBARA LYNN, communications consultant; b. Paterson, N.J., Mar. 16, 1948; d. Albert Raymond and Vivian Betty (Polkoph) Parker; m. Nicholas Solon Gotsopoulos, Mar. 15, 1970. BS, Rensselaer Poly. Inst., 1969. Prin. in wholesale distbg. co. Hollywood, Fla., 1981-84; pvt. practice commodities trading cons. Hollywood, 1984-87; pres. Blue Springs Capital Corp., Hollywood, 1985-86, 1st Fla. Commodities, Inc., North Lauderdale, 1987; ptnr. Multinat. Svcs., Hollywood, 1986-87; br. office mgr. Ind. Brokers Group, Inc., North Lauderdale, 1987; asst. to sr. v.p. E.F. Hutton and Co., Inc., North Miami Beach, Fla., 1987-88, Prudential-Bache Securities, North Miami Beach, 1988; asst. sr. v.p. Telus Communications, North Miami, 1988—. Mem. Nat. Assn. Female Execs. (charter), United Greeks Am. (co-founder), Alpha Psi Omega. Republican. Home: PO Box 183 Hallandale FL 33009

GOTTFRIED, IRA SIDNEY, management consulting executive; b. Bronx, N.Y., Jan. 4, 1932; s. Louis and Augusta (Champagne) G.; m. Judith Claire Rosenberg, Sept. 19, 1954; children: Richard Alan, Glenn Steven, David Aaron. B.B.A., CCNY, 1953, M.B.A., U.S.C., 1959. Sales mgr. Kleerpak Plastics, North Hollywood, Calif., 1956-57; head systems and procedures Hughes Aircraft Co., Culver City, Calif., 1957-60; mgr. corp. bus. systems The Aerospace Corp., El Segundo, Calif., 1960-61; dir. adminstrn. Eldon Industries, Inc., Hawthorne, Calif., 1962; mgr. info. systems Litton Industries Inc., Woodland Hills, Calif., 1963-64; exec. v.p. Norris & Gottfried, Inc., Los Angeles, 1964-69; pres. Gottfried Cons., Inc., 1970-85; exec. ptnr. Coopers & Lybrand, CPA's, 1985-88; v.p. Cresap Consultants, 1988—; chmn., dir. Mgmt. Adv. Services, Inc., 1968—; vice chmn. ACME Inc., 1984-85; dir., mem. exec. com. Blue Cross of Calif., 1968-77. Contbr. articles in field to prof. jours. Bd. dirs. ARC, 1980—, Univ. Synagogue, 1986—. Served with USNR, 1953-56. Recipient Pres.'s award United Hosp. Assn. Mem. Inst. Mgmt. Cons. (cert.), Am. Arbitration Assn., Data Processing Mgmt. Assn. (life), Alpha Phi Omega (life). Jewish. Clubs: Brentwood Country, Palm Valley Country. Lodge: Rotary. Home: 12118 La Casa Ln Los Angeles CA 90049

GOTTFRIED, MAX, medical equipment manufacturing executive; b. Toledo, Aug. 27, 1921; s. Morris and Gussie (Yerzy) G.; student Toledo U., 1939-40, 46-48; children—Brent Morris, Mark Ellis. Sales mgr. Columbus Hosp. Supply Co., Toledo, 1951-60; v.p. Jobst Inst., Toledo, 1960-78; pres. Gottfried Med., Inc., 1981—. Served with AUS, 1940-45. Mem. Aerospace Med. Assn., Assn. for Advancement Med. Instrumentation, Health Care Exhibitors Assn. (dir.). Patentee med. products. Home: 10145 Avienda Del Rio Delray Beach FL 33446 Office: 3350 W Laskey Rd Unit 10 Toledo OH 43623

GOTTLIEB, BARRY NELSON, sales executive; b. Bklyn., Feb. 2, 1944; s. George J. and Anne (Berman) G.; B.A., C. W. Post Coll., 1964; m. Madeline Cotler, July 8, 1967; children—Penni, Stacey. Nat. sales mgr. Mita Copystar, Clifton, N.J., 1973-76; br. sales mgr. Savin Corp., Lake Success, N.Y., 1976; dist. sales mgr. Royal Typewriter, N.Y.C., 1976; v.p. sales Profl. Sports Publs., N.Y.C., 1976—. Office: 600 3d Ave New York NY 10016

GOTTLIEB, JEROME, television production company executive; b. Bklyn., Sept. 4, 1942; s. Saul and Sylvia (Friedman) G.; children: Benjamin, Jonathan. B.A., Hamilton Coll., 1964; J.D., NYU, 1970. Bar: N.Y. 1971. Atty. Screen Gems, N.Y.C., 1971-74; dir. bus. affairs Columbia Pictures TV, Burbank, Calif., 1974-76; bus. affairs exec. William Morris Agy., Beverly Hills, Calif., 1976-78; v.p. bus. affairs Viacom Prodns., Studio City, Calif., 1978-80, Universal TV, Universal City, Calif., 1980-81; exec. v.p. MGM/UA TV, Culver City, Calif., 1982-85; sr. v.p. Lorimar-Telepictures Inc., 1985—. Contbr. articles to profl. jours. Mem. Acad. TV Arts and Scis., Hollywood Radio and TV Soc. Democrat. Jewish. Office: Lorimar-Telepictures Inc 10202 W Washington Blvd Culver City CA 90232

GOTTLIEB, LESTER M., real estate and securities company executive; b. N.Y.C., May 3, 1932; s. Samuel and Eva (Schoenfeld) G.; B.A., CCNY, 1954; postgrad. NYU; m. Sarah Dean Tompkins, Dec. 4, 1967; children—Cynthia Anne, Curtis Tompkins; children by previous marriage—Mark Albert, Alyssa Beth, Adine Julia. With IBM, 1956-69, mgr. bus. planning for systems devel. div., 1967-69; pres. CAMAC Equities, Ltd. and CAMAC Securities, Ltd., Riverside, Conn., 1981—; vice chmn. Data Dimensions, Inc., Los Angeles, 1984—; adj. asst. prof. econs. U. Bridgeport; nat. lectr. Assn. Computing Machinery. Pres., Woodlands-Worthington Taxpayers Assn., 1962-68; bd. dirs. North Greenwich Assn., 1973-74, Center for Internat. Mgmt. Studies, Nat. Bd. YMCA's 1972—, Greater N.Y. YMCA. Served with AUS, 1954-56. Fellow Am. Sociol. Soc.; mem. Acad. Polit. Sci., Am. Arbitration Assn. (comml. arbitrator 1981—), CCNY Alumni Assn. (bd. dirs. 1983—, pres. alumni varsity assn. 1987-88). Republican. Club: Landmark (charter mem.). Lodge: Masons. Mem. editorial bd. Jour. Computer Ops., 1965-69, Mgmt. Tech. mag., 1983-84. Home: 21 Calhoun Dr Greenwich CT 06831 Office: 1212 E Putnam Ave Riverside CT 06878

GOTTSCHALK, FRANK KLAUS, real estate company executive; b. Berlin, Jan. 25, 1932; came to U.S. 1947, naturalized 1953; s. Richard and Grete Johanna (Singer) G.; m. Ellen Ruth Meinhardt, June 16, 1957. Student N.Y. Inst. Banking & Fin., N.Y.C., 1952-53, NYU, 1955-56. Trainee, investment securities Newborg & Co. mem. N.Y. Stock Exchange, N.Y.C., 1951-52; fin. analyst Bendix Luitweiler & Co. Investment Bankers, N.Y.C., 1952-53; assoc. broker, v.p., dir. Peter F. Pasbjerg & Co., Inc., mortgage banker Newark, N.J., 1955-62; v.p., dir. Baldwin Bros., Inc. Real Estate Investors, Erie, Pa., 1962—; v.p., treas., dir. Baldwin-Gottschalk, Inc. Real Estate and Mortgage Financing, N.Y.C., Erie, Charleston, W.Va., 1962—; v.p., treas., dir. Baldwin Gottschalk Properties, Erie, 1967—, Balgot Realty Corp., Erie, 1963—, Balgot Bldg. Corp., Erie, 1967—; pres., dir. Kanawha Realty & Devel. Corp., Charleston, W.Va., 1959—, Assoc. Properties Holdings, Charleston, 1962—; trustee Assoc. Properties Holding Retirement Trust, Charleston, 1982—; mng. ptnr. Kanawha-Monarch Holdings, Erie, 1980—. Trustee, Erie Philharm., 1971—; corporator Gannon U., 1980—. Served with U.S. Army, 1953-55, ETO. Clubs: Erie, Aviation Country of Erie. Office: Baldwin Gottschalk Inc 5 W 10th St Erie PA 16501

GOTTSTEIN, BARNARD JACOB, retail and wholesale food company executive, real estate executive; b. Des Moines, Dec. 30, 1925; s. Jacob B. and Anna (Jacobs) G.; children—Sandra, James, Ruth Anne, David, Robert; m. Rachel Landau, July, 1986. B.A. in Econs. and Bus., U. Wash., 1949. Pres. J.B. Gottstein & Co., Anchorage, 1953—; chmn. bd. Carr-Gottstein Inc., Anchorage, 1974—; dir. United Bank Alaska, Anchorage, 1975-86. Commr. Alaska State Human Rights Commn, 1963-68; del. Dem. Nat. Conv., 1964, 68, 76, 88; committeeman Dem. Nat. Com., 1976-80; v.p. State Bd. Edn., Alaska, 1983-87, pres., 1987—. Served with USAF, 1944-45. Jewish. Office: J B Gottstein & Co 6411 A St Anchorage AK 99518

GOTTWALD, BRUCE COBB, SR., chemical company executive; b. Richmond, Va., Sept. 28, 1933; s. Floyd Dewey and Anne Ruth (Cobb) G.; m. Nancy Hays, Dec. 22, 1956; children: Bruce Cobb, Mark Hays, Thomas Edward. B.S., Va. Mil. Inst., 1954; postgrad., U. Va., Inst. Paper Chemistry, Appleton, Wis. With Albemarle Paper Mfg. Co., from 1956; v.p. Ethyl Corp. (parent), Richmond, Va., 1962-64, sec., 1962-69, exec. v.p., 1964-69, pres., chief operating officer, 1969—; also bd. dirs. Ethyl Corp. (parent); dir. James River Corp., Dominion Resources Inc. Former pres. Va. Mus.; bd. trustees Va. Mil. Inst. Found.; bd. govs. Va. Council Econ. Edn. Mem. Nat. Assn. Mfgrs. (bd. dirs.), Chem. Mfgr. Assn. Home: 4203 Sulgrave Rd Richmond VA 23221 Office: Ethyl Corp 330 S 4th St Richmond VA 23219 *

GOTTWALD, FLOYD DEWEY, JR., chemical company executive; b. Richmond, Va., July 29, 1922; s. Floyd Dewey and Anne (Cobb) G.; m. Elisabeth Morris Shelton, Mar. 22, 1947; children: William M., James T., John D. BS, Va. Mil. Inst., 1943; MS, U. Richmond, 1951. With Albemarle Paper Co., Richmond, 1943-62, sec., 1956-57, v.p., sec., 1957-62, pres., 1962; exec. v.p. Ethyl Corp., Richmond, 1962-64, vice chmn., 1964-68, chmn., 1968—, chief exec. officer, chmn. exec. com., 1970—. Bd. dirs. Nat. Petroleum Council; trustee V.M.I. Found., Inc., U. Richmond. Served to 1st lt. USAR, 1943-46. Decorated Bronze Star, Purple Heart. Mem. Nat. Petroleum Inst. (bd. dirs.), Va. Inst. Sci. Research (trustee), Am. Petroleum Inst. (bd. dirs.), NAM (past bd. dirs.), Chem. Mfgr. Assn. (past bd. dirs.). Clubs: Alfalfa, Country of Va., Commonwealth. Home: 300 Herndon Rd Richmond VA 23229 Office: Ethyl Corp 330 S 4th St PO Box 2189 Richmond VA 23219

GOUGH, MICHAEL W., personnel executive; b. Ft. Sill, Okla., Oct. 12, 1956; s. Elmer W. and Nancy C. (Love) G.; children: Melanie K., Meghann F., Scott R. Student, Bowling Green State U., 1985. Employment service rep. Wood County Dept. Human Services, Bowling Green, Ohio, 1985-86, CWEP coordinator, 1986—. Served with U.S. Army, 1975-81. Mem. Am. Mgmt. Assn., Am. Soc. Tng. and Devel. Office: Econ Opportunities Ctr 1616 E Wooster St Bowling Green OH 43402

GOUILLOUD, MICHEL, oil industry servicing and equipment company executive; b. 1930. Grad., Ecole Normale Superieure, Paris, 1953. With Schlumberger Ltd., 1956—, v.p., 1977—, now exec. v.p. tech. Office: Schlumberger Ltd 277 Park Ave New York NY 10017 *

GOUKE, CECIL GRANVILLE, economist, educator; b. Bklyn., Dec. 5, 1928; s. Joseph and Etheline (Grant) G.; m. Mary Noel, June 19, 1964; 1 son, Cecil Granville. B.A., CCNY, 1956; M.A., N.Y. U., 1958, Ph.D., 1967. Instr. econs. Fisk U., 1958-60; asst. prof. Grambling Coll., 1962-64, asso. prof., 1964-67; prof., chmn. Hampton (Va.) Inst., 1967-73; prof. Ohio State U., 1973—; cons. U.S. Treasury Dept., 1973. Author: Amalgamated Clothing Workers of America, 1940-66, 1972, Blacks and the American Economy, 1987; assoc. editor: Jour. Behavioral and Social Scis, 1974-84. Served with U.S. Army, 1947-49, 50-51. Recipient Founders Day award N.Y. U., 1967; sr. Fulbright scholar, 1979-80. Mem. Am. Econ. Assn., Am. Fin. Assn., Am. Statis. Assn., Indsl. Relations Research Assn., Western Econ. Assn., Nat. Econ. Assn., Hampton NAACP (exec. bd. 1968-70), Ohio Assn. Econs. and Polit. Sci. (v.p. 1986-87), Phi Beta Sigma. Democrat. Episcopalian. Home: 1788 Kenwick Rd Columbus OH 43209 Office: Dept Econs Ohio State U Columbus OH 43210

GOULD, BONNIE MARIE, realtor; b. Cleve., Sept. 3, 1947; d. Edward Louis and Frances Dee (Pavlovich) Marincic; m. Wayne William Gould, June 7, 1969; 1 child, Scott Robert. Student John Carroll U., 1965-66, 76-78. Asst. prodn. mgr. Nelson Stern Advt., Cleve., 1966-73; sec. acctg. S. James Dubin & Assos., Eastlake, Ohio, 1976-78; sec., atty. James Todoroff, Andrews & Todoroff, Eastlake, 1977-78; realtor sales Century 21-Baur, Euclid, Ohio, 1978-82; relocations dir., mgr. Century 21, Euclid, 1979-82; realtor assoc., relocation dir. Century 21-Malone, Inc., Willowick, Ohio, 1982-83, Century 21-William T. Byrne, Euclid, 1983-84, Smythe, Cramer Co., Euclid, 1984-86; v.p., corp. mgr. Acacia Realty Profls., Inc., 1986—; Mem. Realtors Polit. Action Com., Cleve., 1981—; vice chmn. local taxation and legislation com. Cleve. Area Bd. Realtors, 1983-84, vice chmn. polit. affairs, 1987—, chmn. home and flower, 1986, mem. enlarged legis. com., 1986—. Sec., trustee Euclid Gateway Found., 1987—. Recipient Disting. Service award Cleve. Bd. Realtors, 1983, 87. Mem. Cleve. Bd. Realtors (dir. 1984, 85, 86), Ohio Assn. Realtors, Nat. Assn. Realtors, Women's Council Realtors (treas. Cleve. chpt. 1986-87, v.p. 1987—, pres. 1989), North East Roundtable (sec. 1980, chair 1981), Euclid C. of C. (trustee). Republican. Lutheran. Office: Acacia Realty Profls Inc 21801 Lakeshore Blvd Euclid OH 44123

GOULD, DAVID SCOTT, equipment manufacturing company executive; b. Decatur, Ill., Aug. 28, 1926; s. Favre and Helen (States) G.; m. Grace Sitter, June 26, 1955; children: David, Frances. BS, Mo. Sch. Mines, 1951, MS, 1954; PhD, U. Mo., 1957; MS, MIT, 1964; DEng, U. Mo., Rolla, 1986. Registered profl. engr. Metall. engr. Laclede Steel Co., 1950-52; metallurgist Air Craft Engine div. Houdaille-Hershey Corp., 1952-53; with Caterpillar Tractor Co., Peoria, Ill., 1957—, exec. v.p., from 1983; now exec. v.p. Caterpillar Inc., Peoria. Served to sgt. U.S. Army, 1945-47. Fellow Am. Soc. Metals; mem Am. Foundryman's Assn., Soc. Automotive Engrs. Office: Caterpillar Inc 100 NE Adams St Peoria IL 61629 *

GOULD, DONALD EVERETT, chemicals company executive; b. Concord, N.H., May 19, 1932; s. Everett Luther and Gladys (Wilcox) G.; B.S. in Chem. Engring., U. N.H. 1954; postgrad. math. Rutgers U., 1955-59; m. Marilyn Bachelder, June 13, 1953; children—Barbara, Allen, Douglas. Devel. chem. engr. plastics div. Union Carbide Co., Bound Brook, N.J., 1954-59, tech. service engr., Bound Brook and Wayne, N.J. 1959-64, mgr. tech. service indsl. bag dept., Wayne, 1964-66, mgr. tech. services indsl. fabricated products dept. 1966-67, mktg., mgr. indsl. bags, 1967-69, sr. packaging engr., 1969-72, mgr. packaging, 1972-74, mgr. distbn. safety and regulations, 1974-79, staff engr. for packaging, 1980-85, sr. staff engr. packaging, labeling, 1985—. Mem. Packaging Inst. (vice chmn. films, foils and laminations com. 1962-64, chmn. 1964-66, sect. leader bottle containers, chmn. bag com. 1975-78, 85-88), Am. Soc. Quality Control, Chem. Mfrs. Assn. (chmn. distbn. work group), Am. Council for Chem. Labeling, Alpha Chi Sigma. Club: Packanack Lake Country. Contbr. articles profl. jours., also to Ency. Engring. Materials and Processes. Home: 98 Lake Dr E Wayne NJ 07470 Office: River Rd PO Box 670 Bound Brook NJ 08805

GOULD, GLENN HUNTING, marketing professional, consultant; b. Martinsburg, W.Va., June 15, 1949; s. Glenn Hunting Sr. and Margaret Alice (Otto) G.; m. Marilyn Kay Jones, July 12, 1953; 2 children: Courtney Lynn, Angela Pace. BA in Sociology, W.Va. U., 1973, MS in Indsl. Relations, 1974. Cert. life ins. agt. Adminstr. field personnel Ponderosa Systems, Inc., Dayton, 1975-77; adminstr. labor relations Kenner Co. subs. Gen. Mills, Inc., Cin., 1978-79; mgr. human resources Hillenbrand Ind., Batesville, Ind., 1979-81; mgr. human resources, MIAD div. Bausch & Lomb, Balt., 1981-82; dir. human resources Universal Security Inst., Balt., 1982-83; chief exec. officer M.K. Jones & Assocs., Indian Rocks Beach, Fla., 1983—; cons. mktg. Magnolia Fin. Corp., Lake Charles, La., 1985-88, Mktg. Capitol Holding, Inc., Louisville, 1988-89. Contbg. author: Successful Funeral Service Practice, 1987. Served as sgt. USAF, 1967-71, Vietnam. Recipient 13 Addy awards, Am. Advt. Fedn. local awards, 1983; named one of Outstanding Young Men Am., 1980. Mem. Am. Soc. Personnel Adminstrs. (cert. sr. profl.), Alpha Kappa Delta. Democrat. Presbyterian. Home: PO Box 335 Belleair Beach FL 34635 Office: M K Jones & Assocs Inc 107 13th Ave Indian Rocks Beach FL 33535

GOULD, HARRY EDWARD, JR., industrialist; b. N.Y.C., Sept. 24, 1938; s. Harry E. and Lucille (Quartucy) G.; m. Barbara Clement, Apr. 26, 1975; children: Harry Edward, III, Katharine Elizabeth. Student, Oxford U., 1958; B.A. cum laude, Colgate U., 1960; postgrad., Harvard Bus. Sch., 1960-61; M.B.A., Columbia U., 1964. Asso. in corporate fin. dept. Goldman, Sachs & Co., N.Y.C., 1961-62; exec. asst. to sr. v.p. ops. Universal Am., N.Y.C., 1964-65; sec., treas. Young Spring & Wire Corp., Detroit, 1965-67, exec. v.p., chief operating officer, 1967-69, also dir.; v.p. adminstrn. and fin. Universal Am. Corp., 1968-69; mem. exec. com., v.p., sec.-treas. Daybrook-Ottawa Corp., Bowling Green, Ohio, 1967-69; dir., mem. exec. com. Am. Med. Ins. Co., N.Y.C., 1966-74; pres., chmn., chief exec. officer, dir. Gould Paper Corp., N.Y.C., 1969—; chmn. bd., dir. Samuel Porritt & Co., East Peoria, Ill., 1969—, Computer Copies Corp., N.Y.C., 1970-73, Ingalls Mfg., Inc., Ceres, Calif., 1971—, McNair Mfg., Inc., Chico, Calif., 1972—, Hawthorne Paper Co., Kalamazoo, 1974—, Weiss Mfg., Inc., Chico, 1974—, Vrisimo Mfg., Inc., Ceres, 1974—; chmn. bd. Lewis & Gould Paper Co., Inc., Northfield, Ill., 1975-78; pres., dir. Carlyle Internat. Sales Corp., N.Y.C., 1975—; chmn., pres., chief exec. officer Signature Communications Ltd., Los Angeles and N.Y.C., 1986—; dir. Reinhold-Gould GmbH, Hamburg, Germany, 1969—; ltd. ptnr. Hardy & Co. (mem. N.Y. Stock Exchange), N.Y.C., 1973-78. Co-chmn. Pacesetter's com. Boy Scouts Am., 1966-69; participant as U.S. Pres.'s rep. UN E-W Trade Devel. Commn., 1967; mem. N.Y. Gov.'s Task Force on N.Y. State Cultural Life and Arts, 1975—; Pres. Harry E. Gould Found., N.Y.C., 1971—; mem. nat. council Colgate U., 1973-76, trustee, mem. budget, devel., fin. and student affairs coms., 1976—; mem. adv. bd. Columbia U. Grad. Sch. Bus., 1980—; bd. dirs. United Cerebral Palsy Research and Ednl. Found., 1976—, Nat. Multiple Sclerosis Soc., 1977—, N.Y.C. Housing Devel. Corp., 1977—; USO of

Met. N.Y., 1981; bd. dirs. Housing N.Y. Corp., 1986—, vice chmn., 1987—; bd. dirs., chmn. exec. com. Cinema Group, Inc., Los Angeles, 1979-86, chmn., pres., 1982-86; mem. Democratic Nat. Fin. Council, 1974—, also vice chmn. exec. com., chmn. budget and audit coms.; treas. N.Y. State Dem. Com., 1976-77; mem. mayor's citizens com. Dem. Nat. Conv., 1976; mem. U.S. Pres.'s Export Council (exec. com., chmn. export expansion subcom., mem. export promotion subcom.), 1979-82; mem. exec. br. Acad. Motion Picture Arts and Scis., 1985—; nat. trustee, mem. exec. com. Nat. Symphony Orch., Washington, 1978—. Mem. Nat. Paper Trade Assn. (dir., mem. printing paper com. 1973—), Paper Mchts. Assn. N.Y. (dir. 1972—), Young Pres. Orgn., Paper Club N.Y., Fin. Execs. Inst., Columbia U. Grad. Sch. Bus. Alumni Assn. (dir. 1980—), Phi Kappa Tau. Clubs: Pres.'s N.Y. (co-chmn. assocs. div. 1964-68), City Athletic, Harvard, Harvard Business, Friars, Marco Polo (N.Y.C.); Les Ambassadeurs (London); Rockrimmon Country (Stamford, Conn.). Home: 25 Sutton Pl S New York NY 10022 also: Cherry Hill Farm 429 Taconic Rd Greenwich CT 06830 Office: Gould Paper Corp 315 Park Ave S New York NY 10010

GOULD, IRVING, computer company executive; b. Toronto, Ont., Can., 1919. Grad., U. Toronto, 1941. Formerly chmn. Interpool Ltd., N.Y.C.; now chmn., chief exec. officer Commodore Internat. Ltd., West Chester, Pa. Office: Commodore Internat Ltd 1200 Wilson Dr West Chester PA 19380 *

GOULD, JAMES SPENCER, financial consultant; b. Albany, N.Y., Oct. 18, 1922; s. James Spencer and Elsie May (Spiegel) G.; m. Shirley Joan Burrett, June 12, 1948 (div. Oct. 1985); children: Deborah Ann, Jeffrey George, Douglas Spencer; m. Mary White Tredennick, Sept. 6, 1986. BS cum laude, Syracuse U., 1944; grad. advanced mgmt. program, Harvard U., 1958. C.P.A., N.Y., Calif. Ptnr. Arthur Young & Co., Buffalo and Los Angeles, 1949-65, N.Y.C., 1966-82; chief fin. officer, v.p. fin. Stanley Works, New Britain, Conn., 1982-87, v.p., 1987; free-lance cons. 1987—; dir. Imo Industries, Inc., Arrow Electronics, Inc. Served to 1st lt. inf. U.S. Army, 1943-46, ETO, 1st lt. Fin. Corps, 1951-52, Korea. Recipient Disting. Merit award Syracuse U. Sch. Mgmt., 1982, Alumnus of Yr. award, 1987. Mem. AICPA, Fin. Execs. Inst., Nat. Assn. Corp. Dirs., Shuttle Meadow Country Club, Manchester Country Club. Clubs: Manchester Country (Vt.); Farmington Woods Golf. Home: 46 Applewood Ln Farmington Woods Avon CT 06001

GOULD, JAY SHELDON, bank executive; b. Van Nuys, Calif., Sept. 12, 1947. BS, Calif. State U., Northridge, 1969, MS, 1972. Dir. planning and analysis Home Savs. and Loan Assn., Los Angeles, 1969-73; planning cons. Remote Computing Corp., Los Angeles, 1973-75; dir. planning Coast Savs. & Loan, Los Angeles, 1975-77; v.p. planning Security Pacific Nat. Bank, Los Angeles, 1977-82; dir. investor relations Security Pacific Corp., Los Angeles, 1982—. Mem. Bank Investor Relations Assn. (bd. dirs., treas. 1987—), Nat. Investor Relations Inst. Republican. Mem. Church of Nazarene. Office: Security Pacific Corp 333 S Hope St Los Angeles CA 90071

GOULD, JOHN PHILIP, JR., economist, educator, university dean; b. Chgo., Jan. 19, 1939; s. John Philip and Lillian (Jicka) G.; m. Kathleen J. Hayes, Sept. 14, 1963; children: John Philip III, Jeffrey Hayes. BS with highest distinction, Northwestern U., 1960; PhD, U. Chgo., 1966. Faculty U. Chgo., 1965—, prof. econs., 1974—, disting. service prof. econs., 1984—, dean Grad. Sch. Bus., 1983—, v.p. planning, 1988—; vis. prof. Nat. Taiwan U., 1978; spl. asst. econ. affairs to sec. labor, 1969-70; spl. asst. to dir. Office Mgmt. and Budget, 1970; past chmn. econ. policy adv. com. Dept. Labor; bd. dirs. ARCH Devel. Corp., DFA Investment Dimensions Group, Vulcan Materials Co. Author: (with E. Lazear) Microeconomic Theory, 6th edit, 1989; contbg. author: Microeconomic Foundations of Employment and Inflation Theory, 1970; editor: Jour. of Bus. , 1976-83, Jour. Fin. Econs., 1976-83, Jour. Accounting and Econs., 1978-81; contbr. articles to profl. jours. Bd. dirs. United Way/Crusade of Mercy, 1986—; trustee First Lakeshore Funds, 1985—. Recipient Wall St. Jour. award, 1960, Am. Marketing Assn. award, 1960; Earhart Found. fellow. Mem. Am. Econ. Assn., Western Econ. Assn., Econometric Soc. (chmn. local arrangements 1968). Home: 5514 S Kenwood Ave Chicago IL 60637 Office: U Chgo Grad Sch Bus 5801 S Ellis Ave Chicago IL 60637

GOULD, MAXINE LUBOW, lawyer, marketing professional, consultant; b. Bridgeton, N.J., Feb. 28, 1942; d. Louis A. and Bernice L. (Goldberg) Lubow; B.S., Temple U., 1962, J.D., 1968; m. Sam C. Gould, June 17, 1962 (div. Dec. 1984); children—Jack, Herman, David. Head resident dept. student personnel Temple U., 1962-66; dir., treas. Hilltop Interest Program, Inc., Los Angeles, 1973-74; law clk. law firms, Los Angeles, 1975-77; with Buffalo Resources Corp., Los Angeles, 1978-82, corp. sec., 1979-82; corp. sec., securities prin. Buffalo Securities Corp., Los Angeles, 1979-82; corp. sec. LaMaur Devel. Corp., Los Angeles, 1979-82; contracts analyst, land dept. Texaco Inc., Los Angeles, 1982-83; exec. dir. Sinai Temple, West Los Angeles, 1983-85; pres. Cutting Edge, Los Angeles, 1986; adminstr. law firm Robinson, Wolas & Diamant, Century City, 1986, acctg. firm Roth, Bookstein & Zaslow, Los Angeles, 1986-87; project coordinator Cipher, 1987; mktg. dir. Am. Bus. Capital, Beverly Hills, Calif., 1988—. Mem. Roscomare Valley Assn. Edn. Com., Bel Air, Calif., 1975-76; subcom. chmn. Roscomare Rd. Sch. Citizens Adv. Council, Bel Air; active various community drives. Recipient Joseph B. Wagner Oratory award B'nai B'rith, 1959, Voice of Democracy award, 1958-59, award Commentator Club, 1959. Mem. ABA (law office econs. sect.), Los Angeles Bar Assn. (assoc., law office econs. sect.), Nat. Assn. Legal Adminstrs. (Beverly Hills chpt.), Nat. Assn. Female Execs. (network dir.), Nat. Assn. Law Firm Mktg. Adminstrs., Calif. Women Lawyers, Women in Bus. (co-chmn. membership com.), Calif. CPA Soc. (adminstr. com.), Nat. Assn. Synagogue Adminstrs., Am. Assn. Petroleum Landmen, Los Angeles Assn. Petroleum Landmen, Textile Profl. Soc., Comml. Fin. Assn., Phi Alpha Theta, Alpha Lambda Delta. Jewish. Home: 2501 Roscomare Los Angeles CA 90077 Office: Am Bus Capital 400 S Beverly Dr #208 Beverly Hills CA 90212

GOULD, SYD S., publisher; b. Boston, Dec. 16, 1912; s. Charles M. and Cecelia (Duke) G.; student Coll. William and Mary, 1934; m. Grace Leich, May 22, 1938; 1 dau., Nancy Hamilton (Mrs. Lucien M. Gex, Jr.). Radio bus., Buenos Aires, Argentina, 1934, 36; advt. dept. Call-Chronicle Newspapers, Allentown, Pa., 1936-42; v.p. adv. dir. Baytown Sun, Tex. 1943-55; pub.-owner Cleveland Daily Banner, Tenn., 1955—; pres. Cleveland Newspapers, Inc., 1956-67; exec. v.p. So. Newspapers, Inc., 1963-69; pres. Syd S. Gould Assocs., 1966—, Bolivar Newspapers, Inc., 1967—, Ironton Tribune Corp. Ohio, Franklin Newspapers, Inc., La., Comet-Press Newspapers, Thibodaux, La., Milton Newspapers, Inc., Fla. Mem. Regional Small Bus. Adv. Council. Sec., Bradley County (Tenn.) Indsl. Devel. Bd., 1961—; bd. dirs. Providence Hosp.; pres. Bradley County Heart Assn., 1960-61. Served with USNR, World War II. Recipient Disting. Eagle Scout award Boy Scouts Am., 1983. Mem. Newspaper Advt. Execs. Assn., Tenn. Press Assn., Bur. Advt., Am. Newspaper Pubs. Assn., So. Newspapers Pubs. Assn., Gulf Coast Conservation Assn., USCG Aux., U.S. Power Squadron, U.S. Naval Inst., Navy League, Eagle Scout Assn., Sigma Delta Chi. Episcopalian. Clubs: Bayou Country, Mobile Big Game Fishing, Isle Dauphine Country, Capitol Hill, Yachting of Am., Internat. Trade, Bienville, Athelstan, Commodore, Bay Point Yacht, Inc. Home: PO Box 28449 Bay Point Panama City FL 32411 Office: 2111 Thomas Dr Panama City FL 32408

GOULDER, GERALD POLSTER, retail executive; b. Columbus, Ohio, Apr. 30, 1953; s. Norman Ernest and Betty (Polster) G. BA, Ohio State U.; JD, Washington U. Bar: Ohio, N.C. Asst. atty. gen. Ohio Atty. Gen.'s Office, Columbus, 1979-83; atty. James M. Schottenstein & Assocs., Columbus, 1983-84; chmn., chief operating officer Carolina Drug Distrbrs., Inc. and Emporium Stores, Ltd., Greensboro, N.C., 1984—; also dir.; ptnr., cons. Greater Greensboro Indoor Soccer Co., Greensboro Storm. Assoc. editor Washington U. Urban Law Ann., 1977-78; contbr. articles to profl. jours. Bd. trustees Wexner Heritage Village, Columbus, 1983-84; participant Leadership Greensboro, 1985. Mem. N.C. Bar Assn., Greensboro Bar Assn., leadership Greensboro Alumni Assn., Bexley Dem. Club (founder, pres.). Republican. Jewish. Office: Carolina Drug Distrbrs Inc & Emporium Stores Ltd 2803 Battleground Ave Greensboro NC 27408

GOULDEY, GLENN CHARLES, controls manufacturing company executive; b. N.Y.C., July 28, 1952; s. George Howard and Jeannette Ruth Williamson; m. Leslie Jeanne Ruth, Oct. 2, 1982; children: Jeremy Charles, Nicholas Glenn. BS in Bus., Trenton State Coll., 1976; postgrad. Portland State U., 1980; MBA, Rider Coll., 1981. Cert. in purchasing mgmt. Purchasing Mgrs. Assn. Sr. planner Eaton Corp., Flemington, N.J., 1975-77, pricing mgr., distbn., 1977-79, inventory control mgr., 1979-80, materials mgr., purchasing, Beaverton, Oreg., 1980-81, mfg. and materials mgr., 1981-83, mktg. and materials mgr., 1983-87, plant and gen. mgr., 1987-88, v.p. sales and mktg., Carol Stream, Ill., 1988—. Patentee in field. Mem. Am. Prodn. Inventory Control Soc. (cert. in prodn. and inventory control). Republican. Presbyterian. Home: 1195 Brookstone Dr Carol Stream IL 60188 Office: Eaton Corp 191 E North Ave Carol Stream IL 60188

GOULDING, JAYNE MARIE, accountant; b. Oakland, Calif., Mar. 12, 1957; d. Dean Payne and Anita Marie (Stanton) Phillips; m. Donald Rea Goulding, Jan. 31, 1987. AA in Acctg., Sierra Coll., 1979. Acct. clk., sr. acct. clk. Placer County Auditor-Controller, Auburn, Calif., 1974-77, acct.-auditor I and II, 1977-82, acct.-auditor III, tax mgr., 1982—; lectr. in field. Recipient Cert. Placer County Human Rels. Commn., 1979. Mem. World Wildlife Fund (Wash. chpt.), Greenpeace (Wash. chpt.), U.S. Humane Soc. (Wash. chpt.), Animal Protection Inst. Am. (Sacramento, Calif. chpt.), Environ. Def. Fund (N.Y. state chpt.), Calif. Tax Mgrs. Home: 5061 Reservoir Rd Greenwood CA 95635 Office: Placer County Auditor-Contr 135 Fulweiler Ave Auburn CA 95603

GOURGUES, HAROLD WALTER, JR., financial consultant; b. Larose, La., Sept. 23, 1937; s. Harold Walter and Clarabelle (Ducos) G.; m. Geneva Jones, June 25, 1966; children: Katherine Haley, Harold Walter III. BS in Chem. Engring., La. State U., 1960; BS in Meteorology, Pa. State U., 1961. Cert. fin. planner. Account exec. F.I. du Pont and Co., New Orleans, 1963-68; v.p., dir. fin. services Kohlmeyer and Co., New Orleans, 1969-75; sr. v.p., dir. fin. planning Robinson-Humphrey Co. Inc., Atlanta, 1975-83; pvt. practice personal fin. cons. Atlanta, 1983—. Author: Financial Planning Handbook, 1983, Revolution in Financial Services, 1987, Total Financial Planning, 1988; (monthly report) The Gourgues Report, 1984—. Mem. adv. bd. Juvenile Diabetes Found., Atlanta, 1986—. With USAF, 1960-63. Named one of 7 Top Fin. Planners Money mag., 1982; recipient pioneering award Nat. Assn. Profl. Fin. Advisors, 1986. Mem. Internat. Assn. for Fin. Planning, Inst. for Cert. Fin. Planning. Republican. Roman Catholic. Home: 1385 Ragley Hall Rd NE Atlanta GA 30319 Office: The Gourgues Report PO Box 81668 Atlanta GA 30366-1668

GOURLEY, FLETCHER A., dairy company executive; b. Dec. 2, 1912; s. Fletcher and Maude (Prather) G.; m. Lois Holdren, Aug. 29, 1937; children: Stephen A., Barry M. BS in Dairy Industry, Iowa State U., 1937. Mgr. Prairie Farms Dairy, Inc., Carlinville, Ill., 1938-62, gen. mgr., 1962-72, exec. v.p., 1972-88, sr. v.p., 1988—; bd. dirs. Carlinville Nat. Bank. Mem. Dairy Shrine, Rotary. Lodge: Rotary. Office: Prairie Farms Dairy Inc PO Box 499 Carlinville IL 62626

GOURLEY, JAMES LELAND, editor, publisher, business executive; b. Mounds, Okla., Jan. 29, 1919; s. Samuel O. and Lodema (Scott) G.; B.Liberal Studies, U. Okla., 1963; m. Vicki Graham Clark, Nov. 24, 1976; children—James Leland II, Janna Lynn Chancellor, Kelly Clark, Brandon Clark. Editor, pub., pres. Daily Free-Lance, Henryetta, Okla., 1946-73; editor Friday, 1974—; chmn. Nichols Hills Pub. Co., 1974—; v.p. Suburban Grphics, Inc., 1987—; pres. Central Okla. Newspaper Group, 1987; pres. radio sta. KHEN, KHEN-FM, Henryetta, 1955-71; pres. Hugo (Okla.) Daily News, 1953-63; chief of staff gov. Okla., 1959-63; chmn., pres. State Capitol Bank, 1962-69; v.p. radio sta. KXOJ Sapulpa, 1972-75; treas. Okla. Radio Co., Inc., 1962-67. Mem. Pres. Nat. Pub. Advisory Com. to sec. commerce, 1963-66; exec. dir. Gov's Comm. Higher Edn., 1960-61; Democratic candidate for gov. Okla., 1966. Bd. dirs. So. Regional Edn. Bd., 1959-67, Okla. Symphony Soc., 1976-88, Oklahoma City Crimestoppers, 1982—, Salvation Army, Oklahoma City, 1985-87; mem. Gov.'s Reform Com., 1984. Served to maj. AUS, 1942-46. Recipient Best Large City Weekly newspaper awards, 1977, 78, 79, 80, 83, 84, 85, 87, 88; inducted Okla. Journalism Hall of Fame, 1980. Mem. UP Internat. Editors Okla. (pres. 1958-59), Okla. Disciples of Christ Laymen (pres. 1964-65), Suburban Newspapers Am. (dir.), Okla. Press Assn. (pres. 1988-89), Oklahoma City C. of C. (dir.), Okla. State C. of C. (bd. dirs.), Pi Kappa Alpha. Republican. Clubs: Oklahoma City Golf and Country, Econ. (Oklahoma City), Men's Dinner (Oklahoma City); Lodge; Rotary (dir.). Home: 1605 W Wilshire Oklahoma City OK 73116 Office: 10801 N Quail Plaza Dr Oklahoma City OK 73156

GOURLEY, JAMES WALTER, III, natural gas utility executive; b. Los Angeles, Jan. 8, 1941; s. James Walter and Eleanor Mae (Kanel) G.; children: Jennifer Lane, Matthew James; m. Dana C. Matthews, Dec. 20, 1986; stepchildren: Lance, Wendee. AA, Fullerton Coll., 1960; BS in Geology cum laude, U. Redlands, 1962; MS in Geology, U. So. Calif., 1971. Cert. profl. geologist, Calif. Petroleum engr. Standard Oil Calif., 1965-70, devel. geologist, La Habra, 1971-72; supr. energy planning So. Calif. Gas Co., Los Angeles, 1972-76, mgr. energy resources, 1976-80, mgr. supply forecasting, 1980-82, mgr. underground storage, 1982-86, mgr. pub. affairs planning, 1986—, mem. speakers bur., 1978—. Mem. Am. Gas Assn., Soc. Petroleum Engrs., Am. Assn. Petroleum Geologists. Republican. Clubs: Los Angeles Athletic; Candlewood Country (Whittier). Home: 15705 Candelaria Ct Whittier CA 90603 Office: So Calif Gas Co 720 W 8th St Los Angeles CA 90017

GOUVEIA, CHRISTINE SUZANNE, software consultant; b. Syracuse, N.Y., July 2, 1960; d. Samuel Salvatore and Ingrid (Knuth) C.; m. John Joseph Gouveia, Oct. 11, 1986. BS in Biochemistry, BA in Math., U. Maine, 1982. Programmer Syscon Corp., Newport, R.I., 1983-85; software cons. Digital Equipment Corp., East Providence, R.I., 1985—. Office: Digital Equipment Corp 5 Catamore Blvd East Providence RI 02914

GOW, JACK FRANK, management consultant; b. Passaic, N.J., Jan. 25, 1920; s. John M. and Catherine E. (Barney) G.; m. Hilda H. Hulsebos, Sept. 5, 1942; 1 child, N. Holly Gow Thoman. Student, Rutgers U., CCNY. Accredited Pub. Relations Soc. Am. Pub. rels. mgr. Getty Oil Co., N.Y.C., 1946-65; pub. rels. dir. GAF Corp., N.Y.C., 1965-69, v.p. personnel, 1969-75, group v.p., 1975-77, sr. v.p. human resources, 1977-81; pres., owner Pub. Rels./Human Resources Assocs., Inc., Wyckoff, N.J., 1982—. Corr., columnist Evening News, Paterson, N.J., 1935-40; feature writer Sunday Eagle, Paterson., 1952. Alderman City of Paterson, 1948; exec. dir. human rels. commn. City of Paterson, 1951; info. dir. Twp. of Wyckoff, 1963-72; chmn. Wyckoff United Way, 1983-85; bd. dirs. YMCA, Wyckoff, 1983—, past pres. With USNR, 1942-45, PTO. Recipient honor medals Freedom Found., Valley Forge, Pa., 1951,54, 61, 62, Silver Anvil award, 1968, Gold award, 1961, Presdl. citation, 1968 Pub. Rels. Soc. Am., Silver and Gold awards Am. Petroleum Inst., 1950, 65. Mem. Am. Legion. Republican. Club: N.Y. Athletic. Home and Office: 458 Weymouth Dr Wyckoff NJ 07481

GOW, LINDA YVONNE CHERWIN, travel executive; b. Plymouth, N.H., Dec. 15, 1948; d. Roger and Alice Mary (Theriault) Carignan; m. James T. Gow Jr., Aug. 29, 1987; 1 child, M. Alison. Student Rivier Coll., 1966-68, Whittemore Sch. Bus., 1976-79. Asst. mgr. Travel New Horizons, Peterborough, N.H., 1972-76; mgr. Garnsey Bros. Travel, Sanford, Maine, 1976-77; gen. mgr. R-W Travel, Dover, N.H., 1977-84; pres., owner The Travel Pro, Somersworth, N.H., 1984—; owner Cruise Quarters, Somersworth, 1988—. Sponsor, bd. dirs. Internat. Children's Festival, Somersworth, N.H., 1985-86; mem. Gov.'s Pvt. Industry Council. Mem. Am. Soc. Travel Agts., Am. Retail Travel Agts. Assn., Cruise Lines Internat. Assn., Nat. Assn. Cruise Only Agys., Rochester C. of C., Portsmouth C. of C., Dover C. of C., Somersworth C. of C. Office: The Travel Pro 396 High St Somersworth NH 03878

GOWAN, JOSEPH PATRICK, JR., entertainment and food services company executive; b. Bklyn., Sept. 30, 1939; s. Joseph Patrick and Elizabeth C. (Murphy) G.; m. Donna J. DiCostanzo; children—Sheri, Nicole; children by previous marriage—Joseph Patrick III, Thomas, Patricia, Daniel, Sean, Timothy. Student Villanova U., 1961; B.S., Fordham U., 1965. Dir., CBS, N.Y.C., 1964-67; v.p. Metro Media Records Co., N.Y.C., 1967-69; exec. v.p. GRT Record Group, N.Y.C., 1969-71; v.p., chief exec. officer NEC Telephones Inc., Melville, N.Y., 1971-77, pres., dir., 1977-80; v.p. NEC Am. Inc., 1977-80; v.p. Telecom Equipment Corp., Long Island City, N.Y., 1982, chief fin. officer, 1984—, treas., 1986—; exec. v.p., dir., chief fin. officer, treas. TPI Enterprises Inc. (formerly Telecom Plus Internat.), 1982—; pres. Telecom Plus Rental Systems, 1984-87, dir. EVP, various subs., 1984-87; dir. Maxcell Telecom Plus and subs., 1984-87; sec., dir. Alltel Telecommunications Systems Inc., Tel Logic Communications Inc., Pactel Communications Inc., Compath Nat. Inc., 1985-88, TPI Restaurants, Inc., 1988—, TPI Entertainment Inc., 1988—; dir. Shoney's South, Inc. Bd. dirs. Flushing (N.Y.) Community Vol. Ambulance Corps., 1968-73, v.p., 1968-70, treas., 1971-73. Mem. Am. Acad. Scis., Am. Mgmt. Assn., N.Am. Telephone Assns. (dir.), K.C., Kiwanis. Roman Catholic. Home: 102 Ninth St Garden City NY 11530 Office: TPI Enterprises Inc 7300 N Fed Hwy Boca Raton FL 33431 also: 885 3d Ave New York NY 10022

GOZONSKY, EDWIN S., investment banker; b. Laconia, N.H., Mar. 31, 1930; s. Archie and Ida G.; m. Dorothy Adelson, Feb. 28, 1965; children: Judith, Diane. BA, Yale U., 1952; MBA, Harvard U., 1954. With Eastman Dillon, Union Securities (merged with Paine Webber 1980), Boston, 1959—; V.p. Boston office Eastman Dillon, Union Securities (merged with Paine Webber 1980), 1971—; pres. Variable Annuities Provide Personal Security, 1979—; lectr., publicist variable annuities, 1979—. Served with U.S. Army, 1954-56. Mem. Bulldog Soc. (provisional dir.). Home: 118 Irving Ave Providence RI 02906 Office: Paine Webber 265 Franklin St Boston MA 02110

GRABER, HARRIS DAVID, sales executive; b. Bronx, N.Y., Mar. 31, 1939; s. Charles and Ella (Shapiro) G.; AS, Queensborough Community Coll., 1973; BS cum laude, CUNY, 1975; MBA, St. Johns U., 1979; m. Esther Estelle Feldman, Dec. 28, 1957; children: Donald Irwin, Gregory Stuart, Monique Cheryl, Roy Scott. Draftsman, Paramount Designs Co., N.Y.C., 1956-58; design draftsman Milgo Electronic Co., Miami, Fla., 1961-62; design engr. Cons. and Designers Co., N.Y.C., 1958-61, 62-64; with engring. and engring. mgmt. depts. Grumman Aerospace Co., Bethpage, N.Y., 1964-74, mktg. and sales engr., 1974-75, group head customer engring. tech. requirements, 1975-78, internat. bus. analyst, 1978; govt. sales mgr. Systems-East div. Conrac Corp., West Caldwell, N.J., 1978-80; dir. govt. mktg. Telephonics Corp., Huntington, N.Y., 1980-82; regional sales mgr. Measurement Systems div. Gould Inc., Oxnard, Calif., 1982-83; sales mgr. govt. bus. Servonic div. Gulton Industries Inc., Costa Mesa, Calif., 1983-84; dir. mktg. systems ILC Data Device Corp., 1984-88; mktg. mgr. Shipboard and Ground Systems div. Unisys Corp., Great Neck, N.Y., 1988—. Mem. Tech. Mktg. Soc. Am., Assn. MBA Execs., Navy League U.S., Armed Forces Communications and Electronics Assn. Home: 80-51 249th St Bellerose NY 11426 Office: 105 Wilbur Pl Bohemia NY 11716

GRABINSKI, LAWRENCE AUGUST, data processing consultant, designer; b. Chgo., Aug. 10, 1929; s. August Jerome and Pearl Josephine (Wanat) G.; (div.); children: Martin, Thomas. Student U. Md., 1950-52, Ill. Inst. Tech., 1952-54, Morraine Valley Coll., 1980. Quality control engr. Foote Bros., Chgo., 1952-55; designer W.L. Stennsgaard, Chgo., 1955-57; chief draftsman Klemp Corp., Chgo., 1957-65; structural designer Rippel Archt. Metals, Chgo., 1965-74; asst. div. mgr. Pullman Sheet Metal Co., Chgo., 1974-77; computer systems specialist Castle Engring. Co., Chgo., 1977-87; pvt. cons., 1987—. With USAF, 1948-52, ETO. Mem. Am. Fedn. Musicians. Home and Office: 7801 S Lotus Burbank IL 60459

GRABOWSKI, JOSEPH LEON, banker; b. Jersey City, Feb. 28, 1938; s. Joseph J. and Florence (Godlewski) G.; m. Marilyn Brown, Apr. 11, 1964; children: Gayle, Lisa. Cert., Rutgers U., 1980. Enlisted USAF, 1955, advanced through ranks to staff sgt., resigned, 1963; trooper N.J. State Police, Trenton, 1956-57; dist. supr. Household Fin. Corp., N.Y.C., 1957-72; v.p. United Jersey Bank, Hackensack, N.J., 1972-82; pres. Carteret Consumer Credit Co., Parsippany, N.J., 1982—. Author: Automobile Leasing in Banking., 1980. Chmn. Wood-Ridge (N.J.) Planning Bd., 1985; vice chmn., bd. dirs. N.J. Higher Edn. Asst. Authority, Trenton, 1985-87. Mem.. Internat. Credit Assn., Nat. 2d Mortgage Assn., U.S. League of Savs. Insts., Nat. Council Savs. Insts., N.J. League of Savs. Insts. (chmn.), Consumer Credit Assn. Met. N.Y. (bd. dirs., past chmn.), Consumer Bankers Assn. (bd. dirs. 1982—), Morris County C. of C. Lodge: Kiwanis (pres. Hackensack club 1981), KC. Office: Carteret Consumer Credit Co 10 Waterview Blvd Parsippany NJ 07054

GRABSCHEID, WILLIAM HENRY, insolvency and reorganization specialist; b. N.Y.C., May 18, 1931; s. Sidney Oswald and Jeannette (Derdiger) G.; m. Barbara Lee Blam, Dec. 21, 1952 (div. Nov. 1964); children: Paul, Steven, Michael, Karen; m. Carol Sue Birenholtz, Nov. 17, 1964; children: Peter, James, Elizabeth, William Jr. BA in Econs., Lafayette Coll., 1953; MS in Administrv. Mgmt., Columbia U., 1954. Pres. Modern Industries, Inc., N.Y.C., 1954-75, Humphrey's Leather Goodsdiv. Scott & Fetzer, Chgo., 1975-78, E.R. Moore subs. Beatrice Foods, Chgo., 1978-79; mng. dir. William H. Grabscheid and Assocs., Highland Park, Ill., 1979-83; mgr. troubled businesses Friedman, Eisenstein, Raemer & Schwartz, Chgo., 1983-85; mng. dir. midwest region, reorgn. and insolvency div. Arthur Young & Co., Chgo., 1985—; examiner, panel trustee chpts. 7, 11; alt. del. to Insol. Mem. Am. Arbitration Assn., Am. Bankruptcy Inst. (bd. dirs.), Assn. Insolvency Accts. (bd. dirs.), Assn. Bankruptcy Trustees, Assn. for Corp. Growth, Turn Around Mgmt. Assn., Nat. Assn. Accts. Democrat. Jewish. Clubs: Metropolitan, Chgo., Willy's. Home: 3500 University Ave Highland Park IL 60035 Office: Arthur Young & Co One IBM Pla Chicago IL 60611

GRACE, H. DAVID, investment management executive; b. Hornell, N.Y., Sept. 27, 1936; s. H.F. III and Alice (Lamp) G.; B.S., Rensselaer Poly. Inst., 1957; M.B.A., U. Cin., 1963. Staff chem. engr. Procter & Gamble Co., N.Y.C., 1957-58, supr. prodn., quality control, 1959-60, bus. analyst, math. cons., Cin., 1961-63; supr. ops. research, mgmt. econs. Weyerhaeuser Co., Tacoma, 1963-65; dir. ops. research Celanese Corp., N.Y.C., 1965-67; mgr. computer applications Francis I. duPont, N.Y.C., 1968-69, mgr. computer and tech. research, 1969-71, mgr. portfolio analysis and investment adv. depts., 1969-71; v.p., dir. Lenox Capital Mgmt. Corp., N.Y.C., 1971-74, pres., 1973-74; pres., chmn. bd. dirs. Grace-Metro Enterprises, Ltd., 1967-81, Grace Capital Inc., 1974—; pres., dir. Dirs. Capital Inc., 1977-87; mem. faculty Xavier U., 1962-63, Pacific Luth. U., 1964-65. Area counselor Republican party, 1964-65. Mem. Am. Statis. Assn., N.Y. Soc. Security Analysts, Fin. Analysts Fedn., Phi Sigma Kappa. Home: 1 Sherman Sq New York NY 10023 Office: Grace Capital Inc 17 Battery Pl New York NY 10004

GRACE, J. PETER, business executive; b. Manhasset, N.Y., May 25, 1913; s. Joseph and Janet (Macdonald) G.; m. Margaret Fennelly, May 24, 1941. Student, St. Paul's Sch., Concord, N.H., 1927-32; BA, Yale U., 1936; LLD (hon.), Mt. St. Mary's Coll., Manhattan Coll., Fordham U., Boston Coll., U. Notre Dame, Belmont Abbey, Stonehill Coll., Christian Bros. Coll., Adelphi U., Furman U., Rider Coll., Mt. St. Vincent Coll.; D Latin Am. Rels., St. Joseph's Coll.; DSc, Clarkson Coll.; DCS, St. John's U.; LHD, Fairleigh Dickinson U.; LLD (hon.), Assumption Coll., The Citadel, Stevens Inst. of Tech., Union Coll. With W.R. Grace & Co., N.Y.C., 1936—, sec., 1942, dir., 1943—, v.p., 1945, pres., chief exec. officer, 1945-81, chmn., pres., chief exec. officer, 1981—, pres., 1986—; chmn. bd. dirs. Chemed Corp., Taco Villa, Inc.; bd. dirs. Restaurant Enterprises Group, Inc., Canonie Environ. Svcs. Corp., Creative Restaurant Mgmt., Inc., DuBois Chems., Office Warehouse, Inc.; hon. dir. Brascan Ltd.; dir. emeritus Ingersoll-Rand Co.; dir. Stone & Webster, Inc., Omnicare, Inc., Roto-Rooter, Inc., Universal Furniture Ltd., Milliken & Co., Nat. Sanitary Supply Co.; trustee emeritus Atlantic Mut. Ins. Co., Centennial Ins. Co., Atlantic Reins. Co.; chmn. bd., dir. Taco Villa, Inc., Chemed Corp. Bd. dirs., pres. Cath. Youth Orgn. of Archdiocese of N.Y.; bd. dirs. Boys Clubs Am.; pres., trustee Grace Inst.; mem. pres.'s com. Greater N.Y., corp. grants com., trustee emeritus, Notre Dame U.; chmn. coun. nat. trustees Nat. Jewish Ctr. for Immunology and Respiratory Medicine, Denver; chmn. Pres.'s Pvt. Sector Survey on Cost Control in Fed. Govt., 1982-84; co-chmn. Citizens Against Govt. Waste; trustee U.S. Council for Internat. Bus.; bd. govs. Thomas Aquinas Coll.; chmn., dir. Amerishares Found., Inc.; bd. dirs. Americares Found. Recipient Knight Grand Cross, Equestrian Order Holy Sepulchre of Jerusalem; decorated by govts. of Colombia, Chile, Ecuador, Panama, Peru. Mem. Newcomen Soc., Coun. on Fgn. Rels., Knights of Malta (bd. councillors, pres., recipient Sovereign Milt. Order), Madison Sq. Garden Club (gov.),

Links, Meadow Brook Club, Pacific Union Club, Everglades Club, Lotus Club, River Club, Deepdale Club. Office: W R Grace & Co Grace Pla 1114 Ave of the Americas New York NY 10036-7794

GRADE, JEFFERY T., manufacturing company executive; b. 1943. BS, Ill. Inst. Tech., 1966; MBA, DePaul U., 1972. With Plasto Mfg. Corp., 1965-66, Motorola Inc., 1966-67, Bell and Howell, 1967-68, Ill. Cen. Gulf R.R., 1968-73; v.p. fin. IC Industries, 1973-83; with Harnischfeger Corp., Milw., 1983—, pres., chief operating officer, bd. dirs., 1986—. Served with USN, 1865-66. Office: Harnischfeger Industries Corp PO Box 554 Milwaukee WI 53201 *

GRADER, CHARLES RAYMOND, university administrator, mining company executive, retired foreign service officer; b. Marblehead, Mass., May 28, 1931; s. George Wilson and Geneva Frances (Smith) G.; m. Sheila Lillian Humphries, Jan. 2, 1960; children—Mark C. Moses, Sarah Elizabeth. A.B., Boston U., 1954; cert. in internat. studies London Sch. Econs., 1960; Ph.D., Fletcher Sch. Law and Diplomacy, 1967; M.S., MIT, 1974. Budget examiner Exec. Office of Pres., Bur. Budget, Washington, 1961-64; econs. lectr. Northeastern U., Boston, 1964-66; program officer AID mission to Tunisia, Tunis, 1967-69, regional economist West Africa, Dakar, Senegal, 1969-70, dir. Central Africa region, Yaounde, Cameroun, 1970-73; Sloan fellow MIT, Cambridge, 1973-74, dir. AID Mission to Nepal, Kathmandu, 1974-76; assoc. asst. adminstr. for Latin Am., Washington, 1976-77, dir. AID Mission to Afghanistan, Kabul, 1977-79, to Uganda, Kampala, 1979-80, to Zimbabwe, Salisbury, 1980-81; pres. Compagnie des Bauxites de Guinee, Kamsar, Guinea, 1981-85, dir. program for sr. execs. MIT, Cambridge, 1986—. Served to lt. USCG, 1954-57. Home: 11 Highland Terr Marblehead MA 01945 Office: MIT Sloan Sch Mgmt Cambridge MA 02139

GRADISON, HEATHER JANE, government official; b. Houston, Sept. 6, 1952; d. David Lowe Stirton and Dorothy Johanne (Flatt) Cox; m. Willis D. Gradison, Jr., Nov. 29, 1980; children: Maile Jo, Benjamin David, Logan Jane. B.A., Radford U., 1975; postgrad., George Washington U., 1976, 78. Summer intern So. Ry. System, Washington, 1974, mgmt. trainee, market research asst., asst. rate officer, rate officer, 1975-82; mem. ICC, Washington, 1982—; vice chmn. ICC, 1985, chmn., 1985-89. Mem. Rep. Congl. Wives Club, Level IV Presdl. Appointees Orgn., Women's Transp. Seminar. Office: ICC 12th & Constitution Ave NW Washington DC 20423

GRAEFF, DAVID WAYNE, maintenance executive, consultant; b. West Reading, Pa., Oct. 24, 1946; s. Wayne Samuel and Sara (Spohn) G.; m. Linda Ruth Lohrke, Aug. 17, 1968; children—Hether, Rebecca, Matthew. B.S.M.E., Ind. Inst. Tech., 1969. Lic. in sewage treatment plant and waterworks, Pa. Maintenance engr. Central Soya, Decatur, Ind., 1969-71; mfg. engr. Nat. Seal div. Fed. Mogul, Van Wert, Ohio, 1971-73; facilities engr. Kawecki Berylco div. Cabot, Reading, Pa., 1973-76; plant engr. Willson Products div. E.S.B., Reading, 1976-78; maintenance supt. Brush-Wellman Inc., Reading, 1978—; maintenance cons. Maintenance Inc., Fleetwood, Pa., 1976—. Vice comr. USCG Aux., Reading, 1983-84, cert. marine examiner, 1982—, info. system officer, 1984. Mem. Soc. Mfg. Engrs., Am. Water Works Assn., Am. Inst. Plant Engrs., Am. Inst. Chem. Engrs., Theta Xi, Ducks Unlimited. Republican. Lutheran. Lodge: Moose. Avocations: boating; woodworking. Home: 815 Forest St Fleetwood PA 19522 Office: Brush-Wellman Inc Shoemakersville Rd Shoemakersville PA 19555

GRAF, EDWARD LOUIS, JR., lawyer, finance executive; b. Pitts., Sept. 24, 1938; s. Edward Louis and Laura Mae (Flaherty) G.; m. Mary Ann Johnston, July 8, 1961; children: John, Stephen, Timothy. BBA, U. Pitts., 1960; JD, Duquesne U., 1967. Bar: Pa. 1967; CPA, Pa. Auditor, tax accountant Main Lafrentz & Co., Pitts., 1960-65; treas. G.E. Smith Inc., Pitts., 1965-67; controller Cecast div. Combustion Engring. Inc., Pitts., 1967-70; v.p., sec., legal counsel Ketchum, MacLeod & Grove, Inc., Pitts., 1971-75, sr. v.p., corp. sec., 1975-77; exec. v.p. fin. and law Ketchum Communications Inc., Pitts., 1977-88, vice chmn., chief fin. officer, 1988—. Editor quar. PEAL, 1970-78; contbr. articles to profl. jours. Councilman Ben Avon Council, Pitts., 1973-77; treas. Pi Sigma Ednl. Found., 1976—; mem. Three Rivers Youth, Pitts., 1977-79; developer The Priory. Mem. Fin. Execs. Inst. (sec. 1987-88, pres. 1988— Pitts. chpt.), ABA, Pa. Bar Assn., Allegheny Bar Assn., AICPA, Pa. Inst. CPAs, Am. Assn. Advt. Agys. (fiscal control com.). Clubs: Univ. (Pitts.), Ad (Pitts.) (chmn. legal/ethics com.); Duquesne. Office: Ketchum Communications Inc 6 PPG Pl Philadelphia PA 15222

GRAF, JOSEPH CHARLES, foundation executive; b. Jersey City, Sept. 10, 1928; s. John Bernard and Margaret Cecilia (Toomey) G.; B.S., Seton Hall U., 1949, M.B.A., U. Pa., 1954; m. Joleen Schovee; children—Claire Graf Ludwig, Joseph Charles, Michelle, Mary Ellen, Thomas, Richard, stepchildren—Thomas R. Schovee, Stephen W. Schovee, Kathryn L. Schovee. Trainee, Prudential Ins. Co., Newark, 1954-55, systems analyst, 1955-56, asst. research analyst, 1956-58, research analyst, 1958-61, investment analyst, 1961-63, sr. investment analyst, 1963-64, Houston, 1964-67; v.p. So. Nat. Bank, Houston, 1967-69; fin. adv. Quintana Petroleum Corp., Houston, 1969-79, investment mgr., 1979-84; dir. Alamo Group Inc. ; mem. investment com. trust dept. Cullen Bank & Trust; cons. research com. Houston C. of C., 1966-71; exec. sec. Cullen Found., 1974—. Bd. govs., v.p. Center for Retarded, Inc., Houston, 1978-86, trustee, 1982-87; bd. dirs. Alley Theatre, 1981-83. Served with AUS, 1951-53. Mem. Houston Fin. Analysts (pres. 1973-74, dir. 1974-77). Clubs: Houston, Houstonian. Home: 6205 Pickens St Houston TX 77007 Office: 601 Jefferson St Houston TX 77002

GRAFF, STUART LESLIE, accounting executive; b. Bklyn., Nov. 5, 1945; s. Irving and Ruth (Kaplan) G.; BA in Chemistry and Edn., Queens (N.Y.) Coll., 1968; MBA, Loyola U., Chgo., 1972; m. June Hilda Mannheimer, Mar. 2, 1969; children—Ivan Henry, Rachel Caroline. CPA, Md.; cert. mgmt. acct. Chemist, then motor vehicle analyst Atlantic Richfield Co., Harvey, Ill., Chgo. and Phila., 1967-72; cost acct. Nat. Freight, Inc., Vineland, N.J., 1972-75; transp. cost analyst ICC, 1976-80; assoc. A.T. Kearney, Inc., mgmt. cons., Alexandria, Va., 1980-82; systems acct. Arlington County (Va.), 1982-85; systems acct. D.C., Washington, 1985-86; acctg. mgr. Arlington County (Va.), 1986-88; tech. mgr. Am. Inst. C.P.A.s, Washington, 1988—; adj. instr. acctg. Montgomery Coll., Germantown, Md. Pres. Pavilion Tenants Assn., 1980. C.P.A., Md. Mem. Am. Inst. C.P.A.s (Elijah Watt Sells award 1980), Nat. Assn. Accts. (cert. in mgmt. acctg., chpt. treas., Andrew Barr award Washington chpt. 1984-85), D.C. Inst. C.P.A.s, Md. Assn. C.P.A.s. Patentee halide addition and distbn. Jewish. Home: 5901 Montrose Rd Apt N-608 Rockville MD 20852-4753

GRAFFEO, ANTHONY SALVATORE, infosystems executive; b. Bklyn., Dec. 6, 1938; s. Anthony and Clara C. (Inzerillo) G.; m. Angelina Calavetta, Nov. 17, 1962; children: Anthony J., Michael J., John P. BS in Mgmt. and Indsl. Relations, NYU, 1970. Mgr. ops. Shell Oil Co., N.Y.C., 1961-70; svc. pres. Home Ins. Co. Info. Systems, N.Y.C., 1970—; bd. dirs. various cos. Mem. Data Processing Mgmt. Assn. Republican. Roman Catholic. Home: 32 W 7th St Deer Park NY 11729 Office: Home Ins Co 59 Maiden Ln 4th Fl New York NY 10038

GRAGG, SARA ELIZABETH, motel executive; b. Malvern, Ark., Mar. 28, 1930; d. Alymer James and Martha Thelma (Cross) Wells; m. Glen E. Keller, Dec. 18, 1949 (div. 1964); children: Michael, Kathryn, Kim; m. Paris R. Green, Sept. 15, 1968 (dec. 1969); m. Billy Max Gragg, May 14, 1970 (dec. 1987). BA, U. Ark., 1949, MA, 1950, PhD, 1971. Exec. asst. dept. psychiatry U. Ark. Med. Ctr., Little Rock, 1951-56; asst. prof. English Ark. State U., Jonesboro, 1962-66; instr. English dept. U. Ark.-Fayetteville, 1966-69; asst. prof. U. Mo.-Rolla, 1968; pres. Gragg Motels, Inc., Fayetteville, 1970—. Author: The Artistic Unity of Carlyle's French Revolution, 1971. Pres. Ark. Med. Soc. Aux., Jonesboro, 1963-64; Republican county chmn., Jonesboro, 1962-63. Named Woman of Yr., Bus and Profl. Women, Mountain View, Ark., 1961. Mem. Ark. Motel Assn., Am. Hotel and Motel Assn., Ark. Retail Mchts. Assn., Internat. Platform Assn., Fayetteville C. of C., Phi Beta Kappa, Lambda Tau, Psi Chi. Methodist. Avocations: writing, travelling. Home: Route 11 Smokehouse Rd Fayetteville AR 72701 Office: Gragg Motels Inc 215-229 N College St Fayetteville AR 72701

GRAHAM, CAROL ETHLYN, insurance company administrator; b. Guthrie, Okla., Nov. 28, 1941; d. Brance Alma Woodard and Rachel Ione (Brown) Meininger; m. Morton J. Graham Dec. 14, 1965 (div. Apr. 1985); children: Brance D., Kelly L., S. Robert, M. Jeff III. AS in Civil Tech., Okla. State U.-Tech. Inst., 1978; cert. in flood plain analysis, U. Okla., 1979. Cert. premium auditor, Okla. Factory worker Aero Comdr., Bethany, Okla., 1963-66; legal asst. Whit Ingram Atty., Oklahoma City, 1966-75; bookkeeper Joe Roselle Atty., Oklahoma City, 1966-78; hydraulic analyst Cunningham Cons. Inc., Oklahoma City, 1978-80; premium auditor loss control Atwell, Vogel and Sterling, Dallas, 1982-83; premium auditor Mid-Continent Casualty Co., Tulsa, 1983—. Mem. Ins. Auditors Assn. Oklahoma City (sec. 1985-86, pres. 1986-87), Ins. Auditors Assn. of S.W., Nat. Assn. Female Execs., Women Execs. Cen. Okla. Democrat. Home: PO Box 1613 Guthrie OK 73044 Office: Mid-Continent Casualty Co 1646 S Boulder PO Box 1409 Tulsa OK 74101

GRAHAM, DAVID BOLDEN, food products executive; b. Miami Beach, Fla., Feb. 10, 1927; s. Robert Cabel and Bertha Eugenia (Hack) G.; m. Stuart Hill Smith, Sept. 1, 1956; children: Bird, Ellen, Darnall, Lamar, Lyle, Gerard, Barbara, David Bolden. Student Colegio de san Bartolome, Bogota, Colombia, 1946; BS, Georgetown U., 1949; postgrad. Harvard Bus. Sch., 1950. Chmn. Graham Farms, Inc., Washington, Ind., 1950—, Graham Cheese Corp., Washington, 1950—; sec. Bal Harbour Square (Fla.), 1956-57, Graham Bros., Inc., Washington, 1950-72; chmn. Peoples Nat. Bank, Washington. Pres. Washington planning commn., regional planning commn.; bd. dirs. Hist. Landmarks Found., Ind.; mem. Ind. Agrl. Adv. Council; mem. adv. council Bur. Water and Mineral Resources. Served to lt. col. USAF Res., 1949-77. Republican. Roman Catholic. Clubs: Columbia (Indpls.); Rotary (past pres.). Lodge: Elks. Contbr. articles on agr., transp., early fur traders to various publs. Home and Office: PO Box 391 Washington IN 47501

GRAHAM, DUNCAN, construction executive, savings and loan administrator; b. Los Angeles, Mar. 27, 1938; s. John W. and Maxine E. (Smallwood) G.; divorced; children: John D., Valerie A. AA, John Muir Jr. Coll. Chief exec. officer Universal Funds for Edn., Washington, 1966—, Am. Scholarship Rsch. Found., Washington, 1967—, Duncan Graham Inc., Calif., 1972—, Am. I.P.O. Rsch. Found., Calif., 1982—, Box One Soc., Calif., 1983—, Absolute Constrn. Inc., Calif., 1984—; cons. low income housing industry, 1972—; I.P.O.'s, Argo Electronics Inc., 1968—, World Media Verifiers Inc., 1972—, Dividend Ptnrs. Inc., 1986—, Imp. Ltd., 1988—. Asst. scoutmaster Boy Scouts Am., Pasadena, 1982—. Presbyterian.

GRAHAM, FRANCIS RONALD, corporate executive; b. Toronto, Ont., Can., May 6, 1920; s. Francis Ronald and Helen Marguerite (Phelan) G.; m. Renee Beatrice Moncel, Mar. 10, 1942; children: Susan Graham Wild, Ronald, Robert, Margot Graham Heyerhoff, Anthony, Ian. With Bank N.S., 1939-41; pres. Ronmount Holdings Ltd., also bd. dirs.; vice chmn. Scott's Hospitality Inc., also bd. dirs.; bd. dirs. Sulconam Inc. Served with Can. Army, 1941-46. Roman Catholic. Clubs: St. James's (Montreal); Royal Can. Yacht (Toronto). Office: 11 King St W, Ste 1515, Toronto, ON Canada M5H 1A7

GRAHAM, HOWARD HOLMES, manufacturing executive; b. Greensburg, Pa., Apr. 24, 1947; s. Howard B. and Dorothy (Holmes) G.; m. Roberta A. Grant, June 8, 1968 (div. Feb. 1984); m. Linda A. Cossarek, Mar. 14, 1987; 1 child, Christina Ross. BS, Carnegie Mellon U., 1968; MBA, U. Chgo., 1973. CPA, Ill. Various positions Zenith Electronics Corp., Glenview, Ill., 1973-81, dir. acctg., 1981-82, v.p. fin. services, 1982-87, v.p. fin., 1987-88; v.p. fin. Wyse Tech. Inc., San Jose, Calif., 1988—. Mem. adv. bd. acctg. dept. U. Ill. at Chgo., 1982—; bd. dirs. Juvenile Protective Assn., Chgo., 1987—. Served to capt. U.S. Army, 1968-71, Vietnam. Decorated Bronze Star; recipient Elijah Watt Sells award Am. Inst. CPA's, 1982. Mem. Beta Gamma Sigma. Club: Chgo. Yacht. Office: Wyse Tech Inc 3571 N 1st St San Jose CA 95134

GRAHAM, JERRY FISHER, bank executive, accountant; b. Salisbury, Md., Aug. 17, 1939; s. I. Rayner and M. Theresa (Webster) G.; m. Sammi Yvonne Bounds, May 11, 1958; children: David Rayner, Steven Ronald. BS, U. Del., 1969. CPA, Md. Audit mgr. Deloite Haskins & Sells, Balt., 1969-77; lectr. Hartford Community Coll., Bel Air, Md., 1971-85, dean of adminstrn., 1977-80; v.p., chief acct. (controller) Merc. Bankshares Corp., Balt., 1980—. Mem. agy. audit com. United Way, Balt., 1984—; bd. dirs. Meals on Wheels of Cen. Md., Balt., 1985—, treas., 1987-88, v.p., 1988-89, pres. 1989. Mem. Am. Inst. CPA's, Md. Assn. CPA's (pub. relations com., chmn. yr. award 1976), Bank Adminstrs. Inst. Club: Bel Air Athletic, Rock Spring Swim (treas. 1977-78). Lodge: Lions (v.p., sec., 1978, 85). Home: 328 Princeton Ln Bel Air MD 21014 Office: Merc Banksharers Corp 2 Hopkins Pla PO Box 1477 Baltimore MD 21203

GRAHAM, JOHN BRETT, bank executive; b. Washington, Ind., Mar. 9, 1959; s. Ziba F. and Winifred (Heekin) G.; m. Margaret Anne McHugh, Nov. 3, 1984; children: Caitlin A., Laura E. BBA, Xavier U., 1981, MBA, 1983, cert. bank adminstrn., 1988. From mgmt. trainee to ops. officer to asst. v.p. Peoples Nat. Bank and Trust Co., Washington, 1983—; mng. dir. Winco Investment Co., Cin.; bd. dirs. Graham Cheese Corp., Elnora, Ind., Graham Farms, Inc., Washington. Treas. Young Reps. Daviess County, Washington, 1984, Citizens Orgn. Community Devel., Washington, 1984; bd. dirs. Daviess County YMCA, Washington, 1985; co-chmn. Daviess County United Way fund drive, 1988—. Mem. Bank Adminstrn. Inst. (Ind. chpt. sec. 1988), Washington Conservation (corp. sec. 1988—), Elks. Office: Peoples Nat Bank & Trust Co 201 E Main St Washington IN 47501

GRAHAM, JOHN DALBY, public relations executive; b. Maryville, Mo., Aug. 24, 1937; s. Kyle T. and Irma Irene (Dalby) G.; m. Jean Elizabeth Landon, Aug. 30, 1958; children—Katherine Elizabeth, David Landon. B.J., U. Mo., 1959. Editor Hallmark Cards, Inc., Kansas City, Mo., 1959-62; dir. pub. relations St. Louis Met. YMCA, 1962-66; chmn., chief exec. officer Fleishman-Hillard, Inc., St. Louis, 1966—; chmn. Fleishman-Hillard Europe; bd. dirs. Fleishman-Hillard/U.K. Ltd. Bd. dirs. Webster U., St. Luke's Hosp.; mem. exec. bd. St. Louis Area council Boy Scouts Am. Served to capt. U.S. Army, 1959-66. Mem. Pub. Rels. Soc. Am., Internat. Pub. Rels. Assn., Nat. Investor Relations Inst., Round Table, University Club, Noonday Club (St. Louis), Log Cabin Club. Clubs: University, Noonday (St. Louis), Log Cabin. Home: 83 Bellerive Acres Saint Louis MO 63121 Office: Fleishman Hillard Inc 200 N Broadway Saint Louis MO 63102

GRAHAM, JOHN ROBERT, JR., manufacturing company executive; b. Chgo., Oct. 11, 1930; s. John Robert and Grace Beatrice (Strangemen) G.; m. Bettina Abigail Hoffman, Sept. 6, 1958 (div. June 1975); children: Jonathan, Karl; m. Beverly Criley, Dec. 31, 1975. B.S., U.S. Mcht. Marine Acad., 1952; M.B.A., Harvard U., 1959. Ship officer Moore-McCormack Lines, N.Y.C., 1952-53, 55-58; asst. v.p., loan officer Hartford Nat. Bank, 1959-67; asst. treas. Heublein, Inc., Hartford, Conn., 1967-68, treas., 1968-74; sr. v.p. fin. and adminstrn. Sikorsky Aircraft Co., Stratford, Conn., 1974-80; v.p. fin., chief fin. officer Planning Research Corp., Washington, 1980-82; v.p., chief fin. officer Uniroyal Inc., Middlebury, Conn., 1982-88, Uniroyal Holding, Inc., Waterbury, Conn., 1982-88, also bd. dirs.; bd. dirs. Uniroyal Goodrich Tire Co., Akron, Ohio; trustee CDU Holding, Inc. Liquidating Trust, N.Y.C., 1986-89; v.p. Healthware Corp, Seattle, 1989—. Co-author: Nonwoven Textiles-An Unbiased Appraisal, 1959. Corporator, Middlesex Hosp., Middletown, Conn., 1964-85; v.p., treas. Conn. Valley YMCA, Deep River, 1962-64; pres. Essex (Ct.) Bus. Assn., 1964-65. Served as lt. (j.g.) USNR, 1953-55, PTO, Korea. Mem. Harvard (N.Y.C.). Lodge: Masons. Avocations: sailing, skiing. Home: 82 Cascade Key Bellevue WA 98006 Office: Healthware Corp 140 Lakeside Ave Seattle WA 98122

GRAHAM, JOHN WEBB, lawyer; b. Toronto, Ont., Can., Sept. 10, 1912; s. George Wilbur and Rosaline (Webb) G.; m. Velma Melissa Taylor, June 19, 1941 (dec. Nov. 5, 1971); children: Edward Samuel Rogers (stepson), Ann Taylor; m. Natalia Nikolaevna Popowa, July 15, 1976. Student, Upper Can. Coll., 1920-30; B.A., Trinity Coll., U. Toronto, 1933, D.S. Litt., 1981; Barrister-at-law, Osgoode Hall Law Sch., Can., 1936. Bar: Queen's counsel 1956. Corp. trust officer Toronto Gen. Trusts Corp., 1936-39; solicitor Daly, Thistle, Judson & McTaggart, Toronto, 1946-48; gen. counsel Imperial Life Assurance Co. Can., Toronto, 1949-58; partner firm Payton, Biggs & Graham, Toronto, 1958-77, Cassels Brock, 1977-84, Cassels, Brock & Blackwell, 1984—; chmn. bd. Rogers Telecommunications Ltd., Rogers Communications Inc., Rogers Cable TV Ltd., Rogers Broadcasting Ltd.; bd. dirs. numerous cos., including Scorfin Inc., Cantel Inc. Mem. exec. com. Trinity Coll., Toronto, 1960-71, also chmn., 1966-69; Pres. St. Paul's Progressive Conservative Assn., 1957-61. Served with Royal Canadian Armoured Corps, 1939-46, ETO. Decorated Efficiency Decoration, 1944; hon. lt. col. Gov. Gen's Horse Guards, 1970-75. Mem. Canadian Bar Assn., County of York Law Assn., Lawyers Club Toronto, Assn. Life Ins. Counsel, Canadian Tax Found., Estate Planning Council Toronto, Progressive Conservative Bus. Men's Club Met. Toronto (v.p. 1968-70), Sigma Chi (internat. pres. 1971-73). Mem. Conservative party. Mem. Anglican Ch. Can. Clubs: Albany, Toronto Hunt, York, Royal Canadian Mil. Inst. (Toronto); Empire of Can. Home: 2 Wood Ave, Toronto, ON Canada M4N 1P4 Office: 40 King St W Ste 2200, Toronto, ON Canada M5H 1B5

GRAHAM, JOHN WILTON, direct mail marketing executive; b. Chgo., Sept. 18, 1946; s. Joe Wilton and Mary Magdalene (Banister) G.; m. Brenda Bagby, Aug. 6, 1966; children: Scott K., Eric J. BS in Mktg., Murray State U., 1968, MBA, 1969. V.p., gen. mgr. College Mktg. Group, Reading, Mass., 1974-77; v.p. mktg. William C. Brown Pub. Co., Dubuque, Iowa, 1977-79; pres., chief operating officer The Hamilton Group, Jacksonville, Fla., 1980-85; pres. book pub. Coll. Mktg. Group Info. Services, Winchester, Mass., 1986—; cons. Rand McNally, Chgo., 1985-86. Author: (with others) Selling By Mail: An Entrepreneur's Guide, 1985. Vol. Prison Fellowship Job Task Force, Jacksonville, 1981-85. Recipient numerous Addy Awards Am. Advt. Fedn. (representing firm), 1980—. Mem. Am. Mgmt. Assns., Fla. Direct Mktg. Assn., Direct Mktg. Assn. Internat. Democrat. Presbyterian. Office: Coll Mktg Group Info Svcs 50 Cross St Winchester MA 01890

GRAHAM, JUL ELIOT, lawyer, educator; b. Bklyn., June 14, 1953; s. Arnold Harold and Roselle (Lesser) G.; m. Sherry Robin Goldberg, Nov. 2, 1980. B.A. in Polit. Sci. cum laude, NYU, 1975; J.D. magna cum laude, N.Y. Law Sch., 1978. Bar: N.Y. 1979, U.S. Supreme Ct. 1984. Cons. Consumer Law Tng. Ctr., N.Y. Law Sch., 1976, mem. adj. faculty, 1980—; prin. appellate law rsch. asst. appellate div. 1st Dept., Supreme Ct. of State of N.Y., N.Y.C., 1978-79, staff atty., 1979-82, assoc. atty., 1982-83, law asst. to the justices, 1983—, exec. sec. deptl. adv. com. to family ct., 1979-82, editor criminal trial advocacy handbook, 1980—. Assoc. editor N.Y. Law Sch. Law Rev., 1976-78, contbg. author, 1975. Guest lectr. Joe Franklin Show, WOR-TV, 1982—. Mem. N.Y. County Lawyers Assn. (com. on communications and entertainment law 1980—, com. on penal and correctional reform 1980— , spl. com. on practical legal edn. 1979—), Am. Arbitration Assn. (arbitrator 1985—), Internat. Radio and TV Soc., Am. Film Inst., Phi Delta Phi, Phi Sigma Alpha. Home: 249 Adelaide Ave Staten Island NY 10306 Office: NY State Supreme Ct Appellate Div 1st Jud Dept 41 Madison Ave New York NY 10010

GRAHAM, KATHARINE, newspaper executive; b. N.Y.C., June 16, 1917; d. Eugene and Agnes (Ernst) Meyer; m. Philip L. Graham, June 5, 1940 (dec. 1963); children: Elizabeth Morris Graham Weymouth, Donald Edward, William Welsh, Stephen Meyer. Student, Vassar Coll., 1934-36; AB, U. Chgo., 1938. Reporter San Francisco News, 1938-39; mem. editorial staff Washington Post, 1939-45, mem. Sunday, circulation and editorial depts., pub., 1969-79; pres. Washington Post Co., 1963-73, 77, chmn. bd., chief exec. officer, 1973—; co-chmn. Internat. Herald Tribune; bd. dirs. Bowater Mersey Paper Co., Ltd., Reuters Founders Share Co. Ltd., Urban Inst., Fed. City Council, Council for Aid to Edn. Life trustee, U. Chgo.; hon. trustee George Washington U.; mem. sr. adv. bd. of the Joan Shorenstein Barone Ctr. on the Press, Politics and Pub. Policy, Harvard U. Fellow Am. Acad. Arts and Scis.; mem. Am. Soc. Newspaper Editors, Nat. Press Club, Coun. Fgn. Rels., Overseas Devel. Coun., Sigma Delta Chi. Clubs: Cosmopolitan (N.Y.C.); 1925 F Street. Home: 2920 R St NW Washington DC 20007 Office: Washington Post Co 1150 15th St NW Washington DC 20071 *

GRAHAM, MICHAEL JOHN, management consultant, distributor; b. Berwyn, Ill., May 8, 1951; s. John Bernard and Mary Jane (Vynalek) G.; m. Kathleen Evans; children: Meredith, Allison. BA in Geology, Amherst Coll., 1976; M in Internat. Mgmt., Am. Grad. Sch. Internat. Mgmt., 1978. Gen. mgr. Power Group Internat., Houston, 1979-80; dir. corp. devel. Utilities, Inc., Northbrook, Ill., 1980-85; pres. Computer Exchange, Wheeling, Ill., 1984-85; chief operating officer, exec. v.p. The Flyer's Edge, Kenilworth, Ill., 1985-87; pres. Instructional Distbrs., Evanston, Ill., 1986—, It's A Small World, Winnetka, Ill., 1986—, Graham Assocs, Evanston, 1987—, Utility Supply Am., 1988—; corp. sec. Utilities, Inc., Northbrook, 1984-85. Author: Wind Tunnel Testing of SWECS, 1979; inventor automatic peritoneal dialysis machine; exhibitor consumer electronics shows Las Vegas, Chgo., 1986—, video software dealers show, Las Vegas, 1987—. Mem. Chgo. Assn. Direct Mktg., Purchasing Mgmt. Assn., Cons. Roundtable, Am. Mgmt. Assn., Am. Soc. Travel Agts. Republican. Office: Utility Supply Am 2335 Sanders Rd Northbrook IL 60062

GRAHAM, PAMELA SMITH, distributing company executive, artist; b. Winona, Miss., Jan. 18, 1944; d. Douglas LaRue and Dorothy Jean (Hefty) Smith; m. Robert William Graham, Mar. 6, 1965 (div.); children—Jennifer, Eric; m. Thomas Paul Harley, Dec. 4, 1976; stepchildren—Tom, Janice. Student U. Colo., 1962-65, U. Cin., 1974-76. Cert. notary pub., Colo. Profl. artist, craft tchr., art exhibitor Colo., N.J., Ohio, 1968-73; property mgmt. and investor Cin., 1972-77; acct., word processor Borden Chem. Co. div. Borden, Inc., Cin., 1974-78; owner, pres. Hargram Enterprises, Cin., 1977-81; owner, pres. Graham & Harley Enterprises. Morrison, Colo., 1981—; tchr.; cons. County committeewoman Bergen County, N.J., 1972, clk. of session, 1975-79, conv. chmn., 1981; campaign chmn. United Appeal, 1977; lifeline telephone counselor Suicide Hotline, 1985—. Recipient numerous awards for art exhibits, bus. achievements, 1962—. Mem. Nat. Assn. Female Execs., United Sales Leaders Assn., Nat. Museum of Women in Arts, Colo. Artists Assn., Evergreen Artists Assn., Colo. Calligraphers Guild, Foothills Art Ctr., Alpha Gamma Chi, Kappa Kappa Gamma. Republican. Club: Queen City Racquet. Office: Graham & Harley Enterprises 4303 S Taft St Morrison CO 80465

GRAHAM, RICHARD ZOLL, food product executive; b. Ft. Wayne, Ind., Aug. 26, 1929; s. Harold Wilson and Beatrice Elizabeth (Zoll) G.; m. Margaret Louise Brown, June 12, 1951; children: Michael Richard, David Braun, Sharon Elizabeth. BS in Bus., Miami U., Oxford, Ohio, 1951. Sales rep. Libbey Owens Ford Co., Dayton, Ohio, 1954-57, Los Angeles, 1957-60; dist. mgr. Libbey Owens Ford Co., Kansas City, Mo., 1960-67; nat. sales mgr. aircraft def. products Libbey Owens Ford Co., Toledo, 1967-69; v.p., asst. gen. mgr. Brown's Bakery, Inc., Defiance, Ohio, 1969-73, pres., 1973-83, chief exec. officer, ptnr., vice-chmn., 1983—; bd. dirs. Am. Bakers Coop Inc., Clifton, N.J., Ruban Fin. Services, Defiance. Trustee The Defiance Coll., also chmn. bus. affairs. Lt. (j.g.) USN, Korea. Mem. Ind. Bakers Assn. (chmn. 1986-87, bd. dirs.), Am. Inst. Baking (trustee 1980—), Defiance C. of C. (pres. 1974), Am. Soc. Bakery Engrs. (adv. com.), Ohio Bakers Assn. (bd. dirs. 1970—, pres. 1979), Am. Bakers Coop. (bd. dirs. 1973—, chmn. 1983-86), Ketting Country (Defiance (pres. 1980), Masons, Rotary (pres. Defiance chpt. 1981-83), Shriners. Republican. Presbyterian. Club: Kettenring Country (Defiance) (pres. 1982). Lodges: Masons, Shriners, Elks, Rotary (pres. Defiance club). Office: Brown's Bakery Inc 505 Downs St P O Box 1040 Defiance OH 43512

GRAHAM, ROBERT CECIL, information systems executive; b. Richmond, Va., Oct. 23, 1936; s. Raymond V. and Adalena Deane Graham; m. Barbara Roy Graham, Oct. 23, 1971. BS, Hampton Inst., 1958; cert. exec. program, Colgate U., 1969, Stanford U., 1972; grad. advanced mgmt. program, Harvard U., 1981. Supr. student accts. Fla. A&M U., Tallahassee, 1958-60; mgr. data processing, instr. Va. State Coll., Petersburg, 1960-64; systems engr. IBM Corp., N.Y.C., 1964-68; mgr. equal opportunity programs IBM Corp., White Plains, N.Y., 1968-70, br. mgr., Washington, 1970-73; mgr. service ops. planning and analysis Xerox Corp., Rochester, N.Y., 1973-75, service ops. mgr., Washington, 1975-76, region mgr. tech. service, 1976-78, nat. service mgr., 1978-79, v.p. nat. service, field ops., 1979-80, v.p. nat. service ops., 1980-83, region mgr., Atlanta, 1983-86, v.p. nat. tech. support and edn., El Segundo, Calif., 1986-87; v.p. U.S. Mktg. Group Customer Service, Rochester, 1987—.

GRAHAM, ROBERT GRANT, gas company executive; b. Ottawa, Ont., Can., Apr. 8, 1931; B.Comm., McGill U.; Pres., chief exec. officer Inter-City Gas Corp., Toronto, Ont., Can.; bd. dirs. Can. Gen. Ins. Co., Cen. Capital Corp., Conf. Bd. Inc., Fed. Industries Ltd., Gt. West Life Assurance Co., Cen. Guarantee Trust Ltd., Inter-City Gas Corp., MICC Investments Ltd., Moffat Communications Ltd., Mortgage Ins. Co. Can., Trader Group Ltd.; chmn. bd. ICG Utilities Greater Winnipeg Gas Co., ICG Utilities (Ont.) Ltd., KeepRite Inc., Heil Quaker Corp.; past bd. dirs. Conf. Bd. Can., Manitoba Health Scis. Centre, Manitoba Theatre Centre, Winnipeg Found. Office: Inter-City Gas Corp Exec Office, 20 Queen St W Box 32, Toronto, ON Canada M5H 3R3

GRAHAM, STEPHEN MICHAEL, lawyer; b. Houston, May 1, 1951; s. Frederick Mitchell and Lillian Louise (Miller) G.; m. Joanne Marie Sealock, Aug. 24, 1974; children: Aimee Elizabeth, Joseph Sealock, Jessica Anne. BS, Iowa State U., 1973; JD, Yale U., 1976. Bar: Wash. 1977. Assoc. Perkins Coie, Seattle, 1976-83, ptnr., 1983—. Bd. dirs. Wash. Spl. Olympics, Seattle, 1979-83, pres., 1983; mem. Seattle Bd. Ethics, 1982-88, chmn., 1983-88, Seattle Fair Campaign Practices Commn., 1982-88; trustee Cornish Coll. of the Arts, 1986—, exec. com., 1988—; trustee Epiphany Sch., 1987—; mem. exec. com. Sch. Law Yale U., 1988—; bd. dirs. Perkins Coie Community Service Found. Mem. ABA, Wash. State Bar Assn., Seattle-King County Bar Assn. Episcopalian. Clubs: Wash. Athletic, Columbia Tower. Office: Perkins Coie 1201 Third Ave 40th Fl Seattle WA 98101-3099

GRAHAM, WILLIAM B., pharmaceutical company executive; b. Chgo., July 14, 1911; s. William and Elizabeth (Burden) G.; m. Edna Kanaley, June 15, 1940 (dec.); children: William J., Elizabeth Anne, Margaret, Robert B.; m. Catherine Van Duzer, July 23, 1984. S.B. cum laude, U. Chgo., 1932, J.D. cum laude, 1936; LL.D., Carthage Coll., 1974, Lake Forest Coll., 1983; L.L.D. (hon.), U. Ill., 1988; L.H.D., St. Xavier Coll. and Nat. Coll. Edn., 1983. Bar: Ill. 1936. Patent lawyer Dyrenforth, Lee, Chritton & Wiles, 1936-40; mem. Dawson & Ooms, 1940-45; v.p., mgr. Baxter Travenol Labs., Inc., Deerfield, Ill., 1945-53; pres., chief exec. officer Baxter Travenol Labs., Inc., 1953-71, chmn. bd., chief exec. officer, 1971-80, chmn. bd., 1980-85, sr. chmn., 1985—, also dir.; prof., chairperson Weizmann Inst. Sci., Rehoboth, Israel, 1978. Bd. dirs., pres. Lyric Opera Chgo.; vice chmn. bd. dirs. Nat. Park Fedn.; bd. dirs. Chgo. Hort. Soc., Nat. Council U.S.-China Trade; trustee Orchestral Assn., U. Chgo., Evanston (Ill.) Hosp. Recipient V.I.P. award Lewis Found., 1963, Disting. Citizen award Ill. St. Andrew Soc., 1974, Decision Maker of Yr. award Am. Statis. Assn., 1974, Marketer of Yr. award AMA, 1976, Found. award Kidney Found., 1981, Chicagoan of Yr. Chgo. Boys Club, 1981, Bus. Statesman of Yr. award Harvard Bus. Sch. Club Chgo., 1983, Achievement award Med. Tech. Services, 1983, Disting. Fellows award Internat. Ctr. for Artificial Organs and Transplantations, 1982, Chgo. Civic award DePaul U., 1986, Internat. Visitors Golden Medallion award U. Ill., 1988; recognized for pioneering work Health Industry Mfrs. Assn., 1981; inducted Jr. Achievement Chgo. Bus. Hall of Fame, 1986. Mem. Am. Pharm. Mfrs. Assn. (past pres.), Ill. Mfrs. Assn. (past pres.), Pharm. Mfrs. Assn. (past chmn., award for spl. distinction leadership 1981), Chgo. Club (past pres.), Commonwealth Club, Med-Am. Club, Comml. Club, Indian Hill Club, Casino Club, Old Elm Club, Seminole Club, Everglades Club, Bath & Tennis Club, University Club, Links Club, Phi Beta Kappa, Sigma Xi, Phi Delta Phi. Home: 40 Devonshire Ln Kenilworth IL 60043 Office: Baxter Travenol Labs Inc 1 Baxter Pkwy Deerfield IL 60015

GRAHAM, WILLIAM EDGAR, JR., lawyer, utility company executive; b. Jackson Springs, N.C., Dec. 31, 1929; s. William Edgar and Minnie Blanch (Autry) G.; m. Jean Dixon McLaurin, Nov. 24, 1962; children: William McLaurin, John McMillan, Sally Faircloth. AB, U. N.C., 1952, JD with honors, 1956. Bar: N.C. bar. Law clk. U.S. Ct. Appeals 4th Circuit, 1956-57; individual practice law Charlotte, N.C., 1957-69; judge N.C. Ct. Appeals, 1969-73; sr. v.p., gen. counsel Carolina Power & Light Co., Raleigh, N.C., 1973-81, exec. v.p., 1981-85, vice chmn., 1985—. Served with USAF, 1952-54. Mem. Am. Bar Assn., N.C. Bar Assn., Wake County Bar Assn., Edison Electric Inst. Presbyterian. Home: 409 Hillandale Dr Raleigh NC 27609 Office: Carolina Power & Light Co PO Box 1551 Raleigh NC 27602 also: Carolina Power & Light Co 411 Fayetteville St Raleigh NC 27602

GRAINGER, A. JEFFREY, food company executive; b. Bronxville, N.Y., Feb. 21, 1952; s. Edmund Charles Jr. and Virginia (Rocke) G.; m. Moira Dwyer, Dec. 3, 1977; children: Bryan, Andrew, Molly. BA in History, Coll. of Holy Cross, 1974; MBA in Fin., Columbia U., 1980. Program dir. Mass. Dept. Edn., Boston, 1975-76; assoc. in mcpl. fin. E.F. Hutton and Co., N.Y.C., 1976-78; fin. analyst Internat. Paper Co., N.Y.C., 1980-82; sr. fin. analyst United Brands Co., N.Y.C., 1982-83; dir. treasury svcs. Chiquita Brands Inc., N.Y.C., 1983-86, asst. treas., 1986-87; v.p. ops., planning and control Chiquita Brands Inc., N.Y.C. and Cin., 1987-88; v.p. sourcing and ops. Chiquita Tropical Products, Inc., Cin., 1988—; cons. Middle West Svcs. Co., Washington, 1976. Vol. Vista Worcester (Mass.) Consortium for Higher Edn., 1974-75. Named Outstanding VISTA Vol., ACTION, 1975. Home: 8360 Old Stable Rd Cincinnati OH 45243 Office: Chiquita Brands Inc 250 E Fifth St Cincinnati OH 45202

GRALA, JANE MARIE, securities firm executive; b. Phila.; d. Stanley Frank and Anna Stephanie (Yurkiewicz) G. BS, Rutgers U., Camden, 1976; MBA, Winthrop Coll., 1979; postgrad., Am. Mgmt. Assn., N.Y.C., 1980-82, Am. Inst. Real Estate Appraisers, Chgo., 1985. Mgr. acctg. dept. NDI Engring. Co., Pennsauken, N.J., 1968-72, project mgr., 1972-76; rep. sales Am. Cyanamid, Wayne, N.J., 1976-80; dist. mgr. Am. Appraisal Assocs., Phila., 1980-86; fin. advisor Prudential-Bache Securities, Clearwater, Fla., 1986—. Mem. Nat. Assn. Accts. (dir. advt. So. Jersey chpt. 1983-86), Assn. MBA Execs., Bus and Profl. Women's Assn., Nat. Assn. for Female Execs., Chi Delta, Phi Chi Theta. Republican. Office: Prudential-Bache Securities 2920 US Hwy 19N Ste 100 Clearwater FL 34621

GRALLA, EUGENE, natural gas company executive; b. N.Y.C., May 3, 1924; s. Jacob and Anna Ruth (Kleiman) G.; m. Beverly Dorman, Apr. 7, 1946; children: Rhona Gralla Spilka, Steven Stuart. B.S., U.S. Naval Acad., 1945; M.B.A., Harvard U., 1947. Commd. ensign USN, 1945, advanced through grades to comdr., 1961; served sea duty 1947-49, 54-56; control officer (Naval Supply Depot, Guantanamo Bay), Cuba, 1959-61; with (Office Asst. Sec. Def. for Installations and Logistics), 1961-64; ret. 1966; dir. data systems planning Trans World Airlines, N.Y.C., 1966-68; corp. dir. mgmt. info. systems Internat. Paper Co., N.Y.C., 1968; v.p. electronic data processing Columbia Gas System Service Corp., Wilmington, Del., 1969-73; sr. v.p. Columbia Gas Distbn. Cos., Columbus, Ohio, 1973-86, pres., 1986-89, ret., 1989. Trustees Ohio Pub. Expenditure Council. Mem. U.S. Naval Inst., Navy League Columbus, Harvard Bus. Sch., Club Columbus, Agonis Club Columbus. Club: Mason. Home: 5850 Forestview Dr Columbus OH 43213

GRAMM, WENDY LEE, government official. d. Joshua and Angeline (AnChin) Lee; m. Phil Gramm, Nov. 2, 1970; children: Marshall Kenneth, Jefferson Philip. BA in Econs., Wellesley Coll., 1966; PhD in Econs., Northwestern U., 1971. Staff dept. quantitive methods U. Ill., 1969; asst. prof. Tex. A&M U., 1970-74, assoc. prof. dept. econs., 1975-79; research staff Inst. Def. Analyses, 1979-82; asst. dir. Bur. Econs. FTC, 1982-83, dir., 1983-85; adminstr. Office Info. and Regulatory Affairs, OMB, 1985-87; chmn. Commodity Futures Trading Commision, 1988—. Contbr. articles to profl. jours. Office: Commodity Futures Trading Commn 2033 K St NW Washington DC 20581

GRANDE, JOHN JOSEPH, JR., financial services company executive; b. Newark, N.J., Sept. 5, 1942; s. John J. and Dorothy (Knichel) G.; m. Bette Jeanne Miller, Jan. 23, 1964 (div. 1980); children: Cindi, John, Scott, Eric; m. Traudy Fasthuber, Mar. 27, 1987. Student, Fairleigh Dickenson U., 1960-62, Union Coll., 1963; cert., Coll. for Fin . Planning, Denver, 1985. Registered investment advisor. Mgr. Main Savs. and Loan, Bloomfield, N.J., 1966-67; fin. planner Mass. Mut. Life. Ins., Newark, 1967-76; pres. Fin. Group, Inc., Wall, N.J., 1976-80, Tangible Resource Group, Inc., Red Bank, N.J., 1980-81; sr. fin. planner Raymond James & Assocs., Inc., Naples, Fla., 1982-85; prin. Investment Mgm.t and Rsch., Inc., Ocean, N.J., 1985—; pres. Grande Fin. Svcs., Inc., Ocean, 1987—; speaker Rotary Clubs, Fla., N.J., 1984-87. Speaker Am. Heart Assn., Fla., 1983; chmn. fund raising com. Save Our Shores, Monmouth County, N.J., 1986—. Mem. Inst. Cert. Fin. Planning. Office: Grande Fin Svcs Inc 1001 Deal Rd Ocean NJ 07712

GRANDEAU, DAVID MARK, corporate professional; b. Poughkeepsie, N.Y., May 29, 1959; s. Barry and Pearl (Szabo) G. BA, U. Vt., 1981; JD, Albany Law Sch., 1984. Bar: N.Y. 1985. Law clk. N.Y. State Supreme Ct. Appellate Div., Albany, 1984-85; gen. counsel Coradian Corp., Latham, N.Y., 1985-87; sole practice Albany, 1985—; counsel N.Y. State Senate Solid Waste Commn., Albany, 1986—; asst. sec. Coradian Corp., 1985—; sec. First Grafton Corp., Latham, 1987—; bd. dirs. Pureauco Corp.; pres. Pureauco Corp., Loudonville, 1981. Republican. Jewish. Office: Pureauco Corp 253 Osborne Rd Londonville NY 12211

GRANDINETTI, MICHAEL LAWRENCE, management consultant; b. Bklyn., Mar. 7, 1960; s. Francis Mario and Mary Ann (Yelapi) G. BSME magna cum laude, Rutgers U., 1983; M in Pub. and Pvt. Mgmt., Yale U., 1989. Computer systems sales program mgr. Hewlett Packard, Bridgeport, Conn., 1983-85; mgr. market devel. Hewlett Packard, Ft. Collins, Colo., 1985-87; mgmt. cons. Frank Lynn & Assocs., Chgo., summer 1988, McKinsey and Co., N.Y.C., 1989—. Recipient Cert. of Merit award State of N.J. Dept. Higher Edn.; named to Nat. Dean's List; Jess Morrow Johns Meml. scholar Yale U. Mem. Nat. Engring. Honor Soc., Nat. Mech. Engring. Honor Frat., Am. Mgmt. Assn., Local Investment Club (past pres., founder), Colo. Internat. Trade Orgn., U.S. Rowing Assn., Tau Beta Pi, Pi Tau Sigma. Republican. Roman Catholic. Clubs: Rocky Mountain Rowing (Denver), Toastmasters.

GRANDY, BRIAN JOHN, resort company executive, CPA; b. Everett, Mass., Sept. 7, 1954; s. John Anthony and Lillian (Tkachuk) G.; m. Tracy S. Conlon Grandy, July 12, 1986. BS in Acctg., U. Richmond, 1976; postgrad., U. Pa., 1980. CPA. Staff auditor Peat, Marwick, Mitchell & Co., Washington, 1976-78; sr. auditor GAO, Washington, 1978-86, Valley Bank Nev., Las Vegas, 1986-87; contr. Seven Resorts, Inc., Boulder City, 1987—. Mem. Am. Inst. CPA's, Washington CPA's, Inst. Internal Auditors. Home: 2719 Burton AVe Las Vegas NV 89102 Office: Seven Resorts Inc 688 Wells Rd Ste A Boulder City NV 89005

GRANGER, CLIVE WILLIAM JOHN, economist, educator; b. Swansea, Wales, Sept. 4, 1934; came to U.S., 1974.; s. Edward John and Evelyn Agnes (Hessey) G.; m. Patricia Anne Loveland, May 14, 1960; children: Mark, Claire. BA, U. Nottingham, Eng., 1955; MD in Stats., U. Nottingham, 1959. Lectr. in maths. U. Nottingham, 1956-64; profl. statician 1964-74; prof. econs. U. Calif., San Diego, 1976—; bd. dirs. Quantitative Econ. Research Inc., San Diego. Author: Forecasting Stock Markets, 1970; editor: Commodity Markets, 1973. Harkness Fund fellow, 1959-60, Econometric Soc. fellow, 1973. Fellow Royal Statis. Soc.; mem. Am. Econ. Soc., Am. Statis. Assn. (bd. dirs. 1985-87). Office: U Calif San Diego Econs Dept D-008 La Jolla CA 92093

GRANGER, RODNEY J., management executive, industrial engineer; b. Grand Rapids, Mich., Jan. 1, 1935; s. Joseph Stanley and Imogene (Leslie) G.; m. Eugenia Mae Grayson, Mar. 2, 1957; children: David, Leslie. BS in Indsl. Engring., Gen. Motors Inst., 1957; M of Sr. Mgmt., Lewis & Clark Coll., 1971. Gen. foreman Chevrolet div. Gen. Motors Corp., Detroit, 1957-62; chief indsl. engr. H.K. Porter Co., Cleve., 1962-63; quality control mgr. Mattel Toys, Inc., Hawthorne, Calif., 1963-67; mgr. mfg. engring., prodn. control mgr. Precision Castparts, Portland, Oreg., 1967-73; mfg. mgr. Arwood Corp., Cleve., 1973-77; pres. Granger Mfg., Elkhart, Ind., 1977-81, cons., 1982—; plant mgr. ITT Hancock, Jackson, Mich., 1981-82; gen. mgr. Nina Enterprises, Chgo., 1982—. Mem. Am. Mgmt. Assn., Am. Contract Bridge League (nat. master Memphis chpt.). Republican. Methodist. Home: 11128 B NW Rd Palos Hills IL 60465 Office: Nina Enterprises 1350 S Leavitt St Chicago IL 60608

GRANHOLM, JACKSON WALTER, contracting company executive; b. Tacoma, Wash., Nov. 18, 1921; s. John Henry and Elizabeth (Ayres) G.; m. Doris Evelyn Absher, Oct. 14, 1945; children—John Russell, Paul Gregory, Valerie Jo, Patricia Jean, Glen Walter, Dean Jackson. B.S. in Physics, U. Wash., 1947. Lic. engring. gen. contractor, Calif. Pres. Mellonics AV Inc., Tucson, 1961-62; v.p. Informatics, Inc., Sherman Oaks, Calif., 1962-63; sr. v.p. Wolf Research and Devel., Encino, Calif., 1963-65; research scientist Teledyne Systems, Northridge, Calif., 1965-66; chief exec. officer G. J. & A., Thousand Oaks, Calif., 1966—. Author and producer indsl. films. Contbr. articles in field. Mem., pres. Conejo Players, Inc., Thousand Oaks, Calif., 1970-84. Served to capt. USAAF, 1942-45. Decorated D.F.C. Mem. AAAS, Gregor Mendel Bot. Found. (pres. 1973-84). Republican. Episcopalian. Home: 1516 El Dorado Dr Thousand Oaks CA 91362

GRANICK, MICHAEL, computer company executive; b. N.Y.C., Mar. 15, 1932; s. Alexander Joseph and Julia (Greene) G.; m. Ellen M. Davis, May 30, 1953; children: Peter N., Jeremy S., Lisa R. BSChemE, U. Cin., 1955; MSChemE, NYU, 1957; postgrad., Harvard U. Sch. Bus., 1971. Research chem. engr. Texaco, Inc., Beacon, N.Y., 1957-64; dir. applications devel. Texaco, Inc., N.Y.C., 1964-67; mgr. corp. computer and communications services Mobil Corp., N.Y.C., 1967-86; v.p. data and communications services Warner Computer Systems Inc., Fairlawn, N.J., 1986—. Office: Warner Computer Systems Inc 17-01 Pollitt Dr Fair Lawn NJ 07410

GRANNEMANN, GARY W., paper company executive; b. Alburquerque, Jan. 3, 1961; s. Wayne W. and Margaret L. G. BBA, U. N.Mex., 1983; MBA, U. Colo., 1984. Real estate salesperson Tom Stribling & Assocs., Albuquerque, 1980; network control technician Thorn & Co., Englewood, Colo., 1984; mgmt. cons. Dixon Paper Co., Denver, 1985, mgr. research and planning, 1985—. Mem. Am. Fin. Assn., Nat. Eagle Scout Assn. Office: Dixon Paper Co TA Box 5285 Denver CO 80217

GRANNON, CHARLES LEE, investment banking official; b. Lafayette, Ind., Dec. 2, 1915; s. Charles Dale and Verena Ruth (Benedict) G.; m. Alice Fay Conard, Nov. 8, 1941; children: Michael L., Craig C., Charles P., Mark W. B.S., Purdue U., 1939; M.A., U. Iowa, 1941. With Goldman, Sachs & Co., N.Y.C., 1945—, ptnr., 1959-82, ltd. ptnr., 1982-86, ret., 1986. Trustee DePauw U., 1981; trustee Ridgewood YMCA, 1970, Valley Hosp. Found., Ridgewood, N.J., 1981; bd. dirs. U. Iowa Found. Served to lt. comdr. USN, 1942-45, 50-51. Republican. Presbyterian. Clubs: Ridgewood Country, Board St. (N.Y.C.), Broken Sound Golf (Boca Raton, Fla.), Ocean Reef (Key Largo, Fla.). Office: Brethen Christ World Missions PO Box 390 Mount Joy PA 17552

GRANO, JOSEPH DANTE, law educator; b. Olympia, Wash., Nov. 11, 1943; s. Dante J. and Sara R. (Giuffrida) G.; m. Maura D. Corrigan, July 11, 1976; children—Megan, Daniel. A.B., Temple U., 1965, J.D., 1968; LL.M., U. Ill., 1970. Bar: Pa. 1970, Mich. 1977. Asst. dist. atty. Phila. Dist. Attys. Office, 1970-71; asst. prof. U. Detroit, 1971-74, assoc. prof., 1974-75; prof. law Wayne State U., Detroit, 1975—; dep. asst. atty. gen. U.S. Dept. Justice, 1988; vis. prof. law Cornell U., 1978-79, U. Calif.-Berkeley, 1981-82; reporter Mich. Criminal Procedure Rules Comm., 1982—; lectr. Mich. Jud. Inst., 1978—, Am. Jud. Coll., 1986 . Mem. Am. Law Inst., Am. Bar Assn. Author: Problems in Criminal Procedure, 2d edit., 1981; (with James Haddad and Yale Kamisar) Sum and Substance of Criminal Procedure, 1977; contbr. articles in field to profl. jours. Home: 721 Balfour Rd Grosse Pointe Park MI 48230 Office: Wayne State U Sch Law Detroit MI 48202

GRANOFF, GARY CHARLES, lawyer, investment company executive; b. N.Y.C., Feb. 2, 1948; s. N. Henry and Jeannette (Trum) G.; m. Leslie Barbara Resnick, Dec. 21, 1969; children: Stephen, Robert, Joshua. BBA in Acctg., George Washington U., 1970, JD with honors, 1973. Bar: N.Y., 1974, Fla., 1974, U.S. Dist. Ct. (so. dist.) N.Y., 1976. Assoc. Dreyer & Traub, N.Y.C., 1973-75; ptnr. Ezon, Langberg & Granoff, N.Y.C., 1975-78, Granoff & Walker, N.Y.C., 1982—; pvt. practice N.Y.C., 1978-81; pres., also bd. dirs. Elk Assocs. Funding Corp., N.Y.C., 1979—, GCG Assocs., Inc., N.Y.C., 1982—; atty. del. to U.S.-China Joint Session on Trade, Investment and Econ. Law, Beijing, 1987. Campaign vol. Mondale for Pres., N.Y.C., 1984; fundraiser Robert Garcia for Congress, N.Y.C., Dem. Senatorial campaign com., N.Y.C., 1987, 88; active N.Y. Lawyers for Dukakis com., 1988. With USAR, 1969-75. Mem. N.Y. State Bar Assn., Fla. Bar Assn., Assn. Bar City N.Y., People-to-People Internat., North Shore Country Club. Club: North Shore Country. Office: Granoff & Walker 600 3d Ave Ste 3810 New York NY 10016

GRANQUIST, VICTOR MARTIN, environmental scientist, company administrator; b. Pitts., Aug. 26, 1955; s. William Thomas Granquist and Norine Elizabeth (Holt) Jordan; m. Kimberley Anne Obenhaus, Apr. 7, 1984. BS in Microbiology, Tex. A&M U., 1980. Specialist field service Milchem Inc., Houston, 1980-82; mgr. lab. Venture Chem. Inc., Lafayette, La., 1983-87; environ. mgr. Lobeco Products Inc. div. Enterra Corp., Beaufort, S.C., 1987—. Patentee in field. Mem. Emergency Response Team, Beaufort County, 1988; judge Sea Island Sci. Fair, Beaufort County, 1988. Mem. Soc. Petroleum Engrs., Water Pollution Control Fedn. Presbyterian. Club: Broken Paddle, Lafayette (safety dir. 1986). Home: Rt #8 Box 276-I Beaufort SC 29902 Office: PO Box 815 Lobeco SC 29931

GRANSTON, DAVID WILFRED, publishing company executive; b. Schenectady, N.Y., Dec. 5, 1939; s. Arnold Andrew and Edna (Nickerson) G.; B.A., Colgate U., 1958; M.B.A., Syracuse U., 1960; m. Priscilla Day, June 10, 1961; 1 son, David Wilfred. Supr. E.I. DuPont De Nemours & Co., Inc., Parlin, N.J., 1961-62; sr. fin. analyst Bendix Corp., N.Y.C., 1963-69; controller Allied Chem. Corp., N.Y.C., 1969-71; v.p. finance Thomas Borthwick Sons, Ltd., N.Y.C., 1972-78; v.p., chief fin. officer N.Y. Times Syndication Sales Corp., N.Y.C., 1978-82; chief fin. officer, assoc. dir. Consumers Union, Mt. Vernon, N.Y., 1983—. Served with USCGR, 1960. Colgate U. War Meml. scholar, 1954-58. Clubs: Colgate U. Alumni (L.I.) (Pres. 1975-76); Creek (Locust Valley, N.Y.) (bd. govs.); Northport (Maine) Yacht (vice commodore), Windham (N.Y.) Mountain. Home: PO Box 368 Piping Rock Rd Locust Valley NY 11560 Office: Consumers Union Corp 256 Washington St Mount Vernon NY 10553

GRANT, ALBERTA, production company executive, real estate consultant; b. Butler, Ga., Mar. 12, 1946; d. William Grant and Josephine (Tripp) Blasingame; m. James Smith, Feb. 20, 1966 (div. 1988); children—Kerry Jerome, Terry James, Jerry Darnell. B.S., Fort Valley State Coll., 1967. Cert. apt. mgr. Mgr. Hampshire House Apts., College Park, Ga., 1976-79, English Colony Apts., Atlanta, 1979-81; v.p. Southeastern Mgmt., College Park, 1979-81; mgr. Washington St. Apts., Atlanta, 1981-86, Countryside Community, Decatur, Ga., 1986—; owner Turbo Prodns., Atlanta, 1986—; cons. Housing and Phys. Devel., Atlanta, 1981—, real estate dept. AMC, Atlanta, 1981—, Merritt Realty, Atlanta, 1984. Exec. vol. Young for a Greater Atlanta, 1985; mem. dinner com. Martin Luther King, Jr., Ctr. for Non-Violent Social Change, Atlanta, 1985-86; adv. com. Nat. Council Negro Women, mobilization coordinator Black Family Reunion; mem. Nat. Polit. Congress Black Women; co-producer NAACP Radiothon, College Park; mem. exec. com. corp. sales SCLC, Atlanta, 1986; S.E. dist. coordinator for econ. devel., 1986—. Recipient awards Apt. Owners and Mgrs. Atlanta, 1979, Nat. Coop. Housing Partnership, Washington, 1982. Mem. Nat. Assn. Bus. and Profl. Women, Nat. Bd. Realtors (accredited resident mgr.; award 1985), Nat. Assn. Female Execs., Notary Pub. Assn. Ga., Bus. and Profl. Networking Atlanta. Democrat. Baptist. Lodge: Order of Eastern Star. Avocations: tennis; dancing; horseback riding. Office: Turbo Prodns PO Box 20834 Atlanta GA 30320 other: PO Box 20785 Airport Facility Atlanta GA 30320-0785

GRANT, ALICIA BROWN, accountant; b. Dothan, Ala., Apr. 19, 1945; d. Rudolph and Grace (Tyus) B.; m. Paul A. Grant; children: Rodney, Christopher, Adam. BA, Fla. State U., 1970. CPA, Fla. Sr. auditor Peat, Marwick, Mitchell and Co., Tampa, Fla., 1970-73; internal auditor Home Fed. Savs. and Loan Assn., St. Petersburg, Fla., 1973-75; dir. internal audit, v.p. Duval Fed. Savs. and Loan Assn., Jacksonville, Fla., 1984-87; dir. internal audit Fla. Community Coll. at Jacksonville. Chmn. Riverside Avondale Preservation, Inc., Jacksonville; mem. Mayor's spl. task force on recycling, Jacksonville; trustee Meml. Park Assn., Inc., Jacksonville. Mem. AICPA, Fla. Inst. CPA's, Inst. Internal Auditors (bd. govs. N.E. Fla. chpt.), Fin. Mgrs. Soc. (com. fed. regulation), Assn. Coll. and Univ. Auditors, EDP Auditor Assn., Civitans. Republican. Episcopalian. Office: Fla Community Coll 501 W State St Jacksonville FL 32202

GRANT, EDWARD, employment services executive; b. Bklyn., Apr. 10, 1936; s. David and Deborah (Jablow) Gorenstein; m. Helene Clarke, Mar. 12, 1961; children: Robin, Fran, Andrew. BBA in Mktg., Hofstra U., 1958. Pres., chief exec. officer Career Employment Services, Inc., Westbury, N.Y., 1960—. Contbr. articles to bus. jours. Bd. trustees Temple Emanu-el, East Meadow, 1980—; mem. L.I. Com. for Soviet Jewry, Carle Place, N.Y., 1983—; chmn. Nassau Community Coll. Adv. Council, Garden City, N.Y., 1983—, bd. dirs. Nassau Community Coll. Found., 1988—; program chmn. Dist. Citizen award dinner Nassau County Council Boy Scouts Am., 1985. Served with USAFR, 1958-64. Recipient Service award, L.I. Employment Agy. Council, 1977, Ohio Assn. of Personnel Cons., 1980, Outstanding Contbn. award, N.J. Assn. of Personnel Cons., 1982. Mem. Nat. Assn. Personnel Cons. (mem. Speakers Bur. 1977—, bd. dirs. 1968—), Assn. of Personnel Cons. (N.Y. Bd. dirs. 1968—, Service award 1983), Nat. Assn. of Temporary Services, Cert. Personnel Cons. Soc., Hofstra U. Alumni Assn., L.I. Assn., East Meadow C. of C., Am. Diabetes Assn. L.I. Home: 260 Fox Hunt Crescent So Oyster Bay Cove NY 11791 Office: Career Employment Svcs Inc 1600 Stewart Ave Westbury NY 11590

GRANT, EDWIN RANDOLPH, manufacturing executive; b. Stoneham, Mass., Oct. 6, 1943; s. Lauris Levi and Dorothy Hall (Lewis) G.; m. Ruth Louise Kennedy, June 24, 1967; children: Randolph T., George C. BFA, Denison U., 1966; MBA, Syracuse U., 1969. Trainee Sears, Roebuck & Co., Springfield, Mass., 1968-69; asst. to pres. Kennedy Bros., Inc., Vergennes, Vt., 1969-70, v.p., 1970-72, exec. v.p., 1972-74, pres., treas., 1974—; ptnr. Vergennes (Vt.) Shopping Ctr.; mem. exec. bd. Chittenden Trust Co., Vergennes, 1980—; bd. dirs. Middlebury (Vt.) Inn. Incorporator, dir. Addison County Devel. Corp., Vergennes Devel. Corp.; dir. Vt. Attractions Assn., 1975-77, v.p., treas., 1977-78, pres., 1978-80; mem. Vt. Travel-Adv. Council, 1978-80; trustee Burlington Coll., 1980-86, chmn. bd. 1983-84; commr. Vt. Gov.'s Commn. on Status of Women, 1984-85. Served to 2d lt. USAR, 1969-73. Mem. Vergennes Area C. of C. (pres. 1976-81), Vt. State C. of C. (bd. dirs. 1977-78), Addison C. of C. (bd. dirs. 1975-76, 1986—), Lake Champlain C. of C. (bd. dirs. 1977-81), Associated Industries of Vt. Club: Green Mountain Transp. (pres. 1976-77); Lake Champlain Yacht. Lodge: Rotary. Home: RD #2 Box 317 Vergennes VT 05491 Office: 11 Main St Vergennes VT 05491

GRANT, FREDERICK ANTHONY, investment banker; b. Jacksonville, Ill., Sept. 4, 1949; s. Irwin Herbert and Emma Eleanor (Voelker) G.; m. Patricia Johns (div. Dec. 1982); 1 child, Frederick Peter. BA, Ariz. State U., 1972; MBA, U. Chgo., 1975. Assoc. Bacon, Whipple & Co., Chgo., 1976-80; v.p. Security Pacific Capital Markets, N.Y.C., 1980-84, Shearson Lehman Bros., N.Y.C., 1984-86; sr. v.p. C.J. Lawrence, Morgan Grenfell, N.Y.C., 1986—; chmn. commitments com., C.J. Lawrence, Morgan, Grenfell; guest lectr. Columbia U., N.Y.C., 1985-86. Bd. dirs. alumni bd. U. Chgo., 1987—. Clubs: Chicago; Racquet and Tennis (N.Y.C.). Office: CJ Lawrence Morgan Grenfell 1290 Ave of Americas New York NY 10104-0101

GRANT, JAMES DENEALE, health care company executive; b. Washington, July 9, 1932; s. Deneale and Frances (Hoskins) G.; m. Bonnie Carol Johnson, June 14, 1955; children: Glenn James, Bruce William, Scott Stockman. B.S., William and Mary Coll., 1954; M.B.A., Wharton Sch. U. Pa., 1956; postgrad. (Pub. Affairs fellow), Stanford U., 1963-64. Mem. staff AEC, Washington, 1956-64; v.p. Nat. Inst. Pub. Affairs, Washington, 1964-69; dep. dir. White House Conf. Food, Nutrition and Health, 1969-70; dep. commr. FDA, Washington, 1970-72; asst. to chmn. CPC Internat. Inc., Englewood Cliffs, N.J., 1972-73, v.p., 1973-86; chmn., chief exec. officer T Cell Scis., Inc., 1986—; cons. U.S. Bur. Budget, 1965-69, CSC, 1965-69; sci. advisor Syntro Corp., 1985-86. Chmn. Bergen County United Fund, 1974-75; trustee Nutrition Found., 1973-78; chmn. adv. group to sec.-gen. UNCSTD, 1979. Recipient U.S. Govt. Career Edn. award, 1963. Mem. AAAS, N.Y. Acad. Scis., Am. Chem. Soc., Omicron Delta Kappa. Presbyterian. Club: Univ. (N.Y.C.). Home: 860 Fifth Ave New York NY 10021 Office: T Cell Scis Inc 840 Memorial Dr Cambridge MA 02139

GRANT, JOHN CLARENCE, III, oil company executive; b. Providence, Jan. 16, 1934; s. John Clarence Jr. and Florence (Sheehan) G.; m. Nancy Louise Egan, Apr. 4, 1964; children: John, Marion, Carolyn, Kathleen. BA in Econs., U. Del., 1955; JD, NYU, 1960. Bar: Tex. 1961. With Texaco, Inc., 1955—; mgr. equal employment opportunity Texaco, Inc., Houston,

1969-71; dir. labor relations Texaco, Inc., N.Y.C., 1971-79; v.p. personnel Texaco U.S.A., Houston, 1980; gen. mgr. employee relations Texaco, Inc., Harrison, N.Y., 1981—; assoc. Inst. Labor Relations, Ithaca, N.Y., 1980—; dir. AM. Inst. Contemporary German-Am. Studies, Johns Hopkins U., Washington, 1987—. Mem. Tex. Bar Assn., Westchester C. of C. (chmn. bd. dirs. 1987—), Bus. Roundtable, Darien Cotillion Club, Darien Boat Club, Country Club of Darien (Conn.), Ocean Club (Hilton Head Island, S.C.). Home: 370 Mansfield Ave Darien CT 06820 Office: Texaco Inc 2000 Westchester Ave White Plains NY 10650

GRANT, MARICELESTE (MARICELESTE KELLEY), management executive; b. Long Beach, Calif., June 29, 1948; d. Christopher and Beatrice Edwina (Herbert) Mathewson; m. Lawrence Lee Grant, Nov. 22, 1970 (div. 1976); 1 child, Laura S.; m. Robert Paul Kelley Jr., Nov. 28, 1976; children: Robert P. III, Elizabeth R. BA, Loyola U., La., 1970; cert. owner and pres. mgmt. program, Harvard U., 1984. Head pub. affairs dept. Mazda Motors Am., Compton, Calif., 1972-74; mgr. publicity, intertainment and mktg. Knott's Berry Farm, Buena Park, Calif., 1974-76; pres. Strategy Network Corp., Newport Beach, Calif., 1976—; owner, real estate broker All-Am. Properties, Irvine, Calif., 1983-85; chief operating officer, chief fin. officer So. Calif. Tech. Execs. Network, Newport Beach, 1985—; presenter seminars on women's career advancement. Editor-in-chief Execinet Report mag., 1986—. Mem. Wecan Women's Network (founder, pres. 1978-83), Contacts of Orange County, Harvard Bus. Sch. Assn. So. Calif. Republican. Office: Strategy Network Corp 4667 MacArthur Blvd Ste 200 Newport Beach CA 92660

GRANT, MERRILL THEODORE, producer; b. N.Y.C., July 9, 1932; s. Samuel and Rae (Renko) G.; m. Barbara Rosner, May 24, 1961; children: Andrea, Jonathan Samuel. BBA, CCNY, 1953; MS, Columbia U., 1954. V.p., dir. programming Benton & Bowles, N.Y.C., 1957-70; sr. v.p., dir. radio and TV Grey Advt., N.Y.C., 1970-72; v.p. Viacom Internat., N.Y.C., 1972-74; pres. Don Kirshner Prodns., N.Y.C., 1974-78, Grant Case McGrath, N.Y.C., 1978-79, Grant-Reeves Entertainment, N.Y.C., 1979-85; chmn. Reeves Entertainment Group, N.Y.C., 1985—; pres., chief operating officer Reeves Communications Corp., N.Y.C., 1988—. Bd. dirs. U.S. com. for UNICEF; trustee The Berkshire (Mass.) Theatre Festival. Served with AUS, 1954-56. Office: Reeves Entertainment Group 708 Third Ave New York NY 10017

GRANT, MICHAEL PETER, electrical engineer; b. Oshkosh, Wis., Feb. 26, 1936; s. Robert J. and Ione (Michelson) G.; m. Mary Susan Corcoran, Sept. 2, 1961; children: James, Steven, Laura. B.S., Purdue U., 1957, M.S., 1958, Ph.D., 1964. With Westinghouse Research Labs., Pitts., summers 1953-57; mem. tech. staff Aerospace Corp., El Segundo, Calif., 1961; instr. elec. engring. Purdue U., West Lafayette, Ind., 1958-64; sr. engr. Combustion Engring. Corp., Columbus, Ohio, 1964-67, mgr. advanced devel. and control systems, 1967-72, mgr. control and info. scis. div., 1972-74, asst. gen. mgr. indsl. systems div., 1974-76; mgr. system design AccuRay Corp., Columbus, Ohio, 1976-87; v.p., chief scientist SynGenics Corp., Columbus, 1987—; dir. Nat. Ctr. for Mfg. Scis., Ann Arbor, MIch., 1987—. Contbr. articles to profl. jours.; patentee in field of automation. Mem. IEEE, Sigma Xi, Eta Kappa Nu, Pi Mu Epsilon, Tau Beta Pi. Home: 4461 Sussex Dr Columbus OH 43220 Office: Nat Ctr Mfg Scis 900 Victors Way Ann Arbor MI 48108

GRANT, PETER STANLEY, telecommunications executive; b. Tacoma, Feb. 20, 1952; s. Norman F. and Genevieve S. (Shaw) G.; m. Ann Dickman, Aug. 12, 1976; children: Shannon L., Margot A. B of Econs., Brown U., 1976; MPA, U. Oreg., 1977, MA, 1977; MCE, MIT, 1979, MS, 1979. Editor Schlumberger, Paris, 1973; grad. teaching fellow U. Oreg., Eugene, 1977—; logistics analyst Weyerhaeuser Co., Tacoma, 1979, project mgr., 1980-82, planning mgr., 1982-84; dir. internat. mktg. U.S. West/New Vector, Bellevue, Wash., 1984-86; v.p. internat. mktg. U.S. West Internat., Bellevue, Wash., 1986-87; pres., chief exec. officer China Telephone Co. Ltd., Hong Kong, 1987—. Patentee log handling and transport system. Mem. Am. C. of C., Aberdeen Marina Club. Office: China Telephone Co Ltd, 10/F Roxy Ind Ctr, 58-66 Tai Lin Pai Rd, Kwai Chung, Hong Kong Hong Kong

GRANT, PHILLIP DEAN, building supply and construction industry executive; b. Galesburg, Ill., Feb. 10, 1933; s. Richard Roe and Bessie Irene (Baker) G.; m. Reba Joan Vance, Jan. 25, 1925 (div. 1982); children: Richard Roy, Phillip Dean Jr., Lori Irene, Tammy Lynn; m. Darla Jean Dockery, Sept. 3, 1983. Student, U. N.C., 1972, Dartmouth Coll., 1983. Sales mgr. John Mohr and Sons, Chgo., 1962-65; dist. mgr. Varco Pruden, Fayetteville, Tenn., 1965-66; gen. mgr. Varco Pruden, Winston-Salem, N.C., 1966-73; v.p. Varco Pruden, Memphis, 1978-81, sr. v.p., 1981-83; exec. v.p. AMCA Bldgs., Memphis, 1983—. Republican precinct chmn., Winston-Salem, 1972. Served with USN, 1952-56. Mem. Metal Constrn. Assn. (1st v.p. 1985—, chmn. bldgs. council 1986—). Methodist. Home: 8221 Pine Creek Germantown TN 38138 Office: AMCA Bldgs 6000 Poplar Ave Memphis TN 38119

GRANT, WALTER MATTHEWS, lawyer, communications company executive; b. Winchester, Ky., Mar. 30, 1945; s. Raymond Russell and Mary Mitchell (Rees) G.; m. Ann Carol Straus, Aug. 5, 1967; children—Walter Matthews II, Jean Ann, Raymond Russell II. BJ, U. Ky., Lexington, 1967; JD, Vanderbilt U., 1971. Bar: Ga. 1971. Assoc. Alston & Bird, Atlanta, 1971-76, ptnr., 1976-83; v.p., gen. counsel, sec. Contel Corp., Atlanta, 1983—. Editor-in-chief Vanderbilt Law Rev., 1970-71, Ga. State Bar Jour., 1979-82. Mem. Atlanta Bar Assn., Am. Soc. Corp. Secs. Baptist. Home: 1422 Hanover West Dr NW Atlanta GA 30327 Office: Contel Corp 245 Perimeter Center Pkwy Atlanta GA 30346

GRANT, WILLIAM PACKER, JR., banker; b. Orange, N.J., July 18, 1942; s. William Packer and Ruth Katherine (Dwyer) G.; m. Maureen Ann Mele; May 20, 1972; children: William Packer III, Michael Charles. Student, U. Pa., 1960-63. Adminstrv. asst. fiscal services Fed. Res. Bank of N.Y., N.Y.C., 1972-76, spl. asst. fiscal services, 1976-85, chief safekeeping div., 1985-86, chief automated payments div., 1986-87, spl. asst. electronic payments, 1987—. Editor newsletter Update, 1987. Mem. Comdr's Club-Disabled Am. Vets., Washington, 1983—, Am. Space Frontier Com., Washington, 1984—, Rep. Nat. Com., Washington, 1981—; commr. Little Falls Youth Wrestling, 1988—. Wwith U.S. Army, 1964-66. Mem. Am. Security Council, Phi Sigma Kappa. Republican. Roman Catholic. Club: Athletic (Little Falls, N.J.). Home: 159-G Main St Little Falls NJ 07424 Office: Fed Res Bank 33 Liberty St New York NY 10045

GRANTHAM, JOSEPH MICHAEL, JR., hotel executive; b. Smithfield, N.C., Aug. 23, 1947; s. Joseph Michael and Anne Laurie (Hare) G.; student Oak Ridge Mil. Inst., 1965-66, E. Tenn. State U., 1966-70; m. Wilsie Moss Hartman, Nov. 3, 1973 (div. 1982); children: Molly Meade, Joseph Michael III; m. Jean Marie Scully, 1986; 1 child, William Warner. With Grand Hotel, Mackinac Island, Mich., 1966-78, v.p. sales, 1973-74, v.p. and mgr., 1974-78; dir. resort ops., gen. mgr. Pinehurst (N.C.) Hotel and Country Club, 1978-80; pres., chmn. bd. Ind. Fin. Investments, Pinehurst, 1980—; pres., chmn. bd. Carolina Hotels, Inc., 1982—; pres., chmn. Asset Mgmt. & Mktg., Inc., 1986—. Vice chmn. No. Mich. Conv. and Visitors Bur., Mackinac Island; commr. scouting Boy Scouts Am., Pinehurst, 1978—. With USNG, 1970-76. Mem. Mackinac Island C. of C. (dir. 1976-79), Mich. Lodging Assn. (dir. 1976-79), Meeting Planners Internat., Hotel Sales Mgmt. Assn. Internat., Am. Hotel and Motor Hotel Assn., N.C. Restaurant Assn., N.C. Hotel and Motel Assn., Nat. Tour Brokers Assn., Chgo. Assn. Execs., N.C. Innkeepers Assn. (dir. 1978-80), Travel Council of N.C. (dir. 1978-80), Pinehurst Bus. Guild (bd. dirs., pres. 1986), Sandhills Area C. of C. (dir. 1984—), Kappa Alpha. Methodist. Lodges: Shriners (bd. dirs. Moore County club, 1982—, pres. 1986—), Masons. Home: Magnolia Rd Pinehurst NC 28374

GRANTS, VALDIS, engineering manager; b. Liepaja, Latvia, Mar. 5, 1942; came to U.S., 1949, naturalized, 1955; s. Karlis Valdemars and Meta Mudite (Greenvalds) G.; m. Yvette Marie Guhl, June 18, 1966; children: Kristine Marie, Carl Raymond. BS in Sci. Engring., U. Mich., 1964, BS in Engring. Maths., 1965, MS in Elec. Engring., 1967. Rsch. engr. U. Mich., Ann Arbor, 1965-70; sr. design engr. Info. Instrn., Inc., Ann Arbor, 1970-71, Allen-Bradley Co., Highland Heights, Ohio, 1971-76; engring. supr. Allen-Bradley Co., Highland Heights, 1976-77, engr. mgr., 1977—. Patentee in field. Mem. IEEE, Tau Beta Pi, Eta Kappa Nu, Phi Kappa Phi. Office: Allen-Bradley Co 747 Alpha Dr Highland Heights OH 44143

GRANZOW, PAUL H., printing company executive; b. 1927. Student, U. Dayton; LLB, U. Cin, 1950. Ptnr. Turner, Granzow & Hollenkamp; with Standard Register Co., Dayton, Ohio, 1966—, chmn. bd. dirs., 1984—. Served with AUS, 1945-46. Office: The Standard Register Co 600 Albany St Dayton OH 45408 *

GRASS, ALEXANDER, retail company executive; b. Scranton, Pa., Aug. 3, 1927; s. Louis and Rose (Breman) G.; m. Lois Lehrman, July 30, 1950; children: Linda Jane, Martin L., Roger L., Elizabeth Ann; m. Louise B. Gurkoff, Apr. 26, 1974. LLB, U. Fla., 1949. Bar: Fla. 1949, Pa. 1953. Pvt. practice Miami Beach, Fla., 1949-51; v.p. Rite Aid Corp., Shiremanstown, Pa., 1952-66; pres. Rite Aid Corp., 1966-69, 77—, chmn., chief exec. officer, 1969—; chmn. Super Rite Foods, Inc., 1983—; bd. dirs. Hasbro Industries. Mem. nat. exec. com. United Jewish Appeal, 1968-79, nat. vice chmn., 1970-79, gen. chmn., 1984-86, chmn. bd. trustees, 1986-88; pres. Harrisburg (Pa.) Jewish Fedn., 1970-72; chmn. Israel Edn. Fund, 1975-78; bd. dirs. Pa. Right to Work Found., 1972-74, Harrisburg Hosp., 1977-81; vice-chmn. Harrisburg Hosp., 1988—; mem. Pa. Coun. Arts, 1982; bd. dirs. Keystone State Games, 1982—; trustee Jerusalem Inst. Mgmt., 1983; bd. mem. Israel Center Social and Econ. Studies, 1983; mem. exec. com. Jewish Agy. for Israel, 1984-88, bd. govs., 1984—; treas. United Israel Appeal, 1986—. With USNR, 1945-46. Mem. Nat. Am. Wholesale Grocers Assn. (bd. dir. 1971-73), Nat. Assn. Chain Drug Stores (bd. dir. 1972—, chmn. 1986-87). Jewish (dir. temple). Home: 4025 Crooked Hill Rd Harrisburg PA 17110 Office: Rite Aid Corp PO Box 3165 Harrisburg PA 17110

GRASSI, ELLEN ELIZABETH, electronics company service administrator; b. N.Y.C., July 27, 1949; d. Dante J. and Mary D. (Olivieri) G. BA in Teaching, High Point Coll., 1971; postgrad., L.I. U., Brookville, N.Y., 1976, 83-84. Cert. tchr., N.Y. Tchr. Yonkers (N.Y.) Schs., 1971-76; electronics tech. Canon U.S.A., Inc., Lake Success, N.Y., 1977-82, supv. eastern regional service, 1982-84, asst. mgr. nat. serv., 1984-85, mgr. nat. service adminstrn., 1985-88, nat. mgr. customer relations, 1988—. Polling booth elector Bd. of Elections, N.Y.C., 1971-77; founding mem. Little Neck Hills (N.Y.) Assn., 1984. Mem. Nat. Assn. Service Mgrs., Nat. Assn. Female Execs., Douglaston (N.Y.) Civic Assn., High Point Coll. Alumni Assn., Kappa Delta Pi. Club: Tower. Office: Canon USA Inc 1 Jericho Plaza Jericho NY 11753

GRASSO, JAMES ANTHONY, public relation executive, educator; b. Providence, Jan. 12, 1954; s. Eleanor Marie (D'Angelo) Grasso; m. Kimberly I. Maher, Sept. 14, 1986. BS in Pub. Communication cum laude, Boston U., 1976, MS in Pub. Relations, 1983. Land and pub. relations rep. Algonquin Gas Transmission Co., Boston, 1978-83, asst. mgr., 1983-85, mgr. land, pub. relations, govt. relations, 1985—; mem. adj. faculty Coll. Communications, Boston U., 1987—. Mem. Pub. Relations Soc. Am., Interstate Natural Gas Assn. Am. Gas Assn. (natural gas industry exec. rep. World's Fair 1982), New England Council, New Eng.-Can. Bus. Council, New Eng. Broadcasting Assn., Pub. Utilities Communicators Assn., Italian Ams. in Communication (bd. dirs.), Publicity Club Boston, Radio-TV News Dirs. Assn., Capitol Hill Club. Roman Catholic. Office: Algonquin Gas Transmission Co 1284 Soldiers Field Rd Boston MA 02135

GRASSO, RICHARD A., stock exchange executive. BS in Acctg., Pace U.; postgrad. cert. advanced mgmt., Harvard U., 1985. Mem. staff N.Y. Stock Exchange, 1968-73, dir. listing and mktg., 1973-77, v.p. corp. svcs., 1977-81, sr. v.p. corp. svcs., 1981-83, exec. v.p. mktg. group, 1983-86, exec. v.p. capital markets, 1986-88, pres., chief ooperating officer, 1988—; overseer ops. N.Y. Future Exchange; coord. Depository Trust Co., Nat. Securities Clearing Corp.; bd. dirs. Securities Industry Automation Corp. Office: NY Stock Exch 11 Wall St New York NY 10005

GRATER, BETSY, small business owner; b. Chalottesville, Va., Apr. 29, 1933; d. Allan Francis and Eutsler (Isabel) G.; m. Robert S. Runkle, Mar. 26, 1960 (div. June 1984); children: Beth A. Mackey, Brynn A. BEd, Kutztown U., 1955; MEd, Vanderbilt U., 1958; cert., Goucher Coll., 1981. Tchr. various pub. schs., Pa., N.J., Md., 1955-79; devel. coordinator Md. Com. for Children, Inc., Balt., 1979-81; mgr. mktg., user services Info. Network for Occupational Resources in Md., Balt., 1981-83; mktg. support rep. DISC, Inc., Balt., 1983-85; owner, operator Amanda's Bed and Breakfast Reservation Service, Balt., 1985—. Elected mem. Raleigh (N.C.) Bd. Edn., 1971-73. Democrat. Episcopalian. Home and Office: 1428 Park Ave Baltimore MD 21217

GRATTON, PATRICK JOHN FRANCIS, oil company executive; b. Denver, Aug. 28, 1933; s. Patrick Henry and Lorene Jean (Johnson) G.; m. Jean Marie McKinney, June 10, 1955; children: Sara, Vivian, Patrick, Lizabeth. BS in Geology, U. N.Mex., 1955, MS in Geology, 1958. Geologist Westvaco Mineral Devel. Corp., Grants, N.Mex., 1955; mining engr. Utah Internat., Denver, 1956; geologist Shell Oil Co., Roswell, N.Mex. and Tyler, Tex., 1957-62; adminstrv. asst. Delhi-Taylor Oil Corp., Dallas, 1962-64; exploration mgr. Eugene E. Nearburg, Dallas, 1965-70; pres. Patrick J.F. Gratton, Inc., Dallas, 1970—. Contbr. articles to profl. jours. Served with USCG, 1951-53, U.S. Army, 1956-57. Mem. Am. Assn. Petroleum Geologists (v.p. SW sect. 1976-77, del. 1978-81, pres., div. profl. affairs 1989—), Soc. Ind. Profl. Earth Scientists (v.p. 1976-77, pres. 1977-78), Tex. Ind. Producers and Royalty Owners Assn. (exec. com. 1985—), Dallas Geol. Soc. (pub. service award 1985). Roman Catholic. Clubs: Petroleum (Dallas), Explorers (Tex.) (chmn.1987-88). Office: 2403 Thomas Ave Dallas TX 75201

GRAU, MARCY BEINISH, investment banking consultant; b. Bklyn., Aug. 7, 1950; d. Joseph Beinish and Gloria (Rosenbaum) Bennett; m. Bennett Grau, Nov. 19, 1978; 2 children. AB with high honors, U. Mich., 1971; postgrad. Columbia U., 1972, N.Y. Inst. Fin., 1973. Asst. to chmn. Bancroft Convertible Fund, N.Y.C., 1973-75; precious metals trader J. Aron & Co., N.Y.C., 1975-81, mgr. metals mktg., 1981-83; v.p. Goldman, Sachs & Co/J. Aron, N.Y.C., 1983—; bus.-related translator Augustus Clothiers, N.Y.C., 1979—. Editor Precious Metals Rev. and Outlook, 1980—; contbr. article to profl. jours. Vol. worker, pediatrics dept. Lenox Hill Hosp., N.Y.C., 1978-79; asst. The Holiday Project, The Hunger Project, N.Y.C., 1978-83; vol. Yorkville Common Pantry, N.Y.C., 1984; tutor Yorkville Neighborhood Assn., N.Y.C., 1984; assoc. Child Devel. Ctr., N.Y.C. Mem. Phi Beta Kappa. Democrat. Jewish. Avocations: interior design, fashion, cooking, swimming. Home: 300 West End Ave New York NY 10023 Office: Goldman Sachs & Co 85 Broad St New York NY 10004

GRAU, WILFRIED (BILL), hotel executive; b. Fed. Republic Germany, Apr. 9, 1943; came to U.S., 1970; s. Otto and Gretel (Foernzler) G.; m. Christa Meta Fraessle, Apr. 17, 1964; 1 child, Christine S. BS in Fin., Calif. State U., L.A., 1974; MBA, U. So. Calif., 1975. Underwriter real estate fin. Sparkassen Versicherung AG, Stuttgart, 1960-68; mgr. fin. Boorber Enterprises, Winnipeg, Man., Can., 1968-70, Xerox Corp., Rochester, N.Y., 1975-78, Ramada Inc., Phoenix, 1978-80; v.p. fin. and devel. Ramada Inc., Brussels, 1980-82; contr. hotel group Ramada Inc., Phoenix, 1982-83; exec. v.p. Ramada Internat., Phoenix, 1983—. Adv. Am. Internat. Sch. Grad. Bus., Phoenix, 1984-88. Office: Ramada Inc 3838 E Van Buren St Phoenix AZ 85008

GRAUL, DONALD OUELLETTE, JR., import company executive; b. Miami, Fla., Apr. 21, 1944; s. Donald O. and Dorothy Marie (Magnuson) G.; m. Barbara R. Stants, Dec. 31, 1970 (div. 1977); m. Rebecca R. Sawyer, June 13, 1982. BA, Calif. State U., Northridge, 1965, MA, 1968. Reporter Los Angeles Times, 1968-69; editor, writer AP, Detroit, 1969-70; mng. editor Yacht Racing mag., Rowayton, Conn., 1971-74; ptnr. A.M. Hill & Assocs., Washington, 1974-77; assoc. editor Yachting mag., N.Y.C., 1977-81; v.p., gen. mgr. Mariner Resource Corp., Manhasset, N.Y., 1982—. Communications dir. Anderson for Pres. Nat. Com., Washington, 1980. Recipient Civilian Citation for Valor, Detroit Police Dept., 1971. Club: New York Yacht (N.Y.C.). Office: Mariner Resource Corp Box 1039 Manhasset NY 11030

GRAVA, ALFRED H., automotive and business equipment manufacturing company executive; b. 1934. BSME. With Gen. Motors Corp., 1953-73, Rockwell Internat. Corp., 1973-84; with Sheller-Globe Corp., 1984—, formerly exec. v.p., now pres., chief operating officer. Served with U.S. Army, 1958-59. Office: Sheller-Globe Corp 1505 Jefferson Ave PO Box 962 Toledo OH 43697 *

GRAVES, CAROL KENNEY, construction company executive; b. Boise, Idaho, May 3, 1937; d. Elmer Kenney and M. Elizabeth (Rogers) Kenney Stolquist; m. Philip L. Graves, Aug. 6, 1955; children: Steven P., Kenton L., Cynthia M. Owner Carols, Peoria, Ill., 1975-78; realtor Clifton-Strode E.R.A., Peoria, 1978-83; pres. Little Red Hen Outlets Inc., Peoria, 1983—; sec., treas. Asbestos Enviro-Clean Inc., Pekin, Ill., 1987-88; pres. Asbestos Enviro-Clean Inc., Bartonville, Ill., 1988—. Rep. precinct committeeperson, Peoria, 1983-88; funds dir. YWCA, Oconomowoc, Wis., 1965; mem. Girl Scouts U.S., 1963—; active Midwest Asbestos Coun.-PAAC Wis. Mem. Kickapoo Twp. Assn. (bd. dirs. 1984-88), Downtown Bus. Assn. (bd. dirs., pres. 1987—), Heart of Ill. Food Service Assn., Nat. Radon Assn. (midwest asbestos council). Roman Catholic. Home: 4121 N Koerner Rd Peoria IL 61615 Office: Asbestos Enviro-Clean Inc 4322 Entec Dr PO Box 4133 Bartonville IL 61607

GRAVES, EARL GILBERT, publisher; b. Bklyn., 1935; s. Earl Godwin and Winifred (Sealy) G.; m. Barbara Kydd, July 2, 1960; children: Earl Gilbert, John, Michael. B.A. in Econs., Morgan State Coll., Balt., 1958, LL.D., 1973; LL.D., Rust Coll., 1974, Wesleyan U., 1982, Dowling Coll., 1980, Va. Union Coll., 1976, Fla. Meml. Coll., 1978, Baruch Coll., 1984, Morehouse Coll., 1986. Adminstrv. asst. to Senator Robert F. Kennedy, 1965-68; owner mgmt. cons. firm 1968-70; editor, pub. Black Enterprise mag., N.Y.C., 1970—; pres. Earl G. Graves Pub. Co., Inc., Earl G. Graves Mktg. and Research Co., Earl G. Graves Devel. Co., EGG Dallas Broadcasting Co.; bd. dirs. Rolm & Hass Corp., Mag. Pub. Assn., N.Y. State Urban Devel. Corp., Nat. Supplier Devel. Council. Nat. Commr. scouting Boy Scouts Am.; bd. dirs. Coalition N.Y.; bd. govs. Corporate Fund Performing Arts at Kennedy Center; mem. vis. com. Harvard U. John F. Kennedy Sch. Govt.; mem. Pres.'s Com. Small and Minority Bus.; mem. pres. council for bus. adminstrn. U. Vt.; trustee Am. Mus. Natural History and Planetarium Authority. Served to capt. U.S. Army, 1958-60. Recipient Scroll of Honor, Nat. Med. Assn., 1971, Nat. award of excellence U.S. Dept. Commerce, 1972, Silver Beaver award Boy Scouts Am., 1969, Silver Antelope award, 1988, Silver Buffalo award, 1988, Publisher for Freedom award Operation PUSH, Black Achiever award Talk mag., 1972, Key award Nat. Assn. Black Mfrs., 1972, Chgo. Econ. Devel. Corp. award, 1974, Nat. Alliance Black Sch. Educators award, 1974, Silver Antelope award Boy Scouts Am., 1988, Silver Buffalo award Boy Scouts Am., 1988; named One of Ten Most Outstanding Minority Businessmen in Country by Pres. U.S., 1973, Outstanding Citizen of Year, Omega Psi Phi, 1974, also one of 200 Future Leaders of Country, Time mag., Outstanding Black Businessman, Nat. Bus. League, one of 100 influential Blacks, Am. Ebony mag.; Poynter fellow Yale U., 1978. Mem. NAACP, SCLC, Interracial Council Bus. Opportunity (award), Young Pres. Orgn., Mag. Pubs. Assn. (dir.), Advt. Council, Bus. Mktg. Corp. N.Y.C., Sigma Pi Phi, Omega Psi Phi. Democrat. Episcopalian. Club: N.Y. Econ. (trustee). Office: Black Enterprise 130 Fifth Ave New York NY 10011

GRAVES, MELANIE WALLBILLICH, accountant, investment and insurance banker, small business owner; b. New Orleans, Apr. 2, 1963; d. Robert Murphy and Joanna (Charrier) Wallbillich; m. James E. Graves Jr., Oct. 11, 1986. BS in Acctg., U. New Orleans, 1985. Registered rep. Acct. Robert M. Wallbillich, CPA, Metairie, La., 1983-86; owner Taxes & Fin. Planning Services, Metairie, 1987—. Contbr. article to profl. jour. Recipient Sales Talk Champion award Dale Carnegie, Greater New Orleans, 1988. Mem. Women Bus. Owners Assn. of La. (state bd. rep. 1987-88, treas. 1988-89), Bus. and Profl. Women (1st v.p. Jefferson Parish chpt. 1988-89, Young Careerist of Yr. 1988), Internat. Assn. Fin. Planners (symposium com. 1987—), U. New Orleans Alumni (awards and scholarship com. 1987). Club: Premier Athletic. Office: Taxes & Fin Planning Svcs 3525 N Causeway Blvd Ste 728 Metairie LA 70002

GRAVES, RONALD NORMAN, lawyer; b. Caldwell, Idaho, Nov. 11, 1942; s. Vernon E. and Mildred Elizabeth (Norman) G.; m. Diane Jo Plastino, Dec. 29, 1985. BA, Coll. Idaho, 1965; JD, U. Idaho, 1968. Bar: Idaho 1968. Staff lawyer J.R. Simplot Co., Boise, Idaho, 1968-72, corp. counsel, 1972, corp. sec., 1975—, gen. counsel, 1986—; Mem. com. Idaho Corp. Counsel Workshop, Boise, 1987—; corp. sec., v.p. Simplot Livestock Co., Simplot Finl. Corp., Simplot Can. Ltd. Bd. dirs. Idaho Ronald McDonald House, Boise, 1987—; mem. Coll. Idaho Alumni Bd., Caldwell, 1987—. Mem. ABA, Idaho Bar Assn., Am. Corp. Counsel Assn., Mountain States Legal Found. (dir. 1989—). Republican. Presbyterian. Office: JR Simplot Co 999 Main St Suite 1300 Boise ID 83702

GRAVES, THOMAS BROWNING, investment banker; b. Indpls., Feb. 1, 1932; s. Thomas Browning and Erma Sanderson (Lowe) G.; m. Betty Lee MacLeod, June 12, 1954; children: Russell Evan, Bruce Ryan, Jill Graves Van Ness, Jeffrey Hall. BS, Ind. U., 1954; M in Pub. Adminstrn., Harvard U., 1975. Asst. v.p. Penn Cen. Corp., Phila., 1968-72, Union Pacific R.R., Omaha, 1972-77; v.p. fin. and adminstrn. Union Pacific Corp., Omaha, 1977-84; exec. dir. Merrill Lynch, N.Y.C., 1984-85; pres. Pvt. Capital Ptnrs., Inc., N.Y.C., 1985—. Served to maj. U.S. Army, 1955-57, 61-62. Club: Atlantic City Country (Northfield, N.J.). Home: 45 Sutton Pl S Apt #17-C New York NY 10022 also: 110 Beach Rd Ocean City NJ 08226 Office: Pvt Capital Ptnrs Inc 535 Madison Ave New York NY 10022

GRAY, ANN MAYNARD, broadcasting company executive; b. Boston, Aug. 22, 1945; d. Paul Maynard and Pauline Elizabeth MacFadyen; m. Richard R. Gray, Jr.; children: Richard R. Gray III, Dana Maynard. B.A., U. Mich., 1967; M.B.A., N.Y. U., 1971. With Chase Manhattan Bank, N.Y.C., 1967-68; with Chem. Bank, N.Y.C., 1968-73; asst. sec. Chem. Bank, 1971-73; asst. to treas., then asst. treas. ABC, Inc., 1974-76, treas., 1976-81, v.p. corp. planning, 1979-86; v.p. Capital Cities/ABC, Inc. (merged 1986), 1986—; sr. v.p. fin. ABC TV Network Group, 1988—; dir. Carteret Savs. Bank, Morristown, N.J., 1984-88. Trustee Martha Graham Ctr. of Contemporary Dance, N.Y.C., 1989—. Office: Capital Cities/ABC Inc 77 W 66th St New York NY 10023

GRAY, ANN MILLIGAN, interior designer; b. Dallas, July 13, 1942; d. Claude L. and Lois (Morris) M.; m. John D. Gray, May 1, 1971. BFA, U. Colo., 1964; postgrad. in bus., Northwestern U., 1965. Interior designer Marshall Field & Co., Chgo., 1965-70; pres. Ann Milligan Gray, Inc., Chgo., 1971—. Bd. dirs. Big Bros./Big Sisters, Chgo., 1985—; mem. women bd. dirs. Chgo. Boys and Girls Clubs, 1972—. Named to Top 50 Small Bus.'s, Arthur Andersen & Co., 1986, Top 100 Interior Design Firms, Interior Design mag., 1986, 87; recipient Outstanding Achievement award Chgo. Design Source, 1987. Mem. Am. Soc. Interior Designers (bd. dirs. 1970-72, Designer of Yr. 1987). Home: 1416 N Astor St Chicago IL 60610 Office: Ann Milligan Gray Inc 1416 N Astor St Chicago IL 60610

GRAY, CHARLES AUGUSTUS, banker; b. Syracuse, N.Y., Sept. 16, 1928; s. Charles William and Elizabeth Marie (Koch) G.; cert. Am. Inst. Banking, 1958, Sch. Bank Adminstrn., 1961. With Mchts. Nat. Bank & Trust Co. of Syracuse, 1946-77, auditor, 1959-77, v.p., 1970-77; N.Y. State dir. Bank Adminstrn. Inst., 1970-72; regional auditor Central N.Y. region Irving Bank Corp., 1977-82, v.p., 1982—. Treas., Upper N.Y. Synod Luth. Ch. in Am., 1966-87, Upstate N.Y. Synod of Evang. Luth. Ch. in Am., 1988—; treas. Luth. Found. Upstate N.Y., 1972-79, bd. dirs., 1980—; pres. Interfrat. Alumni Council, Syracuse U., 1980-83. Cert. internal auditor. Mem. Bank Adminstrn. Inst. (pres. central N.Y. chpt. 1970-72), Inst. Internal Auditors (treas. central N.Y. chpt. 1974-76, pres. 1985-86). Republican. Clubs: Lions (pres. local club 1973-75), Masons, Shriners. Home: 1321 Westmoreland Ave Syracuse NY 13210 Office: 220 S Warren St Syracuse NY 13201

GRAY, CHRISTOPHER DONALD, software researcher, author, consultant; b. Brookville, Pa., May 18, 1951; s. Donald Garrison and Patricia Lee (Huffman) G.; m. Allison Selby Farragher, Oct. 12, 1974; children: Patrick Xanthe, Colin Christopher. BA in Math., Washington and Jefferson Coll., 1973; MS in Math., Carnegie-Mellon U., 1975. Mfg. systems analyst Ohaus Scale Corp., Florham Park, N.J., 1974-76; systems rep. Software

Internat. Corp., 1976-77, cons. mfg. systems, 1977-78, mktg. rep., 1978-79; v.p. Mfg. Software Systems, Inc., Essex Junction, Vt., 1979-85, pres., 1985; pres. Oliver Wight Software Research, Inc., 1985-88; Gray Rsch., 1988—; assoc. R.D. Garwood, Inc., 1988—, Oliver Wight Edn. Assocs., Newbury, 1982—; cons. Oliver Wight Video Prodns., Essex Junction, Vt., 1980-84; advisor mfg. applications, Software News, Sentry Pub. Co., Hudson, Mass., 1983—. Author: The Right Choice: The Complete Guide to Evaluating, Selecting and Installing MRP II Software, 1987; co-author MRP II/JIT Standard System, 1988, MRP II/JIT Standard System, 1988; contbr. research reports, articles and conf. papers to tech. lit. Fellow Am. Prodn. and Inventory Control Soc. (cert. fellow prodn. and inventory mgmt.; chpt. program chmn. 1978-79, v.p. 1979-80, pres. 1980-81); mem. Data Processing Mgmt. Assn.. Phi Beta Kappa. Republican. Presbyterian. Avocations: gardening, landscaping, house restoration, furniture building. Home and Office: Piscassic Rd PO Box 199 Newfields NH 03856

GRAY, FREDERICK THOMAS, lawyer; b. Petersburg, Va., Oct. 10, 1918; s. Franklin Pierce and Mary Gervase (Pouder) G.; m. Evelyn Helms Johnson: children: Frederick Thomas Jr., Evelyn Cary. BA, U. Richmond, 1949, JD, 1949. Bar: Va. 1949. Asst. atty. gen. Commonwealth of Va., Richmond, 1949-57, atty. gen., 1961-62; ptnr. Williams, Mullen, Richmond, 1957-61, 62-83, Gray, Sinnott, Tucker & Duke, Chesterfield, Va., 1983-85; retired 1985; mem. Va. Ho. of Dels., Richmond, 1966-72, Va. Senate, Richmond, 1972-74. Recipient Medal of Honor DAR, 1981, Disting. Service award U. Richmond Alumni Assn., 1982, Citizen award Am. Legion, 1983, Pub. Service award Am. Acad. Pediatrics, 1983. Mem. Chesterfield-Colonial Heights Bar Assn. (past pres.), Va. State Bar Assn., Richmond Bar Assn , Am. Coll. Trial Lawyers. Democrat. Methodist. Clubs: Meadowbrook Country (Richmond), Jordan Point Country (Hopewell) (pres.). Lodge: Lions. Home: 4701 Bermuda Hundred Rd Chester VA 23831

GRAY, JAMES L., communications company executive. Pres., chief operating officer Warner Cable Communications Inc. subs. Warner Communications Inc., N.Y.C., also bd. dirs. Office: Warner Cable Communications Inc 425 Metro Pl Dublin OH 43017 *

GRAY, JAMES LARRY, metals company executive; b. Southmayd, Tex., Dec. 17, 1932; s. Cecil Lawray and Coquese Adeline (Coe) G.; student Tex. Tech. U., 1954, So. Meth. U., 1956; M.B.A., Pepperdine U., 1978. Sales engr. Simplex Wire & Cable, Cambridge, Mass., 1958-63; pres. Integral Corp., Dallas, 1963—. Served with U.S. Army, 1956-58. Mem. IEEE, Sigma Alpha Epsilon. Republican. Club: Toastmasters (pres. 1966-67), Jaycees (v.p. 1969-70). Home: 3534 Fairmount St Dallas TX 75219 Office: 1424 Barry Ave Dallas TX 75223

GRAY, JAN CHARLES, lawyer; b. Des Moines, June 15, 1947. s. Charles Donald and Mary C. Gray; m. Anita Marie Ringwald, June 6, 1987. B.A. in Econs., U. Calif.-Berkeley, 1969; M.B.A., Pepperdine U., 1986, J.D., Harvard U., 1972. Bar: Calif. 1972, D.C. 1974. Law clk. Kindel & Anderson, Los Angeles, 1971-72; assoc. Halstead, Baker & Sterling, Los Angeles, 1972-75; sr. v.p., gen. counsel external affairs, sec. Ralph's Grocery Co., Los Angeles, 1975—; judge pro tem Los Angeles Mcpl. Ct., 1977—; instr. bus. UCLA, 1976—, Pepperdine MBA Program, 1985—; arbitrator Am. Arbitration Assn., 1977—; media spokesman So. Calif. Grocers Assn., Calif. Grocers Assn.; real estate broker, Los Angeles, 1973—. Trustee, South Bay U. Coll. Law, 1978-79; mem. bd. visitors Southwestern U. Sch. Law, 1983—; mem. Los Angeles County Pvt. Industry Council, 1982—, exec. com. 1984-88, chmn. econ. devel. task force, 1986—; mem. Los Angeles County Martin Luther King, Jr. Gen. Hosp. Authority, 1984—; mem. Los Angeles County Aviation Commn, 1986—; Los Angeles Police Crime Prevention Adv. Council, 1986—; Angelus Plaza Adv. Bd., 1983—; bd. dirs. RecyCAL of So. Calif., 1983—; bd. trustees Santa Monica Hosp. Found., 1986—; mem. Los Angeles County Democratic Central Com., 1980-82 ; del. Dem. Nat. Conv., 1980. Recipient So. Calif. Grocers Assn. award for outstanding contbns. to food industry, 1982; Calif./Nev. Soft Drink Assn. appreciation award for No on 11 Campaign, 1983. Mem. ABA, Calif. Bar Assn., Los Angeles County Bar Assn. (exec. com. corp. law depts. sect. 1974-76, 79—, vice-chmn. 1988—, exec. com. barristers sect. 1974-75, 79-81), San Fernando Valley Bar Assn. (chmn. real property sect. 1975-77, Los Angeles Pub. Affairs Officers Assn., Los Angeles World Affairs Council, Calif. Retailers Assn. (supermarket com.), Food Mktg. Inst. (govt. relations com., govt. affairs council), So. Calif. Businessmen's Assn. (bd. dirs. 1981—, mem. exec. com. 1982—, sec. 1986—), Town Hall Los Angeles, U. Calif. Alumni Assn., Ephebian Soc. Los Angeles, Phi Beta Kappa. Club: Harvard of So. Calif. Contbg. author: Life or Death, Who Controls?, 1976; contbr. articles to legal jours. Home: PO Box 407 Beverly Hills CA 90213 Office: PO Box 54143 Los Angeles CA 90054

GRAY, JOHN BULLARD, manufacturing company executive; b. Boston, Oct. 9, 1927; s. Francis Calley and Helen Rotch (Bullard) G.; m. Virginia Hamilton Tripp, June 25, 1949; children: John Bullard, David M., Lucinda M. AB, Harvard U., MBA. Gen. mgr. Dennison Mfg. Co., Framingham, Mass., 1962-74, sr. v.p., 1974-79, exec. v.p., 1979-86, pres., chief operating officer, 1986—, also dir.; dir. EG&G Inc., Wellesley, Mass., State St. Bank, Boston, Reece Corp., Waltham, Mass., Butler Automatic, Canton, Mass. Selectman, Town of Dover, Mass., 1960-64. Served with USMC, 1945-46. Republican. Unitarian. Club: Dedham Country (Mass.) (pres. 1979-81). Home: 175 Dedham St Dover MA 02030 Office: Dennison Mfg Co 300 Howard St Framingham MA 01701 *

GRAY, JOHN DELTON, retired manufacturing company executive; b. Ontario, Oreg., July 29, 1919; s. Elmer R. and Mabel (Ridgley) G.; m. Elizabeth Neuner, Jan. 4, 1946; children—Anne, Joan, Janet, John Richard, Laurie. B.Secretarial Sci., Oreg. State Coll., 1940; M.B.A., Harvard U., 1947; LL.D., Lewis and Clark Coll., 1967. Asst. to pres. Pointer-Willamette Co., Portland, 1947; asst. gen. mgr. Oreg. Saw Chain Corp. (now Omark Industries, Inc.), Portland, 1948-50; gen. mgr. Oreg. Saw Chain Corp. (now Omark Industries, Inc.), 1950-53, pres., gen. mgr., 1953-67, chmn. bd., 1961-83, vice chmn. bd., 1983-85; chmn. Textronix, Inc., 1985-87, ret., 1987; chmn. Grayco Resources, Inc.; dir. Precision Castparts Corp., First Interstate Bank Oreg., N.A., Standard Ins. Co. Past pres. Portland area council Boy Scouts Am., 1959-61; past mem. exec. bd., also past pres. Columbia-Pacific council; trustee Com. Econ. Devel., 1967-81; mem. Chief Execs. Orgn., 1969—; trustee Reed Coll., Portland, 1961—, chmn., 1968-82, chmn. Steering Com. Capital Campaign, 1983-88; trustee Oreg. Grad. Center. Served from 2d lt. to lt. col. AUS, 1941-46. Decorated Bronze Star medal; recipient Silver Beaver award Portland Area council Boy Scouts Am. Republican. Episcopalian. Lodge: Rotary. Office: Grayco Resources Inc 5331 SW Macadam Ave Suite 200 Portland OR 97201

GRAY, JOHN DOUGLAS, investment banking executive; b. Evanston, Ill., Feb. 15, 1945; s. John D. and Ruth (Campbell) G.; m. April Townley, Oct. 9, 1976 (div. Dec. 1980); m. 2d, Karen Zateslo, June 9, 1984. B.A., Miami U., Oxford, Ohio, 1966; postgrad., U.Chgo., 1966-68; D.H.L. (hon.), Huron Coll., S.D., 1985. With Price Waterhouse, Chgo., Ill., 1969-71; fin. and adminstrn. positions Esmark, Inc-Swift & Co., Chgo., 1971-78; exec. v.p. Swift & Co., 1979-80, Swift Ind. Corp., Chgo, 1980-83; dir., chief fin. officer, pres., chief operating officer Swift Ind. Corp., Chgo., 1983-86; mng. dir. Midwest Morgan Stanley & Co., Inc., Chgo., 1986—. Mem. pres.'s coun. Mus. Sci. and Industry, 1985—; trustee Northwestern Meml. Hosp., Chgo., 1982—; bd. dirs. Rehab. Inst. Chgo., 1984-86, chmn. bd., 1986—; bd. dirs. Chgo. Coun. Fgn. Rels., 1985—, Leadership of Greater Chgo., 1987—. Clubs: Chgo., Comml., The Links (N.Y.C.), Shoreacres (Lake Bluff, Ill.), Glen View (Golf, Ill.), Old Elm. Office: Morgan Stanley & Co Inc 440 S LaSalle 37th Fl Chicago IL 60605

GRAY, JOHN JAMES, JR., finance executive; b. Massena, N.Y., May 4, 1951; s. John James and Madeleine Marie (Montpetit) G.; m. Christine Marie Derouchie, Aug. 23, 1975; children: John III, Kevin, Angela, Jennifer. AS, Jefferson Community Coll., 1971; BS, Clarkson U., 1973, MBA, 1984. Staff acct. Wm. A. Sweeney, CPA, Saranac Lake, N.Y., 1973-76; asst. comptroller Gen. Hosp. of Saranac Lake, 1976-77, chief fin. officer, 1977-86; pvt. practice acct., small bus. cons. Saranac Lake, 1976-87; chief fin. officer Carthage (N.Y.) Area Hosp., 1987—; bd. dirs., treas. St. Bernard's Sch., 1978-85; assessor Village of Saranac Lake, 1979-85. Mem. HANYS Blue Cross Negotiating Com., 1978-86, HANYS MARSAC Statewide Com., 1983-86, Statewide Medicare Billing Liaison Com., 1984-86, State Senate Tech. Adv. Com. of Hosp. Reimbursement, 1985-86. Mem. Saranac Lake Area C. of C. (bd. dirs., treas. 1984-87); advanced mem. Healthcare Fin. Mgmt. Assn. Republican. Roman Catholic. Lodge: Rotary (treas. Saranac Lake club 1984-87), K.C., Elks (exalted ruler 1980-81, hon. life mem. 1981, treas. 1980-86). Home: PO Box 488 Potsdam NY 13676

GRAY, MICHAEL CHARLES, tax consultant; b. Torrance, Calif., Nov. 17, 1951; s. Aubrey Kenneth James and Eleanor Beatrice (Zaich) G.; m. Janet Joy Bowers, Aug. 7, 1971; children: Dawn, Holly, James. AA, West Valley Coll., 1972; BS, San Jose State U., 1974, MS, 1979. CPA, Calif. Acct. Berger, Lewis and Co., San Jose, Calif., 1974-78; sr. tax acct. Hurdman and Cranstoun, San Jose, 1978-80; mgr., tng. coordinator tax div. KMG Main Hurdman, San Jose, 1982-86; founder, ptnr. Hubler, Gray and Assocs., Campbell, Calif., 1986—. Contbr. articles to profl. jours. MBA mentor San Jose State U., 1986—. Named Disting. Alumnus West Valley Coll., 1988. Mem. AICPAs, Calif. Inst. CPAs , Santa Clara County Estate Planning Council, No. Calif. Motor Car Dealers Assn., San Jose C. of C., Phi Kappa Phi. Home: 2482 Wooding Ct San Jose CA 95128 Office: Hubler Gray & Assocs 595 Millich Dr Campbell CA 95008

GRAY, NIGEL GEORGE DAVIDSON, lawyer; b. Chakrata, India, June 16, 1935; s. James Davidson and Barbara Cecilia (Holiday) G.; m. Barbara Johnson Ferguson, Aug. 21, 1964; children: Nicholas, Christopher. BS, Dalhousie U., 1959, LLB, 1964; post grad., Lincoln Coll. Oxford U., 1964-65; AMP, Harvard U., 1986. Bar: N.S. 1966, Que. 1969. Asst. sec., asst. counsel Petrofina Can. Ltd., 1966-69; legal counsel, sec. Capital Mgmt. Ltd., 1969-72; asst. gen. counsel Brinco Ltd., 1972-75, assoc. gen. counsel, 1975; gen. counsel Polysar Energy & Chem. Corp., Toronto, 1978, v.p., 1979—. Fellow Geol. Assn. Can.; mem. N.S. Barristers Soc., Barreau du Québec, Can. Bar Assn., Assn. Profl. Engrs., Geologists & Geophysicists of Alberta. Club: Univeristy (Toronto). Home: 506 Lakeshore Rd E, Oakville, ON Canada L6J 1K5 Office: Polysar Energy & Chem Corp, 444 Yonge St Ste 200, Toronto, ON Canada M5B 2H4

GRAY, RICHARD GORDON, trade association executive; b. Emmett, Idaho, Jan. 11, 1941; s. David D. and Doris (Parrish) G.; m. Catherine Lee Powell, Oct. 10, 1964. BS, U. Idaho, 1964; MBA, U. Ariz., 1967. CPA, Ill. Auditor, cons. Peat Marwick Mitchell and Co., N.Y.C., 1967-70; adminstrv. asst. Am. Standard Co., N.Y.C., 1970-71; group controller Textron Inc., Providence, 1971-74; exec. asst. Merabank, Phoenix, 1974-76; pres. U.S. League Fin. Svcs., Chgo., 1976—, also dir.; bd. dirs. U.S. League Card Svcs., U.S. League Mgmt. Svcs., SAF Systems and Forms, Inc. Capt. U.S. Army, 1964-66, Vietnam. Mem. AICPA, Ill. Soc. CPAs, Young Pres. Orgn., Inst. Fin. Edn., Tavern Club, Knollwood Club. Home: 196 Ahwahnee Rd Lake Forest IL 60045 Office: US League Fin Svcs 111 E Wacker Dr Chicago IL 60601

GRAY, ROBERT APSEY, banker; b. Albuquerque, Jan. 23, 1957; s. Robert Fitzpatrick, Jr. and Jerome (Biddle) G.; m. Carol Goodnow Fox, June 27, 1987. BA, Dartmouth Coll., 1978; MBA, Harvard U., 1980. With Morgan Guaranty Trust Co., N.Y.C., 1979—; v.p. Morgan Guaranty Trust Co., 1985—. Mem. Harvard (N.Y.C.). Home: 1 South Terr, London SWT, England Office: J P Morgan & Co, 1 Angel Ct, PO Box 161, London EC2R 7AE, England

GRAY, ROBERT KEITH, communications company executive; b. Hastings, Nebr., Sept. 2, 1923; s. Garold C.J. and Marie (Burchess) G. BA, Carleton Coll., 1943; MBA, Harvard U., 1949; D.Bus.(hon.), Marymount Coll., 1981; LLD (hon.), Hastings Coll., 1982; HHD (hon.), Creighton U., 1989. Assoc. prof. fin. Hastings Coll., Nebr., 1950-51; prof. U. So. Calif., Los Angeles, 1952; spl. asst. sec. navy 1954; spl. asst. to Pres. Eisenhower White House, Washington, 1955-57, appointments sec., 1958; sec. Eisenhower Cabinet, Washington, 1959-60; v.p. Hill & Knowlton, Inc., Washington, 1961-64, sr. v.p., 1965-70, exec. v.p., 1971-76, vice chmn., 1977-81; founder, chmn. Gray and Co. Pub. Communications Internat. (merger Hill and Knowlton, Inc.), Washington, 1981-86; chmn., chief exec. officer Hill and Knowlton Pub. Affairs Worldwide, Washington, 1986—; chmn., pres. Gray and Co. II, Washington, 1988—; chmn. Gray Investment Properties, Inc., Washington, 1988—; chief exec. officer, pres. Member Services Co., Washington, 1988—; chmn, chief exec. officer Powerhouse Leasing Corp., Washington, 1988—; dir. 1st Am. Bank; chmn. Hill & Knowlton, U.S.A. Author: Casebook on Organization and Operation of a Small Business Enterprise, 1950; Eighteen Acres Under Glass, 1962. mem. pub. info. adv. council World Wildlife Fund; bd. dirs. Freedoms Found., Valley Forge, Pa.; trustee Washington Fed. City Council; mem. nat. adv. bd. Am. U.; mem. bd. Wolf Trap Found., Eisenhower World Affairs Inst.; bd. councilors Sch. Bus. Adminstrn., U. So. Calif.; mem. pvt. sector pub. rels. com. USIA, 1981-88; dir. communications Reagan-Bush Campaign, Washington, 1980; co-chmn. Presdl. Inaugural, Washington, 1981, hon. chmn., 1985; adv. bd. Ctr. Strategic and Internat. Studies, Commn. on Bicentennial of U.S. Constn., 1988; mem. bd. alliance to Save Energy; adv. com. Presdl. Debates, 1988, Pub. Edn. Task Force of Pub./Pvt. Careers Project at the Kennedy Sch. Govt. Harvard U.; mem. steering com. Nat. Air and Space Mus. joint project with the Ctr. for Democracy; prin. benefactor Gray Ctr. Communications Arts, Hastings Coll., Neb. Comdr. USN, 1944-46, now Res. Decorated knight comdr. Order of Merit (Italy); Medaille de Vermeil, Mayor of Paris, 1982; recipient Disting. Nebraskalander award, 1985; named Marketer of Yr., Adweek Mag. Mem. Ctr. Strategic and Internat. Studies. Republican. Episcopalian. Clubs: 1925 F St., George Town (chmn.) (Washington). Lodge: Masons. Home: 4953 Rock Spring Rd Arlington VA 22207 Office: Hill & Knowlton Inc Washington Harbour 901 31st St NW Washington DC 20007-3838

GRAY, ROBERT KEVIN, chemical engineer; b. Huron, S.D., Mar. 22, 1953; s. Buford A. and Ruby E. (Doering) G.; m. Helen M. Kuiper, Aug. 27, 1977; children: Libby K., Molly A. BSChemE, S.D. Sch. Mines and Tech., 1975; MBA, Colo. State U., 1984. Cert. profl. engr., Colo. With Eastman Kodak Co., 1975—; dir. product devel. Plate Mfg. div. Eastman Kodak Co., Windsor, Colo., 1987—. Advisor Jr. Achievement, Ft. Collins, 1984-86; bd. dirs. Am. Cancer Soc., 1983-84; active Leadership Ft. Collins, 1988—. Mem. Am. Soc. Quality Control, Tech. Assn. Graphic Arts, Ft. Collins C. of C. (com. mem.). Methodist. Office: Eastman Kodak Co Bldg C-60 Windsor CO 80551

GRAY, ROBERT WINSTON, portfolio manager; b. Austin, Tex., July 20, 1938; s. Hob and Mary Douglas (Tanner) G.; m. Joyce Y. Eitelman, Jan. 2, 1980; children: Susan Patricia, Lauren Ashley. BS in Petroleum Engring., U. Tex., 1960; MBA, Harvard U., 1963. CPA, Tex.; Chartered Fin. Analyst. Petroleum engr. Conoco, Inc., Sweetwater, Tex., 1960-61; CPA Arthur Young & Co., Houston, 1963-65; security analyst, dir. research Southwestern Regional Securities Cos., Houston and Dallas, 1965-71; stockbroker Schneider, Bernet & Hickman, San Antonio, 1980-85; investment officer MTrust Corp., San Antonio, 1985—. Mem. San Antonio Fin. Analysts Soc. (bd. dirs. 1986—, treas. 1988-89), Inst. Chartered Fin. Analysts, Am. Inst. CPAs, Fin. Analysts Fedn. Republican. Episcopalian. Club: Harvard Bus. Sch. (San Antonio) (pres. 1987-88). Home: 12402 B Autumn Vista San Antonio TX 78249 Office: MTrust PO Box 900 San Antonio TX 78293

GRAY, SANDRA KAY, administrative services company professional; b. Winston-Salem, N.C., Feb. 2, 1959; d. John Ross and Margie (Cook) G. AS, Forsyth Tech. Coll., 1982; BS, High Point Coll., 1988. Cable former AT&T Techs., Winston-Salem, 1979-86; sales rep. Best Western Hotels, Winston-Salem, 1987; sr. acctg. clk. Quality Bus. Cons., Winston-Salem, 1987—; owner, mgr. Profl. Adminstrv. Services, Winston-Salem, 1988—. Mem. Minority Bus. League. Home: 2721 Ludwig St Winston-Salem NC 27107

GRAY, TERRY ALLEN, chemical executive; b. Miami, Aug. 31, 1943; s. Eugene Briggs and Virginia I. (Ingalls) G.; m. Jeanette Marie Eckdahl, Apr. 15, 1972; children: Steven, Michael. BS in Chem. Engring., Princeton U., 1965. Devel. engr., mktg. mgr., product mgr. Dow Chem. Co., various, 1965-81; dir. corp. planning Pakhoed USA, Houston, 1981-83; v.p., corp. devel. and planning Waste Recovery, Inc., Houston, 1983—; pres. WRI-Dade, Miami. Contbr. articles to profl. jours. Community trustee, Houston, 1984-86. Recipient Zeisberg award Delaware Valley Am. Inst. of Chem. Engrs., 1965. Mem. Am. Inst. of Chem. Engrs. Republican. Episcopalian. Office: Waste Recovery Inc 2606 Gaston Ave Dallas TX 75226

GRAY, VINCENT NELSON, banker; b. St. Ann, Jamaica, Jan. 14, 1941; came to U.S., 1969; s. Aston Evans and Ina (Dixon) G.; m. Ina Evadne, Mar. 14, 1964; 1 child, Vincent Jr. AA, Fairleigh-Dickinson U., 1987, student, 1987—. Officer's asst. Chem. Bank, N.Y.C., 1969-80; ops. officer Marine Midland Bank, N.Y.C., 1980-82; asst. v.p. Bank Leumi Trust Co., N.Y.C., 1982-83, v.p., 1984—. Active fund raising Dem. Party of Bklyn., 1971-75. Mem. Montran Users Group (chmn. 1984—). Methodist. Office: Bank Leumi Trust Co 562 Fifth Ave New York NY 10036

GRAY, WALTER FRANKLIN, bank executive; b. Denver, Sept. 25, 1929; s. Walter Franklin and Alice (Fassig) G.; m. Susan Amy Mair, Mar. 26, 1955; children: Constance G. Newhall, Stuart Franklin. BS, Northwestern U., 1951; JD, Loyola U., 1957. V.p. First Nat. Bank of Chgo., 1953-69; exec. v.p., dir. Mercantile Safe Deposit Corp., Balt., 1969-77; exec. v.p. Mercantile Bank, St. Louis, 1977—, adv. dir., 1977—. Chmn. Chancellor's Council U. Mo., St. Louis, 1984—; bd. dirs. St. Louis community Found., 1984—, St. Louis Mercantile Library, 1986—, St. Louis Symphony, 1985—, Arts & Edn. Coun., 1988—. Served with USAF, 1951-53. Mem. ABA, Chgo. Bar Assn., Am. Bankers Assn., Mo. Hist. Soc. (bd. dirs. 1982—). Clubs: Elkridge (Balt.); Noonday, St. Louis Country. Home: 27 Briarcliff Saint Louis MO 63124 Office: Merc Bank Merc Tower 8th & Locust Sts Saint Louis MO 63101

GRAY, WILLIAM ADDISON, financial analyst; b. Upper St. Clair, Pa., Mar. 21, 1960; s. George Hersman and Majorie Mae (Hickey) G.; m. Monica S. Moller, Oct. 20, 1984. Student, W.Va. U., 1978-79; BA in Mktg., U. So. Fla., 1982; MBA in Fin. Investments, George Washington U., 1984. Asset, liability mgmt. analyst 1st Am. Bank N.A., Washington, 1984-86; sr. acct. Mid-Atlantic div. MCI, Arlington, Va., 1986-87; sr. planning analyst Mid-Atlantic div. MCI, Arlington, 1987-88; fin. project cons. Geneva Corp., Costa Mesa, Calif., 1988—. Creator Mid-Atlantic Rep. Productivity Model, 1987. Mem. Pi Sigma Epsilon. Republican. Methodist. Office: The Geneva Corp 575 Anton Blvd Costa Mesa CA 92626

GRAYBEAL, ROBERT CHARLES, comptroller; b. Havre de Grace, Md., Aug. 8, 1947; s. Charles Wilson and Jennie Rosetta (Shepherd) G.; m. Charlotte Belle Toney, June 28, 1969; 1 child, Shannon Michelle. BS, U. Balt., 1977. Acct. clk. Armour Foods, Balt., 1974-75; office mgr., acct. March of Dimes, Balt., 1975-79; comptroller Superior Mgmt., Inc., Mitchellville, Md., 1979—, Food Services, Inc., Annapolis, Md., 1984—, Annapolis Produce & Restaurant Supply Inc., 979—; Pvt. practice tax cons., acctg. services, Annapolis, 1974—. Served with U.S. Army, 1967-70. Mem. Nat. Assn. Credit Mgrs. Office: Annapolis Produce & Restaurant Supply Inc 15 Lee St Annapolis MD 21401

GRAYSON, WALTON GEORGE, III, lawyer, convenience store company executive; b. Shreveport, La., Aug. 18, 1928; s. Walton George and Mary Alice (Lowrey) G.; m. Bennetta McEwen Purse, May 20, 1955; children: Walton Grayson IV, Mark C., Bennett P., Dwight P. AB, Princeton U., 1949; LLB, Harvard U., 1952. Bar: Tex. 1952, Dallas. Asst. counsel Gt. Nat. Life Ins. Co., Dallas, 1954-69; ptnr. Atwell Grayson & Atwell, Dallas, 1961-69, Grayson & Simon, Dallas, 1969-72; v.p., gen. counsel Southland Corp., Dallas, 1965-72; exec. v.p. Southland Corp., 1972—, also bd. dirs.; of counsel Simon & Twombly, 1972-84; chmn. Cityplace Devel. Corp., 1987—. Served with USN, 1952-54. Mem. ABA, Tex. Bar Assn., Dallas Bar Assn. Mem. Christian Ch. (Disciples of Christ). Club: Petroleum. Lodge: Masons. Home: 10525 Strait Ln Dallas TX 75229 Office: Southland Corp 2828 N Haskell Ave Dallas TX 75204

GRAYSON, WILLIAM JACKSON, JR., manufacturing executive; b. Birmingham, Ala., 1930; married;. AB, Birmingham So. Coll., 1953; MBA, Am. U., 1957; postgrad., Harvard U., 1973. Supr. comml. research analytical TCI div. U.S. Steel, 1957-62; market analyst Vulcan Materials Co., Birmingham, 1962-66, sales mgr. S.E. div., 1966-72, v.p. S.E. div., 1972-73, corp. v.p. mktg., 1973-77, exec. v.p. so. div., 1977-79, pres. mideast div., 1979-85, exec. v.p. corp. devel., from 1985, now exec. v.p. constrn. material. Served as lt. USN, 1953-57. Office: Vulcan Materials Co One Metroplex Dr Birmingham AL 35209 *

GRAZIANO, LEONARD FRANK, pump manufacturing company executive; b. Elizabeth, N.J., Oct. 29, 1945; s. Alfred and Virginia Dolores (Donia) G.; m. Alice Laura Kornmeyer, Dec. 2, 1967; children: Leonard A., Jill M., Susan R. BS in Indsl. Engring., Rutgers U.; MBA, Temple U. Dist. sales mgr. WPI-Studebaker Worthington, Wayne, Pa., 1976-77; dir. mktg. WPD-Standard Pump, East Orange, N.J., 1978-79; regional mgr. Worthington Group div. McGraw Edison, Wayne, 1980-82; v.p. sales Worthington Pump div. Dresser Industries, Inc., Wayne, 1982-85; v.p. mktg. and sales Worthington Pump div. Dresser Industries, Inc., Mountainside, N.J., 1986-87, v.p. mktg. Dresser Pump div., 1987—; gen. mgr. Engineer Pump div. Dresser Industries, Inc., Harrison, N.J., 1988—. Roman Catholic. Club: Chester Valley Golf (Frazer, Pa.) (swim/tennis chmn. 1984-86). Home: PO Box 582 Camelot Rd Buckingham PA 18912

GREANEY, JAMES ROBERT, bank executive, financial consultant; b. Woodhaven, N.Y., Aug. 10, 1922; s. James Thomas and Hanora A. (Rigney) R.; m. Eleanor Ann McClosky, Apr. 7, 1943; children: Russell James, Colin Alexander, Dreux Jason. Cert., Am. Coll. CLU; chartered fin. cons. Mgr. Conn. Gen. Life Ins. Co., Boston, 1946-62; pres. Mass. Gen. Life Ins. Co., Boston, 1962-69; agy. dir. Travelers Ins. Co., Hartford, Conn., 1969-73; v.p. Key Bank N.A., Albany, N.Y., 1973—. Dir. Albany chpt. ARC, 1976—. 1st sgt. U.S Army, 1942-45, PTO. Decorated Bronze Star with oak leaf cluster, Purple Heart with oak leaf cluster. Mem. Eastern Am. Soc. CLU's (pres. N.Y. chpt. 1985-86), Albany Assn. Life Underwriters, N.Y. Bankers Assn., Am. Bankers Assn., Found. N.Y. State Nurses Assn., Inc. (trustee). Republican. Roman Catholic. Home: 12 Leaf Rd Delmar NY 12054 Office: Key Bank NA 60 State St Albany NY 12207

GREANEY, PATRICK JOSEPH, electronics executive; b. N.Y.C., Jan. 18, 1939; s. John Joseph and Julia (Dore) G.; m. Susan Kleinermann, Sept. 19, 1970; children: Kathleen M., Patrick J. Jr., John Michael. BEE, Manhattan Coll., Riverdale, N.Y., 1960; MBA, Iona Coll., New Rochelle, N.Y., 1968. Engring. designer Raytheon Co., Norwalk, Conn., 1960-65, mgr. sales/advt., 1965-68, mgr. product planning, 1968-70; mgr. mktg. Am. BOA Inc., N.Y.C., 1970-71; mgr. bus. planning N. Am. Philips Corp., N.Y.C., 1971-77, mgr. corp. planning, 1977-79, dir. corp. planning, 1979-83, corp. v.p., 1983—. Mem. Sch. Bd., Wyckoff, N.J., 1980-82; chmn. United Fund Appeal, Raytheon Co., 1969. Recipient Regents Scholarship, N.Y., 1956. Mem. IEEE, Conf. Bd. Council Planning Execs., Bus. Week's Corp. Planning 100, Assn. for Corp. Growth, Machinery & Allied Products Inst. Corp. Planning Council, Ridgewood (N.J.) Country Club, Union League (N.Y.C.). Republican. Roman Catholic. Office: N Am Philips Corp 100 E 42nd St New York NY 10017

GREBEY, CLARENCE RAYMOND, JR., airline executive; b. Chgo., Mar. 10, 1928; s. Clarence R. and Inez (Fuller) G.; m. Marilyn Irene Isett, Nov. 24, 1951; children—Nancy Virginia, Christine E., Clarence Raymond. B.A., Kenyon Coll., 1949; M.B.A., U. Chgo., 1956. With Inland Steel Co., 1949-56, sr. wage and salary analyst, 1956; with Gen. Electric Co., 1956-78, mgr. wage and salary, 1963-67; mgr. employee relations Gen. Electric Co. (Hotpoint div.), 1967-69, cons. corp. employee relations, mgr. union relations, 1969-74, mgr. corp. planning and strategy, 1974-75, mgr. union relations planning and strategy, 1975-78; chief negotiator corp. employee relations Gen. Electric Co. (EEOC litigation), 1978; dir., sec.-treas. player relations com. Major League Baseball, N.Y.C., 1978-83; exec. scholar-in-residence Grad. Sch. Bus., Washington U., St. Louis, 1983, ret.; sr. v.p. indsl. relations Pan Am. World Airways, N.Y.C., 1984-88; sr. v.p. employee and coop. affairs Trump Shuttle, Inc., N.Y.C., 1989—. Chmn. Personnel Bd. Appeals, City of Stamford, Conn.; bd. advisors Columbia U. Grad. Sch. Bus.

Served with U.S. Army, 1951-52, Korea. Roman Catholic. Clubs: Stanwich (Greenwich, Conn.); University (Washington); Wings Club (N.Y.C.). Office: Trump Tower 725 Park Ave New York NY 10166

GREBSTEIN, STANLEY, accountant; b. Providence, May 16, 1926; s. Louis and Mae (Bereslausky) G.; m. Phyllis Roslyn Pollack, Dec. 26, 1948; children: Lee Alan, Marilyn Joy, Michael Brett. Grad., Bryant Coll., 1949. CPA, R.I. Mgr. acctg. Warwick (R.I.) Sch. Dept., 1974-80; pvt. practice 1980-84; sr. auditor dept. transp. State of R.I., Providence, 1984-87, rate analyst pub. utilities commn., 1987—. Sec., bd. dirs. Lincoln Pk. Cemetery, Warwick, 1970—. Served with USAF, 1944-46, PTO. Mem. AICPA, Jewish War Vets, Masons. Home: 32 Sprague Ave Warwick RI 02889

GRECSEK, MATTHEW THOMAS, software company executive; b. Staten Island, N.Y., Nov. 17, 1963; s. Ernest Edward and Theresa Joan (Lakemann) G. Student, Rensellaer Poly. Inst., 1982-83. Software engr. IBM Corp., Boca Raton, Fla., 1983; pres., chief exec. officer Result Focused Systems Corp., Charlotte, N.C., 1984—, cons. bus., 1984-86, cons. software start-up, 1986-87. Author: (computer software) Cypher, 1984, Admissions Executive, 1985, STAR, 1986, Relocation Manager, 1988. Mem. Assn. for Systems Mgmt., Better Bus. Bur. Republican. Office: Result Focused Systems Corp PO Box 2506 Charlotte NC 28247

GREEHEY, WILLIAM EUGENE, energy company executive; b. Forest Dodge, Iowa, 1936; married. B.B.A., St. Mary's U., 1960. Auditor Price Waterhouse & Co., 1960-61; sr. auditor Humble Oil and Refining Co., 1961-63; sr. v.p. fin. Coastal Corp. (and predecessor), 1963-74; with Valero Energy Corp. (formerly Coastal States Gas Producing Co.), San Antonio, 1974—, pres., chief exec. officer, 1979-83, chmn. bd., 1983—, now also chief exec. officer, dir., also chmn. numerous subsidiaries; pres., chief exec. officer LoVaca Gathering Co. subs., San Antonio, 1974-79. Office: Valero Energy Corp 530 McCullough San Antonio TX 78215 *

GREEK, GENE ALLEN, accountant; b. Princeton, Ind., Sept. 12, 1937; s. Eugene Edwin and Delama Wadina (Geiser) G.; m. Arlie Carolyn Malone, Fed. 17, 1956; children: Rebecca Anne, Margaret Elizabeth. BS, Ea. Ill U., 1959. Adminstrv. clk. U.S. Indsl. Chems. Co., Tuscola, Ill., 1959-64; adminstrv. asst. U.S. Indsl. Chems. Co., Tuscola, 1964-69, office svcs. supr., 1969-71; bus. office mgr. Decatur (Ill.) Meml. Hosp., 1971-73; adminstrv. asst. to dean U. Ill. Coll. Vet. Med., Urbana, 1973—. Sect. leader Champaign (Ill.) County United Way, 1976-87; trustee, Village of Atwood, Ill., 1982, treas., 1983. Mem. Bus. Officers of Colls. of Vet. Med. N.Am. (sec. 1983-84, v.p. 1984-85, pres. 1985-86). Republican. Mem. United Church of Christ. Home: 401 W Orchard Ave Atwood IL 61913 Office: U Ill Coll Vet Med 2001 S Lincoln Ave Urbana IL 61801

GREELEY, ROBERT EMMETT, financial analyst; b. N.Y.C., Jan. 19, 1932; s. Joseph Michael and Mary Cleary G.; m. Joan Hahler, Feb. 19, 1955; children: Shaun Eileen, Madelyn Cammille. AB, Fordham U., 1953; MBA, NYU, 157; postgrad. advanced mgmt. program, Harvard U., 1970. V.p. Smith Barney, N.Y.C., 1959-71; mgr. Gen. Electric Pension Trust, Stamford, Conn., 1971-76; v.p. asset mgmt. Merrill Lynch Asset Mgmt. Co., Stamford, 1977-79; mgr. corp. investments Hewlett Packard Co., Palo Alto, Calif., 1979—. adv. Alaska Permanent Fund, Juneau, 1976—. Served with U.S. Army, 1953-55; Korea. U.S. Steel Fellow, 1955-58. Mem. IEEE (bd. dirs. investors mortgage securities, trustee Equitec Seibel Mutual Funds, Morgan Grenfell small cap fund; advisor William and Flora Hewlett Found.), Fin. Analysts Fedn., N.Y. Soc. Securities Analysts. Clubs: University, Larchmont Yacht, St. Andrews Soc. Home: 25850 Vinedo Ln Los Altos CA 94022 Office: 3000 Hanover St Palo Alto CA 94304

GREELEY, SEAN MCGOVERN, bank executive; b. New Brunswick, N.J., Nov. 8, 1961; s. Horace James, Jr. and Patricia Louise (McGovern) G.; m. Kristin Elisabeth Lindefjeld, June 20, 1987; 1 child, Elisabeth Lindefjeld. BSBA, Monmouth Coll., 1983. With Dean Witter Reynolds, N.Y.C., 1983-85; acct. exec. U.S. Trust Co., N.Y.C., 1985-87, fin. officer, 1987—. Mem. Tau Kappa Epsilon Alumni Assn. (v.p., bd. dirs. 1984—, cons. bd. fin. 1986—). Home: 14 North St Rumson NJ 07760 Office: US Trust Co NY 45 Wall St New York NY 10005

GREELEY, WALTER FRANKLIN, engery, chemicals and metals corporation executive, lawyer; b. Framingham, Mass., July 14, 1931; s. Sidney Foote and Annette (Stiles) G.; m. Alida Daale, Feb. 23, 1957; children—Walter Franklin, Robin, Jennifer, John David. AB cum laude, Harvard U., 1953, LLB, 1960. Bar: Mass. 1960, U.S. Dist. Ct. (ea. dist.) Mass. 1965, U.S. Ct. Appeals (1st cir.) 1969, U.S. Supreme Ct. 1974. With Cabot Corp., Boston, 1960-88, gen. counsel, 1967-86, v.p., 1969-86, dir. human resources, 1982-86, sr. v.p., 1986-88; chmn. High St. Assocs. Inc., Boston, 1988—; bd. dirs. AMT Corp., Reading, Pa., 1987-89, Haynes Internat. Inc., Kokomo, Ind., 1987—. Lt. (j.g.) USN, 1949-56. Mem. ABA, Boston Bar Assn., Harvard Varsity Club (pres. 1985-87, chmn. 1987—). Republican. Unitarian. Avocations: tennis, squash, bird-watching. Home: 17 Maugus Ave Wellesley MA 02181 Office: High St Assocs 50 High St Boston MA 02110

GREEN, ALVIN, lawyer; b. Elgin, Ill., Mar. 13, 1931; s. Samuel and Rose (Brustein) G.; m. Miriam E. Blau, June 13, 1954; children—Andrew, Marie, Jennifer. B.A., U. Mich., 1953, M.A., 1954; LL.B., Harvard U., 1957. Bar: N.Y. bar, Ill. bar. Atty. Eastern Air Lines, Inc., N.Y.C., 1957-65; asst. to gen. counsel C.I.T. Corp., N.Y.C., 1965-70; gen. counsel C.I.T. Corp., 1970-72; v.p. Condren, Walker & Co., N.Y.C., 1972-75; v.p., gen. counsel, sec. Seatrain Lines, Inc., N.Y.C., 1975-81; exec. v.p., sr. counsel Seatrain Lines, Inc., 1981—; exec. v.p. Seatrain Tankers Inc., 1987—, Bay Tankers Inc., 1981—. Woodrow Wilson fellow, 1953-54. Mem. ABA, Assn. Bar City N.Y., Am. Bur. Shipping, Phi Beta Kappa, Phi Kappa Phi. Club: Harvard (N.Y.C.). Home: 22 Arleigh Rd Great Neck NY 11021 Office: 270 Sylvan Ave Suite 100 Englewood Cliffs NJ 07632

GREEN, BERNARD, food products executive. Pres. B. Green & Co. Inc., Baltimore, Md. Office: B Green & Co Inc 3601 Washington Blvd Baltimore MD 21227 *

GREEN, CHARLES KENNARD, JR., computer graphics software executive; b. Bridgeport, Conn., Apr. 8, 1951; s. Charles Kennard Sr. and Shirley (Ford) G.; m. Vickie Spradlin, June 23, 1970 (div. 1973); m. Leslie Jane Carlisle; children: Jeffrey Charles, Robert Ford. Student, Va. Commonwealth U., 1969-71. Art dir. Sta. WTTG-TV, Washington, 1971-73, Riddick Advt. Art, Richmond, Va., 1973-77; designer Freelance Design, Richmond, 1977-82; sr. project dir. Riddick Communications, Richmond, 1982-87; dir. prod. devel. Mktg. Graphics Inc., Richmond, 1987-89, gen. mgr., 1989—. Bd. dirs. Family & Children's Trust Fund of Va., Richmond, 1986-88; active United Way (chmn. advt. task group Va. 1986), judge-nat. advt. competition, Washington, 1986, 88). Office: Mktg Graphics Inc 4401 Dominion Blvd #210 Richmond VA 23060

GREEN, DAVID BRIAN, mortgage company executive; b. Newark, Ohio, June 11, 1957; s. James T. and Marjorie Ann (Robinson) G.; m. Karen E. Lavery, Aug. 25, 1979; 1 child, Shaun D. BBA, Ohio State U., 1980. Regional mgr. to asst. v.p. City Fed. Mortgage Co., Bellview, Wash., 1984—. Mem. Columbus C. of C., Nat. Mortgage Bankers' Assn., Ohio Mortgage Bankers' Assn., Columbus Mortagage Bankers Assn. (chmn. publicity, appraisal coms.). Home: 695 Cardinal Hill Ln Powell OH 43065 Office: City Fed Mortgage Co 475 Metro Ctr N Dublin OH 43017

GREEN, DENNIS JOSEPH, lawyer; b. Milw., Sept. 28, 1941; m. Janet McQueen; children: Karla, Cheryl, Deborah. BS in Mgmt., U. Ill., 1963, JD, 1968. Atty. Monsanto Co., St. Louis, 1968-75, asst. co. counsel, 1975-76, counsel, 1976-79; gen. counsel, sec. Fisher Controls Internat. Inc., Clayton, Mo., 1979-85, v.p., gen. counsel, sec., 1985—; sec. Fisher Svc. Co., Marshalltown, Iowa, 1979—, Permea Inc., St. Louis, 1986—; bd. dirs. Exac Corp., San Jose, Calif. 1st lt. U.S. Army, 1963-65. Office: Fisher Controls Internat Inc 8000 Maryland Ave Clayton MO 63105

GREEN, GEORGE FREDERICK, III, banker; b. Richmond, Va., July 21, 1941; s. George Frederick Jr. and Mary Jeanette (Gibson) G.; m. Ellen Sue Collier, June 13, 1964; children: Eric, Erin, Stacy, Beth. BBA, U. Richmond, 1964, MS, 1969. Asst. auditor Fed. Res. Bank, Richmond, 1964-68; v.p. Signet Bank (formerly Bank of Va.), Richmond, 1968-79; dist. mgr. Tri-Continental Leasing Corp., Mechanicsville, Va. 1979-82; sr. v.p. Sovran Bank/Md., Bethesda, 1982—. Bd. dirs. Richmond Jaycees, 1969-73. Mem. Nat. Comml. Fin. Assn. (bd. dirs. 1982—), Richmond First Club (bd. dirs. 1972-80). Republican. Episcopalian. Home: 4541 Hornbeam Dr Rockville MD 20853 Office: Sovran Bank/Md 6610 Rockledge Dr Bethesda MD 20817

GREEN, HOWARD ALAN, management consultant; b. Los Angeles, Aug. 31, 1938; s. Jack Oscar and Bertha Edith (Blumenthal) G.; B.A., Lehigh U., 1960; J.D., N.Y.U., 1968; m. Joyce Sheila Linn, May 13, 1962; children—Kenneth Ira, Michael Lewis. With IBM, N.Y.C., 1965-67, Keydata Corp., Watertown, Mass., 1967-74, Xerox Computer Services, Los Angeles, 1977-80; mgmt. cons. Coopers & Lybrand, N.Y.C., 1980—; adj. assoc. prof. Iona Coll., New Rochelle, N.Y, 1979—. Served in USMC, 1960. Mem. Am. Prodn. and Inventory Control Soc., Inst. Mgmt. Cons. (cert.), Assn. Systems Mgmt. (cert. systems profl.), Project Mgmt. Inst.

GREEN, JACK ALLEN, lawyer; b. Detroit, Dec. 15, 1945; s. Martin and Frieda Francis (Freeman) G.; m. Pamela Arlene Stern, Aug. 20, 1967; children—Marla Elizabeth, Carrie Lynn. B.B.A., U. Mich., 1967, J.D., 1970. Bar: Ohio 1970, Mass. 1984. Assoc. Schwartz & Schwartz, Columbus, Ohio, 1970-72; gen. counsel Prestolite Co., Toledo, 1972-83; sr. v.p. legal, human resources, facilities, office svcs. and MISConverse Inc., North Reading, Mass., 1983—. Mem. Ohio State Bar Assn., Mass. Bar Assn., ABA, Corp. Counsel Assn. Club: Indian Ridge Country (Andover, Mass.). Avocations: skiing; tennis; running. Office: Converse Inc One Fordham Rd North Reading MA 01864

GREEN, JERRY HOWARD, banker; b. Kansas City, Mo., June 10, 1930; s. Howard Jay and Selma (Stein) G.; BA, Yale U., 1952. m. Betsy Bozarth, July 18, 1981. Pres., Union Chevrolet, 1955-69, Union Securities, Inc., Kansas City, 1969—, Union Bancshares, Inc., Kansas City, 1969-76. chmn. Union Bank, Kansas City, 1976—, Budget Rent-A-Car Mo., Inc., 1961—, Budget Rent-A-Car Memphis, Inc.; pres. Pembroke Bancshares, Kansas City, 1983—; chmn., bd. dirs. Citizens Bank, Ava, Mo., 1980—; bd. dirs. Century City Artists Corp., L.A. Bd. dirs. Boys' Clubs Kansas City, Jackson County Pension Plan Com.; appointed bd. dirs. (by Gov. Ashcroft) Mo. Higher Loan Authority, 1987—; mem. Yale Class of 1952 Reunion Gift. 1st lt. USAF, 1952-55. Mem. Am. Bankers Assn., Yale Alumni Assn. (bd. dirs.). Republican. Clubs: Kansas City, Oakwood Country, Saddle and Sirloin. Home: 5200 Belleview Kansas City MO 64112 Office: Union Bank 12th and Wyandotte Kansas City MO 64105

GREEN, JOHN JOSEPH, banking executive; b. Beverly Farms, Mass., 1931. AB, Harvard U., 1953. From trainee credit dept. to exec. v.p., chief loan officer Shawmut Bank N.A., Boston, 1953—, exec. v.p., chief loan officer, 1983—. Served with USNR, 1951-59. Home: 652 Hale St Beverly Farms MA 01915 Office: Shawmut Corp 1 Federal St 9th Fl Boston MA 02211

GREEN, JOHN ORNE, lawyer; b. Erie, Pa., Jan. 1, 1922; s. John Orne and Harriot Cox (O'Brien) G.; m. Phyllis Booth, Jan. 13, 1945; children—John Orne 3d, Edward Townsend, George Thomas. Grad., Lawrenceville Sch., 1940; A.B., Yale, 1943; J.D., Harvard, 1948. Bar: N.Y. 1950, N.J. 1960, Conn. 1975. Assoc. firm Mudge, Rose, Guthrie & Alexander, N.Y.C., 1948-51; gen. atty., asst. sec. Johnson & Johnson, New Brunswick, N.J., 1951-62; asst. sec., asst. gen. counsel Richardson-Merrell Inc. and Richardson-Vicks Inc., 1962-65, sec., asst. gen. counsel, 1965-66, gen. counsel, 1966-84, v.p., 1970-85; counsel Gregory and Adams, Wilton, Conn., 1986—; Mem. Bd. Improvement Assessors, Princeton Twp., 1961-62; mem. Township Com., Princeton, 1963-65. Served to lt. USNR, 1943-46. Mem. ABA, N.J. Bar Assn., N.Y. State Bar Assn., Conn. Bar Assn., Assn. Bar City N.Y., Am. Soc. Corporate Secs., Westchester-Fairfield Corporate Counsel Assn., Am. Law Inst., Yale Club, Capitol Hill Club, Redding Country Club, Mink Meadows Golf Club, Wilton Riding Club, Vineyard Haven Yacht Club. Home: 54 Village Walk River Rd Wilton CT 06897 Office: Gregory & Adams 190 Old Ridgefield Rd Wilton CT 06897

GREEN, JOYCE, book publishing company executive; b. Taylorville, Ill., Oct. 22, 1928; d. Lynn and Vivian Coke (Richardson) Reinerd; m. Warren H. Green, Oct. 8, 1960. AA, Christian Coll., 1946; BS, MacMurray Coll., 1948. Assoc. editor Warren H. Green, Inc., St. Louis, 1966-78, dir., 1978—; v.p. Visioneering Advt. Agy., 1972—; exec. dir. Affirmative Action Assn. Am., 1977—; pres. InterContinental Industries, Inc., 1980—; asst. to pres. Southeastern U., New Orleans, 1982-86; mem. bd. regents, v.p. adminstrn. No. Utah U., Salt Lake City, 1986—. Mem. Am. Soc. Profl. and Exec. Women, Direct Mktg. Club St. Louis, C. of C. Democrat. Methodist. Clubs: Jr. League, World Trade, Clayton, Media. Home: 12120 Hibler Dr Creve Coeur MO 63141 Office: 8356 Olive Blvd Saint Louis MO 63132

GREEN, JULIE ESTHER, lawyer; b. L.A., Dec. 4, 1958; d. Sheldon Green and Reva (Gurwitz) Camiel. BA, U. So. Calif., 1980; JD, U. Va., 1983. Bar: N.Y. 1984, U.S. Dist. Ct. (ea. and so. dists.) N.Y. 1984. Assoc. Brown & Wood, N.Y.C., 1983—. Vice-chmn. assocs. fundraising com. Lawyers for Legal Aid, N.Y.C., 1985—, capt. Brown & Wood Championship Women's Basketball Team in the N.Y.C. Women's Lawyer League, 1986, 87, 88, 89; bd. dirs.Fairpac, 1989—. Democrat. Jewish. Home: 107 Berkeley Pl #2 Brooklyn NY 11217 Office: Brown & Wood One World Trade Ctr New York NY 10048

GREEN, LINDA LOU, logistics engineer; b. Cape Girardeau, Mo., Sept. 12, 1946; d. Barney Oldfield and Opal (Jeffries) G. BA, East Carolina U., 1967, MA, 1969; postgrad., U. Utah, 1969-70; grad. with honors, Naval War Coll., Newport, R.I., 1985. Cert. in collegiate teaching. Asst. prof. history Jackson (Miss.) State U., 1970-72, Va. State U., Petersburg, 1972-74; commd. 1st lt. U.S. Army, 1974, advanced through grades to maj., 1983; logistics engr. land systems div. Gen. Dynamics Corp., Warren, Mich., 1983-84; systems analyst Raytheon Svc. Co., Huntsville, Ala., 1984-86; pres. Green & Assocs. Inc., Huntsville, 1985-86; logistics engr., cost analyst, br. mgr. Applied Rsch. Inc., Huntsville, 1986—; instr. U. Md., Fed. Republic of Germany, 1975-77. Author: Study Guides for American History, 1969. Mem. Rep. Nat. Com., Washington, 1986—. With USAR, 1983—. Mem. Soc. Logistics Engrs., Assn. U.S. Army (bd. dirs. Redstone, Huntsville chpt. 1988—), Res. Officers Assn., LWV. Baptist. Office: Applied Rsch Inc 5025 Bradford Dr Huntsville AL 35805

GREEN, MARVIN HOWE, JR., communications company executive; b. Syracuse, N.Y., Mar. 30, 1935; s. Marvin Howe and Evelyn (Hougan) G.; m. Catherine Anne Curwain; children: Marvin Howe III, Melissa Perkins, Alexandra Victoria, Allegra Victoria. Student, Bowdoin Coll., 1953-55. Mktg. cons. Xerox, ABC-TV, Am. Express, N.Y.C., 1958-64; pres. Visualscope, N.Y.C., 1964-75; chmn., chief exec. officer Reeves Communications Corp., N.Y.C., 1976—. Chmn. Com. for the Arts of Fairfield County, Stamford, Conn.; bd. dirs. Mayor's Coun. on Motion Picture and TV Prodn., N.Y.C.; trustee Am. Mus. of the Moving Image; bd. overseers Bowdoin Coll., Brunswick, Maine. Served with U.S. Army, 1955-57. Mem. Young Pres.'s Orgn., Nat. Acad. TV Arts and Scis., Stamford Yacht Club (commodore), Royal Bermuda Yacht Club, River Club, N.Y. Yacht Club, Royal Yacht Squadron, Mid Ocean Club. Presbyterian. Home: The Clearing, Tuckertown Bermuda Office: Reeves Communications 708 3d Ave New York NY 10017

GREEN, MEYRA JEANNE, banker; b. Cleve., Oct. 17, 1946; d. Meyrick Evans Green and Jeanne Bynon (Griffiths) Strauss; m. Frank W. Horn, Dec. 10, 1977 (dec. 1983); 1 stepchild, Donna; m. John Joseph Fleming, Aug. 29, 1987; 1 stepchild, Kerry. BA, Lake Erie Coll., 1968; MBA, NYU, 1973. Corp. planner Chem. Bank, N.Y.C., 1968-72, 1st Nat. City Bank, N.Y.C., 1972; security analyst Bank of N.Y., 1972-74; asst. treas. Credit Lyonnais, 1974-84; v.p. 1st Fidelity Bank, N.A., N.J., Newark, 1985—. Vol. Overlook Hosp. Hospice, Summit, N.J., 1985—. Mem. NYU Grad. Sch. Bus. Alumni. Republican. Home: 111 Woodland Rd Madison NJ 07940 Office: 1st Fidelity Bank NA NJ 550 Broad St Newark NJ 07192

GREEN, PHILLIP DALE, banker; b. Longview, Tex., Aug. 17, 1954; s. Horace Green and Gladys Barnes; m. Sandy Koenig, June 12, 1976; children: Jacob Taylor, Laura Ashley, Phillip Michael. BBA, U. Tex., 1977. CPA, Tex. Sr. acct. Ernst & Whinney, San Antonio, 1977-80; contr. Frost Nat. Bank San Antonio, 1981-85; treas. Cullen/Frost Bankers, Inc., San Antonio, 1985—. Bd. dirs. San Antonio Symphony, 1986. Mem. Am. Inst. CPA's, Tex. Soc. CPA's, Fin. Execs. Inst. (v.p. 1988-89). Office: Cullen/Frost Bankers Inc 100 W Houston St San Antonio TX 78205

GREEN, RAYMOND BERT, lawyer; b. Hartford, Conn., July 12, 1929; s. William Gottlieb and Mayme Pauline (Judatz) G.; m. Barbara Louise Miller, Jan. 31, 1955; children: Elizabeth Hollister, William Goodrich. BA, Yale U., 1951, LLB, 1954. Bar: Conn. 1954, U.S. Dist. Ct. Conn. 1959, U.S. Supreme Ct. 1962, U.S. Ct. Appeals (2d cir.) 1966, U.S. Ct. Mil. Appeals 1974, U.S. Dist. Ct. (so. dist.) N.Y. 1976, U.S. Dist. Ct. (ea. dist.) N.Y. 1976. Assoc., Camp, Williams & Richardson, New Britain, Conn., 1954-55; assoc. Day, Berry & Howard, Hartford, Conn., 1958-65, ptnr., 1966—; dir. New Britain Herald; trustee Collinsville Savs. Soc. (Conn.); judge of probate Dist. of Canton, Conn., 1963—. Pres., bd. dirs. Am. Friends of Coll. Cevenol (France); bd. dirs. YMCA Met. Hartford, 1963-84, 86—; sec., bd. trustees Children's Mus. Hartford, 1977-85, Sci. Mus. of Conn., 1985-86; bd. editors Conn. Probate Law Jour. Served with USNR, 1955-58; comdr. JAGC, Res., 1958-79. Mem. Hartford County Bar Assn., ABA, Conn. Bar Assn. (chmn. ins. com. 1978-85, ethics com. 1987—), Judge Advs. Assn., Def. Research Inst., Conn. Def. Lawyers Assn. (bd. dirs. 1985-87), Assn. Trial Lawyers Am., Nat. Coll. Probate Judges, Phi Beta Kappa. Republican. Congregationalist. Clubs: Univ. (Hartford), Officers of Conn., Naval Res. Officers Luncheon (N.Y.C.), Assn. Ex-Mems. Squadron A (N.Y.C.). Home: 120 West Rd Collinsville CT 06022 Office: Day Berry & Howard Cityplace 2500 Hartford CT 06103

GREEN, RAYMOND S(ILVERNAIL), radio station executive; b. Torrington, Conn., Jan. 1, 1915; s. Percy Alexander and Amy (Silvernail) G.; m. Rose Basile, June 20, 1942; children: Carol Rae Green Hoffman, Raymond Ferguson. Student, Julius Hartt Sch. Music, 1934-37; student studied violin with, Sarah Newton, 1925-33; voice with, Royal Dadmun, 1934-38, Giuseppe Boghetti, 1938-41, Alfredo Martino, 1942-50; coached with, Frederick Kitzsinger, 1946, Stuart Ross, 1947, Dr. Ernst Knoch, 1947-50; D.H.L. Cabrini Coll., 1982; D.Mus. (hon.), Combs Coll., 1984; D.F.A. (hon.), New Sch. Music, 1984. Producer, dir. musical programs NBC, N.Y.C., 1941-47; prodn. mgr. NBC, 1948; gen. mgr. Sta. WFLN, Phila., 1949-66; pres. Franklin Broadcasting Co., Phila., 1966-82, chmn. bd., 1982-88; owner, operator conservation tree farm, Washington, Vt. Pres. Phila. Art Alliance, 1966-73, chmn. bd., 1973-77, hon. pres., 1977—; exec. v.p. Schuylkill Valley Nature Center, 1970—; bd. dirs. Presser Found., 1985—, Musical Fund Soc., Union League Phila; v.p. Societa Cavalieri D'Italia, 1987—; chmn. Eugene Ormandy Archive, U. Pa., assoc. trustee, 1989—; trustee Valley Forge Mil. Acad. Found., 1989—. Served to maj. USAAF, 1942-46. Decorated commendatore Order of merit Italian Republic; recipient William Penn Human Rights award, 1982, George Washington Medal Freedoms Found. at Valley Forge. Fellow Royal Soc. Arts (London); mem. Broadcast Pioneers (pres. 1965-66, life dir.), Musical Fund Soc. Phila. (pres. 1983-86, bd. dirs.), Am. Forestry Assn., Pa. Soc. Clubs: Franklin Inn, Philobiblon, Union League (bd. dirs. 1984-88), Phila. Cricket (Phila.). Home: 308 Manor Rd Philadelphia PA 19128 Office: 644 Germantown Pike Lafayette Hill PA 19444

GREEN, RICHARD CALVIN, JR., utility company executive; b. Kansas City, Mo., May 6, 1954; s. Richard Calvin and Ann (Gableman) G.; m. Nancy Jean Risk, Aug. 6, 1977; children—Allison Thompt, Ashley Jean. B.S.B.A., So. Methodist U., 1976. With Mo. Pub. Service, Kansas City, 1976-85, exec. v.p., 1982-85; pres., chief exec. officer UtiliCorp United Inc., Kansas City, 1985-89, chmn. bd., 1989—; bd. dirs. Commerce Bank of Kansas City, BHA Group. Mem. Kansas City C. of C. (bd. dirs. 1983, chmn. bd. 1988). Presbyterian.

GREEN, ROBERT GLENN, investments company executive; b. Kodiak, Alaska, Apr. 14, 1950; s. Wallace Glenn and Phyllis Laverne (Gow) G.; m. Sarah A. Green, June 4, 1977; children: Keith A., Morgan E. BS in Acctg., U. So. Calif., 1972. Cert. fin. mgr. Broker Buckingham Investments, El Segundo, Calif., 1972-77; account exec. Merrill Lynch, Anchorage, 1977-85; portfolio mgr. Hutton Portfolio Mgmt., Anchorage, 1985—. Chmn. bd. dirs. Mabel T. Caverly Sr. Ctr., Anchorage, 1984-85; bd. dirs. Anchorage Employees Retirement Income Security Act Forum, 1986-87; v.p. Turnagain Community Council, Anchorage, 1987-88. Republican. Club: Rotary (bd. dirs. 1987-88) (Anchorage). Home: 2238 Loussac Dr Anchorage AK 99517

GREEN, ROBERT LEONARD, hospital management company executive; b. Los Angeles, Mar. 20, 1931; s. Leonard H. and Helene (Rains) G.; m. Susan Wolf, June 9, 1957; children—Wendy, Julie. B.A., Stanford U., 1952, LL.B., 1956. C.P.A., Calif. Acct. John F. Grieder, San Francisco, 1957-59; assoc. Heller, Ehrman, White & McAuliffe, San Francisco, 1959-61; pres. Sutter Capital Co., San Francisco, 1961-69; chmn. bd. Community Psychiat. Ctrs., San Francisco, 1969—. Trustee Sta. KQED-Pub. TV, San Francisco, 1981-87, Mus. Modern Art, 1984—, Mt. Zion Hosp., 1985-86. Served to 1st lt. U.S. Army, 1954-56. Office: Community Psychiat Ctrs 517 Washington St San Francisco CA 94111

GREEN, ROBERT WAYNE, financial manager, accounting educator; b. N.Y.C., July 2, 1945; s. Donald Edward and Theresa M. (McGuire) G.; m. Carolyn Elvira Casertano, June 17, 1967; children: Mindy Ann, Robert W. Jr. AAS in Acctg., Manhattan Community Coll., 1967; BBA in Acctg., Pace U., 1970. Cert. mgmt. acct., U.S. and Can. Chief acct. Ebasco Services Inc., N.Y.C., 1971-74, mgr. fin. analysis, 1981-87, assst. treas., mgr. fin. planning and analysis, 1987—; mgr. fin. Ebasco Services of Can. Ltd., Toronto, 1974-76, controller, 1976-77; sec.-treas. Ebastec Lavalin Inc., Toronto, 1977-81; asst prof. Pace U., N.Y.C., 1983—. Mem. Inst. Cert. Mgmt. Accts., Controller's Coun., Nat. Assn. Accts. (dir. CMA programs N.Y. chpt. 1987—), Soc. Mgmt. Accts. Alta., Am. Acctg. Assn., Constrn. Fin. Mgmt. Assn. (bd. dirs. N.Y. chpt.), Pace U. N.Y. Undergrad. Alumni Assn. (bd. dirs. 1986), Constrn. Fin. Mgmt. Assn. Republican. Roman Catholic.

GREEN, RUSSELL PETER, investment company executive; b. N.Y.C., Dec. 13, 1942; s. Arthur William and Frances Sarah (Mintz) G.; m. Carolee Madsen, June 21, 1964 (div. June 1981); 1 child, Peter Gregory. AB, Cornell U., 1964, MBA, 1965. Fin. analyst Doubleday & Co., Garden City, N.Y., 1967-72; acctg. mgr. Burroughs Corp., Goleta, Calif., 1972-76; controller MCR Tech., Goleta, 1976-79; dir. fin. Browne Engring., Carpinteria, Calif., 1980-83, Pentabs, Santa Barbara, Calif., 1983-85; v.p. fin. Eyeglasses Unltd., Inc., Santa Barbara, 1985-86; dir. fin. Investors Retirement & Mgmt. Corp., Carpinteria, 1986—; pres. R.P. Green & Assoc., Santa Barbara, 1979—; bd. dirs. MCR Techs., Game Keeper Inc. Home: 230 Alameda Padre Serra Santa Barbara CA 93103 Office: Investors Retirement & Mgmt Corp 1180 Eugenia Pl Carpinteria CA 93013

GREEN, WILLIAM PORTER, lawyer; b. Jacksonville, Ill., Mar. 19, 1920; s. Hugh Parker and Clara Belle (Hopper) G.; m. Rose Marie Hall, Oct. 1, 1944; children: Hugh Michael, Robert Alan, Richard William. B.A., Ill. Coll., 1941; J.D., Northwestern U., 1947. Bar: Ill. 1947, Calif. 1948, U.S. Dist. Ct. (so. dist.) Tex. 1986, Ct. Customs and Patent Appeals 1948, U.S. Patent and Trademark Office 1948, U.S. Ct. Appeals (fed. cir.) 1982, U.S. Ct. Appeals (5th and 9th cirs.), U.S. Supreme Ct. 1948, U.S. Dist. Ct. (cen. dist.) Calif., U.S. Dist. Ct. (so. dist.) Tex., 1986. Practice patent, trademark and copyright law Los Angeles, 1947—; mem. firm Wills, Green & Mueth, 1974-83; of counsel Nilsson, Robbins, Dalgarn, Berliner, Carson & Wurst, Los Angeles, 1984—; del. Calif. State Bar Conv., 1982-88, delegation chair 1986. Bd. editors Ill. Law Rev, 1946. Mem. Los Angeles World Affairs Council, 1975—; del., chmn. Calif. State Bar Conv., 1986. Lt. USNR, 1942-46. Mem. ABA, Calif State Bar, Am. Intellectual Property Law Assn., Los Angeles Patent Law Assn. (past sec.-treas., bd. govs.), Lawyers Club Los Angeles (past treas., past sec., bd. govs., pres.-elect 1985-86, pres. 1985-86), Los Angeles County Bar Assn (trustee 1986-87), Am. Legion (past post comdr.), Phi Beta Kappa, Phi Delta Phi, Phi Alpha. Republican. Presbyn. (deacon 1961-63). Clubs: Big Ten of So. Calif, Northwestern U. Alumni of So. Calif, Phi Beta Kappa Alumni of So. Calif, Town Hall of Calif. Home: 3570 E Lombardy Rd Pasadena CA 91107 Office: Nilsson Robbins Dalgarn

Berliner Carson & Wurst 201 N Figueroa St 5th Floor Los Angeles CA 90012

GREENAWALT, PEGGY TOMARKIN, advertising executive; b. Cleve., Apr. 27, 1942; d. Bernard H. and Gyta Elinor (Arsham) Freed; m. Gary Tomarkin, Aug. 7, 1966 (div. 1981); children: Craig William, Eric Lawrence; m. William Sloan Greenawalt, Oct. 31, 1987. BS, Simmons Coll., 1964. Asst. account exec. Howard Marks/Norman, Craig & Kummel, Inc., N.Y.C., 1964-66; account exec. Shaw Bros. Advt. Co., N.Y.C., 1966-67; copywriter Claire Advt. Co., N.Y.C., 1967; ptnr. Copywriters Coop., Hartsdale, N.Y., 1970-73; copy chief Howard Marks Advt., N.Y.C., 1973-80; sr. copywriter Wunderman, Ricotta & Kline, N.Y.C., 1980-82; v.p., assoc. creative dir. Ayer-Direct (N.W. Ayer), N.Y.C., 1982-84; sr. v.p., creative dir. D'Arcy Direct (D'Arcy, MacManus & Masius), N.Y.C., 1984-86; creative and mktg. cons., 1986-87; pres. Tomarkin/Greenawalt, Inc.; judge Clio Awards. Author: Kiss, The Real Story, 1980. Mem. Direct Mktg. Creative Guild, Direct Mktg. Assn., Direct Mktg. Club N.Y., Westchester Assn. Women Bus. Owners (bd. dirs.). Office: 24 Lewis Ave Hartsdale NY 10530

GREENBERG, ALAN COURTNEY, stockbroker; b. Wichita, Kans., Sept. 3, 1927; s. Theodore H. and Esther (Zeligson) G.; div., Aug. 1976; children: Lynne, Theodore. Student, U. Mo., 1949. With Bear, Stearns & Co., N.Y.C., 1949—, gen. ptnr., 1958—, chmn. bd., chief exec. officer, 1978—, also chmn. exec. com., mng. dir. Recipient Lehman award Am. Jewish Com.; named Man of Yr. NCCJ; winner Nat. Bridge Championship, 1977. Mem. Am. Stock Exch. (gov.), Securities Industry Assn. (governing coun.), Soc. Am. Magicians. Jewish. Clubs: Harmonie, Bond (N.Y.C.); Sunningdale Country (Scarsdale, N.Y.). Office: Bear Stearns Cos Inc 245 Park Ave New York NY 01067

GREENBERG, ARNOLD CHAIM, toys and entertainment products company; b. Hartford, Conn., June 12, 1933; s. Maurice and Frances G. (Milkenstein) G.; m. Beverly Lynn Parks, Oct. 5, 1968; children—Dana Ellen, Sara Beth. A.B. magna cum laude, Harvard U., 1955, LL.B., 1958. Chmn. bd., chief exec. officer Coleco Industries, Inc., West Hartford, Conn., until 1988, remains bd. dirs.; dir. Hartford Nat. Corp.; mem. Harvard Coll. Com. on Univ. Relations. Vice chmn. bd. regents U. Hartford; trustee Wadsworth Atheneum, Horace Bushnell Meml. Hall, Brigham and Women's Hospital; past chmn. Commn. on City Plan of Hartford; co-chmn. Conn.-Western Mass. region NCCJ; mem. Harvard Coll. Com. on Univ. Resources; Conn. chmn. Am. Friends of Hebrew U.; v.p. Greater Hartford Jewish Fedn.; corporator Inst. of Living, St. Frances Hosp., Mt. Sinai Hosp. Democrat. Home: 65 Westwood Rd West Hartford CT 06117 Office: Coleco Industries Inc 999 Quaker Ln S West Hartford CT 06110 *

GREENBERG, ARTHUR WAYNE, financial executive; b. Boston, Jan. 3, 1953; s. Robert Jerome and Betty Lee (Mooren) G.; m. Linda Bearse Popkin, Nov. 7, 1981; children: Evan Jonathan, Stacy Cara. BA, Brown U., 1974; M of Mgmt., Northwestern U., 1976. Fin. analyst The Paperback Booksmith, Inc., Natick, Mass., 1976-77; mgr. fin. analysis Gen. Cinema Corp., Chestnut Hill, Mass., 1977-81; mgr. Arthur Young & Co., Boston, 1981-83; chief fin. officer Hale and Dorr, Boston, 1983—. Interviewer Brown U. Nat. Alumni Sch. Program, Boston, Mass., 1979—. Mem. Assn. Legal Adminstrs. Office: Hale & Dorr 60 State St Boston MA 02109

GREENBERG, FRANK S., textile company executive; b. Chgo., Sept. 11, 1929. Ph.B., U. Chgo., 1949. Asst. to pres. Charm Tred Mills, 1949, v.p., 1953, pres., 1953-59; v.p. Charm Tred Mills div. Burlington Industries, Inc., 1959-61, pres., 1961-62; pres. Monticello Carpet Mill div. Burlington Industries, Inc., N.Y.C., 1962-70, group v.p., mem. mgmt. com., 1970-72, exec. v.p., 1972-78; pres. Burlington Industries, Inc., N.Y.C., now Greensboro, N.C., 1978-86, chmn., chief exec. officer, 1986—, also bd. dirs. Served with AUS, 1951-53. Office: Burlington Industries Inc 3330 W Friendly Ave PO Box 21207 Greensboro NC 27410 *

GREENBERG, GEORGE, mill company executive; b. 1922; married. With Seaberg, Inc. (acquired by Guilford Mills Inc.), to 1967; v.p. mktg. Guilford Mills, Inc., Greensboro, N.C., 1967-70, exec. v.p., 1970-76, pres., 1976—, chief operating officer, from 1976, also dir. Office: Guilford Mills Inc 4925 W Market St Box U-4 Greensboro NC 27401 *

GREENBERG, JACK M., food products executive; b. 1942; s. Edith S. Scher; m. Donna; children: David, Ilyse, Allison. BSc in Acctg., DePaul U., Chgo., 1964, JD, 1968. CPA, Ill.; bar, Ill. With Arthur Young & Co., 1964-82; chief fin. officer, exec. v.p. McDonalds Corp., Oakbrook, Ill., 1982—, also bd. dirs.; bd. dirs. Arthur J. Gallagher & Co., Chgo. Mem. Chgo. Bar Found. (pres.), Chgo. Assn. of Commerce & Industry (bd. dirs.), Am. Inst. Cert. Pub. Accts., Ill. Inst. Cert. Pub. Accts. Office: McDonald's Corp 1 McDonald's Plaza Oak Brook IL 60521

GREENBERG, MAURICE RAYMOND, insurance company executive; b. N.Y.C., May 4, 1925; s. Jacob and Ada (Rheingold) G.; m. Corinne Phyllis Zuckerman, Nov. 12, 1950; children: Jeffrey W., Evan G., L. Scott, Cathleen J. Pre-law cert., U. Miami, Fla., 1948; JD, N.Y. Law Sch., 1950; JD (hon.), New Eng. Sch. Law, 1970. Bar: N.Y. 1953. With Continental Casualty Co., 1952-60; v.p. C.V. Starr & Co., Inc., N.Y.C., 1961-66, exec. v.p., 1966-68, pres., also bd. dirs., 1968—; pres., chief exec. officer, bd. dirs. Am. Internat. Group, N.Y.C., 1967—; bd. dirs. Fed. Reserve Bank N.Y., internat. capital markets adv. com. Chmn. bd. govs. N.Y. Hosp.; mem. Pres.'s adv. com. on trade negotiations Center for Strategic and Internat. Studies. Served to capt. U.S. Army, World War II, Korea. Decorated Bronze Star. Mem. N.Y. Bar Assn., Fgn. Policy Assn., Council Fgn. Relations, , Hoover Inst., ASEAN-US Bus. Adv. Council, N.Y.C Partnership, US-USSR Trade and Econ. Council, Coalition Service Industries, Police Athletic League, Sigma Alpha Mu. Clubs: City Athletic, Sky, India House, Lotus, Harmonie (N.Y.C.); Georgetown (Washington). Office: Am Internat Group Inc 70 Pine St New York NY 10270 *

GREENBERG, MORTON PAUL, lawyer, insurance broker, advanced underwriting consultant; b. Fall River, Mass., June 2, 1946; s. Harry and Sylvia Shirley (Davis) G.; m. Louise Beryl Schindler, Jan. 24, 1970; 1 child, Alexis Lynn. BSBA, NYU, 1968; JD, Bklyn. Law Sch., 1971. Bar: N.Y. 1972. Atty., Hanner, Fitzmaurice & Onorato, N.Y.C., 1971-72; dir., counsel, cons. on advanced underwriting The Mfrs. Life Ins. Co., Toronto, Ont., Can., 1972—; mem. sales ideas com. Million Dollar Roundtable, Chgo., 1982-83; speaker on law, tax, and advanced underwriting to various profl. groups, U.S., Can. Author: (tech. jour.) ManuBriefs. Mem. ABA, N.Y. State Bar Assn., Assn. for Advanced Life Underwriting, Internat. Platform Assn., Alumni Fedn. NYU, Nat. Assn. Life Underwriters, Denver Assn. Life Underwriters, Am. Soc. CLU, Am. Coll. (chartered life underwriter 1975). Office: 7617 E Sunrise Trail Parker CO 80134

GREENBERG, NATHAN, accountant; b. Worcester, Mass., May 17, 1919; s. Samuel and Ida (Katz) G.; m. Mimi Aaron, Mar. 12, 1950 (dec.); children: Henry Aaron, Ruthanne; m. Barbara Rudnick, Feb. 9, 1979. B.S. in Bus. Adminstrn, Boston U., 1942. C.P.A., Mass. With Internal Revenue Service, 1945-47; v.p. finance, dir. Gt. Am. Plactics Co., Worcester, Mass., 1948-68, Gt. Am. Chem. Corp., Fitchburg, Mass., 1968-80; chmn. Greenberg, Rosenblatt, Kull & Bitsoli, P.C., Worcester, 1958—. Trustee Nathan and Barbara Greenberg Charitable Trust, Jewish Home for Aged, Jewish Community Center, Jewish Fedn. Served with AUS, 1942-45, ETO. Decorated Bronze Star. Fellow Am. Inst. C.P.A.'s, Mass. Soc. C.P.A.'s, Controllers Inst. Am.; mem. Mu Sigma. Club: Mt. Pleasant Country (Boylston, Mass.) (v.p. 1962—). Home: 85 Aylesbury Rd Worcester MA 01609 Office: The Day Bldg 306 Main St Worcester MA 01608

GREENBERG, RONALD DAVID, lawyer, educator; b. San Antonio, Sept. 9, 1939. s. Benjamin and Sylvia (Ghetlzer) G. BS, U. Tex., 1957; MBA, Harvard U., 1961, JD, 1964. Bar: N.Y. 1966, U.S. Dist. Ct. (ea. and so. dists.) N.Y. 1970, U.S. Ct. Appeals (2d cir.) 1975, U.S. Supreme Ct. 1975. Engr., bus. analyst Exxon Corp., N.Y.C., 1957-64; atty., engr. Allied Corp., N.Y.C., 1964-67; assoc. Arthur, Dry, Kalish, Taylor & Wood, N.Y.C., 1967-69, Valicenti, Leighton, Reid & Pine, N.Y.C., 1969-70; faculty Columbia U., N.Y.C., 1970—, prof. bus. law and taxation, 1982—; of counsel Delson & Gordon, N.Y.C., 1973-87; lectr., cons. Citibank, Mfrs. Hanover Trust Co., Harcourt, Brace, Jovanovich, Inc., Prudential-Bache, Drexel, Burnham & Lambert, E.F. Hutton; vis. prof. Stanford U., Palo Alto, Calif., 1978, Harvard U., Boston, 1981. Author: Business Income Tax Materials, 1986; editor-in-chief N.Y. Internat. Law Rev., 1988—, Internat. Law Practicum, 1987—; contbr. chpt. to book, articles to profl. jours. Cons. council City of N.Y., 1971-72, Manhattan Community Coll., 1974-76. Lt. USNR, 1957-59. Recipient Outstanding Prof. award Columbia U. Grad. Sch. Bus., 1973. Mem. ABA (chmn. com. on taxation gen. practice sect. 1978-83, chmn. com. on corp. banking and bus. law gen. practice sect. 1985—), NSPE, N.Y. State Bar Assn. (gen. practice sect., chmn. tax law com. 1983—, chmn. bus. law com. 1985-88, internat. law & practice sect., chmn. pubs. com. 1988—), Assn. Bar City of N.Y., N.Y. Acad. Scis., Mensa, Harvard Club, Rye Golf Club. Home: 55 Morton St New York NY 10014 Office: Columbia U 607 Uris Hall New York NY 10027

GREENBERG, SCOTT LEE, marketing professional; b. N.Y.C., Oct. 30, 1949; s. Donald Green and Phyliss (Goldstein) Bartram; m. Irene Susan Weiss, July 16, 1970; children: Melissa Lori, Allison Gayle. Student, Queensborough Community Coll., Bayside, N.Y., 1970, Queens Coll., 1970-71. Dist. sales mgr. Hoover Co., N.Y., North Canton, Ohio, 1972-80; pres., chief exec. officer Courtland Novelty Co., East Stroudsburg, Pa., 1980-86; v.p. br. ops. Curran and Connors, Inc., Morristown, N.J., 1986—. advisor Jr. Achievement, 1982; pres. Temple Israel, 1984-86; bd. dirs. Pocono Mt. C. of C., 1983-85. Recipient Gov.'s Citation Pa. Assn. Rehab. Facilities, 1983. Mem. Morris County C. of C. Democrat. Jewish. Club: Shawnee Country. Lodge: KP. Home: Rd 5 Box 5601 East Stroudsburg PA 18301 Office: Curran & Connors Inc 55 Madison Ave Morristown NJ 07962-1905

GREENBERG, STEVEN MOREY, lawyer; b. Jersey City, N.J., Apr. 9, 1949; s. Joseph and Rhoda (Weisenfeld) G. AB cum laude, Syracuse U., 1971; JD, U. Pa., 1974. Bar: N.J. 1974, U.S. Dist. Ct. N.J. 1974, N.Y. 1980. U.S. Dist. Ct. (so. dist.) N.Y., 1986, U.S. Dist. Ct. (ea. dist.) N.Y., 1986. Assoc. firm Carpenter, Bennett & Morrissey, Newark, 1974-77; assoc. firm Cole, Berman & Belsky, Rochelle Park, N.J., 1977-79; sole practice, Hackensack, N.J., 1979—; atty. Bergenfield (N.J.) Rent Leveling Bd., 1985-89; trustee, past chmn. youth activities com. Jewish Ctr. of Teaneck, 1978—; pres., trustee, past v.p., past sec. Sam Gorovoy Group Care Home for Sr. Adults, Bergenfield, 1983—, mem. gov. bd., 1986—, chmn. personnel com. 1986—; adv. bd. dirs., chmn. personnel com. Jewish Home and Rehab. Ctr. Jersey City and River Vale, 1982—, exec. com., 1987— ; trustee Jewish Family Service Inc. of Bergen County, 1986—, The Solomon Schechter Day Sch. of Bergen County, 1986-87; mem. Jewish Community Relations Council No. N.J., 1986—. Recipient Second Century award Jewish Theol. Sem. Am., 1988. Mem. ABA, N.J. Bar Assn., Bergen County Bar Assn., Assn. Transp. Practitioners, Phi Kappa Phi, Pi Sigma Alpha. Home: 96 Westminster Ave Bergenfield NJ 07621 Office: 2 University Pla Hackensack NJ 07601

GREENBLATT, FRED HAROLD, data processing consultant; b. N.Y.C., Aug. 24, 1938; s. Harry Joseph and Rose (Rosen) G.; m. Marsha R. Mechaneck, Nov. 30, 1963; 1 child, Jay S. BS in Edn., CCNY, 1960; postgrad. Baruch Sch. Bus., 1961-63. Sr. analyst Grosset & Dunlap, N.Y.C., 1969-73; asst. v.p. info. systems GNY Ins., East Brunswick, N.J., 1973-79; cons. J.P. Sedlak Assocs., N.Y.C., 1979-80; adminstr. standards and data ITT, N.Y.C., 1980-81; dir. systems programs Reed, Roberts Assocs., Mitchell Field, N.Y., 1981-83; pres. Data Design, Holliswood, N.Y., 1983—; affiliated cons. ADR, Princeton, N.J., 1985—; affiliated software cons. Software A.G., Reston, Va., 1986—. Served with U.S. Army, 1960-61. Mem. Data Processing Mgmt. Assn. (reviewer 1984, 85, cert. achievement 1984), IEEE (assoc.), N.Y. Personal Computer Club, Soc. Profl. Mgmt. Cons. (assoc.), Assn. Computing Machinery, Personal Engring. Computer Users Soc. Republican. Lodge: B'nai B'rith. Avocations: micro-processors, gardening. Home and Office: 198-14 Epsom Course Holliswood NY 11423

GREENBLATT, MAURICE THEODORE, transportation executive; b. Vineland, N.J., Oct. 2, 1928; s. Benjamin and Emma (Pollock) G.; m. Joan Tobye Bailinger, Apr. 8, 1951; children: David, Daniel. Student, Bucknell U., 1945-48. Pres. Ware's Van and Storage Co., Inc., Vineland, 1958—; chmn., chief exec. officer United Van Lines, Inc., Fenton, Mo., 1984—; vice chmn. Security Savs. and Loan, Vineland, 1977—, also bd. dirs.; bd. dirs. United Van Lines Ltd., Toronto, Can., Am. Movers Conf., Household Goods Carriers Bur. Republican. Jewish. Home: Ocean Pla #417 Longport NJ 08403 Office: Ware's Van & Storage Co PO Box W Vineland NJ 08360 *

GREENE, ALVIN, service company executive, management consultant; b. Pitts., Aug. 26, 1932; s. Samuel David and Yetta (Kroff) G.; B.A., Stanford U., 1954, M.B.A., 1959; m. M. Louise Sokol, Nov. 11, 1977; children—Sharon, Ami, Ann, Daniel. Asst. to pres. Narmco Industries, Inc., San Diego, 1959-62; adminstrv. mgr., mgr. mktg. Whittaker Corp., L.A., 1962-67; sr. v.p. Cordura Corp., L.A., 1967-75; chmn. bd. Sharon-Sage, Inc., L.A., 1975-79; exec. v.p., chief operating officer Republic Distbrs., Inc., Carson, Calif., 1979-81, also dir.; chief operating officer Memel, Jacobs & Ellsworth, 1981-87, 87—; pres. SCI Cons., Inc.; dir. Sharon-Sage, Inc., True Data Corp.; vis. prof. Am. Grad. Sch. Bus., Phoenix, 1977-81. Chmn. bd. commrs. Housing Authority City of L.A., 1983-88 . Served to 1st lt., U.S. Army, 1955-57. Mem. Direct Mail Assn., Safety Helmet Mfrs. Assn., Bradley Group. Office: 10960 Wilshire Blvd Ste 1226 Los Angeles CA 90024

GREENE, CARL WILLIAM, utility company executive; b. N.Y.C., July 29, 1935; B.S., U. Pa., 1957; M.B.A., N.Y.U., 1960; m. Gloria Nissman, June 29, 1958; children—Andrew, Stephen, Suzanne, Nancy. With, Consol. Edison Co., N.Y.C., 1958—, acct., 1966-67, asst. mgr., 1967-68, asst. controller, 1968-74, sr. asst. controller, 1974-75, asst. v.p., 1975-76, controller, 1976—, v.p., 1982—. With U.S. Army, 1957. Mem. Am. Gas Assn. (chmn. fin. and adminstrv. sect. 1986-87, vice chmn. 1985-86, chmn. fin. div. 1983-84, mng. com., acctg. adv. com.), Am. Acctg. Assn., Am. Inst. Corp. Controllers, Fin. Execs. Inst., Planning Execs. Inst., Am. Fin. Assn., Edison Electric Inst. (acctg. exec. adv. com., chmn EEI FERC Liason Group 1982-85), Eastern Fin. Assn., So. Fin. Assn. Avocations: symphonic music, ballet, opera, fgn. travel. Office: Consol Edison Co NY Inc 4 Irving Pl New York NY 10003

GREENE, FRANK S., JR., information systems business executive; b. Washington, Oct. 19, 1938; s. Frank S. and Irma O. (Swygert) G.; m. Phyllis Davison, Jan. 1958 (dec. 1984); children: Angela, Frank; m. Nilene D. Fitzpatrick, Sept. 1985; children: Christopher, David. BS, Washington U., St. Louis, 1961; MS, Purdue U., 1962; PhD, U. Santa Clara (Calif.), 1970. Part-time lectr. Washington U., Howard U., Am. U., 1959-65; dir., chmn. Tech. Devel. Corp., Arlington, Tex., 1985—; pres. Zero One Systems, Inc. (formerly Tech. Devel. of Calif.) Santa Clara, Calif., 1971-87, Zero One Systems Group subs. Sterling Software Inc., 1987—; asst. chmn., lectr. Stanford U., 1972-74; dir. Networked Picture Systems Inc. Author two indsl. textbooks; also articles; patentee in field. Bd. dirs. NCCJ, Santa Clara, 1980—, NAACP, San Jose chpt., 1986—; bd. regents U. Santa Clara, 1983—; mem. adv. bd. Urban League, Santa Clara County, 1986—. Served to capt. USAF, 1961-65. Mem. Assn. Black Mfrs. (dir., 1974-80), Am. Electric Assn. (indsl. adv. bd., 1975-76), Fairchild Research and Devel. (tech. staff, 1965-71), IEEE, IEEE Computer Soc. (governing bd., 1973-75), Bay Area Purchasing Council (dir. 1978-84), Security Affairs Support Assn. (dir. 1980-83), Sigma Xi, Eta Kappa Nu. Office: ZeroOne Systems Group Sterling Software Inc 4401 Great American Pkwy Santa Clara CA 95054

GREENE, GEORGE E., III, utility company executive; b. St. Augustine, Fla., Sept. 27, 1935; s. George E. Jr. and Effie (Floyd) G.; m. Emelyn Boyte, Mar. 1, 1958; children: William E., Katharine, Emelyn, Molly. AA, U. Fla., 1956, BA in Psychology, 1958; MBA, Fla. Atlantic U., 1975. Cert. internal auditor. Personnel dir. Fla. Power Corp., St. Petersburg, 1967-75, asst. dir. internal audits, 1975-76, dir. internal audits, 1976-80, asst. v.p. internal audits, 1980-81, sr. v.p. fin. services, 1983—; pres. Talquin Corp., St. Petersburg, 1981-82; owner, rep. Nuclear Elec. Ins. Ltd., Bermuda. Pres. Woodlawn Presbyn. Ch., Inc., St. Petersburg, 1986—; mem. Leadership Fla. Network, 1986—, Suncoast Tiger Bay, St. Petersburg, 1982—. Capt. USNG, 1958-68. Mem. Southeastern Electric Exchange (chmn. fin. and acctg. div. 1985-86), Edison Electric Inst. (fin. com.), Fin. Execs. Inst. (v.p.), Fla. C. of C. (tax com. 1987, Workers' Compensation Self-Insurers Fund, founding trustee 1988-89, treas., mem. exec. com. 1988—). Republican. Club: St. Petersburg Yacht. Home: 1222 Brightwaters Blvd NE Saint Petersburg FL 33704 Office: Fla Power Corp 3201 34th St S Saint Petersburg FL 33711

GREENE, HERBERT FLOYD, JR., glass manufacturing executive; b. Roaring Spring, Pa., Feb. 25, 1949; s. Herbert F. and Mary Frances (Wright) G.; m. Meredith Millard Macan, Sept. 12, 1970; children: Kristen Lees, Herbert F. III. BS, Pa. State U., 1971. CPA, Pa. Internal auditor Gen. Refractories Co., Phila., 1966-67; mgr. Touche Ross & Co., Phila., 1971-81; fin. dir. Durand Glass Mfg. Co., Millville, N.J., 1981—. Contr. articles to profl. jours. Treas. bd. trustees, Maple Shade, N.J., 1975-77; vol. cons. Community Accts., Phila., 1977-81; counselor alumni admissions Pa. State U., 1982—; founder, coach Greentree Youth Soccer, Mt. Laurel, N.J., 1972-81; mem. Soccer Club, 1987—; pres., Moorestoen Soccer Club; tchr., chmn. com. First United Meth. Ch., Moorestown, N.J., 1984—. Republican. Clubs: Moorestown Field; Toftrees Country (State College, Pa.). Home: 361 W 2d St Moorestown NJ 08057 Office: Durand Glass Mfg Co Inc PO Box 805 Wade Blvd Millville NJ 08332

GREENE, JAMES DOUGLAS, marketing executive; b. Rome, N.Y., June 1, 1957; s. James Douglas and Jacqueline Maggie (Lankford) G.; m. Deborah Susan Barnes, June 16, 1979; 1 child, Andrew James. BBA, U. Ky., 1979. Asst. mgr. Kroger Food Stores, Mt. Sterling, Ky., 1980-82; salesman Tandy Computer Ctr., Lexington, Ky., 1982, sales mgr., 1982-84; sr. sales rep. Computerland of Lexington, 1984; programmer Custom Tool and Mfg. Co., Lexington, 1984-85, mktg. mgr., 1985; dir. mktg. The Automation Group, Inc., Custom Tools, Lexington, 1986—. Republican. Roman Catholic. Office: Automation Group Inc 848 R Nandino Blvd Lexington KY 40511

GREENE, JANELLE LANGLEY, banker; b. Tarboro, N.C., July 27, 1940; d. Romey Roscoe and Stella Louise (Keene) Langley. Student, East Carolina U., 1958-61; cert., Chowan Coll., 1961, U. Ga., 1973, Appalachian U., 1977; diploma, Inst. Fin. Edn. Savs. & Loan, 1976; cert. diploma, Grad. Sch. Savs. and Loan U., 1979. Sec., receptionist Home Savs. & Loan, Rocky Mount, N.C., 1962-67, supr. services, acctg. teller ops., 1967-74, asst. sec., 1969-74, dept. head savs. and mktg., 1974-86, v.p., corp. sec., 1974—; dept. head non-traditional products, v.p., sec. Pioneer Savs. Bank (name formerly Home Savs. & Loan)., Rocky Mount, 1986-88; sr. v.p., mgr. Pioneer Capital Investments, Rocky Mount, 1988—; v.p. bank subsidiaries Pioneer Capital Corp., Rocky Mount, 1988—; asst., sec., dir. HSL Investors, Inc., Rocky Mount, 1972-86; chmn. N.C. Savs. and Loan Conf., 1977. Mem. Rocky Mt. Zoning Bd., 1977-81, YMCA, Rocky Mt., 1976-80; alumni bd. Chowan Coll., Mufreesboro, N.C., 1985—; mem. adv. council N.E.W. Performing Arts; mem. exec. com. N.C. Wesleyan Coll. Recipient Bronze medallion Am. Heart Assn., 1976. Mem. N.C. League Savs. Insts. (outstanding service plaque 1977), , Am. Bus. Women's Assn. (Women of Yr. pres. 1976-77), Rocky Mount C. of C. (ambassador 1976-77, Red Coat 1975-76, 88—), Beta Sigma Phi (pres. 1964-65). Democrat. Baptist. Clubs: Pilot Internat. (lt. gov. N.C. dist., gov. 1986-87), Luncheon Pilot (Rocky Mt.) (pres. 1977-78) (Pilot of Yr/ 1979-80, Pres. award 1982-83). Home: 3004 Wellington Dr Rocky Mount NC 27803 Office: Pioneer Savs Bank 224 S Franklin St Rocky Mount NC 27802

GREENE, JOHN FREDERICK, oil company executive, geologist; b. Muskegon, Mich., Sept. 9, 1940; s. John Percy and Lillian (Klopfenstein) G.; m. M. Jean Pierce, Apr. 24, 1940; children: Karen, John Kenneth. BS in Zoology, U. Mich., 1963, MS in Geology, 1970. Geologist Conoco Inc., Lafayette, La., 1970-72; project mgr. Conoco Inc., Houston, 1972-75; div. mgr. Conoco Inc., Denver, 1976-80; pres. Milestone Petroleum, Denver, 1981-85; exec. v.p. La. Land & Exploration, New Orleans, 1985—. Capital campaign dir. Geosci. Alumni, U. Mich., Ann Arbor, 1985-87. Served to lt. comdr. USN, 1963-68. Mem. Asm. Assn. Petroleum Geologists, Am. Petroleum Inst., New Orleans Geol. Soc. Clubs: Beach (Metairie, La.); Petroleum (New Orleans). Office: La Land & Exploration Co 909 Poydras St Box 60350 New Orleans LA 70160

GREENE, KATHLEEN KING, aircraft corporation and automotive executive; b. West Palm Beach, Fla., June 15, 1932; d. Frederic Worthington and Vera Hilda (Ashburner) King; 1 child, Christopher Tracy. Student Palm Beach Jr. Coll., 1950, Bryant & Stratton Coll., 1963, MIT Lowell Inst., 1967-68, Babson Coll., 1974, 76, Barry U., 1981-84. Sta. mgr. Mackey Airlines, Inc., West Palm Beach, 1954-60; asst. mgr. Dial Employment Bur., Portland, Maine, 1960-62; exec. sec. Neelon Mgmt. Co., Waltham, Mass., 1962-65; div. adminstr. MITRE Corp., Bedford, Mass., 1965-77, asst. planning and analysis, 1977-78, mgr. personnel rels., 1978; div. mgmt. cons. Pratt & Whitney Aircraft Corp., West Palm Beach, 1978-86; dir. employee and civil rights United Tech. Automotive, Inc., 1986—; also mem. adv. com. EEO; cons. in field. Mem. Fla. A&M U. Industry Cluster Com., State Fla. Bd. Regents; co-chmn. Task Force on Equipment and Materials, 1981—; active United Fund/Way drives, Mass., Fla., U.S. Savs. Bonds drive, Mass., Fla., 1970-80, Spl. Olympics Com., 1980—; bd. dirs. Urban League of Palm Beach, Community Action Coun.. Mem. Fla. Mgmt. Assn., NAFE, Urban League, Air Force Assn., Am. Mgmt. Assn., Profl. Bus. Women's Assn. (charter), LWV. Democrat. Home: 7443 Appoline Ave Dearborn MI 48126 Office: United Techs Automotive 5200 Auto Club Dr Dearborn MI 48126-9982

GREENE, R. HUNT, investment banker, venture capitalist; b. Dallas, Dec. 13, 1950; s. Milton J. and Barbara (Huntley) G.; m. Jane E. Piccard, July 11, 1976; children: Christopher, Brennan. BA, Northwestern U., 1971; MBA, Harvard U., 1975. Assoc. Piper Jaffray and Hopwood Inc., Mpls., 1975-77, mng. dir., 1979—; dir. corp. devel. Cardiac Pacemakers Inc., St. Paul, 1977-79; pres. Piper Jaffray Ventures Inc., Mpls., 1983—. Office: Piper Jaffray & Hopwood Piper Tower Minneapolis MN 55402

GREENE, WALTER D., management consultant; b. Brunswick, Ga., Oct. 4, 1936; s. Elliotte E. Greene and Olivia (Moore) Clark; m. Donna M. Pina, May 17, 1986. BA, U. Chgo., 1959; MBA, Nat. U., 1988. Dir. planning Provident Hosp., Chgo., 1976-78; exec. asst. to chancellor N.Y. Bd. Edn., N.Y.C., 1981-83; exec. v.p. Better Chance Inc., Boston, 1984-87; pres. Wherewithal Group Inc., Berkeley, Calif., 1978—. Bd. dirs. Ams. for Dem. Action, Washington, 1972-82. Mem. Data Processing Mgmt. Assn., Assn. Computing Machinery, Exchange, Alpha Phi Alpha. Democrat. Episcopalian. Office: Wherewithal Group Inc 1678 Shattuck Ave Suite 322 Berkeley CA 94709

GREENER, WILLIAM ISAAC, JR., pharmaceutical company public relations executive; b. Memphis, Feb. 18, 1925; s. William Isaac Sr. and Sara (Baer) G.; m. Charlene McPheeters, Aug. 6, 1949; children: William III, Charles, Candice, Thomas, Barbara. BS, U. Mo., 1947; MS, Boston U., 1967. Commd. 2d lt. USAF, 1951, advanced through grades to lt. col., 1968, ret., 1970; dir. congl. pub. affairs IRS, Washington, 1971, 72-73, asst. to commr. congl. pub. affairs, 1972; asst. to sec. pub. affairs HUD, Washington, 1972-74; dep. press sec. to pres. Office of the Pres., Washington, 1974-75; asst. sec. def. Dept. Def., Washington, 1975-76; dep. chmn. for communications Pres. Ford Com., Washington, 1976-77; v.p. Washington office Carl Byoir & Assocs., 1977-79; sr. v.p. pub. affairs G.D. Searle & Co., Skokie, Ill., 1979—. Pres. SSC for Ill., Chgo., 1987—. Recipient Disting. Alumni award Boston U., 1982. Mem. Pub. Relations Soc. Am., Beta Gamma Sigma. Republican. Methodist. Home: 619 Maple Ave Wilmette IL 60091 Office: G D Searle & Co 5200 Old Orchard Rd Skokie IL 60077

GREENFIELD, HELEN MEYERS, real estate executive, publishing company executive, inspection and test service executive; b. Albany, N.Y., Aug. 4, 1908; d. Stephen Ferencevich and Catherine (Bronkov) Meyers; grad. Baker's Bus. Sch., 1924; m. Frank L. Greenfield, Apr. 1, 1929; children—Stuart Franklin, Val Shea. Accounts supr. George G. McCaskey Co., N.Y.C., 1924-29; spl. assignments purchasing dept. McCall's Pub. Co., 1929, Fgn. Affairs Publs., Inc., 1929-31; with purchasing dept. Glidden-Buick Corp., 1931-32; interviewer Civil Works Adminstrn., supr. filing and payroll systems Houston St. Project Center, 1933-36; with dept. accounting Reuben H. Donnelley Co., 1936-37; supr. layouts, makeup prins. of semi-monthly pubs. Tide Publs., Inc., 1939-41; asst. to purchasing agt., supr. maintenance perpetual inventory Hopeman Bros., 1941-43; with money order div., corr. dept. U.S. Govt., P.O. Dept., N.Y.C., 1943-44; v.p. Frank L. Greenfield Co., Inc., N.Y.C., 1945-59; v.p. All Purpose Chair Corp., 1950-55; pres. VAL Equipment, Inc., 1950-62; v.p. Am. Testing Labs., Inc., 1950-63; supr. personnel, purchases Irving Lampert Co., 1951-52; account assignment coordinator, advt. contracts dept. Newsweek, N.Y.C., 1970-78; owner, operator Princess Helen Antiques; pres. Helen M. Greenfield Realty Corp., 1968-79; bus. cons., 1979—. Active New York Heart Assn.; founder, coordinator, show producer, dir. and hostess ann. banquet honor of Dr. Manuel Cabral, composer-dir. Mt. Laurel Ctr. Performing Arts, 1960-84; assoc. mem. Nat. Trust for Hist. Preservation; mem. Statten Island Hist. Soc., Statten Island Inst. of Arts and Scis.; mem. Statue of Liberty-Ellis Island Found. Inc. Named Hon. princess Cherokee Tribe by Chief Rising Sun of Richmond, Va. Mem. Internat. Platform Assn. Club: Order Eastern Star (past matron).

GREENFIELD, ROBERT KAUFFMAN, lawyer; b. Phila., Mar. 30, 1915; s. William I. and Bertha (Kauffman) G.; m. Louise Rose Stern, June 20, 1937; children: Linda Greenfield Baldwin, Mary Greenfield Davenport, William Stern, James Robert. A.B., Swarthmore Coll., 1936; LL.B., Harvard, 1939. Bar: Pa. 1939. Practiced in Phila., 1939—; with firm Goodis, Greenfield, Henry & Edelstein (and predecessors), 1939-77; of counsel firm Montgomery, McCracken, Walker & Rhoads, 1977—; chmn. bd. Phila. Co., 1983-85; dir. Unicorp Am. Corp. Bd. dirs. Conv. and Tourist Bur., Phila., 1942-84; commr., v.p. Phila. Fellowship Commn., 1965-74; pres. Jewish Community Relations Council Phila., 1962-65; pres. Moss Rehab. Hosp., 1969-74, chmn. bd., 1974-77; pres. Alexis Rosenberg Found., 1983—; fin. chmn. Inst. Contemporary Art, 1974-83; exec. com. Council Performing Arts Phila., 1964-70; v.p. Nat. Community Relations Adv. Council, 1965-68; pres. Phila. chpt. Am. Jewish Com., 1966-68; trustee Pa. Coll. Podiatric Medicine, 1967—; v.p. Marriage Council of Phila., 1980-83. Served with USNR, 1945. Mem. ABA, Pa. Bar Assn., Phila. Bar Assn., Phi Beta Kappa, Landings Racquet Club (Sarasota). Home: 1650 Landings Blvd Sarasota FL 34231 Office: 3 Parkway 20th Fl Philadelphia PA 19102

GREENFIELD, SEYMOUR STEPHEN, mechanical engineer; b. Bklyn., July 9, 1922; s. Herman and Yetta (Silfen) G.; m. Eleanor Levy, Oct. 30, 1949; children—Meryl Joy, Bruce Howard. Student, N.Y. U., 1939-40; B.Mech. Engring., Poly. Inst. N.Y., 1944. Registered profl. engr., Calif., Conn., Mass., N.J., N.Y., La., Tex., Ohio. Engr. Percival R. Moses Assos., N.Y.C., 1946-47; sr. engr. and asso. Parsons, Brinckerhoff, Quade & Douglas, N.Y.C., 1947-64; partner Parsons, Brinckerhoff, Quade & Douglas, 1964—, chmn. bd., 1979—; Adviser Manhattan Coll., N.Y.C., 1974—mem. devel. council Tex. A&M Sch. Architecture, 1981; chmn. transp. adv. com. to Pres. of Poly. Inst. N.Y., 1985. Served to lt. USNR, 1944-46. Recipient Engring. News Record Citation for Outstanding Contbns. to Constrn. Industry, 1982; named Transp. Man of Yr., March of Dimes, 1982. Mem. Soc. Am. Mil. Engrs. (nat. pres. 1977, dir. 1975—, pres. N.Y.C. post 1974-75), Nat. Acad. Engring. Bldg. Research (mem. adv. bd. 1972—), N.Y. C. of C. and Industry (vice chmn. Transp. Council 1973—), N.Y. State Soc. Profl. Engrs., ASME, Am. Soc. Heating, Refrigerating and Air Conditioning Engrs., Moles (trustee, pres. 1986). Home: 1600 Parker Ave Fort Lee NJ 07024 Office: Parsons Brinckerhoff Inc 250 W 34th St New York NY 10001

GREENHALGH, MARTHA MORRISON, accountant; b. Dearborn, Mich., Mar. 19, 1962; d. Richard Olcott and Geraldine E. (Schloff) Morrison; m. Donald Albert Greenhalgh, May 3, 1986; 1 child, Sarah Margaret. BS, Boston Coll., 1984. CPA, Mass. Acct. Laventhol & Horwath, Boston, 1984-87; pvt. practice Watertown, Mass., 1987—. Mem. AICPA, Mass. Soc. CPA's. Republican. Roman Catholic. Home: 144 Lovell Rd Watertown MA 02172

GREENHILL, ROBERT FOSTER, investment banker; b. Mpls., June 20, 1936; s. J. Raymond and Mary (Foster) G.; m. Mary Gayle Gussett, Sept. 13, 1958; children: Sarah B., Robert Foster, Mary B. A.B., Yale U., 1958; M.B.A., Harvard U., 1962. Assoc. Morgan Stanley & Co., Inc., N.Y.C., 1962-70, mng. dir., 1970—. Trustee Whitney Mus. Am. Art, N.Y.C.; trustee NYU Med. Ctr. Served to lt. (j.g.) USNR, 1960-62. Mem. Council on Fgn. Relations. Clubs: Ausable (Keene Valley, N.Y.); Field (Greenwich); Links; Union (N.Y.C.). Home: 433 Riversville Rd Greenwich CT 06830 Office: Morgan Stanley Group Inc 1251 Ave of the Americas New York NY 10020 *

GREENMAN, FREDERIC EDWARD, utility executive; b. Cambridge, Mass., Nov. 23, 1936; s. Magnus and Evelyn (Alpert) G.; m. Jocelyn Kuehn, Jan. 26, 1963; children: Jennifer Susan, Laurel Elizabeth. AB, Amherst Coll., 1958; LLB, Columbia U., 1961. Assoc. Titiev, Greenman & Tobin, Boston, 1961-63; asst. atty. gen. Mass. Dept. Atty. Gen., Boston, 1963-69, chief div. health, edn. and welfare, 1967-69; atty. New Eng. Electric System, Westborough, Mass., 1969-73, asst. gen. counsel, 1973-78, assoc. gen. counsel, 1978-84, sec., 1984—, v.p., gen. counsel, 1985-87, sr. v.p., sec., gen. counsel, 1987—; bd. dirs. Conn. Yankee Atomic Power Co., Granite State Electric Co., Maine Yankee Atomic Power Co., New Eng. Electric Transmission Corp., New Eng. Energy Inc., New Eng. Hydro-Transmission Corp., New Eng. Hydro-Transmission Electric Co. Inc., New Eng. Power Co., New Eng. Power Service Co., New Eng. Hydro Fin. Co., Inc., Vt. Yankee Nuclear Power Corp., Yankee Atomic Electric Co., Narragansett Energy Resources Co., New Eng. Hydro Fin. Co., Inc. Chmn. Mental Health-Legal Advisors Com., Mass., 1974-75, Drug Rehab. Adv. Bd. Com., Mass., 1969-73; trustee Franklin Flaschner Found., Boston, 1976—, Samuel Huntington Fund., 1988—, pres., 1989—. Served with U.S. Air Nat. Guard, 1961-67.67. Mem. ABA, Mass. Bar Assn. Republican. Jewish. Office: New Eng Electric System 25 Research Dr Westborough MA 01582

GREENSHIELDS, JACK BROWNING, paper products executive; b. Hartford, Conn., Dec. 7, 1949; s. Jack Browning and Marion Lucille (Clarke) G.; m. Sheila Steinberg, Dec. 26, 1970; children: Tammi, Keith. BSME, Worchester Poly. Inst., 1971; MBA, U. New Haven, 1976. Nuclear engr. Gen. Dynamics, Groton, Conn., 1971-73; with mfg. svcs. Monsanto Co., Stonington, Conn., 1973-76; mgr. purchasing Monsanto Co., St. Louis, 1976-82, bus. mgr., 1982-84, bus. mgr., internat. sales, 1984-86; v.p. materials Waldorf Corp., St. Paul, 1986-87, sr. v.p., 1987—. Dir. Jr. Achievement of Upper Miedwest, 1989—. Maj. USAR, 1971-79. Mem. Boxboard Rsch. & Devel. Assn. (trustee 1988—). Republican. Home: 1719 Laurel Ave Hudson WI 54016 Office: Waldorf Corp 2250 Wabash Ave Saint Paul MN 55114

GREENSPAN, ALAN, economist; b. N.Y.C., Mar. 6, 1926; s. Herman Herbert and Rose (Goldsmith) G. BS summa cum laude, NYU, 1948, MA, 1950, PhD, 1977. Pres., chief exec. officer Townsend-Greenspan and Co., Inc., N.Y.C., 1954-74, 77-87; cons. Council Econ. Advisers, 1970-74, chmn., 1974-77; cons. Congressional Budget Office, 1977-87; mem. Pres.'s Econ. Policy Adv. Bd., 1981-87; chmn. Nat. Commn. on Social Security Reform, 1981-83; mem. Task Force on Econ. Growth, 1969, Pres.'s Fgn. Intelligence Adv. Bd., 1982-85; Commn. on an All-Vol. Armed Force, 1969-70; Commn. on Fin. Structure and Regulation, 1970-71; cons. U.S. Treasury, 1971-74, Fed. Res. Bd., 1971-74; mem. econ. adv. bd. Sec. of Commerce, 1971-72; mem. central market system com. SEC, 1972; mem. GNP rev. com. Office Mgmt. and Budget; sr. adviser panel on econ. activity Brookings Instn., 1970-74, 77-87; chmn. bd. govs. Fed. Res. System, 1987—; mem. bd. economists Time mag., 1971-74, 77-87; adj. prof. Grad. Sch. Bus. Adminstrn., NYU, 1977-87. Mem. Nixon for Pres. Com., 1968-69, dir. domestic policy research; personal rep. of Pres.-elect to Bur. Budget for transition period, chmn. task force on fgn. trade policy.; Bd. overseers Hoover Instn. on War, Revolution and Peace, 1973-74, 77-87. Recipient John P. Madden medal, 1975; joint recipient Pub. Service Achievement award, 1976, William Butler Meml. award, 1977. Fellow Nat. Assn. Bus. Economists (past pres.). Clubs: Hillcrest Country (Los Angeles); Metropolitan (Washington); Century Country, University, Harmonie. Office: Fed Res System 20th & Constitution Ave Washington DC 20551

GREENTREE, JONATHAN PRINCENTHAL, government agency executive; b. Columbus, Ohio, Dec. 15, 1951; s. Leonard Bernard and Edith (Friedman) G.; m. Carol Gene Cheney, May 25, 1986. Student, DePaul U., 1969-71; BA in European History, Ohio State U., 1973, MA in Journalism, 1981. Devel. cons. ARC, Columbus, 1976-80; pres. Greentree Pub. Relations, Columbus, 1981-85; pub. info. officer devel. dept. City of Columbus, 1985-88; mgr. Internat. Trade Devel. Office, Columbus, 1988—. Chmn. pub. relations com. disaster services ARC, Columbus, 1980—; pres. Jr. Council Columbus Mus. Art., 1987-88; bd. dirs. Internat. Visitors Council, Columbus, 1987—. Served to 1st lt. USAR. Mem. Pub. Rels. Soc. Am. (chmn. pub. svc. com., 1985-86, Prism award 1987). Republican. Jewish. Home: 2600 York Rd Columbus OH 43221 Office: Internat Trade Devel Office 37 N High St Columbus OH 43512

GREENWALD, EDWARD HARRIS, mining company executive, mining consultant, researcher; b. Pitts., Mar. 30, 1920; s. Harold Putnam and Sophia (Jones) G.; m. Betty Jean Pelter (div. Apr. 1960); children—Edward H., Jr., Catherine D. Greenwald Perry; m. Charlotte Ann Tomlinson, Apr. 25, 1964. B.S. cum laude, U. Pitts, 1942. Registered profl. engr. Pa., W.Va., Ky. La. Mining engr. Boone County Coal Corp., Sharples, W.Va., 1942-45, chief engr., 1945-47, asst. to v.p., 1947-52, gen. mgr., chief operating officer, 1952-56; ptnr. Eavenson, Auchmuty & Greenwald Cons., Pitts., 1956-57, owner 1967—, chmn. pres., Coraopolis, Pa., 1978—; pres., dir. Washington Energy Processing, Inc., Coraopolis, 1984—; dir., v.p. La. Coal Services, La. Energy Services, U.S. Energy Services, Lafayette, La., 1978-82; dir., exec. v.p. Miller Coal Systems, Houston, 1980-81; pres. Resource engring. and Mgmt., Pitts., 1974-78; v.p., treas. dir. Spruce River Coal Co., Pitts., 1962-70, Aquitaine of Pa., Inc., Pitts., 1973-78, Kanawha Coal Operators Assn., Charleston, W.Va., 1952-56. Contbr. articles to profl. jours. Patentee in field. Mem. Commn. on Mine Safety, State of Pa., 1963-64; bd. dirs. Logan County chpt. ARC, 1952-56, Logan County Tax Payers Assn., 1952-56; v.p. Chief Corn Stock council Boy Scouts Am., Logan, 1954-56. Named Engring. Alumnus of Yr., U. Pitts., 1975. Mem. Am. Inst. Mining and Metall. Engrs., Am. Mining Congress, Coal Mining Inst. Am., Nat. Mine Rescue Assn., W. Va. Coal Mining Inst., Nat. Def. Preparedness Assn., Am. Inst. Mining Engrs. (vice chmn. Central Appalachian sect. 1955-56), Coal River Mining Inst. (pres. 1950). Home: 92 Nancy Ln McMurray PA 15317 Office: Eavenson Auchmuty & Greenwald 420 Rouser Rd Airport Office Park III Coraopolis PA 15108

GREENWALD, GERALD, automotive company executive; b. St. Louis, Sept. 11, 1935; s. Frank and Bertha G.; m. Glenda Lee Gerstein, June 29, 1958; children: Scott, Stacey, Bradley, Joshua. B.A. Cumlaude (Univ. scholar), Princeton U., 1957; M.A., Wayne State U., 1962. With Ford Motor Co., 1957-79; pres. Ford Venezuela; dir. non-automotive ops. Europe; vice chmn. Chrysler Corp., Highland Park, Mich., 1979-85; chmn. Chrysler Motors, 1985-88, vice chmn., 1988—; bd. dirs. Honeywell Inc. Nat. exec. bd. Boy Scouts Am.; bd. dirs. Detroit United Fund, Detroit Renaissance. With USAF, 1957-60. Mem. U.S. C. of C. (bd. dirs.), Motor Vehicle Mfrs. Assn. (exec. com.), Econ. Club Detroit, Chief Execs. Orgn. Clubs: Princeton, Detroit Athletic.

GREENWALD, HERBERT ALLAN, association executive; b. Cleve., May 4, 1919; s. Samuel Edward and Selma (Edelman) G.; m. Gloria Ruth Hersh, Sept. 28, 1943; children—Gary Douglas, Marc Stephen. B.B.A., Western Res. U. Bus. mgr. Cooper Art Studios, Cleve., 1945; advt. mgr. Mayer-Marks Furniture Co., Cleve., 1945-48, Livingston's, Canton, Ohio, 1948-49; dir. mail specialist Ohringer Furniture Co., Pitts., 1949-51; advt. mgr. Kurtz Furniture, Cleve., 1951-66; pres. Herb Greenwald Advt., Cleve., 1967-83; exec. dir. Heights Area C. of C., Cleve., 1968—; cons. in field; exec. dir. Restaurant Row, Cleve., 1974—. Recipient Broadcasting award Hollywood Radio and TV Soc., 1979; Disting. Service award City of University Heights, 1983; Congl. cert. achievement U.S. Congress, 1983; Outstanding Community Service award Gen. Assembly, Ohio Senate, 1983. Mem. Internat. Platform Assn. (bd. govs. 1972—). Jewish. Lodge: Masons.

GREENWALD, JIM CONNEJO, financial consultant; b. Los Angeles, June 26, 1948; s. Robert James and Joan Catherine (McCurrach) G.; m. Judy Capper, Sept. 27, 1988. Cons. Allstate Tax Service, Carson, Calif., 1972-78; owner, ptnr. Jim's Exotic Fish, Westchester, Calif., 1979-80; cons. Frank Andrade & Assocs., Torrance, Calif., 1978-82; owner Jim Greenwald & Assocs., Lawndale, Calif., 1982—; sales leader A.L. williams, Lawndale, 1985-86, div. mgr., 1986-87, sr. regional mgr., 1986-87, regional v.p., 1987—. Contbr. articles and photographs to mags. Democrat. Office: 15900 Hawthorne Blvd Suite A Lawndale CA 90260

GREENWALD, JOHN ROBERT, JR., electronic company executive; b. Ludington, Mich., Sept. 29, 1959; s. John Robert Sr. and Jeanette Marie (Pioszak) G. BS in Engring. Graphics., Western Mich. U., 1983. With computer aided design Upjohn Co., Kalamazoo, 1983; programmer/analyst Magnavox Govt. Electronics Co., Ft. Wayne, Ind., 1983-85; systems engr., group leader Electronic Data Systems, Detroit, 1985—; founder/propr. Wajco Mail Order, Ludington, 1987—. Designer auto motion watch, household products. Mem. Soc. Mfg. Engrs. (cert. mfg. technologist), K.C. Home: 2907 Roundtree Troy MI 48083 Office: Electronic Data Systems 750 Tower Dr PO Box 7019 Troy MI 48007-7019

GREENWALD, MATHEW HENRY, market research company executive; b. N.Y.C., Nov. 6, 1946; s. Daniel Harold and Ethel (Freedman) G.; m. Patricia Ann Gould, Aug. 15, 1971; 1 child, Lisa Joan. BA, SUNY, Binghamton, 1967; MA, Rutgers U., 1970, M in Philosophy, 1971, PhD, 1976; PhD, New Coll. Hofstra, 1976. Instr. Douglass Coll., New Brunswick, N.J., 1970-71; teaching fellow in sociology New Coll. on Hofstra, Hempstead, N.Y., 1971-73; research assoc. Am. Council Life Ins., N.Y.C., 1973-75, program dir., 1975-77; dir. social research Am. Council Life Ins., Washington, 1977-85; pres. Mathew Greenwald & Assocs. Inc., Washington, 1985—. Contbr. articles to profl. jours. NSF traineeship, 1967; Edwin E. Aldwin grantee, 1970, Inst. Life Ins. grantee, 1972; teaching fellow in sociology New Coll. Houston. Mem. Soc. for Ins. Research, Am. Assn. for Pub. Opinion Research, Am. Mktg. Assn., Assn. for Consumer Research, Am. Sociol. Assn. Home: 3420 Garrison St NW Washington DC 20008 Office: Mathew Greenwald & Assocs Inc 4201 Connecticut Ave NW #620 Washington DC 20008

GREENWALT, CHERI ANN, credit union executive; b. Sedro Wooley, Wash., Aug. 3, 1958; d. William Hicks Farnham and Evelyn Louise (Goetzinger) Lynn; m. Bradley Wayne Greenwalt, Sept. 24, 1976; children: Lindsay Jo, Gordon Allen. Student, Wash. State Real Estate Sch., 1978, N.W. Computer Learning Ctr., Salem, Oreg., 1987; student in acctg. and mgmt., Internat. Corr. Schs., 1986. Teller supr. Seattle First Nat. Bank, 1978-81; owner, operator Dessert Delight Catering Svc., Quincy, Wash., 1982-84; adminstrv. asst. Marion and Polk Schs. Maps Credit Union, Salem, 1984-88, svc. mgr., compliance officer, 1988—; mem. capitalization cert. com. Marion and Polk Schs. Maps Credit Union, Salem, 1987-88. Co-author, editor: Capitalization--A Plan for Success, 1987; editor co. newsletter., 1987—. Mem. Oreg. Credit Union League (mem. capitalization com.), PC Users Group, Salem C. of C. (edn. com.). Office: Marion & Polk Schs Maps Credit Union 1900 Hines St SE Salem OR 97302

GREENWOOD, FRANK, data processing educator; b. Rio de Janeiro, Brazil, Mar. 6, 1924; came to U.S., 1935; s. Heman Charles and Evelyn (Heyns) G.; m. Mary Mallas, Oct. 24, 1973; children: Margaret, Ernest, Nicholas. BA, Bucknell U., 1950; MBA, U. So. Calif., 1959; PhD, UCLA, 1963. Cert. systems profl. Various positions The Tex. Co., U.S., Africa and Can., 1950-60; assoc. prof. U. Ga., Athens, 1961-65; chmn. dept. computer systems Ohio U., Athens, 1966-76; dir. computer ctr. U. Mont., Missoula, 1977-84; prof. mgmt. info. systems Southeastern Mass. U., North Dartmouth, 1985-89, Cen. Mich. U., Mt. Pleasant, 1989—; dir. Ctr. for Productivity, Inc., New Bedford, Mass., 1981—. Author: Casebook for Management and Business Policy: A Systems Approach, 1968, Managing The Systems Analysis Function, 1968; (with Nicolai Siemens and C.H. Marting Jr.) Operations Research: Planning, Operating and Information Systems, 1973; (with Mary Greenwood) Information Resources in the Office of Tomorrow, 1980, Profitable Small Business Computing, 1982, Office Technology: Principles of Automation, 1984, Business Telecommunications: Data Communications in the Information Age, 1988; (introduction) Computer-Integrated Manufacturing, 1989; columnist: Computerworld Mag., 1972-73, The Daily Record, 1982-83, (with Mary Greewood) Herald News, 1986, The Beacon, 1986; contbr. monographs, articles to profl. jours. and chpts. to books. Served as sgt. U.S. Army, 1943-45. UCLA Alumni scholar, 1961; Ford Found. fellow, 1962-63. Mem. Assn. for Systems Mgmt. Episcopalian. Club: Wamsutta (New Bedford, Mass.). Home: 100 Spring St New Bedford MA 02740 Office: SE Mass U North Dartmouth MA 02747

GREENWOOD, IVAN ANDERSON, physicist; b. Cleve., Jan. 31, 1921; s. Ivan A. and Mabel (Harlow) G.; m. Jean Elizabeth Siebrecht, June 18, 1949 (dec. Jan. 1983); children: Kyle Ann, Hilary (dec.). BS, Case Inst. Tech., 1942; postgrad., MIT, NYU, Columbia U. Asst. group leader Radiation Lab., MIT, 1942-46; mgr. research dept., assoc. dir. research and advanced devel. GPL div. Gen. Precision Systems Inc., 1946-69; research mgr. physics research ctr. Kearfott div. Singer Co., 1969-81, mgr. advanced research projects, 1981-85; cons., 1985—; cons. on med. research project Bellevue Med. Ctr. NYU, 1956-60, Albert Einstein Coll. Medicine Yeshiva U., 1960-64; incorporating dir. Bio-Instrumentation Inst., Inc., 1962—; bd. dirs., mem. exec. com. Glen Ellen Corp., 1962-70; ptnr. Bus. Trends Publs., Cleve., 1947-49; past dir., mem. exec. com. Syntha Corp. Patentee in field. Mem. Stamford (Conn.) Rep. Town Com., 1981-84, 87—, treas., mem. exec. com., 1981-84, 88—; past mem. bd. dirs. Conn. Ski Council; v.p., incorporator Vt. Recreation Ctr., Inc., 1971-84; trustee 1st Presbyn. Ch., Stamford, 1984-87; treas. Friends of Stamford Symphony, 1986—. Mem. Am. Chem. Soc. (assoc.), Am. Phys. Soc., Am. Inst. Physics, IEEE, Inst. Nav., Fedn. Am. Scientists, AAAS, Case Alumni Assn., Landmark Club, River Hills Ski Club, Cove Island Yacht (vice comdr. 1979-82), Minuteman Yacht Club, Les Amis du Vin, Tau Beta Pi, Theta Tau, Sigma Alpha Epsilon. Presbyterian. Home: 6 Weed Circle Stamford CT 06902

GREENWOOD, JOEN ELIZABETH, economist, consultant; b. Mineral Point, Wis., Aug. 29, 1934; d. John Edward and Lillian Laile (Rohr) G. BS, MA, U. Wis., 1956, 57; postgrad., Newnham Coll. Cambridge U., Eng., 1961-62; diploma in Advanced Mgmt. Program, Harvard U., 1983. Instr. econs. Wellesley (Mass.) Coll., 1962-68; sr. assoc. Charles River Assocs., Boston, 1968-79, v.p., 1979—; mem. bd. editors Energy Jour., 1979-83. Co-author: Folded, Spindled and Mutilated: Economic Analysis and U.S. v. IBM, 1983; contbr. to profl. publs. Mem. Commonwealth of Mass. Pub. Health Coun., Boston, 1973-79; vol. Hospice of Cambridge (Mass.). Earhart fellow U. Calif.-Berkeley, 1960-61; Fulbright scholar U.K., 1961-62. Mem. Internat. Assn. Energy Economists (v.p. 1978-84, exec. v.p. 1981-84), U. Wis. Alumni Assn. (bd. dirs. 1987—), Wis. Alumni Assn. Greater Boston (pres. 1987-89), Boston Club. Home: 108 Chestnut St Cambridge MA 02139 Office: Charles River Assocs 200 Clarendon St Boston MA 02116

GREER, JERRY THOMAS, retail executive, investor; b. Gallipolis, Ohio, Dec. 23, 1948; s. Eugene and Madeline Mary (Ring) G.; m. Rita Ann (Kellermeyer), Dec. 28, 1968. Grad. high sch., Columbus, Ohio. Mgr. Ky. Fried Chicken, Columbus, 1966-69; mgr. sales Buckeye Airstream, Etna, Ohio, 1971-75; pres., gen. mgr. Jerry Greer Airstream Recreational Vehicles, Columbus, 1975—; mem. dealer council Holiday Rambler Corp., Wakarusa, Ind., 1988, Airstream Inc., Jackson Center, Ohio, 1975—; owner, bd. dirs. Knights Worldwide Travel, Columbus; bd. dirs. Horizon Leasing. Served with U.S. Army, 1969-71. Mem. Recreational Vehicle Dealers Assn. (nat. bd. dirs. 1987—). Republican. Roman Catholic. Clubs: Capital (Columbus); Muirfield Country (Dublin, Ohio). Office: 4056 Morse Rd Columbus OH 43230

GREER, MAX WELDON, JR., financial planning executive; b. McAlester, Okla., Sept. 9, 1947; s. Max Weldon Sr. and Alyce G. (Hammond) G.; m. Lois Elaine Stein, Sept. 18, 1970; children: Michele L., Megan Leigh, Michael Weldon. BA, Park Coll., 1970. Cert. fin. planner. Salesman N.Y. Life Ins. Co., Overland Park, Kans., 1970-75; mgr. Mut. Benefit Life Ins. Co., Overland Park, 1975-79, Nat. Life of Vt., Overland Park, 1979-83; pres. Fin. Adv. Svc., Inc., Overland Park, 1983—. Recipient numerous industry awards. Mem. Inst. Cert. Fin. Planners, Internat. Assn. Fin. Planners. Republican. Presbyterian. Home: 12001 Fairway Rd Leawood KS 66209 Office: Fin Adv Svc Inc 10955 Lowell Ave Ste 420 Overland Park KS 66210

GREER, RAYMOND WHITE, lawyer; b. Port Arthur, Tex., July 20, 1954; s. Mervyn Hardy Greer and Eva Nadine (White) Swain; 1 child, Emily Ann. BA magna cum laude, Sam Houston State, 1977; JD, U. Houston, 1981. Assoc. Hoover, Cox & Shearer, Houston, 1980-83, Hinton & Morris, Houston, 1983-85; sole practice Houston, 1985-86; prin. Morris & Greer, P.C., Houston, 1986—; lectr. in field. Mem. ABA, State Bar Tex., Houston Bar Assn., Fort Bend County Bar Assn., Assn. Trial Lawyers Am., Tex. Assn. Bank Counsel. Avocations: golf, water skiing, reading. Office: Morris & Greer PC 952 Echo Ln Suite 110 Houston TX 77024

GREER, ROBERT E., insurance executive; b. Louisville, July 24, 1937; s. William and Marguerite (Fleischaker) G.; m. Helen Dorothy Litton, July 1, 1976; children: Ashley, Alexis. BA, Cornell U., 1959; MBA, Harvard U., 1963. Mktg. research specialist Merrill Lynch, Inc. Co., N.Y.C., 1965-68; v.p. planning Hayden Stone Inc., N.Y.C., 1968-70, Reynolds Securities, Inc., N.Y.C., 1970-75; v.p. Chase Manhattan Bank, N.Y.C., 1975-80; v.p. mktg. research and planning Am. Stock Exchange, N.Y.C., 1980-83; v.p. planning Mcpl. Bond Investors Assurance Corp., White Plains, N.Y., 1983—; mem. exec. com. SEC Conf. on Small Bus. Capital Formation, 1982. Chmn. White Plains Dem. City Com.; treas. Westchester-Putnam Counties chpt. Am. Diabetes Assn. Served with U.S. Army, 1959-60. Mem. The Planning Forum, Wall Street Planning Group, Bus. Execs. for Nat. Security. Home: 20 Cushman Rd White Plains NY 10606 Office: Mcpl Bond Investors Assurance Corp 445 Hamilton Ave White Plains NY 10601

GREESON, JANET ROSEMARY, clinical director, psychotherapist; b. N.Y.C., May 28, 1943; d. Arthur Charles and Rosemary Margaret (Duffy) Durr; m. Eugene W. Boyle, Nov. 28, 1964 (div. 1969); children: Eugene, Jimmy; m. Charles W. Jowers, June 14, 1969 (div. Aug. 1977); 1 child, Rosemary; m. Alden N. Greeson, Apr. 21, 1984 (Mar. 1989). BA in Psychology, U. Cent. Fla., 1978; MA in Clin. Counseling, Rollins Coll., 1979; PhD, Columbia Pacific U., 1987. Cert. addictions, eating disorders, mental health counselor. Counselor alcoholism alcohol rehab. drydock USN, Orlando, Fla., 1978-79, program coordinator alcohol safety action program, 1979-82; assoc. prof. U. West Fla., Pensacola, 1981-82; psychotherapist Met. Alcohol Council Orlando, 1983-85; cons. eating disorders Brookwood Recovery Lodge, Birmingham, Ala., 1985; dir. Alcohol Rehab. Service div. Naval Hosp., Orlando, 1982-86; pvt. practice psychotherapy Orlando, 1981—; founding dir. New Life Ctr. For Depression, Anxiety and Eating Disorders, Orlando, 1986—; trustee exec. bd. Overeaters Anonymous Nat., Torrance, Calif., 1978-85; coordinator conf. on teenage alcohol abuse, Washington, 1983; supr. clin. practice site Rollins Coll., Winter Park, Fla., 1986-87. Mem. adv. bd. Profl. Counselor mag. Pres., treas., trustee Cen. Fla. Intergroup Alcoholics Anonymous, Winter Park, 1977—; bd. dirs. Grove, Altamonte Springs, Fla., 1981-82; mem. Chem. Dependency Network, Orlando, 1983—; founder, corp. dir. Freedom Walk, Inc., 1985; trustee exec. bd. dirs. Overeaters Anonymous, Torrance, Calif., 1978-85; organizer Superwoman Anonymous, cen. Fla., 1986—. Served with USN, 1961-64. Recipient Service to Mankind award Sertoma Club, 1979, appreciation award Lowell State Prison, 1979, cert. achievement U. Tex., 1986, award 30th Fla. Alcoholics Anonymous Conv., 1986. Mem. Internat. Assn. Eating Disorders (bd. dirs.), Am. Eating Disorders Assn. (cert.), Am. Mental Health Counselors (cert.), Am. Counseling and Devel. Assn., Nat. Assn. Alcoholism Counselors, Chem. Dependency Network, Fla. Alcohol and Drug Abuse Assn., Fla. Group Psychotherapy, Fla. Mental Health Counselors, Am. Labor Mgmt. Adminstrs. (sec., presenter conf. 1986-87), Nat. Assn. Female Execs., Am. Orthopsychiat. Assn. Republican. Roman Catholic. Clubs: Rebos (Casselberry, Fla.) (v.p. 1978-85, appreciation award 1983, pres., trustee), Alco-An (Orlando, Fla.). Office: New Life Ctr Depression Anxiety & Eating Disorders 7727 Lake Underhill Orlando FL 32822

GREFE, ROBERT HERMAN, industrial noise control engineer; b. Rockville Center, N.Y., Jan. 5, 1941; s. Herman W. and A. Ruth (Denton) G.; student Va. Poly. Inst., 1958-61; A.A.S., Nassau Community Coll., 1975; B.S., N.Y. Inst. Tech., 1978; m. Dorothy M. Corwin, June 15, 1969; children—James, Jennifer, Janet. Draftsman, Korfund Dynamics Corp., Westbury, N.Y., 1967-69, designer, project mgr., 1969-75, chief acoustical engr., 1975-78, chief engr., 1978-87, div. mgr. Korfund div. ARX Corp., 1987—. Served with U.S. Army, 1964-67. Mem. Acoustical Soc. Am. Presbyterian. Home: 248 Toronto Ave Massapequa NY 11758

GREGG, DAVID, III, investment banker; b. N.Y.C., Jan. 29, 1933; s. David Gregg and Virginia (Wyckoff) Macgregor; m. May Foster Bowers, Dec. 21, 1963 (div. Apr. 1984); children: Justine Simms, David; m. Sarah Choate Massengale, Dec. 8, 1984. Assoc., Eastman Dillon Union Securities & Co., N.Y.C., 1959-67, ptnr., 1967-69; v.p. Blyth & Co., Inc., N.Y.C., 1969-72; 1st v.p. Blyth, Eastman Dillon & Co., N.Y.C., 1972-73; exec. v.p. Overseas Pvt. Investment Corp., Washington, 1973-77; dir. Pierce Internat., Ltd., Washington, 1978-85, mng. dir., 1978-85; mng. dir. Pierce Investment Banking Corp., 1985—; chmn. bd. dirs. Gator Broadcasting Corp., Gainesville, Fla.; bd. dirs. So. Starr Broadcasting, Orlando, Fla., 1983-87. Bd. dirs. Emergency Aid Services, Arlington, Va., 1984—; trustee Calvert Tax Free Res. Fund, 1978-83; dir. 1st Variable Rate Fund, 1978-83. Served with U.S. Army, 1955-57. Mem. Washington Soc. Investment Analysts. Republican. Episcopalian. Clubs: Onteora (dir. 1969-72) (Tannersville, N.Y.); Chesapeake Bay Yacht (Easton, Md.); Amateur Ski of N.Y., Yale (N.Y.C.). Office: Pierce Investment Banking Corp 1910 K St NW Washington DC 20006

GREGG, MARK VAUGHAN, financial executive; b. Denver, Mar. 5, 1945; s. Lowell E. and Novella (Vaughan) Myers; m. Diane D. Heuer, Oct. 31, 1981; children: David, Shellie, Mark, Shad. Student, Cornell U., 1963-66; BA, Ft. Lewis Coll., 1968. CPA, Ariz., Colo. Acct. Haskins & Sells, Denver, 1969-73; cons. Estes Park, Colo., 1973-79; owner, operator Lazy T Resort, Estes Park, 1979-82; asst. controller Rural Metro. Corp., Scottsdale, Ariz., 1982-83; corp. controller Rural Metro. Corp., Scottsdale, 1983—. Mem. AICPAs, Colo. Soc. CPAs, Nat. Assn. Accts., Internat. Soc. Fire Svc. Instrs., Controller's Council, Rotary (pres. Scottsdale chpt.). Home: 8543 E Angus Dr Scottsdale AZ 85251 Office: Rural Metro Corp 3200 N Hayden Rd Scottsdale AZ 85251

GREGG, ROBERT STEVEN, computer company executive; b. Vancouver, Wash., May 17, 1953; s. Cecil Harold and Elizabeth (Moore) G.; m. Cheryl Lynn Gillespie, June 28, 1975; children: Christina Lynn, Robert Matthew. BS, U. Oreg., 1975. CPA, Oreg. Audit mgr. Price Waterhouse Co., Portland, Oreg., 1975-83; v.p. fin. Sequent Computer Systems, Beaverton, Oreg., 1983—; mem. acctg. adv. bd. U. Oreg., 1986—. Mem. Am. Inst. CPA's, Oreg. Soc. CPA's, Sigma Alpha Epsilon. Clubs: Portland Golf, Multnomah Athletic, West Hills Racquet (Portland). Home: 2175 SW Mayfield Ave Portland OR 97225 Office: Sequent Computer Systems Inc 15450 SW Koll Pkwy Beaverton OR 97006

GREGG, WALTER EMMOR, JR., financial corporation executive, accountant, lawyer; b. Utica, N.Y., Sept. 24, 1941; s. Walter Emmor Sr. and Anne (Roberson) G.; m. Pamela Greco, Oct. 25, 1969; children—Ashlee Anne, Marguerite Tadman. B.S. in Psychology, U. Pitts., 1968, J.D., 1973. CPA, Pa. Bar: Pa. 1973. Asst. dist. atty. Allegheny County Dist. Atty. Office, Pitts., 1972-74; resident counsel, asst. sec. PNC Fin. Corp., Pitts., 1975-77, asst. gen. counsel, asst. sec., 1978-83, sr. v.p., treas., chief regulatory counsel, 1983-87, sr. v.p., chief regulatory counsel, 1987, exec. v.p., 1987—; bd. dirs. PNC Capital Corp., PNC Funding Corp., PNC Venture Corp., PNC Bridge Capital Inc., Pitts. Nat. Leasing Corp., Watson Healthcare Inc., Sewickley. Bd. dirs. D.T. Watson Rehab. Hosp., Sewickley, Pa., 1985, Watson Healthcare, Inc., Sewickley, 1988, Sewickley YMCA, 1985—. Mem. ABA, Pa. Bar Assn., Allegheny County Bar Assn., Am. Soc. Corporate Secs., Nat. Assn. Accts., Am. Inst. CPA's, Pa. Inst. CPA's. Republican. Episcopalian. Club: The Duquesne (Pitts.). Office: PNC Fin Corp 5th Ave & Wood St Pittsburgh PA 15222

GREGO, MICHAEL JOSEPH, accounting educator; b. Lebanon, Ill., Jan. 25, 1945; s. Michael Joseph and Anna (Lemke) G. BBA, CUNY, 1967; MBA, St. John's U., Jamaica, N.Y., 1971. CPA, N.Y. Staff acct. Benjamin Kaster & Co., N.Y.C., 1967-69; sr. acct. Deloitte Haskins & Sells, N.Y.C., 1969-75; controller G.A. Thompson & Co., N.Y.C., 1975-78; sr. acct. Patrusky & Weinstein, N.Y.C., 1978-79; assoc. prof. acctg. St. John's U., 1979—; faculty v.p. Beta Alpha Psi chpt., St. John's U., 1983-88; moderator acctg. soc. St. John's U., 1983-88; instr. Convisor-Miller CPA Rev., N.Y.C., 1983-85, Chaykin CPA Rev., N.Y.C., 1987-88. Contbr. articles to profl. jours. Served to sgt. USAR, 1969-74. Mem. Am. Acctg. Assn., Cath. Accts. Guild, Am. Inst. CPA's, N.Y. State Soc. CPA's (edn. com. 1984-88). Roman Catholic. Office: St John's U Coll Bus Adminstrn Grand Central at Utopia Pkwy Jamaica NY 11439

GREGOR, ANDREW, JR., corporate financial executive; b. Greenwich, Conn., Aug. 30, 1948; s. Andrew and Catherine (Mattison) G.; m. Phyllis Rohs, Dec. 27, 1970; children: Andrew III, Jeffrey Victor, Christina. BA in Econs., Wesleyan U., 1970; MBA in Fin., U. Pa., 1972. Sr. investment analyst Aetna Life & Casualty Co., Hartford, Conn., 1972-75; asst. contr. Lone Star Industries, Greenwich, Conn., 1975-81; dep. treas. Diamond Internat. Corp., N.Y.C., 1981-84; v.p., treas. Transway Internat. Corp., White Plains, N.Y., 1984-86; sr. v.p. fin., treas. Rapid-Am. Corp., N.Y.C., 1986—. Home: 11 Lighthouse Ln Old Greenwich CT 06870 Office: Rapid-Am Corp 725 Fifth Ave Trump Tower New York NY 10022

GREGORIO, DANIEL THOMAS, hospital executive; b. N.Y.C., Sept. 10, 1946; s. James and Elizabeth (Enders) G.; m. Dallas Lorraine Stout, Apr. 3, 1983; children: Christina Marie, Dawn Marie, Vicki Lynn. BS in Acctg., St. John's U., 1968; M in Pub. Health Adminstrn., L.I. U., 1975; postgrad. in health care, U. Mich., 1975; postgrad. in mgmt., Northwestern U., 1985. CPA, N.Y., Ill., CLU, Chartered Fin. Cons. Chief acct. Blue Cross/Blue Shield of Greater N.Y., N.Y.C., 1971-73, mgr. acctg., 1973-74, exec. asst. to pres., 1974-75, dir. profl. reimbursement, 1975-78; dir. audit Blue Cross/Blue Shield of Ill., Chgo., 1978-85, officer hosp. contracts and reimbursement, 1985-88; v.p., chief fin. officer Palos Hosp., Palos Heights, Ill., 1988—. Mem. Am. Inst. CPAs, Healthcare Fin. Mgmt. Assn. (advanced), Am. Coll. Healthcare Execs., Ill. CPA Soc. (chmn. hosp. com. 1986-88), Ill. Assn. Preferred Provider Orgns. (bd. dirs. 1986-88). Home: 1560 N Sandburg Terr #3501 Chicago IL 60610 Office: Blue Cross Blue Shield Ill 233 N Michigan Ave Chicago IL 60601

GREGORY, CALVIN, insurance service executive; b. Bronx, N.Y., Jan. 11, 1942; s. Jacob and Ruth (Cherchian) G.; m. Rachel Anna Carver, Feb. 14, 1970 (div. Apr. 1977); children—Debby Lynn, Trixy Sue; m. 2d, Carla Deane Deaver, June 30, 1979. A.A., Los Angeles City Coll., 1962; B.A., Calif. State U.-Los Angeles, 1964; M.Div., Fuller Theol. Sem., 1968; M.R.E., Southwestern Sem., Ft. Worth, 1969; Ph.D. in Religion, Universal Life Ch., Modesto, Calif., 1982; D.Div. (hon.), Otay Mesa Coll., 1982. Notary pub., real estate lic., casualty lic., Calif.; ordained to ministry Am. Baptist Conv., 1970. Youth minister First Bapt. Ch., Delano, Calif., 1964-65, 69-70; youth dir. St. Luke's United Meth. Ch., Highland Park, Calif., 1969-70; tchr. polit. sci. Maranatha High Sch., Rosemead, Calif., 1969-70; aux. chaplain U.S. Air Force 750th Radar Squadron, Edwards AFB, Calif., 1970-72; pastor First Bapt. Ch., Boron, Calif., 1971-72; ins. agt. Prudential Ins. Co., Ventura, Calif., 1972-73, sales mgr., 1973-74; casualty ins. agt. Allstate Ins. Co., Thousand Oaks, Calif., 1974-75; pres. Ins. Agy. Placement Service, Thousand Oaks, 1975—; head youth minister Emanuel Presbyn. Ch., Los Angeles, 1973-74; owner, investor real estate, U.S., Wales, Eng., Can., Australia. Counselor YMCA, Hollywood, Calif., 1964, Soul Clinic-Universal Life Ch., Inc., Modesto, Calif., 1982. Mem. Apt. Assn. Los Angeles, Life Underwriter Tng. Council. Republican. Clubs: Forensic (Los Angeles); X32 (Ventura). Lodge: Kiwanis (club speaker 1971). Home: 3307 Big Cloud Circle Thousand Oaks CA 91360 Office: Ins Agy Placement Svc PO Box 4407 Thousand Oaks CA 91359

GREGORY, DANA GAY, financial planner; b. Beaver Falls, Pa., Feb. 7, 1961; d. Warren Charles and Estelle Maria (Ritchey) G. BA in Fin., BA in Psychology, Mt. Union Coll., Ohio, 1984. Cert. fin. planner. With sales Electronic Circuits, Alliance, Ohio, 1982-84; fin. planner Demming Fin. Services Inc., Aurora, Ohio, 1984-86, Gries Fin. Services Inc., Cleve., 1986—. Mem. Inst. Cert. Fin. Planners. Republican. Roman Catholic. Home: 1167 Homeland Dr Rocky River OH 44116

GREGORY, KATHRINE PATRICIA, food products executive; b. Cornwall, N.Y., Nov. 2, 1952; d. John Theodore and Georgia (Spiliotis) Barbatsuly; m. Paul Gregory, May 17, 1987. BA in Psychology, Hofstra U., 1970-75. Gen. mgr. Au Natural Restaurant, N.Y.C., 1981-84, O'Neals Restaurant, N.Y.C., 1984-87; cons. Orchid Restaurant, N.Y.C., 1986-87; proprietor Argenteuil Restaurant, N.Y.C., 1987-88; cons. N.Y.C., 1988—. Mem. NAFE, Roundtable for Women in Food Svc. (panelist, speaker 1988), Nat. Restaurant Assn., Restaurant Bus. Rsch. Adv. Panel.

GREGORY, MARION F., JR., tool manufacturing executive; b. Denison, Tex., Oct. 26, 1933; s. Marion F. and Nannie (Huseman) G.; m. Fay, Dec. 27, 1975; children: Mark, Gary, Vivian, Nicole, Colette. With Snap-on Tools Corp., 1955—; gen. sales mgr. Snap-on Tools Corp., Kenosha, Wis., 1976-81, v.p., 1977-81, sr. v.p. mfg. and product research and devel., 1981-83, exec. v.p., dir., 1983-85, chief operating officer, dir., 1985—, pres., 1986—, chmn., 1988—; dir. Hand Tools Inst., Tarrytown, N.Y. Served with U.S. Navy, 1951-55. Mem. Wis. Mfg. and Commerce Assn. (bd. dirs. 1985—). Office: Snap-on Tools Corp 2801 80th St Kenosha WI 53140 *

GREGORY, MITCHELL V., steel company executive; b. N.Y.C., Dec. 3, 1935; s. Nicholas and Costandino (Pino) G.; m. Diane C. Brahms, June 7, 1964; children: Michele, William. B.A., Adelphi U., 1957. C.P.A., Pa. With Mathieson Aitken & Co. (C.P.A.s), until 1968; supr., sr. acct. Peat, Marwick, Mitchell, Phila., 1968-72; corp. controller Sharon Steel Co., Miami Beach, Fla., 1972-74; v.p. Sharon Steel Co., 1974—; (also affiliated companies: DWG Corp.), (Pa. Engring. Corp.), (Southeastern Public Service Co), (Wilson Brothers), (NVF Co.); trustee Universal Housing and Devel. Co., 1976—. Elder Miami Shores Presbyn. Ch. Mem. Am. Inst. C.P.A.s, Pa. Inst. C.P.A.s. also: NVF Co Yorklyn Rd Yorklyn DE 19736

GREGORY, ROBERT EARLE, JR., apparel company executive, lawyer; b. Greenville, S.C., May 8, 1942; s. Robert E. and Ellen (Robinson) G.; m. Karen Marie Howard, Apr. 24, 1982; children: Scott, Kelly. B.A., Wofford Coll., 1964; J.D., U. S.C., 1968; Advanced mgmt. program, Harvard Grad. Bus. Sch., Cambridge, Mass., 1978-79. Bar: S.C. 1968, Fed. 1968, U.S. Supreme Ct. 1974. Legal asst. to chief justice S.C. Supreme Ct., Columbia, 1968-70; div. counsel Akzona, Inc., Ashevill, N.C., 1970-72; gen. counsel Spartan Mills, Spartanburg, S.C., 1972-79, group v.p., gen. counsel, 1977-79; exec. v.p., pres. Lee Co. div. VF Corp., Wyomissing, Pa., 1980-83; pres., chief operating officer VF Corp., Wyomissing, Pa., 1983—, dir.; dir. United Mo. Bank Kansas City, N.A., Mo., 1982—. Alumni dir. Wofford Coll., Spartanburg, 1976-81, sec., 1979-80, pres. elect, 1981; trustee Wofford Coll., Spartanburg. Mem. S.C. Bar Assn. Episcopalian. Clubs: Harvard (N.Y.C.); Harvard Bus. Sch. (Phila.). Home: 320 Wyomissing Blvd Wyomissing PA 19610 Office: VF Corp 1047 N Park Rd Wyomissing PA 19610 *

GREGORY, VINCENT LEWIS, JR., retired chemical company executive; b. Oil City, Pa., June 10, 1923; s. Vincent Louis and Celia Viola (Whitling) G.; m. Marjorie Gladys Scott, Feb. 16, 1946; 1 child, Vincent Louis. B.A., Princeton U., 1949; M.B.A., Harvard U., 1949. Fin. asst., asst. plant controller Rohm & Haas Co., Phila., 1949-52; fin. mgr. Minoc S.A.R.L., Paris, 1952-55; asst. mng. dir. Lennig Chems. Ltd., London, 1956-58, mng. dir., 1958-64; dir. European ops. Rohm & Haas Co., London, 1964-68; asst. gen. mgr. fgn. ops. Rohm & Haas Co., Phila., 1968-70, pres., chief exec. officer, 1970-78, chmn., chief exec. officer, 1978-88; dir. Mead Corp. Bd. dirs. Harvard Bus. Sch. Assocs.; chmn. vis. com. Harvard Sch. Pub. Health; active vis. com. Sch. Pub. Health & Community Medicine U. Wash. Served with USAAF, 1942-46. Mem. Chem. Industry Inst. Toxicology, Soc. Chem. Industry (past chmn.), Phi Beta Kappa. Clubs: Harvard, Princeton (Phila.). Office: Rohm & Haas Co Independence Mall W Philadelphia PA 19105

GREGSON, JOHN RANDOLPH, II, real estate development company executive; b. New Orleans, Sept. 10, 1952; s. James Randolph and Mary Isobel (Gannaway) G.; m. Charlotte Lee Thompson, Oct. 23, 1981; children: John Randolph III, Charlotte Reily. Student Princeton U., 1970-72; BA, Tulane U., 1975. Urban policy specialist Office Mayor, New Orleans, 1973-76; project coord. Skid Row, Downtown Devel. Dist., New Orleans, 1976-77; dep. dir. property mgmt. City of New Orleans, 1977-78; exec. asst. to pres. Joseph C. Canizaro Interests, New Orleans, 1978-79; sales and devel. asst. Plantation Bus. Campus, Destrehan, 1979-80; asst. project mgr., program exec. Canal Place 2000, New Orleans, 1980-85; v.p., chief operating officer Lake Forest Inc., 1986—. Bd. dirs. Preservation Resource Ctr. New Orleans, 1976, Neighborhood Improvement Assn. Irish Channel, 1977-79, Met. Battered Women's Program, Inc., 1986-87, sec., 1987, pres., 1987-89, Maple Area Residents, Inc., 1986-87, v.p., 1987, pres., 1987-89; bd. commrs. Community Improvement Agy., 1977-79; bd. dirs. Contemporary Arts Ctr., 1979; trustee La. chpt. Nat. Hemophilia Found., 1977-81, pres. La. chpt., 1979-81, nat. bd. dirs., 1979-80; chmn. Am. Hemophilia Youth, 1980-81. Democrat. Episcopalian.n. Avocation: Tennis. Office: 5690 Eastover Dr New Orleans LA 70189-0546

GREGSON, KEVIN JOSEPH, financial executive; b. Wilmington, Del., July 17, 1959; s. Elwood Varnes and Jeanne Stella (Ogonowski) G.; m. Maria Elena Micovic, June 22, 1985. BA, U. Del., 1981; postgrad., U. Pa., 1986. Employee benefits specialist Crowley Fin. Planning, Wilmington, 1980-84; pension mgr. Lincoln Nat., Phila., 1985-86; pension cons. Unum Corp., Phila., 1986-89; sr. cons. Noble Lowndes Cons. & Actuaries, Phila., 1989—. Mem. exec. com. Rep. Party Birmingham Twp., Pa., 1987—. Mem. Del. Valley Internat. Assn. Fin. Planning (v.p. sponsorships 1984-85), Internat Soc. Cert. Employee Benefit Specialist, Nat. Assn. Securities Dealers (cert.), Newark Jaycees (bd. dirs. 1982-85), U. Del. alumni Assn. (pres. 1986-89), Maxwell Football Club (Phila.). Republican. Home and Office: 1705 N Glen Dr Glen Mills PA 19342

GREGWARE, JAMES MURRAY, financial planner; b. Plattsburgh, N.Y., Dec. 17, 1956; s. John William and Patricia Ann (Murray) G.; m. Kathleen Mary Stanley, June 23, 1979; children: Ryan James, Kailee Michelle. BA in Bus. and Psychology, SUNY, Potsdam, 1979. Cert. investment advisor, stockbroker, fin. planner. Commodities trader The Exchange, Plattsburgh, 1979-82; stockbroker, collections supr., loan officer Champlain Valley Fed. Savs., Plattsburgh, 1982-84; fin. planner, securities instr. New Life Fin. Services, Waterville, Maine, 1984-87; stockbroker Investacorp, Inc., Waterville and Pittsfield, Mass., 1985-89; pres. Fin. Designs & Mgmt., Inc., Manchester, N.H., 1985—; pres. Eastern Fin. Group, Waterville, 1984-87, Pittsfield, 1987—; stockbroker, fin. planner Investment Ctr. Inc., 1989—. Mem. Nat. Assn. Security Dealers, Coll. Fin. Planning. Republican. Roman Catholic. Home: PO Box 1107 Pittsfield MA 01202 Office: Eastern Fin Group Hinsdale Dr Dalton MA 01226

GREIF, EDWARD LOUIS, public relations company executive; b. Bklyn., June 8, 1909; s. Herman and Minnie (Lipschitz) G.; student Coll. City N.Y., 1926-27; LL.B., St. Lawrence U., 1930; m. Mildred Schlamm, Mar. 25, 1939; children: Marion, James David. Sports writer Bklyn. Times, 1926-28; admitted to N.Y. bar, 1932; practice law, N.Y.C., 1932-38; mng. editor Trade Jour. Syndicate, N.Y.C., 1937-38; film critic, columnist Motion Picture Daily, N.Y.C., 1938-42; dir. exploitation NBC, N.Y.C., 1942-45; ptnr. firm Banner & Greif, pub. rels., N.Y.C., 1945-67; pres. Banner & Greif, Ltd., 1968—; cons. mass media edn. USPHS, 1948-52; guest lectr. pub. rels.Columbia, Yale, Temple U., U. Chgo., Sarah Lawrence Coll. Mem. univ. rel. com. Brandeis U., 1948-70, friend Harlan Chapel, 1968-70; mem. adv. com. to communications Nat. Commn. on Community Health Svc., 1964-67. Trustee Gateway Sch. N.Y. Mem. Pub. Rels. Soc. Am. (bd. dirs. pub. affairs sect. 1982-85, chmn. rsch. com. N.Y. chpt. 1980-81). Club: Overseas Press (N.Y.C.). Author: The Silent Pulpit, 1964; contbr. chpt. to Crisis in the Church, 1968. Home: 64 Bradford Rd Scarsdale NY 10585 Office: 370 Lexington Ave New York NY 10017

GREIF, LLOYD, investment banker; b. L.A., May 31, 1955; s. Emile and Herta (Ernst) G.; m. Renee Louise Racicot, Sept. 20, 1986; 1 child, Nicholas Alexander. BA, UCLA, 1977; MBA with honors, U. So. Calif., 1979; JD with honors, Loyola U., L.A., 1984. Bar: Calif. 1984. Ind. mgmt. cons. Hearst Corp., L.A., 1979; assoc. mgmt. cons. Touche Ross and Co., L.A., 1980-81; assoc. corp. fin. Sutro and Co. Inc., L.A., 1982, asst. v.p., 1983-84, v.p., 1985, sr. v.p., 1986-88, exec. v.p. corp. fin., 1988—, also bd. dirs., dir. mergers, acquisitions, and leveraged buyouts group; gen. ptnr. Sutro Investment Ptnrs. I and II. Contbr. to profl. jour. Mem. bd. govs. Law Sch. Loyola U., L.A., 1983-84, adv. coun. entrepreneur program U. So. Calif., L.A., 1984—. Recipient Best New Product Planning And Promotion award U. So. Calif. Food Industry Mgmt. Program, 1979, Am. Jurisprudence awards Bancroft-Whitney Co., N.Y.C., 1982, 83, Alumni Assn. award Law Sch. Loyola U., L.A., 1984; named Outstanding Alumnus of Yr. U. So. Calif. Entrepreneur Program, L.A., 1987. Mem. Calif. Bar Assn., L.A. County Bar Assn., Beverly Hills Bar Assn., Rotary Internat., Beta Gamma Sigma. Republican. Jewish. Office: Sutro & Co Inc 555 S Flower St 34th Fl Los Angeles CA 90071

GRELL, JOSEPH JOHN, III, sales executive; b. Rice Lake, Wis., Nov. 25, 1958; s. Joseph John and Florence Victoria (Kirtcher) G.; m. Nancy Marie Ripplinger, Apr. 26, 1980. Student, U. Wis., Rice Lake, 1977-78. Route salesman Bakerite Bakery, Eau Claire, Wis., 1979-80; custom farmer Rice Lake, Wis., 1980-81; pres. Grell Audio Engring., Barron, Wis., 1981-83; dir. nat. sales Rice Lake Weighing Systems, 1983-89, v.p. product devel., 1989—; lectr. in field. Author: Electronic Scale System, 1987; contbr. articles to profl. jours. Musician, U. Wis. BC Found., Rice Lake, 1984—. Recipient Achievement award Cen. Weights & Measures, 1986, Wis. Weights & Measures, 1987. Mem. Internat. Soc. Weights and Measures. Roman Catholic. Home: 2141 17 1/4 Ave Rice Lake WI 54868 Office: Rice Lake Weighing Systems 230 W Coleman St Rice Lake WI 54868

GRELLER, MARTIN MICHAEL, mamagement consultant; b. Tarrytown, N.Y., July 4, 1950; s. Isadore Morris and Elizabeth (Deely) G.; m. Denise Elena Kollmar, June 10, 1972; children: Christopher M., Katie Ann. BA, Tufts U., 1971; PhD, Yale U., 1975. Lic. psychologist, N.Y., N.J. Supr. tng. AT&T Long Lines, N.Y.C., 1973; asst. prof. mgmt. Grad. Sch. Bus., NYU, N.Y.C., 1974-78; sr. cons. psychologist Rohrer Hibler & Replogle, N.Y.C., 1978-82; dir. human resources planning and devel. N.Y. Times Co., N.Y.C., 1982-86; pres. Pers. Strategies, Inc., Warren, N.J., 1986—; mem. adv. bd. doctoral program in indsl. psychology Baruch Coll., CUNY, 1983—; bd. dirs. multicultural mgmt. program Sch. Journalism, U. Mo., Columbia, 1984—. Author: (with D.M. Herold Feedback Survey, 1975, (with D.M. Nee) From Baby Boom to Baby Bust: How Business Can Meet the Human Resource Challenge, 1989; mem. editorial bd.: The Indsl./Organizational Psychologist, 1982-84; contbr. articles to profl. jours. Vice chair planning com. Passaic Twp. (N.J.) Bd. Edn., 1976-78; chair subcom. Task Force on Employment of Aging, Community Council Greater N.Y., 1984-86. IBM and Beach fellow Inst. Social and Policy Studies, Yale U., New Haven, 1973-74; recipient cert. of appreciation N.Y.C. Police Dept., 1983. Mem. Soc. for Indsl./Organizational Psychology (profl. affairs com. 1980-82), AAAS, Met. N.Y. Assn. for Applied Psychology (bd. dirs. 1979-87, pres. 1983-84), Human Resource Planning Soc. Mem. United Ch. Christ. Club: Yale (N.Y.C.). Office: Personnel Strategies Inc 1 Mountain Blvd Ste 201 Warren NJ 07060

GREMBAN, JOE LAWRENCE, utilities company executive; b. Goodman, Wis., June 3, 1920; s. Joseph and Anna (Kryzyak) G.; m. V. June Smith, June 8, 1945; children: Ronald D., Keith D., Brian D. BBA, U. Wis., 1948; postgrad., U. Mich., 1973, U. Mich., 1974. Spl. acct. in budgeting, income tax reports, analysis Cen. Ill. Electric & Gas Co., Rockford, 1948-62; asst. treas. Sierra Pacific Power Co., Reno, 1962-63, corp. sec., 1963-69, v.p., 1969-71, v.p., sec., treas., 1971-72, fin. v.p., treas., 1972-73, exec. v.p., 1973-75, pres., 1975-76, pres., chief exec. officer, 1976-80, chmn., pres., chief exec. officer, 1980-86, chmn., chief exec. officer, 1986-87, chmn. bd., 1987-89; mem. faculty industry adv. com. Pub. Utilities Edn., U. Mich., 1974; bd. dirs. WEST Assocs., Western Regional Coun., Econ. Devel. Authority of Western Nev., pres. 1988; mem. adv. bd. Coll. Bus. Administrn. U. Nev., Reno. Past pres., past commr., mem. exec. bd. Nev. Area coun. Boy Scouts Am.; past dir. Reno Better Bus. Bur.; dir., past pres. United Way of No. Nev.; bd. dir. Internat. Winter Spl. Olympic Games, 1989; chmn. Salvation Army capital campaign com. With USAAF, 1942-45. Mem. Nat. Assn. Accts. (past pres. Reno chpt.), Reno Execs. Club (past pres.), Edison Electric Inst., Pacific Coast Gas Assn. (past dir.), Pacific Coast Elec. Assn. (past pres., dir.), Greater Reno-Sparks C. of C. Lodge: Rotary. Home: 2865 Juliann Way Reno NV 89509 Office: Sierra Pacific Resources PO Box 30150 6100 Neil Rd Reno NV 89520-3150

GREMBOWSKI, EUGENE, insurance company executive; b. Bay City, Mich., July 21, 1938; s. Barney Thomas and Mary (Senkowski) G.; m. Teresa Ann Frasik, June 27, 1959; children: Bruce Allen, Debora Ann. AA, Allan Hancock U., 1963; BA, Mich. State U., 1967; MBA, George Washington U., 1972. Enlisted USAF, 1955, commd. 2d lt., 1968, advanced through grades to capt., 1971; personnel officer USAF, Goldsboro, N.C., 1968-70; chief of procurement USAF, Cheyenne, Wyo., 1971-73; contract analyst USAF, Omaha, 1973-76; chief of contracting USAF, Atwater, Calif., 1976-79; ret. USAF, 1979; office supr. Farmers Ins. Group of Cos., Merced, Calif., 1980-85, office mgr., 1985-86; fleet mgr. Los Angeles, 1986—. Author: Governmental Purchasing: Its Progression Toward Professional Status, 1972. Cubmaster Boy Scouts Am., Goldsboro, 1968; com. chmn. Am. Heart Assn., Merced-Mariposa, Calif., 1985, sec.-treas., 1986. Recipient Meritorious Service medals Office of the Pres., 1973, 76. Mem. Nat. Contract Mgmt. Assn., Nat. Assn. Fleet Administrs. Home: 14633 Mountain Spring St Hacienda Heights CA 91745 Office: Farmers Ins Group 4750 Wilshire Blvd Los Angeles CA 90010

GRENING, L. KEITH, automotive executive; b. Mt. Vernon, N.Y., June 26, 1957; s. Nancy Jean (Battista) G.; m. Melissa Foster, May 26, 1985. AA, Westchester Community Coll., Valhalla, N.Y., 1977; BA, Westchester Med. Coll., 1980. With chemotherapy x-ray dept. St. Johns Riverside Meml. Hosp., Secaucus, N.J., 1980-84; bus. mgr. White Plains (N.Y.) Nissan, Inc., 1984—.

GRENON, TIMOTHY LOUIS, computer programmer, insurance analyst; b. Barre, Vt., May 10, 1963; s. Louis Roger and Muriel (Butler) G. AS, Champlain Coll., 1985. Analyst Nat. Life Vt., Montpelier, 1986—. Democrat. Roman Catholic. Home: School St PO Box 75 Websterville VT 05678

GRESHAM, ANN ELIZABETH, retailer, horticulturist executive; b. Richmond, Va., Oct. 11, 1933; d. Allwin Stagg and Ruby Scott (Faber) Gresham. Student, Peace Coll., Raleigh, N.C., 1950-52, East Carolina U., 1952-53, Penland Sch., N.C., 1953-54, Va. Commonwealth U., 1960-64. Owner, prin. Ann Gresham's Gift Shop, Richmond, 1953-56; pres., treas. Gresham's Garden Ctr., Inc., Richmond, 1955-79; v.p. Gresham's Nursery, Inc., Richmond, 1959-73, pres., treas., 1973—; pres., treas. Gresham's Country Store, Richmond, 1964—; tchr., 1982—. Bd. dirs. Bainbridge Community Ministry, 1979, Handworkshop, 1984—; class agt. Peace Coll., Raleigh, 1987-88, mem. alumnae council, 1987, 88—, bd. visitors, 1987—; focus group mem. Hand Workshop, Richmond, 1983, bd. dirs., 1984-87. Mem. Midlothian Antique Dealers (treas. 1975-79), Richmond Quilt Guild (chpt. v.p. 1983-84), Nat. Needlework Assn., Quilt Inst., Am. Hort. Soc. Episcopalian. Clubs: Chesmond Women's (v.p. 1979-80), James River Woman's (Richmond). Home: 2324 Logan St Bon Air VA 23235 Office: Gresham's Inc 6725 Midlothian Pike Richmond VA 23225

GRESHAM, GARY STUART, wholesale grocery executive, accountant; b. Boerne, Tex., July 25, 1951; s. Benton Noel and Ida Minnie (Voges) G.; m. Peggy Louise Sears, Aug. 25, 1973; children: Julie Danielle, Leslie Claire. AA, San Antonio Jr. Coll., 1971; BBA, Southwest Tex. State U., 1973. CPA, Tex. Acct. Sweeney and Co., San Antonio, 1973-79, treas., 1979-83, v.p. fin., 1983—. Treas. Cen. Christian Ch. (Disciple of Christ), San Antonio, 1983; adv. com. bus. sch. curiculum San Antonio Jr. Coll., 1986-87. Mem. Am. Inst. CPA's, Tex. Soc. CPA's, San Antonio Chpt. CPA's. Republican. Office: Sweeney & Co 2330 S Roosevelt Rd San Antonio TX 78210

GRESOV, BORIS (VLADIMIR), economist; b. St. Petersburg, Russia, Aug. 7, 1914; s. Paul Vladimir and Maria de Suzor G.; m. Letitia Coxen Graham, June 21, 1945; children: Winston Graham, Christopher Leo. BA with honors, Cambridge U., Eng., 1938, MA with honors, 1952. With Office Econ. Warfare (Unit of War Prodn. Bd.), prodn. mgr. Compania Nacional Minera de Taxco S.A., Mex., 1941-45; v.p. Industrias y Minas S.A., Mex., 1945-49; cons. economist Shields & Co., N.Y.C., 1949-52, G.H. Walker & Co., N.Y.C., 1952-58, E.W. Axe & Co., N.Y.C., 1957-61; dir., mem. exec. com. Western Devel. Co. of Del., Santa Fe, 1954-61; mem. adv. bd. Axe Sci. and Electronics Corp., N.Y.C., 1957-61; dir. The Flying Tiger Line, Inc., Burbank, Calif., 1957-65, Axe-Templeton Growth Fund of Can., Ltd., N.Y.C., 1958-61, Internat. Oil & Gas Corp., Denver, 1961-66; dir., chmn. bd., chief exec. officer Shattuck Denn Mining Corp., N.Y.C., 1958-60, bd. dirs., chmn. exec. com., 1962; founder, pres. Excelsior Fund Inc., 1963—; chmn. Standard Metals Corp., 1963—, pres., chief exec. officer, 1965—; dir. USLIFE Income Fund, Inc., N.Y.C., 1976-86. Mem. Union Soc. (Cambridge, Eng.). Chevalier of Confrerie de la Chaine des Rotisseurs. Mem. Econ. Club N.Y., Nat. Economists Club, N.Y. Soc. Security Analysts Inc.,

Am. Inst. Mgmt. (pres.'s council), N.Y. Assn. Bus. Economists. Roman Catholic. Clubs: Metropolitan, University, Met. Opera (N.Y.C.); The L.I. Wyandanch Club (Eastport, LI., N.Y.); Westhampton Country (Westhampton Beach, L.I.); Surf (Quoque, L.I.). Home: 45 E 72d St New York NY 10021 Office: 45 Rockefeller Pla New York NY 10111

GRESS, EDWARD J(ULES), director university program, consultant; b. Jerusalem, Jan. 11, 1940; came to U.S., 1966; s. Jules Charles and Mary (Alonzo) G.; m. Katie Lorenzo, Sept. 30, 1962; children: Albert, Richard, Alexander. BBA, Am. U. Beirut, 1961, MBA, 1964; PhD, U. Ariz., 1970. Instr. acctg. Am. U. Beirut, 1961-66; lectr. acctg. U. Ariz., Tucson, 1967-70; assoc. prof. acctg. U. Saskatchewan, Saskatoon, Can., 1970-72; vis. assoc. prof. Am. U. Cairo, 1973-74; assoc. prof. Northeast La. U., Monroe, 1972-76; prof. Canisius Coll., Buffalo, 1976-78, chmn. acctg. dept., dir. MBA acctg. program, prof., 1981—, dir. TAG bus. ctr., 1988—. Recipient Faculty award Haskins and Sells Found., 1968, George Washington Honor medal Freedoms Found Valley Forge, 1986, 87; named Hon. Citizen City of Tucson, 1969. Mem. Fin. Execs. Inst. (chmn. acad. relations com.), Arab Soc. Cert. Accountants, Am. Acctg. Assn., Am. Mgmt. Assn., Arab Mgmt. Soc. (founding). Republican. Roman Catholic. Office: Canisius Coll 2001 Main St Buffalo NY 14208

GRESSETTE, LAWRENCE M., JR., utilities executive; b. 1932; married;. BS, Clemson U., 1954; LLB, U. S.C., 1959. With S.C. Electric and Gas Co. subs. SCANA Corp., Columbia, 1982—, now v.p. legal, fin., govt. and regulatory affairs; with SCANA Corp., Columbia, 1982—, pres., 1985—; vice-chmn. S.C. Pipelines Corp., Columbia; bd. dirs. S.C. Nat. Corp., S.C. Nat. Bank. Office: SCANA Corp 1426 Main St Columbia SC 29226 *

GRESSLE, E. MARK, financial advisor; b. Sharon, Pa., Sept. 17, 1950; s. Lloyd E. and Marguerite Louise (Kirkpatrick) G.; m. Deborah G. Feinstein, Sept. 28, 1980. BA, U. Rochester, 1972, MBA, 1980. Officer Chase Manhattan Bank, N.Y.C., 1980-82; co-owner Stern, Stewart & Co., N.Y.C., 1982—. Contbg. editor editor book Blackwell Guide to Wall St., 1988, Corporate Restructuring: Methods and Motives, The Treasurer, 1988. Office: Stern Stewart & Co 450 Park Ave New York NY 10022

GRETZINGER, RALPH EDWIN, III, management consultant; b. Louisville, Sept. 7, 1948; s. Ralph Edwin Jr. and Martha Irene (Jennings) G.; m. Jewel Jean Rocker, Mar. 21, 1970; children: Ralph Edwin IV, Sarah Elizabeth. BS in Applied Math., Ga. Inst. Tech., 1970; MBA, U. Utah, 1974. Group mgr. Prudential Ins. Co., Cin., 1974-76; ptnr., regional office mgr. Hewitt Assocs., Lincolnshire, Ill., 1976-78, Dayton, Ohio, 1978-81, Dallas, 1981—. Trustee Child Care Partnership of Dallas, 1985—. Served with U.S. Army, 1971-74. Mem. S.W. Pension Conf., Ga. Tech. Club of North Tex. (pres. 1986-88), Beta Gamma Sigma. Roman Catholic. Office: Hewitt Assocs 2001 Ross Ave Suite 1150 Dallas TX 75201

GREVE, EINAR, utilities executive; b. Bergen, Norway, 1928. Grad., Tech. Inst. Norway, 1951, MIT, 1953. Formerly pres., chief exec. officer Tucson Electric Power Co., now chmn., pres., chief exec. officer, also bd. dirs.; chmn., chief exec. officer Escavada Leasing Co., Ariz., Valencia Energy Co., Ariz. Office: Tucson Electric Power Co 220 W 6th St Tucson AZ 85701 *

GREVE, MARILYN J., small business owner, interior decorator; b. Indpls., Jan. 13, 1943; d. Harry Winfred and Zylphia Ruth (Romeril) Dickerson; m. Wayne Gordon Greve, June 18, 1964; 1 child, Rodney Wayne. Interior decorator Ortonville, Mich., 1975-77; owner Frames by Marilyn, Ortonville, 1977-85, Flint, Mich., 1984—. Organist, Christ Community Nazerene Ch., Goodrich, Mich., 1972-86. Mem. Profl. Picture Framers Assn. (student 1986-87), Nat. Fedn. Ind. Bus., Ortonville C. of C. (sec. 1983-84, v.p. 1984-85). Republican. Home: 8295 Caribou Tr Clarkston MI 48016 Office: Frames by Marilyn G4215 Miller Rd Flint MI 48507

GREW, ROBERT RALPH, lawyer; b. Metamora, Ohio, Mar. 25, 1931; s. Edward Francis and Coletta Marie G.; m. Anne Gano Bailey, Aug. 2, 1958; 1 son, Christopher Adam. A.B., U. Mich., 1953, J.D., 1955. Bar: Mich. 1955, N.Y. 1958. Assoc., Carter, Ledyard & Milburn, N.Y.C., 1957-68, ptnr., 1968—; lectr. legal problems in banking and in venture capital investments Practising Law Inst. Mem. Pilgrims of U.S., English Speaking Union (nat. v.p. 1989—), Internat. Bar Assn., ABA, N.Y. State Bar Assn. (chmn. health law com. 1986-89), Assn. of Bar of City of N.Y. Republican. Clubs: Union, Down Town Assn., Lansdowne (London). Office: Carter Ledyard & Milburn 2 Wall St New York NY 10005

GREY, FRANCIS JOSEPH, accounting company executive, educator; b. Yeadon, Pa., Nov. 30, 1931; s. William and Delia (Mullen) G.; m. Marlene M. Ward, June 24, 1961; children: Francis Joseph Jr., Melissa Ann. BS in Econs., Villanova U., 1958. CPA. Tax profl. Coopers and Lybrand, Phila., 1958-64; tax ptnr. in charge Coopers and Lybrand, Washington, 1964-72; mng. ptnr. tax Coopers and Lybrand, Phila., 1972—; mem. devel. com. Villanova (Pa.) U., 1972—; bd. dirs. Del. County Hosp., Upper Darby, Pa. Author: Tax Planning for Real Estate, 1978, 88, Pa. Taxation of Corporations, 1980; contbr. articles to profl. jours. Adv. com. Wharton Sch. Tax Conf., Phila., 1970-88, Internat. Bus. Forum, Phila., 1980-88. Sgt. U.S. Army, 1952-53, Korea. Mem. Am. Inst. CPA's, Pa. Inst. CPA's (v.p. 1988), Internat. Fiscal Assn. (treas. 1975—), Phila. C. of C. (bd. dirs. 1975—), Phila. Country Club (bd. dirs. 1980-83), Union League of Phila., Peace Club, Beta Gamma Sigma. Republican. Roman Catholic. Office: Coopers & Lybrand 2400 11 Pennsylvania Ctr Philadelphia PA 19103

GREY, ROCHELLE, banker; b. Reading, Pa., Aug. 10, 1964; d. Robert Harry and Betty Jane Grey. BA, Alvernia Coll., 1986; postgrad., Lehigh U., 1988—. Customer service rep., then asst. mgr. Household Fin. Co., Pottstown, Pa., 1986-87, sr. asst. mgr., 1987; mgmt. trainee Bank of Pa., Reading, 1987, asst. mgr., 1988—. Mem. exec. bd. Citizens for Good Govt., Reading, 1986—; vol. citizen's polit. campaigns, Reading, 1986, 88, United Way, Boyertown, Pa., 1988; asst. campaign mgr. Citizens to Elect Stallone Judge, Reading, 1987. Mem. Bus. and Profl. Women (co-chair ways and means com., personal devel. com. 1988), NAFE, Nat. Assn. Bank Women. Home: 119 W 37th Reiffton PA 19606 Office: Bank of Pa 30 N 5th St Reading PA 19601

GREYTAK, LEE JOSEPH, real estate development company executive; b. Bridgeport, Conn., Sept. 14, 1949; s. Eugene E. and Dorothy B. Greytak; BA in Acctg., Calif. State U., Fullerton, 1973; m. Judy C. Welch, Aug. 31, 1974; children: Marzette Rachelle, Melissa Renee. Sr. acct. Collins Foods Internat., Los Angeles, 1974-75; asst. controller Jack La Lanne European Health Spas, Los Angeles, 1975-77; controller Trammell Crow Co., Los Angeles, 1977-83, corp. sec., 1981-83; v.p., chief fin. officer T.D. Service Fin. 1983—, also bd. dirs., trustee Stock Ownership Plan, 1983—; dir. Guardian Title Agy., 1983—; pres., Territory Devel., 1983—. Mem. Nat. Assn. Accts., Am. Mgmt. Assn., Nat. Cash Mgmt. Assn., So. Calif. Cash Mgmt. Assn., Builders, Owners, and Mgrs. Assn., Aircraft Owners and Pilots Assn., C. of C. of U.S., Young Execs. of So. Calif., Christian Businessmens Com. of USA. Home: 2918 E Shamrock Ave Brea CA 92621 Office: TD Service Fin 601 Lewis St Orange CA 92668

GRIBBLE, CAROLE L., wholesale distributing executive; b. Toppenish, Wash., May 19, 1940; d. Harold Max and Gertrude Louisa (Spicer) Smith; m. Duane E. Clark, Aug. 1959 (div. 1963); 1 child, David Allen; m. Vance William Gribble, May 19, 1966. Student, Seattle Pacific Coll. With B.F. Shearer, Seattle, 1959-60, Standard Oil, Seattle, 1960-62, Seattle Platen Co., 1962-70; ptnr. West Coast Platen, Los Angeles, 1970-87, Waldorf Towers Apts., Seattle, 1970—, Cascade Golf Course, North Bend, Wash., 1970-88, Pacific Wholesale Office Equipment, Seattle and Los Angeles, 1972-87; owner Pacific Wholesale Office Equip.dba Bob Bianco Sales, Seattle and Los Angeles, 1988—, Pac Electronic Service Ctr., Commerce and San Pablo, Calif., 1988—. Republican. Methodist. Office: Pacific Wholesale Equipment 1512 7th Ave Seattle WA 98101

GRIBOW, DALE SEWARD, lawyer, business executive; b. Chgo., June 18, 1943; s. Obby and Norma (Howard) G. BA, U. So. Calif., 1965; JD, Loyola U., Los Angeles, 1968; advanced legal studies UCLA, U. So. Calif. Bar: Calif. 1970. U.S. Dist. Ct. (cen. dist.) Calif. 1970, U.S. Supreme Ct. 1977. Dep. public defender Los Angeles County, 1970-74; sr. partner Gribow, Benjamin & Sandler, Beverly Hills, Calif., 1974-76; sole practice, Beverly Hills, 1976—; pres., chmn. bd. Nutritional Biol. Corp., Los Angeles, 1981-83; owner Exec. Credit Control, Inc., Los Angeles, 1979-83, DDM Properties, Los Angeles, 1981-86; judge pro tem Los Angeles Mcpl. Ct., 1977—, Van Nuys, West Los Angeles, Beverly Hills mcpl. cts., 1983—; dir. Aspen mktg.; mem. adv. bd. Dist. Atty. Los Angeles, 1976-78; city Atty. Los Angeles, 1980-83; guest lectr. univs. Contbr. articles to profl. jours. Mem. U.S. Congressional Adv. Bd., 1982-83; selected 1982 fund raising chmn. Loyola Law Sch. Alumni; founder Concerned Adults for Dubnoff Sch., a sch. for handicapped children, 1972, pres., 1974-77, 80-81, bd. dirs., 1974-83; bd. dirs. Thalians, 1975—, exec. bd., 1983—, exec. v.p., 1984—, exec. vice chmn., 1988—, program chmn., 1983-84, mem. exec. com. Presidents Club, 1980—, chmn. Thalian Ball, 1987, 88; bd. dirs. Guardians Jewish Home for Aged, 1981—, v.p., 1983-84, chmn. spl. events, 1983; bd. dirs. Westside chpt. Kidney Found., West Side Symphony Assn., 1982-84, Ctr. for Improvement Child Caring, 1983-85, Dubnoff Ctr. for Handicapped Children, 1974-85, Boys and Girls Club Los Angeles, 1982-85, founder, chmn. bd. Beverly Hills Men's Charities, 1981—, Scopus Soc., 1983— (award 1988); mem. nat. com. Presdl. Task Force, 1989; founding mem. Children's Liver Transplant Found., 1983-84; contbg. mem. City of Hope, Nat. Jewish Hosp. and Research Center, St. Jude's Hosp., Simon Weisenthal Center for Holocaust Studies, Patrons Art Soc., Greater Los Angeles Zoo Assn., Los Angeles County Mus., Natural History Mus., Earl Warren Inst., Los Angeles World Affairs Council, Mcpl. League Beverly Hills, Am. Film Inst., Commerce Assocs. of U. So. Calif., West Los Angeles Boosters Assn.; v.p. Am. Friends Hebrew U., 1985— (award 1988); trustee U. Judaism Continuing Edn., 1984-86. Recipient David Schloss Meml. award, 1974; plaque City of Los Angeles, 1977, 80, 82; named hon. Ky. Col., 1981; commendation from Gov. Jerry Brown, 1982; resolution Calif. State Assembly and Senate, 1982; award for service Ronald McDonald House for Childrens Cancer, 1984; numerous other commendations and proclamations; Dale Seward Gribow Day proclaimed in Beverly Hills, 1982, 88; Dale Seward Gribow Day declared in Los Angeles, 1988. Mem. Los Angeles Jaycees, U. So. Calif. Law Alumni, State Bar Calif., Los Angeles County Bar Assn. (cert. of appreciation 1984), Beverly Hills Bar Assn. (cert. of appreciation 1984), West Hollywood Bar Assn., San Fernando Valley Bar Assn., Calif. Trial Lawyers Assn., Los Angeles Trial Lawyers Assn., Los Angeles Criminal Cts. Bar Assn., Calif. Attys. for Criminal Justice, San Fernando Valley Criminal Cts. Bar Assn., Scopus Soc. (dir. 1983—, chmn. 1986—), Vikings, Blue Key, Phi Alpha Delta. Democrat. Jewish. Clubs: Friars (membership com.), Variety (dir. 1982-85), Magic Castle, Marbles (dir.), PIPS (v.p., dir. 1982—), J. Daniels. Lodge: B'nai B'rith. Office: 9777 Wilshire Blvd Suite 918 Beverly Hills CA 90212

GRIECH, FREDERICK G., telephone company executive; b. Ridgway, Pa., 1945; married;. BSME, Gannon Coll., 1967. With Elyria (Ohio) Telephone Co. Inc., from 1967, pres., 1978; v.p. Ohio Inc. (formerly Mid-Ohio Telephone Co.) subs. Alltel Corp., Newark, 1979, pres., 1981—, also bd. dirs.; now also pres. telephone ops. Alltel Corp., Hudson, Ohio. Office: Alltel Corp 100 Executive Pkwy Hudson OH 44236 *

GRIESEMER, JOHN N., manufacturing executive; b. Mt. Vernon, Mo., Nov. 30, 1930; s. Joseph John and Margaret (Arend) G.; m. Kathleen A. Poirot, Feb. 7, 1959; children: Margaret, Julia, Joseph E., John F., Stephen. BSCE, U. Mo., 1953. Supt. Griesemer Stone Co., Springfield, Mo., 1956-59, v.p., 1959-74, pres., 1974—; chmn. bd. govs. U.S. Postal Svc., 1987, 88; bd. dirs. Boatmen's Nat. Bank of Springfield. Co-chmn. Sprinfield Cath. Schs. Devel. Fund, 1984-86. With USAF, 1953-56, Japan. Mem. Mo. Limestone Producers Assn. (pres. 1963), Na.t Limestone Inst. (chmn. 1974), Nat. Stone Assn. (Dist. Govt. Svc. award 1988). Republican. Roman Catholic. Home: Rte 2 Box 204-B Springfield MO 65802 Office: Greisemer Stone Co PO Box 2240 Springfield MO 65801

GRIESHOBER, WILLIAM EDWARD, horticulture company executive; b. Erie, Pa., Jan. 10, 1942; s. William Herman and Vera Mae (Guthrie) G.; m. Shelley Alojee Liberg, Sept. 15, 1962; Margaret, William. BBA, Gannon U., Erie, 1969; postgrad., Pa. State U., 1988. CPA, Pa. Staff acct. J.A. Swift, CPA, Erie, 1969-71; internal auditor Massey Ferguson, Inc., Des Moines, 1971-73; audit mgr. Foster & Gallagher, Inc., Peoria, Ill., 1973-77; acctg. mgr. Foster & Gallagher, Inc., Peoria, 1977-78; audit dir. Welch Foods, Inc., Westfield, N.Y., 1978-82; controller Welch Foods, Inc., Westfield, 1982-88; v.p., controller Spring Hill Nurseries Inc., Peoria, Ill., 1988—. Treas. Cystic Fibrosis Assn., Erie County, 1986-87; treas., pres., 1988; treas. St. Gregory Roman Cath. Ch., North East, Pa., 1986-87, pres., 1988; tutor Literacy Vols. of Am., 1988—, Peoria Project Upward. Served with USN, 1960-62. Mem. Fin. Execs. Inst. (ethics and eligibility com.), Inst. Internal Auditors (gov. 1980-81, Dist. Faculty award 1985), Pa. Inst. CPA's (coordinator spring 1986 jour. issue , polit. action com., bus., govt. and edn. com.), Nat. Inst. Accts. for Coops. (pres. northeast region 1985-86). Democrat.

GRIEVE, PIERSON MACDONALD, specialty chemicals and services company executive; b. Flint, Mich., Dec. 5, 1927; s. P.M. and Margaret (Leamy) G.; m. Florence R. Brogan, July 29, 1950; children: Margaret, Scott, Bruce. B.S. in Bus. Adminstrn., Northwestern U., 1950; postgrad., U. Minn., 1955-56. With Caterpillar Tractor Co., Peoria, Ill., 1950-52; staff engr. A.T. Kearney & Co. (mgmt. consultants), Chgo., 1952-55; pres. Rap-in-Wax, Mpls., 1955-62; exec. AP Parts Corp., 1962-67; pres., chief exec. officer Questor Corp., Toledo, 1967-82; chmn. bd., chief exec. officer (NYSE) Ecolab Inc., St. Paul, 1983—; bd. dirs. Diversified Energies, St. Paul Cos. Inc., Norwest Corp., Meredith Corp. Adv. council J.L. Kellogg Grad. Sch. Mgmt., Northwestern U.; bd. overseers Sch. Mgmt., U. Minn.; pres., bd. dirs. Guthrie Theatre. Served with USNR, 1945-46. Mem. Minn. Bus. Partnership (exec. com., pres.), Chevaliers du Tastevin, Beta Gamma Sigma (dirs. table). Episcopalian. Clubs: St. Paul Athletic, Minn. (St. Paul); Mpls. Office: Ecolab Inc Osborn Bldg Saint Paul MN 55102

GRIFFES, ALAN J., finance company executive; b. Louisville, May 15, 1956; s. William A. and Jean V. Griffes; m. M. Dawn Vice, July 25, 1976. AB in Bus., U. Ky., 1976, BLS in Bus., 1980, MAT in Bus., 1984; postgrad., Kensington U. Cert. fin. planner, estate and bus. analyst, registered health underwriter. Bus. mgr. Bldg. Houses and Rehab. Co., Louisville, 1974-79; ind. fin. cons. Louisville, 1979-80; fin. planner Prescott Ball Turben, Louisville, 1980-82; pres. First Fin. Advisors, Louisville, 1982—. Author: Financial Planning for 1990, 1987, Shopper's Guide to New Car Buying, 1987, The Money Mentor, 1988. Chmn. Entrep Soc., Louisville, 1984-86. Named Eagle Scout Boy Scouts of Am., 1972. Mem. Nat. Assn. Accts., Am. Mgmt. Assn., Nat. Assn. Health Underwriters, Nat. Assn. MBA Execs., Internat. Assn. for Fin. Planning (founder, pres. 1984-86), Inst. of Cert. Fin. Planners. Democrat. Presbyterian. Home: 3100 Frankfort Ave Louisville KY 40206 Office: First Fin Advisors 9200 Shelbyville Rd Louisville KY 40206

GRIFFIN, BILLY L., electric utility company executive; b. 1930. B.S., Clemson U., 1952. With Fla. Power Corp. (subs. Fla. Progress Corp.), St. Petersburg, 1954—, dir. div. ops., 1970-71, asst. v.p. div. ops., 1971-72, asst. v.p. constrn. maintenance ops., 1972-73, v.p. systems ops., 1973-77, sr. v.p. engring. constrn., 1977-83, exec. v.p., 1983—. Served to 1st lt. U.S. Army, 1952-54. Office: Fla Power Corp 3201 34th St S Saint Petersburg FL 33711

GRIFFIN, DEWITT JAMES, architect, real estate developer; b. Los Angeles, Aug. 26, 1914; s. DeWitt Clinton and Ada Gay (Miller) G.; m. Jeanmarie Donald, Aug. 19, 1940 (dec. Sept. 1985); children: Barbara Jean Griffin Holst, John Donald, Cornelia Caulfield Claudius, James DeWitt; m. Vivienne Dod Kievenaar, May 6, 1989. Student, UCLA, 1936-38; B.A., U. Calif., 1942. Designer Kaiser Engrs., Richmond, Calif., 1941; architect CF Braun & Co., Alhambra, Calif., 1946-48; pvt. practice architecture Pasadena, Calif., 1948-50; prin. Goudie & Griffin Architects, San Jose, Calif., 1949-64, Griffin & Murray, 1964-66, DeWitt J. Griffin & Assocs., 1966-69; pres. Griffin/Joyce Assocs., Architects, 1969-80; chmn. Griffin Balzhiser Affiliates (Architects), 1974-80; founder, pres. Griffin Cos. Internat., 1980—; founder, dir. San Jose Savs. and Loan Assn., 1965-75, Capitol Services Co., 1964-77, Esandel Corp., 1965-77. Pub. Sea Power mag, 1975-77; archtl. works include U.S. Post Office, San Jose, 1966, VA Hosp, Portland, 1976, Bn. Barracks Complex, Ft. Ord, Calif., 1978. bd. dirs. San Jose Symphony Assn., 1973-84, v.p. 1977-79, pres. 1979-81; active San Jose Symphony Found., 1981-86, v.p. 1988—; bd. dirs. Coast Guard Acad. Found., 1974-87, Coast Guard Found., 1987—; founder, bd. dirs. U.S. Navy Meml. Found., 1978-80, trustee, 1980—; trustee Montalvo Ctr. for Arts, 1982-88. Served to comdr. USNR, 1942-46, 50-57. Recipient Navy Meritorious Pub. Service medal, 1971, Disting. Service medal Navy League of U.S., 1973; Coast Guard Meritorious Pub. Service medal, 1975; Navy Distinguished Pub. Service medal, 1977; Coast Guard Distinguished Pub. Service medal, 1977. Fellow Soc. Am. Mil. Engrs.; emeritus mem. AIA; mem. U.S. Naval Inst., Navy League U.S. (pres. Santa Clara Valley council 1963-66, Calif. state pres. 1966-69, nat. dir. 1967—, exec. com. 1968—, pres. 12th region 1969-71, nat. v.p. 1973-75, nat. pres. 1975-77, chmn. 1977-79), U.S. Naval Sailing Assn., San Francisco C. of C., Naval Order of U.S., Phi Gamma Delta. Republican. Congregationalist. Clubs: St. Francis Yacht, Commonwealth of San Francisco, Island Yacht Club (treas.). Home and Office: 45 Mt Lassen Dr San Rafael CA 94903

GRIFFIN, DONALD WAYNE, defense company executive; b. Evansville, Ind., Mar. 1, 1937; s. Pauline Marie (Rahm) G.; m. Kristanya Johnson; children: Kristanya Anne, Kirstin Alyson. Student, Ind. U., 1954-57; BSBA, Evansville Coll., 1961. Sales rep. organics and explosives Olin Corp., Knoxville, Tenn., 1961-62; sales rep., dist. sales mgr. brass sales dept. Olin Corp., Indpls., 1964-69; dist. sales mgr. Milw., 1969-73; asst. to dir. field sales, s.w. region sales mgr. East Alton, Ill., 1973-77, dir. field sales, 1977-80, dir. internat. bus. devel., 1980-81; v.p. mktg. brass group Olin Corp., East Alton, 1981-83, pres. brass group, 1983-85, pres. Winchester group, 1985-86, pres. def. systems group, 1986-87, exec. v.p., pres. def. systems, 1987—; bd. dirs. Indy Electronic, Manteca, Calif., Ill. State Bank, East Alton. Bd. dirs. Leadership Council S.W. Ill., Edwardsville, 1984—, Alton Meml. Hosp., Ill., 1983—, St. Louis Regional Growth Assn., 1986—. Mem. Assn. U.S. Army, Am. Def. Preparedness Assn., Navy League U.S. (life), Am. Soc. Metals, Small Arms Ammunition Mfrs. (bd. dirs. 1985—), S.W. Ill. Indsl. Assn. (bd. dirs. 1985—), Ill. C. of C. (bd. dirs. 1985—), Wildlife Mgmt. Inst. (bd. dirs. 1986—), Nat. Shooting Sports Found. (bd. dirs. 1985—). Office: Olin Def Systems Group 427 N Shamrock East Alton IL 62024

GRIFFIN, GARY ARTHUR, technological executive; b. Yonkers, N.Y., Nov. 23, 1937; s. William Edmund and Madeline (Lane) G.; student Manhattan Coll., 1956-57, Westchester Community Coll., 1957-62; diploma LaSalle Extension U., 1968; m. Jacqueline Cahill, June 21, 1958; children: Lynn, Elizabeth, Margaret. Engring. cons. IBM Corp., Yorktown, N.Y., 1960-61; engring. cons. Perkin Elmer Corp., Norwalk, Conn., 1961-63; product devel. mgr. Technicon Corp., Tarrytown, N.Y., 1963-69; chmn., pres. Dynacon Research Corp., Rockland, N.Y., 1969-72; with Nat. Patent Devel. Corp., New Brunswick, N.J., 1973-82, corp. group v.p. new technologies, 1977-82, pres. Hydromed Scis. div., 1978-82, pres. NDP Dental Systems, Inc., 1979-82, pres. NPD Epic Systems, Inc., 1979-82, pres., dir. Amalgamated Fin. Services, Inc., 1979-82, v.p., dir. NPD Productos Médicos, S.A., 1979-82, Washburn Ltd., 1979-82; pres., dir. Applied Genetics, Inc., 1981-82; dir. FCS Industries, Inc., Flemington, N.J., 1982—, sr. v.p., 1982-87, treas., 1984-87; chmn. chief operating officer, pres. Circuitech Inc., Eatontown, N.J., 1982-85, now dir.; chmn., pres., treas. Executrex Internat. Inc., Milltown, N.J., 1985—. Served with USNR, 1954-62. Mem. Am. Prodn. and Inventory Control Soc., Am. Mgmt. Assn., IEEE, Am. Assn. Advancement of Med. Instrumentation, Am. Entrepreneurs Assn., Internat. Entrepreneurs Assn., Smithsonian Assn., N.Y. Vet. Police Assn. Republican. Roman Catholic. Patentee in field. Office: Executrex 440 S Main Milltown NJ 08850

GRIFFIN, HARRY FREDERICK, financial executive; b. Birmingham, Ala., Apr. 21, 1951; s. Harry Clay and Osie Virginia (Johnson) G. BS in Mgmt., Fin., U. Ala., 1980; MBA, Samford U., 1983. Cert. Fin. Planner. Owner HFG Fin.Services Co., Birmingham, Ala., 1984-86; registered rep. Waddell & Reed Fin. Co., Birmingham, 1986; account mgr. The Acadia Fin. Group, Birmingham, 1987; cert. fin. planner, v.p. Jefferson Fed. Savs. & Loan, Birmingham, 1988—; instr. Birmingham Adult Edn. Sch., 1986—, U. Ala., Birmingham, 1988—. Capt. U.S. Army, 1970-73; Ala. N.G., 1980—. Republican. Baptist. Office: Jefferson Fed Savs & Loan 215 N 21st St Birmingham AL 35203

GRIFFIN, MELANIE HUNT, accounting firm executive; b. Corpus Christi, Tex., Oct. 25, 1949; d. Roy Albert and Ola Emma (Hunt) G.; m. Robert Thompson; children: Maurice Dale, Donald Dwight, Merideth Thompson, Laura Thompson. BBA summa cum laude, Corpus Christi State U., 1977. CPA, Tex.; cert. fin. planner. Sec.-treas. Roy Hunt, Inc., Corpus Christi, 1970-78, dir., 1970—; v.p. White, Sluyter & Co., Corpus Christi, 1978-80; pres. Whittington & Griffin, Corpus Christi, 1980-82, also dir.; sec.-treas., dir. Sand Express, Inc., Corpus Christi, 1975—; prin. Melanie Hunt Griffin CPA, Corpus Christi, 1982—; ptnr. Fields, Nemec & co., Corpus Christi, 1984—. Devel. chair Am. Heart Assn., 1987, Leadership Corpus Christi Alumni, 1982-83. Mem. Tex. Soc. CPA's (v.p. 1988—, dir. 1987-88, pres. Corpus Christi chpt. 1987-88), Corpus Christi State Univ. Alumni (dir. 1987—), Exec. Women Internat. (chair philanthropy com. 1986-87), Internat. Assn. Cert. Fin. Planners, Internat. Assn. Fin. Planners, Am. Inst. CPA's (personal fin. planning div.), Bus. and Estate Planning Council. Home: 10817 Stonewall St Corpus Christi TX 78410 Office: Fields Nemec & Co Po Box 23067 501 S Tancahoa Corpus Christi TX 78403

GRIFFIN, MERV EDWARD, entertainer, television producer, entrepreneur; b. San Mateo, Calif., July 6, 1925; s. Mervyn Edward and Rita (Robinson) G.; m. Julann Elizabeth Wright, May 18, 1958 (div. June 1976); 1 son, Anthony Patrick. Student, San Mateo Coll., 1942-44; L.H.D., Emerson Coll., 1981. Owner MGP (Merv Griffin Prodns.), TAV, Hollywood, Calif.; owner 3 radio stas. 1965—; v.p., dir. spl. promotions Camelot Inc. subs. Am. Leisure Corp., 1981—, also bd. dirs.; owner Teleview Racing Patrol Inc., Miami, Fla., Beverly Hilton Hotel, Beverly Hills, Calif., various hotels and casinos. Performer, Merv Griffin Show radio sta. KFRC, San Francisco, 1945-48, vocalist, Freddy Martin's Orch., 1948-52; contract player, star: So This is Love, Warner Bros., 1953-55; TV master ceremonies, 1958—, Merv Griffin Show, NBC-TV, 1962-63, Westinghouse Broadcasting Co., 1965-69, CBS-TV, 1969-72, syndication, 1972—; currently producing: Dance Fever and Wheel of Fortune. Trustee Dr. Armand Hammer United World Coll. of Am. S.W. Club: Bohemian (San Francisco). Office: 1541 N Vine St Hollywood CA 90028 *

GRIFFIN, PETER J., finance executive; b. Glen Ridge, N.J., Mar. 31, 1943; s. Peter Cornelius and Kathleen Dolores (Gara) G.; m. Irene F. Hickey, Nov. 25, 1967; children: Kimberley, Allyson, Michael. BA, St. Peter's Coll., 1965; MBA, NYU, 1966. CPA, N.Y. Audit mgr. Price Waterhouse, N.Y.C., 1969-76; controller, mfg. div. Carter-Wallace, Inc., Cranbury, N.J., 1976-79, v.p., internat. fin., 1979-83; v.p., controller Carter-Wallace, Inc., N.Y.C., 1983—. Served as 1st lt. U.S. Army, 1967-69, Vietnam. Mem. Am. Inst. CPA's, Nat. Assn. Accts. Roman Catholic. Club: Bamm Hollow Country. Home: 17 Westminster Dr Colts Neck NJ 07722 Office: Carter-Wallace Inc 767 Fifth Ave New York NY 10153

GRIFFIN, PHILLIP STONE, I, plastics company executive; b. Norfolk, Va., Dec. 6, 1938; s. William Charles and Doris (Stone) G.; m. Carolyn Terretta, Feb. 1, 1964; children: Phillip Stone II, Susan Teretta. BA, U. Va., 1960; postgrad. in bus. adminstrn., NYU, 1964-66. Sales rep. Tiffany Pub. Co., Norfolk, 1960-63; sales service rep. NBC TV, N.Y.C., 1963-65; account exec. Vernard, Torbet and McConnell, N.Y.C., 1965-66; mgr. sales and mktg. O'Sullivan Corp., Winchester, Va., 1966-75, v.p., 1975—; mng. ptnr. G&L Investment Co., Winchester, 1975—. Active Rep. City Com., Winchester, Winchester Airport Commn.; del. Rep. State Conv.; bd. dirs. Shenandoah Area council Boy Scouts Am. Episcopalian. Club: Winchester Golf. Lodge: Rotary. Office: O'Sullivan Corp 1944 Valley Ave Winchester VA 22601

GRIFFIN, SHERRY LUMBERT, stockbroker, financial planner; b. Wichita, Kans., Jan. 5, 1937; s. J. Delos and Volna (Liston) Lumbert; m. Ralph Stephens Griffin, June 4, 1955; children: James D., Ralph E. Diploma, Draughon's Coll., Lubbock, Tex., 1955. Cert. fin. planner. Ops. mgr. Goodbody & Co., Carlsbad, N.Mex., 1967-71; stockbroker Quinn & Co., Inc., Carlsbad, 1971-83; asst. v.p., stockbroker, fin. planner Eppler, Guerin & Turner, Inc., Carlsbad, 1983—; bd. dirs., pres. Carlsbad Found. Mem. Internat. Assn. Fin. Planners, Inst. Cert. Fin. Planners, Carlsbad C. of

C. Republican. Mormon. Club: Millionaires. Home: 802 Elma Dr Carlsbad NM 88220 Office: EGT Inc 302 N Canyon PO Box 1898 Carlsbad NM 88221

GRIFFIN, THOMAS MCLEAN, retired lawyer; b. Lake Placid, N.Y., Sept. 12, 1922; s. Nathaniel Edward and Anne (McLean) G.; m. Hope Wiswall, July 16, 1949; children: Richard Wiswall, Anne McLean, Thomas McLean, David Coggin. AB, Harvard Coll., 1943; LLB, Harvard U., 1949. Bar: Mass. 1950, U.S. Supreme Ct. 1976. Atty. State Life Assurance Co. Am., Worcester, Mass., 1949-58; assoc. counsel Old Colony Trust Co., Boston, 1958-67; sec. bd. dirs. 1st Nat. Bank Boston, 1967-87, gen. counsel, 1971-87, ret., 1987; gen. counsel Bank of Boston Corp., 1973-87, chmn., sec. bd. dirs., 1970-87, ret., 1987. Trustee Morlboro (Vt.) Coll., 1986—, The House of Seven Gables Settlement Assn., Salem, Mass., the First Congregational Soc., Salem, Harmony Grove Cemetery, Salem. Served to lt. j.g. USNR, 1943-46, to comdr., 1960. Mem. ABA, Boston Bar Assn. Democrat. Clubs: Eastern Yacht. Home: 14 Beckford St Salem MA 01970

GRIFFIN, WILLIAM RALPH, business executive; b. Ft. Bragg, N.C., Oct. 30, 1943; s. Henry Ralph Griffin and Annie Maxine (Birmingham) Griffin Straughn; m. Jean Viola, June 12, 1965; children—W. Davis, Drew W. B.S., U.S. Mil. Acad., West Point, N.Y., 1965; M.B.A., Stanford U., Palo Alto, Calif., 1972. Asst. to pres. Chemed Corp., Cin., 1972-74, v.p. group exec., 1983-85, exec. v.p., 1983-85, also dir.; various positions dist. mgr. to v.p. sales, v.p. mktg. Dearborn Chem. Co., Lake Zurich, Ill., 1974-79; pres., dir. Roto-Rooter, Inc., Cin., 1983—. Served to capt. U.S. Army, 1965-70; Vietnam. Decorated Bronze Star, Bronze Star with oak leaf. Mem. Young Pres.' Orgn., Mensa, Phi Kappa Phi. Republican. Club: Cincinnati. Home: 5250 Drake Rd Cincinnati OH 45243 Office: Roto-Rooter Inc 1400 DuBois Tower Cincinnati OH 45202

GRIFFIS, CHARLES BURKS, investment banker; b. Clifton Forge, Va., Dec. 7, 1944; s. Charles and B. Genevieve G.; m. Patricia Ann Ford, Oct. 11, 1975; children: Megan, David. BA, Yale U., 1966; MBA, Columbia U., 1971. Fin. analyst Ford Motor Co., Dearborn, Mich., 1971-72; asst. treas. Joseph E. Seagram & Sons, Inc., N.Y.C., 1972-76; chief fin. officer J. Aron & Co., N.Y.C., 1976-81; ptnr. Goldman Sachs & Co., N.Y.C., 1981-83; pres. Charles Griffis & Co., Inc., Greenwich, Conn., 1983—; ptnr. Griffis, Sandler & Co., Greenwich, 1985—; chmn. bd. dirs. Griffis Metals, Ltd., Mid-Glamongan, Wales, Can. Am. Resources Group, Inc., Houston; bd. dirs. United Wine Producers, Ltd., London, Vesta Tech., Ltd., Ft. Lauderdale, Fla. Bd. dirs. adv. bd. Ctr. for Study of Futures Markets, Columbia U., N.Y.C., 1981—. Lt. USN., 1967-69. Mem. Columbia U. Bus. Sch. Alumnia Assn. (pres. 1978-83), Beta Gamma Sigma, Greenwich Club, Yale Club (N.Y.C.). Republican. Congregationalist. Clubs: Greenwich; Yale (N.Y.C.). Office: Griffis Sandler & Co 60 Arch St Greenwich CT 06830

GRIFFITH, ALAN RICHARD, banker; b. Mineola, N.Y., Dec. 17, 1941; s. Charles Ernest and Amalia (Guenther) G.; m. Elizabeth Ferguson, Nov. 28, 1964; children: Timothy, Elizabeth. BA, Lafayette Coll., Easton, Pa., 1964; MBA, CUNY, 1971. Asst. credit officer The Bank of N.Y., N.Y.C., 1968-72, asst. v.p., 1972-74, v.p., 1974-82, sr. v.p., 1982-85, exec. v.p., 1985-88, sr. exec. v.p., 1988—. Trustee Amyothrophic Lateral Sclerosis Assn., Sherman Oaks, Calif. Club: University (N.Y.C.). Office: Bank NY 48 Wall St New York NY 10286

GRIFFITH, DANIEL ALLEN, software publisher; b. Flint, Mich., July 22, 1951; s. Edwin Willis and Helen Marie (Kraski) G.; m. Diane Marie Skorka, Nov. 24, 1978; children: Alek, Renée, Michael. Student, U. Toledo, 1969-72, Mesa Coll., 1981-83; BSBA, U. Phoenix, 1989. Test leader Michel Electronics, Inc., Scottsdale, Ariz., 1975-77; test supr. Motorola Govt. Electronics, Scottsdale, Ariz., 1977-88; pres. Core Concepts, Inc., Tempe, Ariz., 1983—; cert. software developer Apple Computer Inc. Created software: Work Force II, 1983, Profit Pursuit, 1984; composer Derby Blues, 1977. Republican. Lutheran. Home: 1336 W 11th St Tempe AZ 85281 Office: Core Concepts Inc PO Box 28382 Tempe AZ 85282

GRIFFITH, EMLYN IRVING, lawyer; b. Utica, N.Y., May 13, 1923; s. William A. and Maud A. (Charles) G.; m. Mary L. Kilpatrick, Aug. 13, 1946; children: William L., James R. AB, Colgate U., 1942; JD, Cornell U., 1950; also hon. degrees. Bar: N.Y. 1950, U.S. Supreme Ct. 1954. Gen. practice Lockport, N.Y., 1950-52, Rome, N.Y., 1952—; ptnr. Griffith & Engelbrecht, Rome, N.Y., 1983—; bd. dirs. various corporations and predecessor firms. Contbr. articles to profl. jours. in U.S. and U.K. Mem. N.Y. State Bd. Regents, 1973—, Gov.'s Com. on Libraries, 1976-78, Forum of Edn. Orgn. Leaders, 1978-80, Intergovtl. Adv. Council on Edn., 1982-86; co-chmn. State Conf. on Professions, 1974-77, 85—; del. to China-U.S. Joint Session on Trade and Law, Beijing, 1987, Soviet-Am. Seminar on Comparative Edn., Moscow, 1988; trustee Aerospace Edn. Found., 1979—; v.p. Hon. Soc. Cymmrodorion, London, 1988—; pres. Nat. Assn. State Bds. Edn., 1979-80, Nat. Welsh-Am. Found., 1982-84; mem. exec. com. Bd. Pensions United Presbyn. Ch., 1966-72. Served to maj. USAAC, 1942-46. Recipient Alumni Disting. Service award Colgate U., 1975, Exceptional Service citation Air Force Assn., 1980; Doolittle fellow Aerospace Edn. Found., 1988. Fellow Am. Bar Found., N.Y. State Bar Found. (recipient Root-Stimson award for pub. service 1986, trustee 1989—); mem. ABA (com. pub. edn. 1974—), N.Y. State Bar Assn. (ho. of dels. 1974-76, com. lawyer competency 1986-89, co-chmn. com. atty. professionalism, 1989—, mem. bd. editors Bar Jour. 1986—), Oneida County Bar Assn. (pres. 1974-75), State Coun. County Bar Officers (chmn. 1974-76), Osgoode Soc. Can., Selden Soc. Eng., Phi Gamma Delta (mem. edn. found., pres., trustee 1982-86), Phi Alpha Delta. Clubs: Rome, Fort Orange of Albany, Colgate of N.Y.C. Office: Griffith & Engelbrecht 225 N Washington St Rome NY 13440

GRIFFITH, J(AMES) CLIFFORD, accountant; b. Dallas, Sept. 2, 1948; s. Zack C. and Kaleta Estelle (Ragan) G.; m. Linda Louise Fredrichsen, July 5, 1969; children: James Clifford Jr., Jennifer Cathleen. BBA, N. Tex. State U., 1974; M in Profl. Acctg., U. Tex., Arlington, 1978. CPA, Tex. Sr. mgr. Peat, Marwick, Mitchell & Co., Dallas-Ft. Worth, 1977-86; ptnr. Grant Thornton, Dallas, 1986-89; writer, editor Practitioners Pub. Co., Fort Worth, 1989—; chmn. Dallas Fin. Institutions Practice Grant Thornton, Dallas, 1986-89; mem. Grant Thornton's Nat. Fin. Insts. com. Editor: Currency, 1987. Mem. Tex. Soc. CPA's (savs. and loan com.), Am. Inst. CPA's, North Tex. State U. Alumni Assn. (adv. bd. acctg.), Acctg. Alumni Assn. U. Tex. Arlington (bd. dirs.). Baptist. Home: 5513 Scott Dr Fort Worth TX 76180 Office: Practitioners Pub Co 3221 Collinsworth Fort Worth TX 76107

GRIFFITH, PHILIP T., insurance automation executive; b. Hollywood, Calif., Apr. 23, 1949; s. Everette E. and Dorothy D. (Donaldson) G.; m. Nancy Ellen Winbury, Aug. 3, 1974; children: Julie, Emily. BA, Trinity Coll., 1971. Sr. systems analyst Hartford (Conn.) Ins. Group, 1977-81; 2d v.p. ARC/AMS, Boston, 1981—. Asst. coach Conn. Youth Orgn., Needham, Mass., 1988—. Mem. Acord (industry com. 1981—).

GRIFFITH, RICHARD L., service executive; b. 1931; married. BA, U. Colo.; JD, Georgetown U., 1959. With Cades Schutte Fleming and Wright, 1960-85, Amfac Inc., San Francisco, 1985—; formerly exec. v.p. Amfac Inc., now pres., chief exec. officer, dir.; chmn., chief exec. officer Amfac Hi Inc.; bd. dirs. HAL Inc., Honolulu, Calif. and Hawaiian Sugar Co., Concord, Calif. Office: Amfac Inc 44 Montgomery St San Francisco CA 94104 also: Amfac Inc 700 Bishop PO Box 3230 Honolulu HI 96801 *

GRIFFITH, STEVE CAMPBELL, JR., lawyer; b. Newberry, S.C., June 14, 1933; s. Steve Campbell and Bertie (Hambright) G.; m. Elizabeth Earhardt, May 22, 1976; children: Mary Salley, Elizabeth Jane, Frances Elizabeth, Katherine Earhardt. B.S., Clemson U., 1954; LL.B., U. S.C., 1959. Ptnr. Blease & Griffith Attys., Newberry, 1959-64; asst. gen. counsel Duke Power Co., Charlotte, N.C., 1964-71; sec., assoc. gen. counsel Duke Power Co., 1971-74, gen. counsel, 1975-77, v.p., gen. counsel, 1977-82, sr. v.p., gen. counsel, 1982—, dir., mem. exec. com., 1982—. Mem. S.C. Gen. Assembly, 1961-62. Served to 1st lt. U.S. Army, 1955-57. Mem. ABA, N.C. Bar Assn., S.C. Bar Assn., Mecklenberg Bar Assn. Democrat. Episcopalian. Clubs: Charlotte City, Charlotte Country. Lodge: Masons. Office: Duke Power Co 422 S Church St Charlotte NC 28242

GRIFFITH, STEVEN FRANKLIN, SR., lawyer, real estate title insurance agent and investor; b. New Orleans, July 14, 1948; s. Hugh Franklin and Rose Marie (Teutone) G.; m. Mary Elizabeth McMillan Frank, Dec. 9, 1972; children: Steven Franklin Jr., Jason Franklin. BBA, Loyola U. of the South, 1970, JD, 1972. Bar: La. 1972, U.S. Dist. Ct. (ea. dist.) La. 1975, U.S. Ct. Appeals (5th cir.) 1975, U.S. Supreme Ct. bar 1976. Law offices Senator George T. Oubre, Norco, La., 1971-75; sole practice, Destrehan, La., 1975—. Served to 1st lt. U.S. Army, 1970-72. Mem. ABA, La. Bar Assn., Assn. Trial Lawyers Am., La. Trial Lawyers Assn., New Orleans Trial Lawyers Assn., Fed. Bar Assn., Lions. Democrat.

GRIFFITHS, DAVID NEIL, utility executive; b. Oxford, Ind., Sept. 11, 1935; s. David Scifres and Lorene Francis Griffiths; m. Alice Anne Goodpasture, Aug. 9, 1959 (div. 1972); children—Beth Anne, David Douglas; m. Barbette Suzanne Goetsch, June 7, 1975; children—Michael, Megan. BS in Indsl. Econs., Purdue U., 1957. Various positions Delco Remy div. Gen. Motors Corp., Anderson, Ind., 1957-69; dep. commr. revenue State of Ind., Indpls., 1969-71, adminstrv. asst. to gov., 1971-72; exec. dir. Environ. Quality Control, Inc., Indpls., 1972-75; project mgr. EDP Corp., Sarasota, Fla., 1975-76, v.p. adminstrn., 1977-78; asst. to pres. Citizens Gas and Coke Utility, Indpls., 1978-80, v.p. pub. affairs, 1980—, sr. v.p. adminstrn., 1982—; Mem. Ind. Energy Devel. Bd., Indpls., 1980—, Midwest Govs. Energy Task Force, 1972-75. Pres. Indsl. Mgmt. Club, Anderson and Madison County, Inc., 1961, Cen. Council Indsl. Mgmt. Clubs, 1966; bd. dirs. Environ. Quality Control, Inc., Indpls., 1985—, Better Bus. Bur., Indpls., 1985—, Life/Leadership Devel. Inc.; mem. exec. com. White River Park State Games, Indpls., 1983—. Recipient Exchange Industrialist with USSR award YMCA, 1963; named Sagamore of Wabash, Gov. of Ind., 1971, 75. Mem. Am. Gas Assn. (chmn. pub. rels. com.), Govtl. Affairs Soc. Ind. (bd. govs. pres.), Ind. Gas Assn. (bd. dirs.), Indpls. Pub. Relations Soc. Republican. Methodist. Clubs: Columbia (Indpls.), Downtown Kiwanis (Indpls.). Home: 8158 Brent St Indianapolis IN 46240 Office: Citizens Gas & Coke Utility 2020 N Meridian St Indianapolis IN 46202

GRIFFITHS, ROBERT PENNELL, banker; b. Chgo., May 6, 1949; s. George Findley and Marion E. (Winterrowd) G.; m. Susan Hillman, Jan. 31, 1976. BA, Amherst Coll., 1972; MS in Mgmt., Northwestern U., 1974. Comml. banking officer No. Trust Co., Chgo., 1978-80, 2d v.p., 1980-83, v.p., 1983-85; sr. v.p. comml. lending UnibancTrust Co., Chgo., 1985-88; pres., Ill. Regional Bank of Naperville, Ill., 1988—; sr. v.p. Unibanc Trust/Hawthorne, 1987-89, exec. v.p., 1989—; also dir. Vanguard Fin. Svc., Inc. Mem. University Club (Chgo.), Metropolitan Club. Home: 691 Rockefeller Rd Lake Forest IL 60045 Office: Ill Regional Bank 27W 770 75th St Naperville IL 60540

GRIFFITTS, KEITH LOYD, trust banker; b. Wichita Falls, Tex., July 10, 1942; s. Loyd and Fannie (Moore) G.; m. Dawn Camille Carnes, June 25, 1969; 1 child, Ryan E. BS, Hardin-Simmons U., 1964; MEd, North Tex. State U., 1965. Counselor, adminstr. Dist. #6 Schs., Littleton, Colo., 1965-69; div. mgr. Westamerica Securities, Inc., Denver, 1969-71; project sales mgr. U.S. Home Corp., Denver, 1971-74; comml. real estate salesperson Wilton O. Davis & Co., Dallas, 1974-75; dir. mktg. Schneider Bakery Co., Longview, Tex., 1975-77; nat. account mktg. White Swan, Inc., Dallas, 1977-79; pres. Vantage Petroleum Resources, Inc., Dallas, 1979-82, Western Petroleum Resources, Inc., Dallas, First City,, Tex., 1984—; v.p., mgr. trust devel. 1st City Bank Dallas, 1984—; lectr. North Tex. State U., 1982-86. Author, editor, pub. periodical Oil Patch, 1980-84; editor periodical Trust Trends, 1984—. Trustee Colo. Bapt. Jr. Coll., Denver, 1970-72; vice-chmn. bd. devel. Hardin-Simmons U., Abilene, Tex., 1984—. Served to 2d lt. USAR, 1965-71. Mem. Dallas Pension Soc., Dallas Estate Planning Council. Baptist. Home: 1107 Hillsdale Richardson TX 75081 Office: 1st City Bank Dallas 1700 Pacific Dallas TX 75201

GRIGG, WILLIAM HUMPHREY, utility executive; b. Shelby, N.C., Nov. 5, 1932; s. Claud and Margy (Humphrey) G.; m. Margaret Anne Ford, Aug. 11, 1956; children: Anne Ford, John Humphrey, Mary Lynne. A.B., Duke U., 1954, LL.B., 1958. Bar: N.C. 1958. Gen. practice Charlotte, 1958-63; with Duke Power Co., 1963—, v.p. finance, 1970-71, v.p., gen. counsel, 1971-75; sr. v.p. legal and finance Duke Power Co., Charlotte, 1975-82, exec. v.p. fin. and adminstrn., 1982—; also dir. Duke Power Co. Editor-in-chief: Duke Law Jour, 1957-58; Contbr. articles to profl. jours. Dir. Hatteras Income Fund, Inc.; Trustee Pfeiffer Coll., Aegis Ins. Services, Research Triangle Park; bd. dirs. Charlotte-Mecklenburg YMCA. Served to capt. USMCR, 1954-56. Mem. Am., N.C. bar assns. Methodist. Club: Charlotte Country. Office: Duke Power Co 422 S Church St Charlotte NC 28242

GRIGGS, BENJAMIN GLYDE, JR., transportation executive; b. St. Paul, 1928. BA, Yale U., 1950. With N.W. Airlines, Inc., St. Paul, 1950—, v.p. flight ops., 1964-69, v.p., asst. to pres., from 1969, v.p. ops. svcs., from 1983, exec. v.p. ops., from 1985, exec. v.p., chmn. NWA Cos., 1988—; bd. dirs. St. Paul Cos., 1st Nat. Bank Mpls. Office: NWA Inc Mpls-St Paul Internat Airport Saint Paul MN 55111

GRIGGY, KENNETH JOSEPH, food company executive; b. Suffield, Ohio, Mar. 7, 1934; s. Edward F. and Margaret M. (Rothermel) G.; m. Janice Marie Doetzel, July 30, 1960; children: Jill, Matthew, Mark, Jennifer. B.A., Athenaeum of Ohio, 1956; M.Ed., Xavier U., 1961. With Am. Heart Assn., Cin., 1960-61, Mead Johnson & Co., Evansville, Ind., 1962-64; v.p., dir. consumer product group Ralston Purina Co., St. Louis, 1964-73; pres., dir. domestic ops. Riviana Foods, Inc., Houston, 1973-75; chmn. bd., chief exec. officer Wilson Foods Corp., Oklahoma City, 1975—. Bd. dirs. State Fair Okla. Served with U.S. Army, 1959-60. Mem. Am. Meat Inst. (dir.), Okla. C. of C. Clubs: Oklahoma City Golf and Country, Oak Tree Golf. Office: Wilson Foods Corp 4545 Lincoln Blvd Oklahoma City OK 73105 *

GRIGORCEA, ADRIAN GABRIEL, mineral and chemical company executive; b. Sao Paulo, Brazil, Feb. 7, 1965; came to U.S., 1966; s. John and Stephany (Tautu) Gallard. Diploma, N.Y. Food and Hotel Mgmt. Sch., 1984; grad., Valley Forge Mil. Acad. Mgr. restaurant svc. Sherry Netherlands Hotel, N.Y.C., 1984; v.p. Consol. Brazilian Mines Internat., N.Y.C., 1984-86; pres. Upland Minerals and Chems. Corp., N.Y.C., 1986—; exec. dir. Rio Gam. Min Dourados, Mineral Vale do Rio Santo Antonio, Diamazon Mineracao, Rocha Amarela do Brasil, Royal Minerais do Brasil; cons. mineral processing industries, N.Y.C. Mem. Am. Film Inst. Republican. Roman Catholic. Office: Upland Minerals & Chems 500 Fifth Ave Suite 224 New York NY 10110

GRIGSBY, CHESTER POOLE, JR., oil and investments company executive; b. Ruston, La., Mar. 4, 1929; s. Chester Poole and Vera Aura (Lamkin) G.; B.S., La. Tech. U., 1951; postgrad. U. Ariz., 1953-54; m. Audrey Jane Tombrink, Mar. 27, 1954; children—Jayne, Chester Poole III., Julia, Diana. Accountant, Hudson Gas & Oil Corp., 1955-61; gen. acctg. supr. San Jacinto Gas Processing Corp., 1961-63; v.p., treas., dir. Kinsey Corps., Shreveport, La., 1964—, Kinsey Interests, Inc., Enkay Corp., Alliance Prodn. Co., Norman Corp. Caddo, Inc.; partner Freestate Warehouse Co., 1972—, Freestate Circle Ltd. Served with USAF, 1951-55. C.P.A., La. Mem. Am. Inst. C.P.A.s, Soc. La. C.P.A.s, U.S. Power Squadron, Am. Legion. Home: 5721 River Rd Shreveport LA 71105 Office: 1805 Louisiana Tower Shreveport LA 71101

GRILL, JEFFREY W., furniture manufacturing executive; b. West Reading, Pa., Oct. 14, 1957; s. Harry DeWees and Joanne (Graver) G. BSBA, Bloomsburg State Coll., 1979; MBA, Wilmington Coll., Del., 1985. Acct. The Bachman Co., Reading, 1980-81; corp. acct. INCO, Phila., 1981-82; supr. cost acctg. Knoll Internat., Inc., East Greenville, Pa., 1982, fin. mgr. to dir. fin. systems, 1988; v.p. fin. gen. mgr., ptnr. The Pitts. Furniture Corp., 1988—, also bd. dirs. Vol. Escape Ctr. of Houston, 1986-87. Mem. Am. Mgmt. Assn., Exch. Club (treas., bd. dirs.), Pitts. Harliquins Rugby Club, Brandywine Rugby Club, Pitts. Young Profl. (bd. dirs.). Republican. Home: 6324 Howe St #10 Pittsburgh PA 15206 Office: The Pitts Furniture Corp 625 Liberty Ave CNG Tower Ste 220 Pittsburgh PA 15201

GRILLO, FRANK, office automation company executive; b. N.Y.C., Dec. 13, 1944; s. Frank and Theresa (Santevecchi) G.; m. Deaney Deane Gauntlett, July 21, 1984; 1 child, Michelle. Student, Hofstra U., 1962-65. With IBM Office Products div., 1969-76, mgr., 1976-81; chief exec. officer SCOPE Office Svcs., Inc., Anaheim, Calif., 1981—. With USN, 1965-69, Vietnam. Mem. So. Calif. Office Machine Dealers Assn. (bd. dirs. 1986—), Sierra LaVern Country Club. Office: SCOPE office Svcs Inc 2600 E Katella Ave Anaheim CA 92806

GRIM, PATRICIA ANN, bank executive; b. Everett, Pa., Sept. 7, 1940; d. Harry Grant and Nellie Elizabeth (Koontz) Foor; m. James Woodrow Grim, Feb. 21, 1970. Student, Am. Inst. Banking, Rolling Meadows, Ill., Bank Adminstrn. Inst., The Bus. Women's Tng. Inst. Sec. William H. Snyder, Atty. at Law, Bedford, Pa., 1958-60; sec., loan teller First Nat. Bank of Everett, Pa., 1960-70; teller Orrstown (Pa.) Bank, 1970-81, asst. cashier, asst. sec., 1981-82, v.p., asst. sec., 1982—. Recipient Family Tng. Hour Leader of Yr. award Ch. of God State of Pa., Layman of Yr. award, 1979; nat. nominee Layperson of Yr., 1984. Mem. Ch. of God. Office: Orrstown Bank 3580 Orrstown Rd PO Box 60 Orrstown PA 17244-0060

GRIMALDI, LEONARD NICHOLAS, finance company executive, consultant, arbitrator; b. N.Y.C., Dec. 1, 1942; s. Leonard and Marie Grace (Santillo) G. BA, Fordham Coll., 1966; MA, Fordham U., 1967; Licentiate in Philosophy, Jesuits, N.Y.C., 1969. Registered prin., N.Y. Stock Exchange. V.p. Autex Inc., N.Y.C., 1970-76; sr. v.p., dir. Instl. Networks Corp., N.Y.C., 1979-80; pres. Grimaldi Assocs., N.Y.C., 1976—; v.p. Amivest Corp., N.Y.C., 1982-84, sr. v.p., 1984-86, exec. v.p., pres., 1986—; arbitrator Nat. Securities Dealers, N.Y.C., 1984—. Mem. Internat. Found. Employee Benefit Plans, Atrium Club (N.Y.). Democrat. Roman Catholic. Home: 200 E 24th St New York NY 10010 Office: Amivest Corp 767 Fifth Ave New York NY 10153

GRIMES, JOSEPH RUDOLPH, tractor company executive; b. Monrovia, Liberia, Oct. 31, 1923; s. Louis Arthur and Victoria Elizabeth (Cheeseman) G.; m. Doris D. Duncan, Oct. 31, 1954; children—Dolly, Doris. B.A., Liberia Coll., 1944; J.D., Harvard U., 1949; M.Internat. Affaris, Columbia U., 1951, LL.D. (hon.), 1971. Bar: Liberia 1952. Cons. Liberia Tractor & Equipment Co., 1972-76, pres., 1976-78, chmn., 1978-88, also dir.; chmn. bd. Denco Shipping Lines, Stevfor; dir. West African Explosives & Chem. Co., Ins. Co. Africa, Ins. Co. of Africa, Monrovia Breweries, Inc.; counselor Liberian Dept. State, 1951-56, undersec. state, 1956-60, sec. of state, 1960-72. Chancellor Episcopal Diocese of Liberia, 1976—; mem. Nat. Constn. Commn., chmn. drafting com., 1981-83. Decorated grand cordon Order Pioneers Liberia; grand officer Legion of Honor (France); hon. knight comdr. Order Brit. Empire; recipient Disting. Service citation UN Assn. Mem. Bar Assn. Liberia., Grand Cross, Order Orange Nassau, Masons. Episcopalian. Office: PO Box 299, Monrovia Liberia

GRIMES-FARROW, DOROTHEA D., communications executive; b. New Orleans, Feb. 10, 1952; d. Morris and Rosemary (Birch) Grimes; m. Reginald C. Farrow, July 8, 1978. BS in Physics, So. U., Baton Rouge, 1974; EDD, Rutgers U., 1980. Tchr. physics Piscataway (N.J.) Sch. System, 1975-78; tech. asst. AT&T Bell Labs., Murray Hill, N.J., 1978-80; mem. tech. staff. AT&T Bell Labs., Piscataway, 1980-85; tech. supr. small system devel. lab. AT&T Bell Labs., Middletown, N.J., 1985-88; tech. supr. quality system devel. AT&T Bell Labs., Parsippany, N.J., 1988—. Contbr. articles to profl. jours. Mem. YWCA Mgmt. Forum, Summit, N.J., 1988. Mem. AAAS, IEEE, Assn. Computing Machinery, Am. Ednl. Research Assn., Coalition of 100 Black Women. Office: AT&T 99 Jefferson Rd Rm 1F10 Parsippany NJ 07054

GRIMM, DONALD E., petroleum company executive; b. Charleston, W.Va., 1930. BA, Johns Hopkins U., 1951. With Dept. Commerce U.S. Govt., Washington, 1951-53, with Bur. of Budget, 1957-58, with Office Sec. of Def., 1958-62; with Grace Line, 1962-68, v.p. mgmt. analysis and planning, 1966-67, v.p., treas., also bd. dirs., 1967-68; with W.R. Grace & Co., N.Y.C., 1968—, v.p. adminstrv. controls div., from 1968, v.p., 1971-78, chief operating officer, 1971-86, sr. v.p. natural resources, 1978-86, exec. v.p., group exec. natural resources, 1986; vice chmn. Grace Petroleum Corp. subs. W.R. Grace & Co., Oklahoma City, 1978—. Served with USN, 1953-57. Office: W R Grace & Co 1114 Ave of the Americas New York NY 10036 *

GRIMMIG, ROBERT JOHN, banker, lawyer; b. N.Y.C., Nov. 8, 1928; s. Joseph Andrew and Josephine A. (Mulliner) G.; m. Dorothy Agnes McGrane, May 25, 1957; children—Robert Jr., Diane Marie, Eileen Mary. B.S., Georgetown U., 1950; J.D., Harvard U., 1953. Bar: N.Y. 1953. Asst. U.S. atty. Dept. Justice, Bklyn., 1953-56; assoc. Kissam & Halpin, N.Y.C., 1957-59; sr. v.p. Chem. Bank, N.Y.C., 1960—. Contbr. articles to profl. jours. Mem. ABA, Robert Morris Assocs. Republican. Roman Catholic. Club: Hewlett Point Yacht (commodore 1983) (N.Y.). Office: Chem Bank 300 Madison Ave New York NY 10017 *

GRINBERG, MEYER STEWART, retail company executive; b. New Brunswick, N.J., Aug. 31, 1944; s. Allen Lewis and Edith (Bart) G.; m. Beryll Susan Chackman, May 28, 1967; children: David, Lee, Benjamin. BA, Franklin and Marshall Coll., 1965; JD, U. Pa., 1968; MBA, George Washington U., 1973. Bar: Pa., U.S. Ct. Claims, U.S. Customs Ct., U.S. Ct. Internat. Trade, U.S. Ct. Mil. Appeals, U.S. Supreme Ct.; CPA, Pa. Tax acct. Arthur Andersen & Co., Pitts., 1973-77; v.p., co-owner Buy-Wise, Inc., Pitts., 1977—. Exec. v.p. Cong. B'nai Israel, Pitts., 1982—; v.p. Western Pa. region United Synagogues Am., Pitts., 1984—, mem. nat. adv. bd., 1986—; v.p. Sch. Advanced Jewish Studies, Pitts. 1983—; pres. Community Day Sch., 1988—, former v.p.; bd. dirs. Solomon Schechter Nat. Day Sch. Assn.; co-founder Solomon Schechter Day Sch., Pitts.; bd. dirs. Forward-Shady Housing Project; chmn. Pitts. delegation to The Maccabai Games of Israel, mem. Israel Bond Cabinet, Jewish Com. Ctr., coach Little League; chmn. health and phys. edn. com. Jewish Community Ctr.; mem. N.Am. Youth Maccabar Games Com.; bd. dirs. Hebrew Inst. of Pitts. Served to lt. USCG, 1968-73. Recipient Latterman Vol. Mitzuah award, 1988. Mem. Am. Inst. CPA's, Pa. Inst. CPA's, Pa. Bar Assn., Commn. on Jewish Edn. Democrat. Lodge: Kiwanis. Home: 213 Anita Ave Pittsburgh PA 15217 Office: Buy-Wise Inc 4516 Browns Hill Rd Pittsburgh PA 15217

GRINDE, DOUGLAS, banker; b. Iowa Falls, Iowa, Apr. 30, 1928; s. Sigvald and Mary Agnes (McNabb) G.; m. Mary Ann Hoye, June 25, 1950; children: Carol Lagneaux, Cathy Vickroy, David. BA in Econs., State U. Iowa, 1951. Asst. v.p. Peoples Bank and Trust Co., Cedar Rapids, Iowa, 1951-65; pres. Bettendorf (Iowa) Bank and Trust, 1965-67; pres. Burlington (Iowa) Bank and Trust, 1967-88, chmn., 1988—; bd. dirs. Great Mid-West Fin. Co., Ames, Iowa. Vice-chmn. and dir. Burlington Med. Ctr.; pres. C.B.D., Inc.; bd. dirs. Burlington United Way. Cpl. USMC, 1946-48. Republican. Methodist. Lodge: Rotary (pres. 1986-76). Home: 2713 Clearview Burlington IA 52601 Office: Hawkeye Bank & Trust 222 N Main Burlington IA 52601

GRINDEA, DANIEL, international economist; b. Galatz, Romania, Feb. 23, 1924; came to U.S., 1975; s. Samy and Liza (Kaufman) Grünberg; M.Econs. and M.Law, Inst. Econ. Scis. and Faculty of Law, Bucharest, Romania, 1948; Ph.D. in Econs., Inst. Fin. and Planning, Leningrad, USSR, 1953; m. Lidia Bunaciu; 1 child, Sorin. Asso. prof. Inst. of Econ. Scis., Bucharest, 1953-56, Acad. of Social Scis., Bucharest, 1956-58, U. Bucharest, 1958-62; asso. prof. Inst. of Agronomy, Bucharest, 1962-69, prof., 1969-72; prof. Acad. St. Gheorghiu, Bucharest, 1972-75; cons. State Planning Com., 1953-56, Ministry of Fin., 1956-68; mem. Sci. Council of the Cen. Statis. Office, 1956-68; internat. economist Republic Nat. Bank of N.Y., N.Y.C., 1976-78, sr. internat. economist, dept. head, 1978-79, v.p., sr. internat. economist, 1979-84, sr. v.p., chief economist, 1984—; sr. advisor U.S. Congl. Adv. Bd., 1988; mem. economic adv. bd. of the Inst. of Internat. Fin., Washington; elected mem. sci. coun. L'Ecole Superieure des Sciences Commercieles d'Augerr, 1989; invited vis. prof. l'Institut International de la Planification de l'Education (UNESCO), Paris, 1973; mem. adv. group Com. on Asian Econ. Studies, 1983. Recipient first prize in econ. research Ministry of Edn., Romania, 1969. Mem. Am. Econ. Assn., Nat. Assn. Bus. Economists, Internat. Assn. for Research of Income and Wealth (elected mem.), Internat. Inst. Public Fin. (W.Ger., elected mem.), Acad. Social and Polit. Scis. Bucharest (elected mem. corr.), Soc. Econ. Scis. of Romania (elected, founding mem.). Correct predictions on world economy and individual countries; contbr. articles on forecasts in field U.S. and internat. to publs.; papers presented to profl. confs. U.S., France, Sweden, Ireland. Office: Republic Nat Bank of NY 452 Fifth Ave New York NY 10018

GRINOLS, EARL LEROY III, economist, educator; b. Bemidji, Minn., May 2, 1951; s. Earl Leroy and Betty Annette (Wolfe) G.; m. Anne Dudley Bradstreet, Feb. 2, 1978; children: Kimberly Anne, Lindsay Elizabeth, Daniel Stephen. BS in Econs., BA in Math. summa cum laude, U. Minn., 1973; PhD in Econs., MIT, 1977. Asst. prof. econs. Cornell U., Ithaca, N.Y., 1977-84; assoc. prof. U. Ill., Champaign, 1984-87; sr. economist Coun. of Econ. Advisers, Washington, 1987—; cons. Dept. Labor, Washington, 1985-86. Author: Uncertainty and the Theory of International Trade, 1987. Grad. fellow NSF, 1973-76. Mem. Am. Econ. Assn., Econometric Soc., Assn. Christian Economists, Royal Econ. Soc., Phi Beta Kappa. Home: 4804 Eades St Rockville MD 21853 Office: Econ Advisers Coun Exec Office of Pres Washington DC 20500

GRINSTEIN, GERALD, transportation executive; b. 1932; married. B.A., Yale U., 1954; LL.B., Harvard U., 1957. Bar: D.C., Wash. Counsel to merchant marine and transp. subcoms., chief counsel U.S. Senate Commerce Com., Washington, D.C., 1958-67; adminstrv. asst. U.S. Senator Warren G. Magnuson, Washington, D.C., 1967-69; ptnr. Preston Thorgrimson Ellis & Holman, 1969-83; chmn. bd. Western Air Lines Inc., Los Angeles, 1983-84, pres., chief operating officer, 1984-85, chief exec. officer, 1985-86, chmn., chief exec. officer, 1986-87; vice chmn. Burlington Northern, Inc., Ft. Worth, 1987-88, pres., chief exec. officer, 1988—; pres., chief exec. officer Burlington Northern R.R. Co., 1989—; bd. dirs. Gen. Telephone Co. of Calif., Seattle-First Nat. Bank, Gen. Telephone Co. of Calif., Delta Airlines. Office: Burlington No Inc 3800 Continental Plaza Fort Worth TX 76102 *

GRISANTI, EUGENE PHILIP, flavors and fragrances company executive; b. Buffalo, Oct. 24, 1929; s. Nicholas D. and Victoria (Pantera) G.; m. Anne Couming, June 29, 1953; children: Marylee, Christopher, Eugene Paul. A.B. magna cum laude, Holy Cross Coll., 1951; LL.B., Boston U., 1953; LL.M., Harvard U., 1954. Bar: Mass. 1953, N.Y. 1954. Mem. firm Fulton, Walter & Halley, N.Y.C., 1954-60; gen. atty. Internat. Flavors & Fragrances Inc., N.Y.C., 1960-64, sec., gen. atty., 1964-70, v.p., sec., gen. atty., 1970-74; pres. Internat. Flavors & Fragrances, N.Y.C., 1974-79; sr. v.p., dir. Internat. Flavors & Fragrances Inc., N.Y.C., 1979-85, chmn., pres., chief exec. officer, 1985—. Mem. Fragrance Found. (bd. dirs.), Cosmetic Toiletry and Fragrance Assn. (bd. dirs.). Clubs: Larchmont Yacht, Winged Foot Golf; University (N.Y.C.). Office: Internat Flavor & Fragrances Inc 521 W 57th St New York NY 10019

GRISEUK, GAIL GENTRY, financial consultant; b. Providence, Jan. 24, 1948; d. Marvin Houghton and Gertrude Emma (Feather) Gentry; divorced; 1 child, Christina Deborah. Student (Fla. Power Corp. scholar), Fla. State U., 1966-70. Registry of Fin. Planning Practitioners. Cert. fin. ops. prin.; cert. gen. securities prin.; registered investment advisor. Asst. div. controller Mobile Home Industries, Tallahassee, 1968-70; owner, mgr. BDI Services, Tallahassee and Lake Charles, La., 1970-78; fin. cons. Aylesworth Fin., Inc., Clearwater, Fla., 1978-82; chmn. bd., chief exec. officer Griseuk Assocs. Inc., 1982—; chief exec. officer GAI Internat. Investment Advisors, Inc., 1985—; instr., dir. vet. outreach Angelina Coll., Lufkin, Tex., 1975-76. Contbr. short stories to Redbook, McCall's, Christian Home. Vol., Sunland Tng. Center, 1970-72, George Criswell House, 1969-73. Mem. Inst. Cert. Fin. Planners, Internat. Platform Assn., Internat. Assn. Fin. Planners. Methodist. Home: 1024 Woodcrest Ave Clearwater FL 33516 Office: 5301 Central Ave Saint Petersburg FL 33710

GRISSOM, PAMELA ANN, sales professional; b. Saginaw, Mich., Nov. 13, 1958; d. Alvin Louis and Margaret (Willey) Thiede; m. Stephen Arnold Grissom, June 23, 1984; children: Joshua Stephen Arnold, Ashley Margaret Ann. Grad. high sch., Dearborn, Mich. With First of Mich. Corp., Detroit, 1978-87; sales sec. First of Mich. Corp., Dearborn, 1987—. Office: First of Mich Corp 23400 Michigan Ave Dearborn MI 48124

GRIST, JOHN, goverment official; b. Havana, Cuba, Nov. 17, 1928 (father Am. citizen); s. John Rivers and Raphaela Matilda (Santiesteban) G.; came to U.S., 1945; B.S., Ga. Inst. Tech., 1958; m. Ana Dolores D'Almonte, Nov. 22, 1961; children—Anna Cecilia, John Alexander, Paul Steven. Aircraft indsl. engring. cons. Parr Engring., Atlanta, 1958; food mfg. indsl. engring. cons. U.S. Dept. Agr., Washington, 1958-60; postal mechanization indsl. engr. U.S. Post Office Dept., Washington, 1960-62; hosp. indsl. engr. cons. VA, Washington, 1962-64; bldgs. mgmt. indsl. engr. cons. GSA, Washington, 1964-65; parks mgmt. sr. mgmt. analysis cons. Nat. Park Service, Washington, 1965-71; sr. indsl. engring. cons. U.S. Postal Service, N.Y.C., 1971-74, sr. indsl. engring. cons. Western Mass., Springfield, Mass., 1974—; internat. bilingual export-import tech. cons., 1958—. Pres. parents council Arlington (Va.) Pub. Schs. Deaf Edn. Program, 1970-71; mem. Parents' Council, Lexington Sch. for Deaf, Queens, N.Y., 1972-74; mem. fund raising com. Clarke Sch. for Deaf, Northampton, Mass., 1975-76. Served with USAF, 1951-55. Mem. Nat. Soc. Profl. Engrs., Ga. Inst. Tech. Nat. Alumni Assn. Roman Catholic. Home: 131 Rolling Ridge Rd Amherst MA 01002 Office: Main PO Box 227 Amherst MA 01004

GRISWOLD, BENJAMIN HOWELL, IV, investment banker; b. Balt., Sept. 4, 1940; s. Benjamin Howell and Leith (Symington) G.; m. Page Lee Hufty, May 19, 1979 (div.); children: Belinda J., Anna B., Benjamin H., Alexander P.; m. Wendy Goodyear, Apr. 25, 1987. AB, Princeton U., 1962; MBA, Harvard U., 1967. Security analyst Alexander Brown & Sons, Balt., 1967-70, dir. research, 1971-74, dir. trading, 1975-80, head div. equity, 1981-83, vice chmn., 1984-86, chmn., 1987—; mem. adv. com. regional firms N.Y. Stock Exchange, 1987. Trustee Johns Hopkins U., Balt., 1988, Walters Art Gallery, Balt., 1988, Concord (Mass.) Acad., 1987, Peabody Conservatory, Balt., 1986. 1st lt. U.S. Army, 1963-75. Mem. Links Club N.Y.C., Md. Club. Republican. Episcopalian. Office: Alex Brown & Sons Inc 135 E Baltimore St Baltimore MD 21202

GRISWOLD, FRANK MATTHEW, JR., investment executive; b. Worcester, Mass., June 6, 1944; s. Frank Matthew and Carol (Jaques) G.; m. Paula Garbarino, Sept. 3, 1966; children: F. Matthew III, Christopher, Brooke. BBA, Merrimack Coll., 1966; postgrad., Clark U., 1968-72. Investment officer Mechanics Bank, Worcester, Mass., 1967-72; sr. investment officer Valley Bank, Springfield, Mass., 1973-76; sr. v.p. Boston Safe Deposit and Trust, 1976-84; exec. v.p. John Hancock Advisers, Boston, 1984—, also bd. dirs.; also bd. dirs. John Hancock Advisers Internat., London; Trustee John Hancock Mut. Funds, 1985. Mem. Fin. Analysts Fed., Mcpl. Bond Club (Boston chpt.), Bond Analyst Soc. (Boston chpt.). Clubs: University (Boston), Tennis and Racquet (Boston). Office: John Hancock Bond Trust 101 Huntington Ave 7th Fl Boston MA 02119

GRISWOLD, GARY NORRIS, engineering company executive; b. Fairbanks, Feb. 12, 1947; s. Norris Rockwell and Margaret Moore (Kennedy) G.; m. Lois Ruth Brinkman, June 17, 1967; children: Mark David, Melissa Robin. BS, U. Wash., 1970; MS, Union Coll., 1980. Cert. in data processing. Computer programmer Knolls Atomic Power Lab., Schenectady, N.Y., 1972-75; sr. systems analyst State of N.Y., Albany, 1975-79; mgr. mgmt. info. systems devel. Phoenix Data Systems, Inc., Albany, 1979-85; pres. InfoLogic Software, Inc., Schenectady, 1985—; adj. asst. prof. Union Coll., 1980-83; cons. on mgmt. info. systems. Mem. IEEE, Assn. Computing Machinery.

GRISWOLD, KENT CARRIER, health care company executive; b. Bridgeton, N.J., Mar. 1, 1958; s. Lincoln Tracy and Jean Secord (Coghlan) G. AB, Harvard U., 1980; postgrad. in econs., U. Stockholm, 1984; MBA, U. Pa., 1985. Mgmt. assoc. Sun Co., Radnor, Pa., 1980-81; treasury analyst Phila., 1981-83; systems designer Spl. Care, Inc., Phila., 1984, gen. mgr., v.p., exec. dir., 1987—, also bd. dirs.; rep. Pratt Group, Hong Kong, 1985-86; mgr. treasury Melbourne, Australia, 1986-87; cons. trading A. Johnson & Co., Stockholm, 1984; cons. Mayne Ednl. Fund, Swannanoa, N.C., 1987—. Creator: (bd. game) Mergers and Acquisitions, 1981. Mem. Savoy Co., Phila., 1981, 83, 88; elected mem. Olympus, Phila., 1985—; mem. panel Entrepreneurial Forum, Phila., 1988. Mem. Pa. Health Care Assn., Pvt. Care Assn., Mensa. Republican. Presbyterian. Clubs: Acad. (Ft. Washington, Pa.); Fox (Cambridge, Mass.). Office: Spl Care Inc 707 Bethlehem Pike Philadelphia PA 19118

GRISWOLD, PAUL JOHN, paper company executive; b. N.Y.C., Nov. 27, 1951; s. Leavitt E. and June (Reilly) G.; m. Sharon Griswold; children: Paul J. II, Christopher. BA in Math., Fordham U., 1973; MBA in Fin., MEd, Seton Hall U., 1976. Acct. exec. Internat. Paper, N.Y.C., 1973-75, nat. acct. mgr., 1976, dir. worldwide pulp and paper ops., 1981-84, dir. bus. devel., 1985-86; Midwest regional sales mgr. Internat. Paper, Chgo., 1978-81; pres., chief operating officer Kingston (N.Y.) Systems Inc., 1986-88, also bd. dirs.; v.p. corp. finance Kemper Fin., 1988-89; pres. Bankhouse Capital, Boston, 1989—. Contbg. author: Process Control, 1981. Mem. NCAA Acad. All-Am. Basketball 1973—. Mem. Am. Mgmt. Assn. Home: 2 Broadmoor Dr Rumson NJ 07760

GRIZI, SAMIR AMINE, finance executive; b. Lagos, Nigeria, Feb. 27, 1942; s. Amine R. and Fedwa (Murad) G.; m. Nermine Galeb, Nov. 14, 1964; children: Inji, Inas, Iman. BA in Adminstrv. Studies with honors, York U., 1974. Asst. ops. mgr. Navco Food Services Ltd., Toronto, Ont., Can., 1970-71; office mgr. Electro Mech. Testing Labs. Ltd., Toronto, 1971; asst. chief acct. Janin Bldg. and Civil Works Ltd., Toronto, 1971-74; mgr. ops. acctg. VS Services Ltd., Toronto, 1974-75; exec. prin. Talal Abughazaleh & Co., Dammam, Saudi Arabia, 1975-84; group v.p. fin. Abdulla Fouad & Sons, Dammam, 1984-85; group v.p. ASAS Internat. Group, Riyadh, Saudi Arabia, 1986-88; exec. ptnr. Alsaleh, CPA's, Arkhobar, Saudi Arabia, 1988—; bd. dirs. ASAS Internat., fin. cons.; bd. dirs. Nat. Fire Safety Equipment Co. Ltd., Assil Corp., Saudi Beverages Plant, Cedar House Ltd., Jalloul Internat. Ltd., Chafie O. Aburiche Corp., Saudi Techs. Co. Ltd., SAFIRE, Ltd. Served with C.E. U.S. Army, 1966-70. Fellow Inst .Profl. Mgrs., LEB Assn. Certified Accts., Arab Soc. Protection Indsl. Property; mem. Am. Mgmt. Assn., Nat. Assn. Accts., Am. Acctg. Assn., Arab Soc. Certified Accts. (assoc.), Inst. Internal Auditors (assoc.). Office: Alsaleh CPA's, PO Box 2722, Alkhobar 31952, Saudi Arabia

GROBELNY, LORI JO-ANN, manufacturing executive; b. New Brunswick, N.J., June 14, 1954; d. Stanley Joseph and Rose Marie (Toth) G. BA, Douglass Coll., 1976. Mgr. prod. N.Am. Container Corp. div. The Pratt Group, North Brunswick, N.J., 1976—; bd. dirs. Indsl. Capital Corp., Lawrenceville, Housing Capital Corp., New Hyde Park. Mem. Nat. Rep. Com. Mem. Douglass Coll. Alumnae Assn. Roman Catholic. Club: Douglass Coll. Alumnae Assn. Home: 1 Apple St Edison NJ 08817 Office: N Am Container Corp 501 Finnegans Ln North Brunswick NJ 08902

GROCE, JAMES FREELAN, petroleum engineer; b. Lubbock, Tex., Nov. 24, 1948; s. Wayne Dee and Betty Jo (Rice) G.; m. Patricia Kay Rogers; 1 child, Jason Eric. BS cum laude, Tex. Tech U., 1971. Registered profl. engr., Tex. Petroleum engr. Texaco, Inc., Sweetwater, Tex., 1971-74; drilling and prodn. engr. Texaco, Inc., Wichita Falls, Tex., 1974-77; asst. dist. engr. Texaco, Inc., Midland, Tex., 1977-78; sr. prodn. engr. Bass Enterprises Prodn., Midland, 1978-81; petroleum engr. Murphy H. Baxter Co., Midland, 1981-82, Henry Engring., Midland, 1982-87; petroleum engr. Fasken Oil and Ranch Interests, Midland, 1987, mgr. engring./ops., 1987—. Scoutmaster Boy Scouts Am., Midland, 1980-83, merit badge counselor, 1987; mem. Community Bible Study, Midland, Tex., 1987. Mem. Soc. Petroleum Engrs. (section chmn. 1987), Nat. Assn. Corrosion Engrs., Mensa, Tau Beta Pi. Republican. Presbyterian. Home: 3701 W Michigan Midland TX 79703

GRODY, ALLAN D., financial consultant, investment banker; b. N.Y.C., Feb. 28, 1945; s. Morris and Anna (Klarer) Grodzitsky; m. Deborah Chinitz Grody, June 6, 1970; 1 child, Michael. BS, CUNY, 1972. Bus. specialist GE Credit Corp., N.Y.C., 1965-67; computer analyst Neuberger & Berman, N.Y.C., 1967-69; ops. research analyst Reynolds & Co., N.Y.C., 1969-70; v.p. securities div. Algemene Bank, N.Y.C., 1970-73; ptnr., cons. Coopers & Lybrand, N.Y.C., 1973-85; pres. Fin. InterGroup, N.Y.C., 1985—; faculty advisor Bank Law Inst., N.Y.C., 1982-86, Practice Law Inst. , Washington, 1984; bd. advisors New Sch. Conf. on Commodities and Futures, N.Y.C., 1982-85, Internat. Stock Exchs. Conf. on Computers in the City, 1987-88; moderator Bus. Week Conf. on Fin. Services, N.Y.C., 1983-85; expert witness various fed. cts. Author: (with others) Synergy in Banking in the 1980's, 1981; contbr. monographs and research papers on fin. topics. Mem. NAS (Electronic Automation at the N.Y. Stock Exch. 1988), Am. Bankers Assn., Bank Adminstrn. Inst., Futures Industry Assn., Internat. Assn. Fin. Planners, Electronic Banking Economist Soc., Securities Industry Assn., Wall Street Planning Group. Club: Atrium (N.Y.C.). Office: Fin InterGroup 333 E 30 St New York NY 10016

GROEBER, RICHARD FRANCIS, meteorologist; b. Springfield, Ohio, Apr. 20, 1944; s. Paul Joseph and Catherine Agnes (Walsh) G.; A.A., Urbana Coll., 1966. Meteorologist, Sta. WBLY-AM, Springfield, 1956-62, 1984— Sta. WEEC-FM, Springfield, 1962-72 ; owner, operator Dicks Weather Service, Springfield. Sponsor men's slowpitch softball team. Mem. Am. Meteorol. Soc. (voting privilege), Am. Geophys. Union (supporting mem.). Democrat. Roman Catholic. Home and Office: 1452 N Limestone St Springfield OH 45503

GROESCH, JOHN WILLIAM, JR., oil company executive; b. Seattle, Nov. 22, 1923; s. John William and Jeanette Morrison (Gilmur) G.; B.S. in Chem. Engring., U. Wash., 1944; m. Joyce Eugenia Schauble, Apr. 25, 1948; children—Sara, Mary, Andrew. Engr., Union Oil Co., Los Angeles, 1944-48, corp. economist, Los Angeles, 1948-56, chief statistician, 1956-62, mgr., 1962-68, mgr., Schaumburg, Ill., 1968—. Bd. dirs. Arlington Heights (Ill.) Boy Scouts Am., 1977-88, adv. bd., 1989—, v.p., 1979, 82-85; commr. 1980-81, mem. OakBrook (Ill.) East Cen. Region, 1984—; treas. Scout Cabin Found., Barrington, 1977—. Served with USN, 1944-47. Mem. West Coast Mktg. Research Council (chmn. 1969), Am. Petroleum Inst. (chmn. com. 1970-72). Lodge: Mason. Home: 17 Shady Ln Deer Park Barrington IL 60010 Office: 1650 E Golf Rd Schaumburg IL 60196

GROFF, TIMOTHY JAMES, treasurer; b. Burbank, Calif., May 14, 1949; s. Ralph Downing and Virginia (Atkinson) G.; m. Jeanne Linea, June 23, 1973; children: Kristin L., Lauren N. BS in Fin., U. San Diego, 1971. Regional credit mgr. Gen. Motors Acceptance Corp., San Diego, 1971-79, Rohm & Haas Co., Los Angeles, 1980-82; dir., corp. credit adminstr. Oak Industries, San Diego, 1982-85; treas. Softsel Computer Products, Inc., Inglewood, Calif., 1985—. Mem. Fin. Execs. Inst., Nat. Assn. Credit Mgmt., Credit Research Found., Nat. Microcomputer Credit Assn., Nat. Corp. Cash Mgmt. Assn. Republican. Roman Catholic. Home: 8841 Arcel Circle Huntington Beach CA 92646 Office: Softsel Computer Products 546 N Oak St Inglewood CA 90312

GROGAN, ALICE WASHINGTON, lawyer; b. Richmond, Va., Jan. 25, 1956; d. Thomas Boyd Washington Jr. and Dorothy Jane (Smith) W.; m. Ralph Houston Grogan, Feb. 4, 1989. BS with honors, Va. Poly. Inst., 1978; JD, U. N.C., 1984. Bar: N.C. 1984, U.S. Supreme Ct. 1988. Corp. sec. Piedmont Aviation, Inc., Winston-Salem, N.C., 1984-88; assoc. Womble, Carlyle, Sandridge & Rice, Winston-Salem, 1988—. Mem. ABA (sect. taxation, sect. bus. law, corp. counsel com., subcom. finance and securities), N.C. Bar Assn., Forsyth County Bar Assn., Forsyth Employee Benefits Council, Va. Tech. Alumni Asn., U. N.C. Gen. Alumni Assn., U. N.C. Ednl. Found., Phi Kappa Phi. Episcopalian. Clubs: U.S. Rowing Assn. Office: Womble Carlyle Sandridge and Rice 1 Triad Pk Ste 1600 Winston-Salem NC 27101

GROGAN, ROBERT HARRIS, lawyer; b. Bklyn., Feb. 25, 1933: s. Robert Michael and Nora Howarth (Johnson) G.; A.B., Harvard U., 1955; LL.B., U. Va., 1961; m. Delia Ann Grossi, Dec. 23, 1967 (div. 1982); m. Lynn D. Habian, June 20, 1987. Admitted to N.Y. State bar, 1962, Va. bar, 1961, Ill. bar, 1977, Fla. bar, 1986; assoc. firm Milbank, Tweed, Hadley & McCloy, N.Y.C., 1961-66; counsel Anaconda Co., N.Y.C., 1966-68; asso. firm Shearman & Sterling, N.Y.C., 1968-75; v.p., gen. counsel staff Citibank, N.Y.C., 1975-76; partner Mayer, Brown & Platt, Chgo., 1976-81; of counsel Olwine, Connelly, Chase, O'Donnell & Weyher, N.Y.C., 1981-87, sr. v.p., dep. sr. counsel, Southeast Bank, N.A., Miami, Fla., 1987—; lectr. in field. Sec., bd. dirs. 3d Equity Owners Corp., coop. housing corp., 1975-77, pres., bd. dirs., 1982-86. Served with U.S. Army, 1956-58. Mem. ABA, Va. Bar Assn., Ill. Bar Assn., Fla. Bar, Phi Delta Phi. Club: Harvard N.Y.C. Contbg. author: The Local Economic Development Corporation, 1970.

GROME, RICHARD STANLEY, medical equipment company executive; b. Dayton, Ky., Apr. 2, 1947; s. Richard S. and Anna Mae (Edwards) G.; m. Margaret Ann Kiely, Nov. 15, 1969; children: Sean, Ryan, Mary Elizabeth. BA, Thomas More Coll., Covington, Ky., 1969; MS, U. Cin., 1972. Radiologic adminstr. Carraway Meth. Med. Ctr., Birmingham, Ala., 1972-73; sales rep. X-Ray Sales & Service, Birmingham, 1973-74, Greb X-Ray Co., Lenexa, Kans., 1974-78; radiation therapy product specialist Siemens Med. Systems, Inc., Cin., 1978-85; mgr. regional sales Dornier Med. Systems, Inc., Marietta, Ga., 1985-88; v.p. sales and mktg. Elekta Instruments, Inc., Decatur, Ga., 1988-89, pres., 1989—. U. Cin. fellow, 1972. Republican. Roman Catholic. Office: Elekta Instruments Inc 5028 Covington Hwy Decatur GA 30035

GRONEWOLD, HARLAN LEROY, accountant; b. Beatrice, Nebr., Apr. 24, 1935; s. William W. and Esther Ida (Schuster) G.; m. Alveda Carolyn Meints, Apr. 27, 1956; children: Christy Wood, David, Stephanie. BS in Bus. Adminstrn., U. Denver, 1961. CPA, Cert. fin. planner. Staff acct. Arthur Young and Co., Denver, 1959-61; spl. agt. FBI, Washington, Houston, Mpls., 1962-66; mgr., then ptnr. Dutton, Schmidt, Upp and Co., Red Oak and Atlantic, Iowa, 1966-73; v.p. Dutton and Assocs., P.C., Atlantic, Iowa, 1973-83; pres. Gronewold, Bell, Kyhnn and Co., P.C., Atlantic, 1983—; bd. dirs. Norwest Bank, Atlantic; chmn. Iowa Bd. Accountancy, 1978-80; quality control dir. Internat. Group Acctg. Firms, Dallas, 1977-78. Contbr. articles to profl. publs. Mem. Atlantic Park and Recreation Bd., 1974-76; founder, charter mem. Fact Found., Atlantic, 1972-75. Recipient Service award Atlantic Park and Recreation Bd., 1976, Iowa Bd. Accountancy, 1985. Mem. Am. Inst. CPA's (com. mem. 1981-82), Iowa Soc. CPA's (chmn. personal fin. planning com. 1988-89), Inst. Cert. Fin. Planners. Republican. Lutheran. Club: High Expectations (pres. 1987). Lodge: Elks. Office: Gronewold Bell Kyhnn & Co PC E Hwy 6 and US 71 Atlantic IA 50022

GROOM, DENIS J., airline executive; b. Eng., Feb. 6, 1932; s.Henry J. and Doreen V. (Morrell) G.; m. Valerie F. Thompson, 1961; children—Sharon, Diana, David. B.Commerce, U. Cape Town, Republic of South Africa. Chartered acct. Ptnr. Coopers & Lybrand, London, 1959-66; comptroller, dep. minister fin. Province of Nfld. and Labrador, Can., 1967-70; chmn., chief exec. officer Roneo Vickers Ltd., London, 1970-74, Churchill Falls Corp., Labrador, 1974-78; mng. dir. Cunard Ltd., London, 1978-81; sr. v.p., chief fin. officer Air Can., Montreal, Que., Can., 1981-84, group v.p. mktg. and planning, 1985-86, exec. v.p., head diversified bus. units, 1986—, now exec. v.p., chief fin. officer. Fellow Inst. Chartered Accts. Eng. and Wales; mem. Inst. Chartered Accts. Nfld. Clubs: Mount Bruno Country, Hillside Tennis, Montreal Squash and Badminton. Office: Place Air Can, 500 René Levesque Blvd W, 26th Fl, Montreal, PQ Canada H2Z 1X5 *

GROOM, GARY LEE, recreational vehicle manufacturing executive; b. Rensselaer, Ind., Jan. 3, 1946; s. Robert D. and Margery Ellen (Spain) G.; m. Monica L. Trump, Jan. 30, 1965; children—Richard L., Angela K. B.S.I.M., Purdue U., 1969; M.B.A. (valedictorian), U. Notre Dame, 1971. C.P.A., Fla., Ind. Auditor Arthur Young & Co., Tampa, Fla., 1971-72; exec. v.p. fin., sec. Coachmen Industries, Inc., Elkhart, Ind., 1972—; dir. Coachmen Industries, Inc., Elkhart, 1981—. Mem. Am. Inst. C.P.A.s, Nat. Assn. Accountants. Republican. Methodist. Home: 51007 Beach Dr Elkhart IN 46514 Office: Coachmen Industries Inc 601 E Beardsley PO Box 3300 Elkhart IN 46515

GROOM, JOHN MILLER, food company executive; b. Washington, Dec. 12, 1936; s. Charles Francis and Marjorie (Miller) G.; m. Carolyn Anderson, Sept. 22, 1962; children: John Michael, David Allen. Student, U. of South, 1954-55; B.S., Miami U., Oxford, Ohio, 1958. CPA, Ill. With John Morrell & Co., Chgo., 1960-70; v.p., controller Hygrade Food Products Corp., Detroit, 1970-81; v.p., controller Wilson Foods Corp., Oklahoma City, 1981-85, sr. v.p. ops., 1985-88, sr. v.p. ops., dist., 1985—; exec. v.p., chief fin. officer Daymark Foods, Inc., Russellville, Ark., 1989—. Mem. Am. Inst. CPA's. Home: 2513 Stamford Ct Edmond OK 73034 Office: Wilson Foods Corp 4545 N Lincoln Blvd Oklahoma City OK 73105

GROOM, ROBERT WRAY, data processing executive; b. McAlester, Okla., Aug. 5, 1936; s. Wray Lemuel and Mary Eleanor (Wisely) G.; m. Sarah Jane Goodman, June 20, 1959; children: Leslie Elaine, Laura Elizabeth. BS in Naval Sci. and Engring., U.S. Naval Acad., 1959; MS in Computer Systems Mgmt., Navy Postgrad. Sch., Monterey, Calif., 1970. Various positions U.S. Navy Supply Corps, 1959-79; cons. field office systems div. P&C INA Corp., Voorhees, N.J., 1979-80; mgr. adminstrv. svcs. INA Corp., Voorhees, 1980-83; adminstrv. dir. property & casualty systems div. CIGNA Corp., Voorhees, 1983-85, dir. planning and control property & casualty systems div., 1985-86; dir. personal automobile systems agy. systems div. CIGNA Corp., Phila., 1986-87, dir. planning and control internat. systems div., 1987—. Mem. U.S. Naval Acad. Alumni Assn. Episcopalian. Home: 618 Guilford Rd Cherry Hill NJ 08003 Office: CIGNA Corp 1617 John F Kennedy Blvd Philadelphia PA 19103

GROOME, REGINALD K., hotel executive; b. Montreal, Que., Can., Dec. 18, 1927; s. Cyril T. and Muriel H. (Forbes-Toby) G.; m. Christina M. Walker, June 20, 1953; children: Reginald A., Roderick, Richard. Ed., McGill U., Cornell U. With Montreal Pub. Co., 1945-53; broadcaster CBC Internat. Svc.; also overseas corr. Can. daily newspapers, 1951; dir. advt. and pub. rels., then personnel mgr. hotel chain Montreal, 1953-57; with Hilton Can., 1957, v.p., then exec. v.p., 1965-72, pres., 1972, chmn. bd. dirs., 1978; pres., dir., also gen. mgr. Queen Elizabeth Hotel, Montreal, 1983; v.p. Hilton Internat., N.Y.C., 1982—; cast pres. Montreal Bd. Trade; dir. Crum & Forster Can. Ltd., Herald Ins. Co., Indsl. Alliance Life Ins., Dustbane Enterprises Ltd., Gen. Trust Corp. Can., Palais de la Civilization, Montreal. Hon. pres. Nat. Coun. Boy Scouts Can.; life gov., Montreal Gen. Hosp.; vice chmn., gov. Concordia U. Decorated officer Order of Can.; recipient Silver Wolf award Boy Scouts Can.; Outstanding Citizenship award Montreal Citizenship Coun., 1976. Mem. Tourist Industry Assn. Can. (bd. dirs., past chmn.), Que. C. of C. (dir.).

GROOTHUIS, RICHARD B., insurance executive, lawyer; b. N.Y.C., June 3, 1937; s. Morton B. and Josephine (Bell) G.; m. Jean D. Groothuis, Aug. 3, 1963; children: Kathryn, Carin, Sarah, Meaghan. BA, Columbia U., 1958, LLB, 1961; LLM, NYU, 1966. Bar: N.Y., Conn. Assoc. counsel Mut. Life Ins. Co. N.Y., N.Y.C., 1961-69; counsel Aetna Life & Casualty Co., Hartford, Conn., 1969-73, counsel, sect. head, 1979-82, v.p., corp. counsel, 1982-86, v.p., investment counsel, 1986-89, v.p., sr. counsel, 1989—; gen. counsel, sec. Aetna Bus. Credit, Inc., Hartford, 1973-78; gen. counsel Aetna Realty Group, Hartford, 1978-79. Mem. ABA (commr. Opportunity for Minorities in the Profession, 1987—), Conn. Bar Assn., Am. Corp. Counsel Assn. (pres. Hartford chpt. 1983-86, bd. dirs. 1986—), Assn. Life Ins. Counsel (chmn. corp. sect. 1986-88). Home: 58 Hitchcock Ln Avon CT 06001 Office: Aetna Life & Casualty Co Law Dept YFF1 151 Farmington Ave Hartford CT 06156

GROSE, PETER BOLTON, editor; b. Evanston, Ill., Oct. 27, 1934; s. Clyde Leclare and Carolyn (Trowbridge) G.; m. Claudia Kerr, Sept. 11, 1965; children: Carolyn Bronia, Stephanie Kim. BA, Yale U., 1957, Pembroke Coll., 1959; MA, Oxford (Eng.) U., 1965. Corr. AP, London and Africa, 1959-62, N.Y. Times, N.Y.C., Paris, 1962-63; chief corr. N.Y. Times, Saigon, Republic of Vietnam, 1964-65; bur. chief N.Y. Times, Moscow, 1966-67; diplomatic corr. N.Y. Times, Washington, 1967-70; bur. chief N.Y. Times, Jerusalem, 1970-72; editorial bd. N.Y. Times, N.Y.C., 1972-76, United Nations bur. chief, 1976-77; deputy dir. policy planning staff Dept. of State, Washington, 1977-78; research assoc. Middle East Inst. Columbia U., N.Y.C., 1978-81; dir. studies Seven Springs Ctr., Mt. Kisco, N.Y., 1981-82; sr. fellow Council on Fgn. Rels., N.Y.C., 1982-84; mng. editor Foreign Affairs, N.Y.C., 1984-89, exec. editor, 1989—. Author: Israel in the Mind of America, 1983, A Changing Israel, 1985; co-author: The Soviet Union, 1967, The End of the Palestinian Mandate, 1985. Pres. Pembroke Coll. Found., N.Y., 1986—. Recipient Nat. Jewish Book award Jewish Book Council, 1984, Present Tense award Am. Jewish Com., 1984; named hon. fellow Pembroke Coll., 1987. Mem. Council on Fgn. Rels., The Century

Assn., United Oxford and Cambridge Univ. Club. Office: Coun on Fgn Rels 58 E 68th St New York NY 10021

GROSENBACHER, STEVEN PAUL, insurance company executive; b. Defiance, Ohio, May 15, 1952; s. Paul Russell and Peggy Jean (Bolley) Kemp G.; m. Patricia Ann Meek, June 24, 1972; children: Tracie, Steven Paul, Laura. BS, Defiance Coll., 1974. Chartered property casualty underwriter. V.p. Ins. Ctr. Defiance, Inc., Ohio, 1975—. Mem. Inst. Cert. Fin. Planners, Soc. Chartered Property Casualty Underwriters, Defiance Area C. of C. (v.p. 1988). Republican. Roman Catholic. Club: Sertoma (pres. 1981-82, Sertoman of Yr. 1982), Kettenring Country (Defiance). Lodge: Elks, Masons. Office: Stauffer Mendenhall Agency 507 5th St PO Box 276 Defiance OH 43512

GROSS, JANET LAWSON, financial planner; b. Dover, Del., May 9, 1956; d. Edward Maynard and Nathalie Randall (Smith) Fox; m. Vance T. Gross, Nov. 14, 1981. AA in Psychology and Liberal Arts, Solano Community Coll., 1976; BA, San Diego State U., 1978, MS, 1981. Cert. fin. planner. Career counselor San Diego State U., 1976-80; program dir. San Jose (Calif.) State U., 1980-82; ednl. counselor U. San Francisco, 1982-84; fin. planner Waddell & Reed, Inc., San Jose, 1984—; cons. Cert. Fin. Consulting, San Ramon, Calif., 1987—; speaker various cos. and svc. orgns., San Jose, 1985—. Tchr. dance United Spirit Assn., 1974-76; vol. Spl. Olympics Com., San Jose, 1986; mem. Pacific Neighbors. Mem. Internat. Assn. Fin. Planners, Inst. Cert. Fin. Planners, Internat. Soc. Pre-retirement Planners, Nat. Speakers Assn., Entrepreneur Inst. Republican. Office: Waddell & Reed Inc 1150 N First St Ste 119 San Jose CA 95126

GROSS, JOEL EDWARD, consultant, safety and security executive; b. Paterson, N.J., Mar. 15, 1939; s. Herman and Virginia (Bivens) G.; m. Alma Wilhemi Janner, Aug. 23, 1980. B.A. cum laude, Seton Hall U., 1977; cert. protection profl. Lab. technician Nabisco, Inc., Fairlawn, N.J., 1957-60; detective Lincoln Park (N.J.) Police Dept., 1966-79; tng. specialist Agway, Inc., Syracuse, N.Y., 1980-81; mgr. safety Drake Bakeries-Borden, Inc., Wayne, N.J., 1981-85; dir. risk mgmt. Pinkerton's Inc., N.Y.C., 1986; mgr. safety N.J. Transit, 1986-87; sr. ptnr. Hunter-Rumsen Group, 1987—; lectr. safety, security, risk mgmt., emergency disaster planning. State del. N.J. State Policemen's Benevolent Assn., Silver Life mem. Recipient commendation Sec. of Navy and Mayor of Lincoln Park, Morris County Prosecutors Office; cert. breathalyzer operator, N.J., instr. and instr. trainer defensive driving Nat. Safety Council. Served as petty officer, USN, 1960-65. Decorated Navy Commendation medal. Mem. Am. Soc. Indsl. Security, Am. Soc. Safety Engrs. Computer Security Inst., Fire Protection Assn., Am. Legion, Nat. Rifle Assn. Contbr. articles on fleet safety programs to periodicals. Research on juvenile delinquents. Home and Office: 45 Hopper Ave Pompton Plains NJ 07444

GROSS, LAWRENCE ROBERT, manufacturing executive; b. Washington, Sept. 14, 1941; s. Gerald G. and Pauline M. Gross; m. Ellen Kohn, June 14, 1970; children: Melinda K. BA, Brown U., 1963; postgrad., Georgetown Law Ctr., 1965-67. Dir., mgmt. services Welbilt Corp., New Hyde Park, N.Y., 1967-72, v.p., 1972-74, exec. v.p., 1974—, also bd. dirs.; bd. dirs. Garland Comml. Industries, Freeland, Pa. Trustee Great Neck (N.Y.) Bd. of Edn., 1981—, pres., 1982-85. Served to lt. USN, 1963-67. Office: Welbilt Corp 3333 New Hyde Park Rd New Hyde Park NY 11042

GROSS, NANCY LEE, seeding company executive; b. Crisfield, Md., Jan. 7, 1950; d. Albert Johnson and Edith Marie (Doane) Poole; m. Robert John Gross, June 29, 1968; children: Annette and Alana (twins). Student, Salisbury (Md) State Coll., 1976-77. Office clk. Landreth Seed Co., Balt., 1980-81; telemarketer Seed Corp. of Am., Balt., 1981-82, dir. sales, 1982-84, mgr. office, 1984-86, asst. gen. mgr., 1986-87; gen. mgr. Lofts Seed, Inc., Beltsville, Md., 1988—. Mem. Md. Turfgrass Assn., Md. Seeding Assn., Suburban Md. Bldg. Industry Assn., Md. Landscape Contractors Assn., Va. Landscape Contractors Assn., D.C. landscape Contractors Assn. Republican. Baptist. Office: Lofts Seed Inc 11417 Somerset Ave Beltsville MD 20705

GROSS, OAKFORD W(ILLIAM), III, finance company executive; b. Salem, N.J., Apr. 3, 1956; s. Oakford W. and Ruth O. Gross. B.S., W.Va. State Coll., 1978; m. Jacqueline L. Jones, Oct. 9, 1982; 1 child, Jacqueline L. Jr. internal auditor Community Action Pitts., Inc., 1979-80, sr. internal auditor, 1980, audit supr., 1980-83; controller, Pitts. Community Services, Inc., 1983—; bus. mgr. Three Rivers Youth, 1987-88; investment broker, ins. agt., 1984—; self-employed, acctg., computer & auditing svc. partnership, 1988—; co-owner, operator Miniature Golf Course, Pitts., 1986—, co-owner, investment real estate, 1985—. Democrat. Clubs: Spa Lady/Spa Fitness Ctr. Home: 7341 Bennett St Apt 6 Pittsburgh PA 15208

GROSS, PATRICK WALTER, business executive, management consultant; b. Ithaca, N.Y., May 15, 1944; s. Eric T. B. and Catharine B. (Rohrer) G.; m. Sheila Eve Proby, Apr. 12, 1969; children: Geoffrey Philipp, Stephanie Lovell. Student, Cornell U., 1962-63; B in Engring. Sci., Rensselaer Poly. Inst., 1965; MSE in Applied Math., U. Mich., 1966; MBA, Stanford U., 1968. Cons. info. mgmt. operation Gen. Electric Co., Schnectady, 1965-67; sr. staff mem. Office Sec. Def., Washington, 1968-69, spl. asst., 1969-70; vice chmn., prin. exec. officer Am. Mgmt. Systems, Inc., Arlington, Va., 1970—, also bd. dirs.; chmn. bd. Medlantic Enterprises Inc., 1988—; bd. dirs. Medlantic Healthcare Group, exec. com., 1982—; bd. dirs. Info.-Disc Corp. Trustee Washington Hosp. Ctr., 1977-87, Sidwell Friends Sch., 1980-88; mem. exec. com., treas. Youth for Understanding, 1984—; mem. Econ. Policy Council UNA-USA; mem. Council on Competitiveness. Mem. Fgn. Policy Assn. (bd. govs., bd. dirs., mem. exec. com. 1977-86, 87—), World Affairs Council Washington (bd. dirs., founding vice chmn. 1980—), Council Fgn. Relations, Washington Inst. Fgn. Affairs, Internat. Inst. Strategic Studies (London), Nat. Economists Club, Am. Econ. Assn., Aspen Inst. Soc. Fellows, Pilgrims of U.S., Pres.'s Assn., Smithsonian Luncheon Group, Sigma Xi, Tau Beta Pi. Clubs: Met. (Washington); Chevy Chase (Md.); Univ. (N.Y.C.). Home: 7401 Glenbrook Rd Bethesda MD 20814 Office: Am Mgmt Systems Inc 1777 N Kent St Arlington VA 22209

GROSS, PAUL ALLAN, health service executive; b. Richmond, VA, Oct. 1, 1937; s. Albert and Cynthia (Saxe) G.; m. Gail Byrd, Nov. 19, 1966; children: Lorri, Garry, Randy. Student, U. Richmond, 1956-59; B.A., U. Ga., 1961; M.H.A., Va. Commonwealth U., 1964; cert. in hosp. adminstrn., U. Miami. Cert. hosp. adminstrn., Fla. Resident Tampa Gen. Hosp., Fla., 1964; adminstrv. asst. Dallas County Hosp. Dist., 1964-66, asst. adminstr., 1966-69, sr. asst. adminstr., 1969-70, assoc. adminstr., 1971-72; clin. assoc. prof. hosp. med. care U. Tex. Southwestern Med. Sch., 1964-72, Sch. Allied Health Scis., Dallas, 1964-72; exec. dir. Humana Inc. Suburban Hosp., Louisville, 1972-76; v.p. Fla. region Humana Inc., Miami, 1976-81; sr. v.p. Pacific region Humana Inc., Newport Beach, Calif., 1981-84, exec. v.p., pres. hosp. div., 1984—, trustee acute care gen hosps., 1983—; nat. cons. Surgeon Gen. USAF, 1987—. Contbr. articles to profl. jours. Mem. health adv. com. Senator Paul Carpenter, Cypress, Calif., 1983; mem., asst. chmn. U.S. Selective Service System Local Bd. 154, Newport Beach, 1983, Bd. 113, Louisville; trustee Am. Healthcare Systems, 1981—. Served with USNR, 1955-63. Recipient Humana Club award Suburban Hosp. Central Region, Louisville, 1975, 76; named Outstanding Adminstr. of Yr., 1974. Fellow Am. Coll. Hosp. Adminstrs., Am. Coll. Health Care Execs. (com. ethics); mem. Am. Hosp. Assn. (ho. of dels., regional adv. bd.), Tex. Hosp. Assn., Hosp. Council So. Calif. (chmn. multi-instl. corp. liason com. 1983—), United Hosp. Assn. Calif. Home: 3509 Woodside Rd Louisville KY 40222 Office: Humana Inc 500 W Main St Louisville KY 40201

GROSS, RONALD MARTIN, forest products executive. BA, Ohio State U., 1955; MBA, Harvard U., 1960. With Battelle Meml. Inst., Columbus, Ohio, 1957-58, U.S. Plywood-Champion Paper, Inc., Ohio, 1960-68; with Can. Cellulose Co. Ltd., Vancouver, B.C., 1968-78; pres., chief exec. officer, dir. Can. Cellulose Co. Ltd., 1973-78; pres., chief operating officer, dir. ITT Rayonier, Inc., Stamford, Conn., 1978-81; pres., chief exec. officer, dir. ITT Rayonier, Inc., 1981-84, chmn. bd., 1984—. Office: ITT Rayonier Inc 1177 Summer St Stamford CT 06904

GROSSBARD, ARTHUR S., financial planner; b. N.Y.C., Feb. 5, 1958; s. Henry and Laura (Weissman) G.; divorced; children: Jennifer, Adam. BA in Adminstrn., Queens Coll., 1979; postgrad. in bus., Baruch Coll., 1979-80, Coll. for Fin. Planning, Denver, 1987—. Prin. Pa. Securities, Florham Park, N.J., 1979—; host TV show Fin. Decisions, 1987, radio show Fin. Planning, 1987. Mem. Internat. Assn. Fin. Planners, Inst. Cert. Fin. Planners. Republican. Jewish. Home: 29 Upper Mountain Ave Montclair NJ 07042

GROSSBERG, ESTHER ROSENSTEIN, travel executive, radio commentator; b. Chgo., Mar. 28, 1924; d. Louis E. and Mae (Kazer) Rosenstein; m. Frederick S. Grossberg, Nov. 19, 1944; children—Michael Lee, David Alan. B.A., U. Miami, 1944, postgrad Law Sch., Coral Gables, 1945-46. Sales exec. Seitlin & Co., Miami, 1946-52, Tours & Travel, Houston, 1960-64, Travel Unltd., 1964-66; sales mgr. Houston Travel Ctr., 1966-68; dir. sales Diners Fugazy Travel, Houston, 1968-69; pres. Esther Grossberg Travel Inc., Houston, 1970—, Group Travel Ctr., 1970—. Travel columnist, Texan, Southwestern Argus, Westside News, Forward Times, Pioneer, 1972-79; host weekly radio show Ask the Expert, KTRH, 1970-76, Around the World with Esther, KTSU, 1984—. Mem. Assn. Retail Travel Agts. (nat. bd. dirs. 1980-82, v.p. Tex. region 1980-82), Soc. Incentive Travel Execs., Cruise Lines Internat. Assn., Pacific Area Travel Assn., Houston Exec. Women in Travel. Avocations: Needlepoint; dancing; gourmet cooking. Home: 5555 Del Monte St Apt 505 Houston TX 77056 Office: Esther Grossberg Travel Inc 6300 W Loop S Bellaire TX 77401

GROSSET, A. DONALD, JR., bank executive; b. N.Y.C., Oct. 25, 1932; s. A. Donald and Katharine Skinner (Davis) G.; m. Dorothy Lee Willis, Sept. 10, 1961; children: Alexander Walter, Douglas Ross. BA, Princeton U., 1954. Salesman Oxford Paper Co., N.Y.C., 1957-61; v.p., prin. Leonard A. Frisbie Co., Inc., New Canaan, Conn., 1962-70; v.p. Wood, Gundy & Co., Inc., N.Y.C., 1970-72, Prescott, Ball & Turben, Inc., N.Y.C., 1972-74; co-founder, chmn. Wilderness Sports Corp., N.Y.C., 1974-76; stockbroker Moseley, Hallgarten & Estabrook, Portland, Maine, 1977-78, corp. fin. cons., 1978-84; mng. dir. Bay St. Corp., Palm Beach, Fla., 1984-87; ptnr. Bay St. Ptnrs., Armonk, N.Y., 1986-87; v.p. Bus. Research Co., Palm Beach, 1984—; pres. Bay St. Ventures, Inc., Portland, 1988—; investment advisor Pon Capital Corp., Braintree, Mass., 1987—. Served to 1st lt. U.S. Army, 1954-56. Mem. Small Bus. Assn. New Eng., Newcomen Soc. Am. Republican. Mem. United Ch. of Christ. Clubs: University, Anglers (N.Y.C.); Indian Harbor Yacht (Greenwich, Conn.). Home: Rural Rt 1 Box 1A Yarmouth ME 04096 Office: Bay St Ventures Inc 465 Congress St Suite M Portland ME 04101

GROSSI, BRIAN JOHN, engineer, corporation executive; b. Oakland, Calif., May 10, 1950; s. Bruno John and Sylvia Roring (Garshol) G.; m. Marilyn A. Woods, Oct. 11, 1980. BS in Mech. Engring., Stanford U., 1973, MME, 1973. Design engr. Hewlett Packard, Palo Alto, Calif., 1973-76; rsch. engr. SRI Internat., Menlo Park, Calif., 1976-82; gen. ptnr. Alpha Ptnrs., Menlo Park, 1982—; bd. dirs. Photonics, Campbell, Calif., Biospan, Redwood City, Calif., Answer Computer, Santa Clara, Calif. Contbr. reports to profl jours.; inventor, patentee in field. Mem. ASME, Porsche Club Am. (treas. regional chpt. 1975-76), Phi Beta Kappa, Tau Beta Pi. Republican. Episcopalian. Home: 26030 Elena Rd Los Altos Hills CA 94022 Office: Alpha Ptnrs 2200 Sandhill Rd #250 Menlo Park CA 94025

GROSSI, RICHARD J., electric utility company executive; b. 1935; married;. BS, U. Conn., 1957; MBA, U. New Haven, 1981. Engring. asst. United Illuminating Co., New Haven, 1957-65, chief mech. engr., 1965-70, project mgr. New Haven Harbor Sta., 1970-74, exec. asst. to v.p. engring. planning, then v.p. engring. planning, 1974-81, v.p. corp. planning and devel., 1981-83, exec. v.p., chief operating officer, 1983-87, pres., chief operating officer, 1987—. Office: United Illuminating Co 80 Temple St New Haven CT 06506

GROSSMAN, ANDREW CHARLES, transportation company executive; b. Mpls., Sept. 24, 1951; s. N. Bud and Alene G.; m. Stephanie Chew; children: Alene, Noah. BS, Stanford U., 1974, MBA, 1980; MD, Johns Hopkins Med. Sch., 1978. Dir. devel., exec. v.p. Gelco Travel Service, Eden Prairie, Minn., 1980; pres. Gelco Fleet Mgmt. Group, Eden Prairie, Minn., 1982, Gelco Courier Services, Eden Prairie, Minn., Dec. 1982; pres., chief exec. officer Gelco Fleet Mgmt. Services, Eden Prairie, Minn., 1984-86; exec. v.p. Gelco Corp., Eden Prairie, Minn., 1986-87, pres., chief operating officer, 1987—, also bd. dirs. Bd. govs. Mt. Sinai Hosp; bd. dirs. Metro. Corp. Office: Gelco Corp 1 Gelco Dr Eden Prairie MN 55344 *

GROSSMAN, BURTON E., corporate executive; b. Corpus Christi, Tex., Feb. 15, 1918; s. Edward and Bessie G.; m. Miriam Siegel, Apr. 23, 1980; children—Bruce Edward, Cynthia Helene. B.S. in Bus. Adminstrn., U. Tex., 1940; D.B.A. (hon.), John Dewey U., N.Y., 1981; LL.D., U. Far East, 1983; LL.D. (hon.), Mexican Acad. Internat. Law, 1985; D (hon.), U. of the Ams., Mexico City, 1988. Chmn. bd. Grossman y Asociados, Tampico, Mexico, 1964—, Sociedad Indsl., 1972—, chmn. bd., chief exec. officer Grupo Continental S.A., Tampico, 1977—; chmn. bd., chief exec. officer Asesores de Pensiones S.A., Grabados Fernando Fernandes, Mexico, chmn. bd., chief exec. officer Intercontinental Bankshares Corp., San Antonio. Vice chmn. exec. com. Chancellor's Council, U. Tex. System; mem. investment com. Rotary Internat. Served to capt. U.S. Army, 1942-46. Mem. Inst. Advanced Studies (Tamaulipas) (chmn. bd. trustees), U. Tex. Cancer Found. (bd. visitors), Pres.'s Club U. Tex., Pres.'s Club So. Meth. U., Am. Mgmt. Assn., Conf. Bd., Nat. Advt. Assn. Mexico. Avocations: golf; tennis; big game hunting; collection of cigar bands. Office: InterContinental Bankshares Corp 7710 Jones Maltsberger Suite 200 San Antonio TX 78216

GROSSMAN, EVERETT PHILIP, retail executive; b. Boston, June 10, 1924; s. Joseph B. and Esther L. G.; m. Cynthia E. Rich, Mar. 31, 1979; children: Linsey Grossman Selvitella, Heidi Grossman Soderstrom. AB, Harvard U., 1946. Exec. v.p. real estate and devel. Retail Group div. Grossman's Inc., Braintree, Mass. Served with AUS, 1943-46. Mem. Am. Assn. Mil. Engrs., Northeastern Lumberman's Assn., Mass. Retail Lumber Dealers Assn. (past pres.), South Shore C. of C., Boston C. of C. Clubs: Harvard (Boston). Lodges: Masons, B'nai B'rith. Office: Grossman's Inc 200 Union St Braintree MA 02184 *

GROSSMAN, JAY MITCHELL, publishing executive; b. Hackensack, N.J., Nov. 11, 1954; s. Martin and Joyce (Roberts) G.; m. Vicki Jan Isler, June 12, 1977; children: Lisa, Drew, Jenna. BA, Colgate U., 1976; MBA, NYU, 1982. With Simon & Schuster, Inc., N.Y.C., 1976—, v.p. ops. analysis, 1987; sr. v.p., bus. mgr. sch. group Simon & Schuster, Inc., Morristown, N.J., 1988—. Recipient Founders award Gulf & Western, Inc., 1983. Office: Silver Burdett & Ginn 250 James St Morristown NJ 07960

GROSSMAN, JEROME BARNETT, service firm executive; b. Kansas City, Kans., Sept. 9, 1919; married;. AB, U. Mich., 1941. Exec. v.p., gen. mgr. Helzberg's Diamond Shop Inc., 1941-66; dir. mktg. H & R Block, Inc., Kansas City, Mo., 1966-69, from asst. to pres., 1969-71, exec. v.p., chief operating officer, 1971-88; sr. exec. v.p., chief operating officer H & R Block, Inc., Kansas City, 1988—; also bd. dirs. H & R Block, Inc., Kansas City, Mo.; bd. dirs. CompuServe Inc., Personnel Pool Am. Inc., Path Mgmt. Industries. Served to maj. USAF, 1941-45. Office: H & R Block Inc 4410 Main St Kansas City MO 64111

GROSSMAN, MIKE, retail executive. Chmn. Grossman's Inc., Braintree, Mass., now chmn., pres., chief exec. officer. Office: Grossman's Inc 200 Union St Braintree MA 02184 *

GROSSMAN, N. BUD, personal investments and business development executive; b. 1921; widowed. BA, U. Minn., 1941. Chmn. bd., chief exec. officer Gelco Corp., Eden Prairie, Minn., 1957-87; chief exec. officer Cogel Mgmt. Co., Mpls., 1988—; bd. dirs. Ecolab, Inc., Gen. Mills, Inc., No. States Power Co., The Toro Co. Chmn. Minn. Orchestral Assn.; trustee Carleton Coll.; mem. bd. overseers U. Minn. With USAAF. Office: Cogel Mgmt Co 4670 Norwest Ctr 80 S 7th St Minneapolis MN 55402

GROSSMAN, RICHARD, software development executive; b. N.Y.C., May 29, 1953; s. Eugene M. and Cecelia G.; m. Robbin Grossman, Nov. 14, 1982. Student, U. Pa., 1971-75, CUNY, 1979-80. With McGraw-Hill Info. Systems, Royal Ins., Moore Bus. Systems, Quality Systems and Health Practice Mgmt. Systems, various locations, 1979-84; founder, programmer, pres. Tech III Inc., San Pedro, Calif., 1984—; lectr. in field. Contbr. articles to profl. jours. Mem. Assn. Data Processing Svc. Orgns. Office: Tech III Inc 255 W 5th St San Pedro CA 90731-3003

GROSSMAN, ROBERT ALLEN, transportation executive; b. Port Jervis, N.Y., July 24, 1941; s. George and Helen (Garson) G.; student Cornell U., 1959-60, U. Pa., 1960-62; m. Joan Ward, June 15, 1962 (div.); children—Jeffrey, Wendy; m. Gloria Schwartz, Nov. 22, 1987. Mgr. fin. div. North Shore Packing Co., Inc., North Bellmore, N.Y., 1962-64; mgr. refin. and legal dept. Coburn Corp. Am., Rockville Centre, N.Y., 1964-67; stock broker Weis, Voison & Cannon, Inc., N.Y.C., 1967-69, Nadel & Co., N.Y.C., 1969-70; chmn. bd., chief exec. officer, pres. Emons Industries, Inc., York, Pa., 1970—, Emons Holdings, Inc., 1986—. Mem. York Area C. of C. (dir. 1978-83), Pa. Champer of Bus. and Industry (transp. com.). Office: 96 S George St York PA 17401

GROSSMAN, RONALD, financial executive, lawyer; b. N.Y.C., May 6, 1936; m. Marilynn Pfeiffer, July 2, 1957; children—Andrea, Karen, Bruce, Dana. B.S., NYU, 1958, J.D., 1962, LL.M., 1965. Bar: N.Y. 1962. Tax mgr. Seligman & Latz, Inc., N.Y.C., 1961-62; tax asst. Freeport-McMoRan Inc., N.Y.C., 1962-65, asst. tax mgr., 1965-72, asst. dir. taxes, tax counsel, 1972-74, asst. treas., dir. taxes, 1974-77, v.p. dir. taxes and ins., 1977-83, sr. v.p., prin. fin. officer, controllership ins., mgmt. info. service, taxes and corp. planning, 1983-84, sr. v.p.-controllership, ins., mgmt. info. services and taxes, 1984—; mem. adv. com. Tulane U. Sch. Bus., New Orleans, 1986—, adv. com. tax symposium Sch. Law, 1987, 88—. Contbr. articles to profl. jours. Mem. ABA, Am. Mining Congress (tax com.), Am. Petroleum Inst. (exec. tax com.), , Tax Execs. Inst. Home: 22 Versailles Blvd New Orleans LA 70125 Office: Freeport-McMoran Inc 200 Park Ave New York NY 10166

GROSSMAN, SANFORD J., economics educator; b. Bklyn., July 21, 1953; s. Sloane and Florence G.; m. Naava; children: Shulamite and Aviva. B.A. in Econs. with honors, U. Chgo., 1973, M.A. in Econs., 1974, Ph.D. in Econs., 1975. Asst. prof. econs. Stanford U., Calif., 1975-77; economist Bd. Govs. Fed. Res., 1977-78; assoc. prof. econs. U. Pa., Phila., 1978-79, prof. econs., 1979-81; prof. econs. U. Chgo., 1981-85; John L. Weinberg prof. econs. Princeton U., N.J., 1985-89; trustee prof. fin. U. Pa., Phila., 1989—. Contbr. articles to profl. jours. Guggenheim Meml. fellow; Sloane Found. fellow; recipient Irving Fisher grad. monograph award. Fellow Econometric Soc., Am. Acad. Arts & Scis.; mem. Am. Fin. Assn. (bd. dirs.), Am. Econ. Assn. (John Bates Clark medal, Roger F. Murray First Prize award), Econometric Soc. Office: U Pa Dept Fin 3251 Steinberg-Dietrich Hall 3620 Locust Walk Philadelphia PA 19104-6367

GROSSO, JUDITH ANNE, corporate officer; b. Northampton, Eng., July 22, 1945; came to U.S., 1946; d. William B. and Pamela Hope (Allen) Morse; m. Allan J. Grosso Sr., Jan. 16, 1972; children: Kenneth J., Allan J. Jr., Angela J. Grad. high sch., Montgomery, N.Y. Sec., treas., office mgr. Grosso Equipment and Supply Co. Inc., Montgomery, 1979—. Mem. Grand Juror Assocs. Office: Grosso Equipment RR 02 Box 391 Montgomery NY 12549

GROTE, STEPHEN HENRY, engineering and construction company executive; b. Houston, July 4, 1942; s. Colquitt Baring and Henriette Ida (Daigle) G.; m. Theo Ann Ramsey, June 10, 1967 (div. June 1978); children—Paige, Amanda; m. Peggy Ann Williams, Dec. 12, 1980; children—David, Travis. B.S.M.E., Ga. Inst. Tech., 1964. Registered profl. engr., Tex. Engr., project mgr. Brown & Root, Inc., Houston, 1964-76; v.p. Brown & Root, Inc., 1976-80, sr. v.p., 1980—. Mem. ASME, Project Mgmt. Inst. Republican. Methodist. Clubs: Copperfield Tennis, Petroleum, Houston Engring. and Sci. Soc., Pine Forest Country. Office: Brown & Root USA Inc PO Box 3 Houston TX 77001

GROTEN, STUART, realty appraisal company executive; b. Bklyn.; s. Carl and Edythe (Silver) G.; m. Gail Ellen Goodman, Oct. 17, 1964; children: Erica Maya, Jason Troy, Nicole Lynn. Student, Los Angeles Valley Coll., 1970-73, U. Colo., Denver, 1975-78. Mgr., appraiser Encore Realty, North Hollywood, Calif., 1964-71; sr. appraiser SBA, Los Angeles, 1971-73; loan guaranty officer VA, various locations, 1973-84; pvt. practice real estate appraising Clearwater, Fla., 1984-85; appraiser Donald Nitz Assocs., North Haven, Conn., 1985-86; pres. Stuart Lane Co., Rocky Hill, Conn., 1986—; cons., instr. U. of S. Maine, Portland, 1980—; instr. Post Coll., Waterbury, Conn., 1988—. Mem. Nat. Assn. Rev. Appraisers (cert.), Am. Soc. Appraisers (instr. 1989—); candidate mem. Soc. Real Estate Appraisers. Home: PO Box 132 Rocky Hill CT 06067

GROUSSMAN, DEAN G., manufacturing company executive. With Can. Tire Corp. Ltd., Toronto, Ont., 1986—, formerly pres. and chief operating officer, now pres., chief exec. officer. Office: Can Tire Corp Ltd, 2180 Yonge St, Toronto, ON Canada M4P 2V8 *

GROUSSMAN, RAYMOND G., diversified utility and energy company executive; b. Price, Utah, Dec. 15, 1935; s. Raymond K. and Gene E. (Goetzman) G.; m. Marilyn Kaye Jensen, Mar. 16, 1964; children: Katherine Anne Hajeb, Laura Kaye Hunter, Daniel Ray, Adam J. B.S., U. Utah, 1961, J.D., 1966. Bar: Utah 1965, U.S. Supreme Ct. 1978. Police officer Salt Lake City Police Dept., 1962-66; mem. firm Amoss & Groussman, Salt Lake City, 1966-69; staff atty. Utah Legal Services, 1969-70; chief dep. Salt Lake County atty., 1970-71; assoc. Pugsley, Hayes, Watkiss, Campbell & Cowley, Salt Lake City, 1971-74; gen. counsel Mountain Fuel Supply Co., Salt Lake City, 1974-84; v.p. Mountain Fuel Supply Co., 1977-84; v.p., gen. counsel Questar Corp., 1984—; bd. dirs. Wexpro Co., Celsius Energy Co. Bd. dirs. Children's Service Soc. Utah, 1976-77; trustee Ft. Douglas Mil. Mus., 1976-84 ; bd. advisers Energy Law Center, U. Utah Coll. Law, 1978—; mem. criminal law revision com. Utah Legis. Council; bd. dirs. Utah Legal Services, 1970-78, United Way of Salt Lake City, 1982— Served with U.S. Army, 1957-60; lt. comdr. USCGR, 1967—. Mem. ABA, Fed. Energy Bar Assn., Am. Gas Assn., Pacific Coast Gas Assn. (chmn. legal adv. council 1979-80), Salt Lake County Bar Assn., Salt Lake Legal Defenders Assn. (dir. 1978—), Salt Lake City C. of C., Sigma Alpha Epsilon, Delta Theta Phi. Office: Questar Corp 180 E 100 S St Salt Lake City UT 84139

GROVE, ANDREW S., electronics company executive; b. Budapest, Hungary, 1936; married; 2 children. B.S., CCNY, 1960; Ph.D., U. Calif.-Berkeley, 1963. With Fairchild Camera and Instrument Co., 1963-67; pres., chief operating officer Intel Corp., Santa Clara, Calif., 1967-87, pres., chief exec. officer, 1987—; also dir. Recipient Medal award, Am. Inst. Chemists, 1960; cert. of merit, Franklin Inst.,1975; Townsend Harris medal, CCNY, 1980. Mem. Nat. Acad. Engring.; fellow IEEE (achievement award 1969, J. J. Ebers award 1974). Office: Intel Corp 3065 Bowers Ave Santa Clara CA 95051 *

GROVE, CARL SHIPMAN, chemical company executive; b. Wauscon, Ohio, Nov. 1, 1944; s. Carl and June Joan (Shipman) G.; m. Diana Lea Smith, Feb. 19, 1967; children: Steven Carl, Scott Richard. BSBA, Anderson U., 1971; MA in Mgmt., Ball State U., 1977. Prodn. control supr. GM, Anderson, Ind., 1971-78; adminstrv. asst. Fire Trucks, Inc., Mt. Clemens, Mich., 1978-79; dist. mgr. Am. Dist. Telegraph, Flint, Mich., 1979-80; sales rep. Borden Chem., North Andover, Mass., 1980-86, dist. sales mgr., 1986—. Sgt. USMC, 1966-70, Vietnam. Mem. Evergreen Lodge. Republican. Methodist. Home: 6270 Lindsey Marine City MI 48079 Office: Borden Chem 201 N Riverside Ste 103 Saint Clair MI 48079

GROVE, ERNEST L., JR., utility executive; b. Martinsburg, W.Va., 1924; (married). B.A., Denison U., Granville, Ohio, 1947; M.B.A., U. Pa., 1949; J.D., U. Conn., 1959. Vice pres., chief fin. and acctg. officer Conn. Light & Power Co., 1965-66, All N.E. Utilities Systems Co., 1966-72; exec. v.p. N.E. Utilities Service Co., 1972-75; sr. exec. v.p. fin. Detroit Edison Co., 1975-80, vice chmn. bd., chief fin. officer, 1980—, also dir.; v.p., dir. Midwest Energy Resources Co., St. Clair Energy Corp., Edison Illuminating Co., Detroit, Peninsula Electric Light Co., Washtenaw Energy Corp. Office: Detroit Edison Co 2000 2nd Ave Detroit MI 48226 *

GROVE, RUSSELL SINCLAIR, JR., lawyer; b. Marietta, Ga., Dec. 25, 1939; s. Russell Sinclair and Miriam (Smith) G.; m. Charlotte Mariam Glascock, Jan. 9, 1965; children—Farion Smith Whitman, Arthur Owen Sinclair. B.S., Ga. Inst. Tech., 1962; LL.B. with distinction, Emory U., 1964; postgrad., U. Melbourne Faculty Law, Australia, 1965. Bar: Ga. 1965, U.S. Supreme Ct. 1971, U.S. Ct. Appeals (11th cir.) 1983. Assoc. Smith, Currie & Hancock, Atlanta, 1966-67; assoc. Hansell & Post, Atlanta, 1968-72, ptnr., 1972—; mem. adv. com. Ctr. for Legal Studies; mem. exec. com. real property law sect., sec. 1988—. Author: Word Processing and Automatic Data Processing in the Modern Law Office, 1978, Legal Considerations of Joint Ventures, 1981, Structuring Endorsements and Affirmative Insurance, 1981, Management's Perspective on Automation, 1981, Mineral Law: Current Developments and Future Issues, 1983; co-author: The Integrated Data and Word Processing System, 1981, Georgia Partnership Law: Current Issues and Problems, 1982; (with D.E. Glass) Georgia Real Estate Forms-Practice, 1987; editor-in-chief Jour. Pub. Law, 1963-64. Mem. Central Atlanta Progress, Inc.; bd. dirs. Caribbean Mission, Inc. Served with USMCR, 1960-65. Mem. ABA, Ga. Bar Assn. (exec. com. real property law sect., sec. 1988-89), Atlanta Bar Assn., Bryan Soc., U.S. Marine Corps Assn. Ga. Lawyers, Eastern Mineral Law Found., Am. Coll. Mortgage Attys., Ga. State Bar (mem. joint com. partnership law UPA/ULPA), Am. Coll. Real Estate Lawyers, Ga. Oil and Gas Assn., Ga. Cattlemen's Assn., Nat. Cattlemen's Assn., Am. Scotch Highland Breeders Assn., Can. Highland Cattle Soc., Highland Cattle Soc. U.K., Phi Delta Phi, Omicron Delta Kappa. Episcopalian. Clubs: Dunwoody Country, Commerce, Lawyers of Atlanta, Ashford. Office: Hansell & Post 3300 First Atlanta Tower 2 Peachtree St NW Atlanta GA 30383

GROVE, THOMAS KEITH, periodontist, veterinarian, consultant; b. Pitts., Feb. 9, 1947; s. Thomas Wesley and Mary Louise (Treharne) G.; 1 child, Erin Whitney. BA, U. Pa., 1969, VMD, 1982; DDS, U. Detroit, 1972; MS in Periodontics, U. Mich., 1975. Diplomate Am. Vet. Dental Coll. (chmn. exam. com.). Pvt. practice dentistry Royal Oak, Mich., 1972-73; specializing in periodontics Abington, Pa., 1974-80, Chadds Ford, Pa., 1980-82, Vero Beach, Fla., 1982—; pvt. practice vet. medicine specializing in dentistry Vero Beach, 1982—; instr. Dental Sch., U. Detroit, 1972-73; resident in periodontics U. Mich., Ann Arbor, 1973-75; assoc. in periodontics Sch. Dental Medicine, U. Pa., Phila., 1975-76; cons. in periodontics Abington Meml. Hosp., 1975-80; cons. Upjohn Co., Ft. Dodge Co., Procter and Gamble Co.; lectr. numerous human and vet. dentistry meetings and instns. Former asst. editor, editor Detroit Dental Spectrum; contbr. numerous articles to dental and vet. jour., also reviewer. Fellow Acad. Vet. Dentistry (charter, hon.; past mem. exam. com.); mem. Am. Assn. Implantologists, Am. Vet. Dental Soc., Tri County Dental Soc., Am. Veterinary Dental Coll. (charter diplomate), Omicron Kappa Upsilon. Office: 1956 41st Ave Ste A Vero Beach FL 32960

GROVER, BRENT RICHARD, distribution executive, accountant; b. Cleve., Aug. 7, 1950; s. Jerome E. and Shirley (Bass) G.; m. Candace Lynn Rose, Apr. 24, 1976; children: Robert Carlton, Charles Carlton. BS in Acctg., Case Western Res. U., 1971. CPA, Ohio. Mem. staff Arthur Andersen & Co., Cleve., 1971-75; contr. Nat. Paper & Packaging Co., 1975-78, treas., 1978-84, v.p., 1984-86, exec. v.p., chief operating officer, 1987—. Contbr. articles to profl. jours. Officer Jewish Community Ctr., Cleve., 1980—; pres. United Cerebral Palsy Assn., Cleve., 1985—. Mem. Am. Inst. CPAs, Ohio Soc. CPAs, Nat. Paper Trade Assn. (dir. 1987—), Oakwood Club, Univ. Club. Office: Nat Paper & Packaging Co 1240 E 55th St Cleveland OH 44103

GROVES, FRANKLIN NELSON, business executive; b. Mpls., Dec. 28, 1930; s. Frank Malvon and Hazel Olive (Nelson) G.; m. Carolyn Mary Thomas, July 31, 1954; children: Catherine Mary, Elizabeth Ann Groves Richardson, Franklin N. Jr. B.A., U. Minn., 1954. With S.J. Groves & Sons Co., Mpls., 1954—, v.p., treas., 1964-69, pres., 1969—; chmn. bd. S.J. Groves & Sons Co., 1971—, also dir., pres. subs. corps., 1964—. Pres. trustees Groves Found.; bd. dirs. Groves Learning Center; bd. dirs. Breeder's Cup. Served to 1st lt. USAF, 1954-56. Mem. Am. Saddle Horse Breeders Assn. (dir.), Moles, Beavers, Phi Beta Kappa, Beta Kappa Sigma. Clubs: Mpls. Athletic; Thoroughbred of Am.; LaFayette Country (Wayzata, Minn.). Home: 2730 Woolsey Ln Wayzata MN 55391 Office: S J Groves & Sons Co PO Box 1267 10000 Hwy 55 W Minneapolis MN 55440

GROVES, RAY JOHN, accountant; b. Cleve., Sept. 7, 1935; m. Anne Keating, Aug. 18, 1962; children: David, Philip, Matthew. BS summa cum laude, Ohio State U., 1957. CPA, Ohio. With Ernst & Whinney, Cleve. and N.Y.C., 1957—; ptnr. Ernst & Whinney, 1966-71, nat. ptnr., 1971-77; chmn., chief exec. officer Ernst & Whinney, N.Y.C., 1977—; pres. adv. council Coll. Bus. Ohio State U., 1979-80; mem. adv. council U. Chgo. Grad. Sch. Bus. Councilman City of Lyndhurst, Ohio, 1969-72; chmn. bd. trustees Leadership Cleve., 1977-79; trustee Hawken Sch., 1976-86; mem. exec. com. Tax Found.; mem. bd. overseers Wharton Sch. U. Pa.; mem. exec. com. U. Calif. Securities Regulation Inst.; vice chmn. bd. trustees Ursuline Coll., Cleve., 1970-86; mng. dirs. Met. Opera Assn. Mem. Am. Inst. CPA's (chmn. bd. dirs. 1984-85), Nat. Assn. Securities Dealers (bd. govs. 1981-84), Nat. Assn. Accts., Am. Stock Exchange (bd. govs.). Republican. Clubs: Union, Cleve. Athletic; Pepper Pike (Ohio); Mayfield Country (South Euclid, Ohio); Opera, Board Room, Links (N.Y.C.); Metropolitan (Washington); Blind Brook (Purchase, N.Y.); Laurel Valley Country. Home: 1566 Ponus Ridge New Canaan CT 06840 also: 15 W 53d St Apt 19D New York NY 10019 Office: Ernst & Whinney 787 7th Ave New York NY 10019

GROVES, ROSALIND GANZEL, corporate communications specialist; b. Phila., Aug. 1, 1934; d. John Edward and Flora Edith (Shultz) Ganzel; m. Harold Eber Woodbridge, Dec. 7, 1951 (div. June 1966); children: John Arthur, Martin Alan, June Marie; m. Gary Wayne Groves, Aug. 7, 1975 (div. 1980). AA, Fla. Keys Community Coll., 1972; BA, U. N. Fla., 1975. Cert. profl. Hypnotist, Fla.; registered ins. agt., Fla. Program analyst USN Officer-in-Charge Constrn. Trident, St. Marys, Ga., 1981-83; with acctg. dept. USN Officer-in-Charge Constrn. Trident, St. Marys, 1983-84; telephone communications USN, NAS Jacksonville, Jacksonville, Fla., 1985—; ins. agt. Hill and Co., Jacksonville, 1986—; also freelance writer/editor; dir. Behavior Modification Ctr., Jacksonville, 1983—; cons. hypnosis, Jacksonville, Fla., 1983—. Counselor Vo. Jacksonville, 1975-76; tchr. Duval County Sch. System, 1984; mem. Key West Art & Hist. Soc., 1984—; speaker Naval Air Station Jacksonville Speakers Bur., 1985—; vol. Jacksonville Upbeat Program, 1986—. Named Honorary Fire Reservist #772 Phila. Fire Dept. Mem. Inst. Advanced Hyponology (newsletter editor 1983-85, sec. 1983-85, v.p. 1986-87), Navy League U.S., Fla. Assn. Profl. Hypnosis (newsletter editor 1985-87), The Exec. Female, Assn. to Advance Ethical Hypnosis, So. Bell Large Users Coun. (steering com. 1988-89), Navy League, Jacksonville C. of C., Offshore Power Boat Racing Assn. Republican. Mem. Ch. of Christ. Club: Internat. Toastmistress (sponsored new club). Home: 7212 Cypress Cove Rd Jacksonville FL 32244

GROWICK, PHILIP, advertising executive; b. New York, Dec. 28, 1944; s. Morris and Rose (Tunick) G.; m. Maiju; children: Matthew, Kevin. B.A., Hunter Coll., 1966. Creative dir. Metromedia, N.Y.C., 1968-69; v.p., creative dir. Alan Wolsky & Friends, N.Y.C., 1969-70, SZF, Inc., N.Y.C., 1970-72, Jack Byrne Advt., N.Y.C., 1972-75; pres. Philip Growick Assocs., N.Y.C., 1975—. Author: Hail to the Chief, 1964, Do You Joujou?, 1984. Editor: Nudeniks, 1964. Contbr. Madison Ave. Mag., 1974. Bd. dirs. Tzedake Umpare, N.Y.C., 1981—. Recipient Andy awards, Advt. Club N.Y., 1976, 77, 78, 83, CLIO awards, 1977, 79, 81, Retail Advt. Conf. award, 1977, 78, 81, 83, Art Dirs. Club award, 1981, IMAA award, 1986. Club: Salem Pond & Yacht (Milford, Pa.) (pres. 1983—). Avocations: history studies, political history, scuba, ancient Rome. Home: 5700 Arlington Ave Riverdale NY 10471

GRUBB, DAVID H., construction company executive; b. 1938; married. BCE, Princeton U.; MSCE, Stanford U. With Swinerton and Walberg Co., San Francisco, 1963—, sr. v.p., then exec. v.p. San Structural div., now exec. v.p. ops., also bd. dirs. Office: Swinerton & Walberg Co 580 California St San Francisco CA 94104 *

GRUBB, EDGAR HAROLD, retail food industry executive; b. Harrisburg, Pa., May 8, 1939; s. Harold E. and Ruth (Longenecker) G.; m. Patricia A. Kerwin, Dec. 14, 1963; children: Dennis, Lisa, Mary, Jennifer. BS, Pa. State U., 1961; MBA, Calif. State U., Fullerton, 1967. CPA, Calif. Cons. mgr., auditor Coopers & Lybrand, L.A., 1968-72; group contr. Crown Zellerbach Corp., San Francisco, 1972-75, gen. mgr. packaging papers, 1976-77, dir. planning, 1978-80, v.p. consumer, 1981-82, v.p., contr., 1983-84, sr. v.p., chief fin. officer, 1984-86; sr. v.p., chief fin. officer Lucky Stores, Inc., Dublin, Calif., 1986—; bd. dirs. Goodwill Industries of Alameda/Contra Costa/Solano Counties. Capt. USMC, 1961-65. Mem. AICPA, Calif. Soc. CPAs, Fin. Execs. Inst. Friends of Hearst Gallery, Walnut Creek Open Space Found. Roman Catholic. Home: 41 Comistas Ct Walnut Creek CA 94598 Office: Lucky Stores Inc 6300 Clark Ave PO Box BB Dublin CA 94568

GRUBB, L(EWIS) CRAIG, financial company executive, consultant; b. Canton, Ohio, June 1, 1954; s. Lewis G. and Janet M. (Hornback) G.; m. Carol Elizabeth Norvell, Dec. 19, 1981; children: Carie Lynne, Chelsea Michelle. Student, W.Va. Wesleyan Coll., 1972-74. Regional rep. IDS/Am. Express Corp., Tucson, 1982-84; v.p. Mut. Benefit Fin. Group, Tucson, 1984-86, Am. Fin. Cos. (formerly Estate Fin. Services Ltd.), Tucson, 1986—; also bd. dirs. Estate Fin. Services Ltd., Tucson. Bd. dirs. Desert Survivors Inc., Tucson, 1984-86. Mem. Internat. Assn. Fin. Planners, Gen. Agts. and Mgrs. Assn. Republican. Lodge: Masons. Home: 6573 Calle Herculo Tucson AZ 85710 Office: Estate Fin Svcs Ltd 950 N Finance Center Dr Suite 180 Tucson AZ 85710

GRUBB, NORMEN E., investment planning company executive; b. Battle View, N.D., Apr. 2, 1926; s. Edor S. and Gina (Pladson) G.; m. Lavon O. Nelson, June 18, 1950; children: Nolan, Donelda, Zona, Stanton, Natalie. Cert., Minn. Sch. Bus., 1949. Dist. mgr. I.D.S. Fin. Svcs., Minot, 1959-87; mem. N.D. Ho. of Reps., 1973. Chmn. N.D. Alliance 1989—; bd. dirs. Powers Lake (N.D.) Sch. Dist., 1967-77. With U.S. Army, 1946-47. Mem. Saddle Club (pres. Powers Lake chpt. 1959-64), Better Life Group (Minot, pres. 1978-85). Mem. Assembly of God Ch. Home: 1829 SW Eighth St Minot ND 58701 Office: FSC Securities Corp 900 20th Ave SW Minot SD 58701

GRUBB, WILLIAM FRANCIS X., consumer software executive, marketing executive; b. N.Y.C., Aug. 11, 1944; s. William Martin and Eileen F. (Donnelly) G.; m. Eileen B. O'Leary, Apr. 4, 1964; children: Catherine E., William M., Kerri A., Christopher M. B.A., Fordham U., 1966; M.B.A., Seton Hall U., 1972. Mktg. and sales exec. Black & Decker, Towson, Md., 1968-79; v.p. mktg. Atari, Sunnyvale, Calif., 1979-81; chmn., pres. New West Mktg., Mountain View, Calif., 1981; pres., chief exec. officer, chmn. Imagic, Los Gatos, Calif., 1981-84; exec. v.p. Dataspeed, 1984-85; pres. Axlon Inc., 1985-86; exec. v.p., gen. mgr. Worlds of Wonder, Inc., Freemont, Calif., 1986-87; pres., chief exec. The Complete PC, Milpitas, Calif., 1987—. Home: 12421 Fredericksburg Dr Saratoga CA 95070 Office: The Complete PC 521 Cottonwood Dr Milpitas CA 95035

GRUBBS, DONALD SHAW, JR., actuary; b. Bellvue, Pa., Dec. 15, 1929; s. Donald Shaw and Zora Fay (Craven) G.; m. Margaret Helen Crooke, Dec. 27, 1969; children: David, Deborah, Daniel, Dawson, Dwight, Douglas. AB, Tex. A&M U., 1951; postgrad., Los Angeles State Coll., 1953-54, Fresno State Coll., 1954-55, Boston U., 1955-57, Princeton Theol. Sem., 1959-60, Westminster Theol. Sem., 1960-61; JD, Georgetown U., 1979. Bar: D.C. 1979. Actuarial asst. New Eng. Mut. Life Ins. Co., Boston, 1955-58, Warner Watson, Inc., Boston, 1958-59; cons. actuary John B. St. John, Penllyn, Pa., 1959-65, Grubbs & Co., Phila., 1965-72; v.p. actuary Nat. Health and Welfare Retirement Assn., N.Y.C., 1972-74; dir. actuarial div. IRS, Washington, 1974-76; cons. actuary Buck Cons., Inc., Washington, 1976-86; pres. Grubbs and Co., Inc., Silver Spring, Md., 1986—; chmn. Joint Bd. for Enrollment Actuaries, Washington, 1975-76. Author (with G.E. Johnson): The Variable Annuity, 1967, (with D.M. McGill) Fundamentals of Privated Pensions, 6th ed., 1989. V.p. Ambler (Pa.) NAACP, 1961-61; chmn. Warminster (Pa.) Child Day Care Assn., 1962-64. Served to 1st lt. U.S. Army 1951-53, Korea. Decorated Bronze Star with V U.S. Army, 1953; recipient Employee Benefits Outstanding Achievement award Pension World, 1986. Fellow Soc. of Actuaries (sec. 1983-84), Conf. Actuaries in Pub. Practice; mem. Middle Atlantic Actuarial Club. (pres. 1981-82), ABA. Democrat. Unitarian. Home and Office: 10216 Royal Rd Silver Spring MD 20903

GRUBBS, GERALD REID, furniture company executive; b. Richmond, Va., Oct. 15, 1947. BA, U. Richmond, 1969, M. in Commerce, 1975. Sr. v.p. Sperry & Hutchinson Furniture, High Ponit, N.C., 1979-82; pres. Daystrom Furniture, South Boston, Va., 1983—. Office: Daystrom Furniture Sinai Rd South Boston VA 24592

GRUBE, F. W., refining company executive; b. 1947; married;. BSCE, Rose Humlan Inst., 1970; MBA, Harvard U., 1972. With Rock Island Refining Corp., Indpls., 1972—, v.p. exploration and corp. devel., 1979-83, exec. v.p., 1983—, also bd. dirs. Office: Rock Island Refining Corp PO Box 68007 Indianapolis IN 46268 *

GRUBSTEIN, JEROLD, manufacturing company executive; b. N.Y.C., 1944. BS, CUNY, 1965. Account mgr. IBM Corp., 1965-70; controller Diachem Corp., 1971-73; v.p., controller Petric Stores Corp., 1973-80; v.p., controller Zale Corp., Irving, Tex., 1981-84, sr. v.p., 1984-87, former chief fin. officer; pres., chief operating officer Mich. Gen. Corp., Dallas, 1987—, also bd. dirs. Office: Mich Gen Corp PO Box 819025 Dallas TX 75381-9025 *

GRUE, HOWARD WOOD, insurance company executive; b. Champlain, N.Y., June 5, 1927; s. John A. and Bessie (Wood) G.; m. Marilyn White, Nov. 4, 1950; children: Brian H., David H. AA, Champlain Coll., 1948; BS, U. Vt., 1950; postgrad. in mgmt., Northwestern U., 1981. With LIberty Mut. Ins. Co., 1950—; claims adjustor New Haven, 1950-54, sales rep., 1954-56; mgr. Utica, N.Y., 1956-61; dist. sales mgr. Buffalo, 1961-62; div. dir. hiring and tng. Pitts., 1962-63; dir. hiring Boston, 1963-67, asst. v.p., dir. adminstrn. bus. sales, 1972-75; dist. mgr. Syracuse, N.Y., 1967-72; v.p., mgr. Mid-west div. Chgo., 1975—; bd. dirs. Am. Mut. Reins. Co., Lisle, Ill. Served with USN, 1945-46, PTO. Republican. Presbyterian. Club: Union League (Chgo.). Office: Liberty Mut Ins Co 555 W Pierce Rd Itasca IL 60143-2691

GRUENEWALD, PATRICIA MARY, securities principal; b. St. Louis, Mar. 17, 1953; d. Joseph Charles and Ruth Ann (Mueller) Taschler; m. Gary Allen Gruenewald, Nov. 7, 1975 (div. Apr. 1986); 1 child, Kevin Gary. BSBA, U. Mo., St. Louis, 1975; MA in Computer Data Mgmt., Webster U., 1985. Supr. estates and legal securities Edward D. Jones & Co., St. Louis, 1978-80, mgr. money market fund processing, 1980-84, mgr. mut. fund processing, 1983-84, mgr. gen. prin. funds processing and daily passport cash trust, 1984-88, mgr. trade processing, 1989—; mem. ICI Mut. Fund. Adv. Com., Washington, 1986-88. Campaign worker Kit Bond for Senate, St. Louis, 1986, John Danforth for Senate com., 1987-88. Mem. Single Profls. Assn., NAFE, St. Louis Fin. Assn., Parents without Ptnrs. (sec. 1987-88). Office: Edward D Jones 201 Progress Pkwy Maryland Heights MO 63043

GRUENSTEIN, CELESTE, lawyer; b. Tacoma, May 15, 1959; d. Peter and Ruth Eleanor (Martin) Gruenstein. BA in Philosophy, Maharishi Internat. U., 1980; JD, U. Fla., 1984. Bar: Fla. 1984. Assoc. English, McCaughan & O'Bryan, Ft. Lauderdale, Fla., 1984-86, McCune, Hiaasen, Crum, Ferris & Gardner, Ft. Lauderdale, 1986-88; in house counsel Mini Doro Enterprises, Inc., Plainville, Conn., 1988—. Editor: (manual) Involving Vols., 1988. V.p. Citizens Adv. Com. Community Devel., Gainesville, Fla., 1982-84; mem. Gov. Affairs Task Force, Ft. Lauderdale, 1984; bus. analyst Small Bus. Devel. Ctr., 1987—. Mem. Fla. Bar and Real Property Assn., Nat. Assn. Realtors, Atty.'s Title Ins. Fund, Broward County Women Lawyer's Assn., Phi Delta Phi (outstanding alumna award 1988), Tower Club, Gold Coast Venture Capital Club. Republican. Home: 1850 NW 32d Ct Fort Lauderdale FL 33309 Office: Mini Doro Enterprises Inc PO Box 7001 Plainville CT 06062

GRUENWALD, GEORGE HENRY, new products management consultant; b. Chgo., Apr. 23, 1922; s. Arthur Frank and Helen (Duke) G.; m. Corrine Rae Linn, Aug. 16, 1947; children: Helen Marie Gruenwald Orlando, Paul Arthur. B.S. in Journalism, Northwestern U., 1947; student, Evanston Acad. Fine Arts, 1937-38, Chgo. Acad. Fine Arts, 1938-39, Grinnell Coll., 1940-41. Asst. to pres. Uarco, Inc., Chgo., 1947-49; creative dir., mgr. mdse. Willy-Overland Motors Inc., Toledo, 1949-51; new products, brand and advt. mgr. Toni Co., Chgo., 1951-53; v.p., creative dir., account supr. E.H. Weiss Agy., Chgo., 1953-55; exec. v.p., supr. mgmt. North Advt., Chgo., 1955-71; pres., treas., dir. Pilot Products, Chgo., 1963-71; pres., dir. Advance Brands, Inc., Chgo., 1963-71; exec. v.p., dir. Campbell Mithun Inc., Mpls. and Chgo., 1971-72; pres., dir. Campbell Mithun Inc., 1972-79, chmn., dir., 1979-81, chief exec. officer, dir., 1981-83, chief creative officer, dir., 1983-84; vice-chmn., dir. Ted Bates Worldwide, N.Y.C., 1979-80; mgmt. cons. new products 1984—. Author: New Product Development-What Really Works, 1985; (videos) New Products Seven Steps to Success, 1988, New Product Development, 1989; editor-in-chief Oldsmobile Rocket Circle mag., 1956-64, Hudson Family mag., 1955; expert columnist Mktg. News, 1988—; commentator Am. Pub. Radio, 1989—; contbr. articles to profl. jours.; creator numerous packaged consumer products. Trustee Chgo. Pub. TV Assn., 1969-73, Mpls. Soc. Fine Arts, 1975-83, Linus Pauling Inst. Sci. and Medicine, Palo Alto, 1984—; chmn., v.p., chmn. class reps. Northwestern U. Alumni Fund Council, Chgo., 1965-68; trustee, chmn., pres., chief exec. officer, chmn. exec. com. Twin Cities Pub. TV Corp., 1971-84; trustee Minn. Pub. Radio Inc., 1973-77, vice chmn., 1974-75; bd. dirs., exec. com. Pub. Broadcasting Service, Washington, 1978-86, bd. dirs., 1988—; bd. dirs. St. Paul Chamber Orch., 1982-84,, San Diego Chamber Orch., 1986-88; mem. adv. bd. San Diego State U. Pub. Broadcasting Community, 1986—. Served with USAAF, 1943-45, MTO. Recipient Hermes award Chgo. Federated Advt. Clubs, 1963; Ednl. TV awards, 1969, 71, 86. Mem. Am. Assn. Advt. Agys. (mgmt. com. 1976-84), NSPE (project mem.), Nat. Soc. Profl. Journalists, Internat. Assn. Cooking Profls., Am. Inst. Wine and Food (bd. dirs. 1985—). Office: PO Box 1696 Rancho Santa Fe CA 92067

GRUM, CLIFFORD J., publishing executive; b. Davenport, Iowa, Dec. 12, 1934; s. Allen F. and Nathalie (Cate) G.; m. Janelle Lewis, May 1, 1965; 1 son, Christopher J. B.A., Austin Coll., 1956; M.B.A., U. Pa., 1958. Formerly with Republic Nat. Bank, Dallas; former v.p. fin. Temple Industries, Diboll, Tex.; with Time, Inc., N.Y.C., treas., 1973-75, v.p., 1975-80, exec. v.p., 1980-84, also bd. dirs.; pub. Fortune, 1975-79; pres., chief exec. officer Temple-Inland, Inc., Diboll, 1984—; dir. Cooper Industries, Inc., Premark Internat., Inc. Trustee Austin Coll. Office: Temple Inland Inc 303 S Temple Dr PO Drawer N Diboll TX 75941

GRUNDFEST, JOSEPH ALEXANDER, federal agency administrator, lawyer, economist; b. N.Y.C., Sept. 8, 1951; s. Michael A. and Esther G.; m. Carol Chia-Ming Hsu, Aug. 6, 1978. MSc Program, London Sch. Econs., 1972; BA, Yale U., 1973; JD, PhD (ABD) in Econs., Stanford U., 1978. Bar: Calif. 1978, D.C. 1979, Supreme Ct. 1987. Economist, cons. Rand Corp., Santa Monica, Calif., 1973-78; assoc. Wilmer, Cutler & Pickering, Washington, 1979-84; counsel, sr. economist Council Econ. Advisers, Washington, 1984-85; commr. SEC, Washington, 1985—. Contbr. articles to profl. jours. Research fellow Brookings Inst., 1978-79, Stanford U. fellow, 1974-78, Calif. State law and econs. fellow, 1974-78. Mem. ABA, Am. Fin. Assn., SEC and Fin. Reporting Inst. (adv. council), Heyman Ctr. (adv. council). Office: SEC 450 5th St NW Washington DC 20549

GRUNER, C. GEORGE, financial executive; b. Middletown, N.Y., Apr. 27, 1946; s. Charles Lewis Gruner and Bernice Anita (George) Gruner Morse; m. Christina Wright, Aug. 22, 1986; children by previous marriage: Diane, Shannon; 3 stepchildren. Student, Leo Coll. Field underwriter N.Y. Life Ins. Co., Middletown, 1967-73, mgr., 1973-80; fin. planner G&M Mgmt./N.Y. Life, Middletown, 1981-88, pres., chief exec. officer, 1988—; pres., chief exec. officer Mid Valley Funding In., Middletown, 1988—. Mem. Nat. Assn. Life Underwriters (Nat. Sale Achievement award 1988), Mid Hudson Estate Planning Council, Nat. Assn. Fin. Planners, Coll. Fin. Planning. Republican. Office: G&M Mgmt 22 Mulberry St Ste 1D Middletown NY 10940

GRUNKEMEYER, ROBERT RAYMOND, training professional; b. Winnipeg, Man., Can., Oct. 25, 1951; came to U.S., 1951; s. Robert Franklyn and Hattie (Ferance) G.; m. Carol Ann Klosterkemper, Oct. 4, 1975; 1 child, Christian Robert. Student. U. Cin., 1969-74. Rep. sales Prentice-Hall, Inc., Lexington, Ky., 1979-82; dist. mgr. sales Prentice-Hall, Inc., Cin., 1982-86; nat. tng. dir. Prentice-Hall, Inc., Paramus, N.J., 1986—. Mem. Nat. Assn. Tng. Dirs., Am. Mgmt. Assn. Republican. Roman Catholic. Office: Prentice Hall Info Svcs 235 Frisch Ct Paramus NJ 07652

GRUSH, MARY ELLEN, computer company executive; b. Aurora, Ill., Oct. 28, 1947; d. Byron Edward and Olga Marion (Olson) Grush; m. Kenneth Takagi Takara, Oct. 25, 1981; 1 child, Stephanie Suzanne Grush. B.A., Ft. Wright Coll., 1971; M.A., U. Denver, 1975. Mgr. met. info. retrieval network Bibliog. Ctr. for Research, Denver, 1975-77; customer services rep. tng. Lockheed Dialog Info. Systems, Palo Alto, Calif., 1977-78, computer ops. supr., 1978—. Mem. ALA, Spl. Libraries Assn., Beta Phi Mu, Pi Delta Phi. Home: PO Box 1378 Los Altos CA 94023

GRUSS, MARTIN DAVID, private investor; b. N.Y.C., Mar. 1, 1943; s. Joseph Saul and Caroline (Zelaznik) G.; m. Agneta Peterson; m. Audrey Butvay, June 28, 1988; children: Joshua, Amanda. BSE, U. Pa., 1964; LLB, N.Y. U., 1967. Sr. ptnr. Gruss Ptnrs., N.Y.C. Mem. N.Y. Bar Assn. Office: Gruss & Co 900 3rd Ave New York NY 10022

GRUVER, JAMES DAVID, banker; b. Pottsville, Pa., Feb. 12, 1947; s. John R. and Anna M. (Beneck) G.; m. Susan R. Schoffstall, Feb. 27, 1966; children: Laura R., Lisa M. BA in Math, West Chester (Pa.) U., 1969; diploma, Am. Inst. Banking, Washington, 1979; MBA in Fin., Widener U., 1981. Programming asst. West Chester U., 1965-69; project leader Cen. Pa. Nat. Bank, Phila., 1969-71; with 1st Nat. Bank West Chester, 1971—; sr. v.p. 1st Nat. Bank West Chester, West Chester, 1986—; prof. banking Pa. State U., Media, 1984—; lectr., instr. Am. Inst. Banking, 1978—. Contbr. articles to profl. jours. Pres. West Chester C. of C., 1980. Recipient Gold award Chester County United Way, 1985. Mem. Data Processing Mgmt. Assn. (pres. 1977-78), Am. Inst. Banking, (pres. Valley Forge chpt. 1982-83). Republican. Lutheran. Club: Exchange. Lodge: Rotary. Office: 1st Nat Bank West Chester 9 N High St PO Box 523 West Chester PA 19381

GRUZEWSKI, FRANK RICHARD, controller, accountant; b. Chgo., Nov. 14, 1946; s. Frank W. and Bernice (Kukenis) G.; m. Carol Jean Cozzi, Apr. 19, 1969; children: David, Nicholas, Matthew. BS in Acctg., Roosevelt U., 1975, MBA, 1982. CPA, Ill. Various fin. positons micro-film products div. Bell & Howell, Chgo., 1968-79, asst. controller, 1979-81, mktg. coord., 1981, mgr. sales ops., 1981-83, nat. ops. mgr. micro mgmt. div., 1983-86, controller, 1986-87; controller Heidenhain Corp., Elk Grove, Ill., 1988; contr. Ansco Photo-Optical Products Corp., Elk Grove, 1987—. Served with ensign U.S. Army, 1965-67, Korea. Mem. Assn. for Info. and Image Mgmt., Nat. Assn. for Accts. Home: 525 S Cedarcrest Dr Schaumburg IL 60193

GUADAGNO, BETTY ANN, electrical contracting firm executive; b. N.Y.C., Jan. 6, 1955; d. Matthew Charles and Mary (Settembrini) Benincasa; m. Salvatore Joseph Guadagno III, Feb. 14, 1982. B of Profl. Studies Pace U., 1982. Coordinator bus. affairs RCA Direct Mktg., N.Y.C., 1979-81, adminstr. bus. affairs, 1981-82; mgr. bus. affairs, Inc., N.Y.C., 1982-86; pres. B.S.G. Electric Co., Inc., Hawthorne, N.Y., 1986-89; designers showcase Westchester, Ltd., Yorktown Heights, N.Y., 1989—. Mem. Alpha Chi. Avocations: piano, target shooting. Office: Westchester Ltd PO Box 5 Yorktown Heights NY 10589

GUARINO, SALVATORE FRANK, hotel executive; b. Phila., Mar. 13, 1937; s. Frank and Filomena (Dodaro) G.; m. Marie Louise Mercaldo, Nov. 26, 1960; children: Marc, Marisa. Cert. in acctg., Peirce Jr. Coll., 1956; BA, Drexel U., 1958; postgrad. degree in Profl. Mgmt. Devel., Harvard U., 1984. With Horwath & Horwth, Phila., 1958-65; treas. Shelburne Properties, Atlantic City, N.J., 1965-68; hotel mgr. Prestige Motor Properties, King of Prussia, Pa., 1968-74; asst. to sr. v.p. Hilton Hotels Corp., Chgo., 1974-76, v.p., 1981-86, sr. v.p., 1986—; regional mgr. Hilton Inns, Inc., Chgo., 1976-78, v.p., 1979-81, sr. v.p., 1981—. Bd. dirs. Nazareth Acad., Lagrange, Ill.; pres.'s council St. Mary's Coll., Winona, Minn. Mem. Industry Real Estate Fin. Adv. Council, Am. Hotel/Motel Assn., Urban Land Inst. Home: 5603 Middle Crest Dr Agoura Hills CA 91301 Office: Hilton Hotels Corp 9336 Civic Center Dr Beverly Hills CA 90209

GUCKENHEIMER, DANIEL PAUL, banker; b. Tel Aviv, Oct. 10, 1943; s. Ernest and Eva Guckenheimer; came to U.S., 1947, naturalized, 1957; B.B.A. in Fin., U. Houston, 1970; cert. hosp. adminstrn., Trinity U., San Antonio, 1973; m. Helen Sandra Fox, Dec. 21, 1969; children—Debra Ellen, Julie Susan. Asst. adminstr. Harris County Hosp. Dist., Houston, 1970-76; pres. Mid Am. Investments, Kansas City, Kans., 1976; exec. dir. Allen County Hosp., Iola, Kans., 1977-78; comml. loan officer Traders Bank, Kansas City, Mo., 1979; v.p. and mgr. Traders Ward Pkwy. Bank, 1980, v.p., mgr. installment loans, 1981, v.p., comml. loan officer, 1982; sr. v.p., mgr. comml. loans United Mo. Bank South, 1982—. bd. dirs. Robert Morris Assocs. Bd. dirs. United Way, Iola, Kans., 1977-78, Food Distbn., Inc., 1983-88; adv. bd. Country Side Estate Nursing Home, Iola, 1977-78; clinic adminstr. 190th USAF Clinic, 1977-84; Served with USAF, 1962-66, maj. Res., retired 1984. Mem. Am. Coll. Hosp. Adminstrs., N.G. Assn., C. of C. Kansas City (Mo.), Am. Bankers Assn., Mo. Bankers Assn., Olympic Soc., Internat. Platform Assn., Nat. Assn. Credit Mgmt., Iola Rotary; Kansas City, B'nai Brith (v.p. 1982-83, pres. 1984-85, treas. 1986—). Home: 8439 W 113th St Overland Park KS 66210 Office: 9201 Ward Pkwy Kansas City MO 64114

GUDIS, MALCOLM J., electronic data company executive; b. Newark, Dec. 18, 1941; s. Theodore and Evelyn G.; m. Karen M. McKinstry; 1 child, Mark. BS in Fin. and Mktg., Ohio State U., 1964. Joined Electronic Data Systems Corp., Dallas, 1973, various sales mgr. positions; dir. internat. mktg. Paris, 1978-80; exec. v.p. in charge internat. div. Washington, 1980-83; v.p. mktg. devel. group 1983, group v.p. fin. and comml. group, 1984, sr. v.p., 1986—, also bd. dirs.; mem. Mayor's Commn. on Internat. Trade, Dallas. V.p. bd. dirs. United Cerebral Palsy Assn., Dallas, 1979-81; exec. com. Rep. Party, Paris, 1980. Mem. Assn. Data Processing Service Orgns., Japan Soc. Presbyterian. Clubs: Stonebriar Country (Plano, Tex.) (trustee); American (London, Tokyo, Paris and Republic of Korea). Office: Electronic Data Systems Corp 7171 Forest Ln Dallas TX 75230

GUDORF, KENNETH FRANCIS, services company executive; b. Minster, Ohio, Mar. 3, 1939; s. Norbert Herman and Freda Elizabeth (Moorman) G.; m. Evelyn Margaret Sommer, Aug. 31, 1962; children: Eric, Craig, Caroline. A.B., U. Dayton, 1961; M.B.A., U. Mich., 1967. Dep. treas. Gulf Oil Corp., London, 1970-74; fin. rep. Gulf Corp., Washington, 1974-76; v.p. planning Gulf Oil Corp., Reston, Va., 1976-78; sr. dir. mergers, acquisitions and divestments Gulf Oil Corp., Pitts., 1978-81; sr. v.p. fin., chief fin. officer Diversified Energies Inc., Mpls., 1981-85; v.p. chief fin. officer Carlson Cos., Inc., 1985—; mem. council Minn. State Bd. Investments Adv. Council, St. Paul, 1983—, acctg. adv. coun. U. Minn.; bd. dirs. Sister Kenny Inst., Mpls., 1985—, KTCA 2 Twin Cities Pub. TV. Served to capt. U.S. Army, 1962-65. Mem. Fin. Execs. Inst. (bd. dirs. Twin Cities). Clubs: Minneapolis; Interlachen Country (Mpls.). Home: 5210 Green Farms Rd Edina MN 55436 Office: Carlson Cos Inc 12755 State Hwy 55 Minneapolis MN 55441

GUENTHER, BRENDA MAE, accountant; b. Ft. Scott, Kans., Mar. 27, 1960; d. Henry Emmanual and Doris Kathryn (Graham) Ericson; m. Eric Jerome Guenther, Sept. 3, 1983; children: Amanda Nicole, Ashley Kathryn. BS in Acctg., Kans. State U., 1982. CPA, Kans. Pipeline acct. Koch Industries, Inc., Wichita, Kans., 1982-83; internal/EDP auditor Western Casualty & Surety Co., Ft. Scott, 1983-86; fin. adminstr. Lincoln Nat. Corp., Ft. Scott, 1986—. V.p. St. Patrick Altar Soc., Fulton, Kans., 1986—. Mem. AICPA, Nat. Assn. Accts., Future Farmers Am. Alumni Assn. (treas Uniontown, Kans. chpt. 1986—, sec. 1985-86), Kiwanis. Roman Catholic. Office: Lincoln Nat Corp 102 S National Fort Scott KS 66701

GUENTHER, PAUL BERNARD, securities company executive; b. N.Y.C., May 1, 1940; s. Bernard and Elsie G.; m. Diane Erceg, July 31, 1965; children—Matthew, Elizabeth, Christopher. BS in Econs., Fordham U., 1962; MBA in Fin., Columbia U., 1964. Credit analyst Mfrs. Hanover Trust, N.Y.C., 1964-66; various positions Paine Webber Inc., N.Y.C., 1966-80, exec. asst. to chief exec. officer, 1981, sr. v.p., dir. adminstrn. div., 1981-82, exec. v.p., dir. adminstrv. div., 1982-84, exec. v.p., chief administrv. officer, 1984-87, exec. v.p., adminstrn., ops., systems and consumer markets, 1987-88, pres., 1988—; v.p., bd. dirs. Paine Webber Atlas, Inc., Paine Webber Am. Fund, Inc., Paine Webber Olympus, Inc.; dir. Paine Webber Group Inc., and other numerous co. funds, trusts and portfolios. Mem. N.Y. Social Security Analysts, Inst. Chartered Fin. Analysts, Columbia U. Grad. Sch. Bus. Alumni Assn. (pres). Democrat. Lutheran. Office: PaineWebber Inc 1285 Ave of the Americas New York NY 10019

GUEQUIETTE, JOHN PHILLIP, manufacturing company executive; b. Milw., Sept. 10, 1946; s. Gerald Herbert and Louise Ann (Fenske) G.; m. Mary Rowlands Speer, Aug. 17, 1968; children: William Edward, Robert John, Elizabeth Louise. BA, U. Wis., 1968; MBA, U. Chgo., 1972. Systems analyst Inland Steel Co., East Chgo., Ind., 1968-72; analyst inventory INRYCO, Milw., 1972-73, supr. material planning, 1973-74, mgr. contract adminstrn., 1974-76; mgr. fin. Inland Steel Devel. Corp., Washington, 1976-78; mgr. fin. analysis Inland Steel Urban Devel. Corp., Chgo., 1978-80; v.p. adminstrn. Scholz Homes Inc., Tol., 1980-83; sr. v.p., dir. Schult Homes Corp., Middlebury, Ind., 1983—. Chmn. budget subcom. United Way, Elkhart, Ind., 1983—, bd. dirs. 1989; adult leader 4-H, Elkhart County, 1983—. Mem. Phi Beta Kappa, Phi Kappa Phi, Beta Gamma Sigma. Republican. Presbyterian. Office: Schult Homes Corp PO Bos 151 221 US 20 W Middlebury IN 46540

GUERIN, JOHN P., air transportation company executive. Chmn., dir. PS Group Inc., San Diego; also dir. Pacific Southwest Airlines, San Diego. Office: PS Group Inc 4370 La Jolla Village Dr Ste 1050 La Jolla CA 92122 *

GUERINDON, PIERRE CLAUDE, heavy construction equipment company executive; b. Paris, Apr. 24, 1927; came to U.S., 1980; s. Georges Jean and Marie Antoinette Claudia (Pilon) G.; m. Arlette Jeanne Lagacherie, Aug. 11, 1949; 1 child, Philippe. M.E.,C.E., Ecole National Superieur Arts et Metiers aix France, 1949. Mgr. mfg. Caterpillar France S.A., Grenoble, 1961-68, asst. plant mgr., 1969, pres., 1968-76; mng. dir. Caterpillar Belgium S.A., Gosselies, 1976-80; v.p. Caterpillar Inc. (formerly Caterpillar Tractor Co.), Peoria, Ill., 1980-86; dir. Ateliers de Constructions Electriques de Charleroi, Brussels, 1980-87; exec. v.p. Caterpillar Inc. (formerly Caterpillar Tractor Co.), Peoria, Ill., 1986—. Bd. dirs. Bus. Sch. Inst. Adminstrn. Enterprise, Grenoble, France, 1968-76, Greater Peoria YMCA, 1982-84; v.p. Amis de L' Universite, Grenoble, 1970-76. Served with French Army, 1949-50. Mem. French Civil Engrs., Nat. Engr. Arts et Metiers, Fabrimetal Nat. Metallurgh Profl. Assn. (bd. dirs.), Am. C. of C. (pres. S.E. Region France 1970-76), Soc. Mfg. Engrs. Mfg. Engring. Edn. Found. (bd. dirs. 1985-87). Roman Catholic. Clubs: Ivy (Peoria); Royal Ocean Racing (London); Am. Radio Relay (Newington Conn.). Lodge: Rotary. Home: 242 Detweiller Dr Peoria IL 61615

GUERNSEY, GEORGE THACHER, IV, banker; b. St. Louis, Feb. 13, 1949; s. George Thacher III and Margaret Allen (Marquis) G.; m. Carol Ann Miller, May 28, 1977. BA, Yale U., 1971; MBA, Wharton Sch. U. Pa., 1976. Project mgr. St. Louis Regional Indsl. Devel. Corp., 1971-72; chief of staff Mo. Dept. Adminstrn., Jefferson City, 1973-75; prin. Cresap, McCormick & Paget, N.Y.C., 1976-82; sr. v.p. Rep. Nat. Bank N.Y., N.Y.C., 1982-85, First Chgo. Corp, 1985-87; region mgr. Fin. Instns. Cresap, Chgo., 1988, London, 1989—. St. Louis County coordinator Bond for Gov. campaign, 1972. Mem. Beta Gamma Sigma. Republican. Episcopalian. Clubs: University (Chgo.); Yale (N.Y.C.). Office: Castlewood House, 77-91 New Oxford St, London WC1A 1PX, England

GUERNSEY, NANCY PATRICIA, mechanical engineer; b. Newark, Oct. 12, 1955; d. Orville Wendell and Dorothy Elizabeth (Maccia) Guernsey. BE in Mech. Engring., Manhattan Coll., Riverdale, N.Y. 1977; MS in Nuclear Engring. Poly. Inst., 1986. Cert. aircraft single engine pilot. Asst. engr. systems engring. Grumman Aerospace Co., Bethpage, N.Y., 1977-83; engr. product support, Govt. Support Systems div., Harris Corp., Syosset, N.Y., 1983-86, pub. health engr. Nassau County Dept. Health bur. water pollution control, 1987-88; asst. project coord. N.Y.C. Dept. Trans. Bur. of Bridges, 1988—. Mem. Nat. Rifle Assn., Soc. Women Engrs., Am. Nuclear Soc. (exec. com. L.I. sect.), ASME, The Ninety-Nines (sect. air age edn. chmn. 1982-84), Aircraft Owners and Pilots Assn., Mensa. Republican. Episcopalian. Clubs: Sperry Flying (sec. 1981-85), Long Island Early Fliers. Home: 14 3d St Ronkonkoma NY 11779

GUERNSEY, VAN RIPER, JR., real estate company executive; b. Indpls., July 5, 1909; s. Guernsey and Edith (Longley) Van R.; m. Edna Woodard, Nov. 14, 1988. AB, DePauw U., 1930; MBA, Harvard U., 1932. Advt. copywriter Sidener & Van Riper, Indpls., 1933-40; editor Bobbs-Merrill Co., Indpls., N.Y.C., 1941-48; freelance writer children's books 1949-74; pres. Crooked Stick Devel. Corp., Carmel, Ind., 1972—, Venture Petroleum Drillers (name changed to Vandrill, Inc.), Carmel, Oklahoma City, 1980-88; trustee Ind. Author: (children's Books) Lou Gehrig, Boy of the Sandlots, 1949; Will Rogers, Young Cowboy, 1951; Knute Rockne, Young Athlete, 1952; Babe Ruth, Baseball Boy, 1954; Jim Thorpe, Indian Athlete, 1956; Richard Byrd, Boy Who Braved the Unknown, 1958; Yea Coach! Three Great Football Coaches, 1955; The Game of Basketball, 1967, World Series Highlights, 1970, The Mighty Macs, Three Famous Baseball Managers, 1972, Behind the Plate, Three Great Catchers, 1973; (with J. Newcomb and G. Sullivan) Football Replay, 1973; (with S.B. Epstein and R. Reeder) Big League Pitchers and Catchers, 1973, Golfing Greats, 1975. Mem. Author League of Am., Woodstock Club, University Club. Republican. Episcopalian. Home: PO Box 90289 Indianapolis IN 46290-0289

GUERRA, CHARLES ALBERT, financial consultant and executive; b. Hialeah, Fla., Dec. 4, 1960; s. Charles M. and Elsa Guerra; m. Alicia E. Martell. AA, Miami-Dade Community Coll., 1980; BBA, Fla. Internat. U., 1982; grad., Coll. for Fin. Planning, 1986. CPA, Fla.; cert. fin. planner, Fla., pension plan cons.; lic. real estate agt., investment securities, life ins., health ins., disability ins. Tax auditor IRS, Miami, Fla., 1982; acct. Arthur Young & Co., Miami, 1983-85, Peat, Marwick, Mitchell & Co., Miami, 1985; fin. planner H.M. Barth & Co., Miami, 1985-86, Moring-Armstrong & Co., Miami, 1986-88; fin. svcs. cons. The New Eng. and Integrated Resources Equity Corp., Miami, 1986-89; pres., fin. cons. The Fin. Strategies Group, Miami, 1989—. Mem. Am. Inst. CPA's, Fla. Inst. CPA's (mem. personal fin. planning com. 1988-89), Inst. Cert. Fin. Planners, Internal Assn. for Fin. Planning. Office: Teh Fin Strategies Group 9240 Sunset Dr Ste 100 Miami FL 33173

GUERRERA, EUGENE ROCCO, financial planner; b. Waterbury, Conn., July 17, 1940; s. Rocco and Helen Rose (Soluri) G.; m. Patricia Alice O'Rourke, May 22, 1967; children: Alicia Jean (dec.), Nadine Louise (dec.). AB in Econs., Boston Coll., 1962; student, U. Hartord, 1966-68, Quinnipiac Coll., 1975; cert. fin. planning, Coll. Fin. Planning, 1979. Sales mgr. Waterbury (Conn.) Co. Inc., 1964-68; registered rep. Advest Co. Putnam Coffin Burr, Hartford, Conn., 1968-70; fin. cons. Shearson Lehman Hutton, Waterbury, 1970-88, v.p. investment, fixed income advisor, 1988—. Author: On the Right Side of Wall Street, 1989; columnist: Fin. Planning and You, Cheshire Hearld. Mem. Inst. of Cert. Fin. Planners, Kiwanis (chmn. 1988, dir. local scholarship com.). Home: 32 Williamsburg Dr Cheshire CT 06410 Office: Shearson Lehman Hutton 49 Leavenworth St Waterbury CT 06702

GUERSTER, RENE L., pharmaceutical packaging company executive; b. Basle, Switzerland, Oct. 1, 1938; came to U.S., 1941; s. Eugen and Rose (Haas) G.; m. Miriam Harthen, Nov. 23, 1960; children: Catherine, Jonathan. BSME, U. London, 1960; MS in Mech. Engring., U. Pa., 1966; MBA in Mgmt., Temple U., 1978. Project engr. Armstrong Cork Co., Lancaster, Pa., 1960-62; flight evaluation engr. Gen. Electric Co., King of Prussia, Pa., 1962-66; supr. product devel. Ametek Inc., Hatfield, Pa., 1966-70; exec. v.p. pharm. packaging div. The West Co., Phoenixville, Pa., 1970-84; pres. pharm. packaging div. The West Co., 1984—, pres., chief exec. officer, 1985—; bd. dirs. Teleflex, Inc., Limerick, Pa. Patentee in field (9). Trustee Abington Health Care Corp., Pa., Walnut St. Theatre, Phila. Mem. Pa. Bus. Roundtable. Home: 1000 Limekiln Pike Maple Glen PA 19002 Office: West Co Inc W Bridge St Phoenixville PA 19460

GUEST, FREDERICK EDWARD, II, private investor; b. N.Y.C., Feb. 13, 1938; s. Winston Frederick Churchill and Helena Woolworth (McCann) G.; m. Stephanie Wanger, Oct. 21, 1961 (div. 1982); children: Victoria, Vanessa, Frederick, Andrew; m. Carole Kerr, May 21, 1988. BS, Wharton Sch., U. Pa., 1960. With internat. dept. Smith, Barney & Co., N.Y.C., 1964-69; fin. v.p. N.Y. State Urban Devel. Corp., N.Y.C., 1969-70; instl. salesman Lehman Bros., N.Y.C., 1970-71; ptnr. Singer, Mackie Corp., N.Y.C., 1971-74; vice chmn. Bessemer Securities Corp., N.Y.C., 1974-77, chmn., 1977-82; chmn. F.E. Guest & Co., N.Y.C., 1982—; bd. dirs. Diamond Bathurst, Malvern, Pa., Sunlite, Inc., Atlanta; vice chmn. Bessemer Trust Co., N.Y., N.J., Fla., 1974-82. Trustee Phipps Houses, N.Y.C. Served with USAFR, 1961-67. Republican. Episcopalian. Club: River. Office: F E Guest and Co 630 Fifth Ave New York NY 10111

GUEST, RONALD ANTHONY, telecommunications company executive; b. Dallas, Feb. 19, 1957; s. Roy Maurice and Mildred Jeanette (Hugo) G.; m. Vernell Louise Lee, May 20, 1978. BS, So. Meth. U., 1979; MS, Colo. State U., 1982. Sci. programmer Tex. Instruments Co., Dallas, 1979; mem. tech. staff AT&T Bell Labs., Denver, 1980-84, tech. mgr., 1984—. Patentee data transfer mechanism. Mem. Assn. for Computing Machinery. Republican. Office: AT&T Bell Labs 12110 N Pecos St Denver CO 80234

GUETH, THOMAS FRANKLIN, electrical engineer; b. Columbus, Ohio, Jan. 18, 1950; s. Clarence Francis and Jacqueline (Cummins) G. B.S. in Elec. Engring., Ohio State U., 1973; B.S. in Engring. Mgmt., U. Evansville, 1979. Elec. engr. Warrick ops. Alcoa, Newburgh, Ind., 1974-77, sr. elec. engr., 1978-79; mgr. systems dept. Kinetic Systems Corp., Lockport, Ill., 1979-81, indsl. market dir., 1981-82, v.p. indsl. systems, 1982-83, pres. systems. tech. group., 1983-84; dir. computer engring. Multigraphics div. AM Internat., 1983-84, dir. elec. systems engring., 1984-86; dir. engring. prodn. mail div. Pitney-Bowes Corp., Danbury, Conn., 1987—; evening lectr. U. Evansville, 1979. Mem. Sci. Horizons Planning Com., 1987—; bd. dirs. Meadows Credit Union, Rolling Meadows, Ill., 1986. Mem. IEEE, Instrument Soc. Am., Am. Mgmt. Assn., DECUS, Tau Beta Pi.

GUETZKOW, DANIEL STEERE, computer company executive; b. Ann Arbor, Mich., May 19, 1949; s. Harold S. and Lauris (Steere) G.; m. Diana Gulbinowicz, April, 1979. Student, Columbia U., 1967-70; BS in Bus. and Accountancy, Thomas Edison State Coll., 1989. Prodn. mgr. Rehrig-Pacific, Inc., L.A., 1975-78; maintenance mgr. Setco, Inc., Culver City, Calif., 1978-79; plant mgr. Veneer Tech., Inc., L.A., 1979; co-founder, chief fin. officer, exec. v.p. Netword, Inc., Riverdale, Md., 1981—; also dir. Netword, Inc., Riverdale. Author: (book) Indemnification of Officers and Directors, 1988; author (software): Telemarketing Database Mgr., 1984-86, Systems Acctg. Control, 1985, Electronic Mail Switcher, 1982, 84. Office: Netword Inc PO Box 888 Riverdale MD 20737

GUGEL, CRAIG THOMAS, advertising executive; b. Detroit, Jan. 18, 1954; s. Paul Walter and Patricia Angela (Sullivan) G. BA, U. Windsor, Ont., Can., 1976. Asst. br. mgr. Mich. Nat. Bank, Livonia, 1975-77; analyst media research Kenyon & Eckhardt, Inc., Birmingham, Mich. and N.Y.C., 1977-81; supr. media rsch. Kenyon & Eckhardt, Inc., N.Y.C., 1981-82; v.p., asst. dir. media rsch. McCann-Erickson, Inc., N.Y.C., 1982-84; v.p., dir. media rsch. Foote, Cone & Belding, Inc., N.Y.C., 1984-86; sr. v.p., corp. dir. media resources Bozell, Jacobs, Kenyon & Eckhardt, Inc., N.Y.C., 1986-88; sr. v.p., dir. media research Backer Spielvogel Bates, Inc., N.Y.C., 1988—; bd. dirs. Advt. Info. Svcs., Inc., N.Y.C., 1987—. Mem. Media Rsch. Dirs. Assn., Advt. Rsch. Found. (mem. various couns.), Agy. Media Rsch. Coun., AAA (media rsch. com.), Advt. Club N.Y., Radio and TV Rsch. Coun. Office: Backer Spielvogel Bates Inc 405 Lexington Ave New York NY 10174

GUIDA, RONALD J., sales executive; b. Phila., Aug. 14, 1958; s. Emilio Rocco and Mary (Venuti) G.; m. Jeanne M. Guida, Nov. 10, 1984. BS, Drexel U., 1981. Dir. sales Venusa, Ltd., N.Y.C., 1981-85; sales exec. Covalent Systems, Sunnyvale, Calif., 1985—; cons. Phila. Med., 1983-86. Trustee Sturbridge Lakes, N.J., 1988—. Republican. Roman Catholic. Office: Covalent Systems 600 W Germantown Pike Plymouth Meeting PA 19142

GUILARTE, PEDRO MANUEL, holding company executive; b. Cuba, May 19, 1952; s. Miguel G. and Emma G.; B.S. in Indsl. Engring. (scholar), Northwestern U., 1975; M.B.A., Washington U., St. Louis, 1977; cert. systems dynamics MIT, 1978; m. Zulima Piedra, May 26, 1979. Market analyst Cummins Engine Co., Columbus, Ind., 1976; corp. devel. exec. FPL Group, Miami, 1977—; v.p., Telesat Cablevision, 1985—. Consortium for Grad. Study in Bus. fellow, 1975-77. Mem. Northwestern U. Alumni Admission Council (dir. S. Fla. region 1979—), Planning Execs. Inst. Republican. Methodist. Home: 6464 Wood Lake Rd Jupiter FL 33458 Office: PO Box 88801 North Palm Beach FL 33408-8801

GUILD, RICHARD SAMUEL, trade associations management company executive; b. Boston, Nov. 5, 1925; s. Walter Rayford and Anna (Hollander) G.; BS, Boston U., 1949; m. Susan Jane Coughlin, July 3, 1965; children—Laura Ann, Linda Jean. With Guild Assocs., Inc., Boston, 1949—, mng. dir., 1960-65, pres., 1965—; owner Copypro, 1975—; treas. Resource Matching System, Inc., 1982-83; exec. sec. New Eng. Marine Trade Assn., 1963, Liquified Petroleum Gas Assn. New Eng., 1972-1985; mng. dir. Shoe Pattern Mfrs. Assn., 1951—, Mass. Automatic Merchandising Coun., 1964—, Tel. Answering Assn. New Eng., 1983; exec. v.p. Am. Boat Builders and Repairers Assn., 1979; treas. Wet Ground MICA Assn., 1983-87. With USNR, 1944-45. Cert. assn. exec. Mem. Multiple Assn. Mgmt. Inst. (past pres.), Am. Soc. Assn. Execs. (past bd. dirs.), N.Am. Paddlesports Assn. (exec. v.p. 1987—), Boston Soc. Assn. Execs. (past pres.), Def. Orientation Conf. Assn., Soc. Mgmt. of Profl. Computing (exec. sec. 1985—). Home: 5 Glengarry Rd Winchester MA 01890 Office: 715 Boylston St Boston MA 02116

GUILFOIL, KENNETH VINCENT, financial planner; b. N.Y.C., July 8, 1929; s. Vincent Howell and Isabela Florence (Dunn) G.; m. Catherine Mary McCoole, Aug. 26, 1950; 1 child, Michael Vincent. Grad. high sch., Woodside, N.Y. Registered investment advisor, Conn., real estate broker, Conn., R.I., stockbroker, Conn., R.I., Mass., N.Y. Owner APS Fin. Group, Groton, Conn., 1960—; Registered investment advisor, stock broker, real estate broker, ins. broker. Contbr. articles to profl. jours. Mem. Groton Rep. Town Com., 1978-84; 1st dist. rep. Town of Groton, 1978-82, chmn. 1982-84. Recipient Outstanding Svc. award Rep. Com., 1985. Mem. Internat. Assn. Fin. Planning, Nat. Assn. Realtors, Fin. Profl. Adv. Panel, Am. Assn. Fin. Profls., U.S. Submarine Vets., Fleet Res., Kiwanis (pres. Groton 1974-75, Outstanding Leadership award 1975), Elks. Home and Office: 390 Long Hill Rd Groton CT 06340

GUINN, DONALD EUGENE, retired telephone company executive; b. Wellington, Kans., Oct. 26, 1932; s. Cecil William and Avis Velma (Scoles) G.; m. Marlene Darhl, Mar. 21, 1953; children: Debra Michele, Damon Jeffrey, David Leslie. B.S. in Civil Engring, Oreg. State U., 1954. Various mgmt. positions Pacific Tel. & Tel., Portland, Oreg., 1954-75; v.p. engring. and network sers. Pacific N.W. Bell, 1976; asst. v.p. engring., asst. v.p. customer sers. AT&T, 1976-78, v.p. customer services, v.p. network services, 1978-80; chmn., chief exec. officer Pacific Tel & Tel (now Pacific Telesis Group), San Francisco, until 1988; chmn. Pacific Bell, San Francisco, 1984-88. Bd. dirs. Pacific Sci. Ctr., Seattle, 1975-76. Mem. Profl. Engrs. Oreg., IEEE (communications policy bd.). Republican. Lutheran. Office: Pacific Bell 140 New Montgomery St San Francisco CA 94105 *

GUINN, KENNY C., utility company executive; b. 1934; married. BA, Fresno U., MA; PhD., Utah State U. Supt. Clark County Sch. Dist.; v.p. adminstrn. Nev. Savs. and Loan Assn., 1978-80, pres., chief operating officer, 1980-85, chief exec. officer, 1985—; pres. Southwest Gas Corp., 1987-88, chmn., chief exec. officer, 1988—. Office: Nev Savs & Loan Assn 201 Las Vegas Blvd S PO Box 2191 Las Vegas NV 89125-2191 other: Southwest Gas Corp 5241 Spring Mountain Rd Las Vegas NV 89102 *

GUINN, REUBEN KENT, insurance company executive, business and estate planner; b. Jacksonville, Fla., Dec. 8, 1954; s. Reuben Earl and Margaret Elizabeth (Oliver) G.; m. Sandra Jean Ruelf, June 28, 1980; children: Michael Ryan, Cameron Clark. AA, Cen. Fla. Community Coll., 1976; student, Fla. State U., 1977. With ops. mgmt. dept. Barnett Bank, Ocala, Fla., 1978-80; ops. officer First Marion Bank, Ocala, 1980-82; underwriter Mut. of N.Y., Ocala, 1982—; cre; bd. dirs. Fla. Nat. Bank, Ocala. Arbitrator Juvenile Alternative Svcs. Program, Ocala, 1987-88. Mem. Nat. Estate Planning Coun., Nat. Assn. Life Underwriters, Millon Dollar Round Table (provisional), Exch. Club (Ocala, pres. 1983-84), Kiwanis. Republican. Baptist. Home: 3199 SE 32nd Ln Ocala FL 32677 Office: Mut NY 11 N Magnolia Ave Ocala FL 32670

GUINN, SAM, telecommunications industry executive; b. 1932; married;. Student, Auburn U.; MS, Stanford U., 1969. With AT&T Co. Inc., 1960-78, staff v.p., 1977-78; with Pacific Telephone and Telegraph Co., San Franciso, 1978—, vice chmn. bd., 1983—; vice chmn., dir. Pacific Telesis Group, San Francisco, 1984—. Served to capt. AUS, 1959-60. Office: Pacific Telesis Group 140 New Montgomery St San Francisco CA 94105 *

GUINN, STANLEY WILLIS, accountant; b. Detroit, June 9, 1953; s. Willis Hampton and Virginia Mae (Pierson) G.; m. Patricia Shirley Newgord, June 13, 1981; children: Terri Lanae, Scott Stanley. BBA with high distinction, U. Mich., 1979, MBA with distinction, 1981; MS in Taxation with Distinction, Walsh Coll., 1987. CPA, Mich.; cert. mgmt. acct., Mich. Tax mgr. Coopers & Lybrand, Detroit, 1981-87; tax cons. Upjohn Co., Kalamazoo, Mich., 1987—. Served with USN, 1974-77. Mem. AICPA, Nat. Assn. Accts., Mich. Assn. CPA's, Inst. Mgmt. Acctg., Phi Kappa Phi, Beta Gamma Sigma, Beta Alpha Psi, Delta Mu Delta. Republican. Presbyterian. Home: 8420 Valleywood Ln Portage MI 49002 Office: Upjohn Co Corp Taxes div 8113-242-52 7000 Portage Rd Kalamazoo MI 49001

GUIOL, PATRICE ROLAND, merchant banker; b. Paris, Jan. 14, 1954; came to U.S., 1986; s. Roland R. and Annette (Demandre) G.; m. Veronique M. Thiroloix, Dec. 16, 1980; children: Philippe, Sebastien, Olivier. BA, Paris U., 1974, B in Corp. Law, 1975, M in Corp. Law, 1976, degree in acctg., 1976. Fin. analyst Morgan Guaranty, Paris, 1977-79, 81-82; corp. fin. officer Morgan Guaranty, N.Y.C., 1980; head M&A. for Brazil and Argentina Morgan Guaranty, Buenos Aires, 1982-86; head M&A for Latin Am. Morgan Guaranty, N.Y.C., 1986-89; M&A dir. Concordia, Inc., Rye, N.Y., 1989—. Roman Catholic. Club: Saint Cloud (Paris). Home: 239 Barnard Rd Larchmont NY 10538 Office: Concordia Inc Rye ExecuPlaza Rye NY 10580-1598

GUIST, FREDRIC MICHAEL, minerals and chemicals corporation executive; b. Homestead, Pa., Oct. 8, 1946; s. Thomas John and Clara Hertha (Orend) G.; student in chemistry Juniata Coll., 1964-66; B.S. with high honors in Bus. Adminstrn., U. Md., 1968; m. Barbara Jean Hill, Aug. 4, 1972; children—Heidi Margit, James Fredric. Rate analyst Dow Chem. Co., Midland, Mich., 1968-69, inside sales rep., Saddlebrook, N.J., 1969-70, sales rep. for splty. chems., Chgo., 1970-73, field salesman, 1973-74; product specialist for indsl. chems. Nalco Chem. Co., Oakbrook, Ill., 1974, product mgr. for indsl. chems., 1974-75; mktg. mgr. Engelhard Corp., Edison, N.J., 1975-78, dir. new bus. devel., 1978-79, dir. mktg. and sales worldwide for petroleum catalysts, 1979-81, sr. v.p., gen. mgr. catalyst and chems. group, 1981-85, sr. v.p., gen. mgr. catalysts Specialty Chems. div., 1985, pres. Specialty Chems. div., corp. v.p. 1985-88, pres. engineered materials div., sr. v.p. corp., 1988—, also bd. dirs.; dir. Kali Chemie-Engelhard, Nippon-Engelhard Mem. Nat. Petroleum Refiners Assn. (rep. to bd. dirs. 1979—), Am. Petroleum Inst., Indsl. Specialty Chems. Assn. (dir.), Phi Kappa Phi. Home: 13 Polktown Rd RD 2 Glen Gardner NJ 08826 Office: Engelhard Corp Menlo Park CN 40 Edison NJ 08818

GUITART, MICHAEL HORACIO, educational media consultant; b. Havana, Cuba, Sept. 26, 1935; came to U.S., 1970; s. Miguel Antonio and Emma Rosalia (Tabares) G.; m. Margarita Vargas Gómez, Aug. 16, 1974; children: Virginia, Lillian, Raquel, Diana, Emma, Laura, Patty. BA, U.

Montevallo, Birmingham, 1971; MA, U. Ala., Birmingham, 1973, Specialist of Edn., 1974; postgrad., U. Ala., Tuscaloosa, 1975—. Lic. FCC 3d class radiotelephone operator. Adminstrv. asst. Comml. Enterprises Confiscated, Havana, 1953-57; cartographer Cuban Tourist Commn., Havana, 1960-61; cartography faculty Havana U., 1962-63, lang. faculty, 1964-65; prof. lang. Ministry Pub. Health, Havana, 1965-69; studio specialist Sta. WBRC-TV, Birmingham, 1971-72; media specialist U. Ala., Birmingham, 1972-74; cons. Ala. State Dept. Edn., Montgomery, 1974—; liaison S.E. region Civil Air Patrol, Montgomery, 1985—; historian USAF Hist. Research Ctr., Montgomery, 1985. Contbr.: (newspaper) Ala. Edn., 1974—, (jour.) Dept. Edn. Computer Aims, 1985. Capt. USAFR, 1975—. Scholar Council for Internat. Exchange, 1980, U. Calif., Santa Cruz, 1980. Mem. Ala. Library Media Assn., Ala. State Employees Assn., Ala. Cable TV Assn., Ala. Council for Computer Edn. Democrat. Roman Catholic. Club: Civitans (bd. dirs. Birmingham chpt. 1972-74, chmn. Montgomery chpt. 1975-79). Office: State Dept Edn 304 Dexter Ave Montgomery AL 36104

GULDEN, SIMON, lawyer, foods and beverages company executive; b. Montreal, Que., Can., Jan. 7, 1938; s. David and Zelda (Long) G.; m. Ellen Lee Barbour, June 12, 1977. B.A., McGill U., Montreal, 1959; LL.L., U. Montreal, 1962. P. Adminstrn. Inst. Chartered Secs. and Adminstrs., 1982; Bar: Que. Ptnr. Genser, Philips, Friedman & Gulden, Montreal, 1963-68; sec., legal counsel Pl. Bonaventure, Inc., 1969-72; legal counsel real estate Steinberg Inc., Montreal, 1972-74; solicitor, prime atty. Bell Can., Montreal, 1975-76; v.p., gen. counsel, sec. Nabisco Brands Ltd, Toronto, 1976—. Mem. Internat. Assn. Lawyers and Jurists, Internat. Fiscal Assn., Am. Corp. Counsel Assn., Can. Mfrs. Assn., Can. Bar Assn., Internat. Bar Assn., Lord Reading Law Soc. Que., Osgoode Law Soc., Toronto Bd. Trade, Assn. Conseils Francization Que., Advt. and Sales Execs. Club, Am. Mgmt. Assn., Inst. Chartered Secs. and Adminstrs. (cert.). Clubs: Island Yacht, Canadian, Cambridge (Toronto). Home: 23 Danbury Ct, Unionville, ON Canada L3R 7S1 Office: Nabisco Brands Ltd Box 165, Royal Bank Pla S Tower 2700, Toronto, ON Canada M5J 2J4

GULICK, ROBERT WALTER, financial executive; b. Cortez, Colo., Sept. 1, 1949; s. Robert R. and Betty A. (Muller) G.; m. Susan Mary North, June 9, 1971; children: Laura L., Robert J. BS in Engring., USCG Acad., 1971; MS, MIT, 1976, Ocean Engr., 1976; MBA in Fin., George Mason U., 1981. Registered profl. engr., Va. V.p., treas. Gulick Assocs. Inc., Washington, 1976-82, Brian Watt Assocs. Inc., Houston, 1982-86; v.p. fin., ops. N.Y. Inst. Fin., Simon & Schuster Inc., N.Y.C., 1986-87, pres., 1987—; cons. Houston, Allendale, N.J., 1982-86. Contbr. articles to profl. jours. Served with USCG, 1971-82. Mem. Soc. Naval Architects and Marine Engrs. (panel chmn. 1981-82). Office: NY Inst Fin 70 Pine St New York NY 10270

GULIS, DEAN ALEXANDER, investment banker, broker; b. Chgo., June 27, 1955; s. Alexander Gust and Priscilla Joan (Cooper) G.; m. Cynthia Ann Fonseca, June 27, 1980; children: Phillip, Christopher, Timothy. BA, U. Mich., 1977, MBA, 1982. Fgn. exchange trader Mfrs. Nat. Bank Detroit, 1977-81; investment analyst Roney & Co., Detroit, 1982-85, dir. research, 1985—. Leader Boy Scouts Am., Troy, Mich., 1987-88. Mem. Fin. Analysts Soc. Detroit. Republican. Greek Orthodox. Office: Roney & Co One Griswold Detroit MI 48226

GULKO, EDWARD, health care executive, consultant; b. Paterson, N.J., Nov. 22, 1950; s. Benjamin and Anita (Yankelevsky) G.; m. Judith Ilene Lee, May 29, 1977. BS in Indsl. Engring., N.J. Inst. Tech., 1972; MBA, Temple U., 1974. Health program analyst Morrisania Hosp., Bronx, N.Y., 1974-75; assoc. dir. Mission Health Ctr., San Francisco, 1976; supervising systems analyst Health and Hosp. Corp., N.Y.C., 1977-78; dep. exec. dir. Greenpoint Hosp., Bklyn., 1978-82; assoc. exec. dir. Woodhull Med. Ctr., Bklyn., 1982-84; adminstr. Montclair (N.J.) Med. Group, 1984-87; asst. adminstr. Summit Med. Group, Summit, N.J., 1987—; Med. Service Corps. Officer U.S. Naval Res. Sta., S.I., N.Y., 1983—. Trustee Society Hill Townhouse Assn., 1986—, v.p. 1987-88, pres. 1988—. Mem. Am. Coll. Health Care Execs., Assn. Mil. Surgeons U.S. (exec. com. N.J. chpt., 1985-87, pres. 1987—), Med. Group Mgmt. Assn., Naval Reserve Assn. (dist v.p. 1987—), N.J. Assn. Asst. Hosp. Adminstrs., Inst. Ind. Engrs. Democrat. Jewish. Home: 256 Garth Ct Old Bridge NJ 08857 Office: Summit Med Group 120 Summit Ave Summit NJ 07901

GULMI, JAMES SINGLETON, apparel manufacturing company executive; b. Schenectady, Mar. 16, 1946; s. Henry Charles and June (Singleton) G.; m. Claire Ann Moody, Jan. 16, 1988; children by previous marriage: Bradford Charles, Leah Cole. B.A., Baldwin Wallace Coll., 1968; M.B.A., Emory U., 1971. With Genesco, Inc., Nashville, 1971—, asst. treas., 1974-79, dir. fin. ops., 1978-79, treas., 1979-83, v.p., treas., 1983—, v.p. fin., chief fin. officer, 1986—; mem. young exec. council Nashville City Bank. Chmn. allocations com. United Way, Nashville, 1987-88. Mem. Fin. Execs. Inst. (chpt. dir. 1979-80). Episcopalian. Office: Genesco Inc Genesco Pk Rm 488 Nashville TN 37202

GUMAS, JOHN GEORGE, advertising executive; b. San Francisco, July 22, 1959. AA, City Coll. San Francisco, 1980; BS, San Francisco State U., 1984. Prin. JG&A, San Francisco, 1984-86; pres. Gumas Communications, Inc., San Francisco, 1986—; v.p. H.C. Advt., San Francisco, 1984-85. Mem. Am. Advt. Fedn., San Francisco Advt. Club, Better Bus. Bur., U.S. C. of C., San Francisco C. of C. Office: Gumas Communications Inc 1323 Evans Ave San Francisco CA 94124

GUMMERE, JOHN, insurance company executive; b. Mt. Holly, N.J., Feb. 12, 1928; s. John Westcott and Ruth (Clark) G.; m. Eleanor Frances Greene, Oct. 9, 1954; children: Cynthia Clark, John Greene. B.A., Yale U., 1948. With Phoenix Mut. Life Ins. Co., Hartford, Conn., 1949—; sec. charge underwriting dept. Phoenix Mut. Life Ins. Co., 1961-64, 2d v.p., 1964-65, v.p., 1965-72, sr. v.p., 1972-78, exec. v.p., 1978-81, pres., chief exec. officer, 1981-87, also dir., chmn. bd., chief exec. officer, 1987—; dir. Phoenix Equity Planning Corp., N.Y. Casualty Ins. Co., Phoenix Am. Life Ins. Co., Conn. Nat. Bank, Phoenix Gen. Ins. Co., PM Mortgage Funding Corp., PM Holdings Inc., PML Internat. Ins. Ltd. Mem. exec. com. Med. Info., 1972-77, chmn., 1977; bd. dirs. Hartford Grad. Ctr., Inst. of Living, Old State House, Jr. Achievement. Fellow Soc. Actuaries; mem. Med. Info. Bur. (bd. dirs.), Greater Hartford C. of C. (dir.), Sigma Xi. Office: Phoenix Mut Life Ins Co 1 American Row Hartford CT 06115

GUMUCIO, MARCELO ANDRES, electronics executive; b. Potosi, Bolivia, Oct. 17, 1937; s. Julio Francisco and Delmira (Cortes) G.; m. Carole Lee Burke; children: Shandele, Shelley. BS in Math., U. San Francisco, 1961; MS in Math., U. Idaho, 1963; AMP, Harvard Bus. Sch., 1982. Mgmt. trainee Gen. Electric Co., N.Y.C., 1963-66; product mgr. Hewlett Packard Co., Palo Alto, Calif., 1966-69, mktg. mgr., 1969-71, gen. mgr., 1971-73, regional gen. mgr., 1973-75; v.p. Americas & Asia Memorex Corp., Santa Clara, Calif., 1975-77, pres., 1977-79; exec. v.p. Northern Telecom Inc., Toronto, Can., 1979-80; pres. Northern Telecom Systems, Mpls., 1980-82; exec. v.p. Cray Rsch. Inc., Mpls., 1983-88, pres. and chief oper. officer, 1988—; bd. dirs. Cray Rsch. Inc., 1988, MTS Corp., 1986, Zycao Corp., 1986. Trustee The Blake Sch., Mpls., 1988. Mem. Minneapolis Club, Harvard Bus. Sch. Club (Mpls.). Home: 980 W Ferndale Rd Wayzata MN 55391 Office: Cray Rsch Inc 608 2nd Ave S Minneapolis MN 55402

GUNBY, WILLIAM RICHARDSON, JR., developer, construction educator; b. Tampa, Fla., Feb. 20, 1931; s. William Richardson and Violet (Eversole) G.; children: Robert, Richard, Greer, Adrienne. Student Centre Coll., 1950; BS in Bldg. Constrn., U. Fla., 1953; MBA, Stetson U., 1972; Archtl. engr., Atlanta, 1957-59; archtl. engr., Jacksonville, Fla., 1960-69, constrn. mgr., 1970-71, constrn. cons., 1971-75; pres. Fla. North Cen. Co., Inc., Gainesville, 1979-83; ptnr. Gunby-Halperin Properties, Gainesville, 1977—; pres. Gunby Bldg. Co., 1988—; prof. sch. bldg. constrn. U. Fla., Gainesville, 1973—. Served to 1st lt. USAF, 1953-55; capt. Res. ret. Named Tchr. of Yr., Coll. Architecture, U. Fla., 1978. Mem. Am. Inst. Constructors, Assoc. Schs. Constrn. (pres. 1982-83), Soc. of Cincinnati, Kappa Alpha Order. Episcopalian. Clubs: Heritage (Gainesville); Ponte Vedra. Home: 2415 Costa Verde Blvd #317 Jacksonville Beach FL 32250 Office: Sch Bldg Constrn U Fla Gainesville FL 32611

GUNDERSON, JUDITH KEEFER, golf association executive; b. Charleroi, Pa., May 25, 1939; d. John R. and Irene G. (Gaskill) Keefer; student public schs., Uniontown, Pa.; m. Jerry L. Gunderson, Mar. 19, 1971; children—Jamie L., Jeff S.; stepchildren—Todd G. (dec.), Marc W., Bookkeeper, Fayette Nat. Bank, 1957-59, gen. ledger bookkeeper, 1960-63; head bookkeeper First Nat. Bank Broward, 1963-64; bookkeeper Ruthenberg Homes, Inc., 1966-69; bookkeeper, asst. sec./treas. Pennisular Properties, Inc. subs. Investors Diversified Services Properties, Mpls., 1969-72; comptroller, stockholder, pres. dir. Am. Golf Fla., Inc., dba Golf and Tennis World, Deerfield Beach, 1972—; sec.-treas., stockholder, dir. Internat. Golf, Inc. County committeewoman, Broward County, Fla., 1965-66. Mem. Am. Biog. Inst. Rsch. Assn. (dep. gov., bd. gov.), Nat. Golf Found., C. of C., Beta Sigma Phi.

GUNDLACH, HEINZ LUDWIG, investment banker, lawyer; b. Dusseldorf, Germany, July 6, 1937; came to U.S., 1969, naturalized, 1980; s. Heinrich Otto and Ilse (Schuster) G.; children: Andrew, Annabelle. M.Law, U. Heidelberg, 1962, D.Law, 1962. V.p. Thyssen A.G. Dusseldorf, 1964-68; v.p., partner Loeb, Rhoades & Co., N.Y.C., 1969-75; vice chmn., chief exec. officer Fed-Mart Corp., San Diego, 1975-81; vice chmn., chief execx. officer successor cos. Sunbelt Investment Holdings, Inc., 1981-88; chmn. successor cos. Trucolor Foto Inc., 1981-88, Clearfoto, Inc., 1982-88; mng. dir. Dean Witter Reynolds, Inc., N.Y.C. and London, 1988—. Served with W. Ger. Army, 1958-59. Republican. Clubs: Annabelle's (London), St. James's (London). Office: Dean Witter Reynolds Inc Two World Trade Ctr New York NY 10048

GUNDLACH, HERMAN, civil engineer; b. Houghton, Mich., July 16, 1913; s. Herman and Elvira Amanda (Zenner) G.; m. Barbara Kettle, Apr. 30, 1938 (dec. 1983); children—Gretchen, Martha, Janna, Julie. BCE, Harvard U., 1935. Registered profl. engr., Ga. 1939. Pres. Copper Country Concrete Corp., Houghton, Herman Gundlach, Inc., Houghton, 1945-87; dir. Stonington Realty Co., Inc., Upper Peninsula Power Co.; chmn. Houghton Fin. Corp.; pres. Pilgrim Point Inc. Mem. Mich. Gov.'s Commn. for Architecture. Maj. C.E., U.S. Army, 1941-46, ETO. Past bd. dirs., pres. Mich. Tech. U. Huskies Club; former trustee Jack and Jill Nursery Sch., Ft. Lauderdale, Fla. Fellow ASCE; mem. Assoc. Gen. Contractors (bd. dirs., past pres. Mich. chpt.), Am. Concrete Inst., Upper Midwest Devel. Council, Nat. Football League Alumni (profl.), Upper Peninsula Action, VFW, Chi Epsilon. Home: 1 Woodland Rd Houghton MI 49931

GUNERMAN, THOMAS RICHARD, diemolding company executive; b. Rye, N.Y., Oct. 21, 1950; s. Robert J. and Estelle M. Gunerman; m. Penny A. Bleda, July 7, 1973; children: John Robert, Thomas Joseph. AAS, Westchester Coll., 1975; BS in Acctg., Syracuse U., 1979; postgrad. in mgmt., Pa. State U., 1981. Comml. credit mgr. Kenton Corp., N.Y.C., 1971-75; controller region acctg. Mark Controls Corp., Syracuse, N.Y., 1976-78; corp. controller Diemolding Corp., Canastota, N.Y., 1979-81, sec.-treas., 1982-86, v.p. fin., gen. mgr., 1986—. Mem. Soc. Plastics Industry (fin. mgmt. com.), Nat. Assn. Accts., Fin. Exec. Inst. and Health Industry Mfrs. Assn. Office: Diemolding Corp 125 Rasbach St Canastota NY 13032

GUNJIAN, ARMEN GARO, sales executive; b. Alexandria, Egypt, Jan. 5, 1936; came to U.S., 1976; s. Souren and Zarouhi (Dikranian) G.; m. Chake Benohanian, July 12, 1980; children: Nora, Zaven. Grad. high schs., Oxford and Cambridge, Eng. Pres. Gunjian Mfg. Co. Ltd., Montreal, Can., 1959—, Brushtech, Inc., Plattsburgh, N.Y., 1976—, 124378 Can. Inc., Montreal, 1983—. Patentee barbeque grill brush and battery brush. Mem. Plattsburgh C. of C., Clinton County C. of C. (recipient Bus. of the Yr. award 1984), Nat. Housewares Mfrs. Assn., Nat. Hardware Mfrs. Assn. (recipient Retailer's Choice award 1987). Mem. Christian Orthodox Ch. Club: Royal St. Lawrence Yacht. Home: Crete Blvd near Wall St Plattsburgh NY 12901 Office: Brushtech Inc PO Box 1130 Rt 22 and Wall St Plattsburgh NY 12901

GUNN, JOSEPH RIDGEWAY, III, consulting economist; b. Ross, Calif., Nov. 28, 1928; s. Joseph Ridgeway, Jr. and Melvine Henrietta (Longley) G.; B.S. in Bus. Adminstrn., U. Calif., Berkeley, 1954, M.A. in Econs., 1958; spl. studies Oxford (Eng.) U., 1967; m. Marie Elsie Thurlow, June 16, 1951; children—Dana Carolyn Gunn Winslow, Anita Jayne Gunn Shirley, Janice Marie. Econ. analyst Standard Oil Co., Calif., 1954-61; econ. adv. Ministry Commerce, Govt. Afghanistan, Kabul, 1961-67; cons. economist, 1967—; sr. v.p. Robert R. Nathan Assos., Inc., Washington, 1986—. Chmn. bd. dirs. Terra Linda Community Services Dist., 1954-61. Mem. Am. Econ. Assn., Nat. Assn. Bus. Economists, Washington Internat. Trade Assn., Assn. Transp. Practitioners, Nat. Soc. Rate of Return Analysts, Nat. Economists Club, Asia Soc. Democrat. Episcopalian. Author articles, reports. Home: 10917 Picasso Ln Potomac MD 20854 Office: 1301 Pennsylvania Ave NW Washington DC 20004

GUNN, WENDELL LAVELLE, insurance company executive; b. Stonewall, Miss., Sept. 14, 1932; s. Christopher Clayburn and Lorena (Logan) G.; m. Roberta Anne Ashmore, Mar. 14, 1959; children: Leslie, Katherine. BS in Acctg., Fla. State U., 1958. Actuarial cons. State of Fla. Dept. Ins., Tallahassee, 1957-59; asst. sec.-treas. Ind. Life & Accident, Jacksonville, Fla., 1959-65; v.p. United Educators Life Ins., Miami, Fla., 1965; controller, asst. sec. Ky. Cen. Life Ins., Lexington, 1965-72; v.p. Mobile Home Industries, Tallahassee, 1972-73; sr. v.p., sec.-treas. Ky. Cen. Life Ins., Lexington, 1973—. Charter mem. U. Ky. Sch. Accountancy Adv. Council, Lexington, 1987—; treas., trustee Lexington Pub. Library, 1986—; mem. indsl. revenue bond rev. com. Lexington-Fayette Urban County, 1984—; chmn. Fayette County Rep. Party, Lexington, 1984-86. Served with USN, 1950-53. Mem. Fin. Execs. Inst. (bd. dirs. 1986—), Am. Council Life Ins. (state v.p. 1982—). Republican. Methodist. Home: 217 Clinton Rd Lexington KY 40502 Office: Ky Cen Life Ins Kincaid Towers 300 W Vine St Lexington KY 40507

GUNNELS, LAWRENCE, lawyer; b. Eureka, Kans., May 18, 1931; s. George W. and Sara A. (McComb) G.; m. Beverly A. Ballard, July 3, 1970; 1 child, Warren S. AB, Ottawa (Kans.) U., 1957; LLB, Washington U., St. Louis, 1960. Bar: Mo. 1960, D.C. 1962, Ill. 1963. Law clk. U.S. Supreme Ct., Washington, 1960-62; ptnr. Kirkland & Ellis, Chgo., 1962-78, Reuben & Proctor, Chgo., 1978-83; v.p., gen. counsel Chgo. Tribune Co., 1983-88; ptnr. Mayer, Brown & Platt, Chgo., 1989—. Fellow Am. Coll. Trial Lawyers, Am. Bar Found.; mem. ABA (forum com. communications), Mid-Am. Club. Republican. Episcopalian. Home: 535 N Michigan Chicago IL 60611

GUNNING, FRANCIS PATRICK, lawyer, insurance association executive; b. Scranton, Pa., Dec. 10, 1923; s. Frank Peter and Mary Loretta (Kelly) G.; m. Nancy C. Hill, Aug. 10, 1951; 1 son, Brian F. Student, City Coll. N.Y., 1941-43; LLB, St. John's U., 1950. Bar: N.Y. bar 1950. Legal editor Prentice Hall Pub. Co., N.Y.C., 1950-51; legal specialist Tchrs. Ins. & Annuity Assn. Am., Coll. Retirement Equities Fund, N.Y.C., 1951-53, asst. counsel, 1953-57, assoc. counsel, 1957-60, counsel, 1960-65, asst. gen. counsel, 1965-67, assoc. gen. counsel, 1967, v.p., assoc. gen. counsel, 1967-73, sr. v.p., gen. counsel, 1973-74, exec. v.p., gen. counsel, 1974-88, retired, 1988; mem. N.Y. adv. bd. Chgo. Title Ins. Co.; trustee, mem. exec. and audit coms. Mortgage Growth Investors. Contbr. articles on mortgage financing to profl. jours. With USAAF, 1943-46. Mem. ABA, N.Y. bar assns., Am. Land Title Assn., Am. Law Inst., Assn. Bar City of N.Y., Assn. Life Ins. Counsel, Nat. Assn. Coll. Univ. Attys., Am. Coll. Real Estate Lawyers. Republican. Roman Catholic. Home: 32 Kewanee Rd New Rochelle NY 10804 Office: Tchrs Ins & Annuity Assn Am 730 3rd Ave New York NY 10017

GUNNING, JOSEPH G., chemical company executive; b. N.Y.C., Jan. 8, 1930; s. John J. and Norah (Quinn) G.; m. Jean M. Howell, June 27, 1953; children: Jean-Marie, Gary J., Patrick, Eileen N. BBA, St. John's U., 1953; MBA, NYU, 1956. CPA, N.Y.; cert. fin. planner. Tax. acct. State of N.Y., N.Y.C., 1951-52; sr. acct. Touche Ross, N.Y.C., 1952-56; mgr. corp. reporting Sperry Rand Corp., N.Y.C., 1956-66; mgr. bus. planning Union Carbide Corp., N.Y.C., 1966-69, mgr. internat. acctg., 1973-81; mgr. acctg. research and policies Union Carbide Corp., Danbury, Conn., 1981—; asst. controller Western Union, N.Y.C., 1969-72; asst. prof. St. Francis Coll., N.Y.C., 1956-73; instr. Western Conn. State U., Danbury, 1983-87; dir. Richmond Hill Savs. and Loan, N.Y.C., Whitestone Savs. and Loan, N.Y.C. Lt. U.S. Army, 1947-49. Recipient Pax et Bonum medal St. Francis Coll., 1973. Mem. Am. Inst. CPA's, Nat. Assn. Accts., Fin. Execs. Inst., Inst. Cert. Fin. Planners, N.Y. State Soc. CPA's, Catholic War Vets. Roman Catholic.

GUNST, ROBERT ALLEN, marketing professional; b. Chgo., Apr. 8, 1948; s. Melville A. and Lois Ellibee G.; m. Karen Kemp, Sept. 5, 1970; children: Graham, Katherine. BA in Econs., Dartmouth Coll., 1969; MBA, U. Chgo., 1971. Asst. v.p. First Nat. Bank Chgo., 1969-75; sr. v.p., chief fin. officer Victoria Sta., Larkspur, Calif., 1975-82; v.p. fin. and adminstrn. PepsiCo Foods Internat. div. PepsiCo Inc., Dallas, 1982-84; sr. v.p. La Petite Boulangerie Inc. subs. PepsiCo Inc., Mill Valley, Calif., 1984-86; sr. v.p., chief fin. officer Shaklee Corp., San Francisco, 1987—; mem. adv. bd. Byers Inc., Hartford; bd. dirs. The Good Guys!, San Francisco, Shaklee (Japan). Mem. San Francisco Zool. Soc. (bd. dirs.), Bankers Club, City Club. Office: Shaklee Corp 444 Market St San Francisco CA 94111

GUNTER, EMILY DIANE, communications company executive; b. Atlantic City, N.J., Apr. 5, 1948; d. Fay Gaffney and Verlee (Wright) G.; children: Saliha, Kadir, Amin, Shedia. BA in Mathematical Stats., Am. U., 1970, postgrad. computer sci., 1971; postgrad. mktg., San Diego Community Coll., 1986. Traffic engr. C&P Bell, Washington, 1970-71; market analyst Market Towers Inc., Atlantic City, N.J., 1978-83; outside plant engr. N.J. Bell, Atlantic City, 1979-81; market analyst Empcor Group, Atlantic City, 1981-83; engr. Pacific Bell, San Diego, 1983—; lectr. Princeton (N.J.) U., 1979-81, Atlantic Community Coll., Atlantic City, 1979-81; customer coord. Pacific Bell-Telsam, San Diego, 1983-85. Bd. dirs. Atlantic City Transp. Authority, 1981-83; mem. Atlantic City Urban Area Transp. Commn., 1982-83. Mem. NAFE, Network Exec. Women. Democrat. Islamic. Home: 6005 Hughes St San Diego CA 92115 Office: Pacific Bell 7337 Trade St #5460 San Diego CA 92121

GUNTER, JOHN WADSWORTH, economic consultant; b. Sanford, N.C., Feb. 17, 1914; s. Herbert Brown and Lucy (Betts) G.; m. Lola Hatcher, Sept. 2, 1939 (div. 1960); children: Mary Kensy Ridley, Virginia Clark Krenzke; m. Margaret Jean Dozier, July 15, 1970. BS in Commerce, U. N.C., 1935, MA, 1938, PhD, 1942. Instr. econs. U. N.C., Chapel Hill, 1948-40; economist Office Internat. Fin. Treasury Dept., Washington, 1940-48; assoc. prof. U. Tex., Austin, 1948-49; fgn. mem. Greek Currency Com. Bank Greece, Athens, 1949-51; alt. U.S. mem. Tripartite Commn. on German Debts, London, 1951-53; from asst. dir. to acting dir. Mid. East Dept. Internat. Monetary Fund, Washington, 1953-77; pvt. practice Washington, 1977—; treasury rep. U.S. Treasury Dept., Cairo, 1943-44,, London, 1946-49. Recipient Decorations Govt. of Egypt, 1977. Democrat. Home: 7024 Buxton Terr Bethesda MD 20817 Office: 1627 K St NW Ste 910 Washington DC 20006

GUNTHARP, GRADY ELVIS, real estate executive; b. Vicksburg, Miss., Jan. 25, 1942; s. Grady E. Sr. and Zora B. (Swindoll) G.; m. Patricia A. Moses, Nov. 12, 1944; children: Anthony T., Angelia M. BSBA, Athens State Coll., 1977. Agt. Internal Rev. Service, Dallas, 1977-78; owner, sr. appraiser Grady Guntharp and Assocs., Bedford, Tex., 1978-87; pres., sr. appraiser Grady E. Guntharp, P.C., Bedford, 1987—, Associated Appraisers, Inc., Decatur, Ala., 1987—; pres. Somethin' Poppin', Inc., 1988—. Bd. dirs. Increase Ministry, Inc. Mem. Soc. Real Estate Appraisers, Real Estate Appraisers Tex. (bd. dirs.), Am. Soc. Appraisers, Nat. Assn. Review Appraisers and Mortgage Underwriters. Republican. Lodge: Kiwanis (dir. Bedford club). Home: PO Box 3004 Decatur AL 35602 Office: Associated Appraisers Inc 439 Johnston St SE Decatur AL 35602

GUNTHER, GREG, training and business communications consultant; b. Los Angeles, June 22, 1951; s. Martin and Ethel (Elkin) G.; B.A., Calif. State U., 1973; M.A., Annenberg Sch. Communications, U. So. Calif., 1978; m. Peggy June Rogers, Mar. 21, 1981. Media specialist Tratec Inc., Los Angeles, 1974-78; dir. devel. O.F.I., Guttenberg, N.J., 1978; pres. Enhanced Communications, Inc., Murray Hill, N.J., 1979—. Mem. Am. Soc. for Tng. and Devel., Internat. TV Assn., World Future Soc. Writer, producer: Hit The Ground Running!, 1981-82; developer various computer simulation games for bus. tng.; contbr. articles to profl. jours. Office: Enhanced Communications Inc 180 South St Murray Hill NJ 07974

GUPTA, SURAJ NARAYAN, physicist, educator; b. Haryana, India, Dec. 1, 1924; came to U.S., 1953, naturalized, 1963; s. Lakshmi N. and Devi (Goyal) G.; m. Letty J.R. Paine, July 14, 1948; children: Paul, Ranee. M.S., St. Stephen's Coll., India, 1946; Ph.D., U. Cambridge, Eng., 1951. Imperial Chem. Industries fellow U. Manchester, Eng., 1951-53; vis. prof. physics Purdue U., 1953-56; prof. physics Wayne State U., 1956-61, Distinguished prof. physics, 1961—; researcher on relativity, gravitation, quantum electrodynamics, nuclear physics, high-energy physics; vis. physicist Argonne Nat. Lab., Brookhaven Nat. Lab., NRC Can. Author: Quantum Electrodynamics, 1977. Fellow Am. Phys. Soc., Nat. Acad. Scis. India. Home: 30001 Hickory Ln Franklin MI 48025 Office: Wayne State U Dept Physics Detroit MI 48202

GURASH, JOHN THOMAS, building products manufacturing company executive; b. Oakland, Calif., Nov. 25, 1910; s. Nicholas and Katherine (Restovic) G.; student Loyola U. Sch. Law, Los Angeles, 1936, 38-39; m. Katherine Mills, Feb. 4, 1934; 1 child, John N. With Am. Surety Co. N.Y., 1930-44; with Pacific Employers Ins. Co., 1944-53; pres., organizer Meritplan Ins. Co., 1953-59; exec. v.p. Pacific Employers Ins. Co., 1959-60, pres., 1960-68, chmn., bd., 1968-76; v.p. Ins. Co. N. Am., 1966-70; exec. v.p., dir. INA Corp., 1968-69, chmn., pres., chief exec. officer, 1969-74, chmn., chief exec. officer, 1974-75, chmn. bd., 1975, chmn. exec. com., 1975-79; chmn. bd. Certain-Teed Corp., 1978—, also dir.; dir. Purex Industries Inc., Pic-N-Save Corp. Trustee Occidental Coll., Los Angeles; trustee Orthopaedic Hosp., Los Angeles; bd. dirs. Weingart Found.; mem. nat. Council Pomona Coll., Claremont, Calif. Mem. Pa. Soc., Newcomen Soc. N.Am., Knights of Malta. Clubs: California (Los Angeles); Pine Valley (N.J.) Golf; Los Angeles Country, Sr. Golf Assn. of So. Calif.; Annandale Golf (Pasadena). Office: Certainteed Corp PO Box 860 Valley Forge PA 19482 *

GURFEIN, STUART JAMES, jewelry manufacturing company executive; b. N.Y.C., Mar. 24, 1947; s. Louis J. and Ruthe (Jacobs) G.; divorced; children: Scott Eric, Heather Gill; m. Kathryn Merine, Apr. 4, 1981; children: Kody Allana. BS, Cornell U., 1968; MBA, Columbia U., 1970. Account exec. Cunningham & Walsh Advt., N.Y.C., 1970-71; v.p. Gurfein Bros. Inc., N.Y.C., 1971-82, M. Fabrikant & Sons, N.Y.C., 1983-86; chmn. A.B.L. Jewelers Inc., N.Y.C., 1986—; chmn. Jeffrey Stevens, Inc. N.Y. bd. dirs. Nat. Found. for Advancement in Arts, 1985—. Club: Friars (N.Y.C.). Office: ABL Jewelers Inc 22 W 48th St New York NY 10036

GURIK, DIANE GREEN, personnel company executive; b. Mansfield, Ohio, Apr. 21, 1949; d. Charles Vernon and J. Pauline Green; m. John Carl Gurik, Mar. 13, 1942; children: Jason, Jennifer, Brian, Scott, Christine. Student, Olivet Coll., 1968-69; cert. in nursing, Mid-Ohio Nursing Program, 1972; postgrad., Mansfield Bus. Coll., 1975. Treas. Jet Mgmt. Corp., 1974-78; adminstr. Wee Care Day Care Ctr., Mansfield, 1974-78; dir. nursing Allied Pvt. Duty Nurses Registry, Mansfield, 1978-83; founder, pres., chief exec. officer North Cen. Personnel, Inc., Mansfield, 1983—, also chmn. bd. dirs.; Mem. adv. bd. Pioneer Sch., Shelby, Ohio, 1988. Mem. Better Bus. Bur., Mansfield, 1985—. Recipient Tribute to Women in Industry award YWCA. Mem. Luth. Ch. Nurses (bd. dirs. 1982-86), Mansfield C. of C. Republican. Home: 521 Beech Dr Mansfield OH 44906 Office: North Cen Personnel Inc 491 Lexington Ave Mansfield OH 44907

GURLEY, FRANKLIN LOUIS, lawyer, military historian; b. Syracuse, N.Y., Nov. 26, 1925; s. George Bernard and Catherine Veronica (Moran) G.; m. Elizabeth Anne Ryan, June 17, 1950. A.B., Harvard U., 1949, J.D., 1952. Bar: Mass. 1952, N.Y. 1956, Ill. 1956, Mich. 1956, D.C. 1956. Fgn. service staff officer Dept. State, Washington and Germany, 1953-55; atty. N.Y. Central R.R. Co., 1955-56; asst. dist. atty. New York County, 1956-57; atty. firm Dewey, Ballantine, Bushby, Palmer & Wood, N.Y.C., 1957-63; gen. counsel, sec. IBM Europe Corp., Paris; also mng. atty. IBM Corp., Armonk, N.Y., 1963-68; sr. v.p., gen. counsel Nestle S.A., Vevey, Switzerland, 1968-83; spl. legal adv. Nestle S.A., Vevey, 1984-85; internat. legal cons. 1985—; historian 100th Inf. Div. Assn., 1984—. Author: 399th in Action in World War II, 1946, King Philip's War (play), 1952; contbr. articles to profl. jours. Pres. Tappan Landing Assn. Tarrytown N.Y. 1958-60. Served with inf. AUS, 1944-46, ETO. Decorated Bronze Star, Combat Inf. Badge; set West Point and Heptagonal 1000-yard records in track, 1948. Mem. ABA, N.Y. County Lawyers Assn., SAR (sec., bd. mgrs. N.Y. chpt. 1957-63), Harvard Law Sch. Assn., Harvard Law Sch. Assn. Europe. Clubs: Harvard (N.Y.C., France, Switzerland); Lausanne Golf, Montreux Golf; Am. Internat. (Geneva). Home and Office: 1626 Romanens, Fribourg Switzerland

GURLEY, GERALDINE MARIE, banker; b. Twin Falls, Idaho, Oct. 22, 1947; d. A.L. Jr. and Marie (Gubser) G.; m. Joseph Lamonica, Sept. 14, 1974. BA, Coll. Idaho, 1969; B in Internat. Mgmt., Am. Grad. Sch. Internat. Mgmt., Phoenix, 1970; Cert. de Lingua, U. Madrid, 1971. Adminstrv. asst. to gen. mgr. Arthur J. Fritz, Houston, 1972-73; asst. cashier Bank Am. Internat. of Tex., Houston, 1973-79; v.p. M Bank Houston, 1980—. Mem. Houston Letter of Credit Group, Am. Legion Aux. Office: M Bank Houston 910 Travis St Suite 450 Houston TX 77002

GURLEY, JOHN RAY, banker; b. Mpls., Feb. 5, 1933; s. Roger Allen and Harriett (Stevens) G.; m. Birthe Skovgaard Hansen, May 7, 1961; children: Alice Hansen Gurley Stuttin, John Hansen. AA, Pasadena City Coll., 1953; BA, U. So. Calif., Los Angeles, 1955; postgrad., Stanford U., 1951-52; postgrad. in bus. sch., UCLA, 1957-58. Securities sales Union Bank, Los Angeles, 1958-61; exec. asst. Great Western Fin. Corp, Beverly Hills, Calif., 1961-65; v.p. E.F. Baumer & Co., Los Angeles, 1965-67, Lloyds Bank Calif., Los Angeles, 1967-78; acct. exec. Merrill Lynch Pierce Fenner & Smith, Los Angeles, 1979-80; v.p. City Nat. Bank, Beverly Hills, Calif., 1980-81; sr. v.p. Sanwa Bank Calif, Los Angeles, 1981—. Mem. County Treasurer's Assn., Calif. Mcpls. Treasurer's Assn., Tournament of Roses Assn, Pasadena City Coll. Banking Sch. Adv. Com., Econ. Round Table, Los Angeles Bond Club, Athletic Club, Phi delta Phi. Republican. Protestant. Home: 714 Winthrop Rd San Marino CA 91108 Office: Sanwa Bank Ca 612 S Flower St Los Angeles CA 90017

GURRY, FRANCIS GERARD, international civil servant; b. Melbourne, Victoria, Australia, May 17, 1951; s. Raymond Paul and Eileen (Galbally) G.; m. Sylvie Marie Annick Veit, Aug. 20, 1983; children: Thomas Jerome, Celine Elisabeth. LLB, U. Melbourne, 1973, LLM, 1975; PhD, U. Cambridge, 1980. Solicitor Arthur Robinson & Co., Melbourne, 1974-76; sr. lectr. law U. Melbourne, 1979-83; vis. prof. U. Dijon, France, 1983; solicitor Freehill, Hollingdale & Page, Sydney, Australia, 1984; cons. World Intellectual Property Orgn., Geneva, 1985, sr. program officer, 1986-87, head indsl. property law sect., 1988—. Author: Breach of Confidence, 1984; contbr. articles to profl. jours. Recipient Yorke prize U. Cambridge, 1980. Home: 107 Rue de Lausanne, 1202 Geneva Switzerland Office: World Intellectual Property Orgn, 34 Chemin des Colombettes, 1211 Geneva Switzerland

GUSCIORA, AUDREY JOAN, small business owner; b. Mpls., Dec. 4, 1950; d. Franklin Howard and Clara Josephine Irmen; m. Terrance Gusciora, June 14, 1970 (div.); children: Jeffrey, James; married 1983; children: Jennifer, Joseph. Student, U. Minn., Duluth, 1968-69; BA in Nursing, St. Luke's Coll., Duluth, 1971; student, Normandale Community Coll., Bloomington, Minn., 1985-86, Metro. State U., Bloomington, 1986-87. Dir. Olathe Nursing Home, Kansas, Minn., 1971-73; head nurse St. Michael's Hosp., Sauke Centre, Minn., 1973-75; nurse specialist Minn. Dept. of Health, St. Cloud, 1975-77; supr. Buffalo (Minn.) Meml. Hosp., 1977-79; dir. Olsten, Mpls., 1979-80; br. mgr. Progressive Health, Hopkins, Minn., 1981-82; owner ProTemps, 1981-88; pres. P.T.I., Inc., Mpls., 1983-87, Paycheck Plus of Minn., Inc., 1987—; co-owner A&M Estate and Moving Sales, 1989—; pres. Hennepin Lake Bus. Svcs. Inc., 1989—; med. cons. Headstart, St. Cloud, 1973-75; small bus. cons. Hennepin-Lake Service, Mpls. Author: (manuals) Telemarketing, 1985, Marketing Techniques, 1985; author, artist (children's book) Co-Hug, 1980. Foster parent Hennepin County (Minn.) retarded div., Mpls., 1983-85; active Boy Scouts Am., Annandale, Minn., 1975-78, Assn. for Retarded Citizens, 1976-78; vol. Woman's Resource Ctr., Bloomington, 1985-86. Fellow Nat. Assn. Female Execs., Soc. Behavioral Medicine (small bus. mgmt. award 1986); mem. Nat. Assn. Self Employed, Internat. Platform Assn. Democrat. Roman Catholic. Club: Chart House, Women's Bus. Leads. Home: 11233 Ewing Ave S Bloomington MN 55431 Office: Paycheck Plus Minn Inc 3255 Hennepin Ave S Ste 255 Minneapolis MN 55408

GUSHIKEN, ELSON CLYDE, agricultural technology executive; b. Honolulu, Apr. 22, 1950; s. Nobu and Yoneko (Kaneshiro) G.; m. Aileen Hisako Tanoue, Sept. 7, 1974; children: Kristi, Traci. BFA, U. Hawaii, 1972. Landscape and irrigation design cons. Eckbo, Dean, Austin & Williams, Inc., Honolulu, 1973, Fujiwara & Green, Inc., Honolulu, 1973-74; sales office mgr. water and utilities div. Wisdom Industries, Honolulu, 1974-76; landscape and irrigation design cons. Oberlander, Bush & Cave, Honolulu, 1976-78; sales engr. Kuluwai Irrigation, Haleiwa, Hawaii, 1978, Irrigation Tech. Corp., Haleiwa, 1978-82; v.p., co-owner Irrigation Tech. Corp., 1982—. Mem. Bishop Mus. Assn. Mem. Am. Waterworks Assn., Hawaiian Sugar Techs., World Aquaculture Soc., Irrigation Assn. Home: 95-100 Awiki Pl Mililani HI 96789 Office: Irrigation Tech Corp 66-079 Kamehameha Hwy Haleiwa HI 96712

GUST, (JOHN) DEVENS, JR., chemist, educator; b. Phoenix, Nov. 28, 1944; s. John Devens and Mary Elizabeth (Montgomery) G.; m. Elaine Alice Leachman, Dec. 26, 1969; children: Karen Alison, John Devens III. BS in Chemistry, Stanford U., 1967; MA in Chemistry, Princeton U., 1972, PhD in Chemistry, 1974. Postdoctoral assoc. Calif. Inst. Tech., Pasadena, 1974-75; asst. prof. Ariz. State U., Tempe, 1975-80, assoc. prof., 1980-85, asst. chair for grad. studies, 1986-88, prof., 1985—; vis. prof. biophysics Muséum Nat. d'Histoire Naturelle, Paris, 1982, 85; vis. scientist CEN Saclay, Paris, 1982-83, 84. Contbr. articles to profl. jours. Served to sgt. U.S. Army, 1969-71. Mem. Am. Chem. Soc., Am. Soc. Photobiology, Biophysical Soc., Phi Beta Kappa, Sigma Xi, Phi Lambda Upsilon. Office: Ariz State U Dept Chemistry Tempe AZ 85287

GUSTAFERRO, WILLIAM R., telecommunications industry executive; b. 1929. BSBA, Ohio State U., 1950. Acct. AT&T, 1957-59; with Ohio Bell Telephone, Cleve., 1953-57, 59—, various acctg. and mgmt. positions, 1953-57, 59-75, v.p. rates and revenue, 1975-78, sr. v.p., chief fin. officer, 1978-83, exec. v.p., chief fin. officer, 1983—. Served with AUS, 1950-52. Office: Ohio Bell Telephone Co 45 Erieview Pla Cleveland OH 44114

GUSTAFSON, ALBERT KATSUAKI, lawyer, engineer; b. Tokyo, Dec. 5, 1949; came to U.S., 1951; s. William A. and Akiko (Osada) G.; m. Helen Melissa Laird, July 31, 1971 (div. 1975); m. Karen Jane Ekblad, Dec. 31, 1978 (div. 1987). BA with distinction, Stanford U., 1972; JD, U. Wash., 1980; LLM, 1988. Bar: Wash. 1981, U.S. Dist. Ct. (we. dist.) Wash. 1981, U.S. Ct. Appeals (9th cir.) 1984. Acoustics analyst Boeing Co., Seattle, 1973-74, materiel buyer, 1974; legal editor, Book Pub. Co., Seattle, 1975-76; research analyst Batelle Inst., Seattle, 1975-76; legal intern Office of U.S. Atty., Seattle, 1976; engr. U.P.R.R., 1977-85; corp. counsel Ansette Fin. Corp., Inc., Seattle, 1987—; pres. Albert K. Gustafson, P.S., Seattle, 1981—; corp. counsel Dorden, Inc., Centralia, Wash., 1984—, Ansette Fin. Corp., Inc., Seattle, 1987, Precision Forms, Inc., 1988; prof. internat. bus. law. Sch. Internat. Studies Internat. Edn. Ctr., Tokyo, 1989—. Sec. local 117-E, United Transp. Union, 1984, local vice-chmn., 1984; Dem. precinct chmn., 1984. Kraft scholar, 1968; Calif. State scholar, 1968-72. Mem. Internat. Bar Assn., Asian Bar Assn., Assn. Trial Lawyers Am., Wash. State Trial Lawyers Assn., ABA, Fed. Bar Assn., Seattle-King County Bar Assn., Seattle C. of C., Roppongi Bar Assn., Japan-Am. Soc., Asian Mgmt. Bus. Soc. Democrat. Presbyterian. Clubs: College, City. Lodges: Masons, Shriners, Order of DeMolay (master councilor 1968), Rotary. Home: 4322 Wallingford Ave N Seattle WA 98103 Office: 4100 First Interstate Ctr 999 3d Ave Seattle WA 98104 also: 3d Endo Bldg 3F, 1-17-2 Shinjuku Shinjuku Ku, Tokyo 160, Japan

GUSTAFSON, RONALD ERIC, human resources executive; b. N.Y.C., Jan. 30, 1934; s. Eric N. and Bertha M. (Boehmer) G.; m. Ruth E. Gritzke, Apr. 1, 1956; children: Eric P., David W., Joy E. BBA, U. Buffalo, 1956. Indsl. rels. rep. Union Carbide Corp., Tonawanda, N.Y., 1956-64; supr. tng. and devel. Am. Standard Corp., Buffalo, 1964-66; mgr. pers. Gen. Food Corp., Chgo., 1966-68; mgr. ops. pers. Gen. Food Corp., Kankakee, Ill., 1968-72; mgr. selection and recruitment Gen. Food Corp., White Plains, N.Y., 1972-74; dir. indsl. rels. Burndy Corp., Norwalk, Conn., 1974-77; v.p. human resources U.S. Filter Corp., N.Y.C., 1977-85; v.p. human resources and adminstrn. Bowater Inc., Darien, Conn., 1985—. Capt. USAF, 1956-60. Home: 46 Standish Dr Ridgefield CT 06877 Office: Bowater Inc PO Box 4012 Darien CT 06820

GUT, MICHELE CLAIR, operations facilities planner; b. Pitts., May 11, 1954; d. Francis Thomas G.; divorced. BBA, Western State U., 1987. Supr. Doig Optical Co., Pitts., 1972-76; adminstrn. asst. mktg. Zotos Internat., Darien, Conn., 1976-81; info. facilities trainer Continental Baking Co., Stamford, Conn., 1981-85; asst. to dir. Shearman & Sterling, N.Y.C., 1985-86; ops. facilities planner Wang Fin. Info. Svcs. Corp., N.Y.C., 1986—. Mem. NAFE, Internat. Lotus Users, Internat. Tamdem Users, Am. Mgmt. Assn. Republican. Roman Catholic. Office: Wang Fin Info Svcs Corp 120 Wall St New York NY 10005

GUTELIUS, EDWARD WARNER, marketing professional; b. Pitts., Dec. 28, 1922; s. Edward N. Gutelius and Ruth (Warner) Skinner; m. Dorothy Payne, Apr. 29, 1944; children: Edward Jr., Paul, D.L. Josepha S. Student, U. Pitts., 1943, Western Res. U., 1945-46; BBA, La Salle Extension U., 1965. Asst. mgr., sales promotion Gen. Electric, Cleve., 1946-48; advt. sales promotion mgr. lighting div. Sylvania Electric, N.Y.C., 1952-59; v.p., mktg. devel. mgr. Fuller, Smith & Ross, N.Y.C., 1952-59; dir. new products Gen. Food, White Plains, N.Y., 1959-68; v.p. mktg. Borden Dairy Svcs., N.Y.C., 1968-70; pres., mktg. cons. Edward W. Gutelius & Assocs., N.Y.C., 1971—; broker Esslinger, Wooten & Maxwell, Coral Gables, Fla., 1986—, Richard Bertram & Co., Miami; yacht broker, 1974—. Contbr. articles to profl. jours. Active bd. edn. Tarryton, N.Y., 1958-61; chmn. of bd. Second Ch. of Christian Sci., 1975—. 2nd lt. USAAF, 1943-45. Mem. Am. Mktg. Assn. (program chmn., Miami chpt., 1978-79), Adms. of Fla., N.Y. Yacht Club, Ocean Reef Club, Key Biscayne Yacht Club. Republican. Home: 2727 Hilola St Coconut Grove FL 33133 Office: Richard Bertram & Co 3660 NW 21st St Miami FL 33142

GUTERMUTH, SCOTT ALAN, accountant; b. South Bend, Ind., Nov. 24, 1953; s. Richard H. and Barbara Ann (Bracey) G. BS in Bus., Ind. U., 1976. CPA, Ind. With Coopers & Lybrand, Indpls., 1976-83, supervising auditor, 1980-83, audit mgr., 1983; v.p., controller Society Nat. Group, Indpls., 1983—; instr., nat. update analyst Becker CPA Rev. Course, 1980—. Adv., Jr. Achievement; mem. Marion County Republican Com., 1978—, Rep. Nat. Com., 1972—. Fellow Life Mgmt. Inst.; mem. Am. Inst. CPA's, Nat. Assn. Accts., Ins. Acctg. and Statis. Assn., Ind. Assn. CPA's (ins. com. 1984—), Life Mgmt. Inst. (assoc.). Methodist. Home: 3132 Sandpiper S Dr Indianapolis IN 46268 Office: 9101 Wesleyan Rd Indianapolis IN 46268

GUTFREUND, JOHN H., investment banker; b. N.Y.C., Sept. 14, 1929. B.A., Oberlin Coll., 1951. With mcpl. desk Salomon Brothers, N.Y.C., 1953-62, mgr. syndicate, 1962-63, ptnr., 1963-66, mem. exec. com., 1966-78; mng. ptnr. Salomon Bros., N.Y.C., 1978-81; chmn. bd., chief exec. officer Salomon Bros. Inc., N.Y.C., 1981—; co-chair Phibro Corp., N.Y.C., 1981-83; co-chief exec. officer Phibro-Salomon Inc. (formerly Phibro Corp.), N.Y.C., 1983-84, chief exec. officer, 1984-86; vice chmn. N.Y. Stock Exchange, 1985-87; chmn., chief exec. officer, pres. Salomon Inc. (formerly Phibro-Salomon Inc.), N.Y.C., 1986—; past vice chmn. N.Y. Stock Exchange; past bd. dirs. Securities Industry Assn. Trustee Ctr. for Strategic and Internat. Studies, Com. for Econ. Devel., Joint Council on Econ. Edn.; chmn. Downtown-Lower Manhattan Assn., Inc.; hon. trustee Oberlin (Ohio) Coll.; chmn. Wall St. com. Lincoln Ctr.'s Corp. Fund Campaign, 1986-87; treas. bd. trustees, chmn. fin. com. N.Y. Pub. Library; bd. dirs. Montefiore Med. Ctr. Corp. With U.S. Army, 1951-53. Mem. Downtown-Lower Manhattan Assn. (chmn.). Club: Bond of N.Y. (past pres., past bd. govs.). Office: Salomon Inc 1 New York Pla New York NY 10004

GUTH, MARY ANNE, business communications service company executive; b. Oil City, Pa., Feb. 28, 1954; d. Ralph Joseph and Helen Louis (Hinds) G.; m. Thomas Charles Fulton, Oct. 5, 1985. BA, Holy Cross Coll., 1976. Tech. writer, supr. Travelers Cos., Hartford, Conn., 1977-83; tech. writer, mgr. Coleco Industries, West Hartford, Conn., 1983-85; sr. cons. Courseware Developers, Manchester, Conn., 1985-88; pres. Mentor Communications, Ellington, Conn., 1989—; dir. More Assocs., Coventry, Conn. Author: Adamcalc User Manual, 1984. Mem. Aircraft Owners and Pilots Assn., Sierra Club, Soc. Tech. Communications (cen. Conn. chpt., treas. 1982-83, v.p. 1981-82, pres. 1983-86, membership mgr. 1987—, exec. bd.).

GUTHRIE, CHARLES OWEN, real estate broker, investor, consultant; b. Victoria, Va., Feb. 26, 1928; s. Ernest Franklin and Edythe (Camper) G.; m. Mary Ellen Newman, Apr. 8, 1950; children: Marlene, Susan Charlene. BS in Adminstrn., Va. So. Coll., 1949; course in advt., Internat. Corr. Sch., Scranton, Pa., 1950-52, course in chemistry, 1954-56. With adminstrn. dept. Norfolk-So. Ry., Roanoke, Va., 1945-56; pharm. salesman G. D. Searle and Co., Johnson City, Tenn., 1956-65; pres. Guthrie Med. Services, Roanoke, 1965-67; stock broker Paine & Webber, Roanoke, 1967-72; fin. planner Fin. Corp. Am., Atlanta, 1972; real estate and stock broker Cash Shoaf and Co., Roanoke, 1972-74; real estate broker, pres., cons. Guthrie and Assoc., Inc., Roanoke, 1974—; pres. N-dor Tennis, Inc., Roanoke, 1980—; gen. ptnr. 11 Real Estate Ptnrships, Roanoke, Salem and Daleville, Va., 1974—; fin. cons. N-dor Tennis, Inc., Roanoke, 1980—. Served with USAF, 1946-47. Mem. Nat. Assn. Realtors. Home: 1701 Blair Rd SW Roanoke VA 24015 Office: Guthrie & Assocs Inc 3622 Aerial Way Dr SW PO Box 4145 Roanoke VA 24015-0145

GUTHRIE, EDWARD EVERETT, lawyer, government executive; b. Minot, N.Dak., Aug. 19, 1941; s. James R. and Burnette E. (Olson) G.; m. Denise Ann Hardmeyer, Aug. 18, 1962 (dec. 1986); children: Kristen B., Douglas M.; m. Paulette O. Smith, Aug. 8, 1987. BA, Minot State Coll., 1965; JD, U. Minn., 1972. Bar: N.Dak., 1972. With ICC, Washington, 1972—; atty. advisor Office of Proc., 1972-75, dep. dir., 1980-82; atty. advisor various commrs. 1975-85, mng. dir., 1985—; mem. continuing legal edn. faculty Hamline U. Law Sch., St. Paul, 1981, 83. Served as lt. USN, 1965-69, Vietnam. Republican. Home: 4936 Herkimer St Annandale VA 22003

GUTHRIE, GEORGE RALPH, real estate development executive; b. Phila., Mar. 12, 1928; s. George Ralph and Myrtle (Robertson) G.; m. Shirley B. Remmey; children: Mary Elizabeth, Brenda Ann. BS in Econs., U. Pa., 1948. With I-T-E Imperial Corp., Phila., 1948-70; contr., fin. planner I-T-E Imperial Corp., 1960-68, treas., 1968-69, v.p. fin., 1969-70; pres. N. K. Winston Corp., N.Y.C., 1970-76; exec. v.p. Urban Investment and Devel. Co., Chgo., 1976-78; pres. Urban Investment and Devel. Co., 1978-82, chmn., 1982-88; vice chmn. JMB Instl. Realty Corp., 1987-89; prin. Argyle Enterprises, 1989—; bd. dirs. Zenith Electronics Corp., Ill. Cen. R.R., Chgo. Dock and Canal Trust. Trustee Nat. Coll. Edn.; chmn., bd. trustees Cornerstone Found.; mem. pres.'s coun. Luth. Social Svcs. of Ill.; bd. dirs. Augustana Coll., Jr. Achievement; mem. pres.'s coun., assoc. trustee U. Pa.; co-chmn. Chgo. Devel. Coun.; bd. dirs., exec. com. Chgo. Assn. Commerce and Industry. Mem. Fin. Execs. Inst., Urban Land Inst. (trustee, asst. chmn., mem. urban devel./mixed use coun.), Lambda Alpha Internat. Republican. Clubs: Glen View, Jupiter Hills, Carlton (bd. govs.), Economics, Chicago. Office: 1100 N Lake Shore Dr Chicago IL 60611

GUTIERREZ, MAURICIO EUGENIO, small business owner; b. Santiago, Chile, Feb. 24, 1963; came to U.S., 1986; s. Mario Jorge and Ana (De Gregori) G.; m. Linda Tabor, Aug. 13, 1988. Degree in Bus. Adminstrn. and Comml. Engring., Escuela de Negocios de Valparaiso, Chile, 1985. Mktg. cons. Industrias Ambrosoli S.A., Viña del Mar, Chile, 1985; founder, mgr. Hand Made Internat.-Chile, Santiago, 1986, Hand Made Internat.-USA, Alameda, Calif., 1987—. Roman Catholic. Home and Office: 2019 Shoreline Dr Ste 200 Alameda CA 94501

GUTIN, IRVING, lawyer; b. N.Y.C., Apr. 12, 1932; s. Norman and Eva (Wilf) G.; m. Claire Rosenstein, Mar. 13, 1960 (div. 1974); m. Barbara C. Shannon, June 13, 1982; children: Nina J., Cheryl, Jeffrey A. Student, Bklyn. Coll., 1949-51, LLB, 1954, LLM, 1960. Bar: N.Y. 1954, U.S. Dist. Ct. (ea. and so. dists.) N.Y., U.S. Ct. Mil. Appeals, U.S. Supreme Ct. Assoc. Eckaus & Leader, N.Y.C., 1954-55; atty. Legal Aid Soc., N.Y.C., 1955-57; assoc. M.M. Friedman, N.Y.C., 1957-59; ptnr. Lotwin, Goldman & Gutin, N.Y.C., 1959-73; sr. v.p., gen. counsel Armin Corp., N.Y.C., 1974-81; sr. v.p. Tyco Labs. Inc., Exeter, N.H., 1981—. Bd. dirs. N.Y.C. Assn. Help of Retarded, 1979-85, Greater Portsmouth Charitable Trust, Manchester, 1983—, Seacoast Hospice. Served with U.S. Army, 1954-56. Office: Tyco Labs Inc Tyco Pk Exeter NH 03833

GUTMAN, D. MILTON, advertising agency executive; b. Wheeling, W.Va., Feb. 21, 1933; s. D. Milton and Elizabeth (Henderson) G.; m. Katrine Rempe, Sept. 10, 1955; 1 son, J. Milton. Student U. Pa., 1951-52; B.S. cum laude, W. Va. U., 1955. TV and creative dir. Gutman Advt. Agy., Wheeling, W.Va., 1957-62, pres., 1963—; dir. Security Nat. Bank & Trust Co., 1969—, exec. com., 1974—. Bd. dirs., exec. com. Wheeling Soc. Crippled Children, 1960-87; pres. Oglebay Inst., 1972-75, devel. chmn., 1980—; trustee Linsly Inst., 1968—, v.p., 1975—; bd. trustees Wheeling AAA, 1972—; trustee Ohio Valley Gen. Hosp., 1970-87, pres., 1977-80; sec. Ohio Valley Health Services and Edn. System, 1983-87; pres. Youth Found. Greater Wheeling, 1984—, Chem. People Task Force, 1985-87. Served with U.S. Army, 1955-57. Recipient Silver award Advt. Fedn. Am. and Printers' Ink, 1962; Helen Gaynor Billboard award, 1968-73; Outstanding Shriner award Osiris Temple, 1978; Disting. Service award W.Va. Soc. Crippled Children and Adults, 1976; named Paul Harris fellow Wheeling Rotary, 1981. Mem. Wheeling Area C. of C. (dir. 1967-70), Ohio Valley Ad Club (past pres.). Clubs: Wheeling Rotary (dir., v.p., pres. 1967-68); Blue Pencil (exec. com.), chs, Jesters Office: Gutman Advt Agy 600 Bd of Trade Bldg Wheeling WV 26003

GUTMAN, I. CYRUS, transportation consultant, business executive; b. Perth Amboy, N.J., Mar. 28, 1912; s. Leon and Jennie (Levine) G.; m. Mildred B. Largman, July 21, 1940; children: Harry L., Peggy Sheren, Richard J.S. BS in Econs., Johns Hopkins U., 1932. Dist. mgr. Motor Freight Express, Inc., Phila., 1933-40; v.p., treas., gen. mgr. Modern Transfer Co., Inc., Allentown, Pa., 1940-67, dir. nat. sales, 1967-70; v.p. Atlantic div. Nat. Resource Recovery Corp., 1982—; mem. labor panel Am. Arbitration Assn., 1980—; bd. dirs. Eastern Industries, Inc., Wescosville, Pa., 1967-76. Pres. Lehigh County Indsl. Devel. Corp., 1959-85, Lehigh's Econ. Advancement Project, Inc., 1960-85; chmn. Lehigh County Indsl. Devel. Authority, 1966-82; mem. adv. com. Central Pa. Teamsters Pension and Health and Welfare Funds, 1969-76; mem. nat. resources com., nat. alumni schs. com. Johns Hopkins; mem. Lehigh-Northampton Counties Joint Planning Commn., 1962-82; chmn. Allentown Sch. Dist. Authority, 1966-86; mem. Lehigh and Northampton Transp. Authority, 1972-74; chmn. Allentown Non-Partisan Com. for Local Govt.; mem. Eastern Conf. Joint Area Com.; assoc. mem. Nat. Jewish Welfare Bd.; hon. bd. mem. Allentown Jewish Community Ctr., 1986—; exec. com. Citizens for Lehigh County Progress, 1965—; chmn. central campaign planning com. Lehigh Valley Hosps., 1966-67; adv. com. Good Shepherd Workshop; adv. bd. Allentown citadel Salvation Army, treas., 1971-80; pres. bd. assocs. Muhlenberg Coll., v.p., 1971-73, pres. 1974-76; bd. assocs. Cedar Crest Coll., 1972—; gen. adv. com. Lehigh County Vocat.-Tech. Sch., Lehigh County Community Coll., 1977; mem. Lehigh County Rep. Exec. Com.; trustee Allentown Hosp., 1970-82, hon. trustee, 1982-87, hon. mem., 1987; hon. Lehigh Valley Hosp. Ctr., 1987—; trustee, Swain Sch., 1977-80; bd. dirs. Lehigh Valley Jr. Achievement, United Fund, Allentown, Jewish Fedn. Allentown, 1953-60, Wiley House, 1969-80; bd. dirs. Lehigh Valley Public TV, Sta. WLVT, 1980—, vice chmn., 1984—; past trustee Rabbi Louis M. Youngerman Found., Internat. Assn. Machinists Local 1099 Dist. Pension Plan, Phi Sigma Delta Found; hon. adv. bd. Lehigh Valley Assn. for Retarded Children, 1969-70; mem. adv. bd. Lehigh Valley Ctr. for Performing Arts, 1975-77. Recipient St. Patrick's Day award Lehigh Valley, 1961, Civic Service commendation Whitehall C. of C.; Golden Deeds award Allentown Exchange Club, 1972, Disting. Citizens Sales award Sales and Mktg. Execs., Allentown and Bethlehem, 1976, Outstanding Service award Lehigh Valley Traffic Club, 1978, citation Pa. Ho. of Reps., 1982, City of Allentown, 1982, Americanism award Anti-Defamation League and B'nai Brith, 1985, citation Assn. for Blind and Visually Impaired, 1985, citation Lehigh County Vocat. Tech. Sch., 1986; Jack Houlihan Community Vol. award Lehigh County United Way, 1985, Presdl. proclamation through Gov. Thornburgh, Pa., 1986; Cyrus Gutman Scholarship established by Lehigh County Bus. and Indsl. Community Johns Hopkins U., 1983; I. Cyrus Gutman Day proclaimed in honor Allentown, Bethlehem, Easton, Pa. Mem. Allentown C. of C. (Disting. Service award 1967, past bd. dirs.), Traffic and Transp. Assn. Pitts., Met. Traffic Assn. N.Y., Central Pa. Motor Carriers Assn. (v.p., exec. com.), Pa. Soc., Am. Trucking Assn. (gov. Regular Common Carrier Conf. 1968), Eastern Labor Adv. Assn. (v.p.), Hon. First Defenders, Johns Hopkins Alumni Assn. (past sec., past pres. Phila. area), Lehigh County Hist. Soc. (exec. com. 1968-71), Nat. Fedn. Temple Brotherhoods, Omicron Delta Kappa, Pi Delta Epsilon, Zeta Beta Tau. Clubs: Berkleigh Country (Kutztown, Pa.) (hon. mem., past pres.); Lehigh Valley (Allentown); Locust Midcity, Traffic and Transp., Traffic (Phila.); Traffic (Balt.); N.Y. Traffic (N.Y.C.), Livingston. Lodges: Masons, B'nai B'rith. Home and Office: 1824 Turner St Allentown PA 18104

GUTMAN, RICHARD EDWARD, lawyer; b. New Haven, Apr. 9, 1944; s. Samuel and Marjorie (Leo) G.; A.B., Harvard U., 1965; J.D., Columbia U., 1968; m. Jill Leslie Senft, June 8, 1969 (dec.); 1 son, Paul Senft; m. Rosann Seasonwein, Dec. 10, 1987. Bar: N.Y. 1969, U.S. Ct. Appeals (2d cir.) 1969, U.S. Dist. Ct. (so. and ea. dists.) N.Y. 1975, U.S. Supreme Ct. 1982; asso. firm. Parker Chapin & Flattau, N.Y.C., 1968-72, Marshall Bratter Greene Allison & Tucker, N.Y.C., 1972-76, 78; ptnr. Bartel Engelman & Fishman, N.Y.C., 1976-78; counsel Exxon Corp., N.Y.C., 1978—; pres., dir. 570 Park Ave Apts., Inc., N.Y.C. Fellow Am. Bar Found.; mem. Fed. Regulation Securities Com. ABA, N.Y. State Bar Assn., (exec. com. 1983-86, securities regulation com. 1980—), Assn. Bar of City of N.Y. (securities regulation com. 1980-81, 83-86), N.A.M. (corporate fin. and mgmt. com.). Club: Harvard (admissions com. 1983-86, chmn. 1985-86, nom. com. 1986-87, bd. dirs. 1988—) (N.Y.C.). Home: 570 Park Ave New York NY 10021

GUTMANN, MAX, department store executive; b. Niederwerren, Germany, July 12, 1922; s. Selli and Ida Zeilberger Gutmann; m. Darlene Weller, Oct. 1, 1977; children: Sharon Gutmann Wing, Suzanne Gutmann Groesenek, Jay D., Tod K. Meyer. Chmn. bd., chief exec. officer Elder-Beerman Stores Corp., dept. store chain; co-founder div. Bee-Gee Shoe Corp., 1953, now chmn. bd.; chmn. bd. dirs. Margo's women's splty. chain, El-Bee Chargit Corp.; chmn. bd. div. Office Outfitters; dir. Bank One of Dayton, Dayco Corp., Frederick Atkins, Inc. Vice-chmn. bd. dirs. Good Samaritan Hosp.; bd. dirs. Dayton Art Inst., Urban League, Jewish Fedn. of Greater Dayton; mem. area progress council Downtown Devel. Council; mem. bus. adv. council U. Dayton; past dir. United Way. Mem. Nat. Retail Mchts. Assn. (bd. dirs.), Ohio Council Retail Mchts. (chmn. bd. dirs.), Dayton Area C. of C. (past bd. dirs.). Club: One Hundred. Home: 9556 Bridlewood Trail Spring Valley OH 45370 Office: Elder-Beerman Stores Corp 3155 El-Bee Rd Dayton OH 45401

GUTSHALL, THOMAS L., pharmaceutical company executive; b. Huntingdon, Pa., Feb. 24, 1938; s. Joseph Boyd and Kathryn Pauline (Wear) G.; m. Jane Kipp Taylor, Aug. 22, 1959; children: Jennifer, Douglas, Jodi. BS ChemE, U. Del., 1960. Process engr. Union Carbide Corp., S. Charleston, W.Va., 1960-61, 63-69; mfg. supt. Mallinckrodt, Inc., St. Louis, 1969-72; plant mgr. Mallinckrodt, Inc., Raleigh, N.C., 1972-75; v.p., gen. mgr. Mallinckrodt, Inc., St. Louis, 1975-81; group v.p. Syntex Corp., Palo Alto, Calif., 1981-83, sr. v.p., 1985-86, exec. v.p., 1987—; pres. Syva Co., Palo Alto, Calif., 1983-85. Chmn. City Team Ministries, San. Jose, Calif., 1984—. Served to 1st lt., U.S. Army, 1961-62. Mem. Am. Social Health Assn., Am. Inst. Chem. Engrs., Tau Beta Pi. Republican. Presbyterian. Home: 24968 O'Keefe Ln Los Altos Hills CA 94022 Office: Syntex Corp 3401 Hillview Ave Palo Alto CA 94303

GUTTERMAN, GERALD S., diversified manufacturing company executive; b. Wilkes-Barre, Pa., Jan. 29, 1929; s. Israel and Freda G.; m. Janet Jenkin, Aug. 26, 1954; children: Andrew, Lawrence, David. B.S., U. Scranton, 1950; M.B.A., N.Y. U., 1951. Sr. fin. analyst Allied Chem. Corp., N.Y.C., 1955-58; dir. divs. Am. Mgmt. Assn., N.Y.C., 1958-65; exec. v.p. fin. and adminstrn. Sun Chem. Corp., N.Y.C., 1965—; exec. v.p. fin. and adminstrn., chief fin. officer Sequa Corp. (formerly Sun Chem. Corp.), N.Y.C.; dir. Ault and Wiborg Group, Ltd., London. Served with USN, 1952-55. Mem. Fin.

Execs. Inst. Club: Rolls Royce Owners. Home: 27 Pondfield Pkwy Mount Vernon NY 10552 Office: Sequa Corp 200 Park Ave New York NY 10017 *

GUTTMAN, WILLIAM MICHAEL, communications company executive, lawyer; b. N.Y.C., Apr. 15, 1941; s. Arthur Guttman and Korinne (Shefska) Sobel; m. Jane Ruben (div. Nov. 1971); children: Jennifer L., Catherine R.; m. Susan Gordon, July 29, 1977. AB, Columbia U., 1963, LLB, 1966. Bar: N.Y. 1967. Assoc. Goldstein, Judd & Gurfein, N.Y.C., 1966-68, Moore, Berson & Bernstein, N.Y.C., 1968-78; assoc. gen. counsel Time Inc., N.Y.C., 1978-84, gen. counsel, v.p., sec., 1984—. Mem. ABA, N.Y. State Bar Assn., Assn. of Bar of City of N.Y., Assn. Am. Secs. Democrat. Jewish. Club: Harmonie (N.Y.C.). Office: Time Inc 1271 Ave of the Americas New York NY 10020

GUY, GEORGE A., economist; b. Chuanchow, Foukien, People's Republic of China, Aug. 10, 1933; came to U.S., 1975; s. Sek Tiu Guy and Sekian Ang; m. Decing Chiong, Oct. 10, 1967; children: Athena, Karl, Ann. BS, U. San Carlos, Philippines, 1955, MBA, 1958; MA in Econs., Stanford U., 1960. Asst. to v.p. fin. Gerber Products Co., Fremont, Mich., 1976-85, mgr. fin. projects, 1986-87, corp. economist, 1987-89; analyst Fremont Mut. Ins. Co., 1989—. Fellow Royal Econ. Soc.; mem. Nat. Assn. Bus. Economists (NABE). Club: Fremont Fish and Game. Lodge: Rotary (bd. dirs. Cebu City, Philippines club 1970-75, Fremont club 1976-79). Home: 204 Ramshorn Dr Fremont MI 49412 Office: Fremont Mut Ins Co 933 E Main St Fremont MI 49412

GUYETT, ROBERT LOSEE, petroleum, mining, petrochemical company executive; b. Dobbs Ferry, N.Y., Jan. 10, 1937; s. Howard Lynn Guyett; m. Susan Weisser, Jan. 31, 1959; children: Gregory L., Keith L. BA, Williams Coll., 1958; MBA, Rutgers U., 1959. With Pogson Peloubet (merged with Price Waterhouse, 1963), 1959-63; sr. tax mgr. Price Waterhouse, 1963-76; sr. auditor Stamford, Conn., 1963-65; tax mgr. Europe Brussels, 1968-71; sr. tax mgr. Phila., 1972-76; v.p., treas. LTV Corp., Dallas, 1976-86; dir. taxes 1976-79, asst. treas., fin. and tax, 1979-83, v.p., controller, 1983-86, v.p., treas., 1986; sr. v.p. fin., chief fin. officer Fluor Corp., Irvine, Calif., 1987—, also bd. dirs.; bd. dirs. St. Joe Gold, Clayton, Mo.; founder, dir. Concorde Bank N.A., Dallas, Cntre Reinsurance Holdings, Ltd. Mem. Am. Inst. CPA's, Nat. Assn. Accts., Fin. Execs. Inst., Tax Exec. Inst., Internat. Fiscal Assn., Beta Theta Pi. Clubs: Williams (N.Y.C.); Huntington Valley Country (Phila.) (treas., bd. govs. 1974-76), Santa Ana Country Club. Office: Fluor Corp 3333 Michelson Dr Irvine CA 92730

GUYETTE, JAMES M., airline executive; b. 1945; married. BS, St. Mary's Coll., 1967. With United Air Lines Inc., Chgo., 1967—, various mgmt. positions, 1967-79, v.p. personnel, sr. v.p., 1979-85, exec. v.p. ops., 1985—. Office: United Air Lines Inc PO Box 66100 Chicago IL 60666 *

GUYOT, CHRISTIAN NOEL, chemist; b. Lons-Le-Saunier, France, Dec. 25, 1949; came to U.S., 1987; s. Paul N. and Madeleine (Jacquand) G. Cert. ingenieur agronome, Inst. Nat. Agronomique, Paris, 1973. Chemist Soc. des Usines Chimiques/Rhone-Poulenc, Vitry/Seine, France, 1974-75; chief chemist Rhone-Poulenc Industries, St. Fons, France, 1976-77; sr. chief chemist Rhone-Poulenc Recherches, Antony, France, 1978-84; sect. leader Rhone-Poulenc Agrochimie, Lyon, France, 1984-87; project scientist Rhone-Poulenc AG Co., Research Triangle Park, N.C., 1987—. Contbr. articles to profl. jours.; patentee hardened clay soil conditioning agt., acid treated clay plant growing medium. Mem. Soc. Chimique de France. Roman Catholic. Home: 4609 E Hope Valley Rd Durham NC 27707 Office: Rhone-Poulenc AG Co 2 TW Alexander Dr Research Triangle Park NC 27709

GUZZLE, TIMOTHY L., energy corporation executive; b. Ottumwa, Iowa, Nov. 4, 1936; s. Roy N. and Marcella A. (Turner) G.; m. Kathryn J. Felkel, Aug. 2, 1959; children—Timothy J., Benjamin. B.S. in Physics and Math, U. Okla., 1958, M.S. in Physics, 1959; Ph.D. in Physics, Tex. Christian U., 1965. V.p. engring. AMF Ben Hogan Co., Fort Worth, 1972-77, AMF Tuboscope, Houston, 1977-78; pres. True Temper Sports, Inc., Memphis, 1978-82; pres. spl. tech. group, dir. Allegheny Internat., Inc., Memphis, 1982-84, exec. v.p., dir., 1984-88; pres., chief operating officer TECO Energy, Inc., Tampa, Fla., 1988—, also bd. dirs.; bd. dirs. NCNB Bank of Fla. Contbr. articles to profl. jours. Bd. dirs. Fla. Symphony Orch., Tampa Com. of 100, United Way Tampa. AEC fellow, 1958-59; NSF fellow, 1961-65. Mem. Greater Tampa C. of C. (bd. dirs.), Phi Beta Kappa, Sigma Xi, Sigma Alpha Epsilon. Episcopalian. Clubs: Memphis Country; Allegheny Country (Pitts.); Tampa Club, Palma Ceia Country, University (Tampa), Tampa Yacht. Office: TECO Energy Inc 702 N Franklin St Tampa FL 33602

GWALTNEY, EUGENE C., sportswear company executive; b. Rock Hill, S.C., 1918. BSME, Ga. Inst. Tech., 1940; MS, MIT. With Russell Corp., Alexander City, Ala., 1952—, gen. supt., 1956-59, v.p., gen. supt., 1959-68, chief operating officer, 1968-72, pres., 1968-82, chief exec. officer, 1972—, chmn., 1982—; vice chmn., bd. dirs. First Nat. Bank Alexander City; bd. dirs. Russell Lands Inc. Office: Russell Corp PO Box 272 Lee St Alexander City AL 35010 *

GWILLIM, RUSSELL ADAMS, manufacturing company executive; b. Passaic, N.J., May 4, 1922; m. Elda E. Gwillim; children: Joanne, Linda, Cynthia. BS, MIT, 1948. Sales engr. CR Industries, Elgin, Ill., 1948-58, gen. sales mgr., 1958-64, v.p. mktg., 1964-65, exec. v.p., 1965-69, pres., 1969-84; chmn. bd. Safety-Kleen Corp., Elgin, 1974—; bd. dirs. CR Industries, Elgin, Norwesco Corp., Mpls., Moog Automotive, St. Louis, Sanford Corp., Bellwood, Ill. Chmn. United Way of Elgin, 1980; bd. dirs. Elgin Assn. Commerce, 1978, Ill. C. of C., 1979; mem. adv. bd. St. Joseph Hosp., Elgin, 1984. Served with U.S. Army, 1942-46, PTO. Presbyterian. Clubs: Butler Country (Oak Brook, Ill.); Medinah Country (Itasca, Ill.) (bd. dirs. 1976—). Office: Safety-Kleen Corp 777 Big Timber Rd Elgin IL 60123

GWIN, FRANCIS B., retired cooperative executive; b. Morrowville, Kans., Jan. 13, 1921; s. Roy Elmer and Genevieve Anna (Brooks) G.; m. Mary Arlene Mastin, July 11, 1948 (dec. 1959); 1 child, Francene; m. Margaret Ann Widrig, June 6, 1963; 1 child, Brenda. B.S. in Agrl. Econs., Kans. State U., 1947. Asst. to supr. Farmers Home Adminstrn., Clay Center, Kans., 1948-49; farmer Leoti, Kans., 1949-54; fieldman Consumers Coop. Assn., Kansas City, Mo., 1954-59; fieldman Farmway Coop Inc., Beloit, Kans., 1959-62, elevator dept. mgr., 1962-69, gen. mgr., 1969-86; bd. dirs. Farmland Industries, Inc., Kansas City, 1972-87, chmn. bd., 1981-86; dir. Nat. Coop. Refinery Assn., McPherson, Kans., 1981-87, Farmland Mut. Ins. Co., Des Moines, 1972-81, Far Mar Co., Kansas City, 1977-85, Terra Resources, Tulsa, 1981-83, Coop. League of U.S., Washington, 1974-80, Solomon Valley Feed Lot, Beloit, 1972—, Farmland Industries Inc., Kansas City, chmn. 1981-86; mem. adv. com. Arthur Capper Coop. Ctr. Kans. State U., 1984-86; mem. Kans. Grain Commn., Topeka, 1974-80, Nat. Com. Agrl. Trade and Export Policy, Washington, 1984-86. Served to lt. USAF, 1943-45. Recipient Disting. Agrl. Econ. Alumni award Kans. State U., 1983, Disting. Service award, 1985, Coop. Statesmanship award Am. Inst. Coops., 1985, Meritorious Svc. award Kans. Crops and Soil Ind. Coun., 1987; named Wheat Man of Yr. Kans. Assn. Wheat Growers, 1984. Republican. Methodist. Lodge: Rotary (pres. Beloit 1963-64). Home: 6 Gill Creek Terr Beloit KS 67420 Office: Farmway Coop Inc 204 E Court St Beloit KS 67420

GWIN, JOHN MICHAEL, educator, consultant; b. Montgomery, Ala., June 21, 1949; s. Emmett Brindley Jr. and Irma Rebecca (Watkins) G.; m. Pamela Jane Blair, Sept. 7, 1970; 1 child, Colin Blair. BBA, Auburn U., 1971; MBA, U. Ga., 1973; PhD, U. N.C., 1979. Fiscal officer U. Ga., Athens, 1971-73; ops. mgr. Bedsole & Gwin Inc., Fairhope, Ala., 1973-75; instr. Faulkner Coll., Bay Minette, Ala., 1975-76; research asst. U. N.C., Chapel Hill, 1976-78, vis. instr., 1978-79; asst. prof. Ind. U., Bloomington, 1979-81; asst. prof. U. Va., Charlottesville, 1981-83, assoc. prof., 1983—; instr. many U.S. firms, 1981—; cons. many internat. and U.S. firms, 1983—. Contbr. articles to profl. jours. Inventor LaMaze Timer. Vol. SBA, Charlottesville, 1982-85. Named Fulbright prof. to Dublin, Ireland, U.S. Info. Agy., 1986-87, Sesquicentennial Research Assoc., U. Va., 1986-7, Outstanding Young Man Am., U.S. Jr. C. of C., 1976. Mem. Am. Mktg. Assn. (cen. Va. chpt. conf. coordinator 1986), So. Mktg. Assn., Acad. Mktg. Sci., Boar's Head Sports Club, Colonnade Club. Episcopalian. Home: 1712 Essex Rd Charlottesville VA 22901 Office: U Va McIntire Sch Commerce Charlottesville VA 22903

GWINN, NAOMI JEAN, railroad quality control inspector; b. Greeneville, Tenn., May 10, 1952; d. Robert Walter and Ima Jean (Ferguson) G. Grad. high sch., Greeneville, Tenn., 1974. Cert. journeyman electrician. Supr. Midstate Electronics, Beech Grove, Ind., 1975-77; elec. apprentice Amtrak, Beech Grove, Ind., 1977-80, elec. technician, 1980-86, quality control insp., 1986—. Mem. editorial staff Amtrak co. news, 1985—; contbr. articles to mags. Mem. Nat. Assn. R.R. Bus. Women (Circle City chpt. #74, rec. sec. 1985-86, chmn. pub. affairs, press and publicity 1984-85, chair welfare com. 1986, nominating com. 1986), Nat. Assn. Female Execs., Internat. Brotherhood Elec. Workers. Democrat. Office: AMTRAK 202 Garstang Beech Grove IN 46107

GWINN, ROBERT P., publishing executive; b. Anderson, Ind., June 30, 1907; s. Marshall and Margaret (Cather) G.; m. Nancy Flanders, Jan. 20, 1942; 1 child, Richard Herbert. PhD, U. Chgo., 1929. With Sunbeam Corp., Chgo., 1936-51, gen. sales mgr. elec. appliance div., 1951-52, v.p., dir., 1952-55, pres., chief exec. officer, 1955-71, chmn. bd., chief exec. officer, 1971-82, also bd. dirs.; chief exec. officer, chmn. bd. Ency. Brittanica, Inc., Chgo., 1973—; chmn. bd., chief exec. officer Ency. Britannica; chmn. bd. dirs. William Benton Found., Exploration, Inc., Riverside, Ill., Titan Oil Co., Riverside; bd. dirs. Continental Assurance Co., Continental Casualty Co., CNA/Fin. Corp., Inst. for Philos. Research, Max McGraw Wildlife Found., Alberto-Culver Corp. Trustee Chgo. Zool. Soc., U. Chgo., The Orchestral Assn.; active overseers com. med. sch. and sch. dental medicine Harvard U.; Citizens adv. com., Mus. Contemporary Art. Mem. Elec. Mfrs. Club (hon.), Alpha Sigma Phi. Clubs: Comml. of Chgo., Casino (Chgo.), Execs., Soc. of Chgo., Internat. Food & Wine Soc. of Chgo., Mid-Am., U. of Chgo.; Bird Key Yacht, U. of Sarasota; Confrerie des Chevaliers du Tastevin; Riverside Golf. Office: Ency Brit Inc 310 S Michigan Ave Chicago IL 60604

GWYNN, DAVID WAYNE, stockbroker, financial planner; b. Parkersburg, W.Va., May 26, 1960; s. G. Wayne and Karen E. (Palmer) G. BA, U. Oreg., 1982. Telephonics asst. Xerox Corp., Eugene, Oreg., 1981-82; sales rep. Royal Bus. Machines, Lake Oswego, Oreg., 1982-83; lumber broker Fullmer Lumber Co., Tigard, Oreg., 1983-85, Hancock Lumber Co., Lake Oswego, 1985-87; stockbroker Kidder, Peabody & Co., Phoenix, 1987—. Democrat. Presbyterian. Office: Kidder Peabody & Co 2390 E Camelback Rd Ste 430 Phoenix AZ 85016

HAAB, LARRY DAVID, utility company executive; b. Fairbury, Ill., Sept. 28, 1937; s. Samuel Frances and Sarah Louise (Steidinger) H.; m. Ann Geddes, Aug. 2, 1958; children: Sheryl, David, Julie. B.S., Millikin U., 1959. C.P.A., Ill. Sr. acct. Price Waterhouse, St. Louis, 1959-65; with Ill. Power Co., Decatur, 1965—, now exec. v.p., chief fin. officer; bd. dirs. First Nat. Bank of Decatur, Decatur Meml. Hosp. Pres. Millikin U. Alumni Bd., 1981; pres. Macon County Mental Health Bd., Decatur, 1983-86. Mem. Edison Electric Inst. (fin. com.), Am. Inst. C.P.A.s, Metro Decatur C. of C. (chmn. bd. dirs.). Club: Country of Decatur (bd. dirs.). Office: Ill Power Co 500 S 27th St Decatur IL 62525 *

HAAGENSON, DUARD DEAN, construction company executive, state representative; b. Bonners Ferry, Idaho, Oct. 15, 1941; s. Durward Orlando and Fern Luella (Cady) H.; m. Pamela Lee Beckman, Sept. 14, 1974 (div. July 1977). BS in Mech. Engring., U. Idaho, 1965. Assoc. engr. Boeing Co., Seattle, 1965-66; engr., project mgr. Baugh Constrn., Seattle, 1970-75; constrn. engr. RMK-BRJ, Saigon, Vietnam, 1967-69; pres. Contractors Northwest, Coeur d'Alene, Idaho, 1976—. Rep. state affairs, transp. and def. coms., chmn. resources and conservation com. Idaho Ho. of Reps., Boise, 1982—. Mem. nat. legis. com. Associated Builders and Contractors (chmn. 1984-85, nat. bd. dirs. 1980-83, Idaho Legislator of Yr., 1984-85), Inland Pacific chapt. ABC (pres. 1979-80). Republican. Presbyterian. Lodge: Rotary. Home: Fernan Lake Rd Coeur d'Alene ID 83814 Office: Contractors Northwest Inc PO Box 340 Coeur d'Alene ID 83814

HAAR, ANA MARIA FERNÁNDEZ, advertising, public relations executive; b. Oriente Province, Cuba, Mar. 25, 1951; came to U.S., 1960, naturalized, 1970; d. Gilberto and Esmeralda Emiliana (Diaz) Fernández. Grad. Miami Dade Community Coll., 1971; student Barry Coll., 1972-78. Adminstrv. asst. thru asst. v.p. nat. accounts Flagship Bank, Miami Beach, Fla., 1971-77; v.p. comml. lending Jefferson Nat. Bank, Miami Beach, 1977-78; pres. IAC Advt. Group, Miami, 1978—; instr. Miami Dade Community Coll. Women in Mgmt. Program, 1980-81; hostess Sta. WPBT Program Viva. Mem. Dade County Commn. on Status of Women, 1979-82; chmn. Econ. Devel. Task Force of Commn. on Status of Women, 1979-82; bd. dirs. Downtown Miami Bus. Assn., 1979-82, Fla. Counseling Services, Miami; Internat. Ctr. of Fla., chmn. healthcare com.; mem. Dist. Export Council; hostess (program) Viva, WPBT-TV; mem. community Services Cedars Med. Ctr. Recipient Gran Orden Martiana of Cuban Lyceum for excellence in community service, 1976, Up and Comers award South Fla. Bus. Jour., 1988. Mem. Advt. Fedn. Greater Miami, Greater Miami Advt. Fedn. (bd. dirs.), Asociación de Publicitarios Latino-Americanos (v.p.), Miami Beach C. of C. (hon. life, trustee), Greater Miami C. of C., Hispanic Heritage Festival Com., Home: 2451 Brickell Ave Miami FL 33129 Office: IAC Advt Group 2725 SW 3d Ave Miami FL 33129

HAAS, DEBORAH LYNN, banker; b. Chgo., June 11, 1952; d. William Hermann and Elizabeth Dorothy (Badali) H. BA, U. Dayton, 1973; MA, U. Ariz., 1976; MIM, Am. Grad. Sch. Internat. Mgmt., 1979. Advt. mgr. Flyer News, U. Dayton (Ohio), 1970-73; instr. U. Ariz., Tucson, 1974-79; consumer lending officer Valley Nat. Bank, Phoenix, 1980-82, comml. lending officer, 1982-83, asst. mgr., med. banking specialist, 1984-88; comml. banking officer Sun State Savs. & Loan, 1988—; tchr. ESL, 1975-79; tchr. German, U. Ariz., 1974-76. Mem. Ariz. Sonora Desert Mus., 1984—, Nat. Wildlife Fedn.; sec. Friends of Refugees, 1982; instr. Vols. for Refugee Self-Sufficiency, 1982-83. Mem. Am. Assn. Tchrs. German, Phoenix Thunderbird Alumni Assn. (sec. steering com. 1983-85, balloon race com. 1986—, pres.-elect 1986-87, pres. 1987-88, giving adv. bd. 1989—, chmn. bd. 1988-89, trustee 1989—), Friends of Thunderbird (coordinator fgn. student luncheons, 1986, chmn. bd. 1988-89, mem. planned giving bd. 1989—), Delta Phi Alpha, Phi Beta Alpha. Lodge: Civitan (bd. dirs. local chpt. 1984—, pres.-elect 1985—, pres. 1985-86, chmn. bd. 1987-88). Address: Sun State Savs & Loan 15015 N 7th Pl Phoenix AZ 85022

HAAS, EDWARD LEE, accounting firm executive; b. Camden, N.J., Nov. 9, 1935; s. Edward David and Mildred (Wynne) H.; m. Maryann Lind, Dec. 27, 1958; children: John Eric, Gretchen Lind. B.A., LaSalle U., 1958; post-grad., Temple U., 1960—. Mgr. systems devel. RCA Corp., Cherry Hill, N.J., 1966-71; mgr. computer tech. services Gencorp, Akron, Ohio, 1971-74; sr. mgr. computer applications research and devel. Ernst & Whinney, Cleve., 1974-75; dir. nat. systems group Ernst & Whinney, 1976-77, nat. dir. data processing and software products, 1977, nat. ptnr., 1978—, cons. ptnr., 1983—. Served to 1st lt., arty. U.S. Army, 1958-59. Mem. Data Processing Mgmt. Assn., Assn. Systems Mgmt., Assn. of Inst. for Cert. Computer Profls. Republican. Roman Catholic. Clubs: Phila. Country, Union League of Phila., Hist. Soc. Pa., Phila. Drama Guild, Cotillion Soc. Cleve. Office: Ernst & Whinney 1500 Market St Ste 2900 Philadelphia PA 19102

HAAS, ELEANOR (MRS. PETER RALPH HAAS), business development consultant; b. Jersey City, Mar. 12, 1932; d. Nicholas Mark and Eleanor (Cochran) Alter de Csanytelek; BA, Smith Coll., 1953; cert. N.Y. Sch. Interior Design, 1960; m. Peter Ralph Haas, Oct. 22, 1966. Exec. sec. MCA Artists, Ltd., N.Y.C., 1954-56; exec. sec. Young & Rubicam, Inc., N.Y.C., 1956-58; exec. sec. J. Walter Thompson Co., N.Y.C., 1958-59; exec. sec. Stanford Research Inst., N.Y.C., 1959, Deafness Research Found., N.Y.C., 1960, Earl Newsom & Co., N.Y.C., 1961-65; account exec. Ruder & Finn, Inc., N.Y.C., 1965-68; founder, pres. The Haas Group, Inc., N.Y.C., 1968-87; founder, pres. HTL Ventures, Inc., N.Y.C., 1986-88; v.p., dir. planning The Howard Marlboro Group, N.Y.C., 1988— adj. asso. prof. dept. journalism N.Y. U., 1980-83, lectr. Sch. Continuing Edn., 1981-83. Mem. Info. Industry Assn., Am. Mktg. Assn., Nat. Acad. TV Arts and Scis., Electronic Banking Econs. Soc., Advt. Women N.Y., Hajji Baba Club. Office: 475 10th Ave 12th Floor New York NY 10018-1198

HAAS, GEORGE CHARLES, JR., financial company executive; b. N.Y.C., Sept. 10, 1920; s. George C. and Clara (Simon) H.; m. Dorothy Marston, Aug. 21, 1948; children: Susan Orthwein, Judith Eshelman, Sally Anne Colbert. BA, Yale U., 1942. With Mallard Air Svc., 1946-47, Coca-Cola Co., 1947-49, Pepsi-Cola Co., N.Y.C., 1949-60; pres. Haas Fin. Corp., N.Y.C., 1960—; bd. dirs. Allbev Corp., Charlotte, N.C., Wilson Bottling. Chmn. Polo Tng. Found., Lexington, Ky.; bd. dirs. Nat. Mus. Polo and Hall of Fame, Lake Worth, Fla.; trustee Mus. Hunting and the Horse, N.Y.C. Maj. U.S. Army, 1942-45, ETO. Mem. U.S. Polo Assn. (gov.), Gulfstream Polo Club (v.p.), Sky Club, Yale Club, Explorers Club, Palm Beach Polo and Country Club. Republican. Presbyterian. Home: 4301 Polo Rd Lake Worth FL 33467 Office: Haas Fin Corp 230 Park Ave New York NY 10169

HAAS, HAROLD MURRAY, motion picture company executive; b. Jamaica, N.Y., Apr. 20, 1925; s. Ludwig and Sadie (Borish) H.; m. Henny Notowitz, Dec. 25, 1949 (div. Mar. 1980); children—Gilda Susan, Linda Deborah; m. Beverly Rabinowitz Weingard, Apr. 20, 1980. B.S., Columbia, 1948, M.S., 1951. C.P.A., N.Y., Calif. Jr. acct. Arthur Young & Co. (C.P.A.'s), N.Y.C., 1948-49; audit mgr. Harry Berman & Co. (C.P.A.'s), N.Y.C., 1949-55; asst. controller MCA Inc., N.Y.C., 1955-60; controller agy. div. MCA Inc., Chgo., 1960-62; chief acct. MCA Inc., Universal City, Calif., 1962-65; controller MCA Inc., 1965-75, treas., 1975—, v.p., treas., 1979—; dir. Yosemite Park & Curry Co., 1974—. Bd. dirs. Ebony Showcase Theatrical Workshop, 1971-72, adv. bd., 1972; mem. entertainment industry bd. United Jewish Welfare Fund, 1970-71. Served with AUS, 1943-45. Decorated Combat Inf. Badge. Mem. Columbia U. Grad. Sch. Bus. Alumni Assn. (asso.). Home: 1945 N Normandie Ave Los Angeles CA 90027 Office: MCA Inc 100 Universal City Pla Universal City CA 91608

HAAS, HOWARD GREEN, bedding manufacturing company executive; b. Chgo., Apr. 14, 1924; s. Adolph and Marie (Green) H.; m. Carolyn Werbner, June 4, 1949; children: Jody, Jonathan. Student, U. Chgo., 1942; B.B.A., U. Mich., 1948. Promotion dir. Esquire, Inc., Chgo., 1949-50; advt. mgr. Mitchell Mfg. Co., Chgo., 1950-52; v.p. advt. Mitchell Mfg. Co., 1952-56, v.p. sales, 1956-58; sales mgr. Sealy, Inc., Chgo., 1959-60; v.p. marketing Sealy, Inc., 1960-65, exec. v.p., 1965-67, pres., treas., 1967-86, 87; chmn. Howard Haas Assocs.; vis. scholar U. Chgo. Grad. Sch. Bus., 1988—. Mem. nominating com. Glencoe Sch. Bd.; mem. print and drawing com. Art Inst. Chgo.; chmn. parent's com. Washington U., St. Louis; past bd. dirs. Jewish Children's Bur., NCCJ; pres. Orch. of Ill. Assn.; bd. dirs. Morgan Projects, Colbys Home Furnishings; mem. vis. com. Sch. Social Service Administrn. U. Chgo. Served to 1st lt. USAAF, 1943-45, ETO. Decorated Air medal with 3 oak leaf clusters; recipient Brotherhood award NCCJ, 1970, Human Relations award Am. Jewish Com., 1977. Mem. Nat. Assn. Bedding Mfrs. (past vice chmn., trustee), Print and Drawing Club. Jewish. Club: Birchwood Tennis (Highland Park, Lodge: Masons. Office: Howard Haas Assocs 208 S LaSalle St Suite 900 Chicago IL 60604

HAAS, JAMES E., diversified holding company executive; b. 1936; married. B.S.B.A., Kent State U., 1958. Mgr. distbn. A.M. Castle Co., 1958-65; pres., chief operating officer Nat. Steel Corp., Pitts., from 1982; with Nat. Intergroup Inc., Pitts., 1965—; mgr. A.R. Purdy div., then. exec. v.p. steel ops Nat. Intergroup Inc., Pitts., 1981-83; pres., chief operating officer Nat. Intergroup Inc., Pitts., 1983—, also dir.; v.p., bd. dirs. Steel Service Ctr. Inst. Mem. Nat. Assn. Aluminum Distbrs. (bd. dirs.). Office: Nat Intergroup Inc 20 Stanwix St Pittsburgh PA 15222 *

HAAS, JAMES WAYNE, accountant; b. Merrill, Wis., Sept. 27, 1944; s. Frank Joseph and Verna Antoinette (Beilke) H.; m. Patrice Marie Will, June 2, 1973; children: Christopher Jon, Scott James. Assoc. in Acctg., N. Central Tech. Coll., 1968. Controller, asst. treas. House of Merrill Inc., Merrill, 1968-72; controller Semling Menke Co., Inc., Merrill, 1968-72; treas., dir. North Star Communications, Ltd., Gleason, Wis., 1971-72; pres., dir. Profl. Accounting Systems, Inc., La Crosse, Wis., 1975-88; pres., dir. Haas Enterprises, Inc., 1971-82; pres., treas., dir. Adventure Capital, Ltd., 1971—; treas. Systems, Mgmt., Inc., St. Paul, 1983-84; treas. Gateway Acctg. Services, Inc., Ft. Myers, Fla., 1982-83; v.p., treas. ops. mgr. Accounting Bookkeeping Inc., Wauwatosa, Wis., 1975-76; v.p. Marathon Mining & Mfg. Corp., Wausau, Wis., 1976, pres., 1977-79; treas. controller, prodn. mgr. Moduline Windows, Inc., Wausau, 1977-78; mng. partner Haas Properties, Mosinee Wis., 1979-83; owner Midwest Investments, Winona, Minn., 1980—; pres., bd. dirs. Jim Haas' Triple Check Income Tax Service, Inc., 1986-88, pres., dir. Acctg. Bookkeeping Cons., Ltd., 1987-88; owner Jim Haas Assocs., 1988—. Mem. Adminstrv. Mgmt. Soc., Inst. Internal Auditors, Nat. Notary Assn., Inst. Record Mgrs. and Adminstrs., Am. Soc. Notaries, Nat. Assn. Accts., Am. Inst. Profl. Numismatists (charter mem.), Am. Acctg. Assn. Nat. Soc. Public Accts. Democrat. Roman Catholic. Lodges: K.C., Kiwanis (New Club Bldg. award), Optimists, Winona Lions. Home: 1253 W Broadway Winona MN 55987 Office: 123 N 41th St La Crosse WI 54601

HAAS, JOHN ALLEN, manufacturing company executive; b. Kansas City, Mo., Nov. 29, 1936; s. Norman and Dorothy Haas; m. Carolyn May, AUg. 11, 1958; 1 child, Greg A. BS, Wilmington Coll., 1959; grad., Cin. Milling Machine Indsl. Engring. Sch., 1963. Indsl. engring. grad. program Cin. Milling Machine Co., 1959-63; project engr. Heekin Can, Inc., Cin., 1964-66, personnel mgr., 1966-68, asst. plant mgr., 1968-70, plant mgr., 1970-72, on spl. assignment, 1972-74, mgr. mfg., 1974-76, v.p., gen. mgr., 1976-78, pres. Diamond Internat. div., 1978-82, pres. Wesray div., 1982-88, chmn., pres., chief exec. officer, 1988—. Recipient Chief Exec. Officer Bronze award Wall St. Transcript, 1987. Office: Heekin Can Inc 11310 Cornell Park Dr Cincinnati OH 45242

HAAS, MARC, industrial executive; b. Cin., Mar. 16, 1908; s. Marc and Alice (White) H.; m. Helen Hotze, Feb. 3, 1951. Grad., Horace Mann Sch., 1925, Princeton U., 1929. Ptnr. Emanuel & Co., mems. N.Y. Stock Exchange, 1933-42; dept. dir. Office Def. Transp., Washington, 1942-45; assoc. Allen & Co., N.Y.C., 1945-55; pres. Am. Diversified Enterprises, Inc. and subs., N.Y.C., 1955—; dir. Cave Laurent Perrier. Named Knight Order of St. John. Episcopalian (warden). Club: Princeton (N.Y.C.). Home: 14 E 75th St New York NY 10021 Office: Am Diversified Enterprises Inc 711 Fifth Ave New York NY 10022

HAAS, PAUL RAYMOND, petroleum company executive; b. Kingston, N.Y., Mar. 10, 1915; s. Frederick J. and Amanda (Lange) H.; m. Mary F. Diedrick, Aug. 30, 1936; children: Rheta Marie, Raymond Paul, Rene Marie. A.B., Rider Coll., 1934, LL.D., 1976. C.P.A., Tex. Acct. Arthur Andersen & Co. (C.P.A.s), N.Y.C. and Houston, 1934-41; with La Gloria Oil & Gas Co., Corpus Christi, Tex., 1941-59; v.p., treas., dir. La Gloria Oil & Gas Co., 1947-59; adminstrv. v.p. Tex. Eastern Transmission Corp., Houston, 1958-59; pres., chmn. bd. Prado Oil & Gas Co., 1959-66, Wiltex Corp., 1950-65, Garland Co., 1956-65, Citronelle Oil & Gas Co., 1967-69, Corpus Christi Oil and Gas Co., 1968—, Corpus Christi Exploration Co., 1976—; ltd. partner Salomon Bros., 1973-81; ind. oil and gas operator, 1959—. Trustee Corpus Christi Ind. Sch. Dist., 1951-58, pres., 1956-58; mem. Tex. Bd. Edn., 1962-72, vice chmn., 1970-72; mem. Gov.'s Com. Edn., 1966-69; Trustee Paul and Mary Haas Found., 1954—, Robert T. Wilson Found., 1954-72, Rider Coll., 1959-67, Moody Found., 1966-73, Found. Center, 1970-75, Council on Founds., 1970-76, Commn. on Philanthropy and Pub. Needs, 1973-75, Univ. Cancer Found. M.D. Anderson Hosp. and Tumor Inst., 1975—. Presbyn. (elder). Home: 4500 Ocean Dr Apt 9A Corpus Christi TX 78412 Office: Corpus Christi Exploration Co PO Box 2928 Corpus Christi TX 78403

HAAS, ROBERT DOUGLAS, apparel manufacturing company executive; b. San Francisco, Apr. 3, 1942; s. Walter A. Jr. and Evelyn (Danzig) H.; m. Colleen Gershon, Jan. 27, 1975; 1 child, Elise Kimberly. BA, U. Calif., Berkeley, 1964; MBA, Harvard U., 1968. With Peace Corps, Ivory Coast, 1964-66; with Levi Strauss & Co., San Francisco, 1973—, sr. v.p. corp. planning and policy, 1978-80, pres. new bus. group, 1980, pres. operating groups, 1980-81, exec. v.p., chief operating officer, 1981-84, pres., chief exec. officer, 1984-89, chief exec. officer, 1989—, chmn. bd. dirs.; bd. dirs. Levi Strauss Found. Hon. dir. San Francisco AIDS Found; mem. U.S. adv. coun., Bay are com. '89 Internat. Indsl. Conf. White House fellow, 1968-69. Mem. Am. Apparel Mfrs. Assn. (bd. dirs.), Brookings Inst. (trustee), Bay Area Com., Conf. Bd., Council Fgn. Affairs, Trilateral Commn., Meyer

Friedman Inst. (bd. dirs.), Phi Beta Kappa. Office: Levi Strauss & Co PO Box 7215 San Francisco CA 94120

HAAS, WALTER A., JR., retired apparel company executive, professional baseball executive; b. San Francisco, Jan. 24, 1916; s. Walter Abraham and Elise (Stern) H.; m. Evelyn Danzig, 1940; children: Robert D., Elizabeth Haas Eisenhardt, Walter J. BA, U. Calif., Berkeley, 1937; MBA, Harvard U., 1939; hon. degree, Wheaton Coll., 1983. Hon. chmn. exec. com. bd. dirs. Levi Strauss & Co., San Francisco; owner Oakland (Calif.) Athletics Baseball Co.; dir. Bank of Am., Bank Am. Corp., UAL, Inc., Mauna Kea Properties, Pacific Telephone Co. Active Trilateral Commn.; mem. exec. com., regional chmn. Nat. Alliance Businessman; mem. Presdl. Adv. Council for Minority Enterprise, Presdl. Task Force in Internat. Devel., 1970, Nat. Ctr. for Voluntary Action, Citizens Commn. on Pvt. Philanthropy and Pub. Needs; mem. vis. com. Harvard Bus. Sch.; mem. intercollegiate athletics adv. bd. U. Calif.; dir. Hunters Point Boys' Club, San Francisco Boys' Club, Bay Area Urban League, Mt. Zion Hosp.; campaign chmn. United Bay Area Crusade, 1965, also bd. dirs.; chmn. Radio Free Europe, No. Calif.; commr. San Francisco Parking Authority, 1953; trustee Ford Found., Com. for Econ. Devel.; co-chmn. bus. steering com. Nat. Cambodia Crisis Com. Named a Leader of Tomorrow Time mag., 1953, Chief Exec. Officer of Yr. Fin. World mag., 1976, Alumnus of Yr., U. Calif. at Berkeley, 1984; recipient Jefferson award Am. Inst. Pub. Service, 1977, Alumni Achievement award Harvard Grad. Sch. Bus., 1979, Chancellor's award U. Calif. at Berkeley Found., 1982, The Alexis De Tocqueville Society award United Way Am., 1985. Mem. San Francisco C. of C. (bd. dirs.), Mfrs. and Wholesalers Assn. San Francisco, (pres. 1951), Nat. Urban League (dir.), Phi Beta Kappa, Alpha Delta Phi. Office: Levi Strauss & Co PO Box 7215 San Francisco CA 94120

HAASE, JOHN PETER, financial advisor; b. Green Bay, Wis., Mar. 24, 1961; s. Theodore William and Arvilla Mary (Roskom) H.; m. Kathryn Mae Paul, Oct. 9, 1987. BS in Bus. Adminstrn., U. Wis., LaCrosse, 1983. Cert. Fin. Planner. Investment advisor Source Securities, Green Bay, 1983-85; account exec. Acacia Group, Houston, 1985; fin. advisor New England Fin. Advisors, Houston, 1985-87, Sheffield Fin. Mgmt., Houston, 1987—; cons. Selective Trading, Inc., Memphis, 1986—, M.J.W. Enterprises Inc., 1986—. Mem. Internat. Assn. for Fin. Planning, Internat. Bd. Cert. Fin. Planners. Republican. Clubs: Univ. (Houston). Lodge: Rotary. Office: Selective Trading Inc 3730 Kirby Dr Ste 1200 Houston TX 77098

HABA, LEONARD ALLEN, manufacturing company executive, accountant; b. Carrington, N.D., Aug. 11, 1931; s. Martin and Agnes (Zebd) H.; m. Sherry Marie Kearney, May 19, 1962; children—Linda, Cindy, Matthew, Steven. B.A. in Acctg., U. Wash., 1956; postgrad. U. Pitts., 1972, Stanford U., 1982. CPA, Wash. Sr. auditor Ernst & Ernst, Seattle, 1956-65; internal auditor PACCAR, Inc., Renton, Wash., 1956-65, chief internal auditor , Renton, controller Kenworth div., Seattle, v.p., corp. controller, Bellevue, Wash., 1965-83, sr. v.p., 1983—; also bd. dirs., 1983—. bd. dir. various PACCAR subs. Bd. dirs. Am. Diabetes Assn., N.Y.C., 1982-83, also Wash. affiliate, Seattle; trustee Diabetic Trust Fund, Seattle. Mem. Am. Inst. CPAs, Wash. Soc. CPAs, Fin. Execs. Inst. Avocation: fishing. Office: PACCAR Inc 777 106th Ave NE Bellevue WA 98004

HABACK, H. DONALD, investment banker, consultant; b. N.Y.C., Apr. 17, 1938; s. Harry J. and Leah (Mintz) H.; m. Ann E. Pintow, Mar. 5, 1966; children: Pamela L., Kara C. BEE, Rensselaer Poly. Inst., 1958; MS in Math., Adelphi U., 1963; postgrad., L.I. U., 1969-72. Registered profl. engr., N.Y. Various engrng. and mktg. positions, assorted def. organs contractors 1963-64; tech. dir. Data Dimensions Corp., Greenwich, Conn., 1974-77; v.p. mktg. and cons. Quantum Sci. Corp., N.Y.C., 1977-79; v.p., gen. mgr., cons. Gartner Group, Stamford, Conn., 1979-82; v.p. rsch. Freimark-Blair Co., N.Y.C., 1982-84, Smith Barney, N.Y.C., 1984-86; v.p. mergers and acquisitions Nikko Securities Co. Internat., Inc., N.Y.C., 1986—; cons. French Ministry of Industry, Paris, 1979-82; pres., cons. H.D. Haback, Inc., Gt. Neck, N.Y., 1982-86; speaker at nat. and internat. meetings on tech. and fin. Inventor Haback Oscillator, 1963, patentee communications and detection systems; contbr. articles to profl. jours. Trustee Village of Thomaston, N.Y., 1987—. Mem. IEEE, N.Y. Computer Industry Analyst Group. Democrat. Jewish. Office: 2 Crescent Rd Great Neck NY 11021

HABER, JEFFRY ROBERT, chief financial officer, small officer owner; b. Flushing, N.Y., May 4, 1960; s. Cecil J. and Marilyn L. (Leventhal) H.; m. Linda C. Zane. BS, Syracuse U., 1982, MS, 1982. CPA, N.Y. Acct. Deloitte Haskins & Sells, N.Y.C., 1982-84; contr. Rhinebeck (N.Y.) Country Sch., Inc., 1984-86; chief fin. officer Astor Home for Children, Rhinebeck, 1986—. Mem. AICPA, N.Y. State Soc. CPAs, Mensa. Republican. Jewish. Home: PO Box 686 Rhinebeck NY 12572 Office: Astor Home Children 36 Mill St Rhinebeck NY 12572

HABER, WARREN H., property management company executive; b. Mar. 9, 1941; s. S. Jack and Ruth (Kalish) H.; m. Suellen Green, Nov. 3, 1964; children: Wrenn, Kristin T. BA in Fin., CUNY, 1962. Chmn. Founders Equity, Inc., N.Y.C., 1967—, ptnr., 1969—; chmn. Kenai Corp., N.Y.C., 1974-88, Ocilla Industries, Inc., N.Y.C., 1980-84, 86—, Internat. Power Machines Corp., N.Y.C., 1986—; ptnr. Founders Property Mgmt. Co., Inc., N.Y.C., 1980—; bd. dirs. Lundy Electronics & Systems, Fluid Components Inc., Tulsa, Founders Communications Inc., N.Y.C., Sport Mag. Mgmt. Co., Inc., N.Y.C.; chmn. Watch Hill Group, Inc., 1986—, Direct Action Mktg., Inc., N.Y.C., 1988—; chmn. bd. Meadow Group, Inc., 1988—. Bd. dirs. Internat. Ctr. for Disabled, Barueh Coll. Fund. Served with M.C., USAR, 1962. Recipient Disting. Alumni award CUNY, 1984. Mem. City Athletic Club, University, Econ. Club. Office: Founders Equity Inc 200 Madison Ave New York NY 10022

HABIB, JOSEPH MICHAEL, engineer; b. Lawrence, Mass., Dec. 6, 1932; s. Elias Joseph and Alma Rita (Rashid) H.; m. Janice Kathryn Samia, June 29, 1958; children: Christopher A., Jonathan T. BS in Engring., Lowell Tech. Inst., 1959. Registered profl. engr., Mass. Engr. then sr. engr. AT&T (formerly Western Electric Co.), North Andover, Mass., 1959—; cons. AT&T corp. coms. throughout U.S., 1968—; lectr. on soldering, cleaning fluxes, assembly econs., 1970—. Pres. St. Joseph's Holy Name, Lawrence, 1950-53, Surfside 30 Condo Assn., Hampton, N.H., 1988—; bd. dirs. Salem (N.H.) Boys' Club, 1983-86. Cpl. U.S. Army, 1953-55. Mem. KC. Republican. Melchite. Home: 18 Glen Denin Dr Salem NH 03079 Office: AT&T 1600 Osgood St North Andover MA 01845

HABIG, ARNOLD FRANK, furniture, electronics and piano manufacturing executive; b. Jasper, Ind., May 2, 1907; s. Frank A. and Sarah (Rottet) H.; m. Mary Ann Jahn; children: Thomas, John, Douglas, Nancy, Margaret Ann, Barbara, Marilyn; m. Barbara T. Cukierski. Grad., Spencerian Bus. Coll., 1926; LL.B., U. Evansville, 1978. With Jasper Wood Products Co., 1928-50; founder, pres. Jasper Corp., 1950-63, chmn., 1963-74; chmn. Kimball Internat., Inc., 1974-82, asst. to chief exec. officer, 1982—; with Springs Valley Bank and Trust Co., 1958—, chmn. bd. Office: Kimball Internat Inc 1600 Royal St Jasper IN 47546

HABIG, THOMAS LOUIS, manufacturing executive; b. Jasper, Ind., June 18, 1928; s. Arnold Frank and Mary Ann (Jahn) H.; m. C. Roberta Snyder, Jan. 31, 1953; children: Randall, Julia, Brian, Sandra, Paul. BBA, Tulane U., 1950. With Kimball Internat., Inc. (predecessor firm), Jasper, Ind., 1952—; exec. v.p. Kimball Internat., Inc. (predecessor firm), Jasper, 1960-63, pres., 1963—, chmn., chief exec. officer, 1981—, also bd. dirs.; bd. dirs. Springs Valley Bank & Trust Co. With AUS, 1950-52. Mem. Am. Legion, Sigma Chi. Roman Catholic. Club: K.C. Office: Kimball Internat Inc 1600 Royal St PO Box 460 Jasper IN 47546

HABLUTZEL, PHILIP NORMAN, law educator; b. Flagstaff, Ariz., Aug. 23, 1935; s. Charles Edward and Electa Margaret (Cain) H.; m. Nancy Zimmerman, July 1, 1980; children—Margo Lynn, Robert Paul. BA, La. State U., 1958; postgrad. U. Heidelberg, W.Ger., 1959-60, 60-62; MA, U. Chgo., 1960, JD, 1967. Bar: Ill. 1967, U.S. Dist. Ct. (no. dist.) Ill. 1967. Rsch. atty. Am. Bar Found., Chgo., 1967-68, sr. rsch. atty., 1968-71; asst. prof. law Chgo.-Kent Coll. Law, Ill. Inst. Tech., 1971-73, assoc. prof., 1973-79, prof., 1979—, dir. grad. program in fin. svcs. law, 1985—; cons. OEO Legal Svcs. Program, 1967-69; reporter Ill. sec. state's com. on revision of not-for-profit corp. act, 1984-87. Pres., trustee, Chgo. Sch. Profl. Psychology, 1979-83; reporter Ill. Sec. of State's corp. laws adv. com., 1986—. Rotary Found. Advanced Study fellow, 1959-60. Fellow Chgo. Bar Found.; mem. ABA (chmn. subcom. on adoption of Uniform Trade Secrets Act 1984-86), Ill. State Bar Assn., Chgo. Bar Assn. (chmn. com. on sci., tech. and law 1971-72, sec. corp. law com. 1986-8, vice-chmn. corp. law com. 1987-88, chmn. corp. law com. 1988-89, task force state takeover legis. 1987—, joint com. banking act revisions 1988—). Republican. Episcopalian. Author: (with R. Garrett, W. Scott) Model Business Corporation Act Annotated, 2nd edit., 3 vols., 1971, (with J. Levi) Model Residential Landlord-Tenant Code, 1969. Avocations: travel, sailing, photography. Office: IIT Chgo-Kent Coll Law 77 S Wacker Dr Chicago IL 60606

HACKBARTH, JOHN THOMAS, JR., hospital executive; b. Birmingham, Ala., Apr. 11, 1951; s. John Thomas and Bobbie Ruth (Sweeney) H.; m. Melva Seal, Nov. 27, 1970; children: Mel, Luke, Bobbie. AA, Pearl River Jr. Coll., 1972; BS, U. So. Miss., 1974. CPA, Miss. Sr. acct. Hagaman, Roper, Haddox & Reid, CPA's, Jackson, Miss., 1974-77; mgr. Hagaman, Roper, Haddox & Reid, CPA's, Hattiesburg, Miss., 1979-82; owner, ptnr. Hackbarth & Strahan, Poplarville, Miss., 1977-79; v.p. fin., chief fin. officer Meth. Hosp., Hattiesburg, 1982—. Bd. dirs. Pearl River Community Coll. Found., Poplarville, 1988—, Pine Belt Boys and girls Club, Hattiesburg, 1988—. Mem. AICPA, Am. Coll. Healthcare Execs. (nominee), Hosp. Fin. Mgmt. Assn., Miss. Soc. CPA's, Miss. Hosp. Fin. Mgmt. Assn., Kiwanis. Republican. Baptist. Home: 115 Melton Dr Hattiesburg MS 39402 Office: Meth Hosp Hattiesburg 5001 W Hardy St Hattiesburg MS 39404

HACKEMAN, CALVIN LESLIE, accountant; b. Hanover, N.H., Oct. 6, 1953; s. Leslie B. and Myrtle (Gallup) H.; m. Amy Jo Weissman, May 7, 1978; children: Peter Jonathan Rodger, William Robert Stephan. BS cum laude, Am. U., 1975. CPA, Va. Staff acct. Grant Thornton, Washington, 1975-77, sr. acct., 1977-79, audit supr., 1979-81, mgr. audit, 1981-84, dept. head quality assurance, 1983-84, account mgr., 1984-87, audit ptnr., 1987—. Sec. Manassas Downtown Revitalization Action Com., 1982-85, chmn., 1985-86; chmn. spl. events com. Hist. Manassas, Inc., 1986-87; vice chmn. for Trade Expo '87, chmn. 1988; bd. dirs. Reston (Va.) Bd. Commerce, 1987-88; pres. Greater Manassas Jaycees, 1983-84, chmn. bd. dirs., 1984-86; mem. exec. com. George Mason U. Entrepreneurial Inst., chmn. Grants and Contracts Com., 1988—, profl. svcs. coun., mem. com. Mem. AICPAs, Va. Soc. CPAs, Am. U. Alumni Assn., Prince William County-Gtr. Manassas C. of C. (chmn. seminar com. 1986-87, v.p. membership and programming 1987—, v.p. govtl. rels. 1988-89), Va. Jaycees (Va. Found., trustee 1986—, sec.-treas. 1984-85, v.p. fin. adminstrn. 1985-87, v.p. 1988—), Va. Jaycees Life Mem. Assn. (bd. dirs. 1987), Jaycees Internat. Senate (life, Va. liason 1988-89), Phi Kappa Phi, Omicron Delta Kappa. Home: 8865 Olde Mill Run Manassas VA 22110 Office: Grant Thornton Accts Mgmt Cons 8280 Greensboro Dr Ste 600 McLean VA 22102

HACKETT, GEORGE WHITEHOUSE, industrial engineer, financial planner; b. Youngstown, Ohio, Jan. 17, 1949; s. Paul Edward and Margaret Nancy (Davies) H. BS, BA, Youngstown State U., 1972; MA, Cen. Mich. U., 1974. Methods analyst Sears, Roebuck and Co., Columbus, Ohio, 1973-75; mgr. People's Bank, Youngstown, Ohio, 1975; asst. mgr. Pub. Fin., Youngstown, 1976, Midland Guardian, Youngstown, 1977; indsl. engr. Gen. Am. Transp. Corp., Masury, Ohio, 1977-80, Ohio Rubber Co., Wilby, Ohio, 1981-84; cons. H.B. Maynard and Co., Pitts., 1985; sr. indsl. engr. Kollsman Mfg. Co., Nashua, N.H., 1985-88, Loral Systems Group, Akron, Ohio, 1988—; cons. H.B. Maynard and Co., Pitts., 1985. Counselor Jr. Achievement, Columbus, 1974. Capt. USAR, 1972-80. Mem. Inst. Indsl. Engrs., Inst. Cert. Fin. Planners, Internat. Assn. Fin. Planners., MTM Assn. for Standards & Rsch., The Planetary Soc. Republican. Methodist.

HACKETT, JOHN THOMAS, academic administrator; b. Fort Wayne, Ind., Oct. 10, 1932; s. Harry H. and Ruth (Greer) H.; m. Ann E. Thompson, July 24, 1954; children: Jane, David, Sarah, Peter. B.S., Ind. U., 1954, M.B.A., 1958; Ph.D., Ohio State U., 1961. Instr. Ohio State U., 1958-61; asst. v.p., economist Fed. Res. Bank, Cleve., 1961-64; dir. planning Cummins Engine Co., Columbus, Ind., 1964-66; v.p. finance Cummins Engine Co., 1966-71, exec. v.p., 1971-88, also dir.; v.p. fin. and adminstrn. Ind. U., Bloomington, 1988—; dir. Irwin Union Corp., Corp. for Innovation Devel.; chmn. Ind. Secondary Market for Edn. Loans. Chmn. Ohio State U. Alumni Adv. Council. Served to 1st lt. AUS, 1954-56. Mem. Am. Econ. Assn., Financial Execs. Inst., Am. Finance Assn., Financial Mgmt. Assn., Bus. Economists Assn., Beta Gamma Sigma. Home: PO Box 5487 Bloomington IN 47407-5487

HACKETT, LANCE B., management consultant; b. Warwick, R.I., Sept. 23, 1951; s. Royal E. and Mary K. (Kershaw) H.; m. Ann Fritz, Sept. 8, 1979; children: Conor David, Kelly Susan. BS, Brown U., 1973; MBA, Harvard U., 1979. Mktg. rep. IBM, N.Y.C., 1973-77; v.p. Strategic Planning Assocs., Washington, 1979—. Mem. Strategic Planning Soc. Republican. Clubs: Washington Golf, River Bend Golf. Home: 4500 35th Rd N Arlington VA 22207 Office: Strategic Planning Assocs 2300 N St NW Washington DC 20037

HACKL, DONALD JOHN, architect; b. Chgo., May 11, 1934; s. John Frank and Frieda Marie (Weichmann) H.; m. Bernadine Marie Becker, Sept. 29, 1962; children: Jeffrey Scott, Craig Michael, Cristina Lynn. BArch., U. Ill., 1957, MS in Architecture, 1958. With Loebl Schlossman & Hackl Architects, Chgo., 1963—, assoc., 1967-74, exec. v.p., dir., 1974, pres., dir., 1975—; pres., dir. Dart Hackl Internat. Ltd., Chgo., 1975—; mem. Nat. Council Archtl. Registration Bds.; bd. dirs. Chgo. Bldg. Congress, 1983—, v.p., 1985—; design juries include: Reynolds Metals, Western Mont. Regional Design, Am. Inst. Steel Constrn., Precast Concrete Inst., Okla. Soc. Architects; chmn. Midwest Design Conf., 1983; design critic dept. arch. U. Ill, 1975-76, 81; guest lectr. U. Notre Dame, 1977, 78, 80, 82; adj. faculty Kent Coll. Law, Ill., Inst. Tech., 1983—; cons. Pub. Services Adminstrn., Washington, 1974-76. Prin. works include Water Tower Place, Chgo., 1976, King Faisal Specialist Hosp. and Reserach Ctr., Riyadh, Saudi Arabia, 1978, Household Internat. Hdqrs., Prospect Heights, Ill., 1978, Shriners Hosp. for Crippled Children, Chgo., 1979, Square D Co. Hdqrs., Palatine, Ill., 1979, West Suburban Hosp., Oak Park, Ill., 1981, Allstate Comml. Plaza South, Barrington, Ill., 1981, Sears, Roebuck and Co. stores of tomorrow concept, 1985, Pepper Constrn. Co. Hdqrs., Chgo., 1987, Commerce Clearing House, Riverwoods, Ill., 1986, Physicians Pavilion Greater Balt. Med. Ctr., 1987, Prudential Plaza Two, Chgo., 1987. Mem. Met. Am. Cancer Crusade, 1973; trustee West Suburban Hosp., 1983—, mem. exec. com., 1986-87; trustee North Cen. Coll., 1988—; mem. Pres.' Coun. U. Ill. Found.; mem. curricula adv. com. Dept. Architecture, U. Ill. Fellow AIA (treas. Chgo. chpt. 1978-80, exec. com. 1978-81, v.p. 1980, pres. 1981; bd. dirs. Chgo. AIA Found. 1981-83; bd. dirs. Chgo. Archtl. Assistance Ctr. 1982—; nat. v.p. 1985, 1st v.p. 1986, pres. 1987, chmn. design com. 1985, mem. exec. com. 1985-87, bd. dirs. 1981-84; mem. documents com. 1974-79, chmn. 1980; mem. exec. com AIA Service Corp., 1983-84); hon. fellow Royal Archtl. Inst. Can. , Collegious Architectos Mexicanos; mem. Union Internat. des Architects (bd. dirs., del., 1987—); hon. fellow Royal Arch. Inst. Can., Collegious Architectos Mexicanos; hon. mem. Union of Bulgarian Architects, Soc. of Cuban Am. Architects; hon. prof. of Internat. Acad. of Architects; mem. Chgo. Assn. Commerce and Industry, Greater North Mich. Ave. Assn., Art Inst. Chgo., Field Mus. Natural History, Union Internationale des Architects (dir.),. Clubs: Tavern, Carlton, Economic, Lake Zurich. Office: Loebl Schlossman & Hackl 130 E Randolph Dr Chicago IL 60601 also: Loebl Schlossman & Hackl 845 N Michigan Ave Chicago IL 60611

HACKWORTH, DONALD E., automotive manufacturing company executive; b. 1937. B.S. in Bus. Adminstrn., Ohio State U., 1963; grad. exec. program, Stanford U., 1977. With GM, Detroit, 1963—; various supervisory positions, later mgr. Delco Moraine div. GM, Dayton, Ohio, 1973-77; dir. mfg. facility planning worldwide product planning GM, Detroit, 1978-79, gen. mfg. mgr. Oldsmobile div., 1979-81; corp. v.p., pres., gen. mgr. GM of Can., Ltd., 1981-84; corp. v.p., gen. mgr. Buick Motor div. GM, Flint, Mich., 1984-86; v.p., product mgr. B-O-C Lansing Automotive div. GM, Lansing, Mich., 1986—. Office: GMC B-O-C Lansing Automotive Div 920 Townsend Lansing MI 48921

HACKWORTH, JOHN DENNIS, fund raising, development executive; b. St. Louis, Nov. 9, 1937; s. JOhn Thomas and Pansy Beth (Cole) H.; m. Jeanne Opal Farris, Dec. 26, 1964; children: John Thomas, Jeana Denise. BA, William Jewell Coll., 1959; MA, U. Kans., 1962; MDiv, Midwestern Bapt. Sem., 1966; cert., Coll. for Fin. Planning, 1979. Pastor U. Bapt. Ch., Wichita, Kans., 1968-69; assoc. prof. Southwest Bapt. U., Bolivar, Mo., 1969-73; life underwriter N.Y. Life Ins. Co., Kansas City, 1973-77; assoc. dir. devel. William Jewell Coll., Liberty, Mo., 1977-81; stockbroker Stifel, Nicolaus & Co., Liberty, 1981-85; area dir. Christian Broadcasting Network, Virginia Beach, Va., 1985-87, sr. fin. planning specialist, 1987-88; pres. Capital Creation Concepts, 1988—; dir. estate planning svcs. Midwestern Bapt. Theol. Sem., Kansas City, Mo., 1988—. pres. Liberty High Sch. PTA, 1983; campaign mgr. John Ashcroft for Congress, Polk County, Mo., 1972; mem. Greater Kansas City Coun. on Philanthropy, Kansas City Planned Giving Coun. Mem. Internat. Assn. Fin. Planners (bd. dirs. Kansas City, 1980). Republican. Baptist. Home and Office: 818 Park Ln Liberty MO 64068

HACKWORTHY, CLEMENT ROBERT (CR), II, construction executive; b. Milw., Feb. 21, 1955; s. Robert Durden and Nancy (Lukens) H.; m. Cynthia Simonett, June 9, 1984; children: Nicholas Robert, Sarah Patricia. Student, Mich. Tech. U., 1973-75; BS in Tech. Constrn. Mgmt., U. Wis., 1978. Project mgr. Opus Corp., Mpls., 1978-80; chief exec. officer Con/Spec Corp., Stillwater, Minn., 1980—; bd. dirs. Bank St. Croix; mem. Metro East Devel., St. Paul, 1987—. Dir. bldg. com. St. Paul's Episc. Ch., Hudson, Wis., 1985—, vestry mem., 1985—, also jr. warden. Named Eagle Scout Boy Scouts Am., 1971. Mem. Assn. Gen. Contractors Am., Assn. Bldg. Contractors Am. Club: St. Paul Athletic. Home: 1012 Riverside Dr Hudson WI 54016 Office: Con/Spec Corp 106 E Chestnut Stillwater MN 54016

HADDAD, FRED, lawyer; b. Waterbury, Conn., Sept. 14, 1946; s. Fred Melad and Nancy Anne (Crean) H.; m. Julia Hester, Aug. 2, 1980; 1 dau., Allison Hester; children by previous marriage: Tonja, Tristan, Matthew. Student U. Conn., 1964; BA, U. New Haven, 1971; JD, U. Miami (Fla.), 1974. Bar: Fla. 1974, U.S. Dist. Cts. (so. and mid. dists.) Fla. 1975, U.S. Cts. Appeals (4th, 5th, 6th, 11th cirs.) 1975, U.S. Supreme Ct. 1977, U.S. Dist. Ct. (we. dist.) Tenn. 1982, U.S. Ct. Appeals (10th cir.). Ptnr. Sandstrom & Haddad, Ft. Lauderdale, Fla., 1974—. Mem. Fla. Bar (criminal law, reverse sting coms.), Broward County Criminal Def. Attys. Assn., Fed. Bar Assn. (exec. com.), Nat. Fla. Criminal Def. Attys. Assn., Assn. Trial Lawyers Am., Assn. Criminal Def. Lawyers, Broward County Bar Assn. Democrat. Office: Sandstrom & Haddad 429 S Andrews Ave Fort Lauderdale FL 33301

HADDAWAY, JAMES DAVID, insurance company official; b. Louisville, July 25, 1933; s. Charles Montgomery and Viola (Sands) H.; m. Myrna Lou Harris, June 5, 1954; children: Peggy Ann, Robert Marshall, Susan Gayle. BS in Commerce, U. Louisville, 1961; MBA, Xavier U., 1973. Cert. adminstrv. mgr.; cert. purchasing mgr.; accredited personnel mgr.; sr. profl. human resources. Ins. cons. Met. Life Ins., Louisville, 1955-59; supt. Byck Bros. & Co., Louisville, 1959-61; dir. purchasing Liberty Nat. Bank, Louisville, 1961-63; v.p. and mgr. gen. services adminstrn. Citizens Fidelity Bank, Louisville, 1963-79; asst. v.p. and mgr. human resources Ky. Farm Bur. Ins. Co., 1979—. Founder, chmn. emeritus Kentuckiana Expn. of Bus. and Industry, 1973-85. Served with U.S. Army, 1953-55. Named Boss of Year, Louisville chpt. Nat. Secs. Assn., 1978, 79. Mem. Adminstrv. Mgmt. Soc. (nat. dir. 1979-81), Nat. Assn. Purchasing Mgmt. (dir. nat. affairs 1970-71), Adminstrv. Mgmt. Soc. Louisville (pres. 1975-76, bd. dirs. 1976—), Adminstrv. Mgmt. Soc. Found. (charter), Purchasing Mgmt. Assn. Louisville (pres. 1969-70), Louisville Personnel Assn. (pres. 1983-84), Conf. Casualty Ins. Cos. (chmn. nat. personnel conf. com. 1983), Nat. Eagle Scout Assn. (life), Am. Soc. Personnel Adminstrn. (chmn. conf. com. region 9, 1984, dist. dir. for Western Ky. 1984, v.p. region 9 1985-86), Nat. Assn. Ind. Insurers (mem. personnel com. 1987—), Ky. C. of C. (benefits com., 1987—, chmn. banking and ins. health and welfare sub-com. project 21, 1988), Audubon Soc., Hon. Order Ky. Cols. Baptist. Clubs: Wally Byam Caravan Internat. (treas. 1989), Good Sam Recreational Vehicle, Bass Anglers Sportsman Soc. Lodges: Masons, Shriners. Home: 4015 Wimpole Rd Louisville KY 40218 Office: 120 S Hubbard Ln Louisville KY 40207

HADDOCK, JOHN WOLCOTT, retired industrialist; b. Polo, Ill., Aug. 22, 1904; s. Frank D. and Mabel (Mulford) H.; m. Gladys Baxter, Oct. 2, 1935; m. Patricia Worlton Cosel, May 4, 1974; m. Sibylle Kuhn, May 22, 1987. Mem. Soc. Mining Engrs., Fin. Analysts Soc., Nat. Assn. Bus. Economists, Sons of the Revolution. Clubs: Union League (N.Y.); Tavern (Chgo.); La Jolla (Calif.) Beach & Tennis, Country, Univ. Club (San Diego). Office: 1001 Genter St La Jolla CA 92037

HADDOCK, ROBERT LYNN, data base publishing, marketing professional, writing; b. Vallejo, Calif., May 12, 1945; s. Orville Walter and Lee Ellen (Alexander) H. BA, Union Coll., 1967; postgrad., NYU, 1977-81. Editor So. Pub. Assn., Nashville, 1969-74, controller, 1974-75; mktg. analyst Bus. Publs. div. Prentice-Hall, Englewood Cliffs, N.J., 1975-78, bus. mgr., 1978-81; bus. mgr. Ziff-Davis Pub. Co., N.Y.C., 1981-82, dir. bus. devel., 1982-83; pres. Personal Access, Inc., N.Y.C., 1983-84; v.p., dir. product devel. Citicorp Global Report, N.Y.C., 1984-86; v.p., dir. mktg. Citibank, N.Y.C., 1986-88, v.p., dir. product devel., 1989—. Author: The Broken Web, 1973, How to Stop Smoking, 1974; inventor database accessing system, 1984. Mem. Am. Assn. Artificial Intelligence, Information Industry Assn., Mensa. Home: 105 W 13th St Apt 15F New York NY 10011

HADDOCK, RONALD WAYNE, oil company executive; b. St. Elmo, Ill., July 29, 1940; s. Clarence and Marie (Price) H.; m. Sandra Sue Thomas, Sept. 1957; children: Roni Sue Haddock Fields, Mark Tayler, Rick Wayne. BMechE, Purdue U., 1963. With Exxon Corp., 1963-86; various tech. staff, mgmt. positions Baton Rouge Refinery, 1963-71; specialties econs. coordinator, adminstrv. mgr., planning mgr. Refining Dept. Houston hdqrs., 1971-75; ops. mgr., refinery mgr. Baytown Refinery, 1975-78; corp. planning mgr. then v.p. for refining Houston hdqrs., 1978-81; exec. asst. to chmn. Exxon Corp. Hdqrs. N.Y.C., 1981-82; v.p., dir. Esso Eastern Houston hdqrs., 1982-85; exec. v.p., chief operating officer Am. Petrofina, Inc., Dallas, 1986-88, pres., chief exec. officer, 1988—, also bd. dirs. Mem. Am. Petroleum Inst. (mem. pub. policy com.), Nat. Petroleum Refiners Assn. (bd. dirs.). Methodist. Clubs: Energy, Petroleum (Dallas). Office: Am Petrofina Inc PO Box 2159 Dallas TX 75221 *

HADINATA, RUDY BAMBANG, cigarette company executive; b. Magelang, Central Java, Indonesia, Feb. 24, 1940; s. Paulus Andiko and Paring H.; m. Juliarti Sutanto, Dec. 26, 1964; children—Ariono, Milono, Susilo. Mktg. mgr. Djarum Cigarette Co., Kudus, Central Java, Indonesia, 1964-69, mktg. dir., 1969-82; fin. dir., 1972-84; supervisory dir., 1984—; founder, part owner, dir. P. T. Hadinata Bros. Furniture Co., 1975—. Roman Catholic. Home: IIC/31 AIP KS Tubun, Jakarta Indonesia

HADJIMANOLIS, JOHN, management consultant; b. Athens, Mar. 28, 1950; s. George and Helen (Balaskas) H. BSc, Newcastle U., 1972; DipEng., Athens Nat. Tech. U., 1974, MBA, 1976; MPhil, Cambridge U., 1978. Internat. bus. mgr. Thrace Paper Mill S.A., Athens, 1978-84; tech. mgr. Paragon (Greece) U.S.A., Athens, 1984-85; dir. econ. analysis div. Agrotiki Techniki S.A., Athens, 1985-87; dir. Analysis and Mgmt. Cons., Athens, 1985—; cons. Thrace Paper Mill S.A., Paragon S.A., Compuform S.A., Ronamita Ltd. Author materials in field. Fellow Hellenic Ops. Research Soc.; mem. Hellenic Chamber Engrs., Hellenic Mech. Engring. Assn. Christian Orthodox. Home: 69 Anagnostopoulou St, Athens GR 106 78, Greece Office: Analysis and Mgmt Cons, 39 Didotou St, Athens GR 106 80, Greece

HADLEY, JOHN BART, financial analyst; b. Oil City, Pa., Feb. 17, 1942; s. James Edward and Genevieve A. (Rowley) H.; B.A., Hiram Coll., 1964; M.B.A., (Samuel S. Fels scholar), U. Pa., 1967. Fin. analyst Westinghouse Electric Corp., Bloomington, Ind., 1967-69, mgr. fin. planning, Pitts., Tucson, Richmond, Va., 1969-71, staff asst. corporate fin. planning, Pitts., 1971-74; bus. analyst Farah Mfg. Co., El Paso, Tex., 1974-75, fin. analyst (Treasury), 1975-76, div. controller young men's and boys' div., 1976-77; chief agy. and fin. rev. U.S. Ry. Assn., Washington, 1977-79, chief fin. analysis, 1979-80, spl. asst. to dir. fin. analysis, 1980-82; mgr. ops. budgets NJTRO, 1982-85, mgr. capital budgets, 1986—. Mem. Nat. Assn. Accountants, Transp. Research Forum, Chi Sigma Phi. Episcopalian. Clubs:

Circle K (sec. 1963), Propeller (publicity coordinator 1966-67), Wharton Sch. Home: 52 Gill Ln 1-H Iselin NJ 08830 Office: NJTRO 1160 Raymond Newark NJ 07102

HADLEY, MARK JAMES, office products company executive; b. Wausau, Wis., Oct. 13, 1950; s. Harold Riesberg and Margaret Marion (Burlo) H.; m. Gloria Jean Vilter, Apr. 21, 1975 (div. 1981); 1 child, Matthew Mark; m. Debra Kay Goetsch, Nov. 5, 1982; children: Tyler Harold and Timothy Ardel (twins), Mark Christopher; 1 stepchild, Max Lee Opper. BS in Bus. and Econs., U. Wis.-Stevens Point, 1974. Orderly Wausau Meml. Hosp., 1966-69, St. Mary's Hosp., Wausau, 1969-70; sales clk. Schuler Shoes, Mpls., 1970-71; sales rep. Allen-Hadley Bus. Inc. (name now Hadley Office Products, Inc.), Wausau, 1971-77, ptnr., 1977—; mem. dealer coun. Savin Bus. Machines, Stamford, Conn., 1986—. Mgr., Wausau Little League, 1971-81, bd. dirs., 1978—, pres. 1981-82; bd dirs. Big Bros., Wausau, 1984-86; mem. Citizens Taxpayer Com., Wausau, 1987; chmn. communications Marathon County United Way Campaign, Wausau, 1986, allocations com. 1985—. Fellow Nat. Office Machine Dealers Assn., Nat. Office Products Assn., U.S. C. of C. (mem. recertification program, Small Bus. Person of Yr. 1985), Wausau Area Golf Assn. (bd. dirs. 1979—, pres. 1980-85), Wausau Golf Club, Wausau Curling Club, Wausau Country Club (bd. dirs. 1989—), Elks, Optimist (sec., treas. Wausau chpt. 1979). Roman Catholic. Office: Hadley Office Products Inc 399 S River Dr Wausau WI 54402-1326

HADLEY, STANTON THOMAS, building materials company executive, lawyer; b. Beloit, Kans., July 3, 1936; s. Robert Campbell and Helen (Schroeder) H.; m. Charlotte June Holmes, June 9, 1962; children: Gayle Elizabeth, Robert Edward, Stanton Thomas, Steven Holmes. B.S. in Metall. Engring., Colo. Sch. Mines, 1958; LL.B., U. Colo., 1962. Bar: Colo. 1962, U.S. Dist. Ct. 1962, U.S. Patent Office 1963. Metallurgist ASARCO, Leadville, Colo., 1957; tng. engr. Allis-Chalmers Co., West Allis, Wis., 1958-61; adminstrv. engr. Ball Corp., Boulder, Colo., 1961-62; atty. Ball Corp., 1962-65; patent counsel Scott Paper Co., Phila., 1965-71, USG Corp., Chgo., 1971-76; gen. mgr. metals div. 1976-79, group v.p. indsl. group, 1979-84; sr. v.p. adminstrn., sec. USG Corp., 1984—, sec., 1984-87, sr. v.p. staff services, 1987—; bd. dirs. Masonite Corp., WJE Assocs. Inc., USG Found. Bd. dirs. Ill. Safety Council, North Suburban YMCA, Northbrook Symphony Orch.; mem. founders' council Field Mus.; mem. Chgo. United, Chgo. Assn. Commerce and Industry. Served with U.S. Army, 1959. Mem. Am. Soc. Metals, Licensing Execs. Soc., Assn. Corp. Patent Counsel. Republican. Clubs: Union League, Sunset Ridge Country, Executives. Home: 555 Valley Way Northbrook IL 60062 Office: USG Corp 101 S Wacker Dr Chicago IL 60606

HADLOW, EARL BRYCE, lawyer; b. Jacksonville, Fla., July 29, 1924; s. Earl and Emily (Hadlow) Bryce; m. Nancy Ann Petway, Apr. 5, 1969; children: Richard B., Janet V., Bryce P., Erin. BS, Duke U., 1947, JD, 1950, JD with high honors, 1950. Bar: Fla. 1950. Asst. solicitor Duval County, Jacksonville, 1952-53; ptnr. Mahoney, Hadlow & Adams, Jacksonville, 1953-84; gen. counsel, vice chmn. Barnett Banks Inc., Jacksonville, 1984—; also bd. dirs. Barnett Banks, Inc., Jacksonville; bd. dirs. Barnett Bank Jacksonville. Contbr. articles to profl. jours. Trustee Jacksonville U. Served with U.S. Army, 1943-46. Fellow Am. Coll. Probate Counsel; mem. ABA (house of dels, mem. com. on scope correlation), Fla. Bar Assn. (bd. of govs. 1967-72, pres. 1973-74), Jacksonville Bar Assn. (pres. 1966), Am. Bankers Assn. (govt. relations council, banking leadership conf.), Assn. Res. City Banksrs (govt. rels. coun.), Fla. Bankers Assn. (pres.-elect), Associated Industries Fla. (bd. dirs. 1985—), Fla. Assn. Bank Holding Cos., Jacksonville C. of C. (pres. 1980), Order of Coif, Phi Delta Phi, Alpha Tau Omega. Republican. Episcopalian. Office: Barnett Banks Inc 100 Laura St PO Box 40789 Jacksonville FL 32203-0789

HAEBERLE, WILLIAM LEROY, business educator, entrepreneur; b. Marion County, Ind., May 19, 1922; s. Louis Leroy and Marjorie Ellen (Jared) H.; B.S., Ind. U., 1943, M.B.A., 1947, D.B.A., 1952; m. Yvonne Carlton, June 17, 1947; children—Patricia, William C., David C. Faculty, Ind. U., Bloomington, 1946—, prof. mgmt., 1963—; chmn. bd. Gen. Ill. Investment Corp., 1949—, Century Petroleum Corp., 1957—; dir. Innovest Group, Inc., Transactions Verifications Systems, Inc. ; pres., dir. Nat. Entrepreneurship Found., 1982—; dir. Ind. Inst. for New Bus. Ventures, Inc., 1983—. Served to capt. U.S. Army, 1943-46; lt. col. USAFR, 1947-82. Mem. Air Force Assn., Res. Officers Assn., Am. Legion, VFW, Sigma Alpha Epsilon. Club: Metropolitan (N.Y.C.). Home: 1213 S High St Bloomington IN 47401 Office: Nat Entrepreneurship Found PO Box 5521 Bloomington IN 47402

HAEGER, PHYLLIS MARIANNA, association management company executive; b. Chgo., May 20, 1928; d. Milton O. and Ethel M. H. B.A., Lawrence U., 1950; M.A., Northwestern U., 1952. Midwest editor TIDE mag., 1952-55; exec. v.p. Smith, Bucklin & Assos., Inc., Chgo., 1955-78; pres. P.M. Haeger & Assos., Inc., Chgo., 1978—. Mem. Am. Soc. Assn. Execs., Chgo. Soc. Assn. Execs., Inst. Assn. Mgmt. Cos., Nat. Assn. Women Bus. Owners, Com. of 200, Chgo. Network, Nat. Assn. Bank Women (exec. v.p.).

HAENTJENS, WALTER D., manufacturing company executive; b. Hazleton, Pa., July 25, 1921; s. Otto Haentjens. BSME, Cornell U., 1943; MSME, Case-Western Res. U., 1946. Pres. Barrett, Haentjens & Co., Hazleton, Pa.; bd. dirs. 1st Eastern Corp. Served to capt. U.S. Army, 1943-46. Mem. ASME. Office: Barrett Haentjens & Co PO Box 488 Hazleton PA 18201

HAERER, DEANE NORMAN, marketing and public relations executive; b. N.Y.C., Feb. 14, 1935; s. Frederick Sidney and Florence Agnes (Jackson) H.; AA, Boston U., 1955, BS, 1957; postgrad. NYU Grad. Sch. Bus. and Finance, 1958-60. Drake U. Grad. Sch., 1965-67; m. Polly Ann Dunn, Feb. 24, 1961; children: Jennifer A., Heather J. Account exec. pub. relations and advt. Charles Abbott Assos., Inc., N.Y.C., 1957-60; dir. alumni, community and ch. relations Iowa Wesleyan Coll., 1960-61; tech. editor J.I. Case Co., Burlington, Iowa, 1961-64; dir. publs., asst. dir. pub. relations Drake U., 1964-68; pub. relations account supr. Thomas Wolff Assocs., Des Moines, 1968; dir. sch.-community relations Des Moines Pub. Sch. System, 1968-74; dir. mktg. communications and corp. pub. relations Stanley Consultants, Inc., Muscatine, Iowa, 1974-78, dir. corp. pub. relations and mktg. services, 1978-82; dir. mktg. services Howard Needles Tammen & Bergendoff, Kansas City, Mo., 1982-84; dir. corp. mktg. Robert E. McKee, Inc., 1984-88, pres. DNH/Assocs., Inc., Dallas, 1988—; guest lectr. Sch. Journalism, Drake U., 1970-74, U. Iowa, 1974-78. Bd. dirs. Heart of the Hawkeye council Camp Fire Girls, Des Moines, 1969-72. Recipient 1st place publ. award Univ. div. Mid-Am. Conf., Am. Coll. Public Relations Assn., 1965, 66; nat. awards outstanding ednl. publs. Nations Schs. and Sch. Mgmt. mags., 1972, 73. Mem. Pub. Relations Soc. Am. (accredited; charter mem., co-founder, past pres. and dir. Iowa chpt.; charter mem., co-founder, del. assembly, past chpt. dirand v.p. Quad Cities chpt.), Nat. Sch. Pub. Relations Assn., Acad. Am. Educators, Soc. Mktg. Profl. Services, Am. Mktg. Assn., Tex. Indsl. Devel. Council, So. Indsl. Devel. Council, Pub. Relations Soc. Am., Soc. Am. Mil. Engrs. Nat. Alumni Council of Boston U. Contbr. articles profl. publs. Home and Office: DNH Assocs Inc 17 Cypress Ct Trophy Club TX 76262

HAFER, FREDERICK DOUGLASS, utility executive; b. West Reading, Pa., Mar. 12, 1941; s. Charles Frederick and Irene Naugle (Renninger) H.; m. Martha Louise Gartner, Apr. 6, 1963; children: Frederick, Craig, Keith. Student, Drexel Inst. Tech., 1959-62. With Met. Edison Co., Reading, Pa., 1962-68; with Gen. Pub. Utilities Corp., N.Y.C., 1968-78, asst. treas., 1970, treas., 1970-78; v.p. rates GPU Service Corp., 1977-86; v.p. Met. Edison Co., Pa. Electric Co., 1982-86; pres. Met. Edison Co., 1986—; bd. dirs. Met. Edison Co., GPU Service Corp., GPU Nuclear Corp., Reading Electric Light and Power Co., Utilities Mut. Ins. Co. Mem. pres.'s council Reading chpt. Albright Coll.; mem. endowment com. Atonement Luth. Ch.; bd. dirs. Reading Hosp. and Med. Ctr. Mem. Berks County C. of C. (bd. dirs.), Mfrs. Assn. Berks County (bd. dirs.). Club: Berkshire Country. Office: Met Edison Co PO Box 16001 Reading PA 19640 *

HAFFNER, CHARLES CHRISTIAN, III, printing company executive; b. Chgo., May 27, 1928; s. Charles Christian and Clarissa (Donnelley) H.; m. Anne P. Clark, June 19, 1970. B.A., Yale U., 1950. With R.R. Donnelley & Sons Co., Chgo., 1951—; treas. R.R. Donnelley & Sons Co., 1962-68, v.p. and treas., 1968-83, vice-chmn. and treas., 1983-84, vice-chmn., 1984—, also dir.; chmn. bd. dirs. Lakeside Bank, 1970; dir. DuKane Corp., Protection Mut. Ins. Co. Chmn. Morton Arboretum, Newberry Library; trustee Sprague Found., Art Inst. of Chgo., Latin Sch., Chgo., 1978-84, Ill. Cancer Council, 1984—, Chgo. City Day Sch., Lincoln Pk Zool. Soc., Brooks Sch.; bd. govs. Nature Conservancy., 1973-84, chmn. Ill. chpt., 1984-87; mem. Chgo. Plan Commn., 1986—. Served to 1st lt. USAF, 1952-54. Clubs: Chicago, Commercial, Commonwealth, Racquet, Caxton, Casino, Saddle and Cycle. Home: 1524 N Astor St Chicago IL 60610 Office: R R Donnelley & Sons Co 2223 Martin Luther King Dr Chicago IL 60616

HAFNER, JOSEPH A., JR., food company executive; b. San Bernadino, Calif., Oct. 9, 1944; s. Joseph Albert and Mary Florence (McGowan) H.; m. Merrill Hafner; children—John Michael, Daniel Stephen. A.B. cum laude, Dartmouth Coll., 1966; M.B.A. with high distinction, Amos Tuck Sch. Bus. Adminstrn., 1967. C.P.A. Intern Latin Am. Cornell U.-Ford Found., Lima, Peru, 1967-69; sr. cons. Arthur Andersen & Co., Houston, 1969-71; controller C/A div. Riviana Internat., Inc., Guatemala City, Guatemala, 1972-73; treas., v.p. fin. Riviana Internat., Inc., Houston, 1973-77; v.p. Riviana Foods Inc., Houston, 1977-81, pres., chief operating officer, 1981-84, pres., chief exec. officer, 1984—, dir., 1985—; dir., pres. Rice Millers' Assn., Arlington, Va., 1983—; dir. Tex. Commerce Bank-Richmond Sage, Houston. Recipient C.P.A. Gold medal Ark. State Bd. Pub. Accountancy, 1969. Mem. Am. Inst. C.P.A.s. Clubs: Houston, University (Houston). Office: Riviana Foods Inc 2777 Allen Pkwy Houston TX 77019 *

HAGAN, CHARLES F., corporate lawyer; b. 1923. BS, Georgetown U., 1946; LLB, Fordham U., 1949; LLM, NYU, 1957. Atty. Kerlin, Campbell & Keating, 1949-55; asst. gen. counsel Pfizer Inc., N.Y., 1955-74; gen. counsel Am. Home Products Corp., N.Y.C., 1974-78, v.p., gen. counsel, 1978—. Served to 2d lt. AUS, 1943-45. Office: Am Home Products Corp 685 3rd Ave New York NY 10017

HAGAN, RANDALL LEE, manufacturing executive; b. Columbia, Mo., June 22, 1945; s. Albert R. and Melva (Snodgrass) H.; m. Juanita L. Roberts, Aug. 28, 1972; 1 child, John L. BS in Chem. Engring., U. Mo., 1967; MBA, Harvard U., 1969. Product mgr. Hackney Corp., Birmingham, Ala., 1969-71; dir. distbn. Kem Mfg. Corp., Tucker, Ga., 1971-79; dir. ops. Kem Mfg. Corp., Europe and Rome, 1974-79; project mgr. Am. Filtrona Corp., Richmond, Va., 1979-82, asst. to pres., 1982-83, exec. v.p., gen. mgr., 1983-85, pres., gen. mgr., 1985—, v.p. bonded fiber products, 1985—. Mem. Writing Instrument Mfrs. Assn. (bd. dirs. Washington 1987—). Office: Am Filtrona Co PO Box 34668 Richmond VA 23234

HAGEL, JOHN, III, management consultant; b. Berlin, N.H., Sept. 14, 1950; s. John Jr. and Evelyn Gertrude (Parent) H.; m. Laura Leeann Call, Sept. 11, 1987. BA, Wesleyan U., 1972; PhB, Oxford U., 1974; MBA, Harvard U., 1978, JD, 1978. Bar: Mass. 1978. Cons. Boston Cons. Group, 1978-80; pres. Sequoia Group, Larkspur, Calif., 1980-82; v.p. Atari, Inc., Sunnyvale, Calif., 1982-83, sr. v.p., 1983-84; sr. engagement mgr. McKinsey and Co., N.Y.C., 1984—, ptnr., 1987—. Author: Alternative Energy Strategies, 1976, Assessing The Criminal, 1977; contbr. articles to profl. jours. Keasbey Found. fellow, 1972-74. Mem. ABA, Mass. Bar Assn. Episcopalian.

HAGELSTEIN, ROBERT PHILIP, publisher; b. N.Y.C., Dec. 15, 1942; s. H. Robert and E. Ann (Buhrow) H.; m. Ann G. Linguvic, Apr. 26, 1970; children: Christopher R., Jonathan W. B.A. in English Lit., L.I. U., 1964. Prodn. mgr. Johnson Reprint Corp., N.Y.C., 1965-68; editor-in-chief Johnson Reprint Corp., 1968-70; v.p. Greenwood Press, Inc., Westport, Conn., 1970-73; pres. Greenwood Press, Inc., 1973—; dir. Aldwych Press, London; v.p. Congressional Info. Service; pub. cons. Contbr. articles to scholarly and profl. jours.; author Converticalc computer software program. Mem. Info. Industry Assn., Am. Soc. Info. Sci., Spl. Libraries Assn. (George Polk Awards com.), Scholarly Pub. Assn. Club: Minute Man Yacht. Office: Greenwood Press Inc 88 Post Rd W PO Box 5007 Westport CT 06881

HAGEN, GLENN W., lawyer; b. Detroit, July 8, 1948; s. William A. and Lilian (Abrolat) H.; m. Cynthia Winn, July 21, 1984. BS in Chemistry, U. Ala., 1970; JD, Valparaiso U., 1973. Bar: Mich. 1973, U.S. Dist. Ct. (we. dist.) Mich. 1974, Colo. 1981, U.S. Dist. Ct. Colo. 1982. Ptnr. Peters, Seyburn & Hagen, Kalamazoo, Mich., 1973-76; dir. legal services City of Battle Creek, Mich., 1976-79; staff atty. CF&I Steel Corp., Pueblo, Colo., 1979-81; gen. counsel Commonwealth Investment Properties Corp., Littleton, Colo., 1981-82; assoc. Berkowitz & Brady, Denver, 1982-83, Zarlengo, Mott, Zarlengo & Winbourn, Denver, 1983-87; sole practice Denver, 1987—. Del. Colo. Rep. Party, 1986. Mem. ABA (young lawyers exec. council 1978-81, membership com. 1976-82, gen. practice sect., chmn. small bus. enterprises 1986), Mich. Bar Assn. (young lawyer's exec. coun., 1976-80), Colo. Bar Assn. (chmn. long range planning com. 1983-86, gen. practice exec. coun. 1985—, budget com. 1986-88, chmn., 1987-89, membership svcs. com. 1987—), Arapahoe County Bar Assn., Colo. Lawyers for Arts, Nat. Fedn. Ind. Bus., Am. Arbitration Assn. (mem. panel), South Metro Denver C. of C. Lutheran. Home: 7562 S Monaco Way Englewood CO 80112 Office: 2 United Bank Ctr 1700 Broadway Ste 777 Denver CO 80290

HAGEN, JAMES ALFRED, marketing executive; b. Forest City, Iowa, Mar. 27, 1932; s. Archie M. and Catherine E. (McGuire) H.; m. Mary King, Aug. 16, 1958; children: Joseph Patrick, Margaret Mary. B.A., St. Ambrose Coll., 1956; M.A., Iowa State U., 1958. Asst. gen. freight agt. Mo. Pacific R.R., St. Louis, 1958-62; dir. mktg. research, v.p. corp. devel. So. Rwy., Washington, 1963-71, 76-77; assoc. adminstr. econs. Fed. R.R. Adminstrn., Washington, 1971-74; pres. U.S. Rwy. Assn., Washington, 1974-76; sr. v.p. mktg. and sales Consol. Rail Corp., Phila., 1977-85; exec. v.p. sales and mktg. distbn. services group CSX Transp., 1985-88; pres. distbn. services group CSX Transp., Balt., 1988-89; chmn. bd., pres., chief exec. officer Consol. Rail Corp., Phila., 1989—. Mem. Nat. Freight Transp. Assn. Roman Catholic. Home: 6605 Walnutwood Cir Baltimore MD 21212 Office: Conrail 6 Penn Center Pla Philadelphia PA 19103

HAGER, JOHN ROBERT, landscape architect; b. Ft. Dodge, Iowa, May 20, 1963; s. Robert and Gladyce Jane (Johnson) H. B in Landscape Architecture, Iowa State U., 1986. Landscape architect, draftsman Robert R. Harvey Assocs., Ames, Iowa, 1985-86; civil landscape architect designer Civil Engring. Cons., Des Moines, 1986; landscape designer, estimator Suburban Landscape Assocs., Davenport, Iowa, 1987; civil landscape architect designer Michael Brenneman Assocs., Omaha, 1987-88; landscape architect The Schemmer Assocs., Omaha, 1988—. Mem. Am. Soc. Landscape Architects (assoc.), Omaha Jaycees (chairperson various coms.). Methodist. Home: 11517 Westwood Ln #14 Omaha NE 68144 Office: Faust Howell Architects 14344 Y St Omaha NE 68154

HAGERMAN, JOHN DAVID, lawyer; b. Houston, Aug. 1, 1941; s. David Angle and Noima L. (Clay) H.; m. Linda J. Lambright, June 25, 1975; children: Clayton Robert, Holly Elizabeth. BBA, So. Meth. U., 1963; JD, U. Tex., Austin, 1966. Bar: Tex. 1966, U.S. Dist. Ct. (so. dist.) Tex. 1967, U.S. Ct. Appeals (5th cir.) 1967, U.S. Supreme Ct. 1969. Pres., ptnr. Hagerman & Seureau, Inc., Spring, Tex., 1966—; condr. bank creditor rights seminars. Contbr. articles to profl. jours. Res. dep. sheriff, Montgomery County, Tex.; bd. dirs. Montgomery County Fair Assn., 1978—. Mem. ABA, Tex. Bar Assn., Houston Bar Assn., Houston Outdoor Advt. Assn., Tex. Assn. Civil Trial Specialists, Tex. Assn. Bank Counsel, Beta Theta Pi. Republican. Club: Petroleum (Houston). Avocations: swimming, tennis, jogging, shooting. Office: Hagerman & Seureau Inc 24800 Interstate 45 #100 Spring TX 77386

HAGERSON, LAWRENCE JOHN, health agency executive, consultant; b. Lakewood, Ohio, Dec. 30, 1931; s. John Lawrence and Ruth Evelyn (Watson) H.; m. Shirley Lorraine Carter, July 2, 1955; children: Nancy Lynn, Tracy Ann, Laura Jane. BS in Econs., U. Pa., 1954, postgrad. in Economics, 1957-59. Cons. John Price Jones Co., N.Y.C., 1960-62, U.S Agy. for Internat. Devel. Southeast Asia, 1970-74; asst. to chancellor U. Calif., Santa Barbara, 1962-63, U. Mo., Kansas City, 1967-70; cons. Asia Found., Singapore, Malaysia, 1964-67; exec. v.p. Mid. Am. Health Edn. Consortium, Kansas City, 1970-78; dir. bus. and devel. Inst. Logopedics, Wichita, Kans., 1978-88; dir. devel. The Conservancy, Naples, Fla., 1988—. Mem., officer Kans. City Civic Orchestra Bd., 1976-78; bd. dirs. Greater Kans. City Urban Coalition, 1969-70. Served to lt. USN, 1954-56. Mem. Nat. Soc. Fund Raising Execs. (nat. bd. dirs. 1984-88). Republican. Presbyterian. Avocation: golf. Home: 520 Augusta Blvd #B-202 Naples FL 33962 Office: The Conservancy 1450 Merrimue Dr Naples FL 33942

HAGERUP, RICHARD H., diversified company executive; b. Oak Park, Ill., Dec. 2, 1952; s. Richard Theodore and Joan Alice (Nelson) H. BS, Miami U., Oxford, Ohio, 1975. CPA. Sr. auditor Arthur Andersen & Co., Chgo., 1975-80; mgr. corp. acctg. DWG Corp., Miami Beach, Fla., 1980-82, controller, 1985—; mgr. corp. acctg. APL Corp., Miami Beach, 1983-85. Ernst & Ernst scholar, 1975. Mem. Am. Inst. CPAs. Office: DWG Corp 6917 Collins Ave Miami Beach FL 33141

HAGEY, WALTER REX, banker; b. Hatfield. Pa., July 24, 1909; s. Justus T. and Martha Mabel Hagey; student U. Pa., 1931-36; LLB, La Salle Extension U., 1938; STB, Temple U., 1943; grad. Stonier Grad. Sch. Banking Rutgers U., 1951; LLD, Muhlenberg Coll., 1963; m. Dorothy E. Rosenberger, Oct. 17, 1931; 1 son, Donald C. With Fidelity Bank (formerly Fidelity-Phila. Trust Co.), 1929—, asst. sec., 1948—, asst. v.p., 1957-66, v.p., 1966-74. Supply pastor Eastern Pa. Synod Lutheran Ch. Am., 1950-80, treas., 1950-80, now Luth. Synod S.E. Pa.; treas. Luth. Synod Northeastern Pa., 1969-70; pres., dir. Phila. Luth. Social Union; treas. Luth. Laymens Movement for Stewardship of United Luth. Ch., 1959-63; mem. bd., exec. com. Luth. Council in U.S., 1962-74; mem. bds., treas. home missions, inner missions, Christian edn. Eastern Pa. Synod, Luth. Ch. Am., 1950-69; vice chmn. adminstrn. and fin. Luth. Ch. in Am., 1972-78, mem. bd. pensions, 1978-84 , v.p. Bd. Am. Missions, 1972-78; bd. dirs., adv. bd. Muhlenberg Med. Center; bd. dirs., chmn. Prosser Found., 1968—; bd. dirs., treas. Luth. Retirement Homes, 1978-82; mem. com. for investments Luth. Ch. in Am., 1978-82; bd. dirs., sec. Silver Spring-Martin Luther Sch., 1976—; treas. Bethesda House, 1950-69; treas., registrar Luth. Lay Acad., 1981—; treas. The Auxiliary-Luth. Theol. Sem. at Phila., 1986—, The Religious Tercentenary Com., 1982—. Mem. Am. Inst. Banking, Phila. Estate Planning Council, Pa. Council Chs. (dir. 1954-70), Pa. Soc., Luth. Hist. Soc. Eastern Pa., Men of Mt. Airy Sem. (pres. 1976-86), Pa. Bible Soc. (treas., sec., now pres., dir. 1971—), Rotary, Elm (sec. 1951-63), Midday Club, Anglers (Phila.). Home: 510 E Lawn Ave Lansdale PA 19446

HAGGERTY, ALLEN CHARLES, transportation company executive; b. Bklyn., Apr. 23, 1936; s. Charles Joseph and Florence G. (Cohn) H.; m. Iris May Parkinson, Aug. 13 ,1960; children: Robert, Kathryn, Kenneth. BS in Aero. Engring., Princeton U., 1958; MS in Mgmt., Rensselaer Poly. Inst., 1962; postgrad., Harvard U., 1974. Dir. ops. Boeing Vertol Co., Ridley Park, Pa., 1976-79, dir. comml. helicopter program, 1979-80; sr. v.p. ops. McDonnell Douglas Helicopter Co., Culver City, Calif., 1981, exec. v.p. ops., 1981-85; exec. v.p. engring and ops. McDonnell Douglas Helicopter Co., Mesa, Ariz., 1986—; chmn. rotorcraft adv. group Aerospace Industries Assn. Am., 1987. Co-inventor snap-ring grommet for elec. wiring. Trustee Del. County Community Coll., Media, Pa., 1978-80; pres. bd. of deacons Media Presbyn. Ch., 1977-80, pres. Indian Ln. Jr. High Sch., Media, 1976. Served to lt. USN, 1958-61. Named Mfg. Mgr. of Yr., Soc. Mfg. Engrs., 1984. Mem. Am. Helicopter Soc., Am. Defense Preparedness Assn., Assn. U.S. Army, Soc. Mfg. Engrs. (sr.). Club: McDonnell Douglas Helicopter Mgmt. Home: 30600 N Pima Rd Scottsdale AZ 85262 Office: McDonnell Douglas Helicopter Co 5000 E McDowell Rd Mesa AZ 85262

HAGGETT, DAVID GARDNER, publishing representative; b. Buerne, Mass., Aug. 30, 1964; s. Charles David and Judith Pauline (Firt) H. BS in Mktg. and Fin., U. Utah, 1987. Gen. mgr. Coalition Lodge, Park City, Utah, 1985-87; pubs. rep. Arpin Assocs., Weston, Mass., 1987—. Mem. Golden Key, Fin. Mgmt. Assn., Phi Eta Sigma, Kappa Sigma. Republican. Home and Office: 192 Maple St Springfield MA 01105

HAGGIS, ARTHUR GEORGE, JR., education services executive, publisher; b. Youngstown, Ohio, June 3, 1924; s. Arthur George Sr. and Mary Mildred (Campbell) H.; m. Lewanna Evalyn Strom, Apr. 7, 1944; children: Lynda Lee, Arthur George III, Richard Charles, Douglas Hood, Pamela Sue. BS in Edn., Wayne State U., 1957, MEd, 1959, EdD, 1961. Asst. indsl. engr. U.S. Steel Corp., McDonald, Ohio, 1946-51; bn. survey officer, field arty. U.S. Army, ETO, 1943-46; post dep. comdr., adj. 2d Armored Div. Trains, Bad Kreuznach, Fed. Republic Germany, 1951-54; chief of info., spl. asst. to sec. of army Mich. Mil. Dist., Detroit and Washington, Mich. and D.C., 1954-64; pres., chief exec. officer Haggis Assocs. Inc., Washington and Hollywood, D.C. and Fla., 1964-71, Atlantis Pvt. Schs., Inc., Hollywood, 1971—; chmn., chief exec. officer The Atlantis-Lewart Group, Inc., Hollywood, 1987—; pres., chief exec. officer Ednl. Cons., Washington and Hollywood, 1966—, Atlantis Pub. Co., Hollywood, 1978—; bd. dirs. Atlantis Research Insts., Inc., Hollywood, Perfect Body Products, Inc., Hollywood. Co-editor, Small Business Library, The Government Market, 1966, Selling to the U.S. Government and its Contractors, vol. I, 1966, Bids, Proposals, Contracts, and Contract Administration, vol. II, 1966, Texts of Small Business Enterprise Institute, vol. III, 1966, Bids, Proposals, and Contracts for Small Business Enterprise Course Handbook, vol. IV, 1966; author: Educational Evaluation Program: Predicting College Success, 1967; author: (with others) Atlantis Beginning Language and Number Development Program, Books I and II, 1981-87, Atlantis Basic Spelling Series, Books A-H, 1981-85, Atlantis Computer Series, Books I-VII, 1982-87, Atlantis Health Series, 1981-87. Sustaining mem. Freedoms Found. at Valley Forge, 1985—, Mus. of Art, 1986—, Opera Soc.; founder Performing Arts Ctr. Pacers, 1985; mem. Opera Guild, Inc., 1986—; pres. Wayne State U. Alumni Club Washington D.C., 1963-69; trustee Philharmonic Orchestra Fla., 1987—; mem. Rep. Presdl. Task Force, 1983—, Rep. Senatorial Inner Circle, Rep. Pres.' Club, 1984—. Decorated Bronze Star, Purple Heart; recipient Award City of St. Ignace, 1958, Nat. USO award, 1959, citation City of Detroit, 1959; U.S. Army doctoral scholar Wayne State U., 1960-61; grantee Detroit Edison Co., 1964-65, Litton Industries, 1965-66. Mem. Assn. Am. Pubs., Assn. U.S. Army (regional v.p. 1984-87, sustaining mem. Landpower Edn. Fund, Inc. 1984, chmn. Fla. state exec. council 1985-87, bd. dirs. Fla. Gulf Stream chpt. 1984—), English Speaking Union, Navy League (bd. dirs. Ft. Lauderdale council 1988), USO (pres. Greater Ft. Lauderdale, Inc. council 1988—), Air Force Assn. (Citation 1961), Clan Campbell Soc. of Fla., Inc., Scottish Am. Soc. South Fla. Republican. Lutheran. Clubs: Tower, 110 Tower (Ft. Lauderdale); Army and Navy (washington); Homestead Air Force Base Officers' (Fla.). Lodges: K.T., Masons. Office: Atlantis-Lewart Group Inc 5432 Hallandale Beach Blvd Hollywood FL 33023

HAGIWARA, KOKICHI, steel company executive. Pres. Nat. Steel Corp., Pitts. Office: Nat Steel Corp Nat Steel Ctr 20 Stanwix St Pittsburgh PA 15222 *

HAGOPIAN, LOUIS THOMAS, advertising executive; b. Pontiac, Mich., June 1, 1925; s. Thomas and Sarah (Uligian) H.; m. Joanne Kelly, Dec. 31, 1955; children: Susan Hagopian Goddard, Thomas, Matthew. Student, Northwestern U., 1944; B.A. in Bus. Adminstrn, Mich. State U., 1947. With staff then dist. sales mgr. Pontiac Motor Car Co., 1948-53; with staff then dist. sales mgr. Chrysler Corp., 1953-60, dir. advt. and sales promotion Plymouth div., 1956-60; account supr. NW Ayer Inc., 1960-62, v.p., 1962-66, Detroit mgr., 1963-66, exec. v.p., gen. mgr. N.Y. region, 1967-73, vice chmn., 1973-76, chmn., 1976—, also dir. Mem. exec. com., bd. dirs. Hwy. Users Fedn. for Safety and Mobility; bd. dirs. sports com. USIA, Advt. Council; N.Y. State chmn. Nat. Com. for Employer Support of Guard and Res., 1982-84; sec., trustee YMCA Greater N.Y., 1986—. Served to lt. (j.g.) USNR, World War II. Recipient Disting. Alumnus award Mich. State U., 1978. Mem. Am. Assn. Advt. Agys. (nat. chmn. 1985-86, adv. council 1986—), Am. Council on Arts, Assn. Nat. Advertisers, Adcraft Club Detroit, Kappa Sigma. Clubs: Wee Burn Country, Pine Valley Golf, Jupiter Hills, University; Royal and Ancient Golf of St. Andrews (Scotland). Office: NW Ayer Inc 1345 Ave of the Americas New York NY 10105

HAGRUP, KNUT, aviation consultant; b. Bergen, Norway, Nov. 13, 1913; s. Lie-Svendsen and Ebba (Hagrup) H.; math. degree, 1933; grad. Coll. Royal Norwegian Air Force, 1936; Civil Engr., Darmstadt U., 1940; Dr. Laws (hon.), Pacific Luth. U., 1978; Sc.Dr. (hon.), Northrop U., 1978; Dr.econs., Hochschule fur Verkerswesen, Dresden, Germany, 1979; Dr. tech.,

Stockholm U., 1980; m. Esther Skaugen, Sept. 22, 1944 (dec. 1975); children—Vivi, Bente. Chief engr. Norwegian Civil Aeros. Bd., Oslo, 1945; chief engr. Scandinavian Airlines Systems, Stockholm, 1946, v.p. ops., 1951-56, v.p. engring., 1956-60, v.p. tech. and ops., 1960-62, exec. v.p. tech. and ops., 1962-69, pres., 1969-79; chmn. bd. Saab-Fairchild Airliner program, Stockholm-N.Y.C., 1980-85; cons., dir. various Scandinavian industries; dir. Hennes & Mauritz, Stockholm, SAAB-SCANIA; cons. prof. Pacific Luth. U., Tacoma, 1979; prof., trustee Northrop U., Los Angeles, 1980; chmn. commn. air transport Internat. C. of C., Paris, 1969—; chmn. IATA, 1974-75, Assn. European Airlines, 1975-76 (chmn.); dir. Thai Airways, 1969-76. Served with Royal Norwegian Air Force, 1940-45. Decorated Norwegian War medal; Def. medal; Haakon VII's medal; comdr. Northern Star (Sweden); comdr. Order St. Olav (Norway); grand officer Orange-Nassau (Netherlands); comdr. Legion d'Honneur (France); Brit. Def. medal; comdr. Order White Elephant (Thailand). Fellow Brit. Aero. Soc.; mem. Royal Airforce Club. Author: La Bataille du Transport Aerien, 1978; Die Heutige Weltluftfahrt, 1979; How the Aerospace Industry of Western Europe Will Survive, 1981. Home: 14 rue St-Jean, 1260 Nyon VD, Switzerland

HAGUE, JOHN BRIAN, energy company executive; b. Lethbridge, Alta., Can., Aug. 15, 1944; s. John Rayson and Rose (Knowlden) H. BA in Honors Econs., U. B.C., 1965; postgrad., U. Minn., 1965-66. Bus. analyst Pacific Region Office Imperial Oil Ltd., 1966-69; asst. dir. price rev. div. Prices & Income Commn., Ottawa, Ont., Can., 1969-72; fin. analyst Can. Devel. Corp., Toronto, Ont., 1972-75, mgr. fin. analysis, 1976, v.p., 1976-79, exec. v.p., 1979-86; dir. gen. prices and profits br. Anti-Inflation Bd., Ottawa, 1975-76; pres., chief operating officer Canterra Energy Ltd., Calgary, Atla., Can., 1986—; also bd. dirs. Canterra Energy Ltd., Calgary, Alta., Can.; bd. dirs. Cansulex Ltd., Vancouver, B.C., Can. *

HAHN, CARL HORST, auto company executive; b. July 1, 1926; m. Marisa Traina, 1960; 4 children. Chmn. bd. Continental GummiWerk AG, 1973-81, Volkswagen AG, 1981—; chmn. supervisory bd. Gerling-Konzern Speziale Kreditversicherungs-AG, Cologne, Audi AG; dep. chmn. Supervisory bd. AG fur Industrie und Verkehrswesen, Frankfurt am Main, Gerling-Konzern Zentrale Vertriebs-AG, Cologne; mem. supervisory bd. Gerling-Konzern Allgemeine Versicherungs-AG, Cologne, Wilhelm Karmann GmbH, Norddeutsche Landesbank-Girozentrale, Hanover, Uniroyal Engleberg Reifen GmbH, Aachen. Mem. Fed. Econs. Ministry (adv. com.), Salk Inst. (internat. adv. com. La Jolla, Calif. chpt.), Founders' Assn. German Sci. (bd. mgmt.), Deutsche Bank AG (group cons.), BDI (exec. com., v.p., mem. presidium), VDA (exec. com.), Thyssen AG (bd. dirs.), DLT (bd. dirs.), CCMC (bd. dirs.), Stiftung Volkswagenwerk (bd. trustees). Office: Volkswagen AG, Niedrsachs 1, 3180 Wolfsburg Federal Republic of Germany also: Volkswagen of Am Inc 888 W Big Beaver Troy MI 48007

HAHN, TATIANA C., bank executive; b. Monticello, N.Y., Nov. 26, 1963; d. George and Lubow (Makarenko) C. AS in Bus. Adminstrn., Sullivan County Community Coll., 1983; BS in Mgmt., U. Scranton, 1985. Teller First Nat. Bank of Jeffersonville, N.Y., 1985, installment loan clk., 1985-86, loan officer, 1986-87, br. mgr., 1987—. Advanced first aider Jeffersonville Vol. First Aid Corp., 1987—. Mem. Sullivan County Banker's Assn., Nat. Assn. Women Bankers. Home: RD 1 Box 91B Jeffersonville NY 12748 Office: First Nat Bank Jeffersonville Main St Eldred NY 12732

HAHN, THOMAS MARSHALL, JR., forest products corporation executive; b. Lexington, Ky., Dec. 2, 1926; s. Thomas Marshall and Mary Elizabeth (Boston) H.; m. Margaret Louise Lee, Dec. 27, 1948; children: Elizabeth Hahn McKelvy, Anne Hahn Clarke. BS in Physics, U. Ky., 1945; PhD, MIT, 1950; LLD (hon.), Seton Hall U., 1976, Fla. So. Coll., 1986; PhD (hon.), Va. Poly. Inst., 1987. Physicist U.S. Naval Ordinance Lab., 1946-47; research asst. MIT, Cambridge, 1947-50; assoc. prof. physics U. Ky., Lexington, 1950-52, prof., 1952-54; prof., head dept. physics Va. Poly. Inst., Blacksburg, 1954-59; pres. Va. Poly. Inst. and State U., Blacksburg, 1962-75; dean arts and scis. Kans. State U., Manhattan, 1959-62; exec. v.p. Ga.-Pacific Corp., 1975-76; pres. Ga.-Pacific Corp., Atlanta, 1976-82, pres., chief operating officer, 1982-83, pres., chief exec. officer, 1983-84, chmn. bd., pres., chief exec. officer, 1984-85; bd. dirs. Norfolk So. Corp., Coca-Cola Enterprises, Am. Paper Inst., chmn. 1982-83, Sun Trust Banks; Trust Co. Bank of Ga., former chmn. N.Y. Stock Exchange Listed Co. Adv. Com. Pres. So. Assn. Land Grant Colls. And State Univs., 1965-66; chmn. Va. Met. Area Study Commn., 1966-68, Va. Cancer Crusade, 1972, U.S. Savs. Bond Program, Ga., 1985-87; bd. visitors Air U., 1966-69, Ferrum Jr. Coll.; bd. dirs. Atlanta Arts Alliance, Bus. Coun. Ga., Cen. Atlanta Progress, Keep Am. Beautiful Inc.; mem. adv. bd. Atlanta chpt. Boy Scouts Am.; former chmn. capital funds campaign Atlanta Area Services for Blind, 1984; bd. visitors Callaway Gardens; mem. Atlanta Action Forum, nat. adv. bd. and campaign team greater Atlanta Salvation Army; former campaign chmn. Ga. chpt. Am. Diabetes Assn., 1985-86, United Way of Met. Atlanta Inc., 1987; Ga. chmn. U.S. Savs. Bond Program, 1985-87; trustee Emory U., Inst. Paper Chemistry, Robert W. Woodruff Arts Ctr., Emory U. (adv. coun.). USN, 1945-46. Named Chief Exec. Officer of Yr. for Forest Products and Lumber Industry, Wall St. Transcript, 1984-86, 88, Papermaker of Yr., Paper Trade Jour., 1984, Chief Exec. Officer of Yr., Forest Products and Paper Industry, 1986; recipient Outstanding Citizen Va. award Toastmasters Internat., 1966, Outstanding Profl. Contbns. award Va. Citizens Planning Assn., 1970, MIT Corp. Leadership award, 1976. Fellow Am. Phys. Soc.; mem. The Conf. Bd., Atlanta C. of C., Phi Beta Kappa, Sigma Xi, Omicron Delta Kappa. Republican. Methodist. Clubs: Piedmont Driving, The Links, Shenandoah, Capital City, Ocean Reef, Commerce. Office: Ga-Pacific Corp 133 Peachtree St NE Atlanta GA 30303

HAHN, WILLIAM HARRY, banker; b. Defiance, Ohio, Apr. 6, 1946; s. Robert Harry and Letha Mae (Hellemn) Wehrle H.; m. Cynthia Lou Pauter, June 10, 1967; children: Craig Alan, Jeffrey Alan. BS, Ball State U., 1971; MBA, U. Toledo, 1978; PhD, Columbia Pacific U., 1988. Sr. acct. Ernst & Whitney, Toledo, 1971-74; v.p. chief fin. officer Sylvania (Ohio) Bank, Ohio, 1974-82; exec. v.p., treas. United Vt. Bancorp & Proctor Bank, Rutland, 1982—; bd. dirs. Green Mountain Bank, Bondville, Vt. Contbr. articles to profl. jours. Bd. trustees Coll. St. Joseph, Rutland; bd. auditors Town of Wallingford, Vt. Served with USAF, 1965-69. Scholar Delta Sigma Pi, 1971; recipient award Wall St. Jour., 1971. Mem. Ohio Soc. CPA's, Vt. Soc. CPA's, Am. Bankers Assn. (acctg. task force 1984-86, book rev. com. 1984-89), Vt. Bankers Assn. (chmn. edn. com. 1983-86), Beta Gamma Sigma. Office: United Vt Bancorp 80 West St Rutland VT 05701

HAID, JOHN M., JR., food products executive; b. Ft. Worth, Sept. 15, 1936; s. John M. and Myrtle May (Page) H.; m. Ann Whiteside, Nov. 14, 1959; children: Grayce Michelle Haid Eudy, John Justin, Amy Sue. AS, Akr. Tech. U., 1956; BS in Agriculture, U. Ark., 1959. Gen. mgr. Ark. Poultry Fedn., Little Rock, 1959-61; asst. to pres. Simmons Industries Inc., Siloam Springs, Ark., 1961, 62-68; sr. v.p. mfg. ops. Pilgrims Pride Corp., Pittsburg, Tex., 1968-71, 83—; real estate broker Pittsburg, 1971-83. Served to 1st lt. U.S. Army, 1959, 61-62. Named Man of Yr. Siloam Springs Jaycees, 1963. Mem. Pittsburg C. of C. (bd. dirs. 1987—). Baptist. Home: Roural Route Box 95 Pittsburg TX 75686 Office: Pilgrims Pride Corp PO Box 93 Pittsburg TX 75686

HAIG, ALEXANDER MEIGS, JR., former secretary of state, former army officer, business executive; b. Phila., Dec. 2, 1924; s. Alexander Meigs and Regina Anne (Murphy) H.; m. Patricia Antoinette Fox, May 24, 1950; children: Alexander P., Brian F., Barbara E. Student, U. Notre Dame, 1943; B.S., U.S. Mil. Acad., 1947; M.A., Georgetown U., 1961; grad., Naval War Coll., 1960, Army War Coll., 1966; grad. hon. law degree, Niagara U.; LL.D. (hon.), U. Utah. Commd. 2d lt. U.S. Army, 1947, advanced through grades to gen., 1973; staff officer Office Chief of Staff for Ops. Dept. of Army, 1962-64; mil. asst. to sec. of army 1964, dep. spl. asst. to sec. and dep. sec. of def., 1964-65; bn. and brigade comdr. 1st Inf. Div., Vietnam, 1966-67; regtl. comdr., dep. comdt. U.S. Mil. Acad., 1967-69; mil. asst. to asst. to the Pres. for Nat. Security Affairs, 1969-70; dep. asst. to the Pres. for Nat. Security Affairs Washington, 1970-73; vice chief of staff U.S. Army, Washington, 1973; asst. to Pres., chief White House staff, 1973-74; comdr.-in-chief U.S. European Command, 1974-79; supreme allied comdr. Europe SHAPE, 1974-79; ret. 1979; pres., chief operating officer, dir. United Technologies Corp., Hartford, Conn., 1979-81; sec. state Washington, 1981-82; bd. dirs. Leisure Tech. Inc.; dir. Commodore Internat.; chmn. United Tech. Corp., Atlantic and Pacific Adv. Councils. Decorated D.S.C., Silver Star with oak leaf cluster, Legion of Merit with 2 oak leaf clusters, D.F.C. with 2 oak leaf clusters, Bronze Star with oak leaf cluster, Air medal with 23 oak leaf clusters, Army Commendation medal, Purple Heart U.S.; Nat. Order 5th Class; Gallantry Cross with palm; Civil Actions Honor medal 1st Class; grand officer Nat. Order of Vietnam, Republic of Vietnam; medal of King Abdel-Aziz Saudi Arabia; grand cross Order of Merit W. Ger.; recipient Disting. Service medal Dept. of Def.; Disting. Service medal U.S. Army; Man of Yr. award Air Force Assn.; James Forrestal Meml. award. Mem. Soc. of 1st Div. (v.p.). Office: 1155 15th St NW Suite 800 Washington DC 20005

HAILEY, STEVEN ANDREW, data processing executive; b. Weisbaden, Fed. Republic Germany, Oct. 18, 1953; s. Paul Morgan and Imogene (Rodgers) H.; m. Diane Barr, Nov. 6, 1976; children: Jennifer, Andrew. Diploma, Comml. Coll., 1972. Computer programer Fed. Civil Svc., New Orleans, 1977-78; data processing mgr. Cotton's Holsum Bakery, Alexandria, La., 1978-80, Computer Mgmt. Svcs., 1980-81; v.p. mgmt. info. systems Pub. Investors, Inc., 1981—. Office: Pub Investors Inc One Corporate Sq 2230 S Macarthur Dr Alexandria LA 71301

HAIMOVITZ, JULES, broadcasting company executive; b. Tel Aviv, Dec. 25, 1950; came to U.S., 1955; s. Louis and Josephine (Ratz) H.; m. Susan Lovett, July 3, 1974 (div. Jan. 1978); m. Elizabeth Webster, Apr. 9, 1982. BA in Math., Bklyn. Coll., 1971, MA in Math., 1974. Research analyst ABC TV Network, N.Y.C., 1971-75, mgr. statis. ops., 1975-76; dir. pay TV programming Viacom Internat., Inc., N.Y.C., 1976-77; sr. v.p. Showtime Entertainment, N.Y.C., 1976-81; v.p. Viacom Internat., Inc., N.Y.C., 1981-82; exec. v.p. Viacom Entertainment Group, N.Y.C., 1982-84, pres., 1984-86; pres. Viacom Networks Group, N.Y.C., 1986-87; pres., chief oper. officer Spelling Entertainment, Inc., L.A., 1988—. Office: Spelling Entertainment Inc 1041 N Formosa Ave West Hollywood CA 90046

HAINES, HELEN DRAKE, diversified manufacturing and service company assistant controller; b. Chattanooga, Apr. 2, 1943; d. Charles Barry and Madelyn Lenis (Garner) Neill; m. Stanley Alan Haines, Dec. 20, 1987; BA in Math., Fla. State U., 1966; MBA in Acctg., Ga. State U., 1977. Acctg. clk. Ga. Dept. State, 1962-66; accountant Modern Foods, Inc., Winter Haven, Fla., 1970-72; Staff acct. Nat. Service Industries, Inc., Atlanta, 1972-73, acctg. supr., 1974-75, mgr. corp. acctg., 1975-81, mgr. fin. planning and analysis, 1981-82, asst. to treas., 1982-83, asst. controller, 1983—. C.P.A., Ga. Mem. Am. Inst. CPA's, Ga. Soc. CPA's. Republican. Episcopalian. Home: 1307 Minhinnett Dr Roswell GA 30075 Office: Nat Svc Industries 1180 Peachtree St NE Atlanta GA 30309

HAINES, MICHAEL ROBERT, economist, educator; b. Chgo., Nov. 19, 1944; s. James Joshua and Anne Marie (Welch) H.; m. Patricia Caroline Foster, Aug. 19, 1967 (div. Jan. 1986); children:James, Margaret. BA, Amherst Coll., 1967; MA, U. Pa., 1968, PhD, 1971. Asst. prof. econs. Cornell U., Ithaca, N.Y., 1972-79; vis. lectr. econs. U. Pa., Phila., 1979, rsch. assoc. prof. Sch. Pub. and Urban Policy, 1979-80; assoc. prof. econs. Wayne State U., Detroit, 1980-86, prof., 1986—; cons. NIH, Bethesda, Md., 1980-84, The World Bank, Washington, 1983. Author: Economic-Demographic Interrels. in Developing Agrl. Regions, 1977; Fertility and Occupation, 1979. Contbr. articles to profl. jours. NIH grantee, 1974-77, 78-82. Mem. Internat. Union for Sci. Study Population, Econ. History Assn. (bd. editors 1987—), Social Sci. History Assn. (bd. dirs. 1983-85, treas. 1985—), Am. Econ. Assn., The Cliometrics Soc. (bd. editor 1988—), Population Assn. Am., Am. Statis. Assn. Episcopalian. Avocations: numismatics, wine, book collecting. Office: Wayne State U Dept Econs Detroit MI 48202

HAINES, PERRY VANSANT, cattle company executive; b. Middletown, Ohio, Mar. 14, 1944; s. John Percy and Pendery (Spear) H.; m. Sidonie M. Sexton, 1982; 1 child, Pendery. A.B., Princeton U., 1967; M.B.A., Harvard U., 1970. Research asst. Harvard U., 1970-71; cons. Boston Cons. Group, 1971-74; exec. v.p. IBP, Inc. (formerly Iowa Beef Processors), Dakota City, Nebr., 1974—; dir. IBP, Inc., 1980—; v.p. Occidental Petroleum, Los Angeles, 1981-87. Served with USMCR, 1967-68. Office: IBP Inc PO Box 515 Dakota City NE 68731

HAINLINE, FORREST ARTHUR, JR., retired automotive company executive, lawyer; b. Rock Island, Ill., Oct. 20, 1918; s. Forrest Arthur and Marian (Pearson) H.; m. Nora Marie Schrot, July 7, 1945; children: Forrest III, Jon, Patricia, Judith, Brian, David, Nora. AB, Augustana Coll., Rock Island, Ill., 1940; JD, U. Mich., 1947, LLM, 1948. Bar: Ill. 1942, Mich. 1943, Fla. 1970, U.S. Supreme Ct. 1946. Mem. firm Cross, Wrock, Miller & Vieson and predecessor, Detroit, 1948-71, ptnr., 1957-71; v.p., gen. counsel Am. Motors Corp., Detroit, 1971-84, sec., 1972-84, ret. Chmn., Wayne County Regional Interagy. Coordinating Com. for Developmental Disabilities, Mich., 1972-76; chmn. grievance com. U.S. Tennis Assn., 1970-85, mem. exec. com., 1972-74, 83-85, chmn. constn. and rules, 1983-86, v.p. So. region, 1985-86; arbitrator Men's Internat. Profl. Tennis Council, 1977-85; pres. Cath. Social Services Oakland County, Mich., 1972-75; mem. exec. com. Western Tennis Assn., 1964—, pres., 1972-73, chmn. constn. and rules com., 1976-84; mem. Men's Internat. Profl. Tennis Council, 1985-87; chmn. Internat. Tennis Fedn. rules com., 1987—; pres. Western Improvement Assn., 1969-75; bd. dirs. Augustana Coll., 1974-82, sec., 1975-82; bd. dirs. Providence Hosp., Southfield, Mich., 1975-84, sec. 1980, vice chmn., 1981, chmn., 1982, chmn. exec. com., 1983-84. Served to 1st lt. AUS, 1942-46. Named (with family) Tennis Family of Yr., U.S. Tennis Assn., 1974; recipient Outstanding Service award Augustana Coll., 1977; named to Rock Island High Sch. Sports Hall of Fame, 1977, Mich. Amateur Sports Hall of Fame, 1978, Augustana Coll. Sports Hall of Fame, 1980. Mem. ABA, Fed. Bar Assn., Mich. Bar. Assn., Ill. Bar Assn., Fla. Bar Assn., Am. Judicature Soc., Augustana Coll. Alumni Assn. (pres. bd. dirs. 1973-74), Phi Alpha Delta. Clubs: Suntide Condominiums, Kenmure Golf, Detroit Tennis, Squash. Lodge: KC. Home: 1357 NE Ocean Blvd Stuart FL 34996 also: 148 Overlook Dr Flat Rock NC 28731

HAIR, DANNY G., retail company executive; b. Lancaster, Calif., Sept. 10, 1949; s. Robert L. and Ellen L. (Long) H.; m. Joan K. Worley, Mar. 25, 1975; children: Rochelle R., Danielle R. BBA, U. Okla., 1974. With audit staff Arthur Young & Co., Oklahoma City, 1974-75, Dallas, 1976-78; with audit staff Moak, Hunsaker & Rouse, Oklahoma City, 1975-76; v.p. internal audit Zale Corp., Dallas, 1978-85; v.p. audit dept. Club Corp. Am., Dallas, 1985-87; sr. v.p., chief fin. office Mich. Gen. Corp., Dallas, 1987—; exec. v.p. Diamond Lumber, Inc., Dallas, 1987—. Mem. Am. Inst. CPA's. Office: Mich Gen Corp 12000 Ford Rd Ste 300 Dallas TX 75234

HAIR, DONALD W., real estate investment company executive; b. Canton, Ohio, Nov. 14, 1938; s. Wayne Scott and Marie (Geis) H.; m. Elisabeth Schneider, Aug. 20, 1960; children: Scott, Andrew, William, Susanne. BS, Kent State U., 1960. CPA, Ariz. With Coopers & Lybrand, Cleve. and Phoenix, 1960-66; acct., treas. Motorola, Inc., various locations, 1966-74; internat. and resort controller Ramada Inns, Inc., Phoenix, 1974-77; group internat. controller Gardner-Denver Corp., Dallas, 1977-78; v.p., controller The Victorio Co., Phoenix, 1978-82; v.p., controller Southmark Corp., Dallas, 1983-86, sr. v.p., chief fin. officer, 1986-89, exec. v.p., chief fin. officer, 1989—. Bd. dirs. Richardson (Tex.) Symphony, 1987—, Richardson Chamber Music Soc., 1988—, Dallas Juvenile Diabetes Assn., 1987—. Mem. AICPA, Ariz. Soc. CPA's, Tex. Soc. CPA's, Fin. Execs. Inst. Office: Southmark Corp 1601 LBJ Frwy Ste 800 Dallas TX 75234

HAIRSTON, JOHN THOMAS, JR., food retail executive; b. San Antonio, July 19, 1934; s. John Thomas and Georgia Lucile (Walker) H.; Adrienne Dee Pittman, July 17, 1953 (div. Aug. 1969); m. Carol Ann Graham, Feb. 21, 1970; children—Elizabeth Anne, Andrew Graham, Robert Walker. B.B.A., So. Meth. U., 1955. Mgmt. trainee Tom Thumb Stores Inc., Dallas, 1955-57, store mgr., 1957-59, exec. v.p., 1975-79, pres., 1979-84; exec. v.p., chief oper. officer Cullum Cos. Inc., Dallas, 1984-87, pres., chief oper. officer, 1987—; mem. Coca-Cola Research Council, Atlanta, 1978-84. Chmn. bd. Jr. Achievement of Dallas, 1981-83. Served to 1st lt. USAF, 1955-57. Mem. Supermarket Inst., Am. Mgmt. Assn., Dallas C. of C. (bd. dirs. 1982-84). So. Meth. U. Alumni Assn. (bd. dirs. 1985—). Republican. Presbyterian. *

HAISLIP, DAVID CRAIG, account supervisor; b. Lower Marian Twp., Pa., Mar. 19, 1962; s. Jay R. and Helen (Sobak) H. BA, Ithaca Coll., 1984. Gen. mgr. Pentagon Studios, Belleville, N.J., 1983—; coord. HBM/Creamer Advt., N.Y.C., 1985-86, WCRS Group, 1986-87; account supr., project mgr. Della Femrina and McNamee WCRS, N.Y.C., 1987—; cons. in field. Mem. Am. Mgmt. Assn., Alpha Epsilon Rho, Pi Lamda Chi. Republican. Home: 15 Overlook Ave Belleville NJ 07109 Office: Della Feurina & McNamee WCRS 350 Hudson St New York NY 10014

HAJEK, ROBERT J., lawyer, real estate broker, commodities broker, nursing home owner; b. Berwyn, Ill., May 17, 1943; s. James J., Sr., and Rita C. (Kalka) H.; m. Maris Ann Enright, June 19, 1965; children—Maris Ann, Robert J., David, Mandie. B.A., Loras Coll., 1965; J.D., U. Ill., 1968. Bar: Ill. 1968, U.S. Tax Ct. 1970, U.S. dist. ct. (no. dist.) Ill. 1971, U.S. Ct. Appeals (7th cir.) 1972, U.S. Supreme Ct. 1972. Lic. real estate broker, Ill., Nat. Assn. Securities Dealers; registered U.S. Commodities Futures Trading Commn. ptnr. Hajek & Hajek, Berwyn, Ill., 1968-76; pres., bd. chmn. Hajek, Hajek, Koykar & Heying, Ltd., Westchester, Ill., 1976-85; pres., chief exec. officer Land of Lincoln Real Estate, Ltd., Glendale Heights, Ill., 1985—, also bd. dirs.; ptnr., owner Camelot Manor Nursing Home, Streator, Ill., 1978—, Ottawa (Ill.) Care Ctr., 1981—, Law Centre Bldg., Westchester, 1976—; owner Garfield Ridge Real Estate, Chgo., 1973-78, Centre Realty, Westchester, 1976-85; ptnr. Westbrook Commodities, Chgo., 1983; v.p., bd. mem., gen. counsel DeHart Gas and Oil Devel., Ltd., 1970-73; prin. Northeastern Okla. Oil and Gas Prodn. Venture, Tulsa, 1982—; exec. v.p., gen. counsel Garrett Plante Corp., 1978—, Ottawa Long Term Care, Inc., 1982—; bd. dirs. Land of Lincoln Savs. and Loan, 1981—, Home Title Services of Am., Inc., 1981—, Land of Lincoln Ins. Agy., Inc., 1982—, Medema Builders, Inc., 1983-88 , Ptnrs. of Ill., Inc., 1984—, The Ill. Co., 1984—, Ill. Co. Properties, Inc., subs. of Ill. Co., 1984-87 , Ottawa Long Term Care, Inc., 1982—, Garrett Plante Corp., 1978—, St. Mary's Living Square Chgo., 1985—. Sr. boys' basketball coach Roselle Recreation Assn., Ill., 1981-83. Mem. ABA, Ill. Bar Assn., Nat. Assn. Realtors, Ill. Assn. Realtors, Northwest Suburban Bd. Realtors, Ill. Health Care Assn., Phi Alpha Delta. Republican. Roman Catholic. Clubs: Amateur Radio, No. Ill. DX Assn. Office: Land of Lincoln Real Estate Ltd 2081 Bloomingdale Rd Glendale Heights IL 60139

HAJIM, EDMUND A., financial services executive; b. Los Angeles, July 26, 1936; s. Jack and Sally H.; m. Barbara E. Melnick, Aug. 8, 1965; children: Geoffrey Blair, Jon Bradley, Corey Brooke. B.S., U. Rochester, 1958; M.B.A., Harvard U., 1964. Research analyst Capital Research Co. subs. Capital Group, Inc., N.Y.C., 1964-66, office mgr., 1966-67; v.p., dir. Capital Mgmt. Service, 1967-69; pres. Greenwich Mgmt. Co., Conn., 1969; pres., dir. Growth Fund Am., 1969-70, Income Fund Am., 1970; sr. v.p. E.F. Hutton, Nat. Instl. Equity, N.Y.C., 1974-77; ptnr., mng. dir. Lehman Bros., N.Y.C., 1977, pres. securities div., 1977-79; chmn. Lehman Mgmt. Co., N.Y.C., 1980-83; pres., chmn. Furman, Selz, Mager, Dietz & Birney Inc., N.Y.C., 1983—; ptnr., mng. dir., Lehman Bros Kuhn Loeb & Kuhn Loeb Lehman Bros. Internat., N.Y.C., 1977-83; chmn., dir. Lehman Corp., One William St. Fund, Lehman Cash Mgmt. Fund; chmn. Lehman Capital Fund, Greenwich, Conn., Bd. Trust Fund, Fund Source and FFB Funds Trust; bd. dirs. Xerox Fin. Svcs. Inc. Past chmn. bd. trustees Brunswick Sch., Greenwich; mem. pres. council U. Rochester, 1975—, now trustee. Served with USN, 1958-61. Mem. Inst. Chartered Fin. Analysts, Chief Execs. Orgn., N.Y. Soc. Security Analysts (past dir.), Bond Club, Harvard Club, Wall St. Club, Stanwich Country Club. Office: Furman Selz Mager Dietz & Birney Inc 230 Park Ave New York NY 10169

HAKIM, ALI HUSSEIN, export company executive, consultant; b. Mushref, Lebanon, Aug. 13, 1943; came to U.S., 1973; s. Hussein A. and Sabah (Wazni) H.; m. Raafat M. Siklawi, July 2, 1972; children—Hussein, Ronny, Sameer, Mazen. B.S.B.A., Beirut U., 1970; postgrad. in acctg. Wayne State U., 1975; M.A. in Econs. and Politics, U. Detroit, 1980. Supr. Al-Mouharer Newspaper, Beirut, 1964-67; prin. Lebanese Soc. for Edn., Beirut, 1967-72; field services adviser Chrysler Corp., Detroit, 1973-75; owner, operator H & R Parking Co., Detroit, 1975-81; comptroller Met. Detroit Youth, 1979-82; pres. Hakim Export Import, Detroit, 1979-82, Hakim Export, Detroit, 1983—; pres. Gen. Bus. for Internat. Trade Corp., N.Y.C.; cons. to trading and investment agys., Africa, Middle East; budget cons. Met. Detroit Youth Found., 1983—. Research on U.S./China trade relations, 1980, U.S. monetary policy, 1981, internat. mktg., 1983. Mem. Republican Presdl. Task Force, 1982—. Mem. Am. Mgmt. Assn., Acctg. Aid Soc. Club: Senatorial (Washington).

HAKIM, LOUISE ZALTA, import company executive; b. Mobile, Ala., July 14, 1922; d. Nouri L. and Zahda M. (Lizmi) Zalta; m. Albert S. Hakim, May 24, 1942; children—Saul, Betty, Theda, Eddie, Jack, Joseph, Shirley. Student Northeast U., Monroe, La., 1956-58. Mgr. York Children Shop, Monroe, La., 1942-60; importer, owner Tidy Ties Corp., Monroe, 1960-70, inventor, 1970—, developer, 1974—, researcher, 1980—, dir., 1960—. Designer, developer infant shoe ties, 1965, medicine container, 1965; inventor, designer, developer blanket holder, 1976, squeeze toys, 1976, pacifier, 1980. Mem. U.S. C. of C. Republican. Jewish. Avocations: tennis; golf; fishing, sculpture. Home: PO Box 4826 Monroe LA 71211 Office: Tidy Corp 2813 DeSiard St Monroe LA 71201

HALBERT, ROBERT ORLAF, insurance company executive; b. Denver, May 9, 1937; s. Harold Nolan and Dorothy Irene (Swanson) H.; m. Jean Anne Billigmeier, June 20, 1959; children: John Gregory, Mark Bradford. BA in Sociology, Dartmouth Coll., 1959. CLU, chartered fin. cons. Asst. gen. agt. Equitable of Iowa, Denver, 1962-71; trust officer United Bank of Denver, 1971-75; chmn., pres., chief exec. officer Fidelity Nat. Life Ins. Co., Denver, 1975—; mem. ins. com. Assn. Bank Holding Cos. 1976-85, chmn. 1983-84; speaker Am. Bankers Assn., Colo. Bankers Assn., Colo. Brokerage Assn., 1975—; bd. dirs. Lincoln Agy., Inc., Denver, 1975—; dir. United Bank of Arapahoe, Denver, 1982-85; pres. United Banks Ins. Svcs., Inc., 1975—. Contbr. numerous articles to publs. Chmn. Denver Metro Sports Com., 1984-88. Served to capt. USMC, 1959-62. Mem. Am. Soc. Chartered Life Underwriters, Colo. Assn. Life Underwriters, Colo. Heart Assn. (bd. dirs. 1975-86, Vol. of Yr. 1985), Am. Cancer Soc. (bd. dirs. 1972-85), Colo. Sports Hall of Fame (dir. 1983—), Denver C. of C., Dartmouth Alumnae Assn. (pres. 1972-74), Ins. Fin. Affiliates of Am. (pres. 1987—). Republican. Club: Valley Country (Aurora, Colo.). Home: 6657 E Dartmouth Ave Denver CO 80224 Office: Fidelity Nat Life Ins Co Three United Bank Ctr 1700 Broadway Denver CO 80274

HALBUR, ALVIN ALFRED, JR., advertising executive; b. Racine, Wis., June 21, 1957; s. Alvin Alfred and Doris Mae (Schweitzer) H. BS, U. Wis., 1979, postgrad., 1982-83. Jr. acct. North Shore Savs. and Loan, Milw., 1979-81; staff acct. EZ Painter Corp., Milw., 1981-84; with Pub. Relations Bd., Chgo., 1984-86; controller Doremus/Porter Novelli, Chgo., 1986-87, v.p., 1988—. Republican. Methodist. Home: 1 E Scott Apt 1511 Chicago IL 60610 Office: Doremus Porter Novelli 303 E Wacker Dr Chicago IL 60601

HALBY, ANTHONY WAYNE, insurance agent; b. Mesa, Ariz., Nov. 22, 1949; s. Tony and Linda (Mawson) H.; m. Charlene T. Pavao, Aug. 21, 1971; children: Gabriella Marie, Matthew James, Mark Anthony, Michael Alfred, Joseph Christopher. BS in Mktg., BS in Mgmt., Woodbury U., 1971. Pvt. practice ins. sales La Crescenta, Calif. and Nevada City, Calif., 1971—. Named to Leading Producers Roundtable, Nat. Assn. Health Underwriters, 1982. Mem. (founding) Los Angeles Assn. Health Underwriters (bd. dirs. 1981-83, pres. 1982-83), (charter) Calif. Assn. Health Underwriters, Sacramento Assn. Health Underwriters (pres. 1988—). Republican. Roman Catholic. Home: 11534 Country View Way Grass Valley CA 95945 Office: 206 Sacramento St #304 Nevada City CA 95959 Office: 3131 Foothill Blvd Suite H La Crescenta CA 91214

HALE, CHARLES FRANKLIN, finanical services company executive; b. Betsy Layne, Ky., Jan. 4, 1931; s. Charles E. and Bessie Lee (Vest) H.; m. Joy Lorraine Turner, Aug. 7, 1954; children: Holly Lee, Suzanne. B.S., La Salle U., 1954; J.D., Temple U., 1976. C.P.A., Pa. Mgr. internal audit Ins. Co. N.Am., Phila., 1963-67; asst. controller Ins. Co. N.Am., 1967-72, controller, 1972-74, v.p., controller, 1974-76; v.p., gen. auditor INA Corp., Phila., 1977-82, CIGNA, Phila., 1982—; dir. various INA Corp. cos. Pres.

bd. commrs. Lower Gwynedd Twp., Pa., 1969-83. 1st lt. Fin. Corps. U.S. Army, 1956-58. Recipient Outstanding Achievement award La Salle Acctg. Assn., Phila., 1978; named Citizen of Week Ambler Gazette, Involved Neighbor INA Corp. Mem. Am. Inst. C.P.A.s, Pa. Inst. C.P.A.s, ABA, Pa. Bar Assn. Republican. Presbyterian. Home: 912 Forest Dr Gwynedd Valley PA 19437 Office: Cigna Corp One Logan Sq Philadelphia PA 19103 *

HALE, IRVING, investment executive, writer; b. Denver, Mar. 22, 1932; s. Irving Jr. and Lucile (Beggs) H.; B.A. with distinction, U. Colo., 1964; m. Joan E. Domenico, Dec. 29, 1954; children—Pamela Joan, Beth Ellen. Security analyst Colo. Nat. Bank, Denver, 1955-58; asst. sec. Centennial Fund, Inc., Second Centennial Fund, Inc., Gryphon Fund, Inc., Meridian Fund, Inc., 1959-68; portfolio mgr. Twenty Five Fund, Inc. (formerly Trend Fund, Inc.), Denver, 1969-72; v.p. Alpine Corp., Denver, 1971-72; dir. research Hanifen, Imhoff & Samford, Inc., Denver, 1973-77; v.p. research First Fin. Securities, Inc., 1977-82; arbitrator Nat. Assn. Securities Dealers; contbg. editor Nat. OTC Stock Jour., 1982-83; exec. v.p. research/corp. Fin. R. B. Marich, Inc., 1983—. lectr., Denver Public Schs. Community Talent, 1975—; bd. dirs. Community Resources, Inc., 1981-88, v.p. 1988—. Fellow Fin. Analysts Fedn.; mem. Denver Soc. Security Analysts, Radio Hist. Assn. Colo. (pres. 1977-78), Nat. Assn. of Securities Dealers (abitrator), Mensa, Baker St. Irregulars, Beta Sigma Tau. Republican. Episcopalian. Club: Denver Press (assoc. mem.). Columnist, Denver Post; contbr. articles to profl. jours. Home: 1642 Ivanhoe St Denver CO 80220 Office: R B Marich Inc 1512 Larimer St Suite 800 Denver CO 80202

HALE, JAMES C., III, investment banking executive; b. San Francisco, Feb. 9, 1952; s. James C. and Ruth Hale; m. Donna Jean Dorward, June 28, 1976; children: Kristen, James, Charles. BS, U. Calif., Berkeley, 1974; MBA, Harvard U., 1978. CPA, Calif. Acct. Peat, Marwick, Main, San Francisco, 1974-76; v.p. corp. strategic planning Bank Am., San Francisco, 1978-81, exec. asst. to chmn., 1981-82; gen. ptnr. Montgomery Securities, San Francisco, 1982—. Mem. Am. Inst. CPAs. Office: Montgomery Securities 600 Montgomery St San Francisco CA 94111

HALE, KAYCEE, research marketing professional; b. Mount Hope, W.Va., July 18, 1947; d. Bernard McFadden and Virginia Lucille (Mosley) H. AA, Compton Coll., 1965; BS, Calif. State U., Dominguez Hills, 1981. Fashion model O'Bryant Talent Agy., L.A., 1967-77; faculty mem. L.A. Trade-Tech. Coll., 1969-71, Fashion Inst., L.A., 1969-77, 1975—; pres. The Fashion Co., L.A., 1970-75; co-host The Fashion Game TV Show, L.A., 1982-87; exec. dir. Fashion Inst. Design and Merchandising Resource & Rsch. Ctr., L.A., 1975—, Fashion Inst. Design and Merchandising Mus. and Libr., L.A., 1979—; lectr. in field, internat., 1969—. Author: (brochure) What's Your I.Q. (Image Quotient)?; (tape) Image Builders; contbg. editor Library Mgmt. in Rev. Adv. bd. Calif. State U., Long Beach, 1988-91. Mem. ALA, Spl. Librs. Assn. (pres. elect 1986—, pres. 1987-88, bd. dirs. So. Calif. chpt. 1985—), Spl. Librs. Adv. Coun. (pub. rels. com. 1987—), SLA Libr. Mgmt. Div. (chmn.-elect 1987-88, chmn. 1988-89, pres.'s task force on image of libr./info. profl.), Textile Assn. L.A. (bd. dirs. 1985-87), Calif. Media and Libr. Educators Assn., Am. Mktg. Assn., Western Mus. Conf., Am. Mus. Assn., Costume Soc. Am. Office: Fashion Inst Design and Merchandising 818 W 7th St Los Angeles CA 90017

HALE, RICHARD THOMAS, JR., investment banking company executive; b. Abington, Pa., July 17, 1945; s. Richard Thomas Sr. and Elizabeth (Parrish) H.; m. Eleanor Armsted Gibson, July 27, 1969; children: Delia, Thomas, Gibson. BA, Yale U., 1968; MBA, U. Pa., 1972. Securities analyst Girard Bank, Phila., 1972-74, Robert Garrett & Sons, Balt., 1974, Alex Brown & Sons, Balt., 1974—; v.p. Alex Brown & Sons, 1980-82, prin., 1983-85, mng. dir., 1986—, also bd. dirs.; Treas. Bryn Mawr Sch., Balt., 1983—; pres. Guilford Assn., Balt., 1986—. Lt. USN, 1968-70. Mem. Balt. Security Analysts. Soc. (pres. 1982-83), Maryland Club, Elkridge Club, Brook Club (N.Y.C.), Casino Club (Nantucket). Democrat. Episcopalian. Home: 224 Northway Baltimore MD 21218 Office: Alex Brown & Sons 135 E Baltimore St Baltimore MD 21202

HALE, ROBERT ASHLEY, manufacturing company manager; b. Corning, N.Y., Oct. 6, 1938; s. William Joseph and Louise (McQuigan) H.; m. Donna Jane Wereley, Nov. 10, 1957; children: Robert A. Jr., Michael Joseph. AS in Machine Design, Elmira Coll, 1967, BS in Math. and Physics, 1971. Office clk. Remington Rand, Elmira, N.Y., 1958-60; engr. tech. Corning (N.Y.) Glass, 1960-65, equipment engr., 1965-71; mgr. engring. BMT Mfg., Horseheads, N.Y., 1971-72, SI Handling Systems, Inc., Easton, Pa., 1972—. Patentee material handling equipment, U.S. and Fgn., 1977, 82, 86. Served with U.S. Army, 1955-62. Mem. Soc. Mfg. Engrs., Computer and Automated Systems Assn., Robot Inst. Am., Robotic Internat. (vice chmn. for accessory group 1980-82). Republican. Home: 2651 Northhampton St Easton PA 18042 Office: SI Handling Systems Inc PO Box 70 Easton PA 18042

HALE, ROGER LOUCKS, manufacturing company executive; b. Plainfield, N.J., Dec. 13, 1934; s. Lloyd and Elizabeth (Adams) H.; m. Sandra Johnston, June 10, 1961 (div.); children: Jocelyn, Leslie, Nina. B.A., Brown U., 1956; M.B.A., Harvard U., 1961. With Tennant Co., Mpls., 1961—; pres. Tennant Co., 1975—, chief exec. officer, 1976—, also dir.; dir. First Bank Systems, Donaldson Co., St. Paul Cos., Dayton Hudson Corp.; vice chmn. Minn. Bus. Partnership; co-chmn. Minn. Quality Council. Party sec. Democratic Farm Labor Party, 1968-70; bd. dirs. Citizens League, 1966-68, 81, Walker Art Center, 1970-88; mem. Met. Planning Commn. Mpls., 1965-67; vice-chmn. Minn. Bus. Ptnrship, 1980; chmn. Neighborhood Employment Network, 1980. Served with USN, 1956-59. Named Exec. of Yr. Corp. Report mag., 1988. Office: Tennant Co 701 N Lilac Dr Minneapolis MN 55440

HALE, SELDON HOUSTON, sales executive; b. Jefferson, Tex., June 11, 1948; s. Woster Seldon and Geraldine Leston (Sacra) Hale, Jr.; student San Antonio Coll., 1966-70, East Tex State U., 1970-71, U. Tex., Arlington, 1972-76; m. Kay Ellen Moler, Aug. 7, 1970; children: Emily Michelle, Denise Kathleen. Asst. mgr. service center Phillips Petroleum Co., San Antonio, 1968-69; asst. youth dir. N.W. YMCA, San Antonio, 1969-70; youth dir. Greenville (Tex.) YMCA, 1970-71; asst. mgr. men's and boy's dept. Watson's Dept. Store, Arlington, 1971-76; gen. mgr. Pate's Men's Store, San Antonio, 1976-77; bus. mgr. Bruce Lowrie Chevrolet, Ft. Worth, 1977-80; fin. mgr. Late Chevrolet Co., Richardson, Tex., 1980-84; nat. sales mgr. King Louie Internat., Inc., Grandview, Mo., 1984-89; sales mgr. Melia Assocs., Inc., Knoxville, Tenn., 1989—. Vice chmn. Greenville 4th of July Celebration, 1971; chmn. youth com. Arlington YMCA, 1973-75, sec. bd., 1976; chmn. bd. Tex. Youth and Govt. program, 1976-79; mem. U. Tex. Maverick Club, 1979-80, 82-85, U. Tex.-Arlington Fastbreak Club, 1984-85. Recipient Dedicated Service award Arlington Fellowship of Christian Athletes, 1975-76, Membership Producer award, 1975; Dedicated Service award, Arlington YMCA, 1976; Outstanding Service award Tex. State Youth and Govt. Program, 1970-71. Mem. Am. Mgmt. Assn., Southwestern Men's and Boys' Apparel Club, U.S. Golf Assn., Arlington Fellowship of Christian Athletes (pres.-elect 1976), Chevrolet Soc. Sales Execs., Young Execs. in Splty. Advt. Presbyterian. Home: 12032 Hemlock Overland Park KS 66213 Office: King Louie Internat Inc 13500 15th St Grandview MO 64030

HALE, SHADRACH PAYNE, real estate lawyer; b. Trenton, Ga., Jan. 13, 1912; s. Shabrach Jerome and Clara (Street) H.; m. Margaret Virginia Ashworth, Apr. 16, 1937; children: S. Jerome II, Patricia Elaine. LLB, Chattanooga Coll.Law, 1931, LLM, 1934. Bar: Ga. 1931, Tenn. 1936. Mem. firm Hale & Hale, Trenton, 1931-36, McClure, McClure & Hale(formerly McClure & McClure), Chattanooga, 1938-41, Hale & Ellis, Chattanooga, 1942-80, Hale, Hale & McInturff, Chattanooga, 1980—; sec. Milligan-Reynolds Guaranty Title Agy., Inc., 1941—, exec. v.p., 1975, chmn. bd., chief Exec. officer, 1976—, dir., 1944—. Mem. ABA, Tenn. Bar Assn., Chattanooga Bar Assn., Sigma Delta Kappa. Prebyterian. Clubs: Chattanooga Golf and Country, Mountain City. Lodge: Kiwanis. Home: 1302 Heritage Landing Dr Chattanooga TN 37405 Office: Hale Hale & McInturff 724 Cherry St Chattanooga TN 37402

HALES, JACK, JR., accountant; b. Chillecothe, Tex., Nov. 8, 1933; s. Jack and Frances Esto (Burch) H.; BBA, Pan Am. U., 1957. CPA, Tex.; m. Lula Mae Ivey, Oct. 8, 1954; children: Jack Robert, Pat Lawrence, Lynn Candise, Richard Allen. Staff acct. R.J. Welch, CPA, Weslaco, Tex., 1956-60; ptnr. Welch, White & Co., Weslaco, 1961-85, Hales, Bradford & White, Weslaco, 1985-87, pres. Hales, Bradford & White PC, Weslaco, Brownsville and Harlingen, Tex., 1987-88, ptnr. Hales, Bradford & Allen, CPA, 1989—; v.p., bd. dir. Seal Produce Co., Pharr, Tex., 1975-85. Treas., bd. dirs. Mid Valley Elem. Sch., Weslaco, 1979-84, Magic Valley Pizza Inc., McAllen, Tex., 1986—; bd. dirs. United Fund, 1963. With USAF, 1951-53. Named Boss of Yr. Weslaco Jaycees, 1979. Mem. Weslaco C. of C., Valley C. of C., Aircraft Owners and Pilots Assn., Am. Inst. CPA's, Tex. Soc. CPA's, Am. Acctg. Assn., Am. Taxation Assn. Republican. Baptist. Home: PO Box 8458 Weslaco TX 78596 Office: Hales Bradford & Allen 322 S Missouri Ave PO Box 8458 Weslaco TX 78596

HALEY, BRIAN PAUL, chemical company executive; b. S.I., N.Y., Mar. 1, 1945; s. Frank X. and Marianne (Wieser) H.; m. Bevery L. Leonard, Apr. 12, 1969; children: Christine B., B. Paul. BChemE, U. Del., 1968, MBA, 1972. Mem. prodn. mgmt. staff Allied Chem., Claymont, Del., 1968-73; mem. mktg. rsch. staff Allied Chem., Morristown, N.J., 1973-75; tech. mgr. Allied Chem., Morristown, 1975-77; asst. regional sales mgr. Allied Chem., Phila., 1977-79; regional sales mgr. Allied Chem., Pitts., 1979-81; mgr. mktg. Allied Chem., Morristown, 1981-84, dir. mktg. and sales, 1984-86; v.p., gen. mgr. field ops. Airco Indsl. Gasses div. BOC, Murray Hill, N.J., 1986—. Mem. Fiddler's Elbow Country Club (Lamington, N.J.). Republican. Roman Catholic. Home: 238 Lake Rd Basking Ridge NJ 07920 Office: Airco Indsl Gasses 575 Mountain Ave Murray Hill NJ 07974

HALEY, JOHN F., marketing executive; b. Boston, Mar. 13, 1952; s. Thomas Vincent and Reita Elenore (Doherty) H.; m. Cheryl M. Haley; children: Jennifer, Erin. BS, Bridgewater State Coll., 1977; MBA, U. Pitts., 1980. Project mgr. Akzo Chems., Inc., 1981-82, mgr. dist. sales, 1982-84, mgr. mktg., 1986—; product mgr. Enko Am., Inc., 1984-86.

HALEY, KEVIN JON, mechanical engineer; b. Salem, Oreg., May 2, 1959; s. Bryon Kermith Haley and Janet Claire (Carter) Tolman; m. Karen Louise Terakawa, Sept. 19, 1987. BS in Mech. Engring., U. Wash., Seattle, 1981. Design liason engr. Boeing Aerospace Co., Seattle, 1981-82, mech., design engr., 1982-84; mfg. engr. Intel Corp., Santa Clara, Calif., 1984-85; mfg. engr. supr. Intel Corp., Folsom, Calif., 1985-87; mfg. engr. mgr. Intel Corp., Santa Clara, 1987—. Mem. San Francisco Boardsailing Assn. (charter). Republican. Mem. Unity Ch. Office: Intel Corp 2625 Walsh Ave Santa Clara CA 95052-8122

HALF, ROBERT, personnel recruiting executive, author; b. N.Y.C., Nov. 11, 1918; s. Sidney and Pauline (Kahn) H.; m. Maxine Levison, June 17, 1945; children: Nancy Half Asch, Peggy Half Silbert. B.S., NYU, 1940. C.P.A., N.Y. Staff acct. Ernst & Whinney, 1940-43; mgr. office and personnel Kayser-Roth Corp., 1943-48; founder Robert Half Internat., Inc., N.Y.C., 1948—, Accountemps Inc., U.S., Can., Eng., 1964—; guest speaker Data Processing Mgmt. Assn., Nat. Assn. Accts.; guest on TV and radio shows in, U.S. and Can.; mem. panel of experts Boardroom Reports; pioneer in specialized personnel recruiting. Author: The Robert Half Way To Get Hired in Today's Job Market, 1981, Robert Half on Hiring, 1985, Robert Half's Success Guide for Accountants, 1984, 2d edit. 1987, Making It Big in Data Processing, 1987, How To Hire Smart, How To Keep Your Best People, How to Get Your Employees to Do What They're Supposed To Do, How to Check References When References Are Hard to Check, 52 Good Ideas on Hiring, Firing and More; monthly columnist Nat. Bus. Employment Weekly, Management Accounting, New Accountant, MIS Week, editorial advisor: Jour. Accountancy, Management Accounting, Personnel Jour., Jour. Staffing Recruitment; mem. editorial bd.: CPA Personnel Report, Exec. Productivity; contbr. numerous articles to mags. and newspapers. Expert witness subcoms. U.S. Senate; co-author U.S. tax bill Build Am.; mem. Bd. Appeals Village of Saddle Rock, Great Neck, N.Y., 1956-62. Recipient John Madden award NYU, 1985. Mem. Am. Acctg. Assn., Assn. Personnel Consultants N.Y. (pres. 1963-64, dir. 1960-65, Harold Nelson award 1986), Nat. Assn. Personnel Cons., N.Y. State Soc. CPA's, AICPA, Fla. Inst. CPA's, Nat. Assn. Accts., Am. Mgmt. Assn., Adminstrv. Mgmt. Soc., Am. Soc, Personnel Adminstrs., Assn. Human Resources Cons., Accts. Club Am., Employment Mgrs. Assn., Data Processing Mgmt. Assn., Internat. Platform Assn. Lodge: Toastmasters. Office: Accountemps Inc 111 Pine St San Francisco CA 94111

HALICZER, JAMES SOLOMON, lawyer; b. Ft. Myers, Fla., Oct. 27, 1952; s. Julian and Margaret (Shepard) H.; m. Paula Fleming, Oct. 3, 1987. BA in English Lit., U. So. Fla., 1976, MA in Polit. Sci., 1978; JD, Stetson U., 1981. Bar: Fla. 1982. Assoc. Conrad, Scherer & James, Ft. Lauderdale, Fla., 1982-86, ptnr., 1986—; assoc. Bernard & Mauro, Ft. Lauderdale, 1985-86. Mem. ABA, Fla. Bar Assn., Broward County Bar Assn., Assn. Trial Lawyers Am., Def. Rsch. Inst., Am. Acad. Hosp. Attys., Phi Kappa Phi, Pi Sigma Alpha, Omicron Delta Kappa. Democrat. Methodist. Office: Conrad Scherer & James 633 S Federal Hwy Fort Lauderdale FL 33301

HALKIAS, CHRISTOS CONSTANTINE, electronics educator, consultant; b. Monastiraki, Doridos, Greece, Aug. 23, 1933; s. Constantine C. and Alexandra V. (Papapostolou) H.; m. Demetra Saras, Jan. 22, 1961; children—Alexandra, Helen-Joanna. B.S. in Elec. Engring., CCNY, 1957; M.Sc. in Elec. Engring., Columbia U., 1958, Ph.D., 1962. Prof. elec. engring. Columbia U., N.Y.C., 1962-73; prof. electronics Nat. Tech. U. Athens, Greece, 1973—, Fulbright vis. prof., 1969, dir. infomatics div., 1983-86; dir. Nat. Research Found., Athens, 1983-87; cons. Nat. Bank of Greece, Athens, 1980—, Ergo Bank, Athens, 1975—. Author: Electronic Devices and Circuits, 1967; Integrated Electronics, 1972; Electronic Fundamentals and Applications, 1976, Design of Electronic Filters, 1988; contbr. articles to profl. jours. Recipient D.B. Steinman award CCNY, 1956; Higgins fellow Columbia U., 1958. Mem. IEEE (sr., Centennial medal 1984, chmn. Greek sect. 1982-86), Sigma Xi. Home: 4 Kosti Palama St, Paleo Psyhico, Athens Greece Office: Nat Tech Univ Athens, 42 Patission Ave, Athens Greece

HALKYARD, EDWIN MILTON, diversified industrial company executive; b. N.Y.C., July 20, 1934; s. Edwin Milton and Edna Alice (Franklin) H.; m. Joan Sherwin, Sept. 15, 1956; children: Edwin, Martin, Christopher, Jonathan. A.B. in Econs., Princeton U., 1956. In various employee relations positions PPG Industries, Pitts., 1956-67; mgr. indsl. relations Allied Corp., Morristown, N.J., 1967-68, dir. indsl. relations, labor relations and employee relations, 1968-78, v.p., corp. relations, 1978-79, sr. v.p. human resources, 1979—; bd. dirs. City Fed. Savs. Bank, Bedminster, N.J.; mem. employee relations com. Bus Roundtable, Washington, 1973—. Trustee St. Clare's Hosp., Denville, N.J., 1972—; pres. Arts Council Morris Area, Madison, N.J.; bd. overseers Found. at N.J. Inst. Tech., 1980—. Served to capt. U.S. Army, 1957. Republican. Episcopalian. Club: Princeton (N.Y.C.). Office: Allied Signal Inc PO Box 3000R Morristown NJ 07960

HALL, ANDREW J., oil industry executive. Exec. v.p. Phibro Energy Inc., Greenwich, Conn., until 1987, pres., 1987—. Office: Phibro Energy Inc 600 Steamboat Rd Greenwich CT 06830 *

HALL, ARTHUR EUGENE, JR., financial services company executive; b. Wyandotte, Mich., Sept. 3, 1955; s. Arthur E. and Sally J. (Potter) H.; m. Michaeleen O'Flynn, Feb. 26, 1983; children: Nicholas Adam, Alex Edward, Meredith Lynne. BA in Econs., Albion Coll., 1977; MS in Mgmt., Purdue U., 1979. Bus. planner Hillenbrand Industries, Batesville, Ind., 1979-81; cons. Strategic Mgmt. Assocs., West Lafayette, 1981-82; mgr. Arthur Andersen & Co., Chgo., 1982-85; v.p. strategic planning Community Mut. Ins., Cin., 1985-88; mgr., bus. devel. GE Capital Auto Fin. Svcs., Barrington, Ill., 1988—. Mem. Am. Mgmt. Assn., Planning Forum, Omicron Delta Epsilon, Omicron Delta Kappa. Baptist. Home: 3508 Wisteria Dr Crystal Lake IL 60012 Office: GE Capital 600 Hart Rd Barrington IL 60010

HALL, BEVERLY ELAINE, television director; b. Port Arthur, Tex., Feb. 18, 1957; d. Milton Crawford and Jacqueline Ruth (Pevoto) H. BS in Mass Communications, Lamar U., 1979. Lic. real estate agt., Tex. Tech. dir. Port Arthur Cablevision, 1975-76; prodn. asst. Sta. KJAC-TV affiliate NBC, Port Arthur, 1976-80; word processor The Mansion on Turtle Creek, Dallas, 1980-81; prodn. asst. Sta. KBMT-TV affilate ABC, Beaumont, Tex., 1982; air dir. Sta. KFDM-TV affilate CBS, Beaumont, 1982—; coordinator TV talent Bum Phillips Celebrity Golf Tournament, Bob Hope Birthday Celebration, Port Arthur, 1980; real estate agt. Am. Real Estate, Port Neches, Tex., 1982. Producer, dir.: Life in America, 1982; author: (tng. jour.) Air Director's Manuel, 1987. Republican. Baptist. Home: 2714 S Kitchen Dr Port Neches TX 77651 Office: Sta KFDM-TV 2955 Interstate 10 E Beaumont TX 77706

HALL, BONNIE BAKER, materials management executive; b. Cadiz, Ky., Dec. 20, 1944; d. Bethel Earl and Dorothy Nell (Hall) Baker; m. Robert B. Hall, Apr. 9, 1965. Clk. typist B.F. Goodrich Chemical, Calvert City, Ky., 1966-71, sr. account clk., 1971-78, stores supr., 1978-84, purchasing sec., 1984-85, materials controller, 1985-88, buyer, 1988—; owner, mgr. private resort and lodging facility, 1978-88. Author poetry, songs. Active indentifying job opportunities for handicapped with local industry, 1978-88. Mem. Songwriters Guild, B.F. Goodrich Mgmt. Club (v.p. 1972, plant safety com. 1980-81, program chmn. 1986-87, career day rep. 1987, 88, 89), Land Between the Lakes Assn. Democrat. Baptist. Office: BF Goodrich Hwy 1523 PO Box 527 Calvert City KY 42029

HALL, CHARLES W., bank executive; b. Denver, June 4, 1944; s. Charles F. and Frances (Cockrell) H.; m. Susan Watkins, Aug. 17, 1968; children: Jennifer L., Amy E., Lisa S. BA, Westminster Coll., 1966; MA, U. Mo., 1970. Economist Fed. Res. Bank Cleve., 1970-75, asst. v.p., 1975-77; asst. v.p. Nat. City Bank, Cleve., 1977, v.p., 1978-81; sr. v.p. Nat. City Bank Corp., Cleve., 1981-84, exec. v.p., 1985—; lectr. Case Western Res. U., Cleve., 1977-85. Bd. advisors Ursiline Coll., Cleve., 1987; bd. dirs. Cleve. Ctr. for Econ. Edn., Cleve., 1984-87, Cleve. Edn. Fund, 1985—. Mem. Am. Banking Assn. (funds mgmt. com.), Am. Econs. Assn. Republican. Episcopalian. Clubs: Cleve. Skating, Chagrin Valley Country, Union. Home: 813 Sun Ridge Ln Chagrin Falls OH 44022

HALL, CHERYL ANN, data processing executive; b. San Diego, Sept. 29, 1954; d. Leo Franklin and Anita Lillian (Beuerlein) H. BA, U. Cin., 1979. Intern Lomark, Inc., Middletown, Ohio, 1974-78, mgmt. info. systems operator, 1978-79; dir. accounts Home Care, Inc., West Chester, Ohio, 1979-81; installation dir. SMS, Inc., Malvern, Pa., 1982-85, sr. installation dir., 1985—. Patron Sta. WVXU-FM, Cin., 1984—; sustaining mem. Cin. Zool. Soc., 1984—; advisor youth commn. United Synagogue Youth, Hamilton, Ohio, 1985—; mem. Leadership Council Jewish Fedn., Cin., 1985—, Jewish Community Ctr., Cin.; trustee Congregation Beth Israel, Hamilton, 1985—. Mem. Assn. for Systems Mgmt., Orgn. for Rehab. through Tng. (v.p. 1985-86). Home: 5543 Winton Rd Fairfield OH 45014 Office: SMS Inc 1801 Park 270 Suite 200 Saint Louis MO 63146

HALL, CHRISTOPHER EDWARD, packaging executive; b. Petersburg, Va., Aug. 12, 1962; s. Lawrence Henry and Mary Carlin (Ryan) H.; m. Kaisa Hollingsworth Bowman, Sept. 10, 1988. BA, Boston U., 1984. Sales rep. Bolloré Techs., Stonington, Conn., 1984-88; account mgr. Sonoco Products Co., St. Louis, 1988—. Area rep. alumni schs. com. Boston U., 1985-87; mem. Rep. Nat. Com., 1987—. Mem. Ducks Unltd., Sigma Alpha Epsilon. Roman Catholic. Home: 2317-C S 10th St Saint Louis MO 63104 Office: Sonoco Products Co PO Box 668 Hartselle AL 35640

HALL, DAVID RHEA, bank executive; b. Rogersville, Tenn., May 23, 1952; s. Sam and Anna B. (Woods) H.; m. G. Diane Price, Apr. 15, 1976; children: Matthew David, Callie Rebecca. BS, East Tenn. State U., 1974; grad., Nat. Sch. Retail Banking, Norman, Okla., 1983, Memphis State U., 1984, La. State U., 1987. Office worker, acct. Internat. Playing Card & Label Co., Rogersville, 1976-77; asst. mgr. Svc. Mdse., Kingsport, Tenn., 1977-78; mgr. collections Assocs. Fin. Svcs., Morristown, Tenn., 1978-80, asst. mgr., 1980-81; loan officer Erwin (Tenn.) Nat. Bank, 1981-86, asst. v.p., 1984-86; v.p., br. mgr. First Bank Rhea County, Spring City, Tenn., 1986—. Mem. Mayor's Indsl. Recruiting Com., Spring City; Spring City PTO. Mem. Am. Inst. Banking (rep. Chattanooga chpt. 1987-88), Spring City C. of C. (bd. dirs., treas. 1988—), Kiwanis (pres. Spring City chpt. 1988—). Democrat. Baptist. Home: Sable Hills Subdiv Spring City TN 37381 Office: First Bank Rhea County Front St Spring City TN 37381

HALL, DONALD JOYCE, greeting card company executive; b. Kansas City, Mo., July 9, 1928; s. Joyce Clyde and Elizabeth Ann (Dilday) H.; m. Adele Coryell, Nov. 28, 1953; children: Donald Joyce, Margaret Elizabeth, David Earl. A.B., Dartmouth, 1950; LL.D., William Jewell Coll., Denver U., 1977. With Hallmark Cards, Inc., Kansas City, Mo., 1953—; adminstrv. v.p. Hallmark Cards, Inc., 1958-66, pres., chief exec. officer, 1966-83, chmn. bd., 1983—, chief exec. officer, 1983-85, also dir.; dir. United Telecommunications, Inc., Dayton-Hudson Corp., William E. Coutts Co., Ltd.; past dir. Fed. Res. Bank Kansas City, Mut. Benefit Life Ins. Co., Business Men's Assurance Co., Commerce Bank Kansas City, 1st Nat. Bank Lawrence. Pres. Civic Council Greater Kansas City; past chmn. bd. Kansas City Assn. Trusts and Founds.; Bd. dirs. Am. Royal Assn., Friends of Art, Eisenhower Found.; bd. dirs. Kansas City Minority Suppliers Devel. Council, Kans. City Minority Suppliers Devel. Council, Harry S. Truman Library Inst., Kansas City Symphony; past pres. Pembroke Country Day Sch., Civic Council of Greater Kansas City; trustee, past chmn. exec. com. Midwest Research Inst.; trustee Nelson-Atkins Museum of Art. Served to 1st lt. AUS, 1950-53. Recipient Eisenhower Medallion award, 1973; Parsons Sch. Design award, 1977; 3d Ann. Civic Service award Hebrew Acad. Kansas City, 1976; Chancellor's medal U. Mo., Kansas City, 1977; Disting. Service citation U. Kans., 1980. Mem. Kansas City C. of C. (named Mr. Kansas City 1972, dir.), AIA (hon.). Home: 6320 Aberdeen Rd Shawnee Mission KS 66208 Office: Hallmark Cards Inc 2501 McGee Trafficway PO Box 580 Kansas City MO 64141 *

HALL, DONALD PERRY, utilities company executive, retired naval officer; b. Winthrop, Mass., Dec. 6, 1927; s. John E. and Gertrude (Perry) H.; m. Sarah Cranford, Aug. 4, 1952; 1 child, Donald Roy. BS, U.S. Naval Acad., 1950. Commd. ensign USN, 1950, advanced through grades to rear admiral, 1974; service in nuclear submarines including 1st North Pole crossing 1958; dep. comdr. for fleet support Naval Sea Systems Command, Washington, 1974-77; mgr. Trident Project, Washington, 1977-79; comdr. Submarine Group SIX, Charleston, S.C., 1979-81; retired USN, 1981; v.p. (nuclear) Ill. Power Co., Decatur, 1982—; cons. ASTA Corp., Solana Beach, Calif., 1981-82. Decorated Legion of Merit with 4 gold stars. Mem. Am. Nuclear Soc., Boiling Water Reactor Owner's Group (exec. overview com. 1987—). Republican. Roman Catholic. Office: Ill Power Co 500 S 27th St Decatur IL 62525

HALL, EDWIN HUDDLESTON, JR., investment company executive; b. Bklyn., Sept. 5, 1935; s. Edwin H. and Lois W. Hall; B.S. in Bus. Adminstrn., Boston U., 1957; m. Linda Robbins, July 13, 1958; children—Jeffrey, Lisa, Lesley. With Merrill Lynch, Pierce, Fenner & Smith, 1961-77, v.p., 1973-77, v.p. tax investment mktg., 1978-80, dir. sales support group, 1980-81, v.p., dir. mktg., individual fin. services div., 1982-84, v.p., dir. corp. human resources, 1984-86; chmn., chief exec. officer Merrill Lynch Bank and Trust, 1986-88; chmn., pres. Merrill Lynch Trust Co., 1987, pres. Merrill Lynch Trust Services, Inc., 1987—, pres. Merrill Lynch Fiduciary Services, Inc. 1987; dir. Merrill Lynch Nat. Fin. Corp., 1988—. presdl. interchange exec., Washington, serving as spl. asst. to pres. Govt. Nat. Mortgage Assn., 1977-78. Div. chmn. United Community Chest, Rochester, N.Y., 1975; bd. dirs. Old Colony chpt. ARC, 1966-68; treas. Rochester (N.Y.) Assn. Blind, 1976-77; pres. Opera Theatre Rochester, 1976-77, hon. chmn., 1978. Mem. Nat. Assn. Security Dealers (corp. fin. com. 1978—). Rochester Soc. Analysts, Rochester C. of C. (trustee, chmn. reaccreditation implementation com. 1976), Boston C. of C. (life), Boston U. Alumni Assn. (dir. 1970-72), Washington Valley Community Assn. (pres. 1981-83, chmn. bd. trustees, 1983—), mem. human resource com. SIA, 1984-86; trustee Security Industry Inst. at Wharton, 1986—, chmn., 1989—. Republican. Episcopalian. Clubs: Federal, Fort Hill (Boston); Genesee Valley (Rochester); Club at World Trade Center (N.Y.C.); Spring Brook Country (Morristown), Masons. Address: 173 Washington Valley Rd Morris Township NJ 07960 Office: 800 Scudder Mill Rd Princeton NJ also: World Fin Ctr New York NY also: 5th Ave Naples FL

HALL, GUY HERRING, forester; b. N.Y.C., Feb. 20, 1927; s. Guy Herring and Helen (Travis) H.; m. Barbara Morrison, May 3, 1952; children: Guy T.,

Bruce R., Todd M., Lesa A. BS, U. Calif., Berkeley, 1951. Lic. profl. forester, Calif. Forester Diamond Match Corp., Stirling City, Calif., 1951-53, dist. forester, 1953-57; Calif. timber-land buyer Diamond Match Corp., Chico, Calif., 1957-60; founder, pres. Forest Mgmt., Inc., Chico and Oroville, Calif., 1960—; pres. Cal Oak Lumber Co., Oroville, Calif., 1969—; cons. various state and fed. lumber cos., 1975—; bd. dirs. Cen. Valley Ins., Bermuda; industry advisor Butte County Pollution Bd., Oroville, 1969-71; adv. bd. U. Forest Products Lab., Berkeley, 1974-77. Contbr. articles to profl. jours. Speaker in field. Mem. Gov.'s Hardwood Com., State of Calif., 1981-83. Served to sgt. USAF, 1944-46. Mem. Soc. Am. Foresters, Calif. Lic. Foresters, Forest Products Research (sec. speaker), Hoo-Hoo Lumber Soc. (bd. dirs.). Republican. Club: Chico Tennis (pres. bd. dirs. 1968—). Home: 704 West 8th Ave Chico CA 95926

HALL, JAMES E., computer software executive; b. Phila., Aug. 27, 1933; s. James and Bella (Nottle) H.; m. Evelyn James, June 18, 1955; children: Elizabeth, A. Shelton, James Edward Jr. BS in Econs., Albright Coll., 1955. With IBM Corp., Phila., 1955-65; advisor Japan div. IBM Corp., Tokyo, 1962-63; mktg. mgr. IBM Corp., Syracuse, N.Y., 1963-65; pres Datamedia Corp., Endicott, N.Y., 1965-70, Educators Processing Service, Swathmore, Pa., 1970-74; sr. v.p. Shared Med. Systems Corp., Malvern, Pa., 1974-84; pres. Info. Tech. Corp., Malvern, 1984-87; pres., chief exec. officer, chmn. Rabbit Software Corp., Malvern, 1987—; also bd. dirs. Rabbit Software Corp.; bd. dirs. Fiber Optic Corp., Ann Arbor, Mich. Trustee Bapt. Children's Home, Phila., 1978-83. Mem. Aronomink Country Club. Republican. Office: Rabbit Software Corp 7 Great Valley Pkwy E Malvern PA 19355

HALL, JESSE SEABORN, banker; b. Atlanta, Sept. 26, 1929; s. Jesse Seaborn and Lusu (Ingram) H.; m. Nell Dupree Floyd, Nov. 11, 1951; children—Mark, Laura Hall Vaughn. A.B., Emory U., 1950, LL.B., 1955. Teller Trust Co. Bank, Atlanta, 1950-53, various positions, 1953-75, exec. v.p., 1975—; exec. v.p. Sun Trust Banks, Inc., 1985—; dir. Crawford & Co., Atlanta. Trustee Oglethorpe U., Atlanta, 1976—, Wesley Homes Inc., Atlanta, 1980-86, Egleston Hosp., Atlanta, 1983—. Served to 1st lt. USMCR, 1950-53, Korea. Mem. Am. Bankers Assn. (chmn. trust div. 1985-86). Clubs: Capital City, Commerce. Office: SunTrust Banks Inc PO Box 4418 Atlanta GA 30302

HALL, JOE E., trucking company executive; b. 1938; married. Student, Memphis State U. Dist. mgr. Roadway Express Inc., 1968-73; regional mgr. Spector Freight System Inc., 1973, PIE, 1973-76; terminal mgr. Mason Dixon Lines, 1976-77; with Transcon Lines, 1977—, mgr. Western div., 1978-79, sr. v.p. ops., 1979-82, pres., chief operating officer, 1982-83, pres., chief exec. officer, 1983—; pres., chief exec. officer Transcon Inc., 1983—. Office: Transcon Lines 5700 S Eastern Ave Los Angeles CA 90040

HALL, JOHN BENTLEY, JR., insurance executive; b. Raven, Va., July 13, 1918; s. John Bentley Sr. and Stella Dale (Linkous) H.; m. Madeline June Williams, Mar. 3, 1945; 1 child, Sharon Kay. BSBA, Bluefield (W.Va.) Bus. Coll. Owner J. Bentley Hall Ins. Agy., Pearisburg, Va., 1954—. Master sgt. USAF, 1941-45, PTO. Mem. Masons (sec. 1963-67), Shriners. Republican. Home: PO Box 417 Pembroke VA 24134 Office: 510 Wondrah Ave Pearisburg VA 24134

HALL, JOHN GLENN, litigation technology company executive; b. Boise, Idaho, Feb. 18, 1948; s. Glenn Winford Hall and Mildred Electa Hall. BS in Physics, U. Idaho, 1971. Propr., mgr. John Glenn Hall Co., Boise, 1972—. Office: PO Box 2683 Boise ID 83701-2683

HALL, JOHN RICHARD, oil company executive; b. Dallas, Nov. 30, 1932; s. John W. and Agnes (Sanders) H.; m. Donna S. Stauffer, May 10, 1980. B.Chem. Engring., Vanderbilt U., 1955. Chem. engr. Esso Standard Oil Co., Balt., 1956-58, Ashland Oil Co., Ky., 1959-63; coordinator carbon black div. Ashland Oil Co., Houston, 1963-65; exec. asst. v.p. Ashland Oil Co., 1965-66, v.p., 1966-68, sr. v.p., 1970-71; also dir.; pres. Ashland Chem. Co., 1971-74; exec. v.p. Ashland Oil, Inc., 1974—, group operating officer, 1976—, chief exec. officer petroleum and chems., 1978—, vice chmn., chief operating officer, 1979-81, chmn., chief exec. officer, 1981—; bd. dirs. Banc One Corp., Columbus, Reynolds Metals Co., Richmond, Va. Trustee Vanderbilt U., Nashville, mem. com. visitors Engring. Sch.; bd. curators Transylvania U., Lexington, Ky. Served as 2d lt., Chem. Corps AUS, 1955-56. Mem. Chem. Mfrs. Assn., Nat. Petroleum Refiners Assn., Am. Petroleum Inst., Nat. Petroleum Council, Bus. Roundtable, Tau Delta Pi, Sigma Chi, Delta Kappa. Republican. Home: 99 Stoneybrook Dr Ashland KY 41101 Office: Ashland Oil Inc PO Box 391 Ashland KY 41114 also: Ashland Oil Inc 1000 Ashland Dr Russell KY 41169

HALL, LARRY D., energy company executive; b. Hastings, Nebr., Nov. 8, 1942; s. Willis E. and Stella W. (Eckoff) H.; m. Jeffe D. Bryant, July 5, 1985; children: Scott, Jeff, Mike, Bryan. BA in Bus., Kearney (Nebr.) State Coll.; JD, U. Nebr. Bar: Nebr., Colo. Ptnr. Wright, Simmons, Hancock & Hall, Scottsbluff, Nebr., 1967-71; atty., asst. treas. KN Energy Inc., Hastings, Nebr., 1971-73; dir. regional affairs KN Energy Inc., Hastings, 1973-76; v.p. law div. KN Energy Inc., Lakewood, Colo., 1976-82, sr. v.p., 1982-85, exec. v.p., 1985-88, pres., chief ops. officer, 1988—, also bd. dirs.; bd. dirs. Midwest Gas Assn., Mpls., INCAA. Mem. ABA, Fed. Energy Bar Assn., Nebr. Bar Assn., Colo. Bar Assn., Pres. Assn., Midwest Bar Assn. (bd. dirs. 1986-88), Columbine Country Club, Elks, Masons. Democrat. Presbyterian. Home: 1892 Sugar Bush Dr Evergreen CO 80439 Office: KN Energy Inc PO Box 15265 Lakewood CO 80215

HALL, MARCIA JOY, non-profit organization administrator; b. Long Beach, Calif., June 24, 1947; d. Royal Waltz and Norine (Parker) Stanton; m. Stephen Christopher Hall, March 29, 1969; children: Geoffrey Michael, Christopher Stanton. AA, Foothill Coll., 1967; student, U. Oreg., 1967-68; BA, U. Washington, Seattle, 1969. Instr. aide Glen Yermo Sch., Mission Viejo, Calif., 1979-80; market rsch. interviewer Rsch. Data, Framingham, Mass., 1982-83; adult edn. instr. Community Sch. Use Program, Milford, Mass., 1982-83; career info. ctr. coord. Milford High Sch., 1983-86; corp. rels. dir. Sch. Vols. for Milford, Inc., 1985-86; NE area coord. YWCA of Annapolis and Anne Arundel County, Severna Park, Md, 1987—. Pres. PTO, Mission Viejo, 1979-80, Milford, 1981-84; consumer assistance vol., Calif. Pub. Interest Rsch. Group, 1977-78. Mem. Internat. Platform Assn., AAUW. Club: Toastmasters (treas. 1988—, pres. 1989—). Home: 507 Devonshire Ln Severna Park MD 21146 Office: YWCA NE 17 Cypress Creek Rd Severna Park MD 21146

HALL, MICHAEL ALAN, banker; b. Cheyenne, Wyo., Sept. 14, 1950; s. James Neeley McGill Hall and Rosemary (Marcellus) Cook; divorced; 1 child, Elisabeth Hannah Zeuske Hall. BS in Bus. magna cum laude, Tex. Wesleyan Coll., 1976. Mgr. Howard Blender Co., Dallas, 1976-79; supr. Ernst & Whinney, N.Y.C., 1979-82; prin. Fin. Instns. Cons. Services, Westport, Conn., 1982-83; pres., chief exec. officer, dir. Citizens Bank N.A., Shawano, Wis., 1983—, Citizens Bankshares, Inc., Shawano, 1987—; mem. payment systems policy bd. ABA, Washington, 1986-87. Pres. United Way Shawano County Inc., 1984, Shawano County Arts Council, 1987. With U.S. Army, 1969-72, Vietnam. Mem. Shawano County Bankers Assn. (pres. 1987), Wis. Bankers Assn. (chmn. ops. and procedures com. 1987—). Office: Citizens Bank NA 129 E Division St Shawano WI 54166

HALL, MICHAEL RAY, manufacturing executive; b. Wichita, Kans., Oct. 31, 1956; s. Ira L. and Ruth Ann (Hill) H.; m. Cindy Lee; children: Sean, Jill, Michael. BBA in Acctg., Pittsburg (Kans.) State U. 1978. CPA, Kans. Audit supr. Touche Ross & Co., Topeka, 1977-83; asst. controller profit planning and analysis Volume Shoe Corp., Topeka, 1983-85; pres., chief exec. officer Physio Tech., Inc., Topeka, 1985—. Named Outstanding Young Men of Am., 1987. Mem. Am. Inst. CPAs, Kans. Soc. CPAs, Greater Topeka C. of C. (chmn., pres. 1981). Republican. Office: Physio Tech Inc 1505 SW 42d Topeka KS 66609

HALL, MILES LEWIS, JR., lawyer; b. Fort Lauderdale, Fla., Aug. 14, 1924; s. Miles Lewis and Mary Frances (Dawson) H.; m. Muriel M. Fisher, Nov. 4, 1950; children: Miles Lewis III, Don Thomas. A.B., Princeton U., 1947; J.D., Harvard U., 1950. Bar: Fla. 1951. Since practiced in Miami; ptnr. Hall & Hedrick, Miami, 1953—; dir. Gen. Portland, Inc., 1974-81. Author: Election of Remedies, Vol. VIII, Fla. Law and Practice, 1958. Chmn. 3d Appellate Dist. Ct. Nominating Commn., State Fla., 1972-75; pres. Orange Bowl Com., 1964-65, dir., 1950-84, sec., treas. 1984-86, dir. 1986—; vice-chmn., dir. Dade County (Fla.) ARC, 1961-62, chmn., 1963-64, dir., 1967-73; nat. fund cons. ARC, 1963, 66-68, trustee, 1985—; bd. pres. Ransom Sch. Parents Assn., 1966; chmn. South Fla. Gov.'s Scholarship Ball, 1966; mem. exec. bd. South Fla. council Boy Scouts Am., 1966-67; citizens bd. U. Miami, 1961-66; mem. Fla. Council of 100, vice chmn., 1961-62; mem. Coral Gables (Fla.) Biltmore Devel. Com., 1972-73; mem. bd. visitors Coll. Law, Fla. State U., 1974-77; bd. dirs. Coral Gables War Meml. Youth Ctr., 1967—, pres., 1969-72, bd. dirs; bd. dirs. Salvation Army, Miami, 1968-83, Fla. Citizens Against Crime 1984—; bd. dirs. Am. Found. Inc., 1985-87; sec., treas., dir. Bok Towes Gardens Found. Inc., 1987-89, treas., 1989—. 2d lt. USAAF, 1943-45. Fellow Am. Bar Found.; mem. ABA (Fla. co-chmn. membership com. sect. corp., banking and bus. law 1968-72), Dade County Bar Assn. (dir. 1964-65, pres. 1967-68), Fla. Bar, Am. Judicature Soc., Miami-Dade County C. of C. (v.p. 1962-64, dir. 1966-68), Harvard Law Sch. Assn. Fla. (dir. 1964-66), Kiwanis, Cottage Club, Harvard Club, The Miami Club (v.p., dir. 1989—), City Club of Miami (bd. dirs., v.p. 1989—), Princeton Club So. Fla. (past pres., dir.), Alpha Tau Omega. Methodist (bd. stewards). Home: 2907 Alhambra Circle Coral Gables FL 33134 Office: Hall & Hedrick Republic Nat Bank Bldg 150 SE 2d St Ste 1400 Miami FL 33131

HALL, MILTON REESE, energy company executive; b. Vicksburg, Miss., July 5, 1932; s. Alvin and Adelle (McKay) H.; m. Margaret Louise Bailey, Feb. 17, 1957; children: Mark Russell, Stacy Elaine. B.S. in Acctg., Miss. So. U., 1953; M.B.A. in Acctg., U. Miss., 1956; postgrad., La. State U., 1959-62. C.P.A., Miss. Trainee, div. controller Kaiser Aluminum, various locations, 1957-66; fin. analyst Tex. Instruments, Dallas, 1966-67; v.p. Koch Industries Inc., Wichita, Kans., 1967—. Served to cpl. U.S. Army, 1953-55. Recipient Silver medal Am. Inst. C.P.A.s, 1956. Republican. Baptist. Office: Koch Industries Inc PO Box 2256 Wichita KS 67201

HALL, NEWELL J., chain drug store company executive; b. Clinton, Ind., 1932; married. Pharmacist Hook Drugs, Inc., Indpls., 1961-66, prescription drug buyer, 1966-69, asst. v.p., dir. profl. services, 1969-79, v.p., dir. profl. services, 1972-80, exec. v.p., 1980-88; pres, chief exec. officer Hook Drugs div. Hook SuperX Inc., Indpls., 1988—, also dir., chief operating officer. Office: Hook Drugs Div Hook SuperX Inc 2800 Enterprise St PO Box 26285 Indianapolis IN 46226

HALL, PAMELA S., environmental consulting firm executive; b. Hartford, Conn., Sept. 4, 1944; d. LeRoy Warren and Frances May (Murray) Sheely; m. Stuart R. Hall, July 21, 1967. B.A. in Zoology, U. Conn., 1966; M.S. in Zoology, U. N.H., 1969, B.S. in Bus. Adminstrn. summa cum laude, 1982; student spl. grad. studies program, Tufts U., 1986—. Curatorial asst. U. Conn., Storrs, 1966; research asst. Field Mus. Natural History, Chgo., 1966-67; teaching asst. U. N.H., Durham, 1967-70; program mgr. Normandeau Assocs. Inc., Portsmouth, N.H., 1971-79, marine lab. dir., 1979-81, programs and ops. mgr., Bedford, N.H., 1981-83, v.p., 1983-85, sr. v.p., 1986-87, pres., 1987—. Mem. Conservation Commn., Portsmouth, 1977—, Wells, Estuarine Research Res. Review Commn., 1986—, Great Bay (N.H.) Estuarine Research Res. Tech. Working Group, 1987—. Graham Found. fellow, 1966; NDEA fellow, 1970-71. Mem. Am. Mgmt. Assn., Water Pollution Control Fedn., Am. Fisheries Soc., Estuarine Research Fedn., Nat. Assn. Environ. Profls., ASTM, Sigma Xi. Home: 4 Pleasant Point Dr Portsmouth NH 03801 Office: Normandeau Assocs Inc 25 Nashua Rd Bedford NH 03201

HALL, PATRICIA MARTY, financial executive; b. Stockholm, Jan. 13, 1954; d. William Worth and Elsie Marty (Svedberg) H. BA, Vassar Coll., 1976; MBA, NYU, 1978. Cert. fin. analyst. Fin. analyst Chase Manhattan Bank, N.Y.C., 1978-79; treas., dir. Traid Inc., N.Y.C., 1983—, Working Woman/McCall's Group, N.Y.C., 1987—, Hal Holdings Corp., N.Y.C., 1979—. Mem. N.Y. Soc. Security Analysts, Fin. Women's Wossn., Nat. Soc. Colonial Dames (jr. chair 1982-83), Vassar Club. Republican. Home: 200 E 72nd St #2D New York NY 10021 Office: Hal Holdings Corp 230 Park Ave New York NY 10163

HALL, RICHARD SHAW, corporate executive b. S.I., N.Y., Apr. 21, 1921; s. Raymond Peter and Blanche (Shaw) H.; student Wagner Coll., 1946-48; m. Alice Mary Baker, Feb 12, 1944; children—Richard Shaw, Gregory H. Sales rep. Doyle & Roth Mfg. Co., Inc., Bklyn., 1947-54, sales mgr., 1954-63, v.p., 1963-70; v.p. Walster Corp., Simpson, Pa., 1962-70; asso. Chem-Pro Marketing Services, S.I., 1966-70; v.p. Chem-Pro Assos., Ltd., 1970—; pres. Richard S. Hall & Assos., 1970—. Served to lt. (j.g.), USNR, 1942-46. Decorated Air medal (Navy), D.F.C. Mem. Chemists Club. Home: 72 Roman Ave Staten Island NY 10314 Office: Richard S Hall & Assocs 145 Cortlandt St Staten Island NY 10302

HALL, ROBERT ALAN, manager, finance and administration; b. Montgomery, Ala., Oct. 30, 1958; s. Mack Luverne and Miriam (Johnston) H. BS in Commerce and Bus. Adminstrn., U. Ala., 1981. CPA, Ala. Sr. acct. Jackson and Thronton, CPA's, Montgomery, 1981-83; sr. auditor Vulcan Materials Co., Birmingham, Ala., 1983-86, supr. internal audit, 1986-87; mgr., fin. and adminstrn. Saudi Arabian Vulcan Ltd., Jubail, Saudi Arabia, 1987—. Charter mem. Rep. Presdl. Task Force, Washington, 1984-86. Recipient presdl. achievement award Pres. Ronald Reagan, 1983; named hon. citizen City of Los Angeles, 1984, hon. asst. atty. gen. State of Ala., 1984; named one of Outstanding Young Men of Am., 1986. Mem. Am. Businessmen's Assn. of Saudi Arabia, U. Ala. Sr. Execs. Club, Coll. of Commerce, Am. Inst. CPA's, Ala. Soc. CPA's, Honorable Order Ky. Cols. Baptist. Lodge: Civitan. Home: PO Box 10016, Madinat Jubail 31961, Saudi Arabia

HALL, ROBERT EMMETT, JR., investment banker, realtor; b. Sioux City, Iowa, Apr. 28, 1936; s. Robert Emmett and Alvina (Faden) H.; m. Marna Thiel, 1969. BA, U. S.D., 1958, MA, 1959; MBA, U. Santa Clara, 1976; grad. Am. Inst. Banking, Realtors Inst. Grad. asst. U. S.D., Vermillion, 1958-59; mgr. ins. dept., asst. mgr. installment loan dept. Northwestern Nat. Bank of Sioux Falls, S.D., 1959-61, asst. cashier, 1961-65; asst. mgr. Crocker Nat. Bank, San Francisco, 1965-67, loan officer, 1967-69, asst. v.p., asst. mgr. San Mateo br., 1969-72; v.p., Western regional mgr. Internat. Investments & Realty, Inc., Washington, 1972—; owner Hall Investment Co., 1976—; pres. Almaden Oaks Realtors, Inc., 1976—; instr. West Valley Coll., Saratoga, Calif., 1972-82, Grad. Sch. Bus., U. Santa Clara (Calif.), 1981—. Treas., Minnehaha Leukemia Soc., 1963, Lake County Heart Fund Assn., 1962, Minnehaha Young Republican Club, 1963. Mem. Am. Inst. Banking, San Mateo C. of C., Calif. Assn. Realtors (vice chmn.), Beta Theta Pi. Republican. Roman Catholic. Clubs: Elks, Rotary (past pres.), K.C., Almaden Country, Mercedes Benz Calif. Home: 6951 Castlerock Dr San Jose CA 95120 Office: Almaden Oaks Realtors Inc 6501 Crown Blvd 100 San Jose CA 95120 Home (summer): 8864 Rubicon Bay Lake Tahoe CA 95733

HALL, ROBERT JAMES, marketing professional; b. Ann Arbor, Mich., June 12, 1956; s. Michael Garth and Anne Elizabeth (Elderfield) Shanahan; m. Sheila Ellen Regan, Feb. 28, 1987. Student, Loyola U., 1981-83. Pres. Elderfield & Hall, Chgo., 1979—. Author sales tng. seminars. Alderman W. Chgo. City Council, 1975-79; mem. W. Chgo. Zoning Bd. Appeals, 1979-81, W. Chgo. Planning Commn., 1979-81; chmn. Art Inst. Alliance Fund Raisng Campaign, 1984. Mem. Am. Welding Soc. Club: Union League Chgo. (dir. 1987—).

HALL, ROGER FISHER, JR., insurance executive; b. Lumberton, N.C., Oct. 14, 1951; s. Roger Fisher Sr. and Mary (Hodgin) H.; m. Beverly Egg, Nov. 18, 1984. BA, Catawba Coll., 1975. Job placement officer Employment Security Commn., Carthage, N.C., 1976-78; dir. for state Temperature Restriction Program, Raleigh, N.C., 1978-80; pres., chief exec. officer Safety Ins. Agy., Inc., Hope Mills and Parkton, N.C., 1980—; bd. dirs. So. Nat. Bank, Hope MIlls, 1988—. Mem. exec. council Town of Lumber Bridge, N.C., 1981-87; treas. Robeson County Dem. Party, Lumberton, 1982-86; chmn. Lumber Bridge Zoning Bd., 1985—; bd. dirs. Robeson County Hwy. Commn., Lumberton, 1982-86. Served as major N.C. Nat. Guard, 1970—. Mem. Masons, Shriners, Am. Legion. Presbyterian. Home: 206 N Fayetteville St Lumber Bridge NC 28357 Office: Safety Ins Agy Inc 3109 N Main St Hope Mills NC 28348

HALL, SCOTT MICHAEL, financial planner; b. Harve-de-Grace, Md., Apr. 19, 1950; s. Charles Luther and Frances Mary (Crew) H.; m. Elizabeth Householder, Aug. 5, 1972; 1 child, Kristen Elizabeth. AA, Chesapeake Coll., 1970; BS, James Madison U., 1972. CPA; cert. fin. planner. Acct. Bryce Mountain Resort, Basye, Va., 1973-75, H.P. Cannon & Son, Inc., Bridgeville, Del., 1975-78; also bd. dirs. H.P. Cannon & Son, Inc.; asst. to pres. H.P. Cannon & Son, Inc., Bridgeville, 1979-81, v.p., 1981-82, pres., 1982-84; pvt. practice Seaford, Del., 1984—. Bd. dirs. Seaford Fed. Credit Union. Mem. Am. Inst. CPA's, Inst. Cert. Fin. Planners, Internat. Assn. Fin. Planners. Home: Briar Hook Seaford DE 19973 Office: 111 Warren Rd Hunt Valley MD 21030

HALL, STEPHEN GARDNER, computer executive; b. Evanston, Ill., Jan. 11, 1949; s. Gordon and Charlene (Sowers) H.; m. Cynthia Anne Wood, June 28, 1970; children: Gregory, Kristin. AB, U. So. Calif.; MBA, Dartmouth Coll. Product mgr. Colgate Palmolive Corp., Boston, 1973-79; div. v.p. Millipore Corp., Bedford, Mass., 1979-84; v.p. sales and mktg. Aegis Med. Systems, Marlton, N.J., 1984-86; v.p., gen. mgr. Solarex, Rockville, Md., 1986-87; chief exec. officer Digital Analysis Corp., Reston, Va., 1988—. Republican. Methodist. Office: Digital Analysis Corp 1899 Preston White Dr Reston VA 22091

HALL, SUZANNE MARIE, accountant; b. Watertown, N.Y., Sept. 21, 1962; d. Richard Eugene and Kathryn L. (Towsley) Lawton; m. Thomas Staie Hall, Aug. 22, 1981. BS, Clarkson U., 1984; M of Accountancy, U. North Fla., 1988. Cost acct. Maxwell House div. Gen. Foods, Jacksonville, Fla., 1984-85; auditor Touche Ross & Co., Jacksonville, 1985-87; mgr. fin. reporting, budget and planning Customized Transp. Inc., Jacksonville, 1987—. Mem. NAFE, Am. Mgmt. Assn., Omni Fed. Credit Union (supervisory com.), Beta Alpha Psi, Hidden Hills Country Club, Tournament Players Club (Jacksonville). Home: 11104 Oak Ridge Dr S Jacksonville FL 32225 Office: 9485 Regency Square Blvd N Regency One #500 Jacksonville FL 32225

HALL, WILLIAM EDWARD, JR., insurance agency executive; b. Roanoke, Va., Oct. 15, 1951; s. William Edward and Virginia (Moomaw) H., m. Emily Ayers Rierson, May 27, 1972; children: Amanda Marie, John William. BA in Econs., U. N.C., Chapel Hill, 1973, MBA (Bus. Found. fellow), 1977; MS in Fin. Svcs., Am. Coll., 1989. Coll. agt. Northwestern Mut. Life, Chapel Hill, 1972-73, 75-77, spl. agt., Greensboro, N.C., 1973-75, 78—; staff acct. Price Waterhouse & Co., Charlotte, N.C., 1977-78; partner Sprinkle & Assos., life ins. agy., Greensboro, 1978-87; sr. v.p. John O. Todd Orgn. of Greensboro, 1987— ; CPA, CLU, chartered fin. cons. Active Leadership Greensboro. Mem. AICPA, Nat. Assn. Accts., Estate Planning Council, Am. Soc. CLUs, Greensboro CLU & ChFC Chpt. (bd. dirs. 1980-83, sec., treas. 1988-89) Phi Beta Kappa, Beta Gamma Sigma, Beta Theta Pi, Greensboro Country Club. Republican. Presbyterian. Lodge: Kiwanis. Home: 1005 Country Club Dr Greensboro NC 27408 Office: John O Todd Orgn 620 Green Valley Rd Suite 101 Greensboro NC 27408

HALL, WILLIAM KING, manufacturing company executive; b. Adrian, Mich., Oct. 8, 1943; s. Daniel S. and Jeanne (Isley) H.; m. Valerie Worth Smith, Dec. 26, 1964; children: Stephen Edward, Phillip Andrew, Timothy William, Lesley Michelle. BS in Engring., U. Mich., 1965, MBA, 1967, MS, 1968, PhD, 1969. Prof. bus. adminstrn. U. Mich. Grad. Sch. Bus. Adminstrn., Ann Arbor, Harvard Bus. Sch., Boston, and European Inst. Bus. Adminstrn., Fontainebleau, France, 1970-81; mgmt. cons. to clients including AT&T, Chrysler Corp., Cummins Engine Co., Eastman Kodak, Ford Motor Co., Gen. Electric Co., Gen. Motors, Mobil Oil Co., Republic Steel Corp., Union Carbide Corp., Uniroyal; exec. v.p. N.Am. mktg. and components cos. Cummins Engine Co., Inc., Columbus, Ind., 1981-84, dir. Cummins Engine Found., Columbus; pres., chief operating officer Farley Industries, Chgo., 1984-87; pres., chief op. officer, Eagle Industries, 1987—; dir. Preston Corp., Easton, Md., Huffy Corp., Dayton, Ohio, A.M. Castle & Co., Franklin, Ill. Mem. Planning Execs. Inst., Tau Beta Phi, Beta Gamma Sigma. Presbyterian. Home: 855 Lamson Dr Winnetka IL 60093 Office: Eagle Industries 2 N Riverside Pla Suite 1100 Chicago IL 60606

HALLARD, WAYNE BRUCE, economist; b. Plainfield, N.J., Dec. 28, 1951; s. Donald Jay and Patricia (Adelmann) H.; m. Grace Elizabeth Farrell, Apr. 29, 1972 (div. 1979); 1 child, Travis; m. Deborah Jane Russo, Aug. 16, 1987. Student, Brown U., 1970-71; AA in Bus., Union Coll., 1977; BS in Econs., Fairleigh Dickinson U., 1980, MBA in Econs., 1984; postgrad., N.Y.U., 1984-87. Store mgr. Wine Art of N.J., Watchung, 1972; staff mgr. N.J. Bell Tel., Newark, 1972—; cons. N.J. Coun. of Savs. Instns., West Orange, 1987—. Trustee Lehmen Found., Newark, 1979-84; active, past pres. Newark Young People Orgn., 1979-86; advocate Mental Health Assn., East Orange, 1979-80; mem. Newark Mus., 1987—; trustee Newark Jaycees Internat. Senators Scholarship Found., 1986—; umpire Scotch Plains-Fanwood Youth Baseball Assn., Scotch Plains, N.J., 1982—; trustee, pres. Brotherhood Temple Sharey Tefilo Israel, South Orange, N.J., 1980—. With USAFR, 1971-80. Recipient Cert. of Appreciation 1982 Cts. and Corrections Assn. N.J. 1982; named One of Outstanding Young Men of Am., 1981, 83, 85, 86, 88. Mem. Greater Newark C. of C. (bd. dirs. 1980-82), B'nai B'rith (South Orange chpt. 1988—), Delta Mu Delta, Mastiff Club Am. Republican. Jewish. Home: 518 Jerusalem Rd Scotch Plains NJ 07076 Office: NJ Bell Tel 540 Broad St Newark NJ 07101

HALLBAUER, ROBERT EDWARD, mining company executive; b. Nakusp, B.C., Can., May 19, 1930; s. Edward F. and Lillian Anna (Kendrick) H.; m. Mary Joan Hunter, Sept. 7, 1952; children: Russell, Catherine, Thomas. BS in Mining Engring., U. B.C., 1954. Registered profl. engr., B.C. Various engring. and supervisory positions Placer Devel., Salmo, B.C., 1954-60; mine supr. Craigmont Mines Ltd., Merritt, B.C., 1960-64, mine mgr., 1964-68; v.p. mining Teck Corp., Vancouver, B.C., 1968-79, sr. v.p., 1979—; pres., chief exec. officer Cominco Ltd., Vancouver, 1986—, also bd. dirs.; bd. dirs. Lornex Mining Corp., Vancouver. Recipient Edgar A. Scholz medal B.C. and Yukon Chamber of Mines, 1984. Mem. Assn. Profl. Engrs., Can. Inst. Mining and Metallurgy. Home: 6026 Glenwynd Pl, West Vancouver, BC Canada V7W 2W5 Office: Cominco Ltd, 200 Granville St #2600, Vancouver, BC Canada V6C 2R2

HALLBOM, HAROLD RAYMOND, JR., printing company executive; b. Evanston, Ill., Nov. 8, 1951; s. Harold Raymond and Helen (Hoffman) H.; m. Denise C. Carlson, Oct. 31, 1952; children: Heather Jean, James Erick. BA, Loyola U., Chgo., 1974. Profl. engring. recruiter Profl. div. Businessmaus, Chgo., 1974-76; nat. sales mgr. Control Process Co., Elk Grove Village, Ill., 1975-78; exec. dir. U.V. Process, Inc., Chgo., 1978-82; v.p. Svecia USA, Inc., San Marcos, Calif., 1982—; cons. Argonne Nat. Labs., Batavia, Ill., 1984; advisor Screen Printing Tech. Found., Fairfax, Va., 1986—. Contbr. articles to profl. jours. Recipient Commendation Binday Inst. Am., 1985. Mem. Screen Printing Assn. Internat. (moderator, Commendation 1984), Soc. Mfg. Engrs. (sr., Cert. of Appreciation 1987), Screen Print Tech. Found. (advisor 1986—), Assn. for Finishing Processes, Alpha Delta Gamma (c. mgr. 1971-73). Democrat. Home: O N 626 Lancaster Dr Winfield IL 60190 Office: Svecia USA Inc 220 Distribution St San Marcos CA 92069

HALLE, CLAUS M., beverage company executive; b. 1927; married. With Lemgol Lippe, W.Ger., 1946, Coca-Cola Export Corp. subs., Atlanta, 1950—, Coca-Cola GmbH, Essen, Germany, 1950-56; sales mgr. Coca-Cola GmbH, Germany, 1956-62, mgr., 1962-65; v.p. exprot, area mgr. Central Europe Coca-Cola GmbH, 1965-70; corp. sr. v.p., pres., chief exec. officer Coca Cola Europe, 1970-73; pres., dir. Coca-Cola Export Corp., 1973; v.p. Coca-Cola Co., Atlanta, 1973-74, sr. v.p., 1974-76, exec. v.p., 1976-79; vice chmn. bd. Coca-Cola co., Atlanta, 1979-80; exec. v.p. Coca-Cola Co., Atlanta, 1980-81, sr. exec. v.p., 1981—. Office: The Coca-Cola Co One Coca-Cola Plaza NW Atlanta GA 30313 *

HALLEUX, ALBERT MARTIN JULIEN, motor vehicle inspection company executive; b. Dison, Belgium, Nov. 18, 1920; s. Albert Julien and Marie (Lemaire) H.; Mech. Engr., U. Liege, 1945, Aero. Engr., 1955; m. Arlette Lehyme, May 20, 1967; 1 son, Emmanuel. Engr., then chief engr. Autosecurite, Verviers, 1949-74, pres., 1974—; dep. WP29 experts group Econ. Commn. for Europe, Geneva, 1962—; gen. sec. Internat. Motor Vehicle Insp. Com., 1969—; adj. gen. sec., founder Union Tech. Assistance for Motor Vehicles and Road Traffic, Geneva, 1978—; v.p. Groupement des Organismes de Contrôle Automobile, Brussels, 1979-82, 86—, pres., 1982-85; v.p. Fonds d'Etudes pour la Sécurité Routière, Brussels, 1982-85, Fonds de pré vision et d'utilité publique de l'inspection des véhicules automobiles, Brussels, 1983-85. Decorated chevalier Order de la Couronne, Officier de l'Ordre de Leopold. Mem. Soc. Promoting Traffic Safety. Liberal. Roman Catholic. Home: 2 Rue de Louvain, B-4800 Verviers Belgium Office: 4 Rue de la Marne, B-4800 Verviers Belgium

HALLEY, GEORGE DANIEL, III, construction company executive; b. St. Louis, July 30, 1938; s. George Daniel Jr. and Agnes Florence (Wojtkowski) H.; m. Loretta Marie Bomerito, May 13, 1955 (div. 1960); children: Michael, Donald, Richard, Linda, Jenny; m. Dolores Mary Hirbe, Apr. 17, 1982. BS in Biochemistry, St. Louis U., 1965. Chemist Monsanto Reserach Ctr., St. Louis, 1959-62, Biol. Rsch., Inc., St. Louis, 1962-63, Small Arms Co., St. Louis, 1965-66; researcher St. Louis U. Med. Sch., 1963-65, Los Alamos (N.Mex.) Sci. Labs., 1966-70; engr. various cos., St. Louis, 1970-78, Crown, Cork & Seal, St. Louis, 1978-82; tchr. spl. sch. dist. St. Louis County, 1982-83; chief exec. officer H&H Contracting Co., St. Louis, 1983—. Capt. with USAF, 1954-59, Korea. Democrat. Roman Catholic. Home: 4121 Botanical St Saint Louis MO 63110

HALLIDAY, WILLIAM JAMES, JR., lawyer; b. Detroit, Nov. 16, 1921; s. William James and Katherine Elizabeth (Krantz) H.; A.B. (scholar), U. Mich., 1943, J.D., 1948; m. Lois Jeanne Streelman, Sept. 6, 1947; children—Carol Lynn Halliday Murphy, Richard Andrew, Marcia Katherine, James Anthony. Admitted to Mich. bar, 1948; assoc. Schmidt, Smith & Howlett and successors, Grand Rapids, Mich., 1952-56, ptnr., 1956-66, of counsel Varnum, Riddering, Schmidt & Howlett, 1984—; sec. Amway Corp. Ada, Mich., 1964-84, gen. counsel, 1966-71, v.p., 1970-79, exec. v.p., 1979-84, also dir.; asst. pros. atty., Kent County, Mich., 1949-51; twp. atty., Wyoming Twp., Mich., 1955-57; city atty., Wyoming, Mich., 1961-66. Bd. dirs. Better Bus. Bur. Western Mich., Met. YMCA of Grand Rapids. Served with M.I., U.S. Army, 1943-46, with JAGC, 1951-52. Decorated Bronze Star; recipient William Jennings Bryan award U. Mich., 1943. Mem. ABA, Mich. Bar Assn., Grand Rapids Bar Assn., Phi Beta Kappa, Phi Kappa Phi, Delta Sigma Rho, Phi Eta Sigma. Republican. Presbyterian. Club: Kiwanis. Home: 3020 Uplands Dr SE Grand Rapids MI 49506 Office: Varnum Riddering Schmidt & Howlett 171 Monroe Ave NW Suite 800 Grand Rapids MI 49503

HALLIGAN, THOMAS WALSH, construction company executive; b. Davenport, Iowa, Oct. 20, 1922; s. Eugene Joseph and Gertrude (Walsh) H.; m. Mary E. McClelland, Apr. 17, 1947; children: Carol, Mary Beth, Susan, Nancy, Timothy, Kathleen. A.B., Georgetown U., 1943. With Walsh Constrn. Co., Trumbull, Conn., 1946-80; pres. Walsh Constrn. Co., 1975-80; pres. Guy F. Atkinson Co., South San Francisco, until 1987, now chmn., chief exec. officer. Office: Guy F Atkinson Co of Calif 10 W Orange Ave South San Francisco CA 94080 *

HALLINGBY, PAUL, JR., investment banker; b. Los Angeles, Sept. 27, 1919; s. Paul and Ethel Marie (Sutor) H.; m. Allison Lazo, Oct. 9, 1943 (dec. 1965); children: Leigh H. Platt, Paul Lazo, Allison H. Dodge; m. Mai Vilms, May 18, 1983. BA, Stanford U., 1941; postgrad. Harvard U., 1941-42. Salesman, First Boston Corp., N.Y.C., 1946-48, E.F. Hutton & Co., N.Y.C., 1948-52; v.p. Middle South Utilities Inc., N.Y.C., 1952-58; chmn., chief exec. officer White, Weld & Co. (merger Merrill Lynch, Pierce, Fenner & Smith Inc.), N.Y.C., 1958-78; vice chmn. Merrill Lynch, Pierce, Fenner & Smith, N.Y.C., 1978-80; sr. mng. dir. Bear, Stearns & Co., N.Y.C., 1980—; bd. dirs. Balfour-Maclaine Corp., N.Y.C., MEM Co. Inc., Northvale, N.J., Mass. Mut. Life Ins. Co., Springfield. Chmn. Poly. U. N.Y., 1976—; bd. dirs N.Y. conv. Ctr. Operatin Corp.; trustee Parish Art Mus., Southampton, N.Y., 1981—, Marconi Internat. Fellowship, N.Y.C., 1984—; mem. adv. bd. Skin Cancer Found., N.Y.C. Lt. USNR, 1942-46, comdr. Res. Republican. Presbyterian. Clubs: Links, River, Sky; Meadow, Shinnecock Hills, Bathing Corp. (Southampton, N.Y.); Lyford Cay Club (Nassau, Bahamas). Home: 885 Park Ave New York NY 10021 Office: Bear Stearns & Co Inc 245 Park Ave New York NY 10167

HALLISSEY, MICHAEL, accounting company executive; b. Southampton, England, Mar. 6, 1943; s. John Francis and Mary (Kendall) H. Grad., Magdalen Coll., Oxford U., Eng., 1964. Chartered acct., Eng. With Price Waterhouse, 1964—; asst. mgr. Price Waterhouse, Melbourne, Australia, 1968, Milan, Italy, 1969; ptnr. Price Waterhouse, London, 1974—, head practice devel., 1979-81, head strategic planning, 1981-82, head corp. fin. services, 1983-88; dir. strategy Price Waterhouse Europe, 1988—. Contbr. articles to profl. publs. Fellow Royal Soc. of Arts; mem. Inst. Chartered Accts. Eng. and Wales. Mem. Conservative Party. Mem. Ch. of Eng. Home: 49 Whitelands House, London SW3 4QX, England Office: Price Waterhouse, 32 London Bridge St, London SE1 9SY, England

HALLMON, DOROTHY, insurance company professional, real estate consultant; b. Aiken, S.C., May 30, 1939; d. Willie Lee and Minnie Mae (Robinson) H. BA in Home Econs., Queens Coll., 1976. Decolator Md. Casual Ins. Co., Balt., 1977—; cons. Rainbow Enterprises, Balt., 1986—.

HALLORAN, HARRY RICHARD, contracting company executive; b. Riverside, N.J., July 13, 1902; s. Richard J. and Agnes (Fahy) H.; m. Margaret Schneider, Sept. 8, 1938 (dec. 1980); children: Harry R. Jr., Edward, Richard, Thomas; m. Lorraine Horos, Dec. 1, 1984. BSCE, U. Pa., 1923; D of Comml. Sci. (hon.), Villanova U., 1967; D of Indsl. Rels. (hon.), St. Joseph's U., Phila., 1975. Chmn. bd. dirs. Conduit and Found Corp., Bala Cynwyd, Pa., 1941—; ptnr. N.J. real estate holdings, Deptford, 1956—, Pitman (N.J.) Country Club, 1956—; gen. ptnr. Atlantic City Raceway, 1968-86; vice-chmn. Atlantic City Harness, 1987-88; bd. dirs. City Trusts. Bd. dirs., v.p. Bd. City Trusts, Phila. Recipient Sourin award Cath. Philos. Lit. Inst., Phila., 1979, Alumni award of merit U. Pa. Organized Alumni, 1980, Cresset award Rosemont Coll., 1986. Mem. Assn. Gen. Contractors Am. (treas., life bd. dirs.), Contractors Assn. Eastern Pa. (past pres., chmn. bd. dirs., life bd. dirs.). Republican. Roman Catholic. Clubs: Whitemarsh Valley Country (Lafayette Hill, Pa.) (past pres.); Merion Cricket (Haverford, Pa.); Union (Phila.); N.J. Country. Office: Conduit and Found Corp 33 Rock Hill Rd Bala-Cynwyd PA 19004

HALLORAN, LEO AUGUSTINE, corporate financial executive; b. Schenectady, N.Y., Apr. 2, 1931; s. Leo Augustine Halloran and Helen (O'Hare) Pagel; m. Marilyn Elizabeth Gobeli, Dec. 29, 1956; children: Patricia Garvey, Michael, Kevin. AB in Econs., Union Coll., Schenectady, N.Y., 1953. With fin. mgmt. program Gen. Electric Co., Schenectady, 1956-60, mem. corp. audit staff, 1961-64, mgr. fin., 1965-70; mgr. fin. Consumer Products Group, Fairfield, Conn., 1971-75; sr. v.p., chief fin. officer Gen. Electric Capital Corp., Stamford, Conn., 1976—; bd. dirs. Kidder Peabody, N.Y.C. Sgt. U.S. Army, 1953-55. Mem. Fin. Execs. Inst., Woodway Country Club, Landmark Club. Office: Gen Electric Capital Corp 260 Long Ridge Rd Stamford CT 06902

HALLOWELL, BURTON CROSBY, economist, educator; b. Orleans, Mass., May 2, 1915; s. William George and Sarah Frances (Crosby) H.; m. Pauline Russell, June 7, 1941; 1 son, Robert Crosby. B.A., Wesleyan U., Middletown, Conn., 1936, M.A., 1938, L.H.D., 1969; Ph.D., Princeton, 1949; L.H.D., Boston U., 1969, Tufts U., 1976; LL.D., Northeastern U., 1973, Am. Internat. Coll., 1975. Teller Windham County Nat. Bank, Danielson, Conn., 1936-37; Social Sci. Research Council pre-doctoral field fellow 1940-41; instr. econs. Wesleyan U., 1941-42, asst. prof., 1946-50, assoc. prof., 1950-56, Andrews prof. econs., 1956-67, v.p. for planning and devel., 1962-65, exec. v.p., 1965-67; on leave for research on fed. debt mgmt. Merrill Found. for Advancement Fin. Knowledge, 1956-57; on leave as staff mem. N.Y.C. Commn. for Money and Credit, 1960-61; pres. Tufts U., Medford, Mass., 1967-76; vice chmn. Keystone Custodian Funds, Inc., 1976, chmn. bd., 1977-79, chief exec. officer, 1978-79, also dir., 1971-79; bd. dirs. Oppenheimer & Co. Inc., N.Y.C., Thackeray Corp., N.Y.C.; Econ. cons. Conn. Gen. Life Ins. Co., 1949-62, Com. Econ. Devel., N.Y.C., Washington, 1953-54; Chmn. Mass. Housing Finance Agy., 1968-71; mem. exec. com. New Eng. Colls. Fund, 1968-71; mem. exec. com. Assn. Ind. Colls and Univs. in Mass., 1968-73, pres., 1972-73. Contbr. articles to profl. jours. Trustee Cape Cod Mus., Brewster, Mass., 1982-88, Davis Ednl. Found.; bd. dirs. Friends of Cape Cod Nat. Seashore; trustee Davis Ednl. Found. With OPA and Civilian Supply, 1941. With OSS, 1942; capt. AUS, 1942-46. Mem. Am. Econ. Assn., Am. Finance Assn., Phi Beta Kappa, Sigma Chi. Clubs: Commercial, Algonquin (Boston); Princeton (N.Y.C.). Home: 20 Bufflehead Ln East Orleans MA 02643-0515

HALLOWELL, WALTER HENRY, insurance company executive; b. Rockville Centre, N.Y., Apr. 24, 1943; s. Walter Henry and Anne (Dorman) H.; m. Marilyn Patricia Gallagher, Nov. 28, 1964; children: Denise, Christine. BA, Fordham U., 1964; MBA, St. John's U., Queens, N.Y., 1973. Mktg. supr. Aetna Casualty Co., N.Y.C., 1964-77; prodn. mgr. CNA Ins., N.Y.C., 1977-78; asst. v.p., mgr. Continental Ins. Co., N.Y.C., 1978-82; v.p., mgr. Continental Ins. Co., Livingston, N.J., 1982-83; sr. v.p. Continental Ins. Co., Piscataway, N.J., 1984, pres. agy. group, 1985-86, corp. exec. v.p., 1987-88; corp. exec. v.p. Selective Ins. Group, Branchville, N.J., 1988—. Mem. Casualty and Surety Club N.Y. (sec.-treas. 1984, 2d v.p. 1985, 1st v.p. 1986, pres. 1987). Roman Catholic. Home: 19 Quincy Rd Basking Ridge NJ 07920 Office: Selective Ins Group Inc 40 Wantage Ave Branchville NJ 07890

HALPERIN, ERIC BRIAN, auditor; b. Montreal, Que., Can., Jan. 15, 1959; s. Alexander Harris Halperin and June Hilda (Sanders) Sattler. BA, U. Calif., Santa Barbara, 1982; MBA, George Washington U., 1984. CPA, Calif. Internal auditor Unisource, Long Beach, Calif., 1986-87; dir. internal audit The Nature Conservancy, Arlington, Va., 1987—. Mem. Fin. Analyst Fedn., Inst. Internal Auditors, Assn. Pvt. Vol. Orgns. Fin. Mgrs. Democrat. Jewish. Office: The Nature Conservancy 1815 N Lynn Arlington VA 22209

HALPERIN, JEROME ARTHUR, pharmaceutical company executive; b. Paterson, N.J., Feb. 21, 1937; s. Harry Nathan and Frieda (Niestat) H.; m. Barbara Anne Hott, Sept. 1, 1963; children: Alicia Jennifer, Rachel Elizabeth. BS, Rutgers U., 1958; MPH, Johns Hopkins U., 1962; MS, MIT, 1974. Commd. officer USPHS, 1958; staff pharmacist USPHS Hosps., Dept. HEW, Albuquerque and N.Y.C., 1958-61, advanced through grades to surgeon gen. (rear adm.), 1958-83; radiol. health specialist Calif. Health Dept., Berkeley, 1962-65; dir. states agreement Bur. Radiol. Health, Rockville, Md., 1965-66; dir. indsl. radiation and air hygiene Kans. Dept. Health, Topeka, 1966-68; regional rep. Bur. Radiol. Health, Chgo., 1968-71; dir. Northeastern Radiol. Health Lab., FDA, HEW, Winchester, Mass., 1971-73; dep. assoc. dir. new drug evaluation Bur. Drugs, FDA, HEW, Rockville, Md., 1974-77, dep. dir., 1977-82; acting dir. Office of Drugs Nat. Ctr. for Drugs and Biologies FDA, Rockville, 1982-83; v.p. tech. CIBA Consumer Pharms., Edison, N.J., 1983—; nat. bd. advisors U. Ariz. Coll. Pharmacy, Tucson, 1986—; adv. bd. U. Calif. Drug Studies Unit, San Francisco, 1983—; chmn. Conf. on Pharmacy 21st Century, Va., 1984; cons. WHO, 1979-86. Contbr. articles to profl. jours. Mem. Bd. Health, Hoffman Estates, Ill., 1971; bd. dirs. Perspective Woods Citizen Assn., Olney, Md., 1977-80. Named Alumnus of Yr. Rutgers U., 1981; recipient Outstanding Service award Federally Employed Women's Assn., 1983. Fellow Am. Pub. Health Assn.; mem. AAAS, Am. Assn. Pharm. Scientists (charter), Drug Info. Assn., Am. Pharm. Assn. Jewish. Office: CIBA Consumer Pharms Raritan Plaza III Raritan Ctr Edison NJ 08837

HALPERIN, RICHARD E., lawyer, holding company executive; b. N.Y.C., Dec. 7, 1954; s. Alvin M. and Anne (Beecher) H.; m. Lucy Landesman, Oct. 5, 1980. BS cum laude, Boston U., 1976; JD, New Eng. Sch. of Law, 1979. Bar: N.Y. 1980. Adminstrv. asst. to atty. gen. N.Y. State Exec. Bur., 1979-84; pres. R.O.P. Aviation, Teterboro, N.J., 1984; sr. v.p., spl. counsel to the chmn. Revlon Group Inc., N.Y.C., 1985—, MacAndrews & Forbes Group, Inc., N.Y.C., 1984—; pres. Revlon Found., 1985, MacAndrews & Forbes Found., N.Y.C., 1984—. Office: MacAndrews & Forbes Group Inc 36 E 63rd St New York NY 10021

HALPERIN, RICHARD GEORGE, data processing executive; b. Chgo., Apr. 5, 1948; s. Robert Charles and Phyllis Dorothy (Jewel) H.; m. Carolyn A'Della Bacino, Oct. 5, 1974; children: Nicole, Heidi, Erik. BSBA, Northwestern U., 1970. Mktg. mgr. IBM, Des Plaines, Ill., 1979-83; area dir. Wang Labs., Rolling Meadows, Ill., 1983-85; v.p. sales and svcs. System Software Assoc., Chgo., 1985—; bd. dirs. System Software Assoc., Sydney, Australia; bd. dirs. Adminstrn. EDP, Sydney; ptnrship. CADDO Petroleum, Shreveport, La., 1981-86, BLM, Shreveport, 1981—. Named Top Dist. Mgr., Wang, Chgo., and Rome, 1984. Mem. Internat. Soc. Philosophical Enquiry, Data Processing Mgrs. Assn., Northwestern Club of Chgo., Delta Upsilon, "N" Club Mens (Evanston, Ill.). Address: 641 Golf Rd Crystal Lake IL 60014

HALPERIN, ROBERT MILTON, electrical machinery company executive; b. Chgo., June 1, 1928; s. Herman and Edna Pearl (Rosenberg) H.; m. Ruth Levison, June 19, 1955; children: Mark, Margaret, Philip. Ph.B., U. Chgo., 1949; B.Mech. Engring., Cornell U., 1949; M.B.A., Harvard U., 1952. Engr. Electro-Motive div. Gen. Motors Corp., La Grange, Ill., 1949-50; trust rep. Bank of Am., San Francisco, 1954-56; adminstr. Dumont Corp., San Rafael, Calif., 1956-57; pres. Raychem Corp., Menlo Park, Calif., 1957—; also bd. dirs. Raychem Corp., Menlo Park, 1961—; bd. dirs. Molecular Design Ltd. Trustee U. Chgo.; bd. dirs. Harvard Bus. Sch. Assocs., Stanford U. Hosp. Served to lt. USAF, 1952-53. Club: Harvard of New York City. Home: 80 Reservoir Rd Atherton CA 94025 Office: Raychem Corp 300 Constitution Dr Menlo Park CA 94025

HALPERN, JACK, chemist, educator; b. Poland, Jan. 19, 1925; came to U.S., 1962, naturalized; s. Philip and Anna (Sass) H.; m. Helen Peritz, June 30, 1949; children: Janice Henry, Nina Phyllis. BS, McGill U., 1946, PhD, 1949; DSc (hon.), U. B.C., 1986. Postdoctorate overseas fellow NRC, U. Manchester, Eng., 1949-50; instr. chemistry U. B.C., 1950, prof., 1961-62; Nuffield Found. traveling fellow Cambridge (Eng.) U., 1959-60; prof. chemistry U. Chgo., 1962-71, Louis Block prof. chemistry, 1971-83, Louis Block Disting. Service prof., 1983—; vis. prof. U. Minn., 1962, Harvard, 1966-67, Calif. Inst. Tech., 1968-69, Princeton U., 1970-71, Max. Planck Institut, Mulheim, Fed. Republic Germany, 1983—, vis. prof. U. Copenhagen, 1978; Sherman Fairchild Disting. scholar Calif. Inst. Tech., 1979; guest scholar Kyoto U., 1981; Firth vis. prof. U. Sheffield, 1982; numerous guest lectureships; cons. editor Macmillan Co., 1963-65, Oxford U. Press; cons. Am. Oil Co., Monsanto Co., Argonne Nat. Lab., IBM, Air Products Co., EniChem; mem. adv. panel on chemistry NSF, 1967-70; mem. adv. bd. Am. Chem. Soc. Petroleum Research Fund, 1972-74; mem. medicinal chemistry sect. NIH, 1975-78, chmn., 1976-78; mem. chemistry adv. council Princeton U., 1982—; mem. univ. adv. com. Ency. Brit., 1985—. Assoc. editor: Inorganica Chimica Acta, Jour. Am. Chem. Soc.; co-editor: Collected Accounts of Transition Metal Chemistry, vol. 1, 1973, vol. 2, 1977; mem. editorial bd. Jour. Organometallic Chemistry, Ency. Britannica, Accounts Chem. Research, Catalysis Revs., Jour. Catalysis, Jour. Molecular Catalysis, Jour. Coordination Chemistry, Gazzetta Chimica Italiana, Organometallics, Catalysis Letters; contbr. articles to research jours. Trustee Gordon Research Confs., 1968-70; bd. govs. David and Arthur Smart Gallery, U. Chgo., 1988—. Recipient Young Author's prize Electrochem. Soc., 1953, award in inorganic chemistry Am. Chem. Soc., 1968, award in catalysis Noble Metals Chem. Soc., London, 1976, Wilhelm von Hoffman medal German Chem. Soc., 1988, Humboldt award, 1977, Richard Kokes award Johns Hopkins U., 1978; Alfred P. Sloan research fellow, 1959-63. Fellow Royal Soc. London, AAAS, Am. Acad. Arts and Scis., Chem. Inst. Can. (hon.), Royal Soc. Chemistry London, N.Y. Acad. Scis., Japan Soc. for Promotion Sci.; mem. Am. Chem. Soc. (editorial bd. Advances in Chemistry series 1963-65, 78-81, chmn. inorganic chemistry div. 1971, award for disting. service in advancement inorganic chemistry, 1985, Willard Gibbs medal 1986, Bailar medal U. Ill. 1986), Nat. Acad. Scis. (fgn. assoc. 1984-85, mem. 985—), Max Planck Soc. (sci. mem. 1983—), Art Inst. Chgo., Renaissance Soc. (bd. dirs. 1985—), Sigma Xi. Home: 5630 Dorchester Ave Chicago IL 60637 Office: U Chgo Dept Chemistry Chicago IL 60637

HALPERN, MERRIL MARK, investment banker; b. Bayonne, N.J., May 4, 1934; s. Samuel and Belle (Schwartz) H.; BS, Rutgers U., 1956; MBA, Harvard, 1962; m. Phyllis Goldstein, June 14, 1960; children: Belle Linda, Jennifer, Samuel, Isaac. With Ernst & Ernst, N.Y.C., 1956-60, sr. acct., 1958-60; with McDonnell & Co., Inc., 1962-68, v.p., 1967-68; ptnr. H. Hentz & Co., N.Y.C., 1969—, dir. corp. fin., 1969-70; prin. Merril M. Halpern & Co., N.Y.C., 1970-73; pres. Charterhouse Group Internat., Inc., London, 1973-84, chmn. bd., 1984—; dir. Charter Crellin, Inc., 1986—, Dreyer's Grand Ice Cream, Inc., 1977—, GardenAm. Corp., 1983-84, 85—, Gulf and Miss. Corp., 1986—, Publicker Industries, Inc., 1987—; chmn. bd. Charter Power Systems, Inc., 1986—. Served with AUS, 1957-58. Office: H Hentz & Co 535 Madison Ave New York NY 10022

HALPERSON, MICHAEL ALLEN, rubber company executive; b. Boston, Sept. 11, 1946; s. Bertram David and Rose (Doolan) H. AB, Union Coll., 1968; MA in Teaching, U. Mass., 1970. Asst. to group v.p. Plymouth Rubber Co., Inc., Canton, Mass., 1972—; corp. dir. personnel and indsl. rels. Plymouth Rubber Co., Inc., Canton, 1973-79, mgr. mktg., product cons., 1979-81, dir. sales and mktg., 1981-85, v.p., 1985—; bd. dirs., v.p. The Cape Cod Sea Camps Inc., Camp Wono Inc., Brewster, Capt. Del Assocs. Inc., Brewster, Mass. Bd. dirs. Canton Assn. of Industries Inc., 1977—, Neponset Valley Health System Inc., Norwood, Mass., 1982—, Norwood Hosp., Inc., 1983—, chmn. 1988—, Southwood Community Hosp., Inc., Norfolk, Mass., 1985—, Neponset Valley Nursing Assn., Inc., 1979—. With USAF, 1970-72. Mem. Nat. Office Products Assn., Office Products Mfrs. Assn. (bd. dirs. 1985—), Am. Soc. Personnel Adminstrs., Canton Assn. Industries (bd.dirs. 1977—). Home: PO Box 33 Canton MA 02021 Office: Plymouth Rubber Co Inc 104 Revere St Canton MA 02021

HALPERT, LEONARD WALTER, editor; b. Bklyn., July 7, 1924; s. Daniel and Kate (Hollander) H.; m. Shirley Small, May 25, 1952; 1 child, Melinda. B.A., Bklyn. Coll., N.Y., 1947; M.S. in Journalism, Northwestern U., Evanston, Ill., 1948. Editorial writer Washington Times-Herald, Washington, D.C., 1950-51; reporter Buffalo Evening News, 1948-50, editorial writer, 1951-80, editorial page editor, 1980—. Served with AUS, 1943-45. Mem. Am. Soc. Newspaper Editors, Nat. Conf. Editorial Writers, Sigma Delta Chi. Home: 12 Neumann Pkwy Town of Tonawanda NY 14223 Office: Buffalo News One News Pla Buffalo NY 14240

HALSEY, BRENTON SHAW, paper company executive; b. Newport News, Va., 1927. B.S. in Chem. Engring., U. Va.; postgrad., Inst. of Paper Chemistry. Vice pres. planning Albemarle Paper Co., 1955-66; pres., gen. mgr. Interstate Bag. Co., 1966-68; co-founder James River Corp. of Va., Richmond, 1969, now chmn., chief exec. officer, dir.; dir. Dominion Bankshares, Dominion Nat. Bank, Westmoreland Coal Co. Office: James River Corp Va Tredegar St Box 2218 Richmond VA 23217

HALSEY, JAMES ALBERT, international entertainment impressario, theatrical producer, talent manager; b. Independence, Kans., Oct. 7, 1930; s. Harry Edward and Carrie Lee (Messick) H.; m. Minisa Crumbo; children: Sherman Brooks, Gina. Student, Independence Community Coll., 1948-50, U. Kans. Pres. Thunderbird Artists, Inc., Independence, from 1950; pres. Jim Halsey Co., Inc., Tulsa, from 1952, now chmn., chief exec. officer; pres. Norwood Advt. Agy., James Halsey Property Mgmt. Co., Tulsa Proud Country Entertainment, Stas. KTOW/KGOW, Silverline-Goldline Pub., J.H. Radio Mgmt., Cyclone Records, Tulsa Records, J.H. Lighting and Sound Co., Singin' T Prodns.; v.p. Gen. Artists Corp. now Century City Artists Corp., Beverly Hills, Calif., 1956—; chmn., chief exec. officer Century City Artists Corp., Tulsa, Nashville, Pacific Palisades, Calif.; chmn. Churchill Recs. & Video Ltd., from 1981; personal mgr. various entertainment personalities; internat. jurist Golden Orpheus Festival, Bulgaria, 1981-82; pres. Internat. Fedn. Festival Orgns., Pacific Palisades; producer shows for auditoriums, fairs, rodeos, TV, internat. music fests also others in U.S. and internationally including Tulsa Internat. Music Festival, 1977-80, Neewollah Internat. Music Festival, 1981-83; gen. ptnr. Parker Ranch, Tulsa; bd. dirs. Merc. Bank and Trust, Tulsa, Citizens Nat. Bank, Independence, Farmers & Mchts. Bank, Mound City, Kans. Trustee Philbrook Art Ctr., Tulsa; bd. dirs. Thomas Gilcrease Mus. Assn., Tulsa Philharm. Assn., Roy Clark Celebrity Golf Classic; bd. dirs. UNICEF. Served with U.S. Army, 1954-56. Recipient Disting. Service award U.S. Jr. C. of C., 1959, Ambassador of Country Music award SESAC Corp., 1978, citation Cashbox Mag., 1980, citation Golden Orpheus Festival, 1982, Hubert Long award Mervyn Conn, Eng., 1982, commendation Los Angeles Mayor Tom Bradley, Gov.'s medal Kans. Commn., 1986, Frederic Chopin medal Polish Artist Bur., 1987; named Disting. Kansan Topeka Capital Jour. Mem. Country Music Assn. (bd. dirs. 1963-64, 70-71, v.p. 1979-80, Founding Pres.'s award 1985), Acad. Country Music (bd. dirs. 1969-70, 73-74, v.p. 1975-76, 78-79, 79-80, , 88—, Jim Reeves Meml. award 1977), Internat. Fedn. Festival Orgns. (Am. pres., Oscar Midem award 1982),. Office: Century Cities Artistic Corp 3225 S Norwood Tulsa OK 74135 also: 17351 Sunset Blvd Pacific Palisades CA 90272 also: 24 Music Sq W Nashville TN 37203

HALSTEAD, LESTER MARK, JR., financial planner; b. Las Vegas, Nev., Aug. 13, 1950; s. Lester M. and Eleanor Grace (Bradford) H.; m. Judy Lynn Cook, Apr. 21, 1984; children: Gregory Jason, Justin Mark, Michelle Lynn. Student, U. Nev., Las Vegas, 1969-73, Clark County Community Coll., 1979. Cert. fin. planner. Asst. mgr. Thrifty Drug Store, Las Vegas, 1968-74; mgr. Kentucky Fried Chicken, Las Vegas, 1974-77; clk. supr. Reynolds Elec. & Engring., Las Vegas, 1977-79; dept. mgr. Grand Cen. Stores, Las Vegas, 1979-84; fin. planner Money Concepts of the Gt. West, Las Vegas, 1984-85; sr. account exec., fin. planner Nev. Plan Am. Ctr., Las Vegas, 1985—. Bd. com. mem. Boy Scouts Am., Las Vegas, 1986-88. Recipient Excellence in Fin. Planning award CUNA Mut. Fin. Svcs., Madison, Wis., 1986. Mem. Internat. Assn. Fin. Planning (v.p. pub. rels. Las Vegas chpt. 1986—), Inst. Cert. Fin. Planners. Republican. Mormon. Home: 6232 Espinosa Ave Las Vegas NV 89108 Office: Nev Plan Ctr 3100 W Sahara Ave Ste 207 Las Vegas NV 89102

HALTER, H. JAMES, JR., jewelry company executive; b. Fernandina, Fla., Feb. 28, 1947; s. Henry James and Grace (Bealey) H.; m. Wanda O'Quinn, Mar. 15, 1970; children: Jennifer, John, Elizabeth, Amelia. BS in Mgmt., Valdosta State Coll., 1970. Sales mgr. Southwestern Co., Nashville, 1969; collection mgr. Fla. Title & Mortgage Co., Jacksonville, 1970-72; appraiser Richard Hamilton & Assocs., Jacksonville Beach, 1972-74; exec. v.p. Developers Investors Svc. Corp., Jacksonville, 1975-78; pres. A-Coin and Stamp Gallery, Inc., Jacksonville, 1978-81; ptnr. Jacksonville Precious Metals, 1981, Sidetrack Video Arcade Chain, Ga., 1982-84; pres. Diamond House Corp., Valdosta, Ga., 1985—, J-Mart Jewelry Outlets, Inc., Tifton, Ga., 1988—; also bd. dirs. J-Mart Jewelry Outlets, Inc. Author: May I Help You, 1988. Bd. dirs. Park Ave. United Meth. Ch., Valdosta, 1986—, Alapha Coun. Boy Scouts Am., 1982—. Adm. USN. Recipient Addy award, 1980, 83. Mem. Toastmasters, Sertoma, Vigil Honor, Order of the Arrow, Rotary, Sigma Iota (pres. charter), Alpha Phi Omega. Home: P O Box 2902 Valdosta GA 31604

HALTIWANGER, ROBERT SIDNEY, JR., book publishing executive; b. Winston-Salem, N.C., Mar. 15, 1923; s. Robert Sidney and Janie Love (Couch) H. A.B., Harvard U., 1947. Coll. field rep. Prentice-Hall Inc., Atlanta, 1947-56, Southeast regional mgr., 1956-65; dir. Two Year div. Prentice-Hall Inc., Englewood Cliffs, N.J., 1965-71; v.p. sales Prentice-Hall Inc, Englewood Cliffs, N.J., 1971-80, exec. v.p. coll. div., 1980-85; pres. sales and mktg. coll. div. Prentice-Hall Inc, 1985—. Served to 1st lt. USAF, 1943-46, PTO. Recipient Chmn. award Gulf and Western, 1985, Frank Enenbach award Prentice-Hall Coll. Div., 1987. Mem. Am. Assn. Pubs. (liason com. 1975-82). Democrat. Presbyterian. Home: 1 Horizon Rd Fort Lee NJ 07024 Office: Prentice Hall Inc Englewood Cliffs NJ 07632

HALVERSTADT, ROBERT DALE, engineer, manufacturing company executive; b. Warren, Ohio, Jan. 25, 1920; s. Roscoe B. and Dorothy (Grubbs) H.; B.S. in Mech. Engring., Case Inst. Tech., 1951; m. Maryella Greene, Dec. 31, 1941; children—Marta Jean (Mrs. Michael Carmen), Linda Anne (Mrs. Gary Orelup), Sally Jo. Journeyman machinist Republic Steel Corp., Cleve., 1939-51; design engr. Gen. Electric Co., Evendale, Ohio, 1951-53; supr. Metalworking Lab., 1953-58, corp. cons., N.Y.C., 1958-59, mgr. Thomson Engring. Lab., Lynn, Mass., 1959-63; gen. mgr. engring. Continental Can Co., N.Y.C., 1963-64; group v.p. Booz, Allen & Hamilton Inc., N.Y.C., 1964-73, chief exec. Foster D. Snell Inc. subs., 1964-72, pres. Design & Devel., Inc. subs., 1966-70; v.p. tech. Singer Co., 1973-74; pres. Spl. Metals Corp. subs. Allegheny Ludlum Industries, Inc., New Hartford, N.Y., 1974-81, pres. Materials Tech. Group, 1981-83, mng. dir. Allegheny Ludlum Industries Ltd.; sr. staff v.p. Allegheny Internat., 1983-85; pres. AIMe Assocs., New Canaan, Conn., 1985-87; chmn. bd. Spl. Metal Corp., 1987—; co-chmn. Titanium Metals Corp. Am.; dir. Oneida Nat. Bank, Carus Corp., Centrex Labs., Inc. Pres., Industry, Labor and Edn. Council Mohawk

Valley, Inc. Served with USCGR, 1942-45. Registered profl. engr., N.Y., Ohio. Fellow Am. Soc. Metals (trustee); mem. ASME, Am. Inst. Chem. Engrs., Am. Ordnance Assn., Regional Plan Assn., Am. Water Resources Assn., N.Y. Acad. Scis., Mohawk Valley C. of C. (dir.), Chemists Club, Sigma Xi, Tau Beta Pi, Theta Tau. Mem. United Ch. of Christ. Clubs: Toastmasters; Woodway Country; University (N.Y.C.). Editorial bd. Internat. Jour. Turbo and Jet Engine Tech. Patentee in field. Home: 333 Oenoke Ridge Rd New Canaan CT 06840 Office: Spl Metal Corp PO Box 1649 New Canaan CT 06840

HALVORSON, GEORGE CHARLES, health care insurance company executive; b. Fargo, N.D., Jan. 28, 1947; s. George Charles and Barbara Theone (Paulson) H.; m. Mary Elizabeth Probst, June 27, 1986; children: Jonathan Dale, Seth Gregory, George Charles IV. BA, Concordia Coll., Moorhead, Minn., 1968. Cert. health cons., 1981. Successively mgr. market research, mgr. corp. planning, dir. planning and budget, v.p. planning and budget, sr. v.p. Blue Cross & Blue Shield, St. Paul; exec. dir. HMO Minn., St. Paul; pres. Sr. Health Plan, St. Paul, 1983-86, Health Accord, Inc., Mpls., 1983-86, Group Health, Inc., Mpls., 1986—; ops. dir. HMO/Jamaica, Kingston, 1985-86; cons. AIG/Am. Internat. Health, Washington, 1987-88; lectr. in field. Author: How to Cut Your Company's Health Care Costs; contbr. articles to profl. jours. Chmn. Boy Scout Food Drive, St. Paul, 1988; fund raiser United Way, Mpls., 1987-88. Recipient Internship award Wall St. Jour. Newspaper Fund, 1968. Mem. Nat. Coop. Bus. Assn. (bd. dirs.), Minn. Bus. Partnership (bd. dirs.), Group Health Assn. Am., Minn. Council HMO's (bd. dirs.). Club: Decathlon (Bloomington, Minn.). Office: Group Health Inc 2829 University Ave SE Minneapolis MN 55414

HAMBLETON, GEORGE BLOW ELLIOTT, management consultant; b. Balt., Dec. 20, 1929; s. John Adams Hambleton and Margaret (Elliott) Carey; m. Janet Findlay MacLaren, Mar. 17, 1962; children: Anne Carey, Charles MacLaren, James Elliott. AB, Princeton U., 1952; PMD, Harvard U., 1964. Various positions with Latin American div. Pan Am, 1955-62; asst. div. service mgr. Pan Am, Miami, Fla., 1963-64; dir. USSR Pan Am, Moscow, 1966-70; dir. internat. affairs Pan Am, Washington, 1971-76; dir. comml. sales Pan Am, N.Y.C., 1977-80; v.p. mktg. N.Y. Airways, N.Y.C., 1976-77; exec. dir., vice chmn. Project Orbis, Inc., N.Y.C., 1980-83; pres. Andrews MacLaren, Inc., N.Y.C., 1983-86; dep. asst. sec. U.S. and Foreign Comml. Service, Internat. Trade Adminstrn. U.S. Dept. Commerce, Washington, 1986-88; sr. v.p. Mgmt. Internat. Inc., Westport, Conn., 1988—; bd. dirs. Flight Found., Inc., Washington, Andrews MacLaren Ltd., Northants, Eng. Dir. foreign policy discussion group, Washington, 1975-87; mem. N.J. Conservation Found., N.J., 1987. Served to 1st lt. U.S. Army, 1952-55, Korea. Mem. Foreign Policy Assn., Aircraft Owners and Pilots Assn., Upper Raritan Watershed Assn, U.S. Dept. Commerce (dist. export coun. Conn. 1989). Republican. Episcopalian. Clubs: Brook (N.Y.); Met. (Washington); Naval and Mil. (London); Md. (Balt.); Princeton (N.Y., Washington); Greenspring Valley Hunt (Balt.); Harvard Bus. Sch. (Washington) (v.p. 1973-76); Wings (N.Y.); Aero (Washington). Home: Stone Valley Farm 163 Burrell Rd Lebanon NJ 08833 Office: Mgmt Internat Inc 1853 Post Road E Westport CT 06880

HAMBLETT, STEPHEN, newspaper publishing executive; b. 1937. BA, Harvard U., 1957. With Providence Jour. Co., 1957—, various sales and mgmt. positions, 1957-69, asst. v.p., 1974-79, from v.p. mktg. corp. devel. to exec. v.p., 1979-85, pres., asst. pub., 1985-87, chmn., pub., chief exec. officer, 1987—. Office: Providence Jour Co 75 Fountain St Providence RI 02902

HAMBLEY, DOUGLAS FREDERICK, mining engineer; b. Toronto, Ont., Can., Jan. 14, 1950; s. Fredrick Armstrong and Gwendolyn Shannon (Plant) H. BS in Mining Engring., Queen's U., Kingston, Ont., 1972; MBA, Lewis U., 1986; postgrad., U. Waterloo, Ont., 1988—. Jr. mine engr. Iron Ore Co. Can. Ltd., Schefferville, Que., 1972-73; mining engr. trainee Falconbridge (Ont.) Nickel Mines Ltd., 1974-75; mining engr. Harrison Bradford and Assocs. Ltd., St. Catharines, Ont., 1975-76; project engr. Denison Mines Ltd., Elliot Lake, Ont., 1977-80; sr. mining engr. Engrs. Internat. Inc., Westmont, Ill., 1980-84; mining engr. Argonne (Ill.) Nat. Lab., 1984—; cons. MRAZ Project Cons. Ltd., Saskatoon, Sask., Can. Contbr. articles to profl. jours. Recipient cert. appreciation Office Geol. Repositories Dept. Energy. Mem. Soc. Mining Engr. Inc., Assn. Engring. Geologists, Can. Inst. Mining and Metallurgy (2d prize essay contest 1973), Soc. Explosives Engrs., Internat. Soc. Rock Mechanics. Home: 1051 N Oakley Dr W107 Westmont IL 60559 Office: Argonne Nat Lab EES-362 9700 S Cass Ave Argonne IL 60439

HAMBLEY, SCOTT GLENWOOD, communications executive; b. Providence, Mar. 21, 1955; s. Jackson Wells and Barbara Jean (Fetzer) H.; m. Constance Marie Eugenia Johnson, Nov. 24, 1984. BA, Bowdoin Coll., 1977; MBA, Dartmouth Coll., 1982. Mfg. engr. Split Ball Bearing, Lebanon, N.H., 1978-79; mktg. cons. Summa Four, Inc., Manchester, N.H., 1979-80; telecommunications planner IBM, White Plains, N.Y., 1981; systems mktg. rep. IBM, Burlington, Vt., 1982-85; dir. remarketing C.S.A. Fin. Corp., Boston, 1985; account exec. Computer Intelligence, LaJolla, Calif., 1986—. Program dir. Experiment in Internat. Living, Putney, Vt., 1979; founder Ann. Clean-up Campaign, Bedford, N.Y., 1969. Mem. Computer Dealers and Lessors Assn., Sales and Mktg. Execs. of Greater Boston, Delta Kappa Epsilon. Republican. Episcopalian. Home: 52 Warehouse Ln Rowley MA 01969 Office: Computer Intelligence Prudential Tower Bldg 800 Boylston St Ste 575 Boston MA 02199

HAMBRICK, MARVIN K., energy company executive; b. Cin., 1921. B.A., U. Okla., 1948. Mgr., Arthur Andersen & Co., Houston, 1949-57, mng. ptnr., Oklahoma City, 1957-73; v.p. fin. Kerr-McGee Corp., Oklahoma City, 1973-77, exec. v.p., 1977-87, also dir.; dir. Kendavis Holding Co.; trustee, bd. dirs. Penrod Drilling Corp. Office: PO Box 25861 Oklahoma City OK 73125

HAMBURGER, JEFFREY ALLEN, financial planner; b. N.Y.C., Aug. 17, 1947; s. Erich G. and Inge J. (Kant) H.; m. Linda E. Dubow, May 29, 1969; children: Brian S., Rachael E. BS, Monmouth Coll., 1969. Chartered fin. cons.; registered investment advisor. V.p. Access Assn., Hackensack, N.J., 1976-80; pres. Fin. Roadmaps, Clifton, N.J., 1980-85; v.p. The Fin. Network, Clifton, 1986-87; pres. Access Fin. Planning, Clifton, 1987—; agt. council Lincon Nat., Integrated Resources. Council mem. Cub Scouts, Leonia, N.J., 1982-83; fin. sec. Congregation Sons of Israel, 1985-86. Served as sgt. USNG, 1968-74. Named an Agt. of Yr., Mut. of N.Y., 1977-79, Life Underwriter of Yr., Passaic/Bergen Life Underwriters. Mem. Internat. Assn. for Fin. Planning, Nat. Assn. Life Underwriters (pres. 1977-86), Am. Soc. CLU's and CHFC's, N.J. Estate Planning Council. Jewish. Office: Access Fin Planning 1033 Clifton Ave Clifton NJ 07015

HAMBY, A. GARTH, beverage company executive; b. Oneonta, Ala., 1938. B.A. in Journalism, U. Ala., 1959. Reporter Columbus Ledger News, 1959-61; various positions Ga. Power Co., 1961-67; staff rep. pub. reins. dept. Coca-Cola Co., Atlanta, 1967-70, mgr. editorial group pub. reins. dept., 1970-74, asst. to chmn. bd., 1974-78, v.p., sec., dir., corp. external affairs, 1978-79; sr. v.p., sec., dir. corp. external affairs Coca-Cola Co., 1979-80, exec. v.p., sec., 1980-81; exec. v.p. Coca-Cola Co., Atlanta, 1981—. Office: Coca-Cola Co 1 Coca-Cola Pla NW Atlanta GA 30313 *

HAMEISTER, LAVON LOUETTA, farm manager, social worker; b. Blairstown, Iowa, Nov. 27, 1922; d. George Frederick and Bertha (Anderson) Hameister; B.A., U. Iowa, 1944; postgrad. N.Y. Sch. Social Work, Columbia, 1945-46, U. Minn. Sch. Social Work, summer 1952; M.A., U. Chgo., 1959. Child welfare practitioner Fayette County Dept. Social Welfare, West Union, Iowa, 1946-56; dist. cons. services in child welfare and pub. assistance Iowa Dept. Social Welfare, Des Moines, 1956-58, dist. field rep., 1959-64, regional supr., 1964-65, supr., specialist supervision, adminstrn. Bur. Staff Devel., 1965-66, chief Bur. Staff Devel., 1966-68; chief div. staff devel. and tng. Office Dep. Commr., Iowa Dept. Social Services, 1968-72, asst. dir. Office Staff Devel., 1972-79, coordinator continuing edn., 1979-86; now co-mgr. Hameister Farm, Blairstown, Iowa. Active in drive to remodel, enlarge Oelwein (Iowa) Mercy Hosp., 1952; active in devel. mental health ctrs. in N.E. Iowa in 1950's. Mem. Bus. and Profl. Women's Club (chpt. sec. 1950-52), Am. Assn. U. Women, Nat. Assn. Social Workers (chpt. sec.-elect 1958-59), Am. Pub. Welfare Assn., Iowa Welfare Assn., Acad. Cert. Social Workers. Lutheran.

HAMEL, ALDONA MARY, leasing company executive; b. Lowell, Mass., Oct. 17, 1946; d. Frederick E. and Aldona Mary (Pieslak) H.; m. Robert Louis Gomes, Feb. 1, 1969 (div. 1977); m. David Exton Devendorf, Aug. 12, 1978; children: Hilary Dandridge, Alexandra Exton. BA, Boston U., 1968. Lic. real estate salesman, Conn. Mgr. litigation dept. Pepsico Leasing Corp., Lexington, Mass., 1969-74; mgr. vendor programs Keybank Inc. Leasing, Waltham, Mass., 1974-77; mgr. nat. accounts Pitney Bowes Credit Corp., Norwalk, Conn., 1977-83; v.p. Citicorp N.Am., Harrison, N.Y, 1984—; sr. v.p. mktg. DPF Group Ltd., Woodcliff Lake, N.J., 1986—. Mem. Am. Assn. Equipment Lessors (programming com. 1988, oper. lease com. 1989—), Women in Equipment Leasing (founder and pres. 1987—). Republican. Office: DPF Group Ltd 50 Tice Blvd Woodcliff Lake NJ 07675

HAMEL, LOUIS REGINALD, systems analysis consultant; b. Lowell, Mass., July 23, 1945; s. Wilfred John and Angelina Lucienne (Paradis) H.; AA, Kellogg Community Coll., 1978; m. Roi Anne Roberts, Mar. 24, 1967 (dec.); 1 child, Felicia Antoinette; m. Anne Louise Staup, July 2, 1972; children: Shawna Michelle, Louis Reginald III. Retail mgr. Marshalls Dept. Stores, Beverly, Mass., 1972-73; tech. service rep. Monarch Marking Systems, Framingham, Mass., 1973-74; employment specialist Dept. Labor, Battle Creek, Mich., 1977-78; v.p. corp. Keith Polygraph Cons. and Investigative Service, Inc., Battle Creek, Mich., 1978-79; indsl. engr., engine components div. Eaton Corp., Battle Creek, Mich., 1979-82; tooling and process engr. Kelley Tech. Services, Battle Creek, Mich., Clark Equipment Inc., 1983-84; tooling and mfg. engr., mfg. mgr. Trans Guard Industries Inc., Angola, Ind., 1983-85; facilitator employee involvement program Wohlert Corp., Lansing, Mich., 1985—; systems analysis cons., 1975—. Mem. Calhoun County Com. on Employment of Handicapped, Battle Creek, Mich., 1977-78; mem. U.S. Congl. Adv. Bd., Lansing Area Labor Mgmt. Com., 1986—. With USN, 1963-71, Vietnam. Recipient Services to Handicapped award Internat. Assn. Personnel in Employment Security, Mich. chpt., 1978. Mem. Nat. Geog. Soc., Mich. Assn. Concerned Vets. (dir.), Nat. Assn. Concerned Vets., VFW, Internat. Platform Assn. Democrat. Roman Catholic. Home and Office: 12240 Assyria Rd Bellevue MI 49021

HAMER, JEFFREY MICHAEL, software company executive, consultant; b. Los Angeles, Mar. 11, 1949; s. William Chisdes and Barbara Renee (Wager) H.; BArch. with honors, U. So. Calif., 1971; MArch. with honors, UCLA, 1973; m. Deborah Sue Schwartz, Nov. 29, 1975; children: Stephen Andrew, Jonathan Alan, Jacqueline Paul. Architect/systems analyst Skidmore, Owings & Merrill, Chgo., 1973-74; dir. R&D Group, Cannell-Heumann & Assocs./Albert C. Martin & Assocs., Los Angeles, 1974-78; pres., chief exec. officer The Computer-Aided Design Group, Marina del Rey, Calif., 1978—; mem. faculty Grad. Sch. Architecture and Urban Planning, UCLA, 1974—. Bd. dirs. Speech Pathology Found., 1983—, Internat. Facility Mgmt. Assn., 1987—. Mem. Assn. Computing Machinery, AIA, Assn. for Computers in Design (bd. dirs. 1983-86). Author: Facility Management Systems, 1988, Van Nostrand Reinhold; contbr. numerous articles to tech. publs. Office: 4215 Glencoe Ave Marina del Rey CA 90292

HAMERMESH, RICHARD G., professional society administrator; b. Altadena, Calif., Feb. 10, 1948; s. Bernard and Sylvia (Molberger) H.; m. Lorie Ann Shapiro Hamermesh, June 21, 1970; children: Joshua, Molli. BA, U. Calif., Berkeley, 1969; MBA, Harvard U., 1971, D Bus. Adminstrn., 1976. Asst. prof. sch. bus. Harvard U., Boston, 1976-81; assoc. prof. Harvard U., 1982-88; mng. ptnr. Ctr. for Exec. Devel., Cambridge, Mass., 1987—. Author: Making Strategy Work, 1986; contbr. articles to profl. jours. Pres. Newton (Mass.) Sch. Found., 1986-87. Jewish. Home: 33 Woodland Rd Auburndale MA 02166 Office: Ctr for Exec Devel 124 Mt Auburn St Ste 200 Cambridge MA 02138

HAMILL, JOHN P., bank executive; b. N.Y.C., 1940; married. A.B., Holy Cross Coll., 1961; Master's Degree in Taxation, NYU Sch. Law, 1964. Bar: N.Y., Ohio. Dep. gen. counsel legal dept. Chem. Bank N.Y.; pres., chief exec. officer Galbreath Mortgage Co.; pres., chief exec. officer trust affiliate, pres. mortgage banking affiliate Banc One Corp., Columbus, Ohio, prior to 1980; exec. v.p., gen. counsel Shawmut Corp., Boston, 1980-81, pres., 1981—; pres. Shawmut; dir. Shawmut Bank N.A., 1981—; vice chmn., dir. Shawmut Nat. Corp., Boston, 1988—. Office: Shawmut Bank 1 Federal St Boston MA 02211

HAMILL, JOHN RANSOM, public relations executive; b. Kansas City, Mo., July 18, 1946; s. John Ransom IV and Joyce (Blaizer) H.; m. Mary Margaret Bender, May 20, 1970; children: LeAnne, Barbara. BS in Journalism, Northwestern U., 1968, MS in Journalism, 1969. Reporter Tulsa Tribune, 1969; reporter asst. news dir. KTUL-TV, Tulsa, 1969-70; press sec. U.S. Ho. Reps., Washington, 1970-74; pub. relations mgr. The Williams Cos., Tulsa, 1974-77; v.p. Schnake & Assocs., Tulsa, 1977-80; asst. gen. mgr. Sta. KGCT-TV, Tulsa, 1980-81; dir. corp. relations Facet Enterprises, Tulsa, 1981—. Contbr. articles to mags. Pres. Am. Lung Assn. of Green County, Tulsa, 1979-81, v.p. Theatre Tulsa, 1984-87. Recipient Bronze Leadership award Jr. Achievement, Inc., N.Y.C., 1986. Mem. Pub. Relations Soc. Am. (APR award), Soc. of Profl. Journalists (treas. ea. Okla. chapter 1976-77), Lung Assn. of Okla. (v.p. 1984), Nat. Investor Relations Inst. (pres. Tulsa chpt. 1986—), Sigma Delta Chi. Democrat. Methodist. Club: Meadowbrook Country (Tulsa), Tulsa Press. Home: 9727 S Maplewood Tulsa OK 74137 Office: Facet Enterprises Inc 6100 S Yale Tulsa OK 74136

HAMILL, RICHARD DAVID, medical products company executive; b. Visalia, Calif., Jan. 5, 1939; s. Edward Charles and Elizabeth (Scheidt) H.; m. Mary Lucinda Kilbourne, Aug. 26, 1961; children: Lucinda L., Pamela S., Edward B., Stephanie L. BS, U. Utah, 1960, PhD, 1965. Registered pharmacist, Calif., Utah. Research pharmacist Miles Labs., Elkhart, Ind., 1965-66; from asst. to sr. v.p. research and devel., dir. research and adminstrn., dir. quality assurance Hyland div., corp. dir. product assurance Baxter Travenol Labs., Deerfield, Ill., 1966-76; dir. corp. compliance G.D. Searle & Co., Skokie, Ill., 1976-79; pres. Hamill Assocs. Inc., Northbrook, Ill., 1979-83; pres., chief exec. officer Hycor Biomed., Inc., Garden Grove, Calif., 1983—. Mem. Am. Pharm. Assn. Republican. Home: 22686 Ledana Mission Viejo CA 92691 Office: Hycor Biomed Inc 7272 Chapman Ave Garden Grove CA 92641

HAMILTON, ALLAN CORNING, retired oil company executive; b. Chgo., June 9, 1921; s. Daniel Sprague and Mildred (Corning) H.; m. Edith Johnson, June 3, 1950; children: Kimball C., Scott W., Dean C., Gail W. B.S. in Econs., Harverford Coll., 1943. With Standard Oil Co., N.J., 1946-51, Esso Export Corp., 1951-56; treas. Internat. Petroleum co. Ltd., Coral Gables, Fla., 1956-61, Esso Internat. Inc., 1961-66; with Exxon Corp. (formerly Standard Oil Co., N.J.), N.Y.C., 1966-83; treas., prin. fin. officer Exxon Corp. (formerly Standard Oil co., N.J.), N.Y.C., 1970-83; bd. dirs. Glaxo Enterprises Inc.; chmn. Sullivan Money Mgmt. Inc.; trustee The Common Fund. Mem. vis. com. Grad. Sch. bus. U. Chgo.; chmn. council Grad. Mgmt. Inst., Union Coll. Served to lt. USNR, 1943-46. Clubs: Woodway Country (Darien, Conn.); Explorers, Metropolitan (N.Y.C.).

HAMILTON, BEVERLY LANNQUIST, comptroller; b. Roxbury, Mass., Oct. 19, 1946; d. Arthur and Nancy L. B.A. cum laude, U. Mich., 1968; postgrad., Grad. Sch. Bus., NYU, 1969-70. Prin. Auerbach, Pollak & Richardson, N.Y.C., 1972-75; v.p. Morgan Stanley & Co., N.Y.C., 1975-80, United Technologies, Hartford, Conn., 1980-87; 3d dep. comptroller City of N.Y., 1987—; bd. dirs. Conn. Natural Gas Co., Northeast Savs., Conn. Mut. Investment Mgmt., TWA Pilots Annuity Fund, Nat. Conf. Christians and Jews. Trustee Hartford Coll. for Women, 1981-87; bd. dirs. Inst. for Living, 1983-87. Mem. Fin. Women's Assn., Hartford C. of C. (bd. dirs.). Clubs: Hartford, Economic of N.Y. Office: City Hall Mcpl Bldg 1 Center St New York NY 10007 *

HAMILTON, BOBBY WAYNE, small business owner; b. Kingsport, Tenn., May 25, 1946; s. Charles Robert and Juanita Faye (McClellan) H.; m. Wanda Jean Tankersley, June 7, 1969; children: Rachel Susanne, Bobby Steven. Grad. high sch., Kingsport. Chem. operator Tenn. Eastman Co., Kingsport, 1965-76, prodn. records clk., 1976-86, prodn. records and cost clk., 1986-88; coin dealer B.W. Hamilton Coins, Kingsport, 1972—; cons., authenticator B.W. Hamilton Coins, Kingsport, 1972-88. Mem. Am. Numismatics Assn., Numismatics Internat., Nat. Assn. Investors Corp., Liberty Seated Coin Club, Blue Ridge Numismatic Assn. Republican. Club: Model City Coin (Kingsport). Home: 430 Chesterfield Dr Kingsport TN 37663 Office: Tenn Eastman Co Kingsport TN 37662

HAMILTON, BRUCE HALDENE, financial executive; b. Omaha, July 24, 1951; s. Berwyn Haldene and Mildred Melinda (Heck) H.; divorced; children: Aimee, Brian; m. Karen Ellen Clements, Mar. 31, 1985; children: Beth, Robert. BS, Iowa State U., 1973. Cert. mgmt. acct. Acct. Cen. Soya Co., Marion, Ohio, 1973-75; plant controller Gt. Lake Carbon Corp., Marion, 1975-77, div. controller, 1977-79; budget mgr. EMI Med. Inc., Northbrook, Ill., 1979-80; comptroller EDAX Internat. Inc., Lincolnshire, Ill., 1980-83, SSI Techs. Inc., Janesville, Wis., 1983-87; dir. fin. SSI Techs. Inc., Janesville, 1987—. Mem. Nat. Assn. Accts. (v.p. 1975-76, bd. dirs. 1984-86). Republican. Lodge: Lions (bd. dirs. Janesville club 1987-88). Office: SSI Techs Inc 3330 Palmer Dr PO Box 5002 Janesville WI 53547

HAMILTON, CARL WAYNE, investment banker; b. Burkburnett, Tex., Dec. 18, 1939; s. Raymond Carl and Faye (Crabtree) H.; m. Judith Ann Stever, June 23, 1962; children: Mark, Eric, Cynthia, Jennifer. BS, Calif. Inst. Tech., 1962; MA, UCLA, 1965; PhD, MIT, 1969. Systems engr. IBM, L.A., 1962-66; prof. fin. U. So. Calif., L.A., 1969-85; sr. v.p. Am. Med. Internat., Beverly Hills, Calif., 1985-87, First Interstate Bank, Ltd., L.A., 1987—. Author: Model of a Growth Company, 1971; contbr. numerous articles to profl. jours. Recipient Excellence in Teaching award U. So. Calif. Assocs., 1971, Applied Theory award Inst. Mgmt. Sci., 1979; Alfred Sloan scholar, 1962; Nat. Def. fellow, 1966. Mem. Am. Fin. Assn., Fin. Mgmt. Assn., L.A. World Affairs Council. Republican. Office: First Interstate Bank Ltd 707 Wilshire Blvd Los Angeles CA 90017

HAMILTON, D. STEVEN, comptroller, secretary; b. Bluefield, W.Va., Nov. 30, 1955. BBA, W.Va. U., 1978. Staff acct. Ernst & Whinney, Roanoke, Va., 1978-80; cost acct. Hooker Furniture Corp., Martinsville, Va., 1980-86; comptroller, asst. sec. Rish Equipment Co., Bluefield, 1986—. Mem. Nat. Assn. Accts., Martinsville Henry County C. of C. (local govt. com. 1985-86), Lions. Office: Rish Equipment Co PO Box 330 Bluefield WV 24701

HAMILTON, DENNIS OWEN, architectural and consulting engineering company executive; b. Indpls., Mar. 26, 1951; s. Franklin Curtis and Mary Evelyn (Dye) H.; m. Cathy Ann Burton-Davis, Nov. 17, 1972; children: Sarah Marie, Marianne Elizabeth. BS, Ball State U., 1972, MLS, 1974. Tech. lit. librarian KZF Environ Design Cons. Inc., Cin., 1974-85; adminstrv. svcs. mgr. KZF Inc., Cin., 1985—. Bd. dirs. Mason (Ohio) Pub. Library, 1977-85, SpeciaLink, Cin., 1987—. Mem. Spl. Libraries Assn., Computer Applications for Handicapped Users. Home: 3023 Ash Ct Mason OH 45040 Office: KZF Inc 655 Eden Park Dr Cincinnati OH 45202

HAMILTON, JAMES CARL, insurance company executive; b. Somerville, N.J., Mar. 18, 1941; s. William James and Lillie Catherine (Akers) H.; m. Sharon Bentley, June 15, 1963; children: Daniel James, Brenda Marie, Karen René. B.A., Yale U., 1963, M.A., 1965. Instr. math. Temple U., Phila., 1965-66; mem. actuarial staff Aetna Life & Casualty Co., Hartford, Conn., 1967—, v.p., actuary, 1981—. Fellow Soc. Actuaries; mem. Am. Acad. Actuaries. Lutheran. Office: Aetna Life & Casualty Co 151 Farmington Ave Hartford CT 06156

HAMILTON, JAMES MARVIE, electronic research and development executive; b. Blythe, Calif., Jan. 2, 1950; s. D.L. Hamilton and Mary Elizabeth (Dekens) Charboneau; m. Tracy Parks, Mar. 16, 1985. BSEE, Loyola U., Los Angeles, 1972; MS in Computer Sci., UCLA, 1974. Mem. tech. staff Hughes Aircraft, Los Angeles, 1972-76, group head, 1976-80; sect. head Hughes Aircraft, Irvine, Calif., 1980-84; pres., chief exec. officer Coast Tech., San Diego, 1984-87; sect. head Hughes Aircraft, Rancho Santa Margarita, Calif., 1988—; gen. ptnr. Spectrum Investments, San Diego, 1976-82; bd. dirs. Coast Tech., San Diego. Contbr. articles to tech. jours.; patentee integrated circuits and computerized suspension. Bd. dirs. MSJH, Inc. Home for Handicapped Children, San Diego, 1984-86. Mem. IEEE, Loyola Engring. Alumni Assn. (v.p. 1977-78, pres. 1978-79), Sigma Phi Delta, Tau Beta Pi, Alpha Sigma Nu. Republican.

HAMILTON, JUDITH HALL, computer company executive; b. Washington, June 15, 1944; d. George Woods and Jane Fromm (Brogger) Hall; m. David Hamilton, Oct. 2, 1970 (div. 1980); m. Stephen T. McClellan, Oct. 29, 1988. BA, Ind. U., 1966. Programmer System Devel. Corp., Santa Monica, Calif., 1968-69, dir. programming, 1975-80; systems analyst Daylin, Inc., Beverly Hills, Calif., 1969-71; systems mgr. Audio Magnetics, Gardena, Calif., 1971-73; pres. Databasics, Inc., Santa Monica, 1973-75; v.p. Computer Scis. Corp., El Segundo, Calif., 1980-87; ptnr. Arthur Young & Co., L.A., 1987-89, Manhattan, N.Y., 1989—. Mem. World Affairs Council N.Y. Mem. Assn. Data Processing Service Orgns. (bd. dirs.), Orgn. Women Execs., ADAPSO, Kappa Alpha Theta. Office: Arthur Young & Co 277 Park Ave New York NY 10172

HAMILTON, LYMAN CRITCHFIELD, JR., multi-industry executive; b. L.A., Aug. 29, 1926; s. Lyman Critchfield and Edna Lorraine (Gluck) H.; m. Mary W. Shepard, June 25, 1949 (div. 1984); children: William, Richard, Douglas, David; m. Beverly C. Lannquist, Nov. 17, 1984. Student, U. Redlands, 1944-45; BA, Principia Coll., 1947; MPA, Harvard U., 1949; LLD (hon.), Waynesburg Coll., 1979. Budget exeminer U.S. Bur. of Budget, Washington, 1950-56; asst. adminstr. U.S. Civil Adminstrn. of Ryukyu Islands, Okinawa, Japan, 1956-60; investment officer World Bank & IFC, Washington, 1960-62; with Internat. Telephone & Telegraph Corp., N.Y.C., 1962-79, treas., 1967-76, v.p., 1968-73, sr. v.p., 1973-74, exec. v.p., 1974-77, pres., 1977-79, chief oper. officer, 1977, chief exec., 1978-79; chmn., pres. Tamco Enterprises, Inc., N.Y.C., 1980—; also bd. dirs. Tamco Enterprises, Inc.; chmn. Drive Phone, Inc., Paramus, N.J., 1987—, World TV, Inc., N.Y.C., 1988—; vice-chmn. Am. Med. Inaging Corp., Doylestown, Pa., 1988—; bd. dirs. Imperial Corp. Am., San Diego, Travelers Real Estate Investment Trust, Boston, Internat. Cogeneration Corp., Phila., Internat. Mobile Machines Corp. Lt. (j.g.) USNR, 1944-46. Mem. Econs. Club N.Y., Farmington Woods Country, Univ. Club. Republican. Office: World TV Inc 919 3d Ave 6th Fl New York NY 10022

HAMILTON, PETER BANNERMAN, lawyer, manufacturing company executive; b. Phila., Oct. 22, 1946; s. William George Jr. and Elizabeth Jane (McCullough) H.; m. Elizabeth Anne Arthur, May 8, 1982; children—Peter Bannerman, Jr., Brian Arthur. A.B., Princeton U., 1968; J.D., Yale U., 1971. Bar: D.C. 1972, Pa. 1972, Ind. 1985. Mem. staff Office Asst. Sec. Def. for Systems Analysis and Office Gen. Counsel, Dept. Def., Washington, 1971-74; mem. firm Williams & Connolly, Washington, 1974-77; gen. counsel Dept. Air Force, Washington, 1977-78; dep. gen. counsel HEW, Washington, 1979; exec. asst. to sec. HEW, 1979; spl. asst. to Sec. and Dep. Sec. Def., Washington, 1979-80; partner Califano, Ross & Heineman, Washington, 1980-82; v.p., gen. counsel, sec. Cummins Engine Co., Inc., 1983-86, v.p. law and treasury, 1987-88, v.p., chief fin. officer, 1988—. Articles editor: Yale Law Jour, 1970-71. Served to lt. USN, 1971-74. Recipient Exceptional Civilian Service decoration Dept. Air Force, 1978; Dept. Def. medal for Disting. Public Service, 1981. Democrat. Home: 2717 Riverside Dr Columbus IN 47201 Office: Cummins Engine Co Inc Box 3005 Columbus IN 47202

HAMILTON, PETER OWEN, advertising executive; b. Sydney, Australia, Oct. 22, 1944; came to U.S., 1976; s. Ronald Herriot and Muriel (Flood) H.; m. Christine Anne Lane, Jan. 16, 1970; 1 child, Christian John. Diploma in Advt., Sydney Tech. Coll., 1966; grad. advanced mgmt. program, Harvard U., 1984. With McCann-Erickson, 1962—; mgr. McCann-Erickson, Singapore, 1969-72; dir. McCann-Erickson, Australia, 1974, New Zealand, 1975; v.p. worldwide McCann-Erickson, Atlanta, 1976; asst. to pres. worldwide div. McCann-Erickson, N.Y.C., 1973; sr. v.p. worldwide div. McCann-Erickson, Atlanta, 1980-86; exec. v.p. worldwide div., dir. multinat. accounts McCann-Erickson, N.Y.C., 1987—. Fellow South Inst. Australia; mem. Am. Advt. Fedn. Office: McCann-Erickson Worldwide 485 Lexington Ave New York NY 10017

HAMILTON, ROBERT APPLEBY, JR., insurance company executive; b. Boston, Feb. 20, 1940; s. Robert A. and Alice Margaret (Dowdall) H.; student Miami U. (Ohio), 1958-62; m. Ellen Kuhlen, Aug. 13, 1966; children—Jennifer, Robert Appleby, III, Elizabeth. With Travelers Ins. Co., Hartford, Conn., Portland, Maine and Phila., 1962-65; with New Eng. Mut. Life Ins. Co., various locations, 1965—, regional pension rep., Boston, 1968-71, regional mgr., Chgo., 1972-83, sr. pension cons., 1983—. Producer Sta. WCTV; mem. Republican Town Com., Wenham, Mass., 1970-72, Milton Twp., Ill., 1973-75; mem. Wenham Water Commn., 1970-72. C.L.U.; chartered fin. cons. Mem. Midwest Pension Conf. (chmn. 1989—), Am. Soc. Pension Actuaries (assoc.), Am. Soc. C.L.U.s, Am. Assn. Fin. Planners, Profit Sharing Council Am., Chgo. Council Fgn. Relations, Alpha Epsilon Rho. Republican. Home: 2 S 110 Hamilton Ct Wheaton IL 60187 Office: New Eng Mutual Life Ins Co 10 S Riverside Pla Ste 1710 Chicago IL 60606

HAMILTON, WILLIAM MILTON, industrial company executive; b. Phila., Feb. 5, 1925; s. Louis Valentine and Elsie Marie (Walter) H.; m. Edith Marie Busey, June 9, 1947; children: Barbara Marie, William Milton Jr., Patricia Ann. B.S. in Indsl. Mgmt., Ga. Inst. Tech., 1947. Asst. br. mgr. Swift & Co., Atlanta, 1947-48; treas. R.K. Price Co., Fayetteville, Ga., 1954-55; br. mgr. N.Y. Wire Cloth Co., Atlanta, 1955-56; from ops. mgr. to pres. Premier Indsl. Corp., Cleve., 1956—. Served to lt. USN, 1943-46, 48-54. Methodist. Club: Elyria Country (Ohio). Home: 1585 Greenleaf Circle Westlake OH 44145 Office: Premier Indsl Corp 4415 Euclid Ave Cleveland OH 44103

HAMILTON, WILLIAM VICTOR, tool manufacturing executive; b. Terre Haute, Ind., May 17, 1931; s. Clyde Abraham and Helen Elizabeth (Camp) H.; m. Betty Lou Haynes, Dec. 4, 1955; children: Kimberly Cameron, Mark Haynes. BA in Bus. Econs., U. Nebr., 1961; MBA, George Washington U., 1973. Commd. 2d lt. USAF, 1953; chief data processing br. SAC hdqrs. USAF, Omaha, 1964-67, ops. analyst SAC hdqrs., 1967-69; chief ops. data processor USAF The Pentagon, Washington, 1969-71, retired, 1971; asst. pres. Morris Cafritz Hosp., Washington, 1971-74; mgmt. cons. W.V. Hamilton Assn., Arlington, Va., 1974-83; pres. Am. Machine Systems Corp., Albany, Ind., 1983—; cons. Polaris Data Systems, Arlington, 1974; cons. govt. mktg. Blue Shield Assn., Washington, 1975-77, Optimum Systems Corp., Santa Clara, Calif., 1977; cons. mktg. research Fabergé, N.Y.C., 1979-80. Analyst, Connelly for Pres., Washington, 1980. Mem. Soc. Mfg. Engrs. (treas.), Kiwanis (dir., v.p.), Muncie C. of C. Policy Com., Unitarian Universalist Fin. Com. (bd. dirs.). Lodge: Masons. Home: 1301 N Alden Rd Muncie IN 47304 Office: Am Machine Systems Corp 248 N Broadway St Albany IN 47320

HAMISTER, DONALD BRUCE, electronics company executive; b. Cleve., Nov. 29, 1920; s. Victor Carl and Bess Irene (Sutherl) H.; m. Margaret Irene Singiser, Dec. 22, 1946; children: Don Bruce, Tracy. A.B. cum laude, Kenyon Coll., 1947; postgrad., Stanford U., 1948-49, U. Chgo., 1957. Application engr. S.E. Joslyn Co., Cin., 1947-48; regional sales mgr. Joslyn Mfg. and Supply Co., St. Louis, 1950-52; mktg. mgr. Joslyn Mfg. and Supply Co., Chgo., 1953-55, asst. to pres., 1956-57, mgr. aircraft arrester dept., 1958-62, gen. mgr. electronic systems div., 1962-71; v.p., gen. mgr., dir. Joslyn Mfg. and Supply Co., Goleta, Calif., 1973-78, group v.p. indsl. products, 1974-78, pres., chief exec. officer, 1978-85, chmn., 1979—; chmn. Joslyn Mfg. and Supply Co. named changed to Joslyn Corp., 1986; pres. Joslyn Stainless; pres., dir. Joslyn Stamping Co.; pres., chmn., dir. Joslyn Def. Systems, Inc., 1981—; dir. Brewer Tichener Corp. Served to lt. USNR, 1942-46. Mem. IEEE, Airline Avionics Inst. (pres., chmn. 1972-74). Club: Univ. (Chgo.). Office: PO Box 817 Goleta CA 93017

HAMISTER, MARK EDWARD, health care company executive; b. Buffalo, Oct. 18, 1951; s. George E. and Jane (Hall) H.; m. Lynette C. Miller, Dec. 10, 1972; children: Amy Louise, Daniel Mark, Kathryn Jane. BSBA, Rochester Inst. Tech., 1974. Adminstr. Shire at Culverton Adult Home, Rochester, N.Y., 1973-77; assoc. exec. dir., chief operating officer Presbyn. Homes N.Y., Inc., Buffalo, 1977-80; pres., chief exec. officer Nat. Health Care Affiliates, Buffalo, 1977—; bd. dirs. regional Chabe Lincoln First Bank, Buffalo. Pres. bd. trustees Shea's Buffalo Theater, 1987—; bd. dirs. Studio Arena Theater, Buffalo, 1988—. Mem. Am. Health Care Assn., Pres.'s Assn. Republican. Episcopalian. Home: 14 Deer Rom Ct Williamsville NY 14612 Office: Nat Health Care Affiliates 651 Delaware Ave Buffalo NY 14202

HAMLIN, DENSLO FRANKLYN, JR., venture capitalist; b. Bklyn., May 2, 1948; s. Denslo Franklyn and Elmyra Agnes (Coe) H.; m. Allison Marie Gorcey, Aug. 31, 1970; children: Elizabeth Ann, Garick Lyle. BS in Physics, Rensselaer Poly. Inst., 1970; MBA, Lehigh U., 1973. Pres. Ski Haus Tours, Brewster, N.Y., 1971-74; fin. analyst planning and analysis Inco, Ltd., N.Y.C., 1974-77, fin. analyst spl. projects, 1977-79, sr. fin. analyst spl. projects, 1979-84, fin. advisor, 1980-84; dir. investment mgmt. and fin. analysis Inco Venture Capital Mgmt., N.Y.C., 1984—; bd. dirs. United Tire and Rubber Co., Ltd., Rexdale, Ont., Can. Republican. Methodist. Office: Inco Venture Capital Mgmt One New York Pla New York NY 10004

HAMLIN, DON AUER, financial executive; b. Klamath Falls, Oreg., Oct. 6, 1934; s. Don Fessler and Margaret May (Auer) H.; B.B.A., Loyola U. of South, New Orleans, 1955; grad. USAF Command and Staff Coll., 1967; M.S. in Bus. Adminstrn., George Washington U., 1968; m. Karen Ruth Wagner; children by previous marriage—Michael, Kathryn, Stephen, Mary, Mark, John, Matthew. Commnd. 2d lt. U.S. Army, 1955, advanced through grades to lt. col., 1975; served with inf., ordnance, M.P., various locations, 1955-64; inf. comdr. and staff officer, Alaska, Hawaii, Vietnam, 1964-68; cost analyst and dep. agy. comdr. Pentagon Gen. Staff, Washington, 1968-72; inf. adviser, Vietnam, 1972; comptroller Ft. Sam Houston, Tex., 1972-75; ret., 1975; comptroller Severance & Assos., San Antonio, 1975-81; sec.-treas., dir. Severance Reference Lab., Inc., San Antonio, Tex., 1981-82; co-founder, pres. Engring. Cybernetics, Inc., San Antonio, 1982-85; dir. fin. Whittaker Health Services, Austin, Tex., 1985-86; v.p. fin. Metlife Healthcare Network, 1986-88; Harris Meth. Health Plan, Ft. Worth, 1989—; pvt. investor, 1983—; dir. Data Terminal Corp., San Antonio, 1981; pres. Balance Point Youth Ranch, San Antonio, 1980-81. Pres., St. Pius X Bd. Edn., San Antonio, 1979. Decorated Legion of Merit with oak leaf cluster, Bronze Star with oak leaf cluster, Air medal with oak leaf cluster, Purple Heart with oak leaf cluster, Mem. San Antonio Med. Mgrs. Assn. (pres. 1982-84), Med. Group Mgrs. Assn., San Antonio Mus. Assn., Mexican-Am. Cultural Center, San Antonio C. of C. Home: 2212 Shadywood Ct Arlington TX 76012 Office: Harris Meth Health Plan 1325 Pennsylvania Ave Fort Worth TX 76104

HAMLIN, F(REDERICK) GORDON, JR., real estate company executive; b. Orange, N.J., Apr. 21, 1943; s. F. Gordon and Doris (Keller) H.; m. Julia Keiser, June 29, 1968; children: McCurrah, Andrea. BA, Dartmouth Coll., 1968; MBA, NYU, 1971. Comml. lending officer Bank East, Manchester, N.H., 1971-74; v.p. Canal Nat. Bank, Portland, Maine, 1974-78; pres. Northeast Capital Corp., Portland, 1978-83; pres., bd. dirs. Dartmouth Co., Portland, 1983—; bd. dirs. Sugarloaf Mountain Corp., Kingfield, Maine. Bd. dirs. Maine Osteo. Hosp., Portland, 1976-78, Greater Portland Landmarks, 1978-81; mem. Freeport (Maine) Planning Bd., 1984-86; chmn. Freeport Planning Com., 1985-86. Served with U.S. Army, 1963-66, Korea. NYU Grad. Sch. Bus. scholar, 1971. Mem. Maine Real Estate Devel. Assn. (pres. 1987-88). Republican. Episcopalian. Office: Dartmouth Co 489 Congress St Portland ME 04101

HAMLIN, ORRIN KENNETH, III, financial services principal; b. Coffeyville, Kans., Sept. 1, 1946; s. Orrin Kenneth and Carrie Josephine (Hoppel) H.; m. Sandra Marie Wilson, Jan. 27, 1967; children: Melissa Ann, Heather Marie. Student, Washburn U., Topeka, 1964-66, U. Kans., Lawrence, 1966-68. CLU, ChFC. Agt. Northwestern Nat. Life Ins. Co., St. Joseph, Mo., 1977-79, on-the-job trainer, 1980-81, dist. mgr., 1982, regional mgr., 1985-87; employees benefit cons. Fin. Products, Inc., Wichita, Kans., 1983-85; pvt. practice fin. planning Wichita, 1988—. Sch. bd. mem. Ave City R-9 Sch. Dist. Ave City, Mo., 1986, 87; bd. dirs. Green Acres, Inc., St. Joseph, 1985-87, 1st Christian Ch., St. Joseph, 1984-86; founder fire dist. Maxwell Heights Fire Dist., St. Joseph, 1984. Mem. Life Underwriters Assn. (nat. com. 1978-80, v.p. 1981, pres. 1982), Nat. Assn. Life Underwriters (Nat. Sales Achievement award 1984, 86, 87, Nat. Quality award 1984-87), Am. Soc. Chartered Life Underwriters, Chartered Fin. Counselors, Rotary, Shriners, Masons. Mem. Christian Ch. Office: The Hamlin Agy PO Box 8 Fairleigh Sta Saint Joseph MO 64506 also: ADGH&K Fin Svcs 3306 Dale Ave Saint Joseph MO 64506

HAMM, LLOYD LAWRENCE, JR., banker; b. Boston, Feb. 16, 1960; s. Lloyd Lawrence and Marilyn O. (Rosengren) H.; m. Linda Marie Haeberle, Apr. 16, 1983. BA, Anna Maria Coll., Paxton, Mass., 1981, MBA, 1983; cert. spl. studies, Harvard U., 1984-86. Mgr. trainee, ops. mgr., ops. officer Mechanics Bank, Worcester, Mass., 1981-83; bus. system analyst Multibank Service Corp., Auburn, Mass., 1983-84; system analyst, sr. system analyst, asst. v.p. MTech New Eng., Woburn, Mass., 1984-86; asst. v.p. Ea. Bank, Lynn, Mass. 1986-88, v.p., 1988—; bd. dirs. Alternatives Unltd., Inc., Northbridge, Mass., 1986—, treas., 1987, 88. Mem. Upton (Mass.) Fin. Com., 1981-85, chmn., 1986; com. mem. troop 132 Boy Scouts Am., Upton, 1981—. Republican. Office: Eastern Bank 270 Union St Lynn MA 01901

HAMM, WILLIAM GERALD, aerospace and electronics executive, engineer; b. Charlottesville, Va., May 27, 1931; s. Strother F. and Ruby (Barksdale) H.; m. Nancy B. Adkins, June 14, 1954 (div.); children: William G., Keith E., Alan R., David L.; m. Maria Laqueur, Feb. 12, 1983. B.S. in Mech. Engring., U. Va., 1954. Engr. Douglas Aircraft Co., Santa Monica and Long Beach, Calif., 1954-61; engr. Atlantic Research Corp., Alexandria, Va., 1961-71, v.p., 1971-80, exec. v.p., 1980—, chief operating officer, 1986-88, pres. profl. services group, 1988—, also dir.; bd. dirs. City Nat. Bank of Washington D.C., Profl. Services Coun., Va. Mfrs. Assn. Mem. exec. bd., v.p. Boy Scouts Am. Nat. Capital Area, Washington, 1981—. Mem. Assn. U.S. Army, U.S. Space Found., Armed Forces Communications and Electronics Assn., Am. Soc. Naval Engrs., Navy League, AIAA, Am. Def. Preparedness Assn., Air Force Assn. (patron). Office: Atlantic Rsch Corp Profl Svcs Group 1375 Piccard Dr Rockville MD 20850

HAMMELE, JOSEPH FRANCIS, banker; b. Rochester, N.Y., Dec. 3, 1929; s. Edward Joseph and Helen Elizabeth (Oster) H.; m. Patricia Eileen Murnighan, July 7, 1956; children: Mary, Anne, Margaret, Edward. BA, Holy Cross Coll., 1951; MBA, U. Rochester, 1961. Mortgage loan rep. Prudential Ins. Co., Buffalo and Utica, N.Y., 1955-58; mortgage loan rep. Rochester Savs. Bank, 1958-61, pres. Rochester Leeway Corp subs., 1972-73, sr. v.p., 1973-79, exec. v.p., 1979-84, 1983-84, pres., chief operating officer, 1984—; v.p. H.J. Ludington, Inc., Rochester, 1961-69; pres. Joyce Fla., Inc., Delray Beach, 1969-72; bd. dirs. Rochester Credit Ctr. Bd. dirs. United Way Greater Rochester, 1985—, YMCA Greater Rochester, 1984—, St. Ann's Home, Rochester, 1986—, Rochester Rotary Service Found., Inc., 1985—. Lt. USN, 1951-54. Mem. Rochester Credit and Fin. Mgmt. Assn. Roman Catholic. Club: Toastmasters (pres. 1976-77). Office: Rochester Community Savs Bank 235 Main St E Rochester NY 14604

HAMMER, ARMAND, petroleum company executive, art patron; b. N.Y.C., May 21, 1898; s. Julius and Rose (Robinson) H.; m. Olga von Root, Mar. 14, 1927; m. Angela Zevely, Dec. 19, 1943; m. Frances Barrett, Jan. 26, 1956; 1 child. BS, Columbia U., 1919, MD, 1921, LLD, 1978; LLD, Pepperdine U., 1978, Southeastern U., Washington, 1978, U. Aix-en-Provence, 1981; D in Pub. Service, Salem (W.Va.) Coll., 1979; HHD, U. Colo., Boulder, 1979; DSc (hon.), U. S.C., 1983; PhD (hon.), Tel Aviv U., 1986. Pres. Allied Am. Corp., N.Y.C., 1923-25, A. Hammer Pencil Co., N.Y.C., London and Moscow, 1925-30, Hammer Galleries, Inc., N.Y.C., 1930—, J. W. Dant Distilling Co., N.Y.C. and Dant, Ky., 1943-54; pres., chmn. bd. Mut. Broadcasting System, N.Y.C., 1957-58; chmn. bd., chief exec. officer Occidental Petroleum Corp., Los Angeles, 1957—; chmn. M. Knoedler & Co., Inc., N.Y.C., 1972—, Knoedler-Modarco S.A., N.Y.C., 1977—; dir. Nat. State Bank, Perth Amboy, N.J., 1949-56, City Nat. Bank, Beverly Hills, Calif., 1962-71, Can. Occidental Petroleum Ltd., Calgary, Alta.; dir. Raffinerie Belge de Petroles, Antwerp, Belgium, 1968-79, Cities Service Co., Tulsa; hon. dir. Fla. Nat. Bank of Jacksonville, 1966-72; mem. Nat. Petroleum Council, 1968—, Com. on Arctic Oil and Gas Resources, 1980—. Author: The Quest of the Romanoff Treasure, 1936, autobiography (with Neil Lyndon) Hammer, 1987, (with Neil Lyndon) Hammer: Witness to History, 1987; subject of biography: The Remarkable Life of Dr. Armand Hammer (Robert Considine), 1975; Brit. edit. Larger than Life, 1976; The World of Armand Hammer (John Bryson), 1985. Pres. N.J. Aberdeen Angus Assn., 1948-49; Bd. govs. Monmouth County Orgn. Social Service, Red Bank, N.J., 1949-61, Monmouth Meml. Hosp., Long Branch, N.J., 1946-58, Eleanor Roosevelt Cancer Found., N.Y.C., 1960—, Ford's Theatre Soc., 1970—, UN Assn. U.S.A., 1976—; bd. dirs., exec. com. Internat. Council United World Colls., 1983—; mem. Royal Acad. Trust, Eng., 1980—; mem., fellow Met. Mus. Art, 1985; trustee U. North Africa Assn., 1968-71, Los Angeles County Mus. Art, 1968—, UCLA Found., 1973-76, Nat. Symphony, 1977—, United for Calif., 1977—, Capitol Children's Mus., 1978—; chmn. wine and spirits div. Vis. Nurse Service Greater N.Y., 1946, Am. Aid to France, 1947; mem. Citizens Food Com., 1946-47, Cardinal Spellman's Com. of Laity for Catholic Charities, 1946-48, Public Adv. Com. on U.S. Trade Policy, 1968-69, Am. Com. for Nat. Archives, 1974-76, Los Angeles County-U. So. Calif. Cancer Assos., 1975—, George C. Marshall Assos., James Smithson Soc. of Smithsonian Nat. Assos., 1977—, U. Okla. Assos., 1981—, Bus. Adv. Commn. for 1984 Olympics, 1981—, Los Angeles Olympic Citizens Adv. Commn., 1981—; hon. trustee Denver Art Mus., 1980—; mem. adv. bd. Inst. of Peace, 1950-54, Los Angeles Beautiful, Inc., 1969-75, Com. for a Greater Calif., 1969—, Fogg Art Mus. and Fine Arts Library, Cambridge, Mass., 1977—, The Friendship Force, 1977—, Am. Longevity Assn., Inc., 1980—, Center Strategic and Internat. Studies, Georgetown U., 1981—; mem. fine arts com. U.S. Dept. State, 1981—; chmn. Pres.'s Cancer Panel, 1981—; mem. exec. com. Econ. Devel. Bd. City of Los Angeles, 1968-73; trustee, chmn. exec. com. Salk Inst. Biol. Studies, San Diego, 1969—; bd. dirs. Los Angeles World Affairs Council, 1969—, Planned Parenthood World Population/Los Angeles, 1970—, U.S.-USSR Trade and Econ. Council, 1973—, Assos. Harvard Bus. Sch., 1975—, Calif. Roundtable, 1976—, Century City Cultural Commn., 1977—, Corcoran Gallery Art, Washington, 1978—, Keep Am. Beautiful, Inc., 1979—, Bus. Com. for Arts, N.Y.C., 1980—; bd. visitors Grad. Sch. Mgmt., UCLA, 1957—, UCLA Sch. Medicine Center for Health Scis., 1980—; exec. mem. Energy Research and Edn. Found., 1978—; charter mem. Nat. Visiting Council of Health Scis. Faculties, Columbia U., 1978—; mem. univ. bd. Pepperdine U., 1979—; mem. fellows for life New Orleans Mus. Art, 1980—; bd. dirs. Nat. Coordinating Ctr. forat. support council U.S. Com. for UNICEF, 1980—; founder mem. Pepperdine Assos., 1976—; pres. Found. of Internat. Inst. Human Rights, Geneva, 1977—; mem. exec. bd. dirs. UN Assn. Los Angeles; mem. Bd. Mcpl. Arts Commrs. Los Angeles, 1969-73; mem. budget and fin. com. of bd. trustees Los Angeles County Mus. Art, 1972-74; sponsor Internat. Inst. Human Rights Peace Conf., Oslo, 1978, Campobello Peace Park, 1979, Warsaw, 1980, Aix-en-Provence, France, 1981. Served with M.C. U.S. Army, 1918-19. Endowed Armand Hammer Center for Cancer Biology, Salk Inst., 1969; Armand Hammer prof. bus. and public policy UCLA, 1968; Frances and Armand Hammer wing Los Angeles County Mus. Art, 1969; Armand Hammer Animal Facility Salk Inst., 1976; Calif. Inst. Cancer Research UCLA, 1976; Ann. Armand Hammer Cancer Conf. and Fund Salk Inst., 1976; Harvard/Columbia Russian Study Fund, 1977; Julius and Armand Hammer Health Scis. Center Columbia U., 1977; Five-Yr. Funding Program UN Assn., 1978; Five-Yr. Funding Program Corcoran Gallery Art, 1979; Five-Yr. Funding Program Jacquemart-André Mus., Paris, 1979; Ann. Armand Hammer Award Luncheon Los Angeles, 1980; Los Angeles City Dept. Parks and Recreation, 1981, Armand Hammer Cancer Prize, 1982; Hammer-Rostropovich Cello Scholarship award U. So. Calif., 1982; Theatre du Gymnase, Marseille, France, 1983, Armand Hammer chair Leonardo Ctr., UCLA, 1985; Armand Hammer Ctr. for Advanced Studies in Nucelar Energy and Health, Los Angeles, 1986; recipient Humanitarian award Eleanor Roosevelt Cancer Found., 1962; city commendation Mayor of Los Angeles, 1968; decorated comdr. Order of Crown Belgium, 1962; comdr. Order of Andres Bellos Venezuela, 1975; Order of Aztec Eagle Mex., 1977; officer Legion of Honor France, 1978; Order of Friendship Among Peoples USSR, 1978; Royal Order of Polar Star Sweden, 1979; officer Grand Order of Merit Italy, 1981; Knight Comdr.'s Cross Austria, 1982; comdr. Nat. Order French Legion Honor, 1983; named Hon. Citizen and Seal Bearer of City of Vinci, Italy, 1982; Disting. Honoree of Yr. Nat. Art Assn., 1978; Golden Plate award Am. Acad. Achievement, 1978; Aztec award Mexican-Am. Opportunity Fond., 1978; Appeal of Conscience award N.Y.C., 1978; Spirit of Life award Oil Industry Council of City of Hope, 1979; award Antique Monthly, 1980; Entrepreneur of Yr. award U. So. Calif., 1980; Maimonides award Los Angeles Jewish Community, 1980; Golden Achievement award Andrus Gerontology Center, U. So. Calif., 1981; Ambassador of Arts award State of Fla., 1981; recipient John Jay award Columbia Coll., 1981, Disting. Citizen award Greater N.Y. Councils Boy Scouts Am., 1982, James Ewing Soc. Layman's award, Soc. Surgical Oncology, 1983, Medaille d'Or Mayor of Marseille and French Minister of Interior, 1983, Golda Meir award Israeli Prime Minister, 1984, Hilal-i-Quaid-i-Azam award Pres. Pakistan, 1985, Jubilee Medal Ambassador Zhulev of Bulgaria, 1985, Golden Archigymnaseum Decoration Mayor Renzo Imbeni of Bologna, 1985, Humanitarian award LWV, 1986, Human Achievement award Op. Calif., 1986, Nat. Recognition award Pres. United States Mexico, 1987, 1987 Humanitarian award Internat. Physicians for Prevention of Nuclear War, Inc., 1987, Emma Lazarus Statue Liberty award Nat. Jewish Hist. Soc., 1987, Nat. Arts Medal, 1987, Eleanor Roosevelt Humanitarian award United Nations Assn. San Francisco, 1987, Norman Vincent Peale award Insts. for Religion and Health, 1987, Spl. award Gen. Hosp. Mexico City, Ministry Health, 1987, Franklin and Eleanor Roosevelt Freedom from Fear award, 1988. Mem. Los Angeles Petroleum Club, Royal Acad. Arts (London), hon. corr., Am. Petroleum Inst. (dir. 1975—), Navy League U.S. (Los Angeles council 1980—), Fifty-Yr. Club Am. Medicine, Royal Scottish Acad. (hon.), AMA (life), N.Y. County Med. Assn., Internat. Inst. Human Rights, Alpha Omega Alpha, Mu Sigma, Phi Sigma Delta. Office: Occidental Petroleum Corp 10889 Wilshire Blvd Suite 1500 Los Angeles CA 90024 *

HAMMER, HAROLD HARLAN, oil company financial executive; b. Chgo., May 23, 1920; s. B. James and Frances (Halbren) H.; m. Hannah Richmond, Mar. 1, 1956; children: John, Elizabeth. B.S., Northwestern U., 1941; M.B.A., N.Y. U., 1950, J.D., 1955. Bar: N.Y. State 1955. Accountant U.S. Steel Corp., 1941-42; asst. sec.-treas. Duraloy Co., Scottdale, Pa., 1945-48; financial analyst, asst. controller Port of N.Y. Authority, 1948-50; investment counsel N.Y.C., 1950—, since practiced in; v.p. finance, dir. Control Data Corp., Mpls., 1966-72; chmn. finance com., dir. Gen. Refractories Co., 1963-66; with Gulf Oil Corp., Pitts., 1972—; sr. v.p. Gulf Oil Corp., 1972-73, exec. v.p., 1973-81, chief adminstrv. officer, 1981-85; chmn. MMC Group Inc., 1986—; bd. dirs., chmn. J.C. Horne & Co., Standard-Thomson Corp. Author: Financing the Port of New York Authority, 1957, also articles in field. Bd. dirs. W. Penn Hosp. Served as lt. USNR, World War II. Mem. ABA, Fed., N.Y. Bar Assns., Phi Alpha Delta. Methodist. Clubs: Fox Meadow Tennis (gov. 1966); Duquesne (Pitts.), Fox Chapel Golf (Pitts.); Rolling Rock (Liqonier, Pa.). Home: 212 Schenley Rd Pittsburgh PA 15217 Office: Oliver Plaza Pittsburgh PA 15222

HAMMER, ROBIN JILL, manufacturer's representative; b. N.Y.C., May 29, 1952. Student, Sullivan County Community Coll., S. Fallsburg, N.Y., 1970-71, Fairleigh Dickinson U., 1980-82. Office mgr. Exemplar Internat., Ft. Lee, N.J., 1971-76; mfrs. rep. Sampro, Inc., Hartsdale, N.Y., 1976—. Prog. dir. hotline Am. Social Health Agy., N.Y.C., 1984—. Mem. NOW (task force dir. marriage/div. 1980-83), Nat. Art Material Trade Assn. (prog. com. 1987-88), Garden State Office Products (dir. 1987-88), Met. Office Club. Home: 250 Gorge Rd Cliffside Park NJ 07010 Office: Sampro Inc 38 Joyce Rd Hartsdale NY 10530

HAMMERMAN, IRVING HAROLD, II, real estate executive, banker; b. Trenton, N.J., Sept. 28, 1920; s. Samuel Lawrence and Esther (Boorstein) H.; m. Lois Swimmer, Dec. 14, 1949; children—S.L. Hammerman II, Amy Hammerman, Sandye Nast, Mark Hammerman. BS in Econs., U. Pa., 1942. Pres. The Hammerman Orgn., Inc., Balt., 1966-70, chmn. 1970-86; trustee Morgan Liquidating Ltd. Ptnrship., 1986—; dir. Nat. Corp. for Housing Partnerships, 1972; mem. Home Loan Bank Bd. of Atlanta, 1973. Trustee, The Bancroft Sch., Haddonfield, N.J., 1984—, Loyola Coll., Balt., 1964, Avon Old Farms Sch., Conn., 1970-71; assoc. trustee U. Pa., Phila., 1964-69; pres. Har Sinai Congregation, 1971-73. Served to capt. U.S. Army, 1942-47. Recipient Humanitarian award Am. Cancer Soc., 1970; Disting. Man of Yr. award Am. Mktg. Assn., 1971. Mem. Mortgage Bankers Assn. (pres. 1959-63), Home Builders Assn. Md., Real Estate Bd. Greater Balt. (dir. 1964-65), Advt. Club of Balt. (pres. 1961-63), Beta Gamma Sigma. Republican. Jewish. Clubs: Suburban (Balt. County); Falls (Palm Beach, Fla.). Home: 2000 S Ocean Blvd Palm Beach FL 33480 Office: Hammerman Mortgage Group 105 W Chesapeake Ave Towson MD 21204

HAMMES, TERRY MARIE, advertising executive; b. Chgo., Mar. 27, 1955; d. Howard John and Lorna Marie (Jeans) H. BFA, U. Miami, Coral Gables, Fla., 1976. Lic. real estate broker, Fla. Pres. Hammes Advt. Agy., Coral Gables, Fla., 1978—; pres., broker Hammes Realty Mgmt. Corp., Coral Gables, 1986—; bd. dirs. Coral Gables Bus. Leaders, Ponce de Leon Devel. Assn., Coral Gables. One-woman show includes U. Miami, Fla., 1975; juried art show Lowe Art Mus., 1976. Bd. dirs. Young Democrats, Dade County, 1982-86. Named Miss Minn. Council of State Socs., 1975; Valley Forge Freedom Found. scholar, 1971; recipient Fla. award for Mktg. Excellence in Best Print Campaign, Best Corp. Campaign, Best Print Ad, Best Spl. Event, Best Collateral. Mem. Nat. Assn. Women Bus. Owners (pub. relations chmn. 1986—), Builders Assn. South Fla. (editor, publisher 1986-87), Advt. Fedn. Greater Miami, Coral Gables C. of C., Orange Key, Alpha Lambda Delta. Democrat. Home: 9234 SW 132d St Miami FL 33176 Office: Hammes Advt Inc 896 S Dixie Hwy Coral Gables FL 33146-2674

HAMMETT, WILLIAM M. H., association executive; b. Oldtown, Maine, June 21, 1944; s. Walter Mitchel Howard and Lillian Joyce (Marin) H.; divorced; 1 child, Kelly Marin. BA in Econs., So. Ill. Univ., 1970; MA, U. Chgo., 1976. Pres., trustee Manhattan Inst. for Policy Rsch., N.Y.C., 1980—. Trustee Lehrman Inst., N.Y.C. With U.S. Army, 1968-70. Mem. New York Athletic Club. Office: Manhattan Inst for Policy Rsch 42 E 71st St New York NY 10021

HAMMOND, DEBRA ANN, title examiner, legal secretary; b. Gardner, Mass., Oct. 25, 1964; d. Edward Lenwood Dennis and Nancy Ann (Smith) H. BA in History, North Adams State Coll., 1986. Title examiner Guaranty Title and Abstract Co., Fitchburg, Mass., 1986-87, Guaranty Abstract Co., Worcester, Mass., 1987-88, Mirick, O'Connell, DeMallie & Lougee, Worcester, 1988—. Mem. NAFE. Roman Catholic. Home: Churchill Rd Templeton MA 01468 Office: Mirick O'Connell DeMallie & Lougee 1700 Mechanics Bank Tower Worcester MA 01608

HAMMOND, JERRY NEAL, accountant, financial executive; b. Phenix City, Ala., Dec. 11, 1940; s. Jerry L. Hammond; m. Rita Marie Klingenberger, Mar. 29, 1969; children: Kim, Jerry, Kristi, Kevin. AA, Columbus (Ga.) Coll., 1961; BS, Auburn U., 1963; M in Accountancy, U. S. Fla., 1981. CPA, Fla.; cert. mgmt. acct. Plant acct. West Point (Ga.) Pepperall Inc., 1963-66; sr. acct. West Point (Ga.) Pepperall Inc., Rome, Ga., 1966-69; sr. fin. analyst Cities Service Co., Tampa, Fla., 1970-72; asst. mgr. planning Cities Service Co., Atlanta, 1972-73; mgr. acctg. Gardinier Inc., Tampa, 1973-75, controller, 1975-85, v.p., controller, 1985-86, v.p., treas., 1986—; vice-chmn. Fertilizer Inst., Washington, 1984-85, chmn. fin. mgmt. com., 1985-86; bd. dirs., Chem. and Indsl. Credit Union, Tampa. Mem. AICPA, Fla. Inst. CPAs, Nat. Assn. Accts. Republican. Presbyterian. Office: Gardinier Inc PO Box 3269 Tampa FL 33601

HAMMOND, RALPH CHARLES, real estate executive; b. Valley Head, Ala., Feb. 1, 1916; s. William Bleve and Alice Corina Jane (Holleman) H.; student Snead Jr. Coll., 1938-39, Berea Coll., 1940-41; A.B., U. Ala., 1945; m. Myra Leak, June 20, 1954; children—James, Ben. Press sec. to gov. Ala., Montgomery, 1946-50, exec. sec., 1955-59; gen. rep. ARC, Greensboro, N.C., 1950-54; mayor of Arab (Ala.), 1963-69; pres. City Center, Inc., Arab, 1959—. Commr. from Ala., U.S. Study Commn. S.E. River Basins, 1958-64; bd. dirs. Ala. Tb Assn., 1956-83, pres., 1972-74; hon. Christmas Seal chmn., Ala., 1974; v.p. Ala. Lung Assn., 1980-83. Served with AUS, 1941-45. Mem. Ky. Hist. Soc., Phillip Hamman Family Assn. Am. (pres. 1972-78), Ala. Poetry Soc. (pres. 1981-84, Ala. Poet of Yr. 1985), Ala. Writers' Conclave (pres. 1987—), Nat. Fedn. State Poetry Socs. (treas. 1985-86, 3d v.p. 1987—). Democrat. Methodist. Lodge: Masons. Author: My GI Aching Back, 1945; Ante Bellum Mansions of Alabama, 1951; Philip Hamman, Man of Valor, 1976; Song of Appalachia, 1982; How High the Stars, 1982; Upon the Wings of the Wind, 1982; One Golden Apple a Day, 1983; Collected Poems, 1983; Wisdom Is, 1984; Edging Through the Grass (Book of Yr. Ala.

Poetry Soc.), 1985; contbr. short stories and feature articles to jours., mags.; poems pub. in 40 ed. and poetry jours. Home: 1202 Guntersville Rd Arab AL 35016 Office: PO Box 486 Arab AL 35016

HAMPTON, DELON, engineering consultant company executive; b. Jefferson, Tex., Aug. 23, 1933; s. Uless and Elizabeth (Lewis) H.; m. Janet Elaine Jones, Sept. 19, 1967 (div. 1975). BSCE, U. Ill., 1954; MSCE, Purdue U., 1958, PhD, 1961. Registered profl. engr., Ala., Calif., Colo., Del., D.C., Fla., Ga., Ill., Iowa, Ind., Md., Mich., Miss., N.Y., Tenn., Va., W.Va. Asst. prof. Kans. State U., Manhattan, 1961-64; assoc. rsch. engr. Eric H. Wang Civil Engring. Rsch. Facility, Albuquerque, 1962-63; sr. rsch engr. IIT Rsch. Inst., Chgo., 1964-68; prof. civil engring. Howard U., Washington, 1968-85; pres. Gnaedinger, Baker, Hampton & Assocs., Fairfax, Va., 1972-74; pres., chmn. Delon Hampton & Assocs., Chartered, Washington, 1973—; cons. in field; bd. dirs. Devel. Outer Interstate Thruway Coalition, City Nat. Bank, Washington; mem. Transp. Rsch. Bd., Washington, 1958—. Contbr. over 40 articles to profl. jours. Mem. resource sharing network adv. coun. Montgomery County (Md.) Housing Opportunities Commn., 1983-85; mem. econ. adv. coun. Montgomery County, 1985; mem. transp. coordg. com. Greater Washington Bd. Trade, 1985—; mem. task force Montgomery County Pub. Schs. Human Rels., 1986. Recipient Outstanding Contbn. award L.A. Coun. Black Cons. Engrs., 1983, Disting. Engring. Alumnus and Oldmaster award Purdue U., 1982, 85. Mem. Am. Cons. Engrs. Coun. (v.p. 1987-89), Am. Pub. Transit Assn. (bd. dirs. 1987-89, chmn. awards com. 1988), Am. Rd. and Transp. Builders Assn. (bd. dirs. planning and design div. 1977-87), Am. Soc. Engring. Edn., Am. Soc. Testing and Materials, ASCE (bd. dirs. nat. capital sect. 1976-78, pres. nat. capital sect. 1984-85, active numerous coms. in nat. orgn., Edmund Friedman Profl. Recognition award 1988), Assn. Soil and Found. Engrs., Am. Cons. Engrs. Coun. Met. Washington (pres. 1986-87), Fla. Inst. Cons. Engrs., Internat. Soc. Soil Mechanics and Found. Engring., Nat. Assn. Black Cons. Engrs., Nat. Def. Exec. Res., Nat. Soc. Profl. Engrs., Soc. Am. Mil. Engrs., Urban Land Inst., Washington Soc. Engrs., Washington C. of C. (bd. dirs. 1985-86), Montgomery County C. of C. (v.p. housing and pub. facilities 1983-85), Lakewood Club (Rockville, Md.), City Club (Washington), Sigma Xi, Chi Epsilon. Methodist. Home: 12804 Brushwood Terr Potomac MD 20854 Office: Delon Hampton & Assocs 111 Massachusetts Ave NW Ste 400 Washington DC 20001

HAMPTON, E. LYNN, municipal finance administrator; b. Louisville, Nov. 5, 1947; d. Thomas C. and Estelle (Weeks) H. AA, U. Ky., 1976; BSC, U. Louisville, 1978, MBA, 1983. CPA, Ky., Tex. Systems analyst Courier Jour. and Times, Louisville, 1973-78; sr. auditor Coopers and Lybrand, Louisville, 1978-80; projects adminstr. Atlantic Richfield, Lousiville, 1980-82; dir. fin. and adminstrn. City of Louisville, 1982-85; dir. fin. City of Arlington (Tex.), 1985-89; chief fin. officer Met. Washington Airports Authority, 1989—; dir. Time for Good Food Corp., Alexandria, Va.; assoc. prof. U. Tex., Arlington, 1985-86; mem. Minority Venture Capital Corp., Louisville, 1981-82. Contbg. author: Collective Bargaining, 1984; pub. Labor Law Jour., 1985, RISK Mag., 1986, ARIA Conf. Paper, 1987. Bd. overseers Bellermine Coll., Louisville, 1983-85; grad. Leadership Arlington, 1985-86; treas. Tarrant Council Girl Scouts U.S., 1988—; bd. dirs. Mid-Cities March of Dimes, 1988—. Recipient Vol. Service award Atlantic Richfield, 1981, Cert. Merit Bd. Alderman Louisville, 1985. Mem. Am. Inst. CPA's, Ky. State Soc. CPA's (compufest com. 1981-87), MidCities CPA's, Govt. Fin. Officers Assn. (mem. com. on debt and fiscal policy), Nat. League Cities (FAIR policy com. 1984-85), Bus. and Profl. Women (treas. 1986-87, pres. 1987-88, Citizen of Yr. 1985, Woman of Year 1987, LWV (bd. dirs. Arlington chpt. 1986). Democrat. Roman Catholic. Club: Bull Investment (Arlington) (pres. 1986-87). Office: Met Washington Airports Authority Washington Nat Airport Hanger 9 Washington DC 20001

HAMPTON, JERAL L., banker; b. Booneville, Ark., July 28, 1921; s. John L. and Cara L. (Littlefield) H.; m. Betty Lou Stanfill, Feb. 17, 1944; children—John T., Janie Woolley. B.A., Ouachita Bapt. U., 1944. Commd. 2d lt. U.S. Army; advanced through ranks to lt. col., USMC, ret. 1964; auto dealer Hampton Pontiac Co., Booneville, Ark., 1946-64; with Citizens Bank, Booneville, 1964—, chmn. bd. dirs., pres., chief exec. officer, 1984—. Bd. dirs. Logan County Soil Conservation Service, Paris, Ark., Booneville Indsl. Devel. Corp.; trustee Ouachita Bapt. U.; mem. bd. dirs. Area Agency on Aging; active promotion and establishment Booneville Plant Material Ctr. Decorated Bronze Star, Purple Heart; recipient Disting. Service award Ouachita Bapt. U., 1980, others. Baptist. Mem. C. of C. (bd. dirs.), Rotary (pres.), Masons. Home: Hwy 10 E Booneville AR 72927 Office: Citizens Bank 80 W Main St Booneville AR 72927

HAMPTON, ROBERT K., SR., environmental and industrial specialist, real estate associate, consultant; b. Phila., Nov. 20, 1919; s. John Henry and Helen Louisa (seip) H.; widowed; children: Robert K. Jr., John D., Michael S. Diploma in Civl Engring., Drexel U., 1948. Registered profl. engr. Pres. Hampton Equipment Co., Garden City, N.Y., 1958-81; assoc. Charles R. Velzy Assoc., Inc., Armonk, N.Y., 1982-86; pvt. practice cons. North Myrtle Beach, S.C., 1987—. Inventee ash gate improvement, Can. ash gate, sifting conveyor, refuse claiming. 1st lt. U.S. Army, 1942-46, ETO. Recipient Disting. Teaching award Hofstra U., 1977. Fellow ASME (chmn. incinerator conf. 1972, chmn. solid waste processing div. 1974-75, environment and transp. group 1977-85; bd. dirs., bd. on rsch. 1979-85, Div. Leadership award 1976); mem. Am. Pub. Works Assn. (life 1988, Centennial medal 1980, Div. Achievement Metal 1988), Air Pollution Control Assn., Nat. Assn. Profl. Engrs., Am. Acad. Environ. Engrs. (diplomate). Home: 1004D Edge Dr North Myrtle Beach SC 29582 Office: Robert K Hampton Cons 1004D Edge Dr PO Box 64 North Myrtle Beach SC 29597

HAMRICK, DOUGLAS PAUL, chemical executive; b. Rockford, Ill., Nov. 17, 1963; s. Maurice Wayne and Myra Mignon (Hutchison) H.; m. Laura J. Sala, Oct. 8, 1988. BA, Wartburg Coll., 1986. Research chemist Pierce Chem. Co., Rockford, 1986-87, regulatory control specialist, 1987—. Mem. vol. corps ARC, Rockford, 1981-86. Recipient Nauclér Meml. awards Perstorp AB, 1987, 88, 89. Mem. Am. Soc. Quality Control, Am. Assn. for Advancement Sci., Environ. Quality Control of Rockford Ill. Area C. of C., Am. Chem. soc. (chpt. program chmn. 1987-88, chpt. chmn. 1988—), Fedn. Environ. Technologists, Am. Mgmt. Assn. Republican. Roman Catholic. Office: Pierce Chem Co 3747 N Meridian Rd PO Box 117 Rockford IL 61105

HAN, ITTAH, political economist, high technology, computer engineering and financial strategist; b. Java, Indonesia, Jan. 29, 1939; came to U.S., 1956, naturalized, 1972; s. Hongtjioe and Tsuiying (Chow) H. BS in Mech. Engring. and Elec. Engring., Walla Walla Coll., 1960; MA in Math., U. Calif., Berkeley, 1962; BA in French, U. Colo., 1965, MS in Elec. Engring., 1961; MSE in Computer Engring., U. Mich., 1970; MS in Computer Sci., U. Wis., 1971; MBA in Mgmt., U. Miami, Fla., 1973; BA in Econs., U. Nev., 1977; MBA in Tax, Golden Gate U., 1979, MBA in Real Estate, 1979, MBA in Fin., 1980, MBA in Banking, 1980, MPA in Adminstrv. Orgn. and Mgmt., 1984. Cert. fin. planner. Salesman, Watkins Products, Walla Walla, Wash., 1956-60; instr. Sch. Engring. U. Colo., Denver, 1964-66; systems engr. IBM Corp., Oakland, Calif., 1967-69, Scidata Inc., Miami, Fla., 1971-72; chief of data processing Golden Gate Bridge, Hwy. and Transp. Dist., San Francisco, 1973-74; mgr. info. systems tech. and advanced systems devel. Summa Corp., Las Vegas, Nev., 1975-78; mgr. systems devel. Fred Harvey Inc., Brisbane, Calif., 1978-80; chmn. corp. systems steering com., mgr. systems planning Amfac Hotel & Resorts, Inc., 1978-80; tax strategy planner, innovative turnaround fin. strategy planner, chief exec. Ittahhan Corp., 1980—; exec. v.p. Developers Unltd. Group, Las Vegas, 1982-84; v.p. Fidelity Fin. Co., Las Vegas, 1984-85; exec. v.p. John H. Midby and Assocs., Las Vegas, 1982-84; sec., treas., dir. River Resorts Inc., Las Vegas, 1983-84; sec., treas. Goldriver Ltd., Las Vegas, 1983-84; pres. Weststar Gen. Ptnr. Co., 1984-85, Developers Group Service Co., 1984-86; chief exec. officer, pres. Very High Tech. Polit. Economy Turnaround Management Strategist, Inc., 1986—; chief exec. officer, pres. Artificial Intelligence Computer Engring. and Expert Systems Engring., Inc., 1986—; pres. Orion Land Devel. Co., Las Vegas, 1987—, Very High Tech. Computer Engring., Inc., Las Vegas, 1988—; instr. U. Nev. Sch. Elec. Engring., Reno, 1981; systems designer, cons. in field. Mem. IEEE, Assn. Computing Machinery, Am. Assn. Artificial Intelligence, Am. Math. Assn., Inst. Cert. Fin. Planners, Am. Contract Bridge League. Republican. Home and Office: PO Box 27025 Garside Station Las Vegas NV 89126

HANAHAN, JAMES LAKE, insurance company executive; b. Burlington, Iowa, Aug. 27, 1932; s. Thomas J. and Clarice P. (Lorey) H.; B.S., Drake U., 1955; postgrad. George Williams Coll., 1956; m. Marilyn R. Lowe, Dec. 27, 1952; children—Bridget Sue Bahlke, Erin Rose Hoff. Phys. dir. Monmouth (Ill.) YMCA, 1955-56; mem. community relations staff Caterpillar Tractor Co., Peoria, Ill., 1956-57; rep. Conn. Gen. Life Ins. Co., Des Moines, 1957-59, asst. mgr., 1959-63, mgr. group ins. ops., Tampa, Fla., 1963-80; pres., chief exec. officer WHP, First In Employee Benefits Inc., 1980—, J & H Cons. Group Inc., 1980—; ltd. ptnr. City Ctr. St. Petersburg; ptnr. Crossroads Ltd., Pres.'s Inn; instr. C.P.C.U. courses; seminar leader C.L.U. workshop; cons. ins. seminar Fla. State U.; bd. dirs. Williamsburg Renaissance Co., Shared Administrn. Concepts Corp. Bd. dirs. West Coast Employee Benefit Council, Tampa Sports Found., Jr. Achievement, Tampa Bay Acad.; bd. dirs., past pres. Pinellas Emergency Mental Health Services; mem. Hillsborough County Health Council. Recipient Double D award Drake U., 1978. Mem. Sales Mktg. Execs. Tampa (past pres., Exec. of Yr. 1982), Nat. Risk Mgmt. Soc., Greater Tampa C. of C., Minerat Soc. U. Tampa, Tampa Sports and Recreation Council (bd. dirs.), Self Ins. Assn. Am., Pinellas Econ. Devel. Coun., Health Ins. Inst. Am., Profl. Benefit Adminstrs. Assn., Com. of 100, Suncoast C. of C. (trustee), Phi Sigma Epsilon. Democrat. Roman Catholic. Clubs: 7th Inning (chmn.), Nat. D (Drake U.) (v.p., dir.), Innisbrook Country Resort, Pres.'s Assn. Home: 3301 S Bayshore Blvd #1008 Tampa FL 33629

HANAMIRIAN, VARUJAN, mechanical engineer, educator, journalist, publisher; b. Istanbul, Turkey, June 23, 1952; s. Kurgin and Etil Sona (Azat) H. Dip. in Mech. Engring., U. Stuttgart, Fed. Republic Germany, 1983. Postal mgr. Foto Annemie, Stuttgart, 1977; tchr. Berlitz Sch., Stuttgart, 1980; creative dir. Unver Werbeagentur, Stuttgart, 1986; scientific asst. Fraunhofer-Gesellschaft, Stuttgart, 1987; course leader Volkshochschule, Stuttgart, 1987; educator, cons. Mem. adv. bd. Produktion weekly, 1981-85. Organizer Orgn. Com. EM 1986, Stuttgart; active mem. Freie Demokratische Partei; interviewer various market research assns., 1979—; adminstr. various offices, 1980-87. Mem. Verein Deutscher Ingenieure. Club: Allgemeiner Deutscher Automobil, München.

HANAMURA, NIHACHIRO, airline executive. Chmn. Japan Airlines Co. Ltd., N.Y.C. Office: Japan Air Lines Co Ltd 655 Fifth Ave New York NY 10022 *

HANAU, KENNETH JOHN, JR., packaging company executive; b. Montclair, N.J., Feb. 27, 1927; s. Kenneth John and Elizabeth (Oliver) H.; m. Carol Lee Rossner, July 30, 1949; children: Holly Elizabeth, Jill Ann, Lori Carol, Kenneth John. BA, Wesleyan U., 1951. Salesman Union Bag-Camp Paper Co., N.Y.C., 1951-53; sales rep. Gibraltar Corrugated Paper, North Bergen, N.J., 1953-56; pres. K&H Corrugated Case Corp., Walden, N.Y., 1956—, chmn. bd., 1986—; pres. Vt. Container Corp., Bennington, 1960—, K&H Containers Inc., Wallingford, Conn., 1966—; chmn. bd. dirs. Northeast Packaging, Scranton, Pa., 1987—; bd. dirs. U.S. Home Corp., Houston, chmn. exec. com., 1984—, mem. exec. and compensation coms., 1977—, chmn. nominating and audit coms., 1977—; bd. dirs. Tingue Brown, Englewood, N.J., chmn. compensation com., 1982—; bd. dirs. Cosco Industries Inc., Spring Valley, N.Y., mem. exec., compensation and audit com., 1982—. Chmn. Eastern region Nat. Multiple Sclerosis Soc., 1965. Served with USNR, 1945-46. Mem. Chief Exec. Orgn. Republican. Roman Catholic. Club: Windermere Island (Eleuthera, Bahamas). Home: 2265 W Gulf Dr Apt P1D Sanibel Island FL 33957 also: 8 Bayview Pl Madison CT 06443 Office: K&H Corrugated Case Corp Lake Osiris Rd PO Box 301 Walden NY 12586

HANCOCK, JOAN HERRIN, executive search company executive; b. Indpls., Apr. 16, 1930; d. Roy Silvey and Glenna Olive (Metsker) Herrin; m. John Newton Hancock, May 12, 1951 (div. Feb. 1976); children: Glenna Jill Hancock Smith, Jeri Lee Hancock Moore, John Norman. B.A., Butler U., 1953. Career counselor Career Cons. Inc., Indpls., 1974-82; counselor, corp. officer Unique Alternatives Inc., Indpls., 1982-84, Alternatives Plus Inc., Indpls., 1984—; pres. Herrin & Assocs., 1986—. Precinct Committeeperson Democratic Party, Indpls; pres. Sch. #59 PTA, 1964, C.W.F. Allisonville Christian Ch., also mem. ch. bd., 1987—; active Camp Fire Girls. Mem. Central Ind. Assn. Profl. Cons. (sec. 1984-85, ethics com. 1980-81), Nat. Assn. Personnel Cons., State Assn. Personnel Cons., Am. Mgmt. Assn. (dir. membership 1986), Indpls. C. of C. (mem. community affairs council), Kappa Kappa Gamma (pres. Indpls. Assn. 1967-69; province dir. chpts. 1970-74, Mu club 1958-59, Betty Miller Brown award 1982). Mem. Christian Ch. (Disciples of Christ). Club: Hoosier 500 Toastmistress (pres. 1963) (Indpls.). Home: 4127 Timber Ct Indianapolis IN 46250 Office: Alternatives Plus Inc 9135 N Meridian Suite A8 Indianapolis IN 46260

HANCOCK, JOHN COULTER, telecommunications company executive; b. Martinsville, Ind., Oct. 21, 1929; s. Floyd A. and Catherine (Coulter) H.; m. Betty Jane Holden, Feb. 6, 1949; children: Debbie, Dwight, Marilyn, Virginia. BEE, Purdue U., 1951, MEE, 1955, PhD, 1957. Engr. Naval Avionics Facility, Indpls., 1951-57; asst. prof. elec. engring. Purdue U., West Lafayette, Ind., 1957-60, assoc. prof. elec. engring., 1960-63, prof. elec. engring., 1963-65, head Sch. Elec. Engring., 1965-72, dean Schs. Engring., 1972-84; exec. v.p., chief tech. officer United Telecommunications, Inc., Kansas City, Mo., 1984-86, exec. v.p. corp. devel. and tech., 1986-88, cons., 1988—; cons. Nat. Sci. Bd., 1986—; bd. dirs. Hillenbrand Industries, Batesville, Ind. Author: An Introduction to the Principles of Communications Theory, 1961. Fellow IEEE, AAAS, Am. Soc. Engring. Edn. (pres. 1983-84, Lamme award 1980); mem. Nat. Acad. Engring., Sigma Xi, Eta Kappa Nu, Tau Beta Pi.

HANCOCK, JOHN WALKER, III, banker; b. Long Beach, Calif., Mar. 8, 1937; s. John Walker and Bernice H.; m. Elizabeth Hoien, June 20, 1959; children: Suzanne, Donna, Randy, David. BA in Econs, Stanford U., 1958, MBA, 1960. With Security Pacific Nat. Bank, L.A., 1960—, v.p., 1968-77, sr. v.p., 1977-84, exec. v.p., 1984—. Bd. dirs. Long Beach (Calif.) Meml. Hosp., 1977—, Long Beach Symphony; pres., bd. dirs. Long Beach area coun. Boy Scouts Am., 1972-74; trustee Long Beach City Coll. Found. Mem. Am. Inst. Banking, Stanford U. Alumni Assn., Newcomen Soc. Republican. Clubs: Calif. (L.A.); Va. Country, Balboa Bay Club, Ctr. Club. Home: 258 Roycroft Ave Long Beach CA 90803 Office: Security Pacific Nat Bank PO Box 2097 Terminal Annex Los Angeles CA 90051

HANCOCK, WILLIAM FRANK, JR., business executive; b. Richmond, Va., Jan. 4, 1942; s. William Frank and Gladys Elizabeth (George) H.; B.B.A., U. Iowa, 1964; M.B.A., U. Pa., 1966; postgrad. Columbia Pacific U.; m. Donna G. Hosmer, May 18, 1968; children—Peter James, Jeffrey William, Jennifer Beth. Exec. asst. to exec. v.p. John Hancock Mutual Life Ins. Co., Boston, 1966-69; mgmt. cons. Keane Assos., Boston, 1969-74, regional mgr., 1974-75; v.p., gen. mgr. comml. systems SofTech, Inc., Waltham, Mass., 1975-79; dir. internat. sales and field ops. Nixdorf Computer Co., Burlington, Mass., 1979-80; mgr. mktg. and strategic planning Digital Equipment Corp., 1980—; sr. instr. acctg. and fin. Grad. Sch. Bus., Northeastern U., Boston, 1966—, instr. acctg. Grad. Sch. Bus. Babson Coll., Wellesley, Mass, 1985— . Treas., Pilgrim Ch.; trustee Sherborn Library; chmn. Sherborn council Boy Scouts Am. Served with U.S. Army, 1967-72. C.P.A., C.L.U., C.P.C.U., C.M.A., C.D.P. Mem. Data Processing Mgmt. Assn., Nat. Assn. Accountants, Assn. Computing Machinery, Boston C. of C. Presbyterian. Clubs: Executive (Boston); Wharton Alumni; U. Iowa Alumni. Home: 24 Dexter Dr Sherborn MA 01770 Office: Digital Equipment Corp 199 Riverneck Rd Chelmsford MA 01824

HANCOCK, WILLIAM GLENN, lawyer; b. Richmond, Va., June 3, 1950; s. William Cary and Doris (Glenn) H. BA in Econs., U. Va., 1968-72; postgrad., Tulane U., 1972-73; JD, U. Richmond, 1973-75. Bar: Va. 1975. Assoc. Mays & Valentine, Richmond, 1975-81, ptnr., 1981—; bd. dirs., counsel Home Beneficial Corp., Home Beneficial Life Ins. Co., Richmond. Editorial bd. U. Richmond Law Rev., 1975. Fundraiser United Givers Fund YMCA, Richmond, 1978-80; bd. dirs. Richmond Tennis Patrons, 1978-80; ex-officio bd., Ronald McDonald House, Richmond. Mem. ABA, Va. Bar Assn. (chmn. young lawyers sect. 1985-86), Richmond Bar Assn., St. Christopher's Alumni Assn. (pres. 1983-85). Office: Mays & Valentine 1111 E Main St Richmond VA 23219 also: Home Beneficial Corp 3901 W Broad St Richmond VA 23230

HANCOX, ROBERT ERNEST, financial services company executive; b. Newark, Apr. 6, 1943; s. Ernest E. and Laverne (Bruguiere) H.; B.A., Lycoming Coll., 1965; M.B.A., Fairleigh Dickinson U., 1970; Ph.D., Pace U., 1981; m. Judith Hale, Aug. 6, 1966; children—Jennifer Susan, Elizabeth Jane. Coordinator mgmt. devel. State Farm Ins. Cos., Wayne, N.J., 1965-66, asst. personnel mgr., 1968-70, personnel supt., 1970-72, regional personnel mgr., 1972-76, regional personnel dir., 1976-81; v.p. human resources INA Corp., 1981-83; v.p. human resources Penn Mut. Life Ins. Co., 1983-87; exec. v.p., chief operating officer ICMA Retirement Corp., Washington, 1987—; bd. dirs. The Daro Group Inc.; adj. asso. prof. Seton Hall U., 1970—, Fordham U., 1974—; trustee Lycoming Coll. Mem. Am. Soc. Personnel Adminstrn. (accredited personnel exec.), Acad. Mgmt., Phila. Urban Coalition, Indsl. Gerontology Research Inst. (bd. dirs.), Am. Compensation Assn., Assn. Specialists Group Work, Indsl. Relations Research Assn., Am. Soc. Tng. and Devel. Republican. Methodist. Office: ICMA Retirement Corp 1120 G St NW Washington DC 20005

HAND, ELBERT O., clothing manufacturing and retailing company executive; b. 1939. BS, Hamilton Coll., 1961. With Hart Schaffner and Marx, 1964-83; pres., chief exec. officer men's apparel group Hartmarx Corp., 1983-85, pres., 1985—, now pres., chief operating officer. Office: Hartmarx Corp 101 N Wacker Dr Chicago IL 60606 *

HAND, HERBERT HENSLEY, management educator, executive, consultant, inventor; b. Hamilton, Ohio, July 11, 1931; s. Herbert Lawrence and Berta Elizabeth (Hensley) H.; m. Katharine Harris Gucker, July 26, 1952; children—Stephen Harris, Herbert Gucker. B.S., Ind. U., 1953; M.B.A., U. Miami, 1966; Ph.D., Pa. State U., 1969. Vice pres. Hand Oil Co., 1955-65; instr. Pa. State U., 1968-69; asst. prof. Ind. U., Bloomington, 1969-73, assoc. prof., 1973-76; prof. entrepreneurship U. S.C. Coll. Bus. Adminstrn., Columbia, 1976—; state dir. Small Bus. Devel. Ctr. S.C., 1968-69; exec. v.p. Carter-Miot Engring. Co., Columbia, S.C., 1981; pres. Carolina Consultants, 1973-84; pres. Phronesis, Inc., 1985—, also dir.; cons. to numerous cos., 1973—. Author: (with H.P. Sims, Jr.) Managerial Decision Making in the Business Firm-A Systems Approach, 1972, The Profit Center Simulation, 1975; (with A.T. Hollingsworth) A Guide to Small Business Management, 1979, Practical Readings in Small Business, 1979; contbr. over 90 research articles and papers in field to profl. jours.; mem. editorial bd. Bus. Horizons, 1971-73; patentee in field. Served to 1st lt. USAF, 1953-55. Recipient Western Electric award for most innovative bus. course, 1971; Small Bus. Inst. Regional award SBA, 1976, 80, 81, Small Bus. Inst. Nat. award, 1980; Office Naval Research grantee, 1976, 77, 78. Mem. Acad. Mgmt. (editorial bd. Rev. Jour. 1975-79), So. Mgmt. Assn., Am. Inst. Decision Scis., Internat. Council for Small Bus. Episcopalian. Lodge: Rotary. Office: Phronesis Inc 1517 Gregg St Columbia SC 29201

HAND, SCOTT MCKEE, mining company executive, lawyer; b. San Francisco, May 11, 1942; s. Elbert Osborne Hand and Katherine Andrews (McKee) Stevenson; m. Ellen Foss MacMillan, Aug. 2, 1969; children: David, Elizabeth, Katherine. Diploma, Deerfield Acad., 1960; BA, Hamilton Coll., 1964; JD, Cornell U., 1969. Bar: N.Y. 1970. Tchr. Peace Corp., Ethiopia, 1964-66; assoc. Wickes, Riddell, Bloomer, Jacobs & McGuire, N.Y.C., 1969-73; v.p., gen. counsel, sec. Inco Ltd., N.Y.C. and Toronto, Ont., Can., 1973—, also v.p. stratregic planning and bus. devel., 1987—; bd. dirs. Independence Savs. Bank, Bklyn., Exide Electroncs Group, Inc., Raleigh, N.C. Trustee Bklyn. Hosp-Caledonian Hosp. Mem. ABA, N.Y. State Bar Assn., N.Y. County Lawyers Assn. Clubs: India House (N.Y.C.); Heights Casino (Bklyn.). Home: 43 Remsen St Brooklyn NY 11201 Office: Inco Ltd 1 New York Pla New York NY 10004

HANDEL, MORTON EMANUEL, leisure products company executive; b. N.Y.C., Apr. 12, 1935; s. Benjamin and Mollie (Heller) H.; m. Irma Ruby, Aug. 5, 1956; children: Mark, Gary, Karen. BA, U. Pa., 1956; postgrad., NYU, 1957-59. V.p. Dale Plastic Playing Card Corp., N.Y.C., 1955-57; gen. mgr. Handel Nets & Fabrics Corp., N.Y.C., 1957-62; pres. A.M. Industries, Inc., Farmingdale, N.Y., 1962-68, Allan Marine, Inc., Deer Park, N.Y., 1969-71; chmn. bd. Marlow Yacht Corp., Deer Park, 1969-71; v.p. fin., sec.-treas. Aurora Products Corp. (subs. Nabisco Inc.), 1971-73, sr. v.p., chief fin. officer, 1973-74; v.p. Rowe Industries Inc., 1971-74; v.p., dir. Aurora Nederland N.V., 1971-74, Aurora Plastics Can. Ltd., 1971-74; v.p. fin., chief fin. officer Coleco Industries Inc., 1974-78, sr. v.p., chief fin. officer, 1978-82, exec. v.p. fin. and adminstrn., 1982-83, exec. v.p. corp. com., 1983-85, exec. v.p. corp. devel., 1985-88, chmn., dir., chief exec. officer, 1988—; Coleco Industries, Inc.; trustee Aurora Products Profit Sharing Trust, 1971-74, Coleco Industries Inc. Profit Sharing Trust, 1976-85. Pres. Rochdale Vill. Civic Assn., 1964-65; pres., bd. dirs. Symphony Soc. Greater Hartford, 1976—; bd. dirs. Jewish Children's Service Corp., 1976-78; corporator St. Francis Hosp., 1982—; bd. dirs. One Thousand Corp., 1983—; bd. dir. Greater Hartford Arts Coun., Inc., 1987—. Mem. Am. Mgmt. Assn., Fin. Execs. Inst., Planning Execs. Inst., Alpha Epsilon Pi. Home: 41 Ranger Ln West Hartford CT 06117 Office: Coleco Industries Inc 80 Darling Dr Avon CT 06001

HANDEL, RICHARD CRAIG, lawyer; b. Hamilton, Ohio, Aug. 11, 1945; s. Alexander F. and Marguerite (Wilks) H.; m. Katharine Jean Carter, Jan. 10, 1970. AB, U. Mich., 1967; MA, Mich. State U., 1968; JD summa cum laude, Ohio State U., 1974; LLM in Taxation, NYU, 1978. Bar: Ohio 1974, S.C. 1983, U.S. Dist. Ct. (so. dist.) Ohio 1975, U.S. Dist. Ct. S.C. 1979, U.S. Tax Ct. 1977, U.S. Ct. Appeals (4th cir.) 1979, U.S. Supreme Ct. 1979; cert. tax specialist. Assoc. Smith & Schnacke, Dayton, Ohio, 1974-77; asst. prof. U. S.C. Sch. Law, Columbia, 1978-83; ptnr. Nexsen, Pruet, Jacobs & Pollard, Columbia, 1983-87; ptnr. Moore & Van Allen, Columbia, 1987-88; ptnr. Nexsen Pruet Jacobs & Pollard, Columbia, 1988—. Contbr. articles to legal jours. Served with U.S. Army, 1969-70, Vietnam. Gerald L. Wallace scholar, 1977-78; recipient Outstanding Law Prof. award, 1980-81. Mem. ABA, S.C. Bar Assn., Richland County Bar Assn., Order of Coif. Office: Nexsen Pruet Jacobs & Pollard 1441 Main St Ste 1500 Columbia SC 29202

HANDEL, WILLIAM KEATING, sales executive; b. N.Y.C., Mar. 23, 1935; s. Irving Nathaniel and Marguerite Mary (Keating) H.; m. Margaret Inez Sitton; children: William Keating II, David Roger. BA in Journalism, U. S.C., 1959, postgrad., 1959-60. With Packaging div. The Mead Corp., Atlanta, 1960-64, Ketchum, MacLeod & Grove, Pitts., 1964-67, Rexall Drug & Chem. Corp., L.A., 1967-68; owner Creative Enterprises/Mktg. Communications, L.A., 1968-71; creative dir., sales promotion mgr. Beneficial Standard Life Ins., L.A., 1971-72; mgr. advt. and pub. rels. ITT Gen. Controls, Glendale, Calif., 1972-80; mgr. corp. recruitment advt. Hughes Aircraft Co., L.A., 1980-81; mgr. corp. communications Fairchild Camera and Instrument Corp., 1981-83; dist. mgr. Cahners Pub. Co., 1984—; pub. rels. counsel Calif. Pvt. Edn. Schs., 1978-87; chmn. exhibits Mini/Micro Computer Conf., 1977-78. Bd. dirs. West Valley Athletic League; bd. dir. L.A. chpt. USMC Scholarship Found.; pub. rels. cons. Ensenada, Mexico Tourist Commn., 1978; chmn., master of ceremonies U.S. Marine Corps Birthday Ball, L.A., 1979-82. With USMC, 1950-53. Decorated Silver Star, Bronze Star, Purple Heart (4), Navy Commendation medal with combat V; recipient Pub. Svc. award L.A. Heart Assn., 1971-73. Mem. Bus. and Profl. Advt. Assn. (cert. bus. communicator, past pres.), 1st Marine Div. Assn., Navy League (dir.), Sigma Chi (chpt. adv.). Republican. Roman Catholic. Clubs: AdLinx Golf of So. Calif., Torrey Pines Golf, Griffith Pk. Golf, Nueva España Boat, Baiamar Country, Ensenada Country, Ensenada Fish and Game (Baja, Mexico), Torrey Pines Golf. Home: 2428 Badajoz Pl Rancho La Costa CA 92009

HANDELMAN, DAVID YALE, film company executive, lawyer; b. N.Y.C., July 2, 1938; s. Victor and Ruth (Goodman) H.; m. Janet Kay Tarachow, June 11, 1961; children: Joanna Beth, Peter Henry. BA, U. Pa., 1959; JD, Harvard U., 1962. Bar: N.Y. 1963, Calif. 1977. Atty. SEC, Washington, 1964-66; assoc. Migdal, Low, Tenney & Glass, N.Y.C., 1966-68; sr. v.p., gen. counsel Laird, Inc., N.Y.C., 1968-74, 20th Century-Fox Film Corp., Los Angeles, 1974—. Democrat. Office: 20th Century-Fox Film Corp PO Box 900 Beverly Hills CA 90213

HANDELSMAN, HAROLD S., hotel company executive, lawyer; b. N.Y.C., Oct. 1, 1946. BA, Amherst Coll., 1968; JD, Columbia U., 1973. Assoc. Wachtell, Lipton, Rosen & Katz, N.Y.C., 1974-78; sr. v.p., gen. counsel, sec. Hyatt Corp. Am., Chgo., 1978—. Bd. dirs. Little City Found., 1986—. Mem. ABA, N.Y. State Bar Assn. Office: Hyatt Corp 200 W Madison 38th Fl Chicago IL 60606

HANDER, O. BENJAMIN, retired chemical company executive, consultant; b. Waco, Tex., Feb. 16, 1918; s. Edwin William and Katherine E. (Munz) H.; m. Clariece Sego, May 24, 1942; children: Howard Benjamin, Janet Clariece (Mrs. Robert L. Powers), Robert William. B.S. in Mech. Engring., Rice U., 1942. Chem. engr. Humble Oil Co., 1942-48; mgr. prodn. and control Office Synthetic Rubber, Washington, 1948-51; cons. Exec. Offices Pres. U.S., 1951-52; with Dewey & Almy Chem. Co., 1952-54, asst. to pres., 1953-54; co. merged with W.R. Grace & Co., N.Y.C., 1954; v.p. chem. group W.R. Grace & Co., 1962-65, v.p. gen. devel. group, 1965-71, corporate v.p., 1971-83, corporate sr. v.p., 1983-87, ret., 1987; cons. in field; pvt. investor. Presbyn. Clubs: Baltusrol Golf (Springfield, N.J.); Princeton (N.Y.C.). Home: 30 Colt Rd Summit NJ 07901

HANDLER, LAWRENCE DAVID, financial executive, food products executive; b. Bayonne, N.J., Oct. 12, 1945; s. Nathan and Nettie (Daskal) H.; m. Sharon Rosenthal, June 16, 1968; children: Eric, Hollis. BS in Acctg. cum laude, U. Conn., 1967; MBA in Corp. Fin., NYU, 1969. Audit mgr. Arthur Andersen & Co., Hartford, Conn., 1969-75; treas. Dairy Mart Convenience Stores, Inc., Enfield, Conn., 1975-77, v.p. fin., 1977-79, exec. v.p., 1979—, also bd. dirs.; pres., chief oper. officer Dairy Mart N.E. Div., 1986-89; assoc. bd. dirs. Enfield Nat. Bank. Contbr. articles on bus. to jours. and mags. Co.-campaign chmn. United Way; trustee Emanuel Synagogue, West Hartford, Conn., 1981-89; cons. Project Bus. Jr. Achievement, no. Conn., 1978-80. Recipient Outstanding NYU Faculty award Haskins & Sells Found., 1968, Sr. Acctg. award U. Conn., 1967, bus. law award U. Conn., 1967, author award Nat. Assn. Accts., 1975. Mem. AICPA, Conn. Soc. CPA's (gov. 1987—, named Author of Yr. 1977), Conn. Food Stores Assn. (gov., bd. dirs.), Fin. Execs. Inst., Beta Gamma Sigma. Jewish. Home: 22 Tumblebrook Ln West Hartford CT 06117 Office: Dairy Mart Convenience Stores Inc 240 South Rd Enfield CT 06082

HANDLER, MARK S., retail executive; b. 1933; married. Student, U. Ill.; B.S., Roosevelt U., 1957; M.S., N.Y. U., 1958. With R.H. Macy & Co. Inc., N.Y.C., 1958—; mdse. adminstr. Bamberger's (subs. R. H. Macy & Co., Inc.), Newark, 1962-65, v.p., mdse. adminstr., 1965-67, sr. v.p. merchandising, 1967-71, pres., 1979, chmn., chief exec. officer, 1979-80, also bd. dirs.; pres., dir. R. H. Macy & Co., Inc., N.Y.C., 1980—. Served with U.S. Army, 1953-55. Office: R H Macy & Co Inc 151 W 34th St New York NY 10001

HANDY, CHARLES BROOKS, accountant, educator; b. Coffey, Mo., Apr. 26, 1924; s. Herbert Franklyn and Laura Ada Margaret (Mueller) H.; m. Donna Jean Peters, June 29, 1958; children: William Mark, Karen Lynne. B.A., Westminster Coll., Fulton, Mo., 1947; M.A., U. Iowa, 1956; Ph.D., Iowa State U., 1970. C.P.A., Iowa. Staff acct. McGladrey, Hansen, Dunn & Co. (now McGladrey & Pullen), Davenport, Iowa, 1955-58; instr. acctg. Iowa State U., Ames, 1958-60; asst. prof. Iowa State U., 1960-70, assoc. prof., 1970-75, prof., 1975—, chmn. supervisory com. bus. adminstrv. scis., 1975-78, acctg. coordinator, 1977-78, chmn. dept. indsl. adminstrn., 1978-80, dir. Sch. Bus. Adminstrn., 1980-84, dean Coll. Bus. Adminstrn., 1984-89. Served to lt. (j.g.) USNR, 1943-46. Mem. Am. Inst. C.P.A.s, Iowa Soc. C.P.A.s, Am. Acctg. Assn., Midwest Bus. Adminstrn. Assn., Beta Alpha Psi, Omicron Delta Epsilon. Republican. Presbyterian. Home: 1132 Johnson St Ames IA 50010 Office: Iowa State U Coll Bus Adminstrn Ames IA 50011

HANDY, ROLLO LEROY, educator, research executive; b. Kenyon, Minn., Feb. 20, 1927; s. John R. and Alice (Kispert) H.; m. Toni Scheiner, Sept. 17, 1950; children—Jonathan, Ellen, Benjamin. B.A., Carleton Coll., Northfield, Minn., 1950; M.A., Sarah Lawrence Coll., 1951; postgrad., U. Minn., 1951-52; Ph.D., U. Buffalo, 1954. Mem. faculty U. S.D., 1954-60, prof. philosophy, head dept., 1959-60; assoc. prof. Union Coll., Schenectady, 1960-61; mem. faculty SUNY-Buffalo, 1961-76, prof. philosophy, 1964-76, chmn. dept., 1961-67, chmn. div. philosophy and social scis., 1965-67, provost faculty ednl. studies, 1967-76; pres. Behavioral Research Council, 1976—, Am. Inst. Econ. Research, 1977—. Author: Methodology of the Behavioral Sciences, 1964, Value Theory and the Behavioral Sciences, 1969, The Measurement of Values, 1970, (with Paul Kurtz) A Current Appraisal of the Behavioral Sciences, 1964; (with E.C. Harwood) rev. edit., 1973, Useful Procedures of Inquiry, 1973; Co-editor: (with E.C. Harwood) Philosophical Perspectives on Punishment, 1968, The Behavioral Sciences, 1968, The Idea of God, 1968. Served with USNR, 1945-46. Mem. AAUP (chpt. pres. 1964-65), Am. Anthrop. Assn., Am. Philos. Assn., Mind Assn., Philosophy Sci. Assn. Office: Am Inst Econ Rsch Great Barrington MA 01230

HANEMANN, JOHN H., commodity exchange executive; b. N.Y.C., Aug. 30, 1943; s. Paul A. and Lillian (Blumberg) H.; m. Stephanie D. Haneman, Nov. 14, 1967; children: Jonathan S., Gene P. Student, CUNY, 1962-63. Mgr. order room Orvis Bros., N.Y.C., 1967-69; clk., broker Felix J. Forlenza & Co., N.Y.C., 1969-80; sr. ptnr. Hanemann Commodities, N.Y.C., 1980-82, Prestige Metals Tng. Co., N.Y.C., 1982—; bd. dirs. Comex, N.Y.C., 1979—, pres., 1988—. Office: Commodity Exch Inc Commodities Exchange Ctr 4 World Trade Ctr New York NY 10048

HANES, JOHN T., food products executive; b. 1936. BS, U. Mo., 1958; MBA, U. Chgo., 1969. With Wilson Foods Corp., Oklahoma City, 1961—, v.p., 1977-79, v.p. operating services, 1979, v.p. processed products, 1980-83, from sr. v.p. to pres. retail div., 1983-84, exec. v.p., 1984—. Served to capt. USAF, 1958-61. Office: Wilson Foods Corp 4545 N Lincoln Blvd Oklahoma City OK 73105 *

HANEY, FREDERICK MARION, venture capital executive; b. Columbus, Mar. 5, 1941; s. George Edward and Margaret (Marion) H.; m. Barbara Louise Breig, June 8, 1963; children: Karen Nesbitt, Bradford Jennings. BA, Ohio Wesleyan U., 1963; MS, Colo. State U., 1965; postgrad., Brown U., 1965-66; PhD, Carnegie-Mellon U., 1968. Mgr. Sci. Data Systems div. Xerox Corp., El Segundo, Calif., 1968-75, Computer Scis. Corp., El Segundo, 1975-77; mgr. planning Xerox Corp., El Segundo, 1977-80; gen. mgr., mgr. strategic planning TRW Corp., Westwood, Calif., 1980-84; mgr. ptnr., exec. v.p. 3 1/2 Ventures Inc., Newport Beach, Calif., 1984—; mem. adv. bd. entrepreneurial program U. So. Calif., Los Angeles, 1987—; bd. dirs. Silicon Power Cube Co., Long Beach, Calif., Computer Aided Design Co., Marine Del Ray, Calif., Sensors, Inc., Milpitas, Calif., Speech Systems, Inc., Tarzana, Calif. Contbr. articles to profl. jours. Chmn. Coastline Com., Palos Verdes Estates, Calif., 1973-75; mem. Project Mex., Rolling Hills, Calif., 1974—. Mem. Nat. Assn. Venture Capitalists, Orange Coast Venture Group, So. Calif. Tech. Execs. Network, MBA Group Orange County, Omicron Delta Kappa, Phi Mu Epsilon, Sigma Chi. Republican. Presbyterian. Clubs: Palos Verdes Golf, Palos Verdes Tennis, ; Decathlon (Santa Clara). Office: 3i Ventures Inc 450 Newport Ctr Newport Beach CA 92660

HANISH, ROBERT JOHN, banker; b. Hazelton, Pa., Dec. 27, 1945; s. Albert William and Elizabeth (Chervenak) H.; m. Donna Lee Cadwell, Aug. 17, 1967; children: Brian Robert, Beth Ann. Student, U. Scranton, 1969-71, U. Colo., 1975, U. Va., 1979-81. Quality control engring. aide RCA Corp., Scranton, 1966-68, prodn. technician, 1968-70, foreman screening dept., 1970-72; adjustor Key Bancshares Maine, Augusta, 1972-73, supr. ops., 1973-74, asst. treas., 1974-77, asst. v.p., 1977-80, v.p., 1980-84, sr. v.p., 1984—; instr. Am. Inst. Banking, also pres. bd. dirs. Mem. planning bd. City of Augusta; bd. govs., treas. Salvation Army. USN, 1963-66. Mem. Maine Retailers Assn. (bd. dirs.), Masons, Shriners. Republican. Lutheran. Home: Kenneth St Augusta ME 04330 Office: Key Bancshares Maine PO Box 2029 Augusta ME 04330

HANKE, DOUGLAS PIERSON, financial planning company executive; b. Lakewood, Ohio, Mar. 29, 1948; s. Max J. and Jacqueline (Pierson) H.; m. Eugenia Lee Firday, Sept. 12, 1970; childern: Michael, Michele, Daivd. Student, Emory U., 1966-68; BSBA with honors, U. Fla., 1970; postgrad., Fla. Bankers Assn. Trust Sch., 1978, U. South Fla., 1968-70; cert. property mgmt., Inst. Real Estate Mgmt., Chgo., 1980; cert. fin. planning, Coll. for Fin. Planning, Denver, 1984; postgrad. in fin. planning, U. Tampa, 1984-85. Registered investment advisor SEC; lic. real estate salesman, Fla. Trust real estate officer First Nat. Bank of Fla., Tampa, 1970-74; v.p., trust officer Flagship Bank, Tampa, 1974-80; ptnr., sr. fin. advisor First Commonwealth Assocs., Houston, 1984-82, v.p., sr. fin. planner, 1982-84; pres. Fla. Fin. Advisors, Tampa, 1984—. Mem. legacy com. Tampa chpt. Am. Cancer Soc., 1977-78; lay mem. grievance com. C. Fla. Bar 13th Jud. Cir., 1982. Mem. Nat. Assn. Personal Fin. Advisors, Internat. Assn. for Fin. Planning (bd. dirs. Tampa Bay chpt. 1987-88), Inst. Cert. Fin. Planners, Nat. Assn. Realtors, Fla. Bd. Realtors, Lakeland Bd. Realtors, Tampa Bay Estate Planning Coun. (bd. dirs.) Greater Tampa C. of C. (mem. Leadership Tampa program 1980), Sigma Nu, Commerce Club (bd. dirs., treas. 1978, v.p. 1979). Office: Fla Fin Advisors Inc 330 W Bearss Ave Tampa FL 33613-1224

HANKINS, WILLIAM H., business manager; b. Everton, Mo., Oct. 4, 1942; s. George A. and Mary V. (Myers) H.; m. Paula S. Hall, July 22, 1966; children: Saundra, Heather. BS, SW Mo. State U., 1964. Field advtg. rep. Procter & Gamble Corp., Cin., 1964-66; sales rep. Procter & Gamble Corp., Miami, Fla., 1966-67; personnel specialist Fed. Reserve Bank, Kansas City, Mo., 1967-72; bus. mgr. Sta. KSBH-TV, Scripps Howard Broadcasting Co., Kansas City, Mo., 1972—. Bd. dirs. Children Internat., Kansas City, 1988. Mem. Broadcasting Fin. Mgmt. Assn. (v.p. 1985-86, pres. 1986-87, chmn. bd. dirs. 1987-88), Broadcast Credit Assn., Nat. Assn. Credit Mgmt., Personnel Research Forum (pres. 1980). Republican. Office: Sta KSHB 4720 Oak St Kansas City MO 64112

HANKINSON, JAMES F., business executive; b. Weymouth, Nova Scotia, Sept. 21, 1943; s. J. Scott and Edith Ann (Journeay) H.; m. Grace Mary Buck, July 16, 1966; children—Mary Grace, John Scott. B. Commerce, Mount Allison U., Sackville, N.B., 1964; C.A., Ontario Inst. Chartered Accountants, 1969; M.B.A., McMaster U., Hamilton, Ont., 1970. Asst. to dir. acctg. CP Rail, Montreal, Que., 1973-74, asst. dir., 1974-75; dir. acctg. CP Rail, Montreal, 1975-79; comptroller Can. Pacific Ltd., Montreal, 1979-81; v.p. fin. and acctg. Can. Pacific Enterprises Ltd., 1981-85; chmn., chief exec. officer Can. Pacific Securities Ltd., 1981-85; group v.p. Can. Pacific Ltd., 1985-88; exec. v.p. Can. Pacific Ltd., Toronto, Ont., 1988—; bd. dirs. AMCA Internat. Ltd., Can. Pacific Enterprises Ltd., Can. Pacific Forest Products Ltd., Can. Pacific Securities Ltd., Can. Pacific Securities (Ont.) Ltd., Can. Pacific (U.S.) Inc., Fording Coal Ltd., PanCan. Petroleum Ltd., Processed Minerals Inc., Syracuse China Corp.

HANKS, LARRY BERKLEY, life insurance company executive; b. Idaho Falls, Idaho, Sept. 25, 1940; s. Victor Franklin and Marjorie (Burke) H.; AB, Brigham Young U., 1964; Master in Fin. Sci., Am. Coll., 1982; CLU; chartered fin. cons.; m. Georgia Lee Gammett, Dec. 29, 1965; children—Tiffany, Berkley, Colli, Andrea, Rachel, Jared, Cyrus. Owner, mgr. Larry B. Hanks, CLU, ins. and employee benefits, Salt Lake City, 1969—; pres. Am. Pension Adminstrs. Inc., Salt Lake City 1978—, Integrated Fin. Designs, Inc., 1982—; gen. agt. Mass. Mut. Life Ins. Co., Salt Lake City, 1980—; instr. CLU classes Am. Coll., Bryn Mawr, Pa., 1975—. With U.S. Army, 1968-69. Mem. Am. Soc. CLU (dir. Magic Valley chpt.), Nat. Assn. Life Underwriters, Am. Soc. Pension Actuaries, N.E. Idaho Assn. Life Underwriters (dir., officer), Million Dollar Roundtable, Estate Planning Coun. Boise, Gen. Agts. and Mgrs. Assn. Republican. Mormon. Home: 7628 Riverwood Dr Sandy UT 84092 Office: Integrated Fin Designs Inc 4 Triad Ctr Ste 600 Salt Lake City UT 84180

HANLIN, HUGH CAREY, retired life insurance company executive; b. Chattanooga, Mar. 16, 1925; s. Hugh Carey and Irene (Thompson) H.; m. Wilma Jean Deal, June 23, 1951; children: Timothy Carey, Chris Allan. Student, Emory U., 1942-44, 46-47; BA, U. Mich., 1948. With Provident Life & Accident Ins. Co., Chattanooga, 1948-88, exec. v.p., 1973-77, pres., 1977-87, chief exec. officer, 1979-87, chmn., chief exec. officer, 1988, dir., 1973-88; adv. dir. Am. Nat. Bank & Trust Co., Chattanooga; bd. dirs. Third Nat. Corp.; chmn. Am. Coun. Life Ins., 1988. Bd. dirs. The River City Co., 1986—, Pub. Edn. Found., 1988—, Chattanooga Opera Assn., 1970-79, pres., 1973-74; past pres. Chattanooga-Hamilton County Speech and Hearing Ctr.; bd. dirs. Allied Arts Chattanooga, pres., 1982-84; bd. dirs. Mocassin Bend coun. Girl Scouts U.S., 1971-75, Girls Club Chattanooga, 1976-77, United Way Chattanooga, 1979-82, Chattanooga YMCA, 1980-83; bd. dirs. Chattanooga Area Urban League, 1981-83; trustee U. Chattanooga Found., 1977—, vice chmn., 1988—; trustee Tenn. Ind. Colls. Fund, 1979-80, The Am. Coll., 1981; chmn. bd. trustees Tenn. Aquarium, 1989—; mem. Tenn. Coun. on Econ. Edn., 1978-80; mem. Cherokee Area coun. Boy Scouts Am., 1980—, pres., 1981-82; bd. visitors Berry Coll., Rome, Ga., 1981-84. Lt. (j.g.) USNR, 1943-46. Recipient Silver Beaver award Boy Scouts Am., 1983, Liberty Bell award Chattanooga Bar Assn., 1984, Arthur Vieth Free Enterprise award, 1984. Fellow Soc. Actuaries; mem. Southeastern Actuaries Club (pres. 1956-57), Sertoma Club (Nat. Heritage award), Mountain City Club (bd. dirs. 1977-80, 88—), Phi Beta Kappa, Alpha Tau Omega. Presbyterian (deacon). Home: 3 Glenarn Ct Signal Mountain TN 37377 Office: Provident Life and Accident Ins Co James Bldg Ste 209 735 Broad St Chattanooga TN 37402

HANLIN, JOHN PAUL, general merchandise manager; b. Balt., Sept. 9, 1946; s. Samuel Paul and Billie Louise H.; m. Florence Delores McKaige, Oct. 30, 1971; children: Colleen Louise, Emily Elizabeth, John Paul II, Mary Elaine, Andrew Pierce. BA, U. Pa., 1968; MBA, U. So. Calif., 1982. Ensign USN, 1968, advanced through grades to lt., 1971, resigned, 1976; acad. dir. spl. tng. and instr. USN, Athens, Ga., 1983-86; advanced through grades to capt. USNR, 1988; mgr. Steak & Ale, Norfolk, Va., 1976-77; systems analyst hdqrs. USMC, Quantico, Va., 1977-78; mgr. mdse. exch. USMC, Quantico, 1978-83; gen. mdse. mgr. USMC, 1987—; govt. contracting cons. Author: Government Procurement and Contracting Manual, 1982, 2nd edit., 1986. Pres. Sheraton Hills Civic Assn., Fredericksburg, 1982; cub and webelo leader Boy Scouts Am., Fredericksburg, 1987. Decorated Nat. Def. metal, Vietman Campaign medal, Vietman MUC Gallantry medal. Mem. Am. Mgmt. Assn., Nat. Retail Mchts. Assn. Republican. Roman Catholic. Office: Marine Corps Exch PO Box 229 Quantico VA 22134-0229

HANLIN, RUSSELL L., citrus products company executive; b. Sioux Falls, S.D., 1932; married. Student, U. Wash., Los Angeles City Coll. With Sunkist Growers, Inc., Van Nuys, Calif., 1951—, advt. mgr., 1964-72, v.p. mfg., mkt. research and devel., products group, 1972-78, former chief exec. and chief operating officer, pres., 1978—, also dir. Served with U.S. Army, 1953-55. Office: Sunkist Growers Inc 14130 Riverside Dr Box 7888 Van Nuys CA 91409 *

HANLON, DAVID PATRICK, hotel and casino executive; b. Cin., Nov. 23, 1944; children: Lara Suzanne, David Jeffrey. BS in Hotel Adminstrn., Cornell U., 1966; MBA in Fin., MS in Acctg., U. Pa. Wharton Sch., 1971; cert. advanced mgmt. program, Harvard Bus. Sch., 1986. Salesman Smith, Barney, Harris, N.Y.C. and Los Angeles, 1972-75; dir. project fin., dir. corp. fin. Fluor Corp., 1975-78; treas., chief fin. officer, v.p. ops. and adminstrn., exec. v.p. Caesars World, Inc., Los Angeles, 1978-84; pres. Harrah's East Hotel/Casino, Atlantic City, 1984-88; pres., chief exec. officer Resorts Internat. Casino Hotel, Atlantic City, 1988—. Mem. N.J. Olympic Com., Ptnrship. N.J., Govs. Council Physical Fitness, N.J. Alcoholic Beverage Study Commn. Mem. Casino Assoc. N.J. (chmn.), Casino Reinvestment Devel. Authority. Office: Resorts Internat Hotel Inc N Carolina Ave & Boardwalk Atlantic City NJ 08404 also: Equestrian Ctr Moss Mill Rd Smithville NJ 08201

HANLON, JANET MOORE, financial executive; b. N.Y.C., Sept. 9, 1954; d. Peter Gale and Janet Ruth (Dugan) Moore; m. William R. Hanlon, Aug. 28, 1976; 1 child, William Moore. BA, Coll. William & Mary, 1976; MBA, U. Pa., 1981. CPA, D.C. Acct. Price Waterhouse, Phila., 1977-79; sr. fin. analyst Communications Satellite Corp., Washington, 1981-82, mgr. fin. analysis, 1982-83, dir. fin. ops., 1983-85; dir. fin. Comsat Space Communications div., Clarksburg, Md., 1986-87, Wilmer Cutler & Pickering, Washington, 1987—; bd. dirs. Satellite Fed. Credit Union. Mem. fin. com. YWCA, Washington, 1985. Mem. D.C. Inst. CPA's, NAFE, Assn. Legal Adminstrs. Democrat. Roman Catholic. Office: Wilmer Cutler & Pickering 2445 M St NW Washington DC 20037

HANMAN, GARY EDWIN, dairy company executive; b. Browning, Mo., Jan. 30, 1934; s. John Edwin Hanman and Doris (Crist) Harris; m. Shirley A. Warren, Aug. 16, 1953; children: Vicky, Sandy, Cindy, Ted. BS in Agriculture, U. Mo., 1955, M in Dairy Mktg., 1956. With Fed. Milk Market Adminstrn., St. Louis, 1956-64; gen. mgr. Sq. Deal Milk Producers, Highland, Ill., 1964-68; v.p. fluid mktg. Mid-Am. Dairymen Inc., Springfield, Mo., 1968-70, exec. v.p. mktg., 1970-72; sr. exec. v.p. mktg. Mid-Am. Dairymen Inc., Springfield, 1972-73; sr. corp. v.p. Mid-Am. Dairymen Inc., Springfield, Mo., 1973-75, exec. v.p., gen. mgr., 1975—; vice chmn., bd. advisors Hiland Dairy, Springfield, Mo.; sec., bd. advisors Western Food Processing, Idaho Falls, Idaho; vice chmn., bd. dirs., Robert Dairy, Omaha. Mem. Nat. Council Farmer Coops. (exec. com. vice chair bd. dirs.), Nat. Milk Producers Assn. (exec. com., bd. dirs.). Home: 612 N Elm Marshfield MO 65706 Office: Mid-Am Dairymen Inc 3253 E Chestnut Expwy Springfield MO 65802-2584

HANNA, COLIN ARTHUR, management consultant, executive search consultant; b. Abington, Pa., Dec. 3, 1946; s. Arthur and Jean Victoria (McClure) H.; A.B., U. Pa., 1968; m. Anne Price Hemphill, Dec. 28, 1967; children: Jean Price, Colin Alexander. With CBS, Inc., 1969-76; account exec. CBS Radio Spot Sales, N.Y.C., 1969-70; mgr. creative services CBS-Viacom Group, N.Y.C., 1970-71; account exec. CBS Radio Spot Sales, N.Y.C., 1971-72, sales mgr., Phila., 1974-76; account exec. WCAU Radio, Phila., 1972-74; dir. sales devel. WCAU-TV, Phila., 1976; pres. Hanna & Wile Advt., Wayne, Pa., 1976-77, Tri-State Trade Exchange, Inc., West Chester, Pa., 1978-80, Hanna Enterprises Ltd., 1980—; prin. Whittlesey and Assocs., West Chester, 1980-86; pres. The Cheshire Group, West Chester, 1986—, Vestryman Ch. of Good Samaritan, Paoli, Pa.; mem. bd. overseers Sch. Arts and Scis. U. Pa. With USNR, 1968-69. Mem. Am. Mktg. Assn., Am. Mgmt. Assn., Bank Mktg. Assn., Inter-Fin. Assn., Fin. Instns. Mktg. Assn., Nat. Assn. Corp. and Profl. Recruiters, Phila. Direct Advt. Assn., Shakspere Soc. Phila., Newcomen Soc. N.Am., AMVETS (dir.), Coll. Alumni Soc. U. Pa. (pres.), Gen. Alumni Soc. U. Pa. (v.p.), Alumni Assn. U. Pa. (pres.), Mensa. Republican. Episcopalian. Clubs: Racquet (Phila.); Radley Run Country (West Chester); Tred Avon Yacht (Oxford, Md.). Home: 603 Fairway Dr West Chester PA 19380 Office: 300 S High St West Chester PA 19382

HANNA, FRANK JOSEPH, credit company executive; b. Douglas, Ga., Apr. 20, 1939; s. Frank Joseph and Josephine (Nahoom) H.; B.B.A., U. Ga., 1961; m. Vail Deadwyler, Sept. 15, 1960; children—Frank, Lisa, David. Credit mgr. Sears, Roebeck & Co., Atlanta, 1961-63, Gen. Motors Corp., Atlanta, 1963-65; gen. mgr. Rollins Acceptance Corp., Atlanta, 1965-81; with Credit Claims & Collections, 1981—; real estate developer, 1968. Office: 1140 Hammond Dr Bldg 1 Ste 9250 Atlanta GA 30328

HANNA, HAROLD PUTNAM, JR., accountant, consultant; b. Wareham, Mass., Aug. 2, 1944; s. Harold Putnam and Elsa Louise (Horne) H.; m. Marie Elena Lyons, Sept. 8, 1968; 1 child: Mark Scott. BS, Northeastern U., 1973; MBA, Babson Coll., 1975. CPA, Mass.; cert. internal auditor. Fin. reporter The Boston Traveler, 1963-68; New Eng. reporter Fairchild Publs., Boston, 1968-69; editor The Patriot Ledger, Quincy, Mass., 1969-74; auditor John Hancock Mut. Life, Boston, 1974-78, Air Force Audit Agy., Bedford, Mass., 1978-86; town treas. Canton, 1986—; chmn., controller Canton Cable Access Corp., 1987—; chmn. bd. dirs. Canton (Mass.) Cable Access Corp.; bd. dirs., mem. Supervisory Audit Com., Hanscom Fed. Credit Union, Bedford. Mem. editorial bd. Mass. CPA Review, Boston, 1984-87, editor 1985-86; contbr. articles on fin. and industry to local newspapers. Chmn. Canton Computer Steering Com., 1984-86; mem. Canton Fin. Com., 1983-86, Canton Purchasing Com., 1985-86; mem. Blue Hills Civic Assn., Canton, 1980—. Served with U.S. Army, 1964-69. Mem. Am. Inst. CPA's, Mass. Soc. CPA's, Assn. Govt. Accts., Am. Soc. Notaries. Republican. Episcopalian. Home: 23 Ledgewood Dr Canton MA 02021

HANNA, JOHN A., finance and administration executive; b. Montreal, Que., Can., Nov. 26, 1942; s. Abraham and Marie H.; m. Carol Anne Newton, Sept. 9, 1967; children: Robert, David. B in Commerce, Loyola U., Montreal, 1967, cert. in gen. acctg., 1974. Bus. analyst CGE Co. Ltd., Montreal, 1968-72; v.p. fin. Can. Ports Corp., Montreal, 1972-81; v.p. fin. and adminstrn. Via Rail Can. Inc., Montreal, 1981-87; v.p. fin. and adminstrn. Hydro-Que. Internat., Montreal, 1987—, also bd. dirs.; bd. dirs. Nouveler, SEBJ, Montreal.

HANNAFORD, DAVID CARLYLE, controller; b. Greenville, Ohio, Aug. 20, 1959; s. Paul Emerson and Claudia Lee Hatch. BBA in Acctg., Bus. Adminstrn., Lycoming Coll., 1981. CPA, Ohio, Fla., N.J. Acct. Price, Waterhouse, Toledo, 1981-84; controller Carribbean Gulfstream Co., Boca Raton, Fla., 1984-86, J.W. Charles Realty, Inc., Boca Raton, 1986-87, Burgdoff Realtors, Inc., Murray Hill, N.J., 1987—; cons. Carribbean Gulfstream Co., Boca Raton, Fla. Mem. Am. Inst. CPA's, Fla. Soc. CPA's, N.J. Soc. CPA's, Ohio Soc. CPA's. Republican. Episcopalian. Office: Burgdorff Realtors 560 Central Ave Murray Hill NJ 07974

HANNAFORD, PETER DOR, public relations executive; b. Glendale, Calif., Sept. 21, 1932; s. Donald R. and Elinor (Nielsen) H.; m. Irene Dorothy Harville, Aug. 14, 1954; children: Richard Harville, Donald R. II. A.B., U. Calif., 1954. Account exec. Helen A. Kennedy Advt., 1956; v.p. Kennedy-Hannaford, Inc. (name changed to Kennedy, Hannaford & Dolman, Inc. 1965), San Francisco and Oakland, Calif., 1957-62; pres. 1962-67, Pettler & Hannaford, Inc., Oakland, 1967-69; v.p. Wilton, Coombs & Colnett, Inc., 1969-72; pres. Hannaford & Assos., Oakland, 1973; asst. to Gov. of Calif.; dir. public affairs Govs.' Office, 1974; chmn. bd. Hannaford Co., Inc. (formerly Deaver & Hannaford, Inc.), 1975—; nat. pres. Mut. Advt. Agy. Network, 1968-69; instr. advt. Merritt Coll., Oakland, 1964-67; vice chmn. Calif. Gov.'s Consumer Fraud Task Force, 1972-73. Author: The Reagans: A Political Portrait, 1983; Talking Back to the Media, 1986. mem. Alameda County Rep. Central Com., Rep. State Central Com. Calif., 1968-74; Rep. nominee for U.S. Congress, 1972; mem. governing bd. Tahoe Regional Planning Agy., 1973-74; trustee White House Preservation Fund, 1981—, pres. 1988—; mem. pub. relations adv. com. USIA, 1981—; mem. The Commonwealth Fund's Commn. on Elderly People Living Alone, 1986—; bd. dirs. Wash. Internat. Horse Show, 1986—. Served as 1st lt. Signal Corps AUS, 1954-56. Mem. Theta Xi. Presbyterian. Clubs: University (San Francisco); University, 1925 F St. (Washington); University (N.Y.C.); Potomac Polo (Md.). Office: Hannaford Co Inc 655 15th St NW Washington DC 20005

HANNAH, JOHN ROBERT, SR., accountant; b. Monroe, La., Aug. 11, 1939; s. Robert Ruskin Hannah and Berta (Gilliland) Nelson; m. Elizabeth Girdner, Dec. 26, 1965; children: Allison, John Robert Jr. BS, La. State U., 1960. CPA, Tex. Acct. Arthur Young & Co., Houston, 1960-70; cons. Peters & Smith, Midland, Tex., 1970-71; ptnr. Hannah & Trott, Midland, 1971-72; contr. Western States Producing Co., San Antonio, 1972-73; v.p. fin. Sommers Drug Stores Co., San Antonio, 1973-77; pvt. practice acctg. San Antonio, 1987—; ptnr. Peters, Anders & Hannah, San Antonio, 1978-86; seminar speaker Bexar County Med. Soc., San Antonio, 1981—. Fin. chmn. YMCA, San Antonio, 1975-82, chmn., 1982-83; adminstr. Bible Study Fellowship, San Antonio, 1977-83. Lt. USN, 1961-65. Mem. Am. Inst. CPA's, Tex. Soc. CPa's, Fin. Execs. Internat., Execs. Internat. Club (San Antonio, pres. 1975-76). Methodist. Home: 102 Castle Oaks San Antonio TX 78213 Office: 800 Navarro St Ste 210 San Antonio TX 78205

HANNAN, MYLES, banker, lawyer; b. Rye, N.Y., Oct. 14, 1936; s. Joseph A. and Rosemary (Edwards) H.; m. Gretchen A. Phillips, June 18, 1982; 1 child. BA, Holy Cross Coll., 1958; LLB, Harvard U., 1964. Bar: N.Y. 1964, Mass. 1970. Assoc. Cadwalader, Wickersham & Taft, N.Y.C., 1964-69; v.p., gen. counsel, sec. High Voltage Engring. Corp., Burlington, Mass., 1969-73; v.p., sec. Stop & Shop Cos., Inc., Boston, 1973-79; group v.p. law and adminstrn. Del. North Cos., Inc., Buffalo, 1979-81; v.p., fin., gen. counsel, sec. Anacomp, Inc., Indpls., 1981-84; exec. v.p. Empire of Am. FSB, Buffalo, 1984—. Trustee Studio Arena Theatre, Buffalo, 1986—; bd. dirs. Buffalo Philharm. Orch., 1987—. Lt. USNR, 1958-61. Mem. Saturn Club (Buffalo), Buffalo Canoe Club (Ridgeway, Ont., Can.). Home: 306 Woodbridge Ave Buffalo NY 14214 Office: Empire Am 1 Empire Tower Buffalo NY 14202

HANNAN, ROBERT WILLIAM, retail executive; b. Pitts., Jan. 27, 1939; s. Robert C. and Florence Mae (Swartz) H.; m. Barbara Fordyce, Nov. 26, 1966; children: Karen and Kristen. BS, Slippery Rock U., 1961; postgrad., Duquesne U., 1962-63. Dir. personnel Thrift Drug Co., Pitts., 1969-76, v.p. adminstrn., 1976-80, sr. v.p. adminstrn., 1980-85, sr. v.p. corp. devel., 1985-87, pres., 1987—. Mem. adv. bd. Pitts. Cancer Inst.; mem. nat. adv. council adult illiteracy United Way, Pitts.; chmn. adult illiteracy task force United Way, Pitts., campaign div. United Way, Pitts. Mem. Nat. Assn. Chain Drug Stores (bd. dirs.). Republican. Methodist. Office: Thrift Drug Co 615 Alpha Dr Pittsburgh PA 15238 *

HANNAY, N(ORMAN) BRUCE, chemist, industrial research and business consultant; b. Mt. Vernon, Wash., Feb. 9, 1921; s. Norman Bond and Winnie (Evans) H.; m. Joan Anderson, May 27, 1943; children: Robin, Brooke. BA, Swarthmore Coll., 1942, DSc (hon.), 1979; MS, Princeton U., 1943, PhD, 1944; PhD (hon.), Tel Aviv U., 1978; DSc (hon.), Poly. Inst. N.Y., 1981. With Bell Telephone Labs., Murray Hill, N.J., 1944-82; exec. dir. materials research div. Bell Telephone Labs., 1967-73, v.p. research and patents, 1973-82, ret., 1982; researcher on dipole moments and molecular structure, thermionic emission, mass spectroscopy, analysis of solids, solid state chemistry, semiconductors, superconductors; mem. sci. adv. com. SRI Internat., tech. adv. council Chrysler Corp.; rsch. adv. com. United Techs., Regents' prof. UCLA, 1976, U. Calif., San Diego, 1979; cons. Alexander von Humboldt Found.; bd. dirs. Plenum Pub. Co., Gen. Signal Corp., Rohm and Haas Co., Alex Brown Cash Res. Fund, Tax-Free Investments Trust, and Flag Investors Telephone Income Trust, Internat. Trust, Corp. Cash Trust and Emerging Growth Fund. Author: Solid State Chemistry, 1967, also articles.; Mem. numerous editorial bds.; editor: Semiconductors, 1959, Treatise on Solid State Chemistry, 1974. Recipient Acheson medal, 1976; Perkin medal, 1983; Gold medal Am. Inst. Chemists, 1986. mem. Nat. Acad. Engring. (past fgn. sec.), Nat. Acad. Scis., Am. Acad. Arts and Scis., Mexican Nat. Acad. Engring., Electrochem. Soc. (past pres.), Indsl. Research Inst. (past pres., medal 1982), Dirs. of Indsl. Research (past chmn.).

HANNING, GARY WILLIAM, utility executive, consultant; b. Sherman, Tex., Aug. 30, 1942; s. William Homer and Mary Maxine (Harshbarger) H.; m. Rita Eloise Rech, Apr. 28, 1962 (div. June 1966); 1 child, Tony William; m. Robin Dale Smith, June 8, 1974; children: TJ, Lorissa Diane. BS, Rollins Coll., 1974; MBA, Stetson U., 1976. Mgr., co-owner Hanning Water Systems, Denison, Tex., 1963-66; engring. technician Gen. Dynamics, Ft. Worth, 1966-67; engr. supr. Bendix Field, Pasadena, Calif., 1967-70; engr. Philco-Ford Corp., Cape Kennedy, Fla., 1970-73, Jet Propulsion Lab., Pasadena, Calif., 1973-74; sect. mgr. Planning Research Corp., Kennedy Space Ctr., 1974-77; pres. S.S.S. Water Systems, Inc., Denison, 1978-83, Texoma Services Corp., Pottsboro, Tex., 1980—; bd. dir. Ind. Water and Sewer Co. Tex. Inc., Austin; entrepreneur Bells Discount Supply, Tex., 1983-87. Contbr. articles to profl. jours. Served with USN, 1960-63. Mem. Am. Legion. Democrat. Mem. Ch. of Christ. Office: Texoma Services Corp Hwy 120 PO Box 561 Pottsboro TX 75076

HANNON, JOHN ROBERT, merchant banking executive; b. Atlanta, Aug. 9, 1945; s. George Franklin and Elizabeth (Broadfield) H.; m. Jackie Lyn Wagner, Apr. 28, 1984; children: Kimberly, Melissa. BA, Duke U., 1967. CLU, CPCU. Group sales rep. The Prudential Ins. Co. of Am., Charlotte, N.C., 1967-69, group ins. mgr., 1969-72; assoc. dir. group ins. The Prudential Ins. Co. of Am., Newark, 1972-74; mgr. regional group The Prudential Ins. Co. of Am., Jacksonville, Fla., 1974-79, dir. group mktg., 1979-81; v.p. group credit mktg. The Prudential Ins. Co. of Am., Newark, 1981-83; v.p. group ins. mktg. The Prudential Ins. Co. of Am., Roseland, N.J., 1983-85, v.p. group credit ins. ops., 1985-87, v.p. corp. group mktg. communications, 1987-88; sr. v.p. Prudential Capital Corp., Newark, 1988—; visiting faculty bus. sch. U. North Fla., Jacksonville, 1979-80. Elder Lakewood Presbyn. Ch., Jacksonville, 1977-80; deacon First Presbyn. Ch., Caldwell, N.J., 1987—; vol. campaign U.S. Senate Challenger, State of Fla, 1980. Served with USN, 1963-67. Mem. Consumer Bankers Assn., Mensa. Republican. Clubs: Rudder (commodore 1979-80), University. Home: 45 Stonegate Dr Roseland NJ 07068 Office: Capital Corp S Gateway Ctr 12th fl Newark NJ 07102

HANNON, KITTY SUE, airline pilot; b. San Antonio, Oct. 10, 1954; d. Stanley Edgar and Barbara Lea (Owens) H.; m. Candler Garald Schaffer, June 10, 1976 (div. 1983). MusB, U. Miami, Coral Gables, Fla., 1976. Flight attendant Eastern Airlines, Miami, Fla., 1977-84; pilot, instr. Tibben Flight Lines, Cedar Rapids, Iowa, 1981, Watham Flying Service, Cedar Rapids, 1981; pilot Mid Continent Airlines, Dubuque, Iowa, 1981-83, Cav Air/Jimmy Jet, Ft. Lauderdale, Fla., 1983, Airlift Internat. Airlines, Miami, 1983-84, Larken, Inc., Cedar Rapids, 1984, Life Investors, Cedar Rapids, 1984; pilot Eastern Airlines, Miami, 1984—, check airman, 1987—, instr. Boeing 727, 1985—, supr. pilots, 1985—, co-pilot, 1986—, flight engr., 1984—; speaker in field. Author, producer: Boeing 727 Emergency and Abnormal Training Video, 1988. Vol. pilot Spl. Olympics Fla., Miami, Tallahassee, Fla., 1988; career day guest speaker Miami Schs., 1986, 88. Music and Band Scholar U. Miami, 1972-76; named Honoree, YWCA, 1984. Mem. YWCA Women's Network, Airline Pilots Assn., Aircraft Owners and Pilots Assn., Orange Key, Smithsonian Air and Space, Mortar Bd., Phi Kappa Lambda, Mu Alpha Theta, Phi Kappa Phi, Alpha Lambda Delta. Republican. Lutheran. Home: 3420 Torremolinos Ave Miami FL 33178

HANS, PAUL CHARLES, financial executive; b. N.Y.C., Oct. 10, 1946; s. Charles Sigmund and Eleanore Lydia (Knorowski) H.; B.S. in Materials Sci. Engring., Brown U., 1968; M.B.A., U. Pa., 1972; m. Cynthia L. Troha, Dec. 22, 1977; children—Courtney Marie, Lindsey Taylor, Jesse Paul. Mktg. and tech. analyst advanced planning dept., Pratt & Whitney Aircraft div. United Technologies Corp., East Hartford, Conn., 1968-70; adminstr. fin. analysis and devel. Fairchild Space and Electronics Co. div. Fairchild Industries, Inc., Germantown, Md., 1972-74, mgr. fin. analysis parent co., 1974; dir. fin. analysis and planning Arvin Industries, Inc., Columbus, Ind., 1974-79, asst. treas., 1979-80; corp. mgr. comml. bus. devel. Gen. Dynamics Corp., St. Louis, 1980-82, dir. corp. devel., 1982-83; gen. ptnr. Wolsey & Co., St. Louis, 1983-89; v.p. strategic devel., dir. Sabreliner Corp., St. Louis, 1983-89; pres. P. Hans & Co., Scottsdale, Ariz., 1988—; dir. Indst. Solid Propulsion, Inc., Las Vegas, Nev., 1989—; v.p. corp. devel. AeroTech, Inc. Las Vegas, 1989—. Mem. AIAA. Home and Office: 9688 E Cochise Dr Scottsdale AZ 85258

HANSEL, STEPHEN ARTHUR, holding company executive; b. Long Branch, N.J., Aug. 13, 1947; s. Paul George and Helen (Stephens) H.; m. Sarah Holyfield, Nov. 16, 1985; children by previous marriage—Derek, Andrew, Paula; 1 child by current marriage, Alexander. B.A., Wesleyan U., 1969; M.B.A., Darden Sch. Bus. Adminstrn., 1971; cert. Advanced Mgmt. Program, Harvard Bus. Sch. Mng. dir. Barnett Overseas Fin., N.V., Curaçao, Netherlands Antilles, 1983—; dir. Barnett Computing Co., Jacksonville, Fla., 1980-83, 87—, Barnett People for Better Govt., Jacksonville, 1980-84, Barnett Bank Citrus Co., Crystal River, Fla., 1984-87; also bd. dirs. Barnett Bank Ins. Inc., Jacksonville; dir. Barnett Bank Hernando County, Brooksville, Fla., 1984—, Barnett Ops. Co., Jacksonville, Fla., 1987—. Founder, pres. Found. for Pulmonary Hypertension, Inc.; bd. dirs. Jacksonville Mental Health Clinic, 1978-83; trustee Arlington Congl. Ch., Jacksonville, 1976-80, Jacksonville Art Mus., 1988; com. chmn. Wesleyan Schs., N. Fla., 1973—. Mem. Wesleyan Alumni Assn. (exec. com. 1984—). Republican. Office: Barnett Banks Inc 100 Laura St PO Box 40789 Jacksonville FL 33231

HANSELMAN, RICHARD WILSON, entrepreneur; b. Cin., Oct. 8, 1927; s. Wendell Forest and Helen E. (Beiderwelle) H.; m. Beverly Baker White, Oct. 16, 1954; children: Charles Fielding, II, Jane White. BA in Econs, Dartmouth Coll., 1949. V.p. merchandising RCA Sales Corp., Indpls., 1964-66, v.p. product planning, 1966-69, v.p. product mgmt., 1969-70; pres. luggage div. Samsonite Corp., Denver, 1970-73, pres. luggage group, 1973-74, exec. v.p. ops., 1974-75, pres., 1975-77; sr. v.p. Beatrice Foods Co., Chgo., 1976-77, exec. v.p., 1977-80; pres., chief operating officer, dir. Genesco Inc., Nashville, 1980-86, chief exec. officer, 1981-86, pvt. investor, corp. dir., 1986—; bd. dirs. Becton Dickinson & Co., Arvin Industries, Healthtrust Inc., Truck Components, Inc., Bradford Funds Inc. Trustee Com. for Econ. Devel. Served with U.S. Army, 1950-52. Mem. Denver Country Cub, Belle Meade Country Club, Nashville City Club, Union League, Chgo. Club, Phi Kappa Psi. Office: Genesco Inc 104 Woodmont Blvd Ste 306 Nashville TN 37205

HANSEN, BOBBY JEAN, management consultant, real estate investor and developer; b. Newton, Kans., Jan. 30, 1926; s. Clarence Nielsen and Blanche Eleanore (Andrews) H.; m. Marlene Marie Mendoza, Oct. 18, 1960 (div. May 1986); children: Cherokee E. Stock, Jody K. Abbott, Alyson, Mimi E., Nicole M. BS, U. So. Calif., 1949; MA Pub. Adminstrn., Am. U., 1966. Cert. sailboard instr. U.S. Yacht Racing Union; cert. dingy sailboat sailer Brit. Royal yachting Assn.; cert. open water diver Brit. Sub-Aqua Club, Profl. Assn. Diving Instrs. Pres. Trak-Life Inc., Portland, Oreg., 1957-59; staff specialist Lockheed Missile & Space Co., Sunnyvale, Calif., 1959-61; program mgr. Ops. Research Inc., Silver Spring, Md., 1961-62; exec. v.p. Computer Dynamics Corp., Silver Spring, 1961-65; sr. v.p. John I. Thompson & Co., Washington, 1965-68; pres. Decision Research Corp., Washington, 1968-70; county exec. Prince William County, Manassas, Va., 1970-71; county adminstr. Wythe County, Wytheville, Va., 1971-73; city mgr. Marion, Va., 1973-77; mgr. Williams Crane & Rigging Inc., Wytheville, 1977-80; prin. adminstr. and investors coordinator Royal Commn. Jubail (Saudi Arabia)-Yanbu, 1980-83; div. mgr. Al-Rushaid Investment Co., Dammam, Saudi Arabia, 1980-85; investor Hansen Assocs., Wytheville, 1985—; owner Surfun Co., Tax Shak; adj. faculty professorial lectr. Wytheville Community Coll., The Am. U., New River Community Coll., Golden Gate U., Jubail, Saudi Arabia. Author: Practical Program Evaluation and Review Technique, 1962; guest editor Government Exec. Mag.; former columnist Southwest Va. Enterprise; patentee in field. Mem., former chmn. small bus. adv. council Metro Washington U.S. SBA ; mem. council Luth. Ch.; bd. dirs. No. Va. Police Acad.; founder, chmn. Master Swimming, Kingdom of Saudi Arabia. Served to capt. USNR, 1943-47, WWII, 51-53, Korea, 66-67, Vietnam. Mem. FIABCI-Fedn. Internationale des Professions Immobilieres, Am. Inst. for Mgmt., Am. Mgmt. Assn., Nat. Assn. Real Estate Appraisers (sr. appraiser), Coll. Real Estate Appraisers, Armed Forces Mgmt. Assn. (former v.p.), Def. Orientation Conf. Assn., United Inventors and Scientists, Associated Gen. Contractors, Am. Waterworks Assn., Internat. City Mgrs. Assn., Nat. Assn. County Adminstrs., Nat. Security Indsl. Assn., Am. Arbitration Assn. (nat. panel arbitrators), Naval Res. Officer's Assn., VFW, Am. Legion (China Post 1), DAV, U.S. Yacht Racing Union, U.S. Bd. Sailing Assn., Beta Gamma Sigma, Kappa Mu Epsilon, Sigma Nu. Lutheran. Clubs: Evergreen Country (Haymarket, Va.); Evansham Swim & Racquet (Wythe County); Va. Masters Swimming Assn. (pres. 1979-80); Chantilly (Va.) Country. Lodges: Rotary, Moose. Home: PO Box 777 Wytheville VA 24382-0974

HANSEN, BRUCE W., financial services executive; b. Denver, Apr. 29, 1943; married 1964; children: Kent, Steven, Kristin, Karrin. Grad. high sch., Littleton, Colo. Mgr. trainer Chrysler First, Denver, 1964-67; br. mgr. Chrysler First, Colo., S.D., Kans., 1967-75; area dir. Chrysler First, Jacksonville, Fla., 1975-77, Jackson, Miss., 1977-80; v.p. Chrysler First, Birmingham, Ala., 1980-84; sr. v.p. Chrysler First, Englewood, Colo., 1984—. Office: Chrysler 1st Regional Office 6300 S Syracuse Way Ste 400 Englewood CO 80111-6724

HANSEN, CHARLES, lawyer; b. Jersey City, May 23, 1926; s. Charles Henry and Katherine (Bensch) H.; m. Carolyn P. Smith, Sept. 26, 1953; children: Mark, Melissa. B.S., U. Mich., 1946; J.D., Mich. Law Sch., 1950. Bar: N.Y. 1951, Wis. 1961, Mo. 1980. Engr. Westinghouse Electric Co., 1946; assoc. Mudge, Stern, Williams & Tucker, 1950-53; chief labor counsel, div. counsel Sylvania Electric Products, 1953-61; sec., gen. counsel Trane Co., La Crosse, Wis., 1961-69, exec. v.p., 1968-73; pres. Cutler-Hammer World Trade, Inc., 1973-77; v.p. Cutler-Hammer, Inc., 1973-77, exec. v.p., 1977-79; sr. v.p. law Emerson Electric Co., 1979-84, sr. v.p., sec., gen. counsel, 1984—; adj. prof. Sch. Law St. Louis U., 1987—. Served to lt. (j.g.) USNR, 1943-46. Mem. ABA, Wis., Mo. bar assns., Am. Law Inst., Order of Coif, Tau Beta Pi. Home: 8 Wydown Terr Clayton MO 63105 Office: Emerson Electric Co 8000 W Florissant Ave Saint Louis MO 63136

HANSEN, DAVID FRANKLIN, energy company executive; b. Ada, Minn., Jan. 22, 1928; s. Clifford Franklin and Lumetta Gladys (Swanson) H.; m. Barbara Nichols Bambrick, Dec. 12, 1948 (div. 1976); children: David, Cynthia, Stephen; m. Rosemary Haag, Dec. 11, 1976. BSME, U. Minn., 1951. With Mpls. Gas Co., 1954-72; pres., chief exec. officer Pa. Ent. Inc., Wilkes-Barre, 1972-78, Memphis Light, Gas and Water Co., 1978-84; chmn. Mountaineer Gas Co., Charleston, W.Va., 1984-86; pres., chief operating officer Starmark Energy Industries Inc., Memphis, 1986—; bd. dirs. 1st Nat. Bank NE Pa., Wilkes-Barre. Contbr. articles to profl. jours. Bd. dirs. Edina (Minn.) Pub. Schs., 1968-72; trustee U. Scranton, Pa., 1973-79; bd. visitors Memphis State U., 1979-85; bd. dirs., pres. Memphis Jr. Achievement, 1979-84; bd. dirs. Inst. Power Tech., Sunnyvale, Calif., 1976-82; gen. campaign chmn. Greater Memphis United Way, 1983. Mem. Tau Beta Pi. Republican. Episcopalian. Avocations: skiing, golf, tennis. Home: 6368 Kirby Oaks Dr Memphis TN 38119 Office: Starmark Energy Industries Inc 813 Ridgelake Blvd Memphis TN 38119

HANSEN, DONALD CURTIS, manufacturing executive: b. Marinette, Wis., Mar. 13, 1929; s. Curtis Albert and Dagmar Anne (Johnson) H.; m. Joan Mary Crant, Nov. 9, 1973. BBA, Carroll Coll., 1952. Purchasing agt. Prescott/Sterling Co., Menominee, Mich., 1954-62; mfrs. rep. Don C. Hansen Assocs., Phoenix, 1962-63; sales mgr. Karolton Envelope Co., San Francisco, 1964-72; owner, pres. San Francisco Envelope Co., 1972-79; owner Curtis Swann Cards, San Francisco, 1977-79; pres., owner Don C. Hansen, Inc., San Francisco, 1979—. Mgr., organizer Twin City Civic Chorus, Menominee, 1959; bd. dirs. Menominee C. of C., 1958. Served with U.S. Army, 1952-54. Mem. Envelope Printing Specialists Assn. (bd. dirs. 1983—, pres. 1983-84), San Francisco Lithograph and Craftsmans Club, Printing Industries of No. Calif. (bd. dirs. 1980—). Republican. Clubs: Harbor Point Tennis (Mill Valley, Calif.), San Francisco Tennis Club (bd. govs. 1989-92). Lodges: Masonic, Shriners. Office: The Envelope Co PO Box 77265 San Francisco CA 94107

HANSEN, DONALD WALDEMAR, food products company executive; b. Washington, Oct. 16, 1927; s. Waldemar Conrad and Muriel (Bruggman) H.; m. Janet Eleanor Lines, Sept. 6, 1952; children: Kimberly, Philip, Jeffrey. B.S., Iowa State U., 1951, M.S., 1952; postgrad., NYU Sch. Bus., 1966. Vice pres. Stamats Pub. Co., Cedar Rapids, Iowa, 1953-62; gen. mgr. PDI Internat. (A.B.) Time Inc., London, 1962-67; v.p. Crosfield Electronics Inc., N.Y.C., 1967-68, dir.; with W.W. Grainger Inc., Chgo., 1970-81, pres. Doerr Electric Corp. subs., 1973-76, v.p. ops., 1976-77, v.p. adminstrn. and planning, 1978-81, dir.; exec. v.p., dir. CFS Continental Inc., Chgo., 1981-85; pres. Staley Foodservice Cos., 1985—; pres. Doerr Electric Corp., W. W. Grainger Inc. Mem. Pres.' adv. council Iowa State U. Served with USN, 1946-47. Mem. Internat. Foodservice Mfg. Assn. (chmn., bd. dirs. 1986), Econ. Club Chgo. Office: Staley Foodservice Co 1701 Golf Rd Dr Rolling Meadows IL 60008

HANSEN, EVELYN MARGARET, food products executive; b. Aberdeen, Wash., June 6, 1948; d. Robert Louis and Margaret Issable (Roberson) Hatfield; m. Randall George Hansen, Sept. 19, 1970; 1 child, Margaret Evelyn. Student, Grays Harbor Jr. Coll., 1967, Seattle Pacific U., 1968-69. Instr. in spl. edn. Seattle Pub. Schs., 1970-77; cons. Nat. Seafood Educators, Richmond Beach, Wash.; cons. seafood Quality Food Ctrs., Bellevue, Wash., 1986-87; coord. project Am. Heart Assn., Seattle, 1984-85; educator seafood Safeway, Haggens, various food stores around the N.W. Author: Seafood Treasurers, 1977, Selling Seafood, 1986; co-author: Seafood-A Collection of Heart Healthy Recipes, 1986, Light Hearted Seafood, 1989. Mem. Women's Fisheries Network (v.p. 1986), Coalition Fishermens Wives (v.p. 1982), Puget Sound Gillnetters Wives (pres. 1977-79). Office: Nat Seafood Educators PO Box 60006 Richmond Beach WA 98160

HANSEN, GENEVIEVE EVANS, investment banker; b. Valparaiso, Ind., May 12, 1931; d. Selwyn John and Henrietta (Kitchell) Horan; m. Carl L. Evans, Dec. 30, 1953 (div. June 1982); children: Steven, Jennifer, Michael; m. Keith L. Hansen, Aug. 6, 1983. Student, Stetson U., 1955. Investment broker Hamilton Funds, Denver, 1956-67, FSC Securities-WestAm. Fin., Deltona, Fla., 1967—. Mem. Deltona C. of C. (bd. dirs. 1986—, v.p. 1988—), Internat. Assn. Fin. Planners. Democrat. Baptist. Club: University Women's (Deland). Home: 4075 Hwy 11 N De Land FL 32724

HANSEN, H. JACK, management consultant; b. Chgo., Mar. 28, 1922; s. Herbert Christian John and Laura Elizabeth (Osterman) H.; m. Joan Dorothy Norum, Nov. 28, 1980; children: Marilyn Joan, Gail Jean, Mark John, Jacquelyn Lee. BS in Mech. Engring., Ill. Inst. Tech., 1944; cert. mgmt. cons.; Mech. and indsl. engr. Harper Wyman Co., Chgo., 1944-51; chief plant indsl. engr. Shakeproof div. Ill. Tool Works, Des Plaines, 1951-53; cons., prin. A.T. Kearney & Co., Chgo. and N.Y.C., 1953-71; pres. H.J. Hansen Co., Elk Grove Village, Ill., 1971—; owner, mgmt. cons. Hansen Mgmt. Search Co., Elk Grove Village, 1980—. Pres. Good Sheperd Luth. Ch., Des Plaines, 1988—, pres. Men's Club, 1987—. With AUS, 1945-46. Mem. Inst. Mgmt. Cons. (founding), Methods-Time Measurement Assn. (dir. 1964-70, pres. 1967-68), Am. Arbitration Assn., Soc. Advancement Mgmt. (past dir.), Council for Internat. Progress in Mgmt. (past dir.), Found. Internat. Progress in Mgmt. (past dir.). Office: H J Hansen Co 600 E Higgins Rd Elk Grove Village IL 60007

HANSEN, KENT FORREST, nuclear engineering educator; b. Chgo., Aug. 10, 1931; s. Kay Frost and Mary (Cummins) H.; m. Katherine Elizabeth Kavanagh, June 13, 1959 (dec. Dec. 1975); children—Thomas Kay, Katherine Mary; m. Deborah Lea Hill, June 26, 1977, 1 child, Gordon Benedict. S.B., Mass. Inst. Tech., 1953, Sc.D., 1959. Sr. engr. Sylvania Electric Products, Waltham, Mass., 1957-58; asst. prof. nuclear engring. MIT, Cambridge, Mass., 1960-64, assoc. prof., 1964-68, prof., 1968—, assoc. dean engring., 1979-81, assoc. dir. energy lab., 1984—; bd. dirs. EG&G, Inc., Stone & Webster, Inc.; cons. to industry. Co-author: Numerical Methods of Reactor Analysis, 1964, Advances in Nuclear Science and Technology, Vol. 8, 1975. Ford postdoctoral fellow, 1960-61. Fellow Am. Nuclear Soc. (dir., Arthur Holly Compton award 1978); mem. Soc. Indsl. and Applied Math., Assn. Computing Machines, Am. Soc. Engring. Edn., Nat. Acad. Engring., Sigma Xi, Sigma Chi. Home: Baker Bridge Rd Lincoln MA 01773 Office: MIT Energy Lab Massachusetts Ave Cambridge MA 02139

HANSEN, KRISTEN ELIZABETH, public relations executive; b. Mason City, Iowa, May 17, 1959; d. Richard Fred and Barbara Elizabeth (Mound) H. BA, U. Nebr., 1981; M in Mgmt., Northwestern U., 1989. Reporter Wichita (Kans.) Eagle-Beacon, 1981-82; editorial supr. St. Francis Regional Med. Ctr., Wichita, 1982-84; asst. mgr. pub. rels. Rush Presbyn.-St. Luke's Med. Ctr., Chgo., 1984-86; specialist pub. rels. Am. Hosp. Assn., Chgo., 1986—. Mem. Internat. Assn. Bus. Communicators (bd. dirs. local chpt. 1983-84), Phi Beta Kappa. Republican. Methodist. Office: Am Hosp Assn 840 N Lake Shore Dr 9E Chicago IL 60611

HANSEN, LARRY DAVID, journalist; b. Neenah, Wis., Sept. 11, 1956; s. Mildred Hazel Helgeson. B in Mass Communications, Mankato State U. Sports reporter Redwood Falls (Minn.) Gazette, 1981-82; free lance bus. writer Portsmouth, N.H., 1981-85; bus. writer Northeastern U., Boston, 1985-86; freelance writer Portland, Me., 1986—; pres. Hansen & Adler Pub. Relations, Boston, 1985—. Contbr. articles to popular, profl. bus. publs. Office: Hansen & Adler Pub Rels PO Box 7633 DTS Portland ME 04112

HANSEN, LELAND JOE, communications executive; b. Spokane, Wash., Mar. 26, 1944; s. Herman Johnny and Emma Irene (Borth) H.; m. Jonni Krajeski, Apr. 15, 1979. Cert., Ogden's Broadcast Ops. Sch., 1965. Lic. FCC. Air personality various radio stas., 1960-67; announcer Sta. KLCX, Colfax, Wash., 1960-62; air personality, dir. prodn. Sta. KASH, Eugene, Oreg., 1966-67; air personality, music dir., dir. prodn. Sta. KENO, Las Vegas, Nev., 1967-69; air personality, program dir. Sta. KLUC-AM-FM, Las Vegas, 1969-71; creative dir., dir., producer Mel Blanc and Assocs., Beverly Hills, Calif., 1971-73; creative dir., writer, producer, dir., studio mgr. Watermark Inc., Universal City, Calif., 1973-80; pres., chief exec. officer, writer, producer, dir. Great Dane Entertainment, Sherman Oaks, Calif., 1980—; writer, producer, dir. film, TV and radio GDE Prodns. Inc, Sherman Oaks, Calif., 1980—; voice-over artist nat. TV, and radio commls. Creator, producer, host music program US Entertainment Scene, 1970-71; assoc. dir.: (nat. radio series) American Top Forty, 1973-77, The Elvis Presley Story, 1974, The California Special, American Country Countdown, 1974-78; dir.: (nat. radio series) The Special of the Week, 1977-79, Soundtrack of the Sixties, 1979-80; creator, producer, dir. internat. series Alien Worlds, 1978-80; co-writer (with others), editor, producer, dir. nat. series The Rock Files, 1986; producer, dir. video series Compututor, 1983-84. Founder Am. Forces Radio, Saigon, Socialist Republic of Vietnam, 1963-64. Served with U.S. Army, 1962-65, Vietnam. Recipient Belding award The Advt. Club Los Angeles, 1977; named Speaker of Yr., Oddfellows and Rebeccas, Pullman, Wash., 1962. Mem. AFTRA. Office: GDE Prodns Inc 14755 Ventura Blvd Sherman Oaks CA 91403

HANSEN, N. PETER, manufacturing company executive; b. Elgin, Ill., Mar. 16, 1941; s. Edward Peter and Roberta Adelaide (Bacon) H.; m. Marcia Lynn Wanggaard, Aug. 19, 1962 (div. Dec. 1983); children: Stacy Lynn, Niels Peter, Heather Diane. BS, Purdue U., 1965; MBA, U. Ill., 1980. Sr. quality analyst Johnson Outboard div. Outboard Marine Corp., Waukegan, Ill., 1967-70; quality control mgr. snowmobile div. Outboard Marine Corp., Peterborough, Ont., Can., 1970-73; quality control mgr. outdoor products div. Roper Corp., Bradley, Ill., 1973-74, reliability engring. cons., 1979-80; gen. mgr. Hansen Marine Svc., McHenry, Ill., 1974-79; gen. mgr. quality control, dir. product assurance Mercury Marine, Stillwater, Okla., 1980-82; dir. quality assurance Mercury Marine div. Brunswick Corp., Fond du Lac, Wis., 1982-84, dir. product quality and performance Mercury Marine div., 1984—. Mem. ASME (Gear Rsch. Inst.), Am. Soc. Quality Control, Toastmasters (pres. 1988), SAE. Office: Mercury Marine div Brunswick Corp W6250 W Pioneer Rd Fond du Lac WI 54936

HANSEN, NICK DANE, corporation lawyer; b. Detroit, June 19, 1938; s. Nick F. and Ellen (Adelorn) H.; m. Susan Fox Cohee, Aug. 23, 1963; children: Todd Erik, Dana E. BA, Albion Coll., 1960; JD, Wayne State U., 1964; LLM, Georgetown U., 1970. Bar: Mich. 1964, Ill. 1970, Wis. 1975, Tex. 1985. Law clk. to assoc. justice Mich. Supreme Ct., Lansing, 1964-66; atty. Office of Chief Counsel IRS, Washington, 1966-70; ptnr. McDermott, Will & Emery, Chgo., 1970-74; sr. tax atty. Kimberly-Clark Corp., Neenah, Wis., 1975, tax counsel, 1975-76, staff v.p., 1976-80; v.p., tax counsel Kimberly-Clark Corp., Dallas, 1980—. Sec., bd. dirs. Bergstrom-Mahler Mus., Neenah, 1982-85. Mem. ABA, (vice chmn. com. fgn. activities tax sect.), Tex. Bar Assn., Wis. Bar Assn. Office: Kimberly-Clark Corp 545 E John Carpenter Frwy Irving TX 75062

HANSEN, PER KRISTIAN, management consultant; b. Oslo, Feb. 17, 1932; s. Kristian and Gudrun Marie (Nordal) H.; m. Charlotte Berta Kretzschmar, July 18, 1964; children: Karin, Christian, Elisabeth. BSCE, Stanford U., 1955, MSCE, 1956. Engr., estimator Bechtel Corp., San Francisco, 1957-67, supt., 1967-72; constrn. mgr. Bechtel Power Corp., San Francisco, 1972-78; mgr. of constrn. Bechtel Power Corp., Ann Arbor, Mich., 1978-84; v.p. Bechtel Constrn., Inc., Gaithersburg, Md., 1984-86; pres. CPH Assocs., Inc., Gaithersburg, 1987—; mem. industry adv. com. to sch. of constrn. engring. and mgmt. Purdue U., Lafayette, Ind., 1982-84. Served as lt. C.E., 1950-53. Mem. ASCE, Norwegian Am. C. of C., Contstrn. Mgmt. Assn. Am., San Francisco Engrs. Club. Lutheran. Home: 11604 Flints Grove Ln Gaithersburg MD 20878 Office: CPH Assocs Inc 316 E Diamond Ave Suite 201 Gaithersburg MD 20877

HANSEN, ROBERT ARNOLD, utilities company manager; b. La Crosse, Wis., Mar. 29, 1950; s. Arnold Marinus and Delores (Niedbalski) H.; m. Laurie Jo Lee, June 17, 1972; children: Heather, Hilary. BA in Acctg. and Bus. Adminstrn., Moorhead (Minn.) State U., 1971, MBA, 1983. CPA, Cert. Mgmt. Acct., Minn. Tax examiner II Minn. Dept. Revenue, Crookston, 1971-73; cost acct. FMC-Crane & Excavator, Cedar Rapids, Iowa, 1973-76; from acct. to mgr. tax dept. Otter Tail Power Co., Fergus Falls, Minn., 1976—. Bd. mgrs. Federated Ch., Fergus Falls, 1979-81; county chmn. Minn. Ind. Reps., Fergus Falls, 1987-89. Named one of Outstanding Young Men Am., 1985. Mem. Am. Inst. CPA's (tax div.), Minn. Soc. CPA's, Edison Elec. Inst. (depreciation acctg. div., 1984-87, tax acctg. div., 1987—), Inst. Mgmt. Acctg., Fergus Falls Jaycees, (pres. 1977-83, 3d high state del., 1979, Outstanding Bd. Mem., 1979-81). Congregational. Lodge:

Elks, Kiwanis (Fergus Falls) (treas., asst. sec. 1988-89). Home: Rt 3 Box 426 Fergus Falls MN 56537 Office: Otter Tail Power Co 215 S Cascade Fergus Falls MN 56537

HANSEN, STEVEN LEE, finance executive; b. San Jose, Calif., Feb. 22, 1955; s. Luverne E. and Marguerite O. (Bletz) H.; m. Margaret L. Hansen Sept. 14, 1979; children: Tia, Britt. BS, Mankato (Minn.) State U., 1977; MBA, Nova U., 1986. CPA, Minn., Fla. Auditor Bergeron Booth Machowicz & Co., Mpls., 1978-79, Arthur Young & Co., Mpls., 1979-83; ops. analyst No. Teleom Inc., Mpls., 1983-87; mgr. acctg. and fin. No. Teleom Inc., Miami, Fla., 1987—; chief fin. officer Aurafin Corp., Hollywood, Fla., 1987—. Mem. AICPA, Fla. Inst. CPA's, Weston Athletic Club, Coconut Grove Sailing Club. Republican. Office: Aurafin Corp 3440 Hollywood Blvd Hollywood FL 33021

HANSEN, STEVEN LEO, data processing executive; b. Lehi, Utah, Oct. 23, 1941; s. Darrel and Josephene (Russon) H.; m. Diane Roundy, Oct. 15, 1964; children: Julie, Darrel Jo, Janette, Jennifer, Jessica. Student, U. Nev., 1965-67, Brigham Young U., 1969-70, U. Utah, 1985-86, Salt Lake Community Coll., 1987—. Draftsman Utah County Recorder, Provo, 1984, Chgo. Title, Las Vegas, Nev., 1965-68; plating dept. supr. Utah County Recorder, Provo, 1968-73; mgr. title plant Dynacomp, Las Vegas, 1973-76; mgr. Dynacomp, Salt Lake City, 1976-83; v.p., mgr. Dynacomp of Utah, Salt Lake City, 1983-85; ops. mgr. TRW Real Estate Info. Svcs., Salt Lake City, 1985-87, prodn. mgr., 1988—. Served with Air NG, 1959. Republican. Mormon. Home: 646 N 600 E American Fork UT 84003 Office: TRW Real Estate Info Svcs 330 E 400 S #11 Salt Lake City UT 84111

HANSEN, STEVEN MARK, property manager; b. Salt Lake City, Jan. 14, 1957; s. Harlan E. and Barbara Mae (Dunn) H.; m. M. Tamyra Nielson, Dec. 18, 1984; 1 child, Trevor Steven. BS in Econs., U. Utah, 1981; MBA in Fin., U. Tex., Arlington, 1987. Lic. real estate broker, Utah. Property mgr. Exec. Properties, Inc., Salt Lake City, 1981-84, Dallas, 1984-86; property mgr. Sigma Corp., Salt Lake City, 1986—; adj. prof. mgmt. Salt Lake Community Coll., 1988—. Author: (handbook) Sucessful Apartment Leasing, 1983. Missionary Mormon Ch., Tulsa, 1978-80. Mem. Inst. Real Estate Mgmt. (cert., treas. Utah chpt. 1986-87, chmn. com. 1987—), Apartment Assn. Utah (dir. 1988—), Sigma Gamma Chi (v.p. 1977-78). Republican. Home: 4668 Deer Creek Rd Salt Lake City UT 84124 Office: Sigma Corp 3330 S 700 E Ste 200 Salt Lake City UT 84106

HANSEN, SUSANA, real estate corporation officer, consultant; b. Montevideo, Uruguay, June 21, 1943; came to U.S., 1968; d. Jorge Valdemar and Paula (Maruri) H.; m. Federico Padovan (div. 1974); 1 child, Paola Padovan; m. Rodolfo Careri, 1983. BS in French, Alliance Française, Montevideo, Uruguay, 1964; BS, Fla. Internat. U., 1977. Cert. soc. studies tchr., Fla. Internat. U. Special asst. to pres. Hornblower, Werks, Hemphill, Noyes, Beverly Hills, Calif., 1968-71; v.p. special services Alitalia Airlines, N.Y.C., 1971-74; special asst. to pres. Interterra Inc., Miami, Fla., 1976-78; v.p. Grove Isle Realty, Coconut Grove, Fla., 1979-82; pres., broker Turnberry Realty Corp., Miami Beach, Fla., 1982—; cons. Latin Am. Assn. Real Estate Profl., Buenos Aires, 1978—. Fundraiser Restoration Statue Liberty, N.Y.C., 1985. Mem. Internat. Exec. Women Assn., London, Exec. Women's Edn. Travel, N.Y.C. Republican. Roman Catholic. Home: 19355 Turnberry Way #3D Miami Beach FL 33180 Office: Marina Hansen Klein Realty Corp 20801 Biscayne Blvd #401 Miami Beach FL 33180

HANSEY, RENEE JEANNE, corporate executive; b. Tacoma, Wash., Apr. 24, 1927; d. Francis J. and Genevieve (Hewitt) Payette; m. James Burpee, Mar. 13, 1947 (dec. 1950); children: James, Victoria; m. Orville D. Hansey (div. 1987); children: Dan, Terri, John, Bill. Student in Layout and Design, Art Inst. Chgo., 1943; BS in Psychology, St. John's U., 1988; postgrad. in Graphics, U. Alaska, 1985. Copy writer Sta. KIT, Yakima, Wash., 1942-44; program mgr. Sta. KING, Seattle, 1945-47; advt. mgr. Sequim (Wash.) Press, 1967-70, editor, 1970-76; tv producer Municipality of Anchorage, 1976-86; publisher Voice, Port Angeles, Wash., 1986—; also dir. Retired Sr. Vol. Program, Port Angeles, Wash.; founder Widowed Persons Service, Anchorage, 1983-85; owner Frontier Pub., Anchorage, 1983-85; dir. Far North Network, Anchorage, 1982-86. Author: Go to the Source, 1977, One Way to the Funny Farm, 1978; producer (tv show) Opportunities for Seniors, 1981-86 (TV Prodn. award, 1982-85). Sec. Dem. Cen. Com. Clallam County, Wash., 1965-76; founder Olympic Women's Resource Ctr., Port Angeles, 1966-75; councilwoman City Sequim, 1973-76; active Affirmative Action Clallam County, Wash., 1974, Sr. Companions, Elder Abuse Task Force; bd. dirs. Port Angeles Sr. Ctr. With WAC, 1944. Mem. Alaska Press Women (pres. 1981-82, 85-86), Nat. Fedn. Press Women, Alaska Press Club. Roman Catholic. Home: 235 N Sunnyside Sequim WA 98382 Office: RSVP 215 1/2 S Lincoln Port Angeles WA 98362

HANSFORD, LARRY CLARENCE, computer consultant company executive; b. La Porte, Ind., Oct. 15, 1945; s. Curtis Edgar and Eva Maree (Owens) H.; B.E.E., Ga. Inst. Tech., 1975; m. Mabel Darlene Miller, June 27, 1970; 1 son, Patrick Robert. Asst. purchasing agt. Dobbs House, Inc., Atlanta Airport, 1963-65; enlisted man U.S. Air Force, 1965-75, commd. 2d lt., 1975, advanced through grades to capt., 1975-86; computer systems analyst Mil. Airlift Command, Scott AFB, Ill., 1976-80, Air Force Communications Command, 1980-82; communications liaison officer, Wright Patterson AFB, Ohio, 1982-86; pres., chmn. bd. Milk-N-Honey Acres, Inc., Baldwin, Ill., 1978-79, owner, 1980-82; pres., chmn. bd. Creative Computer Cons., Inc., 1982-86, owner Creative Computer Cons., 1987—; prin. communications cons. Martin Marietta, 1987—. Supt. edn. Skyland United Meth. Ch., Atlanta, 1973-75; sec. enlistment 1st United Meth. Ch., Sparta, Ill., 1978-82, chmn. bd. 1st United Meth. Ch., New Carlisle, Ohio, 1985-87. Mem. Assn. for Systems Mgmt., Assn. Computer Machinery, IEEE. Republican. Home: 11640 Marquart Rd New Carlisle OH 45344

HANSON, DALE S., banker; b. Milw., Nov. 11, 1938; s. Yngve Holger and Evelyn (Johnson) H.; m. Joan Benton, July 15, 1961; children—Thomas S., Tim B. B.A. in Econs., Carlton Coll., 1960; postgrad. Exec. Program, Credit and Fin. Mgmt. Stanford U., 1966-67. Asst. cashier First Bank, St. Paul, 1964-66, asst. v.p., 1966-68, v.p., 1968-82, sr. v.p., 1982-83, exec. v.p., 1983-84, pres., 1984-87; exec. v.p. First Bank System, Mpls., 1987—; mng. ptnr. FBS Merchant Banking Group, 1987—, Matrix Leasing Internat., 1989—; bd. dirs. First Trust Co., First Bank N.A., W.A. Lang Co., Edwards Mfg. Co., C.H. Robinson Co., Delta Beverage Co. Chmn. St. Paul Riverfront Commn.; mem. Corp. Health One, Inc.; bd. dirs. St. Paul Chamber Orch., Twin City Pub. TV. Served to 1st lt. N.G. 1961-67. Mem. Robert Morris Assocs. (pres. 1982-83), Assn. Res. City Bankers, St. Paul Area C. of C. (bd. dirs.). Republican. Presbyterian. Clubs: Somerset Golf, Minnesota, St. Paul Athletic; Minneapolis. Office: FBS Mcht Banking Group 150 S Fifth St Ste 1200 PO Box 512 Minneapolis MN 55480-0512

HANSON, DAVID TENNESON, sales executive, educator; b. Madison, Minn., June 3, 1946; s. Sanford Minton and Cora (Tenneson) H.; m. Lindell Kaye Vellekson, May 27, 1972; children: Kimberly Kaye, Corissa Ann. Student, Minn. Sch. Bus., 1972. Retail sales rep. J.C. Penney, Mpls., 1971-75; engring. sales rep. McCarthy Well Co., Bloomington, Minn., 1975-77; engring. sales rep. Johnson Screen Co., St. Paul, 1977-82, tech. svc. mgr., 1982-83, regional sales mgr., 1983-86, nat. sales mgr., 1987—. Served with USAF, 1967-71, Vietnam. Mem. Nat. Water Well Drillers Assn. Republican. Lutheran. Office: Johnson Screens div Johnson Filtration 1950 Old Hwy 8 Saint Paul MN 55164

HANSON, DIANE CHARSKE, management consultant; b. Cleve., May 15, 1946; d. Howard Carl and Emma Katherine (Lange) Charske; m. William James Hanson, June 30, 1973. BS, Cornell U., 1968; MS, U. Pa., 1989. Home service rep. Rochester Gas and Electric, N.Y., 1968-70; home economist U. Conn., Storrs, 1970-72; job analyst personnel dept. State of Conn., Hartford, 1972-73; sales rep. Ayerst Labs., Waterbury, Conn., 1973-80, sales trainer, 1979-80; dist. sales mgr. Phila., 1980-87; pres. Creative Resource Devel., W. Chester, Pa., 1986—; developer, pres. Womens Referral Network, West Chester, 1987—. Bd. dirs., chmn. spl. events devel. com., aux. pres. Chester County Soc. for Prevention Cruelty to Animals, 1986—. Mem. Great Valley Sales and Mktg. Group, Sales and Mktg. Execs. Phila., West Chester C. of C., Pa. State Tech. Devel. Ctr., Delaware County C. of C. (human services com. 1987), Exton C. of C. Home and Office: 824 W Strasburg Rd West Chester PA 19382

HANSON, DORIS ELIZABETH, healthcare company executive; b. Bowbells, N.D., Mar. 29, 1928; d. Fred and Laure (Finke) H. BS, Wash. State U., 1949; MA, Columbia U., 1958, EdD, 1964. Cert. home economist. Extension agt. Colo. Extension Svc., Ft. Collins, 1949-51; assoc. editor McCall's mag., N.Y.C., 1951-59; advisor Okla.-Pakistan Home Econs. Project, Dacca, East Pakistan, 1959-62; instr. Tchrs. Coll. Columbia U., N.Y.C., 1962-64; asst. dean Sch. Home Econs. Purdue U., West Lafayette, Ind., 1964-67; exec. dir. Am. Home Econs. Assn., Washington, 1967-74; founder HomeCall, Inc., Frederick, Md., 1974—; also chmn. bd. dirs. HomeCall, Inc. Bd. dirs. United Way, Frederick, 1985-87, Ch. Women United, N.Y.C., 1985—. Recipient Alumni Achievement award Wash. State U., 1984. Mem. Am. Home Econs. Assn. (Disting. svc. award 1988), Bus. And Profl. Women's Club (Woman of Yr. award 1981), Frederick County C. of C. (bd. dirs. 1984-86), Nat. Council on Aging. Democrat. Club: Toastmasters (Frederick). Lodge: Zonta (bd. dirs. Frederick 1980-83). Office: HomeCall Inc 30 E Patrick St Frederick MD 21701

HANSON, ERIC ALAN, manufacturer's representative; b. Oslo, Norway, Feb. 4, 1953; s. Frithjof Johan and Geraldine Marie (McMartin) H.; m. Melissa Mae Peachee, 1973 (div. 1977); 1 child, Jason Briscoe; m. Diane Kathleen Cox, Jan. 8, 1983. Student, Tex. Tech U., 1984-86. Asst. motor bank mgr. Shepherd Mall State Bank, Oklahoma City, 1971-73; sr. mgr. Sirloin Stockade Restaurants, Oklahoma City, 1973-76; exec. protection specialist Kerr-McGee Corp., Oklahoma City, 1976-78; sr. patrolman Edmond (Okla.) Police Dept., 1978-81; dir. security Oaktree Golf Club, Edmond, 1981-83; mfr's. rep. J.A. Baldwin Mfg. Co., Inc., Lubbock, Tex., 1983—. Served to capt. Okla. Army N.G., 1972—. Recipient Army Commendation medal U.S. Congress, Minco, Okla., 1982, Okla. Commendation medal Okla. Senate, Marlow, Okla., 1983; named Jr. Officer of Yr., Order World Wars, Oklahoma City, 1985. Life mem. Am. Bus. Clubs, Nat. Rifle Assn., Fraternal Order Police, Am. Defense Preparedness Assn., USAF Assn., Res. Officers Assn., Okla. N.G. Assn., 45th Infantry Div. Assn. Republican. Lutheran. Home: Rte 1 Box 41A Cookville TX 75558-9703

HANSON, FRED B., lawyer; b. Alexandria, Va.; s. August Theodore and Flora Alice (Kays) H.; m. Jane Roberts, Oct. 24, 1934 (dec. Jan. 1971); m. Lucy Merrick, Dec. 10, 1971 (dec. Nov. 1987); children: Linscott, Per, Marta. Student, DePauw U., 1924-26, Northwestern U., 1927-28; LLB, Ill. Inst. Tech., 1932. Bar: Ind. 1925, Ill. 1932, U.S. Dist. Ct. (no. dist.) Ill. 1932. Ptnr. Ross, Berchem & Hanson, Chgo., 1932-34; sole practice Chgo., 1934-37, 52—; atty. Standard Oil Co., Chgo., 1937-46; ptnr. Hanson & Doyle, Chgo., 1946-52, The Firm of Fred B. Hanson Assocs., Chgo., 1952-86; sole practice Chgo., 1986—; gen. counsel., bd. dirs. various banks and cos. Author: Claim Handling, 1956; contbr. articles to profl. jours. atty. Village of Glenview, 1950-54, judge, 1946-50; trustee Bethany Brethren Hosp., Chgo., 1960-71, Maryhaven, Glenview, 1946-72. Served to lt. comdr. USNR, 1943-46, PTO. Mem. ABA, Ill. Bar Assn., Chgo. Bar Assn. Democrat. Clubs: Chgo. Yacht, The Attic; Riverside Country (Menominee, Mich.).

HANSON, FRED T., lawyer; b. Wakefield, Nebr., Feb. 25, 1902; s. Peter H. and Hannah Ulrika (Anderson) H.; LL.B., U. Nebr., 1925; m. Helen Elizabeth Haddock, Nov. 12, 1928; 1 son John Fredrik. Admitted to Nebr. bar, 1925, since in pvt. practice; probate judge, 1931-42, pros. atty., 1927-30, 51-54; spl. asst. to U.S. atty. gen., 1954-62; life mem. Nat. Conf. Commrs. Uniform State Laws from Nebr., com. on uniform probate code. Bd. dirs. Nebr. dist. Luth. Ch.-Mo. Synod, 1976-80. Served as capt. AUS, 1942-46. Mem. Am. Judicature Soc., Am. Coll. Probate Counsel (regent), Am., Nebr., local bar assns., Am. Legion. Office: 316 Norris Ave McCook NE 69001

HANSON, LEILA FRASER, banker; b. Chgo., May 26, 1942; d. Paul and Emily (Dzierzyck) Hucko; m. Joseph Hanson; 1 child, Alec. AB in Polit. Sci. with high distinction, U. Ill., 1964, MA, 1966, PhD, 1971. Teaching asst. Carleton U., Ottawa, Ont., Can., 1967-68; lectr. polit. sci. U. Ky., Lexington, 1970, asst. dir., then acting dir. Office Internat. Programs, 1970-72; staff assoc., then asst. to vice chancellor U. Wis., Milw., 1972-76, asst. vice chancellor, 1976-77, asst. to chancellor, 1977; chief adminstr. to mayor City of Milw., 1977-82; sr. v.p. Banc One Wis. Corp., Milw., 1982—. Mem. adv. com. on women and minorities Office Wis. Commr. Securities, 1976-80; mem. Gov.'s Commn. Wis. Strategic Devel., 1983-85; bd. dirs. Milw. Exposition, Conv. Ctr. and Arena, 1978-82; bd. dirs., chmn. mktg. com. Milw. County Research Park Bd., 1987—, United Performing Arts Fund, 1987—; bd. dirs., exec. com. treas. Milw. Symphony Orch., 1979— , World Festivals Inc., 1982—; bd. dirs. Milw. Urban League, 1984—; mem. corp. bd. adv. com. Milw. Sch. Engring., 1983—; bd. dirs., past pres. Milw. Council Alcoholism, 1979-84; bd. dirs., chmn. mktg. div. United Way Greater Milw., 1987—, mem. campaign cabinet, 1986-87; mem. adv. council Robert M. LaFollette Inst. Pub. Affairs U. Wis., Madison, 1984—; bd. dirs. exec. com. Forward Wis., 1985—, U. Wis., Milw. Found., 1986-87, Bus. Against Drunk Drivers; mem. U. Ill. Bus. Adv. Council, 1987—; mem. Am. Council on Edn. Nat. Commn. on Higher Edn. Issues, 1981-83; telethon co-chmn. United Cerebral Palsy of Southeastern Wis., 1987-88; U.S. rep. 20th Gen. Conf. of UNESCO, Paris, 1978. Recipient Outstanding Achievement award 4th Dist. Wis. Fedn. Women's Clubs, 1978, YWCA of Greater Milw., 1986; fellow Am. Council Edn., 1976-77. Mem. Am. Bankers Assn. (ednl. policy and devel. council 1983-86), Am. Inst. Banking (bd. dirs. 1988—), Bank Mktg. Assn., Phi Beta Kappa, Phi Delta Kappa. Office: Banc One Wisconsin Corp 111 E Wisconsin Ave Milwaukee WI 53202

HANSON, NOEL RODGER, management consultant; b. Los Angeles, Jan. 19, 1942; s. Albert and Madelyne Gladys (Pobanz) H.; B.S. in Indsl. Mgmt., U. So. Calif., 1963, M.B.A. in Fin., 1966; m. Carol Lynn Travis, June 17, 1967; 1 son, Eric Rodger. Asst. dir. alumni fund, then dir. ann. funds U. So. Calif., 1964-66; asst. to Walt Disney for Cal-Arts, Retlaw Enterprises, Glendale, Calif., 1966-68; asst. dir. joint devel. Claremont U. Center, 1968-69; v.p. adminstrn. Robert Johnston Co., Los Angeles, 1969-70; partner Hale, Hanson & Co., Pasadena, Calif., 1970-82, Hanson, Olson & Co., 1982—; pres. Pasadena Services, Inc., 1977—; dir. Pasadena Fin. Cons., Inc., Wilihire Funding, Inc., 1988—. Trustee Oakhurst Sch., Pasadena, 1973-75; bd. advisers Girls Club Pasadena, 1977—; mem. U. So. Calif. Assos., 1979—, U. So. Calif. Commerce Assos., 1965—. Republican. Presbyterian. Club: Jonathan (Los Angeles). Address: 1051 LaLoma Rd Pasadena CA 91105

HANSON, ROBERT ARTHUR, agricultural equipment executive; b. Moline, Ill., Dec. 13, 1924; s. Nels A. and Margaret I. (Chapman) H.; m. Patricia Ann Klinger, June 25, 1955. B.A., Augustana Coll., Rock Island, Ill., 1948. Various positions Deere & Co., Moline, 1950-62; gen. mgr. Deere & Co., Mexico, 1962-64, Spain, 1964-66; dir. mktg. overseas Deere & Co., 1966-70, v.p. overseas ops., 1972, sr. v.p. overseas div., 1973, dir., 1974—, exec. v.p., 1975-78, pres., 1978-85, chief operating officer, 1979-82, chmn., chief exec. officer, 1982—; bd. dirs. Procter & Gamble Co., Merrill Lynch & Co., Texas Instruments Inc.; mem. Internat. Coun. J.P. Morgan, N.Y.C. Trustee Com. for Econ. Devel.; trustee Mayo Found.; bd. dirs. Farm and Indsl. Equipment Inst. Served with USMCR, 1943-46. Mem. Bus. Council. Home: 2200 29th Avenue Ct Moline IL 61265 Office: Deere & Co John Deere Rd Moline IL 61265 *

HANSON, RONALD WILLIAM, lawyer; b. LaCrosse, Wis., Aug. 3, 1950; s. Orlin Eugene and Irene Agnes (Yeske) H.; m. Sandra Kay Cook, Aug. 21, 1971; children: Alec Evan, Corinn Michele. BA summa cum laude, St. Olaf Coll., 1972; JD cum laude, U. Chgo., 1975. Bar: Ill. 1975, U.S. Dist. Ct. (no. dist.) Ill. 1975, U.S. Ct. Appeals (7th cir.) 1978. Assoc. Sidley & Austin, Chgo., 1975-83, ptnr., 1983-88, Latham & Watkins, Chgo., 1988—; ofcl. advisor to Nat. Conf. of Commrs. on Uniform State Laws; lectr. Ill. Inst. Continuing Legal Edn., Springfield, 1979—, Am. Bankruptcy Inst., Washington, 1984—, Banking Law Inst., 1985, Practicing Law Inst., 1985—. Contbr. articles to profl. jours. Mem. ABA, Am. Law Inst., Ill. Bar Assn., Chgo. Bar Assn., Order of Coif, Phi Beta Kappa. Republican. Lutheran. Club: Monroe (Chgo.). Home: 664 58th St W Hinsdale IL 60521 Office: Latham & Watkins 5800 Sears Tower Chicago IL 60606

HANTON, E. MICHAEL, public and personnel relations consultant; b. Gary, Ind.; s. Zachary and Maria (Suciu) H.; A.B., Ind. U., 1951, M.A., 1955; grad. sr. officer's course U.S. Air Force Air War Coll., 1968. Various prodn. positions U.S. Steel Corp., Gary, 1940, 41, 50; prodn. controller Douglas Aircraft Corp., Santa Monica, Calif., 1946-47; classified advt. mgr. Weaver Pub. Co., Santa Monica, 1947-48; reporter Muncie (Ind.) Evening Press, 1952, Gary Post-Tribune, 1952-53; head cashier Office Lake County Treas., Gary, 1955-60; public and personnel relations cons., Gary, 1960—, Plattsburgh, N.Y., 1968—; asst. prof. State U. Coll. Arts and Scis., Plattsburgh, 1966-67; cons. community relations and fund raising. Served with USAAF, 1941-45; mem. Res. Decorated Air medal, Purple Heart. Mem. Am. Med. Writers Assn., Assn. Edn. in Journalism and Mass Communications, Am. Acad. Advt., Gary C. of C., Plattsburgh C. of C., Air Force Assn., Res. Officers Assn., Nat. Arts Club, Steel Club, Caterpillar Club, Flying Boot Club. Author: The New Nurse, 1973. Office: Lake County PO Box 803 Plattsburgh NY 12901

HANWAY, JOHN, III, marketing professional; b. Bronxville, N.Y., June 6, 1952; s. John II and Elena (Garcia) H. BA, Yale U., 1974, M in Pub. Pvt. Mgmt., 1979. Mktg. rep. IBM Corp., N.Y.C., 1974-82; instr. IBM Corp., Poughkeepsie, N.Y., 1982-83; mktg. mgr. IBM Corp., Norwalk, Conn., 1983-86; communications program mgr. IBM Corp., White Plains, N.Y., 1986; account mktg. mgr. IBM Corp., White Plains, 1986-87; account exec. IBM Corp., N.Y.C., 1988—. Club: Yale (N.Y.C.). Home: 217 Bridge St Unit D-1 Stamford CT 06905 Office: IBM Corp 590 Madison Ave New York NY 10022

HARAD, GEORGE JAY, manufacturing company executive; b. Newark, Apr. 24, 1944; s. Sidney Solomon and Irma Miriam (Feigenblatt) H.; m. Beverly Marcia Silverman, June 12, 1966; children—Alyssa Dawn, Matthew Corde. B.A., Franklin and Marshall Coll., 1965; M.B.A. with high distinction, Harvard Bus. Sch., 1971. Staff cons. Boston Cons. Group, 1970-71; asst. to sr. v.p. housing Boise Cascade Corp., Idaho, 1971; asst. to v.p. Boise Cascade Corp., Palo Alto, Calif., 1971; fin. mgr. Boise Cascade Realty Group, Palo Alto, Calif., 1972-76; mgr. corp. devel. Boise Cascade Corp., Idaho, 1976-80, dir. retirement funds, risk mgmt., 1980-82, v.p., controller, 1982-84, sr. v.p., chief fin. officer, 1984—; dir. Allendale Ins. Co. Western Adv. Bd.; dir. bd. trustees Coll. Idaho; mem. fin. mgmt. com. Am. Paper Inst., 1984—. Founder, pres. Boise Council for Gifted and Talented Students, 1977-79; bd. dirs. Boise Philharmonic Assn., 1983-84. Grad. Prize fellow Harvard Grad. Sch. Arts and Scis., 1965-69, Frederick Roe fellow Harvard U. Sch. Bus., 1971; George F. Baker scholar, 1970-71. Phi Beta Kappa. Clubs: Century (Boston); Arid (Boise), Crane Creek Country. Home: 224 E Braemere Rd Boise ID 83702 Office: Boise Cascade Corp 1 Jefferson Sq Boise ID 83728

HARBECK, WILLIAM JAMES, real estate executive, lawyer, international consultant; b. Glenview, Ill., Dec. 16, 1921; s. Christian Frederick and Anna (Gaeth) H.; m. Jean Marie Allsopp, Jan. 20, 1945; children: John, Stephen, Timothy, Mark, Christopher. B.A., Wabash (Ind.) Coll., 1947; J.D., Northwestern U., 1950. Bar: Ill. 1950. Land acquisition atty. Chgo. Land Clearance Commn., 1950-51; with Montgomery Ward & Co., Chgo., 1951-81; asst. to pres., dir. corp. facilities Montgomery Ward & Co., 1968-70, v.p., dir. facilities devel., 1970-81; v.p. Montgomery Ward Devel. Corp., 1972-81; pres., chief exec. officer Montgomery Ward Properties Corp., 1974-81; pres. William J. Harbeck Assocs., 1981—; dir. Randhurst Corp., 1972-81, exec. com., 1975-79; bd. dirs. Internat. Council Shopping Centers, 1972-78, exec. com., 1975-78, govt. affairs com., 1977—, awards com., 1980-83, urban com. 1980-83, lectr., 1969—. Author articles in field; mem. editorial bds. profl. jours. Bd. dirs. Chgo. Lawson YMCA, 1973—, chmn. devel. com., 1979—, mem. exec. com., 1985—; bd. dirs. Greater North Michigan Ave. Assn., Chgo., 1979-81; chmn. constrn. com. Chgo. United, 1979-81; co-chmn. Chgo. Bus. Opportunities Fair, 1980-81; mem. real estate com. Chgo. Met. YMCA, 1982—, chmn. Bldg. Task Force, 1985—; mem. pres.'s council Concordia Coll., River Forest, Ill., 1969-87, mem. bd. regents, 1987—, planning com. Inst. for Philanthropic Mgmt., 1985—; youth Bible and Bethel instr. Redeemer Luth. Ch., Highland Park, Ill., 1965, congregation pres., 1968-70, 85-87, chmn. ch. growth com., 1982—; trustee Lutheran Ch. Mo. Synod Found., 1975-76, 81—, mem. Synodical mission study commn., 1974-75, mem. dist. research and planning com., 1981—, mem. task force on synodical constn. by-laws and structure, 1975-79; mem. research and planning com. No. Ill. Dist. Luth. Ch. Mo. Synod, 1984—; sponsor Luth. Chs. for Career Devel., 1979—; corp. chmn. U.S. Bond drive, Chgo., 1976; chief crusader Chgo. Crusade Mercy, 1976-78; div. chmn. Chgo. Cerebral Palsy campaign, 1977-78. Lt. (j.g.) USNR, 1942-46. Mem. Ill. Bar Assn., Luth. Layman's League, Alpha Sigma Kappa, Phi Alpha Delta, Pi Alpha Chi. Home and Office: 470 E Linden Ave Lake Forest IL 60045

HARBERT, BILL LEBOLD, construction corporation executive; b. Indianola, Miss., July 21, 1923; s. John Murdock and Mae (Schooling) H.; m. Mary Joyce Patrick, June 28, 1952; children—Anne Harbert Moulton, Elizabeth Harbert Cornay, Billy L., Jr. B.S., Auburn U., 1948; Advanced Mgmt. Program, Harvard U., 1966. Lic. profl. engr. and land surveyor, Ala. Exec. v.p. Harbert Constrn. Corp., Birmingham, Ala., 1948-79; pres. Harbert Constrn. Corp., Birmingham, 1979-81; pres., chief exec. officer Harbert Internat., Inc., Birmingham, 1981—. Trustee, co-chmn. Laborers Nat. Pension Fund, Dallas, 1968—; bd. dirs. U. Ala. Health Service Found., Birmingham, 1983—, Met. Devel. Bd. of Birmingham, 1980-83. Served to sgt. U.S. Army, 1943-46. Mem. Birmingham Area C. of C. Methodist. Clubs: Vestavia Country (pres. 1971), Riverchase Country (pres. 1980). Home: 205 Vestavia Circle Birmingham AL 35226 Office: Harbert Corp PO Box 1297 Birmingham AL 35201

HARBISON, EARLE HARRISON, JR., chemical company executive; b. St. Louis, Aug. 10, 1928; s. Earle Harrison and Rose (Hensberg) H.; m. Suzanne Groves Siegel, Nov. 18, 1952; children—Earle Douglas, Keith Siegel. Student, Harvard U., 1960; AB, Washington U., St. Louis, 1949, LLB, 1957. With CIA, Washington, 1949-67; dir. mgmt. info. systems dept. Monsanto Co., 1967-73, dir. corp. orgn. and mgmt. devel. dept., 1973-75, gen. mgr. specialty chem. div., 1975, gen. mgr. plasticizers div., 1976-77, gen. mgr. detergents and phosphates div. and plasticizers div., 1977; v.p., mng. dir. Monsanto Comml. Products Co., 1977, mem. corp. adminstrv. com., 1977; group v.p., mng. dir. Monsanto Chem. Co. (formerly Monsanto Indsl. Chems. Co.), St. Louis, 1979-84; exec. v.p. parent co. Monsanto Co., St. Louis, 1981-86, pres., chief operating officer, 1986—, also bd. dirs.; chmn. bd. G.S. Searle & Co. (subs. Monsanto Co.), Skokie, Ill., 1985-86; dir. Centerre Trust Co.; former chmn. Fisher Controls Internat., Inc. (subsidiary), St. Louis. Bd. dirs., pres. Mental Health Assn. St. Louis, 1973-78; mem. long-range planning com. United Way of Am., 1976—, chmn. NAV Com., 1980—, mem. program evaluation com., 1977—; bd. dirs. Bethesda Gen. Hosp., 1979—, St. Louis Children's Hosp. Served with U.S. Army, 1950-65. Mem. Fed. Bar. Clubs: Old Warson Country, Ponte Vedra, Log Cabin (Ponte Vedra Beach, Fla.). Office: Monsanto Co 800 N Lindbergh Blvd Saint Louis MO 63167 *

HARDER, RAYMOND WYMBS, advertising executive, playwright; b. Mt. Vernon, N.Y., Oct. 25, 1920; s. Raymond Wymbs and Lucie Belden (Scott) H.; B.A., UCLA, 1948; m. Eleanor Lorain Brown, Sept. 4, 1948; children—Daniel Wymbs, Julia Ann. advt. agy. exec., 1964-85, sr. v.p. Michael-Sellers Co., L.A., 1969-86, pres. Marketcomm, , 1986—; lectr. UCLA, 1964-87; cons. SBA, 1966-76. Pres., Westside Village Civic Assn., 1981—. With USCGR, World War II. Mem. Dramatists Guild, Am. Nat. Theatre and Acad., Am. Soc. Composers and Performers. Democrat. Co-playwright: Annabelle Broom, 1956; Good Grief a Griffin, 1960; Sacramento 50 Miles, 1971; How Shall We Sing, 1976, Luann, 1985, others.

HARDIN, CLIFFORD MORRIS, economist; b. Knightstown, Ind., Oct. 9, 1915; s. James Alvin and Mabel (Macy) H.; m. Martha Love Wood, June 28, 1939; children: Susan Carol (Mrs. L.W. Wood), Clifford Wood, Cynthia (Mrs. Robert Milligan), Nancy Ann (Mrs. Douglas L. Rogers), James. B.S., Purdue U., 1937, M.S., 1939, Ph.D., 1941, D.Sc. (hon.), 1952; Farm Found. scholar, U. Chgo., 1939-40; LL.D., Creighton U., 1956, Ill. State U., 1973; Dr. honoris causa, Nat. U. Colombia, 1968; D.Sc., Mich. State U., 1969, N.D. State U., 1969, U. Nebr., 1978, Okla. Christian Coll., 1979. Grad. asst. Purdue U., Lafayette, Ind., 1937-39, 40-41; instr. U. Wis., 1941-42, asst. prof. agrl. econs., 1942-44; asso. prof. agrl. econs. Mich. State Coll., 1944-46, prof., chmn. agrl. econs. dept., 1946-48, asst. dir. agrl. expt. sta., 1948, dir., 1949-53, dean agr., 1953-54; chancellor U. Nebr., 1954-69; sec. U.S. Dept. Agr., Washington, 1969-71; vice chmn. bd., dir. Ralston Purina Co., St. Louis, 1971-80; dir. Center for Study of Am. Bus., Washington U., St. Louis, 1981-83, scholar-in-residence, 1983-85; cons., dir. Stifel, Nicolaus & Co., St. Louis, 1980-87; dir. Nappe-Babcock, Richmond, Halifax Engring., Inc., Alexandria, Va., The Cypress Fund, N.Y.C., Omaha br. Fed. Res. Bank of Kansas City, 1961-67, chmn., 1962-67. Editor: Overcoming World Hunger, 1969. Trustee Rockefeller Found., 1961-69, 72-81, Freedoms Found. at Valley Forge, 1973—, Winrock, Internat., Morrilton, Ark., 1984— , Am. Assembly, 1975—, U. Nebr. Found., 1975—; mem. Pres.'s Com. to Strengthen Security Free World, 1963. Mem. Assn. State Univs. and Land-Grant Colls. (pres. 1960, chmn. exec. com. 1961), Sigma Xi, Alpha Zeta, Alpha Gamma Rho. Home: 10 Roan Ln Saint Louis MO 63124

HARDIN, JAMES, retail food company executive; b. 1936. BBA, East Tex. State U., 1961. Pres. Brookshire Grocery Co. Inc., Tyler, Tex. Office: Brookshire Grocery Co Box 1411 Tyler TX 75701 *

HARDING, ANN MARIE, accountant; b. Reading, Pa., Feb. 2, 1964. BS in Acctg., Albright Coll., 1986. Staff acct. Beard and Co. CPA's Inc., Reading, 1986-88, sr. acct., 1988—; allocations advisor United Way Berks County, Reading, 1987. pres. Muscular Dystrophy Assn. Berks County, Reading, 1987—; fin. sec. Cen. Park United Meth. Ch., 1986-88. Jacob Albright scholar Albright Coll., Reading, 1986. Mem. Nat. Assn. Accts. (sec. 1989—), Nat. Assn. Female Execs., Albright Alumni Assn. (class rep.), Reading Jaycess Inc., Phi Delta Sigma. Democrat. Home: 1015 N 10th St Reading PA 19604 Office: Beard and Co Inc CPAs One Park Plaza PO Box 311 Reading PA 19603

HARDIS, STEPHEN ROGER, manufacturing company executive; b. N.Y.C., July 13, 1935; s. Abraham I. and Ethel (Krinsky) H.; m. Sondra Joyce Rolbin, Sept. 15, 1957; children—Julia Faye, Andrew Martin, Joanne Halley. B.A. with distinction, Cornell U., 1956; M.P.A. in Econs, Woodrow Wilson Sch. of Pub. and Internat. Affairs, Princeton, 1960. Asst. to controller Gen. Dynamics, 1960-61; financial analyst Pfaudler Permutit Inc., 1961-64; staff asst. to controller 1964; mgr. corp. long-range planning Ritter Pfaudler Corp., 1965-68, dir. corporate planning, 1968; treas. Sybron Corp., Rochester, N.Y., 1969—; v.p. fin. Sybron Corp., 1970-77, exec. v.p. fin. and planning, 1977-79; vice chmn., chief fin. and adminstrv. officer Eaton Corp., Cleve., 1979—; dir. Soc. Corp., Soc. Progressive Corp., Soc. Nat., Inc., Nordson Corp., Prog. Cos., Univ. Circle Inc. Past mem. Gov.'s Spl. Task Force on High Tech. Industry; past bd. dirs. Rochester Area Hosp. Corp., Rochester Area Ednl. TV Sta., Genesee Hosp.; trustee Cleve. Clinic, Univ. Circle, Inc. Hathaway Brown Sch. Served with USNR, 1956-58. Mem. Fin. Execs. Inst., Phi Beta Kappa. Office: Eaton Corp 1111 Superior Ave NE Cleveland OH 44114

HARDY, BEVERLEY JANE, controller; b. Windsor, Ont., Can., Aug. 2, 1944; d. Bill and Thelma Viola (Feere) Karpiuk; divorced; children: Kristin Lee, Timothy John. Student, J.L. Forster Collegiate Inst., Can., 1961-63; cert. in bus. mgmt., Western Inst. of Tech., Can., 1964; cert. in bus. tax law, Alvin (Tex.) Jr. Coll., 1978. Acct. Williams and Jamail Elec. Contractors, Houston, 1978-80; compt. So. Tennis Ctrs., Houston, 1980-86; comptroller Brae-Burn Country Club, Houston, 1986—; cons. acctg. and computers 1987—. Leader Girl Scouts of U.S., 1974-78; coach Girls Softball Assn., Tex., 1978-79; band aide Pearland (Tex.) Jr. and Sr. High Schs., 1979-85. Mem. NAFE, Greater Houston Hospitality Accts. Assn. Home: 2710 Grants lake Blvd. #M4 Sugar Land TX 77479

HARDY, DIRK, product designer, consultant; b. Wichita, Kans., Feb. 28, 1956; s. Lyman George and Anabel Marie (Baker) H.; m. Shannon Sutton, Nov. 1, 1980; children: Erik, Jessica. BS in Radio, TV and Film, U. Austin, 1978. Technician CMR reprographics Zytron Inc., Austin, Tex., 1978; Z comp. operator Zytron Inc., Dallas, 1979-80; sales dir. video prodn. Sasco Cosmetics, Dallas, 1980-85; dir. mktg. Smith Howard & Gray CPA, Dallas, 1984-85; v.p. sales Comport Inc., Dallas, 1985-87; v.p. sales, ptnr. Excel Systems Inc., Ft. Worth, 1987—. Republican. Home: 1820 Polstar Plano TX 75093

HARDY, NANCY VISSER, small business owner; b. Syracuse, N.Y., Apr. 18, 1943; d. Henry John and Loata Mae (Benedict) Visser; m. David R. Fitzgibbons, July 8, 1963 (div. 1973); children: David, Kevin, Michael; m. Robert Appleby Hardy, Aug. 24, 1974; children: Paul, Kim, Steve, Scott, Jeff. AA, Rider Coll., 1963. Exec. sec. Stratton Mountain (Vt.) Sch., 1976-81; broker Trask & Waite, Bondville, Vt., 1982-84; prin., pres. Stratton Country Properties, Bondville, Vt., 1984—. Trustee Stratton Mountain Sch., 1976-81; chmn. Town of Stratton Sch. Bd., 1981-84; planning commn. Town of Stratton, 1986—; bd. dirs. Stratton Civic Assn., 1982—. Recipient Excellence award, World Cup Commn., 1978. Mem. U.S. Ski Assn. (nat. race sec. 1980), Eastern Ski Assn. (execellence award 1979), South Cen. Bd. Realtors, Stratton Country Club, Melrose Club (S.C.). Republican. Office: Stratton Country Properties Box 8 Bondville VT 05155

HARDY, RALPH W. F., biochemist, biotechnology executive; b. Lindsay, Ont., Can., July 27, 1934; s. Wilbur and Elsie H.; m. Jacqueline M. Thayer, Dec. 26, 1954; children: Steven, Chris, Barbara, Ralph, Jon. B.S.A., U. Toronto, 1956; M.S., U. Wis.-Madison, 1958, Ph.D., 1959. Asst. prof. U. Guelph, Ont., Can., 1960-63; research biochemist DuPont deNemours & Co., Wilmington, Del., 1963-67, research supr., 1967-74, assoc. dir., 1974-79, dir. life scis., 1979-84; vis. prof. life scis. Cornell U., 1984-86, now pres. Boyce Thompson Inst.; pres. Bio Technica Internat., Inc., Cambridge, Mass., 1984-86; dep. chmn. Bio Technica Internat., Inc., 1986—; mem. exec. com. bd. agr. Nat. Acad. Sci., 1982-88; mem. commn. life scis., bd. biology NRC, com. on biotech., 1988—; mem. com. genetic experimentation Internat. Counc. Sci. Union, 1981—. Author: Nitrogen Fixation, 1975, A Treatise on Dinitrogen Fixation, 3 vols, 1977-79; mem. editorial bd. sci. jours.; contbr. over 100 articles to sci. jours. Recipient Gov. Gen.'s Silver medal, 1956, Sterling Henricks award 1986; WARF fellow, 1956-58; DuPont fellow, 1958-59. Mem. Indsl. Biotech. Assn. (bd. dirs. 1986—), Agriculture Research Inst. (bd. govs. 1988—), Am. Chem. Soc. (exec. com. biol. chemistry div., Del. award 1969), Am. Soc. Biol. Chemists and Molecular Biologists, Am. Soc. Plant Physiology (exec. com. 1974-77), Am. Soc. Agronomy, Am. Soc. Microbiology. Episcopalian. Home: 330 The Parkway Ithaca NY 14850 Office: Bio Technica Internat Inc 85 Bolton St Cambridge MA 02140 also: Boyce Thompson Inst at Cornell Tower Rd Ithaca NY 14853

HARDY, VICTORIA ELIZABETH, cultural organization administrator; b. Marion, N.C., Feb. 26, 1947; d. Milton Victor Roth and Bertha Jean (Norris) R.; m. Grant Thomas Holt Jr., Sept. 14, 1968 (div. 1977); m. Michael Carrington Hardy, June 19, 1983; 1 child, Christopher. BS in Edn., U. Mo., 1970; postgrad., So. Ill. U., 1974-75; postgrad. Mgmt. Devel. Program, Stanford U., 1980-81. Pub. sch. tchr. English and Theater 1970-75; gen. mgr. Miss. River Festival, Edwardsville, Ill., 1975-77; dir. events and svcs. Stanford (Calif.) U., 1977-83; exec. dir. Williams Ctr. for the Arts, Rutherford, N.J., 1983-87; pres., chief exec. officer Music Hall Ctr. for the Arts, Detroit, 1987-89; prin. Hardy and Hardy Counsel for the Arts, Detroit, 1989—; nat. adv. bd. Snowbird (Utah) Inst., 1977—; mem. faculty CUNY, 1986-88. Pres., bd. dirs. New Performance Gallery, San Francisco, 1977-83; bd. dirs. Bay Area Dance Coalition, San Francisco, 1986; mem. Wingspread Conf. Johnson Found., Milw., 1983; mem. USICA study team People's Republic of China, 1981, Mich. Advocates for the Arts (state bd. dirs.). Recipient Gold medal for Community Programs Coun. for Advancement and Support of Edn., Stanford, 1985; named in Creativity in Business Doubleday, 1986. Mem. League of Hist. Am. Theaters. (pres., bd. dirs. 1987—, Ptnrs. for Livable Places, Nat. Trust for Hist. Preservation, Assn. of Coll. Univ. and Community Arts Adminstrs. (exec. bd. dirs. 1977-83). Democrat. Office: Hardy & Hardy Counsel for the Arts 2435 Burns Ave Detroit MI 48214

HARDYMON, JAMES F., electronics company executive. BS, U. Ky., 1956, MS, 1958. With Emerson Electric Co., St. Louis, v.p. corp. group, 1979-83, exec. v.p., 1983-87, vice chmn., chief operating officer, 1987-88, pres., chief operating officer, 1988—. Office: Emerson Electric Co 8000 W Florissant Ave Saint Louis MO 63136 *

HARE, JEFFREY AVERILL, financial advisor; b. Ann Arbor, Mich., Feb. 1, 1937; s. Weldon Parsons and Millicent Averill (Moorman) H.; m. Marie-Rose Lopez, Nov. 13, 1963 (div. 1975). BS, U. N.C., 1959. Cert. fin. planner, N.Y. Mktg. mgr. Owens-Corning Fiberglas, N.Y.C., 1963-82; mktg. dir. Hoechst Fibers Industries, N.Y.C., 1972-82; exec. v.p. Higgins Mgmt. Corp., N.Y.C., 1982-84; pres. The Averill Fin. Group, N.Y.C., 1984; sr. fin. counselor Independent Fin. Svcs., White Plains, N.Y., 1985-89; sr. ptnr. The Capital Planning Group, Greenwich, Conn., 1989—. Lt. USN, 1959-63, Morocco. Mem. Internat. Assn. Fin. Planners, Inst. Cert. Fin. Planners, Taurino Club of N.Y. (treas. 1987-88). Home: 9 Partrick Ln Westport CT 06880 Office: The Capital Planning Group One E Putnam Ave Greenwich CT 06830

HARES, WILLIAM J., electronics executive; b. Auburn, N.Y., Mar. 14, 1949; s. Harlan Arthur and Evelyn Veronica (Wallace) H.; m. Dorothy Jean Wrase, July 23, 1983. BA in Math., SUNY, Oswego, 1972; postgrad. in bus. adminstrn., Syracuse U., 1988—. Vol. U.S. Peace Corps, Liberia, 1972-74; indsl. engr. Singer Co., Auburn, 1976-78, Keith Clark Co., Sidney, N.Y., 1978, Lipe rollway corp., Syracuse, 1979-81; indsl. engr. SL Auburn (N.Y.) Inc., 1982-84, project mgr. mfg. resources planning, 1985-87, project coord. GE programs, 1987-88, project mgr. engring., 1988—. Mem. Inst. Indsl. Engrs., Am. Prodn. and Inventory Control Soc., Internat. Mgmt. Coun., Cen. N.Y. Returned Peace Corps Vols. Assn. (co-chmn. 1987-88). Democrat. Lutheran. Home: 1746 Conners Rd Baldwinsville NY 13027 Office: SL Auburn Inc 89 York St Auburn NY 13021

HARFF, CHARLES HENRY, diversified industrial company executive, lawyer; b. Wesel, Fed. Republic Germany, Sept. 27, 1929; s. Philip and Stephanie (Dreyfuss) H.; m. Marion Haines MacAfee, July 19, 1958; children—Pamela Haines, John Blair, Todd Philip. B.A., Colgate U., 1951; LL.B., Harvard U., 1954; postgrad., U. Bonn, Fed. Republic Germany, 1955. Bar: N.Y. 1955, Pa. 1985. Assoc. Chadbourne & Parke, N.Y.C., 1955-64, ptnr., 1964-84; sr. v.p., gen. counsel, sec. Rockwell Internat. Corp., Pitts., 1984—. Trustee Christian Johnson Endeavor Found., N.Y.C., 1984—. Fulbright scholar U. Bonn, Fed. Republic Germany, 1955. Mem. ABA, N.Y. State Bar Assn., Pa. State Bar Assn., Machinery and Allied Products Inst. (law council 1984—), The Assn. of Gen. Counsel. Clubs: Econ. of N.Y., Harvard, Hemisphere (N.Y.C.); Duquesne, Allegheny Country (Pitts.); Farm Neck (Martha's Vineyard, Mass.). Home: Blackburn Rd Sewickley PA 15143 Office: Rockwell Internat Corp 600 Grant St Pittsburgh PA 15219

HARGETT, LOUIE THOMAS, agricultural chemistry corporation executive, entomologist; b. Wilmington, N.C., Oct. 19, 1932; s. Louie Fulton and Catherine Cordelia (Thomas) H.; m. Anna Catherine Hazel, June 26, 1954; children—Cheryl Ann, Robert Thomas, Catherine Lynn. B.A., Bridgewater (Va.) Coll., 1953; M.S., Va. Poly. Inst., 1958; Ph.D., Oreg. State U., 1962; A.M.P., Harvard Bus. Sch., 1976. Cert. profl. entomologist. Mem. faculty dept. entomology Va. Poly. Inst., Blacksburg, 1955-58, Oreg. State U., Corvallis, 1958-60; dir. field devel., asst. to v.p. mktg. Geigy, Inc., N.Y.C., 1961-70; dir. devel., gen. mgr. Rhodia, Inc., Monmouth Junction, N.J., 1970-77; asst. to pres. Environ. Research and Tech., Concord, Mass., 1977-78; dir. research, devel. crop protection Sandoz, Inc., San Diego, 1979-84; dir. product devel. Zoecon Corp. div. Sandoz Co., Palo Alto, 1984-86, dir. product devel. Sandoz Crop Protection, 1986—. Served with AUS, 1953-55. NIH fellow, 1960-61. Mem. Am. Inst. Biologists, Entomology Soc. Am., Weed Sci. Soc. Am., Sigma Xi. Republican. Protestant.

HARGREAVES, DAVID WILLIAM, communications company executive; b. Akron, Ohio, May 4, 1943; s. William B. and Helen Grace (Slusser) H.; m. Sandra Jean Tessier, Sept. 4, 1965; children: Kristen Elizabeth, Cinda Anne, Gregory David. BSEE, U. Maine, Orono, 1965; MBA, U. Rochester, 1967. Sales engr. Mobile Communications div. Gen. Electric, Lynchburg, Va., 1970-74, mgr. systems projects, 1974-75, mgr. systems bids/proposals, 1975-78; mgr. internat. mktg. Gen. Electric Powerline Carrier Bus., Lynchburg, 1978-80; gen. mgr. Gen. Electric Microwave Link Ops., Owensboro, Ky., 1980-84; mng. dir. Alpha Telecom div. Alpha Industries, Methuen, Mass., 1984-86; pres. Dynatech Tactical Communications, Inc. (formerly Controlonics Corp.), Westford, Mass., 1986—; conductor seminars in field. Contbr. articles to profl. jours. Chmn. bd. Gen. Electric United Way Pacesetter campaign, Lynchburg, 1978; advisor Jr. Achievement project bus., Owensboro, 1982, 83. Served to capt. U.S. Army, 1968-70, Vietnam. Decorated Bronze Star, D.S.C., 1970. Mem. Massibesic Yacht Club, Eta Kappa Nu, Tau Beta Pi. Republican. Home: 191 Buttrick Rd Hampstead NH 03841 Office: Dynatech Tactical Communications Inc 6A Lyberty Way Westford MA 01886

HARGROVES, EDWARD FRANCIS, software company executive; b. N.Y.C., Jan. 30, 1940; s. Edward F. and Mary F. (McLoughlin) H.; m. Patricia A. Daucher, June 3, 1961; children: Kathleen, Kevin, Daniel, Jennifer, Laurie. BS in Mgmt. Engring., C.W. Post Coll., 1969. Bus. systems analyst Republic Aviation, Farmingdale, N.Y., 1959-64, Smith Barney & Co., N.Y.C., 1964-65; mgr. systems programming Fairchild Hiller, Bayshore, N.Y., 1965-67, Union Carbide Corp., N.Y.C., 1967-68; dir. systems Western Union, N.Y.C., 1968-70; owner Firestone franchise, Orlando, Fla., 1970-74; sr. v.p. sales Fla. Software, Orlando, 1974-80; founder, chief exec. officer Credit Card Software, Inc., Orlando, 1980—; mem. Dist. Export Council, Miami, Fla., 1987—, Internat. Trade Council, Orlando, 1988.; bd. dirs. Shared, Inc. Contbr. articles to banking and mktg. publs. Bd. dirs. bus. adv. council Valencia Community Coll., Orlando, 1985-86, Jr. Achievement Orange County, 1988; trustee Pace Sch., Longwood, Fla., 1988. Named Fla. Entrepreneur of Yr. High Tech., 1988. Mem. Pres's. Assn., Exec. Com. Inst. Am. Entrepreneurs, Greater Orlando C. of C. (export council 1988—). Republican. Roman Catholic. Office: Credit Card Software Inc 900 Winderley Pl Maitland FL 32751

HARLAN, LEONARD MORTON, real estate developer, consultant; b. Newark, June 1, 1936; s. Harold Robinson and Doris Harriet (Siegler) H.; BME, Cornell U., 1959; MBA with distinction, Harvard U., 1961, DBA, 1965; m. Elizabeth Nan Kramon, Aug. 27, 1969; children: Joshua, Noah. Security analyst Donaldson, Lufkin & Jenrette, Inc., 1965-69, v.p., 1968-69; founder, chmn. bd. The Harlan Co., Inc. (formerly Harlan, Betke & Myers, Inc.), N.Y.C., 1969—; dir., co-owner San Luis Central R.R., 1970-78; gen. partner Real Estate Partnerships, 1971—; co-owner HBM Properties, Inc., 1976-78; founder, co-owner Mich. Interstate Ry. Co., 1977—; dir. Ryland Group, Inc., 1984-87; pres. Castle Harlan, Inc., 1987—; gen. ptr. Legend Capital Group, 1987—; dir. Del. Group of Mutual Funds, 1988—, Del. Mgmt. Holdings, Inc., 1988—; guest lectr. Harvard U. and Columbia U. grad. schs. bus. adminstrn., 1968—, others; adj. prof. banking and real estate N.Y. U. Real Estate Ist., 1968—, Grad. Sch. Bus. Adminstrn., 1976-80; adj. prof. bus. adminstrn. Columbia U. Grad. Sch. Bus. Adminstrn., 1980—. Mem. Pres.'s Com. on Indsl. Innovation, 1978-80; mem. Urban Devel. Action Grant Task Force, HUD, 1984; mem. exec. com. N.Y. chpt. Am. Jewish Com., 1975-80, Central N.J. chpt., 1980—, nat. budget commn., 1987; mem. Cerberus Soc. (N.Y.C. Citizens Budget Commn.), 1983-88; trustee N.Y.C. Citizens Budget Commn., 1988—. Recipient Charles B. Shatuck Meml. award Am. Inst. Real Estate Appraisers, 1967, 72; Disting. Tchr. award N.Y. U., 1979; Ford Found. fellow, 1964-65; Zurn fellow, 1962-63. Lic. real estate broker, N.Y., N.J. Clubs: Harvard (admissions com. 1973-75), Harvard Bus. Sch. (v.p. 1977-79) (N.Y.C.); Harvard Club N.J. Editorial bd. Real Estate Rev. Jour., 1971-84; contbr. articles to profl. jours. Office: Castle Harlan Inc 150 E 58 St New York NY 10155

HARLAN, NORMAN RALPH, construction executive; b. Dayton, Ohio, Dec. 21, 1914; s. Joseph and Anna (Kaplan) H.; Indsl. Engring. degree U. Cin., 1937; m. Thelma Katz, Sept. 4, 1955; children—Leslie, Todd. Pres. Am. Constrn. Corp., Dayton, 1949—, Mainline Investment Corp., 1951—, Harlan, Inc., realtors; treas. Norman Estates, Inc. Mem. Dayton Real Estate Bd., Ohio Real Estate Assn., Nat. Assn. Real Estate Bds., C. of C., Pi Lambda Phi. Home: 303 Glenridge Rd Kettering OH 45429 Office: Am Constrn Corp 2451 S Dixie Hwy Dayton OH 45409

HARLAN, RIDGE LATIMER, corporate executive; b. Pilot Grove, Mo., Feb. 25, 1917; s. George B. and Dale (Latimer) H.; m. Barbara Hawley, Oct. 7, 1939 (div.); children: Brooke, Holly Ann, Robert Ridge; m. Marjory Folinsbee, June 4, 1976. BJ, U. Mo., 1939; postgrad. Harvard U., 1943, Colo. U., 1945-46, Stanford U., 1965. Pres. Barnes-Hind Pharms., Inc., 1972-76; prin. Harlan & Clucas, Inc., San Francisco, 1968-82; pres. Charila Found., 1969-73; chmn. bd., pres. Flores de las Americas, 1979-81; chmn. Millenium Systems, Inc., 1978-82; pres. Velo-Bind, Inc., 1983-85, chmn., chief exec. officer 1985-87, chmn. 1987—, also bd. dirs.; bd. dirs. Impulflor de Mexico, Velo-Bind Inc., Bishop, Inc.; chmn. Harlan & Dalton, Inc. Lt. (j.g.) USNR, 1943-46. Mem. Nat. Investor Rels. Inst. (dir.), Assn. Corp. Growth (dir.), Alpha Delta Sigma, Kappa Tau Alpha, OlympicClub, Family Club (San Francisco), Boulders Club (Carefree, Ariz.). Home: 839 Seabury Rd Hillsborough CA 94010 Office: Harlan and Dalton Inc 875 Mahler Rd Burlingame CA 96010

HARLAN, WILLIAM GORDON, financial analyst, consultant; b. Oak Park, Ill., Apr. 12, 1938; s. William G. and Pauline (Brush/Prass) H.; m. Arlene J. Halfar, Jan. 25, 1964; children: Heather Anne, William Gordon Jr., Mark Joseph, Dru Elizabeth. BS, Loyola U., Chgo., 1961; MBA, U. Detroit, 1969. CPA, Ill. Staff acct. Price Waterhouse, Chgo., 1961-63; various positions Ford Motor Co., Dearborn, Mich., 1963-75, Congoleum Corp., Milw., 1976-83; sr. v.p. fin. and adminstrn. Kinder div. Congoleum Corp., Elkhart, Ind., 1983-86, pres., 1986; pres. Holiday Holding subs. Holiday Rambler Corp., Wakarusa, Ind., 1987; owner William G. Harlan and Assocs., South Bend, Ind., 1988—. Served with U.S. Army, 1961. Mem. Am. Soc. CPA's, Ind. Soc. CPA's, Fin. Exec. Inst. Home and Office: 1604 E Jefferson Blvd South Bend IN 46617

HARLESS, JAMES WILLIAM, insurance company executive; b. Croton, N.Y., Apr. 24, 1954; s. William Robert and Anne Emma (Weise) H.; m. Esther Julia LeRoy; children: Raphael, Jennifer, Daniel, Stephen. B. in Indsl. Distbn., Clarkson U., 1976. Sales rep. Tex. Instruments Inc., Cleve., 1976-77, mgr. br. sales, 1978-83; v.p. Mut. Health Services Co., Cleve., 1983-85, v.p. mktg., 1985-86, sr. v.p., gen. mgr., 1986-87, pres., chief exec. officer, 1987—. Republican. Methodist. Home: 17339 Long Meadow Trail Chagrin Falls OH 44022 Office: Mut Health Svcs Co 1240 Huron Rd Cleveland OH 44115

HARLEY, SHEILA DAWNE, accountant; b. Santa Rosa, Calif., Apr. 14, 1945; d. Walter I. and Virginia V. (Carlson) R.; m. Jerry L. Harley, Nov. 20, 1977. BS in Bus. Adminstrn., Cen. Mo. U., 1978. CPA, Mo. Mem. audit staff Baird, Kurtz & Dobson, Springfield, Mo., 1977-78; staff accts. Roger Taylor, CPA, Springfield, 1978-79; staff acct. Jackson & Decker CPA, Springfield, 1979; ptnr. Decker & Harley, CPA's, Springfield, 1980—; ptnr. Indsl. Properties Investments, Springfield, 1986—; fin. ptnr. R.B. Investemnts, Springfield, 1985—; bd. dirs. Polar Printing, Inc., Springfield, 1986—. Chmn. Greene County Domestic Violence Shelter Bd., Springfield, 1985-86; treas. Salvation Army adv. bd., Springfield, 1984—, U. Coop. Extension Bd., 1982-86; bd. dirs. Green County Planning and Zoning Commn., Springfield, 1984—, chmn., 1988; bd. dirs. Christian Found., Springfield, 1984—; mem. SBA Adv. Council, Kansas City, Mo. Gen. Hap Arnold scholar USAF, 1963; recipient Advocate of the Yr. award SBA, Kansas City, 1987. Mem. AICPA, Mo. Soc. CPAs, Am. Soc. Women Accts. (treas. 1983-84), Network of Springfield (treas. 1982-83, pres. 1983-84), SBA (mem. adv. bd. Kansas City dist. 1987—, Acct. Adv. of Yr. Kansas City dist. 1987). Republican. Methodist. Lodge: Zonta (pres. 1981-82). Office: Decker & Harley CPA's 805 W Battlefield Springfield MO 65807

HARLING, CARLOS GENE, savings and loan executive; b. Gainesville, Fla., May 11, 1946; s. Hugh Whitman and Hester Elaine (Bonnette) H.; m. Ewa Babara-Maria Hadrych, Dec. 27, 1968; children: Nicole Lara, Audrey Anne. BBA in Acctg., U. Fla., 1968; MBA in Fin., Wayne State U., 1969. CPA, Mich. Mgr.-audit Peat, Marwick, Mitchell & Co., Detroit, 1970-79; chief fin. officer First Fed. of Mich., Detroit, 1979-85, pres., chief operating officer, 1985—, also bd. dirs. Served to 1st lt., U.S. Army, 1969-70. Office: First Fed of Mich 1001 Woodward Ave Detroit MI 48226 *

HARLOW, JAMES GINDLING, JR., utility executive; b. Oklahoma City, May 29, 1934; s. James Gindling and Adalene (Rae) H.; m. Jane Marriott Bienfang, Jan. 30, 1957; children: James Gindling III, David Ralph. B.S., U. Okla., 1957, postgrad., 1959-61. Research analyst Okla. Gas and Electric Co., Oklahoma City, 1961-63; div. auditor Okla. Gas and Electric Co., 1963-65, adminstrv. asst., 1965-66, asst. treas., 1966-68, treas., 1968-69, sec.-treas., 1969-70, v.p., treas., 1970-72, exec. v.p., treas., 1972-73, pres., 1973-76, pres., chief exec. officer, 1976-82, chmn. bd., pres., chief exec. officer, 1982—, also dir.; dir. Mass. Mut. Life Ins. Co., Fleming Cos., Inc., Oklahoma City. Pres. Missouri Valley Electric Assn., 1977-78; bd. dirs. Edison Electric Inst., 1988—, exec. com., 1988—; bd. dirs. State Fair of Okla.; trustee Okla. Zool. Soc., Oklahoma City U.; bd. govs. Kirkpatrick Ctr., pres. 1987—; pres. Allied Arts Found., 1982-84; chmn., trustee U. Okla. Found., Inc., 1986—. Served with USNR, 1957-59. Inducted into Okla. Hall of Fame, 1987. Mem. U.S. C. of C. (dir. 1978-84), Okla. C. of C. (dir. 1973—, pres. 1980), Oklahoma City C. of C. (pres. 1976), Okla. Soc. Security Analysts. Clubs: Petroleum, Oklahoma City Golf and Country, Econ. of Okla. (pres. 1986-87), Men's Dinner, Beacon. Home: 6500 Hillcrest Ave Oklahoma City OK 73116 Office: Okla Gas & Electric Co 321 N Harvey Ave Oklahoma City OK 73102

HARLOW, JOHN GRONBECH, marketing professional; b. Lebanon, Oreg., Aug. 20, 1944; s. Leroy Francis and Agda Sophia (Gronbech) H.; m. Carole Masae, Feb. 5, 1972; children: John Junji, Benjamin Kenzo. BA in Communications, Brigham Young U., 1968; MBA in Mktg., Northwestern U., 1970. Assoc. Booz, Allen & Hamilton, Chgo., 1970-72; prin. Booz, Allen & Hamilton, San Francisco, 1972-78; v.p. Korn Ferry Internat., San Francisco, 1978-81; mng. dir., regional v.p. Korn Ferry Internat., Singapore, 1981-85, mng. v.p., 1985—. Mem. Commonwealth Club, World Affairs Council. Clubs: Tanglin (Singapore), Olympic (San Franciso). Home: 23 Linda Vista Atherton CA 94025

HARLOW, ROBERT DEAN, packaging executive; b. Des Moines, Feb. 23, 1938; s. Gloyd Andrew and Ruth Grace (Hoskins) H.; m. Joyce Wilkins, June 4, 1960; children—Jeffrey, Robert. B.S.E.E., Iowa State U., 1960; M.B.A., Western Mich. U., 1972. Registered profl. engr. Mgr. corp. devel. Tenneco, Houston, 1976-79; v.p. and controller Packaging Corp. Am., Evanston, Ill., 1979-82, v.p. control and planning, 1982-83, v.p. fin., 1983—, sr. v.p., chief fin. officer, 1986-88, sr. v.p. G.M. Molded Fibre Div., 1988—. Author several articles. Dir. White Oaks Assn. Served to capt. U.S. Army, 1960-66. Mem. TAPPI (chmn. engring. com.). Home: 1511 White Oak Rd Lake Forest IL 60045 Office: Packaging Corp Am 1603 Orrington Ave Evanston IL 60204

HARMAN, TOMMY WADE, data processing executive; b. Scottsbluff, Nebr., Sept. 21, 1941; s. Robert Woodson and Kate Linda (Hill) H.; m. Dorothy Ellen Kicker, June 12, 1965; children: Michael Wayne, Timothy Ward. BS in Gen. Engring., U.S. Mil. Acad., 1964. Programmer, analyst Control Data Corp., Sunnyvale, Calif., 1969-73; project mgr. Kaman Scis. Corp., Colorado Springs, Colo., 1973-79; mgr. systems and programming Current Inc., Colorado Springs, 1979-82; dir. div. Nat. Systems & Rsch. Co., Colorado Springs, 1982-88, gen. mgr., 1988—. Mem. governing coun. Pikes Peak YMCA Indian Guides, Colorado Springs, 1980-82; bd. dirs., vice chmn. Colo. Common Cause, Denver, 1975-76; mem. U.S. Audi Owners Adv. Coun., 1989—. With USAF, 1964-68. Mem. Am. Mgmt. Assn., Data Processing Mgmt. Assn. (bd. dirs., vice chmn. 1976-78, seminar leader 1974-82). Democrat. Mem. Ch. Christ. Office: Nat Systems & Rsch Co 5475 Mark Dabling Blvd #200 Colorado Springs CO 80918

HARMON, JACK CLIFFORD, financial planning executive; b. Nashville, July 4, 1937; s. Buford James and Loraine (Poitevint) H.; m. Rebecca Osborne Harwell, Aug. 25, 1961; children: Jack II, Bradley. BA in Econs., Ga. State U., 1971. Cert. fin. planner. Electronic specialist, computer cons. various firms, Atlanta, 1959-74; fin. planner Fin. Services Corp., Atlanta, 1974-75; sr. v.p. Consol. Planning Corp., Atlanta, 1975—. Chmn. subcom. Sec. State's Select Com. on Regulation of Investment Advisors, Atlanta, 1986—. Mem. Ga. Soc. Inst. Cert. Fin. Planners (founding pres. 1984), Internat. Assn. Fin. Planning (nat. bd. dirs. 1985—, pres. Ga. chpt. 1984-85), Inst. Cert. Fin. Planners, Registry Fin. Planning Practitioners. Republican. Lodge: Kiwanis. Home: 3481 Sheridan Chase Marietta GA 30067 Office: Consol Planning Corp 400 Colony Sq Suite 525 Atlanta GA 30061

HARMON, JAMES ALLEN, investment banker; b. N.Y.C., Oct. 12, 1935; s. Bert and Belle (Kirschner) H.; m. Jane Elizabeth Theaman, Aug. 11, 1957; children—Deborah Lynn, Douglas Lee, Jennifer Ann. B.A., Brown U., 1957; M.B.A., Wharton Grad. Sch., U. Pa., 1959. With N.Y. Hanseatic Corp., N.Y.C., 1959-74, sr. v.p., 1969-74; gen. partner Wertheim & Co., Inc., N.Y.C., 1975—, vice chmn., 1980-86, chmn., 1987—, chief exec. officer, 1988—; bd. dirs. Schroders plc, London, Augat, Inc., Mansfield, Mass., Lumex, Inc., Bay Shore, L.I., River Bank Am., N.Y.C., Electra Candover, London, Questar Corp., Salt Lake City; mem. adv. com. on internat. capital markets N.Y. Stock Exchange; non-exec. chmn. of bd. Ames Dept. Stores, Inc., Rocky Hill, Conn. Trustee Brown U.; bd. dirs. Alliance for the Arts; mem. adv. bd. Peggy Guggenheim Collection. Home: 43 Kettle Creek Rd Weston CT 06883 Office: Wertheim Schroder & Co Inc 787 7th Ave New York NY 10019

HARMON, LEE ESTABROOK, manufacturing company executive; b. Milo, Maine, Jan. 2, 1952; s. Cecil F. and Virginia (Estabrook) H.; m. Mary E. Geissler, July 7, 1974; children: Matthew, Patrick, Elizabeth. BS in Acctg., Husson Coll., 1974. Acct. FMC Corp., Rockland, Maine, 1978-80, cost acct., 1981-82, cost acctg. supr., 1982-83, gen. acctg. supr., 1984; sr. internal auditor FMC Corp., Chgo., 1984-87; controller fluid control FMC Corp., Stephenville, Tex., 1987—. Treas. troop 18 Boy Scouts Am., Stephenville, 1987—. Served with U.S. Army, 1974-78. Mem. Inst. Internal Auditors. Roman Catholic. Home: 910 Lydia St Stephenville TX 76401 Office: FMC-Fluid Control Washington St Stephenville TX 76401

HARMON, ROBERT LEE, corporate executive; b. St. Louis, Oct. 31, 1926; s. Jess G. and Lela E. H.; m. Carolyn Metzger, June 9, 1951; children: Robert Lee, Barbara C., Nancy K., Celia A., Julia G., Melinda M. B.S., B.A., Washington U., St. Louis, 1949. Exec. asst. to sales mgr. IBM, N.Y.C., 1949-60; br. mgr. IBM, Chgo., 1960; gen. mgr. McDonnell Automation Ctr., St. Louis, 1960-66; v.p., gen. mgr. McDonnell Automation Co., St. Louis, 1966-70; exec. v.p. comml. McDonnell Douglas Automation Co., St. Louis, 1970-82; corp. v.p. civic affairs. McDonnell Douglas Corp., St. Louis, 1982-88, cons., 1988—; dir. Bank Bldg. Corp.; mem. adv. bd. Boatmen's Bank St. Louis County. Pres. Mo. Bapt. Hosp. Pacesetters, 1973-75; mem. exec. com. bd. trustees Mo. Bapt. Hosp., St. Louis, 1976—, chmn. long range planning com., 1983—; bd. dirs. St. Louis Regional Commerce and Growth Assn., 1983-85, 87-88; moderator Delmar Bapt. Ch., St. Louis, 1969-72, 76-78, mem. exec. council, 1969—, endowment fund dir., 1976—, pres. bd. trustees, 1979—, former deacon, Sunday sch. tchr.; chmn. New Frontiers dist. Boy Scouts Am., 1976-78, 80; bd. chmn.,exec. com. bd. dirs. Jr. Achievement Miss. Valley, Inc.; bd. dirs. Japan Am. Soc., St. Louis; vice chmn. Urban League Met. St. Louis; v.p. exec. com., vice chmn. corp. ptnrs. program Bus. Sch., past mem. bd. trustees Washington U.; bd. dirs. Veiled Prophet Found. past pres. Century Club, Washington U., 1983-85; exec. service Corps. St. Louis Dir. Served as lt. (j.g.) U.S. Mcht. Marines, 1944-47. Mem. Omicron Delta Kappa, Delta Sigma Pi, Beta Gamma Sigma. Club: St. Louis Beta Theta Pi (past pres.). Home: 3 Portland St Saint Louis MO 63131

HARNE, ELEANOR ELIZABETH, restaurateur; b. North Charleroi, Pa., Apr. 2, 1941; d. August Leonard Nicolaus and Marguerite Elizabeth (Headley) Mihalic; m. Carl Francis Rattay (div. 1974); 1 child, Kimberly Renee; m. Carroll Eugene Harne, July 26, 1976. Student bus. sch., Pa., 1959. Teller Household Fin. Corp., Hyattsville, Md., 1966-67; asst. v.p., br. mgr. Md. Fed. Savs. & Loan Assn., Bethesda, 1969-82; co-owner Misty Harbor Seafood Restaurant, Rockville, Md., 1981—. Sponsor Ronald Reagan Congl. Victory Fund, Washington, 1984-87. Mem. Montgomery County Restaurant Assn. Republican. Lutheran. Office: Misty Harbor 1776 E Jefferson St Rockville MD 20852

HARNEDY, EDMUND RICHARD, insurance executive; b. N.Y.C., June 11, 1930; s. Richard Joseph and Margaret (McSweeney) H.; m. Joan Catherine Holland, Dec. 29, 1962; children: Richard, Julia. B.S., U. Ill., 1952; J.D., Fordham U., 1957; LL.M., NYU, 1961. Bar: N.Y. 1957. Atty., New York Life Ins. Co., N.Y.C., 1957-63; asst. counsel New York Life Ins. Co., 1963-66, asso. counsel, 1966-69, asst. gen. counsel, 1969-72, 2d v.p., 1972-73, sec., 1973-82, v.p., sec., 1982—. Served to 1st lt. AUS, 1952-54. Mem. ABA, Am. Soc. Corp. Secs. Home: 611 Knollwood Rd White Plains NY 10603 Office: NY Life Ins Co 51 Madison Ave New York NY 10010

HARNEY, KENNETH ROBERT, editor, columnist; b. Jersey City, Mar. 25, 1944; s. Carroll John and Agnes Theresa (Flanagan) H.; m. Lynne Andrea Leon, Aug. 26, 1967; children: Alexandra Erin, Brendan Leon, Timothy Andrew. AB cum laude, Princeton U., 1966; postgrad. (grad. fellow), U. Pa., 1966-67. Program analyst U.S. Office Econ. Opportunity, 1970-72; exec. editor, ptnr. The Housing & Devel. Reporter, Washington, 1972-82; columnist Washington Post, 1974—; exec. dir. Inst. Profl. & Exec. Devel., Inc., Washington, 1977—; pres. Harney Corp., Bethesda, Md., 1980—; exec. dir. Nat. Real Estate Devel. Ctr., 1983—; pres. Rehab. Investor Corp., 1983—. Author: Beating Inflation with Real Estate, 1979, Guide to Federal Housing Programs, 1982. Councilman Village of Chevy Chase, Sect. 3, Chevy Chase, Md., 1987—. Recipient First prize Nat. Journalism Achievement Competition Nat. Assn. Realtors, 1979, Golden Hammer award Nat. Assn. Home Builders, 1980. Mem. Nat. Assn. Real Estate Editors. Republican. Clubs: Princeton N.Y.C.; Eastern Shore Yacht and Country (Va.). Home: 3801 Bradley Ln Chevy Chase MD 20815 Office: Rehab Investor Corp 6900 Wisconsin Ave Ste 702 Chevy Chase MD 20815

HAROIAN, GARY ELIOT, computer company executive; b. Boston, Sept. 28, 1951; s. Yegazar and Ruth A. (Bosnian) H.; m. Mary Lou Estlinbaum, June 5, 1982. BBA in Acctg., BA in Econs. magna cum laude, U. Mass., 1975. CPA, Mass. Mem. audit sr. staff Laventhol and Horwath, Boston, 1976-78; mem. audit sr. staff Arthur Anderson and Co., Boston, 1978-81, audit mgr., 1981-83; corp. controller Stratus Computer Inc., Marlboro, Mass., 1983-85, chief fin. officer, 1985—. Fellow Mass. Soc. CPAs; mem. fin. Execs. Am., Boston Bus. Assocs., Beta Alpha Psi. Office: Stratus Computer Inc 55 Fairbanks Blvd Marlborough MA 01752

HAROLD, MARK JOSEPH, mechanical engineer; b. Pitts., July 15, 1957; s. Robert Edward and Jeanne Elizabeth (Joyce) H.; m. Kathleen Mary Bonner, July 5, 1987. BCE, Pa. State U., 1979; postgrad., U. Balt., 1985—. Registered profl. engr., Pa. Engr. Boeing Mil. Aircraft Corp., Wichita, Kans., 1979-82, Grumman Flxible Corp., Delaware, Ohio, 1982-83; sr. engr. Martin Marietta Aero and Naval Systems, Balt., 1983—. Mem. Perry Hall Homeowners' Assn., Balt., 1987—. Mem. Soc. Automotive Engrs., Sigma Iota Epsilon. Republican. Roman Catholic. Club: Young Adults. Home: 102 Bourbon Ct Baltimore MD 21234 Office: Martin Marietta Aero & Naval Co 103 Chesapeake Park Pla Baltimore MD 21220

HARP, ROBERT GEORGE, JR., hospitality corporation executive; b. Balt., May 28, 1959; s. Robert George and Delores (Creutzer) H.; m. Jill Stephenson, June 4, 1983; 1 child, Preston Robert. BA in Econs., Wheaton Coll., 1980, MA in Communications with high honors, 1981; ThM, Dallas Theol. Sem., 1985. Lic. real estate broker. Real estate broker The Swearingen Co., Dallas, 1986-87; dir. of devel., v.p. of real estate Global Hospitality Corp., San Diego, 1987—. Contbr. book reviews to jours. in field. Precinct capt. San Diego Count Rep. Com. Named one of Outstanding Young Men of Am., 1985. Mem. Nat. Assn. Realtors, Realtors Nat. Mktg. Inst., Calif. Assn. Realtors, San Diego Bd. of Realtors (edn. com., govt. and polit. affairs com.), Cert. Comml. Investment Mem. (San Diego chpt.). Republican. Baptist.

HARPE, GARY FRANCIS, automotive corporation executive; b. Muskegon, Mich., Dec. 2, 1953; s. Bernard Joseph and Joann (Helman) H.; m. Anne Victoria Surmann, Mar. 9, 1985; children: Emily Elizabeth, Ben Surmann Harpe. BA in Econs. and Polit. Sci., Kalamazoo (Mich.) Coll., 1976; MBA in Bus. Econs. and Mktg., Wayne State U., 1984. From analyst accountable documents to office mgr., sales Rouge Steel-Ford Motor, Dearborn, Mich., 1976-84, mgr. inside sales and services, 1984-85, dir. sales and mktg., 1985—. Home: 22121 Military Dearborn MI 48124 Office: Rouge Steel Ford Motor 3001 Miller Rd Dearborn MI 48121

HARPER, ADRIANE STEWART, broker; b. Charleston, W.Va., May 9. BA in Primary Edn., Nat. Coll. Edn., 1979. Coder, interviewer Mkt. Research, Chgo., 1972-74, project research, 1977-84; agt. Fin. Services, Chgo., 1985-86, v.p., 1986—; jewelry and cosmetics salesperson, Chgo., 1986—; tchr. Chgo. Pub. Schs. Vol. solicitor La Rabida Children's Hosp., Chgo., 1965; beauty cons. Girls Scout Troop, Chgo., 1984. Recipient Top Seller award, Mary Kay Cosmetics, Chgo., 1984; 1st pl. campaign winner Equitable Ins. Agy., 1985, named to agy. honor roll, 1985. Mem. Nat. Assn. Women Bus. Owners, Nat. Assn. Life Underwriters.

HARPER, CHARLES MICHEL, food company executive; b. Lansing, Mich., Sept. 26, 1927; s. Charles Frost and Alma (Michel) H.; m. Joan Frances Bruggema, June 24, 1950; children: Kathleen Harper Wenngatz, Carolyn Harper, Charles Michel, Elizabeth Harper Murphy. BS in Mech. Engring, Purdue U., 1949; MBA, U. Chgo., 1950. Supr. methods engring. Oldsmobile div. Gen. Motors Corp., Detroit, 1950-54; indsl. engr. Pillsbury Co., Mpls., 1954-55; dir. indsl. engring. Pillsbury Co., 1955-60, dir. engring., 1961-66, v.p. research, devel. and new products, 1965-70, group v.p.-poultry, food service and venture businesses, 1970-74; exec. v.p., chief operating officer, dir. ConAgra Inc., Omaha, 1974-76; pres., chief exec. officer ConAgra Inc., 1976-81, chmn. bd., chief exec. officer, 1981—; bd. dirs. Norwest Corp., Valmont Industries, Inc., Peter Kiewit Sons', Inc., Burlington No., Inc.; exec. com. Nat. Commn. on Agrl. Trade and Export Policy, 1984-86. Mem. council Village of Excelsior (Minn.), 1965-70, mayor, 1974; trustee Bishop Clarkson Meml. Hosp.; hon. chmn. Urban League Nebr. Membership Campaign, 1987; bd. dirs. Creighton U., Joslyn Mus.; trustee Com. for Econ. Devel., Washington; pres. Mid Am. Council Boy Scouts Am., 1983-84. Served with AUS, 1946-48. Mem. U.S. C. of C. (bd. dirs., chmn. Food and Agriculture com.), Omaha C. of C. (chmn. 1979), Grocery Mfrs. Am. (bd. dirs. 1985—), Bus. Roundtable, Ak-Sar-Ben (gov.), U. Nebr.-Lincoln Coll. Bus. Admin. Alumni Assn. (hon. life), Beta Theta Pi. Office: ConAgra Inc One Central Park Pla Omaha NE 68102

HARPER, DONALD JACK, manufacturing company executive; b. Chgo., Mar. 10, 1928; s. John L. and Mabel A. (Best) H.; m. Barbara Lighthall, Apr. 14, 1951; children: Laura, Steven, Gregory, Peter. BS in Bus. and Mktg., U. Ill., 1950. Salesman, John I. Paulding Co., 1950-52; with Emerson Electric Co., 1952-72, exec. v.p., then pres. builder products div., 1965-69, pres. Fisher Radio div., 1970-72; with Insilco Corp., Meriden, Conn., 1973—; sr. v.p. Insilco Corp., Meriden, 1978-80, pres., 1980—, chmn. and chief exec. officer, 1986-89, vice chmn., 1989—; chmn. bd., chief exec. officer Internat. Silver Co., Meriden, 1974-77; bd. dir. Hartford Nat. Bank, Rogers Corp. Bd. dirs. Jr. Achievement S. Cen. Conn., 1978-80, Conn. Bus. and Industries Assn., 1981; trustee Conn. Ednl. Telecommunications Corp., 1983—. With AUS, 1945-47. Mem. Electronics Industry Assn. (chmn. audio div. 1972), Home Ventilating Inst. (pres. 1965), Jewelry Industry Coun. (bd. dir. 1977-80), Nat. Assn. Home Builders (dir. 1965-69), Chi Phi. Office: Insilco Corp 1000 Research Pkwy Meriden CT 06450

HARPER, EDWIN LELAND, food processing executive, former government official; b. Belleville, Ill., Nov. 13, 1941; s. Horace Edwin and Evelyn Ruth (Wright) H.; m. Lucy Davis, Aug. 21, 1965; children: Elizabeth Allen, Peter Edwin. B.A. with honors, Principia Coll., 1963; Ph.D., U. Va., 1968. Guest scholar Brookings Instn., Washington, 1965-66; lectr. Rutgers U., 1966-68; staff Bur. of Budget, Washington, 1968-69; sr. cons. Arthur D. Little, Inc., Washington, 1969; spl. asst. to pres. of U.S. 1969-72; asst. dir. Domestic Council, Washington, 1970-72; v.p. INA Corp. (now CIGNA), Phila., 1973-74; pres., chief exec. officer Air Balance, Inc., Chgo., 1975; sr. v.p. strategic planning, chief adminstrv. officer Certain Teed Corp., 1976-78; v.p. Emerson Electric Co., St. Louis, 1978-81; dep. dir. Office of Mgmt. and Budget; asst. to pres. of U.S. Washington, 1981-82, 82-83; chmn. Pres.'s Council on Integrity and Efficiency in Govt., 1982-83, Fed. Property Rev. Bd., 1982-83; dir., exec. v.p. Dallas Corp. (formerly Overhead Door Corp.), 1983-86; sr. v.p., chief fin. officer Campbell Soup Co., Camden, N.J., 1986—; dep. exec. dir. platform com. Republican Conv., 1976; mem. Pres.'s Commn. on Personnel Interchange, Washington, 1976-79, 81-83, Pres.'s Commn. on Indsl. Competitiveness, 1983-86, Pres.' Commn. Exec., Legis. and Judicial Salaries, 1987; bd. dirs. Phila. Suburban Corp., DNA Plant Tech. Contbr. articles to profl. jours. Mem. nat. adv. bd. Goodwill Industries, 1977-81; bd. dirs. Principia Coll., Valley Forge Mil. Acad. Ford Found. grantee, 1965; Recipient Louis Brownlow award, 1969, Exec. Govt. award OICs of Am., 1982, Person of Yr. award Washington chpt. Inst. Internal Auditors, 1982, Spl. Commendation Assn. Fed. Investigators, 1983. Mem. Nat. Acad. Pub. Adminstrn., Fin. Execs. Inst., U.S. C. of C. (econ. policy com.), Union League, Raven Club, Oakwood Club, Phila. Country Club, Omicron Delta Kappa. Republican. Office: Campbell Soup Co Campbell Pl Camden NJ 08103

HARPER, HERBERT CALDWELL, office products distributor, business owner; b. Royston, Ga., Dec. 10, 1912; s. John Frank and Annie (Barnes) H.; m. Elizabeth Legare Stone, Aug. 4, 1934; 1 child, Antony Caldwell. Grad. high sch., Anderson, S.C., 1930. Asst. mgr. Harper Brothers, Inc., Greenville, S.C., 1930-35, mgr., 1935-40, exec. v.p., 1940-50, pres., 1950-80, chmn. bd., 1980-89; pres., chmn. bd. Latone, Inc., Greenville, 1978-89. Vice chmn. The Greenville County Found., 1968; chmn., 1970; trustee Presbyn. Coll., Clinton, S.C., adv. bd. Furman U., Greenville; trustee Greenville County Library Found., 1965, vice chmn., 1966-67, chmn., 1967-68. Mem. Nat. Office Products Assn. (bd. dirs. 1961—, pres. 1961-62, chmn. 1962-63), Greater Greenville C. of C. (v.p. 1956). Republican. Presbyterian. Clubs: Buttonhold Club (pres. 1957), Am. Bus. (pres. 1947-48) (Greenville). Lodge: Rotary (local pres. 1966-67). Home: 11 McDaniel Ct Greenville SC 29605 Office: Harper Brothers Inc 651 S Main St PO Box 9297 Greenville SC 29604

HARPER, JAMES WELDON, III, financial consultant; b. Frederick, Md., Mar. 3, 1937; s. James Weldon, Jr. and Mildred Mary (Conaway) H.; student Duke U. Coll. rep. Time, Inc., 1955-59; jr. exec. trainee Merrill Lynch Pierce Fenner and Smith, N.Y.C., 1959-60; v.p. fin. planning Haight and Co. Inc., Washington, 1961-72; pres. fin. cons. Weldon Enterprises Ltd., Washington, 1972—; pres. U.S. Energy Conservation Service, Inc.; cons. Aries Corp.; nat. coordinator Nat. Planned Giving Assocs., Inc., 1983—; dir. Nat. Real Estate Trust for Health Care, Inc. Served with U.S. Army, 1959. Named Nat. Planned Giving Assocs. Inc. Methodist. Author three manuals on consulting instrumental in the formation of. Office: Weldon Enterprises Ltd PO Box 1061 Main Station Washington DC 20013

HARPER, MICHAEL DENNIS, chemical company executive; b. Denver, Aug. 6, 1947; s. George Everett and Irene Elizabeth (Holmes) H.; m. Barbara Callaway, June 28, 1975; children: Lauren, Brian. BS in Engring., Duke U., 1969; MBA, Cornell U., 1972. Asst. sales engr. Westinghouse Electric Corp., Dayton, Ohio, 1969-70; asst. to pres. Amax Carbon Products Div., Chgo., 1972-74; mgr. spl. products Internat. Minerals and Chems. Corp., Northbrook, Ill., 1974-77, sales mgr., 1977-79, dir. corp. devel., 1979-81, product mgr., 1981-82; asst. to v.p. fin. Velsicol Chem. Corp., Chgo., 1982-85; treas. Velsicol Chem. Corp., Rosemont, Ill., 1985—. Office: Velsicol Chem Corp 5600 N River Rd Rosemont IL 60018

HARPER, W(ALTER) JOSEPH, financial consultant; b. Columbus, Ohio, Apr. 6, 1947; s. J. Joseph and Patricia A. (Whetzle) H.; m. J. Lynn Rutherford, Aug. 1, 1970; children: Tracy, Kelly, Brett. BS in Edn., Ohio State U., 1970. Cert. fin. planner. Tchr., coach Lake Wales (Fla.) Schs., 1970-71, Westerville (Ohio) Pub. Schs., 1971-74; securities salesman, fin. planner Investors Diversified Services, Columbus, 1974-83; fin. planner Harper Assocs., Columbus, 1983—. Mem. Internat. Assn. Fin. Planning, Inst. Cert. Fin. Planners. Republican. Clubs: Scioto Country, Worthington Hills Country, Columbus Athletic. Lodge: Rotary. Home: 4322 Stratton Rd Columbus OH 43220

HARRELD, JAMES BRUCE, food company executive; b. Gallipolis, Ohio, Dec. 12, 1950; s. James Baldwin and Ann Elizabeth (Lascu) H.; m. Mary E. Gillilan; children—Sara Elisabeth, Kelly Lynn, James Christopher. B.S., Purdue U., 1972; M.B.A., Harvard U., 1975. Asst. to exec. sec. Sigma Chi, Evanston, Ill., 1972-73; asst. to pres. Epsilon Data Mgmt., Boston, 1973-74; v.p., dir. Boston Cons. Group, Boston, Munich, Chgo., 1975-82; v.p. Dart & Kraft, Northbrook, Ill., 1982-84; sr. v.p. Kraft, Inc., Glenview, Ill., 1984-88, sr. v.p., chief info. officer, 1988-89; sr. v.p., chief info. officer Kraft Gen. Foods, Glenview, 1989—. Co-author: Survival Manual, 1973. Trustee Westminster Coll. Recipient Balfour Province award Sigma Chi, 1972. Mem. Tau Beta Pi, Alpha Pi Mu. Republican. Presbyterian. Clubs: Harvard (Boston); Barrington Hills Country (Ill.); Va. Hot Springs. Office: Kraft Gen Foods Kraft Ct Glenview IL 60025

HARRELL, HENRY HOWZE, tobacco company executive; b. Richmond, Va., Sept. 18, 1939; s. Theron Rice and Susan Howze (Haskell) H.; m. Jean Covington Camp, Feb. 7, 1970; children—Susan Hampton, Shelby Madison. A.B., Washington and Lee U. V.p. Universal Leaf Tobacco Co., Inc., Richmond, 1974-81, sr. v.p., 1981-82, exec. v.p., 1982-86, pres., 1986-88, pres., chief exec. officer, 1988—; also dir. Universal Leaf Tobacco Co., Inc. (now Universal Corp), Richmond; dir. Jefferson Bankshares Inc., Charlottesville, Va., Lawyers Title Ins. Co., Richmond. Mem. Forum Club, Commonwealth Club, Phi Beta Kappa, Omicron Delta Kappa. Republican. Episcopalian. Clubs: Country of Va., Deep Run Hunt (bd. dirs. 1981-83).

HARRELL, JOHN ELBERT, banker; b. Montgomery, Ala., July 4, 1955; s. Walter Elbert, Jr. and Joyce Lamar (Moncrier) H.; m. Ann Compton, Dec. 10, 1977; children: Margaret Ann, James Wesley. BS in Econs., Auburn U., 1977; postgrad., Stonier Grad. Sch. Banking. Dir. performance Louann, Inc., Clarkesville, Ga., 1980-82; loan officer Cen. Bank of the South, Montgomery, 1983-85; asst. v.p., br. mgr., constrn. loan officer Southtrust Bank, Montgomery, 1985-87; v.p., head real estate loans AmSouth Bank Fla., 1987—. Coach YMCA youth football; bd. dirs. Easter Seal Rehab. Ctr., Montgomery, 1987. Mem. Fla. Bankers Assn. (real estate and tax coms. 1987—), Homebuilders Assn., Bd. Realtors, Mtg. Bankers Assn., Kiwanis. Baptist. Office: AmSouth Bank Fla 100 Main St Destin FL 32541

HARRELL, LINDA DARLYN, accountant; b. Portsmouth, Va., Mar. 29, 1949; d. John Mota Eichholtz II and Hazel Ida (Heimer); divorced; children: James Michael, Stephanie Michelle. BBA, U. Tex., San Antonio, 1985. CPA, Tex. Controller Liberto Splty. Co., San Antonio, 1975-76; acctg. assoc. Hardin Wolff & Bradly, San Antonio, 1976-77; controller Nicholas & Barrera, Inc., San Antonio, 1977-81; sr. bus. assoc. Deloitte Haskins and Sells, San Antonio, 1981-84; staff tax acct. Alexander Grant & Co., San Antonio, 1984; banking service supr. United Services Automobile Assn., San Antonio, 1985-87; supervising sr. tax acct. Touche, Ross & Co., N.Y.C., 1987—; tax cons. Oil and Gas Industries, San Antonio, 1984-85. Acct., panel mem. United Way, San Antonio, 1985—; active with March of Dimes and Youth Soccer Assn., San Antonio. Mem. Nat. Assn. Accts., Am. Inst. CPA's, Tex. Soc. CPA's, Am. Soc. Women Accts., Alliance for Women's Appointments, Beta Gamma Sigma, Alpha Chi. Lutheran. Home: 35 Linden Ln Farmingville NY 11738-1134 Office: Touche Ross & Co 1633 Broadway 7th Fl New York NY 10019

HARRELL, MAXWELL RICHARD, electric power industry executive; b. Marion, Ind., June 23, 1925; s. Maxwell Robert and Mary Gwendolyn (Kelsey) H.; m. Mary Ethel Nicholls, June 3, 1945; children: Susan Patrice Harrell Griffey, Karen Lee Harrell Shumway, Elizabeth Ann Harrell Young. BS in Elec. Engring., Purdue U., 1950; postgrad., Ball State U., 1965, U. Mich., 1966, 76. Registered profl. engr., Ind. Power engr. Ind. & Mich. Electric Co., Marion, 1950-52; indsl. sales engr. Ind. & Mich. Electric Co., Elwood, Ind., 1952-59, div. sr. engr., 1959-60; supr. comml. and indsl. sales Ind. & Mich. Electric Co., Muncie, Ind., 1960-65; area mgr. Ind. & Mich. Electric Co., Hartford City, Ind., 1965-72; dir. area devel. Ind. & Mich. Electric Co., Ft. Wayne, Ind., 1972-74, coordinator pub. svc. commn., 1974-76, dir. comml. and indsl. sales, 1976-80; div. mgr. Ind. & Mich. Electric Co., Marion, 1980—. V.p., bd. dirs. Grant County Econ. Growth Coun., 1981-86; pres. Marion Econ. Devel. Commn., 1982-88, Marion Easter Pageant Bd., 1986-87; pres. bd. dirs. Grant County Community Found., 1984-86, Marion Gen. Hosp., 1987—. With USN, 1943-46. Mem. Marion-Grant County C. of C. (chmn. bd. dirs. 1984, Chmn.'s award 1988), Marion Aero Club (pres. 1985). Republican. Methodist. Home: 1007 Euclid Ave Marion IN 46952 Office: Ind & Mich Power Co 100 S Washington St PO Box 719 Marion IN 46952

HARRELL, SAMUEL MACY, grain company executive; b. Indpls., Jan. 4, 1931; s. Samuel Runnels and Mary (Evans) H.; m. Sally Bowers, Sept. 2, 1958; children: Samuel D., Holly Evans, Kevin Bowers, Karen Susan, Donald Runnels, Kenneth Macy. B.S. in Econs., Wharton Sch., U. Pa., 1953. Pres., chmn. bd., chief exec. officer, chmn., exec. com. Early & Daniel Industries, Cin., 1971—; chmn. bd., chmn. ecec. com. Early & Daniel Co., Cin., 1971—; chmn. bd., chief exec. officer, chmn. exec. com. Tidewater Grain Co., Phila., 1971—; dir. Wainwright Bank & Trust Co., Wainright Abstract Co., Nat. Grain Trade Council, U.S. Feed Grains Council; mem. Chgo. bd. Trade. Served with AUS, 1953-55. Mem. Young Pres.'s Orgn., U. Pa. Alumni Assn. (past pres.), Terminal Elevator Grain Mchts. Assn. (dir.), Millers Nat. Fedn. (dir.), Assn. Operative Millers, Am. Soc. Bakery Engrs., Am. Fin. Assn., Council on Fgn. Relations, Fin. Exec. Inst., N.Am. Grain Export Assn. (dir.), Mpls. Grain Exchange, St. Louis Mchts. Grain Exchange, Buffalo Corn Exchange, Delta Tau Delta (Past prs. Ind. alumni). Presbyterian. Clubs: Columbia, Indpls. Athletic, Woodstock, Traders Point Hunt, Dramatic, Players, Lambs (Indpls.); Racquet (Phila.); University (Washington and N.Y.C.). Lodges: Masons, Rotary. Home: 5858 Sunset Ln Indianapolis IN 46208 Office: Early & Daniel Industries Inc 733 S Missouri St Indianapolis IN 46225 also: Early & Daniel Industries 733 S Missouri St Indianapolis IN 46225

HARRIGAN, KENNETH WILLIAM J., automotive products company executive; b. Chatham, Ont., Can., Sept. 27, 1927; s. Charles A. and Olga Jean (Wallace) H.; m. Margaret Jean Macpherson, June 18, 1955; children: Tara Lynne Harrigan Tomlinson, Stephen Charles. BA with honors, U. Western Ont., 1951. With Ford Motor Co. Can. Ltd., Oakville, Ont., 1951—, regional mgr. Cen. Region, 1965-68, gen. sales mgr., 1968-71; dir. sales and mktg. Ford Asia Pacific Inc., Australia, 1971-73; group dir. So. Europe Ford Europe, Inc., 1973-76, v.p. truck sales and mktg., 1976-78; v.p., gen. mgr. sales Ford Motor Co. Can. Ltd., Oakville, Ont., 1978-81, pres., 1981—, chief exec. officer, 1982—; mem. policy com. Bus. Council on Nat. Issues, Govt. Sectoral Adv. Group on Internat. Trade, 1986-88; mem. Ont. Bus. Adv. Council; bd. dirs. Ford Motor Co., New Zealand, Ltd., New Holland of Can. Ltd., Dome Consortium Investments Inc., London Life Ins. Co., Toronto Ontario Olympic Com. Adv. Bd., Ford Credit Can. Ltd.; mem. Nat. Adv. Council World Energy Conf.; trustee Royal Ontario Mus. Bd. govs. Appleby Coll., Oakville; adv. com. U. Western Ont. Sch. Bus. Adminstrn; mem. adv. bd. Provincial Mcpl. Secretariat for 1988 Toronto Summit. Mem. Conf. Bd. Can. (bd. dirs.), Inst. Corp. Dirs. in Can., Toronto Bd. Trade, Can. C. of C., Motor Vehicle Mfrs. Assn. (bd. dirs.), Ontario Govt. Adv. Com. on Automotive Industry, FTA Select Automotive Panel. Clubs: Mississauga (Ont.) Golf and Country; Canadian; Empire. Office: Ford Motor Co/Can Ltd, Canadian Rd Box 2000, Oakville, ON Canada L6J 5E4

HARRIMAN, MALCOLM BRUCE, residential center executive, healthcare marketing consultant; b. Sandusky, Ohio, Feb. 25, 1950; s. Robert Byron and Catherine (Nicholson) H.; m. Suzan Gwen Alexander, June 27, 1980 (div. Dec. 21, 1985); 1 child, Sasha Bryn; m. Alysa Ellen Gelband, Apr. 19, 1986; 1 child, Sarah Ashley. BA, Antioch Coll., 1976; MA, U. Md., 1981. Child care worker Ft. Wayne (Ind.) Children's Home, 1971-72; adolescent program supr. Taylor Manor Hosp., Ellicott City, Md., 1972-76; program coordinator child and adolescent services Horizon Hosp, Clearwater, Fla., 1981-82, mktg. specialist, 1983-86; v.p., prin. ptnr. Am. Residential Ctrs., Tampa, Fla., 1986—, pres., 1988—; exec. dir. Tampa Bay Acad., Riverview, Fla., 1988—; assoc. Dept. Psychiatry U. S.Fla. Med. Sch., Tampa, 1980-81; mem. severely emotionally disturbed network project adv. council HRS Dist. V, Clearwater, 1984-86, early childhood council, Pinellas County, Fla., 1985-86. Gubernatorial appointee Project Freeway Task Force, HRS Dist. V, Fla., 1985-86, Fla. Alliance for the Mentally Ill. Mem. Council Exceptional Children, Fla. Alcohol and Drug Abuse Assn., Fla. C. of C. (edn. com., del. youth services adv. council), Sales and Mktg. Execs. of Tampa. Republican. Presbyterian. Office: Tampa Bay Acad 12012 Boyette Rd Riverview FL 33569

HARRINGTON, GLENN LEWIS, insurance company executive; b. Fitchburg, Mass., Dec. 18, 1942; s. Lewis Lowe and Eleanor Frances (Mansfield) H.; m. Marcia Ann Browning, Sept. 3, 1971. Student, Suffolk U.,

1963-64, Gordon Coll., 1960-63. Underwriter Hartford Life Ins. Co., Boston, 1964-66; rep. Dentsply Internat., York, Pa., 1966-70; v.p. mktg. Merrill Lynch-Family Life Ins. Cos., Seattle, 1971—; owner Fifth Ave. Books, Seattle, 1979—; pres. Booksellers Internat., Seattle, 1971—. Mem. Am. Booksellers Assn., Greater Seattle C. of C., University (Boston), Coll. (Seattle). Home: PO Box 21189 Seattle WA 98111 Office: Merrill Lynch-Family Life Ins Co 1200 Sixth Ave Seattle WA 98101

HARRINGTON, HERBERT HARRINGTON, accountant; b. Meadville, Pa., Sept. 19, 1946; s. Herbert H. and Sara R. (Rogers) H. Student, Kent U., 1964-69; BS, Memphis State U., 1975; MS in Criminal Justice, Dyersburg State U., 1977. Transp. dir. West Tenn. Easter Seal Soc., 1972-75; compt. So. Trucking, Inc., 1976-77; acct. Cen. So., Inc., 1978-79; compt. Wonder div. ITT Baking Corp., 1980-84; driver N. Fla. Transport, 1985-86; fin. con. Computa-Tax, Inc., 1986—; cons., Covington, Tenn., 1973—. Author 3 textbooks on acctg. procedures and practice. Served with USN, 1963-67. Mem. Covington C. of C. Republican. Episcopalian. Lodges: Lions, Good Fellows, Optimists, Rotary. Home and Office: PO Box 402 Covington TN 38019

HARRINGTON, JESSE MOYE, III, restaurant chain executive; b. Washington, N.C., Sept. 11, 1940; s. Jesse Moye Jr. and Lila Ruth (Bailey) H.; m. Carol Ann Adams, Jan. 31, 1963; children: Paige, Kim, Mary Simmons. BBA, U. N.C., 1963, cert. exec. program, 1984. Staff acct. A.M. Pullen & Co., Greensboro, N.C., 1963-68; dir. acctg. Hardee's Food Systems, Inc., Rocky Mount, N.C., 1968-69, treas., 1969-74, v.p., treas., 1974-85, sr. v.p., treas., 1985—. With N.C. N.G., 1963-69. Mem. Am. Inst. CPA's, Fin. Execs. Inst., N.C. Assn. CPA's., Northgreen Country Club (Rocky Mount) (chmn. 1984-86). Republican. Home: 3705 Sheffield Dr Rocky Mount NC 27803 Office: Hardees Food Systems Inc 1233 Hardees Blvd Rocky Mount NC 27804-2815

HARRINGTON, JOSEPH FRANCIS, educational company executive, educator; b. Boston, Oct. 24, 1938; s. Joseph Francis and Mary Virginia (Lynch) H.; m. Brenda Marie Crowley, Sept. 3, 1966; children: Megan Marie, Christopher Joseph John. BS, Boston Coll., 1960; MA, Georgetown U., 1963, PhD, 1971. Instr. Framingham (Mass.) State Coll., 1966-68, asst. prof., 1968-70, assoc. prof., 1970-72, prof., 1972—, bd. chmn. dept. history, 1972-82; pres. Learning, Inc., Stoughton, 1979—, also bd. dirs.; treas., trustee East European Rsch. Ctr.; pres. MA/AIP, 1987—. Author: Masters of War, Makers of Peace, 1985, Powers, Pawns and Parleys, 1978; contrbr. articles to various jours. Mem. Stoughton, Mass. Sch. Com., 1971-77, 82-87. With U.S. Army, 1962-65. Tchg. fellow Georgetown U., Washington, 1960-62, 65-66, hon. fellow Kennedy Presdl. Libr. 1986—. Mem. Mass. Assn. for Advancement of Individual Potential (bd. dirs., pres. 1988—), Nat. Assn. Creative Children & Adults (bd. dirs. 1985—). Roman Catholic. Home: 119 Holmes Ave Stoughton MA 02072 Office: Framingham State Coll State St Framingham MA 01701

HARRINGTON, MARGUERITE ANN, insurance company executive; b. Phila., Mar. 31, 1949; d. S. Thomas F. and Marguerite Ann (Haggerty) H.; m. Will Charles Shaw, Nov. 28, 1986. Academic Dip., Gwymedd-Mercy Academy, PA, 1967; BA in English Lit., Immaculata Coll., PA, 1971; MBA in Health Care Mgmt., Wharton Sch., Phila., 1976; MS in Social Admin., London Sch. of Econ. Univ. Lon, England, 1977. Field rep. Bureau of Labor Statistics, Phila., 1972-74; ast. dir., graduate health care pem. Wharton-Univ. PA, Phila., 1977-79; asst. secretary Hartford Insurance Group, CT, 1979-86; ast. v.p. Lincoln National Life Ins. Co., Fort Wayne, IN; 2d v.p. Lincoln Nat. Life Ins. Co., Fort Wayne, IN, 1988—; Bd. dirs. Health Care Alumni Assn., phila., 1979--, mem. Youth Service Cmt. YWCA, Hartford, 1979-81, bd. dirs., NCC HMO, Hartford, 1980-83, found. dir. Wharton Alumni Club of Hartford, 1980-86, chair Mbr. Adv. Council, Kaiser Edn. of HEalth Plan of CT, 1983-84, 84-86, founding mem. Bus. Coalition for Health, Hartford, 1983-85, bd. dirs. Ex. Cmt., Wharton alumni Assn., Phila., 1983--. Office: Lincoln Nat Life Ins Co PO Box 2266 Fort Wayne IN 46801

HARRINGTON, PETER TYRUS, public affairs, public relations consultant, author, photographer; b. N.Y.C., Aug. 28, 1951; s. Don and Gerry S. (Spolane) H. BA, Union Coll., 1973, MA in Am. Labor, 1975. Spl. investigator U.S. Dept. of Commerce, 1970; staff dir. N.Y. State Assembly, N.Y.C., 1971-73; editorial staff mem., writer, photographer Nat. Geographic Mag., Washington, 1974-76; ptnr. Don Harrington Assocs., Wilton, Conn., 1977—; pres. Harrington Communications, Wilton, 1980—; cons. IBM, Armonk, N.Y., 1984-85; contbg. editor Taxfax Mktg. Mag., 1985—; spl. cons. So. Conn. Newspaper Syndicate (Greenwich Time, Stamford Advocate); cons. Expeditions Inc., New Canaan, Conn., 1987-88; contbg. corr. Los Angeles Times, Washington Post Syndicate. Author: The Last Cathedral, 1979 (Book of Yr. award 1979), Never Too Old, 1981; author and photographer, The Sailing Chef, 1978, Maine, 1989; contbr. Murdock, Travel Marketing, Intrepid, Discovery, People, Yankee, Video and TV Guide mags., Arizona Republic, Chicago Tribune, Miami Herald, Boston Herald; contbr. and photographer of many articles with expertise in Amazon and Polar Region. Scoutmaster troop, Boy Scouts Am., Albany, N.Y., 1971-73; exec. dir. ACLU, Albany, 1972-73; mem. bd. Annapolis Youth Ctr., Md., 1978; past pres. Wilton Summer Playshop, 1972—; reports officer, exec. asst. fed. coordinating officer, pub. affairs officer Fed. Emergency-Mgmt. Agency, Washington, 1983—. Recipient Pub. Service Citation, Fed. Govt., 1985. Fellow Author's Guild, Nat. Press Found.; mem. Washington Writers Assn., Nat. Press Club, Legis. Councils Assn., Am. Soc. Mag. Photographers. Office: Don Harrington Assocs Merwin Ln Wilton CT 06897

HARRINGTON, SANDRA LYNN GOSSETT, accountant; b. Redwood City, Calif., Feb. 15, 1961; d. Edwin Ralph and Annie Lee (Rackley) Gossett; m. Michael Dawn Harrington, Aug. 2, 1980; children: Dawn Anne, Alisha Dianne, Gregory Lynn. BBA in Acctg., Tex. A&M U., 1983. Acct. non-appropriated funds cen. acctg. div. Red River Army Depot, Texarkana, Tex., 1983—. Troop leader Girl Scouts U.S., New Boston, Tex., 1986—, leader Brownie troop, 1987-88, budget specialist bldg. com., 1988—, del. Conifer coun., Texarkana, 1988—; leader Missions Friends Temple Bapt. Ch., New Boston, 1987—. Mem. Tex. A&M U. Alumni Assn., Texarkana A&M Club. Home: 213 N Ellis St New Boston TX 75570 Office: Red River Army Depot Cen Acctg Div Bldg 116 Texarkana TX 75507-5000

HARRIS, BRUCE EUGENE, finance executive; b. Zanesville, Ohio, Jan. 14, 1950; s. Harold Eugene and Ruth A. (Harbaugh) H.; m. Linda Elaine Vess, Mar. 6, 1971. BS in Acctg., Ohio State U., 1974. Coal miner Peabody Coal Co., New Lexington, Ohio, 1970-72; auditor Boykin Enterprises, 1973-74; cost acct. Ashland Chem. Co., Dublin, Ohio, 1974-76; acct. Ohio State U., Columbus, 1976-78; systems analyst Gulf Oil Corp., Houston, 1978-81; cons. Deloitte Haskins & Sells, Houston, 1981-82; systems mgr. Info. Service Internat. div. Mars, Inc., Houston and Los Angeles, 1982—. Mem. Smithsonian Assocs., Washington, 1986, Citizens Choice, Washington, 1975—, Air Force Mus. Found. Mem. Data Processing Mgmt. Assn. (cert.), Inst. for Cert. of Computer Profls., Mensa. Republican. Roman Catholic. Lodge: Elks. Home: 2419 Moss Hill Dr Houston TX 77080 Office: Mars Inc Info Svcs Internat PO Box 1752 Houston TX 77251-1752

HARRIS, CAROLYN DEE, marketing executive; b. Colfax, Wash., Dec. 13, 1947; d. Hubert Warren and Bettianne (Larsen) Kinney; m. Edward Alan Harris, Feb. 14, 1975; children: Troy Alan, Shane Warren. BS, Portland State U., 1977, MS, 1979. Credit mgr. Dial Fin. Co., Portland, 1978-79; owner, mgr. Z's Deli, Inc., Molalla, Oreg., 1980-81; ops. officer Comml. Bank, Molalla, 1981-83; dir. mktg. Viacom Cablevision, Salem, Oreg., 1983-84, Nashville, 1984-86; v.p. mktg. Dollar Gen. Corp., Nashville, 1986—. Bd. dirs. Nashville Adult Literacy Counc., 1988, Cohn Adult Learning Ctr., Nashville, 1988, W.O. Smith Community Music Sch., Nashville, 1988; active Nashville Literacy Task Force, Robertson Found.-United Way, Nashville, YMCA, Nashville. Named Advocate of Yr. SBA, 1983; recipient Gold medal Cable TV and Advt. Mktg. 1985, gold medal Internat. Radio Festival N.Y., 1987; cited for best radio comml. Advt. Age mag., 1988. Mem. Am. Mktg. Assn., Pub. Rels. Soc. Am., Mktg. and Sales Execs., Nat. Mass Retail Inst., Exec. Women Internat., Sigma Xi. Republican. Episcopalian. Home: 9215 Apache Tr Brentwood TN 37027 Office: Dollar Gen Corp Ste 210 1 Burton Hills Blvd Nashville TN 37215

HARRIS, CHARLES EDGAR, retired wholesale distribution company executive; b. Englewood, Tenn., Nov. 6, 1915; s. Charles Leonard and Minnie Beatrice (Borin) H.; m. Dorothy Sarah Wilson, Dec. 27, 1916; children: Charles Edgar, William John. Office and credit mgr. H.T. Hackney Co., Knoxville, Tenn., 1948-66; v.p. H.T. Hackney Co., Knoxville, Greeneville and Athens, Tenn., 1966-71; treas. H.T. Hacney Co., Knoxville, Greeneville and Athens, Tenn., 1971-72; pres., treas. H.T. Hackney Co., Knoxville, Greeneville and Athens, Tenn., 1972, pres., chmn. bd., chief exec. officer, 1972-82; cons. H. T. Hackney Co., Knoxville, Greeneville and Athens, Tenn., 1982—, hon. dir.; former chmn. bd., chief exec. officer, dir. various corps. in Tenn., Ky., N.C. and Ga. Bd. dirs., v.p., mem. exec. com. Downtown Knoxville Assn., 1979-83; bd. dirs., mem. exec. bd. Greater Knoxville Smoky Mountain coun. Boy Scouts Am. 1956-57, 82-83 ; bd. dirs., mem. exec. com. Met. YMCA, Knoxville, 1971-77, treas., 1975-76; mem. budget fin. com. United Way of Knoxville, 1974-80, bd. dirs., treas., chmn. fin. com., 1979-80; mem. budget com. 1982 World's Fair, Knoxville, 1980-82; deacon, trustee Cen. Bapt. Ch.; active Knox County Assn. Bapt.; mem. exec. bd. Tenn. Bapt. Conv., Nashville, 1976-82; asssoc. chmn. Layman's Nat. Bible Week, Washington, 1977-78; trustee Carson Newman Coll., Jefferson City, Tenn., 1983-89 . Recipient Outstanding Community Leadership award Religious Heritage Am., 1978; recipient Red Triangle award and Silver Triangle award YMCA, 1979. Mem. Greater Knoxville C. of C. (bd. dirs. 1973-76, v.p. 1975-76 Outstanding Corp. Citizenship award), Nat. Assn. Wholesalers-Distrbrs. (trustee 1977-82), LeConte Club (charter mem.), Rotary. Home: 7914 Gleason Dr Unit 1071 Knoxville TN 37919 Office: HT Hackney Co 300 Fidelity Bldg Knoxville TN 37901

HARRIS, CLINTON PAGE, venture capital investor; b. Detroit, Feb. 19, 1947; s. William Page Harris and Gertrude Millar (Howard) Owens; m. Margaret Lynn Gere, Aug. 15, 1972; children: Abigail Howard, Jessica Chamberlain, William Page. BA, Dartmouth Coll., 1969, BS in Engring., 1970; MBA, Harvard U., 1977. Assoc. Mead Corp., Dayton, Ohio, 1976; cons. Bain & Co., Boston, 1977-79; mgr. Bain & Co., San Francisco, 1972-82; v.p. Bain & Co., Munich, 1982-84; v.p. Advent Internat. Corp., Boston, 1984—, sr. v.p., 1988—. Contbr. articles to profl. jours. Served to lt. USN, 1970-75. George F. Baker scholar, 1977. Mem. Nat. Venture Capital Assn., Corp. Assn. for Devel. and Growth. Republican. Episcopalian.

HARRIS, DAVID HENRY, retired life insurance company executive; b. N.Y.C., May 7, 1924; s. Julian A. and May L. (Wilenski) H.; 1 child, Jean Harris Haig. Student, Sherborne (Eng.) Sch., 1937-40. With Prudential Ins. Co. Am., 1940-43; with Equitable Life Assurance Soc. U.S., N.Y.C., 1946-86, exec. v.p., 1973-77; exec. v.p., chief adminstrv. officer Equitable Life Assurance Soc. U.S., 1977-80, exec. v.p., chief staff, 1981-86; pres. Equitable Found., 1986-88, bd. dirs.; chmn. bd. Equimatics, Inc., 1971-73, Informatics, Inc., 1974-75; vice chmn. Equitable Variable Life Ins. Co., 1975-76, chmn., 1976-77; dir. Equitable Life Assurance Soc., 1977-86. Bd. dirs. Am. Council Arts. With AUS, 1943-46. Fellow Soc. Actuaries. Office: 157 E 74th St New York NY 10021

HARRIS, DAVID MICHAEL, financial executive; b. Houston, Mar. 14, 1947; s. Edwin F. and Mary Gayle (McKinney) H.; m. Rachel Anne Williams, June 2, 1970 (div. 1984); 1 child, Matthew Edwin; m. Karol Kaye Kueteman, July 4, 1986. BBA, U. Tex.-Austin, 1970; MS in Accountancy, U. Houston, 1971. CPA, Tex. Staff acct. Arthur Andersen & Co., Houston, 1971-73; with Exxon Co. USA, Houston, 1973-79; v.p., controller Eden Corp./Gen. Homes, Houston, 1979-81; v.p., chief fin. officer, The Johnson Corp., Houston, 1981—; v.p., chief fin. officer Parklane Devel. Co., Houston, 1985—, LDJ Devel. Co. Inc., Houston, 1981—, Instnl. Devel. Corp., Houston, 1986—; cons. in field. Cons., Am. Cancer Soc., Houston, 1982-84; vol. fund raiser U. Houston Acad. Excellence Fund, 1975-82; cons. So. Bible Coll. Named one of Outstanding Young Men Of Am., U.S. Jaycees, 1983. Mem. AICPA, Tex. Soc. CPAs., Beta Theta Pi, Beta Gamma Sigma. Republican. Methodist. Clubs: Houston City, Dorking Sportsmen (pres.), The Houstonian, Yellow Rose Aquatic. Home: One Cape Cod Ln Houston TX 77024 Office: The Johnson Corp 1300 Post Oak Blvd Suite 1800 Houston TX 77056

HARRIS, DAVID TAYLOR, financial anaylst; b. N.Y.C., Apr. 17, 1950; s. David Taylor Harris and Susie (Skidmore) Coxe; m. Laura Thrower, Nov. 11, 1978; children: Taylor Randolph, Patricia Munroe. BS in Econs., U. Pa., 1972. Securities analyst Fahnestock & Co., N.Y.C., 1974-87; securities broker Brean Murray Foster, N.Y.C., 1987—. Mem. investment com. Unitarian Ch., N.Y.C. Mem. N.Y. Soc. Security Analysts, Fin. Analysts Fed., Downtown Assn. Republican. Mem. Unitarian Ch. Clubs: Union (N.Y.C.); Gipsy Trail (Carmel, N.Y.). Home: 325 E 79th St #16B New York NY 10021

HARRIS, DIANE CAROL, optical products executive; b. Rockville Centre, N.Y., Dec. 25, 1942; d. Daniel Christopher and Laura Louise (Schmitt) Quigley; m. Wayne Manley Harris, Sept. 30, 1978. BA, Cath. U. Am., 1964; MS, Rensselaer Poly. Inst., 1967. With Bausch & Lomb, Rochester, N.Y., 1967—, dir. applications lab., 1972-74, dir. tech. mktg. analytical systems div., 1974-76, bus. line mgr., 1976-77, v.p. planning and bus. programs, 1977-78, v.p. planning and bus. devel. Soflens div., 1978-80, corp. dir. planning, 1980-81, v.p. corp. devel., 1981—; v.p. RID-N.Y. State, 1980-83; mem. adv. bd. Merger Mgmt. Report, 1986—; bd. dirs. Delta Labs., Inc. Contbr. articles to profl. jours. Pres. Rochester Against Intoxicated Driving, 1979-83, chmn. polit. action com., 1983, 86; bd. dirs., chmn. long-range planning com. Rochester area Nat. Council on Alcoholism, 1980-84; bd. dirs. Rochester Rehab. Ctr., 1982-84, Friends of Bristol Valley Playhouse Found., 1983-87; mem. Stop DWI Adv. panel to Monroe County Legislature, 1982-87, N.Y. State Coalition for Safety Belt Use, 1984-85. Recipient Disting. Citizen's award Monroe County, 1979, Tribute to Women in Industry and Service award YWCA, 1983; NSF grantee, 1963; selected as one of 50 Women to Watch in Corp. Am. Bus. Week mag., 1987. Mem. Newcomen Soc. N. Am., Am. Mgmt. Assn., Fin. Execs. Inst., Assn. Corp. Growth, C. of C. (pub. safety com. Rochester Area chpt., task force on hwy. safety and legis. 1981-86), Phi Beta Kappa, Sigma Xi, Delta Epsilon Sigma. Home: 60 Mendon Center Rd W Honeoye Falls NY 14472 Office: Bausch & Lomb Inc 1 Lincoln First Sq PO Box 54 Rochester NY 14601-0054

HARRIS, DOUGLAS CLAY, newspaper executive; b. Owensboro, Ky., Oct. 9, 1939; s. Marvin Dudley and Elizabeth (Adelman) H. BS, Murray State U., 1961; MS, Ind. U., 1964, EdD, 1968; grad. advanced mgmt. program, Harvard U., 1987. Counselor, asst. to dean of students Ind. U., Bloomington, 1965-68; mgmt. appraisal specialist United Air Lines, Elk Grove Village, Ill., 1968-69; dir. manpower div. Computer Age Industries, Washington, 1969; area personnel dir. Peat Marwick Mitchell & Co., N.Y.C., 1969-72; v.p. personnel Knight-Ridder, Inc., Miami, Fla., 1972-85, v.p., sec., 1986—. Served to capt. U.S. Army, 1961-62. Mem. Inst. Cert. Fin. Planners, Internat. Assn. Fin. Planners, Am. Psychol. Assn., Fla. Psychol. Assn., Southeastern Psychol. Assn., Am. Soc. Personnel Adminstrs., Newspaper Personnel Relations Assn., Am. Compensation Assn. Democrat. Home: 1408 SE Bayshore Dr Apt 1211 Miami FL 33131 Office: 1 Herald Pla Miami FL 33101

HARRIS, EDWARD MONROE, JR., former office equipment company executive; b. Phila., June 5, 1923; s. Edward Monroe and Grace Ida (Wilson) H.; m. Marion Hoyt Stevens, Sept. 16, 1950; children: Edward Monroe, Marion Olney; 1 foster child: Peter Duncan. BA, Yale U., 1943; LLB, U. Pa., 1949. Bar: N.Y. 1949. Assoc. Sullivan & Cromwell, N.Y.C., 1949-57; assoc. counsel Kennecott Copper Corp., N.Y.C., 1957-62; corp. counsel, sec. MacMillan Inc., N.Y.C., 1963-67; sec., gen. counsel Pitney Bowes Inc., Stamford, Ct., 1967-88, v.p., 1969-88. Dir. Conn. Joint Council on Econ. Edn., 1974-88; trustee Conn. Pub. Expenditure Council, 1979-85, exec. com., 1983-85; dir. Stamford Mus. and Nature Ctr. Inc., 1980—, treas., 1982-84, first v.p., 1984-86, pres., 1986-88; trustee Edward W. Hazen Found., 1981—, mem. adv. com. Conn. Comprehensive Plan for Secondary, Vocat. Career and Adult Edn., 1985. Served to 1st lt. USMCR, 1943-46. Mem. C. of C. U.S. (edn., employment tng. com. 1976-86, environ. com. 1987-88), Conn. Bus. and Industry Assn. (bd. dirs. 1974-77). Republican. Presbyterian. Club: Wee Burn Country (Darien). Avocations: tennis, skiing, golf, travel, gardening.

HARRIS, EMMA EARL, nursing home executive; b. Viper, Ky., Nov. 6, 1936; d. Andrew Jackson and Zola (Hall) S.; m. Ret Haney Marten Henis Harris, June 5, 1981; children: Debra, Joseph, Wynona, Robert Walsh. Grad. St. Joseph Sch. Practical Nursing. Staff nurse St. Joseph Hosp., Bangor, Maine, 1973-75; office nurse Dr. Eugene Brown, Bangor, 1975-77; dir. nurses Fairborn Nursing Home, Ohio, 1977-78; staff nurse Hillhaven Hospice, Tucson, 1979-80; asst. head nurse, 1980; co-owner Nu-Life Elderly Guest Home, Tucson, 1980—. Vol. Heart Assn., Bangor, 1965-70, Cancer Assn., Bangor, 1965-70. Mem. NAFE, Assn. Sr. Resources (cons. 1983—). Democrat. Avocations: theatre; opera. Home: 1082 E Seneca Tucson AZ 85719

HARRIS, HOLLIS LOYD, airline executive; b. Carrollton, Ga., Nov. 25, 1931; s. Clarence L. and Nellie Ruth (Hardegree) H.; m. Joyce Entrekin, July 30, 1955; children—Patricia S., David L., Michael J. B.Aero. Engring., Ga. Inst. Tech., 1961. With Delta Air Lines, Inc., Atlanta, 1954—, asst. v.p. facilities, 1968-71, v.p. engring., 1971-72; asst. v.p. in-flight service dept. Delta Air Lines, Inc., 1972-73, sr. v.p. passenger service, 1973-85, sr. v.p. ops., 1985-87, pres., chief operating officer, 1987—, also bd. dirs.; trustee Delta Air Lines Found.; bd. dirs. Trust Co. Bank, Trust Co. Ga., Am. Bus. Products. Mem. adv. bd. Atlanta Area council Boy Scouts Am., exec. bd. S.E. region, nat. exec. bd.; mem. nat. adv. council Nat. Multiple Sclerosis Soc.; bd. dirs. Ga. Golf Hall of Fame. Served with AUS, 1951-54. Mem. AIAA, Ga. Archtl. and Engring. Soc. Presbyterian. Home: 100 St Andrew Sq Peachtree City GA 30269 Office: Delta Air Lines Inc Hartsfield Atlanta Internat Airport Atlanta GA 30320

HARRIS, IRVING BROOKS, business executive; b. St. Paul, Aug. 4, 1910; s. William and Mildred (Brooks) H.; m. Joan White; children—Roxanne, Virginia, William. AB, Yale, 1931; hon. degree, Loyola U., 1976, Kenyon Coll., 1986, Columbia Coll., 1987, Lesley Coll., 1988, Bank Street Coll. Edn., 1988. Exec. in finance business 1931-42, aircraft part bus., 1944-46; exec. Toni Home Permanent Co., after 1946; (sold stockholdings in Toni Co. to Gillette Safety Razor Co.), 1948; dir. Gillette Safety Razor Co., 1948-60; exec. v.p. Toni Co., 1946-52; chmn. bd. Sci. Research Assos., 1953-58; pres. Michael Reese Hosp. and Med. Center, Chgo., 1958-61, Harris Group, Inc., 1959-76; pres. Standard Shares; chmn. exec. com. Pittway Corp. Trustee U. Chgo., Nat. Center Clin. Infant Programs, Chgo. Ednl. TV Assn.; chmn. emeritus Family Focus; chmn. Harris Found.; pres. emeritus Erikson Inst.; pres., co-founder The Ounce of Prevention Fund, 1982—; trustee Am. Jewish Com., Milton S. Eisenhower Found.; chmn. adv. bd. Ill. Dept. Children and Family Services Tng. Inst., Ill. Competitive Access and Reimbursement Equity Program; vice chmn. Gov.'s Task Force on Future of Mental Health in Ill.; spl. counselor to select com. on children Ill. Gen. Assembly; Served with Bd. Econ. Warfare OPA, 1942-44. Recipient Chgo. UNICEF World of Children award, 1985; hon. membership award Chgo. Pediatric Soc., 1986; Am. Orthopsychiat. Assn. award, 1986; Clifford Beers lectr. Yale U., 1987. Hon. fellow Am. Acad. Pediatrics; mem. Am. Orthopsychiatric Assn. (award 1985), Chgo. Pediatric Soc. (hon. mem. 1983). Clubs: Standard, Lake Shore Country, Midday, Saddle and Cycle, Commercial (Chgo.). Home: 209 E Lake Shore Dr Chicago IL 60602 Office: Standard Shares Inc 2 N LaSalle St Chicago IL 60602

HARRIS, JACK HOWARD, II, consulting firm executive; b. Chgo., Mar. 22, 1945; s. Jack Howard and Myrtice Geneva (Dickson) H.; m. Barbara Beck Czika, Jan. 1, 1983; children: Jack, William, T. Patrick; stepchildren: Joseph C. Czika, Brad D. Czika. AB, U. Chgo., 1966; MPh, George Washington U., 1984. Chief China desk Air Force Intelligence, U.S. Air Force, Washington, 1971-74; dir. policy studies BDM Corp., Washington, 1974-78; sr. assoc. Booz-Allen and Hamilton, Washington, 1979; corp. v.p., govt. ops. Sci. Applications, Inc., Washington, 1980-85; exec. v.p. The Harris Group, Inc., Washington, 1985—; pres. Ctr. for Nat. Program Evaluation, Washington, 1988—. With USAF, 1967-71. Mem. Air Force Assn., Am. Legion, DAV, VFW, Internat. Platform Assn., Phi Gamma Delta. Home: 911 Challedon Rd Great Falls VA 22066 Office: 1801 Robert Fulton Dr Ste 200 Reston VA 22091

HARRIS, JAMES EDWIN, construction company executive, engineer; b. Sept. 1, 1940; s. Pinkney Spratt and Janie Lucille (Wilson) H.; m. Mary Anne Garrison, Aug. 18, 1963; children: James Edwin Jr., John Garrison. BSCE, Clemson U., 1963. Registered profl. engr. N.C., S.C. Engr., project mgr. Crowder Constrn. Co., Charlotte, N.C., 1963-72; v.p. Crowder Constrn. Co., Charlotte, 1972-74; pres. James E. Harris Constrn. Co., Charlotte, 1974—. Mem. Nat. Soc. Profl. Engrs., Profl. Engrs. N.C., Associated Gen. Contractors, Mecklenburg Gen. Contractors Assn. (dir. 1985-86). Republican. Presbyterian. Office: James E. Harris Constrn Co PO Box 25885 Charlotte NC 28229

HARRIS, JOHN ALLEN, information resource analyst; b. Newport News, Va., Nov. 25, 1962; s. John Allen and Billie Marie (Walls) H.; m. Sally Yee-Sue Yuen, Aug. 16, 1986. BS in Acctg., Va. Poly. Inst. and State U., 1985. CPA; cert. info. systems auditor, data processor. Asst. auditor Fed. Nat. Mortgage Assn., Washington, 1985, assoc. auditor, 1985-86, EDP auditor, 1986-87; EDP auditor Am. Tobacco Co., Richmond, Va., 1987-88; auditor info. systems Fla. Power Corp., St. Petersburg, 1988, info. resource analyst, 1988—; cons. in field. Mem. AICPA, Va. Soc. CPAs, EDP Auditors Assn., Am. Inst. Cert. Computer Profls. Democrat. Office: Fla Power Corp Computer Svcs Div MAC B2A 14042 34th St S Saint Petersburg FL 33711

HARRIS, JOHN WOODS, banker, lawyer ; b. Galveston, Tex., Sept. 23, 1893; s. John Woods and Minnie (Hutchings) H.; LL.B., U. Va., 1920; m. Eugenia Davis, June 14, 1917 (dec.); children—Eugenia (Mrs. Archibald Rowland Campbell, Jr.), Anne (Mrs. Donald C. Miller) (dec.), Joan (Mrs. Alvin N. Kelso), Florence (Mrs. Marshall McDonald, Jr.) (dec.). Admitted to Tex. bar, 1920, practiced as atty. and mng. agt. oil, farm, ranch properties in Tex., 1922—; dir. Hutchings Sealy Nat. Bank; chmn. exec. com., chmn. bd., chmn. emeritus First Hutchings Sealy Nat. Bank (merged into First Internat. Bancshares, merged into InterFirst Corp.), Galveston, 1960-74; dir., mem. exec. com. InterFirst Bank Galveston N.A.; pres. Hutchings Joint Stock Assn., 1936-87; dir. Galveston Corp., Cotton Concentration Co., Gulf Transfer Co., Tex. Fiberglas Products Co. Sr. v.p., mem. fin. com., chmn. land com. Sealy and Smith Found. for John Sealy Hosp.; pres. bd. Rosenberg Library, Galveston Orphans Home, Galveston Found.; bd. dirs., v.p., chmn. fin. com. George Ball Charity Fund; trustee Galveston Ind. Sch. Dist., 1927-30; sr. adv. U.S. Congl. Adv. Bd. Served as aviator USN, 1918. Named Rabbi Henry Cohen Humanitarian of Yr., 1981. Mem. Am. Judicature Soc., Early and Pioneer Naval Aviators Assn., Sons of Republic Tex., Am. Legion, Delta Kappa Epsilon. Episcopalian. Clubs: Galveston Artillery; Farmington Country (Charlottesville, Va.); Bob Smith Yacht. Home: 2603 Ave O Galveston TX 77550 Office: 801 InterFirst Bank Bldg 2200 Market St Galveston TX 77550

HARRIS, KAREN KOSTOCK, manufacturing company executive; b. Chgo., Sept. 11, 1942; d. Kenneth P. and Elsie A. (Raffl) Kostock; student Mundelein Coll., 1979; m. Roy Lawrence Harris, Feb. 14, 1981. Clerk, loan dept. Evanston (Ill.) Fed. Savs. and Loan, 1960-63, mgr. collection dept., 1963-65; credit adminstr. Packaging Corp. Am., Evanston, 1965-72, adminstrv. asst. to v.p., 1972-74; credit mgr. trainee Am. Hosp. Supply Corp., McGaw Park, Ill., 1974-75; cash mgr, asst. to treas. Pullman Standard, Chgo., 1975-76; mgr. credit adminstr. Gen. Binding Corp., Northbrook, Ill., 1976-77; treas. C. H. Hanson Co., Chgo., 1977-79, sec.-treas., 1980—, dir., 1980—, adminstr., trustee C. H. Hanson Co. Pension Plan, 1979—, Employees Savs. and Profit Sharing Trust, 1978—; owner Stock Enterprises, Highland Park, Ill., 1980-81; partner Harris Enterprises, 1981—; pres. Sirrah Enterprises, Inc., 1982-88; ptnr. Montana Co., 1984-88; pres. Cottage Keepers Inc., 1986-87; ptnr. Mont. Co., 1984—; cons. in field; lectr. Founder Mundelein Weekend Coll. Scholar Grant. Recipient Cert. of Merit Chgo. Assn. of Commerce and Industry, 1981, 85. Mem. Nat. Fedn. Rep. Women. Clubs: Swedish of Chgo. (sec. 1981-82, steering com. 1982), Venice-Nokomis. Office: C H Hanson Co 3630 N Wolf Rd Franklin Park IL 60131

HARRIS, KAYLENE SLAY, finance executive; b. Santa Barbara, Calif., July 31, 1945; d. Kay Parker Slay and Gwendolyn (Millron) Montgomery; m. William Peyton Harris Jr., June 6, 1964 (div. Aug. 1985); children: William Parker, Russell Slayton, Sara Lorene. Student, Huntingdon Coll., 1963-65, 84. Bookkeeper, designer Dunn's Inc., Prattville, Ala., 1968-76;

pres., owner, mgr. Dunn's, Inc., Prattville, Ala., 1976-81; office mgr., system control operator Profl. Billings, Inc., Montgomery, Ala., 1982—. Cubmaster Boy Scouts Am., dir. Cub Scout Dist. Day Camp, Montgomery, 1972. Mem. Nat. Assn. Female Execs., Ala. Bus. Profl. Women's Assn. (state-wide display artist 1976-78), Ala. Wholesale Floral Assn. (bd. dirs. 1979-81), SE Ala. Floorist Assn., MDS Client Support Group. Republican. Clubs: Jr. Women's (Prattville), Phoenix Christian Singles, Camden Study. Home: 1822 E Autumn Ct Prattville AL 36067

HARRIS, KING W., manufacturing company executive; b. 1943. BA, Harvard U., 1964, MBA, 1965. With Pittway Corp., Northbrook, Ill., 1971—, v.p. alarm div., 1971-75, exec. v.p. electronics div., 1975-80, chmn. bd. dirs., chief exec. officer electronics div., 1980-84, now pres., bd. dirs. Office: Pittway Corp 333 Skokie Blvd Northbrook IL 60065 *

HARRIS, L(AWRENCE) PEYTON, JR., property management executive; b. Gastonia, N.C., Mar. 10, 1947; s. L. Peyton and June Maynard (Trout) H.; m. Kathy Marie Radesky, June 14, 1980; children: Ashley Stewart, L. Peyton III, Sloane Randolph, Lindsay Anderson. Student, The Citadel, 1965-66; BA in Polit. Sci., Western Carolina U., 1971. Pub. relations specialist Rep. Nat. Com., Washington, 1971-72; sr. staff investigator Montgomery County Landlord-Tenant/Rent Control, Rockville, Md., 1972-76; sr. property mgr. Grady Mgmt., Inc., Silver Spring, Md., 1976-81; v.p. Shannon and Luchs Co., Washington, 1981-85; sr. v.p. Zalco Realty Inc., Silver Spring, Md., 1985—; fed. housing liaison Inst. Real Estate Mgmt., Fairfax, Va., 1986; mem. Chief Exec. Officers Com. Community Assn. Inst., Alexandria, 1987—; judge Energy Conservation Competition, Washington, 1984. Pres. McLean (Va.) Youth Assn. sports orgn., 1978-80. Mem. Property Mgmt. Assn. Met. Washington (pres. 1989; named Property Mgr. of Yr. 1983, recipient President's award 1985), Inst. Real Estate Mgmt. (Cert. Property Mgr. 1985), Community Assn. Inst. Republican. Episcopalian. Office: Zalco Realty Inc 8701 Georgia Ave 3rd Fl Silver Spring MD 20910

HARRIS, MICALYN SHAFER, lawyer; b. Chgo., Oct. 31, 1941; d. Erwin and Dorothy (Sampson) Shafer. AB, Wellesley Coll., 1963; JD, U. Chgo., 1966. Bar: Ill. 1966, Mo. 1967, U.S. Dist. Ct. (ea. dist.) 1967, U.S. Supreme Ct. 1972, U.S. Ct. Appeals (8th cir.) 1974, N.Y. 1981, N.J. 1988. Law clk. U.S. Dist. Ct., St. Louis, 1967-68; atty. The May Dept. Stores, St. Louis, 1968-70, Ralston-Purina Co., St. Louis, 1970-72; atty., asst. sec. Chromalloy Am. Corp., St. Louis, 1972-76; sole practice, St. Louis, 1976-78; div. counsel, gen. counsel S.B. Thomas, Inc.; div. counsel CPC N.Am., 1978-84; corp. counsel and asst. sec. CPC Internat., Englewood Cliffs, N.J., 1984-88; ptnr. Weil, Gotshal & Manges, N.Y.C., 1988—. Mem. ABA (co-chmn. subcom. counseling the mktg. function, securities law com., tender offers and proxy statements subcom.), Ill. Bar Assn., N.Y. State Bar Assn. (securities regulation com.), Bar Assn. Met. St. Louis (chmn. TV com.), Mo. Bar Assn. (chmn. internat. law com.), Am. Corp. Counsel Assn. N.J. (bd. dirs., chmn. bus. law com.). Address: 625 N Monroe Ridgewood NJ 07450

HARRIS, MILTON M., distributing company executive; b. San Francisco, Sept. 6, 1916; s. A.H. and Rebecca (Harris) H.; m. Lorraine D. Love, July 3, 1938; 1 child, Jerrold B. Ed. pub. schs. With Braun-Knecht-Heimann Co., San Francisco, 1933-60; v.p. Braun-Knecht-Heimann Co., 1951-60; (co. acquired by Van Waters & Rogers, Inc. (now Univar Corp.)), San Francisco, 1960; sr. v.p., gen. mgr. (co. acquired by Van Waters & Rogers, Inc. (now Univar Corp.)), 1960-61, pres., 1962-66, chmn., 1966-70, vice chmn., 1970—, also dir.; dir. Deep Water Co., VWR Corp., Seattle. Clubs: Cercle de l'Union, Olympic, Lakeside Country, Bohemian (San Francisco); Desert Horizon Country (Indian Wells, Calif.), Bohemian. Home: 75-255 Saint Andrews Ct Indian Wells CA 92210 Office: Univar Corp 1600 Norton Bldg Seattle WA 98104

HARRIS, NEISON, corporate executive; b. St. Paul, Jan. 24, 1915; s. William and Mildred (Brooks) H.; m. Bette Deutsch, Jan. 25, 1939; children: Katherine, King, Toni. AB, Yale U., 1936. Founder Toni Co.; pres. Toni div. Gillette Co., pres. Paper Mate div.; pres., bd. dirs. Pittway Corp., Northbrook, Ill., 1959-84, chmn. bd., 1984—; chmn. bd., chmn. exec. com., dir. Standard Shares, Inc. Named One of Ten Outstanding Young Men U.S., Jr. C. of C., 1948. Clubs: Standard, Lake Shore Country (Chgo.); Boca Rio Country (Boca Raton, Fla.). Office: Pittway Corp 333 Skokie Blvd Northbrook IL 60065

HARRIS, NELSON GEORGE, baking company executive; b. Ridley Park, Pa., Oct. 4, 1926; s. Frank W. and Ruth (Dukes) Harris Hollett; m. Rita Jane Storrie, Sept. 11, 1948; children—Stephen J., Patricia deBarros, David N., William Randall, Nancy, Thomas G. B.S., U. Pa., 1948; LL.B., Temple U., 1953. Bar: Pa. 1954. Vice pres., treas. Tasty Baking Co., Phila., 1959-68; pres. Horn & Hardart Baking Co., Phila., 1968-71; pres., chief exec. officer Central Valley Co., Phila., 1971-79; pres., chief exec. officer Tasty Baking Co., Phila., 1979—, dir., 1979—; bd. dirs. Am. Water Works, Wilmington, Del., 1st Pa. Corp., 1st Pa. Bank, Phila.; Phila. Electric Co. Pres. Blind Relief Fund of Phila., 1968—, Allegheny West Found., 1980—. Served with USN, 1944-45. Mem. ABA, Pa. Bar Assn., Phila. Bar Assn., Am. Inst. C.P.A.s, Pa. Inst. C.P.A.s, Phila. C. of C., Pa. C. of C. Presbyterian. Clubs: Phila. Cricket (pres. 1975-76), Union League (pres. 1978-79). Home: 4130 Presidential Dr Lafayette Hill PA 19444 Office: Tasty Baking Co 2801 Hunting Park Ave Philadelphia PA 19129

HARRIS, NORMAN ALLAN, research and development company executive; b. Los Angeles, Sept. 27, 1933; s. David Jack and Bella (Flack) H.; student (Univ. scholar) U. So. Calif., 1951; B.A. (Coll. scholar), Occidental Coll., 1955; postgrad. Vanderbilt U., 1955-56; grad. Oak Ridge Sch. Radiol. Physics, 1956; m. Sandra Gail Hill, Feb. 22, 1958; children—Todd, Tracy, Wendy. Project engr. Marquardt, Van Nuys, Calif., 1956-60; project mgr. Atomics Internat., Canoga Park, Calif., 1960-62; sr. asso. Planning Research Corp., Los Angeles, 1962-68; prin. scientist advanced sensor systems McDonnell-Douglas, Santa Monica, Calif., 1968-69; mgr. dept. environ. safety EG&G, Goleta, Calif., 1969-74; exec. v.p. Henningson, Durham & Richardson, Santa Barbara, Calif., 1974-83, dir. spl. space shuttle studies, 1974-83, dir. M-X EIS prodn. and spl. systems studies, 1976-83; pres. Motoracing News, 1978-83, Manbourne Inc.; chmn. bd. MI Systems Applications Co. (MISA), Santa Barbara, 1983—; prin. OMI Scis., Santa Barbara, 1984—; pres., chief exec. officer Mgmt. Sci. Inc., Solvang, Calif., 1984—. Mem. com. to establish tchr. qualifications and evaluation standards, Santa Ynez, Calif. AEC fellow, 1955-56. Mem. Health Physics Soc. (charter), Kappa Mu Epsilon, Sigma Pi Sigma. Author tech. monographs in field. Office: PO Box 1310 591 Alamo Pintado Solvang CA 93463

HARRIS, RICHARD ANTHONY SIDNEY, trust company executive; b. Bklyn., Dec. 22, 1940; s. Stanley Sidney and Rose (Franquelli) H.; m. Sharon Lynne Harvey, Dec. 21, 1975; 1 child, Aaron Nathaniel Graeme. Student St. John's U., Jamaica, N.Y., 1958-61. Adminstr. Harris Trust, N.Y.C., 1972—, trustee, 1972—; adminstr. Beehive Trading Co., Provo, Utah, 1980—, Aaron Reseda Med., Calif., 1976—; pres. Reseda Mgmt., 1976—, also dir. Mem. Am. Assn. Individual Investors, Internat. Platform Assn., Heritage Found. Roman Catholic. Office: PO Box 108 Van Nuys CA 91408

HARRIS, RICHARD FOSTER, JR., insurance company executive; b. Athens, Ga., Feb. 8, 1918; s. Richard Foster and Mai Audli (Chandler) H.; m. Virginia McCurdy, Aug. 21, 1937 (div.); children: Richard Foster, Gaye Karyl Harris Law; m. Kari Melandso, Dec. 29, 1962. BCS, U. Ga., 1939. Bookkeeper, salesman 1st Nat. Bank, Atlanta, 1936-40; agt. Vol. State Life Ins. Co., Atlanta, 1940-41; asst. mgr. N.Y. Life Ins. Co., Atlanta and Charlotte, N.C., 1941-44; mgr., agt. Pilot Life Ins. Co., Charlotte and Houston, 1944-63; mgr., agt. bus. planning div.; city agy. Am. Gen. Life Ins. Co., Houston, 1963—; bd. dirs. Fidelity Bank & Trust Co., Houston, 1965-66. Chmn. fund drive Am. Heart Assn., Charlotte, Mecklenburg County, 1958-59, chmn. bd., 1959-61; gen. chmn. Shrine Bowl Promotion, Charlotte Shriners, 1955; v.p., bd. dirs. Myers Park Meth. Ch. Men's Class, 1956-59, bd. stewards, Charlotte, 1959-61; bd. dirs. Houston Polit. Action Com., 1982—; charter mem. Rep. Presdl. Task Force, pres., 1981-88; co-chmn. Christian Community Service Ctr., 1984-88; mem. Mus. of Fine Arts, Houston, 1986—, First Tuesday Group, Houston, 1985—, Ambassadors Club of Rep. Nat. Com. Recipient Pres.'s Cabinet award Am. Gen. Life Ins. Co., 1964-67, 69, 71, 77-83, Disting. Salesman award Charlotte Sales Exec. Club, 1955, 57-59, Bronze Medallion award Am. Heart Assn., 1959, Nat. Quality award Life Ins. Agy. Mgmt. Assn. and Nat. Assn. Life Underwriters, 1965-88. Mem. Assn. Advanced Life Underwriters, Am. Soc. CLU's, Nat. Assn. Life Underwriters, SAR (v.p., bd. dirs. sec. chpt. 5 Tex. 1974—), Life Underwriters Polit. Action Com. (life), Houston Estate and Fin. Forum, English Speaking Union, Mensa Internat., Houston Assn. Life Underwriters, Lone Star Leaders Club, Tex. Leader's Round Table (life), Million Dollar Round Table, Tex. Assn. Life Underwriters, Am. Security Council (nat. adv. bd. 1979—), Nat. Platform Assn., Tex. Crime Prevention Assn., Pi Kappa Phi. Episcopalian. Clubs: Heritage (charter), Warwick, Napoleon, 100, Kingwood Country (Tex.); Deerwood (Tex.); Forum of Houston, Houston Knife and Fork, U.S. Senatorial Bus. Adv. Bd.; Campaigner; Tex. Circle R, 300. Lodges: Kiwanis (bd. dirs. 1979—), Masons (32 degree), Shriners, Sertoma (life; v.p. bd. dirs. Charlotte chpt.), Royal Order Jesters. Home: 2701 Westheimer Rd Houston TX 77098 Office: Am Gen Life Ins Co Wortham Tower 2727 Allen Pkwy Ste 400 Houston TX 77019

HARRIS, RICHARD JOHN, diversified holding company executive; b. Attleboro, Mass., July 19, 1936; s. John Francis and Lauretta Louise (Tharl) H.; m. Carole Mae St. Pierre, May 11, 1963; children—Mark Richard, Pamela Jean. Assoc. Sci. in Acctg., Bentley Coll., 1962. C.P.A., Mass., R.I. Mgmt. trainee Gen. Motors Corp., Wilmington, Del., 1962-65; mem. audit staff Price Waterhouse & Co., Providence, 1965-69; internat. controller metal and electronic products group Tex. Instruments, Inc., Attleboro, Mass., 1969-72; v.p., treas., dir. Nortek, Inc., Cranston, R.I., 1972—. Served with USAF, 1954-59. Fellow Mass. Soc. C.P.A.s; mem. Am. Inst. C.P.A.s. Roman Catholic. Office: Nortek Inc 50 Kennedy Pla Providence RI 02903

HARRIS, RICHARD MAX, corporate executive; b. San Jose, Ill., Mar. 13, 1935; s. James Elmer and Edith Catherine (Leipnick) H.; m. Carole June French, Dec. 22, 1957 (div.); children: Tracy Lynn, Amy French, Richard Max II; m. Susan Rose Varrassi, May 31, 1975. B.S., U. Ill., 1959. Mgr. fin. Gen. Electric Co., Syracuse, N.Y., 1959-71; v.p. Warner Electric, South Beloit, Ill., 1971-73; controller Internat. Paper Co., N.Y.C., 1973-76, v.p., 1976-81, sr. v.p., 1981-87. Active Pres.'s Council U. Ill., Urbana, 1983. Served with USAF, 1955-57. Republican. Presbyterian. Home: 300 E 40th St New York NY 10016 Office: Axel Johnson Inc 110 E 59th St New York NY 10022

HARRIS, RICHARD MICHAEL, electronic systems engineer; b. Balt., Nov. 22, 1941; s. Richard Elmer and Alice Alden (Hartline) H.; m. Ann Harris, Dec. 28, 1963; children: Michael, David, Susan, Catherine, Paul. BSEE, MIT, 1963, MSEE in Ops. Research, 1965; PhD in Engring. and Econ. Systems, Stanford U., 1972. Instr., MIT, 1963-65; cons. celestial navigation Jet Propulsion Lab., Calif. Inst. Tech., Pasadena, 1963-65; tech. staff air transp. systems The MITRE Corp., McLean, Va., 1968-71, group leader advanced airport systems, 1972-74, asso. dept. head systems planning, 1975-78, dept. head advanced systems, 1979-81, dept. head advanced air traffic control automation systems engring., 1981-82, assoc. tech. dir. naval systems engring., 1983-84, tech. dir. navy and info. systems div., 1984-88; chief engr. Washington div., 1988—; seminar lectr. Contbr. articles to profl. jours. Served to lt. USNR, 1965-67. Fellow Ford Found., 1967-68, MITRE, 1969-71. Fellow AIAA (assoc.); mem. Naval Inst., Armed Forces Communications Electronics Assn., Navy League, Sigma Xi, Tau Beta Pi, Eta Kappa Nu, Beta Theta Pi. Home: 2038 Freedom Ln Falls Church VA 22043 Office: 7525 Colshire Dr McLean VA 22102

HARRIS, STEVEN ZOLTAN, consulting company executive; b. N.Y.C., Jan. 3, 1953; s. Zoltan and Irene (Koczerzuk) H. BSEE, MIT, 1974; MBA, U. Chgo., 1975. Mgr. clin. lab. Evanston (Ill.) Hosp., 1975-77, asst. v.p. info. systems, 1977-79; dir. mgmt. info. systems Children's Hosp., Boston, 1979-82; owner Harris Assocs., Durham, N.C., 1982-84; pres. Info. Resource Products, Inc., Woburn, Mass., 1984—. Mem. Echo.

HARRIS, THOMAS L., public relations executive; b. Dayton, Ohio, Apr. 18, 1931; s. James and Leona (Blum) H.; m. JoAnn K. Karch, Apr. 14, 1957; children: James Harris, Theodore Harris. B.A., U. Mich., 1953; M.A., U. Chgo., 1956. Exec. v.p. Daniel J. Edelman Inc., Chgo., 1957-67; v.p. pub. relations Neddham Harper & Steers, Chgo., 1967-72; pres. Foote Cone & Belding Pub. Relations, Chgo., 1973-78; pres. Golin-Harris Communications Inc., Chgo., 1978—, vice chmn., 1989—. Served with U.S. Army, 1953-55. Mem. Public Relations Soc. Am. Home: 241 Melba Ln Highland Park IL 60035 Office: Golin-Harris Communications Inc 500 N Michigan Ave Chicago IL 60611

HARRIS, THOMAS SARAFEN, management consultant; b. Middletown, Ohio, Dec. 17, 1947; s. William Sellers and Ellen Marion (Sarafen) H.; m. Susan Wendy Shuman, Mar. 8, 1968 (div. Apr. 1972); m. Freda Gillian Wooldridge, Dec. 3, 1979; 1 dau., Anna Wooldridge. B.A., Johns Hopkins U., 1969, postgrad., 1969-72. Trainee, Brakeley, John Price Jones, Inc., N.Y.C., 1972-74, account mgr./v.p., 1974-78; directeur service internat. Equip'Contact SARL, Paris, 1978-80; mng. dir. Thos. Harris & Assoc., London, Paris, Essen, Rome, Amsterdam, N.Y.C., 1980—. Contbr. articles to profl. publs. Recipient various awards Boy Scouts Am., 1960-65. Mem. Inst. Fund Raising Mgrs., Nat. Soc. Fund-Raising Execs., Inst. Dirs. (London). Club: Royal Commonwealth.

HARRIS, VERA EVELYN, personnel recruiting and search firm executive; b. Watson, Sask., Can., Jan. 11, 1932; came to U.S., 1957; d. Timothy and Margaret (Popoff) H.; student U. B.C. (Can.), Vancouver; children—Colin Clifford Graham, Barbara Cusimano Page. Office mgr. Keglers, Inc., Morgan City, La., 1964-67; office mgr., acct. John L. Hopper & Assos., New Orleans, 1967-71; office mgr. Elite Homes, Inc., Metairie, La., 1971-73; comptroller Le Pavillon Hotel, New Orleans, 1973-74; controller Waguespack-Pratt, Inc., New Orleans, 1974-76; adminstrv. controller Sizzler Family Steak Houses of So. La., Inc., Metairie, 1976-79; dir. adminstrn. Sunbelt, Inc., New Orleans, 1979-82, sec., dir., 1980—; exec. v.p. Corp. Cons., Inc., 1980-83, pres., 1984-86; pres. Harris Personnel Resources, Arlington, Tex., 1986—, Harris Enterprises, Arlington, 1986—; exec. dir. Nat. Sizzler Franchise Assn., 1976-79. Mem. Am. Bus. Women's Assn., Nat. Assn. Female Execs., La. Assn. Personnel Consultants (treas. 1985-86). Home: 8702 Winding Ln Fort Worth TX 76112 Office: Harris Personnel Resources 2000 E Lamar Blvd Ste 600 Arlington TX 76006

HARRIS, WAYNE MANLEY, lawyer; b. Pittsford, N.Y., Dec. 28, 1925; s. George H. and Constance M. Harris; m. Diane C. Quigley, Sept. 30, 1979; children—Wayne, Constance, Karen, Duncan, Claire. LL.D., Albany Law Sch., U. Rochester, 1951. Bar: N.Y. 1952. Ptnr., Harris, Maloney, Horwitz, Evans & Fox, and predecessors, Rochester, N.Y., 1958—. Pres. Delta Labs., Inc. (non-profit environ. lab.), 1971—, pres. Friends of Bristol Valley Playhouse Found., 1984-87, Monroe County Conservation Council Inc., 1985-87. Served with AUS, 1944-46. Decorated Bronze Star. Recipient Sportsman of Yr. award Genesee Conservation League, Inc., 1960, Conservationist of Yr. award Monroe County Conservation Council, Inc., 1961, Kiwanian of Yr. award, Kiwanis Club, 1965, Livingston County Fedn. of Sportsmen award, 1966, N.Y. State Conservation Council Nat. Wildlife Fedn. Water Conservation award, 1967, Rochester Acad. of Sci. award, 1970, Am. Motors Corp. Conservation award, 1971, Rochester C. of C. award, 1972. Drafter 5 laws passed into law in N.Y. State. Home: 60 Mendon Center Rd Honeoye Falls NY 14472 Office: 700 First Fed Plaza Rochester NY 14614

HARRIS, WILLIAM EDWARD, telecommunications executive; b. Englewood, N.J., July 13, 1961; s. Carl A. and Edna K. (Keane) H.; m. Shelley L. Bowman, June 11, 1983. BS in Econs., U. Pa., 1983. Budget specialist N.J. Bell, Newark, 1983-85; fin. analyst Bell Atlantic Corp., Phila., 1985—. Mem. World Affairs Council. Democrat. Office: Bell Atlantic 1600 Market St 29th Fl Philadelphia PA 19103

HARRIS, WILLIAM MADISON, management consultant; b. Farmville, Va., Feb. 28, 1932; s. William Madison and Ann Holladay (Thackston) H.; m. Marian Leonie Burks, July 27, 1957; children: Ann Holladay Harris Anderson, William Claiborne, Elizabeth Madison, John Spencer Randolph. BS, Coll. of William and Mary, 1953. Sales mgr., engr., dist. traffic supr. Chesapeake & Potomac Telephone Co., Norfolk, Richmond, Lynchburg, Va., 1953-63; v.p., personnel dir. Cen. Fidelity Bank, Richmond, 1963-71; v.p. Planters Nat. Bank, Rocky Mount, N.C., 1971-83; v.p., dir. human resources Ga. Fed. Bank, Atlanta, 1983-86; pres. Harris & Assocs., Atlanta, 1987—; lectr. U. Richmond, 1965-71; chmn. personnel com. N.C. Bankers Assn., Raleigh, 1981-83. Contbr. articles to profl. jours. and speeches. Active Atlanta Human Resources Planning Group, 1987—. Lt. USNR, 1953-56. Mem. Am. Soc. Personnel Adminstrs. (pres. Richmond 1965-66, nat.compensation and benefits com. 1975-84, contbg. editor Handbook, 1980, cert. accredited exec. personnel 1976), Indsl. Relations Research Assn., S.R. (bd. dirs., sec. Richmond 1970-71), Kappa Alpha, Sigma Epsilon Pi. Presbyterian. Clubs: Cosmopolitan (pres. 1959); Fishing Bay Yacht (Deltaville, Va.) (commodore 1970), The Branches (pres. 1986). Home and Office: 6965 Hunters Branch Dr Atlanta GA 30328

HARRISON, CARTER HENRY, banker; b. Washington, Mar. 4, 1935; s. Bernard Johnston and Martha (Kountze) H.; m. Sallie Bourne; children—Carter H., Peter deL. A.B., Harvard U. Mgmt. trainee, comml. loan officer Shawmut Mchts., Salem, Mass., 1958-70, sr. v.p., sr. loan officer, 1970-75, pres., chief exec. officer, 1975-79; pres., chief exec. officer Shawmut Community Bank, Framingham, Mass., 1979-82; sr. v.p., dir. corp. planning Shawmut Corp., Boston, 1982-83; exec. v.p. investment svcs./trust div. Shawmut Corp. and Shawmut Bank, 1983—; bd. dirs. One Fed. Asset Mgmt. Inc. Incorporator, trustee Beverly Hosp., Mass., 1963; mem. exec. com., armory-adhoc, long range planning, mus. com., devel. com., nominating com., trustee Peabody Mus. of Salem. Mem. Mass. Bankers Assn. (immediate past chmn., trust exec. com. Boston), Am. Bankers Assn. (bd. dirs., mem. trust mgmt. seminar Washington), Trustees of Reservations (mem. adv. coun./standing com., northeast regional com., investment rev. com. Beverly), Manchester Yacht Club, Myopia Club, Harvard Club of North Shore , Harvard Club, Union Club. Office: Shawmut Bank 1 Federal St Boston MA 02211

HARRISON, CHARLES PHILIP, pharmaceutical company executive; b. N.Y.C., Feb. 23, 1948; s. Leon Martin and Margaret (Edelstein) H.; m. Esther Kamelgarn, Sept. 1, 1985; 1 child, Matthew Scott. BS in Math., Pa. State U., 1969; MBA, U. Mass., 1971. Product mgr. Organon Inc., West Orange, N.J., 1972-73; mgr. market devel. Organon Diagnostics, West Orange, N.J., 1973-79, mgr. splty. products, 1979-81, dir. mktg., 1981-84; v.p., ptnr. Flair Diagnostics, El Monte, Calif., 1984-85; dir. mktg. Geometric Data div. SmithKline Beckman, Phila., 1985-86; v.p. sales, mktg., bus. devel. Unimed, Inc., Somerville, N.J., 1986-88, exec. v.p., 1989—, also bd. dirs. Mem. communications com. United Way Somerset Valley, 1987-88. Mem. Pharm. Advt. Coun. (membership com. 1988), Licensing Execs. Soc. Home: 465 Channing Ave Westfield NJ 07090 Office: Unimed Inc 35 Columbia Rd Somerville NJ 08876

HARRISON, CLARENCE BUFORD, JR., oil company executive, lawyer; b. Dallas, Sept. 27, 1944; s. Clarence Buford and Clara Janie (Jones); m. Kate Butler, July 19, 1969; children: Amy Elizabeth, Patrick Buford, Amanda Mae. BBA in Fin., U. Tex.-Austin, 1967; JD, U. Tex., 1970. Bar: Tex. 1970. Tax staff Touche Ross & Co., Dallas, 1970-71; assoc. Diamond Goodner Winkle, Wells & Harrison, Dallas, 1971-72; gen. counsel, gen. mgr., dir. Scoggins Petroleum Corp., Dallas, 1972-75; pres. Interam. Oil & Minerals Inc., successor corp., 1981—; ptnr. firm Harrison Vernon & Clark, Dallas, 1975—; speaker profl. seminars including Tri State Oil & Gas, Ind., Ill., Ky., Ind. Oil Producers. Roman Catholic. Club: Dallas Petroleum, Univ. (Dallas). Home: 420 Ridgewood Dr Richardson TX 75080 Office: 12221 Merit Dr Suite 960 Dallas TX 75251

HARRISON, EARL DAVID, lawyer, real estate executive; b. Bryn Mawr, Pa., Aug. 25, 1932; m. Lisa Philippa Wanderman, Oct. 25, 1981; 1 son, H. Jason. BA, Harvard U., 1954; JD, U. Pa., 1960. Bar: D.C. 1960. Sole practice, Washington; exec. v.p. Washington Real Estate Corp., 1986—. Capt. U.S. Army, 1954-57. Decorated Order of Rio Branco (Brazil); Order of Merit (Italy). Mem. ABA, Bar Assn D.C., Washington Assn. Realtors, Montgomery County Md. Assn. Realtors, Nat. Assn. Realtors, Harvard Club of D.C., U. Pa. Club of D.C. Home: 336 Constitution Ave NE Washington DC 20002 Office: 777 14th St NW Ste 305 Washington DC 20005

HARRISON, EARLE, former county official; b. Rainsville, Ala., May 20, 1905; s. Robert Lee and Sarepta Ophelia (Hansard) H.; m. Joan Mary Jackson, Jan. 24, 1942. AB, Northwestern U., 1929, postgrad. in bus. adminstrn., 1942; LLB, Chgo.-Kent Coll. Law, 1935. With Marshall Field & Co., Chgo., 1929-68; div. operating mgr. Marshall Field & Co., 1958-60, v.p. operations, 1960-64, v.p., treas., 1964-68; bd. dirs. Credit Bur. Cook County, 1949-69, pres., 1958-69; mem. bd. suprs., chmn. planning and zoning com. Lake County, Ill., 1970—; cons. finance and adminstrn. to hosps. and health care instns. Commr. Northeastern Ill. Planning Commn., 1970—; pres. Northeastern Ill. Plan Commn., 1973, now mem. exec. com.; ret. pres., bd. dirs. Family Fin. Counseling Service Greater Chgo.; bd. dirs. Condell Meml. Hosp., Libertyville, Ill., 1971—, adminstr., 1973—, pres., 1975-78, bus. cons., 1978—. Mem. Phi Delta Phi. Episcopalian. Home: 2801 N Kentucky Roswell NM 88201

HARRISON, EDWARD JOSEPH, III, financial executive; b. Yonkers, N.Y., June 25, 1936; s. Edward Joseph Jr. and Mary Elizabeth (Hanlon) H.; divorced; children: Deidre Anne, Sean Christopher. AB in Greek, Coll. of the Holy Cross, Worcester, Mass., 1958; JD, Columbia U., 1961. Spl. agt. FBI, 1962-68; atty., chief investigative atty., v.p., dir. Merrill Lynch and subs. cos., 1968-77; sr. v.p. Piper, Jaffray & Hopwood, Mpls., 1977-84; pres., chief exec. officer, chmn. bd. Southmark Fin. Services, Dallas, 1984—; bd. dirs. Hidden Strength Mut. Funds, N.Y.C.; chmn. bd. Global Capital Investors Corp.; pres. Southmark Distbrs. Inc. Contbr. articles to profl. jours. Pfc USMCR, 1961-62. Mem. Internat. Assn. for Fin. Planning (mem. Broker Dealer Com. 1986-87, nat. bd. dirs. 1987—), Securities Industry Assn. (mem. Nat. Mktg. Com. 1987—); Nat. Assn. Security Dealers (mem. Bus. Conduct Com. 1988— Dist. 6); Hackberry Creek Country Club, Las Colinas Sports Club, KC. Republican. Roman Catholic. Home: 2532 Brookside Dr Irving TX 75063 Office: Southmark Fin Svcs 1601 LBJ Freeway Ste 630 Dallas TX 75234

HARRISON, JAMES JOSHUA, JR., food products executive; b. Balt., Sept. 5, 1936; s. James Joshua and Marion Elizabeth (Thompson) H.; divorced; children: James Joshua III, William Darden, Mary Withers, John Theodore, Robert English, Elizabeth Ann; m. Susan Mary Hurley. BCE, Cornell U., 1960; LLB, U. Balt., 1963; MBA, Loyola Coll., Balt., 1976. Bar: Md. 1963, U.S. Supreme Ct. 1975, U.S. Dist. Ct. Md. 1975, U.S. Ct. Appeals (4th cir.) 1975. Project engr. Whiting-Turner Co., Balt., 1960-61; sr. contracts specialist Martin Marietta Corp., Balt., 1962-66; asst. counsel McCormick & Co., Inc., Hunt Valley, Md., 1966-68, asst. sec., 1968-70, assoc. counsel, 1970-73, sec., gen. counsel, 1973-80, v.p., 1980-86, v.p., chief fin. officer, mem. exec. com. 1986—, also bd. dirs; mem. adv. com. U. Balt. Law Sch., 1982—; fundraiser Loyola Coll., 1981; fin. advisor Balt. United Way, 1981—. Mem. ABA. Democrat. Episcopalian. Home: 610 W Timonium Lutherville MD 21093-1824 Office: McCormick & Co Inc 11350 McCormick Rd Hunt Valley MD 21031

HARRISON, J(OHN) MARK, controller; b. Salisbury, Md., Feb. 16, 1958; s. Jack Tarver and Bobbie Lois (McElveen) H.; m. Cynthia Lee Warren, Dec. 29, 1979; children: Dane Michael, Lauren Elizabeth. BS in Bus. Adminstrn. summa cum laude, San Diego State U., 1980. Fin. analyst, programs fin. dept. Litton Data Systems Div., Van Nuys, Calif., 1980-82, sr. fin. analyst, fin. control dept., 1983-84; fin. adminstr., fin. planning/ forecasting dept. Litton Data Systems Div., Van Nuys, 1984-86; controller Litton Data Systems Div., Pascagoula, Miss., 1986—. Mem. Litton DSD Mgmt. Club, Beta Gamma Sigma, Sigma Iota Epsilon (hon.). Republican. Baptist. Office: Litton Data Systems 2810 Old Mobile Hwy Pascagoula MS 39567

HARRISON, KEN L., holding company and electric utility executive; b. Bakersfield, Calif., Oct. 14, 1942. BS, Oreg. State U., 1964, MA, 1966. Cert. fin. analyst. V.p. 1st Interstate Bank, Portland, Oreg., 1966-75; asst. to pres. Portland Gen. Electric Co., 1975-78, v.p., 1978, chief fin. officer, 1978-80, sr. v.p., 1980-87, pres., 1987-88, also bd. dirs., chmn. bd., pres., chief exec. officer; chmn. bd., chief exec. officer Portland Gen. Corp., also bd. dirs. Office: Portland Gen Corp 121 SW Salmon St Portland OR 97204

HARRISON, LOIS SMITH, hospital executive; b. Frederick, Md., May 13, 1924; d. Richard Paul and Henrietta Foust (Menges) S.; m. Richard Lee Harrison, June 23, 1951; children: Elizabeth Lee Boyce, Margaret L. Harrison Wade, Richard Paul. BA, Hood Coll., 1945; MA, Columbia U., 1946. Counselor CCNY, 1945-46; founding adminstr., counselor, instr. psychology and sociology Hagerstown (Md.) Jr. Coll., 1946-51, registrar, 1946-51, 53-54, instr. psychology and orienta, 1954—; registrar, instr. psychology, Balt. Jr. Coll., 1951-54; bus. mgr., acct. for pvt. med. practice Hagerstown, 1953—; trustee Washington County Hosp., Hagerstown, 1975—; chmn. bd. Washington County Hosp., 1986—; bd. dirs. Home Fed. Savs. Bank, Hagerstown, 1983—; speaker ednl. panels and convs. Author: The Church Woman, 1960-65. Trustee Hood Coll., Frederick, 1972—, chmn. bd., 1979—; mem. Md. Gov.'s Commn. To Study Structure and Ednl. Devel. Commn., 1987—; pres. Washington County Coun. Ch. Women, 1970-72; appointee Econ. Devel. Commn., County Impact Study Commn.; bd. dirs. Md. Chs. United, 1975—. Recipient Alumnae Achievement award Hood Coll., 1975, Washington County Woman of Yr. award AAUW, 1984, Md. Woman of Yr. award, 1984, Md. Woman of Yr. award Francis Scott Key Commn. for Md.'s 350th Anniversary, 1984. Mem. Hagerstown C. of C. Democrat. Methodist. Home: 1640 Fountain Head Rd Hagerstown MD 21740 Office: Washington County Hosp Hagertown MD 21740

HARRISON, MARK ALAN, chemical engineer; b. Raleigh, N.C., Oct. 12, 1931; s. Benjamin Sanford and Lillian (Burgur) H.; m. Alice Harrison, May 27, 1957; children: Susan Harrison-Press, Lawrence E., Cindy Ellen. BS in Chem. Engring., N.C. State U., 1953, MS in Phys. Chemistry, 1954. Registered profl. engr. N.J., N.Y. Staff engr. 3M Co., Newark, 1955-61, Standard Dack Corp., Clifton, N.J., 1961-65; plant mgr. Gen. Foam Corp., Carlstadt, N.J., 1965-68; prin. Air-O-Plastic Corp., Edison, N.J., 1968-72; v.p. Tuck Ind. Inc., New Rochelle, N.Y., 1972—. Served to capt. USAF, 1951-57, Korea. Home: 807 Wynetta Pl Paramus NJ 07652 Office: Tech Tape Inc 1 Le Fevre Ln New Rochelle NY 10801

HARRISON, MARY STYRON, accountant; b. Foley, Ala., Dec. 7, 1949; d. Raymond Charles Styron and Vestel Ilene (Wooten) Barnett; m. Dale M. Harrison, May 1, 1974; 1 child, John Dale. AS in Bus. Adminstrn., Faulkner Jr. Coll., 1980; BS in Bus. Adminstrn., Troy State U., 1981. CPA, Ala. Acct. Jerome C. Olsen Co., Mobile, Ala., 1980-83, Johnson, Dees & Montgomery, Foley, Ala., 1983-84; comptroller Vols. Am. S. Ala., Inc., Mobile, 1984-87; controller Lake Forest Yacht and Country Club, Daphne, Ala., 1987—; part-time instr. Faulkner Jr. Coll., Bay Minette, Ala., 1983—. Mem. Am. Inst. CPA's, Ala. Soc. CPA's, Mobile chpt. of Ala. Soc. CPA's. Republican. Mormon. Home: Rt 1 Box 89 Loxley AL 36551 Office: Lake Forest Yacht & Country Club PO Box 1737 Daphne AL 36526

HARRISON, RICHARD DONALD, retired food company executive; b. Salt Lake City, May 19, 1923; s. William Z. and Mary Frances (Sappington) H.; m. Marian D. Fletcher, Feb., 1984; children: Amy Virginia, Leslie Lynn, Julie Fleming, Susan Elizabeth, Alyse Carrie, Richard Donald. B.A., Stanford U., 1946; LL.B., U. Mich., 1949. Bar: D.C., Mich., Utah 1950, Wash. 1952, also U.S. Supreme Ct., other fed. cts 1952. Spl. asst. to atty. tax div., appellate sect. Dept. Justice, 1950-52; pvt. practice Seattle, 1952-54; with Fleming Cos., Inc., Topeka, 1954—, v.p., 1957-64, dir. planning, 1963-64, pres., from 1964, chief exec. officer, 1966-88, chmn., 1981-89, also bd. dirs.; bd. dirs. Fed. Res. Bank, Kansas City, Quaker Oats Co., Chgo., Kerr-McGee Corp., Oklahoma City, Okla. Bd. dirs. United Way; bd. dirs. Oklahoma City YMCA, Oklahoma City Community Found., Food Mktg. Inst., Washington, Nat. Legal Ctr. for Pub. Interest, Washington; bd. govs. Okla. Christian Coll.; past chmn., trustee Oklahoma City U.; mem. nat. adv. coun. U. Utah, Salt Lake City. Mem. Nat. Am. Wholesale Grocers (past pres.), Oklahoma City C. of C. (past pres.), Sigma Chi, Phi Delta Phi. Presbyn. Clubs: River (Kansas City); Beacon (Oklahoma City), Oklahoma City Golf and Country (Oklahoma City), Argyle (San Antonio); Alta (Salt Lake City); Thunderbird (Rancho Mirage, Calif.), Carlton (Chgo.).

HARRISON, ROBERT JOSEPH, former utility company executive; b. St. Charles, Mo., June 21, 1931; s. Daniel Anthony and Marie Elizabeth (Riney) H.; m. Monique Gilbert, June 18, 1955; children: David, Gregory, Elizabeth, Thomas. B.B.A., U. Okla., 1957. With Public Service Co. N.H., Manchester, 1957—; fin. v.p., dir. Public Service Co. N.H., until 1980, pres., 1980-88, chief fin. officer, from 1980, pres., chief exec. officer, dir., 1988, resigned, Sept. 1988; dir. Numerica Fin. Corp., Numerica Savs. Bank, Manchester, Maine Yankee Atomic Power Co., Vt. Yankee Nuclear Power Corp., Yankee Atomic Electric Co.; exec. com. Northeast Power Coordinating Council. Bd. dirs. United Way, 1970-78, mem. exec. com., v.p., 1972—; bd. dir. Am. Heart Assn. N.H. affiliate, Easter Seal Found. of N.H. and Vt.; past pres. St. Catherine's Parish Council. Served with USAF, 1951-55. Office: Pub Svc Co of New Hampshire PO Box 330 1000 Elm St Manchester NH 03105

HARRISON, STEPHEN EARLE, manufacturing executive; b. Little Rock, May 25, 1941; s. Richard G. and Edwin R. (McDaniels) H.; m. Donie Evelyn Brown, Aug. 5, 1960; children: Stephen Brian, Angela Eve. Grad. high sch., Joe T. Robinson, Pulaski County, Ark. Purchasing Welsco Inc., Little Rock, 1959-64, corp. sec., 1964, corp. sec., treas., 1964-80, pres., 1980-85, owner, pres., chief exec. officer, 1985—; bd. dirs. Airgas Inc., Del., 1985-89. Recipient Leonard Parker Poole Safety award Compressed Gas Assn., Washington, 1986. Mem. Internat. Oxygen Mfg. Assn. (pres. 1975-76), Nat. Welding Supply Assn., Compressed Gas Assn. Office: Welsco Inc 9301 Crystal Hill Rd North Little Rock AR 72118

HARRISON, WARREN, finance company executive; b. N.Y.C., Aug. 9, 1951; s. Abraham and Lorraine (Niss) H.; m. Beatrice Schreter, Sept. 8, 1985. BS in Econs., U. Pa., 1973; JD, U. Mich., 1976. Bar: N.Y. 1977. Assoc. Curtis, Mallet-Prevost, Colt & Mosle, N.Y.C., 1976-77, Ullman, Miller & Wrubel, N.Y.C., 1977-78; gen. ptnr. David J. Greene & Co., N.Y.C., 1979-81; spl. ltd. ptnr. L.F. Rothschild, Unterberg, Towbin, N.Y.C., 1981-84; sr. v.p. TSG Holdings, Inc., N.Y.C., 1985-87; gen. ptnr. David J. Greene & Co., N.Y.C., 1987-88; risk arbitrageur Steinhard & Ptnrs., N.Y.C., 1988—. Editor: The Situation Review, 1985. Mem. ABA, N.Y. State Bar Assn. Home: 420 E 72nd St #20E New York NY 10021 Office: Steinhard & Ptnrs 605 3rd Ave New York NY 11581

HARRISON, WILLIAM BURWELL, JR., banker; b. Rocky Mount, N.C., Aug. 12, 1943; s. William Burwell and Katherine (Spruill) H.; m. Anne MacDonald Stephens, Dec. 7, 1985. B.S. in Econs., U. N.C., Chapel Hill, 1966, Spl. student in Bus. Adminstrn., 1966-67; Sr. Mgmt. Program, Harvard Bus. Sch., Vevey, Switzerland, 1979. Trainee Chem. Bank, N.Y.C., 1967-69, Mid-South corp. and corr. banking group, 1969-74, West Coast corp. and corr. banking group, 1974-76; dist. head, Western regional coordinator Chem. Bank, San Francisco, 1976-78; regional coordinator, sr. v.p. Chem. Bank, London, England, 1978-82, sr. v.p., div. head Europe, 1982-83; exec. v.p. U.S. Corp. div. Chem. Bank, N.Y.C., 1983—, group exec. banking and corporate fin. group, 1987—; dir. Kings Entertainment Co., Charlotte, N.C., Dillard Dept. Stores, Little Rock, N.C. Outward Bound Sch., Morganton, N.C. Soc., N.Y.C.; trustee U.S. Council for Internat. Bus., N.Y.C. Bd. visitors U. N.C., U. N.C. Sch. Bus. Mem. Assn. Res. City Bankers, The Brook Club, Racquet Club, Piping Rock Club, The Links Club. Episcopalian.

HARRISON, WILLIAM OLIVER, JR., lawyer, small business owner; b. Corpus Christi, Tex., Oct. 16, 1945; s. William Oliver and Nell Betty (Anderson) H.; m. Cathy Lynn Williams, Dec. 1, 1984. BA, Tex. Christian U., 1967; JD, U. Tex., 1970. Atty. Wood, Burney, Nesbitt and Ryan, Corpus Christi, 1971-75; sole practice Corpus Christi, 1975-78; ptnr. Harrison, Stone and Jordan, Corpus Christi, 1978-84; state rep. Tex. House of Reps., 1979-81, 83-85; ptnr. Parkinson and Assocs., Austin, Tex., 1983—; sec., treas. CompuPrint, Inc., Austin, Tex., 1983-86, Cooper's Alley Restaurant and Saloon, Inc., Corpus Christi, 1983-86; pres. Lighthouse Bar and Grill Inc., Corpus Christi, 1984—; ptnr. Heard Goggan Blair Williams and Harrison, Houston, 1984—. Bd. dirs. Corpus Christi C. of C., Cerebral Palsy Found., 1982-83; selection chmn. Leadership Corpus Christi, 1981-82; mem. steering com. Goals for Corpus Christi; mem. Corpus Christi Conv. and Tourist Bur., LWV, Leadership Corpus Christi Alumni, Governmental Commn. on Efficiency and Economy, 1986. Served to cpl. U.S. Army, 1964-70. Named one of Outstanding Young Men of Am., U.S. Jaycees, 1978. Mem. ABA, Tex. Bar Assn., Nueces County Bar Assn., Nat. Restaurant Assn., Tex. Restaurant Assn. Democrat. Mem. Disciples of Christ Ch. Office: Lighthouse Restaurant 444 N Shoreline Corpus Christi TX 78401

HARRITT, NORMAN L., manufacturing company executive; b. Kansas City, Mo., Mar. 19, 1941; s. Gilbert Norman and Gladys Marie (Henderson) H.; m. Cynthia Marie Lanza, Aug. 14, 1965; children: Kevin, Mark. B.A. in Econs., Duke U., 1963; M.B.A. in Fin., U. Pitts., 1965. V.p. and controller Consol. Foods Corp., Chgo., 1977-78; v.p. fin. and adminstrn. Truck Group Internat. Harvester Co., Chgo., 1978-80; v.p., controller Internat. Harvester Co., 1981-85; v. p. fin., chief fin. officer Savin Corp., Stamford, Conn., 1986-87, exec. v.p. chief fin., adminstrv. officer, dir., 1987—. Served with USAR, 1964-69. Mem. Fin. Execs. Inst. Republican. Episcopalian. Clubs: Economic (Chgo.); Conn. Golf (Easton); Aspetuck Valley Country (Weston, Conn.). Home: 36 Blacksmith Ridge Ridgefield CT 06877 Office: Savin Corp 9 W Broad St Stamford CT 06904

HARROP-WILLIAMS, KINGSLEY ORMONDE, civil engineer, educator; b. New Amsterdam, Guyana, Dec. 12, 1947; came to U.S., 1970, naturalized, 1981; s. Edric Christopher and Adelaide (Jardin) H-W.; m. Lynette Gibson, July 1, 1975; children: Kingsley Audwin, Tippi Ann, Cher Anemone. BE magna cum laude, CUNY, 1975, ME, 1976; PhD, Rensselaer Poly. Inst., 1980. Registered profl. engr., Pa. Adj. lectr. CUNY, 1975-76; research asst. Rensselaer Poly. Inst., Troy, N.Y., 1976-80; geotech. engr. D'Appolonia Cons. Engrs., Pitts., 1981-83; asst. prof. Carnegie-Mellon U., Pitts., 1980-85; prin. Innovation Engring. Inc., Pitts., 1984—; engr. The BDM Corp., McLean, Va., 1985—. Contbr. articles to profl. jours. Coach YMCA Soccer, Penn Hills, Pa., 1984. Recipient J. Charles Rathbun award CUNY, 1974, Univ. fellow, 1975; Rensselaer Poly. Inst. grantee, 1980. Mem. ASCE, Am. Acad. Mechanics, Sigma Xi, Chi Epsilon. Democrat. Roman Catholic. Avocations: personal computer software development, soccer.

HARRY, WILLIAM, III, publishing company executive. V.p. taxes Macmillan Inc., N.Y.C. Office: Macmillan Inc 866 3rd Ave New York NY 10022 *

HARSCH, STEVEN MERRILL, mortgage banker; b. Peoria, Ill., Apr. 20, 1947; s. David Robert and Beth Ardeth (Merrill) H.; m. Kathleen Michele Herbison, Aug. 2, 1969; children: Anne Herbison, Jonathan Merrill. BS in Mktg., U. Ill., 1970; MBA, Old Dominion U., 1975. Analyst mktg. ARINC Research, Annapolis, Md., 1975-76; account exec. Bache, Halsey, Stuart and Shields, Chgo., 1976-79; sr. v.p. Oppenheimer & Co., Chgo., 1979-86, Griffin, Kubik, Stevens & Thompson, Chgo., 1986-87; pres. Harsch & Assocs., Hinsdale, Ill., 1987—; exec. v.p. First Surety Mortgage, Skokie, Ill., 1988; pres. Comml. Security Mortgage Corp., Des Plaines, Ill., 1988—; dir. Citilink Air Parcel, Waukegan, Ill., 1984—, Internat. Laser Machine, Indpls., 1985; cons. Munson Geothermal, Reno, 1986—. Republican. Presbyterian. Home: 19 W Ayres St Hinsdale IL 60521 Office: Comml Security Mortgage Corp 2400 E Devon Ste 246 Des Plaines IL 60018

HARSHA, JACQUELINE GAYLE, marketing professional; b. Fargo, N.D., Dec. 30, 1946; d. Clayton E. and Sylvia (Strickler) Johnson; divorced. Student, Moorhead State Coll., 1964-67; BA in English, Ariz. State U., 1982. Adminstrv. asst. Center for Environ. Studies, Tempe, Ariz., 1980-81; market analyst Pulte Home Corp., Tempe, 1982-85, dir. research, 1985-86; mgr. research, sr. cons. Home Builder Services, Phoenix, 1986—; cons. to Pulte Home Corp., Tucson, Newport Beach, Calif., 1985—. Coordinator, author A Proposal for the Cooperative Devel. of a Water Conservation Program, 1985; appointed mem. Water Quality Adv. Bd. Maricopa County Assn. Govts., Phoenix, 1981—; co-organized Ariz. Clean Air Coalition, Phoenix, 1982; bd. dirs. Laguna Beach Chamber Music Soc. Recipient Outstanding Service in Community and Environ. Issues award Pulte Home Corp., 1985. Mem. Am. Mktg. Assn., Urban Land Inst. Democrat.

HARSHMAN, MORTON LEONARD, physician, business executive; b. Youngstown, Ohio, Apr. 21, 1932; s. Ben and Lllian (Malkoff) H.; m. Barbara Elmore, June 21, 1957; children—Beth, Melissa. B.S., Ohio State U., 1953, M.D., 1957. Diplomate Am. Bd. Family Practice. Intern Grant Hosp., Columbus, Ohio, 1957-58; practice medicine specializing in family practice Cin., 1960—; v.p. med. staff Bethesda Hosp., 1974-75, pres., 1975-77; mem. staff Christ Hosp., Cin., Children's Hosp., Cin., Deaconess Hosp., Cin., Providence Hosp., Cin.; pres. Pacific Isle Co.; pres., bd. dirs. Morton Harshman Inc., 880 Real Estate Co. Trustee Bethesda Hosp. and Deaconess Assn., 1972-79. Served with USNR, 1958-60. Fellow Am. Acad. Family Practice (charter); mem. AMA, Ohio Med. Assn., Cin. Acad. Medicine, Ohio Acad. Family Practice, Southwestern Ohio Acad. Family Practice, Ky. Col. Assn., Phi Beta Kappa, Alpha Epsilon Delta, Phi Delta Epsilon (Cin.). Home: 630 Flagstaff Dr Cincinnati OH 45215 Office: 880 Reynard Dr Cincinnati OH 45231

HART, ALEX WAY, banker; b. Meadville, Pa., June 4, 1940; s. Alex William and Rosemary (Brown) H.; children: Alex, Michael, Gregory, Suzanne, Kiersten; m. Mary Templeton, June 20, 1987. AB, Harvard U., 1962. Asst. v.p. Bank Ohio, Columbus, 1969-73; sr. v.p. First Chgo. Corp., Chgo., 1973-78; pres., chief exec. officer First Interstate Svcs. Co. Inc., L.A., 1978-81; exec. v.p. First Interstate Bancorp, 1981-88; bd. mem. Cirrus Systems, Inc., Chgo., 1982—; pres., chief exec. officer Master Card Internat., N.Y.C., 1988—; also vice chmn. bd. dirs. Master Card, Internat., N.Y.C.; bd. dirs. Regional Inst. So. Calif., Master Card Internat., 1984—, vice chmn. 1988; mem., bd. dir. Eurocard Internat., 1989. Bd. dirs. Mus. Natural History, L.A., 1983, Regional Inst. So. Calif., 1986-87. Mem. Bank Mktg. Assn. (dir. 1977-80). Republican. Roman Catholic. Club: Harvard (L.A.) (bd. dir. 1982); L.A. Athletic. Office: Mastercard Internat 888 7th Ave New York NY 10106

HART, BETTY J(OAN), newspaper columnist; b. Lebanon, Mo., Aug. 27, 1943; d. Francis Rowden and Lorea (Dame) Lindsey; m. Milan Darius Hart, Nov. 16, 1963; 1 child, Mila Jo. Grad., Lebanon High Sch. Exec. sec. Low & Honssinger, Lebanon, 1961-85; field underwriter N.Y. Life Ins. Co., 1985—. Editorial columnist Springfield, Mo. News Leader; contbr. articles to newspapers and religious periodicals. Exec. coun. Lebanon Area Small Bus. Assn., 1987—; commr. Mo. Commn. Human Rights, Jefferson City, 1986—; pres. Lebanon Ministerial Alliance, 1987—, pres., 1988; active Nat. Assn. Evangelists Ch. of God, Anderson, Ind. (ordained 1986); Laclede Co. Rep. Women; bd. dirs. Nat. Assn. Evangelists Ch. of God, Anderson, Ind. Mem. Lebanon C. of C. (gov. affairs com. 1980—), Nat. Assn. Life Underwriters (Nat. Quality award 1987, Nat. Sales Achievement award 1987), Mo. Life Underwriters Assn., Million Dollar Round Table. Home: 481 S Washington Lebanon MO 65536 Office: NY Life Ins Co PO Box 105 Lebanon MO 65536

HART, CHARLES E., health care products executive; b. 1925; married. BS, McGill U., 1948. With A.H. Robins Co., Richmond, Va., 1956-79, 81—, sr. v.p., gen. mgr. pharm. div., 1981-86, exec. v.p., 1987—; pres. Glaxo Inc., 1979-81. Office: A H Robins Co Inc 1407 Cummings Dr Richmond VA 23220

HART, DAVID CHURCHILL, lawyer; b. Galesburg, Ill., Mar. 5, 1940; s. Herbert Edward and Florence (Butterweck) H.; m. Beth Rubinstein, Aug. 11, 1963; children: Melissa, Katherine. BA, Northwestern U., 1962; LLB, Harvard U., 1965. Bar: Ill. 1965, U.S. Dist. Ct. (no. dist.) Ill. 1965. Assoc. Ross & Hardies, Chgo., 1965-69; atty. R.R. Donnelley & Sons Co., Chgo., 1969-85, gen. counsel, 1985-86, v.p., gen. counsel, 1986—, also sec., 1989—. Served to 1st lt. USAR, 1966-71. Mem. ABA (com. on corp. law depts.), Chgo. Bar Assn. Clubs: Law, Univ. (Chgo.). Office: R R Donnelley & Sons Co 2223 Martin Luther King Dr Chicago IL 60616

HART, DONALD RAY, publisher; b. Kansas City, Kans., Aug. 13, 1943; s. Isaac Newton and Lulu Irene (Rollins) H.; m. Jane Marie Vondy, Mar. 13, 1971; children: Bradley Ray, Michael Allan. BA, Colo. State U., 1966. Founder, operator Photo-By Hart Studio, Ft. Collins, Colo., 1962-65; founder, editor, pub. The Campus Tayle, Ft. Collins, 1965-66; salesman Petroleum Pubs., Inc. subs. Bell Publs. Co. (acquired by Data Services Inc. 1970), Denver, 1967-70, pub., 1970-73, editor, 1972-73; editor, pub. Western Oil World and Rocky Mountain Petroleum Directory, Hart Publs., Inc., Denver, 1973—, pub. Southwest Oil World mag., 1976—; founder, pub. Oil and Gas Investor Mag., pub. Northeast Oil World, Northeast Petroleum Directory, Gulf Coast Oil World, MidContinent Oil World, MidContinent Petroleum Directory; pres. Russellville Homeowners and Property Owners Assn., 1980; mem. Douglas County Planning Commn., Colo., 1984—, vice chmn., 1986, chmn., 1987. Recipient Journalism award Rocky Mountain Assn. Geologists, 1983, Downtown Denver Ptnrship. award, 1989. Mem. Rocky Mountain Oil and Gas Assn. (exec. com. 1983—), Ind. Petroleum Assn. (recipient Donald Hart award 1988, Mountain States bd. dirs. 1983—), Assn. Petroleum Writers (bd. dirs. 1981—), Assn. Bus. Publishers, Douglas County Land Conservancy (founder 1988—), Denver Ad hoc Com. To Invite Oil Now (chmn. 1988—). Baptist. Clubs: Denver Petroleum (bd. dirs. 1989—), Pinery Country. Office: Southwest Oil World Mag PO Box 1917 Denver CO 80201

HART, ERIC MULLINS, finance company executive; b. Clanton, Ala., May 6, 1925; s. Eric and Myrtle (Mullins) H.; m. Joy Porter, May 16, 1953; children: Anne Porter, Eric Mullins. BS, U. Ala., 1946; grad., Harvard Advanced Mgmt. Program, 1970. With Internat. Paper Co., 1946-69, asst. to v.p.-treas., 1962-64, comptroller, 1964-69; treas. Red River Paper Mill, Inc., 1964-69; fin. v.p. Lever Bros. Co., 1969-83, dir., 1969-83; dir. Unilever U.S. Inc., 1981-83; exec. in residence Columbia U. Bus. Sch.; bd. dirs. Macmillan Inc. Trustee King Sch., Stamford, Conn., 1970-76. Mem. Sigma Alpha Epsilon. Club: Union League (N.Y.C.). Home: PO Box 2999 Darien CT 06820 Office: Columbia U 117 E 57th St New York NY 10022

HART, JAY ALBERT CHARLES, real estate broker; b. Rockford, Ill., Apr. 16, 1923; s. Jabez Waterman and Monty Evangeline (Burgin) H.; student U. Ill., 1941-42, U. Mo., 1942-43, U. Miami (Fla.), 1952-56, Rockford Coll., 1961-62; m. Marie D. Goetz, July 16, 1976; children—Dale M., Jay C.H. Exec. v.p. Hart Oil Co., Rockford, 1947—; pres. Internat. Service Co., Pompano Beach, Fla., 1952-58; v.p. Ipsen Industries, Inc., Rockford, 1958-61; owner Hart Realtors, Rockford, 1961-86; owner Hart & Assocs., Rockford, 1987—; pres. Rock Cut Corp., 1978—; sec. Intra World, Inc., 1981-83; lectr. in field; trustee, sr. analyst Anchor Real Estate Investment Trust, Chgo., 1971-80. Dir. Winnebago County (Ill.) CD, 1975; dep. coordinator Winnebago County (Ill.) ESDA, 1976-86. Chmn. Rock River chpt. ARC, 1973, nat. nominating com., 1971, disaster chmn. Illiana div., 1972-80; bd. counselors Rockford Coll., 1974-80; emergency coordinator 9th Naval dist. M.A.R.S., USN, 1960-68, civilian adv. council, 1968-78, Ill. area coordinator, 1986-87, lifetime assoc. mem., 1987; net ops. officer 4th region Navy-Marine Corps MARS, 1988—. Office mgr. Citizens for Eisenhower, Chgo., 1952. Served with USAAF, 1943-46. Mem. Rockford Air Guild (pres. 1974, 76-77), Tamaroa Watercolor Soc. (v.p. 1974-80), Rockford Art Guild (dir.), Exptl. Amateur Radio Soc. (pres. 1960-80), Nat. Assn. Real Estate Appraisers, Soc. Indsl. and Office Realtors, Nat. Assn. Rev. Appraisers and Mortgage Underwriters, Nat. Assn. Realtors, Phi Eta Sigma. Mason (Shriner). Clubs: Univ., City. Author: Real Estate Buyers and Sellers Guide, 1961. Paintings in pvt., pub. collections; illustrations in numerous publs. Home: 2406 E Ln Rockford IL 61107 Office: Rock Cut Corp 3701 E State St Rockford IL 61108

HART, LAUREN L., marketing executive; b. Providence, Jan. 30, 1952; d. Giovanni and Ruth Elsie (Schultheis) Luongo; m. Allan Gregory Works, May 26, 1983 (div. Aug. 1985). BS, U. R.I., 1975, MS, 1981. Mktg. asst. Agawam Creative Mktg., Rowley, Mass., 1977-79; asst. sales & mktg. Ocean State Jobbers Inc., North Kingstown, R.I., 1979-81; rsch. assoc. U. R.I., Kingston, 1979-81; with lab supply & chem. sales Ea. Scientific Co., Providence, 1981-82; v.p. corp., v.p. mktg.mgr., ops. officer Alan's Bus. Machines Inc., Barre, Vt., 1982—. Mem. NAFE, Women Bus. Owners Vt., Nat. Women Bus. Owners, Inst. Food Technologists (Z John Ordahl award 1981), Advt./Image/Mktg. Assn. (pres. 1985-86). Home: PO Box 417 Barre VT 05641 Office: Alan's Bus Machines Inc 46 N Main St Barre VT 05641

HART, LEROY BANKS, financial software executive; b. Thompsontown, Pa., July 12, 1954; s. Bill and Helen (Lauver) H.; student Houghton Coll., 1975; m. Virginia Sattazahn, June 26, 1976; children: Peter, Timothy, Michael, Evan. BS Kutztown State U., 1976; postgrad. Pa. State U., 1978-79, St. Joseph's Coll., 1979-81. Acct. Security of Am. Life, Reading, Pa., 1976-78, EDP coordinator, 1978-80, asst. v.p., controller, 1981-82; exec. v.p. Eastern Software Corp., 1984-88; pres. Hart Fin. Svcs., 1982-84, 88—. Trustee Zion Evang. Congl. Ch., 1978-84, 87-88, Lakeside Evang. Congl. Ch., 1987—. Fellow Life Office Mgmt. Assn. Home and Office: 5 Buck Run Mohnton PA 19540 Office: Hart Fin Svcs 61 Shenango Ave PO Box 256 Sharon PA 16146

HART, N. BERNE, banker; b. Denver, Jan. 6, 1930; s. Horace H. and Eva (Saville) H.; m. Wilma Jean Shadley, Sept. 17, 1952; children: Linda Lea Hart Frederick, Patricia Sue Hart Sweeney, David Bruce. B.A., Colo. Coll., 1951; postgrad., Colo. Sch. Banking, 1958-60. Sales trainee U.S. Rubber Co., 1953; exec. trainee United Bank of Denver N.A., 1954-56, asst. operations mgr., 1956-58, asst. cashier, 1958-61, asst. v.p., 1961, cashier, 1961-65, v.p. ops., 1965-69, sr. v.p. personal banking div., 1969, sr. v.p., trust officer, 1969-73; v.p. United Banks Colo. Inc., 1974, exec. v.p., 1975-77, pres., 1977-78, chmn., 1979—; mem. fed. adv. council Fed. Res. Bd., 1983-85. Past chmn. bd. dirs. St. Joseph Hosp., Denver; past chmn. bd. trustees Colo. Sch. Banking. Served to capt. USMCR, 1951-53. Named Denver Met. Exec. of Year Denver chpt. Nat. Secs. Assn., 1968; recipient Torch of Liberty award Anti-Defamation League, 1986, Colo. Bus. Leader of 1988 award, 1988. Mem. Colo. Bankers Assn. (past pres.), Adminstrv. Mgmt. Soc. (past pres. Denver chpt.), Colo. Assn. Commerce and Industry (chmn. 1985-86), Bank Adminstrn. Inst. (chmn. 1980-81), Beta Theta Pi. Republican. Clubs: Rotary (Denver) (pres. 1982-83), University (Denver); Denver Country. Home: 2552 E Alameda Ave #99 Denver CO 80209 Office: United Banks Colo Inc 1 United Bank Ctr 1700 Lincoln Ste 3200 Denver CO 80274-0010

HARTE, CHRISTOPHER MCCUTCHEON, newspaper executive; b. Hanover, N.H., Nov. 20, 1947; s. Edward Holmead and Janet (Wendel) H.; m. Kay Marie Wagenknecht, Feb. 8, 1984; 1 child, William. BA, Stanford U., 1969; MBA, U. Tex., 1974. Assoc. McKinsey and Co., Inc., Dallas, 1974-76; dir. research and promotion Austin (Tex.) Am. Statesman, 1976-79; pvt. practice pub., communications 1979-83; mem. advanced mgmt. devel. program Miami (Fla.) Herald, 1983-85; asst. to pres. newspaper div. Knight-Ridder Inc., Miami, 1985-86; pres., pub. Centre Daily Times, State Coll., Pa., 1986—. Adv. dir. North Shore Weeklies, Ipswich, Mass., 1986—; bd. dirs. Register, Inc., Barnstable, Mass., 1981—, New Eng. Monthly, Haydenville, Mass., 1983—. Trustee Hurricane Island Outward Bound Sch., Rockland, Maine, 1984—. Club: Headliners (Austin). Home: 355 Ridge Ave State College PA 16803 Office: Centre Daily Times Box 89 State College PA 16804

HARTE, HOUSTON HARRIMAN, newspaper, broadcasting executive; b. San Angelo, Tex., Feb. 15, 1927; s. Houston and Caroline Isabel (McCutcheon) H.; m. Carolyn Esther Hardig, June 17, 1950; children: Houston Ritchie, David Harriman, Sarah Elizabeth. B.A., Washington and Lee U., 1950. Partner Snyder (Tex.) Daily News, 1950-52, editor, 1952-54; with Des Moines Register and Tribune, 1954-56; pres. San Angelo Standard, Inc., 1956-62; v.p. Express Pub. Co., San Antonio, 1962-66; pres. Express Pub. Co., 1966-72; chmn. bd. Harte-Hanks Communications, Inc., 1971—. Pres. bd. dirs. San Angelo Symphony, 1960; v.p. Concho Valley council Boy Scouts Am., 1960-62; bd. visitors USAF Acad., 1965-69; bd. regents East Tex. State U., 1970-81; trustee Stillman Coll., 1976—, Washington and Lee U., 1981—; chmn. bd. trustees Tex. Presbyterian Found., 1985-88. Served with USNR, 1945-46. Democrat. Presbyterian. Office: Harte/Hanks Communications PO Box 269 San Antonio TX 78291

HARTEL, STEPHEN ALLEN, telecommunications financial analyst; b. Ft. Worth, Tex., Nov. 4, 1957; s. Bruce and Felicia (Jacobs) H.; m. Lisa Alecci, Apr. 24, 1982. BSBA, U. Denver, 1980, MBA, 1981. Owner, mgr. Rapper's Delight, Denver, 1979-81; cost analyst Mountain Bell, Denver, 1981-84; mgr. access rates United Tel. System, Overland Park, Kans., 1984-87; mgr. costing and pricing United Telecom, Westwood, Kans., 1987-88; staff dir. costing and pricing strategy United Telecom, Westwood, 1988—. Republican.

Methodist. Home: 6513 Bradshaw Shawnee KS 66216 Office: United Telecom 2330 Shawnee Mission Pkwy Westwood KS 66205

HARTER, ROBERT JACKSON, JR., lawyer, transportation holding company executive; b. New Orleans, Nov. 6, 1944; s. Robert Jackson and Anne Marie (Carangelo) H.; m. Ann Eudean Peebles, Mar. 25, 1972; children: Ryan Scott, Ashley Ann. A.B., Stanford U., 1966; J.D., U. So. Calif., 1969. Bar: U.S. Dist. Ct., Calif. 1970. Law clk. to judge U.S. Ct. Appeals (9th cir.), Los Angeles, 1969-70; assoc. Gibson, Dunn & Crutcher, Los Angeles, 1970-76, Shutan & Trost, Los Angeles, 1976-78; assoc. gen. counsel Tiger Internat., Inc., Los Angeles, 1978-79; v.p. law Tiger Internat., Inc., 1979-82, v.p., gen. counsel, sec., 1982-85, sr. v.p. law, sec., 1985, sr. v.p., gen. counsel, sec., 1985—. Mem. ABA, Los Angeles County Bar Assn., Order of Coif.

HARTHUN, LUTHER ARTHUR, lawyer; b. Lansing, Ill., Apr. 25, 1935; s. Herbert and Martha (Loeber) H.; m. Ann Elizabeth Brose, Sept. 24, 1961; children—Matthew James, Nancy Lynn, Jill Marie, Laura Ann. B.A., Valparaiso U., 1957; J.D., U. Chgo., 1960; LL.M., U. Calif., Berkeley, 1961. Bar: Ill. 1961, Calif. 1961, Va. 1985. Assoc. Hopkins, Sutter Owen, Mulroy & Davis, Chgo., 1961-66; gen. counsel, sec. A-T-O Inc. (now Figgie Internat. Inc.), Cleve., 1966-70; v.p., gen. counsel, sec. A-T-O Inc. (now Figgie Internat. Inc.), Willoughby, Ohio, 1970; sr. v.p., internat. gen. counsel Figgie Internat., Inc., Willoughby, Ohio, 1970—. Mem. ABA, Ill. Bar Assn., Calif. Bar Assn., Am. Soc. Corp. Secs., Ohio Bar Assn., Va. Bar Assn. Lutheran. Office: Figgie Internat Inc 4420 Sherwin Rd Willoughby OH 44094

HARTIG, CARL F., JR., financial executive; b. Holyoke, Mass., Apr. 9, 1942; s. Carl F. and Amelia (Gawlik) H.; m. Robina June Hartig, Aug. 22, 1964; children: Scott, Christopher. AS in Bus., Berkshire Community Coll., 1968; BBA, Western New Eng. Coll., 1974, MBA, 1985; MS in Organ. Devel., Am. Internat. Coll., 1987. Data processing supr. Champion Packages Corp., Chicopee, Mass., 1964-65, The Mead Corp., South Lee, Mass., 1965-68; system analyst Combustion Engring., Inc., Windsor, Conn., 1968-70; div. contr. Combustion Engring., Inc., 1970-72; contr., treas. Nonotuck Mfg. Co., South Hadley, Mass., 1972-82; corp. ocntr. Hano Bus. Forms, Inc., Springfield, Mass., 1982-84; corp. contr., dir. Hampden Paper, Inc., Holyoke, 1984—; adj. lectr. Coll. of Our Lady of the Elms, Chicopee, 1985—. Mem. fin. com. Town of Easthampton, Mass., 1973-76; chmn. town Rep. Com., Easthampton, 1975-80. With USN, 1960-64. Mem. Nat. Assn. Accts., Inst. Internal Auditors (cert.), Nat. Assn. Tax Practitioners, Am. Legion, Masons, Order Eastern Star. Republican. United Ch. of Christ. Home: 164 Line St Easthampton MA 01027 Office: Hampden Paper Inc 100 Water St Holyoke MA 01041

HARTKE, NADINE JOYCE, federal agency administrator; b. Falls Church, Va., Dec. 9, 1961; d. Vance and Martha Jane (Tiernan) H. BA in Liberal Studies, MaryMount U., 1988. Fin. analyst Cattle Farm Ops., Aldie, Va., 1980-82; fin. advisor Law Firm, Falls Church, Va., 1982-84; mgmt. analyst Fed. Govt.-OMB, Washington, 1984—. Mem. NAFE, IAHA, AHR, Nat. Arbor Found. Democrat. Lutheran. Home: 7751 Inversham Dr #220 Falls Church VA 22042

HARTL, WILLIAM PARKER, oil company executive; b. Boston, May 9, 1935; s. Emil Martin and Elizabeth (Parker) H.; m. Judith Ford, Feb. 9, 1985. BA, Boston U., 1964. Exec., Ashland Oil Europe, Inc., Geneva, 1968-72, dir. fin. communications Ashland Oil, Inc., N.Y.C., 1972—; dir. Corp. Capital Resources, Westlake Village, Calif., Communications Strategy Group Inc., Boston. Mem. Manhattan adv. bd. Salvation Army. Served to maj. USA, 1956-63, ETO. Recipient Disting. Service award Investment Edn. Inst., 1981, Nat. Assn. Investment Clubs, 1979. Mem. Am. Mgmt. Assn., Nat. Investor Relations Inst. (chmn. bd. 1977-78), Fin. Communications Soc. (pres. 1983), Investor Relations Assn. (exec. com. 1981-86), Pub. Relations Soc. Am., Internat. Assn. Bus. Communicators, Nat. Alumni Council of Boston U. Republican. Presbyterian. Club: University, Metropolitan (N.Y.C.). Lodge: Columbian. Office: Ashland Oil Inc 535 Madison Ave New York NY 10022

HARTLEY, FRED LLOYD, oil company executive; b. Vancouver, B.C., Can., Jan. 16, 1917; came to U.S., 1939, naturalized, 1950; s. John William and Hannah (Mitchell) H.; m. Margaret Alice Murphy, Nov. 2; children: Margaret Ann, Fred Lloyd. BS in Applied Sci., U. B.C., 1939. Engring. supr. Union Oil Co. Calif., 1939-53, mgr. comml. devel., 1953-55, gen. mgr. rsch. dept., 1955-56, v.p. in charge rsch., 1956-60, sr. v.p., 1960-63, exec. v.p., 1963-64, pres., chief exec. officer, 1964-73, chmn. bd. dirs., pres., 1974-85, chief exec. officer, 1985-88, chmn. bd. dirs., 1985-89, chmn. emeritus, 1989—. Bd. dirs. L.A. Philharm. Assn.; sr. trustee Calif. Inst. Tech., Com. Econ. Devel.; ambassador and commr. gen. U.S. exhibition EXPO 86. Mem. Am. Petroleum Inst. (bd. dirs., former chmn. bd. dirs., hon. dir.), Coun. Fgn. Rels., Calif. C. of C. (bd. dirs.). Office: Unocal Corp PO Box 7600 Los Angeles CA 90051

HARTLEY, GRACE VAN TINE, foundation administrator; b. San Francisco, Aug. 24, 1916; d. Ellis Charles and Nadine (Allen) Van Tine; m. Frank Brooke Hartley (div. 1974); children: Shirley Hartley Hill, Linda Hartley Sims, Brooke Hartley Hudson, Jessie Hartley Brady, Frank. Student, De Anza Coll., 1975-77, Coll. of Marin, 1985-86. V.p. Barron & Hartley Builders, Alameda, Calif., 1946-72; pres. Aurley Apt. Houses, Sunnyvale, Calif., 1974-86; exec. dir. George Demont Otis Found., San Francisco, 1974—; pres. Western Arts Acad. Found., San Rafael, Calif., 1982—, Grace Group of Calif., Inc., Corte Madera, Calif. and San Rafael, 1983—. Author, producer: (audio visual) American Artists National Parks, 1976 (Bicentennial award 1976); exhibited in group shows at Golden Gate Collection, 1974 (Soc. Western Artists award 1974), Otis Centennial, 1980 (Calif. History Ctr. award 1980). Pres. Rep. Women's Club, Alameda, 1960-62; active Rep. State Cen. Com., Alameda, 1964, Ronald Reagan Presdl. Task Force, Corte Madera, 1978-80. Recipient cert. Achievement Internat. Platform Assn., Washington, 1982, Presdl. Achievement award Rep. Party, Corte Madera, 1987. Presbyterian.

HARTLEY, HOUSTON LEE, retail executive, director; b. Melissa, Tex., Sept. 9, 1921; s. Elmer Dennis and Laura-Geneva (Davis) H.; m. Ila Mae Jeter, May 15, 1952; children: Donald Ray, Denise Jean. Grad. high sch., McKinney, Tex. V.p. bd. dirs. Nordstrom, Seattle, 1954-83; bd. dirs. Jumping Jacks Shoes, Inc., Monett, Mo.; cons. in field., 1983—. Served with USN, 1942-46. Republican. Home and Office: Rt #4 Box 95 McKinney TX 75070

HARTLEY, JAMES MICHAELIS, manufacturing and printing company executive; b. Indpls., Nov. 25, 1916; s. James Worth and Bertha S. (Beuke) H.; student Jordan Conservatory of Music, 1934-35, Ind. U., Purdue U., Franklin Coll.; m. E. Lea Cosby, July 30, 1944; children: Michael D., Brent S. With Arvin Industries, Inc., 1934-36; founder, pres. J. Hartley Co., Inc., Columbus, Ind., 1937—. Pres., Columbus Little Theatre, 1947-48; founding dir. Columbus Arts Guild, 1960-64, v.p., 1965-66, dir., 1971-74; musical dir., cellist Guild String Quartet, 1963-73; active Indpls. Mus. of Art; founding dir. Columbus Pro Musica, 1969-74; dir. Regional Arts Study Commn., 1971-74; v.p. Ind. Council Republican Workshops, 1965-69, pres., 1975-77; pres. Bartholomew County Republican Workshop, 1966-67. Served with USAAF, 1942-46. Mem. NAM, Nat. Fedn. Ind. Bus., U.S. C. of C., Phi Eta Sigma (honoris causa). Office: J Hartley Co Inc 101 N National Rd Columbus IN 47201

HARTLEY, JOHN T., JR., communications and information processing company executive; b. 1930; married. BSEE, Auburn U., 1955. With Harris Corp., Melbourne, Fla., 1956-60, v.p., 1960-63, v.p., gen. mgr., 1963-73, corp. v.p., group exec., 1973-76, exec. v.p., 1976-78, pres., prin. operating officer, 1978-82, chief operating officer, 1982-86, pres., chief exec. officer, 1986—, chmn., 1987—, also bd. dirs. Office: Harris Corp 1025 W Nasa Blvd Melbourne FL 32919

HARTLEY, PHILIP BOVARD, accounting educator; b. Kansas City, Mo., Nov. 13, 1925; s. Hugh Philip and Mary C. (Bovard) H.; m. Barbara Townley Loudon, June 20, 1952 (div. Mar. 1964); children: Charlton, Susan; m. Isobel Brownlee Duncan, Mar. 20, 1965; children: Stephen, Marnie. BS in Civil Engring., U. Kans., 1947, BS in Bus., 1950; MBA, Harvard U., 1952; PhD, U. Wash., 1966. Registered profl. engr., Kans.; CPA, Kans., Mo., N.J. Prof. emeritus acctg. grad. sch. mgmt. Rutgers U., Newark, 1967-89; bd. dirs. Broad Nat. Bank, Newark; vis. prof. U. San Diego, 1988. Contbr. articles to profl. jours. Served to lt. (j.g.) USN, 1944-45; PTO. Mem. Am. Inst. CPAs, Beta Gamma Sigma. Republican. Home: 2273 Calle Tiara La Jolla CA 92037

HARTLEY, STUART LESLIE, diversified company executive, accountant; b. Luton, Eng., Apr. 3, 1938; emigrated to Can., 1960; s. Leslie and Isobel (Buchan) H.; m. Patricia Holmes, Dec. 27, 1960; children: Stephen, Caroline, Susan. Gen. cert. edn., Royal Liberty Sch., London, 1955. chartered acct. Ont., Eng., Wales, 1960. Controller IBM Can. Ltd., Toronto, Ont., 1971-73; dir. fin. for Latin Am. area IBM Am.'s Far East Corp., Rio de Janeiro, Brazil, 1973-74; v.p. fin. and planning Gen. Bus. Group, IBM Can. Ltd., Toronto, Ont., 1975-79; exec. v.p., chief fin. officer Molson Cos. Ltd., Toronto, Ont., Can., 1979—; mem. Fin. Execs. Council, Conf. Bd. Can., Ottawa, Ont., 1981—; bd. dirs. Can. Malting Co., Ltd., chmn.exec. com. bd. Fellow Inst. Chartered Accts. (Eng. and Wales); mem. Inst. Chartered Accts. (Ont.), Fin. Execs. Inst. (pres. Toronto chpt. 1983-85, v.p. 1987—). Office: Molson Cos Ltd, 2 International Blvd, Toronto, ON Canada M9W 1A2

HARTMAN, DAVID LAWRENCE, marketing professional; b. Buffalo Ctr., Feb. 28, 1942; s. John and Katherine (PresKunitch) H.; m. Mary Elizabeth Jacobi, Jan. 25, 1969; children: Joshua, Jessica. BS in Bus. Adminstrn., Drury Coll., 1983. V.p. sales Teters Floral Products div. U.S. Industries, Bolivar, Mo., 1972-85, Reliance Trading Corp. Am., Chgo., 1985-86; v.p. sales and mktg. Thorco Ind., Lamar, Mo., 1986—. Vol. The Kitchen, Springfield; booster Spring Cath. High Sch. Served to satff sgt., USAF, 1965-68. Republican. Office: Thorco Ind 1801 S Gulf Lamar MO 64759

HARTMAN, TIMOTHY PATWILL, banker; b. Ft. Wayne, Ind., Mar. 1, 1939; s. Harold Albert and Mary Margaret (Sheehan) H.; m. Antoinette Marie Hart, Aug. 1, 1960; children—Melanie, Jeanne-Marie, Andrea. A.B. in Acctg., Xavier U.; Advanced Mgmt. Program cert., Harvard Bus. Sch., 1973. C.P.A., Ohio. Chief internal auditor Baldwin United Corp., Cin., 1966-68, asst. controller, 1968-69, controller, 1969-74, chief fin. officer, 1974-82; chief fin. officer NCNB Corp., Charlotte, N.C., 1982-88; vice chmn. NCNB Tex. Nat. Bank, Dallas, 1988—. Pres. Mercy Hosp. Found., Charlotte, 1984-85; bd. dirs. Charlotte Symphony Orch. 1984-85, 87—; trustee Belmont Abbey Coll., N.C., 1984-85; dir. Ace Charlotte's Repertory Theatre, 1984-85. Mem. Am. Inst. CPA's, Fin. Execs. Inst., Am. Bankers Assn., Assn. Res. City Bankers. Republican. Roman Catholic. Clubs: Quail Hollow Country, Charlotte City, Charlotte Athletic; Litchfield Country (S.C.); Wachesaw Plantation (S.C). Home: 17615 Cedar Creek Canyon Dr Dallas TX 75252 Office: NCNB Tex Nat Bank 1700 Pacific Dallas TX 75201

HARTNESS, SANDRA JEAN, venture capitalist; b. Jacksonville Fla., Aug. 19, 1944; d. Harold H. and Viola M. (House) H. AB, Ga. So. Coll., 1969; post-grad., San Francisco State Coll., 1970-71. Researcher Savannah (Ga.) Planning Commn., 1969, Environ. Analysis Group, San Francisco, 1970-71; dir. Mission Inn, Riverside, Calif., 1971-75; developer, venture capitalist Hartness Assocs., Laguna Beach, Calif., 1976—; ptnr. Western Neuro-Care Ctr., Tustin Calif.; former edu. dir. Laguna Bd. Realtors, 1982. V.p., mem. bd. dirs. Evergreen Homes, Inc.; recipient numerous awards for community service. Democrat. Club: Soroptimists (Riverside, Calif.). Home: 32612 Adriatic Dr Laguna Niguel CA 92677 Office: Hartness Assocs 301 Forest Ave Laguna Beach CA 92651

HARTNETT, JOHN F., manufacturing corporations owner; b. Cleve., July 2, 1937; s. John F. Hartnett and Jean Katherine (Nieman) Mackert; divorced; children: Christine, Heather, Cynthia, John IV. Student, John Carroll U., 1955-63. Salesman Kurt J. Lesker Co., Pitts., 1963-70, gen. mgr., 1970-77; chief exec. officer Molytek, Inc., Pitts., 1977—, Vacuum Research Corp., Pitts., 1987—; bd. dirs. Kurt J. Lesker Co. Mem. Instrument Soc. Am., Sci. Apparatus Mfr. Assn. (mem. exec. com, 1987—). Office: Molytek Inc 2419 Smallman St Pittsburgh PA 15222

HARTNETT, THOMAS PATRICK, health care management executive; b. Dobbs Ferry, N.Y., Sept. 19, 1942; s. Timothy Peter and Anne Marie (O'Neill) H.; m. Mary Elizabeth Brown, July 11, 1971; children: Thomas Walter Timothy, Walter Michael. BBA in Mgmt., Fairfield U., 1963; MBA in Mktg., Iona Coll., 1971; PhD in Health Care Policy, NYU, 1987. Mgr. Shamrock House Restaurant, Dobbs Ferry, 1965-68; med. rep. Burroughs Wellcome Co., Research Triangle Park, N.C., 1969-70, spl. rep., 1971; adminstrv. resident Hosp. for Joint Diseases Orthopedic Inst., N.Y.C., 1972; asst. dir. Bronx Mcpl. Hosp. Ctr., N.Y., 1973-75; adminstr. Westchester Community Health Plan, White Plains, N.Y., 1976-77; exec. dir. HealthWays, Inc., Iselin, N.J., 1978-80, pres., 1981-84; chief exec. officer Health Ways Systems, Inc., Woodcliff Lake, N.J., 1985—, also bd. dirs.; pres. HealthWays Found., Inc., Woodcliff Lake, 1981—; clin. instr. program in health policy and mgmt. grad. sch. pub. adminstrn. NYU, 1985—; adj. prof. grad. program pub. adminstrn. Pace U., White Plains, N.Y., 1983—, Baruch Coll. CUNY, 1974-78; lectr. Mercy Coll., Dobbs Ferry, 1973-74; v.p. Shamrock Liquors Corp., Dobbs Ferry, 1972-84; mktg. cons. Group Health Assn. Am., Washington, 1978; faculty mem. Ctr. to Promote Health Care Studies, Inc., 1975—. Chmn. Boy Scouts Am., Somers, N.Y., 1982-83; v.p. No. Westchester Guidance Clinic, Mt. Kisco, N.Y., 1983—; preceptor grad. sch. pub. adminstrn. NYU, 1977—; mem. Regional Health Planning Council, Newark, 1979-82; sec. Westchester Community Health Plan, 1976-77; bd. dirs. No. Westchester Guidance Clin., Mt. Kisco, 1979-87, chmn. budget and personnel com., 1982-87. Served with U.S. Army, 1964-65. Mem. Acad. Mgmt. (membership com., health care adminstrn. div. 1977-81), Am. Pub. Health Assn., Group Health Assn. Am., Inst. Soc. Ethics and Life Scis. Democrat. Roman Catholic. Office: HealthWays Systems Inc 50 Tice Blvd Woodcliff Lake NJ 07675

HARTON, JOHN JAMES, utility executive; b. Del Rio, Tex., Dec. 26, 1941; s. John Teague and Ara Velva (Boggs) H.; m. Dianne Voss, May 30, 1968; children: Angela Deanne, John Jay. B.S. in Elec. Engring, U. Ark., 1964, M.S. in Elec. Engring, 1965. With Ark. Power & Light Co., 1965—; dir. corp. planning Ark. Power & Light Co., Little Rock, 1974-79; treas., asst. sec. Ark. Power & Light Co., 1979—, v.p., chief fin. officer, 1981-85, treas., 1981—, v.p. fin. services, 1985—; instr. Pines Vocat.-Tech. Sch., Pine Bluff, Ark., 1966-68. Mem. bd. Wesley United Meth. Ch., Pine Bluff, 1971; mem. bldg. com. St. James United Meth. Ch., Little Rock, 1980-81, trustee, 1985-87. Mem. IEEE, Ark. Acad. Elec. Engrs., Nat. Soc. Profl. Engrs. Methodist. Lodge: Shriners.

HARTSHORN, THEODORE SIDNEY, service company executive; b. Lewiston, Idaho, June 2, 1958; s. Teddy Raymond and Yvonne Mae (Dugger) H.; m. Brenda Lee McDonald, Aug. 22, 1981; children: Bradley, Jessica, Kiley. BS in Acctg., U. Idaho, 1979. CPA, Idaho. Mgr. Safeway Stores, Moscow, Idaho, 1975-80; supervising acct. Pannell Kerr Forster, Lewiston, 1980-85; v.p. fin. AIA Services Corp., Lewiston, 1985—; treas. Universe Life Ins. Co., Carson City, Nev., 1988; instr. acctg. Lewis-Clark State Coll., Lewiston, 1984-85. Bd. dirs. Lewis-Clark Valley Boys' and Girls' Clubs, Lewiston, 1982-85. Mem. Idaho Soc. CPA's. Office: AIA Svcs Corp 111 Main St Lewiston ID 83501

HARTSOOK, LARRY D., controller; b. Des Moines, Mar. 30, 1943; s. David Edward and Ruby Lucille (Comp) H.; m. Karen K. Keller, June 16, 1963 (div. 1976); children: Mark W., Danielle R.; m. Lori A. Gramley, Feb. 4, 1983; 1 child, Ken A. BS, Drake U., 1967. CPA, Iowa. Various positions Meredith Corp., Des Moines, 1969-81, controller, 1981—. Pres. Assn. Retarded Citizens of Polk County, Des Moines, 1987-88. Mem. Nat. Assn. Accts. (pres. 1981-82), Iowa Soc. CPA's, AICPA, FEI. Office: Meredith Corp 1716 Locust St Des Moines IA 50336

HARTWELL, PHILIP ALAN, financial planner; b. Syracuse, N.Y., Apr. 5, 1946; s. Peter H. and Gladys (Hawley) H.; m. Kathryn Hitt, July 31, 1983; children: Connor, Grant. BA, Syracuse U., 1970, M Regional Planning, 1972. Cert. fin. planner. Pres. Mountain High Enterprise, Shelburne, Vt., 1973-80; v.p. sales Kilty, Sun Valley, Calif., 1980-83; fin. planner FNI, Torrance, Calif., 1983-85, Christopher Weil & Co., Torrance, 1985-88, Integrated Resources, Rolling Hills Estates, Calif., 1988—; owner, developer Bus. Games & Players, acctg. game for non-accts., Shelburne; frequent speaker to aerospace industry on pre-retirement planning. With USMC, 1965-67. Mem. Internat. Assn. Fin. Planners. Office: Integrated Resources 655 Deep Valley Dr Ste 100 Rolling Hills Estates CA 90274

HARTWIGSEN, NELSON LEROY, rubber company executive; b. Nanticoke, Pa., Mar. 4, 1941; s. Norman L. and Anna (Rowland) H.; B.S., Wilkes Coll., 1963; m. Lucille Bartish, June 11, 1963; children—Dawn Marie, Deborah Ann, Eric Norman. Trade service asst., mech. rubber goods div. UniRoyal, Inc., Buffalo, 1963, salesman, 1964, inside salesman, Pitts., 1964-65, salesman, Balt., 1965-68, asst. mgr. hose sales, Passaic, N.J., 1968-69, dist. sales mgr., Detroit, 1969-70; v.p., gen. mgr. Md. Rubber Corp., Balt., 1970-71, pres., 1971—; pres. Keystone Rubber Corp., York, Pa., 1974—; mng. gen. ptnr. OMR Ltd., gen. ptnr. Key Mar Gen. Ptnrs. Bd. dirs. Bel Air Amateur Sports Assn.; mgr., coach Bel Air Travel League, Little League. Served with Md. Army N.G., 1965-71. Home: 1506 Donegal Rd Bel Air MD 21014 Office: 8661 Towne Courte Ct White Marsh MD 21236

HARTZ, BRADLEY SCOTT, mining engineering specialist; b. Newport, R.I., Sept. 18, 1955; s. James Allen and Katherine (Morran) H.; m. Shirley Ann Miller, Oct. 16, 1962; 1 child, Christina Renee. BS in Mining Engring., Pa. State U., 1980. Registered profl. engr., Ill., Ind. Underground miner Jones & Laughlin Steel Corp., Consolidation Coal Co., Pitts., 1976-79; mining engr. Amax Coal Co., Indpls., 1980-83, Rogers Group, Inc., Plainville, Ind., 1983-86; dir. engring. and govt. affairs Rogers Group, Inc., 1987—. Contbg. author: Design of Supports in Mine, 1983, contbr. articles to tech. publs. Mem. Soc. Mining Engrs., Soc. Explosive Engrs., Vincennes Jaycees (bd. dirs. 1986-87), Ind. State Police Alliance, Ind. Coal Coun. (bd. dirs. 1984-88), exec. sec. 1987-88), Ind. Coal Coun. (vice-chmn. 1988—), Pa. Alumni Assn. Home: 2310 Jerry St Vincennes IN 47591 Office: Rogers Group Inc Rte 1 Box 133 Plainville IN 47568

HARTZ, HARRY J., business consultant; b. Phila., May 11, 1925; s. Joseph and Henrietta (Hoffman) H.; m. Ruth Kapp, Feb. 22, 1959; children: Diane Hartz Warsoff, Eric William. BSChemE, U. Pa., 1948. Dir. corp. planning and devel. INCO ElectroEnergy Corp., Phila., 1966-82; pres. H.J. Hartz & Assocs., Inc., Jenkintown, Pa., 1982—. Contbr. articles to profl. jours.; patentee in field. With USNR, 1944-46. Mem. The Instrument Soc. of Am. (sr. mem.), IEEE, The N.Am. Soc. for Corp. Planning, The Assn. for Corp. Growth, Assn. Polit. Risk Analysts, Tau Beta Pi, Sigma Tau. Home: 512 Saint James Pl Elkins Park PA 19117 Office: HJ Hartz & Assocs Inc One Jenkintown Sta 115 West Ave Jenkintown PA 19046

HARTZ, JOHN ERNEST, JR., lawyer, corporate executive; b. Berkeley, Calif., Apr. 8, 1935; s. John Ernest and Helen (Hower) H.; m. Margaret Ellen Dwyer, Feb. 18, 1966; children: Kimberly Anne, Kevin Earnest. AB, Stanford U., 1957; LLB, U. Calif., Berkeley, 1961; Diploma, Oxford U., 1962. Bar: Calif. 1962, Fla. 1978, D.C. 1978. Assoc. Brobeck, Phleger & Harrison, San Francisco, 1962-64; atty. Formost Diaries, Inc., San Francisco, 1964-66; sr. atty. Crown Zellerbach Corp., San Francisco, 1966-76; sr. v.p. SE Banking Corp., Miami, Fla., 1976-79; sr. v.p., gen. counsel Genstar Co., San Francisco, 1979-87; ptnr. Nossaman, Guthner, Knox & Elliott, San Francisco, 1987—; trustee Fla. Internat. U. Found., Inc., 1978-79; mem. adv. com. Guide Jud. Counsel Arbitration Study, Calif.; mem. com. State Bd. Govs., Calif., 1977; mem. Fla. Comptrollers Task Force on Fgn. Banking, 1977. Capt. USAR, 1957-65. Mem. ABA, Calif. Bar Assn., Fla. Bar Assn., D.C. Bar Assn., Am. Arbitration Assn., Am. Soc. Corp. Secs., Orinda (Calif.) Country Club, United Oxford and Cambridge U. Club, Orinda Country Club, Beefeaters Club. Democrat. Presbyterian. Office: Nossaman Guthner Knox Elliott 100 The Embarcadero 3rd Fl San Francisco CA 94105

HARTZLER, CHERYL ELAINE, financial planner; b. Kokomo, Ind., Feb. 16, 1945; d. Lowell Jay and Juanita Monell (Gasaway) Somsel; m. Edward W. Hartzler, June 11, 1967 (div. June 1981); children: Bryan Joseph, Andrea Lisabeth. BA, Ind. U., 1968; MBA, So. Ill. U., 1985; postgrad., Pacific Luth. U., 1982-83, Seattle Cen. Community Coll., 1979, S.Seattle Community Coll., 1980, Highline Community Coll., 1980-82, U. Washington, 1978, 83, Coll. for Fin. Planning, 1987—. Boutique mgr., jr. asst. buyer trainee Block's, Indpls., 1967-68; tchr. Indpls. Pub. Schs., 1968-71; with sales and inventory dept. Frederick & Nelson's Dept. Store, Seattle, 1971-72; co-owner video store Video World, Inc., Seattle, 1978-81; fin. planner and account exec. Investors Fin. Planning/Southmark Fin. Svcs., Bellevue, Wash., 1983—; pres. C.E. Hartzler & Assocs., 1986—; instr. continuing edn. N. Seattle Community Coll., 1985—; coordinated reorgn. of pvt. med. practice, Seattle, 1976; registered rep. Sun Am., 1989—. Mem. Seattle Repertory Orgn., 1973—; bd. dirs. Seattle Opera Guild, 1978-80; cultural chmn. Highline Sch. Dist. Parent Teachers Students Assn., Seattle, 1978-83. Mem. Internat. Assn. Fin. Planners, Wash. Women United, Women's Bus. Exch., Assn. MBA Execs., NAFE, Am. Soc. Women Accts., Internat. Platform Assn., Alpha Chi Omega Alumni. Clubs: Olympic View Swim (Seattle); Leads (mgmt. team South Seattle chpt.). Home: 718 SW 199th Pl Seattle WA 98166 Office: Investors Fin Planning/Southmark 1300 114th Ave SE Ste 232 Bellevue WA 98004

HARVATH, CHARLES, law firm executive; b. Canonsburg, Pa., Dec. 22, 1932; s. Charles and Pauline (Slyvich) H.; m. Frances B. Tiskiewic, June 16, 1962; children: Charles David, Nancy Lynn, Mark Charles. BS, U. Pitts., 1957, MBA magna cum laude, 1959. Mgr. market research Pitts. Post Gazette, 1959-61; market planner Jones & Laughlin Steel Corp., Pitts., 1961-66; mgr. comml. planning Cyclops Steel Corp., Pitts., 1966-68; mgr. systems, cons. Westinghouse Electric Corp., Pitts., 1968-85; exec. dir. Tucker Arensberg, Pitts., 1985—. Co-author: Bridging the Systems Expectations Gap, 1973. With USAF, 1953-55, maj. USAR. Mem. ABA, Assn. Legal Administrs., U.S. Army Res. Officers Assn., Mensa, Phi Beta Kappa. Republican. Roman Catholic. Home: 1662 Red Mill Dr Pittsburgh PA 15241 Office: Tucker Arensberg 1200 PNC Bldg Pittsburgh PA 15222

HARVEY, EDWIN MALCOLM, manufacturing company executive; b. Hattiesburg, Miss., July 23, 1928; s. Clarence C. and Ezilda (Pegues) H.; m. Charlotte Trewolla, July 7, 1951; children: Sylvia Jane, Sharon Ann, Rebecca Lynn. B.S. in Chem. Enging, La. State U., 1950. With Ethyl Corp., Richmond, Va., 1950-66; mgr. econ. research, dir. econ. evaluation Ethyl Corp., 1963-66; pres., treas. William L. Bonnell Co., Inc. subs. Ethyl Corp., Newnan, Ga., 1966-67, pres., dir., 1967—; v.p. Aluminum div. Ethyl Corp., 1975-85, sr. v.p., 1985—; pres. Capitol Products Corp. (subs.), 1975—; chmn. Fiberlux Inc., 1984—; chmn. bd. First Union Nat. Bank of Newnan, 1987—. Bd. dirs. Newnan Hosp., Bus. Council of Ga. Mem. Ga., Newnan-Coweta chambers commerce., Aluminum Assn. (dir.). Methodist. Club: Newnan Country. Home: 246 Jackson St PO Box 636 Newnan GA 30264 Office: Ethyl Corp PO Box 428 Newnan GA 30264

HARVEY, FRANK W., retail company executive; b. Knoxville, Tenn., Apr. 13, 1931; s. Frank N. and Mildred (Noe) H.; m. Patricia Johnson, Mar. 3, 1963; children: Heather Lea, Frank Whitney. B.S. in Econs., Vanderbilt U., 1957. With Cain-Sloan Co., 1957-76; sr. v.p. Cain-Sloan Co., Nashville, 1966-70, pres., 1970-76; asst. to pres., pres. The Fashion, Columbus, Ohio, 1963-66, Maas Bros. of Fla., Tampa, 1976-87; sr. v.p. Allied Stores, 1984-87; dir. NCNB Nat. Bank of Fla. Bd. dirs. U. South Fla. Found., pres., 1979-81. Served with USMC, 1950-52. Mem. Greater Tampa C. of C. (pres. 1981-82). Methodist. Clubs: Palma Geia Golf and Country, Tampa Yacht, University. Office: Brigantine IV 5210 Interbay Blvd Tampa FL 33611

HARVEY, GEORGE BURTON, office equipment company executive; b. New Haven, Apr. 7, 1931; m. Elizabeth Mary Viola, June 30, 1962; children: Paul, George, David. B.S., U. Pa., 1954. V.p. fin. Pitney Bowes, Stamford, Conn., 1973-76, group v.p. bus. equipment, 1976-78, pres. bus. systems, 1978-81, pres., 1981—, chief operating officer, 1981-83, chmn., pres., chief exec. officer, 1983—; dir. Norton Co., Worcester, Mass., Hartford, Conn., Bus. Equipment Mfrs. Assn., Washington, Bank of New Eng.; trustee Northeast Utilities, Hartford, Conn. Bd. dirs St. Joseph Hosp., Stamford; bd. dirs New Neighborhoods Inc.; trustee King Sch., Conn. Coll., New London. Served with U.S. Army, 1954-56. Mem. Southwestern Area Commerce and Industry Assn. (dir.), Conn. Bus. Industry Assn. (dir.). Home:

663 Ponus Ridge Rd New Canaan CT 06840 Office: Pitney Bowes Inc World Hdqrs Stamford CT 06926 *

HARVEY, HERSCHEL AMBROSE, JR., glass and marketing company executive; b. Steubenville, Ohio, Sept. 16, 1929; s. Herschel Ambrose and Josephine (Bernert) H.; BSBA, U. Notre Dame, 1951; postgrad. Mich. State U., 1958; m. Thelma F. Freeman, July 4, 1974; children: Debera, H.R., Herschel Ambrose III. Indsl. engr. Uniroyal, N.Y.C., 1951-53; indsl. relations mgr. Brunswick Co., Chgo., 1956-64; pres. Harvey Industries, Inc., Clarksburg, W.Va., 1964—, Hersh Harvey Assocs., Inc., Georgetown, S.C., 1974—, Harvey Glass, Inc., Georgetown, S.C., 1986—. Bd. dirs. Am. Cancer Soc. Lt. USNR, 1953-56. Mem. Am. Ceramic Soc., Alumna Club U. Notre Dame. Republican. Roman Catholic. Home: 3 Prospect Ct W DeBordieu Colony Georgetown SC 29440 Office: Harvey Glass Inc PO Box 1099 Georgetown SC 29442-1099

HARVEY, JAMES ROSS, financial company executive; b. Los Angeles, Aug. 20, 1934; s. James Ernest and Loretta Berniece (Ross) H.; m. Charlene Coakley, July 22, 1971; children: Kjersten Ann, Kristina Ross. B.S. in Engring., Princeton U., 1956; M.B.A., U. Calif.-Berkeley, 1963. Engr. Chevron Corp., San Francisco, 1956-61; acct. Touche, Ross, San Francisco, 1963-64; chmn. bd., chief exec. officer, dir. Transamerica Corp., San Francisco, 1965—; bd. dirs. Sedgwick Group, Pacific Telesis Group, McKesson Corp., SRI Internat., Calif. Econ. Devel. Corp., Charles Schwab Corp. Bd. trustees St. Mary's Coll.; bd. dirs. U. Calif. Bus. Sch., Calif. State Parks Found., Bay Area Council, Mt. Land Reliance, Nat. Park Found. Served with AUS, 1958-59. Mem. San Francisco C. of C. (dir., pres.), Bohemian Club, Pacific-Union Club, Union League Club. Office: Transam Corp 600 Montgomery St San Francisco CA 94111

HARVEY, RICHARD CRAIG, educator; b. Morgantown, W.Va., Oct. 27, 1956; s. Clarence and Wilma (Smith) H.; m. Lisa Overfield, May 5, 1984; 1 child, Rachel Elizabeth. BS, W.Va. U., 1977, MBA, 1984. Supr. customer svc. Mountaineer Nat. Bank, Morgantown, W.Va., 1980-82; with customer svc. First Nat. Bank, Morgantown, 1983-84; bus. analyst Small Bus. Devel. Ctr. W.Va. U., Morgantown, 1984-86; mgr. program Small Bus. Devel. Ctr., Fairmont, W.Va., 1986-88; faculty Fairmont State Coll., 1987—; Pres. Venture Mgmt. Corp., Morgantown, 1988—; assoc. Software Valley Corp. Mem. W.Va. Small Bus. Network (bd. advisors), Marion County C. of C. Democrat. Home: 1405 Brockton Dr Morgantown WV 26505 Office: Fairmont State Coll Fairmont WV 26554

HARVEY, RICHARD DUDLEY, marketing consultant; b. Atlanta, Sept. 24, 1923; s. Robert Emmett and June (Dudley) H.; BA, U. Denver, 1947; postgrad. various bus. seminars Harvard U., Stanford U.; m. Donna Helen Smith, Oct. 12, 1944; 1 child, Louise Dudley. Various positions in sales, sales promotion and mktg. The Coca-Cola Co., St. Louis, Denver and Atlanta, 1948-60, v.p., brand mgr., mktg. mgr., mktg. dir., Atlanta, 1965-70, v.p. orgn. and mktg. devel., 1970-75; sr. v.p. mktg. Olympia Brewing Co., Olympia, Wash., 1975-78; with Sound Mktg. Services Inc., Seattle; dir. Lone Star Brewing Co., San Antonio. Mem. mayor's housing resources com., Atlanta, 1968-70; program chmn. United Way, Atlanta, 1969; trustee Episcopal Radio-TV Found., Atlanta, 1961-88, vice chmn. 1975-84, emeritus trustee, 1988—; bd. dirs. Oreg. Shakespearean Festival Assn., 1982-86; chmn. mktg. com., trustee Seattle Symphony, 1983-88; mem. assistance com. Albers Sch. Bus. Seattle U., 1988—; gov.'s adv. com. bus. devel. and job retention, State of Wash., 1988—. Served with USAAF, 1942-45. Mem. Am. Mktg. Assn. (pres. 1983-84), Mktg. Communications Execs. Internat. (pres. 1984-85), Inst. Mgmt. Cons., Phi Beta Kappa, Omicron Delta Kappa. Democrat. Episcopalian. Clubs: The Rainier, Seattle Tennis (Seattle). Home: 3837 E Crockett St Seattle WA 98112-2422 Office: Sound Mktg Svcs Inc PO Box 22443 Seattle WA 98122

HARVEY, WILLIAM ROBERT, university president; b. Brewton, Ala., Jan. 29, 1941; s. Willie D. C. and Mamie Claudis (Parker) H.; m. Norma Baker, Aug. 13, 1966; children: Kelly Renee, William Christopher, Leslie Denise. B.A., Talladega Coll., 1961; D.Ed., Harvard U., 1971. Asst. to dean Harvard U. Grad. Sch. Edn., 1969-70; adminstrv. asst. to pres. Fisk U., Nashville, 1970-72; v.p. student affairs/dir. planning Tuskegee (Ala.) Inst., 1972-75, v.p. adminstrv. services, 1976-78; pres. Hampton (Va.) U., 1978—; owner Pepsi-Cola Bottling Co., Houghton, Mich.; dir. Signet Bank, Richmond, Va., Newport News (Va.) Savs. Contbr. articles to profl. jours. Bd. dirs. Nat. Merit Scholarship Corp.; bd. dirs. United Way, Peninsula Econ. Devel. Council, Presdl. Scholars Commn.; mem., vice-chmn. President's nat. adv. council ESEA; mem. Harvard U. Alumni Council.; trustee U. Va. Served with U.S. Army, 1962-65. Woodrow Wilson Martin Luther King fellow, 1968-70; Woodrow Wilson Found. intern fellow, 1970-72; Harvard U. Higher Edn. Adminstrv. fellow, 1968-70. Mem. Am. Council Edn., Am. Assn. Higher Edn., Nat. Assn. Equal Opportunity in Higher Edn., Va. Assn. Higher Edn., Peninsula C. of C. (dir.), Omega Psi Phi. Baptist. Office: Hampton Inst Hampton VA 23668

HARVIN, LUCIUS H., III, department store company executive, lawyer; b. 1938. B.A., U. N.C., 1961; LL.B., Duke U., 1963. Bar: N.C. Assoc. Wilcox Cooke Savage & Lawrence, 1963-64; asst. mgr. real estate dept. Rose's Stores Inc., Henderson, N.C., 1964-66, mgr. real estate dept., 1966-67, asst. treas., 1967-69, treas., 1969-72, v.p. expansion, 1972-75, sr. v.p., chief operating officer, 1975-80, pres., chief exec. officer, dir., 1980-84, chmn., chief exec. officer, 1984—, also bd. dirs. Office: Rose's Stores Inc 218-220 S Garnett St Henderson NC 27536 *

HARWARD, GARY JOHN, utility holding company executive; b. Sioux City, Iowa, Dec. 2, 1941; s. John Morris and Edith Christine (Falk) H.; m. Linda Readout, Aug. 20, 1960; children: Kimberly Harward Ostler, Nancy Harward Anderson. BBA, Morningside Coll., 1964; MBA, U. S.D., 1982. Ops. officer Livestock Nat. Bank, Sioux City, 1964-68; various mgmt. and supervisory positions Iowa Pub. Service Co., Sioux City, 1968-71, asst. controller, 1971-74, controller, 1974-84; v.p., controller Midwest Energy Co., Sioux City, 1984-85, sr. v.p. fin., chief fin. officer, 1985-88, sr. v.p., chief fin. officer, 1988—; bd. dirs. Midwest Capital Group, Sioux City, 1st Nat. Bank in Sioux City, All-States Quality Foods, Charles City, Iowa. Trustee Buena Vista Coll., Storm Lake, Iowa, 1987—; bd. dirs. Tax Research Conf., Sioux City, 1975—, chmn. bd., 1983-84; bd. dirs. Sioux City Concert Course, 1987, Boys and Girls Home, Family Services, Sioux City, 1987. Republican. Methodist. Lodge: Shriners, Masons. Office: Midwest Energy Co 401 Douglas St PO Box 1348 Sioux City IA 51102

HARWELL, JAMES HENRY, transportation executive; b. Wichita Falls, Tex., May 12, 1953; s. James Clinton and Margret Irene (Gilchrist) H.; m. Cheryl Sampson, Apr. 7, 1978 (div. 1978); m. Brenda Joyce Coffee, Oct. 16, 1987; children: Nancy, Christopher. Grad. high sch., Waco, Tex. Store mgr. Southland Corp., Dallas, 1971-73; ops. mgr. Greyhound Lines, Dallas, 1973-84; asst. city mgr. Greyhound Lines, Austin, Tex., 1984-85; city mgr. Greyhound Lines, Des Moines, 1985-86; owner, operator Harwell Enterprises, Waco, 1986—. Tchr. Jr. Achievement, Des Moines, 1986; cash attendant MDA, Waco, 1978-80. Recipient Merit Achievement award Des Moines ISD, 1986; named Tchr. of Yr. Hoyt Middle Sch., Des Moines, 1986. Republican. Baptist. Office: Greyhound Lines Harwell Enterprises 700 Columbus Waco TX 76701

HARWOOD, RICHARD LEE, journalist, newspaper editor; b. Chilton, Wis., Mar. 29, 1925; s. Luther Milton and Ruby (Heath) H.; m. Beatrice Bottrell Mosby, Dec. 18, 1950; children: Helen, John, Richard, David. A.B., Vanderbilt U., 1950. Reporter Nashville Tennessean, 1947-52; Reporter Louisville Courier-Jour. and Times, 1952-61, Washington corr., 1961-65; nat. corr. Washington Post, 1966-68, nat. editor, 1968-70, asst. mng. editor, 1970-74, dep. mng. editor, 1976—; v.p. Trenton Times Newspapers, 1974-76. Author: Lyndon, a Biography of L.B. Johnson; Contbr. articles to nat. mags. Bd. dirs. Marine Corps Hist. Assn., 1987—. Served with USMCR, 1942-46, PTO. Recipient citation Nat. Edn. Writers Assn., 1957; George Polk Meml. award L.I. U., 1967, 71; Distinguished Service medal Sigma Delta Chi, 1967, 71; Nieman fellow in Journalism Harvard U., 1955-56; Carnegie fellow in journalism Columbia U., 1965-66. Mem. Soc. Nieman Fellows (dir. So. chpt. 1959-61), A.C.L.U. (dir. Ky. 1959-61), Am. Polit. Sci. Assn. (citation 1960). Democrat. Clubs: Nat. Press, Fed. City, Cosmos (Washington). Office: care Washington Post 1150 15th St NW Washington DC 20071

HASAN, WAQAR, computer scientist, researcher; b. Jalaun, India, Apr. 1, 1963; came to U.S., 1984; BS in Computer Sci., Indian Inst. Tech., 1984; postgrad., Stanford U., 1984—. Asst. engr. USDL, Lucknow, India, 1984; research asst. Stanford U., Palo Alto, Calif., 1984-88; research intern DEC, Hudson, Mass., 1985, Intellicorp, Mountain View, Calif., 1986, IBM, Almaden, Calif., 1987; with tech. staff Hewlett Packard Labs., Palo Alto, 1988—. Contbr. articles to profl. jours.; patentee method to intergrate knowledge-based system with arbitrary rel-bd system. Office: Hewlett Packard Labs Bldg 3 Upper 1501 Page Mill Rd Palo Alto CA 94304-1181

HASELMANN, JOHN PHILIP, advertising agency executive; b. Summit, N.J., Feb. 25, 1940; s. John and Elizabeth Haselmann; divorced; children—Terri Lee, Karen Lynn, Guy Philip. BSEE, N.J. Inst. Tech., 1961; MBA in Indsl. Mgmt., Ops. Research and Mgmt. Sci., U. Pa., 1963. Asst. dir. Behavior Systems, Phila., 1961-63; mgr. mgmt. sci. div. Western Electric Co., Princeton, N.J., 1970-73; mgr. mktg. sci. div. AT&T Long Lines, Bedminster, N.J., 1974-78; pres. Info. Mgmt. Group, Morristown, N.J., 1978-83, Trinet Inc., Morristown, N.J., 1984-85, Entity Advt. and Graphics, Inc., Florham Park, N.J., 1986-89, Integrated Mktg. Svcs., Inc., Parsippany, N.J., 1989—. Mem. Am. Mgmt. Assn., Am. Soc. Profl. Cons., Am. Employers Assn. (dir. 1989—). Republican. Lutheran. Office: Integrated Mktg Svcs Inc 1155 Connecticut Ave NW Ste 300 Washington DC 20036

HASELTON, FORREST RONALD, retail company executive; b. Sanford, Maine, Nov. 28, 1938; s. Forrest Sumner and DeLima (Prefontaine) H.; m. Ethel Louise Pinkham, June 20, 1964; children—Forrest Raymond, Eric Pinkham. B.A. in Polit. Sci., U. N.H., 1961. Asst. group mgr. Sears, Roebuck and Co., Wayne, N.J., 1975-77; store mgr. Sears, Roebuck and Co., 1977-80; ter. adminstrv. asst. Sears, Roebuck and Co., St. David's, Pa., 1980-81; group mgr. Sears, Roebuck and Co., Greensboro, N.C., 1981-82; exec. v.p. Sears, Roebuck and Co., Alhambra, Calif., 1982—; dir. Sears Mdse. Group, Chgo. Bd. dirs. N.J. Better Bus. Bur., Wayne, 1978-79, Los Angeles Bldg. Funds, 1982, local council Boy Scouts Am., 1982—, Los Angeles YMCA, 1985—. Served to 1st lt. USAF, 1961-64. Republican. Roman Catholic. Office: Sears Mdse Group Sears Tower Chicago IL 60684 *

HASELTON, WILLIAM RAYMOND, manufacturing executive; b. Glens Falls, N.Y., Jan. 11, 1925; s. Raymond R. and Mary (Vanderwerker) H.; m. Frances C. Crooks, July 10, 1948; children: Susan, Judith, June. B.S. in Chem. Engring, Rensselaer Poly. Inst., 1949; M.S. in Chemistry, Lawrence U., 1951, Ph.D., 1953. With Rhinelander Paper Co. div. St. Regis Paper Co., Rhinelander, Wis., 1953-61; v.p., gen. mgr. Rhinelander Paper Co. div. St. Regis Paper Co., 1956-1961; v.p. St. Regis Paper Co., Tacoma, 1961-69; sr. v.p. St. Regis Paper Co., 1969-71, exec. v.p., 1971-73, pres., 1973-81, chief exec. officer, 1979-84, chmn. bd., 1981-84, also dir.; vice chmn., dir. Champion Internat. Corp., 1984-89; dir. Allendale Ins. Co., Johnston, R.I., Allied-Signal Inc., Morristown, N.J. Served with USNR, 1943-46. Recipient Westbrook Steele award Inst. Paper Chemistry, 1953. Home: PO Box 1300 Live Oak FL 32060 Office: Champion Internat Corp 2000 Sawgrass Village Ste 2303 Ponte Vedra Beach FL 32082 *

HASENOEHRL, ROLAND, retail company executive; b. 1945; married. Student, Sch. Econs., Frankfurt, Fed. Republic Germany. With Coop Binchopheim, Fed. Republic Germany, 1963-78, Fewe Handelsgesellschaft Leibbrand Ong, Fed. Republic Germany, 1978-81; pres. Furr's Inc., Lubbock, Tex., 1981—, also bd. dirs. Served with West German Army, 1956-66. Office: Furrs Inc PO Box 1650 Lubbock TX 79408 *

HASKELL, JOHN HENRY FARRELL, JR., investment banking company executive; b. N.Y.C., Jan. 24, 1932; s. John Henry Farrell and Paulette (Heger) H.; m. Francine G. Le Roux, June 30, 1955; children: Michael J., Christopher E., Diana F. T. B.S., U.S. Mil. Acad., 1953; M.B.A. with distinction, Harvard U., 1958. Assoc. Dillon, Read & Co., N.Y.C., 1958-61; mgr. European office Dillon, Read & Co., Paris, 1961-66; v.p. Dillon, Read & Co., N.Y.C., 1964-75, mng. dir., 1975—; pres., chief exec. officer, dir. The France Fund, Inc., dir. Moet-Hennessy U.S. Corp., Kaydon Corp., Dillon Read Ltd.; mem. adv. council Overseas Pvt. Investment Co., 1972-75. Bd. dirs. Belgian-Am. Ednl. Found, Am. Hosp. Paris Found.; trustee French Inst./ Alliance Francaise. Served with U.S. Army, 1953-56. Decorated Legion of Honor, Ordre National du Merite France; recipient Presdl. Recognition award For Community Service, 1986. Mem. Council Fgn. Relations, French-Am. C. of C. (councillor), Assn. Grads. of U.S. Mil. Acad. (trustee 1984-87), Am. Soc. French Legion of Honor (bd. dirs.). Clubs: Links, University (N.Y.C.); Piping Rock (Locust Valley, N.Y.); Bohemian (San Francisco). Home: 120 East End Ave New York NY 10028 Office: Dillon Read & Co Inc 535 Madison Ave New York NY 10022

HASKELL, PRESTON HAMPTON, III, construction company executive; b. Birmingham, Ala., Oct. 6, 1938; s. Preston Hampton and Mary Wyatt (Rushton) H.; m. Joan Elizabeth Smith, June 9, 1961; children—Elizabeth Rushton, Preston Hampton IV, Sally Milne. B.S. in Engring., Princeton U., 1960; M.B.A., Harvard U., 1962. Registered profl. engr., Fla., Ala., S.C., Va. V.p. S.S. Jacobs Co., Jacksonville, Fla., 1962-65; pres. The Haskell Co., Jacksonville, Fla., 1965—; dir. Barnett Bank Jacksonville, 1978—. Chmn. Jacksonville Electric Authority, 1976-78; chmn., pres. United Way Jacksonville, 1982-85; chmn. Fla. Postsecondary Edn. Commn., Tallahassee, 1980-84. Recipient Top Mgmt. award Sales & Mktg. Execs., Jacksonville, 1978. Mem. Fla. Engring. Soc., Nat. Soc. Profl. Engrs., Fla. Council 100 (dir. 1984-87), Jacksonville Symphony Assn. (dir. 1973—, pres. 1986-87), Soc. Advancement Mgmt. (hon.), Jacksonville C. of C. (pres. 1979), Soc. of the Cin., Beta Gamma Sigma (hon.). Republican. Episcopalian. Clubs: River (Jacksonville) (pres. 1984-85), Fla. Yacht, Timuquana Country. Office: The Haskell Co Haskell Bldg Jacksonville FL 32231-4100

HASKINS, CARYL PARKER, chemical company executive, educator; b. Schenectady, Aug. 12, 1908; s. Caryl Davis and Frances Julia (Parker) H.; m. Edna Ferrell, July 12, 1940. Ph.B., Yale U., 1930; Ph.D., Harvard U., 1935; D.Sc., Tufts Coll., 1951, Union Coll., 1955, Northeastern U., 1955, Yale U., 1958, Hamilton Coll., 1959, George Washington U., 1963; LL.D., Carnegie Inst. Tech., 1960, U. Cin., 1960, Boston Coll., 1960, Washington and Jefferson Coll., 1961, U. Del., 1965, Pace U., 1974. Staff mem. research lab. Gen. Electric Co., Schenectady, 1931-35; research asso. Mass. Inst. Tech., 1935-45; pres., research dir. Haskins Labs., Inc., 1935-55, dir., 1935—, chmn. bd., 1969-87; dir. E.I. du Pont de Nemours, 1971-81; research prof. Union Coll., 1937-55; pres. Carnegie Instn. of Washington, 1956-71, also trustee, 1949—; Asst. liaison officer OSRD, 1941-42, sr. liaison officer, 1942-43; exec. asst. to chmn. NDRC, 1943-44, dep. exec. officer, 1944-45; sci. adv. bd. Policy Council, Research and Devel. Bd. of Army and Navy, 1947-48; cons. Research and Develop. Bd., 1947-51, to sec. def., 1950-60, to sec. state, 1950-60; mem. Pres.'s Sci. Adv. Com., 1955-58, cons., 1959-70; mem. Pres.'s Nat. Adv. Commn. on Libraries, 1966-67, Joint U.S.-Japan Com. on Sci. Coop., 1961-67, Internat. Conf. Insect Physiology and Ecology, 1971-73; panel advisers Bur. East Asian and Pacific Affairs, Dept. State, 1966-68; mem. Sec. Navy Adv. Com. on Naval History, 1971-83, vice chmn., 1975-83. Author: Of Ants and Men, 1939, The Amazon, 1943, Of Societies and Men, 1950, The Scientific Revolution and World Politics, 1964; contbr. to anthologies and tech. papers.; Editor: The Search for Understanding, 1967; Chmn. bd. editors: Am. Scientist, 1971-83 ; chmn. publs. com., 1971-83 . Trustee Carnegie Corp. N.Y., 1955-80, hon. trustee, 1980—, chmn. bd., 1975-80; trustee Rand Corp., 1955-65, 66-75, adv. trustee 1988—; fellow Yale Corp., 1962-77; regent Smithsonian Instn., 1956-80, regent emeritus, 1980—, mem. exec. com., 1958-80; bd. dirs. Council Fgn. Relations, 1961-75, Population Council, 1955-80; bd. dirs. Ednl. Testing Service, 1958-61, 67-71, chmn. bd., 1969-71; trustee Center for Advanced Study in Behavioral Scis., 1960-75, Thomas Jefferson Meml. Found., 1972-78, Council on Library Resources, 1965—, Pacific Sci. Center Found., 1962-72, Asia Found., 1960—, Marlboro Coll., 1962-77, Wildlife Preservation Trust Internat., Inc., 1976—, Nat. Humanities Center, 1977—; trustee Woods Hole Oceanographic Instn., 1964-73, mem. council, 1973—; bd. dirs. Franklin Book Programs, 1953-58; mem. Save-The-Redwoods League, 1943—, mem. council, 1955—; Mem. vis. coms. Harvard, Johns Hopkins; bd. visitors Tulane U. Yale Corp. fellow, 1962-77; recipient Presdl. Cert. Merit U.S., 1948, King's medal for Service in Cause of Freedom Gt. Britain, 1948, Joseph Henry medal Smithsonian Inst., 1980. Fellow Am. Phys. Soc., A.A.A.S. (dir. 1971-75), Am. Acad. Arts and Scis., Royal Entomol. Soc., Entomol. Soc. Am., Pierpont Morgan Library; mem. N.Y. Zool. Soc., Washington Acad. Scis., Nat. Geog. Soc. (trustee 1964-84 , honorary trustee, 1984—, fin. com. 1972-85, com. on research and exploration 1972—, exec. com. 1972-84), Royal Soc. Arts (Benjamin Franklin fellow), Faraday Soc., Met. Mus. Art, Am. Mus. Natural History (trustee 1973—, bd. mgmt. 1973—), Am. Philos. Soc. (councillor 1976-78, 81-83), Brit. Assn. Advancement Sci., Linnean Soc. London, Internat. Inst. Strategic Studies, Asia Soc., Japan Soc., Biophys. Soc., Nat. Acad. Sci., N.Y. Acad. Scis., Audubon Soc., N.Y. Bot. Garden, P.E.N., Pilgrims, Phi Beta Kappa, Sigma Xi (nat. pres. 1966-68, dir. 1966-83), Delta Sigma Rho, Omicron Delta Kappa. Episcopalian. Clubs: Somerset (Boston), St. Botolph (Boston); Century (N.Y.C.), Yale (N.Y.C.); Mohawk (Schenectady); Metropolitan (Washington), Cosmos (Washington) (bd. mgmt. 1973-76); Lawn (New Haven). Home: 22 Greenacre Ln Westport CT 06880 Office: Haskins Labs Inc 1545 18th St NW Washington DC 20036

HASKINS, LUTHER GRANVILLE, III, corporate executive; b. Evanston, Ill., July 22, 1951; s. Luther G. Jr. and Rosemary Haskins. BS in Acctg., U. Ill., Champaign, 1973. CPA, Ill. Auditor Coopers and Lybrand Corp., Chgo., 1972-76; treas. Clear Shield Nat., Inc., Wheeling, Ill., 1976—. Mem. Am. Inst. CPA's, Ill. Soc. CPA's. Office: Clear Shield Nat Inc PO Box 337B Wheeling IL 60090

HASNER, ROLF KAARE, food equipment manufacturing executive; b. Oslo, Mar. 15, 1919; s. Harald Alexander and Henny (Christiansen) H.; m. Edel Jensen, May 26, 1956; children: Richard, Nina. Grad., Norwegian Mil. Acad., 1939; MBA, Norwegian U. Commerce Sci., 1943, U. Chgo., 1947. Clk. Nat. Bank of Norway, Oslo, 1940-41; econ. A.S. Lilleborg Fabrikker, Oslo, 1943-45; bus. cons., newspaper corr. A.S. Lilleborg Fabrikker, N.Y.C., 1951-57; v.p. Globe Slicing Machine Co., Inc., Stamford, Conn., 1957-65; prin. owner, exec. v.p., bd. dirs. Globe Slicing Machine Co., Inc., Stamford, 1965-87, cons., 1987—; also bd. dirs. Globe Slicing Machine Co., Inc., Can. Bd. dirs. Norwegian Am. Mus., Decorah, Iowa; mem. elders bd. Luth. Ch.; bd. dirs. Greenwich (Conn.) Council Boy Scouts Am. Served with Armed Forces, Norway, 1940-45. Rockefeller Found. scholar, 1946-47. Mem. Norwegian Am. C. of C. Internat. (pres. 1985-87), Internat. (pres. 1985-87), Landmark Club, Skytop Club, Greenwich Skating Club, Greenwich Country Club, Rotary (pres. 1978-79). Home: Bobolink Ln Greenwich CT 06830

HASS, JOSEPH MONROE, automotive engineering executive; b. Syracuse, N.Y., July 28, 1955; s. Joseph Monroe and Susan Faith (Betts) H.; m. Lisa Michelle Palmer, Aug. 14, 1982. BS in Secondary Edn., Tenn. Temple U., 1977; postgrad., Tenn. State U., 1986—. Diesel mechanic Cummins Engines Tenn., Chattanooga, 1978-81; mgr. tng. Cummins Engines Tenn., Chattanooga, 1981-85; service floor foreman Cummins Cumberland, Nashville, 1985-86, CompuChek technician, 1986-87, fleet systems support engr., 1987—. Mem. Nat. Arbor Day Found. Office: Cummins Cumberland 706 Spence Ln Nashville TN 37217

HASSAN, AFTAB SYED, financial analyst, educator, researcher; b. Lahore, Punjab, Pakistan, Apr. 20, 1954; came to U.S., 1976; s. Maqsud Syed and Saliha Aktar Hassan. BSCE with distinction, U. Engring. and Tech., Lahore; postgrad. in aerodyns., Colo. State U.; MS, George Washington U., 1977, postgrad. in ocean, coastal and environ. engring.; PhD, Columbia Pacific U., 1985. Tech. asst. George Washington U., Washington, 1979-84, asst. prof., 1980-85; chmn. math. and sci. Emerson Prep. Inst., Washington, 1979-89; acad. coordinator Georgetown U. Med. Sch., Washington, 1983-87; acctg. dir. Met. Acctg. Assocs., Washington, 1987-88; acctg. mgr. Washington Info. Group, 1988—; owner Met. Acctg. and Rsch., 1989—; bd. dirs. French Pastries, Inc., Washington, McPherson News and Gift, Washington, Food for All. Author: Preparation for the MCAT, 1988; author, editor Betz Pub. Co., Bethesda, Md., 1984—. Recipient Merit award Nat. Assn. Chiefs of Police. Mem. ASCE, NSPE, Am. Soc. Engring. Edn., Am. Inst. Profl. Bookkeepers, Am. Mil. Engrs. Home: 2517 K St NW #301 Washington DC 20037

HASSAN, TOM ANDREW, film company executive; b. San Diego, Jan. 11, 1964; s. Mervyn Leslie and Sylvia O.R. (Fry) H. BA in Communications and Broadcasting, Pepperdine U., 1985. Account exec. pub. rels. and mktg. Cooper & Assocs., Santa Monica, Calif., 1984-85; prodn. coord. Lorne Greene Prodns., Santa Monica, 1985-86; asst. mgr. ops. DeLaurentiis Entertainment Group, Beverly Hills, Calif., 1986-87; mgr. ops. TMS Pictures/ The Movie Store, L.A., 1987; dir. film acquisitions TMS Pictures/ The Movie Store, 1988—; guest speaker Pepperdine U., Malibu, Calif., 1988, UCLA; rep. Am. Film Market, L.A., 1988. Creator of Pop-A-Thought greeting cards. Mem. Am. Film Inst., Am. Mgmt. Assn. Republican. Home: 100910 Wellworth Ave #110 West Los Angeles CA 90024 Office: TMS Pictures Inc 11111 Santa Monica Bvld Los Angeles CA 90025

HASSELMAN, RICHARD B., railroad executive; b. Jersey City, Nov. 28, 1926; s. Benjamin R. and Clara A. (Borchert) H.; m. Mildred E. Schaber, May 29, 1954; children: Richard Dwight, James Christopher. B.E. in Mech. Engring., Yale U., 1947; M.B.A., NYU, 1949. Student engr. N.Y. Central R.R., 1947-49, trainee, 1949-52, brakeman, 1952-53, signalman, freight agt., 1953; transp. insp. Eastern region Syracuse, N.Y., 1953-55; trainmaster Mowhawk div. Albany, N.Y., 1955-57; div. trainmaster Syracuse div. 1957; div. supt. Boston & Albany div. Springfield, Mass, 1957-59; dist. transp. supt. Western region Cleve., 1959-60; gen. supt. yards and terminals N.Y. Central System, N.Y.C., 1960-63; gen. mgr. Ind. Harbor Belt and Chicago River & Ind. R.R., Hammond, Ind., 1963; gen. mgr. No. Region N.Y. Cen. R.R., Detroit, 1964; gen. mgr. So. Region N.Y. Cen. R.R., Indpls., 1964-66; gen. mgr. Western Region N.Y. Cen. R.R., Cleve., 1967; asst. v.p. transp. N.Y. Central System, N.Y.C., 1967-68; v.p. transp. Penn. Central, Phila., 1968-76; sr. v.p. ops. Consol. Rail Corp., Phila., 1976—; pres., dir. Ind. harbor Belt R.R. Co., 1968-87; bd. dirs. St. Lawrence & Adirondack Rwy. Co. Home: 669 Dodds Ln Gladwyne PA 19035 Office: Consol Rail Corp 1740 Six Pennsylvania Center Pla Philadelphia PA 19103

HASSELQUIST, MAYNARD BURTON, lawyer; b. Amador, Minn., July 1, 1919; s. Harry and Anna F. (Froberg) H.; m. Lorraine Swenson, Nov. 20, 1948; children—Mark D., Peter L. B.S.L., U. Minn., 1941; J.D.L., U. Minn., 1947. Bar: Minn. 1948. Asst. mgr. taxation Gen. Mills Inc., Mpls., 1947-53; chmn. internat. dept. Dorsey & Whitney, Mpls., 1953-81, sr. ptnr.; dir. Graco Inc., Mpls., McLaughlin Gormley King Co., Mpls., ADC Telecommunications, Inc., Mpls., Wesco Resources, Billings, Mont., Gustavus Adolphus Coll., St. Peter, Minn., Soprea S.A., Paris. Gen. counsel, bd. dirs. Swedish Council Am.; past chmn. Japan-Am. Soc. Minn.; bd. dirs., counsel James Ford Bell Library; past chmn. Fairview Hosps. Internat., Ltd., Cayman Islands. Served with USN, 1941-46. Decorated knight Royal Order of North Star (Sweden). Mem. ABA, Minn. Bar Assn., Internat. Bar Assn., Am. Soc. Internat. Law. Republican. Lutheran. Club: Mpls. Avocations: swimming, fishing, hiking, travel. Office: Dorsey & Whitney 2200 First Bank Pl East Minneapolis MN 55402

HASSELWANDER, ALAN C., telecommunications industry executive. BA, St. Bernard Sem., 1956; MBA, U. Rochester, 1973. With Rochester (N.Y.) Telephone Corp., 1957—, plant mgr., 1968-71, dir. indsl. relations, 1971-72, traffic mgr., 1972-73, v.p. services, 1973-76, pres., chief exec. officer, 1984—. Office: Rochester Telephone Corp 100 Midtown Pla Rochester NY 14646 *

HASSENFELD, ALAN GEOFFREY, toy company executive; b. Providence, Nov. 16, 1948; s. Merrill Lloyd and Sylvia (Kay) H. B.A., U. Pa., 1970. Asst. to pres. Hasbro Industries, Inc., Pawtucket, R.I., 1969-72; v.p. internat. ops. Hasbro Industries, Inc., 1972-78, v.p. mktg. and sales, 1978-80, exec. v.p. ops., 1980-84, pres., 1984—; chmn. bd. Hasbro Canada, 1980—; dir. Hasbro Inc., Hasbro U.K. Ltd. Bd. dirs. Internat. House R.I., Providence, 1974—; mem. R.I. Air Adv. Task Force, The Tomorrow Fund Adv. Bd., 1985; trustee Miriam Hosp., 1984—; mem. exec. com. Deerfield Acad. Alumni Assn., 1985; chmn. Gov.'s Adv. Council on Refugee Resettlement, 1986; bd. overseers U. Pa. Sch. Arts and Scis., 1986—. Served with Air Force N.G., 1967-73. Mem. Toy Mfrs. Assn. (bd. dirs. 1978—, chmn. 1985—). Office: Hasbro Industries Inc 1027 Newport Ave Pawtucket RI 02861

HASSENFELD, STEPHEN DAVID, manufacturing company executive; b. Providence, R.I., Jan. 19, 1942; s. Merrill Lloyd and Sylvia Grace (Kay)

H. Student, Johns Hopkins U., 1959-62; D. Pub. Service, R.I. Coll., 1984; HHD, Bryant Coll., 1985. With Hasbro Industries Inc., Pawtucket, R.I., 1963—; v.p. mktg. Hasbro Industries, Inc., Pawtucket, R.I., 1967-68, exec. v.p., 1968-74, pres., 1974—, chmn. bd., 1980—, also dir.; dir. Am. Stock Exchange; bd. govs. Bank of Boston; bd. dirs. Johns Hopkins U. Past fellow Brandeis U., Waltham, Mass.; past trustee Temple Emanu-El, Providence, R.I., 1981-84, Found. for Repertory Theatre of R.I., 1978-84; bd. trustees R.I. Pub. Expenditures Council, bd. govs., 1986—; bd. dirs. Jewish Fedn. R.I., 1976—, United Way of Southeastern New Eng., Inc., 1985—, Southeastern region NCCJ, 1976—, John H. Chaffee Steering Com., 1975-82, Am. Jewish Joint Distbn. Com., N.Y.C., 1982—; mem. Young Pres. Orgn., 1983—, Am. Jewish Joint Distbn. Com., N.Y.C., R.I. Philharmonic Council, R.I. Commodores, 1978—, R.I. Council of Nat. Jewish Hosp.-Nat. Asthma Center, 1980—, Corp. of R.I. Philharmonic Orch., 1981, Providence Coll. pres. council, 1985—; mem. bus. adv. council U. R.I., 1976-78; bd. dirs. Children's Friend and Service, Providence, 1974-77, Fed. Hill House, 1973-76; mem. adv. com. R.I. Strategic Devel. Commn., 1982-84 ; mem. adv. council Sch. Continuing Studies, Johns Hopkins U., 1983—, dir. advanced internat. studies. Mem. Toy Mfrs. Assn. (dir. 1974-76). Office: Hasbro Inc 1027 Newport Ave Pawtucket RI 02861

HASTIE, K. LARRY, banker; b. Cedar Rapids, Iowa, Apr. 23, 1942; s. Kenneth and Louise Hastie; m. Ruth Gordon; children: Brock, Kevin. BA in Econs., DePauw U., 1964; MBA in Fin., Cornell U., 1966, PhD Managerial Econs., 1969. Fin. analyst Boise (Idaho) Cascade, 1969-71, mgr. budgeting, 1971-72, asst. to controller, 1972; dir. corp. fin. studies Monsanto Co., St. Louis, 1972-73, dir. internat. fin., 1973-74; asst. treas. The Bendix Corp., Southfield, Mich., 1974-76, treas., 1976-77, v.p., treas., 1977-79, v.p. corp. orgn. and human resources, 1979-81, v.p. corp. devel., 1981-82; pres. Hastie and Assocs., Ann Arbor, Mich., 1982-83; chmn., chief exec. officer The Mediclinic Corp., Houston, 1983-85; v.p., chief fin. officer J.P. Industries, Ann Arbor, 1985-86; exec. v.p. Mich. Nat. Corp., Farmington Hills, 1986—. Mem. dean's adv. coun. Krannert Sch. Mgmt. Purdue U., West Lafayette, Ind., 1988—; mem. alumni coun. Johnson Sch. Grad. Mgmt. Cornell U., Ithaca, N.Y., 1988—. Office: Mich Nat Corp 27777 Inkster PO Box 9065 Farmington Hills MI 48018

HASTINGS, SUSAN KAY, auditor, accountant, consultant; b. Mason City, Iowa, Mar. 25, 1952; d. Arnold E. and Mildred E. (Thiemann) Hoveland; m. Robert E. Hastings, June 12, 1971. AA, North Iowa Area Community Coll., Mason City, 1973; BS, Nat. Coll. Bus., 1975. CPA, S.D. Staff acct. McGladrey Hendrickson & Pullen, Rapid City, S.D., 1975-80, mgr., 1980-84, ptnr., 1984-87; v.p., cons. First Fed. Savs. Bank, Rapid City, 1987—; mem. acctg. adv. bd. Nat. Coll., Rapid City, 1985—. Treas., bd. dirs. Rapid City Arts Coun., 1987—, Rapid City Arts Found., 1988—; active YMCA, Rapid City, 1973—. Mem. am. Inst. CPA's, S.D. Soc. CPA's. Fin. Mgrs. Soc., Inst. Internal Auditors, Arrowhead Country Club (Rapid City) (treas., bd. dirs. 1986—). Office: First Fed Savs Bank 909 St Joe St PO Box 8170 Rapid City SD 57709

HASTINGS, WAYNE ALEXANDER, publishing company executive; b. San Bernardino, Calif., Jan. 12, 1949; s. Ray Raymond and Catherine Edith (Stevens) H.; m. Pamela Lorraine Kucera, June 6, 1970; children: Jennifer Rebecca, Zachary Todd. BA cum laude, U. Redlands, 1971. Dept. mgr. Sears Roebuck and Co., San Bernardino, 1971-76; territory mgr. Burroughs Corp., San Bernardino, 1976-78; controller Woelke & Romero, San Bernardino, 1978-82; dir. finance Here's Life Pubs., San Bernardino, 1982-86, exec. v.p., 1986—; bd. dirs. Here's Life Found., San Bernardino. Named one of Outstanding Young Men of Am., U.S. C. of C., 1977. Mem. Am. Mgmt. Assn., Nat. Assn. Accts., Computer Users Assn. Republican. Mem. Evangelical Free Ch. Home: 249 E 34th St San Bernardino CA 92402 Office: Here's Life Pubs 2700 Little Mountain Dr San Bernardino CA 92402

HASWELL, CARLETON RADLEY, banker; b. Milw., May 18, 1939; s. Clayton Lyman and Jane (Radley) H.; m. Almut Haberkamp, Dec. 10, 1966; children—Angela, Robin. B.S., Northwestern U., 1961; M.B.A., NYU, 1967. Chief internat. credit officer Chem. Bank, N.Y.C., 1963-87; dir. Chem. Internat. Inc., N.Y.C., 1981-86, Chem. Internat. Fin., N.Y.C., 1981-84; pres. Carleton Haswell Assocs., 1987—. Dir., United Givers, Wayne, N.J., 1980-83. Served with U.S. Army, 1961-63. Mem. Robert Morris Assocs. Republican. Club: Packanack Yacht (N.J.). Home and Office: 6 Hilltop Terr Wayne NJ 07470

HATCH, ROBERT WINSLOW, food corporation executive; b. Hanover, N.H., Sept. 8, 1938; s. Winslow Roper and Dita Meiggs (Keith) H.; m. Nancy Packard Murphy, June 30, 1962; children: Kristin, Robert Winslow. BA, Dartmouth Coll., 1960, MBA, 1962. Sales rep. Libby Glass Co., N.Y.C., 1961-62; rsch. asst. Amos Tuck Sch., Hanover, 1962-63; with Gen. Mills, Inc., Mpls., 1963-64, product mgr., 1965-68, mktg. dir., 1968-71; exec. v.p. Gorton Corp., 1971-73, gen. mgr. protein div., 1973-75; gen. mgr. Golden Valley div., 1976; gen. mgr. Big G div., 1976-78, group v.p. splty. retailing, 1978-80, exec. v.p. splty retailing, collectibles and furniture, 1980-83, asst. to vice chmn. consumer non-foods, 1984; pres., chief exec. officer Interstate Bakeries Corp., Kansas City, Mo., 1984-87, chmn., pres., chief exec. officer, 1987—; bd. dirs. Leslie Paper Co., Mpls., Sealright Corp., Kansas City. Exec. com. Mpls. Boys Club, 1978-83; pres. bd. East Side Neighborhood Svcs. (Settlement House), 1980—; chmn. Found. Internat. Community Assistance, 1989—. Recipient Mpls. City Coun.'s Com. on Urban Environment award, 1980. Mem. Kansas City C. of C., Calbhoun Beach Club (pres. bd. govs. 1981-83), Kansas City Club, Carriage Club. Republican. Presbyterian. Office: Interstate Bakeries Corp PO Box 1627 Kansas City MO 64141

HATCH, STANLEY THOMAS, accountant; b. Muskegon, Mich., Feb. 4, 1959; s. William Harlos and Margie J. (Harber) H.; m. Sherry Darlene Lafever, June 10, 1978; children: Lindsey E., Emily L. BS in Acctg., Tenn. Tech. U., 1981. CPA, Tenn. Staff acct. Arthur Andersen & Co., Knoxville, Tenn., 1981-83; controller Treetop Enterprises, Inc., Nashville, 1983—. Treas. Ch. of Christ, Nashville, 1986—. Mem. Nat. Assn. Accts., Fin. Mgrs. Assn. Republican. Office: Treetop Enterprises Inc 5100 Linbar Dr Nashville TN 37211

HATCH, STEVEN GRAHAM, publishing company executive; b. Idaho Falls, Idaho, Mar. 27, 1951; s. Charles Steven and Margery Jane (Doxey) H.; BA, Brigham Young U., 1976; postgrad. mgmt. devel. program U. Utah, 1981; m. Rhonda Kay Frasier, Feb. 13, 1982; children: Steven Graham, Kristen Leone. Founder, pres. Graham Maughan Enterprises, Provo, Utah, 1975—. Internat. Mktg. Co., 1980—; dir. Goldbrickers Internat., Inc. Sec., treas. Zions Estates, Inc., Salt Lake City, Kansas City, Mo. Eagle Scout Boy Scouts Am., 1970; trustee Villages of Quail Valley, 1984-88. Recipient Duty to God award, 1970. Mem. Provo Jaycees, Internat. Entrepreneurs Assn., Mormon Booksellers Assn., Samuel Hall Soc. (exec. v.p. 1979), U.S. C. of C., Provo C. of C. (chmn. legis. action com. 1981-82). Republican. Mormon (missionary France Mission, Paris 1970-72, pub. rels. dir. 1972). Club: Rotary. Office: Graham Maughan Pub Co 50 E 500 S Provo UT 84606

HATCHER, DONALD J., manufacturing company executive; b. Scranton, Pa., Jan. 13, 1948; s. Donald H. and Janet M. (Hawley) H.; m. Mary Lyn Padden, Sept. 11, 1975; children: Sara Padden, Brian Padden. AS, Lackawanna Jr. Coll., 1968; BSBA, Bethel Coll., 1970. Clk. Emery Air Freight Corp., Scranton, 1970-71, acct., 1971-72, supr. credit and collections, 1972-73; fin. analyst Emery Air Freight Corp., Wilton, Conn., 1976-78; ins. analyst Emery Air Freight Corp., Wilton, 1978-79, mgr. ins. and safety, 1979-82, risk mgr., 1982-86; gen. mgr. Roberts Cartage, Inc. subs. Emery Air Freight, Akron, Ohio, 1973-76; dir. risk mgmt. Insilco Corp., Meriden, Conn., 1986-89; asst. dir. risk mgmt. Combustion Enging. Inc., Stamford, Conn., 1989—; Editorial advisor Risk and Benefits Mag., Santa Monica, Calif., 1985—. Bd. dirs. New Milford (Conn.) Jaycees, 1979, treas. 1980. Named Jaycee of Yr., 1980. Mem. Risk and Ins. Mgmt. Soc. (sec., dir. Fairfield/Westchester chpt. 1980-86, now v.p. Conn. Valley chpt.), Ins. Inst. Am. (cert. assoc. risk mgmt.). Home: 5 Daniska Dr Bethel CT 06801 Office: Combustion Enging Inc 900 Long Ridge Rd Stamford CT 06904

HATFIELD, JACK KENTON, lawyer, accountant; b. Medford, Okla., Jan. 26, 1922; s. Loate L. and Cora (Walsh) H.; m. D. Ann Keltner, Dec. 5, 1943; children: Susan Kathryn Hatfield Bechtold, Sally Ann Hatfield Clark. BS in BA, Phillips U., Enid, Okla., 1947; BA, Phillips U., 1953; LLB, Oklahoma City U., 1954, JD, 1967. Bar: Okla. 1954; CPA 1954. Sole practice, Enid, Okla., 1954-58; with Dept. Interior, Tulsa, 1958-77. Mem. ABA, Okla. Bar Assn., Tulsa Co. Bar Assn., Am. Inst. CPA's, Okla. Soc. CPA's. Club: Petroleum. Home: 2976 E 75th St Tulsa OK 74136 Office: Jack K Hatfield Atty Inc 7060 S Yale Suite 601 Tulsa OK 74136

HATFIELD, JAMES ROBERT, utilities executive; b. Kansas City, Mo., Oct. 9, 1957; s. Harry Eugene and Barbara Laquita (Breckenridge) H.; m. Gail Francis Neely, May 20, 1980 (div. May, 1984); 1 child, Sara Michelle; m. Rhonda Gail Mcglothlin, Dec. 31, 1984. BSBA in Acctg., Cent. Mo. State U., 1980. Staff acct. Mo. Pub. Service Co., Kansas City, 1980-81, sr. acct., 1981-84, sr. staff analyst, 1984-85; mgr. fin. UtiliCorp United Inc., Kansas City, 1985-87, asst. treas., 1988—. Mem. Nat. Corp. Cash Mgmt. Assn. Republican. Lutheran. Office: UtiliCorp United Inc 2000 Commerce Tower 911 Main St Kansas City MO 64105

HATFIELD, ROBERT SHERMAN, former packaging company executive; b. Utica, N.Y., Jan. 16, 1916; s. Albert R. and Mary (Sherman) H.; m. Roberta Sullivan, May 8, 1937; children: Roberta A. Hatfield Williamson, Suzanne S. Hatfield Miele, Molly J. Hatfield DuPre, Robert Sherman Jr. Student, Cornell U., 1937; LL.B., Fordham U., 1945; postgrad., Advanced Mgmt. Program, Harvard U., 1954. With Continental Group, Inc. (name formerly Continental Can Co.), Norwalk, Conn., 1936-81, chmn., chief exec. officer, 1971-81; chmn. Soc. of N.Y. Hosp., N.Y.C., 1981-88; chmn., chief exec. officer Nat. Exec. Svc. Corps, N.Y.C.; bd. dirs. First Am. Bank N.Y.; past bd. dirs. Am. Health Cos., Providence Washington Ins. Co., Citicorp/Citibank, N.A., Eastman Kodak Co., GM, Johnson & Johnson, Nabisco Brands, Marsh & McLennon, N.Y. Stock Exchange. Mem. Bus. Council, Council on Fgn. Rels.; dir. N.Y.C. Partnership; trustee emeritus Cornell U.; chmn. exec. com. Internat. Exec. Service Corps. Clubs: Links, River; Blind Brook (Port Chester, N.Y.); Pine Valley Golf (N.J.), Augusta Nat. Golf (Ga.); Seminole Golf (Fla.). Office: Nat Exec Svc Corps 600 Third Ave 16th Fl New York NY 10016

HATHAWAY, CARMRID GLASTON, horseman, real estate investor; b. Tarboro, N.C., Feb. 8, 1922; s. Carmrid Glaston and Estelle (Pittman) H.; m. Margaret Tryphena Deese, June 20, 1944; children: Joyce Elaine, Carmrid Glaston III. Student, George Washington U., 1941-42, Naval Air Tng. Ctr., 1944; BS in Mil. Sci. and Bus. Adminstrn., U. Md., 1971. Lic. pilot, real estate, Md. Enlisted USN, 1942, advanced through grades to capt., 1965, ret., 1975; comdg. officer naval air sta. USN, Grosse Ile, Mich., 1967-69; comdg. officer naval tng. ctr. USN, Washington, 1972-75; pres. Harness Racing Inc., Suitland, Md., 1975—; chmn. bd. dirs. Activities Investments Inc., Washington; Md. standard bred racing fund com. Md. Racing Commn., 1984-85. Adv. com. Md. Racing Commn., 1984-85; mem. Md. Standard Bred Race Fund, 1984-85. Mem. Retired Officers Assn., U.S. Trotting Assn., Standard Bred Breeders Md. (bd. dirs. 1980—), Standardbred Race Fund (adv. com.), Md. Harness Horseman's Assn. (bd. dirs. 1979—), Cloverleaf Standard Bred Owners's Assn., U. Md. Alumni Assn. Internat., Md. Racing Commn., Ret. Officers Assn. Baptist. Club: Commd. Officers (Andrews AFB, Md. and Washington D.C.). Home: 4406 Ridgecrest Dr Suitland MD 20746 Office: Activities Investments Inc 3352 Upland Terr NW Washington DC 20015

HATHAWAY, DONALD EUGENE, retail executive; b. Lansing, Mich., May 19, 1932; s. Kenneth A. and Elsa M. (Schroeder) H.; m. Mary E. Roberts, June 18, 1959; children: Stephen, Susan, Sandra. BS in Bus., Mich. State U., 1955. Bid estimator Westinghouse Corp., Detroit, 1958-59; mgr. dept. Jacobson's Stores, Jackson, Mich., 1959-82; v.p., supr. Jacobson's Stores, Fla., 1980—. Pres. Neighborhood Improvement Assn. Served as cpl. U.S. Army, 1955-57. Republican. Methodist. Lodges: Rotary, Elks. Office: Jacobsons Stores Inc 245 Driggs Dr Winter Park FL 32792

HATHAWAY, KEVIN JOSEPH, technology professional, consultant; b. Lynwood, Calif., Aug. 3, 1951; s. Elwood Vernon and Lucy Valerie (Turner) H.; m. Jeanette Kay Ryan, Sept. 15, 1985; children: Geoffrey, Monika. BS in Chemistry, San Jose State U., 1975, MS in Chemistry, 1980. Sr. scientist Microma, Inc., Cupertino, Calif., 1972-78; sr. staff scientist Timex Inc., Cupertino, Calif., 1978-80; pres. Mesophase Inc., Cupertino, Calif., 1980-85, Display Enging., Inc., San Jose, Calif., 1985—; bd. dirs. Altura Corp., Los Angeles. Chmn. Santa Clara County Young Rep. 1986; assisted various polit. campaigns. Mem. Soc. Info. Display, Soc. Photo-Optical Instrumentation Engrs. Clubs: Churchill (Los Altos), Silicon Valley Entrepreneurs (Santa Clara). Office: Display Enging Inc 6472 Camden Ave San Jose CA 95120

HATHAWAY, RAEBURN BURTON, JR., insurance executive, lawyer; b. Newton, Mass., Mar. 20, 1934; s. Raeburn Burton and Christina (Willard) H.; m. Janet Holden, Aug. 30, 1958; children—Karen, Douglas, John. A.B., Colgate U., 1956; LL.B., Harvard U., 1959. Bar: Mass. 1960; C.L.U. Atty. John Hancock Mut. Life Ins. Co., Boston, 1963-68, asst. counsel, 1968-72, assoc. counsel, 1972-79, counsel, 1979-81, v.p., 1981-84, sr. v.p., sec., 1984—. Served to capt. USAF, 1960-63. Recipient Maroon citation Colgate U., 1981. Mem. ABA, Mass. Bar Assn., Assn. Life Ins. Counsel, Am. Soc. Corp. Secs, Mass. Life & Health Ins. Guaranty Assn. Republican. Mem. United Ch. of Christ. Home: 107 Farm St Dover MA 02030 Office: John Hancock Mut Life Ins Co PO Box 111 Boston MA 02117

HATHAWAY, STANLEY KNAPP, lawyer; b. Osceola, Nebr., July 19, 1924; s. Franklin E. and Velma Clara (Holbrook) H.; m. Roberta Louise Harley, Nov. 26, 1948; children—Susan Garrett, Sandra D'Amico. A.B., U. Nebr., 1948, LL.B., 1950; LL.D., U. Wyo., 1975. Bar: Nebr. 1950, Wyo., 1950, U.S. Dist. Ct. Wyo., Nebr., Mont. 1950, U.S. Supreme Ct. 1964. Sole practice, Torrington, Wyo., 1950-66; gov. Wyo., 1967-75; assoc. Hathaway, Speight & Kunz, Cheyenne, Wyo., 1975—; dir. Pacific Power & Light Co., Nerco, Inc., Portland, Oreg., Apache Corp., Mpls., Firt Wyo. Bancorp., Cheyenne, Wyo.; county atty. Goshen County (Wyo.), 1955-62; sec. U.S. Dept. Interior, 1975. Served with USAAF, 1943-45. Decorated Air medals with 5 clusters. Mem. ABA, Wyo. State Bar Assn. Republican. Anglican Orthodox. Clubs: Lions, Masons (Cheyenne); Shriners (Rawlins, Wyo.). Office: Hathaway Speight & Kunz One Pioneer Ctr Cheyenne WY 82001

HATLEY, LESLIE REX, controller; b. Washington, Mar. 1, 1949; s. Harold Rex and Evalyn Rebecca (Ball) H.; m. Cynthia Sue Binsted, Nov. 23, 1975; children: Amanda, Benjamin. BS, U. Md., 1976. CPA. Acct. Gov. Employee Life Ins. Co., Rockville, Md., 1976-80; asst. contr. Acacia Group, Washington, 1980-82; treas. Montgomery Mut. Ins. Co., Sandy Spring, Mo., 1982-88; controller Home Owners Warranty Corp., Washington, 1988—. With USN, 1969-75. Fellow Life Mgmt. Inst. Soc. Washington/Balt.; mem. Ins. Acctg. and Systems Assn. (pres. Mid-Atlantic region 1986-87), Md. Assn. CPAs. Republican. Methodist. Home: 11421 Saddleview Pl Gaithersburg MD 20878 Office: Home Owners Warranty Corp Washington DC 20860

HATLEY-BRICKEY, LAEL ANN, university administrator; b. Pullman, Wash., Sept. 18, 1956; d. James Monroe and Betty Ann (Gillespie) Hatley; m. Randolph Avery Brickey Jr., Oct. 1, 1977; 1 child, James Randolph; 1 stepchild, Brandy. Student, Spokane Community Coll., 1975-76, Wash. State U., 1979—. With The Crescent, Spokane, Wash., 1976-77, Cowles Pub., Spokane, 1977, Keith's Music, Spokane, 1977-78, Myklebust's Clothing, Pullman, Wash., 1978, Wash. State U. Instructional Media Svc., Pullman, summer 1978; office asst. dept. parking svcs. Wash. State U., Pullman, 1978-82, telephone operator, 1982-84, program asst., 1984-87, program mgr. telecommunications, 1987—. V.p. Pullman Meml. Hosp. Found., 1986—. Mem. NAFE, Grange, Jobs Daus., Xi Beta Epsilon (treas. 1987-88, sec. 1989—). Home: Rte 2 Box 368 Pullman WA 99163 Office: Wash State U McCroskey Hall Ste 30 Pullman WA 99164-3412

HATSCHEK, RUDOLF ALEXANDER, electronics company executive; b. Grafenberg, Austria, May 10, 1918; s. Rudolf Bernhard and Maria (Zischka) H.; m. Erika Lucia Satory, Jan. 10, 1946. Student, U. Prague, Czechoslovakia, 1936-40, U. Graz, Austria, 1945-46; Doctorate, U. Graz, 1946. Biochemist Interpharma AG, Prague, 1940-45; head of lab. Fux, Vienna, Austria, 1946-54; v.p. enging. BCF, Vienna, 1954-59; gen. mgr. instrumentation dept. AVL Engine Inst., Graz, 1959-65; v.p. research and devel. Vibro-Meter S.A., Fribourg, Switzerland, 1965-77; v.p. enging. div. ASULAB S.A., Neuchatel, Switzerland, 1978-83; cons. advanced piezo-electric applications in medicine, chronometry, automation and telecommunication; introduced piezo-electric aircraft-engine vibration monitoring. Mem. ASME, IEEE, Swiss Phys. Soc. Home: 3 Rue Vogt, CH1700 Fribourg Switzerland

HATSOPOULOS, GEORGE NICHOLAS, mechanical engineer, thermodynamicist, educator; b. Athens, Greece, Jan. 7, 1927; came to U.S., 1948, naturalized, 1954; s. Nicholas and Maria (Platsis) Hatzopoulos; m. Daphne Phylactopoulos, June 14, 1959; children: Nicholas, Marina. Student, Nat. Tech. U., Athens, 1945-47; B.S., M.S., M.I.T., 1950, M.E., 1954, Sc.D., 1956; Sc.D. (hon.), N.J. Inst. Tech., 1982. Instr. M.I.T., 1954-56, asst. prof. mech. enging., 1956-58, assoc. prof., 1959-62, sr. lectr. in mech. enging., 1962—; founder, pres., chief exec. officer, chmn. bd. Thermo Electron Corp., developer, mfr. and marketer of products based on thermodynamic technologies of heat transfer and energy conversion, Waltham, Mass., 1956—; chmn. bd. Coll. Yr. in Athens; mem. adv. bd. Energy Productivity Center, Carnegie-Mellon Inst., 1978-81; tech. witness numerous Senate and Congl. hearings; mem. enging. edn. com. M.I.T. Center for Policy Alternatives, 1973; mem. policy com. for innovation program NSF at M.I.T., 1973-74; mem. ad hoc com. on air quality and power plant emissions NRC, 1974-75; mem. environ. ad. com. FEA, Washington, 1974-75; dir. Fed. Res. Bank of Boston, Nat. Bur. Econ. Rsch., Am. Bus. Conf., Mass. Ctrs. of Excellence and the Maliotis Found.; adv. bd. Program on Tech. and Econ. Policy, Kennedy Sch. Govt., Harvard U. Author: Principles of General Thermodynamics, 1965, Thermionic Energy Conversion, vol. 1, 1973, vol. 2, 1979; contbr. numerous articles to profl. jours. Recipient Corp. Leadership award M.I.T., 1980. Fellow IEEE, Am. Acad. Arts and Scis., Nat. Acad. Enging., ASME (chmn. exec. com. div. energetics 1968-69); mem. Am. Acad. Achievement (Golden Plate award 1961), Nat. Assn. Mfrs. (regional vice-chmn.), AIAA, Sigma Xi, Pi Tau Sigma (Gold Medal award 1960). Greek Orthodox. Home: Tower Rd Lincoln MA 01773 Office: Thermo Electron Corp 101 1st Ave PO Box 9046 Waltham MA 02254-9046

HATSOPOULOS, JOHN NICHOLAS, high technology company executive, investment advisor; b. Athens, Greece, Apr. 21, 1934; came to U.S., 1953, naturalized, 1964; s. Nicholas George and Maria (Platsis) H.; m. Kathleen Sweeny, May, 1963 (dec. 1970); 1 child, John Constantine; m. 2d, Patricia Lynn Becker, May 5, 1974; children: Alexander John, Nia Marie. Diploma, Athens Coll., 1953; BA, Northeastern U., 1959. Mgr. purchasing Thermo Electron Corp., Waltham, Mass., 1957-63, pres. metals div., Wilmington, Mass., 1963-70, v.p., Waltham, 1970-78, v.p. corp. strategy, 1978-84, sr. v.p., 1984—; exec. v.p., chief fin. officer, 1988—; v.p. Thermedics, Inc., 1983—. Bd. dirs. Thermo Environmental, Inc., Thermo Instrument Systems, Inc., Thermo Process Systems, Inc. Greek Orthodox. Clubs: Regency Whist (dir. 1983—), Lotus (N.Y.). Home: Woodcock Ln Lincoln MA 01773 Office: Thermo Electron Corp 101 1st Ave Waltham MA 02254

HATTIS, ALBERT D., business executive, educator, journalist; b. Chgo., Oct. 12, 1929; s. Robert E. and Victoria C. (Kaufman) H.; m. Fern Hollobow; children: Kim Allyson Hattis Mercer, Kay Arlene Hattis Draper, John Elmore, Michael Allen, Sharon Beth. BS with highest distinction, Northwestern U., 1948, postgrad. in bus. adminstrn., 1950, DD (hon.), 1968. Vice-pres., sec.-treas. Robert E. Hattis Engrs., Inc., Hattis Svc. Co., Inc. (sub. White Motor Corp. also sub. of REH Corp.), Deerfield, Ill., 1950-73; v.p., sec.-treas. Servbest Foods, Inc., Highland Park, Ill., 1973-78; A.C. Equipment Co., 1978-80, Prime Packing Co., Inc., Haitian Am. Meat & Provision Co. SA, Spanish-Am. Foods, Inc., 1973-78; pres., chief exec. officer Frigidmeats, Inc., Chgo., 1978-80; pres. Gits Enterprises, Inc., 1978-80, Double K Bar J Ranch, Inc., 1968—; prof. bus., holder Schwan Endowed Chair for Free Enterprise, S.W. State U., Marshall, Minn., 1981-89, ret. 1989; dir. S.W. Minn. Small Bus. Devel. Ctr., 1984-87, S.W. Minn. Homegrown Economy Local Cooperation Office, 1984-89; chmn. Minn. Small Bus. Procurement Adv. Coun., 1986-87. Exec. dir. The Lambs, Inc., Libertyville, Ill., 1980-81; trustee Orphans of the Storm Found., 1972-74, Cobblers Found., 1972-74; mem. adv. bd. Northwestern Psychiat. Inst., 1972-74; bd. dirs. Marshall Industries Found.; chmn. Marshall Planning Commn., 1982-85. Capt. USAF, 1946-48, 50-52. Mem. Assn. Pvt. Enterprise Edn., Internat. Coun. Small Bus., U.S. Assn. Small Bus. and Entrepreneurship, Minn. C. of C. (small bus. council 1984-87), Marshall Area C. of C. (bd. dirs. 1981-88), Beta Gamma Sigma. Lodges: Lions, Rotary. Syndicated columnist, broadcaster Straight Talk, 900 newspapers, 500 radio stas. Office: 100 E Marshall St Marshall MN 56258-1838

HATTON, JOHN ERNEST, brokerage house executive; b. Melbourne, Australia, Dec. 30, 1938; came to U.S., 1983; s. Ernest Roy and Jean Beryl Christina (Edney) H.; m. Elizabeth Anne Wilkinson, Nov. 19, 1960; children: Jacqueline Anne, Allison Jean, Fiona Jane. Student, Adminstrv. Staff Coll., Henley, U.K., 1977. Mng. dir. Baillieu Bowring, Hobart, Tasmania, 1968-74; mng. dir. Baillieu Bowring, Melbourne, 1974-78, dep. chief exec. officer, 1978-80, chief exec. officer, 1980-83; chief, exec. officer Group IV Marsh & McLennan, Inc., N.Y.C., 1983-85, mng. dir. Pacific Basin ops., 1986-88; dir., chief exec. officer Pacific Basin Ops. Marsh & McLennan Bowring, 1988—; Mem. Law Reform Rev. Council, Melbourne, 1976-77; assoc., bd. dirs. Australian Ins. Inst., 1972-73. Chmn. bd., trustee The Cheshire (Conn.) Acad., 1985—; commr. declarations and affidavits State Law Dept., Victoria, Australia, 1979—. Episcopalian. Clubs: Kew Golf (Victoria, Australia); Australian Club (Melbourne); Pine Orchard Yacht and Country (Branford, Conn.). Home: 15 Hart Ave Pine Orchard Branford CT 06405 Office: Marsh & McLennan Bowring 1221 Avenue Americas New York NY 10020

HATTORI, SHOJI, investment banker; b. Nagoya, Japan, Oct. 19, 1937; s. Hyoichi and Fusako (Okuyama) H.; m. Keiko Nakamura; children: Yuji, Tetsuya. B in Econs., Nagoya U., 1960. Various sales positions Yamaichi Securities Co., Ltd., Tokyo, 1960-72, corp. bus. and fin. dept. gen. mgr., 1979-84, also bd. dirs.; sales mgr. Yamaichi Internat., Tokyo, London, Amsterdam, N.Y.C., 1972-79; pres. Yamaichi Internat., N.Y.C., 1984-89, chief exec. officer, 1988—, chmn., 1989—. Mem. Midwest Stock Exch., Boston Stock Exch., N.Y. Stock Exch., Chgo. Bd. Trade, Chgo. Merc. Exch., Japanese C. of C. and Industry N.Y. (bd. dirs. 1988—), Down Town Assn., Japan Soc., Canyon Club, Scarsdale Golf Club, Nippon Club (bd. dirs. 1988—), Marco Polo Club, Club at World Trade Ctr., Stock Exch. Luncheon Club, Atrium Club. Clubs: Canyon Golf (N.Y.C.), World Trade Ctr. (N.Y.C.). Office: Yamaichi Internat Inc 2 World Trade Ctr Ste 9650 New York NY 10048

HATZIMICHAEL, TASOS CHRIS, financial executive; b. Germansim, Fed. Republic Germany, May 26, 1964; came to U.S., 1968; s. Chris Michael and Sevasti (Konstatin) H.; m. Christine Estella Stephens, Aug. 23, 1982 (div. 1986); children: Sophia, Crystal. Ins. agt. Mut. of Omaha, Concord, Calif., 1982; fin. planner Paine Fin. Co., Oakland, Calif., 1982-83; regional mgr. Paine Fin. Co., 1983, John Hancock Fin. Svcs., Pleasanton, Calif., 1983-85; pres. Consol. Acctg., Walnut Creek, Calif., 1985—, Consol. Fin. Planning Svc. Inc., Walnut Creek, 1985—; pres. Consol. Mortgage Co., Walnut Creek, 1986—, Consol. Ins. Co., Walnut Creek, 1986—, Consol. Real Estate Co., 1987—. Patentee in field. Mem. Nat. Assn. Securities Dealers (registered prin., 1986, registered investment adv. 1986), Internat. Assn. Fin. Planners. Republican. Greek Orthodox. Office: Consol Fin Planning Svc Inc 2255 Ygnacio Valley Rd Ste M Walnut Creek CA 94598

HAUG, SCOTT ERIK, management consultant; b. Oslo, Norway, May 6, 1958; came to U.S., 1959; s. Arne Frithof and Lydia (Boyd) H.; m. Debbe Ann Haupt, Mar. 12, 1988. BS in Econs. and Internat. Relations, U. Calif., Berkeley, 1981; MBA in Fin. and Mktg., UCLA, 1986. Asst. to v.p. Bus. Internat., Inc., San Francisco, 1981-82; rsch. assoc. Haug Internat., Inc., L.A., 1982-83, project dir., 1983-85; assoc. A.T. Kearney, Inc., L.A., 1986-88; cons. Cresap, L.A., 1988—. Contbr. articles to numerous publs. Mem. Am. Mktg. Assn., Am. Mgmt. Assn., Norwegian Am. C. of C., Calif. Club, L.A. Club. Republican. Presbyterian. Office: Cresap 1925 Century Park E Ste 1500 Los Angeles CA 90067

HAUGEN, GERALD ALAN, manufacturing company executive; b. Decorah, Iowa, Nov. 10, 1940; s. Thomas Edgar and Evelyn Lucille (Nelson)

H.; m. Sally Maureen Babb, Nov. 26, 1966; children: Eric, Leif, Dane. BA, Luther Coll., 1962. CPA, Minn. Audit staff Arthur Andersen and Co., Mpls., 1962-69, audit mgr., 1969-72; v.p.-controller Am. Lumber Co., Mpls., 1972-73; internal audit mgr. Jostens, Inc., Mpls., 1973-74, dir. corp. reporting, 1974-75, corp. controller fin., 1975-77, v.p.-controller, 1977-87, v.p. fin., planning and analysis, 1987-88, v.p. fin., chief fin. officer, 1988—. Mem. Am. Inst. CPA's, Minn. Soc. CPA's. Republican. Lutheran. Club: Interlachen Country (Edina, Minn.). Home: 4835 Gaywood Dr Minnetonka MN 55345 Office: Jostens Inc 5501 Norman Center Dr Minneapolis MN 55437

HAUGEN, ORRIN MILLARD, lawyer; b. Mpls., Aug. 1, 1927; s. Oscar M. and Emma (Moe) H.; m. Marilyn Dixon, June 17, 1950; children—Melissa, Kristen, Eric, Kimberly. B.S. in Chem. Engring., U. Minn., 1948, LL.B., 1951. Bar: Minn. 1951. Patent lawyer Honeywell, Inc., Mpls., 1951-59; patent lawyer Univac div. Sperry Rand, 1959-63; pvt. practice patent law Haugen & Nikolai, P.A., Mpls., 1963—. Pres. Arrowhead Lake Improvement Assn., Inc., Mpls., 1958-79. Served with USN, 1945-46. Mem. ABA, Minn. Bar Assn., Am. Patent Law Assn., Minn. Patent Law Assn., Minn. Trial Lawyers Assn., Minn. Acacia Alumni Assn., Inc. (pres. 1961-63), Acacia. Methodist. Lodge: Kiwanis. Home: 6612 Indian Hills Rd Edina MN 55435 Office: Haugen & Nikolai P A Internat Ctr Bldg Minneapolis MN 55402

HAUGH, ROBERT CYRIL, door manufacturing company executive; b. Hammond, Ind., Dec. 28, 1920; s. Cyril M. and Estelle (Lamphere) H.; m. Barbara J. Meek, Oct. 21, 1949; children: Carol, Kristin, Katy. A.B., Ind. U., 1948. Dist. sales mgr. U.S. Gypsum Co., Indpls, 1948-52; regional sales mgr. New Castle (Ind.) Products, 1952-62, v.p. sales, 1962-64, exec. v.p., 1964-67; v.p. ops. Dallas Corp., 1967-68, exec. v.p., 1968-70, pres., chief exec. officer, 1970—; also dir. Dallas Corp., New Castle, Ind.; dir. Mercantile Bank, Dallas, 1985—. . Dir. Youth for Tomorrow, Lewisville, Tex., 1982-88. Served with USN, 1942-46. Fellow, Ind. U. Business Sch., 1984. . Republican. Presbyterian. . Office: Dallas Corp 6750 LBJ Frwy Dallas TX 75240

HAUGHEY, JAMES WILFRED, publishing executive; b. Portland, Oreg., Feb. 3, 1943; s. Clifton Francis and Margaret Catherine (Mustard) H.; m. Barbara Jane Wirsing, Aug. 22, 1964; children: Laura, Brian. BA in econs., U. Mich., 1964; MBA, Eastern Mich. U., 1968; MA in Econs., U. Mich., 1969, PhD in Econs., 1971. Fin. analyst Ford Motor Co., Ypsilanti, Mich., 1965-68; asst. prof. Ohio U., Athens, 1971-72; asst. dir. budget office State of Mich., Lansing, 1972-76; economist Amoco Oil Co., Chgo., 1976-80; v.p. research and econs. Cahners Pub. Co., Newton, Mass., 1980—. Contbr. numerous articles to profl. jours. Mem. Am. Econ. Assn., Am. Mktg. Assn., Assn. Bus. Pubs. (research com. 1987-88). Republican. Episcopalian. Home: 16 Thunder Rd Sudbury MA 01776 Office: Cahners Pub Co 275 Washington St Newton MA 02158

HAUNTY, THOMAS ALEXANDER, financial executive; b. Milw., Apr. 13, 1960; s. Alex. C. and Lucille (Durante) H.; m. Mary Beth Ehlehbach, May 3, 1986. BBA, U. Wis., 1982; cert., Coll. Fin. Planning, 1986. cert. fin. planner Coll. Fin. Planning, 1986; registered health underwriter Northeastern U., 1987. Sr. assoc. Resource Fin. Group, Madison, Wis., 1988—; commentator weekly radio program. Contbr. articles to profl. jours. Evans Coll. scholar Western Golf Assn., 1978-82; recipient New Assoc. of Yr. award Northstar Cons., Inc., 1983, Assoc. of Yr. award Resource Fin. Group, 1983, 84, 86, 88. Mem. Million Dollar Roundtable, Leading Producers Roundtable, Internat. Assn. Fin. Planning, Inst. Cert. Fin. Planners, Greater Madison C. of C., Nat. Assn. Life Underwriters (nat. quality award 1983—, nat. sales achievement award 1983—), Nat. Assn. Health Underwriters (health ins. quality award 1983—). Republican. Club: Cherokee Country (Madison), Madison (Madison). Home: 1143 Emerald St Madison WI 53715 Office: Resource Fin Group 2901 W Beltline Hwy #310 Madison WI 53713

HAUPTFUHRER, ROBERT PAUL, oil company executive; b. Phila., Dec. 31, 1931; s. George J. and Emilie M. (Schoenhut) H.; m. Barbara Ellen Dunlop, May 11, 1963; children—Brenda Lynn, Bruce Andrew, Bryan Dunlop. AB, Princeton U., 1953; MBA, Harvard U., 1957. With Sun Co., Inc., Radnor, Pa., 1957—; pres. Sun Enterprises Group, 1975-79; sr. v.p. Sun Co., Inc., 1979-83; pres. Sun Exploration and Prodn. Co., 1984-86; pres., chief operating officer Sun Co., Inc., 1987-88; chmn., chief exec. officer Oryx Energy Co., Dallas, 1988—; bd. dirs. Quaker Chem. Corp., Nat. Assn. Mfgs., Am. Petroleum Inst. Trustee Princeton U., 1987—; assoc. trustee U. Pa., 1987—; bd. dirs. Dallas Symphony Assn. Lt. (j.g.) USN, 1953-55. Mem. Am. Petroleum Inst. Republican. Presbyterian. Clubs: Union League; Phila. Country (Gladwyne, Pa.); Pine Valley (N.J.) Golf; Merion Cricket (Haverford, Pa.). Home: 602 Old Eagle School Rd Wayne PA 19087 Office: Oryx Energy Co 5656 Blackwell Dallas TX 75221-2880

HAUSER, FRED P., insurance company executive; b. Bronx, N.Y., May 30, 1937; s. Louis and Ruth (Poppel) H.; m. Arlene Harris, Sept. 5, 1965; children: Lisa, Elaine. BS in Math., City Coll., N.Y.C., 1959; cert. Advanced Mgmt., Harvard U., 1986. With actuarial dept. Metropolitan Life Ins., N.Y.C., 1959-70, asst. actuary, 1970-86, sr. v.p., controller, 1986—. Com. person Nassau County Dem. Party, Nassau, N.Y., 1972—; bd. dirs. West Birchwood Civic Assn., Jericho, N.Y., 1975— (pres. 1980-81). Fellow Soc. Actuaries; mem. Am. Acad. Actuaries, Fin. Execs. Inst., N.Y. Actuaries. Democrat. Jewish. Office: Met Life Ins Co 1 Madison Ave New York NY 10010

HAUSER, JOYCE ROBERTA, marketing professional; b. N.Y.C.; d. Abraham and Helen (Lesser) Frankel; BA, SUNY, 1976; PhD, Union Grad. Sch., 1987; divorced; children—Mitchell, Mark, Ellen. Editor, Art in Flowers, 1955-58; pres. Joyce Advt., 1958-65; partner Hauser & Assocs., Pub. Rels., 1966-75; dir. broadcasting Bildersee Pub. Rels., 1973-75; pres. Hauser & Assocs., Inc., Pub. Rels., 1975-78, Hauser-Roberts, Inc., Pub. Rels./Mktg., N.Y.C., 1978-85, Mktg. Concepts & Communications Inc., N.Y.C., 1985—; moderator show Perceptions Sta. WEVD, 1975-77, Speaking of Health Sta. WNBC, 1977—, 97 Health Line, Sta. WYNY, 1980-83, Conversations with Joyce Hauser, Sta. WNBC, 1975-86, What's on Your Mind, Sta. WYNY, 1983-84, Talk-Net, 1983—; entertainment critic Sta. WNBC, 1986—; instr. Baruch Coll., CCNY, 1980-85; asst. prof. NYU, 1987—. Mem. Citywide Health Adv. Coun. on Sch. Health, 1970—, treas., 1980—; mem. adv. bd. degree programs NYU Sch. Continuing Edn.; mediator/artitrator Victim Svcs. Agy., 1986-87, Inst. Mediation & Conflict Resolution, 1985-86. Named one of 10 Top Successful Women Cancer Soc., 1976; recipient Professionalism award Sta. WNBC, 1980. Mem. AFTRA, Am. Women in Radio and TV (corr. sec. 1973, chmn. coll. women in broadcasting 1974), Acad. Family Mediators, Soc. Profl. Dispute Resolutions. Contbg. editor Alive, 1976-77. Home: 115 E 82nd St New York NY 10028 Office: 20 E 53rd St New York NY 10022

HAUSMAN, ARTHUR HERBERT, electronics company executive; b. Chgo., Nov. 24, 1923; s. Samuel Louis and Sarah (Elin) H.; m. Helen Mandelowitz, May 19, 1946; children: Susan Lois, Kenneth Louis, Catherine Ellen. B.S. in Elec. Engring, U. Tex., 1944; S.M., Harvard U., 1948. Electronics engr. Engring. Research Assos., St. Paul, 1946-47; supervisory electronics scientist U.S. Dept. Def., Washington, 1948-60; now advisor, v.p., dir. research Ampex Corp., Redwood City, Calif., 1960-63, v.p. ops., 1963-65, group v.p., 1965-67, exec. v.p., 1967-71, exec. v.p., pres., chief exec. officer, 1971-83, chmn. bd., 1981-87, chmn. bd. emeritus, 1987—; chmn. tech. adv. com. computer peripherals Dept. Commerce, 1973-75; mem. Pres.'s Export Council; chmn. Subcom. on Export Adminstrn.; bd. dirs. Drexler Tech. Inc., T.C.I. Inc., Synthetic Vision Systems Inc., Calif.-Amplifier, Inc. Trustee United Bay Area Crusade; mem. vis. com. dept. math. MIT; Bd. dirs. Bay Area Council. Served with USNR, 1944-54. Recipient Meritorious Civilian Service award Dept. Def. Mem. IEEE, Army Ordnance Assn. (dir. chpt. 1969-71), Am. Electronics Assn. (dir.). Clubs: Commonwealth of Calif.; Cosmos. Office: Ampex Corp 401 Broadway Redwood City CA 94063

HAUSMAN, JERRY ALLEN, economics educator, consultant; b. Weirton, W.Va., May 5, 1946; s. Harold H. and Rose (Hausman) H.; m. Margaretta Stone, Dec. 21, 1968; children: Nicholas, Claire. A.B., Brown U., 1968; B.Phil., Oxford U., 1972, D.Phil., 1973. Mem. faculty MIT, Cambridge, 1973—, prof. econs., 1979—. Contbr. articles to profl. jours. Marshall scholar, 1970-72; recipient Frisch medal Econometrics Soc., 1980; John Bates Clark award Am. Econs. Assn., 1985. Office: MIT Dept Econs Cambridge MA 02139

HAUSMANN, WERNER KARL, pharmaceutical executive; b. Edigheim, Germany, Mar. 9, 1921; came to U.S., 1948, naturalized, 1954; s. Carl and Johanna (Sprenger) H.; m. Helen Margaret Vas, Sept. 29, 1949; 1 child, Gregory. M.S. in Chem. Engring., Swiss Fed. Inst. Tech., 1945, D.Sc., 1947. Cert. quality engr. Research fellow U. London, 1947-48; research assoc. Rockefeller Inst. Med. Research, N.Y.C., 1949-57; research group leader Lederle Labs., Pearl River, N.Y., 1957-66; assoc. dir. quality control Ayerst Labs., Rouses Point, N.Y., 1966-71; dir. quality control Stuart Pharms., Pasadena, Calif., 1971-74; dir. quality assurance, analytical research and devel. Adria Labs., Inc., Columbus, Ohio, 1974-84; cons. Columbus, Ohio, 1985-86, San Diego, 1986—. Patentee in antibiotics; contbr. articles to profl. jours. Pres. Ednl. TV Assn., 1970-71; radiation officer CD, 1962-66; scoutmaster, 1942-45. Served to 1st lt. Swiss Army, 1939-46. Fellow Royal Soc. Chemistry, Chem. Soc. London, Am. Inst. Chemists, N.Y. Acad. Scis., AAAS, Am. Soc. Quality Control (chmn. Columbus sect.); mem. Acad. Pharm. Scis., Am. Soc. Biol. Chemists, Am. Chem. Soc., Am. Soc. Microbiology, Parenteral Drug Assn., Am. Assn. Individual Investors, Nat. Writers Club. Presbyterian. Office: 4332 Post Rd San Diego CA 92117

HAVELKA, CONALD J., chemical sales and service executive, financial consultant; b. Dickinson, N.D., Sept. 3, 1955; s. Joseph L. and Ottilia (Buresh) H.; m. Donna Kaye Hansen, Sept. 3, 1976; children: Joshua, Jessica, Katie Ann. Student, Dickinson State Coll., 1983; BA in Bus. Adminstrn., U. N.D., 1984. Registered drilling fluid engr., well controller. Dept. mgr. JC Penney, Dickinson, 1972-76; supr. sales Western Quality Check'd Dairy, Dickinson, 1976-79; devel. dir. Trinity Schs., Dickinson, 1983-84; field engr. N L Industries, Williston, N.D., 1981-87; ter. mgr. Ecolab Inc., St. Paul, 1986—; v.p. Eiger Inc., Dickinson, 1987—; devel. dir. Trinity Schs., 1983-84. U.S. Edn. Assn. rsch. grantee, 1973. Mem. N.D. Sanitation Bd., N.D. Health Care Assn., Am. Petroleum Inst., Jr. C. of C., KC, Columbian Squires (dep. chief 1973-74), German Hungarian Club. Roman Catholic. Home and Office: 1445 W 2d St Dickinson ND 58601

HAVEMEYER, ROBERT GUSTAV, management consultant; b. Rochester, N.Y.; Gustav A. and Ida (Aufmkolk) H.; m. Florence W. Greaves, Sept. 26, 1953; children: Shelley, Donna, Tara, Roberta. BS, Columbia U., 1950, MS, 1955. Cert. mgmt. cons., mfg. engr. Jr. engr. Neptune Meter Co., L.I., N.Y., 1950-51; budget analyst Sperry Products Co., Danbury, Conn., 1951-53; ptnr. Stevenson, Jordan and Harrison, N.Y.C., 1953-62; sr. v.p. Case and Co. Inc., N.Y.C., 1962-85; mng. ptnr. The Havemeyer Group, Stamford, Conn., 1985—; dir. food industry services Lester B. Knight and Assocs., Chgo., 1987—. Co-author: (books) Industrial Engineering Handbook, 1968, Pricing for Profit and Growth, 1970. Pres. Zion Luth. Ch., Stamford, 1986-88; mem. Coliseum Authority Adv. Panel, Stamford, 1983—; mem. econ. adv. council Grad. Sch. Bus. Columbia U., 1982-85. Mem. Soc. Mfg. Engrs., Inst. Mgmt. Cons. (vice chmn., v.p., bd. dirs. 1986—, cert.). Club: Midtown (Stamford). Home and Office: 16 Prince Pl Stamford CT 06905

HAVEN, GRANVILLE JAMES, utility company executive; b. Barnhart, Mo., Nov. 15, 1927; s. David F. and Matilda E.; m. Joyce Alsmeyer, Apr. 5, 1952; children: Joy Anita Haven Haury, Grant Gilbert. BS in Indsl. Engring., Washington U., St. Louis, 1952, MBA, 1955. With Union Electric Co., St. Louis, 1952—, dir. regional ops., 1967-69, v.p.-regional ops., 1969-73, v.p. transmission and distbn., 1973-85, v.p. engring. and constrn., 1985-88, v.p. R&D, 1988—. Pres., bd. dirs. St. Louis County Indsl. Devel. Authority. Served to lt. U.S. Army, 1946-48, Japan. Mem. Engrs. Club St. Louis, St. Louis Regional Commerce and Growth Assn., Electric Power Rsch. Inst. (chmn. elect. systems div. com. 1979-82, mem. rsch. adv. com. 1979-82, 87—), Edison Electric Inst. (rsch. mgmt. com.), Mo. C. of C. (chmn. econ. devel. council 1978-82, vice chmn. and bd. dirs. 1983-84, 87—, chmn. bd. dirs. 1988—), Bellerive Country Club. Presbyterian. Home: 822 Mason Wood Dr Saint Louis MO 63141 Office: Union Electric Co 18th & Gratoit Saint Louis MO 63166

HAVENS, TIMOTHY MARKLE, investment advisory firm executive; b. New Haven, Oct. 20, 1945; s. Walter Paul and Ida Markle (Hessenbruch) H.; m. Margaret Jean Stockdale, Nov. 1, 1969; children—Paul Markle, David Stockdale. B.A., U. Pitts., 1969. V.p. Drexel Burnham Lambert, Phila., 1970-79; pres. Newbold's Asset Mgmt., Phila., 1979—; bd. dirs. Federal Union, Washington, 1982—, Game Conservation Internat., San Antonio; mem. adv. bd., Phila. Coll. Physicians; trustee Independence Hall Assn., Phila. Served with USAR, 1968-74. Republican. Episcopalian. Clubs: Racquet (Phila.); Merion Cricket (Haverford, Pa.). Avocation: hunting. Home: 418 Fishers Rd Byrn Mawr PA 19010 Office: Newbold's Asset Mgmt Inc 937 Haverford Rd Byrn Mawr PA 19010

HAVER, JURGEN F., marketing consultant; b. Joliet, Ill., July 16, 1932; s. Elmer William and Hermina (Peters) H.; B.A., Wartburg Coll., 1956; m. Jane Suzanne Merrill, Apr. 13, 1985; children: Jason, Kyra. Feature writer Daily Peoples Press, Owatonna, Minn., 1959-60; editor Lyon County Independent, Marshall, Minn., 1960-62; asst. advt. dir. Burpee Seed Co., Phila., 1962-66; advt. mgr. for Organic Gardening, Theater Crafts and Quinto Lingo, promotion dir. for Prevention, Rodale Press, Emmaus, Pa., 1966-67; promotion of electronics mag. staff Kiver Pubs., Chgo., 1968-69; advt. dir. Henry Regnery Co., Chgo., 1969-70; pub. relations dir. Hess's Dept. Stores, Allentown, Pa., 1970-76; cons. Haver Mktg., Bethlehem, Pa., 1976—; faculty mktg. Moravian Coll., U. Pa. Sch. Dentistry, Pa. State U. Mem. Internat. Bus. Writers (past pres.), Am. Mktg. Assn. (past pres.). Author: Personalized Guide to Marketing Strategy, 1982; contbr. articles to profl. jours. Address: 6724 Beck Dr NE Albuquerque NM 87109

HAVERS, ROBERT WILLIAM, auctioneer, consultant, appraiser; b. Onaway, Mich., May 3, 1953; s. William John and Eleanor (Booth) H.; m. Susan Kaye Simpson, Aug. 6, 1977; 1 son, Jason Robert. Student Mo. Auction Sch., Great Lakes Jr. Coll. Bus., Am. Mgmt. Assn. Lic. auction cons., appraiser. Auctioneer Cummins Auction Co., Omaha, Nebr., 1981; franchisee United Auctioneers, Omaha, 1982-84; owner, pres. Bob Havers, Auctioneers, Midland, Mich., 1977—; lectr. Central Mich. U., Mt. Pleasant, 1982; cons. Randy Garner, Auctioneers, Fairfield, Ohio, 1982—; ran benefit auction Scottish Rite, Kansas City, Mo., 1979. Author Procalamtion Nat. Auctioneers Week, 1980, 84. Named largest auction ever conducted in Midland County Midland Daily News, 1982, largest auction ever conducted in Presquele Isle County Cheboygan Buyers Guide, 1983; recipient Cert. Appreciation Trout Unlimited, 1982-85. Mem. Nat. Auctioneers Assn., Nat. Process Svcs. Assn., Am. Pavement Maintenance Assn., Am. Entrepreneurs Assn., Smithsonian Inst., Am. Auction Inst. Democrat. Baptist. Club: Eagles. Avocations: country and bluegrass music, monstor trucks. Home and Office: 700 E Haley St Midland MI 48640

HAVERTY, HAROLD V., forms and check printing company executive; b. 1930. With Deluxe Check Printers, Inc., St. Paul, 1954—, former v.p., now pres., chief operating officer, also chief exec. officer, 1986—, dir. Office: De Luxe Check Printers Inc 1080 W County Rd F PO Box 64399 Saint Paul MN 55112 *

HAVERTY, RAWSON, retail furniture company executive; b. Atlanta, Nov. 26, 1920; s. Clarence and Elizabeth (Rawson) H.; m. Margaret Middleton Munnerlyn, Aug. 25, 1951; children: Margaret Elizabeth, Jane Middleton, James Rawson, Mary Elizabeth, Ben Munnerlyn. B.A., U. Ga., 1941. With Haverty Furniture Co., 1941-42, Haverty Furniture Cos., Inc., Atlanta, 1946—; pres. Haverty Furniture Cos., Inc., 1955—, chmn. bd., chief exec. officer, also dir.; instr. credit and collection So. Retail Furniture Assn. Sch. for Execs., U. N.C., 1950, instr. credits, collections, market analyses, 1951; instr. br. stores Nat. Retail Furniture Sch. for Execs., U. Chgo., 1957—; chmn. bd., dir. Bank of the South, N.A./Bank South Corp.; dir. Central Atlanta Progress. Former chmn. Met. Atlanta Rapid Transit Authority; chmn. bd. trustees St. Joseph's Hosp.; pres. U. Ga. Alumni Soc., 1973-75, mem. exec. com., 1975—, chmn. loyalty fund, 1969-70, 70-71; past pres. bd. trustees St. Joseph's Village; trustee Atlanta Arts Alliance, Westminster Sch., Atlanta, U. Ga. Found.; past pres. bd. sponsors Atlanta Art Sch.; bd. sponsors High Mus. Art; former mem. Fulton Indsl. Authority. Maj. AUS, 1942-46. Decorated Bronze Star medal; Order of Leopold; Croix de Guerre with palms (Belgium); named All Am. Mcht. in retail furniture industry, 1958. Mem. Atlanta Retail Mchts. Assn. (past pres., dir.), Nat. Home Furnishings Assn. (past v.p., dir., Retailer of Year 1979-80), Am. Retail Fedn., Atlanta Jr. C. of C. (hon. life), Assn. U.S. Army (past pres., adv. bd.), Atlanta C. of C. (dir., past pres.), Kiwanis, Piedmont Driving Club, Capital City Club, Ponte Vedra Club, Sigma Alpha Epsilon. Roman Catholic. Home: 3740 Paces Valley Rd NW Atlanta GA 30327 Office: Haverty Furniture Cos Inc 866 W Peachtree St NW Atlanta GA 30308

HAVLICEK, FRANKLIN J., communications executive; b. N.Y.C., July 18, 1947; s. Raymond Joseph and Rosalia Maria (Zona) H.; m. Louise Sferrazza, July 15, 1950. BA, Columbia U., 1968, JD, 1973, MA, 1977, M in Philosophy, 1980; cert., Internat. Inst. Human Rights, Strasbourg, France, 1972. Bar: N.Y. 1974, U.S. Dist. Ct. (so., ea. dists.) 1974, U.S. Ct. Appeals (2d cir.) 1975, U.S. Supreme Ct. 1979. Atty. Battle, Fowler, Jaffin & Kheel, N.Y.C., 1973-78; spl. advisor to Mayor of N.Y.C. 1978-82; ptnr. Seham, Klein, Zelman, N.Y.C., 1982-84; dir. labor relations NBC, N.Y.C., 1984-88; v.p. indsl. relations The Washington Post, 1988—; adj. prof. Sch. Internat. & Pub. Affairs Columbia U., N.Y.C., 1978—; chmn. Sunnyside Found., 1981—. Editor: Collective Bargaining, 1979, Presidential Selection, 1982, Election Communications, 1984; contbr. numerous articles on law, govt. to mags., newspapers. Mem. chmn.'s task force on NLRB, Washington, 1976-77, exec. com. N.Y. Gov.'s Task Force on Schs. and Bus., 1986-88; counsel Vietnam Veterans Meml. Commn., 1982-85, State Commn. on Dioxin, 1983-85; candidate for U.S. Senate in N.Y., 1986, advisor Ctr. for Internat. Leadership, 1986—; mem. U.S.-U.S.S.R. Emerging Leaders Summit, 1988. Served with U.S. Army, 1968-70. Ford Found. fellow, 1977. Mem. ABA, Assn. of Bar of City of N.Y., Am. Polit. Sci. Assn., Am. Acad. Polit. Sci., Czechoslovakian Soc. Arts and Scis., N.Y. Acad. Scis. Democrat. Roman Catholic. Club: City (N.Y.) (trustee 1985-87). Home: 3364 Tennyson St NW Washington DC 20015 Office: Washington Post 1150 15th St NW Washington DC 20071

HAWE, DAVID LEE, consultant; b. Columbus, Ohio, Feb. 19, 1938; s. William Doyle and Carolyn Mary (Hassig) H.; m. Margret J. Hoover, Apr. 15, 1962; children: Darrin Lee, Kelly Lynn. Project mgr. ground antenna systems W.D.L. Labs., Philco Corp., 1960-65; credit mgr. for Western U.S., Am. Hosp. Supply Corp., Burbank, Calif., 1965-74; owner, mgr. Hoover Profl. Equipment Co., contract health equipment co., Guasti, Calif., 1974-75; pres. Baslor Care Services, owners convalescent homes, Santa Ana, Calif., 1975-80; pres. Application Assocs., 1980—; bd. dirs., chmn. of bd. Xiron, Inc., 1984—; dir. Medisco Co., Casa Pacifica, Broadway Assocs. Bd. dirs. Santa Ana Community Convalescent Hosp., 1974-79, pres., 1975-79. With USN, 1954-56. Lic. real estate broker, Calif. Mem. Am. Vacuum Soc. Republican. Roman Catholic. Home: 18082 Hallsworth Cir Villa Park CA 92667

HAWEY, GHISLAIN ARTHUR, accountant; b. Quebec City, Que., Can., Aug. 16, 1931; s. Arthur and Juliette (Lajeunesse) H.; m. Yolande Baril; children: Steven, Douglas, Michael. B of Commerce, Laval (Que.) U., 1952, M of Commerce, 1953, M of Acctg., 1954. Chartered acct., Can. Auditor McDonald, Currie & Co., Toronto, 1953-54, Quebec City, 1954-59; ptnr. Fortier, Hawey & Assocs., Quebec City, 1959-62, Charette, Fortier, Hawey/Touche Ross, Quebec City and Montreal, 1962—. Chmn., pres. Province of Que. Planning and Devel. Council, 1973-78; bd. dirs. Que. Corp. of Indsl. Devel., 1974-80; gov. Laval U. Found., 1975—. Recipient Hermes Trophy Laval U. Dept. Adminstrv. Scis., 1985. Fellow Que. Order Chartered Accts.; mem. Que. Inst. Mgmt. Cons., Can. Inst. Chartered Accts., Que. Profl. Corp. of Chartered Adminstrs., Que. Provincial C. of C. (pres. 1971-72), Rotary (pres. Eastern Que. 1967-68), The Garrison, Royal Que. Golf Club. Roman Catholic. Home: 3336 Arthur Grenier, Beauport, PQ Canada G1E 1G8 Office: Charette Fortier Hawey/, Touche Ross Co, 1 Pl Ville-Marie Bur 3000, Montreal, PQ Canada H3B 4T9

HAWK, DONALD L., banker; b. Massillon, Ohio, Jan. 22, 1947; s. Elroy L. and Mary C. Hawk; m. Anne M. Hawk (div.) 1 child, Brian P. BS, Ohio State U., 1970. Acting ctr. dir. Columbus (Ohio) Bus. U., 1970-73; asst. to v.p. personnel Baster Travenol Labs., Inc., Deerfield, Ill., 1973-78; v.p. programs Ctr. for Creative Leadership, Greensboro, N.C., 1978-81; exec. v.p. Tex. Commerce Bancshares, Inc., Houston, 1981—; bd. dirs. Tex. Commerce Bank, San Antonio, McAllen, Tex., Brownsville, Tex. Contbr. articles to profl. jours. Chmn. fellow adv. com. Coll. Bus. Adminstrn. A&M U., College Station, Tex.; bd. dirs. Houston Job Tng. Partnership Coun., Houston. Mem. Acad. of Mgmt., Am. Psychol. Assn., Houston Club. Office: Tex Commerce Bank 600 Travis 61st Fl Houston TX 77002

HAWK, GEORGE WAYNE, electronics company executive; b. Warren, Ohio, Feb. 21, 1928; s. Oscar Wilmer and Morda Irene (Klingensmith) H.; m. Charline Hines Bond, Feb. 12, 1955; children: George Wayne, David James, John Robert. BS in Aero. Engring, Purdue U., 1951; MS in Mech. Engring., U. So. Calif., 1955; postgrad., U. Tenn. Registered profl. engr., Ind. Asst. research and devel. officer gas dynamics facility Arnold Engring. Devel. Center, Tullahoma, Tenn., 1951-53; project engr. Hughes Research and Devel. Lab., Culver City, Calif., 1953-56; sr. research engr. Goodyear Aircraft Corp., Akron, Ohio, 1956-57; with Moog Inc., East Aurora, N.Y., 1957-81; v.p. aerospace div. Moog Inc., 1968-69, exec. v.p., dir., gen. mgr. controls div., 1969-76, exec. v.p., dir. pres. controls group, 1976-81; pres. G.W. Hawk Inc., 1981-86; pres., chief exec. officer Acme Electric Corp., 1986—; chmn. bd. Comptek Research Inc., 1983-87, M.H.P. Machines, Inc., Buffalo, 1983—; bd. dirs. Acme Electric Corp., Comptek Research Inc., Young & Franklin Inc., Mfrs. Hanover Trust Co. N.A. Contbr. articles profl. jours.; patentee in field. Past chmn. bd. dirs. Buffalo Philharm. Orch.; bd. dirs. Buffalo chpt. ARC; past pres. Greater Niagara Frontier council Boy Scouts Am.; past chmn. bd., pres. Greater Buffalo Devel. Found.; bd. regents Canisius Coll.; bd. dirs. Fluid Power Ednl. Found., Olean Gen. Hosp. Served with AUS, 1946-48; Served to 1st lt. USAF, 1951-53. Fellow AIAA (assoc.); mem. Air Force Assn. (pres. Larry D. Bell chpt. 1978), Navy League, Am. Def. Preparedness Assn., Nat. Fluid Power Assn. (past chmn. bd., past conf. dir.) Buffalo C. of C. (past vice chmn.). Lutheran. Clubs: Buffalo Country, Buffalo, Aero (dir.). Lodge: Masons. Home: 280 Greenwood Ct East Aurora NY 14052 Office: Acme Electric Corp 260 N Union St Olean NY 14760

HAWKES, DAVID R., tax consultant; b. Manchester, Conn., Feb. 12, 1947; s. Ralph W. and Jane (Varrell) H.; m. Kathleen K., May 29, 1983; children: Nathan, Amy, Alison. BS, Thomas Coll., 1969; MBA, Babson Coll., 1975. Staff acct. Price Waterhouse & Co., Boston, 1971-76; mgr. tax Ernst & Whinney, Portland, Maine, 1976-81; ptnr., tax dir. Brooks & Carter, Bangor, Maine, 1981-87; pvt. practice acctg. Ellsworth, Maine, 1987—; instr. Husson Coll., Bangor. Trustee North Yarmouth Acad., Yarmouth, Maine, 1980-82, Thomas Coll., Waterville, 1988; trustee, treas. Portland Mus. Art, 1979-81, Mt. Desert Chamber Music Festival, Northeast Harbor, Maine, 1984—. Recipient Alumni award Thomas Coll. Mem. AICPA, Maine Soc. CPAs, Maine Estate Planning Council. Lodge: Rotary. Office: 75 State St Ellsworth ME 04605

HAWKINS, ADOLPHUS WISE, JR., international business consultant, investment banker, broker; b. Culpeper, Va., Mar. 4, 1922; s. Adolphus W. and Clara (Taylor) H.; m. Bette Worsham; children—John Thomas Worsham, David Telford, Lisabeth Jill. B.A. in Econs., U. Va., 1948; postgrad. U. Paris, 1949, Balliol Coll., Oxford (Eng.) U., 1950; D.C.S., London Inst. Applied Research, 1972. Lic. securities, real estate and ins. broker. Owner A.W. Hawkins, Inc., Culpeper, 1951-59, Ashley Transfer & Storage Co., Charleston, S.C., 1954-56, Hawkins Moving and Storage Co., Fayetteville, N.C., 1954-58; assoc. Elam & Funsten, Richmond, Va., 1960-64; specialist corp. mergers and acquisitions Merrill Lynch, Pierce, Fenner and Smith, Inc., 1966-69; v.p. Anderson & Strudwick Inc., 1969-79, Scott & Stringfellow Inc., Richmond, 1979-83; dir. Doughtie's Foods, Inc.; mem. N.Y. Stock Exchange; pres. Mediterranean Foods S.P.A. Former mem. Richmond Democratic Com.; past mem. bd. dirs. Multiple Sclerosis Soc., bd. assocs. St. Paul's Coll. Served with USN, 1942-46; PTO. Mem. Va. Squash Racquets Assn. (founder, life), U. Va. Alumni Assn., U.S. Squash Racquets Assn., ETA Ednl. Found., Phi Kappa Sigma. Clubs: Westwood Racquet (dir.), Farmington Country, Deep Run Hunt. Home: Windsor Farms 3808 Dover Rd Richmond VA 23221

HAWKINS, JAMES LOWELL, JR., bank executive; b. Kansas City, Mo., Apr. 25, 1950; s. James Lowell and Jean Marion (Schweitzer) H.; m. Linda Faye Cottrill, July 27, 1974; children: Paul Madison, Brian Lowell. BBA, N.Mex.State U., 1973; postgrad., Grad. Sch. Banking, 1982. Fin. intern U. S. Treasury Dept., Denver, 1970-73, asst. nat. bank examiner, 1973-74; asst. cashier Republic Bank & Trust, Tulsa, 1974-76; v.p., cashier Bank Cushing (Okla.) & Trust Co., 1977-83; v.p. Union Bank & Trust, Bartlesville, Okla., 1983-86; sr. v.p. First Nat. Bank Alamogordo, N.Mex., 1987—; bd. dirs., com. on payment systems Fed. Reserve Bank Dallas, 1987—. Dir. Retired Sr. Vol. Program, Alamogordo, 1987; mem. budget com. United Way, Bartlesville and Cushing, 1980-86. Mem. ABA, State U. Alumni Assn. (pres. Otero County 1987), Lions Club (Alamogordo), Rotary (Cushing), Masons. Republican. Prebyterian. Home: 404 Sunglow Ave Alamogordo NM 88310 Office: First Nat Bank Alamogordo 414 10th St Alamogordo NM 88310

HAWKINS, KENNETH EVERETT, insurance executive; b. Louisville, Jan. 6, 1928; s. Wilfor Chester and Flocy (Merideth) H.; m. Charline Myrtle Smith, June 8, 1946; children: Terrell Vance and Cheryl Denise, Geary Lloyd. BA, Olivet Nazarene U., 1953. Lic. ins. advisor. Dist. mgr. Liberty Mut. Ins. Co., Atlanta, 1955-65; pres. Ins. Buyer's Counsel, Atlanta, 1965-72; sr. v.p. R.B. Jones Corp., Kansas City, Mo., 1972-78; owner Hawkins & Assocs., Clearwater, Fla., 1980-81; chmn. Jones & Hawkins Ins., St. Petersburg, Fla., 1981-89, dir., 1981—. With USN, 1946-49, PTO. Mem. Fla. Assn. Ins. Agts. (dir. 1986-89), Nat. Assn. Casualty and Surety Agts., Ins. Agts. Greater St. Petersburg (pres. 1985-86), Harborview C. of C., Fla. Counsel Yacht Club (dir. 1988-89), Treasure Island Tennis and Yacht Club (dir. 1986-89). Home: 5940 Pellican Bay Pla Saint Petersburg FL 33703 Office: Jones & Hawkins Ins 3190 Tyrone Blvd N PO Box 40330 Saint Petersburg FL 33743

HAWKINS, LIONEL ANTHONY, life insurance company executive; b. Jackson, Miss., June 20, 1933; s. Lionel A. and Ruth (Hanna) H.; m. Anne Giesecke, June 29, 1958; children: Lionel A. III, John Randall, Hollie A. Student, U. Tex., Arlington, 1951-54, George Washington U., 1957-59. Ins. agt., asst. mgr. Mut. Ins. of N.Y., Washington, 1959-63; regional supr. and mgr., agy. mgr. Kansas City (Mo.) Life Ins., 1963-69, gen. agt., 1971-73; agy. dir. Jefferson Nat., Indpls., 1969-70, Allied Life Ins., Birmingham, Ala., 1970-71; agy. dir., regional v.p. Mut. Trust Life Ins., Oakbrook, Ill., 1973-87; field v.p. Am. Gen. Life Ins. Co., Oakbrook, 1987—. 1st lt. U.S. Army, 1955-59. Mem. Nat. Assn. Life Underwriters, Gen. Agts. and Mgrs. Assn., Western Agy. Officers Assn. (bd. dirs. 1983-87). Republican. Home: 41 Lynwood Plano IL 60545 Office: Am Gen Life Ins Co 17 W 240 22d St Ste 215 Oakbrook Terrace IL 60181

HAWKINS, PETER GREGORY, certified financial planner; b. Bogota, N.J., Aug. 1, 1951; s. John R. and Loretta (LeBlanc) H.; m. Phyllis Hajduk, Dec. 6, 1975; children: Cannon, Simon. AB, Rutgers U., 1973. Asst. treas. Chase Manhattan Bank, N.Y.C., 1973-77; mortgage broker All Fin. Svcs., Torrance, Calif., 1978-79; pres., fin. planner Hall of Fame Sports, Inc., Darien, Conn., 1980—. Pres. Stamford (Conn.) chpt. Gideon Internat., 1983-86. Mem. Internat. Coll. Fin. Planners, Fellowship Christian Fin. Planners, Delta Phi Epsilon, Dunamis Rugby Football Club (Darien, pres. 1983-85). Episcopalian. Home: 14 Beach Dr Darien CT 06820 Office: Hall of Fame Sports Inc PO Box 2386 Darien CT 06820

HAWKINS, RICHARD SPENCER DADDOW, personnel director; b. Boston, Apr. 29, 1943; s. Joseph Elmer Jr. and Jane Elizabeth (Daddow) H.; m. Roberta Rosenthal, Dec. 24, 1974 (div. Oct. 1984); 1 child, Jessica Clayton. Baccalaureate, Goteborgs Hogre Samskola, Sweden, 1963; BA, Harvard U., 1967; MA, Yale U., 1970. Exec. v.p. Media Engring. Corp., Cambridge, Mass., 1970-73; sales trainer John Hancock Life Ins. Co., Westwood, Mass., 1974-77; dir. employee tng. asst. Commonwealth of Mass., Boston, 1977-78; mgmt. devel. specialist Wang Labs., Lowell, Mass., 1978-80, mgr. mfg. tng., 1980-81; mgr. tng. and devel. electro-optics div. Honeywell Inc., Lexington, 1981-86, mgr. staffing, 1986-87; mgr. mgmt. devel. Otis Elevator Co., Farmington, Conn., 1987—; adj. faculty Northeastern U., Boston, 1983-85, Bryant Coll., 1987—. Contbr. articles to bus. and econs. jours. Harvard U. Scholar, 1961; Nat. Merit scholar, 1961; Fulbright Found. fellow, Singapore, 1967. Mem. Am. Soc. for Tng. and Devel. (bd. dirs. Mass. chpt. 1982-84, chmn. community devel. com. 1982-84, regional conf. program, 1984), Human Resource Planning Soc. Episcopalian. Club: Appalachian Mountain (Boston). Home: PO Box 931 Farmington CT 06034 Office: Otis Elevator Co 4 Farm Springs Farmington CT 06032

HAWKINS, ROBERT LEE, social work administrator; b. Denver, Feb. 18, 1938; s. Isom and Bessie M. (Hugley) H.; A.A., Pueblo Jr. Coll., 1958; B.S., So. Colo. State Coll., 1965; M.S.W., U. Denver, 1967; m. Ann Sharon Hoy, Apr. 28, 1973; children—Robert, Jeanne, Julia, Rose. Psychiat. technician Colo. State Hosp., Pueblo, 1956-58, 1962-63, occupational therapist asst., 1964-65, clin. adminstr. psychiat. team, 1969-75, dir. community services, 1975—, supr. vol. services, 1975—, mem. budget com., 1975—; counselor (part-time) Family Service Agy., Pueblo, 1968-69, exec. dir., 1969-70; mem. faculty U. So. Colo., 1968-75; partner Human Resource Devel., Inc., 1970-75. Mem. Pueblo Positive Action Com., 1970; chmn. adv. bd. Pueblo Sangre de Cristo Day Care Center, 1969-72; chmn. Gov.'s So. Area Adv. Council of Employment Service, 1975-76, chmn. Pueblo's City CSC, 1976-77, Pueblo Community Corrections, 1985-87, Pueblo Civil Service Commn., 1988—; commr. Pueblo Housing Authority, 1986—, Colo. Commn. Higher Edn., 1987—; mem. gov's. adv. com. Mental Health Standards, 1981—; mem. Colo. Juvenile Parole Bd., 1977; bd. dirs. Pueblo United Fund, 1969-74, pres., 1973; bd. dirs. Pueblo Community Orgn., 1974-76, Spanish Peaks Mental Health Center, 1976—, Neighborhood Health Center, 1977-79, Pueblo Community Corrections, 1983—, Pueblo Legal Services, 1983—. Served with U.S. Army 1958-62. Mem. Nat. Assn. Social Workers (nominating com. 1973-76), ACLU (dir. Pueblo chpt. 1980—), NAACP, Broadway Theatre Guild. Democrat. Methodist. Club: Kiwanis. Home: 520 Gaylord St Pueblo CO 81004 Office: Colo State Hosp 1600 W 24 St Pueblo CO 81003

HAWKINSON, GARY MICHAEL, utility holding company executive; b. Chgo., Oct. 30, 1948; s. Roy G. and June M. (Miller) H.; m. Patricia Kaye Schlievert, Jan. 9, 1971; children: Kenneth, Christopher. BBA in Fin., U. Toledo, 1971. Various mgmt. and analytical positions Toledo Edison Co., 1972-79, asst. treas., asst. sec., 1979-86; treas. Centerior Energy Corp., Independence, Ohio, 1986—. Trustee Luth. Med. Ctr. Found. Served to 2d lt. U.S. Army, 1971-72. Club: Cleve. Treas. Home: 26875 Kenley Ct Westlake OH 44145 Office: Centerior Energy Corp 6200 Oak Tree Blvd Independence OH 44131

HAWKINSON, JOHN, investment management company executive; b. Walker, Iowa, May 26, 1912; s. Theodore W. and Gertrude (Nietert) H.; m. Florence Mallaire, Oct. 12, 1946; children—Diane, Judith. A.B., U. Iowa, 1936. With investments dept. Halsey, Stuart & Co., Inc., Chgo., 1936-41; v.p. Halsey, Stuart & Co., Inc., 1946-49; v.p. finance, dir. Central Life Assurance Co., Des Moines, 1950-62; pres., dir. Kemper Fin. Services, Inc., Chgo., 1962-75; chmn. Kemper Fin. Services, Inc., 1975-78; pres., dir. Kemper Group Mut. Funds, 1963-85; bd. dirs. Kansas City So. Industries, La. & Ark. Ry., Ryder Systems, Inc., ALC Communications, LDX Group, Inc., Gaylord Container Corp.; mem. Ill. Securities Adv. Commn. Bd. dirs. U. Iowa Found. Served to col., intelligence AUS, 1942-46, ETO. Mem. Nat. Fedn. Financial Analysts. Clubs: Des Moines (Des Moines); Chicago, Attic, Economic (Chgo.); Glenview (Golf, Ill.). Office: Kemper Group Mutual Funds 120 S LaSalle St Chicago IL 60603

HAWKRIGG, MELVIN MICHAEL, financial company executive; b. Toronto, Ont., Can., Aug. 26, 1930; m. Marilyn Jane Field, June 4, 1954; children: Jane, Michael, Peter, Mary Ann, John. BA in History and Polit. Econ., McMaster U., Can., 1952. Chartered acct. Mgr. Clarkson, Gordon, 1952-59; pres. Fuller Brush Ltd., Hamilton, Ont., Can., 1959-71; vice chmn. Can. Trustco, Toronto, 1972-81; vice chmn. Cen. Ont. region Can. Trustco, 1972-81; exec. v.p. Brascan Fin. Services, Toronto, 1981-82; sr. v.p. Brascan Ltd., Toronto, 1982-83; chief exec. officer, chmn. Trilon Fin. Corp., Toronto, 1983—; chmn. bd. CVL Inc.; bd. dirs. Holden Group, Trilon Bancorp., Inc., Trilon Fin. Corp., May & Baker Can. Inc.; dep. chmn., chmn. exec. com., bd. dirs. Royal LePage Ltd.; bd. dirs. London Life Ins. Co., audit, exec., mgmt. devel., compensation investment coms., chmn.; exec., human resources and compensation, investment rev. coms. Royal Trustco Ltd.; chmn., chief exec. officer Lonvest Corp.; dep. chmn., chief exec. officer, chmn. exec. com., investment com. Wellington Ins. Co.; past chmn., chief exec. officer Can. Depository for Securities; chmn. Triathlon Leasing, Inc., Wellington Ins. Co. Named to McMaster U. Sports Hall of Fame. Fellow Inst. Chartered Accts. Ont.; mem. Inst. Chartered Accts. Anglican. Clubs: Toronto, Beverly Golf, Canadian, Met. Toronto Country Club (chmn. bd. trade). Home: Box 566, 10 First St, Waterdown, ON Canada L0R 2H0

HAWLEY, ALAN, music company executive; b. Bristol, England, Feb. 2, 1950; came to U.S., 1966; s. Arthur Vernon and Frances Patricia (Wood) H.; m. Carol Lynn White, April 2, 1977; 1 child, Morgan Richard. Postgrad., U. Calif., Long Beach, 1968-73. Retail mgr. McCain's Records, Long Beach, Calif., 1974-77; ops. mgr. Decameron Recording Studio, Fullerton, Calif., 1977-78; prodn. mgr. PRC Recording Co., Compton, Calif., 1978-80; warehouse mgr. VHD Mfg., Irvine, Calif., 1980-82; facilities planning, prodn. mgr. Musicland Group, Mpls., 1983—. Mem. Coun. of Logistics. Home: 12570 Porcupine Ct Eden Prairie MN 55344 Office: Musicland Group 7500 Excelsior Blvd Minneapolis MN 55426

HAWLEY, FRANK JORDAN, JR., venture capital executive; b. Roanoke Rapids, N.C., Oct. 3, 1927; s. Frank Jordan and Mary (Miller) H.; m. Alethea Wood, Sept. 12, 1959; children: Frank J. III, Mark R., Andrew D., Stuart W., Alethea S. BS in Physics, U. N.C., 1949; MBA, Harvard U., 1955. Research analyst Eaton & Howard, Inc., Boston, 1955-59; banking assoc. Lazard Freres, N.Y.C., 1959-64; portfolio mgr. Stein, Roe & Farnham, N.Y.C., 1964-69; exec. v.p. Laidlaw Coggeshall, Inc., N.Y.C., 1969-74; gen. ptnr. Foster Mgmt. Co., N.Y.C., 1974-82; mng. ptnr. Saugatuck Capital Co., Stamford, Conn., 1982—; chmn. bd. Morgan Products Ltd, Oshkosh, Wis., Sentinal Group, Inc., Stamford, Med. Rehab Inc., Tallahassee, Fla.; trustee Kenan Inst. Pvt. Enterprise U. N.C., Chapel Hill. V.p., treas. New Canaan (Conn.) YMCA, 1981-85; trustee Chocvua Chapel Assn., Squaw Lake, N.H. Served to lt. (j.g.) USN, 1950-53, Korea. Mem. Conn. Venture Capital Assn. (exec. com. 1983—), Phi Beta Kappa. Republican. Episcopalian. Clubs: Links, Harvard (N.Y.C.); New Canaan Country, New Canaan Field. Home: 613 Silvermine Rd New Canaan CT 06840 Office: Saugatuck Capital Co One Canterbury Green Stamford CT 06901 also: Morgan Products Ltd 601 Oregon St Oshkosh WI 54903

HAWLEY, JEFFREY LANCE, securities executive, accountant; b. Shreveport, La., Aug. 28, 1948; s. Eugene E. Jr. and Opal Marie (Hitchcock) H.; m. Pam Haley, Mar. 7, 1970; children: Suzanne, Allison. BS in Acctg., La. Tech. U., 1970; MBA, N.E. La. U., 1978. CPA, La., Tex.; registered securities rep., La. Sr. acct. Peat, Marwick, Mitchell and Co., Houston, 1970-74; budget dir. Olinkraft, Inc. (now Manville Corp.), West Monroe, La., 1974-77; v.p., treas., chief fin. officer Palomar Fin., San Diego and Monroe, La., 1977-83; v.p., investment broker Legg, Mason, Howard & Weil, Monroe, 1983—. Mem. Am. Inst. CPA's, Soc. La. CPA's (com. chmn. 1986—, past pres. local chpt., 1981-84). Republican. Baptist. Clubs: Tower, Chauvin Racquet (Monroe). Lodge: Rotary, Optimists. Office: Legg Mason Howard & Weil Friedrichs Inc 1401 Hudson Ln Ste 134 Monroe LA 71201

HAWLEY, PHILIP METSCHAN, retail executive; b. Portland, Oreg., July 29, 1925; s. Willard P. and Dorothy (Metschan) H.; m. Mary Catherine Follen, May 31, 1947; children: Diane (Mrs. Robert Bruce Johnson), Willard, Philip M. Jr., John, Victor, Edward, Erin, George. B.S., U. Calif., Berkeley, 1946; grad., Advanced Mgmt. Program, Harvard U., 1967. With Carter Hawley Hale Stores, Inc., Los Angeles, 1958—, pres., 1972-83, chief exec. officer, 1977—, chmn., 1983—, also dir.; bd. dirs. Atlantic Richfield Co., BankAm. Corp., AT&T, The Economist; dir. Johnson & Johnson. Trustee Calif. Inst. Tech., U. Notre Dame, Huntington Library and Art Gallery; bd. dirs. Assocs. Harvard U. Grad Sch. Bus. Adminstrn.; adv. council Grad. Sch. Bus. Stanford U.; vis. com. UCLA Grad. Sch. Mgmt., Bus. Council, Bus. Roundtable, Conf. Bd.; chmn. Los Angeles Energy Conservation Com. 1973-74. Decorated hon. comdr. Order Brit. Empire, knight comdr. Star Solidarity Republic Italy; recipient award of merit Los Angeles Jr. C. of C., 1974, Coro Pub. Affairs award, 1978, Medallion award Coll. William and Mary, 1983; named Calif. Industrialist of Year Calif. Mus. Sci. and Industry, 1975. Mem. Phi Beta Kappa, Beta Alpha Psi, Beta Gamma Sigma. Clubs: California, Los Angeles Country; Bohemian Pacific-Union (San Francisco); Newport Harbor Yacht (Newport Beach, Calif.); Multnomah (Portland); Links (N.Y.C.). Office: Carter Hawley Hale Stores Inc 550 S Flower St Los Angeles CA 90071

HAWLEY, PHILLIP EUGENE, investment banker; b. Tecumseh, Mich., Dec. 9, 1940; s. Paul P and Vadah Arlene (Lawhead) H.; m. Linda Darlene Miller, Feb. 14, 1957; children—Pierre Lee, Paul Marvin, Danny Parke, David Eugene, Martin Edward. Student in mgmt. Yale U., 1959-63; B.S. in Bus. Adminstrn., Northwestern Coll., Tulsa, 1980. With Credit Bur. Fort Myers, Inc., Fl., 1956—, chmn. bd.; pvt. investigator Transworld Investigators, Inc., 1964, now v.p.; mgr., founder real estate co. (now Gold Coast Develop. Corp.), 1965, pres.; pres. Phillip Hawley Investment Banking Co.; bd. dirs. Caribbean Industries Internat. Corp., Future Investment Corp. Cofounder, bd. dirs. Collier-Lee Wrestling Assn., 1974—. Named Outstanding Speaker, Fla. Collectors Assn., 1967; Outstanding Individual, Fla. Fedn. Young Republicans, 1971; recipient Presdl. Sports award, 1979. Author: Law And It's Alternative to Chaos, 1958; The Happiest Man in the World, 1970; The Best Buys In Fort Myers, 1982. Mem. Fla. Collectors Assn., Am. Collectors Assn., Assn. Credit Bur. Am., Med.-Dental Hosp. Burs. Am., Fla. Assn. Mortgage Brokers, Fla. Assn. Pvt. Investigators. Republican. Mem. Nazarene Ch. Clubs: Gideons Internat., Collier Lee Wrestling Assn.; Am. Numismatic Assn. Home: 6435 Winkler Rd Fort Myers FL 33907 Office: 2083 Cleveland Ave Fort Myers FL 33901

HAWLEY, TODD BRYAN, university official, company executive; b. Seattle, Apr. 13, 1961; s. John Paul Hawley and Audrey Gail (Love) Lineman. BA in Econs., Russian Lang. and Lit., George Washington U., 1983, MA in Sci., Tech. and Pub. Policy, 1988. Analyst Intelsat Orgn., Washington, 1983-84; dir. ops. Young Astronaut Coun., Washington, 1984-86; adminstr. Arhur Clarke Found., Washington, 1983; pres., adminstr. Internat. Space U., Boston, 1986—; exec. dirs. Space Generation Found., Washington, 1985—; pres. Hawley Corp., Boston, 1988—; v.p. Diamandis Corp., Boston, 1988—; bd. dirs. Space Devel. Corp., Washington; mgn. dir. Micro Satellite Launch Systems, Houston, 1989—. Editor Z-Axis, 1988; contbr. articles to profl. jours. Space Found. fellow, 1987. Mem. AIAA, Nat. Space Soc., Space Studies Inst. (sr. assoc.), Am. Astron. Soc. (exec. com. 1985). Home: 1126 Boylston St Apt 607 Boston MA 02215 Office: Internat Space U 636 Beacon St Ste 201 Boston MA 02215

HAWORTH, GERRARD WENDELL, office systems manufacturing company executive; b. Alliance, Nebr., Oct. 9, 1911; s. Elmer R. and Lulu (Jones) H.; m. Dorcas A. Snyder, June 22, 1938 (dec.); children: Lois, Richard, Joan, Mary, Julie; m. 2d Edna Mae Van Tatenhove, Feb. 5, 1979. A.B., Western Mich. U., 1937; M.A., U. Mich., 1940. Tchr. Holland High Sch., Mich., 1937-48; chmn. bd. Haworth Inc., Holland, Mich., 1965—. Office: Haworth Inc 1 Haworth Ctr Holland MI 49423

HAWRYLYSHYN, BOHDAN W., business educator; b. Koropec, Ukraine, Oct. 19, 1926; s. Dmytro and Teodosia (Sadowska) H.; M.A.Sc. in Mech. Engring., U. Toronto (Can.), 1954; diploma in indsl. mgmt. Internat. Mgmt. Inst., Geneva, 1958; Ph.D. in Econs., U. Geneva, 1975; hon. degree York U., Alta. U. m. Leonida Hayowsky, June 10, 1950; children—Leslie, Patricia, Christine. Officer UNRRA in Germany, 1946-47; positions in research, engring. and mgmt. in Can., 1954-60; mem. faculty Internat. Mgmt. Inst., Geneva, 1960—, dir., 1968-86, scholar in residence, 1986—; lectr. in more than 40 countries; cons. to govts., internat. orgns. and bds. of transnat. corps.; mem adv. council McGraw-Hill. Trustee Resources for Future. Recipient Gold medal Pres. of Italian Republic, various scholarships and awards. Fellow World Acad. Art and Sci., Internat. Acad. Mgmt., Club of Rome. Ukrainian Catholic. Author: Road Maps to the Future, in six lang. edits., other books and more than 40 articles; editorial bd. several jours. Home: 5 chemin du Reposoir, CH 1255 Geneva-Veyrier Switzerland Office: 4 Chemin de Conches, CH 1231 Geneva-Conches Switzerland

HAWVER, MARY ANNE, marketing executive; b. Weston, W.Va., Jan. 7, 1957; d. Robert Lee and Rose Ann (Calabrese) Swiger; m. Reginald Kyle Hawver, June 4, 1977; 1 child, Emily Rose Elizabeth. BS in Bus., Fairmont (W.Va.) State Coll., 1980; MBA, U. W.Va., 1988. Procurement coordinator U.S. Dept. Energy, Morgantown, W.Va., 1978-80; mktg. rep. Hope Gas Inc., Clarksburg, W.Va., 1980-83, coordinator resdl. mktg., 1983-85; coordinator consumer info. Hope Gas Inc., Clarksburg, 1985-88, mktg. plans specialist, 1988—. Bd. dirs. United Way of Harrison County, Clarksburg, 1987-88; pres. Stonewall Jackson Theatre Co., Weston. Mem. Gas Appliance Mfrs. Assn., Nat. Mgmt. Assn., NAFE, Cath. Daughters Club. Home: 238 Cottage Ave Weston WV 26452 Office: Hope Gas Inc 705 Union Bank Ctr West Clarksburg WV 26301

HAY, ANDREW MACKENZIE, merchant banking and commodities company executive; b. London, Apr. 9, 1928; came to U.S., 1954, naturalized, 1959; s. Ewen Mackenzie and Bertine (Buxton) H.; MA in Econs., St. John's Coll., Cambridge U., 1950; m. Catherine Newman, July 30, 1977. Commodities trader, London and Ceylon, 1950-53; v.p. Calvert Vavasseur & Co. Inc., N.Y.C., 1954-61, pres., 1962-78, pres. Calvert-Peat Inc., N.Y.C., 1978—, Andrew M. Hay, Inc.; chmn. Barretto Peat Inc., N.Y.C., 1974-88; Pacific NW cons. Am. Assn. Exporters and Importers, 1982—; radio and TV appearances. Mem. adv. com. on tech. innovation Nat. Acad. Scis., 1978; bd. dirs. Winston Churchill Found.; treas., trustee World Affairs Coun. Oreg., 1986—; apptd. Her Majesty's hon. Brit. consul., 1987. Capt. Brit. Army. Decorated comdr. Order Brit. Empire. Mem. Am. Importer Assn. (pres. 1977-79), Pacific N.W. Internat. Trade Assn. (exec. dir. 1986—), Brit. Am. C. of C. (pres. 1966-68), Philippine Am. C. of C. (pres. 1977-79), St. George's Soc. (bd. dir.), St. Andrew's Soc. (bd. dir.), Recess Club, Downtown Assn. (N.Y.C.), U. Club, Arlington Club. Episcopalian. Author: A Century of Coconuts, 1972. Home and Office: 3515 SW Council Crest Dr Portland OR 97201

HAY, GEORGE AUSTIN, film actor, producer, director, musician, artist; b. Johnstown, Pa., Dec. 25, 1915; s. George and Mary Louise (Austin) H. B.S., U. Pitts., 1938; postgrad., U. Rochester, 1939; M.Litt., U. Pitts., 1948; M.A., Columbia U., 1948. dir. Jr. League hosp. shows, N.Y.C., 1948-53. Producer, dir. off-Broadway prodns., 1953-55; motion picture casting dir. for Dept. Def. films, Astoria Studios, N.Y., 1955-70, motion picture producer-dir., U.S. Dept. Transp., Washington, 1973—; group exhbns. of paintings and sculpture include, Lincoln Ctr., N.Y.C., 1965, Parrish Art Mus., Southampton, N.Y., 1969, Carnegie Inst., 1972, Duncan Galleries, N.Y.C., 1973, Bicentennial Exhbn. Am. Painters, Paris, 1976, Chevy Chase Gallery, 1979, Watergate Gallery, 1981, Le Salon des Nations a Paris, 1983; rep. permanent collections, Met. Mus. Art, N.Y.C., Library Congress, also, pvt. collections; bibliog. reference to works pub. in History of Internat. Art, 1982. Author, illustrator: Seven Hops to Australia, 1945; Dir.: Bicentennial documentary Highways of History, 1976; dir.: film World Painting in Museum of Modern Art, 1972; Composer: Rhapsody in E Flat for piano and strings, 1950; writer: TV program Nat. Council Chs., 1965; Broadway appearances include: What Every Woman Knows, 1954; original Broadway run of Inherit the Wind, 1955-57; created role of Prof. Fiveash in premiere of The Acrobats, White Barn Theater, Westport, Conn., 1961; feature films include: Pretty Boy Floyd, 1960, The Landlord, 1970, Child's Play, 1971, Chekhov's The Bet, 1978, Being There, 1980, No Way Out, 1986, Her Alibi, 1988; TV appearances include Am. Heritage, 1961, Americans-A Portrait in Verses, 1962, Naked City, 1962, U.S. Steel Hour, 1963, Another World, 1965, Edge of Night, 1968, As the World Turns, 1969, Love Is a Many-Splendored Thing, 1972, The Adams Chronicles, 1976; piano soloist in concerts and recitals, 1937; performer Cruise Ship, Europe, 1938; author, illustrator: The Arts Scene; entrepreneur in mgmt. of property, portfolio of stocks and bonds; contbr. articles to periodicals. Apptd. to pres.'s council Coll. William and Mary; mem. World Affairs Council; bd. govs., trustee Hist. Home of Pres. James Monroe; mus. donor Am. doctor's office turn-of-century period preservation; bd. dirs. Washington Film Council. Served with AUS, 1942-46, PTO. Recipient Loyal Service award Jr. League, 1953, St. Bartholomew's Silver Leadership award, 1966, Gold medal Accademia Italia, 1980, Smithsonian Instn. Pictorial award, 1982; Fed. Govt. Honor award in recognition 30 yrs. dedicated service, 1985; subject of biog. work: Austin Hay Careers of a Christmas Child. Mem. NATAS, AFTRA, SAG, Am. Artists Profl. League, Allied Artists Am., Internat. Bach Soc., Beethoven Soc., Music Library Assn., Actors Equity Assn., Nat. Assn. Investors, Nat. Trust Hist. Preservation, SAR, Nat. Parks and Conservation Assn., Shakespeare Oxford Soc., St. Andrew's Soc., Cambria County Hist. Soc., Am. Philatelic Soc., Am. Mus. of the Moving Image, Fed. Design Coun., Sigma Chi, Phi Mu Alpha. Clubs: Nat. Arts, Players (N.Y.C.); Nat. Travel, Nat. Press, Arts (Washington), English Speaking Union, Classic Car Club of Am. Home: 2022 Columbia Rd NW Washington DC 20009 also: Hay Ave Johnstown PA 15902 Office: US Dept Transp 400 7th St SW Washington DC 20590

HAY, RAYMOND A., steel and diversified manufacturing company executive; b. L.I., N.Y., July 13, 1928; m. Grace Mattson; children: John Alexander, Susan Elizabeth. BS in Econs., L.I. U., 1949; MBA, St. John's U., 1960. Mgr. Northeastern div. Monroe Calculating Machine Co. (now Monroe-Swede), 1958-61; with Xerox Corp., 1961-75; br. mgr. Xerox Corp., N.Y.C., 1961-62, zone mgr. Western Region, also asst. dir. sales ops. and dir. mktg., 1962-68, group v.p. and gen. mgr. info. systems, 1968, exec. v.p., to 1975; pres., chief operating officer LTV Corp., Dallas, from 1975, chief exec. officer, 1982—, also chmn., dir.; bd. dirs. Maxus Energy Corp., MCORP, Nat. Med. Enterprises. Bd. govs. Kennedy Ctr. for Performing Arts; mem. Dallas Citizens' Council, exec. bd. Ed Cox Sch., Pres. Reagan's pvt. sector survey on cost control, Pres. Council for Internat. Youth Exchange, Dallas Roundtable Ctr. for Stategic and Internat. Studies; former trustee Dallas Mus. Fine Arts, Dallas Symphony Orch.; trustee Dallas Better Bus. Bur.; bd. dirs. Dallas Civic Opera Assn. Mem. Salesmanship Club Dallas, SMU Found. for Bus. Adminstrn., Soc. Internat. Bus. Fellows. Club: Dallas C. of C. (council steering com.). Office: LTV Corp 2001 Ross Ave PO Box 655003 Dallas TX 75265-5003

HAY, WILLIAM JEFFREY, insurance company executive; b. Neenah, Wis., Mar. 9, 1953; s. George Hilton Hay and Delores Ellen (Haldeman) Bobinette; m. Susan Faye Woodington; May 16, 1981; children: Laura Katherine, Steven Hilton. BBA, U. Notre Dame, 1975; MBA, U. Wis., 1979. Cert. mgmt. acct. Sr. auditor Peat, Marwick & Mitchell, Chgo., 1975-78; pvt. practice fin. cons. Arlington Heights, Ill., 1978-80; sr. cons. Arthur Andersen & Co., Dallas, 1980-82; fin. mgr. InterFirst Corp., Dallas, 1982-87, Northwestern Mut. Life Ins., Plano, Tex., 1987—. Advisor Jr. Achievement, Dallas, 1981-82; dir. Neighborhood Crime Watch, Dallas, 1983—. Mem. Nat. Assn. Accts. (bus. planning bd. 1985—), Inst. Mgmt. Acctg., Lake Highlands Homeowners Assn., Notre Dame Club. Office: Northwestern Mut Life Ins 4965 Preston Park Blvd Suite 280 Plano TX 75093

HAYASHI, HAJIME, trading company executive; b. San Mateo, Calif., Apr. 13, 1925; s. Kiyoichi and Masue H.; m. Emiko, Feb. 4, 1953; 1 child, Mami. BA, Doshisha U., 1947; student, Stanford U., 1949; BA, San Francisco State U., 1952. Sr. corp. advisor Matsushita Electric Indsl. Co. Ltd., Osaka, Japan, 1953—; chmn. bd. dirs. numerous subs. including Matsubo Equipment and Instrument Corp., Matsubo Electronic Compnonents Co., Matsubo Credit Sales Co., Osaka, 1975—; chmn. AMAC Corp., Los Angeles and N.Y.C., 1981—, Jetro Import Promotion Counc. Osaka. Mem. Japan Machinery Import Assn. Lodge: Lions (decorated insignia of Commdr., Finland, 1983). Home: 700 Okadaura Sennan-City, Osaka 590-05, Japan Office: 3-2 Minamisemba 4-chrome, Minami-Ku, Osaka 542, Japan also: 300 S Grand Ave Suite 3140 Los Angeles CA 90017 also: 375 Park Ave Suite 3708 New York NY 10152

HAYASHI, JOJI, transportation company executive; b. 1939. With Am. Pres. Lines, Ltd., 1964-82, v.p., 1979-82; exec. v.p. Am. Pres. Cos., Oakland, Calif., 1982—, chief oper. officer, also bd. dirs. Office: Am Pres Cos Inc 1800 Harrison St Oakland CA 94612 *

HAYASHI, KEIICHIRO, research company executive; b. Tottori, Japan, Aug. 11, 1929; s. Tomoyuki and Kaoru (Hirotomi) H.; BS, U. Tokyo, 1953; MS, U. Ill., 1956; postgrad. MIT, 1956; m. Ceil Meredith, Mar. 18, 1983; children: Masanari, Shigenari. Came to U.S., 1957. Engr., George G. Sharp, Inc., N.Y.C., 1957-58, Bechtel Assos., N.Y.C., 1958-65, Exxon Research &

Engring. Co., Florham Park, N.J., 1965-82; pres. Keisol, Ltd. Corp., Westfield, N.J., 1982—; dir. computer aided design lab. Stevens Inst. Tech., Hoboken, N.J., 1986—. Mem. ASME, ASCE, Welding Research Council (pressure vessel research com.), Sigma Xi. Research on brittle fracture propagation in steel plate, refinery equipment and future energy sources, computer software development; patentee in field in U.S. Home and Office: 31 Carol Rd Westfield NJ 07090

HAYDEN, JOSEPH PAGE, JR., finance company executive; b. Cin., Oct. 8, 1929; s. Joseph Page and Amy Dorothy (Weber) H.; m. Lois Taylor, Dec. 29, 1951; children: Joseph Page III, William Taylor, John Weber, Thomas Richard. B.S. in Bus, Miami U., Oxford, Ohio, 1951; student, U. Cin. Law Sch., 1952; DL (hon.), Miami U., 1986. With mobile home div. Midland-Guardian Co., Cin., 1952-61; v.p. Midland-Guardian Co., 1954-60; pres., chief exec. officer, dir. Midland Co., Cin., 1961-80; chmn. bd., chief exec. officer, dir. Midland Co., 1980—; dir. Fed. Nat. Mortgage Assn., First Nat. Cin. Corp., First Nat. Bank Cin. Mem. bus. adv. com. Miami U., Oxford, Ohio; mem. pres.'s council Xavier U., Cin.; bd. trustees Miami U. Found. Mem. Bankers Club, Sigma Chi. Clubs: Queen City, Hyde Park Golf and Country, University (Cin.); Boca Grande (Fla.). Office: Midland Co 537 E Pete Rose Way PO Box 1256 Cincinnati OH 45201

HAYDEN, RALPH FREDERICK, retired accountant, corporation executive; b. N.Y.C., Jan. 15, 1922; s. Fred T. and Thrya (Ohlson) H.; m. Gloria McCormick, Feb. 27, 1943; children—Craig O., Glen R. BBA, Pace U., 1951. Sr. ptnr. Hayden & Hayden (accts. and auditors), Huntington, N.Y., 1941—; exec. v.p., sec., treas., dir. King Kullen Grocery Co., Inc., Westbury, N.Y., 1948-88; ret. King Kullen Grocery Co., Inc., Westbury, 1988. Contbr. articles to profl. jours. Pres. Old Chester Hills Civic Assn., 1962-64, Goose Bay Civic Assn., 1975-76; pres. L.I. YMCA, 1976-81; dir. at large, chmn. Suffolk County Co-op. Extension, 1968-76; bd. dirs. L.I. Arthritis Found., L.I. Com. for Crime Control, 1972-82, Bi-County Devel. Corp., 1972-88; mem. Suffolk County Rep. Com., 1958-77; vice-chmn. Suffolk County Airport Adv. Com., 1976-82; former trustee Friends of the Arts; former trustee, past chmn., L.I. Ednl. T.V., Sta. WLIW. With USCGR, 1942-45. Mem. Empire State Assn. Pub. Accts., Nat. Soc. Pub. Accots., Aviation Coun. L.I. (treas. 1971-87), USCG Aux., N.Y. Soc. Ind. Accts., C.W. Post Tax Inst., Real Estate Inst., Acctg. Inst., Huntington C. of C. Clubs: Kiwanis (past pres. local chpt., ret. 1988), Metropolitan. Office: Hayden & Hayden 43 Prospect St Huntington NY 11743

HAYDEN, RICHARD MICHAEL, investment banker; b. Balt., July 31, 1945; s. Richard Taylor and Cecelia (Hense) H.; m. Susan Frances Margolies, June 4, 1978. A.B., Georgetown U., 1967; M.B.A., U. Pa., 1969. Assoc. Goldman, Sachs & Co., N.Y.C., 1969-73, v.p., 1974-80, gen. ptnr., 1980—. Served with USNG, 1968-73. Mem. Phi Beta Kappa. Republican. Episcopalian. Clubs: Quogue Field, The Links, Downtown Assn., Union (N.Y.C.). Office: Goldman Sachs & Co 85 Broad St 24th Fl New York NY 10004

HAYDEN, SPENCER JAMES, management consultant; b. N.Y.C., Sept. 18, 1922; s. Thomas Churchill and Anna May (Forshay) H.; B.S., St. John's Coll., 1942; M.A., Columbia U., 1946; Ph.D., Fordham U., 1951; m. Erica Bannister, Feb. 18, 1950; children—Lisa, Christopher, Robert, Wendy. Cons., Booz, Allen & Hamilton, Genoa, Italy and N.Y.C., 1957-61; v.p., sec. Richardson, Bellows, Henry & Co., Inc., N.Y.C., 1961-63; pres. Spencer Hayden Co., Inc., Hopewell Junction, N.Y., 1963—; prof. mgmt. Rensselaer Poly. Inst., 1967-70; mng. dir. Smith Bros., Ravenel Investment Bankers, Southport, Conn., 1987—. trustee Knickerbocker Hosp., N.Y.C., 1963-70. Served to lt. USAAF, 1942-45. Mem. Am. Inst. Indsl. Engrs., Am. Soc. for Microbiology, Am. Psychol. Assn., AAAS. Clubs: Union League (bd. govs. 1980—), Engrs., Columbia U. (N.Y.C.). Author: Solving the Problems of International Operations, 1970. Home: Creamery Rd Hopewell Junction NY 12533 Office: Spencer Hayden Co Inc 48 Creamery Rd Hopewell Junction NY 12533

HAYDEN, TAYLOR KOCH, karate school executive; b. Gladsen, Ala., Oct. 29, 1948; s. Walter William Sr. and Rosa Amelia (Koch) H. BE, Vanderbilt U., 1970, MS, 1972. Constrn. engr. Armstrong Tire Corp., Madison, Tenn., 1971-74; owner, instr. Taylor Hayden Karate Ctr., Goodlettsville, Tenn., 1973—; instr. math. Vol. State Community Coll., Gallatin, Tenn., 1974-80. Mem. U.S. Eastern Wado Karate Fedn. (bd. dirs. 1978—). Office: Taylor Hayden Karate Ctr PO Box 931 Goodlettsville TN 37072

HAYDEN, WILLIAM JOSEPH, automobile company executive; b. West Ham, Eng., Jan. 19, 1929; s. George and Mary Ann (Overhead) H.; m. Mavis Ballard, Feb. 20, 1954; children—Christopher, Andrew, Elisabeth, Tracey. Student, Romford Tech. Coll., 1939-45. With Ford Motor Co., Briggs Motor Bodies Ltd., Dagenham, Eng., 1950-57; fin. staff Ford Britain, Dagenham, 1957-63; div. controller (Ford Chassis, Transmission and Engine Div.), Dagenham, 1963-67; gen. ops. mgr. transmission and chassis ops. (Ford Chassis, Transmission and Engine Div.), 1967, gen. ops. mgr. truck mfg. ops., 1968, v.p. truck mfg. ops., 1971, v.p. power train ops., 1972; corporate v.p. and v.p. mfg. Ford of Europe Inc., Essex, Eng., 1974—. Served with Brit. Army, 1947-49. Decorated comdr. Brit. Empire. Home: Park House, 259 Brentwood Rd, Herongate, Brentwood Essex, England Office: Ford of Europe Inc, Warley, Brentwood England also: Ford Motor Co The American Rd Dearborn MI 48121

HAYDOCK, MICHAEL PATRICK, manufacturing executive; b. Miami Beach, Fla., Feb. 11, 1951; s. Vincent S. and Patricia L. (Sullivan) H.; m. Debbie R. Dobson, Sept. 5, 1981. AA, Broward Community Coll., Ft. Lauderdale, Fla., 1971; BS, Fla. Atlantic U., 1973, MS, 1976. Tchr. mktg., mgmt. Sch. Bd. Broward County, Ft. Lauderdale, 1973-77; systems mktg. rep. Control Data Corp., Miami, Fla., 1977-78, mktg. rep., 1978-80; asst. area mgr. Control Data Corp., Washington, 1980-81; mktg. mgr. Control Data Corp., Miami, 1981-84; S.E. regional sales mgr. Control Data Corp., Atlanta, 1984-86, nat. accounts sales mgr., 1986-87; mgr. strategic mktg. Control Data Corp., Mpls., 1987-88, dir. environment industry and emerging techs., 1989—. Author: Economic Concepts and Distributive Education, 1976. Mem. Decathlon Athletic Club. Democrat. Roman Catholic. Office: Control Data Corp 8100 34th Ave S Minneapolis MN 55440

HAYES, BARBARA LYNN, publishing company executive; b. Cleve., Mar. 14, 1942; d. Rudolph Frank and Mary Jean Doljack; m. James A. McCormick Hayes, June 16, 1988; student Ohio Dominican Coll., 1960-62, Tobe-Coburn Sch. Fashion Careers, N.Y.C., 1963. With Bloomingdale's, N.Y.C., 1963-66, asst. fashion dir., 1964-66; sr. merchandising coordinator Seventeen Mag., N.Y.C., 1966-69, merchandising editor, 1969-71, merchandising dir., 1971-76; dir. promotion services Seventeen mag., 1976-82, mktg. dir. direct merchandising, pub. relations, promotion, composing and buy-by-mail depts., 1982—; dir. promotion services Panorama mag., 1979-81. Mem. exec. alumnae com. The Tobe-Coburn Sch., 1976-79, also mem. industry adv. com.; mem. various coms. The Floating Hosp., 1978—; pres. exec. com. Friends of Henry St. Settlement, 1976-78, adv. com., 1979—. Recipient Mehitabel award, 1979; The T award Tobe-Coburn Sch., 1968. Mem. N.Y. Jr. League, Mktg. Communications Execs. Internat. (chpt. bd. dirs. 1977-79), Advt. Women of N.Y., Nat. Home Fashions League, Women in Communications, The Fashion Group (v.p. bd. govs. 1981-83). Clubs: Gardiner's Bay Country; Garden of Shelter Island. Home: 310 E 70 St New York NY 10021 Office: Seventeen Mag 850 Third Ave New York NY 10022

HAYES, BERNARDINE FRANCES, computer systems analyst; b. Boston, June 29, 1939; d. Robert Emmett and Mary Agnes (Tague) H. BA in Edn., St. Joseph Coll., 1967; MA in Urban Affairs and Pub. Policy, U. Del., 1973, PhD in Pub. Policy, 1978. Elem. tchr. St. Dominick Sch., Balt., 1960-63; tchr. sci., math. and art St. Mary's Sch., Troy, N.Y., 1963-65, Our Lady Queen of Peace Sch., Washington, 1965-68, St. Patrick Sch., Richmond, Va., 1968-69, St. Peter Cathedral Sch., Wilmington, Del., 1969-71; planner health and social services Model Cities Program, Wilmington, 1971-72; dir. research Del. State Dept. Mental Health, Wilmington, 1972-75; dir. planning and evaluation Mental Health, Mental Retardation Services, West Chester, Pa., 1976-78; instr. Boston U., 1978; div. dir. Systems Architects, Inc., Randolph, Mass., 1979-81; group mgr. Unisys Corp., Cambridge, Mass., 1981—; cons. in field. Contbr. numerous articles to profl. jours. Bd. sec. Model Cities, 1969-70; chairperson bd. State Service Ctr., Wilmington, 1972-75; mem. Human Relations Commn., Washington, 1965-68; co-chmn. State-wide Coalition for Human Services, Del., 1972-74; activist Vietnam protest, Del., 1970-74, Civil Rights Movement, 1965—, numerous polit. campaigns, 1972—; alt. del. Mass. Dem. Conv., 1985; bd. v.p. Women's Action for Nuclear Disarmament, Arlington, Mass., 1982—, fin. com. chmn., 1983-85, 88, treas., 1988—, chmn. polit. action com., 1983-84, dir. nat. voter registration campaign, 1984.; active Mondale for Pres., 1984, John Kerry for Senator campaign, Mass., 1984; del. Com. for an Enduring Peace, Soviet Peace Commn., Moscow, 1987. Fellow NSF, 1966. Mem. Women's Inst. Housing and Econ. Devel. (bd. dirs. 1985—), NAACP, Boston Computer Soc., Boston Mus. Fine Arts, NOW. Roman Catholic. Home: 49 Crane Rd Adams Shore Quincy MA 02169

HAYES, BETTINE J., investment executive; b. Boston, Sept. 6, 1928; d. Reginald W. P. and Ethel (Thomas) Brown; B.A., Wellesley Coll., 1950; m. M. Vinson Hayes, June 10, 1961; children—M. Vinson III, Juliet Dorothy. Security analyst Merrill Lynch, Pierce, Fenner & Smith, Inc., N.Y.C., 1950-60, 76—, portfolio analyst, 1960-73, Canadian research coordinator, 1967-69; mgr. N.Y. Wellesley Club, 1973-74; researcher Nat. Information Bur., Inc., N.Y.C., 1974-76. Mem. D.A.R. (chpt. treas. 1958-59, historian 1961-62, rec. sec. Colonielles 1961-71, 73-77, treas., 1971-73), N.Y. Soc. Security Analysts. Club: New York Wellesley. Home: 39 Gramercy Park New York City NY 10010 also: 11 Spring Close Ln East Hampton NY 11937 Office: Merrill Lynch World Hdqrs North Tower World Fin Ctr New York NY 10281-1215

HAYES, CHARLES A., mill company executive; b. Gloversville, Ky., 1935; married. With Lee Dyeing Co., Inc., to 1961; with Guilford Mills, Inc., Greensboro, N.C., 1961—, exec. v.p., 1961-68, pres., chief exec. officer, 1968-76, chmn. bd., 1976—, chief exec. officer, also dir. Office: Guilford Mills Inc 4925 W Market St Box U-4 Greensboro NC 27401 *

HAYES, CYNTHIA LELA, sales executive; b. Lancaster, S.C., Apr. 22, 1949; d. Wade Heath and Ernestine (Cox) H. BS in Psychology, Fla. Atlantic U., 1971; MS in Psychology, Nova U., 1975, MBA, 1987. Sales rep. Livesavers, Inc. div. Squibb Co., Ft. Lauderdale, Fla., 1974-75; key account mgr. Squibb Co., Tampa and Miami, Fla., 1975-76; sales rep. M & M Mars, Ft. Lauderdale, 1976-78; supr. merchandising M & M Mars, Miami, 1978-79; unit mgr. M & M Mars, Atlanta, 1979-80; nat. accounts mgr. M & M Mars, Hackettstown, N.J., 1980; New Eng. dist. mgr. M & M Mars, Boston, 1981-83; unit mgr. M & M Mars, Miami, 1983—; v.p. sales Decar Designs div. Mars, Inc., N.Y.C., 1980-81; counselor Nova U. Clinic, Ft. Lauderdale, 1974-75. Brevard Community Coll. scholar, 1968. Mem. Network Profl. Women (v.p. Atlanta chpt. 1979-80), Phi Theta Kappa. Republican. Home and Office: 1540 SW 16th St Fort Lauderdale FL 33312

HAYES, DAVID MICHAEL, lawyer; b. Syracuse, N.Y., Dec. 2, 1943; s. James P. and Lillie Anna (Wood) H.; m. Elizabeth S. Tracy, Aug. 26, 1973; children: Timothy T., AnnElizabeth S. AB, Syracuse U., 1965; LLB, U. Va., 1968. Bar: Va. 1968, N.Y. 1969. Assoc. Hiscock & Barclay, Syracuse, 1968-72; asst. gen. counsel Agway Inc., Syracuse, 1972-81, gen. counsel, sec., 1981-87; v.p., gen. counsel, sec. Agway Inc., 1987—. Bd. dirs. Syracuse Boys Club. With Army N.G., 1968-74. Mem. ABA, Onondaga County Bar Assn., N.Y. State Bar Assn., Va. State Bar, Skaneateles Country Club. Democrat. Office: Agway Inc PO Box 4933 Syracuse NY 13221-4933

HAYES, DOROTHY DAMON, controller; b. Concord, Mass., Dec. 10, 1950; d. Henry Orr and Luthena Pearl (Carpenter) Damon; m. Terry Nolan Hayes, Sept. 20, 1980; 1 child, Carolyn. BA, U. Mass., 1972, MBA, 1976; MS in Fin., Bentley Coll., 1986. Cert. Internal Auditor. Cost acct. Data Gen. Corp., Westboro, Mass., 1976-77, internal auditor, 1977-80, cost acct. supr., 1980; asst. to corp. controller Apollo Computer Inc., Chelmsford, Mass., 1980-82, controller tech. ops., 1982-83, dir. group ops., 1983-85, v.p., controller, 1985—. Mem. edn. com. West Concord Union Ch., Concord, 1987—, chancellor's exec. com. U. Mass., Amherst, Mass., 1987—. Mem. Fin. Execs. Inst. Home: 179 Prairie St Concord MA 01742 Office: Apollo Computer Inc 330 Billerica Rd Chelmsford MA 01824

HAYES, DOUGLAS MARTIN, investment banker; b. Cleve., Nov. 27, 1943; s. Douglas Anderson and Anna Carolyn (Martin) H.; m. Constance Anne Maezes, July 22, 1967; 1 child, Stephanie Janet. AB, Dartmouth Coll., 1965; MBA, Harvard U., 1969. Assoc. A.G. Becker Co., Chgo., 1969-72, asst. v.p., 1972-73, v.p., Los Angeles, 1973-77; mng. dir. Warburg, Paribas, Becker, Los Angeles, 1977-82, A.G. Becker Paribas, Los Angeles, 1982-84, Merrill Lynch Capital Markets, Los Angeles, 1984-86; prin., sr. v.p. Donaldson, Lufkin & Jenrette, Los Angeles, 1986—; guest speaker U. Chgo. Bus. Sch., 1972, Harvard U. Bus. Sch., Boston, 1974, UCLA Grad. Sch. Adminstrn., 1982-84. Treas. Calif. Chamber Symphony, Los Angeles, 1981-85, chmn. bd., 1985—; bd. dirs. UCLA Internat. Students Assn., 1982-83, Children's Bur. Los Angeles, 1985—. Clubs: Calif., Regency (Los Angeles). Home: 2545 Roscomare Rd Los Angeles CA 90077 Office: Donaldson Lufin & Jenrette 2121 Ave of Stars Suite 3000 Los Angeles CA 90067

HAYES, JOHN BRUTON, JR., brokerage house executive; b. N.Y.C., Feb. 12, 1942; s. John Bruton and Muriel Mary (Spink) H.; m. Susan Joan Steele, Sept. 11, 1982; children: John B. III, Andrew Steele, Caitlin Corbett. BS, Manhattan Coll., 1964. Retail sales Edwards & Hanly, N.Y.C., 1968-70; retail, dealer sales Merrill Lynch, N.Y.C., 1970-74; nat. dealer sales mgr. Bache Halsey Stuart, N.Y.C., 1974-76; mgr., founder unit trust dept. Weeden & Co., N.Y.C., 1976-79; asst. to pres. Carroll, McEntee, McGinley, N.Y.C., 1978-79; founder, mgr. syndicate, sales unit trusts Bear Stearns & Co., N.Y.C., 1979-82; v.p., mgr. syndicate, sales unit trusts Thomson-McKinnon Securities, N.Y.C., 1982—; v.p. Am. Liquid Trust, N.Y.C., 1978-79. Contbr. to and interviewed for articles in profl. jours. Mem. Mcpl. Bond Club of N.Y., Unit Trust Assn. (bd. dirs. 1980). Republican. Roman Catholic. Clubs: Metropolitan (N.Y.C.); Rockaway Hunting (Cedarhurst, N.Y.); Nat. Golf Links (Southampton, N.Y.); Brooklawn Country (Fairfield, Conn.). Home: 230 Long Meadow Rd Fairfield CT 06430 Office: Thomson McKinnon Financial Sq 14th Fl New York NY 10005

HAYES, JOHN PATRICK, manufacturing company executive; b. Manistee, Mich., May 9, 1921; s. John David and Daisy (Davis) H.; m. Margaret Barbara Butler, Apr. 12, 1947; children—John Patrick, Timothy Michael. Student, U. Detroit, 1939-42, 46-47. With Nat. Gypsum Co., 1947—, group v.p., 1970-75, pres., 1975—, chmn. bd., chief exec. officer, 1983—, also dir.; bd. dirs. Lafarge Coppee, Paris. Served to 1st lt. AUS, 1942-45. Clubs: Brook Hollow Golf (Dallas), Petroleum (Dallas). Office: Nat Gypsum Co 4500 Lincoln Plaza Dallas TX 75201

HAYES, MARY PHYLLIS, savings and loan association executive; b. New Castle, Ind., Apr. 30, 1921; d. Clarence Edward and Edna Gertrude (Burgess) Scott; m. John Clifford Hayes, Jan. 1, 1942 (div. Oct. 1952); 1 child, R. Scott. Student, Ball State U., 1957-64, Ind. U. East, Richmond, 1963; diploma, Inst. Fin. Edn., 1956, 72, 76. Teller Henry County Savs. and Loan, New Castle, 1939-41, loan officer, teller, 1950-62, asst. sec., treas., 1962-69, sec., treas., 1969-73, corp. sec., 1973-84; v.p., sec. Ameriana Savs. Bank (formerly Henry County Savs. and Loan), New Castle, 1984—; exec. sec. Am. Nat. Bank, Nashville, 1943-44; corp. sec. HCSS Corp., New Castle, 1984—; bd. dirs. Ameriana Ins. Co. Treas. Henry County Chpt. Am. Heart Assn., New Castle, 1965-67, 76-87, vol. Indpls. chpt. 1980—; membership sec. Henry County Hist. Soc., New Castle, 1975—; sec. Henry County Chpt. ARC, New Castle, 1976—. Recipient Gold medallian Am. Heart Assn., 1973, diploma of merit Inst. Fin. Edn., 1984, 20-Yr. award, 1983, 25-Yr. award Ind. affiliate Am. Heart Assn., 1987, 40-Yr. award Ind. League of Savs. Instns., 1988, NAPN award Am. Heart Assn., 1989, 15 Yr. Svcs. award Inst. Fin. Edn. Adminstrn., 1989. Mem. Inst. Fin. Edn. (sec., treas. E. Cen. Ind. chpt. 1973—), Ind. League Savs. Insts. (25 Yrs. award 1975, 30 Yrs. Cert. award 1988), Altrusa (past officer, bd. dirs. New Castle chpt.), PEO (past chaplain, sec.), Psi Iota Xi (past sec., treas.). Mem. Christian Ch. Office: Ameriana Savs Bank 2118 Bundy Ave New Castle IN 47362

HAYES, RAWLENE BRIAR WATTERS, accountant; b. Cin.; d. David Albert Watters and Iva (Anderson) Hammond; divorced; 1 child, Laurel Michele Gauna; m. Richard C. Hayes. BA in English, Alma Coll., 1970; MS in Acctg., Cen. Mich. U., 1981. CPA, Colo., cert. mgmt. acct. Staff auditor Scullion, Beekman & Co., CPAs, Denver, 1981-82; chief acct. Interactive Systems Corp., Littleton, Colo., 1982-84; fin. reporting supr. Valleylab, Inc., Boulder, Colo., 1984-86; controller Schmidt-Cannon, Inc., City of Industry, Calif., 1986-88; pvt. practice Boulder, 1988—. Mem. Colo. Soc. CPAs, Nat. Assn. Accts., Inst. Mgmt. Accts., Mensa, Intertel. Democrat.

HAYES, REBECCA ANNE, communications manager; b. Princeton, Ky., June 3, 1950; d. James Luther and Margaret Anne (Sparks) H. AA, Midway Coll., 1970; AB, U. Ky., 1972; MEd, U. Louisville, 1974. Educator Jefferson County Bd. Edn., Louisville, 1972-78; mgmt. asst. S. Cen. Bell, Louisville, 1978-80, engr., 1980-82; engr. AT&T, Tucker, Ga., 1983-84, asst. staff mgr., 1984-87, systems cons. bus. markets group, 1987-88; staff mgr. hdqrs. sales ops. AT&T, Basking Ridge, N.J., 1988—. Advisor Career Explorers S. Cen. Bell, Louisville, 1979-80. Mem. Nat. Assn. Female Execs., Ky. Hist. Soc., U. Ky. Alumni Assn. (life). Democrat. Roman Catholic. Office: AT&T 295 N Maple Ave Basking Ridge NJ 07920

HAYES, ROBERT CUNNINGHAM, financial executive; b. Fall River, Mass., Sept. 10, 1936; s. James Henry and Claire (Short) H.; m. Alia Sklavounou, May 30, 1964; children: Lyena, Claire, John. BS in Engring., U. N.H., Durham, 1958; MS in Fin. Mgmt. with honors, Naval Postgrad. Sch., Monterey, Calif., 1972. Commnd. U.S. Navy, 1958, advanced through grades to lt. commdr., ret., 1979; asst. pub. works officer Hdqrs. Support Activity U.S. Navy, Taipei, Taiwan, 1966-68; tech. officer Naval Constrn. Bn. Ctr. U.S. Navy, Davisville, R.I., 1968-70; staff officer Mac. Dir. Constrn.-LOC U.S. Navy, Saigon, Republic of Vietnam, 1970-71; pub. works officer NAS Lakehurst (N.J.) U.S. Navy, 1972-74; exec. officer Naval Mobile Constrn. Bn. One U.S. Navy, N.Y.C., 1974-76; dep. dir. pub. works Naval Edn. Tng. Ctr. U.S. Navy, Newport, R.I., 1976-79; sr. v.p. fin. N.H. Distbrs., Inc., Concord, 1979—; bd. dirs. First Capital Bank, Concord, 1985—, N.H. the Beautiful, 1983—; trustee Concord Hosp., 1981—. Rep. N.H. Gen. Ct., Concord, 1985-88; mem. Concord Planning Bd., 1981—. Mem. Rotary. Republican. Roman Catholic. Office: NH Distbr Inc 65 Regional Dr Concord NH 03301

HAYES, RONALD GEORGE, manufacturing company executive; b. Battle Creek, Mich., Dec. 29, 1936; s. Leon Sylvester and Mildred Ann (Babic) H.; m. Peggy Jean Smith, Oct. 20, 1957 (div. Oct. 1968); children—Carla, Timothy, Thomas; m. 2d, Pamela Kay Hofmann, Mar. 6, 1971; 1 son, Michael. B.S. in Bus. Adminstrn., U. Evansville (Ind.), 1968. Researcher Gen. Foods Corp., Battle Creek, Mich., 1959-63, research ops., Evansville, Ind., 1963-72, ops., Kanakee, Ill, 1972-80, White Plains, N.Y., 1980-82; sr. v.p. ops. and agr. Am. Crystal Sugar Co., Moorhead, Minn., 1982-85, pres., chief exec. officer, 1986—. Republican. Home: 130 S Prairiewood Dr Fargo ND 58103 Office: Am Crystal Sugar Co 101 N 3rd St Moorhead MN 56560

HAYES-DAVIS, BERTRAM, geologist, oil and gas company executive; b. Colorado Springs, Colo., Dec. 26, 1948; s. Addison and Billy Fern (Sharp) H.-D.; m. Carol Ann Sobona, Feb. 12, 1983; children: Joel Addison, Sarah Taylor. BA, Adams State Coll., 1975; MS, U. Ala., 1980. Geologist Amoco Prodn. Co., New Orleans, 1978-80; geologist Hunt Energy Corp., Dallas, 1980-81, dist. geologist, 1981, div. mgr., 1981-83; mgr. Impel Energy Corp., Denver, 1983-84; onshore geologic mgr. Placid Oil Co., Dallas, 1985-87; geologic mgr. Prosper Energy Corp., Dallas, 1987-88, Petro-Hunt Corp., Dallas, 1988—. Bd. dirs. Papers of Jefferson Davis, Houston, 1987—. With U.S. Army, 1968-70. Mem. Am. Assn. Petroleum Geologists, Davis Family Assn. (pres. Woodville, Miss. 1976—). Republican. Episcopalian. Home: 1514 Jennifer St Richardson TX 75082 Office: Petro-Hunt Corp 2400 Thanksgiving Tower Dallas TX 75201

HAYFORD, JOHN SARGENT, retail executive; b. Balt., Mar. 23, 1940; s. John Enoch and Anne Margaret (Weniger) H.; m. Barbara Jean McGann, Oct. 10, 1964; children: Kathryn, John, Patrick. BBA, Notre Dame U., 1962. CPA, Ind. With Ernst & Whinney, Chgo., 1963-77, ptnr., 1977-84; v.p. fin., treas. Marsh Supermarkets, Inc., Yorktown, Ind., 1984—. Mem. Am. Inst. CPA's (Elijah Watt Sells gold medal, 1966), Ind. Soc. CPA's. Republican. Roman Catholic. Clubs: Indpls. Sailing; Chgo. Yacht. Home: 7715 Candlewood Ln Indianapolis IN 46250 Office: Marsh Supermarkets Inc 501 Depot St Yorktown IN 47396

HAYLE, CLAUDETTE FREDERICA, information services executive; b. Kingston, Jamaica, Jan. 24, 1955; came to U.S., 1974, naturalized; d. Errol and Ruth Amanda (Palmer) Pinnock; m. Carlton Hayle, Mar. 29, 1975 (div. May 1986); children: Keisha, Seretze. BSc, York Coll., 1978; cert., Cornell U., 1982. Supr. fin. systems CBS Inc., N.Y.C., 1980-81, compensation analysis, 1981-82; cons. AT&T, Metro North and Citibank, N.Y.C., 1983; pres., chief exec. officer Goodman and Hayle Info. Systems, N.Y.C., 1984—; cons. in field. Contbr. articles to profl. jours. Trustee Rep. Presdl. Task Force, Washington, 1985; sec. N.Y. del. to Nat. White House Conf., N.Y.C., 1986. Mem. Nat Assn. Women Bus. Owners, Nat. Minority Council, N.Y./N.J. Purchasing Council, Assn. Profl. Women, Chief Exec. Officer's Club. Office: Goodman & Hayle Info Systems Inc 60 E 42d St #1732 New York NY 10165

HAYMAN, ESTHER LYNN, accountant; b. Chgo., Apr. 13, 1952; d. John and Alice Van Til; m. Brian Jonathan Hayman; 1 child, Benjamin. Student, Trinity Christian Coll., Palos Heights, Ill., 1969-71; BS cum laude, St. Joseph's Calumet Coll., Whiting, Ind., 1975; postgrad., Seattle Pacific U. CPA, Wash. Mktg. asst. Scot Lad Foods, Lansing, Ill., 1975-78; office mgr. A.M. Taniguchi, DDS, Redmond, Wash., 1978-81; fin. mgr. B.J. Hayman Construction Co., Bellevue, Wash., 1981-84; acct. Boeing Comml. Airplane Co., Seattle, 1984-87, Boeing Computer Services, Seattle, 1987—. Editor: Heart Beat Newsletter, 1984-86. Mem. Inst. for Christian Studies, Toronto, Ont., Can., 1979—, Friends Alta Vista Coll., Seattle, 1981—, Assn. Children with Learning Disabilities, 1984—. Pride in Excellence award Boeing, 1984-85. Mem. Am. Inst. CPA's, Washington Soc. CPA's, Am. Soc. Women Accts. (book revs. jour. 1983-84, editor 1984-85, v.p. communications 1987-88, v.p. chpt. devel. 1988—), Beta Alpha Psi. Office: Boeing Computer Svcs PO Box 24346 MS 7F-39 Seattle WA 98124-0346

HAYMES, EDWARD A., advertising executive; b. N.Y.C., Dec. 10, 1940; s. Harold and Martha (Boord) H.; widowed; children—Bruce, Karen. B.S., Ohio U., 1961; M.B.A., NYU, 1963. Mgr. budgets CBS, N.Y.C., 1961-68; asst. to treas. Harper & Row, N.Y.C., 1969-86; chief fin. officer Needham, Harper & Steers, Inc., N.Y.C., 1970-87; treas. Omnicom Group Inc., N.Y.C., 1987-88; exec. v.p. fin. and adminstrn. J. Walter Thompson Co., N.Y.C., 1988—. Office: J Walter Thompson Inc 466 Lexington Ave New York NY 10017 *

HAYNE, THOMAS ARTHUR, banker; b. Chgo., July 8, 1937; s. Walter Elliot and Ruth Martha (Langlois) H.; m. Martha Smith Taylor, June 17, 1961; children: Martha Lee, Sarah Taylor. B.A., Williams Coll., Williamstown, Mass., 1959; postgrad., NYU, 1965-68. Trainee Chase Manhattan Bank, N.Y.C., 1962-66, asst. treas., 1966-68, 2d v.p., 1968-70, v.p., 1970-72, sr. v.p., 1972—; bd. dirs. Internat. Art of Jazz, N.Y.C. Served to lt. (j.g.) USN, 1959-62. Mem. Delta Psi (trustee Lamda chpt. 1964-66). Republican. Clubs: Bay Head Yacht (N.J.); Williams (N.Y.C.); Wee Burn, (Darien, Conn.). Home: 11 Pilgrim Rd Darien CT 06820 Office: Chase Manhattan Corp 1 Chase Manhattan Pla New York NY 10081

HAYNES, ARDEN R., oil company executive; b. Sask., Can.. B.Commerce, U. Man., Winnipeg, 1951. With Imperial Oil Ltd., throughout Can., 1951-68, 1972—, Standard Oil Co. (N.J.) (now Exxon Corp.), N.Y.C., 1968-72; v.p., gen. mgr. mktg. dept. Imperial Oil Ltd., Toronto, 1973-74, dir., sr. v.p., 1974-78, pres., chief exec. officer Esso Resources Can. Ltd. subs., 1978-81; chmn. bd. Esso Resources Can. Ltd. subs. Imperial Oil Ltd., 1981-85; exec. v.p. Imperial Oil Ltd., Toronto, 1982, pres., chief operating officer, 1982—, chmn., pres., chief exec. officer, 1985, chmn., chief exec. officer, 1988—; dir. Texaco Can., Inc., Toronto, 1989—; assoc. faculty adminstrv. studies, co-chmn. devel. fund., U. Man.; mem. fed. govt.'s adv. group on energy products and services, fed. govt.'s adv. com. on bus./govt. exec. exchange program; bd. dirs. Royal Bank Can., Power Corp. Can., Moore Corp. Ltd. Chmn. fund-raising campaign Diabetes Can., 1982-87; bd. dirs. Jr. Achievement of Can., Alzheimer Soc. of Can., Centre for Research in Neurodegenerative Diseases at U. Toronto; gov. Olympic Trust Can.; founding mem., bd. dirs. Ont. Trillium Found.; patron Bob Rumball Centre for the Deaf, Toronto; chmn. Nat. Adv. Council for World Energy Congress in Montreal; co-chmn. Can. Ctr. Philanthropy's Imagine campaign. Named Officer of Order of Can., 1989. Office: Imperial Oil Ltd, 111 St Clair Ave W, Toronto, ON Canada M5W 1K3

HAYNES, ELEANOR LOUISE, public relations executive; b. Warrenton, Ga., July 7, 1929; d. Joe Brown and Alma Ruth (Simmons) Crenshaw; m. Kenneth M. Thomas, Jan. 16, 1954 (div. 1963); 1 child, Jeffrey Maynard Thomas. Cert., Fashion Inst. Tech., 1951, Am. Airline Sch., 1976; student, Queensboro Community Coll., 1978, Queens Coll., Flushing, N.Y., 1982-83. Columnist, reporter N.Y. Voice, Flushing, 1968—; columnist St. Thomas (V.I.) Daily News, 1970-74, N.J. Beat, Phila., 1972-74; editor Jamaica (N.Y.) B&P News, 1973-76, Color Report, Roosevelt Island, N.Y., 1979—; columnist, editor Calvary Voice, Jamaica, 1983-85; chief exec. officer Haynes Enterprises, Jamaica, 1960-67; travel cons. Good Svc. & Group Travel, Jamaica, 1970-73; liaison Color Community Adv. Bd.; mem., bd. dirs. Allied Fed. Savs. and Loan Assn., 1981-83. Designer Sipkin Corp., N.Y..C, 1969-74, Petite Frocks, Inc., N.Y.C., 1953-59. Del. N.Y. State Jud. Conv., Laurelton, N.Y., 1981—; mem. 126 St. Black Assn., Laurelton, 1981-84; mem. Vi Vants Inc., N.Y.C., 1983; pub. rels. rep. SE Queens Regular Dem. Club, 1982. Recipient Spl. Recognition award Jamaica Br. NAACP, 1988, Congl. Achievement award Congressman Floyd H. Flake, 1988, Cert. of Recognition Black United Fund of N.Y., 1988. Mem. Nat. Assn. Media Women Inc. (1st v.p. 1983-87), NAFE, L.I. Assn. Media Women (pres., Media Women Yr., 1983), Edges Group, Inc. Lodge: Order Eastern Star. Home: 231-16-126 Ave Laurelton NY 11413 Office: Color Meml Hosp Roosevelt Island New York NY 10044

HAYNES, FRANK MAURICE, business executive; b. Kansas City, Mo., June 1, 1935; s. William John and Marguerite Ida (Brown) H.; B.B.A., U. Colo., 1958; M.B.A. with honors, Roosevelt U., 1974; postgrad. Sch. Mgmt. Northwestern U., 1974-75; m. Arlene Claire Kidd, June 25, 1966; children—Jonathan Frank and Elizabeth Arlene (twins). Owner, operator Frank M. Haynes Ins. Agy., Chgo., 1960-65; pres. Employees Union Health & Welfare Agy., Inc., Chgo., 1965-72; cons. pension, health and welfare plans, Chgo., 1972-75; exec. v.p. W.J. Haynes & Co., Inc., Chgo., 1975-80, pres., 1980—. Served with U.S. Army, 1958-59. Recipient Wall St. Jour. award, 1974; certificate of merit Prudential Ins. Co., 1964; C.L.U. Mem. Am. Risk and Ins. Assn., Am. Soc. C.L.U.s, Internat. Found. Employee Benefit Plans, Beta Gamma Sigma. Home: 427 Sheridan Rd Kenilworth IL 60043 Office: 7045 N Western Ave Chicago IL 60645

HAYNES, FREDERICK LESLIE, industrial engineer, government official; b. Portsmouth, N.H., Oct. 27, 1934; s. James Edwin and Elizabeth (Crankshaw) H.; m. Patricia Marie Griffith, July 29, 1960. BS, Northeastern U., 1960; MBA, Am. U., 1968. Registered profl. engr., Mass. Indsl. engr. Alcoa, Edgewater, N.J., 1962-64; sr. indsl. engr. USAF Mgmt. Engring Program, Pentagon, 1964-72; asst. dir. U.S. Gen. Acctg. Office, Washington, 1972-79; dir. office coop. generic tech. U.S. Dept. Commerce, Washington, 1979-81; assoc. dir. product and market devel. Nat. Tech. Info. Service, Washington, 1981-85, assoc. dir., mktg. and customer services, 1985—; assoc. for research and devel. ltd. partnerships, office of asst. sec. PTI; lectr. in field. Contbr. articles to profl. jours. Served with USN, 1955-57; U.S. Army, 1960-62. Decorated U.S. Army Commendation medal. Fellow Am. Inst. Indsl. Engrs.; mem. Soc. Mfg. Engrs., World Future Soc., Order of the Engr. Home: 3806 Fort Hill Dr Alexandria VA 22310 Office: Nat Tech Info Svcs Springfield VA 22161

HAYNES, HAROLD WALTER, aircraft manufacturer; b. Snoqualmie, Wash., Jan. 23, 1923; s. Ralph and Bertha (Sewell) H.; m. Barbara J. Tatham, Oct. 11, 1943; children—Christine, Steven, Kevin. B.A., U. Wash., 1948. C.P.A., Wash. With Touche, Ross, Bailey & Smart (C.P.A.'s), Seattle, 1948-54; with Boeing Co., Seattle, 1954—, v.p. finance, 1960-70, sr. v.p. finance, 1970-75, exec. v.p., chief finance officer, 1975—, also dir.; dir. First Interstate Bank of Wash., Safeco, Itel Corp. Served as pilot USMCR, 1942-45. Mem. Financial Execs. Inst. Home: Highlands Seattle WA 98177 Office: The Boeing Co 7755 E Marginal Way S Seattle WA 98108

HAYNES, JAMES EARL, JR., association executive; b. Bakersfield, Calif., Oct. 11, 1943; s. James E. and Ruth M. (Campbell) H.; m. Norma Beth Jordan, Feb. 10, 1978; 1 child, Andrew Jordan. B.A. in Journalism, Los Angeles State Coll., 1967. Asst. mgr. West Covina C. of C., Calif., 1966-68; mgr. Monterey Park C. of C., Calif., 1968-72; gen. mgr. ops. San Francisco C. of C., 1972-76; pres. Phoenix C. of C., 1976—; mem. bd. regents Insts. for Orgn. Mgmt. U.S. C. of C.; vice chmn. Western Internat. U. Bd. dirs. Western Internat. U. Mem. Am. C. of C. Execs. (bd. dirs., past chmn.), Ariz. C. of C. Mgrs. Assn. Office: Phoenix C of C 34 W Monroe St Phoenix AZ 85003

HAYNES, JOHN MABIN, retired utilities executive; b. Albany, N.Y., Apr. 22, 1928; s. John Mabin and Gladys Elizabeth (Phillips) H.; m. Marion Enola Hamilton, Apr. 7, 1956; children: John David, Douglas Hamilton, Robert Paul. B.S., Utica Coll., Syracuse U., 1952. Accountant Price Waterhouse & Co., N.Y.C., Syracuse, N.Y., 1953-61; successively auditor, adminstrv. asst., asst. treas., treas., treas. and v.p., sr. v.p. Niagara Mohawk Power Corp., Syracuse, 1961-88; past pres., chmn., dir. N.Y. Bus. Devel. Corp., Syracuse; past dir., pres. N M Uranium, Inc.; past dir., treas. Canadian Niagara Power Co. Ltd.; past treas. Moreau Mfg. Co., St. Lawrence Power Co.; past treas. Empire State Power Resources, Inc.; past dir. and treas. Beebee Island Corp.; past bd. dirs. treas. Opinac Investments Ltd., Opinac Energy Ltd., Opinac Holdings Ltd.; past mng. dir. Niagara Mohawk Fin. N.V. Mem. Westhill Central Sch. Bd. Edn., 1968-73, pres., 1969-71. Served with AUS, 1945-47. Mem. Nat. Assn. Accountants (past dir.), Am. Gas Assn. (fin. com.), Fin. Execs. Inst. Clubs: Bond of Syracuse (past dir.), Masons. Home: 3108 Cove Loop Rd Hendersonville NC 28739 Office: Niagara Mohawk Power Corp 300 Erie Blvd W Syracuse NY 13202

HAYNES, MARTI (MARY ELIZABETH), realtor; b. St. Louis, June 28, 1947; d. Elmer Ellsworth and Doris Elizabeth (Turner) H. BA in Polit. Sci., Roanoke Coll., 1968. Substitute tchr. city and county schs. Roanoke, Va., 1969-71; teller Colonial Am. Nat. Bank, Roanoke, 1971-73; realtor Peery Flora Realtors, Roanoke, 1973-75, Mastin & Assocs., Roanoke, 1975-78, Lugar Inc. Realtors, Roanoke, 1978-80, Mastin, Kirkland, Bolling, Realtors, Roanoke, 1980-88, Owens & Co., Roanoke, 1988—. Mem. Roanoke Valley Bd. Realtors (membership and advt. com. 1989, realtor's polit. action com. 1988, Silver Sales award 1986, Gold Sales award 1988). Republican. Baptist. Home: 2431 Tillett Rd Roanoke VA 24015 Office: Owens & Co Realtors 4216 Brambleton Ave Roanoke VA 24018

HAYNES, THOMAS JOSEPH, marketing executive; b. Grand Haven, Mich., Aug. 4, 1947; s. Donald W. Haynes and Betty L. (Dillinger) Van Hall; m. Wanda L. Doerr, Aug. 17, 1968; children: Terry Sue, Lee Ann. BA, U. Colo., Denver, 1976. Dir. internal affairs Am. Legion Nat. Hdqrs., Indpls., 1976-82; chmn., pres. Haynes and Pittenger Direct, Inc., Indpls., 1982—; chmn. Promotion Mgmt. Co., Indpls., 1982—. Author: (package) Echo award, 1983 (Gold Echo award 1984), Child Support, 1985 (gold Mail Box award 1985); contbr. articles to profl. jours. Sr. v.p. USO, Indpls., 1988—; mem. adv. bd. Wickes for Senate, Indpls., 1988; pres.-elect Ind. Arthritis Found., 1988. Served with USAF, 1965-69, Vietnam. Recipient Nation Achievement award Arthritis Found., Atlanta, 1987. Mem. Am. Mktg. Assn., Direct Mktg. Assn. (pres. Ind. chpt. 1986, agy. council 1986-87, Leader award 1986, 87, Gold Echo award 1986, 87); Indpls. Direct Mktg. Assn. (chmn. 1984-86), Assn. Direct Mktg. Agys., DAV, Am. Legion (dir. rehab.), Am. Mgmt. Assn., Direct Mktg. Creative Guild. Democrat. Lutheran. Office: Haynes & Pittenger Direct Inc 303 N Alabama Indianapolis IN 46204

HAYNIE, RAYMOND RILEY, paper industry executive; b. Childersburg, Ala., Oct. 19, 1943; s. Eugene J. and Leslie S. (Rogers) H.; m. Paula F. Miller, April 18, 1964; children: Michael, Kevin. BS in Pulp and Paper, N.C. State U., 1969; mgmt. program, Emory U., 1979. Research and devel. engr. St. Regis Paper, Cantonment, Fla., 1969-70; mgr. process services St. Regis Paper, Sheldon, Tex., 1981-82; pulp mfg. mgr. Newsprint div. Champion Internat. (acquired St. Regis in 1984), Sheldon, Tex., 1982—; process Engr. Southland Paper, Lufkin, Tex., 1970-73, asst. pulp mill supt., 1973-75; mgr. process engineering Brunswick (Ga.) Pulp and Paper, 1975-81. Co-chmn. United Way Fund Drive BP&P, Brunswick, 1976; nominee Rep. Presdl. Task Force. Recipient Crown Zellerbach award Crown Zellerbach Found., 1968. Mem. TAPPI, N.C. State Pulp and Paper Found., Am. Mgmt. Assn., Phi Kappa Phi, Xi Sigma Pi. Republican. Episcopalian. Club: Fourdrinier Soc. (local program chmn. 1968-69). Lodge: Lions.

HAYS, DIANA JOYCE WATKINS, consumer products company executive; b. Riverside, Calif., Aug. 29, 1945; d. Donald Richard and Evelyn Christine (Kolvoord) Watkins; m. Gerald N. Hays, Jan 30, 1964 (div. Jan. 1970), 1 child, Tad Damon. BA, U. Minn., 1975, MBA, 1982. Dir. environ./phys. sci. Sci. Mus. Minn., St. Paul, 1972-76; dir. mktg. rsch. No. Natural Gas Co., Omaha, 1977-78; mktg, asst., asst. product mgr. Gen. Mills, Inc., Mpls., 1978-81; product mgr. ortho pharms. Consumer Products div. Johnson & Johnson, Raritan, N.J., 1981-82, product dir., 1982-86; mktg. dir. new market devel. Consumer Products div. Becton Dickinson & Co., Franklin Lakes, N.J., 1986—; chmn. energy exhibit com. Assn. Sci.-Tech. Ctrs., Washington, 1974-75. Producer Ecologenie, 1975. Recipient Tribute to Women and Industry award YWCA, 1989. Mem. Beta Gamma Sigma (life). Republican. Roman Catholic. Office: Becton Dickinson & Co Consumer Products Div One Becton Dr Franklin Lakes NJ 07465

HAYS, HERSCHEL MARTIN, electrical engineer; b. Neillsville, Wis., Mar. 2, 1920; s. Myron E. and Esther (Marquardt) H.; E.E., U. Minn., 1942; grad. student U. So. Calif., 1947; children—Howard Martin, Holly Mary, Diane Esther, Willet Martin Hays II. Elec. engr. City of Los Angeles, 1947-60; pres. Li-Bonn Corp. Served as radio officer, 810th Signal Service Bn., U.S. Army, 1942-43; asst. signal constrn. officer, E.T.O., 1943-45, tech. supr. Japanese radio systems, U.S. Army of Occupation, 1945-46; mem. tech. staff, Signal Corps Engring. Labs., U.S. Army, 1946; col. U.S. Army, ret. Signal Officer Calif. N.G. 1947-50. Registered profl. engr. Calif. Mem. Eta Kappa Nu, Pi Tau Pi Sigma, Kappa Eta Kappa. Republican. Episcopalian. Home: 603 Alhambra Venice FL 34285

HAYS, MARILYN PATRICIA, lawyer, rancher, real estate executive; b. Yarrow, Mo., Sept. 19, 1935; d. John Dewey and Ruth (McKim) H.; m. Harold Clifton Ledbetter, Dec. 13, 1953 (div. 1972); children: Latricia Lyn, Lisa Ledbetter Cerio, David Clifton, Laura Lizanne; Harold Clifton, Jr.; m. Dean Leon Fortney, July 21, 1978. BS, Northeast Mo. State U., 1958; broker cert. U. Fla., 1976; MA, U. Mo., 1983; JD, Washburn U., 1987. Lic. real estate broker, Mo., Kans., Fla., Grad. Realtors Inst. Fashion coordinator Ashells, Regina's Co., Kirksville, Mo., 1951-54; instr. pub. schs., Crocker, Novinger, Kirksville and University City, Mo., 1954-61; real estate salestaff Goldman's Assocs., Daytona Beach, Fla., 1975-76; real estate broker Kellogg Century 21, Daytona Beach, 1976-78; pres. M.P. Hays Co., Olathe, Kans., 1978-82, Bucyrus, Kans., 1982—; cons. Goldman, Kellogg, Daytona Beach, 1975-78. Contbr. articles on real estate edn. to profl. jours. Pres. Fla. Osteopathic Med. Assn. Aux., Dist. IV, 1964-65, 73-74, pres.-elect, 1967-68; major chmn. Assn. of Jr. League, Daytona Beach, 1968-69, 72-73; Pan Hellenic del., 1972-78; adviser Ormond Beach Hosp. Guild, Fla., 1972-74; tchr. CCD Holy Rosary Cath. Ch., Bucyrus, 1987-88. Scholar, Mo. Council PTAs, 1953, K.C., 1954; recipient Outstanding Sales Achievement award Kellogg Century 21, 1977. Mem. Kans. Bar Assn., ABA, Miami County Bd. Realtors, Johnson County Bd. Realtors, Nat. Assn. Realtors, Kans. Assn. Realtors, Kans. Farm Bur., Women's Legal Forum, AAUW, Fla. Osteo. Med. Assn. (aux.), Am. Quarterhorse Assn., Holy Rosary Alter Soc., Alpha Sigma Alpha, Phi Delta Phi. Republican. Roman Catholic. Clubs: Ormond Beach Woman's, Oceanside Country. Avocations: photography, cooking, horseback riding. Home: 458 Triton Rd Ormond Beach FL 32074 Office: M P Hays Co 223d St and State Line Rd Bucyrus KS 66013

HAYS, RICHARD MARTIN, steel company executive, lawyer; b. Pitts., Dec. 19, 1927; s. Clarence Martin and Anne (Darby) H.; m. Barbara Ann Gentil, Sept. 5, 1953; children: Richard Martin, Jr., David Willis, Carol Ann, Virginia Louise. AB, Bucknell U., 1949; JD, Cornell U., 1952. Bar: Pa. 1952. Asst. atty. law dept. U.S. Steel Corp., Pitts., 1954-58, asst. sec., gen. atty., N.Y.C., 1964-76, asst. sec., sr. gen. atty.-corp., Pitts., 1976-83, sec., asst. gen. counsel, 1983—; sec., atty. Que. (Can.) Cartier Mining Co., Port Cartier, 1958-64, sec., asst. gen. counsel USX Corp., 1986—. Bd. dirs. Pitts. Coun. for Internat. Visitors, 1986—, River City Brass Band, 1986—. With U.S. Army, 1952-54. Mem. ABA, Pa. Bar Assn., Allegheny County Bar Assn., Am. Soc. Corp. Secs. (bd. dirs. 1978-85, chmn. 1983-84), Am. Corp. Counsel Assn. Republican. Presbyterian. Clubs: Duquesne, Saint Clair Country (Pitts.). Home: 2 Mission Dr Pittsburgh PA 15228 Office: USX Corp 600 Grant St Rm 6116 Pittsburgh PA 15219-4776

HAYS, SALLY UPHAM, business organization executive; b. Ft. Worth, July 15, 1937; d. John Darr and Marjorie Carolyn (Tolhurst) Upham; m. William Auburn Hays, Jr., Apr. 8, 1961 (div. 1985); children: Catherine Carr, Lee Upham. Student, Goucher Coll., 1954-55; BA, Newcomb Coll., 1958; MBA, Tulane U., 1981. Exec. v.p. Metro Area Com., New Orleans, 1981-87; dir. Bus. Task Force on Edn. Inc., New Orleans, 1987—; dir. edn. The Chamber/New Orleans and the River Region, New Orleans, 1987—. Trainer Vol. Leadership Tng. Ctr., New Orleans, 1984—; adv. Jr. League Edn., Community Awareness Project, New Orleans, 1988—; mem. campaign cabinet United Way, New Orleans, 1986. Episcopalian. Office: Business Task Force Edn 301 Camp St New Orleans LA 70130

HAYS, THOMAS A., department store executive; b. Cleve., 1932; married. B.A., Wabash Coll., 1955. Pres. Venture Stores Inc. div. May Dept. Stores Co., St. Ann, Mo., 1972-82, chief exec. officer, 1980-82, chmn., 1982—; pres. The Hecht Co. div. May Stores Co., Washington, 1974—; with May Dept. Stores Co., St. Louis, 1969—, vice chmn., 1982-85, pres., 1985—, dir. dir. Mercantile Trust Co., Mercantile Bancorp. Office: The May Dept Stores Co 611 Olive St Saint Louis MO 63101 *

HAYS, THOMAS CHANDLER, tobacco and holding company executive; b. Chgo., Apr. 21, 1935; s. Marion C. and Carolyn (Reid) H.; m. Mary Ann Jergens, June 8, 1958; children—Thomas, Michael, Paul, Jennifer. B.S., Calif. Inst. Tech., 1957, M.S., 1958; M.B.A. with high distinction (Baker scholar), Harvard U., 1963. Ops. research analyst Lockheed Corp., Los Angeles, 1963-64; product mgr. Andrew Jergens Co. (formerly subs. Am. Brands), Cin., 1964-70; v.p. mktg. Andrew Jergens Co. (formerly subs. Am. Brands), 1970-78, exec. v.p., 1978, pres., chief exec. officer, 1979-80; v.p. mktg. Am. Tobacco Co. (subs. Am. Brands), 1980-81, exec. v.p., 1981-85, pres., 1985-87, pres., chief operating officer, 1985-86, chief exec. officer, 1986-87, chmn., 1987-88; pres., chief operating officer Am. Brands, 1988—, also bd. dirs.; bd. dirs. Am. Tobacco, Acushnet Co., Gallaher Ltd., Golden Belt Mfg. Co., MasterBrand Industries, Inc., MCM Products, Inc., ACCO World Corp., Am. Brands Internat. Corp., Am. Tob. Internat. Corp., Am. Franklin Co., Jim Beam Brands Co., Franklin Life Ins. Co. Trustee, treas. Cin. Country Day Sch., 1978—; trustee The Andrew Jergens Found.; bd. trustees Five-Town Found.; bd. dirs., treas. Meml. Community Center, 1965-75. 1st lt. USAF, 1958-61. Republican. Presbyterian. Clubs: Cin. Country, Darien Country, Bel Air Bay, Tokeneke.

HAYS, THOMAS R., electronics executive; b. MacFarlan, W.Va., July 14, 1915; s. William R. and Myra (Wilson) H.; m. Jeanne Ligney, May 11, 1945; children: Thomas R. Jr., Sharon Hays Stricchiola, Jeanne Anne Hays Nerlino, Bonnie Hays Erlichman. BSEE, Ohio U., 1937; cert., Nothwestern U. Inst. Mgmt., 1959. Registered profl. electrical engr. Student engr. RCA Corp., Camden, N.J., 1937-38, radar and sonar engr., 1938-45; dist. sales mgr. tube div. RCA Corp., Harrison, N.J., 1946-56; sales mgr. picture tube div., receiving tube div., solid state div., memory product div. RCA Corp., Somerville, N.J., 1956-60, mktg. mgr. solid state div., 1960-75; mgr. major accts. RCA Corp., Somerville, 1975-80; pres. Tom Hays, Inc., Madison, N.J., 1980—; realtor Caldwell Banker, 1986—; pres. Tom Hays, Inc., 1980—. Bd. dirs. Madison YMCA, 1982—; bd. dirs., v.p. Madison Meth. Ch., 1985—, pres. bd. trustees, 1988; mem. long range planning com. Morris County Bd. Realtors, 1988—. Republican. Lodge: Rotary (v.p., bd. dirs., 1985—, pres.-elect, 1988, pres., 1989). Home: 20 Beverly Rd Madison NJ 07940 Office: Caldwell Banker 20 Beverly Rd Madison NJ 07940

HAYS, TIMOTHY, newspaper executive; b. Los Angeles, Apr. 13, 1954; s. James F. and Juanita Sayer H. Student, UCLA, 1974-78. Founder, pres. Hays Pub. Co., Los Angeles, 1974-77; sports editor Santa Monica (Calif.) Ind. Jour., 1976-77; mktg. analyst Los Angeles Herald Examiner, 1977-79; sr. account exec. Los Angeles Times, N.Y.C., 1979—, book rev. sales mgr., 1982—; auxiliary dir. Direction Sports Inc., Los Angeles, 1973—; bd. dirs. N.Y. is Book Country. Editor Basketball News, 1974-76; sports editor and journeyman compositor Santa Monica Ind.-Jour., 1976-77. Counselor, dir. sports, Optimist Home for Boys, 1972-75; dep. campaign mgr. Holoman for Assembly, 1974; assoc. mem. Calif. State Rep. Cen. Com., Los Angeles, 1975-76. Mem. Orgn. Am. Historians, Am. Mgmt. Assn., N.Y. is Book Country (bd. dirs.). Republican. Club: Players (N.Y.C.), Chemists. Home: 424 E 52d St New York NY 10022 Office: Los Angeles Times 711 Third Ave New York NY 10017

HAYWARD, CHARLES WINTHROP, railroad company executive; b. Andover, Mass., May 30, 1927; s. Harry W. and Myrtle (Trommer) H.; m. Barbara Burns, Nov. 4, 1952; children: Patricia, John, Paul, Laura, Lee, Linda. BS, U.S. Mil. Acad., 1950; MBA, Syracuse U., 1957. Commd. 2d lt. U.S. Army, 1950, advanced through grades to col., 1968; served in Korea and Vietnam; ret. 1975; budget officer Nat. RR Passenger Corp., Washington, 1976-82, v.p. fin., chief fin. officer, 1982—; pres., chmn. bd. dirs. Chgo. Union Sta. Co., 1986—; bd. dirs. Washington Terminal Co. Mem. Fin. Execs. Inst. (chpt. bd. dirs. 1982—). Home: 7216 Valon Ct Alexandria VA 22307 Office: Amtrak 400 N Capitol St NW Washington DC 20001

HAYWARD, HAROLD, civil engineer, consultant; b. N.Y.C., Jan. 11, 1920; s. Israel and Sadie Lillian (Blum) Horwitz; B.C.E. cum laude, Coll. City N.Y., 1941; M.C.E., N.Y.U., 1949; m. Dorothy Rose Anderson, Aug. 18, 1946; children—H. Garrett, Susan Hayward Wrobel, Rael Joanne Hayward Cantline, Margaret Elizabeth, Carol Anne. Engr.-in-charge Elwyn E. Seely & Co., N.Y.C., 1941-44, Elson T. Killam, N.Y.C., 1946-49; city engr. City of Beacon, N.Y., 1951-54; partner Wiesenfeld Hayward & Leon, N.Y.C., 1954-61, Hayward & Pakan Assos., Poughkeepsie, N.Y., 1961—. Vice chmn. Poughkeepsie Parking Authority, 1965-72, chmn., 1972-76; chmn. bd. dirs. Dutchess County chpt. Am. Heart Assn., 1978—. Bd. dirs. Rehab. Programs Inc., 1965-70, hon. dir., 1970—. Served to lt. (j.g.) USNR, 1943-46. Registered profl. engr., N.Y. Mem. Cons. Engrs. Council, Nat. Soc. Profl. Engrs., Dutchess County Art Assn. (treas. 1967). Clubs: Masons, Rotary (pres.-elect Poughkeepsie 1979), Kevin Barry Irish (Poughkeepsie, treas. 1978, pres. 1980). Works include structural engring. on St. John's Ch., Collegeville, Minn., Arlington Sewage Treatment Plant, Poughkeepsie, Town of Poughkeepsie Water System. Home: 35 Adriance Ave Poughkeepsie NY 12601 Office: Hayward & Pakan Assocs 321 Main Mall Poughkeepsie NY 12601

HAYWOOD, ROBERT CARROLL, manufacturing consultant; b. Albuquerque, Oct. 3, 1950; s. Oliver Garfield and Helen (Salisbury) H.; m. Patricia Ann Howarth, Aug. 22, 1971 (div. 1977); m. Marialys Gadrow, Aug. 28, 1982; children: Jenny Crandall, Ryan Salisbury. BS in Physics with hons., Worcester Poly. Inst., 1973; MBA with distinction, Harvard U., 1977. Research asst. Harvard Bus. Sch., Boston, 1977-79; mng. dir. Tedelex Ltd., Hong Kong, 1979-81; pres. Aspen Internat., Inc., Boulder, Colo., 1981—; assoc. dir. Flagstaff Inst., Ariz., 1985—; bd. dirs. Rocky Mountain Internat. Bus. Service Ctr., Boulder, 1987—. Contbr. articles to profl. jours. Dir. secretariate World Export Processing Zones Assn., Flagstaff, 1986—; mng. dir. Metro Assn. Retarded Citizens, Denver, 1987—. Recipient Community Service award Aspen C. of C., 1982; named Outstanding Young Man Am., 1987. Home and Office: 31251 Eagle Crest Ln Evergreen CO 80439

HAYWORTH, DON CHARLES, pay telephone company executive; b. Clovis, N.Mex., Oct. 15, 1931; s. William Roy and Loma Juanita (Bryant) H.; m. Pauline Hill, Mar. 21, 1950 (div. 1956); children: Banessa Lynn, Bradford Lee. BA, U. Denver, 1951. V.p. data processing payrall services Climax (Colo.) Molybedeum Co., 1951-55; dir. data processing tng. Crocker Nat. Bank, San Francisco, 1955-60; v.p. data processing payrall services Pacific Coast Stock Exchange, Los Angeles, 1960-71, Payfone Systems, Van Nuys, Calif., 1971—. Home: 4151 Tujunga Ave Studio City CA 91406 Office: Payfone Systems 8100 Balboa Blvd Van Nuys CA 91604

HAZAMA, YOSHIKAZU, environmental engineer; b. Tokushima, Japan, Jan. 1, 1948; s. Tamotsu and Toshiko (Iwata) H.; m. Toshi Omori, July 24, 1974; children: Yusuke, Youko. B in Engring., Nagoya (Japan) Inst. Tech., 1972. Engr. Toyo Netsu Kogyo Kaisha, Ltd., Tokyo, 1972-85, chief planning engr., 1986—; cons. in field. Author: Solar System Design Guide, 1981, Knowledge of Solar System, 1982. Mem. Soc. Heating, Air-Conditioning and Sanitary Engrs., Japan Cons. Engrs. Assn. Home: 1-15 Kaijin 3-Chome, Funabashi, Chiba 273, Japan Office: Toyo Netsu Kogyo Kaisha Ltd, 5-12 Kyobashi 2-Chome, Tokyo 104, Japan

HAZARD, ROBERT CULVER, JR., hotel executive; b. Balt., Oct. 23, 1934; s. Robert Culver and Catherine B. H.; m. Mary Victoria Cranor, Jan. 2, 1981; children by previous marriage: Alicia W., Letitia A., Robert Culver, III, Thomas E.J., Anne. B.A. cum laude, Woodrow Wilson Sch., Princeton U., 1956; postgrad., Johns Hopkins U., U. Denver. Mktg. rep. IBM Corp., Denver, 1959-68; with Am. Express Co., 1968-74, v.p. exec. accounts reservations, 1973-74; chief exec. officer Best Western Internat., 1974-80; pres., chief exec. officer Quality Inns Internat., Silver Spring, Md., 1980—, also dir. Served to capt. USAF, 1956-59. Recipient Man of Yr. award Motel Brokers Assn. Am., 1976, Silver Plate award Hospitality mag., 1979. Mem. Am. Hotel and Motel Assn. Office: Quality Inns 10750 Columbia Pike Silver Spring MD 20901

HAZELRIGG, CHARLES RICHARD, banker; b. Cadiz, Ohio, 1933; married. B.S., Miami U., Ohio, 1955. Security analyst United Bank of Denver, 1958-61, portfolio mgr., 1961-65, mgr. bus. devel., 1965-68, v.p., 1968-70, group v.p., 1970-74, sr. v.p., 1974-77, exec. v.p., 1977-81, sr. exec. v.p., 1981-82, pres., 1982-87; with United Banks of Colo., Inc., 1986—, pres., 1986-87, pres., chief operating officer, 1987—, also dir. Served to capt. USAF, 1956-58. Office: United Banks Colo Inc 1700 Lincoln St Ste 3200 Denver CO 80274

HAZELTON, KEITH HARDING, financial services banker; b. Wilmington, Del., Mar. 22, 1956; s. Knox and Joan Burrough (harding) H.; m. Mary Margaret Oliverio, Oct. 9, 1982; 1 child, Jeffrey Adam. BA in Journalism, Ohio State U., 1979, MBA in Fin., 1983. Asst. sr. auditor Banc One Corp., Columbus, Ohio, 1979-81; internat. officer Bank One Columbus NA, Columbus, 1981-83; asst. v.p. BancOhio Nat. Bank, Columbus, 1983-85; v.p. Huntington Nat. Bank, Columbus, 1985-89, Huntington Trust Co., Columbus, 1989—; mem. internat. money transfer com. Mid Am. Council on Internat. Banking, Chgo., 1983-85; mem. fin. team Columbus Export Network, 1988; instr. sales tng. Richardson Group, Phila., 1985-88. Mem. Nat. Assn. Credit Mgrs., Columbus Council on World Affairs, Columbus Sales Execs. Club, World Trade Devel. Club (import com. 1986, exec. com. 1988), Columbus Met. Club (mktg. com. 1987-88), Ohio State U. Internat. Bus. Student Assn. (bd. dirs. 1986-88). Republican. Roman Catholic. Office: Huntington Trust Co 41 S High St HC1131 Columbus OH 43287

HAZEN, PAUL MANDEVILLE, banker; b. 1941; married. BA U. Ariz., 1963, MBA U. Calif., Berkeley, 1964. Asst. mgr. Security Pacific Bank, 1964-66; v.p. Union Bank, 1966-70; chmn. Wells Fargo Realty Advisors, 1970-76; with Wells Fargo Bank, San Francisco, 1979—, exec. v.p., mgr. Real Estate Industries Group, 1979-80, mem. exec. office, 1980, vice-chmn., 1980-84, pres., chief operating offficer, 198—, also dir.; pres., treas. Wells Fargo Mortgage & Equity Trust, 1977-84; with Wells Fargo & Co. (parent), San Francisco, 1978—, exec. v.p., then vice-chmn., now pres., chief operating officer, dir.; trustee Wells Fargo Mortgage & Equity Trust. Office: Wells Fargo & Co 420 Montgomery St San Francisco CA 94163 *

HAZLETON, JOHN VINCENT, financial analyst, consultant; b. Alexandria, La., Dec. 4, 1937; s. Vincent Astor and Sybil (Thompson) H.; m. Frances Jayne Mosley, Aug. 31, 1958 (div. 1988); children: John Vincent Jr., Alice Hazleton Welsh, Stuart Andrew. BA, Northwestern State U., 1960; MA, Kans. U., 1967. Prof. Okla. U., Chickasha, 1968-74; owner Interpersonal Communications, Oklahoma City, 1975—; founder, chmn. bd. TM Communications, Inc., Dallas, 1985—; bd. chmn. Radtech, Inc., Dallas, 1987—; co-founder, bd. dirs. Petra Resources (now Mustang Resources Corp), Oklahoma City and Houston; founder, bd. dirs. Moto Photo, Inc.,

Oklahoma City and Dayton, Ohio, CMS Advt., Inc., Oklahoma City; bd. dirs. Mid Am. Racing Stables, Inc., Norman, Okla., USA Waste Services, Inc., Norman. Author: (play) I Wasn't Listening, 1963. Republican. Methodist. Office: 1101 A Sovereign Row Oklahoma City OK 73108

HAZRA, BILAS KUMAR, industrialist; b. Calcutta, India, Jan. 1, 1946; came to U.S., 1970; s. Bipradas and Annapurna (Mondal) H.; m. Sandra Virginia Lee, Aug. 2, 1969; children: Soma, Amit. Diploma in Prodn. Engring., U. Manchester, Eng., 1966; MME, NYU, 1970; MBA, Rensselaer Poly. Inst., 1974. Registered profl. engr., N.Y. Mfg. engr. Pratt & Whitney Ltd., Longueuil, Que., Can., 1966-68; engr. Gen. Electric Co., Schenectady, N.Y., 1970-77; mktg. mgr. longlines AT&T, Bedminster, N.J., 1977-78; product mgr. Babcock & Wilcox Co., Barberton, Ohio, 1978-81; chief exec. officer Perfeclite Co., Cleve., 1987—, BOF Plastics, Inc., Argos, India, 1985—; chief exec. officer BOF Plastics, Incs., Argos, India, 1985—, Hazra Assocs, Inc., Bath, Ohio, 1982—; bd. dirs. internat. mktg. Pemco, Inc., Cleve., 1983—; internat. cons. Radiation Measurements, Inc., Middleton, Wis., 1983—, TeleDiagnostics, Inc., San Francisco, 1983—; chmn. bd. dirs. Howrah Industries, Ind., Cleve. Mem. ASME, Greater Cleve. Growth Assn. Republican. Hindu. Home: 2996 Burnbrick Rd Bath OH 44210 Office: Perfeclite Co 1457 E 40th St Cleveland OH 44103

HEAD, CHRISTOPHER ALAN, lawyer; b. Buffalo, Nov. 28, 1951; s. Alan S. and Mary Ellen (Carrig) H.; m. Kathleen Rosemarie Meosky, Aug. 22, 1976; children: Matthew, David, Maribeth, Sally, Thomas. BA, Canisius Coll., 1974; JD, U. Akron, 1977. Bar: Ohio 1977, N.Y. 1978, U.S. Dist. Ct. (we. dist.) N.Y. 1979. Adminstr. contracts Comptek Research Inc., Buffalo, 1977-78, corp. counsel, 1978-82, gen. counsel, 1983-85, v.p., gen. counsel, 1985—; corp. counsel Barrister Info. System Corp., Buffalo, 1982-83; bd. dirs. Goldome N.Y. Capital Corp., Wilmington, Del. Mem. ABA, N.Y. State Bar Assn., Erie County Bar Assn., Niagara Frontier Corp. Counsel Assn. (pres. 1984-85). Democrat. Roman Catholic. Home: 3311 Calvano Dr Grand Island NY 14072 Office: Comptek Rsch Inc 110 Broadway Buffalo NY 14203

HEAD, GEORGE EDWARD, SR., finance executive, brokerage executive; b. Louisville; s. Lewis Edward and Josephine (Fox) Horton; m. Helen Smith, Nov. 7, 1958 (div. 1979); children; Helen, George, Lewis, Hannah; m. Dianne Lucille Benoni, July 4, 1982. AA, So. Bapt. Coll., 1968; BA, Ark. State U., 1970. Cert. fin. planner. Health physicist USN, 1958-67; minister 1967-76; various positions Mut. Life Ins. Co., Boston, 1976-85; controller First Bus. Services, Orange, Mass., 1985—; prin. Head & Assocs., Orange, 1985; with Phar Tech, 1987—; cons. in field, 1985—. With USAFR. Mem. Internat. Assn. for Fin. Planning, Inst. Cert. Fin. Planners, Internat. Assn. Registered Fin. Planners (bd. govs. 1988—) GAA Mental Health Assn. (bd. dirs. 1986-87). Lodge: Elks. Home: 222 Walnut PO Box 555 Athol MA 01331 Office: First Bus Svcs Inc 343 E River St Orange MA 01364

HEAD, PATRICK JAMES, lawyer; b. Randolph, Nebr., July 13, 1932; s. Clarence Martin and Ellen Cecelia (Magirl) H.; m. Eleanor Hickey, Nov. 24, 1960; children: Adrienne, Ellen, Damian, Maria, Brendan, Martin, Sarah, Daniel, Brian. A.B. summa cum laude, Georgetown U., 1953, LL.B., 1956, LL.M. in Internat. Law, 1957. Bar: D.C. 1956, Ill. 1966. Asso. firm John L. Ingolsby (and predecessor firm), Washington, 1956-64; gen. counsel internat. ops. Sears, Roebuck & Co., Oakbrook, Ill., 1964-70; counsel midwest ter. Sears, Roebuck & Co., Skokie, Ill., 1970-72; v.p. Montgomery Ward & Co., Inc., Washington, 1972-76; v.p., gen. counsel, sec. Montgomery Ward & Co., Inc., Chgo., 1976-81; v.p., gen. counsel FMC Corp., Chgo., 1981—; bd. visitors Northwestern Law, 1988—. Mem. Chgo. Crime Commn.; bd. regents Georgetown U., Washington, 1981-87; mem. bd. visitors Northwestern U. Law Sch., 1988; chmn. Northwestern Law Corp. Counsel Ctr., 1987—. Mem. ABA, D.C. Bar Assn., Chgo. Bar Assn., Am. Law Inst. Democrat. Roman Catholic. Clubs: Met. (Washington); Chgo, Internat. Office: FMC Corp 200 E Randolph St Chicago IL 60601

HEAD, WILLIAM IVERSON, SR., retired chemical company executive; b. Tallapoosa, Ga., Apr. 4, 1925; s. Iverson and Ruth Britain (Hubbard) H.; m. Mary Helen Ware, June 12, 1947; children: William Iverson, Connie Suzanne, Alan David. BS in Textile Engring. with honors, Ga. Inst. Tech., 1949; D of Textile Engring. (hon.), World U., 1983; PhD in Indsl. Mgmt., Columbia Pacific U., 1988. Research and devel. engr. Tenn. Eastman Co., Kingsport, 1949-56, quality control-mfg. sr. engr., 1957-67, dept. supt., 1968-74; supt. acetate yarn dept. Chems. div. Eastman Kodak Co., Kingsport, 1975-85; info. officer U.S. Naval Acad., 1983—; mem. adv. bd., rsch. assoc. Point One Adv. Group, Inc., 1988—. Patentee textured yarns tech. in U.S., Great Britain, Fed. Republic of Germany, Japan and France. Served with USN, 1943-46, capt. Res., 1946-83. Decorated Navy Commendation medal, Selective Svc. System Meritorious Svc. medal, 1980. Mem. Internat. Soc. Philos. Enquiry (personnel cons. 1978-79, sr. research fellow and internat. pres. 1980-85, diplomate and chmn. bd. trustees 1987—), Am. Chem. Soc., Prometheus Soc., Internat. Platform Assn., Naval Res. Assn., Mil. Order World Wars, Res. Officers Assn. (pres. Tenn. dept. 1981-82), Retired Officers Assn., VFW, Mensa (pres. Upper East Tenn. 1976-79), Cincinnatus Soc., Internat. Legion of Intelligence. Unitarian. Home: 4035 Lakewood Dr Kingsport TN 37663

HEADDEN, LAURA BENSON, banker; b. Butte, Mont., Feb. 15, 1950; d. Fred Melvin and Margaret May (Franks) Benson; m. William D. Headden, June 15, 1974. BBA, Idaho State U., 1972; postgrad., Pacific Coast Banking Sch., 1983-85. Mgmt. trainee 1st Security Bank Idaho, Boise, 1972-73; ops. officer 1st Security Bank Idaho, Payette, 1973-74, Boise, 1974-77; systems analyst 1st Security Co., Salt Lake City, 1977-78; ops. officer, asst. v.p. 1st Security Bank Utah, Salt Lake City, 1978-82, tng. officer, asst. v.p., 1982-85, bus. devel officer, v.p., 1985—; chair 12th Ann. Women and Bus. Conf., Salt Lake City, 1987. Treas., bd. dirs. Utah council Girl Scouts U.S., 1988—; bd. dirs. Utah Heart Assn., Children's Mus. Utah, Salt Lake City; dir. mktg. Jr. League, Salt Lake City, 1987—. Named Woman of Yr. Woman's Info. Network, Salt Lake City, 1986, Woman to Watch Network Publs., Salt Lake City, 1987. Mem. AAUW (chpt. treas. 1985-86). Office: 1st Security Bank Utah PO Box 30004 79 S Main Salt Lake City UT 84130

HEADDING, LILLIAN SUSAN, writer; b. Milw., Jan. 1, 1944; d. David Morton and Mary Davis (Berry) Coleman; m. James K. Hill (div. 1976); children: Amy Denise; m. John Murray Headding (div. 1987). BA, U. Nev., 1975; MA, U. Pacific, 1976. With Gimbels, Milw., 1963-65; retail mgr. Frandisco Corp., N.Y.C., 1965-66; store mgr. Anita Shops, Los Angeles, 1966-68, Clothes Closet, Sunnyvale, Calif., 1969-70; owner Lillian Headding Interiors & Comml. Design, Pittsburg, Calif., 1976-88; instr. 1st degree black belt, 1972—. Author (as Sara Davis): When Gods Fall; short stories. Bd. dirs. Community Action Against Rape, Las Vegas, Nev., 1972-75; self-def. expert Las Vegas Met. Police Dept., 1972-75, North Las Vegas (Nev.) Police Dept.; co. supr. Family & Children's Services, Contra Costa County, Calif., 1985-86. Mem. Walnut Creek Writers Group (pres.), Philippine Hawaiian Black Belters Assn. Republican. Jewish.

HEADLEE, RICHARD HAROLD, insurance company executive; b. Ft. Dodge, Iowa, May 16, 1930; s. William Clarke and Violet Rebecca (Lunn) H.; m. Mary E. Mendenhall, Oct. 21, 1948; children: Mike, Douglas, Kathy, Bruce, Natalie, Carolyn, Laura, Howard, Elaine. BA, Utah State U., 1953; postgrad., Coll. So. Utah, 1983. Spl. account rep. mktg. div. Burroughs Corp., Detroit, 1956-63; with mktg. & sales Burroughs Corp., 1964-66; pres., dir. Morbark Industries, Winn, Mich., 1968-69; pres. Hamilton Internat. Devel. Co., 1970-72; pres., chief exec. officer Alexander Hamilton Life Ins. Co. Am., 1972-88, chmn., chief exec. officer, 1988—; pres., chief exec. officer, Hamilton Internat. Corp., 1972-77; bd. dirs. Wayne Oakland Bank, Automated Tracking Systems, Inc.; chmn. S. Davis United Fund, 1960; mem. steering com. Am. Landmarks Com., 1963-66. Bd. editors: Outstanding Young Men of America, 1964-66. Bishop Mormon ch. 1969-70, stake pres. 1975-80, regional rep. 1983-88; founder S. Davis Welfare Com., 1960; a founder Bountiful Community Concerts Assn., 1961; mem. Nat. Mental Health Adv. Bd.; bd. advisers Project Concern Internat., from 1963; adv. bd. Small Bus. Adminstrn.; del. White House Conf. on Inflation.; Pres. Bountiful (Utah) Jr. C. of C., 1960, Utah Jr. C. of C., 1962; bd. dirs. U.S. Jr. C. of C., 1961-65, v.p., 1962-63, pres., 1963-64, chmn. bd., 1964-65; life mem., senator; chmn. Mich. C. of C., 1980; bd. dirs. Citizen's Choice, Washington, Nat. Multiple Sclerosis Soc., 1963-65; vice chmn. bd. trustees Oakland U., 1980-82, chmn., 1980-81; chmn. Taxpayers Research Inst., 1978, Taxpayers United for Tax Limitation, 1978, Taxpayers United for Mich. Constn., 1984—; bd. dirs., past chmn. Nat. Taxpayers Union, 1984—; asst. campaign chmn. gov. of Mich., 1966; chmn. Citizens for Romney; nat. chmn. Young Civic Leaders for Nixon-Agnew, 1968; mem. exec. com. United Rep. Fund.; nat. co-chmn., chmn. Citizens for Am., Washington, from 1983; mem. exec. com. Voter's Choice, Mich.; mem. president's round table Utah State U., from 1974; Rep. candidate for gov. of Mich., 1982, 88; presdl. appointee Fed. Retirement Thrift Investment Bd., 1988—; mem. exec. com. Commerce and Industry Leaders for Bush, 1988—; mem. area council Boy Scouts Am. Served as 1st lt. U.S. Army, 1953-56. Recipient Outstanding Alumnus award Utah State U., 1964; Distinguished Service award Bountiful, 1960; Recipient Golden Key Oakland U., 1983; named Citizen of Yr. Mich., 1980. Mem. Presidents' Assn., Am. Mgmt. Assn., Nat. Assn. Life Underwriters, Am. Council Life Ins. (exec. round table from 1972), Life Office Management Assn. (nat. bd. dirs. 1988—), U.S. C. of C. (dir. 1964-65), Econ. Club Detroit (bd. dirs. 1987—), Blue Key, Sigma Nu, Beta Gamma Sigma (hon.). Office: Alexander Hamilton Life Ins Co of Am 33045 Hamilton Blvd Farmington Hills MI 48018

HEADLEY, ANNE RENOUF, financier for technology commercialization; b. N.Y.C., Apr. 3, 1937. Student, Emma Willard Sch., 1954, Inst. World Affairs, 1957; AB magna cum laude, Columbia U., 1959; MA, Yale U., 1962, PhD, 1966; JD with honors, Am. U., 1978; postgrad., Duke U. Asst. prof. U. N.C., Chapel Hill, 1966-71; sr. profl. cons. U.S. Govt., Washington, 1972-75; pvt. practice fin. cons. Washington, 1976—; vis. assoc. prof. George Washington U. Sch. Bus. Adminstrn., Washington, 1983-84; gen. ptnr., v.p. Tech. Mgmt. Corp., Montgomeryville, Pa., 1986-88; chmn. Pivot, Inc., 1988—; corp. dir., cons. The Brookings Instn., Washington, 1966, U.S. Dept. State, Washington, 1967; mem. pres. commn. Graduated Edn., 1967-68; vis. scholar Carnegie Endowment for Internat. Peace, N.Y.C., 1968-69; mem. Nat. Chamber Found. Task Force on Space Commercialization, Washington, 1983-86; bd. dirs. Advanced Technology Orgn. Md., 1986—; northeastern dir. Va. Advanced Tech. Assn., 1984-86; advisor D.C. chpt. Internat. Red Cross; speaker on fin. and tech. Contbr. articles on tech. commercialization and fin. to profl. jours. Vice chmn., charter mem. Beijing/Washington Sister City Council, Washington, 1985—; advisor Greater Washington D.C. Bd. Trade, 1985-86, Internat. Red Cross, 1987—; mem. Mayor's Adv. Council on Trade and Investment, 1987—. Woodrow Wilson fellow, 1958, Bushnell fellow, Yale U., 1964, Hon. Officer-Faculty fellow U.S. Dept. State, 1967; recipient citation Washington D.C. Mayor's Office, 1986. Fellow Washington Acad. Scis.; mem. Am. Soc. Internat. Law, Internat. Forum U.S. C. of C., Internat. Energy Seminar-Johns Hopkins Sch. for Advanced Internat. Study, Corcoran Gallery of Art (nat. council), Phi Beta Kappa.

HEADLY, JAY RUTHERFORD, management consultant; b. Phila., July 31, 1930; s. Carroll Rutherford and Charlotte Gwynn (McCarter) H. BA, Penn. St. U., 1953; student, U. Pa., 1956-57, The Principia, St. Louis, 1944-48. Stockbroker Bache & Co., Phila., 1957-62; eastern mgr. Fosdick & Assocs., N.Y.C., 1962-72; v.p. Lippincott & Margulies, N.Y.C., 1972-80; prin. Anspach Grossman Portugal, N.Y.C., 1980-83, Lee & Young, Inc., N.Y.C., 1983-85, Headly & Assocs., N.Y.C., 1985—; cons. Currie, Coopers & Lybrand, Toronto, 1984, The Laurentian Group, Montreal, Que., 1984-85. Bd. mgr. St. Andrew's Soc. of N.Y., N.Y.C., 1984; historian, Scottish-Am. Mil. Soc., Charlotte, N.C., 1984. Warrant Officer arty. U.S. Army, 1953-55, Korea. Mem. Am. Mktg. Assn., Wall St. Planning Group, Internat. Assn. Bus. Communicators, The Explorers Club (chair., media com., 1980-88), Union League (Phila.). Home: 500 E 77th St New York NY 10162 Office: The Explorers Club 46 E 70th St New York NY 10021

HEADMAN, ARLAN OSMOND, JR., lawyer; b. Salt Lake City, Utah, Oct. 22, 1952; s. Arlan O. and Ione (Ficklin) H.; m. Debra Card, Aug. 20, 1973; 1 child, Alexander Oliver. B.S., U. Utah, 1974, J.D., 1977. Bar: Utah 1977, U.S. Dist. Ct. Utah 1977. Cons., Ra-Tek Investment, Denver, 1981-82; sole practice, Salt Lake City, 1982-84; ptnr. Smith & Headman, Salt Lake City, 1984—; mem. rule change com. Ad Hoc Com., Utah State Securities Div., 1984. Del., Utah Democratic Conv., 1972, state and county Dem. Conv., 1986. U. Utah scholar, 1971. Mem. Mt. West Venture Capital Club, Phi Eta Sigma, ABA. Mormon. Office: Smith & Headman 420 E S Temple Suite 334 Salt Lake City UT 84111

HEADRICK, ROGER LEWIS, food company executive; b. West Orange, N.J., May 13, 1936; s. Lewis B. and Marian E. (Rogers) H.; m. C. Lynn Cowell, Sept. 29, 1962; children: Hilary R., Mark C., Christopher C., Heather R. AB, Williams Coll., 1958; MBA, Columbia U., 1960. Fin. analyst Standard Oil (N.J.), Esso Eastern, Inc., N.Y.C., 1960-65; treas. Standard Oil (N.J.), Esso Eastern, Inc., Tokyo, 1965-70; v.p. Standard Oil (N.J.), Esso Eastern, Inc., Manila, 1970-73; treas., mgr. fin. and planning Standard Oil (N.J.), Esso Eastern, Inc., Houston, 1973-78; dep. contr. Exxon Corp., N.Y.C., 1978-82; exec. v.p., chief fin. officer The Pillsbury Co., Mpls., 1982-89; civ; bd. dirs. Tonka Corp., Rahr Malting Co., Crompton & Knowles Corp., Nicolet Instrument Corp.; mem. Fin. Acctg. Standards Adv. Council. Trustee Dunwoody Indsl. Inst., Mpls., 1982—, The Blake Schs., 1983—, Fin. Execs. Rsch. Found.; bd. dirs. The Guthrie Theater, 1985—. With USAFR, N.G., 1960-66. Mem. Fin. Execs. Rsch. Found. (trustee), Coun. Fin. Execs.-The Conf. Bd. Office: 672 TCF Tower Minneapolis MN 55402 Office: Nicolet Instrument Corp 5225-3 Verona Rd Madison WI 53711

HEALEY, ROBERT ELLIOTT, utility company executive; b. New Bedford, Mass., Sept. 22, 1937; s. Walter E. and Helen Blanche (Provencial) H.; m. Ellen Patricia Kershaw. BME, Northeastern U., 1960, MBA, 1968. With Commonwealth Energy Co., 1962—; dist. mgr. Commonwealth Energy Co., New Bedford, 1969-75, asst. v.p., 1976-78; v.p. human resources Commonwealth Energy Co., Wareham, Mass., 1979—; with Canal Electric Co., Sandwich, Mass., Cambridge (Mass.) Electric Co.; Loaned exec. new Bedford United Way, 1972-74;v.p. Housing for New Bedford, Inc., 1970-79. Capt. U.S. Army, 1960-62. Fellow Edison Electric Inst. Human Resource Execs.; mem. New England Utility Group, Kiwanis. Roman Catholic. Office: Commonwealth Electric Co 2421 Cranbetty Hwy Wareham MA 02571

HEALEY, WILLIAM JOHN, III, electronics company executive; b. Boston, Aug. 19, 1940; s. William John Healey Jr. and Ava Maria deCordova. BA, New Coll., Oxford, England, 1958, MA in lit., 1961. Divisional supr. domestic corp. tax div. 1st Nat. City Bank, N.Y.C., 1962-64; officer, office mgr. packing & friction materials div. Johns Manville Corp., N.Y.C., 1969-72; mgr. Orange Bay Estates, Ltd., Montego Bay, Jamaica, West Indies; chmn. Ascarib Ltd., San Francisco. Mem. Ridley Coll. Debating Team, Can. Serve dwith Royal Reserve Corps, Can. Mem. Royal Hist. Assn. Republican. Roman Catholic. Club: Hanover Polo (Jamaica). Home: Montego Bay Jamaica West Indies Office: 209 Stillings Ave San Francisco CA 94131-2843

HEALY, BARBARA ANNE, insurance company executive, financial planner; b. Chgo., May 21, 1951; d. William James Healy and Eileen Mary (Dooley) Dashiell; m. Gerald Lally Angst, June 9, 1973 (div. Sept. 1977). BA, No. Ill. U., 1973; MBA, DePaul U., 1976. Cert. fin. planner. Dept. head, instr. St. Benedict High Sch., Chgo., 1973-76; account rep. Xerox Corp., Chgo., 1976-78, mktg. specialist, 1978-79, high volume sr. sales exec., 1979-81; western dist. mgr. McGraw Hill, N.Y.C., 1981-82; fin. planner United Resources Ins. Service, Torrance, Calif., 1982-83, sales mgr., 1983-85, exec. v.p., 1985-86, regional v.p., 1986—; instr. Trenton Coll., Riverside, Ill., City Coll. Chgo., Northeastern Ill. U., Chgo., Prairie State Coll., Chicago Heights, 1976-81. Author: Financial Planning for Educators, 1987; contbr. articles to prof. jours.; speaker in field. Mem. Internat. Assn. Fin. Planners, Inst. Cert. Fin. Planners, Registry Fin. Planning Practitioners, Nat. Council Fin. Edn. Republican. Roman Catholic. Home: 9 Bellflower Ln San Carlos CA 94070 Office: United Resources Ins Svcs 950 Tower Ln Suite 1120 Foster City CA 94404

HEALY, CARL ROBERT, sales executive; b. Rahway, N.J., Apr. 17, 1941; s. Robert Joseph and Caroline (Cordess) H.; m. Marlene Faye LaMore, July 4, 1980; children: Stacey, Kelly. With Met. Life Ins. Co., Glens Falls, N.Y., 1963—; unit mgr. Met. Life Ins. Co., Glens Falls, 1977-85, sr. account rep., 1985—; also bd. dirs. Met. Life Ins. Co. Rep. committeeman Moreau (N.Y.), 1975, chmn., 1976. Mem. Nat. Assn. Underwriters, Tri-County Life Underwriters Assn. (v.p. 1981-82, 1st v.p. 1982-83, pres. 1983-84), N.Y. Assn. Life Underwriters, Million Dollar Round Table (ct. of table 1988), Nat. Assn. Security Dealers. Roman Catholic. Office: Met Life Ins Co Glen St Glen Falls NY 12801

HEALY, JOHN RUSSELL, education administrator; b. Brookline, Mass., June 6, 1951; s. John James and Dorothy (Johnston) H.; m. Irene Foster, Feb. 20, 1972; 1 child, Melissa Ann. BS, Empire State Coll., New Paltz, 1984; MBA, Manhattan Coll., 1987; PhD, Coll. of New Rochelle, 1988. Asst. mgr. Trefz Mgmt. Corp., Bridgeport, Conn., 1971-73; gen. mgr. Spain Oil Corp., Mahopac, N.Y., 1973-77; pres. DTA Mid-Hudson, Poughquag, N.Y., 1977—; coordinator bus. dept. Beacon (N.Y.) High Sch., 1985-87; adminstr. Pine Bush Cen. Sch. Dist., 1987—; adj. prof. Dutchess Community Coll., 1984-87, Poughkeepsie, SUNY New Paltz, 1984—; guest speaker on half-hour safety talk show, Cablevision Channel 10, Poughkeepsie, 1984; asst. prin. Circleville Mid. Sch., 1987—. Dir. Teen Ctr., Beekman Recreation Assn., Poughquag, 1977. Empire State Challenger fellow, 1986. Mem. Driver Tng. Assocs., So. Dutchess C. of C., Nat. Assn. Secondary Sch. Prins., N.Y. State Middle Sch. Assn., Assn. Sch. Curriculum Devel. Home: RR 2 PO Box 264 Poughquag NY 12570 Office: DTA Mid-Hudson Pleasant Ridge Rd Poughquag NY 12570

HEALY, JOSEPH FRANCIS, JR., lawyer, airline executive; b. N.Y.C., Aug. 11, 1930; s. Joseph Francis and Agnes (Kett) H.; m. Patricia A. Casey, Apr. 23, 1955; children: James C., Timothy, Kevin, Cathleen M., Mary, Terence. B.S., Fordham U., 1952; J.D., Georgetown U., 1959. Bar: D.C. 1959. With gen. traffic dept. Eastman-Kodak Co., Rochester, N.Y., 1954-55; air transp. examiner CAB, Washington, 1955-59; practiced in Washington, 1959-70, 80-81; asst. gen. counsel Air Transport Assn. Am., 1966-70; v.p. legal Eastern Air Lines, Inc., N.Y.C. and Miami, Fla., 1970-80; ptnr. Ford, Farquhar, Kornblut & O'Neill, Washington, 1980-81; v.p. legal affairs Piedmont Aviation, Inc., Winston Salem, N.C., 1981-84, sr. v.p., gen counsel, 1984—. Served to 1st lt. USAF, 1952-54. Mem. ABA, Fed. Bar Assn., Internat. Bar Assn., Am. Soc. Corp. Secs., Am. Irish Hist. Soc., Nat. Aero. Assn., Beta Gamma Sigma, Phi Delta Phi. Clubs: Univ., Internat. Aviation (Washington); Wings (N.Y.C.); Piedmont (Winston-Salem). Home: 236 Heatherton Way Winston-Salem NC 27104 Office: Piedmont Aviation Inc 1 Piedmont Pla Winston-Salem NC 27156

HEALY, PATRICIA, management consultant, educator; b. N.Y.C., Apr. 20, 1951; d. Raymond and Patricia (Manning) H.; m. Michael Hanahoe, Dec. 2, 1972; children: Colin, Terance, Evan. BA, NYU, 1972, postgrad., 1988—; MBA, Rutgers U., 1974. CPA, N.Y. Staff acct. Coopers & Lybrand, White Plains, N.Y., 1975-76; lectr. acctg. Mercy Coll., Dobbs Ferry, N.Y., 1976; lectr. Herbert H. Lehman Coll., Bronx, 1976; asst. chairperson, assoc. prof. Pace U., Pleasantville, N.Y., 1976; pres. H.H. Cons., Peekskill, N.Y., 1980—; cons. endl. tng. IBM, Armonk, N.Y. 1983—. Author: Internal Reporting, 1986. Active Continental Village Property Owners Assn., Peeskill, N.Y., 1978—; mem. Van Cortlandville Sch. Bd., Peekskill, 1981—, legis. adv. com. State of N.Y., Albany, 1982—. Deloitte Haskins and Sells fellow, N.Y.C., 1979, Faculty fellow Coopers & Lybrand, N.Y.C., 1983. Mem. AICPA, Am. Soc. Women Accts., Am. Acctg. Assn., Nat. Assn. Accts., Delta Pi epsilon. Democrat. Roman Catholic. Home: Andre Ln RD3 Box 380 Peekskill NY 10566 Office: Pace U Bedford Rd Pleasantville NY 10570

HEALY, STEVEN MICHAEL, accountant; b. Chgo., July 20, 1949; s. Daniel Francis and Angelina (Massino) H. BA, U. Ill., Chgo., 1971; MBA, Rosary Coll., 1984. Br. mgr. Assocs. Capital Co., Chgo., 1971-74; credit analyst Motorola, Inc., Schaumburg, Ill., 1974-76; office mgr. Triple "S" Steel Corp., Franklin Pk., Ill., 1976-79; accounts payable supr. Zenith Electronics, Chgo., 1979-84; supr. acctg. Village of Oak Park, Ill., 1984-86; bus. analyst Cablevision of Chgo., Oak Park, 1986-87; dir. fin. Village of Maywood, Ill., 1988—. Mem. Oak Park Village Players Group; bd. dirs. Oak Park Employees Credit Union. Mem. Nat. Soc. Pub. Accts., Nat. Govt. Fin. Officers Assn., Ill. Govt. Fin. Officers Assn., U. Ill. Alumni Assn., Rosary Coll. MBA Alumni Assn. (founder, mem. soc. com. 1984—), Oak Park Area Jaycees, Friends of the Oak Park Library, Friends of the Conservatory, Cath. Alumni Club, Village Oak Park Chess Club (pres. 1984-86). Home: 2216 River Rd #202 River Grove IL 60171 Office: Village of Maywood 115 S 5th Ave Maywood IL 60153

HEALY, THOMAS MARTIN, manufacturing company executive; b. Milw., May 9, 1921; s. Thomas and Helen (Galewski) H.; m. Ruth Marcella Johnson, Jan. 30, 1943; children: Kathleen Healy Brey, Maureen Ann Warzon, Timothy James, Eileen Marie, Daniel Michael. Student Milw. Area Tech. Sch., 1945-48; student U. Wisc., 1948-49. Engring. rep. Oilgear Co., Milw., 1952-59; mgr. Houston office, 1959-63, mgr. speciality sales, 1963-73, mgr. corp. devel., 1973-83, v.p. corp. devel., 1984-87; pres. Healy Assocs., Austin, Tex., 1987—. Life mem. Rep. Presdl. Taskforce. Served as non-commissioned officer USN, 1943-45, PTO. Mem. Am. Mgmt. Assn., World Future Soc., Am. Def. Preparedness Assn., Onion Creek Club. Roman Catholic. Avocations: travel, philosophy, business and professional ethics.

HEARD, DAVID DENNIS, snack foods executive; b. Galashiels, Selkirkshire, Scotland, Aug. 25, 1940; came to U.S., 1965; s. Richard and Isabella (Miller) H.; m. Rosemary Helen Waugh; 1 child, Ailsa Margaret. BSc cum laude, U. Edinburgh, Scotland, 1962, PhD, 1965. Assoc. dir. Procter & Gamble, Cin., 1967-77; dir. Am. Cynamid, Clifton, N.J., 1977-81; v.p. research and devel. Frito-Lay Inc., Dallas, 1981-84, sr. v.p. technology, 1984—; bd. advisors Food Research Inst., Madison, Wis. Mem. Indsl. Research Inst. (rep.), Inst. Food Technologists (bd. dirs. office pub. affairs 1986). Office: Frito-Lay Inc 7701 Legacy Plano TX 75093

HEARD, EDWIN ANTHONY, banker; b. N.Y.C., Oct. 31, 1926; s. Edwin Anthony and Frances Weaver (Taylor) H.; m. Phyllis Marie Gregory, Dec. 18, 1948; children: Elizabeth Gregory, Edwin Anthony III. A.B., Princeton U., 1948; grad., Advanced Mgmt. Program, Harvard U., 1966. V.p. Irving Trust Co., N.Y.C., 1960-71; treas. U.S. Trust Co., N.Y.C., 1971-73; exec. v.p. U.S. Trust Co., 1973-76, vice chmn., 1976-88; pres. Excelsior Income Shares, Inc., 1989—; vice chair U.S. Trust Corp., N.Y.C., Royal Life Ins. Co. N.Y. Trustee Collegiate Sch., Trinity Episcopal Sch. Corp. Lt. (j.g.), USNR, 1944-46. Clubs: Down Town Assn. (N.Y.C.), Bond (N.Y.C.). Home: 1133 Park Ave New York NY 10128 Office: Excelsior Income Shares Inc 45 Wall St New York NY 10005

HEARD, WILLIAM ROBERT, insurance company executive; b. Indpls., Apr. 25, 1925; s. French and Estelle (Austin) H.; attended Ind. U.; m. Virginia Ann Patrick, Feb. 6, 1951; children—Cynthia Ann, William Robert, II. With Grain Dealers Mut. Ins. Co., 1948, exec. v.p., Indpls., 1978-79, pres., chief exec. officer, dir., 1979—; pres., chief exec. officer, dir. Companion Ins. Co., 1979—; chmn., dir., exec. and fin. com. Alliance Am. Insurers; chmn., exec. com. IRM; pres., dir. Grain Dealers Mut. Agy., Inc.; chmn. bd. 15 N. Broadway Corp. Served with USNR, 1942-46. Mem. Assn. Mill and Elevator Ins. Cos. (chmn., dir.), Ins. Inst. Ind. (dir., exec. com.), Mut. Reins. Bur. (dir., exec. com.), Indiana Better Bus. Bur. (dir., exec. com., vice chmn.), Excess of Loss Assn. (vice chmn., dir.), Sales and Mktg. Execs. Indpls. (past pres.), Sales and Mktg. Execs. Internat. (past dir.), Fla. 1752 Club (past pres.), Property and Casualty Ins. Council, Ind. Insurors Assn. (dir.), Hoosierland Rating Bur. (dir.), Ind. Mill and Elevator Rating Bur. (dir.), Ins. Claims Service (dir.), Property Loss Research Bur. (dir., chmn.), Mill and Elevator Rating Bur. (dir.), Mill and Elevator Fire Prevention Bur. (dir.), Econ. Club of Indpls., Am. Legion, Hon. Order Ky. Cols., Pi Sigma Epsilon. Club: Indpls. Skyline. Office: Grain Dealers Mut Ins 1752 N Meridian Indianapolis IN 46202

HEARNE, RAETTE SMITH, communications executive; b. Austin, Tex., Oct. 4; d. Raphael Clay and Doris Jean (Patterson)Smith; m. Rayfield Hearne Jr., June 26, 1976; 1 child, Raphael Clayton. BBA, North Tex. State U., 1975; MBAin Permian Basic, U. Tex., 1982. Tng. specialist U. Tex., Austin, 1975-76; asst. v.p. BankOdessa (Tex.), 1977-85. Coord. City of Odessa, 1985-85; communications dir. United Way of Midland, 1989—; active mem. United Way of Odessa, 1988—; pres. West Tex. Adult Lit. Coun., Odessa, 1983—; bd. dirs. Child Abuse Prevention Program, Midland, Tex., 1987—. Named Ida Carter Johnson nominee Bus. & Profl. Women, 1984. Mem. Urban Mgmt. Assts. of West Tex., Women's Ctr., Black C. of C.of the

Permian Basin (mgr. spl. events 1984—). Democrat. Baptist. Home: PO Box 2969 Odessa TX 79760 Office: United Way of Midland 1209 W Wall Ave Midland TX 79701

HEARST, RANDOLPH APPERSON, publishing executive; b. N.Y.C., Dec. 2, 1915; s. William Randolph and Millicent (Willson) H.; m. Catherine Campbell, Jan. 12, 1938 (div. Apr. 1982); children: Catherine, Virginia, Patricia, Anne, Victoria; m. Maria C. Scruggs, May 2, 1982 (div. Oct. 1986); m. Veronica de Uribe, July, 1987. Student, Harvard U., 1933-34. Asst. to editor Atlanta Georgian, 1934-38; asst. to pub. San Francisco Call-Bull., 1940-44, exec. editor, 1947-49, pub., 1950-53; asso. pub. Oakland Post-Enquirer, 1946-47; pres., dir., chief exec. officer Hearst Consol. Publs., Inc. and Hearst Pub. Co., Inc., 1961-64; pres. San Francisco Examiner, 1972—; dir. The Hearst Corp., 1965—, chmn. exec. com., 1965-73, chmn., 1973—; Dir. Hearst Found., 1945—, pres., 1972—; dir. Wm. Randolph Hearst Found., 1950—. Served as capt., Air Transport Command USAAF, 1942-45. Roman Catholic. Clubs: Piedmont Driving (Atlanta); Burlingame Country, Pacific Union. Office: The Hearst Corp 110 5th St San Francisco CA 94103 also: The Hearst Corp 959 8th Ave New York NY 10019

HEATH, WILLIAM CHRIS, accountant, financial planning company executive; b. Yuba City, Calif., Mar. 10, 1938; s. William Gordon Heath and Ann Christine (Spitzer) Kelly; m. Linda Lee Goins, Mar. 4, 1978. BS in Edn., U. So.Calif., 1961; postgrad., U. So. Calif., 1963-68; MBA, U. Houston, 1981. Cert. fin. planner. Staff auditor Haskins & Sells, 1967-69; profl. staff auditor Price Waterhouse Co., Houston, 1970-72; salesperson Finger Office Furniture, Houston, 1972-75; pres., chief exec. officer Ctr. for Fin. Planning, Houston, 1972—; mem. faculty Coll. Fin. Planning, Denver, 1983-86; pres. Pecan Grove POA, Richmond, Tex., 1980. Contbr. articles to profl.jours. Mem. Inst. Cert. Fin. Planners (pres., founder Houston soc. 1985-86, chmn. bd. dirs. 1986-87; bd. dirs. ad hoc com. 1984-86), Internat. Assn. for Fin. Planning, LifeTimeOuts (pres. 1978-83), Skull and Dagger, Delta Chi. Office: Ctr for Fin Planning 4800 Sugar Grove Blvd #200 Stafford TX 77477

HEATHCOCK, JOHN HERMAN, manufacturing company executive; b. Jacksonville, Ala., June 20, 1943; s. John Herman and Fallie Mae (Ford) W.; m. Yvonne Larue Sisk, July 31, 1965 (div. Feb. 1974); 1 child, Deven Scott; m. Janice Carol McCrary, Dec. 31, 1974; 1 child, Johnathan Adam. BBA, Jacksonville State U., 1961-65. CPA, Tenn., Ga. Acct.-in-charge Ernst & Whinney, Chattanooga, 1970-72; acctg. mgr., controller Sykland Internat., Chattanooga, 1973-81; controller Riverside Mfg. Co., Moultrie, Ga., 1981-83, Sunkist Soft Drinks, Inc., Atlanta, 1983-85; v.p., controller Del Monte Franchise Beverages (formerly Sunkist Soft Drinks), Atlanta, 1985-86; v.p. ops., chief fin. officer Digital Transmissions Systems Inc., Duluth, Ga., 1986—; fin. cons. Seabrook Blanching, Inc., Albany, Ga., 1983. Served as capt. U.S. Army, 1965-70, Vietnam. Decorated Bronze Star, Air medal; recipient Outstanding Service plaque Riverside Mfg. Co., 1982. Mem. Tenn. State Soc. CPA's, Ga. State Soc. CPA's, Am. Inst. CPA's, Assn. Corp. Growth, The Planning Forum, Fin. Execs. Inst. Republican. Presbyterian. Home: 3932 Millwood Ln Lilburn GA 30247 Office: Digital Transmissions Systems Inc 4830 Rivergreen Pkwy Duluth GA 30136

HEATWOLE, THOMAS CROMER, healthcare executive; b. Heshey, Pa., July 24, 1948; s. Carroll Cromer and Ethel Mae (Deaven) H.; m. Patricia Ann McWilliams, Feb. 25, 1972 (div. 1981); 1 child, Juliet Ann. BS, Shippensburg U., 1972, MBA, 1983. CPA, Pa. Staff acct. R.M. Newbury & Co. CPA's, Camp Hill, Pa., 1973-77; asst. sec.-treas. Presbyn. Homes, Inc., Camp Hill, 1977-89, asst. contr., 1977-89; chief fin. officer United Meth. Homes for Aging Inc., Camp Hill, 1989—; treas. Presbyn. Apts., Inc., Harrisburg, 1982-89. Mem. Am. Inst. CPA's, Pa. Inst. CPA's, Pa. Assn. Non-Profit Homes for Aging, Healthcare Fin. Mgmt. Assn., Susquehanna Ski Club (treas. 1985—). Republican. Presbyterian. Home: 5332 Oxford Dr #101 Mechanicsburg PA 17055 Office: Presbyn Homes Inc 1217 Slate Hill Rd Camp Hill PA 17011

HEBELER, HENRY KOESTER, aerospace and electronics company executive; b. St. Louis, Aug. 12, 1933; s. Henry and Viola O. (Koester) H.; m. Mirriam Robb, Aug. 12, 1978; children by previous marriage: Linda Ruth, Laura Ann. BS in Aero. Engring., MIT, 1956, MS, 1956, MBA, 1970. Gen. mgr. research/engring. Boeing Aerospace Co., Seattle, 1970-72, pres., 1980-85; v.p. bus. devel. The Boeing Co., Seattle, 1973-74, exec. coun. and corp. v.p. planning, 1988—; pres. Boeing Engring. & Constrn. Co., Seattle, 1975-79, Boeing Electronics Co., Seattle, 1985-87; bd. dirs. Microelectronics and Computer Tech. Corp.; mem. fusion panel Ho. of Reps., 1979-81, energy research adv. bd. Dept. Energy, 1980-81, task force on internat. industry Def. Sci. Bd., 1982-84, adv. com. nat. strategic materials and minerals program U.S. Dept. Interior, 1986—. Patentee in field. Bd. govs. Sloan Sch., MIT, 1980-84; bd. visitors Def. Systems Mgmt. Coll., Ft. Belvoir, Va. Recipient Mead prize for aero. engrs., 1956; Kuljian humanities award, 1954; Sperry Gyroscope fellow, 1956; Sloan fellow M.I.T., 1970. Mem. Nat. Aeros. Assn., Assn. of U.S. Army, Armed Forces Communications and Electronics Assn. (bd. dirs.), Aviation Hall of Fame, AIAA, Ala. Space and Rocket Ctr. (sci. and adv. com. 1980-85), Nat. Space (bd. govs. 1980-85). Clubs: Meridian Valley Country, Burning Tree. Home: 13335 SE 243rd Pl Kent WA 98042 Office: Boeing Co PO Box 3707 Seattle WA 98124

HEBNER, PAUL CHESTER, oil company executive; b. Warren, Pa., Dec. 29, 1919; s. Henry G. and Mabel (Gross) H.; m. Dorothy Farrell, Feb. 16, 1943; children—Richard P., Kathleen D., Susan M., Christine L., Elizabeth A., Jeannie M. Acct., adminstrv. asst. Altman-Coady Co., Columbus, Ohio, 1940-41; mgr. acctg., exec. adminstr. T&T Oil Co. (and assoc. cos.), L.A., 1954-57; with Occidental Petroleum Corp., L.A., 1957—, sec.-treas., 1958-68, v.p., sec., 1968-80, exec. v.p., sec., 1980-88, exec. v.p., 1988—, dir., 1960-88, dir. emeritus, 1988—; bd. dir. subs. cos.; sec.-treas., bd. dir. The Armand Hammer United World Coll. of Am. West. Mem. L.A. Beautiful; trustee Calif. Mus. Found. Maj. USAAF, 1942-45. L.S.B. Leakey Found. fellow. Mem. Am. Soc. Corp. Secs., C. of C. (bd. dir. L.A. Bus. Coun.). Home: 12 Amber Sky Dr Rancho Palos Verdes CA 90274 Office: Occidental Petroleum Corp 10889 Wilshire Blvd Los Angeles CA 90024

HECHINGER, JOHN W., JR., home improvement company executive; b. 1950; married. BBA, Boston U., 1972. With Hechinger Co., Landover, Md., 1972—, v.p. real estate devel., from 1982, now pres., chief operating officer, also bd. dirs. Office: Hechinger Co 3500 Pennsy Dr Landover MD 20785 *

HECHINGER, JOHN WALTER, hardware chain executive; b. Washington, Jan. 18, 1920; s. Sidney Lawrence and Sylvia (Frank) H.; m. June Ross, May 26, 1946; children—Nancy, John Walter, S. Ross, Sally. B.S., Yale U., 1941. With Hechinger Co., Landover, Md.; co-chmn., chief exec. officer Hechinger Co., 1958—, also chief exec. officer. Chmn. D.C. City Council, 1967-69; commnr. D.C. Jud. Nominating Com., 1980-87; chmn. Democratic Nat. Com. chpt. D.C., 1972—; rep. UN, from 1978; bd. dirs. Eugene and Agnes Meyer Found., Nat. Urban Coalition, Handgun Control, Inc. Served with USAAF, World War II. Decorated Air medal. Jewish. Office: Hechinger Co 3500 Pennsy Dr Landover MD 20785

HECHT, EMIL, housing and financial company executive; b. Svalava, Czechoslovakia, July 6, 1924; came to U.S., 1951; s. Leopold and Rebeca-Regina (Herskovits) H.; m. Eva Hecht, Jan. 23, 1950; children: Judy H., Jeffrey J. LHD (hon.), U. Denver, 1987. With M.D.C. Holdings, Denver, 1972—, pres., treas., 1972-82, sr. vice chmn., 1986-87, also bd. dirs.; chmn. emeritus M.D.C. Holdings, 1988—; with Omnibancorp, Denver, 1974—, treas., 1974-87, sr. vice chmn., 1987—, also bd. dirs. Bd. dirs. Allied Jewish Fedn., Denver, 1978-89, Anti-Defamation League, Denver, 1982-89; chmn. Maimonides Soc.-Ctr. of Judaic Studies U. Denver, 1982—. Democrat. Office: MDC Holdings Inc 3600 S Yosemite St Suite 900 Denver CO 80237

HECHT, NORMAN SEYMOUR, electronic media, audience analysis, programming company executive; b. Bronx, N.Y., May 8, 1938; s. David Aaron and Annette (Silverman) H.; m. Elaine Eisenberg, May 7, 1958; children: Sharon, Kenneth, Laura. Student in bus. U. Md., 1959-60; BBA, CUNY, 1966; postgrad. in bus. Hofstra U., 1966-67. Media research supr. Grey Advt., N.Y.C., 1961-63; assoc. media dir. Kenyon & Eckhardt, N.Y.C., 1963-65, v.p. media research Gardner Advt., N.Y.C. and St. Louis, 1965-67; v.p., gen. mgr. Arbitron TV, N.Y.C., 1967-80; pres., founder Info. and Analysis, Hicksville, N.Y., 1980-85; pres. AGB TV Research, N.Y.C. and Boston, 1983-85, Nat. Brand Scanning, Inc., N.Y.C., 1986—, Norman Hecht Research Inc., Hicksville, 1987—; cons. Post-Newsweek Stas., Washington, 1980—, Univision, Westinghouse, Multi-media, Cablevision Systems Inc., N.Y.C., 1981—, Albritton Com., Cox Broadcasting, Hearst Broadcasting, HBO, other leading broadcast and cable TV cos. Contbr. articles to mags. With USAF, 1956-59. Mem. Radio/TV Research Council (hon.), Video Research Council-Advt. Research Found., Cable Advt. Bur., Advt. Agy. Media Research Council. Avocations: sailing, investment analysis, reading, cycling.

HECHT, WILLIAM DAVID, accountant; b. N.Y.C., Nov. 7, 1941; s. Adolph J. and Lillian (Shore) H.; m. Francine Rosen, Aug. 22, 1964; children: Peter, Dana, Allison. BS in Acctg., Queens Coll., 1962; JD, Bklyn. Law Sch., 1971; LLM in Taxation, NYU, 1974. Bar: N.Y. 1972. Ptnr., mem. mgmt. com. M. R. Weiser & Co. CPAs, N.Y.C., 1964—; mem. faculty Found. Acctg. Edn., N.Y.C.; lectr. in field. Contbr. articles to CPA Jour. Mem. Am. Inst. CPAs, N.Y. State Soc. CPAs (mem. profl. ethics com.), ABA, N.Y. State Bar Assn. Democrat. Jewish. Home: 8 Tutor Pl East Brunswick NJ 08816 Office: M R Weiser & Co 535 Fifth Ave New York NY 10017

HECKEL, JOHN LOUIS (JACK), aerospace company executive; b. Columbus, Ohio, July 12, 1931; s. Russel Criblez and Ruth Selma (Heid) H.; m. Jacqueline Ann Alexander, Nov. 21, 1959; children: Heidi, Holly, John. B.S., U. Ill., 1954. Div. mgr. Aerojet Divs., Azusa, Calif., 1956-70, Seattle and Washington, 1956-70; pres. Aerojet-Space Gen. Co., El Monte, Calif., 1970-72, Aerojet Liquid Rocket Co., Sacramento, 1972-77; group v.p. Aerojet Sacramento Cos., 1977-81; pres. Aerojet Gen., La Jolla, Calif., 1981-87; chmn., chief exec. officer Aerojet Gen., 1985-87; pres., chief operating officer GenCorp., Akron, 1987—, also bd. dirs.; dir. WD-40 Corp. Bd. dirs. San Diego Econ. Devel. Corp., 1983-86. Recipient Disting. Alumni award U. Ill. Ann. Alumni Conv., 1979. Fellow AIAA (assoc.); mem. Aerospace Industries Assn. Am. (gov. 1981), Navy League U.S., Am. Def. Preparedness Assn., San Diego C. of C. (bd. dirs.). Office: GenCorp 175 Ghent Rd Fairlawn OH 44313-3300

HECKER, DIANE CLEMENTS, facilities engineering administrator; b. Erie, Pa., Sept. 28, 1945; d. Harold Ralph and Ida Marie (Chimenti) C.; div.; 1 child, Rebecca Elizabeth. Student, So. Methodist U., 1969-72, Tulsa Jr. Coll., 1973-74; MBA, Barry U., 1988, BS in Psychology, 1987, postgrad. in bus., 1987—; postgrad. in bus., Nova U., 1987—. Dept. mgr. Neiman Marcus, Dallas, 1965-69; asst. to v.p. mfg. Lowrance Electronics, Tulsa, 1972-74; flight attendant Braniff Internat., Dallas, 1976-82, night mgr., crew scheduler, 1976-82; coordinator for AIDS Research Labs. U. Miami, Fla., 1984-85; adminstr. Cordis Corp., Miami, 1986-88, supr. adminstrv. and tech. ctr., 1988—, co. quality coord., 1988—; bus. mgr. Carrollton Sch. Sacred Heart, Coconut Grove, Fla., 1989—; cons. Valeries and Valeries Too, Abilene, Tex., 1969-76, Stout Fashions, Midland, Tex., 1976—. Vol. Project Literacy for Every Adult in Dade County. Mem. Nat. Acad. Mgmt., So. Acad. Mgmt., Assn. Pers. Adminstrs., Mothers Against Drunk Drivers, Mensa. Republican. Roman Catholic. Club: Miami Runners. Home: 9151-6 Fontainebleau Blvd Miami FL 33172

HECKER, RICHARD, utility executive; b. N.Y.C., Nov. 25, 1930; s. Harry and Gertrude (Hertzberg) H.; m. Sheila Davis, Sept. 6, 1953; children: Philip Davis, Mark Robert. Student, U. Fla., 1948-49; BBA, U. Miami, 1958; MBA, Nova U., 1976; spl. course, Ga. Inst. Tech., 1976. Chmn. exec. bd. Local 359 Internat. Brotherhood Elec. Workers, 1959-65, pres., 1966, sec., 1967-69; supr. labor relations Fla. Power & Light Co., Miami, 1971-76, mgr. workers' compensation, 1976-78, mgr. safety, 1979; mgr. workers' compensation Fla. Power & Light Co., West Palm Beach, Fla., 1980—; mem. Rules adv. com. of self-insurers Fla. Dept. Labor, 1979—, workers compensation council, 1988—. Pres. U.S.O. Council of Dade County, 1980, bd. dirs. 1965. Mem. Am. Soc. Safety Engrs., Am. Soc. Law Medicine, Acad. Trial Lawyers (safety awards com.), Internat. Assn. Indsl. Accidents Bds. and Commns., Southern Assn. Workers Compensation Adminstrs., Assoc. Self Insurers Fla. (pres. 1983-85, bd. dirs. 1986—). Lodges: Masons, Shriners, K.P. Home: 1012 Green Pine Blvd West Palm Beach FL 33409 Office: Fla Power & Light Co 400 N Congress Ave West Palm Beach FL 33402

HECKERT, RICHARD EDWIN, chemical company executive, chemist; b. Oxford, Ohio, Jan. 13, 1924; s. John W. and Winifred E. (Yahn) H.; m. Barbara Kennedy, 1945; children: Alex Y., Andra Heckert Rudershausen. B.A., Miami U., Ohio, 1944; M.S. in Organic Chemistry, U. Ill., 1947, Ph.D. in Organic Chemistry, 1949. With E.I. DuPont de Nemours & Co., 1949—; research chemist E.I. DuPont de Nemours & Co., Wilmington, Del., 1949-54; from supr. cellophane research and devel. lab. film dept. to asst. mgr. lab. E.I. DuPont de Nemours & Co., Richmond, Va., 1954-57, tech. supt. cellophane plant, 1957-58; tech. supt. cellophane plant E.I. DuPont de Nemours & Co., Clinton, Iowa, 1958-59; plant mgr. E.I. DuPont de Nemours & Co., Circleville, Ohio, 1959-63; dir. supporting research and devel. E.I. DuPont de Nemours & Co., Wilmington, 1963-65, asst. gen. mgr. film dept., 1965-67, asst. gen. mgr. plastics dept., 1967-69, gen. mgr. fabrics and finishes dept., 1969-72, v.p., 1972-73, sr. v.p., dir., 1973-81, pres., 1981-85; vice chmn., chief operating officer DuPont Co., Wilmington, 1981-85, dep. chmn., 1985-86, chmn., chief exec. officer, 1986—; bd. dirs. Provident Mut. Life Ins. Co. Phila. Contbr. articles on cyanocarbon chemistry to sci. jours.; patentee in field. Pres. Longwood Gardens, Inc.; dean's assoc. bus. adv. council Miami U. Sch. Bus. Adminstrn.; chmn. bd. trustees Carnegie Instn. of Washington; trustee Del. Council on Econ. Edn., Med. Ctr. Del., Tuskegee U.; bd. dirs. U. Ill. Found, Nat. Action Council for Minorities in Eng.; mem. Bretton Woods Com., bus. adv. com. to Edn. Com. of States, Conf. Bd., Environ. Assessment Council, Gov.'s High Tech. Task Force, fin. com. of Joint Council on Econ. Edn. Served with U.S. Army, 1944-46. Mem. AAAS, NAM (bd. dirs.), Am. Chem. Soc., Bus. Roundtable. Clubs: Pine Valley Golf, Rodney Sq., Wilmington, Vicmead Hunt. Office: E I Du Pont de Nemours & Co 1007 Market St Wilmington DE 19898 *

HECKLER, JOHN MAGUIRE, stock broker; b. Meriden, Conn., Nov. 11, 1927; s. George Ernest and Mary Catherine (Maguire) H.; A.B., Fairfield U., 1951; postgrad. Fordham Law Sch., 1951-53, Harvard Law Sch., 1953-54; m. Sheryl Jean Bills, Nov. 30, 1985; children—Belinda West, Alison Anne, John Maguire. Exec., Maguire Homes, M. W. Maguire, 1954-62; instl. salesman Harris Upham & Co., Boston, 1962-68; resident mgr. Middendorf, Colgate & Co., Boston, 1968-70; chmn., chief exec. officer Boston Instl. Services, Inc., 1971—; dir. Europension Boston Assocs.; chmn. Boston Overseas Services, Inc., Spur Publs., Inc., 1989; mem. N.Y. Stock Exch., 1970—. Campaign asst. Congressman Bradford Morse, 1960. Served with USCG, 1945-47. Republican. Episcopalian. Clubs: Harvard (Boston); MIddleburg and Piedmont (Va.) Hunt; Capitol Hill (Washington); Downtown (Boston). Office: Boston Instl Svcs Inc Kelvedon Atoka Rd Middleburg VA 22117-1772

HECKMAN, HENRY TREVENNEN SHICK, steel company executive; b. Reading, Pa., Mar. 27, 1918; s. H. Raymond and Charlotte E. Shick H.; AB, Lehigh U., 1939; m. Helen Clausen Wright, Nov. 28, 1946; children: Sharon Anita, Charlotte Marie. Advt. prodn. mgr. Republic Steel Corp., Cleve., 1940-42, editor Enduro Era, 1946-51, account exec., 1953-54, asst. dir. advt., 1957-65, dir. advt., 1965-82; partner Applegate & Heckman, Washington, 1955-56; advt. mgr. Harris Corp., 1956-57. Permanent chmn. Joint Com. for Audit Comparability, 1968—; chmn. Media Comparability Council, 1969-83; chmn. indsl. advertisers com. Greater Cleve. Growth Assn., 1973-76; chmn. publs. com. Lehigh U., 1971-76; pres.'s adv. council Ashland Coll., 1966-76; advt. adv. council Kent State U., 1976-81; exec. com. Cleve. chpt. ARC, 1968-74; mem. Republican Fin. Exec. Com., 1966-87; coord. adv. coun. pub. svcs. campaign Employer Support for Guard and Res., 1973-83. Comdr. USNR, 1942-46, 51-53; Korea. Named to Advt. Effectiveness Hall of Fame, 1967; named Advt. Man of Yr., 1969; recipient G.D. Crain, Jr. award, 1973; Disting. Alumnus award Lehigh U., 1979; elected to Cleve. Graphic Arts Council Hall of Distinction, 1981. Mem. Indsl. Marketers Cleve. (past pres., Golden Mousetrap award 1968), Bus./Profl. Advt. Assn. (pres. 1968-69, Best Seller award 1966), Assn. Nat. Advertisers (chmn. shows and exhibits com. 1966-74, dir. 1969-72), Am. Iron and Steel Inst. (com. chmn. 1961-69), Steel Service Center Inst. (advt. adv. com. 1965-77), SAR (pres. 1979), Mil. Order World Wars (comdr. 1980), Early Settlers, Cleve. Advt. Club (pres. 1961-62, Hall of Fame 1980), Center for Mktg. Communications (chmn. bd. 1965), Internat. Platform Assn. Clubs: Cheshire Cheese (pres. 1982), Cleve. Grays (trustee 1980-82), Mid-Day, Cleve. Skating. Home: 375 Bentleyville Rd Chagrin Falls OH 44022

HECKMAN, JAMES JOSEPH, economist, econometrician; b. Chgo., Apr. 19, 1944; s. John Jacob and Bernice Irene (Medley) H.; m. Lynne Pettler, 1979; children: Jonathan Jacob, Alma Rachel. AB in Math. summa cum laude (Woodrow Wilson fellow), Colo. Coll., 1965; MA in Econs, Princeton U., 1968, PhD in Econs. (Harold Willis Dodds fellow), 1971. Lectr. Columbia U., 1970-71, asst. prof. econs., 1971-73, assoc. prof., 1973-74; assoc. prof. econs. U. Chgo., 1974-76, prof., 1976—, Henry Schultz prof. econs., 1985—; rsch. assoc. Nat. Bur. Econs. Rsch., 1970-77, sr. rsch. assoc., 1977-85, 87—; A. Whitney Griswold prof. econs. Yale U., New Haven, 1988—; treas. Chgo. Econ. Rsch. Assocs.; research assoc. Econs. Rsch. Ctr./NORC, 1979-85, rsch. assoc. Quantitative Econs. Group, NORC, 1985—; Irving Fisher prof. econs. Yale U., 1984. cons. in field; fellow Center for Advanced Study in Behavioral Scis., Palo Alto, Calif., 1978-79; cons. Chgo. Urban League, 1978-86; mem. status Black Ams. com. Nat. Rsch. Coun. Author: Impact of the Economy and The State on the Status of Blacks; assoc. editor: Jour. Econometrics, 1977-83; editor: (with B. Singer) Longitudinal Analysis Labor Market Data, 1985, Labor Economics; Am. editor: Rev. Econ. Studies, 1982-85; editor: Jour. Polit. Economy, 1981-87; assoc. editor Econ. Revs., 1987—; contbr. articles to profl. jours. Founding faculty and curriculum com. U. Chgo. Harris Sch. of Pub. Policy. Recipient L. Benezet Alunmi Prize, Colo. Coll., 1985; J.S. Guggenheim fellow, 1978-79; Social Sci. Rsch. Coun. fellow, 1977-78. Fellow Econometric Soc., Am. Acad. Arts and Scis.; mem. Am. Econ. Assn. (John Bates Clark medal 1983), Am. Statis. Assn., Indsl. Rels. Rsch. Assn., Econ. Sci. Assn. (founder), Phi Beta Kappa. Home: 230 Three Corners Rd Guilford CT 06437 Office: Yale U Dept Econ PO Box 1972 Yale Sta New Haven CT 06520

HECKMAN, RICHARD AINSWORTH, chemical engineer; b. Phoenix, July 15, 1929; s. Hiram and Anne (Sells) H.; BS, U. Calif. at Berkeley, 1950, cert. hazardous mgmt. U. Calif., Davis, 1985; m. Olive Ann Biddle, Dec. 17, 1950; children—Mark, Bruce. With radiation lab. U. Calif. at Berkeley, 1950-51; chem. engr. Calif. Research & Devel. Co., Livermore, 1951-53; assoc. div. leader Lawrence Livermore Nat. Lab., Livermore, 1953-77, project leader, 1977-78, program leader, 1978-79, energy policy analyst, 1979-83, toxic waste group staff engr., 1984-86, waste minimization project leader, 1986—; mem. Calif. Radioactive Materials Forum. Bd. dirs. Calif. Industries for Blind, 1977-80, Here and Now Disabled Services for Tri-Valley, Inc., 1980. Registered profl. engr., Calif. Fellow Am. Inst. Chemists, Acad. Hazardous Materials Mgmt.; mem. AAAS, Am. Acad. Environ. Engrs. (diplomate), Am. Chemistry Soc., Am. Inst. Chem. Engrs., Soc. Profl. Engrs., Water Pollution Control Assn., Air Pollution Control Assn., Internat. Union Pure and Applied Chemistry (assoc.), Nat. Hist. Soc., N.Y. Acad. Scis., Am. Nuclear Soc., Better World Soc., Internat. Oceanographic Soc. Clubs: Commonwealth (San Francisco); Island Yacht (Alameda, Calif.) (commodore 1971), Midget Ocean Racing Club (sta. 3 commodore 1982-83), U.S. Yacht Racing Union, Midget Ocean Racing Assn. No. Calif. (commodore 1972). Co-author: Nuclear Waste Management Abstracts, 1983; patentee in field. Home: 5683 Greenridge Rd Castro Valley CA 94552 Office: Livermore Nat Lab PO Box 808 Livermore CA 94550

HEDBERG, ROBERT DANIEL, venture capitalist; b. Portland, Oreg., Mar. 14, 1922; s. John and Emma Sophia (Gronberg) H.; m. Martha Jane Carr, Oct. 27, 1945 (dec.); children: Hanna, John, Sarah; m. Joan Glover Rohner, Mar. 12, 1988. AB in Math., U. Pa., 1946, MS in Banking and Fin., 1947. Mng. gen. partner Hedberg Assoc., Ltd., Paoli, Pa., 1970-83; chmn., dir. Patrician Paper Co., N.Y.C., 1963-79; trustee Patrician Paper Liquidating Trust, 1979-83; bd. dirs. Betz Labs., Inc., Kappe Assos., Inc., Tamaqua Cable Products, Envirite Corp., Stamford Capital Group, Inc., Infocore, Inc.; cons. corp. fin. planning, 1948—; lectr. investments Wharton Grad. div. U. Pa., 1960. Trustee, treas. Brandywine Hosp., 1985—. Mem. Fin. Analysts Fedn. (chmn. 1974-75). Clubs: Racquet (Phila.); Metropolitan (N.Y.C.); Adirondack League (Old Forge, N.Y.); Wedgefield (Georgetown, S.C.); Whitford (Exton, Pa.). Home: 208 N Ship Rd Exton PA 19341 Office: Stamford Capitol Group Inc 14 Paoli Ct Paoli PA 19301

HEDDEN, ALFRED JOHN, savings and loan executive; b. Stirling, N.J., Jan. 8, 1924; s. Alfred J. and Florence (Hearn) H.; m. Catherine E. Egan, Nov. 4, 1950; children: Thomas, Kathleen. Student spl. courses in banking and mgmt., Ind. U., Rutgers and Seton Hall univs., 1965, Dartmouth Coll., 1975, Harvard U., 1980. With City Fed. Savs. & Loan Assn., Elizabeth, N.J., 1952; asst. loan officer, then v.p. and mortgage officer, sr. v.p., chief loan officer, exec. v.p. investments, exec. v.p. adminstrn. City Fed. Savs. & Loan Assn., now City Fed. Savings Bank, Elizabeth, N.J., 1952-79, pres., chief operating officer, 1979-84, pres., dep. chief exec. officer, 1984, pres., chief exec. officer, 1985, chmn., chief exec. officer; dir. City Fed. Savs. Bank, Bedminster, N.J., 1979—; now also pres., chief exec. officer Cityfed Fin. Corp., Palm Beach, Fla.; former dir. Interstate Service Corp. PAMICO, Blue Bell, Pa. Former Vice-chmn. N.J. Higher Edn. Assistance Authority. Served with AUS, 1943-46. Mem. Garden State Savs. and Loan Inst. Republican. Roman Catholic. *

HEDDINGER, FREDERICK MARTIN, SR., publisher; b. Wilkinsburg, Pa., Jan. 31, 1917; s. William McKinley and Helen Cecelia (Kimmel) H.; student Duquesne U., 1937-46; m. Lillian M. Beatty, Sept. 7, 1940; 1 child, Frederick Martin Jr. With Westinghouse Electric, E. Pitts., 1941-52, contract mgr., Pitts., 1952-54, asst. plant mgr., Youngwood, Pa., 1955-64; pres., founder Pa. Electronics Tech., Inc., Pitts., 1964-69; exec. dir. Sch. Bds. Assn., Harrisburg, 1970-82, sec., trustee Ins. Trust, 1971-82; pres., pub. Martin Frederick Inc., Surfside Beach, S.C., 1982—; trustee Pa. Sch. Employees Retirement System, 1970-82. Pres. Wilkinsburg Sch. Bd., 1951-69; vestryman Zion Lutheran Ch., 1975-82; life mem. N. Huntingdon Twp. Vol. Fire Co.; lectr. Dickinson Law Sch. Forum. Named Paul Harris fellow Rotary Internat., 1986. Mem. IEEE, Am. Assn. Sch. Adminstrs., Am. Soc. Assn. Execs., Nat. Orgn. Legal Problems in Edn., Pa. Soc., SCORE, Long Bay Power Squadron. Republican. Methodist. Club: Litchfield Country (Pawleys Island, S.C.). Lodge: Rotary, Shriners, Omar Temple. Co-inventor series electronic games, 1968; author: Handbook on Public Sector Collective Bargaining, 1971; mng. editor School Law Digest, 1970-82; pub. Kwik-Fax Books, 1983—.3 . Office: Martin Frederick Inc PO Box 14613 Surfside Beach SC 29587

HEDGE, JEANNE COLLEEN, health physicist; b. Scottsburg, Ind., May 30, 1960; d. Paul Russell and Barbara Jean (Belshaw) H. BS in Environ. Health, Purdue U., 1983. Technician chemistry and health physics Marble Hill Nuclear Generating Sta., Pub. Service Ind., Madison, 1983-84; asst. radiation protection Hope Creek Generating Sta., Pub. Service Electric & Gas Co., Hancock's Bridge, N.J., 1984-85, technician radiation protection, 1985-89; health physicist Pub. Service Electric & Gas Co., Hancock's Bridge, 1989—; mem. People to People Internat. Citizen Ambassador Exchange, People's Republic China, 1988. Mem. AAAS, NOW, Am. Nuclear Soc. (assoc.), Health Physics Soc. (plenary mem.), N.Y. Acad. Scis., Tau Beta Sigma (sec. Purdue U. chpt. 1980-81). Democrat. Methodist.

HEDGES, CHARLES FREDRICK, JR., lawyer, petroleum landman; b. Midland, Tex., Oct. 6, 1951; s. Charles Fredrick Sr. and C. Marjorie Frances (Osborn) H.; m. Lee Ann Kay Burke, Feb. 17, 1980; children: Ashley Ann, John David. BS, U. Tex., Austin, 1973; JD, U. Tex., 1976; postdoctoral, London Sch. Econs., 1976. Bar: Tex. 1977, Colo. 1977. Assoc. Ernest S. Baker, Denver, 1976-78, Gorsuch, Kirgis, Campbell, Walker & Grover, Denver, 1979-80; gen. counsel BWAB Inc., Denver, 1980-84; gen. counsel Tom Brown Inc., Midland, Tex., 1984-86, v.p., gen. counsel, 1986—. Mem. ABA, Tex. Bar Assn., Colo. Bar Assn., Denver Bar Assn., Am. Corp. Counsel Assn. Democrat. Episcopalian. Home: 2106 Wydewood Midland TX 79707 Office: Tom Brown Inc PO Box 2608 Midland TX 79707

HEDIEN, WAYNE EVANS, insurance company executive; b. Evanston, Ill., Feb. 15, 1934; s. George L. and Edith P. (Chalstrom) H.; m. Colette Johnston, Aug. 24, 1963; children: Mark, Jason, Georgiana. BSME, Northwestern U., 1956, MBA, 1957. Engr. Cook Electric Co., Skokie, Ill., 1957-64; bus. mgr. Preston Sci., Inc., Anaheim, Calif., 1964-66; security analyst Allstate Ins. Co., Northbrook, Ill., 1966-70, portfolio mgr., 1970-73, asst. treas., 1973-78, v.p., treas., 1978-80, sr. v.p., treas., 1980-83, exec. v.p., chief fin. officer, 1983-85, vice chmn., chief fin. officer, 1986, pres., 1986-89, chmn., chief exec. officer, 1989—, also bd. dirs. Mem. adv. coun. Kellogg Grad. Sch. of Mgmt. Northwestern U. Mem. Inst. Chartered Fin. Analysts (chartered fin. analyst), Newcomen Soc., Econ. Club. Office: Allstate Ins Co Allstate Pla Northbrook IL 60062

HEDIGER, GARY RODDY, property management company executive; b. Elmhurst, Ill., Aug. 7, 1944; s. Adolph M. and Alice Ann (Harrison) H.; m. Gail Marie Hagerty, Apr. 15, 1967; children: Catherine Marie, Carolyn Ann, Christine Michelle, Cynthia Gail. BBA, U. Notre Dame, 1966. Property mgr. Baird and Warner Real Estate Co., Chgo., 1969-71; regional v.p. Kassuba Devel. Corp., Chgo., 1971-73; exec. v.p. U.S. Shelter Corp., Greenville, S.C., 1973—. Bd. dirs. Irish Children's Summer Program, Greenville. Served to lt. USN, 1966-69, Vietnam. Mem. Nat. Multi Housing Council (bd. dirs.), S.C. Inst. Real Estate Mgmt. (pres. 1978), Inst. Real Estate Mgmt. (governing council). Republican. Roman Catholic. Office: US Shelter Corp One Shelter Place PO Box 1089 Greenville SC 29602

HEDLEY, DAVID VAN HOUTEN, investment banker; b. West Chester, Pa., Dec. 21, 1945; s. David Hartas and Helen (Peveril) H.; BA, Upsala Coll., 1968; m. Michele Michaels, Sept. 9, 1967; children—David Van Houten III, Melissa Michele, Peter Caleb. With investment banking div. E.F. Hutton & Co., Inc., N.Y.C., 1968-80; mng. dir., dir. utility fin. Shearson/Am. Express Inc., N.Y.C., 1980-85, corp. dir., 1984-85, also bd. dirs. 1984-85; mng. dir. utility fin. Drexel Burnham, Lambert, 1985—, corp. fin. exec. commn., 1989—. Trustee, Morristown-Beard Sch., 1979—, chmn. 1985-88; active Pete Dawkins for U.S. Sen. Fin. Com. With Army N.G., 1970-76. Mem. N.Y. Soc. Security Analysts. Club: Morris County Golf, Edgartown Yacht, Essex Hunt. Home: Spruce Hill Farm Hardscrabble Rd Mendham NJ 07945 Office: Drexel Burnham Lambert 60 Broad St New York NY 10004

HEDLEY, ROBERT PEVERIL, natural resource company executive; b. Orange, N.J., Aug. 23, 1937; s. David H. and Helen (Peveril) H.; m. Barbara A. King, July 25, 1959; children—Jon P., Susan A., Kenneth G. A.B., Dartmouth Coll., 1959; M.B.A., Amos Tuck Sch., 1960. Mem. exec. tng. program Colgate Palmolive Co., N.Y.C., 1960-63; fin. analyst Texasgulf, Inc., N.Y.C., 1963-65, asst. treas., N.Y.C. and Stamford, Conn., 1965-81, treas., Stamford, Conn., 1981, v.p., treas., 1981—; v.p., treas. Elf Aquitaine, Inc., 1983—; dir. Elf Aquitaine Fin. U.S.A. Inc., Mem. Soc. Internat. Treas., Newcomen Soc., Fairchester Treas. Group. Republican. Clubs: Landmark, Woodway Country (Darien, Conn.). Home: 56 Rilling Ridge New Canaan CT 06840 Office: Elf Aquitaine Inc High Ridge Pk Box 10037 Stamford CT 06904

HEDMAN, FREDERICK ALVIN, accountant, lawyer; b. Evansville, Ind., July 29, 1937; s. Fritz Algot and Marjorie Eugenia (Copenhaver) H. BS in Acctg., U. Balt., 1963, JD, 1969. Bar: Md. 1974, U.S. Supreme Ct. 1980. Operating acct. HUD, Washington, 1964—; sole practice, Bel Air, Md., 1974—. Recipient Silver award Boy Scout Am., N.Y.C., 1955. Mem. Assn. Govt. Accts. (bd. dirs. Montgomery-Prince Georges chpt. 1983—, Certs. of Merit 1977-88, Unsung Hero award 1979), Md. State Bar Assn., Harford County Bar Assn. Republican. Methodist. Home: 218 Fulford Ave Bel Air MD 21014 Office: HUD 451 7th St SW Washington DC 20410

HEDRICK, LOIS JEAN, investment company executive, state official; b. Topeka, Kans., Jan. 25, 1927; d. Arthur Lenard and Nellie Cecelia (Johnson) Lungstrum; m. Clayton Newton Hedrick, Apr. 26, 1949; 1 dau., Carol Beth. Cert., Strickler's Bus. Coll., 1947; student Washburn U., Topeka, 1980-83. Staff sec. Kans. State Senate, Topeka, 1946-65; co-owner Hedrick's Market, Topeka, 1953-67; exec. sec. to sr. legal counsel Security Benefit Life Ins. Co., Topeka, 1963-73; asst. corp. sec. Security Mgmt. Co., Topeka, 1973—, Security Distbrs. Inc., SBL Planning Inc., SBL Fund, Security Action Fund, Security Equity Fund, Security Investment Fund, Security Ultra Fund, Security Bond Fund, Security Cash Fund, Security OmniFund, Security Tax-Exempt Fund, Security Benefit Group, Ins., Security Mgmt. Co.; mgmt. cons. United Way of Greater Topeka, 1981—, mem. pub. relations staff, 1982—, rep. precinct woman. Organizer, chmn. Topeka Crime Blockers, 1976—; vol. fundraiser Am. Heart Assn., Stermont-Vail Hosp. Expansion, 1976-77; chmn. Plant a Tree for Century III, 1976; mem. Greater Topeka Career Edn. Com., 1981—; staff sec., fundraiser Christian Rural Overseas Program, 1951, staff sec. USAF Supply Depot, 1951-53. Named Woman of Year, Am. Bus. Women's Assn., 1970; Sec. of Yr., Profl. Secs. Inc., 1975. Mem. Greater Topeka C. of C. (chmn. edn. com. 1981—, ambassador chmn. high sch. honors banquet, 1982—), Adminstrv. Mgmt. Soc. (dir., pres. 1976—). Republican. Home: 1556 SW 24th St Topeka KS 66611

HEEBNER, ALBERT GILBERT, economist, banker, educator; b. Phila., Mar. 7, 1927; s. Albert and Julia (Zwada) H.; m. Dorothy Mae Kiler, Aug. 16, 1952. A.B., U. Denver, 1948; A.M., U. Pa., 1950, Ph.D., 1967. Instr. econs. Coll. of Wooster, Ohio, 1950-52; with Phila. Nat. Bank subs. Core-States Fin. Corp, 1952-87, economist, 1960-87, asst. v.p., 1961-64, v.p., 1964-70, sr. v.p., 1970-73, exec. v.p., 1973-83; exec. v.p., chief economist Core-States Fin. Corp., Phila., 1983-87; Disting. prof. econs. Eastern Coll., St. David's Pa., 1987—; lectr. in fin. Wharton Sch., U. Pa., 1968-69; spl. asst. to chmn. Council Econ. Advisers, Washington, 1971-72; vis. prof. econs. Swarthmore (Pa.) Coll., 1976; adj. prof. econs. Eastern Coll., St. Davids, Pa., 1982; chmn. econ. adv. com. Am. Bankers Assn., 1978-80; bd. dirs. Nat. Bur. Econ. Rsch., 1983-85; bd. dirs. Global Interdependence Ctr. Author: Negotiable Certificates of Deposit: The Development of a Money Market Instrument, 1969. Served with USNR, 1945-46. Mem. Am. Econ. Assn., Am. Finance Assn., Nat. Assn. Bus. Economists (pres. 1975-76), Conf. Bus. Economists (chmn. 1987-88), Nat. Bur. Econ. Rsch. (bd. dirs. 1983-85). Baptist. Club: Sunday Breakfast (Phila.). Home: 2 Etienne Arbordeau Berwyn Baptist Rd Devon PA 19333 Office: Ea Coll Dept Econs & Bus Adminstrn Saint Davids PA 19087 also: Phila Nat Bank Broad & Chestnut Sts Philadelphia PA 19101-7618

HEEBNER, DAVID RICHARD, technology company executive; b. Hackensack, N.J., Feb. 27, 1927; s. Walter M. and Anne I. (Mountain) H.; m. Marilyn K. Thomte, Sept. 23, 1950; children—Richard, Karen, Kim, Kathleen. A.A., Fairleigh Dickinson U., 1948; B.S.E.E., Newark Coll. Engring., 1950; M.S.E.E., U. So. Calif., 1955. Systems engr. Hughes Aircraft Co., Fullerton, Calif., 1953-60; mgr. Navy systems lab. Hughes Aircraft Co., 1961-68; cons. Nat. Acad. Scis., Washington, 1960-61; asst. dir. sea warfare Office of Sec. of Def., Washington, 1968-70; dep. dir. def. research and engring. Office of Sec. of Def., 1970-75; exec. v.p., vice chmn. bd. Sci. Applications Internat. Corp., San Diego, 1975—; dir. Def. Systems, Inc., McLean, Va.; mem. Def. Sci. Bd., 1987—. Adviser on editorial policy Jour. Def. Research, 1970-75, mem. edit. bd., 1980-86. Served to lt. (j.g.) USN, 1951-53. Decorated Meritorious Civilian Service medal 1975; Comdr.'s Cross of Order of Merit (Fed. Republic Germany); recipient cert. merit for work in antisubmarine warfare NSIA, 1966, Navy Superior Pub. Service award, 1986. Fellow IEEE, AIAA (assoc. fellow); mem. Assn. Unmanned Vehicle Systems (pres. 1976-77, chmn. bd. trustees 1977-78, trustee 1980-83, hon. trustee 1983—), Am. Def. Preparedness Assn. (Bronze medallion for leadership def. R & D 1975), Acad. Model Aeronautics. Republican. Home: 8120 Dunsinane Ct McLean VA 22102 Office: Sci Applications Internat Corp 1710 Goodridge Dr McLean VA 22102

HEENAN, PATRICK MICHAEL, wholesale distribution company executive, consultant; b. Joliet, Ill., Nov. 3, 1946; s. Francis Howard and Ann Marie (Rita) H.; m. Sharon Lynn Eisman, Aug. 17, 1975; children: Lauren, Adam. BA, Coll. St. Thomas, 1968; MBA, No. Ill. U., 1974. Cost acct. electromotivediv. GM, LaGrange, Ill., 1969-73; mgmt. cons. Touche Ross & Co., Mpls., 1974-77; ops. analyst Gould, Inc., Rolling Meadows, Ill., 1977-78; plant controller Gould, Inc., Kankakee, Ill., 1978-80; controller, chief fin. officer Kankakee Indsl. Supply Co., 1980-85, v.p. ops., 1985-87; v.p., gen. mgr. Darter, Inc. (formerly Kankakee Indsl. Supply Co.), University Park, Ill., 1987—. Bd. dirs. Sch. Dist. #111, Kankakee, 1986. With U.S. Army, 1969-71. Recipient Cert. Appreciation Am. Prodn. and Inventory Control Soc., 1986. Mem. Nat. Assn. Accts. (v.p. membership 1985-86). Roman Catholic. Office: Darter Inc 1050 Central Ave University Park IL 60466

HEER, EDWIN LEROY, insurance executive; b. American Falls, Idaho, Aug. 19, 1938; s. Edwin Frederick and Kathryn Irene (Franks) H; m. Jacqulin S. Jefford, May 23, 1960 (div. Mar. 1978); 1 child, Kevin Jack; m. Judith Lee Overton-Jones, Jan. 2, 1980. BS, U. Alaska, 1963; MBA, St. Mary's U. Tex., San Antonio, 1976. Asst. actuary Aetna Life & Casualty Co., Hartford, Conn., 1963-68; assoc. actuary Ins. Co. of N.Am., Phila., 1968-72; asst. v.p. USAA, San Antonio, 1972-78; v.p., corp. actuary W.R. Berkley Corp., Greenwich, Conn., 1978—; bd. dirs. Union Standard Ins. Co., Dallas. Fellow Casualty Actuarial soc.; mem. Am. Acad. Actuaries, Soc. Chartered Property Casualty Underwriters (cert.). Republican. Lutheran. Home: 44 Strawberry Hill Ave Stamford CT 06902 Office: W R Berkley Corp 165 Mason St Greenwich CT 06830

HEER, WILLIAM CHARLES, graphics company executive; b. Columbus, Ohio, Apr. 20, 1921; s. William Charles Heer Sr. and Hilda (Kemery) Herbst; m. Barbara Anna Mitcheltree, Oct. 8, 1958; children: Betsy, William C. III. BS in Printing Mgmt., Carnegie Tech. Inst., 1943. V.p., treas. F.J. Heer Printing Co., Columbus, 1943-68; v.p. Nat. Graphics Corp., Columbus, 1968—; bd. dirs., treas. Scioto Downs Inc., Columbus. Democrat. Congregationalist. Clubs: Columbus Country. Home: 124 Ashbourne Rd Columbus OH 43209-1451 Office: Nat Graphics Corp PO Box 719 Columbus OH 43216

HEFFELBOWER, DWIGHT EARL, engineering services company executive; b. Newton, Kans., Aug. 28, 1925; s. Fred Clifford and Ruby Esther (Garrison) H.; m. Darlene Dorey, Feb. 1, 1948; children: Darl Jay, Kent Lewis, Gail Marie. B.S. in Chem. Engring., Kans. State U., 1949; student, Presbyn. Coll. of S.C., 1943. Engr. Burlington AEC plant Mason & Hanger-Silas Mason Co., Inc., Burlington, Iowa, 1949-56; chief engr. Mason & Hanger-Silas Mason Co., Inc., 1956-63, plant mgr. Iowa Army Ammunition plant, 1963-73; v.p. Mason & Hanger-Silas Mason Co., Inc., Lexington, Ky., 1973-80; exec. v.p. ops. Mason & Hanger-Silas Mason Co., Inc., Lexington, 1980-86; pres. Mason & Hanger-Silas Mason Co., Inc., 1986—, also dir., 1975—; v.p. Mason Co., 1986-87, pres., 1987—, also bd. dirs.; chmn. bd. Mason Chamberlain Inc., Picayune, Miss., pres., 1976-87; chmn. bd. DWC Computer Solutions Inc., Lexington, MCE, Inc.; bd. dirs. Mahco Inc., Mason & Hanger Nat., Inc., Huntsville, Ala., Electronics, Inc., Clute, Tex.; mem. external adv. com. Los Alamos Nat. Lab. M-Div.; mem. Dept Energy Weapons Intelligence Panel, 1983, Indsl. Com. of Ammunition Producers, 1983; chmn. bd. Mason Chamberlain Inc., 1986—, pres., 1976-86. Named hon. Ky. Col. 2d lt. USAAF, 1943-45. Mem. Am. Def. Preparedness Assn. (adv. bd. dirs. 1978—), Lexington C. of C. Home: 1894 Parkers Mill Rd Lexington KY 40504 Office: Mason & Hanger-Silas Mason Co Inc 200 W Vine St Lexington KY 40507

HEFFNER, RALPH H., agricultural products company executive; b. 1938. Farmer Jersey Acres Farm Inc., Pine Grove, Pa.; formerly vice chmn. Agway Inc., now chmn.; bd. dirs. Curtice-Burns Foods Inc. Office: Agway Inc Box 4933 Syracuse NY 13221 *

HEFFNER, RICHARD LOUIS, business consultant; b. St. Louis, Apr. 9, 1933; s. Edward Louis and Esther (Herter) H.; AB, Columbia, 1955; MBA cum laude, U. Tenn., 1965; m. Charlotte Anne Maclellan, Sept. 2, 1961; children—Richard Louis, Thomas Maclellan. Asst. advt. mgr. Richardson-Vicks, Inc., 1957-60; new products market mgr. Chattem Drug & Chem. Co., 1960-64; v.p. mktg. and corp. planning Dorsey Corp., 1964-69; dep. adminstr. Bus. and Def. Svcs. Adminstrn., U.S. Dept. Commerce, 1969-70; chief exec. officer, dir. Chattanooga Glass Corp., subs. Dorsey Corp., 1970-73; exec. v.p. Hamilton Bancshares, Inc., 1973-75; regional secretarial rep. of Sec. Commerce for 8 Southeastern states U.S. Dept. Commerce, 1975-77, mem. Fed. Regional Council, 1975-77; mgmt. cons., 1977-81; pres., dir. Guinness Peat Fin. Svcs., Inc., 1981-82; vice chmn., bd. dir. Guinness Mahon Inc., 1982-83; founder Heffner and Co., 1983—. Regional chmn. Rep. Nat. Fin. Com., 1979-81; bd. dirs. Chattanooga Tb and Respiratory Diseases Assn., 1962-76, pres., 1969-70. Lt. USNR, 1955-57. Mem. Nat. Alliance Businessmen (met. chmn. 1970-71). Home: 3655 Randall Hall NW Atlanta GA 30327 Office: 235 Peachtree St NE Ste 1618 Atlanta GA 30303

HEFFNER, WILLIAM JOSEPH, investment executive; b. Balt., Dec. 6, 1928. BS, Johns Hopkins U., 1961; JD, Mt. Vernon Sch. Law, 1967. V.p. Merc. Safe Deposit & Trust Co., Balt., 1965-74; pres. Redwood Capital Mgmt., Balt., 1974-86, Mt. Vernon Assocs. Inc., Balt., 1986—; bd. dirs. Triangle Industries, Am. Nat. Can. Mem. Nat. Economists, Fin. Analysts Fedn., Indsl. Relations Council. Club: Balt. Country.

HEFNER, CHRISTIE A., international media and marketing executive; b. Chgo., Nov. 8, 1952; d. Hugh Marston and Mildred Marie (Williams) H.; BA summa cum laude in English and Am. Lit., Brandeis U., 1974. Freelance journalist, Boston, 1974-75; spl. asst. to pres. Playboy Enterprises, Inc., Chgo., 1975-78, v.p., 1978-82, bd. dirs., 1979—, vice chmn., 1986-88, pres. 1982-88, chief oper. officer, 1984-88, chmn., chief exec. office, 1988—; bd. dirs. Playboy Found.-Playboy Enterprises, Inc., Ill. chpt. ACLU. Recipient Agness Underwood award Los Angeles chapter Women in Communications, 1984, Founders award Midwest Women's Ctr., 1986, Human Rights award Am. Jewish Com., 1987, Spirit of Life award City of Hope, 1988. Mem. Brandeis Nat. Women's Com. (life); mem. Com. of 200, Young. Pres. Orgn., Chgo. Network, Voters for Choice, Direct Mktg. Assn. (editorial bd.), Nat. Women's Polit. Caucus, Goodman Theatre, Phi Beta Kappa. Democrat. Office: Playboy Enterprises Inc 919 N Michigan Ave Chicago IL 60611

HEFTY, DUANE SEYMORE, management consultant; b. St. Johns, Mich., Dec. 4, 1923; s. Harley E. and Marian G. (Norton) H.; m. Shirley J. Kennedy, Aug. 30, 1947; children: Diane, Paula, Andrea, Britton, Tracy. BS in Mech. Engring., U. Wis., 1946. Chief engr. Chamberlin Products, Detroit, 1946-50; plant mgr. Chamberlin Products, South Whitley, Ind., 1950-53, v.p. mfg., 1953-58, v.p., gen. mgr., 1958-61; dir. ops. Essex Wire Co., Detroit, 1961-73, United Tech., Detroit, 1973-74; v.p. automotive elec. products div. ITT, Detroit, 1974-80; mgmt. cons. pvt. practive Detroit, 1980-83, Traverse City, Mich., 1988—; pres. Fenwick/Woodstream, Westminster, Calif., 1983-88. Active Mizpah Temple, Ft. Wayne, Ind. Ensign USNR, 1943-46, PTO. Mem. Am. Legion, VFW, Lochmoor Country Club, A-GA-Ming Country Club, Mason. Home and Office: Rte 1 Box 312 Rapid City MI 49676

HEGEMAN, JAMES ALAN, corporate executive; b. Indpls., Jan. 8, 1943; s. Frank Anderson and Helene Anna (Sudbrock) H.; BS in Acctg. cum laude, U. Tenn., 1973; MBA, Harvard U., 1975. CPA, Tenn.; m. Catherine Louise Mallers, May 1, 1966 (div. 1973); 1 child, Christopher Scott; m. Janet Lee Scherf Nystrom, May 24, 1986. Pres., chmn. Nat. Rent-A-Cycle, Inc., Indpls., 1964-68, Fairfield Electronics Corp., Indpls., 1965-68; gen. mgr. H & R Block, Inc., Knoxville, Tenn., 1967-73; asst. contr. Rohm & Haas, Inc., Knoxville, 1973-75; v.p. Gerson Co., Middleboro, Mass., 1975-76; contr. Acton Corp. (Mass.), 1976-79; chief exec. officer Acton Films, Inc., N.Y.C., Telaction Phone Corp., Palisades Park, N.J., 1976—; corp. contr. Golden Eye Seafoods, Inc., New Bedford, Mass., 1977-78; chief fin. officer Simon Konover & Assocs., K&P Mgmt., Inc., Anthony Assocs. (all West Hartford, Conn.), 1978-79; v.p. fin. Audio Specialists, Inc. and Sound Playground, Newington, Conn., 1979—; fin./mgmt. cons. Standex Internat. Corp., Salem, N.H., 1979-84; chief cons. APC Skills Co., Palm Beach, Fla., Alexander Proudfoot Co., Chgo., 1984; chief fin. officer State St. Technologies, Hartford, Conn., 1984—; pres. LWC Industries, Inc., Miami, Fla., also dir.; treas., dir. Kenmore Rd. Assn., 1987—; bd. dirs. Window Corp. Am. Mem. Ind. Rep. Cen. Com., 1967-68; bd. govs. U. Tenn., 1975-79; named to Tenn. gov.'s staff Tenn. Col. Continental Grain Co. Fellow, 1973; Cabot fellow, 1974. Mem. Am. Film Inst., Am. Inst. CPA's, Tenn. Soc. CPA's, U. Tenn. Alumni Assn. (pres.), Wally Byam Caravan Club Internat. (bd. dir. 1988, v.p. region I), Beta Alpha Psi. Lutheran. Club: Harvard (Boston). Home: 58 Kenmore Rd Bloomfield CT 06002

HEGGEM, MARK FRANCIS, banker; b. Cin., Sept. 2, 1958; s. David James and Mary Frances (Rank) H.; m. Julie Ann Dieckman, Mar. 15, 1986; 1 child, Jenna Lynne. BBA in Fin. and Mktg., U. Cin., 1981; MBA in Fin., Xavier U., 1987. Assoc. portfolio mgr., analyst trust div. Star Bank, N.A., Cin., 1981-83, portfolio mgr., trust div., 1983-85, coordinator strategic and fin. planning trust div., 1985-87, asst. v.p. pvt. banking, 1987—. Solicitor ann. bus. campaign U. Cin., 1983—; account mgr. United Way, Cin., 1986-88; advisor Ptnrs. in Edn.,Cin., 1987—. Mem. Am. Inst. Banking (v.p. edn. Cin. chpt. 1987-88, pres.-elect 1988—), Internat. Assn. Fin. Planners. Office: Star Bank N A 425 Walnut St ML 9215 Cincinnati OH 45202

HEGGEN, ARTHUR WILLIAM, insurance company executive; b. Eureka, Calif., Aug. 9, 1945; s. Arlo Murray and Edna Marie (Nelson) H.; m. Betty Louise Roddy, Nov. 21, 1970; children: Cherilyn, Christopher. BS in Indsl Adminstrn., Acctg., Iowa State U., 1967. CPA, Iowa, Fla.; chartered property and casualty underwriter. Audit staff mgr. Ernst & Whinney, Des Moines, 1971-84; sr. v.p., treas. Am. Bankers Ins. Co., Miami, Fla., 1984—. Bd. dirs. Metro Dade YMCA, Miami; pres. Iowa Ptnrs. of the Yucatan, Des Moines, 1984; pres., treas. Des Moines Hearing Speech Ctr., 1976-82. Served to capt. USMC, 1967-70, Vietnam. Fellow Life Mgmt. Inst.; mem. AICPA, Soc. Chartered Property and Casualty Underwriters, Fla. Inst. CPAs. Office: Am Bankers Ins Group 11222 Quail Roost Dr Miami FL 33157

HEGGIE, STEVEN WAYNE, banker; b. Louisville, Dec. 20, 1962; s. Niles Warren and Aureda Gale (Shofner) H. With various Citizens Fidelity Corp., Louisville, 1982-87, info. specialist, 1987—. Baptist. Home: 1219 Bourbon Ave Louisville KY 40213 Office: Citizens Fidelity Corp 500 W Jefferson Louisville KY 40296

HEID, KEVIN KEITH, financial analyst; b. Urbana, Ill., Mar. 18, 1958; s. Kermit Keith William and Thelma Irene (Warford) H.; m. Mary Therese Lewis, Dec. 19, 1981; children: Matthew Keith, Christopher Alan. AS in Bus., Lincoln Land Community Coll., 1979; BS in Fin. and Econs., Ill. State U., 1981. Sales rep. Nat. LIfe Vt., Bloomington, Ill., 1981-82; pres. Profl. Planners, Inc., Bloomington, 1982-84; investor services specialist Champion Fed. Savs. and Loan, Bloomington, 1984—; adj. faculty Coll. Fin. Planning, Denver, 1985—; research cons. Ill. Recreation Council, Bloomington, 1979-81. Mem. Inst. Cert. Fin. Planners, Internat. Assn. Fin. Planning, Nat. Assn. Life Underwriters, Ill. State U. Alumni Assn. (bd. dirs. 1982—, v.p. 1987—). Republican. Home: 9 Cove Pointe Ct Bloomington IL 61704 Office: Champion Fed Savs and Loan Assn 115 E Washington St Bloomington IL 61701

HEIDARIAN, KAMBIZ, electrical engineer; b. Kermanshah, Iran, Sept. 11, 1955; came to U.S., 1978; s. Shirali Heidarian and Aghdas Bonyadi; m. Susan Heidarian, Sept. 5, 1985. BSEE, U. Tex., Arlington, 1980, MSEE, 1981; PhD in Elec. Engring., So. Meth. U., 1987. Teaching asst. U. Tex., Arlington, 1981-82; instr. Dallas Community Coll., Irving, Tex., 1982; software engr. Scientific Machines Corp., Dallas, 1982-83; circuit designer United Technologies Mostek, Carrollton, Tex., 1983-84; staff technical specialist United Technical Moster, Carrollton, Tex., 1984-85; mem. tech. staff Electrospace Systems, Richardson, Tex., 1985-87; sr. elec. engr. Teleco Oilfield, Meriden, Conn., 1987-88, project engr., 1988—. Mem. IEEE (communication soc., ASSP soc., automatic control soc., info. theory soc.). Home: PO Box 534 Marion CT 06444 Office: BNR 1150 E Arapaho Rd Richardson TX 75081

HEIDE, THOMAS ROBERT, management consultant; b. Bklyn., Nov. 20, 1949; s. Victor and Eleanor (Mulhearn) H.; m. Darlene Ann Ryan, Jan. 4, 1974; children: Ryan, David, Erin. BS in Mktg., Fairfield U., 1971; MBA, Adelphi U., 1978. CLU. Sales rep., sales mgr. Met. Life Ins. Co., Westwood, N.J., 1971-74; account exec. Johnson & Higgins, Inc., N.Y.C., 1974-77; nat. mktg. specialist Merrill Lynch & Co., N.Y.C., 1978; v.p. Alexander & Alexander, Inc., Greenwich, Conn., 1979-80; pres., chief exec. officer Fin. Mktg. Svcs., Inc., Stamford, Conn., 1980-84; pres., chief oper. officer Security Vault Assocs., Greenwich, Conn., 1984-86; pres., chief exec. officer Vault Plus Ltd., Greenwich, 1986—; mgmt. cons. Sun Mark Capital, Inc., St. Louis, 1984-86, Friedberg Properties, Inc., N.Y.C., 1986—, The Camac Group, Greenwich, 1988—; pres., dir. CLU's of Fairfield Co., 1981-83. Contbr. articles to profl. jours. Pres., dir. Glenhaven Condominium Assn., Stamford, Conn., 1977-80. Mem. Nat. Assn. Securities Dealers. Roman Catholic. Home: 66 Woodway Rd Stamford CT 06907 Office: Vault Plus Ltd 1212 E Putnam Ave Riverside CT 06878

HEIDENRICH, CANDACE, chocolate manufacturing company owner; b. L.A., Dec. 1, 1955; d. Ward Henry Heidenrich and Connie Marie (Peterson) Smith. BA magna cum laude, Coll. of Idaho, 1978; postgrad. in edn., Calif. State U., Long Beach, 1980; postgrad., U. So. Calif., 1982, Otis Parsons Sch. Design, L.A., 1983-88. Tchr. English and theater arts Anaheim (Calif.) Unio High Sch. Dist., 1978-82; dir. rsch. and coll. grad. program Stanley, Barber, Southard, Brown & Assocs., Newport Beach, Calif., 1982-84; gen. mgr. St. Moritz Luxury Chocolates, Beverly Hills, Calif., 1984-88; with Butler's Fine Foods, L.A., 1988—. Mem. Women's Bldg. Home: 691 S Irolo St #1202 Los Angeles CA 90005 Office: Butlers Fine Foods 3377 Wilshire Blvd # 102-17 Los Angeles CA 90010

HEIDER, JON VINTON, lawyer, corporate executive; b. Moline, Ill., Mar. 1, 1934; s. Raymond and Doris (Hinch) H.; m. Barbara L. Bond, Dec. 27, 1960 (div.); children: Loren P., John C., Lindsay L.; m. Mary M. Murray, Jan. 27, 1984. A.B., U. Wis., 1956; J.D., Harvard U., 1961; grad., Advanced Mgmt. Program, 1974. Bar: Pa. 1962, U.S. Dist. Ct. for Eastern Dist. Pa 1962, U.S. 3d Circuit Ct 1962. Assoc. Morgan Lewis & Bockius, Phila., 1961-66; counsel Catalytic, Inc., Phila., 1966-68, Houdry Process & Chem. Co., Phila., 1968-70; counsel chems. group Air Products & Chems., Inc., Valley Forge, Pa., 1970-75, asst. gen. counsel, 1975-76, assoc. gen. counsel, 1976-78; gen. counsel Air Products & Chems., Inc., Allentown, Pa., 1978-80; v.p. corp. affairs, sr. adminstrv. officer-Europe Air Products Europe, Inc., London, 1980-83; v.p. corp. devel. Air Products & Chems., Inc., 1983-84; v.p., gen. counsel BF Goodrich Co., Akron, Ohio, 1984-88, sr. v.p., gen. counsel, 1988—. Trustee St. Thomas Health Corp., St. Thomas Med. Ctr., St. Thomas Found., Akron Regional Devel. Bd.; mem. Akron Art Mus. Served to lt. USNR, 1956-58. Mem. Assn. Gen. Counsel. Club: The Board Room (N.Y.C.); Portage Country (Akron): Union (Cleve.). Home: 2440 Stockbridge Rd Akron OH 44313 Office: B F Goodrich Co 3925 Embassy Pkwy Akron OH 44313

HEIDRICK, GARDNER WILSON, management consultant; b. Clarion, Pa., Oct. 7, 1911; s. R. Emmet and Helen (Wilson) H.; m. Marian Eileen Lindsay, Feb. 19, 1937; children: Gardner Wilson, Robert L. B.S. in Banking and Fin., U. Ill., 1935. Indsl. dist. sales mgr. Scott Paper Co., Phila., 1935-42; dir. personnel Farmland Industries, Kansas City, Mo., 1942-51; assoc. Booz, Allen & Hamilton, Chgo., 1951-53; co-founder partner, chmn. Heidrick & Struggles, Inc., Chgo., 1953-82; co-founder, chmn. Heidrick Ptnrs., Inc., Chgo., 1982—; mem. council Internat. Exec. Service Corp. Bd. dirs. U. Ill. Found. Served with USNR, 1945-46. Recipient Pres.'s award U. Ill. Found., 1979. Mem. U. Ill. Alumni Assn. (past pres., Achievement award 1980), Phi Kappa Sigma. Clubs: Chicago (Chgo.), Tower (Chgo.); Hinsdale (Ill.) Golf (past pres.); University (N.Y.); Little Club (Gulfstream, Fla.); Country of Fla. (Delray Beach), Ocean (Delray Beach). Office: Heidrick Ptnrs Inc 20 N Wacker Dr Chicago IL 60606

HEIDRICK, ROBERT LINDSAY, management consultant; b. Kansas City, Mo., June 8, 1941; s. Gardner W. Sr. and Eileen (Lindsay) H.; m. Deborah Nissen, June 26, 1971 (div.); 1 child, Lindsay T.; m. Raynelle Falkenau, Aug. 4, 1984; stepchildren: Kimberley A., Stephen H. BA, Duke U., 1963; MBA, U. Chgo., 1971. V.p. Am. Hosp. Supply Corp., Evanston, Ill., 1963-75, v.p. Dietary Products div., 1971-75; v.p. Spriggs and Co., Chgo., 1975-77; pres. Robert Heidrick Assocs. Inc., Chgo., 1977-82, The Heidrick Ptnrs. Inc., Chgo., 1982—. Bd. dirs. Glenwood Sch. for Boys, Chgo., 1982—, vice chmn., 1986—. Mem. Duke U. Alumni Assn. (bd. dirs. 1981—, pres. 1988-89), Glenview Club, Chgo. Club, Racquet Club. Office: Heidrick Ptnrs Inc 20 N Wacker Dr Chicago IL 60606

HEIDT, PAMELA ANN, communications company manager; b. Cambridge, Mass., June 5, 1956; d. Carl E. and Catherine M. (Clark) H. BA, Wheaton Coll., Norton, Mass., 1978. Asst. staff mgr. New Eng. Telephone Co., Boston, 1978-81, staff mgr. econometrics, 1981-83, dist. mgr. econ. analysis, 1983-85, dist. mgr. fin., 1985-86, asst. treas., 1986-89, gen. mgr. acctg. ops., 1989—. Mem. coordinating com. advanced workshop in pub. utility econs. Rutgers U., 1981—. Mem. Am. Econ. Assn., Am. Statistic Assn., Nat. Soc. Rate of Return Analysts, Fin. Mgmt., Cash Mgmt. Assn. New Eng. Office: New Eng Telephone Co 99 High St Rm 607 Boston MA 02110

HEIECK, PAUL JAY, wholesale distributing company executive; b. San Francisco, Aug. 6, 1937; s. Erwin N. and Ann C. (Retchless) H.; student Golden Gate Coll., 1958; m. Kathleen Pawela, Oct. 14, 1967; children: Valerie, Yvonne, Elizabeth, Krista, Justin. Sales rep. Heieck & Moran, San Francisco, 1958-63, sec.-treas., 1963-69, Heieck Supply, San Francisco, 1969-76, pres. 1976—; 1st v.p., dir. San Francisco Bd. Trade, 1978-82. Dir., San Francisco Boys Club, 1972—. With U.S. Army, 1955-57. Mem. Nat. Assn. Wholesalers, Am. Supply Assn. (dir. 1984—, v.p. 1987—), Western Supplier's Assn. (pres. 81-83, dir. 1981-85). Republican. Episcopalian. Clubs: Rotary, San Mateo County Mounted Posse, Sharon Heights Country, Olympic. Office: Heieck Supply 1111 Connecticut St San Francisco CA 94107

HEIKENEN, CHARLES EDWARD, financial planning company executive; b. Mpls., Nov. 9, 1950; s. Arnold Isaac and Joyce (Hout) H.; m. Rebecca Hyland, Sept. 6, 1975; children: Rachel, Anna. BA, St. Olaf Coll., 1973; JD, Hamline U., 1979. Bar: Minn. 1979; CLU; chartered fin. cons. Sales agt. Prudential Ins. Co., Mpls., 1973-76; design assoc. CIGNA, Mpls., 1979-82; asst. v.p. mktg. Luth. Brotherhood, Mpls., 1982-87; v.p. Midwest Fin. Mgmt., Mpls., 1987—. Mem. mut. ministry com., Stephen minister Normandale Luth. Ch., Edina, Minn.; mem. adv. bd. Minn. MADD, 1985—. Named one of Outstanding Young Men of Am., 1987. Mem. ABA, Hennepin County Bar Assn., Internat. Assn. Fin. Planning, Twin City Assn. Fin. Planning (regional task force 1988—). Republican. Home: 4809 Larkspur Ln Edina MN 55435 Office: Midwest Fin Mgmt 6600 France Ave S Edina MN 55435

HEIL, TERRY W., defense electronic company executive. BS, Parson Coll., 1960; MS, U. Ariz., Tucson, 1963; PhD, U. Ariz., 1966. With Singer Co., Stamford, Conn., 1966—, v.p. reconaissance services, 1975-78, v.p., programs mgr., 1978-82, v.p., pres. Singer div. products, 1982-83, v.p., pres. HRB Singer div., 1983-84, group v.p., 1984-86, exec. v.p., 1987—. Office: The Singer Co 8 Stamford Forum PO Box 10151 Stamford CT 06904

HEILEMANN, A. DAVID, financial executive; b. Bklyn., July 30, 1943; s. Arthur and Ida Martha (podgus) H.; m. Jo Ann Louise Hubbard, Aug. 14, 1965; children: Karl David, Erich Paul, Marc Eugene. BS in Indsl. Distbn., Clarkson U., 1965; MBA, U. Conn., 1968. Indsl. engr. Gleason Works, Rochester, N.Y., 1965-66; fin. analyst Rogers (Conn.) Corp., 1968-73, sr. fin. analyst, 1973-84, risk mgr., 1984—. Treas. St. John Luth. Ch., Brooklyn, Conn., 1987-88; sec. Town of Brooklyn Ins. Com., 1987-88. Mem. Risk and Ins. Mgmt. Soc. (bd. dirs. Conn. Valley chpt.). Club: Exchange of Danielson, Conn. (bd. dirs. 1987-88). Office: Rogers Corp One Technology Dr Rogers CT 06263

HEILMAN, CARL EDWIN, lawyer; b. Elizabethville, Pa., Feb. 3, 1911; s. Edgar James and Mary Alice (Bechtold) H.; m. Grace Emily Greene, Nov. 29, 1934 (div. 1952); children: John Greene, Elizabeth Greene; m. Claire Virginia Phelps, Oct. 10, 1952. BA, Lafayette Coll., Easton, Pa., 1932, MA, 1933; JD magna cum laude, U. Pa., 1939. Bar: N.Y. 1940, Pa. 1940, Mass. 1973, U.S. Supreme Ct. 1960. Tchr. English, Easton High Sch., 1934-36; assoc. Dwight, Harris, Koegel & Caskey, N.Y.C., 1939-42; atty. OPA, Washington, 1942-43; atty. N.Y. Gov.'s Commn. to Investigate Workmen's Compensation Law, N.Y.C., 1943-44; assoc. Dewey, Ballantine, Bushby, Palmer & Wood, N.Y.C., 1944-59, ptnr., 1959-73; counsel to firm Csaplar & Bok, Boston and San Francisco, 1973—. Trustee Upsala Coll., East Orange, N.J., 1970-73. Fellow Am. Bar Found.; mem. ABA, Boston Bar Assn., Nat. Trust for Hist. Preservation, Order of Coif. Republican. Episcopalian. Club: Down Town (Boston). Home: One Devonshire Pl Apt 2605 Boston MA 02109

HEILMAN, JOHN EDWARD, agribusiness executive; b. Chgo., Mar. 20, 1936; s. Frederick John and Kathryn Grace (Schnider) H.; B.S. in Food Engring., Ill. Inst. Tech., 1961; m. Virginia Lois Anderson, Jan. 28, 1956; children—Wayne John, Warren Wesley. Engr. grocery products div. Armour & Co., Chgo., 1959-61, lab. technician, 1958, foreman, 1958-59; process engr. Central Soya Co., Inc., Ft. Wayne, Ind., 1962-65, supt., Chgo., 1965-68; sr. process engr. Continental Grain Co., Chgo., 1968-75, dir. engring. process div., N.Y.C., 1975-77, asst. v.p. process div., 1977-79, v.p. process div., 1979—. Mem. Nat. Soybean Processors Assn. (tech. com.), Nat. Fire Protection Assn. (sectional com. solvent extraction), Am. Oil Chemists Soc. (mem. bd. govs., pres.). Republican. Methodist. Home: 22 Sugarbush Ct Wilton CT 06897 Office: Continental Grain Co 277 Park Ave New York NY 10172

HEILMEIER, GEORGE HARRY, research electrical engineer; b. Phila., May 22, 1936; s. George C. and Anna I. (Heineman) H.; m. Janet S. Faunce, June 24, 1961; 1 dau., Elizabeth. B.S. in Elec. Engring., U. Pa., 1958; M.S. in Engring., Princeton U., 1960, A.M., 1961, Ph.D., 1962. With RCA Labs., Princeton, N.J., 1958-70; dir. solid state device rsch. RCA Labs., 1965-68, dir. device concepts, 1968-70; White House fellow, spl. asst. to sec. def. Washington, 1970-71; asst. dir. def. rsch. and engring. Office Sec. Def., 1971-75; dir. Def. Advanced Projects Agy., 1975-77; v.p. rsch., devel. and engring. Tex. Instruments Inc., 1978-83, sr. v.p., chief tech. officer, 1983—; mem. Def. Sci. Bd.; mem. adv. group on electron devices Dept. Def.; mem. adv. bd. Stanford Ctr. for Integrated Systems. Pantentee in field. Recipient IEEE David Sarnoff award, 1976; IR-100 New Product award Indsl. Rsch. Assn., 1968, 69; Sec. Def. Disting. Civilian Service award, 1975, 77; Arthur Flemming award U.S. Jaycees, 1974. Fellow IEEE (Outstanding Achievement award Dallas chpt. 1984, Philips award 1985, Founder's award 1986); mem. U. Pa., Princeton U. Grad. alumni assns., Nat. Acad. Engring., Sigma Xi, Tau Beta Pi, Eta Kappa Nu (Outstanding Young Engr. in U.S. award 1969). Methodist. Office: Tex Instruments Inc 13500 N Central Expwy Box 655474 MS 400 Dallas TX 75265

HEIM, DONALD LABARR, financial planner, educator; b. Pitts., Apr. 12, 1945; s. Donald Demms and Mary Ethel (LaBarr) H.; m. Elizabeth May Goughler, May 2, 1969; 1 child, Christopher Ross. BSME, U. Pitts., 1971, MBA, 1978. Engr. Kerotest Mfg. Corp., Pitts., 1968-73; design engr. Fisher Controls, Corapolis, Pa., 1973-76; sr. devel. engr. Rockwell Internat., Pitts., 1976-77, mgr. mktg., 1977-79, mgr. internat. mktg., 1979-80, mgr. engring., 1980-83; fin. planner Allegheny Investments Ltd., Pitts., 1983—; assoc. prof. Community Coll. Allegheny County, Boyce Campus, Monroeville, Pa., 1985—. Served with USAR, 1968-74. Mem. Internat. Assn. Fin. Planning, Inst. Cert. Fin. Planners, Nat. Mgmt. Assn. (pres. Rockwell chpt. 1982-83), East suburban C. of C. Home: 3909 Murry Highlands Circle Murrysville PA 15668 Office: Community Coll Allegheny County 595 Beatty Rd Monroeville PA 15146

HEIMAN, MARVIN STEWART, financial services company executive; b. Chgo., Sept. 16, 1945; s. Samuel J. and Mildred (Miller) H.; m. Adrienne Joy Nathan, Aug. 7, 1966; children: Scott, Michelle, Adam. Student, Roosevelt U., 1963-67. Pres. Curtom Record Co., Chgo., 1969-80, Gold Coast Entertainment, Chgo., 1980-82; ptnr. Profl. Real Estate Securities Co., Lincolnwood, Ill., 1982-86; pres., chmn. bd. Sussex Fin. Group, Inc., Skokie, Ill., 1986—; bd. dirs. Skokie Bank, Drovers Bank, Chgo.; ptnr. Cole Taylor Banks, Chgo., 1984—, bank examining com., 1986—, ptnr. Chgo. White Sox Am. League Baseball Club, 1981—, Gore/Bronson Bancorp, 1988. Mem. Rep. Nat. Com., 1980—, Simon Wiesenthal Ctr., 1988. Mem. Internat. Assn. Fin. Planners, Real Estate Securities Syndication Assn. Am., Nat. Assn. Securities Dealers (registered rep.), Am. Jewish Com. (Humanitarian award 1978), Internat. Platform Assn. Office: Sussex Fin Group Inc 666 Dundee Rd Ste 1903 Northbrook IL 60062

HEIMANN, JOHN GAINES, investment banker; b. N.Y.C., Apr. 1, 1929; s. Sidney M. and Dorothy V.B. (Gainesburg) H.; m. Margaret E. Fechheimer, Dec. 2, 1956 (div.); children: Joshua Gaines, Eliza Faith; m. Anne-Marie Sten, Dec. 31, 1985 (div.). AB, Syracuse (N.Y.) U., 1950. V.p. Smith, Barney & Co., N.Y.C., 1955-66; sr. v.p., dir. E.M. Warburg, Pincus & Co., Inc., N.Y.C., 1967-75; N.Y. State supt. banks 1975-76, N.Y. State commr. housing and community renewal, 1976-77; compt. of the currency Washington, 1977-81; co-chmn. exec. com. Warburg, Paribas, Becker, N.Y.C., 1981-82; dep. chmn. A.G. Becker Paribas Inc., Paribas Internat., 1982-84; vice chmn. Merrill Lynch Capital Markets, N.Y.C., 1984—; chmn. exec. com. Europe/Middle East Merrill Lynch, London, 1988; bd. dir. FDIC, 1977-81, Fed. Nat. Mortgage Assn., 1977-80, Neighborhood Reinvestment Corp., 1978-81, Australis Securities Ltd., Colonial Penn Group Inc., East River Savs. Bank, Merrill Lynch Internat. Bank; chmn. Fed. Fin. Instns. Exam. Coun., 1979-81, Comml. Reinvestment Task Force, 1978-81, 20th Century Task Force on Internat. Debt Crisis; mem. Depository Instns. Deregulation Com., 1980-81; spl. advisor to Gov. on Temporary Commn. Banking, Ins. and Fin. Reform; lectr. Harvard U., Yale U., Columbia U., U. Calif., NYU; trustee Fin. Acctg. Found.; mem. adv. bd. sch. mgmt. Yale U., Fishman-Davidson Ctr. for Study of Svc. Sector; adv. com. internat. markets Fed. Res. Bank, N.Y.; mem. chmn.'s coun. Brit. Mcht. Banking and Securities Houses Assn.; vice chmn., chmn. Securities SubCom. Am. Banking and Securities Assn. of London. Bd. dirs., treas. Group of Thirty; mem. N.Y.C. Housing Partnership, Citizens Com. for Affordable Housing; gov. Atlantic Inst.; bd. dirs. Am. Ditchley Found.; mem. adv. bd. Wharton Sch. Named Housing Man of Yr. Nat. Housing Conf., 1976; recipient Bank Adminstrn. Key for Disting. Svc., 1980, Alexander Hamilton award Treasury Dept., 1981, Brotherhood award NCCJ, 1986, Pacesetter award Nat. Assn. Bank Women, Inc., 1986. Mem. Securities Industry Assn. (bd. dirs.), Fgn. Rels. Coun. Democrat. Club: F Street (Washington). Office: Merrill Lynch Capital Markets World Fin Ctr North Tower D New York NY 10281 also: 25 Ropermaker St, EC2Y London 9LY, England

HEIMBINDER, ISAAC, construction company executive, lawyer; b. Bklyn., May 15, 1943; s. David and Evelyn (Brown) H.; m. Sheila Marie Mooney, Aug. 3, 1970; children: Susan, Daniel, Erin, Michael. BS in Bus., Am. U., 1965; JD, NYU, 1968. Atty. Debevoise and Plimpton, N.Y.C., 1969-72; corp. counsel U.S. Home Corp., Clearwater, Fla., 1973-77; v.p. legal affairs U.S. Home Corp., Houston, 1977-79, chief fin. officer, 1979-86, pres. chief operating officer, 1986—. Mem. N.Y. Bar Assn., Fla. Bar Assn., Tex. Bar Assn., Order of the Coif, Omicron Delta Kappa. Home: 2 Glendenning Houston TX 77024 Office: US Home Corp 1800 W Loop S PO Box 2863 Houston TX 77252

HEIN, SALLY LEE, hospital administrator; b. Cin., May 8, 1951; d. David Edward and Virginia (Herzog) H. B.S., U. Cin., 1973; M.A., Vanderbilt U., 1974; Ph.D., Memphis State U., 1980. Cert. speech pathologist, Tex. Clin. speech pathologist U. Ala. Med. Ctr., Birmingham, 1975-77; asst. prof. N. Tex. State U., Denton, 1980-84; dir. ednl. services Parkland Meml. Hosp., Dallas, 1984—. Vol. Am. Heart Assn., Dallas, 1984—. Recipient Outstanding award for research of handicapped U.S.A. Mil. Order of Purple Heart, 1981. Mem. Am. Speech, Lang., Hearing Assn., N.Y. Acad. Scis., Am. Soc. Tng. and Devel., Am. Hosp. Assn., Tex. Hosp. Assn. Jewish. Avocation: volunteer work. Home: 10723-D Villager Rd Dallas TX 75230 Office: Parkland Meml Hosp 5201 Harry Hines Blvd Dallas TX 75235

HEIN, TODD JONATHAN, financial services executive; b. Encino, Calif., May 11, 1960; s. Walter Adolph Jr. and Valerie Wynan (Phipps) H.; m. Jacqueline Esther Cohen, Oct. 14, 1983. BA in Econs., UCLA, 1982; cert. in fin. planning, U. So. Calif., 1987. CPA; cert. fin. planner. Account analyst Exec. Life Ins. Co., Los Angeles, 1983; acct. Satriano & Young, Los Angeles, 1983-85; personal acct. Barron Hilton; pres. Hilton Hotels Corp., 1985-86; sr. acct. Gursey, Schneider & Co., Los Angeles, 1987-88; v.p. Hein Fin. Services, Inc., Los Angeles, 1988-89; spl. agt. Northwestern Mutual Life, Woodland Hills, 1989—. Mem. Inst. Cert. Fin. Planners, Calif. Soc. CPA's, Am. Assn. CPA's, Corona Investment Affiliates (pres. 1987-88), Sierra Club. Democrat. Office: Nortwestern Mutual Life 6400 Canoga Ave #210 Woodland Hills CA 91367

HEINE, LEONARD M., JR., investment counselor; b. N.Y.C., Nov. 14, 1924; s. Leonard Max and Elise (Frey) H.; B.S. in Econs., U. Pa., 1948; m. Sandra Fleming, Oct. 14, 1966; children—Michael Kenneth, Nancy Ellen, Thomas Charles, Christopher Altman. Salesman, Lehman Bros., N.Y.C., 1952-58; sales mgr. L.F. Rothschild, N.Y.C., 1958-62; gen. partner R.J. Buck & Co., N.Y.C., 1962-70; pres., founder, chmn. Mgmt. Asset Corp., Westport, Conn., 1970—; investment mgr. Philharmonic Symphony Soc. N.Y. Inc., NFL, Xerox Corp., and various Fortune 500 employee benefit funds; chmn., pres. LMH Fund Ltd., 1983—; pres. Heine Mgmt. Group Inc., 1983—; chmn., pub. Weston (Conn.) Voice. Treas., Weston Pub. Library, 1980-81; trustee Norwalk Hosp.; bd. dirs. Fairfield Home Elderly; assoc. nat. commn. ADL, Trustee Weitzman Inst., N.Y.C.; Albert Einstein Coll. Medicine's Soc. Founders. Served with U.S. Army, 1943-46. Decorated Purple Heart, Combat Inf. badge. Mem. Am. Soc. Profl. Cons. Republican. Clubs: Birchwood Country (Westport), U. Pa. (N.Y.C.); Palm Beach Country (Fla.). Office: Mgmt Asset Corp 253 Post Rd W Westport CT 06881

HEINE, RICHARD ATHERTON, financial analyst; b. Cleve., Mar. 10, 1946; s. Richard O. and Jeanette (MacDonald) H.; m. Jill Delhia De Fulgentiis, Sept. 25, 1976. BA in Philosophy, Lehigh U., 1969; cert., Coll. Fin. Planning, 1983. Mgr. Copeland Cos., Armonk, N.Y., 1978-85; sr. counselor Ind. Fin. Svcs., White Plains, N.Y., 1985-86; dir. Income and Asset Adv., Armonk, 1986—. Columnist It's Your Money, 1986-87. Mem. Internat. Assn. for Fin. Planning (v.p. communications Westchester-Rockland chpt. 1987—, bd. dirs. 1987—, program dir. 1987—), Inst. Cert. Fin. Planners. Home: 221 Summit Circle Dr Mahopac NY 10541 Office: Income & Asset Adv 80 Business Park Dr Armonk NY 10504

HEINEN, PAUL ABELARDO, lawyer, executive; b. Teaneck, N.J., Jan. 9, 1930; s. Paul and Encarnacion (Maestu) H.; m. Gloria Newman, Oct. 9, 1952; children—Heidi E., Paul C. B.B.A., U. Mich., 1954, J.D., 1956, M.B.A., 1957; S.M., MIT, 1963. Bar: Mich. 1957, Ill. 1982. Assoc. gen. counsel Chrysler Corp., Detroit, 1968-76, sec., 1969-81, v.p., 1974-81, v.p., gen. counsel, sec., 1976-81; v.p., gen. counsel GATX Corp., Chgo., 1981—. Bd. govs. Met. Planning Council, Chgo. Served to 1st lt. U.S. Army, 1951-53, Korea. Mem. ABA, Mich. Bar Assn., Ill. Bar Assn., Chgo. Bar Assn., Order of Coif, Beta Gamma Sigma. Clubs: Oakland Hills (Birmingham, Mich.); Chicago, Mid-Am. Home: 1780 S Oak Knoll Dr Lake Forest IL 60045 Office: GATX Corp 120 S Riverside Pla Chicago IL 60606

HEINER, CLYDE MONT, energy company executive; b. Wendell, Idaho, Apr. 4, 1938; s. Mont A. and Margaret (Alexander) H.; m. Gail Tanner, Dec. 28, 1966; children: Jeremy, Emily, Sean, Forrest, Joshua, JennyLee, Mandy, Marci. B.A., Columbia U., 1960, B.S. in Structural Engring., 1961; M.B.A., Stanford U., 1966. Registered profl. engr., Utah, Wyo., Idaho, D.C. Budget dir. Mountain Fuel Supply Co., Salt Lake City, 1968-69, dir. rates and planning, 1974-76, mgr. engring., 1976-77, v.p. engring., 1977-80, sr. v.p. corp. devel., 1980-84; sr. v.p. corp. devel. Questar Corp., Salt Lake City, 1984-88, sr. v.p., 1988—; pres., chief exec. officer Questar Devel. Corp., Salt Lake City, 1984—, Interstate Land Corp., Salt Lake City, 1984—; vice chmn., dir. Interstate Brick, Salt Lake City, 1985-87, pres., chief exec. officer, 1987—; asst. adminstr. U. Utah Hosp., Salt Lake City, 1969-74; dir. Entrada Industries, Questar Devel., Interstate Land, Interstate Brick. Mem. adv. council U. Utah Coll. Engring., Salt Lake City, 1980-83, 86—; chmn. bd. Salt Lake chpt. ARC, 1982-84; mem. Clearfield City Council, Utah, 1973-74. Mem. Nat. Soc. Profl. Engrs., Am. Gas Assn., Pacific Coast Gas Assn., Am. Inst. Indsl. Engrs. (past pres. Salt Lake City chpt.). Mormon. Home: 388 W 1150 N Farmington UT 84025 Office: Questar Corp 180 E 1st S St PO Box 11150 Salt Lake City UT 84147

HEINER, DENNIS GRANT, manufacturing company executive; b. Ogden, Utah, Aug. 18, 1943; s. Grant and Mary (Stoker) H.; m. Margo Proctor, Dec. 17, 1970; children: Shalayna, Bryce James, Jillian, Brittnay. BA, Weber State Coll., 1969; MBA, Brigham Young U., 1971; M in Mktg., Northwestern U., 1983; cert. strategic mgkt. mgmt., Harvard U., 1985. V.p. mktg., gen. mgr. Sportplay, Inc., Salt Lake City, 1971-72; dir. mktg. adminstrn. and fin. Sno-Jet, Inc., Burlington, Vt., 1972-74; v.p. fin. Glastron Boat Co., Austin, Tex., 1974-78, v.p. fin. and adminstrn., 1978-79; v.p. fin. Delmar Window Coverings, Westminster, Calif., 1979-81, pres., 1981-84; pres. window coverings div. Beatrice Cos., Inc., Westminster, Calif., 1984-85; group v.p. U.S. Household Prducts div. Black & Decker, Shelton, Conn., 1985-86, pres. Household Products Group World-Wide, 1986—; bd. dirs. Raytech Corp., Trumbull, Conn. Bd. dirs. Jr. Achievement, Austin, 1978-79. Mem. Young Pres.' Orgn. (So. Calif. chpt.). Republican. Mormon. Office: The Black & Decker Corp Household Products Group 6 Armstrong Rd Shelton CT 06484

HEININGER, S(AMUEL) ALLEN, chemical company executive; b. New Britain, Conn., June 13, 1925; s. Alfred D. and Erma Geraldine (Kline) H.; m. Barbara Ashenfelter Griffith, June 16, 1948; children: Janet, Kathryn, Kenneth, Keith. A.B., Oberlin Coll., 1948; M.S., Carnegie Inst. Tech., 1951; D.Sc., 1952. Research chemist Monsanto Chem. Co., Dayton, Ohio, 1952-56, group leader, 1956-58; project mgr. devel. dept. Organic Chems. div. Monsanto Chem. Co., St. Louis, 1958-59, mgr. fine chems. intermediates and market exploration sect., 1959-65, dir. comml. devel., 1965-67, dir. food and fine chems., 1967-71, dir. corp. plans and devel., 1971-74; gen. mgr. plasticizers div. Monsanto Indsl. Chems. Co., St. Louis, 1974-76; dir. corp. research lab. Monsanto Chem. Co., St. Louis, 1977, v.p. research and devel., 1977-79., v.p. corp. plans and bus. devel., 1980-86, v.p. resource planning, 1986—. Contbr. articles to profl. jours. Alderman, City of Warson Woods (Mo.), 1961-65, police commr., 1967-71. Served to lt. USNR, 1943-46. Mem. Am. Chem. Soc., Indsl. Research Inst. (pres., 1987-88), Soc. Chem. Industry, N.Y. Acad. Scis. Republican. Episcopalian. Clubs: Old Warson Country, Creve Coeur Racquet. Office: Monsanto Co 800 N Lindbergh Saint Louis MO 63167

HEINRICH, ELMER G., entrepreneur; b. Grinnell, Kans., Mar. 9, 1934; s. Govel Gaberial and Mary Katherine (Engel) H.; m. Verlene Louise Hoover, May 14, 1954 (div. May 1966); children: Patricia, Larry, Judy, Cathy; m. Shirley Ann Tolson, Nov. 4, 1966; 1 child, Rocky. Student, Ft. Hayes State U., 1953-54. Pres. S&H Drilling Co., Goodland, Kans., 1959-65; mgr. state sales Centennial Life Ins. Co., Pittsburgh, Kans., 1966-68; pres., chmn. bd. The Hotsy Corp., Denver, 1968-73, Citation Mfg. Co., Inc., Siloam Springs, Ark., 1974-79; chmn. bd. Robo Corp., Kansas City, 1976-77; pres., chmn. bd. The Rockland Corp., Tulsa, 1978—, Rockland Internat., Tulsa, 1980—, Liquid Assets, Inc., Tulsa, 1983—; bd. dirs. Hosp. Santa Monica, Rosarita Beach, Mex.; chmn. bd. Body Toddy Mktg. Affairs, Tulsa, 1985—. Patentee in field. Search coord. CAP, Goodland, 1960-66. Recipient Nat. Record for Rookies Life Ins. Assn. Am., 1966, Speaking award, Nat. Assn. Speakers, 1973. Mem. Kans. Well Drillers Assn. (pres. 1964), Nat. Car Wash. Mfrs. (bd. dirs. 1975), Cleaning Equipment Mfg. Assn. (organizer 1977). Democrat. Roman Catholic. Home: 4008 E 80th St Tulsa OK 74136

HEINRICHS, JEFFREY PAUL, gas company executive; b. Pitts., July 12, 1950; s. Andrew N. and Thelma Lee (Collins) H.; m. Patricia Ann Crosely, Aug. 3, 1974; children: Jenni Lee, Sara Leonor. BBA in Acctg., Tex. Tech U., 1972. CPA, Tex. Acct. Transcontinental Gas Pipe Line Corp., Houston, 1976-78, dir. gen. acctg., 1981-85, dir. gas acctg., 1985-86, contr., 1986—; corp. acct. Transco Exploration Co., Houston, 1978, Transco Energy Co., Houston, 1978-81. Mem. AICPA, Tex. Soc. CPA's, Nat. Assn. Accts. Republican. Roman Catholic. Office: Transco Energy Co 2800 Post Oak Blvd Houston TX 77251

HEINTZ, MATTHEW JOSEPH, retail executive; b. Marshfield, Wis., Dec. 22, 1925; s. Joseph Nickolas and Agnes Elizabeth (Wolf) H.; m. Alvia Elizabeth Owens, Dec. 28, 1946; children: Pamela Sue Heintz Robinson, James Allen. Student pvt. schs., Marshfield. Dairy farmer Marshfield, 1940-43; meat cutter Atlantic and Pacific Tea Co., Kenosha, Wis., 1946-53; owner, mgr. Heintz Mobile Homes, Macomb, Ill., 1953—; pres. M.J.L., Inc., Macomb, 1978-82; mobile home park developer Cardinal Paradise, Macomb, 1971—; subdivider Heintz Addition, Macomb, 1974-76. Bd. dirs. Macomb Speedway. Served with USN, 1943-46. Mem. Nat. Manufactured Housing Assn., Ill. Manufactured Housing Assn. Republican. Baptist. Home and Office: 1607 E Jackson Macomb IL 61455

HEINTZE, JULIETTE CHIODO, transportation company executive; b. Rome, Jan. 9, 1947; d. John and Fedora (Giongi) Chiodo; m. Achim J. Heintze, Sept. 25, 1975; 1 child, Christina. BS, Georgetown U., 1968. Dist. corp. rep. Chase Manhattan Bank, N.Y.C., 1968-73; asst. sec. Mfrs. Hanover Trust Co., N.Y.C., 1973-76; asst. v.p. Am. Security Bank, Washington, 1976-77; asst. treas. U.S. Air Inc., Arlington, Va., 1978-83, treas., 1983—; treas. U.S. Air Group Inc., Arlington, 1984—; bd. dirs. United Nat. Bank Washington. Mem. Nat. Bankers Assn. (mem. corp. adv. group 1986—), Washington Assn. Cash Mgrs. (1st v.p. 1980-82), Nat. Assn. Corp. Treas. Roman Catholic. Office: USAIR Inc Washington Nat Airport Washington DC 20001

HEINTZLEMAN, WALTER GRAY, professional engineer; b. Pitts., July 26, 1935; s. Charles R. and Eva J. (Hiner) H.; B.S. in Engring., Carnegie-Mellon U., 1957; M.P.A., U. Pitts., 1963; m. Lynn Baker, June 28, 1958; children—Keith W., Scott A. Chief engr. Urban Redevel. Authority, Pitts., 1957-74 mng. engr. Port Authority of Allegheny County, Pitts., 1974-80; v.p. GAI Cons., Inc., Monroeville, Pa., 1980-87; partner Fortrend, 1981-87; dir. Bus. Devel. Baker Engrs. Served with C.E., AUS, 1957-59. Mem. ASCE (pres. Pitts. sect. 1971), Pa. Soc. Profl. Engrs. (pres. Pitts. chpt. 1979-80), Nat. Soc. Profl. Engrs., Engrs. Soc. Western Pa. Republican. Presbyterian (elder). Home: 1525 Vallimont Dr Mount Lebanon PA 15234 Office: Fortrend 4301 Dutch Ridge Rd Beaver PA 15009

HEINZ, DONALD JAMES, health care executive; b. Appleton, Wis., Aug. 7, 1949; s. Francis Mathew and Lorraine Mary (St. Arnold) H.; m. Mary Elizabeth Hart, May 16, 1987. BBA, U. Wis., 1972, MS, 1982. Acct. U. Wis. Hosps., Madison, 1972-74; asst. to vice chancellor health U. Wis., Madison, 1974-76; controller Meth. Hosp., Madison, 1976-83; v.p., chief fin. officer Bayfront Med. Ctr., St. Petersburg, Fla., 1983—; bd. dirs. Bayfront Enterprises, St. Petersburg, Fla., Hosp. Oxygen Med. Equipment, Clearwater, Fla.; bd. dirs., sec.-treas. Hosps. Home Health Care Pinellas County, Clearwater. Kellogg fellow U. Wis.-Madison, Kellogg Found., 1979-80. Mem. Am. Coll. Healthcare Execs., Am. Mgmt. Assn., Healthcare Fin. Mgmt. Assn. Roman Catholic. Club: Feather Sound Country (Clearwater, Fla.). Office: Bayfront Med Ctr 701 6th St S Saint Petersburg FL 33701

HEINZ, H(ORST) PETER, manufacturing company executive; b. Koenigsberg, Prussia, Germany, Oct. 21, 1942; came to U.S., 1970; s. Josef A. and Irmgard (Klinghammer) H.; m. I. Petra Goedert, Dec. 19, 1970 (div. Oct. 1982); 1 child, Percy; m. JoAnn Holby Hellier, Jan. 21, 1984. BS in Mech. and Elec. Engring., Engring. Coll., Heilbronn, Fed. Republic Germany, 1966; MBA, U. Bridgeport, 1973. Engr. research and devel. dept. Perkin-Elmer Corp., Ueberlingen, Fed. Republic Germany, 1966-70; various positions including project dir., product mgr., internat. mktg. mgr., research and devel. engr. Perkin-Elmer Corp. Instrument Group, Norwalk, Conn., 1970-77; dir. ops. Coulter Electronics, Concord, Mass., 1977-80; gen. mgr., v.p. Karl Suss Am., Inc., Waterbury, Vt., 1980—. Patentee in field. Mem. Rotary. Office: Karl Suss Am Inc PO Box 157 Waterbury VT 05677

HEINZEN, BERNARD GEORGE, lawyer; b. Hendricks, Minn., Sept. 8, 1930; s. Bernard Martin and Thelma Harrington (Bowers) H.; m. Mildred Masters, Dec. 29, 1956 (div. 1975); children: John Masters, Robert Kenneth (dec.), James Warren, William Martin; m. Maryann Mullen, Aug. 25, 1978. BA, Carleton Coll., 1953; LLB, NYU, 1956. Bar: Minn. 1956, U.S. Supreme Ct. 1969, Pa. 1978. Atty., legal adviser U.S. Dept. State, Washington, 1956-58; assoc. Dorsey & Whitney, Mpls., 1960-65, ptnr., 1966-76; spl. asst. atty. gen. State of Minn., St. Paul, 1967-70; gen. counsel Consol. Rail Corp., Phila., 1976-77; counsel Harvey, Pennington, Herting & Renneisen, Ltd., Phila., 1976-83; pres. Bernard G. Heinzen, Ltd., Phila., 1978—; ptnr. Stassen, Kostos & Mason, Phila., 1983-85; adviser U.S. del. to Geneva Conf. on Law of the Sea, 1958. Contbr. Stanford Law Rev., 1959; assoc. editor NYU Law Rev., 1955-56. Mem. Citizens Com. on Pub. Edn., Mpls., 1964-76; exec. com. state cen. com. Minn. Rep. Party, 1967-71. 1st lt. U.S. Army, 1957-60. Mem. ABA, Phila. Bar Assn., Minn. State Bar Assn. (chmn. com. on ins. 1970-73), Hennepin County Bar Assn., Am. Judicature Soc., World Affairs Coun., Mpls. Citizens League, Racquet Club Phila., Union League Phila., Mpls. Club, Phi Beta Kappa. Episcopalian. Home: 1901 Walnut St Philadelphia PA 19103 Office: 2 Mellon Bank Ctr Philadelphia PA 19102

HEINZERLING, LARRY EDWARD, communications executive; b. Elyria, Ohio, Aug. 28, 1945; s. Lynn Louis and Agnes Corinne (Dengate) H.; m. Sharyn Lee Jorgensen, Jan. 11, 1969 (div. 1985); children: Jesse, Kristen, Benjamin; m. Sieglinde Wolf, Aug. 1, 1985; stepchildren: Andreas, Eva. BA, Ohio Wesleyan U., 1967; MA, Ohio State U., 1969. Reporter AP, Columbus, Ohio, 1969-71; corr. AP, Lagos, Nigeria, 1971-74; bur. chief AP,

Johannesburg, Republic of South Africa, 1974-78; mng. dir. AP, Frankfurt, Fed. Republic Germany, 1978-83; dep. dir. world services AP, N.Y.C., 1983—. News coverage includes: coverage West Africa including Sahel drought, 1971-74, coverage Soweto riots, Mozambique independence, Angola, Rhodesia (now Zimbabwe). Recipient Headliners award Headliners Club, Atlantic City, 1977, AP reportorial Performance award Mng. Editors, N.Y.C., 1977; nominated for Pulitzer Prize, 1976. Mem. Internat. Press Inst. of London, Fgn. Press Assn. of N.Y., Sigma Delta Chi, Phi Delta Theta. Roman Catholic. Office: AP 50 Rockefeller Ctr New York NY 10020

HEISEL, RALPH ARTHUR, architect; b. St. Louis, Sept. 17, 1935; s. Ralph Alonzo and Marie Lucille (Hadfield) H.; m. Janet Clevenger Scott, Aug. 4, 1962; children: Jean Marie, Arthur Scott. BS, Ga. Inst. Tech., 1957, BArch, 1958; MArch, U. Pa., 1961. Registered architect, N.Y., Fla. Designer Bodin and Lamberson, Architects, Atlanta, 1961-62, Fry Drew & Ptnrs., Architects, London, 1962-64; sr. assoc. I.M. Pei and Ptnrs., Architects, N.Y.C., 1964-86; pres. Heisel Assocs., Architects P.C., N.Y.C., 1986—; vis. critic various univs. Prin. works include Paul Mellon Ctr. for the Arts, The Choate Sch., Wallingford, Conn., Johnson & Johnson Baby Products Co. Hdqrs., N.J., Sunning Plaza Office and Apt. Complex, Hong Kong, Raffles City Hotel, Office and Shopping Complex, Singapore, The Morton N. Meyerson Symphony Ctr., Dallas, Barell Residence, Kingspoint, N.Y., St. David's Episc. Ch., N.Y. Mem. bd. dirs. Palmer House Group Home for the Handicapped, Larchmont, N.Y., 1980—. Served to 1st lt. USAF, 1958-60. Recipient Design award, N.J. Bus. and Industry Assn., 1982. Mem. AIA (design awards com., scholarship com., Design award 1974), N.Y. State Assn. Architects, Nat. Trust for Historic Preservation, Nat. Council Archtl. Regis. Bds. Club: University (Larchmont). Home: 2 Acorn Ln Larchmont NY 10538 Office: Heisel Assocs Architects PC 611 Broadway New York NY 10012

HEISLER, ELWOOD DOUGLAS, hotel executive; b. Wilmington, Del., June 29, 1935; s. Elwood Dean and Laura Matilda (Hutchison) H.; B.A., Mich. State U., 1957; postgrad. Johns Hopkins U., 1979—. Asst. mgr. Kents Restaurants, Atlantic City, 1957; mgr. Korean Mil. Adv. Group Officers' Club and Housing Office, Tague, 1958-59; innkeeper Treadway Inns Corp., N.Y., Mass., Colo., Ohio, Va., Del., 1960-68, Holiday Inns, Inc., Lansing and Troy, Mich., 1969-77; gen. mgr. Quality Inns, Inc., Towson, Md., 1977—. Mem. St. George's Soc. of Baltimore, German Soc. of Md., L'Amicale-Soc. Francaise de Baltimore, Hist. Soc. of Delaware, Md. Hist. Soc., Nantucket Hist. Assn., Md. Retired Officers Assn., sec. Md. state adv. council Future Bus. Leaders of Am./Phi Beta Lambda; bd. dirs. Gunpowder Youth Camps, Inc.; mem. greater Balt. Com.; chmn. Balt. Country Travel Council; mem. Balt. Council on Fgn. Affairs, Md. Travel Council. Served to 1st lt. U.S. Army, 1957-59. Named Top Ten Innkeeper Holiday Inns Internat., 1975; Md. Bus. Person of the Year, Future Bus. Leaders of Am., 1981, Bus. Person of Year nat. chpt., 1981, award of Merit Baltimore County C. of C., 1982, Paul Harris fellow Rotary Found., 1983, Outstanding Service award Md. Future Bus. Leaders of Am., 1984, Baltimore Mayor's Citation, 1984. Mem. Balt. Econ. Soc., Balt. Public Relations Council, Am. Hotel and Motel Assn., Hotel Sales Mgmt. Assn., Md. Hotel and Motor Inn Assn., Balt. Country Lic. Beverage A Assn., Md. Internat. Trade Assn., Travel and Tourism Research Assn., Balt. County C. of C. (v.p.). Republican. Congregationalist. Clubs: Univ., Towson Rotary (pres.), Advt. of Balt. (bd. govs.). Clubs: Baltimore Yacht. Author manual for resort ops., 1965; author: The Rising Sun of the Japanese Hotel Industry, 1980. Home: 516 Charles Street Ave Towson MD 21204 Office: Quality Inn 1015 York Rd Towson MD 21204

HEISLER, HAROLD REINHART, management consultant; b. Chgo.; s. Harold Reinhart and Beulah Mary (Schade) H.; B.M.E., U. Ill., 1954. Mgmt. cons. Ill. Power Co., Decatur, 1954—, mem. Nuclear Power Group, Inc., Argonne (Ill.) Nat. Lab., 1955-57; chmn. fossil fuel com., West Central region FPC, Chgo., 1966-68; chmn. evaluation com. Coal Gasification Group, Inc., 1971-75; chmn. Decatur Marine Inc., 1964-66; dir. Indsl. Water Supply Co., Robinson, Ill., 1975-77; pub. speaker in field; mem. Ill. Gov.'s Fuel and Energy Bd., 1970, Ill. Commerce Commn. Fuel and Energy Bd., 1971-75, Ill. Energy Resources Commn. Coal Study Panel, 1976-79, evaluation com. of kilngas process, 1976-80; mem. power plant productivity com. Ill. Commerce Commn., 1977-79; mem. com. on nuclear power plant constrn. Inst. Nuclear Power Ops. Mem. ASME, Nat., Ill. socs. profl. engrs., U. Ill. Alumni Assn., Sigma Phi Delta. Conceptual designer power plant sites and recreational lakes, Baldwin and Clinton, Ill. Home: 2350 W Main St Decatur IL 62522 Office: Ill Power Co 500 S 27th St Decatur IL 62525

HEIZER, EDGAR FRANCIS, JR., venture capitalist; b. Detroit, Sept. 23, 1929; s. Edgar Francis and Grace Adelia (Smith) H.; m. Molly Bradley Hunt, June 17, 1952; children: Linda Heizer Seaman, Molly Hunt, Edgar Francis III. BS, Northwestern U., 1951; JD, Yale U., 1954. Bar: Ill. 1954; CPA, Ill. Mem. audit and tax staff Arthur Andersen & Co., Chgo., 1954-56; fin. analyst Kidder, Peabody & Co., Chgo., 1956-58; mgmt. cons. Booz, Allen & Hamilton, Chgo., 1958-62; asst. treas. Allstate Ins. Co., Northbrook, Ill., 1962-69; chmn., founder, chief exec. officer Heizer Corp., Chgo., 1969-85; venture capitalist Tucker's Town, Bermuda, 1985—; bd. dirs. Amdahl Corp., Sunnyvale, Calif., Needham & Co., N.Y., Material Sci. Corp., Elk Grove Village, Ill.; adv. bd. Kellogg Sch. Mgmt., Garrett Isnt., Northwestern U. Chmn. task force on capital formation for White House Conf. on Small Bus., 1978-80. Mem. Delta Upsilon (chmn. bd. dirs. 1985-88), Nat. Venture Capital Assn. (founder, 1st pres., chmn.), Nat. Assn. Small Bus. Investment Cos. Republican. Presbyterian. Clubs: Chgo. Curling, Shoreacres, Econ. of Chgo., Coral Beach and Tennis, Mid-Ocean; Riddells Bay Golf (Bermuda). Home and Office: Dover House, Tuckers Town Bermuda also: 261 Bluffs Edge Dr Lake Forest IL 60045

HEIZER, IDA ANN, real estate broker; b. Oxford, Colo., Mar. 14, 1919; d. Albert Henry and Ella (Engbrook) Ordener; m. Donald Heizer, Apr. 7, 1947; children—Robert John. Diploma, Brown's Bus. Coll., 1939; student Otero Jr. Coll., 1946-47, U. So. Colo., 1962; grad. Realtors Inst., Nat. Assn. Real Estate Bds., 1972. Cert. closer real estate, cert. residential specialist. Clk., Montgomery Ward Co., LaJunta, Colo., 1935-37; bookkeeper Colo. Bank & Trust Co., LaJunta, 1937-38; cashier/bookkeeper Fox Theatre, LaJunta, 1939-40; clk. Civil Service, LaJunta, 1940-45; stenoabstractor Deaf Smith Abstract Office, Hereford, Tex., 1948-50; sec. Otero County Agt. Office, Rocky Ford, Colo., 1953-55; real estate broker Pueblo Realty & Service Co., Inc., Colo., 1958-86; ret., 1988. Mem. Pueblo Bd. Realtors, Nat. Assn. Real Estate Appraisers, Nat. Assn. Realtors, Colo. Assn. Realtors, Women's Council Realtors, Daus. of the Republic Tex., Beta Sigma Phi. Lodge: Quota Internat. Home and Office: 331 Van Buren St Pueblo CO 81004

HEJTMANEK, DANTON CHARLES, lawyer; b. Topeka, July 22, 1951; s. Robert Keith and Bernice Louise (Krause) H.; m. Jenny Jordan, May 26, 1973; 1 child, Brian J. BBA in Acctg., Washburn U., 1973, JD, 1975. Bar: Kans. 1976, U.S. Dist. Ct. Kans. 1976, U.S. Tax Ct. 1976. Ptnr. Schroer, Rice, Bryan & Lykins, P.A., Topeka, 1975-86, Bryan, Lykins, Hejtmanek & Wulz, P.A., Topeka, 1986—. Mem. ABA (rep. young lawyers Kans. and Nebr.), Kans. Bar Assn. (pres. young lawyers 1985), Am. Trial Lawyers Assn., Kans. Trial Lawyers Assn. Republican. Presbyterian. Lodge: Sertoma (pres. 1983). Home: 2800 Burlingame Rd Topeka KS 66611 Office: Bryan Lykins Hejtmanek & Wulz PA 222 W 7th St Topeka KS 66603 also: 222 SW 7th St Topeka KS 66603

HELANDER, JOHN WINSTON, stockbroker, petroleum consulting company executive; b. Tulsa, Oct. 1, 1961; s. Donald Peter and Ella Jane (McCoy) H. BBA, U. Okla., 1985; postgrad., Oral Roberts U., 1987. V.p. fin. Internat. Petroleum Cons., Inc., Tulsa, 1981—, also bd. dirs.; stockbroker Dean Witter Reynolds, Tulsa, 1985-86; chmn., pres. Winston Ventures Internat., Inc., Tulsa, 1986—; stockbroker Stifel, Nicolaus and Co., Inc., Tulsa, 1986-87; chmn., pres., Adam Smith Found., 1989—; mem. adv. bd. small bus. devel. ctr. Tulsa U. Mem. Christian Businessmen's Com., 1985-87, Mayor's Econ.. Devel. Task Force, Tulsa, 1986, Rep. Men's Club, 1985-87; vol., campus dir. Campus Crusade for Christ, 1985-87; escort Internat. Council, Tulsa, 1985-87; 2d vice chmn. Tulsa County Young Reps., 1986, 1st vice chmn., to Nov. 1987, pres. 1987—; del. credentials com. Okla. Young Reps., 1987, vice chmn. precinct, 1987; chmn., 1988; fin. com. Young Reps. Nat. Com., 1987; mem. Okla. Acad. for State Goals, 1987. Named one of Outstanding Young Men Am., 1987. Mem. Fin. Mgmt. Assn., Okla. Pvt. Enterprise Forum, Entrepreneurs of Tulsa (founder and dir.), Assn. Collegiate Entrepreneurs/Young Entrepreneurs Orgn., Met. C. of C., Mensa, Delta Upsilon. Presbyterian. Club: Economics (Tulsa). Home: 4124 E 98th St Tulsa OK 74137 Office: Winston Ventures Internat Inc 4124 E 98th St Tulsa OK 74137

HELBING, EMIL GEORGE, textile executive; b. Wilmington, Del., Dec. 25, 1926; s. Emil and Martha Ellen (Doughten) H.; m. Joan Lorraine Bize, Oct. 6, 1956; children: Matthew, Joseph, Christine, Timothy, James, Thomas. BA in Bus. Adminstrn., Muhlenberg Coll., 1952. Acct. DuPont Co., Wilmington, Del., 1952-54; supr. acct. Jos. Bancroft, Inc., Wilmington, Del., 1954-64, Hewlett-Packard, Avondale, Pa., 1964-69; asst. controller Mannington Mills, Salem, N.J., 1969-71; treas., chief fin. officer Wellco Carpet Corp., Calhoun, Ga., 1971—; bd. dirs. Wellco Carpet Corp., Calhoun, 1973—. Avocations: gardening, golf, exercise. Office: Wellco Carpet Corp PO Box 12281 Calhoun GA 30701

HELDER, BRUCE ALAN, metal products executive; b. Grand Rapids, Mich., July 1, 1953; s. Harry Martin and Margaret (Ditmar) H.; m. Arlene Faye Docter, May 29, 1975; children: Amanda Joy, David Ryan, Joel Brent, Jonathan Bruce, Brandon Michael. Student, Calvin Coll., 1972-73, Grand Valley State Coll., Allendale, Mich., 1974. Lic. realtor assoc.; cert. media specialist. Indsl. sales rep. Newman Communications, Inc., Grand Rapids, 1971-81; nat. sales mgr. Best Metal Products Co., Grand Rapids, 1981—; v.p. Venture Property Mgmt. Co. Mem. Real Estate Bd. Grand Rapids. Republican. Mem. Christian Reformed Ch. Home: 1336 Richwood Dr SE Grand Rapids MI 49508 Office: Best Metal Products Co 3570 Raleigh Dr Grand Rapids MI 49508

HELFINSTEIN, BERT IRA, computer retailing executive; b. N.Y.C., Sept. 23, 1933; s. Jack Helfinstein and Miriam (Lampert) Smith; m. Eileen Carrel, June, 1959 (div. Mar. 1970); children: Paul, Susan, David; m. Judith K. Dimon, June 15, 1970 (div. Oct. 1977); children: Amy; m. Karen Francis, Apr. 1, 1978 (div. 1987); children: Benjamin, Sarah. BSEE, NYU, 1957. Pres. PRC Computer Systems, McLean, Va., 1980-82, CGI Systems, McLean, 1982-83, Source Telecomputing, McLean, 1983-84; v.p. ops. Entre' Computers, Vienna, Va., 1984-86, pres., chief exec. officer, 1986—; bd. dirs. Arena Stage, Washington; chmn. Entre Computer Ctrs., Inc. Served to 1st lt. U.S. Army, 1957-59. Home: 1217 Tottenham Ct Reston VA 22094 Office: Entre Computer Ctrs Inc 1430 Spring Hill Rd McLean VA 22102

HELGESON, EUNICE MAY, machine tool distribution executive; b. Tracy, Minn., Oct. 21, 1947; d. Oscar J. and Louella A. (Rialson) H. BA in Bus. Adminstrn. magna cum laude, Augsburg Coll., 1969; cert. credit and fin. mgmt. with high distinction, U. Minn., 1977. Sec. Tracy (Minn.) Luth. Ch., 1964-65; bookkeeper Milton Granquist Co., Mpls., 1965-68, office mgr., 1968-70, sec., treas., 1970—. Author: Helleson Family History, 1983, Helgeson Family History, 1984. Bd. dirs., treas. Boundary Creek 6th Homeowners Assn., Maple Grove, Minn., 1979-83; coun. mem. Advent Luth. Ch., Maple Grove, 1982-88, treas. 1984-85, v.p., 1986. Mem. Nat. Assn. Credit Mgmt. (bd. dirs. North Cen. chpt., pres. 1984-85, assoc. award with distinction 1972, fellow award with distinction 1977, credit master designation 1987), Credit Womens Group (pres. 1976-77), Am. Soc. Women Accts. (pres. Mpls.-St. Paul chpt. 68, 1974-75), Sons of Norway (pres. Syttende Mai Lodge 1-517 1987-88), Inst. Cert. Mgmt. Accts. (cert. mgmt. acctg. 1980), Cert. Credito Exec. Home: 10943 105 Ave N Maple Grove MN 55369 Office: Milton Granquist Co 3515 48th Ave N Minneapolis MN 55429

HELITZER, MORRIE, publisher; b. N.Y.C., June 8, 1925; s. Abraham and Ethel (Lifschutz) H.; B.S. in Elec. Engring., Cornell U., 1945; A.M. in Polit. Sci., U. Chgo., 1948; postgrad. internat. affairs Columbia U., 1960-61; m. Florence Saperstein, May 29, 1955; m. 2d, Irene Rodman, Sept. 29, 1974; children—Jonathan Aaron, Cynthia Ann, Eve Frances, Elizabeth Sara. Reporter, UP, Madison, Wis., 1946-47, Internat. News Service, Chgo., 1947-48, Paris, 1948, Berlin, 1948-49, Frankfurt, Ger., 1949, bur. chief, Vienna, 1949-50, Belgrade, 1950; freelance writer, Los Angeles, 1950-53; fgn. corr. NBC, India, 1954; news editor ABC, N.Y.C., 1955-56; with McGraw Hill Inc., various locations, 1956-78, v.p. book co., 1966-73, gen. mgr. pub. co., 1976-78; pres. Helitzer Communications, Inc., Sea Cliff, N.Y., 1979—; pres., pub., editor-in-chief New Acct. Co., Glen Cove, N.Y., 1985—; adminstr. McGraw Hill St. Acad., 1968-71. Mem. exec. bd. Princeton Jewish Center, 1970-71. Served with USN, 1945-46. Press fellow Council Fgn. Relations, 1960-61. Mem. Nat. Press Club. Author: The Cold War, 1977; contbr. articles to N.Y. Times Mag., Swiss Rev. World Affairs, Neue Zurcher Zeitung. Address: 72 DuBois Ave Sea Cliff NY 11579

HELLAND, GEORGE ARCHIBALD, JR., equipment manufacturing company executive, management consultnat; b. San Antonio, Nov. 28, 1937; s. George Archibald and Ruth (Gorman) H.; m. Josephine Howell, June 9, 1962 (div. 1989); children—Jane Elizabeth, Thomas Gorman. B.S.M.E., U. Tex., 1959; M.B.A. with distinction, Harvard U., 1961. Registered profl. engr., Tex. With Cameron Iron Works, Inc., Houston, 1961-77, asst. sales mgr., 1963, dist. sales mgr., 1964, mgr. oil tool products, 1968, v.p., 1969-75, exec. v.p., 1975-77; dist. sales mgr. Cameron Iron Works, Inc., U.K., Africa, 1965; product mgr. Cameron Iron Works, Inc., 1966; plant mgr. Cameron Iron Works, Inc., Leeds, Eng., 1967; v.p. Weatherford Internat., Inc., Houston, 1977; pres. Weatherford Internat., Inc., 1977-79, chief exec. officer, dir., 1978-79; pres. McEvoy Oilfield Equipment Co. (name changed to Sii McEvoy div. Smith Internat., Inc. 1980), Houston, 1979-85; pres. McCall Industries, Inc., Houston, 1986-87, also bd. dirs.; gen. mgmt. cons. 1987—; pres. Lockwood Corp., Gering, Nebr., 1986-87; chmn. bd. dirs. SIE Internat., Inc., Ft. Worth; prin. Innova Pontnes, 1988—. Bd. dirs. Briarwood Sch., Houston, Reiton Corp., Houston; trustee SW Research Inst.; mem. exec. com. Jr. Achievement of SE Tex. Recipient Five Outstanding Young Texans award Tex. Jr. C. of C., 1972; named Outstanding Young Houstonian Houston Jr. C. of C., 1972; Disting. Grad. Sch. Engring., U. Tex., 1977. Mem. Am. Inst. Mining, Metall. and Petroleum Engrs., ASME, Am. Petroleum Inst. (dir.), Inst. Gas Engrs. (U.K.), Tex. Soc. Profl. Engrs., Am. Wellhead Equipment Assn. (pres. 1967), Petroleum Equipment Suppliers Assn. (pres. 1976-77), Houston C. of C., Brit. Am. Bus. Assn. (dir.), Tau Beta Pi, Phi Eta Sigma, Pi Tau Sigma, Sigma Nu, Frairs Soc. Presbyterian. Home and Office: 651 Bering Dr #1002 Houston TX 77057

HELLAND, MARK DUANE, small business owner; b. Eldora, Iowa, May 19, 1949; s. Duane J. and Mary Carolyn (Bloomberg) H.; m. Lois Ann Lebakken, Aug. 15, 1970; children: Alissa, Jonathan. BA, Luther Coll., 1971; JD, U. Minn., 1974; postgrad., Harvard U., 1985, 88. Bar: Minn. 1974, Wis. 1980. Assoc. Berg Law Offices, Stewartville, Minn., 1974-77; v.p. Legal Systems, Inc., Eau Claire, Wis., 1977-78; sr. editor Lawyers Coop. Pub. Co., Rochester, N.Y., 1978-80; exec. dir. Profl. Edn. Systems, Inc., Eau Claire, 1980-81, chief exec. officer, 1981-88, pub., 1988—. Author: Minnesota Probate System, 1980, Wisconsin Rules of the Road, 1985. Mem. Greater Eau Claire C. of C. Office: Profl Edn Systems Inc 200 Spring St PO Box 1428 Eau Claire WI 54702

HELLAUER, JAMES CARROLL, insurance company executive; b. Pitts., Feb. 22, 1939; s. Joseph Francis and Margaret Cecelia (Carroll) H.; m. Margaret Ruth Knowles, June 10, 1961 (div. 1981); children: James Douglas, Christine Lynn, Robert Alan; m. Carolyn Donzanti, Nov. 26, 1982. BS, U.S. Naval Acad., 1961; MBA, Harvard U., 1969. V.p., chief fin. officer Kappa Systems, Inc., Arlington, Va., 1970-76; pres., chief exec. officer James C. Hellauer Cons., Danbury, Conn., 1976-78, 80-82, Scholler Bros., Inc., Phila., 1978-80; sr. v.p., chief fin. officer Provident Indemnity Life Ins. Co., Norristown, Pa., 1982-86, pres., chief exec. officer, 1987—; also bd. dirs. Provident Indemnity Life Ins. Co., Norristown; pres., chief exec. officer Provident Am. Corp., Norristown, 1987—, also bd. dirs.; bd. dirs. Automated Scis. Group. Chmn., founding pres. Wellness Council Delaware Valley, 1985—. Served to lt. comdr. USN, 1961-70. Clubs: Sunnybrook golf, Phila. Aviation Country. Office: Provident Indemnity Life Ins Co 2500 DeKalb Pike Norristown PA 19404

HELLENBRAND, SAMUEL HENRY, diversified industry executive, lawyer; b. N.Y.C., Nov. 11, 1916; s. Louis H. and Fannie (Cohen) H.; children: Kathy Noreen, Linda Caryn. LL.B., Bklyn. Law Sch. St. Lawrence U., 1941, LL.M., 1942. Bar: N.Y. 1942. With N.Y. Central R.R., 1942-68, atty., asst. to gen. atty., tax atty., 1942-52, gen. tax atty., 1952-56, dir. taxes finance dept., 1956-63, v.p. planning and devel., 1963-64, v.p. real estate, 1964-68; v.p. indsl. devel. and real estate Penn Central Co., 1968-70, v.p. real estate and taxes, 1970-71; pres. Pa. Co., 1970-71; v.p. exec. asst. to pres., dir. real estate affairs ITT, 1971-81; chmn. fin. com., vice-chmn. AMTRAK, 1982—; dir. Security Capital Corp., 1983—. Mem. ABA, Assn. Bar City N.Y. Home: 177 E 75th St New York NY 10021

HELLER, H(EINZ) ROBERT, federal government official; b. Cologne, Germany, Jan. 8, 1940; s. Heinrich and Karoline (Hermann) H.; m. Emily Mitchell, Dec. 5, 1970; children: Kimberly, Christopher. MA in Econs., U. Minn., 1962; PhD, U. Calif., Berkeley, 1965. Instr. U. Calif., Berkeley, 1965; assoc. prof. econs. UCLA, 1965-71; prof. U. Hawaii, Honolulu, 1971-74; chief fin. studies div. Internat. Monetary Fund, Washington, 1974-78; sr. v.p., dir. internat. econ. rsch. Bank of Am., San Francisco, 1978-86; gov. Bd. Govs. Fed. Res. System, Washington, 1986—; vice chmn. Fed. Fin. Instns. Examination Coun.; mem. Nat. Adv. Coun. on Internat. Monetary and Fin. Policies, 1987—; mem. com. internat. affairs U.S. Coun. on Internat. Bus., N.Y., 1979-86; trustee Inst. Internat. Trade, Berkeley, 1983-86; mem. econ. adv. com. Inst. Internat. Fin.; adv. com. internat. affairs program Golden Gate U., San Francisco; mem. bd. govs. Internat. Mgmt. and Devel. Inst., Washington, 1987-88. Author: International Trade, 1968, rev. edit. 1973, International Monetary Economics, 1974, The Economic System, 1972, Japanese Investment in the U.S., 1974; mem. editorial bd. Jour. Money, Credit and Banking, 1975-83, Internat. Trade Jour., 1985-88; contbr. articles to profl. jours. Ford Found. grantee, 1965-69; NATO fellow, 1973-74. Mem. Royal Econ. Soc., Am. Econ. Assn., Western Econ. Assn. (exec. bd. 1977-81), San Francisco Yacht Club, Tiburon Peninsula Club. Office: Fed Res System 20th and C Sts NW Washington DC 20551

HELLER, JOHN L., II, advertising company executive; b. Galesburg, Ill., Jan. 23, 1953; s. John L. and Wilma (Medows) H.; m. Brenda June Baxter, Nov. 17, 1972; children: Holly Renee, Kelly Susanne. Sales rep. H&K Electric Supply, Inc., Chillicothe, Mo., 1971-73, Schwan Sales Enterprises, Inc., Chillicothe, 1973-79; sales mgr. Schwan Sales Enterprises, Inc., Aurora, Mo., 1979-81; nat. promotions mgr. Schwan Sales Enterprises, Inc., Marshall, Minn., 1981-86; pres. ABar Assocs., Inc., Marshall, 1986—. Mem. Nat. Premium Sales Execs., Minn. Incentive Club, Splty. Advt. Assn. Internat., Marshall C. of C. Republican. Baptist. Office: ABar Assocs Inc 1105 E College Dr Marshall MN 56258

HELLER, JOHN RODERICK, III, lawyer, business executive; b. Harrisburg, Pa., Aug. 14, 1937; s. John Roderick and Susie May (Ayres) H.; m. Nancy Ann Washburn, Aug. 18, 1962; children: Elizabeth, Carolynn, John. AB summa cum laude, Princeton U., 1959; AM in History, Harvard U., 1960, JD magna cum laude, 1963. Bar: D.C. 1964. Assoc. Wilmer, Cutler & Pickering, Washington, 1963-65, 68-71, ptnr., 1971-82, of counsel, 1982-85; spl. asst. to dir. for India, AID, New Delhi, 1966-67, regional legal adviser, Pakistan, 1967-68; pres. Bristol Compressors, Inc. (Va.), 1982-85; pres., bd. dirs. Nat. Corp. for Housing Partnerships, 1985; bd. dirs. Auto-Trol Tech. Corp., Riggs Nat. Bank; prof. law George Washington U., 1976-81. Recipient Meritorious Honor award U.S. Dept. State, 1967. Trustee, bd. dirs. Nat. Trust Hist. Preservation, Washington Opera Soc., Fed. City Council. Mem. ABA, Am. Soc. Internat. Law, Soc. of Cin., Supreme Ct. Hist. Soc. (dir.), Metro. Club (Washington), Chevy Chase Club. Presbyterian. Office: Nat Corp for Housing Partnerships 1225 I St NW Washington DC 20005

HELLER, MELANIE LOUISE, internal auditor; b. Panama City, Fla., Mar. 26, 1948; d. Cary Truman Sr. and Lillian Louise (Bland) Hartzog; m. Jack Carl Miller, June 17, 1973 (dec. Dec. 1983); children: Timothy Jack, Jennifer Melanie, Bryan William. AAS, Gulf Coast Jr. Coll., 1969; BA, U. West Fla., 1973. CPA, Fla. Acct. Escambia County Assn. Retarded Citizens, Pensacola, Fla., 1972-73; prin. Heller Acctg., Birstol, Fla., 1973-81; internal auditor Bay County Sch. Bd., Panama City, Fla., 1981—. Mem. Fla. Assn. Sch. Adminstrs., Fla. Assn. Sch. Bus. Ofcls., Fla. Sch. Fin. Officers Assn., Notary Pub. Assn., Jaycees. Office: Bay County Sch Bd Hwy 98 & Liddon Ave Panama City FL 32401

HELLER, RONALD GARY, manufacturing company executive, lawyer; b. N.Y.C., May 29, 1946; s. Max and Lucy (Weinwurm) H.; m. Joyce R. Mueller, May 29, 1969; children—Caren, Amy, Beth. B.A., CCNY, 1967; postgrad., U. Wis. Law Sch., 1967-68; J.D., Fordham U., 1972. Bar: N.Y. Assoc. Cahill Gordon & Reindel, N.Y.C., 1972-77; asst. sec. Cluett, Peabody & Co. Inc., N.Y.C., 1977-81, sec., 1981-86, v.p., sec., gen. counsel, 1986-87; asst. gen. counsel Ingersoll Rand Co., Woodcliff Lake, N.J., 1988—. Served with USAR, 1969-75. Mem. Am. Soc. Corp. Secs.

HELLER, RONALD IAN, lawyer; b. Cleve., Sept. 4, 1956; s. Grant L. and Audrey P. (Lecht) H.; m. Shirley Ann Stringer, Mar. 23, 1986. AB with high honors, Univ Mich., 1976, MBA, 1979, JD, 1980. Bar: Hawaii 1980, U.S. Ct. Claims 1982, U.S. Tax Ct. 1981, U.S. Ct. Appeals (9th cir.) 1981; Trust Territory of Pacific Islands 1982, Republic of Marshall Islands 1982; CPA, Hawaii. Assoc. Hoddick, Reinwald, O'Connor & Marrack, Honolulu, 1980-84; ptnr. Reinwald, O'Connor & Marrack, 1984-87; ptnr. Torkildson, Katz, Jossem, Fonseca, Jaffe & Moore, Honolulu, 1988—; adj. prof. U. Hawaii Sch. Law, 1981; bd. dirs. Hawaii Women Lawyers Found., Honolulu, 1984-86, Hawaii Performing Arts Co., Honolulu, 1984—. Actor, stage mgr. Honolulu Community Theatre, 1983—, Hawaii Performing Arts Co., Honolulu, 1982—. Mem. AICPA, ABA, Hawaii State Bar Assn., Hawaii Soc. CPAs (chmn tax com. 1985-86, legis. com. 1987-88, bd. dirs. 1988—), Hawaii Women Lawyers, Assn. Trial Lawyers Am. Office: Torkildson Katz Jossem Fonseca Jaffe & Moore 700 Bishop St Ste 1500 Honolulu HI 96813

HELLIWELL, GEOFFREY ERNEST, treasurer; b. Walsall, West Midlands, Eng., Apr. 24, 1951; came to U.S., 1972; s. Ernest Edward and Rae Isabel (Collins) H.; m. Carol Anne Henderson, Apr. 24, 1976; children: Lydia Anne, Ross Edward. BA, U. Sheffield, Eng., 1972; MBA, Standford U., 1974; JD, Suffolk U., 1981. Bar: Mass. 1981. Mgmt. trainee 1st Nat. Bank, Dallas, 1974-75; fin. analyst 1st Nat. Bank, London, 1975-76; various positions Cabot Corp., Boston, 1976-82, asst. treas., 1982-86, treas., 1986—. Mem. Mass. Bar Assn., Fin. Execs. Inst. Home: 40 Lantern Ln Wrentham MA 02093 Office: Cabot Corp 950 Winter St Box 9073 Waltham MA 02254

HELLMAN, F(REDERICK) WARREN, banker; b. N.Y.C., July 25, 1934; s. Marco F. and Ruth (Koshl) H.; m. Patricia Christina Sander, Oct. 5, 1955; children: Frances, Patricia H., Marco Warren, Judith. BA, U. Calif., Berkeley, 1955; MBA, Harvard U., 1959. With Lehman Brothers, N.Y.C., 1959-84; ptnr. Lehman Brothers, 1963-84; exec. mng. dir. Lehman Bros., Inc., 1970-73, pres., 1973-75; ptnr. Hellman Ferri Investment Assocs., 1981—, Matrix Ptnrs., 1981—; gen. ptnr. Hellman & Friedman, San Francisco; bd.dir. DN & E Walter, Alamitos Land Co., Allstar Inns (formerly Shaughnessy Holdings Inc.), Am. Pres. Cos., Ltd., Levi Strauss & Co., Mut. N.Y., Idetek, Inc., Consilium Inc., Williams-Sonoma, Inc., Il Fornaio Inc. Chmn. bd. trustees Mills Coll. 1st lt. AUS, 1955-57. Mem. Explorers Club. Clubs: Bond, Piping Rock, Century Country, Family, Pacific Union. Office: Hellman & Friedman One Maritime Pla 12th Fl San Francisco CA 94111

HELLMAN, HERBERT MARTIN, lawyer; b. Spring Valley, N.Y., Aug. 4, 1943; s. Leon and Gertrude (Schwartz) H.; m. Reva Gaines, Dec. 26, 1965 (div. Aug. 1974); 1 child, Adam D.; m. Monica Deliso, Nov. 6, 1975; 1 child, Andrew D. BA, U. Ariz., 1966; JD, U. Tulsa, 1969. Bar: Okla. 1969, D.C. 1969, N.Y. 1971, U.S. Dist. Ct. (so. dist.) N.Y. 1972, U.S. Dist. Ct. (ea. dist.) N.Y. 1972. Trial atty. FTC, Washington, 1969-70; assoc. Weil, Gotshal & Manges, N.Y.C., 1970-78; sr. atty. J.C. Penney & Co., Inc., N.Y.C., 1978-80; v.p. R.H. Macy & Co., Inc., N.Y.C., 1980-84, sr. v.p., gen. counsel, 1984—. Editor U. Tulsa Law Rev. Recipient Appreciation award Nat. Retail Merchants Assn., N.Y.C., 1985. Mem. ABA (sec. corp. banking and bus. law 1984—), Assn. of Bar City N.Y. (com. on corp. law depts. 1984—), N.Y. State Bar Assn. (task force on simplification 1984—), Retail Industry Trade Action Coalition (mem. steering com. 1984—). Home: 55 E 86th St New York NY 10028 Office: R H Macy & Co Inc 151 W 34th St New York NY 10001

HELLMAN, PETER STUART, technical manufacturing executive; b. Cleve., Oct. 16, 1949; s. Arthur Cerf and Joan (Alburn) H.; m. Alyson Dulin Ware, Sept. 18, 1976; children: Whitney Ware, Garrettson Stuart. BA, Hobart Coll., 1972; MBA, Case Western Res. U., 1984. V.p. Irving Trust Co., N.Y.C., 1972-79; fin. planning assoc. Standard Oil Co., Cleve., 1979-82, mgr. fin. planning, 1982-84, dir. ops. analysis, 1984-85, asst. treas., 1985-86, treas., 1986-88, gen. mgr. crude oil trading, 1987-89; v.p., treas. TRW Inc., Cleve., 1989—. Bd. dirs. Kidney Found. of Ohio, Inc. Clubs: Tavern, Chagrin Valley Hunt (Cleve.). Office: Standard Oil Co 200 Public Sq Cleveland OH 44114

HELLSTROM, JOHN PAUL, JR., investment banker; b. Hartford, Conn., Feb. 22, 1941; s. John Paul and Edith (Oakes) H.; m. Linda Lyall, Sept. 16, 1967; children: Emily Edith, Erika Christie. BA, Hobart Coll., 1964; MBA, Columbia U., N.Y.C., 1970. Asst. Sec. Mfr.'s Hanover Trust Co., N.Y.C., 1964-69; v.p. Blyth Eastman Dillon, N.Y.C., 1970-75; mng. dir. The First Boston Corp., N.Y.C., 1975—; dir. Am. Gas and Oil Ltd., Greeenwich, Conn., 1981—. Trustee Cushing Acad., Ashburnham, Mass., 1984—. Mem. Urban Land Inst. Office: 1st Boston Corp 12 E 49th St New York NY 10017

HELLSTROM, PAMELA DONWORTH, human resource development executive; b. Bangor, Maine, Apr. 4, 1948; d. Clarence Arlowe and Margaret Mary (Donworth) Small; m. Michael Willard Hellstrom, Oct. 12, 1978; 1 child, Kirsten Elyse. BA in English Edn., Merrimack Coll., 1970. Lic. vocat. educator, Wash. Asst. dir. pub. relations, employment counselor Meals-On-Wheels, Seattle, 1970-72; social services asst. Madigan Army Med. Ctr., Tacoma, 1972-73, social work asst., 1974-81; chief counselor drug and alcohol treatment ctr. Am. Lake VA Health Ctr., Tacoma, 1973-74; trainer, cons. alt. chief examiner Gen. Equivalency Diploma program L.H. Bates Vocat. Tech. Inst., Tacoma, 1983-84; founder, pres. Growth Techs., Inc., Tacoma, 1984—, dir. trainer edn. program and ednl. rsch. project. Mem. Am. Mgmt. Assn., Am. Soc. Tng. and Devel., Tacoma-Pierce County C. of C. Democrat. Roman Catholic. Office: Growth Techs Inc 10520 Bridgeport Way SW Ste 102 Tacoma WA 98499

HELM, JOAN MARY, financial planner; b. Springfield, Ill., June 30, 1934; d. Elwood R. and Juanita (Nash) Ressler. Student, Northwestern U., 1972. Cert. fin. planner. With mgmt. engring. dept. Ill. Bell Telephone Co. and So. Bell, 1956-74; agt. Mutual of Omaha, 1974-78; gen. agt. Lafayette Life, 1977-84; pres. Helm Fin. Group, Boca Raton, Fla., 1983—; registered rep., prin. Pvt. Ledger Fin. Services, Boca Raton, 1983—; moderator radio show Sta. WSBR, 1986-87. Active Rep. Party, Chgo., 1972-73. Mem. Internat. Assn. Fin. Planners (pres. Gold Coast chpt. 1986-88), Inst. Fin. Planners, Registry Fin. Planners Practioners, Nat. Assn. Female Execs., Inst. Cert. Fin. Planners, Boca Hotel and Club. Office: Helm Fin Group 400 S Dixie Hwy Ste 411 Boca Raton FL 33432

HELMS, LUTHER SHERMAN, III, bank executive; b. Lubbock, Tex., Dec. 27, 1943; s. Luther S. and Maureen (Williams) H.; m. Gail D. Westover, Aug. 26, 1966; children: Sherman, Peter, Mason. BA, U. Ariz., 1966; MBA, U. Santa Clara, 1968. With Bank of Calif.; assoc. v.p. nat. dept. Seattle First Nat. Bank, Seattle, 1974-76, v.p. U.S. dept., 1976-80, sr. v.p. nat. div., 1980-82, sr. v.p. internat. div., 1982-83, exec. v.p., 1983-87, pres., 1988—. bd. dirs. Fred Hutchinson Cancer Rsch. Found., Eastside Performing Arts, Bellevue, Wash., 1985; trustee Wash. State Research Council, Seattle, 1984—, Pacific Northwest Ballet, Seattle, 1984. Clubs: Broadmoor Golf (Seattle), Columbia Tower, Rainier. Office: Seafirst Corp PO Box 3586 Seattle WA 98124

HELMUTH, NED D., financial planner; b. Kokomo, Ind., Mar. 24, 1928; s. Dewey J. and Mildred C. (Norton) H.; m. Arlene J. Schwartz, Oct. 5, 1952 (div. 1971); children: Pamela M. Jones, Michael J., Gretchen L.; m. S. Patricia Broadhurst Tautfest, Jan. 4, 1973; 1 child, Carol E. Green. BS in Mktg., Ind. U., 1952; MS in Fin. Services, Am. Coll., 1981. Cert. fin. planner, chartered fin. cons., CLU. Agt. Equitable Life Assurance Soc., Houston, 1952-53, Lafayette, Ind., 1953-58; agt. Nat. Life Ins. Co., Lafayette, 1958—; nat. trustee Life Underwriters Tng. Council, Washington, 1975-78. Author: The Client Approach-A Quality Method of Selling, 1963, There's No Fun Like Work, 1989. Bd. dirs. South Side Community Ctr., LAfayette, 1955-57; mem. adv. bd. Salvation Army, Lafayette, 1985-88; bd. dirs. Big Bros./Big Sisters, Lafayette, 1981-83. Cpl. U.S. Army, 1946-48, Korea. Named Underwriter of Yr. Lafayette Assn. Life Underwriters, 1972, Hoosier Underwriter of Yr. Ind. State Assn. Life Underwriters, 1972. Mem. Nat. Assn. Life Underwriters, Am. Soc. CLU's (bd. dirs., v.p. 1965-68), Assn. Advanced Life Underwriting, Am. Inst. Cert. Fin. Planners, Lafayette C. of C., Sarasota C. of C., Phi Gamma Delta, Rotary Club. Home: 1760 Garden St West Lafayette IN 47906 Office: Nat Life Ins Co 1000 Bank One Bldg Lafayette IN 47901

HELTON, SANDRA L., finance executive; b. Paintsville, Ky., Dec. 9, 1949; d. Paul Edward and Ella Rae (Van Hoose) H.; m. Norman M. Edelson, Apr. 15, 1978. BS, U. Ky., 1971; MBA, MIT, 1977. Capital budget adminstr. Corning (N.Y.) Glass Works, 1978-79, fixed assets mgr., 1979-80, controller electronics div., 1980-82, mgr. customer fin. services, 1982-84, dir. fin. services, 1984-86, asst. treas., 1986—. Vol. Mass. Gen. Hosp., Boston, 1976; asst. treas. Corning Mus. of Glass; treas., pres. bd. dirs. Chemung Valley Arts Council, Corning, 1981-87; bd. dirs., mem. fin. com. Clemens Performing Arts Ctr., Elmira, N.Y., 1985—; bd. dirs. Corning Summer Theatre, 1987—, Arnot Hosp. Found., 1988—; mem. adv. bd. Chase Lincoln, 1988—.

HELWIG, ARTHUR WOODS, chemical company executive; b. St. Louis, Feb. 1, 1929; s. Gunther Albert and Emma (Schumacher) H.; m. Evelyn Morgan, July 10, 1954; children: Paul, Katherine, Elizabeth, Mary. BS ChemE, U. Mo.-Rolla, 1950, ChemE (hon.), 1966; MS ChemE, U. Ill., 1952. Process engr. Ethyl Corp., Baton Rouge, 1952-53, econs. engr., 1953-56, supr., 1956-59, gen. supt., 1959-64; dir. planning Ethyl Corp., Baton Rouge and Richmond, Va., 1964-74; v.p. planning Ethyl Corp., Richmond, 1974—; bd. dirs. Solite Corp., Richmond. Trustee Sci. Mus. Va., Richmond, 1987, pres. Found., 1984-87. Served to 1st lt. U.S. Army, 1954-56. Mem. Am. Inst. Chem. Engring., Met. Richmond C. of C. (bd. dirs. 1986). Methodist. Club: Engrs. (v.p. 1987—) (Richmond). Home: 8911 Highfield Rd Richmond VA 23229 Office: Ethyl Corp 330 S 4th St Richmond VA 23217

HEMANN, RAYMOND GLENN, aerospace company executive; b. Cleve., Jan 24, 1933; s. Walter Harold Marsha Mae (Colbert) H.; B.S., Fla. State U., 1957; postgrad. U.S. Naval Postgrad. Sch., 1963-64, U. Calif. at Los Angeles, 1960-62; M.S. in Systems Engring., Calif. State U., Fullerton, 1970, M.A. in Econs., 1972; m. Lucile Tinnin Turnage, Feb. 1, 1958; children—James Edward, Carolyn Frances; m. Pamela Lehr, Dec. 18, 1987.Aero. engring. aide U.S. Navy, David Taylor Model Basin, Carderock, Md., 1956; analyst Fairchild Aerial Surveys, Tallahassee, 1957; research analyst Fla. Rd. Dept., Tallahassee, 1957-59; chief Autonetics div. N.Am. Rockwell Corp., Anaheim, Calif., 1959-69; v.p., dir. R. E. Manns Co., Wilmington, Calif., 1969-70; mgr. avionics design and analysis dept. Lockheed-Calif. Co., Burbank, 1970-72, mgr. advanced concepts div., 1976-82; gen. mgr. Western div. Arinc Research Corp., Santa Ana, 1972-76; dir. future requirements Rockwell Internat., 1982-85; dir. Threat Analysis, Corp. Offices, Rockwell Internat., 1985—; cons. various U.S. govt. agys.; mem. naval studies bd. Nat. Acad. Scis., 1985—; asst. prof. ops. analysis dept. U.S. Naval Postgrad. Sch., Monterey, Calif., 1963-64, Monterey Peninsula Coll., 1963; instr. ops. analysis Calif. State U., Fullerton, 1963, instr. quantitative methods, 1969-72; adj. fellow Ctr. Strategic and Internat. Studies, Washington, 1987—; pres. Asso. Aviation, Inc., Fullerton, 1965-74; lectr. Brazilian Navy, 1980, U. Calif., Santa Barbara, 1980, Yale U., 1985, Princeton U., 1986, U.S. Naval Postgrad. Sch., 1986; cons. to various corps. and govt. agys. Served with AUS, 1950-53. Syde P. Deeb scholar, 1956; Honor awards Nat. Assn. Remotely Piloted Vehicles, 1975, 76. Comml., glider and pvt. pilot. Fellow AAAS; mem. Ops. Research Soc. Am., IEEE, AIAA, Air Force Assn., N.Y. Acad. Scis., Nat. Acad. Scis. (Naval Studies Bd. 1985—), Assn. Old Crows, Phi Kappa Tau (past pres.). Episcopalian. Contbr. articles to profl. jours. and news media. Home: 1215 Hartwood Point Dr Pasadena CA 91107 Office: 2230 E Imperial Hwy El Segundo CA 90245

HEMBREE, HUGH LAWSON, III, diversified holding company executive; b. Fort Smith, Ark., Nov. 16, 1931; s. Raymond N. and Gladys (Newman) H.; m. Sara Janelle Young, Sept. 1, 1956; children—Hugh Lawson IV, Raymond Scott. B.S. in Bus. Adminstrn, U. Ark., 1953, J.D., 1958. In middle mgmt. Ark.-Best Freight Inc., Fort Smith, 1958-61; dir. finance Ark.-Best Freight Inc., 1961-65, v.p., 1965-67; pres., dir. Ark.-Best Corp., Fort Smith, 1967-73, chmn. bd., chief exec. officer, 1973-88; chmn. Sugar Hill Farms, Inc.; mng. ptnr. Sugar Hill Ptnrs., Sugar Hill Interests; chmn. exec. com. Merchants Nat. Bank; bd. dirs. First Mchts. Fin. Corp., Ft. Smith, Okla. Gas and Electric, Oklahoma City, Mchts. Nat. Bank Ft. Smith, Fed. Reserve Bank St. Louis; nat. adv. bd. Comml. Nat. Bank, Little Rock. Sec. Fort Smith/Sebastian County Joint Planning Commn., 1959-72; Ark. past chmn. Radio Free Europe Program; past chmn. devel. council, mem. dean's adv. com. Sch. Bus., U. Ark., past chmn. exec. com. univ. devel. assn.; past mem. Sebastian County Regional Park Commn.; past mem. Democratic Central Com. Ark.; past pres. Westark area council Boy Scouts Am., 1985-88, asst. treas. Nat. Exec. Bd. Boy Scouts Am., 1985-88, treas., 1988—; past area pres., mem. exec. com. South Central region; past Chmn. Ark.-Okla. Livestock and Ednl. Found.; chmn. fund raising program U. Ark., 1973-74; past trustee John Brown U., Siloam Springs, Ark., U. Ark. Found.; trustee U. Ark. Served to capt. USAF, 1953-55. Recipient Silver Antelope award, 1974, Silver Beaver award Boy Scouts Am., 1967, 69, Ark. Leadership and Community Service award, 1970, 75; named Ark. Outstanding Young Man of Year Ark. Jaycees, 1967. Mem. Nat. Assn. of Devel. Orgns. (chmn. adv. com. 1969-72), Ark. C. of C. (1st v.p. 1970-73, pres. 1973, 86-87, dir. 1972-74), Ft. Smith C. of C. (pres. 1970-73, 86), Nat. Young Presidents Orgn., U. Ark. Alumni Assn. (dir., mem. bldg. com.), Am. Trucking Assn., Nat. Assn. Mfrs. (dir. 1976, regional v.p. 1973-75, regional dir. 1976-77), Ark. Arts Center, Scabbard and Blade, Sigma Alpha Epsilon, Beta Gamma Sigma, Phi Eta Sigma, Delta Theta Phi, Alpha Kappa Psi. Episcopalian (vestryman). Clubs: Mason (32 deg., Shriner); Ft. Smith Hardscabble Country and Town (Ft. Smith), Fianna Hills Country (Ft. Smith); Capital (Little Rock); Garden of Gods (Colorado Springs); Texarkana (Ark.) Country. Home: 7 Accomac Pl Texarkana AR 75502 Office: Sugar Hill Farms Inc PO Box 17007 Fort Smith AR 72917

HEMINGER, EDWIN LLOYD, newspaper publisher; b. Findlay, Ohio, July 30, 1926; s. Russell Lowell and Golda (McClelland) H.; m. Barbara Jo Rieck, Sept. 20, 1952; children—Karl Lloyd, Margaret Ann Heminger Gordon, Kurt Frederick. B.A., Ohio Wesleyan U., 1948; M.S., Northwestern U., 1952; D. Jour. (hon.), Bethany Coll., 1980. Field sec. Delta Tau Delta, Indpls., 1948-49; asst. bus. mgr. Courier, Findlay, Ohio, 1952-59, pub., 1965—; v.p. Findlay Pub. Co., 1959-83, pres., 1983-89, chmn. bd. dirs., 1989—; pres. White River Broadcasting Co. Inc., 1983-88, chmn. bd. dirs., 1988—; bd. dirs. AP, 1985—, 5th 3d Bank of Northwestern Ohio, Celina Fin. Corp., Celina Mut. Ins. Co., Nat. Mut. Ins. Co., Nat. Gas & Oil Co. Pres. Findlay YMCA, 1965-67, United Way of Hancock County, 1969-70, Hancock Community Found., 1970-72, Hancock Hist. Mus. Assn., 1970-86; mem. Constl. Revision Commn., State of Ohio, 1970-77; trustee Findlay Coll., 1976, Ohio Wesleyan U., 1977-85. Served with USNR, 1944-45, 50-51. Mem. Am. Newspaper Pubs. Assn. (dir. 1980-88), Am. Newspaper Pubs. Assn. Found. (chmn. 1986-87), Ohio Newspaper Assn. (dir. 1979-88), Newspaper Advt. Bur. (dir. 1980-86), State of Ohio Newspapers Found. (pres. 1979-80), Soc. Profl. Journalists, Nat. Press Club, Toledo Press Club, Ohio C. of C. (chmn. bd. 1977-79), Findlay Area C. of C. (pres. 1959), Rotary, Findlay Country Club, Mid-Ocean Club, Belmont Country Club, Elks, Nat. Interfraternity Conf. (dir. 1979-87 , pres. 1986-87), Delta Tau Delta (nat. pres. 1972-74). Republican. Methodist.

HEMINGWAY, W(ILLIAM) DAVID, banker; b. Los Angeles, Apr. 28, 1947; s. Donald William and Donna (Laws) H.; m. Gay Etta Jorgensen, Apr. 15, 1977; children: Ryan, Jonathan, Jamon. BA, Brigham Young U., 1971; MBA, U. Utah, 1973. Sr. v.p. Zions First Nat. Bank, Salt Lake City, 1982-84, exec. v.p., 1984—; pres. Internat. TV Network, 1986-88, bd. dirs. Nev. State Bank, Las Vegas, Murdock Travel, Inc., Salt Lake City. Candidate Utah Legislature, Salt Lake City, 1972; mem. Electorial Coll., Salt Lake City, 1976, Utah adv. bd. to U.S. Civil Rights Commn., Salt Lake City, 1976—. Mem. Utah State Money Mgmt. Council. Republican. Mormon. Office: Zions First Nat Bank 1 S Main Salt Lake City UT 84111

HEMLEY, EUGENE ADAMS, trade association executive; b. Bklyn., Feb. 20, 1918; s. Benjamin and Fannie (Gottlieb) H.; B.E.E., U.S. Naval Acad., 1940; M.S. in Internat. Affairs, George Washington U., 1968; m. Charlotte McClure, Dec. 22, 1948; children—Philip, Paul, Anne, Margaret. Served as midshipman U.S. Navy, 1936-40, commd. ensign U.S. Navy, 1940, advanced through grades to capt., 1959; comdg. officer USS Bang, 1951, USS Volador, 1952, USS Bristol, 1956-57, USS Taconic, 1961-62, USS Northampton, 1965-66; dir. fleet communications div. Office Chief of Naval Ops., 1958-61, dep. dir. info. systems div., 1968-70; comdg. officer U.S. Naval Communications Sta., Japan, 1962-65; ret., 1970; dir. mgmt. info. systems Nat. Girl Scout Orgn., N.Y.C., 1970-74; computerization mgr. Nat. Council on Internat. Trade Documentation, N.Y.C., 1974-84 (name changed to The Internat. Trade Facilitation Council), assoc. dir., 1984-85, exec. dir., 1985—; U.S. bus. adviser meetings UN Econ. Commn. for Europe, 1982—. Mem. Citizens nominating commn. Town of Scarsdale, 1982-83. Decorated Silver Star. Mem. U.S. Naval Inst., Naval Acad. Alumni Assn. (v.p. N.Y. chpt. 1982-83, pres. 1984-85, trustee 1985—). Clubs: N.Y. Yacht, Army-Navy Country, Scarsdale Town, County Tennis (v.p. 1983-84, pres. 1985-87). Editor: Cardis Standards Manual, 1981, Nat. Council on Internat. Trade Documentation Computerization News, 1982-84. Home: 20 Cohawney Rd Scarsdale NY 10583 Office: UN Econ Commn for Europe 350 Broadway New York NY 10013

HEMMERDINGER, H. DALE, real estate executive; b. Washington, Oct. 31, 1944; s. Monroe Elliott Hemmerdinger and Carol Phyllis (Weil) Haussamen; m. Elizabeth Gould, June 25, 1969; children: Damon John, Katherine Molly. BA, NYU, 1967, postgrad., 1967-68. Cert. real estate broker, N.Y. Pres., chief exec. officer The Hemmerdinger Corp., N.Y.C., 1968—, Atco Properties & Mgmt., Inc., N.Y.C., 1968—; Bd. dirs. Realty Found. N.Y., N.Y.C. Contbr. articles on real estate to Crain's N.Y. Bus., other profl. jours. Commr. conciliation and appeals bd. City of N.Y.C., 1978-84; mem. Dem. County Com., N.Y.C., 1978—, N.Y. State Senate Adv. Com., N.Y.C., 1980—, N.Y. State Fin. Control Bd.; gov. Citizens Housing and Planning Council N.Y., N.Y.C., 1982—; mem. exec. com. Assn. for Better N.Y., N.Y.C., 1984—; trustee, mem. exec. com. Nightingale Bamford Sch., N.Y.C., 1985—; trustee Police Found., N.Y.C., 1986—. Mem. Real Estate Bd. N.Y., Manhattan C. of C., Queens C. of C. Clubs: Harmonie (pres. 1985-86), Sky, Beach Point Yacht, Commanderie de Bordeaux, Town Tennis. Office: Atco Properties & Mgmt Inc 555 Fifth Ave New York NY 10017

HEMMING, WALTER WILLIAM, soft drink company executive; b. Vineland, N.J., Oct. 2, 1939; s. Percy A. and Marguerite E. (Smith) H.; m. Shirley L. Derocher, June 10, 1961; children: Cynthia, Catherine, Walter Jr. BS, Syracuse U., 1961. CPA, N.Y., Conn., N.H. Prin. Arthur Young & Co., Stamford, Conn., 1961-72; controller Coca-Cola Bottling Co. N.Y., Hackensack, N.J., 1972-78; exec. v.p., chief operating officer KW Inc., Manchester, N.H., 1978-81; exec. v.p. fin. and adminstrn., chief fin. officer Coca-Cola Bottling Co. N.Y., Greenwich, Conn., 1981-86, Coca-Cola Bottling Plants of Maine, South Portland, 1987-88; v.p. bus devel. Coca-Cola Bottling Co. No. New Eng., Bedford, N.H., 1989—; mem. fin. rev. com. Coca-Cola Bottlers Assn., Atlanta, 1985—; treas. N.H. Soft Drink Assn., Manchester, 1979-81; bd. dirs. Centerpoint Bank, Manchester. Treas. Clinton (Conn.) United Meth. Ch., 1969-72, Jesse Lee Meth. Ch., Ridgefield, Conn., 1974-77; treas. Hollis (N.H.) Congl. Ch., 1981, asst. treas., 1982—, deacon, 1988—. Mem. AICPA, N.H. Soc. CPAs, Conn. Soc. CPAs, N.Y. Soc. CPAs, Fin. Execs. Inst. Republican. Club: Cumberland (Portland, Maine); Falmouth (Maine) Country. Home: PO Box 141 Hollis NH 03049 Office: Coca-Cola Bottling Co No New Eng 1 Executive Park Dr Bedford NH 03102

HENARD, ELIZABETH ANN, controller; b. Providence, Oct. 9, 1947; d. Anthony Joseph and Grace Johanna (Lokay) Zorbach; m. Patrick Edward Mann, Dec. 18, 1970 (div. July 1972); m. John Bruce Henard Jr., Oct. 19, 1974; children: Scott Michael, Christopher Andrew. Student, Jacksonville (Fla.) U., 1966. Sec. So. Bell Tel.&Tel., Jacksonville, 1964-69; office mgr. Gunther F. Reis Assocs., Tampa, Fla., 1969-71; exec. sec. Ernst & Ernst, Tampa, 1971-72; exec. sec. to pres. Lamalie Assocs., Tampa, 1972-74; exec. sec. Arthur Young & Co., Chgo., 1975; adminstrv. asst. Irving J. Markin, Chgo., 1975; contr., corp. sec. Henard Assocs., Inc., Dallas, 1983—. Mem. Dallas Investors Group (treas. 1986—). Republican. Roman Catholic. Clubs: Bent Tree Country, Stonebriar Country, Hidden Hills (Austin); Willow Bend Polo (Dallas). Home: 5706 Thames Ct Dallas TX 75252 Office: Henard Assocs Inc 15303 Dallas Pkwy Dallas TX 75248

HENBEST, WILLIAM HARRISON, insurance agent; b. Elmira, N.Y., Nov. 14, 1955; s. Robert Leroy and Grace Edith (Rowley) H.; m. Cynthia Jean Rohde, Apr. 26, 1980; 1 child, Danielle Christine. BBA, Rochester Inst. Tech., 1978. Fin. analyst A&P, Horseheads, N.Y., 1979-80; multi-line underwriter Gen. Accident Ins., Syracuse, N.Y., 1980-82; v.p. Henbest & Morrisey Inc., Elmira, 1982—; sec., treas. Chemung County Agts. Assn., Elmira, 1982—. Com. mem. United Way, Elmira, 1986. Mem. Profl. Ins. Agts. Assn., Ind. Ins. Agts. Assn., Chemung County C. of C. (bd. dirs.), Sigma Pi. Republican. Lodge: Kiwanis. Home: 82 Demarest Pkwy Elmira NY 14905 Office: Henbest & Morrisey Inc 305 E Water St Elmira NY 14901

HENCK, DOUGLAS CURRY, insurance executive; b. Knoxville, Tenn., Feb. 14, 1953; s. Frederick Seymour and Martha (McCollum) H.; m. Susan Cornwall Sanders, June 8, 1974 (dec. 1977); m. Suzanne Coakley, Sept. 8, 1979; children: Amanda Curry, Jessica Coakley, Charles Justin. BS in Math., Rensselaer Poly. Inst., 1974. Actuary employee benefits div. Aetna Life & Casualty Ltd., Hartford, Conn., 1975-81, v.p. div. internat. ins., 1981-87; sr. v.p. Aetna Internat. Inc., Hong Kong, 1987—; also bd. dirs. Aetna Internat. Inc.; bd. dirs. Federated Internat. (Far East) Holdings Ltd., East Asia Aetna Ins. Co. (Bermuda) Ltd., Blue Cross (Asia-Pacific) Ins. Ltd., Universal Life & Gen. Ins. Sdn Bhd, Malaysia, Aetna Life Ins. Co. Am., Taiwan. Mem. Task Force for Gov. Related to Pvt. Sector Initiatives on Voluntary Action, Conn., 1986. Fellow Soc. Actuaries; mem. Am. Acad. Actuaries, Internat. Actuarial Assn., Actuarial Assn. Hong Kong, Hong Kong-Am. C. of C. Republican. Office: Aetna Internat Inc, 3508 One Exchange Sq, Hong Kong Hong Kong also: Aetna Life & Casualty Co 151 Farmington Ave Hartford CT 06156

HENDEREK, MICHAEL FRANK, petrochemical company executive; b. Palmerton, Pa., Apr. 13, 1944; s. Frank and Wilma (Arvay) H.; m. Nancy Figgins, Oct. 11, 1969; children: Weston Michael, David Figgins. BSME, Lehigh U., 1966, MSME, 1967. Registered profl. engr., N.J. Process engr. Exxon Research and Engring. Co., Florham Park, N.J., 1967-72; mfg. supr. engr. Exxon Chem. Co., Baton Rouge, 1972-75; bus. and mfg. planner Exxon Chem. Co., Houston, 1975-78; tech. mgr. Esso Chem. Europe, Cologne, Fed. Republic Germany, 1978-80; plant mgr. Esso Chem. AB, Stenungsund, Sweden, 1980-85; v.p. Esso Chem. Norden, Stenungsund, 1980-85; tech. mgr. Exxon Chem. Co., Houston, 1985-86; gen. mgr. tech and engring. Exxon Chem. Polymer Group, Houston, 1986-88; dir. quality devel. Exxon Chem. Co., Darien, Conn., 1988—. Mem. ASME, Am. Soc. Quality Control. Home: 2207 Robinhood Houston TX 77005 Office: Exxon Chem Co Old Kings Hwy S Darien CT 06820

HENDERSON, ALAN CHARLESS, engineering and construction company executive; b. Washington, Feb. 28, 1946; s. Elmer Charless Jr. and Ida Bess (Logan) H.; m. Vicki Lynn, Nov. 16, 1980; children: Logan Charless, Philip Alan. BA, Westminster Coll., 1968; MBA, U. Pa., Wharton, 1970. Auditor Peat Marwick Mitchell & Co., St. Louis, 1970-71; asst. treas. Midland Mortgage Investors Trust, Oklahoma City, 1973-74; mng. cons. Fin. Funding Group, Inc., Salt Lake City, 1978-83; pub., editor Utah Bus. Fin., Salt Lake City, 1978-83; financing mgr. Sverdrup Corp., St. Louis, 1983-88, v.p. fin., 1988—; v.p. fin., chief fin. officer Sverdrup Investments, Inc., 1984-88; mem. adv. bd. Columbine Venture Fund, Denver, 1982-83. Mem. adv. bd. 12th dist. SBA, Salt Lake City, 1983; treas./bd. dirs. Eagle Scout Assn. St. Louis, 1986; mem. round table Arts and Edn. Coun., St. Louis, 1988. 1st lt. inf., U.S. Army, 1971-73. Recipient Vigil Honor, Order of Arrow awards Boy Scouts Am., 1972. Mem. Nat. Assn. Bus. Economists, Nat. Assn. Office and Indsl. Parks, Noonday Club, Mo. Athletic Club. Home: 118 Frontenac Forest Saint Louis MO 63131 Office: Sverdrup Corp 13723 Riverport Dr Maryland Heights MO 63043

HENDERSON, BRUCE ALAN, marine biologist, aquarium executive; b. Newport Beach, Calif., July 12, 1955; s. Robert Frater Henderson and Dortha (Clary) Kellar; m. Susan Lynn Hanneman, Nov. 29, 1985; 1 child, Michele Coleen. BS in Fisheries Sci., Oreg. State U., 1981, MS in Marine Fisheries, 1983. On staff U.S. Marine Fisheries Svc., Seattle, 1979-80; with Fisheries Field Census Nat. Marine Fisheries Svc., Seattle, 1980; research biologist Marine Sci. Ctr. Oreg. State U., Newport, Oreg., 1980-83, edn. specialist Sea Grant Extension Svc., 1983-84; exec. dir. Oreg. Coast Aquarium, Newport, 1984—. Mem. Nat. Marine Edn. Assn., Northwest Assn. Marine Educators, (affiliate) Am. Assn. Zool. Parks and Aquariums, Newport C. of C. (bd. dirs. 1988—), Rotary. Office: Oreg Coast Aquarium 1 Ferry Slip Rd PO Box 78 South Beach OR 97366

HENDERSON, BRUCE DOOLIN, management executive, educator; b. Nashville, Apr. 30, 1915; s. John B. and Ceacy (Doolin) H.; m. Frances Fleming, Sept. 5, 1949; children: Asta, Bruce Balfour, Ceacy, Bruce Alexander.; m. Bess L. Wilson, Oct. 22, 1983. B.E., Vanderbilt U., 1937; postgrad., Harvard U. Bus. Sch., 1940-41; L.L.D. (hon.), Babson Coll., 1983. Trainee Frigidaire div. Gen. Motors Corp., 1937-38; sales Leland Electric Co., 1938-39; buyer Westinghouse Electric Corp., 1941; asst. purchasing agt. Westinghouse Electric Corp., Lima, Ohio, 1942; purchasing agt. Westinghouse Electric Corp., Newark, 1943-46; mgr. purchases, stores Westinghouse Electric Corp., Sharon, Pa., 1946-49; asst. to v.p. Westinghouse Electric Co., Pitts., 1950; gen. purchasing agt. Westinghouse Electric Co., 1951, gen. mgr. purchases and traffic, 1952, v.p. purchasing and traffic, 1953-55, v.p., mem. corp. mgmt. com., gen. mgr. air conditioning div., 1955-59; sr. v.p. in charge mgmt. services div. Arthur D. Little, Inc., 1959-60, sr. v.p. charge mgmt. cons. div., 1960-63; sr. v.p. Boston Safe Deposit & Trust Co., 1963-68; founder Boston Cons. Group, Inc, 1963, pres., 1968-80, chmn. bd., 1980-85, chmn. bd. emeritus, 1985—; prof. mgmt. Vanderbilt U. Owen Grad. Sch. Mgmt.; bd. dirs. Boston Cons. Group Inc., Exide Corp., Abt Assocs. Inc. Author: Henderson on Corporate Strategy, The Logic of Strategy. Clubs: Belle Meade Country (Nashville), University (Nashville); St. Croix (V.I.) Country. Home: 110 Christopher Pl Nashville TN 37205 Office: Vanderbilt U Owen Grad Sch Mgmt 21st Ave S Nashville TN 37203 also: Boston Cons Group Inc Exchange Pl Boston MA 02109

HENDERSON, HAROLD RICHARD, JR., lawyer, transportation executive; b. Washington, Nov. 5, 1942; s. Harold Richard and Channie (Catlett) H.; m. Franzine Moore, Dec. 31, 1965; children: Kimberly Michele, Jessica Nicole, Harold R. III. BS, Mich. State U., 1972; JD, Harvard U., 1976. Bar: D.C. 1976, U.S. Dist. Ct. D.C. 1977, U.S. Ct. Appeals (D.C. cir.) 1977, U.S. Supreme Ct. 1985. Assoc. Morgan Lewis & Bockius, Washington, 1976-80; asst. gen. counsel Amtrak, Washington, 1980-82, dep. gen. counsel, 1982-84, gen. counsel, 1984-86, v.p. law, 1986—. Bd. dirs. Rosemont Daycare Ctr., Washington, 1978—, Children's Hosp. Nat. Med. Ctr., Washington, 1987—. Mem. ABA, Nat. Bar Assn., Com. Ry. and Airline Labor Lawyers, Am. Assn. R.R. (legal affairs com.). Baptist. Home: 10504 Samaga Dr Oakton VA 22124 Office: Amtrak 60 Massachusetts Ave NE Washington DC 20002

HENDERSON, JAMES ALAN, engine company executive; b. South Bend, Ind., July 26, 1934; s. John William and Norma (Wilson) H.; m. Mary Evelyn Kriner, June 20, 1959; children: James Alan, John Stuart, Jeffrey Todd, Amy Brenton. AB, Princeton U., 1956; Baker scholar, Harvard U., 1961-63. With Scott Foresman & Co., Chgo., 1962; staff mem. Am. Rsch. & Devel. Corp., Boston, 1963; faculty Harvard Bus. Sch., 1963; asst. to chmn. Cummins Engine Co., Inc., Columbus, Ind., 1964-65; v.p. mgmt. devel. Cummins Engine Co., Inc., 1965-69, v.p. personnel, 1969-70, v.p. ops., 1970-71, exec. v.p., 1971-75, exec. v.p., chief operating officer, 1975-77, pres., 1977—, also dir.; bd. dir. Cummins Engine Found., Inland Steel Co., Chgo., Ameritech, Chgo., Rohm & Hass Co., Phila., Landmark Communications, Norfolk. Author: Creative Collective Bargaining, 1965. Chmn. exec. com. Princeton U.; pres. bd. trustees Culver Ednl. Found. Lt. USNR, 1956-61. Presbyn. (elder). Home: 4228 Riverside Dr Columbus IN 47203 Office: Cummins Engine Co Inc Box 3005 Columbus IN 47202-3005

HENDERSON, JAMES HAROLD, entrepreneur; b. Knoxville, Tenn., June 18, 1948; s. Harold Alpheus and Joanna Elizabeth (McCammon) H.; m. Jane Frances Dewey, Jan. 22, 1977; children: Jeanette Marie, Joanne Reneé, Jason Harold. BS in Mgmt. and Econs., U. North Ala., 1971; MS in Systems Mgmt., U. So. Calif., Los Angeles, 1981. Registered fin. planner, investment advisor. Commd. U.S. Army, 1971, advanced through grades to capt., 1975, resigned, 1979; owner Worldwide Merchantile and Co., Clarksville, Tenn. and Oscoda, Mich., 1979—; freelance fin. planner Clarksville, Tenn. and Oscoda, Mich., 1979—; registered rep. United Svcs. Planning Assoc., Inc., Clarksville, 1980-83; br. mgr. United Svcs. Planning Assoc., Inc., Oscoda, 1983-86; agt. Ind. Rsch. Agy. for Life Ins., Clarksville, 1980-83; dist. agt. Ind. Rsch. Agy. for Life Ins., Oscoda, 1983-86; gen. agt. North Am. Co. for Life and Health Ins., Oscoda, Mich., 1986—; br. mgr., registered prin. Mut. Service Corp., Oscoda, Mich., 1986—; owner, investment advisor James H. Henderson and Co., Oscoda, Mich., 1987—; counselor Christian Fin. Concepts, Inc., 1985—. Mem. Wurtsmith Mil. Affairs com., Oscoda, 1987—. Served to capt. U.S. Army, 1971-79; res. 1979—. Mem. Internat. Assn. Fin. Planners Inc., Internat. Assn. Registered Fin. Planners, Inc., Nat. Assn. Securities Dealers Inst., Inst. Cert. Fin. Planners (cert.), Officer's Christian Fellowship (area coord. 1984—). Home: 4528 Hillcrest Ave Oscoda MI 48750 Office: James H Henderson and Co 5149 N US 23 Suite 1 Oscoda MI 48750

HENDERSON, KENNETH ATWOOD, investment counseling executive; b. Watertown, Mass., Oct. 18, 1905; s. Charles William and Anna Lyons (Atwood) H.; B.S., Harvard U., 1926; m. Elizabeth Berry Marshall, June 10, 1944; 1 dau., Caroline Marshall. With fgn. dept. Brown Bros. & Co., Boston, 1926-30; analyst Weil McKey & Co., Boston, 1931; salesman, engr. home and comml. heating dept. Standard Oil Co. N.J., Boston, 1932-36; investigator Raymond E. Bell, Inc., N.Y.C., 1936; analyst, editor Poor's, Babson Park, Wellesley, Mass., 1937; investment counsellor Cromwell & Cabot, Inc., Boston, 1937-42, 46-50; sr. v.p. John P. Chase, Inc., Boston, 1950-74; pvt. practice investment counselling, Waban, Mass., 1975—; dir., treas. Henniker Crutch Co. Active investment, fin. coms. 2d Ch., Newton, Mass. Served to comdr. USNR, 1942-46. Fellow Harvard Travellers Club (hon.); mem. Boston Security Analysts Soc., Bond Analysts Soc. of Boston, Public Utility Analysts Boston, Am. (asst. treas., Angelo Heilprin award 1982), Can., London alpine clubs, Harvard Mountaineering Club, Explorers Club, Appalachian Mountain Club (hon.). Author: Handbook of American Mountaineering, 1942; New England Canoeing Guide, 1965, 68, 71; editor: Appalachia, 1947-55; contbr. articles Am. Alpine Jour., Appalachia, Alpine Jour., others. Home: 29 Agawam Rd Waban MA 02168

HENDERSON, MARILYN ANN, communications company executive; b. Scranton, Pa., Aug. 3, 1949; d. William Joseph and Mary Ann (Banick) Delorey; m. William Edgar Henderson, Oct. 23, 1971. Student U. Scranton, 1968; B.S., Pa. State U., 1970; M.B.A., Fairleigh Dickinson U., 1977. With AT&T, 1970-84, dist. mgr., various N.J. locations, 1977-83, div. mgr., Piscataway, N.J., 1983-84; div. mgr. Bell Communications Research, Piscataway, 1984—; editorial bd. Exchange Mag., 1986—. Recipient various corp. awards and recognitions, 1976-85, Clements award Clements Found., 1967, 68, 69, 70. Mem. AAUW, Am. Mgmt. Assn., Assn. Computing Machinery, Telephone Pioneers Am. (v.p. Cen. State council 1987-88, pres. 1988—), Nat. Assn. Female Execs., Morris Mus., Morris County Hist. Soc., Frelinghuysen Arboretum, Hist. Speedwell, Pa. State Alumni Assn., Omicron Nu. Roman Catholic. Avocations: power boating; cats; golfing, historical preservation. Home: Ten Pond Hill Rd Convent Station NJ 07961 Office: Bell Communications Rsch 33 Knightsbridge Rd Piscataway NJ 08854

HENDERSON, ROBERT CAMERON, utility executive; b. Niagara Falls, N.Y., Apr. 5, 1940; s. Robert L. and Marion A. (MacDonald) H.; m. Mary N. Nelson, May 8, 1965; children: Catherine, Robert, Margaret. BS in Acctg., U. Rochester, 1962, MBA, 1977. With Rochester (N.Y.) Gas and Electric Corp., 1963-67, asst. controller, 1967-80, v.p. rates, 1980-86, v.p. rates, controller, 1986-88, sr. v.p., controller, chief fin. officer, 1988—; bd. dirs. Energy Ins. Mut., Ltd., Barbados, Marine Midland Bank, Rochester. Served with U.S. Army, 1962-63. Home: 1305 Middle Rd Rush NY 14543 Office: Rochester Gas & Electric Corp 89 East Ave Rochester NY 14649

HENDERSON, THOMAS JAMES, construction company executive; b. 1931. BS, MIT, 1954, MS. From project mgr. to exec. asst. J.L. Simmons Co., Decatur, Ill., 1958-61; with Guy F. Atkinson Co., South San Francisco, Calif., 1961—, various mgmt. positions, 1961-75, v.p., gen. mgr. Lake Ctr. Industries, 1975-83, sr. v.p., 1983-85, group v.p., 1985-86, exec. v.p., 1986-87, pres., chief oper. officer, 1987-88, pres., chief exec. officer, 1988-89; chmn., pres., chief exec. officer Guy F. Atkinson Co., South San Francisco, 1989—; also bd. dirs. Guy F. Atkinson Co., South San Francisco, Calif. Served to Lt. USN, 1955-58. Office: Guy F Atkinson Co of Calif 10 W Orange Ave South San Francisco CA 94080

HENDERSON, WALTER G., utility company executive; b. Edgemont, S.D., Dec. 19, 1930; s. Andrew M. and Agnes (Galbraith) H.; m. Pamela J. Naeve, Oct. 26, 1974; children: Kevin, Jennifer. B.A. in Bus, U. Nebr., 1953; LL.B., U. Colo., 1957. With El Paso (Tex.) Natural Gas Co., 1957—, asst. v.p., 1974-77, v.p., 1977-79, sr. v.p., 1979-80, exec. v.p., 1980—; dir. various subsidiaries and affiliates of El Paso Natural Gas Co. Served with USMC, 1953-55. Mem. Pacific Coast Gas Assn., So. Gas Assn. Episcopalian. Office: El Paso Natural Gas Co PO Box 1492 El Paso TX 79978

HENDERSON, WILLIAM DONALD, antiquarian, consultant; b. Bluefield, W.Va., June 20, 1914; s. Thomas Ewell and Cordie Ethel (Nelson) H.; B.S.E.E., Va. Poly. Inst., 1936, postgrad. in Mech. Engring., 1938-39; postgrad. in Bus. Adminstrn., U. Pa., 1937, in Edn., U. Md., 1939-40; m. Edythe May Edwards, 1957. Docent, Am. Automobile Assn., Washington; jr. engr. Washington Inst. Tech., College Park, Md., 1940-41; civilian electronics engr. Airborne Communications and Nav., Design Br., Bur. Ships, Navy Dept., Washington, 1941-46; pvt. practice real estate mgmt., Cleveland, Ga., 1946-52, 54—; owner Henderson Lumber Co., 1945—; field service rep. nav. electronic guidance and control of Matador, Glenn L. Martin Co., Essex, Md., 1953; surveyor White County, Ga., 1960-64, 76-80. Mem. AAAS, Am. Def. Preparedness Assn. (life), U.S. Naval Inst. (life), History of Sci. Soc. (life), Tailhook Assn. (life). Developer surveying techniques; inventor entrance lock and deadbolt, doorknocker; author: Minerals of White County, Georgia, 1987. Avocation: genealogy. Office: PO Box 164 Cleveland GA 30528

HENDLEY, DAN LUNSFORD, banker; b. Nashville, Apr. 26, 1938; s. Frank E. and Mattie (Lunsford) H.; m. Patricia Fariss, June 18, 1960; children: Dan Lunsford, Laura Kathleen. B.A., Vanderbilt U., 1960; grad., Stonier Grad. Sch. Banking, Rutgers U., 1969; postgrad., Program Mgmt. Devel., Harvard, 1972. With Fed. Res. Bank Atlanta, 1962-73, v.p., officer in charge Birmingham br., 1969-73; v.p., exec. v.p. AmSouth Bancorp, 1973-77; exec. v.p. First Nat. Bank Birmingham, 1976-77, pres., 1977-79, chmn. bd., chief exec. officer, 1979-83; pres., chief operating officer Am South Bank, N.A., 1983—, also dir.; dir., vice chmn. Am. South Bancorp.; chmn. Am-South Mortgage Co., Inc. Trustee Children's Hosp., Samford U.; v.p. All Am. Bowl. Mem. Tenn. Air N.G., 1961-67. Baptist. Clubs: Kiwanis, Mountain Brook, Vestavia Country, Riverchase Country, Shoal Creek; The Club. Home: 3258 Dell Rd Birmingham AL 35223 Office: AmSouth Bancorp PO Box 11007 Birmingham AL 35288

HENDRAWAN, FRANS, oil company executive; b. Mataram, Indonesia, Nov. 12, 1936; s. Kusuma Widjaya and Bie Nio Kam; m. Yokki Ratnawati Hendrawan, Sept. 4, 1972; children—Albert Mulyadi, Andrew Darmadi, Henry Setiadi. M. Degree in Econs., Parahyangan U., 1971. Lectr. Parahyangan U., Bandung, 1969-71; adminstrn. mgr. PT Astra Internat. Inc., Jakarta, Indonesia, 1972-73, adminstrn., fin. mgr., 1973, gen. mgr., 1973-75; fin., adminstrn. dir. PT Djaya Pirusa, Jakarta, 1976-78; mng. dir. PT Midas Oil, Jakarta, 1978—; pres., dir. PT Woneel Midas Leathers, Jakarta, 1988—, v.p. PT Cheil Samsung Astra, Jakarta, 1988— . Mem. Ikatan Sarjana Ekonomi Indonesia (dep. chmn.), Indonesia Fin. Execs. Assn. (sec. II). Home: Jln Surya Utama 111/7, Kedoya, Jakarta 11520, Indonesia Office: PT Midas Oil, Jln Gaya Motor Raya #6, Sunter II, PO Box 41, Jakarta Utara JKT 14001, Indonesia

HENDRICKS, JESSE ELMER, oil company executive, consulting chemical engineer; b. Dallas, Dec. 23, 1913; s. Jesse Elmer and Grace (Yeargan) H.; m. Margarette Johnson, June 6, 1937 (dec. 1981); m. Fairfax Seward, Oct. 1, 1982; children: Sue Clark, Mary Grace Coates, Evelyn Harrill. AS, U. Tex., Arlington, 1935; BSChemE, Tex. A&M U., 1937. Registered profl. engr., Tex. Process engr. Phillips Petroleum Co., Borger, Tex., 1937-41; asst. dist. mgr. Foxboro Co., Dallas, 1945-46; mgr. reineries and gas plans H.L. Hunt Co., Dallas, 1946-57; v.p. Coastal Corp., Houston, 1957-66; pres. Triton Energy Corp, Dallas, 1966-67, also bd. dirs. Precinct chmn. Dallas Dem. Com., 1948-51; bd. dirs. Nueces County Legal Aid, 1958-64; mem. Corpus Christi (Tex.) Indsl. Devel. Bd., 1958-62. Lt. col. AUS, 1941-45, col. Res. ret. Mem. Oak Cliff Country Club (pres. Dallas chpt. 1986-88). Republican. Home: 1506 Greentree Ln Duncanville TX 75137 Office: Triton Energy Corp 1400 One Energy Sq Dallas TX 75137

HENDRICKS, MAUREEN AGNES, banker; b. Washington, May 29, 1951; d. Donald Michael and Agnes Theresa (Mills) Paris; m. John Kelly Hendricks, Aug. 11, 1973; children: Jennifer, Katharine. BA, Smith Coll., 1973; postgrad., Harvard U., 1980. Trainee Morgan Guaranty Trust Co., N.Y.C., 1973-74, account officer petroleum dept., asst. treas., asst. v.p., 1974-80, capital markets officer, 1980-83, v.p., 1980-84, sr. v.p., 1984—, head comml. paper group, 1983-84, head U.S. banking dept., 1984-88, head specialized fin., 1988—. Republican. Roman Catholic. Office: Morgan Guaranty Trust Co, Morgan House, One Angel Ct, London EC2R 7AE, England

HENDRICKS, RAYMAN MICHAEL, chemical company executive; b. Salt Lake City, Utah, Sept. 14, 1937; s. Rayman Andrew and Cecille Juanita (Wright) H.; m. Marilyn K. Nugent, June 19, 1959; 1 child, R. Matthew. BS in Indsl. Mgmt., MIT, 1959. With Deering-Milliken & Co., Johnston, S.C., 1959-62; with Hercules Inc., Wilmington, Del., 1962-78, mgr. strategy, plastic resins bus. ctr., 1978-81, dir. plastic resins bus. ctr., 1981-83; pres., chief op. officer Himont Inc., Wilmington, 1983—, also bd. dirs.; bd. dirs. Himont U.S.A., Inc., Wilmington, Himont Italia S.P.A., Milan, Montefina S.A., Brussels. Mem. Soc. Plastics Industry, Am. Mgmt. Assn. Office: Himont Inc PO Box 15439 Wilmington DE 19850-5439

HENDRICKS, ROBERT MICHAEL, insurance company executive; b. St. Louis, Aug. 23, 1943; s. Chester Eugene and Reba Eileen (Leake) H.; m. Yvonne Sharon McAnally, Sept. 18, 1971; 1 child, Robert Christian. BA, U. Calif., Berkeley, 1965. Dist. mgr. Am. Gen. Life Ins. Col., L.A., 1965-70; gen. ptnr. Hendricks & Assocs., L.A., 1970-75; v.p. mktg. U.S. Life Corp., L.A., 1975-76; dir. agys. Bankers United Life Assurance Co., L.A., 1976-77; gen. ptnr. Assurance Distbg. Co., Inc., L.A., 1977-83, Diversified Employee Benefits Svcs., Santa Ana, Calif., 1983—; pres., chief exec. officer ADCO Re Life Assurance Co., Santa Ana, 1980-83, also dir.; dir. First Commerce Trust Co., Assurance Distbg. Co., Inc.; instr. CLU and Life Underwriter Tng. Council programs. Recipient various awards in field. Mem. Nat. Assn. Life Underwriters, C. of C., Internat. Platform Assn., Lincoln Club, Silver Circle Club, Balboa Bay Club, Santa Ana Country Club, Masons, Shriners, Rotary. Republican. Office: 1800 E McFadden Ave Ste 260 Santa Ana CA 92705

HENDRICKS, STANLEY MARSHALL, II, executive recruiter, consultant; b. Richmond, Ky., Nov. 15, 1952; s. Stanley Marshall and Margaret Cathleen (Cox) H.; m. Sara Jane Sargent, Aug. 9, 1975; children: Stanley M. III, Elizabeth Jean. BS, Ind. State U., 1976; post baccalaureate degree, Ind. U. Northwest, 1984. Cert. personnel cons. Assoc. A.R. Massena & Assocs., Merrillville, Ind., 1976-77; co-founder, owner Nat. Recruiting Service, Dyer, Ind., 1977—. Council mem. Ind. State U., Terre Haute, 1983-88; pres. Ind. State U. Alumni Coun.; elder Immanuel Presbyn. Ch., Schererville, Ind., 1978—. Mem. Assn. Iron and Steel Engrs., Nat. Assn. Personnel Cons., Fabricating Mfrs. Assn., Ind. State U. Alumni Assn. (v.p., coun. pres.), Am. Tube Assn., Order of Omega (hon.). Club: Sycamore Club of Northwest Ind. (Crown Point) (bd. dirs. 1984—). Home: 301 Blick View Dr Schererville IN 46375 Office: Nat Recruiting Svc 1832 Hart PO Box 218 Dyer IN 46311

HENDRICKS, THOMAS VERNON, finance company executive; b. Cleve., Jan. 30, 1942; s. James Hill and Virginia (Wolcott) H.; m. Judith Mary Jones, Aug. 24, 1963; children: Elizabeth, Kipp. BBA, Ohio U., 1964. CPA, Ohio. Acct. Haskins & Sells, Dayton, 1964-67; controller Greene & Ladd, Dayton, 1967-70; v.p., treas., dir. Fulton, Reid & Staples, Inc., Cleve., 1971-77, The Ill. Co., Inc., Chgo., 1977-78; sr. v.p., treas., sec. Rodman & Renshaw Capital Group, Chgo., 1978—. Mem. Am. Inst. CPA's, Ohio Soc. CPA's. Republican. Congregational. Office: Rodman & Renshaw Inc 120 S LaSalle St Chicago IL 60603

HENDRICKS, WILLIAM N., III, trust company executive; b. Norton, Va., Feb. 27, 1944; s. William N. and Sarah Ruth (Qualls) H.; m. Ruth MacDonald Stevenson, June 23, 1973; children: William, Genevieve, Sarah. BA cum laude, Coll. of William and Mary, 1966; MA, Johns Hopkins U., 1967; PhD, Duke U., 1974; JD, Albany Law Sch., 1981. Bar: N.Y., Fla. Asst. prof. King Coll., Bristol, Tenn., 1967-75, Union Coll., Schenectady, N.Y., 1975-80; v.p. Key Trust Co., Albany, N.Y., 1983—. Trustee Albany (N.Y.) Acad. for Girls, 1987—; bd. dirs. No. Conn. Ballet, Windsor, 1985—; mem. Niskayuna Zoning Bd. Appeals, Niskayuna, N.Y., 1983—. Mem. N.Y. State Bar Assn., Fla. Bar Assn., Estate Planning Council of N.Y. Democrat. Methodist. Club: Mohawk Golf. Office: Key Trust Co 60 State St Albany NY 12201

HENDRICKSON, CHARLES JOHN, corporate executive; b. Glen Cove, N.Y., Apr. 2, 1950; s. Charles John and Adela (Gunthel) H.; m. Marsha Claire McMahon, Jan. 26, 1974; children: Margaret, Matthew. Student, U. Del., 1968-69; BA in Econs., C.W. Post Coll., 1973. Exec. trainee Chase Manhattan Bank, N.A., N.Y.C., 1973-74, mem. credit teaching staff, lending officer, 1974-75, asst. treas., 1975-77, 2d v.p., 1977-79, v.p., 1979-82, v.p. exec. div., 1982; treas. Clarendon Ltd., N.Y.C., 1983-84; sr. v.p., treas. Donaldson, Lufkin & Jenrette, N.Y.C., 1984—. Mem. Nat. Assn. Corp. Treas.'s, N.Y. Treas.'s Group, Wall St. Treas.'s Group. Republican. Episcopalian. Home: 14 Tanager Ln Northport NY 11768 Office: Donaldson Lufkin & Jenrette Inc 140 Broadway New York NY 10005

HENDRICKSON, HARVEY SIGBERT, accounting educator; b. Mpls., July 23, 1928; s. Sigbert and Hilma M. (Johnson) H.; m. Rosanne C. Maddy, Aug. 18, 1962; children: Mary, Erik, Elise. BBA, U. Minn., 1957, MBA, 1962, PhD, 1963. CPA, Minn. Inst. U. Minn., Mpls., 1958-61, vis. assoc. prof., 1969; asst. prof. acctg. SUNY, Buffalo, 1963-68; assoc. prof. acctg. Fla. State U., Tallahassee, 1968-69; asst. dir. exams Am. Inst. CPAs, N.Y.C., 1970-72; chmn. fin., acctg. div. Fla. Internat. U., Miami, 1972-77, prof. acctg., 1972—; acad. acctg. fellow Office of Chief Acct. SEC, Washington, 1980-81; cons. acctg. and budgeting, expert witness, Miami, 1973—. Author: (with others) The Accounting Primer, 1972; editor: (with others) The Accounting Sampler, 1967, 72, 76, 86; mem. editorial bd. The Accounting Rev., 1976-82, book rev. editor, 1984-87; contbr. articles to profl. jours. Active Dade County Pub. Schs., mem. South Area adv. com., 1973-76, chmn. 1973-74; curriculum cons. Palmetto High Sch., Miami, 1983-88; bd. dirs. South Fla. Assn. Accts. Pub. Interest, 1976-80, chmn. 1976-77. Served as sgt. U.S. Army, 1951-52, Korea. Ford found. predoctoral fellow, 1961-62, Arthur Andersen and Co. found. doctoral dissertation fellow, 1962-63; recipient Haskins and Sells found. scholarship, 1957. Mem. AICPA, Am. Acctg. Assn. (SEC liaison com. 1981-83, 85-86, chmn. S.E. Region exec. planning com. 1977-82, chmn. 1978-79), Fin. Execs. Inst. (chmn. acad. relations com. 1983—, sec. and chmn. membership 1988—), Beta Alpha Psi, Beta Gamma Sigma. Democrat. Home: 7865 SW 158 Terrace Miami FL 33157 Office: Fla Internat U Sch of Accounting Miami FL 33199

HENDRICKSON, JEROME ORLAND, trade association executive, lawyer; b. Eau Claire, Wis., July 25, 1918; s. Harold and Clara (Halverson) H.; student Wis. State Coll., 1936-39; J.D., U. Wis., 1942; m. Helen Phoebe Harty, Dec. 27, 1948 (dec.); children—Jaime Ann, Jerome Orland. Bar: Wis., 1942, U.S. Supreme Ct., 1955; sole practice, Eau Claire, 1946; sales and advt. mgr. Eau Claire Coca-Cola Bottling Co., Inc., 1947-48; exec. sec. Eau Claire Community Chest, 1948-49; in charge dist. office Am. Petroleum Inst., Kansas City, Mo., 1950-53, Chgo., 1953-55; exec. dir. Nat. Assn. Plumbing-Heating-Cooling Contractors, 1955-64; sec. Joint Apprentice Text, Inc., 1955-64; exec. v.p. Cast Iron Soil Pipe Inst., Washington, 1964-74; pres. Valve Mfrs. Assn., McLean, Va., 1975-80; exec. v.p. Plumbing and Piping Industry Council, Inc., 1981—. Treas., Wis. Community Chest, 1948-49. Treas., All-Industry Plumbing & Heating Modernization Com., 1956-57; cosec. Joint Industry Program Com., 1958-64. Served to lt. USNR, 1943-46. Mem. ABA, Wis. Bar Assn., Am. Soc. Assn. Execs., Washington Soc. Assn. Execs., Wis. State Soc. Washington (pres. 1966-68), Nat. Conf. Plumbing-Heating-Cooling Industry (chmn. 1967-69), NAM, U. Wis. Alumni Assn., U. Wis. Law Sch. Alumni Assn. Washington (pres. 1970-74), C. of C. of U.S., Gamma Eta Gamma (pres. Upsilon chpt. 1941-42). Episcopalian. Mason (32 deg., Shriner). Clubs: Washington Golf and Country, Internat. (Washington). Home: 4621 N 33d St Arlington VA 22207 Office: Plumbing & Piping Industry Council 501 Shatto Pl Suite 405 Los Angeles CA 90020

HENDRICKSON, ROBERT FREDERICK, pharmaceutical company executive; b. Cambridge, Mass., Jan. 5, 1933; s. Charles H. and Ruth E. (Bjorklund) H.; m. Virginia H. Emery, Apr. 27, 1963; children: Karen, Susan, Douglas. A.B. in Econs. magna cum laude, Harvard U., 1954, M.B.A., 1958. Engaged in prodn. planning, internat. div. Internat. Latex Corp., Dover, Del., 1958-61; mgr. prodn. planning and control Merck Sharp & Dohme, West Point, Pa., 1961-66; dir. long-range planning Merck Sharp & Dohme, 1966-68, exec. sec. new products com., 1968-69, dir. prodn. planning and control, 1969-71, dir. ops., 1971-72, v.p. ops., 1972-80; sr. v.p. Merck & Co., Inc., Rahway, N.J., 1981-85; sr. v.p. mfg. and tech. Merck & Co., Inc., Rahway, 1985—. Bd. dirs. Lenape Valley Mental Health Found., 1972-80, pres., 1976-77; trustee N.J. State Safety Council, 1980—. Served with AUS, 1954-56. Mem. North Penn C. of C. (dir. 1974-77), Pharm. Mfg. Assn. (chmn. prodn. and engring. sect. 1980-81), NOW Legal, Def. and Edn. Fund (dir. 1987—), N.J. State C. of C. (bd. dirs. 1985—). Presbyn. (elder). Home: 204 Gallup Rd Princeton NJ 08540 Office: Merck & Co Inc PO Box 2000 Rahway NJ 07065

HENDRICKSON, ROBERT MELAND, insurance company executive; b. Fargo, N.D., Aug. 23, 1929; s. Reinhard Oscar and Beatrice Harriet (Meland) H.; m. Kathleen McCauley, 1950 (div. 1979); children: David, Nancy; m. Patricia Kruk, 1981. BS, N.D. State U., 1950; DCL (hon.), St. Augustine Coll., 1986; LLD (hon.), N.D. State U., 1987. With Equitable Life Assurance Soc., N.Y.C., 1950—, v.p. investments, 1971-73, sr. v.p., 1973-75, exec. v.p., chief investment officer, 1975-80; pres., chief exec. officer Equitable Holding Corp., N.Y.C., 1977-78; exec. v.p., chief ins. officer Equitable Life Assurance Soc., N.Y.C., 1980-81, exec. v.p., asst. to chief exec. officer, 1981-86, vice chmn., 1986-89, ret., also bd. dirs.; with Pvt. Capital Ptnrs., N.Y.C., 1989—. Chmn. investment com. U.S. Olympic Com., 1980—; former dir. United Student Aid Funds, Burlington No., Inc., Crown Zellerbach Corp.; past mem. N.Y. State Employees Retirement System Adv. Bd., Mfrs. Hanover Trust Co. Adv. Bd. Mem. Am. Econs. Assn., Am. Fin. Assn. Clubs: Econ. N.Y., Huntington Country, Waccabuc Country, Univ. Home: 49 Joan Dr Chappaqua NY 10514 Office: Pvt Capital Ptnrs 535 Madison Ave New York NY 10022

HENDRICKSON, WILLIAM GEORGE, business executive; b. Plainview, Minn., May 31, 1918; s. Clarence and Hildegarde (Heaser) H.; m. Virginia M. Price, Sept. 1, 1942; children: Robert, Thomas, Donald, Julie Ann. BS, St. Mary's Coll., Winona, Minn., 1939; MS, U. Detroit, 1941; PhD, U. Wis., 1946. Scientist Wis. Alumni Research Found., Madison, 1946-54, dir. devel., 1954-61; v.p. Ayerst Labs. div. Am. Home Products Corp., N.Y.C., 1961-67, exec. v.p., 1967-69; group v.p. Am. Home Products Corp., N.Y.C., 1969-80; chmn. bd. St. Jude Med., Inc., St. Paul; bd. dirs. Research Corp. Techs., Tucson. Mem. Am. Chem. Soc., N.Y. Acad. Scis., Sigma Xi., Country Club of N.C. Republican. Roman Catholic.

HENDRIX, DENNIS RALPH, energy company executive; b. Selmer, Tenn., Jan. 8, 1940; s. Forrest Ralph and Mary Lee (Tull) H.; m. Jennie L. Moore, Dec. 28, 1960; children—Alisa Lee, Natalie Moore, Amy Louise. BS, U. Tenn., 1962; MBA, Ga. State U., 1967. CPA, Ga. Staff acct., cons. Arthur Andersen & Co., Atlanta, 1962-65; faculty Ga. Inst. Tech., 1965-67; sr. cons. Touche, Ross & Co., Memphis, 1967-68; pres. United Foods, Inc., Memphis, 1968-73; asst. to pres. Tex. Gas Transmission Corp., Owensboro, Ky., 1973-75, pres., 1976-83, chief exec. officer, 1978-83; vice chmn. CSX Corp., 1983-84; exec. v.p., dir. Halliburton Co., Dallas, 1984-85; pres., chief operating officer, dir. Tex. Eastern Corp., Houston, 1985-87, chief exec. officer, pres., dir., 1987—; bd. dirs. Tex. Med. Ctr. Bd. dirs. Nat. Jr. Achievement, Tex. South Coast United Way, Cen. Houston, Inc., U. Tenn. Devel. Council, Tex. Dept. Corrections, Tex. Med. Ctr., Houston; mem. Ga. State U. Bus. Sch. Adv. Bd. Mem. Am. Petroleum Inst. (bd. dirs.), Conf. Bd., Burning Tree Club, Ramada Club, Houston Ctr. Club, River Oaks Country Club, Forum Club (bd. dirs.), Castle Pines Club. Presbyterian. Office: Tex Eastern Corp PO Box 2521 1221 McKinney Houston TX 77252

HENDRIX, JAMES LEE, physicist, consultant; b. Lompoc, Calif., May 10, 1961; s. James Herman and Ruby Jo (Seals) H.; m. Terri Anne Marie May, Apr. 26, 1983; 1 child, James Thomas V. BS in Physics, U. So. Calif., Los Angeles, 1983. Devel. engr. Apollo Lasers Inc. Allied, Chattsworth, Calif., 1982-84; tech. supr. Hughes Aircraft Co., El Segundo, Calif., 1984—; cons. Santa Barbara (Calif.) Research Ctr., 1984—, Hughes Missile Systems Group, Canoga Park, Calif., 1984—, Hughes Indsl. Products Div., Carlsbad, Calif., 1984—, Computer Solutions, Northridge, Calif., 1988—. Author and editor: LFU Laser Transmitter Module Design, 1988; contbr. articles to profl. jours.; patentee in field. Mem. Am. Phys. Soc., IEEE, Soc. Photo-Optical Instrumentation Engrs., Calif. Scholarship Fedn. Home: 18432 Lemarsh St 56 Northridge CA 91325 Office: Hughes Aircraft Co PO Box 902 El Segundo CA 90245

HENDRIX, JAMES WALTER, accountant; b. Waco, Tex., Nov. 23, 1930; s. Walter Whitworth and Agnes Mary (Robertson) H.; m. Bobbie Joann Hankins, Nov. 27, 1952 (div. Aug. 1983); children—James Walter, John Paul; m. Dehma Lucille Deaver, Sept. 22, 1984. B.B.A., Baylor U. C.P.A., Tex. Staff acct. A.C. Upleger & Co., Waco, 1952-55, ptnr., 1956-65; ptnr.-in-charge KMG Main Hurdman, Dallas, 1965-81, regional mng. ptnr., 1982-83, dep. dir. ops., 1983-85; mng. ptnr. KMG Main Hurdman, N.Y.C., 1985—, mem. policy bd., 1982—; vice chmn. adminstrn. Peat Marwick Main, N.Y.C., 1987—; also bd. dirs. Peat Marwick Main. Bd. dirs. Dallas Council on World Affairs, 1982—. Mem. Am. Inst. C.P.A.s (various coms.), Tex. Soc. C.P.A.s (bd. dirs., various coms.), Govt. Fin. Officers Assn., Nat. Acctg. Assn., Am. Arbitration Assn. (arbitrator 1984—). Republican. Baptist. Clubs: Bent Tree Country, 2001 (Dallas). Lodges: Masons, Shriners, Jesters. Home: 143 Emerson Ct Mahwah NJ 07430 Office: Peat Marwick Main & Co 3 Chestnut Ridge Rd Montvale NJ 07645

HENDRIX, STEPHEN C., financial executive; b. Phila., Feb. 24, 1941; s. Houston W. and Helen B. Hendrix; m. Jean Smith, July 1, 1967; children: Kimberly, Jeffrey, Julie. BA, Tex. Christian U., 1964; M in Internat. Service, Am. U., Washington, 1966; MBA, Ohio State U., 1972. Jr. officer U.S. Dept. State, AID, Washington, 1967-68; mgr. mktg. adminstrn. Amecom div. Litton Industries, College Park, Md., 1968-70; mgr. fin. and planning internat. div. Anchor Hocking Corp., Lancaster, Ohio, 1970-73; mgr. bank relations E.I. Dupont de Nemours & Co., Wilmington, Del., 1973-78; corp. treas., mgr. SmithKline Beckman Corp., Phila., 1978-79, asst. treas. domestic, 1979-82, asst. treas. internat., 1982-87, v.p., asst. treas. internat., 1987—. Contbr. articles to profl. jours. Mem. Fin. Execs. Inst., Nat. Assn. Corp. Treasurers, Phila. Treasurers Club (treas. 1983-84), Am. Mgmt. Assn. Internat. Council. Office: SmithKline Beckman Corp One Franklin Plaza Philadelphia PA 19101

HENDRY, IAIN WILSON MENZIES, lawyer; b. Glasgow, Scotland, June 14, 1927; emigrated to came to Can., 1954; s. James Robertson and May Gold (Bryce) H.; m. Elizabeth Alice Robertson, Apr. 2, 1954; children: Neil Robertson, James Cowan, Ian Douglas, Jill Elizabeth. B.A. with honors, Cambridge U., 1950; LL.B., Glasgow U., 1952. Bar: B.C. 1955, Ont. 1957. Barrister, solicitor Davis & Co., Vancouver, B.C., Can., 1954-56, Norris & Cumming, Vancouver, 1956-57; barrister, solicitor Westinghouse Can., Hamilton, Ont., Canada, 1957-61, asst. gen. counsel, 1962-81, v.p., sec. gen. counsel, 1981—; solicitor Wilson Chalmers & Hendry, Glasgow, 1961-62. Served to lt. Brit. Army, 1945-48. Mem. Assn. Can. Gen. Counsel, Can. Mfrs. Assn., Upper Can. Law Soc., Can. Bar Assn., Hamilton Law Assn.

Progressive Conservative. Presbyterian. Clubs: Hamilton Golf and Country (past pres.); Hamilton. Home: 35 Duke St Apt 3, Hamilton, ON Canada L8P 1X2 Office: Westinghouse Can Inc, 120 King St, West Hamilton, ON Canada L8P 4V2

HENDRY, JAMES E., lawyer, automobile club executive; b. Perry, Fla., Nov. 7, 1912; s. Wesley Alonzo and Mae (Weaver) H.; student St. Petersburg Jr. Coll., 1930-32; J.D., U. Fla., 1935; m. Frances Swope, June 25, 1948; children—James E., Jayne L., Thomas S., John W., David F. Vice pres. Hendry Lumber Co., 1935-42, sec., treas., 1946-60; partner, mgr. Hendry Bldg. Co., 1946-60; practice law as James E. Hendry, atty., 1961—; pres. Gulf Housing Corp., 1946; sec.-mgr. St. Petersburg A.A.A. Motor Club, 1962-67, exec. v.p., gen. mgr., 1967-81; pres., dir. St. Petersburg Motor Club, 1981-86; v.p. Club Ins. Agy., Inc., 1962—; dir. Guardian Bank; adv. bd. First Union Bank Fla., Peninsula Motor Club Am. 1986—. Admitted to U.S. Supreme Ct. bar. Mem. City Planning and Zoning Bd., 1948-57, Pinellas County Sch. Bd., 1957-66, Pinellas Co. Airport Com., 1952, St. Petersburg Planning Commn., 1973-74; mem. citizens adv. com. St. Petersburg Jr. Coll., 1948-68, bd. govs., 1938-48, chmn. dist. bd. trustees, 1968-75, bd. dirs. Devel. Found.; pres. bd. dirs. YMCA, 1951; mem. Mound Park Hosp. Bd., 1953-58, Nat. SSS, local selective service bd.; mem. bd. Pinellas County chpt. Am. Cancer Soc., chmn. Cancer Drive, 1962; pres. Fla. Sch. Bd. Assn., 1964; sec.-treas. Southeastern Conf. AAA Motor Clubs, 1964, v.p., 1965, pres., 1966; exec. com. Continuing Ednl. Council Fla., 1964; State Community Coll. Council, 1974-75; past pres. St. Petersburg Jr. Coll. Found.; past mem. Pinellas Tourist Devel. Council. Lt. comdr. USCG Res. Recipient award of honor Wisdom Soc., 1970; Top Mgmt. award St. Petersburg Sales and Mktg. Execs., 1980; Outstanding Contbn. to Betterment of Community award St. Petersburg C. of C., 1981. Mem. Am., St. Petersburg bar assns., Fla. Bar, Am. Judicature Soc., Nat. Assn. Home Builders (past dir.), Contractors and Builders Assn. of Pinellas County (pres. 1953), Fla. Home Builders Assn. (v.p. 1955), Eastern (treas. 1970-72, vice chmn. 1972-74, chmn. 1975-77), Fla. (chmn. 1974, 79, 80) confs. AAA Motor Clubs, Phi Delta Theta, Phi Alpha Delta. Democrat. Methodist. Clubs: St. Petersburg Yacht, Skal, Quarterback, Presidents, Suncoasters. Home: 409 Snell Isle Blvd Saint Petersburg FL 33704 Office: Peninsula Motor Club Am 1211 1st Ave N Saint Petersburg FL 33705

HENEAULT, ROBERT EDMOND, steel company executive; b. Danielson, Conn., July 4, 1926; came to Can., 1952; s. George J. and Rose Alma H.; m. Mary Theresa Keenan, May 31, 1952; children—Robert George, Suzanne Mary, Pamela Rose, John Keenan, Thomas Maurice, Kathryn Anne. B.A. in Econ., U. Notre Dame. Personnel mgr. Singer Mfg. Co., St. Jean, Que., Can., 1952-54; supt. indsl. relations Montreal Works Stelco Inc., 1954, personnel and indsl. relations adminstr. eastern region, 1959; supt. indsl. relations Hilton Works, Hamilton, Ont., Can., 1960, mgr. prodn. planning, 1962, mgr. field sales central region, 1964, mgr. sheet and strip sales, 1965, v.p. personnel, 1972, v.p. adminstrn., 1976, group v.p., Toronto, Ont., 1984-85, exec. v.p., 1985-88; pres. Stelco Enterprises (div. Stelco Inc.), Toronto, 1988—; Past chmn. Tech. Services Council; dir. St. Lawrence Cement Co., Domtar Inc. Senator Stratford Shakespearean Festival Found. Can. Served with USN, 1944-46. Mem. Internat. Iron and Steel Inst., Am. Iron and Steel Inst., Can. Mfrs. Assn. Roman Catholic. Club: Ontario. Office: Stelco Enterprises, Toronto-Dominion Ctr Box 205, Toronto, ON Canada M5K 1J4

HENEY, JOSEPH EDWARD, environmental engineer; b. Brockton, Mass., Feb. 22, 1927; s. John J. and Nellie A. (Byrnes) H.; m. Frances McElroy, Feb. 22, 1955; children: Mary, John, Edward, Stephen. B.S., Northeastern U., 1952; M.S. in San. Engring, Harvard U., 1954. Diplomate: Am. Acad. Environ. Engrs. With Camp, Dresser & McKee, Inc., Boston, 1950—; now vice-chmn. Camp, Dresser & McKee, Inc.; dir. Camp Scott Furphy Pty. Ltd., Melbourne, Australia; Bd. dirs. Northeastern U. Nat. Council. Trustee Northeastern U., vice chmn. Nat. Commn. Coop. Edn. Fellow Am. Cons. Engrs. Council, ASCE, Instn. Engrs. (Australia), Instn. Water Engrs. and Scientists London; mem. Boston Soc. Civil Engrs., Am. Water Works Assn., New Eng. Water Works Assn., Assn. Cons. Engrs. Australia, New Eng. Water Pollution Control Assn., Inter-Am. Assn. San. Engrs. Home: 26 Winthrop Rd Hingham MA 02043 Office: Camp Dresser & McKee Inc 1 Center Pla Boston MA 02108

HENICK, ALFRED, mechanical contracting executive; b. N.Y.C., Apr. 24, 1925; s. Isadore and Tessie (Posner) H.; divorced; children: Lauren, Donald, Ernest. BME, CCNY, 1945. Registered profl. engr., N.Y. Structural designer Foster-Wheeler Corp., N.Y.C., 1950-55; project engr. J.T. Falk & Co., Inc., N.Y.C., 1955-60; pres. Henick Control, Inc., N.Y.C., 1960-64, Henick-Lane, Inc., N.Y.C., 1964—. Sgt. U.S. Army, 1945-47, ETO. Mem. ASHRAE. Home: 2 Bay Club Dr Bayside NY 11360 Office: Henick-Lane Inc 42-22 9th St Long Island NY 11101

HENICK, STEVEN TITMAN, business executive; b. N.Y.C., July 29, 1942; s. Bernard and Eva (Titman) H.; m. Bette Rosenbaum, Dec. 24, 1964; children: Richard Douglas, Jonathan David, Craig Lawrence, Sara Lynn. AB, Columbia U., 1964; MBA, Harvard U., 1971. With Procter & Gamble, Inc., various, 1971-78; mgr. advt. Procter & Gamble, Inc., Japan, 1979-81; v.p. Atari, Inc., Sunnyvale, Calif., 1982-83; v.p. client svcs. Williams Yarman Advt., 1984; mgr. div. Tambrands, Inc., Lake Success, N.Y., 1985-86; v.p. Tambrands, Inc., Lake Success, 1987—; pres. Physicians Formula Cosmetics (subs. Tambrands Inc.), City of Industry, Calif., 1988—. Bd. dirs. L.I. Stage, 1987. Served as capt. with USMCR, 1964-69, Vietnam. Mem. Delta Phi (Columbia U. chpt. pres. 1963-64). Club: Kobe (Japan). Office: Physicians Formula Cosmetics 230 S 9th Ave City of Industry CA 91746

HENK, FLOYD HENRY, consulting engineer; b. San Marcos, Tex., June 28, 1929; s. Albert P. and Lillie (Bender) H.; m. Ora Ella Rose, Sept. 20, 1951; children: Karen, Floyd, Jr., Robert. BS, Tex. A&MU., 1950; MS, U. Ill., Urbana, 1959. Registered profl. engr., Tex. Commd. 2d lt. U.S. Army, 1950, advanced through grades to col., 1971, ret., 1975; exec. v.p. Yandell and Hiller, Inc., Ft. Worth, 1975—. Decorated Legion of Merit. Mem. Tex. Soc. Profl. Engrs. (pres. Ft. Worth chpt. 1983-84, Engr. of Yr. 1985), Soc. Am. Mil. Engrs. Roman Catholic. Home:: 4200 Harlanwood Dr Fort Worth TX 76109

HENKE, FRANK PAUL, consultant; b. Kansas City, Mo., Nov. 29, 1939; s. Joseph and Mary Gertrude (Thor) H.; m. Carolyn Commer, Apr. 28, 1963; children: Deborah, Susan, Frank Jr., Janet, Steven. AA, Donnelly Coll., 1959; BSBA, Rockhurst Coll., 1961. Cost acct. Western Elec., Lee's Summit, Mo., 1962-65, section chief, 1966-73; dept. chief AT&T, Lee's Summit, 1974-85; cons. AT&T, Kansas City, 1986—. Author: Cost Accounting, 1973, Auditing Reference Guide, 1983, Internal Controls, 1986. Advisor Jr. Achievement, Kansas City, 1969-70; mem. Sch. Bd., Kansas City, 1973-74. Sgt. U.S. Army, 1961-67. Mem. Inst. Internal Auditors (bd. govs. 1980-86). Repbulican. Roman Catholic. Home: 9000 Booth Kansas City MO 64138 Office: AT&T 1100 Walnut Kansas City MO 64141

HENKE, ROBERT JOHN, lawyer, engineer; b. Chgo., Oct. 13, 1934; s. Raymond Anthony and May Dorothy (Driscoll) H.; m. Mary Gabrielle Handrigan, June 18, 1960; children—Robert Joseph, Ann Marie. B.S.E.E., U. Ill., 1956; M.B.A., U. Chgo., 1964; J.D., No. Ill. U., 1979, postgrad. John Marshall Law Sch. Bar: Ill. 1980, Wis. 1980, U.S. Dist. Ct. (no. dist.) Ill. 1980, U.S. Dist. Ct. (we. and ea. dists.) Wis. 1980, U.S. Supreme Ct. 1984; registered profl. engr., Ill., Wis. sr. elec. engr. Commonwealth Edison Co., Chgo., 1956-80; elec. engr. Peterson Builders, Sturgeon Bay, Wis., 1982-83; sr. elec., cost estimating engr. Sargent & Lundy Engrs., Chgo., 1985—; instr. econs. and criminal law NE Wis. Tech. Inst., 1981-82; asst. dist. atty. Door County, Wis., 1981, ct. commr., 1981-82; sole practice, Door County, 1981-84, Lake County, Ill., 1984—; dir. Scand, Door County. Vice chmn. Door County Bd. Adjustment, 1983-84; atty. coach Wis. Bar Found. High Sch. Moot Ct. Competition, Door County, 1984; vol. lawyers program, Lake County, Ill., 1985—. Served with USAR, 1958-63. Mem. ABA, Wis. Bar Assn., Door Kewaunee Bar Assn. (pres. 1983-84), Chgo. Bar Assn., IEEE, Am. Assn. Cost Engrs. Roman Catholic. Home: 891 Garfield Ave #C Libertyville IL 60048 Office: Sargent & Lundy Engrs 55 E Monroe St Chicago IL 60603

HENKEL, ARTHUR JOHN, JR., investment banker; b. Bklyn., Aug. 27, 1945; s. Arthur John and Catherine Rita (Burns) H.; A.B., U. Conn., 1969; M.B.A., U. Chgo., 1971; m. Coralee S. Olicker, Sept. 27, 1981; children: Andrea Rae, Austin Olicker, Reid Baras. USPHS trainee U. Chgo. Hosps. Clinics, 1969-71, adminstrv. asst. fiscal affairs, 1971; cons. Booz, Allen Hamilton, Inc., N.Y.C., 1972-74; asst. dir. ambulatory ops. New Eng. Med. Center Hosp., Boston, 1974-75, dir. ambulatory care, 1975-77; assoc. mcpl. fin. dept. Kidder, Peabody and Co., Inc., N.Y C., 1977-78, asst. v.p., 1978-79, v.p., 1979-80, mng. officer health fin. group, 1980—, dir., 1984-87, mng. dir. 1986-87; v.p. mcpl. fin. dept. Goldman, Sachs & Co., 1987—, instr. community health Tufts U. Sch. Medicine; mem. exec. com. alumni council U. Chgo. Program Hosp. Adminstrn., 1972-76; spl. teaching cons., fin. evaluation hosp. capital projects HEW, 1973. Chmn. investments com. Better Boys Found./Nat. Football League Players Assn. Awards Banquet, 1978, 80—. Recipient Mary Bachmeyer award U. Chgo., 1971; citation Commonwealth Mass., 1976. Office: Goldman Sachs & Co 85 Broad St New York NY 10004

HENKEL, ZANE GREY, retired investor; b. Denison, Iowa, Jan. 19, 1937; s. Franz Henry and Ennice Pearl (Hoskinson) H.; m. Beverly Grace Joy, June 18, 1960; children: Daniel Greyson, Stephen Christopher, Nathan Zachary, Philip Alexander. BA, Drake U., 1970; MEd, Auburn U., 1973. Cert. secondary tchr., Fla., Ga., Ala., Miss., La., Iowa. Freelance musician Des Moines, 1954-62; instr. music Elmer Conservatory, Milw., 1962-65; rehab. supr. State of Iowa, Des Moines, 1974-81; disability investigator and vocat. specialist Social Security Adminstrn., Des Moines, 1981-87. Mem. Cen. Iowa United Profls. (pres. 1984-85), Phi Beta Kappa, Phi Kappa Phi. Home: 1324 Westbrooke Terr Norman OK 73072

HENKELS, PAUL MACALLISTER, engineering and construction company executive; b. Phila., Oct. 7, 1924; s. John Bernard, Jr. and Anne (McCloskey) H.; m. Barbara Brass, Jan. 4, 1958; children—Marin, Paul MacAllister, Christopher B., Andrew M., T. Roderick, Amy, Timothy W., Angela, Carol, Barbara. B.A. in Engring, Haverford (Pa.) Coll., 1947. With Henkels & McCoy, 1947—; v.p., then exec. v.p. Henkels & McCoy, Blue Bell, Pa., 1958-72; pres. Henkels & McCoy, 1972-87, chmn., chief exec. officer, 1987—; bd. mgrs. Beneficial Mut. Savs. Bank, 1978—; Mem. adv. council Coll. Arts and Letters, U. Notre Dame, 1964—, chmn., 1968-70. Mem. Phila. com. United Negro Coll. Fund; chmn. Montgomery County United Way, 1977; vice chmn. Cath. Charities Appeal, Archdiocese of Phila., 1980-84; trustee Temple U., Phila., 1968-72, 1979-83, exec. com., 1969-72; bd. govs. Temple U. Hosp., 1975—, vice chmn., 1975-79; trustee Ind. Colls. Pa., 1976—, exec. com., 1977—, chmn. bd., 1980-83; trustee Chestnut Hill Coll., 1978-84, St. Joseph's U., 1984—, vice chmn., 1987—; exec. com., trustee Ind. Coll. Funds of Am., 1987—. Recipient Man of Yr. award Notre Dame Club, Phila., 1980. Mem. Am. Nat. Standards Inst., Nat. Elec. Contractors Assn. (gov. 1963-67, Coggeshall award 1971), Atlantic Contractors Assn. (1st pres. 1965), Greater Phila. Utility Contractors Assn. (1st pres. 1972-74), Soc. Gas Lighters, Acad. Applied Elec. Sci. (dir. 1980—, exec. com. 1982—). Republican. Roman Catholic. Clubs: Pine Valley Golf, Phila. Cricket. Home: 345 Stenton Ave Plymouth Meeting PA 19462 Office: Henkels & McCoy Inc Jolly Rd Blue Bell PA 19422

HENLEY, JOSEPH OLIVER, manufacturing company executive; b. Sikeston, Mo., June 25, 1949; s. Fred Louis and Bernice (Chilton) H.; B.S.B.A., U. Mo., 1972; M.B.A., Mich. State U., 1973; m. Jane Ann Rhodes, Aug. 21, 1971. Ops. analyst Midland-Ross, Inc., Cleve., 1974, prodn. control mgr., 1974-75, engring. systems mgr. Cameron-Waldron div. Somerset, N.J., 1976; prodn. control mgr., 1976-77; prodn. planning and mfg. systems mgr. ICM div. Massey Ferguson, Inc., Akron, Ohio, 1977-78,; sr. audit specialist (mfg.) United Techs. Corp., Hartford, Conn., 1978-82, mfg. control systems mgr. UT Diesel Systems div., 1983-84, materials mgr., 1983-84, internal cons., 1984-86; inventory mgr. Pratt & Whitney Aircraft div., 1986—. Served with Army N.G., 1970-72. Mem. Nat. Assn. Purchasing Mgmt., Am. Prodn. and Inventory Control Soc., Beta Gamma Sigma, Sigma Iota Epsilon, Omicron Delta Epsilon. Presbyterian. Home: 25 Duncaster Ln Vernon CT 06066 Office: Pratt & Whitney Aircraft div 400 Main St East Hartford CT 06108

HENLEY, PRESTON VANFLEET, former banker, financial consultant; b. Fort Madison, Iowa, July 7, 1913; s. Jesse vanFleet and Ruth (Roberts) H.; m. Elizabeth Artis Watts, Mar. 31, 1940 (div. June 1956); children: Preston Edward VanFleet, Stephen Watts, John vanFleet; m. 2d, Helena Margaret Greenslade, Nov. 29, 1964; 1 adopted son, Lawrence D. Student Tulane U., 1931-34, Loyola U., New Orleans, 1935-36; A.B., Calif. State Coll. at Santa Barbara, 1939; postgrad. U. Wash., 1939-40, N.Y. U., 1943, 46. Teaching fellow U. Wash., 1939-40; sr. credit analyst, head credit dept. Chase Nat. Bank, 45th St. br. N.Y.C., 1942-49; Western sales rep. Devoe & Raynolds, Inc., N.Y.C., 1949-51; v.p., comml. loan officer, mgr. credit dept. U.S. Nat. Bank, Portland, Oreg., 1951-72; loan adminstr. Voyageur Bank Group, Eau Claire, Wis.; v.p. Kanabec State Bank, Mora, Minn., Montgomery State Bank (Minn.), Park Falls State Bank (Wis.), Montello State Bank (Wis.), 1972; v.p., mgr. main office, sr. credit officer So. Nev. region Nev. Nat. Bank, Las Vegas, 1973-75; bus. and fin. cons., 1975—; loan cons. Continental Nat. Bank, Las Vegas, 1983—; instr. Am. Inst. Banking, Portland, 1952-65, Multomah Coll., Portland, 1956-62, Portland State U., 1961-72, Mt. Hood Community Coll., 1971-72, Clark County Community Coll., 1979-83; adv. dir. Vita Plus, Inc., 1979-83; exec. dir. Nev. Minority Purchasing Council, 1979-80; dir., treas. Consumer Credit Counselling Service of Oreg. 1965-72. Treas., Ore. chpt. Leukemia Soc., 1965-66; mem. Menninger Found. 1965-67; trustee, exec. com. St. Rose delima Hosp. Found., 1982-87;dir. So. Nev. chtp. Assn. Part-Time Profls., 1985-87. Served with USNR, 1943-45. Mem. Oreg. Bankers Assn., Robert Morris Assos. (pres. Oreg. chpt. 1959-60, nat. dir. 1961-64), Nat., Oreg. assns. credit mgmt., Credit Research Found., Inst. Internal Auditors, S.A.R., Am. Legion, Navy League, Beta Mu, Leaf and Scarab, Alpha Phi Omega, Portland C. of C., Oreg. Retail Council. Republican. Episcopalian. Mason (32 deg., Shriner), Elk. Club: International. Contbr. articles to profl. jours. Home and Office: 4235 Gibraltar St Las Vegas NV 89121

HENLEY, RICHARD JAMES, healthcare institution financial officer; b. Wroclaw, Poland, May 31, 1956; came to U.S., 1959; s. Henry and Lidia (Alper) Horczak. BA and MA summa cum laude, CCNY, 1978. Asst. to v.p. fin. Mt. Sinai Med. Ctr., N.Y.C., 1978-80, dir. fin. planning, 1980-81, assoc. dir. fin., 1982-84, dir. fin. profl. svcs., 1984-85; v.p. fin., treas. Vassar Bros. Hosp., Poughkeepsie, N.Y., 1985—; treas. VBH Corp., Poughkeepsie, 1986—, Vassar Bros. Hosp. Found., 1986—, VBH Ins. Co., Ltd., 1988—, Riverside Diversified Svces., Inc., 1986—, Riverside Mgmt. Svces., Inc., 1986—. VContbr. articles to profl. jours. Treas. Bardavon 1869 Opera House, Poughkeepsie, 1986—, Family Svces. Dutchess County, Poughkeepsie, 1987-88; com. mem. United Way of Dutchess County, 1987—; pres. Hudson Terr. Owners' Corp., Poughkeepsie, 1987-88. Mem. Am. Coll. Healthcare Execs., Am. Hosp. Assn., Healthcare Fin. Mgmt. Assn. (cost effectiveness award 1979-80, William G. Follmer Merit award 1986). Office: Vassar Bros Hosp Reade Pl Poughkeepsie NY 12601

HENLEY, WILLIAM ARMSTRONG, investment banker; b. Richmond, Va., Apr. 26, 1934; s. William Thomas and Esther (Armstrong) H.; m. Joyce Lee Bass, Mar. 15, 1955; children: Devany, Amy, Jeff. BBA, Washington and Lee U., 1956. Lic. real estate broker, Fla. Acctg. mgr. AT&T, 1956-58; various positions to regional mgr. Lehigh Portland Cement Co., 1958-69; investor, dir., officer pvt. Fla. real estate devels. 1969-76; exec. v.p., dir. Pittway Real Estate, Inc., C&A Investments, Inc., Saddlebrook Resorts, Inc., Clearwater, Fla., 1976-81; founder, pres., dir. Esco Fin., Inc., Esco Capital & Securities, Inc., Esco Realty, Inc., Tampa, Fla., 1981—; sr. v.p., dir. Vanguard Ventures, Inc., Glen Cove, N.Y., 1985—; pres., dir. Vanguard Homes, Inc., Fla., 1985—, Mich. Bapt. Homes, Inc., 1985-87, Am. Vanguard Mgmt. Corp., Mich., 1985—, Vanguard Realty & Mgmt., Inc., Tampa, 1985—; v.p. VVI Securities, Inc., N.Y., 1985—; pres., dir. United Vanguard Homes, Inc., 1988—, Whittier Towers, Inc., Detroit, 1988—, Whitcomb Tower Corp., St. Joseph, Mich., 1988—. Mem. Nat. Assn. Securities Dealers (cert. fin. prin.), Nat. Assn. Realtors, Am. Assn. Homes for Aged, Real Estate Investment Council, U.S. C. of C. Republican. Presbyterian. Clubs: Tampa Yacht and Country, Centre (Tampa). Lodge: Rotary. Office: Vanguard Ventures Inc 4 Cedar Swamp Rd Glen Cove NY 11542

HENNAGE, JOSEPH HOWARD, publisher, printing company executive; b. Washington, Jan. 2, 1921; s. Joseph Howard and Helen (Cook) H.; m. June Elizabeth Stedman, Sept. 29, 1947. Founder, pres. Hennage Creative Printers, Washington, 1945—; pres. Jonage Investment Corp., Washington, 1958—, Highland House Pubs. Inc., Washington, 1969—; mem. adv. bd. First Nat. Bank Washington, 1963-69, Am. Security and Trust Co., Washington, 1969—; chmn. joint govt.-industry adv. bd. Govt. Printing Office, 1972-78; bd. dirs. Graphic Arts Mut. Ins. Co., N.Y.C.; bd. dirs. emeritus United Ins. Co. Ltd., Hamilton, Bermuda, 1975-85, Gadsby's Tarvern; mem. fine arts com. U.S. Dept. State. Bd. dirs. Washington Bd. Trade, 1970-76, Potomacland Amb., 1970. Mem. bus. adv. bd. George Washington U., 1967-75; chmn. Americana com. Nat. Archives, 1972-77, Printing Mgmt. Edn. Trust Fund, 1972—; mem. adv. bd. Am. Freedom Train, 1975-77; trustee Am. Cancer Soc., D.C. Cancer Soc., Balt. Mus. Art; trustee chmn. acquisitions com. Supremem Ct. Hist. Soc.; fellow Va. Mus. Fine Arts; mem. pres.'s house restoration com. Coll. of William and Mary; chmn. bd., trustee Carlyle House Found., 1978—, past pres.; bd. dirs. Boys' Club Washington, 1949-79, local Meth. ch., 1966-70. With USNR, 1942-45. Recipient Disting. Svc. award Boys' Club Washington, 1951, Alumni award Boys', 1959, Freedom Found. award, 1969, Brit. Fedn. Master Printers citation, 1971, Bronze medal Boys' Clubs Am., 1976; named Graphic Arts Man of Yr., 1971. Mem. Master Printers Am. (pres. 1967-69, Man of Yr. 1969), Printing Industries Am. (bd. dirs. 1964-76, exec. com. 1966-76, chmn. bd. 1969-70, v.p. pub. rels. 1970-77, Disting. Svc. award 1972), Printing Industry Washington (pres. 1964-65, bd. dirs. 1960-74, Disting. Svc. award 1969), Creative Printers Am. (pres. 1963-64), Master Printers Washington (pres. 1960-61), Met. Washington Bd. Trade (bd. dirs.-at-large 1972, 78), Raleigh Tavern Soc. of Col. Williamsburg Found., Ash Khan Soc. (King Khan). Clubs: City Tavern of Georgetown (Washington); Columbia Country (Chevy Chase, Md.); Farmington Country (Charlottesville, Va.); Met. (N.Y.C.); La Coquille (Palm Beach, Fla.); Chatmoss (Martinsville, Va.); Med Ocean (Bermuda); Golden Horseshoe (Williamsburg, Va.); Confrerie des Chevaliers du Tastevin. Lodge: Optimist (gov. 1957-58, bd. dirs. Leonard Cheshire Found., Disting. Gov. award 1958). Met. (N.Y.C.); La Coquille (Palm Beach, Fla.); Chatmoss (Martinsville, Va.); Mid Ocean (Bermuda); Golden Horseshoe (Williamsburg, Va.); Confrerie des Chevaliers du Tastevin. Home: 405 S England St Williamsburg VA 23185 Office: Hennage Creative Printers 500 N Henry st Alexandria VA 22314

HENNELLY, EDMUND PAUL, lawyer, oil company executive; b. N.Y.C., Apr. 2, 1923; s. Edmund Patrick and Alice (Laccorn) H.; m. Josephine Kline; children: Patricia A. Anglin, Pamela J. Farley. BCE, Manhattan Coll., 1944; postgrad. Columbia U.; JD, Fordham U., 1950. Bar: N.Y. 1950. Instr., Manhattan Coll., 1947-50; litigation assoc. law firm Cravath, Swaine and Moore, 1950-51, sr. litigation assoc. 1953-54; asst. gen. counsel CIA, Washington, 1951-52; assoc. counsel Time, Inc., N.Y.C., 1954-56; asst. legis. cons. Mobil Oil Corp., N.Y.C., 1956-60, legis. cons., 1960-61, mgr. domestic govt. relations dept., N.Y.C., 1961-67, mgr. govt. relations dept., 1967-73, gen. mgr. govt. relations dept., 1974-78, gen. mgr. pub. affairs dept., 1978-86, pres., chief exec. officer Citroil Enterprises, 1986—; dir. South Cay Trust; dir., mem. exec. com. Home Savs. Bank, N.Y.C. Trustee, vice chmn. Daytop Village Found.; mem. adv. com. N.Y. State Legis. Com. on Higher Edn., Nassau County (N.Y.) Energy Commn., L.I. Citizens' Com. for Mass Transit, N.Y. State Def. Council; mem. White House Conf. on Natural Beauty, 1963; bd. dirs. Nat. Council on Aging; exec. com. Pub. Affairs Research Council of Conf. Bd.; mem. Nassau County Econ. Devel. Planning Council; commr. nat. com. Commn. for UNESCO, 1982-85, head U.S. del. with personal rank of ambassador 22d Gen. Conf., 1983; mem. Pres.' Intelligence Transition Team, 1980-81; cons. Pres.'s Intelligence Oversight Bd.; trustee Austen Riggs Ctr., Pub. Affairs Found. Served from ensign to lt., USNR, 1943-46, PTO, ETO. Decorated Knight of Malta, Knight of Holy Sepulchre. Mem. ABA, Fed. Bar Assn., Assn. Bar City of N.Y., Acad. Polit. and Social Scis., Am. Good Govt. Soc. (trustee), Tax Council (dir.), Pub. Affairs Council (dir.), Freedom House (trustee), Am. Mgmt. Assn., Pi Sigma Epsilon, Delta Theta Phi. Clubs: Army-Navy, Southward Ho Country, Babylon Yacht, Explorers, Metropolitan, International, George Town; Capitol Hill. Lodges: K.M., Knights Holy Sepulcher. Contbr. articles on engring. and law to profl. jours. Home: 84 Sequams Ln E West Islip NY 11795 Office: Citroil Enterprises 275 Madison Ave New York NY 10016

HENNESSEE, MANASSA NIXON, banker; b. Concord, N.C., June 27, 1930; s. Manassa Nixon and Jessie Garland (Jarrell) H.; m. Betty Lee Spainhour, Aug. 20, 1954; 1 child, Nixon Scott. AB, Duke U., 1952. Staff writer, copy editor Twin City Sentinel, Winston-Salem, N.C., 1952-56; mgr. pub. relations Wachovia Bank & Trust Co., Winston-Salem, 1956-69, asst. v.p., then v.p., 1960—, econ. devel. officer, 1969-75, econ. devel. mgr., 1975—; v.p., indsl. econ. devel. mgr. First Wachovia Corp., Winston-Salem and Atlanta, 1986—. Dir. film Caravan to Europe, 1963 (Silver Anvil award 1964); author profl. papers. Pres. Child Guidance Clinic, Winston-Salem, 1967; treas., mem. exec. com. N.C. Council Econ. Edn., 1970—; v.p. United Way Forsyth County, Winston-Salem, 1975-76. Mem. N.C. Indsl. Devel. Assn. (bd. dirs. 1976-78), So. Indsl. Devel. Council, Indsl. Devel. Research Council, Pi Kappa Phi, Omicron Delta Kappa. Democrat. Methodist. Club: Westwood (Winston-Salem). Lodge: Kiwanis. Home: 3400 Paddington Ln Winston-Salem NC 27106-5436 Office: First Wachovia Corp 300 N Main St Winston-Salem NC 27150-3099

HENNESSEY, ALICE ELIZABETH, forest products company executive; b. Havenhill, Mass., May 24, 1936; d. H. Nelson and Elizabeth E. (Johnson) Pingree; A.B. with honors, U. Colo., 1957; cert. with distinction Harvard-Radcliffe Program in Bus. Adminstrn., 1958; m. Thomas M. Hennessey, June 13, 1959; children—Shannon, Sheila, Thomas N. With Boise Cascade Corp. (Idaho), 1958—, sec. to pres., 1958-60, adminstrv. asst. to pres., 1960-61, 65-71, corp. sec., 1971—, v.p., 1974-82, sr. v.p., 1982—. Dir. First Interstate Bank of Idaho. Bd. dirs. Boise Pub. Library Found., U. Idaho Found.; sustaining mem. Boise Jr. League. Mem. Am. Soc. of Corp. Secs., Nat. Investor Relations Inst., Pub. Relations Soc. of Am., Phi Beta Kappa, Alpha Chi Omega. Office: Boise Cascade Corp 1 Jefferson Sq Boise ID 83728

HENNESSEY, DAVID PATRICK, banker; b. Coos Bay, Oreg., Aug. 2, 1950; s. William Patrick and Beverly Ann (Curtis) H.; m. Kathryn Ann McCloskey, Aug. 2, 1975; 1 child, Kristin R. AA, Am. River Coll., 1970; BS, Calif. State U., Sacramento, 1974; MBA, Chico State U., 1978. V.p. Bank of Am. N.T. and S.A., Sacramento, 1974-85; exec. v.p. Sunrise Bank Calif., Curtis Heights, 1985-86; pres., chief exec. officer Sunrise Bancorp Sunrise Bank Calif., Roseville, 1986—, also bd. dirs.; chmn. bd. dirs. Data Corp., Roseville, Western Sunrise Mortgage Corp., Rancho Cordovia, Calif. Advisor Sch. Bus. Calif. State U., Sacramento, 1987. Named Outstanding Alumni Calif. State U., 1987. Republican. Home: 7800 Shelborne Dr Loomis CA 95650 Office: Sunrise Bank 5 Sierragate Pla Roseville CA 95678

HENNESSEY, RAYMOND FRANK, wholesale executive; b. Dover, N.H., Dec. 17, 1925; s. Raymond Joseph and Edith Margaret (Morrissette) H.; grad. high sch. Dover; m. July 23, 1949; children—Donald, Patricia, Raymond, Kathryn, Michael. With Nat. Bisquit Co., Dover, 1944-49; pres., chief exec. officer A. Lipson, Inc., Dover, 1949—; bd. dirs. Strafford Nat. Bank, Dover, Bank of N.H., Manchester; treas. Sta. WTSN, 1983—. Mem. Dover Sch. Bd., 1976-78; mayor pro tem City of Dover, 1978-82, mayor, 1982-84; rep. N.H. Gen. Ct., 1955-56, 80-84. Served with USN, 1942-45. Mem. Dover C. of C. (pres. 1975-76), Nat. Assn. Wholesale Grocers, Am. Legion, VFW, CAP. Democrat. Roman Catholic. Clubs: Moose (gov. 1974-75), K.C. (treas. 1978-80), Rotary (pres. 1976-77), Elks, Eagles. Avocation: boating. Home: 125 Silver St Dover NH 03820 Office: A Lipson Inc 2 Faraday Dr Crosby Ind Park Dover NH 03820

HENNESSY, DEAN MCDONALD, lawyer, manufacturing company executive; b. McPherson, Kans., June 13, 1923; s. Ernest Weston and Beulah A. (Dunn) H.; m. Marguerite Sundheim, Sept. 6, 1946 (div. Sept. 1979); children: Joan Hennessy Wright, John D., Robert D. (dec.), Scott D. (dec.); m. Darlene MacLean, Apr. 4, 1981. A.B. cum laude, Harvard U., 1947, LL.B., 1950; M.B.A., U. Chgo., 1959. Bar: Ill. 1951. Assoc. Carney, Crowell & Leibman, Chgo., 1950-53; atty. Borg-Warner Corp., Chgo., 1953-62; with Emhart Corp., Hartford, Conn., 1962—, asst. sec., 1964-67, sec., gen. counsel, 1967-74, v.p., sec., gen. counsel, 1974-76, v.p., gen. counsel, 1976-86; sr. v.p., gen. counsel, 1986—; dir. Emhart Industries, Inc., Emhart Internat. Corp. Trustee West Hartford Bicentennial Trust, Inc., 1976-77, Friends and

Trustees of Bushnell Meml., Hartford, 1978—. Served to lt. (j.g.) USNR, 1943-46. Sheldon fellow Harvard U. Mem. ABA, Am. Soc. Corp. Secs., Machinery and Allied Products Inst. (vice chmn. law council 1984-87, chmn. 1987—). Republican. Presbyterian. Home: 410 Lovely St Avon CT 06001 also: 48 Wagner Rd Shelter Harbor Westerly RI 02891 Office: Emhart Corp 426 Colt Hwy PO Box 2730 Farmington CT 06032

HENNESSY, EDWARD LAWRENCE, JR., diversified aerospace/automotive products and engineered materials executive; b. Boston, Mar. 22, 1928; s. Edward Lawrence and Celina Mary (Doucette) H.; m. Ruth Frances Schilling, Aug. 18, 1951; children: Michael E., Elizabeth R. BS, Fairleigh Dickinson U., 1955; student, NYU. With Heublein, Inc., Hartford, Conn., 1965-72; v.p. fin. Heublein, Inc., 1965-68, sr. v.p. adminstrn., fin., 1969-72; sr. v.p. fin. and adminstrn. United Techs. Corp., Hartford, 1972-77; chief fin. officer, group v.p. United Techs. Corp. (Systems and Equipment Group), 1977, exec. v.p., 1978-79; chmn., pres., chief exec. officer Allied Corp., Morris Township, N.J., from 1979; chmn., chief exec. officer Allied-Signal Inc., 1985—; bd. dirs. Nova Pharm. Corp., Martin Marietta Corp., Bank of N.Y., Union Tex. Petroleum Holdings, Inc. Trustee Cath. U. Am.; trustee Fairleigh Dickinson U., USCG Found. Served with USNR, 1949-55. Mem. Fin. Execs. Inst., Econ. Club N.Y. Roman Catholic. Clubs: Cat Cay (Bahamas); N.Y. Yacht; Ocean Reef, Anglers (Key Largo, Fla.).

HENNETT, RONALD DENNIS, bank executive; b. Woodruff, S.C., Aug. 3, 1942; s. Ray and Anita Christine (Simpkins) H.; m. Constance Annette Strack, July 8, 1978; children: Elizabeth Blair, Ashley Christine. BA, Furman U., 1965, MA, 1967; diploma in banking, Rutgers U., 1979. Loan officer So. Bank & Trust Co., Greenville, S.C., 1969-71; asst. v.p. 1st Citizens Bank & Trust Co., Greenville, 1972-79; v.p. M.S. Bailey & Son, Bankers, Clinton, S.C., 1979-81, Republic Nat. Bank, Columbia, S.C., 1981-83; sr. v.p. Security Fed. Savs. & Loan, Greenville, 1983-85, Benjamin Franklin Savs. Assn., Houston, 1985-87; pres. Greer (S.C.) State Bank, 1987—, also bd. dirs. Campaign chmn. United Way Greater Clinton, 1980; bd. dirs. YMCA of Clinton, 1980-81, Inst. Fin. Edn., Greenville, 1984-85. Mem. S.C. Bankers Assn., Ind. Bankers Assn. Am. Baptist. Club: Poinsett Sertoma (Greenville). Lodge: Lions. Office: Greer State Bank 1111 W Poinsett St Greer SC 29652

HENNIGAR, DAVID J., investment broker; b. Windsor, N.S., Can., July 5, 1939; s. Dean S. and Jean B. (Jodrey) H.; m. Carolyn Bondra Hiltz, June 8, 1964; children—Brian, Jan. B.Commerce, Mount Allison U., 1960; M.B.A., Queen's U., 1962. Investment analyst Burns Fry Ltd. and predecessor co., Toronto, Ont., Can., 1963-66; br. mgr. Burns Fry Ltd. and predecessor co., Halifax, N.S., Can., 1966-71, Atlantic regional dir., 1971—; pres., bd. dirs. Annapolis Basin Pulp & Power Co. Ltd.; chmn. Crownx, Inc.; vice chmn. Nat. Sea Products Ltd.; bd. dirs. Crown Life Ins. Co., Can. Express Ltd., The Pagurian Corp. Ltd., Ben's Holdings Ltd., Halifax Devel. Ltd., Minas Basin Pulp & Power Co. Ltd., Scotia Investment Ltd., Cobi Foods Inc., Atlantic Shopping Centres Ltd., Landmark Corp., Maritime Paper Products Ltd.; chmn. Extendicare Health Svcs., Inc. Bd. dirs., treas. Izaak Walton Killam Hosp. for Children, Halifax, 1976-82; bd. dirs. Inst. for Research on Pub. Policy, Ottawa, Ont., 1983—, Internat. Inst. Transp. and Ocean Policy Studies; bd. govs. Dalhousie U., 1983—. Mem. Investment Dealers Assn. Can. (nat. bd. dirs. 1985-87). Club: Halifax, Halifax Bd. Trade. Home: 51 Forest Ln, Bedford, NS Canada B4A 1H8 Office: Burns Fry Ltd, PO Box 2408, Halifax, NS Canada B3J 3E4

HENNINGS, DOROTHY ANN, financial planner; b. Spokane, Wash., Mar. 23, 1937; d. Theodore Baza LaRue and Florence Irene (Jaeger) Innes; m. Peter L. Sbarbaro Sr., May 16, 1959 (div. 1973); children: Peter L. Jr., David A., John E. AS in Acctg., Napa Valley Coll., 1974; BS, Calif. State U., Sacramento, 1977. Cert. fin. planner. Acctg. asst. Napa (Calif.) County Counsel for Econ. Opportunity, 1972-73; owner, cons. Dash Enterprises, American Canyon, Calif., 1973-78; owner, bookkeeper Reliable Meats, American Canyon, 1973-74; fin. planner IDS Fin. Services, Napa, 1983—. Vol. Boy Scouts Am., Am. Canyon PTA, Little League, Pop Warner Football; tax preparer Vita, Napa, 1973-74. Served with WAC 1958-59. Mem. Napa C. of C., Nat. Assn. Female Execs. Republican. Club: Soroptomist. Lodge: Women of Moose. Office: IDS Fin Svcs 811 Jefferson Napa CA 94559

HENNION, CAROLYN LAIRD (LYN), financial planner; b. Orange, Calif., July 27, 1943; d. George James and Jane (Porter) Laird; m. Reeve L. Hennion, Sept. 12, 1964; children—Jeffrey Reeve, Douglas Laird. B.A., Stanford U., 1965. Cert. fin. planner, lic. ins. agt. Portfolio analyst Schwabacher & Co., San Francisco, 1965-66; adminstrv. coordinator Bicentennial Commn., San Mateo County Calif., 1972-73; dir. devel. Crystal Springs Uplands Sch., Hillsborough, Calif., 1973-84; tax preparer Household Fin. Corp., Foster City, Calif., 1982, freelance, 1983-87; sales promotion mgr. Franklin Distbrs., Inc., San Mateo, 1984-86, regional sales mgr., 1986—, v.p., 1988—; v.p. Viatech, Inc., 1986—. Editor: Lest We Forget, 1975. Pres. South Hillsborough Sch. Parents' Group, Calif., 1974-75; sec. Vol. Bur. of San Mateo County, Burlingame, Calif., 1975; chmn. Community Info. Com., Town of Hillsborough, 1984-86; mem., subcom. chmn. fin. adv. com., Town of Hillsborough, 1984-86. Recipient awards Council for Advancement and Support of Edn., 1981, Exemplary Direct Mail Appeals Fund Raising Inst., 1982. Mem. Internat. Assn. Fin. Planners (sec. Oreg. chpt. 1988—, bd. dirs.), Inst. Cert. Fin. Planners, Ashland Shakespeare Festival, Jr. League, Rogue Valley Country Club. Republican. Home: 148 Greenway Cir Medford OR 97504 Office: Franklin Distbrs 130 E Main St #282 Medford OR 97501

HENRICH, ROBERT JOHN, JR., stock broker; b. Washington, Sept. 2, 1949; s. Robert John and Mary Virginia (Henry) H. B.S., U. Md., 1975; M.B.A., Fla. Inst. Tech., 1977. Account exec. Jefferson Standard Co., Washington, 1977-79; with E.F. Hutton, Washington, 1979—, v.p., 1985—; mem. membership com. Greater Washington Bd. Trade, 1980—. Republican. Lutheran. Avocations: scuba diving; skiing. Home: 9210 Town Gate Ln Bethesda MD 20817 Office: Shearson Lehman Hutton 1050 Connecticut Ave NW Washington DC 20036

HENRIKSON, LOIS ELIZABETH, photojournalist; b. Lytton, Iowa, Nov. 10, 1921; d. Daniel Raymond and Cora Elizabeth (Thomson) Wessling; m. Arthur Allen Henrikson, July 3, 1943; children: Diane Elizabeth Henrikson Slider, Janet Christine, Michele Charlene Henrikson Smetana. BS, Northwestern U., 1943. Adminstrv. asst. to v.p., dir. ops. bus. communications div. ITT Telecommunications Corp., Des Plaines, Ill., 1980-82; adminstrv. asst. to exec. v.p. Wholesale Stationers' Assn., Des Plaines, 1982-84, membership svcs. coord., editor membership roster, 1984-88; midwest corr. Office World News, Hearst Bus. Communications, Inc., Garden City, N.Y., 1988—; editor membership roster Wholesale Stationers Assn. chair safety com. Cumberland Sch. PTA, Des Plaines, 1957-58, chair publicity, 1960-61; bd. dirs. Maine West High Sch. Music Boosters, Des Plaines, 1967-69; capt. fin. drive YMCA, Des Plaines, 1964; mem. diaconate bd., visitation coord. First Congl. Ch., Des Plaines. Mem. NAFE, Am. Soc. Assn. Execs. (cert. membership mktg. 1986), Chgo. Soc. Assn. Execs. (registrar 1984-85), Am. Soc. of Profl. and Exec. Women, AAUW (chair social com. 1983-84, editor newsletter 1984-85, 88—), Am. Assn. Editorial Cartoonists (aux.), Nat. Soc. Magna Charta Dames (life), Am. of Royal Descent (life), DAR, Art Inst. Chgo., Alpha Gamma Delta. Republican. Home: 27 N Meyer Ct Des Plaines IL 60016 Office: Office World News 645 Stewart Ave Garden City NY 11530

HENRY, DAVID, educational administrator; b. N.Y.C., Dec. 3, 1928; s. Maurice and Regina (Hundert) H.; m. Joanne Greenberg, Aug. 17, 1958; children: Robin Henry, Ilissa Henry, Michael Henry. BBA, Baruch Sch., 1956; MBA, Fordham U., 1974. Cert. Systems Profl. Chief auditor McCrory Corp., N.Y.C., 1957-64; systems project mgr. J.C. Penney, N.Y.C., 1965-74; mgr. manual systems Macy's, N.Y.C., 1974-75; mgr. adminstrn. Mfrs. Hanover Trust, N.Y.C., 1975-87; spl. projects mgr. acad. computing svcs. St. John's U., 1988—; pres. Edn. Challenges, Oceanside, N.Y., 1985—; adj. assoc. prof. NYU, 1970—; instr. Bergtraum Adult Ctr., N.Y.C., 1983—. Author: Handbook of Successful Cost Reduction Techniques, 1985, Companywide Customer Service, 1987. Cons. Citizens Union, N.Y.C., 1979-82. Served with U.S. Army, 1950-52. Recipient Cert. for Contbn. to Edn., Am. Mgmt. Assn., N.Y.C., 1976. Mem. Assn. for Systems Mgmt. (profl., v.p. 1979-82, merit award 1979, achievement award 1982). Republican. Jewish. Club: J.C. Penney Camera (N.Y.C.) (pres. 1973-74); South Shore Camera (Malverne, N.Y.) (treas. 1980-81). Home: 465 Links Dr E Oceanside NY 11572

HENRY, EDWARD FRANK, computer accounting service executive; b. East Cleveland, Ohio, Mar. 18, 1923; s. Edward Emerson and Mildred Adella (Kulow) H.; m. Nicole Annette Peth, June 18, 1977. BBA, Dyke Coll., 1948; postgrad. Cleve. Inst. Music, 1972. Internat. auditor E.F. Hauserman Co., 1948-51; office mgr. Frank C. Grismer Co., 1951-52; Broadway Buick Co., 1952-55; treas. Commerce Ford Sales Co., 1955-65; nat. mgr. Auto Acctg. div. United Data Processing Co., Cin., 1966-68; v.p. Auto Data Systems Co., Cleve., 1968-70; pres. Profl. Mgmt. Computer Systems, Inc., Cleve., 1970—, ComputerEase, Small Bus. Computer Ctrs. div. Profl. Mgmt. Computer Systems, Inc., 1985—, VideoEase Computerized Video Rental Systems div. Profl. Mgmt. Computer Systems, Inc., 1987-89; exec. artisitc dir. NorthCoast Cultural Centre,, 1989. Charter pres. No. Ohio Coun. Little Theatres, 1954-56; founder, artistic and mng. dir. Exptl. Theatre, Cleve., 1959-63; dramatic dir., actor various community theatres, 1955-65; actor Cleve. Playhouse, 1961-63; bd. dirs. Cleve. Philharmonic Orch., 1972-73. With USAAF, 1943-46. Mem. Am. Mgmt. Assn., Nat. Assn. Accts., Mil. Order World Wars, Air Force Assn. (life), Ky. Cols., Data Processing Mgmt. Assn., Mayfield Area C. of C., Phi Kappa Gamma (Gamma charter pres., past nat. pres.). Republican. Presbyterian. Clubs: Acacia Country, Hermit, Univ., Cleve. Grays, Deep Springs Trout, Nat. Sojourners (Nat. Pres.'s cert. 1977-78, pres. Cleve. chpt. #23 1978), Heroes of '76 (comdr. Cleve. 1977). Lodges: Masons, DeMolay (past master Cleve. chpt., Legion of Honor 1970), KT, Grotto, Shriners (dramatic dir. 1968—), Cleve. Ct. #14, Jesters (dir. 1981, impresario 1984—, dramatic dir. 1971—, nat. producer, dir. Nat. Book of the Play Reno, 1988—, Las Vegas, 1989—), Kachina, SOBIB, Rotary. Home: 666 Echo Dr Gates Mills OH 44040 Office: Profl Mgmt Computer Systems Inc 19701 S Miles Ave Cleveland OH 44128

HENRY, JUDITH EULISS, businesswoman; b. Hickory, N.C., May 25, 1940; d. Ned Hartwell and Lucille (Ford) Euliss; m. James Dewitte Henry, Mar. 19, 1983; 1 child, Jennifer. Student Clevenger Bus., 1958-60, Caldwell Community Coll. and Tech. Inst., 1980-82, U. N.C., 1985; various seminars and courses on aging. Owner, pres. Camelot Manor Retirement Home, Inc., Granite Falls, N.C., 1978—, Camelot Manor Nursing Care Facility, Inc., Granite Falls, 1985—, Camelot Comprehensive Out-Patient Rehab. Facility, Camelot Village; instr. therapy for the aged Caldwell Community Coll., 1970-78, mem. nursing adv. bd. Ch. treas., youth dir. St. James Episcopal Ch., Lenoir, N.C.; vol. Social Services, Rest Homes, Sr. Citizens Groups, Hickory Coop. Ministry, Fish, Bloodmobile, Heart Fund, Broughton Hosp., Morganton, N.C.; pres. Granite Falls Am. Field Service; bd. dirs., pres. PTA; bd. dirs. South Caldwell High Sch. Health Occupations Dept.; mem. U. N.C. Nursing Home Adminstrn. Recipient Woman of Yr. award Granite Falls Bus. and Profl. Women's Orgn., 1984. Home: 117 Auld Farm Rd Lenoir NC 28645 Office: Camelot Manor Nursing Care Facility Inc 100 Sunset St Granite Falls NC 28600

HENRY, MARSHALL WEBSTER, JR., trucking company executive; b. Rocky Mount, N.C., Jan. 20, 1946; s. M. Webster and Nancy (Powell) H.; m. Gayle Sims, Sept. 29, 1973; children: Chadwick G. Seymour, Mary Chapman Andrew. grad. Va. Episc. Sch., Lynchburg, 1965, BA, U. N.C., 1969. Gen. mgr. The Entertainers, Ltd., Chapel Hill, N.C., 1965-68; adminstrv. asst. U. N.C. News Bur., 1967-69; ptnr., gen. mgr. All-Star Prodns., Chapel Hill, 1968-69; tchr. Nash County Schs., Nashville, N.C., 1969-70; with C. S. Henry Transfer, Inc., Rocky Mount, 1969—, sec., 1972-74, treas., 1973-74, v.p., gen. mgr., 1975-83, pres., treas., chief exec. officer, 1983-87, pres., chief exec. officer, 1988—, dir., 1972—. Mem. Nash County Transp. Efficiency Council, 1981-84; former gen. chmn. Rocky Mount Spring Arts Festival; mem. adv. com. N.C. D.O.T. Motor Carriers, 1987—; exec. officer local br. U.S. Power Squadron. Mem. N.C. Trucking Assn. (dir. 1973—, pres. 1981-82), N.C. Citizens for Bus. and Industry (ATA bd. dirs. 1986—), Am. Trucking Assns. (dir. ATA Common Carrier Conf.-Irregular Route 1979-81, bd. dirs. 1986—), N.C. Pub. Service Awards Soc., Va. Episc. Sch. Alumni Assn., Rocky Mount Area Personnel Assn., Rocky Mount Area C. of C., Young Pres.' Orgn., U. N.C. Alumni Assn., Delta Nu Alpha. Clubs: Northgreen Country., Rocky Mount Sheep's. Home: 177 Candlewood Rd Rocky Mount NC 27804 Office: C S Henry Transfer Inc PO Drawer 2306 Rocky Mount NC 27802

HENRY, ORMOND LEE, mechanical engineer, manufacturing executive; b. Youngstown, Ohio, July 28, 1937; s. Ormond Lee and Janet (Marshall) H.; m. Margaret M. Mixer, July 1, 1961; children: Betsy, Bruce, Matthew. BSME, Lehigh U., 1959; MBA, U. Mich., 1961; MS in Mech. Engring., Bradley U., 1966. V.p., gen. mgr. Neway Equipment Corp., Muskegon, Mich., 1965-74; group v.p. Bendix Automotive, Detroit, 1974-79; pres. Bendix Automotive, London, 1979-82; pres., chief exec. officer Castolin & Eutectic, Geneva, 1982-83; pres., chief operating officer RTE Corp., Brookfield, Wis., 1983-86; pres., chief exec. officer Champion Spark Plug Co., Toledo, 1986-89. Mem. Phi Kappa Phi. Office: Champion Spark Plug Co 900 Upton Ave Toledo OH 43607

HENRY, PETER YORK, lawyer; b. Washington, Apr. 28, 1951; s. David Howe II and Margaret (Beard) H.; m. Rebecca Jo Csajka, Aug. 1976; children—Ryan York, Zachary Price. B.B.A., Ohio U., 1973; J.D. St. Mary's U., San Antonio, 1976. Bar: Tex. 1976. Sole practice, San Antonio, 1976—. Mem. Tex. Bar Assn., Am. Trial Lawyers Assn., Tex Trial Lawyers Assn., San Antonio Trial Lawyers Assn. (bd. dirs. 1989—), San Antonio Bar Assn., Phi Delta Phi. Home: 6806 Forest Haven San Antonio TX 78240 Office: 224 Casa Blanca San Antonio TX 78215

HENSEL, KATHERINE RUTH, securities analyst; b. Summit, N.J., Nov. 24, 1959; d. John Charles and Carolyn (Bahle) H. BA, Harvard U., 1981, MBA, 1985. Securities analyst Donaldson Lufkin & Jenrette, N.Y.C., 1981-83; investment banker Blythe Easton/Paine Webber, N.Y.C., 1985, Shearson Lehman Bros., N.Y.C., 1986; v.p., securities analyst Shearson Lehman Hutton, N.Y.C., 1987—. Contbr. articles to profl. jours. Mem. Bank and Fin. Analysts Assn., N.Y. Soc. Securities Analysts, Harvard Club N.Y.C. Home: 250 7th St Jersey City NJ 07306 Office: Shearson Lehman Hutton World Financial Ctr New York NY 10285

HENSKE, JOHN M., chemical company executive; b. Omaha, 1923. B.S. in Chem. Engring. and Indsl. Adminstrn, Yale U., 1948. With Dow Chem. Co., 1948-69; v.p., group v.p. chems. Olin Corp., Stamford, Conn., 1969-71, sr. v.p., pres. chems group, 1971-73, pres., 1973-78, 83-87, chief exec. officer, 1978-87, chmn. bd., 1978-88; dir. Harvey Hubbell, Inc., 1987—; dir. Am. Precision Industries, Inc., N.E. Bancorp, Inc., The Hydraulic Co., Sun Co. Bd. dirs. United Negro Coll. Fund. Served with U.S. Army, 1943-46. Mem. Conf. Bd. (dir.), Am. Mgmt. Assn. (dir.), Chem. Mfg. Assn. (chmn., dir.).

HENSLEY, MARGARET ANN, swimming pools distributing company official; b. Knoxville, Tenn., May 6, 1941; d. Herman Geissler and Carrie Lucille (Wilmoth) Ballard; children—Dennis Keith Logan, David Wayne Logan, John Ballard Pecora, Felicia Ann Pecora. Student, Dale Carnegie Sch., 1969, Watterson Coll., Ft. Lauderdale, 1988—. Head subscriptions New Woman mag., Fort Lauderdale, Fla., 1974-75; med. asst. Medi Lab Systems, Fort Lauderdale, 1975-76; mgr. Swimming Pool Owners Assn., Fort Lauderdale, 1976-78; accts. receivable clk. Outdoor World Distbrs., Fort Lauderdale, 1978-81, purchasing agt., 1984, asst. mgr., 1986; credit mgr. Miller Assocs., Miami, Fla., 1981-83, adminstrv. mgr., Miller Miami Br., 1986-87; with Safety Plus, Inc., Louisville, 1987-88; rep. customer service Pool Water Products, 1988; br. mgr. Miller Assocs., 1988—. Named to Hon. Order of Ky. Cols., Gov. of Ky., 1986-87. Mem. Nat. Assn. Female Execs., Gold Coast Women in Credit. Avocations: golfing; bowling; art.

HENSLEY, ROBERT PAUL, manufacturing company executive; b. Dayton, Ohio, Jan. 10, 1931; s. Cecil Paul and Edna Elizabeth (Muddell) H.; m. Carol Jean Kadel, Sept. 13, 1952; children: Diana Lynn, Kimberly Sue, Linda Carol. AA, Miami-Jacobs Jr. Coll., 1951. Acct. Amcast Indsl. Corp., Kettering, Ohio, 1951-63, supr. acctg., 1963-80, asst. treas., 1980-82, asst. sec.-treas., 1982-87, asst. sec., dir. risk mgmt., 1987-88, asst. v.p. risk mgmt., asst. sec., 1989—. Mem. YMCA, Dayton, 1962—, Centerville (Ohio) Tax Appeal Bd., 1976—. Mem. Nat. Assn. Accts. (pres. 1969), Data Processing Mgmt. Assn. (pres. 1970), Risk Ins. Mgmt. Soc. (pres. 1986-88). Republican. Home: 21 Glencroft Pl Dayton OH 45459 Office: Amcast Indsl Corp 3931 S Dixie Ave Kettering OH 45439

HENSON, ARNOLD, lawyer; b. White Plains, N.Y., Oct. 28, 1931; s. Philip Truman and Gwendolen (Bossi) H.; m. Cynthia Madsen, Feb. 27, 1954; children: Philip, Palmer, Drusilla. A.B., Colgate U., 1953; J.D., U. Mich., 1959. Asso. firm Chadbourne, Parke, Whiteside & Wolff, N.Y.C., 1959-66; partner Chadbourne, Parke, Whiteside & Wolff, 1967-81; sr. v.p., gen. counsel, dir. Am. Brands, Inc., N.Y.C., 1981-85; exec. v.p., chief fin. officer Am. Brands, Inc., 1986—. Chmn. Conservation Adv. Bd., New Castle, N.Y., 1972-75; mem. New Castle Planning Bd., 1975-81, chmn., 1981. Served to lt. (j.g.) USNR, 1953-56. Mem. Assn. Bar City N.Y., Namequoit Sailing Assn. (commodore 1979-81). Republican. Clubs: N.Y. Yacht, Camp Fire of Am. Home: 67 Stag Ln Greenwich CT 06831 Office: Am Brands Inc 1700 E Putnam Ave Old Greenwich CT 06870

HENSON, ERNEST EDDIE, real estate company executive; b. Elk City, Okla., June 7, 1936; s. Ernest E. and Ruth S. (Winburn) H.; m. Erma Florence Lilly, Dec. 27, 1956; children: William E., Elizabeth Ruth. BSME, Texas Tech U., 1959; MBA, Harvard U., 1963. V.p. for real estate Helmerich & Payne Inc., Tulsa, 1963-72; pres. Willco Properties Ltd., Tulsa, 1972-75; pres., bd. dirs. Williams Realty Corp., Tulsa, 1975-88; pres. Henson-Williams Realty Inc., Tulsa, 1988—. Past bd. dirs. The Denver Ptnrship., Tulsa chpt. ARC, Tulsa council Boy Scouts Am.; past pres. Downtown Tulsa Unltd. Served to 1st lt. USAF, 1959-62. Mem. Inst. Real Estate Mgmt., Internat. Council Shopping Ctrs. (chmn. bd. dirs. 1988), Urban Land Inst. (trustee, exec. com., chmn. rsch. com. 1988). Office: Henson-Williams Realty Inc 3800 One Williams Ctr Tulsa OK 74102

HENSON, E(RNEST) PAUL, management consultant; b. Knoxville, Tenn., May 1, 1924; s. Ernest P. and Anne (Hall) H.; 2 children. BS in Chem. Engring., U. Tenn., 1948. Registered profl. engr., Tenn. Engr. Procter and Gamble Co., Memphis and Cin., 1949-54; mgmt. positions Gen. Electric Co., Cin., 1954-76; ind. mgmt. cons. Knoxville, 1976—; with Nat. Reactor Testing Sta. (Idaho), Phila. Writer, editor ballistic missile re-entry vehicle manuals. Pres. Northview Community Assn., Kodak, Tenn., 1980. Served with U.S. Army, 1942-45, ETO. Mem. Am. Contract Bridge League (cert. tchr. 1987), Am. Bridge Tchrs. Assn. (cert. tchr. 1988), ELFUN Soc., Toastmasters (pres. Cin. club 1955). Republican. Home: 5700 Pleasant Ridge Rd #206 Knoxville TN 37912

HENSON, PAUL HARRY, communications company executive; b. Bennet, Nebr., July 22, 1925; s. Harry H. and Mae (Schoenthal) H.; m. Betty L. Roeder, Aug. 2, 1946; children: Susan Irene Flury, Lizbeth Henson Barelli. B.S. in Elec. Engring, U. Nebr., 1948, M.S., 1950; hon. doctorates, U. Nebr., Ottawa U., Bethany Coll. Registered profl. engr., Nebr. Engr. Lincoln (Nebr.) Tel. & Tel. Co., 1941-42, 45-48, div. mgr., 1948-54, chief engr., 1954-59; v.p. United Telecommunications, Inc., Kansas City, Mo., 1959-60; exec. v.p. United Telecommunications, Inc., 1960-64, pres., 1964-73, chmn., 1966—, also dir.; bd. dir. Armco, Duke Power, Hallmark Cards; chmn. Pres.'s Nat. Security Telecommunications Adv. Com. Trustee Midwest Research Inst., Tax Found., U. Nebr. Found., U. Mo. at Kansas City. Served with USAAF, 1942-45. Mem. Nat. Soc. Profl. Engrs., IEEE, Armed Forces Communications Electronics Assn., U.S. Telephone Assn. (dir. 1960-76, pres. 1964-65), Masons, Shriners, Sigma Xi, Eta Kappa Nu, Sigma Tau, Kappa Sigma (Man of Yr. 1987). Office: United Telecommunications Inc Box 11315 Kansas City MO 64112

HENYCH, IVO, metal processing company executive; b. Skvorec, Prague, Switzerland, Jan. 12, 1935; s. Rudolf and Vera (Stadelmann) H.; m. Alexandra Spada; 1 child, Blanka. MS in Engring., State U. Mining and Metallurgy, Ostrava, Czechoslavakia, 1962. Metallurgist, mgr. Kralodv Zelezarny, Kraluvdvur, Czechoslovakia, 1961-68; metall. researcher Georg Fischer, Ltd., Schaffhausen, Switzerland, 1968-80, br. mgr., 1980—; mgr. Foundry Tech. Transfer. Contbr. articles to profl. jours.; patentee in field. Mem. Verein Deutsche Giessereifachleute, Lic. Exec. Soc. Home: IM Buel 201, 8234 Stetten Switzerland

HEPTINSTALL, DEBRA LOU, newspaper executive; b. Tacoma, Mar. 5, 1952; d. Fred Bernard and June Isabella (Carter) H.; m. Duval Meade McDaniel, Feb. 16, 1974 (div. Feb. 1978); m. Michael Emory Smith, Sept. 26, 1980. Cert. Cen. Va. Community Coll., 1970, AAS cum laude, 1973; student Longwood Coll., 1971-72. Advt. mgr. Times Record/Roane County Reporter, Spencer, W.Va., 1976-78; advt. clk., sales asst. The Washington Post, 1978-79, advt. mgr. The Reston Times, Va., 1979-80; ind. sales contractor, The Washington Post, 1980-81, advt. sales rep., 1981-85, mktg. analyst (pricing), 1985-87; customer service mgr. Rep. Dominion Bank No. Va., Centreville, 1987; project request clk. Bengtson, DeBell, Elkin & Titus, Ltd., 1988; advt. mgr. The Springfield Connection Newspaper, 1988; mktg. promotional mgr. Def. News, Springfield, Va., 1988; rsch. adminstv. asst. The Times Jour. Co., Springfield, 1989—. Republican. Methodist. Avocation: playing classical piano. Home: 5818 Rock Forest Ct Centreville VA 22020 Office: The Times Jour Co Springfield VA 22159

HERB, SAMUEL MARTIN, manufacturing company executive; b. Yeadon, Pa., Nov. 29, 1938; s. Samuel F. and Mildred V. (Reitz) H.; m. Judith Ann Oesch, July 2, 1966; children: Samuel S., Corinne M., David M., Elizabeth A. BEE, Drexel U., 1969. Registered profl. engr., Calif. Tech. writer Honeywell Corp., Ft. Washington, Pa., 1964-73, applications engr., 1973-76, project engr., 1976-79; product application specialist Leeds & Northrup, N. Wales, Pa., 1979-83, product line mgr., 1983-85; mgr. bus. devel. Leeds & Northrup, N. Wales, 1985-88, systems advt. mgr., 1988—; mem. faculty Spring Garden Coll., Chestnut Hill, Pa., 1976-82. Author: Understanding Distributed Process Control, 1983; contbr. articles to profl. jours. Commr. Boy Scouts Am., 1961—. Named to Legion of Honor Chapel of Four Chaplains, 1985. Mem. Instrument Soc. Am. (sr.). Republican. Roman Catholic. Club: Engineers (Phila.). Home: 117 Pawnee Rd New Britain PA 18901 Office: Leeds & Northrup Systems Sumneytown Pike North Wales PA 19454

HERBERT, DONALD ROY, lawyer, business executive; b. Mpls., Nov. 4, 1935; s. Roy Patrick and Bertha Lydia (Mathre) H.; m. Carol A. Elofson, June 28, 1958; children—Karen, James, Phillip. B.S.L., U. Minn., 1957, LL.B. cum laude, 1959. Mem. firm Dorsey, Owen, Barker, Scott & Barber, Mpls., 1959-62; corp. lawyer Peavey Co., Mpls., 1962-77, v.p., gen. counsel, sec., 1977-85; sr. v.p., gen. counsel, sec. Gelco Corp., Eden Prairie, Minn., 1985—. Mem. ABA, Minn. State Bar Assn. (bd. govs. 1976-77), Corp. Counsel Assn. Minn. (pres. 1975-76). Republican. Lutheran. Club: Mpls. Athletic. Home: 1500 16th Terr NW New Brighton MN 55112 Office: Gelco Corp 1 Gelco Dr Eden Prairie MN 55344

HERBERT, GAVIN SHEARER, JR., health care products company executive; b. Los Angeles, Mar. 26, 1932; s. Gavin and Josephine (D'Vitha) H.; children by previous marriage Cynthia, Lauri, Gavin, Pam; 2d. m. Ninetta Flanagan, Sept. 6, 1986. B.S., U. So. Calif., 1954. With Allergan Pharms., Inc., Irvine, Calif., 1950—; v.p. Allergan Pharms., Inc., 1956-61, exec. v.p., pres., 1961-77, chmn. bd., chief exec. officer, 1977—, pres., from 1977, pres. eye and skin care products group, from 1981; exec. v.p. Smith Kline Beckman Corp., 1986—, also bd. dirs. Trustee U. So. Calif.; bd. dirs. Richard Nixon Presdl. Found., Estelle Doheny Eye Found., Beckman Laser Inst. and Med. Clinic. Served with USN, 1954-56. Mem. Beta Theta Pi. Republican. Clubs: Big Canyon Country, Balboa Bay, Newport Harbor Yacht, Pacific. Office: Allergan Inc 2525 DuPont Dr Irvine CA 92715

HERBERT, IRA C., food processing company executive; b. Chgo., Oct. 5, 1927; s. Solomon David and Helen (Burstyn) Chizever; m. Lila Faye Ellman, Jan. 6, 1951; children: Carrie Jo, Jeffrey, Fred. B.A., Mich. State U., 1950. Account exec. McFarland Aveyard, Chgo., 1951-56; account supr. Edward H. Weiss, Chgo., 1956-63; v.p. McCann Erickson, Los Angeles and Atlanta, 1963-65; sr. v.p. Coca-Cola U.S.A., Atlanta, 1965-74; exec. v.p. Coca-Cola Co., Atlanta, pres. food div., 1975-81, exec. v.p., 1979—, chief mktg. officer, 1981-88, pres., chief exec. officer, 1988—; bd. dirs. Tex. Commerce Bank, T.C.C. Beverages Ltd. Served with USAF, 1945-47; with U.S. Army, 1951-

52. Mem. Advt. Council (dir.). Jewish. Clubs: Standard, Commerce (Atlanta).

HERBERT, JOHN WARREN, forest products executive; b. Columbus, Ohio, June 20, 1924; s. Logan R. and Ruth (Warren) H.; m. Elizabeth Knapp, Oct. 15, 1949; children: Kathryn, Steve, Lisa, David, Laura. B.S., U. Pa., 1948; A.M.P., Harvard U., 1966. Salesman Mead Corp., Dayton, Ohio, 1948-54, regional mgr., 1954-63, v.p., 1963-66, v.p., gen. sales mgr., 1967-70, pres. Mead Paper and exec. v.p. Paper Group, pres. Mead Printing and Writing, 1970-71, group v.p., 1981-85, sr. v.p., 1985—; dir. First Nat. Bank, Dayton, 1977—. Served with U.S. Army, 1943-46. Republican. Presbyterian. Clubs: Moraine Country (bd. govs.), Dayton Racquet. Office: Mead Corp World Hdqrs Courthouse Pla NE Dayton OH 45463

HERBITS, STEPHEN EDWARD, manufacturing company executive; b. Pittsfield, Mass., Mar. 13, 1942; s. Nathaniel R. and Esther (Levin) H.; AB, Tufts U., 1964; JD, Georgetown U., 1972. Adminstrv. asst. for research U.S. Senator Edward W. Brooke of Mass., 1966; staff asst./staff dir. Wednesday Group, U.S. Ho. of Reps., 1967-68; commr. President's Commn. All-Vol. Armed Forces, 1969-70; v.p. fin. devel. Sabre Found., Fond-du-Lac, Wis., 1970; legis. asst. to U.S. Senator Robert T. Stafford of Vt., 1971-73; spl. asst. to asst. sec. def. manpower and res. affairs Dept. Def., 1973-74; cons. Bailey, Deardourff & Assos., Inc., Washington, 1969, 73, 74, 77; spl. asst. to dir. Presdl. Personnel Office, White House, 1974-75; counsel U.S. del. Multilateral Trade Negotiations, Office Spl. Rep. for Trade Negotiations, 1975-76; spl. asst. to sec. and dep. secs. def. Dept. Def., 1976-77; v.p. Seagram Overseas Sales Co., 1977-79; mng. dir. Kirin-Seagram, Japan, 1977-79; v.p. Seagram Europe, 1979-80; pres. Browne Vintners, Joseph E. Seagram & Sons, Inc., N.Y.C., 1980-82; mng. dir. Seagram Far East, 1982-83; v.p. corp. devel. Seagram Co. Ltd., 1983-86, exec. v.p. corp. devel., 1986-88, exec. v.p. corp. policy and external affairs, 1989—; dir. Greenworks, Inc., N.Y.C. Bd. dirs. Nat. Leadership Coalition on Aids, 1987. Mem. D.C. Bar Assn. Republican. Jewish. Author articles. Office: Joseph E Seagram & Sons Inc 375 Park Ave New York NY 10152-0192

HERBST, DAVID GEORGE, finance company executive; b. Joliet, Ill., Oct. 10, 1952; s. James Justin and Betty M. (Wagner) H.; m. Anne L. Zierman, Nov. 14, 1987. BA in History, St. Francis Coll., 1970; MS in Ednl. Adminstrn., Ill. State U., 1980. Cert. fin. planner. Tchr. in history, English Minooka (Ill.) Jr. High Sch., 1977-83; pres. Herbst Fin. Svcs.Inc., Joliet, 1980—. Named mem. Blue Blazer Club All Am. Life Ins. Co., 1986. Mem. Internat. Assn. Fin. Planning, Nat. Assn. Fin. Planning, Nat. Assn. Life Underwriters, Interprofl. Inst., Sec. Club, Phi Alpha Theta. Republican. Evangelical. Home: 10467 N Bell Rd Minooka IL 60447 Office: Herbst Fin Svcs 3077 W Jefferson St Ste 110 Joliet IL 60435

HERBST, LAWRENCE ROBERT, entrepreneur; b. Haverhill, Mass., Aug. 8, 1946; s. Morton and Ruth I. (Cooper) H. Attended UCLA, Alexander Hamilton Bus. Inst.; DVM, N.Am. Sch. Animal Scis.; DD, Missionaries of New Truth, Chgo. Owner, pres. Best-way Records, Data Time Info., Lawrence Herbst Records, Total Sound Records, Beverly Hills Records, Beverly Hills Music Pub. Co., Plus K-Larrco Rec. Studios, Future World Stores, Larry's Family Restaurant, Heavenly Waterbed Showrooms, K-Larrco Satellite Radio and TV Stas.; pres., adminstr. LH Investment Trust Fund of Tex., Inc., Larrco Industries of Tex.; pres., founder House of Robots, Larr Robots, Larry's Merchandising Data Base; founder, pres., dir. chief adminstr. Holy Bible Gospel Ministry of the Body of Christ, 1989—. Author: (book and movie) Legend of Tobby Kingdom, 1975; The Good, The Bad, The True Story of Lawrence Herbst; news columnist World of Investments, 1976. Designer 1st musical electronic amplifier with plug in I.C.'s; inventor Larrco AM/FM satellite car radio, one-man air car, 2-foot satellite dish and system, flat satellite dish and system. Mem. Broadcast Music, Inc.; pres. Lawrence Herbst Farms; producer Spacee the Lion Cartoon. Pres., adminstr. Lawrence Herbst Found. Mem. Nat. Acad. TV Arts and Scis., Los Angeles Press Club, Internat. Platform Assn., Nat. Assn. Broadcasters, Epsilon Delta Chi. Office: PO Box 3842 Houston TX 77253-3842

HERD, JAMES LESLIE, manufacturing executive; b. Lennox Town, Scotland, Mar. 29, 1952; came to U.S., 1979; BSMIE, Luton Tech. Coll., London, 1973, BSIE, 1975; MBA, Gen. Motors Inst., 1977. Engr. apprentice Vauxhall Motors, Luton, Eng., 1968-73, indsl. engr., 1973-75; sr. indsl. engr. Vauxhall Motors, Luton, 1977-79; indsl. engr. Gen. Motors, Flint, Mich. and Detroit, 1975-77; mgr. indsl. engring. Diablo Systems, Hayward, Calif., 1979-81; mgr. indsl. engring. facilities Diablo Systems, Fremont, Calif., 1981-84; mgr. mfg. ops. Xerox Corp., Fremont, 1985-86, mgr. strategic planning, 1986—; cons. various mfrs. Silicon Valley, Calif., 1984—. Contbr. chpt. to book. Mem. Am. Inst. Indsl. Engrs. (sr.), Tau Beta Pi. Office: Xerox Corp 901 Page Ave Fremont CA 94537

HERELD, PETER CLAUDE, management consultant; b. Hanover, Fed. Republic of Germany, Nov. 20, 1920; came to U.S., 1939.; s. John and Alice Herzfeld; m. Ruth Braun, Dec. 24, 1944 (dec. 1980); children: Richard C., Randi A. Cert. of proficiency, Cambridge (Eng.) U., 1939. Exec. v.p. Chemo Puro Mfg. Corp., N.Y.C., 1941-60; v.p. spl. chems. Sequa Corp., N.Y.C., 1960-68; v.p. N.Am. UOP Fragrances, N.Y.C., 1968-69; dir. new ventures Crompton & Knowles Corp., N.Y.C., 1969-71; mng. dir. Hereld Orgn., Hartford, Conn., 1971—; cons. Electrosynthesis Co. Inc., Buffalo, 1987—. Editor food industry directories; patentee in field. Mem. Inst. Food Technologists, Am. Chem. Soc., World Affairs Ctr. Home and Office: Whitney Ctr 200 Leader Hill Dr Ste 330 Hamden CT 06517

HERGENHAN, JOYCE, corporate executive; b. Mt. Kisco, N.Y., Dec. 30, 1941; d. John Christopher and Goldie (Wago) H. B.A., Syracuse U., 1963; M.B.A., Columbia U., 1978. Reporter White Plains Reporter Dispatch, 1963-64; asst. to Rep. Ogden R. Reid Washington, 1964-68; reporter Gannett Newspapers, 1968-72; with Consol. Edison Co. of N.Y., Inc., N.Y.C., 1972-82, v.p., 1977-79, exec. asst. to chmn. bd., 1978, sr. v.p. pub. affairs, 1979-82; v.p. corp. pub. relations General Electric Co., Fairfield, Conn., 1982—. Office: GE 3135 Easton Turnpike Fairfield CT 06431

HERGET, JAMES PATRICK, executive search executive; b. Cleve., Oct. 21, 1944; s. Louis E. and Dorothy R. (Whearty) H. AB, Holy Cross Coll., 1966; MBA, Case Western Res. U., 1969; m. Jane Herget; children: Elizabeth, Lauren. Analyst, Cleve. Trust Co., 1966; sales rep. Xerox Corp., Cleve., 1967, cons., 1968-70, product mgr., Washington, 1971, social service leave, 1972, regional cons. mgr., 1973-75, mgr. sales and sales mgmt. programs, Rochester, N.Y., 1975-76; product mgr. Forward Products, Rochester, 1977-78, asst. to v.p. mktg., 1979—; prin. Spencer Stuart & Assocs., 1980-85; ptnr. Lamalie Assocs., 1985—; cons. Nat. Minority Purchasing Council, Inc., 1973-76; instr. mktg. Cleve. State U., 1970; dir. mktg. Interracial Council for Bus. Opportunity, 1972; treas. Urban Small Bus. Cons., 1970. Co. location chmn. United Way, Arlington, Va., 1973-76; active Big Bros., Washington, 1972-75, Cleve., 1981—; v.p. Genesee Valley Arts Found., Rochester, 1977-78. Recipient Nat. citation Nat. Center for Voluntary Action, 1971; Ace award SBA, 1970. Republican. Roman Catholic. Designer, producer 3 tng. programs for office of minority enterprise Commerce Dept., 1973-76. Mem. Vols. in Partnership, Mensa, Internat. Platform Assn. Clubs: Univ., Playhouse, Skating (Cleve.). Home: 22480 Calverton Rd Shaker Heights OH 44122

HERGUTH, JOHN JAMES, JR., engineering and construction contracting company executive, lawyer; b. Jersey City, Mar. 15, 1947; s. John James and and Lena (Alvarez) H.; m. Ann Marie Senchyshyn, Aug. 16, 1969; 1 child, John James III. BME, Villanova U., 1968, JD, 1975; MBA, U. Utah, 1972. Bar: N.J. 1975, U.S. Patent and Trademark Office 1976. Instr. Golden Gate Coll., San Francisco, 1973-74; patent atty. Foster Wheeler Energy Corp., Livingston, N.J., 1975-80, corp. atty., 1980-84; dir. risk mgmt. Foster Wheeler Energy Corp., Perryville, N.J., 1984—; pres. York Jersey Liability Ltd. and subs., Hamilton, Bermuda, 1986—; mem. Delphi panel ESIS, Inc., Phila., 1988—. Coach Washington Twp. Boys Soccer Leqague, Long Valley, N.J., 1979, Washington Twp. Boys Baseball League, 1986; umpire Washington Twp. Boys Baseball League, 1980. With USAF, 1970-74. Mem. Risk Ins. Mgmt. Soc. (conf. speaker 1987), Pi Tau Sigma. Republican. Roman Catholic. Home: 6 Rosewood Trail Long Valley NJ 07853 Office: Foster Wheeler Corp Perryville Corp Park Clinton NJ 08809-4000

HERING, GUNTHER ERWIN, business executive; b. Munich, Germany, Sept. 22, 1936; came to U.S., 1959; s. Erwin and Wera (Binder) H.; m. Jan T. Turner, Dec. 2, 1978; children: John Gunther, Bren Elizabeth. M.B.A., U. Hamburg, Germany, 1959. Mgmt. cons. McKinsey & Co., N.Y.C., 1971-75; v.p. Fluor Corp., Irvine, Calif., 1975-86; sr. v.p. Shearson Lehmann, N.Y.C., 1986-87; pres., chief exec. officer Harpener AG, Dortmund, Fed. Republic Germany, 1987—; chmn. Wanderer AG, Munich, Bowe GmbH, Augsburg, Fed. Republic Germany; dir. Phenol Chemie, Gladbeck, Fed. Republic Germany; prin., mng. dir. Hering & Co., Greenwich, Conn., 1988—. Adviser Youth for Understanding Found. Recipient Knight of Justice award Johanniter Orden, Bonn, Germany, 1978, Ven. Order St. John, London, 1982. Clubs: N.Y. Yacht, Indian Harbor Yacht, Norddeutscher Regatta Verein, Big Canyon Country. Home: 62 Royal St George Rd Newport Beach CA 92660 also: 45 Greenwich Hills Dr Greenwich CT 06831 Office: Hering & Co 100 Putnam Green Greenwich CT 06830

HERKNESS, LINDSAY COATES, III, securities broker; b. N.Y.C., Feb. 8, 1943; s. Lindsay C. and Harriett (Richard) H. B.A., Trinity Coll., Hartford, Conn., 1965. With Reynolds Securities, Inc. (merged with Dean Witter & Co. 1978), N.Y.C., 1965-78; sr. v.p. investments Dean Witter Reynolds, Inc., N.Y.C., 1978—. Bd. dirs. Manhattan Eye, Ear and Throat Hosp. Clubs: Union, Downtown Assn. (N.Y.C.); Rockaway Hunting; Piping Rock (Locust Valley, N.Y.); Bath and Tennis (Palm Beach, Fla.). Office: 160 E 65th St Ste 31-C New York NY 10021

HERLIHY, ROBERT EDWARD, chemical company executive; b. Lynn, Mass., May 8, 1931; s. Edward Francis and Mary Margaret (Whelan) H.; m. Cornelia Ellen Coan, Sept. 5, 1955; children—Kathleen, Anne, Mary Lou, Robert E. B.S.C.E., Tufts U., Medford, Mass., 1953. With Gen. Electric Co., 1957-68; sr. v.p. W.R. Grace & Co., N.Y.C., 1968—; dir. W.R. Grace Communications Corp., N.Y.C., 1983—. Co-author: Basic Mathematics, 1965; Advanced Methods & Models, 1965; Statistical Inference, 1966; Probabilistic Models, 1968. Served to lt. comdr. USNR, 1953-57. Mem. Inst. Mgmt. Sci., Ops. Research Soc., IEEE. Republican. Roman Catholic. Clubs: Union League (N.Y.C.); Aspetuck Valley Country (Weston, Conn.). Office: W R Grace & Co 1114 Ave of the Americas New York NY 10036

HERLING, MICHAEL, steel company executive; b. Cernauti, Romania; arrived in Canada, 1950; m. Marta Klein; children: Dorothy Herling Chaikelson, Joyce Herling Saifer. B in Econs., U. Vienna, Austria, 1933; D in Econs., U. Florence, 1935. Sr. v.p. Ivaco, Inc., Montreal, Que., Can., 1969—. Office: Ivaco Inc, 770 Rue Sherbrooke Ouest, Montreal, PQ Canada H3A 1G1

HERMAN, BERNARD ALBERT, pharmaceutical company executive; b. Boston, Dec. 11, 1910; s. Michael and Celia Caroline (Pullman) H.; m. Haydée Irma Arevalo, May 14,1938; children: Kathleen Archer Barrow, Bradford Kent II. BA, Yale U., 1934. With R.H. Macy & Co., Inc., N.Y.C., 1934-41; ptnr. Eliot Restaurant Corp., Boston, 1946-52; chmn. bd., chief exec. officer, dir. Herman, Inc., Avon, Mass., 1950—; pres., chief exec. officer, dir. Archer Kent Stores, Avon, 1961—, Trade Winds Inn, Inc., Craigville, Mass., 1972—; ptnr. Kent Realty Co., Boston, 1972-87; trustee Bradford Realty Trust, Avon, 1950—, Archer Kent Realty Trust, Craigville, 1972—. Leader Boy Scouts Am., Newton Highlands, Mass., 1950-52; pres. Little League Baseball, Wellesley Hills, Mass., 1960-63; vestryman St. Paul's Episcopal Ch., Newton Highlands, 1952-55, St. Mary's Episcopal Ch., Newton Lower Falls, Mass., 1963-66. Served to comdr. USN, 1941-46. Military scholar U.S. Army, 1930-34. Mem. Nat. Assn. Service Merchandisers, Nat. Assn. of Drug Chains, Toiletry Merchandisers Assn. (chmn. bd. dirs. 1973-74), Phi Beta Kappa. Republican. Clubs: Yale, Harvard, Wardroom (Boston); Wellesley Country. Lodge: Masons. Home: 57 Damien Rd Wellesly Hills MA 02181 Office: Herman Inc 291 Pond St Avon MA 02322

HERMAN, KURT, financial executive; b. Vienna, Austria, Oct. 27, 1930; came to U.S., 1939, naturalized, 1945; s. Henry and Martha (Feuer) H.; B.A., Pa. State U., 1951; M.B.A., Washington U., 1954; postgrad. Temple U., 1958-59; m. Rosalyn J. Landesberg, May 10, 1953; children—Gayle A., Elise P., Shari E. With Berman Bag Co., Red Hill, Pa., 1954-57, Philco Corp., Phila., 1957-61; corporate controller Esterbrook Pen Co., Cherry Hill, N.J., 1961-68; treas. KDI-Sylvan Pools, Inc., Doylestown, Pa., 1968-72; v.p. fin. TV Facts, Inc., Phila., 1972-74; dir. fin. Fedn. of Jewish Agys., Phila., 1974-83; asst. exec. dir. for fin. and adminstrn. JCCs, Phila., 1983—; dir. Learn Inc.; part-time acctg. instr. Rutgers U., 1966—; cons. in field. United Way coordinator, 1977-83. Served with USCG, 1951-53. C.P.A., Pa. Mem. Nat. Assn. Accts. Contbr. articles to profl. jours. Office: JCCs 401 S Broad St Philadelphia PA 19147

HERMAN, MICHAEL EDWARD, pharmaceutical company executive; b. N.Y.C., May 31, 1941; s. Harris Abraham and Sally (Ruzga) H.; m. Karen May Kuivinen, May 29, 1966; children—Jolyan Blake, Hamilton Brooks. B.Metall. Engring., Renaselaer Poly. Inst., Troy, N.Y., 1962; M.B.A., U. Chgo., 1964. Sr. bus. analyst W.R. Grace & Co., N.Y.C., 1964-66; asst. to pres., v.p. corp. devel. subs. Nuclear Fuel Service, Washington, 1966-68; v.p. Laird, Inc., N.Y.C., 1968-70; founding gen. partner Dryden & Co., N.Y.C., 1970-74; exec. v.p., chief fin. officer, mem. Office of Pres., dir. Marion Labs., Inc., Kansas City, Mo., 1974—; dir. Janus Capital Corp. Boatmen's Bank, Kansas City, Mo., Nordic Labs., Home Office Reference Labs.; chmn. bd. dirs. Tanabe-Marion Labs.; adv. dir. Janus Capital Corp.; vis. lectr. U. Kans. Grad. Sch. Bus.; assoc. prof. Rockhurst Coll. Grad. Sch. Bus. Trustee Kansas City Royals Baseball Club Profit Sharing Trust, Pembroke Hill Sch.; chmn. pension com. Maj. League Baseball Players Relations Com.; pres. Ewing Marion Kauffman Found. Mem. Pharm. Mfrs. Assn. (dir., mem. fin. steering com.). Jewish. Clubs: Kansas City; N.Y. Athletic; Hallbrook Country; Carriage. Home: 6201 Ward Pkwy Kansas City MO 64113 Office: Marion Labs Inc 9300 Ward Pkwy PO Box 8480 Kansas City MO 64114 also: 10236 Marion Park Dr Kansas City MO 64137

HERMAN, ROBERT LEWIS, cork company executive; b. N.Y.C. July 16, 1927; s. Nat W. and Ruth (Stockton) H.; A.B., Columbia, 1948, B.S., 1949; m. Susan Marie Volper, Dec. 10, 1966; children—Candia Ruth, William Neal. Vice pres. Joseph Samuels & Sons, Inc., Whippany, N.J., 1953-62; pres. Dependable Cork Co., Inc., Morristown, N.J., 1962—; chmn. bd. Global Technology Systems. Co., Trevor, Wis., 1980—. Served to comdr. C.E. Corps, USNR, 1949-53. Mem. N.J. Mfrs. Assn., Naval Res. Assn., U.S. C. of C. Clubs: Navy League; Columbia University, Princeton (N.Y.C.). Inventor Corticiera natural cork wallcovering. Home: PO Box 1023 Morristown NJ 07960-1023 Office: PO Box 1102 Morristown NJ 07960-1102

HERMAN, SHIRLEY YVONNE, accountant; b. Jersey City, Nov. 22, 1941; d. Otto and Mary (Erde) H. BA, CCNY, 1963. IRS enrolled agt. Pvt. practice N.Y.C., 1984—. Mem. Nat. Assn. Pub. Accts., Nat. Assn. Tax Practioners, Nat. Assn. Enrolled Agts. Office: 853 Broadway Ste 1101 New York NY 10003

HERMANN, ARTHUR W., controller; b. Detroit, June 22, 1944; s. Arthur George and June (Zeidler) H.; m. Patricia L. Hermann, 1969 (div. 1972); 1 child, Arthur Gregory; m. Margaret Thill, Sept. 23, 1979; children—Anne Catherine, David William. BS in Acctg., Wayne State U., 1972. C.P.A., Mich. Supervising sr. Peat, Marwick, Mitchell & Co., Detroit, 1972-76; asst. to officer Comerica, Inc., Detroit, 1976-77, asst. cashier, 1977-78, asst. v.p., 1978-80, v.p., treas., controller, 1980-83, 1st v.p., controller, 1983-87, sr. v.p., controller, 1987—. Served with USMC, 1966-72. Mem. Fin. Exec. Inst., Bank Adminstrn. Inst., Nat. Assn. Accts., BAI Acctg. and Fin. Commn. Republican. Roman Catholic. Office: Comerica Inc 211 W Fort St Detroit MI 48275-2140

HERMANN, DONALD HAROLD JAMES, lawyer, educator; b. Southgate, Ky., Apr. 6, 1943; s. Albert Joseph and Helen Marie (Snow) H. A.B. (George E. Gamble Honors scholar), Stanford U., 1965; J.D., Columbia U., 1968; LL.M., Harvard U., 1974; M.A. (Univ. scholar), Northwestern U., 1979, Ph.D., 1981. Bar: Ariz. 1968, Wash. 1969, Ky. 1971, Ill. 1972, U.S. Supreme Ct. 1974. Mem. staff, directorate devel. plans Dept. Def., 1964-65; With Legis. Drafting Research Fund, Columbia U., 1966-68; asst. dean Columbia Coll., 1967-68; mem. faculty U. Wash., Seattle, 1968-71, U. Ky., Lexington, 1971-72; mem. faculty DePaul U., 1972—, prof. law and philosophy, 1978—, dir. acad. programs and interdisciplinary study, 1975-76, assoc. dean, 1975-78, dir. Health Law Inst., 1985—; lectr. dept. philosophy Northwestern U., 1979-81; counsel DeWolfe, Poynton & Stevens, 1984—; vis. prof. Washington U., St. Louis, 1974, U. Brazilia, 1976; lectr. law Am. Soc. Found., 1975-78, Sch. Edn. Northwestern U., 1974-76, Christ Coll. Cambridge (Eng.) U., 1977, U. Athens, 1980; vis. scholar U. N.D., 1983; mem. NEH seminar on property and rights Stanford U., 1981; participant law and econs. program U. Rochester, 1974; mem. faculty summer seminar in law and humanities UCLA, 1978; Bicentennial Fellow of U.S. Constitution Claremont Coll., 1986; bd. dirs. Coun. Legal Edn. Opportunity, Ohio Valley Consortium, 1972, Ill. Bar Automated Rsch.Corp., 1975-81, Criminal Law Consortium Cook County, Ill., 1977-80; cons. Adminstrv. Office Ill. Cts., 1975—; reporter cons. Ill. Jud. Conf., 1972—; mem. Ctr. for Law Focused Edn., Chgo., 1977-81; faculty Instituto Superiore Internazionale Di Science Criminali, Siracusa, Italy, 1978-82; bd. dirs. Horizons Community Svcs., 1985-88; cons. Commerce Fedn., State of São Paulo, Brazil, 1975; bd. dirs. Chgo. area AIDS Task Force Inc. Editor: Jour. of Health and Hosp. Law, 1986—, AIDS Monograph Series, 1987—. Bd. dirs. Ctr. for Ch.-State Studies, 1982—, Chgo. Area AIDS Task Force, 1987—. John Noble fellow Columbia U., 1968, Internat. fellow, NEH fellow, Law and Humanities fellow U. Chgo, 1975-76, Law and Humanities fellow Harvard U., 1973-74, Northwestern U., 1978-82, Criticism and Theory fellow Stanford U. 1981; NEH fellow Cornell U., 1982, Judicial fellow U.S. Supreme Ct., 1983-84. Mem. ABA, Ill. Bar Assn., Chgo. Bar Assn., Am. Acad. Polit. and Social Sci., Am. Law Inst., Am. Soc. Law and Medicine, Am. Soc. Polit. and Legal Philosophy, Nat. Health Lawyers Assn., Am. Judicature Soc., Am. Philos. Assn., Soc. for Bus. Ethics, Soc. for Phenomenology and Existential Philosophy, Internat. Assn. Philosophy of Law and Soc., Soc. Writers on Legal Subjects, Internat. Penal Law Soc., Soc. Am. Law Tchrs., Am. Assn. Law Schs. (del., sect. chmn., chmn. sect. on jurisprudence), Am. Acad. Hosp. Attys., Ill. Assn. Hosp. Attys., Evanston Hist. Soc., Northwestern U. Alumni Assn., Signet Soc. of Harvard, Hasty Pudding Club, University Club, Quadrangle Club. Episcopalian. Home: 1243 Forest Ave Evanston IL 60202 also: 880 Lake Shore Dr Chicago IL 60611 Office: De Paul U Coll Law 25 E Jackson St Chicago IL 60604

HERMANN, ROBERT JAY, manufacturing company engineering executive, consultant; b. Sheldahl, Iowa, Apr. 6, 1933; s. John and Ellen Melinda (Ericson) H.; m. Darlene Velda Lowman, Mar. 20, 1954; children: Scott Alan, Sherie Lynn. BSEE, Iowa State U., 1954, MSEE, 1959, PhD, 1963. Dep. dir. research and engring. Nat. Security Agy., Ft. Meade, Md., 1973-75; spl. asst. to supreme allied comr. Europe SHAPE, Casteau, Belgium, 1975-77; dep. under sec. of def. for research and engring. Dept. Def., Washington, 1977-79, asst. sec. of Air Force for research, devel. and logistics, 1979-81, spl. asst. for intelligence to under sec. of def. for research engring., 1981-82; v.p. systems tech. and analysis United Techs., Hartford, Conn., 1982-84, v.p. advanced systems def. and space group, 1984-87, v.p. sci. and tech., 1987—; bd. dirs. Ultra Systems, Inc., Irving, Calif.; cons. Dept. Def., 1982-88. Served to 1st lt. USAF, 1955-57. Recipient Arthur Fleming Washington Jaycees, 1972; recipient Nat. Capital Nat. Capital Area Architects and Engrs., Washington, 1967, Air Force Disting. Service medal USAF, Washington, 1980. Mem. Armed Forces Communications and Electronics Assn. (bd. dirs. 1979-83), Security Affairs Support Assn. (pres. 1983-86), Am. Inst. Aero. and Astronautics, Assn. Old Crows. Home: 5 Stonepost Rd Simsbury CT 06070 Office: United Techs Corp 1 Financial Pla Hartford CT 06101

HERMANN, STEVEN ISTVAN, textile executive; b. Debrecen, Hungary, July 25, 1934; came to U.S., 1957.; s. Zoltan and Maria (Gacs) H.; m. Agnes S. Nadel, Oct. 17, 1958 (div. 1981); m. Elizabeth Takacs, Mar. 11, 1981; children: Roy, George. BS, U. Budapest, 1955. Architect N.Y. Firms, 1958-66; exec. Knitbrook Mills, N.Y.C., 1966-68; exec. v.p. Melena Knitting Co., E. Rutherford, N.J., 1968-69; pres., chief exec. officer Carnaby Mills, Inc., E. Rutherford, 1969-75, Korafab, Inc., N.Y.C., 1973-76; owner, pres. Texpro, Inc., E. Rutherford, 1976-79; v.p. Meadows Knitting Corp., Kearny, N.J., 1979—, Safer Group, Kearney and Newark, 1979—. Contbr. articles to profl. jours. Mem. Kampfe Lake Assn., Bloomingdale, N.J. Served to lt. Hungarian Army, 1952-56. Republican. Home: Kampfe Lake Bloomingdale NJ 07403 Office: Meadows Knitting Corp 650 Belleville Turnpike Kearny NJ 07032

HERNANDEZ, WILLIAM, reprographics company executive; b. Santa Monica, Calif., Oct. 9, 1948; s. Jose Mendez and Beatrice (Saenz) H.; m. Janice Marie Forester, Nov. 30, 1968; children: Novina Marie, Arianna Nicole, Elicia Rene, William Ryan. Dir. ops. Koebig & Koebig, Inc., L.A., 1973-74; asst. controller Koebig, Inc., L.A., 1974-75; mgr. Micro-Device Ford Graphics, L.A., 1975-76, Continental Graphics, L.A., 1975-76, Hughes Helicopter, Inc. (div. Summa Corp.), Culver City, Calif., 1979-83; exec. v.p. Universal Reproductions, Inc., Culver City, 1983—. Staff sgt. USMC, 1967-73. Vietnam. Recipient Cert. Commendation L.A. City Council, 1973, Cert. Commendation Mayor of L.A., 1974. Mem. Am. Legion (fin. officer 1972-73). Republican. Office: Universal Reproductions Inc 5915 Blackwelder St Culver City CA 90232

HEROLD, HOPE ANNE, banker; b. N.Y.C., Aug. 10, 1954; d. Harry and Grace Catherine (McGurn) H.; m. Vincent P. Macaluso, Nov. 29, 1986; 1 child, Vincent Bonaventura IV. B.S., St. John's U., 1976. Mortgage dept. clk. Anchor Savs. Bank, N.Y.C., 1973; work measurement analyst Chase Manhattan Bank, N.Y.C., 1975-76; systems analyst Morgan Guaranty Trust Co., N.Y.C., 1976-79, sr. systems analyst, 1979-80, project mgr., 1980-81; asst. sec., 1981-86, asst. v.p., 1986—. cons. adminstr., 1983—; systems cons. Recipient Pres.'s medal for loyal and disting. service St. John's U. Mem. Am. Mgmt. Assns., St. John's U. Alumni Assn. Roman Catholic. Mem. Lambda Kappa Phi, Alpha Psi Omega. Home: 1091 Cuyama Rd Ojai CA 93023 Office: Morgan Guaranty Trust 23 Wall St New York NY 10015

HEROLD, JOHN DOWNS, director, educator; b. Ann Arbor, Mich., Mar. 21, 1941; s. Griffith Alexander and Mary Bovaird (Downs) H.; m. Sondra Jean Kerr, June 6, 1964; children: Timothy, Rebecca Lyn. BS, U. Mich., 1963, MS in Microbiology, 1965, MA in Counseling, 1968. Teaching asst. U. Mich., Ann Arbor, 1965-66, conf. coord., 1966-67, asst. supr., 1967-69, assoc. supr., 1969-71, dir. confs., 1971-79, liaison dir., 1979-87, asst. dir. indsl. devel., 1987—; mem. com. Mich. Tech. Coun., Ann Arbor, 1979—; chmn. Inventors Coun. Mich., Ann Arbor, 1983-88; bd. dirs. New Enterprise Forum, Ann Arbor, Innovation Ctr., Ann Arbor, Univ. Credit Union, Ann Arbor. Contbr. articles to profl. jours. Bd. dirs. Ann Arbor Area 2000, 1987—. Mem. Nat. Univ. Continuing Edn. (officer 1974-83), Mich. Indsl. Developers, Adult Edn. Assn., Meeting Planners Internat., Rotary (bd. dirs. 1981-85). Presbyterian. Office: U Mich Indsl Devel Div 2200 Bonisteel Blvd Ann Arbor MI 48109

HERON, WESLEY DAVID, treasurer, corporate executive; b. Beckley, W.Va., June 26, 1949; s. Robert W. and Margaret (Turner) H.; m. Lillie Marlene Kasalnak, Aug. 16, 1971 (div. Sept. 1979); m. Beverly Sue Adderholt, Aug. 1, 1980; children: Limberly Blair, Elizabeth Elaine. BBA, U. Fla., 1971, MBA, 1980. CPA, Fla. Staff acct. May, Zima & Co., CPAs, Daytona Beach, Fla., 1972-73; asst. controller U. Fla., Gainesville, Fla., 1973-78; asst. to v.p. J. Hillis Miller Health Ctr., Gainesville, 1978-80; v.p. fin. Richardson (Tex.) Health Systems, Inc., 1980-85, So. Med. Health System, Inc., Mobile, Ala., 1985-86; sr. v.p., treas. Heartland Health System, Inc., St. Joseph, Mo., 1986—. Mem. student fin. aid com. U. Fla., 1976-77. Fellow Hosp. Fin. Mgmt. Assn.; mem. AICPA, Mo. Hosp. Assn. (gov.'s select com. on Medicaid 1987—), Kansas City Area Hosp. Assn. (council on fin. 1987—), Nat. Assn. Accts., Assn. MBA Execs., Acctg. Rsch. Assn., St. Joseph Racquet Club (bd. dirs. 1988—), St. Joseph Country Club. Republican. Roman Catholic. Home: 721 Greenbriar Terr Saint Joseph MO 64506 Office: Heartland Health System Inc 416 N 7th St Saint Joseph MO 64501

HERPST, ROBERT DIX, lawyer, optical company executive; b. Teaneck, N.J., Jan. 23, 1947; s. Harold Dix and Anita Augusta (Adams) H.; children: Katherine Elizabeth, Lauren Gabriel; m. Theresa M. Jacobini, Oct. 24, 1987. BS, NYU, 1969; JD, Rutgers U., 1972. Bar: N.J., U.S. Supreme Ct. Assoc. Pitney, Hardin & Kipp, Morristown, N.J., 1972-77, BOC Group, Inc., Montvale, N.J., 1977-87; div. counsel BOC Group, Inc., Montvale, 1978-80, assoc. corp. counsel, 1980-82, corp. counsel, asst. sec., 1982-88; chmn. bd. Internat. Crystal Labs., Inc., Garfield, N.J., 1988—; pres. Internat. Crystal Labs., Inc., Garfield, N.J., 1982-88, chmn. bd. dirs., 1988—; pres. Nike Syrena Corp., 1989—. Mem. ABA (internat. bus. law com., overseas equity and joint venture investment subcom. of corp., banking and bus. law sect.). Home: 1 Lincoln St Suffern NY 10901 Office: Internat Crystal Labs Inc 11 Erie St Garfield NJ 07026

HERR, EARL BINKLEY, JR., pharmaceutical company executive; b. Lancaster, Pa., Apr. 14, 1928; s. Earl Binkley Sr. and Irene (Zeamer) H.; m. Elizabeth Sydney Hook, June 17, 1950; children: Audrey, Linda. BS, Franklin and Marshall Coll., Lancaster, 1948; MS in Chemistry, U. Del., 1950, PhD in Biochemistry, 1953; postgrad., Cornell U., 1953-55, Brookhaven Nat. Labs., 1955-57. With Lilly Research Labs., Indpls., 1957—, mgr. antibiotic purification devel., 1963-64, head pharm. research, 1964-65, asst. dir. prodn. devel., 1965, dir. antibiotic ops., 1965-68, exec. dir. biochem. and biol. ops., 1968-69, v.p. biochem. ops., 1969-70, v.p. indsl. relations, 1970, v.p. research, devel. and control, 1970-73, pres., 1973—, now exec. v.p., also bd. dirs. Bd. dirs. Ind. Sci. Edn. Fund. Mem. AAAS, Am. Chem. Soc., Sigma Xi. Home: 12011 Eden Glen Dr Carmel IN 46032 Office: Eli Lilly & Co Lilly Corp Ctr Indianapolis IN 46032

HERR, FREDERICK Z., automotive executive; b. Detroit, Dec. 24, 1925; s. Frederick and Irma (Olah) H.; m. Jean Ann Young, Sept. 26, 1953; children: Frederick John, Karen Ann, Laurie Ann. BEE, U. Wis., 1946; MBA, U. Detroit, 1962. Fin. analyst, supr. Ford Motor Co., Dearborn, Mich., 1955-66; mgr. quality control gen. parts div. Rawsonville, Mich., 1966-69; exec. electro-mech. product engring. office Dearborn, 1969-70; mgr. Sheldon Rd. plant Plymouth, Mich., 1970-71; dir. reliability N.Am. automotive div. Dearborn, 1971-72; mgr. Sterling Van Dyke plants Sterling Heights, Mich., 1972-74; chief engr. elec. and electronics div. Dearborn, 1975-78; gen. mgr. elec. and electronics div. Rawsonville, 1981-85; v.p., gen. mgr. electronics div. Aeronutronic Ford Corp., Phila., 1974-75; asst. mng. dir. Ford Australia, Melbourne, 1978-81, v.p. engring., 1985-87, v.p. product assurance, 1987-89. Panel chmn. Career Horizons E. Mich. Univ., 1978, 80, 82. Lt. USN, 1944-46. Recipient Mfg. Tech. Excellence award. Mem. Engring. Soc. Detroit, Am. Soc. Quality Control, Soc. Automotive Engrs., Fairlane Club, Meadowbrook Country Club, Beta Gamma Sigma, Eta Kappa Nu. Office: Ford Motor Co 17101 Rotunda Dr PO Box 1522A Dearborn MI 48121

HERREGAT, GUY-GEORGES JACQUES, banker; b. Oostende, West Flanders, Belgium, July 22, 1939; came to U.S., 1966; s. Georges-Albert Maurice and Marie-Gerard S. (Elleboudt) H. Licence en philosophie, U. Louvain, 1961, licence en philosophie et lettres, 1964; postgrad., Yale U., 1966-67, PhD in Econs., 1972. Rsch. asst. U. Louvain (Belgium), 1964-66; rsch. assoc. Nat. Bur. Econ. Rsch., N.Y.C., 1967-72; internat. economist Brown Bros. Harriman & Co., N.Y.C., 1973-74; asst. v.p. Chem. Bank, N.Y.C., 1974-76; dep. chief econonist European Am. Bank, N.Y.C., 1977-80; sr. advisor, sr. v.p. Societe Generale de Banque, N.Y.C., 1980-85; mgr. Banque Worms, N.Y.C., 1985-86; sr. v.p., dep. gen. mgr. Credit du Nord, N.Y.C., 1986—; cons. Am. Bankers Assn., N.Y.C., 1971, SEIDEIS-Futuribles, PAris, 1967-80, Ford Found., N.Y.C., 1972-73. Author: Managerial Profiles and Investment Patterns, 1972, (with others) The Diffusion of New Industrial Processes, 1974, THe Finances of the Performing Arts, 1974; contbr. articles to profl. jours. Yale U. fellow, 1966-67, Nat. Bur. Econ. Rsch. fellow, 1971-72; named Aspirant de Recherches Fonds National Belge de la Recherche Scientifique, 1967-72. Mem. Am. Econ. Assn., Acad. Polit. Sci., Yale Alumni Assn., Japan Soc., Inst. Internat. Bankers, Belgian-Am. C. of C. (bd. dirs. 1986—). Home: 30 E 81st St New York NY 10028 Office: Credit du Nord 520 Madison Ave New York NY 10022

HERRICK, KENNETH GILBERT, manufacturing company executive; b. Jackson, Mich., Apr. 2, 1921; s. Ray Wesley and Hazel Marie (Forney) H.; m. Shirley J. Todd, Mar. 2, 1942; children: Todd Wesley, Toni Lynn. Student public and pvt. schs., Howe, Ind.; LHD (hon.), Siena Heights Coll., 1974; HHD (hon.), Adrian Coll., 1975, Detroit Inst. Tech., 1980; LLD, Judson Coll., 1975; D Engring. (hon.), Albion Coll., 1981. With Tecumseh Products Co., Mich., 1940-42, 45—; v.p. Tecumseh Products Co., 1961-66, vice chmn. bd., 1964-70, pres., 1966-70, chmn. bd., chief exec. officer, 1970—; bd. dirs. Mfrs. Nat. Bank Detroit. Bd. dirs. Howe Mil. Sch., 1970-81, from Herrick Found., 1970; mem. exec. adv. bd. St. Jude Children's Hosp., from 1978. Served with USAAC, 1942-45. Recipient Hon. Alumni award Mich. State U., 1975; Disting. Svc. award Albion Coll., 1975. Mem. Lenawee Country Club, Elks, Tecumseh Country Club, Masons. Presbyterian. Office: Tecumseh Products Co 100 E Patterson Tecumseh MI 49286 *

HERRICK, PETER, banker; b. White Plains, N.Y., Nov. 10, 1926; s. Harold and Alta (Lake) H.; m. Beatricia Bierau, Oct. 7, 1950; children: David, Wendy. AB, Williams Coll., 1950. With The Bank of N.Y., N.Y.C., 1951—; v.p. The Bank of N.Y., 1967-72, sr. v.p., 1973-79, exec. v.p., chief comml. banking officer, 1979-82, pres., chief operating officer, dir., 1982—; bd. dirs. The Bank of N.Y. Internat. Inc., The Bank of N.Y. Co., Inc., BNY Internat. Investments, Inc., BNY Leasing Inc., BNY Fin. Corp., BNY Holdings Corp. (Del.), ARCS Mortgage Inc., Beacon Capital Mgmt., Inc., Bank of N.Y. Life Ins. Co. Inc., Bank of N.Y. Trust Co., Skandia-Am. Corp., Skandia Am. Reins. Corp., Hudson Ins. Co., MasterCard Internat.; mem. Brit.-N.Am. Com. Vice chmn. mem. exec. com. Better Bus. Bur. Met. N.Y.; trustee Hood Coll., N.Y. Community Trust; bd. govs. Hundred Yr. Assn. N.Y. Served with U.S. Army Air Corps, 1944-46; with USAF, 1950-51. Mem. Assn. Res. City Bankers., N.Y. State Bankers Assn. (bd. dirs.). Clubs: India House, Shenorock Shore, Siwanoy Country, Econ. of N.Y, Pilgrims of U.S. Office: Bank NY Co Inc 48 Wall St New York NY 10286

HERRICK, ROBERT MICHAEL, agricultural products executive; b. Trenton, N.J., Apr. 4, 1951; s. Francis Charles and Mary (Blaner) H.; m. Janet Marie Hartman, June 3, 1972; children: Lisa Marie, Andrea Michelle. BA, Trenton State Coll., 1976; MA, Rider Coll., 1982; MS, Rutgers U., 1984, PhD, 1986. Sci. asst. Am. Cyanamid Co., Princeton, N.J., 1972-77; biologist Am. Cyanamid Co., Princeton, 1977-79, weed scientist, 1979-84, weed research scientist, 1984-86, coordinator product devel., 1986, mgr. product devel., 1986—. Contbr. articles to profl. jours. Patentee in field. Mem. Hamilton Twp. Parks and Recreation Commn., Hamilton, N.J., 1980—. Served as sgt. USAR, 1982-88. Mem. Weed Sci. Soc. Am., So. Weed Sci. Soc., Aquatic Plant Mgmt. Soc., Soc. Am. Foresters, Nat. Agrl. Chem. Assn. Office: Am Cyanamid Co PO Box 400 Clarksville Rd Princeton NJ 08540

HERRICK, TODD W., manufacturing company executive; b. Tecumseh, Mich., 1942. Grad., U. Notre Dame, 1967. Pres., chief exec. officer Tecumseh (Mich.) Products Co. Office: Tecumseh Products Co 100 E Patterson St Tecumseh MI 49286

HERRIN, LEXIE ELBERT, engineering firm executive; b. Donna, Tex., May 17, 1925; s. Lexie E. and Mary Frances (Scates) H.; BSME, U. Mich., 1951, postgrad. 1951; MBA, U. So. Calif., 1964; m. Charlotte Frances Campbell, Mar. 9, 1946; children: Christopher Patrick, Timothy Michael, Bradley Terrence. Commd. 1st lt. USAF, 1951, advanced through grades to lt. col., 1967, ret., 1969; pres. KOHM Mining and Devel., 1966-69; exec. v.p. Oil Producers & Refiners, Glendale, Calif., 1969-70; gen. mgr. Broadmore Homes of Tex., Waco, 1970-72; pres. Exec. Mobile Home Service, Lighthouse Point, Fla., 1972-74; pres. L.E. Herrin Engr. Cons., Redlands, Calif., 1974-76; v.p., gen. mgr., dir. von Haenel-Herrin & Assocs., Glendale, Calif., 1977-83; pres. Herrin-Stanton & Assocs. 1983—; dir. Seagull Industries, 1966-75; chmn. sub-com. on traffic accident reporting Nat. Hwy. Safety Adv. Com.; lectr. U. Calif., Northridge; arbitrator Am. Arbitration Assn., 1978—; del. com. on transp. Calif. Commn. on the Califs. Active, Boy Scouts Am., 1951-64; co-chmn. Reagan for Pres., San Bernardino County, 1976, asst. to chmn., 1980; del. Calif. Rep. Conv., 1981—; presdl. appointee Dept. Transp. 1981-85. Decorated Air Force Commendation medal with oak leaf clusters. Mem. ASME, AIAA, Internat. Soc. Air Safety Investigators, Am. Inst. Indsl. Engrs., Soc. Automotive Engrs., Am. Assn. Automotive Medicine, Triangle, Sphinx, Michigama, Phi Sigma Kappa. Republican. Clubs: Officers, March AFB Flying, Wheeler Flying, Masons. Editor-in-chief U. Mich. Technic, 1949-51. Office: Herrin-Stanton & Assocs 302 Alabama Ste 10 Redlands CA 92373

HERRING, BILL EDWIN, industrial waste management company executive; b. Ft. Worth, July 19, 1942; s. Meldrum Edwin and Mary Lee (Manning) H.; m. Doris Dodd, Dec. 14, 1962; children: Billy Edwin Jr., Russell Todd. BBA, U. Houston, 1970. Pers. mgr. Olin Chem. Corp., Cleveland, Tenn., 1970-73, Joliet, Ill., 1973-77; pers. dir. Olin Chem. Corp., Lake Charles, La., 1977-80, Target So. Dist. Ctr., Maumelle, Ark., 1980-85; owner, mgr. Herring & Assocs., Inc., North Little Rock, Ark., 1985-87, pres., 1985—; v.p. adminstrn. Environ. Systems Co., Inc., Little Rock, 1986—, v.p., 1987—; bd. dirs. Filmed Events Network, Inc., Little Rock. With USAF, 1961-65. Mem. Am. Soc. for Pers. Adminstrn. Baptist. Home: 31 Westwind Dr North Little Rock AR 72118 Office: Environ Systems Co Inc 333 Executive Ct Little Rock AR 72205

HERRING, DAVID M(AYO), engineer; b. Rockport, Tex., Jan. 18, 1929; s. James Clark and Edith Esther (Sneed) H.; m. Nell Adams, Sept. 10, 1955; children—Clark, John, Scott. B.S., U. Tex., Austin, 1955, M.S. in Structures, 1960. Cons. engr. W.P. Moore & Co., Houston, 1955; cons. engr. Chgo. Bridge & Iron Co., Ltd., Caracas, Venezuela, 1956, supt., 1957, asst. mgr. ops., 1958-60, mgr. ops., 1960-64; mgr. internat. ops. Western Hemisphere CBI Co., Oak Brook, Ill., 1964-68, asst. mgr. CBI Nuclear Co., Memphis, 1968-72; constrn. mgr. S.E. div. CBI Co., Birmingham, Ala., 1973-78; pres., dir. Sea-Con Services Inc., New Iberia, La., 1978—; dir. Thermal Designs Inc., Houston, Atlantic Sea-Con, Gloucester, Mass., Sea-Con Services, Ltd., Yarmouth, Eng. Inventor world's largest revolving derrick. Contbr. articles to profl. jours. Served with C.E., U.S. Army, 1950-52, Korea. Mem. Offshore Pipeline Contractors Assn. (founding chmn.), Nat. Ocean Industries Assn., ASCE (Featured Engr. award 1971), Assn. Diving Contractors (bd. dirs. 1986—), Colegio de Ingeneros, Arquetectos and Agrimensores de P.R., Chi Epsilon, Tau Beta Pi. Episcopalian. Office: CBI NA Con PO Box 41146 8900 Fairbanks Houston TX 77064

HERRING, LEONARD GRAY, marketing company executive; b. nr. Snow Hill, N.C., June 18, 1927; s. Albert Lee and Josie (Sugg) H.; m. Rozelia Sullivan, June 18, 1950; children: Sandra Grey, Albert Lee II. BS, U. N.C., 1948. With Dun & Bradstreet, Inc., Raleigh, N.C., 1948-49; with H. Weil & Co., Goldsboro, N.C., 1949-55; pres., chief exec. officer Lowe's Cos., Inc., North Wilkesboro, N.C., 1955—; bd. dirs. First Brands Corp. Danbury, Conn., mem. audit com.; bd. dirs. First Union Nat. Bank, Charlotte, N.C; mem. Lowe's Cos. Inc. Employee Stock Ownership Plan mgmt. com.; mem. bd. vis. U. N.C. Trustee Pfeiffer Coll., Misenheimer, N.C., mem. N.C. Council Mgmt. and Devel., Raleigh; bd. dirs. N.C. Gov.'s Bus. Council Arts and Humanities, Inc., Raleigh; bd. visitors U. N.C. Mem. Chi Psi. Democrat. Methodist. Home: 310 Coffey St North Wilkesboro NC 28659 Office: Lowes Cos Inc Hwy 268 E PO Box 1111 North Wilkesboro NC 28656

HERRING, VICTORIA L., lawyer; b. Des Moines, Nov. 25, 1947; d. Clyde Edsel and Mary Louise (Becker) H.; m. Mark McCormick, June 1, 1985; children: Katharine Herring McCormick, Ryan Mark Herring McCormick. BA, Beloit Coll., 1970; JD, Drake U., 1976; postgrad., Am. U., 1977. Bar: Iowa 1976. Mem. campaign staff Congressman Les Aspin, Janesville, Wis., 1970; intake clk. D.C. Superior Ct., 1971-72; pvt. investigator, process server Martin Security, Inc., Janesville, 1973; assoc. Austin Law Firm, Des Moines, 1976-79; asst. atty. gen. State of Iowa, Des Moines, 1979-83; pvt. practice West Des Moines, Iowa, 1983—; communications specialist Starr & Assocs., Des Moines, 1978-87. Contbr. articles to profl. jours. Vice-chmn. Iowa ERA Coalition, Des Moines, 1979-80; chmn. Iowa Dem. Platform Com., Des Moines, 1982; legis. co-chmn. Iowa Women's Polit. Caucus, Des Moines, 1987-88. Named one of Outstanding Young Women in Am., 1978, 79. Mem. Iowa State Bar Assn., Polk County Bar Assn. (bd. libr. trustees 1987-88), Polk County Women Attys. (pres. 1977-79), The Consortium (founder, pres. 1977-78). Democrat. Home: 4331 Greenwood Dr Des Moines IA 50312 Office: 1200 35th St West Des Moines IA 50265

HERRINGER, FRANK CASPER, diversified financial services company executive; b. N.Y.C., Nov. 12, 1942; s. Casper Frank and Alice Virginia (McMullen) H.; m. Maryellen B. Cattani, Feb. 11, 1989; children: William Laurence, (stepdaughter) Sarah. A.B. magna cum laude, Dartmouth, 1964, M.B.A. with highest distinction, 1965. Prin. Cresap, McCormick & Paget, Inc. (mgmt. cons.), N.Y.C., 1965-71; staff asst. to Pres., Washington, 1971-73; adminstr. U.S. Urban Mass Transp. Adminstrn., Washington, 1973-75; gen. mgr., chief exec. officer San Francisco Bay Area Rapid Transit Dist., 1975-78; exec. v.p., dir. Transamerica Corp., San Francisco, 1979-86, pres., 1986—; dir. Sedgwick Group plc (London), Unocal Corp., Occidental Life Ins. Co., Transam. Ins. Corp., Transam. Fin. Group, Transam. Leasing. Trustee Pacific Presbyn. Med. Ctr., Amos Tuck Sch. Bus. Adminstrn. Dartmouth Coll., Mills Coll. Mem. Phi Beta Kappa. Republican. Clubs: San Francisco Golf, Olympic, Bankers. Home: 224 Hillside Ave Piedmont CA 94611 Office: Transam Corp 600 Montgomery St San Francisco CA 94111

HERRINGTON, JOHN STEWART, government official; b. Los Angeles, May 31, 1939; s. Alan D. and Jean (Stewart) H.; m. Lois Haight, Apr. 10, 1965; children—Lisa Marie, Victoria Jean. A.B. in Econs., Stanford U., 1961; J.D., U. Calif., San Francisco, 1964. Bar: Calif. 1964. Dep. dist. atty. Ventura County Dist. Atty.'s Office, Calif., 1965-66; ptnr. Herrington & Herrington, Walnut Creek, Calif., 1966-81; dep. asst. to Pres. White House, Washington, 1981, asst. to Pres., 1983-85; asst. sec. Dept. Navy, Washington, 1981-83; sec. Dept. Energy, Washington, 1985—; mem. Res. Forces Policy Bd., Washington, 1981-83; chmn. Def. Dept. Per Diem Com., Washington, 1982-83; chmn. U.S. Del. IEA Ministerial Conf.; U.S. Rep. annual gen. conf. IAEA, spl. session on Chernobyl. Trustee Ronald Reagan Presdl. Found., 1985—. Served to 1st lt. USMC, 1962. Recipient Disting. Service medal U.S. Dept. Def., 1983. Mem. U.S. Naval Inst., Calif. Bar Assn., Hastings Alumni Assn., Stanford U. Alumni Assn. Republican. Office: Dept Energy 1000 Independence Ave SW Washington DC 20585

HERRMANN, LACY BUNNELL, investment company executive, financial entrepreneur, venture capitalist; b. New Haven, May 12, 1929; s. James Joseph and Helen Georgia (Bunnell) H.; A.B., Brown U., 1950; postgrad. London Sch. Econs., 1953-54; M.B.A., Harvard U., 1956; m. Elizabeth Ocumpaugh Beadle, May 23, 1953; children—Diana Parsons, Conrad Beadle. Asst. to purchasing mgr. and buyer Westinghouse Elec. Corp., Metuchen, N.J., 1956-60; asst. v.p. Douglas T. Johnston & Co., Inc., N.Y.C., 1960-66; v.p. Johnston Mut. Fund, Inc., N.Y.C., 1964-66; gen. partner Tamarack Assos., N.Y.C., 1966-84; chmn. bd., pres. Family Home Products, Inc., N.Y.C., 1972-84, Buxton's Country Shops, Jamesburg, N.J., 1973-86; pres., dir. STCM Mgmt. Co., Inc., N.Y.C., 1974—; founder, pres. STCM Corp., money market fund, N.Y.C., 1974-76; vice chmn. bd. trustees, v.p. Centennial Capital Cash Mgmt. Trust, N.Y.C. successor to STCM Corp., 1976-81; chmn. bd. trustees, pres. successor fund Capital Cash Mgmt. Trust, 1981—; pres., dir. Incap Mgmt. Corp., 1982—; founder, chmn. bd. trustees, pres. Trinity Liquid Assets Trust, 1982-85, Oxford Cash Mgmt. Fund, 1982-88, Prime Cash Fund, 1982—, Cash Assets Trust, 1984—, Short Term Asset Reserves, 1984—, Hawaiian Tax-Free Trust, 1985—, Churchill Cash Res. Trust, 1985—, Tax Free Trust Ariz., 1986—, Tax Free Trust Oreg., 1986—, Tax Free Fund Colo., 1987—, Churchill Tax-Free Fund Ky., 1987—, Churchill Tax-Free Cash Fund, 1988—, Tax-Free Cash Asset Trust, 1988—, U.S. Treasuries Cash Assets Trust, 1988—; chmn., pres. Aquila Mgmt. Corp., 1983—; v.p. Aquila Distbrs. Inc., 1981—; bd. dirs. Quest for Value Fund Inc., Quest for Value Cash Mgmt. Fund; founder, chmn. bd. trustees, pres. N.Y. Localities Legal Obligations Cash Assets Trust; chmn. Fiduciary Mgmt. Inc.; adviser Access, 1982—; organizer, dir. and/or cons. to numerous small to medium sized corps. and orgns.; founding dir. mgmt. cons. firm merged with Towers, Perrin, Forster & Crosby; instr. Rutgers U., 1958-59. Organizer, trustee endowed award Internat. div. Grad. Sch. Journalism, Columbia U., 1962—; trustee Meml. and Endowment Trust of St. Paul's Ch., Westfield, N.J., 1968—; mem. capital devel. com. St. Luke's Ch., Darien, Conn., 1978-85; mem. coll. scholarship fund com. St. Luke's Ch., Darien, Conn., 1976-85. Served to lt. (j.g.) USN, 1951-54; Korea; lt. USNR ret. Mem. N.Y. Soc. Security Analysts, Harvard Bus. Sch. Alumni Assn. N.Y. (dir. and officer 1958-71), Assn. Alumni Brown U. (dir. 1978-87, exec. com. 1980-85, pres. 1983-85). Republican. Episcopalian. Clubs: Harvard, N.Y. Athletic (N.Y.C.); Brown U., N.Y.C. (bd. dirs. 1981-88); Brown U. of Fairfield County (pres. 1977-82); University (R.I.); Faculty of Brown U. (Providence); Stratton Mountain Country (Vt.). Contbr. articles to profl. jours. Home: 6 Whaling Rd Darien CT 06820 Office: 200 Park Ave New York NY 10017

HERRON, EDWIN HUNTER, JR., energy consultant; b. Shreveport, La., June 7, 1938; s. Edwin Hunter and Helen Virginia (Russell) H.; B.S. in Chem. Engring., Tulane U., 1959, M.S., 1963, Ph.D. (NSF fellow, 1963-64), 1964; m. Frances Irvine Hunter, June 27, 1959; children—Edwin, David, Ashley. Research engr. Exxon Research & Engring. Co., Linden, N.J., 1959-61; sr. research engr. Exxon Production Research Co., Houston, 1964-66; corp. planning advisor Esso Europe, London, Eng., 1966-74; fin. analyst Exxon Corp., N.Y.C., 1974-78; v.p. Gruy Petroleum Tech., Inc., McLean, Va., 1978-84; pres. Petro-Analysis Inc., 1984—; pres. Petroleum Equities, Inc., 1987—. Recipient Levey award, Tulane U., 1970. Mem. Soc. Petroleum Engrs., Am. Inst. Chem. Engrs., Sci. Research Soc., Soc. Tulane Engrs., Tau Beta Pi. Contbr. articles to profl. publs. Office: Petro-Analysis Inc 8700 Old Dominion Dr McLean VA 22102

HERRON, JAMES M., lawyer; b. Chgo., May 4, 1934; s. J. Leonard and Sylvia H.; children: Kathy Lynn, Tracy Ellen, Andrew Ross. A.B., U. Mo., Columbia, 1955; postgrad., Northwestern U., 1958-59; J.D., Washington U., 1961; postgrad., Harvard Bus. Sch., 1982. Bar: Mo. 1961, Ohio 1971, Fla. 1975. Asst. gen. counsel, asst. sec. May Dept. Stores Co., St. Louis, 1961-70; asso. counsel Federated Dept. Stores, Inc., Cin., 1970-71; v.p., sec., gen. counsel Kenton Corp., N.Y.C., 1971-73; gen. counsel Ryder System, Inc., Miami, Fla., 1974-74, v.p., sec., gen. counsel, 1974-78, sr. v.p., sec., gen. counsel, 1978-79, exec. v.p., gen. counsel, 1979—, sec., 1983-86. First v.p., bd. dirs., mem. exec. com. Greater Miami Opera Assn., chmn. corp. devel. com., 1981-82; bd. dirs. Am. Cancer Soc., 1985-87; mem. Washington U. Sch. of Law Nat. Coun.; Served with USMC, 1955-58. Mem. ABA, Mo. Bar Assn., Fla. Bar Assn. Met. St. Louis, Assn. of Bar of City of N.Y., Am. Soc. Corp. Secs., Fla. Bar Assn., Dade County Bar Assn. Club: Royal Palm Tennis (dir.). Home: 2843 S Bayshore Dr #16D Coconut Grove FL 33133 Office: Ryder System Inc 3600 NW 82d Ave Miami FL 33166

HERRON, MICHAEL EDWARD, marketing director; b. Phila., Apr. 10, 1943; s. Thomas David and Walburga Theresa (May) H.; m. Mary Sheila Mahony; children—Michael Thomas, Patrick James. B.S. in English, St. Joseph's U., 1965; M.S. in Communications, Temple U., 1970. Dir. pub. affairs. Rouse (Phila.), Columbia, Md., 1976-77; dir. ins. info. Ins. Fedn. Pa., Phila., 1978-83; dir. mktg. services, Southeastern Pa. Transp. Authority, Phila., 1983—. League dir. and coach Cinnaminson Police Athletic League, N.J., 1975-83; chmn. Cinnaminson Zoning Bd., 1985-87; bd. dirs. pub. relations com. Phila. council Girl Scouts U.S., 1984-86; mem. pub. relations council Rosemont Coll., Phila., 1985—; vice chmn. Phila. Area Council Tourism (PACT), 1986—; mem. pub. info. com. Am. Cancer Soc., Phila. Recipient Merit award Internat. Assn. Bus. Communicators, 1981. Mem. Pub. Relations Soc. Am. (Pepperpot award 1980-82, 87), Phila. Pub. Relations Assn., Am. Pub. Transit Assn. (mktg. com., Adwheel award 1986, 87, 88), Union Internationale des Transports Publics (subcom. Internat. Met. Railways com.), TV/Radio Advt. Club, Mktg. Communications Execs. Internat., Del. Valley Indsl. TV Soc. (pres. 1970), Chestnut St. Assn. (bd. dirs. 1985), St. Charles Holy Name Soc. (dance chmn. 1980-85, carnival chmn. 1979), Downtown Council Phila. C. of C. Democrat. Roman Catholic. Avocations: jogging; golf; tennis. Home: 217 Valley Forge Rd Cinnaminson NJ 08077 Office: SEPTA 714 Market St Philadelphia PA 19106

HERRON, SEAN MICHAEL, realtor; b. Syracuse, N.Y., Dec. 3, 1949; s. Timothy and Mary Ellen (McDonald) H.; m. Kathleen Lawlor, June 16, 1971; children: Patrick, Ellen, Kevin. Student, Syracuse U., 1968-70. Carpenter Herron-Cavanaugh Constrn., Syracuse and Buffalo, 1968-71; with sales dept. Sullivan Oldsmobile, Syracuse, 1971-74, sales mgr., 1974-78; co-owner, pres. Syracuse Rent-To-Own, 1978-81; mgr., realtor Century-21 Realty, Syracuse, 1981-85; prin. Syracuse Real Estate and Mgmt., 1985—. Coach little-league baseball St. Thomas Aquinas, Syracuse, 1982-86; scoutmaster Troop 1200 Boy Scouts Am., Syracuse, 1984; fundraiser Am. Cancer Society, 1985—. With USNG, 1968-72. Mem. N.Y. Assn. Realtors. Roman Catholic. Office: Werik Bldg 915 Erie Blvd Ste 1 Syracuse NY 13210

HERRON, SIDNEY EARL, sales professional; b. Aberdeen, Wash., May 25, 1952; s. Marshall Elbie and Martha Elizabeth (Nicholson) H.; m. Gloria Annette Hanson, Mar. 17, 1973 (div. Mar 1983); children: Jason, Angela; m. Alison Marie Young, Oct. 12, 1985; children: Jeff, Amanda, Shane. Student, U. Washington, Seattle, Grays Harbor Coll., 1970-71, Northwest Coll., 1971-72. Field service engr. Teltone Corp., Kirkland, Wash., 1973-77, sales engr., 1977-80, area sales mgr. component products, 1980-81, area sales mgr. data products, 1981-83, nat. accounts mgr. pvt. label div., 1983-84, western regional sales mgr., 1985—; product mgr. data products Teltone Corp., Kirkland, 1986-87; mgmt. cons. TRC Systems Corp., Federal Way, Wash., 1986-87. Author, editor and actor videotaped tech. tng., 1976; author sales tng. manual for Teltone Corp., 1983. Mem. Internat. Airline Passangers' Assn. Republican. Club: Columbia Athletic (Kirkland, Wash.). Home: 2506 171st Pl SE Bothell WA 98012 Office: Teltone Corp 10801 120th Ave NE Kirkland WA 98033

HERSEY, FRANK JEFFREY, professional engineer; b. Denver, Nov. 30, 1945; s. Frank Parker and Kathryn Frieda (Ziegler) H.; m. Cynthia Ann Wong, June 8, 1967 (div. June 1980); children: Justin Jeffrey, Travis Jay. BS in Engring. Geophysics, Colo. Sch. of Mines, 1967. Registered profl. engr., Tex. Seismologist Western Geophysical, Houston, 1967-70; v.p. and gen. mgr. Sefel Geophysical, Calgary, Alta., Canada, 1970-75; pres. Sefel Geophysical, Houston, 1975-79; founder, pres. Geocenter, Inc., Houston, 1980—, also chmn. bd. dirs. Mem. Soc. of Exploration Geophysicists, Geophysical Soc. Houston. Office: GeoCenter Inc 2 NorthPoint Dr Ste 600 Houston TX 77060

HERSEY, MARIA RUSSO, health facility administrator; b. Balt., June 3, 1943; d. Paul A. and Joanna (Basso) Russo; m. Roscoe Monroe Hersey III, Jan. 3, 1942; children: Sara, Christopher. BA, Loyola Coll., Balt., 1965; MSW, U. Md., Balt., 1970. Clin. social worker Johns Hopkins Hosp., Balt., 1967-68, U. Rochester (N.Y.) Med. Ctr., 1970-72; tng. cons. Rochester Sch. Dist., 1972-75; program mgr. Colo. Perinatal Care Coun., Denver, 1977-79; assoc. program coord. Polyclinic Med. Ctr., Harrisburg, Pa., 1979-84; owner Image Assocs., Hershey, Pa., 1984-86; corp. trainer Pa. Blue Shield, Camp Hill, 1986-88, policy analyst, 1988—; cons. Pa. State U., Harrisburg, 1984-86. Vol. San Joaquin County Com. Action Agy., VISTA, Stockton, Calif., 1965-66, Gov.'s Com. Human Svcs., VISTA, St. Croix, U.S.V.I., 1966-67; bd. dirs. Planned Parenthood, Harrisburg, 1980-84, Infant Devel. Program, Harrisburg, 1983-84, Hershey Pub. Libr., 1981-83. Mem. Am. Soc. Tng. and Devel. (v.p. tech. skills tng. and devel. 1987—). Mem. Soc. of Friends.

HERSH, BARRY FRED, real estate developer, urban planner; b. N.Y.C., May 10, 1947; s. Philip and Ruth (Rubin) H.; m. Jeanne Marie Gasda, July 11, 1972; children: Alayne Sarah, Michelle Heather. BA, CUNY, 1968; M of Urban Planning, NYU, 1972. Lic. real estate broker, N.Y. Dir. planning Chase Assocs., Syracuse, N.Y., 1973-77; prin. planner plan commn. Toledo-Lucas Co., 1977-81; housing planner Stamford (Conn.) Mayor's Devel. Office, 1981-82; exec. dir. Westhab, Inc., Hartsdale, N.Y., 1982-83; project mgr. Reynolds Metals Devel. Co., Orangeburg, N.Y., 1984—; adj. asst. prof. geography and urban planning U. Toledo, 1979-81, Cen. Conn. State U., New Britain, 1982; co-chair fin. The Waterfront Ctr., Washington, 1986—. Author: (with others) Toledo Harbor Area Plan, 1979 (Great Lakes Assn. award 1979); contbr. articles to profl. jours. Mem. pres.'s council Dominican Coll., Orangeburg, 1987; active Trumbull (Conn.) Econ. Devel. Task Force, 1986, Rockland 2000 Planning Group, New City, N.Y., 1987. Recipient Housing for Homeless award N.Y. State, Yonkers, 1983, Econ. Devel. award Rockland (N.Y.) County Exec., 1986; fellow Columbia U., N.Y.C., 1971. Mem. Am. Planning Assn. (sec. Cen. N.Y. chpt. 1976, host com. 1987), Nat. Assn. Office and Ind. Park Developers, N.Y. State Builders Assn., Rockland Builders Assn., Am. Inst. Cert. Planners (cert.), Nat. Assn. Corp. Real Estate Execs., Rockland County Assn., Urban Land Inst., Regional Plan Assn. (Fairfield housing com. 1986). Jewish. Home: 188 Park Ln Trumbull CT 06611 Office: Reynolds Metals Devel Co 17 Corporate Dr Orangeburg NY 10962

HERSHA, KATHRYN LOUISE JAMIESON, system and data analyst; b. Fort Wayne, Ind., Feb. 12, 1940; d. Norval Eugene and Dorothy Ellen (Turflinger) Jamieson. Student St. Francis Coll., Fort Wayne, 1964-65, Fort Wayne Art Inst., 1967-74; AS, Ind. U.-Fort Wayne, 1973; student U. Evansville, 1977-79, Ringling Art Sch., 1984-88. Programmer Lincoln Nat. Bank, Fort Wayne, 1968-74; programmer, analyst Atlas Van Lines, Evansville, Ind., 1974-77; sr. analyst Nat. Sharedata, Evansville, 1977-79; project leader Fla. Software Services, Orlando, 1979-81; system cons. Anacomp, Sarasota, Fla., 1981-86; bus. analyst Electronic Data Systems, Sarasota, 1986—. Active Sarasota Art Assn., Asolo Festival Theatre Assn., Sarasota Arts Council, Women's Caucus for Art, Sarasota Opera Assn. Mem Nat. Assn. Female Execs., Am. Mgmt. Assn. Methodist. Avocations: art, sculpting. Home: PO Box 1235 Sarasota FL 34230 Office: EDS 1680 Third St Ste 400 Sarasota FL 34236

HERSHBERG, DAVID STEPHEN, lawyer, business executive; b. N.Y.C., Nov. 22, 1941; s. Irving and Sophie (Esikoff) H.; m. Karen Jay Subow, July 29, 1965; children: Jared, Rachel. AB, NYU, 1962; JD, Harvard U., 1965. Bar: N.Y. 1966. Assoc. corp. Wolf, Haldenstein, Adler, Freeman & Herz, 1967-72, Finley, Kumble, Wagner, N.Y.C., 1972-76; counsel Am. Express Co., N.Y.C., 1976-78, asst. gen. counsel, 1978-81, dep. gen. counsel, 1981-84; sr. exec. v.p. Shearson, Lehman, Hutton, Inc., N.Y.C., 1984-87, vice chmn., 1987—; also bd. dirs Shearson, Lehman, Hutton, Inc.; bd. dirs. Fin. Guaranty Ins. Co., N.Y.C. Mem. budget com. Village of Larchmont, N.Y, 1986-88; bd. dirs., vice chmn. exec. com. Anti-Defamation League N.Y.C., 1982. Served with mil. Intelligence, 1966-67. Mem. ABA (fed. regulations of securities com., broker-dealer matters subcom.), Assn. of Bar of City of N.Y. (securities regulation com. 1986—), Fairview Country Club (Greenwich, Conn.), Orienta Beach and Yacht Club (Mamaroneck, N.Y.), Phi Beta Kappa. Home: 20 Flint Ave Larchmont NY 10538 Office: Shearson Lehman Hutton Inc Amex Tower World Fin Ctr New York NY 10285-1900

HERSHER, KURT BERNARD, building materials executive; b. Germany, Apr. 4, 1928; s. Bernard and Elsa (Muenzer) H.; came to U.S., 1938, naturalized, 1943; BS in Indsl. Engring., Bradley U., 1951; m. Claire Elovitz, Jan. 29, 1956 (div. Mar. 1970); children: Wayne, Terry, Karen; m. 2d, Edith Doby, Nov. 1975. Chief ops. officer Stevenson Lumber Co. (Conn.), 1954-68; pres. chief exec. officer Stelco Industries, Inc., Stevenson, 1968—; pres. Truss-Tech Inc.; dir., co-founder Builders Supply Credit Bur., Bridgeport, 1960-72. Mem. Bd. of Assocs. U. of Bridgeport, U. Bridgeport Law Sch.; bd. dirs. UJA; co-chmn. "The Circle". With Signal Corps, AUS, 1951-53. Mem. Am. Inst. Indsl. Engrs., Northeast Retail Lumbermens Assn., Fairfield County Home Builders Assn., Monroe (Conn.) C. of C. Home: Stones Throw Rd Easton CT 06612 Office: Stelco Industries Inc PO Box 123 Rural Rt 111 Stevenson CT 06491

HERSHEY, COLIN HARRY, management consultant; b. Everett, Pa., Aug. 31, 1935; s. Harry and Marjorie (Nycum) H.; m. Jacqueline Anderson, June 14, 1974; children: Barclay Harry, Marjorie Anderson. BSCE, Lehigh U., 1957; MBA, U. Pitts., 1967, postgrad., 1968. Registered profl. engr., Pa. Civil engr. contracting div. Dravo Corp., Pitts., 1957-59, cost engr., 1961-63; field engr. Army Corps Engrs., Pitts., 1958-61; mgr. mgmt. info. systems, atomic power div. Westinghouse Electric Co., Pitts., 1964-67; counselor Planning Dynamics, Inc., Pitts., 1968-70, v.p., 1970-72, pres., 1972-77, pres., chmn., 1977—; pres. Planware, Inc., Pitts., 1985—. Author, editor: Strategic Planning Concepts, 1985; contbr. articles to profl. jours. Mem. Am. Mgmt. Assn. (adv. com. Strategic Mgmt. Program), Planning Forum, Duquesne Club, Alpha Tau Omega, Chi Epsilon. Office: Planning Dynamics Inc 135 Industry Dr Pittsburgh PA 15275

HERSMAN, FERD WILLIAM, business owner; b. Cin., Apr. 27, 1922; s. Fernando William and Eliza Ann (Garforth) H.; m. Jill Ann Becker, June 30, 1951; children: Michael S., John A., F. William, Christopher B., Jan (dec.). BSChemE, U. Cin., 1949. Registered profl. engr., Ohio, Ky. Process engr. Frigidaire div. Gen. Motors, Dayton, Ohio, 1949-51; project engr. Vulcan-Cin., 1951-57; R&D engr. U.S. Indsl. Chems. div., Cin., 1957-61; v.p. Fischer Indsl. Equipment, Inc., Cin., 1961-83, pres., owner, 1983—, charter com., 1987-88, trustee, 1985-88. Mem. Mayor's Fin. Com., Greenhills, Ohio, 1983, Charter Commn., Greenhills, 1988—; trustee Greenhills Community Presbyn. Ch., 1985—. Staff sgt. U.S. Army, 1942-45, PTO. Decorated Bronze Star with one oak leaf cluster. Mem. AICE (chmn. Ohio Valley sect. 1966-67), Engring. Soc. Cin., Mfr.'s Agt. Nat. Assn., Mfr.'s Agts. Cin., SAR, Tri-County Racquet Club (Cin.). Republican. Presbyterian. Home: 826 Carini Ln Cincinnati OH 45218 Office: Fischer Indsl Equipment Inc PO Box 46646 Cincinnati OH 45246

HERSZDORFER, PIERRE JACQUES, banker; b. Marseille, France, Apr. 20, 1939; came to U.S., 1955, naturalized, 1960; s. Julius and Paula (Roniger) H.; m. Doris Buntin, Dec. 24, 1968 (div. 1979). BS, NYU, 1968; student Am. Inst. Banking. Mem. staff auditing dept. Irving Trust Co., N.Y.C., 1960-68; mem. staff comptroller's div. Citibank, N.Y.C., 1968-71; v.p. internat. div. Hartford Nat. Bank & Trust Co. (Conn.), 1971-79; v.p. Credit Agricole br. Caisse Nationale de Credit Agricole Paris, 1979-81; v.p. Union Commerce Bank Cleve., 1981; v.p., mgr. internat. banking dept. Norwest Bank Des Moines, N.A., 1981-84; v.p., mgr. internat. banking div. Mchts. Nat. Bank, Cedar Rapids, Iowa, 1984-88; v.p., adminstrn. and fin. Imxport Svcs. Corp., Houston, 1988—; bd. dirs. Des Moines Fgn. Trade Zone Corp.; past lectr. Des Moines Area Community Coll., lectr. Kirkwood Community Coll.; past mem. faculty dept. bus. careers Manchester (Conn.) Community Coll. Mem. Internat. Trade Studies, Kirkwood Community Coll., Internat. Trade Program, Ctr. Indsl. Rsch. and Svc., Iowa State U., Ames; past chmn. fraud detection and safeguard com. Council Internat. Banking. With U.S. Army Res., 1959-65. Mem. Des Moines Com. Fgn. Relations, Internat. Trade Bur., Cedar Falls-NE Iowa Internat. Trade Council, Davenport (Iowa)-Ill. Internat. Trade Assn., Sioux City-Siouxland Internat. Trade Assn., Robert Morris Assocs., Des Moines Art Ctr., Cedar Rapids Mus. Art, NYU Alumni Assn. Home: 1829 Bering Dr #11 Houston TX 77057 Office: 12941 I-45 N Houston TX 77060

HERTZ, MEL ROBERT, finance company executive; b. Toronto, Ont., Can., Feb. 26, 1945; came to U.S., 1954; s. Percy B. and Sandra (Puchkoff) H.; m. Marline Marie Fink, Sept. 4, 1966; 1 child, Marc Aaron. BS, Wayne State U., 1966, MBA, 1968. Asst. buyer J.L. Hudson Co., Detroit, 1966-68, mfr.'s rep., 1968-70; pres. Paper Circus Stores, Detroit, 1969-76; mfr.'s rep. Bob Baum, Mel Hertz Assocs., Detroit, 1970-76; pres. Canterbury Assocs., Inc., Honolulu, 1976-83, v.p., 1983—; v.p. E.A. Buck Co., Inc., Honolulu, 1983-86, pres., 1986—; pres. Western Enterprises, Honolulu, 1986—. Treas. Congregation Sof Maaru, Honolulu, 1983-86, Ptnrs. in Health, Honolulu, 1988—. Mem. Internat. Assn. Fin. Planning (v.p. Honolulu chpt. 1988—), Hawaii United Gift and Garment Salespersons Assn. (treas. 1982). Home: 237 Kuumele Kailua HI 96734 Office: EA Buck Co Inc 900 Fort St Ste 1410 Honolulu HI 96813

HERTZBERG, DANIEL, journalist; b. Quincy, Ill.. Degree, U. Chgo., De Paul U., Harvard U. Formerly with Buffalo Evening News, Cravath Swaine and Moore, N.Y.; formerly exec. editor Am. Lawyer mag.; with Wall St. Jour., N.Y.C., 1977—, now dep. news editor. Recipient Pulitzer Prize for explanatory journalism, 1988. Office: Wall St Jour 200 Liberty St New York NY 10281 *

HERZSTEIN, ROBERT ERWIN, lawyer; b. Denver, Feb. 26, 1931; s. Sigmund Edwards and Estelle Ruth (Borwick) H.; m. Priscilla Holmes, July 11, 1956; children: Jessica Anne, Emily Holmes, Robert Holmes. AB, Harvard U., 1952, LLB, 1955. Bar: Colo. 1956, D.C. 1959, U.S. Supreme Ct. 1962. Sr. ptnr., other positions Arnold & Porter, Washington, 1958-80, sr. ptnr., 1981-89; undersec. for Internat. Trade U.S. Dept. Commerce, Washington, 1980-81; ptnr. in charge Shearman & Sterling, Washington, 1989—; bd. dirs. Survival Tech., Inc., Betheda, Md., mem. exec. com., 1969—. Contbr. articles to profl. jours. Trustee Internat. Law Inst., Washington, 1974—; chmn., bd. dirs. Internat. Human Rights Law Group, Washington. Mem. ABA, Am. Soc. Internat. Law (exec. coun. 1981-84), Coun. on Fgn. Rels. Home: 4710 Woodway Ln Washington DC 20016 Office: Shearmen & Sterling 1001 30th St NW Washington DC 20007-3883

HESS, DAVID GRAHAM, executive; b. Phila., June 20, 1957; s. Carleton and Irene Florence (Ehrle) H.; m. Karen Denise Alke, Apr. 21, 1984; children: Laura Christine, Sarah Elizabeth. BS in Engring., Drexel U., 1980; postgrad., John Hopkins U., 1982-83, U. So. Calif., 1984-85. Metallurgist Howmet Aluminum Corp, Lancaster, Pa., 1976-80; composites engr. Martin Marietta Aerospace, Denver, 1980-81; program mgr. Martin Marietta Aerospace, Balt., 1981-82, liaison engr., 1982-83; mantech sr. engr. Northrop Corp., Pico Rivera, Calif., 1983-84, mfg. tech. specialist, 1984-86, quality assurance specialist, 1986, mgr. div. advanced systems and quality assurance R & D, 1986-88; mfg. engr., mgr. Rayproof Absorber Products, Amesbury, Mass., 1988—; cons. Aero Visions Inc., Irvine, Calif., 1986-87, Rosene Design Inc., Fountain Valley, Calif., 1987—. Contbr. Composites Engineering, 1987; inventor in field. Contbg. mem. Northrop Employees Polit. Action Com., Pico Rivera, 1979—; home donor Life Support for Unwed Mothers, Anaheim, Calif., 1987. Recipient Kerr Cup award Schuylkill Navy, Phila., 1980. Mem. Am. Soc. Metals, Soc. for Advancement of Materials and Process Engrs., U.S. Parachute Club. Republican. Home: 25 Summit Dr Atkinson NH 03811 Office: RayproofAbsorber Products Water St Amesbury MA 01913-4843

HESS, DENNIS JOHN, investment banker; b. Manila, July 7, 1940; s. Carl and Anna (Harris) H.; m. Marilyn Golchert, July 7, 1977; children: Whitney, Christine, Craig. B.S., U. Calif., Berkeley, 1962. With Merrill Lynch & Co., Inc., 1969—, v.p., 1977-80; chmn. bd., chief exec. officer Merrill Lynch, Hubbard, Inc., N.Y.C., 1980—; dir. diversified financial services Merrill Lynch, Pierce, Fenner & Smith, 1985—; pres., chief operating officer ML Realty, 1983—; dir. United First Mortgage Corp., M.L. Huntoon Paige Inc., MLH Puerto, S.A., Family Life Co., Merrill Lynch Life Ins. Co. Served to 1st lt. USAF, 1962-66. Republican. Roman Catholic. Club: Waccabuc Country. Home: 61 Byram Shore Rd Greenwich CT 06830-6906 Office: Merrill Lynch Hubbard Inc 165 Broadway New York NY 10080

HESS, DONALD F., manufacturing executive, accountant; b. Manheim, Pa., Feb. 13, 1919; s. Elam Gross and Marcelia Edna (Farmer) H.; m. Christina Leed Lamparter, Oct. 1, 1937; children: Donald L., David A. Controller Bearings Co. of Am., Lancaster, Pa., 1948-52, prodn. planning mgr., 1952-61; materials mgr. Jamesbury Corp., Worcester, Mass., 1961-64; dir. materials mgmt. Keuffel & Esser Co., Hoboken, N.J., 1964-66; seminar instr. Donald F. Hess Assocs., Lancaster, 1966-72; materials mgr. Rutt Custom Kitchens, Goodville, Pa., 1972—; leader in-plant and pub. seminars throughout U.S. Developer various prodn. and mgmt. publs.; contbr. articles and book chpts. to profl. publs. Mem. Am. Prodn. and Inventory Control Soc. (founding mem., 1st v.p. edn. and research 1959, exec. v.p. 1960, nat. pres. 1961, hon. life mem. 1962; founder, 1st pres. Lancaster chpt. 1958-59, hon. life mem. 1960). Home: 401-L6 Eden Rd Lancaster PA 17601 Office: Rutt Custom Kitchens Rt 23 Goodville PA 17528

HESS, GEOFFREY LAVERNE, accountant; b. Gettysburg, Pa., Dec. 20, 1949; s. Richard LaVerne and Beatrice Geraldine (Brown) H.; BS in Acctg., Mt. St. Mary's Coll., 1976. CPA, Md. Acct. United Bldg. Corp., Germantown, Md., 1976-77; NAD resident auditor U.S. Army Corps Engrs., Balt., 1977-78; sr. acct., Councilor Buchanan and Mitchell, Bethesda, Md., 1979-80; internal auditor George Washington U., 1981; sr. acct. Buchanan and Co., Frederick, Md., 1981-82; acctg. mgr. PATS, Inc., Flight Refueling, Inc., Patrick Aircraft Tank Systems, Inc., 1983-85; contr. Annapolis Fed. Savs. Bank, 1985-88. With USAF, 1968-72. Mem. Am. Inst. CPAs, Md. Assn. CPA's, Internat. Platform Assn., Am. Legion. Republican. Roman Catholic. Home: 1223 Cherrytown Rd Westminster MD 21157 Office: Annapolis Fed Savs Bank 140 Main St Annapolis MD 21404

HESS, KARSTEN, trading company executive; b. Vejle, Denmark, May 20, 1930; came to U.S., 1963; s. Harald Ejnar and Inger Marie (Karsten) H.; m. Lillian Becker-Christensen, May 14, 1960; children: Regitze Marianne, Jannike Julie, Peter Martin. Diploma, Copenhagen Comml. Coll., 1951. Registered indsl. acct., Can. Mgmt. trainee East Asiatic Co., Ltd., Copenhagen, 1948-51; jr. exec., then chief accountant/budget controller East Asiatic Co. (Can.) Ltd., Vancouver, B.C., 1952-63; div. controller East Asiatic Co., Inc., San Francisco, 1963-71; corp. v.p., sec.-treas. East Asiatic Co., Inc., N.Y.C., 1971-83; exec. v.p., sec. EAC USA Inc. (and subs.), N.Y.C., 1983—. Bd. dirs., chmn. fin. com. Day Care Center Tarrytowns, N.Y., 1978—; deacon Second Reformed Ch., Tarrytown, 1978—. Served with Danish Army, 1951-52. Mem. Danish Am. C. of C. (dir., treas. 1980—), Soc. Mgmt. Accountants Can., Am. Acctg. Assn., Nat. Cash Mgmt. Assn., Danish Am. Soc. Clubs: Royal Vancouver Yacht, World Trade Center. Office: EAC USA Inc 73-45 Woodhaven Blvd Glendale NY 11385

HESS, LEE HOWARD, restaurant chain executive; b. Chgo., Mar. 1, 1947; s. Segel Henry and Jane (Kornblith) H.; m. Irene Levine, Nov. 12, 1978; 1 child, Michael. BA, U. Mich., 1968; MA, Stanford U., 1969; MBA, Harvard U., 1972. V.p., chief fin. officer Twenty First Century Corp., N.Y.C., 1972-80; pres. TGI Splty. Restaurants, N.Y.C., 1981; sr. v.p. Wendy's Internat., Dublin, Ohio, 1981—. Home: 324 N Drexel Ave Columbus OH 43209 Office: Wendys Internat Inc 4288 W Dublin Granville Rd Dublin OH 43017

HESS, LEON, oil company executive; b. Asbury Park, N.J., Mar. 13, 1914; (married). With Hess Oil & Chem. Corp. (and predecessor), 1946-69, pres., 1962-65, chmn. bd., chief exec. officer, 1965-69; also dir. Hess Oil & Chem. Corp.; chmn. bd. Amerada Hess Corp. (merger Hess Oil & Chem. Corp. and Amerada Petroleum Corp.), N.Y.C., 1971—, chief exec. officer, 1971-82, 86—, also dir.; co-owner, now sole owner, chmn. bd. N.Y. Jets Football Team, N.Y.C., 1963—; dir. ABC, Mut. Benefit Life Ins. Co., Monmouth Park Jockey Club. Served with AUS, 1942-45. Office: Amerada Hess Corp 1185 Ave of the Americas New York NY 10036 other: NY Jets 598 Madison Ave New York NY 10022 *

HESS, ROBERT, JR., ambulance service executive; b. East Cleveland, Ohio, Oct. 22, 1957; s. Robert and Patricia Lou Hess; m. Susan Hole, Jan. 28, 1983; children: Christine Renee, Robert III, Jessica Marie. Student John Carroll U., 1976-81, Cuyahoga Community Coll., 1977-78. With Physician's Ambulance Service, South Euclid, 1972—, v.p. in charge fin., data processing, med. assurance, 1978-86, sr. v.p., chief operating officer, 1986—; pres., chief exec. officer Medflight, Inc., South Euclid, Ohio, 1986—; dir. Hess Enterprises, Inc.; adj. faculty Cuyahoga Community Coll., vice chmn. Emergency Med. Technician Tng. Dept., 1986—, v.p. Allan R. Sussberg Builders, Inc., Beachwood, Ohio. mem. paramedic admissions com. Cuyahogo Community Coll.; dir. research U.S. Emergency Med. Technician Assn., 1981. Instr. advanced cardiac life support Am. Heart Assn., 1981—; mem. Ohio Bd. Regents Paramedic Adv. Com., 1980-86; alternate mem. emergency med. service adv. com. Ohio Bd. Edn., 1986—; mem. United Way Cleve., eagle com., 1987; paramedic adv. council Hillcrest Hosp.; mem. Ohio EMS Bd Ohio Dept. Edn., 1986-88. Mem. Ohio Ambulance Assn. (pres. 1981-82, trustee 1980-81, chmn. govtl. affairs com. 1985-87), Am. Ambulance Assn. (dir. 1980-83, fin. com. 1987, govtl. affairs com., accreditation com.), Nat. Assn. Emergency Med. Technicians, Ohio Assn. Emergency Med. Services. Republican. Roman Catholic. Office: 4349 Monticello Blvd South Euclid OH 44121

HESS, ROBERT JOHN, toy company executive; b. Aurora, Ill., Sept. 13, 1937; s. Christopher and Marian (Wagner) H.; m. Judith A. Ernst, Aug. 13, 1960 (div. 1982): children: Robert M., Richard C., Patricia K., Margaret M., Marilyn A.; m. Barbara Jean Gentry, Sept. 10, 1983; children: Brittany K., Kristine. BS, Loyola U., Chgo., 1960; MBA, U. Chgo., 1978. CPA, Ill. Cost acct. Automatic Electric Co., Northlake, Ill., 1960-62; gen. acct. Pipe Line Service Corp., Franklin Park, Ill., 1962-68; corp. controller Masonite Corp., Chgo., 1968-84; v.p. fin. Superior Toy & Mfg. Co., Inc., Chgo., 1984-87, exec. v.p. ops. and adminstrn., 1987—. Served to 1st lt. U.S. Army, 1959-60. Mem. Am. Inst. CPA's, Ill. Assn. CPA's. Roman Catholic. Home: 1605 Royal Oak Rd Darien IL 60559 Office: Superior Toy & Mfg Co Inc 3417 N Halsted St Chicago IL 60657

HESS, RONALD L., manufacturing company executive; b. Rensselaer, Ind., Oct. 11, 1942; s. John T. and Eva May (Merchant) H.; m. Sharon Laurent, June 8, 1963 (div. 1977); children: Christina Kathleen, Todd Allen; m. Phyllis Cobb, Sept. 8, 1978. BEE, Purdue U., 1963; MBA, Calif. State U., Fullerton, 1972. Electrical engr. Gen. Dynamics Co., San Diego, 1963-65; mktg. mgr. Borg-Warner Controls, Santa Ana, Calif., 1965-70; gen. mgr. Joy Mfg. Co., Inc., Pitts., 1970-79; v.p. Zero Corp., L.A., 1979—; bd. dirs. Samuel Groves & Co., Ltd., Birmingham, Eng., Air Cargo Equipment Corp., Rancho Dominguez, Calif. Chmn. Jr. Achievement of Lenoir County, Kinston, N.C., 1976-78. Mem. Am. Mgmt. Assn. Republican. Methodist. Office: Zero Corp 444 S Flower St Ste 2100 Los Angeles CA 90071

HESS, WHEELER HERDMAN, insurance executive; b. Shavertown, Pa., Nov. 8, 1931; s. Wheeler H. and Mary (Thomas) H.; m. Lorraine Sickler, June 5, 1954; children: Linda, David, Brenda. A.B., Gettysburg Coll., 1953; M.B.A., U. Conn., 1963; A.M.P., Harvard U., 1979. Asst. sec. Travelers Ins. Co., Hartford, Conn., 1966-67; sec. Travelers Ins. Co., 1967-69, 2d v.p., 1969-71, v.p., 1971-76, sr. v.p., 1976—; pres. Travelers Indemnity and several other subs., 1985—; dir. Ins. Services Office, N.Y.C., 1979—, Nat. Council Compensation Ins., N.Y.C., 1979—. Capt. USAF, 1954-56. Republican. Congregationalist. Home: 422 Lake Rd Andover CT 06232 Office: Travelers Indemnity Co 1 Tower Sq Hartford CT 06183

HESSE, MARGARET MARY, real estate sales management, financial planner; b. Mineola, N.Y., Aug. 19, 1938; d. Donald Purdy Gager and Margaret Helen (Schroeder) Gager; m. John Lamborn Hesse, Jan. 19, 1957 (dec. Jan. 1982); children: John Donald, Judith Anne Young, Shana Marie. BA, San Jose State U., 1969; MA, N.Mex. State U., 1971. Cert. fin. planner, cert. residential broker. Instr. N.Mex. State U., Las Cruces, 1970-72; sales assoc. Drue Self Real Estate, Las Cruces, 1976-77, sales mgr., 1984—; br. mgr. N. Cen. Mortgage Co., Las Cruces, 1977-78; sr. planner Hesse & Assocs. Fin. Planners, Inc., Las Cruces, 1984-88. Bd. dirs. ARC, Dona Ana Chpt., Las Cruces, N.Mex., 1987-88, SMF counselor, Pasadena Chpt., Calif., 1982-83. Mem. Las Cruces C. of C., Nat. Assn. Realtors, Realtors Nat. Mktg. Inst., Realtors Assn. N.Mex. (southwestern chpt.), Internat. Assn. Fin. Planning (pres. 1986-88, v.p. programs 1985-86, v.p. edn. 1984-85) Western Assn. Fin. Planners, Inst. Cert. Fin. Planners, Phi Kappa Phi, Phi Beta Kappa. Republican. Protestant. Home: 3990 Nemesh Las Cruces NM 88005 Office: Drue Self Real Estate Inc 795 S Soland Las Cruces NM 88001

HESSE, NANCY JANE, administrative executive; b. Quincy, Ill., Nov. 2, 1948; d. John William and Geraldine Elaine (Ossian) H. BA, U. Ill., 1970; MEd, Memphis State U., 1971; MBA, Northwestern U., 1980. Program dir. Memphis State U., 1970-75; regional mgr. SEI Info. Tech., Chgo., 1975-80, mgr. cons. ops. sect., 1980-83, mgr. devel. projects, 1983-85, mgr. adminstrn. and fin., 1985-87; dir. adminstrn. Laventhol & Horwath, Chgo., 1987—. Bd. dirs. YWCA Met. Chgo., 1983—. Office: Laventhol & Horwath 300 S Riverside Pla Chicago IL 60606

HESSION, WILLIAM MATTHEW, JR., health care company executive; b. Church Point, La., Feb. 23, 1952; s. William Matthew and Bessie Lee (Cox) H.; m. Carol Anne Blanchard, jan. 9, 1975; children: Michelle, Heather. AS, Nicholls State U., 1976. RN. Dir. nursing Assumption Gen. Hosp., Napoleonville, La., 1976-79; v.p. Profl. Nursing Service, New Orleans, 1979-82; pres. Key Nursing Corp., Thibodaux, La., 1982—; dir. Analytical Nursing Corp., Baton Rouge, Key Nursing Corp. of N.C., Charlotte, Key Nursing Corp. of Tex., Mission, Key Nursing Corp. of Colo., Denver. Patentee on autocath med. device, 1983; inventor protective shroud for IV, 1985, MPB med. device, 1988. Sponsor Louis Infant Ctr., Houma, La., 1988; mem. La. Assn. Bus. and Industry, Baton Rouge, 1988. Served with USMC, 1971-73. Named Small Bus. Person of the Yr., La. Dept. Commerce, Region #3, 1987. Mem. Thibodaux C. of C., La. Assn. Bus. and Industry, Am. Assn. Critical Nurses (chpt. pres. 1988). Republican. Roman Catholic. Home: 627 Fairway Dr Thibodaux LA 70301 Office: Key Nursing Corp 208 Saint Louis St Thibodaux LA 70301

HESSLER, CURTIS ALAN, lawyer; b. Berwyn, Ill., Dec. 27, 1943; s. Robert A. and Ruth T. (Teeter) H.; m. Christine Mary Cocker, Dec. 14, 1968; children: Alexander, Francesca. B.A., Harvard U., 1966; postgrad. (Rhodes scholar), Oxford U., 1966-69; J.D., Yale U., 1973; M.A. in Econs, U. Calif., Berkeley, 1976. Exec. asst. to Sec. Treasury, Dept. Treasury, Washington, 1977-79; asst. sec. for econ. policy Sec. Treasury, Dept. Treasury, 1980; asso. dir. Office Budget and Mgmt., Washington, 1979; ptnr. Paul Weiss Rifkind Wharton & Garrison, 1981-82; exec. v.p. Sears World Trade, Inc., 1982-84; sr. v.p., gen. counsel Unisys Corp., 1985-88, exec. v.p., 1989—. Home: 710 Mill Creek Rd Gladwyne PA 19035 Office: Unisys Corp One Unisys Pl Detroit MI 48232

HESSLUND, BRADLEY HARRY, cost analyst; b. Mpls., June 27, 1958; s. Harry A. and Dorothy (Tishi) H. AA, Normandale Community Coll., 1978; BS, U. Wis., Menomonie, 1981; MBA, U. Pitts., 1984. Indsl. engr. Thermo King Corp. sub. Westinghouse Electric Corp., Bloomington, Minn., 1981-82; quality engr. Westinghouse Electric Corp., Beaver, Pa., 1983; cost engr. IBM Corp., East Fishkill, N.Y., 1984-85; mfg. engring. supr. Hoffman Engring. Co. subs. Pentair Inc., Anoka, Minn., 1985-88; sr. cost analyst Naval Systems div. FMC Corp., Fridley, Minn., 1988—. Mem. Soc. Mfg. Engrs. Republican. Lutheran. Home: 3200 Zane Ave N Crystal MN 55422 Office: FMC Corp Naval Systems Div PO Box 59043 4800 E River Rd Fridley MN 55459-0043

HESTAD, BJORN MARK, metal distributing company executive; b. Evanston, Ill., May 31, 1926; s. Hilmar and Anna (Aagaard) H.; student Ill. Inst. Tech., 1947; m. Florence Anne Ragusi, May 1, 1948; children—Marsha Anne, Patricia Lynn Krueger, Peter Mark. Sales corr., Shakeproof, Inc., Chgo., 1947-50; indsl. buyer Crescent Industries, Inc., Chgo., 1950-51; purchasing agt. Switchcraft, Inc., Chgo., 1951-73, materials mgr., 1973-74, dir. purchasing, 1974-77; pres. Tool King, Inc., Wheeling, Ill., 1977—; pres. H & H Enterprises of Northfield. Mgr. youth orgns. Northfield Jr. Hockey Club, 1968-71, Winnfield Hockey Club, 1972-73; bus. mgr. West Hockey Club, 1973-74. Served as cpl. USAAF, 1944-46. Mem. Tooling and Mfg. Assn., Sons of Norway. Republican. Mem. United Ch. Christ. Clubs: Waukegan Yacht, Lions. Home: 850 Happ Rd Northfield IL 60093 Office: Tool King Inc 275 Larkin Dr Wheeling IL 60090

HESTER, RICHARD GEORGE, accountant; b. Brantford, Ont., Can., July 15, 1940; s. George Ernest and Jean B. (Butcher) H.; m. Elizabeth Anne McCormack, Oct. 9, 1964; children: Robert A., Katherine A., Timothy R. Student, Ont., 1966. Chartered acct., Ont. Acct. McCormack, Barker & Wesbrook, Brantford, 1960-68; ptnr. McCormack, Parker & Hester, Brantford, 1968-74; ptnr. Deloitte, Haskins & Sells, Brantford, 1974-75, mng. ptnr., 1975-79; mng. ptnr. Deloitte, Haskins & Sells, Winnipeg, Man., Can., 1979—. Treas. Health Scis. Ctr. Rsch. Found., Winnipeg, 1984-88; bd. dirs. St. Paul's High Sch., Winnipeg. Mem. Inst. Chartered Accts. Ont., Inst. Chartered Accts. Man., Rotary (bd. dirs. Winnipeg Club), St. Charles Golf and Country Club (Winnipeg), Carleton Club (Winnipeg). Progressive Conservation. Presbyterian. Office: Deloitte Haskins & Sells, 360 Main St Ste 2100, Winnipeg, MB Canada R3C 3Z3

HESTER, THOMAS PATRICK, communications executive, lawyer; b. Tulsa, Okla., Nov. 20, 1937; s. E.P. and Mary J. (Layton) H; m. Nancy B. Scofield, Aug. 20, 1960; children: Thomas P. Jr., Ann S., John L. BA, Okla. U., 1961, LLB, 1963. Bar: Okla. 1963, Mo. 1967, N.Y. 1970, D.C. 1973, Ill. 1975. Lawyer McAfee & Taft, Okla. City, 1963-66, Southwestern Bell Telephone Co., Okla. City, St. Louis, 1966-72, AT&T, N.Y.C., Washington, 1972-75; gen. atty. Ill. Bell Telephone Co., Springfield, 1975-77; gen. solicitor Ill. Bell Telephone Co., Chgo., 1977-83, v.p., gen. counsel, 1983-87; sr. v.p., gen. counsel Ameritech, Chgo., 1987—. Chmn. bd. trustees Taxpayers' Fed. of Ill, Springfield, 1987-88. Served to capt. U.S. Army. Office: Ameritech 30 S Wacker Dr 38th Fl Chicago IL 60606

HETLAND, JOHN ROBERT, lawyer, educator; b. Mpls., Mar. 12, 1930; s. James L. and Evelyn (Lundgren) H.; m. Mildred Woodruff, Dec. 1951 (div.); children: Lynda Lee, Robert John, Debra Ann.; m. Anne Kneeland, Dec. 1972; children: Robin T. Kneeland, Elizabeth J. Kneeland. B.S.L., U. Minn., 1952, J.D., 1956. Bar: Minn. bar 1956, Calif. bar 1962. Practice law Mpls., 1956-59; assoc. prof. law U. Calif., Berkeley, 1959-60, prof. law, 1960—; ptnr. Hetland & Hensen, PC, Berkeley, 1959—; vis. prof. law Stanford U., 1971, 80, U. Singapore, 1972, U. Cologne, Fed. Republic Germany, 1988. Author: California Real Property Secured Transactions, 1970, Commercial Real Estate Transactions, 1972, Secured Real Estate

Transactions, 1974, 1977; co-author: (with Maxwell, Riesenfeld, and Warren) California Cases on Security Transactions in Land, 2d edit., 1975, 3d edit., 1984; contbr. articles to legal, real estate and fin. jours. Served to lt. comdr. USNR, 1953-55. Mem. state bars Calif. and Minn., Am. Bar Assn., Order of Coif, Phi Delta Phi. Republican. Home: 20 Redcoach Ln Orinda CA 94563 Office: 2600 Warring St Berkeley CA 94704

HETSKO, CYRIL FRANCIS, retired lawyer, corporation executive; b. Scranton, Pa., Oct. 4, 1911; s. John Andrew and Anna (Lesco) H.; m. Josephine G. Stein, Nov. 12, 1932; children—Jacqueline V. (Mrs. Charles F. Kaufer), Cyril M., Cynthia F. (Mrs. William J. Rainey). Jeffery F. A.B., Dickinson Coll., 1933; J.D., U. Mich., 1936. Bar: Pa. 1937, N.Y. 1938, U.S. Supreme Ct. 1965. Assoc. Chadbourne, Parke, Whiteside & Wolff (name now Chadbourne & Parke), 1936-55, partner, 1955-64; gen. counsel Am. Brands, Inc.,, 1964-77, v.p., 1965-69, sr. v.p., 1969-77, also former dir.; former dir. Acme Visible Records, Inc., Acushnet Co., Am. Brands Export Corp., Am. Tobacco Internat. Corp., James B. Beam Distilling Co., James B. Beam Distilling Internat. Co., Duffy-Mott Co., Inc., Gallaher Ltd. (Gt. Britain), Master Lock Co., Master Lock Export, Inc., Swingline, Inc., Andrew Jergens Co., Sunshine Biscuits, Inc., Swingline Export Corp., Wilson Jones Co. Mem. ABA, Fed., N.Y. State bar assns., U.S. Trademark Assn. (dir. 1959-67, 68-72, 73-77, pres. 1965-66, hon. bd. chmn. 1966-67, mem. council past presidents 1977—), Order of Coif, Phi Beta Kappa, Phi Delta Theta, Delta Theta Phi. Republican. Presbyterian. Clubs: Intrepids, Explorers, Williams (N.Y.C.); Nat. Lawyers (Washington); Ridgewood (N.J.) Country. Home: 714 Waverly Rd Ridgewood NJ 07450

HEUCHAN, D(ONALD) FRANCIS, JR., real estate investment professional; b. St. Louis, Mar. 7, 1943; s. Donald F. and Florence E. (von Brecht) H.; m. Anne E. Carroll; children: Brecht W., Charles B., Joshua J., Anna C., J. Streckfus, Heidi E. Student, Washington U., St. Louis, 1966. Mgr. farm and land div. Dolan Co. Realtors, St. Louis, Union, Mo., 1970-76; 1st v.p. 1st State Bank, Union, 1975-77; salesman Rodgers & Cummings Inc., Clearwater, Fla., 1977-83; pres., ptnr., comml. investment real estate service Klein & Heuchan Inc., Clearwater, 1983—. Syndicated newspaper columnist, 1983-84. Profl. dir. Pinellas County United Way, 1982; charter mem. property trust bd. U. Tampa, 1984; mem. Rep. Nat. Com., Nat. Rep. Congl. Com. Mem. Nat. Assn. Realtors, Fla. Assn. Realtors (v.p. West coast chpt. 1985), Greater Clearwater Bd. Realtors (sec. 1985), Clearwater-Largo-Dunedin Bd. Realtors (bd. dirs. 1980-84), Nat. Assn. Rev. Appraisers, Cert. Comml. Investors, Aircraft Owners and Pilots Assn., Porsche Club Am. Office: Klein & Heuchan Inc 2040 NE Coachman Rd Clearwater FL 34625

HEUER, RONALD EUGENE, tunneling geotechnical consultant, civil engineer, engineering geologist; b. Pontiac, Ill., Apr. 7, 1940; s. George Ernest and Rosemary (Quinn) H.; m. Debra Lynn Virgens, May 8, 1981; children by previous marriage: Janna Leigh, Garrick Todd. BSCE, U. Ill., 1963, MS in Geology, 1965, PhDCE, 1971. Registered engr., Calif., Ill., Va., N.Y., Wis. Sr. engr., geologist, A.A. Mathews Inc., Arcadia, Calif., 1969-73, Rockville, Md., 1973-74; sr. engr., geologist, Foster Miller Assocs., Alexandria, Va., 1974-75; geotech. cons., Champaign and McHenry, Ill., 1975—; assoc. prof. civil engring. U. Ill., Urbana, 1975-78; mem. Nat. Com. Tunneling Tech., NSF, 1973-78, Nat. Com. Rock Mechanics, 1975-78. Contbr. papers to profl. publs. and confs. Recipient Bronze Tablet, U. Ill., 1963; NSF fellow, 1963-64. Mem. ASCE, Assn. Engring. Geologists, NRA, League Am. Wheelmen. Avocations: bicycle touring, photography, firearms.

HEUSI, JOE DUANE, insurance company executive; b. Defiance, Ohio, June 12, 1942; s. Oscar Joseph and Ernestine (Penrod) H.; m. Frances Jean Hyland, Aug. 15, 1964; children: Richard Duane, Michael David. B.Music, Baldwin Wallace Coll., 1964, B.Music Edn., 1965; M.S., Columbia U., 1979. Tchr. Bedford (Ohio) Pub. Schs., 1965-66, Berea (Ohio) Pub. Schs., 1966-69; career account rep. Variable Annuity Mktg. Co., Cleve., 1968-71; v.p., regional mgr. Variable Annuity Mktg. Co., Cranford, N.J., 1971-80; dir., pres. Variable Annuity Mktg. Co., Houston, 1980-83, dir., chmn., 1983-88; v.p. mktg. services Variable Annuity Life Ins. Co., Houston, 1980-81, sr. v.p. mktg., dir., 1981-83, pres, chief operating officer, 1983-84, pres., chief exec. officer, dir., 1984-88; dir., pres., chief exec. officer Timed Opportunity Fund, VALIC Capital Accumulation Fund, Houston, 1983-85, Separate Accounts One and Two, 1983-87; chmn., dir., chief exec. officer Am. Gen. Series Portfolio Co., 1985-88; pres., chief exec. officer Maryland Casualty Co., Am. Gen. Fire & Casualty Co., Assurance Co. Am., Credithrift Fin. Inc., Hampson, Robert & Son Ltd., Maine Bonding & Casualty Co., Marcasco Co. Inc., Nat. Property Owners Ins. Co., Nat. Standard Ins. Co., Northern Ins. Co. of N.Y., Steadfast Ins. Co., Steadfast Reins Co. Ltd., Valiant Ins. Co. Chmn., bd. dirs. Concert Chorale of Houston, 1983-87; bd. govs. Shepherd Sch. Music, Rice U., 1985-88; trustee Houston Ballet Found., 1987-88. Mem. Am. Mgmt. Assn., Phi Mu Alpha, Sinfonia, Sigma Phi Epsilon. Home: 32 Alderman Ct Timonium MD 21093 Office: Md Casualty Co 3910 Keswick Rd Baltimore MD 21211

HEWITT, JAMES MICHAEL, computer software company executive; b. Seattle, Oct. 24, 1948; s. John Henry and Bonnie Mabel (Anderson) H.; m. Emily DeWitt, Aug, 1975 (div. 1979). Student, Stanford U., 1967-68; BA, U. Wash., 1973; MA, U. Ariz., 1975, postgrad., 1975-78. Assoc. faculty, staff archeologist Pima Community Coll., Tucson, 1976-82, cons., 1982-83; pres. Hewitt-Anderson Co., Tucson, 1983—. Mem. Soc. Profl. Archeologists, Soc. Am. Archeology. Presbyterian. Home: PO Box 41510 Tucson AZ 85717 Office: Hewitt Anderson Co 151 S Tucson Blvd Ste 211 Tucson AZ 85716

HEWITT, THOMAS EDWARD, financial executive; b. West Lafayette, Ind., Sept. 7, 1939; s. Ernest Edward and Katherine (Thelen) H.; BA, Dartmouth Coll., 1961, MBA, 1962; CPA, Ill.; m. Jeraldine Lee Spurgeon, June 16, 1962; children: Debora Lynn, Laura Jean, Gregory Spurgeon. Staff acct. Ernst & Whinney, Chgo., 1966-67, acct. in charge, 1967, sr. acct., 1967-69; controller Thorne United Inc., Addison, Ill., 1969-70, sec.-treas., 1970; supr. Ernst & Whinney, Chgo., 1971-76; controller Waterloo (Iowa) Industries, Inc., 1976-79, v.p. fin., 1979—, also bd. dirs. 1986—. Treas., Salvation Army, Waterloo, 1977-78, 80-82, Cedar Valley United Way, 1983-87, Covenant Med. Ctr., 1986-89, St. Francis Hosp., 1986-89; assoc. campaign chmn. United Way of Black Hawk County, 1981, 82; spl. project chmn. Chgo. Jaycees, 1969; trustee Westminster United Presbyterian Ch., 1984-86, vice-chmn., 1985. Served to capt. USMC, 1962-66. NROTC regular scholar, 1957-62. Mem. Am. Inst. CPAs, Iowa Soc. CPAs, Nat. Assn. Accts., Am. Mgmt. Assn., Sunnyside Country Club (treas. 1984, pres. 1985; trustee, 1986-88), Elks. Home: 1105 Prospect Blvd Waterloo IA 50701 Office: Waterloo Industries Inc 999 Home Plaza Waterloo IA 50701

HEWLETT, WILLIAM (REDINGTON), manufacturing company executive, electrical engineer; b. Ann Arbor, Mich., May 20, 1913; s. Albion Walter and Louise (Redington) H.; m. Flora Lamson, Aug. 10, 1939 (dec. 1977); children: Eleanor Hewlett Gimon, Walter B., James S., William A., Mary Hewlett Jaffe; m. Rosemary Bradford, May 24, 1978. BA, Stanford U., 1934, EE, 1939; MS, MIT, 1936; LLD, U. Calif., Berkeley, 1966, Yale U., 1976, Mills Coll., 1983; DSc (hon.), Kenyon Coll., 1978, Poly Inst. N.Y., 1978; LHD, Johns Hopkins U., 1985; EngD, U. Notre Dame, 1980, Utah State U., 1980, Dartmouth Coll., 1983; PhD, Rand Grad. Inst. Electromed. researcher 1936-39; co-founder Hewlett-Packard Co., Palo Alto, Calif., 1939, ptnr., 1939-46, exec. v.p., dir., 1947-64, pres., 1964-77, chief exec. officer, 1969-78, chmn. exec. com., 1977-83, vice chmn. bd. dirs., 1983-87, emeritus dir., 1987—; mem. internat. adv. council Wells Fargo Bank, 1986—; trustee Rand Corp., 1962-72, Carnegie Inst., Washington, 1971—, chmn. bd. trustees, 1980-86; dir. Overseas Devel. Council, 1969-77; bd. dirs. Inst. Radio Engrs. (now IEEE), 1950-57, pres. 1954. Contbr. articles to profl. jours.; patentee in field. Trustee Stanford U., 1963-74, Mills Coll., Oakland, Calif., 1958-68; mem. Pres.'s Gen. Adv. Com. on Fgn. Assistance Programs, Washington, 1965-68, Pres.'s Sci. Adv. Com., 1966-69; mem. San Francisco regional panel Commn. on White House Fellows, 1969-70, chmn., 1970; pres. bd. dirs. Palo Alto Stanford Hosp. Ctr., 1956-58, bd. dirs., 1958-62; dir. Drug Abuse Council, Washington, 1972-74, Kaiser Found. Hosp. & Health Plan Bd., 1972-78; chmn. The William and Flora Hewlett Found., 1966—; bd. dirs. San Francisco Bay Area Council, 1969-81, Inst. Medicine, Washington, 1971-72, The Nat. Acads. Corp., 1986—, Monterey Bay Aquarium Rsch. Inst., 1987—, Univ. Corp. for Atmospheric Rsch. Found., 1986—. Lt. col. AUS, 1942-45. Recipient Calif. Mfr. of Yr. Calif. Mfrs. Assn., 1969, Bus. Statesman of Yr. Harvard Bus. Sch. No. Calif., 1970, Medal of Achievement Western Electronic Mfrs. Assn., 1971, Industrialist of Yr. (with David Packard) Calif. Mus. Sci. and Industry and Calif. Mus. Found., 1973, Award with David Packard presented by Scientific Apparatus Makers Assn., 1975, Corp. Leadership award MIT, 1976, Medal of Honor City of Boeblingen, Germany, 1977, Herbert Hoover medal for disting. service Stanford U. Alumni Assn., 1977, Henry Heald award Ill. Inst. Tech., 1984, Nat. Medal of Sci. U.S. Nat. Sci. Com., 1985. Fellow IEEE (pres. 1954, Founders medal with David Packard 1973), Franklin Inst. (life, Vermilye medal with David Packard 1976), Am. Acad. Arts and Scis.; mem. Nat. Acad. Scis. (panel on advanced tech. competition 1982-83), Nat. Acad. Engring., Instrument Soc. Am. (hon. life), Am. Philos. Soc., Calif. Acad. Sci. (trustee 1963-68), Assn. Quadrato della Radio, Century Assn. N.Y.C. Clubs: Bohemian, Pacific-Union (San Francisco); Menlo Country (Woodside, Calif.). Office: Hewlett-Packard Co 1501 Page Mill Rd Palo Alto CA 94304

HEWSON, DONNA WALTERS, real estate executive; b. Columbia, S.C., Mar. 28, 1947; d. Jerry William and Rosa (Bryant) Walters; 1 child, Robert Alton Smith Jr.; m. James Robert Hewson, Oct. 1983 (div. 1986). Student, Hollins Coll., 1971-72, Va. Western Coll., 1972, Va. Polytech. and State U., 1972-73, U. S.C., 1978-79, 84, 85. Lic. residential and comml. real estate broker. Sales rep. Russell-Jeffcoat Realtors, Columbia, S.C., 1969-71; broker Russell-Jeffcoat Realtors, Columbia, 1971-72; adminstrv. asst. Roanoke (Va.) Valley Psych. Ctr., 1975-76; sales rep. Moore Bus. Forms, Columbia, 1976-79; project sales mgr. Continental Mortgage Investors, Columbia, 1979-80; broker, project sales mgr. Tom Jenkins Realty, Columbia, 1980-81; sales mgr., broker in charge RELM, Inc., Columbia, 1982-83; sales mgr. So. U.S. Realty/U.S. Shelter, Columbia, 1983-84; pres. WaltersHewson Co., Inc., Columbia, 1984—; v.p. Park Circle Properties, Inc., 1988—. Pub. rels. chmn., bd. dirs. Women's Symphony Assn., 1988; mem. Trinity Episcopal Cathedral, Trinity Cathedral Choir, Hist. Columbia Found., Lyric Opera Guild. Mem. Columbia C. of C. (com. chmn. 1987—), Greater Columbia C. of C.,Nat. Assn. Real Estate Appraisers (cert., sr. mem.), State Assn. Realtors, Nat. Assn. Realtors, Columbia Bd. Realtors (mem. Million Dollar Club, 1981, 84, 86, Grievance com. mem. 1986-88), S.C. Assn. Realtors (Profl. Standards Com. 1986, polit. affairs com. 1987), Realtors Nat. Mktg. Inst. (residential brokerage coun.), Palmetto Real Estate Educators. Episcopalian. Office: Walters Hewson Co Inc PO Box 967 Columbia SC 29202

HEXNER, LILA MAE, business consultant; b. Appleton, Wis., May 14; d. Harold George and Florence Esther (McCabe) Fird; m. Peter E. Hexner (div. 1986); children: Michael T., Holly A., Thomas S. BS in Edn., U. Wis., Madison, 1947; M.Phil.Ed., Boston Coll., 1973 (formerly Newton Coll. Sacred Heart); founder, dir. Women's adv., mem. adminstrn. Middlesex Community Coll., 1971-78, women's center, 1971-75, Widening Opportunity Research Center, 1975-78, founder, Div. Community Svcs., 1978; founder, Edn. for Commercialization div. No. Energy Corp., N.E. Regional Solar Energy Center Edn. Dept., Boston, 1978-82; founder, pres. The Cons. Exchange, Inc., 1982—; bd. dir. Video Research, Inc., Boston. mem. adv. com. Internat. Solar Renewable Energy Conf., 1981; chmn. Bus. Resource Ctr., Small Bus. Assn.; cons. in field. Mem. Mass. Adv. Council on Vocat. Tech. Edn., 1972-79; mem. Mass. Gov.'s Spl. Commn. on Youth Unemployment, 1978—; mem. exec. com. Mass. coordinating com. Internat. Women's Yr., 1978. Recipient Disting. Service award Middlesex Community Coll., 1973; grants include Fund for Improvement Postsecondary Edn., 1976-78. Mem. Women in Solar Energy (nat. adv. bd. 1980-82), Boston Computer Soc., Small Bus. Assn. New Eng. (chmn. first bus. conf., bd. dirs. 1987—), Research Mgmt. Assn. (bd. govs.), Profl. Coun. Avocations: theater, art. Home and Office: 105-1 Trowbridge Cambridge MA 02138

HEY, ANGELA MARGARET, management consultant; b. Horsforth, England, July 23, 1953; came to U.S., 1980; d. Geoffrey Brian and Kathleen Margaret Audrey (McGill) H. MA, Cambridge U., England, 1975; M Math, U. Waterloo, Ont., Can., 1976; PhD, London U., 1980; Diploma of Membership, Imperial Coll. Sci. and Tech., U. London, 1980. Fellow Royal Geographical Soc., London, 1977; research asst. Imperial Coll., London, 1979-80; mem. tech. staff AT&T Bell Labs., Murray Hill, N.J., 1980-83; dept. chief AT&T Techs., Summit, N.J. and Palo Alto, Calif., 1983-85; product mktg. mgr. The Palantir Corp., Santa Clara, Calif., 1985-86; pres. Areva Internat., Foster City, Calif., 1987—. Deacon Menlo Park Presbyn. Ch. Mem. Ops. Research Soc., Assn. Computing Machinery (sec. Princeton, N.J. br. 1981, service award 1981). Club: Decathlon (Santa Clara). Home: 872 Newport Cir Redwood City CA 94065 Office: Areva Internat PO Box 188 Belmont CA 94002

HEYBACH, JOHN PETER, food products executive; b. Oak Park, Ill., Sept. 25, 1950; s. Charles Edward and Muriel Charlotte (DeCleene) H.; m. Mary Susan Conley, Sept. 3, 1971; children: Michelene Conley, Conor Charles. BA, No. Ill. U., 1972, MA, 1974, PhD, 1976; M in Mgmt., Northwestern U. Fellow Nat. Aeronautics & Space Adminstrn., Moffettfield, Calif., 1976-78; research assoc. Bowman-Grey Med. Sch., Winston-Salem, N.C., 1978-79; research scientist Gen. Foods Corp., Whiteplains, N.Y., 1979-85; dir. scientific affairs NutraSweet Co., Skokie, Ill., 1985-86; dir. regional sales NutraSweet Co., Deerfield, Ill., 1986—; dir. corp. liason, asst. gen. mgr. NutraSweet Co., Zug, Switzerland, 1988—. cons. editor Am. Journal Physiology, Physiology and Behavior. Mem. Am. Endocrine Soc., Soc. for Neuroscience, Am. Coll. Nutrition, Am. Inst. Nutrition, Inst. Food Technologists. Roman Catholic. Home: 525 Forest Hill Rd Lake Forest IL 60045 Office: NutraSweet 1751 Lake Cook Rd Deerfield IL 60015

HEYMAN, SAMUEL J., chemicals and building materials manufacturing company executive; b. N.Y.C., Mar. 1, 1939; s. Lazarus S. and Annette (Silverman) H.; m. Ronnie Feuerstein, Nov. 1970; children: Lazarus, Eleanor, Jennifer, Elizabeth. BS magna cum laude, Yale Coll., 1960; LLB, Harvard U., 1963. Bar: Conn. 1963. Atty. U.S. Dept. Justice, Washington, 1963-64; asst. U.S. atty. Dist. of Conn., New Haven, 1964-67; chief asst. U.S. atty. New Haven div., 1967-68; pres. Heyman Properties, Westport, Conn., 1968—; chmn., chief exec. officer GAF Corp., Wayne, N.J., 1983—. Office: GAF Corp 1361 Alps Rd Wayne NJ 07470

HEYNE, GRACE LORRAINE, financial consultant; b. San Marino, Calif., Nov. 12, 1931; d. Wilber Cover and Grace Bertha (Hadley) Thomas; divorced; children: David Richard Baker, Joanne Lorraine Baker Deal, Carolyn Jean; m. Milton William Heyne, July 22, 1982; stepchildren: Katie Heyne Caulk, James, Linda, Rebecca Heyne Pfeiffer, John. BS, UCLA, 1953; MS, U. So. Calif., 1963. Cert. fin. planner; chartered fin. cons.; CLU; lic. stockbroker, real estate broker, ins. agt., income tax preparer, notary pub. Pres. Grace Heyne Fin. Group, San Pedro, Calif., 1987—, Fin. Design Adv. Svcs., San Pedro, 1987—. Mem. Los Angelenas, 1982—; rec. sec. San Pedro Bay Hist. Soc., 1984—. Mem. Internat. Assn. Registered Fin. Planners, Bus. and Profl. Women (rec. sec. San Pedro chpt. 1982—, Woman of Achievement award 1988), AAUW, San Pedro C. of C. (women's div.), Delta Kappa Gamma (pres. Alpha Beta chpt. 1986-88), Pi Lambda Theta (v.p. local chpt., treas., corr. sec. 1963—, mem. nat. investment com. 1986—). Republican. Lutheran. Office: Fin Design Adv Svcs 2184 Passeo del Mar San Pedro CA 90732

HEYSE, WARREN JOHN, publishing company executive; b. Milw., Oct. 13, 1923; s. Raymond Henry and Harriet Margaret (Regner) H.; m. Roxybelle Brown, July 9, 1949; children: Roxanne, Jennifer, Nanette. B.S., U. Wis., 1948; postgrad., Marquette U. Law Sch., 1949; M.S., UCLA, 1950; postgrad., U. Minn., 1952. Classified advt. salesman Milw. Jour., 1952-55, retail advt. supr., 1955-59, classified advt. mgr., 1959-66, asst. advt. dir., 1966-68, v.p., dir. mktg., devel., 1968-73; sr. v.p. Jour. Communications Inc., 1973-77, exec. v.p., 1977-83, pres., 1983—; pres. Jour./Sentinel Inc. (pub. Milw. Jour.), 1977-84, vice chmn. bd., 1984—; bd. dirs. Perry Printing, Midwestern Relay Inc. (all Jour. Co. subs.), 1973—; vice chmn. WTMJ, Inc.; trustee Jour. Stock Trust, 1976—. Gen. chmn. United Way, 1969, bd. dirs., 1970-76; bd. dirs. Vis. Nurses Assn., 1971-76, ARC, 1972-74; bd. dirs. Milwaukee County council Boy Scouts Am., 1975—, pres., 1984-85; bd. dirs. St. Joseph Hosp., 1970-78, Greater Milw. Com., 1977—, U. Wis. Found., 1980—; bd. dirs. United Performing Arts Fund, 1978-86, co-chmn., 1979. Served with inf. U.S. Army, 1943-46, ETO. Recipient McGovern award for classified advt., 1979, Disting. Svc. to Journalism award U. Wis., 1989; named Wis. Newspaper Pub. of Yr. award, 1983, 84. Mem. Sigma Alpha Epsilon, Sigma Delta Chi, Kappa Tau Alpha. Methodist. Clubs: University, Bascom Hill Soc. (U. Wis., Madison), Circumnavigator. Lodge: Rotary. Office: Jour Communications Inc 333 W State St Milwaukee WI 53201

HEYSER, WILLIAM H., landscape contractor; b. Norristown, Pa., Mar. 26, 1928; s. Ellsworth and Ruth (Woodland) H.; m. Janice Marie Knerr, June 27, 1953; children: Susan Marie, Holly Ruth. BS in Horticulture, Pa. State U., 1950. Registered landscape architect, Pa. Mgr. Heyser Landscaping and Tree Service, Norristown, Pa., 1952-62; pres. Heyser Landscaping, Inc., Norristown, 1962-86, chief exec. officer, 1986—; landscape contracting competition judge The Landscape Contractors Assn. of Met. Wash., Inc., 1985. Columnist Tri-State Real Estate Jour., 1986-87. Mem. Worcester Township Planning Commn., Pa., 1968-70, Montgomery County Pvt. Industry Council, Norristown, 1982-83; founder Mid-Atlantic Student Landscape Field Day, 1985; bd. trustees Lower Providence Presby. Ch., 1962-64; pres. Worcester Home and Sch. Assn., 1968-69. Served as staff sgt. U.S. Army, 1950-52. Mem. Pa. Nurserymens Assn (com. chmn. 1983-84, 89—), Associated Landscape Contractors Am. (com. mem. 1983-86), Del. Valley Landscape Contractors Assn. (pres. 1966-67), Pa. Horticultural Soc. (Styer award com. 1984—), Norristown Jaycees (pres. 1960-61). Republican. Clubs: Montgomery Count Pa. State, Penn State (past pres. 1961-62). Lodge: Rotary (pres. 1969-70). Office: Heyser Landscaping Inc 400 N Park Ave Norristown PA 19403

HIBBS, JOHN STANLEY, lawyer; b. Des Moines, Sept. 19, 1934; s. Ray E. Hibbs and Jean Waller (Lackey) Gravender; m. Shirley Jean Moon, June 20, 1958; children: John S. II, Kari S. Hibbs Carroll, Jennifer R. BBA, U. Minn., 1956, JD cum laude, 1960. Bar; Minn. 1960, U.S. Dist. Ct. Minn. 1960, U.S. Ct. Appeals (8th cir.) 1963, U.S. Tax Ct. 1965, U.S. Supreme Ct. 1970. Ptnr. Dorsey and Whitney, Mpls., 1960—; chmn. Adv. Task Force on Minn. corp. law, Mpls., 1979-82, tax policy study group of Minn. Bus. Climate Task Force, Mpls., 1978-80. Author: Minnesota Nonprofit Corporations- A Corporate and Tax Guide, 1979; contrb. over 40 articles to profl. jours. Served to capt. USAR, 1956-66. Fellow Am. Coll. Tax Counsel, ABA (cons. com. on corp. laws 1981-82), Minn. Bar Assn., Hennepin County Bar Assn., Am. Judicature Soc., Am. Soc. Law & Medicine, Nat. Health Lawyers Assn., Am. Acad. Hosp. Attys. Republican. Lutheran. Home: 25 Cooper Circle Edina MN 55436 Office: Dorsey & Whitney 2200 First Bank Pl E Minneapolis MN 55402

HIBBS, STEPHEN HOWARD, telecommunications company executive; b. Medford, Oreg., Feb. 18, 1952; s. Ralph Emerson and Jeanne E. (Howard) H. BS, U. Oreg., 1974; MBA, Harvard U., 1976. Pres. S.M.S. Inc., Portland, Oreg., 1976-81; bus. mgr. Arco Alaska Inc., Prudhoe Bay, 1981-87; ptnr. Telecom Svc. Bur., Sacramento, 1987—; bus. mgr. Tom Bodett Enterprises, Homer, Alaska, 1988—. Contbr. articles to profl. jours. Del. Rep. Nat. Conv., Miami, Fla., 1984. Mem. Entrepreneur Soc.

HIBSHMAN, DAVID THOMAS, financial planner; b. Lancaster, Pa., Dec. 15, 1959; s. Clyde S. and Patricia A. (Hoover) H.; m. Robin Leigh Miller, July 25, 1987. BS in Acctg., Messiah Coll., 1981. CPA, Pa.; cert. fin. planner. Acct. Miller & Miller CPAs, Lititz, Pa., 1981-82, Sager Swisher & Co. CPA, Columbia, Pa., 1982-83; fin. cons. Peat Marwick Mitchell & Co., Phila., 1983-85, Gallers Fin. Group, Bala Cynwyd, Pa., 1985—. Trustee Messiah Coll., 1981-84; bd. dirs. SALT ministries, 1988—. Mem. Am. Inst. CPAs, Pa. Inst. CPAs (2d place award student manuscript, 1981), Internat. Assn. Fin. Planners. Republican. Methodist. Home: 1876 Nanticoke Rd Lancaster PA 17601 Office: Gallers Fin Group 100 Presidential Blvd Ste 300 Bala-Cynwyd PA 19004

HICK, KENNETH WILLIAM, business executive; b. New Westminster, B.C., Can., Oct. 17, 1946; s. Les Walter and Mary Isabelle (Warner) H. BA in Bus., Eastern Wash. State Coll., 1971; MBA (fellow), U. Wash., 1973, PhD, 1975. Regional sales mgr. Hilti, Inc., San Leandro, Calif., 1976-79; gen. sales mgr. Moore Internat., Inc., Portland, 1979-80; v.p. sales and mktg. Phillips Corp., Anaheim, Calif., 1980-81; owner, pres., chief exec. officer K.C. Metals, San Jose, Calif., 1981-87; owner, pres., chief exec. officer Losli Internat. Inc., Portland, Oreg., 1987—; communications cons. Asso. Public Safety Communication Officers, Inc., State of Oreg., 1975-77; numerous cons. assignments, also seminars, 1976-81. Contbr. to numerous publs., 1976—. Mem. Oreg. Gov.'s Tax Bd., 1975-76; pres. Portland chpt. Oreg. Jaycees, 1976; bd. fellows U. Santa Clara, 1983—. Served with USAF, 1966-69. Decorated Commendation medal. Mem. Am. Mgmt. Assn., Am. Mktg. Assn., Assn. M.B.A. Execs., Asso. Gen. Contractors, Soc. Advancement Mgmt. Roman Catholic. Home: 17627 SW Kelok Lake Oswego OR 97034 Office: Losli Internat 8015 SW Hunziker Rd Tigard OR 97223

HICKEY, LADY BARBARA STANDISH, company executive; b. Washington, June 7, 1946; d. Robert Adams and Nell (Green) Thayer; m. Sir Justin Hickey, May 9, 1964; children: Justine, Simon, Portia. Dir. Mrs. World Pagent, Surfers Paradise, Queensland, Australia, 1986, Accident Ins. Mutual, 1986—, Bartinon Securities, 1985—. Patron Lifeline Support Com., Surfers Paradise, Keystone Rehab. Ctr., Brisbane, Australia; found. council mem. Goldcoast Coll. Advanced Edn.; found. mem. Bond U., Queensland. Office: Bartinon Securities Ltd, Gold Coast Mail Centre 4217, PO Box 7370, Queensland Australia

HICKEY, FRANK G., electronic components and equipment manufacturing company executive; b. 1927. B.S. in Bus. Adminstrn., U. Dayton, 1950. Vice pres. Tait Mfg. Co., 1953-63; pres. Fairbanks-Morse Pump div. Colt. Industries Inc., 1963-65; with Gen. Instrument Corp., N.Y.C., 1965—, corp. v.p. capacitor group, 1966-70, exec. v.p. components group, 1970-72, pres., 1972-87, chief operating officer, 1972-74, chmn., chief exec. officer, 1975—, also dir. Served with USN, 1945-46. Office: Gen Instrument Corp 767 Fifth Ave New York NY 10153 *

HICKEY, JOSEPH MICHAEL, JR., investment banker; b. Greensburgh Pa., June 6, 1940; s. Joseph Michael and Margaret (Nelson) H.; m. Suzanne Klempay, July 2, 1970. BS, Ind. U. Pa., 1963. Sales rep. 3M Co., St. Paul, Minn., 1967-69; account exec. Hornblower & Weeks, Hemphill, Noyes, Cleve., 1970-75; pres. Prescott, Ball & Turben, 1976-88; dist. chmn. Nat. Assn. Security Dealers, 1979-81; mem. mktg. com. SIA, N.Y.C., 1982-86, mem. regional firms com., 1989—; chmn. bd. Carnegie Capital Mgmt. Co., Cleve., 1983-88; pres. J.W. Charles Group, 1988—. Capt. U.S. Army, 1963-67. Mem. Kirtland Country Club (Willoughby, Ohio), Hermit Club (Cleve.), Loxahatchee Club (Fla.), Castle Pines Golf Club (Castle Rock, Colo.), Lost Tree Club (Fla.). Office: 980 N Federal Hwy Boca Raton FL 33432

HICKMAN, JAMES CHARLES, business and statistics educator, business school dean; b. Indianola, Iowa, Aug. 27, 1927; s. James C. and Mabel L. (Fisher) H.; m. Margaret W. McKee, June 12, 1950; children—Charles Wallace, Donald Robert, Barbara Jean. B.A., Simpson Coll., 1950; M.S., U. Iowa, 1952, Ph.D., 1961. Actuarial asst. Bankers Life Co., Des Moines, 1952-57; asst. prof. dept. statistics U. Iowa, 1961-64, asso. prof., 1964-67, prof., 1967-72; prof. bus. and statistics U. Wis., Madison, 1972—; dean Sch. Bus. U. Wis., 1985—; mem. panel of cons. on social security fin. Senate Fin. and House Ways and Means Com., 1975-76; mem. adv. com. to Joint Bd. for Enrollment of Actuaries, 1976-78; mem. Actuarial Standards Bd., 1985—. Served with USAAF, 1945-47. Recipient Alumni Achievement award Simpson Coll., 1979; David Halmstad award for actuarial research Actuarial Ednl. Research Fund, 1979, 81. Fellow Soc. Actuaries (v.p. 1975-77); mem. Casualty Actuarial Soc., Am. Acad. Actuaries, Am. Statis. Assn. Presbyterian. Home: 4917 Woodburn Dr Madison WI 53711 Office: U Wis Sch Bus Madison WI 53706

HICKMAN, JOHN HAMPTON, III, entrepreneurial industrialist, investment banker, educator; b. Wilmington, Del., May 19, 1937; s. John Hampton Jr. and Martha (Barnett) H.; m. Barbara Spurlin, 1953; children: Erica Delius Hickman-Downs, Gretchen Leigh Hickman-Jewett, Rochanya Charlotte Hickman-Generous, John Hampton IV. Attended Randolph-Macon Coll., 1954-56; AB, Brown U., 1959; certificate in Chinese, Yale U., 1960, JD, 1962. Dir. internat. dept. McDonnell & Co., N.Y.C., 1964-68; partner investment banking firm The Hickman Corp., 1969—; chmn., chief exec. officer First Bancorp., Reno, 1968—; chmn. bd., chief exec. officer Seilon, Inc., 1968-69, Lockwood Corp., Gering, Nebr., 1968-69; chmn. bd.

Thomson Internat. Co., Thibodaux, La., 1968-69; chmn. bd., pres. Nev. Nat. Bancorp, Las Vegas, 1968-69; pres. Delanair, Inc. (name now Nexus Industries), N.Y.C., 1969-70; chmn. bd. C.R. Burr & Co. (name now United Nurseries Corp.), Middlefield, Conn., 1972-75, Buffalo Capital Corp., 1984—, Palm Beach County Utilities Corp., 1986—; founder, chmn. bd. Peninsula Corp.; prof. bus., chmn. dept. mgmt. Tenn. Wesleyan Coll.; prof., chmn. dept. mgmt. studies Rochester Inst. Tech., 1977-83; mem. faculty U. Conn.; vis. exec. U. N.C., Boone, vis. prof. bus. La. State U., Fordham U. Grad. Sch. Bus., N.Y.C., 1986—; vis. disting. prof. Barry U., Miami, Fla., 1984-85; bd. dirs., mem. fin. com. Aberdeen Petroleum (name now Adobe Oil and Gas Co.), Tulsa, 1970-73; bd. dirs. Dissen & Juhn Corp., Macedon, N.Y., Nat. Health Care Affiliates, Inc., Buffalo; chmn. HTE, Inc., Orlando, Fla., 1986—; founding mng. dir. Acad. for Advancement Corp., Governance, N.Y.C., 1986—. Author: Financing in the Entrepot Capital Market, 1968, East-West Investments, 1969, Spin-Offs As A Management Tool, Corporate Reorganization, 1972; Contbr.: Business Handbook for Photographers, 1980; articles to profl. jours. Founder, trustee Acad. for Advancement Corp. Governance, N.Y.C., 1986—; trustee, treas. Oceanic Soc., Washington, 1972—; trustee N.Y. State Assn. for Human Services, 1977-80; bd. dirs. Genesee Valley Arts Found., Rochester, 1978-84; mem. Yale U. Alumni Assembly, 1976-79; chmn. The Rochester Fund, 1978-81. Mem. Am. Mgmt. Assn. (world coun. pres.'s assn., lectr., editor publs.), Internat. Law Assn. (Am. br.), Fin. Execs. Inst., Acad. Mgmt., Rochester Yacht Club, University Club, Yale (N.Y.C.), Metropolitan, Canadian Club (N.Y.), Arts and Letters Club (Toronto). Office: Mount Morris Rd Geneseo NY 14454

HICKMAN, PAUL THOMAS, sales executive; b. Rock Island, Ill., Oct. 15, 1945; s. Paul Thomas and Mary Louise (Haskell) H.; m. Sandra Kay Munday, Oct. 17, 1970; children: Sheila, Laurie. BA, St. Louis U., 1967, postgrad., 1967-68. Tchr. jr. high sch. Webster Groves, Mo., 1968-69; sales rep. Ralston Purina Co., Peoria, Ill., 1969-71; dist. sales mgr. Ralston Purina Co., New Orleans, 1971-73; regional sales coord. Ralston Purina Co., Clearwater, Fla., 1973-76; dist. sales mgr. Ralston Purina Co., Miami, Fla., 1976-78; regional sales mgr. Ralston Purina Co., Cin., 1978-81, dir. sales, 1981-87; div. dir. Ralston Purina Co., St. Louis, 1987—; judge Students in Free Enterprise, Springfield, Mo., 1988—. With USAF, 1969. Mem. Pvt. Label Mfrs. Assn. (com. chmn. 1980-81), Internat. Mass Retailing Assn., Elks. Republican. Roman Catholic. Home: 428 Claymont Dr Ballwin MO 63011 Office: Ralston Purina Co Checkerboard Sq Saint Louis MO 63164

HICKMAN, ROBERT NORMAN, mining company executive; b. Butte, Mont., Oct. 17, 1935; s. Robert Lemuel and Lucile Elizabeth (McDougal) H.; m. Marilyn Miller, Dec. 28, 1956; children: Cheryl, Pamela, Robert, David. BS in Geol. Engring., Mont. Coll. Mineral Sci. and Tech., 1957. Mining engr. Lucky Mc Mine, Riverton, Wyo., 1960-64; staff engr. Utah Internat. Inc., San Francisco, 1964-69; mine. supt. Island Copper, Can., 1969-72, mine mgr., 1974-76; v.p. engring. ops. Utah Internat. Inc., San Francisco, 1977-84; st. v.p. BHP- Utah Internat. Inc., San Francisco, 1985—. Pres. bd. dirs. Bay Area Sci. Fair, San Francisco. Served to capt. USAF, 1958-69. Mem. Am. Inst. Mining, Metallurgical and Petroleum Engrs. Republican. Club: Bankers San Francisco. Office: BHP Utah Internat Inc 550 California St San Francisco CA 94104

HICKO, SCOTT EDWARD, accountant; b. Hammond, Ind., Dec. 11, 1947; s. Edward J. and Ima (Martin) H.; m. Ruth Ann Greskovich, Apr. 17, 1971; children: Jennifer Lynn, Scott Edward. BS in Acctg., Ind. U., 1971; MBA in Fin., DePaul U., 1979. CPA, Ill., Ind. Ptnr., acct. Louis, Price CPAs, Chgo., 1971-78, Hicko CPA Group, Merrillville, Ind., 1978—. Coach Schererville (Ind.) Soccer Club, 1983-86, Schererville Town Baseball League, 1983-88; adviser St. Michael's Ch., Schererville, 1987—. Mem. Am. Inst. CPA's, Ind. Assn. CPA's, Ill. Soc. CPA's, Internat. Assn. Cert. Fin. Planners. Office: Hicko CPA Group 7891 Broadway Merrillville IN 47030

HICKOK, RAYMOND T., corporate professional; b. Mar. 13, 1918. BS in Bus. Econs., Rollins Coll., 1940; postgrad., Harvard U., 1955. Chmn. bd., chief exec. officer Hickok Mfg. Co., Rochester, N.Y., 1945-71, chmn. bd., 1972-75; chmn. bd. Cape Cod Laundry, Rochester, 1962-72, Carnival Car Washes, Rochester, 1955-75; sr. assoc. Ray Hickok Assocs., Rochester, 1971—. Mem. Young Pres.'s Orgn. (founder, bd. dirs.), World Bus. Council (chmn.). Office: 311 Alexander St Rochester NY 14604

HICKOX, WILLIAM HORACE, III, real estate corporation executive; b. Borger, Tex., May 29, 1941; s. William Horace and Mildred Elizabeth (Barnett) H.; m. Suzanne Lillian Permenter, Nov. 29, 1969; children: William Horace IV, Amy Elizabeth. Student U. Tex., 1959-64. Lic. real estate broker, Tex. Regional mgr. Avis Rent A Car, Dallas and Houston, 1968-74; owner William H. Hickox Investments, Houston, 1974—; pres., chief exec. officer Hickox Devel. Corp., Houston, 1982—; owner Hickox Electronic Group, Houston, 1987—. Pres. Ed White PTO, Houston, 1984-85; mem. fin. com. Gethsemane United Meth Ch., 1977, adminstrv. bd., 1985-87; coach YMCA Youth Program, 1977-81; pres. Band Booster Club Sharpstown High Sch., 1987-88. Named Adm. in the Tex. Navy, Gov. Tex., 1973, Col. and A.D.C., Gov. Miss., 1973, Col. Gov.'s staff, Gov. La., 1973; named hon. mem. KHIVA Temple, Amarillo, Tex., 1984. Mem. Houston Bd. Realtors, U. Tex. Longhorn Singers Alumni Assn. (co-founder, organizer, dir.), Quarter Century Wireless Club, Houston Amateur Radio Club. United Methodist. Office: Hickox Devel Corp 9896 Bissonnet Suite 100 Houston TX 77036

HICKS, CLAIR LLOYD, agricultural educator; b. Payson, Utah, Oct. 9, 1945; s. Theodore McKeen and Evelyn (Lloyd) H.; m. Laurie Elizabeth Hardman, Oct. 12, 1973; children: Chad M., Meg L., Blaine E., Trent W., Dawn C. BS, Utah State U., 1967, MS, 1969; PhD, U. Wis., 1974. Rsch. asst. U. Wis., Madison, 1971-74; asst prof. dept. agrl. sci. U. Ky., Lexington, 1974-80, assoc. prof., 1980-87, prof., 1987—; cons. Corning Glassworks, 1982-84, Genencor, Inc., San Francisco, 1982-86, Hallman Internat., Inc., Lexington, 1982-88, Nordica Internat., Sioux Falls, S.D., 1987—. Contbr. articles to numerous profl. publs. Unit leader Boy Scouts Am., Lexington, 1984—; high councilman Ch. Jesus Christ of Latter day Saints, Lexington, 1983-84, bishop, 1984-88. With U.S. Army, 1969-71. Grantee Nat. Dairy Promotion and Rsch. Bd., 1988, Lifestaff, Inc., 1988; recipient Pfizer award, Am. Dairy Sci. Assn., 1988. Mem. Am. Dairy Sci. Assn. (mem. editorial bd. 1985—), Inst. Food Technologists (mem.-at-large bluegrass sect. 1987-88), Coun. Agr. and Sci. Tech., Sigma Xi. Democrat. Office: U Ky 410 Agriculture Scis S Lexington KY 40546

HICKS, GREGORY STEVEN, economic developer; b. Ft. Wayne, Ind., Dec. 24, 1959; s. Earl Hoyt and Sarah Helen (Bobo) H.; m. Nita Dawn Noblitt, Nov. 9, 1985. BS in Fin., Ind. U., 1983. Asst. v.p. Fidelity Fed. Savs. and Loan, Seymour, Ind., 1983; fin. dir. Devel. Services, Columbus, Ind., 1983-85, account coordinator, 1985-86; exec. dir. Jennings County Econ. Devel., North Vernon, 1986-88; dir. Columbus (Ind.) Econ. Devel. Bd., 1989—. Active Assn. for Retarded Citizens, North Vernon, Ind., 1983—, Jennings County Econ. Devel., North Vernon, 1985-88; head coach Hayden Elementary Girls and Boys Basketball, North Vernon, 1984-86; sec. bd. dirs. Jennings Community Hosp. Found., 1987-88. Mem. South Cen. Savs. and Loan League (v.p. 1983), Kappa Delta Rho (bd. dirs. 1984—). Baptist. Lodge: Kiwanis (treas. local chpt. 1985-86, pres. 1987-88). Home: 615 Riverside Cir Columbus IN 47201 Office: Columbus Econ Devel Bd 500 Franklin St Columbus IN 47201

HICKS, JAMES THOMAS, lawyer; b. Brownsville, Pa., June 5, 1924; s. Thomas A. and Florence Julia (O'Donnell) H.; m. Joanne Elliott, Aug. 25, 1950; children: Ellen, Mary Jo. AB, BS, MS, U. Pitts., 1946; PhD, George Washington U., 1950; MD, U. Ark., 1956; JD, DePaul U., 1975; LLM in Health Law, Loyola U., 1989. Bar: Ill. 1977, Pa. 1977, U.S. Dist. Ct. (no. dist.) Ill. 1977, N.Y. 1988, D.C. 1988, U.S. Supreme Ct. 1980, U.S. Ct. Appeals (D.C. cirs.) 1988, U.S. Dist. Ct. (no. dist.) Ill., 1988. Various teaching positions various colls., 1944-56; intern USPHS Hosp., Balt., 1956-57; resident VA Hosp., Pitts., 1958-60; pvt. practice River Forest, Ill., 1956—. Contbr. editor: Hosp. Mgmt. mag., 1956-70. Asst. surgeon USPHS, 1956-57. Recipient Outstanding Alumnus award De Paul U., 1980. Mem. ABA (com. on professionalism and ethics), Pa. Bar Assn., Ill. Bar Assn., Chgo. Bar Assn., Ill. Trial Lawyers Assn., Am. Trial Lawyers Assn., D.C. Bar Assn., Univ. Club, Elks, Moose. Office: 7980 W Chicago Ave River Forest IL 60305

HICKS, KEN CARLYLE, retail executive; b. Tulsa, Jan. 6, 1953; s. Harold I. and Patricia Ann (Carlyle) H.; m. Lucile Catherine Boland, June 22, 1974. BS, U.S. Mil. Acad., 1974; MBA, Harvard U., 1982. Commd. 2d lt. U.S. Army, 1974, advanced through grades to capt., resigned, 1980; assoc. McKinsey & Co., Dallas, 1982-83; v.p., chief operating officer All-Flow, Inc., Buffalo, 1984; sr. engagement mgr. McKinsey Co., Dallas, 1984-87; sr. v.p. May Dept. Stores Co., St. Louis, 1987—. Class agt. Harvard Bus. Sch., 1982—; co. exec. United Way, St. Louis, 1988. Mem. Media Club, Clayton Club, Harvard Club. Home: 250 N Price Rd Saint Louis MO 63124 Office: May Dept Stores Co Exec Offices 611 Olive St Saint Louis MO 63101

HICKS, PAUL B., JR., petroleum company executive; b. Norfolk, Va., Oct. 3, 1925; s. Paul B. and Maerose (Rausch) H.; m. Lucile Green, Nov. 28, 1953; children: Paul Burton III, Peter David, Thomas Patrick. B.A., U. Va., 1950. Sales rep. Texaco Inc., 1953-57, dist. supr. merchandising, 1957-60; dist. sales mgr. Texaco Inc., Chgo., 1960-62; asst. div. sales mgr. Texaco Inc., 1962; mgr. merchandising Texaco Inc., N.Y.C., 1962; div. sales mgr. Texaco Inc., Columbus, Ohio, 1963-65; asst. to pres. Texaco Inc., N.Y.C., 1965-66; gen. mgr. sales dept. U.S. Texaco Inc., 1966-69; v.p. sales dept. Texaco Inc., U.S., 1969-72; v.p. worldwide sales Texaco Inc., 1972-75, v.p. pub. relations and personnel, 1975-77, v.p. pub. relations and advt., 1977-83; pres. Texaco Europe, 1983—; sr. v.p. Texaco, Inc., 1986; pres., dir. Texaco Services (Europe) Ltd.; dir. Texaco Ltd. Mem. Zeta Psi. Clubs: Winged Foot Golf, Greenwich Country, Farmington (Va.) Country. Home: 3 Cornelia Dr Greenwich CT 06830 Office: Texaco Inc 2000 Westchester Ave White Plains NY 10650

HICKS, STEPHEN DALE, advertising and promotions executive; b. Greensboro, N.C., 1956; s. Earlie Ray and Celia Mae (Wright) H.; m. Angela Rhyne Connor, July 30, 1983; 1 child, Michael Allen. BBA, Cen. Wesleyan U., 1978. Salesperson Telma Electronics GMBH, Pfungstadt, West Germany, 1978-79, mgr. sales, 1979-81, pres., chief exec. officer, 1982-88; mgr. spl. markets, promotions Rios Werbung Gubh Off Duty Mag., Frankfurt, West Germany, 1988—; pres., chief exec. officer Delco Enterprises, Inc., Greensboro and Europe, 1984—; founder Reach UP Internat., Greensboro and Europe, 1984—; bd. dirs. ARCH Prodns., Inc., Greensboro and Europe, 1985—. Mem. Reps. Abroad, Frankfurt, West Germany, 1980—. Mem. Assn. U.S. Army, Am. Logistics Assn. (bd. dirs. exchange com. 1982—), Am. C. of C. Club: Protestant Men of the Chapel (West Germany). Home: Hildebrand Str 7, 6084 Gernsheim Federal Republic of Germany Office: Rios Werbung Gubh, Eschersheimer Landstr, 6000 Frankfurt Federal Republic of Germany

HICKS, TERRENCE HENRY, investment company executive; b. Phila., Mar. 16, 1952; s. William Henry and Charlotte (Jones) H.; m. Gail Elizabeth Brown, Dec. 5, 1976; children: Christian, Lauren. BA in Econs., Swarthmore Coll., 1973; MBA in Fin., La Salle U., 1980. Officer/br. mgr. Fidelity Bank, Phila., 1976-78; v.p. Alliance Enterprise Corp., Phila., 1979—; mem. bus. services adv. com. Advanced Tech. Ctr. Southeastern Pa., 1988—. Instr. Mt. Airy Learning Tree, Phila., 1980—; organizer N.W. Neighborhood Bus. Seminars, Phila., 1988. Mem. Delaware Valley Venture Group (bd. dirs. 1987—). Democrat. Lutheran. Home: 8223 Cedarbrook Ave Philadelphia PA 19150

HIDALGO, MIGUEL, legal administrator; b. Detroit, Nov. 10, 1958; s. Manuel and Ann (Molina) H. BA in Communications, Pepperdine U., 1981; postgrad. in Internat. Bus., Nat. U., 1988—. Owner Pacific Trans Service, Los Angeles, 1981-83; legal adminstr. Hidalgo & Assocs., Los Angeles, 1985—. Contbr. articles to profl. jours. With USN, 1983-85, with Res., 1986—. Mem. Am. Legal Adminstrs., Pepperdine Assocs., Huntington Library. Republican. Roman Catholic. Home: PO Box 80489 San Marino CA 91108 Office: Hidalgo & Assocs 5220 E Beverly Blvd Los Angeles CA 91108

HIDER, WILLIAM OLIVER, broadcasting company executive; b. Binghamton, N.Y., Oct. 1, 1946; s. Albert William and Doris (Grisham) H.; m. Barbara Ann Lubzanski, May 22, 1976; children: Brian Peter, Brittney Leigh. BS cum laude, Capitol Coll., Laurel, Md., 1973; MS, Johns Hopkins U., 1976. Lead engr. Westinghouse Electric Co., Balt., 1973-79; pres., chief operating officer CIRQTEL Inc., Kensington, Md., 1979-80; dir. mktg., planning Am. Satellite Co., Rockville, Md., 1980-81; dir. telecommunications USA Today, Arlington, Va., 1981-83, v.p. telecommunications, 1983-87; v.p. telecommunications Gannett Co., Inc., Arlington, 1987—; adj. prof. Capitol Coll., 1973-80; speaker, presenter to colls., industry, govt. orgns. on satellite communications, internat./domestic facsimile transmission, 1983—. Trustee Capitol Coll., 1984—. Served with USAF, 1966-70, Vietnam. Fellow Inst., Capitol Coll., 1982. Mem. IEEE, Soc. Satellite Profls. (chmn. edn. subcom. 1984). Republican. Episcopalian. Club: Potomac Valley Radio. Office: Gannett Co Inc PO Box 7858 Washington DC 20044

HIELSCHER, UDO ARTUR, educator; b. Ger., Oct. 23, 1939; s. Arthur Paul and Bertha Irmgard (Koehler) H.; Diplom Wirtschaftsingenieur, U. Darmstadt, 1964; Dr. rer. pol., 1968; m. Ursula Hartmann, Jan. 20, 1965. Prof. bus. adminstrn. and fin. Tech. Hochschule Darmstadt, 1971—, exec. dir. Inst. Bus. Adminstrn., 1982-84, dean Faculty of Law and Econs., 1985-86. Mem. European Fin. Assn., German Soc. Fin. Analysts, Soc. U. Profs. Mgmt. Sci., German Soc. Advt. Scis., Soc. German Engrs., Assn. U. Profs. in Germany. Author: Das optimale Aktienportefeuille, 3d edit., 1970, Finanzierungskosten, 1976; Innovationsfinanzierung Mittelstaendischer Unternehmungen, 1982; Historische Amerikanische Aktien, 1987; contbr. articles to sci. jours.; editor: Industrielle Kommunikation, 1978; also various newsletters. Office: 1 Hochschulstrasse, D 6100 Darmstadt Federal Republic of Germany

HIENTON, JAMES ROBERT, lawyer; b. Phoenix, July 25, 1951; s. Clarence J. Jr. and Lola Jean (Paxton) H.; m. Diane Marie DeBrosse, July 22, 1977. BA, U. Ariz., 1972; MBA, Ariz. State U., 1975, JD, 1975; LLM, Washington U., St. Louis, 1977. Corp. atty. Ariz. Pub. Service, Phoenix, 1975-76; asst. prof. Ariz. State U., Tempe, 1977; assoc. then ptnr. Gust, Rosenfeld, Divelbess et al, Phoenix, 1978-85; sr. tax ptnr. Evans, Kitchel and Jenckes, Phoenix, 1985—; bd. dirs. Ariz. Shoe Corp., Phoenix. Officer, bd. dirs. Charter Govt., Phoenix, 1978-82; mem. Phoenix Citizens Charter Rev. com., 1982; participant Phoenix Together, 1st Phoenix Town Hall, 1981, 2d Town Hall, 1982, 3d Town Hall, 1983, Town Hall recorder, 1983, 85; mem. Balanced Govt. com., 1983; dir. Phoenix Police & Fire Pension Bds., 1982—; bd. dirs. Ariz. Theatre Co., 1979—; class mem. Valley Leadership Class V, 1983-84; founding life mem. Ariz. Mus. Sci. and Industry. Mem. ABA, Ariz. Bar Assn., Maricopa County Bar Assn., Phi Kappa Phi. Republican. Club: Phoenix City. Home: 441 W McLellan Blvd Phoenix AZ 85013 Office: Evans Kitchel Jenckes PC 2600 N Central Ave 19th Fl Phoenix AZ 85004-3099

HIERONYMUS, LEONARD CHARLES, securities analyst; b. Jersey City, Sept. 26, 1941; s. Leonard C. and Frances (Mattice) H.; m. Janice Lee, June 5, 1964 (div. 1984); 1 child, Leonard C.; m. Wilma Bott, July 11, 1987. BA, Rutgers U., 1963; MBA, NYU, 1971. Bond analyst Mut. N.Y., N.Y.C., 1966-71, Conn. Mut. Life Ins. Co., Hartford, 1971-84, Unum Life Ins. Co., Portland, Maine, 1984—. Served to capt. U.S. Army, 1962-64. Office: Unum Life Ins Co 2211 Congress St Portland ME 04122

HIGBEE, DONALD WILLIAM, electronics company executive; b. Stonewall, Okla., Jan. 7, 1931; s. James W. and Nannie M. (Driver) H.; m. Joan M. Diamond; children: Bradley, Carter, Phillip, Lisa. AB cum laude, U. So. Calif., 1956, JD, 1962. Bar: Calif. 1963. Acct. Pacific Press, Inc., Los Angeles, 1956-60; sec., treas. Utah Research and Devel. Co., Salt Lake City, 1964; controller Interstate Electronics, Anaheim, Calif., 1960-63; dir. contracts Interstate Electronics, Anaheim, 1965-74, v.p., sec., 1974—, also bd. dirs. Bd. dirs. Silverado (Calif.) Water Dist., 1965-70, Silverado-Modjeska Recreation and Park Dist., 1965-70. Served with USMC, 1950-51, Korea. Decorated Purple Heart, 1951. Mem. Orange County Bar Assn., Nat. Contract Mgmt. Assn., Nat. Assn. Accts., Machinery and Allied Products Inst., Nat. Security Indsl. Assn., VFW. Republican. Lodges: Masons, Moose. Home: 3502 Cazador Ln Fallbrook CA 92028 Office: Interstate Electronics Corp 1001 E Ball Rd Anaheim CA 92803

HIGBY, EDWARD JULIAN, safety engineer; b. Milw., June 9, 1939; s. Richard L. Higby and Julie Ann (Bruins) O'Kelly; m. Frances Ann Knoodle, 1959 (div. 1962); 1 child, Melinda Ann Mozader. BS in Criminal Justice, Southwestern U., Tucson, 1984. Tactical officer Miami Police Dept., Fla., 1967-68; intelligence officer Fla. Div. Beverages, 1968-72; licensing coordinator Lums Restaurant Corp., Miami, 1972-73; legal asst. Walt Disney World, Lake Buena Vista, Fla., 1973-78; loss control cons. R.P. Hewitt & Assocs., Orlando, Fla., 1978-79; safety coordinator City of Lakeland, Fla., 1979—. Author: Safety Guide for Health Care, 1979. Bd. dirs. Tampa Area Safety Council, 1983—, Imperial Traffic Safety Council, Lakeland, 1983—; mem. Bay Lake City Council, 1974-76, mayor, 1975-76; bd. dirs. Greater Lakeland chpt. ARC, 1980-86, chmn. bd. dirs., 1983-84. 85-86, chmn. health services, 1980-86; mem. budget com. United Way Central Fla., 1983-85; mem. Fla. League Cities, 1974-76, Tri-County League Cities, 1974-76, Orange County Criminal Justice Council, 1974-78, Central Fla. Safety Council, 1978-79, Fla. Pub. Health Assn., World Safety Orgn.; mem. Polk County Disaster Coordination Com.; bd. dirs. Employers Health Care Group Polk County, 1987—. Served with U.S. Army, 1963-64. Named Vol. of Yr., Greater Lakeland chpt. ARC, 1983-84. Fellow Am. Biog. Inst. Research Assn., Internat. Biog. Assn.; mem. Fla. Sheriffs Assn. (hon. life), Internat. Assn. Identification, Internat. Assn. Identification (life, Fla. div.), Pub. Risk and Ins. Mgmt. Assn., Nat. Rifle Assn., Imperial Polk Mgmt. Assn., Fla. Fedn. Safety, Risk and Ins. Mgmt. Soc., Am. Soc. Safety Engrs. (chpt. pres. 1984-85, Safety Profl. of Yr. 1984-85), Heartland Safety Soc. (pres. 1983), Fla. Citrus Safety Assn. (pres. 1981-83), Nat. Fire Protection Assn., Am. Indsl. Hygiene Assn., Aircraft Owners and Pilots Assn. Republican. Club: Lakeland Rifle and Pistol. Avocations: hunting, fishing. Office: 1108 E Parker St Lakeland FL 33802

HIGGINS, JEFF DAVID, III, computer company executive; b. Freeport, N.Y., June 15, 1942; s. Jeff David Jr. and Anita Erma (Wyss) H.; m. Cecile Adelaide Cooper, Dec. 21, 1963; children: Timothy David, Michael Gregory. Assoc. in Applied Sci., SUNY, Farmingdale, 1963; BS, Utah State U., 1965; MBA, Pepperdine U., 1976. Programmer Boeing Corp., Seattle, 1965-66; project mgr. Ryan Aero., San Diego, 1966-69; product line mgr. Digital Equipment Corp., Maynard, Mass., 1969-80; v.p. Research Info. Corp., Denver, 1980-82, also bd. dirs.; v.p. Tolerant Systems, Santa Clara, Calif., 1982-83; pres. Ford Higgins Ltd., Longmont, Colo., 1983-87; founder, chief exec. officer Abraham Channing Co., Boulder, Colo., 1987—, also chmn. bd. dirs.; bd. dirs. Minesoft Ltd., Denver. Author: Start at the Top, 1973. Adv. bd. dirs. Tulane U., New Orleans. Lutheran. Home: 321 Gay St Longmont CO 80501 Office: Abraham Channing Co 2975 Valmont Rd Boulder CO 80301

HIGGINS, JOHN JOSEPH, corporate lawyer; b. N.Y., Feb. 6, 1934; m. Susan Maloney, Oct. 6, 1962; children: Timothy A., Sean P., Deirdre E. AB in English, Siena Coll., 1955; LLB, Fordham U., 1958. Bar: Mich. 1982. Atty. GM, N.Y.C., 1959-78, asst. gen. counsel, 1978-81; asst. gen. counsel GM, Detroit, 1981-88; gen. counsel GMAC, Detroit, 1983-88; v.p. gen. counsel Hughes Aircraft Co., L.A., 1988—; mem. Character and Fitness Com. appellate div. N.Y. Supreme Ct., 1978-85. Mem. ABA. Democrat. Roman Catholic. Home: 5739 Ridgebrook Dr Agoura Hills CA 91301 Office: Hughes Aircraft Co PO Box 45066 (CO1/A102) 7200 Hughes Terr Los Angeles CA 90045-0066

HIGGINS, KATHY JEANNETTE, educator; b. New Orleans, Mar. 17, 1948; d. Herbert Joseph and Irma M. (Sconza) H.; m. Terrence F. Verigan, Aug. 28, 1970. BA, U. New Orleans, 1970, MEd, 1979, 86. Cert. tchr., La. Tchr. Jefferson Parish Sch. System, Metairie, La., 1971-78; librarian St. Charles Pub. Sch. System, St. Rose, La., 1979-82; tchr. English Franklin Coll., New Orleans, 1985—. Mem. La. Nature and Sci. Ctr., New Orleans, Jefferson SPCA, Metairie. Allen J. Ellender fellow, 1973; named Outstanding Educator Jefferson Parish Sch. System, 1978. Mem. Am. Hist. Soc., La. Coun. Social Studies, Nat. Coun. for Social Studies, ALA, Phi Delta Kappa, Phi Kappa Phi, Delta Kappa Gamma, Beta Sigma Phi (treas. 1971, pres. 1972, Women of Yr. 1971). Roman Catholic. Office: Franklin Coll 1200 S Clearview Pkwy New Orleans LA 70123

HIGGINS, MARION WEST, real estate executive; b. New Rochelle, N.Y., Jan. 9, 1915; d. James E. and Marion West; m. William F. Higgins (dec. 1983); children: William F. Jr., Robert Kevin. BA in Polit. Sci., Mt. Holyoke Coll., 1937; postgrad., St. John's Coll., N.Y.C. 1942. Chmn. bd. Bill and Marion Higgins Realtors, Hillsdale, N.J., 1947—. Bd. dirs Orange and Rockland Utilities, Bergen County Roman Cath. Youth Orgn., 1987-88, Pascack Valley Hosp. Found., assembly-woman N.J. State Assembly, 1959, rep. majority leader, 1964, speaker of ho., 1965; trustee Penpac Commerce Industry, 1987—, Pascack Valley Hist. Soc., New Concepts for Living; v.p. Rep. Svc. Vol. Program, Bergen coun. Boy Scouts Am.; exec. bd. mem. Bergen County United Way, 1987-88; mem. steering com. Tribute to Women in Industry, 1987-88. Recipient Bronze Pelican Archdiocese Newark. Mem. Ind. Fee Appraisers, Woman's of Hillsdale, Woman's of Westwood, Coll. of Ridgewood, Mt. Holyoke. Home and Office: Werimus Rd & Van Emburgh Ave Hillsdale NJ 07642

HIGGINS, MICHAEL JOHN, consulting company executive, environmental manager; b. Adams, Mass., Feb. 22, 1944; s. John Edward and Shirley Marie (Baker) H.; m. Janet Marion Banas, June 18, 1966; children—Katharine Alane, Deirdre Ann, Jennifer Banas. B.S., U.S. Mil. Acad., 1966; M.S., MIT, 1968. Systems analyst U.S. Dept. Def., Washington, 1971-73; br. chief EPA, Washington, 1973-76; sr. v.p. Sci. Applications Internat. Corp., McLean, Va., 1976—; dir. JRB Architects, Inc., St. Louis. Pres. Kings Park Kings Glen PTA, Springfield, Va., 1976. Served to capt. U.S. Army, 1966-71. Decorated Bronze Star (3), Army Commendation medal. Mem. Assn. Environ. Professionals. Roman Catholic. Home: 8621 Nan Lee Dr Springfield VA 22152 Office: Sci Applications Internat Corp 8400 Westpark Dr McLean VA 22102

HIGGINS, THOMAS JAMES, publishing executive; b. Springfield, Ill., July 20, 1945; s. Thomas A. and Ruth B. (Quinlan) H. BA, St. Ambrose Coll., 1967; postgrad., Iowa State U., 1967-69. Exec. dir. Quint Cities Drug Abuse Council, Davenport, Iowa, 1971-73; mem. Iowa Gen. Assembly, Des Moines, 1973-77; regional dir. HEW, Kansas City, Mo., 1977-79; assoc. commr. Social Security Adminstrn., Washington, 1980; dep. sec. to Cabinet The White House, Washington, 1980-81; dir. Dept. Human Services, Portland, Oreg., 1981-84; pub. The Bus. Jour., Portland, 1984-85; chief operating officer Health Week Publs., Emeryville, Calif., 1985—; bd. dirs. Health Choice, Inc. Portland. Bd. dirs. United Way, Kansas City, Mo., 1978-79; bd trustees St. Luke's Hosp. Found., San Francisco, 1987-88; bd. advisors Ctr. Nat. Policy, Washington, 1981-88. Fellow European Econ. Community, Brussels, 1982, Aspen Inst., Colo., 1983, Carnegie Found., 1983. Democrat. Roman Catholic. Club: City (Portland) (bd. govs. 1985-86). Home: 400 Perkins St Apt 401 Oakland CA 94610 Office: Health Week Publs 2200 Powell St Suite 300 Emeryville CA 94608

HIGGINS, WILLIAM EDWARD, securities analyst; b. Newark, Jan. 18, 1945; s. Joseph Michael Higgins and Katherine (Benko) Higgins Manning. AB cum laude, Georgetown U., 1966; PhD, Harvard U., 1971; MBA, NYU, 1981. Asst. prof. classics Brandeis U., Waltham, Mass., 1971-79; asst. analyst, asst. dir. research Value Line, Inc., N.Y.C., 1981—. Author: Xenophon the Athenian, 1977; contbr. articles to profl. jours. Fellow Ctr. Hellenic Studies; mem. Nat. Assn. Petroleum Investment Analysts, N.Y. Soc. Security Analysts, Am. Philol. Assn. Republican. Roman Catholic. Office: Value Line Inc 711 3d Ave New York NY 10017

HIGGINS, WILLIAM WAUGH, commercial banker; b. Worcester, Mass., July 17, 1935; s. Kenneth Paul and Mary Regina (Waugh) H.; m. Eunice W. Olin, July 18, 1959; children: Barbara O., William W. Jr., Mary H., Richard W., Michael K., James S. B.A., Amherst Coll., 1957; M.B.A., Harvard U., 1959. Asst. treas. The Chase Manhattan Bank, N.Y.C., 1962-65, 2nd v.p., 1965-68, v.p., 1968-83, sr. v.p., 1983—; dir. Olin Corp., Stamford, Conn., 1964—. Home: 54 Byram Dr Greenwich CT 06830

HIGGINSON, JERRY ALDEN, JR., bank executive; b. Mt. Vernon, Ill., July 21, 1957; s. Jerry Alden Sr. and Beverly Joyce (York) H.; m. Leah Jane Murray, June 11, 1983; 1 child, Sara Elisabeth. BA, Graceland Coll., Lamoni, Iowa, 1979; postgrad., So. Ill. U., 1979; postgrad. sch. banking, So.

Meth. U., 1988. Trust officer, asst. cashier Salem (Ill.) Nat. Bank, 1979-80; trust officer MidAm. Bank and Trust, Carbondale, Ill., 1980-82; v.p., trust officer NBC Bank-San Antonio, 1982—; instr. Am. Inst. Banking, San Antonio, 1984—; mem. Estate Planners Coun., San Antonio, 1982—. Pres. San Antonio Symphony Soc., 1985-86; treas., pres. San Antonio Clean and Beautiful Com., 1986-87, pres. bd. dirs. 1987-88; pres. bd. trustees San Antonio Area Found., 1986-87; bd. dirs. Beautify San Antonio, 1987—, pres., 1988-89. Mem. Symphony Soc. San Antonio, San Antonio Baroque Music Soc., San Antonio Conservation Soc., Am. Inst. Banking. Republican. Mem. Reorganized Ch. Jesus Christ of Latter-day Saints. Club: Knife & Fork of San Antonio. Lodge: Rotary.

HIGGINSON, THOMAS JOSEPH, business educator; b. Fall River, Mass., May 18, 1940; s. Thomas Joseph and Susan Frances (Hall) H; B.S. cum laude, Boston Coll., 1962; M.B.A., Boston U., 1963, Ed.D., 1979; m. Anna M. Gardner, July 15, 1978; children—Matthew S., Christopher, Thomas. Prof. bus. adminstrn. Southeastern Mass. U., North Darmouth, Mass., 1963—, instr. div. continuing studies, 1965-83; pres., chief exec. officer A.M.C. Assocs., Westport, Mass., 1980-85; cons. Westinghouse, Stone & Webster Engring., E.H. Hinds, F.L. Collins, Gen. Electric, Perini Corp.; lectr., conductor seminars. Trustee pro-tem Millwright Local 1121, 1980-81; fish commr., Westport, Mass., 1972-73. Recipient Eagle Scout award, Order of Arrow award Boy Scouts Am.; Exec. Bd. award Arnold M. Dubin Labor Edn. Ctr., Southestern Mass. U., 1983. Mem. Am. Soc. Personnel Mgmt., New Eng. Soc. Personnel Mgmt., Nat. Bus. Educators Assn., Eastern Bus. Educators Assn., Assn. MBA Execs., Am. Mgmt. Assn., APICS, Nat. Assn. for Career Edn., Millwright and Machinery Erectors Local 1121, Am. Fedn. Tchrs., United Brotherhood Carpenters and Joiners, Laborers Internat. Union, Mass. Lobsterman's Assn., Beta Gamma Sigma. Clubs: K.C., Lions, Elks. Home: 145 Brayton Point Rd Westport MA 02790

HIGH, DENNY F., retail company executive; b. Milesburg, Pa., July 8, 1939; s. Francis and Ruth (Baine) H.; m. Alta Mae Ralston, Sept. 4, 1960; children: Mark, Kimera, Denise, Kent. Student, Franklin (Ind.) Coll., 1957-60; BS in Acctg., Bentley Coll., 1984. Dept. mgr. J.C. Penney Co., Richmond, Ind., 1962-68, Logansport, Ind., 1968-71; treas. B.L. Ogilvie & Sons Inc., Weston, Mass., 1971—. Advisor Emerson Hosp. Early Intervention Program, Concord, Mass., 1983—; mem. Weston Elderly Housing Com., 1985—. Mem. U.S. Assn. Evening Students (trustee, 1984—, Outstanding Service award, 1984), Bus. Roundtable of Boston (treas. 1985, pres. 1986), Am. Assn. for Adlut Continuing Edn., Smaller Bus. Assn. New Eng. Democrat. Baptist. Home: 510 North Ave Weston MA 02193 Office: B L Ogilvie & Sons Inc 39 Warren Ave Weston MA 02193

HILBER, ROBIN SHOMO, banker; b. Blue Island, Ill., Sept. 14, 1957; d. James Edward and Betty (Foist) Shomo; m. Gary James Hilber; children: Erin, C. Jordan, Jonathan, Justin. BS in Fin., Ind. U., 1980. Cert. fin. planner. Money ctr. officer Irwin Union Bank & Trust, Columbus, Ind., 1980-82, asst. v.p., 1982-84, v.p. investments, 1984-86, chief investment officer, 1986—. Fin. chmn. Ethnic Expo '88, Columbus. Mem. Indpls. Soc. Fin. Analysts, Columbus Area C. of C., Indpls. Econ. Club. Republican. Roman Catholic. Office: Irwin Union Bank & Trust 500 Washington St Columbus IN 47201

HILBOLDT, JAMES SONNEMANN, lawyer, investment advisor; b. Dallas, July 21, 1929; s. Grover C. and Grace E. (Sonnemann) H.; m. Martha M. Christian, Sept. 5, 1953; children: James, Katherine Ann Curtis, Susanna Jean, Thomas. AB in Econs., Harvard U., 1952; postgrad., U. Chgo., 1952-53; JD, U. Mich., 1956. With comml. and trust dept. No. Trust Co., Chgo., 1952-53; sole practice Kalamazoo, 1956—, pvt. practice as registered investment advisor, 1971—; bd. dirs. Lafourche Realty Co., Inc., Kalamazoo, pres., 1969—, dir., 1971—, Am. Nat. Holding Co., Kalamazoo, 1971-86, Hayes-Albion Corp., Jackson, Mich., 1975-86, 86—, Meijer, Inc., Grand Rapids, Mich., Old Kent Bank of Kalamazoo (formerly Am. Nat. Bank & Trust Co., Mich., 1966). Bd. dirs. Kalamazoo Tennis Patrons, Inc., 1974—, Downtown Devel. Authority, Kalamazoo, 1982-88, Downtown Tomorrow, Inc., Kalamazoo, 1985-88, Downtown Kalamazoo, Inc., 1988—. Served as sgt. USMC, 1946-48. Mem. ABA, Kalamazoo County Bar Assn., The Power Found. (sec., treas. 1967—), The W.P. Laughlin Charitable Found. (sec. 1967—). Clubs: Harvard (Kalamazoo, Grand Rapids) (pres. 1972-74), Kalamazoo Country. Home: 4126 Lakeside Dr Kalamazoo MI 49008 Office: Old Kent Bank Bldg 136 E Michigan Ave Ste 1201 Kalamazoo MI 49007-3936

HILBORN, JOHN R., insurance executive; b. Oak Park, Ill., Dec. 15, 1928; s. John T. and Evelyn N. (Newcomer) H.; B.A., DePauw U., 1951; M.B.A., Northwestern U., 1956; m. Shirley S. Butcher, Dec. 22, 1950; children—James, Janet, John, Jeffrey. Vice pres., treas. Easterling Co., Wheaton, Ill., 1959-63; tax mgr. Cory Corp., Chgo., 1963-68; v.p., treas. Page Engring. Co., Chgo., 1968-74; v.p. fin. and personnel Map Internat., Wheaton, Ill., 1974-77; dist. agt. Northwestern Mut. Life Ins. Co., Chgo., 1977—. Pres., LaGrange Highlands Civic Assn., 1957. Served to 1st lt. USMCR, 1951-53. Home: 32 Shawnee Trail Indianhead Park IL 60525 Office: 201 E Ogden Ave Ste 201 Hinsdale IL 60521

HILBY, PAULA BULLOCK, management consultant; b. Memphis, May 20, 1948; d. Leon and Robbie Lee (Stubblefield) Bullock; m. Bruce Titus Hilby, Oct. 28, 1975; children: Anne Titus, Edwin Joseph. Student, U. Miss., 1966-68; BA, Southwestern U., Memphis, 1971; JD, Memphis State U., 1975; postgrad., Ariz. State U., 1977-78; grad. in Pub. Ulitity Exec. Program, U. Mich., 1980. Bar: Ariz.; grad. Pub. Utility Exec. Program, U. Mich., 1980. Atty. law dept. Ariz. Pub. Service Co., Phoenix, 1976-79, mgr. gen. corp. services dept., 1980-81; asst. intergovtl. programs Office of Gov., Phoenix, 1982-83; v.p. Tierra Assocs., Ltd., Phoenix, 1984-86, Hillby & Co., Inc., Phoenix, 1986-87; exec. in residence Ctr. for Pvt., Pub. Sector Ethics, Ariz. State U., Tempe, 1984—; loaned exec. Mayor Terry Goddard, Phoenix, 1984-85. Active Ariz. Pub. Service Polit. Action Com.; sect. chmn. New Dimensions Campaign, Phoenix, 1983; mem. Jr. League Phoenix, 1981—; bd. dirs. Phoenix Symphony, 1980-81. Mem. ABA, Maricopa County Bar Assn. (corp. counsel sect. pres.-elect 1981), Valley Leadership Alumnae Assn. Democrat. Unitarian. Clubs: Phoenix Country, Plaza. Home: 6165 Mimulus PO Box 389 Rancho Santa Fe CA 92067 Office: Hilby & Co Inc 2700 N 3d St Phoenix AZ 85004

HILDEBRANDT, BRADFORD WALTER, consulting company executive; b. Elizabeth, N.J., Dec. 28, 1940; s. Walter Henry and Doris Ann (Zimmermann) H.; B.S., Rutgers U., 1974; postgrad. Pace U., 1975-76; m. Barbara Lynn Frisch, Apr. 29, 1966; children—Christine, Kenneth, Deborah. Adminstr. firm Shanley & Fischer, Newark, N.J., 1966-71; dir. adminstrn. firm. Reavis & McGrath, N.Y.C., 1971-76; chmn. bd., chief exec. officer Hildebrandt, Inc., Somerville, N.J., 1976—; faculty advisor Maryville Coll., St. Louis; dir. Allstate Legal Supply, Cranford, N.J., Served with USAF, 1961-65. Recipient N.Y. State Bar Assn. Spl. award for Edn., 1979. Mem. Assn. Legal Adminstrn. (life, founder, dir., past pres.). Lutheran. Author: Financial Management for Law Firms, 1975; The Successful Lawyer, 1983; columnist: New York Law Journal, 1974-84; contbr. articles to profl. jours. Home: 40 Timber Rock Trail Bernardsville NJ 07924 Office: 501 Post Office Pla 50 Division St Somerville NJ 08876-2943

HILDEBRANDT, FREDERICK DEAN, JR., insurance company executive; b. Upper Darby, Pa., Apr. 17, 1933; s. Frederick Dean and Ruth Taylor (Barry) H.; AB magna cum laude, Dartmouth Coll., 1954, MS, 1955. Engr. Eastman Kodak Co., Rochester, N.Y., 1957-60; systems mgr. J.T. Baker Chem. Co., Phillipsburg, N.J., 1960-63; asso. Booz, Allen & Hamilton Inc., N.Y.C., 1963-72, v.p., 1972-78; sr. v.p. Am. Ins. Assn., N.Y.C., 1978-81; v.p. Travelers Ins. Cos., Hartford, Conn., 1981-89; pres. Dean Hildebrandt & Assocs., Simsbury, Conn., 1989—; adminstr. All-Industry Rsch. Adv. Coun., 1979, dir., 1982-88 , vice chmn. bd. dirs. Workers Compensation Research Inst. 1987-88. With U.S. Army, 1955-57. Mem. Inst. Mgmt. Cons. (cert. mgmt. cons.), Am. soc. Assn. Execs., Soc. Ins. Rsch., Phi Beta Kappa. Home: 38 Lincoln Lane Simsbury CT 06070 Office: One Massaco Pl Simsbury CT 06070

HILFORD, LAWRENCE B., communications company executive; b. N.Y.C., June 17, 1934; s. Norman and Diana Hilford; m. Lynn Sherr, Jan. 11, 1980; children: Jeffrey, Andrew, James. BA, Yale U., 1955; MBA, Harvard U., 1959. Pres. Cartridge Rental Network, N.Y.C., 1972-73; exec. v.p. Viacom Internat., N.Y.C., 1973-77; sr. v.p. Columbia Pictures Industries, N.Y.C., 1979-81; pres., chief exec. officer Sta. CBS/Fox Video, N.Y.C., 1983-85; chmn., chief exec. officer Orion Home Entertainment Corp., N.Y.C., 1986—; adj. prof. program for interactive communications NYU, N.Y.C., 1984-87. Mem. adv. bd. Johns Hopkins U., Balt., 1986—. Office: Orion Home Entertainment Corp 711 5th Ave New York NY 10019

HILGER, FREDERICK LEE, JR., real estate executive, banker, lawyer; b. Dallas, Feb. 17, 1946; s. Frederick Lee Sr. and Maryann Taylor (Ayers) H.; m. Terri Lynn Wilson, May 13, 1984; children: Matthew Charles, Kristen Leigh. BA, U. Pacific, Stockton, Calif., 1967; JD, U. Calif., Berkeley, 1970. Bar: Calif. 1971. Sr. tax acct. Touche Ross and Co., San Francisco, 1971-73; atty. F. L. Hilger Prof. Corp., Eureka, Calif., 1973-75; mng. ptnr. Moses Lake (Wash.) Farms, 1975-78; sr. cons. Sites and Co. Inc., Seattle, 1978-79; v.p. ops. mgmt. U.S. Cruises, Inc., Seattle, 1980-83; pres., chief fin. officer First Nat. Bank, Chico, Calif., 1984-86; pres., chief exec. officer FreeHill Corp., San Marcos, Calif., 1986—. Recipient Outstanding Banker award Am. Bankers Assn. First Nat. Bank, 1984, 85. Mem. ABA, Calif. Bar Assn., Sacramento Bar Assn. Republican. Presbyterian. Clubs: Olympic (San Francisco), Shadowridge Golf. Office: FreeHill Corp Box 1808 San Marcos CA 92069

HILINSKI, ROBERT HARRY, data processing executive; b. Pitts., Aug. 7, 1957; s. Robert Harry and Louise Rose (Hensch) H.; m. Cheryl Lynn Fegely, Sept. 26, 1981; 1 child, Christopher Robert. BS in Info. Processing, Mansfield State U., 1979. Product specialist Pentamation Enterprises, Bethlehem, Pa., 1979-81; supr. Pentamation Enterprises, Bethlehem, 1981-82, account rep., 1982-85, mgr. customer support, 1986-87; mgr. data processing Cen. Bucks Sch. Dist., Doylestown, Pa., 1987—. Mem. Delaware Valley Assn. Sch. Bus. Ofcls. Republican. Methodist. Home: 762 Hawthorne Rd Bethlehem PA 18018 Office: Cen Bucks Sch Dist 315 W State St Doylestown PA 18901

HILL, ALFRED HUMPHREY, JR., financial and investment planner; b. San Antonio, Sept. 25, 1943; s. Alfred H. and Janet (Cory) H.; m. Jo Anne Miller, Aug. 15, 1970; children: Evan, Rachel, Scot. BBA in Mgmt., U. Tex., 1968; B in Acctg., U. Mont., 1972; chartered fin. cons., Am. Coll., 1985. CPA, Colo., Tex.; registered investment adviser. Tax staff mem. Touche Ross & Co., Denver, 1976-77; tax supr. Thomas, Head & Griesen, Fairbanks, Alaska, 1977-80; tax mgr. Thomas, Head & Griesen, Anchorage, 1980-82, Zlotnick, James & Co., Santa Fe, 1983; area coordinator personal fin. planning KMG-Main Hurdman, Odessa, Tex., 1983-86; sole practice San Antonio, 1986—; lectr. estate planning, fin. planning and investments, 1977—; instr. N.Y. U., 1989—. Author: Investment Survival and Growth. Bd. dirs. Grand Junction (Colo.) Pub. Sch. Dist., 1973, Fairbanks Cath. Schs., 1979-80; mem. Commonwealth North, Alaska, 1981-82; mem. Midland-Odessa Bus. and Estate Planning Council, v.p. 1985-86. Served with U.S. Army, 1963-66. Recipient Outstanding Service award Kiwanis, Fairbanks, 1980. Mem. Internat. Assn. Fin. Planners (v.p. Permian Basin chpt. 1985-86), AICPA (instr. personal fin. planning 1988). Republican. Home: 1723 Typhoon San Antonio TX 78248 Office: 1100 NW Loop 410 Ste 617 San Antonio TX 78213

HILL, ALLEN M., public utility executive; b. Dayton, Ohio, June 15, 1945; m. Chris Hill; children: Patricia, Brent. B.S. in Elec. Engring., U. Dayton, 1967, M.B.A., 1972. With Dayton Power & Light Co., 1965—, coordinator rate design, 1975-76, supr. gas services, 1976-78, mgr. planning, 1978-80, asst. v.p., 1980-81, treas., 1981-83, v.p., treas., 1983-86, group v.p., 1986-88, pres., chief ops. officer, 1988—. Treas. Miami Valley Coalition for Health Care Cost Effectiveness. Mem. Edison Electric Inst. Office: DPL Inc Courthouse Pla SW PO Box 1247 Dayton OH 45401

HILL, ARTHUR JAMES, bank executive; b. Jacksonville, Fla., July 4, 1948; s. Charmie Lewis and Patsy (Felder) H.; m. Charlene Taylor, Jan. 27, 1977 (div. Aug. 1984); 1 child, Lolita A. BBA in Econs., Fla. Meml. Coll., 1971; MA in Econs., U. Fla., 1983; diploma in banking, So. Meth. U. V.p. Southeast Bank, N.A., Miami, Fla., 1974-83; regional v.p. Amerifirst Fed. Savs. and Loan, Miami, 1983-84; pres., chief exec. officer, chmn. bd. Peoples Nat. Bank of Commerce, Miami, 1984—; Mem. Miami Herald Economist Bd., 1984—, State of Fla. Bus. Investment Bd., Tallahasse, 1985—; mem. econ. advisers bd. New Miami mag.; cons. econ. devel. U.S. Dept. Housing and Urban Devel. Bd. dirs. Biomedical Research Innovation Ctr., treas., 1985—; campaign co-chmn. United Way of Dade County, Miami, 1985-86, U.S. Paula Hawkins Re-Election, Miami, 1986; mem. Orange Bowl Com.; vice chmn. Fla. Transp. Commn.; mem. adv. bd. Dade County Ptnrs. for Youth, Miami, 1985—; co-chmn. steering com., mem. exec. com. of commerce and industry to elect George Bush pres.; mem. Fla. Electoral Coll.; del. Nat. Rep. Conv., 1988; trustee Barry U. Named Outstanding Young Man of Am., 1983. Mem. Econ. Soc. of S. Fla., Nat. Urban Bankers Assn. (bd. dirs. 1978-79), Nat. Bus. League (bd. dirs. 1985—), Miami Dade Urban Bankers Assn. (bd. dirs., pres. 1978-79, Leadership award), Beacon Council (exec. com., treas 1985—), Greater Miami C. of C. (exec. com. 1987—). Club: City (Miami). Home: 4830 NW 98th Pl Miami FL 33178 Office: Peoples Nat Bank Commerce 3275 NW 79th St Miami FL 33147

HILL, DAVID GARY, management information systems executive; b. Ishpeming, Mich., June 14, 1943; s. David Harris and Zona Rasminnie (Christensen) H.; m. Irene Beverly Borg, July 1, 1967. BS in Physics, S.D. Sch. Mines and Tech., 1965; MS in Indsl. Mgmt., MIT, 1967. Specialist mktg. system Data Gen. Corp., Southboro, Mass., 1975-76; mgr. quantitative mgmt. svcs. Data Gen. Corp., Westboro, Mass., 1976-81; dir. data systems, communications Data Gen. Corp., 1981-86, dir. facilities, ops. div., 1986-88, dir. info. resource mgmt. div., 1988—. Mem. Gov.'s Mgmt. Task Force, Boston, 1975. Mem. Ops. Rech. Soc. Am., Inst. Mgmt. Scis., Assn. for Computing Machinery, Westwood Sq. and Compass Club (Boston), Swedish Sq. and Compass Club (Boston), Masons (worshipful master 1982-83), Shriners. Republican. Congregationalist. Home: 26 Country Ln Westwood MA 02090 Office: Data Gen Corp 4400 Computer Dr Westborough MA 01580

HILL, DEANN GAIL, construction executive; b. Holyoke, Mass., Apr. 25, 1953; d. Cecil Arthur and Drema Aldene (Mundy) H. BA in Sociology, W.Va. State Coll., 1975; postgrad., W.Va. Coll. of Grad. Studies, 1980-85. Case worker Charleston (W.Va.) Guidance Clinic, 1975-77; social worker W.Va. Dept. Mental Health, Huntington, 1977; office mgr. C/D Hill & Son, St. Albans, W.Va., 1978-83, pres. mktg., 1986—; dep. clk. Kanawha County Circuit Ct., Charleston, 1984-86. Co-exec. dir. Kanawha Dem. Club, Charleston, 1987—; active W.Va. Symphony League, Charleston, 1987—, co-chair; active St. Francis Hosp. Aux., chair fundraising com., 1986-87. Mem. Contractors Assn. W.Va. (program com., legis. com., exposition com. 1988—), NAFE, W.Va. U. Alumni Assn. (sec. 1989—), Charleston Regional C. of C. (mem. legis. com.). Roman Catholic. Home and Office: Coal River Rd PO Box 226 Saint Albans WV 25177

HILL, DENNIS PATRICK, communications executive; b. Wilmington, Del., Jan. 28, 1960; s. James A. and Irene P (Kelly) H. BS in Engring., Marquette U., 1982, MSEE and Computer Sci., 1983, postgrad., 1986—. Research engr. Gen. Electric Co., Milw., 1981-82; computer scientist VA Med. Ctr., Wood, Wis., 1982-83, Med. Coll. Wis., Milw., 1982—; dir. computing services Milw. Sch. Engring., 1983-87, exec. dir. Sch. Industry and Govt. Relations, 1987-88, prof. electrical engring. and computer scis., 1984—, exec. dir. industry and govt. rels., 1987-88, v.p., 1988—; pres. Athletic Info. Systems, Milw., 1986—; tech. advisor High Tech. Specialists, Milw., 1984—, Bradford Computer Group, Skokie, Ill., 1983—; TV commentator on computer security for Milw. affiliates NBC, CBS, ABC, 1986—; cons. computer security Honeywell Fed. Systems, HBL-Can., HBL-U.K., 1986—. Author numerous articles. Advisor Milw. Sch. Engring. Explorers Post, 1985; pres. Parc Renaissance Assn., Inc., Milw., 1987—. Recipient Engring. Educator award, Falk Corp., Milw., 1985, Minority Affairs award Milw. Sch. Engring., 1987. Mem. Am. Soc. Engring. Edn. (exec. bd. north midwest sect.), IEEE (exec. bd. Milw.), Soc. Mfg. Engring., Computer and Automated Systems Assn. (program chmn. Milw. sect. 1985-87), Computer Security Inst., Milw. Urban League, Alpha Eta Mu Beta, Eta Kappa Nu, Triangle Frat. (advisor 1984). Republican. Roman Catholic. Lodge: Masons. Home: 4123 W Meinecke St Milwaukee WI 53210 Office: Milw Sch Engring PO Box 644 Milwaukee WI 53201

HILL, HOWARD EARL, liquidations executive; b. Miami, Fla., June 14, 1952; s. John Gibson Hill and Betty Louise (Elam) Nolet. Grad. high sch., Miami. Mgr. Harvey-Howard, Ltd., Miami Beach, Fla., 1983—. With U.S. Army, 1978-79. Democrat. Lutheran. Home: 6865 W Strickland St Douglasville GA 30134

HILL, JAMES EDWARD, insurance company executive; b. Chgo., Mar. 3, 1926; s. George and Mary Luella (Hutchens) H.; student Denver U., 1947; M.S. in Fin. Services, Am. Coll., Bryn Mawr, Pa., 1980; m. Jessie Mae Birmingham, Jan. 29, 1949; children—James R., Ellen M. Office mgr., purchasing agt., acct. Steve Tojek Co., Milw., 1948-54; office mgr., acct. Oreg. Athletic Equipment Co., Portland, 1954-56; spl. agt. Prudential Ins. Co., Portland, 1956-58, div. mgr., 1958-70; gen. agt. Gt. Am. Res. Ins. Co., Portland, 1970—; v.p. Robert A. Amey Co. Inc., mfrs. reps., 1971-75; pres. Diversified Plans, Inc., 1979—. Vice pres. Multnomah County Young Republicans, 1957-58; vice chmn. Washington County Parks Adv. Bd., 1978, chmn., 1979-83; instr. Life Underwriter Tng. Coun. Served with U.S. Army, 1944-47. Recipient Edgar M. Kelly award Prudential, 1967; C.L.U., chartered fin. cons., cert. fin. planner; Mem. Oreg. Life Underwriters Assn. (edn. chmn. 1981-82, pres.-elect 1982-83, pres. 1983-84), Portland Life Underwriters Assn. (dir. 1978-80, chmn. edn. com. 1978-80, pres. 1980-81, Am. Soc. C.L.U.s, (C.L.U. of Yr. award Portland chpt.; instr.), Am. Family Assn. (pres. Beaverton chpt. 1986—), Mem. Christian Ch. (elder). Home: 2045 NW Saltzman Rd Portland OR 97229 Office: Am Res Ins Co 6075 SW 124th Ave Beaverton OR 97005

HILL, JUDY ELLEN, CISA and EDP auditor; b. New Castle, Ind., June 8, 1955; d. Edward Nelson and Bercie Ruth (Sloan) H. AS in Bus. Data Processing, Fla. Jr. Coll., 1979; student, U. North Fla., 1980-82. Computer programmer Am. Heritage Life Ins. Co., Jacksonville, Fla., 1978-79, Peninsular Life Ins. Co., Jacksonville, 1979-80, SAV-A-STOP, Inc. div. Consolidated Foods, Orange Park, Fla., 1980-82; EDP auditor Fla. Nat. Banks, Jacksonville, 1982-83, The Charter Co., Jacksonville, 1983-84, Gulf Life Ins. Co., Jacksonville, 1984-87, First Union Nat. Bank of Fla., Jacksonville, 1987-89, CSX Corp., Jacksonville, 1989—; part-time reservations agt. Delta Air Lines, Jacksonville, 1985-87. Vol. ARC, Rota, Spain, 1975. Mem. Inst. Internal Auditors, Jacksonville Jaycees, Phi Beta Lambda (pres. Fla. Jr. Coll. chpt. 1978). Home: 7098 Beechfern Ln S Jacksonville FL 32244 Office: First Union Nat BAnk Fla PO Box 2080 Jacksonville FL 32231

HILL, LARKIN PAYNE, real estate company data processing executive; b. El Paso, Tex., Oct. 30, 1954; d. Max Lloyd and Jane Olivia (Evatt) H.; m. J. Franklin Graves, July 12, 1975 (div. July 1979). Student Coll. Charleston, 1972-73, U. N.C., 1973. Lic. real estate broker, N.C. Sec., property mgr. Max L. Hill Co., Inc., Charleston, S.C., 1973-75, sec., data processor, 1979-82, v.p. adminstrn., 1982—; resident mgr. Carolina Apts., Carrboro, N.C., 1975-77; sales assoc., Realtor, Southland Assocs., Chapel Hill, N.C., 1977-78; cons. specifications com. Charleston Trident Multiple Listing Service, 1985. Mem. Nat. Assn. Female Execs., Scottish Soc. Charleston (bd. dirs. 1989—), Preservation Soc., Charleston Computer Users Group, N.C. Assn. Realtors. Republican. Methodist. Avocations: reading, crossword puzzles, furniture restoration, T'ai Chi. Home: 7 Riverside Dr Charleston SC 29403 Office: Max L Hill Co Inc 632 Saint Andrews Blvd Charleston SC 29407

HILL, MARY LOU, small business consultant; b. Phila., July 8, 1936; d. Norman Findlay and Gladys Louise (Weigand) Tompkins; m. Ernest Clarke Hill Jr., Mar. 15, 1958; children: Sally, Holly, Randy, Chuck, Jim. Student, U. Miami, 1954-55, U. Okla., 1955-57; BBA, Portland State U., 1979, M in Taxation, 1982. CPA, Oreg. Staff acct. Fordham & Fordham, Hillsboro, Oreg., 1982-84; instr. Portland State U., Oreg., 1984-85; owner The Bookshelf, Sunriver, Oreg., 1985-88; instr. Cen. Oreg. Community Coll., Bend, Oreg., 1986, 88—; small bus. cons. 1988—. Mem. Oreg. Soc. CPAs, Kappa Kappa Gamma. Democrat. Christian Scientist. Home: PO Box 4574 Sunriver OR 97707 Office: PO Box 4574 Sunriver OR 97707

HILL, PAUL DRENNEN, lawyer, banker; b. Bklyn., Jan. 8, 1941; s. John Drennen and Margaret Henrietta (Gens) H.; m. Ann Kilbourne Patch, June 6, 1964; children: Hal Chase, John Andrew. BA, Williams Coll., 1962; LLB cum laude, Columbia U., 1966. Bar: Ga. 1966. Mgmt. asso. Time Inc., 1962-63; partner firm Gambrell, Russell & Forbes, Atlanta, 1970-75; sr. v.p., gen. counsel First Atlanta Corp., 1975-78, exec. v.p., chief fin. officer, 1978-85; exec. v.p. First Wachovia Corp., Atlanta, 1985-87; mng. ptnr. Hansell & Post, Atlanta, 1987-88; exec. v.p., chief operating officer Fed. Home Loan Bank of Atlanta, 1988—; bd. dirs. Builders' Transport, Inc., Camden, S.C.; adj. prof. Emory U. Law Sch., Atlanta, 1975. Mem. Met. Atlanta Crime Commn., 1984—; mem. bd. visitors Grady Meml. Hosp., Atlanta, 1983—; trustee Ga. Inst. Continuing Legal Edn., Atlanta, 1985—, St. Andrew's Sch., Middletown, Del., 1986-88, Paideia Sch., Atlanta, 1980-84; v.p., treas., trustee Atlanta Bot. Garden, 1979—; mem. fin. com., trustee Westminster Schs., Atlanta, 1985-87; chmn. devel. opportunities task force Cen. Atlanta Progress, 1983-84; rep. Williams Coll. Devel. Council, Williamstown, Mass., 1983-85; bd. dirs. Shepherd Spinal Clinic, Atlanta, 1983-84. Served with USAR, 1963-66. Mem. ABA, Am. Inst. Banking, Conf. Board (exec. conf.), Ga. Bar Assn. (chmn. corp. and banking law sect. 1974, mem. corp. counsel sect.), Atlanta Bar Assn. (chmn. continuing legal edn. com. 1981-82), Am. Bankers Assn. Congregationalist. Clus: Piedmont Driving (Atlanta). Office: Hansell & Post 3300 First Atlanta Tower Atlanta GA 30383-3101

HILL, RALPH JAY, automotive company executive; b. Poskin, Wis., July 19, 1932; s. Ralph John and Emma Cecelia (Carlson) H.; m. Patricia Anne Smithwick, Sept. 12, 1964; children: Susan, Steven. BBA, U. Wis., 1955. Jr. acct. A.O. Smith Co., Milw., 1957-59, budget analyst, 1960-64; acctg. supr. A.O. Smith Co., Ionia, Mich., 1964-67; div. controller Sheller-Globe Corp., Keokuk, Iowa, 1967-69; asst. corp. controller Sheller-Globe Corp., Detroit, 1969-72; corp. controller Sheller-Globe Corp., Toledo, 1972-75, v.p. and controller, 1975-86, sr. v.p. fin., chief fin. officer, 1986—. Bd. dirs. Arthritis Found., Toledo, 1987—; trustee Girl Scouts U.S., Toledo, 1979-82, Family Services, Toledo, 1976-80. 1st lt. U.S. Army, 1955-57. Mem. Fin. Execs. Assn. (bd. dirs. Toledo 1985—), Nat. Assn. Accts., Toledo Club, Sylvania (Ohio) Country Club. Home: 5347 Fox Run Toledo OH 43623 Office: Sheller-Globe Corp 1505 Jefferson Ave Toledo OH 43624

HILL, ROBERT WAYNE, utility executive; b. Richmond, Ind., July 10, 1927; s. H. Wayne and Kathryn G. (Weimer) H.; m. Bonnie J. Dishman, June 22, 1948; children: Robert W., Susan Jane Hill deArmendi. BSEE, Purdue U., 1951. Registered profl. engr., Ind. Engr. in charge elec. distn. Indpls. Power & Light Co., 1970-73, asst. v.p. engring. and constrn., 1973-77, v.p. transp. and distbn., 1977-79, sr. v.p. ops., 1979-80, exec. v.p., 1980-81, pres., chief operating officer dir., 1981—, chmn. bd., pres., 1989—; bd. dirs. Indpls. Econ. Devel. Corp.; bd. trustees N.Am. Electric Reliability Coun. Chmn. exec. bd. East Cen. Area Reliability Agreement, Canton, Ohio; bd. dirs. United Way Cen. Ind., Rose-Hulman Indpls. Bd. Assns. Served with USN, 1945-46. Mem. IEEE, Indpls. C. of C., Am. Mgmt. Assn. (pres.'s assn.), The Newcomen Soc. U.S., Ind. Electric Assn., Crooked Stick Golf Club, Columbia Club, Indpls. Athletic Club, Skyline Club, Greenfield Elks, Eta Kappa Nu. Office: Indpls Power & Light Co 25 Monument Cir Indianapolis IN 46204

HILL, W. CLAYTON, management consultant; b. New Hampton, Mo., Sept. 24, 1916; s. Charles A. and Elva E. (Riggins) H.; B.S. in Bus. Adminstrn., U. Mo., 1937; m. Dorothy L. Crosby, Aug. 24, 1938; children—Charles W., Douglas L. Acct., Gen. Elec. Co., Bridgeport, Conn., 1937-41; sales mgmt. IBM Corp., 1941-50; asst. to pres. Gen. Elec. X-Ray Corp., Milw., 1950-53; v.p. Hotpoint Co. div. Gen. Elec. Co., Chgo., 1953-57; mgr. planning Gen. Elec. Co., N.Y.C., 1957-62; dir. planning Am. Can Co., 1962-64; mgmt. cons. C. Hill Assocs., Greenwich, Conn., 1964-80, Prairie Village, Kans., 1980—; instr. Marquette U., 1950-53; cons. RCA Corp., Sperry Co., Ford Motor Co., Pet, Inc., Gen. Elec. Co., Monsanto Co., H&R Block, Inc., Farmland Industries, Inc., United Telecommunications, Inc., others. V.p. Somerset Manor; mem. adv. council Bus. Sch., U.Mo., City of Prairie Village. Served with Signal Corps, AUS, 1943-46. Decorated Army Commendation Medal. Mem. Am. Mktg. Assn., U. Mo. Bus. Sch. Alumni Assn. (Kansas City chpt. pres., Citation Merit award, Outstanding

Achievement and Meritorious Svc. award 1988, Faculty-Alumni award, Disting. Achievements 1988; W. Clayton Hill Innovator of GE Maxiservice award GE Med. Systems, 1989. Office: 8713 Catalina Dr Prairie Village KS 66207

HILL, WILLIAM HAYDON, management consultant; b. Alfreton, Derbyshire, Eng., May 30, 1925; came to U.S., 1958; s. Herbert A. and Doris (Siddown) H.; m. Dorothy M. Lockwood, Sept. 25, 1948; children: Stuart J., Richard A., Malcolm C., Gwendolyn M. Diploma, London Poly. Coll., 1944; FIMA, London Sch. Acctg., 1951; MBA, Harvard U., 1955. Controller Worrmalds & Walker Ltd., Dewsbury, York, Eng., 1950-58; asst. treas. Texton Inc., Providence, 1958-62; exec. v.p. P.H.H. Group, Balt., 1962-76; v.p. fin. Baker Industries Inc., Parsippany, N.J., 1976-77; pvt. practice mgmt. cons. Jacksonville, Fla., 1977—; bd. dirs. Carpco. Inc., Jacksonville, 1980-87. Served with RAF, 1944-47. Fellow Chartered Inst. Mgmt. Accts. Clubs: Menmack, Deerwood (Jacksonville); Ponte Vedra (Fla.). Home: 7841 Woodsdale Ln Jacksonville FL 32256 Office: 3100 University Blvd Jacksonville FL 32216

HILL, WILLIAM HENRY, JR., controller; b. Bennington, Vt., Sept. 8, 1954; s. William Henry and Mildred Jane (Tietjen) H.; m. Beverly Ann Koehler, Sept. 11, 1976; children: Katherine Ann, Andrew Scott. BS, Miami U., 1976. Controller East Weymouth (Mass.) Savs. Bank, 1976-78; asst. controller Vt. Fed. Bank, Burlington, 1978-84, asst. v.p., controller, 1985-86, v.p., controller, 1987—; controller Ea. Bancorp, Burlington, 1987—; mem. Loan Acctg. Devel. Com., Conn. On-Line Computer, Avon, Conn., 1985-87. Bd. dirs. Am. Diabetes Assn. Vt., 1985-87. Mem. Fin. Mgrs. Soc. Home: 197 River Rd Essex Junction VT 05452 Office: Vt Fed Bank 5 Burlington Sq Burlington VT 05402

HILLABRANDT, LARRY LEE, service industry executive; b. Amsterdam, N.Y., Apr. 5, 1947; s. Ronald Edward and Marion Alice (Smith) H.; B.S., Purdue U., 1969, M.S., 1971; m. Beverly Ann Johnson, Jan. 25, 1969; 1 son, Larry Lee. With Mobil Chem. Co., various locations, 1971-84, fin. analyst, Jacksonville, Ill., 1973, sr. systems analyst Macedon, N.Y., 1973-74, fin. analyst, 1974, plant controller, Frankfort, Ill., 1974-77, distbn. supt. NE region, Macedon, 1979-80, div. gen. mgr., Belleville, Ont., Can., 1980-84; bus./fin. mgr. George Heisel Corp., Rochester, N.Y., 1984-85; pres. ZIP Computer Systems, 1985—; owner, mgr. Datemate, 1985—. Mem. Purdue Alumni Assn., Krannert Grad. Sch. Alumni Assn., Mendon Community Orgn. (treas.), Scot-Grove Conservation Club, Zeta Psi Alumni Assn. Club: Lima Gun (bd. dirs.). Home: 53 Stoney Lonesome Rd Honeoye Falls NY 14472

HILLARY, E. MILES, marine engineer; b. Bklyn., Mar. 3, 1922; s. Edwin M. and Florence (Donaldson) H.; married, 1944; children: Sandra Lou Hillary Kunz, Donna Mrie Hillary Cipolla, Thomas Miles, Brendan Miles, Ryan Thomas. BS in Marine Engring., U.S. Mcht. Marine Acad., Kings Point, N.Y., 1943; postgrad., Hofstra Coll., NYU. Pres., chief exec. officer Hill-Pak, Inc., Aston, Pa., 1966—; vice chmn. Packaging Inst., Phila. Served to lt. (s.g.) U.S. Mct. Seamen, 1942-45. Republican. Presbyterian. Club: High 12 (pres. Media, Pa. chpt. 1988). Lodges: Masons, Shriners. Office: Hill-Pak Inc 2 New Rd Suite 301 Aston PA 19014

HILLAS, ROGER S., banker; b. 1927; married. A.B., Dartmouth Coll.; postgrad., Wharton Sch. Fin., U. Pa. With Provident Nat. Bank, Phila., 1951—, v.p., 1960-64, exec. v.p. coml. div., 1964-69, pres., chief adminstrv. officer, 1969-75, chmn. bd., chief exec. officer, 1975—, pres., from 1980; dir. Provident Nat. Bank (now PNC Fin. Corp.), Pitts., from 1973; pres. parent co. Provident Nat. Corp., 1969-75, chief exec. officer, 1973—, chmn. bd., 1975—, dir.; chmn., chief exec. officer Meritor Fin. Corp., Phila., 1988—; dir. Fed. Res. Bank Phila., Lease Financing Corp., P.H. Glatfelter Co., Goodall Co., Phila. Facilties Mgmt. Corp., Consol. Rail Corp., Provident Mut. Life Ins. Co. Treas., bd. overseers William Penn Charter Sch.; trustee Temple U. Office: Meritor Fin Group 1212 Market St Philadelphia PA 19107 also: Provident Nat Bank Broad & Chestnut Sts Philadelphia PA 19101 *

HILLE, STANLEY JAMES, university dean; b. New London, Minn., Mar. 19, 1937; s. Sigurd Munson and Jennie (Stromme) H.; m. Gail Anne Bekowies, Sept. 12, 1964; children: Erik, Peter, Kirsten, Julia, Jennifer. B.B.A. with distinction, U. Minn., 1959, M.B.A., 1962, Ph.D., 1966. Instr. U. Minn., 1962-65; asst. prof. Coll. Bus. and Mgmt. U. Md., 1965-71, prof., chmn. dept. transp., bus. and public policy, 1971-74; prof. transp. U. Ala., 1974-78; dean Coll. Bus. Adminstrn., Kent State U., 1978-81, Coll. Bus. and Public Adminstrn., U. Mo., Columbia, 1981-88; dean coll. bus. and pub. adminstrn. Fla. Atlantic U., Boca Raton, 1988—; cons. to fed. and state gys., pvt. firms; trustee Ctr. for Edn. in Pvt. Enterprise, 1986—; dir. Mo. Engring., Commerce Bank of Columbia;. Contbr. numerous articles to profl. publs. Recipient Teaching award U. Md., 1967; Norfolk and Western fellow, 1967; Gt. No. Ry. Found. fellow, 1974. Mem. Am. Soc. Traffic and Transp., Kent C. of C. (dir.), Delta Nu Alpha (Nat. Man of Yr. 1978). Lodges: Masons; Rotary. Office: Fla Atlantic U Coll Bus & Pub Adminstrn Office of Dean Boca Raton FL 33431

HILLENBRAND, DANIEL A., manufacturing company executive; b. 1923; married. Student, Purdue U. With Hillenbrand Industries, Inc., Batesville, Ind., 1946—, dir. purchasing, 1946-64, v.p., dir. mktg., 1964-69, pres. subs. Batesville Casket Co., 1969-72, chmn. bd., pres., chief exec. officer parent co., 1972-81, chmn. bd., chief exec. officer, 1981—, also dir. Office: Hillenbrand Industries Inc Hwy 46 E Batesville IN 47006 *

HILLER, STANLEY, JR., financial company executive; b. San Francisco, Nov. 15, 1924; s. Stanley and Opal (Perkins) H.; student Atuzed Prep. Sch., U. Calif., 1943; m. Carolyn Balsdon, May 25, 1946; children: Jeffrey, Stephen. Dir. Helicopter div. Kaiser Cargo, Inc., Berkeley, Calif., 1944-45; organized Hiller Aircraft Corp. (formerly United Helicopters, Inc.), Palo Alto, Calif., 1945, became pres. and gen. mgr., pres., 1950-64 (co. bought by Fairchild Stratos 1964), mem. exec. com. Fairchild Hiller Corp., 1965; chmn. bd., chief exec. officer Reed Tool Co., Houston, Nekins, 1980, York Internat., 1985; chmn. bd. Baker Internat. Corp., 1975, Levolor Lorentzen, Inc.; ptnr. Hiller Investment Co.; dir. Boeing Co. Recipient Fawcett award, 1944; Distinguished Svc. award Nat. Def. Transp. Soc., 1958; named 1 of 10 Outstanding Young Men U.S., 1952. Hon. fellow Am. Helicopter Soc.; mem. Am. Inst. Aeros. and Astronautics, Am. Soc. of Pioneers, Phi Kappa Sigma. Office: Hiller Investment Co 3000 Sand Hill Rd Bldg 2 Ste 260 Menlo Park CA 94025

HILLER, WILLIAM ARLINGTON, agricultural executive; b. East Stroudsburg, Pa., Jan. 15, 1928; s. John Jacob and Marguerite Laura H.; m. Joan Drake, June 2, 1947; children: William A., Joel, Jay S. BS cum laude, Upper Iowa U., 1950; MS, Pa. State U., 1952. Mgmt. trainee Agway Inc., Lakewood, N.J., 1951-53, retail store mgr., 1953-71; v.p. corp. mktg. Agway Inc., Syracuse, N.Y., 1971-73, group v.p., 1973-79, asst. gen. mgr., 1979-81, pres., chief exec. officer, 1981—; chmn. Texas City (Tex.) Refining Inc., also bd. dirs.; chmn. bd. Agway Ins. Co.; vice chmn., bd. dirs. Nat. Council Farmer Coops; bd. dirs. Syracuse Research Corp., Chase-Lincoln First Bank, Rochester; corp. adv. council Syracuse U. Sch. Mgmt. Trustee Crouse-Irving Meml. Hosp., Syracuse; trustee Upper Iowa U., Fayette; pres. Hiawatha Council Boy Scouts Am., Syracuse; mem. adv. council Cornell Coll. Agrl. and Life Scis; mem. FFA Sponsors' Adv. Bd.; nat. v.p. admnstrn. Boy Scouts Am. Recipient Silver Beaver award Boy Scouts Am., 1981, Silver Antelope award, Distinguished Citizen award. Mem. Alpha Zeta. *

HILLIER, J(AMES) ROBERT, architect; b. Toronto, Ont., Can., July 24, 1937; came to U.S., 1941, naturalized, 1961; s. James and Florence (Bell) H.; m. Barbara Ann Weinstein, Apr. 7, 1986; children by previous marriage—Kimberly (dec.), James Baldwin. BA, Princeton U., 1959, MFA, 1961. Project designer J. Labatut, Princeton, N.J., 1961-62; project mgr. Fulmer & Bowers, Princeton, 1966-72; prin. J. Robert Hillier, Princeton, 1966-72; pres. The Hillier Group, Princeton, 1972-87, chmn. bd., 1987—; dir. Howard Bank, Livingston, N.J., Harbor Island Devel. Corp., Tampa, Fla., Beneficial Corp., Peapack, N.J. Prin. works include Bryant Coll. campus, Smithfield, R.I., 1969, Rutgers U. Athletic Center, Piscataway, N.J., 1977, Butler Hosp, Providence, 1978, N.J. State Justice Complex, Trenton, 1985, Harbor Island Design, Tampa, Fla., 1981, Beneficial Corp. Complex, 1982, Merritt Tower, 1985, Wharton Sch. Exec. Ctr., 1986. Trustee Peddie Sch., Hightown, N.J., 1981—, McCarter Theatre, Princeton, 1983—. Recipient over 135 design awards from archtl. assns., 1966—; Architect of Yr. award N.J. Contractors Assn., 1976, 87, Disting. Service award Internat. Assn. Conf. Ctrs., 1988, Award of Excellence N.J. Bus. and Industry Assn., 1988. Fellow AIA (v.p. N.J. chpt. 1974); mem. Nat. Council Archtl. Registration Bds. Clubs: Princeton Quadrangle, Nassau (Princeton); Princeton (N.Y.C.). Home: 952 River Rd Washington Crossing PA 18977 Office: Hillier Group 500 Alexander Park Rd Princeton NJ 08540

HILLIKER, RICHARD MYRON, investment security dealer; b. Buffalo, Nov. 15, 1934; s. Donald Burwell and Mildred Angeline (Kieffer) H.; children—Karilea, Darla Jean, Christina Lynn, Nancy A. BA in Fin., Syracuse U., 1956. Salesman, Standard Register, Rochester, N.Y., and Freeport, Ill., 1958-65; registered rep. Doolittle & Co., 1965-68; pres. S.C. Parker & Co., Inc., Lockport, Ill., Elmira, Peekskill, and Rochester, N.Y., St. Petersburg, Fla., also bd. dirs.; treas., dir. Connohio, Inc.; v.p., dir. Tonawanda Share; pres., owner Can Oui Fly, Inc. Bd. dirs. Alcoholism Services of Erie County. Served with AUS, 1957. Mem. Nat. Assn. Securities Dealers (arbitration com.), Bond Club Buffalo (v.p., former bd. dirs.), Aircraft Owners and Pilots Assn., Nat. Rifle Assn. (life), N.Y. Christmas Tree Growers Assn., Syracuse U. Alumni Assn., Buffalo C. of C., Psi Upsilon Alumni. Clubs: Mid-Day of Buffalo, Springville Country, Aero (Western N.Y.). Office: 1031 Ellicott Square Bldg Buffalo NY 14203

HILLINGS, E. JOSEPH, energy company executive; b. Hollywood, Calif., Mar. 6, 1937; s. Edward John and Evangeline (Murphy) H.; m. Yvonne Fox, Jan. 4, 1969; children: Ann-Marie, Teresa, Valerie. AB, U. So. Calif., 1959. V.p. Washington affairs Nat. Airlines, Miami, Fla. and Washington, 1964-80; v.p. pub. affairs Continental Resources, Winter Pk., Fla., 1980-82; v.p. Washington affairs Fluor Corp., Washington, 1982-85; v.p. fed. govt. affairs Enron Corp., Washington, 1985—. Roman Catholic. Home: 3904 Colonel Ellis Ave Alexandria VA 22304 Office: Enron Corp 1020 16th St NW Washington DC 20036

HILLIS, NANCY CASPER, banker; b. Buffalo, Sept. 26, 1954; d. Robert and Dolores (Dick) Casper; m. Mark Hillis, Jan. 5, 1980. BA, Fla. State U., 1976. Mgmt. trainee Trust Co. Bank, Atlanta, 1976-77, comml. officer, 1977-79; sr. credit analyst Contel Credit Corp., Atlanta, 1980, dir. ops., 1981-82, v.p., 1982-84; asst. v.p. Bankers Trust Co. N.Y., Atlanta, 1984-86, v.p., 1986—. Mem. Fla. State U. Alumni Assn. (v.p. bd. dirs. 1987—). Office: Bankers Trust Co NY 133 Peachtree St Ste 3600 Atlanta GA 30303

HILLMAN, DONALD EARL, construction company executive; b. Sioux City, Iowa, Feb. 23, 1928; s. John Walter and Ione Ellen (Boggess) H.; m. Lei Lani Gene Shepp, Sept. 9, 1959; children: John Walter II, Darci Ann, Lance Randall. Student, Calif. State Coll., Los Angeles, 1969; MBA, Golden Gate U., 1971, Golden Gate U., 1976. Safety engr. power div. Bechtel Co., Joppa, Ill., 1953-54; safety engr. Pacific div. Bechtel Co., Masan, Korea, 1954-56; materials supr. Pacific div. Bechtel Co., Sumatra, Indonesia, 1957-59; purchasing agt. Concrete Structures Inc., Sioux City, 1959-60, G.W. Galloway Co., Baldwin Park, 1961-62; purchasing mgr. Arabian div. Bechtel Co., Benghazi, Libya, 1962-67; procurement mgr. Bechtel Co., San Francisco, 1968-70; procurement mgr. South Africa div. Bechtel Co., Johannesburg, 1970-71; field procurement mgr. England div. Bechtel Co., London, 1972-73; mgr. equipment, tool ops. Bechtel Co., San Francisco, 1974-76; v.p. equipment ops. Bechtel Co., Kuwait City, Kuwait, 1977-78, Manama, Bahrain, 1978-81; mgr. internat. equipment ops. Bechtel Co., Louisville, 1982—. Bd. dirs. Am. Sch., Lenghazi, Libya, 1964-66; mem. Ky. Cols., Louisville, 1981—. With U.S. Army, 1947-48. Mem. Assn. Constrn. Equipment Mgrs. (pres. 1988-89). Republican.

HILLMAN, STANLEY ERIC GORDON, former corporate executive; b. London, Eng., Oct. 13, 1911; came to U.S., 1951, naturalized, 1957; s. Percy Thomas and Margaret Eleanor Fanny (Lee) H.; m. May Irene Noon, May 2, 1947; children: Susan, Deborah, Katherine. Educated pub. schs., Eng. With Brit.-Am. Tobacco Co., Ltd., London, Shanghai, 1933-47; dir. Hillman & Co., Ltd., Cosmos Trading Co., FED Inc., U.S.A., Airmotive Supplies Co. Ltd., Hong Kong, 1947-52; v.p. Gen. Dynamics Corp., 1953-61; v.p., group exec. Am. Machine & Foundry Co., N.Y.C., 1962-65; v.p., dir. Gen. Am. Transp. Corp., 1965-67; pres., vice chmn., dir. IC Industries, 1968-78; bankruptcy trustee Chgo., Milw., St. Paul & Pacific R.R., 1978-79; dir. Bandag Corp., Conrail Corp., Axla Corp. Clubs: Chgo., Mid Am.; Onwentsia (Lake Forest, Ill.); Royal Poinciana. Home: 414 Thorne Ln Lake Forest IL 60045

HILLS, ALAN LEE, investment banker; b. Corning, N.Y., May 3, 1954; s. Donald M. and Velma J. (Weir) H.; m. Stephanie L. Miller, Dec. 15, 1984. BA in Acctg., U. South Fla., 1974; MBA in Fin., U. Pa., 1977. C.P.A., Fla. Asst. v.p. The Bank of N.Y., N.Y.C., 1977-79; v.p. E.F. Hutton & Co., N.Y.C., 1979-81, Prudential-Bache Securities, N.Y.C., 1981-84; mng. dir. First Interstate Cogeneration Capital Assocs., San Francisco, 1984-87; sr. mng. dir. Cogeneration Capital Assocs., Larkspur, Calif., 1987—, also bd. dirs. Contbr. (book) Creative Financing for Energy Conservation & Cogeneration, 1984. Scholar Shell Oil Found., 1975-76. Mem. No. Calif. Cogeneration Assn. (bd. dirs. 1975—). Office: Cogeneration Capital Assocs 80 E Sir Francis Drake Blvd Suite 2-A Larkspur CA 94939

HILLS, GEORGE BURKHART, JR., pulp and paper company executive; b. Jacksonville, Fla., July 17, 1925; s. George Burkhart and Anna Donna (McEnerny) H.; m. Sarah Anne Davis, Sept. 6, 1947; children: George Burkhart III, Barrett Davis, Sarah Kathryn (Mrs. William D. McLaughlin), Margaret Anne, Harland Andrew. B.Mech. Engring., Ga. Inst. Tech., 1946; B.Indsl. Engring., U. Fla., 1947, M.S. in Engring., 1949; postgrad., Advanced Mgmt. Program, Harvard Bus. Sch., 1972. With St. Joe Paper Co., Port St. Joe, Fla., 1949-50; with MacMillan Bloedel Ltd., Vancouver, B.C., Can., 1950-61; pres., chief exec. officer MacMillan Bloedel (USA) Inc., Stamford, Conn., 1974-77; with Stone Container Corp., Chgo., 1961-64, sr. v.p., 1977—; with The Continental Group, Inc., N.Y.C., 1964-73. Served to lt. (j.g.) USNR, 1943-46. Mem. TAPPI, Am. Paper Inst., Exmoor Country Club (Highland Park, Ill.), The Landings Club (Savannah, Ga.), Phi Delta Theta, Tau Beta Pi, Phi Kappa Phi. Republican. Episcopalian. Office: Stone Container Corp 150 N Michigan Ave Chicago IL 60601

HILLS, GORDON WESTON, JR., human services executive; b. Waco, Tex., July 14, 1944; s. Gordon Weston and Lula Mae (Hillman) H.; m. Jacquelyn L. Pugh, May 2, 1970; children: Danya C., Gordon Weston. AA, Corning Community Coll., 1970; BA, Elmira Coll., 1972; MA, Mansfield (Pa.) State U., 1979. Therapist Elmira (N.Y.) Psychiat. Ctr., 1972-76; youth program dir. Elmira Neighborhood House, 1976-79; regional health coordinator C.I.D.S., Elmira, 1979-81; exec. dir. Econ. Opportunity Program, Elmira, 1981—; cons. Psychiatric Youth Svcs., 1974-79; cons., trainee Human Svcs., 1972-81; mem. Comprehensive Interdisciplinary Developmental Svcs.; cons. in field. Pres. Family Support Svcs., Inc., 1981, Elmira Sch. Dist. Community Adv. Council, 1987—. Recipient Malcolm X award Corning Community Coll., 1975, Martin Luther King award Elmira Glove House, 1975. Mem. Nat. Assn. Community Action Agencies (bd. dirs.), Human Svcs. Health Care Assn. (pres. 1984-87), Community Action Program Dirs. Assn. (pres. 1986—), Nat. Community Action Found., Rotary. Office: Econ Opportunity Program 318 Madison Ave Elmira NY 14901

HILLSTROM, THOMAS PETER, program manager; b. Lakewood, Ohio, Apr. 20, 1943; s. Harry Edward and Mary Pauline (Mauss) H.; m. Jean Elizabeth Greenfield; children: Edward, Mary. BS in Mech. Engring., Northwestern U., Evanston, 1966; MBA, Northwestern U., Chgo., 1977. Design engr. Internat. Harvester, Hinsdale, Ill., 1966-74, project engr., 1974-78, product safety engr., 1978-82; mgr. engring. FMC, Tipton, Ind., 1982-85; mgr. contract engring. Fire Apparatus div. FMC, Mpls., 1985-87, program mgr., 1988—. Patentee in field. Mem. Soc. Automotive Engrs., Am. Soc. Quality Control, Human Factors Soc., Am. Soc. Agrl. Engrs., System Safety Soc. Republican. Home: 1635 Ranier Circle Plymouth MN 55447 Office: FMC Box 59043 Minneapolis MN 55459

HILMAN, ERIC, infosystems specialist; b. Phila., Aug. 5, 1954; s. Irving William and Sylvia Lilian (Arnold) H.; m. Sharon Ann Stotsky, Sept. 2, 1985; 1 child, Bruce Phillip. BSE, U. Pa., 1975, MS, 1978; MBA, Harvard U., 1980. Engr. Burroughs Corp., Paoli, Pa., 1975-78; product mgr. Prime Computer, Natlick, Mass., 1980-82, TKB Tech. Trading, Waltham, Mass., 1982; product line mgr. CSPI, Billerica, Mass., 1983-84; mktg. mgr. Apollo Computer Co., Chelmsford, Mass., 1984-88; mgr. Digital Equipment, Merrimack, N.H., 1988—. Mem. IEEE. Jewish. Home: 2 Windmere Dr Andover MA 01810

HILTON, ANDREW CARSON, manufacturing company executive; b. D'Lo, Miss., Nov. 20, 1928; s. A.C. and Pearl (Walters) H. B.A., U. Md., 1952; M.A., George Washington U., 1953; Ph.D., Western Res. U., 1956. Former research asso. Personnel Research Inst., Western Res. U.; cons. Psychol. Corp., N.Y.C.; dir. personnel relations Raytheon Co.; then dir. personnel Internat. Tel.& Tel. Corp.; sr. v.p. adminstrn. Colt Industries Inc, N.Y.C., 1963-83; exec. v.p. Colt Industries Inc, 1983—, also bd. dirs., 1985—. Contbr. articles to profl. jours. Corporate trustee Colt Industries Found. Served with USAF, 1946-49. Mem. Am. Psychol. Assn., N.Y. Acad. Scis. Club: University (N.Y.C.). Office: Colt Industries Inc 430 Park Ave New York NY 10022

HILTON, BARRON, hotel executive; b. 1927; s. Conrad Hilton. Founder, pres. San Diego Chargers, Am. Football League, until 1966; v.p. Hilton Hotels Corp., Beverly Hills, Calif., 1954; pres., chief exec. officer Hilton Hotels Corp., Beverly Hills, 1966—, chmn., 1979—, also dir.; mem. gen. adminstrv. bd. Mfrs. Hanover Trust Co., N.Y.C. Office: Hilton Hotels Corp 9336 Civic Ctr Dr Beverly Hills CA 90210 *

HILTON, GREGORY STEVEN, credit manager; b. Haleyville, Ala., Oct. 20, 1956; s. Lester E. and Luvena (Pickard) H.; m. Tracy Wells, Sept. 4, 1982. A in Sci., Walker Coll., 1976; BS in Bus. Adminstrn., Samford U., 1980. Sales rep. Life of Va., Birmingham, Ala., 1980-81; regional credit mgr. Baker Bros., Inc., Birmingham, Ala., 1981-86, corp. credit mgr., 1986—. Named one of Outstanding Young Men Am., 1985, Internat. Dir. Dist. Leadership, 1987. Mem. Nat. Inst. Credit (assoc.), Nat. Assn. Credit Mgmt., Internat. Platform Assn., Fla. Credit Council. Republican. Baptist. Home: 11640 Cape Horn Ave Jacksonville FL 32216 Office: Baker Bros Inc 7892 Baymeadows Way Jacksonville FL 32216

HIMEBAUGH, ARTHUR ELLIOTT, mining company executive; b. Hayden, Ariz., Feb. 28, 1925; s. Claude Edwin and Mary Elizabeth (Elliott) H.; m. Corrine Lee Westervelt, Aug. 26, 1946; children: Deborah Lee Himebaugh Wood, THeodore Arthur. Student, U. Ariz., 1942-43, No. Ariz. U., 1943-44, La. Poly. Inst., 1944-45; BS in Mining Engring., U. Ariz., 1950. Registered profl. engr., Ariz. Engr. Phelps Dodge Corp., Bisbee, Ariz., 1950-55; chief mine engr. Phelps Dodge Corp., Bisbee, 1955-62, chief engr., 1962-67, pit supt., 1967-69; mine supt. Phelps Dodge Corp., Tyrone, N.Mex., 1969-74; gen. supt. Phelps Dodge Corp., Tyrone, 1974-75, mgr., 1975-81, asst. gen. mgr., 1975-81; asst. gen. mgr. Phelps Dodge Corp., Phoenix, 1981-83, gen. mgr., 1983-85, v.p., gen. mgr., 1985—; prof. U. Ariz., 1965. Contbr. articles to profl. jours. Dir. Ariz. Acad., Phoenix, 1988—. With USMCR, 1942-46. Mem. Soc. Mining Engrs. (chmn. Ariz. conf. 1988—), Ariz. Profl. Mining Engrs., Theta Tau, Masons. Republican. Presbyterian. Office: Phelps Dodge Corp 2600 N Central Ave Phoenix AZ 85004

HIMELFARB, RICHARD JAY, securities firm executive; b. Balt., Feb. 3, 1942; s. Jacob and Jennie (Willen) H.; m. Margaret Conn, Sept. 7, 1969; children: Elizabeth Jayne, Michael Ross. BA, Johns Hopkins U., 1962; LLB, Yale U., 1965. Bar: Md., 1965. Employed, then ptnr. Weinberg & Green, Balt., 1967-83; exec. v.p. Legg Mason, Inc., Balt., 1983—, also bd. dirs.; bd. dirs. Phoenix Med. Tech., Andrews, S.C. Bd. dirs. Ctr. Stage, Inc., Balt., 1984—, Balt. Goodwill Industries, Balt., 1984—. Capt. U.S. Army, 1965-67. Mem. Phi Beta Kappa. Home: 116 Taplow Rd Baltimore MD 21212 Office: Legg Mason Inc 111 S Calvert St Baltimore MD 21202

HIMES, KENNETH ALAN, marketing executive; b. Phila., Nov. 2, 1937; s. Kenneth Elwood and Thelma Frances (Dieffenbacher) H.; m. Diane Margaret Zurinsky, Sept. 14, 1959; children: Christine Ann Himes Daly, Susan Leigh. BS in Bus., Lycoming Coll., 1959. With Woolrich (Pa.) Inc., 1959—, sales rep., 1960-85, sr. v.p. mktg., 1985—, also dir. Founder, sec. Woolrich vol. Fire Co., 1960; trustee Lycoming Coll., 1987—, Williamsport Hosp. and Med. Ctr., 1988—. Mem. Nat. Assn. Men's and Boys' Apparel, Somerset Hills Jaycees, Masons, Rotary. Republican. Methodist. Office: Woolrich Inc Mill St Woolrich PA 17779

HIMMEL, HANS BERNARD, service executive; b. Leipzig, Saxony, German Democratic Republic, Aug. 19, 1936; came to U.S., 1954; s. Alexander and Lisbeth Himmel; m. Julia M. Hainey, July 1955 (div. 1986); children: Robert H., Bonnie S., Connie L. Student, XII Oberschule, 1951-54. Gen. mgr. Holiday Inn, Warsaw, Ind., 1972-78; resident mgr. Holiday Star Resort, Merrillville, Ind., 1984, Bonaventure Resort/Spa, Ft. Lauderdale, 1984-86, Omni Internat. Hotel, Miami, Fla., 1986-87; gen. mgr. Sheraton Key Largo (Fla.) Resort, 1987—. Pres. Warsaw Exchange Club, 1981-82. Mem. Am. Hotel Motel Assn., Fla. Hotel Motel Assn., Adv. Council Tourism Devel. Com., Key Largo C. of C. Home: 4759 NW 98 Pl Miami FL 33178 Office: Sheraton Key Largo Resort 97000 S Overseas Hwy Key Largo FL 33037

HIMMELREICH, JANET KNAUFF, medical management consultant; b. N.Y.C., Mar. 1, 1954; d. Edward Franklyn and Carol Janet (Beinert) Knauff; B.A. cum laude, Gettysburg Coll., 1976; M.A., Lehigh U., 1977; M.B.A. in Health and Med. Services Adminstrn., Widener U. 1983; m. William Dickson Himmelreich, May 27, 1978; children; Allison Anne, Douglas Edward. Mktg. rep. Greater Delaware Valley Health Care Inc., Radnor, Pa., 1977-79; cons. for hosp. assoc. physicians Profl. Mgmt. Services Inc., Bala Cynwyd, Pa., 1979-84, sr. cons., 1984-86; prin. Consulting Mgmt., Inc., Wayne, Pa., 1986—. Mem. Gettysburg Coll.-Phila. Alumni, Delta Gamma-Phila. Suburban Alumni. Editor: PMS Mgmt. Update. Office: 940 W Valley Rd Ste 1202 Wayne PA 19087

HINCKS, MARCIA LOCKWOOD, insurance company executive, lawyer; b. N.Y.C., July 3, 1935; d. John Salem and Dorothy Elinor (Tufts) Lockwood; m. John Winslow Hincks, June 14, 1958; children—Rebecca Towne, Jennifer Winslow, John Morris, Benjamin Lockwood. B.A., Bryn Mawr Coll., 1956; LL.B., Yale U., 1959. Bar: Conn. 1960. Atty. Aetna Life & Casualty, Hartford, Conn., 1961-64, 67-70, counsel, 1970-81, v.p., ins. counsel, 1981—. Chmn. United Way Capital Area, Hartford, 1984-85; bd. dirs. Hartford Hosp., 1983—, Conn. Water Co., Clinton, 1983—; trustee Hotchkiss Sch., Lakeville, Conn., 1973-78, Hartford Coll. Women, 1978—. Recipient Community Service award United Way Capital Area, 1982, Alexis de Tocqueville award United Way of Am., 1987. Mem. ABA, Conn. Bar Assn., Assn. Life Ins. Counsel. Democrat. Congregationalist. Club: Hartford Golf. Office: Aetna Life & Casualty Co 151 Farmington Ave Hartford CT 06156

HINDE, EDWARD J., IV, financial consultant; b. Sandusky, Ohio, Feb. 18, 1947; s. Edward J. III and Clara (Tremper) H.; adopted s. Mildred Stang; m. Mary Jane Zinck, Aug. 21, 1976. BA, U. Dayton, 1970; MBA, Ohio State U., 1979. Corp. loan analyst Fidelity Bank, Phila., 1972-73; loan review officer Third Nat. Bank, Dayton, Ohio, 1973-76; asst. to pres. Franklin Bank, Columbus, Ohio, 1976-79; spl agt. Northwestern Mutual Life, Dayton, 1979-83; fin. officer Hiatt Agy., Dayton, 1983-86; prin. Hinde & Hinde, Dayton, 1986—. Mem. Nat. Assn. Accts. Lodge: K.C. Office: Hinde & Hinde 925 Malone Ave Dayton OH 45429

HINDERSMAN, CHARLES HENRY, university administrator; b. Cin., May 2, 1925; s. Charles Peter and Jennie (Van Agthoven) H.; m. Marilyn Justyn Neuhauser, June 14, 1952; children: Gretchen, Christie, Tania. BS in Econs., U. Pa., 1947; MBA, Miami U., Oxford, Ohio, 1954; DBA, Ind. U., 1959. Customer rep. Pitts. Plate Glass Co., Cin., 1947-50; sr. research analyst Shillito's, Cin., 1951-52; asst. dir. research Crosley Broadcasting Corp., Cin., 1952-55; asst. prof. Miami U., 1955-57, 59-60; prof. So. Ill. U., Carbondale, 1960—, dean coll. Bus., 1970-76, acting v.p. univ. relations, 1981-82, v.p. fin. affairs, 1984—; bd. dirs. Home Fed. Savs. & Loan Assn.,

Carbondale. Contbr. articles to profl. jours. Pres. Carbondale #165 Sch. Bd., 1968-76; mem. Gov.'s Comm. on Schs., Springfield, Ill., 1972-73. Served to ensign USN, 1943-46. Mem. Nat. Assn. Coll. and Univ. Bus. Officers, Coll. and Univ. Personnel Assn., Assn. Univ. Planners. Republican. Home: 101 N Lark Ln Carbondale IL 62901 Office: So Ill U Anthony Hall Rm 116 Carbondale IL 62901

HINDERY, LEO JOSEPH, JR., media company executive; b. Springfield, Ill., Oct. 31, 1947; s. Leo Joseph and E. Marie (Whitener) H.; m. Deborah Diane Sale, Feb. 20, 1980; 1 child, Robin Cook. BA, Seattle U., 1969; MBA, Stanford U., 1971. Asst. treas. Utah Internat., San Francisco, 1971-80; treas. Natomas Co., San Francisco, 1980-82; exec. v.p. fin. Jefferies & Co., Los Angeles, 1982-83; chief fin. officer A.G. Becker Paribas, N.Y.C., 1983-85; chief officer planning and fin. Chronicle Pub. Co., San Francisco, 1985-88; mng. gen. ptnr. InterMedia Ptnrs., San Francisco, 1988—; bd. dirs. Bay Area Bus. Devel. Co., San Francisco. Trustee Seattle U. Served with U.S. Army, 1968-70. Club: Olympic (San Francisco). Home: 99 Melanie Ln Atherton CA 94025 Office: InterMedia Ptnrs 235 Montgomery St San Francisco CA 94104

HINES, ANDREW HAMPTON, JR., utilities executive; b. Lake City, Fla., Jan. 28, 1923; s. Andrew Hampton and Louise Dixie (Howland) H.; m. Ann Groover, June 28, 1947; children: Andrew Hampton III, Elizabeth, John Bradford, Daniel Howland. BME with high honors, U. Fla., 1947; degree (hon.), Stetson U., 1987. Registered profl. engr., Fla. Research and devel. Gen. Electric Corp., 1947-51; chmn. bd. Fla. Progress Corp., St. Petersburg, 1982—; chmn. exec. com. of subs. Fla. Power Corp.; bd. dirs., exec. com. Citizens & So. Corp.; bd. dirs. Advanced Reactor Corp.; former chmn. N.Am. Electric Reliability Council; chmn. Com. on Utilities, U.S. Energy Assn.; bd. dirs. Fla. Council of 100. Bd. trustees, exec. com. Rollins Coll.; trustee Asbury Theol. Sem.; bd. dirs. Fla. Council Econ. Edn., U. Fla. Found., PRIDE of Fla.; mem. Fla. State Fair Authority, U.S. Constl. Bicentennial Commn. of Fla.. Served as 2d lt. USAAF, 1943-45; maj. Res. ret. Decorated Air medal, Prisoner of War medal. Fellow ASME; mem. Blue Key, Sigma Tau, Phi Kappa Phi, Tau Beta Pi, Beta Gamma Sigma. Methodist (lay leader and Sunday sch. tchr.). Clubs: St. Petersburg Yacht, Lakewood Country, Presidents (St. Petersburg); Citrus (Orlando, Fla.). Office: Fla Progress Corp 240 1st Ave S PO Box 33733 Saint Petersburg FL 33733

HINES, MICHAEL STEPHEN, auditor; b. Danville, Ill., Apr. 23, 1946; s. Chester G. and Carol E. (Brown) H.; m. Marilyn Kay Jackson, Dec. 12, 1965; children: Michael, Lori. BS, Purdue U., 1971, MS, 1976. Cert. data processing. Programmer Purdue U., West Lafayette, Ind., 1970-71; cons. Snyder Assocs., West Lafayette, 1971-73; coordinator data/research Purdue U., West Lafayette, 1973-75, systems analyst, 1975-77, mgr. devel., 1977-81, auditor electronic data processing, 1982—; mgr. devel. Oberlin (Ohio) Coll., 1981-82; ind. fin. counselor, tax preparer, 1986—; pres. Adminstrv. Bus. Cons. Inc., 1984-88; bd. dirs. Purdue Employees Fed. Credit Union, sec., 1988—. Budget com. Greater Lafayette United Way, 1989—. Served with U.S. Army, 1965-67. Mem. Electronic Data Processing Auditors Assn. (editor newsletter 1984-86, outstanding contributor 1985). Republican. Baptist. Home: 115 Circle Lane Dr West Lafayette IN 47906 Office: Purdue U Freehafer Hall West Lafayette IN 47907

HINES, V. C., newspaper marketing research executive; b. Los Angeles, Oct. 5, 1953; d. Bolden Eugene and Vivian Carrell (Burbridge) Hines. BA, UCLA, 1975, MBA, 1977. Cert. community coll. instr. With May Co., Los Angeles, 1977-84, mgr. regional newspaper advt., 1981-84; mgr. mktg. research project Los Angeles Times, 1984—; bus. seminar instr. Inroads, Inc., 1982-87. Mem. adv. bd. Dean's Council, UCLA Grad. Sch. Mgmt.; exec. advisor Jr. Achievement, 1983-84, tchr. bus. econs. jr. high sch., 1985-87. Named one of Outstanding Young Women Am., 1985. Mem. Am. Soc. Tng. and Devel., Nat. Black MBA Assn. (chair edn. com.), Black Women's Network (chmn. communications com.). Home: 3717 Bagley Ave Apt 111 Los Angeles CA 90034 Office: Mktg Rsch Dept Los Angeles Times Times Mirror Sq Los Angeles CA 90053

HINGORANI, SANJIV GOPAL, securities executive; b. Adipur, Gujarat, India, Jan. 6, 1960; s. Gopal Vasiomal and Krishna (Shahani) H. BSME, U. Bombay, India, 1981; MBA, U. Pa., 1983; postgrad., Stanford U., 1984-85. Cons. Anand & Assocs., Bombay, 1982; sr. prodn. control planner Intel Corp., Santa Clara, Calif., 1983-84, product mgr., 1984-85; tech. analyst Salomon Bros., Inc., N.Y.C., 1985-87, v.p., 1988—. Govt. of India scholar, 1975. Mem. Assn. Computing Machinery, IEEE (assoc.), Am. Soc. Mfg. Engrs., Toastmasters (Wharton pres. 1983), Wharton Grad. Assn. (chmn. student facilities com.). Home: 245 E 40th St Apt 11G New York NY 10016 Office: Salomon Bros Inc 1 New York Pla New York NY 10004

HINKLE, VERNON, JR., finance company executive; b. Hutchinson, Kans., May 4, 1938; s. Vernon Sr. and Florence (Gensman) H.; m. Patricia Ruth Haskard, July 23, 1961 (div. March 1983); children: Cynthia Nellie Hinkle McCoy, Kathleen Ruth. BA, U. Colo., 1960; postgrad., U. Kans., 1979. Cert. securites and real estate broker, Kans. Commd. 2d lt. USAF, 1960, advanced through grades to capt., 1972, resigned, 1971; pres., exec. v.p. Bankers Investment Co. subs. Security Pacific Corp., Hutchinson, Los Angeles, 1976; v.p. Security Pacific Co. Corp., Los Angeles, 1976-78; broker Coldwell-Banker, Hutchinson, 1978-80; prin. broker Hinkle Fin. Services, Hutchinson, 1980—; sec.-treas. Weavers Dept. Stores, Lawrence, Kans., 1982-88; dir. Hutchinson Nat. Bank, 1974-83. Mem. county and state Rep. steering com., 1960, Hutchinson Sch. Bd., 1974-78; mem. Rep. Nat. Com. Mem. Kans. Assn. Fin. Svc. Cons. (pres. 1968), Internat. Assn. Fin. Planners, Am. Indsl. Bankers Assn. (chmn. ops. com. 1968-69, AFC Merit Man 1963), Am. Legion, Young Pres.'s Orgn., Prairie Dunes Country Club (Hutchinson), Elks, Knights of Malta. Episcopalian. Office: Hinkle Fin Svcs P O Box 725 14 W Twelfth St Hutchinson KS 67504-0725

HINNANT, CLARENCE HENRY, III, health care executive; b. Richmond, Va., June 7, 1938; s. Clarence Henry Jr. and Billie Louise (Chewning) H.; m. Barbara Ann Livingston, June 10, 1966 (div. Feb. 1971); children: C.H. IV, W.W. Tuck. BS, Va. Poly. Inst. and State U., 1961; BS magna cum laude, Med. Coll. Va., 1981. Math. tchr. Hopewell (Va.) High Sch., 1961-64; staff mem. Harper & Row Pub., N.Y.C., 1964-67; stockbroker Merrill Lynch & Co., Richmond, Va., 1967-71; pres. Lancaster Corp., White Stone, Va., 1971-81; v.p., treas. Westminster Canterbury, Lynchburg, Va., 1981-89; pres. Westminster Canterbury of Blue Ridge, Charlottesville, Va., 1989—; faculty Am. Coll. Healthcare Adminstrn., Washington, 1982-84. Contbr. articles to profl. jours. Rep. del. to State Conv., Richmond, 1973. Fellow Am. Coll. Healthcare Adminstrs.; mem. Va. Assn. Non-Profit Homes for Aging (bd. dirs. 1983-84), S.R. Republican. Episcopalian. Club: Country of Va. (Richmond). Lodge: Kiwanis. Home: Bulltop Cabin Rt 4 Box 134 D-11 Lynchburg VA 24503 Office: Westminster Canterbury of Blue Ridge S Pantops Dr Charlottesville VA 22901

HINTIKKA, HARRI JUHANI, construction company executive; b. Helsinki, Mar. 27, 1937; s. Vaino Johannes and Maija (Kyrohanka) H.; m. Rita Anja Helena Oila, Aug. 28, 1965; children: Kari Juhani, Anja Kaarina. G-rad., Helsingin Suomalainen Yhteiskoulu Coll., Helsinki, 1955; MSc in Civil Engring., Helsinki U. Tech., 1961. Design engr. Henauer Lee, Zurich, Switzerland, 1961-62, STUP, Paris, 1962-63, Erkki Paloheimo & Co., Helsinki, 1963; tech. mgr. Elementtituote Oy, Helsinki, 1964-67; mgr., pres. Lemminkäien Oy, Helsinki, 1967-83; chmn., chief exec. officer Lemminkäien Oy, 1986—; pres. Polarrakennusosakeyhtio, Helsinki, 1983-86, chief exec. officer, 1986—; bd. dirs. KOP Bank, Pohjola Ins., Uusi Suomi Oy Pub., Finnish-Soviet Econ. Coun., Finn.-Stroi Oy, Scandinavian Link Finska Oy. Mem. Confedn. Finnish Industries, Assn. Gen. Contractors Finland, Assn. Finnish Fgn. Trade. Home: Lyokkiniemi 6, 02160 Espoo 16 Finland Office: Polarrakennusosakeyhtio, Pasilanraitio 9, 00240 Helsinki Finland

HINTON, GEORGE WASHINGTON, systems analyst; b. McLain, Miss., July 23, 1929; s. William Marcus and Mae Annis (McLeod) H.; m. Lorraine Marie Trombly, Nov. 8, 1952; children: Christopher Allan, Jessica Dianne. Student, U. Ill., 1960-61. Enlisted USAF, 1948, resigned, 1947, ret., 1967; systems analyst Boeing Co., Seattle, 1967—; pres., chief exec. officer Hinton Industries, Everett, Wash., 1980—. Mem., fund raiser Rep. Nat. Com., Washington, 1974—, Wash. State Dem. Party, 1980—. Mem. Am. Mgmt. Assn., Columbian Club (pres. 1973-82), KC (Grand Knight 1971-72). Roman Catholic. Home: 5116 Dogwood Dr Everett WA 98203

HINTON BLAKELEY, SHARLANE DIANE, transportation executive; b. Whittier, Calif., July 12, 1947; d. William Charles and Joyce Elaine (Anderson) F.; m. Donald H. Blakeley, May 10, 1986. BA, Calif. State U., 1970; MusM, Tex. Tech., Lubbock, 1976. Buyer Hughes Aircraft, Fullerton, Calif., 1978-81; supr. procurement Hughes Aircraft, Fullerton, 1981-87, acting procurement head, 1987—. Singer profl. concerts, 1986—. Mem. Hughes Mgmt. Club. Mem. Mu Phi Epsilon (pres. 1975-76). Home: 3003 Madison Ave Fullerton CA 92631

HINTSA, MARK LEROY, publishing company executive; b. Duluth, Minn., Dec. 31, 1955; s. LeRoy R. and Maria K. (Taimisto) H.; m. Moira Hearne, June 16, 1985. BS in Communications Mgmt., Ithaca Coll., 1978. Asst. dir. media Benton & Bowles Advt., N.Y.C., 1978-83; assoc. dir. media Lord, Geller, Federico, Einstein Advt., N.Y.C., 1983-85; group mgr. mktg. People Weekly Time Inc., N.Y.C., 1985-87, mktg. mgr. Life, 1987-89, dir. sales devel. Life, 1989—. Home: 25 W 68th St New York NY 10023 Office: Time Inc 1271 Ave of Americas New York NY 10020

HINTZ, BERND JURGEN, consumer goods manufacturing company; b. Tilsit, East Prussia, Fed. Republic Germany, May 3, 1942; came to U.S., 1954; s. Karl-Heinz Hintz and Elsbeth (Horn) Parr; m. Elizabeth Anne Fairbairn, June 11, 1969. BS in Physics, N.C. State U., 1964. Sales trainee, brand asst. Procter & Gamble, Ltd., Newcastle, Eng., 1964, mng. dir., 1979-83; brand mgr. Procter & Gamble Scandinavia, London, 1966-69, mgr. brand promotion, 1971-73; assoc. advt. mgr. Procter & Gamble Germany, Schwalbach, 1973-76; country mgr. Procter & Gamble Holland, Rotterdam, 1976-79; mgr. coffee div. Procter & Gamble Co., Cin., 1983-84, v.p. beverage div., 1984-86, group v.p., 1986—; bd. dirs. Food Industry Safety Council, Chgo., 1986—. Mem. U.K. Soap and Detergent Industry Assn. (chmn. 1980-83), Nat. Coffee Assn. (bd. dirs. 1983-86, advt. subcom. 1985), Am. Health Found. (trustee 1987—).

HINTZ, ROBERT LOUIS, transportation company executive; b. Chgo., May 25, 1930; s. Louis A. and Gertrude V. (Herman) H.; m. Gloria Mae Safbom, Nov. 12, 1955; children—Cary, Leslie, David, Erin. BS in Bus. Adminstrn. magna cum laude, Northwestern U., 1960, MBA, 1965. With Chessie System Inc., from 1963; internal audit officer C.&O. Ry., Cleve., 1963-65; staff asst. to v.p. C.&O. Ry.-B.&O. R.R., Cleve., 1965-68, asst. to v.p., 1968-70; compt. C.&O. Ry.-B.&O. R.R., Balt., 1970-72; asst. to pres. parent co. C.&O. Ry.-B.&O. R.R., Cleve., 1972-74, v.p. corp. svcs., 1974-76, v.p. fin., 1976-78, sr. v.p.-fin., 1978-80; sr. v.p. fin. CSX Corp., Richmond, Va., 1980-83, exec. v.p., 1983-88, ret.; pres., chief exec. officer Tex. Gas Resource Co.(subs.) (now CSX Energy Corp.), Richmond, 1985-88, ret.; chmn., chief exec. officer Sea-Land Corp., Edison, N.J., 1986—; also pres., chief exec. officer Rock Resorts, Inc.; chmn. bd. R.L. Hintz & Assocs.; bd. dirs. Scott & Stingfellow Fin., Inc., Chesapeake Corp., Reynolds Metal Co. Trustee St. Joseph's Villa; bus. adv. coun. Va. Poly. Inst., Va. Commonwealth U.; bd. assocs. U. Richmond. With USAF, 1950-54. Mem. Fin. Exec. Rsch. Found., Fin. Execs. Inst. Roman Catholic. Clubs: Commonwealth, Country Club of Va. Home: 10002 Walsham Ct Richmond VA 23233

HINZ, DOROTHY ELIZABETH, writer, editor, public relations executive; b. N.Y.C., Nov. 28, 1926. AB, Hunter Coll., 1948; postgrad., Columbia U. Copy editor Colliers mag., 1948-53; asst. to dir. devel. Columbia U., N.Y.C., 1953-55; mng. editor Grace Log, econs. researcher-analyst, writer speeches, white papers, com. reports Latin Am. affairs, public relations dept. W.R. Grace & Co., N.Y.C., 1955-64; staff writer Oil Progress, fgn. news media, speeches, films, internat. petroleum ops., pub. relations dept. Caltex Petroleum Corp., N.Y.C., 1964-68; fin. editor Merrill Lynch, Pierce, Fenner & Smith, 1969-74; asst. sec., mgr. publs., asst. speech writer, editor speeches and reports, corp. mktg. and communications dept. Mfrs. Hanover Trust Co., N.Y.C., 1974—. Contbr. articles on multinat. corps., developing nations, trade and fin. to various publs. Mem. Inter-Am. Round Table. Home: 600 W 115th St New York NY 10025 Office: Mfrs Hanover Corp 270 Park Ave New York NY 10017

HIPP, WILLIAM HAYNE, insurance and broadcasting executive; b. Greenville, S.C., Mar. 11, 1940; s. Francis Moffett and Mary Matilda (Looper) H.; m. Anna Kate Reid, June 14, 1963; children: Mary Henigan, Francis Reid, Anna Hayne. BA, Washington and Lee U., 1962; MBA, U. Pa., 1965; grad. mgmt. devel. program, Harvard U., 1971. With Met. Life Ins. Co., 1965-69; v.p. Liberty Life Ins. Co., Greenville, S.C., 1969-74, sr. v.p. investments, 1975-77, exec. v.p., 1977-79, chmn. bd. dirs., 1979-88; vice chmn., chief exec. officer Liberty Corp., Greenville, 1979-81, pres., chief exec. officer, 1981—, also bd. dirs.; bd. dirs. Textile Hall Corp., Cosmos Broadcasting Co., Dan River, Inc., S.C. Nat. Corp., Liberty Life Ins. Co., SCANA Corp. Trustee, vice chmn. Nat. Urban League, 1979—; trustee Com. Econ. Devel., Washington, 1988—, Greenville County Found., 1978-83, Episcopal High Sch., Alexandria, Va., 1982-88; chmn. Greenville YMCA, 1979; trustee Greenville County Sch. System, 1975, Washington and Lee U., Lexington, Va., 1985—, S.C. Fedn. Ind. Colls., 1984—; trustee, chmn. Alliance for Quality Edn., 1986—; bd. dirs. Am. Council Life Ins., 1979-83, S.C. State Devel. Bd., 1980-85, Spoleto Festival, U.S.A., 1984-88; bd. dirs. Greenville Urban League, 1971—, chmn. 1978. Mem. Greenville C. of C. (chmn. 1985). Office: Liberty Corp Wade Hampton Blvd PO Box 789 Greenville SC 29602

HIRAHARA, PATTI, public relations agency executive; b. Lynwood, Calif., May 10, 1955; d. Frank C. and Mary K. Hirahara. A.A., Cypress Coll., 1975; B.A., Calif. State U.-Fullerton, 1977. Pub. affairs dir. United Television, Los Angeles, 1977-80; v.p. Asian Internat. Broadcasting Co., Los Angeles, 1980-81; mktg. cons. Disneyland, Anaheim, Calif., 1982; pub. relations agt. Japan External Trade Orgn., Los Angeles, 1982-86, 87—; owner, pres. Prodns. By Hirahara, Anaheim, 1982—; comml. photographer Hirahara Photography, Anaheim, 1977-83; publicist Tokyo Met. Govt., 1981; advisor State Colo. Trade Mission to Japan, 1986, State Ariz. Trade/Investment Mission to Japan, 1987, County Riverside, Calif. for Japanese trade, investment, tourism, 1986-88; coordinator JETRO's Bus. Study Series, Los Angeles, 1988; advisor Japan External Trade Ordgn., 1987-88. Bd. dirs. Nisei Week Japanese Festival, Los Angeles, 1980-81. Nat. scholar Seventeen Mag. Youth Adv. Council, 1973; named Orange County Nisei Queen, Suburban Optimist Club, Buena Park, Calif., 1975, nat. semi-finalist Outstanding Young Working Women Competititon Glamour mag., 1983-84; recipient service award Suburban Optimist Club of Buena Park, 1975. Mem. Soc. Profl. Journalists (bd. dirs. 1980-81), Nat. Assn. Female Execs., World Trade Ctr. Assn. Orange County, Japanese Am. Citizens League, Am. Women in Radio and TV (bd. dirs. So. Calif. chpt. 1980-82, vice-chair western area conf. 1981), Alpha Gamma Sigma.

HIRANO, KEN-ICHI, metallurgist, educator; b. Hamamatsu-City, Japan, May 18, 1927; s. Etsuhei and Toki (Takabayashi) H.; B.Eng., Tokyo Inst. Tech., 1952; Sc.D., Hokkaido U., 1959; m. Tetsuko Kondo, Dec. 21, 1963; children—Mitsuko, Hiromi. Research asso. M.I.T., Cambridge, Mass., 1957-62; asso. prof. Tohoku U., Sendai, Japan, 1962-69, prof., 1969—, head dept. metallurgy and materials sci., 1971—; vis. prof. univs. including U. Tokyo, Tokyo Inst. Tech., Nat. Cheng-Kung U., Taiwan; also cons. Recipient Achievement award Japan Inst. Metals, 1970. Fellow Am. Soc. Metals; mem. Phys. Soc. Japan, Metal Soc. of AIME, Japan Inst. Metals (trustee), Sigma Xi. Club: Japan Polar Philatelist (pres.). Author: Metal Physics, 1975; editor Jour. Japan Inst Metals, 1971-72, 79-80, 82-83, 87—. Home: 7-5-13 Nakayama, Sendai 981 Japan Office: Dept Material Scis, Tohoku Univ, 980 Aoba Sendai Japan

HIRASAKI, MARSHA PARRISH, industrial sales company executive; b. Sullivan's Island, S.C., Oct. 27, 1945; d. Louis August Rohde and Ruth Ann (Hynes) Nelson; m. John Kiyoshi Hirasaki, Dec. 29, 1968; children: Kitt Nelson, Parrish Nelson. BSME, Duke U., 1967; MSME, U. Houston, 1971. Aerospace engr. TRW Systems, Houston, 1967-72; design engr. Nat. Maritime Research Ctr., Galveston, Tex., 1972-74; sales mgr. Cooper Valve and Fitting, Inc., LaPorte, Tex., 1974-76; pres., gen. mgr. Eurasia Valve Corp., Houston, 1976-79; gen. mgr. Masoneilan div. McGraw Edison, Houston, 1979-84; gen. mgr. Dresser Valve and Controls, Houston, 1985; pres., gen. mgr. Nelson Controls, Inc., Deer Park, Tex., 1985—. Mem. Instrument Soc. Am. (pres. chpt. 1982-83, internat. bd. dirs. 1986—), ISA Svcs., Inc. (chmn. bd. dirs. 1986—). Home: 931 Shady Oak Dr Dickinson TX 77539

HIRATA, GARY DEAN, securities industry executive; b. Seattle, Oct. 16, 1954; s. Satoshi and Meriko (Toda) H.; m. Yu-Shin Valentine, Jan. 8, 1977. BA in History, Yale U., 1976. Account exec. Smith Barney, Seattle, 1978-79, sr. account exec., 1979-80, 2d v.p., 1980-82, v.p., 1982-84; v.p., resident mgr. Smith Barney, Bellevue, Wash., 1984-87; 1st v.p., resident mgr. Smith Barney, Seattle, 1987-89, sr. v.p., resident mgr., 1989—. Mem. Security Industry Assn., Rainier Club. Office: Smith Barney 1301 5th Ave Ste 3229 Seattle WA 98101

HIRSCH, ALAN DAVID, mortgage company exective; b. N.Y.C., June 27, 1958; s. Emanuel M.H.; m. Renee Bowers, Sept. 13, 1987. MA in Exptl. Psychology, Central Wash. U., 1981; cert., Sch. Mortgage Banking, 1982. With mortgage div. Peoples Funding Corp., N.Y.C., 1980-82; account exec. Globe Mortgage Co., Hackensack, N.J., 1982-83; asst. v.p. Globe Mortgage Co., Hackensack and Trumbull, Conn., 1983-85; exec. v.p. Peoples Mortgage Bankers, New City, 1983-85; pres., dir. First Am. Mortgage Corp., New City, 1987—. Mem. N.J. Mortgage Bankers Assn., N.Y. Mortgage Bankers Assn., Conn. Mortgage Bankers Assn. Office: First Am Mortgage Corp 499 S Main St New York NY 10956

HIRSCH, BARRY, lawyer; b. N.Y.C., Mar. 19, 1933; s. Emanuel M. and Minnie (Levenson) H.; m. Myra Seiden, June 13, 1963; children—Victor Terry II, Neil Charles Seiden, Nancy Elizabeth. BSBA, U. Mo., 1954; J.D., U. Mich., 1959; LL.M., N.Y. U., 1964. Bar: N.Y. bar 1960. Assoc., then partner firm Seligson & Morris, N.Y.C., 1960-69; v.p., sec., gen. counsel dir. B.T.B. Corp., 1969-71; v.p., sec., gen. counsel Loews Corp. (and subsidiaries), 1971-86, sr. v.p., 1986—; bd. dirs. Manhattan Fund, Inc. Served to 1st lt. AUS, 1954-56. Mem. ABA, Assn. Bar City N.Y., N.Y. State Bar Assn., Zeta Beta Tau, Phi Delta Phi. Home: 1010 Fifth Ave New York NY 10028 Office: Loews Corp 667 Madison Ave New York NY 10021

HIRSCH, CARL HERBERT, manufacturing company executive; b. Pontiac, Mich., Aug. 24, 1934; s. Robert Reynolds and Charlotte (Zeiss) H.; B.S. in Mech. Engring., U. Mich., 1957; M.Indsl. Engring., U. Toledo, 1962, M.B.A., 1967; grad. Advanced Mgmt. Program, Harvard U., 1974; m. Anne Louise Dearing, June 27, 1959; children—Jeffrey Todd, Gregory Scott. Product engr. Babcock & Wilcox Co., Barberton, Ohio, 1959-60; product engr. Dana Corp., Toledo, 1960-67, mfg. mgr. Perfect Circle div., 1967-69, pres. C.A. Danaven subs. Dana Corp., Valencia, Venezuela, 1969-72, v.p. Latin Am. Dana Internat. div., Toledo, 1972-73, v.p., gen. mgr. Spicer Clutch div., Ft. Wayne, Ind., 1973-75, Spicer Universal Joint div., Toledo, 1975-76, group v.p. Dana Corp., 1977-78, exec. v.p. vehicular, 1979-80, v.p. corp. planning, 1980-85, sr. v.p., 1985—; instr. Earlham Coll., 1967-69, U. Toledo, 1962-65; mem. Machinery and Allied Products Inst. and Internat. Ops. Council; industry adv. com. Coll. Engring., U. Mich, U. Toledo. Bd. dirs. ATA Found., World Trade Ctr. Toldeo, Toledo Area council Boy Scouts Am., NW Ohio Jr. Achievement, Child Abuse Prevention Center, Toledo Zool. Soc., Maumee Valley Country Day Sch., Sta. WGTE-PBS. Served to lt. USN, 1957-59. Registered profl. engr., Mich. Mem. Nat. Mgmt. Assn., Sigma Alpha Epsilon. Presbyterian. Home: 4125 Nantucket Toledo OH 43623 Office: Dana Corp PO Box 1000 Toledo OH 43697

HIRSCH, LAURENCE E., lawyer; b. N.Y.C., Dec. 19, 1945; s. S. Richard and Lillian (Avenet) H.; m. Susan Judith Creskoff, Dec. 23, 1967; children: Daria Lee, Bradford Lyle. BS in Econs., U. Pa., 1968; JD cum laude, Villanova U., 1971. Bar: Pa. 1972, Tex. 1973. Assoc. Wolf, Block, Schoor, Solis Cohen, Phila., 1971-73; assoc., then ptnr. Bracewell & Patterson, Houston, 1973-78; pres. Southdown, Inc., Houston, 1977-85, chief exec. officer, 1984-85; pres. Centex Corp., Dallas, 1985-88, pres., chief exec. officer, 1988—; bd. dirs. NL Industries Inc., NL Chems. Inc., Envoy Corp. Served with USAR, 1968-75. Mem. ABA, Dallas Club. Office: Centex Corp 3333 Lee Pkwy Dallas TX 75219

HIRSCH, LEON CHARLES, medical company executive; b. Bronx, N.Y., July 20, 1927; s. Isidor A. and Roslyn A. (Magnus) H.; m. Irene Karpman, Apr. 8, 1949 (div. Dec. 1969); children: Thomas, Susan, Richard; m. Turi Josefsen. Dec. 24, 1969. Student, Bronx Sch. Sci., 1941-45. Chmn. bd., pres., chief exec. officer U.S. Surg. Corp., Norwalk, Conn., 1964—. Patentee surgical stapling devices. Chmn. adv. bd. Am. Soc. Colon and Rectal Surgeons Rsch. Found. Recipient Surgery award U. Geneva, 1970. Republican. Office: US Surg Corp 150 Glover Ave Norwalk CT 06856

HIRSCH, NORMAN ROBERT, engineer, consultant; b. Cambridge, Mass., May 14, 1944; s. Maurice Bear Hirsch and Evelyn Ruth (Meranus) Hirsch Aub; m. Hanifa Dahela Mezovi, Apr. 6, 1987; 1 child, Solvan Naim. B of Engring. Sci., Rensselear Poly. Inst., 1966; MS, U. Miami, 1971. Registered profl. engr., Wash., N.J. Sr. engr. Gen. Dynamics Electric Boat, Groton, Conn., 1974-78; sr. specialist engr. Boeing Co., Seattle, 1978-84, program mgr., 1982-84; dir. tng. Butler Tng. Ctr., Rahway, N.J., 1984-86; pres. Synergetics, Inc., N.Y.C., 1986—. Office: Synergetics Inc 333 E 79th St Ste 17-S New York NY 10021

HIRSCH, ROBERT ALLEN, lawyer; b. Phila., July 1, 1946; s. Leon Sidney and Harriet Roselyn (Benson) H.; B.S., Pa. State U., 1968; J.D., U. Akron (Ohio), 1974; m. Victoria Ingold, Apr. 23, 1977; 1 child, Courtney Benson. Claims rep. State Farm Ins. Co., Springfield, Pa., 1968-69; claims mgr. Ins. Placement Facility Pa. and Del., Phila., 1970-71; admitted to D.C. bar, 1974; atty. Bur. Enforcement, ICC, 1974-79; assoc. gen. counsel Am. Trucking Assns., Inc., Washington, 1979-87; gen. counsel, dir. govt. affairs Nat. Pvt. Trucking Assn., Washington, 1987-88; gen. counsel, dir. regulatory affairs Nat. Pvt. Truck Council, Washington, 1988—. Mem. bd. Hazardous Materials Adv. Council. Served with USAR, 1969-76. Mem. ABA, Assn. Transp. Practitioners (chmn. D.C. chpt.), Va. Bar Assn., D.C. Bar Assn., Phi Alpha Delta. Democrat. Home: 1540 Malvern Hill Pl Herndon VA 22070 Office: Nat Pvt Truck Coun 2200 Mill Rd Alexandria VA 22314

HIRSCHBERG, GARY EDWARD, computer company executive; b. Mt. Vernon, N.Y., Oct. 2, 1939; s. Sanford Leon and Helen (Felton) H.; m. Peggy Gropper Rosenberg, Nov. 16, 1968; children: Stacy Lynn, Amanda Ruth. BS in Naval Architecture, MIT, 1961. Head computer-aided design Hull Design br. USN Dept. Bur. Ships, Washington, 1961-66, M. Rosenblatt & Son, N.Y.C., 1966-68; pres. Marine Computer Applications Corp., N.Y.C., 1968-70; cons. systems analysis, N.Y.C., 1970-72; v.p. computer ops. Felton Internat. Inc., N.Y.C., 1972-76, v.p. prodn., 1976-82, sr. v.p. fragrance div., 1982-85, sr. v.p. ops., mem. exec. com., dir., 1985-88; chmn. ops. and controls steering group Felton Worldwide, 1986-88; pres. MacinTosh Bus. Systems, Inc., Mamaroneck, N.Y., 1988—. Author, contbr. MacUser mag. Mem. Coastal Zone Mgmt. Commn., Mamaroneck, N.Y. Recipient Superior Performance award USN Dept. Bur. Ships, 1964. Mem. U.S. Naval Inst. Clubs: Beach Point (Mamaroneck, N.Y.) (chmn. entertainment com., bd. govs.), Beach Point Yacht (bd. dirs., purchasing com., protest com., co-chmn.). Home: 3 Country Ln Mamaroneck NY 10543 Office: MacinTosh Bus Systems Inc 599 Johnson Ave Brooklyn NY 11237

HIRSH, NORMAN BARRY, helicopter company executive; b. N.Y.C., Apr. 20, 1935; s. Samuel Albert and Lillian Rose (Minkow) H.; m. Christina M. Poole, Sept. 21, 1957 (div. 1967); children: Richard Scott, Lisa Robin; m. Sharon Kay Girot, Dec. 29, 1973. BSME, Purdue U., 1956; cert. in mgmt., UCLA, 1980. Mech. engr. Ford Motor Co., Dearborn, Mich., 1956-58; design engr. Gen. Dynamics, San Diego, 1958-62; mech. engr. aircraft div. Hughes Tool Co., Culver City, Calif., 1962-65, project engr. aircraft div., 1965-69, engr. mgr. aircraft div., 1969-72; dep. program dir. Hughes Helicopters, Culver City, 1972-79, v.p., 1979-84; v.p., gen. mgr. Hughes Helicopters, Mesa, Ariz., 1984-85; exec. v.p. McDonnell Douglas Helicopter Co., Mesa, 1986—. Served with U.S. Army. Mem. Am. Helicopter Soc. (chmn. 1986-87), Assn. U.S. Army, Army Aviation Assn. Am., Am. Def. Preparedness Assn., Nat. Aeronautic Assn. Office: McDonnell Douglas Helicopter Co 5000 E McDowell Rd Mesa AZ 85205

HISER, HAROLD RUSSELL, JR., pharmaceutical company executive; b. Decatur, Ill., Oct. 21, 1931; s. Harold Russell and Dorothy Marie (Anderson) H.; m. Marguerite Lawrence West, June 20, 1961; children: Elizabeth

Lawrence, Samuel West, John Anderson. B.S.E., Princeton U., 1953. Treas. Inco Ltd., N.Y.C., 1972-77; controller 1977-79; v.p., treas. F.W. Woolworth Co., N.Y.C., 1979-81; sr. v.p. fin. Schering Plough Corp., Madison, N.J., 1981-85; exec. v.p. fin. Schering Plough Corp., Madison, 1986—. Office: Schering-Plough Corp 1 Giralda Farms Madison NJ 07940

HITCH, THOMAS KEMPER, economist; b. Boonville, Mo., Sept. 16, 1912; s. Arthur Martin and Bertha (Johnston) H.; m. Margaret Barnhart, June 27, 1940 (dec. Nov. 1974); children: Hilary, Leslie, Caroline, Thomas; m. Mae Okudaira. Student, Nat. U. Mexico, 1932; A.B., Stanford U., 1934; M.A., Columbia U., 1946; Ph.D., U. London, 1937. Mem. faculty Stephens Coll., Columbia, Mo., 1937-42; spl. study commodity markets Commodity Exchange Adminstrn., Dept. Agr., 1940; acting head current bus. research sect. Dept. Commerce, 1942-43; labor adviser Vets. Emergency Housing Program, 1946-47; economist labor econs. Pres.'s Council Econ. Advisers, 1947-50; dir. research Hawaii Employers Council, Honolulu, 1950-59; sr. v.p., mgr. research div. First Hawaiian Bank, 1959-82; chmn. Hawaii Gov.'s Adv. Com. on Financing, 1959-62; chmn. research com. Hawaii Vistors Bur., 1962-69; chmn. Mayor's Fin. Adv. Com., 1960-68; chmn. taxation and fin. com. Constl. Conv. Hawaii, 1968. Contbr. articles to profl. jours. Trustee Tax Found. of Hawaii, 1955-80, pres., 1968; trustee McInerny Found.; chmn. Hawaii Joint Council Econ. Edn., 1964-68. Served as lt. O.R.C., 1933-38; as lt. USNR, 1943-46. Mem. C. of C. Hawaii (chmn. bd. 1971), Nat. Assn. Bus. Economists, Am., Hawaii econs. assns., Indsl. Relations Research Assn., Am. Statis. Assn., Phi Beta Kappa, Pi Sigma Alpha, Alpha Sigma Phi. Clubs: Waialae Country (pres. 1979), Pacific. Home: 5329 Olapa St Honolulu HI 96821 Office: First Hawaiian Bank Honolulu HI 96847

HITCHCOCK, CHRISTOPHER BRIAN, computer and physical sciences research and development executive; b. Albany, N.Y., Aug. 1, 1947; s. John Dayton and Patricia (Blake) H.; BS in Econs. and Acctg., St. John's U., Collegeville, Minn., 1969; MS with honors in Logistics Mgmt., USAF Inst. Tech., 1975; m. Kathryn Anne Tufte, Dec. 27, 1970; 1 son, Jonathan David. Commd. 2d lt. U.S. Air Force, 1969, advanced through grades to capt. 1973; div. chief, dep. contracting, Hanscom AFB, Mass., 1977-79; sr. tech. rep. Analytical Systems Engring. Corp., Burlington, Mass., 1979-82, bus. devel. mgr., 1982-83, dir. contracts, 1983-84; sr. contracts mgr., Bolt Beranek and Newman, Inc., Cambridge, Mass., 1984-86, dir. contracts, 1986—; speaker, moderator seminars in field. Decorated Air Force Commendation medal (2). Cert. profl. contract mgr., profl. logistician, cost analyst, profl. estimator. Mem. Nat. Contract Mgmt. Assn. (chpt. dir.), Soc. Logistics Engrs., Order Daelalians, Tech. Mktg. Soc. Am., Armed Forces Communications and Electronics Assn. (chpt. dir.), Nat. Estimating Soc., Assn. Old Crows, Inst. Cost Analysis. Roman Catholic. Home: 49 Thomas St Belmont MA 02178-2438 Office: 10 Moulton St Cambridge MA 02238

HITTLE, RICHARD HOWARD, energy company consultant; b. Columbus, Nebr., Apr. 30, 1923; s. Arthur Howard and Frieda Margaret (Poppe) H.; m. Catherine Louise Dethlefsen, May 11, 1951; children: Ann-Louise, Thomas Woodford, Bradley Arthur. Student, Cambridge (Eng.) U., 1945; BS, U. Denver, 1950, LLB, 1951; MBA, Harvard U., 1955. With Conoco Inc., 1955—, mgr. internat. acquisitions, 1964-75; pres. Continental Overseas Oil Co., N.Y.C. also Stamford, Conn., 1969-75; gen. mgr., v.p. internat. govt. affairs Conoco, Inc., Stamford, 1975-83, Wilmington, Del., 1983-87; mem. adv. council Ctr. for Contemporary Arab Studies, Georgetown U., Washington. Mem. president's council on Near East studies NYU; trustee Beirut U. Coll. Served with AUS, 1943-46; with USAF, 1951-53. Mem. Asia Soc., Japan Soc., Norwegian Am. C. of C. (dir.), ANERA (dir.). Republican. Lutheran. Clubs: Harvard (N.Y.C.); Stanwich, Rocky Point (Greenwich, Conn.); Dorset Field. (Vt.); Metropolitan (Washington). Home: 3 Hendrie Dr Old Greenwich CT 06870 Office: PO Box 469 199 Sound Beach Ave Old Greenwich CT 06870

HO, LEO CHI CHIEN, education administrator; b. Tai Hu, An-Wei, Republic of China, Sept. 2, 1940; came to U.S., 1964, naturalized, 1971; s. Yu Yuan and Hung (King) H.; m. Julie Yu-Ling Hou, May 11, 1967; children: Albert, Alexander. BA, Nat. Cheng Chi U., Taipei, Republic of China, 1964; MLS, Atlanta U., 1967; PhD, Wayne State U., 1975. Libr. Tex. Tech U., Lubbock, 1966-69; dir. China Sci. Pub., Taylor, Mich., 1969-77; bus. libr. Detroit Pub. Libr., 1970-75; libr. Washtenaw Community Coll., Ann Arbor, Mich., 1977—; pres. Fin. Brokers' Exch., Farmington Hills, Mich., 1978-87; exec. dir. Sylvan Learning Ctr. Mich., West Bloomfield, 1987—; bd. dirs. Sylvan Learning Ctr. of Mich. Mem. adv. coun. Guide to Ethnic Mus., Librs., and Archives in the U.S., 1984. Bd. govs. Internat. Inst. of Greater Met. Detroit, 1985—; v.p. Mich. Gov.'s Adv. Com. on Asian Affairs, Lansing, 1986—; pres. Detroit Chinese Culture Svc. Ctr., 1984-86, 89—. Recipient Outstanding Svc. award Detroit Chinese Cultural Ctr., 1984, 88. Mem. Assn. Chinese-Ams. (v.p. 1985—, Dedicated Svc. award 1984, 88), Chinese Acad. and Profl. Assn. in Mid-Am. (bd. dirs. 1987—, Outstanding Svc. award 1988). Lodge: Rotary. Home: 3810 Manchester Ct Bloomfield Hills MI 48013 Office: Sylvan Learning Ctr 5755 W Maple Ste 115 West Bloomfield MI 48033

HOADLEY, WALTER EVANS, economist, financial executive; b. San Francisco, Aug. 16, 1916; s. Walter Evans and Marie Howland (Preece) H.; m. Virginia Alm, May 20, 1939; children: Richard Alm, Jean Elizabeth (Mrs. Donald A. Peterson). A.B., U. Calif., 1938, M.A., 1940, Ph.D., 1946; Dr.C.S., Franklin and Marshall Coll., 1963; LL.D. (hon.), Golden Gate U., 1968, U. Pacific, 1979; hon. degree, El Instituto Technologico Autonomo de Mexico, 1974. Collaborator U.S. Bur. Agrl. Econs., 1938-39; research economist Calif. Gov.'s Reemployment Commn., 1939, Calif. Gov.'s Reemployment Commn. (Planning Bd.), 1941; research economist, teaching fellow U. Calif., 1938-41, supr. indsl. mgmt. war tng. office, 1941-42; econ. adviser U. Chgo. Civil Affairs Tng. Sch., 1945; sr. economist Fed. Res. Bank Chgo., 1942-49; economist Armstrong World Industries, Lancaster, Pa., 1949-54; treas. Armstrong World Industries, 1954-60, v.p., treas., 1960-66, dir., 1962-87; sr. v.p., chief economist, mem. mng. com. Bank of Am. NT & SA, San Francisco, 1966-68; exec. v.p., chief economist, mem. mng. com., mem. mgmt. adv. council, chmn. subs. Bank of Am. NT & SA, 1968-81; ret. 1981; sr. research fellow Hoover Inst., Stanford U., 1981—; dir. Transcisco Industries, Inc., Selected Funds; dep. chmn. Fed. Res. Bank, Phila., 1960-61, chmn., 1962-66; chmn. Conf. Fed. Res. Chairmen, 1966; faculty Sch. Banking U. Wis., 1945-49, 55, 58-66; adviser various U.S. Govt. agys.; Wright Internat. Bd. Econ. and Investment Advisors, 1987—; spl. adviser U.S. Congl. Budget Office, 1975-87; mem. pub. adv. bd. U.S. Dept. Commerce, 1970-74; mem. White House Rev. Com. for Balance Payments Statistics, 1963-65, Presdl. Task Force on Growth, 1969-70, Presdl. Task Force on Land Utilization, Presdl. Conf. on Inflation, 1974; gov. Com. on Developing Am. Capitalism, 1977—, chmn. 1987-88. Mem. Meth. Ch. Commn. on World Service and Fin. Phila. Conf., 1957-64, chmn. investment com., 1964-66; bd. dirs., exec. com. Internat. Mgmt. and Devel. Inst., 1976—; trustee Pacific Sch. Religion, 1968—; adviser Nat. Commn. to Study Nursing and Nursing Edn., 1968-73; trustee Duke U., 1968-73, pres.'s assoc., 1973-80; trustee Golden Gate U., 1974—, chmn. investment com., 1977—; trustee World Wildlife U.S.-Conservation Found., 1974-87; mem. periodic chmn. adminstrv. bd. Trinity United Meth. Ch., Berkeley, Calif., 1966-84; mem. adminstrv. bd., advisor Lafayette (Calif.) United Meth. Ch., 1984—; mem. bd. overseers vis. com. Harvard Coll. Econs., 1969-74; chmn. investment com. Calif.-Nev. Meth. Found., 1968-75, mem., 1976-89; mem. Calif. Gov.'s Council Econ. and Bus. Devel., 1978-82, chmn., 1980-82; trustee Hudson Inst., 1979-84; co-chmn. San Francisco Mayor's Fiscal Adv. Com., 1978-81, mem. 1981—; spl. adviser Presdl. Cabinet Com. Innovation, 1978-79; mem. Calif. State Internat. Adv. Com., 1986—, Regent Designate, 1989—. Fellow Am. Statis. Assn. (v.p. dir. 1952-54, pres. 1958), Nat. Assn. of Bus. Economists, Internat. Acad. Mgmt.; mem. Am. Fin. Assn. (dir. 1955-56, pres. 1969), Conf. Bus. Economists (chmn. 1962), Atlantic Council of U.S. (dir. 1985—), Internat. C. of C. (vice chmn. commn. on econ. and fin. policy, trustee, chmn. com. on internat. monetary affairs U.S. council), Commonwealth Club of Calif. (pres. 1987), Internat. Conf. Comml. Bank Economists (chmn. 1978-81), Am., Western Econ. Assns., Am. Marketing Assn., Fin. Analysts San Francisco, Conf. Bd. (econ. forum), Am. Bankers Assn. (chmn. urban and community affairs com. 1972-73, mem. econ. adv. council 1976-78), Nat. Bur. Econ. Research (dir. 1965-81), Western Fin. Assn., dir., mem. steering com., U. Calif. Alumni Assn. (pres. 1989—, chmn. investment com. 1983-89), U.S. Nat. Com. on Pacific Econ. Cooperation (vice chmn. 1984-89), Phi Beta Kappa (dir. 1986—), Kappa Alpha. Clubs: St. Francis Yacht (San Francisco), Commonwealth (San Francisco), Pacific Union (San Francisco), Bankers (San Francisco); Silverado Country. Office: 555 California St Ste 500 San Francisco CA 94104

HOAGLAND, JAMES LEE, electrical distribution company executive; b. Oak Park, Ill., Nov. 2, 1922; s. Walter P. and Lola L. (Lee) H.; m. Florence E., Jan. 15, 1947; children: James, Edward, John, Peter. B.A., Colgate U., 1944. With Graybar Electric Co., 1946—; regional mgr. Graybar Electric Co., Chgo., 1972-75; v.p. Graybar Electric Co., 1975-78; exec. v.p. Graybar Electric Co., N.Y.C., 1979-80; pres., chief exec. officer Graybar Electric Co., 1980—, also dir.; bd. dirs. Centerre Bank N.A., Centerre Bancorp., Laclede Gas Co. Bd. dirs. St. Louis Symphony, United Way, St. Lukes Hosp., Arts and Edn. Council. Served with USNR, 1942-46. Clubs: St. Louis, Log Cabin, Old Warson Country. Office: Graybar Electric Co Inc PO Box 7231 Saint Louis MO 63177 also: Graybar Electric Co Inc 34 N Meramec Ave Clayton MO 63105

HOAGLAND, KARL KING, JR., lawyer; b. St. Louis, Aug. 21, 1933; s. Karl King and Mary Edna (Parsons) H.; m. Sylvia Anne Naranick, July 13, 1957; children: Elizabeth Parsons, Sarah Stewart, Karl King, III, Alison Thompson. B.S. in Econs, U. Pa., 1955; LL.B., U. Ill., 1958. Bar: Ill. 1958, U.S. Dist. Ct. (so. dist.) Ill. 1958. Of counsel Hoagland, Fitzgerald, Smith & Pranaitis, Alton, Ill., 1960-87; v.p., gen. counsel Jefferson Smurfit Corp., St. Louis, 1960—, also bd. dirs.; v.p., gen. counsel Container Cooperation of Am., St. Louis, 1986—; bd. dirs. Millers' Mut. Ins. Assn. Ill. Asst. editor: U. Ill. Law Forum, 1957-58. Trustee, treas. Monticello Coll. Found., 1965—. Served to 1st lt. USAF, 1958-60. Mem. ABA, Ill. Bar Assn., Madison County Bar Assn., Alton-Wood River Bar Assn., Order of the Coif, Beta Gamma Sigma. Republican. Episcopalian. Clubs: Lockhaven Country (Alton); Mo. Athletic (St. Louis). Home: PO Box 130 Alton IL 62002 Office: Jefferson Smurfit Corp 8182 Maryland Ave Saint Louis MO 63130

HOBACK, JOHN THOMAS, chemist, manufacturing company executive; b. La Crosse, Wis., Feb. 12, 1940; s. John Richard and Virginia L. (Thomas) H.; A.B., Gettysburg (Pa.) Coll., 1962; M.S., U. Md., 1966; m. Judy N. Zilker, Feb. 8, 1964; children—Amy N., Peter F. Research chemist, then venture mgr. high temperature composites Gen. Electric Co., Schenectady, 1966-71; market specialist electronic films Am. Hoechst Corp., Delaware City, Del., 1971-72; mgr. bus. analysis and fin. Riston div. duPont Co., Wilmington, 1972-78; mgr. strategic planning chems. group Air Products & Chems. Inc., Allentown, Pa., 1979-82; mgr. strategic planning electronics venture Rohm & Haas, Phila., 1982-83 , mgr. electronics, 1983-84; dir. mktg. EMCA subs Rohm & Haas, 1984-86, v.p. mktg., sales Electro-Kinetic System, Inc., Trainer, Pa., 1986-88; mgr. electronics Amoco Chemicals Co., Chgo., 1988—; bd. dirs. Electro-Kinetic Systems Inc. Sec., Lower Macungie Twp. (Pa.) Authority, 1982-88; bd. dirs. Shepherd Hills Civic Assn., 1982-86. Mem. IEEE, N.Am. Soc. Corp. Planning (v.p., pres. Phila. chpt. 1981—), Am. Chem. Soc., Internat. Soc. Hybrid MicroElectronics, Inst. Republican. Lutheran. Clubs: Lehigh Valley Aquatic (pres. 1980-84), Graylyn Crest Swim (pres. 1975-78). Patentee polymer chemistry. Home: 805 Shanahan Ct Naperville IL 60540 Office: Amoco Chemicals Co 200 E Randolph Dr Chicago IL 60601

HOBBS, CIA HUSTON, communications specialist; b. Charleston, S.C., Nov. 15, 1943; d. Clyde Ramsey and Mary Jo (Baxter) Huston; m. Howard J. Newman, Jan. 3, 1962 (div.); m. Robert George Hobbs, Oct. 14, 1966 (div. June, 1979); children: Michelle, Troy, Cindy, Tracy, Whitney, Amy, Pepper, Sarah. Art dir. Nashville Mag., 1965-67; cons. Home Builders Industry, San Diego, 1972; v.p., creative dir. Pickette, Hobbs & Dyal Inc., Jacksonville, Fla., 1978-79; creative dir. McElfresh & Assoc., Flagstaff, Ariz., 1979-81; founder, pres. Intrinsitec Inc., Jacksonville, 1981—; founder CIAgency, Jacksonville, Central Ark., 1984-87; writer, cons. William Cook Advy., Investment Banking, Jacksonville, 1987-88; cons. polit. pub. relations, Phoenix, 1979-81, Realestate Devel., Jacksonville, 1981-85. Author: Eclectic Ramblings of a Mad Housewife, The Posthumas Revelation of Ms. Callie McQuig; contbr. articles to profl. jour. Pres. Lutheran Sem. Women's Assn., Columbia, So. Carolina, 1975-78; bd. dirs. Mental Health Assn., Shenanodoah County, Va., 1978. Recipient Design Excellence award Advt. Council., Nashville, 1965, 66, 67, Creative Excellence award Advt. Assn., Jacksonville, 1978, Concept and Design award Advt. Assn. Ariz., Phoenix, 1980. Republican. Lutheran. Home and Office: 1104 2d St Neputune Beach FL 32233

HOBBS, GORDON ALAN, horticulturalist; b. Indpls., May 13, 1927; s. Frederick Robert and Helen June (Jones) H.; m. Martha Blake, Sept. 10, 1950 (div. Apr. 1973); children: Sherry Lynn, David Blake, Leslie Carol; m. Norma Lee Blanchard, Aug. 1, 1973. BS, Purdue U., 1949, MS, 1950. Laborer C.M. Hobbs & Sons Inc., Indpls., 1945-54, supt., 1954-75, treas., 1975-86, pres., gen. mgr., 1986—. Mem. exec. com. Cen. Ind. Better Bus. Bur., 1967-69. 1st lt. U.S. Army, 1952-54. Mem. Am. Assn. Nurserymen (bd. dirs. 1988—), Wholesale Nursery Growers Am. (pres. 1983-84), Ind. Assn. Nurserymen (pres. 1968), Indpls. Landscape Assn. (pres. 1961), Toastmasters, Lions, Elks. Republican. Baptist. Office: CM Hobbs & Sons Inc PO Box 31277 Indianapolis IN 46231

HOBBS, JAMES CALVIN, communications executive; b. Harlingen, Tex., May 1, 1938; s. Edward and Bessie Mae (Jackson) H.; student N.Mex. State U., 1955-57; B.J., U. Mo., 1959, B.A. in Math, 1961, M.A. in Journalism, 1961; m. Marijo Caposell, July 11, 1970; children—Rachel Elizabeth, Jared Charles. Publs. editor Trane Co., La Crosse, Wis., 1962-65; publicist Dow Corning Corp., Midland, Mich., 1965-68; account exec., account supr. Ketchum, McLeod & Grove, Pitts., 1968-72; exec. v.p. Dave Brown & Assos., Inc., Oak Brook, Ill., 1972-85; creative dir. Loran Nordgren & Co., Inc., Frankfort, Ill., 1985-87; creative supr., account exec. D.L. Arends Advt., Inc., Oak Brook, 1987—. Served with M.P., U.S. Army, 1962. Recipient Golden Quill award Pitts. Communications Assn., 1971. Mem. Soc. Tech. Communicators (chmn. Pitts. 1971-72), Public Relations Soc. Am., Am. Med. Writers Assn., Chgo. Headline Club, Profl. Photographers Am., Kappa Tau, Phi Alpha Mu, Sigma Alpha Epsilon, Sigma Delta Chi. Presbyterian. Club: Elks. Contbr. articles to profl. jours. Home: 3026 W 76th St Woodridge IL 60517 Office: D L Arends Advt Inc 1000 Jorie St Ste 224 Oak Brook IL 60521

HOBBS, JAMES DANIEL, sales manager; b. Cookeville, Tenn., Dec. 13, 1953; s. James Clarence and Sally Ann (Snyder) H.; m. Sue Marshall Massie, July 31, 1976; children: Sarah Montgomery, James David. BSCE, U. Va., 1975; MBA, Harvard U., 1980. Engr. Va. State Corp. Commn., Richmond, 1975-78; area sales mgr. Raychem, Birmingham, Ala., 1980-82; mktg. mgr. Raychem, Fuquay-Varina, N.C., 1982-84, bus. planner, 1984, production mgr., 1984-85; dist. sales mgr. Raychem, Phila. and Fuquay-Varina, 1985—. Republican. Baptist. Home: 5741 Dutch Creek Dr Raleigh NC 27606 Office: Raychem 2000 Regency Pkwy Cary NC 27511

HOBEN, MICHAEL FRANCIS, financial company executive; b. Torrington, Conn., Dec. 8, 1939; s. Francis Michael and Theresa M. (Bottazzi) H.; m. Elaine Kusako, Jan. 28, 1967 (div. Nov. 1984); children: Susan, Michael, Bradford. BA in Fin., Lehigh U., 1961, MS in Econs., Ariz. State U., 1965; postgrad. econs. PhD program, NYU. chartered investment counselor. Investment officer Chase Manhattan Bank, N.Y.C., 1965-68, 2d v.p., pension fund mgr. Chase Investors, 1968-73; v.p., sr. portfolio mgr. T. Rowe Price Assocs., N.Y.C., 1973-78; mgr. equity portfolios Exxon Corp., N.Y.C., 1978—, mgr. trust investments div., 1983-86; asst. treas. Union Carbide Corp., Danbury Conn., 1986—; pres. Benefit Capital Mgmt. Corp. (subs. Union Carbide Corp.), 1987—. Bd. dirs. Assisting Communities Toward Self-Help, West Palm Beach, Fla., Susan Fund, Westport, Conn. Served to 1st lt. USAF, 1961-65. Decorated Knight of Malta, Nat. Def. Service medal. Fellow Fin. Analysts Fedn.; mem. N.Y. Soc. Security Analysts, Nat. Options and Futures Soc., Investment Counsel Assn. Am., Squadron A Assn. Republican. Roman Catholic. Avocations: architecture, photography sailing, tennis, hiking. Home: 301 Post Rd E Westport CT 06880 Office: Union Carbide Corp 39 Old Ridgebury Rd Danbury CT 06817

HOBERMAN, ANTHONY, real estate and venture capital co. exec.; b. Cape Town, South Africa, Apr. 18, 1939; came to U.S., 1973, naturalized, 1981; s. Isaac and Sonia (Effman) H.; B.S., U. Cape Town, 1959, M.B.A., 1967; M.S., M.I.T., 1974; children—Nicole, Brent. Chief design engr. Plessey South Africa, 1959-66; mng. dir. Top Properties Ltd., Cape Town, South Africa, 1966-73; real estate investment officer Ford Found., N.Y.C., 1974-81; v.p. Alliance Capital Mgmt. Corp., N.Y.C., 1981—. Sloan fellow M.I.T., 1974. Mem. M.I.T. Enterprise Forum (dir.). Office: Alliance Capital Mgmt Corp 1345 Avenue of the Americas New York NY 10105

HOBLIN, PHILIP J., JR., securities company executive; b. S.I., N.Y., July 31, 1929; s. Philip J. and Mary A. (Brown) H.; m. Eileen P. Killilea, Jan. 10, 1959; children: Philip, Monica, Michael. BS, Fordham U., 1951, LLD, 1957. Bar: N.Y. 1957. Regional atty. Bache & Co., N.Y.C., 1958-63; exec. v.p. Shearson Lehman Hutton, Inc., 1963-89; co-chmn. Inst. Fin. Law Ctr., N.Y.C., 1972—; of counsel Gaston & Snow, 1989—; adj. prof. law Fordham U.; mem. Joint Industry Com. Securities Protection, 1969; mem. bd. arbitration N.Y. Stock Exchange; chmn. arbitration com. Chgo. Bd. Options Exchange, 1977-78, mem. conduct com., 1979-80; mem. exec. and nat. arbitration coms. Nat. Assn. Securities Dealers, 1984-85, also mem. bus. conduct com. dist. 12, 1974-77; mem. Securities Industry Conf. on Arbitration, 1977—. Author: Securities Arbitration: Procedures, Strategies and Cases, 1988, also law rev. articles. Bd. advisers Xavier High Sch., N.Y.C., 1969; pres. Sons of Xavier, 1977-79; trustee Village of Suffern, N.Y., 1985-89. Served as spl. agt. USAF, 1951-53; col. Res. (ret.). Mem. Security Industry Assn. (pres. compliance div. 1970-72), ABA, N.Y. County Lawyers Assn., Am. Legion, Res. Officers Assn. (v.p. air N.Y. State chpt. 1973-74, 87-88, pub. rels. sec. judge adv. gen. N.Y.C. chpt., pres. N.Y. state chpt. 1988—), VFW, Military Order of World Wars, Air Force Assn., Mil. Order Fgn. Wars, Tuxedo (N.Y.) Country Club, Skytop Club, Downtown Athletic Club, KC, Elks. Home: 15 Lancaster Dr Suffern NY 10901 Office: Gaston & Snow 14 Wall St New York NY 10005

HOBSON, JAMES RICHMOND, lawyer; b. Atlanta, Sept. 13, 1937; s. Richmond Pearson and Alice Chambers (Carey) H.; m. Nancy Hulbert Saussy, Nov. 29, 1963; children—Kathleen Hunter, Caroline Richmond, Susan Saussy. B.A. in English, Cornell U., 1959; M.A. in Govt., Georgetown U., 1963; J.D., U. San Francisco, 1971. Bar: Calif. 1972, U.S. Ct. Appeals (9th cir.) 1972, U.S. Dist. Ct. (no. dist.) Calif. 1972, D.C., 1973, U.S. Ct. Appeals (D.C. cir.) 1973, U.S. Dist. Ct. D.C. 1973. Staff writer Charlotte Observer, N.C., 1963; researcher, writer Rep. Nat. Com., Washington, 1964-65; info. officer Hoover Instn., Stanford, Calif., 1966-72; atty., mgr. FCC, Washington, 1972-78; asst. v.p. GTE Svc. Corp., Washington, 1978-81; Washington counsel GTE Corp., 1982—. Editor mag. pieces for Med. Econs., 1965. Bd. dirs. Mid-Peninsula Citizens for Fair Housing, Palo Alto, Calif., 1971-72; sr. warden Immanuel Ch. on the Hill, Alexandria, Va., 1977, jr. warden, 88; mem. traffic and parking bd. City of Alexandria, Va., 1980-82. Served with U.S. Army, 1959-60. Mem. ABA, Fed. Communications Bar Assn. (exec. com. 1984-87), Am. Corp. Counsel Assn. (bd. dirs. Washington Met. area 1983-86, mem. bd. editors 1986—), Sigma Alpha Epsilon. Episcopalian. Clubs: Metropolitan (Washington). Home: 3613 Trinity Dr Alexandria VA 22304 Office: GTE Corp 1850 M St NW Suite 1200 Washington DC 20036

HOCH, ORION LINDEL, corporate executive; b. Canonsburg, Pa., Dec. 21, 1928; s. Orion L.F. and Ann Marie (McNulty) H.; m. Jane Lee Ogan, June 12, 1952 (dec. 1978); children: Andrea, Brenda, John; m. Catherine Nan Richardson, Sept. 12, 1980; 1 child, Joe. B.S., Carnegie Mellon U., 1952; M.S., UCLA, 1954; Ph.D., Stanford U., 1957. With Hughes Aircraft Co., Culver City, Calif., 1952-54; with Stanford Electronics Labs., 1954-57; sr. engr., dept. mgr., div. v.p., div. pres. Litton Electron Devices div., San Carlos, Calif., 1957-68; group exec. Litton Components div., 1968-70; v.p. Litton Industries, Inc., Beverly Hills, Calif., 1970, sr. v.p., 1971-74, pres., 1982-88, chief exec. officer, 1986—, chmn., 1988—, also dir.; pres. Intersil, Inc., Cupertino, Calif., 1974-82; bd. dirs. Measurex Corp., Maxim Integrated Products. Trustee Carnegie-Mellon U. Served with AUS, 1946-48. Mem. IEEE, Am. Electronics Assn. (bd. dirs.), Sigma Xi, Tau Beta Pi, Phi Kappa Phi. Office: Litton Industries Inc 360 N Crescent Dr Beverly Hills CA 90210 *

HOCHBERG, FREDERICK GEORGE, accountant; b. L.A., July 4, 1913; s. Frederick Joseph and Lottie (LeGendre) H.; 1 child, Ann C. May. BA, UCLA, 1937. Chief acct., auditor Swinerton, McClure & Vinnell, Managua, Nicaragua, 1942-44; pvt. acctg. practice, Avalon, Calif., 1946-66; designer, operator Descanso Beach Club, Avalon, 1966; v.p. Air Catalina, 1967; treas. Catalina Airlines, 1967; pres. Aero Commuter, 1967; v.p., treas., dir. bus. affairs William L. Pereira & Assocs., Planners, Architects, Engrs., L.A., 1967-72; v.p., gen. mgr. Mo. Hickory Corp., 1972-74; prin. Fred G. Hochberg Assocs., Mgmt. Cons., 1974—; v.p. Vicalton S.A. Mexico, 1976—; v.p., gen. mgr. Solar Engring. Co., Inc., 1977-79; pres. Solar Assocs. Internat., 1979-83. Chmn. Avalon Transp. Com., 1952, Avalon Harbor Commn., 1960, Avalon Airport Com., 1964-66, Harbor Devel. Commn., 1965-66; sec. Santa Catalina Festival of Arts, 1960, Avalon City Planning Commn., 1956-58; pres. Avalon Music Bowl Assn., 1961, Catalina Mariachi Assn., 1961-66; treas. City of Avalon, 1954-62, Catalina Island Mus. Soc., 1964, councilman, 1962-66, mayor, 1964-66; bd. dirs. L.A. Child Guidance Clinic, 1975-86, advisor to bd., 1986—, treas., 1978-79, pres., 1979-81; bd. dirs. Los Aficionados de L.A., 1977—, pres., 1980-83, 87-88; pres. Nat Assn. Taurine Clubs, 1982-85. With USNR, 1944-45. Named Catalina Island Man of Yr., 1956. Mem. Avalon Catalina Island C. of C. (past pres., bd. dirs. 1948-62), Soc. Calif. Accts., Mensa, Am. Arbitration Assn. (panel), El Monte C. of C., Town Hall-West (vice-chmn.). Lodge: Rotary (Avalon pres. 1956). Home: 936 Trout St Staunton VA 24401 Office: PO Box 3173 Staunton VA 24401

HOCHHAUSER, RICHARD MICHAEL, marketing professional; b. N.Y.C., Aug. 25, 1944; s. Stanley and Rita (Weingarten) H.; m. Carole Beth Wasserstein, Sept. 6, 1969; children: Jonathan, Jennifer. BS, Carnegie Mellon U., 1966; MBA, Columbia U., 1968. Systems engr. U.S. Dept. of Navy, Washington, 1968-70; v.p. market research Quayle Plesser & Co., N.Y.C., 1970-75; pres. research RMH Research, Inc. subs. Harte-Hanks Communications, Fort Lee, N.J., 1975-80; pres. mktg. services Harte Hanks, Fairlawn, N.J., 1980-84; pres. direct mktg. Harte Hanks, River Edge, N.J., 1984—; lectr. univ. assns. Mem. Direct Mktg. Assn. Home: 108 Woodcrest Dr Woodcliff Lake NJ 07675 Office: Harte Hanks Direct Mktg 65 Rt 4 River Edge NJ 07661

HOCHHEIMER, FRANK LEO, brokerage executive; b. N.Y.C., Sept. 27, 1943; s. Arthur A. and Alice (Schoenthal) H.; BA in Math., Queens Coll., 1965; MA in Natural Sci., Hofstra U., 1966; MA in Econometrics, New Sch. Social Research, 1973; m. Beverly Widman, Dec. 24, 1967; 1 son, Martin. Instr., chmn. math dept. N.Y. Inst. Tech., 1966-74; mgr. S. Bauer & Sons, N.Y.C., 1974-75; livestock, cotton, citrus analyst Merrill Lynch, N.Y.C., 1975-76, computer applications specialist commodity div., 1976-78, mgr. tech. analysis, 1978-79, v.p., dir. research, 1980-83, v.p., dir. Futures Info. Services, 1983-85, v.p., mgr. global data and pricing Fin. Strategies Group, 1985—. Mem. Am. Econs. Assn., Nat. Assn. Bus. Economists, Market Technicians Assn., Futures Industry Assn. (former dir., treas. research div.). Contbr. articles to profl. jours.

HOCHSCHWENDER, HERMAN KARL, management consultant; b. Heidelberg, Federal Republic Germany, Mar. 1, 1920; came to U.S., 1930, naturalized, 1935; s. Karl G. and Maria (Recken) H.; B.S., Yale U., 1941; postgrad. Harvard U. Bus. Sch.; m. Jane Elliott (div. 1961); children—Lynn Anne Hochschwender McGowin, Herman Karl, Irene Hochschwender Pate, James E.; m. 2d, Mary Koger, July 3, 1965; 1 son, J. Michael. Asst. indsl. relations mgr. Sargent & Co., New Haven, 1943-45; mgr. corp. planning Firestone Tire & Rubber Co., Akron, Ohio, 1945-56; pres. Mohawk Rubber Co., N.Y.C., 1959; founder, pres. Hochschwender & Assocs., Akron, 1959-72, Smithers Sci. Services, Inc., Akron, 1972—; lectr. in field. Contbr. articles to profl. jours. Vice-chmn. Bd. Trustees Akron Gen. Med. Ctr. Mem. Am. Council Ind. Labs., Union Internat. des Laboratoires Independents (pres., bd. govs.), ASTM, Soc. Automotive Engrs., Am. Assn. Lab. Accreditation, Yale U. Alumni Assn. Clubs: Akron City (trustee), Portage Country (Akron); Yale (N.Y.C.); Naples Yacht; Royal Poinciana Golf. Lodge: Rotary. Home: 2400 Gulfshore Blvd N Apt #603 Naples FL 33940 Office: 425 W Market St Akron OH 44303

HOCHSCHWENDER, KARL ALBERT, government relations consultant; b. Mannheim, Ger., Feb. 1, 1927; came to U.S., 1931, naturalized, 1938; s. Karl Georg and Maria Irma (Recken) H.; m. Lilli Gettinger, July 4, 1964. BA, Yale U., 1947, MA, 1949, PhD, 1962. Instr. polit. sci. Fla. State

U., Tallahassee, 1949-51; assoc. Mott of Washington & Assocs., Washington, 1954-58; research analyst U.S. govt., 1959-60; asst. to mgmt. Am. Hoechst Corp., Bridgewater, N.J., 1961-63, mgr. govt. relations, 1963-68, dir. public relations, 1968-72, dir. public affairs, 1972-83; prin. Palatine Assocs., Princeton, N.J., 1983—; mem. Roster of Tech. Specialists, Office of Spl. Rep. for Trade Negotiations, Exec. Office of Pres., 1964-67. Trustee United Fund of Somerset Valley (N.J.), 1969-75. Yale U. fellow, 1952-54; recipient Am. Polit. Sci. Assn. Leonard D. White Meml. award, 1963. Mem. Am. Assn. Exporters and Importers (bd. dirs. 1963—, v.p. 1967-83, pres. 1983, chmn. 1983-85), Am. Polit. Sci. Assn., Chem. Communications Assn. (bd. dirs. 1976-80), Soc. Plastics Industry, Inc. (chmn. food, drug & cosmetics packaging material com. 1972-76). Club: Yale of N.Y.C. Office: Palatine Assocs PO Box 1466 Princeton NJ 08542

HOCHSTADT, ARNOLD LAWRENCE, investment broker; b. N.Y.C., Jan. 6, 1961; s. Seymour Jacob and Malvina (Kasserman) H.; m. Heidi Gayle Adelman, Aug. 31, 1986. BA, Colgate U., 1983. Asst. sales Lehman Bros., N.Y.C., 1983-84; assoc. v.p. Drexel Burnham Lambert, N.Y.C., 1984—. Mem. Am. Mgmt. Assn. Home: 1-705 High Point Dr Hartdale NY 10530 Office: Drexel Burnham Lambert 555 Madison Ave New York NY 10022

HOCHWALT, WILLIAM JOSEPH, stockbroker, financial planner; b. Dayton, Ohio, Apr. 14, 1955; s. Thomas Charles and Lois Jean (Breidenbach) H.; m. Deborah Leigh Rose, Sept. 6, 1985; 1 child, Tyler James. BBA, Ariz. State U., 1982. Cert. fin. planner. With Paine Webber, Inc., Scottsdale, Ariz., 1984—; v.p. investments Paine Webber, Inc., Scottsdale, 1987—; treas. Abalone Internat., Crescent City, Calif., 1988—. Mem. Inst. Cert. Fin. Planners, Toastmasters. Republican. Office: Paine Webber Inc 6750 E Camelback Scottsdale AZ 85251

HOCKADAY, IRVINE O., JR., greeting card company executive; b. Ludington, Mich., Aug. 12, 1936; s. Irvine Oty and Helen (McCune) H.; m. Mary Ellen Jurden, July 8, 1961; children: Wendy Helen, Laura DuVal. A.B., Princeton U., 1958; LL.B., U. Mich., 1961, J.D., 1961. Bar: Mo. 1961. Atty. firm Lathrop, Righter, Gordon & Parker, Kansas City, 1961-67; atty., asst. gen. counsel, asst. to pres., v.p. Kansas City So. Industries, Inc., 1968-72, pres., chief ops. officer, 1972-81, pres., chief exec. officer, 1981-83; pres., chief exec. officer, dir. Hallmark Cards, Inc., 1983—; Bd. dirs. Ford Motor Co.; past chmn. bd. dirs. 10th dist. Fed. Res. Bank. Chmn. Civic Council Kans. City, 1987-89. Club: Kansas City Country. Office: Hallmark Cards Inc PO Box 419580 2501 McGee Kansas City MO 64141

HOCKMAN, KARL KALEVI, transportation and management services executive; b. N.Y.C., Jan. 17, 1924; s. John Laakso and Fanny Maria (Wirtanen) H.; m. Betty Lou Heyle, June 24, 1970; children: William, James Karol, Thomas, David, Kathleen. BA, Shelton Coll., 1956; BD, Bibl. Sem., 1958; cert. in indsl. relations U. Calif.-Berkeley, 1968; cert. in personnel devel. U. Calif., Santa Barbara, 1972. V.p. Schroeder Distbg. Co. No. Calif., Oakland, 1960-66; controller Inland Cities Express, Inc., Riverside, Calif., 1967-70; data processing mgr. Moss Motors, Ltd., Goleta, Calif., 1970-73; controller LKL Industries, Fontana, Calif., 1973-82; mng. ptnr. Hockman & Hockman Assocs., Rialto, Calif., 1982—; chmn. bd. Computer Networking Specialists, Inc., 1983—; sec./treas. Moreno Valley Constrn., Inc., 1986—, also bd. dirs.; bd. dirs. Raemont & Co., Inc., MI Sueno Ranch Nursery, Inc., Quest Electronics Corp. Served with AUS, 1942-45, ETO. Mem. Assn. Computing Machinery, Data Processing Mgmt. Assn., IEEE, Nat. Def. Transp. Assn., N.Y. Acad. Scis., Bibl. Archeol. Soc. Republican. Adventist. Club: Valley Transp. Office: Hockman & Hockman Assocs 1325 N Fitzgerald Ste E Rialto CA 92376

HOCKSTADT, ANDREW KEITH, security consultant, polygraph examiner; b. N.Y.C., July 26, 1951; s. Norman and Roslyn (Steinfeld) H. BS, Northeastern U., 1974. Polygraph examiner ACE Plygraph Co., N.Y.C., 1984—; pres. ACE Polygraph and Protective Svcs., Inc., N.Y.C., 1985—. Negotiator 67-69 8th Ave. Tenant's Com., 1986. Mem. Soc. Profl. Investigators, Am. Polygraph Assn., Empire State Polygraph Assn., Fraternal Order of Police, N.Y. Vets. Police Assn., Knights of Malta. Home: 259 W 21st St #2 New York NY 10011 Office: ACE Protective Svcs 200 W 24th St New York NY 10011

HOCOTT, JOE BILL, chemical engineer, educator; b. nr. Big Flat, Ark., Sept. 19, 1921; s. Jeiks Edmonds and Frances Clara (Berry) H.; B.S., U. Ark., 1945; M.S., Okla. State U., 1951. Insp. Maumelle Ordnance Works, U.S. Army Ordnance Dept., Little Rock, 1942-43; head sci. dept. Joe T. Robinson High Sch., Little Rock, 1945-46; instr. chemistry U. Tulsa, 1946-47; teaching fellow Okla. A. and M. Coll., Stillwater, 1947-49; research chem. engr. Deep Rock Petroleum Corp., Cushing, Okla., 1950, Kerr-McGee Oil Corp., Stillwater, 1951; chem. engr. cons. Joe Bill Hocott, Little Rock, 1952-55, 63—; med. technician U. Ark. Med. Center, Little Rock, 1955-56, research asso., 1956-57, instr. internal medicine, 1957-62; head chemistry dept. Little Rock Central High Sch., 1963-66; head sci. dept. Met. Vocat.-Tech. High Sch., Little Rock, 1967-73. Asst. scoutmaster Boy Scouts Am., 1945-46, troop committeeman, 1945-46, 57-58, neighborhood commr., 1969-70. Bd. dirs. Ark. Jr. Sci. and Humanities Symposium, 1965-75, asst. dir., 1972. Mem. Am. Inst. Chem. Engrs., Nat. Soc. Profl. Engrs., Ark., Ark. Jr. (dist. dir. 1966-70) acads. sci., Sigma Xi, Phi Lambda Upsilon, Unitarian. Home: 1010 Rice St Little Rock AR 72202

HODAPP, DON JOSEPH, food company executive; b. Madelia, Minn., Dec. 24, 1937; s. Phillip Henry and Katherine Lillian (Quinn) H.; m. Dorothy Ann Berg, Sept. 7, 1959; children: Don Jr., Jennifer, Paul, Patrick, Laurie. BA in Math., St. John's U., Collegeville, Minn., 1959. Adv. mktg. rep. IBM Corp., Mpls., 1959-66; dir. data processing Geo. A. Hormel & Co., Austin, Minn., 1966-69, asst. controller, 1969-81; gen. mgr. Geo. A. Hormel & Co., Fremont, Nebr., 1981-85; v.p. strategic planning Geo. A. Hormel & Co., Austin, 1985-86, group v.p., 1986—, also bd. dirs., 1986—. Republican. Roman Catholic. Lodge: Rotary. Office: Geo A Hormel & Co Po Box 800 Austin MN 55912

HODDER, EDWIN CLIFTON, investment company executive; b. Denver, July 1, 1955; s. Edwin James and Ruth Lowell (Lierd) H.; m. Susan L. Benson, 1984. BA cum laude, U. Denver, 1977; MBA, U. Pa., 1979. Founder, pres., bd. dirs. Hodder Sinclair Enterprises, Inc., Casper, Wyo., 1980-88; founder, mgr. Car Wash Supply Co., Casper, 1981—, Mountain Soft, 1982—; founder, mgr., bd. dirs. Hodco, Inc., Casper, 1982—; account exec. Wyo. Fin. Securities, Inc., 1988—; asst. dir. internat. affairs, Wharton Sch. U. Pa., 1978-79. Inventor turn-key box system for self-service timed bus. Francis Ferris Meml. scholar; U. Pa. Wharton fellow. Mem. Rotary, Omicron Delta Epsilon. Republican. Christian Scientist. Home: 1652 Begonia Casper WY 82604 Office: Wyo Fin Securities PO Box 407 Casper WY 82602

HODDER, WILLIAM ALAN, fabricated metal products company executive; b. Lincoln, Nebr., May 6, 1931; s. Ernest Chesley and Velma Catherine (Warren) H.; m. Suzanne Holmes, Apr. 3, 1954; children: Kent, Laurie, Susan, Mark, Beth. BA, U. Nebr., 1954; postgrad., Harvard U., 1961. Mktg. positions IBM Corp., 1954-66; v.p. orgn. planning and devel. Dayton Co., Mpls., 1966-68; sr. v.p. Dayton Hudson Corp., 1970-73, dir., 1971-73; pres. Target Stores, 1968-73; pres., dir. Donaldson Co., Inc., Mpls., 1973—, chief exec. officer, 1982—, chmn. bd., 1984—; bd. dir. Norwest Corp., Tennant Co., Network Systems Corp., Cowles Media Co., NNLI Cos., Inc., Moniterm Corp.; mem. Minn. Bus. Partnership. Trustee Macalester Coll.; bd. overseers Carlson Sch. of Mgmt. U. Minn. With AUS, 1954-56. Mem. Chief Execs. Orgn., Inc., Soc. Automotive Engrs., Harvard U. Bus. Sch., Club Minn. (bd. dir., past pres.). Clubs: Minneapolis, Minikahda. Home: 11 Circle West Edina MN 55436 Office: Donaldson Co Inc 1400 W 94th St Minneapolis MN 55431

HODGE, NETA ANN, advertising executive; b. Springfield, Ill., Jan. 4, 1948; d. Earl Leo and Mary Elizabeth (Evans) Lard. BS, St. Louis Coll. Pharmacy, 1971; PharmD, U. Ky., 1978. Pharmacist in charge S&C Drugs, Peoria, Ill., 1971-72; mgr. pharmacy Wal-Mart Drugs, Manhattan, Kans., 1972-75; pharmacist in residence A.B. Chandler Med. Ctr., U. Ky., Lexington, 1975-78; instr. clin. pharmacy Phila. Coll. Pharmacy, 1978-79, asst. prof., 1979-86; adj. asst. prof. in medicine U. Pa., Phila., 1980-86; account exec. Deltakos, USA (J. Walter Thompson), N.Y.C., 1986-87; account supr. Sudler & Hennessey div. Young & Rubicam, N.Y.C., 1987-89, Lavey/Wolff/Swift Inc., N.Y.C., 1989—; clin. pharmacist, cons. U. Pa. Sch. Medicine, Phila. Pa. Diabetic Task Force, Phila., 1985-86. Contbg. editor Pa. State Health Plan, 1986-87; contbr. articles to profl jours. Mem. Pa. Gov's Adv. Bd. on Arthritis, 1985—; vice chair Profl. Edn. Com., 1985-87; mem., vice chair Patient/Pub. Edn. Com., 1985-87. Named one of Outstanding Young Women of Am., 1980, 84. Mem. Am. Soc. Hosp. Pharmacists, St. Louis Coll. Pharmacy Alumni Assn., Univ. City Hist. Soc., Green Thumb Gardeners Assn. (sec. Phila. chpt. 1986—), Rho Chi, Lambda Kappa Sigma. Democrat. Roman Catholic. Home: 434 S 42d St Philadelphia PA 19104

HODGE, ROBERT JOSEPH, retail executive; b. St. Louis, July 5, 1937; s. Joseph Edward and Alberta Marie (Oehler) H.; m. Carmen Maria Villalobos, Sept. 1, 1960; children: Ralph, Robert, Carmen. BS in Indsl. Relations, St. Louis U., 1959. Meat dept. merchandiser Kroger Co., Cleve., 1972-74; corp. v.p. deli/bakery Kroger Co., Cin., 1981-83; v.p. Atlanta div. Kroger Co., 1983-85; meat merchandiser Kroger Co., St. Louis, 1977-80; v.p. gateway region Kroger, St. Louis, 1985-87; v.p. meat ops. Ralph's Grocery Co., Los Angeles, 1974-77; gen. mgr. Super X Drug, Melbourne, Fla., 1980-81; sr. v.p. Dillon Co., Hutchinson, Kans., 1987—. Sgt. U.S. Army, res., 1959-66. Home: 2844 Cypress Cir Wichita KS 67226 Office: Dillon Cos Inc PO Box 1266 Hutchinson KS 67504-1266

HODGES, C(LIFTON) TOM, financial planner; b. Scottsboro, Ala., Oct. 13, 1937; s. Laudra Clifton and Olive Elizabeth (Thomas) H.; m. Lee Ann Boyd, July 2, 1960; children: Frank Thomas, Donald Lee, Robert Greer. BS in Chemistry, U. Ala., Tuscaloosa, 1960, BSCE, 1962; grad., La. State U., 1974. CLU; chartered fin. cons.; cert. fin. planner. Research chemist Freeport Sulphur, Belle Chase, La., 1962-66, Rhom-Haas, Redstone Arsenal, Huntsville, Ala., 1966; chief chemist Freeport Chem., Uncle Sam, La., 1967-69, Revere Copper and Brass, Scottsboro, Ala., 1969-72; owner, mgr. C. Tom Hodges, CLU, ChFc, CFP, Scottsboro, Ala., 1972—; instr. fin. planning course Northeast State Coll., Rainsville, Ala., 1986—; tng. council instr. Life Underwriter Tng. Council, 1985. Columnist weekly fin. planning column Daily Sentinel newspaper, North Jackson News, Sand Mountain News. Pres., Scottsboro C. of C., 1979-80, Scottsboro Jackson County C. of C., 1980-81; eagle scout rev. bd. Scottsboro Council Boy Scouts Am., 1988—; bd. dirs. North Ala. Better Bus. Bur., 1982-83. Recipient Silver Beaver award, Boy Scouts Am., 1975, Vigil Honor, 1960, Eagle Scout, 1954. Mem. Internat. Assn. Fin. Planning, Inst. Cert. Fin. Planners, Million Dollar Round Table, Life Underwriters Assn. Republican. Episcopalian. Home: Rte 6 PO Box 190 Scottsboro AL 35768 Office: C Tom Hodges 808 John T Reid Pkwy Scottsboro AL 35768

HODGES, EDWIN C., consultant; b. Montgomery, Kans., July 9, 1940; s. Charles E. and Mary R. (Marvel) H.; m. Rebecca Carlisle; children: Mark E., Elaine L., Kelly M., Sherry, Bill. BA, U. Kans., 1964. Commd. 2nd lt. U.S. Army, 1964, advanced through grades to maj., 1974; with Adv. Team 33, Republic Vietnam, 1968; ret. U.S. Army, 1985; founder Genesis Cons. Ltd., Inc., Arlington, Tex., 1985-88; pres., chmn. bd., chief exec. officer def. concepts Quantitative Systems Internat., Inc. (formerly Genesis Cons., Ltd. Inc.), Arlington, 1988—; chief force devel., test and evaluation, U.S. Army, Ft. Knox, Ky., 1974, chief operational test and evaluation, 1976, exec. office dir. chief Requirements team for Armored Gun System, 1980-83; security asst. officer, Ankara, Turkey, 1983-85. Contbr. articles and reports profl. jours. Mem. Am. Def. Preparedness Assn., Am. Cons. League. Republican. Lodge: Masons (32 degree). Office: Quantitative Systems Internat 2307 Roosevelt Dr Ste B 6411 Saddle Ridge Rd Ste 101 Arlington TX 76016

HODGES, H(ERBERT) ANTHONY, investment management executive; b. Manchester, Eng., Jan. 25, 1919; s. Herbert and Annie Agnes (Rankin) H.; came to U.S., 1963, naturalized, 1975; student Manchester Coll. Tech., 1935-37; B.A., Victoria U. Manchester, 1940; m. Mary Press, Sept. 6, 1940 (div. 1970); children—Beverley Anne, Andrea Jane, Thomas Anthony; m. 2d, Joan Bannerot Lappe, Aug. 25, 1973 (div. 1979); m. 3d, Donna Kinneman Hasley, Aug. 5, 1979. Econ. asst. Joint Com. Cotton Trade Orgns., Manchester, 1935-40; asst. treas. Sun Life Can., Montreal, Que., 1946-63; v.p. Mellon Bank, Pitts., 1963-79; v.p., dir. mktg. Fort Hill Investors Mgmt. Corp., 1979-82; v.p., cons. Muhlenkamp & Co., Inc., 1982-86; advisor, bd. dirs. Envirospec Inc., 1984—; founder, pres. Herodane Investments, Inc., 1987; lectr. fin. Sir George Williams U., 1949; pres. Gt. Dane Club Western Pa. Served with Royal Navy, 1940-46. Decorated knight comdr. Order St. Lazarus Jerusalem. Mem. Pitts. Soc. Security Analysts. Republican. Roman Catholic. Clubs: Westchester K.C.; Duquesne; Gt. Harbour (B.W.I.). Home: 5513 Howe St Pittsburgh PA 15232

HODGIN, DAVID TIMBERLAKE, service executive; b. Buffalo, June 8, 1932; s. David Reid Hodgin and Elva (Timberlake) Twamley; m. Claire Evelyn Arnold, July 19, 1953; children: David Arnold, Kathryn Anne, Elizabeth Claire, Amanda Claudia. Student, Wesleyan U., 1950-51; BA in Econs., U. Calif., Santa Barbara, 1954; B in Fgn. Trade, Am. Grad Sch. Internat. Mgmt., Phoenix, 1961; postgrad., NYU, 1964-65. Asst. to v.p. internat. div. Paul Hardeman, Inc., Stanton, Calif., 1961; dir. adminstrn. Paul Hardeman, S.A., Buenos Aires, 1962-63; supr. office svcs. Owens Corning Fiberglas Corp., N.Y.C., 1964-65; v.p. adminstrn. Fibraglas S.Am., Bogota, Colombia, 1965-67; bus. analyst Owens Corning Fiberglas Corp., Toledo, 1967-68, Daire Assocs., Walnut Creek, Calif., 1968-78; pres. Am. Powerwash Corp., Concord, Calif., 1969-78; pres. Pathfinder Cos., Scotts Valley, Calif., 1977-88, chmn., 1989—; pres. Am. Holiday Resorts, Inc., Scotts Valley, 1983—, Compustudy Inc., 1989—; v.p., gen. mgr. Sunset Recreation, Inc., Menlo Park, Calif., 1973-77; sr. cons. Leisure Mgmt. Cons., Inc., Concord, 1975-77; bd. dirs. Evergreen Holding Co., Ltd., Barbados, W.I., Conifer Reinsurance, Ltd., Barbados. Contbr. numerous articles to profl. jours. Mem. Senate and Assembly Select Coms. on Small Bus., Sacramento, 1982—, Santa Cruz County (Calif.) Rep. Cen. Com., 1988—; chmn. dist. adv. council U.S. Small Bus. Adminstrn., San Francisco, 1983-87; advisor small bus. edn. program Cabrillo Coll., Aptos, Calif., 1983—; pres. Santa Cruz County Conv. and Vis. Bur., 1984, Calif. State Conf. on Small Bus., Sacramento, 1986-88, Calif. Small Bus. United, 1988—. Mem. Nat. Campground Owners Assn. (bd. dirs. 1974-83, v.p. 1976-78, pres. 1978-80), Calif. Travel Pks. Assn. (pres. 1974-76), Calif. State C. of C. (vice chair small bus. com. 1983-84), Santa Cruz Area C. of C. (bd. dirs. 1983-84), Scotts Valley C. of C. (bd. dirs. 1979-84), Exchange Club (pres., dir. Calif. and Nev. dists 1980-82). Republican. Office: Am Holiday Resorts Inc 100 Santa's Village Rd Scotts Valley CA 95066

HODGKIN, CHRISTOPHER, management consultant; b. Phila., May 22, 1944; m. Margaret Scott Bryan, Aug. 26, 1980; children: David Winton, Dorothy Scott and Katharine McCurdy (twins). BA, St. John's Coll., Annapolis, Md., 1966; MS, Union Coll., 1976. V.p. fin. Cogent Data Techs., Friday Harbor, Wash., 1980-84; bus. mgr. Inter-Island Med. Ctr., Friday Harbor, 1984-86; sr. ptnr. Madrona Group, Friday Harbor, 1985—; pres. N.W. Ctr. Nonprofit Mgmt., 1987—. Author (with others) Annual Economic and Demographic Almanac of Washington Counties, 1986—; contbr. articles to mags.. Pres. San Juan Islands Libr. Dist., 1985—; com. chmn. Mt. Baker Coun. Cub Scouts Am., 1987—; bd. dirs. San Juan Islands Econ. Devel. Coun., 1985—. Mem. Soc. of Friends. Office: Madrona Group PO Box 1635 Friday Harbor WA 98250

HODGKINSON, WILLIAM JAMES, marketing company executive; b. Bklyn., July 31, 1939; s. William James and Augusta Anne (Botka) H.; A.B., Bucknell U., 1961; M.B.A., Columbia U., 1963; m. Virginia Evelyn Humphreys, Sept. 7, 1963; 1 dau., Elizabeth Anne. Mktg. research analyst Singer Co., N.Y.C., 1963-66; asst. adminstrn. Writing Paper div. Am. Paper Inst., N.Y.C., 1966-67; market research mgr. Diners Club, N.Y.C., 1967-68; with Dun & Bradstreet Cos., Inc., 1968—, mgmt. cons. William E. Hill Co. div., N.Y.C., 1971-73, mgr. fin. services group Donnelley Mktg. div., Stamford, Conn., 1973-86, v.p., 1987—. Bd. dirs. Bklyn. Pub. Library br., 1974-79, Enlightenment Together, Inc., 1971-76; research coordinator Presdl. Task Force on Improving Small Bus., 1969-70; v.p., trustee Montessori Sch. Bklyn., 1975-79; trustee Greens Farms Congl. Ch., 1983-85; co-chmn. Save Fairfield Com., 1984—. Served with U.S. Army, 1963. Grantee Columbia U., 1962-63; recipient Brotherhood award Bucknell U., 1960. Mem. Bank Mktg. Assn., Am. Mktg. Assn., Direct Mail Mktg. Assn., Phi Lambda Theta. Congregationalist. (bd. deacons 1971-78, pres. 1977-78). Club: Princeton of N.Y. Contbr. articles to profl. jours. Home: 4454 Black Rock Turnpike Fairfield CT 06430 Office: Donnelley Mktg div Dun & Bradstreet 1515 Summer St Stamford CT 06905

HODGSON, ALLAN ARCHIBALD, aluminum company executive; b. Montreal, Can., Oct. 13, 1937; s. Jonathan Archibald and Anne Churchill (Hyde) H.; m. Margaret Victoria Webster, Apr. 12, 1978; children: Lucinda Nora, Jonathan Welbourn, Anne Gregory. BA with honors, McGill U., 1958. Dir. research C.J. Hodgson & Co., Montreal, 1961-67; shareholder rels. officer Alcan Aluminium Ltd., Montreal, 1967-69, asst. treas., 1969-72, treas., 1980-83, v.p., chief fin. officer, 1982—, also bd. dirs., 1987—; fin. dir. Indian Aluminium Co., Ltd., Calcutta, India, 1972-76; treas. Aluminum Co. of Can., Ltd., Montreal, 1976-80; bd. dirs. Spar Aerospace Ltd., Toronto; adv. bds. Allendale Mut. Ins. Co., Toronto, Can., 1983—, Banco de Montreal Investimento, S.A., Rio de Janeiro, 1983—. Club: University of Montreal. Office: Alcan Aluminum Ltd, 1188 Sherbrooke St W, Montreal, PQ Canada H3A 3G2

HODGSON, JAMES DAY, corporate executive; b. Dawson, Minn., Dec. 3, 1915; s. Fred Arthur and Casaraha (Day) H.; m. Maria Denend, Aug. 24, 1943; children: Nancy Ruth, Fredric Jesse. AB, U. Minn., 1938; LLD (hon.), Temple U., 1970, U. Cin., 1972. Sr. v.p. Lockheed Corp., Burbank, Calif., 1946-68; sec. Dept. Labor, Washington, 1970-73; amb. to Japan Tokyo, 1974-77; chmn. bd. Pathfinder Mines Co., San Francisco, 1977-82; bd. dirs. Alliance Capital Mgmt., N.Y.C., ARA Services Inc., Phila., United TV Inc., L.A., Am. Health Properties, L.A., Trust Svcs. Am., L.A. Author: Looking for a Pearl Harbor, 1980; contbg. author: Industrial Relations Public Policy, 1974, The Nations Dilemnas, 1978; contbr. articles to profl. jours. Chmn. Presdl. Commn. on Productivity, Washington, 1971-73; dep. chmn. Presdl. Commn. on U.S.-Japan Rels., Washington, 1983-85; bd. dirs. ARC, Washington, 1971-73, Council Am. Ambs., Washington, 1983—. Decorated 1st class Order of the Rising Sun (Japan), 1982; recipient Disting. Svc. award U. Minn., 1970-78. Mem. Nat. Acad. Pub. Adminstrn., Nat. Alliance Businessmen (bd. dirs. 1973-74), Coun. on Fgn. Rels., Japan Soc., Pacific Forum (bd. dirs. 1980-88), U.S. Comm. Pacific Econs. Coop., Pacific Basin Inst. (bd. dirs. 1981—), Fedn. 21 Century (bd. dirs. 1987—), L.A Country Club, Univ. Club (N.Y.C.), Capitol Hill Club (Washington). Home: 10132 Hillgrove Dr Beverly Hills CA 90210 Office: Pacific Sci Co 1350 S State College Blvd Anaheim CA 92806

HODGSON, THOMAS RICHARD, chemical company executive; b. Lakewood, Ohio, Dec. 17, 1941; s. Thomas Julian and Dallas Louise (Livesay) H.; m. Susan Jane Cawrse, Aug. 10, 1963; children: Michael, Laura, Anne. BSChemE, Purdue U., 1963; MSE, U. Mich., 1964; MBA, Harvard U., 1969. Devel. engr. E.I. Dupont, 1964; assoc. Booz-Allen & Hamilton, 1969-72; with Abbott Labs., North Chicago, Ill., 1972—; gen. mgr. Faultless div. Abbott Labs., North Chicago, 1976-78, v.p. gen. mgr. Hosp. div., 1978-80, pres. Hosp. div., 1980-83, group v.p., pres. Abbott Internat. Ltd., 1983-84, exec. v.p. parent com., 1985—; also dir. Abbott Labs. Mem. Lake Forest (Ill.) Bd. Edn. Served with Chem. Corps U.S. Army, 1965-67. Baker scholar; NSF fellow; recipient Disting. Engring. Alumni award Purdue U., 1985. Mem. Chgo. Coun. Fgn. Rels., Econ. Club, Knollwood Club, Phi Eta Sigma, Tau Beta Pi. Home: 1015 Ashley Rd Lake Forest IL 60045 Office: Abbott Internat Ltd 1 Abbott Park Rd Abbott Park IL 60064

HODKINSON, STEVEN FRANCIS, controller; b. Detroit, Aug. 24, 1952; s. Francis William and Rita Eileen (Stoll) H.; m. Renee Ann Malinowski, Apr. 23, 1976; children: Emily Frances, William Francis. BBA, U. Mich., 1974. CPA, Mich. Supr., acct. Coopers & Lybrand, Detroit, 1974-78; mgr. corp. acctg. Guardian Industries, Northville, Mich., 1978-79, mgr. fin. reporting, 1979-81, asst. corp. controller, 1981-84, corp. controller, chief acctg. officer, 1984—. Mem. Am. Inst. CPA's, Mich. Assn. CPA's, Fin. Execs. Inst., Nat. Assn. Accts., Controllers Council and Bus. Planning Bd. Office: Guardian Industries Corp 43043 W Nine Mile Rd Northville MI 48167

HODOUS, ROBERT POWER, bank holding company executive; b. Zanesville, Ohio, July 29, 1945; s. Robert Frank and Nancy Aurelia (Power) H.; m. Susan Cottrell Birkhead, Feb. 1, 1969; children: Robert Everett, Shannon Alycia. B.A., Miami U., Oxford, Ohio, 1967; J.D., U. Va., Charlottesville, 1970. Bar: Va. 1970. Assoc. firm McGuire, Woods & Battle, Charlottesville, 1970-71; asst. trust officer Nat. Bank & Trust Co., Charlottesville, 1971-72, trust officer, 1972-75, sec., 1975-79; sec. Jefferson Bankshares, Inc. (formerly NB Corp.), Charlottesville, 1979—, v.p., sec., 1985—, sr. v.p., sec., 1987—; asst. to pres. Jefferson Nat. Bank, Charlottesville, 1987—. Chmn. profl. div. Thomas Jefferson Area United Way, 1973, vice-chmn., 1978-79, campaign chmn., 1979-80, v.p. planning, 1981, pres., 1983; bd. dirs. Central Va. chpt. ARC, 1972-78, treas., 1972-75, chmn., 1975-77; commr. Charlottesville Redevel. and Housing Authority, 1974-78; mem. Region X Community Mental Health and Retardation Services Bd., 1973-79, chmn., 1974-76, mem. exec. com., 1976-78; v.p. Soccer Orgn. of Charlottesville-Albemarle, 1985-86, pres., 1986-88; co-pres. Greenbier Sch. PTA, 1985-86; chmn. recreation precinct Charlottesville City Democratic Com., 1971. Mem. Am., Charlottesville-Albemarle Bar Assns., Va. State Bar, Va. Bankers Assn. (com. drafted Va. Trust Subs. Act 1973, trust com. 1974-77, legal affairs com. 1986—, large bank legis. coordinator, 1987—). Roman Catholic. Club: Fairvie (pres. 1974-75) (Charlottesville). Home: 1309 Lester Dr Charlottesville VA 22901 Office: 123 E Main St Charlottesville VA 22901

HODOWAL, JOHN RAYMOND, holding company executive, utility company executive, lawyer; b. Dayton, Ohio, Feb. 16, 1945; m. Virginia A. Hall, 1966. B.S. in Indsl. Engring., Purdue U., 1966; J.D., Ind. U., 1960. Bar: Ind. 1971, U.S. Dist. Ct. (so. dist.) Ind. 1971, U.S. Ct. Appeals (7th cir.) 1973. Jr. engr. Indpls. Power and Light Co., 1968-69, assoc. engr., 1969-71, atty., 1971-73, asst. sec., assoc. gen. counsel, 1973-76, asst. sec., asst. treas., 1976-77, treas., 1977-79, v.p., treas., 1979; sr. v.p. fin. Indpls. Power and Light subs. IPALCO Enterprises, 1979-87, exec. v.p., 1987-89, chief exec. officer, 1989—; v.p., treas. IPALCO Enterprises Inc., Indpls., 1984-89, chmn. bd., pres., 1989—; pres. Mid-Am. Capital Resources Inc. subs. IPALCO Enterprises, Indpls., 1984—; pres., chmn. bd. Mid-Am. Capital Resources Inc. subs. IPALCO Enterprises, 1989—; bd. dirs. Banc One Ind. Corp., Bank One, Indpls., N.A. Bd. dirs. Circle Theatre Assocs., Ind. State Symphony Soc., Crossroads of Am. Counc. Boy Scouts Am., Indpls. Neighborhood Housing Ptnrship., Ltd., Corp. Community Coun., Greater Indpls. Progress Com., Cathedral Arts, Inc., Community Leaders Allied Superior Schs., Regional Ctr. Plan II Task Force; chmn. fund drive, chmn. investment com. Indpls. Symphony Orch.; trustee Hanover Coll., Ind. Mem. Indpls. Zool. Soc. (bd. dirs., exec. com.), Ind. Bar Assn., Indpls. Bar Assn., Purdue U. Alumni Assn., Ind. U. Alumni Assn., Edison Electric Inst. (fin. com.), The Conf. Bd. (fin. com.), Phi Delta Phi. Clubs: Woodstock, Columbia, Athletic, Skyline. Home: 5136 E 74th Pl Indianapolis IN 46250 Office: IPALCO Enterprises Inc 25 Monument Cir PO Box 1595 Indianapolis IN 46206-1595

HODSDEN, JOHN BURGESS, food products executive; b. Gary, Ind., Jan. 19, 1948; s. Stephen Kenneth and Margaret Elizabeth (Maybaum) H.; m. Jacquelyn Patricia Kornas, Apr. 27, 1973; children: Jeffrey Burgess, Jerelyn Michele. BS in Physics summa cum laude, Rose Polytech. Inst., 1970; MBA in Fin., U. Chgo., 1974. Engr. Inland Steel Co., Indiana Harbor, 1970-74; mgr. production control Waukesha (Wis.) Engine Div. Dresser Ind., 1974-76; mgr. ops. Foundry Products Div. Gould Inc., Eau Claire, Wis., 1976-80; pres. Markon Mfg. Inc., Golden, Colo., 1980-85, Carts Colo. Inc., Denver, 1986—; dir. Jaffe Baking, N.Y.C., 1983. Contbr. articles to profl. jours. Inventor in field. Co-founder, v.p. Jr. Achievement, Eau Claire, 1976-79; bd. dirs. Luther Hosp., Eau Claire, 1977-79; mem. Pvt. Industry Council Econ. Devel. Com., Jefferson County, Colo., 1985, Econ. Devel. Council Adams County, Colo., 1988. Recipient Kelly award Am. Inst. Steel Engrs., 1974. Mem. Assn. Iron and Steel Engrs., Am. Prodn. and Inventory Control Soc. Office: Carts Colo Inc 5750 Holly St PO Box 16249 Denver CO 80216

HODSON, BETH ANN, diversified manufacturing company executive; b. Muncie, Ind., Oct. 7, 1953; d. Ivan Ellis and Ruby Eleanora (Rhoades) H. Student Ball State U. Instr. Eleanor Coles Dance Studio, Muncie, 1969-76; supply clk. Marsh Supermarkets, Inc., Yorktown, Ind., 1972, offset press operator, 1972-77; instr. tap dance Gale Kim's Dance Studio, Muncie, 1977-

80; graphic stripper-platemaker Ball Corp., Muncie, 1977-79, supr. reprographic services, 1979-80, supr. office services, 1980-84, mgr. office services, 1984—, mem. human resource devel. team, 1980—, leader, 1983, bd. dirs. Employees Credit Union, 1985—, sec., 1986; judge printing contest Vocat. Indsl. Clubs Am., 1978, 82, 84, 87, 88. Corp. vol. United Way Campaign, 1971—, grocery supplier team capt., 1983-85; vol. Salvation Army, 1979—, Ind. Renaissance Fair, 1984; chair 473 Postal Customer Council, 1982-84, bd. dirs., 1984—; pco-chair Sta. WIPB-TV Telesale, 1983; judge, regional v.p. mktg. Jr. Achievement, 1984; actress, choreographer, costume coordinator, asst. dir., bd. dirs. Muncie Civic Theatre, 1984-85; chair program Am. Cancer Soc., 1985, 87, 88; bd. dirs. Cambridge House, Muncie, 1987—, pub. rels. chmn., 1988, 89. Recipient cert. of appreciation Union City (Ind.) Kiwanis Club, 1983, Muncie Clean City award, 1983, Channel 49's Telesale award, 1983, cert. of appreciation Ind. Renaissance Fair, 1984, Women of Achievement award East Cen. Ind. chpt. Women in Communications, INc., 1985; named one of Outstanding Young Women in Am., 1983, Top 100 In-Plant Printing Ops. Among Indsl. Cos. Mem. In-Plant Printing Mgmt. Assn. (communicator 1980—, exemplary mem. 1981—, pres. 1985—, Mem. of Yr. 1985), Advt. Club Muncie (bd. dirs. 1982-85), Muncie-Delaware County C. of C., Acad. Community Leadership. Club: Riley Jones' Women's. Lodge: Elks. Avocations: bowling, dancing, skiing, tennis, body building. Home: 1904 Duane Rd Muncie IN 47304 Office: Ball Corp 345 S High St Muncie IN 47305

HOE, RICHARD MARCH, insurance executive; b. Plainfield, N.J., June 16, 1939; s. Arthur James Hoe and Marjorie (Vandergrift) Beeson; m. Lynne Hovell, Sept. 26, 1964; children: Joshua Blake, Susan Brooke, Seth Jamieson. Student, Pace U., 1964-67, U. Tenn., 1976. CLU. Asst. to controller, fleet mgr., asst. purchasing agt. Hoe & Co. Inc., Bronx, N.Y., 1964-66; pres. OJS Mfg. Co., Bklyn., 1966-68, Fresh Impressions Inc., N.Y.C., 1968; agt. Fidelity Mut. Life, N.Y.C., 1968-72; asst. mgr. Fin. Life, N.Y.C., 1972-73; brokerage mgr. Am. Life N.Y., N.Y.C., 1973-75; exec. Provident Life & Accident Ins. Co., Chattanooga, 1975-78; mgr. Jefferson Standard, Tulsa, 1978-81; pres. Hoe & Co. Inc., Tulsa, 1981—; lectr. Tulsa Pub. Schs. Project Bus., 1983, 85, cons., 1984-86; lectr. in field; founder employee and exec. benefit plans: residual split-dollar; money purchase flexible spending acct. plans, pvt. sector social security alternative portable plan, satellite split-dollar, satellite supplemental pensions. Columnist (monthly) Broker World, 1985-86, Probe, Life Assn. News; contbr. articles to profl. jours. Chmn. fund raising Grimes Elem. Sch., Tulsa Pub. Schs., 1984-87; mem. gifted and talented com. Tulsa Pub. Schs., 1982; bd. dirs. Nat. ALS Found., N.Y.C., 1971-82. Fellow Life Underwriter Tng. Council (moderator 1979-86); mem. Am. Soc. CLU's, Tulsa Estate Planning Forum, Million Dollar Round Table. Republican. Episcopalian. Home: 5843 E 50th St Tulsa OK 74135 Office: Hoe & Co Inc 4835 S Fulton Ave Suite 103 Tulsa OK 74135

HOECK, DARLENE B., credit analyst; b. Balt., Aug. 26, 1956; d. Harry C. and Nora Francis (Clark) Schreck; m. Michael Joseph Hoeck, June 19, 1986; children: Justin Edward, Brian Michael. Credit and collection mgmt. cert., U. Balt., 1982; credit-fin. analyst cert., Dun & Bradstreet, N.Y.C., 1987. Key account analyst Noxell Corp., Hunt Valley, Md., 1979-87; sr. credit analyst EIL Instruments Inc., Sparks, Md., 1987—; fin. analyst, agt. A.L. Williams, Atlanta, 1986—. Mem. Balt. Credit Womens Group. Home: 3938 Grimm Rd Jarrettsville MD 21084 Office: EIL Instruments Inc 10 Loveton Circle Sparks MD 21152

HOEFT, PAMELA ANN, small business executive; b. Detroit, Sept. 26, 1946; d. Anthony Roy and Bernice Rosella (Kreibich) H.; m. Charles Harris Wylie, Apr. 12, 1969 (div. Mar. 1976); Daniel Stephen Morse, Sept. 23, 1988. Student, Cen. Mich. U., 1964-66; BS, Eastern Mich. U., 1968; MA, U. Mich., 1975. Lic. realtor, Washington, DC. Librarian Wayne-Westland Community Schs., Wayne, Mich., 1968-70; librarian, media specialist, dist. coordinator Pinckney (Mich.) Community Schs., 1970-78; cons. Fed. Grant Library Services to Penal Instns. Petoskey Pub. Library, 1975-78; owner Media Innovations, Arlington, Va., 1975—, Hoeft Assocs. Info. Brokerage, Patent Searches, Arlington, 1978—; owner, sec. Common Man Motion Picture Corp., Arlington, 1984—; fin. dir. The Pentan Co., Arlington, 1985—; pres. Legendary Pictures, Ltd., Washington, 1989—. Contbg. author: Automotive Engineering and Litigation, 1984; author (booklet): Information for Inventors, 1986; producer: Bertel Assocs. Internat., 1985; assoc. producer 35mm film, feature length motion picture Beyond the Rising Moon, 1988. Mem. ALA, Am. Chem. Soc., Internat. Platform Assn., Arlington C. of C. (small bus. adv. council 1979-84). Roman Catholic. Home and Office: PO Box 2323 Arlington VA 22202

HOEFT, RICHARD JAMES, financial executive; b. Wausau, Wis., Mar. 13, 1946; s. Clarence C. and Doris A. (Bowers) H. BS, U. Wis., La Crosse, 1969; MS, U. Wis., 1970; Grad., Real Estate Inst. Cert. fin. planner; chartered life underwriter, chartered fin. cons.; registered investment advisor and assoc. Counselor, educator Western Wis. Tech. Coll., La Crosse, 1969-80; real estate cons., mgr., owner Sunworld Enterprises Area Investments, La Crosse, 1980-83; br. mgr., acct. exec. Security Spring and Boe, La Crosse, 1983-84; provisional fin. planner Fin. Options, La Crosse, 1984; fin. planner equity qualified agy. Equitable Fin. Cos., La Crosse, 1985—; also bd. dirs. Equitable Fin. Cos., LaCrosse. Bd. dirs. LaCrosse Tourist and Convention Bur., 1975-82, LaCrosse Festivals, 1976—; chmn. LaCrosse Bicentannial, 1976. Recipient Nat. Quality award, National Leader Corp. award, Nat. Sales Achievement award. Mem. Inst. Cert. Fin. Planners, Internat. Assn. Fin. Planning, Nat. Assn. Life Underwriters, Am. Soc. CLU's, Am. Soc. Chartered Fin. Cons. Lutheran. Home: W5798 State Hwy 33 La Crosse WI 54601 Office: Equitable Fin Cos 505 King St #223 La Crosse WI 54601

HOELLEN, JOHN JAMES, lawyer; s. John J. and Mame F. (Skellinger) H.; m. Mary Jane McMeans, Apr. 24, 1948; children: Elizabeth J. Hoellen Ward, Robert B. BA, Northwestern U., 1935, JD, 1938; LittD (hon.), North Park Coll., 1988. Bar: Ill. 1938, U.S. Dist. Ct. (no. dist.) Ill. 1938, U.S. Ct. Appeals (7th cir.) 1966. Assoc., Willner & Horwitz, Chgo., 1938-46; atty. Ill. Dept. Registration and Edn., 1946-47; ptnr. Leonard, Hoellen & Raszus, Chgo., 1947-54, Hoellen & Willens, Chgo., 1954-68, John J. Hoellen and Assocs., Chgo., 1968-75, Hoellen, Lukes & Halper, Chgo., 1975-88; spl. asst. atty. gen., 1969-75; ptnr. Hoellen & Lukes, 1988—; dir., gen. counsel Bank of Ravenswood, Chgo., 1962—; dir., gen. counsel Ravenswood Fin. Corp.; bd. dirs. Chgo. Transit Authority, 1979—, vice chmn. 1986—; alderman City of Chgo., 1947-75; del. Republican Nat. Conv., 1972, 76, 80, 84, 88; mem. Rep. Central Com. Cook County, 1964-87, Rep. nominee for mayor of Chgo., 1975; pres. Sulzer Family Found., 1958—. Lt. U.S. Navy, 1941-46. Mem. ABA, Ill. Bar Assn., Chgo. Bar Assn., Am. Judicature Soc., Chgo. Club, Kiwanis. Methodist. Office: 1940 Irving Park Rd Chicago IL 60613

HOENICKE, EDWARD HENRY, lawyer, corporate executive; b. Chgo., Apr. 12, 1930; s. Edward Albert and Henrietta Christina (Hameister) H.; m. Janice Armande Gravel, Aug. 14, 1954; children—Jeanne E., Anne L. A.B., Cornell U., 1950; J.D., U. Mich., 1956. Bar: N.Y. 1956. Assoc. Cravath, Swaine & Moore, N.Y.C., 1956-59; div. counsel Olin Corp., N.Y.C., 1959-68; v.p., gen. counsel Beechnut, Inc., N.Y.C., 1968-69; pres. Beechnut Lifesavers Internat., N.Y.C., 1969-76; v.p., asst. gen. counsel Squibb Corp., N.Y.C., 1976-77; sr. v.p., gen. counsel, UAL, Inc. and United Airlines, Inc., Elk Grove Village, Ill., 1977—. Bd. dirs. Care, Inc., 1971—. Served with USAF, 1951-53. Mem. ABA. Club: Exmoor Country (Highland Park, Ill.). Office: United Airlines 1200 Algonquin Rd Elk Grove Village IL 60007

HOESCHLER, LINDA LOVAS, investments business executive; b. Joplin, Mo., July 19, 1944; d. Stephen Edward and Hildur (Wederquist) Lovas; m. John Gregory Hoeschler, Aug. 27, 1966; children: Kristen Bowe, Frederick Reeves. B.A., Barnard Coll., 1966; M.A., New Sch. for Social Research, 1968. Free-lance writer, editor, lectr. 1969-76; mng. editor Minn. Gov's Commn. on Arts, St. Paul, 1976-77; arts grants coordinator Dayton-Hudson Found., Mpls., 1977-78; dir. communications Dayton-Hudson Corp., Mpls., 1978-80, v.p. communications, 1980-82; regional mgr. B. Dalton Bookseller (subs. Dayton-Hudson Corp.), Mpls., 1982-83; mem. adv. bd. Nat. Computer Systems, Mpls., 1981-83, group v.p., 1983-87; pres. Landmark Investors, Ltd., St. Paul, 1987—; bd. dirs. Personal Decisions Rsch., Inc. Author music, dance and book criticism, Mpls. Star and St. Paul Pioneer Press; author (with Jimmie Powell), Minnesota: State of the Arts, 1977. Pres. Lark Quartet, 1987-88; bd. dirs. Minn. Dance Theatre, Mpls., 1979-81, Plymouth Music Series, 1979-86, Ordway Music Theatre, 1988—; mem. exec. com., fin. com. and books com. Am. Council for Arts, N.Y.C., 1981-87; mem. adv. bd. grad. programs in mgmt. Coll. of St. Thomas, St. Paul, 1986—; mem., subcom. chair Minn. Gov.'s Commn. on Edn. for Econ. Growth, 1983-85; mem. North Cen. Regional Ednl. Lab., 1985—. Herbert Lehman fellow, 1966-68. Mem. Women's Econ. Roundtable. Mem. Democratic Farm Labor Party. Congregationalist. Club: Mpls. Home: 1630 Edgcumbe Rd Saint Paul MN 55116 Office: Landmark Investors Ltd W-1390 First Nat Bank Bldg 332 Minnesota St Saint Paul MN 55101

HOFER, CHARLES WARREN, strategic management educator, consultant; b. Phoenixville, Pa., Nov. 11, 1940; s. Charles Emil and Alice May (Howard) H.; m. Judith Racella Millner, Oct. 22, 1980. BS in Engring. Physics summa cum laude, Lehigh U., 1962; MBA in Mktg. with distinction, Harvard U., 1965, MS in Applied Math., 1966, D in Bus. Policy, 1969. Research asst. Harvard Bus. Sch., Boston, 1965-66; asst. prof. Northeastern U., Boston, 1968-69; vis. lectr. Singapore Inst. Mgmt., 1969-70; asst. prof. Northwestern U., Evanston, Ill., 1970-75; assoc. prof. Northwestern U., 1975-76; vis. assoc. prof. Stanford (Calif.) U., 1976-77, Columbia U., N.Y.C., 1978, NYU, 1978-80; vis. prof. U. Calif., Riverside, 1980; prof. U. Ga., Athens, 1981—; lectr. Chgo. C. of C., 1976-78; campaign cons. Congressman (now Senator) Donald W. Riegle, Jr., Flint, Mich., 1968-72. Author: Toward a Contingency Theory of Business Strategy, 1975 (ranked 16th in world Acad. Mgmt. survey 1985), Strategy Formulation: Analytical Concepts, 1978 (ranked 30th in world Acad. Mgmt. survey 1985); co-author: Strategic Management: A Casebook in Policy and Planning, 1980, 84; co-editor: Strategic Management: A New View of Business Policy and Planning, 1979 (ranked 6th in world Acad. Mgmt. survey 1985); editor: Strategic Planning Mgmt., 1987—; assoc. editor: Jour. of Bus. Strategy, 1980-85; contbg. editor Am. Jour. Small Bus., 1987—. Pa. Scholar, 1958-62, Baker Scholar Harvard U., 1965; NSF fellow, 1962-63, Ford Found. Fellow, 1966-67. Mem. Acad. Mgmt. (chmn. policy div. 1977-78), Strategic Mgmt. Soc. (charter), Decision Scis. Inst. (policy track chmn. 1985-86), Inst. Mgmt. Scis., Am. Econ. Assn., Phi Beta Kappa, Phi Eta Sigma, Pi Mu Epsilon, Tau Beta Pi, Sigma Iota Epsilon, Beta Gamma Sigma. Republican. Lutheran. Clubs: Harvard Bus. Sch. of Atlanta, Harvard of Ga.; Lehigh Chess (pres. 1961-62). Home: 4445 Stonington Cir Dunwoody GA 30338 Office: U Ga Mgmt Dept Athens GA 30602

HOFF, CHARLES WORTHINGTON, III, banker; b. Balt., Mar. 1, 1934; s. Charles Worthington Jr. and Sarah Durant (Yearley) H.; m. Margaret Elizabeth Ober, Sept. 7, 1967; children: Zoe Carey, Alexandra Yearley, Juliana Macgill, Margaret Frazier, Charles Worthington IV. BS in Bus., Johns Hopkins U., 1961; postgrad., Stonier Sch. Banking, 1964-66. With First Nat. Bank Md., Balt., 1955-77, div. v.p., 1968-77; exec. v.p. Farmers & Mechanics Nat. Bank, Frederick, 1977-81, pres., 1981—, also bd. dirs.; bd. dirs. Yankee Engring. Co., Balt. Br. Fed. Res. Bank Richmond. Bd. dirs. Children's Aid and Family Service Soc. Balt., 1972-77, exec. com., fin. com. 1974-76; pres. Oriole Advocates, Inc., 1963, treas., 1964-65; trustee FredericK Meml. Hosp., 1983—, Hood Coll., 1985—, Community Found. Frederick County, Md., 1987—. Mem. Maryland Bankers Assn. (bd. dirs. 1988—), Am. Bankers Assn. (council, v.p. for Md. 1983), Am. Inst. Banking, Frederick County C. of C. (bd. dirs. 1980-82). Republican. Methodist. Clubs: Elkridge, Holly Hills Country, Cap and Gown (Princeton, N.J.), Bachelors Cotillon. Lodge: Rotary. Home: 5512 Bootjack Dr Frederick MD 21701 Office: Farmers & Mechanics Nat Bank 110 Thomas Johnson Dr Frederick MD 21701

HOFF, LAURETTA ELAINE, city finance official; b. Grenville, S.D., Jan. 2, 1932; d. Henry Advin and Blanche Marie (Jones) Ellingson; m. LaVoid Charles Hoff, June 22, 1949; children: Neil, Randy, Kevin. Dep. auditor City of Watertown, S.D., 1959-73, city auditor, 1973-78, fin. officer, 1978—. Bd. dirs. Watertown Community Found., sec., 1979—; bd. dirs. S.D. Retirement System, Pierre, 1987—. Mem. Govt. Fin. Officers Assn. (numerous awards S.D. chpt.), Internat. Inst. Mcpl. Clerks. Lutheran. Office: City of Watertown 23 2d St NE Watertown SD 57201

HOFF, LAWRENCE CONRAD, pharmaceutical company executive; b. Fresno, Calif., Jan. 19, 1929; s. Conrad and Katherine H.; m. Jacqueline Goodyear, Jan. 27, 1950; children: M. Catherine, Frederick L., Lisa J. AB in Econs., Stanford U., 1950; ScD in Pharmacy (hon.), Mass. Coll. Pharm. & Allied Health Sci., 1981; LLD (hon.), Kalamazoo Coll., 1987. With sales The Upjohn Co., Kalamazoo, 1950-66, dir. domestic pharm. ops., 1966-69, v.p. domestic pharm. mktg., 1969-74, v.p., gen. mgr. domestic pharm. ops., 1974-77, exec. v.p., 1977-84, pres., 1984-87, pres., chief operating officer, 1987—; bd. dirs., mem. exec. com. Coun. on Family Health, N.Y.C., 1976; trustee, chmn. Nat. Found. Infectious Diseases, Washington, 1976-81; bd. dirs., mem. exec. com., v.p. Proprietary Assn., Washington, 1979-85; nat. adv. com. Kellogg Pharm. Clin. Scientist Program, Mpls., 1980; bd. dirs. 1st Am. Bank Corp. Trustees Borgess Med. Ctr., Kalamazoo, 1982. Mem. Pharm. Mfrs. Assn. (chmn. 1987-88, bd. dirs. 1984), Am. Fedn. Pharm. Edn. (bd. dirs. 1980-84), Kalamazoo Country Club. Republican. Episcopalian. Office: The Upjohn Co 7000 Portage Rd Kalamazoo MI 49001

HOFFMAN, EDWARD FRANCIS, controller; b. Topeka, Dec. 16, 1948; s. Jerome J. and Loretta A. (Herman) H.; m. Sherel A. Dyer, Oct. 21, 1967; children: Shawn E., Michelle A. BBA in Acctg., Wichita (Kans.) State U., 1980. CPA, Kans. Engring. designer The Boeing Co., Wichita, 1967-72, Gates Lear Jet Corp., Wichita, 1972-80; sr. acct. Baird, Kurtz & Dobson, CPA's, Wichita, 1980-82; audit supr. Markel, Koch & Siedhoff, CPA's, Wichita, 1982-84; controller Precision Pattern Inc., Wichita, 1984-86, Doskocil Foods Group, Hutchinson, Kans., 1986—; bd. dirs. Humphrey Products Inc., Wichita, 1986—. Mem. Am. Inst. CPA's, Kans. Soc. CPA's. Republican. Home: 202 Green St Hutchinson KS 67502 Office: Doskocil Foods Group PO Box 1570 Hutchinson KS 67504

HOFFMAN, EDWARD SULLIVAN, insurance company executive; b. N.Y.C., May 5, 1947; s. Albert L. and Florence (Meyer) H.; m. Megg Picoli, Aug. 29, 1970; children: Amy B., Carrie L. BSBA, Babson Coll., 1970. Asst. sec. Wilcox Baringer, N.Y.C., 1975-77; sr. v.p. N.Y. Marine Mgrs., N.Y.C., 1978-84; exec. v.p. Navigators Ins. Co., N.Y.C., 1983—;, also bd. dirs.; sr. v.p. Navigators Group Inc., N.Y.C., 1983—, also bd. dirs.; pres. Navigators Mgmt. Corp., N.Y.C., 1984—, also bd. dirs.; bd. dirs. Navigators Ins. Svcs., San Francisco, J.H. Blades, Houston. Mem. Am. Inst. Marine Underwriters. Office: Navigators Mgmt Corp 84 William St New York NY 10038

HOFFMAN, EDWIN PHILIP, banker; b. Allentown, Pa., Sept. 13, 1942; s. Donald Brooks and Margaret Jane (Gruber) H.; m. Marie Rose Ann Smuldis, Aug. 14, 1965 (div. Mar. 1973); m. Sandra Fay Norsworthy, Mar. 31, 1973; children—Lara, Edwin Alexander, Jamie. B.S., Muhlenberg Coll., 1964; M.S., Yale U., 1966, Ph.D., 1968. Exec. trainee Citicorp, N.Y.C., 1969-70, asst. v.p. computer services, 1970-72, v.p., head Colombia, 1972-74, sr. v.p., div. head Middle East and N. Africa, 1974-80, exec. v.p. individual bank, 1980-84, group exec. Latin Am., 1984-87; pres., chief op. officer Household Internat., Prospect Heights, Ill., 1988—; bd. dirs. Eljer Industries, Scotsman Industries, Schwitzer Inc. Trustee Presbyterian Ch., Mt. Kisco, N.Y., 1984-87, Muhlenberg Coll., Allentown, Pa., Rassias Found., Hanover, N.H.; bd. dirs. Manhattan Inst., Chgo. Symphony Orch., 1988—. Mem. Exec. Club Chgo. (bd. dirs. 1989—). Republican. Home: 1580 Kathryn Ln Lake Forest IL 60045 Office: Household Internat Inc 2700 Sanders Rd Prospect Heights IL 60070

HOFFMAN, GENE, food company executive, consultant; b. East St. Louis, Ill., July 29, 1927; s. Edmund H. and Bee (Hood) H.; m. Nancy P. Claney, Oct. 27, 1951; children: Kim Elizabeth, Keith Murdock. B.J. in Advt, U. Mo., 1948. Asst. advt. mgr. Montgomery Ward Co., 1948; copywriter, asst. mgr. advt. promotion Chgo. Tribune, 1949-50; mgr. promotion Phila. Bull., 1951-56; with The Kroger Co., 1956-77, gen. mgr. St. Louis div., 1956-61; dir. mktg. processed foods div., Cin., 1961-63, v.p., gen. mgr., 1964-66; corp. v.p. St. Louis, 1966, v.p. food mfg. divs., 1966-69; pres. Kroger Food Processing Co., 1969-72, Kroger Brands Co., 1972-74; sr. corp. v.p. parent co. 1974-75, corp. pres., bd. dirs. parent co., 1975-77; with Super Valu Stores, Inc., Mpls., 1977-88; pres. Super Valu Wholesale Food Cos., 1977-87, chmn., 1985-88; sr. corp. v.p. Super Valu Stores Inc.; chmn., chief exec. officer Food Giant, Inc.; pres. Corp. Strategies Internat., Mpls., 1987—, Mktg. Assocs., Inc., Mpls., 1987—, LeaderShape, Inc., Champaign, Ill., 1987—; bd. dirs. Novate Enterprises Inc., Americana Mag., Rural Ventures, Inc., Rural Ventures Inc., Lewis Grocer Co., Vital Resources Inc., West Coast Grocery Co., U.S. Quality Plastics Co., The Liggett Group, Inc., Confab Corp. Chmn., Leader Shape Inst.; bd. govs. ATO Found. Served with AC USNR, 1945-46. Mem. Am. Mgmt. Assn., Food Mktg. Inst., Greater Cin. C. of C. (v.p., dir.), AIM, Alpha Delta Sigma, Alpha Tau Omega. Episcopalian. Clubs: Interlachen Country (Mpls.), Comml., Cin., Hyde Park Golf and Country, Queen City, Bankers (Cin.); Tonka Racquets, Camargo Racquet. Office: Corp Strategies Internat 6482 Carlson Dr Minneapolis MN 55346

HOFFMAN, GLORIA LEVY, communications executive; b. Norfolk, Va., Feb. 8, 1933; d. Maxwell Lewis and Jessie (Mashbitz) Levy; m. Frank Katz Hoffman (dec.); children: Daniel L., L. Stephen, Victoria Anne, Jonathan M. (dec.). BA in Speech and Radio, U. Wis., 1954. Pres. Creative Concepts in Communications, Ltd., Kansas City, Mo., 1984—, Peoplehood Products, Kansas City, 1987—. Author: I Belong to ME!, 1984. Promotional and pub. relations dir. Menorah Med. Ctr., Trans-Menorahs, Brandeis Books Drives; vol. Nelson Gallery Art, Kansas City Art Inst., Young Woman's Philharmonic, Children's Mercy Hosp. Recipient Commemorative Medal of Honor Hallmark, 1987. Republican. Jewish. Home and Office: 1250 W 63rd St Kansas City MO 64113

HOFFMAN, JAMES ZANTESON, consulting executive; b. La Grange, Ill., May 15, 1930; s. Harold L. and Alma M. (Zanteson) H.; m. Barbara L. Rundell, Nov. 21, 1959; children: Elizabeth C., James Z. Jr. BS in Chem. Engring., U. Ill., 1953; MBA, Purdue U., 1958. Tech. sales rep. Spencer Chem. Co., Kansas City, Mo., 1955-60; prin. Techno-Econ. Services Co., Los Altos, Calif., 1960-64; mgr. ventures Internat. Minerals & Chem. Co., Skokie, Ill., 1964-70; mng. dir. Coromandel Fertilizers Ltd, Secunderabad, India, 1967-69; corp. v.p. Reliance Universal Co., Louisville, 1970-82; pres. Zanchem Internat. Co., Louisville, 1982—. Contbr. articles to profl. jours. Dir., officer Stage One, Louisville, 1975—. Lt. U.S. Army, 1953-55. Home: 132 Council Rd Louisville KY 40207 Office: Zanchem Internat Inc PO Box 7411 Louisville KY 40207

HOFFMAN, LOWELL MARTENS, food company executive; b. Chgo., Dec. 27, 1940; s. Howard D. and Muriel (Martens) H.; m. Ruth E. Weber, Sept. 4, 1965; children: Laura, Bruce, Catherine. BS in Metall. Engring., U. Ill., 1963; MBA in Prodn. Mgmt., Ind. U., 1965. Prodn. mgr. Cummins Engine Co., Columbus, Ind., 1965-69, Voplex Corp., Lapeer, Mich., 1969-71; v.p. materials Nat. Can Corp., Chgo., 1971-84; v.p., dir. material mgmt. Kraft, Inc., Glenview, Ill., 1985—. Bd. dirs. Glen Ellyn Children's Chorus, Glen Ellyn, Ill., 1984-88, Glen Ellyn United Way, 1985-88, Chgo. Econ. Devel. Corp., 1986-88. Mem. Council Logistics Mgmt., Nat. Assn. Purchasing Mgmt., Beta Gamma Sigma, Omicron Delta Kappa. Congregationalist. Home: 571 Hawthorne Glen Ellyn IL 60137 Office: Kraft Inc 2211 Sanders Rd Northbrook IL 60062

HOFFMAN, MILTON BERNARD, television executive; b. Mineola, N.Y., Apr. 20, 1946; s. Sol Walter and Dorothy (Sokolowsky) H.; m. Stephanie Elan Cherry, Nov. 4, 1983. BS, Columbia U., 1969. Dir. drama and lit. Sta. WBAI-FM, N.Y.C., 1970-72; producer, dir. Sta. WNET-TV, N.Y.C., 1972-76; exec. producer Sta. WVIZ-TV, Cleve., 1978-81; v.p. prodn. Pacific Mountain Network, Denver, 1981-86; pres., exec. producer Milton B. Hoffman Prodns. (formerly TVI Prodns.), Denver, 1986—; judge Columbia Univ. Film Festival, N.Y.C., 1974; prodn. cons. NPO Task Force, N.Y.C., 1976-78. Producer: (marathon radio reading) War and Peace, 1970 (selected for Mus. Broadcasting collection), (home video) Perestroika Papers, 1988, The Profl. Server, 1988, (radio series) Not Without Art: Arts and the Handicapped, 1976, (cable TV series) American Viewpoints, 1984-86 (Ace award 1987); producer, dir.: (TV spls.) Lucy and the First Family, 1981, Legends of Laughter: Dick Cavett Remembers Groucho Marx and Jack Benny, 1987. Recipient Silver Anvil award Pub. Relations Soc. Am., 1976, Spl. Ace award Nat. Acad. Cable Programming, 1985. Mem. Nat. Acad. TV Arts and Scis. (judge Cleve. chpt. 1980, Denver chpt. 1987, Emmy award 1981), Solstice Arts Found. (founder 1975). Office: TVI Prodns 368 S High St Denver CO 80209

HOFFMAN, MITCHELL WADE, corporate executive; b. Newport News, Va., Sept. 27, 1954; s. Joseph and Sarah (Goldberg) H.; m. Patrice Lynn Bare, Dec. 2, 1978; 1 child, Loren Kimberly. BA in Psychol., U. Va., 1975; MBA, Coll. Wm. and Mary, 1978; MS in Fin., Va. Commonwealth U., 1988. Cert. purchasing mgr., Nat. Assn. Purchasing Mgmt. Sr. buyer Harvey Hubbell Inc., Christiansburg, Va., 1978-79; agt. purchasing Ingersoll Rand Inc., Roanoke, Va., 1979-82; supr. distbn. HoN Industries Inc., Richmond, Va., 1983; agt. capital purchasing Brockway Inc., Richmond, 1983-88; ops. fin. analyst Philip Morris, Inc., Richmond, 1988—; cons. purchasing Ingersoll Rand Inc., Roanoke, 1982-83; adj. prof. fin. Va. Commonwealth U., 1988-89. Mem. Nat. Assn. Purshasing Mgmt., Nat. Assn. Fin. Mgmt., Alpha Iota Delta, Beta Gamma Sigma, Phi Kappa Phi. Home: 4218 Brixton Rd Chesterfield VA 23832

HOFFMAN, RICHARD M., lawyer; b. N.Y.C., Oct. 22, 1942; s. Simon and Pearl (Lancet) H.; children—Mark, Michael. Grad., CCNY, 1964; LL.B., Bklyn. Sch. Law, 1967. Bar: N.Y. 1968. Law clk. to presiding judge U.S. Dist. Ct. (ea. dist.) N.Y., N.Y.C., 1967-69; assoc. Kramer, Lowenstein, Nessen & Kamin, N.Y.C., 1969-73; various positions legal dept. Gen. Instrument Corp., N.Y.C., 1973-82, v.p., gen. counsel, 1982-86, v.p. gen. counsel, sec., 1986—. Mem. N.Y.C. Bar Assn. (com. corp. law depts. 1981-84). Home: 60 Brite Ave Scarsdale NY 10583 Office: Gen Instrument Corp 767 Fifth Ave New York NY 10153

HOFFMAN, RICHARD SCOTT, retail executive, financial consultant; b. Salisbury, N.C., Mar. 16, 1956; s. Charles Alfred Sr. and Lillie Mae (Hardiman) H.; m. Sheree Jo Fuller, Sept. 7, 1985. Student, Wake Forest U., 1975-76; BBA in Acctg., Appalachian State U., 1980. CPA, N.C. Staff acct. Peat Marwick Mitchell & Co., Roanoke, Va., 1980-81; sr. acct. Daniel, Pulliam, McKee & Co., CPA's, Winston-Salem, N.C., 1981-83; fin. cons. Merrill Lynch, Greensboro, N.C., 1983—; owner I Natural Cosmetics, Greensboro and Raleigh, N.C., 1986—; bd. dirs. Many Faces Ltd., Raleigh. Mem. AICPA (div. personal fin. planning), N.C. Assn. CPA's, Acctg. Club (treas. Boone, N.C. chpt. 1978-79), Sportime Club, Greensboro City Club, Beta Gamma Sigma, Beta Alpha Psi, Gamma Beta Phi. Republican. Presbyterian. Office: Merrill Lynch 200 N Elm St Greensboro NC 27401

HOFFMAN, STANLEY JOHN, credit company executive; b. Balt., May 18, 1935; s. Bernard Leroy and Catherine Mary (Rosemer) H.; m. Cathy Renee Meyr; children: Deborah, Catherine, Lorraine, Gina. With Beneficial Corp., Peapack, N.J., 1955-84; operating v.p. Wayne, N.J., 1975; mem. exec. com., mgmt. com., corp. systems steering com., bd. dirs; v.p. Spiegel Corp., Farifacts Corp., BWS Services subs. Beneficial Corp., Chgo., Louisville, and Oakbrook, Ill., 1975-77; corp. v.p., dir. Western Auto Supply Corp. subs. Beneficial Corp., Kansas City, Mo., 1977-84; sr. v.p., corp. officer Gordon Jewelry Corp., Houston, 1984—. Mem. Mcths. Research Council. Office: Gordon Jewelry Corp 820 Fannin St Houston TX 77002 also: Gordon Jewelry Corp 1617 Richey Rd Houston TX 77073

HOFFMAN, SUSAN E. FLANNERY, lawyer; b. Akron, Ohio, Nov. 9, 1950; d. Frank A. Flannery and Elizabeth Ann (McLaughlin) Flannery; m. John H. Hoffman Jr., May 7, 1988. BA, Bowling Green (Ohio) State U., 1972; MA, No. Mich. U., 1976; JD, Duquesne U., 1983. Bar: Ohio 1983, Pa. 1983, N.J. 1988. Instr. biology No. Mich. U., Marquette, 1972-76; environ. specialist Western Res. Econ. Devel. Agy., Youngstown, Ohio, 1976-79; regulatory analyst Jones & Laughlin Steel Corp., Pitts., 1979-83; asst. atty. gen. State of Ohio, Columbus, 1983-85; assoc. Squire, Sanders & Dempsey, Columbus, 1985-88, Cohen, Shapiro, Polisher, Shiekman & Cohen, Lawrenceville, N.J., 1988—; chair OEPA Constrn. Grants Task Force, Columbus, 1987-88. Mem. ABA, Ohio Bar Assn., Columbus Bar Assn. Home: 225 Alberts Way Langhorne PA 19047 Office: Cohen Shapiro Polisher Shiekman & Cohen 977 Lenox Dr Bldg 3 Lawrenceville NJ 08648

HOFFMANN, CAROL TOMB, financial planner; b. Balt., Nov. 3, 1952; d. Richard John and Doris Elaine (Shoemaker) Tomb; m. Michael R. Hoffmann, July 29, 1973; children: Kurt M., Kristen E., Kevin R. Student, Drake U., 1972; AS, Harcum Jr. Coll., 1973. Cert. fin. planner. Various retailing positions N.Y. and Iowa, 1973-76; store opening area supr. Brandeis, Des Moines, 1976-77, Peterson, Harned Von Maur, Des Moines, 1977-78; adminstrv. asst. Clk. Iowa Supreme Ct., Des Moines, 1978-79; retirement fund advisor Jones, Hoffmann and Davison, Des Moines, 1978-83; fin. advisor Michael R. Hoffmann, P.C., Des Moines, 1983—; pres. Nouveau Riche, Ltd., Des Moines, 1986—. Mem. Internat. Bd. Standards and Practices for Cert. Fin. Planners, Internat. Assn. for Fin. Planning, Am. Assn. Individual Investors, Blank Park Zoo, Nat. Rifle Assn., Des Moines Art Ctr., Des Moines Sci. Ctr., Friends Iowa Pub. Television. Office: Nouveau Riche Ltd 9632 Quail Ridge Des Moines IA 50322

HOFFMANN, CHRISTOPH LUDWIG, corporate lawyer; b. Elsterwerda, Fed. Republic Germany, Oct. 9, 1944; came to U.S., 1965; s. Gunther and Ruth (Hornschuh) H.; m. Susan Magnuson, June 18, 1983. Student, Freie U. Berlin, 1964-65; BA, U. Wis., 1966; JD, Harvard U., 1969. Bar: Mass. 1969, R.I. 1977. Assoc. Bingham, Dana & Gould, Boston, 1969-76; asst. gen. counsel Textron Inc., Providence, 1976-83; v.p., gen. counsel, sec. Pneumo Corp., Boston, 1983-85; sr. v.p., gen. counsel, sec. Pneumo Abex Corp., Boston, 1985—; instr. bus. law Barrington (R.I.) Coll., 1981-82. Bd. dirs. R.I. Citizens Energy Conservation Corp., Providence, 1979-83. Mem. ABA, Mass. Bar Assn., R.I. Bar Assn., Am. Corp. Counsel Assn., Machinery and Allied Products Inst. Law Council. Office: Pneumo Abex Corp 4800 Prudential Tower Boston MA 02199

HOFFMANN, MANFRED WALTER, oil company executive; b. Bklyn., Apr. 21, 1938; s. Hermann Karl and Emilie (Talmon) H.; B.S., Cornell U., 1960; M.Ed., Temple U., 1972, Ph.D., 1977; m. Barbara Ann Kenvin, Aug. 5, 1961; children—Lisa Joy, Lauren Kimberly, Kurt William. Mktg. rep. H. T. Heinz Co., N.Y.C., 1960-61; regional mgr. Swift & Co., Curtis Bay, Md. and Reading, Pa., 1961-63; salesman Sun Oil Co., Syracuse, N.Y., 1963-67, personnel mgr., 1967-71, mgr. mktg. devel., Rosemont, Pa., 1971-72, mgr. tng., 1973-77, dir. orgn. and mgmt. devel., 1977-79; dir. human resources and adminstrn. Sun Prodn. Co., Dallas, 1979-83; dir. human resources Sun Exploration & Prodn. Co., 1983-86; gen. dir. World Wide Human Resources Services, Dallas, Tex., 1986—; lectr. Grad. Sch., U. Tex., Dallas, 1979—. Pres., PTA, bd. mem. Beechwood Sch., 1975-77; cons. exec. com. Orgns. Industrialization Congress Am., 1975-79; bd. dirs. Job Opportunity for Youth, 1980-81; bd. dirs. Dallas SER, 1986—. Served with USMCR, 1956-62. Mem. Am. Soc. Tng. and Devel. (mgr. petroleum industry spl. interest group 1977-78, cert. of Appreciation 1977), Am. Soc. Personnel Adminstrn. (cert. of Appreciation 1977, 78), Am. Psychol. Assn. Republican, Am. Mgmt. Assn. Am. Petroleum Inst. Episcopalian. Home: 2210 Forest Creek McKinney TX 75069

HOFFMANN, ROBERT EDWARD, JR., business owner; b. Latrobe, Pa., July 8, 1959; s. Robert E. Sr. and Jane E. (Flack) H. BS, E. Stroudsburg (Pa.) U., 1982; postgrad., N.Y.U., 1983-85. Dir. beverage div. Sky Top (Pa.) Club and Resort, 1982; dir. foods and beverage div. Galley Restaurant, Wind Cap, Pa., 1983; beverage specialist T.G.I. Fridays, Pitts., 1984; mgr. Summit House Restaurant, Jersey City, 1985, Sporting Club Restaurant, N.Y.C., 1986; group mgr. Caliente Cab Co. Mexican Cafe, N.Y.C., 1987-88; owner Systematic Restaurant Analysis, Jersey City, 1986—; dir. ops. Exchange Enterprises, Jersey City, 1985—. Recipient Eagle Scout award Boy Scouts Am., 1974. Mem. Am. Inst. Wine and Food, Tasters Guild. Office: Systematic Restaurant Analysis 21 Lembeck Ave Jersey City NJ 07305-4716

HOFFSTOT, HENRY PHIPPS, JR., lawyer; b. Pitts., Nov. 13, 1917; s. Henry Phipps and Marguerite (Martin) H.; m. Barbara Drew, Apr. 17, 1948; children: Thayer Drew Hoffstot Unterman, Henry Phipps, III. A.B., Harvard U., 1939, LL.B., 1942. Bar: Pa. 1942. Assoc. firm Reed Smith Shaw & McClay, Pitts., 1946-55, ptnr., 1956-87, of counsel, 1987—; pres., dir. Pennsgrove Water Supply Co., 1967-84; Adv. bd. Biltmore Co., 1985—. Active Commn. for Study of Common Body of Knowledge for C.P.A.s, N.Y., 1965-67, Nat. Parks Centennial Commn., 1971-73; trustee Carnegie Library, Pitts., 1966—, v.p., 1970—; trustee Carnegie Inst., 1966—, sec., 1968—; supervising com. Bellefield Boiler Plant, 1967—, chmn., 1978—; trustee Family and Children's Service, 1962-68, 69-75, 77-83, pres., 1964-66; trustee Pitts. Regional Library Center, 1967—; trustee St. Edmunds Acad., 1964-72, pres., 1968-70; bd. dirs. Community Chest of Allegheny County, 1962-68, exec. com., 1968-69; bd. dirs. Mendelssohn Choir, Pitts., 1958-85, treas., 1959-61; bd. dirs. Pitts. Chamber Music Soc., 1968—; bd. dirs. Vis. Nurse Assn. of Allegheny County, 1948—, pres., 1957-60, 66-67, 79-83; mem. council Am. Mus. in Britain, 1979—; trustee Phipps Friends, 1985—, pres., 1988—; bd. dirs. Pitts. chpt. World Federalist Assn., 1967—. With inf. AUS, 1942-46. Fellow Am. Bar Found.; mem. ABA, Pa. Bar Assn., Allegheny County Bar Assn., Am. Coll. Probate Counsel, Am. Law Inst., SAR (pres. Pitts. chpt. 1978-79). Presbyterian. Clubs: Duquesne (Pitts.), Harvard-Yale-Princeton (Pitts.), Pitts. Golf (Pitts.); Rolling Rock, Harvard (N.Y.C.); Bath and Tennis, Everglades (Palm Beach). Home: 5057 5th Ave Pittsburgh PA 15232 Office: Reed Smith Shaw & McClay Mellon Sq 6th Ave & William Penn Way Pittsburgh PA 15219-1886

HOFGESANG, PAUL JOSEPH, electronics company executive; b. Princeton, N.J., May 17, 1957; s. Edward G. and Anna S. (Schettino) H.; m. Carolyn J. Reiff, June 4, 1988. BSME, U. Vt., 1979; MBA, Villanova U., 1988. Registered profl. engr., Va. With Gen. Electric Co., 1979; program mgr. microelectronics Gen. Electric Co., Valley Forge, Pa., 1985-87; mgr. mech. shops Gen. Electric Co., Valley Forge, 1987-88; prodn. mgr. Gen. Electric Co., Phila., 1988—. Mem. Am. Prodn. and Inventory Control Soc. Home: 2494 Fieldcrest Ave West Norriton PA 19403 Office: GE Chestnut St Philadelphia PA 19101

HOFSTAD, RALPH PARKER, agricultural cooperative executive; b. Phila., Nov. 14, 1923; s. Ottar and Amelia (Davis) H.; m. Adeline Smedstad, June 14, 1947; children: Diane (Mrs. Roger Dunker), Barbara (Mrs. Dan McClanahan), James, Ron, Tom, Susan. Student, Hamline U., 1942-43, Gustavus Adolphus Coll., 1943-44, Northwestern U., 1944, U. Minn., 1946-47; B.B.A., Northwestern U., 1948. Accountant F S Services, Bloomington, Ill., 1948-51; mgmt. ops. F S Services, 1953-65; pres. Farmers Regional Coop (Felco), Ft. Dodge, Iowa, 1965-70; sr. v.p. agrl. services Land O' Lakes Inc., Ft. Dodge, 1970—; pres. Land O' Lakes Inc., Mpls., 1974—; bd. dirs. Hon Industries, Muscatine, Iowa, Control Data Corp., Mpls., First Interstate Bank, Des Moines;. Trustee Hamline U., St. Paul, U. Minn. Found., St. Paul; bd. dirs. Goodwill Industries Am., 1977—. Served with USNR, 1943-46. Mem. Grocery Mfrs. Am. (bd. dirs. 1983), Nat. Council Farmer Coops. (bd. dirs. 1973—), Mpls. C. of C. Methodist. Home: 7724 Pondwood Dr Edina MN 55435 Office: Land O'Lakes Inc PO Box 116 Minneapolis MN 55440

HOFSTATTER, STEPHEN LEWIS, marketing executive; b. Marlborough, Mass., Aug. 19, 1958; s. Lewis Albert and Joan Carol (Ahlin) H.; m. Kelly Patrice Keener, Nov. 22, 1986. Health physics cons. Numanco Inc., Barrington, R.I., 1979-85; mktg. rep. Resource Tech. Svcs. Inc., Toledo, 1985-87; mktg. mgr. Applied Radiol. Control Inc., Marietta, Ga., 1987—; pres., bd. dirs. Advent Devel. Corp., Charlotte, N.C. Mem. Am. Nuclear Soc. Democrat. Home: 915 Magnolia Ave Charlotte NC 28203 Office: Applied Radiol Control Inc 830 Franklin Ct Marietta GA 30067

HOFSTEAD, JAMES WARNER, laundry machinery company executive; b. Jackson, Tenn., Feb. 3, 1913; s. Harry Oliver and Agnes Lucile (Blackard) H.; m. Ellen Frances Bowers, Dec. 27, 1940; 1 dau., Eda Lucile. A.B., Vanderbilt U., 1935, LL.B., 1938. Bar: Tenn. Sole practice law; v.p., dir. United Telephone Co., 1969—; pres., dir. Wishy Washy, Inc., Nashville, 1946—; pres., dir. Wishy Sales Inc., 1959—. Served to capt. USMC, 1942-45. Mem. SAR (nat. committeeman, state pres.), So. Srs. Golf Assn., Soc. of the Cincinnati, English Speaking Union (chmn.), Soc. Colonial Wars, C. of C., Sigma Chi. Methodist. Clubs: Belle Meade, Cumberland, 200, Exchange (Nashville); Eccentric (London). Home: 215 Deer Park Cir Nashville TN 37205 Office: 3729 Charlotte Ave Nashville TN 37209

HOGAN, BRIAN JOSEPH, editor; b. Aberdeen, S.D., Apr. 11, 1943; s. Arthur James and Magdalena (Frison) H.; m. Jamie Isabelle Schwingel, June 21, 1987. BS, U. Ariz., 1965, 68; MS, U. Utah, 1972. Rsch. asst. U. Va. Rsch. Labs for Engring. Scis., Charlottesville, 1965-66; exploration geophysicist Anaconda Co., Tucson, 1968-71; assoc. editor Benwill Pub. Co., Brookline, Mass., 1973-74; asst. editor Design News, Boston, 1974; midwest editor Design News, Chgo., 1974-87; sr. editor Design News, Newton, Mass., 1987-89; mng. editor DesignNews, Newton, Mass., 1989—. Author stage plays including The Young O'Neil, 1983, Awakening, 1984. Precinct worker Cook County Rep. Com., Oak Park, Ill., 1986; interpreter Frank Lloyd Wright Home and Studio Found., Oak Park, 1981-87. Mem. Am. Soc. Bus. Press Editors, Am. Hist. Print Collectors Soc. Roman Catholic. Office: Design News 275 Washington St Newton MA 02158

HOGAN, CURTIS JULE, union executive, industrial relation consultant; b. Greeley, Kans., July 25, 1926; s. Charles Leo and Anna Malene (Rousselo) H.; m. Lois Jean Ecord, Apr. 23, 1955; children—Christopher James, Michael Sean, Patrick Marshall, Kathleen Marie, Kerry Joseph. B.S. in Indsl. Relations, Rockhurst Coll., 1950; postgrad., Georgetown U., 1955, U. Tehran, 1955-57. With Gt. Lakes Pipeline Co., Kansas City, 1950-55; with Internat. Fedn. Petroleum and Chem. Workers, Denver, 1955-85; gen. sec. Internat. Fedn. Petroleum and Chem. Workers, 1973-85; pres. Internat. Labor Relations Services, Inc., 1976—; cons. in field; lectr. Rockhurst Coll., 1951-52. Contbr. in field. Served with U.S. Army, 1945-46. Mem. Internat. Indsl. Relations Assn., Indsl. Relations Research Assn., Oil Chem. and Atomic Workers Internat. Union. Office: PO Box 6565 Denver CO 80206

HOGAN, DAVID EARL, telecommunications executive; b. Ruston, La., Oct. 5, 1949; s. Frank Earl and Roberta Ruth (Morgan) H.; m. Cathey Dee O'Donnell, Apr. 10, 1971; children: Grant, Todd. BSME, La. Tech. U., 1971, MBA, 1973. Mktg. rep. IBM Corp., Shreveport, La., 1976-78, regional mktg. rep., 1978-79; adv. regional mktg. rep. IBM Corp., Dallas, 1979; mktg. mgr. IBM Corp., Ft. Worth, 1980-82; adminstrv. asst. to v.p. plans and controls IBM Corp., White Plains, N.Y., 1982-83; v.p., gen. mgr. Mobilecom of Ill., Chgo., 1983-84; v.p. mktg. Mobile Communication Corp. of Am. (MCCA), Jackson, Miss., 1985-86; sr. v.p. Century Tel., Monroe, La., 1986-87; pres. bus. group Century Telephone, Monroe, La., 1987-89; pvt. practice Monroe, 1989—; bd. dirs. Async, Inc., Atlanta. Mem. Cellular Tel. Industry Assn. (bd. dirs.). Republican. Baptist.

HOGAN, DAVID J., banker; b. McKees Rocks, Pa., Dec. 18, 1939; s. James A. and Sophie (Vrusk) H.; m. Patricia Ann Liberatore, Feb. 17, 1962; children: David J. Jr., Jeffrey, Brian. BA in Econs., Juniata Coll., 1961. From asst. treas. to dir. corp. planning Sara Lee Corp., Chgo., 1970-74; treas. Fleet Fin. Corp., Providence, 1974-76; v.p. Citicorp, N.Y.C., 1976-83; gen. mgr. N.Am. Saudi Internat. Bank subs. J.P. Morgan, 1983—; mem. sources and uses com., credit policy com. and mng. com. Saudi Internat. Bank, London, 1988—. Mem. Com. for Selection Sch. Dirs., Bronxville, N.Y., 1972-85; pres. Council for Devel. Juniata Coll., Huntingdon, Pa., 1988—; bd. dirs. Chgo. Forum, 1974. Mem. Fin. Execs. Inst., Inst. Internat. Bankers, Univ. Club (N.Y.C.). Democrat. Roman Catholic. Office: Saudi Internat Bank 520 Madison Ave New York NY 10022

HOGAN, DONALD ROBERT, publishing executive; b. Chgo., Mar. 10, 1936; s. Elmer Niles and Lillian E. (Holmes) H.; m. Marie E. DuCote, Jan. 7, 1957 (dec. July 1978); children: Teresa, Robert, Lisa, Christopher; m. Dixie Lee Lash, July 25, 1981. BA, Northeastern Ill. U., 1986. Lic. computer data processor; cert. systems profl. Supr. Jewel Co., Chgo., 1962-65; cons. Namar Inc., Wheaton, Ill., 1966; mgr., then v.p. Hitchock Pubs., Wheaton, 1966; v.p. ABC Pub. Co., Midwest Group, Wheaton, 1966—. Served with U.S. Army, 1955-56. Mem. West Suburban chpt. Data Processing Mgmt. Assn. (pres. 1969-70, bd. dirs. 1967-76, chmn. ABP Data Processing com., individual performance award 1970, meritorious service award 1976). Congregationalist. Home: 1116 Dunstan Rd Geneva IL 60134 Office: ABC Pub Midwest Group 191 S Gary Ave Carol Stream IL 60188

HOGAN, JAMES MICHAEL, management consultant; b. Boston, Aug. 6, 1946; s. Coleman Francis and Margaret Marie (Lawrence) H.; m. Sharon Marie Robinson, Aug. 24, 1968; children: Katherine, John, Elizabeth. AB, Holy Cross Coll., 1970; MBA, Rutgers U., 1971. CPA. Cons. Price Waterhouse and Co., N.Y.C., 1971-76; fin. mgr. Perkin Elmer Data Systems, London, 1976-79; sr. assoc. Theodore Barry and Assocs., N.Y.C., 1979-82; pres. Hogan and Co., Madison, N.J., 1982—. Mem. Inst. Mgmt. Cons. (cert.), Inst. Cert. Mgmt. Accts. (cert.), Am. Inst. CPA's (cert.). Club: Beacon Hill (Summit, N.J.). Office: Hogan & Co 2 Shunpike Rd Suite 32 Madison NJ 07940

HOGAN, JOHN DONALD, college dean, finance educator; b. Binghamton, N.Y., July 16, 1927; s. John D. and Edith J. (Hennessy) H.; m. Anna Craig, Nov. 26, 1976; children—Thomas P., James E. A.B., Syracuse U., 1949, M.A., 1950, Ph.D., 1952. Registered prin. Nat. Assn. Securities Dealers. Prof. econs., chmn. dept. Bates Coll., Lewiston, Maine, 1953-58; dir. edn. fin. research State of N.Y., 1959, chief mcpl. fin., 1960; staff economist, dir. research Northwestern Mut. Life Ins. Co., Milw., 1960-68; v.p. Nationwide Ins. Cos., Columbus, Ohio, 1968-76; dean Sch. Bus. Adminstrn. Central Mich. U., Mt. Pleasant, 1976-79; v.p. Am. Productivity Ctr., Houston, 1979-80; pres., chmn., chief exec. officer Variable Annuity Life Ins. Co., Houston, 1980-83; sr. v.p. Am. Gen. Corp., Houston, 1983-86; dean, prof. fin. Coll. Commerce U. Ill., Champaign, 1986—; dir. First Busey Corp., Urbana, Ill., Mercy Hosp., Champaign, Sinfonia de Camera, Champaign;. Author: American Social Legislation, 1965, U.S. Balance of Payments and Capital Flows, 1967, School Revenue Studies, 1959, Fiscal Capacity of the State of Maine, 1958, American Social Legislation, 1973; editor: Dimensions of Productivity Research (2 vols.), 1981; contbr. articles to jours., abstracts to profl. meetings. Bd. dirs. Goodwill Industries, Columbus, 1972-76, chmn. capital fund drive, 1974-75; mem. Houston Com. on Fgn. Rels., 1980—, Chgo. Coun. on Fgn. Rels., 1986—, Chgo. com., 1987—. Served with U.S. Army, 1944-46, ETO; capt. (ret.) USAR. Maxwell fellow Syracuse U., 1950-52; recipient Best Article award Jur. Risk and Ins., 1964; Maxwell Centennial lectr. Maxwell Grad. Sch., Syracuse U., 1970. Mem. Acad. Mgmt., Am. Econ. Assn., Inst. Mgmt. Scis., Nat. Assn. Bus. Economists, Nat. Tax Assn. (dir. 1981-85, treas., exec. com. 1988—), Inst. Research in Econs. of Taxation (dir. 1984—), Columbus C. of C. (chmn. econ. policy com. 1972-76), Phi Kappa Phi, Beta Gamma Sigma. Clubs: Columbus Athletic; Heritage (Houston); University (Chgo.), Lincolnshire Fields Country (Champaign). Home: 3301 Stoneybrook Dr Champaign IL 61821 Office: Univ Ill Coll Commerce Bus Adminstrn 1206 S 6th Champaign IL 61820

HOGAN, RONALD P., forest products company executive; b. 1940. BS, U. Houston. Sales rep. Houston distbn. div. Georgia-Pacific Corp., Atlanta, 1965-68, mgr. Wichita, Kans. br., 1968-70, mgr. Houston br., 1970-73, mgr. western region, 1973-76, mgr. northeast region, 1976-78, v.p. distbn. div. northeast region, 1978-82, v.p. distbn. div., 1982-83, group v.p. distbn. div., 1983-85, sr. v.p. distbn. div., 1985-87, exec. v.p. ops., 1987-88, exec. v.p. bldg. products, 1988—. Office: Ga-Pacific Corp 133 Peachtree St NE Atlanta GA 30303 *

HOGAN, THOMAS DENNIS, III, metals company executive; b. St. Paul, Mar. 13, 1930; d. Thomas Dennis, Jr. and Charlotte (Bork) H.; B.S. in Econs., Yale U., 1953; m. Elizabeth Mansfield Bowen, Apr. 27, 1960; children—Thomas IV, Kerry, Elizabeth. Gen. mgr. Consol. Industries S.A., Caracas, Venezuela, 1955-61; dir. diversification Singer Sewing Machine Co., N.Y.C., 1962-64; pres. Univest Corp., N.Y.C., 1964-71; dir. Proventa S.A., Mexico City, 1972-75; chmn., dir. Oilfunds Investments, Inc., Miami, Fla., 1976-82; chmn. Reliance Petroleum Corp., Denver, 1983-85; pres. Bretton Corp., pres. Precious Metals Mines, 1987—, TDH Cons. Corp., 1980—. Served to 1st lt. USAF, 1953-55. Mem. Am. Petroleum Inst., Internat. Assn. Fin. Planners. Republican. Roman Catholic. Clubs: Riviera Country, Yale of N.Y.; Bankers (Miami). Home: 7135 SW 109th Terr Miami FL 33156

HOGAN, THOMAS V., insurance company executive; b. Jay, Okla., Feb. 1, 1936; s. Thomas Victor and Eula Mae (Cating) H.; m. Patsy Lynn Weir, June 12, 1955; children: Terry Michael, Jeffrey Robert. MS in Fin. Services, The Am. Coll., 1986. CLU, chartered fin. cons. Agent Northwestern Nat. Life, Wichita, Kans., 1955-61; field supr. Northwestern Nat. Life, Dallas, 1961-64; dist. mgr. Northwestern Nat. Life, Houston, 1964-67; mktg. mgr. Northwestern Nat. Life, St. Louis, 1967-72; supt. of agys. Northwestern Nat. Life, Mpls., 1972-75; br. mgr. Northwestern Nat. Life, Dallas, 1975-83; pres. Metroplex Fin. Services, Dallas, 1983—; also bd. dirs. Metroplex Fin. Services. Contbr. articles to profl. jours., tape series. Loan exec. United Way Mpls., 1973; treas. Royal Oaks Bapt. Ch., Dallas, 1979-87. Merit scholar Phillips U., 1954. Mem. Am. Soc. CLUs and Chartered Fin. Cons. (pres. 1986, bd. dirs. 1983—), Gen. Agts. and Mgrs. Assn. (bd. dirs. 1980-83), Dallas Estate Planning Council, N. Dallas Fin. Forum. Republican. Home: 2703 N Surrey Carrollton TX 75006 Office: Metroplex Fin Svcs Inc 4004 Beltline Rd Suite 220 LB14 Dallas TX 75244

HOGE, JAMES FULTON, JR., newspaper publisher; b. N.Y.C., Dec. 25, 1935; s. James Fulton and Virginia (McClamroch) H.; m. Alice Patterson Albright, June 2, 1962 (div. 1971); children—Alicia McClamroch, James Patrick, Robert Warren; m. Sharon King, Jan. 4, 1981. BA in Polit. Sci., Yale U., 1958; MA in Modern Am. and European History, U. Chgo., 1961; grad. Advanced Mgmt. Program, Harvard U. Grad. Sch., Bus., 1980. Fin. writer Chgo. Sun Times, 1958-62; Am. Polit. Sci. Assn. Congl. fellow, 1962-63; Washington corr. Chgo. Sun Times, 1963-65, city editor, 1965-67, mng. editor, 1967-68, exec. editor, 1968, editor, 1968-76; editor-in-chief, 1976-78; exec. v.p., editor-in-chief, 1978-80, pub., 1980-84; chmn., pub. N.Y. Daily News, 1984-85, pub., pres. 1985—. Mem. Pulitzer Prize Bd., N.Y.C.; trustee Eisenhower Exchange Fellowships, 1978—; bd. govs. Columbia U. Media & Society Seminars, 1983—; mem. adv. bd. Ctr. for Fgn. Journalists, Gannett Media Ctr.; mem. editorial bd. Fgn. Affairs Quar., Congl. Fellows, 1962; mem. Overseas Devel. Council, 1988; chmn. Regional Plan Assn. Open Spaces Prog., 1988, N.Y.C. Partnership Com. Devel. Commn., 1988; chmn. adv. bd. Queens Coll. Jour., 1988; bd. dirs. Newspaper Advt. Bur., N.Y.C., 1981—, N.Y.C. Ptnrship., 1984—. Recipient Pub. Service award U. Chgo., 1977, Am. Heritage award B'nai B'rith Anti Defamation League, 1981, Disting. Journalism award Better Govt. Assn., 1983, Civic Commn. award Daily News, Anti Defamation League, 1985. Mem. Council Fgn. Relations, Am. Council on Germany, Soc. Profl. Journalists, Commercial Club, Century Assn., Sky Club, Pilgrims of the U.S. Club, Sigma Chi. Office: NY Daily News 220 E 42d St Ste 817 New York NY 10017-5858

HOGG, DAVID CALVERT, engineer, consultant; b. London, Ont., Can., Nov. 16, 1940; s. Calvert Douglas and Eillene Gertrude (McMurray) H.; m. Beverley Frances Barnes, July 9, 1966; children: Stuart David, Gillian Leslie. Student, Hamilton Inst. Tech., 1964; Bachelors of Applied Sci., U. Waterloo. Engring. asst. Canadian Westinghouse, Hamilton, Ont., 1963-67; engring. asst. turbine & generation div. Canadian Westinghouse, Kitchener, Ont., 1967-70; faculty Conestoga Coll., Kitchener, 1970-74, curriculum planning cons., 1978-80, chmn. technology div., 1980-83; mktg. mgr. Unitron Industries, Kitchener, 1974-78; dir. ednl. services Ont. Ctr. for Adv. Mfg., 1983-87; v.p., gen. mgr. ProSync div. Intrasyst, Inc., Cambridge, Ont., 1987—; cons. Ont. govt. and industry. Contbr. articles to profl. jours. Dir. Kitchener/Waterloo Counsellin Services, 1973; co-founder Waterloo Sci. and Engring. Fair. Mem. Assn. Profl. Engrs. Ont., IEEE (Centenial medal, 1984), Soc. Mfg. Engrs. (Pres.'s award, 1988), Computer and Automated Systems Assn. (chmn. 1988), Cambridge C. of C. (dir.), U. Waterloo Engring. Alumni (founding pres.), Cambridge Club, Toastmasters (founding pres. Cambridge chpt.). Home: 138 Blueridge Ave, Kitchener, ON Canada N2M 4E1 Office: ProSync div Instrasyst Inc, 18 Jarvis St, Cambridge, ON Canada N1R 1G8

HOGLUND, FORREST EUGENE, petroleum company executive; b. Lawrence, Kans., July 1, 1933; s. Roy A. and Edna M. (McMichael) H.; m. Sally Sue Roney, June 19, 1956; children—Kelly M., Shelly L., Kristan K. B.S. in Mech. Engring, U. Kans., 1956. Registered profl. engr. Tex., Kans. With Exxon Corp., N.Y.C., 1957-1977; mgr. Exxon Corp. (E. Tex. div.), N.Y.C., 1970-73; v.p. ops. Exxon Corp. (Middle East), N.Y.C., 1973-76, v.p. gas, 1976-77; pres., chief operating officer Tex. Oil and Gas, Dallas, 1977-83, pres., chief exec. officer, 1983-87; dir. USX Corp., Pitts., 1986-87; chmn., chief exec. officer Enron Oil & Gas Co.(subs. Enron Corp.), Houston, 1987—; bd. dirs. Mid Continent Oil and Gas, Tex., (Houston) Tex. Commerce Bancshares. Mem. Bd. Visitors of The U. Cancer Found. (assoc.); area v.p. Kans. U. Endowment Assn. Served with C.E. U.S. Army, 1957-58. Mem. Am. Petroleum Inst., AIME, Soc. Petroleum Engrs., Independent Petroleum Assn. Am., Tex. Independent Producers and Royalty Assn., Tau Beta Pi, Pi Tau Sigma, Sigma Tau, Omicron Delta Kappa. Presbyterian. Club: Petroleum, Dallas Country. Office: Enron Oil & Gas Corp 1400 Smith Ste 5020 Houston TX 77002

HOGLUND, WILLIAM ELIS, automotive executive; b. Stockholm, Sweden, Aug. 22, 1934; came to U.S., 1940; s. Elis Sterner and Helen (Klinger) H.; m. Beverly Jane Scales, Feb. 1, 1958; children—Lynne Melissa Effler, Cynthia A. Shannon, Peter K. A.B., Princeton U., N.J., 1956; M.B.A., U. Mich., Ann Arbor, 1958. Various fin. positions Gen. Motors Corp., Kansas City, Detroit, and N.Y.C., 1958-74; div. comptroller Pontiac Motor Div. Gen. Motors Corp., Pontiac, Mich., 1974-78; comptroller Gen. Motors Corp., Detroit, 1978-80; v.p., gen. mgr. Pontiac Motor Div. Gen. Motors Corp., Pontiac, 1980-84; v.p., group exec. Gen. Motors Corp., Detroit, 1984-85; pres. Saturn Corp.-Gen. Motors Corp., Troy, Mich., 1985-86; v.p., group exec. Buick-Oldsmobile-Cadillac Group/Gen. Motors Corp., Warren, Mich., 1986-88; exec. v.p. Gen. Motors Corp., Detroit, 1988—. Trustee, Skillman Found., 1984—, William Beaumont Hosp., 1984—; mem. U. Mich. Grad. Sch. Bus.-Vis. Com., 1984—. Clubs: Bloomfield Hills Country (bd. govs. 1980-87), Bloomfield Hills; Detroit Athletic. Office: Gen Motors Corp 3044 W Grand Blvd Detroit MI 48202

HOHN, HARRY GEORGE, insurance company executive; b. N.Y.C., Mar. 1, 1932; s. Harry George and Violia (Meehan) H.; m. Janet Jean LaRosa, June 19, 1954; children: Cynthia, Jennifer, Nancy, Patricia. B.S., NYU, 1953, LL.M., 1959; J.D., Fordham U., 1956. Bar: N.Y. 1956, U.S. Supreme Ct. 1976. With N.Y. Life Ins. Co., N.Y.C., 1974—, sr. v.p., gen. counsel, 1977-82, exec. v.p., gen. counsel, 1982-83, exec. v.p., 1983-86, vice chmn. bd. dirs., 1986—. Editor: Fordham Law Rev, 1955-56. Trustee Found. Ind. Higher Edn., The Am. Coll., L.O.M.A. Mem. Assn. Life Ins. Counsel (bd. govs.). Republican. Roman Catholic. Office: NY Life Ins Co 51 Madison Ave New York NY 10010

HOHNER, KENNETH DWAYNE, fodder company executive; b. St. John, Kans., June 24, 1934; s. Courtney Clinton and Mildred Lucile (Forrester) H.; m. Sherry Eloi Anice Edens, Feb. 14, 1961; children: Katrina, Melissa, Steven, Michael. BS in Geol. Engring., U. Kans., 1957. Geophysicist Mobil Oil Corp., New Orleans, Anchorage, Denver, 1957-72; sr. geophysicist Amerada Hess Corp., Houston, 1972-75, ARAMCO, London, 1975-79; far east area geophysicist Hamilton Bros., Denver, 1979-83; owner Hohner Poultry Farm, Erie, Colo., 1979—; pres. Hohner Custom Feed, Inc., Erie, Colo., 1982—. Mem. Soc. Exploration Geophysicists. Home and Office: 3398 Weld County Rd 4 Erie CO 80516

HOIGAARD, JAN CHRISTIAN, electronics executive; b. Stavanger, Rogaland, Norway, May 1, 1933; came to U.S., 1959; s. Jonas and Signy Leonora (Olsen) H.; m. Iris Christiansen, June 26, 1959; children: Jane Leonora, Kim Joann, Lisa Diann. BSEE, Olso Sch Tech., Oslo, 1959. bd. dirs. Equicapital Corp., Denver. Design engr. Polytronic Rsch., Rockville, Md., 1960-61, Def. Electronics, Rockville, Md., 1961-64; sr. devel. mgr. Vitro Corp., Silver Springs, Md., 1964-67; engring. mgr. Singer Instrumentation, Los Angeles, 1967-69, Vari-L Comp. Inc., Denver, 1969-73; program mgr. TRW, Colorado Springs, Colo., 1973-84; pres., chief exec. officer SpectraScan, Inc., Colorado Springs, 1984—. Patentee in field; contbr. articles to profl. jours. Republican. Lutheran. Office: SpectraScan Inc 1110A Elkton Dr Colorado Springs CO 80907

HOISINGTON, CHARLES WILLIAM, commodity trading advisor; b. Columbus, Ohio, Feb. 4, 1939; s. Charles William and Helen Marie (Warner) H.; m. Patricia Ann Smith, June 3, 1963 (div. Aug. 1981); children: Amy B., Charles W. Jr. BS in edn., Ohio State U., 1967. Registered commodity trading advisor. Real estate salesman Preston Cooke & Co., Columbus, 1960-64; real estate broker Columbus, 1964—; profl. educator Columbus City Schs., 1967-70; gen. mgr. Cring Marine, Westerville, Ohio, 1970-78; commodity trading advisor Columbus, 1978—; cons. in field; tchr. Ohio State U. Contbr. articles to profl. jours. Officer, trustee Fathers and Children for Equality, 1988, Father's and Children's Equity Found. Nat.

Merit scholar, 1957; recipient Outstanding Service award Am. Mensa Assn. and Big Bros. Assn. Mem. C. of C., Better Bus. Bur., Parents without Ptnrs.

HOKE, KATHLEEN KAREN, accountant, business owner; b. San Francisco, Jan. 13, 1944; d. Milton Charles and Edith Adina (Lunn) Hess; m. Jerry Allen Palinsky, Nov. 13, 1961 (div. May 1975); children: Jerry Allen Jr., Joel A., Karaleen K.; m. Charles Clarence Hoke, Apr. 15, 1978; stepchildren: Linda Misnar, Roy, Patricia, Charles A. Grad. high sch., Tacoma. With bus. dept. Knoght, Vale & Gregory, CPAs, Tacoma, 1969-77; mem. staff Gilbert W. Gimbel, CPAs, Hillsboro, Oreg., 1984—; pvt. practice Beaverton, Oreg., 1984—; instr. tax agt. Jewitt & Hoke Partnership, Beaverton, 1984. Mem. Nat. Assn. Tax Cons. (chmn. state edn. com. 1987-88), Oreg. Assn. Tax. Cons. (chmn. state edn. com. 1983-85, state pres. 1985-87, conv. chmn. 1987-88, Outstanding Service award Westside chpt. 1984), Beaverton Area C. of C. Republican. Lutheran. Home: 12275 SW Davies Rd Beaverton OR 97005 Office: 8285 SW Nimbus Ave Suite 106 Beaverton OR 97005

HOLBERTON, PHILIP VAUGHAN, theater company financial executive; b. N.Y.C., Sept. 29, 1942; s. Robert Maynard and Charlotte Metcafe (Stone) H.; m. Gale Russell, May 16, 1970 (div. 1980); children—Matthew Russell, Alexandra; m. Anne Meigs Blodget, June 6, 1987. A.B. in Acctg., Franklin and Marshall Coll., Lancaster, Pa., 1964. CPA, N.Y. Auditor Peat Marwick Main CPA's, N.Y.C., 1964-72, mgr. audit services, 1975-79; investment profl. McDonald & Co., N.Y.C., 1972-75; asst. controller Becton Dickinson & Co., Paramus, N.J., 1979-81, group controller, 1981-85; v.p. finance Gen. Cinema Theatres, Chestnut Hill, Mass., 1985—; outside dir. Mgmt. Decision Lab., N.Y.C., 1981-84. Chmn. strategic planning panel United Way of Bergen County, Paramus, 1983-85; dir. Poppenhusen Inst., College Point, N.Y., 1983-85. Mem. Am. Inst. CPA's, Fin. Execs. Inst., Rockway Hunting Club. Republican. Episcopalian. Office: Gen Cinema Theatres 1280 Boylston St Chestnut Hill MA 02167

HOLBROOK, ANTHONY, manufacturing company executive; b. 1940; married. With Advanced Micro Devices Inc., Sunnyvale, Calif., 1973—, former exec. v.p., chief operating officer, pres., chief operating officer, 1986—. Office: Advanced Micro Devices Inc 901 Thompson Pl Sunnyvale CA 94086 *

HOLCOMB, CONSTANCE L., sales executive; b. St. Paul, Oct. 28, 1942; d. John E. Holcomb and Lucille A. (Westerdahl) Hope. BS, U. Minn., 1965; MA in Intercultural Edn., U. of the Americas, Puebla, Mex., 1975. Rsch. analyst U.S. Dept. Def., Washington, 1965-66; br. gen. mgr. Berlitz Lang. Schs., Mexico City, 1966-68; pres., gen. mgr. Centro Lingüistico, Puebla, 1968-72; gen. mgr., prof. Lang. Ctr. Am. Sch. Found., Puebla, 1972-74; assoc. prof., dir. lang. programs U. of the Americas, Puebla, 1974-76; prof., dean faculty of langs. Nat. Autonomous U. Mex., Mexico City, 1976-78; dir. sales & mktg. Longman Pub. Co., N.Y.C., 1978-80, dir. internat. sales & mktg., 1980-84; mng. dir. ESL Pub. Div. McGraw-Hill Book Co., N.Y.C., 1984-85; dir. mktg. mgmt. McGraw-Hill Tng. Systems and Book Co., N.Y.C., 1985-86; dir. mktg. electronic bus. McGraw-Hill Book Co., N.Y.C., 1986-87; cons. info. industry, bus. mgr., ind. contractor info. businesses N.Y.C., 1987—; v.p. MexTESOL, Mexico City, 1977-78. Editor: English Teaching in Mexico, 1975; contrb. articles to profl. jours. Mem. Assn. Am. Pub. (com. chairperson internat. div. 1980-84, exec. com. 1980-84), Info. Industry Assn. Office: 66 Madison Ave Ste 9E New York NY 10016

HOLCOMB, PHILO III, steel company executive; b. Atlanta, Nov. 8, 1936; s. Philo Jr. and Mabel Marie (List) H.; m. Erika Hedwig Bairer, June 28, 1963; 1 child, Kristina E. AB, Harvard U., 1958; postgrad., U. Tuebingen, Fed. Republic of Germany, 1962-63; MBA, Columbia U., 1968. Various positions Bell Telephone Labs., Murray Hill, N.J., 1963-67; fin. dir. FHS Stahlverformung, Iserlohn, Fed. Republic of Germany, 1972-78; adminstrv. assoc. USX Corp., Pitts., 1968-72, mgr. corp. strategic planning, 1978-80, dir. corp. strategic planning, 1980—. Mem. mgmt. adv. bd. Laroche Coll.; bd. dirs. U.S. Good Fellowship Club. With U.S. Army, 1958-62. Mem. Assn. Corp. Growth (pres.), Planning Forum (bd. dirs. Pitts. chpt.), Beta Gamma Sigma. Home: 375 Jefferson Dr Pittsburgh PA 15228 Office: USX Corp 600 Grant St Pittsburgh PA 15230

HOLCOMB, RICHARD DALE, sales executive; b. Wadsworth, Ohio, July 11, 1946; s. Dale Overholt and Olive Jean (Stauffer) H.; m. Helen Linda Kirby, Apr. 23, 1977 (div.); children: Ian Eric, Jordan Taylor; m. Kerry Jean Bublitz, May 2, 1987. BS, SUNY, Saratoga Springs, 1976; MA, Columbia Pacific U., 1987, PhD, 1988. News dir. Sta. WBBF Radio, Rochester, N.Y., 1969-70; asst./exec. v.p. Jaco Enterprises, Rochester, 1970-72; sales mgr. Sta. WAXY Radio, Rochester, 1972-76; gen. mgr. Sta. WTCR Radio, Huntington, Va., 1976-79; v.p., gen. mgr. Stereo Broadcasting Corp., Fresno, Calif., 1981-83, Sta. WBCS AM-FM Radio, Milw., 1983-84, Sta. KKSS/KAFE Radio, Albuquerque, 1984-87; v.p. sales Vision Interfaith Satellite Network, Albuquerque, 1987—; mgmt. cons. RIK Communications, Albuquerque, 1985—. Author: Ultimate Radio Manager, 1987; pub. Parenteen, 1988. Bd. dirs. Lebanon Community Hosp., Oreg, 1982-83, HackEstep Home for Boys, 1976-79. With USAF, 1964-68.

HOLCOMB, STEPHEN FRENCH, banker; b. Austin, Minn., Dec. 17, 1945; s. Hansel Hanley and Janet (French) H.; m. Joan von Maur, May 24, 1972; children: Jennifer French, Hanley Maddock. BSc in Econs., U. Pa., 1969. Successively asst. treas./asst. v.p. U.K. Dept., v.p. Can. Dept., v.p., head loan syndication group, mng. dir. Soc. Fin Valinvenca J.P. Morgan & Co., 1970-83; v.p., Asia dept. head J.P. Morgan & Co., N.Y.C., 1983-86, v.p., head product devel. Investor Services Group, 1987-88; mng. dir. J.P. Morgan Australia Ltd., Sydney, 1988—. Mem. Indonesian-Am. C. of C. (bd. dirs. 1983-86), Philippine-Am. C. of C. (bd. dirs. 1983-86), Arcola Country Club, Upper Ridgewood Tennis. Republican. Presbyterian. Office: JP Morgan & Co 23 Wall St New York NY 10015

HOLDEN, GEORGE FREDRIC, brewing company executive, public policy specialist, consultant; b. Lander, Wyo., Aug. 29, 1937; s. George Thiel Holden and Rita (Meyer) Zulpo; m. Dorothy Carol Capper, July 5, 1959; children: Lorilyn, Sherilyn, Tamilyn. Adminstr. BSChemE, U. Colo., 1959, MBA in Mktg., 1974. Plastics lab. EDP, indsl chems. plant, prodn. process engring., tool control supervision, aerospace (Minuteman, Polaris, Sparrow), Parlin, N.J., Salt Lake City, Cumberland, Md., 1959-70; by-product sales, new market and new product devel., resource planning and devel. and pub. relations Adolph Coors Co., Golden, Colo., 1971-76; dir. econ. affairs corp. pub. affairs dept., 1979-84, dir. pub. affairs research, 1984-86; owner Phoenix Enterprises, Arvada, 1986—; mgr. facilities engring. Coors Container Co., 1976-79; instr. brewing, by-products utilization and waste mgmt. U. Wis.; cons., speaker in field. Del. Colo. Rep. Conv., 1976—; bd. dirs. Colo. Pub. Expenditures Council, 1983-86, Nat. Speakers Assn., Colo. Speakers Assn. (bd. dirs. 1987—), Nat. Assn. Bus. Economists, Colo. Assn. Commerce and Industry Ednl. Found. Mem. U.S. Brewers Assn. (chmn. by-products com., Hon. Gavel, 1975), Am. Inst. Indsl. Engrs. (dir. 1974-78). Co-author: Secrets of Job Hunting, 1972; The Phoenix Phenomenon, 1984, TOTAL Power of ONE in America, 1989; contbr. articles to Chem. Engring. Mag., 1968-76, over 200 published articles, white papers in field; over 400 speeches. Regular guest columnist La Voz, Colo. Statesman. Spkr. Heritage Found. Guide to Pub. Policy Experts, Spkrs. Bur., Commn. on the Bicentennial, U.S. Constn. Home: 6463 Owens St Arvada CO 80004 Office: Phoenix Enterprises PO Box 1900 Arvada CO 80001

HOLDEN, WILLIAM VAUGHN, controller; b. Newton, N.J., Dec. 25, 1949; s. James Henry and Helen (Valentine) H.; m. Sharon Schuh, Aug. 14, 1971; children: W. Andrew, Kevin, Rebecca. BS, Georgetown Coll., 1972. CPA, Ky. Contr. Pauly & Pauly Constrn. Co., Cin., 1972-73; sr. acct. Charles F. Pelfrey, CPA, Cin., 1973-75, Wasserman & Noe, CPAs, Louisville, 1975-78; audit mgr. Deming, Malone, Livesay & Ostroff, CPAs, Louisville, 1978-85; contr. KFC Nat. Purchasing Coop., Louisville, 1985-89, v.p., contr., 1989—. Mem. AICPA, Ky. Soc. CPAs, Nat. Assn. Accts., Nat. Soc. Accts. Coops. Office: KFC Nat Purchasing Coop 950 Breckenridge Ln Ste 300 Louisville KY 40207

HOLDEN-BROWN, SIR DERRICK, food executive; b. Surrey, Feb. 14, 1923; s. Harold Walter and Beatrice Florence (Walker) H.; m. Patricia Mary Ross Mackenzie, 1950; 2 children. Ed Westcliff. Chartered acct., Scotland. Joined Hiram Walker & Sons, 1949-54;; dir. Ind Cooper Ltd., 1962; chmn. Victoria Wine Co., 1964; dir. Allied Breweries Ltd., 1967; chief exec. SVPW, 1969; fin. dir. Allied Breweries, 1972; chmn. and chief exec. Allied-Lyons, 1982—. Chmn. FDF, 1984-85, pres. 1985-86; dir. Sun Alliance and London Ins., 1977, Midland, 1984-88; chmn. 87; dep. chmn. Food From Britain Council, 1986; mem. Confederation of British Industry/Industry Task Force, 1986. Mem. Brewers' Soc. (chmn. 1978-80, pres. 1980). Address: Copse House, Milford-on-Sea Hampshire, England Office: Allied Lyons PLC, 156 St John St, London EC1P 1AR, England

HOLDER, HOWARD RANDOLPH, SR., broadcasting corporation executive; b. Moline, Ill., Nov. 14, 1916; s. James William and Charlotte (Brega) H.; m. Clementi Lacey-Baker, Feb. 21, 1942; children: Janice Clementi Holder Collins, Susan Charlotte Holder Mason, Marjory Estelle Holder Turnbow, Howard Randolph. BA, Augustana Coll., 1939. With radio stas. WHBF, Rock Island, Ill., 1939-41, WOC, Davenport, Iowa, 1945-47, WINN, Louisville, 1947, WRFC, Athens, Ga., 1948-1956, WGAU & WNGC, Athens, 1956—; pres. Clarke Broadcasting Corp., Athens, 1956—; v.p. and treas. H. Group, Inc., 1986—; mem. adv. bd. U. Georgia Coll. Journalism and Mass Communication, 1973-78; pres. Mid-West Ga. Broadcasting, Inc., 1983—; bd. dirs. AP Broadcasters Inc. Chmn. adv. bd. Salvation Army, 1962-63, mem., 1952—; chmn. Athens Parks and Recreation Bd., 1952-62; chmn. Cherokee dist. Boy Scouts Am., 1966-67, bd. N.E. Ga. council, 1950— (Disting. Citizens award 1989); regent for life Nat. Eagle Scout Assn., 1989; mem. fine arts task force U. Ga., 1989; mem. adv. bd. Clarke County Juvenile Ct., 1960-72; chmn. region IV Ga. div. Am. Cancer Soc., 1968; bd. dirs. Athens Crime Prevention Com., 1960-70; mem. Georgians for Safer Hwys., 1970; mem. adv. bd. Athens-Clarke County ARC, 1950-70; trustee Ga. Rotary Student Fund, Inc., 1969—; mem. Model Cities Policy Bd., 1970-71, Ga. Criminal Justice Coordinating Com.; mem. Ga. Productivity Bd., 1984-85; mem. bicentennial alumni activities com. U. Ga., 1982; co-pres. Friends U. Ga. Mus. Art, 1973-75; state bd. advisors Ga. Mus. Art, 1984—; sec. adv. bd. Henry W. Grady Sch. Journalism, U. Ga., 1973-74, mem., 1972-76; mem. adv. com. Ga. Commn. for Nat. Bicentennial, 1976; bd. dirs. Rec. for the Blind, 1977-83, Athens Symphony, 1981-85; mem. Ga. Gov.'s Jail/Prison Overcrowding Com., 1982. Served with AUS, 1941-46, ETO, maj. USAR ret. Named Boss of Yr., Athens Jr. C. of C., 1959, Broadcaster-Citizen of Yr., Ga. Assn. Broadcasters, 1962, Employer of Yr., Bus. and Profl. Women's Club, 1969, Athens Citizen of Yr., Rotary Club, 1971, Athens Citizen of Yr., Athens Woman's Club, 1971; recipient Silver Beaver award Boy Scouts Am., 1973, Liberty Bell award Athens Bar Assn., 1977, Robert Stolz medaille, 1973, Nat. DAR medal of Honor, 1983, cert. of Merit United Daus. of the Confederacy, 1983; Paul Harris fellow, 1978, Will Watt fellow, 1984. Mem. Res. Officers Assn. (pres. Athens chpt. 1962), Am. Ex-prisoners War, Ga. Assn. Broadcasters (pres. 1961), Athens Area C. of C. (pres. 1970), Ga. AP Broadcasters (pres. 1963), Augustana Coll. Alumni Assn. (bd. dirs. 1973-76; Outstanding Achievement award 1973), Golden Quill, Gridiron, Sigma Delta Chi, Alpha Psi Omega, Alpha Delta Sigma, Di Gamma Kappa (Ga. Pioneer Broadcaster of Yr. award 1971), Phi Omega Phi. Club: Touchdown (Athens) (pres. 1963-64). Lodge: Rotary (pres. Athens club 1957-58, gov. dist. 692, 1969-70, internat. pub. relations com. 1987—). Home: 383 Westview Dr Athens GA 30606 Office: H Group Inc 850 Bobbin Mill Rd Athens GA 30610

HOLDER, ROBERT JAMES, management consultant; b. Alton, Ill., June 19, 1955; s. Robert L. and Ann (Wrobel) H. BA in History and Govt., So. Ill. U., 1980, M in Pub. Adminstrn., 1982. Adminstrv. asst. community devel. Nameomi Twp., Granite City, Ill., 1978-81; quality assurance and orgnl. devel. specialist Avco Services, Houston, 1982-86; cons., pres. Human Energy Design Systems, Edwardsville, Ill., 1986—. Contbr. articles to various publs. Mem. Orgnl. Devel. Inst., Orgnl. Devel. Network, Am. Soc. Tng. and Devel. Home and Office: 620 Roosevelt Dr Edwardsville IL 62025

HOLGUIN, MICHAEL JOHN, securities broker; b. Milw., Aug. 18, 1955; s. Tony and Ann M. (Ronnebaum) H.; m. Ellen Jo Gronski, Dec. 6, 1975; children: Jacob J., Barbara A. Student, U. Wis., Stevens Point, 1973-75. Printer Marshfield (Wis.) Clinic, 1977-84; registered rep. Offerman and Co., Inc., Stevens Point, 1984—. Mem. Nat. Assn. Securities Dealers. Roman Catholic. Lodge: Lions. Home: 608 Locker Rd Mosinee WI 54455 Office: Offerman & Co Inc 101 Division St N Stevens Point WI 54481

HOLIDAY, PATRICK JAMES See MANFRO, PATRICK JAMES

HOLIEN, KIM BERNARD, historian; b. Bad Cannstadt-Stuttgart, Fed. Republic of Germany, Mar. 10, 1948; s. Maurice Joel and Margaret Alice (Wild) H. BS, Bethel Coll., 1970; MA, George Mason U., 1984. With Dept. State, Washington, 1971-73; adjudicator GAO, Washington, 1975-76; with Nat. Archives, Washington, 1977-79; mil. historian Dept. Army, Washington, 1979—; historian Nat. Guard Bur., 1984; officer First North-South Brigade, Inc., 1974-84. Recipient Letter of Commendation, Dept. State, 1971, Disting. Service award Va. div. Sons of Confederate Vets., 1980; Outstanding Service award, 1980, Sustained Outstanding Service award and Spl. Service award, 1981 (all Dept. Army); Comdr.-in-Chief's award Sons Confederate Vets., 1982, Comdr.'s award Sons Union Vets., 1982; cert. of achievement U.S. Army Ctr. Mil. History, 1984. also letters of commendation/appreciation Dept. Army, Sec. Def., 1983, spl. service award Chief of Mil. History, 1986, official commendation, 1988. Author: Battle at Ball's Bluff, 1985, Battle at 1st Manassas, 1988; asst. editor The Sharpshooter,, 1976-79; editor Clarion's Call, 1980-83, Ann. Rev. N.G. Bur., 1984. Mem. Am. Hist. Assn., Co. of Mil. Historians, D.C. Civil War Round Table (past pres.), Am. Mil. Inst., No. Va. Assn. of Historians, Alexandria Civil War Round Table (past pres.), Sons of Norway, Bethel Coll. Alumni Assn. (dir.), Heritage of Honor (pres.). Lutheran.

HOLINGSWORTH, JOAN DIANNE, banker; b. Anniston, Ala., Oct. 20, 1950; d. Lester Thomas and Myrtle (Dobbins) Bible; m. Robert Marshall Hollingsworth, Dec. 19, 1970; 1 child, Robert Clark. BS Human Resource Mgmt., U. Ala., 1981. staff asst. U. Ala., Tuscaloosa, 1970-80; group leader supr. Gulf Oil Corp., Houston, 1981-82; instr. New World Bus. Coll., Anniston, Ala., 1982-84, Cen. Tex. Jr. Coll., Ft. McClellan, Ala., 1984-85; tng. and devel. specialist Cen. Bank of South, Birmingham, Ala., 1985—. Mem. Am. Inst. Banking (bank rep. 1988—). Home: 2824 Altadena S Way Birmingham AL 35233 Office: Cen Bank of the South 701 S 32d St Birmingham AL 35233

HOLLAND, CHARLES EDWARD, corporate executive; b. Pottstown, Pa., Aug. 31, 1940; s. Charles Edward and Ethel Viola (Ludwig) H.; m. Linda Beth VandeBerg, Nov. 20, 1982. Student, Messiah Coll., 1962-63; BS in Biology and Chemistry, Albright Coll., 1966; PhD in Zoology, Rutgers U., 1974. Clin. lab. technician Reading Hosp., West Reading, Pa., 1962-66; rsch. assoc. dept. biochemistry St. Louis U. Sch. Medicine, 1972-75; rsch. assoc. dept. pharmacology and surgery U. Ill.Med. Ctr., Chgo., 1975-77; clin. project mgr. Am. Critical Care (Am. Hosp. Supply), McGraw Park, Ill., 1977-81; asst./assoc. dir. clin. rsch. Glaxo, Inc., Research Triangle Park, N.C., 1981-84; dir. planning and project mgmt. Glaxo, Inc., Research Triangle Park, 1984-86, dir. human resources, 1986-87, dir. strategic planning, 1987-88, dir. bus. expansion, 1988-89, dir. dermatology bus., product devel., 1989—; mem. indsl. adv. bd. Pharmacotherapy jour., 1986—, Geriatric Medicine jour., 1986—; bd. trustees Glaxo Bus. Sch., 1986—, chmn. 1986-88. Contbr. articles to profl. jours. USPH fellow Rutgers U., 1966-71; grad. teaching fellow Rutgers U., 1971-72; NIH fellow St. Louis U. Sch. Medicine, 1973-75, U. Ill., 1975-77. Mem. Project Mgmt. Inst. (editor newsletter 1986-87), AAAS, Human Resource Planning Soc., Lic. Exec. Soc., N.Y. Acad. Sci., Sigma Xi. Office: Glaxo Inc 5 Moore Dr Research Triangle Park NC 27709

HOLLAND, CHARLES LEE, energy industry executive; b. Shelby, N.C., Nov. 17, 1941; BS in Nuclear Engring., N.C. State U., 1965; postgrad. U. Va., 1969-70; children: Angelia, Charles L. Asso. engr. Boeing Co., Seattle, 1965-66; mgr. svc. products Babcock & Wilcox Co., Lynchburg, Va., 1967-74; bus. devel. mgr. Brown & Root, Inc., Houston, 1974-79; v.p. mktg. Blount Inc.- Constrn. Group, Montgomery, Ala., 1979-83, ; pres. MBF-Blount, Kuala Lumpur, Malaysia, 1984-85; exec. v.p. Engery Am. South East sub. Blount, 1988—. Mem. ASME, Am. Mgmt. Assn., Newcomen Soc. Republican. Clubs: Arrowhead Golf and Country. Office: 4520 Executive Park Dr Montgomery AL 36116

HOLLAND, GARY ALEXANDER, oil company executive; b. Winnipeg, Man., Can., Dec. 24, 1933; s. Alexander Fredercik and Queenie (Sinclair) H.; 1 child, Mark Douglas. BA, U. Man., 1955, LLB, 1959. Mem. adv. council Govt. of Can. Dept. of Justice, Ottawa, Ont., 1959-62; atty. Gulf Can., Calgary, Alta., Can., 1962-66; econ. advisor Gulf Can., Toronto, Ont., 1966-69; solicitor Gulf Can., Calgary, 1967-76, assoc. gen. counsel, 1976-85, sec., v.p. gen. counsel, 1985—. Contbr. articles to profl. jours. Mem. Can. Inst. Resource Law (chmn. 1979-86), Can. Petroleum Law Found. (pres. 1978, bd. dirs. 1972-88), Internat. Bar Assn. (energy sect. council 1984—), Law Soc. of Alta., Law Soc. of Man., Petroleum Club of Calgary, Calgary Golf and Country Club. Conservative. Anglican. Office: Gulf Can Resources Ltd, 401 9th Ave SW, Calgary, AB Canada T2P 2H7

HOLLAND, GARY RICHARD, electronics company executive; b. Willow Springs, Mo., Feb. 23, 1942; s. John Grayson and Voneta Erma (McCracken) H.; m. Ruth Gretchen Stadler, Oct. 10, 1970; 1 dau., Heidi Suzanne. B.S. in Mech. Engring., U. Mo., 1964; M.S. in Indsl. Adminstrn., Purdue U., 1965. Dir. mktg. MPL Inc., Chgo., 1965-68; nat. sales mgr. Maremont Inc., Chgo., 1968-71; v.p. mktg. Coleman Co., Witchita, Kans., 1971-73; v.p. Toro Co., Mpls., 1973-79; pres. CPT Corp., Mpls., 1979-82; pres., chief operating officer Data Card Corp., Mpls., 1982-88, pres., chief exec. officer, 1988—. Mem. Minn. High Tech. Council, Mpls., 1984—, dist. export council Dept. Commerce, Mpls., 1978-83; bd. dirs. Med. Payment Systems, Cleve. Recipient Disting. Alumni award U. Mo., 1969; named one of Outstanding Young Men in Am., 1975-76. Mem. Am. Electronics Assn. (chmn. Minn. chpt. 1984-86, bd. dirs.). Mem. Ch. of God. Home: 6312 Indian Hills Rd Edina MN 55435 Office: Data Card Corp Corp Tech & Devel 11111 Bren Rd W Box 9355 Minneapolis MN 55440

HOLLAND, JAMES MICHAEL, accountant, oil drilling executive; b. Stamford, Tex., Apr. 24, 1945; s. Leo Harold and Margie Allin (Cooper) H.; m. Sandra kay St. Clair, June 24, 1966; children: Sheri Ann, James Michael Jr., Brain. BBA, Tex. Tech. U., 1967, MBA, 1970. CPA, Tex. Staff acct. Arthur Andersen & Co., Houston, 1970-71, sr. acct., 1972-74, mgr., 1975-76; controller Atwood Oceanics, Inc., Houston, 1977-79, treas., 1980, v.p. fin., 1981—. Served with U.S. Army, 1968-69, Vietnam. Mem. Am. Inst. CPAs., Tex. Soc. CPAs, Fin. Execs. Inst. Republican. Baptist. Home: 5107 Boyce Springs Houston TX 77066 Office: Atwood Oceanics Inc 15835 Park Ten Pl Dr Houston TX 77218

HOLLAND, JAMES RICHARD, JR., business executive; b. Conway, Ark., Nov. 22, 1943; s. James R. and D. Mildred Holland; m. Cherie Holland; 1 child, Jeff D. BS in Chem. Engring., Okla. State U., 1966; MS in Indsl. Adminstrn., Carnegie-Mellon U., 1969. Assoc. Booz, Allen & Hamilton, Inc., Chgo., 1969-72; v.p. Tex. Industries, Inc., Dallas, 1972-77; pres. KSA Industries, Inc., Houston, 1977-80, Western Services Internat., Inc., Ft. Worth, Tex., 1980-85; exec. v.p. TGI Friday's, Inc., Dallas, 1985-87, Coast Am. Corp., Denver, 1987—; bd. dirs. Cryomec, Inc., Anaheim, Calif.; chmn. pension trust 1982-84, investment com. 1984-85, WCNA, Ft. Worth. Author: Information for Marketing Management, 1971. Mem. Leadership Ft. Worth, 1982, Forum Ft. Worth, 1983—; vice chmn. Grad. Sch. Indsl. Adminstrn., Pitts., 1984, allocations United Way, Ft. Worth, 1983. Mem. Nat. Assn. Corp. Real Estate Execs., Planning Forum. Clubs: Windsor, Shady Oaks (Ft. Worth). other: Dollar Gen Corp 427 Beech St Scottsdale KY 42164

HOLLAND, JOHN BEN, clothing manufacturing company executive; b. Scottsville, Ky., Mar. 26, 1932; s. Elbridge Winfred and Lou May (Whitney) H.; m. Margaret Irene Pecor, Jan. 31, 1954; children: John Sandra, Robert. B.S. in Acctg., Bowling Green Bus. U., 1959. With Union Underwear Co., Inc., Bowling Green, Ky., 1961—, v.p.-adminstrn., 1972-74, vice chmn., 1975, chmn., chief exec. officer, 1976—; dir. 1st Ky. Nat. Corp., Louisville, Dollar Gen. Corp.; mem. N.Y. Cotton Exchange, 1985—. Bd. dirs. Ky. Council Econ. Edn., Louisville, 1981—, Ky. Advocates for Higher Edn. Inc., 1985—, Camping World Inc., 1985-88; chmn. corp. council Western Ky. U., also mem. devel. Steering com.; bd. dirs. Ky. C. of C., 1987-88. Mem. Bowling Green-Warren County C. of C. (bd. dirs. 1981-85), Am. Arbitration Assn. (panel 1985—). Office: Fruit of the Loom Inc 1 Fruit of the Loom Dr Bowling Green KY 42101

HOLLAND, JOHN DEAL, corporate executive; b. Poplar Bluff, Mo., Sept. 1, 1937; s. Ernest Rudolph and Alphia Emma (Brown) H.; m. Catherine Arrendale Sheets, Mar. 9, 1963; children: Timothy, Daniel, Heather. BBA, U. Mo., 1959. Commd. ensign USN, 1959, advanced through grades to comdr.; officer in charge Navy Occupational Devel. and Analysis Ctr., Washington, 1974-81, resigned, 1981; analyst Data Design Lab, 1981; bus. mgr. Poplar Bluffs (Mo.) Sch. Dist., 1981—; bd. dirs. Mo. United Sch. Ins. Council, St. Louis. Chmn. bd. adjustment City of Poplar, 1982—; treas. Sr. Olympics Bd., Poplar Bluff, 1984—; bd. dirs. Poplar Bluff C. of C., 1984-86. Mem. Mo. Assn. Sch. Bus. Officials, Assn. Sch. Bus. Officials, Rotary Club (v.p. 1984-85, pres. 1985-86). Republican. Methodist. Home: 225 S 6th St Poplar Bluff MO 63901 Office: Poplar Bluff Sch Dist PO Box 47 Poplar Bluff MO 63901

HOLLAND, JUDITH RAWIE, producer; b. Long Beach, Calif., Jan. 25, 1942; d. Wilmer Ernest and Margaret Jane (Towle) Rawie; m. John Allen Holland, July 11, 1964 (div.); children: Daryn Kirsten, Dawn Malia. BBA, Marymount Coll.; BA in Visual Arts and Communication, U. Calif., San Diego, 1978; MD in Bus. Adminstrn. Producer/writer PBS series Achieving (Emmy award 1982, ACE nominee), asst. dir. rsch. and video/producer IABC, San Francisco, 1982; bd. dir. programming Group W Cable, Westinghouse Co., 1983-85; ptnr. RH Positive Prodns. Co., 1986-87; mgr. video programming Nelson/Embassy Home Entertainment, 1986-87; ptnr. Real Magic, Studio City, Calif., 1988-87. Recipient You Make the Difference award Group W, 1983. Mem. Am. Film Inst., Women in Film, INDCP Features Assn. Democrat. Episcopalian.

HOLLAND, LYMAN FAITH, JR., lawyer; b. Mobile, Ala., June 17, 1931; s. Lyman Faith and Louise (Wisdom) H.; m. Leannah Louise Platt, Mar. 6, 1954; children: Lyman Faith III, Laura. BS in Bus. Adminstrn, U. Ala., 1953; LLB, 1957. Bar: Ala. 1957. Assoc. Hand, Arendall & Bedsole, Mobile, 1957-62; ptnr. Hand, Ardendall, Bedsole, Greaves & Johnston, 1963—. Mem. Mobile Historic Devel. Com., 1965-69, v.p., 1967-68; Bd. dirs. Mobile Azalea Trail, Inc., 1963-68, chmn. bd., 1963-65; bd. dirs. Mobile Mental Health Ctr., 1969-76, v.p., 1972, pres., chmn. bd., 1973; bd. dirs. Mobile chpt. ARC, vice chmn., 1975-77, exec. vice chmn., 1978-80, chmn., 1980-82; bd. dirs. Deep South coun. Girl Scouts U.S., 1965-71, Gordan Smith Ctr. Inc., 1973, Bay Area Coun. on Alcoholism, 1973-76, Community Chest, Coun. of Mobile County, Inc., 1976-81; bd. dirs. Greater Mobile Mental Health-Mental Retardation, 1975-81, pres., 1975-77; mem. exec. com. Mobile Estate Planning Coun., 1988—. 1st lt. USAF, 1953-55; lt. col. Res. ret. Mem. ABA, Mobile County Bar Assn., Ala. State Bar (chmn. sect. corp., banking and bus. law 1978-80), Am. Counsel Assn., Am. Coll. Probate Counsel, Ala. Law Inst. (coun.), Pi Kappa Alpha, Phi Delta Phi. Baptist (deacon, ch. trustee 1968-73, chmn. trustees 1971-73). Clubs: Athleston (Mobile); Country Club of Mobile, Bienville. Lodge: Lions (Mobile). Home: 717 Westmoreland Dr W Mobile AL 36609 Office: Box 123 Mobile AL 36601

HOLLAND, ROBERT CARL, economist; b. Tekamah, Nebr., Apr. 7, 1925; s. Carl Luther and Gretchen (Thompson) H.; m. DeEtte Harriet Hedlund, Sept. 7, 1947; children: Joan DeEtte Holland Geltz, Nancy Gretchen Holland Kerr, Timothy Robert. Student, U. Nebr., 1942-43, 46; B.S. in Fin., U. Pa., 1948, M.A. in Econs., 1949, Ph.D. in Econs., 1959. Instr. money and banking U. Pa., 1948-49; with Fed. Res. Bank Chgo., 1949-61, v.p., 1959-61; with bd. govs. Fed. Res. System, 1961-76; mem. bd. govs. FRS, 1973-76, sec. of bd., 1968-71, exec. dir., 1971-73, sec. to fed. open market com., 1966-73; pres. Com. for Econ. Devel., Washington, 1976—. Bd. dirs. Nat. Bur. Econ. Research, Council on Fgn. Relations, Ctr. for Excellence in Govt., Congl. Econ. Leadership Inst., Council for Community-Based Devel.; sr. mem. The Conf. Bd., Inc.; mem. UN Assn.'s Bus. and Labor Econ. Policy Council. Served with AUS, 1943-45. Mem. Am. Econ. Assn., Am. Fin. Assn., Nat. Acad. Pub. Adminstrn., Beta Theta Pi. Clubs: Cosmos (Washington); Univ.

of N.Y. (N.Y.C.); Kenwood Country (Bethesda, Md.). Home: 5508 Cromwell Dr Bethesda MD 20816 Office: Com Econ Devel 1700 K St NW Ste 700 Washington DC 20006

HOLLAND, WILLIAM RAY, diversified company executive; b. Ada, Okla., Dec. 19, 1938; s. Arthur Bruce and Artie Mary (Hood) H.; m. Donna Ruth Albright, Jan. 25, 1959; children—Donna Kristen, William Dallas, John Foster. B.S., U. Denver, 1960, J.D., 1962. Bar: Colo. bar 1963, Ark. bar 1964. With Met. Area Planning Commn. Little Rock, 1959-63; atty. Southwestern Bell Telephone, Little Rock, 1964-66; assoc. firm Bridges Young Matthews & Davis, Little Rock, 1966-73; with AMCA Internat. Ltd. (formerly Dominion Bridge Co. Ltd.) and AMCA Internat. Corp., Hanover, N.H., 1973—, exec. v.p., 1981-85, pres., chief exec. officer, 1986—, chmn., 1987—. Served to capt., JAGC USAF, 1968. Mem. Am. Bar Assn., Ark. Bar Assn. Republican. Baptist. Home: 13 Pine Dr Hanover NH 03755 Office: AMCA Internat Ltd Dartmouth Nat Bank Bldg B 44 S Main Hanover NH 03755

HOLLANDER, GERHARD LUDWIG, computer company executive; b. Berlin, Feb. 27, 1922; s. Ernst Julius and Cecilie H.; m. Marianne Schempp, Dec. 24, 1957; children—Susan, Carolyn, Jeffrey. B.S. in Elec. Engring., Ill. Inst. Tech., 1947; M.S., Washington U., St. Louis, 1948; E.E., MIT, 1953. Registered profl. engr., Ill. Radio buyer Spiegel, Inc., 1940-42; research engr. McDonnell Aircraft Co., 1947; asst. prof. engring. St. Louis U., 1948-49; sr. engr. servo lab. Raytheon Mfg. Co., 1949-51; mem. research staff servomechanisms lab. MIT, Cambridge, 1952-54; sect. head data processing systems Clevite Research Ctr., 1954-57; sect. mgr. computer systems Philco Corp., 1957-60; mgr. gen. purpose computer dept. Hughes Aircraft Co., 1960-61; pres., tech. dir. Hollander Assocs., Fullerton, Calif., 1961—; cons. govt. agys., indsl. firms, 1953—, Argonne Nat. Lab., 1957, USAF Hdqrs., 1959-60, IBM, 1976, Dept. Def., 1976; U.S. del. Internat. Fedn. of Automatic Control Congresses, Moscow, Russia, 1960; bd. dirs. WINCON, 1975-79, chmn., 1978-79; founding dir. Elec. and Electronics Exhibits, Inc., 1974. Fellow Inst. for Advancement Engring., Nat. Contract Mgmt. Assn. (vice chmn., program chmn. 1975-78), IEEE (chmn. computing devices com., vice-chmn. computer group, 1962-65, gen. chmn. joint nat. conf. maj. systems 1971, gen. chmn. Westex '86 Expert Systems conf., chmn. bd. dirs. Westex, 1986—, Centennial medal 1984); mem. Am. Computer Machinery, Ops. Research Soc. Am., Am. Fedn. Info. Processing Socs. (nat. joint computer com. 1959-61, dir. 1962-65, Cosati rep. NSF, 1965-68), Am. Automatic Control Council (control adv. com. 1960-62), Sigma Xi, Sigma Alpha Mu. Editor: Computer in Control, 1961; chmn. editorial bd. Computer Design, 1969-73; contbr. numerous articles to profl. jours.; patentee in field. Pioneer in hierarchical memory concept used in computers. Office: Hollander Assocs PO Box 2276 Fullerton CA 92633

HOLLANDER, STANLEY CHARLES, marketing educator; b. Balt., Aug. 2, 1919; s. Abraham A. and Selma (Langfeld) H.; m. Selma Dorothy Jacobs, Dec. 16, 1956. BS, NYU, 1941; MA, Am. U., 1946; PhD, U. Pa., 1954. Trainee, asst. mgr. Neisner Bros., various locations, 1941-43; analyst U.S. Office Price Adminstrn., Washington, 1943-45, cons., 1946; analyst Charles Stoen Co., N.Y.C., 1945-47; instr. dept. mktg. U. Buffalo, 1947-49; instr. dept. mktg. U. Pa., Phila., 1949-54, assoc. prof., 1956-58; asst. prof. Sch. Bus. U. Minn., Mpls., 1954-56; assoc. prof. mktg. Mich. State U., East Lansing, 1958-59, prof., 1959—. Author: Retail Price Policies, 1958; Multinational Retailing, 1958; Restraints on Retail Competition, 1965; author (with D.J. Duncan) Modern Retailing Management, 1972, 77, (with R. Savitt), 83; editor: Exploration in Retailing, 1959; (with R. Moyer) Markets and Marketing in Developing Countries, 1968; (with J. Boddewyn) Public Policy Toward Retailing, 1972; Passenger Transportation, 1968; Business Consultants and Clients, 1963; Management Consultants and Clients, 1972; also articles. Recipient NYU Inst. Retail Mgmt. award, 1964; named disting. scholar Mich. State U., 1982; essays written in honor of Stanley Holland in Festschrift Historical Perspectives in Marketing, 1988. Mem. Am. Mktg. Assn., Am. Coll. Retailing Assn. (pres. 1986-88), Am. Econ. Assn., Acad. Mktg. Sci. (bd. govs. 1986—), Bus. History Conf., AAUP (co-chmn. mktg. history confs.), Phi Kappa Phi, Beta Gamma Sigma, Eta Mu Pi. Jewish. Club: University (Lansing). Office: Mich State U 321 Eppley Ctr East Lansing MI 48824

HOLLANDSWORTH, KENNETH PETER, management consultant; b. York, Pa., Jan. 18, 1934; s. Dover Daniel and Sarah Kathryn (Meyers) H.; B.A. in Econs., Gettysburg Coll., 1956; m. Edith D. Butera, Oct. 15, 1960; children—Stephanie, Tracy. Purchasing clk. Certain-Teed Products Corp., York, 1958-59; territorial salesman Todd div. Burroughs Corp., Allentown, Pa., 1959-61; dir. presentation and incentive sales, then nat. dir. retail sales Hamilton Watch Co., Lancaster, Pa., 1962-69; gen. mgr. Vendome Watch div. Coro Inc., N.Y.C., 1969-71; pres., chief exec. officer Jules Jurgensen Corp. subs. Downe Communications, Inc., N.Y.C., 1972-75; exec. v.p., sec. to corp. Optel Corp. Princeton, N.J., 1975-76, also dir.; pvt. fin. and gen. mgmt. cons., 1976-80, 82—; pres., dir. Thomas-Pond Bus. Devel. Group, Inc., 1978-80; v.p. consumer products Commodore Internat. Ltd., 1980-82; gen. cons. to v.p. ops. Timex Computer Corp., also cons. to exec. v.p. Timex Corp., 1983—; bus. devel. cons. AT&T Consumer Products Group, 1984. Mem. Conn. Task Force on Computers and Instrn., 1983. Served with U.S. Army, 1956-58. Author: The Emerging Watch Industry, 1978. Home: PO Box 296 Yardley PA 19067

HOLLEMAN, JOHN ALBERT, mortgage company executive; b. San Antonio, Jan. 15, 1939; s. Samuel Brooks and Martha (Blair) H.; m. Barbara Ann Hilburn, July 14, 1964 (div. Mar. 1983); m. Angelyn Head Berry, Aug. 29, 1986. BS, U. Ala., 1960; Diploma in Banking, La. State U., 1972; JD, Jones Law Inst., 1974. Registered rep. Hugo Marx & Co., Birmingham, Ala., 1961-68; sr. investment officer First Ala. Bancshares, Montgomery, 1968-80; pres., chmn. bd. Real Estate Financing, Inc., Montgomery, 1980—. Mem. Mortgage Bankers Assn. Baptist. Club: Arrowhead Country (Montgomery). Home: 1640 Cairnbrook Dr Montgomery AL 36106 Office: First Ala Real Estate Financing PO Box 669 Montgomery AL 36195

HOLLENDER, JOHN EDWARD, infosystems, planning and marketing executive; b. Massillon, Ohio, Mar. 16, 1941; s. Edward Clarence and Grace Rebecca (Rohr) H.; m. Darleen Kay Lewis, Oct. 16, 1978; children: John, Rebecca, Matthew. BS, Ohio State U., 1964, MBA, 1965. Gen. mgr. systems devel. Montgomery Ward & Co., Chgo., 1967-80; sr. v.p. planning, fin. and info. systems Signature Group, Schaumburg, Ill., 1981-85; sr. v.p., gen. mgr. Metronet Metromail Corp., Lombard, Ill., 1985—; bd. dirs. Montgomery Ward Life Ins. Co., 1981-85, Forum Ins. Co., 1981-85. Chmn. Montgomery Ward Crudade of Mercy, Chgo., 1974-78; chmn. bd. dirs. Chgo. Chamber Choir, 1976-80. With USNR, 1960-66. Fellow Life Office Mgmt. Inst.; mem. Direct Mktg. Assn., Chgo. Direct Mktg. Assn., Credit Card Mktg. Co. Council, DuPage Club. Home: 23655 W Juniper Ln Barrington IL 60010 Office: Metromail Corp 360 E 22d St Lombard IL 60148

HOLLER, DAVID GLENN, accountant, minister; b. Hyattsvill, Md., Aug. 3, 1964; s. Victor Earl and Verly Gale (Krausse) H. BS in Acctg., Frostburg State Coll., 1985. Ordained to ministry, Watchtower Bible, Tract Soc. N.Y. Crew head 4-M Corp., Lavale, Md., 1983-84; mgr. student activities Frostburg (Md.) State Coll., 1984; mgr. catering Marriott Corp., Frostburg, 1984-85; acctg. controller Marriott Corp., Bethesda, Md., 1985-86; acct. Jeremiah Connor, PC, Rockville, Md., 1986-87, Lightening Maid, P.C.S., Cumberland, Md., 1987—; pres., cons. Pioneer Support Svcs., 1988—; pres. FSC Acctg. Assocs., Frostburg, 1984-85.

HOLLINGSWORTH, DAVID SOUTHERLAND, chemical company executive; b. Wilmington, Del.. BS in Chem. Engring., Lehigh U., 1948. Chem. engr. research ctr. Hercules Inc., Wilmington; chem. engr. lab. Hercules Inc., Kalamazoo, Mich.; tech. rep. sales office Hercules Inc., New Orleans and Wilmington, 1953-61; asst. sales mgr. paper chems. Hercules Inc., Wilmington, 1961-63, sales mgr. specialty chems., 1963-65, mgr. specialty paper chems. pine and paper chem. dept., 1965-67, dir. sales paper chems., 1967-72, from dir. mktg. to asst. gen. mgr., 1972-74, gen. mgr. new enterprise dept., 1974-75, gen. mgr. food and fragrance devel. dept., 1975-78, dir. worldwide bus. ctr. organics, 1978-79, v.p. planning, 1979-82, group v.p. water-soluble polymers, 1982-83, also bd. dirs., divisional v.p. mktg., 1983-84; pres. Hercules Specialty Chems. Co., Wilmington, 1984-86, vice chmn., 1986; chmn., chief exec. officer Hercules Inc., Wilmington, 1987—; bd. dirs. Del. Trust Co. Trustee Grand Opera House Inc.; bd. dirs. Med. Ctr. Del., Del. Symphony. Mem. Chem. Mfrs. Assn. (bd. dirs.), Conf. Bd. Club: Hercules Country. Office: Hercules Inc 1313 N Market St Wilmington DE 19894 *

HOLLINSHEAD, PETER DONALD, marketing professional; b. Rochester, N.Y., Apr. 30, 1952; s. G. Donald and Marjorie (Killian) H.; m. Julie Beth Rattner, Oct. 28, 1984. BA, George Washington U., 1974; MA, John Hopkins U., 1982. Clk. Pa. Dept. Revenue, Phila., 1974-75, tax examiner, 1975-77; field investigator Pa. Dept. Revenue, Media, Pa., 1977-80; automotive editor Springfield (Pa.) Press., 1978-82; account exec. Sandy Corp., Troy, Mich., 1982-84, Ross Roy, Inc., Detroit, 1984-85; mgr. Chrysler Satellite Network Chrysler Motors Corp., Highland Park, Mich., 1985-86; shows and meetings coord., with merchandising dept. Chrysler Motors Corp., Highland Park, 1986-87, dealer sales promotion specialist Dodge car and truck div., 1987—. Alcan fellow Johns Hopkins U., 1981. Democrat. Home: 1659 Stanley Blvd Birmingham MI 48009 Office: Chrysler Motors Corp 12000 Chrysler Dr Highland Park MI 48288-0857

HOLLIS, DONALD ROGER, banker; b. Warren, Ohio, Mar. 4, 1936; s. Louis and Lena (Succo) H.; m. Marilyn G. Morganti, Aug. 23, 1958; children—Roger, Russell Kirk, Gregory, Heather. B.S., Kent State U., 1959. Regional mgr. Glidden Corp., San Francisco, 1959-65; dir. mgmt. info. services Glidden Corp., Cleve., 1965-68, SCM Corp., N.Y.C., 1968-71; v.p. Chase Manhattan Bank, N.Y.C., 1971-81; sr. v.p. First Chgo. Corp., 1981-85, exec. v.p., 1986—, now head customer services and service products; mem. customer council AT&T; dir. Chgo. Info. Industry Council; mem. systems com. Chgo. Bd. Options Exchange; bd. govs. Fed. Res. Systems' Large Dollar Payments Systems Adv. Group; mem. bd. advs. Bankers Mag. Mem. exec. com. Ill. Inst. Tech. Bd. Trustees, chmn. bd. overseers Sch. Bus. Adminstrn. Mem. Am. Bankers Assn. (past chmn. exec. com. ops. and automation div., daylight overdraft task force), Am. Mgmt. Assn. (info. systems and tech. council), Nat. Assn. Check Safekeeping (past pres.). Clubs: Chgo.; Barrington Hills Country (Ill.). Office: First Chgo Corp 1 First National Pla Chicago IL 60670

HOLLIS, KATHLEEN SUE, accountant, auditor, state official; b. Champaign, Ill., Sept. 18, 1955; d. James R. and Ellen Louise (Woods) H. Student, DePaul U., 1978-79; BA, U. Ill., Chgo., 1982; student, Columbia Pacific U., 1989—. Acct. Champaign Nat. Bank, 1978; supr. aircraft services Dept. Def., Chgo., 1978-83; methods and procedures analyst Alexander Proudfoot Co., Chgo., 1983-84; security cons. Excalibur & Assocs., Bridgeview, Ill., 1984-86; examiner Ill. Dept. Fin. Instns., Chgo., 1986—. Contbr. articles to profl. publs. With USAF, 1974-78, lt. USNR. Ill. Air NG scholar, 1979-82. Mem. Soc. Fin. Examiners, Ill. Soc. Fin. Examiners, Nat. Assn. Female Execs., U.S. Naval Inst., Air Force Assn., Naval Res. Assn., Am. Mgmt. Assn., Ill. NG Assn. (legis. comm. 1979-83, membership com. 1981-83). Republican. Episcopalian. Office: Ill Dept Fin Instns 100 W Randolph St Suite 15-700 Chicago IL 60601

HOLLISTER, CHARLOTTE ANN, computer systems design-implementation consultant; b. Santa Fe, Jan. 1, 1940; d. Bertram Keats and Sara Evelyn (Vaughn) H.; m. Donald Carl Clagett, June 22, 1968; children: Jennifer, Sarah, Emma. BA, Vassar Coll., 1961; PhD, Yale U., 1965. Rsch. asst. NYU, N.Y.C., 1965-68; programmer Harvard U. Observatory, Cambridge, Mass., 1969; sr. applications scientist Bolt Beranek and Newman, Inc., Cambridge, 1969-78, sr. scientist, 1980-84; product planner GE, Schenectady, 1979-80; dep. mgr. BBN Labs., Inc. Cambridge, 1984—. Contbr. articles on computer systems to profl. jours. Vol. Berkshire Ballet, Pittsfield, Mass., 1984-86. Mem. Assn. for Computing Machinery, Am. Chem. Soc. (com. chmn. N.E. sect. 1975-77, sec. 1977-79, svc. award 1979). Democrat. Episcopalian. Home: 193 Bartlett Ave Pittsfield MA 01201 Office: BBN Labs Inc 10 Moulton St Cambridge MA 02138

HOLLOWAY, CARL MAURICE, banker; b. Raleigh, N.C., Jan. 24, 1947; s. Carl Milner and Julia Mae (Mitchell) H.; m. Brenda Diann Lindsey, Nov. 26, 1970; children: David, Nathan, Kristen. AA, Meridian Jr. Coll., 1967; BS in Fin., U. So. Miss., 1970. Mgmt. trainee First Nat. Bank, Meridian, Miss., 1969-70; asst. nat. bank examiner compt. of currency U.S. Treasury Dept., Montgomery, Ala., 1970-74; exec. v.p. adminstrn. and ops. Nat. Bank Commerce Miss., Starkville, 1974—. Formerly active Boys Scouts Am., United Way, also others. Named Outstanding Young Man Starkville Jaycees, 1982, One of 30 Outstanding Young Leaders in Miss. Miss. Econs. Coun., 1982. Mem. Am. Bankers Assn. (edn. com., 1979-81), Miss. Bankers Assn. (chmn. ops. com. 1981-82), Starkville C. of C. (bd. dirs. 1980-83). Republican. Baptist. Home: 107 Dunbrook Dr Starkville MS 39759 Office: Nat Bank Commerce Miss 301 E Main St Starkville MS 39759

HOLLOWAY, CINDY, mortgage company executive; b. Queens, N.Y., Aug. 8, 1960; d. Richard Stephen and Beverly Bunny (Harris) Tannenbaum; m. David Milton Holloway (div. Mar. 1986); 1 child, Benjamin Jerome. BA, Calif. State U., Fullerton, 1981. Lic. real estate broker. Waitress Bob's Big Boy, San Bernardino, Calif., 1984-85; receptionist RNG Mortgage Co., San Bernardino, 1985; loan processor Quality Mortgage Co., Colton, Calif., 1985-88, loan officer, 1988—. Mem. San Bernardino Bd. Realtors spl. events com., 1988—. Mem. San Bernardino Bd. Realtors (spl. events com. 1988—). Home: PO Box 3187 Crestline CA 92325 Office: Quality Mortgage Co 1060 E Washington Ste 125 Colton CA 92324

HOLLOWAY, DOUGLAS JAY, marketing executive; b. Sacramento, June 21, 1945; s. Lowell Winford and Freda Marie (Kudart) H.; m. Teresa May Arnold, Mar. 24, 1973 (div. Apr. 1978); m. Deborah Marie Johnson, July, 24, 1981; children: Amy Katherine, Elizabeth Marie. Grad. high sch., Sacramento. Customer svc. agt. Delta Airlines, San Francisco, 1965-69; flint instr. Kenharber Flying, San Carlos, Calif., 1968-71; airport salesman Continental Air Lines, San Francisco, 1970-75; proprietor Columbia Mktg. Ltd., Burlingame, Calif., 1975-81; sales mgr. Am. Audio Corp., South San Francisco, 1978-81; rep. assoc. Seaport Mktg, Inc., Beaverton, Oreg., 1981—; rep. prin. Columbia Mktg., Beaverton, 1987—; pres. The Movie Mart, Inc., Portland, Oreg., 1988—. Republican. Roman Catholic. Home: 7935 Carol Glen Pl Beaverton OR 97007 Office: The Moive Mart Inc 10302 NE Sandy Pl Portland OR 97220

HOLLOWAY, DOUGLAS PATRICK, banker; b. Las Vegas, Nev., Dec. 21, 1938; s. Walker Lee and Frances Marguerite (Webber) H.; divorced; children: Gregory Stephen, Thomas Welling. B.A., U. San Francisco, 1962. Loan examiner Bank Calif., San Francisco, 1960-67, asst. v.p., 1960-70, asst. mgr., 1967-69, mgr., 1969-70; loan examiner Wells Fargo Bank, San Francisco, 1971-73, asst. v.p., 1973-76, v.p., 1976-82, dep. chief loan examiner, 1977-79, chief loan examiner, 1979—, sr. v.p., 1982—; mem. com. corp. responsibility Wells Fargo Bank, 1981-84, chmn., 1981-84. Bd. dirs. Am. Blood Commn., Arlington, Va., 1984—, chmn. fin. and audit com., 1985—, mem. exec. com., 1985—, planning com. 1986—, transition com. 1987—; bd. dirs. Irwin Meml. Blood Ctrs. of Med. Soc. San Francisco, 1984—, treas. 1984-89, pres., 1989—, chmn. fin. and audit com., 1984-89, mem. exec. com., 1984—, chmn., 1989—, mem. pers. com., 1988—, long range planning com. 1987—, chmn. community awareness task force, 1988—; bd. dirs. Blood R & D Found., 1986—; bd. dirs. Shanti Project, 1988—, chmn., 1989—, mem. fin. com., fundraising/pub. edn. coms., 1988—, chmn. vol. and direct svcs. com., 1988—, mem. nominating and bylaws coms., 1988—. Republican. Roman Catholic. Office: Wells Fargo & Co 111 Sutter St 13th Fl San Francisco CA 94163

HOLLOWAY, EUGENE CLEVELAND, III, lawyer; b. Murfreesboro, Tenn., July 6, 1942; s. Eugene Cleveland Jr. and Carolyn Christobel (Cook) H.; m. Sally Ann Dusbabek, Sept. 29, 1973; children: Elizabeth Anne, Carolyn Price. BS, U.S. Naval Acad., 1964; JD, George Washington U., 1973, LLM, 1975. Bar: D.C., N.Y. Assoc. Covington & Burling, Washington, 1973-79, Harris, Beach, Wilcox, Rubin & Levey, Rochester, N.Y., 1981-83; sr. counsel GTE Sylvania Inc, Batavia, N.Y., 1977-81; asst. gen. counsel Schlegel Corp., Rochester, 1983-86; gen. counsel, sec. Amerace Corp., Parsippany, N.J., 1986—. Mem. ABA, Am. Soc. Corp. Secs. Office: Amerace Corp 8 Campus Dr Parsippany NJ 07054

HOLLOWAY, JAMES DAVID, steel company executive; b. Lancaster, Pa., Oct. 11, 1943; s. J. Phillip and Antoinette (Regan) H.; m. Carol A. Lapp, May 17, 1947; children: Kristen Carol, Beth Ann. BBA, Va. Poly. Inst. and State U., 1965; postgrad., Dartmouth Coll., 1984. Trainee steel plants Lukens Steel Co., Coatesville, Pa., 1965-67, sales estimator, 1968-69, claims negotiator, 1972-78, credit rep., 1978-81, regional credit mgr., 1981—; office mgr. Lukens Steel Co., Atlanta, 1969-72. Mem. planning commn. East Fallowfield Twp., Coatesville, 1972-78, twp auditor, 1985—. Mem. Credit Research Found., P.E.P. Investment Club (v.p. 1969-70). Republican. Presbyterian. Office: Lukens Steel Co S 1st Ave Coatesville PA 19320

HOLLOWAY, WENDELL MONDOZA, automobile company executive; b. Washington, Feb. 25, 1933; s. John Henry and Fannie Esther (Simpson) H.; m. Kay Gwendolyn Trent, June 8, 1957; children: Brian D., Karen J., Jonathan S. BA, Ohio Wesleyan U., 1954; MSSM, U. So. Calif., 1967, MPA, 1973, PhD, 1975. Commd. 2d lt. USAF, advanced through grades to lt. col., pilot and ops. officer, Ohio, Nebr., Hawaii, Calif., 1955-69, contracting officer, Bedford, Mass., 1970-71, chief prodn., 1971-73; mem. faculty Air War Coll., Montgomery, Ala., 1973-74; adminstrv. asst. Rep. Y.B. Burke, Washington, 1974-77; legis. mgr. Ford Motor Co., Washington, 1977—; mem. research adv. bd. Joint Ctr. Polit. Studies, Washington, 1985; mem. Plowman and Fisherman, Montgomery County, Md., 1984—; Del. Democratic Nat. Conv., Montgomery County, 1984; Chmn. bd. trustees Md. State U. and Coll., 1986—; bd. trustees Suburban Hosp., Bethesda; mem. adv. bd. Big Bros., Washington, 1983—; campaign worker Gilchrist for County Exec., 1976-82, Barnes for Congress, 1978—, Mondale for Pres., 1984; candidate for U.S. Ho. of Reps. from 8th dist. Md., 1986. Decorated Bronze Star, Air medals. Mem. Calif. State Soc. (pres., bd. dirs., 1984), Am. League Lobbyists, Nat. Indsl. Transp. League, Thursday Group. Methodist. Avocations: photography; camping; motorcycling; boating. Home: 11805 Canfield Rd Potomac MD 20854 Office: Ford Motor Co 815 Connecticut Ave NW Washington DC 20006

HOLLOWELL, THOMAS RALPH, infosystems specialist; b. Ann Arbor, Mich., Jan. 29, 1958. BBA, U. Mich., 1980. Account exec. Mich. Bell, Detroit, 1981-83; account exec., industry cons. AT&T, Detroit, 1983-85; sr. mgmt. cons. Diversitec, New Hudson, Mich., 1985-86, cons. mgr., 1986, product mgr., 1987—; cons. in field. Mem. Nat. Mgmt. Assn., Ind. Computer Cons. Republican. Office: Diversitic 53200 Grand River New Hudson MI 48165

HOLLSTEIN, BRIAN RAY, manufacturing executive; b. Peekskill, N.Y., Dec. 3, 1939; s. Raymond C. and Ethel (Starks) H.; m. Catherine Tinger, Sept. 22, 1962; children: Theresa Derr, Christian P., Stefan P. BA, NYU, 1961. Spl. agt. FBI, Washington, 1967-77; security mgr. Latin Am. Xerox Corp., Stamford, Conn., 1977-80, with security ops., 1980-83, with govt. relations Latin Am., 1983-84, dir. security, 1984—. Served to capt. U.S. Army, 1962-67. Mem. Am. Soc. for Indsl. Security (sr. v.p. 1988, pres. 1989), Internat. Security Mgmt. Assn., Soc. Former Agts. FBI. Office: Xerox Corp 800 Long Ridge Rd Stamford CT 06904

HOLM, DONALD GODFREY, utility company executive; b. Chgo., Aug. 19, 1927; s. Godfrey F. and Adeline (Carlson) H.; m. Geraldine Sliger, Sept. 5, 1949; children: Carol, Mark, John. BBA, Northwestern U., 1949; MBA, U. Chgo., 1961. Asst. treas. Peoples Energy Corp., Chgo., 1971-74, asst. sec., 1974-75, asst. treas., asst. sec., 1975-81, v.p., sec., treas., 1981-87, v.p., controller, sec., treas., 1987—. Bd. dirs. ARC Mid-Am. chpt., Chgo. Served to sgt. U.S. Army, 1952-54. Mem. Am. Soc. Corp. Secs., Am. Gas Assn. Presbyterian. Office: Peoples Energy Corp 122 S Michigan Ave Chicago IL 60603

HOLMAN, FRANCIS W(ADE), JR., lawyer; b. Long Branch, N.J., Sept. 24, 1939; s. Francis Wade and Helen Augusta (Shafto) H.; m. Rose Elizabeth Donahue, July 17, 1965; children: Elise Anne, Craig Alan. AB, Columbia U., 1960, MBA, 1962; JD, Boston Coll., 1965. Bar: Mass., U.S. Supreme Ct. Assoc. Finn & Brownell, Northampton, Mass., 1965-66; atty. Machinery and Allied Products Inst., Washington, 1967-68, 70-74, counsel, 1974-78, sec., 1978-82, v.p., sec., 1982—, chmn. various confs., 1984—; tax lawyer The Singer Co., N.Y.C., 1969; mgr., lectr. exec. seminars; presenter testimony to IRS, Dept. Treasury. Author numerous policy studies. Vol. Peter Bent Brigham Hosp., Boston, 1964, Newton (Mass.)-Wellesley Hosp., 1964-65; active Manor Citizens Assn., Rockville, Md., 1981—. Figure skating competitor/medalist, N.Y.C., Lake Placid, N.Y., Buffalo, 1957, 60, nat. competitor, Seattle, 1960. Mem. ABA, Nat. Lawyers Club, Planning Forum, Columbia Alumni Assn., Boston Coll. Alumni Assn., Nat. SAR, Manor Country Club (mem. social com. 1982-85). Home: 14620 Chesterfield Rd Rockville MA 20853 Office: Machinery & Allied Products Inst 1200 18th St NW Ste 400 Washington DC 20036

HOLMAN, LARRY DEAN, health care administrator; b. Lincoln, Nebr., Nov. 1, 1940; s. Clarence Woodford and Ethel Elizabeth (Remmenga) H.; m. Setsuko Umekawa, Dec. 5, 1960 (div. Aug. 1978); children: Lori Akiko, Yuko Donna; m. Debbie Joan Berkowitz, Dec. 8, 1980; children: Andrew Joseph, Jodi Michelle, Matthew Jacob. AA, Palomar Community Coll., San Marcos, Calif., 1971; BS, George Washington U., 1974; MBA, LaSalle U., 1989, postgrad., 1989—. Enlisted USN, 1958, advanced through grades to lt. comdr., ret., 1982, hosp. corpsman, 1958-71; with USN Med. Service Corps, 1971-82; purchasing dir. St. Francis Country House, Darby, Pa., 1982-85; bus. mgr. Stapeley Hall, Phila., 1985-86; bus., program mgr. Seaman's Ch. Inst., Phila., 1986-87, Grad. Hosp., Phila., 1988-89; buyer Grad. Health System, Phila., 1989—. Mem. Beth Emeth Synagogue Mens' Club, Phila. Mem. Assn. Mil. Surgeons U.S., Am. Soc. Mil. Comptrollers, VFW, AMVETS, Vietnam Vets. Am., Am. Legion. Jewish. Lodge: B'nai B'rith. Home: 6746 Souder St Philadelphia PA 19149 Office: Grad Health System Purchasing Dept 1 Graduate Pla Philadelphia PA 19146

HOLMBERG, BRANTON KIETH, management consultant; b. Tacoma, Mar. 6, 1936; s. Victor August and Ann Irene (Warren) H.; B.A., Central Wash. U., 1962, M.Ed., 1964; Ed.D., U. Idaho, 1970; m. Margaret Ann Nelson, Sept. 17, 1960; children—James Michael, Ann Marie, Nelson John. Asst. prof. Pacific Lutheran U., 1964-70; asso. prof. Central Wash. U., Ellensburg, 1970-76, asso. dir. Orgn. Devel. Center, 1972-73; Ph.D. program dir. U.S. Internat. U., McChord AFB, 1977-78; pres. Holmberg Assoc., mgmt. and orgn. devel. cons., Bellingham, 1975—, Northpoint Corp., geriatric care centers, Bellingham, 1978-84, Northwest Horticulture, Inc., 1979—, Internat. Highpoint Corp., 1983—, Advanced Laundry Service, 1984-88. Mem. Ellensburg Criminal Law and Justice Planning Com., 1972-73. Served with USAF, 1954-58. U. Idaho fellow, 1968. Mem. Am. Psychol. Assn., Am. Mgmt. Assn., Am. Personnel and Guidance Assn., Internat. Assn. Quality Circles, Internat. Registry Orgn. Devel. Cons., Acad. Mgmt., AAUP, Orgn. Devel. Network, Phi Delta Kappa. Home: 205 North Shore Dr Bellingham WA 98226

HOLMES, CHARLES EVERETT, lawyer; b. Wellington, Kans., Dec. 21, 1931; s. Charles Everett and Elizabeth Francis (Bergin) H.; m. Lynn Lacy, Jan. 2, 1954; children: Anne Lacy, Charles Everett, Rebecca. BA, Wichita U., 1953; LLB, U. Okla., 1961. Bar: Okla. 1961. Practice, Tulsa, after 1961; sec. Sinclair Oil & Gas Co., Sinclair Can. Oil Co., Mesa Pipeline Co., Border Pipe Line Co., Sinclair Transp. Co., Ltd.; ptnr. Rogers, Bell & Robinson, Tulsa, 1969-71; v.p. Nat. Bank of Tulsa, 1971-78; atty. Petro-Lewis Corp., Denver, 1978-87; v.p. Mc Mo Ran Oil & Gas Co., 1987—. Served with USAF, 1954-56, 61-62. Mem. ABA, Okla. Bar Assn., Colo. Bar Assn., Denver County Bar Assn. Roman Catholic. (del. Okla. Council Cath. Diocese 1966—, chmn. Cath. Parish Governing Body 1968—, bd. dirs. Youth Services, Travelers Aid, Com. Fgn. Relations). Home: 1643 Josephine #318 New Orleans LA 70130 Office: 1615 Poydras New Orleans LA 70112

HOLMES, CHRISTOPHER FRANCIS, advertising agency executive; b. Boston, Dec. 3, 1959; s. William Burton and Marie F. (Crowley) H. BBA in Mktg., Suffolk U., 1984. Account exec. Doyle Realty corp., Boston, 1979-82; account exec. Ski Ad Internat. Inc., Boston, 1983-85, v.p., treas., 1985, pres., chief exec. officer, 1985-89; chmn. Ski Ad Mktg. Group, Boston, 1989—; bd. dirs. Manning Industries, Boston, SAI, Inc., Boston; adviser Neman Internat., Boston, A.S.&D., Inc., Norwell, Mass., 1989—. Mem. Am. Mktg. Assn., Nat. Ski Areas Assn., Ski Industries Am. Roman

Catholic. Home and Office: Ski Ad Internat Inc 47 Candia St Weymouth MA 02189

HOLMES, CLAIRE COLEMAN, real estate broker; b. Ruston, La., Sept. 14, 1931; d. Eusel Monroe and Mabel Claire (Cahoon) Coleman; m. Major Joe Holmes, Dec. 20, 1951; children: George David, Claire Anne, William Gray. BA cum laude, U. Ark., 1952. Tchr. Pulaski (Ark.) County Spl. Sch. Dist., 1952-53, Pine Bluff (Ark.) Sch. Dist., 1953-55; real estate salesman Sullivant-Cross Realty, Pine Bluff, 1979-83; legal sec. Joe Holmes, Atty., Pine Bluff, 1985—; real estate broker C & J, Inc., Pine Bluff, 1985—. Mem. DAR, Soc. Mayflower Descendants, Jr. League, Pine Bluff Duplicate Bridge Club, Am. Contract Bridge League. Home: 22 So Pines Dr Pine Bluff AR 71603 Office: C & J Inc 514 Nat Bldg Pine Bluff AR 71601

HOLMES, DAVID RICHARD, computer and business forms company executive; b. Salt Lake City, Aug. 10, 1940; s. John Rulon and Evelyn Nadine (Schettler) H.; m. Nancy Alice Lewis, Sept. 11, 1965; children: David Matthew, Stephen Michael, Jeffrey Alan. BA, Stanford U., 1963; MBA, Northwestern U., 1965. Category mgr., strategic planning mgr. Gen. Foods Corp., White Plains, N.Y., 1965-77; dir. mktg. Standard Brands Inc., N.Y.C., 1977-78; mktg. mgr. Gen. Electric, Fairfield, Conn., 1978-81; v.p., gen. mgr. Nabisco Brands Inc., N.Y.C., 1981-84; pres. computer systems div. Reynolds & Reynolds Co., Dayton, Ohio, 1984-87, pres., chief operating officer, 1987—, also bd. dirs. Bd. dirs. St. Elizabeth Med. Found., Dayton, 1986, Dayton Pub. Radio, 1986, Dayton Met. YMCA, 1988—. Served with USNR, 1966-74. Mem. Am. Mgmt. Assn., Dayton Phil. Orch. Assn. (trustee 1988-91). Republican. Presbyterian. Clubs: Am. Yacht (Rye, N.Y.); Dayton Country. Office: Reynolds & Reynolds Co 115 S Ludlow St Dayton OH 45402

HOLMES, ELLEN CAROLYN, banker, data processing executive; b. Memphis, Sept. 14, 1946; d. Thomas Phillips and Geraldine L. (Scurr) Hemphill; m. Harold Edward Holmes, June 27, 1981; 1 child, Jason Edward. Student, Ind. U., Gary, 1963-65, Glendale (Ariz.) Community Coll., 1968-78, Phoenix Coll., 1981-82, Scottsdale Community Coll., 1983. Lead systems analyst Valley Nat. Bank, Phoenix, 1966—. Mem. Unity Ch. Home: 610 E Port Au Prince Phoenix AZ 85022 Office: Valley Nat Bank of Ariz PO Box 71 Q-493 Phoenix AZ 85001

HOLMES, HARRY DADISMAN, health facility administrator; b. Houston, Aug. 8, 1944; s. Harry newton and Ruth Eleanor (Dadisman) H.; m. Patricia Ann Hunt, Aug. 23, 1969; children: Hillary Hunt, Ashley Elizabeth. BA, Rice U., 1966; MA, La. State U., 1968; PhD, U. Mo., 1973. Asst. prof. urban devel. U. Tenn., Knoxville, 1973-76; asst. to exec. v.p. Tex. Med. Ctr., Inc., Houston, 1976-80; dir. govt. affairs, orgnl. liaison U. Tex. System Cancer Ctr., Houston, 1980—, asst. to pres., 1981—; mem. select com. on pub. issues Greater Houston Hosp. Council, 1983—; mem. exec. adv. bd. White, Petrov and McHone, 1987—; mem. pub. relations adv. council Tex. Med. Ctr., 1985—, chair South Tex. Legis. Conf., 1985, 87, founder Biotech. Assn., 1986. Mem. adminstrv. bd. St. Luke's Meth. Ch.; mem. Mayor's Task Force on Pvt. Sector Initiatives for Houston, 1981-82; mem. exec. bd. Leadership Houston, 1983-86; mem. exec. bd. Houston Ctr. for Humanities, 1983-86; mem. govt. relations com. Greater Houston Hosp. Council, 1985—; mem. com. Harris County Sesquicentennial, 1986, Institutional Task Force on Oncology in Chile, 1986-87, exec. com. Institutional Strategic Planning Com., 1986—, pub. issues com. Engring. Council of Houston, 1986; div. chmn. United Way of Houston, 1983. White fellow U. Mo., 1972. Mem. So. Hist. Assn., Young Hosp. Adminstrs., Houston C. of C. (co-chmn. govt. relations com. 1982-83, chmn. voting record task force 1983-84), Rice U. Alumni Assn. (exec. bd., chmn. publs. com. 1982-83), Phi Alpha Theta. Home: 2018 Suffolk St Houston TX 77027 Office: U Tex System Cancer Ctr 1515 Holcombe Houston TX 77030

HOLMES, JAMES PARKER, investment executive; b. Chgo., Nov. 6, 1940; s. Parker M. and Dorothy (Thomas) H.; m. Barbara A. Marshall; 1 child, Elizabeth K. BS, Marquette U., 1962; MBA, Northwestern U., 1963. Investment analyst Equitable Life Assurance Co., N.Y.C., 1963-66; mgr. investments CBS Inc., N.Y.C., 1966-69; sr. investment analyst Dean Witter, N.Y.C., 1969-72, portfolio strategist Ford Found., 1972-82; ptnr. Value Quest, N.Y.C., 1982-86; mng. dir. Dreman Value Mgmt., N.Y.C., 1986—. Contbr. chpts. to books. Treas. Ridgewood Republican Club, 1982-84. Mem. N.Y. Soc. Security Analysts (Vol. of Yr. award 1985), Am. Rhododendron Soc. (pres. Tappan Zee chpt.), Inst. Chartered Fin. Analysts, Am. Iris Soc., Garden State Iris Soc. (sec.). Republican. Roman Catholic. Avocations: gardening, reading. Home: 210 Greenway Rd Ridgewood NJ 07450 Office: Dreman Value Mgmt 70 Pine St New York NY 10005

HOLMES, JAY THORPE, lawyer; b. Waukesha, Wis., Aug. 4, 1942; s. Oliver Wendell and Lillian (Thorpe) H.; m. Karen E. Johnston, Sept. 9, 1962; children: Jayne, Jay Daniel, Susan. BA in History, U. Alaska, 1964; JD, U. Wis., 1967. Bar: Wis. 1967, Minn. 1967, Ill. 1972, N.Y. 1982. Corp. atty. Cargill, Inc., Mpls., 1967-71; gen. counsel A.E. Staley Mfg. Co., Decatur, Ill., 1971-81; sr. v.p., sec. Bausch & Lomb Inc., Rochester, N.Y., 1981—, also bd. dirs. Bd. dirs. various civic and charitable orgns. Mem. N.Y. Bar Assn., Monroe County Bar Assn. Presbyterian. Home: 75 Douglas Rd Rochester NY 14610 Office: Bausch & Lomb Inc 1 Lincoln Sq Rochester NY 14604

HOLMES, MALCOLM HERBERT, telecommunications company executive; b. London, Nov. 11, 1934; came to U.S., 1975; s. Harold and Gladys H.; m. Veronica Menezes, June 26, 1982. Grad. Sch. Accountancy, Scotland, 1956. Pres. Jamaica Telephone, Kingston, 1970-75; v.p. eastern region Continental Telephone, Washington, 1975-79; v.p. fin. Continental Telephone, Atlanta, 1979-82; exec. v.p. fin. Continental Telecom. Inc., Atlanta, 1982-83, exec. v.p. ops., 1983-85, exec. v.p., chief fin. officer, 1985—. Mem. Fin. Execs. Inst., Brit. Inst. Mgmt., Inst. Chartered Accts. Scotland. Home: 120 Laurel Dr Atlanta GA 30342 Office: Contel Corp 245 Perimeter Center Pkwy PO Box 105194 Atlanta GA 30348

HOLMES, OPAL LAUREL, publisher; b. Laurens, Iowa, Oct. 14, 1913; d. Ila Laurel and Jessie Merle (Hesselgrave) Holmes; ed. pub. and pvt. schs.; m. Vardis Fisher, Apr. 16, 1940. Publisher, Opal Laurel Holmes, Pub. Co-author: Gold Rushes and Mining Camps of the Early American West. Recipient Golden Spur award, 1969. Mem. Authors Guild, Authors League Am., Nat. Soc. Lit. and Arts, Internat. Platform Assn. Office: PO Box 2535 Boise ID 83701

HOLMES, ROBERT DESMOND, manufacturing company executive; b. Lisburn, County Antrim, Ireland, Feb. 3, 1945; s. Nora A. (Barclay); m. Janet B. Stuart, Apr. 4, 1970; children: Stuart, Kathryn, Andrew. Trainee acct. Coopers & Lybrand, Dublin, Ireland, 1961-68; audit mgr. Coopers & Lybrand, Dublin, 1968-69; fin. acct. Hely Group, Dublin, 1969-70; fin. acct. Jefferson Smurfit Group p.l.c., Dublin, 1970-72, fin. dir. Smurfit Corrugated div., 1972-75, asst. group fin. controller, 1975-78, group fin. controller, 1978-83, chief. fin. officer, 1983—. Fellow Inst. Chartered Accts. Office: Jefferson Smurfit Group, Beech Hill Clonskeah, Dublin 4, Ireland

HOLMES, WALTER S., JR., retired accountant; b. South River, N.J., May 23, 1919; s. Walter Stephen and Frances (Heckman) H.; m. E. Jean Pringle, Aug. 20, 1941; children—W. Stephen, Richard Alan. BS, Lehigh U., 1941, LLB, 1977; MBA, NYU, 1947. CPA, N.J. Staff acct. Haskins & Sells CPA's, Phila., 1941-42, Franke, Hannon & Withey, CPA's, N.Y.C., 1946-47; contr. RCA Corp., N.Y.C., 1947-59; contr., v.p., exec. v.p., pres., chmn., chief exec. officer CIT Fin. Corp., Livingston, N.J., 1959-84, ret., 1984; chmn. UNC Inc., Annapolis, Md., 1984-89; ret. UNC Inc., Annapolis, 1989. Mem. Presdl. Commn. on Structure of Fin. Instn., Washington, 1975; trustee Lehigh U., 1974—. Lt. USN, 1942-45. Mem. Inst. CPA's, Little Club. Home: 1225 S Ocean Blvd Delray Beach FL 33483

HOLMES À COURT, (MICHAEL) ROBERT (HAMILTON), oil company executive; b. July 27, 1937; s. Peter Worsley and Ethnée Celia Holmes à Court; m. Janet Lee Ranford, 1966; 4 children. Grad., U. West Australia. Barrister, solicitor Supreme Ct. Western Australia, 1965-82; chmn. Associated Communications Corp., Australia, 1982—, Weeks Petroleum Co., Australia, 1984—, Bell Group Ltd., Australia, 1970-88, The Bell Group Internat. Ltd., 1982—, Bell Resources Ltd., Australia, from 1983; bd. dirs. Standard Chartered Bank, joint dep. chmn., 1987—. Office: Bell Group Internat Ltd, 22 Esplanade Peppermint Gro, WA 6011 Perth Australia *

HOLMGREN, THEODORE JOSEPH, food company executive; b. N.Y.C., May 2, 1927; s. Oscar F. and Madeline (Thompson) H.; m. Miriam Brady, June 3, 1950; children: Miriam Jane (Mrs. James C. McCrea III), Barbara Lynn (Mrs. Benjamin Fowler), Theodore Douglas. A.B., Brown U., 1949; M.B.A., Harvard U., 1955. Asst. to Donald Deskey, Indsl. Designer, 1955-60; sr. product mgr. Gen. Foods Corp., White Plains, N.Y., 1960-64, dir. of design, 1964-68; sr. v.p. Curtis Burns Foods, Inc., Rochester, N.Y., 1968—; mng. trustee Curtis Burns/ProFac Found., Rochester, 1968—; co. rep. to Grocery Mfrs. Am., Washington. Pres. Community Council Chs. Irvington, Ardsley, Dobbs Ferry, Hastings, and Hartsdale, N.Y., 1961-63; trustee Orphan Asylum Soc. City N.Y., 1962-68, Curtice-Burns Charitable Found., 1970—; mem. corp. bd. United Way of Greater Rochester; life assoc. Pres.'s Soc. U. Rochester. Served to lt. (j.g.) USNR, 1951-53. Mem. Nat. Food Processors Assn. (alt. dir.), Rochester Acad. Sci., Alpha Delta Pi. Clubs: Harvard Bus. Sch. (Rochester); U. Rochester Faculty. Home: 16 Esternay Ln Pittsford NY 14534 Office: Curtice-Burns Foods Inc 1 Lincoln First Sq PO Box 681 Rochester NY 14603

HOLOWESKO, MARK GORDON, investment counsellor; b. Washington, Mar. 12, 1960; s. William Paul and Lynn (Pyfrom) H.; m. Nancy Ann Schoeb, May 20, 1983; children: Lauren Elizabeth, James Peter. BA in Econs., Coll. Holy Cross, 1982; MBA in Fin., Babson Coll., 1984. Cert. investment counsellor; chartered fin. analyst. Portfolio mgr. NatWest Trust Internat. Ltd., Nassau, Bahamas, 1984-85; dir. Templeton, Galbraith & Hansberger Ltd., Nassau, 1985—. Active Bahamas Nat. Trust, Nassau, 1978—. Mem. Internat. Soc. Fin. Analysts (founding mem.), Fin. Analyst Fedn. S. Fla. Roman Catholic. Clubs: Lyford Cay, Royal Nassau Sailing. Home: PO Box N-4406, Nassau The Bahamas Office: Templeton Galbraith & Hansberger Ltd, PO Box N-7776, Lyford Cay, Nassau The Bahamas

HOLSCLAW, ROBERT GRAYDON, oil and gas company executive; b. Auburn, Calif., July 26, 1934; s. Arthur Graydon and Frona Emaline (Meadows) H.; m. Kay Anne Ottmann, Aug. 3, 1952 (div. 1975); children; Barbara Anne, Robert Arthur, Elizabeth Gay; m. Steppie Rice Filbert, Sept. 18, 1975. AA, Sierra Coll., 1957; BA, Sacramento State U., 1959. Mgmt. analyst USAF, Sacramento, Calif., 1959-63; indsl. engr. Aerojet Gen., Sacramento, 1963-66; with Coastal Corp., Corpus Christi, Tex., Houston and London, 1966—, successively systems analyst, supr., asst. v.p. mktg., dir. internal auditing, asst. corp. controller, exec. asst. eastern hemisphere supply div., exec asst to pres., v.p. info. systems, now corp. v.p. systems and fin. services; bd. dirs. Colbourne Ins., Ltd., London. Office: The Coastal Corp 9 Greenway Pla Houston TX 77046

HOLSTEIN, JENS CHRISTIAN, pharmaceutical company executive; b. Hamburg, Federal Republic of Germany, June 16, 1930; s. Christian A. and Helene E. (Esser) H.; m. Margarete O. born Weth, Aug. 28, 1956; children: Cecil, Claudine, Peter, Gabriele. BA in Econs., Heidelberg U., 1954. Bd. dirs. Holstein Co. Group, Hamburg, Federal Republic of Germany, 1955; chief exec. officer C. Holstein Co., Osaka, Japan, 1956, chief operating officer, chief exec. officer, 1957—; v.p., bd. dirs. German C. of C. in Japan, 1970-83. Contbr. articles to profl. jours. Mem. Japan Pharm. Assn., Japan C. of C. Clubs: Rotay (Osaka) (bd. dirs. 1980-81); Kobe (Japan) (pres. 1976-80). Home: 24-31 Rokurokuso-cho, Ashiya City 659, Japan Office: C Holstein Co, Doshomachi, 541 Osaka Japan

HOLSTROM, CARLETON ARTHUR, financial executive; b. Appleton, Wis., Aug. 18, 1935; s. Carl W. and Nettie O. (Casterton) H.; m. Evan Grant Cameron, June 29, 1957 (div. 1978); children: Christina, Marcia, Cynthia Cawthorne; m. Mary Beth Kineke, Nov. 19, 1988. B.S., U. Wis., 1957; M.A., Rutgers U., 1962. Asst. v.p. Irving Trust Co., N.Y.C., 1962-66, Bank of Commonwealth, Detroit, 1966-69, Bear, Stearns & Co., N.Y.C., 1969-73; ptnr. Bear, Stearns & Co, N.Y.C., 1973-87; sr. v.p. fin. The Bear Stearns Cos. Inc., 1985-87, spl. assoc. dir., 1987—; Dir. Custodial Trust Co., Trenton, N.J., View Master Ideal Group Inc. Bd. overseers Rutgers U. Found., New Brunswick, 1975—; bd. trustees New Brunswick Cultural Ctr.; overseer Jane Voorhees Zimmerlee Mus.; trustee Rutgers U., vice chmn., 1985-88, chmn., 1988-89, gov., 1989—; bd. dirs. U. Wis. Found., 1989—. Served to lt. USNR, 1957-61. Club: Ht. Casino (Bklyn.). Home: Iron Bridge Rd Pipersville PA 18947 Office: Bear Stearns & Co 245 Park Ave New York NY 10167

HOLSWORTH, WILLIAM C., food company executive; b. N.Y.C., June 18, 1944; s. William Charles and Katherine Rose Holsworth; m. Helen Mary Moore; children: Casey, Kristy. Grad., Montclair State Coll., 1966. Regional fin. analyst Grand Union, Hialeah, Fla., 1976-78, dist. sales mgr., 1978-80, supt. stores ops., 1980-82, area v.p., 1982-83, regional v.p., 1983-84; v.p. ops. and planning Grand Union, Elmwood Park, N.J., 1984-85; pres. Lowe's Food Stores, Inc., Wilkesboro, N.C., 1985—. Office: Lowe's Food Stores Inc PO Box 700 Wilkesboro NC 28697

HOLT, GORDON ARTHUR, broadcast executive, media broker; b. Austin, Tex., Oct. 27, 1951; s. Arthur Henry and Phyllis Imogen (Jones) H. BFA, North Tex. U., 1971. With pub. relations dept. Universal Studios, Los Angeles, 1971-72; print salesman Sta. WTMI-FM, Miami, 1972-73; dir. gen. Holt Corp. Internat., Bogota, Colombia, 1977-78; v.p. Holt Corp., Bethlehem, Pa., 1974-86; exec. v.p., chief operating officer, Holt Media Group, Holt Tech. Service, Stas. WZZO-FM, Bethlehem, Pa., WUSQ-AM/FM, Winchester, Va., 1986—; exec. v.p. Holt Communications Corp., Del. including Stas. WJMI, WOKJ, Jackson, Miss., WGCM-AM/FM, Biloxi, Miss., WTKX, WBOP, Pensacola, Fla., 1986—; pres. Holt Communications Corp., Pa., 1986—; dir. Pa. Assn. Broadcaster, 1985-86; v.p. KMXQ, Socorro, N.Mex.; v.p. WBNE-FM, Benton, Pa. Contbr. articles to profl. jours. Mem. Inter-Am. Assn. Broadcasters, Internat. Inst. Communications, Nat. Assn. Broadcasters, Fla. Broadcasters Assn., Pensacola Broadcasters Assn.. Republican. Office: Holt Corp Pa Inc Suite 205 Westgate Bethlehem PA 18017 also: 111 N Baylen St Pensacola FL 32501

HOLT, LEON CONRAD, JR., business executive, lawyer; b. Reading, Pa., June 19, 1925; s. Leon Conrad and Elizabeth (Bright) H.; m. June M. Weidner, June 30, 1947; children: Deborah Holt Weil, Richard W. B.S. cum laude in Metall. Engring, Lehigh U., 1948; LL.B., U. Pa., 1951. Bar: N.Y. 1952. With firm Mudge, Stern Williams & Tucker (attys.), N.Y.C., 1951-53; atty. Am. Oil Co. (and predecessor co.), N.Y.C., 1953-57; gen. atty. Air Products & Chems., Inc., Allentown, Pa., 1957-61; v.p. Air Products & Chems., Inc., 1961-76, v.p. adminstrn., 1976-78, gen. counsel, 1961-78, vice chmn. bd., chief adminstrv. officer, 1978—, also dir., mem. exec., finance, pub. policy coms.; dir. VF Corp. Vice chmn. Lehigh Centennial Fund, 1964-65; chmn. Allentown Bd. Ethics, 1970-74; bd. dirs. Lehigh County United Fund, 1971-83, mem. exec. com., 1971-74, campaign chmn., 1972; Bd. dirs. Allentown YMCA, 1965-69, trustee, 1972-79; trustee, pres. Allentown Art Mus.; mem. Allentown Sch. Dist. Authority, 1976-86; mem. exec. com. Machinery and Allied Products Inst.; mem. adv. bd. U. Pa. Inst. Law and Econs.; bd. overseers U. Pa. Law Sch.; trustee Dorothy Rider-Pool Health Care Trust, Rider-Pool Found., Com. Econ. Devel. Lt. (j.g.) USNR, 1943-46. Mem. Allentown C. of C. (gov. 1965-68), ABA, Assn. Bar N.Y.C., Pa. Soc., Tunkhannock Creek Assn., Alpha Tau Omega. Republican. Episcopalian. Clubs: Lehigh Country (Allentown) (bd. govs. 1970-77); USEPPA Island. Home: 3003 Parkway Blvd Allentown PA 18104 Office: Air Products & Chems Inc PO Box 538 Allentown PA 18105 also: Pocono Lake Preserve PA 18348

HOLT, THOMAS ROBERT, infosystems specialist; b. Spartanburg, S.C., Jan. 20, 1957; s. Robert Earl and Margaret Louise (Dedmond) H.; m. Janet Lynne Strawhorn, Sept. 20, 1980; children: Jessica Michelle, Nicholas Paul. BS in Computer Sci., U. S.C., 1979. Systems analyst Bigelow Sanford, Inc., Greenville, S.C., 1982-83, mgr. EDP support, 1983-84, dir. EDP services, 1984-87; mgr. info. services carpet and rug div. Fieldcrest Cannon, Inc., Greenville, 1987—. Treas. Chestnut Lake Homeowners Assn., Spartanburg, 1987—. Mem. Data Processing Mgmt. Assn. Methodist. Home: 176 Ridgewood Dr Spartanburg SC 29303 Office: Fieldcrest Cannon Inc PO Box 3089 Interstate 85 and White Horse Rd Greenville SC 29602

HOLT, TIMOTHY ARTHUR, insurance executive; b. Hartford, Conn., Mar. 16, 1953; s. Ralph and Elizabeth (Leonard) H.; m. Beverly Charney, Aug. 17, 1975; children: Melissa, Laura, Alexander. BA, U. Conn., 1975; MBA, Dartmouth Coll., 1977. Chartered fin. analyst. Securities analyst AEtna, Hartford, 1977, investment officer, 1980, asst. v.p., 1983, v.p., 1987—. Named Edward Tuck scholar Tuck Sch. Dartmouth Coll. Mem. Phi Betta Kappa. Office: Aetna Life & Casualty Co CityPlace Hartford CT 06103

HOLTER, MARVIN ROSENKRANTZ, research and development executive, physicist; b. Fairport, N.Y., July 4, 1922; s. Frank Marcus and Florence (Zonnevylle) H.; m. Frances Elizabeth Jenkins, July 15, 1955; children: Christine E., Ann F. BS in Physics, U. Mich., 1949, MS in Math., 1951, MS in Physics, 1958. Prof. remote sensing U. Mich., Ann Arbor, 1968-70, head infrared lab., 1964-70; dep. dir. Willow Run lab. U. Mich., Ann Arbor, 1972-73; div. chief earth obs. div. NASA Johnson Space Ctr., Houston, 1970-72; exec. v.p. Environ. Research Inst. Mich., Ann Arbor, 1973-86, sr. v.p., 1986—; invited lectr. univs. Stockholm, Upsalla, Lund, Sweden, 1969; mem. USAF Sci. Adv. Bd., 1963-79; mem. com. on remote sensing programs for earth resources surveys Nat. Acad. Sci.-NRC, 1973-77; mem. U.S.A.-USSR Working Group on Remote Sensing, 1971-77; advisor Def. Intelligence Agy., 1978-81; mem. U.S. Army Sci. Bd., 1986—. Co-author: Fundamentals of Infrared Technology, 1962, Remote Sensing, 1970; editorial bd.: Remote Sensing of Environ., 1968-75. Recipient Exceptional Civilian Service award USAF, 1979; recipient Sci. Achievement award NASA, 1973; co-recipient William T. Pecore award Dept. Interior, 1976, Interpretation award Am. Soc. Photogrammetry, 1969. Mem. Explorers Club, Sigma Xi. Club: Cosmos (Washington). Lodge: Masons. Home: 493 Orchard Hills Dr Ann Arbor MI 48103 Office: Environ Rsch Inst Mich PO Box 8618 Ann Arbor MI 48107

HOLTZ, DANIEL MARTIN, banker; b. Havana, Cuba, July 2, 1959; came to U.S., 1961; s. Abel and Fana (Sklar) H. Student, U. Fla., 1977-78, BS, 1978-81; student, Fla. Internat. Sch. Banking, 1983-84. V.p. Hemisphere Nat. Bank, Washington, 1981-82; sr. v.p. Capital Bancorp, Washington, 1982—; pres., chief exec. officer Capital Trading Group, Inc., Miami, Fla., 1984—; sr. v.p. Capital Bank of Calif., Los Angeles, 1985, exec. v.p., 1985-87, pres., chief exec. officer, 1987—; sr. v.p. Capital Bank, Miami, 1985—; bd. dirs. Capital Bank of Calif., Los Angeles. Regional bd. dirs. Anti-Defamation League, Miami, 1986—; vice chmn. City of Miami (Fla.) Beach Zoning Bd., 1984—. Recipient Young Leadership award Anti-Defamation League, N.Y., 1986, Profl. Achievement award Outstanding Young Men of Am., 1985, Outstanding Service award Young Pres.' Assn. Mt. Sinai Hosp., Miami Beach, 1985, Outstanding Pub. Service award Police Athletic League; named New Generation Leader United Way of Dade County, Miami, 1986. Democrat. Jewish. Club: The Palm Bay (pres., chief exec. officer). Home: 2128 N Bay Rd Miami Beach FL 33140 Office: Capital Bancorp 1221 Brickell Ave Miami FL 33131

HOLTZ, GILBERT JOSEPH, steel company executive; b. N.Y.C., Jan. 23, 1924; s. Al S. and Carrie (Schindler) H.; student N.Y.U., 1940-42; m. Carla Kahn, July 18, 1948; children—Steven J., Robert A. Vice pres. Hanger Service Co., Yonkers, N.Y., 1946-48; owner Economy Sales Co., Yonkers, 1948-50; v.p. Belvedere Space Saving Products, Inc., 1951-72; pres. Walnut Metal Industries, Inc., Yonkers, 1955-72, Belvedere Home Products Inc. (formerly 411 Walnut St. Corp.), 1962—, Holtz Realty Corp., 1962—, Walnut Assn. Inc., 1961—, Belvedere Internat. Ltd., 1970—. Ward leader 2d Ward Republican County Com., Yonkers. Served with AUS, 1943-46. Mem. Yonkers C. of C. Club: Kiwanis. Patentee in field. Home: 182 Tibbetts Rd Yonkers NY 10705 Office: 937 Saw Mill River Rd Yonkers NY 10710

HOLTZ, GLENN EDWARD, band instrument manufacturing executive; b. Detroit, Jan. 15, 1938; s. Edward Christian and Evelyn Adele (Priehs) Foutz H.; m. Mary Eleanor Russell, Nov. 25, 1981; children by previous marriage—Robert, Kimberly, Rene, Letitia, Kimberly, Pamela. B. Mus. Edn., U. Mich., 1960, M. Mus. Edn., 1964; cons. motivation student Personnel Dynamics, Mpls., 1980. Mus. tchr. Middleville High Sch. (Mich.), 1960-62; dist. mgr. Selmer Co., Elkhart, Ind., 1965-74, sales mgr., 1974-76; pres. Knapp Mus. Co., Grand Rapids, Mich., 1976-80; v.p. mktg. sales Gemeinhardt/CBS, Elkhart, 1981-83, gen. mgr., 1983—, also pres. CBS Columbia Music Div., 1984, v.p. CBS, 1985; pres. Steinway Music Properties (formerly CBS Columbia Music Div.), 1985; pres. Gemeinhardt Co., Inc. seminar leader Sch. Band Movement Phase II Gemeinhardt, Elkhart, 1982-83. Dist. gov. Lion's Internat., Jackson, Lansing, Battle Creek, Mich., 1970-71; pres. Middleville Bd. Edn., 1964-66. Recipient Disting. award Lion's Internat., Mich., 1971. Mem. Nat. Assn. Band Instrument Mfrs. (pres. 1986-88), Am. Music Conf. (bd. dirs. 1987—). Republican. Office: Gemeinhardt PO Box 788 Elkhart IN 46515

HOLTZMAN, GARY YALE, retail executive; b. N.Y.C., Aug. 7, 1936; s. Abram and Pearl (Kashetsky) H.; m. Alice A. Lang, Sept. 5, 1958; children: Bruce, Sheri, Michele. B.B.A., CCNY, 1958. Exec. v.p. control and ops. Jordan Marsh Co., Miami, Fla., 1967-87; sr. v.p. ops. and stores L. Luria & Sons Inc., Miami, 1987—; bd. advisers Universal Nat. Bank. Bd. dirs. Dade County Safety Council, Miami, 1978—, Jewish Community Ctr. Greater Miami, 1983—, Fla. Bus. Roundtable, 1975-80, Anti-Defamation League of B'nai B'rith, 1983—; bd. advisers Opportunities Industrialization Ctr., 1982-84; pres. Michael Ann Russell Jewish Community Ctr., 1984—; life bd. dirs. Temple Adath Yeshurun, 1970—; active Greater Miami Jewish Fedn.; com. chmn. United Way of Dade County. Served to lt. U.S. Army, 1958-59, capt. Res., 1959-65. Recipient Americanism award Anti-Defamation League, 1983; recipient Adath Yeshurun Man of Yr. award, 1978. Mem. Greater Miami C. of C., Fla. Retail Fedn. Democrat. Home: 851 NE 182d St North Miami FL 33162 Office: L Luria & Sons Inc Miami Lakes Dr Miami Lakes FL 33014

HOLWAY, JAMES COLIN, steel company executive; b. Youngstown, Ohio, Nov. 14, 1927; s. Robert G. and Marie W. (Kane) H.; BS, Ohio State U., 1950; MBA, Pa. State U., 1952; m. Patricia Ann Touscany, Aug. 31, 1957; children: Moira Ann, Colin A., Brent Patrick, Jamesin McAndrew, Jonathan Lynch. Sales trainee U.S. Steel Corp., 1951-55; salesman Republic Steel Corp., Cleve. and Detroit, 1955-58; dist. sales mgr. Tenn. Products & Chem. Corp., Detroit, 1958-60; dist. sales mgr. Nat. Steel Corp., Charlotte, N.C., 1960-72; founder, pres. Southeastern Steel Rolling Mills, Charlotte, 1972-73; co-founder, pres. Decker-Holway Steel Co., 1973-77; chmn. bd. Mid-Atlantic Industries, Inc., 1979—; adj. prof. corp. fin., bus. policy, econs. Queens Coll., Charlotte, 1987-88; cons. venture capital to industry. Served with USNR, 1945-46. Mem. AIME (asso.). Clubs: Country of Detroit (Grosse Pointe, Mich.); Charlotte City, Charlotte Country. Home: 2312 Pembroke Ave Charlotte NC 28207 Office: Mid-Atlantic Industries Inc PO Box 15057 Charlotte NC 28211

HOLZER, ROBERT LEE, Mortgage banker; b. Chgo., Jan. 16, 1938; s. Philip and Vera (Konya) H.; m. Ruth E. Rechtoris, June 24, 1961; children: Linda, John, Paul, Ann. BS in Mgmt., U. Ill., 1960. With Northwest Fed. Savs., Chgo., 1958-82, sr. v.p., to 1982; pres. Serve Corps Mortgage Corp., Downers Grove, Ill., 1983—; advisor Savs. and Loan Commn., Ill., 1987. Dir. YMCA, Park Ridge, Ill., 1976, North River Commn., Chgo., 1965-70. Served to 1st lt. USAR, 1960-68. Mem. Soc. of Loan Underwriters (pres. 1984), Ill. Mortgage Bankers Assn., Kiwanis (pres. 1976). Republican. Lutheran. Office: Serve Corps Mortgage Corp 1430 Branding Ln Ste 129 Downers Grove IL 60515

HOLZINGER, JAMES JAY, bank executive; b. Newark, July 11, 1935; s. Joseph L. and Rose A. (Morsch) H.; m. Phyllis Margaret Marx, Sept. 22, 1962; children: Linda Jane, James Jr., Kathryn, Arthur Christopher. BS, Villanova U., 1957; postgrad., NYU, 1960-61. Asst. v.p. Bank of N.Y., N.Y.C., 1960-66; corp. fin. asst. Burnham and Co., N.Y.C., 1966-70; exec. v.p. United Jersey Banks, Princeton, N.J., 1970—. Trustee Daytop Village, N.Y.C., 1987—; chmn. membership com. Bergen Counc. Boy Scouts Am., 1987. Sgt. U.S. Army, 1958-60. Mem. Essex Fells Country Club (trustee 1987—, N.J.). Republican. Roman Catholic. Office: United Jersey Bank 301 Carnegie Ctr PO Box 2066 Princeton NJ 08543-2066

HOLZMAN, IRWIN B., finance company executive; b. Portland, Oreg., Jan. 4, 1930; s. Jerome L. and Lena (Kleinberg) H.; m. Renee Rosenberg,

July 3, 1958; children: Jay, Larry, Lee. Postgrad., U. Wash., 1954; BS, U. Oreg., 1952, postgrad. Adjuster Comml. Credit Corp., Portland, 1955-57; asst. mgr. Doug Gerow Fin., Portland, 1958; mgr., pres. Reliable Credit Assn. Inc., Portland, 1958—. Served capt. inf. U.S. Army, 1952-59, res. 1954-59, Korea. Mem. Portland Lenders Exchange (pres. 1973-75), Oreg. Fin. Services Assn. (pres. 1983-85), Am. Fin. Services Assn. (chmn. independents sect. 1985-86). Office: Reliable Credit Assoc Inc PO Box 42205 Portland OR 97242

HOMBURGER, FRANK PETER, controller; b. Lancaster, Pa., Aug. 22, 1952; s. Fred R. and Lore (Marck) H. BS in Econs., U. Pa., 1974; MBA, Northwestern U., 1978. CPA, Va. Assoc. fin. exec. devel. program GTE, Stamford, Conn., 1974-77; mgr. budgets and forecasting Telenet Communications Corp., Vienna, Va., 1979-80; sr. acct. MCI Telecommunications Corp., Washington, 1978-79; supr. acctg. Potomac Electric Power Co., Washington, 1980-88; controller Bengtson, DeBell, Elkin & Titus Ltd., Centerville, Va., 1988—; chmn. supervisory com. Potomac Electric Power Co. Fed. Credit Union, 1985-87. Fellow D.C. Inst. CPA's; mem. AICPA, Nat. Assn. Accts. (bd. dirs. Washington chpt. 1987-88). Home: 4437 Chase Park Ct Annandale VA 22003 Office: Bengtson DeBell Elkin & Titus Ltd 5900 Centerville Rd Centerville VA 22020

HOMEYER, HOWARD C., energy company executive; b. Caldwell, Tex., Jan. 16, 1933; s. George A. and Bettie (Mueller) H.; m. Dorothy Bahr, Mar. 4, 1961; children—Michael, Paul, Jonathan. B.S. in Indsl. Engring., Tex. A&M U., 1955; M.B.A., Northwestern U., 1963. Registered profl. engr., Tex. Indsl. engr. Hughes Tool Co., Houston, 1955-59; dir. rates So. Union Corp., Dallas, 1963-68; project analyst Tex. Eastern Corp., Houston, 1959-61, mgr. corp. planning, 1968-71, mgr. coal activities, 1971-76, dir. corp. planning, 1977-78, dir. new ventures, 1979-80, dir. synfuels, 1980-82, v.p. fin. planning, 1982-83; exec. v.p. Tex. Eastern Gas Pipeline Co., Houston, 1983-85; sr. v.p. Tex. Eastern Corp., Houston, 1985-88; with Algonquin Gas Transmission Co., Houston, 1988—. Served to capt. U.S. Army, 1957. Lutheran. Home: 201 Vanderpool #130 Houston TX 77024 Office: Algonquin Gas Transmission Co 201 Vanderpool #130 Houston TX 77024

HOMMEN, JAN H. M., aluminum company executive; b. 's Hertogenbosch, The Netherlands, Apr. 29, 1943; came to U.S., 1978; s. Joseph W. H. and Johanna J.C. (Van Herpen) H.; m. Tucke Van Enschot, June 25, 1969; children: Liselotte, Jan Pieter, Maarten, Merel. Graduate, U. Tilburg, The Netherlands, 1970. Controller Alcoa Nederland B.V., Drunen, The Netherlands, 1970-74, fin. dir., 1974-78; mgr. corp. fin. Aluminum Co. Am., Pitts., 1978-79, asst. treas., 1979-86, v.p., treas., 1986—; bd. dirs. Grupo Aluminio, Mexico City, ACO S.A., Venezuela. Mem. Fin. Execs. Inst., Nat. Investor Relations Inst., Machinery and Allied Products Inst.(fin. council), Nat. Assn. Corporate Treas. Office: Aluminum Co Am 1501 Alcoa Bldg Pittsburgh PA 15219

HOMPERTZ, MELBA ANN, financial planner; b. Chgo., July 11, 1936; d. John Joseph and Elizabeth (Conway) H. BSC, Loyola U., Chgo., 1959. Cert. in banking and fin. planning. Asst. ops. officer Cen. Nat. Bank, Chgo., 1971-79; auditor, compliance mgr. 1st Arlington (Ill.) Nat. Bank, 1980-82; auditor, compliance mgr. LaGrange (Ill.) Bank and Trust, 1982-84, asst. v.p., 1984-86; pres., chief exec. officer 1st Ill. Adv., LaGrange, 1986-87; fin. planner Key Concepts, Bensenville, Ill., 1987—. Tax asst. for elderly Am. Assn. Ret. Persons, Bensenville, 1988—, IRS, Bensenville,,1988—; entrepreneurial workshop leader Breakfast Forum, Arlington Heights, 1983-85. Mem. Greater Ohara Assn., Inst. Cert. Fin. Planning, Chgo. So. Suburban Internat. Edn. Assn. (v.p. 1986-87), Internat. Assn. Fin. Planners, Assn. Fin. Planning (pres. 1987-88), Bus. and Profl. Women (v.p. Downers Grove chpt. 1979-81, pres. 1981-82). Office: Key Concepts 200 W Devon Ste 6 Bensenville IL 60106

HONEYWELL, LARRY G., publishing company executive, travel company executive; b. Clinton, Iowa, Jan. 4, 1935; s. Robert L. and Anna F. (Hansen) H.; m. Carol J. Skidmore, Aug. 22, 1957; children: Kenneth, Karen, Diane, Thomas, Steven. BS in Commerce, State U. Iowa, 1957. Credit reporter Dun & Bradstreet, N.Y.C., 1959-62, computer programmer trainee, 1962-68, mgr. systems, 1968-69; dir. data processing Moody's Investor Svc., N.Y.C., 1969-71, v.p., 1971-72; sr. v.p. Official Airline Guides Inc., Oak Brook, Ill., 1972-86; v.p. fin. A.C. Nielsen, Northbrook, Ill., 1986-88; exec. v.p., chief operating officer Nielsen Clearing House, Clinton, 1988-89; pres. Official Airline Guides, Thomas Cook Travel, Oak Brook, 1989—. Pres. Coll. DuPage Found., Glen Ellyn, Ill., 1983-85. Lt. U.S. Army, 1957-59. Mem. Travel Industry Assn. (bd. dirs.). Office: Official Airline Guides 2000 Clearwater Dr Oak Brook IL 60521

HONG, JAMES MING, consumer product company executive; b. Macao, Portuguese Colony, Oct. 1, 1940; came to U.S., 1955; s. William L.T. and Siu Jung Hong; children: Diana, Paula, Susanna. BBA in Acctg., Pace U., 1965, PhD (fellow) in Econs., Mktg., Internat. Bus., 1973; MBA in Fin. NYU, 1966; PhD in Econs., Mktg., Internat. Bus., 1973. Sr. corp. planning and devel. mgr. Mobil Corp., N.Y.C., 1965-70; mgr. fin. systems McGraw Hill Inc., N.Y.C., 1970-72, dir. fin. and systems, 1972-74; v.p., corp. controller Beverage Mgmt. Inc., Columbus, Ohio, 1974-75, v.p. fin., treas., chief fin. officer, 1976-79; sr. exec. v.p., chief fin. officer Mid Atlantic Coca Cola Bottling Co., Inc., Harrisburg, Pa., 1980-87, pres. chmn., chief exec. officer Sav-A-Stop Inc., Orange Park, Fla., 1987—; bd. advs. Deutschman & Co., Los Angeles; dir. First Jardin Group, Hong Kong; dep. dir. Belmont Group (USA) Ltd.; chmn. exec. dir. com. Lim Tech. Labs., Richmond; dirs. Aneco Mut. Ins. Co., bd. dirs. Mut. Indemnity Ins. Ltd., Bermuda. Bd. dirs. Va. Council Econ. Edn., Va. Commonwealth U., United Coll. Fund, Soc. Prevention Blindness, Richmond Symphony. Recipient Woodrow Wilson fellow, Regent scholar NYU, Trustee fellow. Mem. Pace Alumni Assn. (trustee), Nat. Accts. Assn. (dir. manuscripts Central Ohio chpt.), Nat. Assn. Bus. Economists, Inst. Mgmt. Accts., Inst. Corp. Controllers, Nat. Public Relations Inst., Fin. Execs. Inst., Columbus Soc. Fin. Analysts, Nat. Mgmt. Assn. (fiscal policy and monetary com.), Worthington Hills Country, Univ. (Washington), NYU. Home: PO Box 2790 Orange Park FL 32067 Office: Hong & Co PO Box 11431 Richmond VA 23230

HONIG, LAWRENCE EDWARD, retail executive; b. Spartanburg, S.C., Jan. 19, 1948; s. O. Charles and Jean Gates (Davis) H.; m. Ellen Stokes, Aug. 7, 1971. B.A., Washington and Lee U., 1970, B.S., 1970; M.A., U. Tex.-Austin, 1972; M.B.A., Harvard U., 1975. Assoc. Loeb, Rhoades & Co., N.Y.C., 1972-73; prin. McKinsey & Co., Chgo., 1975-82; exec. v.p. May Dept. Stores Co., St. Louis, 1982-85, vice chmn., 1986—, also bd. dirs. Author: John Henry Brown, 1972. Served to capt. U.S. Army, 1971-72. Club: St. Louis Country; Capital City (Atlanta). Office: The May Dept Stores Co 611 Olive St Saint Louis MO 63101

HONKE, SUE ANN, financial executive; b. Flint, Mich., Feb. 4, 1948; d. Ivan L. and Frances E. Tuttle; grad. Victor Bus. Sch., 1969; student U. Mich., 1970-73; m. Alfred A. Honke, June 27, 1981; children—Victoria Sue, Byron D. Med. sec. Univ. Hosp., 1966-69; adminstrv. asst. Inland Scholtz Modular Housing, 1971-72; adminstr., acct. Washtenaw County Rd. Commn., 1972-76; office mgr. Moehrle, Inc., Ann Arbor, Mich., 1976-79; fin. mgr. Lovejoy Tiffany & Assocs., Inc., Ann Arbor, 1979-80, dir. fin. and adminstrn., 1980-83, v.p., gen. mgr., 1983—. Mem. Nat. Assn. Female Execs., Nat. Assn. Accts., Am. Mgmt. Assn., Credit Women Internat. Office: Lovejoy Tiffany & Assocs Box 8259 Ann Arbor MI 48107

HONLEY, RUSSELL LORAN, accountant; b. Harrisonville, Mo., June 15, 1948; s. Loran Francis and Mary Louise (Russell) H.; m. Donna Kay Courtney, May 24, 1972 (div. June 1982); m. Robin Denise Gibbons, Aug. 11, 1983; children: William Russell, Mary Elizabeth. BBA, Cen Mo. U., 1973; MBA, U. Mo., 1979. CPA, Mo. Controller EMCO, Inc., Lenexa, Kans., 1973-74, Greiner-Fifield, Inc., Kansas City, 1974-75; staff acct. Robert K. Williams CPA, Kansas City, 1976-79; pvt. practice Grandview, Mo., 1979-85; chief fin. officer Automotive Distbrs., Inc., Kansas City, 1985—. Mem. Am. Inst. CPAs, Mo. Soc. CPAs, Phi Kappa Phi, Phi Eta Sigma. Methodist. Home: 1208 Elm St W Greenwood MO 64034 Office: Automotive Distbrs Inc 3155 Terr PO Box 410769 Kansas City MO 64141

HOOD, EDWARD EXUM, JR., electrical manufacturing company executive; b. Boonville, N.C., Sept. 15, 1930; s. Edward Exum and Nellie (Triplett) H.; m. Kay Transou, Dec. 30, 1950; children: Lisa Kay, Molly Ann. M.S. in Nuclear Engring., N.C. State U., 1953. Registered profl. engr., Ariz. Powerplant design engr. Gen. Electric Co., 1957-62, mgr. supersonic transport engine project, 1962-67, v.p., gen. mgr. comml. engine div., from 1968, v.p., group exec. internat. group, 1972-73, v.p., group exec., power generation group, 1973-77, sr. v.p., sector exec. tech. systems and materials sector, from 1977, vice-chmn., 1979—, now also exec. officer, bd. dirs. Served with USAF, 1952-56. Fellow AIAA (assoc.); mem. Nat. Acad. Engring., Aerospace Industries Assn. (chmn. 1981). Home: Woods End Rd New Canaan CT 06840 Office: GE 3135 Easton Turnpike Fairfield CT 06431

HOOD, JEANINE K., accountant; b. Amarillo, Tex., Apr. 4, 1961; d. Carl Julius and Norva Jeanne (Yoder) Kuper; m. Thomas E. Hood, Aug. 24, 1985. BBA in Acctg., Tex. Tech U., 1983, MS in Taxation, 1984. CPA, Tex. Sr. acct. Arthur Young & Co., Amarillo, 1985-89; interim fin. dir. Campfire, Amarillo, 1989—. Loaned exec. United Way, Amarillo, 1987; bd. dirs. women's health adv. bd. High Plains Bapt. Hosp., Amarillo, 1987—; mem. Children's Learning Ctr. Aux., Amarillo Symphony Guild, Amarillo Area Estate Planning Coun., Polk St. United Meth. Ch. Mem. AICPA, Am. Bus. Women's Assn. (bulletin chmn.), Tex. Soc. CPA's (chpt. membership chmn.), Lawyer's Aux. Amarillo Club, Kappa Alpha Theta. Office: Arthur Young & Co 900 S Fillmore Amarillo TX 79105

HOOD, JOHN EDWARD, steel company executive; b. Gananoque, Ont., Can., Oct. 31, 1925; married; 3 children. B.A.Sc. in Mech. Engring., Queen's U., Kingston, 1946. With Swansea Works, Toronto, Ont., 1946; with steelmaking dept. Stelco Inc., Toronto, various posts, apptd. raw materials mgr., 1970, gen. supt. Lake Erie devel., 1973, v.p. mfg. primary ops., 1976, exec. v.p., 1985-88, vice chmn., 1988—. Office: Stelco Inc, 79 Wellington St W, IBM Tower, Toronto, ON Canada M5K 1J4 also: Toronto Dominion Ctr, PO Box 205, Toronto, ON Canada M5K 1J4

HOOD, MATHER DANIEL, manufacturing company executive; b. Newnan, Ga., Dec. 23, 1946; s. Robert Lee and Margaret (Johnson) H.; m. Susan Diane High, Dec. 21, 1968 (div. 1985); children: William Daniel, Dana Cary. BS, Auburn U., 1968, MBA, 1973. Pers. mgr., supt. Classe Ribbon Co., Anniston, Ala., 1973-77; mgr. employee rels. Heil Co., Athens, Tenn., 1977-82, Matushita Electronic Components Co., Knoxville, Tenn., 1982-83; pers. mgr. Athens Furniture Co., 1983-85; mgr. human resources Nat. Seating Co., Vonore, Tenn., 1985—; prof. Tenn. Wesleyan Coll., Athens, 1983, Hiwassee Coll., Madisonville, Tenn., 1987—, Cleveland (Tenn.) State Jr. Coll., 1988—. Bd. dirs. YMCA, Athens, 1980—. Capt. USAF, 1969-73. Mem. Inst. Bus. and Industry (bd. dirs. 1980—), Am. Soc. Pers. Adminstrn., Tenn. Valley Pers. Assn., Loudon County Pers. Assn., Internat. Mgmt. Club (v.p. 1972-73), Kiwanis, Phi Psi. Methodist. Home: 401 Gallaher View Rd #305 Knoxville TN 37919 Office: Nat Seating Co 200 National Dr Vonore TN 37884

HOOD, PAUL FORRESTER, investment consultant; b. Phila., Aug. 13, 1926; s. William Paul and Kathryn Holler (Henderson) H.; m. Anita May Montali, June 4, 1955; children: Bradford Forrester, Tracy Anne. AB in Econs., Brown U., 1949. Sr. cons. A.S. Hansen, Inc., N.Y.C., 1965-69; v.p. Lionel D. Edie & Co., Inc., N.Y.C., 1969-76; 1st v.p. Schroder Capital Mgmt., N.Y.C., 1976-80; v.p. H T Investors Inc., Providence, 1980-82; pres. P.F. Hood and Assocs. Inc., Providence, 1982—; state chmn. Assn. Pvt. Pension and Welfare Plans, Washington, 1981-82. Served with USN, 1943-46, PTO. Fellow Fin. Analysts Fedn.; mem. N.Y. Soc. Fin. Analysts. Republican. Congregationalist. Home: 9 Shore Dr Warren RI 02885 Office: PF Hood & Assocs Inc One Custom House St Providence RI 02903

HOOD, WILLIAM DOUGLAS, financial executive; b. Frankfort, Fed. Republic Germany, Mar. 19, 1959 (parents Am. citizens); s. William Robert and Mattielene (Abercrombie) H.; m. Leslie Marilea Spivey, June 15, 1979. BBA, North Ga. Coll., 1981. Bank officer Bank South, Forest Park, Ga., 1981-83; loan officer Atlantic Bank, Orlando, Fla., 1983-84; S.E. rep. ITT Small Bus. Fin. Corp., Atlanta, 1984-86; v.p. Bus. Devel. Corp. Ga., Atlanta, 1986-87; v.p. Chattahoochee Bus. Group, 1987—, Ga. Dome Com., 1988; speaker, cons. SBA, Orlando and Atlanta, 1984—; guest lectr. Emory U., Atlanta. Exec. dir. Jr. Achievement, 1982; bd. dirs. Am. Cancer Soc., 1983, United Way, 1983. Recipient Ga. Gov.'s citation for work with Jr. Achievement, 1983. Mem. Sigma Chi (founding pres. local chpt.). Avocations: refinishing antiques, remodeling houses, fishing. Home: 4662 Collins Ave Acworth GA 30101 Office: The Chattahoochee Bank 1640 Powers Ferry Rd Bldg 29 Marietta GA 30067

HOOGEVEEN, LINDA LORRAINE, bank executive; b. Jacksonville, Fla., Aug. 12, 1958; d. Henry William and Phyllis Evelyn (Roberts) H. AA cum laude, ST. Johns River Community Coll., 1978; BBA, U. N.Fla., 1979, MBA, 1982. CPA, Fla. Mgmt. trainee Southeast Banking Corp., Miami, Fla., 1980; br. mgr. Century Bank of Gainesville, Fla., 1981; auditor Touche Ross and Co., Orlando, Fla., 1983-84; v.p., regional comml. credit mgr. Fla. Nat. Bank, Orlando, 1984—. Mem. Orange County Young Reps.; vol., chmn. com. various state and local polit. campaigns, 1986—; trustee, treas. Orlando Community Concert Assn., 1985-86; founding pres. Bravo!; mem. Transp. Task Force-Goals 2000, 1987—; vol. Spl. Olympics and Summer Day Camp, 1975-76, Scout World Expo, 1983; vol. judge Orange County Regional Sci. Fair, 1985; fund-raiser pub. TV, 1983—, adv. bd., 1987—, Orange Park Women's Aux., 1978; mem. Community Adv. Bd., 1987—; active Future Leaders Council of Cen. Fla., 1987—. Recipient Blue Key Community Coll. Leadership award, 1978; named one of Outstanding Women of Am., 1984, one of People to Watch in 1988, Orlando Mag., to St. John's River Community Coll. Hall of Fame, 1978. Mem. AICPA, Fla. Inst. CPAs, U. North Fla. Alumni Assn. (bd. dirs. 1980-84), The Women's Network (corp. rep.), Phi Theta Kappa (chpt. pres. 1977-78). Clubs: Bally Health and Racquet, Tiger Bay (Orlando), Bay. Home: 400 E Colonial #606 Orlando FL 32803 Office: Fla Nat Bank 800 N Magnolia Ave Box 3593 Orlando FL 32803

HOOGSTEDEN, ALOYSIUS FRANCISCUS, manufacturing company executive; b. Rotterdam, The Netherlands, Dec. 5, 1936; s. Fredericus Josephus and Cornelia Maria Christina (Baerveldt) H.; m. Johanna Christina Henrica Floris (Baerveldt), Nov. 23, 1973; children: Aloysius Franciscus Jr., Maurice Danielle Frederique. BA, Rotterdam High Sch. Jr. clk. Shipping & Forwarding Co., Rotterdam, 1952-62; mgr. various shipping lines, trading houses, Rotterdam, 1962-74; dir. Freight Forwarding Group, Rotterdam, 1974-80; pres. Intern. Freight Specialists B.V., Gravenzande, Netherlands, 1980—, A.F. Hoogsteden Holding B.V., Gravenzande, 1980—, Globe Trading B.V., Gravenzande, 1982—; pres. Globe Oilfield Services, Gravenzande, 1985—, dir., 1985—; dir. Anembo Trading and Forwarding Inc., Latham, N.Y., 1980—, Hoco Mfg. Co., Ltd., Sunninghill, Eng., 1984—, Hoco Shipping Co. Ltd., Sunninghill, 1984—. Home: Frejo Parallelweg 27, 2691 JM 's-Gravenzande The Netherlands Office: AF Hoogsteden Holding BV, PO Box 58, 2690 AB's- Gravanzande The Netherlands

HOOK, HAROLD SWANSON, insurance company executive; b. Kansas City, Mo., Oct. 10, 1931; s. Ralph C. and Ruby (Swanson) H.; m. Joanne T. Hunt, Feb. 19, 1955; children: Karen Anne, Thomas W., Randall T. BS in Bus. Adminstrn., U. Mo., 1953, MA, 1954; grad., So. Meth. U. Inst. Ins. Mktng., 1957; postgrad., NYU, 1967-70; LLD (hon.), U. Mo., 1983, Westminster Coll., 1983. CLU. Faculty U. Mo. Sch. Bus., 1953-54; asst. to pres. Nat. Fidelity Life Ins. Co., Kansas City, Mo., 1957-60, dir., 1959-66, adminstrv. v.p., 1960-61, exec. v.p., investment com., 1961-62, pres., exec. com., 1962-66; sr. v.p. U.S. Life Ins. Co., N.Y.C., 1966-67, dir., 1967-70, exec. v.p., mem. exec. com., 1967-68, pres., 1968-70; pres., mem. bd., exec. com. Calif.-Western States Life Ins. Co., Sacramento, 1970-75, chmn., 1975-79, sr. chmn., 1979—; mem. exec. com. Am. Gen. Corp., Houston, 1975—, pres., 1975-81, chmn., chief, exec. officer, 1978—, also bd. dirs.; founder, pres. Main Event Mgmt. Corp., Sacramento, 1971—; bd. dirs. Panhandle Eastern Corp., Houston, Texas Commerce Bancshares, Inc., Houston, United Telecommunications, Inc., Kansas City, Mo, Cooper Industries, Inc., Houston, Chem. Banking Corp., N.Y.C. Founder, mem. Naval War Coll. Found.; trustee, chmn. fin. com. Baylor Coll. Medicine, Houston; vice chmn. council of overseers Jesse H. Jones Grad. Sch. Adminstrn., Rice U., Houston; pres. nat. exec. bd. Boy Scouts Am., mem. adv. bd. Sam Houston Area council; bd. dirs. Tex. Research League, Soc. for Performing Arts, Houston., Houston Area Research Ctr.; bd. dirs. Am. Council of Life Ins., Tex. Med. Ctr. Served to lt. USNR, 1954-57. Recipient Citation of Merit, U. Mo. alumni award, 1965, Faculty-Alumni award U. Mo., 1978, Silver Beaver award Boy Scouts Am., 1974, Disting. Eagle Scout award, 1976, Chief Exec. Officer award Fin. World mag., 1979, 82, 84, 86; named Man of Year Delta Sigma Pi, 1969, Outstanding Chief Exec. Officer in Multiline Ins. Industry Wall St. Transcript, 1981-87. Fellow Life Mgmt. Inst.; mem. Philos. Soc. Tex., Houston C. of C. (chmn. bd. dirs. 1983-84), U.S. C. of C. (bd. dirs.), Tex. Assn. Taxpayers (bd. dirs.), Nat. Assn. Life Underwriters, Houston Assn. Life Underwriters, Beta Gamma Sigma Dirs. Table (mem. 1976, Nat. honoree 1984), Forum Club (bd. govs.), University Club, River Oaks Country Club, Petroleum Club, Ramada Club, Heritage Club of Houston, Economic Club of N.Y.C., Eldorado Country Club, Rotary. Presbyterian. Home: 2204 Troon Rd Houston TX 77019 Office: Am Gen Corp 2929 Allen Pkwy Houston TX 77019-2115

HOOKER, BILLIE JUNE, fundraising executive; b. Port Gibson, Miss., Nov. 29, 1938; d. William and Hazel (Routh) Shaifer; m. William Edward Hooker, May 4, 1958 (div. 1971); 1 child, Brian Casey. BA in English, Albany State Coll., 1957; MLS, Atlanta U., 1967; PhD in Edn., Ohio State U., 1982. Project dir. So. Assn. Colls. and Schs., Atlanta, 1969-70; asst. prof. library sci. Ft. Valley (Ga.) State Coll., 1970-72; program assoc. Office Advancement Pub. Negro Colls., Atlanta, 1972-74; asst. dir. pub. relations and devel. Atlanta U. Ctr., Inc., 1974-77; dir. devel. U. Ark. Pine Bluff, 1977-80; grad. research assoc. Ohio State U., Columbus, 1980-82; area devel. dir. United Negro Coll. Fund, Chgo., 1982-84; dir. instl. advancement Interdenom. Theol. Ctr., Atlanta, 1984—; cons. Positive Futures, Inc., Washington, 1977-78, United Negro Coll. Fund, N.Y.C., 1988. Mem. adv. bd. Benjamin E. Mays Sci. and Math. Acad., Atlanta, 1984-88; vol. Alonzo Herndon Home, Atlanta, 1985-88; chmn. internat. task force So. Christian Leadership Conf. Women, Atlanta, 1986-87; youth council advisor NAACP, Atlanta, 1986-88; mem. Leadership Atlanta, 1989—. Rockefeller fellow Atlanta U., 1966; recipient Earl A. Anderson award, Coll. Edn., Ohio State U., 1980, John A. Ramseyer award, 1981. Mem. AAUW, Nat. Soc. Fund Raising Execs. (sec. bd. dirs. 1988-89), Nat. Assn. Media Women, Council Advancement and Support Edn., Beta Phi Mu. Democrat. Methodist. Home: 653 Peeples St SW Atlanta GA 30310 Office: Interdenom Theol Ctr 671 Beckwith St SW Atlanta GA 30314

HOOKER, NATHAN HARVEY, sales executive; b. Leachville, Ark., Mar. 29, 1939; s. Vann and Opal Faye (Harvey) H.; m. Alice Anne Henderson, Aug. 10, 1962; children: John Mark, Patrick Ed. BA, Hendrix Coll., 1964. Pres. Pruitt & Hooker Pub. Relations, Houston, 1974-76; mgr. circulation Cordovan Pub., Houston, 1975-80; v.p. Corp. Services Inc., Houston, 1980-84, Charles P. Young Inc., Houston, 1984-86; sales mgr. The Beasley Co., Houston, 1986-87, Champagne Fine Printing and Lithographing, Houston, 1987—. Named Man of the Yr., Gulf Coast Direct Mail Assn., 1982. Mem. Bus. Profl. Advt. Assn., Houston Direct Mail Mktg. Assn. Home: PO Box 924291 Houston TX 77292-4291

HOOKSTRATTEN, EDWARD GREGORY, lawyer; b. Whittier, Calif., June 12, 1932; s. E.G. and Winona (Hewitt) H.; children: Jon Crowley, Ann. B.S., U. So. Calif., 1953; J.D., Southwestern U., Los Angeles, 1957; LL.D., Southwestern U., 1984. Bar: Calif. 1958, U.S. Supreme Ct. 1974. Individual practice law Beverly Hills, Calif., 1960—; pres. Broadcast Artists, Ltd.; dir. Nat. Athletic Health Inst., Los Angeles Rams Football Co., 1973-79; mem. Dist. Attys. Adv. Council. Commr. bd. adminstrn. Los Angeles Retirement System, 1970-71; commr. Los Angeles Dept. Pub. Utilities and Transp., 1971-73, v.p., 1973; commr. Los Angeles Dept. Recreation and Parks, 1973-75, v.p., 1974; commr. State of Calif. Motion Picture Council, 1979—; bd. dirs., life mem. U. So. Calif. Assocs.; bd. dirs. Los Angeles Police Meml. Found.; trustee Southwestern U., 1984—. Mem. Los Angeles County Bar Assn., Beverly Hills Bar Assn. Clubs: Bel Air Country, Bohemian (San Francisco), Beverly Hills Tennis (pres. 1988—). Office: 9489 Dayton Way Beverly Hills CA 90210

HOOLEY, JOHN HADRATH, food retailing executive; b. Stillwater, Minn., Dec. 14, 1951; s. Jack Wright and Joyce (Hadrath) H.; m. Colleen Colwell, June 14, 1980; children: J. Benjamin, Meghan Maureen, Ryan Michael. BA in Econs., St. John's U., 1974; JD, Wm. Mitchell Coll. Law, 1979. Buyer, mdse. dir. Cub Foods Hooley's Inc., Stillwater, 1974; advt. and mktg. dir. Cub Foods Hooley's Inc., Stillwater, Minn., 1976, advt. and mktg. dir. super store ops., 1978; dir. store ops. Cub Foods, Stillwater, 1979—, sr. v.p. merchandising and mktg., 1989—; bd. dirs. Taylor Investment, Inc., Two Kis Inc.; mng. ptnr. Tower Properties Ptnrship.; mem. food retailers Ad Hoc Legis. com. Contbr. articles to profl. jours. Instr. Bus. Econ. Edn. Found., 1980; bd. dirs. United Way, 1980-85; mem. St. Croix Cath. Sch. Bd., St. Michael's Ch. Fundraiser Com., 1985. Recipient Leadership award, Am. Legion, 1976. Mem. ABA, Interstate Bridge Constrn. Com., Stillwater Devel. Com. Roman Catholic. Club: White Bear Racquet and Swim. Home: 9770 Old Deer Trail Stillwater MN 55082 Office: Cub Foods 127 Water St Stillwater MN 55082

HOOPER, DAVIS LEE, manufacturing company executive; b. Balt., Nov. 3, 1943; s. Fred Lee and Ottilie Lina (Baker) H.; m. Fredda Jo White, Aug. 26, 1972 (div. Dec. 1973). Student, Franklin and Marshall Coll., 1961-63, Strayer Coll., Washington, 1963-66, 70-71. Staff acct. Robert K. Sutton, CPA, Fairfax, Va., 1970-72; asst. mgr. acctg. Marsh & McLennan Cos., Washington, 1972-78; mgr. gen. acctg. Woodward & Lothrop, Washington, 1978-83; controller Schinnerer & Younger, Inc., Washington, 1983-86; comptroller EMDS, Inc., Gaithersburg, Md., 1986-89, v.p. fin., 1989—. Served with USN, 1966-70, Vietnam. Democrat. Methodist. Office: EMDS Inc 16618 Oakmont Ave Gaithersburg MD 20877

HOOPER, JAMES ANDREW, III, electric utility executive; b. Dallas, Sept. 24, 1937; s. James Andrew, Jr., and Lucille (Hicks) H.; student U. Ark., 1955-57; student UCLA, 1958-60; student public utility exec. program U. Mich., 1977; m. Dorothy Ann Blackford, Feb. 1, 1958; children: LuClare, Cheryl, Deanna, James Andrew IV. Acct., So. Calif. Edison Co., 1957-64, auditor, L.A., 1965-68, supervising auditor, Long Beach, Calif., 1969-70, mgr. audits, Rosemead, Calif., 1971—; lectr. internal auditing, nat. and internat. levels. Pres. Hacienda Heights Youth Football Program, 1979-80; dir. Hacienda Heights Little League, 1978-79; treas. So. Calif. Baton Assn., 1976-78; pres. Hacienda Heights Bobby Sox Program, 1975, nat. commr., 1975-76; mem. So. Calif. Acctg. Careers Coun., 1974-76; loaned exec. United Way, 1963; mem. bus. coun. Calif. State Poly. U., Dominguez Hills, 1989—; mem. adv. coun. acctg. dir. Calif. State Poly. U. and La. State U. Cert. internal auditor, info. systems auditor. Mem. Pacific Coast Elec. Assn., Inst. Internal Auditors (internat. treas., dir., sr. vice chmn. 1982-83, chmn. 1983-84, pres. Los Angeles chpt., Disting. Service award 1987), Edison Electric Inst. (internal auditing com. chmn. 1981-82). Republican. Roman Catholic. Clubs: K.C. (grand knight 1974-75, faithful navigator 1976-77, keynote speaker, lectr.). Contbr. articles to internal auditing jour. Home: 1817 S Blazing Star Dr Hacienda Heights CA 91745 Office: So Calif Edison Co 2244 Walnut Grove Ave Rosemead CA 91770

HOOPER, SIDNEY F., business executive; b. Lexington, Mass., May 9, 1941; s. Sidney and Doris (Blaser) H.; m. Helen E. McAndrew, Aug. 7, 1966; children: Frank, Stephen, Robin. BSBA, Northeastern U., 1964. Ops. mgr. Arlington Trust Co., Lawrence, Mass., 1964-66; acct. mgr. Profl. Hosp. Equip. Co., Lawrence, 1967; controller Alco Electronic Products, Inc., North Andover, Mass., 1967-74; v.p. fin. Augat/Alcoswitch, North Andover, 1974-86, v.p., gen. mgr., 1986—. Sec. North Andover Soccer Assn., 1985-87, coach, 1977-87; coach North Andover Boosters Assn., 1983—. Mem. Nat. Assn. Controllers, Am. Mgmt. Assn. Home: 30 Barco Ln North Andover MA 01845 Office: Augat Alcoswitch 1551 Osgood St North Andover MA 01845

HOOPES, SPENCER WENDELL, manufacturing executive; b. Safford, Ariz., Apr. 13, 1947; s. Spencer P. and Mary Anne (Ray) H.; m. Barbara Lynn Colvin, Dec. 14, 1983; 1 child, Lindsay Blair. BA, U. So. Calif., 1969; JD, U. Calif., Davis, 1972. Bar: Calif. 1972, U.S. Dist. Ct. (no. dist.) Calif. 1972, U.S. Ct. Appeals (10th cir.) 1972. Antitrust counsel Safeway Stores, Oakland, Calif., 1972-73; fin. analyst Curtis Fin. Corp., San Francisco, 1973-77; mng. dir. Churchill Internat., San Francisco, 1977-83; chief exec. officer

Xytec Internat. Industries, Inc., Burlingame, Calif., 1983—. Patron Mont. Land Reliance, Helena, 1985; active Nature Conservancy, San Francisco, 1983. Capt. USAR, 1972-80. Mem. Calif. Bar Assn., Sierra Club, Young Pres. Orgn. Home: 449 Parker Ave San Francisco CA 94118 Office: Xytec Internat Industries Inc 433 Airport Blvd #212 Burlingame CA 94118

HOORWITZ, MARK IRA, marketing general manager, consultant; b. Schenectady, N.Y., Nov. 25, 1961; s. Bernard and Marion (Kagan) H.; m. Robin Misikoff, Aug. 26, 1984. BA in Psychology, SUNY, Albany, 1983; MBA in Mktg. and Mgmt., U. Conn., 1984. Small bus. cons. Small Bus. Devel. Ctr., Storrs, Conn., 1983-84; mktg. asst. Eastern Display Products, Port Washington, N.Y., 1984-85; mktg. mgr. Stratocom Corp., N.Y.C., 1985—, gen. mgr., 1986—. Mem. Am. Mktg. Assn., Nat. Office Products Assn., Nat. Office Machine Assn. Home: 510 DuBois Ave Apt 1B Valley Stream NY 11581 Office: Stratocom Corp 45 W 36th St New York NY 10018

HOOTKIN, PAMELA NAN, apparel company executive; b. N.Y.C., Nov. 14, 1947; d. Louis Arthur and Sally (Perlman) Mash; BA, SUNY, Binghamton, 1968; MA in Econs., Boston U., 1970; m. Stephen Allen, Aug. 2, 1972; 1 dau., Julie Beth. Diversification analyst Champion Internat., N.Y.C., 1971-75; sr. fin. analyst Squibb Corp., N.Y.C., 1975-77, mgr. fin. analyst, 1977-79, dir. fin. planning, 1979-82; asst. controller Charles of The Ritz Group Ltd., N.Y.C., 1982-83, v.p., treas., 1983-87; sr. v.p. fin. Yves St. Laurent Parfums Corp., N.Y.C., 1987-88; v.p., treas., sec. Phillips Van Heusen Corp., N.Y.C., 1988—; lectr. econs. U. York, Heslington, Eng., 1970-71. Mem. Fin. Women's Assn. of N.Y. Office: Charles of Ritz Group Ltd 40 W 57th St New York NY 10028

HOOVEN, WENDY LEE, corporate professional; b. Phila., June 5, 1963; d. William David and Carolyn Mae (Herring) H. Student, U. Charleston, 1981-82, Cen. Piedmont Community Coll., 1985—. Cons. Nat. Travel Svc., Charleston, W.Va., 1982-83; cons. So. Travel Agy., Charlotte, N.C., 1985-86, mgr. corp. sales, 1986-87; mgr. corp. sales Travel/Unltd., Charlotte, N.C., 1988—. Champion State Fair W.Va., Lewisburg, 1982-84, Tri-State Horseman's Assn., Columbus, Ohio, 1983-84. Mem. Travel Agts. Carolinas, Bus. & Profl. Women's Orgn. (chmn. 1987—, pres. elect 1988—), Charlotte C. of C. (connector 1986-87), Alpha Xi Delta (quill chmn. 1982). Republican. Presbyterian. Home: 7926 Greenside Ct Charlotte NC 28226 Office: Travel Unltd 2422 N Tryon St Charlotte NC 28206

HOOVER, ANNETTE LOUISE, appliance manufacturing company official; b. Dayton, Ohio, Dec. 2, 1944; d. Joseph Vincent and Mary Frances (Dinus) De Saro; m. Clonta Fox, Dec. 5, 1964 (div. Jan. 1976); children: C. Steven, Rodney W.; m. H. Alan Hoover, June 14, 1986. Student, Wright State U., U. S.C., Purdue U. Dental asst. Dayton, 1963-64, realtor, 1966-77; asst. to dir. sales tng. Frigidaire div. Gen. Motors Co., Dayton, 1977; dist. mgr. SE region Charlotte zone Frigidaire div. WCI Home Appliance Co., Columbia, S.C., 1977-87; dist. mgr. Midwest region Indpls. zone Frigidaire div. WCI Home Appliance Co., Ft. Wayne, Ind., 1987—. Named Realtor Assoc. of Yr. Dayton Area Bd. Realtors, 1972. Mem. Am. Bus. Women's Assn. Democrat. Roman Catholic. Home: 411 Deep Wood Cove Fort Wayne IN 46845 Office: WCI Appliance Co Frigidaire Div 300 Phillipi Rd Columbus OH 43288 also: 846 E Algonquin Rd Schaumburg IL 60173

HOOVER, C(HARLES) JACKSON, SR., investment executive; b. Boston, Oct. 24, 1929; s. Walter Boyd and Lorna A. (Lelley) H.; m. Joan Kathryn Salvucci, Feb. 19, 1972; children: C. Jackson Jr., Reid Allen. BA, Wesleyan U., 1952; MBA, U. Colo., 1971. Enlisted USAF, 1952, advanced through grades to maj., 1967, command pilot, ret., 1972; with Bank of Boston, 1972-76; broker Kidder Peabody, Boston, 1976-79; broker, portfolio mgr. Buttonwood Securities, Boston, 1979-80; v.p. spl. investments and tax shelters Bank of Boston, 1980-86; founder, pres. Pegasus Group, Inc., Boston, 1986—; lectr. Ctr. for Life Long Learning, Harvard U., Cambridge, Mass., 1983—; mem. adv. panel Total Partnership Mgmt., Inc., Oklahoma City, Okla., 1985—. Decorated D.F.C., Air medal with eleven oak leaf clusters. Clubs: Duxbury Yacht (Mass.), Blue Water Sailing (New Eng.). Home: PO Box 338 SHS Duxbury MA 02331

HOOVER, CHARLIE BEUFORD, JR., insurance company executive; b. Salisbury, N.C., June 10, 1950; s. Charlie Beuford Sr. and Dorcas Victoria (Milholen) H.; m. Debra Lynn Strickland, Sept. 6, 1970; children: Kevin Charles, Daniel Allen. AA in Bus. Administrn., Wingate Coll., 1970; BA in Bus. Administrn., U. N.C., 1972. With Kemper Ins., Charlotte, N.C., 1973-77; supr. underwriting Kemper Ins., Charlotte, 1976-77; mgr. commercial lines Piedmont Ins. Agy., Davidson, N.C., 1977-79; v.p. Conder, Setzer, Hoover and Assocs., Davidson, 1979—; agt. adv. bd. Jackson, Sumner and Assocs., Boone, N.C., 1983—. Asst. chmn. planning bd. Town of Mooresville; bd. dirs. Mooresville Spl. Olympics; mem. bd. adjustment Town of Mooresville; coach soccer, baseball, basketball with Mooresville Recreation Dept.; deacon First Presbyn. Ch., Mooresville. Mem. Charlotte-Mecklenburg Independent Agts. Assn., Mooresville-S. Iredell C. of C., N. Mecklenburg C. of C. Democrat. Home: 919 Stoneycrest Ct Mooresville NC 28115 Office: Conder Setzer Hoover and Assocs 116 S Main St Davidson NC 28036

HOOVER, DONALD LEROY, construction executive; b. Lancaster, Pa., May 28, 1952; s. E. Leroy and Arlene M. (Pickel) H.; m. Sharon Lee Horne, Aug. 15, 1973; children: Steven, Andrew. Student, Millersville U., 1970-71, U. Wis., 1977. Analyst materials Schick Inc., Lancaster, 1970-75; mgr. bus. Reitz Concrete Constrn., Neffsville, Pa., 1976-77; pres. Hoover-Kemp Inc., Lancaster, 1977-83; sec./treas. Oberholtzer Constrn. Inc., East Petersburg, Pa., 1987-88; pres. Indsl. Restorations Ltd., East Petersburg, 1983—; dir. Teen Challenge Tng. Ctr., Rehresburg, Pa., 1983—, sec., mem. exec. com., 1989—; mem. adv. bd. High Constrn. Inc., Lancaster, 1987—. Treas. New Life Assembly of God, Lancaster, 1982-86, 88—, also bd. dirs., 1987-88. Served in USAR, 1972-78. Mem. Associated Builders and Contractors, Bldg. Industry Assn. Lancaster, Painting and Decorating Contractors Am., Lancaster C. of C. Republican. Club: Hammers & Gravels. Home: 1909 Edisonville Rd Strasburg PA 17579 Office: Indsl Restorations Ltd PO Box 406 East Petersburg PA 17520

HOOVER, WILLIAM R(AY), computer service company executive; b. Bingham, Utah, Jan. 2, 1930; s. Edwin Daniel and Myrtle Tennessee (McConnell) H.; m. Sara Elaine Anderson, Oct. 4; children—Scott, Robert, Michael, James, Charles. B.S., M.S., U. Utah. Sect. chief Jet Propulsion Lab., Pasadena, Calif., 1954-64; v.p. Computer Scis. Corp., El Segundo, Calif., 1964-69, pres., 1969—, chmn. bd., 1972—, now also chief exec. officer, also bd. dirs. Office: Computer Scis Corp 2100 E Grand Ave El Segundo CA 90245 *

HOPE, LAWRENCE WINSTON, banker; b. Norfolk, Va., Nov. 3, 1943; s. Winston and Alice (Burroughs) H.; m. Suzanne Turnbull, June 18, 1966; children: R. Winston, Jane Lawrence. BA, U. Va., 1966; cert. in bank mktg., U. Colo., 1975; cert., Coll. Fin. Planning, Denver, 1986. Cert. fin. planner. Trust officer Bank Va., Newport News, 1970-80; asst. v.p. new bus. devel. United Va. Bank, Harrisonburg, 1980-87; v.p., regional fin. svcs. group mgr. Cen. Fidelity Bank, Charlottesville, Va., 1987—. Pres. Girls Club Va. Peninsula, Newport News, 1975-78, Peninsula Ballet Inc., 1978-80; Alpine ofcl., tech. del. U.S. Ski Assn.; selectee Leadership Charlottesville 1988. Lt. col. USAR. Mem. Inst. Cert. Fin. Planners, Cen. Va. Estate Planning Coun., Pa. Alpine Racing Assn., Rotary (bd. dirs. club svc.). Episcopalian. Home: 1613 King Mountain Rd Charlottesville VA 22901 Office: Cen Fidelity Bank 200 E Main St PO Box 138 Charlottesville VA 22901

HOPKINS, BARBARA PETERS, writer, editor; b. Santa Monica, Calif., Sept. 26, 1948; d. Philip Rising and Caroline Jean (Dickason) Peters; m. Philip Joseph Hopkins, May 23, 1981. AA, Santa Monica Coll., 1971; BS, San Diego State U., 1976; postgrad. UCLA, 1981-82, 84. Gen. ptnr. Signet Properties, Los Angeles, 1971-85; tech. editor C. Brewer & Co., Hilo, Hawaii, 1975-76; editor The Aztec Engineer mag., San Diego, 1976-77; regional publicist YWCA, San Diego, 1977-78; campaign cons. Rep. Congl. and Assembly Candidates San Diego; Pollster, Los Angeles Times, 1983; pres. Humbird Hopkins Inc., Los Angeles, 1978—; pub. relations cons. ASCE, San Diego, 1975-76, Am. Soc. Mag. Photographers, San Diego, 1980. Author: The Layman's Guide to Raising Cane: A Guide to the Hawaiian Sugar Industry, 1975, The Student's Survival Guide, 1976, 2d edit. 1977. Council mem. Mayor's Council on Libraries, Los Angeles, 1969; mem. Wilshire Blvd. Property Owners Assn., Santa Monica, 1972-78; docent Mus. Sci. and Industry, Los Angeles, 1970; founding mem. Comml. and Indsl. Properties Assn., Santa Monica, 1982—. Recipient Acting award Santa Monica Coll., 1970. Mem. Internat. Assn. Bus. Communicators, Sales and Mktg. Execs. Assn. Avocations: travel, opera.

HOPKINS, CHARLES PETER, II, lawyer; b. Elizabeth, N.J., June 16, 1953; s. Charles Peter Sr. and Josephine Ann (Battaglia) H.; m. Elizabeth Anna Altinger, Jan. 21, 1984; 1 child, Courtney Alexandra. AB summa cum laude, Boston Coll., 1975, JD, 1979; MBA, Rutgers U., 1987. Bar: N.J. 1979, U.S. Dist. Ct. N.J. 1979, U.S. Ct. Appeals (3d cir.) 1982, U.S. Supreme Ct. 1985, U.S. Tax Ct. 1988. Assoc. Gagliano, Tucci & Kennedy, West Long Branch, N.J., 1980; sole practice West Long Branch, 1980-81; assoc. Richard J. Sauerwein (formerly Sparks & Sauerwein), Shrewsbury, N.J., 1981-83; trial atty. Sparks & Sauerwein, Shrewsbury, N.J., 1983-87, sr. trial atty., 1987—; arbitrator U.S. Dist. Ct. N.J., 1985—, N.J. civil arbitrator program, 1987—. Mem. West Long Branch Sch. Bd., 1980-82. Mem. ABA, N.J. Bar Assn., Monmouth Bar Assn., N.J. Def. Assn., Phi Beta Kappa. Republican. Roman Catholic. Office: Sparks & Sauerwein 655 Shrewsbury Ave Shrewsbury NJ 07701

HOPKINS, EDWARD DONALD, manufacturing executive; b. Little Rock, Apr. 16, 1937; s. Edward J. and Mildred Irene (Thompson) H.; m. Dawn Dee Fritz, June 12, 1965; children—Mark Edward, Scott Edward, Paige Noel. Student, Purdue U., 1955-56; B.S., U.S. Air Force Acad., 1960; M in Aero. Ops. Mgmt., U. So. Calif., 1966. Commd. lt. USAF, 1960, advanced through grades to capt., resigned, 1967; prodn. mg. Gen. Electric Co., Cin., 1967-70; v.p. sales Tri-City Bldg., Cin., 1970-71; group v.p. Rochester Inst. Systems, N.Y., 1971-74; div. pres. Gould Inc., Pa., Mo., Ind., 1974-80; group v.p. Sherwin Williams Co., Cleve., 1980-83; exec. v.p. Interlake Corp. and Sealed Power Corp., Oak Brook, Ill., 1983-88, pres., chief operating officer, 1983-88; also bd. dirs. Interlake Corp. and Sealed Power Corp., Oak Brook; bd. dirs. Sealed Power Corp., Muskegon, Mich., 1985—. Bd. dirs. March of Dimes, Chgo., 1984—, Glenwood Sch. for Boys, Chgo., 1988—. Named one of Outstanding Young Men Am., 1965. Mem. Ill. Mfrs. Assn. (bd. dirs. 1985—). Office: Interlake Corp 701 Harger Rd Oak Brook IL 60521

HOPKINS, GEORGE MATHEWS MARKS, lawyer, business executive; b. Houston, June 9, 1923; s. C. Allen and Agnes Cary (Marks) H.; m. Betty Miller McLean, Aug. 21, 1954; children: Laura Corrigan, Edith Cary. Student, Ga. Sch. Tech., 1943-44; B.S. in Chem. Engring, Ala. Poly. Inst., 1944; LL.B., J.D., U. Ala., 1949; postgrad., George Washington U., 1949-50. Bar: Ala. 1949, Ga. 1954; Registered profl. engr., Ga. registered patent lawyer, U.S., Can. qualified deep-sea diver. Instr. math. U. Ala., 1947-49; assoc. firm A. Yates Dowell, Washington, 1949-50, Edward T. Newton, Atlanta, 1950-62; asst. dir. research, legal counsel Auburn (Ala.) Research Found., 1954-55; ptnr. firm Newton, Hopkins and Ormsby (and predecessor), Atlanta, 1962-87; sr. ptnr. Hunt, Richardson, Garner, Todd & Cadenhead, Atlanta, 1987—; spl. asst. atty. gen. State of Ga., 1978; chmn. bd. Southeastern Carpet Mills, Inc., Chatsworth, Ga., 1962-77, Thomas-Daniel & Assocs., Inc., 1981-85, Eastern Carpet Mills, Inc., 1983-87; dir. Xepol Inc. Served as lt., navigator, Submarine Service USNR, 1944-46, 50-51. Mem. ABA, Ga. Bar Assn. (chmn. sect. patents 1970-71), Atlanta Bar Assn., Am. Intellectual Property Law Assn., Am. Soc. Profl. Engrs., Submarine Vets. World War II (pres. Ga. chpt. 1977-78), Phi Delta Phi, Sigma Alpha Epsilon. Episcopalian. Clubs: Nat. Lawyers (Washington); Atlanta Lawyers, Phoenix Soc, Cherokee Town and Country, Atlanta City. Home: 795 Old Post Rd NW Atlanta GA 30328 Office: Hunt Richardson Garner Todd & Cadenhead SW 1400 999 Peachtree St Atlanta GA 30303

HOPKINS, LEANN ELISABETH, sales representative; b. Oklahoma City, Sept. 15, 1960; d. Donald Ray and Janyth Lee (Stanmire) H. B.A. in Motion Picture Journalism, U. Okla., 1982. Okla. Asst. dist. retail mgr. Fox-Stanley Photo, Inc., Oklahoma City, 1978-82; media cons. Okla. pari-mutuel horse racing state campaign, Okla. Horsemen's Assn., 1982; ter. mgr. ArtCarved Class Rings, Inc., Austin, Tex., 1982-85; sales rep. Met. Ins. Co., Oklahoma City, 1985-86, sales exec. Am. Sportswear Co./ Southwest Athletics, Inc., Dallas, 1986—; account specialist Southwestern Bell Yellow Pages, Inc., 1987—. Producer, asst. dir. and cinematographer: The Complete Works of Christopher Brandon (Silver award Okla. Internat. Film Festival), 1982. Mem. NOW, Am. Mensa, World Wildlife Fund, Greenpeace, Am. Film Inst., Nat. Assn. Female Execs. Democrat. Home: 9313 Maypark Dr Oklahoma City OK 73159

HOPKINS, THOMAS MOORE, small business owner; b. Beloit, Wis., June 8, 1952; s. Guy Moore and Patricia Louise (Weeks) H.; m. Elizabeth Ellen Lowery, July 8, 1978; children: Katherine Casey, Maureen Elizabeth, Patrick Thomas. BS in Architecture, U. Ill., 1974. Registered architect, Ill., Wis. Draftsman Home Plan Service, Rockford, Ill., 1974-78, Olsen-New & Assocs., McHenry, Ill., 1978-79, Don New, Architect, Sharon, Wis., 1980-81; owner Thomas M. Hopkins, Architect, McHenry, 1982—. Contbr. house designs to mag., 1983, 88, 89. Mem, cons. city of McHenry Landmark Commn., 1985, McHenry Downtown Revitalization Com., 1988—. Mem. Nat. Trust for Hist. Preservation, McHenry Area C. of C. Roman Catholic. Office: 1402 N Riverside Dr McHenry IL 60050

HOPPE, ROBERT RODERICK, accountant; b. Carlisle, Pa., Sept. 15, 1951; s. Barton Walker and Marion (Whitman) H.; m. Susan Lewis, July 31, 1971; children: Lindsay Christine, Trevor Alexander, Derek Whitman. BS in Acctg., U. N.C., 1973. CPA, N.C., S.C. Mem. audit staff Coopers and Lybrand, Charlotte, 1973-82; mng. ptnr. Columbia, S.C., 1982—; past pres. Columbia Forum. Mem. exec. com. Better Bus. Bur. Midlands, Columbia, 1983—, past chmn. bd. dirs.; chmn. bd. dirs., mem. exec. com. Salvation Army of the Midlands, 1983—; bd. dirs. Arthritis Found., Columbia, 1988—; trustee United Way Midlands. Recipient Outstanding Pres. award Mecklenburg Jaycees, 1980. Mem. Am. Inst. CPA's, N.C. Assn. CPA's, S.C. Assn. CPA's, Greater Columbia C. of C. (bd. dirs., treas.). Republican. Methodist. Clubs: Summit, Capital (Columbia). Office: Coopers & Lybrand 1401 Main St Suite 500 Columbia SC 29201

HOPPER, WALTER EVERETT, lawyer; b. Houghton, Mich., Oct. 29, 1915; s. Walter E. and Maude (Crum) H.; m. Jeannette Ross, Aug. 23, 1941 (dec. 1947); 1 dau., Nancy Cameron Hopper Marcovici; m. Diana Kerensky, Sept. 24, 1958; 1 stepdau., Nicole Sudrow Hopper Neilan. A.B., Cornell U., 1937, J.D., 1939. Bar: N.Y. 1939, U.S. Supreme Ct. 1946, D.C. 1959. Practice in Ithaca, 1939-42, N.Y.C., 1946—; chmn., chief exec. officer Fort Amsterdam Corp., 1973-81; dir. Davis Brake Beam Co. Chmn. trustees Loyal Legion Found.; trustee Inst. on Man and Science, 1969-71, Signal Hill Ednl. Center; bd. dirs. U.S. Flag Found. Served from 1st lt. to lt. col. inf. AUS, World War II, ETO; col. U.S. Army Res. ret. Decorated Army Commendation medal with oak leaf cluster; N.Y. State Conspicious Service Cross with Maltese Cross; Order Ruben Dario Nicaragua; comdr. Order Orange-Nassau, Netherlands; Order St. John of Jerusalem. Mem. Internat. Assn. Protection Indsl. Property (exec. com. Am. group 1958-71), Internat. Fiscal Assn., Nat. Fgn. Trade Council (mem. coms.), Internat. C. of C. (U.S. council 1949-71, mem. coms.), Am. Arbitration Assn. (panelist), U.S. Trademark Assn. (past v.p., dir., chmn. internat. com.), UN Assn. (dir. N.Y. chpt. 1964-66), Holland Soc. (pres. 1966-71), Loyal Legion (comdr.-in-chief 1964-67), Assn. Bar City N.Y., N.Y. State Criminal Bar Assn., Res. Officers Assn. (pres. N.Y. State 1949), Confrerie des Chevaliers du Tastevin, Pilgrims, Soc. War 1812, Founders and Patriots of Am., Mayflower Descs., Soc. Colonial Wars, St. Nicholas Soc. (pres. 1982-84), S.R., Huguenot Soc. Am. (pres. 1972-75), Mil. Order Fgn. Wars, Soc. of Cincinnati. Clubs: Explorers (N.Y.C.), University (N.Y.C.), Leash (N.Y.C.); Metropolitan (Washington), Army-Navy (Washington). Home: 715 Park Ave New York NY 10021

HOPPES, HARRISON NEIL, corporate executive, chemical engineer; b. Lehighton, Pa., Aug. 11, 1935; s. Charles Harold and Margaret Lois (Troxell) H.; m. Friederike Witte, June 20, 1959; children: Anne Marie, Charles Victor, Michael David, Margaret Louise, John Christian, Daniel James. BS in Chem. Engring., Pa. State U., 1957; MS in Indsl. Mgmt., MIT, 1959; PhD in Bus. Administrn., Am. U., 1968. Ops. analyst, project dir. Rsch. Analysis Corp., Bethesda, Md., 1961-69; dir. European field office Rsch. Analysis Corp., Heidelberg, Fed. Republic Germany, 1969-73; dir. div. Gen. Rsch. Corp., McLean, Va., 1973-76; v.p. Gen. Rsch. Corp., McLean, 1976-80; pres. Am. Tech. Assistance Corp., McLean, 1977-80; v.p. Flow Labs, McLean, 1980-85; v.p., pres. facilities group ERC Internat., Fairfax, Va., 1985—; chmn. bd. dirs. Logistics Ops., Fairfax, ERC Internat. Service Corp., Fairfax; bd. dirs. D-K Assocs., Inc., Fairfax. Author: Happes Family to 1800, 1985. Mem. Am. Mgmt. Assn., Pa. German Soc., Wash. Ops. Rsch. and Mgmt. Sci. Council. Republican. Lutheran. Home: 15716 Jones Ln Gaithersburg MD 20878 Office: ERC Internat 3211 Jermantown Rd Fairfax VA 22030

HOPPIN, THOMAS EDWARD, transportation executive; b. Bois D'Arc Township, Ill., Aug. 15, 1941; s. Curtiss and Frances (Witt) H.; m. Marvalene Ann Shanks, June 5, 1965; children: Elizabeth Ann, Robert Curtiss. BS, Eastern Ill. U., 1969. Pub. relations exec. Penn Cen. Transp. Co., Phila., 1969-75; media relations coordinator Conrail, 1975-76, dir. media relations, 1976-78, dir. corp. communications, 1978-81; dir. fin. communications CSX Corp., Richmond, Va., 1981-83, asst. v.p. corp. communications, 1983-86, v.p. corp. communications, 1986—; mem. Nat. Advt. Rev. Bd., 1988—. Bd. dirs. Boys Club Richmond, 1986—, Met. Richmond Pvt. Industry Council, 1986—. With U.S. Army, 1959-62, Korea. Mem. Assn. Nat. Advertisers (corp. communications com. 1986—, nat. advt. rev. bd. 1988—), R.R. Pub. Relations Assn. (pres. 1986-87, bd. dirs. 1985—), Brandermill Country Club, Bull and Bear Club of Richmond. Home: 4001 McIntyre's Cove Rd Midlothian VA 23313 Office: CSX Corp 901 E Cary St Richmond VA 23219

HORAN, JUSTIN THOMAS, association executive; b. Manchester, N.H., Feb. 6, 1927; s. Richard and Helen (Lenihan) H.; m. Helen Raymah Cook, Mar. 20, 1952; children: Catherine Helen, Carol Ann, Justin Thomas, Steven Edward, Daniel Kevin, Mark Gregory, Virginia Louise, Paul David. B.S., U. N.H., 1950; postgrad., Yale U., 1958, Syracuse U., 1961, Mich. State U., 1964. Asst. v.p. Manchester C. of C., 1955-57; exec. v.p. Newton (Mass.) C. of C., 1957-66, Greater Lawrence (Mass.) C. of C., 1966-69; pres. Greater Waterbury (Conn.) C. of C., 1969-75, Greater Pitts. C. of C., 1975—; chmn. bd. regents Inst. Orgn. Mgmt., 1966—. Contbr. articles to profl. publs. Met. chmn. Western Conn., Nat. Alliance Businessmen, 1973-75; mem. Mayor's Com. on Econ. Devel., Pitts., 1976—; trustee LaRoche Coll.; mem. corp. North Hills Passavant Hosp. Served to capt. U.S. Army Res., 1950-59. Mem. Am. C. of C. Execs. (dir., vice chmn. 1981-82, chmn. 1983-84), New Eng. Assn. C. of C. Execs. (past pres.), Mass. Assn. C. of C. Execs. (past pres.). Clubs: Duquesne (Pitts.), Allegheny (Pitts.). Home: 103 Camden Ct Pittsburgh PA 15237 Office: Greater Pittsburgh C of C 3 Gateway Ctr Pittsburgh PA 15222

HORAN, LAWRENCE JAMES, securities analyst, economist; b. Aurora, Ill., July 29, 1950; s. Lawrence James and Florence Katherine (Pitz) H.; m. Elaine Christine Cuddihy, Dec. 21, 1974; children: Christopher Edward, Marielle Christine. BS, U. Santa Clara, 1972; PhD, Columbia U., 1980. Economist Equitable Life Ins. Co., N.Y.C., 1973-83; securities analyst Smith Barney Harris Upham & Co., N.Y.C., 1983—. Mem. Constrn. and Bldg. Analyst Group (treas. 1987-88). Republican. Office: Smith Barney Harris Upham & Co 1345 Ave of Americas New York NY 10105

HORDEMAN, AGNES MARIE, real estate professional, investment company executive; b. Phila., May 19, 1929; d. Hector and Victoria (Charais) Hill; m. Walter George Hordeman, Sept. 28, 1947; children: Phyllis, Kim, Henry, Rex, Gary. BA in Social Sci., Thomas Edison U., 1978. Relief dir. New Chgo. Trustee's Office, Hobart Twp., Ind., 1962-64; exec. sec. Real Estate Office, Pine Beach, N.J., 1964-65; office mgr. Crestwood Village, Whiting, N.J., 1965-67; reporter Ocean County Daily Times, Lakewood, 1967-69; real estate agt. De-Bow Agy., Lakewood, 1972-73, Century 21 Sullivan Agy. and Centurion and Rimm Howell, 1973-79; dir. Counteract Agy. for Children, Jackson, N.J., 1974-75; pres. Blue Sky Realty, Jackson, 1979—; appraiser Garden State Bank, Jackson, 1986-87; pres. Brassica Inc., Jackson, 1986-87. Contbr. articles to profl. jours. Mem. com. Jackson Twp. Rep. Orgn., 1964-76; rep. to People's Republic China amb. program SBA. Named Woman of Yr. Girl Scouts U.S., 1975. Mem. Nat. Assn. Real Estate Appraisers, Ocean County Bd. Realtors, Monmouth County Bd. Realtors, N.J. Bd. Realtors, Nat. Bd. Realtors, NAFE, Jackson C. of C. (v.p., directory chmn., pres. 1989). Republican. Roman Catholic. Clubs: Legion Mary (v.p. 1962-64) (New Chgo.); Rosary Sodality (v.p. 1967) (Jackson). Home: RD #4 121 Cooks Bridge Jackson NJ 08527 Office: 277 County Line Rd Jackson NJ 08527

HORE, JOHN EDWARD, commodity futures educator; b. Kingston-on-Thames, Surrey, Eng., Dec. 13, 1929; came to Can., 1954; s. Ernest and Doris Kathleen (Horton) H.; m. Diana King, May 3, 1958; children: Edward John Bruce, Celia Kathleen Hore Milne, Timothy Frank. B.A. with honors, King's Coll., Cambridge, Eng., 1952, M.A., 1957. Chartered fin. analyst. Asst. sales mgr. Borthwicks, London, 1952-54; security analyst Dominion Securities, Toronto, Ont., Can., 1955-57; asst. mktg. mgr. Rio Algom, Toronto, 1957-61; dir. Bell, Gouinlock & Co., Toronto, 1961-75; v.p., dir. futures Can. Securities Inst., Toronto, 1979—, seminar leader, 1980—; founding sec. Can. Nuclear Assn.; past v.p. Brit. Can. Trade Assn.; chmn. 1st Can. Internat. Futures Research Seminar, 1985, also editor Proc., 2 vols., 1986; chmn. Can. Futures Conf., 1986, 88; chmn. 3d and 4th Can. Internat. Futures Conf. and Research Seminars, 1987, 88 (mng. editor Selected Papers, 1988, 89), chmn. proposed 5th Conf., 1989. Author: Trading on Canadian Futures Markets, 1984, 3rd edit., 1987, 4th edit., 1989; co-editor Canadian Securities Course, 1980—; co-author Fin. Analysts Fedn. Standards of Practice Handbook, 1982 (Pres. Reagan citation 1984). Gov. Montcrest Sch., 1970-73; mem. internat. com. Futures Industry Assn., Washington (appointed), rowing com. Upper Can. Coll., Toronto, 1982-86; pres. St. George's Soc. Toronto, 1978-80, chmn. edn. com., 1987. Served with Royal Army Ednl. Corps., 1948-49; Singapore. Mem. Toronto Soc. Fin. Analysts (bd. dirs. 1968-71), Fin. Analysts Fedn. (bd. dirs. investment analysis standards 1974-85, emeritus 1985). Progressive Conservative. Anglican. Clubs: University (bd. dirs. 1980-83) (Toronto); Leander (assoc.) (Henley-on-Thames), United Oxford, Cambridge U., Hurlingham, Royal Overseas League (hon. corr. sec. for Toronto) (London). Avocations: historical research, squash, choral music. Office: Can Securities Inst, 33 Yonge St, Toronto, ON Canada

HORGAN, JAMES EDWARD, financial planner; b. Pitts., Sept. 22, 1953; s. James Woodside Zepfel and Joan Louise (Hennessy) Horgan; m. Diane Louise Dukes, Nov. 4, 1977; children: Ryan James, Ashley Diane. BA in Communications and Mktg., Duquesne U., 1976; postgrad., Cleve. State U., 1977. Software developer Control Data Corp., Cleve., 1979-84; fin. planner Life-Work Planning, Cleve., 1984-87; pres., fin. planner Horgan Adv. Services, Spring, Tex., 1987—; v.p., fin. planner Ameriway Fin. Advisors, Houston, 1987—. Author software, 1984, 86. Mem. Internat. Assn. Fin. Planners, Inst. Cert. Fin. Planners, Houston Consortium Cert. Fin. Planners, Cleve. Investment (sec. 1986-87), Masons (jr. daecon 1985-88). Republican. Roman Catholic. Home: PO Box 6020 #122 Spring TX 77391

HORINE, MERRILL CACERES, food company executive; b. S.I., N.Y., Apr. 29, 1925; s. Merrill Castleberry and Grace (Caceres) H.; m. Grace Moerling, 1948; 1 child, Richard Merrill. BS, Wagner Coll., 1949; postgrad. in personnel adminstrn., NYU, 1951-55. Asst. mgr. adminstrn., plans and compensation div. Exxon Co.-USA, N.Y.C., 1948-62; pension and ins. supr. Ford Instrument Co. div. Sperry Rand Corp., N.Y.C., 1962-66; mgr. employee benefits Amerada Hess Corp., N.Y.C., 1966-77; dir. benefit planning and med. cost mgmt. Hershey (Pa.) Foods Corp., 1977—; chmn. Internat. Found. Employee Benefits, 1987-88; lay mem. Pa. Blue Shield, 1987—. Mem. editorial adv. bd. Pension World. Dist. rep. S.I. Republican Com., 1958-62; pres. Great Kills Little League, S.I., 1962-64; bd. dirs., mem. exec. com. Health Care Alliance, Harrisburg, Pa., 1984—. Served with inf., AUS, 1943-45, ETO. Mem. Council on Employee Benefits, NAM (employee benefits com.). Republican. Club: Hershey Country. Home: RD 1 Box 234A Hummelstown PA 17036 Office: Hershey Foods Corp Corp Hdqrs Hershey PA 17033

HORKY, REGINALD PATRICK, manufacturing jeweler, designer; b. Flint, Mich., July 18, 1952; s. Stanley Joseph and Helen Mary (Gasparovic) H.; m. Melinda Ellen Mizikow, April 18, 1977; children: Reginald,

Elisa. Cert. diamond grading. Goldsmith Diamond Exchange, Flint, 1975-77; owner R. Horky Co., Flint, 1977-80, Swartz Creek, Mich., 1980-83; owner Reginalds Fine Jewelry, Swartz Creek, 1983-85, Elegance in Diamonds, Grand Blanc, Mich., 1985-89; with Robsons Goldsmith Ltd., Flint, 1989—; apprenticed to Paul Marciszewski, M. Paul & Sons, Flint, 1971, Jim Alphin, Jim Alphin Mfg. Jeweler, Inc., Dallas, 1975. Patentee methods of mfg. Roman Catholic. Home: 4449 Van Vleet Swartz Creek MI 48473

HORN, CHARLES G., textile executive; b. Decatur, Ill., June 10, 1939; s. Charles Henry and Constance Pauline (Fryman) H.; m. Myrna Marie Motta, Aug. 22, 1959 (div. 1975); children: Melissa, Matthew. BS in Personnel and Industrial Relations, U. So. Calif., 1961; advanced mgmt. program, Harvard U., 1983. Sales rep./regional mgr. Fieldcrest, Los Angeles, Houston, San Francisco, Chgo., 1963-77; v.p., dir. sales Karastan Rug Mills, N.Y.C., 1977-83, pres., 1983-85; pres. bed and bath div. Fieldcrest Mills, N.Y.C., 1985-86; pres. bed and bath div. Fieldcrest Cannon, Inc., N.Y.C., 1986-87, pres., 1987—. Served in U.S. Army, 1961-64. Club: Harvard (N.Y.C.). Office: Fieldcrest Cannon Inc 1271 Ave of the Americas New York NY 10020

HORN, CHRISTIAN FRIEDRICH, venture capital company executive; b. Dresden, Germany, Dec. 23, 1927; came to U.S., 1954, naturalized, 1959; s. Otto Hugo and Elsa H.; m. Christa Winkler, Feb. 13, 1954; 1 child, Sabrina. M.S., Technische Hochschule, Dresden, 1951; Ph.D., Technische Hochschule, Aachen, Germany, 1958. Rsch. scientist German Acad. Sci., Berlin, 1951-53, Farbwerke Hoechst, Germany, 1953-54; research mgr. Union Carbide, N.Y.C., 1954-65; pres. Polymer Tech. Inc., N.Y.C., 1965-74; mem. bd. mgmt. Zimmer A.G., Frankfurt, Fed. Republic Germany, 1971-73; v.p. W.R. Grace & Co., N.Y.C., 1974-81; sr. v.p. W.R. Grace & Co., 1981—, dir., 1985—; pres. Grace Ventures Corp., Cupertino, Calif., 1983—; mng. ptnr. Horn Venture Ptnrs, Cupertino, 1987—; chmn. bd. dirs. Interlink Electronics, Inc.; bd. dirs. Interfax, Inc., Biocare, Inc. Patentee in field. Served with German Army, 1944-45. Decorated Iron Cross. Mem. Am. Chem. Soc. Lutheran. Home: 27827 Via Feliz Los Altos Hills CA 94022 Office: Grace Horn Ventures 20300 Stevens Creek Blvd Cupertino CA 95014

HORN, JERRY DEAN, health products executive; b. Bloomfield, Iowa, June 29, 1937; s. Ervin Floyd Horn and Mildred Helena (Stump) Bayless; m. Marsha Kay Whitaker, Aug. 6, 1960; children—Gregory, Douglas, Stacy. B.S., Drake U., 1962. With Sears Roebuck & Co., Chgo., 1959-79; pres., chief exec. officer Recreational Equipment Inc., Seattle, 1979-83, Thousand Trails Inc., Seattle, 1983-85; chief exec. officer Gen. Nutrition Inc., Pitts., 1985—, chmn. bd., pres., 1986—, also bd. dirs.; chmn. bd. GNC; dir. Pay N Pak Corp., Seattle. Bd. dirs. Jr. Achievement, San Francisco, 1978-79, Seattle Symphony, 1980-83, Pub. TV, Seattle, 1980-83, Coop. League of U.S.A., Washington, 1980-83, United way, Allegheny County, 1987—; mem. fin. com. Republican Party, Seattle, 1981-82. Served with U.S. Army, 1956-58. Clubs: Duquesne, Rivers (Pitts.), Oakmont Country; Overlake Country (Seattle). Home: 4162 187th Ave SE Issaquah WA 98027 Office: Gen Nutrition Inc 921 Penn Ave Pittsburgh PA 15222

HORN, JOHN CHISOLM, management consultant; b. N.Y.C., Jan. 16, 1915; s. William M. and Marguerite E. (Jacobs) H.; A.B., Cornell U., 1936, postgrad., 1937; LL.D., Susquehanna U., 1965; m. Solveig E. Wald, June 22, 1938; children—Phyllis Downing, John Chisolm, Stephen Lunde, Eric Laurens, Robert Gregg, Thomas Wald, Dorothy Traill, James Melchior. With John R. Wald Co., 1937-39; sec. Prismo Safety Corp., 1939-45, sec., treas., 1945-49, v.p., 1949-57, exec. v.p., 1957-62, pres., 1962-69; pres. John C. Horn Assos., 1970—; pres. Prismo Universal Corp., 1969-70, vice chmn. bd., 1970—; asst. sec. Wald Industries, Inc., 1950-51, pres., 1951-69; exec. dir. Church Mgmt. Service, Inc., 1971—; dir. Long Siding Corp., Prismo France, Paris, Prismo Universal Ltd., Eng. cooperating cons. Tech. Diversification Services, 1972—; dir. Springfield Corp. Dir. Huntingdon Bus. and Industry, Inc., 1958—; chmn. Indsl. Devel. Commn., 1959-60, area devel. chmn., 1960-62. Bd. dirs., vice chmn. Wald Found., 1954-63; mem. nat. council Boy Scouts Am., 1950—, nat. com. on cubbing, 1961-68, nat. com. exec. profl. tng., 1971—, exec com Region III, 1961—, v.p. Juniata Valley council 1951-57, pres., 1957—; pres., bd. dirs. Huntingdon County United Fund, 1959-68; mem. indsl. and profl. council Pa. State U. Bd. dirs. Juniata Valley Schs., St. James Huntingdon Choir; pres. bd. dirs. Susquehanna U.; mem. bd. publ. Luth. Ch. Am., 1968-74. Recipient Silver Beaver, Lamb and Silver Antelope awards Boy Scouts Am., also Outstanding Civic Leader award, 1967. Mem. Army Ordnance Assn., NAM, AIM, Am. Mgmt. Assn., Am. Road Builders Assn., Internat. Bridge Tunnel and Toll Rd. Assn., Inst. Traffic Engrs., C. of C. (dir. 1955), Juniata Mountains Devel. Assn. (pres. 1956). Lutheran (home mission bd. Central Pa. Synod 1948—, com. on music and worship; synodical proposal com. 1957—, exec. bd. 1962-67, higher edn. com. 1967—). Clubs: Huntingdon Music, Huntingdon Country. Home: Killmarnock Hall Alexandria PA 16611 Office: Huntingdon Bus and Industry Inc 301 Penn St Huntingdon PA 16652

HORN, JOHN F., transportation company executive; b. 1941; married. BA, Lawrence U., 1963. With N.W. Airlines Inc., St. Paul, asst. v.p. properties, 1976-80, v.p. properties, 1980-81; v.p. Orient region Tokyo, 1981-85; exec. v.p. St. Paul, 1985-86, pres., chief operating officer, 1986—; also bd. dirs. Served as lt. (j.g.) USN, 1966. Office: NW Airlines Inc Mpls-St Paul Internat Airport Saint Paul MN 55111 *

HORN, RUSSELL EUGENE, engineering executive, consultant; b. Yoe, Pa., May 4, 1912; s. Eugene M. and Charlotte (Snyder) H.; m. Eleanor B. Baird, Jan. 12, 1934; children: Russell Eugene, Ralph Elliot, Rosalind Emily (Mrs. Lee Kunkel), Robert Errol. BS, Pa. State U., 1933. Foreman Pa. Dept. Hwys. dist. office, York, Pa., 1933-35; draftsman, supr., designer C.S. Buchart, architect, 1935-41; exec. v.p., chief engr. Buchart Engring., 1945-59, pres., chief engr., 1959-61; pres., chief engr. Buchart-Horn, Inc., cons. engrs., 1961-72, chmn. bd. dirs., 1972—; pres. PACE Resources, Inc., 1970-87, chmn. bd. dirs., 1970—, chief exec. officer, 1987-88; dir. emeritus Dauphin Deposit Bank and Trust Co.; dir. emeritus adv. bd. So div. Dauphin Deposit Bank & Trust Co.; bd. dirs. AAA White Rose Motor Club, chmn., 1975-78; bd. dirs. Auto Club So. Pa., bd. dirs. York County chpt. ARC; bd. dirs. emeritus Retirement Homes of Meth. Ch., 1978—. Served to col. AUS, 1940-45. Mem. Soc. Am. Mil. Engrs., NSPE, Pa. Soc. Profl. Engrs. (pres. Lincoln chpt. 1961), Pa. Assn. Cons. Engrs. (pres. 1965, bd. dirs. 1966), Pa. Hwy. Information Assn. (bd. dirs.), Am. Soc. Hwy. Engrs. (nat. pres. 1962), Tech. Socs. Council Southeastern Pa. (chmn. 1963), Engring. Soc. York, Profl. Engrs. Pvt. Practice, Am. Concrete Inst., Assn. Pa. Constructors, Assn. Hwy. Ofcls. N. Atlantic States, Assn. U.S. Army, Res. Officers Assn., ASCE, VFW, Cons. Engrs. Council, Am. Rd. Builders Assn., Am. Legion, Pa. State U. Alumni Club York County. Clubs: Univ., Lake, Dutch, Exchange ((Golden Deeds award 1979), Mt. Nittany Soc. Pa. State U. Lodges: Masons (32 deg.; Order of the Double Eagle award, 1983, Legion of Freedom award 1986), Moose. Home: 1270 Brockie Dr York PA 17403 Office: Pace Resources Inc 40 S Richland Ave York PA 17405

HORNBERGER, FREDERICK CHARLES, JR., management consultant; b. New Orleans, Feb. 1, 1960; s. Frederick Charles and Jerry Margaret (Jung) H.; m. Roxann Anita Schaffhausen, May 23, 1987; 1 child, Sasha Michelle. BA in Econs., Loyola U., New Orleans, 1981; MBA, Loyola U., 1985. Cert. personnel cons. Sales cons. A.L. Williams Ins., New Orleans, 1979-81; account exec. Engring. Personnel Cons., New Orleans, 1981-82; exec. v.p. Kimmel and Fredericks Inc., Asheville, N.C., 1983—; cons., writer, speaker Omega Enterprises Ltd., Asheville, 1985—; lectr. in field. Author: Maximum Career Advancement, 1988; contbr. articles to profl. jours. Bible instr. B.C. Bapt. Ch., Asheville, 1986—. Mem. Nat. Assn. Personnel Cons., Soc. Mktg. Profl. Svcs., Nat. Speakers Assn., Asheville C. of C., Lions, Sigma Nu. Republican. Baptist. Office: Kimmel & Fredericks Inc Rte 1 PO Box 147 Fairview NC 28730

HORNE, SCOTT JEFFREY, recycling company executive, lawyer; b. Bklyn., Jan. 5, 1955; s. Seymour M. Judie (Saffer) H.; m. Judith Theresa Stachniak, May 22, 1983. BA in Econs., Emory U., 1976; JD, John Marshall Law Sch., 1981. Bar: Ill. 1981, Md. 1982, Va. 1983, U.S. Ct. Appeals (4th cir.) 1983. Mem. sales and mgmt. staff AAA Brands Plastics Co., Atlanta, 1976-77; customer svc. rep. Davis Industries, Arlington, Va., 1977-78; asst. to pres. Davis Industries, Arlington, 1981, v.p., counsel, 1982-84; v.p., gen. counsel Prince Georges Scrap, Inc., College Park, Md., 1984—; also dir. Prince Georges Scrap, Inc., College Park, 1984—. Mng. editor John Marshall Law Rev., 1981, assoc. lead articles editor, 1980. Bd. dirs., crusade chmn. Am. Cancer Soc., College Park, 1987—, pres. Western Prince George Unit, 1988—; bd. dirs. Northwood Four Corners Civic Assn., 1988—. Mem. ABA, Inst. Scrap Recycling Industries (bd. dirs., pres. seaboard chpt. 1988—), Ill. State Bar Assn., Md. State Bar Assn., Va. State Bar Assn. Home: 107 Snowy Owl Dr Silver Spring MD 20901 Office: Prince Georges Scrap Inc PO Box 626 College Park MD 20740

HORNE, TOM LEE, III, entrepreneur; b. Athens, Ga., Dec. 21, 1950; m. Skeater Jane Doster, July 24, 1953 (div. 1985). BA, Stetson U., 1972. Mechanic Durham Motors, New Orlrans, 1973-74; parts man Ferguson Pontiac, Daytona Beach, Fla., 1976-80, Noels Salvage, Orlando, Fla., 1980-84; owner, mgr. Dourphous Enterprises, Orlando, 1984-86, Franklin, La., 1986—. Trustee Brumby Family Trust, Franklin, 1985—. Liberatarian. Unitarian. Office: Dourphous Enterprises 519 Main St PO Box 999 Franklin LA 70538

HORNECKER, WENDELL E., retail company executive; b. Geneseo, Ill., June 18, 1941; s. Earl E. and Mildred (Radue) H.; m. Betty J. Sprung, Sept. 5, 1964; children: Gina T., James R., Benjamin E. BS in Bldg. Constrn., Bradley U., 1963. Registered architect, 30 states. Project architect Eagle Food Ctr., Inc., Milan, Ill., 1964-66; salesman Weyerhauser, Rock Island, Ill., 1967-70; regional engring. mgr. Montgomery Ward, Orlando, Fla., 1970-75; sr. v.p. design and constrn. Albertson's Inc., Boise, Idaho, 1975—. Served with Ill. Air N.G., 1963-69. Mem. AIA, Architects in Industry, Internat. Council Shopping Ctrs., Nat. Council Archtl. Registration Bds., Sigma Nu. Republican. Lutheran. Home: 1044 Harcourt Dr Boise ID 83702 Office: Albertson's Inc 250 Parkcenter Blvd Boise ID 83726

HORNER, WILLIAM FREDERICK, bank executive; b. Detroit, Jan. 25, 1946. BBA, Wayne State U., Detroit, 1969; MBA, Eastern Mich. U., 1984; grad., Stonier Sch. Banking, Rutgers U. 2d v.p. Mfrs. Bank, Detroit, 1973-76; v.p. lending Mfrs. Bank, Southfield, Mich., 1977-82; v.p. loan workouts Mfrs. Bank, Detroit, 1982-84; sr. v.p. Mfrs. Bank of Lansing, Mich., 1984-87; pres. Mfrs. Bank of Coopersville, Mich., 1985-87; exec. v.p. Mfrs. Bank, Lansing, 1987—; mem. bd. trustees, chmn. planning com., fin. and exec. coms. St. Lawrence Hosp., Lansing, 1986—. Bd. dirs. Impressions Five Mus. Sci., Lansing, 1987—. Mem. Robert Morris Assocs. (bd. dirs. Mich. chpt.). Lodge: Kiwanis (pres. Plymouth, Mich. chpt. 1983-84). Office: Mfrs Bank of Lansing 101 N Washington Lansing MI 48933

HORNIG, DONALD FREDERICK, scientist; b. Milw., Mar. 17, 1920; s. Chester Arthur and Emma (Knuth) H.; m. Lilli Schwenk, July 17, 1943; children: Joanna, Ellen, Christopher, Leslie. B.S., Harvard U., 1940, Ph.D., 1943; LL.D., Temple U., 1964, Boston Coll., 1966, Dartmouth Coll., 1974; D.H.L., Yeshiva U., 1965; D.Sc., U. Notre Dame, 1965, U. Md., 1965, Rensselaer Poly. Inst., 1965, Ripon Coll., 1966, Widener Coll., 1967, U. Wis., 1967, U. Puget Sound, 1968, Syracuse U., 1968, Princeton U., 1969, Seoul Nat. U., Korea, 1973, U. Pa., 1975, Lycoming Coll., 1980; D.Eng., Worcester Poly. Inst., 1967. Research asso. Woods Hole (Mass.) Oceanographic Instn., 1943-44; scientist, group leader Los Alamos Lab., 1944-46; asst. prof. chemistry Brown U., 1946-49, asso. prof., 1949-51, prof., 1951-57; dir. Metcalf Research Lab., 1949- 57, asso. dean grad. sch., 1952-53, acting dean, 1953-54; vis. prof. Princeton U., 1957, prof. chemistry, 1957-64, chmn. dept., 1958-64, Donner prof. sci., 1959-66; spl. asst. sci. and tech. to Pres. U.S., 1964-69; dir. Office Sci. and Tech., 1964-69; chmn. Fed. Council Sci. and Tech., 1964-69; v.p., dir. Eastman Kodak Co., 1969-70; prof. chemistry U. Rochester, 1969-70; pres. Brown U., Providence, 1970-76; hon. research asso. in applied physics Harvard U., 1976-77, prof. chemistry in pub. health, dir. Interdisciplinary Programs in Health, 1977—, Alfred North Whitehead prof. chemistry (public health), 1981—; pres. Radiation Instruments Co., 1946-48; bd. dirs. W.A. Benjamin, Inc., Upjohn Co., Westinghouse Electric Corp.; Mem. Pres.'s Sci. Adv. Com., 1960-69, chmn., 1964-69; chmn. Project Metcalf, Office of Naval Research, 1951-52; bd. dirs. Chem. Industry Inst. Tech., 1983—. Author articles sci. jours. Bd. overseers Harvard U., 1964-70; bd. dirs. Overseas Devel. Council, 1969-75; trustee George Eastman House, 1969-71, Manpower Inst., 1969-76; bd. dirs., treas. Overseas Devel. Network, 1984—. Decorated Disting. Civilian Service medal Korea; Guggenheim fellow, 1954-55; Fulbright fellow, 1954-55; recipient Charles Lathrop Parsons award Am. Chem. Soc., 1967, Engring. Centennial award, 1967, Mellon Inst. award, 1968. Fellow Am. Phys. Soc., Am. Acad. Arts and Scis.; mem. Nat. Acad. Scis., Am. Chem. Soc., AAAS, Am. Philos. Soc., Romanian Acad. (fgn.), Sigma Xi. Home: 16 Longfellow Pk Cambridge MA 02138 Office: Harvard U Sch Pub Health 665 Huntington Ave Boston MA 02115

HORNSTEIN, MARK, financial executive; b. N.Y.C., Dec. 7, 1947; s. Joseph and Anne (Fox) H.; BBA, Pace U., 1969; postgrad. N.Y.U., 1973. Staff acct. Peat, Marwick, Mitchell & Co., N.Y.C., 1969-70; sr. acct. Robert J. Cofini & Co., N.Y.C., 1972-74; asst. v.p. United Va. Factors Corp., N.Y.C., 1974-77; asst. v.p., adminstrv. head mortgage loan div. James Talcott, Inc., N.Y.C., 1977-78; v.p., dir. Talcott of P.R., Inc. and subs.; loan adminstrn. officer Aetna Bus. Credit, Inc., East Hartford, Conn., 1978-79; asst. v.p. A.J. Armstrong Co. Inc. (now Security Pacific Bus. Credit Inc.), N.Y.C., 1979-83; v.p. Leucadia Nat. Corp., N.Y.C., 1983—; treas. Am. Investment Co., St. Louis, 1984—; asst. v.p. Cardiff Equities Corp., La Jolla, Calif., 1984-86; v.p. Charter Nat. Life Ins. Co., St. Louis, 1985—, PHLCORP, Inc. (formerly Baldwin United Corp.), Phila., 1987—; sec. Bolivian Power Co., Ltd., Salt Lake City and LaPar, Bolivia, 1988—. Served with USNR, 1970-72. Home: 25 Sutton Pl S New York NY 10022 also: Killington Gateway Mendon VT 05701 Office: 315 Park Ave S New York NY 10010

HOROWITZ, BEN, medical center executive; b. Bklyn., Mar. 19, 1914; s. Saul and Sonia (Meringoff) H.; m. Beverly Lichtman, Feb. 14, 1952; children: Zacjary, Jody. BA, Bklyn. Coll., 1940; LLB, St. Lawrence U., 1935; postgrad. New Sch. Social Research, 1942. Bar: N.Y., 1941 Dir. N.Y. Fedn. Jewish Philanthropies, 1940-45; Eastern regional dir. City of Hope, 1945-50, nat. exec. sec., City of Hope Los Angeles, 1950-53, exec. dir., 1953-85, gen. v.p. of bd. dirs. City of Hope, 1985-87, pres., bd. dirs. City of Hope Nat. Med. Ctr., 1986-87; bd. dirs. Beckman Research Inst. City of Hope, 1980—. Mem. Gov.'s Task Force on Flood Relief, 1969-74. Bd. dirs., v.p. Hope for Hearing Found., UCLA, 1972—; bd. dirs. Forte Found., 1987—, Ch.-Temple Corp. for Homeless, 1988—. Recipient Spirit of Life award, 1970, Gallery of Achievement award, 1974, Profl. of Yr. award So. Calif. chpt. Nat. Soc. Fundraisers, 1977; Ben Horowitz chair in research established at City of Hope, 1981. Los Angeles City street named in his honor, 1986. Jewish (dir. temple 1964-67, 1986—). Home: 221 Conway Ave Los Angeles CA 90024 Office: City of Hope 208 W 8th St Los Angeles CA 90014

HOROWITZ, GEORGE C., controller; b. Bklyn., June 11, 1952; s. Max and Charlotte H. BA, NYU, 1974, MBA, 1975. Asst. controller Am. Sponge & Chamois Co., L.I., N.Y., 1975-77; inventory acct. Avon Products Inc., N.Y.C., 1977-78, sr. inventory acct., 1978-79, supr. gen. acctg., 1979-80, mgr. worldwide acct., 1980-84; mgr. corp. acctg. Tambrands Inc., Lake Success, N.Y., 1984-87; corp. controller Kentek Info. Systems Inc., Allendale, N.J., 1987—. Mem. Nat. Assn. Accts. Office: Kentek Info Systems Inc 6 Pearl Ct Allendale NY 07471

HOROWITZ, IRVING LOUIS, educator, publisher; b. N.Y.C., Sept. 25, 1929; s. Louis and Esther (Tepper) H.; m. Ruth Lenore Horowitz, 1950 (div. 1964); children: Carl Frederick, David Dennis; m. Mary Curtis Horowitz, 1979. B.S.S., CCNY, 1951; M.A., Columbia U., 1952; Ph.D., Buenos Aires (Argentina) U., 1957; postgrad. fellow, Brandeis U., 1958-59. Asst. prof. sociology Bard Coll., 1960; assoc. prof. social theory Buenos Aires U., 1955-58; chmn. dept. sociology Hobart and William Smith Colls., 1960-63; assoc. prof., then prof. sociology Washington U., St. Louis, 1963-69; chmn. dept. sociology Livingston Coll., Rutgers U., 1969-73; prof. sociology grad. faculty Rutgers U., 1969—, Hannah Arendt prof. social and polit. theory, 1979—; vis. prof. sociology U. Caracas, Venezuela, 1957, Buenos Aires U., 1959, 61, 63, SUNY, Buffalo, 1960, Syracuse U., 1961, U. Rochester, fall 1962, U. Calif., Davis, 1966, U. Wis., Madison, 1967, Stanford U., 1968-69, Am. U., 1972, Queen's U., Can., 1973, Princeton U., 1976; vis. lectr. London Sch. Econs. and Polit. Sci., 1962; Prin. investigator for numerous sci. and research projects. Author: Idea of War and Peace in Contemporary Philosophy, 1957, Philosophy, Science and the Sociology of Knowledge, 1960, Radicalism and the Revolt Against Reason: The Social Theories of Georges Sorel, 2d edit, 1968, The War Game; Studies of the New Civilian Militarists, 1963, Historia y Elementos de la Sociologia del Connocimento, 1963, Professing Sociology: The Life Cycle of a Social Science, 1963, The New Sociology: Essays in Social Science and Social Values in Honor of C. Wright Mills, 1964, Revolution in Brazil: Politics and Society in a Developing Nation, 1964, The Rise and Fall of Project Camelot, 1967, rev. edit., 1976, Three Worlds of Development: The Theory and Practice of International Stratification, 1966, rev. edit., 1972, Latin American Radicalism: A Documentary Report on Nationalist and Left Movements, 1969, Sociological Self-Images, 1969, The Knowledge Factory: Masses in Latin America, 1970, Cuban Communism, 1970, 6th edit., 1986, Foundations of Political Sociology, 1972, Social Science and Public Policy in the United States, 1975, Ideology and Utopia in the United States, 1977, Dialogues on American Politics, 1979, Taking Lives: Genocide and State Power, 1979, Beyond Empire and Revolution, 1982, C. Wright Mills: An American Utopian, 1983, Winners and Losers, 1985, Communicating Ideas, 1987; pres., editor-in-chief: Transaction/SOCIETY; pres. transaction books and periodicals. Fellow AAAS; mem. AAUP, USIA (bd. advisors), Am. Polit. Sci. Assn., Am. Sociol. Assn., Authors Guild, Center for Study The Presidency, Council Fgn. Relations, Internat. Studies Assn., Latin Am. Studies Assn., Internat. Soc. Polit. Psychology (founder), Council on Fgn. Relations, Soc. Internat. Devel., Soc. Study Social Problems (chmn. awards com. 1964-66). Assn. Am. Pubs. (exec. dir.), U.S. Gen. Acctg. Office (exec. adv. bd.). Home: Rt 206 1247 State Rd Blawenburg Rd/Rocky Hill Intersection Princeton NJ 08540 Office: Rutgers U Transaction Pubs Bldg #4051 New Brunswick NJ 08903

HORRELL, KAREN HOLLEY, insurance company executive; b. Augusta, Ga., July 10, 1952; d. Dudley Cornelius and Eleanor (Shouppe) Holley; m. Jack E. Horrell, Aug. 14, 1976. B.S., Berry Coll., 1974; J.D., Emory U., 1976. Bar: Ohio 1977, Ga. 1977. Corp. counsel Great Am. Ins. Co., Cin., 1977-80, v.p., gen. counsel, sec., 1981-85; sr. v.p., gen. counsel, sec. Great Am. Ins. Co., 1985—; counsel Am. Fin. Corp., 1980-81; gen. counsel numerous subsidiaries Great Ins. Co.; sec., asst. sec. numerous other fin. and ins. cos. Trustee Community Chest, 1987—; mem. cabinet City of Cin., 1984; bd. dirs. YWCA, 1984—, v.p. fin., 1986—. Mem. ABA, Ohio Bar Assn., Cin. Bar Assn. (admissions com. 1978—, nominating com. 1987—), Am. Corp. Counsel Assn. Democrat. Presbyterian. Home: 3733 Vineyard Pl Cincinnati OH 45226 Office: Great Am Ins Co 580 Walnut St Cincinnati OH 45202

HORRIGAN, EDWARD A., JR., food and consumer products company executive; b. N.Y.C., Sept. 23, 1929; s. Edward A. and Margaret V. (Kenny) H.; m. Elizabeth R. Herperger, June 27, 1953; children: Ellen, Christopher, Gordon, Brian. B.S. in Bus. Adminstrn, U. Conn., 1950; grad., Advanced Mgmt. Program, Harvard U., 1965. Mgr. sales Procter & Gamble Co., N.Y.C., 1954-58; gen. mgr. Ebonite Co., Boston, 1958-61; div. v.p. T.J. Lipton Inc., 1961-73; chmn. bd., pres. Buckingham Corp., N.Y.C., 1973-78; chmn. bd., chief exec. officer R.J. Reynolds Tobacco Internat., Inc., Winston-Salem, N.C., 1978-80; chmn. bd., pres., chief exec. officer R.J. Reynolds Tobacco Co., Winston-Salem, 1980-81, chmn., chief exec. officer, 1987—; exec. v.p. RJR Nabisco, Inc., 1981-84, pres., chief operating officer, 1984-85, vice chmn. bd., 1985—; chmn., chief exec. officer R.J. Reynolds Tobacco Co., 1987—. Served as officer, inf. U.S. Army, 1950-54. Decorated Silver Star, Purple Heart, Combat Inf. badge, Parachute badge. Mem. Knights of Malta. Clubs: Old Town Country, Vintage. Home: 2815 Bartram Rd Winston-Salem NC 27106 Office: R J Reynolds Tobacco Co 401 N Main St Winston-Salem NC 27102 *

HORSLEY, JACK EVERETT, lawyer, author; b. Sioux City, Iowa, Dec. 12, 1915; s. Charles E. and Edith V. (Timms) H.; m. Sallie Kelley, June 12, 1939 (dec.); children: Pamela, Charles Edward; m. Bertha J. Newland, Feb. 24, 1950 (dec.); m. Mary Jane Moran, Jan. 20, 1973; 1 child, Sharon. AB, U. Ill., 1937, JD, 1939. Bar: Ill. 1939. Ptnr. Craig & Craig, Mattoon, Ill., 1939—, sr. counsel, 1983—; vice-chmn. bd. dirs. Cen. Nat. Bank, 1976—, chmn. trust com., mem. exec. com., 1986—, Harlan Moore Heart Rsch. Found., 1968—; mem. lawyers adv. coun. U. Ill. Law Forum, 1960-63; lectr. Practising Law Inst., N.Y.C., 1967-73, U. Ill., Champaign, 1974, Ct. Practice Inst., Chgo., 1974—, Coll. Law Inst. Continuing Legal Edn. U. Mich., 1968; vis. lectr. Orange County (Fla.) Med. Soc., 1975, San Diego Med. Soc., 1970, U. S.C., 1976, Duquesne Coll., 1970; U. Ill. Law Forum, 1972; chmn. rev. com. Ill. Supreme Ct. Disciplinary Commn., 1973-76. Narrator: Poetry Interludes, Sta. WLBH-FM; author: Trial Lawyer's Manual, 1967, Voir Dire Examinations and Opening Statements, 1968, Current Development in Products Liability Law, 1969, Illinois Civil Practice and Procedure, 1970, The Medical Expert Witness, 1973, The Doctor and the Law, 1975, The Doctor and Family Law, 1975, The Doctor and Business Law, 1976, The Doctor and Medical Law, 1977, Testifying in Court, 1973, 2d edit., 1983, 3d edit., 1988, Anatomy of a Medical Malpractice Case, 1984; contbr. articles to profl. jours. including RN Mag. and Forensic Scis.; cons., contbr. Med. Econs., 1969—; legal cons. Mast-Head, 1972—, Contri., A.L.L. Life, Stafford, Va., 1988—. Pres. bd. edn. sch. dist. 100, 1946-48; bd. dirs. Harlan Moore Heart Rsch. Found., 1968—; vol. reader in recording texts Am. Assn. for Blind, 1970-72. Lt. col. U.S. Army, 1942-46. Fellow Am. Coll. Trial Lawyers; mem. ABA, Ill. Bar Assn. (exec. coun. ins. law 1961-63, lectr. law course for attys. 1962, 64-65, sr. counsellor, 1989—, Disting. Svc. award 1982-83), Coles-Cumberland Bar Assn. (v.p. 1968-69, pres. 1969-70, chmn. com. jud. inquiry 1976-80, chmn. meml. com. 1981—), Am. Arbitration Assn. (nat. panel arbitrators), U. Ill. Law Alumni Assn. (pres. 1966-67, Alumni of Month Sept. 1974), Ill. Def. Counsel Assn. (pres. 1967-68), Soc. Trial Lawyers (chmn. profl. activities 1960-61, bd. dirs. 1966-67), Adelphic Debating Soc., Assn. Ins. Attys., Internat. Assn. Ins. Counsel, Am. Judicature Soc., Appellate Lawyers Assn., Masons , Scribes, Delta Phi (exec. com. alumni assn. 1960-61, 67-68), Sigma Delta Kappa. Republican. Home: 50 Elm Ridge Mattoon IL 61938 Office: Craig & Craig 1807 Broadway PO Box 689 Mattoon IL 61938

HORSMAN, DAVID A. ELLIOTT, author, educator, financial services executive; b. Calvert County, Md., June 28, 1932; s. Alvin W. and Bessie L. (Elliott) H.; student U. Chgo.; B.A., San Francisco State U., 1964; M.A., N.Y. U., 1967, Ph.D., 1970, M.Div., Episcopal Div. Sch., 1984. Floor dir., stage mgr. WTOP-TV, Washington, 1959-61; TV writer/producer Insight, Nat. Council Chs., Washington, 1961-62; English master, dir. studies Searing Sch., N.Y.C., 1965-67; asst. prof. humanities Acad. Aeros., Flushing, N.Y., 1967-68; instr. humanities Rensselaer Poly. Inst., Troy, N.Y., 1969-70; asso. prof., founder and coordinator film sequence U. South Fla., Tampa, 1970-80; adj. prof. Union Grad. Sch., Yellow Springs, Ohio, 1976—; headmaster All Hallows Acad., Alexandria, Va., 1985-87; asst. mgr., sr. account exec. Blinder, Robinson and Co., Columbia, Md., 1987-88; pres. Elliott Horsman & Assocs., 1988-89; fin. cons. Shearson, Lehman, Hutton, Inc., 1989—. Served with U.S. Army, 1957-59. Recipient Founders Day award N.Y. U., 1971. Fellow Intercontinental Biog. Assn. (Cert. of Merit 1974); mem. MLA, Nat. Soc. Hist. Preservation, Univ. Film Assn., Am. Film Inst., Internat. Platform Assn., Soc. Edn. in Film and TV, Alcuin Club. Episcopalian. Author: The Liturgy as Communication, 1970; (novel and screenplay) Pilgrims on Strange Strands, 1979; Introduction to Structural Description of Liturgical Dromena, 1979. Office: PO Box 1682 Baltimore MD 21203

HORSMAN, NANCY JANE, real estate company official; b. Louisville, Aug. 31, 1938; d. Edwin A. and Arnella (Kendall) Lyskowinski; m. David C. Horsman, Mar. 9, 1960 (div. 1978); 1 child, Kathryn Elizabeth Copeland. BS, Ball State U., 1962. Cert. English tchr., Inc. Tchr. Perry Twp. High Sch., Southport, Ind., 1962-64, Ctr. Grove High Sch., Greenwood, Ind., 1964-69; saleswoman Kettler Bros. Inc., Gaithersburg, Md., 1971-78, Washington, 1984—; saleswoman U.S. Homes Corp., N. Bethesda, Md., 1978-82, Milton Co., Fairfax County, Va., 1983-84. Mem. Nat. Assn. Homebuilders (Million Dollar club). Democrat. Methodist. Home: 10625 Muirfield Dr Potomac MD 20854 Office: Kettler Bros Inc Stewartown Rd Gaithersburg MD 20879

HORST, DAVID LESTER, publishing executive; b. Hummelstown, Pa., Oct. 21, 1939; s. David L. and Puline Louise (Ricker) H.; m. Judith Lorene Wetzed, June 9, 1967. BS in Edn., Shippensburg U., 1961; LLB, LaSalle U., 1974; MA in Edn., Pa. State U., 1976. Tchr. Conewago Valley Sch. Dist., New Oxford, Pa., 1961-62; tchr., dept. chmn. Derry Twp. Sch. Dist., Hershey, Pa., 1962-77; tng. and communications adminstr. Lebanon (Pa.) Steel Foundry, 1977-81; personnel adminstr. Lebanon (Pa.) Steel Foundry, 1979-81; mgr. employee relations Sci. Press, Ephrata, Pa., 1981-84, pres., gen. mgr., 1984—; bd. dirs. Nat. Assn. Printers. Lithographers, Teaneck N.J., Graphic Arts Tech. Found., Pitts. Mem. council Mt. Gretna (Pa.) Borough, 1975-82, Palmyra (Pa.) Borough, 1987. Mem. Graphic Arts Assn., Soc. Am. Valve Engrs., Hamilton Club, Masons, Shriners. Republican. Methodist. Office: Sci Press 300 W Chestnut St Ephrata PA 17522

HORTILLOSA, RAUL PAMPLONA, financial and accounting executive; b. Iloilo City, Philippines, Jan. 3, 1941; came to Guam, 1967; s. Heracleo Bayona and Rosalina (Pamplona) H.; m. Erlinda Geraldo, Dec. 9, 1972; children: Ronald, Rodney, Leia. Student, Divine Word U., Tacloban, Philippines, 1961-65; BS in Commerce, U. Iloilo, 1971. Cert. fin. planner. Bookkeeper Commd. Officers' Mess, Agana, Guam, 1967-69, fiscal acctg. supr., 1969-74; acctg. supr., mgr. Common Support Service Office NAS, Agana, 1974—; sole practice acctg. and bookkeeping Agana, 1979—; agt. Comml Bankers Life Ins. Co., Agana, 1980-85; regional mgr. A. L. Williams Inc., Agana, 1985—; registered rep. 1st Am. Nat. Securities Inc., Duluth, Ga., 1987—; tax preparer H&R Block, Agana, 1983-84. Treas. Baroctac Nuevo, Iloilo Families Assn. Guam, Agana, 1986—, SVS PTA, Barrigada, Guam, 1987—. Mem. Inst. Cert. Fin. Planners. Roman Catholic. Home: PO Box 21606 GMF Agana GU 96921 Office: AL Williams Inc Tumon Guam Agana GU 96911

HORTON, ALDEN, III, communications executive; b. Bennington, Vt., Aug. 11, 1960; s. Alden Jr. and Elizabeth Mansur (Davis) H.; m. Janet Andrews, June 20, 1987. BA, Bowdoin Coll., 1982. Account exec. Bride Broadcasting, Portland, Maine, 1982-84; gen. sales mgr. Porter Broadcasting, Bath, Maine, 1984; v.p., dir. sales Rebs, Inc., Nashville, 1984-88; gen. sales mgr. GMX Communications, Inc., Nashville, 1988—. Democrat. Home: 2113 Ashwood Ave Nashville TN 37212 Office: Sta WRLT Radio 215 Canterview Dr #351 Brentwood TN 37027

HORTON, FINIS GENE, bank auditor; b. Batesville, Ark., Jan. 3, 1953; s. Allie George and Zelda (Brooks) H. BA, Ark. Coll., 1974; postgrad., Ark. State U., 1974-75, U. Cen. Ark., 1976. Asst. v.p., cost mgr. Worthen Bank, Little Rock, 1975-81; controller First Fed. Bank of Morrilton, Ark., 1981-82; auditor Superior Fed. Bank, Little Rock, 1982—, Ft. Smith, Ark., 1988—; bd. dirs. WRV Constrn. Co., Jacksonville, Ark. Mem. Inst. Internal Auditors, Assn. MBA Execs. Lodge: Kiwanis (pres. Little Rock chpt., 1978-79, bd. dirs. 1979-81). Home: 5 Palmer Dr Conway AR 72032 Office: Superior Fed Bank FSB 5000 Rogers Ave Fort Smith AR 72903

HORTON, GARY BRUCE, transportation company executive; b. Vallejo, Calif., Aug. 27, 1943; s. John Vernon and Della Leona (Shock) H.; m. Janice DeLoach, Oct. 31, 1987; children: Cody Jacob, Dillon Edward, Rocky. Student, Ea. Ariz. Coll., 1964-65, Ariz. State U., 1965-68. Cost acct. Motorola, Inc., Mesa, Ariz., 1968-69; acct. supr. Arcoa, Phoenix, 1969-70, fin. acctg. mgr., 1970-77; fin. mgr. U-Haul Internat., Phoenix, 1977-82; v.p. fin. U-Haul Internat., 1987—; treas. AMERCO-U-Haul Internat., Phoenix, 1982—; asst. treas. U-Haul Can., Ltd., Burlington, Ont., 1982—; pres., dir. U-Haul Credit Corp., 1984—; bd. dirs. Amerco Lease, Las Vegas, Nationwide Comml. Co., Phoenix. Republican. Lutheran. Home: 5227 W Freeway Ln Glendale AZ 85302 Office: Amerco U-Haul Internat PO Box 21502 Phoenix AZ 85036

HORTON, MADELINE MARY, financial executive, consultant, financial and estate planner; b. Chgo., Mar. 1, 1939; d. James P. and Priscilla Mary (Caruso) Fiduccia; m. Richard J. Dickman, July 7, 1962 (div. 1981); children: James Earl, Suzanne Dickman Noel; m. Larry B. Horton, June 30, 1984; stepchildren: Michele Rene, Margot Lyn Parsons. BA in Math. cum laude, Rosary Coll., River Forest, Ill., 1960; MS in Math., U. Miami, Coral Gables, Fla., 1962; postgrad., U. Va., 1974-78. Instr. in math. U. Miami, Coral Gables, 1962-63; prin. Dickman Deductions, Charlottesville, Va., 1974-77; instr. devel. math. Piedmont Community Coll., Charlottesville, Va., 1974-78; health affairs planner U. Va. Med. Ctr., Charlottesville, 1978-80; zone mgr. Investors Diversified Svcs., Inc., Charlottesville, 1980-83; fin. cons. Merrill Lynch, Charlottesville, 1983-86; mgr., fin. cons. Prudential-Bache Securities, Inc., Charlottesville, 1986-87; investment broker Wheat First Securities Inc., Charlottesville, 1987; pres., fin. cons., co-founder Horton Fin. Svcs. Inc., Charlottesville, 1987—. Humor columnist Charlottesville Daily Progress, 1971; featured in article Va. Bus. jour., 1988. Mem. Internat. Mgmt. Coun. (sec. Charlottesville chpt. 1986-88, v.p. 1988-89). Republican. Roman Catholic. Home: 3866 Lake Park Rd Earlysville VA 22936 Office: Horton Fin Svcs Inc One Morton Dr Ste 100 Charlottesville VA 22901

HORTON, PAUL BRADFIELD, lawyer; b. Dallas, Oct. 19, 1920; s. Frank Barrett and Hazel Lillian (Bradfield) H.; m. Susan Jeanne Diggle, May 19, 1949; children: Bradfield Ragland, Bruce Ragsdale. B.A., U. Tex., Austin, 1943, student Law Sch., 1941-43; LL.B., So. Methodist U., 1947. Bar: Tex. 1946. Ptnr. McCall, Parkhurst & Horton, Dallas, 1951—; lectr. mcpl. bond law and pub. finance S.W. Legal Found.; drafter Tex. mcpl. bonds legislation, 1963—. Mem. Gov.'s Com. Tex. Edn. Code, 1967-69. Served to lt. USNR, 1943-46. Mem. Am., Dallas bar assns., Nat. Water Resources Assn., Tex. Water Conservation Assn., Govt. Finance Officers Assn., The Barristers, Delta Theta Phi, Beta Theta Pi. Clubs: Dallas Country, Crescent, Tower, 2001 (Dallas). Home: 5039 Seneca Dr Dallas TX 75209 Office: McCall Parkhurst & Horton 717 N Harwood St Ste 900 Dallas TX 75201

HORTON, ROBERT BAYNES, petroleum company executive; b. Bushey, Eng., Aug. 18, 1939; s. William H. Horton and Dorothy Joan (Baynes) Dunn; m. Sally Doreen Wells, July 28, 1962; children: Simon, Ruth. BSME, U. St. Andrews, Scotland, 1960; MS, MIT, 1971. With Brit. Petroleum Ltd. (now BP plc), London, 1957—; gen. mgr. BP Tankers, London, 1975-76, gen. mgr. corp. planning, 1976-79; mng. dir. BP Co. plc, 1983-86, 1988—; vice chmn., chief exec. officer BP Am. Inc., 1987-88; chmn., chief exec. officer Standard Oil Co., Cleve., 1986-88, also bd. dirs.; dep. chmn. British Petroleum Co., 1989; bd. dirs. API, Nat. City Corp., Emerson Electric Co. Trustee Case Western Res. U., Cleve.; mem. Com. for Econ. Devel., MIT Corp. Fellow Royal Soc. Arts; mem. Nat. Petroleum Council, Chem. Industries Assn. (pres. 1982-84), Bus. Roundtable, British Inst. Mgmt. (companion, vice chmn. 1984—), Musical Arts Assn. (trustee), Univ. Circle Inc. (trustee). Anglican. Clubs: Carlton (London); Leander (Henley, Eng.); Union, Pepper Pike (Cleve.). Office: Brit Petroleum Co Ltd, Britannic House, Moor Ln, London EC24 9BU, England other: BP Am Inc 200 Public Sq Cleveland OH 44114 *

HORTON, THOMAS R., association executive; b. Fort Pierce, Fla., Nov. 17, 1926; s. Charles Montraville Horton and Ruby Mae (Swain) Warren; m. Marilou Deeming, Dec. 19, 1947; children—Susan, Jean, Marilyn. B.S., Stetson U., 1949, L.H.D. (hon.), 1982; M.S., U. Fla., 1950, Ph.D., 1954; LL.D. (hon.), Pace U., 1976; D.Litt. (hon.), U. Charleston, 1980. Instr., asst. headmaster Bolles Sch., Jacksonville, Fla., 1950-52; with IBM Corp., Armonk, N.Y., 1954-82; v.p. data processing div. IBM Corp., Armonk, 1966-67, dir. univ. relations, 1968-82; pres., chief exec. officer Am. Mgmt. Assn., N.Y.C., 1982—; dir. Perrigo Co., Allegan, Mich., Charlesbridge Pub., Watertown, Mass. Author: What Works for Me, 1986; editor: Traffic Control--Theory and Implementation, 1965; columnist Mgmt. Rev., 1982—. Mem. adv. bd. Salvation Army, White Plains, N.Y. and N.Y.C., 1968—; trustee Bethune-Cookman Coll., Daytona Beach, Fla., 1971-82, hon., 1982—; trustee Pace U., N.Y.C., 1975—, Am. Grad. Sch. Internat. Mgmt., Glendale, Ariz., 1982—. Served with U.S. Army, 1944-46, ETO. Fellow Internat. Acad. Mgmt. (vice chancellor); mem. European Found. for Mgmt. Devel., Japan Mgmt. Assn. (hon.), Korean Mgmt. Assn. (hon.), Pres'. Assn. N.Y.C. (chmn. 1982—), Mgmt. Exec. Soc., The Conf. Bd. (sr.), Westchester Country Club, University Club, Army and Navy Club, Commonwealth of Calif. Club, DeLand Country Club. Mem. United Ch. of Christ. Office: Am Mgmt Assn 135 W 50th St New York NY 10020

HORVATH, MARGARET MARY, insurance agency executive; b. New Haven, Aug. 13, 1935; d. Joseph and Irma Elizabeth (Szabo) H. Student, Quinnipiac Coll., 1963-65. CPCU; cert. profl. ins. counselor, Conn. Sec. to office mgr. Podoloff Ins. Agy., New Haven, 1953-67; mgr. Jos. Golden Ins. Agy., Inc., New Haven, 1967—; pres. Wm. H. Hull Agy., Inc., West Haven, Conn., 1986—; speaker various ins. convs. throughout country; liaison mem. Ins. Inst. Rsch./ACORD, 1977-86. Contbr. articles to ins. trade publs. Former treas. New Haven Assn. Retarded Citizens; mem. ins. adv. com. on med. malpractice study HEW, 1971-72. Mem. Nat. Assn. Ins. Women (nat. pres. 1969-70), New Haven Assn. Ins. Women (pres. 1962-63, 81-82), Profl. Secs. Assn. (pres. Quinnipiac chpt. 1966-67, 80-81), Profl. Ins. Agts. (bd. dirs. Conn. 1972-81, Woman of Yr. 1979), CPCU (pres. So. Conn. chpt. 1985-86), Woodbridge County Club (sec. 1983—, sec. bd. govs. 1984—, entertainment chmn. 1986-88). Office: Joseph Golden Ins Agy 23 Maiden Ln North Haven CT 06473

HORVATH, RONALD FRANK, financial executive; b. Bethlehem, Pa., Aug. 18, 1950; s. Frank Louis and Theresa (Shelanick) H.; m. Denise Kathleen Bugger, July 28, 1973 (div. 1976); m. Donna Grace Iobst, Feb. 25, 1978. BA in Math. and Urban Studies, Lehigh U., 1972. Cert. fin. planner. Asst. planner Lehigh U., Bethlehem, 1972-74; jr. planner City of Bethlehem, 1974-80, grant adminstr., 1980-86; owner, prin. R. Horvath and Assocs., Allentown, Pa., 1980—; fin. planner Boyer Fin. Group, Allentown, 1986—; tax preparer H&R Block, Bethlehem, 1976-78. Officer Community Action Com. Lehigh Valley, Bethlehem, 1975-86, Southside '76 Housing Devel. Corp., Bethlehem, 1980-86; sec. Friends of Bethlehem Area Pub. Library, 1984—; bd. dirs. Bethlehem Area Sr. Citizens Council, 1987—. Mem. Northeastern Pa. Soc. Inst. Cert. Fin. Planners (pres. 1986-87, chmn. 1987—), Bethlehem Area Jaycees. Democrat. Home: 822 Prospect Ave Bethlehem PA 18018 Office: Boyer Fin Group 1259 S Cedar Crest Blvd Allentown PA 18103

HORVITZ, HARRY RICHARD, newspaper publisher, cable television company executive; b. Elyria, Ohio, Mar. 14, 1920; s. Samuel Aaron and Harriet (Mendelson) H.; m. Lois Unger, Dec. 9, 1947; children: Michael, Pam Horvitz Schneider, Peter. BS in Econs., U. Pa., 1942; LittD (hon.), Siena Coll., 1985. Pub., pres. Mansfield Jour. Co., Valley View, Ohio, 1956—; pres. Multi-Channel TV Cable Co., Valley View, 1965—; bd. dirs. First Buckeye Bank, Mansfield, Ohio. Pres. Soc. Crippled Children, Cleve., 1981-84; trustee Mt. Sinai Hosp., Cleve., 1976-85. Served to lt. USN, 1942-46, PTO. Mem. Soc. Profl. Journalists. Jewish. Clubs: Oakwood (Cleve.); Vintage (Indian Wells, Calif.). Home: 16700 Parkland Dr Shaker Heights OH 44120 Office: 25201 Chagrin Blvd Ste 170 Beachwood OH 44122

HORWITZ, ALLAN BARRY, publisher, franchiser; b. Bklyn., July 10, 1947; s. Gerard and Rhoda Horwitz; m. Elizabeth Ruth Farkas, June 22, 1975; children: Aaron, Robert, Tara, Blake. BA, U. Hartford, 1969; postgrad., Coll. William and Mary, 1970, The New Sch. for Social Research, 1973. Account exec. Wall Street Jour., N.Y.C., 1970-72, sales strategy planner, 1972-74; acquisitions and new bus. ventures analyst Dow Jones & Co., Inc., N.Y.C., 1974-76; pub. TV News, N.Y.C., 1973—; chmn., chief exec. officer Modular Publs., Inc., N.Y.C., 1974—, also bd. dirs.; pres., chmn., bd. dirs. Community Publs. of Am., Inc., N.Y.C., 1979—. Served on Blue Ribbon Panel of Judges Emmy Awards, 1987, 88, 89. Mem. Nat. Acad. TV Arts and Scis., Assn. Free Community Papers, Consumers Union, TV Critics Assn. Democrat. Jewish. Office: Community Publs of Am Inc 80 Eighth Ave New York NY 10011

HORWITZ, DONALD PAUL, restaurant chain executive; b. Chgo., Feb. 5, 1936; s. Theodore J. and Lillian H. (Shlensky) H.; m. Judith Robin, Aug. 23, 1964; children—Terry Robin, Linda Diane, Gail Elizabeth. BS, Northwestern U., 1957; JD, Yale U., 1960. Bar: Ill. bar 1961, D.C. bar 1961, U.S. Supreme Ct 1966; C.P.A., Ill. With atty. gen.'s honors program Dept. Justice, 1961-63; atty. firm Gottlieb & Schwartz, Chgo., 1963-66; with Arthur Young & Co. (C.P.A.'s), Chgo., 1966-72; ptnr. Arthur Young & Co. (C.P.A.'s), 1971-72; exec. v.p., sec., dir. McDonald's Corp., Oak Brook, Ill., 1972—; lectr. Grad. Sch. Commerce, DePaul U., Chgo. Contbr. articles to profl. jours. Mem. Ctr. for Excellence in Govt.; mem. caucus nominating com. Village of Glencoe, Ill., 1975-78, vice chmn., 1988—; bd. dirs. Chgo. Med. Sch./U. Health Scis., 1984-88; bd. dirs., chmn. bd. Highland Park Hosp., Lakeland Health; chmn. bd., hon. trustee St. Augustine Coll., Chgo. Mem. Am. Bar Assn., Ill. Bar Assn., Chgo. Bar Assn., Am. Inst. CPA's, Ill. Soc. CPA's. Club: Northmoor Country. Office: McDonald's Corp 1 McDonald's Pla Oak Brook IL 60521

HORWITZ, MURRAY LEE, data processing executive; b. Chgo., Dec. 17, 1957; s. David L. and Dolores R. (Krandel) H.; m. Patricia C. Kowalski, Nov. 1, 1986. BS in acctg., U. Ill., 1980; MBA, Loyola U., Chgo., 1981. CPA, Ill.; Cert. Prodn. and Inventory Mgr. Mgmt. cons. Arthur Andersen & Co., Chgo., 1981-84, Beatrice Foods, Chgo., 1984-85; mgmt. info. systems dir. Coleman Cable Systems Inc., North Chicago, Ill., 1985—. Mem. Ill CPA Soc., Am. Prodn. and Inventory Control Soc. Home: 15463 W Fairlane Libertyville IL 60048

HOSBACH, HOWARD DANIEL, publishing company executive; b. North Bergen, N.J., Mar. 9, 1931; s. Howard D. and Marjorie V. (Hoffer) H.; m. Eugenia Elizabeth Paracka, Apr. 10, 1954; children: Susan Hosbach Murray, Cynthia Hosbach Miezeiewski, Beth Ann, Alyssa. BS, Fairleigh Dickinson U., 1953, MBA, 1967. Advt. mgr. McGraw-Hill Book Co., N.Y.C., 1958-62; dir. mktg. McGraw-Hill Book Co., 1962-66, gen. mgr. dealer and library sales, 1966-69; group v.p. Standard & Poor's Corp., N.Y.C., 1970-73; exec. v.p., chief operating officer Standard & Poor's Corp., 1973-80, pres., chief exec. officer, 1981-84, chmn., chief exec. officer, 1985-88; exec. v.p. ops. McGraw-Hill, Inc., 1985-88; bd. dirs. Interlake Corp., Chgo., Harbinger Corp., Teaneck, N.J. Trustee Fairleigh Dickinson U., Peirce Jr. Coll.; mem. Governing Bds. of Univs. and Colls., 1983—. With AUS, 1953-55. Recipient Alumni medal for disting. service Fairleigh Dickinson U. Mem. Pinnacle Soc. Roman Catholic. Home: 104 Green Way Allendale NJ 07401

HOSIE, STANLEY WILLIAM, foundation executive, writer; b. Lismore, New South Wales, Australia, Apr. 28, 1922; came to U.S., 1945; s. Stanley James and Catherine Clare (Chisholm) H. BA, U. Queensland, Brisbane, Australia, 1945; Lic. in Theology, Cath. U., Washington, 1947, MA, 1948. Dean of studies Marist Coll., Lismore, 1949-57; pres., founder Chanel Coll., Geelong, Victoria, Australia, 1958-62; writer-in-residence Casa Generalitia Societatis Mariae, Rome, 1963-66; exec. dir. The Found. for the Peoples of the South Pacific, Inc., N.Y.C., 1966—; theologian for Conf. of Pacific Cath. Bishops, 2d Vatican Council, Rome, 1963-65; dir. Am. Council of Vol. Agys., N.Y.C., 1976—, treas. 1983-84; dir. Pvt. Agys. Collaborating Together, 1977—; mem. Presdl. Adv. Com. on Vol. Aid, 1988—. Author: The Swiss Conspiracy, 1976, The Boomerang Conspiracy, 1978, (biography) Anonymous Apostle, 1966, also numerous screenplays. Recipient Best Article Vatican II award Nat. Cath. Periodicals Assn., 1964. Mem. Writers Guild Am. East, Soc. des Oceanistes, Australian Coll. Edn. Democrat. Roman Catholic. Home: 720 Palisades Beach Rd Santa Monica CA 90402 Office: Found for Peoples South Pacific 3200 Wilshire Blvd 14th Floor Los Angeles CA 90010

HOSKINS, W. LEE, banker; b. Los Angeles, Feb. 7, 1941; s. E. W. and Mary E. (Taylor) H.; m. Gail Entrekin, Oct. 23, 1964. B.A. in Econs., UCLA, 1962, M.A., 1964, Ph.D. in Econs., 1969. With Fed. Res. Bank Phila., 1969-80, research officer, economist, 1972-73, v.p., dir. econ. research, 1973-80; sr. v.p., chief economist PNC Fin. Corp. and Pitts. Nat. Bank, 1980-87; pres. Fed. Res. Bank, Cleveland, 1987—. Contbr. articles to profl. and bus. publs. Trustee Cleve. Tomorrow, Greater Cleve. Roundtable; mem. Com. on Fgn. Rels., Cleve. Com. on World Affairs. Mem. Nat. Assn. Bus. Economists (past pres.), Am. Bankers Assn. (past mem. econ. adv. com.), Union Club, Duquesne Club. Office: Fed Res Bank Cleve 1455 E Sixth St Cleveland OH 44114

HOSKINS, WILLIAM KELLER, pharmaceutical company executive, lawyer; b. Cin., Feb. 22, 1935; s. John Hobart and Gertrude Louise (Keller) H.; m. Elizabeth Ann Grimm, Aug. 5, 1961; children: Bruce, Andrew, John, Elizabeth, Allison. BA, Yale U., 1956; LLB, Harvard U., 1962. Bar: Ohio 1962, U.S. Dist. Ct. (so. dist.) Ohio 1963, U.S. Tax Ct. 1963, U.S. Ct. Appeals (6th cir.) 1964, N.Y. 1982, Mo. 1983. Assoc., Frost & Jacobs, Cin., 1962-68; gen. counsel Drackett Co., Cin., 1968-71, v.p., gen. counsel, 1971-81; assoc. gen. counsel Bristol Myers Co., N.Y.C., 1981, spl. counsel, 1982; v.p., gen. counsel, sec. Marion Labs., Kansas City, Mo., 1982—, also bd. dirs.; chmn. household div. Soap and Detergent Assn., N.Y.C., 1978-79; chmn. Chem. Spltys. Mfg. Assn., Washington, 1982. Mem. Hamilton County Republican Central Com., Ohio, 1970-81; sec.-treas. Marion Labs. Polit. Action Com., 1982—; sec.-treas. polit. action com. Mid-Am. Com. Sound Govt., Lake Quivira, Kans., 1982-86. Served to lt. (j.g.) USN, 1956-59. Mem. ABA, Mo. Bar Assn., Ohio Bar Assn., Cin. Bar Assn., Lawyers Assn. of Kansas City. Republican. Roman Catholic. Home: 1101A W 47th St Kansas City MO 64112 Office: Marion Labs Inc 9300 Ward Pkwy Kansas City MO 64114

HOSSFELD, WALTER EDWARD, JR., insurance company executive; b. Seattle, June 30, 1932; s. Walter Edward and Ruth Dagney (Peterson) H.; m. Jean Marilyn Rue, Mar. 17, 1955; children: Kimberly, Karin, Kristen, Karla. BA, U. Wash., 1954. CLU. Agt. N.Y. Life Ins. Co., Seattle, 1954-56, asst. mgr., 1956-60, regional supt., 1964-69, regional v.p., 1972-82; gen. mgr. N.Y. Life Ins. Co., Anchorage, 1960-64; dir. agys. N.Y. Life Ins. Co., N.Y.C., 1969-72; pres. Can. ops. N.Y. Life Ins. Co., Toronto, Ont., 1982—; pres., bd. dirs. N.Y. Life Can. Ltd., Toronto, 1987—, N.Y. Life Fund Mgmt. Ltd., Toronto, 1987—, N.Y. Life Ins. Co. Can., Toronto, 1984—; mem. Toronto Bd. Trade, 1982. Mem. Am. Coll. Life Underwriters (Toronto chpt.), Can. Life and Health Ins. Assn. (bd. dirs. 1986). Club: Toronto. Home: 65 Harbour Sq, Ste 1408, Toronto, ON Canada M5J 2L4 Office: NY Life Ins Co, 121 Bloor St E, Toronto, ON Canada M4W 3N2

HOSTER, WILLIAM HENRY, JR., steel company executive; b. Chillicothe, Ill., Nov. 13, 1912; s. William Henry and Gertrude (Schuenemann) H.; m. Eleanor M. Tersip, Dec. 7, 1935; children—William Henry (dec.), Jeffrey Vernon, Karen Barbara, Bruce Richard. Ph.B., U. Chgo., 1933. Pres., Star Mfg. Co., Oklahoma City, 1945-50; pres., chmn. bd. Okla. Steel Corp., Oklahoma City, 1951-66, Kans. Steel Corp., Wichita, 1958-66, Confederate Steel Corp., Houston, 1959-66, Little Rock, 1962-66, Columbia Steel Co., Magnolia, Ark., 1962-66, Magnolia Steel Corp., Stamps, Ark., 1963-66; farmer, rancher, Yukon, Okla., 1966-73; v.p., gen. mgr. Lofland Steel Mill, Inc., Oklahoma City, 1973-77; pres. Okla. Steel Mill, Oklahoma City, 1977-82, Comml. Steel Mill Corp., Glassport, Pa., 1984-87. Bd. dirs. Tulsa REBAR, Inc., Hoster Steel Co. Mem. Concrete Reinforcing Steel Inst., Am. Forestry Assn., ASTM, Assn. Iron & Steel Engrs., Smithsonian Inst., Nat. Audubon Soc., Nat. Wilderness Soc., Consumers Union, Confederate Air Force, Nat. Hist. Preservation Soc., Aircraft Owners and Pilots Assn., Oklahoma City C. of C. Clubs: Oklahoma City Golf and Country; Petroleum, International, Cork (Houston). Lodge: Rotary.

HOTCHKISS, HENRY WASHINGTON, banker; b. Meshed, Iran, Oct. 31, 1937; s. Henry and Mary Bell (Clark) H. BA, Bowdoin Coll., 1958. French tchr. Choate Sch., Wallingford, Conn., 1959-62; v.p. Chem. Bank, N.Y.C., 1962-80, v.p. Chem. Bank Internat. San Francisco, 1973-80; dir. corp. rels., mgr. Crédit Suisse, San Francisco, 1980-87; dir. Indonesia-U.S. Bus. Seminar, Los Angeles, 1979. Assoc. bd. regents L.I. Coll. Hosp., 1969-71, pres., 1971, bd. regents, 1971-73, pres., bd. dirs. Gordonstown Am. Found, 1986—. Capt. USAR, 1958-69. Mem. Explorers Club (treas. North Calif. chpt. 1984-86), Calif. Council Internat. Trade (dir. 1976-87, chmn. membership com. 1977-79, treas. 1978-79), New Eng. Soc. in City Bklyn. (v.p., dir. 1968-73). Clubs: Heights Casino (bd. govs. 1971-73) (Bklyn.); St. Francis Yacht (San Francisco), Internat. Folkboat Assn. San Francisco (cruise chmn. 1976-77, pres. 1977-79, membership chmn. 1979-84, historian 1984-86). Home: 1206 Leavenworth St San Francisco CA 94109

HOTTENSTEIN, EVELYN JEANETTE KENNY, communications executive; b. Glasgow, Mont., Mar. 4, 1948; d. Daniel Patrick and Miriam (Phelan) Kenny; m. Glenn Hottenstein, 1969 (div.); children: Erin, Kimberly. BA, Carroll Coll., 1970-72. Cert. tchr. English tchr. Mont. State Sch. for Girls, Helena, 1970-72; exec. dir. Camp Fire Council, Helena, 1972-73; mgr. exec. orientation program Camp Fire, Inc., Englewood, Colo., 1974-76; owner, mgr. H&G Devel Co., Cheyenne, Wyo., 1976-78; owner Lifework Assocs., Denver, 1978—; prin. Pub. Speaking for the Profl., Denver, 1979—, pres., 1979—; pres. The Ctr. for Intercultural Communication, Denver, 1987—; pub. speaker, instr. U. Colo., Denver, 1982—. cons. Assn. for Vol. Adminstrn.; mem. Gov.'s Commn. on Status of Women, Mont., 1973-79; bd. dirs. Unitarian Universalist service com. Mem. Am. Soc. Tng. and Devel. (career devel. tng. group), Nat. Assn. Women Bus. Owners, Nat. Speakers Assn. Office: Pub Speaking for Profl 1776 Lincoln #614 Denver CO 80203

HOTZ, ROBERT HENRY, investment banking executive; b. Hackensack, N.J., June 11, 1944; s. Kenneth John and Lucille Marie (Levitzki) H.; m. Dorothy Alice Leiding, Dec. 1966; children—Robert, Bradford, Jonathan, Jeffrey, Kimberly. BA, Rutgers U., 1966; MBA, Cornell U., 1968. Assoc. Smith Barney, N.Y.C., 1968-70, officer, 1971-75, 1st v.p., 1976-80, sr. v.p., 1981-84, exec. v.p., 1985-88, sr. exec. v.p., 1988—; bd. dirs. Smith Barney Harris Upham, Smith Barney, Inc., mem. exec. com., 1989—. Bd. regents Georgetown Univ. Mem. N.Y.U. Jour. Venturing, Am. Stock Exchange (firm adv. com.). Office: Smith Barney Harris Upham & Co Inc 1345 Ave of the Americas New York NY 10105

HOUCK, LEWIS DANIEL, JR., management consultant; b. Cleve., July 9, 1932; s. Lewis Daniel and Mary Clark (Dowds) H.; A.B., Princeton U., 1955; M.B.A. with distinction, N.Y. U., 1964, Ph.D., 1971; m. Ellen Dorothy Thayer, Sept. 8, 1962 (div. 1975); children—Marianne Jennifer, Leland Daniel. Mgr. spl. research Young & Rubicam, Inc., N.Y.C., 1957-59; mktg. mgr. Selling Research, Inc., N.Y.C., 1959-62; ednl. projects mgr. Nat. Assn. Accts., N.Y.C., 1969-71; spl. cons. U.S. Dept. Agr., Washington, 1971-73; project leader nat. econ. analysis div. Econ. Research Service, 1973-79; pres. Houck Mktg. and Mgmt. Cons., Inc., 1979-85; pres. Houck & Assocs. Inc., Kensington, Md., 1986—; instr. N.Y.U. Grad. Sch. Bus. Adminstrn., 1966-69; trustee World U., 1982—, v.p., 1983—. Served as 1st lt., AUS, 1955-56. Recipient Founders Day award N.Y.U. Grad. Sch. Bus. Adminstrn., 1971. Ford Found. fellow, 1964-66. Fellow Am. Biog. Inst. (Medal of Honor 1986), Internat. Biog. Assn. (hon. editorial adv. bd. 1981—); mem. Am. Acctg. Assn., Am. Econ. Assn., AIM, Am. Mktg. Assn., Am. Statis. Assn., AAAS, Acad. Polit. Sci., Am. Acad. Polit. and Social Sci., Internat. Platform Assn., Ind. Cons. Am., Internat. Council Small Bus. Episcopalian. Club: Princeton (Washington). Author: A Practical Guide to Budgetary and Management Control Systems, 1979. Home: 11111 Woodson Ave Kensington MD 20895 Office: Houck & Assocs Inc PO Box 356 Kensington MD 20895

HOUGEN, EVERETT DOUGLAS, tool manufacturing company executive; b. Sceptre, SK, Canada, July 7, 1916; came to U.S. 1936; s. Louis Oscar and Corinna (Brillon) H.; m. Therese Yvonne Perrault, July 5, 1941; children: Douglas, Victor, Randall, Bradley. Student Dominion Bus. Coll., Winnipeg, Canada; apprenticeship Gen. Motors Inst., Fint, Mich. Quality control bd. Curtis Wright, Clifton, N.J., 1942-45; managed body shop Kaiser-Frazier, Paterson, N.J., 1946-48; instr. Gen. Motors Inst., Flint, Mich., 1948-58, also pres.'s council; pres. Hougen Mfg. of Flint, Mich., 1959-83, Blair Equipment Co., Flint, 1953-78; dir. Hougen Mfg. of Fla., Largo; lectr. in field. Patentee many inventions including holecutter, 1972, magnetic drill, 1976, rotabroach, 1975. Mem. Nat. Soc. Mfg. and Engring., Motor and Equipment Mfg. Assn., Nat. C. of C., Presdl. Task Force. Republican. Office: Hougen Mfg Inc G-5072 Corunna Rd Flint MI 48501-2005

HOUGH, FREDERICK JOHN, II, chiropractic coll. ofcl.; b. Chgo., Sept. 14, 1936; s. Frederick John and Eleanora Francis (Cyra) H.; A.A., Coll. of DuPage, 1975; B.A., Elmhurst Coll., 1976; divorced; children—Frederick, Michael, Neil, Linda, Laura. Cost acct. Wilson Sporting Goods Co., 1957-58; office mgr. Howell Tractor and Equipment Co., 1958-60; pres. Great Lakes Sci. Corp., Lombard, Ill., 1960-74; corp. v.p., chief fiscal officer, v.p. adminstrn., Nat. Coll. Chiropractic, Lombard, 1974-88; instr. investing, fin., bus. and law, 1974-88; lectr., bus. and investment adv., 1974-88; pres. Marquette Realty Inc., Oxford, Wis., 1988—. With USMC, 1954-57. Lic. real estate broker, Ill., Wis. Mem. 1st Marine Brigade, Fleet Marine Force, Delta Mu Delta. Republican. Methodist. Home: 326 S Monterey St Villa Park IL 60181 Office: Marquette Realty Inc 112 Ormsby St Oxford WI 53952

HOUGH, JAMES EMERSON, engineer, geologist, educator; b. Paducah, Ky., July 25, 1930; s. Winfred Cyril and Goldie Bernice (Stewart) H.; m. Valeska Marie Runge, Aug. 11, 1956; children: Jerome Kevin, Christopher Kendall. AS, Paducah Jr. Coll., 1951; BS, U. Ky., 1953, MS, 1958. Registered profl. engr., Ohio, Ill., Ky., Va., Pa., Ind., profl. geologist, Del. Geologist TVA, Lexington, Ky., 1958-59; soils engr. Ky. Dept. Hwys., Lexington and Frankfurt, Ky., 1959-60; asst. dist. soils engr. Ill. Div. Hwys., Paris, 1960-63; geol. engr. Geo-Engring. Labs., Mt. Vernon, Ill., 1963; chief soils engr. Earth Sci. Labs., Cin., 1963; owner James E. Hough & Assocs., Cin., 1963—, JV Enterprises, Cin., 1983—, Home Inspection Cons. Greater Cin., 1985—; instr. geology, U. Cin. Reviewer ref. book, 1987; contbr. tech. papers and books. Co-chmn. Earthwork Regulations Task Force, City of Cin., 1973-74, mem. Earth Movement Working Team, 1982-83, Earthwork Regulations Team, 1982-88, Geotech. Subsection Com., City Cin., 1988-89; cons. land use com. Cin. Hillside Trust, 1988—; advisor Earth Movement Task Force, Hamilton County, Ohio and Cin., 1982. Served with U.S. Army, 1953-55. Fellow Geol. Soc. Am.; mem. ASCE, Am. Cons. Engrs. Council, Assn. Soil and Found. Engrs., Assn. Engring. Geologists, Internat. Soc. Soil Mechanics and Found. Engrs., Internat. Assn. Engring. Geologists, Order of Engr., DAV, Sigma Gamma Epsilon, Masons. Republican. Presbyterian. Home and Office: 10936 Gosling Rd Cincinnati OH 45252

HOUGHTALING, PAMELA ANN, business machines company executive; b. Catskill, N.Y., July 8, 1949; d. Stanley Kenneth and Mildred Edythe (Fyfe) H. BA, Princeton U., 1971; cert. Russian Inst., Columbia U., 1976, M in Internat. Affairs, 1974. Internat. relations analyst Library of Congress, Washington, 1974-75, U.S. GAO, Washington, 1976-77; pub. affairs specialist IBM Corp., Washington, 1977-81; sr. external programs analyst IBM World Trade Americas/Far East Corp., North Tarrytown, N.Y., 1981-82; mgr. labor affairs/bus. practices U.S. Council Internat. Bus., N.Y.C., 1982-84; communications specialist-advt. IBM Corp., Boca Raton, Fla., 1984-86; staff communications specialist IBM Corp., White Plains, N.Y., 1986—. Mem. Women in Communications, Nat. Trust Historic Preservation, Nature Conservancy, Am. Mktg. Assn.

HOUGHTON, AMORY, JR., congressman; b. Corning, N.Y., Aug. 7, 1926; m. Ruth West, 1950; 4 children. BA, Harvard U., 1950, MA, 1952; hon. docotorate, Alfred U., 1963, Albion Coll., 1964, Cen. Coll., 1966, Clarkson Coll. Tech., 1968, Elmira Coll., 1982, Hartwick Coll., 1983, Houghton Coll., 1983. Exec. officer Corning Glass Works, 1951-86; mem. 100th Congress from N.Y., 1987—; mem. Grace Commn., Bus. Council N.Y. State, Bus. Adv. Commn. for Gov. N.Y., Labor-Industry Coalition for Internat. Trade. Trustee Brookings Instn. Served with USMC, 1945-46. Mem. Corning C. of C. Republican. Lodge: Rotary. Office: US Ho of Reps Office of House Members Washington DC 20515 *

HOUGHTON, JAMES RICHARDSON, glass manufacturing company executive; b. Corning, N.Y., Apr. 6, 1936; s. Amory and Laura (Richardson) H.; m. May Tuckerman Kinnicutt, June 30, 1962; children: James DeKay, Nina Bayard. AB, Harvard U., 1958, MBA, 1962. With Goldman, Sachs & Co., N.Y.C., 1959-61; v.p., European area mgr. Corning Glass Internat., Zurich, Switzerland, Brussels, Belgium, 1964-68; with Corning Glass Works (name changed to Corning Inc. 1989), 1962—, v.p., gen. mgr. consumer products div., 1968-71, vice chmn. bd., dir., chmn. exec. com., 1971-83, chmn. bd., chief exec. officer, 1983—; bd. dirs. Met. Life Ins. Co., J. P. Morgan Co. Inc., Dow Corning Corp., CBS, Inc., Owens-Corning Fiberglas Corp. Trustee Corning Glass Works Found., Corning Mus. Glass, Pierpont Morgan Library, N.Y.C., The Bus. Council of N.Y. State, Met. Mus. Art; mem. Bus. Com. for Arts, N.Y.C., Council on Fgn. Relations.; bd. dirs. US-USSR Trade and Econ. Council. Served with AUS, 1959-60. Mem. Bus. Council, Bus. Roundtable. Episcopalian. Clubs: Corning Country; River, Harvard, Univ., Links (N.Y.C.); Brookline (Mass.) Country; Tarratine (Dark Harbor, Maine); Augusta (Ga.) Nat. Golf; Rolling Rock, Laurel Valley Golf (Ligonier, Pa.). Home: Field 36 Spencer Hill Rd RD 2 Corning NY 14830 Office: Corning Glass Works Houghton Pk Corning NY 14831

HOUGLAND, ETSON, financial executive; b. Scottsburg, Ind., Jan. 17, 1949; s. George Elson Hougland and Gertie Irene (Perdiew) Baker; m. Nancy Criswell, Apr. 16, 1977 (div. 1983); m. Rita Ann Minich, Mar. 18, 1985; 1 child, Taylor Etson. BS in Acctg., U. Evansville, 1971; MBA in Fin., So. Meth. U., 1973. CPA, Tex. Program contr. Bell Helicopter div. Textron, Hurst, Tex., 1973-75; sr. fin. analyst Western Co. N.Am., Ft. Worth, 1975-79; mgr. fin. planning United Tech. Corp., Ft. Wayne, Ind., 1979-82, asst. contr., 1982-85, mgr. fin., 1985—. Republican. Methodist. Home: 1721 Marietta Dr Fort Wayne IN 46804 Office: United Tech Corp PO Box 1500 Fort Wayne IN 46801

HOULIHAN, PATRICIA POWELL, financial planner; b. Emporia, Va., Dec. 16, 1947; d. John Cyrus and Hazel Wright (Hines) Powell; m. Dennis Finley Houlihan, Oct. 13, 1973; children: Sean Finley, Ryan Patrick. BS, U. Richmond, 1969. Cert. fin. planner. Tchr. math. Fairfax County Schs., McLean, Va., 1970-74; fin. planner Cavill & Co., Washington, 1985—; panelist TV Washington Forum on Fin. Planning, Fairfax, Va., 1987-89, TV Money Watch, Washington, TV The Money Makers, PBS, Video Fin. Planning, The Internat. Found. of Employee Benefit Plans; adj. prof. Coll. Fin. Planning, George Washington U. Pres. Homeowners Assn., Oakton, Va., 1984; treas. Navy Elem. PTA, Fairfax, 1984; chmn. Creative Playground Project, Fairfax, 1982. Recipient Disting. Svc. award Va. Congress Parents and Tchrs., 1985. Mem. Internat. Assn. Fin. Planning, Registry Fin. Planning Practitioners (1st place award 1987), Inst. Cert. Fin. Planners, Internat. Bd. Standards and Practicesfor Cert. Fin. Planners. Methodist. Office: Cavill & Co 1225 Eye St NW Ste 1200 Washington DC 20005

HOUSEHOLDER, CALVIN REY, clergyman, business owner, engineer; b. Maywood, Calif., Feb. 24, 1941; s. Frank Emerson and Anna Minerva (Atha) H.; m. Ruth Emmi Shorn, May 21, 1966; children: Angela Rae, Jennifer Ann. AS in Engring., Glendale City Coll., 1960. Engr. Allied/Bendix, Columbia, Md., 1961-88; evangelist minister Maranatha Ministries, Severna Park, Md., 1984—; owner, mgr. Marantha Cassette Svcs., Severna Park, 1987—; co-pastor Fullness of Christ Fellowship, 1989—; field rep. Full Gospel Bus. Mens Fellowship, Costa Mesa, Calif., 1983-87. 4th Congl. dist. coord. Freedom Coun., Virginia Beach, Va., 1985-86. Mem. World Ministry Fellowship. Republican. Home and Office: 600 Kensington Ave Severna Park MD 21146

HOUSER, DONALD EUGENE, financial planner; b. Dearborn, Mich., May 14, 1948; s. Albert C. and C. Inez (Smith) H.; m. June Long, May 5, 1967; children: Jacqueline Anne, Donald Eugene Jr., Elizabeth Long. AA, Williamsport (Pa.) Area C.C., 1969. Registered fin. planner. Ins. agt. Equitable Iowa, Des Moines, 1970-83; ptnr. Davis & Houser Fin. Planners, Lock Haven, Pa., 1983—. treas. Clinton County Rep. Com., 1980—. Named Republican of Yr. Clinton County Rep. Com., 1984; recipient Nat. Sales Achievement award Nat. Assn. Life Underwriters. Mem. Pa. Assn. Life Underwriters (regional v.p. 1985—, Pres.'s Cup 1987), West Br. Assn. Life Underwriters (pres. 1982-83, 86), Million Dollar Round Table (life), Equitable Iowa Pres.'s Club. Baptist. Lodge: Kiwanis (mem. chmn. Lock Haven). Club: Clinton Country. Home: 331 W Main St Lock Haven PA 17745 Office: Davis & Houser Fin Planners 208 E Church St Lock Haven PA 17745

HOUSMAN, HARRY J., pharmaceutical company executive; b. Chgo., July 12, 1942; s. John G. and Winifred L. (Streelman) H.; m. Susan G. Godley, Sept. 3, 1966; children: Christopher, Molly. BS, Iowa State U., 1965; postgrad., U. Chgo., 1970-71, Western Carolina U., 1977-78. With data processing systems dept. Armour and Co., Chgo., 1965-67; data processing mgr. Armour Indsl., Chgo. and Alliance, Ohio, 1967-71; programming mgr. Akzona Inc., Asheville, N.C., 1971-76, asst. to controller, 1976-79; v.p. fin. Organon Inc., West Orange, N.J., 1979—. Mem. Nat. Assn. Accts., Fin. Execs. Inst., Data Processing Mgmt. Assn. Methodist. Home: 42 Stonehenge Rd Morristown NJ 07960 Office: Organon Inc 375 Mount Pleasant Ave West Orange NJ 07052

HOUSTON, ALEXANDER MACDOWELL, airline executive; b. Summit, N.J., July 15, 1955; s. William James and Clayre (MacDowell) H.; m. Debra Kay Kammeyer, June 15, 1985. BBA, U. N.C., 1978; MBA, U. Houston, 1989. Account exec. Ea. Airlines, Houston, 1980-83, supr. sales, 1983-84; dist. mgr. sales Ea. Airlines, Orlando, Fla., 1984-86, Houston, 1986; dist. mgr. sales Continental-Ea. Sales, Houston, 1987-89; regional sales mgr. Continental Airlines, Houston, 1989—. Mem. Am. Soc. Travel Agts., Sales and Mktg. Execs., Tex. Passenger Traffic Assn., Houston Airline Mgrs. Assn., SKAL, Cypress Creek Club (Orlando), Houston City Club. Home: 855 Pecanwood Ln Houston TX 77024 Office: Continental Airlines 9999 Richmond #100 Houston TX 77042

HOUSTON, E. JAMES, JR., financial consultant; b. Highland Park, Mich., Sept. 25, 1939; s. Ernest James and Frieda Mary (Milligan) H.; m. Ann Draper, Dec. 16, 1961; children: James Lee, Jay Douglas. B.S. in Finance, Wayne State U., 1964, M.B.A., 1967. Asst. v.p. Bank of the Commonwealth, Detroit, 1957-69; v.p. Birmingham Bloomfield Bank, Mich., 1969-70; pres. Birmingham Bloomfield Bank, 1970-71; exec. v.p. Fidelity Bank Mich., Birmingham, 1971; pres. Houston & Assos., Inc., Birmingham, 1971—, Houston Funding, Inc., Houston Mgmt. Corp.; chmn. bd., pres. Xylem Corp.; sec. Hacht Sales & Mktg., Ltd., Farmington Hills, Mich.; lectr. fin. Wayne State U. Sch. Bus. Adminstrn., Detroit, 1971—; dir. Sutherland Leather & Felt Co., Inc., Troy, Mich. Active Bloomfield Hills Hockey Assn.; pres. pro tem Village of Bingham Farms Village Council; chmn. Southfield Twp. Citizens' Com.; v.p. Hickory Hollow Homeowners Assn.; trustee Southeastern Oakland County Water Authority; mem. Community House Assn., Birmingham; bd. dirs. CATV, Birmingham YMCA; mem. parents council Brookside Sch., Cranbrook, Mich.; pres. Brookside Sch. Dads Club; mem. Cranbrook Arena Com. Mem. Birmingham-Bloomfield C. of C., Greater Detroit C. of C. Republican. Presbyterian. Club: Wayne State U. Alumni; Lodge: Rotary. Home: 9 Hickory Hollow Birmingham MI 48010 Office: Houston & Assoc 1471 S Woodward Ave Ste 210 Bloomfield Hills MI 48013-1446

HOUSTON, GEARY DEWAYNE, real estate developer, general contractor; b. Las Vegas, Nev., Sept. 25, 1953; m. Rebecca N. Noble, June 10, 1975; children: Clint Michael, Julie Ann. ATA, Edmonds (Wash.) Community Coll., 1979. Constrn. supr. J. C. Milne Constrn. Co., Portland, Oreg., 1975-81; constrn. mgr. D. L. Constrn., Phoenix, 1981-82, The DuPaul Co., Phoenix, 1982-87; pres. DuPaul Mgmt. Co., Phoenix, 1986-87, DuPaul Constrn. Co., Phoenix, 1984-87; pres./owner Intrinsic Devel. & Constrn. Co., Tempe, Ariz., 1987—; cons. Continental Cirs. Corp., Phoenix. Active Boy Scouts Am., YMCA. Mem. Associated Builders & Contractors Safety Com.; Japan Am. Soc. Republican. Home: 1309 E Donner Dr Tempe AZ 85282 Office: Intrinsic Devel & Constrn 2121 S Mill Tempe AZ 85282

HOVEY, ALAN EDWIN, JR., personnel executive; b. Burlington, Vt., Apr. 23, 1933; s. Alan Edwin and Jessie Miller (Emerson) H.; BSBA, U. Fla., 1956; postgrad. Cornell U. Law Sch.; m. Sue S. Weeks, Aug. 28, 1987; children: Alison Clair, Kimberly Ann, Christopher Owen, Adam Kimball. Civilian mgmt. anaylst Dept. Army, Orleans, France, 1958-60; with Century Housewares Co., 1961-80, dir. human resources, Buffalo, 1979; dir. personnel Everfast, Inc., Wilmington, Del., 1980-83; v.p. human Resources Mr. Goodbuys, Inc., Phila., 1983—; mem. personnel policies forum Bur. Nat. Affairs, Inc., 1987-88; bd. dirs. Del. Valley Project with Industry, 1989—. Mem. East Aurora (N.Y.) Bd. Edn., 1976-80; chmn. Wilmington Gt. Am. Smokeout, Am. Cancer Soc. Served with AUS, 1956-58. Accredited Sr. Profl. Human Resources. Personnel Accreditation Inst. Mem. Greater Phila. C. of C. (chmn. retail coun. 1988-89), Am. Mgmt. Assn., Am. Soc. Personnel Adminstrs. Republican. Unitarian. Home: 3019 Oakwood Dr Norristown PA 19401-3025 Office: Mr Goodbuys Inc 9901 Bluegrass Rd Philadelphia PA 19114

HOWARD, DONALD SEARCY, banker; b. Leadville, Colo., Aug. 13, 1928; s. Paul Parker and Amanda Jane (Searcy) H.; m. Phyllis Havey, Oct. 1, 1955; children: Steven, Julie, Rebecca, Martin. BSBA, Northwestern U., 1950; MBA, Harvard U., 1955. Rsch. assoc. Bus. Sch., Harvard U., Boston, 1955-57; ofcl. asst. overseas div. Citibank, London, 1957; asst. cashier Citibank, N.A., N.Y.C., 1959-60; asst. v.p. Citibank, N.A., 1960-63, v.p., 1963-69, dep. comptroller, 1969-72; sr. v.p.-fin. Citicorp-Citibank, 1972-79, exec. v.p., chief fin. officer, 1980-88; chief fin. officer Salomon Inc., N.Y.C., 1988—; bd. dirs. N.Y. Futures Exchange, N.Y.C., 1980—; mem. fin. acctg. standards adv. coun. Fin. Acctg. Found., Stamford, Conn., 1985-88; mem. Internat. Acctg. Standards Adv. Commn., London, 1986—. Co-Author: Managing The Liability Side of the Balance Sheet, 1976, Evolving Concepts of Bank Capital Management, 1980. Lt. comdr. USNR, 1950-57, Korea. Mem. Fin. Execs. Inst., Nat. Assn. Corp. Treas., Am. Bankers Assn. (chief fin. officer's exec. com. 1984-87). Presbyterian. Office: Salomon Inc 1 New York Pla New York NY 10004

HOWARD, ERNEST E., III, lawyer, natural resource company executive; b. Vicksburg, Miss., Mar. 26, 1943; s. Ernest E. and Joy Gamlin (Webb) H.; m. Brenda Lee Brock, July 26, 1969; children: Meredith, Michael, Ellen. BBA, U. Miss., 1965, JD, 1968. Mem. tax staff Peat Marwick Mitchell & Co., Dallas, 1969-71; asst. v.p., asst. sec. Dallas Bus. Capital Corp., 1971-74; exec. v.p., chief fin. officer McMoRan Oil & Gas Co., Metairie, La., 1974-84; sr. v.p. Freeport-McMoRan Inc., New Orleans, 1984-87, sr. v.p., gen. counsel, treas., 1988—; bd. dirs. McMoRan Oil & Gas Co., New Orleans. Bd. dirs. S.E. La. council Girl Scouts Am., Metairie, 1986—, Cystic Fibrosis Found., Metairie, 1986-87, St. Martin's Episcopal Sch., Metairie, 1988—, Archbishop Rummel High Sch., 1988—; mem. adv. bd. Opera Ball, New Orleans, 1984-86; mem. fin. com., adminstrv. bd. Munholland United Meth. Ch., Metairie, 1984—. Mem. Miss. Bar Assn., Tex. Bar Assn., Am. Mining Congress, Metairie Country Club, Petroleum Club New Orleans, English Turn Golf and Country Club. Republican. Methodist. Home: 3716 Rue Emilion Metairie LA 70002 Office: Freeport-McMoRan Inc 1615 Poydras St New Orleans LA 70112

HOWARD, HOMER LAMAR, JR., medical clinic administrator; b. Greenwood, Miss., May 11, 1939; s. Homer Lamar and Inez (Bailey) H.; m. Linda Lee Covington, Mar. 15, 1969; children: Lisa Anne, Homer Lamar III. BA, U. Miss., 1962; MBA, Miss. Coll., 1970. Project dir. family planning U. Miss. Med. Ctr., Jackson, 1970-74; health maintenance orgn. dir. Mercy Hosp., Vicksburg, Miss., 1974; admnistr. Smith County Gen. Hosp., Raleigh, Miss., 1974-76; dist. adminstr. Miss. State Bd. Health, Greenville, 1976-78; adminstr. Gamble Bros. and Archer Clinic P.A., Greenville, 1978—. Active Delta council, Greenville, Greenville United Way, exec. bd.; bd. dirs. Delta Area Council Boy Scouts Am., Clarksdale, adminstrv. bd. and pastoral parish relations com. 1st United Meth. Ch., v.p. Washington sch. PTA. Served to lt. USN, 1961-67. Mem. Med. Group Mgmt. Assn., Am. Assn. Med. Assts., Navy Res. Assn., Med. Group Mgmt. Assn. of Miss., Res. Officer Assn. (bd. dirs.), Greenville C. of C., Pi Kappa Alpha. Home: 1526 Woodcrest Cove Greenville MS 38701 Office: Gamble Bros and Archer Clinic 344 Arnold Ave Greenville MS 38701

HOWARD, JACK ROHE, newspaperman; b. N.Y.C., Aug. 31, 1910; s. Roy Wilson and Margaret (Rohe) H.; m. Barbara Balfe, Apr. 5, 1934 (dec. 1962); children: Pamela, Michael; m. Eleanor Sallee Harris, 1964. A.B., Yale U., 1932. Reporter Japan Advertiser, Tokyo, Shanghai (China) Evening Post and Mercury, 1932-33; reporter Indpls. Times, 1933-34; asst. telegraph editor, telegraph editor and news editor Washington Daily News, 1935; with program dept. Sta. WNOX, Knoxville, Tenn.; also Washington and N.Y.C. offices Continental Radio Co. (now Scripps-Howard Broadcasting Co.), 1936-39; asst. exec. editor Scripps Howard Newspapers, 1939-42, 1946-48, gen. editorial mgr., 1948-75; pres., dir., mem. exec. com. Scripps-Howard Newspapers (E.W. Scripps Co.), 1953-75, chmn. exec. com., 1976-85; pres., dir., chmn. exec. com. Scripps-Howard Broadcasting Co., 1937-42, 45-74, chmn. bd., mem. exec. com., 1974—; Mem. adv. bd. U.S. Post Office, 1955-61. Trustee Village of Centre Island, Oyster Bay, N.Y., 1977-88; bd. dirs. Wildlife Preservation Trust Internat., Gen. Douglas MacArthur Found., Boys' Clubs Am. Commd. lt. (j.g.) USNR, 1942; active duty 1943, Washington; sea duty 1944-45, PTO; now lt. comdr. USNR; ret. Fellow Inst. Jud. Adminstrn.; mem. Am. Soc. Newspaper Editors, Am. Newspaper Pubs. Assn. (dir. 1964-72), Inter Am. Press Assn. (pres. 1965-66, mem. adv. council), Phillips Exeter Alumni Assn. (pres. 1958-60), Beta Theta Pi, Sigma Delta Chi. Clubs: Dutch Treat, River, Pilgrims (N.Y.C.); Bohemian (San Francisco); Seawanhaka Corinthian Yacht (Oyster Bay, N.Y.). Office: Scripps-Howard Broadcasting Co 200 Park Ave New York NY 10166

HOWARD, JAMES JOSEPH, III, utility company executive; b. Pitts., July 1, 1935; s. James Joseph Jr. and Flossie (Wenzel) H.; m. Donna Joan Fowler, Aug. 31, 1955; children: James J. IV, Catherine A., Christine A., William F. BBA, U. Pitts., 1957; MS, MIT, 1970. With Bell Telephone of Pa., Pitts., 1957-78, v.p., gen. mgr., 1976-78; v.p. ops. Wis. Telephone Co., Milw., 1978-79, exec. v.p., chief operating officer, 1979-81, pres., chief exec. officer, 1981-83, chmn., chief exec. officer, 1983; pres., chief operating officer Ameritech, Chgo., 1983-87, dir.; pres., chief exec. officer No. States Power Co., Mpls., 1987—, chmn., 1988—; bd. dirs. Equitable Life Assurance Soc., N.Y. Bd. Overseers, Carlson Sch. Mgmt. U. Minn., Walgreen Co., Deerfield, Ill., No. States Power Co., Mpls., Am. Nuclear Energy Coun. Bd. trustees Coll. of St. Thomas, St. Paul, Minn., Minn. Safety Council; bd. overseers Carlson Sch. Mgmt., Greater Mpls. Met. Housing Corp., Am. Com. on Radwaste Disposal. Sloan fellow MIT, 1969. Mem. Conf. Bd. N.Y., Greater Mpls. C. of C., Am. Nuclear Energy Coun. (bd. dirs.). Clubs: Chgo., Comml., Econ.; Milw. Country; Duquesne, Oakmont Country (Pitts.), Minn., Mpls. Athletic (Minikahda).

HOWARD, JAMES WEBB, investment banker, lawyer, engineer; b. Evansville, Ind., Sept. 17, 1925; s. Joseph R. and Velma (Cobb) H.; m. Phyllis Jean Brandt, Dec. 27, 1948; children: Sheila Rae, Sharon Kae. B.S. in Mech. Engring, Purdue U., 1949; postgrad., Akron (Ohio) Law Sch., 1950-51, Cleve. Marshall Law Sch., 1951-52; M.B.A., Western Res. U., 1962; J.D., Western State Coll. Law, 1976. Registered profl. engr., Ind., Ohio. Jr. project engr. Firestone Tire & Rubber Co., Akron, 1949-50; gen. foreman Cadillac Motor Car div. Gen. Motors Corp., 1950-53; mgmt. cons. M.K. Sheppard & Co., Cleve., 1953-56; plant mgr. Lewis Welding & Engring. Corp., Ohio, 1956-58; underwriter The Ohio Co., Columbus, 1959; chmn. Growth Capital, Inc., Chgo., 1960—; pres. Meister Brau, Inc., Chgo., 1965-73; others. Co-chmn. Chgo. com. Ill. Sesquicentennial Com., 1968. Served with AUS, 1943-46. Decorated Bronze Star, Parachutist badge, Combat Inf. badge. Mem. ASME, ABA, Nat. Assn. Small Bus. Investment Cos. (past pres.), State Bar Calif., Grad. Bus. Alumni Assn. Western Res. U. (past gov.), Tau Kappa Epsilon, Pi Tau Sigma, Beta Gamma Sigma. Methodist. Club: Masons.

HOWARD, JAMES WESLEY, JR., sales executive; b. Valdosta, Ga., Nov. 20, 1959; s. James Wesley and Carolyn (Daniels) H.; m. Mary-Lynda Brown, Dec. 2, 1983. BS in Indsl. Mgmt., Ga. Inst. Tech., 1982. Ops. mgr. Merona div. Oxford Industries, Toccoa, Ga., 1982-83; SE sales rep Merona div. Oxford Industries, Atlanta, 1984; SE sales rep. Lanier div. Oxford Industries, Atlanta, 1985, SE account exec., 1985—; mgr. corp. sales, editor Corp. Club Catalogue, 1986—. Mem. Am. Mgmt. Assn., Direct Mktg. Assn., Jaycees (dir. 1984). Baptist. Club: Neuman Country. Office: Oxford Industries 222 Piedmont Ave NE Atlanta GA 30308

HOWARD, JOHN LINDSAY, lawyer, forest industry company executive; b. Drumheller, Alta., Can., Nov. 18, 1931; s. Lindsay Lee and Nancy (Martin) H.; m. Jeannette Huguenin, Nov. 21, 1969. B.Comm., U. B.C., 1959, LL.B., 1961; LL.M., Harvard U., 1968; postgrad., McGill U., Montreal, Can., 1967. Bar: B.C. 1962, Que. 1967, Fed. Queen's Counsel 1977. Mem. Brahan, Dickerson & Howard, Vancouver, B.C., 1962-67, Tansey, de Grandpre, Montreal, 1968-71; asst. dep. minister Fed. Dept. Consumer and Corp. Affairs, Ottawa, Ont., 1971-79; sr. v.p. law and corp. affairs MacMillan Bloedel Ltd., Vancouver, 1979—; head Can. del. U.S.-Can. bilateral bankruptcy treaty, Ottawa, 1978. Co-author: Proposals for a New Corporation Law for Canada, 1971, Proposals for a Securities Market Law for Canada, 1979. Mem. Can. Bar Assn., Assn. Can. Gen. Counsel, Can. Inst. Chartered Accts. (chmn. acctg. research adv. bd. 1981-83). Home: 1955 W 33rd Ave Apt 214, Vancouver, BC Canada V6M 1B6 Office: MacMillan Bloedel Ltd, 1075 W Georgia St, Vancouver, BC Canada V6E 3R9

HOWARD, JOHN LORING, trust banker; b. Auburn, N.Y., Apr. 12, 1935; s. Chauncey Frisbie and Ruth Dorothea (Burrows) H.; m. Catherine Edith Swaffin, July 1, 1961; children: John Loring, Jr., Sarah Catherine. BS, Cornell U., 1957; postgrad., NYU, 1961-62; grad. with distinction, Southwestern Grad. Sch. Banking, 1968-70. V.p. Chase Manhattan Bank, New York, 1961-77; sr. v.p., div. mgr. RepublicBank Houston, 1978-82; sr. v.p., group mgr. RepublicBank Trust Co., Houston, 1983-87, NCNB Tex. Nat. Bank, Dallas, 1988—. Elder, Munn Ave. Presbyn. Ch., East Orange, N.J., 1963-64; troop com. chmn. Boy Scouts Am., New Providence, N.J., 1975-77; dist. chmn. Friends of Scouting, Houston, 1980-82; fin. com. chmn. Spring Woods United Meth. Ch., Houston, 1981-84. Served to 1st lt. USMC, 1957-60. Mem. Stock Transfer Assn., Southwest Stock Transfer Assn. (bd. dirs. 1980-81), Am. Soc. Corp. Secs. (sec. southwest regional group 1984-85). Republican. Club: Plaza Athletic (Dallas). Office: NCNB Tex Nat Bank PO Box 2964 Dallas TX 75221

HOWARD, JOHN RAYMOND, insurance company executive; b. Coffeyville, Kans., Aug. 27, 1938; s. John R. and Vivian A. (Schertzer) H.; m. D. Jane Moore, July 3, 1965; children: Janna R., Jolie M. Student, Coffeyville Jr. Coll., 1956-57; BA, U. Kans., 1960, MS, 1962. Acct. Peat, Marwick, Main, Kansas City, Mo., 1962-68; treas., controller I.C.H. Corp., Kansas City, 1968-72; v.p. Nat. Western Life Ins. Co., Austin, Tex., 1972—; bd. dirs. Westcap Corp., Houston, ICO Inc., Ft. Worth. Mem. Jr. C. of C., Austin, 1972-73; bd. dirs. Balcones Village Homeowners Assn., Austin, 1974-78. Mem. Austin C. of C., Fin. Exec. Inst. (bd. dirs. 1986—), Tex. Soc. CPA's (Austin chpt.), Ins. Acctg. and Stats. Assn., Balcones Country Club (bd. dirs. 1974-78). Republican. Presbyterian. Office: Nat Western Life Ins Co 850 E Anderson Ln Austin TX 78752-1602

HOWARD, KATHLEEN, computer company executive; b. Norman, Okla., Nov. 3, 1947; d. Robert Adrian and Jane Elizabeth (Morgens) Howard; m. Lawrence W. Osgood, Aug. 10, 1968 (div. Sept. 1970); m. Norman Edlo Gibat, Oct. 15, 1971. Student U. Okla., 1966-68. Typesetter, Selenby Press, Norman, 1968-72; owner, pres. Noguska Industries, Fostoria, Ohio, 1973—; co-founder Home Wine Mchts., Chgo., 1976; cons. Bechtel Corp., Ann Arbor, Mich. and Gaithersburg, Md., 1980—; chairperson Am. Software Project, 1985. Co-author, illustrator: Lore of Still Building, 1972; co-author: Making Wine, Beer and Merry, 1973, Computer Comix Mag., 1986; also jours. and bus. mgmt. software. Treas. United Way of Fostoria, 1986-88, 2d v.p. 1988—; bd. dirs. Pvt. Industry Council, 1988—. Recipient Disting. Service award Bechtel Corp., 1983, Founders award Home Wine and Beer Trade Assn. Chgo., 1976. Mem. Better Bus. Bur., Nat. Fedn. Ind. Bus., C. of C. (bd. dirs. 1986—), Employer's Assn. Toledo. Club: Altrusa Internat. (sec. Fostoria 1984-85, pres. 1986-88). Avocations: painting, printing, travel, reading. Office: Noguska Industries 735-741 N Countyline Fostoria OH 44830

HOWARD, MARGUERITE EVANGELINE BARKER (MRS. JOSEPH D. HOWARD), business executive, civic worker; b. Victoria, B.C., Can., July 30, 1921; d. Reuel Harold and Frances Penelope (Garnham) Barker; brought to U.S., 1924, naturalized, 1945; BA, U. Wash., 1943; m. Joseph D. Howard, June 16, 1952; children: Wendy Doreen Frances, Bradford Reuel. Vice pres., dir. Howard Tours, Inc., Oakland, Calif., 1953—; co-owner, gen. mgr. Howard Travel Service, Oakland, 1956—, mng. dir. Howard Hall, Berkeley, Calif., 1964-75; co-owner, asst. mgr. Howard Investments, Oakland, 1960—; sec., treas. Energy Dynamics Inc. Bd. dirs. Piedmont council Campfire Girls, 1969-79, pres., 1974-79, mem. nat. council, 1972-76, zone chmn., 1974-76, 77-83, zone coordinator, 1976, nat. v.p., 1975, nat. bd. dirs., 1976-83, bd. dirs. Alameda Contra Costa council, 1984—; bd. dirs. Oakland Symphony Guild, 1969-87, pres., 1972-74; trustee Piedmont Campfire Camp Agusta, 1988—; mem. exec. bd. Oakland Symphony Orch. Assn., 1972-74, bd. dirs., 1972-86; 1st pres. Inner Wheel Club of East Oakland, 1983-84; bd. dirs. Piedmont Jr. High Sch. Mothers Club, 1968-69. Recipient Wohelo Order award Campfire, Inc, 1985. Mem. Oakland Mus. Assn., U. Wash. Alumni Assn., East Bay Bot. and Zool. Soc., Young Audiences, Am. Symphony Orch. League, Assn. Calif. Symphony Orchs., Chi Omega Alumni Seattle, Chi Omega East Bay Alumni Berkeley. Republican. Clubs: Womens Univ. (Seattle); Womens Athletic (Oakland) (bd. dirs. 1986—). Home: 146 Bell Ave Piedmont CA 94611 Office: Howard Tours Inc 526 Grand Ave Oakland CA 94610

HOWARD, MELVIN, office equipment and financial services company executive; b. Boston, Jan. 5, 1935; s. John M. and Molly (Sagar) H.; m. Beverly Ruth Kahan, June 9, 1957; children: Brian David, Marjorie Lyn. BA, U. Mass., 1957; MS, Columbia U., 1959. Fin. exec. Ford Motor Co., Dearborn, Mich., 1959-67; v.p. adminstrn. Shoe Corps. of Am., Columbus, Ohio, 1967-70; asst. controller Bus. Products group Xerox Corp., Rochester, N.Y., 1970-72; v.p. fin. Bus. Devel. group Xerox Corp., 1972-74, sr. v.p., sr. staff officer, 1974-75, corp. v.p., controller, 1975-77, corp. v.p. fin., 1977-78, sr. corp. v.p.

fin., 1978-81, sr. v.p., chief fin. officer, 1981-84, exec. v.p., pres. fin. services, 1984-86, vice chmn., 1986; chmn. Xerox Fin. Services, Inc.; also bd. dirs. Xerox Corp.; bd. dirs. LMH Fund Ltd., Crum and Forster, Inc., Van Kampen Merritt, Inc., Gould Pumps, Inc., Xerox Credit Corp., Bond Investors Group, VMS Realty Ptnrs. Trustee Norwalk Hosp. Served to 1st lt. AUS, 1957. Mem. AIA (conf. bd.), Fin. Execs. Inst., Am. Mgmt. Assn., Beta Gamma Sigma. Club: Birchwood Country. Home: 42 Red Coat Rd Westport CT 06880 Office: Xerox Corp 800 Long Ridge Rd Stamford CT 06904

HOWARD, MURRAY, manufacturing, real estate, property management executive, farmer, rancher; b. Los Angeles, July 25, 1914; s. George A. J. and Mabel (Murray) H. B.S., UCLA, 1939. C.P.A., Calif. Mgr. budget control dept. Lockheed Aircraft, 1939-45; pres., chmn. bd. Stanley Foundries, Inc., 1945-59, Howard Machine Products, Inc., 1959—, Murray Howard Realty, Inc., 1959—, Murray Howard Devel., Inc., 1969—, Howard Oceanography, Inc., 1967—, Ranch Sales, Inc., 1968—, Murray Howard Investment Corp., 1961—; owner, gen. mgr. Greenhorn Ranch Co., Greenhorn Creek Guest Ranch, Spring Garden, Calif.; pres., chmn. bd. Murray Howard Cattle Co., Prineville, Oreg.; dir. Airshippers Publ. Corp., LaBrea Realty & Devel. Co., Shur-Lok Corp. Served as mem. Gov. Calif. Minority Com. Mem. Nat. Assn. Cost Accts. (dir., v.p.), NAM (dir.). Office: 1605 W Olympic Blvd Ste 404 Los Angeles CA 90015

HOWARD, PHILIP MARTIN, insurance agent; b. Chgo., Dec. 16, 1939; s. Anthony Gerald and Mary Elizabeth (Smith) H.; m. Diane R. Miller, Sept. 12, 1964; children: Anne Marie, Philip Martin II, Kevin Vincent. Student Chgo. parochial schs. Laborer, tree trimmer Chgo. Bur. Forestry, 1963-66; sales rep. O.H. div. Bell & Howell, Chgo., 1966; sr. account agt. Allstate Ins. Co., Chgo., 1967—; ins. officer Mt. Greenwood Youth Baseball, Chgo., 1981-86. With USMCR, 1962-67. Republican. Roman Catholic. Home: 11324 S Lawndale Ave Chicago IL 60655 Office: Allstate Ins Co 7000 W 111th St Worth IL 60482

HOWARD, ROBERT CLARK, energy company executive; b. Cin., Jan. 4, 1931; s. Loren Eastman and Frances (Madden) H.; m. Mary Louise Maloney, Oct. 4, 1980; children: Loren Hazard, Ashley Madden; children from previous marriage: Timothy, Robert, Peter, Christopher, Mary, Patrick, Brooke. BS in Engring., U. Mich., 1953; MS, MIT, 1955. Nuclear Engr. Argonne Nat. Lab., Lemont, Ill., 1955-57; research staff mem. Gen. Atomic Co., LaJolla, Calif., 1957-62; exec. v.p. Thermo Electron Corp., Waltham, Mass., 1962—; bd. dirs. Thermedics, Inc., Thermo Environ. Corp., Thermo Instrument Systems, Inc., Tecogen Inc., Thermo Cardiosystems, Inc. Contbr. articles to profl. jours.; patentee nuclear fuel elements. Club: Brae Burn Country. Home: 230 Windsor Rd Waban MA 02168 Office: Thermo Electron Corp 101 1st Ave Waltham MA 02254

HOWARD, SAMUEL HOUSTON, communications company executive, health care executive; b. Marietta, Okla., May 8, 1939; s. Houston and Nellie M. (Gaines) H.; m. Karan Anica Wilson, Dec. 29, 1962; children: Anica Lynne, Samuel H. II. BS, Okla. State U., 1961; MA, Stanford U., 1963. Chmn. Phoenix Communications Group., Inc., Nashville, 1972—; v.p. fin. and bus. Meharry Med. Coll., Nashville, 1973-77; v.p. planning Hosp. Affiliates Internat., Nashville, 1977-80, v.p., treas., 1980-81; v.p., treas. Hosp. Corp. Am., Nashville, 1981-85, sr. v.p. pub. affairs, 1985-88; chmn. Phoenix Holdings, Inc., 1987—. Trustee Fisk U., Nashville, 1984—; mem. Tenn. Indsl. and Agrl. Devel. Commn., 1985-88; chmn. Nashville Conv. Ctr. Commn., 1986-87. Recipient Gov.'s Outstanding Tennessean award State of Tenn., 1981, Disting. Businessman of Yr. U. Tenn., 1985; Samuel H. Howard Day named in his honor City of Nashville, 1981; named to Bus. Hall of Fame, Okla. State U., 1983. Mem. Fedn. Am. Health Systems (bd. dirs. 1980—, past pres., Pres.'s Achievement award 1980, 84), Am. Hosp. Assn. (select del.), Fin. Execs. Inst. (so. v.p. 1979-86), Alpha Phi Alpha, Sigma Pi Phi, Rotary Club. Baptist. Home: 5320 Cherry Blosom Trail Nashville TN 37215 Office: Phoenix Communications Group Inc 2100 W End Ave#780 Nashville TN 37215

HOWARD, SUZANNE MARIE, finance company executive; b. Detroit, Dec. 8, 1941; d. David Eli and Ann Julia (Pilisko) Johnson; m. David George Howard, Jan. 21, 1961 (div. Nov. 1987); children: Lorrie Ann, Susan Lynn, Steven David. BBA, Oakland U., 1972. With comml. real estate sales dept. Shepard Realty, Rochester, Mich., 1972-74; v.p., owner Brant & Cochran Tool, Centerline, Mich., 1974-81; asst. to pres., controller AMS Mgmt. Corp., Troy, Mich., 1981-83; mgr. adminstrn. services, div. controller Vuebotics Corp., Troy, 1983-84; mgr. acctng. adminstrn. DUATEK Corp., Greenbelt, Md., 1984-86; dir. fin. DUATEK Corp., Greenbelt, 1986-87, v.p. fin., 1987—. Bd. dirs., treas. AIDS Edn. Bur., Va., 1987—. Mem. Nat. Assn. Female Execs., Am. Mgmt. Assn. Republican. Roman Catholic. Home: 309 Yoakum #1409 Alexandra VA 22304 Office: Duratek Corp 6700 Alexander Bell Dr Columbia MD 21046

HOWARD, WILLIAM BARKER, JR., financial planner; b. Winston-Salem, N.C., Apr. 12, 1956; s. William Barker and Betty (Price) H.; m. Sonya Ellzey, Aug. 29, 1981; 1 child, Elizabeth Caldwell. BBA in Ins., U. Miss., 1979. Cert. fin. planner. Account exec. John Hancock Fin. Services, Memphis, 1979-85; prin. Wray, Fugitt and Howard Fin. Advisors, Inc., Memphis, 1985—. Mem. Inst. Cert. Fin. Planners, Internat. Assn. Fin. Planners (bd. dirs.), Kiwanis. Republican. Baptist. Office: Wray Fugitt & Howard 755 Crossover Ln Memphis TN 38117

HOWARTH, DAVID H., banker; b. Lafayette, Ind., Apr. 3, 1936; s. C.H. and Dorothy Howarth; m. Mary Alice Fisher; children: Lynn Howarth Easton, David P. Student, Wabash Coll., 1955-56; BS in Indsl. Econs., Purdue U., 1958; postgrad. banking, U. Wis., 1970; grad. exec. program, Columbia U., 1975. With Lafayette Nat. Bank, 1958-61, 64—, pres., 1978-83, pres., chief exec. officer, 1983—; ptnr. McVay and Howarth, Lafayette, 1961-64; bd. dirs. Lafayette Life Ins. Co.; chmn., bd. dirs. Union Bank & Trust, Delphi, Ind., 1985—. Mem. Ind. Econ. Devel. Council, Indpls.; bd. dirs. N. Cen. Health Services, Lafayette. Named Sagamore of the Wabash, Gov. Ind., 1986. Mem. Ind. Bankers Assn. (pres., bd. dirs. 1985-86, trustee), Greater Lafayette C. of C. (pres. 1976-77), Ind. State C. of C. (bd. dirs.), Rotary, Masons. Home: 2117 S 8th St Lafayette IN 47905 Office: Lafayette Nat Bank 437 South St PO Box 789 Lafayette IN 47902

HOWARTH, ROBERT RUELL, manufacturing executive; b. Newkirk, Okla., Mar. 28, 1931; s. Raymond Lee and Audrey Irene (Davidson) H.; m. Marjorie C. Wilson, June 18, 1960; children: Cindy, Brent, Gregory, Todd, Jeffrey. Student, Okla. U., 1955-56; BS, Ottawa (Kans.) U., 1958. Mem. supt.'s staff Mo. Pacific R.R., Kansas City, Mo., 1952-60; acctg. mgr. Parkview-Gem, Inc., Kansas City, 1960-70, O'Sullivan Industries, Inc., Lamar, Mo., 1970-73; controller O'Sullivan Industries, Inc., Lamar, 1973-86, v.p., controller, 1986—; v.p. O'Sullivan Industries Va., South Boston, 1988—. Chmn. bd. dirs. Oakton United Meth. Ch., Lamar, 1987—. Cpl. USMC, 1952-54. Republican. Home: 100 Gulf St Lamar MO 64759 Office: O'Sullivan Industries Inc 1900 Gulf St Lamar MO 64759

HOWE, ALAN EUGENE, computer company executive; b. Lebanon, Pa., Mar. 22, 1946; s. Lloyd Russell and Beatrice (Farling) H.; m. Mary Lou Keegan, June 21, 1975; children: Stephen Alan, Bess Caroline. BS in Acctg., Elizabethtown (Pa.) Coll., 1968. Acct. Kuntz, Hipple, Broggs and Co., Lancaster, Pa., 1968-69, Ernst and Ernst, Lancaster, Pa., 1969-71; owner Pub. Acct. Firm, Lebanon, Pa., 1971—74; pres., chief executive officer Alan E. Howe, Inc., Lebanon, 1974—, Howe Turnkey Systems, Inc., Lebanon, 1974—. Contbr. articles to profl. jours. Mem. Soc. Industry Oriented Profls. Office: Howe Development Systems Inc 761 Poplar St Lebanon PA 17042

HOWE, CARROLL VICTOR, construction equipment company executive; b. Kearny, N.J., Dec. 12, 1923; s. Wright and Ada (Hodge) H,; m. Nancy Osborne Stivers, Nov. 24, 1951 (div.); m. 2d, Prscilla Howland Greene, Mar. 1, 1957 (div.); children: Gregory Carroll, Christopher David; m. 3d Eilene Crawley Pierson, Apr. 14, 1984. BA, Princeton U., 1947; MFA, Yale U., 1950. Writer, producer Pemeho Prodns., N.Y.C., 1950-51; free lance actor, writer Pemeho Prodns., 1952-54; salesman Atlas Rigging Supply Corp., Newark, 1954=56, office mgr., 1956-57, sales mgr., 1957-58, v.p., 1958=62, pres., 1962—; pres. Arsco Industries, Inc., Newark, 1966—; bd. dirs. Select Ins. Group of North Am., 1987—. Author: (play) Long Fall, 1950, 1957. Bd. dirs., pres. 15 Tenant Shareholders, Inc., N.Y.C., 1978-81, Alumni Coun. Yale U. Grad. Sch. Drama, 1988—; mng. ptnr. Crollar Assocs. Newark, 1983—. Served from pvt. to 2d lt. USMCR, 1942-46, 1st lt. to capt., 1951-52. Recipient Applause award N.J. Theatre Group, 1989. Mem. Newark C. of C., English-Speaking Union, Mensa, Alumni Council, Yale U. Grad. Sch. Drama. Episcopalian. Clubs: Quandrangle, Princeton; La Ronde; Westhampton Yacht Squadron (treas. 1970-72, vice commodore 1972-74, commodore 1974-76, dir. 1976-80). Home: 31 Ilford Ave N Arlington NJ 07032 also: 4511 Ocean Blvd Highland Beach FL 33444 Office: 181 Vanderpool St Newark NJ 07114

HOWE, JAMES EVERETT, investment company executive; b. N.Y.C., Mar. 30, 1930; s. Ernest Joseph and Gladys Montgomery (Sills) H.; m. Judith DePuy Keating, May 9, 1959; children—James E., Jr., David K. B.A., Williams Coll., 1952; M.B.A., Columbia U., 1954. Chartered fin. analyst. Statistician J.P. Morgan & Co., N.Y.C., 1956-59; investment research officer Morgan Guaranty Trust Co., N.Y.C., 1959-65; sr. analyst Tri-Continental Corp., N.Y.C., 1965-80; asst. v.p., shareholder J&W Seligman & Co., N.Y.C., 1980-81; chmn. investment com. Charles Edison Fund, East Orange, N.J., 1981—; trustee Brook Found., N.Y.C., 1966-72, Charles Edison Fund, 1972—; bd. deacons Brick Presbyn. Ch., N.Y.C., 1963-66. Served to 1st lt. USAF, 1954-56, ETO. Recipient Fin. award Wall St. Jour., 1954, award of Appreciation Thomas A. Edison Found., 1977. Mem. N.Y. Soc. Security Analysts, Inst. Chartered Fin. Analysts, Machinery Analyst of N.Y. (pres. 1967-68, charter mem.), Environ. Control Analysts of N.Y. (pres. 1975, charter mem.), Steel Analysts Group, Jamestown Soc. (charter), Alpha Kappa Psi (pres. 1953-54). Republican. Presbyterian. Clubs: Genesee Valley (Rochester, N.Y.); Short Hills (N.J.). Avocation: photography. Home: 33 Keats Rd Short Hills NJ 07078 Office: Charles Edison Fund 101 S Harrison St East Orange NJ 07018

HOWE, JOHN PRENTICE, III, health science center executive, physician; b. Jackson, Tenn., Mar. 7, 1943; s. John Prentice and Phyllis (MacDonald) H.; m. Jill Olmsted, Aug. 19, 1967; children—Lindsey Warren, Brooke Olmsted, John Prentice IV. B.A., Amherst Coll., 1965; M.D., Boston U., 1969. Diplomate Am. Bd. Internal Medicine, internal medicine and cardiovascular disease. Research assoc. cellular physiology Amherst Coll., 1963-64; research assoc. cardiovascular physiology Boston U. Sch. of Medicine, 1966-67, lectr. medicine, 1972-73; intern Boston City Hosp., 1969-70, asst. resident, 1970-71; research fellow in medicine Harvard U., 1971-73, Peter Bent Brigham Hosp., 1971-73; survey physician Framingham Cardiovascular Disease Study, Nat. Heart and Lung Inst., 1971; asst. clin. prof. medicine U. Hawaii, 1973-75; asst. prof. medicine U. Mass., 1975-77, assoc. prof., 1977-85, vice chmn. dept. medicine, 1975-78, asst. dean continuing edn. for physicians, 1976-78, assoc. dean profl. affairs and continuing edn., 1978-80, acad. dean, 1980-85, vice chancellor, 1980-85, acting chmn. dept. anatomy, 1982-85; pres., prof. medicine U. Tex. Health Sci. Ctr., San Antonio, 1985—; assoc. chief div. medicine U. Mass. Hosp., 1975-78, dir. patient care studies dept., 1975-80, chief of staff, 1978-80; bd. dirs. First RepublicBank, San Antonio. Contbr. numerous articles to profl. jours., chpts. to books. Pres., trustee, mem. exec. com. Am. Heart Assn., San Antonio, 1986—; mem. med. adv. com. Hospice San Antonio; trustee SW Found. for Biomed. Research, San Antonio Med. Found., S.W. Research Inst., Worcester Found. Exptl. Biology. Served to maj. M.C., U.S. Army, 1973-75. Alfred P. Sloan scholar Amherst Coll., 1962-65; recipient Ruth Hunter Johnson award Boston U. Sch. of Medicine, 1969. Fellow Am. Coll. Cardiology, Am. Coll. Chest Physicians, ACP, Council on Clin. Cardiology of Am. Heart Assn.; mem. Bexar County Med. Soc. (exec. com. 1985—), Japan-Am. Soc. San Antonio (bd. dirs.), Assn. Am. Med. Colls. (group on med. edn. 1978—), Assn. Acad. Health Ctrs., AMA.

HOWE, RICHARD J., oil company executive; b. Mpls., Oct. 15, 1928; s. Chauncey Eugene and Mildred (Rall) H.; m. Charlotte Relf, June 15, 1951; children—Richard Jr., Dwight, Roger. BME, U. Minn., Mpls., 1950, MME, 1951, PhD, 1953; MS in Indsl. Mgmt., MIT, 1965. Registered profl. engr., Tex., Okla. Engr. Shell Oil Co., Houston, 1953-59; gen. mgr. prodn. research Exxon Co. USA, Houston, 1959-78; pres., chief operating officer Pennzoil Co., Houston, 1978-87; adv. dir. Pennzoil Co.; dir. Battle Mountain Gold Co., Houston, Fugro-McClelland, Netherlands. Patentee offshore drilling systems. Contbr. articles to profl. publs. Bd. dirs. Florence Crittendon Home, Houston, 1974-76; bd. trustees Kelsey-Seybold Found., Houston, 1984-88, United Way Tex. Gulf Coast, 1987-88; v.p. Houston Grand Opera, 1985-88. Served to 1st lt. USAF, 1955-57. Mem. Soc. Petroleum Engrs. (Disting. Lectr. 1969), Sigma Xi, Tau Beta Pi, Pi Tau Sigma. Republican. Methodist. Club: Petroleum (Houston). Office: Pennzoil Co PO Box 2967 Houston TX 77252

HOWE, TIMOTHY FURNIVALL, venture capitalist; b. Hartford, Conn., Feb. 18, 1958; s. Ralph Sawyer and Nancy (Furnivall) H.; m. Anne Elizabeth Berry, May 29, 1982. BA, Columbia U., 1980, MBA, 1985. Fin. analyst J. Henry Schroder Bank & Trust Co., N.Y.C., 1980-82; treasury officer Nat. Westminster Bank USA, N.Y.C., 1982-83; assoc. Schroder Venture Mgrs., N.Y.C., 1984-88; asst. v.p. J. Henry Schroder Corp., N.Y.C., 1985-86; ptnr. Shroder Venture Mgrs., N.Y.C., 1986—; bd. dirs. GD Acquisition Corp., N.Y., Gerard Daniel and Co., Inc., Nuclean, Inc., McBride's for Kids Inc., Ill. Mem. Beta Gamma Sigma. Office: Schroder Venture Managers 787 Seventh St New York NY 10019

HOWE, WESLEY JACKSON, medical supplies company executive; b. Jersey City, June 7, 1921; s. Wesley Veith and Phyllis (Jackson) H.; m. Suzanne Rodrock, July 20, 1946; children: Marc Edward, Richard Douglas, Suzanne. ME, Stevens Inst. Tech., Hoboken, N.J., 1943, MS, 1953; DEng (hon.), Stevens Inst. Tech., 1981; LHD, U. N.J. Medicine & Dentistry (hon.), 1988. With Becton, Dickinson and Co., Rutherford, N.J., 1949—, group v.p., then exec. v.p., 1970-72, pres., chief exec. officer, dir., 1972-80, chmn. bd., 1980—, chief exec. officer, dir., 1980-89, pres., 1983-87; dir. First Fidelity Bank, N.A., N.J., First Fidelity Bancorp., Ecolab Inc., Lukens Inc.; chmn. N.J. Mfrs. Ins. Co., N.J. Re-Ins. Co., N.J. Bus. and Industry. Chmn. bd. trustees Stevens Inst. Tech.; trustee Found. of Univ. Medicine and Dentistry N.J. Served to 1st lt. AUS, 1944-46, 51-52. Mem. N.J. C. of C. (dir.). Clubs: Arcola (N.J.) Country, Upper Montclair (N.J.) Country; University (N.Y.C.). Office: Becton Dickinson & Co 1 Becton Dr Franklin Lakes NJ 07417

HOWE-ELLISON, PATRICIA MARY, investment banker; b. Chgo., Sept. 14, 1928; d. Harry Michael and Helen Mary (Maloney) Howe; student Barat Coll., Lake Forest, Ill., 1944-47, Goodman Theatre, Chgo., 1947; m. Ernest O. Ellison, Sept. 23, 1977. Instl. sales asst. Blyth & Co., 1954-55; with L.F. Rothschild & Co., 1957-82, mgr. San Francisco br., 1965-82, partner, 1968-82; pres. Ellmark Assocs., San Francisco, 1982—; chmn. Corp. Capital Investment Advisors, 1984—; mng. dir. Thrift Investment Services, 1984—. Trustee U. San Diego, Women's Forum West. Mem. Securities Industry Assn., San Francisco Bond Club, Equestrian Order Holy Sepulchre, Opera Guild. Republican. Roman Catholic. Clubs: World Trade, Metropolitan, Bankers, Villa Taverna, Bankers (dir.), Bel Air Bay. Home: 1080 Chestnut St San Francisco CA 94109 Office: Ellmark Assocs 550 Kearny St San Francisco CA 94108

HOWELL, BARTON JOHN, JR., sales executive; b. Ann Arbor, Mich., Apr. 13, 1944; s. Barton John and Lorraine (Cortese) H.; children: John, Rosemary, Catherine, Henry, Scott, Amy. BA, Brigham Young U., 1969. Sales rep. Shell Oil Co., Sacramento, 1969-73; div. mgr. ADP Dealer Svcs., Portland, Oreg., 1973-78; v.p. SCS/Compute, St. Louis, 1979—. Contbr. articles to profl. jours. Mem. Nat. Rep. Com., 1979—. Mem. Sales and Mktg. Execs. Mormon. Office: SCS/Compute 1714 Deer Tracks Trail Saint Peters MO 63376

HOWELL, DONALD LEE, lawyer; b. Waco, Tex., Jan. 31, 1935; s. Hilton Emory and Louise (Hatchett) H.; m. Gwendolyn Avera, June 13, 1957; children—Daniel Liege, Alison Avera, Anne Turner. BA cum laude, Baylor U., 1956; JD with highest honors, U. Tex., 1963. Bar: Tex. 1963. Assoc. Vinson & Elkins, Houston, 1963-70, ptnr., 1970—, mem. mgmt. com., 1980—. Served to capt. USAFR, 1956-59. Woodrow Wilson fellow U. Tex., 1959-60. Fellow Am. Bar Found., Tex. Bar Found., Houston Bar Found.; mem. ABA, Houston Bar Assn., Am. Law Inst., Nat. Assn. Bond Lawyers (pres. 1981-82, bd. dirs. 1979-83), Tex. Research League (bd. dirs. 1987—), Order of Coif, Phi Delta Phi. Democrat. Episcopalian. Clubs: Houston Ctr., Ramada (Houston).

HOWELL, GREGORY JOSEPH, engineering company executive; b. East St. Louis, Ill., Nov. 24, 1939; s. Jesse Allan and Rita Claire (LePere) H.; m. Yvonne Elizabeth Mallett, Aug. 22, 1959; children: Joseph K., Christopher G., Yvette M., Jeanine M., Rita C., Madelon L. BS in Acctg., St. Louis U., 1965, MBA, 1973. Acct./data processor Sverdrup Corp., St. Louis, 1957-82, dir. info. systems ctr., 1982-83, chief acct., 1983-85, corp. controller, 1986—; instr. acctg. McKendree Coll., Lebanon, Ill., 1976-81. Roman Catholic. Home: 881 Meadowview Ln Columbia IL 62236 Office: Sverdrup Corp 801 N 11th St Saint Louis MO 63101

HOWELL, HARLEY THOMAS, lawyer; b. Chgo., June 5, 1937; s. Harley W. and Geneva (Engelmann) H.; m. Aliceann A. McLaughlin, Apr. 23, 1983; children by previous marriage: Shelley A., Rebecca L., Emily S. A.B., Princeton U., 1959; J.D., Yale U., 1962. Bar: Md. 1962, U.S. Supreme Ct. 1966, D.C. 1972. Law clk. to chief judge U.S. Ct. Appeals (4th cir.) 1962-63; assoc. Semmes, Bowen & Semmes, Balt., 1966-72, ptnr., 1972—; mem. Gov.'s Commn. to Revise Annotated Code Md., 1975-85; mem. standing com. on rules of practice and procedure Ct. Appeals of Md., 1985—. Bd. dirs. Balt. Symphony Orch., 1975—, sec., 1986—; trustee Edn. Ctr. of Sheppard Pratt, 1986—. Served to capt. JAG Corps, U.S. Army, 1963-66. Decorated Army Commendation medal. Mem. ABA, Md. State Bar Assn., Balt. City Bar Assn., D.C. Bar Assn., Fed. Bar Assn. Democrat. Clubs: Center, Wine and Food Soc., Wranglers Law (Balt.). Home: 1012 Chestnut Ridge Dr Lutherville MD 21093 Office: Semmes Bowen & Semmes 250 W Pratt St Baltimore MD 21201

HOWELL, HENRY WARDWELL, JR., banker; b. N.Y.C., Feb. 19, 1942; s. H. Wardwell and Margaret Grant (Noyes) H.; m. Barbara Connell, June 7, 1969; children: Margaret Colby, Olivia Wardwell. BA, Yale U., 1964. Asst. treas. Morgan Guaranty Trust Co., N.Y.C., 1968-70, asst. v.p., 1970-72, v.p., 1972-73; v.p. Morgan Guaranty Trust Co., Frankfurt am Main, Fed. Republic of Germany, 1973-77, Sydney, Australia, 1977-79; mng. dir. Australian United Corp., Melborne, 1979-82; mng. dir. Australian United Corp., N.Y.C., 1982-86, sr. v.p., 1986—; bd. dirs. Morgan Securities Svcs. Trading Corp., N.Y.C., Morgan Bank, Wilmington, Del. Steward Power Ten, N.Y.C., 1986-88, pres., 1988—. Mem. Links Club (N.Y.C.), Round Hill Club, Leander Club (Eng.). Office: Morgan Guaranty Trust Co 60 Wall St New York NY 10015

HOWELL, JAMES BURT, III, technical sales consultant; b. Bridgeton, N.J., Dec. 11, 1933; s. James Burt and Catharine Stanger (Sparks) H. BS with high honors, Rutgers U., 1956; MBA, U. Del., 1980. Agrl. sales rep. Allied Chem. Corp., Phila., 1957-59; sales cons. Asgrow Seed Co. subs. Upjohn Co., Vineland, N.J., 1960—; bd. dirs. Advance Weight Systems, Inc., LaGrange, Ohio. Mem. ofcl. bd. (session) 1st Presbyn. Ch. of Cedarville (N.J.), 1960—; admissions liaison officer U.S. Mil. Acad., West Point, N.Y., 1973—. Served with U.S. Army, 1957, served to col. U.S. Army Res. Recipient Burpee Hort. award Rutgers U., 1955. Mem. Am. Def. Preparedness Assn., Vegetable Growers Assn. N.J., Pesticide Assn. N.J. (bd. dirs.), Res. Officers Assn. U.S., Phi Beta Kappa, Alpha Gamma Rho, Alpha Zeta. Home: Sayres Neck Cedarville NJ 08311 Office: Asgrow Seed Co 1740 E Oak Rd Vineland NJ 08360

HOWELL, JOHN ALFRED, chemical company executive; b. Montreal, Que., Can., July 2, 1929; s. John Charles and Barbara MAry (Green) H.; m. Lorna Grant, May 16, 1953; children: Barbara, Elaine, Grant, Valerie, David. BSc, Concordia U., 1952; diploma in mgmt., Western U., 1967, Oxford U., 1969. With C-I-L Inc., Montreal and Toronto, Can., 1950-80; v.p. comml. C-I-L Inc., Toronto, 1980-82, v.p., 1982-87, sr. v.p. corp. devel. and info. tech., 1987—; bd. dirs. Bapco Partnership, Toronto. Leader, exec. Scouts Can., Toronto, 1962—. Recipient medal of merit Scouts Can., 1988. Mem. Bd. Trade. Office: C-I-L Inc, 90 Sheppard Ave E, North York, ON Canada M2N 6H2

HOWELL, MARY ELIZABETH, small business owner; b. Galesburg, Ill., Feb. 19, 1942; d. John A. Shaner and Elizabeth N. (Bowen) Knowles; m. Murrell D. Howell, Dec. 22, 1969; children: Cherie, Thomas, Dean, Murrell. Cert., Alamo Beauty Coll., 1961; student, Jane Grace Sch. Dress Design, 1973; BS in Bus. Adminstrn., U. Redlands, 1985. Owner, operator Howell's Acctg., Minot, N.D., 1972-78; gen. mgr. Gravel Products, Inc., Minot, 1978-80; controller Bluebird Internat., Inc., Denver, 1981-83; owner, pres. Magnetic Power Systems, Huntington Beach, Calif., 1984—; free-lance cons. Huntington Beach, 1984—; cons. for mfg., health care, real estate, electronics, academia and personal svcs.; owner Cosmetics For Me, Huntington Beach, 1987—; cons., sr. fin. analyst U. Calif., Irvine, 1987—. Copyright Thin Graille of Insanity etching; patentee rail system, ground effect vehicle; designer award winning needlework, costumes and hairstyles for amateur theater groups; developer cosmetic cream. Leader Girl Scouts USA, Minot, 1973-75, den mother Boy Scouts Am., Minot, 1974, fund raiser Minot AFB Little League and Youth Orgn., 1975; active Hadassah, 1975—, Temple Sharon sisterhood, Costa Mesa, Calif., 1986—. Mem. Nat. Assn. Female Execs., Nat. Assn. Accts. Orange Coast (dir. 1982, 83, v.p. edn. and profl. devel. 1984, 86, sec. 1985, v.p. adminstrn. 1987, pres. 1988), Toastmasters, CTM. Republican. Jewish. Office: Magnetic Power Systems PO Box 1115 Huntington Beach CA 92647

HOWELL, RICHARD PAUL, SR., transportation engineer; b. Sarasota, Fla., Nov. 20, 1927; s. Paul Augustus and Mary Amanda (Snead) H.; m. Judith Kay Eshelman, Sept. 6, 1958; children: Richard Paul, Thomas Bradford, Robert Greggson, Mary Amanda. BSCE, Mich. State U., 1949. Registered profl. engr., Ohio, Mass., R.I., Conn., N.Y., N.J., Pa., Del., D.C., Md. Track supr. to div. engr. Pa. R.R. and successor co. Penn Central R.R., 1949-71; from chief r.r. engr. to v.p. Deleuw, Cather & Co., Washington, 1971— ; mem. Mich. State U. Alumni Engring. Council, East Lansing, 1968-72. Contbr. articles on transp. to profl. publs. Dist. chmn. Md. gubernatorial campaign, 1967. Served to lt. USN, 1945-46, Civil Engr. Corp. USNR. Recipient Toulmin medal Am. Soc. Mil. Engrs., 1979; named Railroader of Mo., Progressive Railroads, 1979. Mem. Am. Ry. Engring. Assn., Transp. Research Bd., Camp Hill Jr. C. of C. (pres. 1961-62), Masons, Phi Delta Theta. Republican. Presbyterian. Avocations: golf, racquetball, sailing, skiing, travel. Home: 15205 Hannans Way Rockville MD 20853 also: 27 South Terr Chautauqua NY 14722 Office: De Leuw Cather & Co 1133 15th St NW Washington DC 20036

HOWELL, R(OBERT) THOMAS, JR., food company executive; b. Racine, Wis., July 18, 1942; s. Robert T. and Margaret Paris (Billings) H.; m. Karen Wallace Corbett, May 11, 1968; children: Clarinda, Margaret, Robert. AB, Williams Coll., 1964; JD, U. Wis., 1967; Advanced Mgmt. Program, Harvard U., 1981. Bar: Wis. 1968, Ill. 1968, U.S. Dist. Ct. (no. dist.) Ill. 1968, U.S. Tax Ct. Assoc. Hopkins & Sutter, Chgo., 1967-71; sr. atty. The Quaker Oats Co., Chgo., 1971-77, counsel, 1977-80, v.p., assoc. gen. corp. counsel, 1980-84, v.p., gen. corp. counsel, 1984—. Editor: (mags.) Barrister, 1975-77, Compleat Lawyer, 1983-87. Bd. dirs., v.p. Neighborhood Justice of Chgo., 1985-88; bd. dirs., sec. Infant Welfare Soc. Chgo., 1984—; bd. dirs., v.p. Chgo. Bar Found., 1987—. Served to capt. U.S. Army, 1966-72. Mem. ABA (bd. dirs., council mem. gen. practice sect. 1987—), Ill. Bar Assn., Wis. Bar Assn., Chgo. Bar Assn. (bd. mgrs. 1977-79, chmn. young lawyers sect. 1974-75), Food and Drug Law Inst. (bd. dirs. 1986—). Presbyterian. Clubs: Law of Chgo., Econ. of Chgo., Univ. (Chgo.) (bd. dirs. 1982-85, 87—, v.p.); Pewaukee (Wis.) Yacht. Home: 853 W Chalmers Pl Chicago IL 60614 Office: Quaker Oats Co 321 N Clark Chicago IL 60610-4714

HOWELL, WILLIAM ASHLEY, III, lawyer; b. Raleigh, N.C., Jan. 2, 1949; s. William Ashley II and Caroline Erskine Greenleaf; m. Esther Holland, Dec. 22, 1973. BS, Troy State U., 1972; JD, Birmingham Sch. Law, 1977; postgrad. U. Ala.-Birmingham. Bar: Ala. 1977, U.S. Dist. Ct. (no. dist.) Ala. 1977, U.S. Ct. Appeals (5th cir.) 1977, U.S. Supreme Ct. 1982, U.S. Ct. Appeals (11th cir.) 1983, U.S. Dist. Ct. (mid. dist.) Ala. 1987. Atty. pub. defender div. Legal Aid. Soc. of Birmingham, 1977-78, later civil div.; dist. office atty. SBA, Birmingham, 1980-82, dist. counsel Ala. Dist., 1982—; spl. asst. U.S. Atty. (Middle Dist.), Ala., 1988—. Bd. dirs. Hoover

Homeowners Assn., 1977-81. Recipient Am. Jurisprudence Criminal Procedure Book award. Mem. ABA, Fed. Bar Assn. (sec. Birmingham chpt. 1980-81), Ala. Bar Assn. (com. on future of the profession 1978-81, 83-84), Birmingham Bar Assn., Comml. Law League, Sigma Delta Kappa (Outstanding Sr. award 1977). Episcopalian. Office: US SBA 2121 8th Ave N Room 200 Birmingham AL 35203

HOWELL, WILLIAM ROBERT, retail company executive; b. Claremore, Okla., Jan. 3, 1936; s. William Roosevelt and Opal Theo (Swan) H.; m. Donna Lee Hatch, June 7, 1956; children: Ann Elizabeth, Teresa Lynn. BBA, U. Okla., 1958. With J.C. Penney Co., Inc., 1958—, store mgr. J.C. Penney Co., Inc., Tulsa, 1968-69, dist. mgr., dir. Treasury Stores subs., Dallas, 1969-71, div. v.p., dir. domestic devel., N.Y.C., 1973-76, regional v.p., western regional mgr., 1976-79, sr. v.p., dir. merchandising, mktg. and catalog, 1979-81, exec. v.p., 1981-82, vice chmn. bd. dirs., 1982-83, chmn., chief exec. officer, 1983—, also bd. dirs.; bd. dirs. Exxon Corp., Warner-Lambert Corp., NYNEX Corp., Bankers Trust Co. Trustee Nat. Urban League. Mem. Am. Mgmt. Assn., Bus. Council, Bus. Roundtable, Am. Retail Fedn., Retail Tax Com. of Common Interest, Am. Soc. of Corp. Execs., Nat. Retail Mchts. Assn. (bd. dirs.), Dirs.' Table, Delta Sigma Pi, Beta Gamma Sigma, Economic Club. Baptist.

HOWES, ALFRED SPENCER, business and insurance consultant; b. Troy, N.Y., Sept. 10, 1917; s. Alfred G. and Frances (Youngs) H.; m. Elizabeth Hoffner, Oct. 10, 1942; children: Wendy, Mary Lee, Constance Ellen. Student, Brown U., 1934-35, U. Ala., 1935-36, Syracuse U., 1943-44. Agt., advanced underwriting cons. for N.Y. and Vt. with Conn. Mut. Life Ins. Co.; owner bus. cons. co., 1946; pres. Employee Incentive Plans of Am., Inc.; chmn. bd. Utica Duxbak Corp., 1956-86; pres., dir. Hyden, Inc., 1970-80, Outdoor Outfitters, 1960-86; bd. dirs. Emerson Plastics Corp., Insulating Shapes, Inc., Bering Trading Corp., Scotsmoor Co., Inc., Killip Laundering & Dry Cleaning Co., Inc., Killip Services, Inc., Smiley Bros., Inc., Mech. Tech., Inc., SVM Inc., Nursing Homes, Inc., Broad St. Realty Co. Pub. Gray Letter. Past sec., bd. dirs. N.Y.C. Estate Planning Council; bd. dirs. Placid's Parkas, Inc., 1956-82, Winchestor Knitting Mills, Inc., 1960-75, J.A. Firsching & Son, IN.c, 1976-85. mem. N.Y. State Temporary Commn. on Banking, Ins. and Fin. Services. Served with U.S. Army, ETO, 1943-46. Mem. Nat. Assn. Life Underwriters (life, pub. relations chmn. Million Dollar Round Table), N.Y. State Assn. Life Underwriters (chmn. com. to revise laws concerning decedents and their estates, pres. 1966-67), N.Y.C. Assn. Life Underwriters (bd. dirs., pres.), Am. Philatelic Soc., Assn. for Advanced Life Underwriting (pres. 1970-71). Clubs: Collectors, Brown (N.Y.C.); University (Albany); Fort Schuyler (Utica). Home: 42 Fenimore Rd Scarsdale NY 10583 Office: 551 Fifth Ave New York NY 10176

HOWES, WILLIAM BROWNING, forest products company executive; b. Washington, Apr. 22, 1937; s. William and Mildred (Browning) H.; m. Carey Green, June 4, 1959 (div. Apr. 1978); children: William, Heather; m. Mary McCall Howes. BA, Furman U., 1959; grad. advanced mgmt. program, Harvard U., 1977. With Union Camp Co., 1962—; salesman Spartanburg, S.C., 1963-68; nat. accounts mgr. Atlanta, 1968-69; various sales and managerial positions Wayne, N.J., 1968-78, v.p., gen. mgr. bags, 1978-83, v.p. gen. mgr., containers, 1983-84, sr. v.p., 1984—. 1st lt. U.S. Army, 1960-62. Mem. Am. Paper Inst., Paper Bag Inst. (pres. 1976-77), Paper Shipping Sack Mfrs. Assn., Paperboard Packaging Council, Furman U. Alumni Assn. (bd. dirs. 1986), Ridgewood Country Club. Presbyterian. Home: 30 E Saddle River Rd Saddle River NJ 07458 Office: Union Camp Corp 1600 Valley Rd Wayne NJ 07470

HOWEY, GREGORY BLAIR, diversified manufacturing company executive; b. Sandwich, Ill., 1942; married. BS, U. Wis., 1964; MBA, Harvard U., 1966. With Torrington (Conn.) Co., 1966-79; v.p. needle div., hand tool div. Ingersoll Rand, Fullerton, Calif., 1979-83; v.p. Insilco Corp., Meriden, Conn., 1983-87, exec. v.p. adminstrn. and planning, 1987—. Office: Insilco Corp 1000 Research Pkwy Meriden CT 06450

HOWKINS, JOHN BLAIR, mining company executive; b. Falkirk, Stirlingshire, Scotland, Feb. 12, 1932; immigrated to Can., 1965; s. George and Jemina Maclaren (Brown) H.; m. Heather Ferguson Nicoll, Jan. 8, 1955; children: Blair Nicoll, John Alexander, Cecilia Anne. B.S. with honors, U. Edinburgh (Scotland), 1953, Ph.D., 1961. Registered profl. engr., Ont. Sr. geologist Anglo Am. Corp., Central Africa, 1965; chief geologist Hudson Bay Mining and Smelting, Ont., Can., 1965-68, v.p. exploration, 1968-76, sr. v.p., 1978-82, 83-86; sr. v.p., group exec. Inspiration Resources Corp., N.Y.C., 1986—; dir. Farley Gold, Inc., Hudson Bay Gold, Inc., Hudson Bay Mining, Tantalum Mining Corp. of Can., Inspiration Gold, Inc.; dir., pres. Hudson Holdings Corp.; chmn. bd. dirs. Black Pine Mining Co., Phoenix, Terra Internat. Inc., Sioux City, Iowa. Mem. Canadian Inst. Mining and Metallurgy, Assn. Profl. Engrs. Ont., AIME, Geol. Assn. Can.

HOWLAND, ALLEN HATHAWAY, soap company executive; b. Walpole, Mass., Jan. 3, 1921; s. Ralph S. and Laura A. (Garby) H.; m. Katharine L. McFarland; children: John H., Pater A., Frances Gammell, Janet Gorod. BA, Amherst Coll., 1942. Treas. Original Bradford Soap Works Inc., West Warwick, R.I., 1960-70, pres., 1970-80, chief exec. officer, 1970—, chmn. bd. dirs., 1980—; bd. dirs. Old Stone Corp., Providence, Providence Energy Corp. Served to lt. USN, 1942-46, PTO. Office: Original Bradford Soap Works 200 Providence St West Warwick RI 02893

HOWLETT, JULIE A., corporate communications specialist. AA in Bus. Adminstrn., Broward Community Coll.; BS in Profl. Studies, Barry U. With Eastern Airlines, mng. editor Flight Line mag., supr., sr. analyst, project mgr.; assoc. exec. dir. BJ Assocs., Miami, Fla., sr. assoc.; speaker, instr. seminars. Mem. instructional tech. and ednl. media adv. bd. U. Cen. Fla., Orlando. Mem. Assn. for Edn. Communications and Tech., Internat. TV Assn., Assn. Women in Mgmt., Am. Soc. Tng. and Devel. Home: 2740 Egret Way Cooper City FL 33026 Office: Audio Visual Mgmt Assn 7907 NW 53d St Ste 346 Miami FL 33166

HOXTER, CURTIS JOSEPH, international economic adviser, public relations counselor; b. Marburg, Germany, July 20, 1922; s. Jacob and Hannah (Katzenstein) H.; AB, NYU, 1948, MA, 1950; m. Grace Lewis, Feb. 4, 1945 (dec.); children: Ronald Alan, Victoria Ann Finder, Audrey Theresa Strecker; m. 2d, Allegra Branson. Staff contbr. AUFBAU-Reconstn., N.Y.C., 1939-40; feature writer, reporter L.I. Daily Press, 1940-42; editor, writer OWI, 1943-45; public info. officer Dept. State, 1945-47; info. cons. ECA, 1950-55; public relations cons. various cos.; dir. public relations Internat. C. of C., U.S. Council Internat. C. of C., 1948-53; freelance columnist Scripps-Howard Newspapers; exec. v.p. George Peabody and Assos., Inc., 1953-56; pres. Curtis J. Hoxter, Inc., internat. public relations counsels and econ. and fin. advs. Adviser, U.S. Com. for UN Day; adv. on internat. econ. and fin. problems to govt. agys.; adv. U.S. Del. Disarmament Conf., London. Served with AUS, World War II. Mem. Public Relations Soc. Am. Clubs: Metropolitan, Overseas Press (N.Y.C.), Nat. Press, University (Washington), Bonnie Briar Country. Author weekly column Scripps-Howard papers, The Foreign Economic Scene; sr. advisor Internat. Economy mag.; contbr. articles to nat. mags. Office: 350 Lexington Ave New York NY 10016

HOYT, BRADLEY JAMES, financial executive; b. Spokane, Wash., Sept. 26, 1949; s. Delmar W. and Katherine (Bjerke) H.; m. Carolyn Nirk (div.); 1 child, Bret; m. Christine M. Loomis, Nov. 28, 1977; 1 child, Harley. BA in Bus. Adminstrn., Eastern Wash. U., 1976; cert., Coll. Fin. Planning, 1987. Adminstrv. asst. Boise Cascade Homes, Post Falls, Idaho, 1976-77, dealer, coordinator, 1977-78; direct sales rep. Boise Cascade Homes, Boise, 1978-80, territorial sales mgr., 1980-81; v.p., office mgr. Cascade Homes, Post Falls, 1981-82; registered rep. Waddell & Reed, Spokane, 1982-84, sr. acct. exec., 1984—; pres. Hoyt Ranch, Inc., Spokane, 1978—, Riviera Travel, Spokane, 1987—. Mem. Inst. Cert. Fin. Planners, Spokane C. of C. (mem. prodn. com. 1987—, 1st v.p. 1988). Office: Waddell & Reed E 9016 Indiana Spokane WA 99212

HOYT, CHARLEE ILDORA, management executive; b. Bluefield, W.Va., May 21, 1936; d. Charles Ives Van Cleve and Kathryn Margarete (Harden) Perrow; m. Ronald Reiner Hoyt, 1959 (div. 1983); children: Dean Christopher, Jason Allen. BA in Edn., U. Fla., 1959, MEd, 1962, postgrad., 1963-64. Cert. spl. edn. tchr. Tchr. Amherst County Schs., Elon, Va., 1958; tchr. spl. edn. Marion County Schs., Ocala, Fla., 1959-61; counselor Univ. Counseling Ctr., Gainesville, Fla., 1962-63, Sunland Tng. Ctr., Gainesville, 1963; mem. community faculty Minn. Met. State Coll., Mpls., 1972-83; mem. council City of Mpls., 1975-86; ptnr. Van Cleve Assocs., 1980-87; pres. Van Cleve, Doran & Bruno, Inc. 1987—; corp. officer BAM Leasing Co., Inc., 1987—; dir. human resources Pascua Yagu Tribe; mem. faculty Govt. Tng. Service, St. Paul, 1978-86, Ariz. Govt. Tng. Services; pres. Minn. Women in City Govt., St. Paul, 1978-79; mem. Met. Land Use Adv. Bd., St. Paul, 1978-83; bd. dirs. Transp. Adv. Bd., St. Paul, 1979-81; mem. conf. faculty League of Minn. Cities, St. Paul, 1979-82; bd. dirs. Met. Council Criminal Justice Adv. Bd., St. Paul, 1979-82; pres. Women in Mcpl. Govt., Nat. League of Cities, Washington, 1980-81, founder minority caucus coalition, 1982, dir., 1982-84; curriculum cons. Nat. Women's Edn. Fund, Washington, trainer, 1982—. Presenter numerous workshops; contbr. articles to profl. jours. Mem. Women Helping Women YWCA, 1987—; various offices with Republican Party, Minn., 1970-86 ; pres. Burroughs Elem. Sch. PTA, Mpls., 1973-74; panelist White House Conf., 1981; chmn. Senator Durenburger's Task Force on Women's Issues, Mpls., 1981-84; bd. dirs. Nat. Conf. Rep. Mayors and Council Mems., 1984-85; mem. Senator Durenburger's Intergovtl. Relations Adv. Com., Mpls., 1984-86; bd. dirs. Twin Cities Internat. Program, Mpls., 1983-86; participant Women's Dialogue US/USSR, Moscow, 1985; trustee Council Internat. Programs, Cleve., 1985—; bd. dirs. At the Foot of the Mountain Theater, Mpls., 1985-86, Tucson Ctrs. for Women and Children, 1988—; bd. dirs. GOP Feminists, Hamline U. Ctr. for Women in Govt.; mem. Nat. Women's Polit. Caucus, Hennepin County Women's Polit. Caucus; mem. Tucson Support for Success Team, 1986—, Tuscon YWCA Women Helping Women; bd. dirs. Tucson Ctrs. Women and Children. Mem. Am. Soc. Training and Devel., Minn. Women Elected Ofcls. (pres. 1983-85), Izaak Walton League, Tucson C. of C. Methodist. Club: Remington Investment (pres. 1968-70) (Mpls.). Avocations: lapidary, music, handwork, camping, science fiction. Home: 6932 E Second St Tucson AZ 85710

HOYT, HENRY HAMILTON, JR., pharmaceutical and toiletry company executive; b. Orange, N.J., Aug. 10, 1927; s. Henry Hamilton and Anna Clark (Orcutt) H.; m. Muriel Virginia Christie, Feb. 5, 1960. A.B. cum laude, Princeton U., 1949. With Carter-Wallace Inc., N.Y.C., 1950—; chmn. bd., chief exec. officer Carter-Wallace Inc., 1975—, also bd. dirs. Trustee Princeton Elm Club, 1959—, Overlook Hosp., Summit, N.J., 1976—; bd. dirs. Deafness Research Found., 1977—; trustee Pingry Sch., Hillside, N.J., 1970-78, pres. bd., 1972—. Served with Transp. Corps U.S. Army, 1946-47. Mem. Cosmetic, Toiletry and Fragrance Assn. (dir. 1965—, treas. 1966-76), Pharm. Mfrs. Assn. (dir. 1971-75), Proprietary Assn. (dir. 1970—). Episcopalian. Clubs: Univ, Met, Princeton of N.Y; Baltusrol Golf (Springfield, N.J.); Oyster Harbors (Osterville, Mass.). Office: Carter-Wallace Inc 767 Fifth Ave New York NY 10153

HRIBERNIK, ROBERT MARTIN, distribution executive; b. St. Louis, July 23, 1945; s. Anthony Martin and Dorothea Harriet (Bridwell) H.; m. Mary Kathleen Daniels, Oct. 1974 (div. 1982); children: Leigh Kathleen, Susan Elizabeth; m. Jo Ann Surmont, July 3, 1982. BSBA, U. Mo., St. Louis, 1969; MS in Mgmt., Duke U., 1974. Account rep. Mallinckrodt, Inc., St. Louis, 1969-70; sr. account rep. Mallinckrodt, Inc., Raleigh, N.C., 1970-73, adminstrv. mgr., 1973-77; mgr. customer service Borden, Inc., Columbus, Ohio, 1977-80; mgr. sales service and user info. systems Anaconda Wire & Cable Co., Indpls., 1980-84; dir. distbn. and customer service Fisher Cheese Co., Wapakoneta, Ohio, 1984-87; mgr. distbn. services Bausch & Lomb, Greenville, S.C., 1987—; cons. Ind. Bell, Indpls., 1984. Mem. Council Logistics Mgmt., Warehouse Edn. and Research Council, Am. Prodn. and Inventory Control Soc. Presbyterian. Lodges: Sertoma (v.p. 1986-87), Elks. Home: 201 Eastcrest Dr Simpsonville SC 29681 Office: Bausch & Lomb 130 Commerce Dr Greenville SC 29615

HRUBY, F. MICHAEL, marketing executive; b. Cleve., Feb. 2, 1946; s. Frank M. and Pollee Menoher (Phipps) H.; m. Leslie Marie Clift, July 20, 1974; children: Emily Rose, Pollee Jeanne. BA in History, U. Rochester, 1968; MS in Resource Econs., U. N.H., 1972. Policy analyst N.Y. State Senate, Albany, 1975-76; tech. sales rep. graphic arts industry, 1976-78; cons. The MAC Group, Cambridge, Mass., 1978-81; mktg. mgr. Gregory Fossella Assoc., Boston, 1981-83; dir. new product mktg. Foster Grant Corp., Leominster, Mass., 1983-84; pres. Tech. Mktg. Group Inc., Acton, Mass., 1984—; bd. dirs. Internat. Polarizer Inc., Marlborough, Mass., 1987—. Trustee Nashoba-Brooks Sch., Concord, Mass. Author: But We Can't Get a Mortgage, 1975; What's Missing at the "T"?, 1981. Mem. tax com. SBA New Eng., Waltham, Mass., 1985—. Mem. Soc. Competitor Intelligence Profls. (v.p.), Nat. Speakers Assn. Am. Mktg. Assn. Republican. Avocations: economic history, railroads, travel, hiking, skiing. Office: Tech Mktg Group Inc 77 Great Rd Suite 202 Acton MA 01720

HRUBY, PAUL JAMES, sales and marketing services executive; b. Cleve., July 30, 1927; s. John and Jennie (Matousek) H.; m. Theresa M. Tulcewicz, Oct. 3, 1964; children: Maria, Faith Ann, Paul James. BBA, Western Res. U., 1951, MBA, 1967. Asst. product mgr. Harshaw Chem. Co., Cleve., 1951-61; mktg. analyst Shell Oil Corp., Cleve., 1962; tech. sales rep. N.Am. Mogul Products Co., Cleve., 1963-64; mktg. and sales mgr. Marlin Mfg. Corp., Cleve., 1964-76; pres. Pathon Co., Cleve., 1976—. Active Big Bros., 1963-67; former cons., judge Jr. Achievement. Served with USNR, 1945-46. Mem. Sales and Mktg. Execs. Internat., Soc. Plastic Engrs., Cleve. Bd. Area Realtors. Republican. Roman Catholic. Club: Cayomaw (hon., past pres., trustee). Home and Office: 4352 Brendan Ln North Olmsted OH 44070

HRUSKA, ELIAS NICOLAS, financial executive; b. San Francisco, July 7, 1943; s. Nicholas Emanuel Hruska and Silvia Maria (Cortés) Warren; m. Maria De Simone, Jan. 29, 1966; children: Sonia K., Shala M., Karim M. BA with honors, U. Calif.-Berkeley, 1966, MA, 1968. Cert. fin. planner. Acct. exec. Apex Fin. Planners, Los Altos, Calif., 1978-79, v.p. ins., 1979-80, pres., 1980-81; br. mgr. Fin. Network Investment Corp., San José, Calif., 1981—; investment advisor Fin. Network Adv. Corp., San José, 1980—. Author numerous poems. Parent-student liaison student coun. Fisher Jr. High Sch., Los Gatos, Calif., 1987—. Mem. Internat. Assn. Fin. Planning. Democrat. Roman Catholic. Office: Fin Network Investment Corp 51 University Ave Ste G Los Gatos CA 95030

HRYCAK, PETER, mechanical engineer, educator; b. Przemysl, Poland, July 8, 1923; came to U.S., 1949, naturalized, 1956; s. Eugene and Ludmyla (Dobrzanska) H.; m. Rea Meta Limberg, June 13, 1949; children: Maria (dec.), Michael Paul, Orest W.T., Alexandra Martha. Student, U. Tubingen, Germany, 1946-48; B.S. with high distinction, U. Minn., 1954, M.S., 1955, Ph.D., 1960. Registered profl. engr., N.J. Adminstrv. asst. French Mil. Govt. in Germany, 1947-49; instr. engring. U. Minn., Mpls., 1955-60; mem. tech. staff Bell Telephone Labs., Murray Hill, N.J., 1960-65; sr. project engr. Curtiss-Wright Corp., Woodridge, N.J., 1965; assoc. prof. mech. engring. N.J. Inst. Tech., 1965-68, prof., 1968—; Participant in Internat. Conf. on Engring. and Applied Sci. Contbr. articles to profl. jours.; one of original Telstar designers. Bd. dirs. Ukrainian Congress Com. Am., Mpls., 1956-60, Plast Camp, East Chatham, N.Y., 1963-68; v.p. Ukrainian Music Found., 1977-86. NASA grantee, 1967-68; NSF grantee, 1982-84. Sr. mem. Inst. Environ. Scis.; mem. ASME, AIAA, Am. Soc. Engring. Edn., Ukrainian Engrs. Soc. Am. (pres. 1966-67), Am. Geophys. Union, AAUP, Shevchenko Sci. Soc., Ukrainian Acad. Arts and Scis. in U.S.A., Am. Chem. Soc., U. Minn. Alumni Club, Pi Tau Sigma, Tau Beta Pi, Sigma Xi. Home: 19 Roselle Ave Cranford NJ 07016 Office: New Jersey Inst Tech 323 Martin Luther King Blvd Newark NJ 07102

HSIAW, HENRY CHING-YE, engineering executive; b. Taipei, Taiwan, Sept. 14, 1955; came to U.S., 1977; m. Shiaw-Fen Hwang, Oct. 16, 1980; children: Alice, Jennifer. BSEE, Nat. Chiao-Tung U., Taiwan, 1977; MS, MIT, 1980, PhD, 1987. Staff engr. Advanced Micro-Devices, Inc., Sunnyvale, Calif., 1980-82; project mgr. Hewlett Packard Labs., Palo Alto, Calif., 1982-84; mgr. Digital Equipment Corp., Littleton, Mass., 1986-88; engring. mgr. Kinetics Inc., Walnut Creek, Calif., 1988—; cons. Modem Tech., Inc., Los Altos, Calif., 1982-85. Contbr. articles to profl. jours.; inventor fiber optic clock recovery circuit, 1988. Naval Rsch. Lab. fellow, 1985. Mem. IEEE, Soc. Photo-Optical Instrumentation Engrs., Lions Club, Sigma Xi. Office: Kinetics Inc PO Box 30476 Walnut Creek CA 94598

HSIEH, MICHAEL THOMAS, venture capitalist; b. Hong Kong, Mar. 9, 1958; came to U.S., 1968; s. Ching Chi and Za Za (Suffiad) H.; m. Tonia Chao, Sept. 6, 1987. BA, Harvard U., 1980, MBA, 1984. Analyst Merrill Lynch Capital Markets, N.Y.C., 1980-81; assoc. Sun Hung Kai Securities, N.Y.C., 1981-82, Chappell and Co., San Francisco, 1984-86; pres. LF Internat. Inc., Burlingame, Calif., 1986—; bd. dirs. Millworks Trading Co. Ltd., N.Y.C., Wilke Rodriguez, N.Y.C., West Bay Design, Inc., San Francisco. Mem. Harvard Club, Bay Club (San Francisco). Office: LF Internat Inc 1355 Market St Ste 501 San Francisco CA 94103

HSIEH, RUDY RU-PIN, banker; b. Taipei, Taiwan, July 6, 1950; came to U.S., 1976; s. Yu-Fu and Lan-Ying (Wu) H. B.S., Fu-Jen Catholic U., Taiwan, 1973; M.B.A., Long Island U., 1978. Credit officer Cathay Bank, Los Angeles, 1979; asst. v.p., Monterey Park, Calif., 1979-81, asst. v.p., asst. mgr., 1981-84, v.p., mgr., 1984—; fin. cons. Super Success Co., Ltd., Los Angeles, 1983-87; legislator, Republic of China, 1987—. Pres. Taiwan Benevolent Assn. of Calif., Monterey Park, 1983; bd. dirs. Taiwan Benevolent Assn. of Am., Bethesda, Md., 1982, v.p., 1983, pres., 1984. Mem. Chinese Am. Profl. Soc. Office: #1 Chung-San S Rd, Taipei Republic of China

HSIUNG, JAMES CHIEH, political science educator, consultant; b. Kaifeng, Honan, China, July 23, 1935; came to U.S., 1958, naturalized, 1973; s. Kungchieh Hsiung and Yungchih Hsieh; children: Susette Lyn, Eric Paul, Cynthia Cheryl. BA, Nat. Taiwan U., 1955; MA, So. Ill. U., 1960; PhD, Columbia U., 1967. Asst. prof. Columbia U., N.Y.C., summer 1967; asst. prof. polit. sci. NYU, N.Y.C., 1967-69, assoc. prof., 1969-75, prof. 1975—; pres. U.S.-Asia Research, Inc., N.Y.C., 1981—, Contemporary U.S.-Asia Research Inst., N.Y.C., 1982—. Author: Ideology and Practice, 1970; Law and Policy in China's Foreign Policy, 1972; editor: U.S.-Asian Relations, 1983; Beyond China's Foreign Policy, 1985, Human Rights in East Asia: A Cultural Perspective, 1986; contbr articles to profl. publs. Mem. Am. Assn. Chinese Studies (bd. dirs.), Am. Polit. Sci. Assn., Internat. Studies Assn., Assn. Asian Studies, Am. Soc. Internat. Law. Democrat.

HUANG, JENNMING STEPHEN, chemical engineer; b. Changhua, Taiwan, July 30, 1947; came to U.S., 1970; s. Ho-yian and Chung-Mei (Hsu) H.; m. Y. Sue Shy, Dec. 25, 1969; children: Raymond, Rayleen. BS in Chem. Engring., Nat. Taiwan U., 1969; MS, Syracuse U., 1972, PhD, 1975. Research engr. Internat. Flavors and Fragrances, Inc., Union Beach, N.J., 1976-78, sr. research engr., 1978-79, project leader, 1979-80, mgr. corp. engring. tech., 1980-83, dir. corp. engring. tech., 1983—. Contbr. articles to profl. jours. Mem. Am. Inst. Chem. Engrs. Office: Internat Flavors Fragranc Inc 1515 Hwy 36 Union Beach NJ 07735

HUBBARD, C(HARLES) RICHARD, financial consultant; b. Roanoke, Va., Feb. 2, 1954; s. Richard E. Hubbard and Anne H. (Hairfield) Todd; m. Pamela P. Vanderschoot, Apr. 23, 1978; 1 child, David R. AB in Econs. and Acctg. magna cum laude, Duke U., 1975. CPA, N.C.; cert. fin. planner. With Duke Power Co., Charlotte, N.C., 1975-77; sr. acct. Peat, Marwick, Mitchell and Co., Charlotte, 1977-79; prin., co-founder Carroll, Hubbard and Assocs., Charlotte, 1980-84; prin. MD Evans Fin. Cons., Charlotte, 1984—. Mem. Humane Soc., Charlotte, 1984—, People for Ethical Treatment of Animals, Washington, 1986—, Animal Welfare Inst., 1986—. Fellow N.C. Assn. CPA's (com. chmn. personal fin. planning 1985-87); mem. Am. Inst. CPA's, Internat. Assn. Fin. Planning, Registry for Fin. Planning Practitioners. Methodist. Office: M D Evans Fin Cons PO Box 30335 Charlotte NC 28230-0335

HUBBARD, CHARLES RONALD, engineering executive; b. Weaver, Ala., Feb. 4, 1933; s. John Duncan Hubbard and Athy Pauline (Lusk) Thorpe; m. Betty Lou McKleroy, Dec. 29, 1951; 1 son, Charles Ronald Hubbard II. BSEE, U. Ala., 1960. Mktg. mgr. Sperry Corp., Huntsville, Ala., 1969-71, head engring. sect., 1971-74; sr. staff engr. Honeywell Inc., Clearwater, Fla., 1974-76, mgr., 1976-79, chief engr., West Covina, Calif., 1979-83, assoc. dir. engring., 1983-84, assoc. dir. advanced systems, 1984-87, assoc. dir. programs, 1987-88; v.p. govt. systems div. Integrated Inference Machines, Anaheim, Calif., 1988—. Served as staff sgt. USAF, 1953-57. Mem. IEEE (sect. chmn. 1972-73). Methodist. Home: 5460 Willowick Circle Anaheim CA 92807 Office: Integrated Inference Machines 1468 E Katella Ave Anaheim CA 92805

HUBBARD, HYLAN THOMAS, III, insurance company executive; b. Lynchburg, Va., Jan. 26, 1947; s. Hylan Thomas Jr. and Florine (Morris) H.; m. Christine Richardson, Feb. 11, 1967; children: Hylan T. IV, Carmen D. AB, Bowdoin Coll., 1969. Mktg. trainee Aetna Life & Casualty Co., Washington, 1970-71; mktg. rep. Aetna Life & Casualty Co., Providence, 1971-74; instr., adminstr. Aetna Life & Casualty Co., Hartford, 1974-75; mgr. mktg. and personnel ins. Aetna Life & Casualty Co., Buffalo, 1975-78; regional dir. field mgmt. Aetna Life & Casualty Co., Hartford, 1978-80; gen. mgr. Aetna Life & Casualty Co., Harrisburg, Pa., 1980-82; gen. agt. Aetna Life & Casualty Co., Washington, 1982, gen. mgr., 1982-85; regional v.p. Aetna Life & Casualty Co., Hartford, 1985—; Mem., co. rep. D.C. Assigned Claims Bd., 1982-83, Commr.'s Task Force on Take-Out, Harrisburg, 1981-82. Co-chmn. campaign Am. Cancer Soc., Harrisburg, 1981; chmn. bd. counsellors U. D.C., 1985; bd. dirs. Greater Hartford YMCA, 1988-89; trustee Clark Atlanta U. Named One of Am.'s Best and Brightest Dollars & Sense Mag., Chgo., 1987. Mem. IMPACT (com. 1988), Sigma Pi Phi (bd. dirs. 1987-88), Hartford chpt. Kappa Alpha Psi Fraternity Inc.

HUBBARD, MICHAEL CHARLES, health science association administrator; b. Cortland, N.Y., Nov. 7, 1949; s. Gerald D. and Gloria Janet (Newman) H.; m. Janet Sue Martin, Dec. 30, 1972 (div. 1984); m. Jeanette Rosemary Moore, Nov. 16, 1985. AA, Tompkins-Cortland Community Coll., 1971; student, SUNY, Cortland, 1971-72; BS, Empire St. Coll., 1975. Lab. technologist Upstate Med. Ctr., Syracuse, N.Y., 1972-75; med. technologist, asst. supr. Oreg. Health Scis. U., Portland, 1975-80; co-founder, ptnr. Immunologic Assn., Portland, 1979-81, pres., chief exec. officer, dir., 1981-83; pres., chief exec. officer, dir. Epitope, Inc., Beaverton, Oreg., 1983—; ptnr. Oisinn Farms and Vineyards, Hillsboro, Oreg., 1987; bd. dirs. Purification Techs., Inc., Wilsonville, Oreg. Contbr. articles to profl. jours. Editor Portland Highland Games Assn., 1985-87. Mem. Nortwest Regional Lab., 1985 (com. on high tech.), Confrerie des Vignerons Club (Portland), Clan MacLeay Pipe Band Club, Pipe Major Club. Office: Epitope Inc 15425 SW Koll Pkwy Beaverton OR 97006

HUBBARD, THOMAS EDWIN (TIM), lawyer; b. Roseboro, N.C., July 10, 1944; s. Charles Spence and Mary Mercer (Reeves) H.; m. Leslie Howard, July 20, 1985; 1 child, Marvin Gannon. BS in Biomed. Engring., Duke U., 1970, postgrad., 1970-71; JD, U. N.C., 1973. Bar: N.C. 1973. Regulation writer, med. devices FDA, Washington, 1974-75; asst. dir. clin. affairs Zimmer USA, Warsaw, Ind., 1975, dir. regulatory affairs, 1975-76; house counsel Gen. Med. Corp., Richmond, Va., 1976-79; pvt. practice, Pittsboro, N.C., 1979—; pres. Chathamborough Research Group, Inc., Pittsboro, 1979—, Chathamborough Farms Inc., 1982—; sec., treas. Hubbard-Corry, Inc., Pittsboro, 1981—; chmn. Hubbard Bros., Inc., Chapel Hill, N.C., 1982-87; bd. dirs. No. State Legal Service, Hillsborough, N.C., 1980—, pres., 1986—; adj. instr. U. N.C. Law Sch., 1983. V.p. N.C. Young Dems. 4th Congl. Dist., 1970-71; mem. State Dem. Exec. Com., 1972-73; mem. paralegal adv. com. Cen. Carolina Community Coll., Sanford, N.C., 1987—, legal svcs. N.C. Long Range Planning Com., 1987—. Sgt. USMC, 1963-68. Named Top N.C. Young Dem., 1971. Mem. ABA, N.C. Bar Assn. (legal svcs. planning com. 1988—), Chatham County Bar Assn., Assn. for Advancement Med. Instrumentation (govt. affairs com. 1976). Democrat. Methodist. Office: PO Drawer 929 Pittsboro NC 27312 also: Chathamborough Research Group Inc 105 West St Pittsboro NC 27312

HUBBS, RONALD M., retired insurance company executive; b. Silverton, Oreg., Apr. 27, 1908; s. George W. and Ethel (Burch) H.; B.A., U. Oreg.; LL.D. (hon.), William Mitchell Coll. Law, Macalester Coll. H.L.D., (hon.), Carleton Coll., m. Margaret S. Jamie, Sept. 9, 1935; 1 son, George J. With St. Paul Fire & Marine Ins. Co., 1936-77, asst. to pres., 1948-52, v.p., 1952-59, exec. v.p., 1959-63; pres., chief exec., 1963-68, chmn., 1968-73; pres., chief exec. officer St. Paul Cos., Inc., 1968-73, chmn., 1973-77; past dir. Western Life Ins. Co., chmn. Toro Credit Co.; past chmn. AFIA Worldwide Ins. Past bd. dirs. Minn. Coun. on Econ. Edn.; bd. dirs., founding trustee Twin Cities

Pub. TV Corp., James H. Hill Reference Libr.; adv. bd. U. Minn. Sch. Mgmt.; task force U. Minn. Writing Standards, Lt. Gov. Minn. on Womens' History Ctr.; Gov.'s Adv. Com. on Literacy; bd. dirs. emeritus William Mitchell Coll. Law; trustee emeritus Coll. St. Thomas, Carleton Coll.; retired chmn. bd. trustees F.R. Bigelow Found.; past trustee, past chmn. Ins. Inst. Am.; mem., past chmn. pres.'s coun. St. Catherine's Coll.; gov. Internat. Inst. Seminars, Inc.; bd. dirs. Charles Lindbergh Fund, Cath. Digest; bd. overseers emeritus U. Minn. Sch. Mgmt.; bd. dirs. Inst. Philos. Rsch.; hon. trustee St. Paul Found., North Star Found.; bd. overseers Hill Monastic Manuscript Libr. and Univ. Without Walls; trustee Sci. Mus. Minn. elector Ins. Hall Fame. Served from 1st lt. to col. AUS, World War II. Decorated Legion of Merit; recipient St. Thomas Aquinas medal Coll. St. Thomas; creative leadership in adult edn. award MACAE; Life-long learning award Met. State U.; Disting. Community Builder award Indianhead coun. Boy Scouts Am.; Great Living St. Paulite award St. Paul C. of C.; Pres. Coun. award Minn. Pvt. Colls.; King's medal Carl XVI Gustaf of Sweden; Disting. Svc. award Minn. Humanities Commn.; Humanitarian award St. Paul YWCA; John Myers award for community svc.; Heckman award Minn. Coun. Founds. Mem. Am. Inst. Property and Liability Underwriters (past chmn., trustee), Orgn. Am. Historians, Minn. Hist. Soc. (past pres.), Co. Mil. Historians, Sherlock Holmes Soc. of London, Orchid Soc., Minn. Club (past pres., Alpha Tau Omega, Phi Delta Phi, Scabbard and Blade, Friars, Beta Gamma Sigma. Episcopalian (past trustee diocese Minn.). Home: 689 W Wentworth Ave #102 Saint Paul MN 55118 Office: 385 Washington St Saint Paul MN 55102

HUBER, JOAN MACMONNIES, frozen food co. exec.; b. N.Y.C., Dec. 15, 1927; d. Wallace and Marguerite Adele (Searing) MacMonnies; m. Don Lawrence Huber, June 23, 1951. BS in Biochemistry, Northwestern U., 1949; postgrad. N.Y. U., CCNY, 1950-57, Northwestern Transp. Inst., 1974; cert. fin. planner, Adelphi U., 1980. Research chemist Continental Baking Co., Jamaica, N.Y., 1949-57, research supr., 1953-57; co-owner, asst. mgr. Sta. KALE, Richland, Wash., 1957-59; new products mgr., Southland Frozen Foods, Mitchel Field, N.Y., 1959-62, asst. mktg. mgr., 1962-69, mktg. mgr., 1969-72, v.p. distbn. and corp. planning, 1972-86; pres. East Coast Services subs. Southland Frozen Foods, 1986—. Mem. Am. Chem. Soc., Am. Mgmt. Assn., Inst. Food Technologists, Am. Frozen Food Inst. (chmn. modularization task force, past chmn. distbn. council), Council of Logistics Mgmt., Internat. Assn. Fin. Planners. Home: 24 Rolling Dr Brookville NY 11545 Office: East Coast Svcs subs Southland Frozen Foods 50 Charles Linbergh Blvd Mitchel Field NY 11553

HUBER, RICHARD ALAN, financial planning executive; b. Peoria, Ill., Jan. 16, 1949; s. Robert and Dorothy Marie (Getz) H.; m. Margarete Helene Loos, Oct. 29, 1977; children: Renee, Jesse. AAS, DeVry Inst. Tedh., Chgo., 1969; BS, Elmhurst Coll., 1975. Cert. fin. planner. Messenger, phone clk. Merrill Lynch, Pierce, Fenner & Smith, Inc., Chgo., 1967-69; engr. Western Electric co., Rolling Meadows, Ill., 1969-73; ind. trader Merc. Exch., Chgo., 1973-82; owner, mgr. Richard A. Huber, Ltd., investment advisors, Northfield, Ill., 1983-88; reg. prin. Integrated Resources Equity Corp., N.Y.C. Mem. Internat. Assn. for Fin. Planning, Inst. Cert. Fin. Planners. Mem. Community Ch. Home: 2689 Birchwood Ln Deerfield IL 60015 Office: One Northfield Pla Northfield IL 60093

HUBER, RICHARD LESLIE, banker; b. Brevard, N.C., Nov. 2, 1936; s. William Worden and Marion (Griffith) H.; m. Roberta Palmer, June 10, 1960; children—Benjamin Philip, Alexander Leslie, Marcus Sebastian. BS, Harvard U., 1958. V.p. Citibank, N.A., Sao Paulo, Brazil, 1973-77; sr. v.p. Citibank, N.A., Tokyo, 1977-82; group exec. Citibank, N.A., N.Y.C., 1982-87; exec. v.p. Chase Manhattan Bank, N.Y.C., 1988—; bd. dirs. Chase Manhattan Capital Fin. Corp., Chase Manhattan Investment Holdings, Inc., Bank Capital Markets Assn., bd. dir.; chmn. bd. Chase Manhattan Futures Corp. Lt., USCG, 1959-60. Mem. Japan Soc. (treas.).

HUBER, THOMAS ARTHUR, business executive, administrator; b. Los Angeles, Apr. 3, 1959; s. John Roger and Louise Anne (Wombacher) H. BS, Pepperdine U., 1980. Programmer/analyst Pepperdine U., Malibu, Calif., 1979-81; tech. dir Masterfile, Santa Monica, Calif., 1980-84; v.p. Masterfile Inc., Santa Monica, Calif., 1984-86; ops. dir. A V Tronics, Azusa, Calif., 1984-86; data base adminstr. Calif. State U., Los Angeles, 1986—; tech. cons. C.H. Berger Corp. Tech. advisor: (book) Age Reduction System, 1985. Home: 3217 Utah #C Elmonte CA 91731 Office: Calif State U 5151 State University Dr Los Angeles CA 90032

HUBERT, JEAN-LUC, chemical executive; b. Metz, Moselle, France, Mar. 13, 1960; s. Andre and Franziska (Schmidt) H. Diplome Ingenieur, Ecole Centrale Paris, 1982, advanced engring., 1982; MS in Mech. and Nuclear Engring., Northwestern U., 1985. Simulation engr. Didier Werke, Wiesbaden, Fed. Republic Germany, 1981; engr. Iron and Steel Rsch. Inst., Metz, France, 1983; applications engr. L'Air Liquide, Paris, 1985-86; R&D mgr. cryogenic refrigeration processes Liquid Air Corp., Countryside, Ill., 1986-89; mgr. innovation and devel. bulk gases div. Liquid Air Corp., Countryside, 1989—; new process devel. cons. Liquid Air Corp./Energy Systems, Lake Charles, La. Patentee in field. 2d lt. French Navy, 1982-83. Tuition fellow Georges Lurcy Found., 1984, Henri Blanchenay fellow French Inst., 1984, Bieneck/Didier fellow, Fed. Republic of Germany, 1984. Mem. ASME (assoc.), Internat. Inst. Refrigeration (assoc.), Inst. Food Technologists. Home: 6103 Knollwood Rd Willowbrook IL 60514 Office: Liquid Air Corp Applied Tech Ctr 5230 S East Ave Countryside IL 60525

HUBLER, BRUCE ALBERT, management professional; b. Bridgeport, Conn., July 3, 1944; s. Julius Albert and Grace (Cass) H.; m. Michele A. Labonte, Dec. 12, 1975. BA, U. Bridgeport, 1967; MA, Fairfield (Conn.) U., 1970; MBA, Columbia U., 1975. Mgr. dealer relations Videorecord Corp., Conn., 1970-73; mgr. market devel. Sony Corp., N.Y.C., 1973-74; mgr., cons. Booz Allen & Hamilton, N.Y.C., 1975-76; corp. dir. staffing and manpower planning Heublein (Conn.) Inc., 1976-81; dir. mgmt. devel. GTE Corp., Conn., 1981-82; dir. exec. staff Celanese Inc., N.Y.C., 1982-83; dir. exec. staff Dun & Bradstreet Corp., N.Y.C., 1983-85, dir. mgmt. staffing and succession planning, 1985-87, sr. v.p. mgmt. resources planning and devel., 1987—. Mem. Nat. Assn. Corp. and Profl. Recruiters (bd. dirs.). Roman Catholic. Clubs: Bd. Room (N.Y.C); Patterson (Fairfield); Black Rock (Conn.) Yacht. Home: 149 Old Battery Rd Bridgeport CT 06605 Office: Dun & Bradstreet Corp 299 Park Ave New York NY 10171

HUBLITZ, SUE, sales professional; b. N.Y.C., June 6, 1940; d. Lincoln and Katherine (Daly) H. BA in Speech Therapy, Hofstra Coll., 1962; M, Columbia U., 1968. Head occupational therapy dept. St. Agnes Hosp., White Plains, N.Y., 1971-76; program coordinator devel. disabilities North Shore U. Hosp., Manhasset, N.Y., 1976-78; sales rep. Becton-Dickinson, Rutherford, N.J., 1978-81, Argus Surg. Co., Inc., Mt. Vernon, N.Y., 1981—. Mem. Am. Assn. Occupational Therapist (cert.). Home: 765 N Broadway 18B Hastings-on-Hudson NY 10706 Office: Argus Surg Co Inc 6 North St Mount Vernon NY 10550

HUCAL, STEPHEN JOSEPH, financial services company executive; b. Utica, N.Y., Aug. 10, 1952; s. Julian Stephen and Helen Mary (Ziober) H.; m. Louise Ann Case, May 2, 1981. BA, Syracuse U., 1974; MBA, Wharton Sch. U. Pa., 1979. CPA, 1980. Auditor Arthur Young and Co., N.Y.C., 1974-77; various positions from fin. analyst to mgr. fin. analysis Internat. Harvester Corp., Chgo. and Tulsa and Ft. Wayne, Ind., 1979-82; mgr. corp. fin. planning and analysis Am. Hosp. Supply Corp., Evanston, Ill., 1982-85; dir. fin. planning and analysis Sears Consumer Fin. Corp., Riverwoods, Ill., 1985-88; dir. mgmt. reporting and fin. analysis Dean Witter Fin. Svcs. Group, N.Y.C., 1988—. Patentee in med. field. Mem. Am. Inst. CPAs. Republican. Roman Catholic. Club: Lake Forest (sec., treas. 1986-87, pres. 1988—). Home: 1253 Breckenridge Ct Lake Forest IL 60045 Office: Sears Consumer Fin Corp 2500 Lake Cook Rd Riverwoods IL 60015

HUCKINS, VERNON DALE, financial executive; b. Thomas, Okla., May 14, 1944; s. Dean and Nida (Marshall) H.; m. Ellen Hopkins Huckins, Apr. 4, 1976; children: Matthew, Ernest, Teresa. BSBA, Okla. Panhandle State U., 1968; postgrad., U. Okla., 1969. Teller, asst. to cashier City Nat. Bank, Guymon, Okla., 1966-68; staff acct., audit Elmer Fox & Co., CPA's, Wichita, Kans., 1970-71; mgr. internal ops. Medicare reimbursement dept. Kans. Blue Cross Blue Shield, Topeka, 1971-82; mgr. health care third party reimbursement, mgmt. adv. services and small bus. acctg. Baird, Kurtz & Dobson CPA's, Wichita, 1982-85; chief fin. officer Golden Plains Inc., Hutchinson, Kans., 1984-86; v.p., chief fin. officer Install Inc. Colo., Lafayette, 1985—, Trautmann Millwork Inc., Lafayette, 1985—; chief fin. officer Install Inc. Kans., Tulsa, 1986—, Lahoma Ltd. Inc., Hutchinson, 1985—; v.p. adminstrn., chief fin. officer D.C. Inc., Hutchinson, 1985—; v.p., chief fin. officer, chief ops. officer Archtl. Millwork Inc., Hutchinson, 1985—; v.p., chief fin. officer Dick Currie Leasing Inc., Hutchinson, 1985—; cons. Cherokee Farms, Hutchinson, 1985—; fin. cons. Sandy Inc., Hutchinson, 1985—, C-K Supply Inc., Hutchinson, 1985—, Golden Plains Convalescent Ctr. Inc., Hutchinson, 1983-84; treas., bd. dirs. Golden Plains Inc., Hutchinson, Trautmann Millwork Inc., Lafayette, Colo., Install Inc., Lafayette and Tulsa, Lahoma Ltd. Inc., Hutchinson. Founder Y-Indain Princess program YMCA, Topeka, 1975—, treas. Y-Indain Guides program, 1974. Served with USN, 1962-66. Mem. Archtl. Woodwork Inst., Healthcare Fin. Mgmt. Assn. Home: 1311 N Covington Circle Wichita KS 67212 Office: Archtl Millwork Inc 401 S Adams St PO Box 1007 Hutchinson KS 67504

HUDAK, BARBARA MARGARET, securities company executive; b. East Orange, N.J., Aug. 11, 1944; d. Edmond J. and Rosemary B. (Hewett) Kennedy; m. Henry A. Hudak, July 29, 1967; children: Margaret, Matthew, Michele, Maureen. BA, St. Joseph Coll., 1966; MLS, Rutgers U., 1982. Library clk. U. Rochester (N.Y.), 1966-67; asst. librarian Mobil Chem. Co., Edison, N.J., 1967-69, 75-82; info. mgr. Morgan Guaranty Trust Co., N.Y.C., 1982-86; v.p. J.P. Morgan Securities, Inc., N.Y.C., 1987—. Mem. Spl. Libraries Assn., Assn. of Info. and Image Mgmt., Assn. of Records, Mgrs. and Adminstrs., Phi Beta Mu. Roman Catholic. Office: JP Morgan Securities 23 Wall St New York NY 10015

HUDGINS, CATHERINE HARDING, business executive; b. Raleigh, N.C., June 25, 1913; d. William Thomas and Mary Alice (Timberlake) Harding; m. Robert Scott Hudgins IV, Aug. 20, 1938; children: Catherine Harding, Deborah Ghiselin, Robert Scott V. BS, N.C. State U., 1929-33; grad. tchr. N.C. Sch. for Deaf, 1933-34. Tchr. N.C. Sch. for Deaf, Morganton, 1934-36; sec. Dr. A.S. Oliver, Raleigh, 1937; tchr. N.J. Sch. for Deaf, Trenton, 1937-39; sec. Robert S. Hudgins Co., Charlotte, N.C., 1949—, v.p., treas., 1960—, also bd. dirs. Mem. Jr. Service League, Easton, Pa., 1939; project chmn. ladies aux. Profl. Engrs. N.C., 1954-55, pres., 1956-57; pres. Christian High Sch. PTA, 1963; program chmn. Charlotte Opera Assn., 1959-61, sec., 1961-63; sec. bd. Hezekiah Alexander House Restoration, 1949-52, Hezekiah Alexander House Aux., 1975—, treas., 1983-84, v.p., 1984-85, pres., 1985—; sec. Hezediah Alexander Found., 1986—; past chmn. home missions, annuities and relief Women of Presbyn. Ch., past pres. Sunday Sch. class. Mem. N.C. Hist. Assn., English Speaking Union, Internat. Platform Assn., Mint Mus. Drama Guild (pres. 1967-69), Internat. Biog. Ctr. Eng. (dep. dir. gen.), Daus. Am. Colonists (state chmn. nat. def. 1973-74, corr. sec. Virginia Dare chpt. 1978-79, 84-85, state insignia chmn. 1979-80), DAR (mem. nat. chmn.'s assn., nat. officers club; chpt. regent 1957-59, chpt. chaplain 1955-57 N.C. program chmn. 1961-63, state chmn. nat. def. 1973-76, state rec. sec. 1977-79, state regent 1979-82, hon. state regent 1982—), Children Am. Revolution (N.C. sr. pres. 1963-66, sr. nat. corr. sec., 1966-68, sr. nat. 1st v.p. 1968-70, sr. nat. pres. 1970-72, hon. sr. nat. pres. life 1972—; 2d v.p. Nat. Officers Club, 1st v.p. 1977-79, pres. 1979-81), Huguenot Soc. N.C. Club: Carmel Country (Charlotte), Viewpoint 24 (v.p. 1986, pres. 1987). Home: 1514 Wendover Rd Charlotte NC 28211 Office: Robert S Hudgins Co PO Box 17217 Charlotte NC 28211

HUDGINS, DUDLEY RODGER, pharmaceutical company official; b. Chgo., Nov. 4, 1937; s. Dudley Wallace and Helen (Sterling) H.; B.A. in Psychology, Kans. U., 1959; m. Pegge Resch, Aug. 8, 1975; children—Brian, Randy; stepchildren—Todd Woods, Mianne Woods. With Marion Labs., Inc., 1961—, tng. mgr., also bids and contracts mgr., 1970-72, dir. pharm. div., 1972-82, dir. sales tng. and devel. for entire co., Kansas City, Mo., 1982—; cons. in field. Pres. Zion Luth. Ch., 1980; condr. chapel service City Union Mission, Kansas City. Served with AUS, 1960. Recipient Nat. Builder's award Marion Labs., 1979, 85, Marion Presdl. award, 1985. Mem. Nat. Soc. Pharm. Sales Trainers (chpt. pres. 1978-79, nat. pres. 1979-80, hon. life). Home: 511 W 123d Terr Kansas City MO 64145 Office: Marion Labs Inc 10236 Bunker Ridge Rd Kansas City MO 64137

HUDIBURG, JOHN JUSTUS, JR., utility executive; b. Raleigh, N.C., Jan. 16, 1928; s. John Justus and Lucille (Pearson) H.; m. Joan Helen Adams, Apr. 24, 1954; children: Lee Ann, Carol Joan, John Justus, Mark Adams. B.S., Ga. Inst. Tech., 1951; grad., Advanced Mgmt. Program, Harvard U., 1972. Registered profl. engr., Fla. With Fla. Power & Light Co., Miami, 1951—; dir. mgr. Fla. Power & Light Co., 1969-71, v.p., 1971-72, exec. v.p., 1973-79, pres., 1979-86, chmn., chief exec. officer, 1986—; chmn. Fla. Electric Power Coordinating Group, 1983-84. Mem. Fla. Prison Industries Commn., 1977-79; chmn. West Palm Beach United Fund campaign, 1967; pres. United Fund Palm Beach County, 1968; v.p. Goodwill Industries, West Palm Beach, 1968; campaign chmn. Dade County United Way, 1984; v.p. Malcolm Baldrige Nat. Quality Award Found. Served with USNR, 1946-47. Mem. IEEE (chpt. chmn. 1964), Nat. Soc. Profl. Engrs., Fla. Engring. Soc., Malcolm Baldridge Nat. Quality Award Found. (v.p.)., Internat. Club, Harvard Bus. Sch. So. Fla. Club (pres. 1976), Exec. Club. Episcopalian. Office: Fla Power & Light Co PO Box 029100 Miami FL 33102-9100

HUDIK, MARTIN FRANCIS, hospital administrator, educator; b. Chgo., Mar. 27, 1949; s. Joseph and Rose (Ricker) H; 1 child, Theresa Abraham. BS in Mech. and Aerospace Engring., Ill. Inst. Tech., 1971; BPA, Jackson State U., 1974; MBA, Loyola U., Chgo., 1975; postgrad. U. Sarasota, 1975-76. Cert. health care safety mgr., hazard control mgr., hazardous materials mgr.; cert. police and security firearms instr., Ill. and Nat. Rifle Assn. With Ill. Masonic Med. Ctr., Chgo., 1969—, dir. risk mgmt., 1974-79, asst. adminstr., 1979—; lt. tng. div. Cicero (Ill.) Police Dept., part-time 1971—; instr. Nat. Safety Council Safety Tng. Inst., Chgo., 1977-85; cons. mem. Council Tech. Users Consumer Products, Underwriters Labs., Chgo., 1977—; instr., lt. U.S. Def. Civil Preparedness Agy. Staff Coll., Battle Creek, Mich., 1977-85; leason officer Emergency Svcs. and Disaster Agy., 1988—, asst. dir. Town Cicero. Pres. sch. bd. Mary Queen of Heaven Sch., Cicero, 1977-79, 84-86; pres. Mary Queen of Heaven Ch. Council, 1979-81, 83-86; pres. I.M.M.C. Employee Club, 1983-86. Ill. State scholar, 1969-71. Mem. Am. Coll. Healthcare Execs., Am. Soc. Hosp. Risk Mgmt., Nat. Fire Protection Assn., Am. Soc. Safety Engrs., Am. Soc. Law and Medicine, Ill. Hosp. Security and Safety Assn. (co-founder 1976, founding pres. 1976-77, hon. dir. 1977-82), Cath. Alumni Club Chgo. (bd. dirs. 1983-84, 86), Mensa, Pi Tau Sigma, Tau Beta Pi, Alpha Sigma Nu. Republican. Roman Catholic. Lodges: KC (Cardinal council), Masons. Office: Ill Masonic Med Ctr 836 W Wellington Ave Chicago IL 60657

HUDNUT, DAVID BEECHER, leasing company executive, lawyer; b. Cin., Feb. 21, 1935; s. William Herbert and Elizabeth Allen (Kilborne) H.; m. Robin Fraser, Apr. 12, 1958; children: David Beecher, Marjorie Elizabeth, Joshua Fraser, John Marshall, Benjamin Parker. A.B., Princeton U., 1957; J.D., Cornell U., 1962. Bar: N.Y. 1962, U.S. Supreme Ct. 1967. Assoc., Hughes, Hubbard & Reed, N.Y.C., 1962-67; with Ind. & chem. prodn. div. Ford Motor Co., 1967-69; v.p. U.S. Leasing Internat., Inc., San Francisco, 1969-76, sr. v.p., 1976—; bd. dirs. San Francisco chpt. Assn. for Corp. Growth, 1977-79, Donaldina Cameron House, 1969-76, 80—, Services for Srs., 1970—, No. Calif. Presbyn. Homes, 1971-77, chmn., 1973-76, 79-86; bd. dirs. Edgewood Children's Ctr., 1979-86, Ind. Colls. No. Calif., 1981-84, Calif. Hist. Soc., 1986—. Republican. Presbyterian. Office: US Leasing Internat Inc 733 Front St San Francisco CA 94111

HUDOBA, GREGORY JOSEPH, controller, tax consultant; b. Mnpls., Aug. 25, 1951; s. Louis Robert and Sophia Marie (Tomczyk) H.; m. Mary Ellen Terhaar, June 1973 (div. June 1980); children: Jeremy Louis, Genine Marie, Shavaun Ann; m. Meri Frances Moore, July 25, 1981; 1 child, Aubree Danielle. BA, Carroll Coll., 1985. CPA, Mont. Med. lab. technician St. Peter's Hosp., Helena, Mont., 1972-81; staff acct. Todd Lindberg, CPA, Helena, Mont., 1976-77; sr. staff acct. Anderson ZurMuehlen & Co., PC, Helena, Mont., 1977-85; corp. controller Visocan Petroleum Co., Helena, Mont., 1985—. Mem. Am. Inst. CPA's, Mont. Soc. CPA's. Club: Mont. Boat and Ski (sec.-treas. 1988—). Lodge: Rotary (treas. Helena Sunrise club 1985-87). Home: 1430 Shirley Rd Helena MT 59601 Office: Visocan Petroleum 3180 Prospect PO Box 5564 Helena MT 59604

HUDSON, AMY, banker; b. San Diego, Aug. 2, 1954; d. James Robert and Susan Elizabeth (Forth) H.; m. Michael Caldwell, Apr. 2, 1976 (div. Jan. 1980). BA in English, UCLA, 1976; MBA, Stanford U., 1984. Copy editor L.A. Times, 1978-80, reporter, 1981-84; v.p. mktg. First Nat. Bank San Francisco, 1984-88; prin. Bay Area Investments, San Francisco, 1988—. Mem. San Francisco Art Mus., Bay Area Devel. Assn.; vol. Peace Corps, Columbia, 1976-78. Mem. Soc. Calif. Investment Advisors, NOW, Phi Beta Kappa. Office: Werik Ctr 936 Wisconsin St Ste B San Francisco CA 94107

HUDSON, BOBBY GILEN, railway equipment manufacturing executive; b. Roanoke, Va., Apr. 17, 1930; s. Walter Gilen and Elsie May (Lane) H.; B.S. in Civil Engring., Va. Poly. Inst. and State U., 1952, M.S. in Civil Engring., 1958; m. Eleanor Dean Harrison, Mar. 21, 1952; children—David Alan, Robert Steven, Catherine Lynn. Asst. supr. bridges and bldgs. Norfolk & Western Ry., Roanoke, Va., 1957-59, roadmaster, 1959-64, div. engr., Crewe, Va., 1965-67; div. engr. Akron, Canton & Youngstown Ry., Akron, Ohio, 1964-65; design supr. Newport News Shipbuilding & Dry Dock Co. (Va.), 1967-70; chief engr. Fla. East Coast Ry., St. Augustine, 1970-77; v.p. sales Speno Rail Services, East Syracuse, N.Y., 1977-79, exec. v.p., gen. mgr., 1979-85; gen. mgr. sales and service Railway Maintenance Products div., Portec, Inc., Pitts., 1985—. Mem. Crewe (Va.) Town Council, 1969-70. Served with U.S. Army, 1954-56. Mem. Am. Ry. Engrs. Assn., Roadmaster and Bridge and Bldg. Assn. Democrat. Methodist. Home: 1941 Red Coach Rd Allison Park PA 15101-3228 Office: Railway Maintenance Products div Portec Inc PO Box 38250 Pittsburgh PA 15238-8250

HUDSON, CHARLES DAUGHERTY, insurance executive; b. La Grange, Ga., Mar. 17, 1927; s. J.D. and Janie (Hill) H.; m. Ida Cason Callaway, May 1, 1955; children: Jane Alice Hudson Craig, Ellen Hudson Hardenstein, Charles Daugherty, Ida Hudson Hughes. Student Auburn U., 1945-48; LLD, La Grange Coll.; LHD (hon.) Mercer U., 1987. Ptnr. Hudson Hardware Co., La Grange, 1950-57; ptnr. Hammond-Hudson Ins. Agy., La Grange, 1957-58, owner, 1958-78; pres. Hammond, Hudson & Holder Inc., 1978—; bd. dirs., mem. exec. com. Citizens & So. Nat. Bank, La Grange, 1963—; acting pres. La Grange Coll., 1979-80; v.p., bd. dirs. La Grange Industries, Inc., 1956—, Hudson Maddox Enterprises, 1965—; ptnr. PCH Properties, 1981—; bd. dirs. C&S Investment Advisors, Inc., Atlanta, 1986—; chmn. bd. dirs. First Annuity Corp., LaGrange, Ga. Mem. exec. com. Camp Viola, La Grange, 1956—, chmn. bd. trustees, 1988— ; mem. pres. adv. council Ga. State U.; v.p., trustee Callaway Found., Inc., 1965—, Fuller E. Callaway Found., 1957—; former chmn. La Grange chpt. United Fund; trustee, chmn. Florence Hand Home Charitable Trust, 1982—, Scottish Rite Children's Hosp., Atlanta, 1988—; mem. La Grange Bd. Edn., 1967-88, chmn., 1971-74, 81-83; trustee Ga. Bapt. Found., 1980-85; chmn. endowment com. Ga. Bapt. Conv., 1983-85; chmn. bd. trustees La Grange Coll., 1970—; trustee, chmn. bd. Ga. Bapt. Hosp., Atlanta, 1973, 76-77; former trustee West Ga. Med. Ctr., La Grange, chmn., 1977, 80-81, treas., 1978-79; trustee, past pres. Troup County Hist. Soc., 1975—, mem. staff Ga. gov., 1959-62, 63-66, 71-74, Ala. gov., 1975; mem. Downtown La Grange Devel. Authority, 1976—; trustee Ga. Trust for Historic Preservation, 1981—, Callaway Ednl. Assn., 1968-80; mem. La Grange Bicentennial commn., 1975-76, George E. Sims Nursing Scholarship Fund; mem. bd. dirs., v.p. Ga. Dept. of Corrections, 1983—, sec., 1983-84, vice chmn., 1985, chmn., 1986—; chmn. Hosp. Equipment Fin. Authority, 1985—; trustee West Ga. Youth Council, 1970—; bd. dirs. Auburn U. Fund, 1987—; leader Aetna Life & Casualty, 1980-81, 86-87; pres. adv. council Ga. State U. Recipient Pres.'s award Colonial Life Ins. Co., 1966, 69-70, 75-80, Disting. Alumni award Ga. Mil. Acad., 1971, Disting. Alumni award Woodward Acad., 1971, Disting. Service award Ga. Hosp. Assn., 1980, Respect Law award Optimists Assn., 1977, Pub. Service award Ga. Assn. of AIA, 1977, Leading Producer award Aetna Life and Casualty, 1979; Paul Harris fellow, 1984. Mem. Ga. Assn. Ind. Ins. Agts., Ga. Sch. Bd. Assn. (area dir.), SAR, Amicale de Groupe LaFayette (hon.), Chattahoochee Valley Art Assn., La Grange C. of C. (bd. dirs.), Newcomen Soc. N.Am., Ga. Hosp. Assn. (trustee 1980—), U. Ga. Gridiron Secret Soc., Sigma Alpha Epsilon, Beta Gamma Sigma. Clubs: Highland Country, Lafayette (LaGrange); Commerce (Atlanta); Aetna Life and Casualty Pres.'s. Lodges: Masons, Shriners, Elks, Rotary (pres. 1964-65). Home: 407 Country Club Rd La Grange GA 30240 Office: Hammond Hudson & Holder Inc 206 W Haralson St La Grange GA 30240

HUDSON, EDWARD GORDON, real estate development corporation executive; b. Seattle, Feb. 20, 1950; s. Edward S. and Ruth (Gordon) H.; m. Karen L. Bennett, Oct. 15, 1977 (dec. Dec. 1981). BBA, U. Wash., 1973, MBA, 1974. Project mgr. McKern Devel. Co., San Mateo, Calif., 1974-77; v.p. Demonet Industries, Los Angeles, 1977-84; pres. Hudson Industries, Santa Monica, Calif., 1984—; cons. Town & Country Constrn. Co., Sacramento, 1981—. Vol., Mission Rescue Ctr., Los Angeles, 1980—, Am. Cancer Soc., Los Angeles, 1981—. Home: 10505 Sandal Ln Bel Aire CA 90077

HUDSON, JOHN BOSWELL, condominium corporation executive; b. Decatur, Ill., June 1, 1930; s. George Taylor and Margaret Shirley (Boswell) H.; student Reed Coll., 1948-51; BA, U. Oreg., 1952; MA, U. Wash., Seattle, 1956; postgrad. Cornell U., 1957-60, PhD, 1963; m. Sandra Lee Cermak, Mar. 16, 1957; children: Scott Martin, Bradford Taylor. Asst. prof. sociology Humboldt State U., Arcata, Calif., 1960-61, Cornell U., Ithaca, N.Y., 1961-64, Lehigh U., Bethlehem, Pa., 1964-65, Syracuse (N.Y.) U., 1965-66; research assoc. Harvard U., 1966-67; research sociologist Mass. Dept. Mental Health, Boston, 1967-68; sr. sociologist Abt Assocs., Inc., Cambridge, Mass., 1968-69; prof. sociology Trent U., Peterborough, Ont., Can., 1969-73; asst. adminstr. Brockton (Mass.) Multi-Service Center, 1973-74; lectr. Northeastern U., Boston, 1974-76; cons., Cambridge, 1976-78; pres., treas. Cambridge Condominium Collaborative, Inc., 1978—; vis. scientist dept. behavioral scis. Harvard Sch. Public Health, summers 1971, 72, winter-spring 1973. Mgmt. com. Sch. Nursing, Peterborough Civic Hosp., 1970-72; bd. dirs. Brockton Area Assn. for Retarded Citizens, 1974-75; mem. City Mgr.'s Cable TV Adv. Com., Cambridge, 1979-85; chmn. Cambridge Condominium Network, 1979—; mem. adv. com. Scarborough Chamber Players, 1987—. Social Sci. Research Council fellow Stanford U., summer 1964; recipient award of merit Peterborough Assn. for Mentally Retarded, 1972. Mem. Am. Sociol. Assn., Mass. Sociol. Assn. (treas. 1979-82, v.p. 1987—), Community Assns. Inst. (named Colleague of Yr. New Eng. chpt. 1985), Nat. Assn. Realtors, Mass. Assn. Realtors, Greater Boston Real Estate Bd. Unitarian. Club: Harvard Faculty. Lodge: Rotary (Cambridge). Author: Creativity and Innovation, 1966; Policy-Oriented Basic Research, 1969; Social Policy and Theoretical Sociology, 1970; The Structure of Innovation, 1971; A Proposal for a Center for Innovation, 1971; The Interface Between Theory and Practice, 1979. Home: 988 Memorial Dr Cambridge MA 02138 Office: 20 University Rd Cambridge MA 02138

HUDSON, KEITH HENRY, personnel executive; b. Leicester County, England, Nov. 6, 1939; came to U.S., 1980; s. Harry and Agnes Mary (Langman) H.; m. Jacqueline Marie Suter, Sept. 5, 1964; children: Jeremy, Yvonne, Kathryn. Cert. in elec. tech., City and Guilds of London Inst., 1962; diploma in indsl. engring., Inst. Work Study Practitioners (now Inst. Mgmt. Svcs.), 1965; diploma in mgmt. studies, British Inst. of Mgmt., 1968. With Partridge Wilson & Co., Ltd., Leicester, Eng., 1958-64; cons. indsl. engr. Leicester, 1964-70; with W. Symingtons Ltd., Northants, Eng., 1970-71; gen. mgr. Transworld Pubrs., Ltd., Northants, 1971-74; mgr. indsl. engring. Bowaters Consumer Pkgs., Kent, Eng., 1974-77; mgmt. cons. supr. Metra/Proudfoot, Brussels and Paris, 1977-80; dir. indsl. relations thru v.p. ops. Rock of Ages Corp., Vt., 1980-84; dir. pensions, benefits Nortek Inc., Providence, 1985—. Sec., chmn. Vt. Coalition for Health, Montpelier, 1982-84. Mem. Brit. Inst. Mgmt., Inst. Mgmt. Services U.K., Inst. Indsl. Engrs. Anglican. Home: 52 Wisteria Dr Coventry RI 02816 Office: Nortek Inc 50 Kennedy Pla Providence RI 02903

HUDSON, MYRA LINDEN FRANK, consultant; b. Richmond, Va., Oct. 26, 1950; d. J. C. and Myra Teresa (Lanzarone) Frank; m. Timothy Franklin Long (div. Jan. 1981); m. Robert Andrew Hudson. BA, Erskine Coll., 1972; student, Inst. Fin. Edn., 1982-88. Chief activities therapist S.C. Dept. Corrections, Columbia, 1973-75, acting prin., 1975-77, coll. coord., 1977-78; owner, operator Carolina Coast Seafood, Aiken (S.C.) and Beaufort (S.C),

1978-80; from teller to savs. counselor Security Fed. Savs. & Loan, Aiken, 1981-83; customer svc. rep. Bankers 1st Savs. & Loans, Augusta, Ga., 1983-84, mgr. br. adminstrn., 1984-85; coord. automated teller machines, banking officer 1st Fed. Savs. Bank, Brunswick, Ga., 1985-88; ptnr., cons. electronic banking/computer programming RAH Systems, Brunswick, Ga., 1988—; lectr. S.C. Edn. Tchrs. Assn., Columbia, 1974, S.C. Assn. Social Workers, Columbia, 1975, Bus. & Profl. Women's Club, Columbia, 1978; small bus. owner, distbr. Nuskin product line, 1987—; ind. mktg. rep. Network 2000/U.S. Sprint. Appeared with Aiken Community Theatre, 1981. Mem. hospice com. Am. Cancer Soc., Augusta, 1981; lectr. St. John's United Meth. Ch., 1981-82. Mem. NAFE, Internat. Platform Assn., Brunswick-Golden Isles C. of C. Democrat. Home: 32 Seminole Rd Brunswick GA 31520

HUDSPETH, JOHN ROBERT, bank executive; b. Greenville, Tex., July 23, 1938. BA, Rice U., 1960; MA, U. Tex., 1966. With CitiBank, N.Y.C., 1966-73; with NCNB Tex., Dallas, 1973—, now exec. v.p., 1988—; mem. adv. bd. Pvt. Export Funding Corp., N.Y.C. Bd. dirs. Dallas Opera, 1983-88, Family Guidance Ctr., Dallas, 1988. Lt. comdr. USN, 1960-64. Mem. Am. Bankers Assn. (internat. com. 1983-86), Bankers Assn. for Fgn. Trade (bd. dirs. 1986-89), Univ. Club of Dallas, Pi Sigma Alpha. Office: NCNB Tex PO Box 830302 Dallas TX 75283

HUEBNER, KURT WALTER, real estate executive; b. San Mateo, Calif., May 20, 1960; s. Herbert W. and Louise (How) H. BA, Coll. of the Holy Cross, Worcester, Mass., 1982. Owner Huebner Enterprises, Worcester, 1980-83; pres., chief exec. officer, chmn. bd. Huebner Fin. Corp., Houston, 1983—; devel. bd. Woodcreek Bank, Houston. Mem. Houston N.W. C. of C. (chmn. SICA com. 1985), Tex. Real Estate Commn. (broker). Lodge: Optimists (adminstrv. v.p. local club 1985-86). Office: Huebner Fin Corp PO Box 682123 Houston TX 77268-2123

HUEBSCHMAN, MARTIN JOHN, JR, corporate executive, lawyer; b. Balt., Apr. 25, 1947; s. Martin John and Elizabeth (Rosenberger) H.; m. Carol Ann Hall, Jan. 15, 1967 (div. Aug. 1971); 1 child, Martin John III; m. Barbara Kathleen Cummings, June 23, 1973; children: Eric Sean, Kevin James. BBA, Cleve. State U., 1972; JD, Cleve. Marshall Law Sch., 1976. Bar: Ohio, 1976. Asst. treas. Nordson Corp., Cleve., 1976-80, treas., 1980-84; sr. v.p. fin. and planning Met-Coil Systems Corp., Cedar Rapids, Iowa, 1984-86, pres., chief oper. officer, 1986-88, pres., chief exec. officer, 1988—; also bd. dirs. Met-Coil Systems Corp., Cedar Rapids. Pres., v.p., treas. Lake of the Falls Condominium, Olmsted Falls, 1973-76; trustee Lake Ridge Acad., Elyria, 1984; bd. dirs., pres., campaign chmn. United Way of Greater Lorain County, 1982-84. Mem. Nat. Machine Tool Builders' Assn., ABA, Nat. Investor Relations Inst. Risk & Ins. Mgmt. Soc., Young Pres. Orgn. Republican. Methodist. Clubs: Elmcrest Country, Investment. Home: 130 Tomahawk Trail SE Cedar Rapids IA 52403 Office: Met-Coil Systems Corp 425 2d St SE 11th Floor Cedar Rapids IA 52401

HUELSMAN, WALTER JOHN, management consultant; b. St. Louis, Feb. 22, 1937; s. Cornelius John and Leona Ann (Bohn) H.; m. Patricia Ann Davis, Jan. 21, 1961; 1 child, Holly Marie. BSIE, Washington U., 1960; MBA, Wayne State U., 1964. Mfg. engr. Westinghouse Corp., Pitts., 1960-61; computer analyst Gen. Am. Life, St. Louis, 1961-63; systems analyst Burroughs Corp., Detroit, 1963-64; ptnr. Coopers & Lybrand, Washington, 1964—; with Maximus. Author: Environmental Auditing, 1985. Mem. Solid Waste Adv. Com., Montgomery County, 1983-86. Mem. Inst. Mgmt. Cons. (pres. 1980—), Am. Water Works (assoc. mem.), Assn. Metro. Sewer Agys. Home: 8145 Buckspark Lane E Potomac MD 20854 Office: Maximus 7799 Leesburg Pike Falls Church VA 22043

HUENEFELD, THOMAS ERNST, banker; b. Cin., July 7, 1937; s. Carl Ernst and Catherine Louise (Messer) H.; B.S. in Bus. Adminstrn., U. Fla., 1961; grad. Nat. Comml. Lending Grad. Sch., U. Okla., 1975; m. Catherine Ann Cogburn, Feb. 5, 1960; children—Richard Ernst, Amy Cogburn. Mgmt. trainee Huenefeld Co., Cin., 1961-62, asst. sec., buyer, 1963-65; credit analyst First Nat. Bank Cin. (now Star Bank, N.A.), 1966-68, asst. cashier, 1968-69, asst. v.p., 1969-75, v.p., 1975-83, sr. v.p., 1983—; dir. Wolf Machine Co., S. Eastern Materials Corp., Archiable Electric Co., Eastern Machinery Co., Ninth St. Garage, Inc., Logan & Kanawha Coal Co., Inc. Bd. mgrs. Emanuel Community Center, Cin., 1965-70, pres., 1968-70; trustee Huenefeld Meml., Inc., Cin., 1965-72, treas., 1965-69; trustee Funds for Self Enterprise, Cin., 1972-76, pres., 1973-76; trustee Cin. Musical Festival Assn., 1976-82, mem. exec. com., 1977-79; trustee Community Ltd. Care Dialysis Center, Cin., 1978-85, Merc. Library, 1979—, v.p., chmn. fin. com. 1983-88; trustee MagnaCare Health Plan, 1988—, v.p., chmn. fin. com., 1983—. Cert. comml. lender Am. Bankers Assn. Mem. Am. Fin. Assn. (life), Fin. Mgmt. Assn. (life), Robert Morris Assos., Cin. Assn. Credit and Fin. Mgmt. (dir. 1972-76), Am. Inst. Banking, Newcomen Soc. N.Am., Ohio (life), Cin. (life; trustee 1979—, mem. exec. com. 1983—) hist. socs., Cincinnatus Assn. (exec. com. 1983-84), Cin. Country Club (bd. govs. 1982—), Queen City Club, Bankers Club, The Assemblies (chmn. 1972-73), Univ. Club (bd. govs. 1982-89), Fanfare (pres. 1979-80), Sigma Chi. Republican. Methodist. Home: 3440 Principio Ave Cincinnati OH 45208 Office: Star Bank NA 5th and Walnut Sts Cincinnati OH 45202

HUEPPCHEN, HAROLD EDWARD, food products executive; b. Plymouth, Wis., Aug. 9, 1931; s. Edwin Edward and Verna Rose (Hahn) H.; m. Maureen Agnes Krieg, Oct. 25, 1958; children: Nancy Ann, Daniel Howard, Kathleen Rose. BArch, Chgo. Tech. Coll., 1958; cert. in food industry mgmt., Cornell U., 1982; cert. CAD-CAM, Clayton State U., 1988. Archtl. draftsman Robert Taylor AIA, Oak Park, Ill., 1955-57; mgr. produce A&P Tea Co., Chgo., 1956-58; asst. maintenance supt. A&P Tea Co., Milw., 1959-71; dir. store engring. A&P Tea Co., Columbus, Ohio, 1971-76; constrn. engr. A&P Tea Co., Detroit, 1976-77, Nat. Supermarkets, New Orleans, 1977-78; dir. store engring. Roundy's United Foods, Inc., Milw., 1978-83; dir. store engring., devel. Associated Grocers Coop., Inc., College Park, Ga., 1983—. Advisor 4-H Club, New London, Wis., 1982, Columbus, Ohio, Boy Scouts Am., 1976; active Beautiful Fayette, Peachtree City, Ga., 1988. Decorated Bronze Star. Mem. Grocers' Fixtures and Equipment (mem. edn. sems. 1978—). Republican. Roman Catholic. Lodge: Kiwanis (bd. dirs. 1986—). Home: 200 Shadowood Ln Peachtree City GA 30269 Office: Associated Grocers Coop Inc 2225 Shurfine Dr College Park GA 30337 *

HUETTNER, RICHARD ALFRED, lawyer; b. N.Y.C., Mar. 25, 1927; s. Alfred F. and Mary (Reilly) H.; children—Jennifer Mary, Barbara Bryan; m. 2d, Eunice Bizzell Dowd, Aug. 22, 1971. Marine Engrs. License, N.Y. State Maritime Acad., 1947; B.S., Yale U. Sch. Engring., 1949; J.D., U. Pa., 1952. Bar: D.C. 1952, N.Y. 1954, U.S. Ct. Mil. Appeals 1953, U.S. Ct. Claims 1961, U.S. Supreme Ct. 1969, U.S. Ct. Appeals (fed. cir.) 1982, also other fed. cts, registered to practice U.S. Patent and Trademark Office 1957, Canadian Patent Office 1968. Engr. Jones & Laughlin Steel Corp., 1954-55; assoc. atty. firm Kenyon & Kenyon, N.Y.C, 1955-61; mem. firm Kenyon & Kenyon, 1961—; specialist patent, trademark and copyright law. Trustee N.J. Shakespeare Festival, 1972-79, sec., 1977-79; trustee Overlook Hosp., Summit, N.J., 1978-84, 86—, vice chmn. bd. trustees, 1980-82, chmn. bd. trustees, 1982-84; trustee Overlook Found., 1981—, chmn. bd. trustees, 1986—; trustee Colonial Symphony Orch., Madison, N.J., 1972-82, v.p. bd. trustees 1974-76. pres. 1976-79; chmn. bd. overseers N.J. Consortium for Performing Arts, 1972-74; mem. Yale U. Council, 1978-81; bd. dirs. Yale Communications Bd., 1978-80; chmn. bd. trustees Center for Addictive Illnesses, Morristown, N.J., 1979-82; rep. Assn. Yale Alumni, 1975-80, chmn. com. undergrad. admissions, 1976-78, bd. govs., 1976-80, chmn. bd. govs., 1978-80; chmn. Yale Alumni Schs. Com. N.Y., 1972-78; assoc. fellow Silliman Coll., Yale U., 1976—; bd. dirs., exec. com. Yale U. Alumni Fund, 1978-81; mem. Yale Class of 1949 Council, 1980—; bd. dirs. Overlook Health Systems, 1984—. Served from midshipman to lt. USNR, 1945-47, 52-54; cert. JAGC 1953; Res. ret. Recipient Yale medal, 1983. Fellow N.Y. Bar Found.; mem. Am., N.Y. State bar assns., Assn. Bar City N.Y., N.Y. Patent-Trademark-Copyright Law Assn. (chmn. com. meetings 1961-64, chmn. com. econ. matters 1966-69, 72-74), AAAS, N.Y. Acad. Scis., N.Y. County Lawyers Assn., Am. Intellectual Property Law Assn., Internat. Patent and Trademark Assn., Am. Judicature Soc., Yale Sci. and Engring. Assn. (v.p. 1973-75, pres. 1975-78, exec. bd. 1972—), Fed. Bar Council. Clubs: Yale (N.Y.C.); Yale of Central N.J. (Summit) (trustee 1973-88, pres. 1975-77), Morris County Golf (Convent, N.J.); The Graduates (New Haven). Home: 150 Green Ave Madison NJ 07940 Office: Kenyon & Kenyon One Broadway New York NY 10004

HUEY, JOHN WESLEY, JR., editor; b. Atlanta, Apr. 18, 1948; s. John Wesley and Helen (Cahill) H.; m. Kathryn White (div. 1981); m. Sue Yeargan (dec. Dec. 1986); 1 child, John Wesley IV. BA in English, U. Ga., 1970. Reporter DeKalb New Era, Decatur, Ga., 1972-74, Atlanta Constn., 1974-75, Wall St. Jour., Dallas, 1975-79; bur. chief Wall St. Jour., Atlanta, 1979-82; mng. editor Wall St. Jour., Brussels, 1982-83, editor, 1983-84; sr. spl. writer Wall St. Jour., Atlanta, 1984-86, bur. chief, 1986-88, mng. editor, 1988—; contbg. editor Fortune Mag., 1988. Contbg. editor Fortune mag., 1988—. Served to lt. (j.g.) USN, 1970-72. Methodist. Office: Wall St Jour 11 Piedmont Ctr NE Suite 300 Atlanta GA 30305

HUFF, NANCY RUTH, citrus groves administrator, investments executive; b. Cin.; d. Norman Vincent and Marie (Voss) H.; m. William H. Brady, Sept. 9, 1961 (div. Apr. 1971); children—William Huff, Sherry Lynn. B.A., Newton Coll. of the Sacred Heart, Mass., 1961. Asst. to pres. Star Fruit Co., Lake Alfred, Fla., 1961-71; mgr., pres. Huff Groves, Winter Haven, Fla., 1971—; pres Star Investments, Winter Haven, 1980—; v.p. Allapattch Operating Co., Fort Pierce, Fla., 1982—, pres. Alpat Grove care Co., Fort Pierce, 1982—. Mem. Fla. Citrus Mutual, Indian River Citrus League (com. mem.), Women in Citrus, Fla. Citrus Women. Republican. Clubs: Lake Region Yacht and Country, Gardania Garden. (v.p. 1974-78) (Winter Haven); Citrus (Orlando, Fla.). Avocations: photography; dance; tennis. Office: PO Box 7167 Winter Haven FL 33883

HUFF, NORMAN NELSON, investor, computer consultant, educator; b. San Diego, Apr. 22, 1933; s. George Kleineberg Peabody and Norma Rose (Nelson) H.; BS, San Diego State U., 1957; cert. UCLA, 1972; MBA, Golden Gate U., 1972; AA, bus. cert., Victor Valley Coll., 1972; Cultural D, World U., 1987; m. Sharon Kay Lockwood, Sept. 30, 1979. Chemist, Convair, San Diego, 1954-55, astrophysicist, 1955-56; mgmt. trainee, chem. engr. U.S. Gypsum Co., Plaster City, Calif., 1957-58; instr. data processing Victor Valley Coll., Victorville, Calif., 1967-70, chmn. data processing, 1970-81; owner High Desert Data Systems, 1972-82, chmn. Computer Sci., 1984-88; dir. Deputy Gen. Internat. Biog. Ctr., 1987, Congress Proclamation, 1987; mgmt. info. systems cons. Pfizer Inc., 1970-72, Mojave Water Agy. Calif., 1972-74. With USNR, 1950-54, to capt. USAF, 1954-67; Vietnam. Decorated Life Sav. award (Spain); recipient Life Sav. award Mil. Forces Spain, 1961, Tchr. of Yr. award, 1967-68, Presdl. Achievement award, 1982, Presdl. Medal of Merit, 1983, 86. Mem. Calif. Ednl. Computing Consortium, Am. Mgmt. Assn., Calif. Bus. Edn. Assn. (treas. 1967-73), Inst. Aero. Sci. (pres. 1956-57), Soaring Soc. Am. (life). Author 5 computer sci. texts. Home and Office: 16173 Rimrock Rd Apple Valley CA 92307

HUFFINGTON, ROY MICHAEL, geologist; b. Tomball, Tex., Oct. 4, 1917; s. Roy Mackey and Bertha (Michel) H.; m. Phyllis Gough, Oct. 26, 1945; children: R. Michael, Terry Lynn Huffington Dittman. BS, So. Meth. U., 1938; MA, Harvard U., 1941, PhD, 1942, grad. advanced mgmt. program, 1976. Teaching fellow Harvard U., 1939-42, instr. geology, 1942; sr. geologist, div. exploration geologist Humble Oil and Refining Co., 1946-56; pres. Roy M. Huffington, Inc., Houston, 1956-83, chmn. bd., 1956—. Contbr. articles to profl. jours. Dir. Houston Ballet Found., U. Tex. Health Sci. Ctr. at Houston, Tex. Med. Ctr.; vice chmn. Interferon Found.; trustee Baylor Coll. Medicine; sec. bd. visitors U. Tex. M.D. Anderson Cancer Ctr.; trustee Com. Econ. Devel. Lt. comdr. USNR, 1942-45. Decorated Bronze Star. Recipient Alumni Achievement award Harvard Bus. Sch., 1982, Oil Drop award petroleum div. ASME, 1985, Gold Medallion Oil Pioneer award Indonesian Govt., 1985, John Rogers award Southwestern Legal Found., 1987, Disting. Alumni award So. Meth. U., 1988, Internat. Businessman of the Yr. award Houston World Trade Assn., 1988. Fellow Geol. Soc. Am. (trustee), AAAS; mem. Am. Assn. Petroleum Geologists, Ind. Petroleum Assn. Am., Am. Petroleum Inst. (bd. dirs.), Mid-Continent Oil and Gas Assn., Tex. Ind. Producers and Royalty Owners Assn., Tex. Mid-Continent Oil and Gas Assn. (bd. dirs., Disting. Svc. award 1988), Houston Geol. Soc., Am. Inst. Profl. Geologists, Geochem. Soc., Marine Tech. Soc., All-Am. Wildcatters (former chmn.), The Asia Soc. (past chmn., hon. life trustee), Tex. Rsch. League, The Brookings Instn. (hon. trustee), Coun. Fgn. Rels., Navy League U.S., U.S. C. of C., S.A.R., Nat. Petroleum Coun., Houston Country Club, Ramada Club, Houston Petroleum Club, Houston Club, New Orleans Petroleum Club, Met. Club, Indonesian Petroleum Club, Dr.'s Club Houston, Alpha Tau Omega (Disting. Alumnus award 1987). Republican. Presbyterian. Office: Roy M Huffington Inc 5500 InterFirst Pla PO Box 4455 Houston TX 77210

HUFFMAN, GARY CLAUDE, finance company executive; b. Springfield, Ill., Dec. 4, 1944; s. Claud A. and Eula L. (Fritsch) H.; m. Susan P. Beville, Sept. 27, 1969; children: Heather, Claudia. BS in Bus. Adminstrn., Olivet Nazarene U., 1966; MBA, Sangamon State U., 1981. Sales exec. Glidden-Durkee/SCM, Balt. and Chgo., 1969-71; branch mgr. Huffman Fin. Co., Springfield, 1971-73, pres., 1978—; nat. acct. mgr. Xerox Corp., Springfield, 1973-78; mem. adv. bd. Consumer Credit Counseling Svc., Springfield, 1979—. Mem. com. Gov.'s Prayer Breakfast, Springfield, 1979—, Ill. Task Force Fin. Services, Springfield, 1985-86; bd. dirs. Am. Cancer Soc., Springfield, 1986—. Served to 1st lt. U.S. Army, 1966-69. Mem. Am. Fin. Svcs. Assn. (vice-chmn. ind. sect. 1988, chmn. 1989), Ill. Fin. Svcs Ins. (pres. 1983-85, chmn. 1986-88), Am. Bus. Club (bd. dirs. 1978-80). Republican. Methodist. Lodge: Sertoma Internat. (treas. 1986-88). Home: 107 Pinehurst Dr Springfield IL 62704 Office: Huffman Fin Co 424 E Monroe Springfield IL 62701

HUFFNAGLE, NORMAN PARMLEY, physicist; b. Honolulu, Dec. 26, 1941; s. Norman Sylvester and Helen Louise (Parmley) H.; m. Cleda May Walker, June 7, 1980; children: Mitchell Walker, Norman Walker, Donley Walker Jr., Kent Norman, Craig Benjamin, Christian Thomas. BA, Drake U., 1963; MS in Sci. Edn., U. Nebr., 1969. Physicist Mine Def. Lab. USN, Panama City, Fla., 1963-66; mem. tech. staff Hughes Aircraft, Canoga Park, Calif., 1969-72; staff engr. Martin Marietta Corp., Orlando, Calif., 1972-78; mgr. Electro-Optics Systems div. Boeing Mil. Airplane Co., Huntsville, Ala., 1978-83, sr. staff engr. Honeywell Def. Systems div., 1983-87; mgr. advanced concepts Northrop Electro-Mech. Div., Anaheim, Calif., 1987—; dir. Village Green Lighting Dist. Contbr. articles to profl. publs. including IEEE Jour., Acoustical Soc. of Am., and USN Auto Testcon; holder 7 patents in sonar, electronics, lasers, fuzing, signal processing, and fiber optics control systems. Mem. Acoustical Soc. Am., Soc. Auto. Test Engring., Martin Marietta Mgmt. Club, Boeing Mil. Airplane Co. Mgmt. Club, Honeywell Mgmt. Club, Sigma Xi. Republican.

HUFFSTETLER, PALMER EUGENE, transportation company executive, lawyer; b. Shelby, N.C., Dec. 21, 1937; s. Daniel S. and Ethel (Turner) H.; m. Mary Ann Beam, Aug. 9, 1958; children: Palmer Eugene, Ben Beam, Brian Tad. BA, Wake Forest U., 1959, JD, 1961. Bar: N.C. 1961. Practiced in Kings Mountain, N.C., 1961-62, Raleigh, N.C., 1962-64; with State Farm Ins. Co., Orlando, Fla., 1962; gen. legal counsel Carolina Freight Carriers Corp., Cherryville, N.C., 1964—; sec. Carolina Freight Carriers Corp., 1969—, sr. v.p., 1981-85, exec. v.p., 1985—, also dir.; dir. Carolina Freight Corp. Author, composer: Senior Man on Carolina Line, Fifty Years Ago. Chmn. Cherryville Zoning Bd. Adjustment, 1967-70; mem. N.C. Gasoline and Oil Insp. Bd., 1974-76; Class chmn. Wake Forest Coll. Fund, 1972-79, decade chmn., 1981-82; mem. governing body, chmn. adminstrv. com. So. Piedmont Health Systems Agy., 1975-77; mem. Cherryville Econ. Devel. Commn., 1982-87; pres. Cherryville Devel. Corp., 1986; bd. dirs. Schiele Mus., Gastonia, 1985-88; mem. N.C. Gov.'s Hwy. Safety Commn., 1985-88; bd. trustees Brevard Coll., 1987—. Mem. N.C. State Bar, ABA., N.C. Bar Assn. (corp. counsel com.), Am. Soc. Corp. Secs., S.C. Motor Truck Assn. (dir.), Central and So. Rate Bur. (v.p., dir.). Methodist (mem. adminstrv. bd. 1965-69, 71-72, chmn. adminstrv. bd. 1969-70, 79, trustee 1970-73). Club: Rotarian (past pres.). Home: 2141 Fairways Dr Cherryville NC 28021 Office: Carolina Freight Corp PO Box 545 NC Hwy #150 East Cherryville NC 28021 also: Carolina Freight Carriers Corp PO Box 697 Cherryville NC 28021

HUGEL, CHARLES E., industrial equipment and services executive; b. Plainfield, N.J., Aug. 9, 1928; s. Charles Emil and Alice (Durr) H.; m. Cornelia Fischer, Apr. 11, 1953; children: Jeffrey, Christian. A.B., Lafayette Coll., 1951. With N.J. Bell Telephone Co., 1952-66, 70-73, gen. mgr. So. area, 1964-66, v.p. ops., 1970-73; gen. mgr. N.E. region Western Electric Co., Newark, 1966-70; v.p. ops. New Eng. Telephone Co., Boston, 1974-75; pres. Ohio Bell Telephone Co., Cleve., 1975-78; exec. v.p. AT&T, Basking Ridge, N.J., 1978-82; pres., chief operating officer, dir. Combustion Engring., Inc., Stamford, Conn., 1982-84, pres., chief exec. officer, dir., 1984-88, chmn., chief exec. officer, dir., 1988—; bd. dirs. Eaton Corp., Pitney Bowes Inc., RJR Nabisco, Inc. Chmn. bd. trustees Lafayette Coll. Served with U.S. Army, 1951-52. Office: Combustion Engring Inc 900 Long Ridge Rd PO Box 9308 Stamford CT 06904

HUGG, JAMES WILLIAM, JR., physicist; b. Raceland, La., Nov. 10, 1952; s. James William Sr. and Emily Jo (Boyd) H.; m. Olivia Brooks, June 30, 1973. BS in Physics and Econs., Calif. Inst. Tech., 1973, MS in Physics, 1974; MS in Physics, Stanford U., 1976, PhD in Physics, 1978. 2nd chef, asst. mgr. Casa Bonita Restaurant, Oklahoma City, 1967-70; systems programmer Kerr-McGee Oil Co., Oklahoma City, 1971-72; translator sci. German Sci-Tran, Santa Barbara, Calif., 1974-76; sr. research physicist Shell Devel. Co., Houston, 1978-82; staff research geophysicist Sohio Petroleum Co., Dallas, 1982-84; staff exchange scientist Brit. Petroleum, London, 1984; mgr. applied research Sohio Petroleum Co., Dallas, 1984-85; research assoc. ARCO Oil and Gas Co., Plano, Tex., 1985-88; cons., founder Bio-Physical Sci. Inst., McKinney, Tex., 1988—; expert witness Creation Sci. Trial, La., 1981-87. Contbr. articles to profl. jours. Patentee in field. Vice chmn. and bd. trustees Lamb and Lion Ministries, McKinney, Tex., 1981—; mem. steering com. Palmer Drug Abuse Program, Houston, 1979-82. Fellow NSF, 1974-78. Mem. Fedn. Am. Scientists, Union Concerned Scientists, Soc. Exploration Geophysicist (research com., jour. referee), Am. Physical Soc. (jour. referee), Am. Geophysical Union, AAAS, N.Y. Acad. Scis., IEEE (sr. mem.), Stanford Alumni, Caltech, MENSA, Planetary Soc., Sigma Xi, Tau Beta Pi. Home and Office: 513 W Louisiana McKinney TX 75069-4445

HUGGINS, DAVID GLENN, investment company executive; b. Balt., Oct. 2, 1932; s. Maurice and Dorothy (Gettell) H.; m. Mary Ann Williamson, June 26, 1954; children: David Glenn Jr., Cynthia Huggins Tidd, Clayton. AB, Amherst Coll., 1954. Cert. fin. planner. Stockbroker Dean Witter Reynolds, San Mateo, Calif., 1958—. 1st lt. USAF, 1954-57. Office: Dean Witter Reynolds 181 E 2d Ave San Mateo CA 94401

HUGGINS, KENNETH MILLARD, educator, financial executive; b. Geddes, S.D., Apr. 18, 1932; s. Ben F. and Nellie Mae (Haney) H.; m. Florence J. McCreesh, Aug. 8, 1964; children: Ronald, Suzanne, Sean, Brian. BA, Dakota Wesleyan Coll., 1960; MBA, Ind. U., 1962; PhD, Tex. Tech. U., 1973. Cert. fin. planner. Mgmt. trainee Crown-Zellerback Co., San Francisco, 1961-63; acct. exec., advt. mgr. Castro Realty Co. Inc., San Francisco, 1963-66; prof. Dakota Wesleyan U., Mitchell, S.D., 1966-70, U. Nebr., Omaha, 1970-78, Metro State Coll., Denver, 1987—; chief fin. officer Farm Credit Banks, Omaha, 1978-84; head acad. dept. Coll. Fin. Planning, Denver, 1984-87; cons. fin. planning Greenwood Village, Colo., 1987—; vis. prof. in fellowship Chgo. Mercantile Exchange, 1976. Named one of Outstanding Young Men Am., 1968, Outstanding Educator Am., 1974-75; recipient Excellence in Consultation award U. Nebr., 1978. Mem Fin. Mgmt. Assn., Midwest Fin. Assn., Soc. Fin. Analysts, Internat. Assn. Fin. Planners, Inst. Cert. Fin. Planners. Presbyterian. Home: 4319 S Alton Way Englewood CO 80111

HUGGINS, MARION DIXON, JR., manufacturing company executive; b. Durham, N.C., Apr. 20, 1941; s. Marion Dixon and Edith (Slayton) H.; m. Linda Faye Williams, Jan. 10, 1967 (div. Apr. 1980); 1 child, Pamela Carol; m. Holly See Egan, Apr. 2, 1980; children: Michele Diane, Mark David. BS in Applied Math., N.C. State U., 1963. Various positions Colonial Flooring Co., Durham, 1963-66; various mfg. positions Rockwell Internat. Co., Raleigh, N.C., 1966-71; mktg. mgr. Rockwell Internat. Co., Pitts., 1971-72; bus. mgr. Digital Equipment Corp., Westfield, Mass., 1972-74; v.p. Sybron Corp., Asheville, N.C., 1974-80; pres., chief exec officer Erie Mfg. Co., Milw., 1980-85; v.p. RTE Corp., Waukesha, Wis., 1985—; bd. dirs., officer Alpex Computer Corp., Hartford, Conn., 1980-82, Erie Controls, NV, Herentials, Belgium, 1980-85; bd. dirs. Exec. Solutions Inc., Brookfield, Wis. Gen. chmn. Waukesha United Way, 1987—; bd. dirs. Asheville C. of C., 1979-80, Edn. and Research Found., Washington, 1976-80. Served to sgt. U.S. Army, 1966-72. O'Connor Found. scholar N.C. State U., 1959-63. Mem. Am. Prodn. and Inventory Control Soc. (pres. 1976), Exec. Com., Am. Mgmt. Assn. Republican. Lutheran. Club: Western Racquet (Elm Grove, Wis.). Office: RTE Corp 1319 E Lincoln Ave Waukesha WI 53186

HUGGINS, RANDALL D., construction company executive; b. Amarillo, Tex., Aug. 9, 1959; s. Harold Don and LaJuana Lee (Ward) H. BArch, Tex. Tech. U., 1983. Intern architect Ensign and Tunnell Architects, Amarillo, 1977-81; head draftsman Charles Freeburg and Assocs., Lubbock, Tex., 1981-82; project architect Shepherd & Boys USA, Dallas, 1983-85; mgr., architect Cen. Constrn. Co. div. Trammell Crow Co., Dallas, 1985-86, pres., 1986-88, ptnr., 1988-89; exec. v.p. Remington Interiors, Dallas, 1989—. Mem. Assn. Builders and Contractors (chmn. polit. action com. 1987—), Assn. Builders and Contractors Tex. (bd. dirs. 1988—). Republican. Presbyterian. Home: 527 Lee Dr Coppell TX 75019 Office: Remington Interiors PO Box 551521 Dallas TX 75355

HUGHES, BRADLEY JAMES, manufacturing executive; b. El Paso, Tex., Oct. 10, 1940; s. Oscar M. and Josephine C. (Frericks) H.; m. Mary Ann Zaegel, Apr. 22, 1967; children: Julie, Ann. BS in Acctg., Quincy Coll., 1962. Audit mgr. Arthur Andersen & Co., St. Louis, 1962-74; asst. controller Combustion Engring. Inc., Stamford, Conn., 1974-78; v.p. fin. NATCO div. Combustion Engring. Inc., Tulsa, 1978-82, v.p. fin. oil and gas group, 1982-84; v.p. gen. auditor Combustion Engring. Inc., Stamford, 1984-85; v.p., controller The Dexter Corp., Windsor Locks, Conn., 1985-87; v.p. fin. Nat. Spinning Co., Inc., N.Y.C., 1988—. Served with USAF, 1963-69, Res. Mem. Am. Inst. CPA's, Fin. Execs. Inst. Republican. Roman Catholic. Office: Nat Spinning Co Inc 183 Madison Ave New York NY 10016

HUGHES, BRADLEY RICHARD, marketing executive; b. Detroit, Oct. 8, 1954; s. John Arthur and Nancy Irene (Middleton) H.; AA, Oakland Coll., 1974; BS in Bus., U. Colo., 1978, BJ, 1979; MBA in Fin. and Mktg., 1981; MS in Telecommunications U. Colo., 1988; m. Linda McCants, Feb. 14, 1977; children: Bradley Richard Jr., Brian Jeffrey. Cert. Office Automation Profl. Buyer, Joslins Co., Denver, 1979; mktg. adminstr. Mountain Bell, Denver, 1980-82, tech. cons. AT&T Info. Systems, mktg. exec. AT&T, 1983-86, acct. exec., 1986-87; mktg. mgr. U.S. West, 1987—. Bd. dirs. Brandychase Assn.; state del., committeeman Republican Party Colo. Mem. Assn. MBA Execs., U.S. Chess Fedn., Internat. Platform Assn., Mensa, Intertel, Assn. Telecommunications Profls., Am. Mgmt. Assn., Am. Mktg. Assn., Info. Industry Assn., Office Automation Soc. Internat., World Future Soc., Internat. Soc. Philos. Inquiry. Republican. Methodist. Home: 5759 S Jericho Way Aurora CO 80015 Office: US West 6200 S Quebec Ste 310 Englewood CO 80111

HUGHES, DAVID H., manufacturing executive; b. Kansas City, Mo., Sept. 9, 1928; s. Hilliard W. and Mary (Histed) H.; m. Dorothy H. Halsey, Dec. 19, 1950; children: David, Avery, Steven, Betsey. B.S.E., Princeton U., 1949; M.B.A., Harvard U., 1952. Vice chmn. Hallmark Cards, Kansas City, Mo., also bd. dirs.; bd. dirs. Yellow Freight Systems, Overland Park, Kans. Trustee Hall Family Found., Kansas City, Mo.; chmn. Midwest Research Inst., Kansas City; past chmn. bd. Sunset Hill Sch., Kansas City; past pres. Jr. Achievement Greater Kansas City; past bd. dirs. Boys' Club Kansas City, INROADS, Kansas City; bd. dirs., trustee Children's Mercy Hosp., Kansas City; pres. St. Luke's Hosp. Found. Served to 2d lt. USAF, 1952-53. Mem. Greater Kansas City C. of C. (past v.p., past dir.). Republican. Presbyterian. Clubs: Kansas City Country (pres. 1982) (Mission Hills, Kans.); River (dir. 1981-83) (Kansas City, Mo.). Office: Hallmark Cards Inc 2501 McGee Trafficway Box 580 Kansas City MO 64141 *

HUGHES, DAVID HENRY, manufacturing company executive; b. Orlando, Fla., Dec. 20, 1943; s. Harry C. and Pauline B. Hughes; m. Rebecca Wilkins; 1 child, Kristin E.; m. 2d, Linda Cooper, Apr. 26, 1986. BS, U. Fla., 1965, JD, 1967. Mgmt. trainee Hughes Supply Inc., Orlando, 1968-72, pres., chief operating officer, 1972-74, pres., chief exec. officer, 1974-86, chmn., pres., chief exec. officer, 1986—; bd. dirs. Sun Banks Inc., Orlando, SunTrust Banks Inc., Atlanta. Bd. dirs. U. Cen. Fla. Rsch. Pk., Orlando, Orlando Regional Med. Ctr.; trustee U. Cen. Fla.; mem. bd. overseers Rollins Coll., Winter Park, Fla., Young Pres.'s Orgn. Mem. Fla. Bar Assn., Fla. Coun. of 100. Republican. Office: Hughes Supply Inc 521 W Central Blvd Orlando FL 32801

HUGHES, DAVID MICHAEL, oil service company executive; b. Knoxville, Tenn., Mar. 20, 1939; s. Cleo L. and Lucille (Farmer) H.; m. Louise Love, Mar. 17, 1960 (div. 1971); children: David Michael Jr., Sheryl Lynn; m. Elizabeth Grove, Mar. 16, 1974; children: Christopher Grove, Andrew Carter. BCE, U. Tenn., 1962. Founder, owner World Wide Divers, Inc., Morgan City, La., 1962-69; founder, chmn. bd. Oceaneering Internat., Inc., Houston, 1969—; founder, owner Broken Arrow Ranch, Ingram, Tex., 1975—; founder, pres. Tex. Wild Game Coop., Ingram, 1981—, Game Ranching, Inc., Ingram, 1986—; Bd. dirs. Oceaneering Internat., Inc., 1969—. Author: Broken Arrow Ranch Cookbook, 1984; patentee underwater corrosion meter and underwater camera. Mem. Hist. Preservation Com., Ingram, 1986-87; mem. Adv. Council Tex. Marine Sci. Inst., 1980—. Mem. Assn. Diving Contractors (pres. 1967-71, Galletti award 1981); Exotic Wildlife Assn. (pres. 1987—), Chi Epsilon (nat. conv. del. 1961). Republican. Home: Broken Arrow Ranch PO Box 530 Ingram TX 78025 Office: Tex Wild Game Coop 102 Hwy 27 W PO Box 530 Ingram TX 78025 also: Oceaneering Internat Inc 16001 Park Ten Place Houston TX 77084

HUGHES, DONALD R., textile executive; b. 1929; married. MBA, Harvard U., 1957. Mem. controller staff Burlington Industries, Inc., Greensboro, N.C., 1959-63, mgr. ops. research dept., 1963-66, asst. controller, 1966-70, sr. asst. controller, 1970-73, controller, 1973-75, treas., controller, 1975-76, v.p. fin., controller then exec. v.p., chief fin. officer, 1976, now vice chmn., dir., chief fin. officer. Served with USN, 1946-50. Office: Burlington Industries Inc PO Box 21207 Greensboro NC 27420

HUGHES, EDWIN LAWSON, management consultant; b. Pittsburg, Kans., Aug. 11, 1924; s. Edwin Byron and Vera (Lawson) H.; m. Ann Turner Nolen, Oct. 21, 1961; 1 child, Andrew George; children from previous marriage: John Lawson, James Prescott. BSEE, Mo. Sch. Mines, 1949; MSEE, U. Ill., 1950. Registered profl. engr. Fla. Group leader Systems Devel. Corp., Santa Monica, Calif., 1957-60; tech. dir. Gen. Motors, Oak Creek, Wis., 1960-71; v.p. engring. Xerox Corp., Webster, N.Y., 1971-81, Santec Corp., Amherst, N.H., 1981-82; chmn., pres., chief exec. officer Fla. Data Corp., Melbourne, 1982-83; pvt. practice cons. Melbourne, 1984-88; ret. Contbr. articles and papers to profl jours.; inventor computers, copiers; patentee in field. Com. mem. Boy Scouts Am., Pittsford, N.Y., 1974-76. Served with U.S. Army, 1943-46, ETO. Mem. IEEE, AAAS, Fla. Engring. Soc., Nat. Soc. Profl. Engrs., Space Coast PC User's Group (sec. 1988), Coast Club, Space Coast Ski Club (asst. sec. 1988), Suntree Country Club. Republican. Home and Office: 447 Pauma Valley Way Melbourne FL 32940

HUGHES, GENE WYATT, construction company executive; b. Dayton, Ohio, Feb. 20, 1926; s. John Clayborne and Catherine (Wyatt) H.; Julie Clare Loeffel, May 22, 1964; children: Robert, Meredith, John. BA, Williams Coll., 1950; MS, Stanford U., 1960; MBA, U. San Francisco, 1970. Registered profl. engr., Ohio. Project engr. Hughes Simonson, Dayton, 1954-59; dept. mgr. Scott Co. of Calif., Oakland, 1960-67; project mgr. Swinerton-Walberg, San Francisco, 1967-70; v.p. Hughes Bechtol, Dayton, 1970-82, pres., chief exec. officer, 1982-84; pres. Frebco, Inc., Dayton, 1984—. Adv. com. Sinclair Community Coll., 1980—. Served with USNR, 1944-46, PTO. Mem. ASHRAE, (chpt. v.p. 1974-75), Internat. Exec. Service Corps, Mech Contractors Assn. (bd. dirs.), Am. Arbitration Assn. Republican. Presbyterian. Club: Dayton Country. Lodge: Rotary (pres. Oakwood chpt. 1983-84). Office: Frebco Inc 1395 Olive Rd Dayton OH 45426

HUGHES, GEORGE DAVID, business educator; b. Collingswood, N.J., Jan. 27, 1930; s. Edgar M. and Lillie C. (Snyder) H.; m. Elizabeth Jane Barrett, Sept. 15, 1966; 1 child, David Barrett. B.S. in Bus. Adminstrn., Drexel U., 1952; M.B.A., U. Pa., 1960, Ph.D., 1963. Sales rep. Burroughs Corp., Phila., 1955-58; vis. lectr. Johns Hopkins U., Balt., 1960-61; vis. assoc. prof. U. Calif., Berkeley, 1966-67; asst. prof. Cornell U., Ithaca, N.Y., 1963-66, assoc. prof., 1966-72; Burlington prof. bus. U. N.C., Chapel Hill, 1972—; vis. prof. Harvard U., 1978, 83; cons. on jury trials, evaluation of advertising, TV programs, movies; founder, pres. Decision Labs, Ltd., 1987—;. Author numerous books on consumer behavior, mktg. strategy, microcomputer applications; contbr. articles to profl. jours. Served to lt. j.g. USNR, 1952-55. Mem. Am. Acad. Mgmt., Am. Mktg. Assn., Am. Psychol. Assn., Assn. Consumer Research, Inst. Mgmt. Scis.

HUGHES, GEORGE FARANT, JR., safety engineer; b. Roanoke, Va., June 22, 1923; s. George Farant and Pattie (Shafer) H.; m. Frances Miriam Perdue, July 1, 1950. BS, Va. Mil. Inst., 1948. Registered profl. engr., Va., Calif.; cert. safety profl. With roadway maintenance dept. N. & W. Ry. Co., Roanoke, 1948, with Liberty Mut. Ins. Co., Roanoke, Balt., 1949-61, asst. div. mgr., Pitts., 1962-63; safety supr. Westinghouse Electric Corp., Balt., 1963-64; supr. safety and accident prevention, Buffalo, 1965-67; safety dir. U.S. Naval Weapons Sta., Yorktown, Va., 1967-73; head occupational safety U.S. Naval Safety Center, Norfolk, Va., 1973-83, dep. dir. shore safety programs, 1984—. Served with AUS, 1943-46, 50-52. Decorated Bronze Star with oak leaf cluster, Purple Heart. Mem. Am. Soc. Safety Engrs. (profl. mem.), Western N.Y. Safety Conf. (dir. 1966-67), Nat. Soc. Profl. Engr., Va. Safety Assn. (bd. dirs. 1979—), Nat. Eagle Scout Assn., SAR, Assn. Presevation Va. Antiquities (bd. dirs. 1984-87), Vets. Safety. Home: 520 Randolph St Williamsburg VA 23185 Office: Naval Safety Center Norfolk VA 23511-5796

HUGHES, GEORGE MAXWELL KNIGHT, pharmaceutical company executive; b. Wallasey, Eng., July 10, 1928; came to U.S., 1954; s. Arthur Trevor and Gwendolyn Mary (Jones) H.; m. Christine Anne Rofe, Sept. 21, 1954; children: Jane K., Mark K. BA, Cambridge U., Eng., 1950, PhD, 1954. Research chemist, asst. to v.p. research, then dir. research adminstrn. Pfizer-Research, Groton, Conn., 1959-69; dir. systems and planning Pfizer Pharms., N.Y.C., 1969-71, v.p. adminstrn., 1971-75; v.p. diagnostics products Pfizer Pharms., Columbia, Md., 1980-81; v.p. systems and communications Pfizer Pharms., N.Y.C., 1981—; v.p., gen. mgr. Pfizer Med. Systems, Columbia, 1975-80; bd. dirs. Interdatum Inc., N.Y.C.; mem. panel on healthcare tech. assessment Inst. Medicine, Washington, 1986—. Patentee in chemistry; contrb. papers to numerous publs. Served to capt. U.S. Army, 1946-48. Home: 627B Onondaga Ln Stratford CT 06497 Office: Pfizer Pharms 235 E 42d St New York NY 10017

HUGHES, HEIDI, retail executive; b. Orange, N.J., Feb. 23, 1948; d. John Walker and Dorothy Eloise (Walker) H; m. Thomas Michael Valega, Mar. 15, 1988. BS, Skidmore Coll., 1971; MA in Journalism, Am. U., 1983. Edn. curator II L.A. Zoo, 1977-78; outdoor recreation planner U.S. Fish and Wildlife Svc., Washington, 1978-80; pub. relations dir. Dept. of Wildlife, Washington, 1981-82; news assignment staff Sta. WRC-TV, Washington, 1984; pres. sec. to Congressman Don Bonker Ho. of Reps., Washington, 1985; profl. lectr. Am. U., Washington, 1987; pres. News Speak Pub. Relations, Rockville, Md., 1986—, Am. Wild Bird Co., Rockville, 1988—; dir. edn. Raccoon Ridge Bird Obs., Layton, N.J., 1976-83; cons. in field; lectr. in field. Co-author: Bird Gadgets Galore: Your Guide to Everything for the Birds, 1989; contbr. articles to profl. jours.; photographer. Recipient Merriman award Writers Guild Am., 1983, Image award Nat. Assn. Remodeling Industry, 1986. Mem. Wild Bird Feeding Inst., NATAS (Davis award 1983), Nat. Press Club, Md. Ornithol. Soc. Democrat. Pantheist. Home: 802 Cabin John Pkwy Rockville MD 20852 Office: Wild Bird Co 617 Hungerford Dr Rockville MD 20850

HUGHES, JAMES CAMERON, animal breeder; b. Columbus, Ohio, Jan. 4, 1935; s. Printen James and Alma May (Wray) H.; m. Sharon Sue Moore, Oct. 25, 1959; children: Douglas, Robert, Trisha. BS, Calif. Poly. State U., 1957. Chemist Dept. Agr. State of Ohio, Columbus, 1958-59, San Bernardino, Calif., 1960-64; dairyman Purdy, Mo., 1964-73; canine breeder, broker Do Bo Tri Kennels, Ltd., Purdy, 1960—. With U.S. Army, 1957-63. Republican. Mem. Ch. of Christ. Home: Rte 1 Purdy MO 65734

HUGHES, JOHN FARRELL, finance company executive; b. Bridgeport, Conn., Aug. 12, 1946; s. John Hubbell and Alice Catherine (Farrell) H.; m. Patricia Nancy Wetzel, July 10, 1971; children: Michael John, Jonathan Wetzel, Katherine Farrell. B.B.A., U. Notre Dame, 1968; M.B.A., U. Ga., 1973. Banking officer Commerce Union Bank, Nashville, 1974-75; asst. v.p. Commerce Union Bank, 1975-77, v.p., 1977-78; asst. tres. Assocs. Corp., Dallas, 1978-79; asst. v.p., asst. treas. Assocs. Corp., 1979-80, v.p., asst. treas., 1980-81, v.p., treas., 1981-83, sr. v.p., treas., 1983—. Vice chmn. St. Paul Hosp. Found. Drive, Dallas, 1982. Lt. USN, 1968-72, Vietnam. Mem. Fin. Execs. Inst., U.S. Naval Inst. Roman Catholic. Office: Assocs Corp N Am PO Box 660237 Dallas TX 75266-0237

HUGHES, KEITH WILLIAM, banking and finance company executive; b. Cleve., July 1, 1946; s. Delmar Vern and Margaret Virginia Hughes; m. Cheryl F. Hughes, Aug. 30, 1969; 1 dau., Amy. BS, Miami U., Oxford, Ohio, 1968, MBA, 1969. Mktg. mgr. Continental Bank, Chgo., 1970-73; exec. v.p. broker/dealer subs. Assos. Corp., 1973-74; v.p. mktg. Northwestern Nat. Bank, 1974-76; sr. v.p. Crocker Bank, San Francisco, 1976-81; exec. v.p., dir. Assos. Corp., Dallas, 1981-85; sr. exec. v.p. Assos. Corp., 1985-88, vice-chmn., 1988—. Active Big Bros. Am.; bd. dirs. Dallas Opera. Mem. Am. Bankers Assn., Bank Mktg. Assn., Consumers Bankers Assn., Nat. Consumer Fin. Assn., lympic club (San Francisco), Los Colinas Country Club (Tex.), Lincloln City Club (Dallas), Ocean Reef Club (Key Largo). Office: Assocs Corp N Am 250 Carpenter Frwy Irving TX 75062

HUGHES, PATRICIA TANNER, management consultant; b. Syracuse, Dec. 3, 1940; d. Kenneth R. and Bernadine Tanner; 1 child, D. Scott. BS, SUNY-Brockport, 1962; MEd, Kent State U., 1974. Tchr. pub. schs., Ravenna and Hiram, Ohio, 1962-71; asst. dir., prof. human relations Kent State U., 1971-77; mgr. orgn. devel. and tng. Norton Co., Akron, 1977-80; orgn. devel. adv. Exxon Research & Engring. Co., Florham Park, N.J., 1980-83; mgr. orgn. devel. Lockheed, Burbank, Calif., 1985—. Bd. dirs. Community Action Council Ravenna, Ohio, 1965-70. Mem. Cert. Cons. Internat., Organizational Devel. Network, Internat. Registry Organizational Devel. Cons., Am. Soc. Tng. and Devel.

HUGHES, PHILLIP RALPH, software designer; b. Colo. Springs, Colo., Oct. 31, 1940; s. Herbert Harold and Dorothy Garrison (Phillips) H.; m. Jacky Jeanette McDonald, Oct. 3, 1975 (div. Apr. 1977). B in Music, N. Tex. State U., 1962, M in Music, 1962; postgrad., Brandeis U., 1962-65. Entertainment dir. Dept. of Army, Leesville, La., 1965-68; systems analyst Southland Life Ins. Co., Dallas, 1968-70; internal cons. Informatics, Inc., Dallas, 1970-79; v.p. Incepts, Inc., Dallas, 1979-87, prin. cons., 1987—. Mem. Assn. for Computing Machinery, IEEE Computer Soc.

HUGHES, ROBERT J., bank executive; b. N.Y.C., Dec. 9, 1946; s. Harry and Kathleen (Wilde) H.; m. Marie Di Pietro, May 28, 1975; 1 child, Christopher J. B.B.A., Manhattan Coll., 1968. C.P.A., N.Y.; cert. mgmt. acct. Audit mgr. Coopers & Lybrand, N.Y.C., 1968-78; v.p., asst. comptroller Am. Express Co., N.Y.C., 1978-83; exec. v.p., chief fin. officer Am. Savs. Bank, FSB, White Plains, N.Y., 1983—; mem. acctg. & fin. mgmt. com. Nat. Council of Savs. Instns., Washington, 1984—, mem. taxation com., 1986—; mem. com. acctg. and taxation Savs. Bank Assn. of N.Y. State, 1987—. Mem. AICPA, N.Y. State Soc. CPAs, Fin. Execs. Inst. Republican. Roman Catholic. Office: Am Savs Bank 99 Church St White Plains NY 10601

HUGHES, ROBERT MERRILL, mining engineer; b. Glendale, Calif., Sept. 11, 1936; s. Fred P. and Gertrude G. (Merrill) H.; AA, Pasadena City Coll., 1957; 1 child, Tammie Lynn Cobble. Engr. Aerojet Gen. Corp., Azusa, Calif., 1957-64, 66-74; pres. Automatic Electronics Corp., Sacramento, 1964-66; specialist Perkin Elmer Corp., Pomona, Calif., 1974-75; gen. mgr. Hughes Mining Inc., Covina, Calif., 1975-76; project mgr. L&A Water Treatment, City of Industry, Calif., 1976-79; dir. Hughes Industries Inc., Alta Loma, Calif., 1979—; pres. Hughes Devel. Corp., Carson City, Nev.; chmn. bd. Hughes Mining Inc., Hughes Video Corp. Registered profl. engr., Calif; lic. gen. bld. contractor. Mem. AIME, Nat. Soc. Profl. Engrs., Instrument Soc. Am., Am. Inst. Plant Engrs. Republican. Patentee in field. Home: 10039 Bristol Dr Alta Loma CA 91701 Office: Box 723 Alta Loma CA 91701

HUGHES, ROBERT STANLEY, machine manufacturing company executive; b. Richmond, Va., Feb. 13, 1930; s. Robert Stanley and Eva Estelle (Turner) H.; m. Katherine M. Edwards, July 8, 1950; children: Kathy Roberta Hughes Bulifant, Robert Stanley III. BS, U. Richmond, 1953, MC, 1981. Asst. sec., asst. treas. Molins Machine Co. Inc., Richmond, 1952—, contr. Richmond div., 1987—; sec., treas., bd. dirs. Molins Richmond, Inc., 1987—. With U.S. Army, 1956-58. Mem. Am. Mgmt. Assn., Richmond Export-Import Club, Masons. Democrat. Baptist. Home: 8005 Galaxie Circle Richmond VA 23228 Office: Molins Machine Co Inc 3900 Carolina Ave Richmond VA 23222

HUGHES, SARAH GILLETTE, software company executive; b. Detroit, Jan. 24, 1947; d. William R. and Virginia M. (Sloan) Gillette; m. Robert Denis Hughes, June 28, 1969. BS in Math., U. Mich., 1969; MBA in Fin., U. Chgo., 1976. Programmer analyst U. Mich., Ann Arbor, 1969-71; mgr. systems and programming Am. Hosp. Assn., Chgo., 1972-82; dir. software devel. SPSS Inc., Chgo., 1982-84; dir. systems devel. InnerLine, Arlington Heights, Ill., 1984-86; dir. product devel. Pansophic Systems, Inc., Lisle, Ill., 1986—. Mem. Lakeview Citizens' Council, Chgo. Mem. Inst. Indsl. and Electronics Engrs., Assn. Computing Machinery, Data Processing Mgmt. Assn., U. Chgo. Women's Bus. Group (past dir.), Execs. Club Chgo., Beta Gamma Sigma. Office: Pansophic Systems Inc 2400 Cabot Dr Lisle IL 60532

HUGHES, SPENCER EDWARD, JR., utility executive; b. Bklyn., Sept. 6, 1933; s. Spencer Edward and Marie (Carey) H.; m. Diane E. Woods, June 15, 1963; children: Spencer Edward III, David Charles, Charles Woods. BA, Columbia Coll., 1955; postgrad., NYU, 1959-60; MBA in Fin., Hofstra U., 1961. Mem. staff L.I. Lighting Co., Hicksville, N.Y., 1958-64, mgr. investor relations, 1964-83, asst. treas., 1984—. 1st lt. USAF, 1955-57. Mem. Securities Industry Assn., Corp. Transfer Agts. Assn. (bd. dirs. 1968-75), Am. Gas Assn. (investor relations com. 1985—). Home: 11 Highland St W Massapequa NY 11758 Office: LI Lighting Co 175 E Old Country Rd Hicksville NY 11801

HUGHES, THOMAS H., health care executive; b. Muncie, Ind., Feb. 23, 1929; s. Ray Myers and Dorothy (Stewart) H.; m. Judy A. Manning, Aug. 26, 1956; children: Theodore M., Elizabeth. BS, Ind. U., 1951. Dir. mktg. communications Zimmer, Inc., Warsaw, Ind., 1964-67; dir. mktg. Zimmer, Inc., Warsaw, 1967-68, v.p. mktg., 1968-71, exec. v.p., 1971-79, pres., 1979-88; v.p. Bristol-Myers Co., N.Y.C., 1980-81, sr. v.p., 1981-88, pres. health care group, 1988—. Mem. Pres.'s Adv. Com. Grace Coll., Warsaw, 1987; mem. Ind. U. Dean's Adv. Council, 1984. Fellow Ind. U. Sch. Bus. Acad. Alumni; mem. Ind. State C. of C. (bd. dirs.).

HUGHS, RICHARD EARL, utilities holding company executive; b. Rochester, N.Y., Jan. 2, 1936; s. Earl Leaman and Frances Rose H.; m. Gretchen Markwardt, Mar. 31, 1959; children—Mark Allen, Grant Evan. B.S. in Physics, U. Rochester, 1957; M.S. in Math, Purdue U., 1959, Ph.D., 1962. Systems analyst Sandia Corp., Albuquerque, 1962-64; asst. prof. Carleton Coll., 1964-66; pres. Math. Service Assos., Inc., Edwardsville, Ill., 1966-69; asso. prof. applied math. and info. systems So. Ill. U., 1966-69; sr. cons. Cresap, McCormick & Paget, Inc., 1968-70; assoc. dean Grad. Sch. Bus. Adminstr., NYU, 1970-77; dean Coll. Bus. Adminstrn., U. Nev., Reno, 1977-84; v.p. corp. affairs Sierra Pacific Resources, Reno, 1984—; bd. dirs. Sierra Pacific Resources, Sierra Energy Co., Inc., Lands of Sierra, Inc., Bonnel Fund Inc., Reno Rotary Club, Citizens for Pvt. Enterprise, also chmn. 1986—; mem. com. on edn. C. of C. and Industry N.Y.C., 1970-74; mem. adv. com. Medgar Evers Coll., City U. N.Y., 1971-74; NSF research fellow Purdue U., 1958-60. Mem. deferred compensation com., State of Nev., 1978-84; ; mem. Nev. Gov.'s Commn. on Econ. Diversification, 1981-83. Mem. Assn. Corp. Growth, Western Indsl. Nev., Nev. Fin. Soc., Western Assn. Collegiate Schs. Bus. (dir. 1977-84), Sigma Xi, Beta Gamma Sigma. Club: Rotary (Reno). Office: Sierra Pacific Resources 6100 Neil Rd PO Box 30150 Reno NV 89520

HUGIN, ADOLPH CHARLES EUGENE, lawyer, engineer, inventor, educator; b. Washington, Mar. 28, 1907; s. Charles and Eugenie Francoise (Vigny) H. BS in Elec. Engring., George Washington U., 1928; MS in Elec. Engring., MIT, 1930; cert. in patent law and practice, JD, Georgetown U., 1934; cert. radio communication (electronics) Union Coll., 1944; cert. better bus. mgmt. Gen. Electric Co., continuing edn. program, 1946; LLM, Harvard U., 1947; SJD, Cath. U. Am., 1949; cert. in Christian Doctrine and Teaching Methods, Conf. of Christian Doctrine, 1960; cert. in social svcs. and charity Ozanam Sch. Charity, 1972. Bar: D.C. 1933, U.S. Ct. Customs and Patent Appeals 1934, U.S. Supreme Ct. 1945, Mass. 1947, U.S. Ct. Claims, 1953, U.S. Ct. Appeals (fed. cir.) 1982; registered U.S. Patent and Trademark Office Atty. Bar, 1933; registered profl. elec. and mech. engr., D.C.; examiner U.S. Patent and Trademark Office, 1928. With Gen. Electric Co., 1928-46, engr. Instruments R&D Lab., West Lynn Works, Mass., 1928, engr.-in-charge Insulation Lab. River Works, Lynn, 1929, Engine-Electric Drive Devel. Lab., River Works, 1929-30, patent legal asst., Schenectady, 1930, patent investigator, Washington, 1930-33, patent lawyer, Washington, 1933-34, Schenectady, 1934-46; engr.-in-charge section aeros. and marine engring. div., Schenectady, 1942-45; organizer, instr. Gen. Electric patent practice course, 1945-46; pvt. practice law, cons. engring., Cambridge and Arlington, Mass., 1946-47; vis. prof. law Cath. U. Am., Washington, 1949-55; assoc. Holland, Armstrong, Bower & Carlson, N.Y.C., 1957; pvt. practice law, cons. engr. Washington and Springfield, Va., 1947—. Author: International Trade Regulatory Arrangements and the Antitrust Laws, 1949; editor-in-chief Bull. Am. Patent Law Assn., 1949-54; editor notes and decisions Georgetown U. Law Jour., 1933-34, staff, 1930-34; contbr. articles on patents, copyrights, antitrust, radio and air law to profl. jours.; inventor dynamoelectric machines, insulation micrometer calipers, ecology and pollution controls, musical instruments, dynamometers, heavy-duty inherent constant voltage characteristic generators, water-cooled eddy-current clutches, brakes, and others; 12 U.S. and several fgn. patents. Mem. Schenectady N.Y. Com. Boy Scouts Am., 1940-42, North Springfield Civic Assn.; charter mem., 1st bd. mgrs. Schenectady Cath. Youth League, 1935-38, hon. life mem., 1945; mem. adv. bd. St. Michael's Parish, Va., 1974-77, lector, commentator, 1969-80; bd. dirs. St. Margaret's Fed. Credit Union, 1963-67, 1st v.p., 1965-67; chmn. St. Margaret's Bldg. Fund, 1954; lector St. Margaret's Parish, 1966-69, retreat group capt., 1965-68, Parish Council, 1969-71; mem. legis. com. Schenectady C. of C., 1940-46. Recipient Dietzen Drawing prize, George Washington U., 1926, Georgetown U. Law Jour. Key award, 1934, Aviation Law prize Cath. U. Am., 1948, Radio Law prize Cath. U. Am., 1949, Charities Work award St. Margaret's Ch., 1982; elected to Gen. Electric Co. Elfun Soc. for Disting. Exec. Svc., 1942. Mem. Am. Intellectual Property Law Assn. (life; cert. of Honor for 50 Yrs. Svc.), ABA (life), John Carroll Soc., Nat. Soc. Profl. Engrs., D.C. Soc. Profl. Engrs., St. Vincent de Paul Soc. (parish conf. v.p. 1949-65, pres. 1965—, pres. Prince Georges County, Md. council 1958-61, founding pres. Arlington, Va. Diocesan council 1975-77, nat. trustee 1975-77), Nocturnal Adoration Soc., St. Margaret's Parish Confraternity Christian Doctrine (pres., instr. 1960-61), Archdiocesan Council Cath. Men (pres. So. Prince George's County deanery 1956-58, 65-68), Holy Name Soc. (pres. parish 1950-52, Prince George's County section 1953, Washington Archdiocesan Union 1953-55), Retired Tchrs. Assn., Men's Retreat League (Wash. exec. bd. 1954-58), Delta Theta Phi (Georgetown U. Law Sch. Scholarship Key award 1934). Avocations: travel, photography, sketching, horticulture. Address: 7602 Boulder St North Springfield VA 22151

HUHMAN, PETER WILLIAM, finance executive; b. Phila., Nov. 15, 1960; s. Louis E. and Margaret (Maher) H. BA, Rutgers Coll., 1984. Computer technician Atlantic Fin., Phila., 1984-86; mgmt. trainee GC Svc., Woburn, Mass., 1986-87; account rep. Citicorp Acceptance, Marlton, N.J., 1987; div. mgr. Trans Union Credit, Phila., 1988. Republican. Roman Catholic. Home: 246 Willow Dr Cinnaminson NJ 08077 Office: Trans Union 1211 Chestnut St Philadelphia PA 19105

HUITT, JIMMIE L., oil, gas, real estate investor; b. Gurdon, Ark., Aug. 21, 1923; s. John Wesley and Almedia (Hatten) H.; m. Janis C. Mann, Oct. 30, 1945; children—Jimmie L., Jr., Allan Jerome. B.S. in Chem. Engring., La. Tech. U., 1944; M.S. in Chem. Engring., U. Okla., 1948, Ph.D., 1951. Registered profl. engr., La. Research engr. Mobil Oil Corp., Dallas, 1951-56, Gulf Research Co., Pitts., 1956-67; ops. coordinator Kuwait Oil Co., London, 1967-71; gen. mgr. Gulf Oil-Zaire, Kinshasa, 1971-74; mng. dir. Gulf Oil-Nigeria, Lagos, 1974-76; sr. v.p., exec. v.p. Gulf Oil Exploration and Prodn. Co., Houston, 1976-81, pres., 1981-85; rancher Four Jays Ranch, Industry, Tex., 1986—. Contbr. articles to profl. jours.; patentee in field. Served to 1st lt. U.S. Army, 1944-47. Mem. Soc. Petroleum Engrs. (chmn. various coms. 1956—). Republican. Lodges: Masons, Shriners. Office: Four Jays Ranch PO Box 236 Industry TX 78944

HULBERT, BRUCE WALKER, corporate executive, banker; b. Evanston, Ill., Feb. 5, 1937; s. Bruce Walker and Mary Alice (Utley) H.; m. Linnette Ott, June 19, 1963; children: Christina, Jennifer, William. B.S. in Bus., Northwestern U., 1961. Sr. v.p. 1st Interstate Bank of Calif., Los Angeles and San Francisco, 1962-78; pres., chief exec. officer, dir. First Interstate Bank of Denver, 1978-84; exec. v.p. Western Capital Investment Corp., 1984—; chmn bd. Shelter Am. Corp., 1986—; pres. PV Mortgage Corp., 1988—. Mem. nat. bd. trustees, exec. com., former Denver regional chmn. Inst. Internat. Edn., 1979—; adv. bd. Jr. League Denver, 1980—; trustee, exec. com. Denver Art Mus., 1985—; bd. dirs. Denver Partnership, 1978—, Denver Civic Ventures, Inc., 1982-88, chmn., 1984-86; exec. bd. Denver Area council Boy Scouts Am., 1981—, Nat. Jewish Ctr. Immunology and Respiratory Medicine, 1982-88; mem. exec. bd. AMC Cancer Research Ctr., 1984—, vice chmn. bd., 1988—; trustee Mile High United Way, Denver, 1980—, chmn. bd., 1987-89; bd. dirs., exec. com. NCCJ, 1983—. Mem. Colo. Assn. Bank Holding Cos. (exec. com., dir., 1978-84), Am. Bankers Assn., Mortgage Bankers Assn., Denver Clearing House Assn. (pres. 1982-83), Denver C. of C. Republican. Clubs: Confrerie des Chevaliers du Tastevin, Cherry Hills Country, Denver Petroleum. Office: Western Capital Investment Corp 1675 Broadway #1700 Denver CO 80202

HULCE, CRAIG GERALD, real estate, investment and management consulting company executive; b. Wausau, Wis., Mar. 9, 1961; s. Gerald Lee and Patricia Anne (Shea) H. BS, U. Wis., La Crosse, 1985; BA in Psychology, U. Wis., Green Bay, 1988. Pres. PCL Properties, Green Bay, Wis., 1985—. Vol. Village Vol. Fire Dept., Ashwaubenon, Wis., 1983. Roman Catholic. Home and Office: 2431 Kubale Ln Green Bay WI 54303-4088

HULEN, MARJORIE JANE, medical center executive; b. Denver, Sept. 23, 1921; d. Perry E. and Garnet W. (Doty) Kellogg; student pub. schs., Redondo Beach, Calif.; m. Ray Romaine Hulen, June 10, 1950; 1 child, Lynn Robert. With A. O. Smith Corp., Los Angeles, 1948-60, exec. sec., 1956-60; exec. sec. Sterling Electric Motors, Los Angeles, 1960-61; research sec. Pasadena (Calif.) Found. for Med. Research, 1961-65; exec. sec. Profl. Staff Assn., Los Angeles County/U. So. Calif. Med. Center, Los Angeles, 1965-70, office mgr., 1970-74, bus. mgr., 1974-79, exec. dir., 1979—. Instl. rep. Los Angeles Regional Family Planning, 1977-79. Nat. Pub. Relations award Nat. Assn. Accts., 1979. Mem. Am. Soc. Assn. Execs., Nat. Secs. Assn., Soc. Research Adminstrs., Nat. Assn. Accts., Nat. Council Univ. Research Adminstrs., Assn. Ind. Research Insts., Nat. Assn. Female Execs. Democrat. Home: 2311 El Paseo St Alhambra CA 91803 Office: 1739 Griffin Ave Los Angeles CA 90031

HULL, AARON, office furniture company executive; b. Chgo., Nov. 20, 1928; s. Joseph and Esther H.; m. Ann Greenberg, May 21, 1951; children: Helene, Leonard, David. MA, U. Ill., 1951. Salesman Chgo. Office Supply Co., 1951-54; mgr. Town Office Furniture Co., Chgo., 1954-57; owner, pres. Aaron's Office Furniture Co., Lincolnwood, Ill., 1957—. Bd. dirs. office products chpt. City of Hope, Chgo., 1983—;, Am. Soc. to Prevent Blindness, Schaumburg, Ill., 1987—. Recipient Spirit of Life award City of Hope, 1983. Mem. Masons, Shriners. Home: 351 Little Melody Lake Forest IL 60635 Office: Aarons Office Furniture Co 6700 N Lincoln Ave Lincolnwood IL 60645

HULL, CORDELL WILLIAM, business executive; b. Dayton, Ohio, Sept. 12, 1933; s. Murel George and Julia (Barto) H.; m. Susan G. Ruder, May 10, 1958; children: Bradford W., Pamela H., Andrew R. B.E., U. Dayton, 1956; M.S., MIT, 1957; J.D., Harvard U., 1962. Bar: Ohio 1962; Registered profl.

engr., Mass. Atty. Taft, Stettinius & Hollister, Cin., 1962-64, C & I Girdler, Cin., 1964-66; gen. counsel, treas., pres. C&I Girdler, Internat., Brussels, 1966-70; v.p. Bechtel Overseas Corp., San Francisco, 1970-73; pres., dir. Am. Express Mcht. Bank, London, 1973-75; v.p., treas. Bechtel Corp. and Bechtel Power, San Francisco, 1975-80; pres. Bechtel Fin. Services, San Francisco, 1975-82; v.p., chief fin. officer Bechtel Group Inc., 1980-85, mem. exec. com.; dir. Bechtel Investments Inc., Sequoia Ventures, Inc., Bechtel prin. operating cos., Bechtel Financing Services, Bechtel Devel. Co.; pres. Bechtel Power Corp.; exec. v.p., dir. Bechtel Group, Inc.; mem. services policy com. Office of the U.S. Trade Rep.; bd. dirs. Fed. Res. Bank of San Francisco. Mem. adv. com. Am. Enterprise Inst. for Pub. Policy Research; mem. Inst. Internat. Studies, U. Calif.-Berkeley Schs., Pacific Basin Coun.-Dominican Coll., Nuclear Power Oversight Com.; co-chmn. Coalition for Employment through Exports; trustee Com. for Econ. Devel., Western Regional Council; mem. U.S.-Japan Bus. Council, U.S. Coun. for Energy Awareness, The Atlantic Coun. of U.S. Served with U.S. Army, 1956. Clubs: Bankers, Knickerbocker, Pacific Union, Links, San Francisco Golf, Menlo Country. Office: Bechtel Group Inc 50 Beale St PO Box 3965 San Francisco CA 94105

HULL, JAMES DONALD, financial executive; b. Reading, Pa., July 4, 1946; s. Robert Floyd and Florence Weiler (Wealand) H.; m. Linda Ann Hill, Nov. 2, 1968; children: Julie, James, Jeffrey. BSBA, Pa. State U., 1968. Mgr. acctg. Firestone Plastics Co., Perryville, Md., 1971-82; contr. Seaboard Foods, Inc., Cecilton, Md., 1983-84; dir. adminstrn., chief fin. officer Nat. Aquarium in Balt., Inc., 1985—. Lt. (j.g.) USN, 1968-71. Republican. Presbyterian. Home: 309 Elkton Blvd Elkton MD 21921 Office: Nat Aquarium in Balt Inc Pier 3 501 E Pratt St Baltimore MD 21202

HULL, LARRY WAYNE, coal company executive; b. Welch, W.Va., Oct. 1, 1950; s. Marlin Philip and Mabel May (Triplett) H.; m. Lydia Marie Kish, Dec. 11, 1971; children: Stephanie, Courtney. AS, Bluefield Coll., 1970; BS in Mining Engring., Va. Poly. Inst. & State U., 1972; MS in Mgmt., MIT, 1987. With Consolidation Coal Co., Pitts., 1970—, tech. asst. to v.p., 1983-85, v.p., 1985—. Republican. Baptist. Home: PO Box 1536 Bluefield WV 24701 Office: Consolidation Coal Co PO Box 68 Pocahontas VA 24635

HULL, ROBERT GLENN, financial administrator; b. Ottumwa, Iowa, Sept. 14, 1929; s. C. Glenn and DeElda L. (Davidson) H.; m. Donna Marie Hastriter, Jan. 26, 1951; children: Cynthia Ann Hull Williams, Steven Kent. B.A., Friends U., 1956; M.S., Emporia Kans. State U., 1966. With Nat. Coop. Refinery Assn., McPherson, Kans., 1957—; treas., comptroller Nat. Coop. Refinery Assn., 1968-76, v.p. finance, 1976—; dir. Jayhawk Pipeline Corp., Clear Creek Cos. Bd. dirs. Central Coll., McPherson. Served with USAF, 1951-55. Mem. Fin. Execs. Inst., Nat. Assn. Accountants for Coops., Am. Petroleum Inst., Delta Pi Epsilon. Republican. Methodist. Clubs: Petroleum, McPherson Country. Home: 417 S Grand St McPherson KS 67460 Office: Nat Coop Refinery Assn PO Box 1404 McPherson KS 67460

HULLIN, TOD ROBERT, chemical company executive; b. Seattle, May 28, 1943; s. Jack Elmer and Floretta Elizabeth (Light) H.; BA in Bus. Adminstrn., U. Wash., 1966; m. Susan Lee Kanz, May 6, 1967. Staff asst. domestic coun. White House, Washington, 1973-74, assoc. dir. domestic coun. for housing and community devel., 1974-76; prin. dep. asst. sec. def. for pub. affairs, Washington, 1976-77; v.p. Interstate Gen. Corp., St. Charles, Md., 1977-83; pres. Interstate Condominiums, Inc., 1981-83; v.p. communications/pub. affairs G.D. Searle Pharms., Skokie, Ill., 1983-86; v.p. corp. affairs SmithKline Beckman Labs., Phila., 1986—. Bd. dirs. Phila. Drama Guild, Balch Inst. for Ethnic Studies. 1st lt. U.S. Army, 1967-69. Decorated Army Commendation medal; recipient Outstanding Pub. Sfc. award Sec. of Def., 1977. Mem. Nat. Assn. Home Builders, Urban Land Inst., Greater Washington Bd. Trade, U. Wash. Alumni Assn. (pres. San Francisco Bay Area chpt. 1982-83), Eureka (Ill.) Coll. Arts Coun., Army Navy Country Club, Sigma Nu. Republican. Presbyterian. Office: SmithKline Beckman Labs One Franklin Pla Philadelphia PA 19101

HULSEBOSCH, CHARLES JOSEPH, truck manufacturing company executive; b. N.Y.C., Dec. 14, 1933; s. Albert J. and Marie (Gough) H.; m. Elizabeth Ferguson, July 6, 1957; children—Albert, Daniel, Joseph, Kristine, Thomas, Howard, John. A.B., Dartmouth, 1955; M.B.A., Amos Tuck Sch., 1956. Fin. analyst Ford Motor Co., 1956-60; from budget mgr. to controller Renault, Inc., N.Y.C., 1960-63; with United Fruit Co., 1963-69, treas., 1967-69; v.p., treas. Libby, McNeill & Libby, 1969-74, v.p. fin., 1974-77; also dir.; v.p. fin., treas., dir. Oshkosh Truck Corp., Wis., 1978—; former owner Wis. Flyers, Continental Basketball Assn. Mem. Oshkosh City Council, 1981-85; treas. Lourdes Acad. Found., Inc., Oshkosh. Mem. Fin. Execs. Inst., Newcomen Soc., Zeta Psi. Republican. Roman Catholic. Club: Oshkosh Power Boat, Oshkosh Country. Home: 5059 Valley Heights Rd Oshkosh WI 54904 Office: Oshkosh Truck Corp 2307 Oregon St Oshkosh WI 54901

HULTQUIST, TIMOTHY ALLEN, investment banker; b. Faribault, Minn., Apr. 1, 1950; s. Wayne Burdette and Helen Sorg (Armitage) H.; m. Cynthia Marie Mealhouse, May29, 1972; children: Kirsten Lee, Matthew Anton, Andrew Thomas. BA summa cum laude, Macalester Coll., 1972; MBA, U. Chgo., 1975. Asst. mgr. First Nat. Bank Chgo., London, 1975-76; asst. v.p. First Nat. Bank Chgo., N.Y.C., 1976-79; v.p., fgn. exchange mgr. First Nat. Bank Chgo., Chgo., 1979-81, sr. v.p. fgn. exchange, 1981-82; prin. Morgan Stanley & Co., Inc., N.Y.C., 1982—, mng. dir., 1985-88; chief London office, mem. mgmt. com. Morgan Stanley Group Inc., 1988—. Trustee Macalester Coll., St. Paul, Minn., 1985—. Mem. Westchester Hills Golf Club (White Plains), Wentworth Golf Club (Va. Water, U.K.), Phi Beta Kappa. Congregationalist. Club: Westchester Hills Golf (White Plains), Wentworth Golf, Virginia Water (England). Office: Morgan Stanley Internat, Kingsley House 1A Wimpole St, London W1M 7AA, England

HUMBERT, ROGER, food products executive. married. Grad., DePaul U., 1961. With Kroger Co., 1955-66, Jewel Food Co., 1966-67, Shurfine-Cen. Corp., Melrose Park, Ill., 1967—; v.p. advt. mktg. Shurfine-Cen. Corp., Northlake, Ill.; now exec. v.p., sec. mktg. Northlake, Ill. Office: Shurfine-Cen Corp 2100 N Mannheim Rd Northlake IL 60164

HUME, HORACE DELBERT, manufacturing company executive; b. Endeavor, Wis., Aug. 15, 1898; s. James Samuel and Lydia Alberta (Sawyer) H.; student pub. schs.; m. Minnie L. Harlan, June 2, 1926 (dec. May 1972); 1 son, James; m. 2d, Sarah D. Lyles Rood, Apr. 6, 1973 (dec. Jan. 1988). Stockman and farmer, 1917-19; with automobile retail business, Garfield, Wash., 1920-21, partner and asst. mgr., 1921-27; automobile and farm machine retailer, Garfield, partner, mgr., 1928-35, gen. mgr. Hume-Love Co., Garfield, 1931-35, pres., 1935-57; partner, gen. mgr. H.D. Hume Co., Mendota, Ill., 1944-52; pres. H.D. Hume Co., Inc., 1952—; partner Hume and Hume, 1952-72; pres. Hume Products Corp., 1953—; pres., dir. Hume-Fry Co., Garden City, Kans., 1955-73; dir. Granberry Products, Inc., Eagle River, Wis. Mayor, Garfield, Wash., 1938-40. Bd. dirs. Mendota Hosp. Found., 1949-73, pres., 1949-54; bd. dirs. Mendota Swimming Pool Assn.; mem. City Planning Commn., 1953-72, chmn., 1953-69; mem. Regional Planning Commn., LaSalle County, Ill., 1965-73, chmn., 1965-71; mem. Schs. Central Com., 1953—, LaSalle County Zoning Commn., 1966—, LaSalle County Care and Treatment Bd., 1970-73; chmn. Mendota Watershed Com., 1967-73. Recipient Key to City City of Mendota, 1988, Cert. of Appreciation City of Mendota, 1988. Mem. Am. Soc. Agrl. Engrs., Eagle River (Wis.) C. of C. (pres., dir. 1962-63), Mendota C. of C. (pres. 1948-49, dir. 1946-49, Community Service award 1972). Republican. Presbyterian (elder). Clubs: Kiwanis (pres. 1953, dir. 1954), Masons, Shriners, Order Eastern Star, Elks. Patentee in various fields. Home: 709 Carolyn St PO Box 279 Mendota IL 61342 Office: 1701 1st Ave Mendota IL 61342

HUMES, GRAHAM, investment banker; b. Williamsport, Pa., Oct. 8, 1932; s. Samuel and Elenor (Graham) H.; m. Elizabeth Schwartz Hershey, June 17, 1978; children: Margaret, Kathryn, Malcolm, Elizabeth, John Hershey, Lisa Hershey. BA, Williams Coll., 1954; MBA, Harvard U., 1958. Mng. ptnr. Butcher & Singer, Inc., Phila., 1958-74; sr. v.p. Girard Bank-Mellon Bank, Phila., 1974-87; mng. dir. Legg Mason Wood Walker, Inc., Phila., 1987—; also bd. dirs. Legg Mason Wood Walker, Inc., Balt.; bd. dirs. Avant-Garde Computing, Inc., Mt. Laurel, N.J., Brunschwig & Fils, Inc., North White Plains, N.Y., Technitrol, Inc., Flourtown, Pa., Phila. Industries, Inc. Chmn. Com. of 70, Phila., 1988—; bd. dirs. UNICEF, Phila., 1985—; mem. Phila. Com. on Jud. Selection, 1986—. Mem. Am. Arbitration Assn., Locust Club, Harvard Bus. Sch. Club (bd. dirs. Phila. chpt. 1982—), Merion Cricket Club. Republican. Home: 262 Radnor-Chester Rd Radnor PA 19087 Office: Legg Mason Wood Walker Inc Five Penn Center Pla Philadelphia PA 19103

HUMES, ROBERT ERNEST, pharmaceutical company executive; b. Erie, Pa., Sept. 30, 1943; s. Millard and Mildred Rosemary (Sabatino) H.; m. JoAnn Florence Malanka, May 29, 1965; children: Christine Marie, Robert Ernest Jr. B.A., St. John's U., 1967; M.B.A., NYU, 1974. With Met. Life Ins. Co., N.Y.C., 1961-67; asst. to v.p. sales U.S. Life Ins. Co., N.Y.C., 1967-68; supr. ins. Bristol-Myers Co., N.Y.C., 1968-71; mgr. personnel planning Squibb Corp., N.Y.C., 1971-72, dir. personnel planning, 1972-75; exec. asst. to chmn. Squibb Corp., 1975-79; v.p. exec. asst. to chmn. Squibb Corp., N.Y.C., 1979-82; sr. v.p. human resources Squibb Corp., Princeton, 1982—. Chmn. Mayor's Task Force on Pvt. Sector Intiatives, Lawrence Twp., N.J., 1982—; bd. dirs. Princeton chpt. ARC; trustee, v.p. adminstrn. United Way Princeton Area Communities; mem. state corp. cabinet N.J. chpt. Am. Heart Assn. Mem. N.Y. Indsl. Relations Assn. (pres. 1981-83), Am. Soc. Personnel Adminstrn., Am. Pension Conf. (steering com. 1981-83). Home: 87 West Shore Dr Pennington NJ 08534 Office: Squibb Corp PO Box 4000 Princeton NJ 08540

HUML, DONALD SCOTT, distribution executive; b. Lake Geneva, Wis., May 8, 1946; s. Robert Francis and Shirley (Roberts) H.; m. Joyce Cora Featherstone, Oct. 2, 1965; children: Tiffany Lynn, Alison Michelle, Andrew Scott. BBA, Marquette U., 1969; MBA, Temple U., 1980. Mgr. treasury ops. Allis-Chalmers Corp., West Allis, Wis., 1970-73; dir. fin. services CertainTeed Corp., Valley Forge, Pa., 1973-75, asst. treas., 1975-78, v.p., treas., 1978-81, v.p., comptroller, 1981-83, v.p., group pres., 1983—; chmn. Precision Meters, Inc., Orlando, 1984—. Mem. Am. Mgmt. Assn., Fin. Execs. Inst., Am. Water Works Assn., Beta Gamma Sigma. Republican. Roman Catholic. Home: 340 Wyllpen Dr West Chester PA 19380 Office: Certainteed Corp 750 E Swedesford Rd Valley Forge PA 19482

HUMMEL, CHARLES LEROY, accountant; b. Detroit, Jan. 22, 1947; s. Ward Luther and Ethel Virginia (Hoffman) H.; A.A. in Bus. Adminstrn., Mesa Community Coll., 1972; B.S. in Acctg. with distinction, Ariz. State U., 1974, M.B.A., 1980; m. Janice Claire Gray, Oct. 26, 1968; children—Katherine Elizabeth, Michael Jason. Auditor, Price Waterhouse & Co., Phoenix, 1975-77; dir. acctg. Samaritan Health Service, Phoenix, 1977-80; v.p., chief fin. officer Camelback Hosps., Inc., Phoenix, 1980-86; pres. Delta Cons., Inc., Scottsdale, Ariz., 1986-88, Hummel & Baer, Mesa, Aria., 1988—. Served with USAF, 1968-72. C.P.A., Ariz. Fellow Healthcare Fin. Mgmt. Assn. (cert. mgr. patient accounts); mem. Am. Inst. C.P.A.s, Ariz. Soc. C.P.A.s. Nat. Assn. Accts., Inst. Mgmt. Acctg. (cert. mgmt. acct.). Home: 1063 N Cherry Mesa AZ 85201

HUMPHREIS, EDWARD VARNER, manufacturing engineer; b. Notasulga, Ala., Nov. 23, 1939; s. Shadrick Stephan and Isabelle (Ackimon) H.; m. Olivia Gray, Apr. 4, 1964; children: Deborah K., E. Christopher. BS, Auburn U., 1963; MS, U. Tenn., 1975. Registered profl. engr. Staff supr. Newport News (Va.) Shipbldg., 1964-66; with Monsanto Co., Decatur, Ala., 1966—; engring. specialist Monsanto Co., 1980—. Pres. Morgan County Vol. Action Ctr., 1982-85; dist. program chmn. Huntsville coun. Boy Scouts Am., 1985-88, dist. explorer chmn., 1988—; campaign asst. Rep. Presdl. Election, 1984; Rep. candidate state senate, 1985. With U.S. Army, 1961-62. Recipient Dist. Merit award Huntsville coun. Boy Scouts Am., 1984, Three Bead Wood Badge, 1986. Mem. Indsl. Engrs. (sr.), Soc. Mfg. Engrs. (sr. mem., cert.), Kiwanis (pres. local chpt. 1984-85), Masons, Order Ea. Star. Baptist. Home: 1021 Way Thru the Woods SW Decatur AL 35603 Office: Monsanto Co PO Box 2204 Decatur AL 35602

HUMPHREY, BINGHAM JOHNSON, chemical company executive; b. Proctor, Vt., Feb. 9, 1906; s. Albert Parmlee and Angie T. (Tenney) H.; B.S., U. Vt., 1927, hon. LL.D., 1978; Ph.D., Yale U., 1930; m. Esther R. Stanley, Oct. 25, 1930; children—Eugene B., James R., Sarah. Sr. research chemist Firestone Corp., 1930-42; tech. dir. Conn. Hard Rubber Co., 1942-49; pres. Humphrey-Wilkinson, Inc., 1949-64; pres. The Humphrey Chem. Co., Hamden, Conn., 1964-72, chmn. bd., 1972—; dir. Milfoam Corp. Chmn., Hamden Bd. Edn., 1958-66; trustee U. Vt., 1968-74, chmn. trustees, 1973-74. Mem. Am. Chem. Soc., U. Vt. Nat. Alumni Assn. (pres. 1969-70), Sigma Xi. Clubs: N.Y. Chemists, Rotary. Office: Humphrey Chem Co PO Box 325 North Haven CT 06473

HUMPHREY, BLAKE B., electronics company executive. Pres. Mallory Timers Co., Indpls., to 1988; pres. electronic/elec. group Emhart Corp., Farmington, Conn., 1988—. Office: Emhart Corp 426 Colt Hwy Farmington CT 06032

HUMPHREY, JEFFREY HAUGER, property tax specialist; b. Vancouver, Wash., Dec. 8, 1957; s. John Foulk and Bonnie (Hauger) H.; m. Linda Ann Gallaher, Nov. 23, 1985; children: Amber, Keith. BS in Acctg., St. Mary's Coll., 1981. Owner, mgr. Design Woodcraft, Walnut Creek, Calif., 1981-83; ltd. ptnr. Sacramento Satellite Systems, 1983-85; dir. property tax dept. Equitec Fin. Group, Inc., Oakland, Calif., 1985—. Mem. Inst. Property Taxation (mem. subcom. on computer use), Toastmasters. Republican. Presbyterian. Home: 291 Biddleford San Ramon CA 94583 Office: Equitec Fin Group Inc 7677 oakport St Oakland CA 94621

HUMPHREY, R. BRUCE, investment banking executive; b. Atlanta, Sept. 22, 1951; s. Harold Grady and Frances Adelle (Bryant) H.; 1 child, Brandon Scot. Student, San Jacinto Coll., 1972-75. Estimator Sullivan Transfer Co., Houston, 1975-77, Machinery Movers, Inc., Houston, 1977-79; ind. ins. salesman Houston and Atlanta, 1979-82; investment banker Blinder Robinson & Co., Inc., Atlanta and Chgo., 1982—. Office: Blinder Robinson & Co Inc 5455 S Yosemite St Englewood CO 80111

HUMPHREYS, ANTHONY MICHAEL, financial consultant; b. Bklyn., May 1, 1932; s. Michael A. and Rose Ann (McHugh) H.; m. Ann Marie Weaver, Sept. 10, 1960; children: Michael A., Francis P., Rose Ann M. BBA, St. John's U., 1958. CPA, N.Y. Auditor Deloitte Haskins and Sells, N.Y.C., 1958-62; corp. acct. Internat. Playtex Corp., Dover, Del., 1962-68; staff acct. Glen Alden Corp., N.Y.C., 1968-70; corp. controller Monroe Group Inc., N.Y.C., 1971-73; prin. Gen. Bus. Services, Hightstown, N.J., 1974—. Served as cpl. U.S. Army, 1953-54, Korea. Mem. Nat. Soc. Pub. Accts., Hightstown-East Windsor C. of C. (pres. 1981). Republican. Roman Catholic. Lodge: KC. Office: Gen Bus Svcs 131 S Main St Hightstown NJ 08520

HUMPHRIES, ROMILLY HELFENSTEIN, manufacturing executive; b. Newton, Mass., Jan. 25, 1930; s. Floyd Thurston and Anna Trail (Helfenstein) H.; m. Elizabeth Beryl Prescott, Aug. 13, 1955; children: Lisa, Jennifer, Charles, William. BA, Trinity Coll., Hartford, Conn., 1953. Instr. Hawaii Prep. Acad., Kamuela, 1955-57; assoc. Arthur D. Little, Inc., Cambridge, Mass., 1957-63; v.p. Henry Lewis Co., Attleboro, Mass., 1963-68; pres. Diamond Drug, Inc., Revere, Mass., 1968-70; v.p. Burns & Towne, Inc., Leominster, Mass., 1970-76; pres., chief exec. officer SAY Industries, Inc., Leominster, 1976—, also bd. dirs.; bd. dirs. Vulsay Industries, Inc., Branford Ont., Can., Accent Systems, Inc., Pitts. Inventor oil container; patentee in field. Pres. PTA, Dover, Mass., 1970; active Youth Ch. Group, Dover, 1972; chmn. Youth Soccer Orgn., Dover, 1972-82. Mem. The Packaging Inst. Internat., Petroleum Packaging Com.

HUMPHRIES, WELDON R., real estate executive; b. Lampasas, Tex., Aug. 17, 1937; s. Weldon L. and Ruth Beatrice (Ballard) H.; m. Nancy Carol Sandy; children: Weldon R. Jr., Nanette, Walter. BBA, U. Houston, 1959; MBA, U. Hartford, 1971. Sr. mortgage analyst Conn. Gen. Life Ins. Co., Hartford, 1962-69; v.p. real estate Arvida Corp., Miami, 1969-72; v.p. investments Mortgage Investments Services Inc., Coral Gables, Fla., 1972-78; sr. v.p. real estate Manor Care Inc., Silver Spring, Md., 1978—. Sch. bd. Spencerville Jr. Acad., Silver Spring, 1987—; bd. dirs. Spencerville Seventh Day Adventist Ch., Silver Spring, 1984—. Served to 1st lt. USMC, 1959-62. Republican. Home: 2118 Sondra Ct Silver Spring MD 20904 Office: Manor Care Inc 10750 Columbia Pike Silver Spring MD 20901

HUMPHRIES, WILLIAM DARLINGTON, venture capital company executive; b. Allendale, S.C., Mar. 19, 1927; s. Gilliam Gee and Martha Elizabeth (Darlington) H.; m. Mignon Jacqueline Faget, Oct. 12, 1957 (div. June 1971); children: William, Jacqueline, John; m. Barbara Sears Pitts, Oct. 19, 1974. BA in Fgn. Affairs, U. Va., 1951. Sales rep. Proctor & Gamble Co., New Orleans, 1951-55; v.p. fin. Royal Street Corp., New Orleans, 1955-82; pres., chief exec. officer Royal Street Investment Corp., New Orleans, 1962-82; pres. Royal Street Devel. Co., New Orleans, 1974-82, Mission Hills Ranch, Inc., Newport Beach, Calif., 1975-82; v.p. Royal Street Land Co., Park City, Utah, 1974-82, Stanford Ct. Hotel Mgmt. Co., San Francisco, 1975-82; mng. gen. ptnr. Walnut Street Capital Co., New Orleans, 1982—; bd. dirs., chmn. fin. and audit coms. GTS Corp., Houston, 1969—; bd. dirs., chmn. audit com. Cucos, Inc., New Orleans, 1983—; com. dir. Cartrex Corp., Grand Rapids, Mich., 1984—. Bd. dirs. Urban League, New Orleans, 1964-68; active United Way, New Orleans, 1955-75; Bur. Govtl. Research, New Orleans, 1987—; various other civic orgns. Served with U.S. Army, 1945-46, ETO. Republican. Methodist. Clubs: New Orleans Lawn and Tennis, Bienville (New Orleans). Office: Walnut St Capital Co 2330 Canal St New Orleans LA 70119

HUNDLEY, CHARLES MORGAN, pension administrator; b. Champaign, Ill., Feb. 10, 1942; s. Charles E. and June E. H.; student So. Ill. U., 1960-63, Cameron Coll., 1965, U. Ill., 1974-75; degree Life Underwriter Tng. Council, 1970-72; m. Barbara S. Shelton, Sept. 9, 1974. Supr. communications Kentron Hawaii, Ltd., Port Hueneme, Calif., 1966-68, Fed. Elec. Corp., Lompoc, Calif., 1968-69; ins. cons. Met. Life Ins. Co., Decatur, Ill., 1969-74; benefits coordinator U. Ill.-Urbana, 1974-80; assoc. dir. State Univs. Retirement System Ill., Champaign, 1980-86; v.p. strategic investment services No. Trust Co., Chgo., 1986—. Treas. local United Way, 1975-76; bd. dirs. Levis Faculty Center, 1976—, also corp. sec.; treas. Developmental Services Center, 1977-81, Disabled Citizens Found., 1977-81. Served with Security Agy., U.S. Army, 1963-66. Mem. Univ. Risk Mgmt. and Ins. Assn. (editor, pub. newsletter 1975-80), Nat. Assn. Securities Internat. Found. Employee Benefit Plans, Mcpl. Fin. Officers Assn., U. Ill. Round Table (pres. 1981-82). Club: Rotary. Home: 1129 Johnson Dr Naperville IL 60540 Office: Northern Trust Co 50 S La Salle St 4th Floor W Chicago IL 60674

HUNG, MIMI WONG, electronics company executive; b. Shanghai, China; d. James and Diana (Chu) Wong; m. Raymond K. Hung, Apr. 22, 1971; children: Renee, Nina, Marcus. ScB in Econs., Purdue U., 1971. Exec. dir. Applied Electronics Ltd., Hong Kong, 1966—, Applied Toys, Hong Kong, 1984; bd. dirs. Applied Internat. Ltd., Hong Kong, Applied E&T Inc., N.J. Clubs: Royal Hong Kong, Jockey, Marina, Clear Water Bay Country (Hong Kong). Office: Applied Electronics Inc, Good Prospect Indsl Bldg, 33-35 Wong Chuk Hang Rd, Hong Kong Hong Kong

HUNGER, J(OHN) DAVID, business educator; b. New Kensington, Pa., May 17, 1941; s. Jackson Steele and Elizabeth (Carey) H.; m. Betty Johnson, Aug. 2, 1969; children: Karen, Susan, Laura, Merry. BA, Bowling Green (Ohio) State U., 1963; MBA, Ohio State U., 1966, PhD, 1973. Selling supr. Lazarus Dept. Store, Columbus, Ohio, 1965-66; brand asst. Procter and Gamble Co., Cin., 1968-69; asst. dir. grad. bus. programs Ohio State U., Columbus, 1970-72; instr. Baldwin-Wallace Coll., Berea, Ohio, 1972-73; prof. U. Va., Charlottesville, 1973-82; strategic mgmt. prof. Iowa State U. Coll. Bus., Ames, 1982—; prof. bus. George Mason U., Fairfax, Va., 1986-87; cons. to bus., fed. and state agys. Capt. Mil. Intelligence, U.S. Army, 1966-68. Decorated Bronze Star. Mem. Acad. Mgmt., N.Am. Case Rsch. Assn. (pres.), Midwest Case Rsch. Soc. (pres.), Strategic Mgmt. Soc. Author: (with T.L. Wheelen) Strategic Management and Business Policy, 1983, rev. edit., 1986, 89, An Assessment of Undergraduate Business Education in the U.S., 1980, Strategic Management, 1983, rev. edit., 1987, Cases in Strategic Management and Business Policy, 1987; contbr. articles to publs. Office: Iowa State U Coll Bus 300 Carver Hall Ames IA 50011

HUNGER, MELVYN IRWIN, electronics executive; b. Bklyn., Sept. 20, 1940; s. David Joseph and Fay R. (Mack) H.; m. Michele Helene Kroll, Nov. 9, 1969; 1 child, Wayne Foster. BA in Econs., Fairleigh Dickinson U., 1963. Audio buyer E.J. Korvette Stores, N.Y.C., 1963-66; product mgr. for home entertainment Singer Co., N.Y.C., 1966-71; dir. mktg. CBS Masterworks, N.Y.C., 1971-72; v.p. mktg. Benjamin Electronics, Farmingdale, N.Y., 1972-73; sr. v.p. Teknika Electronics Corp., Fairfield, N.J., 1973—, also bd. dirs. Inventor automatic announcing machine, on site video vending replicating. Trustee Temple Beth Tikvah, Wayne, N.J., 1987. With USAR, 1962-68. Mem. NARDA (adv. bd.). Home: 8 Welsh Ct Wayne NJ 07470 Office: Teknika Electronics Corp 353 Rt 46 W Fairfield NJ 07006

HUNNEWELL, WALTER, JR., investment banker; b. Boston, Dec. 14, 1956; s. Walter and Maria Luisa (de la Borbolla) H. AB, Harvard U., 1979; MBA, U. Chgo., 1985. Media planner McCann-Erickson, Houston, 1980-81; ter. mgr. Continental Cablevision, Boston, 1981-83; rsch. dir. Veronis Suhler & Assocs. Inc., N.Y.C., 1985, assoc., 1985—. Club: Harvard (N.Y.C.). Office: Veronis Suhler & Assocs Inc 350 Park Ave New York NY 10122

HUNSCHER, WILLIAM HOMER, SR., entrepreneur; b. Lansdale, Pa., Apr. 18, 1938; s. Homer Leroy and Martha Anne (Alderman) H.; m. Anne Weadon, Jan. 23, 1959 (div. 1981); children: Liza Anne Hunscher Cautino, William Homer Jr., Karen Beth. BSChemE, Lafayette Coll., 1960; MBA, Babson Coll., 1970. Product mgr. Union Carbide Corp., N.Y.C., 1964-68; co-founder, v.p. Data Terminal Systems, Inc., Maynard, Mass., 1968-72; founder, pres. Fasfax Corp., Nashua, N.H., 1973-78, Calcogen Corp., San Francisco, 1981-83; chief exec. officer Eloquent Systems Corp., Manchester, N.H., 1983—. Libertarian candidate for Pres. Nomination, 1979, Party N.H. com., 1976-78; rep. candidate N.H. Primary for U.S. Senate, 1980. 1st lt. U.S. Army, 1960-63. Linde scholar, 1959, NSF scholar, 1958. Mem. Lafayette Coll. Alumni Assn. (pres., Mayfield Outstanding Alumni award 1974), Boston Area Alumni (pres. 1967-70). Office: Eloquent Systems Corp PO Box 6235 Manchester NH 03108

HUNSICKER, RONALD JAY, health care executive; b. Norristown, Pa., Sept. 8, 1945; s. Christian D. and Florence H. (Gottshall) H.; m. Joyce M. Brunner, June 22, 1968 (div. June 1985); children: Jonathan Jay, Angela Dawn; m. Kendall P. Keech, Dec. 14, 1985. BA, Bluffton Coll., 1967; MDiv., Mennonite Bibl. Sem., 1971; DMin., Princeton Theol. Sem., 1982. Pastor Charleswood Mennonite Ch., Winnipeg, Man., Can., 1971-75; dept. dir. Oaklawn Psychiatric Ctr., Elkhart, Ind., 1975-81; v.p. for behavioral health Meml. Hosp., South Bend, Ind., 1981-88; exec. dir. ARC Westchester, Yorktown Heights, N.Y., 1988—; cons. Coll. Chaplains, Chgo., 1984. Contbr. various articles on marriage and family issues to profl. jours. Fellow Nat. Assn. Addiction Treatment Providers (bd. dirs. 1986—), Coll. Chaplains; mem. Am. Assn. Marriage and Family Therapists (clin.), Assn. Clin. Pastoral Edn. (cert. supr. 1977—). Home: 5 Richard Dr RR #4 Mahopac NY 10541 Office: ARC Westchester PO Box 37 Route 118 Yorktown Heights NY 10598

HUNSINGER, DOYLE J., electronics executive; b. Hazelton, Pa., Nov. 12, 1947; s. Doyle J. and Doris Adele (Price) H.; m. Diane Barbara Trivigno, Oct. 12, 1968; children: Doyle III, Dana. BS in Mktg., Fairleigh Dickinson U., 1974. Various positions Sears, Roebuck & Co., Watchung, N.J., 1966-79; mdse. asst. Sears New York Group, Wayne, N.J., 1979-81; v.p., treas. CMF Key Services, Kenilworth, N.J., 1983-85; pres. CMF Bus. Supplies, Garwood, N.J., 1985—, DSI Delivery Systems, Inc., 1987—; mem. distbr. council Memorex Corp., Santa Clara, Calif., 1983-86. Committeeman Somerset County Rep. Orgn., Watchung, 1974—, mcpl. chmn. 1980; treas. Watchung Candidates Com., 1983—; cons. Union County (N.J.) Dist. 1 Adv. Bd., 1985; capt. Watchung Fire Dept., 1980-83; v.p., coach Watchung Little League baseball, 1982-83; scoring chmn. N.J. Synchronized Swimming, 1982-84; bd. dirs. Wilson Meml. Ch., Watchung, 1977-79, 83—, fin. chmn. 1984—. Served with USNG, 1967-74. Mem. Data Processing Mgrs. Assn. N.J. Exempt Firemans Assn., Nat. Bus. Forms Assn. Club: Watchung Fire (pres. 1979). Lodge: Optimists (sec. Watchung club 1975-76). Home: 701 Valley Rd Watchung NJ 07060 Office: CMF Bus Supplies Inc 116 South Ave Garwood NJ 07027

HUNT, FREDERICK TALLEY DRUM, JR., association executive; b. Martinque, French West Indies, Sept. 19, 1947; s. Frederick Talley Drum and Eleanor Conly H.; BA, Vanderbilt U., 1970; m. Acacia Lynn Graham,

Dec. 4, 1976. Dir. program devel. Manufactured Housing Inst., Washington, 1973-74; pres. Hunt Assos., Washington, 1974-75, asst. dir. field services, Nat. Assn. Life Underwriters, 1975-77; dir. communications, govt. liaison Am. Acad. Actuaries, Washington, 1977-80; pres. Soc. Profl. Benefit Adminstrs., 1980—; pres., owner Hunt Mgmt. Systems, 1982—. speaker in field. Mem. Am. Soc. Assn. Execs. (chmn. employee benefits subcom. of govt. affairs com., vice chmn.), Greater Washington Soc. Assn. Execs. (liability ins. task force), Internat. Found. Employee Benefit Plans (govt.-industry relations com.), Soc. of the Cin., Mil. Order Loyal Legion, Aztec Club of 1847, Met. Club. Republican. Anglican. Home: 5308 Blackistone Rd Westmoreland Hills Bethesda MD 20816 Office: Hunt Mgmt Systems 2033 M St NW Ste 605 Washington DC 20036

HUNT, JAMES MUNSON, management consultant; b. New Britain, Conn., Sept. 16, 1947; s. Stanley Mills and Dorothy Adams (Kinkade) H. BA, Bates Coll., 1969; JD, Willamette U., 1976. Bar: Calif. 1976. Pvt. practice Oakland, Calif., 1976-80; ptnr. Legal Productivity Resources, Cambridge, Mass., 1981-86, Found. for Integrating Systems and Human Resources, Cambridge, Mass., 1983—, Heller and Hunt, Legal Cons., Brookline, Mass., 1986—. Author Practicing Law and Managing People: How to Be Successful, 1988; editor Heller and Hunt Law Practice Mgmt. Report, 1987—. Active in Boston Youth at Risk Program, 1986—; bd. dirs. Berkeley Ecology Ctr. 1971-72, 1976-77. Served alt. mil. duty nat. service, 1969-71. Mem. Mass. Bar Assn. Democrat. Office: Found for Integrating Systems and Human Resources 1753 Massachusetts Ave Cambridge MA 02140

HUNT, JOHN EDWIN, insurance company executive, consultant; b. Ozark, Ala., Jan. 13, 1918; s. Tim Atticus and Ada (Arnold) H.; m. Winnifred Prichard; children: Jacqueline, John Edwin Jr., Geoffery, Scott, Richard. Student, Columbus U., Washington, 1938-40, Pace U., 1940-41; diploma in banking, Am. Inst. Banking, 1942; diploma in ins., Travelers Ins. Co., 1944. Aide to regional adminstr., chief auditor Fed. Housing Adminstrn., Washington, 1938-40; with trust dept. Riggs Nat. Bank, Washington, 1940-42; asst. trust officer Fla. Nat. Bank, Jacksonville, 1942-44; asst. mgr. Travelers Ins. Co., Jacksonville, 1944-45, gen. agt. regional br., 1945-58; pres. John E. Hunt & Assocs., Tallahassee, 1972-84; chmn. bd. dirs. Hunt Ins. Group-Spl. Law Enforcement Agy. and Self-Ins. Fund Adminstrn., Tallahassee, 1984—; pres. John Hunt & Assocs., Miami, Fla., 1958-72; ptnr. The Five; pres. Ins. Cons. and Analysts, Tallahassee, 1972—; sec. Home Escort Sales, Tallahassee, 1986—; treas., bd. dirs. Mission Rd. Properties; pres., bd. dirs., vice chmn. bd. dirs. Bankers Savs. Bank, Miami; bd. dirs. Home Intensive Care, Nantahala Village Resort. Past chmn. pvt. industry counsel Pres. Reagan's Job Tng. Ptnrship Act; past mem. Gov.'s Advisors Coun. for Ins.; trustee, chmn. bd. St. Paul's United Meth. Cu., Tallahassee; trustee Fla. Police Chiefs Edn. Rsch. Found.; trustee and mem. pres.'s council Fla. So. Coll., Lakeland, 1986—. Mem. Fla. Assn. Surplus Lines, Fla. Assn. Ins. Agts., Com. of 99 (past pres. and bd. dirs. law enforcement com. 1984-85), Greater Miami Mortgage Brokers Assn. (pres. 1964-65), Fla. Jr. C. of C. (nat. dir., state pres. 1950-52), Killearn Golf and Country Club, Fla. Econs. Club, Govs. Club, Masons, Shriners, Elks. Democrat. Methodist. Clubs: Fla. Econs., Tiger Bay, Govs., Killearn Country, Lodges: Masons, Elk's (lifetime), Shriners (Tallahassee chpt.). Home: Rte 3 PO Box 582 Tallahassee FL 32308 Office: Hunt Ins Group Inc 2324 Centerville Rd Tallahassee FL 32308

HUNT, JONATHAN TODD, real estate appraiser, consultant; b. Sacramento, Nov. 30, 1959; s. Jack Burrell and Ruth Arlene (Larsen) H. Student, Am. River Coll., 1977-79. Salesman Emigh Hardware & Bldg., Sacramento, 1977-78; appraiser J.B. Hunt & Assocs., Fair Oaks, Calif., 1978-86; sales, value cons. Red Carpet Realty, Fair Oaks, 1985-86; appraiser Westland div. Imperial Corp. Am., Sacramento, 1986—; chief appraiser, asst. v.p. ICA Mortgage Corp., Sacramento, 1987—; cons. Red Carpet Realty, Fair Oaks, 1985-86. Bd. dirs. Citizens for a Better Sacramento, 1985-86; mem. Rep. Presdl. Task Force, Washington, 1984-86. Mem. Nat. Fedn. Ind. Bus., Soc. Real Estate Appraisers, Sacramento Bd. Realtors, Calif. Assn. Realtors, Nat. Assn. Realtors, The Comstock Club. Republican. Clubs: 20/30 Internat. (Sacramento); Capital Athletic. Home: 1614 11th St Sacramento CA 95814 Office: ICA Mortgage Corp 3046 Prospect Park Dr Ste 6 Rancho Cordova CA 95670

HUNT, MARY LOU, counselor, small business owner; b. Bell, Calif., Apr. 23, 1932; d. David Allen and Ruth Irene (Bolton) Smith; m. Earl Busby Hunt, Dec. 20, 1954; children: Robert David, Susan Mary, Alan James, Steven Thomas. BA in Psychology, Stanford U., 1954, MA in Psychology, 1954. Tchr., counselor Women's Guidance Ctr. U. Wash., Seattle, 1972; from sec. to pres., cons. counselor Individual Devel. Ctr. Inc., Seattle, 1972—, also bd. dirs. Contbr. chpt. to book Management Preparation for Women, 1978. Bd. dirs. Seattle Day Nursery Assn., 1974-76, Focus on Part-Time Employment, Seattle, 1976, Together in Employment, Seattle, 1982-85, Classical Music Supporters, 1987—. Mem. Am. Assn. Counseling and Devel., Wash. State Assn. Counseling and Devel., Am. Soc. for Tng. and Devel. (bd. dirs. Seattle 1979-82, membership dir. 1980-82), Am. Soc. Personnel Adminstrn., Assn. Measurement and Evaluation in Guidance, Puget Sound Career Devel. Assn. (pres. 1988—). Office: Individual Devel Ctr 1020 E John St Seattle WA 98102

HUNT, PHILIP GARDNYR, food service company executive; b. Mobile, Ala., Dec. 29, 1935; s. Robert Lewis Hunt and Agnes Eve (Herrmann) Weir; m. Ann Carolyn Chamberlain, May 16, 1959; children—Philip Jr., John, Samuel. B.S. in Geology, Fla. State U., 1960, M.S. in Bus. Adminstrn., 1961; J.D., Stetson U., 1966. Bar: Fla. 1967. Asst. v.p. adminstrn. Fla. State U., Tallahassee, 1963-65. 66-68; asst. v.p. food services Morrison Inc., Mobile, Ala., 1968-72, asst. v.p. corp. affairs., 1972, v.p. corp. affairs., 1972-81, v.p., gen. counsel, 1981-84, v.p., gen. counsel, sec., 1984-85, sr. v.p., gen. counsel, sec., 1985—. Coach, Mobile Youth, Baseball and Football, 1969-78; chmn. Morrison Polit. Action Com., 1977—; lay dir. Scout Olympics, Boy Scouts Am., 1978-79; v.p. UMS Prep. Sch. Boys Athletic Assn., 1981, 83-84; pres., 1984-85. Fellow Internat. Bus. Fellows; mem. Fla. Bar Assn., ABA, Internat. Bar Assn., U.S. C. of C. (mem. pub. affairs com. Washington, mem. Southeastern legis. task force), Foodservice and Lodging Inst. Washington (Pres. 1973, 74, dir. 1975—, chmn. legal com. 1981-84), Nat. Restaurant Assn. Washington, Nat. Right to Work Com., Am. Mgmt. Assn., Am. Soc. Corp. Secs., Associated Industries Ala. Republican. Christian Scientist. Clubs: Capitol Hill (Washington); Lake Toxaway (N.C.) Country. Lodge: Rotary of Mobile (bd. dirs. 1982-86). Home: 203 Tuthill Ln Mobile AL 36608 Office: Morrison Inc 4721 Morrison Dr Mobile AL 36625

HUNT, RONALD FORREST, lawyer; b. Shelby, N.C., Apr. 18, 1943; s. Forrest Elmer and Bruna Magnolia (Brackett) H.; m. Judy Elaine Shultz, May 19, 1965; 1 child, Mary. A.B., U. N.C., 1966, J.D., 1968. Bar: N.C., D.C. Mem. staff SEC, Washington, 1968-69, legal asst. to chmn., 1970-71, sec. of commn., 1972-73; dep. gen. counsel, sec. Student Loan Mktg. Assn., Washington, 1973-78, sr. v.p., gen. counsel, sec., 1979-83, exec. v.p., gen. counsel, 1983—; vice chmn., dir. 1st Capital Corp., Southern Pines, N.C., 1984—; bd. dirs. Connie Lee Ins. Co., Washington, 1987—. Mem. Montgomery County Commn. Landlord and Tenant Affairs, Md., 1976-81, chmn., 1979-81; bd. dirs. D.C. chpt. ARC, 1976-83; trustee Arena Stage, Washington, 1984—; trustee Washington Theatre Awards Soc., 1988—. Mem. ABA, Fed. Bar Assn., Order of Coif. Republican. Presbyterian.

HUNT, ROSS STUART, financial planner; b. Garden Grove, Calif., June 30, 1959; s. Ross S. and Dorothy (Walker) H. BS, Miami U., Oxford, Ohio, 1981. Cert. fin. planner. Pres. Progressive Fin. Concepts, Inc., Columbus, Ohio, 1983—; registered rep. Chubb Securities Corp., Concord, N.H., 1982—; adj. faculty Coll. for Fin. Planning, 1988—. Active Columbus Landmarks Found., 1983—. Mem. Internat. Assn. Fin. Planning (pres. bd. trustees 1986—), Inst. Cert. Fin. Planners, Nat. Assn. Securities Dealers (cert.). Office: Progressive Fin Concepts Inc 3677 Karl Rd Columbus OH 43224

HUNT, SUE WHITTINGTON, accountant; b. Greenville, Miss., Nov. 23, 1952; d. Robert Bryan Sr. and Dale (Montgomery) W.; m. Ronnie Charles Hunt, Dec. 28, 1974; children: Andrew W., Emily P. AA in Bus., Holmes Jr. Coll., 1972; BBA, Delta State U., 1974; MBA, Miss. Coll., 1985. Acct. J. Milton Newton, Inc., Jackson, Miss., 1975-76; acct., auditor Dept. of Pub. Welfare, Jackson, Miss., 1976-81; chief fiscal officer Miss. Worker's Compensation Commn., Jackson, Miss., 1982-85; budget analyst IV Fiscal Mgmt. Bd., Jackson, Miss., 1985—. Mem. Clinton Park (Miss.) PTA, 1986—. Mem. Assn. Govt. Accts. (sec. Jackson chpt. 1986, pres.-elect Jackson chpt. 1986-87, pres. Jackson chpt. 1987-88, named Outstanding Chpt. Pres. for Southcentral Region 1988-89), Am. Soc. Women Accts. (pres. Jackson chpt. 1986—, 1st v.p. Jackson chpt. 1985-86, treas. Jackson chpt. 1985-86), Career Forum, Miss. Assn. Govt. Purchasing Agts., MBA Club of Jackson Miss. Methodist. Home: 1707 Melrose Pl Clinton MS 39056 Office: Fiscal Mgmt Bd 901 Walter Sillers Bldg Jackson MS 39201

HUNT, TERRENCE MICHAEL, small business owner; b. Oklahoma City, Dec. 9, 1947; m. Mary Jo Hunt, Nov. 21, 1981; children: Dana, Brian, Taryn, Zachary, Christopher. BS in Bus., So. Meth. U., 1972. Pres., founder Houston Wire & Cable Co., 1975—. Republican. Roman Catholic. Office: Houston Wire & Cable Co PO Box 23221 Houston TX 77228

HUNTER, CHARLES DAVID, retail company executive; b. Alameda, Calif., Dec. 3, 1929; s. Adin Wesley and Bertha Anna (Mayer) H.; m. Alice Betty Trinski, Nov. 6, 1954 (dec. 1970); children: Jeffrey Paul, Karen Sue, Brian David, Robert Stephen; m. Joy Ann Morris, Jan. 12, 1973. A.A., Modesto Jr. Coll., 1949; B.S., U. Calif.-Berkeley, 1951. Staff auditor, mgr. Arthur Andersen & Co., Chgo., 1955-66; asst. controller Walgreen Co., Chgo., 1967-69; controller Walgreen Co., 1969-71, v.p. adminstrn., 1971-78, exec. v.p., chief fin. officer, 1978—. Served to lt. USNR, 1952-55. Mem. Financial Execs. Inst., Am. Inst. C.P.A.s, Ill. Soc. C.P.A.s, Chgo. Retail Financial Execs. Assn. (pres. 1971-72). Home: 1589 S Garden St Palatine IL 60067 Office: Walgreen Co 200 Wilmot Rd Deerfield IL 60015

HUNTER, DOUGLAS LEE, elevator company executive; b. Greeley, Colo., May 3, 1948; s. Delmer Eural and Helen Converse (Haines) H.; m. Janet Lee Snook, May 26, 1970; children: Darin Douglas, Joel Christopher, Eric Andrew, Jennifer Lee. Student, Phillips U., Enid, Okla., 1966-70; BA cum laude, Sioux Falls Coll., 1979; postgrad., N.Am. Bapt. Sem., Sioux Falls, 1977-79. Elevator constructor Carter Elevator Co., Inc., Sioux Falls, S.D., 1971-72, rep., 1972-74, controller, 1974-78, sec.-treas., 1978-82, v.p., 1982-87, pres. 1987—; ptnr. Lifters Ltd., Sioux Falls, S.D., 1984—, chief exec. officer 1987—. Creator, editor: Body Building Manual for the Christian Church in the Upper Midwest, 1983. Mem. gen. bd. Christian Ch., Indpls., 1984-88; mem. regional bd. Christian Ch. in the Upper Midwest, Des Moines, 1985-87; bd. dirs. Glory House, Sioux Falls, 1983-86; teaching leader Bible Study Fellowship, Sioux Falls, 1981—; vice chmn. Greater Sioux Empire Billy Graham Crusade, 1986-87; bd. dirs. Sioux Coun. Boy Scouts Am., 1989. Named Outstanding Young Religious Leader, Sioux Falls Jaycees, 1974; recipient Alumni Pacesetter award Sioux Falls Coll., 1988. Mem. S.D. Family Bus. Coun., Sen. Larry Pressler's Small Bus. Adv. Com., Nat. Assn. Elevator Contractors, Nat. Assn. Elevator Safety Authorities, Constrn. Specifications Inst., Christian Businessmen's Com. U.S., Sioux Falls C. of C. Republican. Lodge: Rotary. Avocations: golf, tennis, reading, music. Home: 1605 Shafer Dr Sioux Falls SD 57103 Office: Carter Elevator Co Inc 2504 S Duluth Ave Sioux Falls SD 57105

HUNTER, EMMETT MARSHALL, lawyer, oil investments company executive; b. Denver, Aug. 18, 1913; s. Emmett Marshall and Pearl Joe (Hubby) H.; m. Marjorie Louise Roth, Nov. 21, 1941; children—Marsha Louise, Marjorie Maddin, Margaret Anne. LL.B., So. Meth. U., 1936, grad. U.S. Naval Mine Warfare Sch. Bar: Tex. 1936. Assoc. Vaughan & Work, Dallas, 1936, Thornton & Montgomery, 1937; sole practice, Dallas, Longview, Houston, 1937-42; with Humble Oil & Refining Co., and successor firm Exxon Co. USA, 1945-78; pres., gen. counsel Internat. Oil Investments, Tyler, Tex., 1978—. Bd. dirs. Tex. Rose Festival, Tyler; bd. mgrs. SAR Tex., state registrar, 1973-85, registrar emeritus, pres. Tyler chpt., 1973. Served with USN, 1942-45; PTO. Recipient Gold Good Citizenship medal SAR, 1979, Patriot's medal, Meritorious medal, 1984. Mem. Am. Petroleum Inst., State Bar Tex., U.S. Naval Inst., Pi Upsilon Nu, Lambda Chi Alpha. Author: Adventuring Abroad on a Bicycle, 1938; Marinas, A Boon to Yachting, 1948. Office: Internat Oil Investments Co PO Box 7402 Tyler TX 75711

HUNTER, JACK DUVAL, lawyer; b. Elkhart, Ind., Jan. 14, 1937; s. William Stanley and Marjorie Irene (Upson) H.; m. Marsha Ann Goodsell, Nov. 14, 1958; children: Jack, Jon, Justin. BBA, U. Mich., 1959, LLB, 1961. Bar: Mich. 1961, Ind. 1962. Atty. Lincoln Nat. Life Ins. Co., Ft. Wayne, Ind., 1961-64, asst. counsel, 1964-68, v.p., gen. counsel, 1975-79, sr. v.p., gen. counsel, 1979-86, exec. v.p., gen. counsel, 1986—; asst. gen. counsel, asst. sec. Lincoln Nat. Corp., Ft. Wayne, 1968-71, gen. counsel, 1971-72, v.p., gen. counsel, 1972-79, sr. v.p., gen. counsel, 1979-86, exec. v.p., gen. counsel, 1986—. Trustee Ind. Nature Conservancy. Mem. ABA, Mich. Bar Assn., Ind. Bar Assn., Allen County Bar Assn., Assn. Life Ins. Counsel., Am. Corp. Counsel Assn., Ind. Nature Conservancy. Office: Lincoln Nat Corp 1300 S Clinton St PO Box 1110 Fort Wayne IN 46801

HUNTER, JAMES D., food products company executive. Pres., chief exec. officer Can. Packers, Inc., Toronto, Ont., Can., also bd. dirs. Office: Can Packers Inc, 30 St Clair Ave W, Toronto, ON Canada M4V 3A2

HUNTER, JAMES DAVID, treasurer; b. Dumont, N.J., Sept. 30, 1954; s. John Jr. and Sylvia (Wightman) H.; m. Mary Ellen Sprigg, May 26, 1985; children: Alexander, Robert. BSBA, U. Vt., 1976. CPA, Vt. Staff acct. Touche Ross & Co., Boston, 1976-78; controller Skis Dynastar, Inc., Colchester, Vt., 1978-80; fin. analyst Skis Rossignol, S.A., Voiron, France, 1980-82; treas. Rossignol Ski Co., Williston, Vt., 1982—. Treas. Lake Champlain Islands Trust, 1984-88. Mem. Am. Inst. CPA's, Vt. Soc. CPA's. Home: 37 Buckingham Dr Colchester VT 05446 Office: Rossignol Ski Co Inc Industrial Ave Williston VT 05495

HUNTER, JAMES MICHAEL, computer systems company executive; b. Richmond, Calif., Oct. 21, 1943; s. George Banks and Norma (Leavitt) H.; children: George Todd, Christine Anne. Ops. mgr. Fox Theatre Corp., Kansas City, Mo., 1963-66; computer systems engr. USN, Port Hueneme, Calif., 1966-71; mgr. computer systems engring. Am. Embassy, Bangkok, 1971-75, Mariannas Island, 1975-77; dir. engring. field office Am. Embassy, Port Hueneme, 1977-82; dir. info. ctr. Warner Bros. Music, Hollywood, Calif., 1982-84; exec. dir. spl. projects Infotec Devel. Inc., Camarillo, Calif., 1984—; bus. cons. Hunter Communications Inc., Fillmore, Calif., 1980—, tchr. computer sci. Ventura Community Coll.; mem. speakers bur. Ventura Community Coll. Candidate for Fillmore City Coun., 1978; commr. Area Housing Authority, Ventura County, Calif., 1978-79; pres. adv. group accreditation Fillmore Union High Sch., 1980-81; mem. mission group to Nigeria World Bible Sch., 1982. With USAF, 1961-63, Korea. Mem. Data Processing Mgmt. Assn., Nat. Contract Mgmt. Assn. Home: 7007 E Gold Dust Ave #2032 Scottsdale AZ 85253 Office: Infotec Devel Inc 150 Camino Ruiz Camarillo CA 93010

HUNTER, JEFFREY SCOTT, accountant; b. Moorhead, Minn., May 6, 1959; s. William Gerald and Marie (Francis) H.; m. Kimberly Jane Green, June 13, 1981; children: Marissa, Brittany. Student, N.D. State U., 1977-80; BS cum laude, Moorhead State U., 1983. Salesperson Connco Shoes, Fargo, N.D., 1980-82; universal comml. teller Dakota Bank & Trust, Fargo, 1982-83; sr. acct. Charles Bailly & Co., Bismarck, 1983-86; internal auditor MDU Resources Group, Inc., Bismarck, 1986-87; fin. analyst budget regulatory acctg., acctg. control Williston Basin Interstate Pipeline Co. subs. MDU Resources Grp, Inc., Bismarck, 1987—; ptnr. Paytech Data Services, Fargo, 1987—; cons. Small Bus. Inst., Moorhead, 1983. Mem. Am. Inst. CPA's, N.D. Soc. CPA's, Inst. Cert. Mgt. Accts. Lutheran. Club: Highnooners Toastmasters of Bismark. Lodge: Optimists (youth com. activities bd. 1985-86, chmn. essay contest). Home: 1841 Wood Moor Pl Bismarck ND 58501-2587 Office: Williston Basin Interstate Pipeline Co Inc 400 N 4th St Bismarck ND 58501

HUNTER, JUDY LAVERNE, air transportation executive; b. Amherst, Tex., May 24, 1944; d. Arthur Laverne and Edith Grace (Enloe) B.; m. William J. Hunter, Aug. 11, 1962 (div. Mar. 1981); remarried Aug. 24, 1984. Student, Levelland (Tex.) Jr. Coll., 1964, Tex. Tech U., 1967. Supr. scheduling Weber Aircraft, Gainesville, Tex., 1974-78, supr. purchasing, 1978-81, mgr. purchasing, 1981—. Mem. Purchasing Mgmt. Assn. Dallas (program dir. 1987-88), Kiwanis (bd. dirs. Gainesville chpt.). Republican. Baptist. Home: 1002 Aspen Rd Gainesville TX 76240 Office: Weber Aircraft 2000 Weber Dr Gainesville TX 76240

HUNTER, KENNETH JAMES, federal agency adminstrator; b. L.A., Jan. 23, 1944; s. David Earl and Florence Lillian (Brewster) H.; m. Lucinda Lynn Fischer, Sept. 3, 1964 (div. 1984); children: Mark, Mike, Eric, John; m. Lynette Joy Darmody, Aug. 3, 1985; children: Troy, Robyn. Student, Colo. U., 1961-64; BS in Math., Colo. State U., 1969; student, Stanford U., 1981. Postal inspector U.S. Postal Svc., Chgo., 1969-74; gen. mgr. postal inspection svc. U.S. Postal Svc., Washington, 1974-78; dir. Postal Data Ctr. U.S. Postal Svc., Mpls., 1978-85; asst. postmaster gen. U.S. Postal Svc., Washington, 1985-86, sr. asst. postmaster gen., 1986-88, assoc. postmaster gen., 1988—. Chmn. Fed. Exec. Bd. Twin Cities, Minn., 1985; water safety chmn. ARC, Larimer County, Colo., 1964-69; mem. Friends of the Kennedy Ctr. Mem. Stanford Alumni Assn., Wolf Trap Assn., Colo. Mountain Club. Presbyterian. Home: 1632 Montmorency Dr Vienna VA 22180-2021 Office: US Postal Svc 475 L'Enfant Plaza SW Washington DC 20026-3567

HUNTER, LARRY LEE, electrical engineer; b. Versailles, Mo., Mar. 5, 1938; s. Donnan Kleber and Molly Opal (Roe) H.; m. Marcella Ann Avey, Feb. 1, 1959; children: Cynthia Lynn Hunter Chapman, Stuart Roe. BSEE, U. Mo., 1963; MBA, Fla. Inst. Tech., 1984. System test engr. McDonnell Aircraft Corp., St. Louis, 1963-65; design engr. Magnavox Co., Urbana, Ill., 1965-66, research and devel. engr., 1966-68; project engr. LTV Electrosystems, Garland, Tex., 1968-69, systems engr., 1969-70; program mgr. Dorsett Electronics, Tulsa, 1970-73; program mgr. Harris Corp., Melbourne, Fla., 1973-75, bus. area mgr., 1975-85; v.p. mktg., engring., program mgmt. Teledyne Lewisburg, Tenn., 1985—. Inventor thermometer; contbr. articles to profl. jours. Mem. IEEE, Eta Kappa Nu. Republican. Methodist. Home: 1204 Sunnyside Dr Columbia TN 38401

HUNTER, ROBERT WILLIAM, portfolio manager; b. Boston, July 23, 1950; s. Lawrence Joseph and Brigid M. (Sheehy) H.; m. Kathryn Haynes; 1 child, Erin E. BA in Polit Sci., Assumption Coll., 1972; MBA in Fin., Clark U., 1985; grad., Northwestern U.-Mortgage Bankers Am., 1976. Cert. mortgage banker. Loan officer 1st Fed. Savs. & Loan, Worcester, Mass., 1973-76; asst. v.p. Freedom Fed. Savs. & Loan, Worcester, 1976-79, v.p., 1979-82; % N.E. Savs., F.A., Hartford, Conn., 1982-86; 1st v.p. N.E. Savs., F.A., Hartford, 1986—. Mem. Cath. Charities Housing Commn., Worcester, 1980-81. Mem. Inst. Fin. Edn. (bd. dirs. 1980-84, treas. 1984-85, pres. 1985-86). Home: 26 Whispering Rod Rd Farmington CT 06032 Office: NE Savs FA 50 State St Hartford CT 06103

HUNTINGTON, EARL LLOYD, lawyer, natural resources company executive; b. Orangeville, Utah, Sept. 2, 1929; s. Lloyd S. and Hannah Annette (Cox) H.; m. Phyllis Ann Reed; children: Jane, Ann, Stephen. BS, U. Utah, 1951, JD, 1956; LL.M., Georgetown U., 1959. Bar: Utah 1956, D.C. 1959, N.Y. 1966, Conn. 1988. Trial atty. Dept. Justice, Washington, 1956-63; counsel Texasgulf Inc., N.Y.C., 1963-74, v.p., gen. counsel, 1974-81, sr. v.p., gen. counsel, 1981—, also bd. dirs.; also sr. v.p., gen. counsel, dir. Elf Aquitaine Inc. Case note editor U. Utah Law Rev., 55-56. Served with U.S. Army, 1951-53. Mem. ABA; mem. Assn. Bar City N.Y., Westchester-Fairfield Corp. Counsel Assn., Order of Coif, Phi Delta Phi, Beta Gamma Sigma. Clubs: Landmark; Country of Darien. Home: 1 Maywood Ct Darien CT 06820 Office: Elf Aquitaine Inc High Ridge Pk Box 10037 Stamford CT 06904

HUNTINGTON, JAMES CANTINE, JR., equipment manufacturing company executive; b. Detroit, Mar. 21, 1928; s. James Cantine and Joanna (Donlon) H.; m. Bettyanne Hopkins, Sept. 21, 1973; children: James, Ann, Patricia, Carol, Judith, Amy. B.E.E., Cornell U., 1950. Mktg. exec. Harnischfeger Corp., Milw., 1953-62; cons. Milw., 1962-64; mgr. Colt Industries, Beloit, Wis., 1964-67; v.p., dir. Clark Equipment Co., Buchanan, Mich., 1967-76; sr. v.p. Am. Standard, Inc., 1976-88; ret. 1988; bd. dirs. SPX Corp., Anax Inc., Dravo Corp. Served with AUS, 1945-47, 50-53. Mem. Constrn. Industry Mfrs. Assn., Delta Kappa Epsilon, Tau Beta Pi, Eta Kappa Nu. Home: 613 Twin Pine Rd Pittsburgh PA 15215

HUNTINGTON, ROBERT HUBBARD, advertising agency executive; b. Sept. 28, 1937; s. Robert Hubbard and Katherine (Wolf) H.; m. Eleanor K. Gallagher, Mar. 18, 1961; children: Robert Hubbard III, Thomas Andrew, Elizabeth. B.S., Cornell U., 1959; M.B.A., U. Pa., 1961. With Saatchi & Saatchi Compton Group Inc. (formerly Compton Advt., Inc.), N.Y.C., 1962-88, account handling, 1962-69, asst. treas., 1969-75, treas., sr. v.p., 1975-78, exec. v.p., chief adminstrv. officer, 1978-80, exec. v.p., chief operating officer, 1980-83, chmn., chief exec. officer, 1983-88; vice-chmn., chief operating officer, dir. DDB Needham Worldwide, Inc., N.Y.C., 1988—; bd. dirs. Omnicron Group, Inc. Served with U.S. Army, 1961. Clubs: University (N.Y.C.); Apawamis (Rye, N.Y.), Manursing Island (Rye, N.Y.). Office: DDB Needham 437 Madison Ave New York NY 10022

HUNTOON, ROBERT BRIAN, chemist, food company official; b. Braintree, Mass., Mar. 1, 1927; s. Benjamin Harrison and Helen Edna (Worden) H.; BS in Chemistry, Northeastern U., 1949, M.S., 1961; m. Joan Fairman Graham, Mar. 1, 1952; children: Brian Graham, Benjamin Robert, Elisabeth Ellen, Janet Lynne, Joelle. Analytical chemist Mass. Dept. Public Health, microbiologist Met. Dist. Commn., Boston, 1950-53; research and devel. chemist Heveatex Corp., Melrose, Mass., 1953-56; with Gen. Foods Corp., 1956-70, acting quality control mgr., Woburn, Mass., 1965-67, head group research and devel., Tarrytown, N.Y., 1967-70; dir. quality control U.S. Flavor div. Internat. Flavors & Fragrances, Teterboro, N.J., 1970-83, mgr. tech. services, 1983-87, mgr. product devel., 1987—. Served with USCG, 1945-46. Com. mem. Essential Oils Assn., Flavor and Extracts Mfg. Assn.; mem. Am. Chem. Soc., Inst. Food Technologists, Internat. Platform Assn. Republican. Lutheran. Clubs: Indsl. Mgmt. (v.p. 1967) (Woburn); Croton Yacht, Saugus River Yacht (treas. 1967-68). Contbr. articles on flavor and food quality control to profl. and co. publs.; patentee gelatin compositions and mfg. processes. Home: 252 Livingston Ave Apt 1 New Brunswick NJ 08901-3058

HURD, G. DAVID, financial services executive; b. Chgo., Dec. 14, 1929; s. Gerald Walton and Hilldur Ingabore (Hallgren) H.; m. Patricia Ann Lamb, Feb. 12, 1955; children—Janet Susan, Sally Jane, Michael David. B.A., Mich. State U., 1951. With The Prin. Fin. Group (formerly Bankers Life Co.), Des Moines, 1954—, officer, 1960-71, v.p., 1971-83, sr. v.p., 1983-85, exec. v.p., 1985-87; pres. The Prin. Fin. Group, 1987-88, pres., chief exec. officer, 1989—; bd. dirs. Prin. Mut. Life Ins. Co., Des Moines ; mem. Pension Research Council, U. Pa. Wharton Sch. Bus., 1979-85. Mem. Adv. Council on Employee Welfare and Pension Benefit Plans, Dept. Labor, Washington, 1977-80; bd. dirs. Drake U., 1986—, Nature Conservancy; chmn. Group Assurance Internat. Network, 1987-89; mem. steering com. Bus. for Peace. Served to 2d lt. C.E., U.S. Army, 1951-53, Korea. Mem. Employee Benefit Research Inst. (bd. dirs. 1979-86), Assn. Pvt. Pension and Welfare Plans (chmn. bd. 1985-87), Des Moines C. of C. (bd. dirs. 1985—). Clubs: Prairie, Des Moines. Home: 3930 Grand St Apt 406 Des Moines IA 50312 Office: Prin Mut Life Ins Co 711 High St Des Moines IA 50309

HURD, RICHARD NELSON, pharmaceutical company executive; b. Evanston, Ill., Feb. 25, 1926; s. Charles DeWitt and Mary Ormsby (Nelson) H.; m. Jocelyn Fillmore Martin, Dec. 22, 1950; children: Melanie Gray, Suzanne DeWitt. BS, U. Mich., 1946; PhD, U. Minn., 1956. Chemist, Gen. Electric Co., Schenectady, 1948-49; research and devel. group leader Koppers Co., Pitts., 1956-57; research chemist Mallinckrodt Chem. Works, St. Louis, 1956-63, group leader, 1963-66; group leader Comml. Solvents Corp., Terre Haute, Ind., 1966-68, sect. head, 1968-71; mgr. sci. affairs G. D. Searle Internat. Co., Skokie, Ill., 1972-73, dir. mfg. and tech. affairs, 1973-77, rep. to internat. tech. com. Pharm. Mfrs. Assn., 1973-77; v.p. tech. affairs Elder Pharms., Bryan, Ohio, 1977-81; v.p. research and devel. U.S. Proprietary Drugs & Toiletries div. Schering-Plough Corp., Memphis, 1981-83; v.p. sci. affairs Moleculon Inc., Cambridge, Mass., 1984-88; v.p. regulatory affairs Pharmaco, Inc., Austin, Tex., 1989—. Patentee in field; contbr. articles to profl. jours. Mem. Ferguson-Florissant (Mo.) Sch. Bd., 1964-66; bd. dirs. United Fund of Wabash Valley (Ind.), 1969-71. Served with USN, 1943-46, 53-55. E. I. DuPont de Nemours & Co., Inc. fellow, 1956. Mem. Am.

Acad. Dermatology, Soc. Investigative Dermatology, Am. Soc. Photobiology, Am. Chem. Soc., N.Y. Acad. Sci., Am. Pharm. Assn., Am. Assn. Pharm. Scientists, AAAS, Sigma Xi. Presbyterian. Club: Mich. Shores (Wilmette, Ill.). Home: 49 Austin Rd Sudbury MA 01776 Office: Pharmaco Inc 2 Park Pl 4009 Banister Ln Austin TX 78704

HURET, BARRY S., marketing professional; b. N.Y.C., May, 1938; s. Benjamin and Anna (Berko) H.; B.A. with honors, Cornell U., 1961; M.B.A. with distinction, N.Y. U., 1970; m. Marilynn Moskowitz, Feb., 1961; children—Abbey, Eric. Asst. sales engr. Westinghouse Corp., Pitts., 1962-64; sales engr. MultiAmp Corp., Cranford, N.J., 1964-65; sales engr., regional mgr., nat. sales mgr. Gould, Inc., St. Paul, 1965-77; successively mktg. mgr., dir. mktg., dir. new bus. ventures, v.p. new bus. and govt. sales, dir. splty. product mktg. Exide Corp., Horsham, Pa., 1977-82; nat. sales mgr. battery sales div. Panasonic Indsl. Co., Secaucus, N.J., 1982-86; asst. gen. mgr. battery sales group, 1986—. Served to lt. U.S. Army, 1961-62. Recipient Hector Lazo Meml. Mktg. award N.Y. U., 1970, Alumni Key, 1970. Mem. Cornell U. Alumni (v.p. class of '59), Phi Beta Kappa. Author: A User Friendly Guide to Selcting Rechargeable Batteries. Home: 484 Kings Rd Yardley PA 19067

HURFORD, GARY THOMAS, oil company executive; b. Woodson, Tex., Aug. 24, 1936; s. William B. and Alta Nita (Gardner) H.; m. Thelma G. Salinas, Aug. 5, 1962; children: Gary Michael, David Thomas, Michelle Ann. BS in Petroleum Engring., U. Tex., 1959. Registered profl. engr., Tex., Okla., La. Petroleum engr. Mobil Oil Co., Corpus Christi, Tex., 1959-62; dist. engr. Hunt Oil Co., Arp, Tex., 1962-65; unit engr. Hunt Oil Co., Tyler, Tex., 1965-68; coordinator east Tex. ops. Hunt Oil Co., Tyler, 1971-75; staff reservoir engr. Hunt Oil Co., Dallas, 1968-71, chief engr., 1975-80, v.p. drilling and prodn., 1980-84, exec. v.p. energy, 1984-86, pres., 1986—; bd. dirs. Hunt Consol., Inc., Dallas. Contbr. articles to profl. jours. Mem. Soc. Profl. Engrs. of AIME (dir. East Tex. sect. 1974-76), Am. Petroleum Inst. Clubs: Dallas Petroleum, Ft. Worth Petroleum. Office: Hunt Oil Co 2900 InterFirst One Bldg 1401 Elm Dallas TX 75202

HURLBUT, ROBERT HAROLD, health care services executive; b. Rochester, N.Y., Mar. 9, 1935; s. Harold Leroy and Martha Irene (Fincher) H.; student Coll. Hotel Adminstrn. Cornell U., 1953-56; m. Barbara Cox, June 14, 1958; children—Robert W., Christine A. Adminstr., dir. Pillars Nursing Home, Rochester, 1956—, Elmcrest Nursing Home, Churchville, N.Y., 1960—, Elm Manor Nursing Home, Canandaigua, N.Y., 1960—, Penfield Nursing Home, Rochester, 1963—, Avon (N.Y.) Nursing Home, 1964—, Newark (N.Y.) Nursing Home, 1965—, Lakeshore Nursing Home, Rochester, 1972—, others; organizer, adminstrv. dir. Rohm Services Corp., hdqrs. Rochester, 1964—organizer, pres. Vari-Care, Inc., hdqrs. Rochester, 1969—; adv. bd. mem. long-term healthcare planning program Monroe Community Coll.; mem. nat. adv. bd., Rochester Inst. Tech. Sch. Hotel and Tourism Mgmt. Trustee, bd. dirs. St. John Fisher Coll.; trustee, bd. dirs. Eastman Dental Ctr.; mem., bd. dirs. Rochester Area Found.; bd. dirs. Finger Lakes Health Systems Agy., Rochester Philharm. Orch.; bd. mgrs. Strong Meml. Hosp, Marine Midland Bank; mem. exec. adv. bd. Roberts Wesleyan Coll.; mem. N.Y. State Sen. Lombardi's Task Force on Hosp. Alternate Care. Fellow Am. Coll. Health Adminstrs.; mem. N.Y. State Health Facilities Assn. (multi-facility com.); bd. trustees Rochester Area C. of C. , Lambda Chi Alpha. Clubs: Genesee Valley, Oak Hill, Cornell (Rochester). Home: 200 Sheldon Rd Honeoye Falls NY 14472 Office: 277 Alexander St Rochester NY 14607

HURLEY, FRANK THOMAS, JR., realtor; b. Washington, Oct. 18, 1924; s. Frank Thomas and Lucille (Trent) H.; A.A., St. Petersburg Jr. Coll., 1948; B.A., U. Fla., 1950. Reporter St. Petersburg (Fla.) Evening Independent, 1948-53; editor Arcadia (Calif.) Tribune, 1956-57; reporter Los Angeles Herald Express, 1957; v.p. Frank T. Hurley Assos., Inc. realtors, 1958-64, pres., 1964—; sec., dir. Beau Monde, Inc., 1977-79. Elected St. Petersburg Beach Bd. Commrs., 1965-69; chmn. Pinellas County Traffic Safety Council, 1968-69; pres. Pass-A-Grille Community Assn., 1963, Gulf Beach Bd. Realtors, 1969; mem. St. Petersburg Mus. Fine Arts; bd. govs. Palms of Pasadena Hosp., 1979-86. Served with USAAF, 1943-46. Mem. Fla. Assn. Realtors (dir., dist. v.p. 1971), St. Petersburg Beach C. of C. (dir., pres. 1975-76; Citizen of Yr. award 1983), Vina del Mar Island Assn., Am. Legion, Sigma Delta Chi, Sigma Tau Delta. Author: Surf, Sand and Post Card Sunsets, 1977. Home: 2808 Sunset Way Saint Petersburg Beach FL 33706 Office: 2506 Pass-A-Grille Way Saint Petersburg Beach FL 33706

HURLEY, JAMES DONALD, JR., printing company executive, lawyer; b. La Salle, Ill., June 11, 1935; s. James Donald and Emily Elizabeth (Reinhard) H.; B.A., U. Ill., 1957, LL.B., 1959; m. Judith A. Hurley; children—Katherine, Mary, James Donald III, Ellen. Bar: Ill. 1959, U.S. Cts. Appeals, U.S. Dist. Ct., U.S. Tax Ct. Chief exec. officer Reilley, Inc., La Salle, 1986—; mem. nat. MIS printing com. Postal Instant Press. Trustee Hurley Family Trust. Recipient Golden Apple award for Unltd. Design Postal Instant Press, L.S., 1987-88, Disting Svc. award U.S. Jr. C. of C., 1968. Mem. Printing Industry Ill. and Ind., Graphic Arts Tech. Found., Nat. Assn. Quick Printers, IVAC (past pres.), Ill. C. of C., La Salle C. of C., Mensa, Union League Club (Chgo.), Lions. Home: 617 Fifth St La Salle IL 61301 Office: 210 Marquette St La Salle IL 61301

HURLEY, JOHN KENNETH, real estate and exporting executive; b. Washington, Nov. 28, 1931; s. Frank T. and Lucille (Trent) H.; m. June Carol Morgan, June 19, 1954 (div. 1976); children: Sean Kenneth, Kathleen Patricia; m. Joyce Carol Winemiller, Mar. 30, 1980; stepchildren: Donna, Kelly, Tracy. AA, St. Petersburg Jr. Coll., 1952; BS, Fla. State U., 1954. V.p. Frank T. Hurley Assocs., Inc., St. Petersburg Beach, Fla., 1954—; pres. Hurley Marine Corp., St. Petersburg Beach, 1980—, Pass-a-Grille Trading Co., St. Petersburg Beach, 1982—, J. Kenneth Hurley Co., St. Petersburg Beach, 1984—; ptnr. Joyce Hurley Natural Food Products, St. Petersburg Beach, 1982-84; guest lectr. over 40 colls., univs. Pub. Palma Ceia - MacDill News, Tampa, Fla., 1972-76; pub. poet in numerous periodicals and anthologies. Bd. dirs. Orthomolecular Research Ctr., St. Petersburg Beach, 1955-85; chmn. Zoning and Planning Bd., St. Petersburg Beach, 1968-71; pres. Friends St. Petersburg Beach Library, 1976-78. Mem. Nat. Assn. Mortgage Brokers, Gulf Beach Seminole Bd. Realtors, Slocum Soc. Republican. Mem. United Ch. of Christ. Club: Pass-a-Grille (Fla.) Yacht (sec. 1978-80). Home: 2122 W Vina del Mar Blvd Saint Petersburg Beach FL 33706 Office: 2506 Pass-a-Grille Way Saint Petersburg Beach FL 33706

HURLEY, SAMUEL CLAY, III, investment executive; b. Peoria, Ill., Jan. 25, 1936; s. Samuel Clay Jr. and Wilmina Marie (Loveless) H.; m. Dorothy Jane Atkinson, Aug. 19, 1967; children: Samuel C. IV, Bruce Hilliard. AB in Econs., Brown U., 1958; MBA in Fin., Northwestern U., 1960. Portfolio mgr. Continental Ill. Nat. Bank, Chgo., 1960-62; mgr. bank relations Internat. Harvester Co. (later Navistar), Chgo., 1962-71; asst. treas. Internat. Harvester Credit Corp., Chgo., 1962-71; asst. treas. Anchor Hocking Corp. (now owned by Newell Corp.), Lancaster, Ohio, 1971-74, treas., 1975—, v.p., 1983-87; v.p., chief fin. officer, dir. Fabstar Internat., Inc., Humble, Tex., 1988—; gen. ptnr. Steele and Co. Ltd., Columbus, Ohio, 1988—. Mem. Columbus Council World Affairs; trustee Lancaster-Fairfield Community Hosp., 1984—; bd. dirs. Fairfield County Bd. Mental Retardation and Devel. Disabilities, Lancaster, 1981—. Mem. Fin. Execs. inst. (bd. dirs. Columbus chpt. 1984-85). Republican. Episcopalian. Clubs: Lancaster Country; Univ., Treas.'s (Columbus). Lodge: Rotary (Lancaster club). Home: 148 E Wheeling St Lancaster OH 43130 Office: Steele & Co Ltd 40 E Gay St Columbus OH 43215-3119

HURLEY, WILLIAM JOSEPH, information systems executive; b. N.Y.C., June 14, 1939; s. William and Anna Rita (Hubschman) H.; m. Dorothy Ann Mellett, Sept. 23, 1961 (dec.); children: William, Terrianne, Barbara, Daniel. BBA, Pace U., 1968, MBA, 1973. Dir. info. system Gen. Foods Corp., White Plains, N.Y., 1973-79; dir. systems devel. Securities Industry Automation Corp., N.Y.C., 1979; dir. mgmt. info. systems Schering Plough Corp., Kenilworth, N.J., 1979-81, sr. dir. mgmt. info. systems, 1981-83, v.p. mgmt. info. service, 1983-88; v.p. world wide info. systems Technicon Corp., Tarrytown, N.Y., 1988—. Pres. New City (N.Y.) Vol. Fire Engine Co. 1, 1979-81; commr. New City Fire Dist, 1983—. Served with USMC, 1956-59. Mem. Soc. Info. Mgmt. (pres. 1968—), Assn. Systems Mgmt. (v.p. 1981), Am. Legion. Republican. Roman Catholic. Home: 10 Rugby Rd New City NY 10956 Office: Technicon Instruments Corp 511 Benedict Ave Tarrytown NY 10591

HURST, BOYD EDWIN, management consultant, banker; b. Tenaha, Tex., Nov. 15, 1928; s. Clarence Ezra Hurst and Mable Lois (Crump) Hurst McElyea; m. Patsy Ruth Dorsey, Jan. 27, 1950 (div. 1967); children: Boyd Edwin Jr., Christi Kay Hurst Becker, Daryl Scot, Alan Todd. BBA in Personnel Mgmt., So. Meth. U., 1957; cert., U. Houston, 1960. Personnel asst. Employers Ins. Co., Dallas, 1957-61; asst. to pres. World Gift Co., Inc., Dallas, 1961-62; personnel dir. Fed. Res. Bank Dallas, 1962-67; facilities mgr. Recognition Equipment, Inc., Dallas, 1967-69; asst. personnel dir. Mercantile Nat. Bank, Dallas, 1969-79; v.p., personnel dir. Oak Cliff Bank & Trust Co., Dallas, 1979-82, Abilene (Tex.) Nat. Bank, 1982-86; pres. Hurst-Texas, Abilene, 1986—; mem. adv. com. Okla. State Tech. Inst., Okmulgee, 1975-79; chmn. adv. com. vocat. office edn. Abilene Ind. Sch. Dist., 1985—. Author employment and banking pubis. Mem. adminstrv. bd. First United Meth. Ch., Abilene, 1983—. sgt. with USAF, 1951-56. Mem. Big Country Personnel Assn. (pres. 1986-87), Abilene C. of C. (mem. mil. affairs com., edn. com., aviation com.). Lodges: Optimists; Rotary. Home: 4633 Royal Ct Cir Abilene TX 79606 Office: HurstTexas 4633 Royal Ct Circle Abilene TX 79606

HURST, JOHN EMORY, JR., retired airline executive; b. Phoenix, Feb. 9, 1928; s. John Emory and Kathryne Ann (Prechtel) H.; m. Sara Waugh; children—Craig K., Susan M., John J. BS, U.S. Mil. Acad., 1950; MS, U. Ill., 1956; MA, Columbia U., 1960; grad., U.S. Army Command and Gen. Staff Coll., 1964, Naval War Coll., 1968. Registered profl. engr., N.Y., Fla. Commd. 2d lt. U.S. Army, 1950, advanced through grades to col., 1970; served in U.S. Army, Korea, 1950-51, Vietnem, 1964-65; mem. Dept. of Army Staff, 1969-71; ret. U.S. Army, 1971; from v.p. to sr. v.p. Eastern Airlines, Miami, Fla., 1971-86. Mem. ASCE. Republican. Episcopalian. Lodge: Masons.

HURST, PATRICIA WINIFRED, computer information scientist, consultant; b. Savannah, Ga., Sept. 19, 1942; d. Enoch Henry and Moselle (Walker) H.; m. Robert Marion Baucom, Aug. 25, 1972 (div. 1983); children: Patricia Josie Baucom, Jessica Marion. BA in Math., Winthrop Coll., 1963; MS in Computer Sci., U. Va., 1985. Mathematician NASA, Hampton, Va., 1963-66; systems analyst Lockheed Missiles & Space Co., Sunnyvale, Calif., 1966-67, Univac Internat., London, 1967-69; sr. analyst Univac, Atlanta, 1969-71; sr. analyst Control Data Corp., Hampton, 1973-74, project mgr., 1975-79; cons. Hampton, 1979-82, Charlottesville, Va., 1982—. Editor, pub. Deadline newsletter, 1987—. Mem. IEEE, Assn. Computing Machinery. Home and Office: 12 Georgetown Green Charlottesville VA 22901

HURST, ROBERT JAY, securities company executive; b. N.Y.C., Nov. 5, 1945; s. Kurt and Jeanette (Sachs) H.; m. Fern Karesh, Dec. 13, 1970; children: Alexander, Amanda. BA, Clark U., 1966; M in Govt. Adminstrn., U. Pa., 1968. With investment banking div. Merrill Lynch, Pierce, Fenner & Smith, Inc., N.Y.C., 1969-74, v.p., 1974; v.p. Goldman, Sachs & Co., N.Y.C., 1974-80, gen. ptnr., 1980—; bd. dirs. E-Z-EM, Inc., USF&G Corp. Bd. dirs. Henry Street Settlement, N.Y.C., 1982; trustee Clark U., 1983—, mem. adv. coun. grad. sch.; trustee Com. Econ. Devel. With USAR, 1969-74. Mem. Securities Industry Assn. (trustee found., 1985), Com. Fin. Econ. Devel. (trustee). Clubs: University, India House (N.Y.C.). Office: Goldman Sachs & Co 85 Broad St New York NY 10004

HURT, DANIEL I., manufacturing executive, real estate executive, consultant; b. St. Louis, Dec. 30, 1951; s. Irvin E. and Virgina R. (Krebeck) H.; m. Rhonda K. Overton, Nov. 15, 1975; children: Justin I., Jenna N. BSMechE, Washington U., St. Louis, 1975, MBA, 1981. Registered profl. engr., Mo.; lic. real estate agent, Mo. Coop. research engr. McDonnell-Douglas Aircraft, St. Louis, 1970-74; utilities design engr. Monsanto Corp., St. Louis, 1975-79; mktg. specialist Watlow Electric Co., St. Louis, 1979-81; capital investment analyst Sherwood Med. Co., St. Louis, 1981-84, internat. mktg. mgr., 1984-85; co-owner, pres. Wermke Spring Mfg. Co., St. Louis, 1985—; cons. Hurtculean Enterprises, Inc., St. Louis, 1985—, owner, pres., 1986—; cons. Hurtculean Enterprises, St. Louis, 1985—. Head coach St. Louis YMCA, 1985—; active Chesterfield Bd. Adjustment, 1988-89; mem. Chesterfield City Coun., 1989—. Recipient Eagle Scout award, Boy Scouts Am., St. Louis, 1966. Mem. Spring Mfrs. Inst., Sigma Alpha Epsilon. Roman Catholic. Office: Wermke Spring Mfg Co 4229 N Broadway Saint Louis MO 63147

HURT, ROBERT GLENN, retired investment banker; b. Pasadena, Calif., Jan. 31, 1919; s. Leslie Milton and Effie Mae (McKim) H. AB, U. So. Calif., 1940; postgrad. Harvard, 1941. With sales dept. Calvin Bullock, Ltd., N.Y.C., Los Angeles, 1946-50, No. Calif. mgr., San Francisco, 1950-65, west coast mgr., San Francisco, 1965-66, v.p., San Francisco, 1967-87. Mem. pres.'s circle U. So. Calif. Served from pvt. to lt. col. AUS, 1941-46. Named Ky. Col. Mem. Los Angeles Stock Exchange Club, Mil. Order World Wars, Am. Legion. Clubs: Commonwealth (San Francisco), San Francisco City, San Francisco Comml., San Francisco Engrs.; (Andreas Canyon (Palm Springs, Calif.). Home: 937 Ashbury St San Francisco CA 94117 Other: 38000 S Palm Canyon Dr Palm Springs CA 92262

HURTT, CALEB BROWN, aerospace company executive; b. Ridley Pk., Pa., Aug. 15, 1931; s. Spencer Merritt and Marietta Dashiel (Waller) H.; m. Maryan Forbes; children: Dana Ayn, Kisa Forbes, George Caleb. ME, Stevens Inst. Tech., 1953; postgrad., Harvard U., 1971. With Martin Marietta Denver Aerospace, 1956-80, pres., 1980-82; exec. v.p. Martin Marietta Corp., Bethesda, Md., 1982-87; dir., pres., chief oper. officer Martin Marietta Corp., Bethesda, 1987—; chmn. Denver Branch Fed. Res. Bank, 1981-82. Trustee Stevens Inst. Tech., 1988—. 1st lt. USAF, 1953-55. Recipient Pub. Svc. award NASA; Am. Astronautical Soc. fellow, Pub. Affairs fellow Brookings Inst., 1964. Mem. Aerospace Industries Assn. (bd. govs. 1982—, chmn. 1989), Bethesda Country Club, Cherry Hills Country Club (Denver). Republican. Episcopalian. Home: 11205 Tack House Ct Potomac MD 20854 Office: Martin Marietta Corp 6801 Rockledge Dr Bethesda MD 20817

HURTT, CLAUDE DAVID, risk management executive; b. Birmingham, Ala., May 6, 1947; s. Oscar Lee, Jr. and Florrie (Thompson) H.; m. Betty Dougherty, Aug. 9, 1969; children: Laurie, Amy. BSBA, Samford U., 1969; MBA, Ind. U., 1971. Staff acct. Ala. Power Co., Birmingham, 1971-72; asst. v.p. fin. The Bapt. Med. Ctr., Birmingham, 1972—; treas. Employee Benevolent Fund, Birmingham, 1972—, sec., treas. Ala. chpt. Risk and Ins. Mgmt. Soc., Birmingham, 1974-75. Sponsored exec. United Way, 1982. With U.S. Army Res., 1969-71. Mem. Birmingham Bapt. Assn. Chs. (treas. 1979-80, mem. exec. bd. 1987—), Hosp. Fin. Mgmt. Assn., Am. Soc. Hosp. Risk Mgmt., Employee Benefit Forum, Ala. Hosp. Assn. Republican. Baptist. Office: The Bapt Med Ctr 3201 Fourth Ave South Birmingham AL 35222

HURWITZ, IRVING LEONARD, lawyer; b. Boston, Feb. 25, 1941; s. Saul and Pauline Josephine (Goldin) H.; m. Barbara Ruth Sidel, Aug. 14, 1966; children: Cheryl, Jeffrey. BA, U. Mass., 1963; LLB cum laude, Boston U., 1966; LLM, N.Y.U., 1967. Atty. Nat. Labor Relations Bd., Buffalo, 1967-72; ptnr. Carpenter, Bennet and Morrissey, Newark, 1973—. Author, editor: Boston U. Law Review, 1965-66. V.p. Mataman-Aberdeen Regional Bd. Edn., 1984-85, pres. 1985-87. Mem. ABA, N.J. Bar Assn., Essex County Bar Assn. (dist. ethics com. 1987—), Indsl. Relations Research Assn. Home: 39 Poet Dr Matawan NJ 07747 Office: Carpenter Bennett & Morrissey Gateway 3 100 Mulberry St Newark NJ 07102

HUSAIN, MAZHAR, cement company executive; b. Karachi, Pakistan, Aug. 18, 1949; s. Irshad and Subhun (Nisa) H.; m. Rukhsana Karimuddin, May 20, 1982; children: Salman, Maria . BS, Middle East Tech. U., Ankara, Turkey, 1972, MBA, 1974; MS, Union U., Schenectady, N.Y., 1976. Mgmt. counselor Pakistan Inst. of Mgmt., Karachi, 1977-79; mgr. purchasing-mktg. dept. So. Province Cement Co., Abha, Saudi Arabia, 1979—. Contbr. articles to profl. jours. Merit scholar Cen. Treaty Orgn., 1968-74; research fellow Union U., 1974-76. Mem. Pakistan Inst. Engrs. Home: PO Box 826, Abha Saudi Arabia also: 35-IV Saba Ave, Phase V Ext, DHA, Karachi Pakistan

HUSBAND, WILLIAM SWIRE, computer industry executive; b. Hinsdale, Ill., Dec. 18, 1939; s. William Thompson and Arlene Martha (Frey) H.; m. Janet Goatley, Nov. 26, 1965; children—Scott, Andrea. B.S., Iowa State U., 1962. Mktg. rep. IBM, San Francisco, 1966-70; dist. mktg. mgr. DPF, Des Plaines, Ill., 1971-78; v.p. Celtic Computer Investment Co., Palatine, Ill., 1978; pres. 20th Century Systems, Inc., Palatine, 1978—; presenter symposium for U. Calif.-Berkeley Systems Technology Inst., Milan, 1987, 88, 89; speaker World Congress of Computing, Chgo., 1988. Author, pub.: Computer Acquisition and Disposition Planning, 7th edit., 1987; editor COMPUTALK mag., 1987—. IBM Technology and Product Strategies in the 80's, 1986; contbg. editor Computer Econs. mag., 1986—. Active Buehler YMCA, Palatine Boys' Baseball, 1978-85. Served to lt. (j.g.) USN, 1962-66. Republican. Presbyterian. Office: 20th Century Systems Inc 647 E Carpenter Dr Palatine IL 60067

HUSER, KIMBERLY ELIZABETH, respiratory therapist; b. Eastliverpool, Ohio, Dec. 6, 1956; d. John Michael and JoAnn Faye (Christensen) Karaffa; m. Robert Gene Huser, Aug. 6, 1977; 1 child, Jacqueline Marie. Tech. cert., Meth. Hosp., Indpls., 1977. Regional dir. Rehab. Health Svcs., Indpls., 1978-85; v.p. Nat. Therapy Svcs., Inc., Carmel, Ind., 1985—. V.p. The Breath of Life Guild Inc., Indpls., 1987-88, pres., 1988-89. Mem. Am. Assn Repiratoiry Care, Ind. Thoracic Soc. Roman Catholic. Home: 1202 N Audubon Rd Indianapolis IN 46219 Office: Nat Therapy Svcs Inc PO Box 132 Carmel IN 46032

HUSER, LAWRENCE ROY, sales and marketing executive; b. Detroit, Apr. 24, 1945; s. Walter George and Mildred Elenor (Rhodel) H.; m. Mary Ellen Gammicchia, May 9, 1970; children: Jenna Lynn, Jessica Lee. BS in Engring., Western Mich. U., 1967; MBA, Wayne State U., Detroit, 1971. Sales engr. Ingersoll-Rand Co., Kalamazoo, 1971-75; br. mgr. Ingersoll-Rand Co., Detroit, 1975-80; internat. mktg. mgr. Ingersoll-Rand Co., Charlotte, 1980-84; pres., dir. Program World Inc., Charlotte, 1984-85; v.p. sales and mktg. Connell L.P., Mayville, Wis., 1985—; cons. Air Systems, Charlotte, N.C., 1984;. Mem. Charlotte Ambassadors, 1984-85. Mem. Sales and Mktg. Execs. Milw., Reef Point Yacht Club. Republican. Lutheran. Home: 19165 Killarney Way Brookfield WI 53005 Office: Connell LP PO Box 28 Mayville WI 53050

HUSI, DONALD LESTER, retirement community administrator; b. Milw., Jan. 31, 1963; s. James William and Judith (Zirbel) H.; m. Rebecca Margaret Brown, July 25, 1987. BS in Health Care Adminstrn., U. Wis.-Eau Claire, 1985. Lic. nursing home adminstr. Adminstrv. intern Walker Meth. Residence & Health Services, Inc., Mpls., 1985; coordinator spl. projects Am. Retirement Corp., Nashville, 1986; acting exec. dir. Richmond Place Am. Retirement Corp., Lexington, Ky., 1986; ops. mgr. Williamsburg (Va.) Landing Am. Retirement Corp., 1986—. Mem. Am. Coll. Health Care Adminstrs., Va. Assn. Non-Profit Homes for Aging (mem. strategic long-range planning com.), Am. Assn. Homes for Aged, Kiwanis. Home: 5314 Sloan Sq Williamsburg VA 23185 Office: Williamsburg Landing 5700 Williamsburg Landing Dr Williamsburg VA 23185

HUSKINS, ROBERT GARY, brokerage house executive; b. Scott AFB, Ill., Feb. 2, 1953; s. Sam J. and Veda Sybil (Wright) H.; m. Robin Anne Barker, June 11, 1977; children: Sean Christopher, Ashley Lauren. BS in Fin., Fla. State U., 1975; MBA, U. Cen. Fla., Orlando, 1981. Cert. fin. planner. With S.E. Bank Corp., Satellite Beach, Fla., 1976-80; fin. planner, assoc., v.p. A. G. Edwards & Sons, Inc., Melbourne, Fla., 1981—. Mem. Brevard County Estate Planning Council, Melbourne, 1987. Mem. Internat. Assn. Cert. Fin. Planners. Republican. Methodist. Home: 3202 Wind Song Ct Melbourne FL 32935 Office: A G Edwards & Sons Inc 930 S Harbor City Blvd Melbourne FL 32901

HUSLIN, CYNTHIA L., marketing representative; b. Phila., May 19, 1961; d. Stanley C. and Bette Ann (Wehmeyer) H. BS, Pa. State U., 1983, MBA, 1985. Mktg. rep. IBM Corp., Radnor, Pa., 1985—; IBM liaison Deleware Valley Computer Users, Phila., 1987—. Office: IBM Corp 580 E Swedesford Rd Wayne PA 19087

HUSS, CHARLES MAURICE, municipal building official; b. Chgo., Nov. 11, 1946; s. Charles Maurice and June Pierce (Bailey) H.; m. Winifred Louise Traughber, Dec. 24, 1973; children—Amber Elaine, Ra Ja Lorraine, Micah Alexander, Gabriel Joe, Cameron M., Jordan Charles. AA, Kendall Coll., 1984; student Oregon State U., Western Oreg. State Coll., U. Cinn., U. Alaska, Western Ill. U., City U., Nat. Fire Acad., Ohio U. Traffic mgr. The Harwald Co., Evanston, Ill., 1966-67, asst. v.p., 1968-69; traffic mgr. Northwestern U. Press, Evanston, 1969-71; fire chief City of Kotzebue (Alaska), 1971-76, asst. city mgr., 1973-76; dir. maintenance USPHS Hosp., Kotzebue, 1976-79; pres., gen. mgr. Action Builders, Inc., Kotzebue, 1979-82; gen. mgr. Husky Maintenance Svcs., 1982—; chief bldg. insp. City of Kotzebue, 1985—; adj. faculty Nat. Fire Acad., Emmitsburg, Md. Chmn., Kotzebue Planning Commn., 1978-82, Kotzebue Sch. Bd., 1974-79, 83—; founding vice chmn. Kotzebue chpt. ARC; mem. Alaska Criminal Code Revision Commn., 1976-78; mem. Fire Marshal's Sprinkler Task Force; mem. Alaska Fire Fighter Tng. Commn.; asst. chief Kotzebue Vol. Fire Dept., 1972-76, 82—; bd. dirs., instr. Alaska Craftsman Home Program 1986—; instr. Kotzebue Regional Fire Tng. Ctr., 1982—. Pullman Found. scholar, 1964-65, Blackburn Coll. scholar, 1964-65, Ill. State scholar, 1964-66. Mem. ASHRAE, AACED, Constrn. Specifications Inst., Internat. Soc. Fire Svc. Instrs., Fire Marshalls Assn. N.Am., Bldg. Ofcls. and Code Adminstrs. Internat., Alaska Firefighters Assn., Internat. Assn. Fire and Arson Investigators, Western Fire Chiefs Assn., Internat. Conf. Bldg. Ofcls. (cert. bldg. ofcl., fire, plumbing and mech. insp.), Am. Soc. Safety Engrs., Internat. Assn. Plumbing and Mech. Ofcls., Internat. Assn. Elec. Insps., Internat. Assn. Fire Chiefs, Home Builders Assn. Alaska, Nat. Fire Protection Assn., Soc. Nat. Fire Acad. Instrs., Coalition for Home Fire Safety, Kotzebue C. of C. Guest essayist: Seven Days and Sunday (Kirkpatrick), 1973; contbr. Alaska Craftsman Home Building Manual. Home and Office: PO Box 277 Kotzebue AK 99752

HUSSEY, JOHN F., public affairs executive; b. Dallas, July 27, 1940; m. Nancy Riegle. Grad., U. S.C.; postgrad., Columbia U. Dir. U.S. Senate Nat. Ocean Policy Study, 1972-76; mem. nat. adv. com. on coastal zone mgmt. Sec. of Commerce, 1977-80; correspondent, bur. mgr., regional exec. UPI; spl. asst. to U.S. Sen. Ernest F. Holling; dir. legis. affairs Monsanto Co., Washington, dir. corp. pub. relations; v.p. pub. affairs Monsanto Co., St. Louis, 1985-87; sr. v.p. and mng. dir. Hill and Knowlton, Inc., Washington, 1987—. Office: Hill and Knowlton Inc 901 31st St NW Washington DC 20007

HUSSEY, JOHN GREGORY, manufacturing company executive; b. Providence, July 29, 1946; s. Walter Joseph and Evelyn Louise (Hobin) H.; m. Sharon Lee Clay; children: Janet C., John Gregory, Corinne P. BA, Providence Coll., 1968; postgrad., U. N.H., 1984. Fleet specialist Fram Corp., Providence, 1968-72, mgr. dist. sales, 1972-75, head mgr. sales, 1975-82, dir. o.e. sales, 1982-85; dir. heavy duty sales Allied Aftermarket Div., Providence, 1985—; lectr. in field. Mem. 52 Assn.-Confidence Thru Sports, Handicapped, N.Y.C., 1986-87; active Rober Kennedy for Pres. campaign, Providence, 1968. Mem. Automotive Svc. Ind. Assn., The Maintenance Coun., Heavy Duty Mfrs. Assn. (planning com.), The Am. Trucking Assn., Motor Vehicle Suprs. Tng. Assn., Heavy Duty Mktg. and Sales Coun. Democrat. Roman Catholic. Home: 1 Edgewood Farm Rd Wakefield RI 02879 Office: Allied Aftermarket Div 105 Pawtucket Ave Providence RI 02916

HUSTING, PETER MARDEN, advertising agency executive; b. Bronxville, N.Y., Mar. 28, 1935; s. Charles Ottomar and Jane Alice (Marden) H.; m. Carolyn Riddle, Mar. 26, 1960; children: Jennifer, Gretchen, Charles Ottomar. B.S., U. Wis., 1957; grad., Advanced Mgmt. Program, Harvard U., 1974. Sales rep. Crown Zellerbach Corp., San Francisco, 1958-59; media analyst Leo Burnett Co., Chgo., 1959-61, time buyer, 1961-62, asst. account exec., 1962-63, account exec., 1963-68, v.p., account supr., 1968-72, sr. v.p., account dir., 1972-79, group exec., 1979—, exec. v.p., 1979—, dir. human relations internat., 1986—, also bd. dirs. Trustee Shedd Aquarium Soc., Chgo., 1980—; bd. dirs. Chgo. Better Govt. Assn., 1976—. Leadership Council Met. Open Communities, Chgo., 1980—, Lyric Opera Guild, 1971-78, Chgo. Forum, 1969-76. Served with AUS, 1958. Mem. Chgo. Advt. Club. Republican. Clubs: Indian Hill (Winnetka) (bd. govs. 1975-79); Univ.,

Mid-Am., Les Nomad, Internat., Lincoln Pk. Trap (Chgo.); Bull Valley Hunt. Office: Leo Burnett Co Inc 35 W Wacker Dr Chicago IL 60601

HUTA, HENRY NICHOLAUS, manufacturing and service company executive; b. Traunstein, Bavaria, Fed. Republic of Germany, Nov. 16, 1947; came to U.S., 1963; s. Mykola and Berta (Hoffmann) H.; m. Kay C. Crouch (div. 1985); stepchildren: David, Scott; m. Sharon L., Jan. 2, 1986; 1 child, Nicholaus Henry. AS with honors, Suffolk County Community Coll., 1976; BS magna cum lude, L.I. U., 1976; MS with honors, West Coast U., 1980; postgrad., Claremont Coll., 1986. CPA, Calif. Sr. cons. Arthur Young & Co., N.Y.C., 1976-78; pres. R&B Info. Systems, Inc., Los Angeles, 1978-80; mgr. cons. Price Waterhouse & Co., Los Angeles, 1980-81; v.p. fin. and ops. Bay Distbrs., Los Angeles, 1981-83; v.p., gen. mgr. Cal Fruit Inc., Los Angeles, 1983-84; v.p., asst. to chmn. Ducommun Inc., Los Angeles, 1984-86; exec. v.p., chief oper. officer Pacific Diversified Capital Co. (subs. San Diego Gas & Electric), San Diego, 1986—; bd. dirs. Phase One Devel. Inc., San Diego, Integrated Info. Systems Inc., San Diego, Wahlco., Inc., Los Angeles, Moch Resources Inc., Los Angeles, Creative Nail Design Inc. Lance cpl. USMC, 1964-67, Vietnam. Mem. Calif. State Soc. CPA's, Fin. Exec. Inst., Am. Inst. CPA's, Am. Mgmt. Assn. Republican. Mem. Christian Ch. Home: 12324 Avenida Consentido San Diego CA 92128

HUTCHEON, CHRISTA MARIE, trust company executive; b. Providence, Sept. 10, 1957; d. Alexander and Marianne Eva (Deitchmann) H.; m. John Philip O'Meara, Feb. 14, 1987. BA, Colby Coll., 1979; postgrad., So. Maine U., 1980-81, Fla. Atlantic U., 1983-85. Cert. employee benefit specialist. Trust adminstr. Key Bank So Maine, Portland, 1979-81; project mgr. SEI Corp., Wayne, Pa., 1981-83; trust officer Chem. Bank & Trust Co. Fla., Palm Beach, 1983—. County rep. Maine State Rep. Com., 1974-80; mem. Falmouth Town Rep. Com., 1974-81, Falmouth Emergency Rescue Squad, 1980-82. Mem. Nat. Trust Aid Systems Assn. Office: Chem Bank & Trust Co Fla 251 Royal Palm Way Palm Beach FL 33480

HUTCHERSON, JOHN ROGERS, financial planner; b. Cleve., Sept. 29, 1943; s. Joseph R. and Betty (Foley) H.; children: Jay Rogers, Joy Elizabeth. BA, Allegheny Coll., 1965; MS, Fla. State U., 1967; PhD, U. Md., 1972. Exec. dir. Regional Mental Health Complex, Starkville, Miss., 1972-81; health benefit cons. Health Benefit Assocs., Starkville, 1982-83; fin. planner Waddell & Reed Inc., Starkville, 1983-84, San Antonio, 1984-85; personal fin. planner I.D.S. Fin. Svcs., San Antonio, 1985—; cons. NIMH, Atlanta, 1975-81, State of S.C., 1980, State of Fla., 1980. Maj. USAF, 1967-72. Mem. Internat. Assn. Fin. Planning, Inst. Cert. Fin. Planners, Toastmasters (ednl. v.p. San Antonio 1988). Methodist. Home: 8515 Village Creek San Antonio TX 78151 Office: IDS Fin Svcs 84 NE Loop 410 San Antonio TX 78216

HUTCHINS, GENE ROBERT, manufacturing company executive; b. St. Louis, June 26, 1949; s. Clyde Joseph and Virginia (Klee) H.; m. Nancy Lee Kisslinger, Apr. 3, 1971; 1 child, Robert. BBA, U. Mo., 1975; MA in Fin., St. Louis U., 1984. Credit mgr. Armour Foods Co., St. Louis, 1975-78; acctg. supr. ITT Continental Baking Co., St. Louis, 1978-79; corp. credit mgr. Coca-Cola Bottling Co., St. Louis, 1979-81; credit mgr. Processing div. Con Agra Grain Merchandising, St. Louis, 1981; corp. credit mgr. Falcon Products, St. Louis, 1982-83; owner Hutchins & Assocs., St. Louis, 1983-84; corp. credit mgr. Watlow Electric Mfg. Co., St. Louis, 1984—. Truste N.E. Webster Neighborhood Improvement Assn., Webster Groves, Mo., 1876-77; mem. Jefferson Twp. Reps., 1984—. With U.S. Army, 1967-71, Vietnam. Mem. St. Louis Assn. Credit Mgmt. Avocations: shortwave radio, collecting writing instruments. Office: Watlow Electric 10001 Lackland Rd Saint Louis MO 63146

HUTCHINS, JOHN M., fiber company executive; b. Gardiner, Maine, Sept. 7, 1942; s. Gordon and Helen (Alexander) H.; m. Barbara G. Perkins, Feb. 24, 1968; children: Beth A., Michael D., Suzanne E. BSME, U. Maine, 1964; MBA, Rutgers U., 1970. Prodn. supr. Union Carbide Corp., Wayne, N.J., 1964-66, process engr., 1966-69; fin. analyst Allied Chem. Corp., Morristown, N.J., 1969-72, planning mgr., 1972-74, mktg. mgr., 1974-76, asst. controller, 1976-79, div. controller, 1979-80; gen. mgr. Allied Corp., Morristown, N.J., 1980-82; v.p., gen. mgr. Allied-Signal Inc., N.Y.C., 1982—. Democrat. Roman Catholic. Office: Allied-Signal Inc Fibers Div 1411 Broadway New York NY 10018

HUTCHINS, JOHN RICHARD, III, fiber optics electronic company executive. m. Jane Ide; children: John IV, Jane E., James, Jeffrey. BS in Physics, Rensselaer Poly. Inst., 1955; ScD in Ceramics, MIT, 1959; grad. program for mgmt. devel., Harvard U., fall 1968; ScD (hon.), Rutgers U., 1984. Research asst. dept. metallurgy MIT, Cambridge, 1955-59; research physicist Knox Labs., Inc., Rahway, N.J., 1959-60; with Corning (N.Y.) Glass Works, 1960-80, dir. research and devel., corp. v.p., 1973, sr. v.p., 1980; exec. v.p. of staffs Siecor Corp., Hickory, N.C., 1985-88, exec. v.p., dir. tech. and new bus. devel., 1988; chmn. bd. Broadband Techs. Inc., Research Triangle Pk., N.C., 1988—; areas of expertise and/or responsibility include hypodermic syringes mfg., solid state reactions, gases in glass, dissolution studies, foam glass, cement chemistry, synthetic marble, inorganic materials, electro-luminescent materials, organosilanes, oxidation kinetics, glass-plastic composites, anticoagulants, immobilized biologically active materials, ion selective electrodes, radioimmunoassays, chromatography, detergent enzymes, optical waveguides, medical instrumentation, single crystals, autoemission control substrates, specialty glass manufacture, glass ceramics, fusion cast and bonded refractories, laminated glass, photosensitive glasses, optic cables; past mem. adv. groups at N-Cor, Ltd., Siecor Corp, U. Rochester, Atlanta Research Ctr., Cornell U., MIT, Case Western Reserve U., Dept. Energy, NRC, N.Y. State. Contbr. articles to profl. jours. Previously active Boy Scouts Am., YMCA Indian Guides, Corning-Painted Post Sch. Dist. Long Range Planning Task Force, First United Meth. Ch.; past bd. trustees Alfred U., Catawba Valley Community Coll. Fellow Am. Ceramic Soc. (past trustee, past chmn. glass div., other coms.); mem. Nat. Inst. Ceramic Engrs., Soc. Glass Tech. (Eng.), Am. Chem. Soc., AAAS, Indsl. Research Inst. (corp. rep., past bd. dirs.), Am. Mgmt. Assn. (research and devel. council), Dirs. Indsl. Research, Electronic Industries Assn. (mem. tech. council ITG), Sigma Xi (past pres. local chpt.). Office: Broadbrand Techs Inc PO Box 23737 Research Triangle Park NC 27709

HUTCHINSON, ALBERT NEWHALL, bank executive; b. Northampton, Mass., Aug. 5, 1939; s. Albert Savage and Eleanor (Newhall) H.; m. Susan Jaquith, June 18, 1963; children—Scott, Julie. B.S., Nasson Coll., 1962; M.B.A., Columbia U., 1964. Asst. treas. Chase Manhattan Bank, N.Y.C., 1968-70, 2nd v.p., 1970-71, v.p., 1971-82, sr. v.p., 1982-87; exec. v.p. Chase Bank of Fla., St. Petersburg, 1987—; also sr. v.p. Chase Manhattan Corp. Republican. Club: Isle of Springs Assn. (Boothbay Harbor, Maine) (v.p. 1983—). Home: 4950 62nd Ave S Saint Petersburg FL 33715 Office: Chase Bank PO Box 12408 Saint Petersburg FL 33715

HUTCHINSON, GEORGE J., insurance company executive; b. Boston, Feb. 24, 1937; s. Edmund A. and Agnes B. (Crehan) H.; m. Carol A. Svensen, June 18, 1956 (dec. Dec. 1985); children: Karen, David, Kevin, Bryan; m. Dorothy B. Garofoli, Oct. 10, 1987. BS, Northeastern U., 1960. CPCU. Underwriter Liberty Mutual Ins. Co., Boston, 1960-62; asst. chief underwriter Liberty Mutual Ins. Co., Atlanta, 1962-67; asst. sec. Liberty Mutual Ins. Co., Boston, 1967-84, asst. v.p., 1984-86, v.p., 1986—. Office: Liberty Mut Ins Co 175 Berkeley St Boston MA 02117

HUTCHINSON, JULIUS STEVEN, financial services company executive; b. Greensboro, N.C., Oct. 10, 1952; s. Jimmie Wayne and Geneva (Chester) H.; m. Karen Barber, Apr. 2, 1982; children: Cassandra, Raymond, Jason, Bryant, Aaron, Andrew. Student, Guilford Tech. Community Coll., 1981-86. Cert. fin. planner. Enlisted USMC, 1969, advanced through grades to sgt., 1976, resigned, 1978; mgr. Food Dimensions, Inc., San Francisco, 1978-81, Macke Co., Greensboro, 1981-83; v.p. Fin. Group, Greensboro, 1983-84; exec. v.p. Cornwallis Investment Corp., Greensboro, 1984-86; pres., chief exec. officer Delta Internat. Investment Corp., Greensboro, 1986—. Mem. Internat. Assn. Fin. Planning, Internat. Cert. Fin. Planners. Republican. Baptist. Office: Delta Internat Investment Corp 125 S Elm St Ste 510 PO Box 3032 Greensboro NC 27402

HUTCHINSON, PEMBERTON, coal company executive; b. Charlotte, N.C., 1931. Grad., U. Va. Exec. v.p. Westmoreland Coal Co., Phila.; also pres. subs. Gen. Coal Co., 1979-81; pres., chief exec. officer, dir. Westmoreland Coal Co., Inc., 1981—; bd. dirs. Teleflex, Inc., Mellon Bank. Office: Westmoreland Coal Co 700 The Bellevue 200 S Broad St Philadelphia PA 19102

HUTCHINSON, THOMAS NELSON, JR., small business owner; b. Lubbock, Tex., Dec. 26, 1950; s. Thomas Nelson and Barbara Ann (Lunceford) H.; m. Di Ann Rutherford, Jan. 25, 1974; 1 child, Hilary. BEd, Tex. Tech. U., 1977. Mgr. Cycle Ctr., Lubbock, 1971-72; salesman Robert's Bicycle Shop, Lubbock, 1972-73; mgr. Peytons Bicycle Shop, Odessa, Tex., 1974-75; tchr. Estacado High Sch., Lubbock, 1978-79; owner Hutchinson Cycles, Lubbock, 1979—; 3d category ofcl. U.S. Cycling Fedn., Colorado Springs, Colo., 1988—. Named Tex. Rd. Racing Champion, U.S. Cycling Fedn., Tex., 1972, Tex. Sprint Champion, 1978, Silver medallist, 1978, Bronze medallist, 1973. Mem. Lubbock Bicycle Club (bd. dirs. 1977—, editor newsletter 1988), Chaparral Cycling Club (founder 1988). Office: Hutchinson Cycles 2420 Broadway Lubbock TX 79401

HUTCHINSON, VIRGINIA NETTLES, librarian; b. Richmond, Va., Feb. 7, 1936; d. Joseph and Virginia (Davies) Nettles; m. John Michael Robin H., Oct. 3, 1959; children: Catherine Pierce, Peter Anthony. BA in English Lit., Mary Washington Coll., 1958. Librarian D.C. Pub. Library, Washington, 1958-59, 66-67; asst. to communications cons. Govt. Employees Ins. Co., Washington, 1973-78, librarian, 1978—. Mem. Am. Soc. Personnel Adminstrn., Special Libraries Assn. Democrat. Club: Book Discussion Group (Chevy Chase, Md.). Home: 113 Hesketh St Chevy Chase MD 20815 Office: Goodwin Learning Ctr GEICO Plaza Washington DC 20076

HUTCHISON, CRAIG AUSTIN, printing company executive; b. Davenport, Iowa, Mar. 4, 1952; s. John Manvel and Lois Elaine (Leeds) H.; m. Ann Christine Schneiter, May 8, 1976; children: Blake, Alan, Lindsay. BS, Ind. U., 1974. Sales rep. Am. Hosp. Supply Co., McGaw Park, Ill., 1974-76; rep. Perry Printing Corp., Waterloo, Wis., 1976-80, dir. mktg., 1980-82, v.p. mktg., 1982-84, sr. v.p. mktg., 1984-86, sr. v.p., chief operating officer Web div., 1986-89, pres., coord., 1989—. Mem. Leslie Paper Adv. Bd. Office: Perry Printing Corp PO Box 97 Waterloo WI 53594

HUTCHISON, THEODORE MURTAGH, insurance company executive; b. Iowa City, Iowa, May 19, 1932; s. Theodore Call and Helen Louise (Murtagh) H.; m. Susan K. Starman, July 30, 1954; children: Holly Hutchison Ardinger, Hilary Hutchison Wright, Theodore Thomas. BA, U. Iowa, 1954, JD, 1956; LLM, U. Mich., 1958. Bar: Iowa 1956. Law clk. U.S. Ct. Appeals 8th Cir., St. Louis, 1956-57; instr. law U. Mich., Ann Arbor, 1958-59; asst. prof. law Boston U., 1959-62, assoc. prof., 1962-63; atty., asst. counsel Prin. Mut. Life Ins. Co. (formerly Bankers Life Co.), Des Moines, 1963-71, assoc. counsel, 1971-73, assoc. gen. counsel, 1973-77, v.p., counsel, corp. sec., 1977-84, sr. v.p., counsel, sec., 1984-85, sr. v.p., gen. counsel, sec., 1985-88, sr. v.p., gen. counsel, 1988—. Mem. Iowa Nat. Heritage Found., Des Moines Urban Renewal Bd., 1971-82, chmn., 1973-75, 80-82; bd. dirs. United Way, 1976-82, Iowa Law Sch. Found., 1974—, Hawley Found., 1980—, Grand View Coll., 1988—. W.W. Cook fellow, 1957-58. Mem. ABA, Iowa Bar Assn., Polk County Bar Assn., Assn. Life Ins. Counsel, Iowa Supreme Ct. Commn. Continuing Legal Edn. (chmn. 1983-88), Order of Coif, Des Moines Club, Prairie Club, Rotary. Republican. Presbyterian. Home: 4019 Oak Forest Dr Des Moines IA 50312 Office: Prin Fin Group 711 High St Des Moines IA 50309

HUTCHISON-HALL, WILLIAM ELLSWORTH HENRY, IV, merchant banker; b. Jersey City, May 21, 1963; s. Wiiliam Frederick and Mary Ruth (Hall) Ellinger; m. Andrea Lynn Bryant, May 28, 1988; 1 child, Iain Henry William Bryant Ellinger. Trainee, assoc. R. Kovi & Co., Ltd., London, 1979-81; mng. dir. R. Kovi & Co., Ltd., Berlin, 1986-87, N.Y.C., 1987—; mng. dir. R. Kovi et Cie, Limitee, Ottawa, Ont., Can., 1981-86; bd. dirs. Charlworth Devels., N.Y.C. Mem. Falkville (Ala.) Zoning Bd. Adjustment, 1988—. Republican. Episcopalian. Home: Bryant House Falkville AL 35622-0510 Office: R Kovi & Co Ltd 40 Wall St New York NY 10005

HUTSON, ALAN ROBERT, apparel company executive; b. Boston, Apr. 16, 1945; m. Jane Palmour, Dec. 16, 1967; 1 child, Alan Jr. BBA, U. Fla., 1968; MBA, Harvard U., 1973. Nat. sales mgr. Work Wear Corp., Cleve., 1977-80, v.p. mktg. div., 1980-86; exec. v.p. U.S. ops. Work Wear Corp., Chagrin Falls, Ohio, 1986—. Served to 1st lt. U.S. Army, 1968-71. Republican. Episcopalian.

HUTT, ERIC JOHN VILLETTE, accountant; b. Royston, Eng., May 14, 1915; s. John and Olive Villette (Gillespie) H.; law student London U., 1939; m. Jadwiga de Sulerzyska, Jan. 29, 1949; children—Anthony Villette, Timothy Patrick de Sulerzyski, Clive Karl. Office boy, 1933; jr. accountant, 1934; accountant's articled clk., 1935-39; chief accountant China Engrs. Ltd., Shanghai, 1946-48; mgr. Lowe, Bingham & Thomsons, chartered accountants, Tokyo and Kobe, Japan, 1949-50, partner, 1951-65; adviser, exec. dir. Jardine Matheson & Co., Ltd., Hong Kong, 1966-84; dir. Jardine Fleming & Co., Ltd., Mcht. Bankers, 1970-84, prof., non-exec. dir., fin. cons., 1984—. Served with Brit. Army, 1940-45. Fellow Inst. Chartered Accountants in Eng. and Wales, Huguenot Soc. London; mem. Am. Inst. C.P.A.s (internat. asso.). Clubs: East India, Sports and Schools, St. James St. (London); Hong Kong. Home: 22 Braga Cir, Kowloon Hong Kong Office: Jeatac Ltd, World Fin Ctr North Tower, Suite 1410, Canton Rd, Kowloon Hong Kong

HUTTO, TERRELL DON, corrections management company executive; b. Sinton, Tex., June 8, 1935; s. Terrell Sanford and Winnie (Custer) H.; m. Nancy Sue Moore, June 10, 1960; children: Jennifer Marie, Robyn Suzanne, Shelley Anne. BS, East Tex. State U., 1958; postgrad., So. Meth. U., 1958-59, Am. U., 1963-64, Sam Houston State U., 1956-67. Correctional officer Tex. Dept. Corrections, Huntsville, 1964-65, asst. warden, 1965-67, warden, 1967-71; commr. correctioners State of Ark., Little Rock, 1971-76; dir. corrections State of Va., Richmond, 1977-82; correctional cons. Richmond, 1982-83; exec. v.p., bd. dirs. Corrections Corp. Am., Nashville, 1983—; pres. CCA Internat., Nashville, 1986—. Del. Tex. Dem.Conv., 1957; pres. Foresdale Civic Assn., Chesterfield, Va., 1980-81. With U.S. Army, 1960-62. Mem. Am. Correctional Assn. (life, pres. 1984-86, E.R. Cass Correctional Achievement award 1987), So. State Correctional Assn. (life, pres. 1978-79), Assn. State Correctional Adminstrs. (pres. 1979-80). Democrat. Methodist. Office: Corrections Corp Am 28 White Bridge Rd Ste 206 Nashville TN 37205

HUTTON, EDWARD LUKE, chemical company executive; b. Bedford, Ind., May 5, 1919; s. Fred and Margaret (Drehobl) H.; m. Kathryn Jane Alexander; children—Edward Alexander, Thomas Charles, Jane Clarke. B.S. with distinction, Ind. U., 1940, M.S. with distinction, 1941. Dep. dir. Joint Export Import Agy. (USUK), Berlin, 1946-48; v.p. World Commerce Corp., 1948-51; asst. v.p. W.R. Grace & Co., 1951-53, cons., 1960-65, exec. v.p., gen. mgr. Dubois Chems. div., 1965-66, group exec. Specialty Products Group and v.p., 1966-68, exec. v.p., 1968-71; cons. internat. trade and fin. 1953-58; fin. v.p., exec. v.p. Ward Industries, 1958-59; pres., chief exec. officer Chemed Corp., Cincinnati, 1971—, dir.; chmn. Omnicare, Inc., Cincinnati, 1981—; dir. Omnicare, Inc.; chmn., dir. Roto-Rooter, Inc., 1984—, DuBois Chem. Co.; dir. Am. States Ins. Co., Nat. Sanitary Supply Co. Co-chmn. Pres.'s Pvt. Sector Survey on Cost Control, exec. com., subcom.; bd. advisors U. Cin. Coll. Bus. Adminstrn. Recipient Disting. Alumni Service award Ind. U., 1987. Mem. Internat. Platform Assn., U. Cin. (CBA bd. advisors), Dirs.' Table, AAUP (governing bd. dirs. 1958—), Newcomen Soc., Cin. Club, Downtown Assn., Econs. Club, Princeton Club, Univ. Club, Queen City Club, Bankers Club. Home: 6680 Miralake Dr Cincinnati OH 45243 Office: Chemed Corp 1200 DuBois Tower Cincinnati OH 45202

HUTTON, HELEN MARION WAY, data processing executive; b. Burlington, Vt., Apr. 2, 1948; d. Harry Abel and Edwina Laura (Hinds) Way; m. Greg Alan Hutton, Oct. 9, 1976; children: Brittany, Robert Scott. BS, U. Mass., 1971. Community organizer City of Springfield, Mass., 1971-72; engring. asst. New. Eng. Instrument Co., Natick, Mass., 1974-78; programmer, analyst Mgmt. Decision Systems Inc., Waltham, Mass., 1978-84; owner, mgr. Personalized Bus. Systems, Ashland, Mass., 1984-87; pres. Personalized Bus. Systems, Ashland, 1987—; guest lectr. recreation dept. U. Mass., Amherst, 1971-73. Mem. Assn. Computing Machinery, Metrowest C. of C. Office: Personalized Bus Systems Inc 23 Tower Rd Ashland MA 01721

HUTTON, SHEILA RAE, pension fund administrator; b. Burien, Wash., July 29, 1965; d. Patrick Eugene and Judith M. (Lysne) Boone; m. Clifford Ralph Hutton, June 15, 1985; 1 child, Conrad Ryan. BS in Acctg., Lake Washington Vocat. Tech., 1983. Office mgr. Dan Sweeney & Assocs., Inc., Bellevue, Wash., 1983—; v.p. ops. Davis-Bacon Pension Adminstrn., Inc., Bellevue, 1987—. Mem. Associated Bldg. Contractors. Methodist. Home: 15102 111th Ave NE Bothell WA 98011 Office: Davis-Bacon Pension Adminstrn 11911 NE First St #102 Bellevue WA 98005

HUTTON, THOMAS J., engineer; b. Pitts., Sept. 8, 1938; s. Thomas J. and Betty (Galbraith) H.; m. Ellen Guzum, Oct. 16, 1959; children: Jennifer, Kimberley, Holly. BSEE, Carnegie-Mellon U., 1960; MBA, U. Pitts., 1976. Registered profl. engr., Pa. With Vectran Corp., Pitts.; chmn bd., pres., chief exec. officer Vectran Corp. Inventor in field; patentee in field. Mem. IEEE (dir. 1980-81, pres. 1979-83). Unitarian-Universalist. Office: Vectran Corp 261 Kappa Dr Pittsburgh PA 15238

HUYNH, KIET TUAN, clothing executive; b. Phnom Penh, Cambodia, Dec. 21, 1952; came to U.S., 1982; s. Thanh Long and Diep Hue (To) H.; m. Carole Madeleine Palfray, Dec. 15, 1986. Tchr. Acad. Paris, 1979-80, 1981-82; programmer Mfr. Michelin, Clermont, France, 1980-81; computer info. mgr. Joseph Love Inc., N.Y.C., 1983-86, comptroller, 1986—. Office: Joseph Love Inc 131 W 33d St #802 New York NY 10001

HYATT, KENNETH E(RNEST), building materials company executive; b. Canton, Ga., Aug. 14, 1940; s. Spurgeon Ernest Hyatt and Grace Marian Lorentzen; m. Anne King Rogers, Nov. 19, 1966; children: Ava Rogers, Grace Marian, Kenneth Ernest Jr. BSCE, Ga. Inst. Tech., 1962, MS in Indsl. Mgmt., 1966. Plant engr. Ga. Marble Co., Tate, 1966-68; div. mgr. Ga. Marble Co., Sylacauga, Ala., 1968-71; v.p. Ga. Marble Co., Atlanta, 1971-76, pres., 1976-84; v.p. Jim Walter Corp., Tampa, Fla., 1984-86, exec. v.p., chief operating officer, 1986-88, pres., chief exec. officer, 1988—; bd. dirs. Barnett Bank of Tampa. V.p. Sylacauga Ala. Rotary Club, 1969-70, pres., 1970-71. Served to lt. USN, 1962-65. Episcopalian. Office: Jim Walter Corp 1500 N Dale Mabry Hwy Tampa FL 33607

HYCLAK, JOSEPH GERARD, accountant, consultant; b. Cleve., Dec. 17, 1957; s. Benny Andrew and Catherine Ann (Kurzeja) H. BBA, Cleve. State U., 1981. CPA, Ohio. Intern Ernst & Whinney, Cleve., 1979, Touche Ross & Co., Cleve., 1980; sales bookkeeper Revco Drug Stores, Inc., Cleve., 1974-85; acct. Cuyahoga Valley Ry. Co., Cleve., 1981-85; pvt. practice cons., acctg. Cleve., 1984—; acctg. mgr. Aero Services Internat., Cleve., 1985-86; controller Arnco Corp., Cleve., 1986-88, Packaging Specialties, Inc., Cleve., 1988—; cons. KDJ, Inc., Cleve., 1984-87. active Big Brother, Cath. Big Bros., Cleve., 1981. Mem. Am. Inst. CPA's, Ohio Soc. CPA's. Democrat. Home: 31 Garfield Ln Bratenahl OH 44108 Office: 9520 Richmond Ave Cleveland OH 44105

HYDE, PAUL EUGENE, mining company executive, geological engineer; b. Coeur d'Alene, Idaho, Mar. 14, 1929; s. Charles Sheldon and Eleanor Mae (Murray) H.; m. Beverly Allayne Marble, June 13, 1954; children: Sonya, Sandra, Bret, Shelly. BS in Geol. Engring., U. Idaho, 1954. Registered geol. engr., Idaho. Geologist Hecla Mining Co., Wallace, Idaho, 1954-81; landman Hecla Mining Co., 1981-86; mgr. lands Hecla Mining Co., Coeur d'Alene, 1986—. Pres. United Crusade Shoshone County, 1979-80; mem. United Way Kootenai County, 1986—; commr. Idaho Panhandle Coun. Boy Scouts Am., 1988—. With F.A. U.S. Army, 1951-52. Recipient Silver Beaver award Idaho Panhandle Coun. Boy Scouts Am., 1974. Mem. Soc. Mining Engrs. of AIME., Idaho Profl. Geologists Assn., Elks, Kiwanis (past pres. Wallace, Idaho). Republican. Home: 428 Ross Point Rd Post Falls ID 83854 Office: Hecla Mining Co 6500 Mineral Dr Coeur d'Alene ID 83814-1931

HYDE, ROBERT WILLIAM, JR., accountant; b. Rome, Ga., May 26, 1956; s. Robert William and Charlotte Marie (Winslett) H.; m. Glynis Elizabeth Jones, May 12, 1978; children: Robert William III, Jennifer Elizabeth. AA, Pensacola Jr. Coll., Fla., 1976; BS, U. Ala., 1978. CPA, Ala. Staff acct. Smith, Dukes & Buckalew CPA's, Mobile, Ala., 1978-81; fin. analyst Autlan Manganese, Mobile, 1981-82; controller Crawford Beverage, Inc., Mobile, 1982-85; sr. acct. Delchamps, Inc., Mobile, 1985-86, acctg. mgr., 1986—; bd. dirs., mem. audit com. Delchamps Credit Union, Mobile. Loan exec. United Way, Mobile, 1987, mem. audit com., 1985-86; bd. dirs. Adopt-A-Sch. Com. Scarbrough Middle Sch., Mobile, 1987-88. Mem. Nat. Assn. Accts. (bd. dirs. 1987-89). Republican. Baptist. Office: Delchamps PO Box 1668 Mobile AL 36633

HYDOK, JOSEPH THOMAS, utility company executive; b. Nyack, N.Y., Sept. 23, 1928; s. Joseph Bernard and Mary Rose (McGovern) H.; m. Eleanor Patricia Bednar, May 3, 1952; children: Paul, Joanne Hydok Woolgar, Janice Hydok Maitre. BS, L.I. U., 1950; MBA, CCNY, 1958. Jr. auditor Price Waterhouse, N.Y.C., 1947-50; with Con Edison, N.Y.C., 1950-78, 80—, v.p., 1969-78, sr. v.p., 1980-89, exec. v.p., 1989—; dir. Mayor's Office of Ops., N.Y.C., 1978-80; mem. exec. com. N.Y. Gas Group. Dir. Mayor's Office of Operation, N.Y.C., 1978-80; mem. Mayor's Mgmt. Adv. Com., 1978—; bd. dirs. Indsl. Home for Blind, Bklyn., 1981—; pres. Fulton Mall Improvement Assn., 1978—. Served to capt. U.S. Army, 1950-53, ETO. Named Man of Yr., YMCA, 1974, Alumnus of Yr., L.I. U., 1982; recipient Service award St. Patrick's Home for Aged, Bronx, N.Y., 1976, Service award Kings County Am. Legion, N.Y., 1978. Mem. Am. Gas Assn. (bd. dirs. 1980—), Assn. Gas Distbrs. (vice chair exec. com.). Roman Catholic. Home: 80 Bocket Rd Pearl River NY 10965 Office: Consol Edison Co NY Inc 4 Irving Pl New York NY 10003

HYER, DOUGLAS KEITH, financial consultant, banker; b. St. Louis, Apr. 18, 1943; s. Ralph August and Florence (Elizabeth) H.; m. Jill Susan Miller, Feb. 19, 1972; children: Corry Elizabeth, Melanie Lauren. BA, U. Mo., 1966; MS in Fin. Services, Am. Coll., 1985. Chartered fin. cons., CLU. Mktg. rep. Baxter Travenol, N.Y.C., 1967-69; pvt. practice, N.Y.C., 1969-75; pres. Asset Adv. Services, Great Neck, N.Y., 1975—. Author: Employee Benefits Seminar, 1983. Pres., chmn. bd. dirs. People's Nat. Bank, Monsey, N.Y., 1985. Dep. Mayor, trustee Village of Plandome Manor, N.Y., 1988. Mem. N.Y. Fin. Planning Mgrs. Group (pres. 1985-87), Internat. Assn. Registered Fin. Planners (Master 1985), Registered Fin. Planners L.I. (pres.), Nat. Assn. Accts., Estate Planning Council N.Y.C. (bd. dirs. 1982-84), Am. Assn. Ind. Investors (sect. head N.Y.C. chpt. 1987-88), CLU Assn. (Sect. head N.Y.C. chpt. 1987-88), CPA Club of Toastmasters Internat. (pres.), Manhasset N.Y. Sailing (commodore), Yacht. Republican. Mem. Universal Unitarian Ch. Avocations: sailing, tennis, skiing, triathlons. Home: 5 Gulls Cove Manhasset NY 11030 Office: Asset Adv Svc 233 E Shore Rd Great Neck NY 11023

HYER, FREDERICK LEWIS, JR., insurance company executive; b. Plainfield, N.J., July 19, 1940; s. Frederick Lewis Hyer and Elizabeth (Runnells) Cornelius; m. Christine Datri (div. 1971); children: Frederick III, Susan, Nancy, Andrew; m. Patricia McLaughlin, July 3, 1979. AB, Princeton U., 1961; MBA, U. Chgo., 1966. Various positions Chubb & Son Inc., Chgo. and Los Angeles, 1961-83; sr. v.p., mng. dir. Chubb & Son Inc., Sherman Oaks, Calif., 1983-88; dir. Pacific Indemnity subs., mgr. U.S. and Can. branch ops. Chubb & Son Inc., Warren, N.J., 1988—. V.p. City of Hope Ins. Coun., Los Angeles, 1985—. Mem. Ins. Edn. Assn. (bd. dirs. 1988—), Princeton Club N.Y.C., Panther Valley (N.J.) Country Club. Republican. Office: Chubb & Son Inc 15 Mountain View Rd Warren NJ 07061 Also: Pacific Indemnity Co 6500 Wilshire Blvd Los Angeles CA 90048

HYERS, KEMPER KENT, lawyer; b. Charleston, S.C., July 8, 1929; s. Samuel Kent and Carlotta (Johnson) H.; m. Audie Delores Martin, Jan. 20, 1962; children: Kemper Kent Johnson, William Borden Martin, Samuel Thomas Campbell. Student, The Citadel, 1946-49; BS, U. S.C., 1952, LLB,

1956; grad. student law, NYU, 1964. Bar: S.C. 1956, Va. 1965, U.S. Supreme Ct. 1974. Claim agt. Seaboard Air Line R.R., Charleston, 1956-62; asst. gen. claims atty. Seaboard Air Line R.R., Richmond, Va., 1963-66, gen. claims atty., 1967-70, asst. gen. solicitor, gen. solicitor, 1975-78, dir. state govt. affairs, 1979-82; asst. v.p. legal and pub. affairs Seaboard Air Line R.R., Washington, 1971-72; v.p. govt. relations Seaboard Air Line R.R., Jacksonville, Fla., 1983-87; v.p. CSX Corp., Richmond, Va., 1987-88; of counsel McQuire, Woods, Battle and Boothe, Richmond, 1988—. Served to comdr. USNR. Mem. ABA, Richmond Bar Assn., Va. Bar Assn., ICC, Naval Res. Assn. Republican. Clubs: Country of Va., Bull and Bear (Richmond). Lodge: Masons, Order of Eastern Star. Office: McQuire Woods BattleBooth 1 James Ctr Richmond VA 23219

HYETT, DOYLE GREGORY, economist, city planner, author, consultant; b. Anniston, Ala., Nov. 7, 1948; s. Robert Ivan and Margaret Elizabeth (Murray) H.; m. Dolores P. Palma, Apr. 12, 1986; 1 child, Hillery. BS, U. Ala., 1971; M in City Planning, Ga. Inst. Tech., 1973. Dir. planning B.G. Sanders and Assocs., Atlanta, 1971-74, City of Anniston, Ala., 1975-80; dir. community devel. City of Steamboat Springs, Colo., 1981-82; v.p. Sanbury Corp., Atlanta, 1983-85; prin. Hyett-Palma, Inc., Washington, 1985—; adj. prof. Auburn (Ala.) U., 1980; instr. Ga. Tech. Continuing Edn., Atlanta, 1986—; pvt. practice cons. prof., 1971—. Author: (books) RFP for Economic Development, 1986, Small Business Enhancement, 1986, Parking Analysis, 1987, Retail Market Analysis, 1988. Chmn. Met. Planning Orgn., Anniston, Ala, 1979-80; rep. APA Colo.-Western Slope, Steamboat Springs, 1980. Named one of Outstanding Young Men of Am., 1977, 79, 80, 81; Carnegie-Mellon fellow, 1971, 72, Rotary Internat. fellow, 1979. Mem. Am. Inst. Cert. Planners, Am. Planning Assn. (mem. chpt. pres.'s coun. 1979-80). Office: Hyett Palma Inc PO Box 65881 Washington DC 20035

HYLAND, J. BRIAN, government official. BS, Fordham U., 1960; MBA, George Washington U., 1972. Insp. gen. U.S. Dept. of Labor, Washington. CPA. Office: US Labor Dept 200 Constitution Ave NW Washington DC 20210

HYLAND, VIRGINIA LING, small business owner; b. North Plainfield, N.J., Sept. 20, 1947; d. James C. and Juliet (Tchou) Ling.; m. Dale J. Hyland, June 7, 1967; children: Devin K., Christopher. Cert. in Ct. Reporting, Tampa Coll., 1975. Dep. ofcl. Conley & Swain, St. Petersburg, Fla., 1975-76; reporter Jud. Reporters, St. Petersburg, 1976-77; reporter, owner Suncoast Reporting Svcs., St. Petersburg, 1977—. Mem. Fla. Shorthand Reporters Assn. (bd. dirs. 1983-85, 87—, chief examiner 1986—), Nat. Shorthand Reporters (chief examiner 1986—). Democrat. Office: Suncoast Reporting Svcs 501 First Ave Ste 503 Saint Petersburg FL 33701

HYLAS, ROBERT EDWIN, management consultant; b. N.Y.C., Nov. 14, 1953; s. Albert Edwin and Anna Kathleen (Higgins) H.; m. Ellen Catherine Downey, July 31, 1982; 1 child, Catherine Joan. BA, Hamilton Coll., 1975; MBA, NYU, 1980. CPA, N.Y. Staff acct. Peat, Marwick, Mitchell & Co., N.Y.C., 1975-79, sr. mgmt. cons., 1979-85; mgr. Touche Ross & Co., N.Y.C., 1985-86; sr. prin. Am. Mgmt. Systems, N.Y.C., 1986—. Contbr. articles to profl. jours. and mags. Mem. Am. Inst. CPAs, N.Y. Soc. CPAs. Democrat. Roman Catholic. Home: 480 Hillsdale Ave Allendale NJ 07401 Office: Am Mgmt Systems 85 Livingstone Ave Roseland NJ 07068

HYMAN, BRUCE, securities analyst, engineer; b. N.Y.C., Jan. 8, 1944; s. Walter and Clara M. (Schoenberg) H.; m. Arlene Sondra Cash, Sept. 5, 1965; children: Wendy, Jennifer. B in Mech. Engring., CCNY, 1965; MS in Engring., Columbia U., 1967; postgrad., Seton Hall U., 1985-90. Registered profl. engr., N.Y. Staff mem. Bell Labs., Holmdel, N.J., 1965-68; sr. staff mem. Bell Labs., Piscataway, N.J., 1970-76; sr. cons. Booz, Allen & Hamilton, Bethesda, Md., 1968-70; mktg. mgr. AT&T, Bedminster, N.J., 1976-84; pvt. practice Millburn, N.J., 1984-85; analyst Fitch Investors Service, N.Y.C., 1985-88; asst. v.p. Standard & Poor's, N.Y.C., 1988—. Mem. Fixed Income Soc. (program com. 1987-88), IEEE (sr.), Nat. Soc. Rate Return Analysts. Home: 6 Marion Ave Short Hills NY 07078 Office: Standard & Poor's 25 Broadway New York NY 10004

HYMAN, GLENN CARTER, insurance company executive; b. Bristol, Pa., Dec. 22, 1958; s. Julius and Helen (Gerber) H. BBA in Acctg., Franklin and Marshall Coll., 1980. Fin. acct. Ins. Co. N.Am., Phila., 1980-81, fin. systems analyst, 1981-84; mgr. statis. and data control CIGNA Worldwide, Inc., Phila., 1984-85, mgr. fin., 1985-87, mem. spl. task force, 1987-88; dir. corp. fin. CIGNA Corp., Phila., 1988—. Mem. Youth Aid Panel, Middletown Township, Pa., 1987—. Office: CIGNA Corp 1 Logan Sq Philadelphia PA 19103

HYMAN, KEVIN MICHAEL, communications executive; b. Dallas, Mar. 8, 1950; s. Joseph Raymond and Mary Angela (Dwyer) H.; m. Marianna Mercer, July 17, 1983; children: Colleen, Chasen, Katelynn. BA in Econs., U. No. Colo., 1972; MA in Econs., U. R.I., 1974. Asst. prof. econs. Nasson Coll., Springvale, Maine, 1974-78; v.p. Boettcher & Co., Colorado Springs, Colo., 1978-85; chief exec. officer, pres. Citizens' Cable, Colorado Springs, Colo., 1985—; also bd. dirs. Citizens' Cable, Colorado Springs. coordinator West El Paso Little League, Colorado Springs; coach Pikes Peak Amateur Hockey Assn., Colorado Springs, 1987-88; dir. Profile Theatre, Portland, Maine, 1974-76. Mem. Colo. C. of C. Roman Catholic. Club: Plaza (Colorado Springs). Office: Citizens Cable 2833 Dublin Blvd Colorado Springs CO 80918

HYMAN, LEONARD STEPHEN, financial executive, economist, author; b. N.Y.C., June 5, 1940; s. Milton and Elsie (Reiter) H.; m. Judith N. Siegel, July 4, 1965; children: Andrew S., Robert C. BA, NYU, 1961; MA, Cornell U., 1965. Fin. analyst Chase Manhattan Bank, N.Y.C., 1965-72; ptnr. H.C. Wainwright & Co., N.Y.C., 1972-77; v.p. Wainwright Securities, N.Y.C., 1977-78; v.p., head utility research group Merrill Lynch Capital Markets, N.Y.C., 1978—, first v.p., 1987—; Author: America's Electric Utilities, 1983, The New Telecommunications Industry, 1987; (with others) Electric Power Strategic Issues, 1983, The Future of Electrical Energy, 1986, Deregulation and diversified of Utilities, 1988; contbr. article to profl. jours. mem. Pa. Task Force on Electric Utility Efficiency, Harrisburg, 1982-83; mem. adv. com. U.S. Congress-Office Tech. Assessment, Washington, 1983-84, 86-87, 87-88. Mem. NASA (lunar energy enterprise case study task force 1988—), N.Y. Soc. Security Analysts, Fin. Analysts Fedn., Inst. Chartered Fin. Analysts, AAAS, Phi Beta Kappa. Democrat. Jewish. Avocations: photography; travel; music; canoeing. Home: 34 Fremont Rd North Tarrytown NY 10591 Office: Merrill Lynch World Hdqrs World Fin Ctr North Tower New York NY 10281-1391

HYMAN, MORTON PETER, shipping company executive; b. N.Y.C., Jan. 9, 1936; s. Irving S. and Dora (Pfeffer) H.; m. Chris Oliphant Stern, Mar. 18, 1979. B.A., Cornell U., 1956, LL.D. with distinction, 1959; D.H.L. h.c., N.Y. Med. Coll. Bar: N.Y. 1960. Assoc. Proskauer Rose Goetz & Mendelsohn, N.Y.C., 1959-63; officer, dir. Overseas Discount Corp., N.Y.C., 1963—, pres., 1983—; officer, dir. Overseas Shipholding Group, Inc., N.Y.C., 1969—; pres. Overseas Shipholding Group, Inc., 1971—. Bd. editors Cornell Law Rev. Vice chmn. N.Y. State Health Planning Commn., 1977-78; mem. Pub. Health Council N.Y., 1971—, vice-chmn., 1977-85, chmn., 1985—; co-chmn. N.Y. State Health Issues Forum ; mem. Pub. Health Care Capital Policy Adv. Com., 1982—; chmn. bd. trustees Beth Israel Med. Center, Doctors Hosp.; trustee Mt. Sinai Med. Center; chmn. N.Y. State Joint Exec. and Legis. Task Force on Delivery of Health Care, 1977-80; co-chmn. N.Y. State Health Issues forum; chmn. N.Y. State Joint Exec. and Legis. Com. on Residential Health Care Facilities, 1977-80; bd. dirs. United Jewish Appeal Fedn. 2d lt. AUS, 1956-57. Fellow N.Y. Acad. of Medicine. Fellow N.Y. Acad. Medicine; mem. N.Y. Bar Assn., Harmonie Club, Order of Coif, Phi Kappa Phi. Republican. Home: 998 Fifth Ave New York NY 10028 Office: Overseas Shipholding Group Inc 1114 Ave of the Americas New York NY 10036

HYMAN, SIGMUND M., investment company executive; b. Balt., Aug. 4, 1921; m. Mary Bloom, Nov. 28, 1947; children: Carol A. Hyman Williams, Nancy L. BS in Econs., Franklin and Marshall Coll., 1947. CLU. Chmn. S.M. Hyman Co., Balt., 1956-77, S.M. Hyman Co. Ltd., London, 1971-77, Bus. Data Services, Balt., 1963-77; gen. agt. New Eng. Life Ins. Co., Boston, 1960-79; v.p. William M. Mercer, Inc., Balt., 1977-80; benefits cons. Balt., 1980—; bd. dirs. Control Data Corp., Mpls.; assoc. Council Profit-Sharing Industries, 1960-82, Am. Pension Conf., 1960-82; mem. faculty Pension and Profit-Sharing Inst. Purdue U., 1961-82, Balt. Mayor's Pension Study Com., 1966—, Mayor's Bus. Adv. Council, 1977—. Mem. exec. com. Greater Balt. Com., 1960-80; vice chmn. Md. Acad. Scis., 1970—; bd. dirs. Balt. Mus. Art, 1973-79, Goodwill Industries Balt., 1981—; trustee, bd. overseers Franklin and Marshall Coll., Lancaster, Pa., 1973—; chmn. internat. affairs com. Johns Hopkins U., Balt., 1979-80. 1st lt. AUS, 1941-46, ETO, 1951-53, Korea. Named Disting. Citizen City of Balt., 1976, Outstanding Alumni Franklin and Marshall Coll., 1981. Mem. Balt. C. of C. (v.p. 1970-78), Balt. Center Club, Suburban Balt. Country. Office: PO Box 248 Stevenson MD 21153

HYMS, KEVIN L., safety professional; b. Bklyn., Nov. 5, 1955; s. Murray A. and Suzanne Z. (Miller) H.; m. Gail L. Golden, Sept. 4, 1983. BS in Chemistry, SUNY-Stony Brook, 1977; MBA, N.Y. Inst. Tech., 1986. Cert. safety profl. Chemist County of Suffolk DPW, Yaphank, N.Y., 1979-82; with Pulmosan Safety Equipment, Flushing, N.Y., 1983-86, Nytest Environ. Inc., Port Washington, N.Y., 1986; tech. writing cons. Bayside, N.Y., 1986-87; tech. cons. The Home Ins. Co., N.Y.C., 1987—; teaching/rsch. asst. SUNY, Stony Brook, 1977-78. Mem. ACS, AAAS, ASSE, Am. Inst. Chemists, N.Y. Acad. Sci., Delta Mu Delta. Home: 212-79 16th Ave Bayside NY 11360 Office: The Home Ins Co Loss Dontrol Dept 59 Maiden Ln New York NY 10038

HYNES, JAMES PATRICK, banker, corporate telecommunications executive; b. N.Y.C., Sept. 16, 1947; s. John M. and Dorothy (Heaney) H.; m. Anne Marie Nichol, May 29, 1971; children: Alanna, Katherine. BA, Iona Coll., 1969; MBA, Adelphia U., Garden City, N.Y., 1978. Communications cons. N.Y. Tele., 1969-73; mgr. Bache & Co. Inc., N.Y.C., 1973-77; v.p. Continental Corp., N.Y.C., 1977-86, Chase Manhatten Corp., N.Y.C., 1986—; bd. advisors Data Pro Reports, Princeton, N.J., 1986-88; bd. dirs., v.p. alumni Iona Coll., New Rochelle, N.Y., 1987-89. Mem. Internat. Communications Assn. Republican. Roman Catholic. Club: Milbrook (Greenwich, Conn.). Home: 83 Overlook Dr Greenwich CT 06830 Office: Chase Manhattan Bank One World Trade Ctr 38th Floor New York City NY 10048

HYNES, MARY ANN, lawyer, publishing executive; b. Chgo., Oct. 26, 1947; d. Ernest Mario and Emma Louise (Noto) Iantorno; m. James Thomas Hynes, Jan. 25, 1969; children: Christina, Nicholas. B in Math. and Polit. Sci., Loyola U., 1967; JD, John Marshall Law Sch., 1971, LLM in Taxation, 1975. Bar: Ill. 1971, U.S. Dist. Ct. (no. dist.) Ill. 1971. Exec. editor, law editor Commerce Clearing House, Inc., 1971-79, asst. sec, counsel, 1979-80, v.p., gen. counsel, 1980—. Chief crusader United Way/Crusade of Mercy; v.p., bd. dirs., legis. and policy chmn., chmn. membership Chgo. Crime Commn.; mem. nat. strategy forum Midwest Council Nat. Security; adv. council Chgo. Symphony Orch. Chorus; deanery del. Chgo. Archdiocesan Pastoral Council; pres. local sch. bd., 1984-87; bd. dirs. local YWCA.; pres. corp. council inst. planning com. Northwestern U. Sch. Law. Mem. ABA (chmn. publs. com., corp. law depts. com., sect. corp., banking and bus. law sect., 1987—; membership chair, computer law com., litigation sect.), Ill. State Bar Assn. (corp. law dept. sect. coun.), Chgo. Bar Assn., Internat. Bar Assn., Internat. Fedn. Women Lawyers, Nat. Assn. Women Lawyers (corp. counsel reporter coordinator), Women's Bar Assn. Ill. (former dir., found. adv. bd. mem.), Am. Corp. Counsel Assn., Am. Soc. Corp. Secs., Computer Law Assn., Justinian Soc. Lawyers, Law Club of the City of Chgo., Legal Club of Chgo. (exec. com. 1987), Execs. Club of Chgo., Chgo. Club. Roman Catholic. Office: Commerce Clearing House Inc 2700 Lake Cook Rd Riverwoods IL 60015

IACOBELLI, JOHN LOUIS, economist; b. Cleve., Dec. 24, 1931; s. Joseph and Theresa (Caporaso) I.; m. Eleanor M. Mandala, Sept. 3, 1956; children: Joseph, Andrew, Christopher. BBA, Kent State U., 1955, MS in Econs., 1965; PhD in Econs., U. Tex., 1969. Sr. sales rep. National Cash Register Co., Cleve., 1957-64; asst. prof. labor and indsl. relations Cleve. State U., 1968-71, assoc. prof. mgmt. and labor, 1971-76; prof. econs., chmn. dept. econs. Wright State U., 1976-79; pres., economist Delphi Assocs., Inc., Cleve., 1972-76; economist, spl. rep. Columbus Mut. Life Ins. Co., 1980-86; v.p. Advance Planning Concepts, Inc., Cleve., 1984-85; registered rep. Integrated Resources Equity Corp., Cleve., 1983-85; registered rep., registered prin. Lowry Fin. Svcs. Corp., 1985-89, Mut. Svc. Corp., 1989—; broker, dealer, 1985—; economist, pres. I.A. Bell Fin. and Econ. Planning, Inc., Cleve.; registered investment advisor, 1986—; gen. agt. various life ins. cos., 1986—; cons. in field. Contbr. articles to profl. jours. With U.S. Army, 1955-57. U.S. Dept. Labor grantee, 1967-68. HUD and Nat. League of Cities grantee, 1973-74; named Top of Table, Million Dollar Round Table, 1985. Mem. Nat. Assn. Life Underwriters, Cleve. Assn. Life Underwriters, Am. Econ. Assn., Indsl. Relations Rsch. Assn., Internat. Assn. Fin. Planning, Nat. Assn. Security Dealers, Securities Investor Protection Corp., Christian Family Movement (pres. Cleve. chpt. 1984-85). Avocations: yachting, swimming. Home: 19953 Idlewood Trail Strongsville OH 44136 Office: IA Bell Fin & Econ Planning Inc 11925 Pearl Rd #103 Cleveland OH 44136

IACOBUCCI, GUILLERMO ARTURO, chemist; b. Buenos Aires, Argentina, May 11, 1927; s. Guillermo Cesar and Blanca Nieves (Brana) I.; m. Constantina Maria Gullich, Mar. 28, 1952; children: Eduardo Ernesto, William George. MSc, U. Buenos Aires, 1949, PhD in Organic Chemistry, 1952. Came to U.S., 1962, naturalized, 1972. Research chemist E.R. Squibb Research Labs., Buenos Aires, 1952-57; research fellow in chemistry Harvard U., Cambridge, Mass., 1958-59, prof. phytochemistry U. Buenos Aires, 1960-61; sr. research chemist Squibb Inst. Med. Research, New Brunswick, N.J., 1962-66; head bio-organic chemistry labs. Coca-Cola Co., Atlanta, 1967-74, asst. dir. corp. research and devel., 1974-87, mgr. biochemistry and basic organic chemistry group, 1988—; adj. prof. chemistry Emory U., 1975—. John Simon Guggenheim Meml. Found. fellow, 1958. Fellow Am. Inst. Chemists; mem. AAAS, Assn. Harvard Chemists, Am. Chem. Soc., N.Y. Acad. Scis., Am. Soc. Pharmacognosy, Sigma Xi. Contbr. articles on organic chemistry to sci. jours. Patentee in field. Home: 160 North Mill Rd NW Atlanta GA 30328 Office: Coca Cola Co PO Drawer 1734 Atlanta GA 30301

IACOCCA, LIDO ANTHONY (LEE IACOCCA), automotive manufacturing executive; b. Allentown, Pa., Oct. 15, 1924; s. Nicola and Antoinette (Perrotto) I.; m. Mary McCleary, Sept. 29, 1956 (dec.); children—Kathryn Lisa Hentz, Lia Antoinette Nagy. BS, Lehigh U., 1945; ME, Princeton U., 1946. With Ford Motor Co., Dearborn, Mich., 1946-78; successively mem. field sales staff, various merchandising and tng. activities, asst. dirs. sales mgr. Ford Motor Co., Phila.; dist. sales mgr. Ford Motor Co., Washington, 1946-56; truck mktg. mgr. div. office Ford Motor Co., 1956-57, car mktg. mgr., 1957-60, vehicle market mgr., 1960, v.p.; gen. mgr. Ford Motor Co. (Ford div.), 1960-65, v.p. car and truck group, 1965-69, exec. v.p. of co., 1967-69, pres. of co., 1970-78; also pres. Ford Motor Co. (Ford N.Am. automobile ops.); pres., chief operating officer Chrysler Corp., Highland Park, Mich., 1978-79, chmn. bd., chief exec. officer, 1979—. Author: Iacocca: An Autobiography, 1984, Talking Straight, 1988. Past chmn. Statue of Liberty-Ellis Island Centennial Commn. Wallace Meml. fellow Princeton U. Mem. Tau Beta Pi. Club: Detroit Athletic. Office: Chrysler Corp 12000 Chrysler Dr Highland Park MI 48288

IACONE, MARGE, small business owner; b. Bklyn., Feb. 13, 1943; d. Thomas and Margaret Lucy Fiore; children: Donna Avanti, Debra Iacone. Student, Adelphia Sch. Bus., 1958, Morris County Vocat. Sch., 1977, Caldwell Coll., 1989. Gen. mgr. Guaranteed Premium Loan Co., Bklyn., 1963-65; claims inspector Universal Car Loading & Distbn., N.Y.C., 1965-68; quality motor control insp. Nash Controls, Fairfield, N.J., 1968-69; gen. mgr. Roman's Mobile Elec. Co., Caldwell, N.J., 1969-72; gen. mgr. Exptl. Plastic Molds Corp., Fairfield, 1972-86, owner, pres., 1986—. Contbr. articles to profl. jours. Indsl. commr. Fairfield Indsl. Commn., 1986-87; vice chmn. Mayor's Adv. Com., Fairfield, 1987-88; mem. The Steeple Fund Com., 1986-88. Fellow Soc. Plastics Industry, West Essex C. of C.; mem. Fairfield Bus. Industrialists (pres. 1986-89), Rotary (treas. 1987—, v.p. 1989—). Office: Exptl Plastic Molds Corp 3 Spielman Rd Fairfield NJ 07006

IAMS, JOSEPH THOMAS, accountant; b. Hamilton, Ohio, Dec. 6, 1954; s. John Winder and Helena Rita (Schott) I.; m. Ann Marie Thomas, June 2, 1979; children: Benjamin, Sean, Matthew. BBA, Xavier U., 1977. CPA, Ind. Acct. McGladrey Hendrickson Co., South Bend, Ind., 1982; controller Universal Bearings, Inc., Breman, Ind., 1982—. Blair Hills Community Assn. Recreation Com., Mishawaka, Ind., 1988. Mem. AICPAs, Ind. Soc. CPAs, Am. Mgmt. Assn., South Bend-Michawaka Area C. of C. Democrat. Roman Catholic. Office: Universal Bearings Inc 431 N Birkey Dr Breman IN 46506

IANZITI, ADELBERT JOHN, industrial designer; b. Napa, Calif., Oct. 10, 1927; s. John and Mary Lucy (Lecair) I.; student Napa Jr. Coll., 1947, 48-49; A.A., Fullerton Jr. Coll., 1950; student UCLA, 1950, Santa Monica Community Coll., 1950-51; m. Doris Moore, Aug. 31, 1952; children—Barbara Ann Ream, Susan Therese Shifflett, Joanne Lynn Lely, Jonathan Peter, Janet Carolyn Kroyer. Design draftsman Basalt Rock Co. Inc. div. Dillingham Heavy Constrn., Napa, 1951-66, chief draftsman plant engring., 1966-68, process designer, 1968-82, pres. employees assn., 1967; now self-employed indsl. design cons. Vice-pres., Justin-Siena Parent-Tchr. Group, 1967. Mem. Aggregates and Concrete Assn. No. Calif. (vice-chmn. environ. subcom. 1976-77), Am. Ordinance Assn., Constrn. Specifications Inst., Italian Catholic Fedn., Native Sons of the Golden West, World Affairs Coun. No. Calif. Republican. Roman Catholic. Clubs: Toastmasters, Commonwealth of Calif. Home and Office: 2650 Dorset St Napa CA 94558

ICAHN, CARL C., arbitrator and options specialist, corporation executive; b. Queens, 1936; m. Liba Icahn; 2 children. B.A., Princeton U., 1957; postgrad., NYU Sch. Medicine. Apprentice broker Dreyfus Corp., N.Y.C., 1960-63; options mgr. Tessel, Patrick & Co., N.Y.C., 1963-64, Gruntal & Co., 1964-68; chmn., pres. Icahn & Co., N.Y.C., 1968—; chmn., chief exec. officer ACF Industries Inc., Earth City, Mo., 1984—, also dir.; chmn. Trans World Airlines Inc., N.Y.C., 1986—, also dir. Office: Icahn & Co Inc 100 S Bedford Rd Mount Kisco NY 10549 other: ACF Industries Inc 3301 Rider Trail S Earth City MO 63045 *

ICE, JOAN ELIZABETH, real estate sales associate; b. Olympia, Wash., Aug. 9, 1938; d. Ira James McCullough and Myrtle Elizabeth (Nefstad) McCullough Shriner; m. Rodney Dean Ice, Mar. 21, 1958; children: Randal Dean, Rex Daryl, Ronald Dale. BS, Cen. State U., Edmond, Okla., 1981. V.p. Triar Enterprises, Edmond, 1976—. Lectr. Christian women's groups, 1971—. Baptist. Home: 1211 Johnson Dr Miami OK 74354 Office: Triar Enterprises PO Box 3042 Edmond OK 73083

ICHIKAWA, YOSHIO, wood trade company executive; b. Koriyama, Japan, Feb. 12, 1914; s. Keisaburo and Eyi I.; law degree U. Tokyo, 1938; m. Shizuko Satoh, May 26, 1946; children—Yoshiro, Shigeo. Mem. staff Ministry of Fin., 1938-48, chief investigator research dept., 1947-54; chief acct. Tobata Chem. Co., Ltd., Tokyo, 1954-74; mng. dir. Kinugasa Co., Ltd., Tokyo, 1964—; mng. dir. Daiwa Shoji Co., Tokyo. Buddhist. Mem. Tokyo C. of C. and Industry. Buddhist. Avocation: travel. Home: 1-1-2-913 Oyada, Adachi-ku, Tokyo 120, Japan Office: 219 Koskudoro Bldg, 10 Ginzanishi-8 chuo-ku, Tokyo 104, Japan

IDLEMAN, LARRY LYNN, utility company executive; b. Chanute, Kans., Dec. 13, 1938; s. Charles Lee and Hazel Adelle (McCoy) I.; m. Edith Marie Maher, Apr. 4, 1959; children: Jana Lynne, Jay Dee. AA, Independence (Kans.) Community Coll., 1965; BSEE, BBA, Kans. State U., 1969. Elec. engr. Ill. Power Co., Decatur, 1969-73; asst. mgr. Ill. Power Co., Champaign, Ill., 1973-75; dir. environ. affairs Ill. Power Co., Decatur, 1975-78, mgr. energy supply, 1978-83, mgr. indsl. relations, 1983-86, v.p., 1986—; bd. dirs. Council of Owners & Constrn. Assocs. Inc., Maryville, Ill., vice chmn., 1986, chmn. bd., 1987. Chmn. Employees Polit. Involvement Com., Decatur, 1982; bd. dirs. Jr. Engring. Tech. Soc., State of Ill., 1983. Served with USAF, 1959-63. Mem. IEEE, Ill. State C. of C., Metro Decatur C. of C., Edison Electric Inst., Am. Legion, Farm Bur., Etta Kappa Nu, Sigma Tau. Republican. Clubs: Southside Country. Office: Ill Power Co 500 S 27th St Decatur IL 62525

IDLEMAN, LEE HILLIS, investment company executive; b. Washington, June 13, 1933; s. Holland Beecher and Marion (Cox) I.; m. Sue Ann O'Connor, May 7, 1960; children: Douglas Lee, Christopher Holland, Scott Clark. BS in Commerce and Fin., Bucknell U., 1954. Chartered financial analyst. V.p., research analyst Merrill Lynch, Pierce, Fenner & Smith, N.Y.C., 1957-69; exec. v.p., dir. research Dean Witter Reynolds, N.Y.C., 1969-84; ptnr., dir. rsch., pension fund portfolio mgr. Neuberger and Berman, N.Y.C., 1984—; guest appearances on Today Show, Wall Street Week, Fin. News Network, CBS Radio, others. Contbr. articles to profl. jours. and newspapers. Trustee Bucknell U., vice chmn., exec. com., 1980—; chmn. troop com., treas. Boy Scouts Am., Madison, N.J., 1972-83. Served with U.S. Army, 1954-56. Named One of Top Five Wall St. Research Dirs., Instl. Investor, 1984. Mem. N.Y. Soc. Security Analysts, Inst. Chartered Fin. Analysts, N.Y. Stock Exchange (allied), Delta Mu Delta, Kappa Delta Rho (ordo hon.). Republican. Unitarian. Clubs: Williams (N.Y.C.); Noe Pond (Chatham, N.J.); Bison (Lewisburg, Pa.) (exec. com. 1988—). Home: 35 Winding Way Madison NJ 07940 Office: Neuberger & Berman 522 Fifth Ave New York NY 10036

IGNASIK, ADAM, financial planner; b. Tarnow, Poland, Sept. 13, 1958; came to U.S., 1981; s. Marion and Stanislava (Klusek) I. BA, Oxford U., England, 1981. Analyst PKO-Polish Nat. Bank, N.Y.C., 1982-84; amalyst mkt. Drezdener Bank, N.Y.C., 1984-87; with estate-fin. planning Met. Life Ins. Co., N.Y.C., 1987—. Republican. Home: 128 2nd Ave New York NY 10003 Office: Met Life Ins Co 6027 Broadway Suite C New York NY 10471

IHLE, HERBERT DUANE, food company executive; b. Ames, Iowa, July 8, 1939; s. Joe and Martha Marie (Larson) I.; m. Catherine Eileen Klein, Dec. 27, 1959; children: Brenda Kirsten, Valerie Anne, Michael David. AA, Waldorf Jr. Coll., Forest City, Iowa, 1959; BA, Concordia Coll., Moorhead, Minn., 1961; MS, U. Minn., 1963. Dir. fin. planning Pillsbury Co., Mpls., 1976-78, sr. v.p. fin. Burger King, 1979-80, v.p. fin. foods, 1980-81, v.p., controller, 1981-82, exec. v.p., chief fin. officer Burger King, 1982-83, sr. v.p., controller, 1983—, sr. v.p., controller, treas., 1987—, exec. v.p. fin., 1989—; bd. dirs. Pillsbury Commodity Svcs., Chgo. Mem. Fin. Execs. Inst. (com. on corp. reporting, SEC subcom., com. on corp. fin.), Nat. Assn. Corp. Treas. Bd. dirs. Luth. Brotherhood, Mpls. Republican. Club: Mpls. Avocation: tennis. Home: 7782 Lochmere Terrace Edina MN 55435 Office: Pillsbury Co 4057 Pillsbury Ctr Minneapolis MN 55402

ILACQUA, ROSARIO S., securities analyst; b. Albany, N.Y., Aug. 12, 1927; s. Anthony and Carmela (Gerasia) I.; B.S., Siena Coll., 1950; M.S., Columbia, 1955. With L.F. Rothschild, N.Y.C., 1957-87 , ptnr., 1972-87, Nikko Securities, 1987—. Served with USNR, 1945-46. Chartered fin. analyst. Mem. Nat. Assn. Petroleum Investment Analysts (pres. 1977), N.Y. Soc. Security Analysts, Oil Analysts Group N.Y. (pres. 1972). Club: N.Y. Athletic. Home: 2 Horatio St New York NY 10014 Office: One World Fin Ctr A New York NY 10281

ILSTAD, GEIR (ARE), investment banker; b. Mo i Rana, Norway, Mar. 19, 1955; s. Johan Julius and Rønnaug Synnøve (Kristensen) I.; m. Prudence Burnett Herman, Dec. 1, 1984; 1 child, Bergen Burnett. Degree in Econs., U. de Fribourg, Switzerland, 1980; BS, MBA, Menlo Sch. Bus., Atherton, Calif., 1982. Fin. advisor Ilstad Group, Menlo Park, 1981; mgr. Bergen Bank A/S, Oslo, 1982-85; registered rep. First Investors Corp., San Francisco, 1984; project mgr. corp. fin. A.S. Factoring Finans, Oslo, 1985-86; pres., chmn. Prudent Mgmt., Inc., Menlo Park, 1986—. Sec. Nesodden Speed Skating Club, 1969-75, Unge Høyre, Nesodden, Norway, 1971. Served with paratroopers Norwegian Army, 1975-76. Mem. Norwegian Bus. Forum, Swedish-Am. C. of C. Home: 12620 Viscaino Ct Los Altos Hills CA 94022 Office: Prudent Mgmt Inc 683 Live Oak Ave Menlo Park CA 94025

IMBER, BRIAN LEE, electronics executive; b. Denver, June 9, 1959; s. Burton Moss and Mona (Adsley) I.; m. Victoria Patricia Cook, Sept. 4, 1988. BA, U. Colo., 1983; postgrad., U. San Francisco, 1987—. Geophys. technician Robert Klipping Cons., Denver, 1981-83; geologist Willard Owens Cons., Denver, 1984-85; systems engr. Electronic Data Systems, San

Francisco, 1985-86; program mgr. Nat. Semicondr., Santa Clara, Calif., 1986-88; mktg. project mgr. Hewlett-Packard Corp., 1988—. Mem. World Affairs Council, Bay Area Soc. Info. Ctrs. Club: Commonwealth (San Francisco). Office: Hewlett-Packard Corp Mountain View CA 95051

IMERSHEIN, RICHARD EDWARD, sales executive; b. N.Y.C., Dec. 6, 1927; s. Louis E. and Rosetta Charlote (Kaufman) I.; m. Virginia Lee Mize, June 21, 1952; children: Deborah, Diane, Deidre. BA in Mech. Engring., Clemson Coll., 1948. With svc. sales and mktg. and comml. analysis Regional Div. and Corp. Hdqrs. Br. Office IBM, various cities, U.S. and Fed. Republic of Germany, 1956-64; v.p. corp. RAS, Stamford, Conn., 1982-86, sr. v.p. internat. sales and mktg., 1986-88; sr. v.p. quality and edn. Gartner Group Inc., Stamford, Conn., 1989—; chmn. U.S. com. for Internat. Fedn. Info. Processing 9th World Computer Congress of Am. Fedn. Info. Processing Soc., Reston, Va., 1981-89, advisor 10th and 11th congresses. bd. dirs. Union Am. Hebrew Congregations, N.Y.C., 1982-90; pres. REFRESH, Stamford, 1980-86. 1st lt. USAF, 1951-53, capt. USAFR. Mem. Assn. for Computing Machinery. Republican. Jewish. Lodge: Temple Brotherhood. Office: Gartner Group Inc 56 Top Gallant Rd Stamford CT 06902

IMHOFF, RICHARD JAMES, bank officer, financial planner; b. Boonville, June 4, 1958; s. James Alvin and Clara Mae (Hurt) I.; m. Angela Marie Hutchinson, Dec. 28, 1979; children: Anna Michelle, Danielle Dominique. Student, Columbia (Mo.) Coll., 1976-78; grad., Coll. for Fin. Planning, 1987; student, Nicholls State U., 1988—. Rep., fin. planner NIS Fin. Svcs. Inc., Kansas City, Mo., 1979-84, Waddell and Reed Fin. Svcs./United Investors Life Ins. Co., Kansas City, Mo., 1984-85, IDS Fin. Svcs., Houma, La., 1985; trust officer, fin. planner Premier Bank South La., Houma, 1985—. Lay minister Maria Immacolata Cath. Ch., Houma, 1985—, chmn. fin. com., 1987—; speaker various civic and social orgns. Mem. Inst. Cert. Fin. Planners, Internat. Assn. for Fin. Planning, K.C. Republican. Office: Premier Bank South La 720 E Main St PO Box 5036 Houma LA 70361

IMMESBERGER, HELMUT, lawyer; b. Bad Durkheim, W.Ger., Feb. 24, 1934; s. Friedrich Wilhelm and Luise Klara (Schaumloeffel) I.; student U. Mainz, 1953-57, Speyer Coll. Adminstrn., 1959; LL.D., Fed. Acad. Fiscal Mgmt., Siegburg, 1962; m. Doris Pillat, June 24, 1957; children—Jutta, Stephan, Thomas, Petra. With Bad Kreuzhach Taxation Dept. 1961-62; with Kaiserslautern Taxation Dept., 1962-85, adminstrn. dir., 1972-85 . Chmn. Christian Democratic Union parliamentary deputation Kaiserslautern Municipal Council, 1978-85, mng. bd., Kaiserlautern Gas Works, Inc., 1986—. Author: Zur Problematik der Abgeordneten im Deutschen Bundestag, 1962; Das Recht der Konzessionsabgaben, 1988; contbr. articles to profl. jours. Named hon. citizen Davenport, Iowa. Home: 72 Rostocker Strasse, D-6750 Kaiserslautern Federal Republic of Germany

INADOMI, ROBERT JOHN, supermarket executive; b. Los Angeles, Mar. 1, 1948; s. Yosh and Ruth K. Inadomi; m. Peggy Ann Ishikawa, July 24, 1971; children: Mary Catherine, Robert Yosh. BBA, U. Calif., Berkeley, 1969; MS in Mgmt., MIT, 1971. Asst. to gen. mgr. Boise Cascade Corp., Honolulu, 1971-74; dir. corp. devel. JonSons Markets, Inc., Los Angeles, 1974-78; gen. mgr. Jonsons Markets, Inc., Los Angeles, 1978-85, pres., 1985—; Mem. Coca Cola Retailing Research Council, Atlanta, 1985—. Mem. adv. bd. Mexican-Am. Grocers Assn., Los Angeles, 1985—, Food For All, Los Angeles, 1986—. Mem. Calif. Grocers Assn. (bd. dirs. 1987—) So. Calif. Grocers Assn., Food Mktg. Inst. (mem. operating execs. council 1985—), Cert. Growers Calif. (bd. dirs. 1989—), Beta Gamma Sigma. Clubs: MIT of So. Calif. (Los Angeles), Santa Monica Tennis. Office: JonSons Markets Inc 3425 Whittier Blvd Los Angeles CA 90023

INATOME, RICK, retail computer company executive; b. Detroit, July 27, 1953; s. Joseph T. and Atsuko Nan (Kumagai) I.; m. Joyce Helene Kitchen, Aug. 18, 1979; children: Dania Lynn, Evan Richard, Blake Everett, Jaron Grant. BA in Econs., Mich. State U., 1976. Vice pres., gen. mgr., founder Computer Mart, Inc., Clawson, Mich., 1976-82, pres., chief exec. officer, 1982—; lectr., cons. computers; mem. AT&T Adv. Council, 1987—, Microsoft Dealer Council , 1983-85, Ashton Tate Adv. Bd., 1987—, IBM Exec. Council, 1985-86, Apple Dealer Adv. Bd., 1983-84, Computer Reseller Mag. Avd. Bd. Mem. Mich. Minority Bus. Adv. Council, 1986—, Mich. Lottery Commn., 1988—, Mich. Small Bus. and Entrepreneur Commn., 1989—; bd. gov's. Cranbrook Inst. Sci., 1985—; mem. adv. bd. Ctr. for Entrepreneurship, Ea. Mich. U., 1986-88, Gov's. Entrepreneurial & Small Bus. Commn., 1989—. Recipient Entrepreneur Yr. award Harvard U. Bus. Club, Detroit, Leadership award Mich. State U. Grad. Sch. Bus., 1986; named Oustanding Young Man of 1984, Jaycees, Michiganian of Yr. Detroit News, 1985. Mem. Engring. Soc. Detroit, Am. Mgmt. Assn., ACM, Lotus Dealer Council, Software Publishing Exec. Council, Mich. State U. Alumni Assn. (bd. dirs. 1989—), Phi Delta Theta. Office: Inacomp Computer Ctrs Inc 1800 W Maple Rd Troy MI 48084

INCANDELA, JOSEPH JOHN, manufacturing company executive; b. Bklyn., Oct. 31, 1946; s. Gasper and Adeline (Riena) I.; m. Deborah Jean Wilson, Oct. 9, 1982; children: Cara Beth, Jonathon Lee. BS in Econs., Wagner Coll., 1968; postgrad., U. Detroit, 1970-71, Loyola U., Chgo., 1972. Personnel asst. Thomas & Betts Corp., Raritan, N.J., 1968, mgr. bus. unit, 1980-81; sales rep. office equipment Thomas & Betts Corp., Mich. and Chgo., 1969-72; several mktg. mgmt. positions Thomas & Betts Corp., Calif., 1972-79, div. gen. mgr., 1981-83; pres., chief exec. officer Conductron Corp., Leominster, Mass., 1983-86; chmn., chief exec. officer Amerace Corp., Parsippany, N.J., 1986—; bd. dirs., advisor JMMC, Jamestown, N.Y., Middco Corp., Conn., Kopflex Corp. Mem. Rep. Nat. Com., Washington, 1984-86; pres. MAPI council. Mem. Am. Mktg. Assn., Am. Elect. Assn. (bd. dir. 1985-87, chmn., capt. forum task force 1985-86), Young Pres. Orgn. Roman Catholic. Office: Amerace Corp 8 Campus Dr Arbor Cir S Parsippany NJ 07054

INDIEK, VICTOR HENRY, finance corporation executive; b. Spearville, Kans., Nov. 15, 1937; s. Ben W. and Helen Ann (Schreck) I.; m. Marlene Gould, June 2, 1962; children: Kathy, Kevin. Student, U. Nebr., 1955-57; BS in Bus., U. Kans., 1959; postgrad., U. Nebr., 1955-57. CPA, Kans. Audit mgr. Arthur Andersen & Co., Kansas City, Mo., 1961-70; pres., chief exec. officer Fed. Home Loan Mortgage Corp., Washington, 1970-77; pres., dir. Builders Capital Corp., Los Angeles, 1977-84; chief fin. officer, exec. v.p. Fin. Corp. of Am., Irvine, Calif., 1984-88; pres., chief exec. officer FarWest Savs. and Loan Assn., Newport Beach, Calif., 1988—; v.p. and pres. regional Assn. Small Businesses Investment Cos., 1979-81, bd. govs. nat. assn., 1982. Mem. Selective Service Bd., Santa Monica, Calif., 1978; capt. United Fund, Kansas City, 1968. Served with USN, 1959-61. Republican. Roman Catholic. Office: FarWest Savs & Loan Assn 4001 MacArthur Blvd Newport Beach CA 92660

INFUSO, JOSEPH, printing executive; b. Bklyn., May 19, 1927; s. Joseph and Rosalia (Marcantonio) I.; m. Josephine Rose Arcuria; children: Joseph, Louis, Glen, Rosalie. Grad. high sch., Bklyn. V.p. Queens Group of Calif., Inc., Hollywood, 1957—. Democrat. Roman Catholic. Home: 763 Lynnmere Dr Thousand Oaks CA 91360 Office: Queens Group Calif Inc 6290 Sunset Blvd Hollywood CA 90028

INGAGLIO, MICHAEL LOUIS, sales and marketing executive; b. Bklyn., Apr. 29, 1960; s. Alfred Joseph and Christina Ann (Caldararo) I. AASET, Queensborough Community Coll., 1981; BS in Elec. Engring. cum laude, Fairleigh Dickinson U., 1985. Sales rep., mgr. Radio Shack, Bklyn., 1977-80; crystal technician Frequency Electronics, Inc., L.I., N.Y., 1980-81; project leader Bell Labs. div. AT&T, Whippany, N.J., 1981-83; nat. program mgr. Hamilton/Avnet div. AT&T, Culver City, Calif., 1987-89; engr. telecommunications Bell Communications Rsch., Morristown, N.J., 1983-85; design engr., project mgr. Hughes Aircraft Co., Canoga Park, Calif., 1985-86; sales engr. Nat. Semiconductor Co., L.A., 1987; mgr. S.W. regional sales Sony Corp., Cypress, Calif., 1989—; pres., counselor Career Counseling Svcs., Irvine, Calif., 1986—, Home Based Solutions, 1989—; tchr. Learning Tree, Career Counseling, Chatsworth, Calif., 1987, Learning Activity, Bus. Consulting, Anaheim, Calif., 1989—. Patentee in field. Named Eagle Scout Boy Scouts Am. Democrat. Roman Catholic. Home: 60 Alicante Aisle Irvine CA 92714 Office: Sony Corp 10833 Valley View St Cypress CA 90630

INGALLS, STEPHEN DAVID, finance executive; b. Wilmington, Del., Feb. 25, 1954; s. David Peabody and Beverly (Watt) I.; m. Elizabeth Mary Ceilestino, Apr. 16, 1988. BBA in Acctg. magna cum laude, U. Mass., 1976; MS in Fin., Bentley Coll., 1981. CPA, Mass. Acct. Laventhol & Horwath CPA's, Boston, 1976-78; controller Lynn Plastics Corp., Mass., 1978-80, John Solomon, Inc., Somerville, Mass., 1980-81; fin. con. Digital Equipment Corp., Maynard, Mass., 1981-83; strategic fin. mgr. Digital Equipment Corp., Littleton, Mass., 1983-85; mfg. controller Digital Equipment Corp., Westfield, Mass., 1985-87; mfg. fin. mgr. Digital Equipment Corp., Marlboro, Mass., 1987—; cons. Interactive Bus. Systems, Waltham, Mass., 1979-81. Leader Jr. Achievement, Salem, Mass., 1978. Mem. Am. Inst. CPA's. Republican. Home: 130 Webster St Arlington MA 02174 Office: Digital Equipment Corp 200 Forest St Marlborough MA 01752-3011

INGERMAN, MICHAEL LEIGH, business consultant; b. N.Y.C., Nov. 30, 1937; s. Charles Stryker and Ernestine (Leigh) I.; m. Madeleine Edison Sloane; Nov. 24, 1984; children by previous marriage: Shawn Marie, Jenifer Lyn. BS, George Washington U., 1963. Health planner, Marin County, Calif., 1969-70, 70-72; regional cons. Bay Area Comprehensive Health Council, San Francisco, 1972-73; hosp. cons. Booz, Allen & Hamilton, San Francisco, 1974; health planning coordinator Peralta Hosp., Oakland, Calif., 1975-76; pres. Discern, Inc., hosp. cons., Nicasio, Calif., 1976-88; ptnr. Decision Processes Internat., 1988—; instr. Golden Gate U., 1981-88. Capt. Nicasio Vol. Fire Dept., 1976-88; coord. Nicasio Disaster Commn., 1988—; dep. coroner Marin County, 1980-83; nat. bd. dirs. Am. Friends Svc. Com., 1980-81, bd. dirs. Hospice of Marin, 1983—, pres. bd. dirs., 1988—; bd. dirs. Friends Assn. Svc. for the Elderly, 1984—, pres. 1988—. Mem. Marin County Civil Grand Jury, 1977-78; mem. Nicasio Design Rev. Com., 1979-83; bd. dirs. John Woolman Sch., 1980-87. Office: Decison Processes Internat 2101 Nicasio Valley Rd Nicasio CA 94946

INGERSLEW, NEILL DENNIS, printing co. exec.; b. Kirksville, Mo., Oct. 6, 1934; s. John P. and Lissa (Madsen) I.; B.S. in Edn., U. Mo., 1958; m. Shirley Ann Bareis, Oct. 8, 1954; children—John, Susan, Cheryl, Nancy. With Western Pub. Co., Hannibal, Mo., 1956—, mgr. Data Page div., St. Charles, Mo., 1969-77, sr. v.p., mgr. Metomail div. R.R. Donnelley & Son, 1977—. Republican. Lutheran. Club: Masons (32 deg.). Home: 404 Lincoln St Seward NE 68434 Office: R R Donnelley & Son 901 W Bond St Lincoln NE 68521

INGHAM, GEORGE ALEXANDER, sales executive; b. Wakefield, Yorkshire, Eng., Feb. 14, 1936; s. Joseph Stanley and Katherine (Rennie) I.; m. Mavis Wood, Mar. 19, 1955; children: Veronica Ann, Janet Elizabeth, Martin Graham. Diploma in Mktg. and Econs., Leeds Sch. Commerce, 1959. Ptnr. Family Bus., Horbury, Eng., 1952-53; mgr. sales Granada TV, York, Eng., 1956-57; mgr. regional sales Lincoln Floor Maintenance, Farnborough, Eng., 1957—; bd. dirs. Bridge Mill Autos, Wakefield, Eng. 1984—. Served to sgt. Coldstream Guards, 1953-56. Fellow Inst. Mktg. and Sales Mgmt. Anglican. Club: Century (Ossett, Eng.) (pres. 1983—). Home: Grange View, Healey Rd, Ossett England Office: Lincoln Floor Maintenance, 4 Eelmoor Rd, Farnborough England GU14 7QR

INGRAHAM, JOHN WRIGHT, banker; b. Evanston, Ill., Nov. 10, 1930; s. Harold Gillette and Mildred (Wright) I.; m. Barbara Gaye Barker, Nov. 8, 1967; children—Kimberly, Elizabeth, Scott. A.B., Harvard U., 1952, M.B.A., 1957; postgrad., NYU Grad. Sch. Bus., 1963-68. Jr. lending positions Citicorp, N.Y.C., 1957-66, sr. lending positions, 1966-70, head instl. recovery mgmt., 1970-78, dep. chmn., credit policy com., 1979—, sr. v.p. oversight N.Am lending, 1979-84, sr. v.p. oversight Latin Am. lending, 1985-88, sr. v.p. oversight global pvt. bank lending and investing, 1988—; bd. dirs. Sprague Techs., Inc., Greenwich, Conn., Ark. Best Corp., Ft. Smith, 1984-88; chmn. audit com. Presto Industries, Houston, 1986-88; vice chmn. bd. Penn Central Corp., Cin., 1978—, chmn. fin. com., bd. dirs.; bd. dirs. Ark. Best Corp., Ft. Smith, 1968-75, 84-88; rep. of banking industry before House and Senate coms. and hearings, 1976-78. Trustee Noble and Greenough Sch., Dedham, Mass., 1987—; mem. bus. adv. council to dean U. Ark. Grad. Sch. Bus., Fayetteville, 1985—. Served to lt. USN, 1952-55, Korea. Recipient Disting. Service award Robert Morris Assocs., Phila., 1978. Mem. Fin. Acctg. Standards Bd. (task forces 1974-81), Robert Morris Assocs. (bd. dirs. 1972-75). Republican. Christian Scientist. Clubs: Union (N.Y.C.); Rockaway Hunting, Sleepy Hollow Country (N.Y.); Gulfstream Bath and Tennis (Fla.); Quogue Field; Ocean (Fla.). Home: 950 Park Ave New York NY 10028 Office: Citicorp 399 Park Ave New York NY 10043

INGRAHAM, SEARS WILSON, cosmetics company executive; b. Providence, Mar. 11, 1927; s. Earle Nye and Eunice Pauline (Wilson) I.; m. Laura King Ely, Feb. 3, 1951; children: Laura, Robert, Taylor. AB, Brown U., 1950. With Colgate Palmolive Co., 1951-62; exec. v.p. Noxell Corp., Balt., 1974—, also bd. dirs. Served to lt. (j.g.) USNR, 1945-54. Club: Camp Fire (Chappaqua, N.Y.) (treas. 1985-88); Wee Burn Country (Darien, Conn.). Office: Noxell Corp 200 Park Ave Ste 4404 New York NY 10166

INNES, JOHN PHYTHIAN, II, steel company and insurance company executive, lawyer; b. Indpls., Feb. 26, 1934; s. John Phythian and Eleanor (Tilton) I.; m. Marianne Berger, Oct. 29, 1966; children: Valerie Alexandra, James Walker, John Phythian. B.A., William Coll., 1955; J.D., Temple U., 1971. Bar: Pa. 1971, N.Y. 1973; airline transport rated pilot. Commd. U.S. Navy, 1955, advanced through grades to lt. comdr., 1966; served with U.S. Navy, Vietnam; ret. U.S. Navy, 1966; with U.S. Steel Co., 1966-68; atty. Asso. Aviation Underwriters, N.Y.C., 1971-73; asso. firm Speiser & Krause, N.Y.C., 1973-76; sec., gen. counsel Gulfstream Aero Corp., Savannah, Ga., 1976-86; mng. dir., pres. Boxhall Group, Inc., Houston, 1986—, Sabre Ins. Co. Ltd., Guernsey, Channel Islands, 1986—; vice chmn., bd. dirs. Wheeling-Pitts. Steel Corp.; bd. dirs. Wheeling-Nisshin Inc. Mem. ABA, Assn. of Bar of City of N.Y., Ft. Henry Club (Wheeling, W.Va.), Duquesne Club (Pitts.), Marshallwood at the Landings Club. Episcopalian. Home: 3 Barnwell Ln Savannah GA 31411 Office: Boxhall Group Inc 5718 Westheimer Ste 2100 Houston TX 77057

INSALACO, JOSEPH STEPHEN, financial services executive; b. Bklyn., Nov. 2, 1946; s. Michael and Pauline (Ambrosecchia) I.; m. Cheryl Phylis Thristino, May 31, 1969; children: Joseph, Michael, Corinne. BBA, Hofstra U., 1969; MBA, Adelphi U., 1984. CPA, N.Y. Auditor Arthur Anderson & Co., N.Y.C., 1970-76; fin. controller Citicorp Retail Services, N.Y.C., 1976-79, chief fin. officer, 1979-83; chief fin. officer Citibank, N.A., N.Y.C., 1983-85, regional fin. dir., 1985-87, dir. fin., 1987—. Mem. Am. Inst. CPA's, N.Y. State Soc. CPA's, Am. Mgmt. Assn. Republican. Office: Citibank 100 Baylis Rd Melville NY 11747

INSLEY, RICHARD WALLACE, lawyer, business executive; b. Tampa, Fla., Sept. 27, 1918; s. Levin Irving and Sadie Bell (Waddell) I.; m. Eleanor Jane Robinson, Oct. 22, 1945; children: Glen Thomas, Anne Insley McCausland. AB, Trinity Coll., Hartford, Conn., 1946; JD, U. Va., 1970; MBA, Harvard U., 1948. Bar: Mich. 1956. Mem. Richard W. Insley, Atty.-at-Law, St. Joseph, Mich., 1950—; pres. Southwestern Developers Inc., St. Joseph, 1960—, also bd. dirs.; pres. Whinco Inc., Pizza Hut franchisee, St. Joseph, 1969—, also bd. dirs.; v.p., sec. Jan Barb, Inc., Holiday Inn franchisee, St. Joseph, 1970—, also bd. dirs. Trustee Barat Coll., Lake Forest, Ill., 1972-82; mem. U.S. Senate Bus. Adv. Bd., Washington. Served to lt. USN, 1942-45. Decorated Silver Star. Mem. ABA, Mich. State Bar Assn., Berrien County Bar Assn. Republican. Episcopalian. Clubs: Point O'Woods Country, Berrien Hills Country (Benton Harbor, Mich.). Home: 278 Ridgeway Saint Joseph MI 49085 Office: 421 Main St PO Box 63 Saint Joseph MI 49085

IRAHA, MICHAEL MASAICHI, financial planning company executive; b. Honolulu, Dec. 23, 1948; s. Masao and Kay (Arakaki) I.; m. Jocelyn Ikeda, June 10, 1977; children: Kerensa Kendall, Christopher Michael. BBA in Mgmt., U. Hawaii, 1970. Cert. fin. planner, 1984. Mgmt. trainee Territorial Savs. and Loan, Honolulu, 1971; br. mgr., asst. v.p. Am. Savs. and Loan, Honolulu, 1971-76; sales agt. Investors Equity Life Ins., Honolulu, 1976-82; fin. planner Chamberlain and Assocs., Inc., Honolulu, 1982-86, Iraha Fin. Group, Honolulu, 1986—. Mem. Internat. Assn. for Fin. Planning (bd. dirs., v.p. edn. Hawaii chpt. 1987-88), Hawaii Soc. Inst. Cert. Fin. Planners (bd. dirs. 1987-88). Office: Iraha Fin Group 1001 Bishop St Pauahi Tower Ste 860 Honolulu HI 96813

IRANI, RAY R., chemical company executive; b. Beirut, Lebanon, Jan. 15, 1935; came to U.S., 1953, naturalized, 1956; s. Rida and Naz I.; m. Joan D. French; children: Glenn R., Lillian M., Martin R. BS in Chemistry, Am. U. Beirut, 1953; PhD in Phys. Chemistry, U. So. Calif., 1957. Sr. research group leader Monsanto Co., 1957-67; assoc. dir. new products, then dir. research Diamond Shamrock Corp., 1967-73; with Olin Corp., 1973-83, pres. chems. group, 1978-80; corp. pres., dir. Olin Corp., Stamford, Conn., 1980-83; exec. v.p. Occidental Petroleum Corp., Los Angeles, 1983-84, pres., chief operating officer, 1984—, also dir.; chmn., chief exec. officer subs. Occidental Chem. Corp., Norwalk, Conn., 1983—; bd. dirs. Am. Petroleum Inst. Author: Particle Size; also author papers in field; numerous patents in field. Trustee St. John's Hosp. and Health Ctr. Found., Natural History Mus. Los Angeles County. Mem. Soap and Detergent Assn., Chem. Mfrs. Assn. (bd. dirs.), Am. Inst. Chemists (hon. fellow award 1983), Am. Chem. Soc., Scientific Research Soc. Am., Indsl. Research Inst., Los Angeles C. of C. (bd. dirs.). Home: 250 Lost District Dr New Canaan CT 06840 Office: Occidental Petroleum Corp 10889 Wilshire Blvd Los Angeles CA 90024 also: Can Occidental Petroleum Ltd, 500 635 8th Ave S W, Calgary, AB Canada T2P 3Z1 •

IRELAND, JAMES DUANE, III, broadcasting company executive; b. Montgomery, W.Va., Jan. 1, 1950; s. James Duane and Cornelia (Allen) I.; m. Anne Hollis, Jan. 5, 1980; 1 child, James Duane IV. BA, Columbia U., 1972, postgrad., 1974-75. V.p. Salomon Bros. Inc., N.Y.C., 1975-82; gen. ptnr. RRY Ptnrs., Pineville, Pa., 1982-87; chmn. bd. dirs. Olympic Broadcasting Co., Seattle, 1985—; bd. dirs. Cleveland Cliffs Inc., Merrill-Ring, Seattle, Am. Water Devel. Co. Clubs: Racquet and Tennis, Brook (N.Y.C.); Piping Rock. Office: Olympic Broadcasting 605 First Ave Seattle WA 98104

IRMIERE-MARCHITTO, AMY FRANCES, securities trader; b. Paterson, N.J., Apr. 23, 1961; d. Frank Nicholas and Amedia Delores (Contini) Irmiere; m. Michael Otto Marchitto, Aug. 23, 1987. BS in Pub. Health Adminstrn. and Econs., Livingston Coll., 1984. With Drexel Burnham Lambert, N.Y.C., 1983—, N.Y. stock exchange options fl. broker, asst. v.p., 1987—. Republican. Roman Catholic. Home: 4 Avery Dr Old Bridge NJ 08857 Office: Drexel Burnham Lambert 60 Broad St New York NY 10004

IRMINGER, EUGENE HERMAN, telecommunications executive; b. Boise, Idaho, Feb. 16, 1929; s. Carl Eugene and Clara (Hirsbrunner) I.; m. Beatrice Evelyn Lawrence, June 20, 1953; children: Charles W., Steven E., Betticlare. Student, Boise Jr. Coll., 1948-49; BBA in Acctg. with honors, U. Wis., 1953. CPA, Ill. Staff auditor Arthur Andersen & Co., Chgo., 1956-61; mgr. adminstrv. services Arthur Andersen & Co., Indpls., 1961-66; comptroller Boise Cascade, 1966-72; v.p. fin. Permaneer Corp., St. Louis, 1972-73; v.p., controller Centel Corp., Chgo., 1973-82, sr. v.p., chief fin. officer, 1982—; pres. Centel Credit Co., Chgo., 1985-88. Mem. adv. coun. Northeastern Ill. U. Lt. (j.g.) USN, 1953-56. Mem. Fin. Execs. Inst. (bd. dirs. 1980-83, area v.p. 1982-83, pres. Nebr. chpt. 1975-76), AICPA, Ill. Soc. CPAs, Nat. Assn. Accts. (acctg. practices com. 1984-87, fin. com. 1987—). Republican. Methodist. Home: 1 W Onwentsia Rd Lake Forest IL 60045 Office: Centel Corp 8725 Higgins Rd Chicago IL 60631

IRVIN, GERARD THOMAS, retail executive; b. Mpls., Sept. 28, 1958; s. Richard Eugene and Valerie Ann (Mellberg) I.; m. Janet Grace Grove, Oct. 15, 1983; 1 child, Katie Scarlett. Student, Macalester Coll., 1977-78. Warehouse clk. The Musicland Group, Mpls., 1975-78, group leader, 1978-80, supr. purchasing, 1980-84, mgr. purchasing, 1984—. Roman Catholic. Home: 11974 70th Pl N Maple Grove MN 55369 Office: Musicland Group 7500 Excelsior Blvd Minneapolis MN 55426

IRVINE, RICHARD HAMLIN, entertainment company executive; b. Los Angeles, May 28, 1941; s. Richard F. and Ann (Nerney) I.; m. Elizabeth Thompson, May 19, 1962; 1 child, Elizabeth Ann. Student, U. So. Calif., 1959-63. Pres. Walt Disney Ednl. Media Co., Burbank, Calif., 1970-75, Straight Arrow Pubs., San Francisco, 1974-75; exec. v.p. IDC Services, Los Angeles, 1975-78; pres. Aurora Prodns., Los Angeles, 1978-85; exec. v.p. Internat. Game Tech., Reno, 1985—; bd. dirs. Channel 5 TV Pub. Broadcasting, Reno. Exec. producer (films) Secret of Nimh, 1981, Eddie and The Cruisers, 1983, Heart Like A Wheel, 1983, Maxi, 1985. Home: 6319 Windy Meadow Dr Reno NV 89509 Office: Internat Game Tech 520 S Rock Blvd Reno NV 89502

IRVING, EDWARD MUIR, corporate executive, chemical engineer; b. London, Ont., Canada, Sept. 6, 1928; came to U.S., 1947; s. Edward and Rose A. (McEwan) I.; m. Catherine Ann Aloia, June 14, 1953. B.S. in Chem. Engring., N.J. Inst. Tech., 1955. With Inmont Corp., 1947-83, on internat. assignment, 1963-70; in sr. mgmt. positions Inmont Corp., Clifton, N.J., 1970-80; pres., chief exec. officer Inmont Corp., Clifton, 1980-83; corp. officer United Techs. Corp., Hartford, Conn., 1982—; sr. v.p. Indsl. Group, United Techs. Corp., Hartford, 1983—. Mem. Am. Chem. Soc., Am. Inst. Chem. Engrs., Tau Beta Pi. Clubs: Bloomfield Hills (Mich.) Country; Detroit Athletic. Office: United Techs Corp United Techs Bldg Hartford CT 06101

IRVING, ROBERT CHURCHILL, safety engineer, manufacturing company executive; b. Waltham, Mass., Sept. 15, 1928; s. Frederick Charles and Emily Alvina (Churchill) I.; A.S., Franklin Inst. of Boston, 1965; cert. of profl. achievement Northeastern U., 1975; children—Robert F., John W. Sr. draftsman Mason-Neilan, Boston, 1948-54; mgr. design services Kinney Vacuum Co., Gen. Signal Corp., Boston, 1955-69; mgr. engring. services Sturtevant div. Westinghouse Electric Corp., Hyde Park, Mass., 1969-81, supr. quality assurance, 1981-84; mgr. engring. services Am. Davidson, Inc., Hyde Park, Mass., 1984-87, mgr. quality control, 1987—. Served with U.S. Army, 1946-48. Mem. Am. Def. Preparedness Assn., Am. Soc. for Quality Control (sr.), Am. Security Council, Am. Legion. Home: 11 Linda Ave Brockton MA 02401 Office: One Westinghouse Pla Hyde Park MA 02136

IRWIN, DIANE LOIS, administrator; b. Plattsburgh, N.Y., Apr. 27, 1932; d. Donald Herbert and Alberta Marion Prevost. BA in English, SUNY, Plattsburgh, 1969, cert. in Psychology and Counseling, 1973. Field dir., exec. dir. North Country Girl Scouts U.S.A., Plattsburgh, N.Y., 1970-72; exec. dir. Sr. Citizens Coun. Clinton County, 1974-79; dir. adult edn., counselor Saratoga/Warren Bd. Coop. Ednl. Svcs., N.Y.C., 1978-80; exec. dir. svcs. Montgomery (Ala.) Area on Aging, 1979-80, exec. dir., 1981-82; bus. mgr. Danville (Va.)/Pittsylvania Dept. Mental Health, 1983-86; mgr., adminstr. Greensboro (N.C.) C. of C., 1987—. Mem. Adminstrv. Women's Soc. Am., Assn. Counselors and Coll. Educators. Office: 5605 Virgilwood St Greensboro NC 27409 Office: Greensboro C of C PO Box 3246 Greebsboro NC 27402

IRWIN, JOE ROBERT, banker; b. Madison, Wis., Feb. 2, 1936; s. Malcolm Robert and Margaret (House) I.; m. Mary Lee Richardson, Aug. 16, 1958; children—Julie, Tom, Molly, Laurie. B.S., U. Wis., Madison, 1958, U. Wis., Madison, 1963. Exec. v.p. Pitts. Nat. Bank, 1963—; lectr. U. Wis., Madison, 1978—; instr. Bankers Assn. Sch. Fin. Mgmt.; dir. Blue Cross of Western Pa. Mem. exec. com. Pa. Economy League, Inc.; ruling elder Westminster Presbyn. Ch. Served to lt. (j.g.) USN, 1958-61. Clubs: Pitts. Sportsmen's Luncheon (treas. 1975-88), Duquesne, Ruffed Grouse Soc. (nat. dir.), St. Clair Country, Ruffed Grouse Soc. (bd. dirs. Pa. chpt. 1987—). Office: Pitts Nat Bank 5th Ave & Wood St Pittsburgh PA 15265

IRWIN, JOHN ROBERT, oil and gas drilling executive; b. Melbourne, Australia, July 24, 1945; came to U.S., 1969; s. Robert and Daisy (Minnie) I.; m. Margo Mayon, 1979; children: Joshua, Elizabeth. BE with honors, Melbourne U., M Engring. Sci., 1969; MS in Indsl. Adminstrn., Purdue U., 1970. Chartered engr. Various fin. positions Kerr-McGee Corp., Okla, Wis., Tex., La., 1970-72; engring. positions Kerr-McGee Corp., Wales, Scotland, Denmark, Singapore and Burma, 1972-75; mgr. ops. Transworld Drilling Co. (subs. Kerr-McGee Corp.), Sharjah, Nigeria and La., 1975-79; mgr. ops. Atwood Oceanics, Inc., Houston, 1979-80, gen. mgr., 1980, v.p., 1980-88, exec. v.p., 1988—; bd. dirs. Internat. Assn. Drilling Contractors, Gt. Atwood, Ltd. Fellow Inst. Engrs. Australia; mem. Coll. Civil Engrs., Soc. Petroleum Engrs., Inst. Mining, Metallurg., Petroleum Engrs., Westlake Club (Houston). Office: Atwood Oceanics Inc Box 218350 Houston TX 77218

IRWIN, JOSEPH AUGUSTUS, banker; b. Cleve., Apr. 3, 1936; s. Joseph Tilden and Naomi Eleanor I.; m. Barbara Joan Clever, July 9, 1960; children: Linda, Donald, Phillip. B.A. magna cum laude, Dyke Coll., Cleve., 1960. C.P.A., Ohio. With IRS, Cleve., 1960-68; mgr. tax dept. Sherwin-Williams Co., Cleve., 1968-71; corp. tax dir. Burroughs Corp., Detroit, 1971-74; sr. v.p. Security Pacific Nat. Bank, Los Angeles, 1974—, Security Pacific Corp., 1981—. Served with U.S. Army, 1955-58. Mem. Internat. Fiscal Assn., Tax Execs. Inst., Nat. Assn. Rev. Appraisers, Am. Inst. C.P.A.s, Am. Bankers Assn., Calif. Bankers Assn., Ohio Soc. C.P.A.s, Calif. Taxpayers Assn. (dir.), Los Angeles Internat. Tax Club. Clubs: Los Angeles Internat., Jonathan (Los Angeles).

IRWIN, LAWRENCE BURTON, accountant; b. Cleve., Mar. 21, 1947; s. Lawrence M. and Barbara L. (Boer) I.; m. Shirley Kay Meece, Feb. 27, 1971; children: Shane, Lesley, Margaret. BS in Acctg., U. Ill., 1969; MBA in Fin., Ohio State U., 1970. CPA, Ill.; lic. real estate broker, Ill.; cert. fin. planner, Ill. Acct. Arthur Andersen & Co., Chgo., 1971-72; dir. fin. planning Advance Schs., Inc., Chgo., 1972-74; sr. fin. analyst Baxter Travenol, Deerfield, Ill., 1974-76; pres. Burton Group, Schaumburg, Ill., 1976—; real estate broker Burton Investment Properties, Inc., Schaumburg, 1981—; fin. planner Burton Fin. Planning, Inc., Schaumburg, 1985—. Pres. Barrington (Ill.) PTA, 1982; mem. sch. bd. adv. com. Barrington, 1985. Served to lt U.S. Army, 1970-71. Named Eagle Scout, Boy Scout Am., 1960. Mem. Am. Inst. CPAs, Ill. CPA Soc., Barrington (Ill.) C. of C., NW Suburban Assn. of Commerce. Republican. Episcopalian. Home: 206 Otis Rd Barrington IL 60010 Office: Burton Assocs 921 N Plum Grove Rd Schaumburg IL 60173

IRWIN, MIRIAM DIANNE OWEN, miniature book publisher, writer; b. Columbus, Ohio, June 14, 1930; d. John Milton and Miriam Faith (Studebaker) Owen; m. Kenneth John Irwin, June 5, 1960; 1 child, Christopher Owen Irwin. BS in Home Econs., Ohio State U., 1952, postgrad. in bus. adminstrn., 1961-62. Editorial asst. Am. Home Mag., N.Y.C., 1953-56; salesman Owen Realty, Dayton, Ohio, 1957-58, Clevenger Realty, Phoenix, 1958-59; home economist Columbus and So. Ohio Electric Co., 1959-60; pub. Mosaic Press, Cin., 1977—; owner Bibelot Bindery, 1987—. Author: Lute and Lyre, 1977, Forty is Fine, 1977, Miriam Mouse's Survival Manual, 1977, Miriam Mouse's Costume Collection, 1977, Miriam Mouse's Marriage Contract, 1977, Miriam Mouse, Rock Hound, 1977, Silver Bindings, 1983; editor: Tribute to the Arts, 1984; contbg. author Publisher's Favorite, 1988; illustrator: Corals of Pennekamp, 1979. Daytime crew chief Wyoming Life Squad, Ohio, 1966-71. Mem. Internat. Guild Miniature Artisans, Miniature Book Soc. (bd. dirs. 1983—, chairperson 1987-89), Am. Philol. Assn., DAR, Soc. for Promotion of Byzantine Studies, Wyo. Women's Club. Republican. Presbyterian. Avocation: book collecting. Home and Office: 358 Oliver Rd Cincinnati OH 45215

ISAACS, KENNETH S(IDNEY), psychoanalyst, educator; b. Mpls., Apr. 7, 1920; s. Mark William and Sophia (Rai) I.; m. Ruth Elizabeth Johnson, Feb. 21, 1951 (dec. 1967); m. Adele Rella Bodroghy, May 17, 1969; children—Jonathan, James; stepchildren—John, Curtis, Peter and Edward Meissner. B.A., U. Minn., 1944; Ph.D., U. Chgo., 1956; postgrad., Inst. Psychoanalysis, 1957-63. Intern Worcester State Hosp., Mass., 1947-48; trainee VA Mental Hygiene Clinic, Chgo., 1948-50; chief psychologist outpatient clinic system Ill. Dept. Pub. Welfare, 1949-56; research assoc., assoc. prof. U. Ill. Med. Sch., Chgo., 1956-63; practice psychoanalysis Evanston, Ill., 1960—; supr. psychiat. residency program Evanston Hosp., Northwestern U., 1972-81, Northwestern Meml. Hosp.; pres. Chgo. Ctr. Psychoanalytic Psychology, 1984-87; cons. to schs., hosps., clinics, pvt. practitioners and industry; sr. cons. Bata Consulting Ltd.; pres. Kenisa Drilling Co., Kenisa Securities Co., Kenisa Oil Co. Author: (book) Again with Feeling, (syndicated newspaper column) A Psychologist's Notebook; contbr. articles to profl. publs. Served with AUS, 1943-45, ETO. Mem. Am. Psychol. Assn. (bd. dirs. div. psychoanalysis), AAAS, Chgo. Psychoanalytic Soc., Am. Bd. Psychoanalysis (sec. bd. dirs.), N.Y. Acad. Sci., Sigma Xi.

ISAACS, ROBERT WOLFE, structural engineer; b. Clayton, N.Mex., Sept. 22, 1931; s. Robert Phillip and Eva Estella (Freeman) I.; student So. Meth. U., 1949-50, Amarillo Jr. Coll., Tex. Tech U.; BS in Civil Engring., UCLA, 1959; m. Ruth Marie Peffley, Jan. 12, 1951; children: Robert Philip, Jeannette Lucille Isaacs Darlington, Charlotte Ruth Isaacs Frye, Rebecca Grace Isaacs Brund. Structural engr. N.Am. Aviation, Rockwell Internat., L.A., 1959—. Asst. scoutmaster, com. mem., fund raiser, Order of Arrow Gt. Western council Boy Scouts Am., 1964—; patron L.A.County Mus. Art; active Rep. Party. With U.S. Army, 1955. Lic. profl. engr., Tex. Recipient Pride award N.Am Aviation Orgn., 1984; named Pacemaker of Scouting, 1966. Mem. ASCE, NRA (life), Calif. Rifle and Pistol Assn. (life), Nat. Muzzleloading Rifle Assn. (endowment life, So. Calif. rep. 1976—), Western States Muzzleloading Rifle Assn. (life, charter, sportsman award 1983), Calif. Muzzleloading Rifle Assn., Colo. State Muzzleloading Rifle Assn., Bakersfield (Calif.) Muzzleloaders, Nat. Assn. Primitive Riflemen, High Desert Muzzleloaders., Santa Fe Trail Rendezvous Assn. (Bourgeous 1988), Piute Mountain Men, Sante Fe Trail Gun, Rockwell Rod and Gun, Burbank Muzzle Loader, Masons. Condr. rsch. design and devel. press diffusion bonding of titanium, aircraft design and structure; underwing and overwing inflatable seals (structure liaison B-1B, final mate, asst. checkout B-1B). Home: 1028 H-1 Lancaster CA 93534 Office: AF Plant 42 Site 9 Palmdale CA 93550 also: NAm Aircraft Ops Palmdale Facility 2825 E Ave P Palmdale CA 93550

ISAACS, S. TED, engineering company executive; b. Louisville, July 13, 1914; s. Max and Rose (Kaplan) I., m. Ann Fabe, June 7, 1939; children: Marjorie McKelvey, Susan L. Freund. BS in Chem. Engring., U. Cin., 1936, AA, 1944. Registered profl. engr. , Ohio; cert. sr. grade fluid power tech. Instrument engr. Standard Oil Co. Ohio, Latonia, Ky., 1936-41; instrumentation mgr. Wright Aero. Corp., Lockland, Ohio, 1941-45; sr. process engr. Drackett Co., Cin., 1945-48; pres. The Isaacs Co., Cin., 1948-86; mng. gen ptnr. AFTI Systems, Cin., 1986—; v.p. sales, pres. Indsl. Engring. Corp., Louisville, 1951-55. Contbr. articles to profl. jours. Energy commn. chmn. City Environ. Task Force, Cin., 1970-72. Mem. Instrument Soc. Am. (sr., life, local bd. dirs. 1946-47), Engring. Soc. Cin. (life, pres. jr. chpt. 1947-48), Fluid Power Soc., Metric Assn. (v.p. 1962-65), Sierra Club., Ohio Assn. Railway Passengers. Democrat. Jewish. Home: 8080 Springvalley Dr Cincinnati OH 45236 Office: AFTI Systems 1840 Amberlawn Dr Cincinnati OH 45237

ISAACSON, ARLINE LEVINE, food and beverage/hotel executive; b. Bklyn., Jan. 28, 1946; d. Harry and Sally (Fogelman) Levine; m. Leslie Robert Isaacson, Oct. 31, 1964 (div. July 1970); 1 child, Eric Michael. A.A.S. in Hotel and Restaurant Mgmt., N.Y.C. Tech. Coll., 1983. Restaurant and lounge mgr. Holiday Inn, N.Y.C., 1982-83; mgr. Astors, St. Regis Hotel, N.Y.C., 1983-84; banquet and conf. mgr. Mariner 15 Conf. Ctr., N.Y.C., 1984-85; dir. banquets, confs. and sales Sardi's Restaurant Corp., N.Y.C., 1985-87; dir. catering sales Days Inn Hotel, N.Y.C., 1987—. Dem. vol. Koch Relection Campaign, N.Y.C., 1985. Mem. Food and Beverage Mgrs. Assn. (sec. 1984-88), Roundtable for Women in Food Service (treas. 1986-87), Meeting Planners Internat., Soc. Incentive Travel, Hotel Sales and Mktg. Assn., Internat. Food Service Execs., N.Y.C. Tech. Coll. Alumni Assn. (bd. dirs. 1986—, v.p. 1986-87). Jewish. Avocations: dancing; travel; theatre; gourmet cooking. Home: 1836 E 18th St Brooklyn NY 11229 Office: Days Inn Hotel 440 W 57th St New York NY 10019

ISAACSON, BURTON CHARLES, electronics company executive; b. Chgo., July 30, 1943; s. Julius and Isabelle (Newman) I.; B.S. in B.A., Roosevelt U., 1966; m. Aug. 15, 1971; 2 children. Sr. acct. Peat, Marwick, Mitchell & Co., Chgo., 1968-70; controller, asst. sec. 1st Nat. Bank of Highland Park (Ill.), 1970-73; v.p. fin. and adminstrn. Jefco Labs., Inc., Chgo., 1973-79; asst. treas. Helene Curtis Industries, Inc., Chgo., 1979-84; asst. treas. Western Pub. Co., Racine, Wis., 1984-88; chief fin. officer Mortara Instrument, Inc., Milw., 1988— . Served with Fin. Corps, U.S. Army, 1966-68.

ISAACSON, GARY ALAN, television producer; b. Dayton, Ohio, Apr. 6, 1952; s. Howard Benton and Rita Jane (Katz) I. BA, Oberlin (Ohio) Coll., 1974; MBA, Ind. U., 1976. Pres. Isaacson Communications, Inc., Dayton, 1976—. Writer, producer TV documentary: 21st Century Dayton, 1981 (nominated IRIS and Emmy awards 1982), Making Things Happen, 1985 (nominated Emmy 1986); TV series: Economic Outlook, 1982, The Pen of Mike Peters, 1988. Mem. Citizens Advisory for Dayton Pub. TV, 1984—; mem. Montgomery County Dem. Party, Dayton, 1988—. Recipient Gratitude award, The Spl. Olympics, 1981. Mem. Nat. Acad. TV Arts and Scis. (gov. Ohio 1980-84), Meadowbrook Club (Dayton), Dayton Racquet Club, Metro West Country Club, Citris Club (Orlando, Fla.). Jewish. Office: Isaacson Communications Inc 4385 Tam O'Shanter Kettering OH 45429

ISELY, HENRY PHILIP, association executive, integrative engineer; b. Montezuma, Kans., Oct. 16, 1915; s. James Walter and Jessie M. (Owen) I; m. Margaret Ann Sheesley, June 12, 1948; children—Zephyr, LaRock, Lark, Robin, Kemper, Heather Capri. Student S. Oreg. Jr. Coll., Ashland, 1934-35, Antioch Coll., 1935-37. Organizer, Action for World Fedn., 1946-50, N.Am. Coun. for People's World Conv., 1954-58; organizer World Com. for World Constl. Conv., 1958, sec. gen., 1959-66; sec. gen. World Constn. and Parliament Assn., Lakewood, Colo., 1966—, organizer worldwide prep. confs., 1963, 66, 67, 1st session People's World Parliament and World Constl. Conv. in Switzerland, 1968, editor assn. bull. Across Frontiers, 1959—; co-organizer Emergency Coun. World Trustees, 1971, World Constituent Assembly at Innsbruck, Austria, 1977, Colombo, Sri Lanka, 1978-79, Provisional World Parliament 1st session, Brighton, Eng., 1982, 2d Session New Delhi, India, 1985, 3d Session Miami Beach, Fla., 1987, mem. parliament, 1982—; sec. Working Commn. to Draft World Constn., 1971-77; pres. World Svc. Trust, 1972-78; ptnr. Builders Found., Vitamin Cottages, 1955—; pres. Earth Rescue Corps, 1984—; sec.-treas. Grad. Sch. World Problems, 1984—; cabinet mem. Provisional World Govt., 1987—; pres. World Govt. Funding Corp., 1986—; sec. preparatory com. 1990 World Constituent Assembly, 1988—; sec., preparatory com. for the 1990 World Constituent Assembly; organizer Differential Greenhouse Action Network, 1989. Author: The People Must Write the Peace, 1950; A Call to All Peoples and All National Governments of the Earth, 1961; Outline for the Debate and Drafting of a World Constitution, 1967; Strategy for Reclaiming Earth for Humanity, 1969; Call to a World Constituent Assembly, 1974; Proposal for Immediate Action by an Emergency Council of World Trustees, 1971; Call to Provisional World Parliament, 1981; People Who Want Peace Must Take Charge of World Affairs, 1982; Plan for Emergency Earth Rescue Administration, 1985; Plan for Earth Finance Credit Corporation, 1987; Climate Crisis, 1989; handbook for provisional world govt. and provisional world parliament, 1988; co-author, editor: A Constitution for the Federation of Earth, 1974, rev. edit., 1977; also author several world legis. measures adopted at Provisional World Parliament; co-author Plan for Collaboration in World Constituent Assembly in 1990; Climat Crisis, 1989. Designer prefab modular panel system of constrn., master plan for Guacamaya project in Costa Rica. Candidate, U.S. Congress, 1958. Recipient Honor award Internat. Assn. Educators for World Peace, 1975, Gandhi medal, 1977. Mem. Soc. Internat. Devel., World Union, World Federalist Assn., World Future Soc., Earth Island Inst., Internat. Assn. for Hydrogen Energy, Global Edn. Assocs., Friends of Earth, Wilderness Soc., Denver Symphony Soc., Planetary Soc., Sierra Club, SANE, Global Futures Network, Amnesty Internat., ACLU, Am. Acad. Polit. and Social Sci., Nat. Nutritional Foods Assn., Environ. Def. Fund, Greenpeace, Internat. Studies Assn., War Resistors League, Audubon Soc., Worldwatch Inst., Nation Assocs., Debt Crisis Network, Mt. Vernon Country Club. Home: 241 Zephyr Ave Lookout Mountain Golden CO 80401 Office: 1480 Hoyt St Ste 31 Lakewood CO 80215

ISEMAN, MURRAY, insurance company executive; b. Phila., Mar. 13, 1943; s. Samuel M. Iseman and Ilene (Moskowitz) Goldstein; m. Eileen Barr, Dec. 19, 1964 (div. Feb. 1982); children: Sherri, Stephani, Wendi; m. Reva I. Goldman, Mar. 6, 1982; children: Mara, Randy. BA, Rider Coll., 1965; MA in Fin. Svcs., Am. Coll., 1980, MA in Mgmt., 1986. Chartered fin. cons.; registered fin. planner; CLU. Agt., Occidental Life Ins. Co. Am., Broomall, Pa., 1969-71; brokerage supr. Reliance Standard Life Ins. Co., Haddonfield, N.J., 1971-74; advanced sales cons. INA, Phila., 1974-76; dir. advanced sales Continental Am. Life Ins. Co., Wilmington, Del., 1976-79; v.p. mktg. Bankers Security Ins. Co., Arlington, Va.,1979-87; pres. U.S. Equities Corp., 1987—. Contbg. author: Seminar Selling, 1988; contbr. articles to Barrons' and profl. jours. Mem. D.C. Soc. CLU's (award 1981), Life Ins. Mktg. Rsch. Assn. (chmn. advance sales com. 1983-84), Eastern Agy. Officers Assn. (chmn.), Nat. Assn. Life Underwriters, Internat. Assn. Registered Fin. Planners (bd. govs.), Estate Planning Council, Cherry Hill Jaycees (v.p. 1973-77, Jaycee of Yr. 1975), Am. Soaring Soc. Republican. Jewish. Club: Mid-Atlantic Soaring Assn. Avocations: soaring, custom car construction, public speaking. Home: 11808 Rosalinda Dr Potomac MD 20854

ISHERWOOD, JOHN S., beverage company executive; b. 1940. BS, Groves City Coll., 1963. With Pitts. Brewing Co., 1963-78; gen. mgr. Cleve. Coca Cola Bottling Co. Inc., 1978-79; with G. Heileman Brewing Co. Inc., LaCrosse, Wis., 1979—, sr. exec. v.p., 1984—, also bd. dirs. Office: G Heileman Brewing Co Inc 100 Harborview Pla La Crosse WI 54601

ISHIKAWA, HIROSHI, reliability engineering educator; b. Kotohira, Kagawa, Japan, Nov. 29, 1941; s. Asataro and Fusano (Ohnishi) I.; m. Setsuko Kojima, Sept. 26, 1971; children: Chie, Yoko, Emiko. B.Sc., Kyoto U., 1964, M.S., 1966, Ph.D., 1969. Rsch. assoc. Kyoto U., 1969-76; rsch. assoc. Columbia U., N.Y.C., 1973-74, 77-79; assoc. prof. dept. info. sci. Kagawa U., Takamatsu, Japan, 1976-87, prof. 1987—; chmn. conf. organizing com. Internat. Conf. on Structural Safety and Reliability '85, 1983, 89, mem. conf. sci. com., 1986, sec.-gen. steering com., Japan Conf. on Structural Safety and Reliability '87, 1986; vice chmn. Com. on Promotion of Tech., Kagawa Prefecture, Takamatsu, Japan, 1985; editorial bd., Internat. Jour. Probabilistic Engring Mechanics C.M.L pubs., Eng. Co-author: Fatique of Metals and Machine Design, 1977; Introduction to Statistics, 1982; Structural Safety and Reliability, 1984; Linear Algebra, 1985, Practice of Reliability Engring., 1987. Ishikawajima-Harima Heavy Industries Ltd. grantee, 1982. Mem. Japan Soc. Materials Sci. (editorial bd. jour. 1979—), Japan Soc. Mech. Engrs. (reviewer 1980—), ASTM, Internat. Assn. for Structural Safety and Reliability, Japan Soc. Steel Constructions, Shikoku Soc. Materials Sci. (v.p. 1981—), Japan Statis. Soc. Home: 2-4-1 Tokiwa-cho, Takamatsu City, Kagawa 760, Japan Office: Kagawa U Dept Info Sci, 2-1 Saiwai-cho Takamatsu, Kagawa 760, Japan

ISNARD, ARNAUD JOSEPH, venture capitalist; b. Paris, Dec. 8, 1956; came to U.S., 1980; s. Louis and Jacqueline (Rongieras) I. Student, U. Arts and Metiers, Paris, 1978, Sch. Commerce and Industry, Paris, 1979. Ptnr. Barracuda SARL, Paris, 1978-80; bus. development exec. Thomson CSF, Los Angeles, 1980-83; internat. fin. exec. Thomson CSF, Paris, 1983-84; mng. dir. Venture Capital Fund Am. Inc., N.Y.C., 1984—, gen. ptnr., 1988—. Served with French Navy, 1977-78. Mem. Nat. Venture Capital Assn., N.Y. Venture Capital Forum. Office: Venture Capital Fund Am Inc 509 Madison Ave New York NY 10022

ISRAEL, VIVIANNE WINTERS, nurse; b. Inglewood, Calif., Mar. 29, 1954; d. Robert Reynolds and Annie Laura (Ripley) Winters; m. Richard Clyde Israel, May 30, 1976 (div. 1985); 1 child, Tiffany Carissa. RN, El Camino Coll., Torrance, Calif. Fashion model Los Angeles, 1957-70; critical care nurse Northridge Med. Ctr., Reseda, Calif., 1977-80, St. Joseph Med. Ctr., Burbank, Calif., 1980-81; exotic animal handler, trainer Gentle Jungle, Corona, Calif., 1980-81; coronary care nurse Mercy Med. Ctr., Reading, Calif., 1981-85; critical care nurse Norrell/CCSI, Los Angeles, 1985-87; pres. Pacific Coast Publs., Rolling Hills Estates, Calif., 1986—. Vol., co-dir. edn. Wildlife Way Sta., Little Tajunga, Calif., 1987—. Mem. Pubs. Mktg. Assn., Book Publicists of So. Calif., Book Publicists of San Diego, Execs. of S. Bay, Nat. Assn. Female Execs., Womens Internat. Network, Walters Internat. Speakers Bur., Internat. Assn. of Ind. Pubs. Baptist. Home: 1180 W Locust Ave Anaheim CA 92802 Office: Pacific Coast Pubs 710 Silver Spur Rd Ste 126 Rolling Hills Estates CA 90274

ISRAELOV, RHODA, financial planner, writer; b. Pitts., May 20, 1940; d. Joseph and Fannie (Friedman) Kreinen; divorced; children—Jerome, Arthur, Russ. BS in Hebrew Edn. Herzlia Hebrew Tchr.'s Coll., N.Y.C., 1961; BA in English Language and Lit. U. Mo.-Kansas City, 1965. Cert. Fin. Planner, Chartered Life Underwriter. Tchr. Hebrew, various schs., 1961-79; ins. agt. Conn. Mut. Life, Indpls., 1979-81; fin. planner Shearson, Lehman, Hutton, Inc., Indpls., 1981—, v.p., 1986—; instr. for mut. fund licensing exams. Pathfinder Securities Sch., Indpls., 1983-87; cons. channel 6 News, 1984-85. Weekly fin. columnist Indpls. Bus. Jour., 1982—; bi-weekly fin. columnist Jewish Post & Opinion, 1982-86; weekly regular guest WTVX Radio and WRTV-TV. Recipient Gold Medal award Personal Selling Power, 1987; named Bus. Woman of Yr. Network of Women in Bus., 1986. Mem. Inst. Cert. Fin. Planners, Nat. Assn. Life Underwriters, Women's Life Underwriters' Conf. (treas. Ind. chpt. 1982, v.p. chpt. 1983), Internat. Assn. Fin. Planners (v.p. Ind. chpt. 1983-84, bd. dirs.), Am. Soc. Chartered Life Underwriters, Women's Life Underwriters Conf., Nat. Council Jewish Women, Nat. Assn. Profl. Saleswomen (nat. bd. dirs.), Nat. Speakers Assn. (pres. Ind. chpt. 1986-87, treas.), Registry Fin. Planning Practitioners. Lodge: Toastmasters (chpt. ednl. v.p. 1985-86), Soroptimists (bd. dirs.). Avocations: piano; folk and square dancing; theatre. Office: Shearson Lehman Hutton 201 N Illinois #400 Indianapolis IN 46204

ITTELSON, MARY ELIZABETH, museum director; b. Dayton, Ohio; d. Richard W. and Lois (Koblitz) I.; m. Richard Carl Tuttle. BA, NYU, 1979; MBA, Stanford U., 1985. Dir., choreographer Premiers Dance Theatre, N.Y.C., 1976-78; exec. dir. Crossroads Inc., N.Y.C., 1978-79; asst. prof. dance Northwestern U., Evanston, 1979-83; assoc. McKinsey & Co., Inc., Chgo., 1985-88; acting dir. Mus. Contemporary Art, Chgo., 1988—. Choreographer: (dance) In Three Places, 1977, Garland Epitaphium, 1981, Sir Gawain and the Green Knight, 1982, Little Children Lost, 1983. Am. Dance Festival fellow, 1980. Office: Mus Contemporary Art 237 E Ontario St Chicago IL 60611

ITZ, SHIRLEY ANNE, small business owner; b. Fredericksburg, Tex., Oct. 6, 1946; d. Marvin Louis Elmon and Ruby (Miller) Grona; m. Charles E. Itz, Apr. 30, 1966; children: Tanya, Jared, Lorne. Student, Austin Coll., 1966. Sec. Community Savs. and Loan, Fredericksburg, 1966-71; co-mgr., bookkeeper Itz Electric, Fredericksburg, 1969—. Adult leader Cave Creek 4-H, Fredericksburg, 1988. Named Outstanding Woman Leader, Cave Creek 4-H, 1987, 88. Republican. Roman Catholic. Office: 804 E Main St Fredericksburg TX 78624

IVANYI, THOMAS PETER, bank executive, lawyer; b. Budapest, Hungary, Feb. 26, 1944; came to U.S., 1946; s. Walter A. and Fanny (Margulies) I.; m. Mary Elias, Dec. 22, 1968; children: Peter Livingston, Julie Gilman. BS, NYU, 1965; JD, Fordham U., 1969; cert. in program mgmt. devel., Harvard Bus. Sch., 1976. Account officer, asst. v.p. Citibank, N.Y. and Brussels, Belgium, 1965-73; v.p., dept. head investor relations Citibank, N.Y.C., 1973-74, v.p. dept. head personal trusts, estates and pvt. banking, 1974-77; v.p., head strategic planning Citibank Internat. Fin. Instn., N.Y.C., 1977-79; v.p., div. head corp. banking Citibank, Paris, 1979-82; v.p., region head corp. banking Citibank India/Nepal, New Delhi, 1982-84; v.p., region head Asia, internat. pvt. banking Citicorp Investment Bank, Hong Kong, 1984-86; sr. mng. dir., chief exec. officer Mitsubishi Trust & Banking Corp. (U.S.A.), N.Y.C., 1986—. Mem. ABA, N.Y. State Bar Assn. Clubs: Cercle de l'Union Interalliee (Paris); Hampshire Country (Mamaroneck, N.Y.); University (N.Y.C.). Office: Mitsubishi Trust & Banking Corp (USA) 520 Madison Ave New York NY 10022

IVERSON, CARL JOHN, data processing executive; b. La Crosse, Wis., Oct. 20, 1940; s. Clem J. and Natalie (Heintz) I.; m. Rhea J. Hundt, June 13, 1964; children: Traci Lee, Erik Jon, Craig Jason. BS, U. Wis., La Crosse, 1969. Clk. property records and billing Univac, St. Paul, 1964-65, programmer, 1965-67; programming analyst, mgr. data processing La Crosse Garment Co., 1969-71; mgr. data processing Peerless Chain Co., Winona, Minn., 1971-77, dir. data processing, 1977-86, v.p. info. systems, 1986—; founder, pres. Group Homes of Winona, Inc., 1975-85, computer cons., 1987-88. Pres. Winona County ARC, 1974-75, bd. dirs., 1974-87. Named Outstanding Vol. Minn. Assn. Retarded Citizens, 1982. Home: RR 4 PO Box 67 Winona MN 55987 Office: Peerless Chain Co 1416 E Sanborn St Winona MN 55987

IVERSON, FRANCIS KENNETH, metals company executive; b. Downers Grove, Ill., Sept. 18, 1925; s. Norris Byron and Pearl Irene (Kelsey) I.; m. Martha Virginia Miller, Oct. 24, 1945; children: Claudia (Mrs. Wesley Watts Sturges), Marc Miller. Student, Northwestern U., 1943-44; B.S., Cornell U., 1946; M.S., Purdue U., 1947. Research physicist Internat. Harvester, Chgo., 1947-52; tech. dir. Illium Corp., Freeport, Ill., 1952-54; dir. mktg. Cannon-Muskegon Corp., Mich., 1954-61; exec. v.p. Coast Metals, Little Ferry, N.J., 1961-62; v.p. Nucor Corp. (formerly Nuclear Corp. Am.), Charlotte, N.C., 1962-65, pres., chief exec. officer, dir., 1965-85, chmn., chief exec. officer, 1985—, also bd. dirs.; bd. dirs. C.H. Heist Co., Cato Corp., Wachovia Bank and Trust Co., Rexham Corp. Contbr. articles to profl. jours. Served to lt. (j.g.) USNR, 1943-46. Named Best Chief Exec. Officer in Steel Industry Wall St. Transcript, 1986. Mem. NAM (dir.), Steel Joist Inst., Am. Soc. Metals, AIME, Am. Foundrymens Soc. Clubs: Quail Hollow Country (Charlotte). Office: Nucor Corp 4425 Randolph Rd Charlotte NC 28211 *

IVES, GEORGE ALLEN, JR., real estate and investments executive; b. New Bern, N.C., Aug. 15, 1931; s. George Allen and Dorothy (Gregory) I.; m. Gisela Nora von zur Muehlen, Feb. 21, 1956; children: Caroline, Tanya, Dorothy, Allen. BA, Princeton U., 1953. Various positions Dept. State, Washington, 1959-64; sales mgr. Ives Oil Co., New Bern, 1964-71, pres., chief exec. officer, 1971-84; pres., chief exec. officer Ives Transport, Inc., New Bern, 1971-84; pres. Ives Enterprises, Inc., New Bern, 1984—; pres. Carolina Oil Fuel Inst., Raleigh, 1971; chmn. bd. First Fed. Savs. and Loan Assn., New Bern, 1975-81. Vice chmn. New Bern/Craven County Bicentennial Celebration, 1974; mem. Tryon Palace Commn., New Bern, 1974—, chmn., 1985—; trustee, mem. exec. com., treas. Chatham (Va.) Hall Sch., 1975-79, N.C. Symphony, Raleigh, 1971-75, 86—. Trustee Kellenberger Hist. Found., 1985—, sec., treas. 1988—. Served to lt. (j.g.) USNR, 1953-55. Mem. N.C. Oil Jobbers Assn. (v.p. 1973; named Fuel Oil Man of Yr. 1971). Republican. Episcopalian. Clubs: New Bern Golf and Country (pres. 1971), Coral Bay (Atlantic Beach, N.C.), Raleigh City. Avocations: tennis, sailing, boating.

IVES, J. ATWOOD, financial executive; b. Atlanta, May 1, 1936; s. Stephen Bradshaw and Ellen (Atwood) I.; m. Elizabeth Saalfield; children: Ian, Anna, Benjamin. B.A. in Econs., Yale U., 1959; M.B.A., Stanford U., 1961; A.M.P., Harvard U., 1975. C.P.A., Calif. Acct. Price, Waterhouse & Co., San Francisco, 1961-64; fin. analyst Textron, Inc., Providence, 1964-66; ptnr., v.p. Paine Webber Jackson & Curtis, 1966-74; dir. Gen. Cinema Corp., Chestnut Hill, Mass., 1970—, sr. v.p. fin., 1974-83, exec. v.p., chief fin. officer, 1983-84, vice chmn., chief fin. officer, 1985—, mem. office of chmn., 1983; vice chmn., chief fin. officer The Neiman Marcus Group, Inc., 1987—, also bd. dirs.; bd. dirs. Barry Wright Corp., 1986; trustee Property Capital Trust, Boston. Mem. corp. adv. com., overseer Mus. Fine Arts; trustee Buckingham, Browne & Nichols, Sch., Cambridge, Mass., 1983—. Served with U.S. Army, 1961-62. Recipient award Haskins and Sells Found., 1961. Mem. Fin. Execs. Inst., Treasurers Club. Home: One Bennington Rd Lexington MA 02173 Office: Gen Cinema Corp 27 Boylston St Chestnut Hill MA 02167

IVEY, HARRIET MARGARET, foundation executive; b. Dodgeville, Wis., Jan. 17, 1949; d. Harry S. and Patricia (Ludden) I. MusB, U. Wis., 1972. Devel. officer San Francisco Opera, 1977-80; dir. devel. The Washington Opera, 1980-84; v.p. Brakeley John Price Jones Inc., Stamford, Conn., 1984-86, Fed. Nat. Mortgage Assn., Washington, 1986—. Trustee Washington Performing Arts Soc., 1987—. Mem. Nat. Soc. Fund Raising Execs. (cert.). Office: Fed Nat Mortgage Assn 3900 Wisconsin Ave NW Washington DC 20016

IVIE, LESLIE TODD, elevator company executive; b. San Diego, June 30, 1960; s. Lloyd E. and Florence J. (Ojeda) I.; m. Susan E. Shannon, Nov. 5, 1960. BS in Econs., Portland State U., 1982; MBA, U. Denver, 1987. Sr. svc. cons. Otis Elevator Co., San Francisco, 1982-83; sr. new equipment cons. Otis Elevator Co., Denver, 1983-87; product mgr. geared elevator and escalator div. Otis Elevator Co., Farmington, Conn., 1987—; pres., chief exec. officer LSI Rsch., Hartford, Conn., 1986—. Mem. Rep. Nat. Com., Washington, 1986—. Office: Otis Elevator Co 1 Farm Springs Rd Farmington CT 06032

IVISON, DONALD ALEXANDER STUART, chemical company executive; b. Ottawa, Ont., Can., June 3, 1932; s. E. H. Stuart and Marjorie (Simmers)

I.; m. M. Elizabeth (Betty) Mann, July 30, 1955; children—Deborah, Robert, Duncan. B.A., McMaster U., 1953; M.B.A., U. Western Ont., 1955; student, Nat. Def. Coll., 1966. Various positions Du Pont Can. Inc., Mississauga, Ont., 1955-74, v.p., treas., from 1975; sr. v.p., dir. corp. plans dept. E.I. du Pont de Nemours & Co., Wilmington, Del., 1982-84; sr. v.p. Du Pont Can. Inc., Wilmington, 1984—; dir. corp. plans dept. E.I. duPont de Nemours & Co., Wilmington, Del., 1982-84. Baptist. Club: Forest and Stream (Dorval, Que., Can.). Office: Du Pont Can Inc, PO Box 2200, Streetsville, ON Canada L5M 2H3

IVY, CONWAY GAYLE, paint company executive; b. Houston, July 8, 1941; s. John Smith and Caro (Gayle) I.; student U. Chgo., 1959-62; m. Diane Ellen Cole, May 25, 1973; children: Brice McPherson, Elizabeth. BS in Natural Scis., Shimer Coll., 1964; postgrad. U. Tex., 1964-65; MBA, U. Chgo., 1968, MA in Econs., 1972, postgrad. 1972-74. Geol. asst. John S. Ivy, Houston, 1965-72; securities analyst Halsey Stuart & Co. and successor Bache & Co., Chgo., 1973-74, Winmill Securities Inc., Chgo., 1974; econ. and fin. cons., Chgo., 1974-75; dir. corp. planning Gould Inc., Rolling Meadows, Ill., 1975-79; v.p. corp. planning and devel. Sherwin-Williams Co., Cleve., 1979-88, v.p., treas., 1989—; pres. Ivy Minerals Inc., Boise, Idaho, 1978—; bd. dirs. CorrIm Door Systems Inc., dep. chmn., 1989—. Trustee Cleve. Inst. Music, 1983—, treas., 1987—; trustee Michelson-Morley Centennial Celebration, 1987. Mem. Am. Econs. Assn., Soc. Mining Engrs., Am. Inst. Mining Engrs., Phi Gamma Delta. Republican. Author of numerous analytical reports for brokerage industry. Office: Sherwin-Williams Co 101 Prospect Ave NW Cleveland OH 44115

IX, ROBERT EDWARD, food company executive; b. Woodcliffe, N.J., Oct. 15, 1929; s. William Edward and Helen Elizabeth (Gorman) I.; m. Mildred Gilmore, June 27, 1959; children: Helen Adele, Alesia Gilmore, Robert Owens Gilmore, Julia Ryan, Christopher Prouty. A.B., Princeton U., 1951; M.B.A., Wharton Grad. Sch., U. Pa., 1956; LL.D. (hon.), Marymount Coll., 1978, Sacred Heart U., Conn., 1984. Mgmt. cons. Arthur D. Little Inc., Cambridge, Mass., 1956-63; mktg. dir. Browne-Vintners Co., Distillers Corp.-Seagrams Ltd., N.Y.C., 1963-66; v.p. mktg. Schweppes (USA) Ltd., N.Y.C., 1966-68; pres. Schweppes (USA) Ltd., 1968; pres., chief exec. officer Cadbury Schweppes Inc., Stamford, Conn., 1970-78; chmn., chief exec. officer Am. region Cadbury Schweppes P.L.C., 1976-86; dir. Cadbury Schweppes P.L.C., London, N.E. Bancorp Inc., Union Trust Co., Hendries, Inc., Loctite Corp., Chase Packaging Co., Health Waters Inc. Trustee Marymount Coll., also chmn.; trustee Greenwich (Conn.) Acad., Trinity Pawling Sch. (N.Y.); mem. adv. council N.Y. Med. Coll., Valhalla, N.Y. Served to lt. comdr. USNR, 1951-55. Decorated Knight Sovereign Mil. Order Malta. Mem. Young President's Orgn., World Bus. Council, Chief Execs. Forum, Southwestern Area Commerce and Industry Assn. Conn. (dir. 1970-80 , chmn. bd. 1976-77), Def. Orientation Conf. Assn. (dir.), Grocery Mfrs. Am. (dir. 1981-85), U.S. Navy League (dir. Conn.). Roman Catholic. Clubs: Univ. (N.Y.C.); Belle Haven (Greenwich); Greenwich Country; Landmark (Stamford) (chmn. bd. govs.). Office: 60 Arch St Greenwich CT 06830 also: Loctite Corp 705 N Mountain Rd Newington CT 06111

JABARA, MICHAEL DEAN, telecommunications company executive; b. Sioux Falls, S.D., Oct. 26, 1952; s. James M. and Jean Marie (Swiden) J.; m. Gundula Beate Dietz, Aug. 26, 1984; children: James Michael, Jenna Mariel. Student, Mich. Tech. U., 1970-72; BSBA, U. Calif., Berkeley, 1974; MBA, Pepperdine U., 1979. Mgr. Sprint project So. Pacific Communications Corp., 1976-78; network product mgr. ROLM Corp., 1978-81; cons. McGraw Hill Co., Hamburg (Fed. Republic of Germany) and London, 1982-83; founder, chief exec. officer Friend Techs. Inc. (merger VoiceCom Systems, Inc.), San Francisco, 1984-88; pres. VoiceCom Ventures, San Francisco, 1988—. Patentee in field. Mem. Pepperdine Bus. Alumni, U. Calif. Berkeley Bus. Alumni. Home: 340 St Francis Blvd San Francisco CA 94127 Office: VoiceCom Systems Inc 222 Kearny St San Francisco CA 94108

JABBOUR, C. L., accountant; b. McKeesport, Pa., Sept. 20, 1932; s. Louis and Mary (Thomas) J.; widowed; children: Renee, Maura, Dana. Assoc., Robert Morris Coll., 1960. Lic. Pub. Accountant, Pa. Pvt. practice acctg. West Mifflin, Pa., 1960—; mgr. Riverview Homes Assn., West Mifflin, 1973—. Councilman West Mifflin Borough, 1977-78, 79-83, 85—. Served to cpl. U.S. Army, 1953-55, Japan. Recipient Bronze Keystone award Boys/Girls Clubs Am., 1979. Mem. nat. Soc. CPA's, Pa. Soc. CPA's, Duquesne-West Mifflin C. of C. (pres. 1983-84, bd. dirs. 1988—). Club: Prince Humbert (sec. Duquesne Pa. chpt. 1958—). Home and Office: 2501 Pennsylvania Ave West Mifflin PA 15122

JABIN, MARVIN (MARK), real estate developer, investor, lawyer; b. N.Y.C., Mar. 28, 1929; s. Sol and Belle Jabin; BA in Biology and Chemistry, NYU, 1952; BS in Engring., UCLA, 1954, JD, 1957; m. Lelia Honig, May 13, 1952; children: Valerie, Gregory, Anthony, Desiree. Bar: Calif. 1958, U.S. Supreme Ct. 1961; ptnr. Jabin & Jabin, Monterey Park, Calif., 1958—; v.p. CVJ Constrn. Inc., Monterey Park, 1977— ; pres. Jabin Corp., Monterey Park, 1979—; ptnr. several real estate devel. cos. in Los Angeles County, 1979—; judge protem Alhambra Mcpl. Ct., Calif., 1981-82; asst. prof. bus. law Calif. State U., Los Angeles, 1972-75; bd. dirs. Golden Security Thrift & Loan Assn., 1983—, chmn. 1988—. Adv. council Calif. State U., Los Angeles, 1971-76. Served with U.S. Army, 1946-49. Mem. Am. Arbitration Assn. (arbitrator 1963-80), San Gabriel Valley Bar Assn. (pres. 1975), Los Angeles County Bar Assn. (trustee 1975-77), Monterey Park C. of C. (bd. dirs. 1982-85). Lodge: Rotary (bd. dirs. Monterey Park club 1982-83). Office: 701 S Atlantic Blvd Monterey Park CA 91754

JABLIN, LAURIE CLARK, real estate company executive; b. Hall County, Ga., May 9, 1921; d. Joseph Thomas and Josephine (Jones) Clark; m. Frederick Jablin, Feb. 4, 1944 (div. 1973); children: Jo Anne, Juliana. Student, Catawba Coll., 1940, Realtors Inst., Chgo., 1973. Cert. accredited land counselor Realtors Land Inst.; broker N.J. Real Estate Commn., Ga. Real Estate Commn. With various radio stas. 1947-57; owner, prin. broker Radium Realty, Albany, Ga., 1965-79, Century 21-Radium Realty, Albany, 1979-80; broker Doane Western, Inc., St. Louis and Albany, 1980-81; ind. broker, appraiser, Albany, 1981-85; sr. counselor mktg. rsch. Yankelovitch, Skelly & White, N.Y.C., 1985-87; broker VTY Realty, Atlantic City, 1986-87; broker, land specialist Price Real Estate, Ventnor City, N.J., 1987—; broker Mercado Realty, Pleasantville, N.J., 1988—. Pres. Radium Springs Civic Assn., 1977; reader for blind Libr. of Congress, 1976. Mem. Nat. Assn. Realtors (real estate fin. com. 1988—), Ga. Realtors Inst. (gov. 1971-73), Ga. Assn. Realtors (bd. dirs. 1971-73), Woman's Coun. Realtors (pres. 1971), Albany Bd. Realtors (ednl. dir. 1975-76), Realtors Land Inst. (accredited cons.), Nat. Audubon Soc. (life, bd. dirs. 1983-85, Albany), Nat. Hist. Trust, Internat. Toastmistress Club (pres. Albany chpt. 1962-63). Democrat. Presbyterian. Home: 16 S Rosborough Ave Ventnor City NJ 08406 Office: Mercado Realty 1416 N Main St Pleasantville NJ 08232

JABLONSKI, LOUIS JOHN, JR., communications executive; b. Bklyn., Aug. 28, 1950; s. Louis John Sr. and Vincenza Helen (DiLustro) J.; m. Mary Beth Gigantelli, July 28, 1973; children: Louis III, Andrew, Peter. BS, Manhattan Coll., 1972, postgrad., 1974-76. Customer service mgr. N.Y. Telephone Co., 1972-76, mgr. strategic planning, 1976-79; mgr. ops. planning N.Y. Telephone/AT&T, 1979-81; mgr. data systems AT&T, Parsippany, N.J., 1982-85; dist. mgr. ops. and fin. AT&T/EDS Venture, Parsippany, 1985-87; dist. mgr., EDP Architecture Planning AT&T, Bedminster, N.J., 1987—; bd. dirs. Aversa-Martin, Inc., N.Y. V.p. Bd. Edn., Haworth, N.J., 1981-83; bd. dirs. Little League, Basking Ridge, N.J., 1985-86. Mem. Am. Mgmt. Assn., Manhattan Coll. Alumni Assn., Omicron Delta Epsilon. Lodge: Kiwanis (v.p. Bronx chpt. 1973-76). Home: 124 Penwood Rd Basking Ridge NJ 07920

JABLONSKI, ROBERT ANTHONY, automotive engineer; b. Parma, Ohio, July 7, 1963; s. Leo Joseph and Audrey Marie (Ross) J.; m. Diane Marie Michaux, Nov. 8, 1986. BSEE, U. Cin., 1986. Application engr. Packard Electric div. Gen. Motors Corp., Warren, Ohio, 1986-87; elec. devel. engr. Lansing (Mich.) Auto div. Gen. Motors Corp., 1987—. Mem. Tau Beta Pi, Eta Kappa Nu, Alpha Lambda Delta. Republican. Roman Catholic. Club: Comsee Soccer (mgr. 1987). Office: GM Lansing Automotive Div 920 Townsend M/S 6616 Lansing MI 48921

JACCARD, WALTER BRYCE, lawyer; b. Seattle, July 6, 1953; s. Gilbert W. and Shirley M. (Jones) J.; m. Debra J. Rappe, May 31, 1976 (div. 1984); children: Erik, Kaitlen. AB, Whitman Coll., 1975; JD, Columbia U., 1980. Bar: Wash. 1980. Assoc. Hillis, Clark, Martin & Peterson, Seattle, 1980-83; v.p., gen. counsel, corp. sec. Thousand Trails, Inc., Bellevue, Wash., 1983—. Mem. Seattle Bar Assn., King County Bar Assn., Wash. State Bar Assn., ABA. Home: 7414 125th Pl SE Renton WA 98056 Office: Thousand Trails Inc 12301 NE 10th Pl Bellevue WA 98005

JACEY, CHARLES FREDERICK, JR., accounting company executive; b. Staten Island, N.Y., Feb. 16, 1936; s. Charles Frederick and Marie A. (Coakley) J.; children: Lauren, David, Curtis; m. Arlene Theresa Biele, Jan 14, 1984; 1 child: Jonathan. BBA, Pace U., 1957. CPA. Mem. audit staff Coopers & Lybrand, N.Y.C., 1957-69, ptnr., 1969, mng. ptnr. N.Y. metro region, 1976-87, vice chmn., 1982—. V.p., treas. Police Athletic League, N.Y.C., 1980—; trustee Pace U., N.Y.C., 1986—. Mem. Baltusrol Golf Club. Office: Coopers & Lybrand 1251 Ave of the Americas New York NY 10020

JACHIMOWICZ, LUCIAN GARY, marketing executive; b. New Britain, Conn., July 10, 1955; s. Lucian James and Irene (Samojeden) J.; m. Diane Lynn Courey, Nov. 17, 1984. BS in Acctg., Cen. Conn. State U., 1977; MBA, U. Conn., 1978; postgrad., Loyola U., Balt., 1988—. Asst. controller Harte Hanks Communications, Inc., Framingham, Mass., 1979-80; acct./data processing mgr. Fred Locke Stereo Inc., Berlin, Conn., 1981-82; acctg. mgr. Imprint Inc., West Hartford, Conn., 1982-84; controller Harte-Hanks Communications, Inc., Glastonbury, Conn., 1984-85, Miami, Fla., 1985-87; v.p. fin. Harte-Hanks Communications, Inc., Balt., 1987—. Roman Catholic. Home: 3402 Font Hill Dr Ellicott City MD 21043

JACKEL, LAWRENCE, publishing company executive; b. N.Y.C., July 25; s. Solomon and Sylvia (Fisher) J.; children: Kenneth Isaac, Molly Laurie. BBA, CCNY, 1961, MBA, 1966. Acct. Aviquipo, Inc., N.Y.C., 1961-62; fin. exec. Litton Industries, N.Y.C., 1962-68; group controller Alloys Unltd., Inc., N.Y.C., 1968-69; v.p. fin. Litton Ednl. Pub., Inc., N.Y.C., 1969-72, sr. v.p., 1972-75, exec. v.p., 1975-76, pres., 1976-80; pres., owner TAB Books Inc., Blue Ridge Summit, Pa., 1980—; pres. Delmar Pubs. div., Albany, N.Y., 1973-80. Democrat. Jewish. Club: University. Home: 17411 Sunshine Trail Sabillasville MD 21780 Office: TAB Books Inc Blue Ridge Summit PA 17214

JACKEL, SIMON SAMUEL, food products co. exec., tech. cons.; b. N.Y.C., Nov. 11, 1917; s. Victor and Sadie (Ungar) J.; A.M., Columbia, 1947, Ph.D., 1950; B.S., Coll. City N.Y., 1938; postgrad. U. Ill., 1941-42; m. Betty Carlson, Jan. 22, 1954; children—Phyliss Marcia, Glenn Edward. Head fermentation div. Fleischmann Lab., Stamford, Conn., 1944-59; v.p. research and devel. Vico Products Co., Chgo., 1959-61; dir. lab., research and devel. v.p., dir. lab. and tech. research Quality Bakers of Am. div. Sunbeam Baked Foods, Greenwich, Conn., 1961-84, v.p., research dir., 1980-84; dir. research and devel., mem. operating com. Bakers Research Devel. Service, Greenwich, 1969-84; pres. Plymouth Tech. Services, Westport, Conn., 1951—; dir. hearing aid audiology Jewish Home and Hosp. for Aged, N.Y.C., 1951-76. Mem. sci. adv. com. Am. Inst. Baking, 1970—, mem. sanitation edn. adv. com., 1978-81. Mem. industry adv. com. N.D. State U., 1971-85; chmn. Am. Bakers Assn. tech. liaison com. to U.S. Dept. Agr., 1975-87. Recipient USAAF Exceptional Civilian Service award, 1943; USPHS research grantee, 1947-50. Fellow Am. Inst. Chemists, AAAS; mem. Am. Chem. Soc., Am. Assn. Cereal Chemists (chmn. milling and baking div. 1973-74, chmn. N.Y. sect. 1973-74; Charles N. Frey award 1981; bakery columnist Cereal Foods World 1984—), Am. Soc. Bakery Engrs. (chmn. tech. info. service com. 1979—), ASTM, Am. Bakers Assn. (nutrition com. 1971—, chmn. tech. liaison com. to U.S. Dept. Agr. 1975-87, food tech. regulatory affairs com. 1977—; alt. gov. 1978-87, gov. 1988—), Assn. for Environ. Protection, Ind. Bakers Assn. (cons., food safety com. 1977—, labeling com. 1978—, tech. affairs com. 1978—, chmn. labeling and good mfg. practices com. 1984—), Inst. Food Technologists, Am. Mgmt. Assn., Nutrition Today Soc., Soc. Nutrition Edn., Environ. Mgmt. Assn., N.Y. Acad. Sci., N.Y.C. Chemists Club, Sigma Xi, Phi Lambda Upsilon. Jewish. Author tech. articles; tech. editor Bakery Prodn. and Mktg. Mag., 1968-85; contbr. articles to tech. jours. Patentee in field. Home: 46 Kings Highway North Westport CT 06880 also: 14024 Capital Dr Tampa FL 33613 Office: 191 Post Rd W Westport CT 06880

JACKELEN, HENRY RICHARD, banker, financial analyst, consultant; b. São Paulo, Brazil, Jan. 10, 1952; came to U.S., 1979; s. Henry James and Mary Theresa (Frost) J. BS, Boston Coll., 1973; MA, Johns Hopkins U., 1981. Loan officer Bank of Boston, São Paulo, 1973-77; mgr. Bank of Boston, Rio de Janeiro, 1977-79; lectr. Fgn. Service Inst., Washington, 1981-83; country officer Appropriate Tech. Internat., Washington, 1982-84, dir., 1984-85; pvt. practice cons. Washington, 1985-89; sr. tech. adviser UN Capital Devel. Fund, 1989—; cons. World Bank, UN Devel. Program, Interam. Devel. Bank, U.S. Aid. Author: Commercial Analysis of Snall Scale Projects, 1983, Banking on the Informal Sector, 1988; co-author: Micro Enterprise Development in the Urban Informal Sector, 1984. Home: 2605 Mill Rd Washington DC 20009

JACKMAN, FRANCIS SWEET, electrical engineer, manufacturing executive; b. Bristol, Vt., Apr. 5, 1921; s. Glenn Everett and Ila Belle (Sweet) J.; m. Rose Bogdan; children: Glenn, Arlene, Carol, Ronald, Kenneth. Cert. in engring., Coast Guard Acad., 1942. Chief fin. officer, chmn. bd. dirs. Holiday Sportswear Miami, Miami, Fla., Vt. and N.Y., 1946—. Advisor Senatorial Adv. Bd., Washington, 1980—, Presdl. Task Force, Washington, 1980—. With Mcht. Marines, 1942-45. Recipient Task Force award Pres. Reagan, 1984. Republican. Roman Catholic. Home: 3158 N Bay Rd Miami Beach FL 33140 Office: Holiday Sportswear Miami 537 NW 24th St Miami FL 33127

JACKMAN, ROBERT ALAN, retail executive; b. N.Y.C., Mar. 22, 1939; s. Joseph and Kate Queenie (Silverman) J.; m. Lois Wiederschall, June 10, 1962; children: Jennifer Sharon, Deborah Lynn. BS, U. Bridgeport, 1961. Dir. sales Mattel Inc., Hawthorne, Calif., 1963-75; sr. v.p. mktg. and sales Tyco Industries Inc., Moorestown, N.J., 1975-78; gen. mgr. Aurora Products Inc., Stamford, Conn., 1978-80; ptnr. Scott Lancaster Jackman Mills Atha, Westport, Conn., 1980-83; pres., chief exec. officer Leisure Dynamics Inc. div. Coleco Industries, Westport, 1983—; exec. v.p. Coleco Industries Inc., West Hartford, Conn., 1986-89; bd. dirs. Leisure Dynamics Inc., Westport, 1983-86, Oak Tree Publs., San Diego, 1983-87; cons. Harvard U. Bus. Sch. Club, N.Y.C., 1984. Patentee in field. With USAR, 1961-62. Recipient Disting. Alumni award U. Bridgeport (Conn.), 1986. Mem. U. Bridgeport Mktg. Coun., Mission Hills Country Club (Rancho Mirage, Calif.). Home: 5 Hedgerow Common Weston CT 06883

JACKSON, ANDREW SIMON, auditor; b. Washington, Mar. 27, 1955; s. Floyd and Claretta (Britt) J. BS, Bowie State Coll., 1979; MA in Pub. Adminstrn., No. Ill. U., 1983. Legislative intern Md. Ho. Dels., Annapolis, 1976-79; acct. Re-BAR Constrn. Co., Washington, 1980-81, Hagler Mgmt. Co., Washington, 1983-84; paralegal asst. McKenna, Conner & Cuneo, Washington, 1984-85; auditor City of Washington, 1985—. Tutor, counselor Upward Bound program, No. Ill. U., DeKalb, 1981-83; instr. The Close-up Found., Washington, 1979-80; bd. deacons Greater Triedstone Bapt. Ch., Washington, 1983-86, asst. chmn., 1986. Named Outstanding Young Man of Am., 1986. Mem. Nat. Assn. Black Accts., Golden Spinal Inst. (bd. dirs. 1986). Home: 1307 Buchanan St NW Washington DC 20011 Office: Office DC Auditor 415 12th St NW Washington DC 20004

JACKSON, ARTHUR GILBERT, drilling company executive; b. Lebanon, Tenn., July 2, 1949; s. Arthur Ilo and Winne Edith (Vaughn) J.; m. Teresa Ann Stacy, Feb. 19, 1987; 1 child, Laura Leah. BS, Vanderbilt U., 1972. Dist. sales rep. Ingersoll-Rand Corp., Elkridge, Md., 1972-75; project dir. Eatherly & Jackson, Lebanon, 1975-76; v.p. Jackson Drilling, Lebanon, 1976-85; pres. Jackson Enterprises, Lebanon, 1985—; v.p. Am. Geosearch, Lebanon, 1984-85; cons. in industry, 1979—; several directorships. Contbr. articles to profl. jours. Mem. Internat. Assn. Air Drilling Contractors, So. Air Drilling Assn. (pres. 1981-86), Ducks Unltd. (founder Wilson County, Tenn. chpt.). Republican. Presbyterian. Office: Jackson Enterprises 204 S Maple St Lebanon TN 37087

JACKSON, BOBBY L., financial corporate executive; b. Jacksonville, Fla., Jan. 15, 1930; s. Walter Drew and Vernie Belle (Knowles) J.; m. Martha Lydia Whiddon, Dec. 23, 1950; children: Debra Lee Danyus, Murray Steven. BS in Bus. Mgmt., Jones Coll., Jacksonville, 1959; BS in Acctg., Jacksonville U., 1974; MBA, U. No. Fla., 1978. CPA, Fla.; cert. assoc. in risk mgmt., Ins. Inst. Am. Asst. credit acctg. supr. Standard Oil of Ky., Jacksonville, 1951-55; staff acct. Humphreys Mining Co., Jacksonville, 1955-62; bus. mgr. Massey Tech. Inst., Jacksonville, 1962-63; chief acct. Jacksonville Shipyards Inc., subs. Fruehauf, 1963-64, corp. controller, 1964—. Mem. Rep. Exec. Com., Jacksonville, 1970-73. Served to cpl. U.S. Army, 1947-48, 1950-51. Mem. Am. Inst. CPAs, Risk and Ins. Mgmt. Soc. (dir. Jacksonville/No. Fla. chpt. 1980-85; pres. 1981nat. soc. dir. 1980-85), Nat. Assn. Accts. (chpt. pres. 1968-69, Most Valued Mem. award 1963-65, Manuscript award 1978). Democrat. Baptist. Lodge: Woodmen of World (Fla. state pres. 1969-71). Home: 9178 Tottenham Ct Jacksonville FL 32257 Office: Jacksonville Shipyards Inc 750 E Bay Jacksonville FL 32203

JACKSON, DAVID R., publishing company executive; b. Salt Lake City, July 8, 1952; s. Junius M. and Margaret (Romney) J.; m. Karen Leigh Madsen, Dec. 30, 1975; children: Christopher, Stephen, Richard, Elizabeth. BA in Psychology cum laude, U. Utah, 1976; MBA in Fin. and Investments, George Washington U., 1982. Legis. asst. Office of Senator Orrin G. Hatch, Washington, 1977-82; bus. planner PepsiCo, Inc., Purchase, N.Y., 1982-83, sr. bus. planner, 1983-84, mgr. investor relations, 1984-86, dir. investor relations, 1986-87; v.p. investor relations Macmillan, Inc., N.Y.C., 1987-88; v.p. corp. Maxwell Communication Corp. N.Am., Macmillan, Inc., N.Y.C., 1988—. Scouting coordinator Fairfield County (Conn.) Boy Scouts Am. Mem. Nat. Investor Relations Inst. (bd. dirs. 1986-87, v.p. membership Fairfield/Westchester chpt., mem. spring conf. com. 1987, co-chmn. spring conf. 1988), Sigma Chi. Republican. Mormon. Office: Macmillan Inc 866 3rd Ave New York NY 10022

JACKSON, DONALD EUGENE, municipal administrator; b. Washington, July 8, 1952; s. Albert S. and Jean D. (Fairfax) J.; m. Cheryl D. Whitten, Aug. 26, 1972 (div. 1980); 1 child, Chante. Student in engring. tech., Prince Georges Community Coll., Largo, Md., 1974-76; BS in Mech. Engring. Tech., Prairie View A&M U. Tex., 1985. Lic. mech. contractor. Project engring. mgr. Computer Scis. Corp., Falls Church, Va., 1980-81, Prairie View A&M U. Tex., 1981-83; prin. Don Jackson Systems and Service, Houston, 1983-85; dep. chief engr. City New Orleans, 1985—; exec. dir. Ctr. Career Devel. and Research, New Orleans, 1988—. Recipient Mayor's Meritorious award City New Orleans, 1986. Mem. Refrigerating Engrs. and Techs. Assn. (past chpt. pres., regional mgr.), Nat. Fire Protection Assn., Nat. Fire Code Com., Bldg. Owners and Mgrs. Inst. Internat., ASME, Sigma Tau.

JACKSON, ELMER MARTIN, JR., publishing executive; b. Hagerstown, Md., Mar. 9, 1906; s. Elmer Martin and Blanche Beatrice (Bower) J.; m. Mary W. A. Conard, Aug. 27, 1929 (div.); children: Elmer Martin III, Allen Conard, Pamela Conard; m. Doris C. Grace, Apr. 18, 1972. A.B., St. John's Coll., Annapolis, Md., 1926. Reporter, sports editor, city editor Hagerstown and Annapolis, Md., 1920-30; editor Evening Capital and Md. Gazette, Annapolis, 1933-41; v.p., editor and gen. mgr. Evening Capital and Md. Gazette Newspapers, 1947-69; pres., pub. Anne Arundel Times, 1969—; owner-pub. Worcester Democrat, Pocomoke City, Md.; gen. mgr., editor Capital-Gazette News, also County News, 1961-69; pres. and pub. Carroll County Times, Westminster, Md., Jackson Printing, Inc., Annapolis and St. Michael's, Md., 1975—; owner Scott Book Ctr., Annapolis; bd. dirs. Md. Nat. Bank. Author: The Rat Tat, 1927, Annapolis, Three Centuries of Glamour, 1938; (nature study) The Baltimore Oriole; Maryland Symbols, 1964, (genealogy) Keeping the Lamp of Remembrance Lighted, 1985. Past pres. dist. and state press assns.; mem. evaluating commn. Instns. Higher Learning.; mem. bd. Fed. Council State Govt., Chgo. Alderman, Annapolis, 1932-36; del. Md. Legislature, 1937-41; pres. Anne Arundel Pub. Library Assn., 1945-87, Fine Arts Festival Found.; chmn. Anne Arundel County Econ. Devel. Commn., State Capital Planning Commn.; pres. Md. Gov.'s Prayer Breakfast Soc., 1967-76. Served as comdr. USNR, 1941-47. Named hon. adm. U.S. Naval Acad., 1965; recipient Man of Yr. award Anne Arundel County, 1965, Trustee of Yr. award ALA, Dallas, 1984. Mem. Am. Soc. Newspaper Editors, Newcomen Soc., Md. Hist. Soc. (dir.), Mil. Order World Wars (comdr.), Md. Soc. of SAR (pres. 1985-86), Polit. Sci. Club, Sigma Delta Chi. Democrat. Episcopalian. Clubs: Nat. Press (Washington); Annapolis Athletic (past pres.), Annapolitan (sec.-treas.), Thirteen, Annapolis Yacht, Annapolis Roads Golf and Beach, Naval Academy Officers, Naval Academy Golf, Naval Academy Beach, Young Democratic of Anne Arundel County (past pres.); Army-Navy (Washington); University, So. Md. Soc, Propeller. Lodges: Elks, Civitan (past pres. and dist. gov. internat. club). Home: 219 Claude St Wardour Annapolis MD 21401 also: Rousby Hall Lusby MD 20657 Office: Anne Arundel Times Bldg 208-10 West St Annapolis MD 21401

JACKSON, GORDON ALEXANDER, manufacturing executive; b. Melbourne, Victoria, Australia, July 1, 1913; s. William and Annie Rose (Uphon) J.; m. Patricia Winifred Skates, Aug. 10, 1969; children by previous marriage—Diane, Robert, Graeme, Marjory. Music degree, London Coll. Music, 1932. Profl. pianist, Victoria, 1933-45; mng. dir. Klipspringer Pty. Ltd., Victoria, 1950—; chmn. music bd. Australia Council, New South Wales, 1977-83; mng. dir. Corio Meat Packing Co., Victoria, 1965-71, Jackson's Wool and Skin Co., Victoria, 1984—. Mem. Ch. of Eng. Clubs: Athenaeum, Annabels, Victoria Racing. Home: 52 Saint Georges Rd, Toorak, Melbourne, Victoria 3142, Australia Office: Klipspringer Pty Ltd, 37 Cranwell St, Braybrook, Melbourne, Victoria 3019, Australia

JACKSON, HORACE FRANKLIN, state official, accountant; b. Dillon, S.C., Oct. 1, 1934; s. Redden Haney and Daisy Belle (Moody) J.; m. Margie Jan Phillips, June 1, 1955; children: Margie Jan, Horace Darrin. BS, U. S.C., 1961, MBA, 1971. Staff acct. J.W. Hunt & Co., CPA's, 1961-64; staff auditor State Auditor S.C., Columbia, 1964-68, sr. budget analyst, 1968-70; dir. fin. S.C. Dept. Social Services, Columbia, 1970-72, dep. commr. fin. mgmt., 1973-75, dep. commr. fiscal ops., 1975-78, exec. asst. for fin. mgmt., 1978-80; fin. dir. S.C. Commn. on Aging, 1980-85, dir. fin. and support services, 1985-87, dir. fiscal and mgmt. services, 1987—; mem. Gov.'s Task Force on Nursing Home Reimbursement, 1969, on Medicaid, 1970, Gov.'s Health Planning Com., 1973, HEW Task Force on Welfare Cost Allocation, 1979-81, City of Forest Acres Planning Commn., 1985—. Served with AUS, 1957-61. Mem. S.C. State Employees Assn. (dir. 1976-77, 83-86), Nat. Assn. Enrolled Agts., S.C. Assn. Pub. Accts., U. S.C. Alumni Assn. Methodist. Office: 400 Arbor Lake Dr Ste B-500 Columbia SC 29223

JACKSON, JEFFREY LEWIS, data processing executive; b. Dayton, Ohio, Mar. 10, 1955; s. Merle Eugene and Hazel Irene (Wehneman) J.; m. Julie Mary Bauer, Oct. 1, 1977 (div. July 1983). BS in Computer Sci., Mich. State U., 1977; MBA, Boston Coll., 1987. Programmer, analyst Am. Motors, Detroit, 1977-82; programmer, database analyst Euclid, Inc., Cleve., 1982-84; database analyst Kendall Co., Boston, 1984-85; database tech. specialist Fiedlity Investments, Boston, 1985—. Asst. scoutmaster Boy Scouts Am., Cleveland Heights, 1983-84; asst. post advisor Explorers (BSA), Norton, Mass., 1988. Mem. IDMS Users Assn. (rep. 1982-88, rep. large users spl. interest group 1988—). Lutheran. Home: PO Box 3328 Boston MA 02101 Office: Fidelity Investments 82 Devonshire St F 4A Boston MA 02101

JACKSON, JOHN ROBERT, financial company executive; b. N.Y.C., May 21, 1946; s. John Hynes and Irma (Wagner) J.; m. Elizabeth Alice Whittle, Nov. 12, 1966; 1 child, John Courtney. AA, Daytona Beach Coll., 1974. Cert. fin. planner. Asst. trust officer Fla. Nat. Bank, Daytona, Beach, 1972-74; asst. v.p., trust officer Flagship 1st Nat. Bank, Ormond Beach, Fla., 1973-78; v.p., dist. trust mgr. Sun Bank, Vero Beach, Fla., 1978-85; fin. planner A.G. Edwards & Sons Inc., Vero Beach, 1985—. With USN, 1965-69, Vietnam. Mem. Inst. Cert. Fin. Planners, Indian River Estate Planning Council (acting sec.), Rotary Club (bd. dirs. Vero Beach chpt. 1987-88). Republican. Lutheran. Home: 1048 Orchid Oak Dr Vero Beach FL 32963 Office: AG Edwards & Sons Inc 333 17th St Vero Beach FL 32960

JACKSON, KAREN SUE, electrical engineer; b. Wrightstown, N.J., Apr. 15, 1958; d. Lloyd William and Olivia Bernice (Pickens) J. BSEE, U. Okla., 1981. Engr. I, Pub. Service of Okla., Tulsa, 1981-83, elec. engr., Jenks,

1983—; prin. Simply Original Designs, Inc. U. Okla. scholar, 1975. Mem. IEEE, Nat. Assn. Female Execs., Nat. Soc. Black Engrs., Am. Craft Coun., Am. Quilter's Soc. Democrat. Baptist. Office: Pub Svc Co Okla Riverside Sta 116th St and Arkansas River Jenks OK 74037

JACKSON, KENNETH WAYNE, academic program director; b. Kingsport, Tenn., July 5, 1958; s. Alfred James and Dorothy Eloise (Tyler) J.;m. Debra Owens, Oct. 22, 1988. Student, The Citadel, 1975-76; BS, Francis Marion Coll., 1984. Asst. foreman Seaboard Coastline R.R., Jacksonville, Fla., 1977-80; cons. edn. and leadership Kappa Alpha Order Ednl. Found., Lexington, Va., 1984-85, dir. devel., 1985-88; dir. devel. Coker Coll., Hartsville, S.C., 1988—. Editor Kappa Alpha Jour., 1986, dir. devel. 1985-88. Mem. Coun. for Advancement and Support of Edn.; mem. steering com. Campaign for KA; tutor Florence Area Literacy Coun. Recipient Comdr.'s Accolade award, 1988. Mem. Rotary. Office: Coker Coll Hartsville SC 29550

JACKSON, LYNDA KAY, leasing company executive; b. Ottumwa, Iowa, Sept. 26, 1949; d. James Leon and Evelyn Melosina (Hartwig) J. Student, Iowa State U., 1967-70. From sec. to state comptroller Iowa State Dept. Transp., Ames, 1967-70; cash analyst McCall Pattern Co., Manhattan, Kans., 1970-71; credit analyst Beneficial Fin., Manhattan, 1971-72; mgmt. trainee CIT Fin. Services, Des Moines, 1973-75; loan mgr. CIT Fin. Services, Ft. Dodge, Iowa, 1975-76; dist. sales mgr. CIT Fin. Services, St. Louis, 1976-80; v.p. sales TriContinental Leasing Corp., Paramus, N.J., 1980-86; v.p. Copelco Credit Corp., Upper Saddle River, N.J., 1986—. Republican. Baptist. Home: 24 Peach Hill N Ramsey NJ 07446 Office: Copelco Credit Corp 10 Mountainview Rd Upper Saddle River NJ 07458

JACKSON, RICHARD BRINKLEY, metal company executive; b. Wilmington, N.C., July 3, 1929; s. Lloyd Franklin and Lelia (Jones) J.; m. Betty Hodnett, June 28, 1958; 1 child, Richard Alan. BS in Indsl. Rels., U. N.C., 1956. Div. personnel mgr. Dan River, Inc., Danville, Va., 1956-63; div. dir. personnel Reynolds Metals Co., Richmond, Va., 1963-77; v.p. personnel and labor rels. Reynolds Internat., Inc., Richmond, 1977—. With USAF, 1947-52. Mem. Nat. Fgn. Trade Coun., Machinery and Allied Products Inst. (Human Resource Coun.). Club: Stonehenge Golf and Country (Richmond). Home: 1236 Shirlton Rd Midlothian VA 23113 Office: Reynolds Internat Inc 6603 W Broad St Richmond VA 23261

JACKSON, RICHARD LYNN, accounting executive; b. Joplin, Mo., Apr. 12, 1950; s. James K. and Wanda J. (Pearson) J.; m. Jenise L. Williams, June 5, 1970; children: Matthew, Julie. BS, Southwest Mo. State U., 1972. CPA, Mo. Mgr. mgmt. adv. services Lipscomb & Preston, CPA, Springfield, Mo., 1972-74; owner, mgr. Rick Jackson, CPA, Springfield, 1974-80; ptnr. Jackson & Docker, CPA's, Springfield, 1980-89, Jackson & Jackson, PC, CPA's, Springfield, 1989—. Mem. Am. Inst. CPA's, Mo. Soc. CPA's. Baptist. Office: 3029 E Sunshine Ste E Springfield MO 65804

JACKSON, ROBERT JOHN, industrial engineer; b. Los Angeles, Dec. 24, 1922; s. John M. and Ona Blanche (Hill) J.; m. Ethel K. Beecher, Dec. 1, 1950; children: Kathryn, Bradley, Diane, Margaret, Shirley, Kelly, Riley. AA, Pasadena Coll., 1958. Supr. assembly dept. Lockheed Aircraft Co., Burbank, Calif., 1941-51; time standards engr. Bendix Pacific Co., North Hollywood, Calif., 1951-53; indsl. engr. Walsco Electronic Co., Los Angeles, 1953-55; methods and time standards engr. Lockheed-Calif. Co., Burbank, 1955-69, dir. hours rep., 1969—. Dir. Modal Investment Co., Eagle Rock, Calif., 1955-56. Served with AUS, 1944-46; PTO. Decorated Purple Heart with oak leaf cluster, Bronze Star, Silver Star. Mem. Am. Inst. Indsl. Engrs. Lodge: Masons. Home: 415 N Plymouth Blvd Los Angeles CA 90004 Office: Lockheed-Calif Co 2555 N Hollywood Way Burbank CA 91503

JACKSON, ROBERT SHERWOOD, petroleum company executive; b. Sept. 14, 1945; married. BS, U. Ill., 1968, MBA, 1971. Mgr. pricing and devel. sales analyst dept. Ford Motor Co., 1971-81; dir. operational plans analysis Champlin Petroleum Co., Ft. Worth, 1981-84, v.p. fin., 1984-87; exec. v.p., chief fin. officer Union Pacific Resources Co., Ft. Worth, 1987—. Home: 4424 Westridge Ave Fort Worth TX 76116 Office: Union Pacific Resources Co 801 Cherry St Fort Worth TX 76102

JACKSON, ROBERT WILLIAM, utility company executive; b. Beaumont, Tex., June 22, 1930; s. Robert and Elizabeth (Watler) J.; m. Theta Ann Watt, Aug. 14, 1959; 1 child, Robert W. Jr. BBA, U. Tex.; MBA, U. Ill. With Gulf States Utilities Co., Beaumont, Tex., 1955-79, sec., chief fin. officer, 1972-74, sec., treas., chief fin. officer, 1974-75, v.p. fin., chief fin. officer, sec., 1975-79; v.p. fin., chief fin. officer, sec. Cen. Ill. Pub. Svc. Co., Springfield, 1979-80, sr. v.p. fin., chief fin. officer, corp. sec., 1980—, also bd. dirs.; bd. dirs. 1st Bank of Ill., Inc., Springfield, 1st Nat. Bank Springfield. Mem. bus. adv. coun. U. Ill.; bd. dirs. Springfield Symphony Orch., United Way of Sangamon County; adv. bd. St. John's Hosp., Springfield. Served with U.S. Army, 1953-55. Mem. Am. Soc. Corp. Secs., Fin. Execs. Inst., Edison Electric Inst. (fin. exec. com.). Methodist. Office: Cen Ill Pub Svc Co 607 E Adams St Springfield IL 62739

JACKSON, WILLIAM ELMER, JR., packaging company administrator; b. Washington, Pa., Oct. 25, 1935; s. William Elmer and Hazel Celestine (Moore) J.; BS in Indsl. Engring., Okla. U., 1966; MBA in Fin., U. Mo., Kansas City, 1970; children: Randall Lee, Barry Howard. With Sealright Co. Inc., Kansas City, Mo., 1966—, corp. econ. evaluation engr., 1966-69, process engr. central div., 1969-72, profit evaluation specialist, cen. div., 1972-74, corp. mgr. econ. evaluation, 1974-75, corp. ops. analysis mgr., 1975-78, adminstrv. mgr. cent. div., 1978-81, mfg. and control mgr. cen. div., 1981-83, corp. planning and devel., 1983—, chmn. eastern div. operational study project, 1976, chmn. corp. mfg. info. requirements study project, 1978, chmn. western div. operational study project, 1984, Kansas City plant relocation project, 1987, mem. bus. profile study team; sec., treas., dir. Agrl. Tech. Internat. Mktg., Inc., Louisburg, Kans., 1984-85. Com. chmn., merit badge counselor Troop 278 Heart of Am. coun. Boy Scouts Am., 1972-74; adv. Jr. Achievement of Greater Kansas City, 1974-75; caravan dir. Overland Park Nazarene Ch., 1968-74, ch. bd., 1976-79, 88—, ch. treas., 1977-78, fin. com., 1976-78, house com., 1978-79, mem. choir, 1968-81; chmn. adv. bd. mid-mgmt. program Penn Valley Community Coll., Kansas City, Mo., 1980-84, 87—; mem. Johnson County Assn. Retarded Citizens. With USAF, 1955-59. Mem. Inst. Indsl. Engrs. (sr.), Fishing Club Am. Republican. Office: 8300 Ward Pkwy Ste 500 Kansas City MO 64114

JACKSON, WILLIAM RICHARD, SR., steel company executive; b. Des Moines, May 25, 1908; s. William H. and Minnine (Long) J.; m. Lucilla Scribner, June 4, 1932; children—William Richard, Mary, Polly (Mrs. G.B. Townsend). Student, Ohio Wesleyan U., 1925-27; B.S. in Bus. Adminstrn, MIT (1930). With Am. Bridge div. U.S. Steel Corp., 1930-36; with Pitts.-Des. Moines Steel Co., 1936—, sec.-treas., 1943-59, pres., 1959-71, chmn. bd., 1971—, also dir. Trustee Dollar Savs. Bank, Pitts.; Councilman Borough Sewickley Heights, Pa., 1958—; v.p., bd. dirs. Allegheny council Boy Scouts Am., 1961—, life mem., 1987—. Mem. Am. Inst. Steel Constrn. Presbyterian (elder). Clubs: Duquesne (Pitts.); Allegheny Country (Sewickley). Office: Pitt-DesMoines Inc Neville Island Pittsburgh PA 15225

JACOBI, JOHN ALBERT, lawyer, engineer; b. Columbus, Ohio, June 28, 1947; s. James Henry and Annabelle Marie (Koenig) J.; m. Jane Alice Rohrer, Aug. 26, 1967; children: Jill Ann, James Andrew. BSME with honors, Rose-Hulman Inst. Tech., 1969; MS in Indsl. Engring., Tex. A&M U., 1970; JD, U. Mo.-Kansas City, 1975. Bar: Mo. 1976, Tex. 1979, Fla. 1980, U.S. Patent and Trademark Office, 1982, U.S. Supreme Ct. 1985. Registered profl. engr., Mo., Tex., Fla. Civilian gen. engr. Red River Army Depot, Texarkana, Tex., 1969-71; indsl. engr. U.S. Army Aviation Systems Command, St. Louis, 1971-72; chief engr. Lake City Army Ammunition Plant, Independence, Mo., 1973-78; phys. scientist Office Dir. Army Rsch., Pentagon, fall 1977; mgr. environ. affairs Tenneco Inc., Houston, 1978-79, planning mgr., 1979-80, atty., 1980-84; gen. atty. Tenn. Gas Transmission, Houston, 1985-88; mgr. tech. svcs. Tenneco Gas Transp., Houston, 1988—. Bd. dirs. Independence Fed. Credit Union, 1973-78, Tenneco Inc. Fed. Credit Union, 1985-88; mem. presdl. exch. exec., 1978-79. Olin rsch. grantee, 1968. Mem. ABA, Tex. Bar Assn., Mo. Bar Assn., Fla Bar Assn., Fed. Energy Bar Assn., NSPE, Tex. Soc. Profl. Engrs., Nat. Rifle Assn. (life), Exptl. Aircraft Assn., Blue Springs (Mo.) Jaycees (bd. dirs. 1975-77, 1st v.p. 1977), Aircraft Owners and Pilots Assn., Blue Key, Tau Beta Pi, Pi Tau Sigma, Alpha Pi Mu, Alpha Tau Omega. Office: PO Box 2511 Houston TX 77252

JACOBS, ARTHUR DIETRICH, health services executive, educator; b. Bklyn., Feb. 4, 1933; s. Lambert Dietrich and Paula Sophia (Knissel) J.; m. Viva Jane Sims, Mar. 24, 1952; children: Archie (dec.), David L., Dwayne C., Dianna K. BBA, Ariz. State U., 1962, MBA, 1966. Enlisted USAF, 1951, commd. 2d lt., 1962, advanced through grades to maj., 1972, ret., 1973; indsl. engr. Motorola, Phoenix, 1973-74; mgmt. cons. state of Ariz., 1974-76; mgmt. cons. Productivity Internat., Tempe, Ariz., 1976-79; faculty assoc. Coll. Bus. Adminstrn., Ariz. State U., Tempe, 1977—; productivity advisor Scottsdale (Ariz.) Meml. Health Services Co., 1979-84. Bd. dirs. United Way of Tempe, 1979-85. Mem. Ariz. State U. Alumni Assn. (bd. dirs. 1973-79, pres. 1978-79), Inst. Indsl. Engrs. (pres. Central Ariz. chpt. 1984-85), Am. Soc. for Quality Control, Ops. Research Soc. Am., Sigma Iota Epsilon, Beta Gamma Sigma, Delta Sigma Pi. Club: Optimist (life) (Tempe). Contbr. articles to profl. jours.

JACOBS, BARBARA FRANK, risk management consultant; b. Mt. Kisco, N.Y., June 17, 1942; d. Howard and Mary (Brown) F.; m. Stewart M. Jacobs, Aug. 30, 1964 (div. 1979). BA, U. Rochester, 1963; MS, Queens Coll., 1970. Tchr. various schs., Eastchester, Scarsdale, Harrison, N.Y., 1963-64, 67-74; editor, coll. textbook dept. David McKay Co., N.Y.C., 1964-65; hosp. adminstr. Downstate Med. Ctr., N.Y.C., 1965-67; programmer Anistics, N.Y.C., 1975-77, project mgr., 1978-82, asst. v.p., 1982-83, v.p., 1983—; systems analyst Blue Cross/Blue Shield, N.Y.C., 1977-78. Editor: The Past Recaptured, 1975. Mem. Am. Mgmt. Assn. Republican. Jewish. Avocations: classical piano playing, jewelry making, bridge, tennis. Home: 4 Field End Ln Eastchester NY 10709 Office: Anistice 220 E 42d St New York NY 10017

JACOBS, HARRY ALLAN, JR., investment firm executive; b. N.Y.C., June 28, 1921; s. Harry Allan and Elsie (Wolf) J.; m. Marie Stevens, Dec. 31, 1942; children: Nancy (Mrs. William F. Haneman, Jr.), Harry Allan III. B.A., Dartmouth Coll., 1942. With Bache Group Inc. (now Prudential-Bache Securities, Inc.), N.Y.C., 1946—; partner Bache Group Inc. (now Prudential-Bache Securities, Inc.), from 1956, dir., from 1966, pres., 1968-86, chief exec. officer, 1976, chmn., 1977-86; now sr. dir. new bus. devel. Bache Group Inc. (now Prudential-Bache Securities, Inc.), N.Y.C.; bd. govs. N.Y. Stock Exchange, 1969-72; dir. Carteret (N.J.) Savs. Bank. Trustee Trudeau Inst., Lake Placid, N.Y.; dir. Dem. Nat. Com., Ctr. Nat. Policy; former chmn. Dem. Bus. Council. Served to 1st lt. USAAF, 1942-45. Mem. Bond Club N.Y. (past gov., sec.), Assn. Stock Exchange Firms (past com. chmn., mem. exec. com.), Investment Bankers Assn. (past gov., chmn. pub. relations com.), Investment Assn. N.Y. (past pres.). Clubs: Wall Street, Univ., Econ., N.Y. Stock Exchange Luncheon (N.Y.C.); Ardsley (N.Y.) Country; Lake Placid (N.Y.). Office: Prudential-Bache Securities Inc 100 Gold St New York NY 10292

JACOBS, HERBERT HOWARD, investor; b. Freeport, N.Y., Mar. 23, 1923; s. Murray and Anna (Deutsch) J.; m. Blanche Goldman, Jan. 26, 1947; children: Lynne, Janis, Neil, Nancy. BS in Chem. Engring., Cornell U., 1944; MS in Engring., Columbia U., 1947, PhD, 1955. Assoc. Dunlap & Assocs., Inc., N.Y.C., 1949-53; v.p. Dunlap & Assocs., Inc., Stamford, Conn., 1956-62; asst. prof. Columbia U., N.Y.C., 1953-56; v.p. Hallmark Cards, Inc., Kansas City, Mo., 1962-72; pres. April House, Inc., Lenexa, Kans., 1972-77, Jacobs Co., La Jolla, Calif., 1977—; cons. Surgeon Gen. U.S., Bethesda, Md., 1956-63, Am. Greetings Corp., Cleve., 1982—, bd. dirs.; vis. prof. Waseda U., Tokyo, 1958. Contbr. numerous articles to profl. jours. Bd. trustees U. Kansas City, 1965-72. Lt. (j.g.) USNR, 1943-46, PTO. Fellow Ops. Research Soc. Am. (founder, Lanchester prize 1956); mem. Inst. Mgmt. Scis. (founding), Joint Engring Socs. (accreditation com. 1966-72), Midwest Research Inst. (trustee, exec. com.).

JACOBS, IRWIN LAWRENCE, diversified corporate executive; b. Mpls., July 15, 1941; s. Samuel and Rose H. Jacobs; m. Alexandra Light, Aug. 26, 1962; children: Mark, Sheila, Melinda, Randi, Trisha. Student pub. schs. Pres., chief exec. officer Jacobs Industries, Inc., Mpls., 1977—; chmn. bd. Fed. Fin. Corp., Mpls., 1976—; chmn. Arctic Enterprises, Inc. (now Minstar, Inc.), Mpls., from 1977, Watkins Products, Winona, Minn., 1978—; owner Grain Belt Properties, 1976—, Countryside Estates, 1978—; v.p. Northwestern Bag Corp., Mpls.; pres. Jacobs Bag Corp., 1977—, Harper-Crawford Bag Co., Charlotte, N.C., 1978—, JYJ Corp., Mpls. Shareholders Co., 1976—, JII Air Service, Inc., Mpls., 1978—, Regional Accounts Corp., Mpls., 1976—, FFC Realty, 1977—, Nationwide Collection Service, Inc., 1977—, Nationwide Accounts Corp., 1977—; chmn. Kodicor, Inc., Mpls., 1979—. Clubs: Minneapolis, Mpls. Athletic, Lafayette Country, Belle Aire Yacht, Oakridge Country. Office: Minstar Inc 100 S 5th St Minneapolis MN 55402 *

JACOBS, JOSEPH JOHN, engineering company executive; b. June 13, 1916; s. Joseph and Afiffie (Forzley) J.; m. Violet Jabara, June 14, 1942; children: Margaret, Linda, Valerie. B.S. in Chem. Engring, Poly. Inst. N.Y., Bklyn., 1937, M.S., 1939, Ph.D., 1942. Registered profl. engr., N.Y., N.J., La., Calif. Chem. engr. Autoxygen, Inc., N.Y.C., 1939-42; sr. chem. engr. Merck & Co., Rahway, N.J., 1942-44; v.p., tech. dir. Chemurgic Corp., Richmond, Calif., 1944-47; pres. Jacobs Engring. Co., Pasadena, Calif., 1947-74; chmn. bd., chief exec. officer Jacobs Engring. Group Inc., Pasadena, 1974—. Contbr. tech. articles to profl. jours. Area bd. dirs. United Way, 1978—; bd. trustees Poly. Univ. N.Y.; trustee Harvey Mudd Coll.; mem. Assocs. Calif. Inst. Tech.; bd. dirs. Genetics Inst., Inst. Contemporary Studies, Calif. Round Table, Bank Audi, Calif. Recipient Herbert Hoover medal United Engring. Socs., 1983. Fellow Am. Inst. Chem. Engrs., Am. Inst. Chemists, Inst. for Advancement Engring.; mem. Am. Chem. Soc., AAAS, Los Angeles C. of C., Pasadena C. of C., Sigma Xi, Phi Lambda Upsilon. Clubs: Altadena Town and Country, California, Annandale Golf, Pauma Valley Country. Office: Jacobs Engring Group Inc 251 S Lake Ave Pasadena CA 91101

JACOBS, LEO HERMAN, real estate investor; b. Des Moines, Nov. 19, 1902; s. Moses and Elizabeth Clara (Byoir) J. Student U. Iowa, 1921-24, U. Calif. So. Branch (now UCLA), 1924-25; A.B., U. So. Calif., 1926. Real estate salesman, 1926-27; pres., dir. Am. Gear and Parts Co., Ltd., San Francisco, 1928-34; owner, mgr. Advance Co., 1935—, bldg. contractor, 1935-75; pres., dir. Laurel Valley Devel. Co., Dallas, 1960-82. Worker, Pres. Birthday Ball, N.Y.C., 1935. Mem. Presidents Club, Old Gold Capital Club, U. Iowa Found., Phi Epsilon Pi. Lodges: Masons (Fifty Yr. award), Shriners. Recognized as most sr. Eagle Scout in U.S.

JACOBS, LINDA CARROL, computer consultant; b. Long Beach, Calif., June 26, 1946; d. Scott Willard and Darlene Ell (Wolfe) Busselle; m. Albert Stickley Jacobs, June 6, 1981; stepchildren: Bruce, Kenneth, Don, Randy, Kevin, Cynthia; m. George Henry Martin, Nov. 6, 1963 (div.); 1 child, Michael. Student Pierce Community Coll., 1971-73. Programmer, Olga Co., Inc., Van Nuys, Calif., 1971-75; programmer analyst Idaho Power Co., Inc., Boise, 1975-78; systems analyst Morrison-Knudsen Co., Boise, 1978-86; sales mktg. v.p. Delta Group, Inc., Boise, 1986-87; computer cons., Boise, 1981-87, Macintosh cons., Donnelly, Idaho, 1985—. Mem. publicity staff Rep. senatorial campaign, Boise, 1979-80. Mem. Assn. Systems Mgmt. (cert.). Republican. Methodist. Avocations: camping, hiking, snowmobiling, sailing, skiing. Home: Lake Cascade Ranch Donnelly ID 83615 Office: PO Box 564 Donnelly ID 83615

JACOBS, MARK NEIL, financial services corporation executive, lawyer; b. Ogdensburg, N.Y., Apr. 2, 1946; s. Al Milton and Alma (Rothwein) J.; m. Susan Ruth Sadowsky, Aug. 17, 1968; children: Melanie Beth, Andrew Lawrence, Jonathan Alexander. B.A., Wagner Coll., 1967; J.D., N.Y. Law Sch., 1971. Bar: N.Y. Law clk. Goldman, Frier & Altesman, N.Y.C., 1971-72; trial atty. U.S. SEC, N.Y.C., 1972-75, supervisory trial atty., br. of enforcement, 1975-77; asst. gen. counsel Dreyfus Corp., N.Y.C., 1977-82, sec., assoc. gen. counsel, 1982—; sec. The Dreyfus Third Century Fund, Inc., N.Y.C., 1977—, Dreyfus Growth Opportunity Fund, Inc., 1977—, Dreyfus Mgmt., Inc., 1977—, Dreyfus Life Ins. Co., 1982—, Daiwa Money Fund, Inc., 1981—, Gen. Money Market Fund Inc., 1981—, Gen. Govt. Securities Money Market Fund, Inc., 1982—, L.F. Rothschild Earnings and Liquidity, Inc., N.Y.C., 1982—, Dreyfus Calif. Tax Exempt Bond Fund, Inc., Dreyfus Intermediate Tax Exempt Bond Fund, Inc., N.Y.C., 1983, Dreyfus N.Y. Tax Exempt Bond Fund, Inc., 1983—, Dreyfus Capital Value Fund, Inc., 1985—, Dreyfus Cash Mgmt., Inc., 1985—, Dreyfus Consumer Life Ins. Co., 1984—, Dreyfus GNMA Fund, Inc., 1985—, Dreyfus Govt. Cash Mgmt., Inc., 1985—, Dreyfus Insured Tax Exempt Bond Fund, Inc., 1985—, Dreyfus Mass. Tax Exempt Bond Fund, 1985—, Dreyfus New Leaders Fund, Inc., 1985—, Dreyfus Personal Mgmt., Inc., 1983—, Dreyfus Tax Exempt Cash Mgmt., 1985—, Dreyfus Calif. Tax Exempt Money Market Fund, 1985—, Gen. Aggressive Growth Fund, Inc., 1984—, Gen. Tax Exempt Bond Fund, Inc., 1984—, Gen. Tax Exempt Money Market Fund, Inc., 1983, 1st Lakeshore Tax Exempt Money Market Fund, 1985, 1st Lakeshore Money Market Fund, 1985, Premier GNMA Fund, 1986, Dreyfus Taxable Mcpl. Fund, 1986, Dreyfus Treasury Cash Mgmt., 1986, Dreyfus N.Y. Insured Tax Exempt Bond Fund, 1986—, Dreyfus N.Y. Tax Exempt Intermediate Bond Fund, 1987—, Dreyfus N.Y. Tax Exempt Money Market Fund, 1987—, Dreyfus N.J. Tax Exempt Money market Fund, Inc., 1988—, various others. Mem. ABA. Home: 297 Lupine Way Short Hills NJ 07078 Office: Dreyfus Corp 885 3d Ave Suite 1600 New York NY 10022

JACOBS, NORMAN ALLAN, biotechnology executive; b. Providence, Aug. 17, 1937; s. Daniel and Bertha (Fain) Jacobs; m. Elaine Marcia Kritz, Aug. 16, 1959; children: Marjorie Ilene, Alan Jeffrey. BE in Chem. Engring., Yale U., 1958; SM in Chem. Engring., MIT, 1959; MBA, Harvard U., 1961. Comml. developer Rohm and Haas Co., Phila., 1961-62; v.p., founder Amicon Corp., Lexington, Mass., 1962-71, pres., 1971-83; pres. Amicon div. W.R. Grace & Co., Lexington, Mass., 1983-85; pres., chief operating officer BioTechnica Internat. Inc., Cambridge, Mass., 1986-88, pres., chief exec. officer, 1988—; bd. dirs. Symbion, Inc., Salt Lake City, IMRE Corp., Seattle. Co-editor: The Law and Business of Licensing, Vols. 7 and 8, 1987-88; contbr. articles to profl. jours. NSF fellow, 1958-59; Baker scholar Harvard Bus. Sch., 1961. Mem. Licensing Exec. Soc. (U.S. treas. 1971-74, U.S. pres. 1975-76, internat. treas. 1981-84), Indsl. Biotech. Assn., Am. Assn. Artificial Internal Organs, Sigma Xi, Tau Beta Pi. Jewish. Home: 141 Worthen Rd Lexington MA 02173 Office: Biotechnica Internat Inc 85 Bolton St Cambridge MA 02140

JACOBS, RICHARD MOSS, consulting engineer; b. N.Y.C., Jan. 19, 1925; s. Joseph and Rhoda E. (Levine) J.; m. Esther Rosalyn Siegal, Dec. 19, 1948; children: George Howard, Miriam Wendy, Robert Allan. BS in Indsl. Engring., Syracuse U., 1949, MS in Indsl. Engring., 1952. Registered profl. engr., N.J., Calif. Mgr. reliability engring. RCA, Moorestown, N.J., 1951-59; mgr. reliability, quality control, safety Sylvania Electric, Waltham, Mass., 1959-63; asst. dir. reliability Westinghouse Electric Co., Pitts., 1963-69; prof. indsl. engring. N.J. Inst. Tech., Newark, 1969-77; pres. Cons. Services Inst., Inc., Livingston, N.J., 1970—; mem. faculty Syracuse U., Villanova U., Drexel U., Boston U., Air Force Inst. Tech.; past internat. sec. reliability com. Internat. Electrotech. Commn., U.S. chief del., chmn. Formal Design Rev.. Com., 1969—. Mem. editorial rev. bd. Reliability Transactions IEEE, Microelectronics and Reliability. Served with USN, 1943-46. Fellow Am. Soc. Quality Control, Israel Soc. for Quality Assurance; mem. IEEE (former sec. reliability group), ANSI, ASME, ASTM, Am. Soc. Safety Engrs. Democrat. Jewish. Office: Cons Svcs Inst Inc 651 W Mt Pleasant Ave Livingston NJ 07039

JACOBS, SAMUEL, entrepreneur; b. Ainring, Fed. Republic Germany, Feb. 1, 1947; came to U.S., 1950; s. Jacob and Bronia (Band). SBEE, MIT, 1969. Assoc. engr. fed. systems div. IBM, Owego, N.Y., 1969-74; spl. products div. IBM, Endicott, N.Y., 1974-75; test engr. BG Labs., Binghamton, N.Y., 1975-76; project engr. Wyle Labs., Hampton, Va., 1976-79; reliability assurance engr. GE, Portsmouth, Va., 1979-83; dir. engring. Superior Engring. Co., Norfolk, Va., 1983-84; owner, pres. Sam's Comics and Collectibles, Newport News, Va., 1984—. Home: 1 Bonita Dr Newport News VA 23602 Office: Sams Comics & Collectibles 13262 Warwick Blvd Newport News VA 23602

JACOBS, SELWYN, marketing, sales professional; b. Paterson, N.J., Mar. 2, 1930; s. Alexander and Anna (Levine) J.; m. Marjorie Slater, Nov. 8, 1953; children: Randi S., Scott S. BS, Rutgers U., 1951. Cert. CLU, ChFC. Buyer L. Bamberger Co., Newark, 1954-56; buyer, sales adminstrn. Slaters Inc., Paterson, 1956-66; agt., supr. Mutual Benefit Life Ins. Co., N.Y.C., 1966-74; v.p. VIP Agy., Teaneck, N.J., 1974-78; pres. Creative Fin. Programs, Teaneck, 1978—; trustee North Jersey CLU, ChFCs, 1983-84. 2nd lt. U.S. Army, 1951-54. Mem. Internat. Assn. Fin. Planners, Nat. Assn. Life Underwriters, Million Dollar Round Table, Teaneck City Club. Republican. Jewish. Office: Creative Fin Program 363 Cedar Ln Teaneck NJ 07666

JACOBSEN, DANIEL TOWER, banker; b. Brookings, S.D., Oct. 15, 1932; s. Daniel Herman and Veta May (Tower) J.; m. Diane Marie Curtis, Dec. 20, 1964; children—Christopher Susannah. B.A., Knox Coll., 1954; B.F.T., Am. Grad. Sch. Internat. Mgmt., 1959; cert., Sloan Sch., MIT, 1975. Mgr. Citicorp-Citibank, Seoul, Korea, 1968-69; v.p. Citicorp-Citibank, Tokyo, 1969-72, Hong Kong, Brit. Crown Colony, 1972-75; sr. v.p. Hong Kong, Manila, 1975-80; chief auditor Hong Kong, N.Y.C., 1980—. Contbr. chpt. to book. Served with U.S. Army, 1954-57, PTO. Mem. Bank Adminstrn. Inst. (audit commn. 1980-83), Am. C. of C. (bd. dirs., v.p. 1977-80). Congregationalist. Home: 23 Hyatt Rd Briarcliff Manor NY 10510 Office: Citicorp 399 Park Ave 37th Fl New York NY 10043

JACOBSEN, DONALD MARTIN, manufacturing company executive; b. Chgo., Sept. 17, 1931; s. Martin George and Irene Francis J.; B.S. in Commerce, Roosevelt U., 1952; postgrad. Northwestern U., 1953-54; C.P.A., Ill.; m. Sally, 1985; children by previous marriage—William, Mark, Valerie, Diane, Nancy. Plant acct. Ill. Tool Works, Chgo., 1955-58; mgr. fin. analysis U.S. Industries, N.Y.C., 1958-60; dir. ednl. services div. Sci. Research Assocs. div. IBM, Chgo., 1960-65; v.p. fin. MSL Industries, Los Angeles, 1965-67; pres. Computer Programming Center, Salem, Oreg., 1967-71; v.p. Research Rev. Service div. ITT, Indpls., 1971-72; pres. Varsity House div. NSM Industries, Columbus, Ohio, 1972-75; mgmt. cons., Libertyville, Ill., 1975-80; chmn. bd., pres., chief exec. officer Cardinal Tech., Inc., St. Louis, 1981—; lectr. UCLA, So. Ill. U. Active United Way; chmn. Salem Budget Com., 1973-75. Mem. Nat. Soc. Bus. Budgeting, Assn. Data Processing Service Orgns., Am. Mgmt. Assn. Presbyterian. Clubs: Mo. Athletic, Algonquin Golf. Inventor fabric measuring device. Home: 12651 Bradford Woods Dr Sunset Hills MO 63127 Office: Cardinal Tech Inc 10820 Sunset Office Dr Suite 202 Saint Louis MO 63127

JACOBSEN, ERIC KASNER, consulting engineer; b. N.Y.C., July 21, 1932; s. Henry and Caroline (Kasner) J.; BSCE, U. Iowa, 1956; m. Dorothy H. Caldwell, Mar. 30, 1957; 1 son, Steven. Registered profl. engr., Ill., N.Y., Iowa, Mo., Wis. Structural engr. Stanley Engring. Co., Muscatine, Iowa, 1956-59; asso. dept. mgr. R. W. Booker & Assos., St. Louis, 1959-63; plant mgr. Tri-Cities Terminal div. Nat. Marine Service, Inc., Granite City, Ill., 1963-65; sr. engr. Monsanto Co., 1965-69; chief structural engr. Weitz-Hettalsater Engrs., Kansas City, 1969-72; supr. structural and archtl. engring. Austin Co., Cleve., 1972-78; mgr. Engring. Mining and Metals div., 1978-87, chief structural engr. western dist., 1987—; cons. engr. structural and archtl. engring., 1960—; owner/mgr. Jacobsen Farms. Recipient Eagle Scout award Boy Scouts Am., 1951. Mem. ASCE, ASME, Chgo. Farmers, Chi Epsilon. Presbyterian. Home: 25071 Paseo Cipres El Toro CA 92630 Office: 18800 Von Karman Ave Irvine CA 92715

JACOBSEN, JOHN CHARLES, oil company executive, lawyer; b. Detroit, Apr. 12, 1929; s. Edward Hastings and Marie (Thomas) J.; m. Frances Jane Dickey, Oct. 18, 1952; children: Scott Thomas, Kathleen Marie. B.A., Mich. State U., 1951; LL.B., Wayne State U., 1958. Bar: Mich. 1958. With Shell Oil Co., 1953—; asst. treas. Shell Oil Co., Houston, 1970-75, treas., 1975-77, controller, 1977-82, spl. assignment, 1982-83, v.p. fin., 1983—. Served to 2d lt. U.S. Army 1951-53. Mem. Mich. Bar Assn., Fin. Execs., Am. Petroleum Inst. (fin. and acctg. com.), Paton Acctg. Ctr. U. Mich. (emeritus mem.), Lambda Chi Alpha. Republican. Presbyterian. Clubs: Lakewood Yacht (Seabrook, Tex.); Houston. Office: Shell Oil Co 1 Shell Pla PO Box 2463 Houston TX 77252

JACOBSON, ALLEN FRANK, manufacturing company executive; b. Omaha, Oct. 7, 1926; s. Alma Frank and Ruth Alice (Saalfeld) J.; m. Barbara Jean Benidt, Apr. 18, 1964; children: Allen F., Holly Anne, Paul Andrew. B.S. in Chem. Engring., Iowa State U., 1947. Product engr. tape lab. 3M Co. (Minn. Mining & Mfg. Co.), St. Paul, 1947-50, tech. asst. to plant mgr., Hutchinson, Minn. and Bristol, Pa., 1950-55, tape prodn. supt., Bristol, Pa., 1955-59, plant mgr. tape, 1959-61, plant mgr. tape and AC&S, 1961-63, tape prodn. mgr., 1963, mfg. mgr. tape and allied products, 1963-68, gen. mgr. indsl. tape div., 1968-70, div. v.p. indsl. tape div., 1970-72, exec. v.p., gen. mgr., 1973-75, v.p. European ops., 1975, v.p. tape and allied products group, 1975-81, exec. v.p. indsl. and consumer sector, 1981-84, pres. U.S. ops., 1984-86, chmn., chief exec. officer, 1986—, dir., 1983—; exec. v.p., gen. mgr. 3M Can., Ltd., 1973-75; bd. dirs. Valmont Industries Inc., Valley, Nebr., U.S. West Inc., Denver, No. States Power Co., Mpls., Mobile Corp., N.Y.C. Recipient Profl. Achievement citation in engring. Iowa State U., 1983, Marston medal Iowa State U., 1986. Office: Minn Mining & Mfg Co 3M Ctr 220-14W-04 Saint Paul MN 55144-1000 *

JACOBSON, ALLEN H., economist; b. N.Y.C., July 5, 1939; s. Jack Joseph and Mary (Laxman) J.; m. Gladys Cecile Safier, Sept. 20, 1970; children: Gennifer Ann, Allison Lindsay. BA, NYU, 1962, MA, 1965. Economist Lional D. Edie & Inc., N.Y.C., 1966-69; sr. economist U.S. Trust Co., N.Y.C., 1969-79; ptnr. Washington Analysis Corp., 1979-87; v.p. County NatWest USA, Washington, 1988—. Mem. Nat. Economists Club (v.p. 1982-83), Nat. Assn. Bus. Economists (council mem. nat. chpt. 1985-86), Washington Assn. Money Mgrs., Lakewood Club, Norbeck Club. Home: 13140 Bushwood Way Potomac MD 20854 Office: County Securities Corp USA 1612 K St NW Washington DC 20006

JACOBSON, ALLEN MARTIN, controller; b. Mpls., Aug. 10, 1945; s. Arthur Emelius and Esther Amanda (Martinson) J. BA, Antioch Coll., 1969; MBA, NYU, 1981. Asst. dir. overseas ops. AFS Intercultural Programs, N.Y.C., 1970-73, sr. acct., fin. analyst, asst. treas., 1973-86; controller, v.p. for ptnr. fin., sr. v.p. fin. United Way of Tri-State, N.Y.C., 1986—. Lutheran. Home: 35-30 81st St Jackson Heights NY 11372 Office: United Way Tri-State 99 Park Ave New York NY 10016

JACOBSON, ANNA SUE, finance company executive; b. Ft. Smith, Ark., Aug. 13, 1940; d. Ray Bradley and Joy Anna (Person) McAlister, (stepfather) Cleve J. McDonald, Sr.; m. Lyle Norman Jacobson, Nov. 23, 1958; children: Lyle Michael, Daniel Ray, Julie Anne, Eric Joseph. B in Fin. Planning, Coll. for Fin. Planning, 1984. Cert. fin. paraplanner. Office mgr. Twin Cities Lithographic Inst., St. Paul, 1963-66; sec., St. Paul, Mpls., 1971-78; asst. to pres., office mgr. Planners Fin. Svcs., Mpls., 1978-85, asst. corp. treas., 1987—; fin. paraplanner McAlmont Investment Co., Mpls., 1985-88, office mgr., 1988—; rep. McAlmont Investment Co., 1989—; bd. dir. Planners Fin. Svcs.; mem. bd. advisors Coll. for Fin. Planning, Denver, 1982—; speaker various orgns. Co-creator Paraplanning Profession Advisor; asst. sales cons. Skie & Assocs., St. Louis Park, Minn., 1987—. Del. Dem. Farmer Labor Com., St. Paul, 1980; campaign chmn. mayoral election, Roseville, Minn., 1983, county commr., city coun. election, Roseville, 1980, 84; local chmn. for passage of ERA, Minn.; chmn. Am. Lung Assn., St. Paul; past. pres. PTA, Minn.; mem. exec. coun. Boy Scouts Am., 1977-81; mem. adv. bd. Sch. Dist. 623, Roseville, Minn., 1978-81; fund raising com. mem. Twin Cities Pub. TV Sta., 1975—. Recipient Volunteerism award State of Minn., 1981, Cert. of Appreciation Minn. Bicentennial Com., 1976. Mem. Internat. Assn. Fin. Planning, Twin Cities Assn. Fin. Planners, Internat. Assn. Bus. and Profl. Women (bd. dirs. 1977-86, pres. 1980-82, Woman of Yr. 1982), Concordia Acad. Booster Club, Beta Sigma Phi Nu Phi Mu Chpt. Democrat. Lutheran. Avocations: tennis, riding, reading, piano, fencing. Office: McAlmont Investment Co Shelard Pla N Minneapolis MN 55426

JACOBSON, BARRY STEPHEN, lawyer, administrative judge; b. Bklyn., Mar. 30, 1955; s. Morris and Sally (Ballaban) J. Cert. in drama, Sch. of Performing Arts, N.Y.C., 1973; BA, CUNY, 1977, MA, 1980; JD, Bklyn. Sch. Law, 1980. Bar: N.Y. 1981, U.S. Dist. Ct. (ea. and so. dists.) N.Y. 1981, U.S. Ct. Appeals (2d cir.) 1981, U.S. Supreme Ct. 1984, D.C. 1985, U.S. Ct. Claims 1985, U.S. Ct. Internat. Trade 1985, U.S. Ct. Mil. Appeals 1985, U.S. Ct. (we. and no. dists.) N.Y. 1988, U.S. Tax Ct., U.S. Ct. Appeals (fed. cir.), U.S. Ct. Appeals (D.C. cir.), U.S. Dist. Ct. D.C. Sole practice Bklyn., 1981; asst. corp. counsel N.Y.C. Law Dept., Bklyn., 1981-84; asst. dist. atty. Borough of Queens, Kew Gardens, N.Y., 1984-85; judge adminstrv. law N.Y. Dept. Motor Vehicles, Bklyn., 1985-86, 87—; assoc. counsel N.Y. State Dept. Health, N.Y.C., 1986; arbitrator N.Y.C. Small Claims Ct., 1986—; gen. counsel Amersfort Flatlands Devel. Corp., Bklyn., 1981-82; arbitrator N.Y.C. Civil Ct. 1987—; adminstrv. law judge N.Y.C. Parking Violators Bur., 1987—; mem. Indigent Defenders Appeal Panel, 1988—. Mem. Roosevelt Dem. Party, Bklyn., 1984—, mem. adv. bd., 1989—; mem. Kings Hwy. Dem. Party, Bklyn., 1982—; King's County Dem. com., 1986—; active King's County Young Dems., 1985-86; gen. counsel, Bklyn. Coll. Hillel, Bklyn. Coll. Student Govts., 1980—, also advisor; treas. local div. dept. motor vehicles pub. emplpoyees fedn. AFL-CIO; chmn. Bklyn. Traffic Employee Assistance Program, 1989—. Named one of Outstanding Young Men Am., 1983, 85, 86, 87, 88. Mem. ABA, N.Y. State Bar Assn. (spl. com. juvenile justice), Bklyn. Bar Assn. (family ct. com., chmn. young lawyers section), N.Y. County Lawyers Assn. (family ct. com.), Am. Judicature Soc., Bklyn. Coll. Alumni Assn. (gen. counsel student govt. affiliate 1983—, bd. dirs. 1985—), Jaycees (named one of Outstanding Young Men of Am. 1983, 85, 85, 87, 88), Am. Arbitration Assn. (arbitration forums 1988—), Assn. Administrv. Law Judges (pres. N.Y. state dept. motor vehicles, v.p. 1989—), NRA, Am. Judges Assn., Am. Inns of Ct. Found. (charter mem. Bklyn. chpt.), Phi Delta Phi (hon.). Jewish. Lodges: B'nai B'rith, Hillei (bd. dirs. 1983—, gen. counsel 1987—). Home: 2912 Brighton 12th St Brooklyn NY 11235 Office: NY State Dept Motor Vehicles 350 Livingston St 4th Fl Brooklyn NY 11217

JACOBSON, BONNIE BROWN, energy and utility company executive, statistician; b. Annapolis, Md., Feb. 15, 1952; d. Albert Robert and Ruth Marie (Puhak) Brown; m. Peter Roy Jacobson, Apr. 28, 1979. BS cum laude, LaRoche Coll., Pitts., 1974; MS, U. Pitts., 1976. Research scholar U. Pitts., 1974-76; research assoc. Squibb Inst. Med. Research, Princeton, N.J., 1976-78; assoc. statistician N.E. Utilities Service Co., Hartford, Conn., 1978-80, statistician, 1980-82, sr. statistician, 1982-83, mgr. consumer research, 1983-87, corp. statistician, 1987-89; project mgr. energy dept. ICF Resources Inc., Fairfax, Va., 1989—; cons. stats., Hartford, 1976-89; adviser Electric Power Research Inst., Palo Alto, Calif., 1978-89. Research plan developer Conn. Energy Assistance Study Project, Hartford, 1983-84. Mem. Am. Statis. Assn., Am. Mktg. Assn., Nat. Assn. Female Execs., Electric Utility Market Research Council. Club: Sport and Leisure (Wallingford, Conn.). Avocations: golf, skiing, racquetball, gardening, reading. Home: 12302 Sleepy Lake Ct Fairfax VA 22033 Office: ICF Resources Inc 9300 Lee Hwy Fairfax VA 22031

JACOBSON, CHARLES MAY, financial planning executive; b. Summit, N.J., Oct. 28, 1941; s. Saul Baum and Carolyn (Schwed) J.; m. Ruth Ellen Fink; children: Sarah Garner, Lee Schwed. BS in Bus., U. Del., 1965; MBA, Seton Hall U., 1967, cert. internat. bus., 1969. Cert. fin. planner. Supr. fin. analysis Atlantic-Richfield Corp., N.Y.C., 1967-71; mgr. budgets Warnaco, Bridgeport, Conn., 1971-73; sr. cons. Xerox Corp., Stamford, Conn., 1973-75; mgr. capital budgets Warner Lambert Co., Morris Plains, N.J., 1975-80; dir. planning Sterling Drug Co., Montvale, N.J., 1980-82; ptnr. Midwest Fin. Mgmt. Corp., Edina, Minn., 1982-88; founder Jacobson & Assocs., Edina, 1988—; Frequent lectr. to civic orgns. Contbr. articles to profl. jours. Mem. Inst. Cert. Fin. Planners, Twin Cities Assn. Fin. Planners (bd. dirs. 1984-87), Am. Arbitration Assn. (apptd.). Jewish. Lodge: Rotary. Home: 6801 Chapel Ln Edina MN 55435 Office: Jacobson & Assocs 6800 France Ave Ste 178 Edina MN 55435

JACOBSON, DENNIS LEONARD, business executive; b. Stoughton, Wis., May 19, 1945; s. Leonard Harold and Elaine Marie (Folbrecht) J.; B.S. in Bus. Adminstrn. and Econs., U. Wis., 1967; m. Jane Marie McGill, June 3, 1967; children—Timothy Dennis, Darren Todd. Price analyst Caterpillar, Geneva, 1967-71, pricing supr., Peoria, Ill., 1971-73; mgr. pricing Overseas div. Internat. Harvester Co., Chgo., 1973-76, asst. to mng. dir. Internat. Harvester Germany, Neuss/Rhine, W. Ger., 1976-78, mgr. distbr. mktg. Internat. Harvestor Agrl. Equipment Europe, Paris, 1978-81, dir. export mktg. Equipment Group, 1978-84; v.p. mktg. Internat. Group Internat. Harvestor, 1984-85, v.p. sales and mktg., Fed. Signal Corp., 1985-86; dir. internat. ops. Outboard Marine Corp., Waukegan, Ill., 1986-88, v.p., corp. officer, 1988—. Pres., parent faculty assn. Am. Internat. Sch., 1977-78. Bd. dirs. St. Therese Hosp., Waukegan, 1987—. Club: Am. Men's. Home: 1420 Lawrence Ave Lake Forest IL 60045

JACOBSON, ELI ASHER, financial management company executive; b. N.Y.C., July 17, 1947; s. Nathan and Claire (Gottfried) J.; m. Kristina Lilja, 1982; children: Scott, Lori. BA, U. Akron, 1969; postgrad., Cleve. State U., 1969-70. CLU; cert. fin. cons. Agt., asst. supr., then supr. Aetna Life & Casualty Co., Cleve., 1969-75; agy. dir. Res. Life Ins. Co., Dallas, 1975-78; regional sales mgr. Time Ins. Co., Milw., 1983-86; v.p. group mktg. Interstate Cos., Columbus, Ohio, 1987—; prin., chief exec. officer, bd. dirs. Jacobson Mgmt. Trust, Columbus, 1970—; pres., chief exec. officer Columbus Basketball Inc.; bd. dirs. Coshocton Valley Mfg. Corp., West Lafayette, Ohio, chmn. bd.; chief exec. officer Columbus Basketball, Inc. Mem. devel. bd. Columbus Children's Hosp.; bd. dirs. Arthritis Found. Mem. Chartered Fin. Counselors, Am. Inst. CLU's, Nat. Assn. Life Underwriters, Nat. Assn. Health Underwriters. Republican. Jewish. Home: 2014 Collingswood Rd Columbus OH 43221 Office: Jacobson Mgmt Trust 6649 N High St Ste LL5 Worthington OH 43085

JACOBSON, ISHIER, utility executive; b. Worcester, Mass., June 21, 1922; s. Aaron and Mollie (Mallor) J.; m. Maria Bohm, Dec. 18, 1948; children: Joanna M., Jonathan B., Paula R. B.A., Clark U., 1946; M.S. in Mech. Engring, Harvard U., 1947, LL.B., 1951. Bar: Conn. bar. Asst. to pres., gen. counsel Connor Engring. Corp., Danbury, Conn., 1951-53; with Citizens Utilities Co., Stamford, Conn., 1954—; exec. v.p. Citizens Utilities Co., 1970, pres., chief operating officer, 1970-81, pres., chief exec. officer, 1981—, also dir.; dir. subs. cos. Citizens Utilities Co.; dir. Vt. Electric Co. Served to lt. USNR, 1942-46. Home: 326 Four Brooks Rd Stamford CT 06903 Office: Citizens Utilities Co High Ridge Pk PO Box 3801 Stamford CT 06905

JACOBSON, JAMES BASSETT, financial services executive; b. San Francisco, Nov. 16, 1922; s. James Peter and Bertha (Bassett) J.; m. Janice Isabel Meilstrup, Aug. 29, 1949; children: Steven Blair, Karen Christine, Richard Barlow. BS, UCLA, 1947; student, Wharton Sch. U. Pa., 1947-48; MBA, U. So. Calif., Los Angeles, 1954. CLU. Dir. group sales and service Prudential Ins. Co. Am., Newark, N.J., 1964-66; exec. dir. group ins. Prudential Ins. Co. Am., Newark, 1966-67, v.p. group pension mktg., 1967-70, sr. v.p. in charge group ins., 1970-73; pres., western ops. Prudential Ins. Co. Am., L.A., 1973-83; exec. v.p. CalFed Inc. and Calif. Fed. Savs. & Loan Assn., L.A., 1983-87; chmn., chief exec. officer Beneficial Standard Life Ins. Co., L.A., 1987-88, chmn. bd. dirs., 1984-88; chmn. bd. dirs. Direct Mktg. Corp. Am., 1984-88, Celluloid Corp, 1988—; bd. dirs. Am. Med. Internat., Beverly Hills, Calif., Internat. Lease Fin. Corp., Beverly Hills, Bonneville Internat. Corp., Salt Lake City; Turnaround Mgmt. Assn., Wherehouse, Inc., N.W. Pipe and Casing; pres. Peterson Outdoor Advt., 1988, AMA Mgmt. Corp., 1988—, Stoody Corp., 1987. Author: An Analysis of Group Creditors Insurance, 1954. V.p. Los Angeles Philharmonic Assn., 1977-83, bd. dirs., 1975-83; vice chmn. Community TV of So. Calif., Los Angeles, 1983, bd. dirs., 1979-83; chmn. bd. dirs. Orthopaedic Hosp., Los Angeles, 1981-84, trustee, 1980-84; chmn. bd. Los Angeles Ballet, 1974-79, bd. dirs. 1974-83; bd. councilors U. So. Calif. Grad. Sch. Bus., 1977-85; vice chmn., mem. fin. com. Los Angeles Bicentennial Com., 1979-81; pres. Hollywood Turf Club Assoc. Charities, 1981-82. Served to 2d lt. U.S. Army, 1943-46, res. 1951, ETO. Recipient Silver Beaver award Los Angeles council Boy Scouts Am., 1984. Mem. Am. Coll. CLU's, Calif. Round Table, UCLA Alumni Assn. (community service award 1985), Calif. C. of C. (bd. dirs. 1974-83), L.A. C. of C. (bd. dirs. 1981-83), Beta Gamma Sigma. Clubs: Calif., Los Angeles Country, The 100 (Los Angeles), Lochinvars (pres. 1981-84), Lincoln (Los Angeles).

JACOBSON, JAMES LAMMA, JR., data processing company executive; b. Washington, May 19, 1946; s. James Lamma Jacobson Sr. and Hazel Virginia (Howard) Jacobson Tatelman; m. Dayle Barbara Jackson, Dec. 30, 1972; children: Julie, Christie, Jennie. BBA, Drexel U., 1969. Systems engr. IBM Corp., Arlington, Va., 1969-70, mktg. rep., 1970-74; mktg. instr. IBM Corp., Atlanta, 1975-76; mktg. mgr. IBM Corp., Akron, Ohio, 1977-79; founder, pres. Jacore Technologies, Inc., Atlanta, 1979-84, chmn., 1985—. Mem. Ch. of God. Home: 2535 Johnson Ferry Rd Marietta GA 30062

JACOBSON, LARRY, finance company executive; b. Balt., Aug. 9, 1943; s. Sidney and Mildred (Hoffman) J.; m. Paula Quartel, June 29, 1975; children: Owen Paul, Paul Austin. BS in Labor Studies, SUNY, N.Y.C., 1981. Apprentice electrician local union #3 Internat. Brotherhood Elec. Workers, N.Y.C., 1961-69, journeyman electrician, 1969-81; asst. to chmn. joint industry bd. Electric Industry, N.Y.C., 1981—; mem. pension investment policy group N.Y. State AFL-CIO, N.Y.C., 1984—; bd. dirs. Community Capital Bank. Mem. polit. dist. orgn. Internat. Brotherhood Elec. Workers, Flushing, N.Y., 1979-81. Mem. Allied Union Social Club (Queens, N.Y.), Leonia Tennis Club (N.J., bd. dirs. 1985—). Democrat. Jewish. Home: 308 Park Ave Leonia NJ 07605 Office: Joint Industry Bd Elec Industry 158-11 Jewel Ave Flushing NY 11365

JACOBSON, LEWIS MICHAEL, manufacturing executive; b. Chgo., Aug. 7, 1942; s. Mandel and Edna (Story) J. BS, Ill. Inst. Tech., 1964. CLU. Health underwriter, cost analyst Prudential Ins. Co., Chgo., 1964-70; mgr. individual plans devel. and sales, office adminstrn. CNA, Chgo., 1970-75; mgr. corp. personnel, benefit plans adminstr. Joslyn Corp., Chgo., 1975—. Pres. Tempo Homeowners Assn., Hanover Park, Ill., 1972-74; active Chgo. Heart Assn., 1985—; area co-chmn. Ravinia Coupon Com., Chgo., 1987-88; bd. dirs., treas. Friday Night Group, Chgo., 1987-88, 89—. Fellow Life Mgmt. Inst.; mem. Am. Soc. Personnel Adminstrn., Soc. for Human Resource Profls. (bd. dirs. 1986, sec. 1987, pres.-elect 1988, pres. 1989). Republican. Jewish. Home: 6033 N Sheridan Rd Apt 45C Chicago IL 60660 Office: Joslyn Corp 30 S Wacker Dr Chicago IL 60606

JACOBSON, MILTON MURRAY, auditor; b. Pitts., Sept. 21, 1952; s. Sidney and Dena Ruth (Ferguson) J. BSBA, Duquesne U., 1975; MBA, U. Ariz., 1981. CPA, Md.; cert. data processor; cert. info. systems auditor. Civilian auditor U.S. Army, Washington, 1978-79; rsch. asst. U. Ariz., Tucson, 1980; sr. auditor Def. Contract Audit Agy., Columbia, Md., 1981-88; staff auditor Health Care Fin. Admnstrn., Balt., 1988—. Pres. Consumers Orgn. for Hearing Impaired, Silver Spring, Md., 1985-86. Mem. Assn. Govt. Accts., EDP Auditors Assn., Am. Inst. CPA's. Club: Merritt Athletic. Home: 3000 G Fallstaff Manor Ct Baltimore MD 21209

JACOBSON, MIRIAM NACHAMAH, lawyer; b. Westfield, Mass., Feb. 25, 1941; d. Bernard and Rose (Heller) J.; m. S. David Scher, Apr. 23, 1978. BA summa cum laude, CUNY, 1975; JD, Yale U., 1978. Bar: Pa. 1978, U.S. Dist. Ct. (ea. dist.) Pa. 1978. Assoc. Mesirov, Gelman, Jaffe, et al, Phila., 1978-82, Cohen, Shapiro, Polisher, et al, Phila., 1983; v.p., assoc. counsel Fidelity Bank, N.A., Phila., 1984-87; prin. Law Offices of Miriam N. Jacobson, Phila., 1987—. Co-founder, treas. Lawyers Com. Reproductive Rights, Phila., 1981-85; bd. dir. Yale Law Sch. Fund, New Haven, Conn.; active Nat. Abortion Rights Action League, Planned Parenthood. Mem. ABA, Pa. Bar Assn. (real property and banking sects.), Phila. Bar Assn. (real property and banking sect.), Women Real Estate Attys. (organizer, coordinator 1979—), ACLU, Nat. Orgn. for Women; Nat. Assn. of Women Lawyers, Bus. Women's Network, Nat. Women's Polit. Caucus, Nat. Assn. Women Bus. Owners. Office: Law Offices Miriam N Jacobson 30 South 15th St Ste 1200 Philadelphia PA 19102

JACOBSON, RICHARD NORMAN, chemical engineer; b. Neenah, Wis., Dec. 21, 1942; s. Randolph N. and Lorraine A.J.; m. Elaine Hamilton, Mar. 22, 1969 (div. July 1986); children: Eric, Christopher; m. Margaret Evans Reid, May 7, 1988; 1 child, David. BS, Mich. State U., 1965; PhD, Calif. Inst. Tech., 1970. Registered profl. engr., Pa. Sr. chem. engr. Occidental Petroleum Corp., LaVerne, Calif., 1970-74; with Foote Mineral Co., Malvern, Pa., 1974-88; dir. engring. Foote Mineral Co., Exton, 1981-82, v.p., 1983-88; v.p. engring. Cyprus Foote Mineral Co., Malvern, Pa., 1988—. Mem. Am. Inst. Chem. Engrs., Soc. Mining Engrs. Republican. Lutheran. Office: Cyprus Foote Mineral Co 301 Lindenwood Malvern PA 19355-1740

JACOBUS, RUSSELL LEE, retail store executive; b. Bossier City, La., Aug. 8, 1953; s. Lawrence R. and Patricia Jane (Kelleher) J.; m. Holly Hess, July 31, 1976 (div. 1979); m. Patricia Margaret Oppenheimer, Sept. 13, 1987. BA, Santa Clara U., 1975, JD, 1978; MBA, St. Mary's Coll., 1983. Bar: Calif. 1975. With Safeway Stores Inc., Oakland, Calif., 1971—; now v.p. asset fin. Safeway Stores Inc., Oakland. Office: Safeway Stores Inc 201 4th St Oakland CA 94660

JACOCKS, HENRY MILLER, bank executive; b. Hampton, Va., Mar. 14, 1953; s. Wilbur Harrell and Gussie Anita (Cox) J.; m. Barbara Alexander Van Vleck, Sept. 13, 1975; children: Caitlin, Laura. BS in Pub. Adminstrn., Va. Poly. Inst., 1976. Dist. mgr. Automatic Data Processing, Inc., Richmond, 1984-86; loan officer Cardian Mortgage Corp., Richmond, 1986—, br. mgr., 1986-88; agt. New York Life, Richmond, 1988—. Named one of Outstanding Young Men Am., U.S. Jaycees, 1980, 81, 85. Mem. Richmond Assn. Life Underwriters, Jaycees (bd. dirs. Richmond club 1979-83). Republican. Presbyterian. Home: 8026 Spottswood Rd Richmond VA 23229 Office: New York Life 9501 Arboretum Pkwy Ste 350 Richmond VA 23236

JACOX, JOHN WILLIAM, mechanical engineer and consulting company executive; b. Pitts., Dec. 12, 1938; s. John Sherman and Grace Edna (Herbster) J.; 1 child, Brian Erik. BSME in Indsl. Mgmt., Carnegie Mellon U., 1962, BS in Indsl. Mgmt, 1962. Mfg. engr. Nuclear Fuel div. Westinghouse Elec. Co., Pitts., 1962-64; rsch. engr. Continental Can Co. Metal R&D Ctr., Pitts., 1964-65; dataprocessing sales engr. IBM, Pitts., 1965-66; mktg. mgr. nuclear products MSA Internat., Pitts., 1966-72; v.p. Nuclear Cons. Svcs., Inc., Columbus, Ohio, 1973-84; v.p. NUCON Internat., 1981-84; bd. dirs. NUCON Europe Ltd., London, 1981—; pres. Jacox Assocs., Inc., 1984—; div. mgr. Space Techs. div. Fiber Materals Inc., 1988—; cons., lectr. Nat. Ctr. for Rsch. in Vocat. Edn., 1978-84 ; author, presenter, session chmn. DOE/Harvard Nuclear Air Cleaning Confs., 1974—; lectr. Harvard Sch. Pub. Health Air Cleaning Lab., 1986—; co-chmn. program subcom. Tech. Alliance Cen. Ohio, 1984-85, vice-chmn., chmn.-elect dir. subcom., 1986-87, chmn. bd. trustees, 1986; program com. World Trade Devel. Club; mem. legis. svcs. com. coop. edn. adv. com. Otterbein Coll., 1978-82. Mem. ASME (code com. nuclear air and gas treatment, main exec. com., chmn. subcom. field test procedures), Am. Nuclear Soc. (pub. info. com.), N.Y. Acad. Scis. (life), Ohio Acad. Sci. (life), Inst. Environ. Scis., Electric Overstress-Electrostatic Discharge Assn., ASHRAE, Inc. (standards com.), Air Pollution Control Assn., Am. Nat. Standards Inst., Columbus Area C. of C. (tech. roundtable 1983), ASTM (F-21), ASM, Air Force Assn. (life), Mensa, Nat. Rifle Assn. (patron), Sun Bunch (pres. 1980-81). Club: Capitol. Home: 5874 Northern Pine Pl Columbus OH 43229 Office: PO Box 29720 Columbus OH 43229

JAEGER, IRWIN JEROME, real estate developer; b. N.Y.C., Sept. 18, 1931; s. Phillip and Emma (Zussman) J.; m. Patricia Heit, June 12, 1977; children: Michael, Wendy, Jeffrey. Student, U. Mich., 1948-50; BBA, U. Cin., 1953; MBA, NYU, 1954. V.p. United Dept. Stores, Cin., 1950-63; pres. Jaeger Corp., L.A., 1963—, Jaeger Industries, Inc., L.A., 1963—, SG&T, Inc., L.A., 1982—; mng. ptnr. WMJ Partnership, L.A., 1983—, Jaeger Family Partnership, L.A., 1984—; pres. Jaeger Devel. Co., L.A., 1984—; mng. ptnr. Jaeger Enterprises, L.A., 1987—, Rose Canyon Bus. Park Partnership, San Diego, 1987—; cons. MRA Cons. Orgn., N.Y.C. Pres. Big Bros. of Cin., 1968, Irwin J. Jaeger Found., L.A., 1988—; treas. So. Calif. Counseling Ctr., L.A., 1988—; bd. dirs. Para Los Ninos Found., L.A., 1988—, Jewish Fedn., Cin., 1969; mem. planning and allocations com. Jewish Fedn., L.A., 1988—. Mem. Losantiville Club of Cin., Beta Gamma Sigma. Democrat. Office: Jaeger Corp 2121 Avenue of the Stars Ste 1575 Los Angeles CA 90067

JAEGER, THOMAS, financial executive; b. Augsburg, Fed. Republic Germany, Dec. 15, 1946; came to U.S., 1983; s. Johannes and Ilse (Tscheuschner) J.; m. Susanne Margarete Waibel, Feb. 17, 1977; children: Nikolaus, Magdalene, Federica, Moritz. PhD in Law, U. Innsbruck, 1975, MBA in Bus., 1976. Asst. to Dr. Oetker Bielefeld, Fed. Republic Germany, 1977-80; sr. contr. beverage div. R.A. Oetker Zentral-Verwaltung, Bielefeld, Fed. Republic Germany, 1980-83; sr. v.p. fin. Hapag-Lloyd (Am.) Inc., N.Y.C., 1983—; sec.-treas. Hapag-Lloyd Travel (Am.), Inc., N.Y.C., 1983—; sec. Hapag-Lloyd Travel, Inc., N.Y.C., 1987—. Mem. Deutscher Controller Verein West Germany, Coveleigh Club (Rye, N.Y.). Home: 12 Maplewood Ln Port Chester NY 10573 Office: Hapag-Lloyd (Am) Inc One Edgewater Pla Staten Island NY 10305

JAFFE, ANDREW MARK, editor; b. Boston, Aug. 2, 1938; s. Henry Leslie and Diana (Gaines) J.; divorced; 1 child, Christopher. BA, Pomona Coll., 1960; MS, Columbia U., 1962. Newsman AP, L.A., 1964-66; corr. Newsweek mag., Atlanta, 1966-69; African bur. chief Newsweek mag., Nairobi, Kenya, 1969-76; bur. chief Newsweek mag., Miami, 1976-77; bus. editor L.A. Herald Examiner, 1978-84; v.p. Spl. Expdns., N.Y.C., 1984-85; editor Adweek/SouthEast, Atlanta, 1985-88; editorial dir. Adweek, AdDay, Winners mags., N.Y.C., 1988—; instr. UCLA Extension, 1979-84, Atlanta Portfolio Ctr., 1987-88. Author: (with others) Alaska: Southeast to McKinley, 1986; contbg. editor Atlanta mag., 1987-88. Bd. dirs. Atlanta Virtuosi, 1986-88. 1st lt. U.S. Army, 1962-64, Korea. Mem. Am. Soc. Mag. Editors, Overseas Press Club, Sigma Delta Chi. Office: Adweek Mag 49 E 21st St New York NY 10010

JAFFE, AUSTIN JAY, business administration educator; b. Chgo., Aug. 15, 1952; s. Aaron and Shirley (Davis) J.; m. Lynn Laiken, June 12, 1977; 1 child, Alexander M. BS in Fin., U. Ill., 1974, MS in Fin., 1975, PhD in Fin., 1978. Fellow Coll. Bus. Adminstrn., U. Ill., Urbana, 1974-75; asst. prof. fin. and real estate Coll. Bus. Adminstrn., U. Oreg., Eugene, 1977-80; vis. asst. prof. Coll. Bus. Adminstrn., Pa. State U., University Park, 1980-81, assoc. prof., 1981-87, prof., 1987—, dir. research Inst. for Real Estate Studies, 1985—; vis. prof. dept. real estate econs. Royal Inst. Tech., Stockholm, 1987-88; pres. JS & Assocs., State College, Pa., 1987—; advisor and cons. real estate. Author: Fundamentals of Real Estate Investment (2d edit.), 1988, Complete Real Estate Investment Handbook, 4th edit. 1988, Analyzing Real Estate Decisions Using Lotus 1-2-3, 1985; functional editor: Interfaces, 1987-88; editor book of research papers on law and econs., 1987; mem. editorial rev. bd. Jour. of Managerial Issues, 1988—; developer computer software Real Estate Invest Templates, 1987; contbr. articles to profl. and acad. jours. Rsch. grantee Swedish Inst., 1987, S.W. Council for Bldg. Rsch./S.W. Fedn. Rental Property Owners, 1988; Homer Hoyt Advanced Studies Inst. fellow, 1988—. Mem. Am. Real Estate and Urban Econs. Assn. (bd. dirs. 1984-86, 89—, mem. editorial rev. bd. 1984-87), Am. Real Estate Soc. (mem. editorial rev. bd. 1986—), Research in Real Estate (mem. editorial review bd., 1987—), Nat. Tchg. Faculties, Am. Inst. Real Estate Appraisers, Lincoln Inst. Land Policy, Am. Fin. Assn., European Fin. Assn., Fin. Mgmt. Assn., Internat. Ctr. for Land Policy Studies, Beta Gamma Sigma. Jewish. Home: 505 W Nittany Ave State College PA 16801 Office: Pa State U Coll Bus Adminstrn University Park PA 16802

JAFFE, DAVID ROYCE, investment executive; b. Stamford, Conn., June 27, 1959; s. Elliot Stanley and Roslyn (Solomon) J. BSE/BA with honors, U. Pa., 1981; MBA, Stanford U., 1985. Portfolio mgr. Merrill Lynch Asset Mgmt., N.Y.C., 1981-83; gen. ptnr. Chem. Venture Ptnrs., N.Y.C., 1985—; mem. adv. bd. Mgmt. Horizons; bd. dirs. Office Depot, Boca Raton, Fla., Superior Coach, Lima, Ohio, VCA/Teletronics, N.Y.C., Erik Chandler Communications, L.A.; assoc. dir. Pentacle, N.Y.C. Mem. steering com. Am. Jewish World Svc., N.Y.C. Mem. Nat. Venture Capital Assn., Nat. Assn. Small Bus. Investment Cos., N.Y. Venture Capital Forum (event co-chmn. 1988). Office: Chem Ventures Ptnrs 277 Park Ave 11th Fl New York NY 10172

JAFFE, EDWIN HENRY, financial consultant; b. West Memphis, Ark., Feb. 7, 1960; s. Eli H. Jaffe and Rosemary (Sullivan) Croker. BBA, Ark. State U., 1981. Owner Edwin H. Jaffe Photography, Rogers, Ark., 1982-83; trainee to sr. compliance specialist Merrill Lynch, Memphis, 1983-85; registered rep. N. Y. Life Ins. Co., Memphis, 1985-86; fin. cons. Shearson Lehman Hutton Inc., Memphis, 1986-88, Jonesboro, Ark., 1988—. Counselor Boy Scouts Am., Memphis, 1986-88. Recipient Eagle Scout award Boy Scouts Am., 1975. Mem. Lambda Chi Alpha Alumni Assn. Republican.

Home: PO Box 335 Jonesboro AR 72403 Office: Shearson Lehman Hutton Inc 411 S Main St Ste 604 Jonesboro AR 72401

JAFFE, ELLIOT S., women's clothing retail chain executive; b. Paterson, N.J., May 3, 1926; s. Samuel and Frieda (Wolf) J.; m. Roslyn S. Solomon, July 6, 1952; children: Elise, Richard, David. BS, U. Pa., 1949. Merchandise mgr. R.H. Macy & Co., N.Y.C., 1949-62; pres., chmn. bd. The Dress Barn, Stamford, Conn., 1962—; bd. dirs. Shearson Lehman Hutton family of funds, Zweig Total Return Fund. Treas. Stamford Mus. and Nature Ctr., 1979-80; chmn. bd. trustees Family & Children's Services, Stamford, 1987—; bd. dirs. Stamford Hosp., 1987—. Served with U.S. Army, 1943-46. Recipient Chief Exec. Officer Yr. Bronze medal award Fin. World mag., N.Y.C., 1986, Bronze Chief Exec. Officer of Decade award Apparel div., 1989; named one of top 1000 chief exec. officers (Corp. Elite) Bus. Week mag., 1987. Mem. Am. Bus. Conf. Clubs: Harmonie, Princeton (N.Y.C.); Rockrimmon Country (Stamford). Office: The Dress Barn Inc 88 Hamilton Ave Stamford CT 06902

JAFFE, LEONARD MAURICE, financial planner, consultant; b. Kankakee, Ill., June 25, 1934; s. Benjamin Harry and Henrietta (Kleinhammer) J.; m. Sandra Gayle Barnbaum, Nov. 3, 1957; children: Loryn Hope, Melissa Suzanne. BS, U. Ill., 1957; cert., Coll. Fin. Planning, 1982. Owner Snowite Laundry, Kankakee, 1960-72; v.p. John Shannon Assocs., Chgo., 1972-83; sr. assoc. Capital Analysts, San Diego, 1983-87; prin. C.I.T.E. Fin. Svcs., San Diego, 1987—; Past pres. Ill. Laundry Assn., 1965. Contbr. mag. articles on fin. planning. Mem. seminar com. San Diego Cancer Soc., 1986; Rep. precinct capt., south suburbs Chgo., 1972-76; mem. Automotive Service Council. Mem. Internat. Assn. Fin. Planning (bd. dirs. 1982-83), Inst. Cert. Fin. Planners, San Diego C. of C. (seminar com. 1983-87). Club: Univ. of San Diego (chmn. Speaker's Forum). Lodge: Rotary (North San Diego). Home: 14683 Woodhue Ln Poway CA 92064

JAFFE, MARK MAIER, investment advisor; b. Cheboygan, Mich., Sept. 22, 1935; s. Morris and Bessie Helen (Diamond) J.; m. Barbara G. Wolff (div. Aug. 1970); children: Lynne, Ellen; m. Judith Maureen Phillips, Mar. 21, 1971; 1 child, David. BBA, U. Mich., 1957, MBA, 1958. Treas. Valley Oxygen Co., Bay City, Mich., 1958-74, pres., 1974-84; pvt. practice investment adviser Bay City, 1984—; chief exec. officer Cinderella Inc., Bay City, 1987—; bd. dirs. First of Am. Bank, Bay City, Hamilton Electric Co., Saginaw, Mich.; chmn. bd. dirs. Bay Health Systems, Bay City. Pres. bd. edn. Essexville-Hampton Sch. Dist., 1969—. Named Boss of Yr. Am. Bus. Women's Assn., 1979; recipient Golden Frog award Bay Area C. of C., 1981. Mem. Inst. Cert. Fin. Planners, Internat. Assn. Fin. Planning, Nat. Assn. Personal Fin. Advisors, Bay City Country, Rotary. Office: 307 Phoenix Bldg Bay City MI 48708

JAGOW, CHARLES HERMAN, lawyer, finance consultant; b. Winona, Minn., Jan. 23, 1910; s. Walter Paul and Anna Marie (Thode) J.; m. Alice MacFarlane, Aug. 3, 1940 (dec. 1967); children—Paul M., Richard C. Student LaCrosse (Wis.) State Tchrs. Coll., 1928-30; A.B. cum laude, U. Wis., 1932, LL.B. cum laude, 1934; LL.M., Columbia U., 1936. Bar: N.Y. 1937. Assoc., Cravath, Swaine & Moore, N.Y.C., 1936-52; atty. Met. Life Ins. Co., N.Y.C., 1952-75, assoc. gen. counsel, 1957-75, v.p., 1967-75; dir. corp. debt financing project Am. Bar Found., Chgo., 1975-81; cons. in corp. fin., N.Y.C., 1975—; counsel Am. Assn. Gifted Children, 1975-85; project dir. Mortgage Bond Indenture Form, English text, 1981, Japanese text, 1982. Elder Presbyn. Ch. Mem. Assn. Life Ins. Counsel, ABA, Assn. Bar City N.Y., Order of Coif, Phi Kappa Phi, Delta Sigma Rho. Home: RD 3 Smalley Corners Rd Carmel NY 10512 Office: 510 E 23d St 1F New York NY 10010

JAHNCKE, REDINGTON TOWNSEND, investment banker; b. N.Y.C., Dec. 27, 1949; s. Ernest Lee Jr. and Cornelia Redington (Dickerman) J.; m. Robin Davis, July 23, 1983; children: Amanda Davis, Redington Townsend II, Ashley Dickerman, Alexander Stanton. Grad., Deerfield Acad., 1968; BA, Harvard U., 1972, MBA, 1976. V.p. Prudential Bache, N.Y.C., 1976-82; 1st v.p. E.F. Hutton & Co., Inc., N.Y.C., 1983-87; pres. Townsend Group, N.Y.C., 1987—. Republican. Episcopalian. Club: University (N.Y.C.). Home: 630 Park Ave New York NY 10021 Office: Townsend Group 122 E 42d St Ste 1021 New York NY 10168

JAHNCKE, THOMAS BOOK, securities executive; b. Detroit, May 21, 1946; s. Donald Edward and Vivienne Althea (Book) J.; m. Barbara Jahncke, Sept. 6, 1975 (div. Nov. 1987); children: Thomas A.W., Daniel P. BS, Cornell U., 1969; MBA, U. Mich., 1971. Cert. fin. planner. Mortgage loan officer Comerica Bank, Detroit, 1971-77; v.p. acquisitions Hall Real Estate Group, Southfield, Mich., 1977; dir. acctg. and personnel Sports Illustrated Clubs, Southfield, 1978; v.p., prin. Hall Securities Corp., Southfield, 1979, sr. v.p., 1981, regional v.p., 1982; pres. Dallas, 1986—; bd. dirs. Planned Investments, Inc., San Francisco. Mem. Internat. Assn. Fin. Planning (pres. S.E. Mich. chpt. 1985-86, bd. dirs. Dallas chpt. 1986—), Inst. Cert. Fin. Planning, Econ. Club Detroit. Club: Otsego Ski (Gaylord, Mich.). Office: Hall Securities Corp 10100 N Central Expwy Dallas TX 75231

JAHNKE, ERIC RICHARD, financial planner; b. San Francisco, Feb. 12, 1954; s. Richard Bruce and Marie Christine (Voreyer) J. AA, Cabrillo Coll., 1975-77; MS in Fin. Planning, Am. Coll., 1987. Cert. fin. planner. Ops. mgr. Spinnaker Corp., Redwood City, Calif., 1978-82; owner, prin. Jahnke FIn. Ctr., Grand Junction, Colo., 1982—; tchr. Colo. Mountain Coll., Rifle, 1988—. Treas. Mesa County Rep. Central Com., 1987-88. Mem. Inst. Cert. Fin. Planners, Internat. Bd. Standards and Practices Cert. Fin. Planners, Grand Junction C. of C. (chmn. aviation task force 1984-86). Republican. Office: Jahnke Fin Ctr 715 Horizon Dr Ste 401 Grand Junction CO 81506

JAIN, ADISH, engineer; b. Delhi, India, Nov. 3, 1939; came to U.S., 1966; s. Kishori Lal and Kapoori Devi Jain; m. Asha Jain, June 4, 1966; children: Sam, Cindy. BSME, U. Delhi, 1961; MSME, U. Minn., 1963; MBA, U. Wis., 1977. Registered profl. engr., Wis. Lectr. Indian Inst. Tech., New Delhi, 1963-66; project engr. White Farm Equipment, Mpls., 1967-72; sr. project engr. Waukesha (Wis.) Engine, 1972-77; project mgr. Deere & Co., Waterloo, Iowa, 1977-80, mgr. engring. dept., 1981—. Pres. Indo-American Club, Milw., 1970-71; chmn. Energy Conservation Commn., Cedar Falls, 1980-84. Mem. Soc. Automotive Engrs., Am. Soc. Mech. Engrs., Soc. Mfg. Engrs., Beta Gamma Sigma. Jain. Club: Indo-Am. (pres. 1970-71). Home: 910 Juanita Ave Cedar Falls IA 50613 Office: John Deere Product Engring Ctr 6725 Deere Rd Waterloo IA 50704

JAISWAL, ARVIND KUMAR JAY, marketing executive; b. Nadiad, Gujarat, India, Apr. 14, 1943; came to U.S., 1969; s. Navnitlal and Vidyadevi J.; m. Cornelia Elizabeth Ringle, Nov. 16, 1972. BEE, M.S.U., Baroda, India, 1964; MEE, Mich. Technol. U., 1972; mktg. advanced mgmt. program, Harvard, 1984. Mgr. computer systems Burroughs Corp., Detroit, 1973-79, corp. dir., 1981-85; mgr. market planning Xerox Corp., El Segundo, Calif., 1979-81; v.p., gen. mgr. mktg. and alternate channels Keyword Office Techs., Calgary, Alta. Can., 1985—. Mem. Eta Kappa Nu (pres. 1970). Republican. Office: Keyword Office Techs 7929 Jones Branch Dr McLean VA 22102

JALKUT, RICHARD ALAN, telecommunications executive; b. Boston, Apr. 5, 1944; s. Albert Sidney and Cathleen Ellen (Hannon) J.; m. Mary Elizabeth Honan, Jan 28, 1981; children: Stephen Alan, Mark William. BA, Boston Coll., 1966; postgrad., Northeastern U., 1969-70. Dist. mgr. AT&T Co., N.Y.C., 1970-72; mgr. New Eng. Telephone Co., Boston, 1966-70, dist. mgr., 1973-77; div. mgr. New Eng. Telephone Co., Maine, 1977-79, Boston, 1979-81; state v.p. New Eng. Telephone Co., Maine, 1981-85; v.p. New Eng. Telephone Co., Boston, 1985-88, exec. v.p., 1988—. Pres. New. Eng. region Boy Scouts Am., 1984, v.p. N.E. region, 1985—; chmn. Maine Devel. Found., 1983-85, U.S. Olympic Com., Maine, 1981-84, United Way, Portland, Maine, 1984-85. Home: 15 Bubbling Brook Rd Walpole MA 02081

JAMAL, MOEZ AHAMED, bank executive; b. Mombasa, Kenya, June 15, 1955; s. Ahamed and Shamsultan (Kalyan); m. Nadia Eboo, June 23, 1979; children: Nijhad, Shazia. BA in Economics with honors, Manchester U., 1976; MBA, NYU, 1979. V.p. Lloyds Bank, N.Y., 1979-85, Credit Suisse, London, 1985—. Mem. R.A.C. Club, Overseas Bankers Club, City Swiss Club. Moslem. Home: 3 The Fairway, New Malden Surrey KT3 4SP, England

JAMES, CHARLES GRANT, entrepreneur; b. Washington, Oct. 18, 1928; s. Charles Grant and Maude (Casey) J.; m. Elizabeth Y. Cunningham, Oct. 5, 1985. BBA, Bowling Green State U., 1950; student U.S. Naval Schs. Aviation and Justice, 1951-52. Treas., Sea Pines Co., Hilton Head, S.C., 1960-64; v.p. devel. Rockresorts, N.Y.C., 1964-69; group v.p. Heizer Corp., Chgo., 1970-74; pres. Sci. Advances, Inc. subs. Battelle Meml. Inst., Columbus, Ohio, 1975—, also dir.; pres. Comml. Ops. Group Battelle Meml. Inst., 1988—; bd. dirs. Small Bus. High Tech. Inst., Washington, Olentangy Mgmt. Co., Columbus, Columbus, Geosafe Corp., Info. Dimensions, Inc. Served to lt. USN, 1951-55, retired comdr. USNR. Decorated Air medals. Mem. Nat. Venture Capital Assn., Delta Tau Delta. Club: Athletic of Columbus. Office: Scientific Advances Inc 601 W 5th Ave Columbus OH 43201

JAMES, EDITH JOYCE, steel company executive; b. Chgo., May 22, 1926; d. John and Rebecca Miriam (Fischer) Shaiova; m. W. Ivan James, Dec. 29, 1958 (div. 1970). Student, Hunter Coll., 1944-45, Northwestern U., 1945-47, Ill. State U., 1963-66, Washington U., 1966-70. Acctg. supr. Panelit, Inc., Skokie, Ill., 1958-62; compt. Johnstone Constrn., Bloomington, Ill., 1962-66; asst. dir. housing Washington U., St. Louis, 1966-70; v.p., gen. mgr. William A. Miller Machine and Elevator, St. Louis, 1970-76; founder, pres. James Elecvator Co. and E.J. Elevator Co., St. Louis, 1977-85; pres. J & J Installers, Inc., St. Louis, 1976—; pres. Erector and Riggers St. Louis, 1986—. Mem. Am. Sub-contractors Assn. (sec., bd. dirs. St. Louis chpt.), St. Louis Cou. Constrn. Employers (sec., bd. dirs. St. Louis Goaltenders), Nat. Assn. Miscellaneous Ornamental Archtl. Porducts Contractors (bd. dirs.). Democrat. Jewish. Office: J & J Installers Inc 4301 Arco Ave Saint Louis MO 63110

JAMES, GENE ALBERT, farmers cooperative executive; b. Jan. 16, 1932. B.S., Va. Poly. Inst., 1953. With So. States Coop. Inc., Richmond, Va., 1953—; trainee, then asst. mgr. Cumberland Coop., acting mgr., asst. mgr. farm supply warehouse Roanoke So. States Coop. Inc., 1956-60; mgr. seed and farm supply warehouse So. States Coop. Inc., Clarksburg, 1960-66; product and promotional mgr. catalog service So. States Coop. Inc., 1966-69; regional mgr. So. States Coop. Inc., Winchester, Va., 1969-72; dir. planning So. States Coop. Inc., 1972-75, sr. v.p. ops., 1975-80; pres., chief exec. officer So. States Coop. Inc., Richmond, 1980—; vice chmn., dir. Texas City Refining, Inc., Tex.; bd. dirs. CF Industries Inc., Nat. Council Farmer Coops., Crestar Fin. Corp.; bd. dirs., trustee Grad. Inst. Coop. Leadership. Home: 11515 Edenberry Dr Richmond VA 23236 Office: So States Cooperative Inc PO Box 26234 Richmond VA 23260

JAMES, GEORGE BARKER, II, apparel industry executive; b. Haverhill, Mass., May 25, 1937; s. Paul Withington and Ruth (Burns) J.; m. Beverly A. Burch, Sept. 22, 1962; children: Alexander, Christopher, Geoffrey, Matthew. AB, Harvard U., 1959; MBA, Stanford U., 1962. Fiscal dir. E.G. & G. Inc., Bedford, Mass., 1963-67; fin. exec. Am. Brands Inc., N.Y.C., 1967-69; v.p. Pepsico, Inc., N.Y.C., 1969-72; sr. v.p., chief fin. officer Arcata Corp., Menlo Park, Calif., 1972-82; exec. v.p. Crown Zellerbach Corp., San Francisco, 1982-85; sr. v.p., chief fin. officer Levi Strauss & Co., San Francisco, 1985—; bd. dirs. Pacific States Industries, Inc., Sequoia Pacific Systems, Inc. Author: Industrial Development in the Ohio Valley, 1962. Mem. Andover (Mass.) Town Com., 1965-67; mem. Select Congl. Com. on World Hunger; adv. council Calif. State Employees Pension Fund; chmn. bd. dirs. Towle Trust Fund; trustee Nat. Corp. Fund for the Dance, Cate Sch., Levi Strauss Found., Stern Grove Festival Assn.; mem. San Francisco Com. on Fgn. Relations; trustee Zellerbach Family Fund, Mid-Peninsula High Sch.; chmn. bd. trustees San Francisco Ballet Assn.; bd. dirs. Stanford U. Hosp.; mem. adv. bd. Protection Mut. Ins. Co. Served with AUS, 1960-61. Mem. Newcomen Soc. N.Am., Fin. Execs. Inst. Clubs: Pacific Union, Commonwealth Calif., Family (San Francisco); Menlo Circus (Atherton, Calif.); Harvard (Boston and N.Y.C.); Harvard (San Francisco) (bd. dirs.). Home: 207 Walnut St San Francisco CA 94118 Office: Levi Strauss & Co Levi's Pla 1155 Battery St San Francisco CA 94111

JAMES, JENNIFER AUSTIN, information service company executive; b. N.Y.C., Aug. 26, 1943; d. Francis Wadsworth and Dorothy (Muller) James; m. Jeffrey Pritchard Parker, Mar. 25, 1966 (div. July 1975); children: Lisa Lynn and Lora Paige (twins). BA, Marietta Coll., 1965. Founder, pres. GLOBALDATA Services, Inc., New Canaan, Conn., 1985—. Mem. Am. Chem. Soc. (nat. affiliate), Info. Industry Assn., Nat. Assn. Female Execs. Republican. Episcopalian. Office: GLOBALDATA Services Inc Valley Ln New Canaan CT 06840

JAMES, JOHN ALAN, management consultant; b. Pocahontas, Iowa, Apr. 11, 1927; s. Clarence Grant and Blanche (Westholm) J.; S.B., Northwestern U., 1950; M.B.A., U. Chgo., 1957, postgrad., 1958-59; m. Diane Margot Thomas, Dec. 26, 1955; children—Carolyn, Cynthia, Alison. Partner, Hewitt Assos., Chgo., 1950-57, McKinsey & Co., N.Y.C., 1960-61; exec. counsellor CPC Internat., N.Y.C., 1961-67; pres. Mgmt. Counsellors Internat., Brussels, 1967—; chief exec. officer Shared Techs. Internat.; dir. Shared Techs., Inc., European trade relations State of Conn., 1975-79; vis. lectr. Northwestern U., European Sch. Bus. Adminstrn., Fontainebleau, Centre d'Etude Industrielle, Geneva. Served with USAAF, 1944-46. Mem. Beta Gamma Sigma, Delta Phi Epsilon. Republican. Episcopalian. Clubs: Met., Doubles (N.Y.C.); Wee Burn (Darien, Conn.). Author: Industrial Democracy in Europe, 1975; Termination of Employment Laws in Europe, 1976; also articles; editor, publisher publs. on European labor law, collective bargaining. Home: 12 Contentment Island Rd Darien CT 06820

JAMES, MARION RAY, editor, publisher; b. Bellmont, Ill., Dec. 6, 1940; s. Francis Miller and Lorraine A. (Wylie) J.; m. Janet Sue Tennis, June 16, 1960; children: Jeffrey Glenn, David Ray, Daniel Scott, Cheryl Lynne. BS, Oakland City Coll., Ind., 1964; MS, St. Francis Coll., Fort Wayne, Ind., 1978. Sports and city editor Daily Clarion, Princeton, Ind., 1963-65; English tchr. Jac-Cen-Del High Sch., Osgood, Ind., 1965-66; indsl. editor Whirlpool Corp., Evansville and LaPorte, Ind., 1966-68, Magnavox Govt. and Indsl. Electronics Co., Fort Wayne, 1968-79; editor, pub. Bowhunter mag., Kalispell, Mont., 1971-89, 1989—; instr. Ind.-Purdue U., Ft. Wayne, 1980-88. Author: Bowhunting for Whitetail and Mule Deer, 1975, Successful Bowhunting, 1985; editor: Pope and Young Book World Records, 1975, Bowhunting Adventures, 1977. Recipient Best Editorial award United Community Svc. Publs., 1970-72; named Alumnus of Yr., Oakland City Coll., 1982, to Hall of Fame, Mt. Carmel High Sch., Ill., 1983. Mem. Outdoor Writers Assn. Am., Fort Wayne Assn. Bus. Editors (Fort Wayne Bus. Editor of Yr. 1969, pres. 1975-76), Toastmasters (Able Toastmaster award), Alpha Phi Gamma, Alpha Psi Omega, Mu Tau Kappa. Home: 600 Bayou Rd Kalispell MT 59901

JAMES, MICHAEL THAMES, data processing executive, consultant; b. Gulfport, Miss., Feb. 16, 1949; s. William Denning and O. Christell (Cruthirds) J.; m. Debra Lynn Bryant, May 21, 1983; children: William Bryant, Shelley Christine. BS, U.S. Naval Acad., 1971; MS, U. S. Calif., 1978. Commd. ensign USN, 1971, advanced through grades to lt., 1975, resigned, 1978; mktg. rep. IBM, South Bend, Ind., 1978-79; cons. Price Waterhouse, Houston, 1979-85; internal cons. Shell Oil, Houston, 1985-86; mgr. systems devel. & support Carolina Power & Light, Raleigh, 1986—. Computer studies adv. bd. Meredith Coll., 1987-89; sec./treas. U.S. Naval Acad. Alumni Assn. Triangle area chpt., Raleigh, 1987-89. Mem. Inst. Mgmt. Cons (sec./treas. Houston chpt. 1984-85). Republican. Presbyterian. Home: 9405 Greenfield Dr Raleigh NC 27615

JAMES, PAUL CHARLES, tire company executive; b. New Cumberland, Pa., Jan. 31, 1935; s. Joseph Bauchman and Ruth (Troutman) J.; m. Brenda Bock, June 30, 1962; children: Eric Arnold, Kimberley Jill. BA in Chemistry, Cornell U., 1956. V.p. research and devel. tire group, BF Goodrich Co., Akron, Ohio, 1956-82; v.p. research and devel. Armtek Rubber Co. (formerly Armstrong Rubber Co.), New Haven, 1982-85, sr. v.p., 1987—; pres. Pirelli Armstrong Tire Co. (formerly Armstrong Tire Co.), New Haven, 1985—; exec. v.p. Armteck Corp., New Haven, 1987—. Bd. dirs. New Haven Council for Arts, 1982—; bd. visitors bus. sch. U. Conn. Served with Chem. Corps U.S. Army, 1957. Mem. Soc. Automotive Engrs., Am. Chem. Soc. (rubber group). Republican. Clubs: Grads. (New Haven); Pine Orchard Yacht and Country (Branford, Conn.). Home: 4 Hillside Pl Madison CT 06443 Office: Pirelli-Armstrong Tire Co 500 Sargent Dr New Haven CT 06536-0201

JAMES, ROBERT LEO, advertising agency executive; b. N.Y.C., Sept. 23, 1936; s. Leo Francis and Mildred Virginia (Schaffa) J.; m. Anne Krapp, Feb. 2, 1968; children: Robert Leo, Victoria, Jeffrey. A.B., Colgate U., 1958; M.B.A., Columbia U., 1961. Field researcher Farm Jour., Inc., Cleve., 1956-57; salesman Procter and Gamble Co., Schenectady, 1958-59; office head sales mgr. Procter and Gamble Co., Syracuse, N.Y., 1959-60; product mgr. household products, brand mktg. and new product devel. Colgate Palmolive Co., N.Y.C., 1961-64; account exec. Ogilvy and Mather, Inc., N.Y.C., 1964; account supr Ogilvy and Mather, Inc., 1965-66, v.p., account supr., 1967-69; sr. v.p., mgmt. service dir. Marschalk Co., Inc., N.Y.C., 1968; dir. Marschalk Co., Inc., 1969—, exec. v.p., 1970, gen. mgr., 1971, pres., 1974, chmn. bd., chief exec. officer, 1975-80; vice chmn. Interpub. Group of Cos., Inc., 1980—, also dir.; vice chmn. McCann-Erickson Worldwide, 1981-85, chmn., chief exec. officer, 1985—, also bd. dirs.; adj. asso. prof. mktg. Fordham U., 1968-69; dir. Broadlands Farm (thoroughbred horses.). Nat. service council Colgate U.; trustee Fordham Preparatory Sch., 1977-83, South Street Seaport Mus.; bd. dirs. March of Dimes, N.Y.C., 4A's. Mem. Am. Assn. Advt. Agys., Young Pres.'s Orgn. Internat., Greenwich Power Squadron, Columbia Bus. Sch. Alumni Assn. (bd. dirs.), Delta Kappa Epsilon. Clubs: Milbrook (Greenwich, Conn.); N.Y. Yacht, Indian Harbor Yacht (dir.), Clove Valley Rod and Gun, NY40 Assn. (chmn.), Colgate U. Pres.'s, River. Home: 68 W Brother Dr Greenwich CT 06830 Office: McCann-Erickson Worldwide 750 3d Ave New York NY 10017

JAMES, WILLIAM W., banker; b. Springfield, Mo., Oct. 12, 1931; s. Will and Clyde (Cowdrey) J.; A.B., Harvard U., 1953; m. Carol Ann Muenter, June 17, 1967; children—Sarah Elizabeth, David William. Asst. to dir. overseas div. Becton Dickinson & Co., Rutherford, N.J., 1956-59; stockbroker Merrill Lynch, Pierce, Fenner & Smith, Inc., St. Louis, 1959-62; with trust div. Boatmen's Nat. Bank of St. Louis, 1962—, v.p. in charge estate planning, 1972—, sr. v.p., 1984—; dir. Heer-Andres Investment Co., Springfield. Mem. gift and bequest council Barnes Hosp., St. Louis, 1963-67, St. Louis U., 1972-78; dir. Mark Twain Summer Inst., St. Louis, 1987—. Served with U.S. Army, 1953-55. Mem. Estate Planning Council St. Louis, Mo. Bankers Assn., Bank Mktg. Assn., Am. Inst. Banking, Harvard Alumni Assn. (bd. dirs. 1987—). Republican. Clubs: Harvard (pres. 1972-73), Mo. Athletic, Noonday (St. Louis). Office: Boatmen's Nat Bank PO Box 7365 Saint Louis MO 63177

JAMESON, JAY MARSHALL, financial executive; b. Coatesville, Pa., Dec. 30, 1943; s. Delmar K. and Hagar A. (Heston) J.; B.A. in Bus., Parsons Coll., 1966; m. Barbara Vukmanic, Jan. 14, 1977; children—Jacqueline, Jay M., John and Ann Marie (twins). Acct., Johnston, Young & Ofria, CPA's., Bala Cynwyd, Pa., 1967-69; acct. Yaverbaum & Co., CPA's., Harrisburg, Pa., 1969-70; chief acct. Polyclinic Med. Center, Harrisburg, 1970-79; v.p. fin. Horsham Hosp., Ambler, Pa., 1979-84; pres. Jameson and Co., Gwynedd, Pa., 1984—. Served with USAR, 1966-72. Mem. C. of C. (small Bus. council), Hosp. Fin. Mgmt. Assn., Med. Group Mgmt. Assn., Nat. Staff Network. Lodge: Rotary (Norristown). Home: 604 Brookwood Ln North Wales PA 19454 Office: Jameson & Co PO Box 1 Gwynedd PA 19436

JAMIN, GERALD ALAN, petroleum company executive; b. N.Y.C., Dec. 27, 1941; s. Morris Phillip and Hannah (Chasen) J.; children—Meridith, Michael. B.A., CCNY, 1962; M.B.A., Columbia U., 1963. Mgr. planning, analysis and control Mobil Oil Corp., N.Y.C., 1964-69; fin. mgr. Amerada Hess Corp., N.Y.C., 1970-73, asst. to chmn., 1974, treas., 1976—; chief fin. officer Bio Med. Scis., Inc., Fairfield, N.J., 1975-76. Active Big Brothers Am. Served with U.S. Army, 1963-69. Republican. Jewish. Office: Amerada Hess Corp 1185 Ave of the Americas New York NY 10036

JAMISON, ROBERT LOWERY, university administrator; b. Newark, Ohio, June 15, 1925; s. Robert L. and Hazel J. (Wilson) J.; m. Marie H. Omo, Aug. 30, 1975. BA, Calif. State U., Northridge, 1972. Supr. inventory supply Glendale (Calif.) Adventist Med. Ctr., 1964-76; dir. purchasing Northern Inyo Hosp., Bishop, Calif., 1976-78; dir. material mgmt. Santa Monica (Calif.) Hosp. Med. Ctr., 1978-81; asst. dir. bus. mgmt. Calif. State U., Northridge, 1981—. Mem. Nat. Assn. Ednl. Buyers, Calif. Assn. Pub. Purchasing Officers, Assn. Claif. State U. Profs., Moose. Democrat. Office: Calif State U Northridge 18111 Nordhoff St Northridge CA 91330

JAMISON, SHEILA ANN, finance company executive; b. Hattiesburg, Miss., July 19, 1950; d. Stanley Gear and Vivian (Gillis) English; m. Troy James Creel, Dec. 21, 1968 (div. 1980); m. Richard Allen Jamison, Oct. 24, 1981. BS in Mgmt. magna cum laude, Fairleigh Dickinson U., 1986. Purchasing asst. Dept. Hosps. State La., Independence, 1973-77; sales rep. Fisher Sci., Houston, 1977-79; account v.p. Paine Webber, Clifton, N.J., 1981-87; asst. br. mgr., assoc. v.p. Dean Witter Reynolds, Inc., N.Y.C., 1987—; speaker The Cons. Firm, Saddle Brook, N.J., 1987. Dir. Gene Michael Scholarship Fund, Bergenfield, N.J., 1986; mem. fund raising com. Tomorrow's Children Fund, Hackensack, N.J., 1987; mem. Group Against Smoking Pollution, 1987—. Mem. Direct Investment Adv. Bd., Phi Zeta Kappa, Delta Mu Delta, Phi Omega Epsilon, Barron's High Tech Round Table. Baptist. Office: Dean Witter Two World Trade Ctr 73rd Fl New York NY 10048

JANEK, ADELINE, company executive, consultant; b. San Antonio, Sept. 30, 1942; d. Norbert Steohen and Lena Annie (Siebold) Richter; m. Victor P. Janek, May 6, 1961; children: Melissa Janek Helms, Russell, Jennifer, Shelley. Student pub. schs., Pleasanton, Tex. Owner, mgr. Hitchin Post, San Antonio, 1978-80; with ops. dept. Prudential Bache Securities, San Antonio, 1980-83; ops. sec. So. Steel Co., San Antonio, 1983-84; account exec. Paulsen Investments, San Antonio, 1984; rep. Waddell & Reed, Inc., San Antonio, 1984-87, dist. mgr., 1987; div. mgr. Waddell & Reed, Inc., Houston, 1987—. Founder Tower Lake 4-H Club, Floresville, Tex., 1973. Mem. Toastmasters (San Antonio) (organizer, pres. 1987, Outstanding Toastmaster 1986). Roman Catholic. Office: Waddell & Reed Inc 654 N Belt E #140 Houston TX 77060

JANES, WILLIAM MICHAEL, sales executive; b. Centralia, Ill., July 1, 1940; s. Orville Ardell and Helen Maxine (Kell) J.; m. Mary Alice Noble, July 30, 1966; children: David Michael, Merrill Michelle. BS in Mgmt., So. Ill. U., 1964. Sales rep. Mudsingwear, Grand Rapids, Mich., 1964-67, Cluett Peabody, Des Moines, 1967-70, Inland Container Corp., Atlanta, 1970-79; sales mgr. Inland Container Corp., Ft. Smith, Ark., 1979-85; sales mgr. MacMillan Bloedel Containers div. MacMillan Bloedel of Am., Little Rock, 1985—, sales mgr. Ark. Containers div., 1988—; gen. mgr., sales exec. MacMillan Bloedel Containers div. MacMillan Bloedel of Am., Chgo., 1989—. Active Big Bros./Big Sisters, Atlanta, 1978-79. With USAR, 1963-69. Mem. Sales and Mktg. Execs. Assn. Home: 14240 Streamstown Orland Park IL 60462 Office: MacMillan Bloedel Containers 5555 W 73d St Chicago IL 60638

JANES, WILLIAM SARGENT, real estate corporation executive; b. Cambridge, Mass., Mar. 24, 1953; s. G. Sargent and Ann (Brown) J.; m. Alice Maxine Rowley, June 19, 1982; children: Pack Sargent, Maxine Cotton. BA, Bowdoin Coll., 1976. Sr. sales cons. coldwell Banker, Washington, 1976-84; ptnr. Lincoln Property Co., Washington, 1984—. Mem. Soc. Indsl. Realtors, Nat. Assn. Industrial and Office Pks., Cathedral Coll. of Laity (devel. com.), Decade Soc. Office: Lincoln Property Co 1455 Pennsylvania Ave NW Washington DC 20004

JANIS, JAY, savings and loan executive; b. L.A., Dec. 22, 1932; s. Ernest and Diana (Friedman) J.; m. Juel Mendelsohn, 1954; children: Laura, Jeffrey. AB with high honors, Yale U., 1954. Ptnr., community developer Janis Corp. (named changed to MGIC-Janis Properties 1970) and related cos. in pvt. bldg. industry), South Fla., 1956-64, 69-75; with Dept. Commerce, Washington, 1964-66; exec. dir. nat. citizens' com., community rels. svc. Dept. Commerce, 1964-65; dir. OEO, spl. asst. to under sec. Commerce, 1965-66; exec. asst. to sec. HUD, Washington, 1966-69; under sec. HUD, 1977-79; chmn. Fed. Home Loan Bank Bd., Washington, 1979-80; pres.

Calif. Fed. Savs. and Loan Assn., Los Angeles, 1981-82; chmn. exec. com. Gibraltar Savs. Corp., Beverly Hills, Calif., 1983-88; chmn. bd. Gibraltar Savs., Beverly Hills, Calif., 1988; chmn. bd. Flagship Fed. Savs; bd. dirs. Mortgage Guaranty Ins. Corp., Coast Savs., L.A.; sr. v.p. for mgmt. and bus. affairs U. Mass., 1976-77; former prin. housing adviser to gov. Fla.; former bd. dirs. Nat. Assn. Home Builders, Nat. Com. against Discrimination in Housing; former mediator labor disputes in constrn. industry. Past pres. bd. trustees Fla. Internat. Univ. Found., Miami. Served with Intelligence Corps U.S. Army, 1954-56. Office: Gibraltar Fin Corp 9111 Wilshire Blvd Beverly Hills CA 90213

JANKUN, ROBERT EDWARD, chemical engineer; b. Somerville, Mass., June 19, 1949; s. William Walter and Grace Agnes (Kelley) J.; M. Betty Jean Randle, Aug. 21, 1971; children: Teresa, Matthew. BS in Chem. Engring., Case Western Res. U., 1971; MBA, Loyola U., Balt., 1981. Process and product devel. engr. Procter & Gamble, Cin., 1971-76; process devel. engr. Noxell Corp., Balt., 1976-78, quality engr., dept. head, 1978-81; sr. group leader Amway Corp., Ada, Mich., 1981-82; mgr. process rsch. and devel. Amway Corp., Ada, 1982-86; mgr. product engring. Richard-Allan Med., Inc., Richland, Mich., 1986-87; dir. lab. products Richard-Allan Med., Inc., Richland, 1987-88; dir. quality assurance DLP, Inc., Grand Rapids, Mich., 1988—. Pres. Waycross Condominiums, Cin., 1976; v.p. New Freedom Library, Pa., 1980; adviser Grand Rapids Jr. Achievement, 1985. Mem. Am. Inst. Chem. Engrs., Rockford Jaycees (pres. 1986), Toastmasters (treas. 1985). Home: 6173 Archer St Rockford MI 49341 Office: DLP Inc 620 Watson SW Grand Rapids MI 49504

JANKURA, DONALD EUGENE, hotel executive, educator; b. Bridgeport, Conn., Dec. 20, 1929; s. Stephen and Susan (Dirga) J.; m. Elizabeth Deborah Joynt, June 20, 1952; children: Donald Eugene Jr., Stephen J., Daria E., Diane E., Lynn M. BA in Hotel Adminstrn., Mich. State U., 1951. Asst. sales mgr. Pick Fort Shelby Hotel, Detroit, 1951-53; steward Dearborn Inn and Colonial Homes, Dearborn, Mich., 1953-54; sales mgr. Dearborn Inn and Colonial Homes, 1954-60, resident mgr., 1960-62; gen. mgr. Stouffer's Northland Inn, Southfield, Mich., 1962-64; staff adv. Stouffer Motor Inns, Cleve., 1964-66; v.p. Stouffer Motor Inns, 1966-68, Assoc. Inns & Restaurants Co. Am., Denver, 1968-76; exec. v.p. Assoc. Inns & Restaurants Co. Am., 1976-81, sr. v.p., 1981—; dir. sch. hotel and restaurant mgmt. U. Denver; disting. spl. lectr. hospitality U. New Haven, Conn.; pres. Am. Hotel Assn. Directory Corp., 1986; guest lectr. Mich. State U., 1964, Fla. Internat. U., 1968, Cornell U., 1983, Denver U., 1986-87; mem. industry adv. bd. U. Denver, Mich. State U.; bd. dirs. Vend Right Service Co., Kansas City, Kans., Beverage Retailers Ins. Co., Washington. Recipient Alumnus of the Year award Mich. State U. Hotel Sch., 1986. Mem. Am. Hotel and Motel Assn. (dir. 1978-80, vice chmn. industry adv. council 1980-81, sec.-treas. 1985, v.p. 1986, pres. 1987—) Colo./Wyo. Hotel and Motel Assn. (dir., bd. dirs. 1984—, Disting. Svc. award 1983), Coalition Lic. of Beverage Retailers Assn. (bd. dirs. 1987—), Hotel Sales Mgmt. Assn. (bd. dirs. 1984—), Council Hotel, Restaurant and Instnl. Educators, Internat. Platform Assn., Denver C. of C., Pinery Country Club, Pres.'s Club, Masons, Phi Kappa Tau. Episcopalian. Home: 7445 Windlawn Way Parker CO 80134 Office: AIRCOA Cos Inc 4600 S Ulster St Ste 1200 Denver CO 80237

JANOVIC, MICHAEL JOHN, management consultant, educator; b. Paterson, N.J., Mar. 31, 1941; s. Victor and Maria (Letvin) J.; m. Mary Jo Ryan; children: Andrea, Ryan. BS, U. Akron, 1963, MBA, 1969. Prof. Xavier U., Cin., 1966-70; dir. strategic planning internat. div. Gen. Corp., Akron, Ohio, 1970-81; pres. N.Am. div. Charles Zub & Assocs., Akron, 1981-82; v.p. Predicasts div. Thyssen Bornemisza, Cleve., 1983-84; pres. Group Am. Cos. Inc., Akron, 1984—; bd. dirs. Archbishop Hoban H.S. Corp., Akron, Ohio, 1981-83. Fellow Acad. of Mgmt., British Inst. of Mgmt. Roman Catholic. Office: Group Am Cos Inc 1862 Akron-Peninsula Rd Akron OH 44313

JANSEN, JON DAVID, construction company executive; b. Milw., Oct. 22, 1964; s. Georgie and Sue J. BS in Archtl. Engring., Milw. Sch. Engring., 1986. Registered engr. in tng. Project mgr., estimator Hunzinger Constrn. Co., Brookfield, Wis., 1986—. Home: 475 Concord Rd #67 Pewaukee WI 53072 Office: Hunfeinger Constrn Co 21100 Enterprise Ave Brookfield WI 53005

JANURA, JAN AROL, apparel manufacturing executive; b. Chgo., May 12, 1949; s. Harold Charles and Violet Mary J.; B.S., Colo. State U., 1971; M.A., Fuller Theol. Sem., 1973. Area dir. Young Life Campaign, Seattle, 1973-76; chief exec. officer, dir. Carol Anderson, Inc., Los Angeles, 1977—; chief fin. officer Fresh Retail Chain, 1988—, Outdoor Videos Inc., 1988—; pres. Los Angeles Electric Motorcar Co., 1979-80; bd. dirs. Western Leadership Found., Starr Leadership Found., SW Leadership Found., NW Fellowship, Rivergate Fellowship, Crested Butte, Colo., Glendale (Calif.) Fellowship; mem. Presl. Task Force, 1986; founder Janura Library, 1986. Mem. Rep. Nat. Com., 1986, Rep. Presdl. Task Force, 1984-86; trustee Janura Library, Glendale, Colo. Weyerhaueser fellow, 1972-73; recipient Salesman of Yr. award, 1983, 84. Clubs: Snowcreek Athletic, Los Angeles Athletic, Wash. Athletic, N.Y. Athletic, Admirals (life), Solomon Hill Hunt, Scootney Farms Hunting. Office: 5770 Anderson St Vernon CA 90058

JARMOLOW, KENNETH, aerospace company executive; b. Lebanon, Conn., Sept. 15, 1924; s. Rose (Lubetsky) J.; m. Shirley Sara Mendoza, Jan. 31, 1947; children: Elizabeth, Janet. BS, MIT, 1948. Engr. Balt. div. Martin Marietta Corp., 1948-58, dir. research Balt. div., 1958-83; v.p. research Martin Marietta Corp., Balt., 1983-84; pres. energy systems Martin Marietta Corp., Oak Ridge, Tenn., 1984-88; v.p. tech. Martin Marietta Corp., Bethesda, Md., 1988—; bd. dirs. Chiron Corp., Emeryville, Calif. Contbr. articles to profl. jours. Mem. tech. adv. panel HBCU Office of Pres., Washington, 1985—; bd. dirs. Knoxville (Tenn.) Symphony Orch., 1985—; mem. Chancellor's Assocs. U. Tenn., Knoxville, 1985—. Served to 2d lt. U.S. Army Air Corps, 1943-45. Home: 100 Windgate Pl Oak Ridge TN 37830

JARNAGAN, HARRY WILLIAM, JR., project control engineer; b. Cedar Rapids, Iowa, Nov. 7, 1953; s. Harry William and Virginia Lillian (Grusy) J.; m. Anne Therese Tompkins, June 7, 1975; children: Douglas William, Michael Patrick, Marianne Virginia. BS, U.S. Mil. Acad., 1975; M of Engring., Tex. A&M, 1984. Registered profl. engr., Tex. Project mgr. Dunbar & Dickson, Inc., Clute, Tex., 1980-83, 84-85; grad. teaching asst. Tex. A&M U., College Station, 1983-84; cost. engr. Bechtel Power Corp., Houston, 1985-87; project control engr. Tenn. Valley Authority, 1987-88, Fluor-Daniel, Inc., Rochester, N.Y., 1988—. From 2d lt. to capt. U.S. Army, 1975-80. Mem. Am. Assn. Cost Engrs., Tau Beta Pi. Lutheran. Home: 171 St James Dr Webster NY 14580 Office: Fluor Daniel Inc 30 Corporate Woods Ste 100 Rochester NY 14623

JAROS, ROBERT JAMES, insurance company executive; b. Port Reading, N.J., June 30, 1939; s. Michael and Marian (Kurta) J.; m. Margaret Efthin, May 19, 1974; children: Marian Reilly, Jennifer, Christina,. Student, Rutgers U., 1957-60. With Prudential Ins. Co., Newark, 1957-77; sr. systems analyst, project leader Ins. Svcs. Office, N.Y.C., 1977-81; project mgr. Shearson Lehman Bros. Inc., N.Y.C., 1981-88; mgr. The Guardian Life Ins. Co. of Am., N.Y.C., 1988—. Mem. Middletown Twp. Transp. Com., 1988—, Rolling Knolls Civic Soc. (past pres.); mem. U.S. Power Squadron, Watchung Power Squadron. With USAR, 1962-68. Fellow Life Mgmt Inst. Soc. of Greater N.Y.; mem. Am. Soc. CLU's, Am. Legion. Greek Orthodox. Home: 12 Jocarda Dr Middletown NJ 07748

JARRETT, JERRY VERNON, banker; b. Abilene, Tex., Oct. 31, 1931; s. Walter Elwood and Myrtle Elizabeth (Allen) J.; m. Martha Ann McCabe, June 13, 1953; children: Cynthia Ann, Charles Elwood, Christopher Allen, John Carlton. B.B.A., U. Okla., 1957; M.B.A., Harvard U., 1963. Gen. sales mgr. Tex. Coca-Cola Bottling Co., Abilene, 1957-61; exec. v.p. Marine Midland Bank, N.Y.C., 1963-73; exec. v.p. Ameritrust Co., 1973-76, vice chmn., 1976-78, chmn., chief exec. officer, 1978—; chmn., chief exec. officer Ameritrust Corp. Co-author: Creative Collective Bargaining, 1964. Served with USAAF, 1950-54. Mem. Phi Gamma Delta. Home: 2751 Chesterton Rd Shaker Heights OH 44122 Office: AmeriTrust Corp 900 Euclid Ave PO Box 5937 Cleveland OH 44101 *

JARVIS, EDWARD CURTIS, manufacturing company executive; b. Malden, Mass., Jan. 6, 1951; s. John Albert and Shirley Ann (Fronduto) J.; m. Nancy Jean Cotoia, June 24, 1973; 1 child, Ryan Edward. BA in History and Psychology, Bridgewater State Coll., 1972; postgrad., Salem State Coll., 1973-74; exec. MBA, Suffolk U., 1983. Mfg. and personnel mgr. Cape Dory Yachts, Tanton, Mass., 1974-77; plant mgr. Am. Alumninum Inc., Malden, 1977-80; mgr. human resources Prime Computer, Natick, Mass., 1980-81; orgn. and manpower rep. aircraft engine bus. group Gen. Electric Co., Lynn, Mass., 1981-83, mgr. profl. compensation and human resources systems, 1983-84; dir. human resources U.S. ops. Scitex Am. Corp., Bedford, Mass., 1984-85; corp. dir. human resource planning Scitex Corp. Ltd., Herzlia, Israel, 1985-86; corp. v.p. Towle Mfg. Co., Burlington, Mass., 1986-88; exec. v.p., gen. mgr. Demakes Enterprises, Lynn, Mass., 1988—. Mem. Am. Compensation Assn., Am. Soc. Personnel Adminstrn., New Eng. Human Resources Planning Group, New Eng. Human Resources Mgmt. Group, Route 128 Internat. Personnel Group, Beach Club. Democrat. Roman Catholic. Home: 90 Farragut Rd Swampscott MA 01907 Office: Towle Mfg Co 144 Addison St East Boston MA 02128

JASICA, ANDREA LYNN, mortgage banking executive; b. Orlando, Fla., Aug. 21, 1945; d. Walter S. and Florence E. (Pasek) J. AA in Pre Bus. Adminstrn. cum laude, Orlando Jr. Coll., 1965; BS with honors, Rollins Coll., 1976. Sec. Am. Mortgage Co. Fla. Inc., Orlando, 1965-68; closing specialist Charter Mortgage Co., Orlando, 1968-70, Gen. Guaranty Mortgage Co. Inc., Winter Park, Fla., 1971; sr. loan processor C.E. Brooks Mortgage Co. Inc., Orlando, 1971-79; v.p. mktg. Twin Homes Ltd., Orlando, 1980-83; asst. v.p., mgr. region Atlantic Mortgage and Investment Corp. subs. Atlantic Nat. Bank, Orlando, 1984-86; v.p. Commerce Nat. Mortgage Co., Winter Park, 1987-88; real estate assoc. Atlantic-to-Gulf Realty Inc., 1972-73, Medel Inc., Maitland, Fla., 1973-74; instr. Mortgage Personnel Svcs. Inc. Contbr. articles to profl. jours. Mem. Valencia Community Coll. Alumni (bd. dirs. 1983-85), Home Builders Assn. Mid-Fla. (assoc., mem. mortgage fin. com., pubs. chmn. 1985, 88, mem. aux. 1985, mem. sales and mktg. council 1984, 85), Orlando Area Bd. Realtors (affiliate, mem. edn. com. 1988), Greater Orlando Assn. Profl. Mortgage Women (chartered, chmn. scholarship com. 1986-87), Mortgage Bankers Assn. Cen. Fla., Fla. Assn. Mortgage Brokers, Nat. Secs. Assn. (asst. treas. Orlando chpt. 1965-71, chmn. future secs. com. 1971).

JASON, JAY FRANCIS, lawyer; b. Worcester, Mass., Mar. 31, 1952; s. Vitie J. and Carolyn (Simmons) J.; m. Jan Blei, May 19, 1973; children: Greer, Kyle, Leigh, Quinn. AB, Duke U., 1973; LLB, JD, Boston U., 1976. Bar: Mass. 1977, U.S. Dist. Ct. Mass. 1977, N.Y. 1980, U.S. Dist. Ct. (ea. and so. dists.) N.Y. 1981, U.S. Ct. Appeals (2d cir.) 1981. Asst. corp. counsel City of Boston, 1976-79; assoc. Morgan, Lewis & Bockius, N.Y.C., 1979-81; pvt. practice Pearl River, N.Y., 1981-84; prin., ptnr. Lexow, Berbit & Jason, Suffern, N.Y., 1984—; adj. prof. Sch. Indsl. and Labor Rels., Cornell U., Ithaca, N.Y., 1985—. Contbr. articles to legal jours. Mem. N.Y. State Bar Assn. (labor rels. subcom.), Am. Arbitration Assn. Office: Lexow Berbit & Jason 56 Park Ave Suffern NY 10901

JAUDES, WILLIAM E., lawyer; b. St. Louis, May 6, 1937; s. August William and Gertrude Johanna (Simon) J.; m. Carol Joan Hurtgen, June 30, 1961; children: Phyllis Anne, Richard William, Suzanne Louise. AB, U. Mo., 1958; JD, St. Louis U., 1962, MBA, 1969. Atty. Union Electric Co., St. Louis, 1963-73, gen. atty., 1973-80, gen. counsel, 1980-85, v.p., gen. counsel, 1985—. Author: introduction to Mo. Bar Assn. book, Administrative Law, 1979. Mem. Ill. State Bar Assn., Mo. Bar Assn., St. Louis Bar Assn., Am. Corp. Counsels Assn., Edison Electric Inst. Legal Com. Mem. United Ch. Christ. Home: 3873 Holly Hills Blvd Saint Louis MO 63116 Office: Union Electric Co 1901 Chouteau Ave PO Box 149 Saint Louis MO 63166

JAVITCH, GARY RICHARD, banker; b. Cleve., June 27, 1947; s. Samuel and Dorothy (Baxt) J.; m. Sandra Jeanne Freeman, Jan. 9, 1975. BBA, U. Wis., 1969, MS in Fin., 1969. CPA, Ill. Staff officer, project mgr. First Nat. Bank Chgo., 1974-79; contr., v.p. MeraBank Fed. Savs. Bank, Phoenix, 1980-83, sr. v.p., treas., 1983-86, sr. v.p., chief fin. officer, treas., 1986, exec. v.p., chief fin. officer, 1986—. Mem. Am. Inst. Pub. Accts., Stock and Bond Club Phoenix, Assn. for Corp. Growth. Office: MeraBank Fed Savs Bank 3003 N Central Ave Ste 2400 Phoenix AZ 85012

JAY, CAROL ANN, accountant; b. Balt., Mar. 14, 1950; d. Raymond and Ingeborg (Binner) Gramiak; m. John Henry Jay, Oct. 30, 1971 (div. 1978). Student, Elmira Coll., 1968-70; BA, SUNY, Buffalo, 1972; BS, George Mason U., 1976. CPA, N.Y. Auditor C.L. Brovitz & Co., Rochester, N.Y., 1976-78; sr. auditor Metzger, Wood & Sokolski, Rochester, 1978-81; contr. Rochester Manpower, Inc., 1981-82; sr. fin. analyst Instruments & Systems div. Bausch & Lomb, Inc., Rochester, 1982-83, sr. internal auditor corp. dept., 1983-84, mgr. internat. treasury ops., 1984-86, mgr. fin. planning and analysis internat. div., 1986-87, dir. fin. planning and analysis, 1987-88, dir. fin. acctg. planning and reporting, 1988—. Student counselor St. John Fisher Coll., Rochester, 1986-87; vol. United Cerebral Palsy Found., Rochester, 1987. Mem. AICPA, N.Y. State Soc. CPAs (com. mem. 1978-83) Rochester Women's Roundtable (sec. 1984-85). Republican. Home: 20 Hollyvale Dr Rochester NY 14618 Office: Bausch & Lomb Inc 42 East Ave Rochester NY 14604

JAY, DAVID JAKUBOWICZ, management consultant; b. Danzig, Poland, Dec. 7, 1925; s. Mendel and Gladys Gitta (Zalc) Jakubowicz; came to U.S., 1938, naturalized, 1944; B.S., Wayne State U., 1948; M.S., U. Mich., 1949, postgrad., 1956-57; postgrad. U. Cin., 1951-53, Mass. Inst. Tech., 1957; m. Shirley Anne Shapiro, Sept. 7, 1947; children—Melvin Maurice, Evelyn Deborah. Supr. man-made diamonds Gen. Electric Corp., Detroit, 1951-56; instr. U. Detroit, 1948-51; asst. to v.p. engring. Ford Motor Co., Dearborn, Mich., 1956-63; project mgr. Apollo environ. control radiators N.Am. Rockwell, Downey, Calif., 1963-68; staff to v.p. corporate planning Aerospace Corp., El Segundo, Calif., 1968-70; founder, pres. PBM Systems Inc., 1970-83; pres. Cal-Best Hydrofarms Coop., Los Alamitos, 1972-77; cons. in field, 1983—. Pres., Community Design Corp., Los Alamitos, 1971-75; life master Am. Contract Bridge League. Served with USNR, 1944-46. Registered profl. engr., Calif., Mich., Ohio. Fellow Inst. Advancement Engring.; mem. Inst. Mgmt. Sci. (chmn. 1961-62), Western Greenhouse Vegetable Growers Assn. (sec.-treas. 1972-75), Tau Beta Pi. Jewish. Patentee in air supported ground vehicle, others. Home: 13441 Roane Circle Santa Ana CA 92705

JAY, JAMES ALBERT, insurance company executive; b. Superior, Wis., Aug. 24, 1916; s. Clarence William and Louie (Davies) J.; student pub. schs., Mpls.; m. Margie Hoffpauir, Dec. 23, 1941; 1 son, James A. Franchise with The Stauffer System of Calif., 1946-49; Ala. dist. mgr. Guaranty Savs. Life Ins. Co., Montgomery, Ala., 1949-51, state mgr. La., 1951-—, dir., 1952-—, La. gen. agent, 1964-—; La. gen agt. Gen. United Life Ins. Co. of Des Moines (merged with Lincoln Liberty Life Ins. Co., Des Moines, with All Am. Life Ins. Co., Chgo. 1984), 1969-—. Com. chmn. Attakapas council Boy Scouts Am., Alexandria, La., 1955, council commr., 1961-62, commr. Manchac dist., 1967-—. Served as cpl. USMC, 1942-45, PTO. Decorated Purple Heart. Mem. Nat., Baton Rouge life underwriters assns., Gen. Agts. and Mgrs. Conf., Internat. Platform Assn. Methodist. Elk. Home: 5919 Clematis Dr Baton Rouge LA 70808 Office: 2279 Main St Baton Rouge LA 70802

JAY, PETER, publishing company executive, writer; b. Feb. 7, 1937; s. Baron Jay; m. Margaret Ann Callaghan, 1961 (div. 1986); 3 children; m. Emma Thornton, 1986; 1 child. Student, Winchester Coll., Eng.; MA with 1st class honors, Oxford U., Eng., 1960; LittD (hon.), Wake Forest U., 1979; LHD (hon.), U. Calif., Berkeley, 1979. Asst. prin. Her Majesty's Treasury, London, 1961-64, pvt. sec., 1964, prin., 1964-67; econs. editor The Times, London, 1967-77; assoc. editor Times Bus. News, London, 1969-77; amb. to U.S. Washington, 1977-79; dir. Economist Intelligence Unit, Washington, 1979-83; chmn., chief exec. officer TV-am Ltd., 1980-83, pres., 1983—; chief of staff to chmn. Mirror Group Newspapers Ltd., London, 1986—; vis. scholar Brookings Inst., Washington, 1979-80; Wincott Meml. lectr., 1975, Copland Meml. lectr., Australia, 1980, Shell lectr. Glasgow, 1985; cons. Economist Group, 1979-81; chmn., chief exec. officer TV-am News, 1982-83; bd. dirs. Maxwell Communication Corp., Mirror Holdings Ltd., Pergamon Holdings Ltd. Author: The Budget, 1972; (with others) America and the World 1979, 1980, The Crisis for Western Political Economy and Other Essays, 1984; (with Michael Stewart) Apocalypse 2000, 1987; TV broadcaster A Week in Politics, 1983-86, Weekend World, 1972-77, The Jay Interview, 1975-76; supervising editor Banking World, 1986, editor, 1984-86. Mem. feasibility studies steering com. United Way U.K., 1982-83, adv. com. United Funds, 1983-85, coun. Cinema and TV Benevolent Fund, 1982-83, coun. St. George's House, Windsor, Eng., 1982—; chmn. Working Party on Children and Young Persons in Custody, 1976-77, Charities Effectiveness Rev. Trust, 1986-87; gov. Ditchley Found., 1982—; bd. dirs. New Nat. Theater, Washington, 1979-81. Sub-lt. Royal Navy, 1956-57. Named Polit. Broadcaster of Yr., 1973, Harold Wincott Fin. and Econ. Journalist of Yr., 1973, Male Personality of Yr. (Pye award) Royal TV Soc., 1974; recipient Berkeley citation U. Calif., 1979, SFTA Shell Internat. TV award, 1974. Mem. Royal Naval Sailing Assn., Royal Cork Yacht Club, Garrick Club. Home: 39 Castlebar Rd, London England W5 2DJ

JEANNIOT, PIERRE JEAN, airline executive; b. Montpellier, France, Apr. 9, 1933 . BS, Concordia U., Montreal, Can., 1957; postgrad., McGill U., Montreal; hon. doctorate, Que. U., 1988. With Sperry Gyroscope, to 1955; with Air Can., 1955—, dir. systems adminstrn. and operational research, 1968-70, v.p. computer and systems services, 1970-76, head corp. planning office, 1971-76, v.p. Eastern region, exec. in charge subs. and associated cos., 1976-79, sr. v.p. mktg. and planning, 1979-80, exec. v.p., chief airline ops., 1980-82, exec. v.p., chief operating officer, 1982-84, pres., chief exec. officer, 1984—; chmn. bd. La Revue du Commerce, 1979-83. Contbr. articles to profl. jours. Chmn. bd. U. Que., Can., 1972-77; chmn. bd. U. Que. Found., 1979—. Decorated officer Order of Canada; recipient Mgmt. Achievement award McGill U., 1988. Mem. Can. Operational Rsch. Soc. (past nat. pres.), Can. Air Transport Assn. (v.p., chmn. bd.), Mount-Royal Club, Montreal Traffic Club. Roman Catholic. Clubs: Saint-Denis, Mt. Stephen, Laval-sur-le-Lac. Office: Air Can, Pl Air Canada, Montreal, PQ Canada H2Z 1X5

JECKOVICH, GARY, senior business consultant; b. New Kensington, Pa., Aug. 3, 1953; s. Stephen and Mildred (Halvonik) J.; m. Diane M. Shedlosky, Nov. 29, 1986. BS, Pa. State U., 1974; MBA, Temple U., 1982. Prodn. planner packaging machinery FMC Corp., Horsham, Pa., 1976-77, chief planner, 1977-79, mgr. prodn. control, 1979-80, materials mgr., 1980-82; spl. project engr. ordnance div. FMC Corp., Aiken, S.C., 1983; cons. Xerox Computer Services, Cherry Hill, N.J., 1984—. Sec. Friends of St. Christopher's Hosp. for Children, Phila., 1987-89. Mem. Am. Prodn. and Inventory Control Soc. (cert. 1982). Republican. Office: Xerox Computer Cons 365 W Passaic St Rochelle Park NJ 07662

JEDLICKA, WILLIAM JOSEPH, management consultant; b. Chgo., Feb. 27, 1947; s. William Francis and Mary Agnas (Zarish) J.; m. Candy Jedlicka, Aug. 1974; children: Julie, Michael. BBA, John Carroll U., 1970; MBA, No. Ill. U., 1971; PhD, Ill. Inst. Tech., 1984. Registered psychologist. Mgr. prodn. Pan Am. Gyro Tex., Franklin Pk., Ill., 1971-72; mgr. ops. Trane Co., Westchester, Ill., 1972-75; chmn. mgmt. dept. Harper Coll., Palatine, Ill., 1975—; sr. cons. Performance Improvement, Norwood Pk., Ill. 1977—. Contbr. articles to profl. jours. 1st lt. U.S. Army, 1969-70. Mem. Am. Psychol. Assn. Home: 416 Lauder Dr Inverness IL 60067 Office: Harper Coll Algonquin & Roselle Rds Palatine IL 60067

JEFFE, SIDNEY DAVID, automotive engineer; b. Chgo., May 6, 1927; s. J.I. Jeffe; children: Robert A., Leslie A. B.S. with honors in Mech. Engring., Ill. Inst. Tech., 1950; M.S. with honors in Automotive Engring., Chrysler Inst. Engring., 1952; grad. program for execs., Carnegie-Mellon U., 1968. With Chrysler Corp., 1950-80, v.p. engring. and research, 1976-80; sr. v.p. ops. Sheller Globe Corp., Detroit, 1982-86, sr. v.p. internat. bus. and tech. devel. and implementation, head customer and govt. relations activities, 1986—; exec. dir. Transp. Research Center Ohio, E. Liberty; prof. mech. engring. Ohio State U., 1980-82; sec.-treas. Transp. Research Bd. Ohio, 1980-82; mem. bd. Engring. Sch., Oakland U., 1977—; bd. dirs. Sheller-Ryobi Corp. Responsible for devel. Chrysler's first line front-wheel drive cars, 1976-80; author papers in field. Served with AUS, 1945-47. Fellow Engring. Soc. Detroit, Soc. Automotive Engrs. (Russell Springer award 1957, Coll. Fellows 1985—); mem. Tau Beta Pi (Outstanding New Mem. award 1948), Pi Tau Sigma (Outstanding New Mem. award 1948). Unitarian. Clubs: Orchard Lake Country, Detroit Athletic, Ren Cen. Home: 3673 Quail Hollow Bloomfield Hills MI 48013 Office: Sheller-Globe Corp 1641 Porter St Detroit MI 48216

JEFFERIES, ROBERT AARON, JR., furniture company executive; b. Richmond, Ind., June 30, 1941; s. Robert Aaron and Roberta June (Hart) J.; m. Sylvia Mae Gilmore, Apr. 16, 1962; children—David E., Michael S., Stephen R. A.B. with honors in Govt, Earlham Coll., Richmond, 1963; J.D. with distinction (Herman C. Krannert scholar 1963-65), Ind. U., 1966. Bar: Ohio bar 1966, Ind. bar 1966, Ill. bar 1970, Mo. bar 1970. Assoc. firm Shumaker, Loop & Kendrick, Toledo, 1966-69; asst. gen. counsel, asst. sec. May Dept. Stores Co., St. Louis, 1969-77; v.p., gen. counsel, sec. Leggett & Platt, Inc., Carthage, Mo., 1977—. Contbr. articles to legal jours.; bd. editors law jour., Ind. U., 1965-66. Mem. Am. Bar Assn., Ind. Bar Assn., Ohio Bar Assn., Ill. Bar Assn., Mo. Bar Assn., St. Louis Bar Assn., Order of Coif. Office: Leggett & Platt Inc PO Box 757 Carthage MO 64836

JEFFERSON, NANCY ZANDERS, engineer; b. Winter Garden, Fla., Sept. 10, 1936; d. William Napoleon Jr. and Grace (Williams) Zanders; m. Sam James Jefferson, June 11, 1953; children: Wendy Alicia, Samuel James, Patricia Ann, Charlotte Gail. Cert. in engring., Iowa State U., 1977; AS in Bus. Adminstrn., Bryant Coll., Smithfield, R.I., 1978. Key punch operator So. Bell Telephone Co., Orlando, Fla., 1965-70; key punch operator New Eng. Telephone, Providence, 1970-72, reports clk., 1972-76; asst. engr. New Eng. Telephone, Boston, 1976-77; engr. New Eng. Telephone, Pawtucket, R.I., 1977—. Pres. missionary circle Olney St. Bapt. Ch., Providence, 1978-84; company rep. Jr. Achievement of R.I., Providence, 1986—; bd. dirs. Bryant Coll. Alumni Assn., 1988—. Mem. Telephone Pioneers of Am. (Cert. of Participation 1984), Minority Mgrs. Assn. (sec. 1983), Greater Providence Bowling Assn. (bd. dirs. 1988—). Democrat. Lodges: Order of Eastern Star (Providence chpt. worthy matron 1972-83), Cyrene Crusaders (Providence chpt. Royal Magdalene 1986-87), Queen of Sheba (treas. 1985—, worthy matron 1983, Royal Martha 1987, Royal Commandress 1988—). Home: 101 Apulia St East Providence RI 02914 Office: New Eng Telephone 85 High St Pawtucket RI 02860

JEFFREDO, JOHN VICTOR, aerospace engineer, manufacturing company executive, inventor; b. Los Angeles, Nov. 5, 1927; s. John Edward and Pauline Matilda (Whitten) J.; m. Elma Jean Nesmith, (div. 1958); children: Joyce Jean Jeffredo Ryder, Michael John; m. Doris Louise Hinz, (div. 1980); children: John Victor, Louise Victoria Jeffredo-Warden; m. Gerda Adelheid Pillich. Grad. in Aerospace Engring. Cal-Aero Tech. Inst., 1948; AA in Machine Design, Pasadena City Coll., 1951; grad. in Electronics The Ordnance Sch. U.S. Army, 1951; AA in Am. Indian Studies, Palomar Coll., 1978; postgrad. U. So. Calif., 1955-58; MBA, La Jolla U., 1980, PhD in Human Rels., 1984. Design engr. Douglas Aircraft Co., Long Beach and Santa Monica, Calif., 1955-58; devel. engr. Honeywell Ordnance Corp., Duarte, Calif., 1958-62; cons. Honeywell devel. labs., Seattle, 1962-65; supr. mech. engr. dept. aerospace div. Control Data Corp., Pasadena, Calif., 1965-68; project engr. Cubic Corp., San Diego, 1968-70; supr. mech. engring. dept. Babcock Electronics Co., Costa Mesa, Calif., 1970-72; owner, operator Jeffredo Gunsight Co., Fallbrook, Calif., 1971-81; chief engr. Western Designs, Inc., Fallbrook, 1972-81, exec. dir., 1981-88, chief exec. officer, 1988—; owner, operator Western Designs, Fallbrook, 1981-87; exec. dir. JXJ, Inc., San Marcos, Calif., 1981-88, chief exec. officer, 1988—; mgr. Jeffredo Gunsight div., 1981—, chief engr. JXJ, Inc., 1987—; owner, mgr. Energy Assocs., San Diego, 1982-86; pres. Jeffredo Internat., 1984-88; chief exec. officer John-Victor Internat., San Marcos, Calif., Frankfurt, Fed. Republica Germany, 1988—; engring. cons. Action Instruments Co., Inc., Gen. Dynamics, Alcyon Corp., Systems Exploration, Inc. (all San Diego), Hughes Aircraft Co., El Segundo, Allied-Bendix, San Marcos; bd. dirs. Indian World Corp., JXJ., Inc. Author: Wildcatting; contbr. articles to trade jours. and mags.; guest editorial writer Town Hall, San Diego Union; patentee agrl. frost control, vehicle off-road drive system, recoil absorbing system for firearms, telescope sight mounting system for firearms, breech mech. sporting firearm, elec. switch activating system, 33 others. Mem. San Diego County Border Task Force on Undocumented Aliens, 1979-80, 81-82; chmn. Native Californian Coalition, 1982—; bd. dirs. Nat. Geog. Soc., 1968. With U.S. Army, 1951-53. Recipient Superior Svc. Commendation award U.S. Naval Ordnance Test Sta., Pasadena, 1959. Mem. Am. Soc. for Metals, Soc. Automotive Engrs., Nat. Rifle Assn. (life), San Diego Zool. Soc., Sierra Club (life), Nat. Wildlife Fedn., The Wilderness Soc., Rocky Mountain Elk Found. Avocations: sculpture, chess, music, conservation, travel. Home: 1629 Via Monserate Fallbrook CA 92028 Office: 133 N Pacific St Ste D San Marcos CA 92069

JEFFREY, CHARLES ALAN, sales executive; b. Chgo., July 4, 1950; s. Thomas Edward and Charlotte Gladys (Dragstedt) J. BS, U. Md., 1973; BEE, Ga. Inst. Tech., 1977; MBA, Emory U., 1985. Sales engr. Stallings Inc., Atlanta, 1975-81, sr. sales engr., 1981-83; v.p. Stallings of Ga., Atlanta, 1983-84; area mgr. Indsl. Data Techs., Columbus, Ohio, 1985-87, sr. area mgr., 1987—, govt. mktg. task force, 1987-88, new product mktg. task force, 1988. Mem. Instrument Soc. Am., Eta Kappa Nu, Delta Sigma Phi. Republican. Baptist. Home: 1438 Merriman Ln Atlanta GA 30324

JEFFREY, DAVID GORDON, marketing executive; b. Pawtucket, R.I., July 31, 1946; s. David Gordon and Clara Ellen (Wilson) J.; m. Pamela J. Kunatz, Jan. 25, 1980; children: Alexandra Elizabeth, James Johnstone, MacAllister George David. BA, Furman U., 1968; MBA, Wake Forest U., 1971. With mktg. staff Hanes Corp., Winston-Salem, N.C., 1969-71, Levi Strauss & Co., San Francisco, 1972-74; pres., chief exec. officer Caledonia Group Inc. and subs. British Am. Trading Co., Inc., England, Jeffrey Advt., Inc., San Francisco, 1974—; bd. dirs. San Francisco Advt. Softball League, 1978-80, commr., 1981-83. 1st lt. airborne rangers U.S. Army, 1967-69. Decorated Silver Star, Bronze Star, Purple Heart. Republican. Episcopalian. Lodge: Rotary.

JEFFREY, FRANCIS, software developer, forecaster; b. Calif., 1950. BA in Computational Neurophysiology, U. Calif., Berkeley, 1972. Research assoc. U. Calif., San Diego, 1972-73; cons. Sci. Applications, Inc., La Jolla, Calif., 1973-75; entrepreneur Big Sur, Calif., 1973-77; cons. Alive Systems Info. Scis., San Francisco, 1978-87; founder, pres., chief exec. officer Alive Systems, Inc. and Elfnet, Inc., Malibu, Calif., 1987—; cons. Inst. for Advanced Computation, Sunnyvale, Calif., 1973-75, Human-Dolphin Found., 1980-82, 87-89, Esalen Inst., 1982-83. Author: (with others) Handbook of States of Consciousness, 1986, The Biography of Dr. John C. Lilly, 1989; co-author: In the Provence of the Mind, 1989; designer computer co-pilot software; patentee isolation module. Co-founder New Forum, Monterey, Calif., 1984, Gt. Whales Found., San Francisco, 1987, Big Sur chpt. L5 Nat. Space Soc. Mem. Computer Soc. of IEEE, Control Systems Group Am. Soc. for Cybernetics (charter). Home: PO Box 6847 Malibu CA 90264

JEFFREY, LOUIS ROBERT, JR., retail executive; b. East Orange, N.J., Mar. 7, 1927; s. Louis R. Sr. and Mabel E. (Fagley) J.; m. Susan Skilling, Dec. 5, 1953; children: Richard, David, Mark, Sarah. BA, Williams Coll., 1950; MBA, Harvard U., 1953. Pres. Nat. Ultrasonic Corp., Sommerville, N.J., 1964-69; v.p. Pres.'s Assn. div. AMA, N.Y.C., 1970-74; pres., chief exec. officer Square Two Golf, Fairfield, N.J., 1974—. Ltd. USAF, 1944-45. Home: 50 Gloucester Rd Summit NJ 07901 Office: Square Two Golf 18 Gloria Ln Fairfield NJ 07006

JEFFREYS, ELYSTAN GEOFFREY, geologist, oil company executive; b. N.Y.C., Apr. 26, 1926; s. Geoffrey and Georgene Frances Theodora (Littell) J.; m. Pat Rumage, May 1, 1946; children: Jeri Lynn, David Powell; m. 2d, Peggi Villar, Feb. 28, 1975. Geol. Engr., Colo. Sch. Mines, 1951, grad. Econ. Evaluation and Investment Decision Methods, 1972. Registered profl. engr., Miss.; registered land surveyor, Miss. Ptnr. G. Jeffreys & Son, 1951-53, Jeffreys and Launius, 1953-55; instr. structural geology U. So. Miss., 1955; pvt. practice petroleum exploration, 1954-77; exploration mgr. Arrowhead Exploration Co., Mobile and Brewton, Ala., 1977-83; cons. geologist, 1964—; pres., chmn. bd., chief exec. officer Major Oil Co., Jackson, Miss., 1961-84; pres., chief exec. officer The Jeffreys Co., Inc., Mobile, Ala. Trustee Nat. Eye Found. Served with 281st Combat Engrs., U.S. Army, 1944-46, ETO. Mem. Miss. Geol. Soc., New Orleans Geol. Soc., Am. Assn. Petroleum Geologists, Gulf Coast Assn. Geol. Socs. (treas. 1960, cert. of service 1971), Soc. Petroleum Engrs. AIME, Soc. Petroleum Evaluation Engrs., Am. Assn. Petroleum Landmen, Ind. Petroleum Assn. Am., Assn. Petroleum Landmen of Ala., Soc. Ind. Profl. Earth Scientists, English Speaking Union, Mobile-Bristol Soc. (treas.), Pi Kappa Alpha. Clubs: Athlestan; Capital City Petroleum, Bienville. Lodges: Masons (32 degree), Shriners. Home: 1810 Old Government St Mobile AL 36606

JEFFS, THOMAS H., II, banker; b. Grosse Pointe Farms, Mich., July 11, 1938; s. Thomas Raymond and Geraldine (Bogan) J.; m. Patricia Lucas, June 20, 1964; children—Leslie, Laura, Caroline. B.B.A. in Gen. Bus., U. Mich., 1960, M.B.A., 1961. With Nat. Bank Detroit, 1962—, now vice chmn.; dir. Hwy. Users, Washington, Maccabees Mut., Southfield Mich., MasterCard Internat., N.Y.C. Bd. dirs. Detroit Symphony, St. John Hosp., Detroit, St. Clair Health Services Corp., Detroit. Served with U.S. Army, 1960-62. Republican. Episcopalian. Clubs: Detroit (pres. 1982), Detroit Country, Yondotega. Home: 27 Waverly Ln Grosse Pointe Farms MI 48236 Office: NBD Bancorp Inc 611 Woodward Ave Detroit MI 48226

JEGOU, CAROL KULINA, retail store executive; b. Somerville, N.J., Aug. 23, 1949; d. Stephen and Helen (Zeban) K.; m. Peter John Jegou, March 4, 1973; 1 child, Alyse Ann. BS, W.Va. U., 1971. Head buyer Reynolds, Inc., Perth Amboy, N.J., 1971-73; advtg. acct. exec. Princeton (N.J.) Packet Group, Inc., 1973-75; exec. v.p., chief exec. officer Creative Learning Products, South Plainfield, N.J., 1986—. Creator, producerline of childrens' cards, stationery, paper activity products and video cassettes, 1986—. Mem. AAUW. Republican. Methodist. Office: Creative Learning Products Inc 3567 Kennedy Rd South Plainfield NJ 08070

JEHLE, MICHAEL EDWARD, banker, lawyer; b. Lawrence, Kans., Apr. 2, 1954; s. Edwin Paul and Catherine Claire (Cragoe) J.; m. Kimberly Ellen Davis, Aug. 4, 1979; 1 child, Kathryn Anne. BS, S.W. Mo. State U., 1976; JD, Stanford U., 1979. Bar: Calif., Ill., Pa. Atty. The First Nat. Bank of Chgo., 1979-84, sr. atty., 1984-86; v.p., gen. counsel Equibank, Pitts., 1986-87, sr. v.p., gen. counsel, sec., 1987; sr. v.p., gen. counsel, sec. Equimark Corp., Pitts., 1987-89, exec. v.p., chief fin. officer, 1989—. Co-author: Sovereign Lending, 1984. Mem. ABA. Republican. Presbyterian. Home: 411 Maple Ln Sewickley PA 15143 Office: Equimark Corp 2 Oliver Pla Pittsburgh PA 15222

JELINSKI, LEONARD SEYMOUR, financial planner; b. Bklyn., Jan. 17, 1940; s. Irving and Rose (Alterman) J.; m. Barbara Miller, Dec. 23, 1965; children: Jeffrey, Michael. BS, Ariz. State U., 1965; MBA, Farleigh Dickinson U., 1969. Lic. real estate broker, N.J. V.p. Airwick, Inc., Carlstadt, N.J., 1966-77, Garden State Group, Clinton, N.J., 1977-84; fin. planner IDS Fin. Svcs./Amex, Wayne, N.J., 1984-87, dist. mgr., 1988—. Asst. chmn. Town of Wayne Indsl. Commn., 1986—; coach Police Athletic League, Wayne, 1974-84, Young Men/Young Women's Hebrew Assn., Wayne, 1974-84. Mem. Internat. Assn. Fin. Planning, Wayne Valley Basketball Booster Club. Home: 27 Andover Dr Wayne NJ 07470 Office: IDS Fin Svcs Inc Amex 22 Riverview Dr Wayne NJ 07470

JELINSKY, LEONARD SEYMOUR, financial planner; b. Bklyn., Jan. 17, 1940; s. Irving and Rose (Alterman) J.; m. Barbara Miller, Dec. 23, 1965; children: Jeffrey, Michael. BS, Ariz. State U., 1965; MBA, Fairleigh Dickinson U., 1969. Lic. real estate broker. V.p. Airwick Inc., Carlstadt, N.J., 1966-77, Garden State Group, Clinton, N.J., 1977-84; fin. planner IDS Fin. Svcs., Wayne, N.J., 1984-87, dist. mgr., 1988—. Asst. chmn. Wayne Indsl. Commn., 1986—; coach Police Athletic League, Wayne, 1974-84, YM-YWHA, Wayne, 1974-78. Mem. Internat. Assn. Fin. Planners, Wayne Valley Basketball Boosters. Office: IDS Fin Svcs Inc 500 Valley Rd Wayne NJ 07470

JENEFSKY, JACK, wholesale executive; b. Dayton, Ohio, Oct. 27, 1919; s. David and Anna (Saeks) J.; m. Beverly J. Mueller, Feb. 23, 1962; 1 child, Anna Elizabeth; 1 stepchild, Cathryn Jean Mueller. BSBA, Ohio State U., 1941; postgrad. Harvard Bus. Sch., 1943; MA in Econs., U. Dayton, 1948. Surplus broker, Dayton, 1946-48; sales rep. Remington Rand-Univac, Dayton, 1949-56, mgr. AF account, 1957-59, br. mgr. Dayton, 1960-61, regional mktg. cons. Midwest region, Dayton, 1962-63; pres. Bowman Supply Co., Dayton, 1963—. Selection adv. bd. Air Force Acad., 3d congl. dist., chmn., 1974-82; chmn. 3d. dist. screening bds. Mil. Acad., 1976-82; coordinator Great Lakes region, res. assistance program CAP, 1970-73. Served from pvt. to capt. USAAF, 1942-46; CBI, maj. USAF, 1951-53; col Res. Mem. Air Force Assn. (comdr. Ohio wing 1957-58, 58-59), Res. Officers Assn. (pres. Ohio dept. 1956-57, nat. council 1957-58, chmn. research and devel. com. 1961-62), Dayton Area C. of C. (chmn. spl. events com. 1970-72, chmn. rsch. com. on mil. affairs 1983-87), Miami Valley Mil. Affairs Assn. (trustee 1985—, pres. bd. trustees 1987-88), Ohio State U. Alumni Assn. (pres. Montgomery County, Ohio, 1959-60), Nat. Sojourners (pres. Dayton 1961-62). Jewish. Club: Harvard Bus. Sch. Dayton (pres. 1961-62). Lodge: Lions. Home: 136 Briar Heath Cir Dayton OH 45415 Office: Bowman Supply Co PO Box 1404 Dayton OH 45401

JENG, CHAWN-YAW, transportation engineer; b. Taipei, Taiwan, July 16, 1956; came to U.S., 1982; s. Kao-Ming and Huei-Chiao (Lin) J.; m. Shwu-Ching Chen, Dec. 19, 1982; 1 child, Karen J.R. BS, Nat. Chiao-Tung U., Hsinchu, Taiwan, 1978; MS, Nat. Taiwan U., 1980; PhD in Engring., U. Calif., Berkeley, 1987. Cert. engr. in tng. Research asst. Inst. Transp. Studies U. Calif., Berkeley, 1982-85, research assoc., 1986; tchg. assoc. Dept. Civil Engring. U. Calif., Berkeley, 1985-86; transp. system analyst Masami Sakita & Assocs., Mt. View, Calif., 1986-87; transp. analyst Comsis Corp., Silver Spring, Md., 1987—. Assoc. mem. ASCE, Inst. Transp. Engrs., Operation Research Soc. Am., Transp. Research Bd, Phi Tau Phi. Home: 1925 Morningmist Dr Silver Spring MD 20906 Office: Comsis Corp 8737 Colesville Rd Ste 1100 Silver Spring MD 20910

JENKINS, BENJAMIN LARRY, insurance company executive; b. Washington, Aug. 17, 1938; s. Benjamin Joseph and Ruth Elizabeth (deButts) J.; m. Catherine O. Hungerford, June 30, 1956; children: Lynne, Lisa, Larry, Laine, Lacy, Lexy. B.S., Mt. St. Mary's Coll., Emmitsburg, Md., 1960. C.L.U. Dist. agt. Peoples Life, Waldorf, Md., 1959-62, sales mgr., 1962,65; mgr. Peoples Life, Newport News, Va., 1965-69; supt. agys. Peoples Life, Washington, 1969-71; v.p. Peoples Life, 1971-74, sr. v.p., 1974-76, exec. v.p., 1976-77, pres., 1977-78, chmn. bd., pres., 1978-82; vice chmn. Monumental Life Ins. Co., Balt., 1982-83; chmn. bd., pres. Monumental Life Ins. Co., 1983—; dir. Mercantile Bankshares, Balt., 1982—; vice chmn. Life Insurers Conf., Richmond, Va., 1982-83. Trustee Balt. Mus. of Art, 1983-86, Coll. Notre Dame of Md.; campaign chmn. Unied Way Cen. Md., 1986. Fellow Life Office Mgmt. Assn. (cert. life mgmt. inst.); mem. Am. Council Life Ins., Am. Soc. Chartered Life Underwriters, Nat. Assn. Life Underwriters, Life Insurers Conf. (chmn. 1984-85). Republican. Roman Catholic. Home: 8530 Park Heights Ave Baltimore MD 21208 Office: Monumental Life Ins Co 2 E Chase St Baltimore MD 21202

JENKINS, BRUCE ARMAND, manufacturing company executive; b. Lansing, Mich., June 4, 1933; s. George H. Jenkins and Margaret E. (Hoeflinger) Tinlin; m. Peggy A. Unruh, July 22, 1967; children: David, Mark. With Gen. Motors Corp., Lansing, 1953-83, supr. tech. tng., 1984-86; pres. Advanced Tech. Seminars, Inc., Eagle, Mich., 1986—; chmn. bd. Allied Tech. Tooling, Inc., Potterville, Mich., 1987—, Advanced Tech. Innovations, Inc., Potterville, Mich., 1988—. Author: Automotive Plastics, 1985, Plastics Repair, 1986, Cast Plastic Tooling Techniques, 1986; contbr. numerous articles to profl. jours. Pastor Foursquare Gospel Ch., Eagle, 1983—. Served to 1st lt. U.S. Army, 1950-1961. Republican. also: Allied Tech Tooling Inc 570 E Main St Potterville MI 48876

JENKINS, JOHN LOGAN, financial planning company executive; b. San Diego, Dec. 17, 1950; s. Lyle Ervin and Emily Patricia (Lyons) J.; children: Justin, Kristen; m. Margaret Sprotte, Apr. 2, 1983. Bs, San Diego State U., 1977, MA, 1982; grad., Coll. for Fin. Planning, Denver. Tchr. Encinitas (Calif.) Union Sch. Dist., 1978-83; salesman Mass. Indemnity Life Ins. Co., San Diego, 1982-83, Am. Capital Securities Co., Houston, 1983-85, Am. Gen. Life Ins. Co., Houston, 1983-85, MONY Securities Corp., N.Y.C., 1983-85, Mut. of N.Y., N.Y.C., 1983-85; securities rep. Anchor Nat. Fin. Svcs. Inc., Phoenix, 1985-87; officer Clyman and Jenkins Inc., Encinitas, 1985-88; v.p., prin. Christopher Weil and Co. Inc., Encinitas, 1987-88; owner Jenkins Fin. Planning Svcs., San Diego, 1988—; prin. W.S. Griffith and Co. Inc., San Diego, 1988—; instr. Nat. Inst. Fin., South Plainfield, N.J., 1985—; cons. Soc. CLU, Great Falls, Mont., 1988. Guest pub. broadcasting systems Money Makers series, 1989. Mem. Inst. Cert. Fin. Planners, Internat. Assn. for Fin. Planners, Encinitas C. of C., San Diego C. of C. Democrat. Office: Jenkins Fin Planning Svcs 1455 Frazee Rd #802 San Diego CA 92108

JENKINS, JOHN MARSHALL, sales executive; b. N.Y.C., May 2, 1921; s. Rouget deLisle and Patricia (Abernethy) J.; m. Mary Mecklin, Feb. 28, 1944; children: Patricia, Mary Shelton, John Jr., Robert. BA, Dartmouth Coll., 1942. Sales rep. La France Industries, N.Y.C., 1946-55, nat. sales mgr., v.p. sales, bd. dirs., 1955-60; nat. sales mgr. consumer products div. Standard Packaging Corp., N.Y.C., 1960-68; gen. sales mgr., bd. dirs. Imperial-Schrade Corp., N.Y.C., 1968—, v.p. sales, 1984—. Chmn. Westport Railroad Parking Com. 1st lt. USAF, 1942-46. Democrat. Home: 156 Roseville Rd Westport CT 06880 Office: Imperial-Schrade Corp 99 Madison Ave Ste 1500 New York NY 10016

JENKINS, MADGE MARIE, management educator, consultant; b. Dearborn, Mich., Oct. 19, 1938; d. Lem and Margaret Mary (Tulloch) VicKroy; m. Robert Eugene Brennan, Dec. 28, 1958 (div. 1965); 1 child, Richard; m. George Henry Jenkins, Aug. 15, 1967. Student Systems Inst., Detroit, 1965, Henry Ford Community Coll., 1965-67; B.A. cum laude, U. Mich., 1976; M.P.A., Wayne State U., 1978. Ops. mgr. Custom Lab., Dearborn, Mich., 1967-68; mgr. Jenkins Wedding Studies, Dearborn, 1968-74; unit dir. dept. recreation City of Dearborn, 1976-78; enumerator Dept. Agr., Seattle, 1978-79; coordinator Stillaguamish Ctr., Arlington, Wash., 1979-80; asst. prof. mgmt., coordinator mgmt. dept. Lima Tech. Coll., Ohio, 1980—; mem. Adv. Bd. Continuing Edn., Bellingham, Wash., 1978-80, Marysville, Wash., 1979-80; mgmt. cons. Jenkins & Jenkins, Cario, Ohio, 1984—; cons. Ctr. for Bus. and Econ. Research, Western Wash. U. 1979-80. Elder, Columbus Grove Presbyterian Ch., Ohio, 1982-83. Mem. Acad. Mgmt., Am. Mgmt. Assn., Am. Assn. Pub. Adminstrn., Am. Soc. Tng. and Devel., Am. Assn. Personnel Adminstrn. Republican. Club: 8-16 Cine (Detroit). Lodge: Toastmasters (v.p. local chpt. 1981-82). Office: Ohio State U Lima Tech Coll Campus Lima OH 45804

JENKINS, PHILLIP LANE, manufacturing executive; b. Bridgewater, Mass., Jan. 19, 1923; s. H. Loring and Etta (Lane) J.; m. Nancy McGrath, Oct. 26, 1948 (div. 1975); children: Phillip Lane, Geoffrey Holbrook; m. Henrietta Mary Ferris, Oct. 8, 1983. Student, Amherst Coll., 1941-42, Northeastern U., 1946-56. With George O. Jenkins Co., Bridgewater, 1946-48, v.p. ops., 1948-64; owner Jenkins Corp., Quincy, Mass., 1964-65; plant mgr. Hollingsworth & Vose Co., Greenwich, N.Y., 1965-73, East Walpole, Mass., 1973-83; dir. purchasing Hollingsworth & Vose Co., East Walpole, Mass., 1983-87, v.p. mfg., 1987—. Chmn. adv. bd. Salvation Army, Brockton, Mass., 1953-65; chmn. Rep. Com., Brockton, 1958-60. Mem. Glen Falls Country Club, Blue Water Sailing Club, Masons. Republican. Congregationalist. Home: 241 Elm St Waldole MA 02081 Office: Hollingsworth & Vose Co 112 Washington St East Walpole MA 02032

JENKINS, RICHARD LEE, manufacturing company executive; b. Lynchburg, Va., July 20, 1931; s. Robert Julian and Beulah Vivian (Crews) J.; m. Doris E. Rucker, Dec. 24, 1958; children: Terena M., Richard C. BA, Lynchburg Coll., 1957; MBA, U. Mass., 1970. Various fin. mgmt. positions Gen. Electric Co., Lynchburg, Schenectady, N.Y., and Pittsfield, Mass., 1957-72; controller, mgr. Mfg. Transformer div. Allis-Chalmers, Pitts., 1972-75; gen. mgr. Indsl. Pump div. Allis-Chalmers, Cin., 1975-79; sr. v.p. Lynchburg Foundry, 1979-81; gen. mgr. service div. Siemens-Allis, Inc., Atlanta, 1981-84; sr. v.p. adminstrn. and internat. ops., chief fin. officer Diversified Products Corp., Opelika, Ala., 1984—; treas., bd. dirs. Micah Corp. of Berkshire County, Pittsfield, 1968-72; bd. dirs. Va. Nat. Bank, Lynchburg, 1979-81. Auditor ARC, Pittsfield, 1966; bd. dirs., exec. on loan United Community Services, Pittsfield, 1972; campaign chmn. Piedmont Heart Assn., Lynchburg, 1980. Served with USN, 1950-54, Korea. Clubs: Cherokee Country (Atlanta), Saugahatchee Country (Opelika). Home: 2127 Hamilton Pl N Opelika AL 36801 Office: Diversified Products Corp 309 Williamson Ave Opelika AL 36801

JENKINS, ROBERT RICHARD, leasing company executive; b. Chgo., June 1, 1938; s. Matthew N. and Marion (Shelby) J.; B.S., Loyola U., 1960, M.A., 1962; m. Mary Ellen Thulis, May 31, 1969; children—Tracy Jane, David Robert. Product mgr. Nat. Steel Corp., Evanston, Ill., 1965-69; sales mgr. Xerox Corp., Chgo., 1969-71; regional mgr. Gelco Corp., N.Y.C., 1971-77, v.p. mktg., Eden Prairie, Minn., 1977-80; v.p. The Van Arnem Co., Bloomfield Hills, Mich., 1980-81; exec. v.p. Republic Fin. Corp., Denver, 1981-89, Ill. Capital Group, Inc., Chgo., 1989—. Mem. Planning Commn. City of Westport, Conn., 1975-77. Served to lt. USNR, 1963-65. Mem. Sales Exec. Club N.Y., Am. Equipment Leasing Assn., Western Assn. Equipment Leasors, Sales and Mktg. Exec. Mpls., Denver Area Lessors Assn. (bd. dirs.), New Eng. T Register, Colo. MG T Club, Am. Automotive Leasing Assn. Clubs: Heather Ridge Country, Denver Athletic, Colo. Racquet. Home: 420 Fullerton Pkwy Chicago IL 60614

JENKINS, ROYAL GREGORY, manufacturing executive; b. Springville, Utah, Dec. 11, 1936; s. Chester W. and Sarah E. (Finch) J.; m. Donna Jeanne Jones, Aug. 3, 1957; children: Brad, Kent. BS in Engring., San Jose State U., 1959; MBA, U. Santa Clara, 1968. With Lockheed Corp., Sunnyvale, Calif., 1959-64; contr. ICORE Industries, Sunnyvale, 1964-68; div. v.p. fin. Dart Industries, Los Angeles, 1968-74; dir. planning, div. v.p. Avery Label Group, Avery Internat., Los Angeles, 1974-81, group v.p. Materials Group, Painesville, Ohio, 1981-87, sr. v.p. tech. and planning, Pasadena, Calif., 1987-88, sr. v.p. fin., 1988—. Republican. Avocations: golf, racquetball. Office: Avery Internat 150 N Orange Grove Blvd Pasadena CA 91103

JENKINS, RUBEN LEE, chemical company executive; b. Beggs, Okla., Nov. 27, 1929; s. William Arnold and Myrtle (Kimble) J.; m. Sylvia Griffin, July 17, 1956; children: Amy, Kimble Lee, William Griffin. BA, U. Okla., 1952, LLB, 1956; LLM, NYU, 1959. Bar: Okla. 1956. Law clk. to presiding justice U.S. Dist. Ct. (we. dist.) Okla., Oklahoma City, 1956; clk. U.S. Ct., Oklahoma City, 1956-58; research asst. in internat. law NYU, N.Y.C., 1958-59; assoc. Allende & Brea, Buenos Aires, Argentina, 1959-60; exec. v.p., gen. counsel White Eagle Internat., Midland, Tex., 1960-65; v.p. corp. devel. Plough, Inc., Memphis, 1965-71, dir, 1970, sr. v.p. hdqrs., 1972-73, exec. v.p., 1973-76, pres., 1976-80; dir. Schering-Plough Corp., Madison, N.J., 1971, sr. v.p., 1976-80, exec. v.p., 1980—; dir. 1st Am. Bankshares, Washington. Bd. dirs. Chickasaw Council Boy Scouts Am., Memphis, Council on Family Health, N.Y.C.; trustee Memphis Univ. Sch., Rhodes Coll., Memphis. Served to capt. USMC, 1952-54. Mem. ABA, Tenn. Bar Assn., Okla. Bar Assn., Proprietary Assn. (bd. dirs. 1976—). Presbyterian. Club: Union League (N.Y.C.). Office: Schering-Plough Corp 3030 Jackson Ave Memphis TN 38151

JENKINS, WILLIAM, building materials and property development company executive; b. Mystic, Iowa, Feb. 15, 1920; s. William and Agnes (Gallager) J.; m. Barbara Jane Crafts, June 4, 1944; children—Kathryn Ann, Thomas William. B.A., Drake U., 1941. Acct. Gen. Motors Corp., Kansas City, Kans., 1941-42; acct. Menasco Mfg. Co., Los Angeles, 1946-47; pres., chief exec. officer Conrock Co., Los Angeles, 1947-84; chmn. bd., chief exec. officer CalMat Co. (merger Conrock Co. and Calif. Portland Cement), 1984-88, chmn. bd., 1988—; bd. dirs. CalMat Properties Co., L.A., CalMat of Ariz., Phoenix, Calmet of Central City, Allied Concrete and Materials Co., Calif. Portland Cement Co. Trustee United for Calif., Costa Mesa. Lt. USN, 1942-46. Mem. Calif. Mfrs. Assn. (bd. dirs., chmn. 1980-81), So. Calif. Ready Mixed Concrete Assn. (bd. dirs., past pres.), Portland Cement Assn. (dir., pres., chmn.1985-88), Nat. Sand and Gravel Assn. (dir., chmn. bd. dirs. 1982-83), Calif. Club, Jonathan Club, Hacienda Golf Club, Beavers (bd. dirs.). Republican. Home: 3274 Canal Point Rd Hacienda Heights CA 91745 Office: CalMat Co 3200 San Fernando Rd Los Angeles CA 90065

JENKS, RONALD H., public accounting management consulting company executive ; b. Chillicothe, Ohio, Dec. 16, 1945; s. Truman P. and Lydia Louise (Lyghtle) J.; B.S.I.S.E., Ohio U., 1968, postgrad., 1969; cert. office automation profl.; m. Cheryl J. Stauffer; children—Brett, Jill, Beth. Indsl. engr. Wearever Aluminum Co., Chillicothe, Ohio, 1968; system research analyst Ohio U., Athens, Ohio, 1969; mgmt. cons. Touche Ross & Co., Detroit, 1969-72, Washington, 1972-78, ptnr., dir. info. services, N.Y.C., 1978—. Vice pres. and mem. bd. dirs. Am. Cancer Soc. of Essex County, N.J. Mem. Inst. Mgmt. Cons. (cert.), Infosystems, N.Y. Users Council, Tau Beta Pi. Contbr. articles to profl. jours., researcher and interview subject on using advanced info. system techs. in bus.; bd. editorial advisors Microcomputer Software Letter. Office: 1633 Broadway New York NY 10019

JENNINGS, CHRISTINE LOUISE, banker; b. Portsmouth, Ohio, Nov. 26, 1945; d. Kenneth Franklin and E. Louise J. Student, Ea. Ky. U., 1964-65, Franklin U., 1982-83. Asst. v.p. Huntington Nat. Bank, Columbus, Ohio, 1970-84; v.p. S.E. Bank, Sarasota, Fla., 1984-85, N.C.N.B., Sarasota, 1985-87; sr. v.p. Liberty Nat. Bank, Bradenton, Fla., 1987—, also bd. dirs. Inventor product to remove labels from glass, plastic, metal. Pres., bd. dirs. Mental Health Assn. Sarasota County, 1988—; pres.'s coun. Am. Lung Assn., Bradenton, 1988—; bd. dirs., exec. com., chmn. agys. rels. United Way Manatee County, 1988—; active Big Bros./Big. Sisters; treas. Community Orch., 1980. Mem. NAFE, Fla. Women's Network, Worthington C. of C. (pres. 1981-82), Sarasota City Club, Fla. Westcoast Music (bd. dirs. 1989—), Sarasota-Manatee Community Orch. (bd. dirs. 1989—). Republican. Home: 888 Blvd of the Arts Apt 602 Sarasota FL 34236 Office: Liberty Nat Bank 6001 26th St W Bradenton FL 34207

JENNINGS, DENNIS RAYMOND, accountant, consultant; b. Coleman, Tex., Sept. 28, 1942; s. Raymond Earl and Montie Elizabeth (Moore) J.; m. El Wanda Key, Oct. 31, 1964; children: Jon Marc, Jamie Dennis, Amy Elizabeth. BBA cum laude, Tex. Tech U., 1970. CPA, Tex., La. Mgr. Peat, Marwick, Mitchell & Co., Dallas, 1970-76; mgr. Coopers & Lybrand, Tulsa, 1976-79; mgr. Coopers & Lybrand, New Orleans, 1979, ptnr., 1979-88; ptnr. Coopers & Lybrand, Dallas, 1988—; quality control team leader Cooper & Lybrand, 1981-85; quality control coordinator, west region, 1988—; chmn. personnel com., SW region, 1983-84; mem. personnel com., 1985—, oil and gas com., 1985—. Contbg. author brochure The Revised Petroleum Accounting Rules, 1980. Bd. dirs. U. New Orleans Oil and Gas Conf., 1985-88; mem. acctg. adv. council A.B. Freeman Sch. of Bus. Tulane U., New Orleans, 1986; mem. audit adv. com. New Orleans Parish Sch. Bd., 1980-83. Mem. Am. Inst. CPA's, Tex. and La. Soc. CPA's (bd. dirs. New Orleans chpt., Cert. of Merit 1985, 87), New Orleans C. of C. (chmn. govtl. affairs com. 1984-88, West Bank Council, edn com. 1985-86, West Bank council 1987 (exec. com., Outstanding Svc. award 1985), Open, Inc. (bd. dirs., treas.), Royal Oaks (Dallas) C. of C. Republican. Clubs: Aurora Garden, Petroleum (New Orleans). Office: Coopers & Lybrand 1999 Bryan St Ste 3000 Dallas TX 75201

JENNINGS, DIANE BONNIE, accountant; b. Cedar Rapids, Iowa, July 14, 1953; d. William C. and Patricia Rose (Proskovec) Jennings. BS, Mt. Mercy Coll., 1975; student Coe Coll., 1971-73; postgrad. U. Iowa, 1981-88. MBA, CPA, Iowa. Bookkeeper (part-time) Eagles Grocery Store, Cedar Rapids, 1969-75; sr. acct. Bell & Van Zee, P.C., Cedar Rapids, 1975-81; treas. (part-time) Kenwood Park Ch., Cedar Rapids, 1977-78; controller LeaseAm. Corp., Cedar Rapids, 1981-82, asst. treas., 1982-84, v.p., chief fin. officer, 1984-87, v.p. info. mgmt., 1988—. Mem. selection com. for Ramsey Scholarship Coe Coll., 1973, vol. Growth Fund Drive, 1981; vol. sr. citizen Thanksgiving dinner, 1983-88, Life Investors Inc., 1983-87, Cedar Rapids, 1983-87; fin. review com. United Way, 1986-88, adminstrv. com., 1989; mem. exec. com. Alumni Phonathon, Mt. Mercy Coll., Cedar Rapids, 1985, fin. com. Indian Creek Nature Ctr., 1988—, bd. dirs., 1989, fin. com. YWCA, Cedar Rapids, 1988—, treas., 1989; alumni career cons., 1984—. Mem. Nat. Assn. Accts., 1978-88 (Storm award 1985, 87), Iowa Soc. CPAs, Am. Women's Soc. CPAs, Am. Inst. CPAs, Nat. Assn. Female Execs. Roman Catholic. Avocations: running, golf, racquetball, bicycling, reading. Office: LeaseAm Corp 4333 Edgewood Rd NE Cedar Rapids IA 52499

JENNINGS, FRED EDWARD, management consultant; b. Englewood, N.J., Apr. 7, 1954; s. Frederick Edward and Edith (Vozza) J.; m. Cynthia

Ann Norbut, May 24, 1987; children: Lindsay Elizabeth, Lauren Alyssa. BS in Civil Engring., Tufts U., 1976; MBA, U. Pa., 1979. Project engr. Camp Dresser & McKee, Boston, 1976-77; ptnr. Theodore Barry & Assocs., N.Y.C., 1979-86; pres. F.E. Jennings & Co., Vienna, Va., 1986—. Chmn. Oakton Glen Design Rev. Com., Vienna, 1986—; mem. Fairfax (Va.) Land Use Task Force, 1986; vol. Make-a-Wish Found., Bethesda, Md., 1987—. Mem. Cen. Fairfax C. of C. (small bus. com. 1986—), Inst. Mgmt. Cons. (assoc.). Roman Catholic. Home and Office: 2764 Chain Bridge Rd Vienna VA 22180

JENNINGS, JAMES BURNETT, oil company executive; b. Temple, Tex., Sept. 20, 1940; s. William Donald and Ruth Imogene (Dodson) J.; m. Sharon Marie Lewis, Aug. 7, 1964 (div. 1982); 1 child, James Christopher; m. Regina Ann Richter, Nov. 5, 1983; 1 child, Michael Thomas. AA, Del Mar Coll., Corpus Christi, Tex., 1961; BS, Trinity U., 1963; MS, Purdue U., 1966; postgrad., Cornell U., 1967. Tchr. Burbank High Sch., San Antonio, Tex., 1963-65; tchr., coach Munster (Ind.) High Sch., 1965-69; geophysicist Shell Oil Co., Houston, 1969-74; chief geophysicist Columbia Gas Devel. Corp., Houston, 1974-79; exploration mgr. Hunt Oil Co., Houston, 1979-84; sr. v.p. Hunt Oil Co., Dallas, 1984-88, group v.p. worldwide exploration, 1988—. Contbr. articles to mags. Mem. Soc. Exploration Geophysicists, Am. Assn. Petroleum Geologists, Am. Petroleum Inst. (gen. com. exploration affairs 1987—), Independent Petroleum Assn. Am. (bd. dirs. 1986—). Republican. Office: Hunt Oil Co 1400 Elm St Ste 2900 Dallas TX 75202

JENNINGS, JEFFREY HOWELLS, lawyer; b. Pitts., Feb. 16, 1919; s. Elroy Jeffrey and Bertha Marie (Howells) J.; m. Patricia Walmsley, Oct. 26, 1945; children—Randolph, Sharon, Thomas, Andrea, Alison. A.B., Columbia U., 1941, J.D., 1944. Bar: N.Y. 1944. Assoc. to counsel Columbia U., N.Y.C., 1944-55; asst. U.S. atty. Eastern Dist. N.Y., 1961-66; now sole practice, Smithtown, N.Y.; librarian Old Mill Sch., N.Y.C., 1973. Prin. clk. Smithtown Hwy Dept., 1961. Recipient Cross of Honor Order of DeMolay, 1972. Mem. Columbia U. Secondary Sch. Com., Friends Assn. for Higher Edn., Smithtown C. of C. (pres. 1959-60), Phi Delta Phi. Republican. Quaker. Clubs: Dramatists Guild (N.Y.C.). Works include: Battle of the Andes, The Classmate, 1934; Laws into Song, The Fossil, 1963; Manhattan 2, New Oberammergau Players, 1982, India Or Bust, The Countersign, 1987. Home: 1348 Bridgewater Ct Wichita KS 67209 Office: 11 Rainbow Dr Hauppauge NY 11788

JENNINGS, JOSEPH LESLIE, JR., textile executive; b. LaGrange, Ga., 1937. BSBA, U. Okla., 1961. Plant mgr. Dixie div. West Point Pepperell; with Mt. Vernon Mills Inc., Greenville, S.C., 1974—, v.p., 1976-80, exec. v.p., 1980-82, pres., 1982, also chief operating officer, bd. dirs.; bd. dirs. Textile Hael Corp. Served to capt. USMC, 1961-64. Mem. Am. Textile Mfrs. Inst. (bd. dirs.). Office: Mt Vernon Mills Inc 1 Shelter Pl Box 3478 Greenville SC 29602

JENNINGS, MADELYN PULVER, communications company executive; b. Saratoga Springs, N.Y., Nov. 23, 1934; d. George Joseph and Martha (Walsh) Pulver. BA in Bus. and Econs., Tex. Woman's U., 1956. Asst. dir. pub. relations Slick Airways, Dallas, 1956-58, VIP Svcs., Inc., N.Y.C., 1958; asst. to pres. Smith, Dorian & Burman, Hartford, Conn., 1959; bus. mktg. planning GE, Bridgeport, Conn., 1960-68, mgr. manpower planning, 1968-71, mgr. environ. support operation, 1971-73, mgr. employee relations, 1973-76; v.p. human resources Standard Brands, Inc., N.Y.C., 1976-80; sr. v.p. personnel Gannett Co., Arlington, Va., 1980—; NOW legal def. and edn. fund/corp. adv. bd.; bd. dirs. Detroit News. Bd. sponsor trustees U. Va. Colgate Darden Sch. of Bus. Adminstrn.; trustee Russell Sage Coll., Gannett Found.; bd. dirs. Am. Press Inst., Tex. Woman's Univ. Found., Labor Policy Assn. Mem. Am. Soc. Personnel Adminstrn., Human Resources Roundtable, Sr. Personnel Execs. Forum, Human Resources Planning Soc., Newspaper Personnel Relations Assn., Sr. Personnel Execs. Roundtable, Conf. Bd. (mem., chmn. adv. coun. human resources mgmt.), Am. Newspaper Pubs. Assn. (chair human resources com.), Bus. Roundtable (employee relations com.), Ctr. Pub. Resources (human resources exec. program). Home: 3520 Duff Dr Falls Church VA 22041 Office: Gannett Co Inc Box 7858 Washington DC 20044

JENNINGS, MARCELLA GRADY, rancher, investor; b. Springfield, Ill., Mar. 4, 1920; d. William Francis and Magdalene Mary (Spies) Grady; student pub. schs.; m. Leo J. Jennings, Dec. 16, 1950 (dec.). Pub. relations Econolite Corp., Los Angeles, 1958-61; v.p., asst. mgr. LJ Quarter Circle Ranch, Inc., Polson, Mont., 1961-73, pres., gen. mgr., owner, 1973—; dir. Giselle's Travel Inc., Sacramento; fin. advisor to Allentown, Inc., Charlo, Mont.; sales cons. to Amie's Jumpin' Jacks and Jills, Garland, Tex. investor. Mem. Internat. Charolais Assn., Los Angeles County Apt. Assn. Republican. Roman Catholic. Home and Office: 509 Mt Holyoke Ave Pacific Palisades CA 90272

JENNINGS, ROBERT MARTIN, JR., accountant, financial planner; b. Jeffersonville, Ind., June 4, 1953; s. Robert M. and Mary R. (Julius) J.; m. Jean L. McMurry, June 25, 1976; 1 child, Ryan M. BS, Ind. U., 1977; MS, Colo. State U., 1978. CPA, Ind., Ky.; cert. fin. planner. Fin. analyst Shell Oil Co., Chgo., 1978-79; staff acct. Coopers & Lybrand, CPA's, Louisville, 1979-80; mgr. Melhiser & Endres, CPA's, New Albany, Ind., 1980-84; prin. Robert Jennings, CPA, Jeffersonville, 1984—; vis. lectr. Ind. U. Southeast, New Albany, 1979—. Contbr. articles to profl. jours. Mem. com. United Way, Jeffersonville, 1984-86. Fellow Am. Acctg. Assn.; mem. Am. Inst. CPA's, Ind. CPA Soc., Ky. CPA Soc., Nat. Assn. Accts. Democrat. Office: Spring Hill Ctr Ste 109 Jeffersonville IN 47130

JENNINGS, THOMAS PARKS, lawyer; b. Alexandria, Va., Nov. 16, 1947; s. George Christian and Ellen (Thompson) J.; m. Shelley Corrine Abernathy, Oct. 30, 1971; 1 child, Kathleen Eayre. BA in History, Wake Forest U., 1970; JD, U. Va., 1975. Bar: Va. 1975. Assoc. Lewis, Wilson, Lewis & Jones, Arlington, Va., 1975-78; atty. First Va. Banks, Inc., Falls Church, 1978-80, gen. counsel, 1980—; adj. prof. George Mason U. Sch. Law, Arlington, 1987-88. Deacon Georgetown Presbyn. Ch., Washington, 1979-82, elder, 1982-85, trustee, 1988—. With U.S. Army, 1970-71. Mem. ABA, Va. State Bar Assn., Va. Bankers Assn. (legal affairs com.), Fairfax County Bar Assn., Am. Corp. Counsel Assn., Washington Met. Area Corp. Counsel Assn. (bd. dirs. 1984-87). Office: First Va Banks Inc 6400 Arlington Blvd Ste 420 Falls Church VA 22042-2336

JENNINGS, TODD KYLE, investment banker; b. Los Angeles, Mar. 10, 1949; s. William Randolph and Jeanne Burton (Englemann) J.; m. Mary Mallory Kountze, June 30, 1973; children: Barton, William, Mary Mallory. AB, Harvard Coll., 1971; MBA, Harvard U., 1973. Investment banker E.F. Hutton & Co. Inc, N.Y.C., 1973-82, group head, investment banking, mktg., 1982-87, dep. head, corp. fin. dept., 1987; pvt. practice investment banking N.Y.C., 1988—; prin. Source Capital, Ltd., McLean, Va., 1988—; pres. SCL Mgmt., Inc., N.Y.C., 1988—. Clubs: Round Hill (Greenwich, Conn.), Wianno (Osterville, Mass.). Home: 145 Clapboard Ridge Rd Greenwich CT 06831

JENRETTE, RICHARD HAMPTON, financial and insurance company executive; b. Raleigh, N.C., Apr. 5, 1929; s. Joseph M. and Emma V. (Love) J. B.A., U. N.C., 1951; M.B.A., Harvard U., 1957; Litt.D. (hon.), U. N.C. With Brown Bros. Harriman & Co., N.Y.C., 1957-59; with Donaldson, Lufkin & Jenrette, Inc., N.Y.C., 1959—, now chmn. bd.; chief investment officer The Equitable Life Assurance Soc. U.S., N.Y.C., 1986—; chmn., dir. Equitable Life Assurance Soc. U.S., N.Y.C., 1987—; pres., chief exec. officer Equitable Investment Corp., from 1986; dir. Bus. Found. N.C., Advanced Micro Devices, Rockefeller Found., Hist. Hudson Valley Restorations. Served to 2d lt. USAR, 1953-55. Mem. Securities Industry Assn. (dir., exec. com.), Inst. Chartered Fin. Analysts, N.Y. Soc. Security Analysts, Phi Beta Kappa. Democrat. Episcopalian. Clubs: University, Brook, Harvard, Harvard Bus. Sch., Links (N.Y.C.); Carolina Yacht (Charleston, S.C.). Office: Equitable Life Assurance Soc US 787 7th Ave New York NY 10019

JENSEN, DENNIS MARK, marketing executive; b. Lawrence, Kans., Oct. 26, 1946; s. Keith E. and Betty M. (Gardner) J.; m. Wendalyn A. Dennis, Mar. 21, 1969 (div. Nov. 1987); 1 child, Michael Shawn; m. Joyce M. Halt, Feb. 20, 1988; children: Melody J. Krueger, Melinda J. Krueger. Student, Ind. State U., 1964, Ind. U., 1964-66; BA, Adrian Coll., 1968; MA, U. Fla., 1970; postgrad., U. Mo., 1970-71, 74-77. Teaching asst. English U. Fla., Gainesville, 1968-70; teaching asst. speech and dramatic art U. Mo., Columbia, 1970-71, 74-77; project analyst Pfizer Pharms., N.Y.C., 1977-80, mgr. communications devel., 1980-81; mgr. tech. com. Pfizer Internat., N.Y.C., 1981-86, mgr. profl. rels., 1986—. Elder Pleasantville Presbyn. Ch., N.Y., 1981-83. With USN, 1971-74. Recipient tng. grants NIH, USPHS, Ind. U. Med. Ctr., 1964, Am. Cancer Soc. Adrian Coll., 1966. Mem. AAAS, Am. Soc. Microbiology. Methodist. Office: Pfizer Internat 235 E 42nd St New York NY 10017

JENSEN, EDMUND PAUL, bank holding company executive; b. Oakland, Calif., Apr. 13, 1937; s. Edmund and Olive E. (Kessell) J.; m. Marilyn Norris, Nov. 14, 1959; children—Juliana L., Annika M. B.A., U. Wash., 1959; postgrad., U. Santa Clara, Stanford U., 1981. Lic. real estate broker, Oreg., Calif. Mgr. fin. plan and evaluation Technicolor, Inc., Los Angeles, 1967-69; group v.p. Nat. Industries & Subs, Louisville, 1969-72; v.p. fin. Wedgewood Homes, Portland, 1972-74; various mgmt. positions U.S. Bancorp, Portland, 1974-83; pres. U.S. Bancorp, Inc., Portland, 1983—; dir. U.S. Bancorp, U.S. Nat. Bank of Oreg., VISA, U.S. Bank Washington. Bd. dirs. United Way, Portland, 1982—, chmn. campaign, 1986; bd. dirs. Saturday Acad., Portland, 1984—, Providence Child Ctr. Found., Portland, 1984—, Marylhurst Coll., Oreg. Bus. Council, Oreg. Art Inst.; bd. dirs. Oreg. Ind. Coll. Found., 1983—, treas., 1986—, chmn. 1988—; chmn. N.W. Bus. Coalition, 1987—; mem. Oreg. Tourism Alliance, 1987—, bd. visitors law sch. U. of Oreg., 1987—. Mem. Portland C. of C. (bd. dirs. 1981—, chmn. 1987), Assn. Res. City Bankers, Assn. for Portland Progress (pres. 1988). Club: Waverly country, Multnomah Athletic. Lodge: Rotary. Office: US Nat Bank Oreg 111 SW 5th St PO Box 4412 Portland OR 97204 also: US Bancorp PO Box 8837 Portland OR 97208

JENSEN, HAROLD SHERWOOD, real estate executive; b. Detroit, Aug. 29, 1930; s. Harold Soren and Lyndon Elizabeth (Neddermeyer) J.; m. Dona Bernard, Apr. 26, 1958; children: Barbara, Lyndon, Susan, Karl. B.S. in Civil Engring. cum laude, Mich. Tech. U., 1952, D. Engring. (hon.), 1978; postgrad., Wayne State U., 1954; M.B.A., Harvard U., 1957. Chief survey party Brennan Constrn. Co., Detroit, 1955-56; asst. structural engr. Metcalf & Eddy, Boston, 1956-58; mgr. fin. and devel. Gilbane Bldg. Co., Providence, 1958-62; exec. v.p. Lumbermen's Co., Austin, Tex., 1962-66; asst. v.p. real estate Penn Central, Phila., 1967-69; group v.p. real estate I.C. Industries, Inc., Chgo., 1970-77; gen. ptnr. Met. Structures, 1977—; pres. Urban Land Inst., 1977-79; bd. dirs. Lake Forest Hosp., Family Focus Inc.; cons. U. Pa. Sch. Urban Design, Northern Trust Bank, Lake Forest, Ill., Lake Forest Hosp. Served with C.E. AUS, 1952-54. Mem. Tau Beta Pi, Chi Epsilon, Theta Tau. Clubs: Tavern (Chgo.); Onwentsia; California (Los Angeles). Office: Met Structures 111 E Wacker Sr Ste 1200 Chicago IL 60601

JENSEN, JENS ANKER, banker; b. Chgo., June 27, 1944; s. Anker and Florence (Warther) J.; (div.). BS in Fin., No. Ill. U., 1967; postgrad., Loyola U., Chgo., 1980-81. Asst. v.p. lending Skokie (Ill.) Fed. Savs., 1973-78, Talman Home Fed. Savs., Chgo., 1978-81; self employed 1981-84; v.p. mortgage lending Liberty Fed. Savs., Chgo., 1984—. Mem. Soc. Loan Underwriters (dir. 1985-87). Republican. Lutheran. Club: Union League (Chgo.). Home: 612 Cedar Ave Elmhurst IL 60126 Office: Liberty Fed Savs 5700 N Lincoln Ave Chicago IL 60659

JENSEN, JERRY KIRTLAND, industrial engineer, operations manager; b. Chgo., Sept. 27, 1947; s. Harry Dybdahl and Violet May (Nowak) J. BS, Cornell U., 1969, M in Indsl. Engring., 1971. Cert. in prodn. and inventory mgmt. Pres., Jensen's Cinema 16, Western Springs, Ill., 1970—; indsl. engr. Gen. Foods, Chgo., 1970-72, sr. indsl. engr., 1972-73, prodn. scheduling supr., 1973-74, prodn. control mgr., 1974-76; mgmt. systems specialist Beatrice Cos., Chgo., 1976-77, operating services project mgr., 1977-79, mgr. indsl. engring., 1980-84, mgr. mfg. services dir. Louver Drape, Inc. div. Home Fashions Inc., Memphis, 1984-85, dir. ops., 1985-88; mgr. mgmt. cons. svcs. Coopers and Lybrand, N.Y.C., 1989—; v.p., sec. Country Residential, Inc., Western Springs and Crystal Lake, Ill., 1978-86. Author: (with Dr. Joel Ross) Productivity, People and Profits, 1981; contbr. Productivity Improvement: Case Studies of Proven Practice, 1981. Film festivals chmn. Western Springs Recreation Commn., 1969-70, 73-84; active Theatre of Western Springs, 1983—, Theatre Memphis, 1984—, Germantown Theatre, 1985— (bd. dirs., treas. 1987, 2d v.p. 1988). Mem. Am. Prodn. and Inventory Control Soc. (program chmn. Memphis chpt. 1986, v.p. 1986-87, pres. 1987-88), Am. Inst. Indsl. Engrs. (nat. productivity com. 1982-85, v.p. services Chgo. chpt. 1984), Great Lakes English Springer Spaniel Breeders Assn. (pres. 1979-81), English Springer Spaniel Field Trial Assn., Alpha Phi Omega, Beta Theta Pi. Methodist. Clubs: Cornell, Variety. Home: 2828 Treasure Island W Memphis TN 38115 Office: Coopers and Lybrand 1251 Avenue of the Americas 3d Fl New York NY 10020

JENSEN, PETER L., accounting company executive; b. Tucson, Aug. 18, 1943; s. Lyman M. and Mary K. (Sell) J.; m. Judythe Anne Dora, June 5, 1965 (div. Aug. 1985); children: Kelly A., Holly L.; m. Mary Ann McGovern, May 9, 1987. BS in Acctg., U. Ariz., 1965. CPA, Colo. Various positions Deloitte Haskins & Sells, Denver, 1965-83, area mng. ptnr., 1983—. Chmn. Jr. Achievement Metro Denver, 1988; treas. Boys Clubs Metro Denver, 1986-88, Colo. Bus. Com. for the Arts, 1986-88. Recipient Bronze Leadership award Jr. Achievement, 1987; U. Denver fellow, 1987-88. Mem. Am. Inst. CPA's, Colo. Soc. CPA's, Rotary (pres. Denver club 1978-79), Univ. Hills Denver Country Club. Office: Deloitte Haskins & Sells 1560 Broadway Ste 1800 Denver CO 80202

JENSEN, ROBERT P., bank executive; b. Chgo., Dec. 29, 1925; s. Louis P. and Ellen (Goede) J.; m. Anne Fletcher, June 15, 1980; children—Erik P., Curtis R. BS in Mech. Engring., Iowa State Coll., Ames, 1947; postgrad., U. Mich., 1953-54; grad., advanced mgmt. program Harvard U., 1965. Salesman, br. and dist. mgr., gen. sales mgr., operations mgr. Kaiser Aluminum & Chem. Sales, Inc., 1954-61, gen. mgr. bldg. products div., 1963-66, dir. bus. planning aluminum div., 1967; exec. v.p., gen. mgr. Olin Foil Packaging Corp. (subsidiary Olin Mathieson Chem. Corp.), 1961-63; v.p. aluminum group Howmet Corp., N.Y.C., 1967-68, exec. v.p., 1968-70, chief operating officer, dir., 1970, pres., chief exec. officer, 1971-72, also dir.; chief operating officer, pres., chief exec. officer, dir. Gen. Cable Corp. (now GK Technologies, Inc.), Greenwich, Conn., 1973-83; chmn. bd. Gen. Cable Corp. (now GK Technologies, Inc.), after 1978; chmn., chief exec. officer EF Hutton LBO Inc., 1983-85; chief exec. officer, pres., dir. Tiger Internat., Inc., 1985—, chmn., 1986-87; chmn., chief exec. officer, dir. Flying Tiger Line Inc., 1985—, pres., chief operating officer, 1986-87; dir. Irving Bank Corp., Irving Trust Co., Jostens, Inc., EF Hutton LBO Inc., Arrow Electronics, Aerospace Corp., Singer Co.; trustee Aerospace Corp. Served to lt. (j.g.) USNR, 1944-46. Clubs: Board Room (N.Y.C.), Greenwich Country (Greenwich, Conn.), Indian Harbor Yacht (Greenwich, Conn.); Landmark (Stamford, Conn.); La Cumbre Golf and Country (Santa Barbara, Calif.); Los Angeles Country. Office: EF HUtton LBD Inc 8 E Figueroa St Santa Barbara CA 93101

JENSEN, RODGER BLAINE, farming executive; b. Parlier, Calif., Sept. 12, 1920; s. Chris B. and Edna L. (Peterson) J.; m. Margaret Roberts, Dec. 28, 1941; children: Douglas Blaine, Marjorie Brand. BA, Fresno State Coll., 1941. V.p. S&J Ranch, Inc., Fresno, Calif., 1948-70, pres., 1970—; pres. Earlibest Orange Assn., Exeter, Calif., 1972—, San Joaquin Citrus Co., Clovis, Calif., 1974—; co-chmn. bd. dirs. T.M. Duche Nut Co, Inc., Orland, Calif., 1979-86; chmn. bd. dirs. T.M. Duche Nut Co., Inc., Orland, Calif., 1986-88; commr. Calif. Pistachio Commn., Fresno, 1981-87; bd. govs. Agrl. Found., Calif. State U., Fresno, 1965—, chmn. 1976-79; bd. govs. Fresno Found. at Calif. State U., 1984—. Commr. Calif. Commn. Agr., Sacramento, 1978-82; bd. dirs. Calif. C. of C., Sacramento, 1978—, Calif. State U. Ag One Boosters, 1979-83, Bus. Adv. Bd., 1980-84, Fresno C. of C., 1974-78, Fresno County Farm Bur., 1950-60, Fresno Met. Mus., 1985-87, St. Agnes Hosp. Found., Fresno, 1984, Sequoia Council Boy Scouts Am., 1960-78, Valley Children's Hosp., Fresno, 1955-65. Decorated Air medal; named Citrus Farmer of Yr. TV series Agriculture USA, 1964; recipient Outstanding Achievement award, Calif. State U., 1980. Mem. Am. Soc. Farm Mgrs. and Rural Appraisers. Republican. Lodge: Rotary (pres. North Fresno club 1977-78). Home: 5476 N Parrish Way Fresno CA 93711 Office: S & J Ranch Inc PO Box 3347 Pinedale CA 93650

JENSEN, TERESA ELAINE, financial planner; b. Honesdale, Pa., Aug. 11, 1948; d. James Bernard Jensen and LaVaughn Beatrice (Tomlinson) Nixon; m. Nolan Stanley Lapsley Jr., May 29, 1982. Student, San Antonio Coll., 1966-67. Cert. fin. planner; registered investment advisor. V.p. Outdoor Sports Ctr., San Antonio, 1968-73; tchr. New Age Sch., San Antonio, 1973-76; organizer, negotiator Nat. Maritime Union, Galveston, Tex., 1973-76; agt., sales mgr. B&B Assocs., San Antonio, 1977-78; pvt. practice San Antonio, 1978-80; pres. Money Mgrs. Inc., San Antonio, 1981—; adj. instr. Coll. Fin. Planning, Denver, 1985—, St. Mary's U., San Antonio, 1985—; expert witness for legal community. Mem. Big Sister Alamo Area Big Bros. & Big Sisters, San Antonio, 1981, bd. dirs. 1985. Recipient Presdl. Citation C. of C., 1982. Mem. Inst. Cert. Fin. Planners (chmn. 1988-89, pres. 1987-88, v.p. Cen. Tex. soc. 1986-87), Internat. Assn. Fin. Planners, Internat. Bd. Standards and Practices for Cert. Fin. Planners. Republican. Office: Money Mgrs Inc 7800 IH 10 W Ste 636 The Lincoln Ctr San Antonio TX 78230

JENSEN, WALTER EDWARD, JR., law educator, lawyer; b. Chgo., Oct. 20, 1937. A.B., U. Colo., 1959; J.D., Ind. U., 1962, M.B.A., 1964; Ph.D. (Univ. fellow), Duke U., 1972. Bar: Ind. 1962, Ill. 1962, D.C. 1963, U.S. Tax Ct. 1982, U.S. Supreme Ct. 1967. Assoc. prof. Colo. State U., 1964-66; assoc. prof. Ill. State U., 1970-72; prof. bus. adminstrn. Va. Poly. Inst. and State U., beginning 1972, now prof. fin., ins. and law; with Inst. Advanced Legal Studies, U. London, 1983-84; prof. U.S. Air Force Grad. Mgmt. Program, Europe, 1977-78, 83-85; Duke U. legal research awardee, researcher, Guyana, Trinidad and Tobago, 1967; vis. lectr. pub. internat. law U. Istanbul, 1988, Roberts Coll. U. of Bospouous, Istanbul, Uludag Univ. , Turkey, 1988; researcher U. London Inst. Advanced Legal Studies, London Sch. Econs. and Inst. Commonwealth Studies, summers, 1969, 71, 74, 76, winter 1972-73; Ford Found. research fellow Ind. U., 1963-64; faculty research fellow in econs. U. Tex., 1968; Bell Telephone fellow in econs. regulated pub. utilities U. Chgo., 1965. Recipient Dissertation Travel award Duke U. Grad. sch., 1968; Ind. U. fellow, 1963, 74, scholar, 1963-64. Mem. D.C. Bar Assn., Ill. Bar Assn., Ind. bar Assn., ABA, Am. Polit. sci. Assn., Am. Soc. Internat. Law, Am. Judicature Soc., Am. Bus. Law Assn., Alpha Kappa Psi, Phi Alpha Delta, Pi Gamma Mu, Pi Kappa Alpha, Beta Gamma Sigma. Contbr. articles to profl. publs.; staff editor Am. Bus Law Jour., 1973—; vice chmn. assoc. editor for adminstrv. law sect. young lawyers Barrister (Law Notes), 1975-83; book rev. and manuscript editor Justice System Jour: A Mgmt. Rev., 1975—; staff editor Bus. Law Rev., 1975—. Home: PO Box 250 Blacksburg VA 24060 Office: Va Poly Inst and State U Blacksburg VA 24060

JENTNER, BRUCE ALAN, financial planning consultant; b. Cleve., Sept. 13, 1954; s. Thomas A. and Solveig B. (Hildebrandt) J.; m. Bonnie N. Manzo, June 13, 1975; children: Seth, Matthew, Briana. BS in Edn., Kent State U., 1977. Cert. fin. planner, cert. estate bus. and fin. analyst. Sales mgr. Berea Pre Hung Door, Inc., Medina, Ohio, 1977-79; asst. dir. Fin. Analysts Ohio, Inc., Akron, 1980-84; pres. Profit Resource Equity Planning Corp., Akron, 1984—. Mem. Internat. Assn. Fin. Planning, Inst. Cert. Fin. Planners, Akron Tax and Estate Planning Coun., Akron Pension Coun., Registry Fin. Planning Practitioners, Toastmasters Internat. (Fairlawn, Ohio). Republican. Office: Prep Corp 1540 W Market St Ste 300 Akron OH 44313

JEPPESEN, M. K., university administrator; b. Logan, Utah, Dec. 31, 1935; s. Moses A. and Afton (Hillyard) J.; m. Carol Jenkins, June 10, 1955 (dec. Nov. 1963); children: Steven, Juliane, Karen, Jennifer; m. Ellen Rae Burtenshaw, July 14, 1966; children: Christine, Craig, David, Nanette. BS, Utah State U., 1957, MBA, 1971. Cert. profl. contracts mgr. Mgr. bus. Utah Sci. Found., 1958-60; rep. controllers Utah State U., Logan, 1960-69, dir. contracts/grants, 1972—, mem. patent com., investment adv. com., research council, 1978—; auditor Peat Marwick Main, Salt Lake City, 1969-71; pres. Nat. Calibration Co., Logan, 1978-87; treas., chief fin. officer, treas. Space Dynamics Lab., Logan, 1987—; cons. in field; lectr. in field; conductor seminars, workshops in field. Trustee Utah State U. Found., 1987—. Lt. U.S. Army, 1957-63. Fellow Nat. Contracts Mgmt. Assn. (cert., chmn. program com. 1983-84); mem. Soc. Research Adminstrs. (pres. 1986-87, pres. Mountain chpt. 1983-85), Nat. Council Univ. Rsch. Adminstrs. (profl. devel. com. 1982-85, mem. nominating com. 1987-89), Nat. Assn. Coll. and Univ. Bus. Officers, Soc. Pub. Accts., Western Assn. Coll. and U. Bus. Officers, Cache C. of C., Logan Country Club. Republican. Mormon. Home: 1050 E 2000 N Logan UT 84321 Office: Utah State U UMC 1415 Logan UT 84322

JEPPSON, JOHN, corporate professional, director; b. Worcester, Mass., Dec. 10, 1916; s. George Nathaniel and Selma Ulrika (Swanstrom) J.; m. Julie Armstrong, June 6, 1939 (div. 1946); children: John III, Julie Jeppson Stout; m. Marianne Jenner Shellabarger, Jan. 15, 1947; children: Eric Shellabarger, Ingrid Georgia Selma Jeppson Mach. Student, Deerfield Acad., 1934; B, Amherst Coll., 1938, DCS, 1963; MBA, Harvard U., 1940; LLD, Clark U., 1968. Dir., chmn. Norton Co., Worcester, 1940-85; chmn. bd. Guaranty Bank & Trust Co., Worcester, 1973-87, Crompton & Knowles Corp., N.Y.C., 1965-87, Kennecott Copper Corp., N.Y.C., 1972-77; dir. The Foxboro (Mass.) Co., 1966-88. Pres. Am. Antiquarian Soc., 1977-87; chmn. trustee emeritus Clark U.; dir. Worcester County Music Assn.; hon. trustee Worcester Art Mus. Lt. comdr. USN, 1942-45. Recipient Isaiah Thomas award for distinguished community svc. Worcester Advt. Club, 1977. Mem. Worcester Fir Soc., St. Wulstan's Soc, Amherst Alumni Assn.

JEPSEN, JOHN ROBERT, paper and forest products company executive; b. Boston, Dec. 19, 1955; s. Robert J. and Mary J.; m. Joann M. Bottoni, Oct. 17, 1987. BS, Boston Coll., 1977; MBA, U. Va., 1981. Sr. auditor Arthur Andersen & Co, Boston, 1977-79; mfg. analyst Internat. Paper Co., N.Y.C., 1981-83; controller Internat. Paper Co., San Leandro, Calif., 1983-85; portfolio mgr. Internat. Paper Co., N.Y.C., 1985-86; mgr. corp. fin. Internat. Paper Co., Purchase, N.Y., 1986—. Office: Internat Paper Co 2 Manhattanville Rd Purchase NY 10577

JEPSON, HANS GODFREY, investment company executive; b. Spencer, W.Va., July 24, 1936; s. Hans G. and Juanita Imogene (Shears) J.; m. Barbara Gayle Keller, Dec. 3, 1966. A.B. magna cum laude, Princeton U., 1958. Exec. editor Arnold Bernhard & Co., N.Y.C., 1961-68; v.p., research dir. Dominick & Dominick, Inc., N.Y.C., 1968-70; dir., sr. v.p., research dir. Alliance Capital Mgmt. Corp., N.Y.C., 1970-76; exec. v.p., chief investment officer U.S. Trust Co. N.Y., N.Y.C., 1976-80; pres. Valquest Assocs., Inc., N.Y.C., 1980—, Lafayette Enterprises, Inc., N.Y.C., 1983—; dir. United States Newspapers, Inc., The Stanton Corp. Bd. dirs. J. Aron Charitable Found., The 1331 Found.; v.p., bd. dirs. Fedn. of Petanque U.S.A. Inc. Served to 2d lt. U.S. Army, 1958-59. Mem. Fin. Analysts Fedn., N.Y. Soc. Security Analysts. Clubs: Dial (N.Y.C.), Princeton (N.Y.C.), Economic (N.Y.C.). Home: 11 Fifth Ave New York NY 10003 Office: Lafayette Enterprises Inc 126 E 56th St New York NY 10022

JEPSON, LINDA JEAN, financial planner; b. Erie, PA, Oct. 7, 1951; d. Edward Joseph and Dorothy Emily (Csencsics) J. BA, Allegheny Coll., 1973; MPA, Syracuse U., 1975. Cert. fin. planner. Dir. employee benefits Robert Griewahn & Assocs., Erie, 1977-80; v.p. Jeffrey Evans & Assocs., Erie, 1980-85; prin. Lillis, McKibben & Co., Erie, 1985-87; ptnr. Lillis, McKibben & Jepson, Erie, 1987—. Pres. Am. Cancer Soc. Erie County unit, 1986-88. Mem. AAUW (treas. 1986-87), Am. Soc. CLU's and ChFC's, Nat. Assn. Fin. Planning Councils, Inst. Cert. Fin. Planners, Internat. Assn. Fin. Planning. Republican. Baptist. Lodge: Zonta (pres. 1987-89). Office: Lillis McKibben & Jepson 246 W 10th St Erie PA 16501

JEPSON, ROBERT SCOTT, JR., international investment banking specialist; b. Richmond, Va., July 20, 1942; s. Robert Scott and Inda (Hodges) J.; BS, U. Richmond, 1964, M.Commerce, 1975; LLD (hon.), Gonzaga U., 1986; DCS, U. Richmond, 1987; HHD (hon.), Hamline U., 1988;LLD Tusculuh Coll., 1989. m. Alice Finch Andrews, Dec. 28, 1964; children—Robert Scott, John Steven. With Va. Commonwealth Bankshares, Richmond, 1966-68; v.p. corp. fin. Birr Wilson & Co., Inc., San Francisco, 1968-69; with Calif. Capital Mgmt. Corp., Irvine, 1970-73; pres. Calcap Securities Corp., Los Angeles, 1970-73; v.p., dir. corp. fin. Cantor Fitzgerald

& Co., Beverly Hills, Calif., 1973-75; dir. corp. planning and devel. Campbell Industries, San Diego, 1975-77; v.p., mgr. merger and acquisition div. Continental Ill. Bank, Chgo., 1977-82; sr. v.p., group head U.S. Capital Markets Group, 1st Nat. Bank Chgo., 1982-83, 83—; chmn. bd. Jepson Corp., Chgo., Signet Armorlite, Inc., San Marcos, Calif., Emerson Quiet Kool Corp., Woodbridge, N.J., Air-Maze Corp., Bedford Heights, Ohio, Hedstrom Corp., Bedford, Pa., Gerry Sportswear Corp., Seattle, Atlantic Industries, Inc., Nutley, N.J., Jepson-Burns Corp., Winston-Salem, N.J., Farwest Garments, Inc., Seattle, Jepson Vineyards Ltd., Ukiah, Calif., Trans-Aero Industries, Inc., Los Angeles, Denman Tire Corp., Warren, Ohio; vice chmn. bd. Hill Refrigeration, Trenton, N.J.; bd. dirs. Hecla Mining Co. Inc., Coeur d'Alene, Idaho, 1989—; asst. prof. fin. Nat. U., 1976. Trustee, Gonzaga U., Spokane, Wash., 1982-86; bd. trustees, Hamlin U., St. Paul, Minn., 1987; bd. advisors Jepson Found., Elmhurst, Ill., 1988—; lectr. numerous schs. including U. Richmond, U. Chgo., Northwestern U., Kansas U., Luthr Coll., Wake Forest U. Served to 1st lt. M.P. Corps., AUS, 1964-66. Mem. Omicron Delta Kappa, Alpha Kappa Psi, Beta Gamma Sigma. Republican. Clubs: Mid-Am., Chicago (Chgo.); DuPage (Oakbrook, Ill.); Commonwealth (Richmond, Va.); Marshwood (Savannah, Ga.). Office: Jepson Corp 360 W Butterfield Rd Elmhurst IL 60126

JERAULD, GORDON OTIS, utility executive; b. Hyannis, Mass., Mar. 11, 1921; s. Bruce Kempton and Lucile (Thayer) J.; m. Ruth Johnson, June 29, 1946; children: Curtis A., Ann E., Steven B. BS in Chem. Engring., Northeastern U., 1943. Chief chemist Gas Co., Haverhill, Mass., 1947-50; gen. supt. Wash. Natural Gas Co., Tacoma, 1950-57; sr. cons. Stone and Webster Mgmt. Cons, N.Y.C., 1957-66; mgr. dir. Stone and Webster Svc. Ltd., Melbourne, Australia, 1966-69; v.p. ops. Fla. Pub. Utilities Co., West Palm Beach, 1969-76, sr. v.p., 1976—, also bd. dirs. Bd. dirs. West Palm Beach Salvation Army, 1973—. Lt. USNR, 1943-46, PTO. Mem. Fla. Natural Gas Assn. (bd. dirs. pres. 1972-74), Rotary. Republican. Office: Fla Pub Utilities Co 401 S Dixie Hwy West Palm Beach FL 33402

JERDE, JON, architect. Degree, U. So. Calif. Formerly with Charles Kober Assocs.; founder Jerde Partnership. Prin. works include Seventh Market Pl., L.A., Horton Pla., San Diego, Westside Pavilion, West Los Angeles, Fashion Island, Newport Beach, Calif. Office: The Jerde Partnership 2798 Sunset Blvd Los Angeles CA 90026 *

JERNIGAN, EDDIE DEAN, brokerage house executive; b. Sparta, Tenn., Mar. 18, 1956; s. Edward Martin and Johonnie Margaret (McCoin) J.; m. Sandy Gale, Apr. 5, 1986. BS, Middle Tenn. State U., 1978. Account exec. Thomson McKinnon Securities, Nashville, 1980-82; commodity broker Maduff and Sons, Inc., Nashville, 1982-84, Donaldson, Lufkin, Jenrette Co., N.Y.C., 1984-85; sr. v.p. investments Prudential- Bache Securities, Inc., Nashville, 1985-88; v.p. Thomson McKinnon Securities Inc., 1988—. Editor Jernigan's Cotton Sheet Newsletter, 1986; contbr. articles to profl. jours. Mem. Am. Cotton Shippers Assn., Western Cotton Shippers Assn., So. Cotton Assn., Tex. Cotton Assn., Am. Agrl. Editors Assn., Am. Security Council. Presbyterian.

JERNIGAN, FINITH EWIN, II, architect; b. Wichita Falls, Tex., Oct. 2, 1952; s. Finith Ewin and Vanita Ruth (Uthe) J.; m. Beth Susan Raymond, June 17, 1978. Student Tex. A&M U., 1971; B.S. in Environ. Design, Okla. U., 1975; M.Arch., 1976. Registered architect, Md., Va., Del., D.C., Pa.; cert. Nat. Council Archtl. Registration Bds. Architect NASA, Wallops Island, Va., 1976-77, George, Miles & Buhr, Salisbury, Md., 1977-82, architect, ptnr., 1984—; asst. prof. King Faisal U., Dammam, Saudi Arabia, 1982-84; cons. Washington Adventist Hosp., Takoma Park, Md., 1985, Dunes Manor Hotel, Ocean City, Md., 1987—, Horn Point Envirn. Lab., 1987—. Author JFK Redevel. Study, 1976, N.Am. Wildfowl Mus. master plan, 1982. Pres. Newtown Hist. Dist. Assn., Salisbury, 1982-83; mem. Downtown Long Range Planning Com., Salisbury, 1985; ex officio mem. R/Udat Action Group, Salisbury, 1980—. Recipient design in Concrete award Md. Ready-Mix Concrete Assn., 1982; Lew Wentz scholar, 1972-76. Mem. Nat. Fire Protection Assn., 1986—, Mktg. Profl. Services, 1985—, Inst. for Urban Design (charter mem.), Constrn. Specifications Inst. (Mason Dixon chpt.) (charter mem., v.p. 1978-79), Am. Planning Assn. (charter mem.), AIA (award for excellence in scholarly achievement 1976), Salisbury-Wicomico C. of C., Mensa, Wicomico Arts Council, Tau Sigma Delta Archtl. Honor Soc., 1974. Democrat. Baptist. Avocations: sailing, painting, reading. Office: George Miles & Buhr 724 E Main St Salisbury MD 21801

JERNSTEDT, RICHARD DON, public relations executive; b. McMinnville, Oreg., Feb. 26, 1947; s. Don and Catherine (Anderson) J.; m. Jean Diane Woods, Dec. 28, 1969; children—Ty Parker, Tiffin Kay. B.S., U. Oreg., 1969. Mgr. mktg. com. Container Corp. Am., Chgo., 1976-78; pres., chief oper. officer Golin/Harris Communications, Inc., Chgo., 1978—. Bd. dirs. Off the Street Club, Chgo., 1984—, Am. Liver Found., 1988; mem. adv. bd. Barrington Area Arts Council, 1986—; mem. nat. steering com. U. Oreg. Capital Campaign, 1988. Served to lt. (j.g.) USNR, 1968-72. Recipient Golden Trumpet award Publicity Club of Chgo.; named Outstanding Jr., U. Oreg., 1968. Mem. Internat. Assn. Bus. Communications, Pub. Relations Soc. Am. (Silver Anvil award 1986). Republican. Presbyterian.

JERRITTS, STEPHEN G., computer company executive; b. New Brunswick, N.J., Sept. 14, 1925; s. Steve and Anna (Kovacs) J.; m. Audrey Virginia Smith, June 1948; children: Marsha Carol, Robert Stephen, Linda Ann; m. 2d, Ewa Elizabet Rydell-Vejlens, Nov. 5, 1966; 1 son, Carl Stephen. Student, Union Coll., 1943-44; B.M.E., Rensselaer Poly. Inst., 1947, M.S. Mgmt., 1948. With IBM, various locations, 1949-58, IBM World Trade, N.Y.C., 1958-67, Bull Gen. Electric div. Gen. Electric, France, 1967-70, merged into Honeywell Bull, 1970-74; v.p., mng. dir. Honeywell Info. Systems Ltd., London, 1974-76; group v.p. Honeywell U.S. Info. Systems, Boston, 1977-80; pres., chief operating officer Honeywell Info. Systems, 1980-82, also bd. dirs.; pres., chief exec. officer Lee Data Corp., 1983-85, also bd. dirs.; with Storage Tech. Corp., 1985-88, pres., chief operating officer, 1985-87, vice-chmn. bd. dirs., 1988; pres., chief exec. officer NBI Corp., 1988—, also bd. dirs.; bd. dirs. First Bank, Mpls. Bd. dirs. Guthrie Theatre, 1980-83, Charles Babbage Inst., 1980—, Minn. Orch., 1980-85; trustee Rensselaer Poly. Inst., 1980-85. Served with USNR, 1943-46. Mem. Computer Bus. Equipment Mfrs. (dir. exec. com. 1979-82), Assoc. Industries Mass. (dir. 1978-80). Clubs: Wellesley (Mass.) Country; Minneapolis. Home: 650 College Ave Boulder CO 80302 Office: Storage Tech Corp 2270 S 88th St Louisville CO 80028

JESANIS, PETER JOSEPH, financial planner; b. Rockville, Conn., May 21, 1958; s. Edward W. and Madeline E. (Daneau) J.; m. Laura Jean Esten, Sept. 24, 1982; 1 child, Larissa Noelle. Student, Am. Internat. Coll., 1976-80. Cert. fin. planner; registered fin. planner. Rep. IDS Fin. Svcs., Wethersfield, 1983-87, Key Fin. Concepts, Ellington, Conn., 1987—. Mem. Inst. Cert. Fin. Planners, Internat. Assn. Registered Fin. Planners, Internat. Assn. Registered Fin. Planners. Office: Key Fin Concepts 56 Main St PO Box 367 Ellington CT 06029

JESCHKE, MARK WALTER, trade association administrator; b. Kenitra, Morocco, Oct. 31, 1956; s. Walter George and Rose Margaret (Fabrizio) J.; m. Teresa Ann Maloney, June 11, 1983. BA, St. John's Coll., 1978. With community affairs Prince George's County Govt., Upper Marlboro, Md., 1978-80; coordinator econ. devel. sect. Bowie (Md.) City Govt., 1980-81; mgr. yearbook Broadcasting Pubs. Inc., Washington, 1981-85; dir. mktg. pubs. Nat. Tooling and Machining Assn., Ft. Washington, Md., 1985-88, mgr. pub. rels. and publs., 1989—. Rep. alumni St. John's Coll., Annapolis, Md. Mem. Washington Directory Assn. (bd. dirs.), Am. Soc. Assn. Execs. Roman Catholic. Home: 5204 W Boniwood Turn Clinton MD 20735 Office: Nat Tooling & Machining 9300 Livingston Rd Fort Washington MD 20744

JESESEKE, ELLEN FRANCES, computer programmer, corporate computer graphic artist; b. Saddle Brook, N.J., Sept. 3, 1954; d. Frank Alexander and Helen (Kandravy) J. BA in Fine Arts, certs. in art edn. and computer sci., magna cum laude, William Paterson Coll., 1976; cert. in comml. art, Sch. Advt. Art, Bloomfield, N.J., 1977; certs. in microcomputers, CES Tng. Sch., River Edge, N.J., 1985; certs. in computer graphics, Pratt Inst., The New Sch., N.Y.C., 1985-86; VAX cert., Digital Equipment Corp., N.Y.C., 1987; cert. in computer documentation, Am. Mgmt. Assn., 1988. Tchr. art N.J. Sch. Systems, 1976-79; visual merchandising artist Hahne's & Co., Montclair, N.J., 1979-80; health aide, art therapy asst. John F. Kennedy Rehab. Ctr., Edison, N.J., 1980-81; interior designer Carriage House, River Edge, N.J., 1981-82; mainframe programmer PDP 11/70, data processing tech. writer and documentation coord., corp. comml. artist, graphic project coord. Christian Salvesen, Secaucus, N.J., 1982—, co. rep. computer and graphic seminars, confs. and tradeshows, 1984—, corp. computer graphics artist, 1987—, personal computer and computer graphics rsch. coord., writer and artist employee newsletter, mainframe programmer VAX cluster 8250, 1988—, company art library coord., company art photographer, 1989—. Mem. Nat. Computer Graphics Assn., Digital Equipment Computers Users Soc., Nat. Assn. Desktop Pubs., Am. Mgmt. Assn., Nat. Assn. Female Execs., Assn. for Women in Computing, Nat. Tng. and Computer Network, Pi Lambda Theta. Russian Orthodox. Home: 260 Fourth St Saddle Brook NJ 07662 Office: Christian Salvesen 1 Enterprise Ave Secaucus NJ 07094

JESSEE, JAMES ANDREW, financial executive; b. Detroit, Jan. 7, 1958; s. Walter Jennings and Diane Elizabeth (Trimborn) J.; m. Kimberly Sie Bowles, July 19, 1980; children: Megan Elizabeth, Ryan Jennings. BS, U. Richmond, 1980. CLU. Region mgr. Minn. Mut. Life, St. Paul, 1980-86; region v.p. Mass. Fin. Svcs., Boston, 1987—. Republican. Roman Catholic. Home: 2736 Rosegate Ln Charlotte NC 28226 Office: Mass Fin Svcs 500 Boylston St Boston MA 02116

JESSUP, JOE LEE, educator, management consultant; b. Cordele, Ga., June 23, 1913; s. Horace Andrew and Elizabeth (Wilson) J.; m. Genevieve Quirk Galloway, Aug. 29, 1946; 1 child, Gail Elizabeth. B.S., U. Ala., 1936; M.B.A., Harvard U., 1941; LL.D., Chung-Ang U., Seoul, Korea, 1964. Sales rep. Proctor & Gamble, 1937-40; liaison officer bur. pub. relations U.S. War Dept., 1941; spl. asst. and exec. asst. Far Ea. div. and office exports Bd. Econ. Warfare, 1942-43; exec. officer, office deptl. adminstrn. Dept. State, 1946; exec. sec. adminstr.'s adv. council War Assets Adminstrn., 1946-48; v.p. sales Airken, Capitol & Service Co., 1948-52; assoc. prof. bus. adminstrn. George Washington U., 1952, prof., 1952-77, prof. emeritus, 1977—, asst. dean Sch. Govt., 1951-60; pres. Jessup and Co., Ft. Lauderdale, Fla., 1957—; bd. dirs. Giant Food, Inc., Washington (audit comm. 1974-75), 1971-75, Am. Equity Investors, Inc., 1986-87, Hunter Assn. Labs, Fairfax, Va., 1964-69 (exec. comm. 1966-69, exec. v.p. 1967, gen. mgr. 1969), coordinator air force resources mgmt. program, 1951-57; del. in edn. 10th Internat. Mgmt. Conf., Sao Paulo, Brazil, 1954, 11th Conf., Paris, 1957, 12th Conf., Sydney and Melbourne, Australia, 1960, 13th Conf., Rotterdam, Netherlands, 1966, 14th Conf., Tokyo, 1969, 15th Conf., Munich, Germany, 1972; mem. Md. Econ. Devel. Adv. Commn., 1973-75. Mem. nat. adv. council Center for Study Presidency, 1974; mem. Broward Bd. Trustees Philn. Orch. Fla., 1986—; mem. Chaine des Rotisseur, 1987—; mem. Civil Service Commn., Arlington County, Va., 1952-54; trustee Tng. Within Industry Found., Summit, N.J., 1954-58. Served from 2d lt. to lt. col. AUS, 1941-46. Decorated Bronze Star; recipient cert. of appreciation Sec. of Air Force, 1957. Mem. Acad. Mgmt. Clubs: Harvard (N.Y.C.); University (Washington); Coral Ridge Yacht; Tower (Ft. Lauderdale). Home: 2420 NE 34th Ct Lighthouse Point FL 33064

JESSUP, WILLIAM WALKER, accountant; b. Greensboro, N.C., Sept. 2, 1938; s. William L. and Mollie (Walker) J.; m. Patricia Proctor, June 17, 1961; children: Ann Elizabeth, John Walker. BS, U. Ala., 1960. Cert. fin. planner, CPA, Ala. Staff acct. Gafford & Webb CPA, Sylacauga, Ala., 1962-64, Morrison & Smith CPA, Tuscaloosa, Ala., 1964-68; ptnr. Morrison & Smith CPA, Tuscaloosa, 1968-70, Jessup & Palmer CPA, Tuscaloosa, 1970-79; pres., co-mng. dir. Jessup, Palmer & Co., Tuscaloosa, 1979—; bd. dirs. Holmes Fin. Assocs. Inc., Memphis, Thrift Found. Inc., Tuscaloosa, Greene Group, Inc., Tuscaloosa. Pres., bd. dirs. YMCA of Tuscaloosa County, 1986; treas. Tombigbee council Girl Scouts Am., 1980; mem. fin. adv. com. City of Tuscaloosa, 1980; bd. dirs. Tuscaloosa Rotary Meml. Found., 1975—. Served with USAF, 1961-62. Mem. Inst. Cert. Fin. Planners, Am. Inst. CPA's, Ala. Soc. CPA's (pres. Tuscaloosa chpt. 1970-71), Tuscaloosa Estate Planning Council (pres. 1987-88), North River Yacht Club, Rotary (pres. 1977-78, Paul Harris fellow 1980). Methodist. Home: 1224 High Forest Dr N Tuscaloosa AL 35406 Office: Jessup Palmer & Co 2704 8th St Tuscaloosa AL 35401

JESTER, ROBERTS CHARLES, JR., engineering services company executive; b. Atlanta, July 12, 1917; s. Roberts Charles and Lynwood (Waters) J.; children: Rita (Mrs. Charles B. Jones, Jr.), Carol (Mrs. John M. Sisk, Jr.), Janelle (Mrs. Michael C. Patty). B.S., U. Ga., 1940; grad., Advanced Mgmt. Program, Harvard, 1957. Chief clk. Ga. R.R., 1936-40; project mgr. Mich. Design & Engring. Co., 1941-42; partner Allstate Engring. Service Co., Dayton, Ohio, 1943-45; pres. Allstates Engring. Co., 1945—; chmn., chief exec. officer Allstates Engring. Co. Inc., Allstates Design & Devel. Co. Inc., Trenton, N.J., 1954—; dir. N.J. Nat. Bank. Bd. dirs., vice chmn. Greater Trenton Symphony Assn.; bd. dirs. George Washington council Boy Scouts Am.; bd. govs. Hamilton Hosp.; mem. lay adv. bd. St. Francis Hosp.; trustee YMCA, Trenton. Mem. Greater Trenton C. of C. (bd. dirs.). Republican. Presbyterian. Clubs: Mason (Shriner, Jester), Engineers, Trenton Country (past pres.); Metropolitan (N.Y.C.); Pitts. Athletic; Little Egg Harbor Yacht (N.J.). Office: Allstates Engring Co Inc Allstates Design Devel Co Inc 367 Pennington Ave Trenton NJ 08608

JETER, KATHERINE LESLIE BRASH, lawyer; b. Gulfport, Miss., July 24, 1921; d. Ralph Edward and Rosa Meta (Jacobs) Brash; m. Robert McLean Jeter, Jr., May 11, 1946. BA, Newcomb Coll. of Tulane U., 1943; JD, Tulane U., 1945. Bar: La. 1945, U.S. Dist. Ct. (we. dist.) La. 1948, U.S. Tax Ct. 1965, U.S. Supreme Ct. 1971, U.S. Dist. Ct. (ea. dist.) La. 1975, U.S. Ct. Appeals (5th cir.) 1981, U.S. Dist. Ct. (mid. dist.) La. 1982. Assoc. Montgomery, Fenner & Brown, New Orleans, 1945-46, Tucker, Martin, Holder, Jeter & Jackson, Shreveport, 1947-49; ptnr. Tucker, Jeter, Jackson and Hickman and predecessors, Shreveport, 1980—; judge pro tem 1st Jud. Dist. Ct., Caddo Parish, La., 1982-83; mem. adv. com. to joint legis. subcom. on mgmt. of the community; pres. YWCA of Shreveport, 1963; hon. consul of France; Shreveport; pres. Little Theatre of Shreveport, 1966-67; pres. Shreveport Art Guild, 1974-75; mem. task force crim justice La. Priorities for the Future, 1978; pres. LWV of Shreveport, 1950-51. Recipient Disting. Grad. award Tulane U., 1983. Mem. La. State Law Inst. (mem. coun. 1980—, adv. com. La. Civil Code 1973-77, temp. ad hoc. com. 1976-77), Pub. Affairs Rsch. Coun. (bd. trustees 1976-81, exec. com. 1981—, area exec. committeeman Shreveport area 1982), ABA, La. Bar Assn., Shreveport Bar Assn. (pres. 1986), Nat. Assn. Women Lawyers, Shreveport Assn. for Women Attys., C. of C. Shreveport (bd. dirs. 1975-77), Order of Coif, Phi Beta Kappa. Baptist. Contbr. articles on law to profl. jours. Home: 3959 Maryland Ave Shreveport LA 71106 Office: 401 Edwards St Ste 905 Shreveport LA 71101-3146

JETT, RICHARD JAMES, bank executive; b. South Gate, Calif., May 7, 1940; s. Artie Richard and Evelyn Clara (Tuksbre) J.; m. Deborrah C. Wiesman, July 14, 1975 (div. Sept. 1982); m. Michelle Diane Hall, Oct. 25, 1984; children: Sandi, Teri, Richi. Diploma in retail banking, U. Va. Collector Dial Fin., Alhambra, Calif., 1960-62; v.p. 1st Interstate Bank, Los Angeles, 1962-79; exec. v.p. Citrus State Bank, Covina, Calif., 1979-82; pres., chief exec. officer Empire Bank, N.A., Ontario, Calif., 1982—, also bd. dirs. Mem. Am. Bankers Assn. (advisor 1979-83,), Am. Inst. Banking (bd. dirs. 1983—), Independent Bankers Assn. So. Calif. (bd. dirs. 1984—, pres. 1989), Calif. Bankers Assn. (bd. dirs. 1985-87, 88—), Covina C. of C. (pres. 1986-87, named Dir. of Yr. 1984), Western States Consu,er Law Adv. Group (dir. 1980—). Republican. Lutheran. Lodges: Lions, Masons. Home: 646 Chaparro Rd Covina CA 91724 Office: Empire Bank NA 800 N Haven Ave Ontario CA 91764

JEWELL, GEORGE HIRAM, lawyer; b. Fort Worth, Jan. 9, 1922; s. George Hiram and Vera (Lee) J.; m. Betty Jefferis, July 21, 1944; children: Susan Jewell Cannon, Robert V., Nancy Jewell Wommack. B.A., U. Tex., 1942, LL.B., 1950. Bar: Tex. 1950. Geophysicist Gulf Research and Devel. Corp., Harmarville, Pa., 1946-47; assoc. Baker & Botts, Houston, 1950-60, ptnr., 1960-70, sr. ptnr., 1970—; dir. Schlumberger Ltd., N.Y., Paris; dir. Pogo Producing Co., Houston. Contbr. articles to profl. jours. Trustee Tex. Children's Hosp., Houston, 1977—, pres., 1982-83, chmn., 1984-86; bd. dirs. Schlumberger Found., N.Y.C., 1982—; mem. adv. council Coll. Natural Scis., U. Tex. Served to lt. USNR, 1943-46, 50-51. Fellow Am. Coll. Tax Counsel, Am. Bar Found.; mem. ABA, Order of Coif, Phi Beta Kappa, Phi Delta Phi. Clubs: Houston Country, Coronado (pres. 1976-77), Tejas, Old Baldy, Eldorado Country. Home: 6051 Crab Orchard Ln Houston TX 77002 Office: Baker & Botts 3000 One Shell Pla Houston TX 77002

JEWELL, ROBERT BURNETT, engineering company executive; b. Binghamton, N.Y., Mar. 20, 1906; s. Howard Clinton and Anne Bersina (Burnett) J.; m. Helen Louise Pflug, May 18, 1935; children—Robert William, Linda Louise. B.S. in Civil Engring., Lehigh U., 1928. Registered profl. engr., N.Y., Ky. Asst. engr. Friestedt Found. Co., N.Y.C., 1928-30; asst. engr. Port of N.Y. Authority, N.Y.C., 1930-39; with Mason & Hanger Co., 1939-43; resident engr. for constrn. Bklyn. Battery Tunnel, 1942-43; with Silas Mason Co., 1943-55; project mgr. Ft. Randall Tunnels, 1949-51, AEC Nev. Test Site, 1951-53; chief engr., co. rep. constr. Harvey Canal Tunnel, New Orleans, 1953-55; with Mason & Hanger-Silas Masons Co., Inc., 1955—; v.p., chief engr. Mason & Hanger-Silas Masons Co., Inc., Lexington, Ky., 1959-64; v.p. ops. Mason & Hanger-Silas Masons Co., Inc., 1964-75, exec. v.p., 1975-76, pres., 1976-86, vice chmn., 1986-87, chmn., 1987—; also dir. Mason Chamberlain Inc.; pres. The Mason Co., 1986-87, chmn., 1987—; fellow U. Ky., 1972—; Van Meter fellow Lees Coll., 1979—, trustee, 1977. Recipient Disting. Service award Dept. Energy, 1981. Fellow ASCE; mem. AIAA, Nat. Soc. Profl. Engrs., The Moles, Beavers, Tau Beta Pi. Presbyterian. Clubs: Lexington Country, Lafayette, Keeneland, Rotary. Office: Mason & Hanger-Silas Mason Co 200 W Vine St Lexington KY 40507

JILANI, ATIQ AHMED, industrialist; b. Amroha, India, Feb. 1, 1948; came to U.S., 1970; s. Siddiq Ahmed and Nasima (Khatoon) J.; m. Khalida Bano Naqvi, Dec. 25, 1975; children: Hussain, Ibrahim. Student D.J. Sci. Coll., Karachi, Pakistan, 1965; BE, NED Engring. Coll., Karachi U., 1969; MS, Tuskegee Inst., Ala., 1971; cert. in mgmt., Purdue U., 1978, Northwestern U., 1980, U. Pa., 1982. Registered profl. engr., Ill. Script writer Karachi (Pakistan) TV, 1967-70; mem. research staff AEC, Tuskegee, Ala., 1970-71; design engr. Lummus Industries, Columbus, Ga., 1971-73; product engr. Borg-Warner Corp., Chgo., 1974-78, mgr. engring. Chgo. Marine Containers div. Sea Containers, Broadview, Ill., 1978-80; v.p. operations Borg-Erickson Corp., Chgo., 1980-81, chief operating officer, v.p., gen. mgr. 1981-85; pres., chief exec. officer, Circuit Systems Inc., 1985-87, chmn. bd. dirs., 1986—, dir. 1988—; pres., chief exec. officer Bright Image Corp., 1988—; chmn. bd., chief exec. officer Tri-Lite Electronics, Inc., 1988—; cons. in industry and agr. UN, including work in South Asia, 1981. Contbr. articles to profl. jours.; patentee (U.S. and internat.) in field agrl. equipment. Mem. Rep. Precinct Com., York Twp., Du Page County, Ill., 1988—; organizer Voter registration campaign for Asian-Am. voters in Du Page County, 1987—; chmn., pub. rels. com. York Township Rep. Committeeman's Orgn., 1988—; treas. Forest Glen Homeowners Assn., Oak Brook, Ill., 1988—; trustee bd. Islamic Found., Villa Park, Ill., 1989—. Recipient Asian Human Services of Chgo. Honor award 1988. Mem. Inst. Printed Circuits, Assn. Energy Engrs. (charter), Thinkers Forum (pres. 1967-70). Home: PO Box 3212 Oak Brook IL 60521

JINKS, JILL KAREN, insurance company executive; b. Atlanta, Nov. 13, 1957; d. John Gordon Jr. and Carolyn Irene (Nelms) J. BBA in Fin. and Econs. cum laude, Stetson U., 1979; MBA in Fin., NYU, 1986; postgrad., Ga. State U., 1986—. Comml. underwriter trainee Chubb & Son, Atlanta, 1979-80, comml. liability underwriter, 1980-82; comml. accounts underwriter Chubb & Son, N.Y.C., 1982-83, mgr. comml. lines unit, 1983-86; comml. liability underwriter/broker Ins. House/So. Gen. Ins. Co., Atlanta, 1986, mgr. comml. liability underwriting, 1987—. First Fed. Savs. & Loan Fla. scholar, 1979. Mem. Nat. Assn. Profl. Surplus Lines, Ga. Assn. Surplus Lines Brokers, Soc. CPCUs (program dir. Ga. chpt. 1986—), Atlanta Track Club (race food coord. 1986—, event com.), N.Y. Road Runners Club (food and baggage coord. 1985 N.Y.C. Marathon). Republican. Home: 1521 Fordham Ct NE Atlanta GA 30306 Office: Ins House Inc PO Box 28155 Atlanta GA 30328

JOAQUIM, RICHARD RALPH, hotel executive; b. Cambridge, Mass., July 28, 1936; s. Manuel and Mary (Marrano) J.; m. Nancy Phyllis Reis, Oct. 22, 1960; 1 dau., Vanessa Reis. BFA, Boston U., 1955, MusB, 1959. Social dir., coordinator summer resort, Wolfeboro, N.H., 1957-59; concert soloist N.H. Symphony Orch., Vt. Choral Soc., Choral Arts Soc., Schenectady Chamber Orch., 1957-60; coordinator performance functions, mgr. theatre Boston U., 1959-60, asst. program dir., 1963-64, dir. univ. programs, 1964-70; gen. mgr. Harrison House of Glen Cove; dir. Conf. Service Corp., Glen Cove, N.Y., 1970-74, sr. v.p., dir. design and devel.; v.p. Arltec, also mng. dir. Sheraton Internat. Conf. Center, 1975-76; v.p., mng. dir. Scottsdale (Ariz.) Conf. Center and Resort Hotel, 1976—; pres. Internat. Conf. Resorts, Inc., 1977, chmn. bd., 1977—; pres. Western Conf. Resorts; concert solist U.S. Army Field Band, Washington, 1960-62. Creative arts cons., editorial cons., concert mgr. Commr. recreation Watertown, Mass., 1967—; mem. Spl. Study Com. Watertown, 1967—, Glen Cove Mayor's Urban Renewal Com., Nat. Com. for Performing Arts Ctr. at Boston U., Jacob K. Kavits Fellows Program Fellowship Bd. Bd. dirs. Nat. Entertainment Conf.; trustee Boston U., 1983—, Hotel and Food Adminstrn. Program Adv. Bd., Boston U., 1986—. Served with AUS, 1960-62. Mem. Assn. Coll. and Univ. Concert Mgrs., Am. Symphonic League, Am. Fedn. Film Socs., Assn. Am. Artists, Am. Personnel and Guidance Assn., La Chaine des Rotisseurs, Knights of the Vine, Nat. Alumni Council Boston U. Clubs: The Lotos (N.Y.); The Arizona (Phoenix). Office: scottsdale Conf Ctr & Resort Hotel 7700 McCormick Pkwy Scottsdale AZ 85258

JOBS, STEVEN PAUL, computer corporation executive; b. 1955; adopted s. Paul J. and Clara J. (Jobs). Student, Reed Coll. With Hewlett-Packard, Palo Alto, Calif.; designer video games Atari Inc., 1974; co-founder Apple Computer Inc., Cupertino, Calif., chmn. bd., 1975-85, former dir.; pres. NeXT, Inc., Palo Alto, Calif., 1985—. Co-designer: (with Stephan Wozniak) Apple I Computer, 1976. Office: NeXT Inc 3475 Deer Creek Rd Palo Alto CA 94304 *

JOCHMANN, SISTER ROSE, treasurer of religious order; b. Appleton, Wis., Mar. 31, 1943; d. Edward Joseph and Rosella Mary (Hoelzel) J. BS, St. Norbert Coll., 1969; MSA, Notre Dame U., 1986. Tchr. various grade schs., Green Bay, Casco, De Pere, Wis., 1963-81; prin. Holy Cross Grade Sch., Green Bay, 1981-83; treas. Sisters of St. Francis of the Holy Cross, Green Bay, 1983—; coordinator Oneida (Wis.) Indian Summer Session, 1977-80; pres. Green Bay Diocese Sisters Council, 1979-81; mem. Just Labor Relations Task Force, 1983-87; coordinator Social Justice Coordinator, Sisters of St. Francis of the Holy Cross, 1985-88. Chairperson Fiscal Concerns Com., 1986—. Mem. Nat. Assn. Treasurers of Religious Insts., Corp. Responsibility Coalition for State of Wis. Roman Catholic.

JODSAAS, LARRY ELVIN, computer components company executive; b. Lisbon, N.D., May 11, 1935; s. Elvin Bernard Jodsaas and Elizabeth Louise (Kingren) Wiederholt; m. Beverly Ann Levang, Dec. 27, 1959; children: Sherry, Rick, Kimberly. ASEE, Wahpeton State Sch. Sci., N.D., 1960; BSEE, U. N.D., 1962. Pres. computer systems and services Control Data Corp., Mpls., 1987—, cons. product line mgmt., 1970-72, gen. mgr. computer devel., 1972-74, v.p. computer devel., 1974-78, v.p. new product programs, 1978-79, v.p. product mgmt. and strategic planning, 1979-81, v.p. ops., peripheral products, 1981-82, v.p. computer systems, 1982-85, pres. computer systems and services, 1985-86, sr. v.p. quality and ops. effectiveness, 1986—; bd. dirs. ETA Systems Inc., St. Paul, Norwest Bank Bloomington, Minn. Mem. U. N.D. Adv. Council. Served with USN, 1954-58. Lutheran. Home: 1700 19th Terr NW New Brighton MN 55112 Office: Control Data Corp 8100 34th Ave St Minneapolis MN 55440

JOHANSEN, ROBERT JOSEPH, consulting actuary; b. N.Y.C., May 2, 1922; s. Irving Joseph and Margaret (McKee) J.; B.A., Manhattan Coll., 1943; M.A., Columbia U., 1974; m. Mary Carroll Hayes, June 27, 1964; children—Mary Carroll, Robert Hayes, David McKee. With Met. Life Ins. Co., N.Y.C., 1947-82, 3d v.p., 1964-68, 2d v.p., 1968-69, v.p. personal ins. adminstrn., 1969-70, v.p., 1970-72, v.p., actuary, 1972-82; cons. actuary, 1982—; sec. Council Profl. Assns. on Fed. Stats., 1980-83, chmn., 1984. Trustee Dominican Coll., Blauvelt, N.Y., 1970-87; former pres. Van Cortlandt Terr. Assn.; mem. Mayor's Com. for Community Relations, Yonkers, N.Y., 1978-86. Served with USAAF, 1943-46. Fellow Soc. Actuaries (treas. 1980-83, chmn. com. on govt. stats. 1980-81, 86—, chmn. com. to recommend a new mortality basis for individual annuity valuation 1980-83, com. on nonforfecture and valuation mortality problems, individual life ins. and annuities, chmn. 1983-85), com on research mgmt., 1988—, com. on experience studies, 1988—; mem. Am. Acad. Actuaries, Am. Statis. Assn., N.Y. Acad. Sci., Internat. Actuarial Assn., N.Y. Actuaries Club (treas. 1978-81), Actuarial Studies in Non-Life Ins. Roman Catholic. Contbr. articles to profl. jours. Office: Life Actuarial Svcs 56 Pershing Ave Yonkers NY 10705

JOHANSEN, WILFORD WOODRUFF, government organization executive, lawyer; b. Salt Lake City, Apr. 15, 1928; s. Wilford W. and Olive Louise (Vincent) J.; m. Patricia A. Rund, May 2, 1959; children: Eric, Evan. BA, Idaho State U., 1951; LLB, George Washington U., 1957; grad. mgmt. training, Fed. Exec. Inst., Charlottesville, Va., 1972. Bar: D.C., 1957. Dep. asst. gen. counsel Office of Gen. Coun., Washington, 1961-71; Region 21 dir. Office of Gen. Coun., L.A., 1971-85; acting. gen. counsel NLRB, Washington, 1984-85, bd. mem., 1985—; mem. L.A. Fed. Exec. Bd. Served with U.S. Army, 1952-55, Korea. Mem. D.C. Bar Assn. (labor law sect.), L.A. County Bar. Assn. (advisor ann. labor law symposium, chmn. labor rels. com., mem. policy com.), So. Calif. Indsl. Rels. Rsch. Assn. (past pres.), NLRB-Orange County Indsl. Rels. Rsch. Assn. (founder, co-sponsor ann. labor law conf.), Adminstrv. Conf. U.S. Home: 3117 Northampton St NW Washington DC 20015-1608 Office: NLRB 1717 Pennsylvania Ave NW #650 Washington DC 20570

JOHANTGEN, NICHOLAS DARWIN, systems engineer; b. Indpls., May 22, 1953; s. Harold Nicholas and Alice Jeanette (Dowds) J.; m. Mary Carol Heiselman, Nov. 4, 1978; 1 child, Andrew. BA, Miami U., Oxford, Ohio, 1975. Loan officer BancOhio Nat. Bank, Cin., 1976-80; systems mgr. Shelby (Ohio) Mut. Ins. Co., 1980-85; mgr. systems engring. Electronic Data Systems, Dallas, 1985-87; sr. systems engr. Teradata Corp., Cin., 1987—. Mem. Soc. CPCUs. Office: Teradata Corp 211 Grandview Ste 303 Fort Mitchell KY 41017

JOHLER, JOSEPH RALPH, physicist; b. Scranton, Pa., Feb. 23, 1919; s. Joseph Jacob and Lillian (Dietzel) J.; B.A., Am. U., 1941; B.S.E., George Washington U., 1950; m. Nora Stella Callahan, Sept. 16, 1953; children—Dennis Ralph, Mark Stephen, Paul Norman, Annette Diane. Ballistic mathematician Ballistic Research Lab., Aberdeen Proving Grounds, Md., 1942-45; with Nat. Bur. Standards, Washington, 1946-51, electronic engr. Boulder Labs., 1951-65, chief electromagnetic theory sect., 1961-65; program leader, electromagnetic theory program Environmental Sci. Services Adminstrn., Inst. Telecommunication Scis. and Aeronomy, U.S. Dept. Commerce, Boulder, 1965-70, physicist, project scientist Office Telecommunications 1970-72, chief nav. and D-Region Sci. sect., 1972-76; pres. Colo. Research and Prediction Lab., Boulder, 1976-86; cons. Johler Assocs., 1986—. Served with USNR, 1944-46. Research Nat. Bur. Standards Disting. Authorship award, 1963, 66. Mem. Internat. Union Radio Sci., IEEE (sr. mem., life mem.), Internat. Radio Consultative Com., Wild Goose Assn. (Gold Medal of Merit award 1982). Contbr. articles to profl. jours. Home: 16796 W 74th Pl Golden CO 80403

JOHNS, EMERSON THOMAS, chemical company executive; b. Phila., June 24, 1947; s. Charles and Sophia (Milak) J.; m. Marlene Catherine Giorello, Oct. 9, 1971; children: Tracey, Jeffrey. BS in Acctg., Mt. St. Mary's Coll., 1969; MBA in Fin., Widener U., 1980. Auditor DuPont Co., Atlanta, Parlin (N.J.), and Wilmington (N.C.), 1969-77; fin. analyst internat. dept. DuPont Co., Wilmington, Del., 1978-80, mgr. acctg. and internal controls, 1981-82; mgr. acctg. and bus. analysis dept., petrochems. dept. Savannah River plant Dupont Co., Aiken, S.C., 1983-85; mgr. adminstrv. svcs. atomic energy div. DuPont Co., Wilmington, 1986-89, mgr. govt. contracting fin. dept., 1989—. Bd. dirs. St. Mary Help of Christians Sch., Aiken, 1985, chmn.-elect, 1986; bd. dirs. Foxchase Civic Assn., Aiken, 1986; advisor Jr. Achievement, Wilmington, 1987-88; mem. Christian formation St. John the Beloved, Wilmington, 1988-89. Roman Catholic. Club: Foxchase Swim (Aiken) (pres. 1985). Home: 1105 Kelly Dr Yeatman Estates Newark DE 19711 Office: DuPont Co Fin dept govt contracting DuPont Bldg 3030 Wilmington DE 19898

JOHNS, HYLAND R., tree company executive, mayor; b. Westfield, N.J., July 13, 1925; s. Hyland R. and Edith (Hughes) J.; m. Beth Synnestvedt, Sept. 10, 1950; children: Deanne, Kara, Judy, Bradley, Sherryn. BS, Purdue U., 1950; MS, Mich. State U., 1951. Sr. v.p. Asplundh Tree Expert Co., Willow Grove, Pa., 1950—; mayor Borough of Bryn Athyn (Pa.). Bd. dirs. Holy Redeemer Hosp., Acad. of New Church. Mem. Nat. Arbor Assn. (ann. award 1988), Internat. Soc. Arborists (pres. 1976-77), Soc. Am. Foresters, Arbor Rsch. Trust (bd. dirs.). Republican. Home: PO Box 336 Bryn Athyn PA 19009 Office: Asplundh Tree Expert Co 708 Blair Mill Rd Willow Grove PA 19090

JOHNSEN, RICHARD ALAN, finance executive; b. Richmond, Va., Mar. 9, 1946; s. Richard Louis and Madeline Ann (Gonsalves) J.; m. Pamela Gail Kruse, May 20, 1968; children: Scott Adam, Kristin Elizabeth. BA, Whitman Coll., 1968; MBA, U. Wash., 1971. CPA, Wash. Fin. mgmt. program Gen. Electric, Pittsfield, Mass., 1968-70; sr. internal auditor PACCAR Inc., Bellevue, Wash., 1971-72, asst. to v.p., controller, 1972-77, corp. acctg. mgr., 1977-81, dir. strategic planning, 1981-84, dir. fin., 1984-85, treas., 1986—. Office: PACCAR Inc PO Box 1518 Bellevue WA 98009

JOHNSEN, WALTER CRAIG, venture capitalist; b. N.Y.C., Dec. 15, 1950; s. Walter S. Johnsen and Therese L. (Nissen) J. BS, Cornell U., 1973, MS in Eng., 1974; MBA, Columbia U., 1978. Gen. ptnr. First Century Partnerships, N.Y.C., 1981-85; v.p. Smith Barney Venture Corp., Upham, N.Y., 1978-85; mng. ptnr. Johnsen Securities, N.Y.C., 1985—; bd. dirs. Marshall Products, Inc., Lincolnshire, Ill., Marine Med. Corp., San Diego, Buffalo Med. Specialties, Clearwater, Fla., N.J. Mem. St. Francis Yacht Club, Cornell Club. Office: Johnsen Securities 767 3d Ave, 7th Fl New York NY 10017

JOHNSON, ALAN CLAIR, process engineer; b. Washington, Jan. 1, 1946; s. Clair Warren and Margaret Leone (Powell) J.; m. Maria Teresa Sancho, Dec. 28, 1981; 1 child, Alan Antonio. BA, Colgate U., 1967; MS, Tulane U., 1971, PhD, 1975. Assoc. engr. Westinghouse Electric Corp., Balt., 1967-69; lectr. physics U. New Orleans, 1975-79; process engr. Rockwell Internat., Newport Beach, Calif., 1979-83, Commodore Internat., Costa Mesa, Calif., 1985-86, Holt Inc., Irvine, Calif., 1986—; cons. L.A. Power and Light Co., 1977. Mem. Am. Phys. Soc. Home: 274 E 22nd St Costa Mesa CA 92627 Office: Holt Inc 9351 Jeronimo Rd Irvine CA 92718

JOHNSON, ANITA WATSON, finance company executive; b. Murfreesboro, Tenn., Dec. 27, 1949; d. Robert Lee and Grace Lynn (Hayes) Watson; m. Thomas W. Drennan, Aug. 31, 1974 (div. May 1981); m. Jerry Wayee Johnson, Oct. 20, 1982. BS, Western Ky. U., 1973; postgrad., Tenn. State U., 1981. Staff acct. J. Alan Hopper CPA, Nashville, 1973-74; staff acct. Fidelity Fed. Savs. and Loan, Nashville, 1974-75, acctg. mgr., 1975-77, asst. treas., 1977-78; pvt. practice cons. Lebanon, Tenn., 1978-80; asst. comptroller Steiner Liff Iron and Metal Co., Nashville, 1980-84, comptroller, 1984-86, sec.-treas., bd. dirs., 1986—; sec.-treas. M.Cohen Iron and Metal Co., Nashville, 1985—; bd. dirs., sec.-treas. Diversified Sci. Svcs. Inc., Kingston, Tenn., 1987—; bd. dirs. Sci. Ecology Group Inc., Oak Ridge, Tenn., Roane Acquisition Corp., Rockwood, Tenn., Tenn. Valley Acquisition Corp., Harriman, Shredders Inc., Birmingham, Ala. Mem. Am. Mgmt. Assn. Republican. Methodist. Office: Steiner Liff Iron & Metal Co PO Box 1182 Nashville TN 37202

JOHNSON, ASHMORE CLARK, JR., oil company executive; b. Phila., Dec. 7, 1930; s. Ashmore Clark and Elsie (Carstens) J.; m. Myra Lee Wheeler, Dec. 2, 1967; 1 dau., Elyse Charlotte. B.A., Haverford Coll., 1952; M.B.A., U. Pa., 1954. V.p. mktg. Union Tex. Petroleum div. Allied Chem. Corp., Houston, 1972-76, exec. v.p. div., 1976-77; pres. specialty chems. div. Allied Chem. Corp., Houston, 1977-79; exec. v.p. Allied Chem. Co. div. Allied Chem. Corp., Morristown, N.J., 1979-82, pres., 1982-83; pres., chief operating officer Union Tex. Petroleum Corp. div. Allied Chem. Corp., Houston, 1983-84; chmn., chief exec. officer Union Tex. Petroleum Corp., Houston, 1985—. Republican. Episcopalian. Office: Union Tex Petroleum Holdings Corp 1330 Post Oak Blvd Houston TX 77252

JOHNSON, BRAD HART, transportation systems planner; b. Dowagiac, Mich., Oct. 2, 1951; s. Irving Julius and Marjorie June (Hart) J.; m. Rosemary Christoff, June 23, 1979. AS, Kalamazoo (Mich.) Valley Community Coll., 1976; BS, Mich. State U., 1978. Regional planner Cheyenne-Laramie County Regional Planning Office, Wyo., 1978-80; city planner City of Longmont, Colo., 1980; transp. planner County of Kalamazoo, Mich., 1980-81; transp. program dir. Pikes Peak Area Council of Govts., Colorado Springs, Colo., 1982-86; transp. mgr. Planning Research Corp. (now P&D Techs.), Colorado Springs, 1986-87, gen. mgr., 1987—; com. mem. Transp. Research Bd., Washington, 1983—. Contbr. tech. reports to profl. publs. Served with USAF, 1970-74. Recipient Letter of Appreciation, Pikes Peak Area Council Govts., 1986, Letter of Appreciation, Transp. Adv. Com., 1986; named One of Outstanding Young Men of Am., 1986. Mem. Urban and Regional Info. Systems Assn., Am. Planning Assn., Internat. City Mgmt. Assn. Home: 130 E Kelly Rd Woodland Park CO 80863-8358

JOHNSON, BRUCE ALLAN, marketing professional; b. Flint, Mich., Jan. 17, 1958; s. Harold Norgen and Opal Emma (King) J.; m. Laurie Anne Wiedemer, May 3, 1986. BS with honors, Mich. State U., 1981. Packaging engr. Eastman Kodak Co., Rochester, N.Y., 1981-84, quality engr., 1984-87, mktg. coordinator, 1988—. Bd. dirs. YMCA Greece, N.Y., 1984-85, chmn. com., 1983-85; com. mem. YMCA, Pittsford, N.Y., 1987—; mem. Rochester Landmark Soc., 1987—. Mem. Am. Soc. Nondestructive Testing, Pi Kappa Gamma, Alpha Zeta. Republican. Office: Eastman Kodak Co 343 State St Rochester NY 14608

JOHNSON, BRUCE ALVIN, photo company executive; b. Hibbing, Minn.; s. Alvin J. and Taimi O. Johnson. AS, Hibbing Community Coll., 1978; BSCE, U. Minn., 1980. Engr. U.S. Steel Co., Mt. Iron, Minn., 1980-84; supt. Range Photo, Chisholm, Minn., 1984—. With U.S. Army, 1971-73. Mem. Engrs. Club No. Minn. Office: Range Photo 311 W Lake St Chisholm MN 55719

JOHNSON, BRUCE EDWARD, distribution company executive; b. Hempstead, N.Y., Dec. 29, 1959; s. William David and Diane Kathryn (Ryan) J.; m. Lee Luise Wurster, July 18, 1981. B in Acctg., Dowling Coll., 1980; MBA in Fin., U. So. Calif., 1983. Facility controller ElectroSound Group, Sun Valley, Calif., 1980-84; corp. controller, chief acctg. officer ElectroSound Group, Hauppauge, N.Y., 1984-86; v.p. fin., chief fin. officer Syscomm Internat. Corp. (previously Info. Tech. Services, Inc.), Hauppauge, 1986—; ind. fin. cons., Ridge, N.Y., 1985—; acctg. internship instr. Dowling Coll., Oakdale, N.Y., 1984—. V.p. Ridge Vol. Fire Dept., 1985. Mem. Nat. Assn. Accts., U. So. Calif. Alumni Assn., Dowling Coll. Alumni Assn. Republican. Office: Syscomm Internat Corp 275 Marcus Blvd Ste F Hauppauge NY 11788

JOHNSON, CALVIN KEITH, research executive, chemist; b. Litchfield, Minn., Dec. 15, 1937; s. Delphin J. and Iva Mae (Watkins) J.; m. Constance S. Hoffman, June 18, 1960; children—Eric O., Judd. F., Malinda K. B.A., Olivet Nazarene Coll., Ill., 1959; Ph.D. in Chemistry, Mich. State U., 1963. Postdoctoral fellow Columbia U., N.Y.C., 1963-64; research chemist 3M Co., St. Paul, 1964-67; group leader CPC Internat., Summit, Ill., 1967-69; mgr. research and devel. Acme Resin Corp. subs. Borden, Inc., Forest Park, Ill., 1969-71, tech. dir., 1971-76, v.p., tech. dir., 1977-85, sr. v.p., tech. dir., 1985—. Patentee in field (10). Contbr. articles to tech. jours. Mem. ch. bd. 1st Ch. of Nazarene, Lemont, Ill., 1969—, Sunday Sch. supt., 1977-83; chmn. bd. Olivet Research Assocs., Kankakee, Ill., 1982—; mem., fundraiser Chickasaw Homeowners Assn., Lockport, Ill., 1979—. NSF fellow, 1961; NIH fellow, 1963. Mem. Am. Chem. Soc., Am. Foundrymen's Soc. (chmn. com.), Soc. Petroleum Engrs., AAAS, Research Dirs. Assn. Chgo., Sigma Xi. Republican. Avocations: gardening; fishing. Home: 1006 E Division St Lockport IL 60441 Office: Acme Resin Corp 1372 Circle Ave Forest Park IL 60130

JOHNSON, CHARLES FOREMAN, architect, architectural photographer, planning, architecture and systems engineering consultant; b. Plainfield, N.J., May 28, 1929; s. Charles E. and E. Lucile (Casner) J.; student Union Jr. Coll., 1947-48; B.Arch., U. So. Calif., 1958; postgrad. UCLA, 1959-60; m. Beverly Jean Hinnendale, Feb. 19, 1961 (div. 1970); children—Kevin, David. Draftsman, Wigton-Abbott, P.C., Plainfield, 1945-52; architect, cons., graphic, interior and engring. systems designer, 1952—; designer, draftsman with H.W. Underhill, Architect, Los Angeles, 1953-55; teaching asst. U. So. Calif., Los Angeles, 1954-55; designer with Carrington H. Lewis, Architect, Palos Verdes, Calif., 1955-56; grad. architect Ramo-Wooldridge Corp., Los Angeles, 1956-58; tech. dir. Atlas weapon system Space Tech. Labs., Los Angeles, 1958-60; advanced planner and systems engr. Minuteman Weapon System, TRW, Los Angeles, 1960-64, div. staff ops. dir., 1964-68; cons. N.Mex. Regional Med. Program and N.Mex. State Dept. Hosps., 1968-70; prin. Charles F. Johnson, architect, Los Angeles, 1953-68, Sante Fe, N.Mex., 1968-88, Carefree, Ariz., 1988—; free lance archtl. photographer, Sante Fe, 1971—; tchr. archtl. apprentice program, 1974—. Major archtl. works include: residential bldgs. in Calif., 1955-66; Bashein Bldg. at Los Lunas (N.Mex.) Hosp. and Tng. Sch., 1969, various residential bldgs., Santa Fe, 1973—, Kurtz Home, Dillon, Colo., 1981, Whispering Boulders Home, Carefree, 1981, Hedrick House, Santa Fe, 1983, Kole House, Green Valley, Ariz., 1984, Casa Largo, Santa Fe (used for film The Man Who Fell to Earth), 1974, Rubel House, Santa Fe, 1986, Smith House, Carefree, Ariz., 1987, Klopfer House, Sante Fe, 1988, Janssen House, Carefree, 1988, Art Start Gallery, 1988. Pres., Santa Fe Coalition for the Arts, 1977; set designer Santa Fe Fiesta Melodrama, 1969, 71, 74, 77, 78, 81; designed Jay Miller & Friends Fiesta float 1970-88 (winner of 20 awards). Mem. Delta Sigma Phi. Club: El Gancho Tennis. Contbr. articles on facility planning and mgmt. to profl. publs.; contbr. archtl. photographs to mags. in U.S., Eng., France, Japan and Italy, contbr. articles on facility mgmt., planning info. systems, etc. to profl. jours. Recognized for work in organic architecture and siting buildings to fit the land. Club: El Gancho Tennis. Avocations: music, photography, collecting architecture books, Frank Lloyd Wright works. Home: 9100 Clubhouse Cir The Boulders PO Box 6070 Carefree AZ 85377

JOHNSON, CHARLES M., banker; b. 1941; married. BS, Ohio State U., 1963; MA, Stanford U., 1978. With Wells Fargo Bank, San Francisco, 1967—, personnel officer, 1969-70, internat. banking officer, 1970-71, asst. v.p., Nicaragua rep., 1971-74, asst. v.p., Hong Kong rep., 1974-75, v.p. real estate indsl. group, 1975-78, v.p., mgr. constrn. loan dept., 1978-79, sr. v.p. retail banking group, dep. head group, 1979-80, sr. v.p. comml. banking group, 1980-83, exec. v.p., 1983—. Office: Wells Fargo Bank 660 Newport Center Dr Ste 1300 Newport Beach CA 92660

JOHNSON, CHARLES REED, real estate developer; b. Columbus, Ohio, Oct. 25, 1954; s. Charles White and Lillian (McCain) J.; m. Cynthia O'Quinn, June 6, 1981. BS, BA, Ohio State U., 1982. Dir. mktg. Ball & Galloway Indsl. Devel., Columbus, 1980-82; assoc. Ball & Galloway, Columbus, 1982-87; exec. v.p. G.W. Banning Assocs. Inc., Worthington, Ohio, 1987—; pres. Charles R. Johnson Co. Inc., Columbus, 1987—; dir. devel. Airborne Commerce Park, Wilmington, Ohio, 1987—. Mem. chmns. club Franklin County Rep. Party. Mem. Nat. Assn. Realtors, Ohio Assn. Realtors, Columbus Bd. Realtors (govt. affairs com. 1986-88), Nat. Found. for Hist. Preservation, Worthington C. of C. (bd. dirs.), Rivera Country Club (Columbus), Maennerchor Club (Columbus), Agonis Club. Republican. Episcopalian. Clubs: Columbus Maennerchor, Riviera Country, Agonis. Home: 1567 Sandringham Dr Columbus OH 43220 Office: 685 High St Worthington OH 43085

JOHNSON, CHARLES SIMONS, candy company executive; b. Topeka, Kans., Dec. 8, 1940; s. Harry F. and Dorothea A. (Simons) J.; children—Elizabeth, Steve, Scott; BA, U. Kans., 1962; JD, U. Va., 1965. Bar: Mo. 1965. Assoc., Stinson, Mag & Fizzell, Kansas City, Mo., 1965-67, ptnr., 1968-76; pres. Price Candy Co., Kansas City, 1976—; dir. Chaz Investment Corp., Kansas City. Bd. dirs. Kansas City Boy's Club (Mo.), 1974-76, Greater Kansas City YMCA, 1981-83, Starlight Theatre, Kansas City, 1984. 1st lt. USAF, 1965-71. Mem. ABA (exec. com. Young Lawyers sect.), Mo. Bar Assn. Republican. Presbyterian. Home: 6601 Willow Ln Mission Hills KS 66208 Office: Price Candy Co South & Wellington PO Box 378 Richmond MO 64085

JOHNSON, CHARLES WAYNE, mining engineer, mining executive; b. Vinita, Okla., Feb. 7, 1921; s. Charles Monroe and Willie Mae (Hudson) J.; m. Cleo Faye Wittee, 1940 (div. 1952); m. Genevieve Hobbs, 1960 (dec. Sept. 1985); m. Susan Gates Johnson, Apr. 19, 1986; 1 child, Karen Candace Limon. BE, Kensington U., 1974, ME, 1975, PhDE, 1976. Owner El Monte (Calif.) Mfg. Co., 1946-49; co-owner Anjo Pest Control, Pasadena, Calif., 1946-56, Hoover-Johnson Cons. Co., Denver, 1956-59; pres. Vanguard Chem. Co., Denver, 1957-61, Mineral Products Co., Boise, Idaho, 1957-61; owner Crown Hill Meml. Park, Dallas, 1959-61, Johnson Engring., Victorville, Calif., 1961-86; pres. Crown Minerals, Victorville, 1985-87; owner J&D Mining Co., Victorville, 1977—. Contbr. articles to profl. pubs.; patentee in field. Active Rep. VIP Club. Served with USN, 1941-45. Recipient Outstanding Achievement award East Pasadena Bus. Assn., 1948. Mem. Ch. Ancient Christianity. Office: Johnson Engring Crown Minerals PO Box 641 Wrightwood CA 92397

JOHNSON, CHAUNCEY PAUL, banker; b. Detroit, Oct. 25, 1931; s. Chauncey Frederic and Lois Jean (Hon) J.; m. Anne Gayman, June 1949; children: Julianne, Deborah, Rebecca. Student, Denison U., 1949-51; B.S., Mich. State U., 1953. Account exec. Robert W. Baird, Milw., 1956-59; pres. Wis. Capital Corp., Milw., 1959-64, Reef Club Hotel, Ocho Rios, Jamaica, 1964-66, Maru Imports, Inc., 1959-66; sr. v.p., dir. Milw. Western Bank, 1967-70; pres. Growth Capital, Inc., Chgo., 1970-72; chmn. bd., chief exec. officer Colonial Bank & Trust Co., Chgo., 1972—; chmn., chief exec. officer 1st Colonial Bankshares, Chgo.; chmn. bd. Bankers Tech., Mid-States Leasing; pres. Popo Agie Ranch Ltd., Lander, Wyo.; chmn. bd. N.W. Commerce Bank, Rosemont, Ill., Community Bank of Edgewater, Ave. Bank of Oak Park, Ill; vice chmn. Mich. Ave. Nat. Bank; chmn. First Colonial Mortgage Co., First Escrow Co. Trustee Am. Field Service, Chgo. Acad. Sci.; bd. dirs. Adler Planetarium, Chgo., Crow Canyon Archeology Ctr.; mem. exec. bd. Chgo. area Boy Scouts Am. Served as 1st lt. USAF, 1953-56. Mem. Ill. Bankers Assn. (past pres. Chgo. dist.), Northside Bankers Assn. (past pres.), Belmont Central C. of C. (past pres.), Ridgemore Country Club, Milw. Athletic Club, Union League Club, Lambda Chi Alpha. Office: 1st Colonial Bankshares 30 N Michigan Ste 300 Chicago IL 60602

JOHNSON, CHLOE RENE, community economic developer; b. Dallas, Oct. 18, 1939; d. William Porter and Vera Lee (Skinner) Riggs; m. Doyle K. Chaddick, Dec. 1, 1956 (div. July 1976); 1 child, Susan Kay; m. Walter Lee Johnson Jr., Apr. 30, 1983. Cert. indsl. developer; registered chamber executive. Exec. v.p. Quitman (Tex.) C. of C., 1973-76, Waxahachie (Tex.) C. of C., 1976-78, Grand Prairie (Tex.) C. of C., 1978-80; mgr. community devel. Tex. Econ. Devel. Commn., Austin, 1980-86; prin. Johnson & Assocs., Austin, 1986—. Recipient Community Svc. award Plano C. of C., 1971, Community Svc. award County of Wood, 1975. Mem. Tex. Indsl. Devel. Council (dir., com. chmn. 1975—), So. Indsl. Devel. Council (com. chmn. 1981—), Am. Indsl. Devel. Council (com. chmn. 1983—). Democrat. Baptist. Home and Office: 8308 Tecumseh Dr Austin TX 78753

JOHNSON, CLAYTON ERROLD, poultry company executive; b. DeSota, Wis., Apr. 20, 1921; s. James and Louella (Goodin) J.; student U. Wis., 1940-41, Tex. A. and M. Coll., 1946; m. Betty J. Higenbotham, May 23, 1943; children—Roderick and Ronald (twins), Richard. Pres. Flavor Fresh Brand, Inc., 1949—; Calif. gen. bldg. contractor, 1947—. With USAAF, 1942-45. Home: 1008 Pine Hurst Dr Las Vegas NV 89109 Office: 830 E Sahara #3 Las Vegas NV 89104

JOHNSON, DALE SPRINGER, financial executive; b. Westport, Tenn., Dec. 28, 1932; s. Joseph B. and Thelma S. (Springer) J.; m. Diane E. Wagner, Aug. 7, 1961 (div. Mar. 1972); children: Carlyle, Kelmie, Rachele; m. Patricia A. Beck, Aug. 25, 1984. BA, Rhodes Coll., Memphis, 1955; postgrad., U. Strasbourg, France, 1956-57; MA, Tulane U., 1959; PhD, U. Mich., 1968. Cert. fin. planner. Lectr. Lycée Bartholdi Colmar, France, 1956-57; instr. Park Coll., Parkville, Mo., 1960-62; asst. prof. Centenary Coll., Shreveport, La., 1962-65; instr., lectr. U. Mich., Ann Arbor, 1966-68; asst. prof. U. Colo., Boulder, 1968-75; account exec. Merrill Lynch Pierce Fenner and Smith, Albuquerque, 1976-78; dean Coll. for Fin. Planning, Denver, 1979-80; asst. prof. Am. Coll., Bryn Mawr, Pa., 1981-84; pvt. practice fin. planning Villanova, Pa., 1984—; vis. exchange prof. Laval U., Quebec City, Que., Can., 1973-74; bd. dirs. PFM Investment Corp., Tampa, Fla.; cons. in field. Author: Managing The Computerized Financial Planning Practice, 1989; co-author, editor Readings in Financial Services, 1982; co-author Financial Planning: Practice and Procedure, 1988; author handbook; contbr. articles to profl. jours. Danforth Found. fellow, 1965. Mem. Internat. Assn. Fin. Planning, Assn. Fin. Counseling and Planning Edn. (bd. dirs. 1984-87), Inst. Cert. Fin. Planners, Phi Kappa Phi. Episcopalian. Home and Office: 105 Radnor Ave Villanova PA 19085

JOHNSON, DAVID EARL, agri-business executive; b. Minn., Jan. 26, 1937; m. Patricia L., Sept. 6, 1958; children—Darren, Denise, Dodd, Dana. B.S., U. Minn., 1959. Salesman Cenex, St. Paul, 1959-65; salesman Monsanto Co., St. Louis, 1965-66; mgr. plant food dept. Cenex, St. Paul, 1966-72, v.p. agri-products, 1972-81, sr. v.p. ops., 1981—; pres. Cenex/Land O'Lakes Agronomy Co., St. Paul, 1987—; vice chmn. Minn. Agri-Growth Council, Bloomington, 1972—; chmn. bd. Universal Coops., Bloomington, 1981—; vice chmn. bd. C.F. Industries, Long Grove, Ill., 1981—. Bd. dirs. St. Paul Area YMCA. Recipient Disting. Achievement award U. Minn., 1983. Lutheran. Home: 2280 Ocala Ct Mendota Heights MN 55120 Office: Cenex/Land O'Lakes Agrl Svcs 5500 Cenex Dr Inver Grove Heights MN 55075

JOHNSON, DAVID GALE, economist, educator; b. Vinton, Iowa, July 10, 1916; s. Albert D. and Myra Jane (Reed) J.; m. Helen Wallace, Aug. 10, 1938; children: David Wallace, Kay Ann. BS, Iowa State Coll., 1938, PhD, 1945; MS, U. Wis., 1939; student, U. Chgo., 1939-41. Research assoc. Iowa State Coll., 1941-42, asst. prof. econs., 1942-44; with dept. econs. U. Chgo., 1944—, beginning as research assoc., successively asst. prof., assoc. prof., 1944-54, prof., 1954—, now emeritus prof., assoc. dean div. social scis., 1957-60, dean, 1960-70, chmn. dept. econs., 1971-75, 80-84, acting dir. library, 1971-72, dir. Office Econ. Analysis, 1975-80, v.p., dean of faculties, 1975, provost, 1976-80; economist OPA, 1942, Dept. State, 1946, Dept. Army, 1948; mem. food adv. com. Office of Tech. Assessment, U.S. Congress, 1974-76; cons. TVA and Rand Corp., AID, 1962-68; pres. Nat. Opinion Research Center, 1962-75, 79-85; agrl. adviser Office of Pres.'s Spl. Rep. for Trade Negotiations, 1963-64; mem. Pres.'s Nat. Adv. Commn. on Food and Fiber, 1965-67; adv. bd. Policy Planning Council State Dept., 1967-69, Nat. Commn. on Population Growth and the Am. Future, 1970-72; mem. steering com. Pres.'s Food and Nutrition Study, Nat. Acad. Scis., 1975-77; chmn. bd. dirs. Univ. Savs. and Loan Assn., 1986-88, chmn. exec. com., 1988—; co-chmn. working group on population growth and econ. devel. Nat. Acad. Scis., 1984-86. Author: Forward Prices for Agriculture, 1947, Agriculture and Trade: A Study of Inconsistent Policies, 1950, (with Robert Gustafson) Grain Yields and the American Food Supply, 1962, The Struggle Against World Hunger, 1967, World Agriculture in Disarray, 1973, World Food Problems and Prospects, 1975, (with Karen Brooks) Prospects for Soviet Agriculture in the 1980's, 1983. Bd. dirs. Wm. Benton Found., 1980—; pres. S.E. Chgo. Commn., 1980—. Fellow Am. Acad. Arts and Scis.; mem. Social Sci. Research Council (dir. 1953-56), Am. Econ. Assn., Am. Farm Econ. Assn. (pres. 1964-65), Phi Kappa Phi, Alpha Zeta. Home: 5617 S Kenwood Ave Chicago IL 60637 Office: U Chgo Dept Econs 1126 E 59th St Chicago IL 60637

JOHNSON, DEANE FRANK, communications company executive; b. Des Moines, Sept. 2, 1918; s. Frank Joseph and Alma Odessa J.; m. Anne McDonnell, Nov. 9, 1968; 1 son, Deane Frank. A.B., Stanford, 1939, J.D., 1942. Bar: bar. Mem. firm O'Melveny & Myers, 1942-49, partner, 1949-81, mng. partner, 1977-81; pres. Warner Communications, Inc., N.Y.C., from 1980, now mem., office of the pres.; also dir. Warner Communications, Inc. Trustee Am. Film Inst., Calif. Inst. Tech. Mem. Am. Bar Assn., Order Coif. Episcopalian. Clubs: Los Angeles Country (Los Angeles), Calif. (Los Angeles); The Links (N.Y.C.); Nat. Golf Links (Southampton, L.I.); Lyford Cay (Bahamas); Mt. Kenya Safari. Office: Warner Communications Inc 75 Rockefeller Pla New York NY 10019 *

JOHNSON, DOUGLAS VERNON, manufacturing executive; b. David City, Nebr., Sept. 4, 1944; s. C. Vernon and Renata Marie (Schroeder) J.; m.

Glenna Kay Whetstine, July 9, 1966; children: Shale Kaye, Shaun Douglas. AA, BBA, U. Iowa, 1966, postgrad., 1968; postgrad., U. Akron, 1970. Foremen Kelly Springfield Tire Co., Freeport, Ill., 1967-76; v.p. engring. Welles Products Co., Roscoe, Ill., 1985-86; chief engring., gen. mgr. Ronalco, Inc., Louisville, 1986-87; pres., chief exec. officer Electrologic Inc., Prospect, Ky., 1987—. Designer vaccuum seals Voyager Space Craft, 1965, space frame INGUN V Space Craft, 1966. Lt. USAF, 1962-66. Named to Winners Circle Litchfield Com., 1972; recipient Pres. award Belvedere Co. Exec. Bd., 1981. Mem. Planetary Soc., Soc. Automotive Engrs. Lutheran. Home: 13006 Tattersall Ln Prospect KY 40059 Office: Electrologic Inc PO Box 787 Prospect KY 40059

JOHNSON, EARL DALLAM, aviation and financial consultant; b. Hamilton, Ohio, Dec. 14, 1905; s. Sidney Cornelius and Marion Esley (Felton) J.; B.A., U. Wis., 1928; grad. Randolph and Kelley Fields, 1931; m. Mytle O. Vietmeyer, Nov. 3, 1932; children—Raud Earl, Susan Lynne, Cynthia Lee. Vice pres., dir. Loom- Sayles & Co., Boston, 1947-50; ; asst. sec. army Dept. Army, Washington, 1950-51, undersec. army, 1952-54, also chmn. bd. Panama Canal, 1952-54, pres. Air Transport Assn. and Air Cargo Inc., Washington, 1954-55; sr. v.p., exec. v.p., pres., vice chmn. bd. Gen. Dynamics Co., N.Y.C., 1955-63; exec. v.p. Delta Airlines, Atlanta, 1963-64; cons. aviation, Greenwich, Conn., 1964—; dir. numerous corps., including Gen. Dynamics, Damson Oil, Menasco Mfg. Co. Ltd.; lectr. in field; Def. Dept. sr. ofcl. on Japanese Peace Treaty. Trustee Air Acad. Found., Colorado Springs, Bataan Meml. Hosp., Albuquerque, Lovelace Med. Found., Albuquerque; past pres. Wings Club, N.Y.C.; past gov. Union League Club, N.Y.C. Served to col. AC, U.S. Army, 1931-33, 1941-45. Mem. Navy League (life), Nat. Security Indsl. Assn., Nat. Transp. Assn., Air Force Assn., Phi Beta Kappa, Pi Kappa Alpha. Clubs: Greenwich Country; Rolling Rock (Ligonier, Pa.); Explorers (N.Y.C.); Club Limited. Home: 36 W Brother Dr Greenwich CT 06830

JOHNSON, EDWARD ALDEN, dean of college; b. Palmerton, Pa., May 11, 1937; s. John Alden and Mary (Ronemus) J.; m. Beryl Ann Benschop, June 26, 1966; 1 child, Edward Blaine. BA in Psychology, Antioch Coll., 1960; M of Indsl. Relations, Cornell U., 1962; PhD in Mgmt., Mich. State U., 1968. From asst. to assoc. prof. W.Va. U., Morgantown, 1966-72; dean Coll. of Bus. Rochester (N.Y.) Inst. Tech., 1972-79, M.J. Neeley Sch. Bus. Tex. Christian U., Ft. Worth, 1979-86, Coll. Bus. and Adminstrn. U. Colo., Boulder, 1986—; Bd. dirs. Residential Mortgage Investments, Ft. Worth, Colo. Council Econ. Edn., Denver. Contbr. articles to profl. jours. Mem. human resources and personnel task force Commn. on Govt. Productivity, Denver, 1988—; chmn., bd. dirs. Blue Cross of Rochester area, 1976-78. Mem. Fin. Execs. Inst., Rotary, Golden Key Soc., Beta Gamma Sigma, Phi Kappa Phi, Delta Sigma Pi. Republican. Methodist. Home: 543 Linden Park Dr Boulder CO 80302 Office: U Colo Coll Bus Adminstrn Campus Box 419 Boulder CO 80309-0419

JOHNSON, EDWARD CROSBY, III, financial company executive; b. Boston, June 29, 1930; s. Edward Crosby and Elsie (Livingston) J.; m. Elizabeth Bishop Hodges, Oct. 8, 1960; children: Abigail Pierrepont Johnson, Elizabeth Livingston, Edward Crosby. A.B., Harvard U., 1954. With Fidelity Mgmt. & Research Co., Boston, 1957—, pres., chief exec. officer, 1972-77; chmn. bd., chief exec. officer parent co. FMR Corp., 1977—. Mem. coun. Mass. Hist. Soc., 1971-78, 87, Essex Inst., 1967-78. Served with AUS, 1954-56. Mem. Am. Acad. Arts and Scis., Fin. Analysts Fedn. Office: Fidelity Investments 82 Devonshire St Boston MA 02109

JOHNSON, EDWARD FULLER, investment banker, consultant; b. Princeton, N.J., Sept. 14, 1921; s. Rankin and Kate Gilbert (Fuller) J.; m. Joan Van Alstyne, Apr. 1, 1950; children: Susan, Keats, Kate, Kimball, David, Edward; m. 2d, Zoé Van Antwerp Wells, June 10, 1988. ME, Cornell U., 1946. With J.G. White Constrn. Co., Venezuela, 1947-48, George S. Armstrong, Mgmt. Cons. Engrs., N.Y.C., 1948-50; ptnr. Van Alstyne Noel Co., N.Y.C., 1952-61; dir. Johnson Redbook Service, Prescott, Ball & Turben, N.Y.C., 1970—; cons. to diversified industries; mem. polymers panel Nat. Acad. Scis., 1980-82. Chmn. No. Valley Red Cross Fund Drive, Englewood, N.J., 1964-65; councilman, Englewood, 1967-70; chmn. bd. dirs. Englewood Community Chest, 1976-78. Served to capt. USAF, WWII and Korea. Decorated Air medal with 2 oak leaf clusters. Mem. N.Y. Analysts Soc., Apparel and Textile Analysts Group (pres. 1987-88), Chem. Analysts Group, Merchandising Analyst Group (pres. 1986-87), Home Furnishing Analysts Group. Republican. Presbyterian. Clubs: Englewood Field; Bayhead (N.J.) Yacht; Mantoloking (N.J) Yacht; Bond, Cornell. Home: 821 East Ave Bayhead NJ 07631 Office: One World Trade Ctr 56th Floor New York NY 10048

JOHNSON, ELLEN CHRISTINE, marketing executive; b. St. Paul, Mar. 10, 1948; d. Arnold Elwood and Betty Jane (Bruening) Damsgaard; m. Neal Frank Johnson, June 21, 1969; 1 child, April Holly. BA in Advt., U. Minn., 1971; MBA, Coll. St. Thomas, 1985. Dir. pub. rels. Children's Home Soc. Minn., St. Paul, 1971-73, asst. dir. devel., 1973-78; coord. pub. rels. Minn. Hosp. Assn., Mpls., 1978-80; dir. mktg., pub. rel. Unity Med. Ctr., Mpls., 1980-83; exec. dir. Unity Health Found., Mpls., 1983-85; mgr. mktg. product Health One Corp., Mpls., 1985-87; pres., chief exec. officer Notch/Bradley of Minn., Inc., Mpls., 1987—. Contbg. author: Fifty Effective Print Ads for Hospitals, 1986, Profiles in Hospital Marketing, 1984; editor (newsletter) Women in Sr. Mgmt., 1987. Recipient Mpls. YWCA Leadership award, 1985, MacEachern citation Acad. Hosp. Pub. Rels., 1979. Fellow Am. Soc. for Hosp. Mktg. and Pub. Rels. (pres. 1985); mem. Pub. Rels. Soc. Am. (accredited, pres. Minn. chpt. 1982, Silver Anvil award 1983), Minn. chpt. Am. Mktg. Assn. Presbyterian. Office: Notch/Bradley Minn Inc Ct Internat 238N 2550 University Ave W Saint Paul MN 55114

JOHNSON, ELLSWORTH LEVINE, business executive; b. Osakis, Minn., July 3, 1918; s. Bennett M. and Beatrice J. (Meinstead) J.; ed. U. Minn.; m. Lucille M. Hanson, Feb. 11, 1939; children—Beverly L. Anderson, Robert E., Joan I. Berthiaume, Barbara L. Mace, Nancy S. Johnson Nelson, Jennifer A. Store mgr., zone supt., then asst. v.p. franchise stores Gamble Skogmo, Inc., Mpls., 1939-59; dir. sales and public relations Apache Corp., Mpls., 1959-60; exec. v.p. Western Devel. Corp., Mpls., 1960-67; v.p. Federal's Inc., Detroit, 1967-69; pres., dir. Rembrandt Enterprises, Inc., Mpls., 1970-74; chmn., chief exec. officer, dir. Wickes Cos., Inc., 1980. First Am. Cos., 1974—. Founder, chmn., pres. Boys & Girls Club Found. Mpls, 1984—; chmn., Minn. Devel. Com., 1957-58. Mem. Minn. Gov.'s Adv. Commn. to Dept. Bus. Devel., 1958-62; pres., dir. Community Centers, Inc., 1960-67; adviser SBA, Washington, 1970-76; chmn bd. dirs. Boy's Clubs of Mpls., 1983—. Recipient Order of North Star, State of Minn., 1958; Outstanding Citizen award Mpls. 1959; Community Chest award, 1957; Nat. Gold Key award Minn. Jaycees, 1956; Golden Boy award Boys' Clubs Mpls., 1964; Bicentennial certificate SBA, 1976; named commodore Mpls. Aquacentennial, 1958. Mem. Am. Legion. Lutheran. Clubs: InterInterlaken Country, Masons, Shriners, Mpls. Home: 6304 Westwood Ct Edina MN 55436 Office: First Am Cos Southdale Pl Bldg 3400 W66 Edina MN 55435

JOHNSON, EUGENE MANFRED, marketing educator; b. Milford, Del., Oct. 21, 1940; s. Willis Moore and Elizabeth (Duling) J.; m. Carolyn Passwaters, July 7, 1962; children: Laura, Greta. BS, U. Del., Newark, 1962; MBA, U. Del., 1964; DBA, Wash. U., 1969. Asst. prof. U. Del., Newark, 1968-71; assoc. dean U. R.I., Kingston, 1971-76, acting dean, 1976-77, assoc. dean, 1977-79, prof. mktg., 1979—; cons. R.I. Hosp. Trust Nat. Bank, Providence, 1979-80; v.p. mktg. DVC Ind., Bay Shore, N.Y., 1984. Author: Sales Management, 1986, Profitable Service Marketing, 1986, Managing Your Sales Team, 1986, Successful Marketing for Service Organizations, 1986. Mem. Am. Mktg. Assn., AAUP. Mem. United Ch. of Christ. Lodge: Lions (pres. 1985). Home: 877 Saugatucket Rd Wakefield RI 02879 Office: Univ RI Dept Mktg Kingston RI 02881

JOHNSON, F. ROSS, former food products and tobacco company executive; b. Winnipeg, Man., Can., Dec. 13, 1931; s. Frederick Hamilton and Caroline (Green) J.; m. Laurie Ann Graumann; children: Bruce, Neil. B-Comm, U. Man., 1952; MBA, U. Toronto, Ont., Can., 1956; LLD (hon.), St. Francis Xavier U., Antigonish, 1978, Meml. U. Nfld., 1980. Tchr. U. Toronto, 1962-64; dir. mktg. CGE, Toronto, 1964-66; mgr. mdse. T. Eaton Co., 1966-67; exec. v.p. GSW Ltd., 1967-71; pres. Standard Brands Ltd., Toronto, 1971, pres., chief exec. officer, 1972; v.p. Standard Brands, Inc., N.Y.C., 1973, sr. v.p., dir., 1974, pres., 1975-81, chief exec. officer, 1976-81, chmn., 1977-81, chmn., chief operating officer, 1981; pres., chief operating officer Nabisco Brands, Inc. (formerly Standard Brands, Inc. and Nabisco, Inc.), Parsippany, N.J., 1984-85, vice chmn., 1985-86; pres. R.J. Reynolds Industries Inc. (known as RJR Nabisco, Inc. as of 1986), Winston-Salem, N.C., 1985-89, chief operating officer, 1985-87; chief exec. officer RJR Nabisco, Inc., Winston-Salem, N.C., 1987-89; dir. Wosk's Ltd., Vancouver, Bank of N.S., Toronto. Mem. adv. council Columbia U. Bus. Sch., N.Y.C.; chmn. bd. N.Y.C. chpt. Nat. Multiple Sclerosis Soc., 1980—. Served to lt., Ordance Corps Royal Can. Army. Mem. Grocery Mfrs. Assn. (dir.), Young Pres.'s Orgn., Phi Delta Theta (pres. 1951). Clubs: Mt. Bruno Country; Brook (N.Y.C.), The Links (N.Y.C.), Blind Brook (N.Y.C.), Econ. (N.Y.C.); Conn. Golf (Easton). Office: RJR Nabisco Inc 1100 Reynolds Blvd RJR World Hdqrs Bldg Winston-Salem NC 27105 *

JOHNSON, FRANK STANLEY, JR., government official; b. N.Y.C., Dec. 24, 1930; s. Frank Stanley and Alice Claire (Stern) J.; m. Lavern Schlemeyer, Aug. 19, 1978; children: Kenneth F. (dec.), Scott D.; stepdaughter: Lisa Lam. B.S. in Mktg. with honors, Ind. U., Bloomington, 1955. Reporter, then edn. editor Newsday, Garden City, N.Y., 1955-59; asst. to pres. Daniel & Florence Guggenheim Found. and Solomon R. Guggenheim Found., N.Y.C., 1959-61; asst. dir., then dir. info. Sci. Research Assos., Inc. (subs. IBM), Chgo., 1962-66; asst. to pres., dir. public affairs Rodman Job Corps Tng. Center (subs. IBM), New Bedford, Mass., 1966-68; mgr. communications IBM Corp., Endicott, N.Y., 1968-69; v.p. Chgo. Bd. Trade, 1969-72; dir. public affairs U.S. Dept. Labor, Washington, 1972-73; dir. public affairs and advt. Gen. Dynamics, Inc., St. Louis, 1974-78; v.p. public affairs Revlon, Inc.; also pres. Revlon Found., Inc., N.Y.C., 1978-81; pres. Frank Johnson & Assocs. Ltd., 1981—; v.p. Newport News Shipbldg. & Dry Dock Co. (Va.), 1981-83; dir. pub. affairs NASA, asst. assoc. adminstr. external relations, 1983-86; asst. postmaster gen. U.S. Postal Service, 1986—; founder, 1st chmn. Internat. Grad. Achievement, Inc., 1960-63. Bd. dirs. Susquenango County (N.Y.) council Boy Scouts Am., 1968-69, St. Louis chpt. Nat. Multiple Sclerosis Soc., 1974-78, Acting Co., Inc., N.Y., 1980—82, Goodwill Industries Am., Washington, 1982-88 , Va. Opera Assn., Norfolk, 1982-84; adv. bd. Adelphi Coll., Garden City, N.Y., 1957-59, trustee Manhattanville Coll., 1982-88; adv. bd. European Pub. Relations Roundtable, 1978-82. Served with USMC, 1950-53. Recipient Golden Trumpet award Publicity Club Chgo., 1969, Outstanding Shareholder Communications award Nat. Security Traders Assn., 1969; Best in Industry award Fin. World mag., 1975, 76, 2d best, 1962. Mem. Pub. Relations Soc. Am. Clubs: Capitol Hill, Nat. Press (Washington); Overseas Press Am. (N.Y.C.), Wings (N.Y.C.). Home: 6639 Madison-McLean Dr McLean VA 22101-2902 Office: US Postal Svc 475 L'Enfant Pla SW Washington DC 20260-3100

JOHNSON, FRANK WILLIAM, marketing professional; b. Sumter, S.C., Sept. 20, 1948; s. John William and Dorothy (Ferrigan) J.; m. Sally Gattshall, Nov. 25, 1970; children: Lauren Elizabeth, Mark William. BA in Polit. Sci., The Citadel, 1970; MS in Ops. Mgmt., U. Ark., 1976. Sales rep. Union Carbide Corp., Dallas, 1976-78; product mgr. Union Carbide Corp., N.Y.C., 1979-82; sales mgr. Steelcase Inc., Dallas, 1982-83; dir. mktg. VECTA div. Steelcase Inc., Dallas, 1984-86; dir. sales and mktg. Lista Internat., Dallas, 1986-87, Kewaunee Sci. Corp., Lockhart, Tex., 1987—. Served to capt. USAF, 1970-76. Mem. Sales and Mktg. Club. Republican. Presbyterian. Lodge: Shriners. Home: 6407 Indian Canyon Dr Austin TX 78746 Office: Kewaunee Sci 901 FM 20 Lockhart TX 78644

JOHNSON, FREDERICK DEAN, former food company executive, consultant; b. Shreve, Ohio, Feb. 27, 1911; s. Harry H. and Grace Marcella (Cammarn) J.; A.B., Coll. Wooster (Ohio), 1935; m. Haulwen Elizabeth Richey, June 19, 1937; children—Frederick Dean II, Mary Haulwen, Grace Elizabeth. Dir. research Bama Co. (now Bama Products Borden Foods div. Borden Inc.), Birmingham, Ala., 1961-65, dir. research, Houston, 1965-76, dir. product devel. and tech. adviser, 1976-78, cons., 1978—; U.S. del. FAO/WHO Codex Alimentarius Commn. Processed Fruits and Vegetables, 1973, 74, 75. Bd. dirs. Afton Oaks Civic Club, 1967-70, 82—. Mem. Internat. Jelly and Preserve Assn. (chmn. quality control adv. com. 1969-73, chmn. standards com. 1973-76, citation and plaque 1974), Inst. Food Technologists (charter), Am. Chem. Soc. (past sec., chmn. Wooster sect.), AAAS. Republican (precinct chmn. 1981—). Presbyterian (ruling elder). Home: 4546 Shetland Ln Houston TX 77027

JOHNSON, GARY EVAN, engineer; b. Balt., July 3, 1936; s. Emil Leonard and Jesse Lillian (Reynolds) J.; m. Lillian Marie Chumley, Apr. 19, 1958; children: Linda Wright, Deborah Smith, Gary Jr., Gregory Evan. BS in Engring., John Hopkins U., 1970. Registered profl. engr., Md. Draftsman Henry Adams Inc., Balt., 1955-57, jr. engr., 1957-61, project engr., 1961-70, project mgr., 1970-85, v.p., 1985—. Chmn. com. Boy Scouts Am., Balt., 1972-81; pres. Harford Park Little League, Balt., 1975-76; bd. overseers Balt. Polytechnic, 1985. Mem. Balt. Polytechnic Inst. Alumni Assn. (pres. 1985-87), ASHRAE (pres. 1975-76), Soc. Mktg. Profl. Svcs. (dir. 1985-87), Am. Soc. Plumbing Engring., Engring. Soc. Balt., Am. Rose Soc. Republican. Roman Catholic. Home: 129 Sunnydale Way Reisterstown MD 21136 Office: Henry Adams Inc 600 Baltimore Ave Baltimore MD 21204

JOHNSON, GARY HAROLD, sales and marketing executive; b. Elk River, Minn., Aug. 31, 1943; s. Harold August Johnson and Bernice Elizabeth (Stevens) Johnson Lavin; m. Sara Kathryn Wildman, Feb. 27, 1982; 1 child, Charles Bryant. BA, U. Minn., 1969. Nat. sales mgr. Snow Sports Publs., Mpls., 1970-74; dist. mgr. Kawasaki Motors USA, Mpls., 1974-78; regional mgr. Kawasaki Motors USA, Arlington, Tex., 1978-82; v.p. sales Kawasaki Motors USA, Irvine, Calif., 1982—. Host Inter Study program, San Francisco, 1988; mem. presdl. task force Rep. Com., 1982-86. With USMC, 1962-66. Mem. Internat. Jet Ski Boating Assn. (sec.-treas. 1985-89), Toastmasters (pres. 1986-87, Spirit of Merit award 1987). Office: Kawasaki Motors USA 9950 Jeronimo St Santa Ana CA 92718

JOHNSON, GARY KENT, management education company executive; b. Provo, Utah, Apr. 16, 1936; s. Clyde LeRoy and Ruth Laie (Taylor) J.; m. Mary Joyce Crowther, Aug. 26, 1955; children—Mary Ann Johnson Harvey, Gary Kent, Brent James, Jeremy Clyde. Student Brigham Young U., 1954-55, U. Utah, 1955-58, 60-61, U. Calif.-Berkeley, 1962. Sales rep. Roche Labs., Salt Lake City, 1958-61, sales trainer, Denver, 1962, sales trainer, Oakland, Calif., 1962, div. mgr., Seattle, 1962-69; sec.-treas. Western Mgmt. Inst., Seattle, 1969-71; pres. WMI Corp., Bellevue, Wash., 1971—, Provisor Corp., 1983-86; speaker, cons. various nat. orgns. Bd. dirs. Big Bros.; del. King County Republican Com. Served with U.S. N.G., 1953-61. Walgreen scholar, 1955-58; Bristol scholar, 1958. Mem. Am. Soc. Tng. and Devel., Internat. Platform Assn., Phi Sigma Epsilon. Mormon. Club: Bellevue Athletic. Author: Select the Best, 1976; Antitrust Untangled, 1977; The Utilities Management Series, 1979; Performance Appraisal, A Program for Improving Productivity, 1981. Office: WMI Corp 1309 114th Ave SE Ste 212 Bellevue WA 98004

JOHNSON, GENE EDWARD, financial planner; b. Melvern, Ark., Jan. 25, 1953; s. Eugene and Mary (Nelson) J.; m. Julia Mae Mitchell, Oct. 3, 1973; children: Marquis, Monique. AA, Menlo Coll., 1973; BS, U. Santa Clara, 1976. Salesman Met. Ins., Cupertino, Calif., 1976-79; asst. controller Allstate Ins., Menlo Park, Calif., 1979-82; mgr. Variable Annuity Life An Am. Gen. Co., Houston, 1982-84; asst. v.p., asst. controller Variable Annuity Life, Houston, 1984-86, 2d v.p., 1985—; instr. Main Event Mgmt. Corp., Houston, 1986—. Inst. In Roads/Houston, Inc., 1986; ofcl. Southwest Basketball Ofcls. Assn., Houston, 1982—. Named a Jr. Coll All-Am., UPI Sportswriters, 1973, One of Outstanding Young Men of Am., 1985; recipient Community Service award United Way, 1984. Mem. Internat. Assn. Fin. Planners, Internat. Soc. Planning and Strategy, Survey Fin. Profls. (panel mem. 1982—). Democrat. Roman Catholic. Lodge: Kiwanis (founder, pres. Met. Houston club 1985-87). Office: Variable Annuity Life Ins Co 2929 Allen Pkwy Houston TX 77019

JOHNSON, GERARD G., apparel company executive; b. Evanston, Ill., Feb. 13, 1941; s. Gerard Burkhardt and Alice (Griffin) J.; m. Jean Hill, Aug. 16, 1967; children—Matthew, Sarah, Christopher. S.B., U.S. Naval Acad., Annapolis, 1963; M.B.A., Harvard U., Boston, 1969, D.B.A., 1972. Asst. prof., instr. Harvard Bus. Sch., Boston, 1969-75; dir. indsl. engring. Electric Boat-Gen. Dynamics, Groton, Conn., 1975-77; cons. self-employed, Old Saybrook, Conn., 1977-78; asst. treas. The Continental Group Inc., Stamford, Conn., 1978-82; v.p., treas. Gen. Instrument Corp., N.Y.C., 1982-85, v.p. fin., chief fin. officer, 1985-88; v.p. fin., chief fin. officer VF Corp., Wyomissing, Pa., 1988—; instr. Internat. Tchrs. Program, Fountainbleau, France, 1973. Creative cons. annual editions Readings in Business, 1973-74. Vice pres. Liberty Corner Assn., N.J., 1984-85. Served to lt. USN, 1963-67. Baker scholar Harvard Bus. Sch., 1969. Mem. Century Club (Harvard Bus. Sch.), Fin. Execs. Inst. Roman Catholic. Office: VF Corp 1047 N Park Rd Wyomissing PA 19610

JOHNSON, GRANT LESTER, lawyer, manufacturing company executive; b. Virginia, Minn., Aug. 16, 1929; s. Ernest and Anna Elizabeth (Nordstrom) J.; m. Esther Linnea Nystrom, June 16, 1956, (dec. July 1985); children—Karen Elisabeth, Elise Ann. A.B., Cornell U., 1951; LL.B., Harvard, 1957. Bar: Ohio 1958, Ill. 1972. Asso. Squire, Sanders & Dempsey, Cleve., 1957-58; atty. Pickands Mather & Co., Cleve., 1958-71, assoc. gen. counsel, 1967, gen. counsel, 1968-71, sec., 1969-71; corporate counsel Interlake, Inc., Chgo., 1971-73, v.p. law, 1974-78, v.p. law and adminstrn., 1978-84, sr. v.p., gen. counsel, 1984-86; sr. v.p., gen. counsel The InterLake Corp., 1986—. Served to lt. (j.g.) USN, 1951-54. Home: G-205 4 Oak Brook Club Dr Oak Brook IL 60521 Office: Interlake Corp 701 Harger Rd Oak Brook IL 60521

JOHNSON, H. ARVID, lawyer; b. Chgo., Aug. 21, 1936; s. Harold A. and Agnes B. (Lorenzen) J.; m. Janice Meeg Alison, Oct. 15, 1982; children: Susan Joy, Steven Lee. B.A., Northwestern U., 1958, J.D., 1961. Bar: Ill. 1961, U.S. Dist. Ct. (no. dist.) Ill. 1961, U.S. Ct. Mil. Appeals 1962, U.S. Supreme Ct. 1963, U.S. Ct. Appeals (7th cir.) 1965, Va. 1988. Atty. Ross, Hardies & O'Keefe, Chgo., 1961-67; assoc. gen. counsel R.R. Donnelley & Sons, Chgo., 1967-71; gen. counsel, sec. Stanray Corp., Chgo., 1971-73; sr. v.p., gen. counsel Container Corp. Am., Chgo., 1973-86; sr. v.p., gen. counsel, corp. sec. A.H. Robins Co., Inc., Richmond, Va., 1986-88; sr. v.p., gen. counsel Am. Nat. Can Co., Chgo., 1988—; bd. dirs. T.R. Miller Mill Co., Brewton, Ala., 1974-84, Pioneer Paper Stock Co., Chgo., 1974-86, Calif. Paper Corp., 1974-86; bd. dirs. Ctr. Pub. Resources, 1982—. Contbr. articles to profl. jours. Capt. USAF, 1962-65. Northwestern U. scholar, 1956-58, 58-61; recipient Am. Jurisprudence award, 1960. Mem. ABA, Ill. Bar Assn., Va. Bar Assn., Chgo. Bar Assn., Am. Soc. Corp. Secs., Assn. Corp. Counsel, Northwestern U. Sch. Law Alumni Assn. (bd. dirs. 1984—). Republican. Presbyterian. Clubs: Law, Legal, Mid-Day, University (Chgo.). Home: 1345 Deerpath Rd Lake Forest IL 60045 Office: 8770 W Bryn Mawr Chicago IL 60631

JOHNSON, HAROLD EARL, personnel executive; b. Lincoln, Nebr., July 11, 1939; s. Earl W. and Evelyn Jean (Sipp) J.; m. Carol Louise Schmidt, Aug. 17, 1971; children—Andrew Brian, Daniel Earl. B.S., U. Nebr., 1961. From indsl. relations trainee to mgr. profl. employment Am. Can Co., 1961-68; dir. recruitment/devel. metal mining div. Kennecott Copper Corp., 1968-73; v.p. personnel Am. Medicorp Inc., 1973-75; v.p. employee relations. devel., then sr. v.p. employee relations and corp. adminstrn. INA Corp., 1975-79; sr. v.p. human resources Federated Dept. Stores, Inc., Cin., 1979-85; sr. v.p. corp. personnel and adminstrn. The Travelers Cos., Hartford, Conn., 1985—; mem. exec. com. Hartford Whalers Hockey Club. Bd. dirs. Hartford Inst. Social Justice. Mem. Am. Mgmt. Assn., Conf. Board, Human Resources Roundtable, Bus. Roundtable (employee relations com.). Republican. Presbyterian. Clubs: University (N.Y.C.); Kenwood Country Cin.); Hartford Golf (West Hartford, Conn.), Hartford, N.Y. Athletic. Office: The Travelers Corp 1 Tower Sq #30CR Hartford CT 06183

JOHNSON, HENRY ARNA, mail order company executive; b. Chgo., Mar. 26, 1919; s. John J. and Sigrid (Jorgensen) J.; m. Darlene H. Green, Oct. 11, 1973; children: Nancy, Martin, Roy; step-children: Pamela, James, Kristine. Student, Northwestern U., 1940-43; MBA, U. Chgo., 1964. With mdse. div. Montgomery Ward & Co., Chgo., 1939-49; exec. v.p. Aldens Inc., Chgo., 1949-74; pres. Family Fashions by Avon, Hampton, Va., 1974-76; pres. Spiegel, Inc., Oak Brook, Ill., 1976-85, chief exec. officer, 1976-85, vice chmn., 1985-88. Mem. nat. exec. bd. Boy Scouts Am., pres. Area 3 region Boy Scouts Am., pres. Chgo. Area council, 1980-81. Served with USAF, 1943-45. Decorated Air medal; recipient Disting. Citizens award, 1982, Horatio Alger award, 1985. Mem. Direct Mail Mktg. Assn. (dir.), Am. Retail Fedn. (dir.), Nat. Retail Merchants Assn. Clubs: Butterfield Country, Mid-Am., Chgo. Yacht. Office: Spiegel Inc 1515 W 22d St Oak Brook IL 60522

JOHNSON, HORACE RICHARD, electronics company executive; b. Jersey City, Apr. 26, 1926; s. Horace Adam and Grace (Lower) J.; m. Mary Louise Kleckner, July 29, 1950; children: Lucinda Louise, Karen Ann, Richard Adam, Russell Kleckner, David Thorp. B.E.E. with distinction, Cornell U., 1946, postgrad., 1947; Ph.D. in Physics, M.I.T., 1952. Mem. tech. staff Hughes Aircraft Co., 1952-57; co-founder Watkins-Johnson Co., Palo Alto, Calif., 1958; pres. Watkins-Johnson Co., 1967-87, vice chmn. bd. dirs., 1988—; lectr. engring. UCLA, 1956-57, Stanford U., 1958-68; chmn. Los Angeles Profl. Group on Electron Devices, 1955-56; dir. WEMA, 1971-72, Vols. Internat. Tech. Assistance, 1971-73. Patentee in field; contbr. articles to profl. jours. Pres. Stanford Area council Boy Scouts Am., 1968-70, bd. mem., 1967-77; campaign chmn. Palo Alto-Stanford chpt. United Fund, 1967. Served with USNR, 1943-46. Research Lab. for Electronics fellow, 1947-51. Fellow IEEE; mem. Nat. Acad. Engring., NAM (dir. 1983—), Am. Phys. Soc., Newcomen Soc. N.Am., Sigma Xi, Eta Kappa Nu, Tau Beta Pi, Phi Kappa Phi, Gamma Alpha. Club: Commonwealth of Calif. Office: Watkins-Johnson Co 3333 Hillview Ave Palo Alto CA 94304

JOHNSON, J. MITCHELL, communications executive; b. Dallas, May 12, 1951; s. J. Edward and Blanche (Dabney) J.; m. Kira Alexandrine Harris; 1 child, Philip Louis. BS, U. Tex.; MS, U. So. Calif. Prodn. asst. Guggenheim Prodns., Washington, 1975-77; pres. Fort Worth Prodns., 1977—; producer, chief exec. officer TravelWorld Video, Ft. Worth, 1986—; mng. ptnr., bd. dirs. Frontier Broadcasting, Ft. Worth, 1985—. Producer, dir. TV films including Gymnast, Pub. Broadcasting System, 1980 (JQ award 1981), Artist and Athlete, ABC, 1980; producer TV films Moses Pendleton Presents Moses Pendleton, ABC, 1983 (1st place award San Francisco Film Festival 1984), Mondale for America, 1984. Exec. producer Mondale for Am.-Cons. '84, Washington, 1984; pres. Southwest Pub. Communications, Ft. Worth, 1985-86; chmn. media panel Tex. Commn. for Arts and Humanities, Austin, 1986. Recipient Gold award N.Y. TV Film Festival, 1981, Golden Eagle award Council on Internat. Nontheatrical Events, Washington, 1983, Best Documentary and Film awards N.Mex. Film Festival, Albuquerque, 1984, Best Documentary award USA Film Festival, Dallas, 1984. Mem. Internat. Music Ctr. (pres. 1987-88), Motion Picture Producers Tex. (pres. 1987-88). Democrat. Methodist. Club: Ft. Worth. Office: J Mitchell Johnson Prodns Inc 1423 W Terrell Fort Worth TX 76104

JOHNSON, J. WAYNE, truck leasing company executive; b. Greensboro, N.C., Jan. 24, 1941; s. J.P. and Bertha A. (May) J.; m. Shirley Anderson, Oct. 9, 1965; 1 child, Jennifer Marie. BBA in Acctg., Pace U. With Price Waterhouse & Co., N.Y.C., 1969-72; mgr. NBC div. RCA, N.Y.C., 1972-74; dir. Ryder Truck Rental, Inc. div. Ryder System, Inc., Miami, Fla., 1974-77; asst. treas. Ryder System, Inc., 1977-80; v.p., controller Ryder Truck Rental, Inc., 1980—; instr. bus., colls. Bd. dirs., pres. Jr. Achievement Greater Miami, Inc. Office: Ryder Truck Rental Inc 3600 NW 82nd Ave PO Box 020816 Miami FL 33102

JOHNSON, JACKSON MELVIN, computer company executive; b. Bemidji, Minn., Oct. 23, 1940; s. Melvin Sigurd and Margaret Marie (Hendershot) J.; m. Karen F. Winegarten, Aug. 15, 1981; children: D. Scott, Kim, Julia M., Lisa, Cyndra E. BS in Bus. Adminstrn., Wright State U., 1978; BS, U.S. Naval Acad., 1965; AS in Bus. Adminstrn. with honors, Sinclair Coll., 1974. CPA, Ohio. Dir. mgmt. info. systems United Aircraft Products, Dayton, Ohio, 1969-70; fin. EDP sales mgr. NCR, Los Angeles, 1970-77; regional sales mgr. Calcomp/Sanders, Dayton, 1977-82; v.p. sales Universal Data, Inc., Dayton, 1982-87; sales mgr. Western Region, Lowry Computer Systems LaGuna Hills, Calif., 1987—; pres., chief exec. officer Jaxxon Industries, Irvine, 1988—; assoc. prof. EDP Sinclair Coll. Served with USMC, 1958-67. Mem. Data Processing Mgmt. Assn., NCR Speakers' Bur. Republican. Lutheran. Home: 19532 Misty Ridge Ln Trabuco Canyon CA 92679 Office: 130 Business Center Dr Irvine CA 92715

JOHNSON, JAMES ERLING, insurance executive; b. Waseca, Minn., May 19, 1942; s. Erling Olaf and Geneva Eleanor (Nyberg) J. BA cum laude, Carleton Coll., 1964; MS, U. Iowa, 1966. With Minn. Mut. Life Ins. Co., St. Paul, 1968—, 2d v.p., actuary, 1976-79, v.p., actuary, 1979—; pres., chief exec. officer Minn. Mut. Fire & Casualty, Minnetonka, 1984—, also bd. dirs.; pres., chief exec. officer Adjustable Life Ins. Co., St. Paul, 1988—, also bd. dirs. Mem. alumni bd. Carleton Coll., Northfield, Minn., 1988—, council, 1988—; campaign cabinet St. Paul United Way, 1988—; dir. Minn. Landmarks, 1988—. Served to sr. asst. health services officer Commd. Corps, USPHS, 1966-68. U. Iowa fellow, 1964-66. Fellow Soc. Actuaries; mem. Am. Acad. Actuaries, Phi Beta Kappa, Pi Mu Epsilon. Episcopalian. Clubs: St. Paul Athletic; Decathlon Athletic (Bloomington, Minn.); Twin Cities Actuarial (chmn. 1978-79). Home: 2367 Apache Ct Mendota Heights MN 55120 Office: Minn Mut Fire & Casualty Co 10225 Yellow Circle Dr Minnetonka MN 55343 also: Minn Mut Life 400 N Robert St Saint Paul MN 55101

JOHNSON, JAMES HAROLD, lawyer; b. Galesburg, Ill., May 3, 1944; s. Harold Frank and Marjorie Isabel (Liby) J.; m. Judith Eileen Moore, June 5, 1966; children: Todd James, Tiffany Nicole. BA, Colo. Coll., 1966; JD, U. Tex., 1969. Bar: N.Y. 1970, Colo. 1971, Tex. 1975. Assoc. Winthrop, Stimson, Putnam & Roberts, N.Y.C., 1969-70, Sherman & Howard, Denver, 1970-72; corp. counsel Tex. Instruments, Inc., Dallas, 1972-85; v.p., gen. counsel, sec. Am. Healthcare Mgmt., Dallas, 1985-86, Rep. Health Corp., Dallas, 1986—. Mem. ABA, Am. Soc. Corp. Secs., Am. Acad. Hosp. Attys., Dallas-Ft. Worth Metroplex Gen. Counsel Assn., Tex. Bar Assn., N.Y. State Bar Assn., Colo. Bar Assn. Republican. Methodist. Home: 2724 Dunwick Dr Plano TX 75023 Office: Republic Health Corp 15303 Dallas Pkwy Ste 1400 Dallas TX 75248

JOHNSON, JAMES LAWRENCE, telephone company executive; b. Vernon, Tex., Apr. 12, 1927; s. Samuel Lonzo and Adeline Mary (Donges) J.; m. Ruth Helen Zweig, Aug. 5, 1949; children: James Lawrence, Helayne, Barry, Todd. BBA in Acctg., Tex. Tech Coll., 1949. Acct. Whiteside Laundry, Lubbock, Tex., 1949; with Gen. Telephone Co. SW, San Angelo, Tex., 1949-59; asst. controller Gen. Telephone Co. SW, 1953-59, v.p., controller, treas., 1966-69; controller Gen. Telephone Co. Mich., Muskegon, 1959-63; asst. controller telephone ops., then chief acct. consol. ops. GTE Service Corp., N.Y.C., 1963-66; v.p., controller telephone ops. GTE Service Corp., 1969-74; v.p. revenue requirements Gen. Telephone & Electronics Corp., Stamford, Conn., 1974-76; pres. Gen. Telephone Co. Ill., Bloomington, 1976-81; also dir., also group v.p. Gen. Telephone Co. Ill. (No. region); pres. GTE telephone operating group Gen. Telephone & Electronics Corp., from 1981; sr. v.p. GTE Corp., until 1986; pres., chief operating officer, dir. GTE Corp., Stamford, Conn., 1986-88, chmn., chief exec. officer, 1988—; dir. First Fed. Savs. & Loan Assn., Bloomington.; Mem. adv. council Coll. Bus., Ill. State U., Normal. Trustee, adv. council Mennonite Hosp., Bloomington; bd. dirs. Bloomington Unlimited; mem. Wesleyan Assos., Ill. Wesleyan U., Bloomington. Served with USNR, 1945-47. Mem. Nat. Accts. Assn., Fin. Execs. Inst., Ill. Telephone Assn. (dir.), McLean County Assn. Commerce and Industry (dir.). Republican. Methodist. Clubs: Bloomington Country, Crestwicke Country (Bloomington); Woodway Country (Darien, Conn.). Lodge: Rotary. Office: GTE Corp 1 Stamford Forum Stamford CT 06904 *

JOHNSON, JAMES MACK, III, banker; b. Mobile Ala., Dec. 18, 1945; s. James Mack and Annie Mae (Edmonson) J.; m. Marie Eubanks, Feb. 24, 1968. BS, Auburn U., 1969; MBA, U. W. Fla., 1975; postgrad. U. Fla., 1972-74, 76-78; cert. fin. planner, Coll. Fin. Planning, Denver, 1981. Adminstrv. asst. Valparaiso Bank & Trust Co., Ft. Walton Beach, Fla., 1972, asst. trust officer, 1973, trust officer, 1976, asst. v.p., trust officer, 1978, v.p., trust officer, 1979-84; pres. Vanguard Bank & Trust Co., Mary Esther, Fla., 1984-86, exec. v.p., 1987—; instr. banking and fin. Okaloosa-Walton Jr. Coll., 1976—; sr. dir. Fla. Bankers Assn. Comml. Lending Sch. at U. of S. Fla., Tampa. Treas. Ft. Walton (Fla.) YMCA, 1982. Served to capt., U.S. Army, 1969-72. Decorated Bronze Star. Mem. Soc. Advancement Mgmt. (pres. 1969), N.W. Fla. Estate Planning Council (sec.), Inst. Cert. Fin. Planners, Am. Inst. Banking (Banker of Yr. Okaloosa County chpt. 1985), Fla. Bankers Assn. (pres. Okaloosa-Walton County chpt., 1988—), Ft. Walton Life Underwriters Assn., Ft. Walton C. of C. (treas. Mil. Affairs Com.), Scabbard and Blade, Omicron Delta Kappa, Delta Sigma Pi. Club: Krewe of Bowlegs (first mate), Fort Walton Yacht. Lodges: Rotary (pres. 1978-79), Sertoma (pres. Ft. Walton Beach club 1986-87).

JOHNSON, JANET LOU, real estate executive; b. Boston, Aug. 22, 1939; d. Donald Murdoch and Helen Margaret (Slauenwhite) Campbell; m. Walter R. Johnson, Mar. 31, 1962; children—Meryl Ann, Leah Kathryn, Christa Helen. Student Boston U., 1959, Gordon Coll., Hamilton, Mass., 1962-64. Adminstr., account exec. Fuller/Smith & Ross, Boston, 1958-63; adminstr. Walter R. Johnson, P.E., Gloucester, 1970-76; broker Realty World, Gloucester, 1976-77, Hunneman & Co., Gloucester, 1977-79; pres., owner Janet L. Johnson Real Estate, Gloucester, 1979—. Mem. Mass. Assn. Realtors (bd. dirs. 1985-87), Nat. Assn. Realtors, Cape Ann C. of C. (state dir. 1986-87), Cape Ann Bd. Realtors (pres. 1984-85, state dir. 1985-86), Greater Salem Bd. Realtors. Home: 35 Norseman Ave Gloucester MA 01930 Office: Janet L Johnson Real Estate 79 Rocky Neck Ave Gloucester MA 01930

JOHNSON, JOHN ALLEN, real estate executive; b. San Antonio, Aug. 8, 1950; s. William Alton and Lillian T. (Kelley) J.; m. Marijon McLeroy, Mar. 5, 1973; children: Robert, Renea, Jeff, Michael. Student, San Antonio Jr. Coll., 1968-70; BS in Math., U. Houston, 1972. Store mgr. Shop Rite Foods, San Antonio, 1973-74; supr. U.S. Home Corp., San Antonio, 1974-77; div. pres. U.S. Home Corp., Houston, 1977-80, v.p. ops., 1980-83, v.p. constrn., 1988—; pres., chmn. bd. Homecraft Devel. Corp., Houston, 1983-87. Office: US Home Corp 1800 W Loop S Ste 2100 Houston TX 77027

JOHNSON, JOHN C., petroleum company executive. Pres. Steuart Petroleum Co., Washington, Eastern Seaboard Petroleum Co. Inc., Jacksonville, Fla. Office: Eastern Seaboard Petroleum Co Inc 6531 Evergreen Ave Jacksonville FL 32206 *

JOHNSON, JOHN DOEPPERS, nuclear physicist; b. Petoskey, Mich., Nov. 27, 1963; s. John Howard and Mary Elizabeth (Doeppers) J. BS in Physics, Mich. Tech. U., 1986; MS in Physics, Mich. State U., 1988. Cons. Mich. Tech. U., Houghton, 1986; instr. physics Mich. State U., East Lansing, 1986-88; nuclear physicist Nat. Superconducting Cyclotron Lab., East Lansing, 1988—; assoc. counselor Soc. Physics Students, 1983, nat. bd. dirs., 1983-85; v.p. ops. and fin. PPSA Internat., East Lansing, 1983-86, chief exec. officer, Houghton, 1986—. Editor: PPSA Newlsetter, 1986—. Pres. MTU Coll. Reps., Houghton, 1984; active Rep. Nat. Com. Mem. The Heritage Found., Am. Phys. Soc., Am. Assn. Physics Tchrs., Sigma Pi Sigma. Presbyterian. Office: Nat Superconducting Cyclotron Lab East Lansing MI 48824-1321

JOHNSON, JOHN F., manufacturing executive; b. N.Y.C., Sept. 17, 1947; s. George Francis and Margaret Eileen (Sproat) J.; m. Nancy Johnson; children: Ted, Katie. BS in Econs., Tufts U., 1970; MS, Columbia U., 1972; M in Mgmt., Northwestern U., 1985. Registered profl. engr., Ill. Mem. tech. staff Bell Labs., Holmdel, N.J., 1970-72; dist. mgr. Illinois Bell, Chgo., 1973-82; br. mgr. AT&T, Chgo., 1983-84, div. mgr., Morristown, N.J., 1985; exec. v.p. mfg. div. Anixter Bros. Inc., Skokie, Ill., 1986-87, pres. mfg. div., 1987—. Bd. dirs. United Way, Wilmette, Ill., 1983-85. Mem. Elec. Industries Assn. Office: Anixter Bros Inc Anixter Mfg Div 4711 Golf Rd Skokie IL 60076

JOHNSON, JOHN FRANK, professional recruitment executive; b. Bklyn., Apr. 23, 1942; s. John Henry and Sirkka (Keto) J.; m. Martha Lear Fryer, Aug. 31, 1963 (div. Apr. 1988); children: Kristin Lin, Heather Alane. BS in Econs., Tufts U., 1963; MBA in Indsl. Relations, Columbia U., 1964. Indsl. relations analyst Ford Motor Co., Dearborn and Livonia, Mich., 1964-67; various human resources positions Gen. Electric Co., Chgo. and Louisville, Ky., 1967-76; successively assoc., v.p., mng. dir., exec. v.p. and mng. dir. Lamalie Assocs., Inc., Cleve., 1976-84; pres., chief op. officer Lamalie Assocs., Inc., N.Y.C. and Cleve., 1984-87; pres., chief exec. officer Lamalie Assocs., Inc., Cleve., 1987—. Rep. zone capt., Livonia, 1964-67. Mem. Human Resource Planning Soc., The Planning Forum, Assn. for Corp. Growth, Nat. Assn. of Corp. and Exec. Recruiters, Union Club (Cleve.), Hudson Tennis Club (Ohio). Clubs: Union (Cleve.), Hudson Tennis (Ohio). Home: 12550 Lake Ave #1607 Lakewood OH 44107

JOHNSON, JOHN WILLIAM, securities company official; b. Jersey City, May 8, 1937; s. J. Ward and Marie (Murphy) J.; m. Norma Jean Le Bedz, July 20, 1958 (div. June 1974); children: Phyllis, Christopher; m. Karen Marie Nielson, Nov. 29, 1975; 1 child, Marie. BSBA, Monmouth Coll., 1962. Securities analyst Merrill Lynch, Pierce, Fenner & Smith, 1961-68, Composite Rsch. & Mgmt., Spokane, Wash., 1968-69, Nomura Securities Internat., N.Y.C., 1974-77; chief investment officer Lexington Mgmt., Saddle Brook, N.J., 1977-85; securities analyst Cable Howse & Ragen, Seattle, 1985-88; sr. v.p. Kennedy Assocs., Seattle, 1988—. Served with USN, 1955-59. Mem. N.Y. Soc. Securities Analysts, Chartered Fin. Analyst, Overlake Country, Bellevue Athletic Club. Home: 1431 86th St NE Bellevue WA 98004 Office: Kennedy Assoc 2400 Financial Ctr Bldg Seattle WA 98161

JOHNSON, JOHNNY GAYLE, manufacturing executive; b. Portsmouth, Va., July 18, 1948; s. George William and Dorothy Derring (Desmond) J.; m. Diane Puckett, Oct. 12, 1969; children: John Douglas, Jeffrey David. BS in Fin., Old Dominion U., 1977, MBA, 1984. Store mgr. Albano's, Norfolk, Va., 1969-71; pres., owner Trans-Am., Norfolk, 1971-79; traffic mgr. Kransco, Virginia Beach, Va., 1979-84; plant mgr. Kransco, Virginia Beach, 1984-87, dir. of ops., 1987—; v.p. Hampton Roads Transp. Assn., Norfolk, 1977-79. Patentee piggyback suspension system. Bd. dirs. Middle Plantation Civic League, Virginia Beach, 1982-88; mem. Lynnhaven Borough Adv. Council, Virginia Beach, 1982-88. Cpl. USMC, 1967-69, Vietnam. Decorated Purple Heart. Mem. Am. Soc. Transp. and Logistics (cert.), Am. Prodn. and Inventory Control Soc. (cert.), Am. Soc. Personnel Adminstrn. (cert.), Soc. Mfg. Engrs. (sr. mem.). Republican. Presbyterian. Home: 3352 Glen Eden Quay Virginia Beach VA 23452 Office: Kransco 5816 Ward Ct Virginia Beach VA 23455

JOHNSON, KEITH WINDSOR, financial planning company executive; b. Winston-Salem, N.C., Feb. 16, 1952; s. Alden L. and Lottie (Windson) J.; m. Richene R. Metzger, June 14, 1975; children: Robyn M., Jennifer D. BS, Phila. Coll. Bible, 1975; postgrad., Seton Hall U., 1978; grad., Coll. for Fin. Planning, Denver, 1984. Registered investment advisor. Police officer Ocean City (N.J.) Police Dept., 1975-80; asst. minister Linwood (N.J.) Community Ch., 1980-83; minister Milford (Pa.) Bible Ch., 1983-86; pres. North Easter Fin. Planning, Reading, Pa., 1981—; sr. resident mgr. Anchor Nat. Fin. Svcs., Reading, 1985—; owner KRJ and Assocs., Reading, 1987—; ornanizer fin. seminars. Chmn. bd. Tri-State Bible Conf., 1983—; bd. dirs. Christian Missionary Tech. Svcs., 1987—; treas. Schuylkill Valley Bible Ch., Reading, 1987—; mem. Pa. Better Bus. Bur., 1987-88. Mem. Inst. Cert. Fin. Planners, Internat. Assn. for Fin. Planning, Nat. Assn. Tax Practitioners, Pa. Soc. of Internat. Cert. Fin. Planners (treas. 1987-88, bd. dirs. 1987—), Berks County C. of C. Republican. Office: 420 Park Rd N Ste 103 Reading PA 19610

JOHNSON, KENNETH ODELL, aerospace engineer; b. Harville, Mo., Aug. 31, 1922; s. Kenneth D. and Polly Louise (Wilson) J.; B.S. in Aero. Engring., Purdue U., 1950; m. Betty Lou Jones, Aug. 5, 1950; children—Cynthia Jo, Gregory Alan. Engr., design, quality and production mgmt. Gen. Lamp Co., Elwood, Ind., 1950-51; mem. staff aircraft gas turbine engine design Allison div. Gen. Motors Corp., Speedway, Ind., 1951-66; mem. turbofan aircraft engines plus marine, indsl. gas turbine engine design mgmt. staff Gen. Electric Co., 1966-86, dir. aerospace engring. Belcan Corp., Cin., 1986—. Served to capt. USAF, 1942-45. Assoc. fellow AIAA. Republican. Methodist. Holder over 20 patents in field. Recipient UDF Pioneer & Extraordinary Service award for unducted fan invention and patent, Gen. Electric Co., 1985, cert. recognition NASA, 1987; named to Gen. Electric Aircraft Engines Propulsion Hall of Fame, 1987. Home: 8360 Arapaho Ln Cincinnati OH 45243 Office: Belcan Corp Aerospace Engring 10200 Anderson Way Cincinnati OH 45242

JOHNSON, KENNETH OSCAR, oil company executive; b. Center City, Minn., Apr. 11, 1920; s. Oscar W. and Sigrid (Hollsten) J.; m. Margery Wheeler, Apr. 18, 1945; 1 child, Eric W. B.S. in Chem. Engring., U. Minn., 1942. With Exxon Corp., Houston, 1942-74; heavy fuels mgr. supply dept. Exxon Corp., 1968-72, wholesale fuels sales mgr., mktg. dept., 1972-74; chmn., chief exec. officer Belcher Oil Co., Miami, Fla., 1974-88; sr. v.p. Coastal Corp., Houston, 1988—, also bd. dirs.; dir. S.E. 1st Nat. Bank, Petroleum Industry Found. Patentee in field. Mem. Fla. C. of C.. Clubs: Port Royal (Naples); Petroleum (Houston). Home: 845 Admiralty Parade Naples FL 33940 Office: Coastal Corp 9 Greenway Plaza Houston TX 77046

JOHNSON, KENNETH STUART, publisher and printer; b. Chgo., Aug. 22, 1928; s. William Moss and Lucille (Carsellio) J.; student Wright Jr. Coll., 1949-50, U. Ill., 1951-52; children—Cynthia Diane, Randall, Andrew, Peter. Dir., chmn. Free Press, Inc., Carpentersville, Ill., 1965-83; pres. Johnson Enterprises Inc. Served with U.S. Army, 1946-47. Named Man and Boy of Year, 1963. Mem. Cook County Pubs. Assn. (pres. 1963, dir.), Profl. Journalistic Soc., Sigma Delta Chi. Home: 44 Park Ln Park Ridge IL 60068

JOHNSON, KENNETT CONRAD, advertising agency executive; b. Crystal City, Mo., Feb. 5, 1927; s. Robert Winthrop and Gladys Agnes (Butler) J.; m. Noreen Ellen Driscoll, July 25, 1953; children: Lydia, Burke. BA in Journalism, U. Mo., 1950. State editor Binghamton Press, N.Y., 1950-55; advt. supr. Southwestern Bell, St. Louis, 1955-59; sr. v.p. Gardner Advt., N.Y.C., 1959-63, St. Louis, 1966-75; v.p. Butler & Gardner Ltd., London, 1964-65; exec. v.p. Kenrick Advt., St. Louis, 1975-77, 1975-77; exec. v.p. BHN Advt. and Pub. Relations Inc. (formerly Batz Hodgson Neuwoehner), St. Louis, 1977-81, pres., chmn., chief exec. officer, 1981-88, chmn., 1988—. Campaign communications chmn. United Way, St. Louis, 1981-83, co-chmn., 1984—, bd. dirs., 1982—; bd. dirs. Arts and Edn. Council Greater St. Louis, 1988—, Better Bus. Bur. Eastern Mo. and So. Ill., 1988—, chmn. advt. rev. com., 1985—. Served in CIC, 1946-47, Japan. Recipient Clio award Am. TV and Radio Commls. Festival N.Y., 1971. Mem. Am. Assn. Advt. Agys. (chmn. Mo. council 1973-74), Advt. Club Greater St. Louis (gov. 1976—, pres. 1985-86), Am. Advt. Fedn. (gov. 9th dist. 1988—, Advt. Man of Yr. 1986). Club: Bellerive Country (St. Louis). Home: 13330 Thornhill Dr Saint Louis MO 63131 Office: BHN Advt & Pub Rels 910 N 11th St Saint Louis MO 63101

JOHNSON, KENT ROBERT, physician; b. Joliet, Ill., Dec. 12, 1946; s. Robert N. and Helen Charlotte Johnson; m. Sarah Jane Kough, Oct. 25, 1980; 1 child, Wylie Crawford. BA, Harvard U., 1969; MA, Oxford U., 1971; MD, Johns Hopkins Med. Sch., 1976. Diplomate Am. Bd. Internal Medicine. Pvt. practice medicine specializing in rheumatology Bethesda, Md., 1982—; chmn. Rheumatic Therapeutics Rsch. and Devel. Group, Bethesda, 1987—; med. officer Fed. Drug Adminstrn., Rockville, Md., 1985—. Mem. Am. Rheumatism Assn., Harvard Club (Boston). Home: 6311 Newburn Dr Bethesda MD 20816 Office: 5415 W Cedar Ln #106B Bethesda MD 20814

JOHNSON, KIM BRADLEY, infosystems specialist; b. Mpls., Sept. 7, 1949; s. Carl Raymond and Dorothy Jeanne (Sadler) J.; m. Sally Denise Rinal, Sept. 3, 1971; children: Samuel Trew, Erin Kathleen. BS in Elem. Edn., U. Minn., 1972; MBA, Coll. St. Thomas, 1988. Systems analyst Hypro, Inc., New Brighton, Minn., 1973-81; materials mgr. Carter-Day, Fridley, Minn., 1981-86; sr. analyst Sinclair & Valentine, Mendota Heights, Minn., 1986-88; prodn. mgr. I.C. System, Vadnais Heights, Minn., 1988—. Den, pack leader Cub Scouts Boy Scouts Am., St. Anthony, Minn., 1985—; youth coach, St. Anthony, 1984—. Sgt. USAR, 1971-77. Home: 3304 Skycroft Dr Saint Anthony MN 55418 Office: IC System 44 E Hwy 96 Saint Paul MN 55110

JOHNSON, KIRK ALAN, auditor; b. Lansing, Mich., Dec. 29, 1963; s. Tony Edward and Ruth (Richardson) J. BS in Acctg., Miami U., Oxford, Ohio, 1986. CPA, Ohio. Computer auditor Ernst and Whinney, Columbus, Ohio, 1986—. Big brother, Columbus Big Bros./Big Sisters, 1987—. Mem. Nat. Assn. Accts., Ohio Soc. CPAs, Beta Alpha Psi. Republican. Club: Outdoor (Columbus). Office: Ernst and Whinney 2400 Nationwide Blvd Columbus OH 43215

JOHNSON, LAEL FREDERIC, lawyer; b. Yakima, Wash., Jan. 22, 1938; s. Andrew Cabot and Gudney M. (Fredrickson) J.; m. Eugenie Rae Call, June 9, 1960; children: Eva Marie, Inga Margaret. A.B., Wheaton (Ill.) Coll., 1960; J.D., Northwestern U., 1963. Bar: Ill. 1963, U.S. Dist. Ct. (no. dist.) Ill. 1964, U.S. Ct. Appeals (7th cir.) 1966. Sr. v.p., sec., gen. counsel Abbott Labs., Abbott Park, Ill., 1966—; chmn. adv. bd. corp. counsel ctr. Northwestern U. Sch. Law. Fellow ABA, Am. Bar Found.; mem. Chgo. Bar Assn., Ill. State Bar Assn. Office: Abbott Labs 1 Abbott Park Rd Abbott Park IL 60064-3500

JOHNSON, LESTER OSCAR, JR., securities and insurance company executive, financial planner; b. Niagara Falls, N.Y., Oct. 20, 1933; s. Lester Oscar and Angela (Dargis) J.; m. Ardath Louise Smith, June 2, 1958; children: Carol Anne, Terry Elizabeth. BS, U.S. Naval Acad., 1958; MBA, U. So. Ill., 1976. Cert. fin. planner; registered fin. planner; prin., options prin. Commd. ensign USN, 1958, advanced through grades to commdr., 1972, ret., 1982; rep. Waddell & Reed, Inc., San Diego, 1982-85, Wedbush Securities, Inc., San Diego, 1985-87; prin., pres. Golden Triangle Equities, San Diego, 1987—. Office: Golden Triangle Equities PO Box 22212 San Diego CA 92122

JOHNSON, LINDA JOYCE, sales executive; b. Lowell, Mass., Nov. 6, 1956; d. Emil and Esther Muriel (Ayer) Zabierek; m. James M. Johnson, Sept. 5, 1975 (div. Nov. 1979). Mfg. adminstr., M/A-Com., Inc., 1979-81, sales administr., 1979-81, sales specialist, 1981-84; regional sales mgr. Hyletronics, Inc., Littleton, Mass., 1984; regional sales mgr. Frequency Sources, Chelmsford, Mass., 1984-86; regional sales mgr. Sanders Assocs., Manchester, N.H., 1986-88; v.p., co-owner Computer Decisions, Inc., Derry, N.H., 1988—. Mem. Nat. Contract Mgmt. Assn., Nat. Assn. Female Execs., Women in Electronics, Women In Def., Computer Decisions, Inc. (bd. dirs.), Assn. Old Crows. Avocations: golf, piano, reading. Home: 5 Walnut Hill Rd Derry NH 03038 Office: Computer Decisions Inc PO Box 368 E Derry NH 03041

JOHNSON, LLOYD PETER, banker; b. Mpls., May 1, 1930; s. Lloyd Percy and Edna (Schlampp) J.; m. Rosalind Gesner, July 3, 1954; children: Marcia, Russell, Paul. B.A., Carleton Coll., Northfield, Minn., 1952; M.B.A., Stanford U., 1954. With Security Trust & Savs. Bank, San Diego, 1954-57; vice chmn. charge corp. banking, fiduciary svcs., internat. banking Security Pacific Nat. Bank, L.A., 1957-84; chmn., chief exec. officer Norwest Corp., Mpls., 1985—; mem. faculty Pacific Coast Banking Sch., 1969-72, chmn., 1979-80; bd. dirs. Minn. Bus. Partnership; mem. Internat. Monetary Conf.; trustee Minn. Mutual Life Ins. Co.; mem. fed. adv. council of Fed. Reserve System. Trustee Carleton Coll., Mpls. Inst. Arts; bd. dirs. United Way Mpls., Minn. Orchestral Assn.; mem. U. Minn. Bd. Overseers; adv. coun. Fed. Reserve System. Mem. Assn. Res. City Bankers, Calif. Bankers Assn. (pres. 1977-78), Assn. Bank Holding Cos. Office: Norwest Corp Northwest Ctr 6th & Marquette Minneapolis MN 55479-1060

JOHNSON, MANUEL HOLMAN, JR., government official, economics educator; b. Troy, Ala., Feb. 10, 1949; s. Manuel Holman and Ethel Lorraine (Jordan) J.; m. Mary Lois Wilkerson, June 10, 1972; children—Marshall, Merritt. Student, U. Ala., 1967-68; B.S., Troy State U., 1973; M.S., Fla. State U., 1974, Ph.D., 1977. Instr. econs. Fla. State U., Tallahassee, 1975-76; asst. prof. econs. George Mason U., Fairfax, Va., 1977-79, assoc. prof. econs., 1979-81; dep. asst. sec. U.S. Treasury Dept., Washington, 1981-82, asst. sec., 1982-86; vice chmn. Fed. Res. Bank, Washington, 1986—; mem. Pres.'s Commn. on Indian Econs., 1983-84; dir. Solar Energy Bank, Washington; mem. adv. bd. Heritage Found., Washington, Synthetic Fuels Corp., Washington. Co-author: Political Economy of Federal Government Growth, 1980, Better Government at Half Price, 1981, Deregulating Labor Relations, 1981; assoc. editor Jour. Labor Research, 1979-81 contbr. articles to profl. jours. Youth chmn. Winton Blount for Senate, Montgomery, Ala., 1972; mem. Scholars for Reagan, Los Angeles, 1980; chmn. Treasury United Way Campaign, 1983. Served with U.S. Army, 1968-71. Recipient Alumnus of Yr. award Troy State U., 1982, named hon. pres., 1982; Sec.'s Honor award U.S. Treasury Dept., 1982; U.S. Nuclear Regulatory Commn. fellow, 1975. Mem. Am. Econ. Assn., Western Econ. Assn., So. Econ., Assn. Pub. Choice Soc., Regional Sci. Assn. Republican. Presbyterian. Club: Phila. Soc. (Chgo.). Home: 10512 Dillard Ct Fairfax VA 22032 Office: Fed Res System 20th and C Sts NW Washington DC 20551 *

JOHNSON, MARC KIMBALL, marketing executive; b. Ft. Leonardwood, Mo., Aug. 27, 1954; s. Harlan Warren and Norma Darlene (Pleines) J. BS in Fin., U. Ill., 1976; MAS, Johns Hopkins U., 1983. Locomotive engr. Balt. and Ohio R.R., St. Louis, 1976-77; account exec. Chesapeake & Ohio R.R., Pitts., 1978-80; market mgr. chems. Chesapeake & Ohio R.R., Balt., 1981-82, group mgr. agrl., 1982-85; dir. mktg. Seaboard Coast Line R.R., Jacksonville, Fla., 1986, CSX Transp., Inc., Balt., 1987; pres., v.p. Stensel Corp./Agmark Internat. Systems, Jacksonville, 1987—, v.p. mktg., 1987—; pres., owner Stensel Corp., Jacksonville and Balt., 1985—, Agmark Foods, Nashville, 1985—; owner Marc Johnson Farms, 1985—; bd. dirs. various cos. Lloyd Morey grantee U. Ill., 1975-76. Mem. Ill. Grain and Feed Assn. (transp. com. 1985—), Plummers Cove Yacht Club of Jacksonville, Johns Hopkins Alumni Assn., U. Ill. Alumni Assn., Alpha Kappa Lambda, Balt. Orioles Hit and Run Club (Balt. Best Bus. award 1985). Republican. Roman Catholic. Home: 2724 Cove View Dr N Jacksonville FL 32217

JOHNSON, MARGARET HELEN, welding executive; b. Chgo., June 3, 1933; d. Harold W. and Clara J. (Pape) Glavin; m. Odean Jack Johnson, Nov. 18, 1950; children: Karen Ann, Dean Harold. Student Moody Bible Inst., 1976-78. V.p., sec. Seamline Welding, Inc., Chgo., 1956—, also dir.; trustee SWCEPS, Chgo., 1963—. Author: Living Faith, 1973, 80, Lord's Ladder of Love, 1976, God's Rainbow, 1982; contbr. articles to religion mags. Life mem. Rep. Presdl. Task Force, 1982—, trustee, 1986-88; charter founder Ronald Reagan Rep. Ctr., 1987; mem. Lake View Neighborhood Group, Chgo., Small Group Ch. Community; active Mary, Seat of Wisdom Cath. Women's Club, 1970—, renew facilitator 1986-88, co-chairperson 1986-88; Sunday sch. tchr., 1985. Mem. ASCAP, Fedn. Ind. Small Bus., Internat. Platform Assn. Home: 101 S Summit Unit 405 Park Ridge IL 60068

JOHNSON, MARLENE A., business executive; b. Hoonah, Alaska, Aug. 4, 1935; d. Robert N. and Elsie (Douglas) Greenwald; children from previous marriage: Donald, Robert, Howard, Lynell Starbard; m. Clifford Leo Johnson, Feb. 11, 1964; 1 child, Jodi Michelle. BA, Oreg. State U., 1989. Acct. Dept. Interior, Juneau, Alaska, 1953-54, Fed. Market, Ketchitan, Alaska, 1954-57; mgr. Tom and Jerry's, Ketchitan, 1958-60; acct. Hoonah Seafoods, 1960-66; mgr., owner Wings of Alaska, Hoonah, 1969-82; chmn. bd. SeaLaska, Juneau, 1982—; bd. dirs. Huna Totem, Inc., Hoonah. Bd. dirs. State of Alaska Personnel Bd., Juneau, 1984—, Pub. Employee's Retirement Bd., Juneau, 1984—; commr. Alaska Labor Relations Agy., Juneau, 1984—, Gov.'s Interim Commn. on Children and Youth, 1987—, Alaska R.R. Labor Relations Agy., 1987—. Mem. Nat. Assn. Corp. Dirs. Democrat. Roman Catholic. Club: Alaska Native Sisterhood. Home: PO Box 218 Hoonah AK 99829 Office: Sealaska Corp 1 Sealaska Pla Juneau AK 99801

JOHNSON, MARLYS DIANNE, utility holding company executive; b. Akron, Iowa, Mar. 31, 1948; d. Harry J. and Alvina (Jurgensen) Nannen; m. Randall Lee Johnson, June 27, 1970; children: Amy Lyn, Ann Marie. BS, Augustana Coll., 1970; MBA, U. S.D., 1985. Clk. City of Sioux City, Iowa, 1970-74; ops. mgr. Dain Bosworth, Sioux City, 1974-77; mgmt. trainee Iowa Pub. Service Co., Sioux City, 1977-79, adminstrv. asst. to treas., 1979-81; asst. treas. Midwest Energy Co., Sioux City, 1981-85, v.p., treas., 1985—; bd. dirs. Sioux City Stationary Co. Sec.-treas. Akron Pub. Library, 1970-80; chmn. fin. YWCA, Sioux City, 1983; investments subcom. Marian Health Ctr., Sioux City, 1985-88; vice chair Immanuel Luth. Ch., Akron, 1984; bd. dirs. Girls' Club of Siouxland, Siouxland River-cade. Mem. Nat. Assn. Corp. Treas., Assn. Fin. Analysts, Electrical Women's Round Table, NAFE, Siouxland River-Cade Assn. Republican. Lutheran. Clubs: Quota Internat. (treas. 1982-83), Toastmasters (historian 1979-80), Sioux City Girls. Home: 521 Reed St Akron IA 51001 Office: Midwest Energy Co 401 Douglas St Sioux City IA 51101

JOHNSON, MARVIN MELROSE, industrial engineer; b. Neligh, Nebr., Apr. 21, 1925; s. Harold Nighram and Melissa (Bare) J.; m. Anne Stuart Campbell, Nov. 10, 1951; children: Douglas Blake, Harold James, Phyllis Anne, Nighram Marvin, Melissa Joan. B.S., Purdue U., 1949; postgrad., Ill. Inst. Tech., 1953; M.S. in Indsl. Engring, U. Iowa, 1966, Ph.D., 1968. Registered profl. engr., Iowa, Mo., Nebr. Quality control supr., indsl. engr. Houdaille Hershey, Chgo., 1949-52; indsl. engr. Bell & Howell, Chgo., 1952-54; with Bendix Aviation Corp., Davenport, Iowa, 1954-64; successively chief indsl. engr., staff asst., supr. procedures and systems Bendix Aviation Corp., 1954-63; reliability engr. Bendix Aviation Corp. (Pioneer Central div.), 1963-64, cons., 1964—; lectr. indsl. engring. State U. Iowa, 1963-64; instr. indsl. engring. U. Iowa, 1965-66; asso. prof. U. Nebr., 1968-73, prof., 1973-88; emeritus prof., 1988—; vis. prof. Ind. Engrs. S.D. Sch. Mines and Tech., 1989—; AID adv., mgmt. engring. and food processing Kabul (Afghanistan) U., 1975-76; vis. prof. indsl. engring. U. P.R., Mayaguez, 1982-83; NSF trainee U. Iowa, 1964-67. Editor The Johnson Reporter, 1980-88. Served with AUS, 1943-46, ETO. Fellow Am. Inst. Indsl. Engrs.; Mem. Am. Soc. Engring. Educators, Am. Statis. Assn., ASME, Ops. Research Soc. Am., Inst. Mgmt. Sci., Sigma Xi, Tau Beta Pi, Pi Tau Sigma, Alpha Pi Mu. Presbyterian. Home: 329 Fox Run Dr Rapid City SD 57701 Office: Sch Mines & Tech Indsl Engring 501 E St Joseph St Rapid City SD 57701-3995

JOHNSON, MAURICE VERNER, JR., agricultural research and development executive; b. Duluth, Minn., Sept. 13, 1925; s. Maurice Verner Sr. and Elvira Marie (Westberg) J.; m. Darlene Ruth Durand, June 23, 1944; children: Susan Kay, Steven Dale. BS, U. Calif., 1953. registered profl. engr. From research engr. to dir. research and devel. Sunkist Growers, Ontario, Calif., 1953-84; v.p. research and devel. Sunkist Growers, Ontario, 1984—; v.p., dir. Calif. Citrus Quality Council, Claremont. Contbr. articles to profl. pubs.; patentee in field. Sgt. U.S. Army, 1944-46, ETO. Fellow Am. Soc. Agrl. Engrs. (dir. 1969-70); mem. ASME, Am. Inst. Indsl. Engrs., Am. Assn. Advancement Sci., Nat. Soc. Profl. Engrs., Tau Beta Pi. Republican. Home: 1344 Taylor Way Upland CA 91786 Office: Sunkist Growers 760 E Sunkist St PO Box 3720 Ontario CA 91761

JOHNSON, MILLER ALANSON, II, paper company executive; b. Williamsport, Pa., June 1, 1933; s. Miller Alanson and Naomi (Plitt) J.; m. Delores Secrist, June 18, 1955; children—Miller Alanson III, Christopher R., Keith F. A.B., Haverford Coll., 1955. Budget trainee, then asst. controller budgets Hamilton Watch Co., Lancaster, PA, 1958-67; comptroller P.H. Glatfelter Co., Spring Grove, Pa., 1967-68, v.p., treas., dir., 1968-78, exec. v.p., treas., chief, fin. officer, dir., 1978—. Chmn. bd. York Hosp., Pa., 1982-85, bd. dirs. 1978-88; vice-chmn. bd. dirs. York Hosp. Found., 1988—; bd. dirs. Tax Found., 1985—, vice-chmn. bd. dirs., 1988—. Served to lt. (j.g.) USN, 1955-58. Republican. Presbyterian. Home: 1745 Hillock Ln York PA 17403 Office: P H Glatfelter Co 228 S Main St Spring Grove PA 17362

JOHNSON, PAUL JOSEPH, manufacturing company executive; b. Pittsfield, Mass., Dec. 20, 1923; s. Samuel Walsh and Kathryn (Nash); m. Winnefred Ryan, Aug. 31, 1949 (div. Mar. 1978); children: Paul Geoffrey, Barbara Jane Johnson Salance, Mary Jill Johnson Watts, Peter Ryan, Christopher Joseph. Acct. Standard Oil (N.J.) Inc., Boston and Talara, Peru, 1947-48; chief acct. Planters Nut & Chocolate Co., Toronto, 1948-55; comptroller Bate Chem. Corp., Toronto, 1955-60; v.p., treas. Trans Union Corp., Chgo., 1960-81; exec. v.p. fin. Am. Invesco, Chgo., 1981-82; pres. Paul J. Johnson Assoc., Chgo., 1982-84; treas., cons. Bally Mfg. Corp., Chgo., 1984-87, v.p., chief fin. officer, 1987—. Bd. dirs. Mid-Am. chpt. ARC, Chgo., 1982—. Served with U.S. Army, 1943-45. Office: Bally Mfg Corp 8700 W Bryn Mawr Chicago IL 60631

JOHNSON, PAUL OREN, lawyer; b. Mpls., Feb. 2, 1937; s. Andrew Richard and LaVerne Delores (Slater) J.; m. Georgene Howalt, July 1, 1961; children: Scott, Paula, Amy. BA, Carleton Coll., 1958; JD cum laude, U. Minn., 1961. Bar: Minn. 1961. Atty. Briggs & Morgan, St. Paul, 1961-62; atty. Green Giant Co., Le Sueur, Minn., 1961-66, asst. sec., 1967-74, sec., 1975-79, v.p., gen. counsel, 1971-79, v.p. corporate rels., 1973-79, mem. mgmt. com., 1976-79; gen. counsel H.B. Fuller Co., St. Paul, 1979-84, sr. v.p., sec., 1980—, mem. mgmt. com., 1981—, chmn., 1988—; chmn. bd. dirs. Sta. WCAL-PBS, Northfield, Minn. Coun. mem. at large Boy Scouts Am., chmn. Rep. County Com., 1965; bd. dirs. Minn. State U., 1979-82 , v.p., 1980-82. Served with U.S. Air N.G., 1961. Mem. ABA., Minn. Bar Assn., Ramsey County Bar Assn., Assn. Corp. Secs.

JOHNSON, PHILIP MARTIN, lawyer; b. Boston, Feb. 22, 1940; s. Philip E. and Catherine (Martin) J.; divorced; children: Charles T., Jennifer M., Melissa C.; m. Carolyn Moxley, Feb. 14, 1981. BA, Colgate U., 1963; LLB, Union U., 1966, JD, 1968; grad., Nat. Coll. Trial Advocacy, 1973. Bar: N.Y. 1967, U.S. Dist. Ct. (we. dist.) N.Y. 1967, Vt. 1970, U.S. Dist Ct. Vt. 1970, U.S. Dist. Ct. N.H. 1975. Asst. dist. atty. County of Livingston, N.Y., 1968-70; ptnr. Niles, Johnson & Brush, Woodstock, Vt., 1970-80; sr. ptnr. Johnson & Dunne, Norwich, Vt., 1980-84; sole practice Taftsville, Vt., 1985—. Justice Village of Dansville, 1967-68, moderator, 1971-73; justice Village of Woodstock, 1972-79; moderator Town of Woodstock; chmn. Woodstock Village Zoning Bd. Adjustment, 1972-74, fin. com., 1986-87; bd. dirs. Woodstock Recreation Assn., 1972-79, chmn. 1973-76, 78-79; bd. dirs. Woodstock Union High Sch., 1974-79, chmn. 1975-79; trustee Ottaquechee Health Ctr., 1979-83, chmn. 1980-83; judge moot ct. competition U. Vt. Law Sch. Mem. N.Y. Bar Assn., Vt. Bar Assn. (coms. bus. cop. law, unauthorized practice). Home and Office: 1 River Rd PO Box 67 Taftsville VT 05073

JOHNSON, QULAN ADRIAN, software engineer; b. Gt. Falls, Mont., Sept. 17, 1942; s. Raymond Eugene and Bertha Marie (Nagengast) J.; m. Helen Louise Pocha, July 24, 1965; children—Brenda Marie, Douglas Paul, Scot Paul, Mathew James. B.A. in Psychology, Coll. Gt. Falls, 1964. Lead operator 1st Computer Corp., Helena, Mont., 1966-67; v.p., sec.-treas. Computer Corp. of Mt., Great Falls, 1967-76, dir., 1971-76; sr. systems analyst Mont. Dept. Revenue, Helena, 1976-78; software engr. Mont. Systems Devel. Co., Helena, 1978-80; programmer/analyst III info. systems div. Mont. Dept. Adminstrn., Helena, 1980-82; systems analyst centralized services Dept. Social and Rehab. Services State of Mont., 1982-87, systems and programming mgr. info systems, Blue Cross and Blue Shield of Montana, Helena, 1987—. Mem. Assn. for Systems Mgmt., Mont. Data Processing Assn., Data Processing Mgmt. Assn., Mensa. Club: K.C. (rec. sec. 1975-76). Home: 2231 8th Ave Helena MT 59601 Office: Blue Cross & Blue Shield Info Systems 404 Fuller Ave Helena MT 59604-4309

JOHNSON, RADY A., oil company executive; b. Omaha, July 23, 1936; s. Walter Richard and Mary Violet (Burt) J.; m. Mary Alice Fitzpatrick, Aug. 6, 1960; children: Rady A. II, Ann, Patrick W., Frederick F., Mary. B.A., U. Nebr., 1959, J.D., 1964; A.M.P., Harvard U., 1979. Bar: U.S. Supreme Ct. 1967. Adminstrv. asst. to Rep. David T. Martin U.S. Ho. of Reps., Washington, 1965-68; mgr. fed. govt. affairs PPG Industries, Washington, 1968-71; asst. to sec. of defense Dept. Def., Washington, 1971-73; mgr. Amoco Corp., Washington, 1973-79, v.p. govt. affairs, 1979-86; v.p. pub. and govt. affairs Amoco Corp., Chgo., 1986—. Mem. ABA, Nebr. Bar Assn. Republican. Roman Catholic. Home: 1130 N Lake Shore Dr Chicago IL 60611 Office: Amoco Corp 200 E Randolph Dr Chicago IL 60601

JOHNSON, RALPH RAYMOND, federal agency administrator; b. Portland, Oreg., Mar. 31, 1943; s. Ralph Wilson and Margaret Mary (Munly) J.; m. Ann Frances Huetter, Aug. 19, 1967; children: David, Timothy. BA in Polit. Sci., Seattle U., 1965; MA in Internat. Rels., Columbia U., 1965. Mgmt. trainee Seattle First Nat. Bank, 1968-69; vice-consul U.S. Embassy, Georgetown, Guyana, 1969-71; econ. officer U.S. Embassy, Warsaw, Poland, 1973-76, Lapaz, Bolivia, 1977-79; asst. chief indsl. and strategic materials U.S. Dept. State, Washington, 1979-81, chief trade agreements div., 1981-83, office dir. European regional polit./econ. affairs, 1985-86, dep. asst. sec. state, 1986—; dep. trade rep. bilateral affairs Japan-Europe Trade Rep.'s Office, Washington, 1983-85. Sgt. U.S. Army, 1965-68. Mem. Am. Fgn. Svc. Assn. Roman Catholic. Office: Econs & Bus Affairs Bur Dept State 2201 C St NW Washington DC 20520

JOHNSON, REID STUART, financial advisor; b. Pitts., July 22, 1951; s. Ross H. and Marjorie J. M in Fin. Services, Am. Coll. CLU, Cert. Fin. Planner, employee benefits specialist; chartered fin. cons.; registered health underwriter, investment advisor, gen. prin. Assoc. regional mgr. Old Heritage Life Ins. Co., Lincoln, Ill., 1972-74; regional v.p. Lincoln Heritage Life Ins. Co., Springfield, Ill., 1974-76; pres. First Line Brokerage Inc., Champaign, Ill., 1976-83, First Line Fin. Planning, Inc., Champaign, 1981—; fin. advisor Shearson Lehman Hutton Inc., Mesa, Az., 1986—; faculty council mem. Coll. Fin. Planning, Denver, Parkland Coll., Champaign; ednl. cons. Nat. Ctr. Fin. Edn., Inc., San Francisco. Conbtr. weekly articles on fin. planning and money mgmt. to area newspapers and profl. publs.; mem. rev. com. Longman Pub. Mem. Am. Soc. CLU's, Soc. Chartered Fin. Cons., Internat. Assn. Fin. Planners (registered), Eastern Ill. Estate Planning Council, Inst. Cert. Fin. Planners, Am. Assn. Fin. Planning. Home: 1055 W Baseline #1085 Mesa AZ 85210 Office: Shearson Lehman Hutton 1901 E University Dr Ste #100 Mesa AZ 85203

JOHNSON, RHEUBEN CLIFFORD, financial consultant; b. M, Red Oak, Iowa, Mar. 9, 1937; s. Rheuben Clifford and Pauline (Swoboda) J.; m. Janice Lee Briggs, Nov. 2, 1979; children: Lori, Greg, Rheuben III, Deborah, Mellisa. BA in Actuarial Math., U. Mich., 1958, MBA, 1962. V.p., actuary Bus. Mens Assurance Co., Kansas City, Mo., 1962-84, sr. v.p. tech. services, 1984-85, sr. v.p. mktg. and tech. services, 1985-86, sr. v.p. fin. mgmt., 1986-87; fin. cons. R.C. Johnson & Assocs., Leawood, Kans., 1987—. Served to 1st lt. U.S. Army, 1958-60. Fellow Soc. Actuaries; mem. Am. Acad. Actuaries, Conf. Actuaries in Pub. Practice (assoc.). Home: 8904 Pawnee Ln Leawood KS 66206

JOHNSON, RICHARD DARREL, lumber company executive; b. Charlotte, Mich., Aug. 30, 1931; s. Darrel E. and Josephine (Richard) J.; m. Donna Evelyn Walker, Oct. 5, 1952; children: Mark Richard, Sheryl Ann, Timothy Walker. Student, Albion Coll., 1949-51; BS in Bus., Ferris U., 1952. Lic. electrician. Pres. L.L. Johnson Lumber Mfg., Charlotte, Mich., 1970-80, chmn. bd., 1980—. Mem. Charlotte City Council, 1964-67, Charlotte Planning Commn., 1968—. Named Charlotte's Outstanding Young Man, Charlotte Jaycees, 1962; recipient Disting. Service award Charlotte Rotary Club, 1986. Mem. Charlotte C. of C. (past pres.). Republican. Congregationalist. Lodge: Rotary (pres. Charlotte club 1973-74), Masons, K.T., Shriners. Home: 117 Cambridge Dr Charlotte MI 48813 Office: L L Johnson Lumber Mfg Co 563 N Cochran Charlotte MI 48813

JOHNSON, RICHARD EDWARD, gas company executive; b. Milw., May 23, 1954; s. Robert G. and Betty M. (Moeller) J.; m. Suzanne M. Altmann, Nov. 13, 1976; children: Joseph, Timothy. BBA, U. Wis., Milw., 1976. CPA, Wis. Staff acct. Arthur Andersen & Co., Milw., 1976-1981, mgr., 1981-85; treas. Wis. So. Gas Co. Inc., Lake Geneva, Wis., 1985-87, v.p., treas., 1988—. Mem. AICPA, Wis. Inst. CPA's. Office: Wis So Gas Co Inc 120 E Sheridan Springs Rd Lake Geneva WI 53115

JOHNSON, RICHARD NED, automotive research executive, mechanical engineer; b. Perry, Iowa, Jan. 4, 1942; s. Harding Richard and Dorothy Marjarita (Nelson) J.; m. Lila Lee Herron, June 24, 1978 (dec. Oct. 1984); children: Jana, David; m. Karen L. Friedman, May 18, 1986. BS in Applied Math., U. Wis., 1964; MS in Engring. Mechanics, Case Inst., Cleve., 1968; PhD in Engring. Mechanics, U. Wis., 1972; MBA with honors, Roosevelt U., Chgo., 1980. Project mgr. Lewis Research div. NASA, Cleve., 1964-70; teaching asst. U. Wis., Madison, 1970-71; dept. mgr. Gen. Am. Research Div./GATX Corp., Niles, Ill., 1971-82; sect. mgr. Borg-Warner Research, Des Plaines, Ill., 1982-87; dept. mgr. Borg Warner Automotive Rsch., Des Plaines, Ill., 1987-88, Burr Ridge, Ill., 1988—; cons. Gen. Dynamics, San Diego, 1969, Psych Systems, Virginia Beach, Va., 1979-80; mem. Computer Aided Design/Computer Aided Mfg. com. Harper Coll., Rolling Meadows, Ill., 1983-84, Ill. State CAD/CAM Edn. Bd., 1984-86, N.W. Material Sci. Adv. Com., Evanston, Ill., 1987-88. Author: Handbook of Manufacturing High Technology, 1986; co-inventor tire degradation monitor, rubber bond inspection. NASA research grantee, 1970. Mem. Soc. Mfg. Engrs., Robot Industries Assn., ASTM, Sigma Xi. Home: 15W755 Shepard Dr Burr Ridge IL 60521 Office: Borg-Warner Research 15 W755 Shepard Ln Burr Ridge IL 60521

JOHNSON, RICHARD TENNEY, lawyer; b. Evanston, Ill., Mar. 24, 1930; s. Ernest Levin and Margaret Abbott (Higgins) J.; m. Marilyn Bliss Meuth, May 1, 1954; children: Ross Tenney, Lenore, Jocelyn. A.B. with high honors, U. Rochester, 1951; postgrad., Trinity Coll., Dublin, Ireland, 1954-55; LL.B., Harvard, 1958. Bar: D.C. 1959. Trainee Office Sec. Def., 1957-59; atty. Office Gen. Counsel. Dept. Def., 1959-63; dep. gen. counsel Dept. Army, 1963-67, Dept. Transp., 1967-70; gen. counsel CAB, 1970-73, NASA, 1973-75, ERDA, 1975-76; mem. CAB, 1976-77; chmn. organizational integration Dept. Energy Activation, Exec. Office of Pres., 1977; ptnr. firm Sullivan & Beauregard, 1978-81; gen. counsel Dept. Energy, 1981-83; ptnr. firm Zuckert, Scoutt, Rasenberger & Johnson, 1983-87, Law Offices of R. Tenney Johnson, Washington, 1987—; v.p., gen. counsel Ohio Ont. Clean Fuels, Inc., 1987—. Served to lt. USNR, 1951-54. Mem. ABA, Fed. Bar Assn., Phi Beta Kappa, Theta Delta Chi. Office: 2300 N St NW Suite 600 Washington DC 20037

JOHNSON, ROBERT DAVID, mechanical engineer; b. Alexandria, Va., Dec. 14, 1957; s. Edward William and Irmgard Maria (Zeisberg) J. BME, Ill. Inst. Tech., Chgo., 1979; MME, Oakland U., Rochester, Mich., 1986. Research asst. Ill. Inst. Tech., Chgo., 1978-79; jr. exptl. engr. Gen. Motors Truck & Coach, Pontiac, Mich., 1979-81; exptl. engr. Gen. Motors Truck & Bus, Pontiac, 1981-84, sr. exptl. engr., 1984—. Gen. Motors scholar, 1977. Mem. Soc. Automotive Engrs., Pi Tau Sigma, Tau Beta Pi. Republican. Lutheran. Home: 1951 Ridge Ct Royal Oak MI 48073

JOHNSON, ROBERT E., financial executive; b. Manchester, Conn., Oct. 25, 1936; m. Barbara Lappen; 2 children. BS in Accounting, U. Conn., 1961; postgrad., Lehigh U., 1966, Hartford Grad. Center, 1971, Harvard Bus. Sch., 1984. CPA, Conn. With Coopers & Lybrand, CPA's, 1961-64, Air Products & Chems., Inc., 1964-67; audit mgr. The Stanley Works, New Britain, Conn., 1967-72; dir. planning and control The Stanley Works, 1973-76, dir. treasury svcs., 1976-77, dir. internat. finance, 1977-81, asst. treas., 1981-82, v.p., treas., 1982—; mem. adv. bd. Conn. Nat. Bank, Allendale Mut. Ins. Co. Trustee Conn. Pub. Expenditure Coun.; incorporator Manchester (Conn.) Meml. Hosp., New Britain YMCA. Mem. AICPA, Fin. Execs. Inst., Nat. Assn. Corp. Treas., So. New Eng. Chpt. Inst. Internal Auditors (pres.). Home: 139 Tunxis Village Farmington CT 06032 Office: Stanley Works PO Box 7000 New Britain CT 06050

JOHNSON, ROBERT G., city official, financial consultant; b. Marion, S.C., May 19, 1940; s. Albert B. and Edna D. (Davis) J.; m. Beatrice E. Mason, June 24, 1961; chidren: Robert G. Jr., Brian E., Duane L., Charles S., Albert K. ABS in Acctg., Columbia Inst., Phila., 1967; BSBA, LaSalle U., Phila., 1975. Clk., typist Phila. Dept. Pub. Property, 1958-60; acctg. clk. Office City Controller, Phila., 1960-62; acctg. assoc. Phila. Water Dept., 1962-67; chief acct. Phila. Housing Devel. Corp., 1967-68; acct. Phila. Model Cities Program, 1968-70, asst. controller, 1970-75, fiscal dir., 1975-78; fiscal dir. Phila. Allied Action Commn., 1978-80; budget dir. Phila. City Council, 1980—; pvt. practice tax planning and acctg., Phila., 1975—; fin. cons. Mgmt. Reports, Inc., Phila., 1978—. Fin. sec. Hwy. Ch. of Christ, Sharon Hill, Pa., 1970; treas. Phila. Citywide Devel. Corp., 1975; active Phila. Home and Sch. Assn., 1980, Boy Scouts Am., Phila., 1981. Democrat. Mem. Apostolic Ch. Office: Phila City Coun 564 City Hall Philadelphia PA 19107

JOHNSON, ROBERT LEWIS, JR., retail company executive; b. Chgo., June 17, 1935; s. Robert Lewis Sr. and Gladys (Cherry) J.; m. Rose Harris; children—Rhonda, Rosalyn. B.A., Roosevelt U., 1958. Asst. mgr. Chgo. Housing Authority, 1960-65; v.p. specialty sales Sears, Roebuck and Co., Chgo., 1965—; dir. Rymer Corp., Chgo. Bd. dirs. Evanston Hosp., Ill., 1983-87, Suburban United Way, Chgo., 1987—, Voices for Ill. Children, 1987—; chmn. Evanston Civil Service commn., 1981-88; trustee Roosevelt U., Chgo., 1986—, mem. alumni bd., 1984-88; mem. Sch. of Bus. Round Table Fla. A&M U., 1987—. Served with U.S. Army, 1958-60. Club: Druids. Home: 310 Barton Ave Evanston IL 60202 Office: Sears Roebuck & Co Sears Tower Chicago IL 60684

JOHNSON, ROBERT N., metallurgical engineer, consultant; b. Belgrade, Minn., Feb. 17, 1934; s. Nobel Odin and Catherine Rebecca (Reese) J.; m. Anne Claudia Pechacek, Aug. 19, 1961; children: Wendy, Julie, Mark. Degree in Metallurgy, Colo. Sch. of Mines, 1957; MBA, Colo. State U., 1987. Mgr. bus. devel. Stearns Catalytic Corp., Denver, 1982-84; mgr. projects Stearns Roger div. United Engring., Denver, 1987—; metall. engr. Cleve. Cliffs Iron Co., Ishpeming, Mich., 1965-67; mech. design engr. Stearns Roger Corp., Denver, 1963-65, project engr., 1967-70; resident engr. Stearns Roger Corp., Aso, Ariz., 1970-73; project engr. Stearns Roger Corp., Denver, 1973-76, project mgr., 1973-82; mgr. bus. devel. Stearns Catalytic Corp., Denver, 1982-84; mgr. projects Stearns Roger div. United Engring., Denver, 1984-87; cons. process engring. and project mgmt. Denver, 1987—. Vol. Boy Scouts Am., Lakewood, Colo., 1978—, Spl. Olympics, Lakewood, 1984—. Mem. AIME (vice chmn. ext. met. subsect. 1987-88, chmn. 1988—), Project Mgmt. Inst. Republican. Home: 1650 S Estes St Lakewood CO 80226 Office: Johnson HYYPPA Ltd 2255 S Wadsworth Ste 101 Lakewood CO 80227

JOHNSON, RONALD ALAN, plastics company executive; b. Chgo., May 30, 1948; s. Raymond Alfred and Ellen Mae (Clauson) J.; m. Helen Margaret Katlun, June 8, 1969 (div. Mar. 1980); children: Richard Andrew, Ryan David, Scott Gregory; m. Mary Ann Dragovich, Nov. 20, 1982; children: Daniel Nicholas, Katherine Marie. BA in History, Columbia U., 1970. Terr. mgr. Procter & Gamble Co., Cin., 1970-72; plastics specialist Baxter Travenol Labs., Deerfield, Ill., 1972-75; mgr. nat. sales Klapat, Union, S.C., 1975-86; v.p. sales and mktg. Wellington-Klapat Co., Madison, Ga., 1986-87; sales mgr. spl. markets Duraco Products Inc., Streamwood, Ill., 1987—. Republican. Presbyterian. Office: Duraco Products Inc 1109 E Lake St Streamwood IL 60103

JOHNSON, RONNIE, industrial engineer, motivational trainer; b. Jasper, Ala., Dec. 27, 1948; s. James Alex and Elsie (Hollis) J.; m. Iris Smiley, Nov. 19, 1969 (div. Mar. 1975); 1 child, Ronnie Jr. Certs. in mgmt., Clayton State Coll., 1986, 87. Machine operator 3-M Co., Cleve., 1970-72; steel sawman Crusible Steel Co., Solon, Ohio, 1972-73; machinist mate Farmers Marine Co., Galveston, Tex., 1973-76; analyst time study Reed Tool Co., Houston, 1976-78; technician methods and standards Daniel Industries, Houston, 1978-80, Weatherford/DMC, Houston, 1980-83; indsl. engr. Porex Techs., Fairburn, Ga., 1984—, trainer, 1987—; cons. Ga. Dept. Labor, 1987; cons., trainer Atlanta Chs., 1987—. Active in Big Bros./Big Sisters of Atlanta, 1987—; vice chmn. programs New Life Presbyns. Ch., mem. of caucus. With USN, 1968-69. Mem. Inst. Indsl. Engrs. Democrat. Home: 5058 Jonesboro Rd Union City GA 30291 Office: Porex Techs 7380 Bohannon Rd Fairburn GA 30213

JOHNSON, SAMUEL CURTIS, wax company executive; b. Racine, Wis., Mar. 2, 1928; s. Herbert Fisk and Gertrude (Brauner) J.; m. Imogene Powers, May 8, 1954; children: Samuel Curtis III, Helen Johnson-Leipold, Herbert Fisk III, Winifred Johnson Marquart. BA, Cornell U., 1950; MBA, Harvard U., 1952; LLD (hon.), Carthage Coll., 1974, Northland Coll., 1974, Ripon Coll., 1980, Carroll Coll., 1981, U. Surrey, 1985, Marquette U., 1986. With S.C. Johnson & Son, Inc., Racine, 1954—; internat. v.p. S.C. Johnson & Son, Inc., 1962-63, exec. v.p., 1963-66, pres., 1966-67, chmn., pres., chief exec. officer, 1967-72, chmn., chief exec. officer, 1972-88, chmn., 1988—; bd. dirs. Johnson Wax Cos., Eng., Japan, Germany, Switzerland, Can., Australia, France, Mex., Deere & Co., Moline, Ill., Mobil Corp., N.Y.C.; chmn. bd. dirs. Johnson Heritage Bancorp, Ltd., Racine, Wis., Johnson Worldwide Assocs., Inc., H.J. Heinz Co., Pitts., Johnson Internat. Bancorp, Ltd. Chmn. The Mayo Found., Johnson's Wax Fund, Inc., Johnson Found., Inc.; trustee emeritus, presdl. councillor Cornell U.; founding chmn. emeritus Prairie Sch., Racine; mem. adv. council Cornell U. Grad. Sch. Mgmt.; bd. regents Smithsonian Assn.; mem. Bus. Coun., Internat. Coun. of J.P. Morgan. Mem. Chi Psi. Clubs: Cornell (N.Y.C., Milw.); Univ. (Milw.); Racine Country; Am. (London). Home: 4815 Lighthouse Dr Racine WI 53402 Office: S C Johnson & Son Inc 1525 Howe St Racine WI 53403

JOHNSON, SANKEY ANTON, manufacturing company executive; b. Bremerton, Wash., May 14, 1940; s. Sankey Broyd and Alice Mildred (Norum) J.; m. Carolyn Lee Rogers, Nov. 30, 1968; children: Marni Lee, Ronald Anton. B.S. in M.E, U. Wash.; M.B.A., Stanford U. Vice pres. gen. mgr. Cummins Asia Pacific, Manila, Philippines, 1974-78; v.p. automotive Cummins Engine Co., Columbus, Ind., 1978-79; v.p. North Am. Bus., 1979-81; pres., chief exec. officer Onan Corp., Mpls., 1981-85; exec. v.p. Pentair Inc., St. Paul, from 1985, chief operating officer, 1985—, pres., 1986-89; pres., chief exec. officer Johnson Industries, Mpls., 1989—; bd. dirs. Roger's Electromatics Inc., Donaldson Co., Hitchcock Industries. Bd. dirs. Twin Cities Jr. Achievement. Mem. Am. Mgmt. Assn. Clubs: Minneapolis, Wayzata Country. Home: 2709 Hidden Creek Ln Wayzata MN 55391 Office: Johnson Industries 4806 IDS Ctr Minneapolis MN 55402 *

JOHNSON, SCOTT WILLIAM, manufacturing company executive, lawyer; b. St. Paul, Apr. 10, 1940; s. Clark William and Ruth (McCulloch) J.; AB, Harvard U., 1962; JD, U. Minn., 1966; m. Marjorie Anne Rex, June 13, 1964; children: Matthew Rex, Katharine Brooke. Bar: Colo. 1966, Wis. 1970, Minn. 1976. Tchr., Maumee Valley Country Day Sch., Toledo, 1962-63; atty. firm Sherman & Howard, Denver, 1966-70; asst. gen. counsel Trane Co., LaCrosse, Wis., 1970-72; gen. counsel, sec. Western Empire Fin., Denver, 1972-75; asst. gen. counsel Bemis Co., Mpls., 1975-78; v.p. gen. counsel Am. Hoist & Derrick Co., St. Paul, 1978-88; bd. dirs. Vac Tec Systems, Inc., Amhoist, 1982-87; chmn. bd. Farwell Ozmun, 1986-87, Kirk and Co.; v.p., gen. counsel, corp. sec. Bemis co., Mpls., 1988—. Mem. ABA, Wis., Colo., Minn. bar assns. Republican. Congregationalist. Club: Interlachen Country. Office: Bemis Co 800 Northstar Ctr Minneapolis MN 55402

JOHNSON, SHERREL EDMUND, broadcasting company executive; b. Los Angeles, Nov. 9, 1945; s. Joseph Edmund and Miney Oleta (Stanley) J.; m. Dorothy B. Lopez, Nov. 12, 1966 (div. Apr. 1983); 1 child, Carl Edmund; m. Terry Ann Kimber, July 27, 1983 (div. Apr. 1987). Grad. high sch., Oakland, Calif. Staff technician overseas radio div. Am. Telephone and Telegraph, Oakland, 1963-68; staff engr. Sta. KGO-TV, San Francisco, 1968, mgr. R.F. facilities, 1984-86, dir. engring., 1986—; staff engr. Sta. KBHK-TV, San Francisco, 1968-69, various ABC TV and radio stas., San Francisco, 1969-77; chief engr. Sta. KSFX-FM, San Francisco, 1977-81, Sta. KGO-AM, San Francisco, 1981-82; chmn. bd. dirs., chief exec. officer Madzar Corp., Fremont, Calif., 1982-84; chmn. bd. dirs., chief exec. officer No. Calif. Frequency Coordinating Com. Inc., San Francisco, 1985—; asst. treas. Sutro Tower, Inc., San Francisco, 1986—. Served as sgt. USMCR, 1966-71. Mem. Soc. Motion Picture and TV Engrs., Soc. Broadcast Engrs., IEEE, Soc. Bay Area Broadcast Engrs. Republican. Lutheran. Office: Sta KGO-TV 900 Front St San Francisco CA 94111

JOHNSON, SHIRLEY ANN, health care executive; b. Detroit, Apr. 12, 1944; d. Edward James and Verdia (Kegler) Joseph; children: Cynthia Elaine, Gerald Essex, Natalie Ann. AS, Highland Park Coll., Mich., 1975; BS, Mercy Coll., Detroit, 1982; MS, U. Detroit, 1984. Lab. technician Children's Hosp. of Mich., Detroit, 1964-69, med. lab. technician, 1973-84; mgr. implementations Comprehensive Health Svcs., Detroit, 1985-86, adminstr., 1987—. Mem. Am. Acad. Med. Adminstrs., Nat. Assn. Female Execs., Greater Detroit Area Health Council, Soc. Healthcare Planning & Mktg. Democrat. Methodist. Home: 15390 Hubbell Detroit MI 48227 Office: Comprehensive Health Svcs 6500 John C Lodge Detroit MI 48227

JOHNSON, TERRILL B., insurance company executive; b. Galesburg, Ill., Dec. 1, 1942; s. Arthur August and Lenore May (Pugh) J.; m. Susan Johnson, Dec. 29, 1963; children: Terrill B. Jr., Timothy, Brett C. Bachelors, Augustana U.; Masters, Am. Coll. Cert. fin. planner, chartered fin. cons., CLU; lic. ins. agt. Iowa. Agt. Conn. Mutual Life Ins., Davenport, Iowa, 1964-67, supr., 1967-70, gen. agt., 1970—; bd. dirs. Bi-State Packaging, Rock Island, Ill. Mem. Am. Soc. CLU's, Chartered Fin. Cons. (pres.-elect), Gen. Agt. Mgrs. Assn. (pres. 1977-78), Quad City Estate Planning Coun. (pres. 1985-86), Davenport Assn. Life Underwriters (pres. 1980-81), Pinnacle Country Club. Republican. Lutheran. Office: River Bend Fin Group 111 Perry St Davenport IA 52801

JOHNSON, THOMAS ALLIBONE BUDD, pension fund administrator, consultant; b. Washington, Nov. 11, 1955; s. William D. and Susan A. (Budd) J.; m. Hannelore B. Langener, Oct. 29, 1981; children: Jason Ellis,

Ashley. BA, Davidson Coll., 1978. With Merrill Lynch, Houston, 1982-84; cons. group assoc. E.F. Hutton Cons. Group, Houston, 1984-88; pension cons. Shearson Lehman Hutton Cons. Group, Houston, 1988—. Contbr. articles to profl. jours. Asst. troop leader Sam Houston Coun. Boy Scouts Am., 1986-87. 1st. lt. U.S. Army, 1978-82. Mem. Internat. Found. Employee Benefit Plans, Investment Mgmt. Cons. Assn. Episcopalian. Home: 1806 Copperwood Ln Richmond TX 77469 Office: Shearson Lehman Hutton Cons Group 580 W Lake Park Blvd Ste 1700 Houston TX 77079

JOHNSON, THOMAS S., banker; b. Racine, Wis., Nov. 19, 1940; s. H. Norman and Jane Agnes (McAvoy) J.; m. Margaret Ann Werner, Apr. 18, 1970; children: Thomas Philip, Scott Michael, Margaret Ann. A.B. in Econs., Trinity Coll., 1962; M.B.A., Harvard U., 1964. Instr. Ateneo de Manila U. Grad. Bus. Sch., Philippines, 1964-66; spl. asst. to controller U.S. Dept. Def., Washington, 1966-69; with Chem. Bank, N.Y.C., 1969—, pres., dir., 1983—; dir. Pan Atlantic Re, Chem. Banking Corp., Tex. Commerce Bankshares. Chmn. bd. dirs. Union Theol. Sem.; bd. dirs. Montclair Art Mus. (N.J.), Phelps Stokes Fund, N.Y.C., Inst. Internat. Edn.; trustee Trinity Coll.; v.p., bd. dirs. Cancer Research Inst. Mem. Assn. Res. City Bankers, The Group of 30, Council Fgn. Relations, Bond Club N.Y., Econs. Club N.Y. Democrat. Roman Catholic. Clubs: Montclair Golf; Palm Beach Polo & Country; Harvard Bus.; River (N.Y.C.), The Links; Chgo. Office: Chem Banking Corp 277 Park Ave New York NY 10172

JOHNSON, VERNON EUGENE, history educator, educational administrator; b. Norfolk, Va., Oct. 25, 1930; s. Ellis Moses and Maude Louvenia (Wilkins) J.; m. Barbara Lucy Wynder, June 6, 1959; children: Kevin Bertram, Troy Eugene, Stacy Yvette. AB with distinction, Va. State Coll., 1951; MA, U. Pa., 1964; diploma with honors U.S. Army Command and Gen. Staff Coll., 1968; postgrad. Old Dominion U., 1977-78; advanced cert. in edn. Coll. William and Mary, 1979, EdD, 1982. Commd. 2d lt. U.S. Army, 1951, advanced through grades to lt. col., 1966, ret., 1979; adminstr., univ. collection mgr., adj. instr. Hampton (Va.) U., 1980—; sr. prof. Tidewater Va. Ctr.; St. Leo Coll. of Fla., 1980—. Active Boys' Clubs. Decorated Legion of Merit with oak leaf cluster; recipient Brotherhood award, 1981, Jefferson Cup, 1982; named Man of Yr., 1981. Mem. Am. Assn. of Higher Edn., Am. Hist. Assn., Assn. for the Study Higher Edn., Nat. Hist. Assn., Assn. U.S. Army, Alpha Kappa Mu, Phi Alpha Theta, Omega Psi Phi (3d dist. rep.). Methodist. Club: Beau Brummell Civic and Social. Office: Hampton Univ Stone Bldg Hampton VA 23668

JOHNSON, WALTER GILES, III, marketing executive; b. Jackson, Miss., Feb. 14, 1947; s. Walter Giles Jr. and Bettie (Horrell) J.; divorced; 1 child, Stephanie Grace. BS, Miss. State U., 1971. CLU; chartered fin. cons.; cert. fin. planner. Life agt. Mass. Mut. Life Ins. Co., Jackson, 1984-87; dir. investment mktg. C.M. Alliance, Jackson, 1987—. Mem. Internat. Assn. Fin. Planning, Internat. Assn. Cert. Fin. Planning, Nat. Assn. Life Underwriters, Kiwanis (bd. dirs. Jackson chpt. 1988—). Office: CM Alliance 850 E River Pl Ste 403 Jackson MS 39202

JOHNSON, WANDA FAYE, waste disposal company executive; b. Houston, June 23, 1959; d. Wesley J. and Lillie (Jackson) J. Student Houston pub. schs. Sales mgr. Johnson & Sons Disposal Svcs., Houston, 1970-85; pres. Johnson's Disposal Svcs., Houston, 1985—. Mem. NAACP (Houston chpt.), Houston Apt. Assn., Buy Freedom, Houston Restaurant Assn., Greater C. of C. of Houston, Houston Urban League, LWV (Houston chpt.). Home: 4706 Trail Lake Houston TX 77045 Office: Johnson's Disposal Svc 8400 Lawler St Houston TX 77051

JOHNSON, WARREN RICHARD, aerospace company executive, retired marine corps officer; b. Stillwater, Minn., Sept. 25, 1928; s. Seymour Evan Richard and Ethel Christine (Hallen) J.; m. Violet L. Bergquist, June 11, 1950; children—Karen C., Warren R., Matthew E., Paul W. B.A., U. Minn., 1950; student, Indsl. Coll. Armed Forces, 1969-70; M.S.B.A., George Washington U., 1970. Commd. 2d lt. U.S. Marine Corps, 1950, advanced through grades to maj. gen., 1976; served as supply officer First Marine Div. Korea, 1952-53; exec. officer Supply Sch. Co. Camp Lejeune, N.C., 1954-57; served with 3d Marine Div. Okinawa, Japan, 1957-58; at Marine Corps Supply Ctr. Barstow, Calif., 1958-61; at Marine Corps. Hdqrs. 1961-64, marine aide to asst. sec. Navy for installations and logistics, 1965-67; supply officer 9th Marine Amphibious Brigade Vietnam, 1967-68; served at Marine Corps Supply Activity Phila., 1968-69; dir. supply ops. div., dir. tech. ops. div. and dep. chief of staff for ops. 1970-73; comdr. 2d Force Service Regt., Fleet Marine Force Atlantic, 1973-74; comdg. gen. Marine Corps Supply Ctr. Albany, Ga., 1974-76; asst. dep. chief of staff for installations and logistics Marine Corps. Hdqrs. Washington, 1976-77; dep. chief of staff 1977; comdg. gen. Marine Corps Logistics Base Albany, Ga., 1977-80; ret. U.S. Marine Corps, 1980; program dir. Fairchild Republic Co., Farmingdale, N.Y., 1980-87; tech. advisor Grumman Aerospace Corp., Bethpage, N.Y., 1987—. Decorated Legion of Merit, Bronze Star. Mem. Marine Corps Assn., U.S. Naval Inst., Am. Def. Preparedness Assn. Lutheran. Home: Tulip Dr R R #1 Box 149A Huntington NY 11743 Office: Grumman Aerospace Corp Bethpage NY 11714

JOHNSON, WENDY ROBIN, retail buyer; b. N.Y.C., Dec. 26, 1956; d. Clarence Woodson Jr. and Dolores Elizabeth (Dominguez) J. AAS in Bus., Elizabeth Seton Coll., 1981; BA in Fin., Marymount Manhattan Coll., 1983; MBA in Mgmt., Manhattan Coll., 1987. Receptionist RCA Records, N.Y.C., 1976-79, purchasing clk., 1979-81, buyer, 1981-83; mgr. purchasing PolyGram Records, N.Y.C., 1983-85; buyer Gen. Foods U.S.A., White Plains, N.Y., 1985—. Mem. Delta Sigma Theta. Home: 187 Elm Ave Teaneck NJ 07666-2320 Office: Gen Foods USA 250 North St White Plains NY 10625

JOHNSON, WILLIAM C., direct mail marketing company executive; b. 1940; married. BS, U. Kans., 1962. Mgr. Direct Mail Promotions, Look Mag., 1961-71; asst. v.p. Fingerhut Corp., Minnetonka, Minn., 1971-73, v.p., 1973-81, pres., chief operating officer, 1981-86, chmn., chief exec. officer, 1986. Bd. dirs. Better Bus. Bur. Mem. Direct Mktg. Assn. (chmn. 1987), Greater Mpls. C. of C. (bd. dirs.). Office: Fingerhut Corp 4400 Baker Rd Minnetonka MN 55343

JOHNSON, WILLIAM KELLY, controller; b. San Antonio, July 1, 1943; s. William Alton and Lillian Theresa (Kelly) J.; m. Lillian Jane Rowland, Nov. 18, 1962; children: W. Kelly, James A., Michelle J., Stephanie N. BBA summa cum laude, St. Mary's U., San Antonio, 1975. Store mgr. Nat. Convenience Stores Inc., San Antonio, 1971-75; sr. acct. Tex. Pacific Oil Co., Dallas, 1975-78; auditing mgr. Pool Well Servicing Co., Houston, 1979-80, acctg. mgr., 1980-82; controller Global Marine Prodn. Systems, Houston, 1982-83, Applied Drilling Technology Inc., Houston, 1983—. Mem. Nat. Assn. Accts., Am. Inst. CPAs, Tex. Soc. CPAs, Controller's Council, Bus. Planning Bd., Delta Epsilon Sigma, Kappa Pi Sigma. Democrat. Roman Catholic. Home: 7610 Weatherhill Ln Houston TX 77041 Office: Applied Drilling Tech Inc 10777 Westheimer Ste 700 Houston TX 77042

JOHNSON, WILLIAM POTTER, newspaper publisher; b. Peoria, Ill., May 4, 1935; s. William Zweigle and Helen Marr (Potter) J.; m. Pauline Ruth Rowe, May 18, 1968; children: Darragh Elizabeth, William Potter. AB, U. Mich., 1957. Gen. mgr. Bureau County Rep., Inc., Princeton, Ill., 1961-72; pres. Johnson Newspapers, Inc., Sebastopol, Calif., 1972-75, Evergreen, Colo., 1974-86, Canyon Commons Investment, Evergreen, 1974—; pres., chmn. bd. dirs. Johnson Media, Inc., Winter Park, Colo., 1987—. Author: How the Michigan Betas Built a $1,000,000 Chapter House in the '80s. Alt. del. Rep. Nat. Conv., 1968. Lt. USNR, 1958-61. Mem. Colo. Press Assn., Nat. Newspaper Assn., Suburban Newspapers Am., San Francisco Press Club, Beta Theta Pi, Sigma Delta Chi. Roman Catholic. Clubs: Hiwan Country (Evergreen); Oro Valley Country, Cañada Hills Country (Tucson). Home: 445 W Rapa Pl Tucson AZ 85737 Office: PO Box 409 Winter Park CO 80482

JOHNSON, WILLIAM RAY, insurance company executive; b. West Union, Ohio, Feb. 12, 1930; s. A. Earl and Helen (Walker) J.; B.S. in Edn., Wilmington Coll., 1951; m. Anne Abrams, Mar. 27, 1954; children—Elizabeth Anne, William Randall. Tchr., theater dept. Miami U., Oxford, Ohio, 1951; div. mgr. Prudential Ins. Co. of Am., Waco, Tex., 1956-60; nat. tng. cons. Paul Revere Life Ins. Co., Dallas, 1960-65; health and accident ins. cons., Dallas, 1965-68; pres. MSP Service Corp., Dallas, 1974—; partner Wiedemann & Johnson, Cos., Dallas, 1965—; bd. dirs. Cullen Frost Bank of Dallas. Bd. dirs. Suicide Prevention of Dallas, 1973-81, pres., 1975-76; bd. dirs. Routh St. Ctr., 1975-78, Turtle Creek Manor, 1977-79, Sr. Citizens of Greater Dallas, Inc., 1977-81, Dallas Child Guidance Clinic, 1977-83; mem. Bishops Adv. Com. on Planning and Devel., Episcopal Diocese of Dallas, 1976-81; sr. warden St. Michael's Episcopal Ch., 1979-81; trustee Episcopal Theol. Sem. of SW, Austin, Tex., 1981-87, mem. exec. com., 1984-86; mem. bd. theol. edn. Episcopal Ch., N.Y.C., 1982-88; mem. exec. council Episcopal Diocese of Dallas, 1983-86, standing com., 1987—; trustee St. Michael Sch., 1989—, Greater Dallas Community of Chs., 1986-89, mem. exec. com. 1987-88. Served to 1st lt. USAF, 1951-55. Mem. Multiple Sclerosis Soc. (bd. dirs. N. Texas Div. 1987-89), Anglican Sch. Theology (bd. trustees 1986-89). Clubs: Dallas City, Dallas Country. Office: 3500 Oak Lawn Ave Suite 300 Dallas TX 75219-4216

JOHNSTON, ALLAN FREDRICK, controller, educator; b. Pawhuska, Okla., Nov. 22, 1942; s. Fred and Ferol (Lamb) J.; m. Suzanne O'Neil; children: David, Lisken, Jeffrey. BS, U. Okla., 1965, MBA, 1970. Mgmt. cons. Arthur Andersen & Co., Dallas, 1970-71; mgr. corp. inventory acctg. Union Carbide Co., Tarrytown, N.Y., 1971-76, mgr. fixed asset acctg., 1976-79; asst. div. contr. Union Carbide Co., Danbury, Conn., 1979-81; contr., dir. fin., instr. Pacific N.W. div. Battelle Meml. Inst., Richland, Wash., 1981—; instr. U. Wash., Seattle, 1986—. Bd. dirs. Mid-Columbia Arts Council, Richland; mem. allocations com. United Way, Richland, 1982-85, campaign bd. dirs., 1987; treas. Mid-Columbia Hosp., Richland, 1984. With U.S. Army, 1965-68. Mem. Fin. Execs. Inst. Republican. Office: Pacific NW Labs PO Box 999 Richland WA 99352

JOHNSTON, BENNIE WADE, accountant; b. Plantersville, MIss., Nov. 25, 1936; s. Elger Wade and Ellie Dee (Clayton) J.; m. Nancy Jo Davis, Dec. 22, 1968. BBA, U. Miss., 1961, MBA, 1962. Acct. Ben F. Mitchell & Assocs., Cleveland, Miss., 1962-63; chief acct. Oldberg Mfg. Co., Dyersburg, Tenn., 1963-68, Day Brite Lighting Co., Tupelo, Miss., 1968-69, Trenton Mills, Inc., 1969-77; prin. Johnston Bookkeeping Svc., Dyersburg, 1977-86; mgr. One Way Bookkeeping Svc., Inc., Dyersburg, 1986—; instr. acctg. Cumberland U., Lebanon, Tenn., 1986—. With U.S. Army, 1955-58. Mem. Ch. of God. Home: 2049 Crossgate Rd Dyersburg TN 38024 Office: One Way Bookkeeping Svc Inc PO Box 546 Dyersburg TN 38025-0546

JOHNSTON, CHRISTINA JANE, real estate executive, mortgage broker, educator; b. Toronto, Ont., Can., June 3, 1952; d. George Elmer and Mary Selina (Northey) J. B.A. with honors, U. Western Ont., London, 1975. Researcher, writer House of Commons, Ottawa, Ont., 1975-77; adminstrv. mgr. sales Marco Beach Realty, Marco Island, Fla., 1977-79; pres., owner Marco Summit Realty, Marco Island, 1979-82; v.p., mortgage broker Windjammer of Marco, Marco Island, 1979—; instr. Realty World Acad., St. Petersburg, Fla., 1979-81 ; pres., mgr. Fla. Sun Realty Co., Sarasota, 1982-86; v.p., mgr. Fla. Home Properties & Comml. Realty, Inc., 1986-87; mgr. 1st So. Trust Realty Corp., 1987—; bd. dirs., chmn. edn. com. Sarasota Bd. Realtors, 1985-86, also mem. realtors polit. action com. 1985—; pres. So. Gulf Council Realty World, 1980-82; bd. dirs. First Fla. region Broker's Council, Realty World, 1982-84; pres. Women's Council of Realtors, Marco Island, 1988; dir. Marco Island Bd. Realtors, 1987—; pres. Marco Multi-List, 1989. Contbr. articles to profl. jours. Pres. Young Progressive Conservatives, Cambridge, Ont., 1968-70; Recipient Office of Yr. award Realty World, 1980, Top Listing Office award, 1981, Spl. award for Prodn., 1981, Million Dollar Sales Awards Marco Beach and Realty World, 1979-81. Mem. Sarasota C. of C., Marco Island C. of C. (chmn. Expo '82). Home: 829 W Elkcam Cir #107 Marco Island FL 33937

JOHNSTON, DANIEL WEBSTER, banker, investment company executive; b. Dickson County, Tenn., Sept. 30, 1903; s. James C. and Dixie (White) J.; m. Elizabeth Sudekum, Dec. 28, 1943; children—Frances Earthman, Dan W., Anthony S. Student Indsl. and Tng. Sch., Huntington, Tenn.; diploma in banking, Rutgers State U. Founder, asst. cashier Third Nat. Bank, Nashville, 1927, various positions to sr. chmn. bd., until 1970; dir. Mountain Life Ins. Co., Bank of Commerce, Woodbury, Tenn.; chmn. bd., Farmers and Mchts. Bank, White Bluff, Tenn.; past pres. Nashville Clearing House, Am. Inst. Banking (Nashville chpt.). Mem. Nashville Area C. of C. Methodist. Clubs: Belle Meade, City (Nashville). Lodges: Mason, Shriners. Home: 400 Jackson Blvd Nashville TN 37205 Office: Third Nat Bank Nashville TN 37244

JOHNSTON, DENNIS ROY, facility management consultant, corporation interior design company executive; b. Wahoo, Nebr., June 29, 1937; s. Roy Alfred and Wilma Jean (Weidensall) J.; Student U. Nebr., 1955-56, 57-58, U. Colo., 1961-64; m. Dorothy McLay Carr, June 19, 1965; children—Kristin Anne, Ami Carr. City planner Denver Urban Renewal Authority, 1965-69; dir. graphics Haines, Lundberg & Waehler, N.Y.C., 1969-72; sr. v.p., sr. project mgr. LCP Assos., Inc., N.Y.C., 1972—. Mem. Adminstrv. Mgmt. Soc. (cert. of merit), Am. Mgmt. Assn., Fish and Game Assn. Chatham. Republican. Methodist. Home: 3 Sussex Ave Chatham NJ 07928 Office: LCP Assos Inc 25 Tudor City Pl New York NY 10017

JOHNSTON, DONALD WALTER, retail department store executive; b. New Orleans, Nov. 25, 1936; s. Alex Henry and Henrietta (Moreci) J.; m. Sally Elizabeth Staub, Jan. 28, 1973; children—Donna, David, Denis, Christi. B.S., La. State U. Trainee, asst. buyer D.H. Holmes Co. Ltd., New Orleans, 1959-63, buyer, 1963-67, div. mdse. mgr., 1967-72, v.p. merchandising, 1972-78, sr. v.p. mdse. and advt., 1978-86, exec. v.p. mdse. and advt., 1985—, pres., chief exec. officer, 1986-87, chmn. bd. dirs. Mem. Nat. Retail Mchts. Assn. Democrat. Roman Catholic. Clubs: New Orleans Athletic, Metairie Country. Office: D H Holmes Co Ltd 819 Canal St New Orleans LA 70112

JOHNSTON, DONNA FAYE, color consultant, production art director; b. Stromburg, Nebr., Oct. 16, 1941; d. Verlin James and Roberta Carola (Larsen) Fellows; m. Robert Carl Johnston, May 2, 1964 (div. 1965); 1 child, Karla Kathliene. BFA, Kansas City Art Inst., 1963; journeyman cert., Graphic Communications Union, 1980; cert. color correction, Vocat. Tech. Edn., 1980. Prodn. mgr. H.H. Harney Advt., Lincoln, Nebr., 1966-68; lead mech. art and trainer Bozell & Jacobs Advt., Omaha, 1968-70; mech. art spl. account Dudycha Studio, Omaha, 1970-72; prodn. mgr. Oliver Advt., Kansas City, 1972-73; prodn. and color correction artist Vile/Goller Fine Arts, Kansas City, 1973-79; color correction artist K&A Lithographing, Kansas City, 1979-80, Chroma-Graphics, Kansas City, 1980-81; color correction artist and quality control Orent Graphic Arts, Omaha, 1981-86; color correction supr. Epsen-Hillmer Graphics Co., Omaha, 1986—; printing cons. Margo Kries-Entrepreneur, Stromsburg, 1987—, Willie Plith-Photographer, Omaha, 1987—. Author monthly newsletter Am. Singles, 1986. Mem. Landmarks, Omaha, 1986-87, Westport Art Assn., Kansas City, 1979-80, Earthwatch, Watertown, Mass., 1985-87, Nat. Geographic Soc., 1984-85. Mem. Omaha Club Printing House Craftsmen (bd. dirs.), Nat. Assn. Female Execs., Am. Singles of Omaha (pub. relations dir. 1986-87, author monthly newsletter 1986), Parents Without Ptnrs. (Outstanding Service award 1986). Methodist. Office: Epsen-Hillmer Graphics Co 2000 California Omaha NE 68102

JOHNSTON, DOUGLAS FREDERICK, industrial holding company executive; b. Phila., Nov. 18, 1930; s. Douglas Miller and Ellen Eudora (Brewer) J.; m. Marilyn Jane March, Nov. 25, 1955 (div. Jan. 1985); children: Douglas Jr., Leslie Ann, Dina Louise, Kim Marie. BS, Yale U., 1952; MBA, Harvard U., 1958. Portfolio mgr. Investors Diversified Svcs., Mpls., 1958-66; exec. v.p. TICOR, L.A., 1966-73, The Pittston Co., Greenwich, Conn., 1973-78; chmn. Majestic Wood Products, Walden, N.Y., 1979-84; pres. Rivondale Oil Co., Oklahoma City, 1983-88, also bd. dirs.; pres., chief exec. officer Sudbury, Inc., Cleve., 1988—, also bd. dirs.; bd. dirs. Arrow Dynamics, Inc. Lt. USN, 1952-56. Office: Sudbury Inc 25800 Science Park Dr Cleveland OH 44122

JOHNSTON, EDWIN JOSEPH, JR., utility company executive; b. N.Y.C., Nov. 11, 1937; s. Edwin Joseph and Elizabeth Marie (Keller) J.; m. Irene Mary Klukowski, Aug. 13, 1966; children: Jennifer Ann, Jacqueline Rose, Janelle Marie. BSME, Villanova U., 1962; MBA, U. Conn., 1967. Performance engr. Pratt & Whitney Aircraft, East Hartford, Conn., 1962-65; indsl. sales engr. Conn. Light & Power Co., Willimantic, Conn., 1966-73; mgr. energy mgmt. services Conn. Light & Power Co., Danielson, Conn., 1973-80; mgr. ems dept. Conn. Light & Power Co., Enfield, Conn., 1980; mgr. new bus. Northeast Utilities, Hartford, Conn., 1980-87, mgr. mktg., 1987—; instr. Quinebaug Valley Community Coll., Killingly, Conn., 1973-79; chmn. comml./indsl. com. Electric Council New Eng., Bedford, Mass., 1985-87. Chmn. St. Columba Parish Council, Columbia, Conn., 1973-77, Columbia Planning and Zoning Commn., 1982—; sec. Shetucket Valley Devel. Corp., Willimantic, 1972-73. Mem. ASME. Republican. Roman Catholic. Club: Norwich (Conn.) Power Squadron (treas. 1980-81, vice comdr. 1981-82). Lodge: Lions (pres. Columbia 1976-77). Home: Erdoni Rd Columbia CT 06237 Office: Northeast Utilities PO Box 270 Hartford CT 06141

JOHNSTON, FRED BALCH, II, graphic company executive; b. Evanston, Ill., Feb. 28, 1938; s. Fred Balch and Evelyn (Weber) J.; m. Linda Wiseman, Aug. 8, 1964; children: Fred Balch III, Scott G., Allison B. Student, Cornell U., 1956-59; BBA, Northwestern U., 1961. Salesman Weisz Decalcomania Inc., Chgo., 1963-65, sales mgr., 1965-68, v.p. sales, 1968-74; pres., chief operating officer Weisz Graphics, Chapin, S.C., 1974-80; pres., chief exec. officer Fred B. Johnston Co. Inc., Chapin, 1980—; mem. graphics communications adv. group Clemson (S.C.) U., 1986—. Mem. adv. bd. fed. program Job Partnership Tng. Act, Lexington S.C., 1985-86., Clemson, S.C. Served with U.S. Army, 1961-63. Home: 1406 Beaver Dam Rd Columbia SC 29212 Office: Weisz Graphics B280 Chapin SC 29036

JOHNSTON, GARY RALPH, financial executive; b. East Orange, N.J., Nov. 25, 1942; s. Ralph and Elsie Beatrice (Buchanan) J.; m. Sandra Ann St. Julian, May 21, 1971; children: Gwyn, Renee, Shawn. BS, Fairleigh Dickinson U., 1965; MBA, U. Toledo, 1979. Cert. internal auditor. Auditor field Gen. Corp. (formerly Gen. Tire & Rubber), Akron, Ohio, 1965-66, 68-70; sr. internal auditor Sterling Drug Inc., N.Y.C., 1970-72; mgr. audit & tech. support Libbey-Owens-Ford, Inc., Toledo, 1972-84; mgr. corp. internal auditing Easco Corp., Balt., 1984-86; sec./treas., chief fin. officer Custom-Bilt Machinery Inc., York, Pa., 1986-88; chief fin. officer, controller Custom-Bilt Machinery, div. Am. Internat., Inc., York, 1988—. Served with USMC, 1966-68. Mem. Inst. Internal Auditors (com. chmn. 1978-81, dir. 1980-81 and numerous other positions). Home: 31 Leader Dr Jacobus PA 17407 Office: Am Internat Inc Custom-Bilt Machinery div 419 Norway St York PA 17405

JOHNSTON, GEORGE ELMER, real estate developer; b. Brockville, Ont., Can., Jan. 31, 1927; came to U.S., 1977; s. George Elmer and Jane (Drew) J.; m. Mary Selina Northey, Aug. 1, 1951; children: Christina, Patricia, Shelly, Teri. Grad., Brockville Collegiate High Sch., Ontario, Can. Lic. real estate agt., Fla. Pres., chief exec. officer Williams Shoe Ltd., 1949-65; v.p. J.A. Johnston Co., Ltd., Brockville, Ont., Can., 1951-65; pres., chief exec. officer Jarman Shoes, Cambridge, Ont., Can., 1953-65; chief exec. officer Genesco (Can) Ltd., Cambridge, 1965-67; pvt. practice real estate Cambridge, 1967-68; chmn., chief exec. officer Diversco Holdings Ltd., Cambridge, 1968-74; v.p. Ontario Trust Co., Toronto, Ont., Can., 1972-74; pres., chief exec. officer Windjammer Corp., Marco Island, Fla., 1977—; pres. Johnco Investments Inc., Marco Island, 1977—; chmn., chief exec. officer Diversco Holdings Ltd., 1968-74, Franklin Lumber Co. Ltd., 1968-74, Vascan Securities, 1968-74, Leaseway Transit, 1968-74, Thainen Securities, 1968-74, Woolley Shoes Ltd., 1968-74, Knolls Printing Ltd., 1968-74, Funcraft Vehicles Ltd., 1968-74; pres. Resorts Recreational, 1977-81, Skico Inc., 1980-82, Smokey Mountain Investments, 1981—, Northey Investments Inc., 1981—, Chez Shel Inc., 1977—; chief exec. officer Continental Overseas Devel., 1979-81, Gatlinburg Summit Realty, 1981-82, Club Tenn Ptnrs., 1980—; v.p., cons. polit. organizer Ontario Trust Co., 1972-74; cons. mgmt. 1977—. Chmn. fund raising campaign Peel Meml. Hosp., 1954-56; bd. dirs. Waterloo Cancer Soc., Ont., 1966-67; chmn. Plebisite Com., Galt., Ont., 1966-67; campaign dir. then chmn. Prog. Conservatives of Ont., Waterloo County, 1968-74; campaign chmn. providence of Ont. Prog. Conservatives of Can. Served with Royal Can. Naval Res., 1944-45. Distinctive Merit award Graphics Club of Can., 1969, Merit award Premier of Ont., 1972, Special Sales award Marco Beach Realty, Inc. 1978, Comml. Salesman of Yr. Marco Beach Realty, 1979. Mem. Marco Island Area Bd. Realtors, Fla. Assn. of Realtors, Nat. Assn. Realtors. Anglican. Clubs: International (assoc.). Home: PO Box 806 Marco Island FL 33969

JOHNSTON, GERALD ANDREW, aerospace company executive; b. Chgo., July 17, 1931; s. Gerald Ervan and Mary Henrietta (Dowell) J.; married; children: Jan, Colleen, Jeffrey, Gregory, Steven. Student, San Bernardina Jr. Coll., 1950-51; BS in Engring., U. Calif., L.A., 1956, Cert. of Bus. Mgmt., 1968, MS in Engring., 1972. Jr. engr. Shell Oil Co., 1952-54; test engr. Robinson Aviation, 1955-56; stress analyst N. Am. Aviation, 1955-56; assoc. engr. Douglas Aircraft Co., Santa Monica, Calif., 1956-68; dir., v.p. gen. mgr. McDonnell Douglas Astronautics, Huntington Beach, Calif., 1968-87; pres. McDonnell Douglas Corp., St. Louis, 1988—, also bd. dirs. Trustee St. Louis U., 1988—. Mem. Inst. Elec. and Electronic Engrs., Armed Forces Communications and Electonics Assn., Am. Inst. Aeronautics and Astronautics, Lambda Chi Alpha. Roman Catholic. Office: McDonnell Douglas Corp PO Box 516 Saint Louis MO 63166

JOHNSTON, GERALD MCARTHUR, food company executive; b. Atkins, Ark., Apr. 19, 1942; s. Finis and Beatrice (Virden) J.; m. Charlotte Raye Boren, May 31, 1963; children—Cheryl, Monte, Charity. BS, Ark. Poly. Inst., 1965. C.P.A., Ark. Bus. mgr. Morrilton Sch. Dist., Ark., 1965-66; pub. acct. Douglas Walker & Co., Fort Smith, Ark., 1968-70; cost and budget mgr. Tyson Foods, Inc., Springdale, Ark., 1970-74, sec.-treas., 1974-80, exec. v.p. fin., 1980—, also trustee fringe benefit plans; dir. First State Bank of Springdale. Mem. alumni bd. dirs. Ark. Tech. U., Russellville, 1985—. Served with U.S. Army, 1966-68. Mem. Am. Inst. C.P.A.s, Ark. Soc. C.P.A.s. Home: 3805 Valley View Dr Springdale AR 72764 Office: Tyson Foods Inc 2210 W Oaklawn Springdale AR 72764

JOHNSTON, JAMES BRUCE, steel company executive; b. Pitts., Oct. 7, 1930; s. Scott and Grace Elizabeth (Ford) J.; m. Rose Marie Silko, Feb. 16, 1957; children—J. Bruce, Jr., Gordon Scott, Harrison Charles, Jesse Cousins, Andrew Kirk. Student in govt. and econs., U. Pitts., 1948-52, J.D., 1955; student, Harvard U., 1952-53. Gen. mgr. labor relations U.S. Steel Co., Pitts, 1966-73, v.p. labor relations, 1973-77, v.p., gen. mgr. employee relations, 1977-81, sr. v.p. employee relations, 1981-83, exec. v.p. employee relations, 1983—; chief negotiator for basic steel industry; chmn. U.S. Employer Delegation-ILO steel sector; bd. dirs. Equimark Corp.;. Bd. trustees Robert Morris Coll., Pitts., Children's Hosp. of Pitts., Sta. WQED Pub. Broadcasting, Pitts. Served with U.S. Navy, 1955-57. Mem. Nat. Assn. Mfrs. (bd. dirs.), Bituminous Coal Operators Assn. (bd. dirs.), Am. Arbitration Assn. (bd. dirs.), Labor Policy Assn. (bd. dirs.). Republican. Presbyterian. Clubs: Duquesne (Pitts.); Rolling Rock (Ligonier, Pa.). Office: USX Corp 600 Grant St Pittsburgh PA 15219-4776

JOHNSTON, JAMES CANNON, financial executive; b. Ogden, Utah, May 6, 1955; s. Peter Budge and Charlotte (Cannon) J.; m. Mary Hazen, June 5, 1979; childrn: Rachel, Peter, Matthew, David. AB with high honors, Princeton U., 1979; MBA, U. Chgo., 1981. Fin. analyst Cummins Engine Co., Columbus, Ind., 1981-85; dir. fin. Cadec Systems Inc., Londonderry, N.H., 1985-86; regional mgr. Aqua Tek Inc., Manchester, N.H., 1986-87; prin. Saunders Capital Corp., Boston, 1987-88; chief fin. officer Embassy Microtech. and Packaging Inc., Framingham, Mass., 1988, DiscWorks Inc., Cambridge, Mass., 1988; chief fin. officer Handi-Van of Lowell (Mass.) Inc., 1988—, also bd. dirs. sec. Highland Goffe's Falls Sch. Support Assn., Manchester. Republican. Mormon.

JOHNSTON, JAMES D., automobile manufacturing company executive; b. McCook, Nebr., May 6, 1930; s. Glenn Raymond and Neville Regina (Daggett) J.; m. Margaret Mary Conrad; 1 child, Mary M.; children by previous marriage—Lynn M., Sandra S., Stephen T., Julie A. B.S. in Fgn. Service, Georgetown U., 1953; M.S. in Pub. Adminstrn., UCLA, 1957. With Fgn. Service, Dept. State, Washington, Mexico, Nicaragua, 1957-66; spl. asst. to pres. Motor Vehicles Mfrs. Assn., Detroit and Washington, 1966-71; adminstrv. coordinator, dir. Washington office Gen. Motors Corp., 1971-82; v.p. industry-govt. relations Gen. Motors Corp., Washington, 1982—. Bd.

govs. Ford's Theatre, Washington, 1982—; bd. dirs. Traffic Safety Now, Detroit, 1984—; pres. Am. Coalition Traffic Safety, 1986. Mem. Bus.-Govt. Relations Council, Fed. City Council (bd. dirs.), Nat. Assn. Mfrs. (bd. dirs.), Traffic Safety Assn. Mich. (bd. dirs.), Mich. Mfrs. Assn. (bd. dirs.). Clubs: Carlton, Economic (Washington); Recess (Detroit). Home: 2029 Connecticut Ave NW Washington DC 20036 Office: GM Corp 1660 L St NW Suite 401 Washington DC 20008

JOHNSTON, JERRY WILSON, banker; b. Port-au-Prince, Haiti, Sept. 25, 1932 (parents American citizens); s. James Wilson and Pauline (Claussner) J.; m. Katharine Mayer, June 8, 1957; children—Jennifer, Alexander. BA, U. So. Calif., 1954; MA, Fletcher Sch. Law and Diplomacy, Harvard U./Tufts U., 1957; Advanced Mgmt. Program, Harvard U., 1979. Joined Chase Manhattan Bank, N.Y.C., 1957, asst. treas., 1959-61, asst. v.p., 1961-65; mgr. Banco Continental, Lima, Peru, 1965-67, v.p., 1967-70; pres. Chase Manhattan Internat. Banking Corp., L.A., 1970-74; sr. v.p., sec. pac Security Pacific Nat. Bank, L.A., 1975-87, exec. v.p., sec. pac, 1986—. Bd. dirs. Hillsides Home for Children, Pasadena, Calif., 1984—; bd. dirs. Calif. Mus. Sci. and Industry, L.A.; trusee Diocesan Investment Trust, L.A. Mem. Calif. Club, San Gabriel Country Club, Jonathan Club (L.A.). Episcopalian. Office: Security Pacific Nat Bank PO Box 2097 Terminal Annex Los Angeles CA 90051

JOHNSTON, JOHN PAUL, real estate developer; b. L.A., Dec. 18, 1948; s. Donald Carlyle and Mary (Arena) J.; m. Susan Kelly Guengerich, June 6, 1970 (div. Dec. 1982); 1 child, Jonathan Mathew; m. Teri Kay Lybbert, Sept. 4, 1982; children: Mary Caherine, Sarah Elizabeth. BA, Fullerton (Calif.) State U., 1975. Pres. Johnston Devel. Corp., Park City, Utah, 1971-85, Golden Eagle Racing Group, Park City, Utah, 1979-83; v.p. Master's Fin. Corp., Newport Beach, Calif., 1981-83; pres. Exec. Domaine Inc., Sacramento, Calif., 1985—. Mem. Bldg. Industry Assn., Placer County Contractors Assn. Republican. Office: Exec Domaine PO Box 4 Rocklin CA 95677

JOHNSTON, JOHN WAYNE, educational administrator; b. McAlester, Okla., Oct. 8, 1943; s. Cecil Wayne and Hazel Elena (Robinson) J.; m. Lynda Faith Gee, Feb. 4, 1971 (div.); 1 son, Ian Sean. Student Graceland Coll., 1961-62, William Jewell Coll., 1962-63; B.S. in Journalism, Kans. U., 1964; M.A. in Edn. and Sociology, U. Mo.-Kansas City, 1966; M.A. in Polit. Sci., History and Econs., Goddard Coll., 1972; Ph.D. (hon.), Calif. Western U., 1975; Ph.D. in Social Psychology, Internat. U., 1975. Instr. Central Mo. State U., Independence, 1969-72; founder, chancellor The Internat. U., Independence, 1973—; Editor: Internat. U. Press, 1973—. Bd. dirs. Good Govt. League, Independence, Com. for County Progress, Jackson County, Mo.; asst. varsity soccer coach Ft. Osage High Sch., 1983-89. Republican. Mem. Reorganized Church of Jesus Christ of Latter Day Saints (ordained minister). Lodge: Lions (Independence). Author: Divided for Plunder, 1984; Turmoil in the North, 1984, Crisis in Northern Ireland, 1985, The University of the Future, 1985.

JOHNSTON, LAWRENCE FITZGERALD, insurance company executive; b. El Reno, Okla., May 6, 1935; s. Frank Lynn and Ann Lucile (Fitzgerald) J.; m. Mary Frances Kerber, May 27, 1961; children: Kathleen, Christine, Stephen, Cynthia, Karen, Charlene. BA, Aquinas Inst., 1958; MBA, U. Colo., 1976, D Bus. Adminstrn., 1981; MS, Am. Coll., 1977. CLU, Cert. fin. planner. Agt., supr. Great West Life Ins. Co., Denver, 1964-72; prin. Lawrence F. Johnston Inc., Denver, 1972-78; pres. Phifer-Johnston, Denver, 1978-81; br. mgr. E.F. Hutton Fin. Services, Denver, 1981-83; acct. exec., asst. v.p. E.F. Hutton & Co. Inc., Denver, 1981-85; dir. fin. planning Transamerica Fin. Resources, Denver, 1985—; cons. Transamerica Life Cos., Denver, 1987—; instr. grad. tax program U. Denver, 1987—; bd. dirs. Info. Solutions, Denver, Kellogg Corp., Littleton, Colo. Author: Investment Planning, 1984, How to Successfully Provide Personal Financial Planning, 1987, Case Studies in Personal Financial Planning. Past treas. Colo. Ins. Edn. Found., Denver; past pres. Denver Estate Planning Council; mem. Nat. Eagle scouts. Served with USAF, 1958-62. Recipient Disting. Life award Denver Gen. Agts. and Mgrs. Conf., Flight Instr. of Yr. award Denver Gen. Aviation Dist. Office FAA. Mem. Internat. Assn. Fin. Planners, Beta Gamma Sigma, Sigma Iota Epsilon. Office: Transamerica Life Cos 303 E 17th Ave Ste 420 Denver CO 80203

JOHNSTON, MARION ELIZABETH, financial company executive; b. Tulsa, Mar. 18, 1946; d. William Wade and Lena (Reed) J.; m. James Quentin Knight, Dec. 19, 1970 (div. May 1979); 1 child, David Travis Knight. BS, Mich. State U., 1970, MA, 1973. Registered fin. planner; registered investment advisor; chartered fin. cons. Food service dir. YWCA, Lansing, Mich., 1970-71; sr. prodn. supr. Mich. State U., East Lansing, 1971-73; asst. prof. Ariz. State U., Tempe, 1974-76; with research and devel. div. Greyhound Food Mgmt., Phoenix, 1976-78; assoc. Mfrs. Fin. Services, Phoenix, 1978-83; pres. Johnston Fin. Services, Inc., Phoenix, 1983—; mgr. Integrated Resources Equity Corp., N.Y.C., 1982—; cons. Mich. Dept. Labor, East Lansing, 1970-71, Ariz. Dept. Edn., Tempe, 1975, Utah State U., Logan, 1975; advisor Citibank, Phoenix, 1985—; membership chairperson Current Tax Discussion Group; pres. The Sourcr Group, 1987—. Active Madison Sch. Dist., Phoenix, 1978—; mem. fundraising com. Planned Parenthood, Phoenix, 1982; mem. Home Economists in Bus., 1976-78; mem. allocations com. United Way, Valley of the Sun, 1987-88. Named Outstanding Life Underwriter of Yr. Gen. Agts. Mgrs. Assn, 1979, Outstanding Alum of Yr. Mich. State U. Coll. Human Ecology, 1988. Mem. Nat. Assn. Life Underwriters Assn. (Nat. quality award 1982), Greater Phoenix Life Underwriters Assn., Am. Soc. Chartered Life Underwriters, Scottsdale C. of C., Nat. Assn. Women Bus. Owners, Faculty Women's Assn. (estate planning council 1974-76), Internat. Assn. Fin. Planners, Omicron Nu. Home: 5530 N 10th St Phoenix AZ 85014 Office: Johnston Fin Svcs 4747 N 7th Suite 428 Phoenix AZ 85014-3663

JOHNSTON, ROBERT LLOYD, JR., food products executive; b. L.A., Nov. 23, 1931; s. Robert Lloyd and Minnie (Hovland) J.; m. Gail Embury, Feb. 15, 1931; children: Denise, Diane. Student, L.A. City Coll., 1951. Salesman, ter. mgr. Gerber Products, L.A., 1955-67, asst. dist. mgr., 1967-69; product mgr. Gerber Products, Fremont, Mich., 1969-71, group product mgr., 1971-80; mgr. sales div. Gerber Products, Chgo., 1980-83; plant mgr. Gerber Products, Asheville, N.C., 1983-84; v.p. mktg. Gerber Products, Fremont, 1984-85, corp. v.p. gen. mgr., 1985-86, exec. v.p. gen. mgr., 1986-89, pres., 1989—; bd. dirs. Gerber Co. Found., Fremont. Tech. sgt. USAF, 1951-54. Mem. Ramshorn. Republican. Office: Gerber Products Co 445 State St Fremont MI 49412

JOHNSTON, RONALD VERNON, stockbroker; b. Los Angeles, Dec. 27, 1942; s. Arthur Vernon and Lillian Kristine J.; m. Patricia Joan Westerlind, Sept. 8, 1963; 1 child, Michael Arthur Roland. AA, Pasadena Coll., 1963; BA, Kensington U., 1977, MBA, 1978, PhD, 1979. Investment exec., asst. mgr., then mgr. Hornblower Weeks Hemphill Noyes, Glendale, Calif., 1968-74; v.p., resident mgr. Reynolds Securities, San Diego, 1974-78; v.p., resident mgr. Blyth Eastman Dillon/Paine Webber, San Diego, 1978-80; resident mgr., Crowell Weedon & Co., San Diego, 1985-86; pres. Trademark Investment of Am., 1986-87; regional dir. GNA/Investment Network Am., So. Calif., 1987—. Mem. Los Angeles County Dem. Cen. Com., 1966, Calif. State Dem. Cen. Com., 1968; Dem. candidate for assemblyman, 1968. Mem. Nat. Assn. Security Dealers (bd. arbitration), San Diego Stock and Bond Club. Methodist. Office: 8949 Claremont Mesa Pl San Diego CA 92123

JOHNSTON, SAMUEL MERRITT, sales executive; b. New Haven, Apr. 24, 1948; s. Wilbur Dexter and Elizabeth Merritt J.; B. Indsl. Engring. Tech., So. Tech. Inst., 1971; M.B.A., U. Utah, 1978; m. Marian Elizabeth Hayes, Oct. 23, 1971; children—Brandi Elizabeth, Courtney Lynne. Methods engr. Tex. Instruments, Dallas, 1978-79; sales engr., UPA Tech., Inc., Syosset, N.Y., 1979, regional sales mgr., 1979-80 dir. Central and South Am., 1980-81, field sales mgr., 1980-84, dir. internat. sales, 1981-84; territory mgr. Micro Component Tech., St. Paul, 1984-85, key account mgr., 1985-87; gen. mgr. Micro Component Tech.-Asia, 1987—. Pres., park Forest Homeowners' Assn., Plano, Tex., 1979-80. Served with USAF, 1971-78. Named Salesman of Year, UPA Tech., Inc., 1980. Mem. Am. Mgmt. Assn., Am. Electroplaters' Soc. Republican. Home: 235 Arcadia Rd, Unit A10-01, Singapore 1128, Singapore other: 1600 Interstate 35E N Carrolton TX 75006

JOHNSTON, THOMAS JOHN, management consultant; b. Oak Park, Ill., Nov. 2, 1922; s. John J. and Helen J. (Gilmore) J.; m. Elaine Berger, Feb. 16, 1946; children—Elene Johnston Kapp, Molly, Anne Johnston Gardner, Karen, John. B.S., St. Marys Coll., 1943; Postgrad., Columbia U., 1943. Personnel analyst Western Electric Co. Inc., Chgo., 1946-49; retail personnel mgr. Montgomery Ward & Co., Chgo., 1949-54; dir. personnel Panellit Inc., Chgo., 1954-56; assoc. Heidrick & Struggles Inc., Chgo., 1956-60, dir. in charge West Coast ops., 1960-70; pres., chief exec. officer Heidrick & Struggles Inc., Calistoga, Calif., 1970—; chmn. Heidrick & Struggles Inc., Calistoga, 1978—; bd. dirs. Chalone, Inc. Mem. U. Redland's Pres.'s Adv. Council, 1968-73; mem. Pres.'s Commn. on White House Fellows, 1971-76; trustee Robert Louis Stevenson Sch., Pebble Beach, Calif., 1977—, chmn. bd. dirs., 1984—. Served to lt. USNR, 1942-46, PTO. Republican. Roman Catholic. Clubs: Calif., University, Annandale Golf, San Francisco Yacht. Lodge: Knights of Malta.

JOHNSTON, THOMAS WARREN, engineering executive; b. Salem, Oreg., May 24, 1951; s. Hugh Marion and Helen Louise (Thayer) J.; m. Janet Marie Watkins, June 10, 1972. BSME, Oreg. State U., 1973. Registered profl. engr., Ariz., Oreg., Calif. Project engr. Marquess Engring. Co., Springfield, Oreg., 1973-78, v.p. comml. engring., 1978-82; sr. engr., project mgr. Brown & Caldwell Cons. Engrs., Eugene, Oreg., 1982-87, prin. engr., 1987—; mgr. mech. engring. Brown & Caldwell Cons. Engrs., Phoenix. Mem. ASHRAE (1st place award energy conservation in institutional design), Constrn. Specifications Inst., Toastmasters (sgt. at arms Springfield chpt., 1987), Beaver Club. Republican. Methodist. Home: 9650 E Pershing Scottsdale AZ 85260 Office: Brown & Caldwell 2025 N 3d St Phoenix AZ 85004

JOHNSTONE, CHAUNCEY OLCOTT, pharmaceutical company executive; b. N.Y.C., Sept. 11, 1943; s. Edmund F. and Janet (Olcott) J.; B.A., Jacksonville U., 1965; m. Patricia E. Porter, May 30, 1971; children—Carolyn Ann, Jessica Olcott. Fin. analyst Dun & Bradstreet, Inc., Jacksonville, Fla., 1965-68; co-founder, v.p. Trinity Industries, Inc., Mount Kisco, N.Y., 1968-77; product mgr. Beiersdorf, Inc., Norwalk, Conn., 1978-81, mktg. mgr., from 1982, v.p. and mem. mgmt. bd., 1984-88, sr. v.p., mem. mgmt. bd. 1988—. Bd. dirs. Wilton (Conn.) chpt. ARC, 1976-81; charter mem. Wilton Vol. Ambulance Corps, 1976—; corp. mem. Dublin Sch., N.H., 1986—; founding mem. Healthcare Mktg. Coun., 1988—. Club: Wilton Riding (Conn.). Home: 19 Hillbrook Rd Wilton CT 06897 Office: Beiersdorf Inc BDF Plaza PO Box 5529 Norwalk CT 06856

JOHNSTONE, DONALD FREDERICK, electronics executive; b. Ocean City, N.J., May 25, 1930; s. Lari Johnstone and Helen (Bielicki) Jones; m. Nancy Brewner, Mar. 25, 1977; children from previous marriage: Helen Beyer, David, Dwight, Eileen. BS, Cornell U., 1953; MBA, Harvard U., 1957. With sales and mktg. dept. G.E. Major Appliance Group, Louisville, 1958-80; v.p. mktg. Litton Industries, Mpls., 1980-83; sr. v.p. mktg. Phillips Consumer Electronics Co. (formerly NAP Consumer Electronics), Knoxville, 1983-84, pres., chief exec. officer, 1984—. Served to 1st lt. U.S. Army, 1953-55, Korea. Republican. Roman Catholic. Home: 138 Champions Point Knoxville TN 37922 Office: Phillips Consumer Electronics Co PO Box 14810 Knoxville TN 37914

JOHNSTONE, JOHN WILLIAM, JR., chemical company executive; b. Bklyn., Nov. 19, 1932; s. John William and Sarah J. (Singleton) J.; m. Claire Lundberg, Apr. 14, 1956; children—Thomas Edward, James Robert, Robert Andrew. B.A., Hartwick Coll., Oneonta, N.Y., 1954; grad., Advanced Mgmt. Program, Harvard U., 1970. With Hooker Chem. Corp., 1954-75, group v.p., 1973-75; pres. Airco Alloys div. Airco, Inc., 1976-79; v.p., gen. mgr. indsl. products, then sr. v.p. chems. group Olin Corp., 1979-80; corp. v.p., pres. chems. group Olin Corp., Stamford, Conn., 1980-85; pres. Olin Corp., 1985-87, chief operating officer, 1986-87, pres., chief exec. officer, chmn., 1988—, also chmn. bd.; bd. dirs. Home Life Ins. Co., Research Corp., Am. Brands, Inc. Bd. dirs. SPUR, Niagara Falls, N.Y., 1974-79, United Way Niagara Falls, 1974-77; trustee Hartwick Coll., 1983—. Mem. Am. Mgmt. Assn., Soc. Chem. Industry, Soap and Detergent Assn. (former chmn. bd. dirs.), Chem. Mfrs. Assn. (vice chmn. bd. dirs. 1988—). Episcopalian. Clubs: Landmark; Duquesne (Pitts.); Woodway Country, Blind Brook; Links (N.Y.C.). Office: Olin Corp 120 Long Ridge Rd Stamford CT 06904

JOICE, JOHNNY, transportation executive; b. Selma, Calif., Jan. 21, 1943; s. Buford and Cloretta Joice; m. Claudette Cleystene Gray, July 29, 1971; children: Jacqueline Marie, Kiesha M. AA, La. Trade Tech., 1976; BS in Mgmt., Pepperdine U., 1982; MBA, U. Redlands, Calif., 1984. Mem. Interstate Commerce Practitioners (com. chmn. 1976-78, attendance chmn. 1977-79), Fed. Maritime Practitioners, Am. Soc. for Traffic and Transp., Nat. Council Logistics Mgmt. Office: 3204 N Rosemead Blvd Ste 201 El Monte CA 91731

JOINES, JAMES EMORY, JR., management consultant; b. Mountain City, Tenn., Jan. 14, 1946; s. James Emory and Josephine (Banner) J.; student U. Tenn., 1964-66; B.S., Appalachian State U., 1968, postgrad., 1969-70; m. Mary Christine Hill, May 28, 1970; children—Stephanie Denise, James Emory III. Office mgr. Computer Bus. Service, Greensboro, N.C., 1969-70, regional mgr., 1970; prof. econs. Croft Coll., Greensboro, 1970; with Profl. Cons., Inc., Greensboro and Lynchburg, Va., 1971—, area mgr., 1971-78, pres., Lynchburg, 1978—, also dir.; vis. prof. U. Va., Charlottesville, 1975—. Mem. vestry Grace Meml. Episcopal Ch., 1975-79, sr. warden, 1977-78. Mem. Soc. Profl. Bus. Cons. (nat. public relations dir. 1978-80; chmn. stats. com. 1980-82, bd. dirs. 1985—, pres. 1987-88), Inst. Cert. Profl. Bus. Cons. Am. Inst. Profl. Cons. Clubs: Boonsboro Country, Lions (pres. 1980). Contbg. editor Physicians Mgmt., 1974—, The Dentist, 1986—. Home: 2103 Link Rd Lynchburg VA 24503 Office: 1928 Thomson Dr Lynchburg VA 24501

JOLICOEUR, TIMOTHY J., communications executive; b. Burbank, Calif., Feb. 27, 1961; s. Edward Thomas and Lorraine (Daigle) J. Student, Calif. State. U., Hayward. Gen. mgr. Tandy Corp., Santa Maria, Calif., 1979-85; sales mgr. Taft Telecommunications, Ventura, Calif., 1985-87; regional mgr. GTEL, Thousand Oaks, Calif., 1987—. Mem. Boys Club of Am. Mem. Am. Mgmt. Assn. Democrat. Home: 1414 Lexington Ct Camarillo CA 93010

JOLLEY, WELDON BOSEN, surgery educator, research executive; b. Gunnison, Utah, Sept. 8, 1926; s. Edward Mckinley Jolley and Rosella (Elvira) Bosen; m. Dorothy Timms, Dec. 21, 1954 (dec. Jan. 1983); children: Elizabeth Price, Kathleen Cope, Phillip Jolley; m. JoLane Laycock, Aug. 20, 1983; children: Jessica, Brian. BA, Brigham Young U., 1952; PhD, U. So. Calif., 1959; postdoctoral, UCLA, 1960. Prof. surgery, physiology and biophysics Loma Linda (Calif.) U., 1969—, assoc. dir. surg. research lab., 1969—; dir. surg. research VA Hosp., Loma Linda, 1979-85; pres. Nucleic Acid Research Inst., Costa Mesa, Calif., 1985—; bd. dirs. SPI Pharms., Inc.; sr. v.p., bd. dirs. ICN Pharms., Inc.; sci. adv. Viratek, Inc. Contbr. tech. articles to pubs. Named McPherson Soc. Clin. Prof. of Yr., 1982. Home: 3825 E Woodbine Rd Orange CA 92667 Office: Nucleic Acid Rsch Inst 3300 Hyland Blvd Costa Mesa CA 92626

JOLLIFF, ROBERT ALLEN, corporate executive; b. Wooster, Ohio, Sept. 12, 1943; s. Samuel Martin and Ethel May (Eschliman) J.; m. Marcella Joanne BAttig, AUg. 31, 1968; children: John Douglas, Laura Joanne. BS, Kent State U., 1965; MBA, U. Akron, 1974. Asst. cash mgr. B.F. Goodrich, Akron, Ohio, 1968-73; cash mgr. Aladdin Industries, Nashville, 1973-74; cash mgr. McDermott Inc., New Orleans, 1974-78, treas., 1978—; owner Catlin Energy Corp., Cord Energy Resources Inc. Trustee Blood Ctr. SE La., New Orleans, 1986—. Served to 1st lt., U.S. Army, 1966-68. Mem. Nat. Assn. Corp. Treas., Winchester Arms Collectors Assn. Republican. Methodist. Lodge: Masons. Office: McDermott Inc 1010 Common St New Orleans LA 70112

JOLLY, BRUCE DWIGHT, manufacturing company executive; b. Wheeling, W.Va., Aug. 27, 1943; s. Edward and Martha Elizabeth (Glass) J.; m. Alice Marie O'Beirne, May 25, 1974; children—Mara O'Beirne, Brock Thomas. A.B., Dartmouth Coll., 1965; M.B.A., U. Va., 1967. Systems engr. IBM Corp., Richmond, Va., 1967-68; financial analyst Keystone Consol. Industries, Peoria, Ill., 1970-73; controller HON Industries, Inc., Muscatine, Iowa, 1973-76, sec., treas., 1976-79; v.p. fin. Hawkeye Steel Products, Inc., Waterloo, Iowa, 1979-83, Cosco, Inc., Columbus, Ind., 1983—. With AUS, 1968-70, Vietnam. Decorated Bronze Star. Mem. Phi Kappa Psi. Republican. Presbyterian. Home: 3610 Oriole Dr Columbus IN 47203 Office: Cosco Inc 2525 State St Columbus IN 47201

JONASSEN, GAYLORD D., product development, manufacturing executive; b. East Orange, N.J., Oct. 13, 1932; s. Jonas M. and Alma M. (Stelter) J.; B.S. in M.E., Ariz. State U., 1960; m. Shirley Ann Christophel, June 15, 1956; children—Glenn, Brenda, Devel. engr. Motorola Semiconductor, Phoenix, 1956-60; plant and facilities research and devel. engr. Western Electric, N.Y.C., 1960-65; new products mgr. Deutsch Relays, Long Island, N.Y., 1965-67; new product mktg./sales mgr. Kinemotive Corp., Farmingdale, N.Y., 1967-69; div. mgr. Atlantic Sci. Corp., Plainview, N.Y., 1969-70; exec. v.p., tech. dir. Telecommunications Industries, Inc., Copaigue, N.Y., 1970-73; founder, pres., Internat. Protein Industries, Inc., Hauppauge, 1973-84, chmn. bd., 1973-84; mgmt. cons. Gaylord Jonassen Assocs., 1984-85; systems engring. project mgr. Norden Systems, 1985—. Served with U.S. Navy, 1950-54. Recipient Disting. Achievement award, Coll. Engring. and Applied Sci., Ariz. State U., 1982; ASTM fellow, 1958. Mem. L.I. Assn. Commerce and Industry. Baptist (deacon). Patentee in field. Contbr. articles to various publs. Home: 9 Wood Ln Smithtown NY 11787 Office: 75 Maxess Rd Melville NY 11747

JÓNATANSSON, HALLDÓR, utility company executive; b. Reykjavik, Iceland, Jan. 21, 1932; s. Jónatan Hallvarðsson and Sigurrós Gísladóttir; m. Gudrún Dagbjartsdóttir, May 3, 1958; children: Dagny, Rósa, Jórunn, Steinunn. JD, U. Iceland, Reykjavik, 1956; MA, Fletcher Sch. Law and Diplomacy, Medford, Mass., 1957. Sec. Ministry of Justice, Reykjavik, 1957; div. chief Ministry of Commerce, Reykjavik, 1957-65; office mgr. Landsvirkjun, Reykjavik, 1965-71, dep. gen. mgr., 1971-83, gen. mgr., 1983—. Recipient Knights Cross Order the Falcon, Pres. Iceland, 1970; Order Merit Grand Duke of Luxembourg, 1986. Mem. Assn. Icelandic Electric Utilities (dep. chmn.), NORDEL (leading people active in electric energy in Nordic countries) (bd. dirs.). Home: Thinghólsbraut 46, 200 Kópavogur Iceland Office: Landsvirkjun, Nat Power Co, Háaleitisbraut 68, 103 Reykjavik Iceland

JONCKOWSKI, DAVID LAWRENCE, food store chain Executive; b. Fargo, N.D., Nov. 14, 1948; s. Lawrence Andrew and Alma (Lange) J.; m. Diane Rose Rediske, Sept. 9, 1972; children: Joshua, Julie. BS in Commerce and Mktg., Mont. State U., 1972. Warehouseman Associated Food Stores, Inc., Billings, Mont., 1971-72, asst. produce mgr., 1972-74, produce mgr., 1974-84, retail devel. mgr., 1984-87, div. mgr., 1987—. Office: Associated Food Stores Inc PO Box 2513 Billings MT 59103

JONDAHL, JAMES OWEN, tax preparation company executive; b. Fargo, N.D., Aug. 18, 1951; s. Gerald O. and Gladys A.M. (Jungnitsch) J.; m. Lori Jo Theurer Jondahl, Aug. 11, 1983; children: Justin, Jamie. BS, N.D. State U., 1973. Sales rep. Swift & Co., Punxsutawney, Pa., 1973-75; tax profl. Fargo, McGill Co., Grove City, Pa., 1975; truck driver Red Owl Stores, Fargo, 1976-82; tax profl. Woell & Woell Law Office, Casselton, N.D., 1976, Jondahl Fin. Service, West Fargo, N.D., 1977-86; registered securities rep. Offerman & Co., Mpls., 1983-85; ins. sales Jondahl Ins., West Fargo, 1979—; real estate sales, cons. West Fargo Investment Corp., 1985—; tax profl. Taxman Inc., West Fargo, 1986—. Mem. Nat. Soc. Pub. Accts. (del. 1985—). Home: 1127-24th Ave S Moorhead MN 56560 Office: Taxman Inc 1042-14th Ave E West Fargo ND 58078

JONES, ANNETTE, health care executive; b. Winterville, Miss., July 21, 1944; d. Roy and Ophelia (Washbrook) T.; m. Bennett Neil Jones Jr., July 23, 1943; children: Bennett Neil, Douglas Bernard. BA, Youngstown State U., 1967. With Mahoning Nat. Bank, Youngstown, Ohio, 1965-67; auditor E.L.A.S., Youngstown, 1968-81; travel agt. Ramex Travel, Youngstown, 1982-84; adminstrv. asst. Econ. Devel., Youngstown, 1984-85; founder AB&J Comprehensive Mgmt., Youngstown, 1985—; claims mgr. MedCare HMO, Columbiana, Ohio, 1986-88. Mem. Assoc. Neighborhood Ctrs., Delta Sigma Theta. Home: 1029 Genesee Youngstown OH 44511 Office: AB&J Comprehensive Mgmt 322 W Earl Ave Youngstown OH 44511

JONES, ARTHUR JAMES, program manager; b. Meridian, Miss., Oct. 15, 1938; s. Sam and Lula (Mason) J.; divorced; children: V. Bernard, Shawn S., J. Fitzgerald. Student, Tenn. State U., 1970, Tex. So. U., 1975, Troy (Ala.) State U., 1980. Enlisted USAF, 1956, advanced through grades to capt., 1974; comdr. squadron sect. USAF, Griffiss AFB, N.Y., 1970-71; chief base adminstrn. and logistics for recruiting services USAF, Houston, 1971-75; chief, weapons controller USAF, Wallace Air Sta., 1975-76; comdr. squadron sect. USAF, Hurlburt AFB, Fla., 1976-79; chief base adminstrn. USAF, Hurlburt AFB, 1979-81; ret. USAF, 1981; specialist EEOC, Birmingham, Ala., 1981; mgr. data/configuration EEOC, Eglin AFB, Fla., 1981-86; logistics mgmt. specialist EEOC, Eglin AFB, 1986-87, data mgmt. specialist, 1987—. V.p. Okaloosa County Blacks in Govt., Ft. Walton Beach, Fla., 1986—. Mem. NAACP, Am. Def. Preparedness Assn., Am. Mgmt. Assn., Sigma Rho Sigma (Zeta chpt.). Democrat. Baptist. Home: 2407 Dunn Ct Niceville FL 32578 Office: Armament Div/YBP Eglin Air Force Base FL 32542

JONES, ARTHUR MCDONALD, SR., financial executive; b. Hattiesburg, Miss., Aug. 26, 1947; s. Henry Thomas and Ethel (McDonald) J.; m. Trudy Canant, Jan. 15, 1972; children—Sally, Robin, Art. B.S. in Acctg., Miss. State U., 1969. C.P.A., Miss. Staff and sr. acct. Arthur Andersen & Co., New Orleans, 1969-70, 72-75; asst. controller Bruno's Inc., Birmingham, Ala., 1975-77; v.p. fin., sec.-treas. Big B, Inc., Birmingham, 1977-85, exec. v.p., 1985— , also dir., Deacon and trustee Shadescrest Baptist Ch., Birmingham; past pres. Bluff Park Elementary P.T.A., Birmingham; dir., past treas. Shadescliff Swim Club, Birmingham. Served to capt. U.S. Army, 1970-72. Mem. Am. Inst. C.P.A.s, Nat. Assn. Accts. Office: Big B Inc PO Box 10166 Birmingham AL 35202

JONES, BARRY KENNARD, insurance brokerage executive; b. San Francisco, July 2, 1933; s. Kennard and Burnette (Grimes) J.; m. Carole Jo Cooke, June 25, 1955; children: Scott Kennard, Craig Steven, Todd Cooke. BBA, Wash. State U., 1955. CPCU. Commd. 2d lt. U.S. Army, 1955, advanced through grades to capt., 1961, resigned, 1965; v.p. Cen. Bus. Property Co., Spokane, Wash., 1957—; pres., chief exec. officer Fidelity Assocs., Inc., Spokane, 1968-88, chmn. chief exec. officer, 1988—; pres. Fidelity Assocs. Fin. Services, Spokane, 1982-88, chmn., 1988—. Chmn., treas. Spokane Dist. 83 Levy, 1984—; bd. dirs. Spokane C. of C., 1982—. Named Ins. Leader of Yr., Spokane Ins. Women, 1985, Dad of Yr., Wash. State U., 1978; fellow Paul Harris Found., 1985. Mem. Alpha Tau Omega (province dir. 1961-68, pres. house corp. 1966-82, Alumni of Yr. 1966). Republican. Episcopalian. Clubs: Spo Knife and Fork (Spokane) (exec sec. 1960-81), Knife and Fork Internat. (Topeka) (pres. 1982-89, treas. 1976-81). Lodges: Rotary (pres. Spokane club 1984-85), Shriners, Divan. Home: 1914 E 25th Ave Spokane WA 99203 Office: Fidelity Assocs Ins Brokers PO Box 3144 Spokane WA 99220

JONES, BERNARD LEE, engineer, construction company executive; b. Spokane, Wash., Aug. 31, 1939; s. Alfred Frederick and Yvonne Elizabeth (Ball) J.;m. Mary Jessie McKay, Apr. 28, 1961; children: Geraldine, Craig, Margaret, Paul. LPN, St. Joseph's Sch. Nursing, Lewiston, Idaho, 1959; BS in Safety Engring., Northwestern Coll., Tulsa; cert. Occupational Health and Safety Tech. Heavy constrn. safety-med.-security-fire supr., 1959-65; from safety engr. to chief safety engr. Morrison Knudsen Co., Inc., Saigon, South Vietnam, 1965-72; safety-fire supr. Crystal River (Fla.) nuclear power plant J.A. Jones Inc., 1972-74; from safety rep. to safety dir. Alyeska Pipeline Service Co., Fairbanks, Alaska, 1974-78; safety security-fire supr. Bechtel Inc., San Francisco, Hassi R'Mel, Algeria, 1978-79, safety-fire supr., Jubail, Saudi Arabia, 1979-81, mgr. project safety and fire (petrochem. complex), Yanbu, Saudi Arabia, 1981-85; project safety supr., Western Space Shuttle Launch Complex, Vandenburg AFB, Calif., 1985-86, Pilgrim Nuclear Power Sta., Mass., 1986—. Mem. Am. Soc. Safety Engrs., Idaho Lic. Practical Nurse Assn., Nat. Fire Protection Assn., Nat. Safety Mgmt. Soc. Roman Catholic. Home: 13 Regents Gate Sandwich MA 02563 Office: Bechtel Inc Safety Div 50 Beale St San Francisco CA 94119

JONES, CHARLES DAVIS, insurance consultant; b. Abraham, W.Va., Jan. 6, 1917; s. Benjamin Franklin and Mary Catherine (Smith) J.; student Beckley Coll., 1936-37, Concord Coll., 1937-38; A.B., Marshall U., 1947; postgrad. Columbia U., 1947; M.A., N.Y.U., 1956; postgrad. Am. U., 1957; m. Letha Arbell Plumley; children—Charles Davis, Irvin Howard; m. 2d, Margaret Lee Greene, Aug. 4, 1951. With Social Security Adminstrn., 1951-77, field rep., Charleston, W. Va., 1951-54, policy examiner, sect. chief, state ops. officer, Balt., 1954-66, area chief field ops. Bur. Disability Ins., Balt., 1966-71, dir. gen. policy coordination and liaison, 1971-75, chief eligibility policy to Office of Policy and Regulations, 1975-77; disability ins. cons., 1977—; mem. staff sec's. task force on medicaid and related programs HEW, 1969; mem. Social Security Adminstrn. Task Force on Social Security Adminstrn. Regional Orgns. and Functions, 1970. Active Balt. Mus. Art. Served to 1st lt. USAF, 1942-45. Decorated 4 Air medals. Mem. Nat. Assn. of Disability Examiners, Mensa, VFW, Nat. Trust for Historic Preservation, Eighth Air Force Hist. Soc. (life), 96th Bomb Group Assn. (life), Nat. Hist. Soc., Md. Hist. Soc. Home: 3904 Elm Ave Baltimore MD 21211

JONES, CHARLES HILL, JR., banker; b. N.Y.C., July 14, 1933; s. Charles Hill and Susan Roy (Johnston) J.; grad. Groton (Mass.) Sch., 1952; BA in Econs., U. Va., 1956; m. Hope Haskell, Jan. 28, 1961; children: Hope H., Charles Hill III, Henry M.T. With Wood, Struthers & Winthrop, Inc., N.Y.C., 1956-73, gen. ptnr., 1968-69, v.p., dir., dir. rsch., 1969-73; sr. v.p., chief investment officer Midlantic Nat. Bank, Edison, 1974-87; pres., dir. McBee Jones Corp., 1964-86; gen. ptnr. Jones Ellwood & Co. (now Edge Ptnrs.), 1987—. Treas., N.Y. chpt. R.E. Lee Meml. Found., 1964-69; trustee, chmn. fin. com. Monmouth Med. Center, 1975-81; pres. bd. trustees Rumson (N.J.) Country Day Sch., 1982-85. With AUS, 1956-57. Chartered fin. analyst. Mem. Inst. Chartered Fin. Analysts, N.Y. Soc. Security Anaylsts, Met. Squash Racquets Assn. (bd. govs. 1964-69), Bond Club, City Midday Club (trustee, treas. 1965-71, v.p. 1972-74). Author: (with Joseph D. Davis) Toll Road Bonds, 1959, The Growth Rate Appraiser, 1968. Home: PO Box 441 Rumson NJ 07760 Office: Edge Ptnrs PO Box 7511 Shrewsbury NJ 07702

JONES, CLARENCE WHITEHEAD, bank and trust company executive; b. Columbia, S.C., Oct. 13, 1933; s. Clarence W. and Arizona (Waites) J.; m. Carole Joanne Medlin, June 13, 1959; children: Kenneth, Scott, Leah. BS in Acctg., U. S.C., 1955. Agt. Liberty Life Ins. Co., Columbia, 1955-56; mgr. Universal C.I.T. Credit Corp., various locations, 1958-71; adminstr. 1st Nat. Bank S.C., Columbia, 1971-84; dep. adminstr. S.C. Nat. Bank, Columbia, 1984-86; sr. v.p., adminstr. consumer credit div. 1st Citizens Bank & Trust Co., Columbia, 1986—. Coach Little League Baseball,Columbia, 1970-71, Pee Wee League Football, Columbia, 1972-73. With U.S. Army, 1956-58. Republican. Baptist. Home: 9528 Highgate Rd Columbia SC 29223 Office: 1st Citizens Bank & Trust Co PO Box 29 Columbia SC 29201

JONES, CURTIS HARVEY, finance executive; b. Springfield, Ill., Apr. 22, 1929; s. J. Barclay and Anna (Harvey) J.; m. Betty Warren Sager, June 14, 1952; children: C. Barclay Jones-Kopchak, Curtis Harvey Jr., Stanley Warren. AB, Harvard U., 1950, MBA, 1952, DBA, 1962. Labor economist Mutual Security Agy., Oslo, Norway, 1952-56; prodn. planner Kaiser Aluminum and Chem. Corp., Newark, Ohio, 1956-59; assoc. prof. Harvard Bus. Sch., Boston, 1962-71; dir. evaluation Peace Corps, Washington, 1971-72; dir. price policy Price Commn., Washington, 1972-73; nat. coordinator wage and price controls Arthur Young & Co., N.Y.C., Conn., 1973; chief fin. officer MBXL Corp., Wichita, Kans., 1973-79; ptnr. Synergistic Services, Wichita, 1979-82; treas. Eaton Vance Corp., Boston, 1982—. Contbr. articles to profl. jours. Mem. Religious Soc. Friends. Club: Harvard.

JONES, D. PAUL, JR., banker, lawyer; b. Birmingham, Ala., Sept. 26, 1942; s. D. Paul and Virginia Lee (Mount) J.; m. Charlene Dale Angelich, Aug. 1964; children—Elizabeth Holly, Allison Leigh, D. Paul, III. B.S., U. Ala., 1964, J.D., 1967; LL.M., N.Y. U., 1968. Bar: Ala. Mem. firm Balch, Bingham, Baker, Hawthorne, Williams & Ward, Birmingham, 1970-78; of counsel Balch, Bingham, Baker, Hawthorne, Williams & Ward, 1978-86; exec. v.p., gen. counsel, dir. Central Bancshares South, Inc., Birmingham, 1978-84; vice chmn. Central Bancshares South, Inc., 1984-89, pres., chief oper. officer, 1989—; dir. Central Bank of South, Marathon Corp., Russell Lands Co. Trustee Advent Episcopal Day Sch., Birmingham, 1969-71; bd. dirs. Ala. Symphony Orch. Assn., 1985-88. Mem. ABA, Ala. Bar Assn. (chmn. sect. corp., banking and bus. law 1973-75, bd. bar examiners 1975-78), Birmingham Bar Assn., Am. Bankers Assn. (mem. govt. relations council 1985-88), Ala. Bankers Assn. (pres. 1989-90). Clubs: Rotary, Downtown (Birmingham); Country of Birmingham; Willow Point Golf and Country (Alexander City). Home: 3148 Guilford Rd Birmingham AL 35233 Office: Cen Bancshares S Inc 701 S 20th St Birmingham AL 35205

JONES, DALE P., oil field service company executive; b. Gillham, Ark., Oct. 19, 1936; s. Ray Elgin and Alma Lee (Wheeler) J.; m. Anita Ruth Collier, Dec. 28, 1963; children: Lee Anna, Leisa. BS, U. Ark., 1958; postgrad., So. Meth. U., 1966, U. Okla., 1970. CPA, Ark., Tex., Okla. Sr. auditor Arthur Andersen & Co., 1958-59, 62-65; corp. auditor Halliburton Co., Dallas, 1965-66; fin. coordinator Halliburton Services, London, 1967-69; asst. to controller Halliburton Services, Duncan, Okla., 1970-84; pres. Welex Div., Houston, 1985-87; sr. v.p. Halliburton Co., Dallas, 1987, exec. v.p. oil field services, 1987—. Chmn. bd., pres. Duncan Regional Hosp. Inc., 1977-80. Served to capt. USAF, 1959-62. Mem. Am. Petroleum Inst., Fin. Execs. Inst., Tex. Soc. CPA's, U. Ark. Coll. Bus. Adminstrn. Assocs. Republican. Baptist. Clubs: Petroleum, Plaza Athletic (Dallas); Westlake (Houston). Office: Halliburton Co 500 N Akard St 3600 Lincoln Pla Dallas TX 75201

JONES, DAVID ALLEN, health facility executive; b. Louisville, Aug. 7, 1931; s. Evan L. and Elsie F. (Thurman) J.; m. Betty L. Ashbury, July 24, 1954; children: David, Susan, Daniel, Matthew, Carol. BS, U. Louisville, 1954; JD, Yale U., 1960. Bar: Ky. 1960. Founder, chief exec. officer Humana Inc. (formerly Extendicare Inc.), Louisville, 1961—, also chmn., dir.; ptnr. Greenebaum, Doll and McDonald and predecessor, Louisville, 1965-69, of counsel, 1969-74; dir. Royal Crown Cos., Inc.; dir., exec. com. 1st Ky. Nat. Corp. and affiliates, 1st Ky. Trust Co., First Nat. Bank Louisville. Served as lt. (j.g.) USN, 1954-57. Mem. Louisville Area C. of C. Office: Humana Inc 500 W Main St PO Box 1438 Louisville KY 40201 *

JONES, DAVID EUGENE, pharmaceutical company executive; b. Bassett, Va., Nov. 18, 1942; s. Thaddeus Eugene and Bessie (Mason) J.; m. Carole Leigh Jones, Sept. 3, 1966; children: Candace, Michael. BS in Pharmacy, Med. Coll. Va., 1966; MS in Bus., Va. Commonwealth U., 1969. Registered pharmacist, Va. Mktg. research analyst A.H. Robins Co., Richmond, Va., 1969-70, sr. mktg. research analyst, 1970-72, mgr. pharm. mktg. research, 1972-75, mgr. research and devel. project cost analysis, 1975-77, mgr. research and devel. budgets and planning, 1977-79, mgr. planning and bus. devel., 1980-82, dir. animal health group spl. projects div., 1982-85, v.p. ops. spl. products div., 1985-86, corp. v.p. spl. products div., 1986—. Mem. Planning Forum (pres. 1983), Computer Users Club (newsletter 1987). Club: Toastmasters (adminstrv. v.p. 1985). Office: AH Robins Co 1405 Cummings Dr Richmond VA 23220

JONES, DAVID KELLY, resort executive, environmental and outdoor education specialist; b. Seattle, June 30, 1962; s. Robert Neale and Irene Sharon (Whitney) J.; m. Karin Margaret Bucy, Aug. 9, 1986. BA in Recreation and Parks, Case Western Res. U., 1985; BA in Environ. Edn., Wash. U., 1985. Dir. outdoor edn. program Western Wash. U., Bellingham, 1984-85; mgr. program Highline Sch. Dist. #401, Seattle, 1985-86; mgr. Thousand Trails, Seattle and San Diego, 1986—; cons. Highline Sch. Dist. #401, Seattle, 1984-85. Cons. Camp Lutherwood-Luth. Ch., Bellingham, 1984; mem. Jamul (Calif.) Planning Commn., 1987-88. Mem. Nat. Recreation and Parks Assn., Wash. Recreation and Parks Assn., Hwy. 94 Club. Republican. Home: 325 Division St #301 Leavenworth WA 98826 Office: Thousand Trails 20752-4 Chiwawa Loop Rd Leavenworth WA 98826

JONES, DAVID LEE, banker; b. Des Moines, Sept. 3, 1948; s. Alfred Leroy and Lois Lorraine (Miller) J.; m. Mirta Stavisky; children from previous marriage: Douglas, Kimberlee. BS in Bus. Adminstrn., The Citadel, 1972; ThM in Psychology Luther Rice Seminary, 1975. Fin. analyst Am. Nat. Bank, Jacksonville, Fla., 1973-75; coml. loan officer Flagship Bank of W. Palm Beach (Fla.), 1975-77; asst. v.p., br. mgr. Barnett Banks of Fla., Inc., W. Palm Beach, 1977-78; v.p., dir. mktg. First Nat. Bank in Palm Beach, 1978-83; pres. employee Ins. Group, Inc., Boca Raton, Fla., 1989—; v.p. regional mktg. Centrust Savs. Bank, Miami, 1984-86 ; v.p. regional admnstrn Carteret Savings, Delray Beach, Fla.; instr. Palm Beach Jr. Coll., Palm Beach Atlantic Coll. Served with USN, 1966-69. Mem. Bank Mktg. Assn. (recipient cert. of merit 1980), Fla. Bank Mktg. Assn., Am. Inst. Banking, Nat. Assn. Nouthetic Counselors. Republican. Baptist. Office: 200 E Palmetto Park Rd Boca Raton FL 33432

JONES, DENNIS RAY, banker; b. Elkhart, Ind., Nov. 2, 1945; s. Robert L. and Opal C. (Sanders) J.; B.S., Ind. U., 1967, MBA, 1969; m. Beth A. Weideman, Dec. 23, 1966 (dec. Feb. 1984); children—Brenton W., Ryan T.; m. Christine Lydon, Apr. 11, 1987. CPA. Sr. acct. Touche Ross & Co., Detroit 1969-72; v.p., contr. Mich. Nat. Bank, Lansing, 1972-77; contr. Ind. Bank Group, Waukesha, Wis., 1977-80, exec. v.p., treas., chief fin. officer, 1980-85; v.p., contr. Marshall and Ilsley Corp., Milw., 1985-89, v.p., regional mgr., 1979—. Pres. PTO, Waukesha, 1978-79. Recipient sr. scholarship award, 1967. Mem. AICPA, Nat. Assn. Accts., Fin. Exec. Inst., Beta Alpha Psi, Beta Gamma Sigma. Presbyterian. Avocations: golf, photography. Office: Marshall & Ilsley Corp 770 N Water St Milwaukee WI 53202

JONES, DOROTHY JUNE, data processing executive; b. New Brighton, Pa., July 20, 1942; d. John Leroy Sr. and Ethel Vivian (Hennessey) Black; m. Charles William Jones, Sept. 20, 1959 (div. 1972); children: Deborah, Linda Sue, Rebecca, Charles. BS, W.Va. State Inst., 1972; M in Engring., W.Va. U., 1974. Instr. W.Va. U., Morgantown, 1972-73; systems analyst State of W.Va., Charleston, 1973-77; sr. systems analyst Am. Express, Phoenix, 1977-79; sr. systems analyst Comml. Union, Boston, 1979-81, cons., 1987-88; sr. systems analyst Sheraton Corp., Boston, 1981-82; mgr. Unisys, Cambridge, Mass., 1981-82; pres., chief exec. officer Proficiency Inc., Cambridge, 1985—; cons. Blue Cross Mass., Braintree, 1988—. Mem. Ind. Computer Cons. Assn. (Greater Boston chpt.), Alpha Kappa Mu. Office: Proficiency Inc Cambridge MA 99990

JONES, E. STEWART, JR., lawyer; b. Troy, N.Y., Dec. 4, 1941; s. E. Stewart and Louise (Farley) J.; m. Constance M., Dec. 28, 1968; children: Christopher, Brady, Erin. BA, Williams Coll., 1963; JD, Albany Law Sch., 1966. Bar: N.Y. 1966, U.S. Dist. Ct. (no. dist.) N.Y. 1966, U.S. Supreme Ct. 1970, U.S. Ct. Appeals (2d cir.) 1976, U.S. Dist. Ct. (we. dist.) N.Y. 1987; cert. specialist in civil and criminal trial advocacy. Asst. dist. atty. Rensselaer County (N.Y.), 1968-70, spl. prosecutor, 1974; ptnr. E. Stewart Jones, Troy, N.Y., 1974—; lectr. in field; mem. com. on profl. standards of 3d jud. dept. State of N.Y., 1977-80; mem. merit selection panel for selection and appointment of U.S. magistrate for No. Dist. N.Y., 1981; bd. dirs., The Univ. Found. at Albany, trustee Troy Savs. Bank. Contbr. numerous articles to profl. jours. Served with USNG, 1966-72. Fellow Am. Bar Found., Internat. Acad. Trial Lawyers, Am. Bd. Criminal Trial Lawyers, Am. Coll. Trial Lawyers, Roscoe Pound Assn.; mem. N.Y. State Bar Assn. (Outstanding Practitioner award 1980, mem. continuing edn. com. 1977-78, mem. exec. com. of criminal justice sect. 1977—, mem. exec. com. trial lawyers sect. 1981—, mem. spl. com. med. malpractice, other coms.), N.Y. State Trial Lawyers Assn. (dir. 1982—, co-chmn. com. on med. jurisprudence 1973-74, vice chmn. com. criminal law and procedure 1974-76, co-chmn. criminal law sect. 1978), Capital Dist. Trial Lawyers Assn. (dir. 1973-76), ABA (numerous coms.) Calif. Attys. for Criminal Justice, Practising Law Inst., Am. Judicature Soc. (sustaining), Rensselaer County Bar Assn., Am. Soc. Law and Medicine, ACLU, N.Y. Civil Liberties Union, Lawyer to Lawyer Consultation (panel), Albany County Bar Assn., N.Y. State Defenders Assn., Nat. Orgn. for Reform of Marijuana Laws, Am. Arbitration Assn., Fed. Bar Council, Upstate Trial Attys. Assn., Inc., Nat. Bd. Trial Advocacy (diplomate). Clubs: Schuyler Meadows, Troy Country, Troy, Steuben Athletic, Fort Orange, Wychmere Harbor; Stone Horse Yacht (Harwich Port, Mass.); Equinox Country (Manchester, Vt.). Home: 46 Schuyler Rd Loudonville NY 12211 Office: 28 2d St Troy NY 12181

JONES, EBEN LEE, insurance executive; b. Augusta, Ga., June 6, 1949; s. Roy Alva and Sydney (Smith) J.; m. Jeanne Marie Jones, Mar. 5, 1983; childrne: Erin Marie, Carrie Elizabeth. AB, Ga. State U., 1971. Nat. risk supr. Liberty Mut. Ins. Co., Atlanta, 1973-79; asst. to v.p. ins. Grand Union Co., Atlanta, 1979-82; dir. ins. and risk mgmt. Rollins Inc., Atlanta, 1982—. With U.S. Army, 1971-73. Mem. Nat. Risk and Ins. Mgmt. Soc. (pres. Atlanta chpt. 1986-87, chmn. nat. membership 1987-88). Republican. Methodist. Home: 1329 Oakcrest Ct Lilburn GA 30247 Office: Rollins Inc 2170 Piedmont Rd NE Atlanta GA 30324

JONES, EBON RICHARD, retailing executive; b. Oak Park, Ill., Aug. 23, 1944; s. Ebon Clark and Marilyn B. (Dow) J.; m. Sally Samuelson, Jan. 27, 1968; children: Stephanie Blythe, Heather Denise. B.A., Priceton U., 1966; M.B.A., Stanford U., 1968. Adminstrv. asst. Nat. Air Pollution Control Adminstrn., Washington, 1968-70; cons. McKinsey & Co., San Francisco and Paris, 1970-83; exec. v.p. Safeway Stores Inc., Oakland, Calif., 1983-86, group v.p., 1986-88, exec. v.p., 1988—. Chmn. bd. San Francisco Zool. Soc., 1979-84, pres. 1985—; trustee San Francisco Trust; Crystal Springs Uplands Sch., 1986—; gov. Uniform Code Council, 1984—. Served to lt. USPHS, 1968-70. Mem. Phi Beta Kappa. Home: 58 Chester Way San Mateo CA 94402 Office: Safeway Stores Inc 201 4th St Oakland CA 94660

JONES, EDWARD AMES, contractor; b. Sherbrooke, Que., Can., Oct. 30, 1952; came to U.S., 1953; s. Charles Henry and Beverly (Ames) J.; m. Michele Miskiv, Oct. 7, 1978; 1 child, Tad Michael. Student, Nichols Coll., 1971-72. Pres., chief exec. officer Belmont Contracting Inc., Ridgewood, N.J., 1976-87; chmn. Belmont Constrn. and Devel. Corp., Ridgewood, 1988—. Contbr. articles to profl. jours. Mem. Am. Soc. Interior Design, Guild Profl. Paper Hangers (pres. N. Jersy chapter 1982-83). Republican. Episcopalian. Lodges: Rotary (bd. dirs. Ridgewood 1984-85), Masons. Home: 242 W Glen Ave Ridgewood NJ 07450

JONES, EDWARD MARSHALL, automotive parts distributing company executive; b. Decatur, Ga., Feb. 3, 1926; S. Henry L. and Stella (Moessner) J.; m. Shirlie McCleary, June 13, 1947; children—Glenn Steven, Gary Lynn, Michael Alan. Student, Ga. Inst. Tech., 1946-48, Ga. State Coll., 1948-49. With Genuine Parts Co., Atlanta and Jacksonville, Fla., 1947—; asst. to pres. Genuine Parts Co., 1961-65, treas., 1965-67, v.p. ops., 1967-79, sr. v.p. ops., 1979-81, group v.p., 1981-84, exec. v.p. adminstrn., 1985-88, vice chmn. bd. dirs., 1988—; mem. S.E. adv. bd. Allendale Ins. Co. Active United Way; bd. dirs. YMCA Met., Atlanta. Served with USAAF, 1944-45. Lutheran. Home: 4170 Thunderbird Dr Marietta GA 30067 Office: Genuine Parts Co 2999 Circle 75 Pkwy Atlanta GA 30339

JONES, EDWARD THOMAS, accountant, regional planning commission adminstrator; b. Mechanicville, N.Y., Nov. 12, 1933; s. Jesse and Loula (Whitfield) J.; B.B.A., Siena Coll., 1961; M.B.A., Pace U., 1979; m. Rachel Manley, Aug. 22, 1970; children—Mark, Kimberly, Julie, Antonio. Ins. examiner N.Y. State Ins. Dept., N.Y.C., 1961-65; asst. sec. treas. dept. Crum & Forster Ins. Co., N.Y.C., 1965-71; chief acct. N.Y. Fair Plan, N.Y.C., 1971-72; controller, chief fiscal officer United Negro College Fund, Inc., N.Y.C., 1972-80; dep. exec. dir. adminstrn. and fin. Tri-State Regional Planning Commn., N.Y.C., 1980-82; cons. fin. services non-profit orgns., 1982-83; controller, chief fiscal officer NAACP, Bklyn., 1983-85; chief fin. officer, treas. Community Action for Legal Services, Inc., N.Y.C., 1985—. Served with U.S. Army, 1952-55. Mem. Nat. Assn. Black Accts. (past nat. sec.). Democrat. Baptist. Home: 47 E 56th St Brooklyn NY 11203 Office: 335 Broadway New York NY 10013

JONES, GASTON C(ARLISLE), adminstrative executive; b. Gulfport, Miss., May 31, 1918; s. Henry Hugh and Hilda (Gaston) J.; m. Carolyn Dupre Latta, Feb. 22, 1951. BSC, U. Miss., 1940; student, Northwestern u., 1941. CPA, Tex. With tax. dept. Arthur Andersen & Co., accts. and auditors, Houston, 1941-50; v.p., dir. F.A. Callery, Inc., Houston, 1950-66, pres., 1966-75; pres. C&J Services, Inc., Houston, 1975-84; v.p., bd. dirs. Callery Properties, Inc.; chmn. bd. Seminole Harvesting, Inc.; mng. partner Callery Judge Grove. Pres. Seminole Water Control Dist. Mem. Am. Inst. Accts., Phi Kappa Psi. Clubs: Beach Club, Palm Beach Polo and Country, Pundits. Home: 170 Chilean Ave Palm Beach FL 33480 Office: 612 Comeau Bldg West Palm Beach FL 33401

JONES, GENE KERRY, finance company executive; b. Farmville, N.C., July 17, 1928; s. Samuel Lester and Estelle Adelaide (Piercy) J.; m. Lee Blankenship, June 29, 1951. BS, U. Ala., 1956, MS in Mktg. with honors, 1961; postgrad., U. Calif., Berkeley, 1961; PhD in Fin. with honors, U. Tex., 1964. Corp. dir. acquisitions Rockwell Internat., Pitts., 1965-67; chief fin. officer Chapman Chem. Co., Memphis, 1967-70; chief exec. officer Vam, Ltd., Sydney, Australia, 1970-71; pres., chief exec. officer Dream Air, Inc., Birmingham, Ala., 1971-74; prof. fin. U. N.D., Minot, 1974-77, U. Wis., Eau Claire, 1977-80, Temple U., Phila., 1980-83; pres. G & L Mortgage Corp., Atlanta, 1983—. Contbr. articles to profl. jours. Tchr. Sunday sch. Meth. Ch., Tuscaloosa, Ala., 1960; trustee Presbyn. Ch., Phila., 1982; mem. fin. and budget com., Stephen minister 1st Presbyn. Ch., Atlanta. Served as sgt. U.S. Army, 1952-54. Woodrow Wilson fellow, 1961, Flood fellow in Bus. Adminstrn., 1961, Bus. Adminstrn. Found. fellow, 1963. Mem. Fin. Mgmt. Assn., Beta Gamma Sigma. Republican. Home: 1606 Runnymeade Dr Atlanta GA 30319 Office: G & L Mortgage Corp PO Box 467158 Atlanta GA 30346

JONES, GERRE LYLE, marketing and public relations consultant; b. Kansas City, Mo., June 22, 1926; s. Eugene Riley and Carolyn (Newell) J.; m. Charlotte Mae Reinhold, Oct. 30, 1948; children: Beverly Anne Jones Putnam, Wendy Sue. BJ, U. Mo., 1948, postgrad., 1953-54. Exec. sec. Effingham (Ill.) C. of C., 1948-50; field rep. Nat. Found. Infantile Paralysis, N.Y.C., 1950-57; dir. pub. relations Inst. Logopedics, Wichita, Kans., 1957-58; owner Gerre Jones & Assocs., Pub. Relations, Kansas City, Mo., 1958-63; info. officer Radio Free Europe Fund, Munich, Federal Republic of Germany, 1963-65, spl. asst. to dir. pub. relations, 1965-66; exec. asst. pub. affairs Edward Durell Stone, 1967-68; dir. mktg. and communications Vincent C. Kling & Ptnrs., Phila., 1969-71; mktg. cons. Ellerbe Architects, Washington, 1972; v.p. Gaio Assocs., Ltd., Washington, 1972-73, exec. v.p., 1973-76; exec. v.p. Bldg. Industry Devel. Services, Washington, 1973-76; pres. Gerre Jones Assocs. Inc., Albuquerque, 1976—; sr. v.p. Barlow Assocs., Inc., Washington, 1977-78; lectr. numerous colls. and univs. Author: How to Market Professional Design Services, 1973, 2d edit., 1983, How to Prepare Professional Design Brochures, 1976, (with Stuart H. Rose) How to Find and Win New Business, 1976, Public Relations for the Design Professional, 1980; contbr. articles to profl. jours. Served with USAAF, 1944-45, maj. USAF (ret.). Mem. Internat. Radio and TV Soc., Nat. Assn. Sci. Writers, Am. Soc. Tng. and Devel., AIA (hon.), Sigma Delta Chi, Alpha Delta Sigma, Phi Delta Phi. Republican. Clubs: Kansas City Press; Overseas Press; Deadline (N.Y.C.). Lodge: Masons.

JONES, H. W. KASEY, financial planning executive, author, lecturer; b. Burlington, Iowa, Feb. 11, 1942; s. Herbert Warren and Mary Kathryn (Gardner) J.; m. Ellen E. Toon, Mar. 11, 1961 (div. Dec. 1969); children: Kari Lynne, Kevin C., Anthony W. Student, Bradley U., 1960-61, Coll. Fin. Planning, 1988. Cert. fin. planner. Gen. mgr. sales Wickstrom Chevrolet, Roselle, Ill., 1967-80; v.p. Re-Direct Svcs., Villa Park, Ill., 1980-81, pres., chief exec. officer, 1982—; also chmn. bd. dirs. Re-Direct Svcs., Villa Park; founding sponsor, mem. speakers' bur. Nat. Ctr. for Fin. Edn., San Francisco, 1984—. Bd. dirs. Indian Trails Homeowners Assn. Mem. Internat. Assn. Fin. Planners, Inst. Cert. Fin. Planners, Profl. Ins. Agts. Ill. Club: Chief Exec. Officers' (N.Y.C.), The Pres.'s Assn. Home: 940 Indian Boundary Westmont IL 60559 Office: Re-Direct Svcs 721 E Madison St Villa Park IL 60181

JONES, HOMER WALTER, JR., statistician; b. N.Y.C., Sept. 3, 1925; s. Homer Walter and Margaret (Campbell) J.; M.E., Stevens Inst. Tech., 1947, M.S., 1950; M.B.A., Am. U., 1959; M.S., George Washington U., 1965; m. Shirley Jean Dabbs, June 15, 1957; children—Laura Gwen, Linda Margaret. Cost estimator Standard Oil Devel. Co., Linden, N.J., 1947-51; engr. Wallace and Tiernan Co., Belleville, N.J., 1957-58; sr. math. statistician U.S. Treasury Dept., Internal Revenue Service, Washington, 1959-88; ret., 1988. ltd. partner Vista Lakes Estates, Alta Vista, Va. Pres., IRS Chess Club, 1968-78; team capt. D.C. Chess League, 1963-86; nat. tournament dir. U.S. Chess Fedn., 1978—, rated expert, 1984—; mem. exec. com. Va. Chess Fedn., 1975-78; organizer Region III Chess Championship, 1974-77, 79; dir. U.S. Jr. Chess Championship, Memphis, 1978; dir. USAF Chess Team Qualification Tournament, 1983—; dir. USAF Chess Championship, 1988—. Mem. and host family Am. Field Service, 1977-78, 87; elder Presbyn. Ch., 1973-76, 78; treas. Performing Arts Assn. of Alexandria, 1985-87. Served with USNR, 1944-45. Recipient Certificate of Award, U.S. Treasury Dept., 1978, 84. Mem. U.S. Chess Fedn. (regional v.p. 1973-76, voting mem. 1973-83), Assn. U.S. Chess Journalists (sec.-treas. 1976-79), Chess Journalists Am., Am. Statis. Assn., Am. Assn. Ret. Persons, DAV, Tau Beta Pi. Editor: Kings File mag., 1974. Asst. editor Va. Chess Fedn. Newsletter, 1976-83, games editor, 1978, 80-82. Home: 607 Pulman Pl Alexandria VA 22305 Office: 1201 E St NW Washington DC 20224

JONES, JAMES GRAHAM, communications and information systems executive; b. Detroit, Dec. 1, 1948; s. James Graham and Eddythe (Collins) J.; m. Sally Hemenway, Dec. 19, 1970; children: Shaun Graham, Christopher Allen. BS in Edn., Mich. State U., 1970, MBA, 1974. Dist. exec. Boy Scouts Am., LaGrange, Ill., 1970-72; mktg. mgr. McDonnell Douglas Corp., St. Louis, 1974-77; br. mgr. Tymshare Corp., Chgo., 1977-80; regional mgr. IBM/Rolm, Chgo., 1980-87; pres., chief exec. officer RNW Inc., Chgo., 1988—. Author TV seminars on data processing, microwave communications, fiber optics communications, 1984. Mem. Am. Mgmt. Assn., Aircraft Owners and Pilots Assn. Home: 307 Whitfield Dr Geneva IL 60134 Office: RNW Inc 175 N Franklin Chicago IL 60606

JONES, JAMES RONALD, accountant; b. Picayune, Miss., June 4, 1947; s. James Harold and Beatrice (Germany) J.; m. Janice S. King, Apr. 24, 1950; children: Cooper, Karen. BS, Miss. Coll., 1969; MBA, Miss. State U., 1971. CPA, Miss., Tenn. With Peat, Marwick, Main and Co., Jackson, Miss., 1971-78, Washington, 1978-80; With Peat, Marwick, Main and Co., Nashville, 1980-85, 87—, ptnr., 1981—; with Peat, Marwick, Main and Co., Greenville, S.C., 1985-87, Nashville, 1987—. Mem. Am. Inst. CPA's, Tenn. Soc. CPA's. Baptist. Office: Peat Marwick Main & Co Nashville City Ctr Nashville TN 37219

JONES, JAMES THOMAS, hospital administrator; b. Glen Dale, W.Va., Nov. 13, 1949; s. James H. and Rose (Antonacci) J.; m. A. Jane Byrne, Sept. 4, 1971; children: Christopher, Jennifer. BS, W.Va. U., 1971; MHA, U. Minn., 1973. Resident W.Va. U. Hosp., Morgantown, 1972-73; asst. adminstr. Wheeling (W.Va.) Hosp., 1973-79, assoc. adminstr., 1979—; instr. health adminstrn., Wheeling Coll., 1977; lectr. W.Va. U., Wheeling, 1982; bd. dirs. No. Panhandle Mental Health Ctr., Wheeling, 1978-82. Bd. dirs. Bridgeport (Ohio) Area C. of C., 1983-85. Named one of Outstanding Young Men Am., U.S. Jaycees, 1980. Mem. Am. Coll. Health Adminstrs., W.Va. Hosp. Assn., W.Va. Hosp. Edn. and Research Found. (pres. 1984-86), Wheeling C. of C. (bd. dirs. 1986—). Republican. Roman Catholic. Home: 124 Rogers Rd Wheeling WV 26003 Office: Wheeling Hosp Inc Medical Park Wheeling WV 26003

JONES, JENKIN LLOYD, newspaper publisher; b. Madison, Wis., Nov. 1, 1911; s. Richard Lloyd and Georgia (Hayden) J.; m. Ana Maria de Andrada Rocha, July 30, 1976; children: Jenkin Lloyd, David, Georgia; step-children: Maria Alice Rocha, Paulo Rocha. PhB, U. Wis., 1933; various hon. degrees. Reporter Tulsa Tribune, 1933, mng. editor, 1938, editor, 1941-88, pub., 1963—; dir. Newspaper Printing Corp., Tulsa. Author: The Changing World, 1966; writer syndicated weekly column. Served to lt. comdr. USNR, 1944-46, PTO. Recipient William Allen White award Okla. Hall of Fame, 1957; Fourth Estate award Am. Legion, 1970; Freedom Leadership award Freedoms Found., 1969; Disting. Service award U. Wis., 1970; Disting. Service award U. Okla., 1971; Disting. Service award Okla. State U., 1972. Mem. Am. Soc. Newspaper Editors (pres. 1957), Inter Am. Press Assn., U.S. C. of C. (pres. 1969), Internat. Press Inst. Republican. Unitarian. Clubs: So. Hills Country (Tulsa), Summit (Tulsa). Home: 6683 S Jamestown Pl Tulsa OK 74136 Office: Tulsa Tribune Box 1770 315 S Boulder Ave Tulsa OK 74103

JONES, JOHN EARL, construction company executive; b. June 24, 1934. B.A., Carleton Coll., 1956; postgrad., U. Chgo., 1958-60, Northwestern U., 1960-61. Sr. v.p. Continental Ill. Nat. Bank and Trust Co., Chgo., 1957-80; with CBI Industries, Inc., Oak Brook, Ill., 1980—, exec. v.p., treas.,

1982—; vice chmn. bd. CBI Industries, Inc., 1985-88, pres., chief operating officer, 1988—, also dir.; bd. dirs. Allied Products Corp. Trustee Glenwood Sch.; mem. bus. adv. council U. Ill. Office: CBI Industries Inc 800 Jorie Blvd Oak Brook IL 60521

JONES, JOSEPH LOUIS, retired manufacturing company executive; b. Farmville, Va., Feb. 27, 1923; s. Joseph Louis and Edna (Elcan) J.; m. Dorothy Jeanne Jennings, June 21, 1949; children: Joseph, Catherine, Carolyn. B.A., Va. Poly Inst., 1947. With Armstrong World Industries, Lancaster, Pa., 1947-88, prodn. mgr., 1961-66, v.p. carpet ops., 1966-74, exec. v.p., dir., 1974-83, chmn., pres., chief exec. officer, 1983-88, bd. dirs.; bd. dirs. Carpenter Technology, Reading, Pa., Armstrong World Industries. Trustee Lancaster Gen. Hosp. Served to capt., inf. AUS, 1943-46. Decorated Bronze Star. Mem. Lancaster C. of C., NAM (dir.). Republican. Presbyterian (trustee). Club: Lancaster Country. Home: 121 Eshelman Rd Lancaster PA 17601

JONES, LARRY T., manufacturing executive, consultant; b. Lexington, Okla., Mar. 9, 1934; s. Lemuel Thomas and Emma Ann (Anderson) J.; m. Donna Lou Moore, Dec. 19, 1953 (div. Aug. 1979); children—David, Linda, Daniel, m. Joyce Ann Shortridge, Aug. 7, 1983; children—Lisa, Charlotte, Gabrielle, Jonathan. Project leader Singer Co., Reston, Va., 1974-76; contract publ. engr. IBM, Manassas, Va., 1976-77, Sperry Univac, Bristol, Tenn., 1977-78, Westinghouse Co., Hunt Valley, Md., 1978-81, Gen. Electric, Syracuse, 1981-84, project leader, 1984—; fin. advisor for non-profit orgn., 1984-87; dir. Keeper Publs., Christian Acres. Author short story, poetry, tech. manuals, 1966—. Adviser, Am. Security Council, Washington, 1974—. Served as airman 1st class USAF, 1953-57. Mem. IEEE. Republican. Avocations: chess; bowling; computer technology. Office: PO Box 391 Liverpool NY 13088

JONES, LEONADE DIANE, financial executive; b. Bethesda, Md., Nov. 27, 1947; d. Leon Adger and Landonia Randolph (Madden) J. BA with distinction, Simmons Coll., 1969; JD, Stanford U., 1973, MBA, 1973. Bar: Calif. 1973, D.C. 1979. Securities analyst Capital Rsch. Co., L.A., 1973-75; asst. treas. Washington Post Co., 1975-79, 86-87, treas., 1987—; dir. fin. services Post-Newsweek Stas., Inc., Washington, 1979-84, v.p. bus. affairs, 1984-86. Treas., bd. dirs. Big Sisters Washington Met. Area, 1984-85; bd. dirs. D.C. Contemporary Dance Theatre, 1987-88. Mem. ABA, Calif. Bar Assn., D.C. Bar Assn., Stanford Bus. Sch. Alumni Assn. (bd. dirs. 1986-88, pres. Washington-Balt. chpt. 1984-85). Office: Washington Post Co 1150 15th St NW Washington DC 20071

JONES, MALINDA THIESSEN, telecommunications company executive; b. Perryton, Tex., Jan. 23, 1947; d. Chester Francis Thiessen and Bobbye Pearson (Wallis) Schwalm; m. Hollis Bass Jones, Mar. 21, 1969 (div. 1972); 1 child, Reshad. B.A. in Psychology, U. Mo.-Kansas City, 1975. Research asst. U. Kans. Med. Ctr., Kansas City, 1975-77; owner, mgr. Metro Shampoo Co., Kansas City, Mo., 1977-79; regional mgr. U.S. Telecom, Dallas, 1981-82, staff asst. to pres., Dallas, 1983-84, sr. planner, 1984-85; dir. mktg. Telinq Systems Inc., Richardson, Tex., 1985-86, dir. bus. devel. and corp. communications, 1986—; v.p. Dakota Group, Inc., 1988—; cons. in field. Editor conf. presentations, bus. plans. Vol. tchr. Sch. for Learning Disability, Operation Discovery, Kansas City, 1973-75; corp. liaison exec. assistance program Dallas C. of C./Dallas Ind. Sch. Dist., 1984; chmn. com. Therapeutic Riding Tex., Dallas, 1985. Recipient Outstanding Contbr. award Dallas Ind. Sch. Dist., 1984. Mem. NAFE, Nat. Mus. Assn. for Women in Arts, Assn. Women Entrepreneurs Dallas. Home: 1122 Overlake Dr Richardson TX 75080 Office: Telinq Systems Inc 1651 N Glenville Dr Richardson TX 75081

JONES, MARY DELLA, accountant; b. Clarksville, Pa., June 2, 1949; d. Will and Maggie E. (Claytor) J.; m. James David West, Dec. 31, 1981; 1 child, Eugenia Michelle (dec.). Student, Community Coll. Allegheny County, Pitts.; BA in Econs., U. Pitts., 1989. Sales clk. Sears Roebuck and Co., Pitts., 1967; file clk. Blue Cross/Blue Shield, Pitts., 1967-68; recruiter, bookkeeper Bidwell Tng. Ctr., Pitts., 1968-69; receptionist Homewood Brushton Health Ctr., Pitts., 1969-70; exec. sec. Recreation Ctr. Bidwell Street United Presbyn. Ch., Pitts., 1970-71; cashier, sr. acctg. clk. U. Pitts., 1971-78; data analyst, acct. Volkswagen Am., New Stanton, Pa., 1978—; bookkeeper Black Medium Coffee Shop, Inc., Pitts., 1969-70; fin. chair Sch. Gen. Studies U. Pitts., 1978; chair staff adv. bd. fin. Volkswagon Am., 1985; mem. staff adv. bd. U. Pitts, 1978; mem. James Cleveland Gospel Music Workshop, Pitts. Pres., bd. trustees Mt. Ararat Bapt. Ch., Pitts., 1984—, personnel chmn., 1987. Recipient Community Service award Homewood Brushton YWCA, 1980. Mem. Nat. Assn. Female Execs., Internat. Platform Assn., Nat. Negro Bus. and Profl. Women's Clubs, Inc. (publicity chmn. Pitts. area 1978-79, pres. 1980, Club award 1979), Phi Chi Theta (pres. U. Pitts. chpt. 1977). Democrat. Baptist. Home: 104 Old Farm Dr Pittsburgh PA 15239 Office: Volkswagen Am Hwy 119 New Stanton PA 15672

JONES, MICHAEL WADE, accountant, financial and real estate consultant; b. Pawhuska, Okla., Oct. 16, 1947; s. Wade Prentice and Leota Euphemia (Rennick) J.; m. Linda Lee O'Dell, Aug. 2, 1969; children: Wade, Mary-Margaret, Jennifer. BS, U.S. Mil. Acad., 1969; MBA, U. Okla., 1976. CPA, Okla.; lic. real estate broker. Engr., acct. Phillips Petroleum Co., Bartlesville, Okla. and Dallas, 1976-81; pvt. practice acctg. Pawhuska, Okla., 1981-88; chief fin. officer Potomac Realty Advs. Inc., Arlington, Va., 1988—; pres., chmn. Mgmt. Solutions, Inc., Bartlesville, 1981—. Served to capt. U.S. Army, 1969-74, Vietnam. Decorated Bronze Star, Air medal. Mem. Okla. Soc. CPA's. Office: Potomoc Realty Adv Inc 520 Leahy PO Box 1567 Pawhuska OK 74056

JONES, NANCY LANGDON, certified financial planner; b. Chgo., Mar. 24, 1939; d. Lewis Valentine and Margaret (Seese) Russell; m. Lawrence Elmer Langdon, June 30, 1962 (div. 1970); children: Laura Kimberley, Elizabeth Ann; m. Claude Earl Jones, Jan. 1, 1973. BA, U. Redlands, Calif., 1962. Bookkeeper Russell Sales Co., Santa Fe Springs, Calif., 1962-70; office mgr. Reardon, McCallum & Co., Upland, Calif., 1970-77; broker, assoc. ERA Property Ctr., Upland, 1977-84; registered rep. Am. Pacific Securities, Pasadena, Calif., 1984—; pvt. practice fin. planning Upland, 1984—; adj. faculty Coll. Fin. Planning, Denver, 1986—. Leader Spanish trails coun. Girl Scouts Am., 1974-81; Asst. League of Upland. Recipient Hon. Svc. award Valencia Elem. Sch., 1978. Mem. Internat. Assn. Fin. Planners (pres. San Gabriel Valley chpt. 1987-88), Am. Bus. Women's Assn. (sec. Upland chpt. 1984-85, Woman of Yr. award 1988), Inst.Cert. Fin. Planners, Nat. Coun. Exchangers (sec. 1986-87), Women's Bus. Network (pres. 1987-88), Registry of Fin. Planning Practitioners, Upland C. of C., Screen Actors Guild. Home and Office: 2485 Mesa Ter Upland CA 91786

JONES, NEIL EDWARD, communications executive; b. Jackson Center, Pa., July 31, 1928; s. Alvin R. and Viola G. (Jenkins) J.; m. Elaine K. Anderson, July 24, 1962; children: Dana Kathleen, Lisa Elaine, Stephen Neil. B.S. in Nautical Sci., U.S. Mcht. Marine Acad., 1952. Sales mgr., officer various cos. engaged to prin. underwriters for oil and gas drilling programs, 1965-72; v.p. devel., dir. Jones Intercable, Inc., Englewood, Colo., 1972-83; pres. Jones Intercable Securities, Englewood, 1978-83; exec. v.p. Communications Properties, Inc., Englewood, 1983-86; pres., chief exec. officer, Pioneer Paging, Inc., Englewood, 1986—; pres., Cellular Cons's., Inc., Naples, Fla., 1988—. Mem. Republican Nat. Fin. Com., 1964-69. Served with USN, 1953-55. Contbr. articles to profl. jours. Office: 3333 S Bannock St Ste 660 Englewood CO 80110

JONES, NORMAN THOMAS, service executive; b. Herrin, Ill., Feb. 21, 1936; s. Thomas Henry and Mary Frances (Beckner) J.; m. Nevelyn J. Childers, Apr. 11, 1955; children: David, Debra, Deanna. BS in Commerce, U. Ill., 1962. CPA. Auditor Peat Marwick and Mitchell, St. Louis, 1962-63; with mgmt. devel. GE, Bloomington, Ill., 1963-64; various mgmt. positions GROWMARK Inc., Bloomington, 1964-80, exec. dir. human resources, 1980-84, v.p. corp. services, 1984-86, sr. v.p. fin., 1986-87, exec. v.p., chief exec. officer, 1987—; bd. dirs. Agri-Trans Corp., Long Grove, Ill., Mut. Svc. Ins., St. Paul, ADM/GROWMARK Inc., Decatur, Ill., CF Industries, Inc., Nat. Coun. Farmer Coops. chmn. Bd. Police and Fire Commissioners, Bloomington, 1970—; mem., pres. Dist. 87 Sch. Bd., Bloomington, 1974-84; mem. Ill. Sch. Bd. Assn., Springfield, 1979-84. Sgt. U.S. Army, 1954-57. Mem. Ill. Soc. CPA's, Exchange Club (pres. 1980-81, disting. service award 1980). Republican. Baptist. Office: GROWMARK Inc 1701 Towanda Ave PO Box 2500 Bloomington IL 61702-2500

JONES, OWEN J(OHN), III, laser sales executive; b. Harrisburg, Pa., Oct. 12, 1949; s. Owen J. Jr. and Tamea Ann (Mixell) J.; m. Penny A. Jones, 1982. BS in Chemistry, Lehigh U., 1971, MBA, 1972. Sales engr. Enthone, Inc., New Haven, 1973-78, UPA Tech., Syosset, N.Y., 1979-80; sales engr., sales mgr. Allied Corp./Apollo Lasers, Chatsworth, Calif., 1981-82; sales mgr. Lumonics Marking Corp., Camarillo, Calif., 1982-89; nat. sales mgr. A-B Lasers Inc., 1989—. Mem. Laser Inst. Am., Am. Electroplaters and Surface Finishers Soc., Am. Soc. Metallurgists, Nat. Assn. Realtors, Porsche Club Am. Republican.

JONES, RAYMOND EUGENE, financial executive; b. Chillicothe, Mo., Apr. 30, 1941; s. Merl L. and Mary F. (Saccaro) J.; m. M. Karol Hawkins, May 31, 1964; 1 child, Andrea Rae. BSBA, Cen. Mo. State U., 1964. From agt. to dist. sales mgr. MFA Ins. Co., Columbia, Mo., 1964-65, supr. budgeting and planning, 1965-67, mgr. budgeting and planning, 1967-75; conv. planning mgr. MFA Ins. Co., Columbia, 1975-81; adminstrv. asst. to pres. Shelter Ins. Co., Columbia, 1981-82, v.p. adminstrn., 1982-86, v.p. adminstrn., sec. bd. dirs., 1986—. Chmn. Columbia Tomorrow, 1987, Columbia Planning and Zoning Com., 1978-84. Served with USAR, 1968-74. Mem. Ins. Conf. Planners, Conf. of Casualty Ins. Cos., Nat. Assn. Ind. Insurers, Columbia C. of C. (v.p., 1985-86). Lodge: Rotary. Home: 1207 Torrey Pines Dr Columbia MO 65203 Office: Shelter Ins Cos 1817 W Broadway Columbia MO 65218

JONES, REID, JR., supply company executive, farmer; b. San Antonio, Jan. 18, 1916; m. Margaret Garris, Jan. 16, 1947 (div. July 1982); 1 child, Margaret Jones Irvin. Student, Columbia U., 1937-40. From clk. to salesman Linde div. Union Carbide Corp., St. Louis and other locations, 1935-49; owner, mgr. Jones Welding Supplies, Roanoke, Va., 1949-74; owner, pres. Jones Safety Supply, Inc., Roanoke, 1959—, Safehouse Signs, Inc., Roanoke, 1980—; owner, mgr. Joco Farms, Roanoke, 1965—. Co-chmn. Roanoke Valley United Fund., 1972. Served with USAAF, 1943-46. Mem. Nat Welding Supply Assn. (pres. 1964-65). Republican. Episcopalian. Office: Jones Safety Supply Inc 719 Gainsboro Rd NW Roanoke VA 24006

JONES, RENEE KAUERAUF, healthcare administrator; b. Duncan, Okla., Nov. 3, 1949; d. Delbert Owen and Betty Jean (Marsh) Kauerauf; m. Dan Elkins Jones, Aug. 3, 1972. BS, Okla. State U., 1972, MS, 1975; PhD, Okla. U., 1989. Statis. analyst Okla. State Dept. Mental Health, Okla. City, 1978-80, divisional chief, 1980-83, adminstr., 1983-84; assoc. dir. HCA Presbyn. Hosp., Okla. City, 1984—; adj. instr. Okla. U. Health Sci. Ctr., 1979—; assoc. staff scientist Okla. Ctr. for Alcohol and Drug-Related Studies, Okla. City, 1979—; cons. in field. Assoc. editor Alcohol Tech. Reports jour., 1979-84; contbr. articles to profl. jours. Mem. Am. Pub. Health Assn., Assn. Health Services Research, Alcohol and Drug Problems Assn. N.Am., N.Y. Acad. Scis., So. Sleep Soc. Democrat. Methodist. Home: 215 NW 20th Oklahoma City OK 73103 Office: HCA Presbyn Hosp NE 13th at Lincoln Blvd Oklahoma City OK 73104

JONES, RICHARD CYRUS, lawyer; b. Oak Park, Ill., Oct. 20, 1928; s. Ethler E. and Margaret S. (Stoner) J.; m. Betty Jane Becker; children: Richard C., Carrie, William. PhB, DePaul U., 1960, JD, 1963. Bar: Ill. 1963. Dept. mgr. Chgo. Title & Trust Co., 1947-64; mem. Sachnoff, Schrager, Jones, Weaver & Rubenstein Ltd. and predecessor firms, Chgo., 1964-81; of counsel Sachnoff & Weaver, Chgo., 1981—; instr. Real Estate Inst., Chgo., 1970—; trustee, sec., exec. v.p. Income Properties and Equity Trust, 1974—; trustee, chmn. Ind. Dirs. of Wis. Real Estate Investment Trust, 1980—. Mem. alumni bd. Wayland Acad., 1983-87, trustee, 1986—. Decorated Bronze Star. Mem. ABA, Ill. Bar Assn., Chgo. Bar Assn. (com. chmn. real property law 1980-82, 76—), Chgo. Council Lawyers, Delta Theta Phi. Lodge: Kiwanis (past pres.). Home: 1044 Forest Ave River Forest IL 60305 Office: Sachnoff & Weaver 30 S Wacker Dr 29th Fl Chicago IL 60606

JONES, RICHARD LEE, accountant; b. San Antonio, Feb. 4, 1961; s. Leroy and Beatrice (Starustka) J. BBA in Acctg., U. Tex., San Antonio, 1983. With Army & Air Force Exchange Svc., 1984—; cash ops. specialist Golden Gate Exchange Region, San Francisco, 1984-85; acctg. ops. specialist Golden Gate Exchange Region, Tacoma, 1985-87; chief fin. planning Pacific Hdqrs. Honolulu, 1987—. Mem. Honolulu Jaycees. Mem. Hawaii Soc. CPA's, Am. Soc. Mil. Comptrollers, Am. Inst. CPA's. Roman Catholic.

JONES, RICHARD M., bank executive, former retail executive; b. Eldon, Mo., Nov. 26, 1926; m. Sylvia A. Richardson, 1950; 3 children. B.S. in Bus. Adminstrn., Olivet Nazarene Coll., 1950, LL.D. (hon.), 1983; grad. Advanced Mgmt. Program, Harvard U., 1973. With Sears, Roebuck & Co., 1950-89, store mgr., 1963-68; gen. mgr. Sears, Roebuck & Co., Washington and Balt., 1974; exec. v.p.-East Sears, Roebuck & Co., 1974-80, corp. v.p., 1980, vice chmn., chief fin. officer, 1980-85, pres., chief fin. officer, 1986-89; chmn., pres., chief operating officer Guaranty Fed. Savs. Bank, Dallas, 1989—; dir. Sears Roebuck Found.; bd. of govs. indsl. issuer adv. council Standard & Poor's, Com. for Econ. Devel., Conf. Bd. Chmn. bd. trustees Field Mus. Natural History, Chgo.; bd. dirs. Council for Aid to Edn., Inc., bd. govs. Am. Red Cross, Northwestern Univ. Assocs., Chgo., ARC, Washington, Fishman-Davidson Ctr. adv. bd. Wharton Sch. of U. Pa.; bd. of govs. adv. council J.L. Kellogg Grad. Sch. Mgmt. at Northwestern U. Club: Comml. (bd. of govs.). Office: Guaranty Fed Savs Bank 10440 N Central Expwy Ste 500 Dallas TX 75231 *

JONES, RICHARD M., management professional; b. Newark, Sept. 15, 1946; s. David Arthur and Jessie (Brown) J.; m. Joan Straayer (div. May 1977); m. Elsie Ann Fassl; children: Dana, Jennifer, Richard Jr., Zachary, Bryan. BS, St. Francis Coll., 1968; MBA, Lehigh U., 1982. Pres., chief exec. officer Collegiate Mgmt. Systems Inc., Bethlehem, Pa., 1986—. Sec. City Line Little League, Bethlehem, 1987-88. With USN, 1969-70. Mem. Fraternity Mgmt. Assn. Lehigh U. (exec. dir. 1975-86), Rotary (chmn. conv. com. 1987-88), Saucon Valley Country Club. Republican. Roman Catholic. Office: Collegiate Mgmt Systems Inc 840 Stefko Blvd Bethlehem PA 18017

JONES, ROBERT ALONZO, economist; b. Evanston, Ill., Mar. 15, 1937; s. Robert Vernon and Elsie Pierce (Brown) J.; m. Kathleen Mary Bush, Aug. 16, 1958; children: Lindsay Rae, Robert Pierce, Gregory Alan, William Kenneth. AB, Middlebury Coll., 1959; MBA, Northwestern U., 1961. Sr. research officer Bank of Am., San Francisco, 1969-74; v.p., dir. fin. forecasting Chase Econometrics, San Francisco, 1974-76; chmn. bd. Money Market Services, Inc., Belmont, Calif., 1974-86; chmn. bd. MMS Internat., Redwood City, Calif., 1986—, Market News Service, Inc., N.Y.C., 1987—; dir. Money Market Services, Ltd., London, Money Market Services, Ltd., Hong Kong; dir. Market News Service, Inc., Washington; chmn. bd. trustees Internat. Inst. Econ. Advancement, Incline, Nev., 1982—; instr. money and banking, Am. Inst. Banking, San Francisco, 1971, 72. Councilman, City of Belmont (Calif.), 1970-77, mayor, 1971, 72, 75, 76; dir. San Mateo County Transit Dist., 1975-77; chmn. San Mateo County Council of Mayors, 1975-76; trustee Incline Village Gen. Improvement Dist., 1984-85. Author: U.S. Financial System and the Federal Reserve, 1974, Power of Coinage, 1987. Named Hon. Life Mem., Calif. PTA, to Kappa Delta Rho Nat. Hall of Fame. Mem. Nat. Assn. Bus. Economists, San Francisco Bond Club. Republican. Methodist.

JONES, ROBERT ROLAND, JR., physicist; b. Houston, Sept. 1, 1942; d. Robert R. and Rubye Laura Frances (Burch) J.; children—Regina Renee, Robert R. III. B.S. in Physics, U. Tex.-Austin, 1967, B.A. in Math., 1967; M.A. in Physics, 1970; postgrad. U. Houston, Tex. So. U., 1960-61. Teaching and research asst. U. Tex., Austin, 1967-70; instr. physics and math. Houston Community Coll. and Lockheed Electronics, 1970-72; instr. physics and math. Tex. So. U. and Community Coll., 1972-74; teaching asst. U. Houston, 1974-76; teaching and research asst. Howard U., Washington, 1976-77; sr. engr. assoc. Lockheed Electronics, Inc., Houston, after 1978; owner, operator Trebore Industries, Trebore Medi-Ctr. Recipient Award of Merit, Greater Houston Sci. Fair, 1958; grantee Fisk U., Nashville, 1960; Worthing Scholar, Houston, 1960. Mem. Am. Phys. Soc., Am. Chem. Soc. (cert. of honor and plaque 1965), Sigma Pi Sigma. Republican. Baptist.

JONES, ROBYN A., insurance company executive, accountant; b. N.Y.C., June 14, 1944; children: Lindsay Draper, Christopher Austin. Student, U. Montpellier, France, 1964; Deuxième Degré in French, U. Paris, 1965; BA cum laude in Foreign Languages, Elmira Coll., 1966; MA in French, Duke U., 1969; postgrad., St. Andrews Presbyn. Coll., 1977. Instr. French Duke U., Durham, N.C., 1967-69, Scotland Country Schs., Laurinburg, N.C., 1973-75; staff acct. Integon Life Ins. Inc., Winston-Salem, N.C., 1977-79, sr. acct., 1979-80, dir. budgeting and planning, 1980-81, v.p. planning and budgeting, 1981, v.p., exec. asst. to chief exec. officer, 1982-84, v.p. spl. mktg. adminstrn., 1984-87, v.p. mktg. svcs., 1988—. Contbr. articles to profl. jours. Pres., bd. dirs. Coun. on Status of Women, Winston-Salem, 1984-87. Mem. AICPA, N.C. Soc. CPA's, Am. Coll. Bryn Mawr, Life Office Mgmt. Assn. (chmn. corp. planning com., fin. planning and control bd. 1988-89). Home: 751 Roslyn Rd Winston-Salem NC 27104 Office: Integon Life Ins Inc 500 W 5th St Winston-Salem NC 27152

JONES, RODDIS STEWART, construction and land development company executive; b. Marshfield, Wis., Jan. 11, 1930; s. Henry Stewart and Sara (Roddis) J.; m. Anne Crook Orum, Jan. 7, 1955; children: Patricia, Jeffrey, Jennifer. BSME, Auburn U., 1952; PMD, Harvard U., 1960; postgrad., U. Wis., Madison, 1959. Lic. realtor, Wash. Project ngr. Marathon Corp., Rothschild, Wis., 1955-57; prodn. supt. indsl. engring., mgr. cost acctg. Roddis Plywood Corp., Marshfield, 1957-60; br. mgr. Weyerhauser Co., Hancock, Vt., Oakland, Calif., Federal Way, Wash., 1960-78; pres., gen. mgr. Roddis Jones Cos., Solarcrete N.W., Investment Bldg. & Devel. Co., Mgmt. Cons. Fin., Prodn. 1978—. Served as officer USN, 1952-55. Mem. Seattle Master Builders. Republican. Episcopalian. Lodges: Rotary, Elks, Masons. Home: 104 Cascade Key Bellevue WA 98006

JONES, SHALLEY ANN MATTHEWS, banker; b. Moorehead, Miss., Sept. 17, 1954; d. Robert Lee and Rosie Lee (Taylor) Matthews; m. Ernest Jones, June 17, 1977; children: Shantea K., Ernest J. BA, U. Miami, 1975; MS in Mgmt., Fla. Internat. U., 1983. Lic. mortgage broker, Fla. Asst. v.p., mgr. loan processing Flagler Fed. Savs. and Loan Assn., Miami, Fla., 1976-84; asst. v.p., regional mgr. 1st Union Nat. Bank, Pompano Beach, Fla., 1984-85; v.p. loan adminstrn. Chase Fed. Bank, Miami, 1985—; instr. Inst. Fin. Edn., Miami, 1983—, Miami-Dade Community Coll., 1987—; mortgage counselor Neighborhood Housing Services, Inc., Miami, 1984—; mem. loan com. Miami Capital Devel., Inc., 1984—. Instr. Presdl. Classroom/Young Ams., Washington, 1983—; mem. vol. recognition program com. Dade County (Fla.) United Way, 1988; mem. Planned Process to Stimulate Black Econ. Devel. in Dade County, 1988—; mem. loan com. Dade Employment & Econ. Devel. Corp.; bd. dirs., chairperson Metro-Miami Action Plan; pres. Bapt. Young Women Glendale Bapt. Ch., Miami, 1980-84. Recipient Black Achiever award Family Christian Assn. Am., Up & Comers award Banking and Fin. Mem. Miami-Dade Urban Bankers Assn. (nat. rep. 1983-87, pres. 1987-89, Banker of Yr. 1986), Nat. Assn. Urban Bankers (so. regional v.p.), Inst. Fin. Edn. (bd. dirs. 1988—), Alpha Kappa Alpha. Democrat. Home: 11255 SW 127th St Miami FL 33176

JONES, SONIA JOSEPHINE, advertising agency executive; b. Belize, Brit. Honduras, Nov. 9, 1945; came to U.S., 1962, naturalized, 1986; d. Frederick Francis and Elsie Adelia (Gomez) Alcoser; m. John Marvin Jones, Mar. 21, 1970; children—Christopher William Edward, Joshua Joseph Paul. Student Lamar U., 1964-66. With Foley's Federated Dept. Store, Houston, 1965-67; media buyer Vance Advt., Houston, 1967-68; media buyer, planner O'Neill & Assocs., Houston, 1968-75; media supr. Ketchum Houston, 1975-76; v.p., media dir. Rives Smith Baldwin Carlberg/Y & R, Houston, 1976-86; sr. v.p. media dir. Black Gillock & Langberg, Houston, 1986—; lectr. U. Houston, 1983—, mem. journalism adv. bd., 1983—. Vol., Women in Yellow, Houston, 1966; mem. sch. bd. St. Cecilia Cath. Sch.. Mem. Houston Advt. Fedn., Houston Area Media Council. Republican. Office: Black Gillock & Langberg 5851 San Felipe Suite 100 Houston TX 77057

JONES, STEPHEN CRAIG, marketing professional; b. Highland Park, Mich., July 23, 1952; s. Harold Stephen and Winnifred (Gould) J.; m. Beth Barefoot, Aug. 25, 1973; children: Griffin Stephen, Meredith Beth. BS in Communications, Emerson Coll., 1974. Sales rep. Underwriters Ins. Agy., Farmington Hills, Mich., 1978-79; chief exec. officer Metro Newswire, Detroit, 1980-81; news dir. Sta. WJZZ-FM, Detroit, 1981-82; reporter Sta. WWJ-AM/ Detroit News, 1982-83; v.p. sales and mktg. Jordan Bay Co., Raymond, Maine, 1984—; mem. com. Cable TV, New Gloucester, 1987—; bd. dirs. New Gloucester (Maine) News. Congregationalist. Office: Jordan Bay Co Rte 302 PO Box 640 Raymond ME 04071

JONES, STEVE JUSTIN, dairyman, farmer, rancher; b. Rush Springs, Okla., Dec. 26, 1952; s. Jack Jervis and Dorothy Pauline (Lutonsky) J.; m. Amy Renee Beard, June 19, 1957; children: Kyle Jerome, Stephen Kyle, Jamie Renee. Grad., Pan Am. Breeders Embryo Transfer Sch., Terrel, Tex., 1983. Farmer, rancher Rush Springs, 1971-75; soil conservation technician Soil Conservation Svc., Duncan, Okla., 1975-79; owner, chief exec. officer Sooner J Dairy, Rush Springs, 1980—; young cooperator sec. so. region Assoc. Milk Producers, Inc., 1983—; sec. Grady County Farm Bur., Chickasha, Okla., 1988—. Agr. advisor to U.S. Senator Don Nickles of Okla., 1988—. Mem. Holstein Assn. Am., Okla. Far Bur. (sec., bd. dirs. 1988—), Grady County Dairy Herd Improvement Assn. (v.p., bd. dirs. 1988—, Highest Producing Dairy Herd award 1986), Lions. Democrat. Roman Catholic. Home and Office: Sooner J Dairy Rte 1 Box 28A Rush Springs OK 73082

JONES, STEVEN GIBB, finance executive; b. Newton, Mass., Apr. 23, 1949; s. Roland D. and Nancy (Gibb) J.; m. Danelle C. Molphy, Aug. 21, 1971; children: Bradley, Rebecca. BA, Cornell U., 1972, MBA, 1974. CPA, Ohio. Staff acct. Arthur Andersen & Co., Cin., 1974-76; sr. fin. analyst forms div. Mead Corp., Chillicothe, Ohio, 1976-78, mgr. mktg., 1981-82; fin. analyst internat. div. Mead Corp., Zurich, Switzerland, 1978-81; v.p. fin. Yuba div. Avondale Industries, Tulsa, 1982-84; v.p. fin. Danly div. Avondale Industries, Cicero, Ill., 1984-86, v.p. fin., 1986-87; v.p. fin. Carriage Industries, Calhoun, Ga., 1987—. Office: Carriage Industries Inc South Industrial Blvd Calhoun GA 30701

JONES, THEODORE LAWRENCE, lawyer; b. Dallas, Nov. 29, 1920; s. Theodore Evan and Ernestine Lucy (Douthit) J.; m. Marion Elizabeth Thomas, Feb. 29, 1944; children: Suzanne Maas, Scott Evan, Stephen Lawrence, Shannon Ritter. BBA, U. Tex., 1944, JD, 1948; postgrad., So. Meth. U., 1950-52, Am. U., 1965-66. Bar: Tex. 1948, U.S. Supreme Ct. 1962, D.C. 1988. Assoc. Carrington, Gowan, Johnson & Walker, Dallas, 1948-51; gen. counsel W. H. Cothrum & Co., Dallas, 1951-54; pvt. practice law Dallas, 1955-56; asst. atty. gen., chief ins., banking and corp. div. Atty. Gen. Office, Tex., 1957-60; ptnr. Herring & Jones, Austin, Tex., 1960-61; gen. counsel maritime adminstrn. U.S. Dept. Commerce, 1961-63; dep. gen. counsel Dept. Commerce, 1963-64, dep. fed. hwy. adminstr., 1964-66; pres. Am. Ins. Assn., N.Y.C., 1967-86; counsel Hunton & Williams, Washington, 1986—; chmn. interdeptl. com. for bilateral agreements for acceptance of nuclear ship, Savannah, 1962-63; lectr. Fgn. Service Inst., 1962-64; alt. U.S. rep. 11th session Diplomatic Conf. on Maritime Law, Brussels, 1962; advisor U.S. del. 6th session Coun., Intergovtl. Maritime Consultative Orgn., London, 1962; mem. maritime subsidy bd. U.S. Dept. Commerce, 1962-63; acting hwy. beautification coord., 1965-66; del. White House Conf. on Internat. Cooperation; mem. Property-Casualty Ins. Coun., 1976-86, Internat. Ins. Adv. Coun., 1980-87; mem. adv. com. Pension Benefit Guaranty Corp., 1977; mem. Time Newstour, Ea. Europe and Persian Gulf, 1981, Mexico and Panama, 1983, Pacific Rim, 1985; bd. dirs. Nat. Safety Coun., 1967, Ins. Inst. for Hwy. Safety, 1967-86. Contbr. articles to profl. jours. Lt. (j.g.) USNR, 1944-46. Mem. ABA, D.C. Bar Assn., Fed. Bar Assn. (chmn. nat. speakers bur. 1964), Tex. Bar Assn., Am. Judicature Soc., Friars, Phi Delta Phi, Beta Gamma Sigma, Phi Eta Sigma, Met. Club, Nat. Lawyers Club (Washington), Gt. Oaks Country Club (Floyd, Va.), World Trade Ctr. Club (N.Y.C.). Democrat. Presbyterian. Home: 648 S Carolina Ave SE Washington DC 20003 also: Camp Creek Farm Rt 3 Box 182-B Floyd VA 24091 Office: Hunton & Williams 2000 Pennsylvania Ave NW Ste 9000 Washington DC 20006

JONES, THOMAS BRANCH, JR., electronics company executive; b. Richmond, Va., Mar. 13, 1930; s. Thomas B. Sr. and Lucy (Robinson) J.; m. Dorothy W., June 1, 1953; children: Robert, William. Student, Bridgewater Coll., 1946-48. Cert. drug abuse counselor. Engr. sales Broadcast Electronics, Silver Springs, Md., 1974-76; mgr. sales Multronics Inc., Ft. Lauderdale, Fla., 1976-81; asst. to pres. Antenna Research Assocs. Inc., Beltsville, Md., 1981—. Counselor Profl. Alcohol and Drug Abuse Counselors Assn. D.C., 1986—. Served in U.S. Navy, 1948-51. Mem. Suburban Md. Internat. Trade Assn. (bd. dirs. 1984-86, 88—), Md. Mfr. Assn. (founding mem., pres. 1983-85). Episcopal. Club: Amateur Radio, W 3 HMB. Lodges: Elks, Mason, Shriners. Home: 11459 Cherry Hill Rd #204 Beltsville MD 20705-3609 Office: Antenna Rsch Assocs Inc 11317 Frederick Ave Beltsville MD 20705-2088

JONES, THOMAS (FRANK), management and investments company executive; b. Los Angeles, June 25, 1937; s. Frank Kemon and Cordelia Esther (Renard) J.; m. Louise Annette Agee, June 19, 1964; children: Suzanne, Kevin, Jeffrey. BS, Calif. State Poly. U., 1959; MBA, UCLA, 1964; MS, Claremont Grad. Sch., Calif., 1983, PhD, 1986. Plant engr. GT&E, Santa Monica, Calif., 1965-67; ptnr. Rodriquez, Jones Co., Anaheim, Calif., 1967—; founding pres. Jonescorp, Pasadena, Calif., 1984—; chmn. bd. dirs. COS Endowment, San Gabriel, Calif.; mem. bd. visitors John E. Anderson Grad. Sch. Mgmt. UCLA; bd. dirs. Childrens Hosp. of Los Angeles. Author: Entrepreneurism: The Mythical, The True and The New. Fellow Huntington Library, 1978—, Claremont U. Ctr. and Grad. Sch., 1986—; founder Music Ctr. of Los Angeles; assoc. Pres.'s Circle 1982; adv. bd. Pasadena Library Found; mem. bd. fellows Claremont U. Ctr. and Grad. Sch. Served with U.S. Army, 1960-62, ETO. Republican. Episcopalian. Clubs: Jonathan (Los Angeles); Univ. (Pasadena), San Gabriel Country. Office: Jonescorp 350 W Colorado Blvd Pasadena CA 91105

JONES, THOMAS VICTOR, aerospace company executive; b. Pomona, Calif., July 21, 1920; s. Victor March and Elizabeth (Brettelle) J.; m. Ruth Nagel, Aug. 10, 1946; children: Ruth Marilyn, Peter Thomas. Student, Pomona Jr. Coll., 1938-40; BA with distinction, Stanford U., 1942; LLD (hon.), George Washington U., 1967. Engr. El Segundo div. Douglas Aircraft Co., 1941-47; tech. adviser Brazilian Air Ministry, 1947-51; prof., head dept. Brazilian Inst. Tech., 1947-51; staff cons. Air Staff of USAF, Rand Corp., 1951-53; asst. to chief engr. Northrop Corp., Los Angeles, 1953, dep. chief engr., 1954-56, dir. devel. planning, 1956-57, corp. v.p., 1957, sr. v.p., 1958-59, pres., 1959-76, chief exec. officer, 1960—, chmn. bd., 1963—; bd. dirs. MCA Inc., Universal City, Calif. Author: Capabilities and Operating Costs of Possible Future Transport Airplanes, 1953. Bd. dirs. Los Angeles World Affairs Council, Calif. Nature Conservancy; trustee Inst. for Strategic Studies, London. Fellow AIAA (hon.); mem. Los Angeles C. of C., Navy League U.S. (life), Aerospace Industries Assn., U. So. Calif. Assocs., Town Hall, Nat. Acad. Engring. Clubs: California; The Beach (Santa Monica); Georgetown, California Yacht, Bohemian. Home: 1050 Moraga Dr Los Angeles CA 90049 Office: Northrop Corp 1840 Century Park E Century City Los Angeles CA 90067 *

JONES, THOMAS WATSON, accountant, financial planner; b. Louisville, Ga., Aug. 9, 1951; s. A.P. Jr. and Kathryne (Arrington) J.; m. Victoria Norman, July 11, 1970; children: Kathryne E., Thomas Watson Jr. BBA in Acctg., Ga. So. Coll., 1973. CPA, Ga.; cert. fin. planner. Sr. acct. Spillane, Rhoads, Lebey and Sieg, Savannah, Ga., 1973-76; controller B.F. Diamond Constrn. Co. Inc., Savannah, Ga., 1976-77; pres. Purvis Jones Polhill and Prescott, Louisville, 1978—; treas. Indsl. Devel. Corp., Louisville, 1986—. Mem. AICPA, Inst. Cert. Fin. Planners, Ga. Soc. Cert. Pub. Accts. (estate planning com. 1983-88), Jefferson County C. of C. (bd. dirs. 1982-86). Presbyterian. Office: Purvis Jones Polhill & Prescott 220 E Fifth St Louisville GA 30434

JONES, WALTER LEON, accountant; b. Ft. Worth, Apr. 5, 1955; s. William Leroy and Mary Lynne (Bigby) J.; m. Laurie Ann Friedson, July 23, 1978; children: Jessica Blair, Jaclyn Bigby. BBA in Acctg., U. Tex., Arlington, 1978. CPA, Tex. Staff acct. George, Morgan & Simpson, CPA's, Weatherford, Tex., 1978-79, sr. acct., 1979-80, mgr., 1980-84; mgr. Tittle & Assocs., CPA's, Ft. Worth, 1984-86; pvt. practice acctg. Ft. Worth, 1986—. Mem. bd. dirs. Weatherford Community Edn. Council, 1985. Mem. Am. Inst. CPA's (personal fin. planning div., tax div.), Tex. Soc. CPA's (Ft. Worth chpt. Young CPA Involvement com. 1984), White Settlement Area C. of C. (bd. dirs. 1987, treas. 1988). Baptist. Home: 416 Couts Weatherford TX 76086 Office: 7451 Chapel Ave Fort Worth TX 76116

JONES, WILLIAM FRANK, investment manager, security analyst; b. Lakehurst, N.J., June 29, 1951; s. William Frank and Martha Frances (Williams) J.; m. Mary Ellen Elizabeth Hennessy, Oct. 13, 1984. AB in Econs., Princeton U., 1973; JD, Georgetown U., 1976; MBA in Fin., U. Pa., 1980. Bar: Wash. 1976; chartered fin. analyst, 1987. Dir. ops. and fin. INA Diversified Svcs. Div., Phila., 1980-82; corp. planning analyst Becton, Dickinson & Co., Paramus, N.J., 1982-84; investment mgr. J. Bush & Co., Inc., N.Y.C., 1984—. Mem. N.Y. Soc. Security Analysts, D.C. Bar Assn. Office: J Bush & Co Inc 641 Lexington Ave New York NY 10022

JONES, WILLIAM HOUSTON, stock brokerage executive, financial consultant; b. Woodruff, S.C., May 28, 1932; s. Walter H. and Inez (Ray) J.; m. Delores Edna Emmett, Dec. 5, 1959 (div. Apr. 1983); children: Sheila L., Brenda R. BS, Clemson U., 1955; diploma, Air War Coll., 1974. Cert. fin. planner. Commd. officer USAF, 1955, advanced through grades to lt. col., 1971; flight inst. USAF, Greenville AFB, Miss., 1956-60; inst. instrument pilot sch. USAF, Randolph AFB, Tex., 1960-64; a.d.c. to comdr. AEC USAF, Washington, 1964-66; pilot 460th Tactical Reconnaissance Wing USAF, Saigon, Vietnam, 1966-67; asst. exec. officer Comptroller of Air Force USAF, Washington, 1967-70; ops. officer 7101th Airborne Wing USAF, Weisbaden, Fed. Republic of Germany, 1970-71; a.d.c. to U.S. rep. Nat and Joint Chiefs Staff, Am. Embassy USAF, Brussels, 1971-75; chief resources div. USAF, Sheppard AFB, Tex., 1975-77; ret. USAF, 1977; asst. v.p. Merrill Lynch, Wichita Falls, Tex., 1977—. Decorated Air medal with five oak leaf clusters, Legion of Merit. Mem. Air Force Assn., Daedalions, Toastmasters (pres. Wichita Falls 1979, area gov. 1980), Masons, Shriners, Rotary. Republican. Baptist. Home: 3614 Glenwood Wichita Falls TX 76308 Office: Merrill Lynch 3711 Maplewood PO Box 4887 Wichita Falls TX 76308

JONES, WILLIAM SHAW, housing finance executive; b. Grenada, Miss., Oct. 30, 1934; s. Robert Walton and Mary Elizabeth (Knight) J.; m. Jean Martin, Dec. 28, 1956; children: Cheryl, Timothy, Stephen. BA, Okla. State U., 1956; BD, McCormick Theol. Sem., 1960. Asst. pastor Roanoke Presbyn. Ch., Kansas City, Mo., 1960-64; pastor Calvary United Presbyn. Ch., Asheville, N.C., 1964-69; with Fed. Nat. Mortgage Assn., Atlanta, 1970—, various positions, 1970-77, regional underwriter, 1977-83, mgr. loan adminstrn., 1983-84; v.p. quality control, ops. Dallas, 1985—. Office: Fed Nat Mortgage Assn 13455 Noel Rd Ste 600 Dallas TX 75240-5003

JONES-GORDON, CHERYL ANNE, controller; b. Detroit, Dec. 8, 1944; d. Paul M. and Millie V. (Holden) Aldhizer; m. Michael G. Jones, June 15, 1963 (div. 1968); children: Catherine Anne (dec.), Carie Anne. Student, Valdosta (Ga.) State Coll., 1962-63, Miami-Dade Community Coll., Miami, Fla., 1982-83. Asst. head bookkeeper, supr. customer service Nat. Bank Albany, Ga., 1966-69; sr. customer advisor Simon & Mogilner, Inc., Birmingham, Ala., 1969-71; asst. to contr. Fla. Fed. Savs. & Loan Assn., St. Petersburg, 1971-72; owner Wall Decorating by Cherie, St. Petersburg, 1971-74; dist. mgr., buyer Bentley's Luggage & Shoes, St. Petersburg, 1972-74; prodn. asst., designer Breezy Point, Inc., Pompano Beach, Fla., 1974-79; sales/office mgr. Eagle Industries, Miami, 1979-84; sec. Neiworth & Neiworth, Miami, 1979; corp. contr. Vokes Equipment, Inc., Miami, 1983—; owner, data processing cons. Computer Services by Cherie, Miami, 1986—; ptnr., pres. Qui Can Assocs., Miami, 1988—; ptnr., pres. desk top publishing BC Computer Svcs., Miami, 1989—; ptnr. B&C Assoc., Miami, 1989—. Active Children's Hosp. Helping Friends program, 1988—; bd. dirs. North Miami chpt. Compassionate Friends, 1988—. Mem. NAFE, Bus. and Profl. Women (fin. chmn. Hialeah-Miami Springs chpt. 1986-87, ways and means chmn., 2d v.p. 1987-88, pres. 1988-89, Speak Off prize 1988, Vina Betterly award 1987, 88, asst. dist. dir. 1989—), Nat. Assn. Parliamentarians. Republican. Home: 20316 NW 52d Pl Miami FL 33055 Office: Vokes Equipment Inc 3595 NW 74th St Miami FL 33147

JONES-PARKER, JANET, professional association executive; b. Berkeley, Calif., Dec. 27, 1942; d. Elmo Dewey and Audrey May (Johnson) Jones; m. Larry Arthur Lynn, Aug. 12, 1966 (div. 1974); 1 child, Jessica Lynn; m. Thomas Garcin Parker Sr., Mar. 24, 1977; 1 child, Thomas Garcin Parker Jr.; stepchildren: Haile, Knox. Student, Brigham Young U., 1960-61; cert., U. de Dijon, France, 1961-62; BA, Drew U., 1965. Supr. group Trans World Airlines, Queens, N.Y., 1965-73; chmn. Parker Hyde, Inc., Greenwich, Conn., 1973-88; pres. Assn. Exec. Search Cons., Inc., Greenwich, 1982—. Contbr. articles on women in mgmt. to profl. jours. Exec. v.p. Greenwich Adv. Council on Youth and Drugs, 1983—; bd. dirs. Greenwich YWCA, 1982—. Mem. Women in Mgmt., Women's Forum (bd. dirs.), Commn. on Status of Women (commr. N.Y.C. chpt. 1976-80), Com. of 200. Republican. Mormon. Office: Assn Exec Search Cons Inc 17 Sherwood Pl Greenwich CT 06830-5606

JONSSON, GISLI, electrical power engineering educator; b. Reykjavik, Iceland, June 6, 1929; s. Jon and Elin (Gisladottir) G.; m. Margret Gudnadottir, Jan. 9, 1930; children—Elin Gisladottir, Gudni Gislason, Ingunn Gisladottir. M.Sc. in Elec. Engring., Danish Tech. U., Copenhagen, 1956. Elec. engr. Iceland Elec. Authority, Reykjavik, 1956-60; cons. engr., Reykjavik, 1960-61; directing mgr. Mcpl. Elec. Works, Hafnarfjordur, Iceland, 1961-69, Assn. Electricity Systems in Iceland, Reykjavik, 1969-75; prof. elec. power engring. U. Iceland, Reykjavik, 1975—, chmn. engring. dept., 1978-79, electrical engring dept., 1984-85, Engring. Research Inst., 1988—; cons. Elec. State Inspection, Reykjavik, 1981-84; chmn. Assn. Mcpl. Electricity Utility Work's Mgrs., 1963-60. Author: (booklet) Electric Space Heating, 1968; (report) Use of Electric Car in Iceland, 1984, Ripple Control Systems. Mem. Assn. Chartered Engrs. Iceland (chmn. elec. sect. 1971-72), The Consumer Assn. (bd. dirs. 1979-82). Club: Rotary (Hafnarfjordur, pres. 1975-76, Paul Harris fellow). Home: Brekkuhvammur 4, IS-220 Hafnarfjordur Iceland Office: U Iceland, Hjardarhagi 2-6, IS-107 Reykjavik Iceland

JOPLIN, ALBERT FREDERICK, transportation executive; b. Victoria, B.C., Can., Feb. 22, 1919; s. Albert Edward and Emily Eliza (Norford) J.; B.A.Sc. in Civil Engring., U. B.C., 1948; m. Margaret McMorragh-Kavanaugh, May 26, 1947 (dec.); 1 dau., Mary Lynn Barbara; m. 2d, Dorothy Anne Cook, July 29, 1977. With Can. Pacific Ltd., 1947-87 , spl. engr., Calgary, 1962-65, devel. engr., Vancouver, 1965-66, mgr. spl. projects, 1966-68, system mgr. planning and devel., Montreal, Que., 1968-69, dir. devel. planning, 1969-71, v.p. mktg. and sales CP Rail, 1971-74, v.p. operation and maintenance, 1974-76; gen. mgr. Marathon Realty, 1965-66; pres., chief exec. officer Canadian Pacific (Bermuda) Ltd., 1976-84; Shaw Industries, Ltd., Toronto, Ont., Straits Oil and Gas Ltd., pres. Straits Oil and Gas U.S.A. Ltd.; Sydney, Superburn Systems Ltd., Vancouver; chmn., bd. dirs. Leaders Equity Corp., Vancouver. Commr., gen. dir. Can. Pacific Pavilion Expo '86, 1984-87; pres. and chief exec. officer Cen. Ocean Industries Ltd.; active Boy Scouts Can. Served with RCAF, 1941-45. Mem. Assn. Profl. Engrs. B.C. (life), Engring. Inst. Can. (life), Can. Soc. Civil Engrs., Internat. Soc. for Planning and Strategic Mgmt., Can. Maritime Law Assn., Vancouver Maritime Arbitrators Assn., Inst. Corp. Dirs. Can., Air Force Officers Assn., Beta Theta Phi. Clubs: Engrs. (Vancouver), Royal Montreal Golf, Traffic, Mount Stephen (Montreal); Canadian Railway; Western Canada Railway; Mid-Ocean, Maritime Museum, Nat. Trust (Bermuda). Lodge: Rotary (Vancouver, B.C.), Order of St. John. Home: 4317 Staulo, Vancouver, BC Canada V6N 3S1 Office: 140-200 Granville St, Vancouver, BC Canada V6C 2R3

JORDAN, CHARLES MORRELL, automotive designer; b. Whittier, Calif., Oct. 21, 1927; s. Charles L. and Bernice May (Letts) J.; m. Sally Irene Mericle, Mar. 8, 1951; children: Debra, Mark, Melissa. BS, MIT, 1949. With Gen. Motors Co., Warren, Mich., 1949—; chief designer Cadillac Studio, 1957-61, group chief designer, 1961-62, exec. in charge automotive design, 1962-67; dir. styling Adam Opel A.G., 1967-70; exec. in charge Cadillac, Oldsmobile, Buick Studios, Warren, 1970-73; exec. in charge Chevrolet, Pontiac and Comml. Vehicle Studios, 1973-77, dir. design, 1977-86; v.p. Gen. Motors Design Staff, 1986—; ednl. councillor MIT. Served as 1st lt. USAF, 1952-53. Recipient First Nat. award Fisher Body Craftsman's Guild, 1947. Mem. Soc. Automotive Engrs., Calif. Scholastic Fedn. (life). Clubs: Mass. Tech. Detroit Alumni, Ferrari of Am. Home: 3955 Kirkland Ct Bloomfield MI 48013 Office: Gen Motors Design Staff Detroit MI 48090

JORDAN, DON D., electric company executive; b. Corpus Christi, Tex., 1932; married. BBA, U. Tex., 1954; JD, So. Tex. Coll. Law, 1969. With Houston Lighting & Power Co. subs. Houston Industries, Inc., 1956—, mgr. comml. sales, 1967-69, mgr. personnel relations, 1969-71, v.p., asst. to pres., 1971-73, group v.p., 1973-74, pres., 1974-82, chief exec. officer, also bd. dirs., 1977—, chmn., 1982—; also chmn., chief exec. officer Houston Industries, Inc., also bd. dirs.; bd. dirs. Hughes Tool Corp. Office: Houston Industries Inc PO Box 4567 Houston TX 77210

JORDAN, DONALD DERRICK, pest control company executive; b. Newark, Mar. 4, 1958; s. Miller and Hazel (Jeffrey) J.; m. Karren Lynette Moore, June 28, 1986. BS in Indsl. Mgmt., N.J. Inst. Tech., 1985. Gen. mgr. Nationwide Pest Control Co., East Orange, N.J., 1983-85; dist. exec. Essex Council Boy Scouts Am., Newark, 1986-88; owner, v.p. adminstrn. Nationwide Termite and Pest Control, Orange, N.J., 1988—. Mem. NAACP. Democrat. Home: 44 19th Ave Newark NJ 07103 Office: Nationwide Termite & Pest Control 19 High St Newark NJ 07050

JORDAN, DONALD LAGERMAN, finance executive, marketing consultant; b. Phila., Dec. 21, 1941; s. Joseph Richard and Josephine (Lagerman) J; m. Janet Irene Wasserman, May 12, 1980; children: Geoffrey, Jeremy. BS in Econs., U. Pa., 1964; MBA, Harvard U., 1970. Dep. dir. staff domestic bus. policy analysis White House, Washington, 1975, cons. task force on product liability, 1975-77; govt. affairs officer Alliance Am. Insurers, Washington, 1978-80; exec. dir. Nat. Assn. Ins. Brokers, Washington, 1980-84; sr. cons. Temple Barker Sloane, Lexington, Mass., 1984-86; sr. v.p. corp. planning Brit. Am. Corp., Raleigh, N.C., 1986-88, also bd. dirs.; pres. VMA Corp., Raleigh, 1988—; fed. lobbyist Alliance Am. Ins., Washington, 1977-80, Nat. Assn. Ins. Brokers, Washington, 1980-84; bd. dirs. Brit. Am. Nigeria Ltd, Lagos. Contbr. articles to profl. jours. V.p. com. social concerns Holy Trinity Ch., 1978—; mem. planning forum Md. Right to Life. Republican. Roman Catholic. Clubs: Harvard Bus. Sch. (v.p. 1977—), Wharton Sch., Ferrari, ALPHA. Home: 405 Bridgetender Dr Raleigh NC 27615 Office: VMA Corp Raleigh NC 27615

JORDAN, HENRY HELLMUT, JR., management consultant; b. Heidelberg, Germany, May 31, 1921; came to U.S., 1934, naturalized, 1940; s. Henry H. and Johanna (Narath) J.; m. Hildegarde C. Dallmeyer, Mar. 11, 1942 (dec. 1987); children: Sandra, Michael, Patric, Henry Hellmut. Student U. Cin., 1938-39. Commd. 2d lt. U.S. Army, 1942, advanced through grades to maj., 1956; staff officer Ordnance Corps; ret., 1961; mgr. prodn. and inventory control Sperry Corp., N.Y.C., 1961-66, dir. quality control and field service engring., 1967-68; mgmt. cons. Wright Assos. Inc., N.Y.C., 1969-70; pres. Henry Jordan & Assos., N.Y.C., 1970-74; mng. partner Cons. Services Inc., Atlanta, 1975-88; chmn. Center for Inventory Mgmt., Stone Mountain, Ga., 1975—; chmn. bd. Crugers Services Corp., Atlanta. Editorial bd. Jour. Prodn. and Inventory Mgmt.; editor: Production and Inventory Control Handbook, 1986, Cycle Counting for Record Accuracy, 1985, System Implementation Handbook, 1982. Mem. Am. Inst. Indsl. Engrs. (sr.), Inst. Mgmt. Cons. (cert.), Am. Prodn. and Inventory Control Soc. (chmn. curricula and cert. council; Presdl. award of Merit 1974), Am. Radio Relay League. Methodist. Club: Yacht Hilton Head. Home and Office: 941 Carlisle Rd Stone Mountain GA 30083

JORDAN, JERRY L., economist, banker; b. Los Angeles, Nov. 12, 1941; s. Robert L. and Josephine L. (Adams) J.; children: Mark, Trisha, Michael. BA, Calif. State U., Northridge, 1963; PhD, UCLA, 1969. Asst. prof. econs. Calif. State U., Northridge, 1966-67; sr. v.p. FRB-St. Louis, 1967-75, PNC Corp., Pitts., 1975-80; dean U. N.Mex., Albuquerque, 1980-85; pres. council econ. advisers White House, Washington, 1981-82; sr. v.p., chief economist FI-Bancorp, Los Angeles, 1985—. Fellow Nat. Assn. Bus. Econs. (pres. 1986-87, bd. dirs. 1978-81, 85-89). Office: First Interstate Bancorp 707 Wilshire Blvd W30-48 Los Angeles CA 90017

JORDAN, JOHN R., JR., accountant; b. Houston, Jan. 7, 1939; m. Anne Jordan; children—John Jennifer, Stephanie, Anne-Marie, Suzanne. B.A. with highest honors, U. Tex.-Austin, 1961; M.B.A. with high distinction, Harvard Bus. Sch., 1963. With Price Waterhouse, St. Louis, regional vice chmn. mng. ptnr., mem. mgmt. com. Contbr. articles to profl. jours. Trustee Barnes Hosp., St. Louis; bd. dirs. Washington U. Med. Ctr.; former pres. Cath. Charities, Archdiocese of St. Louis; mem. Archdiocese Devel. Coun., bd. dirs. YMCA of Met. St. Louis; mem. acctg. adv. council U. Tex.-Austin; exec. bd. St. Louis Area council Boy Scouts Am. Mem. AICPA, Mo. Soc. CPA's, St. Louis Regional Commerce and Growth Assn. (bd. dirs.), Phi Beta Kappa, Beta Gamma Sigma. Clubs: Bogey, Noonday, Old Warson Country, St. Louis, Harvard Bus. Sch. Avocations: golf; tennis; jogging; photography; reading. Office: Price Waterhouse PO Box 1097 Saint Louis MO 63188

JORDAN, KENNETH GARY, textiles executive; b. Anderson, S.C., Nov. 18, 1935; s. Samuel Woodrow and Dorothy (Wakefield) J.; m. Joyce Huckaby, June 8, 1957; 1 child, Kenneth Gary Jr. BS, Clemson U., 1957, MS, 1961, PhD, 1963. Sr. chemist DuPont Co., Kinston, N.C., 1957, 63-67; sr. rsch. chemist DuPont Co., Wilmington, Del., 1967-75, devel. assoc., 1975-78, sr. mktg. rep., 1978-81, account mgr., 1982-86, sr. account mgr., 1986—. Capt. U.S. Army, 1957-59. Home and Office: 4502 Lanier Ave Anderson SC 29624

JORDAN, LOUIS RICHARD, financial executive; b. Bklyn., Mar. 1, 1940; s. Richard Franklin and Clara (Simpler) J.; m. Joanne Clemente, Sept. 5, 1965; 1 child, Stephanie Arianne. BS in Acctg., U. Ill., 1964. CPA, Oreg. Supervisory acct. Price Waterhouse and Co., N.Y.C., 1964-69; adminstrv. v.p. U.S. Real Estate Corp., Portland, Oreg., 1969-70; v.p. fin. HEICO Inc., Hollywood, Fla., 1970-72; investment counselor Skiver and Assocs., Portland, 1972-75; pres. Profl. Real Estate Svcs., Lake Oswego, Oreg., 1975-84; controller, chief fin. officer Pacific Marquis Spas, Independence, Oreg., 1984-88; chief fin. officer Color and Design Exhibits Inc., Portland, 1988—. With U.S. Army, 1959-61. Mem. AICPA, Oreg. Soc. CPAs, U. Ill. Alumni Assn., Lake Oswego Jaycees (treas. 1971), N.Y.C. Illini Club (pres. 1967-68). Republican. Episcopalian. Office: Color & Design Exhibits Inc 3625 N Mississippi Ave Portland OR 97227

JORDAN, MICHAEL HUGH, food products company executive; b. Kansas City, Mo., June 15, 1936; m. Kathryn Hiett, Apr. 8, 1961; children: Kathryn, Stephen. B.S. in Chem. Engring., Yale U., 1957; M.S. in Engring., Princeton U., 1958. Cons., prin. McKinsey & Co., Toronto, London, Cleve., 1964-74; dir. fin. planning PepsiCo, Purchase, N.Y., 1974-76; sr. v.p. planning and devel. PepsiCo Internat., Purchase, N.Y., 1976-77; sr. v.p. mfg. ops. Frito-Lay, Dallas, 1977-82, pres., chief exec. officer, 1983-85; pres. PepsiCo Foods Internat., 1982-83; exec. v.p., fin. and adminstrn. PepsiCo Inc., Purchase, 1985-86, pres., 1986, also bd. dirs.; pres., chief exec. officer PepsiCo Worldwide Foods, Plano, Tex., 1987—; bd. dirs. 1st RepublicBank, Dallas, Melville Corp. Bd. dirs. United Negro Coll. Fund, 1986—. Recipient cert. nuclear engring. Bettis Labs. AEC, Pitts. Office: PepsiCo Inc 7701 Legacy Dr Plano TX 75024-4099

JORDAN, REGINALD CLEVELAND, environmental scientist; b. Washington, Mar. 12, 1946; s. Oscar Royce and Mary Elizabeth (Craver) J.; m. Gayle Anne Steger, June 8, 1968; children: Erin, Kelly, Megan. BS, Salem Coll., 1968; MS, Temple U., 1970. Diplomate Am. Acad. Indsl. Hygiene. Chemist Gillette Rsch. Inst., Rockville, Md., 1968-69; chief lab. sect. Pa. Bur. Air Quality and Noise Control, Harrisburg, 1970-73; chief chemist Gen. Environments Corp., Springfield, Va., 1973-74; project scientist TRW Environ. Engring., McLean, Va., 1974-76; dep. program mgr. EPA Air Pollution Tng. Inst., 1976-79; mgr. quality assurance and environ. monitoring programs Northrop Services, Inc., Research Triangle Park, N.C., 1979-84; pres., chief exec. officer EnviroScis., Inc., Raleigh, N.C., 1984—; adj. prof. environ. health Ctr. for environ. studies Temple U. Contbr. articles to profl. jours. Mem. Am. Indsl. Hygiene Assn., N.C. Acad. Sci., Air Pollution Control Assn., Am. Mgmt. Assn., Soc. Occupational and Environ. Health, Am. Soc. Quality Control, ASTM. Home: 3120 Julian Dr Raleigh NC 27604 Office: EnviroScis Inc 3509 Haworth Dr Ste 310 Raleigh NC 27609

JORDAN, RICHARD THOMAS, promoter; b. Flushing, N.Y., Apr. 16, 1948; s. Thomas Robert and Emma Rose (Haas) J. BA, Iona Coll., 1970; PhD, NYU, 1974. Head NYU Library Acquisitions Bibliographic Searchers, N.Y.C., 1972-77; pres. Jordanbooks, N.Y.C., 1972—, Jordanventures, N.Y.C., 1977—; tchr. legal proofreading Proofreading Dynamics Inc, N.Y.C., 1987; devel. dir. St. Paul's Episcopal Ch., Staten Island, N.Y., 1985-87; spl. asst. to the dir. Miami Art Deco Weekend, 1987; U.S. coordinator to Internat. Congress, Hannover, Fed. Republic Germany, 1987; chmn. bd. dirs. Jordan Music Mgmt., N.Y.C., 1987—. Author: How to Transform Yourself Through Legal Proofreading, 1985. V.p. Concerned Citizens Speak, Inc., N.Y.C., 1984—; mem. World Citizen's Assembly, Communications Coordinating Com. UN, UN Environment Programme, Environ. Sabbath Rest Day Com. 1988—; internat. del. to peace conf. Anuvibha Jain U.; chmn. bd. dirs. The Inst. for the Recycling of N.Y.C., 1986—; Ladnun, India, 1988; participant Rainforest Preservation Conf., Seattle, 1988, Common Security Through New Structures of Peace Conf., Washington, D.C., 1989, speaker, Peace Conf. U. for Peace, Escazu, Costa Rica, 1989. Recipient Award for Zeal in the Pursuit of Excellence Grand St. Boys' Assn., N.Y.C., 1966. Mem. Nat. Assn. for Olmsted Parks, ALA, MLA, Teilhard de Chardin Soc., Nat. Trust Hist. Preservation, Martha's Vineyard Hist. Soc., Mass. Reservations (trustee), ABA. Episcopalian. Club: Nat. Arts (N.Y.C.) (admissions com., younger mems. com.). Home: 26 Gramercy Park New York NY 10003 Office: Jordanventures PO Box 807 Woodside NY 11377-0807

JORDON, DEBORAH ELIZABETH, lawyer; b. Pitts., June 24, 1951; d. Joseph Mitchell and Marjorie Odessa (Glaude) J. BA, Brown U., 1972; JD, Yale U., 1975. Bar: Pa. 1975, N.Y. 1978, U.S. Dist. Ct. (ea. and so. dists.) N.Y., 1978. Law clk. to presiding justice U.S. Dist. Ct. (ea. dist.) Pa., Phila., 1975-77; assoc. Paul, Weiss, Rifkind, Wharton & Garrison, N.Y.C., 1977-79; asst. to mayor City of N.Y., 1979-82; counsel to pres. CCNY, 1982-84; sr. atty. NBC, N.Y.C., 1984-87, asst. gen. atty., 1987-88, gen. atty., 1988-89, sr. gen. atty., 1989—; chmn. bd. dirs. Harlem Legal Svcs. Inc., N.Y.C.; bd. dirs. Met. Assistance Corp., N.Y.C. Bd. dirs. N.Y.C. Sports Commn., Bennett Coll., Greensboro, N.C., 1985—, Lifelong Learning Program, N.Y. 1981-82, Marymount Manhattan Coll., N.Y.C., 1984-87. Named Achiever in Industry Harlem YMCA, N.Y.C., 1988. Mem. Phi Beta Kappa. Roman Catholic. Home: 200 W 79th St New York NY 10024 Office: NBC Inc 30 Rockefeller Plaza New York NY 10112

JORGE, NUNO MARIA ROQUE, architect; b. Macau, Portugal, Feb. 9, 1947; s. Adolfo Adroaldo and Edith (Roque) J.; m. Maria de Fátima da Costa Azevedo, Sept. 14, 1975; children: Edith Azevedo, Alexandra Azevedo, Filipa Azevedo. Cert Bus. Mgmt., Inst. Superior de Novas Profissoes, Lisbon, 1972; diploma in architecture, Higher Sch. Fine Arts, Lisbon (Portugal) U., 1974. Architect trainee Ministério do Ultramar, Lisbon, 1972-73; computer programmer, systems analyst Cen. Mecanografico de Exercito, Lisbon, 1973-75; pvt. practice architecture Macau, 1975—; pvt. practice bus. mgr., cons., Macau, 1981—; pvt. practice acct., Macau, 1981—; tech. dir. Sao Tiago Hotel and Tourism Co., Ltd., Macau, 1982—; mng. ptnr. Soc. Geral de Comercio e Industria Ltd., Macau, 1983—. Del. Portuguese Red Cross, Macau, 1986—; mem. Santa Casa de Misericordia, Macau, 1980—. Served with Portugese mil., 1973-75. Recipient Spl. award for Heritage Preservation, Pacific Area Travel Assn., 1982, Decoration of Profl. Merit, Govt. of Macau, 1984, Decoration of Commendation (Portuguese Red Cross, 1988). Mem. Soc. de Geografia de Lisbon (effective 1972—), Macau Assn. Architects in Pvt. Practice (founder, charter mem. 1983—), Portuguese Assn. Acct. (charter mem. v.p., chmn. gen. assembly Macau chpt. 1981—), Macau Mgmt. Assn. (charter mem., advisor 1985—, life), Portuguese Assn. Architects, Portuguese Assn. Mktg., Portuguese Assn. Quality Control, Alliance Francaise de Macao (charter mem. 1987—). Clubs: Tenis Civil (pres. 1976-77), Macau Trotting, Skal, PATA (treas. Macau chpt. 1983-84), Elos (chmn. 1988—). Home: Estrada de D Joao Paulino, # 26 28 30, Macau Macao Office: 61 Ave de Amizade, 18th Floor C Cam Fai Coc Bldg, Atterros do Porto Exterior, Macau Macao

JORGENSEN, GORDON DAVID, engineering company executive; b. Chgo., Apr. 29, 1921; s. Jacob and Marie (Jensen) J.; B.S. in Elec. Engring., U. Wash., 1948, postgrad. in bus. and mgmt., 1956-59; m. Nadina Anita Peters, Dec. 17, 1948 (div. Aug. 1971); children—Karen Ann, David William, Susan Marie; m. 2d, Barbara Noel, Feb. 10, 1972 (div. July 1976). With R.W. Beck & Assos., Cons. Engrs., Phoenix, 1948—, ptnr., 1954-86; pres. Beck Internat., Phoenix, 1971—. Served to lt. (j.g.) U.S. Maritime Service, 1942-45. Recipient Outstanding Service award Phoenix Tennis Assn., 1967; Commendation, Govt. Honduras, 1970. Registered profl. engr., Alaska, Ariz., Calif., Colo., Nev., N.Mex., N.D., Utah, Wash., Wyo. Mem. IEEE (chmn. Wash.-Alaska sect. 1959-60), Nat. Soc. Profl. Engrs., Am. Soc. Appraisers (sr. mem.), Ariz. Cons. Engrs. Assn., Ariz. Soc. Profl. Engrs., Internat. Assn. Assessing Officers, Southwestern Tennis Assn. (past pres.), U.S. Tennis Assn. (pres. 1987-88, chmn. U.S. Open com.); chmn. U.S. Davis Cup com.; chmn. Internat. Tennis Fed., Davis Cup com. Presbyterian (elder). Project mgr. for mgmt., operation studies and reorgn. study Honduras power system, 1969-70. Home: 5329 N 25th St Phoenix AZ 85016 Office: RW Beck & Assocs 3003 N Central Phoenix AZ 85012

JORGENSON, EVERETT THOMAS, computer engineer, executive; b. St. Louis, Aug. 27, 1952; s. Everett Henry and Josephine Mary (Haake) J.; divorced; 1 child, Timothy Michael Twillman. Assoc. in Elec. Engring., Florrisant Valley Coll., 1972. Test engr. Emerson Electric Co., St. Louis, 1973-77; elec. design engr. McDonnell-Douglas Aircraft, St. Louis, 1977-78; sr. engr. test systems div. Bendix Corp., Saint Charles, Mo., 1978-81; pres., founder Software Wizardry, Inc., Saint Peters, Mo., 1981—, First Capitol Computer, Saint Peters, 1985—, Computer Ad Designs, Inc., Saint Peters, 1987—; system operator, co-founder Heath User's Group, SIG & CP/M User's Group, SIG Compuserve; system operator, founder Night Owl BBS System, Saint Charles. Supporter Young Republicans, Saint Charles County, 1970, St. Louis Regional HUG Conv., 1986; organizer Saint Peters Area Computer Enthusiasts, 1987—. Named 500 Fastest Growing Cos., Inc. Magazine, 1987. Mem. Saint Peters C. of C., Regional Commerce and Growth Assn., Saint Charles C. of C., Mensa, Heath User's Group, SPACE (pres. 1987—). Roman Catholic. Office: First Capitol Computer 16 Algana Saint Peters MO 63376

JORGENSON, RONALD MARK, automotive executive; b. LaCrosse, Wis., June 4, 1955; s. Harold and Joan Shirley (Kenyon) J.; m. Joy Ellen Minnick, Oct. 16, 1976; children: Daniel, Matthew, Kathryn. Bachelor of Indls. Adminstrn., Gen. Motors Inst., 1978; MBA, Harvard U., 1980. Fin. analyst comptroller's staff Gen. Motors, Detroit, 1980-83; adminstr. product cost Saturn project Gen. Motors, Warren, Mich., 1983-85; fin. mgr. Saturn Corp. div. Gen. Motors, Troy, Mich., 1985—. Pres. Our Saviour Luth. Ch., Westland, Mich., 1982-88, se., 1981-82.

JORGESON, BRENT WILSON, management executive; b. Atlanta, Aug. 29, 1950; s. Charles Milton and Arleen Irma (Marshall) J.; m. Mary Elizabeth House, June 9, 1973. BS, Ga. Inst. Tech., 1973; MBA, Harvard U., 1975. With Advance Mortgage Corp., Southfield, Mich., 1975-76; v.p. ops. Hosp. Investors, Inc., Atlanta, 1977-80; sr. assoc. Booz, Allen & Hamilton, Inc., Atlanta, 1980-81; v.p. devel. Healthcare Internat., Inc., Austin, Tex., 1981-83, v.p. ops., 1984—. Served 1st lt. U.S. Army, Mil. Intelligence, 1975. Clubs: Harvard Bus. Sch., Harvard. Home: 6206 Lost Horizon Dr Austin TX 78759 Office: PO Box 4008 Austin TX 78765

JORNDT, LOUIS DANIEL, drug store chain executive; b. Chgo., Aug. 24, 1941; s. Louis Carl and Margaret Estelle (Teel) J.; m. Patricia McDonnell, Aug. 1, 1964; children—Kristine, Michael, Kara. B.S. in Pharmacy, Drake U., 1963; M.B.A., U. N.Mex., 1974. Various mgmt. positions Walgreen Co., Chgo., 1963-68, dist. mgr., 1968-75; regional dir. Walgreen Co., Deerfield, Ill., 1975-79; regional v.p. Walgreen Co., Deerfield, 1979-82, v.p., treas., 1982-85, sr. v.p., treas., 1985—. Bd. dirs. Better Bus. Bur. Chgo., 1982—, Chgo. Assn. Commerce and Industry; nat. chmn. Drake U. Pharmacy Alumni Fund. Mem. Nat. Assn. Corp. Treas., Fin. Execs. Inst. Clubs: Economic (Chgo.); Glen View (Ill.) Golf. Office: Walgreen Co 200 Wilmot Rd Deerfield IL 60015

JOSCELYN, KENT BUCKLEY, research scientist, lawyer; b. Binghamton, N.Y., Dec. 18, 1936; s. Raymond Miles and Gwen Buckley (Smith) J.; B.S., Union Coll., 1957; J.D., Albany Law Sch., 1960; m. Mary A. Komoroske, Nov. 20, 1965; children—Kathryn Anne, Jennifer Sheldon. Bar: N.Y. 1961, U.S. Ct. Mil. Appeals 1962, D.C. 1967, Mich. 1979. Atty., adviser Hdqrs. USAF, Washington, 1965-67; asso. prof. forensic studies Coll. Arts and Scis., Ind. U., Bloomington, 1967-76, dir. Inst. Research in Pub. Safety, 1970-75; head policy analysis div. Hwy. Safety Research Inst., U. Mich., 1976-81, dir. transp. planning and policy, Urban Tech., Environ. Planning Program, 1981-84; partner firm Joscelyn & Treat, P.C., 1981—; cons. Law Enforcement Assistance Adminstrn., U.S. Dept. Justice, 1969-72; Gov.'s appointee as regional dir. Ind. Criminal Justice Planning Agy., also vice chmn. Ind. Organized Crime Prevention Council, 1969-72; commr. pub. safety City of Bloomington, 1974-76. Capt. USAF, 1961-64. Mem. Transp. Research Bd. (chmn. motor vehicle and traffic law com. 1979-82), NAS, NRC, Am. Soc. Criminology, Assn. for the Advancement Automotive Medicine, Soc. Automotive Engrs., Am. Soc. Pub. Adminstrn., Acad. Criminal Justice Scis., ABA, D.C., Mich., N.Y. State bar assns., Internat. Assn. Chiefs Police (asso.), Nat. Safety Council, Sigma Xi. Editor Internat. Jour. Criminal Justice. Office: Joscelyn & Treat P C 325 E Eisenhower Pkwy Ann Arbor MI 48108

JOSEFSEN, TURI, medical supply company executive; b. Apr. 6, 1936; d. Hans and Birgit Josefsen; m. Leon C. Hirsch, Dec. 24, 1969. Student, Hammerfest (Norway) Real Sch., 1953. With U.S. Surg. Corp., 1965—; asst. to pres. N.Y.C., 1965-68, mgr. prof. cons., 1968-70, nat. sales mgr., 1970-72, v.p. sales, 1972, v.p. mktg., 1972-77; sr. v.p. mktg. Norwalk, Conn., 1977-81, exec. v.p. mktg., 1981—, also bd. dirs., domestic and internat.; cons. Auto Suture products. Co-author Auto Suture product tech. tng. manual, 1970; editor Surgical Stapling Atlas, 1976, 85; patentee hematocrit measurements by elec. conductivity, 1979, liquid conductivity measuring system, 1981. Lutheran. Office: US Surg Corp 150 Glover Ave Norwalk CT 06856

JOSEPH, A. DAVID, automotive parts corporation executive; b. Chgo., Aug. 3, 1931; s. E. Paul and Ann (Rush) J.; m. Browina Grove, July 24, 1954; children: Peter, Ann. BS, Alfred U., 1949, MS, 1954. Engr. Pratt & Whitney Aircraft, united Tech. Corp., Hartford, Conn., 1960-68; gen. mgr. Howmet Corp., Whitehall, Mich., 1969-71; v.p. SPX Corp. (formerly Sealed Power Corp.), Muskegon, Mich., 1972—. Served to lt. (j.g.) USNR, 1955-59.

JOSEPH, EARL CLARK, futurist; b. St. Paul, Nov. 1, 1926; s. Clark Herbert and Ida Bertha (Schultz) J.; AA, U. Minn., 1947, BA, 1951; m. Alma Caroline Bennett, Nov. 19, 1955; children: Alma (Mrs. Richard Chadner), Earl, Vincent, René (Mrs. Brian Leer). Mathematician/programmer Engring. Rsch. Assocs., Remington Rand Univac, Arlington, Va., 1951-55, supr., St. Paul, 1955-60, systems mgr. Sperry Univac, St. Paul, 1960-63, staff scientist-futurist, 1963-82; pres. Anticipatory Scis., Inc., 1981—; bd. dirs. Dorn, Swensen & Myer, Inc. and Corp. Capital Resources, Inc.; lectr. Coll. St. Thomas, 1985-87, Met. State U., 1978—, Kotz Sch. Mgmt., 1987—; instr. Walden Univ., 1985—; scholar Scholar Leadership Enrichment Program, Okla. U., 1984; vis. lectr. U. Minn., Mpls., 1971—; mem. Sci. and Mgmt. Adv. Com., U.S. Army, 1972-74. Futurist-in-residence Sci. Mus. of Minn., 1973-82; chmn. bd. Future Systems, 1979-81. Chmn., Met. Young Adult Ministry, 1967-69; mem. Gov.'s Planning Commn. for City Center Learning, 1968. Served with USNR, 1944-46. Disting. lectr. IEEE Computer Soc., 1971-72, 76-82, Assn. Computer Machinery. Mem. IEEE (sr.), Minn. Futurists (founder, dir., past pres.), World Future Soc., Soc. for Gen. Systems Research (founding chpt. pres., bd. dirs. 1978—), Assn. Computer Machinery (gen. chmn. 1975, pres. chpt. 1976-77, 86-87), AAAS, Data Processing Mgmt. Assn., Beta Phi Beta. Patents, publs. in field; co-author 50 books; founding editor jour. Futurics; editor Future Trends Newsletter, System Trends Newsletter; adv. editor Jour. Cultural and Ednl. Futures, Jour. Futures, Futures Rsch. Quarterly. Home: 365 Summit Ave Saint Paul MN 55102 Office: Anticipatory Scis Inc 245 E 6th St Ste 700 Saint Paul MN 55101

JOSEPH, EDNA WHITEHEAD (MRS. LAWRENCE J. JOSEPH), tax financial consultant, former banker; b. Everett, Mass., Feb. 4, 1924; d. Alfred Edward and Mary Kathleen (Butler) Whitehead; attended Winthrop Schs., Boston U., Am. Inst. Banking; m. Lawrence James Joseph, May 30, 1958. With Nat. Shawmut Bank (name now Shawmut Bank of Boston, N.A.), 1941-55, 57-84, asst. tax officer, 1965-69, tax officer, 1969-79, sr. trust officer, 1979-84; owner The Old Looking Glass, antiques; income tax mgr. Sam C. Charlson, Manhattan, Kans., 1955-57. Bd. dirs. Found. of Hope, Boston; mem. Republican Nat. Com., Women's Rep. Club Essex County, Nat. Fedn. Rep. Women. Mem. Fiduciary Tax Assos., Mass. Bankers Assn. (vice chmn. taxation com. 1971-72, chmn. 1972-73, tax cons. com. 1975-84), Nat. Assn. Bank Women, Am. Inst. Banking, Nat. Early Am. Glass Club (founders chpt.), North Shore Antique Assn., Soc. Preservation New Eng. Antiquities, Friends of Sandwich Mus., Woman 76 (Boston organizing com.), Soc. Jesus in New Eng. (liaison com. 1974-75, exec. com. 1975-76), Mus. Fine Arts, Bostonian Soc., Victorian Soc., Essex Inst., Peabody Mus., Jones Gallery Glass and Ceramics. Home: 8 Laurel Rd Lynnfield MA 01940

JOSEPH, FREDERICK HAROLD, investment banker; b. Boston, Apr. 22, 1937; s. Edward M. and Sarah (Mostowitz) J.; m. Susan Ferran, Aug. 27, 1960; children—Melissa, Melinda, Amy, Tommi Beth, Mark. B.A., Harvard, 1959, M.B.A., 1963. With E.F. Hutton Co., N.Y.C., 1963-70, Shearson Hamill Co., N.Y.C., 1970-74; with Drexel Burnham Lambert Inc., N.Y.C., 1974—; sr. exec. v.p. Drexel Burnham Lambert Inc., 1981-85, vice chmn., chief exec. officer, 1985—; pres. Drexel Burham Lambert Group, 1987—. Served with USNR, 1959-61. Home: 60 Lakeview Ave Short Hills NJ 07078 Office: Drexel Burnham Lambert Inc 60 Broad St New York NY 10004

JOSEPH, MICHAEL ANTHONY, marketing executive; b. Darlington, England, Nov. 4, 1944; s. Helmut and Joan (Lister) J.; m. Johanna Cornelia de Wijs, Mar. 15, 1969; children: Dominique Annabella, Charlotte Nathalie. Licence es Sciences Economiques, U. Neuchâtel, Switzerland, 1967. Sales rep. IBM United Kingdom, Croydon, 1968-70, Systems Internat., Kegworth, England, 1970-71; mktg. exec. RCA Computers, London, 1971, CMC Ltd., Maidenhead, England; mktg. mgr. Winton Labs., Brussels, 1972-74; country mgr. Standard Chartered Leasing, Brussels, Paris, 1974-77; sr. v.p. Comdisco Europe S.A., Paris, Morges, Switzerland, 1977—. Home: Rte de Mex, 1036 Sullens, Vaud Switzerland Office: Comdisco Inc 6111 N River Rd Rosemont IL 60018 also: Comdisco SA, 11 Rue de la Gare, 1110 Morges Switzerland

JOSEPH, MICHAEL THOMAS, broadcast consultant; b. Youngstown, Ohio, Nov. 23, 1927; s. Thomas A. and Martha (McCarius) J.; m. Eva Ursula Boerger, June 21, 1952. BA, Case Western Res. U., 1949. Program dir. Fetzer Broadcasting, Grand Rapids, Mich., 1952-55; nat. program dir. Founders Corp., N.Y.C., 1955-57; program cons. to ABC, CBS, NBC, Capital Cities, Infinity, Malrite, Cox and the N.Y. Times 1958—; v.p. radio Capital Cities, N.Y.C., 1959-60, NBC, N.Y.C., 1963-65. Mem. Internat. Radio and TV Soc., Nat. Assn. Broadcasters. Roman Catholic. Home and Office: 11 Punchbowl Dr Westport CT 06880

JOSEPHS, MARVIN MURRAY, retail company executive; b. Pitts., Mar. 6, 1923; s. Charles and Clara (Richter) J.; m. Lois Rose Shoop, Nov. 3, 1946 (div. Jan., 1969); children—Daniel W., David M.; m. Eileen Shirley Lisowitz, May 25, 1969 (div. Apr. 1988). Student U. Pitts., 1940-42. Sec., King's Clothes, Inc., Pitts., 1941-56, pres. The Coach House, Inc. (formerly King's Clothes, Inc.), 1956—. Pres. Rodef Shalom Brotherhood, Pitts., 1968; v.p. Rodef Shalom Congregation, Pitts., 1985, sr. v.p. 1988. Served with U.S. Army, 1942-45; ETO. Mem. Menswear Retailers Am. (dir. 1967-74), Nat. Assn. Sportswear Buyers (adv. council 1981—), Golden Triange Assn. (vice pres.). Democrat. Jewish. Club: Rivers (Pitts.). Avocations: tennis; photography; swimming, travel. Office: 300 6th Ave Suite 200 Pittsburgh PA 15222

JOSEPHSON, JOHN ERIC, food retail executive; b. Chgo., May 12, 1947; s. Iver A. and Pearl Louise (Seiler) J.; m. Sandra K. Nichols, Dec. 9, 1972; children: Megan, Andrew. BBA, Ohio U., 1969. Asst. contr. Kroger Columbus, Ohio, 1976-80, contr., 1980-83; v.p. fin., chief fin. officer P&C Foods, Syracuse, N.Y., 1983-87, sr. v.p. fin., chief fin. officer, 1987—. Treas. Cub Scouts Am., Marcellus, N.Y.; bd. dirs. Friends Zoo, Syracuse, 1987-90. Mem. Fin. Execs. Inst., Empire Appaloosa Assn. Club (treas.). Republican. Lutheran. Office: P&C Food Markets Inc PO Box 4965 Syracuse NY 13221 also: P & C Food Markets Inc PO Box 4965 Syracuse NY 13221

JOSLIN, ROGER SCOTT, insurance company executive; b. Bloomington, Ill., June 21, 1936; s. James Clifford Joslin and Doris Virginia (McLaflin) Joslin Browning; m. Stephany Moore, June 14, 1958; children—Scott, Jill, James. B.S. in Bus., Miami U., 1958; J.D., U. Ill., 1961. Bar: Ill. 1961. Assoc. Davis, Morgan & Witherell, Peoria, Ill., 1961-63; controller Union Ins. Group, Bloomington, Ill., 1963-64; asst. v.p. State Farm Mut., Bloomington, 1964-69, v.p., controller, 1969-77, v.p., treas., 1977-87, sr. v.p., treas., 1987—; chmn. bd. State Farm Fire and Casualty Co.; v.p., bd. dirs. State Farm Gen. Ins. Co.; bd. dirs. State Farm Mutual; treas. State Farm County Mut. Co. Tex.; v.p., treas., bd. dirs. State Farm Lloyds, Inc., State Farm Internat. Services, Inc., State Farm Investment Mgmt. Corp., State Farm Growth Fund, Inc., State Farm Balanced Fund, Inc., State Farm Interim Fund, Inc., State Farm Mcpl Bond Fund, Inc.; bd. dirs. State Farm Life Ins. Co., State Farm Life and Accident Assurance Co., State Farm Annuity and Life Ins. Co. Mem. Bloomington Bd. Edn., 1980—, pres. 1983-84, 85-86; trustee 2d Presbyn. Ch., 1971-74, pres. bd. trustees 1973-74; bd. dirs. Brokaw Hosp., 1981-84; pres. BroMenn Healthcare, 1984-86, bd. dirs. 1984—; Western Ave. Community Ctr., 1979-85, pres. 1981-83. Mem. ABA, Ill. State Bar Assn., McLean County Bar Assn., Ill. Soc. C.P.A.s, Miami U. Alumni Assn. (exec. council 1971-74). Presbyterian. Home: 2001 E Cloud St Bloomington IL 61701 Office: State Farm Mut Automobile Ins Co One State Farm Pla Bloomington IL 61710

JOSS, FREDERICK AUGUSTUS, energy and natural resources company financial executive; b. Mexico City (parents Am. citizens), Sept. 5, 1932; s. John H. Joss and Elizabeth Eleanor (Taylor) Hume; m. P. Caroline F. Bingham, Aug. 15, 1959 (div. Jan. 1980); children—John B., Caroline H., Elizabeth F.; m. Diana B. Dickey, Apr. 19, 1980; 1 child, Taylor Dickey. B.A., Williams Coll., 1954; M.B.A., U. Pitts., 1967. Fin. dir. CIA Minera de Aluminio-Alcominas, Sao Paulo, Brazil, 1967-73; asst. treas. Aluminum Co. Am., Pitts., 1973-76; v.p., treas. Dravo Corp., Pitts., 1976-82, v.p., chief fin. officer, 1982-87, contr., 1984-86, v.p., treas., 1987-88. Bd. dirs. Mt. Lebanon Sch. Dist., Pa., 1975-77, Opportunities and Resources, Pitts., 1978—; trustee Mercy Hosp., Pitts., 1980—, Pitts. Expt., 1979-82. Served as 1st lt. USAF, 1955-57. Mem. Fin. Execs. Inst. Republican. Clubs: Duquesne (Pitts.), Pittsburgh Golf; Chevy Chase (Md.). Home: 433 Denniston Ave Pittsburgh PA 15206 Office: Dravo Corp 1 Oliver Pla Pittsburgh PA 15222

JOST, ROBERT ALAN, academic administrator; b. Oceanside, N.Y., June 13, 1952; s. Richard Henry and Helen (Von Brook) J.; m. Kayren Prosser, May 5, 1973. BBA, Stetson U., 1975, MBA, 1987. Dir. adminstrv. svcs. Human Resources Ctr. Volusia County, Inc., Daytona Beach, Fla., 1975-81; budget dir. Embry-Riddle Aero U., Daytona Beach, 1981—. Mem. Nat. Assn. Coll. and Univ. Bus. Officers. Republican. Lutheran. Office: Embry-Riddle Aero U Daytona Beach FL 32014

JOTCHAM, THOMAS DENIS, marketing communications consultant; b. Llandudno, Wales, Feb. 21, 1918; s. George James and Marion (Brand) J.; m. Margaret Jean Thirlwell, Aug. 10, 1940; children: Patricia, Douglas, Joy, Candace (dec.). Student Lower Can. Coll., 1929-36, McGill U., 1937-39. Sales rep. Montreal Lithographing Co., Ltd., Montreal, 1945-47; sales mgr. Wesco Waterpaints Can., Ltd., Montreal, 1947-48; advt. mgr. Pepsi-Cola Co. Can., Ltd., 1948-52, mgr., Montreal, 1952-54; asst. advt. mgr. Reader's Digest Assn., Ltd., Montreal, 1954-56; mgr., v.p. Foster Advt. Ltd., Montreal, 1956-73, exec. v.p., 1973-75, pres., 1976-81, vice chmn., 1981-86; vice chmn. Sherwood Communications Group Ltd., 1981-83; mem. council Montreal Bd. Trade, 1973-75, v.p., 1977-78, pres., 1979, hon. chmn., 1980-81. Bd. dirs. Grace Dart Hosp., 1973-83, pres., 1979-83; bd. dirs. Can. Council Christians and Jews, 1978-81, Les Grands Ballets Canadien, 1976-77; mem. Venetion Condominium, Inc., pres. 1984, 88—. From lt. to maj. U.S. Army, 1940-45. Recipient ACA Gold medal, 1978; charter recipient McGill Mgmt. Achievement award, 1981. Fellow Inst. Can. Advt. (pres. 1976-77); mem. Can. Advt. and Sales Assn. (pres. 1960-61), Advt. and Sales Execs. Club (pres. 1956-58), Advt. and Sales Assos. Montreal (pres. 1948-49), Advt. Agy. Council Que. (pres. 1975-76), Can.-S. African Soc. (dir. 1980-89, chmn. 1983-86), Mount Stephen (pres. 1967-68), St. James's Club (com. chmn. 1979-81), Royal Montreal Golf Club, Ontario, Thistle Curling (pres. 1977-78), Fort Lauderdale (Fla.) Golf and Country Club, Psi Upsilon. Home: 1 Las Olas Cir #1101 Fort Lauderdale FL 33316

JOURNEY, DREXEL DAHLKE, lawyer; b. Westfield, Wis., Feb. 23, 1926; s. Clarence Earl and Verna L. Gilmore (Dahlke) Journey Gilmore; m. Vergene Harriet Sandsmark, Oct. 24, 1952; 1 child, Ann Marie. BBA, U. Wis., 1950, LLB, 1952; LLM, George Washington U., 1957. Bar: Wis. 1952, U.S. Dist. Ct. (we. dist.) Wis. 1953, U.S. Supreme Ct. 1955, U.S. Ct. Appeals (4th cir.) 1960, U.S. Ct. Appeals (5th cir.) 1961, U.S. Ct. Appeals (D.C. cir.) 1965, U.S. Ct. Appeals (7th and 9th cirs.) 1967, U.S. Ct. Appeals (1st cir.) 1969, D.C. 1970, U.S. Dist. Ct. D.C. 1970, U.S. Ct. Appeals (2d, 3d, 6th, 8th and 10th cirs.) 1976, U.S. Ct. Appeals (11th cir.) 1981. Counsel FPC, Washington, 1952-66, asst. gen. counsel, 1966-70, dep. gen. counsel, 1970-74, gen. counsel, 1974-77; ptnr. Schiff, Hardin & Waite, Washington, 1977—. Author: Corporate Law and Practice, 1975; contbr. articles to profl. jours. Pres. Am. U. Park Citizens Assn., Washington, 1970-72; trustee Lincoln-Wesmoreland Housing Project, Washington, 1978-79. Served with Mcht. Marine Res. USNR, 1944-46, USNG, 1948-50. Knapp scholar U. Wis., 1952. Mem. ABA, Fed. Bar Assn., Fed. Energy Bar Assn., Nat. Lawyers Club, Phi Kappa Phi, Phi Eta Sigma, Theta Delta Chi. Republican. Congregationalist. Lodge: Masons. Home: 4540 Windom Pl NW Washington DC 20016 Office: Schiff Hardin & Waite 1101 Connecticut Ave NW Washington DC 20036

JOVANOVICH, PETER WILLIAM, publishing executive; b. N.Y.C., Feb. 4, 1949; s. William Illya and Martha Evelyn (Davis) J.; m. Robin Adair Thrush, Feb. 14, 1976; children—Nicholas, William. B.A., Princeton U., 1972. Dir. trade dept. Macmillan Pub. Co., N.Y.C., 1977-78; dir. trade dept. Harcourt Brace Jovanovich, Inc., N.Y.C., 1980-83; exec. v.p. Harcourt Brace Jovanovich, Inc., San Diego, 1985—; mng. dir. Acad. Press, London, Eng., 1983-84, pres. AP Jours., 1984-85. *

JOVANOVICH, WILLIAM, publisher; b. Louisville, Colo., Feb. 6, 1920; s. Iliya M. and Hedviga (Garbatz) J.; m. Martha Evelyn Davis, Aug. 21, 1943. AB, U. Colo., 1941; grad. study, Harvard, 1941-42, Columbia, 1946-47; LittD (hon.), Colo. Coll., 1966, U. Colo., 1971, Adelphi Coll., 1971, Middlebury Coll., 1971, Ohio State U., 1971; LLD (hon.), U. Alaska, 1971, Grinnell Coll., 1984, U. Nebr., 1987. With Harcourt Brace Jovanovich, Inc. (formerly Harcourt, Brace & Co.), N.Y.C., 1947—, assoc. editor, 1947-53, v.p., dir., 1953-54, pres., chief exec. officer, dir., 1955-70; chmn., chief exec. officer, dir. Harcourt Brace Jovanovich, Inc. (formerly Harcourt, Brace & Co.), Orlando, Fla., 1970-88; pres., chief exec. officer, dir. Harcourt Brace Jovanovich, Inc. (formerly Harcourt, Brace & Co.), San Diego, 1976-88, chmn bd., exec. com., 1989—; Regent prof. U. Calif.-Berkeley, 1967; lectr. Adelphi U., 1973. Author: Now Barabbas, 1964, Madmen Must, 1978; also essays. Regent State of N.Y., 1974-77. Fellow Morgan Library, N.Y.C. (life). Office: Harcourt Brace Jovanovich Inc 1250 6th Ave San Diego CA 92101

JOYCE, BURTON MONTGOMERY, natural resources company executive; b. Evanston, Ill., Feb. 16, 1942; s. Edwin M. and Helen (Van Riper) J.; m. Marlene Anderson, Nov. 21, 1964; children: Matthew Lodge, Sarah Anne. Student, Beloit Coll., 1959-61; BSBA in Acctg., Miami U., Oxford, Ohio, 1964. Auditor Ernst & Ernst, Cleve., 1964-66; various positions Airco, Inc., Montvale, N.J., 1967-76; corp. controller Compugraphic Corp., Wilmington, Mass., 1976-77; corp. controller United Technologies Corp., Hartford, Conn., 1977-80, v.p. fin. electronics sector, 1980-82, exec. v.p. Essex Group, 1982-84, v.p. investor relations, 1984-85, exec. v.p. Mostek, 1985-86; chief exec. officer Terra Internat., Inc. subs. Inspiration Resources Corp., Sioux City, Iowa, 1986—; sr. v.p. Inspiration Resources Corp., N.Y.C., 1986-88, chief operating officer, 1987—; exec. v.p., chief operating officer Inspiration Resources Corp., 1988—; also bd. dirs. Inspiration Resources Corp., N.Y.C.; bd. dirs. Hudson Bay Mining and Smelting, Toronto, Ont., Can. Bd. dirs. Niagara Falls C. of C., N.Y., 1975-76, Swiss Am. C. of C., Zurich, Switzerland, 1982-84. Served with USAR, 1964-70. Mem. Fin. Execs. Inst. Republican. Club: Whippoorwill (Armonk, N.Y.).

JOYCE, H(ARRY) RICHARD, JR., food service executive; b. Winston-Salem, N.C., Mar. 21, 1950; s. Harry Richard and Ruby Elizabeth (Johnson) J.; m. Ruth Ellen Crowell, June 15, 1974; children: David Austin, Charles Bradford, Leigh Ellen. BS in Econs., Guilford Coll., 1972. Gen. mgr. Joyce Bros. Co., Inc., Winston-Salem, 1976-82, v.p., 1982—; dir. All Kitchens, Boise, Idaho; bd. advisers Food Bank N.W., Winston-Salem, 1987-88, dir. 1988—. Chmn. bd. trustees, Fairview Moravian Ch., Winston-Salem, 1988. Mem. United Comml. Travelers. Office: Joyce Bros Co Inc 1501 S Stratford Rd Winston-Salem NC 27103

JOYCE, MALLORY CARTER, financial executive, advisor; b. Martinsville, Va., Jan. 16, 1948; d. Frances Mallory (Power) Carter; m. Richard Lee Joyce, Aug. 9, 1969; children: Elizabeth Anne, Richard Carter. BS, Radford Coll., 1969; MEd in Adminstrn., Coll. of William and Mary, 1975; Cert., Am. College, 1985. CLU; chartered fin. cons. Elem. tchr. York County Sch. Bd., Yorktown, Va., 1969-76; elem. adminstr. Hampton (Va.) Sch. Bd., 1976-80; agt. Mass. Mut. Life Ins. Co., Newport News, Va., 1980—; owner Summit Fin. Resources, Inc., Newport News, 1982-85; pres., owner Contemporary Fin. Designs, Inc., Newport News, 1985—; reg. rep. MML Investors Services, Inc., Springfield, Mass., 1982—. Producer 3 TV programs: Ednl. Perspectives for Title IX: Implications for Daily Living, 1973. Bd. govs., parlimentarian, leadership devel. team Jr. Woman's Club of Hilton Village, Newport News, 1971-82; bd. dirs., treas. Guild of Peninsula Nature & Sci. Ctr., Newport News, 1978-80; bd. dirs. Peninsula Nature & Sci. Ctr. 1984-85; trustee Newport News Pub. Libraries, 1983—; mem. fin. com. First United Meth. Ch., Newport News, 1970—. Recipient Disting. Service award York Edn. Assn., Yorktown, 1974, Va. Edn. Assn., Richmond, 1977, Freshman Five award Mass. Mut. Life Ins. Co., 1981; named Outstanding Young Woman of Am., 1978. Mem. Peninsula Assn. Life Underwriters, Peninsula chpt. CLU's, Jr. League of Hampton Rds., Internat. Assn. Fin. Planners, Internat. Assn. Registered Fin. Planners (charter). Home and Office: 9 Burns Dr Newport News VA 23601

JOYCE, WALTER JOSEPH, retired electronics company executive; b. Pitts., Sept. 23, 1930; s. John Joseph and Olive Dorothy (Boyle) J.; BBA, Duquesne U., 1957; MBA, Columbia U., 1961; m. Dolores Marchessault, Dec. 2, 1961; children: Kevin, Jacqueline. CPA, Pa. Sr. acct. Coopers & Lybrand, Pitts., 1957-59; div. acct. Singer Co., N.Y.C., 1961-64; asst. factory controller Singer Co., Bonnieres, France, 1964-65, controller, 1966-67; asst. controller Singer Consumer Products, Paris, 1968-70; corp. controller Conrac Corp., Stamford, Conn., 1973-83, v.p. indsl. group, 1984-87 , also bd. dirs. Bd. dirs. Red Cross Youth, Conn., 1979; mem. New Canaan (Conn.) Concert Band. Served with AUS, 1953-55. Recipient Father/Son award Cub Scouts Am., 1972. Mem. Am. Mgmt. Assn., AICPA, Nat. Assn. Accts., Landmark Club, Columbia U. Alumni Bus. Club. Home: Box 33021 Saint Petersburg FL 33707

JOYCE, WILLIAM ROBERT, textile machinery company executive; b. Springfield, Ohio, Mar. 18, 1936; s. Robert Emmet and Christel Beatrice (Beekman) J.; m. Betty Arlene Provonsha, Aug. 29, 1959; children—Jennifer Lynn, Janet Cathleen. BA in Bus., Calif. Western U., 1982; MBA, Calif. Coast U., 1984. Cert. mfg. engring. technician Soc. Mfg. Engrs., 1975. Mgr. engring. Heinicke Instruments, Hollywood, Fla., 1964-68; div. mgr. Jensen Corp., Pompano Beach, Fla., 1969-72; pres. Textiles Supply, Inc., Gerton, N.C., 1972-80; v.p., gen. mgr. Tex-Fab, Inc., Gerton, N.C., 1980-82; pres. Tex-nology Systems, Inc., Gerton, N.C., 1982—; owner Corrib Enterprises, Automation Cons., Gerton, 1981—. Mem., co-founder Assoc. Woodland Owners N.C.; Upper Hickory Nut Gorge Vol. Fire Dept., Gerton. Served with USAF, 1958-64. Recipient innovative devel. award, 1985, award Optimist Club, 1953-54. Mem. Guild Master Craftsmen (internat. mem.) Nat. Rifle Assn., Soc. Mfg. Engrs., Am. Inst. Design and Drafting, Western

Carolina Entrepeneurial Council. Republican. Baptist. Club: Gerton Community Civic. Patentee in field.

JOYNER, CALVIN BRUCE, telecommunications executive; b. Farmville, N.C., Jan. 10, 1938; s. Jarvis and Agnes Irene (Boswell) J.; m. Sandra Gail Crouch, Apr. 13, 1963; children: Cynthia Gail, Jay Anthony. Cert., Fayetteville (N.C.) Tech. Sch., 1959, Wilson (N.C.) Tech. Inst., 1963. Cert. engr., gen. radiotelephone operator. With Carolina Telephone and Telegraph Co., 1956-78; various positions with Carolina Telephone and Telegraph Co., Fayetteville, Rocky Mount, New Bern, Tarboro, N.C., 1978; gen. plant supr. Carolina Telephone and Telegraph Co., Tarboro, N.C., 1980-84, asst. v.p. customer service, 1987, asst. v.p. network service, 1985—; dir. network engrng. and planning United Telecommunications, Inc., Kansas City, Mo., 1985. Mem. IEEE, N.C. World Trade Assn., Ind. Telephone Pioneers Assn., Armed Forces Communications Electronics Assn. (pres. N.C. chpt. 1987-88), Vocat./Tech. Edn. Found of N.C. (bd. dirs. 1988—). Republican. Methodist. Lodge: Kiwanis (Tarboro) (bd. dirs. 1986-88, pres. 1988—). Office: Carolina Telephone & Telephone 122 E St James St Tarboro NC 27886

JOYNER, DEE ANN, county official; b. Alton, Ill., Feb. 26, 1947; d. T. Claxton and Dorothy M. (Troeckler) Burroughs; m. Orville Joyner, Mar. 15, 1973; 1 child, Dawn L. Kotva. BA in Govt., So. Ill. U., 1971, MS in Govt., 1973; MBA, St. Louis U., 1985. Adminstrv. asst. So. Ill. U., Edwardsville, 1970-72; staff assoc. Marshall Kaplan, Gans and Kahn, Washington, 1972-73; dir. community affairs East-West Gateway Coordinating Council, St. Louis, 1973-78; exec. dir. Coro Found., St. Louis, 1978-80, St. Louis County Econ. Council, Clayton, Mo., 1985—; planning dir. St. Louis County, 1980-84. Bd. dirs. Confluence St. Louis, 1983—, Civil Svc. Bd. University City, Mo., 1984—; treas. St. Louis Counts, 1987—; chmn. St. Louis Econ. Devel. Campaing, 1988—. Named Alumnus of Yr. So. Ill. U., 1984; recipient spl. leadership award YWCA, St. Louis, 1987. Mem. St. Louis Regional Commerce and Growth Assn. (vice chmn. mktg. 1988), Leadership St. Louis, St. Louis Forum, Rotary, Lambda Alpha. Office: St Louis County Econ Coun 121 S Meramec Ave Clayton MO 63105

JOYNER, WEYLAND THOMAS, physicist, educator, business consultant; b. Suffolk, Va., Aug. 9, 1929; s. Weyland T. and Thelma (Neal) J.; m. Marianne Steele, Dec. 3, 1955; children: Anne, Weyland, Leigh. B.S., Hampden-Sydney Coll., 1951; M.A., Duke, 1952, Ph.D., 1955. Teaching fellow Duke, 1954, research asso., 1958; physicist Dept. Def., Washington, 1954-57; research physicist U. Md., 1955-57; asst. prof. physics Hampden-Sydney Coll., 1957-59, asso. prof., 1959-63, prof., 1963—, physics chmn., 1968-82, 85—; research asso. Ames Lab. AEC, 1964-65; vis. prof. Pomona Coll., 1965; staff Commn. on Coll. Physics, Ann Arbor, Mich., 1966-67; vis. fellow Dartmouth Coll., 1981; mem. Panel on Preparation Physics Tchrs., 1967-68; nuclear phys. cons. Oak Ridge Inst. Nuclear Studies, 1960-67; NASA-Lewis faculty fellow, 1982-84; pres. Piedmont Farms, Inc., 1958-75; ednl. cons. numerous colls. and univs., 1965-75; pres. Windsor Supply Corp., 1966-82, Three Rivers Farms, Inc., 1971—; mgmt. cons., 1966—; pres. Windsor Seed & Livestock Co., 1969-83; v.p. Software Plus Inc., 1986—, Tidewater F&G, 1982—. Contbr. articles profl. jours. Bd. dirs. Prince Edward Acad., 1971—, exec. com., 1975—; trustee Prince Edward Sch. Electoral Bd., 1979-80. NASA prin. investigator, 1985-87. Fellow AAAS; mem. Am. Phys. Soc., Am. Assn. Physics Tchrs., IEEE, Va. Acad. Sci. (past mem. council, sect. pres.), Am. Inst. Physics (regional counselor, past dir. Coll. Program), Phi Beta Kappa, Sigma Xi, Lambda Chi Alpha. Presbyn. (elder). Home: Venable Pl Hampden-Sydney VA 23943

JOYNES, RALPH CARLISLE, construction material company executive; b. Cheriton, Va., May 15, 1928; s. Ralph Havord and Irma Blanche (Sexton) J.; m. Roxanna Edge, June 7, 1952; children: Linda Carter, Ralph Carlisle, Jr., Karen Edge. B.A. in Econs., U. Va. Sales rep. U.S. Gypsum Co., 1952-60, dist. sales mgr., 1960-63; div. sales mgr. U.S. Gypsum Co., Charlotte, N.C., 1964-69; mgr. sales U.S. Gypsum Co., Atlanta, 1970-74; mgr. mktg. U.S. Gypsum Co., 1975-77; gen. mgr. U.S. Gypsum Co., Chgo., 1977-80, group v.p., 1980-84; chmn. bd. U.S. Gypsum Co., 1984—; exec. v.p., dir. USG Corp. (parent), Chgo., pres., chief operating officer, 1987—. Served with USMC, 1950-52. *

JOZOFF, MALCOLM, consumer products company marketing executive; b. Allentown, Pa., May 2, 1939; s. Martin and Frieda (Wiener) J.; m. JoAnne Flynn, May 7, 1963; 1 son, Matthew James. B.A., Columbia U., 1961. With Procter & Gamble, 1967—, v.p. packaged soap and detergent div., 1981, v.p. So. Europe, 1982-85, group v.p., 1985—. Bd. dirs. Arthristis Found. Southwestern Ohio, Cin., 1980; trustee Cin. Symphony Orch., 1981. Served to capt. USAF, 1962-67. Clubs: Queen City (Cin.); Briarwood (Bellefontaine, Ohio); American (Brussels). Home: 8375 Eustis Farm Ln Cincinnati OH 45243 Office: Procter & Gamble Co One Procter & Gamble Pla Cincinnati OH 45202

JOZWICKI, EDWARD MARCELLUS, electronics company executive; b. N.Y.C., Dec. 30, 1937; s. Alexander and Cecilia (Fiust) J.; m. Maureen Ann Jozwicki, July 6, 1973; 1 child, Matthew Edward. BS, Davis & Elkins Coll., 1959; JD, St. John's U., 1967. Bar: N.Y. 1965, Fed. bar 1968, U.S. Cir. Ct. (2nd cir.), U.S. Dist. Ct. (ea. dist.) N.Y. Mng. atty. The Travelers Ins. Co., N.Y.C., 1965-70; assoc. counsel The Chase Manhattan Bank, N.Y.C., 1970-81, contract officer, 1981-83, corp. real estate officer, 1983-87; real estate mgr. The Bowery Savs. Bank, N.Y.C., 1987-88; mgr. gen. adminstrn. svcs. Digital Equipment Corp., N.Y.C., 1988—. Home: 44 Old Town Ln Huntington NY 11743 Office: Digital Equipment 2 Penn Pla New York NY 10017

JUAREZ, DIANA MARTINEZ, computer company executive; b. Laredo, Tex., Oct. 1, 1952; d. Manuel and Lina (Villarreal) M.; m. Jesus Padilla, Dec. 15, 1975 (div. 1980); 1 child, Anna Christina; m. Amador A. Juarez, Aug. 17, 1982; 1 child, Amador Santiago. BA summa cum laude, Laredo State U., 1982. Computer programmer Laredo Jr. Coll., 1972-76, Daniel B. Hastings Co., Laredo, 1977-78; pres. S.U.M.S., Inc., Laredo, 1979—. Mem. Laredo Mfrs. Assn., Laredo C. of C., Latin Bus. Assn., Laredo Profl. Women Assn., Phi Theta Kappa. Office: SUMS Inc 1001 Bristol Rd Laredo TX 78041

JUDD, DANIEL STEWART, finance and management consultant; b. West Asheville, N.C., Mar. 6, 1924; s. Oscar John and Mabel (Moyers) J.; m. Margaret Norvelle Shipman, Dec. 8, 1946; children: Daniel Stewart, Mary Margaret Judd Wood, Oscar Herbert. Student Berea (Ky.) Coll., 1941-43, U. Okla., 1943, U. N.C., Asheville, 1946. Ptnr. Judd Furniture & Supply Co., West Asheville, 1949-54; owner Judd Supply Co., West Asheville, 1954-64; pvt. practice acctg., West Asheville, 1962-68; acct. Columbia (S.C.) Coll., 1968-73; fin. and mgmt. cons., Irmo, S.C., 1973—; instr. extension div. Asheville-Buncombe Tech. Inst., 1966-67; mem. adv. bd. 1st Union Nat., Irmo. Pres. Buncombe County (N.C.) Rep. Club, 1950; charter pres. Buncombe County Young Rep. Club; sec. Buncombe County Rep. Exec. Com., 1954-60; chmn. 12th Dist. N.C. Rep. Com., 1960-62; dist. dir. 1960 Census for for 11th congressional dist. N.C.; mem. Buncombe County Bd. Elections, 1948-50, N.C. Bd. Elections, 1961-62; bd. dirs. Lexington County Health Svcs. Dist., Inc.; pres. Health Investment Group (Rikard Nursing Home).; mem. adv. bd. Greenwood (S.C.) Meth. HomeSunday sch. tchr., adminstrv. bd., lay speaker, conf. del. Meth. ch. Served with Armed Forces, 1943-45. Decorated Bronze Star. Mem. Nat. Assn. Accts., Nat. Assn. Pub. Accts. (Columbia chpt.), S.C. Tax Council (pres. 1980-82), Berea Alumni Assn. (pres. Asheville chpt. 1957). Club: Mid-Carolina. Lodges: Lions (pres. West Asheville 1955-56, pres. Seven Oaks Columbia 1970-71, editor bulls. 1964-67, 68—), Masons (master West Asheville chpt. 1953). Home: 612 Old Friars Rd Columbia SC 29210 Office: 7349 Nursery Rd PO Box 68 Irmo SC 29063

JUDD, JAMES THURSTON, savings and loan executive; b. Hurricane, Utah, Dec. 13, 1938; s. Finley MacFarland and Bessie (Thurston) J.; m. Janis Anderson, July 15, 1960; children: Juliet, Brian. BS, Utah State U., 1961; postgrad., Los Angeles State U., 1962-63, U. Detroit, 1963-64. Cert. flight instr. Fin. analyst automotive assembly div. Ford Motor Co., Detroit, 1961-64; sales mgr. Xerox Corp., Rocester, N.Y., 1966-75; loan mgr. Golden West Fin. Corp. Savs. and Loan, Oakland, Calif., 1975—; pres. Judd Ranch. Chmn. northbay Bringing Entertainment To The Elderly, Saratoga, Calif., 1972—; chmn. Beef for the Poor, Oakland, 1983-87. Mem. Nat. Assn. Real Estate Appraisers, Calif. Assn. Real Estate, Exptl. Aircraft Assn., Simga Nu. Republican. Mormon. Home: 3284 Blackhawk Meadow Dr Danville CA 94526 Office: Golden W Fin Corp 1901 Harrison St Oakland CA 94612

JUDGE, JOANNE M., hospital administrator; b. Kingston, Pa., July 10, 1952; d. Michael Joseph and Mary (Koval) J. BS in Acctg., St. Joseph U., Phila., 1974. CPA. Audit staff Touche Ross & Co., Phila., 1974-76; controller Community Hosp. Lancaster, Pa., 1976-78, dir. fiscal affairs, 1978-83, v.p. fin., 1983-86, acting adminstr., 1986-87, pres., 1987—; bd. dirs. Heritage Savs. Assn., Lancaster, Pa. Contbr. articles to profl. jours. Bd. dirs., treas. YMCA, 1985-88, Emergency Health Services Fedn. South Cen. Pa., EHSF Found., 1984-88, treas. 1985-88; bd. dirs., chmn. planning com. Vis. Nurse Home Care Assn., 1983-88; treas. Lancaster County Emergency Med. Services Council, 1978-88; mem. conceptual team and faculty Leadership Lancaster, 1984-88; mem. coms. on capital planning, Non-Profit vs. For-Profit Competition Agy. Evaluation, 1982-88, div. chmn., 1988; mem. Task Force on Info. Systems and Cost Effectiveness, Profl. Adv. and Planning Com., 1986-87; bd. dirs. C. of C. Found, 1987-88. Mem. Healthcare Fin. Mgmt. Assn. (nat. bd. dirs. 1986—, nat. sec. 1988—), Nat. Assn. Accts. (pres. Lancaster chpt. 1984-85), Accts. 52 Club, Am. Inst. CPAs, Pa. Soc. CPAs, Hosp. Assn. Pa., Lancaster C. of C. (bd. dirs. 1989), Rotary. Democrat. Roman Catholic. Home: 1939 N Eden Rd Lancaster PA 17604 Office: Community Hosp Lancaster 1100 E Orange St PO Box 3002 Lancaster PA 17604

JUDGE, JOHN EMMET, manufacturing company marketing executive; b. Grafton, N.D., May 5, 1912; s. Charles and Lillian (Johnson) J.; m. Clarita Garcia, Apr. 18, 1940; children: Carolyn Judge Stanley, John Emmet, Maureen Judge Barron, Eileen Judge Horowitz, Susan Judge Lloyd. B.S. in Elec. Engring., U. N.D., 1935. Asst. to adminstr. Ruarl Elctrification Adminstrn., 1937-39, Fed. Works Agy., Washington, 1939-42; staff specialist Exec. Office Pres., Washington, 1942; staff Wallace Clark & Co. (mgmt. cons.), N.Y.C., 1943-46; v.p. Morgan Furniture Co., Asheville, N.C., 1946-48; mgr. financial analysis Lincoln-Mercury div. Ford Motor Co., 1949-53, asst. gen. purchasing agt., 1953-55, mgr. mdsg. and product planning, 1955-58, marketing mgr., 1958-60; product planning mgr. Lincoln-Mercury div. Ford Motor Co., Dearborn, Mich., 1960-62; v.p. mktg. services Westinghouse Elec. Corp., Pitts., 1963-67; v.p. mktg. Indian Head, Inc., 1967-68; mktg. cons. 1969—; dir. Capital Corp. of Am. (investments), Intertek Industries, Kratos, Inc., Cashiers Plastics Corp., Cambridge Instruments, Inc.; Mem. adv. com. to U.S. sec. of commerce. Chmn. Birmingham Library Com., 1957; mem. bd. Boysville of Mich., 1957—. Named to Order of the Holy Sepulchre of Jerusalem. Mem. Am. Ordnance Assn., Soc. Advancement Mgmt., AAAS, N.A.M. (chmn. marketing com.), Am. Soc. M.E., Engring. Soc. Detroit, Nat. Assn. Accountants, Soc. Automotive Engrs., U. N.D. Alumni Assn. (pres.), KC, Sigma Tau, Alpha Tau Omega. Roman Catholic. Clubs: Detroit Athletic, Economic; Orchard Lake (Mich.). Address: S Lake Shore Dr Harbor Springs MI 49740

JUDGE, THOMAS JOSEPH, engineering and construction executive; b. Green Island, N.Y., Oct. 18, 1927; s. Thomas Francis and Mary Ann (Lemieux) J.; m. Eileen Frances Dunn, Oct. 10, 1953; children: Mary Kathleen, Thomas Peter, Elizabeth Frances. BArch, Rensselaer Poly. Inst., 1951. Registered profl. engr. 48 states, D.C., 5 Can. Provinces. Engr. The Austin Co., N.Y.C., 1951-59; gen. sales mgr. The Austin Co., Cleve., 1970-72, v.p., dir., 1972-81, sr. v.p. internat., 1981-83, sr. v.p. domestic, 1983-85; exec. v.p., chief operating officer The Austin Co., Cleve., 1985-86; pres., chief exec. officer The Austin Co., Cleve., 1986—; chief engr. The Austin Co. Ltd., Montreal, Que., Can., 1959-63; v.p., gen. mgr. The Austin Co. Ltd., Toronto, Ont., Can., 1963-70. Served to cpl. USAF, 1946-47. Mem. Nat. Soc. Profl. Engrs., Sigma Xi, Tau Beta Pi. Club: Shaker Heights (Ohio) Country. Office: The Austin Co 3650 Mayfield Rd Cleveland OH 44121

JUDKINS, CHARLES IRA, JR., technical services company executive; b. Worcester, Mass., Feb. 24, 1931; s. Charles I. and Amy F. (Friden) J.; m. Nancy Brandon Kaufman, Nov. 24, 1956; children: Lynn F., Peter B., Eric T. AB, Brown U., 1954; MBA, Columbia U., 1958. Sales rep. IBM, N.Y.C., 1958-62; dir. adminstrn., treas. Travelers Research Conf. Ctr. Inc., Hartford, Conn., 1962-68; owner, pres. Geomet Techs. Inc., Germantown, Md., 1968—; v.p. Versar Inc., Springfield, Va., 1986—. Chmn. exec. com. Geneva Presbyn. Ch., Rockville, Md., 1983—. Served to lt. j.g. USN, 1954-56. Mem. Am. Mgmt. Assn., Am. Meteorological Soc. Republican. Office: Geomet Techs Inc 20251 Century Blvd Germantown MD 20874

JUDY, PAUL RAY, entrepreneur, investor; b. Portland, Ind., Feb. 18, 1931; s. Paul R. and Mary Ellen (Hanlin) J.; m. Mary Ann Dorsey, Nov. 27, 1954; children: Carol, Hannah, John, Beth. AB, Harvard U., 1953, MBA, 1957. Assoc. A.G. Becker & Co., Chgo., 1958-62, v.p., 1962-65, pres., chief exec. officer, 1967-78, co-chmn., 1978-81; bd. dirs. Internat. Minerals & Chem. Corp., Northbrook, Ill., NICOR, Inc., Naperville, Ill., The Raymond Corp., Greene, N.Y., De Kalb & Genetus (Ill.) Corp., Ft. Dearborn Income Securities, Inc., Chgo. Life trustee, Chgo. Symphony Orch. Served with USMC, 1953-55. Republican. Clubs: Ft. Sheridan, (Ill.), Chgo., Sanhaty Head (Nantucket, Mass.).

JULIN, JOSEPH RICHARD, lawyer, educator; b. Chgo., July 5, 1926; s. George Allan and Jennie Elizabeth (Carlsten) J.; m. Dorothy Marie Julian, Oct. 18, 1952; children: Pamela, Thomas, Diane, Linda. Student, Deep Springs Coll., 1944, George Washington U., 1946-49; B.S.L., Northwestern U., 1950, J.D., 1952. Bar: Ill. 1952, Mich. 1960. Assoc. firm Schuyler, Stough & Morris, Chgo., 1952-57; ptnr. Schuyler, Stough & Morris, 1957-59; assoc. prof. law U. Mich., Ann Arbor, 1959-62; prof. law U. Mich., 1962-70, assoc. dean, 1968-70; dean, prof. law U. Fla. Coll. Law, Gainesville, 1971-80; dean emeritus and prof. law U. Fla. Coll. Law, 1980—, Chesterfield Smith prof. law, 1985—; spl. Master U.S. Dist. Ct. 1985—. Author: (with others) Basic Property Law, 1966, 72, 79. Trustee Ann Arbor Bd. Edn., 1966-69, pres., 1968-69. Served with U.S. Army, 1944-46. Fellow Am. Bar Found.; mem. Legal Club of Chgo., Mich. Bar Assn., Ill. Bar Assn., Chgo. Bar Assn., Am. Bar Assn. (chmn. sect. on legal edn. and admissions to the bar 1977-78), Assn. Am. Law Schs. (pres. 1984), Order of Coif., Phi Beta Kappa. Republican. Home: 1657 NW 19th Cir Gainesville FL 32605 Office: U Fla Coll Law Gainesville FL 32611

JUNCHEN, DAVID LAWRENCE, pipe organ manufacturing company executive; b. Rock Island, Ill., Feb. 23, 1946; s. Lawrence Ernest and Lucy Mae (Ditto) J.; B.S. in Elec. Engring. with highest honors, U. Ill., 1968. Founder, owner Junchen Pipe Organ Service, Sherrard, Ill., 1968—; co-owner Junchen-Collins Organ Corp., Woodstock, Ill., 1975-80; mng. dir. Baranger Studios, South Pasadena, Calif., 1980-81. Named Outstanding Freshman in Engring. U. Ill., 1963-64. Mem. Am. Inst. Organbuilders (bd. dirs. 1986—), Am. Theatre Organ Soc. (Tech. Excellence award 1986), Mus. Box Soc., Automatic Mus. Instrument Collectors Assn., Tau Beta Pi, Sigma Tau, Eta Kappa Nu. Author: Encyclopedia of American Theatre Organs; contbr. to Ency. Automatic Mus. Instruments; composer, arranger over 100 music rolls for self-playing mus. instruments. Office: 280 E Del Mar Ste 311 Pasadena CA 91101

JUNEAU, PIERRE, broadcasting company executive; b. Verdun, Que., Can., Oct. 17, 1922; s. Laurent Edmond and Marguerite (Angrignon) J.; m. Fernande Martin, Mar. 17, 1947; children: Andre, Martin, Isabelle. BA, College Sainte-Marie, Montreal, 1944; student philosophy, Sorbonne, Paris, 1949; licentiate in Philosophy, Institut Catholique, Paris, 1949; LLD (hon.), York U., Toronto, 1973, Trent U., Peterborough, Ont., 1987. With Nat. Film Bd. Can., 1949-66; dist. rep., asst. regional supr. of Que., chief internat. distbn. Nat. Film Bd. Can., Montreal, 1951; asst. head European office Nat. Film Bd. Can., London, 1952-54; sec. Nat. Film Bd. Can., Montreal, 1954-64, sr. asst. to commr. and dir. French Lang. prodn., 1964-66; vice chmn. Bd. Govs., Ottawa, 1966-68; chmn. Can. Radio-TV Commn., Ottawa, 1968-75; minister communications Govt. Can., Ottawa, 1975, adviser to Prime Minister, 1975; chmn. Nat. Capital Commn., 1976-78; under sec. state Govt. Can., 1978-80, dep. minister communications, 1980-82; pres. CBC, Ottawa, 1982—; co-founder Cité libre, periodical, 1949; co-founder, 1st pres. La Federation des Mouvements de jeunesse au Que., early 1950s. Co-founder Montreal Internat. Film Festival, 1950's, pres., 1959-68; former sec., former bd. dirs. Albert-Prevost Psychiat. Inst., Montreal, 1960s; former chmn. bd. Ecole nouvelle St.-Germain; co-founder, bd. dirs. Institut Canadien d'Education des Adultes; bd. dirs. Nat. Arts Centre. Decorated officer Order Can. Mem. Royal Soc. Can., Club of Rome. Office: CBC, 1500 Bronson Ave PO Box 8478, Ottawa, ON Canada K1G 3J5 also: Sta CBW, PO Box 160, Winnipeg, MB Canada R3C 2H1 also: CBOFT, PO Box 3220 Sta C, Ottawa, ON Canada K1Y 1E4

JUNEJA, DILJIT SINGH, management consultant; b. Peshawar, India, Nov. 14, 1922; became Can. citizen, 1970; came to U.S., 1982; s. Kartar Singh and Rawel J. (Ahuja) J.; m. Gulshan Raj Chug, Oct. 23, 1943; children: Ravinder Singh, Vinita M. BA, Punjab U., India, 1943; MA in Math., Islamia Coll., India, 1945. Exec. v.p. William M. Mercer Ltd., Toronto, Ont., Can., 1976-80, pres., 1980-82, also bd. dirs.; pres., chief exec. officer William M. Mercer, Inc. div. Marsh and McLennan Cos., Inc., N.Y.C., 1982-87, also bd. dirs.; bd. dirs. Marsh & McLennan Cos., Inc., N.Y.C., William M. Mercer-Meidinger-Hansen, Inc., William M. Mercer Fraser Ltd., U.K., William M. Mercer Ltd., Can., William M. Mercer-Campbell Cook & Knight Pty. Ltd., Australia, 1982-88. Fellow Inst. Actuaries (U.K.), Can. Inst. Actuaries, Conf. Actuaries in Pub. Practices; mem. Internat. Assn. Cons. Actuaries, Am. Acad. Actuaries, Soc. Actuaries (assoc.), Granite Club, Nat. Club (Toronto), Can. Met. Club (N.Y.C.). Home and Office: 24 Parkfield Rd Scarsdale NY 10583

JUNG, JUERGEN ALFRED, data processing executive; b. Frankfurt, Fed. Republic Germany, Jan. 2, 1951; came to U.S., 1958; s. Arthur Powell and Ingeborg J.; m. Ruby Cadena, Nov. 3, 1973; 1 child, Michelle Marie. Student, El Camino Coll., 1970-72. Tech. illustrator Info. Handling Svcs., Hawthorne, Calif., 1972-75, supr., 1975-80; product mgr. Auto-Graphics Inc., Pomona, Calif., 1980-82, v.p. ops., 1983—. With USMC, 1968-70, Vietnam. Home: 11 Skyline Ln Pomona CA 91766 Office: Auto-Graphics Inc 3201 Temple Ave Pomona CA 91788

JUNGBLUTH, CONNIE CARLSON, investment banker; b. Cheyenne, Wyo., June 20, 1955; d. Charles Marion and Janice Yvonne (Keldsen) Carlson; m. Kirk E. Jungbluth, Feb. 5, 1977; 1 child, Tyler. BS, Colo. State U., 1976. CPA, Colo. Sr. acct. Rhode Scripter & Assoc., Boulder, Colo., 1977-81; mng. acct. Arthur Young, Denver, 1981-85; asst. v.p. Dain Bosworth, Denver, 1985-87, George K. Baum & Assocs., Denver, 1987—; bd. dirs. Security Diamond Exchange, Denver. mem. Denver Estate Planning Council, 1981-85, organizer Little People Am., Rocky Mountain Med. Clinic and Symposium, Denver, 1986; adv. bd. Children's Home Health, Denver, 1986—; fin. adv. bd. Gail Shoettler for State Treas., Denver, 1986; bd. advisors U. Denver Sch. Accountancy, 1986-89; campaign chmn. Kathi Williams for Colo. State Legis., 1986. Named one of 50 to watch, Denver mag., 1988. Mem. AICPA, Colo. Soc. CPAs (strategic planning com. 1987-89, instr. bank 1983, trustee 1984-87, pres. bd. trustees, 1986-87, bd. dirs. 1987-89, Pub. Service award 1985-87, chmn. career edn. com. 1982-83), Colo. Mcpl. Bond Dealers, MetroNorth C. of C. (bd. dirs. 1987—), Pi Beta Phi. Club: Denver City (bd. dirs. 1987-88).

JUNIA, EDWARD XAVIER, attorney; b. Cleve., Aug. 20, 1948; s. Joseph J. and Johanna G. (Petack) J.; m. Mary Ann Beskid, Sept. 1, 1973; children: Heather Lee, Jonathan Edward. B of Engring. Scis., Cleve. State U., 1970; MS in Indsl. Engring., U. Toledo, 1973, JD, 1986. Bar: Ohio; registered profl. engr.; cert. safety profl. Sales engr. Duriron Co. Inc., Cleve., 1970-71; safety cons. Aetna Life & Casualty, Cleve., 1971-74; safety/plant mgr. Midland Ross Corp., Cleve., 1974-76; safety/risk mgr. Cleve. Cliffs Iron, Ishpeming, Mich., 1976-78; risk mgr. Andersons Mgmt. Corp., Maumee, Ohio, 1978-88; assoc. Eastman & Smith, Toledo, 1988—; adj. prof. Med. Coll. Ohio, Toledo; environ./safety cons. Contbr. numerous articles on safety. Mem. Lucas County (Ohio) Emergency Planning Com., 1987, Toledo Area Council Govts. Remedial Water Action Com., 1987-88; mem. adv. bd. Salvation Army. Mem. ABA, Ohio Bar Assn., Toledo Bar Assn., Am. Soc. Safety Engrs. (chpt. pres. 1984-85), Risk Ins. Mgmt. Soc., Am. Trial Lawyers Assn., Order of Coif, Toledo Club, KC, Sigma Pi Sigma. Republican. Roman Catholic. Club: Toledo Country. Office: Eastman & Smith Attys-at-Law 800 United Savings Bldg Toledo OH 43604-1141

JUNION, ROBERT DONALD, financial planner, broker; b. Sturgeon, Wis., Oct. 15, 1931; s. Raymond A. and Loretta M. (Strahen) J.; m. Veronica M. Roessler, Aug. 17, 1957; children: Jaci, Don, Richard, David, Dianne, Janine, Lisa, Kathy. BS, St. Norbert Coll., 1953; MS, U. Wis., 1957. Tchr., coach Cath. Cen. High Sch., Green Bay, Wis., 1953-54, Tigerton (Wis.) High Sch., 1957-59, D.C. Everest High Sch., Schofield, Wis., 1959-68; sales mgr. House of Merrill, Schofield, 1968-77; fin. planner Investors Diversified Services, Wausau, Wis., 1978—. 1st. lt. U.S. Army, 1954-56. Mem. Internat. Coll. Fin. Planners (cert.). Home: 1413 Everest Ave Schofield WI 54476 Office: Investors Diversified Svcs 2424 Stewart Sq Wausau WI 54401

JUNKIN, WILLIAM WAKEMAN, advertising agency executive; b. N.Y.C., July 13, 1943; s. George de Forest and Alice Gertrude Maslin J.; m. Janet Grace Blass, Feb. 28, 1968 (div. May 1973); children: Jennifer Noel, Drew deForest; m. Pamela Brewer, June 21, 1981; children: Devon deForrest, Trent Brewer. BS, Fordham U., 1965. Asst. mgr. customer relations Hertz Corp., N.Y.C., 1965-67; advt. mgr. Diners Club, N.Y.C., 1967-70; acct. supr. N.W. Ayer Co., N.Y.C., 1970-75; v.p. mktg. Cally Curtis Co., Hollywood, Calif., 1975-78; sr. v.p., mgmt. supr. Cochran Chase Livingston, Newport Beach, Calif., 1978-81; exec. v.p. Gillen Stone, Newport Beach, 1981—; pres. Wakeman & deForrest, Newport Beach, 1981—. Mem. Calif. Rep. Assembly, Newport Beach. Served to lt. USMC, 1962-68. Mem. Direct Mktg. Assn. Roman Catholic. Office: Wakeman & deForrest 2601 Main St Irvine CA 92714

JUNKINS, ANITA GOLL, insurance company executive; b. Bronx, N.Y., Nov. 17, 1956; d. Edward Charles and Margaret Elizabeth (Hayes) Goll; m. Kevin Dexter Junkins, Dec. 30, 1978; 1 child, Raymond Edward. BS in Zoology, U. Md., 1978; MS in Biology with honors, Fairleigh Dickenson U., 1983. Chem. technician Ledoux & Co., Teaneck, N.J., 1978; assoc. analytical chemist Henkel Corp., Hoboken, N.J., 1978-80; chemist Am. Cynamid Co., Pearl River, N.Y., 1980; rsch. biologist Am. Cynamid Co., Pearl River, 1980-83, clin. data coord., 1983-85; mgmt. sci. analyst Pfizer Inc., N.Y.C., 1985-86; asst. to v.p. Group Health Inc., N.Y.C., 1986—; founder, cons. Integrated Bus. Solutions, Washingtonville and N.Y., 1988—; cons. Advanced Design Tech., Croton-on-Hudson, N.Y., 1986—. Chmn. site com. Matteson Hist. Congress, Shaftsbury, Vt., 1988; mem. Tappan Hill Homeowners Assn. Mem. N.Y. Acad. Scis., SAS Users Group Internat. Home: 173 Barnes Rd Washingtonville NY 10992 Office: Integrated Bus Solutions 173 Barnes Rd Washington DC 10992

JUNKINS, JERRY RAY, electronics company executive; b. Ft. Madison, Iowa, Dec. 9, 1937; s. Ralph Renaud and Selma Jennie (Kudebeh) J.; m. Marilyn Jo Schevers, June 13, 1959; children—Kirsten Dianne, Karen Leigh. B.E.E., Iowa State U., 1959; M.S. in Engring. Adminstrn., So. Methodist U., 1968. Engr., mgr. Mfg. group Tex. Instruments, Inc., Dallas, 1959-73, asst. v.p., mgr. radar div., 1973-75, v.p., mgr. equipment group, 1975-81, exec. v.p., mgr. data systems and indsl. systems, 1981-85, pres., chief exec. officer, 1985-88, chmn, pres., chief exec. officer, bd. dirs., 1988—; bd. dirs. Proctor and Gamble Co., Caterpillar Inc. Bd. dirs. Dallas Citizens Coun. Mem. Nat. Acad. Engring., Greater Dallas C. of C. (bd. dirs.). Methodist. Office: Tex Instruments Inc 13510 N Central Expwy PO 655474 MS236 Dallas TX 75243

JUON, LESTER ALLEN, utility executive; b. Webster City, Iowa, Sept. 7, 1938; s. Alfred J. and Fern A. (Taylor) J.; m. Shirley A. Rinehimer, June 10, 1962; children: Melissa Louise, Thomas Jay. BS in Indsl. Adminstrn., Iowa State U., 1962; MBA, U. S.D., 1981. Various mktg. positions Iowa Pub. Service Co., Sioux City, 1962-66; area mgr. Clarion and LeMars, Iowa, 1966-72; dist. cons. svc. mgr. LeMars, Iowa, 1972-78; asst. to the pres. LeMars, Sioux City, 1978-79, v.p. adminstrn., 1979-83, v.p. staff svcs., 1983-85, v.p. gas div., 1985-87, v.p. electric div., 1987-88, sr. v.p. electric div., 1988—. Div. chmn. United Way of Siouxland, Sioux City, 1982; chmn. bd. trustees Westmar Coll., 1983-87; mem. exec. coun. Prairie Gold Area Boy Scouts Am., Sioux City, 1983-84; bd. dirs. Florence Crittenton Home, Sioux City, 1982-88, Sioux City Art Ctr., 1987—. Mem. Sertoma Club (pres. 1986-87), Indsl. Devel. Coun. Sioux City (pres. 1983-84), Sioux City C. of C. Mem.

Evang. Covenant Ch. Office: Iowa Pub Serv Co 401 Douglas St PO Box 778 Sioux City IA 51102

JURDANA, ERNEST J., banker, accountant; b. Friday Harbor, Wash., Oct. 30, 1944; s. Ernest and Thelma Hannah (Starr) J.; m. Mary Ellen Patterson, Feb. 5, 1966; children: Jeanette, Brian. BS, City U., Seattle, 1985. CPA, Wash. Trainee, acct. Wash. Mut. Savs. Bank, Seattle, 1966-72, acctg. officer, 1972-77, controller, 1977-86, sr. v.p., 1986—, sr. v.p. fin. mgmt., 1986—. Bd. dirs., treas. City Swimming and Exercise Orgn., Mill Creek, Wash., 1985—. Served with USAF, 1963-66; PTO. Mem. Nat. Assn. Accts., Bank Adminstrn. Inst., Fin. Execs. Inst. Clubs: Jaycees (pres. 1974) (Lynwood, Wash.); Toastmasters (pres. 1976) (Seattle). Home: 2922 152d SE Mill Creek WA 98012 Office: Wash Mut Savs Bank 1101 2d Ave Seattle WA 98101

JUREDINE, DAVID GRAYDON, insurance company executive; b. Rahway, N.J., Aug. 26, 1937; s. Gordon Mounier and Ruby Fern (Thomas) J.; m. Carol Marie Nemec, Feb. 7, 1970; children: Adam, Jason. BS, Bowling Green State U., 1960; postgrad., Cleve.-Marshall Law Sch., 1963-66. Sales rep. Sperry Rand Corp., Cleve., 1960-62; claims rep. CNA Ins. Co., Cleve., 1962-66; div. mgr. Progressive Corp., Cleve., 1966-73; exec. v.p. Ohio Indemnity Co. (subs. of Bancins Corp.), Columbus, Ohio, 1973—, Bancinsurance Corp., Columbus, 1980—. Mem. Am. Mgmt. Assn., Downtown Sertoma. Office: Bancins Corp 50 W Broad St Columbus OH 43215

JUREN, DENNIS FRANKLIN, petroleum company executive; b. Ellinger, Tex., Apr. 4, 1935; s. Daniel Arthur and Ellen Emily J.; m. Ruth Birmingham, Oct. 7, 1961; children—Patrick Edward, Ellen Emily, Anne Elizabeth. B.A. in econs., U. Tex., 1966; M.B.A. in fin., U. Houston, 1969. Mgr. supply Eastern States Petroleum Co., Houston, 1956-60; owner Bonded Petroleum Co., Houston, 1960-62; v.p. mktg. and supply Coastal States Petrochem. Co., Houston, 1962-70; pres. Tesoro Petroleum Corp., San Antonio, 1970—, chief operating officer, 1987—, also dir. Bd. dirs. YMCA, San Antonio, 1979. Served with U.S. Army, 1954-55. Mem. San Antonio C. of C. (dir. 1982), Nat. Petroleum Refiners Assn. (dir.), Am. Petroleum Inst. Methodist. Clubs: Oakhills Country, Univ. Lodge: Masons. Office: Tesoro Petroleum Corp 8700 Tesoro Dr San Antonio TX 78286 *

JUSTICE, BOB JOE, economist; b. Ardmore, Okla., Dec. 14, 1946; s. Jesse William and Nora Estell (Boston) J.; B.B.A., U. Okla., 1970; M.B.A., Coll. William and Mary, 1973; m. Patricia Ann Thorpe, Dec. 26, 1970; children—Chad Andrew, Melanie Katherine, Kimberly Ann. Landman, Mobil Oil Co., Oklahoma City, 1970-71; planning analyst DuPont Corp., Wilmington, Del., 1973-75; planning specialist Houston Oil & Minerals Corp., Houston, 1976-79; mgr. planning and econs. Dome Petroleum Corp., Denver, 1979-82; mgr. investment and bus. analysis Union Pacific Resources, Ft. Worth, 1982—. Served with U.S. Army, 1971-73. Am. Assn. Petroleum Landmen scholar, 1968-70. Mem. Planning Forum, Assn. Corp. Growth, Am. Petroleum Inst. Republican. Methodist. Club: Woodhaven Country. Home: 6150 Silverleaf Ct Fort Worth TX 76112 Office: PO Box 7 Fort Worth TX 76101

JUSTICE, BRADY R., JR., medical products executive; b. Albertville, Ala., Dec. 20, 1930; s. Brady R. and Kate (McEachern) J.; m. Sandra Gearner, Dec. 29, 1956; children: David, Michael, Lori Blankenship, Kathy Baker. BBA, Baylor U., 1953. CPA. Ptnr. Arthur Andersen & Co., Dallas, 1953-64, Indpls., 1964-72; exec. v.p. Basic Am. Industries, Inc., Indpls., 1972-83; pres. Basic Am. Med., Inc., Indpls., 1983—, also bd. dirs. Mem. Columbia Club, Lions (pres. Indpls. chpt.). Republican. Baptist. Home: 5435 Hedgerow Dr Indianapolis IN 46226 Office: Basic Am Med Inc 4000 E Southport Rd Indianapolis IN 46227

JUSTIN, L(EMBIT) PETER, accountant; b. Tallinn, Estonia, Apr. 4, 1928; came to U.S., 1949, naturalized, 1955; s. Heinrich and Sophia (Malt) Jurgenson; m. Maryellen Wagner, Apr. 26, 1957 (div. 1978); children: Bradford, Janet, Diann, Cristofer; m. Luz Mercedes Arnao, June 7, 1985; children: Eugene, Edward. BA, Columbia U., 1957, MBA, 1959. CPA, Pa. Ptnr. E. Charles Conway and Assocs., Ardmore, Pa., 1955-57; pres. L. Peter Justin and Assocs., Bryn Mawr, Pa., 1957—; IRS liaison officer Pa. Soc. Pub. Accts.; dir. Matos Enterprises Ltd., Bryn Mawr, Pa., Dennis Assocs., Inc., Las Vegas; cons. joint com. taxation, U.S. Congress. Mem. Nat. Soc. Pub. Accts., Pa. Soc. Pub. Accts. (pres. 1983-85), Am. Mgmt. Assn. Republican. Club: Vesper (Phila.). Lodge: Lions (pres. Bryn Mawr, Pa. 1982-83, Man of Yr. award 1981, 82, 83). Avocations: boating, skiing, philately. Home and Office: 5555 Calle Miramar Ste 101 La Jolla CA 92037

JUSTUS, JACK GLENN, farm organization executive, livestock farmer; b. Lead Hill, Ark., Oct. 29, 1931; s. Charles A. and Nancy C. (Mooneyham) J.; m. Freda Sue Anderson, Sept. 23, 1950; children: Michael, Thomas. AS, Ark. Poly. Coll., 1951; BS, U. Ark., 1953. County agt. coop. extension bur. USDA, Jonesboro, Melbourne and Piggott, Ark., 1954-60; dist. dir. field svcs. Ark. Farm Bur. Fedn., Little Rock, 1960-71, 1960-71, legis. dir., 1971-75, adminstrv. v.p., 1975-82, exec. v.p., 1982—; bd. dirs. Ark. Blue Cross/Blue Shield, Little Rock, 1st Comml. Banking Corp., Little Rock. Active Future Farmers Found., 4-H Club Found. Mem. Ark. C. of C. (bd. dirs. 1982—), Nat. Future Farmers Am. (hon. Am. farmer), Pleasant Valley Country Club. Mem. Ch. of Christ. Office: Ark Farm Bur Fedn PO Box 31 Little Rock AR 72203

KACEK, DON J., management consultant; b. Berwyn, Ill., May 4, 1936; s. George J. and Rose (Krizik) K.m. Carolyn K. Hiner, July 22, 1961; children: Scott M., Stacey M. B.S. in Mech. Engring, Ill. Inst. Tech., 1958. Engring. sect. mgr. Sunstrand Corp., Rockford, Ill., 1958-72; group v.p. Kysor Indsl. Corp., Cadillac, Mich., 1972-76, 1975-76; dir. product devel. Ransburg Corp., Indpls., 1976-77; pres. Ransburg Corp., 1977-88, chmn. bd., chief exec. officer, 1978-88; mgmt. consulstant Indpls., 1988—; bd. dirs. Arvin Industries Inc., Columbus, Ind., 1982—, Ind. Corp. for Sci. and Tech., Indpls., 1982—. Inventor Burn Rate Control Valve, 1966. Served with AUS, 1960. Recipient Sagamore of the Wabash award Gov. Ind., 1985.

KACLIK, DEBI LOUISE, construction executive; b. Pitts., May 15, 1953; d. John G. and Dolores J. (Grekalskis) K. BA, West Liberty State Coll., 1975; Cert. in Computer Aided Drafting and Design, Pitts. Tech. Inst., 1982; postgrad., Horry-Georgetown Tech. Sch., 1987-88, Columbia Pacific U., 1988—. Program dir. YMCA, Pitts., 1975-78; regional supr. United Republic Life Ins. Co., Harrisburg, Pa., 1977-80; phys. therapy asst. The Verland Found., Pitts., 1980-81; estimator, mgr. PPS Enterprises, Inc., Pitts., 1981-83; mgr. Wild Sisters Restaurant, Inc., Pitts., 1983-84; v.p., project mgr. Kreisle Bros. Masonry, Ltd., Georgetown, S.C., 1984-85; owner, ptnr., constrn. mgr. Mastco Masonry/Steel, Georgetown, 1986-87; owner, pres. The Brick People, Inc., Surfside Beach, S.C., 1988—; presenter news spl. Sta. KDKA-TV, Pitts., 1977; guest speaker Sta. WTAE-TV, Pitts., 1978, Sta. WBTW-TV, Myrtle Beach, S.C., 1987. Instr. water safety, first aid and disaster shelters ARC, Myrtle Beach and Pitts., 1969-85; coordinator regional and internat. Cerebral Palsy Games, Pitts., 1981; bd. dirs. North Am. Riding for the Handicapped, Pitts., 1982; team coordinating asst. nat. telethon teamwalk Am. March of Dimes, Myrtle Beach, 1986-88. Mem. Am. Assn. Subcontractors, U.S. Sidewinder Assn. Democrat. Roman Catholic. Home: 28 Bay Dr Salters Cove Murrells Inlet SC 29576 Office: The Brick People Inc South Point Exec Offices 1012 16th Ave NW Ste 114 Surfside Beach SC 29575

KADZIELSKI, MARK ANTHONY, lawyer; b. Cleve., July 1, 1947; s. Karl A. and Ann T. (Krol) K.; m. Marilyn E. Manis, Dec. 17, 1977; children: John, Mary, Paul. AB, John Carroll U., 1968; JD, U. Pa., 1976. Bar: Calif. 1976. Assoc. Lawler, Felix & Hall, Los Angeles, 1976-78, Buchalter, Nemer, Fields, Chrystie & Younger, Los Angeles, 1978-81; ptnr. Weissburg and Aronson, Inc., Los Angeles, 1981—; prof. law U. West Los Angeles, 1978-85; vice chmn. State Bar Commn. to Confer with Calif. Med. Assn., Los Angeles, San Francisco, 1979-84. Vice chmn. bd. editors Los Angeles Lawyer mag., 1980-84; contbr. articles to legal jours. Sec. sect. on legislation and adminstrn. of justice, Town Hall Calif., Los Angeles, 1977-81, bd. dirs. 1981—. Mem. Los Angeles County Bar Assn., U. Pa. Alumni Club So. Calif. (bd. dirs. 1985—). Roman Catholic. Office: Weissburg and Aronson Inc 2049 Century Park E Ste 3200 Los Angeles CA 90067

KAEGEL, RAY MARTIN, real estate and insurance broker; b. St. Louis, Dec. 7, 1925; s. Ray E. and Loyola (Mooney) K.; B.S. in Secondary Edn., Washington U., St. Louis, 1948, M.B.A., 1955; m. Daniel Marilyn Dugger, July 2, 1943. Mgr., St. Louis Amusement Co., Inc., 1941-43, 46-52; gen. mgr. Md. Real Estate & Ins. Agy., Inc., Granite City, Ill., 1953-60; pres., gen. mgr., dir. Kaegel Real Estate & Ins. Agy., Inc., Granite City, 1961—; dir. Comfort Air-Conditioning & Heating, Inc., Granite Center. Sec., Granite City Bd. Realtors, 1959-63, 66-77, pres, 1964-65, 79-81, 86-87. Vice chmn. Tri-Cities Area Red Cross, 1972; bd. dirs., v.p. Lighthouse for Blind, St. Louis, 1985-87, vice-chmn. 1987—. Served to lt. (j.g.) USNR, 1943-46. Mem. Nat. (exec. officer's council 1959-77), Ill. assns. real estate bds., Tri-Cities Ind. Ins. Agts. Assn. (pres. 1971-73), Ind. Ins. Agts. Ill., Tri-Cities C. of C., Granite City Multiple Listing Service, Inc. (sec.-treas. 1971-82, 88—, pres. 1982-88). Optimist. Home: 660 Pine Creek Dr Chesterfield MO 63017 Office: Kaegel Real Estate & Ins Agy 2001-A Adams Ave Granite City IL 62040

KAEMPF, ROBERT FRANCIS, leasing company executive; b. Rockville Center, N.Y., May 17, 1953; s. Robert F. and Irma (Morris) O.; m. Diane T. Dudley, Feb. 17, 1979; children: Brian P., Christine A. AS in Programming Sci., N.Y. Inst. Tech., 1973; AAS in Acctg. and Fin., Nassau Community Coll., 1979, BS in Acctg., 1983. Acct. All Island Lease A Car, Garden City, N.Y., 1975-78, Hempstead Bank, N.Y.C., 1978-79; acct. Transvc. Lease Corp., Lake Success, N.Y., 1979-82, asst. controller, 1982-83, controller, 1984—; cons. Diane's Data Service, North Bellmore, N.Y., 1987—. Mem. Acctg. Soc. Republican. Office: Transvc Lease Corp 5 Dakota Dr Lake Success NY 11042

KAESER, CLIFFORD RICHARD, food service industry executive, lawyer; b. Boise, Idaho, Feb. 17, 1936; s. Clifford Morgan and Bertha Marie (Minton) K.; m. Marjorie Ann, Sept. 21, 1959; children: Richard L., Cynthia M., Kenneth R.; m. Carol L. Roach, May 11, 1979. BA, Coll. of Idaho, 1959; JD, Yale U., 1962. Bar: Calif. 1962, Tenn. Assoc. Lawler, Felix & Hall, Los Angeles, 1962-63; asst. div. counsel Lockheed Missiles & Space Co., Sunnyvale, Calif., 1963-64; group counsel Litton Industries, Beverly Hills, Calif., 1964-66, acquisition counsel, 1966-68; gen. counsel, v.p. Hitco, Los Angeles, 1968-70; pres. Chapparel Inc., Denver, 1970-72; gen. counsel, v.p. Conroy, Inc., San Antonio, 1972-80; gen. counsel, v.p. Dobbs Houses, Inc., Memphis, 1980-84; sr. v.p., gen. counsel Howard Johnson Co., North Quincy, Mass., 1984-86; v.p., gen. counsel Delaware North Cos., Inc., Buffalo, 1986—; dir. Sportservice Corp., APCOAm Inc., Concession Air Corp. Served with USMCR, 1954-61. Mem. ABA, State Bar Calif., State Bar Tenn., Nat. Restaurant Assn., Multi Unit Food Industry Assn., Am. Mgmt. Assn. Republican. Home: 31 Viscount Dr East Amherst NY 14221 Office: Del North Cos Inc 700 Delaware Ave Buffalo NY 14209

KAGAN, STEPHEN BRUCE (SANDY), travel agency executive; b. Elizabeth, N.J., Apr. 27, 1944; s. Herman and Ida (Nadel) K.; m. Susan D. Kaltman, July 3, 1966; children—Sheryl, Rachel. B.S. in Econs., U. Pa., 1966; M.B.A. in Fin., Bernard Baruch Coll., 1969. Chartered fin. analyst. Security analyst Merrill Lynch Pierce Fenner & Smith, N.Y.C., 1966-68; dir. research Deutschmann & Co., N.Y.C., 1968-70; v.p. Equity Sponsors, Inc., N.Y.C., 1970-72; v.p., investment counselor Daniel H. Renberg & Assocs., Inc., Los Angeles, 1972-78; exec. v.p. Ask Mr. Foster Travel Svc., Van Nuys, Calif., 1978—. Vice pres. bd. Temple Beth Hillel, North Hollywood, Calif., 1976-83. Mem. Inst. Cert. Fin. Analysts, Beta Gamma Sigma. Home: 13952 Weddington St Van Nuys CA 91401 Office: Ask Mr Foster Travel Svc 7833 Haskell Ave Van Nuys CA 91406

KAGAWA, KATHLEEN HATSUYO, entrepreneur; b. Honolulu, June 9, 1952; d. Shinso and Jane Fumiko (Murata) K.; m. Masamichi Irimajiri (div. 1977). Student, U. Hawaii, Honolulu, 1970-73, Sophia U., Tokyo, 1973; BSBA, U. Beverly Hills, 1977, MBA, 1979, PhD in Internat. Bus., 1982. Mgr. Flipside Record Shop, Honolulu, 1969-70; producer, singer Victor Records, Tokyo, 1973-76; actress Hawaii Five-O, Honolulu, 1976; co-owner Images Internat. of Hawaii, Honolulu, 1976-79; v.p., sec., hostess East-West Connection TV Show, Los Angeles, 1980-81; dir. pub. relations Fendi, Beverly Hills, 1981-82; pres. Sky Prodns., Inc., Honolulu, 1982-86; adminstrv. exec. New Tokyo-Hi Restaurants, Honolulu, 1983—; v.p., treas. Born Internat., Inc., Honolulu, 1986—; cons. Schlossberg-Cassidy and Assoc., Washington, 1983-86, Yamada Group, Japan and U.S.A., 1987—; sponsor State of Hawaii Nat. Aquaculture Assn., Washington, 1983-86; admissions counselor U. Beverly Hills, Honolulu, 1984-86; adminstrv. exec., corp. sec. New Tokyo-Hawaii Restaurant Co, Ltd., 1981—; pres. K & H Devel. Co., Ltd.; realtor Diamond Head Group subs. New Tokyo Restaurant, 1986, bd. dirs; sec.-treas. Azabu Enterprises Ltd., 1989—, bd. dirs. Sponsors State of Hawaii Nat. Aquaculture Assoc., Washington, 1983-86. Named Best in Backstroke, State of Hawaii Swim Competition, 1968. Mem. Gemological Inst. Am. Alumni Assn., Japan-Am. Soc. of Honolulu, Honolulu Bd. Realtors, Mortgage Broker Assn., Pacific and Asian Affairs Council, Internat. Ladies Benevolent Assn., Punahou Alumni Assn. Baptist. Club: Oahu Country (Hawaii). Home: 3215 Kaohinani Dr Honolulu HI 96817

KAHALAS, HARVEY, business educator; b. Boston, Dec. 3, 1941; s. James and Betty (Bonfeld) K.; m. Dianne Barbara Levine, Sept. 2, 1963; children: Wendy Elizabeth, Stacy Michele. BS, Boston U., 1965; MBA, U. Mich., 1966; PhD, U. Mass., 1971. Data processing coordinator Ford Motor Co., Wayne, Mich., 1963-66; lectr. Salem (Mass.) State Coll., 1966-68; asst. prof. bus. Worcester (Mass.) Polytech. Inst., 1970-72; asst. prof. Va. Polytech. Inst., Blacksburg, 1972-75, assoc. prof., 1975-77; assoc. prof. SUNY, Albany, 1977-79, assoc. dean, 1979-81, prof., 1979—, dean, 1981-87; cons. Aspen Inst. for Humanistic Studies/Fund for Corp. Initiatives, N.Y.C., 1980—, Gen. Electric, Schenectady, N.Y., 1981-85, Gen. Motors, Tarrytown, N.Y., 1987—. Contbr. articles to profl. jours. Bd. dirs. Fund for Corp. Initiatives, N.Y.C., 1980—, Nat. Found. Ileitis and Colitis, Albany, 1982—, Blue Cross Northeastern N.Y., Albany, 1983—, Capital Dist. Bus. Rev., Albany, 1984—. Named Disting. Alumni, U. Mass., 1982, Disting. Lectr. USIA, 1985, Am. Participant USIA, 1989, Fulbright Coun., 1988. Mem. Acad. Mgmt. (treas. 1971-73, mem. exec. com.), Human Resource Planning Soc. (hon.), Human Resource Systems Profls. (hon.), Beta Gamma Sigma, Delta Tau Kappa. Home: 500 Stratton Pl Delmar NY 12054 Office: SUNY Sch Bus 1400 Washington Ave Albany NY 12222

KAHLENBECK, HOWARD, JR., lawyer; b. Fort Wayne, Ind., Dec. 7, 1929; s. Howard and Clara Elizabeth (Wegman) K.; m. Sally A. Horrell, Aug. 14, 1954; children: Kathryn Sue, Douglas H. BS with distinction, Ind. U., 1952, LLB, U. Mich., 1957. Bar: Ind. 1957. Ptnr. Krieg, DeVault, Alexander & Capehart, Indpls., 1957—; sec., bd. dirs. Maul Tech. Corp. (formerly Buehler Corp.), Indpls., 1971-81, Am. Monitor Corp., Indpls., 1971-86, Am. Interstate Ins. Corp. Wis., Milw., 1973-84, Am. Interstate Ins. Co. Ga., Am. Underwriters Group, Inc., Indpls., 1973-86, Pafco Gen. Ins. Co., 1987-88. Served with USAF, 1952-54. Mem. ABA, Ind. Bar Assn., Indpls. Bar Assn., Alpha Kappa Psi, Delta Theta Phi, Beta Gamma Sigma, Delta Upsilon Internat. (sec., bd. dirs. 1971-83, chmn. 1983-86, trustee found. 1983—). Lutheran. Home: 6320 Old Orchard Rd Indianapolis IN 46226 Office: Krieg DeVault Alexander & Capehart 2800 Indiana National Bank Tower Indianapolis IN 46204

KAHLER, LOUISE SANTOS, real estate developer; b. New London, Conn., Feb. 16, 1939; d. Anthony and Belva Margaret (Frechette) Santos; m. William E. Kahler, Jan. 27, 1971 (div. 1984); 1 child, Laura Anne. AS, Mitchell Coll., 1971; BSBA, U. New Haven, 1972; postgrad., U. Conn., 1988—. Sec. Electric Boat div. Gen. Dynamics Co., Groton, Conn., 1957-62, adminstrv. asst., 1963-67, market analyst, 1970-72, long-range planner, 1972-74; adminstrv. asst. Conn. Correctional Ctr., Niantic, 1968-70; owner, mgr. Timeless Treasures Antique Shop, Mystic, Conn., 1976-79, K&L Painting Contractors, Mystic, 1979-83; prin. LaBelle Ins., Oakdale, Conn., 1984-88; pres. Laurel Assocs., Groton, Conn., 1988—; agt., rep. comml. lines Allyn Agy., Gales Ferry, Conn., 1983-88. Chmn. long-range planning Pine Point Sch., Stonington, Conn., 1982-85, Town Coun., Stonington, 1985-87. Mem. NAFE, Nat. Assn. Real Estate Appraisers (cert.), Profl. Ins. Agts. Assn., Conn. Child and Family Svcs., Norwich C. of C. Republican. Congregationalist. Home: 639A Wolcott Ave Stonington CT 06378 Office: Laurel Assocs 495 Rt 184 Suite 305 Groton CT 06340

KAHN, ALAN BRUCE, real estate development and construction executive; b. Columbia, S.C., Apr. 15, 1940; s. Irwin and Katie Kahn; m. Charlotte Segelbaum, Feb. 28, 1965: children: Kevin A., Monique B., Charles B. BA in History, Duke U., 1962; MBA in Fin., George Washington U., 1965. Pres. Kahn Devel Co., Columbia, 1968—; v.p.-sec. M.B. Kahn Constrn. Co., Inc., Columbia, 1968—; mem. adv. bd. NCNB/SC, Columbia, 1970—. Bd. dirs. Columbia Area Mental Health Ctr., 1968-72, 74-78, chmn. 1971; sec. adv. bd. dirs. Providence Hosp., Columbia, 1973-80; bd. dirs. Columbia Jewish Community Ctr., Hist. Columbia Found., 1974-78, Salvation Army, 1983-85, Friends of Richland County Pub. Libr., 1981-84, Columbia Philharm. Orch., 1970-78, S.C. Arts Found., 1974-76; trustee Columbia Mus. Art and Sci., 1982-85; bd. dirs. Columbia Jewish Welfare Fedn., 1982—, treas. 1982-83, 88—, 2d v.p., 1984, chmn. endowment, 1985—; mem. partnership bd. U. S.C. Sch. Medicine, 1985—. Recipient (with wife) Lyre award City of Columbia, 1978, Order of Palmetto Sate of S.C., 1988, State of Israel Bonds award, 1988. Mem. B'nai B'rith (Community Leadership award 1982). Office: Kahn Devel Co Hwy 555 and Flintlake Rd Columbia SC 29223

KAHN, CHESTER DENNIS, real estate developer; b. Boston, Jan. 18, 1947; s. Leonard and Perl (Meyers) K.; m. Linda Sue Thaler, June 8, 1976; children: Michelle, Jamie-Beth, Joshua. Student, Babson Coll., 1965-66, Boston Coll., 1967-68. Pres. Mallard Realty Group Inc., developers and cons., Framingham, Mass.; bd. dirs. Blackstone Bank & Trust Co., Boston. Mem. Wayland (Mass.) Zoning Bd. Appeals, 1988. With U.S. Army. Named Developer of Yr., Community Assns. Inst., Boston, 1987. Mem. Am. Power Boat Assn. (Driver of Yr. 1988). Office: Mallard Realty Group Inc 463 Worcester Rd Framingham MA 01701

KAHN, HYMAN R., health science administrator; b. N.Y.C., May 16, 1931; m. Sara Kahn; children: Mark, Joel, Ellen. BS magna cum laude, Franklin-Marshall Coll., Lancaster, Pa., 1952; MD, Jefferson, Phila., 1956. Sr. med. dir. U.S. Healthcare, Blue Bell, Pa. Served as capt. USAF, 1960-62. Mem. Phi Beta Kappa. Office: US Healthcare Inc 980 Jolly Rd PO Box 1109 Blue Bell PA 19422

KAHN, JAN EDWARD, manufacturing company executive; b. Dayton, Ohio, Aug. 29, 1948; s. Sigmond Lawrence and Betty Jane K.; m. Deborah Ann Deckinga, Nov. 28, 1975; children: Jason Edward, Justin Allen, Julie Ann. BS in Metall. Engring., U. Cin., 1971. Mgmt. trainee U.S. Steel Corp., Gary, Ind., 1971-72; plant metallurgist Regal Tube Co., Chgo., 1972-74, gen. foreman, 1974-76, supt., 1976-77, mgr. tech. service, 1978-80, materials mgr., 1980-81; mgr. quality control Standard Tube Co., Detroit, 1977-78; dir. ops. Boye Needle Co., Chgo., 1981-82, v.p. ops., 1982-83, v.p., gen. mgr., 1984-85, pres., 1985-88; v.p. sales and mktg. Caron Internat., Rochelle, Il., 1988—. Mem. Am. Soc. Metals, AIME, ASTM, Ravenswood Indsl. Council (bd. dirs. 1983-84, pres. 1985), Hand Knitting Assn. (chmn. 1986-88), Triangle Club. Republican. Mem. Christian Reformed Ch. Home: 13909 S Teakwood Lockport IL 60441 Office: Caron Internat 150 Ave E Rochelle IL 61068

KAHN, LESLIE RUTH, service executive; b. N.Y.C., Jan. 15, 1947; d. Murrey and Florence (Marine) Kahn; child from previous marriage: Steven Craig Ringelheim; m. John Schwartz. AAS, N.Y. Tech. Coll., N.Y.C., 1972; BA, CUNY, 1981. Adminstr. coll. dentistry NYU, N.Y.C., 1967-71; dental hygienist Dr. Steven S. Baron, DDS, Rego Park, N.Y., 1974-79; office mgr. Dr. Jerome Levine, DDS, N.Y.C., 1973-74; dental hygienist Dr. Steven S. Baron, DDS, Rego Park, N.Y., 1974-78; pres. Craig Med. and Dental Pers. Agy., Inc., N.Y.C., 1980—; adj. lectr. CUNY Med. Assts. Sch., 1981, Greater N.Y. Dental Meeting, 1980-86; cons. in field. Mem. N.Y. State Dental Hygiene Soc. (hons.), Fla. State Dental Hygienist Soc., Fla. Dental Soc. Office: Craig Pers Agy Inc 25 W 43d St Ste 405 New York NY 10036

KAHN, MARK LEO, arbitrator, educator; b. N.Y.C., Dec. 16, 1921; s. Augustus and Manya (Fertig) K.; BA, Columbia U., 1942; MA, Harvard U., 1948, PhD in Econs., 1950; m. Ruth Elizabeth Wecker, Dec. 21, 1947 (div. Jan. 1972); children: Ann Mariam, Peter David, James Allan, Jean Sarah; m. Elaine Johnson Morris, Feb. 12, 1988. Asst. economist U.S. OSS, Washington, 1942-43; teaching fellow Harvard U., 1947-49; dir. case analysis U.S. WSB, Region 6-B Mich., 1952-53; mem. faculty Wayne State U., Detroit, 1949-85, prof. econs., 1960-85, prof. emeritus, 1985—, dept. chmn., 1961-68, dir. indsl. relations M.A. Program, 1978-85; arbitrator union-mgmt. disputes, specializing in airline industry. Bd. govs. Jewish Welfare Fedn. Detroit, 1976-82; bd. dirs. Jewish Home for Aged, Detroit, 1978—. Served to capt. AUS, 1943-46. Decorated Bronze Star. Mem. Indsl. Relations Research Assn. (pres. Detroit chpt. 1956, exec. sec. 1979-89; exec. bd. 1986-88), AAUP (past chpt. pres.), Nat. Acad. Arbitrators (bd. govs. 1960-62, v.p. 1976-78, chmn. membership com. 1979-82, pres. 1983-84), Soc. Profls. in Dispute Resolution (v.p. 1982-83, pres. 1986-87). Co-author: Collective Bargaining and Technological Change in American Transportation, 1971; contbr. articles to profl. jours. Home and Office: 4140 2d Ave Detroit MI 48201

KAHN, PAUL MARKHAM, actuary; b. San Francisco, May 8, 1935; s. Sigmund Max and Alexandrina K. (Strauch) K.; m. Linda P. McClure, May 20, 1968. BS, Stanford U., 1956; MA, U. Mich., 1957, PhD, 1961. Asst. actuary Equitable Life Assurance Soc., N.Y.C., 1961-71; v.p., life actuary Beneficial Standard Life, Los Angeles, 1971-75; v.p., actuary Am. Express Life Ins. Co., San Rafael, Calif., 1975-77, P.M. Kahn & Assocs., 1977-. Editor Dictionary of Actuarial and Life Ins. Terms, 1972, 2d edit., 1983, Credibility: Theory and Practice, 1975, Computational Probability, 1980. Fellow Soc. Actuaries (Triennial prize 1961-64), Can. Inst. Actuaries, Conf. Actuaries in Pub. Practice; mem. Am. Acad. Actuaries, Internat. Actuarial Assn., Inst. Actuaries (Eng.), Spanish Actuarial Assn., Swiss Actuarial Assn., German Actuarial Assn., Italian Actuarial Assn., Am. Antiquarian Soc. Clubs: Zamorano (Los Angeles); Roxburghe; Concordia-Argonaut, Comml. (San Francisco); Pacific, Waikiki Yacht (Honolulu). Address: 2430 Pacific Ave San Francisco CA 94115

KAHN, ROBERT IRVING, management consultant; b. Oakland, Calif., May 17, 1918; s. Irving Herman and Francesca (Lowenthal) K.; m. Patricia E. Glenn, Feb. 14, 1946; children: Christopher, Roberta Anne. BA cum laude, Stanford U., 1938; MBA, Harvard U., 1940; LLD (hon.), Franklin Pierce Coll., 1977. Exec. researcher R.H. Macy's, Inc., N.Y.C., 1940-41; controller Smith's, Oakland, 1946-51; v.p., treas. Sherwood Swan & Co., Oakland, 1952-56; prin. Robert Kahn & Assocs. (mgmt. cons.), Lafayette, Calif., 1956—; pres. Kahn and Harris Inc. (investment bankers), San Francisco, 1971—; v.p. Hambrecht & Quist (investment bankers), San Francisco, 1977-80; prin. Pacific Area Corp. Exchange, 1986—; cons. to comdr. gen. U.S. Army and USAF, 1987—; dir. Wal-Mart Stores Inc., Components Corp. Am.; dir., chief fin. officer, v.p. Lipps, Inc.; dir., v.p. Marc Paul Inc.; v.p., dir. Piedmont Grocery Co. Publisher: newsletter Retailing Today, 1965—; author: weekly newspaper column Pro and Kahn, 1963-77, 86—; editorial bd.: Jour. of Retailing. Mem. Nat. Eagle Scout Assn., Boy Scouts Am., past dir. Oakland Coun.; past bd. dirs. Oakland Area ARC; bd. dirs., officer, mem. exec. com. Unitd Way Bay Area, 1946-81, chmn. allocations, membership, fin., by-laws, and personnel coms.; trustee Kahn Found.; past sec. League to Save Lake Tahoe; founder Lafayette Forward, 1970, sec., 1976—; mem. adv. com. Retail Mgmt. Inst. Santa Clara U., 1983—. Served with USAAF, 1941-46; with USAF, 1951-52; lt. col. Res. ret. Recipient Mortimer Fleishhacker award as outstanding vol. United Way Bay Area, 1980, Best Article award Jour. Mgmt. Cons., 1984-85; founding mem. Baker Scholar Harvard U., 1939. Mem. Assn. Mgmt. Cons. (pres. 1977), Inst. Mgmt. Cons. (a founder), Nat. Retail Mchts. Assn. (asso. cons. mem.), Mensa, Phi Beta Kappa. Home: 3684 Happy Valley Rd Lafayette CA 94549 Office: PO Box 249 Lafayette CA 94549

KAHN, STEPHEN LOUIS, soft drink bottling company executive; b. Memphis, Nov. 10, 1955; s. Jay and Ruth Joan (Manis) K.; m. Debra Ilene Losner, June 9, 1985; 1 child, Jason Carey. BS in Bus., U. Tenn., 1977; M in Accountancy, U. Ga., 1979. CPA, Ga.; Cert. info systems auditor, data processor. Cons. Price Waterhouse, Atlanta, 1979-81, sr. cons., 1981-82; EDP auditor The Coca-Cola Co., Atlanta, 1982-84, sr. EDP auditor, 1984-85, staff cons., 1985-88, account exec., 1988; mgr. planning and adminstrn. Coca-Cola Inf. Svcs., Atlanta, 1988—. Mem. EDP Auditors Assn. Office: The Coca Cola Co PO Drawer 1734 Atlanta GA 30301

KAHN, WARREN ROBERT, trust officer, financial planner; b. N.Y.C., May 8, 1949. BA, Bowling Green U., 1971; diploma, Northwestern U., 1977. Cert. fin. planner; registered investment advisor. Trust adminstr. Mfrs. Nat. Bank, Detroit, 1971-74; trust officer Belmont County Nat. Bank, St. Clairsville, Ohio, 1974-78; sr. v.p. Comml. Nat. Bank, Tiffin, Ohio, 1978-88; v.p., sr. trust officer Bay Bank & Trust Co., Panama City, Fla., 1988—. Treas. Seneca County chpt. ARC, 1981-84, Community Hosp. Assn., Tiffin, 1987-88. Mem. Inst. Cert. Fin. Planners. Episcopalian. Home: 2710 Woodmere Dr Panama City FL 32405 Office: Bay Bank & Trust Co 509 Harrison Ave Panama City FL 32401

KAISER, BO PAUL, consultant in trade promotion, researcher; b. Stockholm, Feb. 5, 1917; m. Gerny Tenström, Jan. 1, 1944; 1 child, Sten. Student, Royal Mil. Acad., 1939; BA, Stockholm U., 1940-43, PhD, 1975-78; postgrad., Harvard U. Bus. Sch., 1981. Asst. in orgn. dept. Civil Adminstrn. Nat. Def., 1943-45; research mgr. Swedish Gallup Poll, 1946-48, sales mgr., 1949-51, mng. dir., 1952-54; mng. dir. Swedish Retail Research Inst., 1954-58; pres., chief exec. officer Affarsindex AB, Solna, Sweden, 1958-74; spl. cons. A.C. Nielsen Mgmt. Services SA, Lucerne, Switzerland, 1975-80; cons. Unctad-Gatt. Internat. Trade Ctr., Geneva, 1980—; dir. Svenska Johnson's Wax AB, Stockholm; chmn. bd. A.C. Nielsen Co. AB, Stockholm; dir. Marketindex OY, Helsinki; chmn. bd. Marketindex Group, Helsinki, Nielsen Nordic Arco Bd. Contbr. articles to profl. jours. Swedish rep. Fedn. Internat. des Societes d'Aviron, 1947-59; mem. exec. com. Swedish Olympic Com., 1956-65; internat. umpire Olympics Helsinki, 1952, European Championships, Copenhagen, 1953, Amsterdam, 1954. Decorated by Pres. Finland, 1953, Swedish Sports Fedn., 1954. Mem. Nat. Index Bd., Internat. C. of C. (commn. on mktg. 1957—), Fedn. Swedish Market Research Insts. (chmn. bd. 1963, 67, 71, 72), European Soc. Opinion and Mktg. Research (Swedish rep. 1964-74), Swedish Rowing Assn. (pres. 1950-55, hon. pres. 1988). Home: Hammarbacken 14, S 18235 Danderyd Sweden Office: Marketindex AB, Box 1032, S 16421 Kista Sweden

KAISER, GEORGE CHAPIN, investment company executive; b. Chgo., Jan. 20, 1933; s. George Chapin and Grace (Betz) K.; m. Jeanne Aurelius, June 1972 (div.); children: Mark A., Richard A., Charles M.; m. Jane Elizabeth Leicht, June 16, 1973. BS, U. Ill., 1954. CPA, Wis. Mgr. Arthur Andersen & Co., Milw., 1957-64, ptnr., 1969-84; sec. adminstrn. State of Wis., Madison, 1965-67; exec. v.p., chief fin. officer Arandell-Schmidt Corp., Menomonie Falls, Wis., 1985-87; owner George Kaiser & Co., Milw., 1988—; chief exec. officer, chmn. bd. dirs. Hanger Tight Co., Wheeling, Ill., 1988—; bd. dirs. Roundy's Inc., Gazette Printing Co., Luitink Inc., P & S Investments, Mail Advt. Supply Co., Breakfall, Inc. Treas. Rep. Party Wis., Madison, 1969-74; trustee Pub. Policy Forum, Milw., 1982—; treas., bd. dirs. Competitive Wis., Inc., Milw., 1982—, U. Wis.-Milw. Found., 1979—; v.p., bd. dirs. Florentine Opera Co., Milw., 1978—; bd. dirs. Columbia Hosp., 1987—. Lt. (j.g.) USNR, 1954-56. Mem. AICPA, Wis. Inst. CPA's (pub. svc. awd. 1986), Fin. Execs. Inst., Milw. Country Club, Lake Geneva Country Club (gov., treas.), Jupiter Hills Golf Club, Univ. Club. Office: George Kaiser & Co 759 N Milwaukee #608 Milwaukee WI 53202

KALAFUT, GEORGE WENDELL, distribution company executive, retired naval officer; b. Chgo., Feb. 21, 1934; s. George Andrew and Ann Catherine (Panak) K.; m. Alice Quinn, Nov. 9, 1957; children: Katherine, Tracy. AB in Econs., St. Joseph's Coll., Rensselaer, Ind., 1955; MBA, Harvard U., 1969. Commd. USN, 1956, advanced through grades to capt.; asst dir. air equipment purchasing div. Naval Air Systems Command, Washington, 1969-71; dep. dir. F14/Grumman rev. team Naval Air Systems Command, Washington and Bethpage, N.Y., 1971; dir. airframes purchasing div. Naval Air Systems Command, Washington, 1972-73; supply officer USS Ranger CV61, San Francisco, 1973-75; dir. plans and budget Naval Supply Systems Command, Washington, 1976-78; retired USN, 1978; dir. inventories Motion Industries, Birmingham, Ala., 1979, v.p., 1980-83, v.p. fin., chief fin. officer, 1983-85, sr. v.p., 1985—, also bd. dirs. Baker scholar Harvard Bus. Sch., 1969. Home: 4216 Stone River Circle Mountain Brook AL 35213 Office: Motion Industries Inc 741 Alton Rd Birmingham AL 35210

KALAKOS, JOHN EMMANUEL, metal executive; b. Pitts., June 11, 1943; s. Theodore and Margaret (Zafereo) K.; m. Judith K. Allison, Jan. 23, 1980; 1 child, Kristen. BA, Calif. State Coll., 1965. Exec. v.p., sales exec. Three Rivers Aluminum Co., Warrendale, Pa., Pitts., N.Y.C. and Chgo., 1969—; bd. dirs. VekaPlast USA, Pa., Venango, Warrendale. Mem. Am. Archtl. Mfrs. Assn. (mem. div. council 1983-87). Democrat. Greek Orthodox. Office: TRACO Cranberry Industrial Pk Warrendale PA 15095

KALAN, GEORGE RICHARD, venture capitalist; b. Cleve., Dec. 13, 1944; s. Edward George and Betty Virginia (Triska) K.; m. Cheryl Ann Fine, Aug. 27, 1976; children: Gavin Richard, Jonathan Edward. BEE, Case Inst. Tech., 1966; MEE, MIT, 1968; MBA, Harvard U., 1978. Project mgr., engr. Charles Stark Draper Lab. (formerly MIT Instrumentation Lab.), Cambridge, 1968-76; mgmt. cons. Booz, Allen & Hamilton, Inc., Sao Paulo, Brazil and N.Y.C., 1978-81; pres. Kalan Sutton McGraw, Inc., Short Hills, N.J., 1981-85; pres., mng. gen. ptnr. Orien Ventures, Inc./Orien Ptnrs., L.P., New Canaan, Conn., 1985—; dir. Sigma Circuits, Inc., Santa Clara, Calif., BioGrowth, Inc., Richmond, Calif., ImmunoSci. Corp., N.Y.C., Phys. Optics Corp., Torrance, Calif. Recipient MIT Cert. Commendation for contbn. to design and devel. of Apollo lunar module autopilot, 1969, Apollo Achievement award, NASA, 1969, Presdl. Medal Freedom for participation in Apollo 13 mission rescue operation, 1970. Home: 72 Good Hill Rd Weston CT 06883 Office: Orien Ventures Inc 36 Grove St New Canaan CT 06840

KALELKAR, ASHOK SATISH, consulting company executive; b. Ahmedabad, India, June 10, 1943; came to U.S., 1960; s. Satish Dattatrey and Chandan (Parekh) K.; m. Joanne Bottiglieri, June 21, 1969 (div. Sept. 1983); children: Dorian, Jessie, Milan. BS in Math., George Wash. U., 1963; SB & SM In Mech. Engring., MIT, 1964, postgrad., 1966; PhD in Engring., Brown U., 1969. Sr. scientist Factory Mut. Rsch. Co., Norwood, Mass., 1969-71; staff Arthur D. Little Inc., Cambridge, Mass., 1971-76, sr. staff, 1976-80, v.p., 1980-85, sr. v.p., 1985—; bd. dirs. Program Systems Mgmt. Co., Cambridge; chmn. Opinion Rsch. Co., Princeton, N.J. Contbr. articles to profl. jours. Mem. Soc. for Risk Mgmt., Combustion Inst., Ops. Research Soc. Am. Unitarian. Office: Arthur D Little Inc 25 Acorn Park Cambridge MA 02140

KALEN, THOMAS HARRY, banker; b. Balt., Mar. 14, 1938; s. Harry Lawrence and Angela Carolyn (Nockels) K.; BS, UCLA, 1960; m. Judith L. Cochran, Aug. 29, 1959; children—John Merrill, Bonnie Jean. Account exec. Dean Witter & Co., San Bernardino, Calif., 1966-69; v.p. Chase Investment Mgmt. Co., N.Y.C., 1969-71, Transamerica Corp., L.A., 1971-77, No. Trust Co., Chgo., 1977-82; v.p. Mellon Bank, Pitts., 1982-84; sr. v.p. Boston Safe Deposit & Trust Co., L.A., 1984-88, sr. v.p. U.S. Trust Co., 1988—. V.p., chmn. pub. rels. Calif. Jaycees, 1968; dist. chmn. UCLA Scholarship Soc., 1974-77; chmn. pub. rels. com. Mass Transit for L.A., 1976; Mem. adv. bd. Ctr. Entrepreneurial Studies NYU; bd. dir. Venture Capital Studies, NYU, 1983-85. With USAF, 1960-66, Vietnam. Named Calif. Outstanding Jaycees, 1968. Mem. Nat. Assn. Security Dealers, Western Pension Conf., Instl. Investor Conf., Pension and Investment Conf. Club: Union League (Chgo.).

KALFON, FREDERICK GEOFFREY, biomedical company executive; b. N.Y.C., Nov. 8, 1941; s. William Neuman and Linda (Zelman) K.; m. Carol F. Moskwitz, Aug. 29, 1965 (div. July 1975); children: Stephanie Jill, Deborah Michelle; m. Judith F. Goldstein, Aug. 29, 1977; 1 child, Lee Heather. BS in Biology, Norwich U., 1963; M in Marine Biology, U. Md., 1965. Tech. sales rep. Pharmacia Fine Chems., Piscataway, N.J., 1967-69, regional sales mgr., 1969-75, mgr. sales tng., 1975-76; mgr. nat. sales div. Pharmacia Diagnostics, Piscataway, N.J., 1976-78, product mgr., 1978-82; sr. product mgr. Organon Diagnostics, East Orange, N.J., 1982; dir. mktg. Surgidev Corp., Mpls., 1982-85; v.p. mktg. Eye Tech. Inc., St. Paul, 1985-88; pres. ICEO Advanced Med. Techs., Inc., Bloomington, Minn., 1988—; cons. Eye Sat, Sarasota, Fla., 1985. Patentee hydrogen internal combustion engine. With U.S. Army, 1965-67. Decorated Bronze star. Republican. Jewish. Home: 8125 Telegraph Rd Bloomington MN 55438 Office: AMTI 8125 Telegraph Rd Bloomington MN 55438

KALIKA, DALE MICHELE, financial corporation executive; b. N.Y.C., Dec. 30, 1948; d. Albert and Ida K.; BA in Psychology with high honors cum laude, Queens Coll., 1970; MA in Communication Arts and Scis., U. Wis., Madison, 1974; MBA, N.Y. U., 1981; m. Robert David McPhee, Mar. 21, 1982. Teaching asst. U. Wis., 1971-73; orgn. cons., asst. treas. Chase Manhattan Bank, N.Y.C., 1974-76, sr. project mgr., 1976-77, mgr. customer service, 2d v.p., 1977-79; supr. personnel devel. Quaker Oats Co., Chgo., 1979-83; v.p. planning and adminstrn. Midway Motor Lodges Service Co., 1983-84; mktg. mgr. First Wisconsin, Milw., 1986—. Mem. Am. Mktg. Assn., Am. Soc. Tng. and Devel. Home: 4407 N Murray Shorewood WI 53211 Office: First Wis Milw 777 E Wisconsin Ave Milwaukee WI 53202

KALINOWSKI, RAYMOND J., investment company executive; b. 1929. Gen. ptnr., then exec. v.p., treas. vice chmn. and dir. A.G. Edwards & Sons, Inc., St. Louis, 1951-89; bd. dirs. A.G. Edwards & Sons., Inc. Office: AG Edwards & Sons Inc 1 N Jefferson Ave Saint Louis MO 63103

KALISTA, JAMES ALEXANDER, accountant; b. Erie, Pa., Apr. 10, 1947; s. Walter Thomas and Casmira (Wasielewski) K.; m. Jodee Ann Taraski, Jan. 20, 1968; children: James W., Bryan E., Timothy D., Michael A., Julie A. BS in Bus. Adminstrn., Gannon U., 1968. CPA, Ohio. Sr. acct. Ernst & Whinney, Cleve., 1968-72; mgr., tax ins. traffic Chase Metals Service, Cleve., 1972-75; treas., controller FLX Corp., Beachwood, Ohio, 1975-80; freelance cons. Solon, Ohio, 1980-83; corp. budget mgr. Ferro Corp., Cleve., 1983-86, mgr. corp. acctg., 1986-89; group controller Specialty Plastics, Cleve., 1989—. Mem. Am. Inst. CPAs, Ohio Soc. CPAs. Roman Catholic. Home: 6560 Brookland Ave Solon OH 44139 Office: Ferro Corp 4150 E 56th St Cleveland OH 44101

KALL, GAYLE ANN, marketing professional; b. Bristol, Conn., Apr. 6, 1954; d. Russell Oscar and Anna Marie (Heidkamp) K. BA, Upsala Coll., E. Orange, N.J., 1976; MBA, Rutgers U., 1981. Market rsch. analyst Luning Prak Assocs., Montvale, N.J., 1976-79, assoc., 1979-81; owner, v.p. Info. Dynamics, West Chester, Pa., 1981—. Mabel Fitzgerald scholar Upsala Coll., 1972; recipient Luth. Brotherhood honor, 1972. Democrat. Office: Info Dynamics F&M Bldg High and Market Sts West Chester PA 19382

KALLAY, MICHAEL FRANK, II, medical devices company official; b. Painesville, Ohio, Aug. 24, 1944; s. Michael Frank and Marie Francis (Sage) K.; BBA, Ohio U., 1967; m. Irma Yolanda Corona, Aug. 30, 1975; 1 son, William Albert. Salesman, Howmedica, Inc., Rutherford, N.J., 1972-75, Biochem. Procedures/Metpath, North Hollywood, Calif., 1975-76; surg. specialist USCI div. C. R. Bard, Inc., Billerica, Mass., 1976-78; western and central regional mgr. ARCO Med. Products Co., Phila., 1978-80; Midwest regional mgr. Intermedics, Inc., Freeport, Tex., 1980-82; Western U.S. mgr. Renal Systems, Inc., Mpls., 1982—; pres. Kall-Med, Inc., Anaheim Hills, Calif., 1982—. Mem. Am. Mgmt. Assn., Phi Kappa Sigma. Home and Office: 6515 Marengo Dr PO Box 17248 Anaheim Hills CA 92817-7248

KALLMAN, THEODORE WILLIAM, corporate executive; b. Shirley, Mass., Feb. 28, 1952; s. James T. and Mildred E. Kallman; m. Claudia A. Sherwood, July 28, 1974; children: Benjamin B., James S., Isaiah J., Etta E. Student, Alma Coll., 1970, Spring Arbor Coll., 1972-74; BA with honors, Mich. State U., 1976. CLU, Chartered Fin. Cons., L.I.C. Agy. mgr. Farm Family Ins. Cos. Eastern Mass., Bridgewater, 1979-84; owner, operator Spartan Ins. Agy., Inc., Lansing, Mich., 1984—; pres. Kallman Ltd., Spartan Premium Fin. Co., Inc. Youth retreat speaker and musician, 1970—; area capt. Capital Area United Way Drive, 1976; bd. dirs. Trinity Sch. of Cape Cod, 1981; bd. deacons Osterville Bapt. Ch., 1981, chmn. bd., 1983, 84; pres. Com. Against Display of Pornography, 1982-85; mem. Statewide Task Force for Justice Fellowship, 1986-87; chmn. Teen Suicide Prevention Taskforce of Mich.; mem. State Cen. Com., Republican Party, 1989—; county Rep. exec. com. 1984-85, chmn. fin. com., 1987; bd. dirs. Greater Lansing Salvation Army, 1988—. Mem. Ind. Ins. Agts. of Greater Lansing (bd. dirs.), Aircraft Owners and Pilots Assn., Rotary (charter mem., bd. dirs., past pres. 1986-88). Republican. Baptist. Home: 3941 Belding Ct Okemos MI 48864 Office: Kallman Bldg 205 W Saginaw Lansing MI 48933

KALM, MAX JOHN, pharmaceuticals company executive; b. Munich, Bavaria, Germany, Nov. 27, 1928; came to U.S. Dec. 7, 1938; s. Emil and Emmy (Berliner) K.; m. Louise Nickel (div. July 1969); children: Denise, Deborah; m. Lila Crosby Dayhoff, Aug. 2, 1969; children: Stephen R. Crosby, Rita Sue MacFee. BS, U. Calif., Berkeley, 1952, PhD, 1954. Rsch. assoc. U. Mich., Ann Arbor, 1954-55; rsch. scientist G.D. Searle & Co., Skokie, Ill., 1955-65; dir. scientific liaison Cutter Labs., Berkeley, 1965-70, dir. control, 1970-72, mgr. quality assurance, 1972-73, dir. quality assurance, 1973-77, v.p. quality assurance, 1977-82; v.p. quality assurance Schering Corp., Union, N.J., 1982—. Author numerous articles; patentee in field. Dir. Jr. Achievement, Elizabeth, N.J., 1986—. Midshipman, USN, 1947-48. Mem. Parenteral Drug Assn. (dir. 1987—), Pharmaceutical Mfrs. Assn. (adv. bd. 1978-84), Am. Chemical Soc., Am. Inst. Chemists, Am. Assn. Advancement Sci., Sigma Xi. Republican. Methodist. Home: 9 Bennett Pl Westfield NJ 07090 Office: Schering Corp 1011 Morris Ave Union NJ 07083

KALMBACH, JOHN HENRY, chemical company executive; b. Drexel Pa., Oct. 17, 1952; s. Charles Frederic and Elizabeth (Uhl) K.; BSE with high honors, Princeton U., 1973; AM with distinction, Harvard U., 1975; m. Cecilia Elizabeth Rice, June 22, 1974; children: Hilary Elizabeth, Whitney Alison, Eliot Ramsay. Cons. geologist, Boston, 1976-78; geologist, credit exec. First Nat. Bank Boston, 1978-80; asst. to pres., corp. officer Pauley Petroleum, Inc., L.A., 1980-87; pres., chief operating officer Polymorphic Polymers Corp., Miami Shores, Fla., 1987—; v.p. KTA Ltd., Frazer, Pa., 1987—. Author: Notes on the Upper Cretaceous Invertebrate Fauna of Haddonfield, 1969. NSF grad. fellow, 1973-76. Mem. Jonathan Club, Princeton Ivy Club, Harvard Club of Boston, Sigma Xi, Tau Beta Pi. Office: KTA Ltd 7 Roselawn Ln Malvern PA 19335

KALNICK, STEPHEN MICHAEL, controller; b. Bklyn., Apr. 23, 1943; s. Calvin and Charlotte (Kipling) K.; m. Martha Eve Ashkenasy, Dec. 22, 1966; children: Abbe, Adam. BS in Acctg., L.I. U., 1965. CPA, N.Y. Auditor Clarence Rainess & Co. CPA's, N.Y.C., 1966-78, Brout & Co. CPA's, N.Y.C., 1978-80; controller Yves St. Laurent div. Bidermann Industries Inc., Secaucus, N.J., 1980-86, QUI Designer Collection Inc., Secaucus, 1980-86, Jason Tynan & Co., N.Y.C., 1988—. Served to sgt. USAR, 1965-71. Mem. Am. Inst. CPA's, N.Y. State Soc. CPA's. Jewish. Office: Jason Tynan & Co 525 Seventh Ave New York NY 10018

KALTINICK, PAUL R., trust company executive; b. N.Y.C., Dec. 1, 1932; s. Morris and Vera (Halpern) K.; m. Alice Levy, Dec. 26, 1954; children—Vera, Marjorie, Pamela. B.B.A. in Acctg., Pace U., 1954. Accountant Peat, Marwick, Mitchell, N.Y.C., 1959-61; mgmt. cons. Peat, Marwick, Mitchell, 1961-63; exec. v.p. Flowerized Presentations, N.Y.C., 1963-64; with J.C. Penney Co., Inc., N.Y.C., 1964-80; v.p. J.C. Penney Co., Inc., 1974-80, dir. fin. mgmt., 1976-78, dir. tech. support ops., 1978-80; pres., chief exec. officer Frank Russell Trust Co., Tacoma, 1980-88, chmn., chief exec. officer, 1988—. Served with USMC, 1954-56. Mem. Am. Inst. C.P.A.s, Fin. Execs. Inst., Treasurers Club. Home: 12713 54th Ave NW Gig Harbor WA 98335 Office: First Interstate Pla 909 A St PO Box 1454 Tacoma WA 98402

KAMAN, CHARLES HURON, diversified technologies corporation executive; b. Washington, June 15, 1919; s. Charles W. and Mabel (Davis) K.; m. Helen Sylvander, Oct. 20, 1945 (div.); children: Charles William II, Cathleen, Steven Wardner; m. Roberta C. Hallock, Sept. 1, 1971. BS in Aero. Engring. magna cum laude, Cath. U. Am., 1940; DSc (hon.), U. Colo., 1984, U. Hartford, 1985; LLD (hon.), U. Conn., 1985. With Hamilton Standard Propellers div. United Aircraft Corp., East Hartford, Conn., 1940-45; pres. Kaman Corp., Bloomfield, Conn., 1945—, chmn. bd., 1945—, chief exec. officer, 1986—; chmn. Vertical Lift Aircraft council of Aerospace Industries Assn., 1964, Helicopter council, 1954; former mem. The World Affairs Ctr. Honors adv. bd. Bd. govs. Cath. U. Am.; bd. dirs. Inst. of Living; founder, pres., bd. dirs. Fidelco Guide Dog Found., Inc.; founder, Am. Leadership Forum, U. Hartford; former trustee Western New England Coll.; former mem. Catholic U. bd. govs.; past corporator Health Care Facilities Planning Council of Greater Hartford; past indsl. com. mem. Greater Hartford YMCA. Recipient Disting. Service award Conn. Jr. C. of C., 1953, Engr. of Year award Conn. Soc. of Profl. Engrs. inc., 1961, Alumni Achievement award Cath. U. Am., 1961, Outstanding Young Man of Yr. award Hartford Jr. C. of C., 1948, Assoc. award Navy Helicopter Assn., 1975, Nat. Human Relations award Nat. Conf. of Christian and Jews, 1987, The Fleet Adm. Chester W. Nimitz award Navy League of the U.S., 1986. Fellow Am. Helicopter Soc. (pres. 1958, dir. 1959-61, Dr. Alexander Klemin award 1981), AIAA; mem. Conn. Bus. and Industry Assn. (dir., exec. com.), Nat. Acad. Engring., Conn. Soc. Profl. Engrs., Aviation Hall of Fame (charter), Navy Helicopter Assn. (hon.), Newcomen Soc. Am., 1983, Navy League of U.S. (nat. adv. council), Pi Tau Sigma (hon.), Beta Gamma Sigma, Am. Helicopter Soc., Conn. Acad. Sci. and Engring., Conn. Aero. Hist. Assn., Catgut Acoustical Soc., The Internat. Transactional Analysis Assn. Office: Kaman Corp 1322 Blue Hills Ave Bloomfield CT 06002 *

KAMBA, CHARLES JAMES, III, electronics company executive; b. Chgo., Oct. 9, 1935; s. Charles J. II and Bernice (Niedzielski) K.; m. Gloria Diane Broska, Oct. 13, 1962 (dec. June 1983); children: Valerie Anne, Charles J. IV. BS in Commerce, DePaul U., 1957. Internal auditor Crane Co., Chgo., 1957-60; internal auditor Zenith Electronics Corp., Chgo., 1960-72, mgr. corp. payables, 1972-82, mgr. corp. risk, 1982—. Served with U.S. Army, 1958. Mem. Risk and Ins. Mgrs. Soc. Republican. Presbyterian. Office: Zenith Electronics Corp 1900 N Austin Ave Chicago IL 60639

KAMBER, VICTOR S., political consultant; b. Chgo., May 7, 1944; s. Samuel J. and Cordelia A. Kamber. BA, U. Ill., 1965; MA, U. N.Mex., 1966; JD, Am. U., 1969; LLM, George Washington U., 1971. mem. adv. bd. Dem. Media Ctr., Washington, Women Make Movies V, Washington; mem. Washington adv. bd. and communications dept. Am. U.; bd. dirs. D.C. Pub. Access Corp., Washington, Nat. Resource Ctr. adv. bd., Washington; mem. sr. adv. bd. Am. League Lobbyists, Washington. Adminstrv. asst. Congressman Seymour Halpern, Washington, 1969-72; asst. to pres. Bldg. & Constrn. Trades Dept., Washington, 1974-78; dir. AFL-CIO Labor Law Reform Task Force, Washington, 1978-80; pres., chief exec. officer The Kamber Group, Washington, 1980—. Served with U.S. Army, 1972-74. Mem. Internat. Assn. Polit. Cons., Am. Assn. Polit. Cons. (bd. dirs. 1987-88), Coalition of Labor Union Women, Indsl. Relations Research Assn., ACLU, NOW, Nat. Press Club, Nat. Dem. Club, Local 35 The Newspaper Guild, Phi Gamma Delta. Democrat. Presbyterian. Home: 129 11th St NE Washington DC 20002 Office: Kamber Group 1920 L St NW #700 Washington DC 20036

KAMER, JOEL VICTOR, insurance company executive, actuary; b. N.Y.C., Nov. 2, 1942; s. Archie Harry and Helen Lillian (Unick) K.; m. Jane Edith Casdin, Aug. 20, 1967; children—Wendy Lynn, Allen Samuel. B.S., CCNY, 1963; M.A., Pa. State U., 1964; M.S., Northeastern U., 1967. Actuarial asst. John Hancock Mut. Life Ins. Co., Boston, 1964-69, actuarial assoc., 1969-71, asst. controller, 1971-75, assoc. controller, 1975-70, gen. dir., 1979-82, 2d v.p., 1982-85, v.p., group ins. actuary 1985-87, sr. v.p., group ins. actuary, 1988—. dir. John Hancock Health Plans Inc., John Hancock Property and Casualty Co. Recipient Goldman Meml. award CCNY, 1963. Fellow Soc. Actuaries, mem. Am. Acad. Actuaries. Jewish. Office: John Hancock Mut Life Ins Co PO Box 111 Boston MA 02117

KAMERSCHEN, ROBERT JEROME, consumer products executive; b. Laurium, Mich., Feb. 16, 1936; s. Robert Raymond Kamerschen and Elsie D. (Barsanti) K. Barkell; m. Judith A. Campbell, July 26, 1958; children: Kathryn, Carol, Jean. B.S., Miami U., Oxford, Ohio, 1957, M.B.A., 1958. Exec. sales trainee Nat. Cash Register, Gary, Ind., 1958-59; mgmt. trainee Foote Cone & Belding, Chgo., 1959-60; dir. consumer mktg. Scott Paper Co., Phila., 1960-71; v.p. mktg. Revlon Inc., N.Y.C., 1971-73; sr. v.p. mktg. ops. Dunkin Donuts Inc., Randolph, Mass., 1973-77; pres., chief operating officer Chanel Inc. and Christian Dior Parfums Inc., N.Y.C., 1977-79; sr. v.p. Norton Simon Inc., N.Y.C., 1979-80; pres., chief exec. officer Max Factor & Co., Hollywood, Calif., 1979-83; exec. v.p., office of chmn. sector exec. Norton Simon Inc., 1980-84; pres., chief operating officer Mktg. Corp. of Am., 1984-87; pres., chief exec. officer RKO Six Flags Entertainment, Inc. div. Wesray Capital Corp., N.Y.C., 1987-88; chmn., chief exec. officer ADVO-System Inc., Windsor, Conn., 1988—; disting. practitioner/lectr. Coll. Bus. Adminstrn., U. Ga., 1978-80; guest lectr. various univs., trade assns.; bd. dirs. Electrolux Corp., Playboy Enterprises, Inc., Six Flags Corp. Mem. bus. adv. council, exec.-in-residence Miami U., 1979—; trustee, 1st vice chmn. Emerson Coll., 1984—. Mem. Beta Gamma Sigma, Delta Sigma Pi, Sigma Alpha Epsilon. Clubs: N.Y. Athletic, Metropolitan, Can. (N.Y.C.), Hartford. Home: 204 Parade Hill Rd New Canaan CT 06840 Office: ADVO-System Inc One Univac Ln Windsor CT 06095-0755

KAMINSKI, CHARLES ANTHONY, portfolio manager; b. Norwich, Conn.; m. Elizabeth Carbery Wick, Oct. 19, 1985; children: Catherine, Ian. BEE, MIT, 1970, MEE, 1972; MBA, Harvard U., 1974. Chartered fin. analyst. Assoc. John Barry and Assocs., Newport Beach, Calif., 1974-75; sales mgr. N.Am. Video, Acton, Mass., 1975-79; v.p. mktg. Creare Innovations, Hanover, N.H., 1979-82; pres. Commtech, Cambridge, Mass., 1982-84; group mktg. mgr. Instrumentation Lab. (Allied), Lexington, Mass., 1983-84; portfolio mgr. Baring Am. Asset Mgmt., Boston, 1984—. Mem. Inst. Chartered Fin. Analysts, Boston Security Analysts Soc., Bond Analysis Soc., Sigma Xi, Eta Kappa Nu, Tau Beta Pi. Home: 19 Thackeray Rd Wellesley Hills MA 02181 Office: Baring Am Asset Mgmt 77 Franklin St Boston MA 02110

KAMM, JACOB OSWALD, economist; b. Cleve., Nov. 29, 1918; s. Jacob and Minnie K. (Christensen) K.; m. Judith Steinbrenner, Apr. 24, 1965; children: Jacob Oswald II, Christian P. A.B. summa cum laude, Baldwin-Wallace Coll., 1940, LL.D., 1963; A.M., Brown U., 1942; Ph.D., Ohio State U., 1948; LL.D., Erskine Coll., 1971. Asst. econs. Brown U., 1942; instr. Ohio State U., 1945; instr. Baldwin-Wallace Coll., 1943-46, asst. prof., 1947-48, assoc. prof., 1948; prof., dir. Baldwin-Wallace Coll. (Sch. Commerce), 1948-53; econ. cons. to U.S. Post Office, 1951; exec. v.p. Cleve. Quarries Co., 1953-55, pres., 1955-67, chmn. bd., chief exec. officer, dir., 1967-88; chmn. bd., pres., chief exec. officer Electric Furnace Co., 1985—; pres., treas., dir. Am. Shipbldg. Co., 1967-69, pres., 1973-74; dir. Nordson Corp., McDonald Money Market Fund, McDonald Tax-Exempt Fund, Oatey Co., United Screw and Bolt Corp. MTD Products, Inc.; bd. dirs., chmn. Canefco Ltd. Author: Decentralization of Securities Exchanges, 1942, Economics of Investment, 1951, Making Profits in the Stock Market, 3d rev. edit, 1966, Investor's Handbook, 1954; contbg. author: An Introduction to Modern Economics, 1952, Essays On Business Finance, 1953; weekly columnist econ. affairs Cleve. Plain Dealer, 1964-68; contbg. editor: Webster's New World Dictionary of the American Language; contbr. articles to profl. jours. Exec. bd. Lorain County Met. Park Bd., 1961-66; hon. mem. Mental Health Com., 1964-69; mem. St. Luke's Hosp. Assn., 1967—; mem. adv. council Cleve. Mus. Natural History, 1967—; bd. regents State of Ohio, 1969-72; pub. mem. Underground Gas Storage Com. Ohio, 1964-73; chmn. Lorain County Republican Finance Com., 1968-70, mem. exec. com., 1969-70; mem. Ohio Rep. Finance Com., 1969-70; charter life mem. bd. counselors Erskine Coll., 1962—; life fellow Cleve. Zool. Soc., trustee, 1966-77; trustee Fairview Gen. Hosp., 1966-68; trustee Baldwin-Wallace Coll., 1953-78, mem. exec. and investment coms., 1956-78, chmn. investment com., 1974-78, hon. life trustee, 1979—; mem. pres.'s club Ohio State U.; mem. com. grad. edn. and research Brown U., 1978-80, Red Cross of Constantine. Recipient Alumni Merit award Baldwin-Wallace Coll., 1956, Wisdom award of honor, and election to Wisdom Hall of Fame, 1970, Pro Mundi Beneficio medal Acad. Humanities, Sao Paulo, Brazil, 1975, Winston Churchill Medal of Wisdom, 1988; named an Eminent Churchill fellow of the Wisdom Soc., 1988; inducted into the Hall of Excellence for the Ohio Found. of Ind. Colls., 1988. Mem. Am. Econs. Assn., Royal Econ. Soc., Am. Finance Assn., AAUP, Indsl. Assn. North Central Ohio (pres. 1960), Ohio Mfrs. Assn. (exec. com. 1970—, trustee, chmn. bd. trustees 1975-77), Early Settlers Assn. of Western Res. (life mem.), Newcomen Soc. N.Am., Assn. Ohio Commodores, Nat. Alumni Assn. Baldwin-Wallace Coll. (pres. 1961-63), John Baldwin Soc., Ohio Soc. N.Y., Phi Beta Kappa, Phi Alpha Kappa, Delta Phi Alpha, Delta Mu Delta, Beta Gamma Sigma. Methodist. Clubs: Brown University (N.Y.C.); Valley of Cleve. (treas. emeritus), Union (Cleve.); Duquesne (Pitts.); Clifton (Lakewood, Ohio). Lodges: Masons (33 degree), Shriners, Jesters. Home: PO Box 718 Sanibel FL 33957 Office: 435 W Wilson St Salem OH 44460

KAMMAN, ALAN BERTRAM, communications consulting company executive; b. Phila., Jan. 25, 1931; s. Daniel Lawrence and Sara Belle K.; m. Madeleine Marguerite Pin, Feb. 15, 1960; children: Alan Daniel, Neil Charles. BCE, Swarthmore Coll., 1952. With Bell Tel. Co. Pa., Phila., 1952-69; with Arthur D. Little, Inc., Cambridge, Mass., 1969-85, v.p. telecommunications scis., 1977-81, v.p. corp. staff, 1981-85; pres. Telematix Intern. Ltd., Boston, 1985-87, Gand A Unltd., 1985-88; nat. dir. telecommunications markets KPMG Peat Marwick, Lexington, Mass., 1987—; mem. adv. bd. grad. program telecommunications U. San Francisco, Intelevent, Europe, Telecom 75, Telecom 79, Telecom 83; world rep. KPMG Peat Marwick to Internat. Telecommunications Union, UN; bd. dirs. Modern Gourmet, Inc. Mem. adv. bd. Telecommunications mag., Telecommunications Abstracts; contbr. articles to jours. in field. Bd. dirs. U.S. Coun. World Communications Yr.; v.p. ops., bd. dirs. N. Country. Mem. Royal Geophys. Soc. (London), Appalachian Club (v.p. ops., bd. dirs.), World Link. Office: Nolan Norton & Co 1 Cranberry Hill Lexington MA 02173

KAMP, ALISSA DENISE, transportation company executive; b. Alexandria, Va., Dec. 9, 1965; d. Rainer Werner and Marsha Jane (Shugrue) K.; m. Dan Unruh, June 11, 1988. BA, Wichita State U., 1987. Sales clk. J.C. Penney Corp., Kansas City, Kans., 1981-83; advt. sales rep. Sunflower Newspaper Co., Wichita, Kans., 1984-85; intern F.H. Kaysing Co., Wichita, 1987; intern internat. dept. Coburger Sparkassen Bank, Coburg, Fed. Republic of Germany, 1987; br. mgr. Oxford Transp. Co., Wichita, 1987—; owner Global Trading Enterprises, Wichita, 1987—; regional mgr. Oxford Transpn. Co., Wichita, 1989—. Mem. Internat. Assn. Students in Econs. and Welfare (bd. advisors 1987—), World Trade Coun., Traffic Club Wichita, World Trade Ctr. Mid-Am. Republican. Methodist. Office: Oxford Transp Inc 6075 Air Cap Dr Ste 232 Wichita KS 67219

KAMP, THOMAS GEORGE, computer corporation executive; b. Detroit, July 22, 1925; s. James and Frances (Van Zanten) K.; m. Janette Louise Schermer, Sept. 2, 1949; children: Jennifer, Pamela, Thomas, Nancy. Student, Calvin Coll., 1942-43, Middlebury Coll., 1943-44, Columbia U., 1945; B.S. in Elec. Engring., U. Minn., 1949. Registered profl. engr., Minn. With A.C. Spark Plug div. Gen. Motors Corp., Milw., 1949-52; with Lear Siegler, Inc., Grand Rapids, Mich., 1952-56, asst. chief prodn. engr., 1956-57; with Control Data Corp., Mpls., 1957-84, gen. mgr. peripheral equipment group, 1961-65, v.p. mfg., 1965-68, group v.p. peripheral products and computer mfg. group, 1968-69, sr. v.p., group exec. peripheral products, 1969-73; pres. Control Data Peripheral Products Co., Control Data Corp., Mpls., 1973-84; chief exec. officer, chmn. Centronics Data Computer Corp., Hudson, N.H., 1984—; chmn. Premeir Computer Corp., Mpls., Rodime, Inc., Glen Rothes, Scotland. Served to lt. (j.g.) USNR, 1943-46. Mem. Christian Reformed Ch. Club: Decathlon Athletic (Bloomington, Minn.) (bd. dirs.). Office: Premier Computer Corp 8200 Normandale Blvd Ste 424 Minneapolis MN 55437

KAMPFER, JOHN BRENNAN, data processing administrator; b. Albany, N.Y., May 10, 1939; s. Franklyn Frederick and Jeanne Marie (Fleming) K.; m. Joyce Elizabeth Boiser, Dec. 6, 1963; children: Valerie, Robert, Regina, Elizabeth. BS, U.S. Mil. Acad., 1961; MS in Computer Systems Mgmt., U.S. Naval Postgrad. Sch., 1969; MBA, U. South Fla., 1976. Commd. 2d lt. U.S. Army, 1961, advanced through ranks to lt. col., 1977, ret., 1981; mgr. personnel actions div. U.S. Army Vietnam AG Office, Long Binh, Republic of Vietnam, 1971-72; staff officer data processing U.S. Readiness Command, Tampa, Fla., 1972-76; mgr. automation mgmt. 25th Data Processing Unit, Heidelberg, Fed. Republic Germany, 1977-80; mgr. data processing Rapid Devel. Joint Task Force, Tampa, 1980-81; with Bank of Hawaii, Honolulu, 1981—, mgr. facilities and data security data processing div., 1987—. Elected mem. Wahiawa Neighborhood Bd., Hawaii, 1985—; mem. cen. com. Dem. Party of Hawaii, 1986—, treas. 1988—; mem. adv. com. Hawaii State Elections, 1987—; sch. bd. Our Lady Sorrows Cath. Sch., Wahiawa, Hawaii, 1988—. Decorated Bronze Star. Mem. Assn. Computing Machinery, Data Processing Mgmt. Assn. Honolulu (pres. 1986, Outstanding Service award 1987). Roman Catholic. Lodge: Lions (past dir., v.p., pres.). Office: Bank of Hawaii 800 Nunanu Ave Honolulu HI 96817

KAMPMEIER, DONALD GEORGE, livestock association executive; b. Morris, Minn., Feb. 22, 1944; s. Walter Emil and Loretta Helen (Fritsch) K.; m. Barbara Elaine Murphy, Sept. 3, 1966; children: Jeffrey Jon, Kevin Dean, David James. BA, U. Minn., 1966. Produce broker C.H. Robinson Co., Des Moines, 1966-68; field rep. Cen. Livestock Assn., Inc., South St. Paul, Minn., 1968-75; dir. pub. rels. Cen. Livestock Assn., Inc., South St. Paul, 1975-76, v.p. ops., 1976-83, v.p. mem. services, 1983-85, pres., gen. mgr., 1985—. Webelo leader Boy Scouts Am., Inver Grove, Minn., 1976-82; coach Little League, Inver Grove, 1987-88; del. Senate 52B Republican Conv., Inver Grove, 1980-84; adv. com. U. Minn., Waseca, 1980-88; pres. Livestock Market Inst., South St. Paul, 1978-80; trustee Am. Inst. Cooperation, Washington, 1984-86. Named Hon. State FFA Farmer Future Farmers Assn., 1983. Mem. Nat. Cattlemen's Assn., Nat. Feeder Pig Mktg. Assn., K.C. (3rd degree). Republican. Roman Catholic. Office: Cen Livestock Assn Inc PO Box 419 South Saint Paul MN 55075

KAMPOURIS, EMMANUEL ANDREW, corporate executive; b. Alexandria, Egypt, Dec. 14, 1934; came to U.S., 1979; s. Andrew George and Euridice Anne (Caralli) K.; m. Myrto Stellatos, July 4, 1959; children—Andrew, Alexander. O and A Level, King's Sch., Burton, Somerset, U.K., 1953; M.A. in Law, Oxford U., 1957; cert. in ceramic tech., North Staffordshire Coll. of Tech., U.K., 1962. Plant mgr., dir. "KEREM", Athens, Greece, 1962-64; dir. "HELLENIT", Athens, Greece, 1962-65; mng. dir. Ideal Standard, Athens, 1966-79; v.p., group exec. internat. and export Am. Standard Inc., New Brunswick, N.J., 1979-84; sr. v.p. bldg. products Am. Standard Inc., New Brunswick, 1984-89, pres., chief exec. officer, 1989—; dir. Ideal Refractories SAI, Athens, Ideal Standard Mexico, Am. Standard Sanitaryware (Thailand) Ltd., INCESA, San Jose, Costa Rica. Bd. dirs. Greek Mgmt. Assn., Athens, 1975-77, Fedn. of Greek Industries, Athens. Mem. Young Presidents Orgn., Chief Execs. Orgn., Econ. Club of N.Y., Oxford Union, Oxford Law Soc., Am. Hellenic C. of C. (gen. sec. 1975-79). Greek Orthodox. Clubs: Spring Brook Country (Morristown, N.J.); Quogue Field, Quogue Beach (L.I., N.Y.). Office: Am Standard Inc 1 Centennial Pla Piscataway NJ 08855-8820 also: Am Standard Inc 40 W 40th St New York NY 10018

KAMPSCHROEDER, KATHY PEARCE, security company executive, polygraph examiner; b. Las Cruces, N.Mex., June 26, 1953; d. Guy Edward and Elizabeth Katherine (Billington) P.; m. John Charles Kampschroeder, Jan. 3, 1974 (div. June 1988); 1 child, Gretchen Virginia. BS, Tex. Wesleyan U., 1975. Cert. tchr., Tex. Tchr. Kennedale (Tex.) Ind. Sch. Dist., 1976-80; polygraph examiner Macho & Assocs., Dallas, 1982-83; pres. Tex. Indsl. Security, Ft. Worth, 1983—; bd. dirs. United Security Assocs. Ins. Co., Grand Oayman, W.I. Mem. Am. Soc. Indsl. Security, Am. Polygraph Assn., Tex. Assn. Polygraph Examiners. Democrat. Methodist. Office: Tex Indsl Security 1 Summit Ave Ste 106 Fort Worth TX 76102

KAMUDA, CAROLYN ANNE, real estate company executive; b. Hanover, N.H., Apr. 20, 1955; d. Edward Albert and Theodore Vieno (Moiseo) K. BS in Chemistry and Biology, Keene State Coll., 1977; postgrad., Northeastern U., 1981-82, Boston U., 1985, Antioch New Eng. Grad. Sch., 1985. Lic. real estate broker, Mass. Saleswoman Century 21-Gateway Assocs., Dover, N.H., 1984, Century 21-Jennings Agy., Keene, N.H., 1985, Century 21-Westward Home, North Grafton, Mass., 1986; news dir. Sta. WGAW, Gardner, Mass., 1987; owner, prin. Kamuda Real Estate, Gardner, 1987—, Surroundings Custom Framing Gallery, Gardner, 1987—. Sec. Mass. Arts Lottery Coun., Gardner, 1987-88. Mem. Nat. Assn. Realtors, Mass. Assn. Realtors, No. Worcester County Bd. Realtors, Greater Gardner Artists Assn. (founder, bd. dirs. 1988, pres. 1988), Franklin-Hampshire County Bd. Realtors. Home: 61 W Broadway Apt 305 Gardner MA 01440 Office: Kamuda Real Estate 16 Main St Gardner MA 01440

KAN, KON CHEONG, architect; b. Singapore, Apr. 15, 1954; s. Kan Yew and Chew Sui Fong. BArch, U. Singapore, 1980. Registered architect, Singapore. Architect Housing and Devel. Bd., Singapore, 1980-81; sr. architect Ong Chin Bee Architects, Singapore, 1981-86; prin. architect KC Kan and Assocs. Architects, Singapore, 1986—. Contbr. monthly articles on archtl. design and geomancy. Mem. Singapore Inst. Architects (corporate, com. mem. 1985-88), Royal Australian Inst. Architects (assoc.), Malaysia Inst. Architects (acad.), Singapore Inst. Mgmt., Nat. U. Singapore Soc. Home: Block 27 Telok Blangah Way, 02-1014, Singapore 0409, Singapore Office: KC Kan & Assocs Architects, 585 N Bridge Rd, 10-11 Blanco Ct, Singapore 0718, Singapore

KAN, PAUL MAN-LOK, computer company executive; b. Canton, China, Feb. 12, 1947; came to Hong Kong, 1947; s. Joseph and Winnie (Mok) K.; m. Maria Chan; children—Katherine, Joanne. M.B.A., Chinese U. of Hong Kong. Cert. data processing Programmer, Govt. Hong Kong, 1967-70; systems analyst Swire Group, Hong Kong, 1970-72; sr. systems analyst, Asiadata, Hong Kong, 1972-74, cons., 1974-76, sr. cons., 1976-78, mktg. mgr., 1978-85, gen. mgr., 1985-87; computer programmer compere TVB (HK) Ltd., Hong Kong, 1983, pres. Champion Group, Champion Techs. Ltd., Chinese Computers Ltd., Chinese Data Processing Co., Ltd., Chinese Paging Co., Ltd., Macintosh Computer Co., Ltd., Lisa Computer Co., Ltd., bd. dirs. Y. S. Kan & Co., Good Time Pub. Ltd., Jockey Daily News, Inside Racing News, Showa Info. Co. (Hong Kong) Ltd., Chinese Paging Co. Ltd., Kantone Paging Co. Ltd., KTT Group, 1988—. Founding chmn. MBA (Chinese U.) Assn., Hong Kong, 1978. Fellow Inst. Data Processing; mem. Brit. Computer Soc., Inst. Mgmt. Services; assoc. Chartered Inst. Transport, Inst. Bankers. Clubs: Royal HK Jockey, Royal HK Golf (Hong Kong). Contbr. articles to profl. jours. Home: PO Box 20003, Hong Kong Hong Kong Office: Champion Group Gloucester, 1 Ning Fu St 9th and 10th Fls, Hong Kong Hong Kong

KANARKOWSKI, EDWARD JOSEPH, advertising/public relations executive; b. Jersey City, May 5, 1947; s. Joseph Anthony and Lillian Dorothy (Pietrowicz) K.; BA, St. Peter Coll., 1969; m. Carol Ann Miller, Sept. 14, 1969; children—Edward, Kelly, Paul, Karen, Kevin. Grad. U.S. Army Command and Gen. Staff Coll., Ft. Leavenworth, Kans., 1985. Corp. communications cons., N.J., 1973-75; staff writer Daily and Sunday Register, Shrewsbury, N.J., 1975-77; with ADP, Roseland, N.J., 1977—, dir. corp. communications, 1983-88, v.p. corp. communication, 1988—; adj. vis. prof. communications St. Peter's Coll., 1985—; corp. career adv. grad. sch. bus. Rutgers U., N.J. With U.S. Army, 1969-73, to maj. N.G., 1978-84; maj. USAR, 1984—. Decorated Army Commendation medal (3); named Hon. Ky. Col. Commonwealth of Ky., 1988. Mem. Internat. Assn. Bus. Communicators, Meeting Planners Internat., 3d U.S. Inf. Div. Assn., N.J. Mil. Acad. (assoc.). Roman Catholic. Home: 132 Yellowbank Rd Toms River NJ 08753 Office: One ADP Blvd Roseland NJ 07068

KANE, ALICE THERESA, lawyer; b. N.Y.C., Jan. 16, 1948. AB, Manhattanville Coll., 1969; JD, NYU, 1972; grad., Harvard U. Sch. Bus. Program Mgmt. Devel., 1985. Bar: N.Y. 1973, U.S. Dist. Ct. (so. dist.) N.Y. 1974. Atty. N.Y. Life Ins. Co., N.Y.C., 1972-83, v.p., assoc. gen. counsel, 1983-85, v.p. dept. personnel, 1985, sr. v.p., gen. counsel, 1986—. Mem. ABA (chmn. employee benefits com., tort and ins. practice sect. 1984-85, mem. corp., banking and bus. law sects., tort and ins. practice sects.), Assn. of Life Ins. Counsel. Office: NY Life Ins Co 51 Madison Ave New York NY 10010

KANE, E(DWARD) LEONARD, electronics company executive; b. Danvers, Mass., Sept. 23, 1929; s. Edward Benedict and Rachael Mary (Lyons) K.; m. Anne Tracy Ronan, Apr. 26, 1958; children: James Ronan, Tracy Anne, Edward Leonard, Rosamond Marie, Thomas Henry, Matthew Noel. B.S. in Bus. Adminstrn., Boston Coll., 1951; J.D., Harvard U., 1954. Bar: Mass. 1954, U.S. Supreme Ct. 1970. With Raytheon Co., Lexington, Mass., 1957—, atty., 1957-63, dir. labor relations, 1963-75, v.p. indsl. relations, 1975-88, v.p. human resources, 1988—; dir. Assoc. Industries Mass., vice chmn. 1986—. Trustee Mass. Taxpayers Assn., 1978—; dir. Better Bus. Bur. Mass., 1976—, Mass. Indsl. Devel. and Employment Com., 1984—; bd. dirs. Greater Boston YMCA, 1976—, vice chmn., 1982-87; corporator Waltham Hosp., 1977—, trustee, 1977-85; trustee New Eng. Aquarium, 1984—. Served as agt. CIC U.S. Army, 1955-57. Knight Comdr. Order of the Holy Sepulchre; recipient Cardinal Cushing award for excellence in labor relations, 1971. Mem. ABA, Boston Bar Assn., Aerospace Industries Assn. (human resources council), Indsl. Relations Research Assn., Roman Catholic. Clubs: Annisquam Yacht; Harvard (Boston). Office: Raytheon Co 141 Spring St Lexington MA 02173

KANE, JACK ALLISON, physician, county administrator; b. Meadville, Pa., Feb. 28, 1921; s. Thomas Emery and Mildred (McMahon) K.; m. Virginia Joanne Casque, Sept. 28, 1946; children: Jeffrey, Marsha, Sharman, Cheryl. BS, Allegheny Coll., Meadville, Pa., 1943; MD, Case Western Res. U., 1949. Diplomate Am. Bd. Preventive Medicine. Intern U.S. Naval Hosp., 1949-50; fellow Sch. of Pub. Health U. Mich., 1950-51; med. dir. Cen. Foundry div. GM, Defiance, Ohio, 1954—, Defiance County Health Dept., 1975—; pres. J. Kane MD, Inc., Defiance, 1977—; pres. Defiance County Bd. Health, 1962-82, Defiance County Lung Assn., 1968-78. Lt. USNR, 1952-54. Fellow Am. Coll. Occupational Medicine; mem. AMA, Ohio State Med. Assn., Ohio Thoracic Soc. Republican. Home: PO Box 201 Defiance OH 43512 Office: GM Cen Foundry Div PO Box 70 Defiance OH 43512

KANE, JAMES ROBERT, financial systems analyst; b. Pitts., Mar. 22, 1959; s. John William Sr. and Helen Mary (Neimeier) K. AS, Allegheny County Community Coll., 1979; BBA, Robert Morris Coll., 1981. CPA, Tex. Staff acct. UCCEL Corp., Dallas, 1982-83, fin. reports analyst, 1983-85, fin. systems analyst, 1985-86, fin. reporting, analysis supr., 1986; acct. Zoecon Corp., Dallas, 1986, sr. acct., 1987—; cons. in field. Recipient Achievement award UCCEL Corp., 1985. Mem. Am. Inst. CPA's, Tex. Soc. CPA's. Republican. Methodist. Club: Pres.'s. Home: 9812 N MacArthur #601 Irving TX 75063 Office: Zoecon Corp 12005 Ford Rd #800 Dallas TX 75234

KANE, JOSEPH CHARLES, management consultant; b. Jackson, Wyo., July 9, 1935; s. Maxwell J. and Ethel M. (Read) K.; A.B., Rutgers U., 1957; M.B.A., U. Pa., 1963; Ph.D., Harvard U., 1974; m. Janet Allis, Aug. 28, 1982. With Gen. Motors Corp., Detroit, 1957-61; cons. McKinsey & Co., Phila., 1961-63; prin. Joseph Kane Assocs., N.Y.C., 1963-70; cons. Cambridge Consulting Group, Lexington, Mass., 1970—, prin., 1970—; pres. CMA Products, Stoneham, Mass., 1982—, High Tech Leasing Corp., N.Y.C., 1982—; pres. Charles River Advisors, 1988; lectr. Purdue U., SUNY. Mem. Am. Mgmt. Assn., Nat. Assn. Mgmt. Consultants. Author: To Merge? Why, Why Not, 1972; Small Business: Characteristics of the Successful Entrepreneur, 1982; The Negotiation Process in the Successful Merger Buyout, 1982. Home: 56 Ledgeways Wellesley Hills MA 02181 Office: Cambridge Cons Group 33 Bedford St Ste 12 Lexington MA 02173

KANE, ROBERT JOSEPH, floracultural company executive; b. Centralia, Wash., July 26, 1929; s. McKinley and Josephine Marie (Thompson) K.; m. Sally Jean Schilling, Aug. 24, 1957; children: Barbara Jo, Michael M. BBA, U. Oreg., 1950; AMP, Harvard U., 1971. CPA, Oreg. Sr. acct. Goldrainer Carmichael & Swanson, CPA's, Portland, Oreg., 1950-58; div. controller RTE Corp., Portland, 1958-61; sr. v.p. Omark Ind., Inc., Portland, 1961-86; fin. cons. Grayco Resources, Inc., Portland, 1986—; chmn. bd. dirs. Melridge Inc., Aurora, Oreg.; bd. dirs. Howard Cooper Corp., Portland, Hydroelectric Devel., Inc., Noninvasive Tech. Inc. Mem. Oreg. Bus. Coun., 1985; mem. adv. bd. dept. accts. U. Oreg., 1983. 1st lt. USAF, 1953-55. Mem. Fin. Execs. Inst., Oreg. Soc. CPA's, AICPA, Waverley Country Club, Univ. Club. Republican. Office: Grayco Resources Inc 5331 SW Macadam Ave Portland OR 97201

KANE, SAM, meat company executive; b. Spisske Podhradie, Czechoslovakia, June 23, 1919; s. Leopold and Bertha (Narcisenfeld) Kannengiesser; grad. Rabbinical Coll. Galanta, 1939; m. Aranka Feldbrand, Jan. 15, 1946; children—Jerry, Harold Ira, Esther Barbara. Came to U.S., 1948, naturalized, 1953. Pres., Sam Kane Wholesale Meat, Inc., Corpus Christi, Tex., 1956—, Sam Kane Meat, Inc., Corpus Christi, 1956—, Sam Kane Packing Co., Corpus Christi, 1962—, Kane Enterprises, Inc., Corpus Christi, 1956—; pres., chmn. bd. Sam Kane Beef Processors, Inc., 1975—; dir. First City Bank Corpus Christi. Pres., Jewish Welfare Appeal, 1962—; pres. Combined Jewish Appeal, 1968, chmn. bd., 1962-64; mem. nat. cabinet United Jewish Appeal; bd. dirs. Tex. Council on Econ. Edn. mem. Gov. Tex. 2000 Commn.; Recipient award chmn. bd. edn. B'nai Israel Synagogue, 1965; Israel Service award, 1966; Koach award State of Israel, 1976; Prime Minister of Israel Peace Medal, 1980; Brotherhood award Corpus Christi chpt. NCCJ, 1984, Torch of Liberty award Anti Defamation League, 1984; named Outstanding Jewish Citizen of Corpus Christi, 1969. Mem. Tex. Council on Econ. Edn. (bd. dirs.), Tex. Taxpayers Assn. Jewish (pres. synagogue 1964-65; Mem. Tex. Taxpayers Assn. Lodge: B'nai B'rith. Home: 27 Hewit Dr Corpus Christi TX 78404 Office: 9001 Leopard St Corpus Christi TX 78409

KANE, STANLEY BRUCE, food products executive; b. N.Y.C., June 5, 1920; s. Jacob and Anna (Epstein) K.; m. Janet Marilyn Haas, May 23, 1948; children: Katherine, Betsy, Priscilla. Student, NYU, 1938-39. With Kane-Miller Corp., N.Y.C., 1938—, chmn. bd., 1959-77, pres., chief exec. officer, 1977—, also bd. dirs. Served with USAAF, 1942-45. Home: 741 Hideaway Bay Dr Longboat Key FL 33548 Office: Kane-Miller Corp 555 White Plains Rd Tarrytown NY 10591

KANER, HARVEY SHELDON, corporate lawyer, executive; b. June 26, 1930; s. Rueben and Lillian Kaner; m. Caren Lee Gross, June 5, 1960; children—Amy B., Daniel E., Jason M., Joshua A. B.B.A., U. Minn., 1952, LL.B., 1955. Bar: Minn. Sole practice Mpls., 1956-58; asst. corp. counsel Farmers Union GTA, St. Paul, 1958-59, corp. counsel, 1959-77, v.p. law, 1977-82, sr. v.p., corp. counsel, 1982—; past sec. St. Louis Grain Corp.; lectr. extension program U. Wis., Madison; past dir. Farmers Export Co.; trustee Corp. Pension Funds. Author pubsl. Products Liability, 1977. Served with USNG, 1947-49. Mem. ABA, Minn. State Bar Assn., Hennepin County Bar Assn., Nat. Council Farmer Coops. (mem. legal, tax and acctg. com.). Jewish. Home: PO Box 718 Hudson WI 54016 Office: Harvest States Coops 1667 N Snelling Ave Saint Paul MN 55164

KANE-VANNI, PATRICIA RUTH, lawyer, consultant; b. Phila., Jan. 12, 1954; d. Joseph James and Ruth Marina (Rameriz) Kane; m. Francis William Vanni; Feb. 14, 1980; 1 child, Christian Michael. AB, Chestnut Hill Coll., 1975; JD, Temple U., 1985. Bar: Pa. 1985, U.S. Ct. Appeals (3d cir.) 1988. Free-lance art illustrator Phila., 1972-80; secondary edn. instr. Archdiocese of Phila., 1980-83; contract analyst CIGNA Corp., Phila., 1983-84; jud. aide Phila. Ct. of Common Pleas, 1984; assoc. atty. Anderson and Dougherty, Wayne, Pa., 1985-86; atty. cons. Bell Telephone Co. of Pa., 1986-87; assoc. corp. counsel Independence Blue Cross, 1987—; cons. Coll. Consortium on Drug and Alcohol Abuse, Chester, Pa., 1986—. Contbr. articles and illustrations to profl. mags. Committeewoman Dem. Party, Lower Merion, Pa., 1983-87; judge Delaware Valley Sci. Fairs, Phila., 1986, 87. Recipient Legion of Honor award Chapel of the Four Chaplins, 1983. Mem. ABA, Phila. Bar Assn., Pa. Bar Assn., Brehon Law Soc., Phila. Assn. Def. Counsel, Nat. Health Lawyers Assn., Phi Alpha Delta. Democrat. Roman Catholic. Home: 32 E Levering Mill Rd Bala Cynwyd PA 19004 Office: Independence Blue Cross Widner Bldg 133 Chestnut St Philadelphia PA 19107

KANGAS, CLARE MICHELE, accountant; b. Detroit, June 9, 1956; d. John Eugene and Irene Marjorie (Sanford) K. BS in Bus. magna cum laude, Wright State U., 1985. CPA, Ohio. Mgr. Deloitte Haskins & Sells, Dayton, Ohio, 1978—. Vol. Soc. Improvement Conditions Stry Animals, Dayton, 1986—; treas. Dayton March of Dimes Found., 1987—; bd. dirs. Big Bros.-Big Sisters Am., Dayton, 1988—. Mem. Nat. Assn. Accts., Toastmasters Internat., Dayton Microcomputer Assn. Office: Deloitte Haskins & Sells 2200 Kettering Tower Dayton OH 45423

KANIA, ARTHUR JOHN, lawyer; b. Moosic, Pa., Feb. 11, 1932; s. Stanley J. and Constance (Jerry) K.; m. Angela Volpe, Apr. 24, 1954; children: Arthur Sandra, Kenneth, Karen, James, Linda, Steven. B.S., U. Scranton, 1953; LL.B., Villanova U., 1956. Bar: Pa. bar 1956. Acct. Peat, Marwick, Mitchell & Co., Phila., 1954-55; ptnr. Davis, Marshall & Crumlish & Kania (now Kania, Lindner, Lasak & Feeney), Phila., 1961—; pres., dir. Greate Bay Hotel Corp. (and affiliated corps.), 1979-81; sec.-treas., dir. Piasecki Aircraft Corp., 202 Data Systems, Newton St. Rd. Assoc.; sec., dir. Indsl. Ops. Corp., Consol. Mortgage Co.; dir. Continental Bank; chmn. bd. dirs. U. Scranton. Mem. chmn.'s adv. com. dept. health adminstrn. Temple U.; mem. Phila. Com. of 70.; Bd. dirs. Piasecki Found.; former vice chmn. bd. trustees Villanova U.; former chmn. bd. trustees Hahnemann Med. Coll., 1978. Mem. Fed. Bar Assn., ABA, Pa. Bar Assn., Phila. Bar Assn. Clubs: Pine Valley (N.J.) Golf; Overbrook (Bryn Mawr, Pa.); Squires Golf (Phila.); Boca Raton (Fla.), Jupiter Hills Golf (Fla.). Home: 1030 Mount Pleasant Rd Bryn Mawr PA 19010 Office: Kania Linder Lasak & Feeney 2 Bala-Cynwyd Pla Bala-Cynwyd PA 19004

KANN, PETER ROBERT, journalist; b. N.Y.C., Dec. 13, 1942; s. Robert A. and Marie (Breuer) K.; m. Francesca Mayer, Apr. 12, 1969 (dec. July, 1983); m. Karen Elliott House, 1984; children: Hillary Francesca, Petra Elliott. B.A., Harvard U., 1964. With The Wall St. Jour., 1964—; journalist N.Y.C., 1964-67, Vietnam, 1967-68, Hong Kong, 1968-75; pub., editor Asian edit. 1976-79, assoc. pub., 1979-88; formerly asst. to chmn. and mem. exec. com., now exec. v.p. Dow Jones & Co., 1986—, pres. internat. and mag. groups, 1986—, also bd. dirs., 1987—; pub. Wall Street Journal, 1989—; dir. Group Expansion, Paris, 1987—; chmn. bd. Far Eastern Econ. Review, 1987—; elected mem. Pulitzer Prize Bd., 1987—. Recipient Pulitzer prize for internat. reporting, 1972. Club: Spee (Cambridge, Mass.). Office: Dow Jones & Co Inc 200 Liberty St New York NY 10281

KANNRY, SYBIL, psychotherapist, consultant, b. Tulsa, Okla., Oct. 1, 1931; d. Julius and Celia Bertha (Triger) Zeligson; m. Daniel Kannry, June 12, 1977; children by previous marriage: Jeffrey Alan Shames, Erica Leslie Shames, Jonathan Adam Shames. Student U. Colo., 1949-51; BA, U. Okla., 1953; MSW, NYU, 1974. Diplomate in Clin. Social Work; cert. clin. social worker, N.Y.; credentialled alcoholism counselor; cert. employee assistance profl. Tchr. piano, Tulsa, 1956-61; psychiatric social worker Essex County Hosp., Cedar Grove, N.J., 1974-75, Rockland Psychiat. Ctr., Spring Valley, N.Y., 1975, adult team supr., 1975-78, adult team supr., Haverstraw, N.Y., 1978, clinic supr., Orangeburg, N.Y., 1978-83, clinic dir., Yonkers, N.Y., 1983-84; founder, dir. Indsl. Counseling Assocs., South Nyack, N.Y., 1982-84, Ctr. for Corp. and Community Counseling, South Nyack, 1984—; founder, pres. Tulsa Assn. for Childbirth Edn., 1957-59. Fellow Soc. Clin. Social Work Psychotherapists; mem. Am. Assn. Marriage and Family Therapy (clin. mem.), N.Y. Milton H. Erickson Soc. for Psychotherapy and Hypnosis, Nat. Assn. Social Workers, Am. Orthopsychiat. Assn., Acad. Cert. Social Workers, Assn. Labor-Mgmt. Adminstrs. and Cons. on Alcholism, Soc. Clin. and Exptl. Hypnosis. Home and Office: 2 Clinton Ave South Nyack NY 10960

KANO, OSAMU, management executive; b. Obama, Japan, Feb. 5, 1937; came to U.S., 1968; s. Seijiro and Taka Kano; m. Yumiko Inoue, Dec. 12, 1964; children: Hajime, Akiko. Degree in Law, Kyoto (Japan) U., 1961. With Mitsubishi Oil Co. Ltd., Tokyo, 1961-68; program coordinator Japan Productivity Ctr., Washington, 1968-70; pres. Toyota Internat. Sales (U.S.A.) Inc., Tulsa, 1971-76; exec. v.p. Tel Am. Inc., Mountain View, Calif., 1977-84; dir. venture devel. Nikko Securities Co. Ltd., Tokyo, 1984-87; sr. v.p. LAM Rsch. Corp., Fremont, Calif., 1988—, also dir.; cons. in field. Home: 455 Old Oak Ct Los Altos CA 94022 Office: LAM Rsch Corp 4650 Cushing Pkwy Fremont CA 94538

KANTOR, EDWIN, investment company executive; b. Bklyn., May 24, 1932; s. William and Ann (Friedlander) K.; m. Madeline Liebstein, Sept. 10, 1955; children: Steven Lloyd, Jay Scott, Stacey Lynn. B.S. in Fin, N.Y. U., 1960. With L.F. Rothschild Co., N.Y.C., 1950-55; with Drexel Burnham Lambert & Co. Inc., N.Y.C., 1955—; now vice chmn., also dir. Drexel Burnham Lambert & Co. Inc.; v.p. Drexel Bond Fund; chmn. Drexel Burnham Lambert G.S.I. Served with AUS, 1952-54. Decorated Bronze star. Mem. Corp. Bond Traders of N.Y. Club: Bond of N.Y. Home: 16 Palatine Ct Oyster Bay Cove Syosset NY 11791 Office: Drexel Burnham Lambert Inc 60 Broad St New York NY 10004

KANTOR, GERALD L., retail company executive. Pres. Marshalls Inc., Wakefield, Mass. Office: Marshalls Inc 30 Harvard Mill Sq Box 1000-34 Wakefield MA 01880 *

KANTOR, NATHAN, communications company executive; b. N.Y.C., Aug. 22, 1942; s. Harry and Bertha (Levey) K.; m. Etta S. Rosenbach, June 13, 1965; children—Kenneth, Karen, Jennifer. B.S. in Engring., U.S. Mil. Acad., West Point, N.Y., 1965; M.S. in Bus. Mgmt., Fla. State U., 1968. Vice pres. adminstrn. MCI Telecommunications, 1972-77, v.p. ops., Washington, 1977-82, pres. MCI Internat., Rye Brook, N.Y., 1982-84, pres. N.E. div. MCI Telecommunications, Rye Brook, 1984—. Author: Contractual Aspects of Value Engineering, 1968. Mem. exec. council Westchester (N.Y.) Boy Scouts; chmn. March of Dimes, N.Y. Boy Scouts. Served to capt. USAF, 1965-69. Mem. Am. Mgmt. Assn. Home: 4 Pilgrim Trail Westport CT 06880 Office: MCI Telecommunications Corp 5 International Dr Rye Brook NY 10573 also: MCI Telecomunications Corp 1133 19th St NW Washington DC 20036

KANUCK, MARIE ELECTA, savings bank executive; b. Rutland, Vt., June 2, 1941; d. David and Electa Lucinda (Bass) MacDougall; children: Tammy Marie, Robin Dean; m. Robert Landes Kanuck, May 20, 1979; children: Rebecca Diane, Andrew Owen. Basic cert., No. New Eng. Sch. Banking, U. N.H., 1972. Br. mgr. Northfield (Vt.) Savs. Bank, Waterbury, 1976-80; v.p., sr. loan officer Northfield (Vt.) Savs. Bank, 1980-81, v.p., sr. ops. officer, 1981-82; v.p. consumer lending Home and City Savs. Bank, Albany, N.Y., 1983-86, v.p. residential lending, 1986—. Mem. Am. Inst. Bankers, Mortgage Bankers Assn., DAR, Soc. Mayflower Desc. Methodist. Lodge: Eastern Star. Office: Home and City Savs Bank PO Box 160 Latham NY 12110

KAPADIA, VINODCHANDRA SHIVDAS, machine tool company executive; b. Surat, Gujarat, India, Sept. 7, 1936; s. Shivdas and Lilavati S. (Chevli) K.; m. Pushpa M. Vakharia, Nov. 26, 1963; children: Dharmendra, Anish. Intermediate of Arts, Univ. Calcutta, India, 1957; B. Commerce, U. Rangoon, Burma, 1959. CPA, Calif., N.J., N.Y. Audit sr. Dalal & Shah, Bombay, India, 1959-64; controller Gokul Enterprise Pvt., Ltd., Bombay, 1965-69; audit mgr. Seidman & Seidman, N.Y.C., 1969-77, Edward Isaacs & Co., N.Y.C., 1977-78, Mitchell, Titus & Co., N.Y.C., 1978-79; v.p., controller Wotan Machine Tools, Fairfield, N.J., 1979—, also sec., treas. Fellow Inst. Chartered Accts. of India; mem. AICPA, Calif. Soc. CPAs. Home: 10 Cypress Ct Edison NJ 08820 Office: Wotan Machine Tools Inc 14-45 Madison Rd Fairfield NJ 07006

KAPATKIN, FRED, accountant, lawyer; b. Bklyn., Sept. 22, 1927; s. Herman and Pearl (Rosner) K.; m. Selma Levy; children: Keith B., Amy Sue. Student, Bklyn. Coll., 1943-45; BBA in Acctg., CCNY, N.Y.C., 1949; JD, Bklyn. Law Sch., 1953. Bar: N.Y. 1954; CPA, N.Y.C. Assoc. acct., legal cons. Bernstein & Freedman, N.Y.C., 1963-69, 1970-78; chief fin. officer, contr. W.A. Di Giacomo Assoc., N.Y.C., 1969-70, Lehr Assocs., N.Y.C., 1978-85; acct., legal cons. Fred Kapatkin, CPA, N.Y. Met. area, 1985—; adj. prof. acctg. N.Y. Inst. Tech., 1976-78. With USMC, 1945-47. Mem. Nat. Soc. Pub. Accts., YMHA, Am. Assn. Ret. Persons. Club: Wayne Merrick Tennis (Seaford, N.Y.). Home: 4024 Demont Rd Seaford NY 11783 Office: 226-A Post Ave Westbury NY 11590

KAPCHE, RONALD ANTHONY, personnel agency executive; b. Milw., Mar. 21, 1941; s. Fred George and Mary Ann (Janovec) K.; divorced; children: Jeffrey, Jennifer, Jessica. Student, U. Wis., 1958-60; BA in Psychology, Tex. Christian U., 1962. Jr. electric engr. Louis Allis Co., Milw., 1964-65; indsl. psychologist Motorola, Chgo., 1965-68; franchise operation mgr. Manpower Internat., Milw., 1968-73; v.p. sales Manpower, Inc. Houston, 1973-75, pres., chief exec. officer, 1975—; pres., chief exec. officer Manpower, Inc. San Antonio, Tex., 1980—; chief exec. officer Manpower Inc., Bryan/College Station, Tex., 1982—. Contbr. articles to profl. mags. including Employment Trends, Sales and Mktg. Mag. Del. Rep. Dist. Conv., Houston, 1986, Rep. State Conv., Dallas, 1986; candidate Tex. Ho. of Reps., 1986; mem. Harris County Pvt. Industry Council, 1988; dist. chmn. Boy Scouts Am., 1988—, bd. dirs. Sam Houston Coun.; bd. dirs. Harris County Pvt. Industry Coun., 1988—. Named Outstanding Texan, Tex. Dept. Labor and Standards, 1986, Hon. Citizen, City of Leon, Mexico, 1986. Mem. Am. Diabetes Assn., 1987—, Temporary Help Services Assn. Tex. (chmn. legis. com., 1985-87, chmn. ins. com. 1985-87, lobbyist Austin 1975—, bd. dirs. Houston 1976-79, pres. Houston 1982-84), Houston C. of C. (chmn. internat. program Houston 1985-87, mem. internat. steering com. Houston 1987, vice chmn. internat. bus. com. 1988—, fgn. trade del. Mexico and Argentina, 1986-87, mem. Leadership Houston 1984-85), Houston Livestock Show and Rodeo (vice chmn. steer auction com. 1988—, Outstanding Texan 1987). Roman Catholic. Clubs: Governors, Houstonian, West Houston Republican Men. Home: 15615 Memorial Dr #6 Houston TX 77079 Office: Manpower Inc 10000 Memorial Dr Ste 320 Houston TX 77024

KAPLAN, ARNOLD HARVEY, chemical company executive; b. Pitts., Nov. 28, 1939; m. Deanne G. Lesher, Dec. 23, 1961; children: Katherine Kendall, Pamela. BS in Commerce and Engring., Drexel U., 1962; MS in Indsl. Engring., Carnegie-Mellon U., 1964. With Air Products & Chems., Inc., Allentown, Pa., 1964—, corp. controller, 1976-82, v.p., corp. controller, 1982-88, v.p. energy and materials, 1988—. Mem. Fin. Execs. Inst., Bus. Forum of Phila. (bd. dirs.), Drexel U. Alumni Assn. (chmn. bd. govs. 1988—), Lehigh County Hist. Soc. (bd. dirs.). Home: 500 Orchid Circle Emmaus PA 18049 Office: Air Products & Chems Inc Allentown PA 18195

KAPLAN, BEN AUGUSTUS, financial services company executive; b. Toronto, Ont., Can., Nov. 15, 1952; came to U.S., 1974; m. Ann R. Ginsberg, Aug. 6, 1974; children: Jennifer, Andrew, Eric. BA, Fla. Internat. U., 1976; MBA, NYU, 1981. Budget analyst Consol. Edison Co., N.Y.C., 1979-81; fin. analyst Bector Dickinson Co., Paramus, N.J., 1981-85; fin. mgr. IMNET, Princeton, N.J., 1986; budget mgr. Merrill Lynch, N.Y.C., 1987—. Mem. NYU Fin. Club. Home: 83 Moore Ave Waldwick NJ 07463 Office: Merrill Lynch 225 Liberty St New York NY 10281

KAPLAN, BRADLEY S., financial analyst; b. Chgo., July 4, 1960; s. Irving and Gloria Lee (Hellerman) K.; m. Judith Ann Frei, Mar. 6, 1982; children: Patrick Marcus, Rachel Marie. BS in Acctg., Met. State Coll., 1982. CPA, Colo. Acct. Deloitte, Haskins & Sells, Denver, 1982-84; controller Internat. Tubular Supply, Englewood, Colo., 1984-85; mgr. fin. results U.S. West, Inc., Englewood, 1985—. Mem. Am. Inst. CPA's, Nat. Assn. Accts. (bd. dirs. 1987—), Colo. Soc. CPA's. Home: 4760 E Dartmouth Denver CO 80222 Office: US West 7800 E Orchard Englewood CO 80111

KAPLAN, CHARLES PAUL, real estate development association executive, educator, geographer, consultant; b. Chgo., Nov. 16, 1942; s. Charles Basil and Theresa (Shabatura) Fedun; m. Patricia Ann Barnett, Apr. 6, 1968 (div. July 1976); m. Carol Ann Willoughby, Sept. 1, 1979; children: Nicholas Paul Fedun, Nathan Charles Willoughby. BA, DePaul U., 1968; MA, U. Chgo., 1972, PhD, 1976. Cert. assn. exec. Product scheduling mgr. IBM, Chgo., 1960-68; rsch. assoc. U. Chgo., 1969-75, Mellon Found. fellow Ctr. for Urban Studies, 1970-75; prof. U. Houston, 1975-79; program mgr. U.S. Census Bur., Washington, 1979-81; dir. policy planning U.S. Synthetic Fuels Corp., Washington, 1981-84; exec. dir. Nat. Assn. Indsl. and Office Pks., San Antonio, 1984—; con. Indsl. Rels. Ctr., U. Chgo., 1970-74, Internat. Survey Rsch. Corp., Chgo., 1974-87; mem. faculty Grad. Sch. Social and Policy Scis., U. Tex., San Antonio, 1987—, cons. to dean Sch. Engring., 1987—; pres. CPK & Assocs., 1989—. Co-author: Land Use, Urban Form and Environmental Quality, 1974, The Social Burdens of Environmental Pollution, 1977, Census '80, 1980; contbr. over 100 articles on urban and regional change to profl. publs. Bd. dirs., mem. exec. com. Target '90: Goals for An Antonio, 1985—; mem. adv. bd. U. Tex. Sch. Architecture, 1988—; chmn. Pub. Affairs Council San Antonio, 1985—; chmn. Brooks AFB devel. opportunities com. San Antonio City Council, 1986-87, chmn. fin. and adminstrv. incentive to retain and rehabilitate landmark resources com., 1987—. With USN, 1966-68. Mem. Concord Club. Mem. Ukrainian Cath. Ch. Home: 8710 Sagebrush San Antonio TX 78217 Office: Nat Assn Indsl and Office Pks 1777 NE Loop 410 San Antonio TX 78217

KAPLAN, DANIEL I., service executive; b. Newark, Jan. 18, 1943; s. Edward and Blanche (Bernstein) K.; m. Doris Elaine Weiler, Apr. 15, 1967; children: Tammy G., Bradley E. BS, Rider Coll., 1965; MBA, Fairleigh Dickinson U., 1969. Buyer Foster Wheeler Corp., Livingston, N.J., 1966-69; purchasing agent Allied Chem. Corp., Morristown, N.J., 1969-73; gen. mgr. supply and distbn. New Eng. Petroleum Corp., N.Y.C., 1973-74, 78; pres. equipment rental The Hertz Corp., Park Ridge, N.J., 1978-82; exec. v.p. The Hertz Corp., 1988—; guest lectr. Am. Mgmt. Assn., N.Y.C., 1977-78, Am. Rental Assn.; mem. adv. bd. Round Table, editorial adv. bd. Rental mag.; mem. Rental Equipment Register, L.A., 1987—. Mem. Am. Rental Assn. (guest lectr. 1986—, achievement award 1986), N.J. Rental Assn. Office: Hertz Equipment Rental Corp 225 Brae Blvd Park Ridge NJ 07656-0713

KAPLAN, JEFFREY GENE, pediatrician, health services company executive; b. Bayonne, N.J., Apr. 20, 1943; s. Daniel D. and Toby Kaplan; m. Marie A. Levinson, June 26, 1966; children: Daniel, Mathew, Heather. MD, SUNY, Syracuse, 1969; MPS in Health Service Adminstrn., New Sch., Syracuse, 1985. Diplomate Am. Bd. Pediatrics. Intern then resident in pediatrics Children's Hosp., Phila., 1969-72; exec. v.p. med. affairs Health Svcs. Med. Corp., Syracuse, 1975—. Contbr. articles on productivity, health-risk appraisals, econometrics, mktg. and performance evaluation procedures to profl. publs. Lt. comdr. USPHS, 1972-75. Fellow Am. Acad. Pediatrics. Jewish. Home: 105 Edenberry Circle Syracuse NY 13224 Office: Health Svcs Med Corp 8278 Willet Pkwy Baldwinsville NY 13027

KAPLAN, JOCELYN RAE, financial planning firm executive; b. Lynbrook, N.Y., Apr. 23, 1952; d. Eugene S. and Adeline (Dembo) K. B.S., Northwestern U., 1975. Cert. fin. planner. Ins. agt. Fidelity Union Life Ins. Co., College Park, Md., 1976-77, Bankers Life Ins. Co., Rockville, Md., 1977-80; fin. planner Reutemann & Wagner, McLean, Va., 1980-82; fin. planning casewriter McLean Fin. Group, 1982-83; dir. fin. planning DeSanto Naftal Co., Vienna, Va., 1983-85; pres. Advisors Fin., Inc., Vienna, 1985—. Founding mem., treas. Congregation Bet Mishpachah, Washington, 1981, v.p., 1982, pres., 1983. Recipient Nat. Quality award Nat. Assn. Life Underwriters, 1978; Agt. of Yr. award Gen. Agt. and Mgrs. Assn., 1978. Mem. Internat. Assn. Fin. Planners, Inst. Cert. Fin. Planners, Registry of Fin. Planning Practitioners. Home: 5000 N 17th St Arlington VA 22207 Office: Advisors Fin Inc 8321 Old Courthouse Rd Ste 250 Vienna VA 22182

KAPLAN, JONATHAN HARRIS, management consultant, health care and infosystems specialist; b. N.Y.C., Apr. 29, 1957; s. Bernard and Arlene (Lavender) K.; m. Lorraine Caryl Weiss, Aug. 6, 1983. AB, Cornell U., 1979; MPH, U. Pitts., 1980. Cert. data processor, mgmt. cons., systems profl. Statistician Nat. Ctr. Health, Hyattsville, Md., 1980; assoc. installation dir. Shared Med. Systems, N.Y.C., 1981, installation dir., 1981-82; cons. Ernst & Whinney, N.Y.C., 1982-83, sr. cons., 1984, supr., 1985, mgr., 1985-86, sr. mgr., 1986—. Speaker in field. USPHS grantee for achievement in pub. health studies, Washington, 1979, 80, Westinghouse Sci. award, Shared Med. Systems Field Svc. award. Mem. Inst. Mgmt. Cons., IBM User Group, Healthcare Fin. Mgmt. Assn., Am. Hosp. Assn., N.Y. Acad. Sci., Inst. Cert. Computer Profls., Am. Coll. Healthcare Execs., Met. Healthcare Adminstrs. Assn., Cornell U. Alumni Assn., Pelham Country Club. Office: Ernst & Whinney 787 Seventh Ave New York NY 10019

KAPLAN, JUDITH HELENE, corporate professional; b. N.Y.C., July 20, 1938; d. Abraham and Ruth (Kiffel) Letich; m. Warren Kaplan, Dec. 31, 1958; children: Ronald Scott, Elissa Aynn. BA, Hunter Coll., 1955; postgrad., New Sch. for Social Rsch., 1955-56. Registered rep. Herzfeld & Stern, N.Y.C., 1963; agt. New York Life Ins. Co., N.Y.C., 1964-69; registered rep. Scheinman, Hochstin & Trotta, 1969-70; v.p. Alpha Capital Corp., N.Y.C., 1970-74; pres. Tipex, Inc., N.Y.C., 1966-84; v.p. Alpha Pub. Relations, N.Y.C., 1970-73; pres. Utopia Recreations Corp., 1971-73, Howard Beach Recreation Corp., 1972-73; chmn. bd. Alpha Exec. Planning Corp., 1970-72; field underwriter N.Y. Life Ins. Co., 1974-75; pres. Action Products Internat. Inc., 1978-87, chairperson, 1980—, Ronel Industries, Inc., 1982-84; participant White House Conf. on Small Bus., 1979. Author: Woman Suffrage, 1977; co-author: Space Patches-from Mercury to the Space Shuttle, 1986; contbg. editor: Stamp Show News, M & H Philatelic Report; creator, producer Women's History series of First Day Covers, 1976-81; contbr. articles to profl. jours. Active Wyo. adv. on woman suffrage; trustee Found. for Innovative Lifelong Edn. Inc., 1986-88. Named Outstanding Young Citizen Manhattan Jaycees, Small Bus. Person of Yr. State of Fla, 1986. Mem. NOW (ins. coord. nat. task force on taxes, v.p. N.Y. chpt., co-founder Ocala/Marion County chpt. 1982, bd. women's adv. coun. Ocala and Marian Counties 1986-88), Nat. Women's Polit. Caucus, Women Leaders Round Table, Nat. Assn. Life Underwriters, Assn. Stamp Dealers Am., Am. First Day Cover Soc. (life), Am. Philatelic Soc. (life), Bus. and Profl. Women, AAUW. Home: 577 Silver Course Circle Ocala FL 32672 Office: 344 Cypress Rd Ocala FL 32672

KAPLAN, KENNETH FRANKLIN, manufacturing company financial executive; b. N.Y.C., July 14, 1945; s. Harold and Jeannette (Rubin) K.; m. Judith Zacharias, Aug. 26, 1967; children: Teri, Joshua. BS in Math., U. Mich., 1967; MBA in Mgmt., UCLA, 1969. Fin. analyst Northrop Corp., L.A., 1969-71; sr. fin. analyst Dart Industries, L.A., 1971-74; asst. controller consumer products group West Bend (Wis) Co., 1974-76, dir. fin. planning and analysis, 1976-77; controller Graham Co., Milw., 1977-81, v.p. fin. and adminstr., 1981-85; treas. Gehl Co., West Bend, 1986—, corp. controller, 1985-87, v.p. fin., 1988—. Bd. dirs., chmn. fin. com. Kettle Moraine YMCA, West Bend, 1981—; bd. dirs., vice chmn. camping svcs. Milw. YMCA, 1985—; bd. dirs. West Bend C. of C., 1988—. Office: Gehl Co 143 Water St West Bend WI 53095

KAPLAN, MADELINE, law firm administrator; b. N.Y.C., June 20, 1944; d. Leo and Ethel (Finkelstein) Kahn; m. Theodore Norman Kaplan, Nov. 14, 1982. AS, Fashion Inst. Tech., N.Y.C., 1964; BA in English Lit. summa cum laude, CUNY, 1982, postgrad. Free-lance fashion illustrator N.Y.C., 1965-73; legal asst. Krause Hirsch & Gross, Esquires, N.Y.C., 1973-80; mgr. communications Stroock & Stroock & Lavan Esquires, N.Y.C., 1980-86; dir. adminstrn. Cooper Cohen Singer & Ecker Esquires, N.Y.C., 1986-87; mgr. adminstrv. svcs. Donovan Leisure Newton & Irvine Esquires, N.Y.C., 1987—. Contbr. articles to profl. jours. Founder, pres. Knolls chpt. of Women's Am. Orgn. Rehab. Through Tng., Riverdale, N.Y., 1979-82, v.p. edn., Manhattan region, 1982-83. Mem. Women Info. Processing, Assn. Legal Adminstrs., Am. Soc. Tng. and Devel., Adminstrv. Mgmt. Soc.

KAPLAN, NEAL, securities analyst; b. Boston, Dec. 2, 1951; s. Ralph and Elinor Mildred (Rubin) K.; m. Frances Olga Camera, Apr. 9, 1983. BA in History and Polit. Sci., U. Rochester, 1973; MS in Mgmt., MIT, 1976. Economist Sanford C. Bernstein & Co., Inc., N.Y.C., 1976-83; securities analyst Interstate Securities Corp., Charlotte, N.C., 1983—. Mem. N.C. Soc. Securities Analysts, Inst. Chartered Fin. Analysts, Audubon Soc. Democrat. Jewish. Clubs: Cedarwood Country, Sierra. Home: 10417 Rocking Chair Rd Matthews NC 28105 Office: Interstate Securities 2700 NCNB Pla Charlotte NC 28280

KAPLAN, RONALD V., financial executive; b. N.Y.C., Oct. 23, 1930; s. Morris and Ethel (Glass) K.; B.B.A., N.Y. U., 1951; M.B.A. in Accounting, Columbia, City U. N.Y., 1956; m. Bette Wise, June 27, 1954; children—Bruce, Jerry, Michael. Acct. Ernst & Whinney, C.P.A.s, N.Y.C., 1954-66; treas., chief fin. officer Gen. Hose & Coupling Co., Caldwell, N.J., 1966-68; v.p., treas., chief fin. officer Midland Capital Corp., N.Y.C., 1968-82; v.p., treas., chief fin. officer Belding Heminway Co. Inc., 1982—. C.P.A., N.Y. Chmn. bd. pres. Flight Servies, Inc., Ft. Lauderdale, Fla., 1977-81. Mem. Am. Inst. C.P.A.s, N.Y. State Soc. C.P.A.s, Beta Gamma Sigma. Club: K.P. Home: 21 Tammy Terr Wayne NJ 07470 Office: Belding Heminway Co Inc 1430 Broadway New York NY 10038

KAPLER, A. WILLIAM, III, consulting partner, manufacturing industries; b. Beach Haven, N.J., June 15, 1951; s. William Jr. and Isabel (Harms) K. BS in Elec. Engring., Princeton U., 1973. Analyst Arthur Andersen & Co., N.Y.C., 1973-75, sr. analyst, 1975-77, mgr., 1977-83, ptnr., 1983-87, ptnr., div. head, 1987—. Bd. dirs. MS Soc. N.Y.C., 1985—; treas. Princeton Class of 1977, 78—; treas. Princeton Alumni Assn., Essex County, 1987. Fellow Am. Prodn. and Inventory Control Soc. Clubs: Athletic, Princeton (N.Y.C.). Office: Arthur Andersen & Co 1345 Ave of the Americas New York NY 10105

KAPLOW, JONATHAN, controller; b. Englewood, N.J., Apr. 25, 1957; s. Milton and Riena (Leopold) K. BS in Labor Rels., Cornell U., 1979; MBA in Fin., U. Mich., 1984. Sr. financial analyst Am. Airlines, Dallas, 1984-87, contr. Capture div., 1987-88; contr. Iroquois Brands Ltd., Houston, 1988—. Mem. Toastmasters. Jewish. Office: Iroquois Brands Ltd 20405 FM 149 Ste 700 Houston TX 77070

KAPLOWITZ, ANDREW JOEL, investment banking and finance company executive; b. Vancouver, B.C., Can., May 10, 1964; came to U.S., 1976; s. Harold Jules Kaplowitz and Linda Shirley (Coane) Copeland. BA in Econs. and Fin., Rutgers U., 1985. Adminstrv. asst. Chase Manhattan Bank, N.Y.C., 1985-86, credit analyst, 1986-88; assoc., credit tng. profl. devel. program Chase Nat. Corp. Svcs., Inc., Atlanta, 1988—. Precint capt. Edward Kennedy Presdl. campaign, Bellingham, Wash., 1979-80; vol. Gary Hart Presdl. campaign, N.H., N.Y., N.J., Washington, 1983-84. Mem. Sigma Phi Epsilon. Jewish. Home: 1407 Harbor Pointe Pkwy Dunwoody GA 30350 Office: Chase Nat Corp Svcs 2 Ravinia Dr Ste 200 Atlanta GA 30346

KAPNICK, HARVEY E., JR., corporate executive; b. Palmyra, Mich., June 16, 1925; s. Harvey E. and Beatrice (Bancroft) K.; m. Jean Bradshaw, Apr. 5, 1947 (dec. 1962); m. Mary Redus Johnson, Aug. 5, 1963; children—David Johnson, Richard Bradshaw, Scott Bancroft. Student, James Miliken U., 1942-44; B.S., Cleary Coll., 1947, D.Sc. in Bus. Adminstrn. (hon.), 1971; postgrad., U. Mich., 1947-48; D.H.L. (hon.), DePauw U., 1979. C.P.A., Ill. Mem. staff, mgr. Arthur Andersen & Co. (C.P.A.'s), Chgo., 1948-56, partner, 1956-62; partner in charge Arthur Andersen & Co. (C.P.A.'s), Cleve., 1962-70; chmn., chief exec. Arthur Andersen & Co. (C.P.A.'s), 1970-79; dep. chmn. 1st Chgo. Corp., 1st Nat. Bank Chgo., 1979-80; pres. Kapnick Investment Co., 1980-84; chmn., pres., chief exec. officer Chgo. Pacific Corp., 1984—, also bd. dirs.; mem. Adv. Com. on Internat. Investment, Tech. and Devel., Adv. Com. for Trade Negotiations. Pres.'s Commn. on Pension Policy, Ill. Fiscal Commn., 1977; Adv. Com. Fed. Consol. Fin. Statements, 1976-78; Chmn. Ill. crusade Am. Cancer Soc., 1972; chmn. campaign Met. Crusade of Mercy, Chgo., 1976; trustee, Meninger Found., Mus. Sci. and Industry, Northwestern U.; bd. dirs. Orchestral Assn., Lyric Opera Chgo., council U. Chgo. Grad. Sch. Bus.; adv. council Stanford Grad. Sch. Bus. Served to 2d lt. USAAF, 1943-46. Mem. Assn. Ohio Commodores, U.S. C. of C. (govt. ops. and mgmt. com.; dir. 1973-76), Ill. C. of C. (dir. 1970-74), ASEAN-U.S. Bus. Council (exec. com. U.S. sect.), Iran-U.S. Bus. Council. Clubs: Met. (Washington); Mid-America (gov. 1971-76, treas. 1974-76), Chgo., Carlton, Univ., Execs., Indian Hill, Econ., Comml. (Chgo.), Naples Yacht, Hole-in-Wall, Port Royal. Home: 1425 Sheridan Rd Wilmette IL 60091 Office: Chgo Pacific Corp 200 S Michigan Ave Chicago IL 60604 *

KAPNICK, RICHARD BRADSHAW, lawyer; b. Chgo., Aug. 21, 1955; s. Harvey E. and Jean (Bradshaw) K.; m. Claudia Norris, Dec. 30, 1978; children: Sarah Bancroft, John Norris. BA with Distinction, Stanford U., 1977; M Philosophy in Internat. Relations, U. Oxford, 1980; JD with honors, U. Chgo., 1982. Bar: Ill. 1982, U.S. Dist. Ct. (no. dist.) Ill. 1982. Law clk. to justice Ill. Supreme Ct., Chgo., 1982-84; law clk. to Justice John Paul Stevens U.S. Supreme Ct., Washington, 1984-85; assoc. Sidley & Austin, Chgo., 1985-89, ptnr., 1989—. Mng. editor U. Chgo. Law Rev., 1981-82. Governing mem. Chgo. Symphony Orch., 1988—; mem. Marshall Scholarship Selection Com. Midwest Region, 1988-89. Marshall scholar, 1978-80. Mem. Order of Coif., Phi Beta Kappa. Republican. Episcopalian. Clubs: University, Econ. of Chgo. Home: 565 Willow Rd Winnetka IL 60093

KAPNICK, STEWART, investment company executive; b. N.Y.C., Mar. 10, 1956; s. Charles and Ruth Kapnick. BA with honors, George Washington U., 1978; MBA, Baruch Coll., 1986. Summer internship IBM Corp., White Plains, N.Y., 1977-78; acct. exec. L & C Pub. Inc., Los Angeles, 1979-82, 3M Corp., N.Y.C., 1982-83; pres., fin. ops. prin. Ulysses Capital, N.Y.C., 1983-86; lease fin. cons. SK Capital, N.Y.C., 1986—; regional sales mgr. Equity Placement IBL Corp., Stamford, Conn., 1986-87; assoc. dir. product devel. and lease fin. CIS Corp., N.Y.C., 1987-89; dir. equity fin. Info. Processing Systems Inc. subs. USF&G Financial Svcs. Corp., Hackensack, N.J., 1989—. Mem. Internat. Assn. Fin. Planners, Nat. Assn. Security Dealers, Internat. Platform Assn., Assn. Equipment Lessors, Computer Dealers and Lessors Assn., Community Leaders Am. Home: 336 West End Ave Ste 7E New York NY 10023 Office: Info Processing Systems Inc Continental Pla III 433 Hackensack Ave Hackensack NJ 07601

KAPOOR, ASHOK, management consultant; b. Lahore, Punjab, India, Nov. 21, 1940; came to U.S., 1960; s. Chaman Lal and Rano (Devi) K.; m. Catherine Donelda, Apr. 15, 1966; children: Sonya Catherine, Celina Elizabeth. BA, St. Stephen's Coll., Delhi, India, 1960; MBA, U. N.C., 1962, PhD, 1966. Prof. NYU, N.Y.C., 1966-80; founder, pres. Internat. Negotiation Inst., Princeton, N.J., 1980—; asst. prof. internat. mktg., bus. NYU, 1966-70, assoc. prof., 1970-73, prof., 1974-78; pres. Internat. Negotiation Inst., Inc., Princeton, N.J., 1978—. Author: International Business Negotiation, 1971; co-author: Multinational Enterprises, 1973, Strategy and Negotiation, 1975. Mem. World Leisure and Recreation Assn. (bd. dirs. Can. chpt.). Office: Internat Negotiation Inst 301 N Harrison St Bldg B Ste 347 Princeton NJ 08540

KAPP, ROGER W., lawyer, corporate executive; b. N.Y.C., Oct. 8, 1936; s. Julian S. and Sophie (Wolfe) K.; m. Marcia Mittleman, Dec. 25, 1970; 1 child, Roberta. BA, CUNY, 1958; JD, U. Mich., 1961. Bar: U.S. Dist. Ct. D.C. 1962, U.S. Dist. Ct. (so. dist.) N.Y. 1962, U.S. Ct. Appeals (D.C. cir.) 1962, U.S. Ct. Appeals (2d cir.) 1962, U.S. Supreme Ct. 1962, N.Y. 1965. Atty. SEC, Washington, 1961-65, Donovan, Leisure, Newton & Irvine, N.Y.C., 1965-88; sr. v.p., gen. counsel Am. Home Products Corp., N.Y.C., 1988—. Office: Am Home Products Corp 685 Third Ave New York NY 10017

KAPPES, PHILIP SPANGLER, lawyer; b. Detroit, Dec. 24, 1925; s. Philip Alexander and Wilma Fern (Spangler) K.; m. Glendora Galena Miles, Nov. 27, 1948; children: Susan Lea, Philip Miles, Mark William. BA cum laude, Butler U., 1945; JD, U. Mich., 1948. Bar: Ind. 1948, U.S. Supreme Ct. 1970. Pvt. practice Indpls., 1948; assoc. Armstrong and Gause, 1948-49, C. B. Dutton, 1950-51; ptnr. Dutton, Kappes & Overman, 1952-85, of counsel, 1983-85; ptnr. Lewis Kappes Fuller & Eads, Indpls., 1985—, Labeco Properties Creston Group, Indpls.; sec., dir. Lab. Equipment Co., Mooresville, Ind.; sec., dir. Labsonics, Inc.; dir. Premier Distbg. Co., Labthermics, Inc., Mid Am. Chem. Corp.; instr. bus. law Butler U., 1948-49, chmn. bd. govs., 1965-66. Bd. dirs. Crossroads Am. coun. Boy Scouts Am. (life), 1965—, v.p. fin., mem. exec. com then pres. 1977-79, chmn. trustees endowment fund; bd. dirs. Fairbanks Hosp., Indpls., 1986—, chmn. bd., 1988—; trustee Butler U., 1987—, Children's Mus., Indpls., 1969-88, pres. bd. trustees, 1984-85. Mem. Am. Judicature Soc., ABA (ho. of dels. 1970-71), Ind. Bar Assn. (ho. dels. 1959—, mem. chmn. pub. rels. exec. com. 1966-69, sec. 1973-74, bd. mgrs. 1975-77), Indpls. Bar Assn. (treas., 1st v.p. 1965, pres. 1970, bd. mgrs. 1968-71, 75-77), Indpls. Legal Aid Soc., Indpls. Jr. C. of C. (past 1st v.p., dir.), Butler U. Alumni Assn. (past pres.), Mich. Alumni Assn, Masons (33 degree, most wise master Indpls. chpt. Rose Croix 1982-84), Shriners, Meridian Hills Country Club, Lawyers Club, Gyro Club (pres. 1966), Mystic Tie Club (worshipful master 1975), Phi Delta Theta, Tau Kappa Alpha. Republican. Presbyterian (deacon, elder, past pres. bd. trustees). Home: 624 Somerset Dr Indianapolis IN 46260 Office: 1210 One American Sq Indianapolis IN 46282-0003

KAPPLER, ROGER HOMER, mechanical contracting executive, consultant; b. Tecumseh, Mich., Nov. 18, 1946; s. Paul Wallace and Margaret Claudine (Wheeler) K.; m. Dulce May Greene, Dec. 17, 1977; children: R. Paul D., Karl N.D., Lindsey Anne. BS, U. Mich., 1968, MS, 1978. Budget analyst Townsend and Bottum, Inc., Monroe, Mich., 1969-70, asst. controls mgr., 1970-71, procurement supr., 1971-75, dir. procurement, 1975-79, mgr. equipment div., 1979-82; pres. Lindendale Venture Devel., Inc., Ann Arbor, Mich., 1982-88; dir. fin. services Townsend and Bottum Capital Fund, Ann Arbor, 1986-87, v.p., 1987; pres., chief exec. officer C & H Piping, Inc., Romulus, Mich., 1988-89; pres. R.H. Kappler Assocs., Inc., Ann Arbor, 1989—; bd. dirs. chmn. Peterson, Williams & Bizer, Inc., Ann Arbor, Gt. Lakes Moving & Storage Co., Ann Arbor; cons. T & B Computing, Inc., Ann Arbor, 1988—, Kerr Constrn., Inc., N.J., 1988—. Editor Kappler Report newsletter, 1986-87. Mem. Mich. Tech. Council, 1982-86. Served with U.S. Army, 1968-69. Presbyterian. Home: 19163 Bethel Church Rd

Manchester MI 48158 Office: RH Kappler Assocs Inc 5025 Venture Dr Ann Arbor MI 48108

KAPSAR, ROBERT CHARLES, financial executive; b. Cleve., Sept. 27, 1952; s. Robert Francis and Joan Mercedes (Cook) K.; m. Nancy Lynn Buice, May 12, 1978; children: Rebecca Joann, Joanna Elizabeth. BS, N. Tex. State U., 1979. Owner Preferred Parking, Dallas, 1978-79; reg. v.p. A.L. Williams Corp., Atlanta, 1979—. Precinct chmn. Kaufman Co. Rep. Party, Tex., 1988. Home: Rte 3 PO Box 569 Kaufman TX 75142 Office: AL Williams Kapsar Region 402 WIH 30 #100 Garland TX 75142

KARAGOSIAN, FRED JACK, financial planner; b. Bronx, N.Y., Mar. 30, 1943; s. Souren Jack and Grace (Tatarian) K.; m. Jean Marie Lauro, Sept. 3, 1972; 1 child, Kimberly. MBA, Fairleigh Dickinson U., 1975. Cert. fin. planner, CPA, N.J. Pension acct. Irving Trust Co., N.Y.C., 1972-74; asst. contr. Trascott, Alyson, Craig, Inc., Teaneck, N.J., 1975-78; pub. acct., cons. various CPA and mgmt. consulting firms, 1978-79; mgr. acctg. Bijur Lubricating Corp., Oakland, N.J., 1979-80; contr. Precision Multiple Controls, Midland Park, N.J., 1980-84; prin. Fred J. Karagosian, Englewood Cliffs, N.J., 1984—; owner, pres. Karagosian Fin. Svcs., Englewood Cliffs, 1985—; broker, dealer Fin. Product Resources, Inc., Englewood Cliffs, 1988—; speaker various pub. seminars and classes. With U.S. Army, 1966-68. Named to Century Club, Anchor Nat. Fin. Services, 1987. Mem. Internat. Assn. Fin. Planners, Inst. Cert. Fin. Planners, Knights of Vartan. Office: Karagosian Fin Svcs Inc 550 Sylvan Ave Englewood Cliffs NJ 07632

KARALIS, JOHN PETER, computer company executive; b. Mpls., July 6, 1938; s. Peter John and Vivian (Deckas) K.; m. Mary Curtis, Sept. 7, 1963; children: Amy Curtis, Theodore Curtis. BA, U. Minn., 1960, JD, 1963. Bar: Minn. 1963, Mass. 1972, Ariz. 1983, N.Y. 1985, Pa. 1986. Pvt. practice Mpls., 1963-70; assoc. gen. counsel Honeywell Inc., Mpls., 1970-83, v.p., 1982-83; pvt. practice Phoenix, 1983-85; sr. v.p., gen. counsel Sperry Corp., N.Y.C., 1985-87; v.p., gen. counsel Apple Computer Inc., Cupertino, Calif., 1987—; mem. bd. advisors Ariz. State U. Ctr. for Study of Law, Sci. and Tech., Tempe, 1983—. Recipient Disting. Achievement award Ariz. State U., Tempe, 1985. Clubs: Metropolitan (N.Y.C.), Gainey Ranch Golf Club (Scottsdale, Ariz.). Office: Apple Computer Inc 20525 Mariana Ave Cupertino CA 95014

KARAPOSTOLES, DEMETRIOS ARISTIDES, civil engineer; b. Larissa, Greece, Mar. 2, 1936; s. Aristides Demetrios and Zoi-Lili Aristides (Papadimitriou) K.; m. Toula Haralambos Giagtzoglou, Oct. 24, 1976; children—Zoi-Lili, Aristides. Diploma Cathedral Sch. St. Paul, Garden City, N.Y. 1954, student pre-engring. Bethany Coll., W.Va., 1954-56; B.S. in Civil Engring. U. Mich., 1961; profl. degree in civil engring Nat. Tech. U., Athens, 1962. Registered engr. Cons. profl. civil engr., Thessaloniki, 1964-75; assoc. prof. civil engring. Larissa's Inst. Tech., 1975; asst. head hydraulics div. Ministry Pub. Works, Larissa, 1976—. Served to lt. C.E., Greek Army, 1962-64. Fellow ASCE; mem. Tech. Chamber of Greece. Greek Orthodox. Avocations: photography; short-wave radio.

KARATSU, OSAMU, large scale integration researcher; b. Tokyo, Apr. 25, 1947; s. Hajime and Sumako (Narumi) K. B.S., Tokyo U., 1970, M.S., 1972, Ph.D. in Physics, 1975. Researcher Nippon Telegraph and Telephone Pub. Corp., Musashino Labs., Tokyo, 1975-79, staff researcher, 1979-83; sr. staff researcher NTT Atsugi Labs., Atsugi, Japan, 1983-86; research group leader NTT LSI Labs, Atsugi, 1987—. Author: Introduction to Very Large Scale Integration Design, 1983; Microelectronics Series, 1985. Mem. Japan Soc. Applied Physics, Am. Phys. Soc., IEEE, Inst. Electronic and Communication Engrs. Japan, Inst. Elec. Engring. Japan. Avocations: playing and listening to classical music. Home: 5-19-2 Hiroo #501, Shibuyaku, Tokyo 150A, Japan Office: NTT LSI Labs 3-1 Morinsato, Wakamiya, Atsug-shi, Kanagawa 243-01, Japan

KARCH, ROBERT E., real estate company executive; b. Bklyn., May 30, 1933; s. Charles H. and Etta R. (Becker) K.; AB, Syracuse U., 1953, MBA, 1958; student in Russian, Army Lang. Sch., Monterey, Calif., 1953-54; m. Brenda Schechter, Sept. 7, 1958; children: Barry S., Karen D., Brian D. With Nationwide Beauty & Barber Supply Co., Syracuse, N.Y., 1956-87, pres., 1966-74, chmn., 1974-87, also dir.; sales mgr. Helen of Troy Corp., El Paso, Tex., 1974-76, v.p. sales and mktg., 1976-79, also dir.; v.p., dir. Bormex Constrn. Inc., 1980-81; pres. BKB Properties, 1978—; ptnr. BKB Ins. Agy., 1987—; instr. investment real estate Acad. Real Estate, 1984-88. Pres. Syracuse Hebrew Day Sch., 1972-73. Served with U.S. Army, 1953-56. Lic. real estate broker, Tex., N.Mex., Colo.; lic. comml. pilot. Mem. Beauty and Barber Supply Inst., Direct Mail/Mktg. Assn., Aircraft Owners and Pilots Assn., Real Estate Securities and Syndication Inst., El Paso Real Estate Investment Club (pres. 1985), Jewish War Vets., El Paso Aviation Assn., El Paso Bd. Realtors (comml. investment div., mem. Exchangers Club, Top Vol. Producer award 1984, 85, 86, Best Real Estate Exchange award 1986), El Paso Apt. Assn. Clubs: Coronado Country, Lancer's. Author: Data Processing for Beauty/Barber Dealers, 1968. Pub. Real Estate Investor's Newsletter, 1982—, Property Mgmt. Newsletter, 1985—. Home: 6016 Torrey Pines El Paso TX 79912 Office: BKB Properties Inc 10622-A Montwood Dr El Paso TX 79935

KARCHER, JOHN DRAKE, textile, apparel company executive; b. Washington, Sept. 10, 1939; s. Raymond Edward and Mary Frances (Drake) K.; B.B.A., Wake Forest U., 1961; M.B.A., Wharton Sch., U. Pa., 1964; m. Lois Allison Lynch, Apr. 3, 1965; children—Kimberly Price, John Drake, II, Christopher Brett. Exec. v.p., dir. Spectrum Textured Fibers, Inc., N.Y.C., 1971-72; pres. Wamsutta Decorative Fabrics, N.Y.C., 1972-77, Baxter/Kelly, Inc., N.Y.C., 1977-80; pres., dir. Scorpio Ventures, Inc., cons. and investment firm, Darien Conn., 1981-83; v.p. mktg. home fashions div. Dan River Inc., N.Y.C., 1983-84; pres., mktg. dir. Soc. Brand Industries, Inc., N.Y.C., 1985-87; chmn. bd., pres., chief exec. officer, dir. P.L. Industries, Inc., N.Y.C., 1987—. Co-chmn. Ox Ridge Sch. PTA, Darien, 1977-78; mem. bldg. fund drive Darian YMCA, 1977; head coach Darien Youth Hockey, 1977-79, Darien Little League, 1977-79, Darien Babe Ruth League, 1981-83; active fund raising Wake Forest U., New Canaan Country Sch. Named Darien Little League Coach of Yr., 1977. Presbyterian. Club: Wee Burn Country. Home: 2 Dew Ln Darien CT 06820 Office: PL Industries Inc 350 Fifth Ave New York NY 10118

KARCZMAR, MIECZYSLAW, economist; b. Lodz, Poland, Jan. 22, 1923; s. Henryk and Franciszka (Lubicz) K.; came to U.S., 1973; M.S. in Econs. Commerce, Acad. Commerce, Poznan, Poland, 1945-48; Ph.D. in Econ., Main Sch. Planning Statistics, Warsaw, Poland, 1949-51, 60; postgrad. banking seminar London Sch. Econs., 1958; m. Gabriela Bogucka, Dec. 22, 1947; children—Thomas, Peter. With Nat. Bank Poland, Warsaw, 1949-62, dep. dir. planning dept., 1955-58, dep. dir. internat. dept., 1958-62; dir. fin. dept. Polish Ministry Fgn. Trade, Warsaw, 1962-69, trade commr., comml. counsellor to Can., Montreal, 1969-73; sr. v.p., chief economist European Am. Bank & Trust Co., European Am. Banking Corp., N.Y.C., 1974-86; economic adviser Deutsche Bank, N.Y.C., 1986—; dir. Bank Handlowy, Warsaw, 1962-69; mem. supervisory bd. Warta—Ins. Reins. Co., Warsaw, 1962-69; lectr., asst. prof. Main Sch. Planning Statistics, Warsaw, 1951-68; lectr. vocat. courses in fin. planning and credit system, 1950-56. Author: (with W. Pruss) Credit in Trade, 1956; (with others) Accountant's Guidebook, 1956; (with others) Money and Credit, 1960; contbr. articles to profl. jours.; researcher money, credit theory, internat. monetary system, banking. Office: European Am Bank 10 Hanover Sq New York NY 10005

KARHOFF, MARJORIE PHILOMENA, accountant, consultant; b. Lima, Ohio, Dec. 21, 1948; d. Walter F. and Agnes M. (Maag) K. BS, U. Dayton, 1971; MS, Bowling Green State U., 1975. CPA, Ohio. Tchr. Sidney (Ohio) City Sch., 1972, Kalida (Ohio) Local Sch., 1972-75; high sch. tchr. Westerville (Ohio) Schs., 1975-77; probate acct. Porter, Wright, Columbus, Ohio, 1977-85; acctg. cons. Porter, Wright, Morris & Arthur, Columbus, 1986—. Mem. Columbus Mus. Art Soc., Friends of Columbus Zoo. Mem. Am. Inst. CPA's, Ohio Soc. CPA's, Pub. Acct. Soc. Ohio, Columbus Bar Assn. Club: Columbus Ski. Office: Porter Wright Morris & Arthur 41 S High St Columbus OH 43215

KARIS, JAMES MICHAEL, management consultant; b. Hammond, Ind., May 1, 1948; s. Peter J. and Virginia (Lukasik) K.; m. Joanne Rita Kukanza, June 6, 1975; children: Matthew, Timothy. BS in Indsl. Mgmt., Purdue U., 1970; MA in Econs., The Am. U., 1979. Officer Am. Fletcher Nat. Bank, Indpls., 1970-73; v.p. Lester B. Knight and Assoc., Inc., Chgo., 1973-81, Continental Bank, Chgo., 1981-82, Baxter Internat., Inc., Deerfield, Ill., 1982-87, The Heidrick Ptnrs., Inc., Chgo., 1987-88; v.p., ptnr. The Chgo. Tokyo Group, Inc., Deerfield, 1988—; dir. Chgo. Tokyo Group, Inc., Chgo., 1988—; owner, Heartland Mgmt. Corp., Chgo., 1987—. Mem. Japan Am. Soc., Union League Club (Chgo.). Republican.

KARL, JAMES LAWRENCE, II, lawyer; b. Stamford, Conn., June 9, 1956; s. Wayne Frederick Karl and Audrey (Newstad) Shaff. Student, Oxford U., 1976-77; BA in Econs., Washington Coll., Chestertown, Md., 1978; JD, Cornell U., 1983. Bar: Conn. 1983, N.Y. 1984, Fla. 1987. Assoc. Rogers and Wells, N.Y.C., 1982-85; assoc. Kelley, Drye and Warren, N.Y.C., 1985-87, Frost and Jacobs, Marco Island, Fla., 1987—; bd. dirs. Conn. Real Estate Corp., Stamford, Gulf View Realty Co., Naples, Fla. Atty. Young Republicans, 1983—. Mem. ABA, N.Y. Bar Assn., Conn. Bar Assn., Fla. Bar Assn., Collier Bar Assn., Internat. Real Estate Fedn. Roman Catholic. Lodge: Rotary. Office: Frost and Jacobs 985 N Collier Blvd Marco Island FL 33937

KARL, RONALD JOSEPH, engineer; b. Saginaw, Mich., Apr. 4, 1956; s. Harry Frederick and Mary Elizabeth (Knox) K.; m. Jody Lynn Rohrbacher, Apr. 28, 1979; children: Adam, Rachael, Michelle. BME, GM Inst., 1979; MS in Mgmt., MIT, 1984. Supr. mfg. Saginaw div. GMC, 1979; maintenance engr. GMC, Saginaw, 1979-82, sr. mfg. engr., 1984, asst. supt. mfg. engring., 1984—. Organizer Can.-Am. Games Com., Saginaw, 1982. GM fellow, 1984-86. Mem. IEEE. Roman Catholic. Office: GMC Saginaw Div 3900 Holland Saginaw MI 48601-9494

KARLSON, BEN EMIL, kitchen design company executive; b. Hedemora, Sweden, Aug. 27, 1934; came to U.S., 1954, naturalized, 1960; s. Emil W.J. and Ester Linnea (Hellman) Karlsson; student bus. mktg. Alexander Hamilton Inst., N.Y.C., 1967, Am. Inst. Kitchen Designers, 1972; m. Susan Jo Kaupert, Feb. 7, 1958; children—David, Kristine, Thomas. Salesman, Edward Hines Lumber Co., Chgo., 1954-63; v.p., gen. mgr. Lake Forest Lumber Co. (Ill.), 1963-67; pres. Karlson Home Center, Inc., Evanston, Ill., 1967—, Poggenpohl-Midwest/USA, Inc., Evanston, Atag USA Corp., Evanston; dir. tng. U.S. Poggenpohl, Herford, W. Ger., 1981-86 ; pres. Bank Lane Investors, Lake Forest, 1971-72; founder chmn. Evanston Home Show, 1973, 74; judge, Nat. Design Contest, 1974; showroom design cons., Ill., Poggenpohl Kitchens Germany; speaker in field; lectr. on kitchen bus. and design at univs. and convs. Mem. steering com. Covenant Meth. Ch., Evanston, 1968-69; bd. dirs. Evanston Family Counseling Service, 1973-75, Evanston United Community Services, 1974-75, mid-Am. chpt. No. region ARC, 1974; chmn. bus. div. Evanston United Fund, 1974, gen. campaign chmn., 1975. Recipient awards for community service. Cert. kitchen designer. Mem. Nat. Kitchen and Bath Assn. (bd. dirs. 1987), Evanston Inventure (bd. dirs. 1987—, exec. com. 1988—), Am. Inst. Kitchen Designers (pres. 1975-76), Soc. Cert. Kitchen Designers, 1987— (bd. govs., sec. 1987—), Evanston C. of C. (dir. 1973-74, v.p. 1975, pres. 1976), Westmoreland C. of C., Nat. Fed. Ind. Bus., Mid-Am. Swedish Trade Assn., Evanston Rotary (pres. 1984-85). Contbr. kitchen designs to nat. mags. Home: 2311 Central Park Ave Evanston IL 60201 Office: 1815 Central St Evanston IL 60201

KARLSON, LAWRENCE CARL, technology company executive; b. Canora, Saskatchewan, Can., Dec. 29, 1942; s. Carl Louis and Katherine (Novakowski) Kulchyski; m. Margo Thompson, Sept. 28, 1963; children: Graydon, Stephen. Diploma in engring., Ryerson Polytech. Inst., 1963; MBA with distinction, U. Pa., 1980. Mng. dir. Fischer & Porter Pty Ltd., Melbourne, Australia, 1973-77; v.p. mktg. Fischer & Porter Co., Warminster, Pa., 1977-78, v.p. mfg., 1978-80, dir., pres. U.S. ops., 1980-83; pres., chief exec. officer Nobel Electronics, Inc., Blue Bell, Pa., 1983-86; pres., chief exec. officer Pharos AB, Blue Bell and Stockholm, 1986—, also bd. dirs.; pres., chief exec. officer Karlson Corp., Blue Bell, 1986—; bd. dirs. Dynisco, Inc., Norwood, Mass., Vidar Systems, Inc., Herndon, Va., ABB Robotics, Inc., New Berlin, Wis., CDI Corp., Phila. Contbr. articles to profl. jours. Bd. dirs. Warminster Gen. Hosp., 1980-86. Griffith Labs. scholar, 1961, Texaco scholar, 1962. Mem. Young Pres.'s Orgn., Union League. Republican. Roman Catholic. Club: Cedarbrook Country (Blue Bell). Home: 1024 Woods Ln Ambler PA 19002 Office: Pharos USA Inc 595 Skippack Pike Ste 300 Blue Bell PA 19422 also: Pharos AB, Box 5226, S-102 45 Stockholm Sweden also: Flat 1 Rosebery Ct, 14-15 Charles St, London WIX7HB, England

KARMAN, KENNETH ALLEN, accountant; b. St. Louis, July 20, 1943; s. Allen V. and Ivy M. (Myer) K.; m. Patricia C. Baumann, Mar. 28, 1964 (div. 1979); m. Carolyn J. Wheeler, May 24, 1980; children: Ronald L. Squires II, Ryan L. Squires, Kendra S. Karman. BBA, U. Mo., St. Louis, 1972; MS in Accountancy, Western Ill. U., 1979. CPA, Mo., Ill. Audit staff Ernst & Whinney, St. Louis, 1972-76; asst. controller Broadcast Products div. Harris Corp., Quincy, Ill., 1976-78; instr. Western Ill. U., Macomb, 1978-80; mgr. acctg. Foster & Gallagher, Inc., Peoria, Ill., 1980-83, controller, 1983-87, v.p., 1987-88; pvt. practice acctg. Chillicothe, Ill., 1988—; mem. Acctg. Adv. Bd. ICC; bd. dirs. 1st Chillicothe Corp. Served to staff sgt. USAF, 1966-70. Named one of Outstanding Young Men in Am., 1975. Mem. Am. Inst. CPA's, Mo. Soc. CPA's, Ill. CPA Found., U. Mo. St. Louis Alumni Assn. (life), Ill. Soc. CPA's, Beta Alpha Psi. Lodge: Lions (sec. Chillicothe club 1983-84, bd. dirs. 1984—, pres. 1987—). Home: 1213 W Pine Chillicothe IL 61523 Office: 1007 N Second St PO Box 275 Chillicothe IL 61523

KARNES, TIMOTHY JOSEPH, hospital administrator, consultant; b. Buffalo, Feb. 21, 1956; s. John Richard and Margaret Mary (Beck) K.; m. Michelle Jean Suchsland, Oct. 23, 1982; children: Caitlin Marie, Courtney Colleen. BA in Psychology, SUNY, Buffalo, 1979; M in Health Svcs. Adminstrn., George Washington U., 1982. Systems analyst Health Resources Adminstrn., Hyattsville, Md., 1980-81; adminstrv. resident Richland Meml. Hosp., Columbia, S.C., 1981-82; adminstrv. fellow William S. Hall Inst., Columbia, 1982; asst. adminstr. Cypress Hosp., Hosp. Corp. Am., Lafayette, La., 1982-83; asst. chief exec. officer Iredell Meml. Hosp., Statesville, N.C., 1983-85; asst. v.p. profl. svcs. Indian River Meml. Hosp., Vero Beach, Fla., 1985-87; v.p. Meml. Hosp., Danville, Va., 1987—; pres. Tommy R. McDougal Symposium on Healthcare Adminstrn., Montgomery, Ala., 1987-88. Recipient Traineeship award U.S. Dept. Health, Edn. and Welfare, 1980, Leadership award Cypress Hosp., 1983, Kidney Dialysis Orgn. Iredelle County, 1985. Mem. Am. Coll. Healthcare Execs., Kiwanis. Republican. Roman Catholic. Home: 2833 Finch Dr Danville VA 24540 Office: Meml Hosp Danville 142 S Main St Danville VA 24541

KARNIA, JACK J., sales executive; b. Chgo., Feb. 6, 1955; s. Joseph E. and Dolores (Bobber) K.; m. Monika Felgenhauer, Oct. 21, 1978. Lab analyst Faber Labs., Chgo., 1973-74; prodn. mgr. Lowrey Organ Co., Romeoville, Ill., 1974-78; sales rep. J.R.C. Industries, Hillside, Ill., 1978-80; sales mgr. Wash. Nat. Ins., Evanston, Ill., 1980-85, Hinckley & Schmitt, Inc., Chgo., 1985—. Author: Sales Manual, 1986. Campaigner George Wallace for Pres., Chgo., 1968. Office: Hinckley & Schmitt Inc 6055 S Harlem Ave Chicago IL 60638

KARNOS, CHARLOTTE ESGATE, manufacturing executive, controller; b. Riverside, Calif., June 7, 1945; d. Richard Minard and Maryetta (Youtsler) Esgate; m. Joe Wilson Floyd Jr., Apr. 20, 1970 (div. Apr. 1979); m. Patrick Raymond Karnos, Jan. 3, 1981; children: Patrick, Kathryn, Gregory. BA in Mgmt., Sonoma State U., 1974; BA in Math., UCLA, 1967. Acct. Codding Enterprises, Rohnert Park, Calif., 1974-78; controller Young Am. Homes, Rohnert Park, 1979; controller, sec. treas. Corner Pockets of Am., Inc., Billings, Mont., 1980—. Republican. Office: Corner Pockets Am PO Box 20878 Billings MT 59104

KAROLAK, DALE WALTER, aerospace company executive; b. Detroit, Sept. 18, 1959; s. Walter Joseph and Betty Jane (Bugala) K.; m. Lorraine Kay Theunissen, June 24, 1984; children: Jessica Ann, Ryan Walter. BS, Cen. Mich. U., 1981; MBA, U. Phoenix, 1985. Computer programmer Lowry and Assocs., Brighton, Mich., 1980-81; engr. GTE Communication Systems, Phoenix, 1981-85; mgr. optical div. ITT Aerospace, Ft. Wayne, Ind., 1985—. Mem. IEEE, Assn. Computing Machinery, Assn. MBA Execs. Office: ITT Aerospace Optical Div PO Box 3700 Fort Wayne IN 46801

KARP, PETER SIMON, corporate marketing executive; b. New City, N.Y., Dec. 9, 1935; s. Joseph Bernard and Esther (Wexler) K.; m. Mona Leea Pecheux; children: Matthew Henry, Mark Andrew. BA, Hobart Coll., 1954; MFA, Columbia U., 1957. Reseacher Bur. Advt., Am. Newspaper Pubs. Assn., N.Y.C., 1954-56; media dir. Smith, Hager & Knudsen, Inc., N.Y.C., 1957-59; media and research dir. CAG Advt., Inc., N.Y.C., 1960-62; exec. v.p. Bennett-Chaiken, Inc., N.Y.C., 1963-66; pres., founder Bus. Sci. Internat., N.Y.C., 1967—; mng. dir. The Concept Testing Inst., N.Y.C., 1972—; chair, chief exec. officer Pimi. Inc., N.Y.C., 1986—; dir. Office of the Future Panel, N.Y.C., 1976—; co-dir. The Genesis Group, N.Y.C., 1983—. Editor The BSI Newsletter, 1976—. Pollster Ken Keating Campaign, State of New York, 1964; vol. Grand Cen. YMCA, N.Y.C., 1964-82. Recipient Thomas T. Semon Creative Research award BMD Found., 1977. Mem. Am. Mktg. Assn., Advt. Research Found., Artificial Intelligence Assn., N.Y. Acad. Sci. Jewish. Club: Palisades Tennis. Home: 157 Tweed Blvd Upper Grandview NY 10960

KARP, RICHARD M., advertising executive; b. N.Y.C., Aug. 17, 1929; s. Harry and Jo Golden (Bosk) K.; m. Jane Hausman, Nov. 26, 1978; 1 son, David. B.S., B.A., N.Y. U., 1950; postgrad., Boston U. Publicist 20th Century Fox Film Corp., 1954-56; sr. writer Donahue & Coe Advt., N.Y.C., 1956-58; asso. creative dir., account supr. Reach, McClinton Advt., N.Y.C., 1958-63; exec. v.p., creative dir. Grey Advt., N.Y.C., 1963—; guest lectr. Baruch U., 1977-79. Author: monograph The Films of Buster Keaton, 1949. Bd. dirs. United Cerebral Palsy. Served with AUS, 1950-51, USAF, 1951-54. Decorated Commendation medal; recipient Clio award, Internat. Advt. award, Screen Advt. award, Copywriters Club award. Mem. Brit. Inst. Practitioners in Advt. Home: 455 E 57th St New York NY 10022 Office: Grey Advt Inc 777 3rd Ave New York NY 10017

KARPEN, MARIAN JOAN, financial executive; b. Detroit, June 16, 1944; d. Cass John and Mary (Jagiello) K.; A.B., Vassar Coll., 1966; postgrad. Sorbonne, Paris, N.Y. U. Grad. Sch. Bus., 1974-77. New Eng. corr. Women's Wear Daily, Fairchild Publs.-Capital Cities Communications, 1966-68, Paris fashion editor, TV and radio commentator Capital Cities Network, 1968-69; fashion editor Boston Herald Traveler, 1969-71; nat. syndicated newspaper columnist and photojournalist Queen Features Syndicate, N.Y.C., 1971-73; account exec. Blyth Eastman Dillon, N.Y.C., 1973-75, Oppenheimer, N.Y.C., 1975-76; v.p., mcpl. bond coordinator Faulkner Dawkins & Sullivan (merged Shearson Hayden Stone), N.Y.C., 1976-77; mgr. retail mcpl. bond dept. Warburg Paribas Becker-A.G. Becker (merger Becker Paribas and Merrill Lynch), N.Y.C., 1977-79, sr. v.p. and prin., 1977-84; sr. v.p., ltd. ptnr. Bear Stearns & Co., 1984-87, assoc. dir., 1987—; lectr. fin. seminars, 1978—; mem. bus. adv. council U.S. Rep. Senate. Mem. benefit com. March of Dimes, 1983; mem. Torchlight Ball com. Internat. Games for Disabled, 1984, other benefit coms.; friend vol. Whitney Mus. Am. Art. Recipient Superior Prodn. award Becker Paribas, 1983. Mem. Nat. Assn. Securities Dealers (registered rep.), N.Y. Stock Exchange (registered rep.), N.Y.C. Women's Econ. Roundtable, Am. Soc. Profl. and Exec. Women, AAUW, U.S. Figure Skating Assn., Fishing Club of Am. (angler's honor roll), English Speaking Union. Clubs: Vassar, Skating (N.Y.C. and Boston). Past editorial bd. Retirement Planning Strategist; contbr. articles and photographs to newspapers and mags. Home: 233 E 69th St New York NY 10021 Office: Bear Stearns & Co 245 Park Ave New York NY 10167

KARPINSKI, JACEK, computer company executive; b. Torino, Italy, Apr. 9, 1927; s. Adam and Wanda (Cumft) K.; m. Eulalia Gryniecka, Mar. 1, 1955 (div. 1975); children: Dorota, Ewa; m. Ewa Stepien, July 11, 1978; children: Adam, Daniel, Sylvan. Spl. student Harvard U., 1961-62; M.Sc.E.E., Politechnika Warsaw, 1951. System engr. Electronic Systems Mfg., Warsaw, 1951-54; adj. prof. Polish Acad. Scis., Warsaw, 1955-65; head computer lab. Warsaw U., 1965-70; mng. dir. Minicomputer R & D & Prodn., Warsaw, 1970-73; asst. prof. Warsaw Politechnic U., 1973-81; mng. dir. Karpinski Computer Systems, Le Mont, Switzerland, 1983-85; cons. in field of artificial intelligence and computer systems, 1985—. Author numerous computer systems. Served to lt. Polish Armed Forces, 1941-44. Decorated Cross of Valor (3), Polish Underground Army, 1944, AK Cross, 1944. Mem. IEEE, State Comity for Computers. Roman Catholic. Home: Champ-Soleil, CH-1055 Froideville Switzerland

KARR, JAMES BARRY, financial programmer; b. Elmhurst, Ill., May 30, 1945; s. John Melvin and Katherine Karr; m. Laurel Ann Spruth, May 3, 1966; children: Lisa A., Alison L., Jamie R., Samuel J. BBA, Elmhurst (Ill.) Coll., 1973; MBA in Prodn. Mgmt., Fla. Inst. Tech., 1977. Commd. 2d lt. U.S. Army, 1967, advanced through grades to lt. col., 1967-86; registered rep. and agt. USPA & IRA, Ft. Worth, 1986—. Decorated Bronze Star. Mem. Nat. Assn. for Def. Preparedness., Manhattan (Kans.) C. of C. (mil. relations com. 1986, 87, 88). Republican. Mem. Christian Ch. Clubs: Ducks Unltd., N.Am. Versatile Hunting Dog Assn. Home: Rte 1 Box 662 Saint George KS 66535 Office: USPA & IRA 315 Houston St Ste L Manhattan KS 66502

KARR, JOHN DANIEL, controller; b. St. Louis, Apr. 13, 1944; s. John Mayo and Rozanne Mary (Tenny) K.; m. Sue Elizabeth Cox, Dec. 15, 1978; children: Frank, Tina, Ned. BS in Acctg., So. Ill. U., 1966. Acct. Country Mut. Ins. Co., Bloomington, Ill., 1968-69; acct. The Eureka Co., Bloomington, 1969-71, br. acctg. supr., 1971, mgr. gen. acctg., 1971-87, controller, 1987—. Served with U.S. Army, 1966-68. Republican. Roman Catholic. Office: The Eureka Co 1201 E Bell St Bloomington IL 61701

KARRO, WILLIAM STUART, chemical corporation executive; b. N.Y.C., Mar. 31, 1944; s. William G. and Bessie (Philips) K.; m. Patti Sue Entzminger, May 26, 1973; children: Jason F., Jared Q., Matthew P. BS in Chem. Engring., Ill. Inst. Tech., 1972. Tech. svc. rep. Ciba-Geigy Corp., Ardsley, N.Y., 1965-67, Portland, Oreg., 1967, Chgo., 1968-72; sales rep. Kalamazoo, Mich., 1972—. Patentee multicolored paper, 1969. Mem. Paper Indsl. Mgmt. Assn., Tech. Assn. Pulp and Paper Industries. Home: 3728 Bronson Blvd Kalamazoo MI 49008 Office: Ciba-Geigy Corp 410 Swing Rd Greensboro NC 27419

KARRON, RONALD ARTHUR, mutual fund company executive; b. Bklyn., Feb. 3, 1934; s. Jack Karron and Miriam (Slutskin) Leider; m. Kristin A. Mattson, Mar. 6, 1982; children: Michael, Melissa, Lee. BSBA in Fin., NYU, 1952. CLU; chartered fin. cons. Agt. Mut. of N.Y., Stamford, Conn., 1958-60, Occidental Life Ins. Co., Bridgeport, Conn., 1960-62; supr. Phoenix Mut., Norwalk, Conn., 1962-65; agy. mgr. Phoenix Mut., Denver, 1966-69, 73-81; v.p. Planned Equity Corp., Denver, 1969-73; br. mgr. E.F. Hutton Fin. Svcs., Denver, 1981-84; v.p., nat. mktg. dir. Transam. Fin. Resources, L.A., 1984-87; sr. v.p., sales mgr. RNC Mut. Fund Group, L.A., 1987—; guest speaker to life ins. agts. Author: (book and videotape) Financial Planning, 1986, Finding the Money, 1986; editor Colo. Life Underwriter's Assn. newsletter, 1981-82. Vice chmn. Colo. Conservative Union, 1982; former arbitrator Denver Better Bur. Mem. Internat. Assn. for Fin. Planning. Republican.

KARSON, ALLEN RONALD, aerospace company executive; b. Chgo., June 18, 1947; s. Bruno Stanley and Rose Jean (Nowakowski) Kasprzyk; m. Bonnie Jean Pazdziora, Sept. 1, 1968. BS in Acctg., Bradley U., 1970; postgrad. DePaul U., 1972. CPA, Ill. Corp. controller Time Industries, Inc., Chgo., 1973-77; controller U.S. ops. Indal, Inc., Toronto, Ont., Can., 1977; v.p. fin. affairs Rentco Internat., Inc., subs. Fruehauf Corp., The Hague, The Netherlands, 1977-83; pres., chief exec. officer Ideal Aerosmith, Inc., Cheyenne, Wyo., 1983-84, East Grand Forks, Minn., 1984—. Apptd. hon. consul of The Hague, 1985; pres. Bus. Devel. Bd., East Grand Forks, Minn., Econ. Devel. Corp., East Grand Forks, 1985—, East Grand Forks Devel. Authority, 1986—. Mem. Am. Inst. CPA's, Ill. Soc. CPA's, Minn. Soc. CPA's, Planning Execs. Inst., Nat. Assn. Accts. (bd. dirs. Netherlands chpt. 1981-83). Roman Catholic. Lodge: Elks. Office: Ideal Aerosmith Inc Hwy 2 East Grand Forks MN 56721

KASAVANA, TOBY STUART, financial services executive; b. Stamford, Conn., Apr. 29, 1946; s. Louis Uban and Dorothy Naomi (Lipshutz) K.; m.

Kathleen Brigid Trainor, Feb. 23, 1977; children: Dagan, Brian, Kara. BBA, U. Mass., 1969, MBA, 1971. CPA, N.Y. Instr. bus. Berkshire Community Coll., Pittsfield, Mass., 1971-73; rsch. economist U. Mass., Amherst, 1973-74; bus. mgr. Saw Graphics, Westbury, N.Y., 1974-76; acct. L.I. Jewish Hillside Med. Ctr., New Hyde Park, N.Y., 1976-79; assoc. spl. auditor, investigator State of N.Y., N.Y.C., 1979-80; mgr. costs and budgets Emerson Hosp., Concord, Mass., 1980-83; svc. cons. Peat, Marwick, Mitchell & Co., Boston, 1983-85; dir. internat. acctg. John Hancock Property & Casualty Co., Boston, 1985—. Bd. dirs. Regional Family YMCA, Framingham, Mass., 1985-88. Home: 20 Strawberry Hill Rd Natick MA 01760 Office: John Hancock Property & Casualty Co PO Box 854 Boston MA 02117

KASCHAK, LILLIAN ANNE, financial fund executive; b. Plymouth, Pa.; d. Stanley and Mary Christine (Sinkiewicz) Javer; student Wyo. Sem., Dean Sch. Bus., 1946-47, Wilkes Coll., 1952-53; m. Joseph V. Kaschak; 1 son, Thomas J. Sr. clk. Prudential Ins. Co., Kingston, Pa., 1953-58; with advt. dept. Wyoming Valley Distbg. Co., Wilkes-Barre, Pa., 1968-69; adminstrv. mgr. Keystone Welfare & Pension Funds, Wilkes-Barre, 1969-82; with Sheetmetal Workers Welfare Fund, Wilkes-Barre, 1982—; partner Kaschak & Slesinski, 1977—. Mem. Eastern Pa. Adminstrs. Assn. (sec.-treas. 1975-79), Tri-County Personnel Assn. (publicity chmn. 1976-78), Madam Curie Soc. Roman Catholic. Clubs: Quota (membership chmn. 1972-79), Wyoming Valley Ski. Home and Office: 306 Stephanie Dr Plymouth PA 18651

KASEVICH, LAWRENCE STANLEY, management consultant; b. Hartford, Conn., July 22, 1952; s. Stanley George and Mildred Agnes (Knebel) K.; m. Debra Lona Metcalf, Jan. 29, 1972; children: Cheryl, Alissa. BSEE, U. Conn., 1974; MS in Mgmt., Hartford Grad. Ctr., 1986. Engr. UTC div. Hamilton Standard, Windsor Locks, Conn., 1974-75; engr. Dynamic Controls Corp., South Windsor, Conn., 1975-78, project mgr., 1978-85, dir. mgmt. info. systems, 1985-88; cons. Computer Mktg. Concepts, South Windsor, 1981-85, KAZ Assocs., South Windsor, 1985—; adj. prof. Hartford Grad. Ctr. Sch. Mgmt., 1988—. Author: (books) Using Framework, 1985, Controlling Your Resources, 1986, Framework II, 1986, Mastering Framework III, 1988; contbr. articles to mags. Mem. Am. Prodn. & Inventory Control Soc., Project Mgmt. Inst., Lions. Episcopalian. Home: 55 Juniper Ln South Windsor CT 06074 Office: KAZ Assocs 55 Juniper Ln South Windsor CT 06074

KASHMERI, SARWAR AGHAJANI, management consulting company principal; b. Bombay, India, Nov. 2, 1942; came to U.S., 1964; s. Aghajani and Khursheed (Kazi) K.; m. Deborah Kellogg Ellis, May 23, 1981. B.S., Parks Coll., St. Louis U., 1967, M.S., St. Louis U., 1971. Faculty, St. Louis U., 1967-72; pvt. practice info. systems mgmt., 1972-73; co-founder, dir. REJIS Commn., St. Louis, 1973-76; spl. cons. dep. mayor criminal justice, N.Y.C., 1976-78, Div. Criminal Justice Services, State of N.Y., 1978-82; founder, pres. Sabzevar, Inc., N.Y.C., 1982-85; founder, pres. Niche Systems Inc., Corp. Cons., N.Y.C., 1985—. Writer book, host TV program, Sta. KETC-TV, St. Louis, 1972; reviewer books, St. Louis Post Dispatch, 1972-76; author papers. Mem. gov.'s adv. com. criminal justice standards and goals, Mo., 1974-76. Recipient Cert. of Appreciation, Dept. Pub. Safety State of Mo., 1976. Home: 1 Leonard St Mount Kisco NY 10549 Office: Niche Systems Inc 274 Madison Ave New York NY 10016

KASLOW, JOHN FRANCIS, utility executive; b. Lawrence, Mass., June 24, 1932; s. Charles Michael and Helen Veronica (Minihan) K.; m. Barbara J. Fox, Apr. 14, 1956; children: Charles M., John Francis, Thomas W. BS, Lowell Tech. Inst., 1953; Advanced Mgmt. Program Harvard U., 1980. Project mgr. Yankee Atomic Electric Co., 1966-73; v.p. New Eng. Electric System, Westborough, Mass., 1973-79, sr. v.p., 1979-84, exec. v.p., chief operating officer, 1984—; pres. New Eng. Power Co., Westborough, 1979—; dir. New Eng. Power Co., New Eng. Power Service Co., New Eng. Electric System, Doble Engring. Co. Bd. dirs. Holy Family Hosp., Lawrence, 1981—; trustee Merrimack Coll., 1986. Served with AUS, 1954-56. Recipient Eminent Grad. award U. Lowell, 1980. Mem. ASME. Home: 15 Duston Dr Methuen MA 01844 Office: New Eng Electric System 25 Research Dr Westborough MA 01581

KASMIR, GAIL ALICE, insurance company official, accountant; b. N.Y.C., Aug. 19, 1958; d. Fred and Evelyn Silvie (Mailman) K. BSBA summa cum laude, U. Cen. Fla., 1979. CPA, Fla. Acct. Ernst and Whinney, Orlando, Fla., 1979-83; fin. mgr. Harcourt Brace Jovanovich (Harvest Life Ins. Co.), Orlando, Fla., 1983-85; sr. v.p., treas., sec. LifeCo Investment Group, Inc and subs. Nat. Heritage Life Ins. Co., Farmers and Ranchers Life Ins. Co., Maitland, Fla., 1985—, cons. to bd. dirs., mem. investment com., 1985—. Vol. Am. Cancer Soc., 1987—, Am. Soc. for Cancer Research, 1987—. Fellow Life Office Mgmt. Assn.; mem. Am. Inst. CPAs, Fla. Inst. CPAs, Ins. Acctg. and Systems Assn., Beta Alpha Psi, Beta Gamma Sigma. Republican. Jewish. Home: 1160 Woodland Terr Trail Altamonte Springs FL 32714 Office: LifeCo Investment Group Inc 1101 N Lake Destiny Dr Suite 200 Maitland FL 32751

KASPAR, ROBERT STEPHEN, investment executive; b. Chgo., Oct. 3, 1958; s. Adolph Edward and Kathryn Ann (Arns) K.; m. Rhonda Lorraine Newport, May 8, 1982. BS in Acctg., Ball State U., 1981, BS in Mgmt., 1981. CPA, Ind. Acct., auditor Ernst & Whinney, CPAs, Indpls., 1981-84; v.p., contr. Irwin Union Bank, Columbus, Ind., 1984-87, Irwin Union Corp., Columbus, 1985—; mng. dir. Irwin Union Capital Corp., Columbus, 1987—. Chmn. United Way Fund Irwin Union Corp., Columbus, 1987; treas. Ind. Dance Conv., Greenwood, 1984—; treas., bd. dirs. Columbus Pro Musica, 1985—, Southside Youth Coun., Indpls., 1982-85. Named one of Outstanding Young Men of Am., 1987. Mem. AICPA, Ind. Soc. CPAs, Nat. Assn. Securities Dealers (prin.). Roman Catholic. Office: Irwin Union Capital Corp 500 Washington St Columbus IN 47201

KASPER, HORST MANFRED, lawyer; b. Dusseldorf, Germany, June 3, 1939; s. Rudolf Ferdinand and Lilli Helene (Krieger) K. Diplom-Chemiker, U. Bonn., 1963, Dr. rer. nat., 1965; J.D., Seton Hall U., 1978. Bar admittee: N.J. 1978, U.S. Patent Office, 1977. Mem. staff Lincoln Lab., M.I.T., Lexington, 1967-69; mem. tech. staff Bell Telephone Labs., Murray Hill, N.J., 1970-76; asso. Kirschstein, Kirschstein, Ottinger & Frank, N.Y.C., 1976-77; patent atty. Allied Chem. Corp., Morristown, N.J., 1977-79; sole practice, Warren, N.J., 1980-83; with Kasper and Weick, Warren, 1983—. Mem. ABA, N.J. Bar Assn., Internat. Patent and Trademark Assn., Am. Patent Law Assn., N.J. Patent Law Assn., Am. Chem. Soc., Electrochem. Soc., Am. Phys. Soc., AAAS, N.Y. Acad. Scis. Contbr. numerous articles to profl. jours.; patentee semicondr. field.

KASPERCZYK, JÜRGEN, business executive; b. Pitschen, Germany, Mar. 4, 1941; arrived in Luxembourg, 1980; s. Gerhard Max and Edith Clara (Utta) K.; m. Katrin Schimbke, Apr. 25, 1968; children: Martin, Kristina. MSc in Mining Engring., Tech. U., West Berlin, 1968, PhD in Chem. Engring., 1970. Research scientist Bergbauforschung GmbH., Essen, Fed. Republic Germany, 1968-72; mgr. coking plant Rhodesian Iron and Steel Co., Ltd., Redcliff, Rhodesia, 1972-74; project mgr. Exploration und Bergbau GmbH., Düsseldorf, Fed. Republic Germany, 1974-76; tech. mgr. Hansen Neuerburg GmbH., Essen, 1976-78; mng. dir. CARBOMINA Rohstoffhandel GmbH., Essen, 1978-80; pres., chief exec. officer ENSCH S.àr.l., Luxembourg, 1980—. Contbr. papers to tech. mags., internat. confs. Clubs: Golf Grand-Ducal (Luxembourg), Cercle Munster (Luxembourg). Lodge: Old Tablers. Office: ENSCH Sarl, 12-14 Bd d'Avranches, PO Box 2132, L-1021 Luxembourg Luxembourg

KASPERKO, JEAN MARGARET, chemical economic analyst; b. Wheeling, W.Va., Aug. 17, 1949; d. John Richard and Jean Eleanor (Ebersole) K. Student, Carnegie-Mellon U., 1967-69; BS in Chem., U. Pitts., 1972, MLS, 1974, MBA, 1983. Computer sci. librarian U. Pitts., 1974-75; info. specialist Calgon Corp., Pitts., 1975-79, supr. purchasing svcs., 1979-84, planning analyst, 1984—. Named Nat. Merit Scholar Ford Found., 1967-72; recipient Warner Prize in Chem. Carnegie-Mellon U., 1969; NSF grantee Carnegie-Mellon U., 1969. Mem. Am. Chem. Soc., Am. Inst. Chemists, Spl. Libraries Assn., Ohio Valley Coll. Club, Beta Phi Mu, Beta Gamma Sigma. Democrat. Presbyterian. Home: 14 Vigne Rd Coraopolis PA 15108 Office: Calgon Corp PO Box 1346 Pittsburgh PA 15230

KASPRICK, LYLE CLINTON, private investor; b. Angus, Minn., Aug. 23, 1932; s. Max Peter and Mary (Taus) K.; BS in Bus. Adminstrn. magna cum laude, U. N.D., 1959. CPA, Minn., N.D.; m. Harriet Susan Lydick, July 14, 1953; children—Susan, Michael, John; m. Kathleen M. Westby, June 4, 1977; 1 stepchild, Kristin Westby. Tax mgr. Arthur Andersen & Co., Mpls., 1959-69; v.p. Search Investments Corp., Mpls., 1969-77; financial v.p., treas. Tropicana Hotel and Country Club, Las Vegas, 1970-72; chief operating officer Key Pharms., Inc., Miami, Fla., 1972-76, bd. dir., 1976-86; bd. dir. Search Investments Corp., 1973-77, Mo Am Co Corp., 1975-76; v.p. MEI Corp., Mpls., 1977-86; v.p. MEI Diversified, Inc., Mpls., 1986-88; dir. IVAX Corp., Miami, Fla., 1987—; bd. dir. Am. Vaccine Corp., Laurel, Md., 1988—. Speaker before profl. and civic groups., dist. and city convs. Del. Rep. Com., 1964, 66, 68, 70. With USN, 1951-55. Mem. Am. Inst. CPA's, Minn. Soc. CPA's, Am. Legion. Republican. Roman Catholic. Lodge: KC. Home: 1067 Linden Ln Orono MN 55364-9754 Office: IVAX Corp 8800 NW 36th St Miami FL 33178-2404

KASPUTYS, JOSEPH EDWARD, corporate executive, economist; b. Jamaica, N.Y., Aug. 12, 1936; s. Joseph John and Henrietta Viola (Derenthall) K.; m. Marilyn Patricia Kennedy, Oct. 29, 1953; children—Clare Victoria, Patricia Jeanne, Jacqueline Ann, Veronica Joy. B.A. magna cum laude, Bklyn. Coll., 1959; M.B.A. with high distinction, Harvard U., 1967, D.B.A., 1972. Dep. dir. data automation U.S. Dept. Def., Washington, 1967-69, asst. to def. comptroller, 1969-70; dir. Office of Policy and Plans U.S. Maritime Adminstrn., Washington, 1972-73, asst. adminstr., 1973-75; asst. sec. U.S. Dept. Commerce, Washington, 1975-77; exec. v.p., chief operating officer Data Resources, Inc., Lexington, Mass., 1977-81, pres., chief exec. officer, 1981-84; exec. v.p. McGraw-Hill, Inc., N.Y.C., 1984-87; pres., chief operating officer Primark Corp. Inc., McLean, Va., 1987-88; chmn., chief exec. officer Primark Corp. Inc., McLean, 1988—; lectr. Am. U., Washington, 1967-68, Bentley Coll., Boston, 1971-72; assoc. prof., lectr. George Washington U., Washington, 1967-77; bd. dirs. Lifeline Systems, Inc., Boston. Bd. dirs. Hitachi Found., Washington; mem. Com. for Econ. Devel., Washington. Served to comdr. USN, 1956-76. Decorated Legion of Merit; recipient Outstanding Young Comptroller award Am. Soc. Mil. Comptrollers, 1968; Warren G. Harding Aerospace fellow, 1971. Mem. Nat. Economists Club, Nat. Assn. Bus. Economists, Assn. for Corp. Growth, Phi Beta Kappa. Republican. Roman Catholic. Clubs: Harvard Bus. Sch. (Boston); Capitol Hill (Washington). Home: 398 Simon Willard Rd Concord MA 01742 Office: Primark Corp Inc 8251 Greensboro Dr McLean VA 22102

KASRIEL, BERNARD L., gypsum products manufacturing company executive; b. Lyon, France, 1946. Grad., Ecole Polytechnique, 1965; MBA, Harvard U., 1970. Cons. Institut de Developement Industriel, 1970-72; chief operating officer Établissements Braudet Benac, 1972-75; chief exec. officer Allia Co., 1975-77; exec. v.p. Allia and Lafarge Refractaires, 1982-84, Lafarge Coppee Ciments et Betons, France, 1984-87, Lafarge New Materials; pres. Nat. Gypsum Co., Dallas, 1987—, also bd. dirs. Office: Nat Gypsum Co 4500 Lincoln Pla Dallas TX 75201 *

KASS, BENNY LEE, lawyer; b. Chgo., Aug. 20, 1936; s. Herman and Ethel (Lome) K.; m. Salme Lundstrom, Aug. 30, 1963; children: Gale, Brian. B.S., Northwestern U., 1957; LL.B., U. Mich., 1960; LL.M., George Washington U., 1967. Bar: D.C. 1960. Atty. Maritime Adminstrn., 1960-61; counsel House Info. Subcom., 1962-65; asst. counsel Senate Adminstrv. Practice Subcom., Washington, 1965-69; pvt. practice law Washington, 1969—; mem. firm Kass, Skalet, Segan, & Spevack, P.C.; prof. communication law Am. U.; pub. mem. Nat. Advt. Rev. Bd., 1971-74; commr. D.C. Conf. on Uniform State Laws. Columnist: Washington Post; contbr. articles to profl. jours. Chmn. consumer affairs subcom. Mayors Econ. Devel. Com., 1968-70; chmn. Ad Hoc Com. on Consumer Protection, 1965—. Served with USAF, 1961-62. Am. Polit. Sci. Assn. Congl. fellow, 1966. Mem. Am., Fed. bar assns., Am. Polit. Sci. Assn., Sigma Delta Chi. Office: Kass Skalet Segan & Spevack PC 1050 17th St NW Ste 1100 Washington DC 20036

KASSING, KIRK ANDREW, industrial engineer; b. Ft. Wayne, Ind., Aug. 24, 1962; s. Anton Frederick and Nancy Gertrude (Petersen) K.; m. Michele Marie Smith, Oct. 24, 1987. BS in Acctg. and Fin., Ind. U., 1984. Sr. credit analyst Summit Bank, Ft. Wayne, 1985-86; indsl. engr. Wayne Home Equipment Co., Ft. Wayne, 1986-88, sr. buyer pump div., 1988—. Mem. Inst. Indsl. Engrs. Home: 644 Prospect Ave Fort Wayne IN 46805 Office: Wayne Home Equipment Co 801 Glasgow St Fort Wayne IN 46803

KASTEN, RICHARD JOHN, accounting company executive; b. Chgo., July 4, 1938; s. Victor and Margaret Dorothy (Madertz) K.; m. Karen Linet' Weindorf, June 23, 1962; 1 child, Kent Lane. BS in Mktg. Rsch., U. Ill., 1960, M in Commerce, 1962. CPA, Ill. Staff acct. Ernst & Whinney, Chgo., 1962-63, advanced staff acct., 1963-64, sr. acct., 1964-65, sr. cons., 1965-67, supr., 1967-68, mgr., 1968-72, ptnr., 1972-80; vice-chmn. cons. services Ernst & Whinney, Cleve., 1980-85; regional dir. mgmt. cons. svcs. Ernst & Whinney, Chgo., 1985-86, mng. ptnr. midwest cons., 1986-88, ptnr. in charge healthcare Great Lakes region, 1988—. Chmn. fin. com. St. Joseph's Hosp., Chgo., 1978-80; active Gov. Walker's Com. on Health, Chgo., 1977. Sgt. USNG, 1962-68. Mem. AICPA (exec. com. 1981-84), Anderson com. 1983-86), Ill. CPA Soc., Hosp. Fin. Mgmt. Assn., Chgo. Club, Inverness Golf Club (fin. com. 1979-80). Republican. Lutheran. Office: Ernst & Whinney 150 S Wacker Dr Chicago IL 60606

KATA, EDWARD JOHN, industrial products manufacturing company executive; b. N.Y.C., Aug. 24, 1941; s. Edward John and Rita Dolores (Kelleher) K.; m. Lorraine Frances Verunac, Nov. 11, 1942; children: Scott, Glenn, Gregg, Todd, Bradd. BA, Fordham U., 1963; MBA, L.I. U., 1972. Mgr. bus. devel. Olin Corp., Stamford, Conn., 1963-72; dir. corp. devel. Thyssen Bornemisza Group S.A., Monaco, 1972-81; v.p. Dover Corp., N.Y.C., 1981—; bd. dirs. K&L Microwave Inc., Salisbury, Md., Nurad Inc., Balt., Dover Resources Inc., Tulsa, Pathway Bellows Inc., El Cajun, Calif., Dover Techs., Inc., Binghamton, N.Y. Pres. St. Edwards Christian Youth Orgn., Syosset, N.Y., 1982-85. Mem. Assn. Corp. Growth (mem. internat. com. 1985), Excelsior Club, Marco Polo Club. Roman Catholic. Home: 75 Belvedere Dr Syosset NY 11791 Office: Dover Corp 277 Park Ave New York NY 10172

KATAI, ANDREW ANDRAS, chemical company executive; b. Gyor, Hungary, Sept. 17, 1937; came to U.S., 1956; s. Ivan and Clara (Szel) K.; m. Debbie Judwin, May 12, 1963 (div. 1970); children: Alisa, Gregory; m. Joan Eleanor Klein, July 30, 1972; children: Peter, Daniel. BS, Juniata Coll., 1960; MS, PhD, Syracuse U., 1965; MS, PhD in Chemistry, SUNY, Syracuse, 1965. Internat. mktg. asst. Esso chem. Co., N.Y.C., 1965-66; asst. prof. Hunter-Lehman Coll. N.Y.C., 1965-70; research chemist Union Carbide Corp., Tarrytown, N.Y., 1966-67; internat. assoc. prodn. mgr. Union Carbide Corp., N.Y.C., 1967-69, internat. product mgr., 1969-71; new bus. devel. mgr. W.R. Grace Constrn. Co., Cambridge, Mass., 1971-73; bus. mgr. internat. div. Inolex Corp., Chgo., 1973-77; Far East devel mgr. Eschem (Swift) Inc., Chgo., 1977, gen. mgr. internat. div., 1977-81, dir. internat. div., 1981-82, v.p. internat. div., 1982-83; pres. Swift Adhesives subs. Reichhold Chem. Co., Downers Grove, Ill., 1983—. Contbr. articles to profl. jours. Chmn. coll. fundraising dr., Westchester County, N.Y., 1969; co-chmn. Homeowners' Assn., Flossmoor, Ill., 1981-82. Mem. Adhesive Mfrs. Assn. (treas. 1986-88, pres. elect 1988), Am. Chem. Soc., Sigma Xi, Phi Lambda Upsilon. Home: 1105 Johnson Dr Naperville IL 60540 Office: Reichhold Chem Co Swift Adhesives Subs 3100 Woodcreek Dr Downers Grove IL 60515

KATELEY, RICHARD, real estate consultant; b. Niagara Falls, N.Y., June 1, 1944; s. Lawson M. and Mary T. Kateley. BA, U. Tex., 1966; MA, U. Chgo., 1973. Chief adminstrv. asst. office of lt. gov. State of Ill., Chgo., 1973-77; sr. v.p., chief operating officer Real Estate Rsch. Corp., Chgo., 1981-86, exec. v.p., 1986-89, pres., chief exec. officer, 1989—; bd. dirs. JW Holdings, N.Y.C. Co-author: America's High-Rise Office Buildings, 1986, Emerging Trends in Real Estate, 1986; contbr. articles to profl. jours. Bd. dirs. The Woodlawn Orgn., Chgo., 1985; mem. Gov.'s Film Fin. Task Force, 1986—. Fulbright fellow, 1971. Mem. Urban Land Inst., Econ. Club Chgo., Am. Polit. Sci. Assn., Lambda Alpha Internat. Democrat. Club: University (Chgo.). Office: Real Estate Rsch Corp 72 W Adams St Chicago IL 60603

KATES, HENRY E., life insurance company executive; b. Denver, Feb. 18, 1939; s. I. Allen and Dorothy K.; B.S. in Fin., U. Colo., 1960; children—Dorianne, Bradley; m. Alison Selover, Sept. 12, 1987. Agt., Mut. Benefit Life, Newark, 1960-67, gen. agt., 1967-81; pres. Mut. Benefit Fin. Service Co. (subs.), Providence, 1981-85; exec. v.p. Mut. Benefit Life Ins. Co., 1985-87, pres., 1987—. Bd. dirs. Holiday Corp., Revco D.S., RKO pictures, Carnegie Hall, U. of Colo. Found., Lincoln Ctr. Theaters, Newark Mus., Am. Coun. for the Arts. Mem. Newark C. of C. Author: Body Language in Sales, 1980. Home: 435 E 52d New York NY 10022 Office: Mut Benefit Life Ins Co 520 Broad St Newark NJ 07102

KATLIC, JOHN EDWARD, electric utility company executive; b. Washington, Pa., Nov. 3, 1928; s. Frederick John and Dorothy Ann (Gideon) K.; m. Nancy Jean Nicely, Aug. 26, 1950; children: Mark Richard, Kerry Leigh, Kevin Edward, Kathleen Diane, Nancy Ellen. B.S.E.M., W.Va. U., 1955, M.S.E.M., 1961. Mine surveyor Rochester & Pittsburgh Coal Co., Indiana, Pa., 1948-49; mine supt. Consolidation Coal Co., Morgantown, W.Va., 1959-62; gen. supt. Consolidation Coal Co., 1962-66; v.p. Consolidation Coal Co., Pitts., 1973-75; sr. mining engr. Eastern Assn. Coal, Pitts., 1967-68; div. mgr. Eastern Assn. Coal, 1969, v.p. personnel safety and indsl. relations, 1970; also dir.; v.p., gen. mgr. coal Allied Chem. Co., Morristown, N.J., 1970-73; exec. v.p. engring. and govt. relations Island Creek Coal Co., Lexington, Ky., 1975-83; sr. v.p. fuel supply Am. Electric Power Service Corp., 1983—; pres. So. Ohio Coal, Cen. Ohio Coal, Windsor Coal, Conesville Coal (all subs.), 1983—; mem. negotiating team Nat. Bituminous Coal Wage Agreement, Joint Industry Devel. Com., 1978. Patentee mining machine indicator, dust control in longwall mining. Mem. Morgantown City Council, 1964-66, Marshall U. Found., 1979; bd. dirs. W.Va. Edn. Found.; mem. steering com. W.Va. U. Served with inf. U.S. Army, 1946-47; C.E. 1950-52, Japan; C.E. Germany. Named Coal Age Man of Yr., 1987, Ohio Mining and Reclamation Coal Man of Yr., 1988. Mem. Nat. Mine Rescue Assn., Mine Rescue Vets. of Pitts. Dist. Republican. Presbyterian. Clubs: King Coal, Ky. Cols, Cherry River Navy, Buckeye Lake Yacht, Exec. Order of Ohio Commodores. Lodges: Masons; Shriners. Home: 1233 Ridgewood Way NE Lancaster OH 43130 Office: PO Box 700 Lancaster OH 43130

KATZ, ABRAHAM, retired foreign service officer; b. Bklyn., Dec. 4, 1926; s. Alexander and Zina (Rabinowitz) K.; children: Tamar, Jonathan, Naomi. B.A. cum laude, Bklyn. Coll., 1948; M.I.A., Columbia U., 1950; Ph.D., Harvard U., 1968. Commd. fgn. service officer Dept. State, 1951; 1st sec. U.S. missions to NATO, OECD, Paris, 1959-64; counselor Am. Embassy, Moscow, 1964-66; dir. office of OECD European Communities and Atlantic Polit. Econ. Affairs, Washington, 1967-74; dep. chief of mission OECD, Paris, 1974-78; dep. asst. sec. for internat. econ. policy and research Dept. Commerce, Washington, 1978-80; asst. sec. internat. econ. policy Dept. Commerce, 1980-81; U.S. rep., ambassador OECD, Paris, 1981-84; pres. U.S. Coun. Internat. Bus., 1984—. Author: The Politics of Economic Reform in the Soviet Union, 1972. Decorated grand officier Ordre National du Merite (France). Mem. Assn. Advancement Slavic Studies, Am. Fgn. Service Assn., Am. Assn. Comparative Econ. Studies, Council on Fgn. Relations. Clubs: Cosmos, B'nai B'rith, Harvard. Office: US Coun Internat Bus 1212 Sixth Ave New York NY 10036

KATZ, ARNOLD MARTIN, brokerage firm executive; b. Schenectady, N.Y., Mar. 22, 1940; s. David and Minna Katz; m. Marsha Katz, Sept. 4, 1969; 1 child, Sharon. BS in Pub. Relations, Boston U., 1962. Cert. life underwriter, Pa. Sales rep. Mass. Gen. Life Ins. Co., Hartford, Conn., 1964-66, sr. sales rep., 1966-67, asst. mgr., 1967; mgr. Phila., 1967-72; v.p. Boston, 1972-76; pres. Brokerage Concepts, Inc., Phila., 1977—; bd. dirs. Brokers Service Inc., N.Y.; pres. Atlantic Adminstrs., Waltham, Mass.; v.p. Group Source, Phila. Contbr. articles to profl. jours. Bd. dirs. Moss Rehab. Hosp., Phila., 1985—, Police Athletic League, Phila., 1986—; exec. com. Einstein Hosp., Phila., 1987—; v.p. Phila. Psychiat. Hosp. 1987—. Served to maj. U.S. Army, 1962-73. Mem. Life Underwriter Assn., CLU (bd. dirs. Phila. chpt.). Jewish. Office: Brokerage Concepts Inc 651 Allendale Rd King of Prussia PA 19406

KATZ, HILDA, artist; b. June 2, 1909; d. Max and Lina (Schwartz) K. Student, Nat. Acad. Design; student (3 awards; New Sch. Social Research scholarship), 1940-41. Author: (under pen name Hulda Weber) poems including numerous anthologies, spl. ltd. edit., 1987-88; anthologies include The Bloom, 1984-85, Perfume & Fragrance, 1988, Lightning & Rainbows, 1989; contbr.: numerous poems, short stories to books and mags. including Humpty Dumpty's Mag. (publ. for children); contbr. commemorative poetry to mus. and govt. including Pres. Ronald W. Reagan, 1985; one-woman exhbns. include: Bowdoin Coll. Art Mus., 1951, Calif. State Library, 1953, Print Club Albany, N.Y., 1955, U. Maine, 1955, 58, Jewish Mus., 1956, Pa. State Tchrs. Coll., 1956, Massillon Mus., 1957, Ball State Tchrs. Coll., 1957, Springfield (Mass.) Art Mus., 1957, Miami Beach (Fla.) Art Ctr., Richmond (Ind.) Art Assn., 1959, Old State Capitol Mus. La., other exhbns. include: Corcoran Bienniale Library of Congress, Am. in the War Exhbn, 26 mus., Am. Drawing anns. at: Albany Inst., Nat. Acad. Design, Conn. Acad. Fine Arts, Bklyn. Mus., Delgado Mus., Art-U.S.A., 1959, Congress for Jewish Culture, Met. Mus. Art., Springfield (Mo.) Art Mus., Children's Mus. Hartford, Conn., Miniature Printers, Peoria (Ill.) Art Ctr., Pa. Acad. Fine Arts, Originale Contemporate Graphic Internat., France, Bezalel Nat. Mus., Israel, Venice (Italy) Bienniale, Royal Etchers and Painters Exchange Exhibit, Eng., Bat Yam Mus., Israel, Paris, France, 1958, 59, Am.-Italian Print Exchange, numerous libraries, artists socs., invitational exhbns. include, Rome, Turin, Venice, Florence, Naples (all Italy), Nat. Academe Muse, France, Israel, USIA exhbns. in, Europe, S. Am., Asia, Africa; represented spl. collections, U.S. Nat. Mus., 1965, U. Maine, 1965, Library of Congress, 1965-71, Met. Mus. Art, 1965-66, 80, Nat. Gallery Art, 1966, Nat. Collection Fine Arts, 1966-71, 78, Nat. Air and Space Mus., 1970, N.Y. Pub. Library, 1971, 78, U.S. Mus. History and Tech., 1972, Naval Mus., 1972, Ft. Lewis Coll., Durango, Colo., 1980-81, Boston Pub. Library, 1980-81, Israel Nat. Mus., Jerusalem, 1980-81, State Mus. Albany, N.Y., 1980, N.Y. State Mus. Archives, Albany, 1979-89; also represented in permanent collections Balt. Mus. Art, Franklin D. Roosevelt, Fogg Mus., Harvard, Santa Barbara (Calif.) Art Mus., Syracuse U., Colorado Springs Fine Arts Ctr., Pennell Collection, Am. Artists Group Prize at Samuel Golden Coll., U. Minn., Calif. State Library, Pa. State Library, Bezalel Nat. Mus., Archives Am. Art Smithsonian Instn. (art and poetry), Washington, Archives and State Mus. Albany, N.Y. (120 works), Newark Pub. Library, Addison Gallery Am. Art, Bat Yam Municipal Mus., Safed Mus., Israel, Pa. State Tchrs. Coll., Richmond Art Assn., Peoria (Ill.) Art Ctr., Boston Pub. Library, St. Margaret Mary Sch. Art, Musee Nat. d'Art Modern, Yad Vashem Meml. Archives, Jerusalem (poetry), 1987, N.Y. State Mus. and Archives, 1989; spl. collections paintings, drawings and prints acquired by 19 nat. and internat. mus./archives. Represented as artist and poet: Miss. Art Assn. Internat. Water Color Club award 1947, 51, New Haven Paint and Clay Club, purchase award Peoria Art Ctr. 1950, Print Club Albany 1962, also Library of Congress, U. Minn., Calif. State Library, Met. Mus. Art, Pa. State Tchrs. Coll., Art Assn. Richmond, Ind., N.Y. Pub. Library, Newark Pub. Library, St. Margaret Mary Sch. Art Coll., landscape award Soc. Miniature Painters, Gravers and Sculpture, James Joyce award Poetry Soc. Am. 1975; presented spl. commemoration to Yad Vashem Meml. Hist. Site, Jerusalem, 1987; named Dau. of Mark Twain 1970; life fellow Met. Mus. Art; named to Exec. and Profl. Hall of Fame (plaque of honor 1966). Recipient World Order of Narrative Poets; named Membro Honoris Causa dell'Accademia di Scienze, Letteri, Arti Classe Accademica "Nobel", Milan, 1974, 75, Classe Storia Letter-Atura Americana, Milan, 1978, Exec. and Profl. Hall of Fame-Life, 1966; named A Daughter of Mark Twain, 1970; Met. Mus. fellow, 1966. Fellow Internat. Acad. Poets (founder 1977); mem. Soc. Am. Graphic Artists (group prize 1950), Print Club Albany (N.Y.), Boston Printmakers (award 1955), Washington Printmakers (exhbns.), Conn. Acad. Fine Arts, Am. Color Print Soc., Audubon Artists (group exhbns., award 1944), Phila. Water Color Club (group exhbns.), Nat. Assn. Women Artists (award 1945, 47), Print Council Am., Hunterdon Art Center, Internat. Platform Assn., Poetry Soc. Am., Artists Equity N.Y., Authors Guild, Inc., Accademia Di Scienze, Lettere, Arti-Milano, Italy (Consigliere, named hon. mem. as artist 1974, author/poet 1975, Nobel designate 1978); Academia Di Scienze. Lettere, Arti, Classe. Office: 915 W End Ave Apt 5D New York NY 10025

KATZ, IRWIN, marketing executive; b. N.Y.C., Oct. 6, 1942; s. Sam and Ethel (Weinstein) K.; m. Beatrice Eva Kraus, July 11, 1985; children: Ivan

Todd, Andrew Craig. BBA, Ohio U., 1964. Sales analyst J.B. Williams Co., N.Y.C., 1964-67; product mgr. Thayer Knomark div. Revlon Co., N.Y.C., 1967-69; supr. accounts Rumrill-Hoyt Advt. Agy., N.Y.C., 1969-71; exec. v.p., ptnr. Popofsky Advt. Agy., N.Y.C., 1971-78; v.p. mktg. Commerce Drug Co. div. Del Labs. Inc., Plainview, N.Y., 1979-81; v.p. strategic planning Del Labs Inc., Farmingdale, N.Y., 1981-83; sr. v.p. Ansell-Ams. Inc., Tinton Falls, N.J., 1983-88, Eatontown, N.J., 1988—. Jewish. Lodge: Free Sons. Home: 12 Geanne Way Marlboro NJ 07746 Office: Ansell-Ams Inc Cranberry Commons 446 State Hwy 35 Eatontown NJ 07724

KATZ, LEON, paper company executive; b. Springfield, Mass., Aug. 27, 1921; s. Frederick and Sarah (Kirsner) K.; m. Blossom Shirley Zeidman, June 8, 1947; children: Stanley G., Barbara D., Nancy L. B.S., Trinity Coll., 1944; Ph.D. in Organic Chemistry, U. Ill., 1947. With GAF Corp., 1953-70; v.p. research and devel.; exec. v.p. Rockwood Industries, 1970-72; v.p. comml. devel. Polychrome Corp., 1972-73; v.p. research and devel. packaging div. Am. Can Co., 1973-80, v.p. gen. mgr. recovery systems and research and devel. fiber, 1980-82; sr. v.p. corp. research and devel. James River Corp., Norwalk, Conn., 1982-85, v.p. corp. tech., 1985-88, cons., 1989—. Patentee in field; contbr. articles to profl. jours. Served with AUS, 1943-44. Mem. Am. Chem. Soc., AAAS, N.Y. Research Dirs., Am. Mgmt. Assn., Sigma Xi, Pi Mu Epsilon, Phi Lambda Upsilon. Office: James River Corp PO Box 6000 Norwalk CT 06856

KATZ, MARC ELLIS, industrial engineer; b. Phila., May 14, 1947; s. Henry and Sylvia C. (Sosnov) K.; m. Patricia L. Ritunnano, Jan. 23, 1968 (div. 1977); 1 child, Alan D.; m. Elizabeth A. Cattrall, Sept. 24, 1977; 1 child, Nathan S. BS in Commerce & Engring. Sci., Drexel U., 1969. Indsl. engr. Hooker Chem. Co., Niagara Falls, N.Y., 1969-70; sr. indsl. engr. Carborundum Co., Niagara Falls, 1970-73; supr. corp. indsl. engring. Hooker Chem. Co., Niagara Falls, 1973-76; dept. head raw material prodn. Hooker Chem. Co., Columbia, Tenn., 1976-79; sr. group indsl. engr. Air Products & Chems. Inc., Allentown, Pa., 1974-84, distrbn. mgr. field support, 1984-86; dir. indsl. engring. Rollins Environ. Svcs., Wilmington, Del., 1987—; pvt. practice cons., 1983—. Mem. Inst. Indsl. Engrs. (dir. 1988—, v.p. 1971-72)., Packaging Inst. (chem. packing com. 1980-86), Rotary, Branmar Racquetball and Fitness Club. Republican. Jewish. Home: 1021 Jeffrey Rd Wilmington DE 19810 Office: Rollins Environ Svcs 400 Bellevue Pk Wilmington DE 19809

KATZ, NORMAN, manufacturing company executive; b. Zwickau, Fed. Republic Germany, Apr. 10, 1925; came to U.S., 1940; naturalized, 1944; s. Paul and Dora (Ungar) K.; children: Ira and Stephen (twins); m. Sandra H. Hendricks, Dec. 22, 1988. BA in Econs., Columbia U., 1943. Exec. v.p. John Weitz Jrs., Inc., N.Y.C., 1947-52; pres. Norman Katz, Inc., N.Y.C., 1952-58, At Home Wear, Inc., N.Y.C., 1959-75, I. Appel Corp., N.Y.C., 1976—; instr. econs. CCNY, 1947-51. Trade chmn. Fedn. Jewish Philanthropies, 1957-71. Served with AUS, 1943-46. Recipient Torch Liberty award Anti Defamation League, 1987, Femmy Intimate Apparel Industry award, 1988. Clubs: Saugatuck Harbor Yacht (Westport, Conn.), Harrow U.S.A. (N.Y.C.). Home: 160 E 38th St New York NY 10016 also: Timberlake Estate Jackson TN 38305 Office: I Appel Corp 136 Madison Ave New York NY 10016

KATZ, RAUL LUCIANO, management consultant; b. Buenos Aires, Aug. 11, 1953; came to U.S., 1980; s. Jorge Manuel and Flora (Marinansky) K.; m. Barbara Christie Samuels II, Mar. 21, 1982. Lic. in history, U. Paris, 1979, M in Polit. Sci., 1980; M in Polit. Sci., M in Info. Scis., U. Paris II, 1980; MS in Polit. Sci., MIT, 1981, PhD in Polit. Sci., Mgmt., 1985. 2d v.p. Chase Manhattan Bank, N.Y.C., 1982-84; assoc. Booz, Allen & Hamilton, Inc., N.Y.C., 1984-87, sr. assoc., 1987—; cons. UNESCO, Paris, 1979, Kalba Bowen Assocs., Cambridge, Mass., 1982, Govt. of Argentina, Buenos Aires, 1983-87, UN, N.Y.C., 1985; advisor Nat. Commn. on Informatics, Buenos Aires, 1983-84. Author: The Information Society: An International Perspective, 1988; contbr. articles to profl. jours. Mem. Internat. Communications Assn. (K. Kyoon Hur Meml. Dissertation award 1986), Internat. Telecommunications Soc. Jewish. Office: Booz Allen & Hamilton Inc 101 Park Ave New York NY 10178

KATZ, ROBERT FRANCIS, film producer; b. N.Y.C., Feb. 7, 1941; s. Arnold Gilbert and Laura (Levine) K.; m. Pamela Ferol Rice, Mar. 27, 1982; 1 child, Victoria. Producer Los Angeles, 1965-70; exec. v.p., producer Medcom, Los Angeles, 1970-76; pres. Robert Katz Video Entertainment, Los Angeles, 1976-84; pres., bd dirs. Saints and Sinners Film Devel. Co., Los Angeles, 1984—; pres. Esparza-Katz Prodns., Los Angeles, 1984—; cons. Embassy Home Video, Los Angeles, 1984-85. Producer: (videos) Pritikin Diet, 1985, Shape Up With Arnold Swarzeneggar, 1985, Quick Dog Training With Barbara Woodhouse, 1985, (film) The Telephone starring Whoppi Goldberg, 1987. Bd. dirs. Santa Monica (Calif.) Airport Commn., 1987. Served to lt. USMC, 1961-64. Jewish. Home: 11313 Gladwin St Los Angeles CA 90049

KATZ, ROBERT HERMAN, insurance company executive; b. Balt., Sept. 20, 1925; s. Louis and Julia (Levitz) K.; m. Frances Frank, Nov. 5, 1966; children: Cheryl Lynn, Lauren Rebecca. BS, U. Md., 1950. Agt. Columbus Mut. Life Ins. Co., Balt., 1949-56; underwriter Chesapeake Life Ins. Co., Balt., 1956-57, asst. sec., 1957-58, sec., 1958-70, 72-73, 78-83, exec. v.p., 1963-73, pres., 1973-77, v.p., 1977—; also bd. dirs. Chesapeake Life Ins. Co.; v.p. Mut. Security Life Ins. Co., Ft. Wayne, Ind., 1988—; bd. dirs. Mut. Security Life Ins. Co. Active small craft com. ARC, Balt. Sgt. U.S. Army, 1943-45, ETO. Mem. Life Office Mgmt. Inst., Nat. Assn. Life Cos. (dir.-treas. 1987-88, sec. 1980-83, Claude H. Poindexter award 1984). Democrat. Jewish. Office: Mut Security Life Ins Co 3000 Coliseum Blvd E Fort Wayne IN 46805

KATZ, ROGER MARTIN, infosystems engineer; b. Jamaica, N.Y., Oct. 25, 1945; s. Joseph Morton and Helen (Bodner) K.; m. Gila Iris Slavin, Feb. 14, 1985; children: Adam, Karin. B.E.E. cum laude, Rensselaer Poly. Inst., 1967, M.E., 1968, Ph.D., 1974. Mem. faculty Rensselaer Poly. Inst., Troy, N.Y., 1967-72; mem. staff Mitre Corp., McLean, Va., 1972-82; sect. head Sperry Corp., Great Neck, N.Y., 1982-85; advanced systems engr. Norden Systems, Norwalk, Ct., 1986, mgr. project, Singer Co., Little Falls, N.J., 1987— ; owner Precision Techniques, Westbury, N.Y., 1983—; cons. to U.S. Congress, Office Tech. Assessment, 1983. Contbr. articles to profl. jours. Recipient Wynant James Williams award Rensselaer Poly. Inst., 1967. Mem. AAAS, Armed Forces Communications and Electronics Assn., IEEE, Sigma Xi, Tau Beta Pi, Eta Kappa Nu. Address: 11 Meadow Rd Old Westbury NY 11568

KATZ, WILLIAM EMANUEL, chemical engineer; b. Honesdale, Pa., June 12, 1924; s. Edward David and Aimee Helen (Rosenfelder) K.; m. Martha Elizabeth Legg, Feb. 13, 1960; children, Susan Katz Miller, Martha A., E. David II, James A.L. BSCE, MIT, 1948, MSCE, 1949. With Ionics Inc., Watertown, Mass., 1949—, chem. engr., 1949-51, asst. treas., 1951-53, treas., 1953-58, v.p. and dir., 1958-81, exec. v.p. and dir., 1981—; pres. Ionics Ultrapure Water Corp., Campbell, Calif., 1984—. Author chapter in AWWA Manual of Water Quality and Treatment, 1964, and 30 articles on water and waste treatment; patentee in field. With U.S. Army, 1942-46, PTO. Mem. Am. Inst. Chem. Engrs., Am. Water Works Assn., Nat. Water Supply Improvement Assn., Internat. Desalting Assn. Home: 11 Sunset Rd Weston MA 02193 Office: Ionics Inc 65 Grove St Watertown MA 02172

KATZENBACH, NICHOLAS DEBELLEVILLE, lawyer; b. Phila., Jan. 17, 1922; s. Edward Lawrence and Marie Louise (Hilson) K.; m. Lydia King Phelps Stokes, June 8, 1946; children—Christopher Wolcott, John Strong Minor, Maria Louise Hilson, Anne deBelleville. B.A., Princeton U., 1945; LL.B., Yale U., 1947; Rhodes scholar, Balliol Coll., Oxford (Eng.) U., 1947-49. Bar: N.J. 1950, Conn. 1955, N.Y. 1972. With firm Katzenbach, Gildea & Rudner, Trenton, N.J., 1950; atty.-adviser Office Gen. Counsel Air Force, 1950-52, part-time cons., 1952-56; asso. prof. law Yale Law Sch., 1952-56; prof. law U. Chgo. Law Sch., 1956-60; asst. atty. gen. Dept. Justice 1961-62, dep. atty. gen., 1962-64, acting atty. gen., 1964, atty. gen., 1965-66, under sec. state, 1966-69; sr. v.p., gen. counsel IBM Corp., 1969-84, sr. v.p. law and external relations, 1984-86, also bd. dirs.; ptnr. Riker, Danzig, Scherer & Hyland, Morristown, N.J., 1986—. Author: (with Morton A. Kaplan) The Political Foundations of International Law, 1961; editor-in-chief: Yale Law Jour, 1947; contbr. articles to profl. jours. Served to 1st lt. USAAF, 1941-45. Decorated Air medal with three clusters; Ford Found. fellow, 1960-61. Mem. Am. Law Inst., Am. Bar Assn., Am. Judicature Soc. Democrat. Episcopalian. Home: 906 The Great Rd Princeton NJ 08540 Office: Riker Danzig Scherer & Hyland 1 Speedwell Ave Hdqrs Pla Morristown NJ 07960

KATZMAN, ELLIOT MARK, accountant; b. Boston, Oct. 15, 1956; s. Myer and Marilyn (Rosenthal) K.; m. Donna M. Frangimone, Aug. 5, 1979; children: Matthew Adam, David Steven. BBA, Salem (Mass.) State Coll., 1978. CPA, Mass. Sr. acct. Touche Ross & Co., Boston, 1978-81; mgr. corp. acctg. Wheelabrator Frye, Inc., Hampton, N.H., 1981-83; controller Prime Leasing, Prime Computer, Natick, Mass., 1983-84; dir. fin. Cadlcam Bus. Group, Natick, Mass., 1984-87, dir. fin., customer svc., 1987-88; v.p., fin., chief fin. officer Vitronics Corp, Newmarket, N.H., 1988—. Mem. AICPA (North Andover adv. bd.), Mass. Soc. CPA's. Democrat. Jewish. Home: 50 Willow Ridge Rd North Andover MA 01845 Office: Vitronics Corp Newmarket Industrial Park Newmarket NH 03845

KAUFFMAN, EWING MARION, pharmaceutical executive; b. Mo., Sept. 21, 1916; s. John S. and Effie May (Winders) K.; m. Muriel Irene McBrien, Feb. 28, 1962; children: Larry, Sue, Julia. AS, Kansas City Jr. Coll.; BS, Union Coll., Schenectady, N.Y. Founder, chmn. Marion Labs., Inc., Kansas City, Mo., 1950—; co-owner, chmn. Kansas City Royals Baseball Club, 1969—. Mem. Civic Council, Kansas City.; pres. Ewing M. Kauffman Found.; bd. dirs. Mayor's Corps Progress. Served to ensign USNR. Recipient Horatio Alger award Am. Schs. and Colls. Assn., Golden Plate award Am. Acad. Achievement, Mktg. Man of Year award Sales and Marketing Execs. Internat., Disting. Service award Fellowship Christian Athletes, Disting. Eagle award Boy Scouts Am. Mem. Kansas City C. of C. (Man of Yr. award 1986). Clubs: Indian Hills Country, Kansas City, Eldorado Country. Office: Marion Labs Inc 9300 Ward Pkwy PO Box 8480 Kansas City MO 64114 also: Marion Lab Inc 10236 Marion Park Dr Kansas City MO 64137 *

KAUFFMANN, NORMAN JACQUES, JR., manufacturing company executive; b. New Orleans, Mar. 12, 1923; s. Norman J. and Edna Frances K.; B.S. in M.E., Tulane U., 1947; m. Carol Elizabeth Brown, Oct. 31, 1970; children—Norman S., Alan J., John E. Salesman, Westab div. Mead Corp., Dayton, Ohio, 1947-54, sales mgr., 1954-61, v.p., 1961-69; v.p. Nat. Blank Book Co. div. Dennison Mfg. Co., Holyoke, Mass., 1969-78; chmn. bd., pres. Norcom, Inc., Norcross, Ga., 1978-88; chmn. bd. Norex Inc., 1988—. Served to capt. USAAF, 1943-45. Mem. Paper Converters Assn. (dir. 1975-77), Springfield (Mass.) C. of C., Sales and Mktg. Execs. Club Springfield, Rotary, Commerce Club, Georgian, Ashford Club, Colony of Springfield, Buckhead Club, World Trade Club. Republican. Home: 2565 Habersham Rd Atlanta GA 30305 Office: 100 Galleria Pkwy #400 Atlanta GA 30339

KAUFMAN, DAVID GRAHAM, construction company executive; b. North Canton, Ohio, Mar. 20, 1937; s. DeVere and Josephine Grace (Graham) K.; student Kent State U., 1956; grad. Internat. Corr. Schs., 1965; grad. N.Y. Inst. Photography, 1983; postgrad. Calif. Coast U.; m. Carol Jean Monzione, Oct. 5, 1957 (div. Aug. 1980); children—Gregory Allan, Christopher Patrick. Machinist apprentice Hoover Co., North Canton, Ohio, 1955-57; draftsman-designer Goodyear Aircraft Corp., Akron, Ohio, 1957-60, Boeing Co., Seattle, 1960-61; designer Berger Industries, Seattle, 1961-62, Puget Sound Bridge & Drydock, Seattle, 1963, C.M. Lovsted, Seattle, 1963-64, Tracy, Brunstrom & Dudley, Seattle, 1964, Rubens & Pratt Engrs., Seattle, 1965-66; founder, owner, Profl. Drafting Svcs., Seattle, 1965, Profl. Take-Off Svcs., Seattle, 1966, Profl. Representation Svcs., Seattle, 1967, pres. Kaufman Inc., Seattle, 1967-83, Kaufman-Alaska Inc., Juneau, 1975-83 , Kaufman-Alaska Constructors, Inc., Juneau, 1975-83. Trustee, advisor Kaufman Internat., The Kaufman Group, Kaufman Enterprises; constrn. mgr. U. Alaska, 1979-84; constrn. cons. Alaskan native and Eskimo village corps., 1984—; prin. Kaufman S.W. Assocs., N. Mex., 1984—. Mem. Constrn. Specifications Inst., Associated Gen. Contractors Seattle Constrn. Council, Producers Council Oreg., Wash., Idaho, Hawaii, Alaska, Portland C. of C. Republican. Roman Catholic. Club: Toastmasters (past gov.). Lodge:Lions. Home and Office: PO Box 2390 Chinle AZ 86503

KAUFMAN, ERIC J., real estate investor; b. Bklyn., Sept. 4, 1956; s. Malvin and Joan K. AB, Vassar Coll., 1978; MBA, Wharton Sch., 1979. Cert. fin. planner, registered investment advisor. Fin. planning mgr. Am. Can Co., Edison, N.J., 1979-81; banker's cons. Bankers Trust Co., N.Y.C., 1981; chief exec. officer Creative Capital Group, Creative Capital Cons., Ltd., CCM Brokerage, Inc., Creative Capital Contracting Corp., CREA Real Estate Group, Inc., N.Y.C., N.Y.C., 1981—; bd. dirs. coop. corps., condominium assns. Composer improvisational classical and jazz music. Mem. Inst. Cert. Fin. Planners, Internat. Assn. Fin. Planners, Vassar Club, Wharton Club. Office: Creative Capital Group 27 E 38th St New York NY 10016

KAUFMAN, FRANK JOSEPH, lawyer; b. N.Y.C., July 16, 1944; s. Joseph F.X. and Carmen (Beatty) K.; m. Diane M.M. Laurendeau, July 28, 1973; 1 child, Elizabeth. BA, Hamilton Coll., 1966; JD, Harvard U., 1972. Assoc. Malcolm A. Hoffman Law Firm, N.Y.C., 1973-74; tax atty. McGraw Hill Inc., N.Y.C., 1974-80, dir. taxes, 1980-81, v.p. tax, 1981-87, sr. v.p. tax, 1987—. Mem. Phi Beta Kappa. Home: 50 E 89th St New York NY 10128 Office: McGraw-Hill Inc 1221 Ave of the Americas New York NY 10020

KAUFMAN, HARVEY, telecommunications equipment company executive; b. Boston, Nov. 10, 1931; s. Hyman M. and Sophie (Spear) K.; A.B., Harvard U., 1953. Product mgr. Gen. Electric Co., Auburn, N.Y., 1964-69, mgr. overseas bus. devel., Syracuse, N.Y., 1969-72; eastern regional mgr. NEC Telephones, Inc., Glen Cove, N.Y., 1972-77, dir. large systems mktg., Melville, N.Y., 1977-79; v.p. applications engring. Telecom Plus Internat., Inc., Long Island City, N.Y., 1979-83, v.p. strategic planning and product mgmt., 1984-87, exec. dir. mktg. Siemens Info. Systems Inc., Tel Plus Communications Inc., 1987—. Past bd. dirs. Internat. Center of Syracuse, Lynchburg Sci. Engring. and Sci. Served with Signal Corps, U.S. Army, 1953-55. Mem. IEEE. Club: Harvard of The Palm Beaches; Harvard of N.Y.C. Home: 2000 S Ocean Blvd #17C Boca Raton FL 33432 Office: 5500 Broken Sound Blvd Boca Raton FL 33487

KAUFMAN, HOWARD JACK, lawyer; b. Montreal, Que., Can., Dec. 22, 1942; s. Max and Jessie (Prashker) K.; children: Stuart David, Stephanie Reisha, Joshua Michael. BA, Concordia U., Montreal, 1963; B in Civil Law, McGill U., 1967. Bar: Que. 1971. Analyst Sun Life Assurance Co. Can., Montreal, 1968-69, sr. analyst, 1969-70; assoc. La Fleur, Brown, De Grand Pre, Montreal, 1970-77; staff counsel Xerox Can., Inc., Toronto, 1977-79, sr. staff counsel, 1979-80, v.p., sec., gen. counsel, 1980—; bd. dirs. Xerox Can. Fin. Inc., Toronto, Xerox Can. Holdings Inc., Xerox Can. Acceptance Inc., Xerox Can. Realty Inc.; lectr. seminars. Commr. Laval (Que.) Sch. Bd., 1973-77; 2d v.p., bd. govs. , 2d v.p. Beth Tikvah Synagogue, Toronto. Served to lt. RCAF, 1960-63. Recipient H.E. Herschon award Faculty of Law McGill U., 1967. Mem. Can. Bar Assn. (vice chmn. corp. counsel sect. 1983-85, chmn. 1985-87), Que. Bar Assn., Assn. Can. Gen. Counsels, Am. Corp. Counsel Assn., Info. Tech. Assn. Can. (chair legal affairs 1985-88), Can. Mfrs. Assn. (bd. dirs., chair legis. com. 1988—). Liberal. Hebrew. Clubs: Lawyers; Richmond Hill (Ont.) Country. Office: Xerox Can Inc, 5650 Yonge St, Toronto, ON Canada M2M 4G7

KAUFMAN, IRA JEFFREY, investment banker; b. Chgo., Mar. 4, 1928; s. Hy and Gertrude (Schwartz) K.; m. Audrey Becker, Jan. 12, 1969; children—Stephen, Stacy, Elizabeth, Jonathan. Student, Chgo. Mil. Acad., 1938-41, Northwestern Mil. and Naval Acad., 1941-45, U. Ill., 1945-46. With Rodman & Renshaw, Inc., 1958—, pres., 1969-79, chmn. bd., 1969—; past chmn. exec. com. Skyline Corp.; dir. emeritus Dan River Mills, Inc.; Mem. Chgo. Bd. Trade; mem. Chgo. Bd. Options Exchange, Midwest Stock Exchange; chmn. bd. Exchange Nat. Bank Chgo., 1979—, Exchange Bancorp Inc., 1979—. Past trustee, mem. exec. adv. bd. St. Joseph Hosp. Clubs: Standard, Chgo. Yacht, Attic (Chgo.); Jockey (Miami, Fla.); Fisher Island (Fla.); Ocean Reef (Key Largo, Fla.). Home: 2479 Woodbridge Ln Highland Park IL 60035 Office: Exch Bancorp Inc 120 S LaSalle St Chicago IL 60603-3499

KAUFMAN, PHYLLIS CYNTHIA, lawyer, author, theatrical producer; b. Phila., Nov. 4, 1945; d. Harry and Gertrude (Friend) K. BA cum laude, Brandeis U., 1967; JD, Temple U., 1974. Bar: Pa. 1974, U.S. Dist. Ct. (ea. dist.) Pa. 1974. Pvt. practice entertainment law, Phila., 1977—; exec. producer Playhouse in the Park, Phila., 1979; dir. entertainment Caesar's Hotel-Casino, Atlantic City, N.J., 1980-81; v.p. entertainment Sands Hotel-Casino, Atlantic City, 1981-83; v.p. Kanadus Entertainment Inc., Toronto, 1982—, Bright Techs., Inc., N.Y.C. and Phila., 1989—. Co-author: No-Nonsense Financial, Real Estate, Career and Legal Guides, 1985—; assoc. editor Temple Law Quarterly. Bd. dirs. Phila. Coll. Performing Arts, 1977-85, Creative Artists Network, 1986—. Ford Found. grantee, 1965-67. Mem. Phila. Bar Assn. Democrat. Office: Bright Techs 1500 Locust St #3805 Philadelphia PA 19102

KAUFMAN, RICHARD, investment services executive; b. White Plains, N.Y., July 10, 1936; s. Max Kaufman and Anne Kaufman Kaplan; m. Joanne Marie Ippolito, Apr. 29, 1976; children—Shari Ellen, Kenneth Craig. B.A. in Econs., Brandeis U., 1958. Regional v.p. Dupont Walston, Boston, 1966-74; exec. v.p. Paine Webber, N.Y.C., 1974-84; mng. dir. investment services group Donaldson, Lufkin & Jenrette, N.Y.C., 1984—; dir. Empire State Coll. Found. Parent chmn. Skidmore Coll., Saratoga Springs, 1981-85; bd. dirs. 75th Street Tenants Assn., N.Y.C. Served with U.S. Army, 1960-66. Mem. Securities Industry Assn. (com. mem.). Club: Rolling Hills. Home: 1 Strawberry Hill Ave Apt 16A Stamford CT 06902 Office: Donaldson Lufkin & Jenrette Inc 140 Broadway New York NY 10005

KAUFMAN, ROBERT MAX, lawyer; b. Vienna, Austria, Nov. 17, 1929; came to U.S., 1939, naturalized, 1945; s. Paul M. and Bertha (Hirsch) K.; m. Sheila Seymour Kelley, Nov. 20, 1959. B.A. with honors, Bklyn. Coll., 1951; M.A., NYU, 1954; J.D. magna cum laude, Bklyn. Law Sch., 1957. Bar: N.Y. 1957, U.S. Supreme Ct. 1961. Successively jr. economist, economist, sr. economist N.Y. State Div. Housing, 1953-57; atty. antitrust div. U.S. Dept. Justice, 1957-58; legis. asst. to U.S. Senator Jacob K. Javits, 1958-61; asso. Proskauer Rose Goetz & Mendelsohn, N.Y.C., 1961-69, partner, 1969—; chmn. bd. Pirelli Cable Corp., Pirellie Armstrong Tire Corp.; dir. Haseg (S.A.), Roytex, Inc.; mem. N.Y. State Legislature Adv. Com. on Election Law, 1973-74; chmn. adv. com. N.Y. State Bd. Elections, 1974-78; chmn. N.Y. State Bd. Pub. Disclosure, 1981-82; mem. adminstrv. conf. of U.S., U.S. Army Chief of Staff's Spl. Commn. on Honor System, N.Y. Chief Judge's Com. on Availability of Legal Svcs.; referee Commn. on Jud. Conduct; chmn. Exec. Com. for Modern Cts. Co-author: Congress and the Public Trust, 1970, Disorder in the Court, 1973. Bd. dirs., mem. exec. com. Lawrence M. Gelb Found., Inc., Volunteers of Legal Service, N.Y. Lawyers in the Pub. Interest; bd. dirs., sec. Community Action for Legal Services, Inc., 1976-78; dir., mem. exec. com. Legal Aid Soc.; mem. platform com. N.Y. Rep. State Com., 1974; mem. jud. selection adv. coms. Senator Javits, 1972-80, and Senator Moynahan, 1977—; mem. distbn. com. N.Y. Community Trust; bd. dirs. N.Y. Community Funds, James Found., Fairfield, Conn. Community Found.; treas., mgr., counsel various polit. campaigns; presdl. appointee mem. bd. visitors U.S. Mil. Acad., 1977-79; mem. Adminstrv. Conf. U.S., 1988—, chief of sheriff's commn. on West Point nominating system, 1988-89. With U.S. Army, 1957-58. Fellow Am. Bar Found., N.Y. State Bar Found.; mem. ABA, Assn. of Bar of City N.Y. (pres. 1986-88, past chmn. com. on 2d Century; past chmn. exec. com., past chmn. com. profl. responsibility, past chmn. spl. com. on campaign expenditures, past chmn. com. civil rights, past vice chmn. com. grievances, chmn. delegation to state bar ho. dels.), N.Y. State Bar Assn. (ho. of dels. 1978, 1986—), N.Y. County Lawyers Assn. (past chmn. com. on civil rights), Am. Law Inst., Assn. Bar Fund, Inc. (v.p.). Office: Proskauer Rose Goetz & Mendelsohn 300 Park Ave New York NY 10022

KAUFMAN, STEPHEN P., electronics company executive; b. Cambridge, Mass., Nov. 19, 1941; s. Arthur Samuel and Dorothy Ethel (Birman) K.; m. Sharon Kay Malin, Sept. 28, 1969; 1 child, Jeremy Scott. BS, MIT, 1963; MBA, Harvard U., 1965. Asst. to pres. Grand Steel & Mfg. Co., Clawson, Mich., 1965-67; group controller Chase, Brass & Copper Co., Cleve., 1967-69; assoc. McKinsey & Co., Cleve., 1969-75, ptnr., 1976-80; group v.p. Midland Ross Corp., Cleve., 1980-82; exec. v.p. Arrow Electronics, Inc., Melville, N.Y., 1982-84, pres., 1984—, chief operating officer, 1984-86, chief exec. officer, 1986—; also bd. dirs. Arrow Electronics, Inc. Bd. dirs. L.I. Philharm., Melville, 1984—; trustee L.I. U., Brookville, 1985—. Recipient Corp. Leadership award MIT, 1987. Clubs: Mill River (Oyster Bay, N.Y.); Lloyd Neck Bath (N.Y.). Office: Arrow Electronics Inc 25 Hub Dr Melville NY 11747

KAUFMANN, BEN COMBS, financial services company executive; b. Clay County, Ky., June 1, 1943; s. Maurice and Sara (Combs) K.; m. Stacia Yadon, Aug. 6, 1966 (div.); m. Janet L. Zusman, Apr. 13, 1986. Student, Transylvania U., 1961-64; BA, Eastern Ky. U., 1966; postgrad., U. Tenn., 1966-67; cert., Coll. Fin. Planning, Denver, 1982. CLU; chartered fin. cons. Sr. ptnr. Kaufmann & Michalove, Lexington, Ky., 1967-85, Kaufmann Bros. Properties, Lexington, 1971—, A.P.T. Real Estate, Lexington, 1976—; pres. Kaufmann Realty & Assocs, Lexington, 1968—, Kaufmann Properties, Lexington, 1968—; owner, mgr. Kaufmann Ins. Co., Lexington, 1968—; sec. Interconnect Tel. System, Lexington, 1979-85; chief exec. officer Capital Creation Co., Lexington, 1981—, Kaufmann Devel. Co., Inc., Lexington, 1986—; sec., treas. Nat. Pavers Inc., Nashville, 1987—. Contbr. articles on life ins. to profl. publs. Bd. dirs. YMCA, Lexington, Boy Scouts Am., Lexington, Adath Israel Temple, Lexington. Mem. Am. Soc. CLU, Inst. Cert. Fin. Planners, Internat. Assn. Fin. Planning, Nat. Assn. of Life Underwriters. Republican. Home: 125 Sycamore St Lexington KY 40502 Office: 326 Woodland Ave Ste 2 Lexington KY 40508

KAUFMANN, MARK STEINER, banker; b. N.Y.C., Dec. 3, 1932; s. Milton L. and Elsa S. (Steiner) K.; B.S. cum laude in Bus. Adminstrn., Lehigh U., 1953; m. Carole Richard, June 16, 1957; children—Jon Richard, Susan Helen. Vice pres., dir. mktg. Standard Fin. Corp., N.Y.C., 1958-64; sr. v.p., dir. Milberg Factors, Inc., N.Y.C., 1964-73; dir. corp. devel. Chase Manhattan Bank, N.Y.C., 1973-87, sr. v.p., 1987—; chmn. Lower Manhattan Cultural Council, Wall St. Planning Group. Past treas. bd. trustees Calhoun Sch., N.Y.C.; trustee Temple Israel, N.Y.C. Served as 1st lt. USAF, 1953-55. Recipient Human Relations award Anti-Defamation League, 1973, Human Relations award Am. Jewish Com., 1987. Mem. Am. Arbitration Assn., Beta Gamma Sigma, Lambda Mu Sigma, Pi Gamma Mu, Omicron Delta Kappa. Club: Old Oaks Country (dir.). Home: 124 W 79th St New York NY 10024 Office: Chase Manhattan Bank One Chase Manhattan Pla New York NY 10081

KAUL, KENNETH LEE, marine company marketing executive; b. Beaver Dam, Wis., Oct. 17, 1945; s. Willie Jr. and Harriet (Lembrich) K.; m. Elaine E. Friedrich, Aug. 21, 1965; 1 child, Corey. Bus. cert., U. Wis., Milw., 1969, 71. Sales fin. mgr. Chrysler Corp., Hartford, Wis., 1965-84; mktg. mgr. U.S. Marine Corp., Hartford, 1984—; pres., chmn. Nat. Leisure Products Group, Mpls., 1982-83. Mem. Sales and Mktg. Execs., Nat. Marine Mfrs. Assn., Lions (pres. Allenton, Wis. 1983-84). Lutheran. Office: US Marine Corps 105 Marine Dr Hartford WI 53027

KAUSEL, THEODORE CARL, metal processing executive; b. Lynn, Mass., Mar. 5, 1941; s. Robert Livingston and Mary Elizabeth (Legro) Benford; m. Virginia d' Elseaux, June 6, 1963; children: Mark Christian, Christopher Scott. BSME, U. Maine, 1961; MBA, Dartmouth U., 1969. Mgr. material control NCR, Millsboro, Del., 1969-72; plant supt. Handy & Harman, Fairfield, Conn., 1972-77; controller Torin Corp, Torrington, Conn., 1977-82; mgr. mfg. Clevepak Corp., Torrington, 1982-86; v.p. fin. and systems The Stanley Works Steel Div., New Britain, Conn., 1986-87; v.p., gen. mgr. Cold Metal Products Co., Inc., New Britain, 1987—. Capt. U.S. Army, 1963-67, ETO. Home: 86 Harmony Hill Rd Harwinton CT 06791 Office: Cold Metal Products Co Inc PO Box 6000 New Britain CT 06050-6000

KAUSHIK, SURENDRA KUMAR, economist; b. Malsisar, India, June 21, 1944; came to U.S., 1970; naturalized, 1980; s. Lakminarain Sharma and Rathi Chaturvedy; m. Helena Pokornicki, Sept. 12, 1973. BS in Commerce, U. Rajasthan, India, 1965, MA in Econs., 1967; PhD in Econs., Boston U., 1976. Research asst., instr. Inst. Econ. Growth, Delhi, India, 1968-70; tchg. fellow, research asst., then sr. tchg. fellow and lect. Boston U., 1971-75; lectr. Lowell Technol. Inst., Boston State Coll., 1973-74; asst. prof. Babson Coll.,

Wellesley, Mass., 1976-81; dir. Inst. Internat. Banking, Lubin Grad. Sch. Bus., 1981—; prof. Pace U., White Plains, 1984—; instr. Northeastern U., Bosron, 1972-73; cons. UN, 1976-77. Condr. research internat. banking and fin.; editor: Banking, Money Markets and Monetary Policy, 1980, International Banking and Global Financing, 1983, Debt Crisis and Financial Stability: The Future, 1985, Internal Banking and World Economic Growth, 1987, The Practical Financial Manager, 1988; co-author: The Practical Financial Manager, 1988. Mem. Am. Econ. Assn., Am. Fin. Assn., AAUP, Western Econ. Assn., Eastern Econ. Assn., Atlantic Econ. Soc. Office: Pace U Lubin Grad Sch Bus 1 Martine Ave White Plains NY 10606

KAUTT, GLENN GREGORY, financial planner; b. Arlington, Va., Jan. 25, 1948; s. Elmer Curtis and Phyllis Ruth (Schmalz) K.; m. Elisabeth B. Emerson, Aug. 19, 1973 (div. 1975); 1 child, Christopher Curtis. BS, Purdue U., 1973; MBA, Harvard U., 1979. Commd. lt. USN, 1969, resigned, 1977; sr. assoc. ICF, Inc., Washington, 1979-81; mng. dir. The Challenger Group, Silver Spring, Md., 1981-85; sr. planner Fin. Svc. Group, Vienna, Va., 1985-88; prin. Capitol Fin. Cons., Inc., Vienna, 1988—. Co-author, editor Inside the Real Estate Business, 1981; contbr. articles to profl. mags. Mem. Registry Financial Planning Practitioners, Internat. Assn. Fin. Planning, Inst. Cert. Fin. Planners, Nat. Assn. Life Underwriters, Internat. Assn. Registered Fin. Planners. Republican. Mormon. Office: Capitol Fin Cons Inc 1577 Spring Hill Rd Ste 400 Vienna VA 22180-2223

KAUTZ, JAMES CHARLES, investment banker; b. Cin., Mar. 3, 1931; s. Paul Daniel and Marie M. (Fisher) K.; m. Caroline Miller, June 15, 1957; children: Leslie Barnes, Daniel Paul. A.B., U. Cin., 1953; M.B.A., U. Pa., 1957. With food advt. dept. Procter & Gamble Co., Cin., 1957-59; corp. sec. Main Supply, Cin., 1959-66; gen. ptnr. Goldman, Sachs & Co., N.Y.C., 1978-87, ltd. ptnr., 1987—. Trustee, chmn. investment com. Vassar Coll.; hon. trustee U. Cin. McMicken Found.; trustee Nat. Geographic Soc. Edn. Found., 1988—, Greater N.Y. council Boy Scouts Am., 1983—. Served with U.S. Army, 1953-55. Clubs: Bond (N.Y.C.); Beacon Hill (Summit, N.J.). Home: 251 Oak Ridge Ave Summit NJ 07901 Office: Goldman Sachs & Co 85 Broad St New York NY 10004

KAVANAGH, CHERYL ELIZABETH, investor, consultant; b. Marlborough, Mass., May 30, 1949; d. Joaquim Michael Costa and Alice Delores (Morris) Kasaras; m. Richard Patrick Kavanagh, Nov. 10, 1967; children: Richard Christopher, Christopher Noel. Student, Mt. Wachusett Coll., 1972-74. Investor real estate, property mgr. Hudson, Mass., 1973—; part-time fin. cons. Hudson, 1985—. Freelance writer. Chairperson parent adv. council Marlborough Sch. Dept., 1982-87; vol. polit. candidates, 1972-74, Right to Life, Marlborough, 1972-75; sponsor Save the Children; tchr. religious instrn., Marlborough, 1981-83, contbg. editor newsletter, 1982-87; coordinator Marlborough Chapter I program, 1985-87. Republican. Roman Catholic. Clubs: Paradise Island, Golf and Tennis (St. Petersburg). Home and Office: 95 White Pond Rd Hudson MA 01749

KAVEE, ROBERT CHARLES, global investment research executive; b. N.Y.C., Aug. 9, 1934; s. Julius and Kate K.; m. Donna Helen Auld, Jan. 31, 1959; children: Andrew L., Patti M., Stacie R. AB in Math., U. Rochester, 1956; MS in Elec. Engring., Columbia U., 1959; postgrad., U. Pa., 1974. Def. space electronics, systems engr. ITT Labs. & Sperry Rand Systems Group, Nutley, N.J. and Great Neck, N.Y., 1959-66; NSF sr. rsch. fellow Poly. Inst., Bklyn., 1966-68; sr. systems specialist ITT Data Svcs., Paramus, N.J., 1968-70; mgr. ops. rsch. ITT World Hdqrs., N.Y.C., 1970-75; mgr. instl. applications devel. Merrill Lynch, Pierce, Fenner & Smith, N.Y.C., 1975-84; v.p., mgr. fixed income portfolio optimization Merrill Lynch Capital Markets, N.Y.C., 1984-88; sr. v.p. Intersec Rsch. Corp., Stamford, Conn., 1988—. Mem. Rep. Town Meeting, Greenwich, Conn. Mem. Am. Fin. Assn., Inst. Quantitative Rsch. Fin., Bond Quantitative Group,IEEE, Old Greenwich Yacht. Home: 51 Mary Ln Riverside CT 06878 Office: Intersec Rsch Corp 48 Signal Rd Stamford CT 06902

KAVIN, REBECCA JEAN, health science facility executive, medical consultant; b. Dodge, Nebr., June 29, 1946; d. William Wilber Walsh and Dorothy Eleanor (Watson) Williams; m. Paul Babcock, May 15, 1965 (div. Sept. 1976); m. E. Iraj Kavin, Apr. 23, 1977; children: Mark Bijan, Seana Shereen. Cert., Ohio U., 1963. Claims adjuster San Found. for Med. Care, San Diego, 1968-70; adminstrv. asst. Friendly Hills Med. Group, La Habra, Calif., 1971-77; office mgr. Robert M. Peck and Sergio Blesa, M.D., Pasadena, Calif., 1978-81; pres. Provider Mgmt. Assocs., La Canada, Calif., 1981—; speaker Continuing Edn. Dept. UCLA, 1985, Hosp. Council of So. Calif., Los Angeles, 1986, Am. Acad. Med. Preventics, Los Angeles, 1986. Contbr. articles to profl. jours. Mem. Am. Guild Patient Account Mgrs. (speaker Los Angeles chpt. 1986). Republican. Presbyterian. Office: Provider Mgmt Assocs 2418 Honolulu Ave Montrose CA 91020

KAWANO, JAMES CONRAD, pharmaceutical company executive. Student, U. Calif., Berkeley, 1972-73; PharmD, U. Calif., San Francisco, 1978; postgrad., U. Pa., 1986—. Registered pharmacist. Clin. pharmacist Med. Coll. Pa. and Hosp., Phila., 1978-82; med. devel. coordinator E.R. Squibb and Sons, U.S., Princeton, N.J., 1982-84, mktg. research supr., 1984-85, mktg. research mgr., 1985-86; mgr. strategic planning and bus. analysis Squibb U.S., Princeton, 1986-87, bus. devel. mgr., 1987-88; mgr. product planning worldwide bus. devel. Squibb Operating Group, Princeton, 1988—. Mem. Am. Soc. Hosp. Pharmacists, Pa. Soc. Hosp. Pharmacists, Calif. Pharmacists Assn.

KAWANO, RANDALL TOSHIO, banker; b. Honolulu, Sept. 27, 1959; s. Toshio and Tokiye (Kato) K.; m. Suzanne C. Harada, Feb. 15, 1986. BBA in Acctg. with distinction, U. Hawaii, 1982; student, Sch. for Bank Adminstrn., 1987—. CPA, Hawaii; cert. mgmt. acct. Auditor Ernst and Whinney, Honolulu, 1983-84; acctg. officer First Hawaiian Creditcorp., Honolulu, 1984-86; asst. v.p. and asst. controller City Bank, Honolulu, 1986—. Mem. Nat. Assn. Accts., Nat. Assn. Bank Cost and Mgmt. Accts., Fin. Mgmt. for Data Processing. Home: 98-615 Kilinoe St Aiea HI 96701 Office: City Bank 201 Merchant St Honolulu HI 96813

KAYE, BARRY, insurance company executive; b. N.Y.C., May 20, 1928; s. Herbert and Blanche (Sabin) K.; C.L.U., Am. Coll. Life Underwriters, 1966; m. Carol Golison, Mar. 16, 1962; children—Fern L., Alan L., Howard S. Pres., Barry Kaye, Inc., 1960—; owner Barry Kaye Assos., Century City, Calif., 1970—. Mem. faculty Practicing Law Inst., 1969—; lectr. U. Calif., Los Angeles, 1970—. Mem. adv. bd. Eddie Cantor Charitable Found., 1973—. Bd. govs. Diamond Circle of Hope, Sinai Temple; bd. trustees City of Hope. Fellow, Ben Gurion Soc., Ben Gurion U. of the Negev. Recipient Founders award Diamond Circle City of Hope, 1972, Lifetime Achievement award Ben-Gurion U. of the Negev, 1987; Man of Year award Gen. Agts. and Mgrs. Conf., 1965, 66, 67. Mem. NCCJ, Am. Soc. C.L.U.s, NCCJ (trustee, bd. dirs.). Mem. B'nai B'rith. Clubs: Presidents of the Thailians, Uncles of Vista del Mar. Author: How to Save a Fortune on Your Life Insurance, 1987. Office: Barry Kaye Assocs 1840 Century Park E Ste 600 East Los Angeles CA 90067

KAYE, IRA B., wholesale distributor executive; b. Bklyn., June 28, 1937; s. Phillip and Renee (Diamond) K.; m. Valencia Marie Wolf, Mar. 5, 1983; children: Dana, Paul, Jordan, Justin. Student, Calif. State U., San Francisco, 1959-60. Salesman A.H. Meyer, San Francisco, 1959-61; salesman Calectron, San Francisco, 1961-68, merchandise mgr., 1968-71; dist. mgr. RCA Corp., Indpls., 1971-72; gen. sales mgr. RCA Distbg. Corp., San Francisco, 1975-84; v.p., gen. mgr. D&H Distbg. Co. N/W, Seattle, 1985—. Served to sgt. USMC, 1955-59. Mem. Electric Gas Industry Assn. (pres. 1978-79). Republican. Jewish. Office: D&H Distributing Co NW 5920 S 180th St Seattle WA 98188

KAYE, LORI, travel academy executive, consultant; b. N.Y.C.; d. Eldin Bert and Katherine Angeline Onsgard; student Detroit Inst. Art, 1951, 56, U. N.Mex., 1960. Actress, radio and TV commls., 1951-82; actress Warner Brothers, 1960-64; dir., v.p. John Robert Powers Schs., Los Angeles, 1961-71; v.p. Electron Industries, Torrance, Calif., 1963-65; owner, v.p., Lawrence Leon Photography Studio, Los Angeles, 1964-68; pres. Lori Kaye Cosmetics, Hollywood, Calif., 1964-70; co-owner, v.p. K and S Employment, Calif. Fashion Mart, 1965-67; dir., internat. cons. Airline Schs. Pacific, Van Nuys, Calif., 1972-74; dir. Caroline Leonetti Ltd. Sch., Hollywood, 1976-79; pres., dir. Internat. Travel Acad., North Hollywood, Calif.; internat. cons. Internat. Career Acad., Van Nuys, 1978—, Glendale Coll. Bus. and Paramed. (Calif.), 1980—, Acad. Pacific, Hollywood, 1981—; pres. Molori Publs., Studio City, Calif., 1981—; cons. A&T Inst. Travel and Tourism, 1982; lectr., 1969—. Dir. project Camarillo State Hosp., 1963-69; cons. Job Corps. Recipient Mental Health Achievement award, 1967. Mem. Nat. Assn. Female Execs., Assn. for Promotion of Tourism Africa, AAU, Screen Actors Guild, AFTRA, Smithsonian Assocs., Calif. Assn. Pvt. Postsecondary Schs., U.S. Masters-Internat. Swim Club, Nat. Geog. Soc., Internat. Platform Assn., Better Bus. Bur. (also arbitrator), Universal City- No. Hollywood C. of C. Paintings included in UNICEF collection, 1957; hostess TV talk show The New You, KTTV, Hollywood, 1964-65. Office: Molori Publs 11684 Ventura Blvd Ste 134 Studio City CA 91604 Office: Internat Travel Acad 12123 Magnolia Blvd North Hollywood CA 91607

KAYE, RICHARD MICHAEL, accounting company executive; b. Chgo., Feb. 23, 1945; s. Harry J. and Bertha (Forman) K.; m. Ellen Kaye, 1967; children: Martin, Joel, Heather. B in Math, U. Mich., 1967, M in Acturial Sci., 1968. CPA, Mich., Ill. Tchr. Grove Sch., Northbrook, Ill., 1968-69; acct. Peat Marwick Mitchell & Co., Chgo., 1969-70, actuary, 1970-72; supr. actuarial div. Coopers & Lybrand, Chgo., 1972-73, sr. cons. actuarial div., 1973-75; mng. ptnr. actuarial, benefits and compensation cons. div. Coopers & Lybrand, Detroit, 1975—. Fellow Soc. Actuaries; mem. Am. Inst. CPA's, Am. Acad. Actuaries, Knollwood Country Club, Am. Contract Bridge Club. Jewish. Home: 5644 Apple Ridge Trail West Bloomfield MI 48322 Office: Coopers & Lybrand 400 Renaissance Ctr Ste 3900 Detroit MI 48243

KAYNE, JON BARRY, industrial psychologist; b. Sioux City, Iowa, Oct. 20, 1943; s. Harry Aaron and Barbara Valentine (Daniel) K.; m. Bunee Ellen Price, July 25, 1965; children: Nika Jenine, Abraham; m. 2d Sandra Kay Fossbender, Jan. 5, 1985; 1 child, Shay-Marie Kathryn. BA, U. Colo., 1973; MSW, U. Denver, 1975; PhD, U. No. Colo., 1978. With spl. services Weld County Sch. Dist. 6, Greeley, Colo., 1975-77; forensic diagnostician Jefferson County (Colo.) Diagnostic Unit, 1977-78; assoc., dir. mktg. 1 Dow Ctr., assoc. prof. psychology Hillsdale (Mich.) Coll., 1978-87; pres. Jon B. Kayne, P.C., Hillsdale, 1980-87; chmn. bd. dirs., chief exec. officer Am. Internat. Mgmt. Assocs., Ltd., Denver, 1984-87; v.p. continuous edn. and profl. studies, prof. bus. adminstrn. and psychology Bellevue (Neb.) Coll., 1987—. Chmn. bd. dirs. Domestic Harmony, 1979-82; dir. religious sch., Greeley, 1975-77; candidate for sheriff of Boulder County, 1974. Served with USAR, 1962. Mem. Am. Psychol. Assn., Am. Soc. Clin. Hypnosis, Am. Statis. Assn., Internat. Neuropsychol. Soc., Mich. Soc. Investigative and Forensic Hypnosis (chmn. bd., pres. 1982), N.Y. Acad. Scis., Phi Delta Kappa, Psi Chi, Alpha Gamma Sigma. Office: Bellevue Coll Galvin Rd at Harvell Dr Bellevue NE 68005

KAYSER, DONALD ROBERT, financial executive; b. Chgo., Oct. 7, 1930; s. Harold William and Catherine (Spillane) K.; m. Mary King, Oct. 13, 1956; children—Catherine E. Blazer, D. Robert, Kevin C., Jean K., William H., Christopher J. B.S.E.E., Fournier Inst. Tech., 1952; M.B.A., Harvard U., 1956. V.p., gen. mgr. southern ops. La.-Pacific Corp., Portland, Oreg., 1972-73, Vice pres., chief fin. officer, 1973-82, dir., 1972—; sr. v.p., chief fin. officer Bendix Corp., Southfield, Mich., 1982-83; v.p fin. Allied Corp., Morristown, N.J., 1983-84; sr. v.p., chief fin. officer Allied-Signal Inc., Morristown, N.J., 1984-88; exec. v.p., chief fin. officer Morrison Knudsen Corp., Boise, Idaho, 1988—, also bd. dirs.; Bd. dirs. La. Pacific Corp. With Signal Corps, U.S. Army, 1952-54. Baker scholar, Harvard U., 1956. Mem. Nat. Assn. Mfrs. (bd. dirs. 1986—). Roman Catholic. Office: Morrison Knudsen Corp Box 73 Boise ID 83707

KAZARIAN, JEAN ANN, technical-scientific writer, editor; b. San Francisco, July 13, 1948; d. George Abraham Kazarian and Carmen Lorraine (Moore) Surratt. BA in Physiology, San Francisco State U., 1977, MA in Physiology, 1985. Research asst., dir. mktg., writer, editor supr. Creative Strategies, San Jose, 1982-84; database writer, editor Coalesce Corp., Saratoga, Calif., 1986; publisher, owner, chief exec. officer Act-Now Enterprises, Santa Clara, Calif., 1986-88; owner, pres. wholesale products J. Kazarian & Assocs., Santa Clara, 1986-88; tech. writer/editor Lockheed Missiles and Space Co., Hewlett-Packard Co., Anaerobe Systems, 1987—; prodn. mgr. CopyMat, Santa Clara, 1986. San Francisco State U. grantee, 1967. Mem. Nat. Specialty Merchandisers Assn. Democrat. Armenian Orthodox.

KEAN, CHARLES THOMAS, dental manufacturing company executive; b. Boston, July 21, 1941; s. Charles Theodore and Katherine (Mooney) K.; m. Ulrike G. Klenkler, May 12, 1984; children: Lisa, Stephanie, Michael. BS, Boston Coll., 1963; MBA, Boston U., 1968; JD, Suffolk U., 1976. Analyst The Gillette Co., Boston, 1968-69, fin. planner, internat. mgr., 1970-72, project mgr. chmn.'s office, 1973-74; controller Can. div. The Gillette Co., Montreal, Que., 1975-76; diversified group controller The Gillette Co., Boston, 1977-79; gen. mgr. European div. Jafra Cosmetics Co., London, 1980-84; internat. controller Dentsply Internat., York, Pa., 1985, v.p., gen. mgr., 1986—; bd. dirs. Dental Products of India, Bombay, Somadent, Kharkov, U.S.S.R. Served to capt. USMC, 1963-66. Office: Dentsply Asia Inc, Hop Hing Centre, 8-12 Hennessy Rd, Hong Kong Hong Kong

KEAN, JOHN, utility company executive; b. N.Y.C., Oct. 28, 1929; s. John and Mary Alice (Barney) K.; m. Joan E. Jessup, June 25, 1952; children: Mary Lita, John, Katharine, Susan; m. Pamela A. Summers, Sept. 10, 1983. B.A., Harvard U., 1953; student, N.Y. Inst. Fin., 1954-55. Security analyst Kean, Taylor & Co., N.Y.C., 1953-55; comml. and gas cadet Pub. Service Elec. & Gas Co., Newark, 1955-56; adminstrv. asst. Pub. Service Elec. & Gas Co., 1956-59, v.p. sales and pub. relations, 1959-63; pres. Elizabethtown (N.J.) Gas Co., 1963-80, chmn. bd., chief exec. officer, 1980; pres., dir. Nat. Utilities & Industries Corp., Elizabeth, N.J., 1969—; also bd. dirs. NUI Corp., Bedminster, N.J.; hon. pres. Internat. Gas Union (sci. and tech. fedn. representing 46 countries); bd. dirs. City Gas Co. Fla., Utility Billing Svcs., City Fed. Savs. Bank, Cityfed Fin. Corp. Elizabethtown Water Co., E'town Corp., numerous others. Mayor, Bedminster Twp., N.J., 1962-69, committeeman, 1970—; pres. N.J. State League of Municipalities, 1969-70, mem. exec. com., 1962—; Hon. chmn. bd. dirs. Deborah Hosp.; trustee Kean Coll. N.J., St. Mark's Sch. Served with USMCR, 1948-50. Mem. Am. Gas Assn. (dir. 1967-80, chmn. bd. 1978-79), N.J. Gas Assn. (pres. 1962), N.J. Utilities Assn. (dir.). Club: Mason. Home: Klines Mill Rd Box 62 Bedminster NJ 07921 Office: NUI Corp 550 Rte 202-206 Box 760 Bedminster NJ 07921-0760

KEAN, JOHN VAUGHAN, lawyer; b. Providence, Mar. 12, 1917; s. Otho Vaughan and Mary (Duell) K.; A.B. cum laude, Harvard, 1938, J.D., 1941. Admitted to R.I. bar, 1942; with Edwards & Angell, Providence, 1941—, partner, 1954-87; of counsel, 1987—. dir., sec. The Robbins Co., Attleboro, Mass. Chmn., Downtown Providence YMCA, 1964-67. Bd. dirs. Greater Providence YMCA, 1964-76. Served to capt. AUS, 1943-46, 50-52, brig. gen. Decorated Legion of Merit. Mem. Am., R.I. bar assns., N.G. Assn., Res. Officers Assn., Assn. U.S. Army, R.I. Army N.G. (brig. gen. 1964-72). Episcopalian. Clubs: Harvard R.I. (pres. 1964-66), Agawam Hunt, Hope, Providence Art, Turks Head; Army and Navy (Washington); Sakonnet Golf (Little Compton, R.I.). Home: 2 Angell St Providence RI 02903 Office: Edwards & Angell 2700 Hospital Trust Tower Providence RI 02903

KEANE, GERALD JOSEPH, toy company executive; b. Detroit, Oct. 24, 1947; s. Bernard Patrick and Jovita Mary (Tolksdorf) K.; m. Margaret Ann Wray, May 8, 1970; children: Daniel, Patrick, Katherine, Dennis. BBA, U. Toledo, 1973; MBA, U. So. Calif., 1988. Sales rep. Procter & Gamble, Toledo, 1971-73, Louisville, 1973-74; sales rep. M&M/Mars, Louisville, 1974-76; unit sales mgr. M&M/Mars, Cleve., 1976-78; bus. mgr. western div. M&M/Mars, Los Angeles, 1984—; sales mgr. western div. Kal Kan Foods, Los Angeles, 1978-81; bus. mgr. ea. div. Mars Broker div., Detroit, 1981-84; dir. nat. sales spl. market Mattel Toys co., Hawthorne, Calif., 1988—; lectr. in field. Head coach Washington Jr. Football League, Toledo, 1968-72; coach Mission Viejo (Calif.) Little League, 1985, 86, NJB Basketball, 1988-89; athletic dir. Saddleback Valley Pop Warner, 1986, 87; v.p. Santa Margarita High Sch. Football Boosters Club; vice-chmn. St. Catherines Endowment Com., Laguna Beach, Calif., 1986—. Mem. Nat. Candy Wholesalers Assn. Republican. Roman Catholic. Home: 22452 Canaveras Mission Viejo CA 92691 Office: Mattel Toys Co 5150 Rosecrans Ave Hasthorne CA 90250-6692

KEANE, MICHAEL, investment banker; b. Bronx, N.Y., July 18, 1960; s. Maurice Aloysius and Margaret Mary (Hutchinson) K. AB, U. So. Calif., 1982; MBA, U. Chgo., 1984. Fin. analyst AMR, Dallas and Ft. Worth, Tex., 1984-85; assoc. Lovett Mitchell Webb & Garrison, Inc. (fomerly Boettcher & Co.), Houston, 1985-87, v.p., 1987—; bd. dirs. Williams & Mettle Co., Houston. Roman Catholic. Home: 2226 Mimosa Apt 7 Houston TX 77019 Office: Boettcher & Co Inc 700 Rusk PO Box 4348 Houston TX 77210

KEAR, MARIA MARTHA RUSCITELLA, lawyer; b. Phila., May 9, 1954; d. Ulysses Thomas and Joan Marie (Hagner) Ruscitella; m. Daniel John Kear, May 31, 1988. BA, Elmira Coll., 1975; JD, Delaware Law Sch., Wilmington, 1978. Bar: Pa. 1979, Md. 1985. Pvt. practice, Wayne, Pa., 1979-80; corp. counsel C.D.M. Inc., Hatboro, Pa., 1980-82; sole practice, Paoli, Pa., 1982-83; gen. counsel Theriault's Inc., Annapolis, Md., 1983-85, corp. counsel Devel. Resources, Inc., Alex, Va., 1985-87; sr. atty., asst. corp. sec. People's Drug Stores, Inc., Alexandria, 1987—. Contbr. monthly newsletter The Dollmasters, 1983; contbr. The Law Forum, 1976—. Mem. Annapolis Law Ctr., 1983—; treas. Women's Law Ctr. Anne Arundel County. Mem. ABA, Pa. Bar Assn., Md. Bar Assn., Women's Bar Assn. Md., Delta Theta Phi. Republican. Roman Catholic. Home: 6801 Tepper Dr Clifton VA 22024 Office: Peoples Drug Stores Inc 6315 Bren Mar Dr Alexandria VA 22312

KEARLEY, RICHARD IRVEN, III, electronics company executive; b. Nashville, Apr. 13, 1953; s. Richard Irven Jr. and Josephine Clarice (Wells) K. BBA, So. Meth. U., 1974; MBA, North Tex. State U., 1976. Gen. contractor Sta. DKTV-TV, Dallas, 1976; gen. mgr. Sta. KCIR, Corsicana, Tex., 1976-77; store mgr. Tandy Corp., Dallas, 1977-78; exec. v.p. ABE Corp., Dallas, 1978—. Active with First Bapt. Ch., Richardson, Tex., 1986—. Mem. IEEE, Dallas Zool. Soc., Nat. Arbor Day Soc. Lodge: Rotary. Office: ABE Corp 10923 Indian Trail #105 Dallas TX 75229

KEARNEY, AUSTIN EUGENE, JR., finance company executive; b. Jersey City, May 15, 1952; s. Austin Eugene Sr. and Virginia (Gomber) K.; m. Joanne Holt, May 26, 1979. BBA, U. Notre Dame, 1974; MBA, U. Chgo., 1976. Comml. lending officer Chem. Bank, N.Y.C., 1976-80; account mgr. HBO & Co., Atlanta, 1980-81; dir. investor rels. HBO & Co., 1981-84, asst. treas., 1984—. Mem. Nat. Investor Rels. Inst. (lectr.), Ashford Club (Atlanta). Roman Catholic. Home: 4947 Buckline Crossing Dunwoody GA 30338 Office: HBO & Co 301 Perimeter Ctr N Atlanta GA 30349

KEARNEY, JOHN JOSEPH, JR., utility executive; b. Bklyn., June 28, 1924; s. John Joseph and Kathryn Virginia (Diamond) K.; m. Regina C. Welsh, Feb. 21, 1952; children: John J., David W., Elizabeth L., Peter A. B.S., Coll. of Holy Cross, 1945; J.D., Bklyn. Law Sch., 1957. Bar: N.Y. 1958; C.P.A., N.Y. Accountant J.K. Lasser & Co., David Fields & Co., N.Y.C., 1945-51; tax accountant Charles Pfizer & Co., Bklyn., 1951-56; asst. div. controller IBM, N.Y.C., 1956-59; sec., gen. auditor L.I. Lighting Co., Mineola, N.Y., 1959—. Trustee St. Joseph's Coll., 1976—; trustee, faculty advisor SUNY, Farmingdale. Served with USNR, 1942-44. Mem. AICPA, N.Y. State Soc. CPA's. Club: Cherry Valley (Garden City, N.Y.); Manchester (Vt.) Country. Home: 35 Russell Rd Garden City NY 11530 Office: LI Lighting 175 E Old Country Rd Hicksville NY 11801

KEARNEY, RICHARD JAMES, marketing consultant; b. Kansas City, Mo., Aug. 25, 1927; s. Emmett Leo and Irene Elizabeth (Ruddock) K.; B.S. in Chem. Engring., U. Mich., 1951; m. Caroline Hamilton Archer, Sept. 19, 1953; children—Caroline Hamilton, Richard James. Chem. purchasing agt. Hercules, Inc., Wilmington, Del., 1954-62; chmn. bd., pres., sr. v.p. Kearney Chems. Inc., Tampa, Fla., 1962-80; sr. v.p. Royster Chems., Inc., Tampa, 1980-82; mktg. cons., Tampa, 1982—. Served with USNR, 1945-46, to 1st lt. AUS, 1951-53, Korea. Mem. Am. Chem. Soc., Pershing Rifles, Scabbard and Blade Honor Soc., Decorative Arts Soc., Tampa Art Mus. Soc., Sigma Chi. Episcopalian. Clubs: U. Mich. Pres.'; Tampa Yacht and Country, Bath, Tower. Office: Caroline Kearney Antiques 4301 El Prado Blvd Tampa FL 33629

KEARNEY, SHIRLEY JOHNSON, management consultant; b. Terre Haute, Ind., Sept. 15, 1946; d. Mervil Ray and Sarah Kathryn (Tucker) W.; m. Richard E. Johnson Jr., Sept. 23, 1964 (div. 1974); children: Richard Alan, Gary Michael Sr.; m. Paul R. Kearney, Oct. 17, 1989. AA, Coll. Dupage, 1980; student, DePaul U., 1988—. Sec. to v.p. fin. Cenco Inc., Oak Brook, Ill., 1972-74, exec. asst. to group pres., 1974-75, asst. to chmn., 1975-77, corp. personnel/office mgr., 1977-80; corp. sec. Acadia Petroleum Corp., Denver, 1980-82; mgr. office Chapman, Klein & Weinberg, PC, Denver, 1982-84; asst. to chmn. The Heidrick Ptnrs., Inc., Chgo., 1984—. Mem. Am. Mgmt. Assn., Am. Soc. Personnel Adminstrs., DuPage Personnel Assn. (sec. 1979), Exec. Women Internat., Nat. Assn. Female Execs. Home: 7309 Hartford Downers Grove IL 60516 Office: The Heidrick Ptnrs Inc 20 N Wacker Dr Ste 4000 Chicago IL 60606

KEARNS, DAVID TODD, business products and systems company financial services executive; b. Rochester, N.Y., Aug. 11, 1930; s. Wilfrid M. and Margaret May (Todd) K.; m. Shirley Virginia Cox, June 1954; children—Katherine, Elizabeth, Anne, Susan, David Todd, Andrew. B.S., U. Rochester, 1952. With IBM Corp., 1954-71, v.p. mktg. ops., data processing div., until 1971; with Xerox Corp., Stamford, Conn., 1971—; group v.p. for info. systems Xerox Corp., 1972-75; group v.p. charge Rank Xerox and Fuji Xerox, 1975-77, exec. v.p. internat. ops., 1977; pres., chief exec. officer Xerox Corp., 1977-85, also dir., pres., chief operating officer, 1977-82, pres., chief exec. officer, 1982-85, chmn., chief exec. officer, 1985—, also chmn. exec. com.; bd. dirs. Rank Xerox Ltd., Time Inc., Fuji Xerox., Chase Manhattan Corp., Dayton Hudson Corp.; chmn. Pres.'s Commn. on Exec. Exchange. Bd. visitors Grad. Sch. Bus., Duke U.; bd. dirs. U. Rochester; trustee Stamford Hosp., Inst. Aerobics Research; bd. dirs. Jr. Achievement; bd. trustees Nat. Urban League. Served with USNR, 1952-54. Mem. Bus. Roundtable, Council on Fgn. Relations, Com. Exec. Exchange (chmn., pres.). Office: Xerox Corp PO Box 1600 Stamford CT 06902

KEARNS, JAMES FRANCIS, textile technology company executive; b. Cleve., July 18, 1928; s. Allen Edward and Mildred Helen (Kilrain) K.; m. Rita Lawless, Aug. 4, 1951; children—Patricia J. Kearns Connell, James F., Thomas G. B.Chem. Engring., U. Del., 1950. Mktg. dir. textile fibers div. E.I. du Pont de Nemours Co., Wilmington, Del., 1973-74, prodn. mgr., 1974-77, bus. dir., 1977-81, gen. mgr., 1981-83, sr. v.p. materials and logistics, 1983-85, group v.p. textile fibers, 1985-88, exec. v.p., mem. exec. com., 1988—; bd. dirs. Textile/Clothing Tech. Inc., N.Y.C.; chmn. engring. adv. com. U. Del. Trustee U. Del. Rsch. Found.; bd. dirs. Easter Seal Soc. Del-Mar, Inc., March Dimes. Mem. Am. Fiber Mfrs. Assn. (bd. dirs., exec. com.). Clubs: Du Pont Country, Wilmington, Wilmington Country. Office: E I Du Pont de Nemours & Co Chestnut Run Pla Walnut Run 2147 Wilmington DE 19880-0722

KEARNS, WILLIAM MICHAEL, JR., investment banker; b. Orange, N.J., June 26, 1935; s. William Michael and Doris Mae (Hodgkinson) K.; m. Patricia Anne Wright, Aug. 17, 1957; children: William Michael III, Susan Elizabeth, Kathleen Anne, Michael Patrick, Elizabeth Anne. AB, U. Maine, 1957; AM, NYU, 1960; LLD (hon.), Gonzaga U., 1988; student, Boston Coll. Law, 1957-58, NYU Grad. Sch. Bus. Adminstrn., 1960-64. With Chase Manhattan Bank, 1958-59; security analyst Hayden, Stone & Co., Inc., N.Y.C., 1960-62; assoc. instl. sales and syndicate dept. Kuhn, Loeb & Co., N.Y.C., 1962-64, asst. v.p., 1964-66, v.p., 1966-68, sales mgr., 1968-69, gen. partner, 1970-75; mng. dir. Kuhn, Loeb & Co., Inc., 1976-77, Lehman Bros. Kuhn Loeb Inc., 1977-84, Shearson Lehman/Am. Express Inc., N.Y.C., 1984-85, Shearson Lehman Bros. Inc., N.Y.C., 1985-88, Shearson Lehman Hutton Inc., 1988—; bd. dirs., chmn. fin. com. Selective Ins. Group, Inc., Branchville, N.J.; bd. dirs. The Jepson Corp., Elmhurst, Ill.; investment advisor G.D. Young & Co., Phoenix; mem. faculty Fairleigh Dickinson U. Coll. Bus. Adminstr., 1959-68; instr. security analysis N.Y. Inst. Finance, 1961-67; adj. prof. Grad. Sch. Bus. Adminstrn., NYU, 1971-72, chmn. Forum on Fin., 1971. Trustee Drumthwacket Found. Inc., 1985—, Morris Mus. Arts and Sci., 1968-86, Rider Coll., 1981-88, Morristown-Beard Sch.,

1982-88; trustee Tri-County Scholarship Fund 1982—, v.p. 1985-86, pres. 1987—; bd. dirs. Greater N.Y. Councils Boy Scouts Am. 1986—; mem. N.J. Republican Fin. Com.; mem. adv. bd. Internat. Tennis Hall of Fame, 1984-86, dir. 1986—; mem. exec. com. William E. Simon Grad. Sch. Bus. Adminstrn., U. Rochester, 1986—; mem. diocesan investment com. Diocese of Paterson, N.J., 1986—; mem. Cardinal's Com. of Laity, N.Y.C. Served with USMCR, 1955-61. Decorated Knight Sovereign Mil. Order Malta, Knight of St. Gregory The Great. Mem. Nat. Assn. Security Dealers (corp. fin. com. 1976-80), Securities Industry Assn. (minority capital com. 1978-86, exec. com. N.Y. dist. 1970, vice chmn. 1973, chmn. 1974), New Eng. Soc., Beta Theta Pi, Kappa Phi Kappa. Roman Catholic. Clubs: University (trustee 1978-81), Bond of N.Y., Econ. (all N.Y.C.); Morris County Golf (Convent, N.J.) (gov. 1976-82, treas. 1978-82; Log Cabin Gun (Sterling, N.J); Twin Oaks (Morristown, N.J.); Wellington (Fla.); Mid-Ocean (Bermuda), Palm Beach (Fla.) Polo and Country. Office: Shearson Lehman Hutton Inc Am Express Tower World Fin Ctr New York NY 10285

KEATING, CORNELIUS FRANCIS, record company executive; b. Boston, Aug. 3, 1925; s. Cornelius Francis and Mary (Grey) K.; children: Cecily, Gregory, Christopher, David, Elisabeth. AB, Harvard U., 1947, LLD, 1950. Bar: N.Y. 1951. Atty. Thayer & Gilbert, N.Y.C., 1951-53, Life Ins. Assn. Am., 1953-55; atty. Columbia Records, 1955-57, gen. atty., 1957-58; gen. mgr. Columbia Record Club, 1958-60, v.p., gen. mgr., 1960-67; pres. CBS Direct Marketing Services (div. CBS), N.Y.C., 1967-70, Columbia House div., N.Y.C., 1970-79, CBS/Columbia Group, 1979-80; sr. v.p. CBS/Records Group, 1980-88; sr. v.p. direct mktg. CBS Records Inc., 1988—; bd. dirs. 3d Class Mail Assn., chmn. bd. 1968-72; bd. dirs. GRI Corp. Mem. Am. Theatre Wing Bd. Advisors; trustee Rheedlen Found. Served to ensign USNR, 1943-46. Mem. Harvard Law Sch. Assn., Confrerie des Chevaliers du Tastevin, Commanderie de Bordeaux, Harvard CLub. Home: 1161 Ponus Ridge New Canaan CT 06840 Office: CBS Records Inc 51 W 52d St New York NY 10019

KEATING, DONALD FRANCIS, human resources executive; b. Bklyn., Oct. 16, 1931; s. Timothy Francis and Catherine Dolores (Moore) K.; m. Patricia Ann Mahoney, Apr. 25, 1953; children: Kevin Patrick, Keith Patrick, Kerry Ann. BA, St. John's U., 1952; MBA, NYU, 1959. Asst. personnel mgr. Intertype Corp., Bklyn., 1956-61; labor relations specialist Republic Aviation, Farmingdale, N.Y., 1961-64, personnel dir., 1977-79; asst. labor relations mgr. Chem. Constrn. Corp., N.Y.C., 1964-67; labor relations mgr. Borden Co., N.Y.C., 1967-71; personnel dir. Kollsman Instrument, Syosset, N.Y., 1971-74, Keene Corp., N.Y.C., 1974-77; v.p. human resources Burndy Corp., Norwalk, Conn., 1979—. Prin. Confraternity Edn. Program, St. Rose of Lima, Massapequa, N.Y. Comdr. USNR, 1952-56. Mem. Am. Soc. Personnel Adminstrs., Fairfield County Roundtable. Republican. Roman Catholic. Home: 174 Turner Rd Stamford CT 06905 Office: Burndy Corp Richards Ave Norwalk CT 06856

KEATING, EDWARD THOMAS, banker; b. Evergreen Park, Ill., Feb. 26, 1961; s. Charles Joseph and Dolores Patricia (Shannon) K.; m. Doreen Ruth Leydon, Apr. 26, 1986. BA, U. Ill., 1983. Cert. fin. planner. Portfolio analyst Feldman Securities Corp., Chgo., 1983-85; asst. portfolio mgr. State Nat. Bank, Evanston, Ill., 1985-87; trust investment officer Old Second Nat. Bank, Aurora, Ill., 1987—. Mem. Inst. Cert. Fin. Planners, Chgo. Coun. on Fgn. Rels., Investment Analysts Soc. Chgo. Home: 732 Garfield Ave Batavia IL 60510 Office: Old Second Nat Bank 37 S River St Aurora IL 60507

KEATING, THOMAS EDWARD, insurance company executive; b. Atlantic City, July 24, 1933; s. Francis J. and Beatrice M. (Scholler) K.; m. Lynne R. Engelhardt, July 26, 1980; children: Cynthia, Susan, Sally, Nancy, Jennifer. BS in Econs., Villanova U., 1956; cert. exec. mgmt. program, Stanford U. With Travelers Corp., Hartford, Conn., 1968—, v.p., 1980-85, sr. v.p., 1985—; pres. Travelers of Bermuda; vice chmn. Travelers Investment Mgmt. Co. Contbr. numerous articles to trade periodicals. Mem. Assn. Investment Mgmt. Sales Execs. (bd. dirs., mem. exec. com., adv. council 1984—, program chmn. 1986, pres. 1986—), Am. Pension Conf., Profit Sharing Council Am., Internat. Found. Employee Benefits, Employee Benefits Research Inst. (sustaining, trustee). Club: Glastonbury (Conn.) Hills Country (v.p., dir. 1975-78). Lodge: Optimist (pres. 1966). Office: The Travelers Corp 1 Tower Sq Hartford CT 06183

KEATING, THOMAS PATRICK, health care administrator, educator; b. Cleve., Jan. 5, 1949; s. Thomas Wilbur and Margaret (Gahllagher) K.; m. Carolyn Elizabeth Kraft, Sept. 4, 1976; children: Jerrod Patrick, Kerri Ann. BS in Bus., Cleve. State U., 1971; MS in Bus., U. Toledo, 1973. Lic. nursing home adminstr.; cert. health care materials mgr. Asst. dir. facilities U. Kans. Med. Ctr., Kansas City, 1977-80; dir. mgmt. services Charleston (S.C.) County Park and Recreation Commn., 1980-84; dir. support services Med. U. of S.C., Charleston, 1984—; adj. instr. Cen. Mich. U., Mt. Pleasant, 1979—; accreditted cons. SBA, Charleston, 1980—; adj. prof. Webster U., St. Louis, 1981—; nursing home cons. Charleston County Mental Retardation Bd., Charleston, 1987-88. Contbr. articles to profl. jours. Vol. Driftwood Health Care Ctr., Charleston, 1981-83; mem. Buist Acad. PTA, Charleston, 1986—. Served to capt. with U.S. Army, 1973-77; with USAR, 1978—. Mem. Health Care Materials Mgmt. Soc., Internat. Assn. of Cen. Service Mgmt., Environ. Mgmt. Assn. (com. mem. 1986—), Nat. Assn. of Purchase Mgmt., Am. Coll. of Health Care Execs., Sigma Phi Epsilon (com. chmn. 1970-71), Alpha Kappa Psi (com. chmn. 1972-73). Roman Catholic. Club: Toastmasters (adminstrv. v.p. 1985-86). Lodge: KC. Home: 575 Hobcan Bluff Dr Mount Pleasant SC 29464 Office: Med U of SC 171 Ashley Ave Charleston SC 29425

KEATINGE, RICHARD HARTE, lawyer; b. San Francisco, Dec. 4, 1919; m. Betty West, Apr. 20, 1944; children: Richard West, Daniel Wilson, Nancy Elizabeth. A.B. with honors, U. Calif., Berkeley, 1939; M.A., Harvard U., 1941; J.D., Georgetown U., 1944. Bar: D.C. 1944, N.Y. 1945, Calif. 1947, U.S. Supreme Ct. 1964. Sr. economist, sr. indsl. specialist WPB, Washington, 1941-44; practice law N.Y.C., 1944-45, Washington, 1945-47, Los Angeles, 1947—; sr. ptnr. Keatinge, Pastor & Mintz (and predecessor firms), 1948-79, Reavis & McGrath, 1979-88, Fulbright Jaworski & Reavis McGrath, 1989—; spl. asst. atty. gen., State of Calif., 1964-68; public mem. Adminstrv. Conf. of U.S., 1968-74. Mem.: Georgetown Law Jour, 1943-44. Mem. Calif. Law Revision Commn., 1961-68, chmn., 1965-67; trustee Coro Found., 1965-73; bd. trustees, mem. exec. com. U. Calif. Berkeley Found., 1973-87, chmn. bd. trustees, 1983-85, mem. The Berkeley Fellows, 1989—. Fellow (life) Am. Bar Found., Am. Coll. Tax Counsel; mem. ABA (bd. govs. 1978-79, mem. ho. of dels. 1974-81, 82—, mem. council 1961-64, 65-69, 74-78, 82—, chmn. adminstrv. law sect. 1967-68, mem. standing com. on resolutions 1973-74, chmn. com. on sales, exchanges and basis taxation sect. 1963-65, mem. council econs. of law practice sect. 1974-75, mem. commn. on law and economy 1976-78, vice chmn. 1977-78, mem. spl. com. on housing and urban devel. law 1968-73, vice chmn. adv. commn. on housing and urban growth 1974-77, nat. sec. Jr. Bar Conf. 1949-50), State Bar Calif. (del. conf. of dels. 1966-67, 77—, mem. exec. com. public law sect. 1976-78), Los Angeles County Bar Assn. (chmn. taxation sect. 1966-67, mem. fair jud. election practices com. 1978-79, mem. exec. com. law office mgmt. sect. 1977-85, mem. housing and urban devel. law com. 1971-80, mem. arbitration com. 1974—, mem. new quarters com. 1979-80), Assn. Bus. Trial Lawyers (bd. govs. 1974-79, pres. 1978-79), Inter-Am. Bar Assn., Internat. Bar Assn., Am. Judicature Soc., Am. Law Inst., Am. Arbitration Assn. (nat. panel of arbitrators 1950—), Com. to Maintain Diversity Jurisdiction, Lawyers Club Los Angeles, Berkeley Fellows, Phi Beta Kappa. Home: 220 S San Rafael Ave Pasadena CA 91105 Office: Fulbright Jaworski & Reavis McGrath 700 S Flower St Sixth Fl Broadway Pla Los Angeles CA 90017

KECK, ALBERT PHILIP, computer executive; b. Pitts., Oct. 3, 1934; s. Richard Anthony and Gertrude Anna (Dipple) K.; m. Evelyn Eileen Haines, June 30, 1962; children: Leslie Marie, Cynthia Lynn, Bruce Allen. BS in Bus. Mgmt. and Acctg., U. Balt., 1959; cert. in mgmt. info., Am. U., 1970; M of Pub. Adminstrn., Southeastern U., Washington, 1983, MBA in Info. Resource Mgmt., 1983. Data processing specialist Olin Corp., Balt., 1959-61; systems engr. Burroughs Corp., Washington, 1961-62; assoc. scientist Dunlap and Assocs., Stanford, Conn., 1962-63; systems analysis dir. Fed. Power Commn., Washington, 1963-78; project mgr. Dept. of Energy, Washington, 1978-82, program mgr., 1982-85; sr. cons. Acumenics Rsch. & Tech., Fairfax, Va., 1985—. Contbr. articles to profl. jours. Founder Oaklands Citizen Assn., Laurel, Md., 1970. Served as sgt. USAF, 1954-58. Mem. Soc. Advancement of Mgmt. (program dir. 1959-62), Jr. C. of C. (state delegate, Committeeman of Year award 1960), Soc. Adv. of Mgmt. (v.p. membership 1962-64), Assn. Fed. Info. Resource Mgrs. (program chmn. 1978-80), Data Processing Mgmt. Assn. Democrat. Methodist. Lodge: KC (grand knight 1975-76, dep. grand knight 1974-75, chancellor, warden 1972-74). Home: 3314 Sharp Rd Glenwood MD 21738

KECK, PHILIP WALTER, transportation executive; b. Wyandotte, Mich., Feb. 6, 1947; s. George and Genevieve (Baranowski) K.; m. Janice Dallas, Aug. 31, 1969; children: Derek James, Lisa Tiffany. BS, USAF Acad., 1969; MBA, U. Colo., 1982; postgrad., U. Tex., 1987—. Commd. 2d lt. USAF, 1969, advanced through grades to capt., 1972; instr. pilot USAF, Beale AFB, 1970-75, DaNang AFB, Vietnam, 1972; instr. USAF Acad. USAF, Colorado Springs, Colo., 1975-77; resigned USAF, 1977; pilot Braniff Internat. Airlines, Dallas, 1977-81; flight data supr. Denver Air Route Traffic Control Ctr., Longmont, Colo., 1981-82; account exec. Merrill Lynch, Denver, 1982-83; pilot Regent Air Corp., L.A., 1983-85; flight mgr. Am. Airlines, Dallas, 1985—; fin. planner Merrill Lynch, Denver, 1982-83. Co-author (study guide) Windshear Microburst, 1987. Decorated D.F.C., Vietnam. Republican. Lutheran. Home: 786 Windmere Way Keller TX 76248 Office: Am Airlines PO Box 619617 Dallas-Fort Worth Airport TX 75261

KECK, RICHARD JOSEPH, banker, accountant; b. Mattoon, Ill., July 21, 1963; s. Vincent George and Anna Marie (Mammoser) K. BS, U. Ill., 1985; postgrad. in fin., U. Chgo., 1985—. CPA, Ill. Banking officer Continental Bank, NA, Chgo., 1985—. V.p. Champaign County Young Reps., 1984; active Young Friends of ARC. Mem. Ill. CPA Soc., U. Ill. Alumni Assn., Delta Upsilon (sec. bd. dirs. Ill. chpt. 1985-86). Roman Catholic. Office: Continental Bank NA 231 S La Salle St Chicago IL 60697

KECK, ROBERT CLIFTON, lawyer; b. Sioux City, Iowa, May 20, 1914; s. Herbert Allen and Harriet (McCutchen) K.; m. Ruth P. Edwards, Nov. 2, 1940 (dec.); children: Robert, Laura E. Simpson, Gloria E. Sauser; m. Lauryne E. George, June 20, 1987. A.B., Ind. U., 1936; J.D., U. Mich., 1939; L.H.D., Nat. Coll. Edn., 1973. Bar: Ill. 1939. Since practiced in Chgo; mem. firm Keck, Mahin & Cate, 1939—, partner, 1946—; sec., dir. Methode Electronics, Inc.; bd. dirs. Schwinn Bicycle Co., Ill. Masonic Med. Ctr., 1630 Sheridan Corp. Chmn. bd. trustees Nat. Coll. Edn., 1955—; trustee Sears Roebuck Found., 1977-79. Served with USNR, 1943-45. Fellow Am. Coll. Trial Lawyers; mem. ABA, Fed. Bar Assn., Ill. Bar Assn., Chgo. Bar assn. Seventh Fed. Circuit (past pres.), Phi Gamma Delta. Republican. Methodist. Clubs: Westmoreland Country (Wilmette);Metropolitan, Chgo.; Biltmore Forest Country (Asheville, N.C.); Glen View (Golf, Ill.). Lodge: Masons. Office: Keck Mahin & Cate Sears Tower 83d Fl Chicago IL 60606

KECKEL, PETER J., advertising executive; b. Berlin, Dec. 13, 1942; came to U.S., 1956; s. F. Paul and Frieda G. (Schmidt) K.; m. Katherine Alice Brown, Nov. 27, 1971. BS in Polit. Sci., U. Md., 1966, postgrad., 1966; grad., U.S. Infantry Sch., Ft. Benning, Ga., 1967; grad. advanced officers course, Adjutant Gens. Sch., Ft. Ben Harrison, Ind., 1971. Exec. dir. Med. Personnel Pool, Oklahoma City, 1973-74; regional dir. Medox div. Drake Internat., Oklahoma City, 1974-78; pres., owner Okla. Communities, Inc., Edmond, 1978—, Okla. Gold Jewelry, Inc., Edmond, 1982—; mktg. cons. to various orgns. and groups, 1978—. Bd. dirs. Edmond YMCA, 1980-81. Served to capt. U.S. Army, 1966-73, Vietnam. Decorated Bronze Star; recipient Presdl. Vietnam Veterans Outstanding Community Achievement award Pres. Carter, 1979; received Key to the City of Garland, Tex. Mem. Am. Bus. Clubs (life; bd. dirs. 1979—, pres. 1985-86, chmn. bd. dirs. 1986-87, regional big hat chmn. 1986-87, dist. gov. 1989-90, mem. nat. new club bldg. com., Mr. Ambucs awards 1980-1981, 83-84, 87-88, dist. 1987-88, Top Nat. Membership Recruiter 1982—, Top Nat. Fundraiser, Excellence award 1982-83, #1 Club Pres. in Country 1985-86, chartered New Ambucs chpt., 1988), U. Md. Alumni Assn. (life), POW-MIA Orgn., Edmond C. of C. (life; bd. dirs. 1979-81, medal of merit 1979, Top Nat. Membership Recruitment award 1979-81, Life Mem. award 1982). Republican. Lutheran. Club: Edmond Soccer (v.p., bd. dirs. 1977-79, coach, referee 1976-82). Home: 908 SE 10th Edmond OK 73034 Office: Okla Communities Inc 3409-C S Wynn Dr Edmond OK 73013

KEDING, ANN CLYRENE, free-lance copywriter; b. Ft. Benning, Ga., Aug. 31, 1944; d. Porter Bill and Clyrene (Stull) Maxwell; children from previous marriage: Robert, Jeff. BA in Psychology, Calif. State U., Fullerton, 1973, MA in Psychology, 1975; postgrad., U. So. Calif., 1980-83. Instr. psychology Calif. State U., Fullerton, 1974-76, Golden West Coll., Huntington Beach, Calif., 1976-78; mktg. research project dir. Foote, Cone & Belding, Los Angeles, 1978-80; copywriter Yuguchi & Krogstad, Los Angeles, 1980-82, Hamilton Advt., Los Angeles, 1982-84, Grey Advt., Los Angeles, 1984-85; freelance copywriter Los Angeles, Eugene, Calif., Oreg., 1985—; asst. prof. U. Oreg., Eugene, 1986—. Writer TV commls, advt. campaigns, brochures. Mem. adv. council Los Angeles Commn. on Assaults Against Women, 1985—. Recipient Pub. Citation Govt. Calif., 1985, Humanitarian award Los Angeles Commn. Assaults Against Women, 1986; Gannett fellow, Ind. U., 1987, 88. Mem. Am. Acad. Advt., Calif. State U. Fullerton Alumni Assn., Phi Kappa Phi (bd. dirs. 1974-75). Office: U Oreg Sch Journalism Eugene OR 97403

KEEFE, HARRY V., JR., investment banking executive; b. Boston, Apr. 9, 1922; s. Harry V. and Catherine T. (Dennis) K.; m. Jean M. Mulcahy, Sept. 25, 1943 (dec. Sept. 83); children: Kathleen K. Raffel, Harry V. III; m. Anita de Lesseps, Dec. 21, 1985. BA, Amherst Coll., 1943; postgrad., Boston U., 1946; LLD (hon.), Lafayette Coll., 1985, Amherst Coll., 1987. Analyst R.L. Day & Co., Boston, 1946-47; mgr. of local office R.L. Day & Co., Hartford, Conn., 1947-56; ptnr. R.L. Day & Co., Hartford, 1952-56, Tucker, Anthony & R.L. Day (result of 1956 merger), N.Y.C., 1956-62; founder, chmn., chief exec. officer, dir. Keefe, Bruyette & Woods, Inc., N.Y.C., 1962-89. Author: Banking, A Vital and Stable Industry. Co-chmn., founder First Ins. City Open Golf Tournament, greater Hartford area; former trustee Boston Latin Sch., Brunswick Sch.; trustee Wheaton Coll.; vice chmn. bd. trustees Lafayette Coll. Served with USN, 1943-46. Mem. Securities Industry Assn. (bd. dirs.), Am. Assn. Sovereign Mil. Order of Malta. Roman Catholic. Clubs: Indian Harbor Yacht, John's Island, Fairfield County Hounds (past sr. master). Office: Keefe Bruyette & Woods Inc 2 World Trade Ctr Ste 8566 New York NY 10048

KEEFE, JAMES MICHAEL, alarm and security company executive; b. Framingham, Mass., June 29, 1951; s. John Joseph and Carmen Alicia (Dorian) K.; m. Clarita Eugenio Perias, Oct. 7, 1983. Grad. high sch., Northboro, Mass. Exec. chef Kona Galley Restaurant, Kailua-Kona, Hawaii, 1970-78; v.p., gen. mgr. W. Hawaii Alarm Inc., 1978-83; v.p. Alert Alarm Inc., Honolulu, 1983—. Coord. Advs. for Self-Govt., Hilo, Hawaii, 1988—; advisor Jr. Achievement Kona, Kailua-Kona, 1980-83; chmn. county Libertarian Party, Island of Hawaii, 1980—. Mem. Nat. Fire Protection Assn., Hawaii Burglar and Fire Alarm Assn., Assn. Soc. Indsl. Security. Office: Alert Alarm Inc 9 Shipman St Hilo HI 96720

KEEFE, ROGER MANTON, former banker, financial consultant; b. New London, Conn., Feb. 26, 1919; s. Arthur T. and Mabel (Foran) K.; m. Ann Hunter, June 4, 1949; children: Christopher Hunter, Matthew Foran, Michael Devereux, Susan Ann, Robin Mary, Victoria Morrill. Student, Coll. St. Gregory, Downside Abbey, Eng., 1936-37; B.A. in History and Internat. Relations, Yale, 1941. With Chase Manhattan Bank, N.Y.C., 1945-71; sr. v.p. charge div. financing devel. and tech. services Chase Manhattan Bank, 1966-71; exec. v.p. Conn. Bank & Trust Co., Hartford, 1971-76; vice chmn. Conn. Bank & Trust Co., 1976-80, CBT Corp., Hartford, 1976-83; chmn. exec. com. CBT Corp., 1980-83, Conn. Bank & Trust Co., 1980-83; pres. R.M. Keefe Assocs., Inc., 1983—; dir. Callahan Mining Co., Maritime Ctr. Mem. exec. council Yale Class of 1941, 1962—, treas., 1966-71, mem. bd. edn., Norwalk, Conn.; mem. Nat. Rep. Fin. Com., 1961—, also treas. adv. fin. com.; mem. N.Y. State Rep. Fin. Com., 1961-69; trustee St. Thomas More Corp., 1962—, treas., 1964-69; trustee Greens Farms Acad., 1978-88, Fairfield U., 1982-88; bd. dirs. St. Joseph's Med. Ctr., 1978—. Served to maj. AUS., World War II, ETO. Decorated Silver Star, Bronze Star with cluster, Purple Heart., Knight of St. Gregory. Mem. Fin. Execs. Inst., Assn. Res. City Bankers, Am. Arbitration Assn., Southwestern Area Commerce and Industry Assn. (dir. 1978). Clubs: Yale (N.Y.C.); Wee Burn Country, Harbor, Norwalk Yacht; Internat. (Washington). Home: Nathan Hale Rd Wilson Point South Norwalk CT 06854

KEEGAN, JANE ANN, insurance executive, consultant; b. Watertown, N.Y., Sept. 1, 1950; d. Richard Isidor and Kathleen (McKinley) K. BA cum laude, SUNY-Potsdam, 1972; MBA in Risk Mgmt., Golden Gate U., 1986. CPCU. Comml. lines mgr. Lithgow & Rayhill, San Francisco, 1977-80; risk mgmt. account coordinator Dinner Levison Co., San Francisco, 1980-83; ins. cons., San Francisco, 1983-84; account mgr. Rollins Burdick Hunter, San Francisco, 1984-85; account exec. Jardine Ins. Brokers, San Francisco, 1985-86; ins. cons., San Francisco, 1986-87, ins. adminstr. Port of Oakland, 1987—. Vol. San Francisco Ballet vol. orgn., 1981—, Bay Area Bus., Govt. ARC disaster conf. steering com., 1987-88, 89; mem. Nob Hill Neighbors Assn., 1982—. Mem. Nat. Safety Mgmt. Soc., Soc. Chartered Property Casualty Underwriters (spl. events chairperson 1982-84; continuing profl. devel. program award 1985, 88), Risk and Ins. Mgr. Soc. (dep.). Democrat. Roman Catholic. Home: 1635 Clay St Apt 1 San Francisco CA 94109

KEEGAN, PETER WILLIAM, broadcast company executive; b. Providence, Sept. 11, 1944; s. James Francis and Lucile (Bowers) K.; m. Jane Louise Carpenter, Oct. 19, 1985. BA, Brown U., 1966; MBA, Columbia U., 1970. With CBS, Inc., N.Y.C., 1970—, dir., fin. analyst Broadcast Group div., 1972-74, asst., contr. then v.p., contr. Records div., 1974-76; v.p., contr. CBS, Inc., 1976-83, sr. v.p. fin., 1988—; bd. mgrs, CBS/MTM Co., Studio City, Calif., CBS/Fox Co., N.Y.C. Served with U.S. Army, 1966-68. Office: CBS Inc 51 W 52nd St New York NY 10019

KEEGAN-CORSELLO, ROBYN, financial planner; b. Worcester, Mass.. AAS, Fashion Inst. Tech., N.Y.C., 1973; Cert. in Fin. Planning, Adelphi U. Registered investment advisor. V.p. Keegan Fin. Cons., Seaford, N.Y., 1983-87; pres. Keegan Fin. Planning, Inc., Seaford, 1988—. Mem. Internat. Assn. Fin. Planning, Inst. Cert. Fin. Planners. Office: Keegan Fin Planning Inc 3560 Tuscala St Seaford NY 11783

KEEHNER, MICHAEL ARTHUR MILLER, banker; b. Cedar Rapids, Iowa, Nov. 15, 1943; m. Diane Temple; children: Brigham, Jonathan. BS in Nuclear Physics, MIT, 1965; MBA in Fin. with high distinction, Harvard U., 1971. Registered securities rep. Engring. mgr. Gen. Dynamics Corp., Quincy, Mass., 1965-69; pres., chief exec. officer K P Exploration, Inc., N.Y.C., 1982-88; mng. dir., mem. mgmt. com., bd. dirs. Kidder Peabody Group, Inc., N.Y.C., 1971; bd. dirs. Kidder Peabody Group Inc., Fin. Guaranty Ins. Co. Trustee Bklyn. Mus. Baker scholar Harvard U.; Loeb Rhodes fellow Harvard U. Mem. Securities Industry Assn. Clubs: Coronado (Houston); Point O'Woods (N.Y.); India House (N.Y.C.); Heights Casino, Rembrandt (Bklyn.).

KEELE, LYNDON ALAN, electronics company executive; b. Clyde, Tex., Nov. 3, 1928; s. Theadore Fannin and Zada (Sikes) K.; B.B.A., U. Tex., 1951; m. Muriel Alice Murphy, June 1, 1968; children—Carolyn Chase, Tiffany Ames. With York div. Borg-Warner Co., York, Pa., 1953-58, asst. gen. plant mgr., 1956-58; program mgr. Sylvania Elec. System div. Gen. Telephone & Electronics Co., Needham, Mass., 1958-62; program mgr. ITT Fed. Labs., Nutley, N.J., 1962-68; exec. v.p. TeleScis., Inc., Moorestown, N.J., 1968-73; pres. Sci. Dynamics Corp., Cherry Hill, N.J., 1973—. Served with AUS, 1946-47, USAAF, 1951-53. Mem. IEEE. Club: Riverton Country. Office: Sci Dynamics Corp 1919 Springdale Rd Cherry Hill NJ 08003

KEELEY, JOHN LEMUEL, JR., brokerage house executive; b. New Orleans, May 20, 1940; s. John Lemuel and Mary S. K.; m. Barbara Geary, Jan. 2, 1960; children: John Lemuel III, Mark, Kevin, Christopher. BA, U. Notre Dame, 1962; MBA, U. Chgo., 1965; BA, U. Notre Dame, 1962; MBA, U. Chgo., 1965. Asst. bank examiner dept. fin. instns. State of Ill., Chgo., 1963-64; asst. bank examiner FDIC, Chgo., 1964-65; fin. analyst investment div., treas. dept. Standard Oil Co., Ind., Chgo., 1966-68; v.p. research analysis Chgo. Corp., 1968-70; sr. v.p., dir., supervisory analyst U.S. div. James Capel and Co., London, 1970-74; sr. v.p., treas., chief fin. officer, dir. Seward Securities Corp., Chgo., 1974-77; pres., treas. Keeley Investment Corp., Chgo., 1977—, Keeley Asset Mgmt. Corp., Chgo., 1981—. Mem. Investment Analysts Soc. Chgo., Securities Industry Assn., Notre Dame Club Chgo., Bond Club. Roman Catholic. Home: 4304 Hampton Ave Western Springs IL 60558 Office: Keeley Investment Corp 401 LaSalle St Chicago IL 60605

KEEN, LEONARD, computer consultant; b. Miami, Fla., May 15, 1957; s. Joseph and Libby (Kopetman) Kishinisky; m. Jodi Lynn Globerman, Oct. 18, 1980; children: Justin, Ryan, Kevin. BS, U. Miami, Fla., 1978; postgrad., U. Fla., 1980. Asst. researcher U. Miami Sch. of Medicine, 1978-79; med. technologist Jackson Meml. Hosp., Miami, 1978-79; programmer Am. Helicopter, Gainesville, Fla., 1979-80; automation tech. specialist Coulter Electronics, Miami, 1979-80, software engr., 1980-82; sr. support cons. Arrow Electronics, Boca Raton, Fla., 1982-84; unix div. mgr. Computer Trade Devel., Ft. Lauderdale, Fla., 1984-85; pres. Keen Cons., Inc., Coral Springs, Fla., 1985—. Patentee. Mem. Assn. Computing Machinery, C Users Group, Ind. Computer Cons. Assn., IEEE, South Fla. Ind. Computer Cons. Assn. Office: Keen Cons Inc PO Box 8514 Coral Springs FL 33075

KEENAN, DEIRDRE ANN BRADBURY, manufacturing executive, employee relations, total quality consultant; b. Providence, Mar. 7, 1952; d. John Joseph and Marion Damon (Shute) Bradbury; m. Thomas Keenan, Nov. 15, 1975 (div. Dec. 1980); 1 child, Victoria Irene. BA in Govt. and Law, Lafayette Coll., 1973. Supr. Procter & Gamble Mfg. Co., S.I., N.Y., 1973-76; mgr. warehouse dept. Procter & Gamble Mfg. Co., 1976-79, mgr. shortening and oils dept., 1979-81, cost mgr. food plant, 1981-82, mgr. health & safety, 1982-86, mgr. total quality and pub. affairs, 1986—; cons. Procter & Gamble, S.I., 1982—, Cin., 1982—, Greensboro, N.C., 1983-86, Gen. Motor/AC Spark Plug, 1988. Trustee Lafayette Coll., 1985—. Recipient Clifton P. Mayfield award Lafayette Coll. Alumni Assn. Roman Catholic. Club: Maroon (Easton, Pa.) (pres. 1987—). Office: Procter & Gamble Mfg Co 40 Western Ave Staten Island NY 10303

KEENAN, MICHAEL HARRY, insurance executive; b. Columbus, Ohio, Sept. 27, 1951; s. John J. and Dolores (Frederick) K.; m. Jill Hall, July 28, 1972; children: Ryan Michael, Kelley Marie. BS in Fin., Ohio State U., 1976. Assoc. realtor Kent Real Estate, Columbus, 1975-76; assoc. appraiser John W. Peck & Assocs., Columbus, 1976-77, Donald Casey Hambleton & Assocs., Columbus, 1977-78, Jean Littlejohn & Assocs., Columbus, 1978-82; v.p. The Hutchinson Agy. Inc., Columbus, 1978-81; pres. The Keenan Agy. Inc. and The Hutchison Keenan Serra Agy., Columbus, 1981—; chmn. CNA Pacer, Columbus, 1986. Trustee Washington Twp., Franklin County, Ohio, 1983—. Mem. Ind. Ins. Agts. Ohio, Dublin Youth Assn., Ohio State U. Pres.'sClub, Ohio State U. Alumni Assn., Columbus C. of C., Dublin C. of C., Franklin County Twp. Trustees and Clks. Assn. Office: Hutchison Keenan Serra Agy 500 W Wilson Bridge Rd 306 Worthington OH 43085

KEESEE, ROGER N., family entertainment company executive; b. 1937; married;. BSEE, Va. Poly. and State U., 1960. With Gen. Electric Co., 1960-83, gen. mgr. dept. mfg. div. video products bus., 1981-83; exec. v.p. sales and mktg. engring. Bally Mfg. Corp., Chgo., 1983-88, now chief operating officer, pres., 1988—; now pres., chief exec. officer Six Flags Corp. subs. S.F. Acquisition Inc., Chgo., also bd. dirs. Office: Bally Mfg Corp 8700 W Bryn Mawr Chicago IL 60631 *

KEEVIL, NORMAN BELL, JR., mining executive; b. Cambridge, MA, Feb. 28, 1938; s. Norman Bell and Verna ruth (Bond) K.; m. Nancy J. Brown, 1957 (div.); children: Scott, Laura, Jill, Norman III; m. Catherine E. Taylor, July 5, 1970. BA in Sci., U. Toronto, Ont., Can., 1959; PhD, U. Calif., Berkeley, 1964. Registered profl. engr., Ont. V.p. exploration Teck Corp., Vancouver, B.C., Can., 1962-68; exec. v.p. Teck Corp., Vancouver, B.C., 1968-81, pres., chief exec. officer, 1981—; chmn. Cominco Ltd., Vancouver, 1986—. Named Mining Man of Yr. No. Miner, 1979. Mem. Mining Assn. Can. (chmn. 1988), Can. Inst. Mining and Metallurgy, Soc. Exploration Geophysicists, Vancouver Club, Shaughnessy Golf and Country

Club (Vancouver). Office: Teck Corp, 1199 W Hastings St, Vancouver, BC Canada V6E 2K5

KEFFALAS, JOHN SPERO, financial planner, lawyer; b. Grove City, Pa., Jan. 16, 1950; s. Spero John and Elizabeth Jane (Lichman) K. BS, Pa. State U., 1971, MBA, 1973; JD, Syracuse U., 1979. CLU, Cert. Fin. Planner. Advt. mktg. cons. Chubb/Colonial Life, Parsippany, N.J., 1979-82; asst. to regional v.p. Penn Mutual Life, Rochester, 1982-83; gen. legal counsel Coordinated Fin. Resources, Pitts., 1984-86; pres. So. Calif. div. New Eng. Fin. Advisors, L.A., 1986-88; mgr. Ordinary Agys., Mktg., Devel. and Tng. The Prudential Ins. Co. Am., Woodland Hills, Calif., 1988—. Mem. bd. editors Syracuse Jour. Internat. Law and Commerce, 1978-79. Mem. Thalians Fundraisers, Cedars-Sinai Hosp., Beverly Hills, Calif. Named S.P.O.K.E. of Yr. Jaycees, 1976. Mem. Am. Soc. CLU's, Chartered Fin. Cons. (bd. dirs.), Inst. Cert. Fin. Planners. Lutheran. Home: 623 Park Shadows Ct Baldwin Park CA 91706

KEGEL, WILLIAM GEORGE, mining company executive; b. Pitts., Mar. 15, 1922; s. William G. and Gertrude (Holl) K.; m. Jacqueline Treacy, Feb. 17, 1942; children: Kathy, Danyele, Janice, Jacqueline, William, Madeline, Colleen, Lisa, Brian. Student elec. engring, U. Pitts., 1940-43. Mgr. mech. and elec. depts. Lee Norse Co., 1941-50; with Jones & Laughlin Steel Corp., Pitts., 1950-76, gen. mgr. raw materials and traffic, 1975-76; pres. Cerro Marmon Coal Group, 1976-79; pres., chief exec. officer Rochester & Pitt. Coal Co., Indiana, Pa., 1979-88, chmn. bd., 1988—; dir. Savs. & Trust Co. Pa., Indiana. Mem. Indiana (Pa.) Airport Authority, 1980; bd. dirs. Brownsville Gen. Hosp., 1964-71; mem. Centerville Borough Council, 1952-60. Mem. Pitts. Coal Mining Inst., Coal Mining Inst. Am., Am. Mining Congress (dir.), AIME. Republican. Roman Catholic. Clubs: Duquesne Indiana Country, Laurel Valley Golf. Home: 100 Croyhill Dr Indiana PA 15701 Office: Rochester & Pitts Coal Co 655 Church St Indiana PA 15701

KEGERREIS, ROBERT JAMES, management consultant, marketing educator; b. Detroit, Apr. 2, 1921; s. I.G. and A.M. (Merry) K.; m. Katherine L. Falknor, Oct. 30, 1943; children: Merry, Duncan, Melissa. BA, Ohio State U., 1943, BS, 1943, MBA, 1946; EdD (hon.), U. Dayton, PhD, 1968; LLD (hon.), U. Akron, Wilberforce U.; ScD (hon.), Cen. State U. Economist Fed. Res. Bank, Cleve., 1946-49; pres. KV Stores, Inc., Woodsfield, Ohio, 1949-69; v.p., sec. KBK Devel. Co., Inc., 1955-62; assoc. prof. Ohio U., Athens, 1967-69; dean Coll. Bus. and Adminstrn. Wright State U., Dayton, Ohio, 1969-71; v.p. adminstrn. Wright State U., Dayton, 1971-73, pres., 1973-85; cons. RJK Co., Dayton, Ohio, 1985—; bd. dirs. DPL, Inc., Dayton, Robbins & Myers, Dayton, Bank One, Dayton, N.A.; chmn. bd. Moto Photo, Inc., Dayton. Served to lt. (j.g.) USN, 1943-46, PTO. Methodist. Clubs: Moraine Country, Bicycle (Dayton); Pelican Bay Country (Naples, Fla.). Office: 1850 Kettering Tower Dayton OH 45423

KEHOE, PAUL JEROME, human resources executive; b. Toronto, Ont., Can., Mar. 2, 1931; s. Jerome Lachland and Madeline (Thomson) K.; came to U.S., 1982; m. Jo Anne Beaupre, May 28, 1955; children—Paul James, Peter, Mary Jo. B.Commerce, U. Toronto (Ont., Can.), 1954. Dir. personnel Burroughs Corp., Toronto and Detroit, 1954-68; internat. ptnr. Hay Assocs. Canada Ltd., Toronto, 1968-82; sr. v.p. human resources Genstar Corp., San Francisco, 1982-87; sr. v.p. Clark/Bardes Orgn., San Francisco, 1988—. Mem. Personnel Assn. Toronto (dir. 1973-74). Roman Catholic. Clubs: Bankers (San Francisco); Peninsula Golf & Country (San Mateo, Calif.). Office: Clark/Bardes Orgn 2100 Geng Rd Ste 203 San Francisco CA 94303

KEHOE, STEVEN C., financial planner; b. Plymouth, Ind., Feb. 27, 1955; s. M. Frederick and Barbara Ann (Drake) K.; m. Amy T. Timmers, Sept. 7, 1985; children: Bryn, Steven C. BS, Ball State U., 1977; MS, Ind. U., 1978; postgrad., Ill. State U., 1981-82, Coll. of Fin. Planning. Cert. fin. planner. Tchr. Bartholomew Sch. System, Columbus, Ind., 1978-79; dir. Muncie (Ind.) YMCA, 1979-82; dist. mgr. IDS/Am. Express, Cin., 1982-85; fin. planner Oxford Fin. Group, Cin., 1985—; cons. Citizens Fed. Savs. and Loan, Cin., 1987—. Mem. Westwood (Ohio) Civic Assn., 1987, Concerned Citizens for Community Values, Cin., 1987. Mem. Internat. Assn. Fin. Planners, Miami Valley Inst. Cert. Fin. Planners, Kiwanis. Democrat. Home: 2614 Fleetwood Ave Cincinnati OH 45211 Office: Total Fin Planning 5907 Glenway Ave Cincinnati OH 45238

KEHRLI, RONALD LOUIS, insurance company executive; b. Albany, N.Y., 1932. BA, Cornell U., 1952. Agt. sales Bus. Mens Assurance Co., 1956-60; field supt. Safeco Life Ins. Co., 1960-66; dir. sales Congl. Life Ins. Co., 1966-70; pres., chief exec. officer Somerset Capital Corp., 1970-75; sr. v.p. Franklin Life Ins. Co., 1975-82; exec. v.p. USLIFE Corp., 1982-84; pres., chief exec. officer Exec. Life Ins. Co. N.Y., Jericho, 1984-86, also bd. dirs.; pres., chief exec. officer Lincoln Liberty Life Ins. Co. (affiliate Exec. Life Ins. Co. N.Y.), Omaha, 1986—; dir. Life Ins. Cos. Council of N.Y. Served to capt. USAF, 1952-56. Office: Exec Life Ins Co NY 390 N Broadway Jericho NY 11753

KEIFFER, EDWIN GENE, defense industry company executive; b. Dallas, Aug. 25, 1929; s. Edwin L. and Eunice Alpha (Foster) K.; m. Carole Ann Porter; children: Edwin Paul, Cheri Ann, Judith Susan, Amy Lynn. BEE, So. Meth. U., 1955, MEE, 1962. Lead systems design engr. Chance Vought Co., Grand Prairie, Tex., 1955-58, engring. specialist, 1958, sr. engring. specialist, 1958-59, sect. chief antenna systems, 1959-60, chief antenna and microwave design, 1960-62; br. mgr. communications and tracking systems Chance Vought Co., Garland, Tex., 1962-63; dep. mgr. Radiation Lab., 1963-66; product line dir. spl. projects LTV Electrosystems (name changed to E-Systems, Inc.), 1966-70; successively v.p. electronic systems, v.p., gen. mgr., Garland div. E-Systems, Inc., 1970-83; sr. v.p. group exec. E-Systems, Inc., Dallas, 1983-87, corp. pres., chief operating officer, 1987—, also bd. dirs. Mem. chancellor's century council Tex. A&M U., College Station, 1988. With USMC, 1948-50. Recipient Disting. Alumni award So. Meth. U., 1989. Mem. IEEE (sr.), Am. Def. Preparedness Assn., Armed Forces Communications and Electronics Assn., Army Aviation Assn. Am., Assn. Old Crows, Assn. U.S. Army. Republican. Office: E-Systems Inc PO Box 660248 Dallas TX 75266

KEIL, JAMES HUGH, sales executive; b. Phila., Jan. 21, 1943; s. Howard McIntyre and Mae (Cromie) K.; children: Kevin James, Kellye Ellen, Kristen Elizabeth. BS in Secondary Edn., Westchester U., 1966. Mktg. rep. Armstrong Cork Co., Lancaster, Pa., 1968-72; sales mgr. Scott Paper Co., Phila., 1972-74, AMP Spl. Industries, Valley Forge, Pa., 1974-77; proprietor Naples Bootery, Maine, 1977-81; gen. slaes mgr. Blue Rock Industries, Westbrook, Maine, 1981—. Author: Real Salesmen Drive Company Cars, 1988; contbr. articles to profl. jours. Founder Naples Bus. Assn., Maine, 1980; mem. Naples Budget Com., 1978-82, Transp. Rsch. Bd.; chmn. Jetport Study Com., Portland, Maine, 1987-88. With USN, 1966-68. Mem. Portland C. of C. (bd. dir. 1988), Sales and Mktg. Execs. Internat. (v.p. 1985-87), Maine Better Transp. Assn. (treas. 1986-88). Home: 369 Capisic St Portland ME 04102 Office: Blue Rock Industries 58 Main St Westbrook ME 04092

KEIL, JEFFREY C., banker; b. West Orange, N.J., 1943. Grad., U. Pa., 1965; MBA, Harvard U., 1968. Vice chmn. Republic Nat. Bank, N.Y.C., also bd. dirs.; pres., bd. dirs. Republic N.Y. Corp. Office: Republic NY Corp 452 Fifth Ave New York NY 10018

KEIL, ROBERT MATTHES, chemical company executive; b. Bloomefield, N.J., Apr. 5, 1926; s. Wiliiam August and Myra (Maguire) K.; m. Betty Jane Appar, May 3, 1952; children: Barbara Lynn, Nancy Lee. B.S., Syracuse U., 1948. Gen. mgr. olefin plastics Dow Chem. U.S.A., Midland, Mich., 1969-76, v.p. consumer goods and services, 1976-78, v.p. mktg., 1978-79, exec. v.p., 1979-80; fin. v.p. Dow Chem. Co., Midland, Mich., 1980-82, exec. v.p., 1982—, also bd. dirs.; bd. dirs. Dow Corning Corp., Midland, Comerica Bank, Detroit; chmn. Dow Chem. Que. Ltd., 1978-82. Pres. Midland Community Ctr., 1976-77. Served to lt. U.S. Army, 1943-46, 51-52. Office: Dow Chem Co 2030 Willard H Dow Ctr Midland MI 48674

KEIM, CARROLL STEPHEN, corporate executive; b. Bronxville, N.Y., Jan. 6, 1946; s. Carroll Ralph and Attrude (Gillies) K.; m. Carol Jane Chisholm; children: Lisa, Heather, Beth, Pam, Jennifer, Victoria. BA, Wesleyan U., 1967; MBA, Harvard U., 1974. Brand asst. Procter & Gamble Co., Cin., 1974-77, brand mgr., 1978; dir. advt. Deltona Corp., Miami, Fla., 1979-81; v.p. mktg. Citibank, N.Y.C., 1981-82; pres. Belmont Springs Water Co. Foods div. Coca-Cola Co., Boston, 1983-85; v.p. mktg. Foods div. Coca-Cola Co., Houston, 1985-87; chmn. Aquarius Spring Water Co., Houston, 1987—; dir. mktg. Bottled Water div. Anjou Internat., Phila., 1987—; pres. Sierra Springs Water Co. subs. Anjou Internat., Houston, 1988—. Served to capt. inf. U.S. Army, 1968-71, Vietnam. Mem. Internat. Bottled Water Assn. (bd. dirs.). Club: Am. Contract Bridge League. Home: 4127 Cypress Lake Dr Spring TX 77388 Office: Sierra Spring Water 16630 Imperial Valley Dr Ste 161 Houston TX 77060

KEIPI, KARI JUHANI, forestry investment analyst; b. Porvoo, Finland, Oct. 6, 1946; came to U.S., 1980; s. Paavo and Kerttu Saara Ilona (Valanne) K.; m. Aila Toini Marjukka Ketolainen, Dec. 26, 1983; children: Teo Aleksi, Sakari Ensio, Aaro Juhani, Tapani Artturi. BSc in Agr. and Forestry, Helsinki U., Finland, 1969, MSc, 1971, Dr. Agr. and Forestry, 1978; PhD, Oreg. State U., 1976. Researcher Finnish Forest Research Inst., Helsinki, 1969-71; cons. ATK Suunnittelu-Kop Bank Oy, Helsinki, 1971; researcher Finnish Forest Research Inst., Helsinki, 1972, project leader, 1976-80; rsch. asst. Oreg. State U., Corvallis, 1974-75; cons. Crown Zellerbach Co., Portland, 1975;; asst. prof. Helsinki U., 1979-80; cons. Resource Devel. Tech., 1987-88; forestry specialist Inter-Am. devel. Bank, Washington, 1980—; vis. economist Royal Forestry Coll. Sweden, Stockholm, 1969, Royal Forestry Coll. Norway, 1969, U. Ljubljana, Yuoslavia, 1978; cons. in field. Author: Wood Procurement Planning, 1978, Transfer Pricing in Forest, 1979; contbr. articles to profl. jours. Vol. Internat. Students, Inc., Washington, 1981; mem. adv. bd. The Navigators, Inc., Washington, 1988—; deacon Barcroft Bible Ch., 1988—. Kellogg Found. grantee, 1972-74, Acad. Finland grantee, 1977, 78. Mem. Soc. Forestry of Finland (grantee 1978), Soc. Am. Foresters, Soc. Profl. Foresters of Finland, Internat. Soc. Tropical Foresters, Nordic Forest Econs. Seminar. Home: 6019 Shaffer Dr Alexandria VA 22310 Office: Inter-Am Devel Bank 1300 New York Ave Washington DC 20577

KEISER, HENRY BRUCE, lawyer, publisher; b. N.Y.C., Oct. 26, 1927; s. Leo and Jessie (Liebeskind) K.; BA with honors in Econs., U. Mich., 1947; JD cum laude, Harvard U., 1950; m. Jessie E. Weeks, July 12, 1953; children: Betsy Cordelia Keiser Smith, Matthew Roderick. Admitted to N.Y. bar, 1950, D.C. bar, 1955, Fla. bar, 1956, U.S. Supreme Ct bar, 1954; trial atty. CAB, Washington, 1950-51; head counsel alcoholic beverages sect. OPS, 1951-52; legal asst. to Judge Eugene Black, Tax Ct. U.S., 1953-56; practice in Washington, 1956—; founder, chmn. bd., pres., Fed. Pubs., Inc., 1959-85; chmn. bd. Gene Galasso Assos., Inc., Washington, 1963—; founder, chmn. Crown Eagle Communications Ltd., London, 1978-84; chmn. bd. The Arkhon Corp., Cherry Hill, N.J., 1983—; chmn. Empire Carriages, London, 1984—; chmn. bd., pres. Keiser Enterprises, Inc., Washington, 1985—; chmn. Lion Worldwide, London, 1985—; chmn. bd. U.S. Telemktg., Inc., Atlanta, 1986—; chmn. bd., chief exec. officer Phila. Inst., 1986—; chmn., sec. adv. com. on Constrn. Contract Document Reform, HUD, 1983-85; dir. Nat. Bank of Commerce, Washington, 1983-84; mem. adv. cabinet Southeastern U.,1965-75; judge, bd. of contract appeals, AEC, 1965-75; profl. lectr. Dept. Agr., 1960-77, George Washington U., 1961-79, U. San Francisco, 1965-82, Coll. William and Mary, 1966-75, Calif. Inst. Tech., 1967-72, U. So. Calif., 1973-74, U. Denver, 1975-85, Air Force Inst. Tech., 1975-76, U. Santa Clara, 1975-81, trustee Touro Coll., 1979—. Served to 1st lt. Judge Adv. Gen. Corps, USAF, 1952-53; maj. Res. (ret.). Lord of Tuxford (hereditary), Nottinghamshire, Eng. Fellow Am. Bar Found., Nat. Contract Mgmt. Assn.; mem. Am. (council pub. contract law sect. 1972-75, fellow), N.Y., Fla., D.C. (dir. 1965-66, chmn. adminstrv. law sect. 1964-65) bar assns., Cosmos, Nat. Press, Army Navy, Harvard (Washington); Crockford's (London). Jewish. Home: 7200 Armat Dr Bethesda MD 20817 Office: 2828 Pennsylvania Ave Washington DC 20007

KEISER, NORMAN MICHAEL, securities company executive; b. Binghamton, N.Y., Sept. 15, 1919; s. Norman George and Helen Elizabeth (Clinton) K.; m. Louise Knight Belcher, June 26, 1943; children: Michael Lewis, Bruce Norman, Thomas Clinton, Stephen Knight. B.S., Wharton Sch., U. Pa., 1941. Mem. sales staff Armstrong Cork Co., Lancaster and Buffalo, Pa., 1941-42, 45-47; with George D.B. Bonbright Co., Buffalo, 1947-50; exec. v.p. Hugh Johnson & Co., Buffalo, 1950-69, pres., 1969-74, vice chmn., 1974-76; v.p. First Albany Corp., Buffalo, 1977—; exec. v.p., dir. Johnson's Charts, Buffalo, 1949—; pres. Binghamton Credit Corp., N.Y., 1951-80, also dir. Served as aviator USNR, 1942-45. Decorated Navy Cross, Silver Star, D.F.C. (3), Air medal (3). Mem. Beta Gamma Sigma (capt. of varsity crew), Phi Gamma Delta. Republican. Presbyterian (elder). Club: Bond (Buffalo). Home: 39 Hillcrest Rd East Aurora NY 14052 Office: First Albany Corp 69 Delaware Ave Buffalo NY 14202

KEISOGLOU, ABRAHAM NIKOLAOS, engineering company executive; b. Salonica, Greece, June 10, 1945; came to U.S., 1956; s. Nikolaos and Elizabeth (Kamalakidou) K.; m. Marie Frances Scott, Dec. 28, 1968; children: Christa, Nicole, Laura. BS, Mich. State U., 1969. Structural engr. Chrysler Corp., Highland Park, Mich., 1970-76; project engr. Rockwell Internat., Troy, Mich., 1976-78; sr. project engr. Ford Motor Co., Dearborn, Mich., 1978-81; owner, pres. Keis Assocs., Southfield, Mich., 1981-83; pres. Enging Tech. Assocs., Troy, 1983—; cons. Gen Motors Corp., Warren, Mich., 1981-84, Ford Motor Co., Dearborn, 1981-83. Mem. Soc. Automotive Engrs. Greek Orthodox. Office: Enging Tech Assocs 1895 Crooks Rd Troy MI 48084

KEISTLER, BETTY LOU, accountant, tax consultant; b. St. Louis, Jan. 2, 1935; d. John William and Gertrude Marie (Lewis) Chancellor; m. George E. Keistler, Aug. 4, 1957 (div. Mar. 1981); children: Kathryn M. Morrissey, Deborah J. Birsinger. AS, St. Louis U., 1956; BBA, U. Mo., 1986. Asst. treas. A. G. Edwards & Sons, St. Louis, 1956-57; owner, mgr. B. L. Keistler & Assoc., St. Louis, 1969-82; contr. Family Resource Ctr., Inc., St. Louis, 1982-87; registered rep. Equitable Fin. Svcs., Mo., 1987; bus. mgr. Mo. Bapt. Coll., St. Louis, 1987-88, Barnes Hosp. Sch. of Nursing, St. Louis, 1989; cons. in field, St. Louis, 1982—; registered rep. Equitable Fin. Services, 1987—. Treas. Pkwy. Townhouses At Village Green, Chesterfield, Mo., 1985—; exec. core United Way Greater St. Louis, 1984—; mem. U. Mo. Alumni Assn., 1987—; rep. to the bd. alumni assn. U. Mo., St. Louis., 1988-89. Scholar Phillip Morris Corp., St. Louis, 1982-84. Mem. Am. Bus. Women Assn. (v.p. 1978-79, pres. 1979-80, treas. nat. conv. 1981, Woman of Yr. 1979-80), Am. Soc. Women Accts., Ind. Accts. of Mo. (sec. 1978-79, v.p. 1980-81, state sec. 1978-79), St. Louis Women's Commerce Assn., 1904 World's Fair Soc., Internat. Platform Assn., Am. Biog. Inst. (hon. advisor, rsch. bd. advisors nat. div. 1989), Alpha Sigma Lambda (life, treas. 1985-87), NAFE. Republican. Baptist. Home: 14524 Bantry Ln Chesterfield MO 63017

KEITER, WILLIAM EDWARD, insurance company executive; b. Orange, N.J., Dec. 7, 1929; s. Ernest R. and Florence H. (Reineke) K.; m. Jeanne D. Flauss, May 16, 1953; children: Nancy, John, Susan. B.A., Muhlenberg Coll., 1951; M.B.A., U. Pa., 1952. With N.Y. Life Ins. Co., N.Y.C., 1954—; 2d v.p. N.Y. Life Ins. Co., 1964-67, v.p., 1967-74, sr. v.p. in charge investment dept., 1974-79, exec. v.p., 1979—. Trustee Episcopalian Diocesan Investment Trust, Newark, Muhlenberg Coll., United Student Aid Funds. Served with fin. corps AUS, 1952-54. Office: NY Life Ins Co 51 Madison Ave New York NY 10010

KEITH, GARNETT LEE, JR., investment insurance company executive; b. Atlanta, Nov. 27, 1935; s. Garnett Lee and Agnes (Roark) K.; m. Martha Holmes, Oct. 12, 1957; children: Suzanne, Geoffrey. B.Indsl. Engring., Ga. Inst. Tech., 1957; M.B.A., Harvard U., 1962. Asst. sec. Irving Trust Co., 1962-64; v.p. Irwin Mgmt. Co., 1964-75; pres. Irwin Union Corp., 1975-76; vice chmn. investments Prudential Ins. Co., Newark, 1977—; bd. dirs. Super Valu Stores, Minn., Inland Steel Industries Inc. Mem. Inst. Chartered Fin. Analysts. Republican. Club: Harvard (N.Y.C.). Office: The Prudential Ins Co Am 24 Prudential Pla 745 Broad St Newark NJ 07101

KELAHAN, JOHN ANTHONY, JR., financial planner; b. Newport, R.I., Feb. 19, 1952; s. John Anthony and C. Joanne (Greider) K.; m. Rosalind Tariello, Apr. 12, 1975. Student, Rensselaer Poly. Inst., 1970-72; BS in Fin., Northeastern U., 1982; postgrad., Coll. Fin. Planning, 1985, Am. Coll., 1986-87. CLU; chartered fin. cons.; cert. fin. planner. Mgr., various mgmt. positions Bradlees div. Stop and Shop, Braintree, Mass., 1975-83; counselor CIGNA Individual Fin. Services Co., Boston, 1983-85, asst. mgr., 1986—; instr., Ins. and Fin. Services Inst. Northeastern U., 1988—. Mem. Internat. Assn. for Fin. Planning, Inst. of Cert. Fin. Planners, Am. Soc. CLU/Chartered Fin. Cons., Nat. Assn. Life Underwriters, Retail Fin. Execs. New England (bd. dirs. 1985-87), Am. Assn. Ind. Investors (bd. dirs. 1986), Sigma Epsilon Rho (scholarship award 1982, pres. Northeastern U. chpt. 1985-86). Home: 126 Cabral Circle Stoughton MA 02072 Office: CIGNA 260 Franklin St Suite 510 Boston MA 02110

KELAIDITIS, ANESTIS, construction company executive; b. Cairo, Egypt, Feb. 28, 1948; s. Stylianos and Anastasia (Christodoulou) K.; m. Stefania Zaglaras, July 2, 1977; 1 child, Stylianos. Diploma in Civil Engring., Nat. Tech. Univ. Athens, 1971; student Mgmt. Tng. and Devel. program Urwick Mgmt. Ctr., London, 1985. Site engr. Edok S.A.-Eter S.A., Agrinion, Greece, 1972-73, GETEM S.A., Piraeus, Greece, 1973-74; market survey and tenders staff Hydrotechnic S.A., Athens, 1974-75; site engr. Odon & Odostro Maton S.A., Saudi Arabia, 1975-79, bridge engr., 1979-80, project mgr., 1980-85; comml. mgr. Itihad Al Tatwir Wal Tanmia Al Saoudia Ltd., Saudia Arabia, 1986—. Greek Orthodox. Avocations: boy scouts, photography, painting. Home: 88 Rovertou Galli-Kato Heliopolis, 16346 Athens Greece Office: Itihad Al Tatwir Wal, Tanmia Al Saoudia Co Ltd, PO Box 8825, Riyadh 11492, Saudi Arabia

KELBLEY, STEPHEN PAUL, consumer products and health care executive; b. Tiffin, Ohio, Aug. 31, 1942; s. Ralph John and Clara Ann (Ridenour) K.; m. Kathleen Ann Williams, Sept. 5, 1964; children—Monica, John, Jay. B.A. in Econs., Heidelberg Coll. Various fin. positions Gen. Electric Co., 1964-81; mgr. fin. air conditioning div. Gen. Electric Co., Louisville, 1981-83; sr. v.p. and adminstrn. Moog Automotive, St. Louis, 1983-84; sr. v.p. fin. Bausch & Lomb Inc., Rochester, N.Y., 1984—. Bd. dirs. Geva Theatre, Rochester, 1985—, United Way campaign, Rochester, 1985—; trustee Nazareth Coll., 1987. Mem. Fin. Execs. Inst. Republican. Roman Catholic. Clubs: Genesee Valley, Country of Rochester. Home: 109 Ambassador Dr Rochester NY 14610 Office: Bausch & Lomb Inc One Lincoln First Sq Rochester NY 14601

KELEHER, PAUL DONALD, investment banker; b. Lowell, Mass., Mar. 27, 1931; s. John Leo and Anna (Shipsey) K.; m. Virginia Jean Griffin, Aug. 25, 1956; children: Joanne, James, David, Peter. BA in Econs., Boston Coll., 1958; MBA in Fin., U. Pa., 1959. Gen. mgr. investments Prudential Ins. Co. Am., Newark, 1959-70; sr. ptnr. Danes, Cooke & Keleher, Inc., N.Y.C., 1970-80; sr. v.p., dir. corp. fin. W.H. Newbolds Son & Co., Inc., Phila., 1980-89; pres. Oxford Investment Ptnrs., Inc., Phila., 1989—. Served with U.S. Army, 1952-54. Clubs: Racquet (Phila.), Aronimink Golf (Newtown Sq.). Home: 3660 Wyola Dr Newtown Square PA 19073

KELLAR, LORRENCE THEODORE, retail food and manufacturing executive; b. Burlington, Iowa, Aug. 10, 1937; s. William Paul and Grace Alberta (Mathews) K.; m. Susan Stewart, Aug. 10, 1958 (div. 1976); children: Kevin, Katherine, Nicholas; m. Barbara Ann Weeks, Aug. 26, 1977; 1 child, Ainsley. B.S., U. Iowa, 1958; M.B.A., U. Va., 1962. With 3M Corp., St. Paul, 1962-65; with Kroger Co., Cin., 1965—, beginning as mgr. fin. planning, successively asst. treas., v.p. corp. devel., v.p. capital mgmt., 1965-82, v.p., treas., 1982-85, v.p. corp. real estate, 1985—, group v.p., 1986—; bd. dirs. U.S. Shoe Corp., Multi-Color Corp.; trustee Bartlett Mgmt. Trust. Pres., chmn. bd. Cin. Ballet Co., 1976—; bd. dirs. WCET Pub. TV, Cin., 1982—, Cin. Symphony Orch., 1983—; Cin. Charter Com., 1970-78; trustee City of Cin. Retirement System Bd., 1985—; pres. Queen City Assn., 1969. Recipient Corbett award in fine arts Cin. Post, 1983. Mem. Fin. Execs. Inst. Clubs: Cin. Country, Queen City (Cin.). Office: Kroger Co 1014 Vine St Cincinnati OH 45201

KELLEHER, HERBERT DAVID, lawyer, airline executive; b. Camden, N.J., Mar. 12, 1931; s. Harry and Ruth (Moore) K.; m. Joan Negley, Sept. 9, 1955; children—Julie, Michael, Ruth, David. B.A. cum laude (Olin scholar), Wesleyan U., 1953; LL.B. cum laude (Root Tilden scholar), NYU, 1956. Bar: N.J. 1957, Tex. 1962. Clk. N.J. Supreme Ct., 1956-59; assoc. Lum, Biunno & Tompkins, Newark, 1959-61; ptnr. Matthews, Nowlin, Macfarlane & Barrett, San Antonio, 1961-69; sr. ptnr. Oppenheimer, Rosenberg, Kelleher & Wheatley, Inc., San Antonio, 1969—; founder, gen. counsel, pres. chmn., dir. S.W. Airlines Co., Dallas, 1967—, now also chief exec. officer; dir. M Corp., Dallas, Merc. Tex. Corp. Chmn. adv. bus. council Trinity U., San Antonio; vice chmn. bus. adv. council U. Tex. Sch. Bus.; campaign coordinator Connally for Gov., 1961, 63, 65; Bexar County dir. Bentsen for Senator, 1970, 76, state co chmn., 1975-76; chmn. Senate Dist. 19 Democratic Com., 1968-70; del. Dem. Nat. Conv., 1964, 68; mem. state steering com. Bentsen for Pres., 1975-76; pres. bd. trustees St. Mary's Hall, San Antonio; pres. Travelers Aid Soc., San Antonio. Named Chief Exec. Officer of Yr., The Fin. World, 1982, Best Chief Exec. Regional Airline Industry Wall St. Transcript, 1982, Airline Industry Svc. award, 1988, Tex. bus. Hall Fame, 1988; Recipient Fin. Mgmt. award Air Transport World, 1982. Fellow Tex. Bar Found. (life); mem. ABA, San Antonio, N.J. bar assns., State Bar Tex., San Antonio C. of C. (dir.), Order of Alamo, Tex. Cavaliers. Home: 144 Thelma Dr San Antonio TX 78212 Office: SW Airlines Co PO Box 37611 Dallas TX 75235

KELLEHER, JAMES RAYMOND, health care corporation executive; b. N.Y.C., Sept. 14, 1948; s. James Raymond and Constance (Roche) K.; m. Anne Gilmartin, May 6, 1972; children: Brian James, Michael Patrick. BS, Fairfield U., 1970; MBA, St. John's U., N.Y.C., 1975. Plant controller Gen. Foods, Topeka, 1976-79; owner Rutland Corp., Newport, R.I., 1979-81; asst. controller C.R. Bard-Davol, Cranston, R.I., 1981-83; controller cardiopulmonary div. C.R. Bard, Santa Ana, Calif., 1983-84; v.p., controller cardiosurgery div. C.R. Bard, Billerica, Mass., 1984-88, asst. corp. controller, 1988—. Served with U.S. Army N.G., 1970-76. Roman Catholic. Home: 12 Green Way Chelmsford MA 01824 Office: Bard Cardiosurgery Div 129 Concord Rd Box M Billerica MA 01821

KELLEHER, KATHLEEN, financial services marketing specialist; b. Suffern, N.Y., May 3, 1951; d. John James and Carol (Re) K. BA, Fairleigh Dickinson U., 1973. CLU, chartered fin. cons. Ins. sales adminstr. Blyth Eastman Dillon & Co., 1977-79; product mktg. assoc. Dean Witter Reynolds, N.Y.C., 1980-82; mgr. product mktg. annuities and ins. dept. Kidder, Peabody & Co., 1982-85; v.p. nat. sales mgr. ins. Paine Webber, 1985-88; v.p., dir. mktg. Landmark Fin. Corp., Okla. City, 1988—. Mem. Am. Mgmt. Assn., Internat. Fin. Planners. Republican. Club: Coll. of Ridgewood. Home: 5506 Inverary Dr Edmond OK 73034 Office: Landmark Fin Corp 6307 Waterford Blvd Oklahoma City OK 73118

KELLEN, STEPHEN MAX, investment banker; b. Berlin, Germany, Apr. 21, 1914; came to U.S., 1936, naturalized, 1944; s. Max and Leonie (Marcuse) Katzenellenbogen; m. Anna-Maria Arnhold, Mar. 7, 1940; children: Marina Kellen French, Michael. Grad., Royal French Coll., Berlin, 1932. With Berliner Handels-Gesellschaft, Berlin, 1932-35, Lazard Bros. Ltd., London, Eng., 1936, Loeb, Rhoades & Co., N.Y.C., 1937-40; with Arnhold and S. Bleichroeder, Inc., N.Y.C., 1940—; pres. Arnhold and S. Bleichroeder, Inc., 1955—; dir. Pittway Corp., Siemens Western Fin. N.V.; mem. adv. com. on internat. capital markets N.Y. Stock Exchange. Trustee WNET/13, Trust for Cultural Resources City of N.Y., Carnegie Hall Soc.; mem. trustees council Nat. Gallery Art, Washington. Mem. Investment Bankers Assn. Am. (bd. govs. 1969-71, chmn. fgn. investment com. 1967-72), Securities Industry Assn. (bd. govs. 1972-73, chmn. internat. finance com. 1972-73). Clubs: Bond, Wall Street, Metropolitan (N.Y.C.). Home: 784 Park Ave New York NY 10021 also: Ridgefield CT 06877 Office: Arnhold & S Bleichroeder Inc 45 Broadway New York NY 10006

KELLER, DONALD JOHN, textile and apparel company executive; b. Chgo., Feb. 14, 1932; s. Philip F. and Gertrude (Rice) K.; m. Virginia Wilson, July 22, 1955; children: Ann Keller Springborn, Edward Wilson, Amy Margaret. A.B., Princeton U., 1954; M.B.A., Northwestern U., 1958. Account exec. Leo Burnett Co., Chgo., 1958-63; various positions to exec. v.p., dir. Gen. Foods Corp., White Plains, N.Y., 1963-86, group v.p., 1977-79, exec. v.p., 1979-86, dir., 1981-86; pres., chief operating officer, dir. West Point Pepperell, Inc., N.Y.C., 1986-89; bd. dirs. Sysco Corp., Houston, Hartwell Growth Fund, Inc., N.Y.C., Hartwell Emerging Growth Fund,

Inc., N.Y.C.; bd. visitors Fuqua Sch., Duke U., Durham, N.C. Bd. trustees The Hosp. Chaplaincy, Inc., N.Y.C., 1987—; ruling elder Presbyn. Ch. Served to sgt. U.S. Army, 1954-56. Republican. Clubs: Riverside (Conn.) Yacht; Blind Brook (Purchase, N.Y.), John's Island (Vero Beach, Fla.), Riomar Bay Yacht (Fla.). Office: 95 Rowayton Ave Bldg A Rowayton CT 06853

KELLER, ERIC MARTIN, underwriter; b. Chgo., Apr. 17, 1951; s. Carl and Mary Ann (Kilzer) K.; B.S., Elmhurst Coll., 1979; m. Carol Ann Boyle, Jan. 21, 1978; children: Erica Elizabeth, Ryan Kristopher. Mgr., Ponderosa, Niles, Ill., 1973-74; ter. mgr. Burroughs Corp., Oak Brook, Ill., 1974-77; controller Bally/Diemasters, Inc., Elmhurst, Ill., 1977-86, agt. N.Y. Life, Oakbrook Terr., Ill. CPA, Ill. Mem. Am. Inst. CPAs, Ill. CPAs Soc., Nat. Assn. Life Underwriters, Tau Kappa Epsilon. Republican. Mem. Christ Ch. Home: 6919 Richmond St Darien IL 60559 Office: Keller-Savaiano Assocs 15660 Midwest Rd Ste 270 Oakbrook Terrace IL 60181

KELLER, GEORGE MATTHEW, oil company executive; b. Kansas City, Mo., Dec. 3, 1923; s. George Matthew and Edna Louise (Mathews) K.; m. Adelaide McCague, Dec. 27, 1946; children: William G., Robert A., Barry R. BS in Chem. Engring., MIT, 1948. Engr. Standard Oil Calif. (now Chevron Corp.), San Francisco, 1948-63, fgn. ops. staff, 1963-67, asst. v.p., asst. to pres., 1967-69, v.p., 1969-74, dir., 1970—, vice-chmn., 1974-81, chmn., chief exec. officer, 1981-88; bd. dirs. First Interstate Bancorp., First Interstate Bank Calif., Boeing Co., McKesson Corp., SRI Internat., Met. Life Ins. Co. Trustee Notre Dame Coll., Belmont, Calif. Served to 1st lt. USAAF, 1943-46. Mem. Bus. Council, Trilateral Commn., Coun. Fgn. Rels. Office: Chevron Corp 555 Market St San Francisco CA 94105

KELLER, JIMMY RAY, military officer; b. Fayetteville, Tenn., Nov. 2, 1952; s. J.D. and Irene (Bennett) K.; m. Rungrawee Musikaphan, May 8, 1975. Student, Liberty U., 1987—. Enlisted USAF, 1970, advanced through grades to capt., 1982; adminstrn. specialist Office of Spl. Investigations, Bolling AFB, DC, 1971-78; stock control officer 401 Supply Squadron, Torreson AB, Spain, 1979-81; customer support officer 3345 Supply Squadron, Chanute AFB, Ill., 1982-83; weapons dir. 964 and 966 Airborne Warning and Control Tng. Squadron, Tinker AFB, Okla., 1984—. Chmn. bd. overseers Calvary Bible Ch., Okla. City, 1985—. Decorated Air medal. Mem. Air Force Assn. (life). Republican. Baptist. Home: 5332 Vandenberg St Tinker AFB OK 73145 Office: 966 Airborne Warnings and Tng Squadron Tinker AFB OK 73145

KELLER, RICHARD CHARLES, banker; b. Buffalo, Apr. 12, 1937; s. Walter F. and Katherine D. K.; m. Diane M. Henry, June 30, 1962; 2 children. B.S., U. Buffalo, 1969. With Marine Midland Bank, N.A., 1959—, exec. v.p. money mgmt., chmn. asset-liability com., sr. exec. v.p. fin. markets sector, now exec. dir. Served with USAF, 1961-62. Mem. Treasury Securities Luncheon Group, Bond Club of N.Y.C. Club: City Midday (N.Y.C.). Office: Marine Midland Banks Inc Marine Midland Bldg 140 Broadway New York NY 10015

KELLER, RONALD EUGENE, association executive; b. Lancaster, Ohio, May 6, 1955; s. Glenn Eugene and Mary Francis (Hedges) K.; m. Kitty Lea Nicewanger, Aug. 11, 1979; children: Adam Eugene, Katie Lea, Jordan Glenn. B in Gen. Studies, Ohio U., 1978. Mem. legis. staff Ohio Ho. Reps., Columbus, 1976-81; adminstrv. asst. Ohio Tech. and Community Coll. Assn., Columbus, 1981—. Treas. Sweet Corn Festival, Inc., Millersport, Ohio, 1982—; mem. Ohio Amusement Ride Safety Bd., Columbus, 1985—; pres. Bd. Pub Affairs, Millersport, 1983—; bd. dirs. Ohio Festivals and Events Assn., 1985—, v.p. 1987-89, pres. 1989—; mem. Dawes Arboretum. Democrat. Methodist. Home: 12395 Lancaster St Millersport OH 43046

KELLER, SUSAN AGNES, insurance officer; b. Moline, Ill., July 12, 1952; d. Kenneth Francis and Ethel Louise (Odendahl) Hulsbrink; m. Kevin Eugene Keller, June 20, 1981; 1 child, Dawn Marie. Grad. in Pub. Relations, Patricia Stevens Career Coll., 1971; grad. in Gen. Ins., Ins. Inst. Am., 1986. CPCU. Comml. lines rater Bitiminous Casualty Corp., Rock Island, Ill., 1973-78; with Roadway Express, Inc., Rock Island, 1978-81; front line supr. Yellow Freight System, Inc., Denver, 1982-83; supr. plumbing and sheet metal prodn. Bell Plumbing and Heating, Denver, 1983-84; underwriter Golden Eagle Ins. Co., San Diego, 1985—; cons. real estate foreclosure County Records Service, San Diego, 1986—. Vol. DAV, San Diego, 1985—. Mem. Soc. Chartered Property and Casualty Underwriters, Profl. Women in Ins., Nat. Assn. Female Execs. Roman Catholic. Home: 449 Jamul Ct Chula Vista CA 92001 Office: Golden Eagle Ins Co 7175 Navajo Rd San Diego CA 92119

KELLER, THOMAS FRANKLIN, management science educator; b. Greenwood, S.C., Sept. 22, 1931; s. Cleaveland Alonzo and Helen (Seago) K.; m. Margaret Neel Query, June 15, 1956; children: Thomas Crafton (dec.), Neel McKay, John Caldwell. A.B., Duke U., 1953; M.B.A., U. Mich., 1957, Ph.D., 1960; HHD, Clemson U., 1987. C.P.A., N.C. Mem. faculty Fuqua Sch. Bus. Duke U., 1959—, assoc. prof., 1962-67, prof., 1967-74, R.J. Reynolds Industries prof., 1974—, also vice provost, 1971-72, dean Fuqua Sch. Bus., 1974—, chmn. dept. mgmt. scis., 1974—; editorial bd. Duke Univ. Press, 1970-87; vis. assoc. prof. Carnegie Mellon U., 1966-67, U. Wash., 1963-64; cons. govt., industry; Fullbright-Hays lectr., Australia, 1975; dir. Southeast Growth Fund, Inc., Hatteras Income Securities, Inc., Pennwalt, Inc., Ladd Furniture Inc. Author: Accounting for Corporate Income Taxes, 1961, Intermediate Accounting, 1963, 68, 74, Advanced Accounting, 1966, Financial Accounting Theory vol. 1, 1965, 73, 85, vol. 2, 1970, Earnings or Cash Flows: An Experiment on Functional Fixation and the Valuation of the Firm, 1979; editor: monographs Financial Information Needs of Security Analysts, 1977, The Impact of Accounting Research on Practice and Disclosure, 1978; Contbr. articles to profl. jours. Served with AUS, 1953-55. Mem. Am. Accounting Assn. (v.p. 1967-68, editor jour. 1972-75), N.C. Assn. C.P.A.s, Am. Inst. C.P.A.s, Financial Execs. Inst., Phi Kappa Sigma, Beta Gamma Sigma, Alpha Kappa Psi. Presbyn. (elder). Home: 1024 W Markham Ave Durham NC 27701 Office: Duke U Fuqua Sch Bus Durham NC 27706

KELLER, THOMAS MICHAEL, construction company executive; b. St. Paul, July 11, 1950; s. Austin P. and Florence Keller; m. Susan Elizabeth Sweet, Nov. 24, 1982; children: Alexander, Nicholas, Brett, Madison. BA, St. Cloud State Coll., 1972. Laborer A.G. Keller Constrn. Co., St. Paul, 1965-72, estimator, 1972-74, chief estimator, 1975-77, v.p., 1977-78, controller, 1978-84, pres., chief exec. officer, 1984—. Bd. dirs. St. Paul Winter Carnival, 1987-91. 1989 Guinness Book of World Records entrant for World's Tallest Ice Palace. Mem. A.G.C. Minn. (v.p. St. Paul, 1985, nat. committeeman, 1986), Minn. Moles, Tau Kappa Epsilon. Republican. Roman Catholic. Lodge: Royal Guard (comdr. St. Paul 1982). Office: AP Keller Constrn Co 481 Front Ave Saint Paul MN 55117

KELLEY, ALBERT JOSEPH, manufacturing company executive; b. Boston, July 27, 1924; s. Albert Joseph and Josephine Christine (Sullivan) K.; m. Virginia Marie Riley, June 7, 1945 (dec. June 1945); children: Mark, Shaun, David. BS, U.S. Naval Acad., 1945; BSEE, MIT, 1948, ScD, 1956; postgrad., U. Minn., 1954, Carnegie-Mellon U., 1974. Commd. ensign USN, 1945, advanced through grades to comdr., 1961; carrier pilot USN, Korea, 1950-51; exptl. test pilot Naval Air Test Ctr. USN, 1951-53, program engr. F-4 aircraft Bur. Aeros., 1956-58, mgr. Eagle missile program Bur. Weapons, 1958-60; mgr. Agena program NASA, 1960-61, dir. electronics and control, 1961-64, dep. dir. Electronics Research Ctr., 1964-67; dean sch. mgmt. Boston Coll., 1967-77; pres. Arthur D. Little program Systems Mgmt. Co., Cambridge, Mass., 1977-85, chmn., 1985-88; sr. group v.p. Arthur D. Little Inc., Cambridge, Mass., 1985-88; sr. v.p. strategic planning United Techs. Corp., Hartford, Conn., 1988—; chmn. Bd. Econ. Advisors Commonwealth of Mass., 1970-74; chmn. bd. dirs. Arthur D. Little Valuation Inc., 1985-86; corp. mem. C.S. Draper Lab. Corp., Cambridge, 1975—; cons. White House; mem. Nat. Research Council Space Applications Bd., 1976-82, bd. visitors Def. Systems Mgmt. Coll., 1970-82; bd. dirs. Perini Corp., Framingham, Mass., State St. Boston Corp., State St. Bank & Trust Co., Boston. Author: Venture Capital, 1977, New Dimensions of Project Management, 1982; contbr. articles to profl. jours. Trustee Milton (Mass.) Acad., 1975-83; bd. dirs. Mass. Bus. Devel. Corp., Boston, 1969-78, Mass. Tech. Devel. Corp., Boston, 1979-82, Am. Assembly Collegiate Schs. Bus., 1970-76. Fellow IEEE, AIAA (assoc.); mem. Internat. Acad. Astronautics, Armed Forces Communications and Electronics Assn. (v.p. 1962-65), Sigma Xi, Tau Beta Pi. Clubs: Algonquin (Boston); Army Navy Country (Arlington, Va.); Wollaston Golf, Milton-Hoosic (Boston); Hop Meadow Country (Simsbury, Conn.). Home: 31 Saddle Ridge Bloomfield CT 06002 Office: United Techs Corp United Techs Bldg Hartford CT 06101

KELLEY, EDWARD WATSON, JR., federal agency administrator; b. Eugene, Oreg., Jan. 27, 1932; s. Edward Watson and Allie (Autry) K.; widowed; children: Kinsloe K. Queen, James M., Michael. BA, Rice U., 1954; MBA, Harvard U., 1959. Pres., chief exec. officer Kelley Industries, Inc., Houston, 1959-81; chmn. bd. Investment Advisors, Inc., Houston, 1981-87; gov. FRS, Washington, 1987—. Lt. (j.g.) USNR, 1954-56. Mem. Houston Country Club (bd. dirs. 1984-87), Bayou Club. Methodist. Office: FRS 20th & Constitution Ave NW Washington DC 20551

KELLEY, JAMES FRANCIS, lawyer; b. Dec. 30, 1941; s. James O'Connor and Marcella Cecilia (Salb) K.; m. Anne Rachel Keeney, June 27, 1970; children: Sarah, Leah. AB, Yale U.; JD, U. Chgo. assoc. Breed, Abbott & Morgan, N.Y.C., 1967-75; dep. gen. counsel United Tech. Corp., Hartford, Conn., 1975-81; sr. v.p., gen. counsel Diamond Shamrock Corp. (name now Maxus Energy Corp.), Dallas, 1981-88; ptnr. Jones, Day, Reavis & Pogue, Dallas, 1988—. Gov. Dallas Symphony Assn., 1985—; bd. dirs. North Tex. Pub. Broadcasters Found., Dallas, 1983—. Mem. ABA, Tex. Bar Assn. Clubs: Dallas; Bent Tree Country. Home: 3800 Shenandoah Dallas TX 75205 Office: 2300 Trammell Crow Ctr 2001 Ross Ave Dallas TX 75201

KELLEY, JAMES OLIVER, real estate appraiser; b. Deerlodge, Mont., Jan. 8, 1951; s. James O. and Dorothy L. (Wickberg) K. BA, U. Mont., 1975. Real estate appraiser First Bank Western, Missoula, Mont., 1975-77; real estate loan officer First Fed. Savs. Bank, Kalispell, Mont., 1977-79, Charter First Mortgage, Kalispell, 1979-81; real estate salesman Chuck Olson Real Estate, Kalispell, 1981-83; prin. James O. Kelley Appraisals, Kalispell, 1983—; Instr. real estate Flathead Valley Community Coll., Kalispell, 1980—. Bd. dirs. United Way of Flathead County (Mont.), 1979-82, 87—, pres. 1980, chmn. 1981. Mem. Mont. Assn. Real Estate Exchangers. Republican. Clubs: Exchange, North Flathead Yacht (Kalispell) (treas.). Lodge: Elks. Home: 99 Hawthorn W Kalispell MT 59901 Office: PO Box 1633 Kalispell MT 59903

KELLEY, JOHN HENRY, electronics company executive; b. Somerville, Mass., May 6, 1941; s. John Dennis and Mary Agnes (Barry) K.; m. Melanie Ann Groszko, July 12, 1969; children: John Dennis, Dennis Barry. AB, Boston Coll., 1967, MBA, 1969; MS in Mgmt., MIT, 1980; JD, Suffolk U., 1971. Chief fin. officer M/A-COM, Inc., Burlington, Mass., 1979-83; pres., chief executive officer Lawrence Lab. Inc., Chatsworth, Calif., 1983-84; exec. v.p., chief operating officer Azonix Corp., Burlington, Mass., 1984-86; pres., chief exec. officer Cyborg Corp., Newton, Mass., 1986-87, also bd. dirs., 1986—; chmn. bd. Fidelis Group Inc., Newton, Mass., 1983—, pres., chief exec. officer, 1986—. Served to capt. USMC, 1960-66, Vietnam. Decorated Silver Star with oak leaf cluster. Mem. Am. Mgmt. Assn., Am. Electronics Assn. Republican. Roman Catholic. Home: 39 Juniper Ave Wakefield MA 01880 Office: Fidelis Group Inc 94 Bridge St Newton MA 02158

KELLEY, LYLE ARDELL, insurance company executive; b. Milan, Mo., Aug. 8, 1944; s. Azel Farril and Anne Ellen (King) K.; m. Carol Ann Clark, Nov. 26, 1966; children: Julie Kay, Kristie Lynn. BS in Mgmt. and Acctg., NE Mo. State U., 1967. Acct. Skelly Oil Co., St. Louis, 1967; claims adjuster State Farms Ins., St. Louis, 1967-77; auditor State Farms Ins., Bloomington, Ill., 1977-83, computer systems design analyst, 1983-86; asst. claims supt. State Farms Ins., Madison, Wis., 1986-87; supt. Wis. property State Farms Ins., Milw., 1987—; Pres. Crime Stoppers McLean County, Bloomington, Ill., 1986, treas. 1984, v.p., 1985; sec. Madison Area Crime Stoppers, 1987; dist. 10 rep. McLean County Bd., Bloomington, 1985-86. Republican. Roman Catholic. Home: 367 Birch Rd Delafield WI 53018 Office: State Farm Ins 2747 Mayfair Rd Milwaukee WI 53213

KELLEY, MARICELESTE See GRANT, MARICELESTE

KELLEY, MICHAEL JAMES, financial services executive; b. Columbus, Ohio, Oct. 27, 1955; s. James Robert and Shirley Ann (Adams) K.; m. Linda May Wagner, Mar. 18, 1988. BS, Fla. Atlantic U., 1976, MBA, 1980. Advisor to prime minister Turks and Caicos Islands, Brit. West Indies, 1978-79; mktg. dir. Intercollegiate Video Clearinghouse, Boca Raton, Fla., 1979-80; chief adminstr. Ft. Lauderdale (Fla.) Eye Inst., 1980-87; v.p. Ambassador Real Estate Equities Corp., Tamarac, Fla., 1984—, also bd. dirs.; v.p. Ambassador Fin. Group Inc., Tamarac, Fla., 1985—; project mgr. Envoy Funding Corp., Tamarac, 1987—, also bd. dirs.; bd. dirs. Ambassador Savs. and Loan, Tamarac, Astrum Funding Corp., Great Neck, N.Y., Amb. Homes, Inc. Mem. Med. Group Mgmt. Assn., MBA Assn. (pres. Boca Raton chpt. 1980), Ft. Lauderdale Art Inst., Coral Ridge Club, Stonebridge Country Club. Office: Ambassador Fin Group 8201 N University Dr Tamarac FL 33321

KELLEY, RICHARD EVERETT, management consultant; b. El Paso, Tex., Sept. 9, 1927; s. Lawrence E. and Sue (Spanton) K.; A.B., Harvard U., 1948. Sales mgr. Goodyear Co., Brazil, 1956; mgmt. cons. Robert Heller & Assos. Inc., Cleve., 1956-61; v.p. Bell Intercontinental Corp., N.Y.C., 1961-64; dep. group exec. internat. group AMF Inc., London, 1964-66; pres. Pacific div. W.R. Grace & Co., 1967-69; mgmt. cons., 1970—. Office: 37 Soundview Rd PO Box 331 Guilford CT 06437

KELLEY, WENDELL J., utilities executive; b. Champaign, Ill., May 2, 1926; s. Victor W. and Erma (Dalrymple) K.; m. Evelyn Kimpel, June 12, 1947; children: Jeffrey, David, Alan, Stephen, John. B.S. in Elec. Engring, U. Ill., 1949. Registered profl. engr., Ill. With Ill. Power Co., Decatur, 1949—, operating eng., 1954, mgr. personnel, 1959-61, v.p., 1961-66, pres., 1966-76, chmn. and pres., 1976-89, chief exec. officer, chmn., 1989—, also bd. dirs.; bd. dirs. Am. Brands, Inc., Old Greenwich, Conn., Edison Elec. Inst., Washington, Magna Millikin Bank of Decatur, NA, Electric Energy, Inc., Joppa, Magna Group Inc., Belleville, Ill., Franklin Life Ins. Co., Springfield, Ill. Chmn. Mid-Am. Interpool Network, 1969-71, vice chmn., 1975-77, past mem. exec. com.; bd. dirs. Edison Electric Inst., Washington, 1974-77, 80-83, Assn. Edison Illuminating Cos., N.Y.C., 1985-87; trustee Millikin U., Decatur; past trustee No. Am. Reliability Council, vice chmn., 1975-77, chmn., 1978-80; past mem. Ill. Council on Econ. Edn., citizens com. U. Ill., U. Ill. Found.; past mem. adv. council St. Mary's Hosp., Decatur, pres., 1972-73; past mem. Shults-Lewis Children's Home, Valparaiso, Ind. Served with USAAF, 1944-45. Recipient Disting. Alumnus award, 1973, Alumni Honor award Coll. Engring., U. Ill., 1974, Alex Van Praag, Jr. Disting. engring. award, 1983. Fellow IEEE (past chmn. central Ill. sect., Centennial medal and cert. 1984); mem. Nat. Soc. Profl. Engrs., Elec. Engring. Alumni Assn. U. Ill. (past pres., Disting. Alumnus award 1973), Ill. State C. of C. (chmn. 1973-74, past dir.), U. Ill. Alumni Assn. (past dir.), Nat., Ill. socs. profl. engrs., Eta Kappa Nu. Mem. Ch. of Christ (elder). Home: 65 Dellwood Dr Decatur IL 62521 Office: Ill Power Co 500 S 27th St Decatur IL 62525

KELLEY-CRESCI, MARILYN V., bookkeeping service owner; b. Tucson, Jan. 13, 1937; d. Marion and Lovetta (Merchant) Adkins; children: Russell D., Wanda L. (dec.), James H.; m. Frank V. Cresci, Sept. 13, 1986. Student Heald Bus. Sch., 1977, Regional Occupational Ctr., 1981. Bookkeeper Barbary Coast, San Jose, Calif., 1980-82, Argon Steel, San Jose, 1982-83, Indsl. Chimney, Hayward, Calif., 1984-85; owner Marilyn's Bookkeeping Service, Union City, Calif., 1983—; corp. sec.-treas. Rod's Trucking, Inc., Newark, Calif., 1985—; corp. v.p., sec. Newark Wreckers, 1987—; bookkeeper R&D Resume Services, Fremont, Calif. 1983—. Fellow Nat. Assn. Female Execs. Republican. Episcopalian. Lodge: Order of Demolay (pres. mother's club 1979-80). Avocations: fishing, camping. Address: 118 Madrone Way Union City CA 94587

KELLING, DAVID HENRY, bank executive, accountant; b. Pasadena, Tex., Oct. 6, 1953; s. Henry Adolf Walter and Bonnie Ruth (Cayton) K.; m. Rebecca Sue Harper, May 24, 1983 (div. Feb. 1987). BBA in Acctg., Tex. A&M U., 1975. CPA, Tex., chartered bank auditor. Acct. Lower Colo. River Authority, Austin, Tex., 1976-78; sr. auditor Tex. Comml. Bancshares, Austin, 1978-81; controller, v.p. First Victoria (Tex.) Nat. Bank, 1981-83; chief fin. officer, sr. v.p. Bay Bancshares, Inc., La Porte, Tex., 1983-87; prin. David H. Kelling, CPA, La Porte, 1983-87; acct. Tiller & Co., Baytown, Tex., 1987—; Bd. dirs. Bay Banc Data Services, La Porte. Treas. Good Shepherd Luth. Ch., Leander, Tex., 1981-83. Mem. Am. Inst. CPA's, Tex. Soc. CPA's (Houston chpt), Nat. Assn. Accts., Bank Adminstrn. Inst., Soc. Chartered Bank Auditors, Beta Alpha Psi (v.p. 1974-75, Outstanding chpt. mem. 1975), Phi Kappa Phi. Republican. Lodge: Optimist (v.p. Victoria chpt. 1980-81). Home: 3823 Youpon La Porte TX 77571 Office: Tiller and Co 1300 Rollingbrook Baytown TX 77522

KELLNER-ZINCK, SUZANNE, marketing consultant, real estate entrepreneur; b. Mt. Kisco, N.Y., Sept. 24, 1961; d. Philip Kellner and Carol Ann (Strauss) Clark; m. Robert Charles Zinck, Jr., Aug. 23, 1986. BA, Curry Coll., 1983. Lic. real estate salesperon. Office asst. Spaulding Co., Boston, 1983-84; clk. Olston Temporary Svcs., Boston, 1984-85; receptionist-sec. Meehan, Boyle & Cohen, Boston, 1985; adminstrv. asst. Atty. Robert Petrow, Boston, 1985-86; saleswomen Burlington (Mass.) Homes, Inc., 1987-88; with customer svc. and mktg. depts. VERIBANC, Inc., Wakefield, Mass., 1987-88; co-owner, mgr. Z&Z Concepts Inc., Percept Mktg. Cons. Inc., Providence, 1988—; Vol. George Bush for Pres. campaign, Boston, 1979-80. Mem. Nat. Assn. Female Execs., Am. Mgmt. Assn. Home and Office: 260 Vermont Ave Providence RI 02905

KELLOGG, C. BURTON, II, financial analyst; b. Plainfield, N.J., June 22, 1934; s. Chester M. and Alice (Luellen) K.; m. Dorothy E. Harasty, July 31, 1954; children: Katharine E., Patricia A., Peter B. BA in Econs., Dartmouth Coll., 1956; MBA in Fin., Columbia U., 1958. With A.M. Best Co., N.Y.C., 1958-68; v.p. A.M. Best Co., Oldwick, N.J., 1968-81, sr. v.p., 1981—, also bd. dirs. Editor: Best's Insurance Reports, 1963—. Sec. Westfield, N.J. YMCA, 1972-76. Mem. Assn. Ins. and Fin. Analysts. Club: Echo Lake Country (Westfield) (trustee 1983—). Office: AM Best Co Ambest Rd Oldwick NJ 08858

KELLOGG, DEAN LUNDT, communications executive; b. North Platte, Nebr., Apr. 14, 1922; s. George Henry and Wilma Louise (Lundt) K.; m. Charlotte Anne Chamberlin, July 10, 1954; children: Dean L. Jr., James C., Paul B., Scott S. BS, U.S. Naval Acad., 1946; MS, U. Kans., 1963; postgrad., U. Md., 1966-68. Commd. ensign USN, 1946, advanced through grades to comdr., 1970; fin. adv. U.S. Naval Acad., 1965-70; petroleum, marine economist Amerada Hess, Corp., Woodbridge, N.J., 1971-85; bd. dirs. Tech Communication Corp., Concord, Mass., 1968—. Author: Optimization Techniques in Petroleum Industry, 1963. Sloan fellow, 1960. Mem. U.S. Naval Acad. Alumni Assn. Republican. Home: 37 Robin Rd Rumson NJ 07760 Office: Tech Communications Corp 100 Domino Dr Concord MA 01742

KELLOGG, E. SUSAN, financial services marketer, educator; b. Cin., July 11, 1945; d. Joseph A. and G. Louise (Bewersdorf) Petering; m. Joseph A. Kellogg, Aug. 23, 1974 (div. 1980); m. Walter A. Frankhauser, Apr. 15, 1984. BA in Pub. Address, U. Cin., 1967; MA in Student Personnel, Syracuse U., 1969; MBA, Loyola Coll., Balt., 1979. Dir. residence hall Boston U., 1969-70; asst. dean students Framingham (Mass.) State Coll., 1970-73; dean students Wheaton Coll., Norton, Mass., 1973-76, Hood Coll., Frederick, Md., 1976-83; acct. exec. Met. Life, Rockville, Md., 1983-86; dir. mktg. Met. Life, N.Y.C., 1986-88; ins. commr. State of Md., Balt., 1988—; cons. Optima Tng. and Research, Frederick, 1978—; grad. adj. faculty Mt. St. Mary's Coll., 1983-88, Johns Hopkins U., 1988—. Mem. Mature Market Inst. (dir. Info. Resources Com., 1988), Am. Soc. Aging, Internat. Assn. Fin. Planning, Nat. Assn. Life Underwriters (Nat. Sales Achievement award 1985). Republican. Christian Scientist. Home: 6220 White Oak Dr Frederick MD 21701 Office: State of Md Ins Commr 501 Saint Paul Pl Baltimore MD 21202

KELLOGG, THOMAS RUSSELL, utility executive; b. Gulfport, Miss., Jan. 25, 1961; s. Thomas Alfred and Eunice Joan (Geiger) K.; m. Lorie Lynn Vowell, Feb. 20, 1982; 1 child, Ashleigh Claire. AS in Bus., Jefferson Davis Jr. Coll., 1981; BSBA in Acctg., U. So. Miss., 1984, postgrad. in bus. adminstrn., 1984—. Drilling rig supr. Braden Pump & Well Drilling Co., Gulfport, 1980-82; adminstrv. asst. Miss. Power Co., Gulfport, 1982, computer operator, 1982-83, systems info. specialist, 1983-84, systems analyst, 1985-86, supr. info. svc., planning and adminstrn., 1986—, mem. polit. action group, 1986-88. V.P. adminstrv. bd. Ramsey Meml. United Meth. Ch., Gulfport, 1986. Mem. Data Processing Mgmt. Assn., Nat. Mgmt. Assn., Am. Mgmt. Assn., Computer Security Inst. Republican. Office: Miss Power Co 2992 W Beach Blvd Gulfport MS 39501

KELLUM, CARMEN KAYE, apparel company executive; b. Greensburg, Pa., Oct. 15, 1952; d. Bruce Lowell and Mildred Louise (Montgomery) Taylor; m. John Douglas Kellum, Aug. 2, 1975 (div. May 1987). Student, MacMurray Coll., 1971-72, Elgin Community Coll.; AA, Coll. DuPage, 1975; BA with honors, Nat. Coll. Edn., 1978. Cert. tchr. Aide occupational therapy Mercy Ctr., Aurora, Ill., 1972-76; tchr. behavior disorders Lake Park High Sch., Roselle, Ill., 1978-80, Salk Pioneer Sch., Roselle, 1980-81; mgr. So-Fro Fabrics Stores, Chgo., Lombard and Joliet, Ill., 1981-84; offshore coordinator Florsheim Shoe Co., Chgo., 1984—. Mem. Orton Dyslexia Soc., Nat. Assn. Female Exec., Kappa Delta Pi. Lutheran. Home: 30 W 156 Wood Ct and Hwy 59 Bartlett IL 60103 Office: Florsheim Shoe Co 130 S Canal St Chicago IL 60606

KELLY, ANTHONY ODRIAN, carpet manufacturing company executive; b. Dublin, Ireland, June 12, 1935; s. John Peter and Delia Mary (Finnegan) K.; m. Sheila Josephine Clancy, Sept. 4, 1963; children—Barbara Anne, Adrienne Elizabeth, Damian Anthony. Grad., Coll. Commerce, Dublin, 1958; M.B.A., Columbia U., 1965, doctoral degree, 1971. Adj. asst. prof. Columbia U., N.Y.C., 1968-69; dir. econ. studies Sperry & Hutchinson Co., 1969-71, asst. to pres. furnishings div., 1975; dir. mktg. Irish Agrl. Devel. Co., 1971-74; sr. v.p. mktg. Bigelow-Sanford, Inc., Greenville, S.C., 1976-79; exec. v.p., chief operating officer Bigelow-Sanford, Inc., 1979-85, pres., chief exec. officer, 1985-86; cons. in field. Ford Found. fellow; Samuel Bronfman fellow. Mem. Inst. Cost and Mgmt. Accts., Beta Gamma Sigma. Club: Greenville Country. Office: Bigelow-Sanford Inc PO Box 26411 Greenville SC 29616-1411

KELLY, ARTHUR LLOYD, management and investment company executive; b. Chgo., Nov. 15, 1937; s. Thomas Lloyd and Mildred (Wetten) K.; B.S. with honors, Yale U., 1959; M.B.A., U. Chgo., 1964; m. Diane Rex Cain, Nov. 25, 1978; children: Mary Lucinda, Thomas Lloyd, Alison Williams. With A.T. Kearney, Inc., 1959-75, mng. dir., Dusseldorf, W.Ger., 1964-70, v.p. for Europe, Brussels, 1970-73, internat. v.p., London, 1974-75, ptnr., dir., 1969-75, mem. exec. com., 1972-75; pres., chief operating officer, dir. LaSalle Steel Co., Chgo., 1975-81; pres., chief exec. officer, dir. Dalta Corp., Chgo., 1982—; mng. ptnr. KEL Enterprises Ltd., Chgo., 1983—; vice chmn., bd. dirs. ARCH Devel. Corp., Chgo., 1986—; dir. Snap-on Tools Corp., Kenosha, Wis., Twin Disc Inc., Racine, Wis., Georgetown Industries, Inc., Charlotte, N.C., Cimlinc, Inc., Elk Grove Village, Ill., Crosspoint Venture Ptnrs., Palo Alto, Calif., DataCard Corp., Minnetonka, Minn., Bankhaus Trinkaus & Burkhardt KGaA, Dusseldorf, Fed. Republic of Germany, Northern Trust Corp., Chgo., Internet Systems Corp., Chgo., chmn. vis. com. div. phys. scis., also mem. council Grad. Sch. Bus.; mem. bd. trustees U. Chgo.; mem. adv. council Ditchley Found., Oxford, Eng.; bd. dirs. Chgo. Council Fgn. Relations (mem. exec. com.), Am. Council on Germany, N.Y.C. Mem. Young Pres.'s Orgn., World Bus. Council, Beta Gamma Sigma. Clubs: Chgo., Racquet, Casino (Chgo.), Brook, Yale (N.Y.C.), Econ., Comml. Office: 135 S La Salle St Ste 1117 Chicago IL 60603

KELLY, BERNARD NOEL, banker; b. Brussels, Apr. 23, 1930; s. David and Marie Noele de Vaux Kelly; m. Mirabel Fitzalan Howard, July 11, 1952; 7 sons, 1 dau. Student Downside Sch., Somerset, Eng. Solicitor, ptnr. Simmons, Simmons, London, 1950-63; dir. S.G. Warburg & Co., Ltd., London, 1963-75; mng. dir. Compagnie Monegasque de Banque, Monaco, 1975-80; bd. dirs. Lazard Bros. & Co. Ltd., London, 1980—; chmn. First Equity Holding Ltd; bd. dirs. Barnes Group Inc., Bristol, Conn., Pheonix Re., N.Y., Highcross PLC. Served to capt. Queens Royal Irish Hussars, 1948-50. Mem.

The Athenaeum Club, Brooks's Club, Kildare Street Club, University Club. Office: Lazard Bros & Co Ltd, 21 Moorfields, London EC2, England also: Insilico Corp 1000 Research Pkwy Meriden CT 06450

KELLY, DONALD PHILIP, enterpreneur; b. Chgo., Feb. 24, 1922; s. Thomas Nicholas and Ethel M. (Healy) K.; m. Byrd M. Sullivan, Oct. 25, 1952; children: Patrick, Laura, Thomas. Student, Loyola U., Chgo., 1953-54, De Paul U., 1954-55, Harvard U., 1965. Mgr. tabulating United Ins. Co. Am., 1946-51; mgr. data processing A.B. Wrisley Co., 1951-53; mgr. data processing Swift & Co., 1953-65, asst. controller, 1965-67, controller, 1967-68, v.p. corporate devel., controller, 1968-70, fin. v.p., dir., 1970-73; fin. v.p., dir. Esmark, Inc., Chgo., 1973, pres., chief operating officer, 1973-77, pres., chief exec. officer, 1977-82, chmn., pres., chief exec. officer, 1982-84; pres. Kelly, Briggs & Assocs., Inc., Chgo., 1984-86; chmn. BCI Holdings Corp., Chgo., 1986-87; chmn., chief exec. officer E-II Holdings Inc., Chgo., 1987-88; chmn. Beatrice Co., Chgo., 1988, also bd. dirs.; pres., chief exec. officer D.P. Kelly & Assocs., L.P., Oak Brook, 1988—. Trustee Com. for Econ. Devel., Washington, Mus. Sci. and Industry, Chgo.; mem. Conf. Bd. N.Y.; trustee U. Notre Dame. Served in USNR, 1942-46. Mem. Fin. Execs. Inst. Clubs: Chgo. (Chgo.), Comml. (Chgo.), Econ. (Chgo.). Office: 701 Harger Rd Ste 190 Oak Brook IL 60521

KELLY, EILEEN PATRICIA, management educator; b. Steubenville, Ohio, Oct. 24, 1955; d. Edward Joseph and Mary Bernice (Cassidy) K. BS, Coll. Steubenville, 1978; MA, U. Cin., 1979, PhD, 1982. LPA, Ohio. Lectr. U. Cin., 1981-82; asst. prof. bus. Creighton U., Omaha, 1982-87, chmn. mgmt., mktg. and systems dept., 1986-88, assoc. prof., 1987-88, coordinator project Minerva, 1987-88; assoc. prof. La. State U., Shreveport, 1988—, chmn. dept. mgmt. and mktg., 1988—; comml. arbitrator, 1988—. Author: Reindustrialization and Employee Stock Ownership Plans: The Case of the Weirton Steel Corporation, 1986, The AIDS Epidemic, 1987, Worker Ownership in the United States: Two Centuries of Participation, 1988, Employee Ownership and Industrial Democracy: The Pursuit of Free Enterprise, 1988. Mem. Indsl. Relations Research Assn., Am. Arbitration Assn., Acad. Mgmt., Am. Soc. Personnel Adminstrs., Beta Gamma Sigma (faculty advisor 1985-88). Roman Catholic. Office: La State U Coll Bus 8515 Youree Dr Shreveport LA 71115

KELLY, FRANK J., service company executive; b. Atlanta, May 5, 1948; s. Francis J. and Addie (Murphy) K.; m. Susan Dawson Kelly, Dec. 6, 1969; children: Katy, Patrick, Kevin. BS in Urban Mgmt., Ga. State U., 1973; JD, Atlanta Law Sch., 1978. Br. mgr., loan officer Nat. Bank Ga., Atlanta, 1973-76; sales mgr. German Auto Parts, Atlanta, 1976-77; numerous positions in sales and mgmt. leading to group v.p. Cintas Corp., Cin., 1977—, mem. exec. com., 1981—. Served to sgt. U.S. Army, 1969-71, Vietnam. Decorated Bronze Star. Republican. Roman Catholic. Office: Cintas Corp 11803 Grant Rd Ste 206 Cypress TX 77429

KELLY, GERALD WAYNE, chemical coatings company executive; b. Charleston, W.Va., May 21, 1944; s. Wayne Woodside and Sarrah (Myers) K.; m. Nancy Butenhoff, Sept. 5, 1965 (div. June 1983); children: Scott Wayne, Lauren Melissa; m. Elizabeth Long, Nov. 18, 1983. BS, W.Va. U., 1966. From sales corr. to regional mgr. duPont Corp., various locations, 1966-83; bus. mgr. Decatur (Ala.) div. Whittaker Corp., 1983-85, v.p. Decatur (Ala.) div., 1985-86, pres. Decatur (Ala.) div., 1986—; pres. Piedmont div. Whittaker Corp., Greenville, S.C., 1988—. Bd. dirs. Ind. Cystic Fibrosis Found., Indpls., 1971-73. Mem. Nat. Coil Coaters Assn., Nat. Paint and Coatings Assn., Beta Theta Pi. Republican. Methodist. Home: Rte 2 Box 131 Trinity AL 35673 Office: Whittaker Corp Decatur Div PO Box 2238 Decatur AL 35602

KELLY, HARLEY LAWRENCE, retail executive; b. Monterey, N.Y., Aug. 12, 1937; s. Jacob Darwin and Grace Mae (Putnam) K.; m. Grace Cook, June 21, 1957 (div. 1960); 1 child, Shawn L.; m. Linda Crone, Oct. 19, 1967; 1 child, Jacob Darwin. BA in Religion, Northeastern Bible Inst., 1969; DD, Ohio State U., 1972. Mgr. W.T. Grant Co., N.Y.C., 1957-64, Leggets Dept. Store, Newport News, Va., 1964-67, Sydner and Hundley Furniture Stores, Richmond, Va., 1967-79; mgr., asst. v.p. Haverty Furniture Stores, Richmond, Va., 1979-83; salesman Grand Piano Furniture, Staunton, Va., 1983-85; v.p., gen. mgr. Furniture City, Christiansburg, Va., 1985—. cons. Ch. of Brethren, Staunton, 1983-84; dir. Distbv. Edn. Va., 1968. Named Distbv. Edn. Employer of Yr., 1963, Furniture Retailer of Yr., 1987. Mem. Christiansburg C. of C. Republican. Home: 770 Tower Rd Christiansburg VA 24073 Office: Furniture City 125 Bristol Dr Christiansburg VA 24073

KELLY, JACK ROBERT, accountant; b. Muskegon, Mich., Oct. 30, 1952; s. Bill Glen and Elaine Bertha (Johnson) K. AA in Bus., Muskegon Bus. Coll., 1972; BS in Bus. Adminstrn., Aquinas Coll., 1982, M in Mgmt., 1984. Acct. office mgr. Vets Clothing, Inc., Muskegon, 1973-79; acct. Jacobson, Touri & Miedona, Muskegon, 1979-80, Shaw Walker, Inc., Muskegon, 1980-81; dir. fin. Gospel Films, Muskegon, 1981-86, dir. fin. ops., 1986—; instr. bus. Grace Bible Coll., Grand Rapids, 1986—. Bd. dirs. Youth for Christ, Muskegon, 1985-87, also former treas. Mem. Nat. Assn. Accts. Republican. Home: 1428 Marcoux Ave Muskegon MI 49442 Office: Gospel Films Inc 2735 E Apple Ave Muskegon MI 49442

KELLY, JAMES EDWARD, banker; b. Phila., Aug. 18, 1944; s. John J. and Teresa B. (Ragan) K.; m. Ellen M. Lombard, Apr. 20, 1968; children—Kristen, Jeanine, Gavin Paul. B.S., LaSalle U., 1970, M.B.A., 1980. C.P.A., Pa. Acct. Mobil Oil Co., Phila., 1965-67; auditor Gino's, Inc., King of Prussia, Pa., 1967-69, acctg. mgr., 1969-75; treas. Lincoln Bank, Phila., 1975-82; sr. v.p., treas. Continental Bank, Phila., 1982-88, exec. v.p., chief fin. officer, 1988—. Mem. Pa. Inst. C.P.A.s. Republican. Roman Catholic. Office: Continental Bancorp 515 Pennsylvania Ave Fort Washington PA 19034

KELLY, JANET LEE, educator; b. Akron, Ohio, Jan. 19, 1943; d. Milo M. and Alice (Marksity) Ratkovich; m. Patrick J. Kelly, July 25, 1981. BA, U. Wis., 1964; MBA, George Washington U., 1980. Mem. staff Ho. of Reps., Washington, 1965-68; counselor Dunhill Personnel, Washington, 1968-69; mem. staff Tobacco Inst. Inc., Washington, 1970-73; adminstrv. asst. Delta Group Ltd., Washington, 1973-76; legal adminstr. Moss, Frink & Franklin, P.C., Washington, 1976-79; adminstrv. aide Va. Energy & Land Co., Washington, 1979-81; mem. staff div. community services Mont. Dept. Social Rehab., Miles City, 1982-85; instr. mgmt. Miles Community Coll., Miles City, 1985-88; county commr. Custer County, Miles City, 1989—. Vice chmn. Miles City Study Commn., 1984-86. Home: 602 S Strevell Miles City MT 59301

KELLY, JOHN KEVIN, financial planner; b. Little Rock, Aug. 5, 1959; s. William Thomas and Lucille (Metrailer) K.; m. Christy Snowden, Nov. 27, 1982; 1 child, A. Elaine. BA in Fin., U. Ark., Little Rock, 1982. Cert. fin. planner. Fin. planner First Fin. Planners, Little Rock, 1982—. Mem. Inst. Cert. Fin. Planners. Republican. Roman Catholic. Home: 5200 Country Club Little Rock AR 72207 Office: First Fin Planners 1100 N University Ste 230 Little Rock AR 72207

KELLY, JOHN LOVE, public relations executive; b. N.Y.C., Jan. 30, 1924; s. Joseph John McDermott and Mary Florence Keenan (Love) K.; m. Helen M. Griffin Hanrahan, June 28, 1952; children: Janet Ann Kelly Alegi, J. Scott. BS, St. Peter's Coll., 1951. Buyer exec. tng. program Macy's, N.Y.C., 1951-53; mktg. exec. Sanforized div. Cluett Peabody Co., N.Y.C., 1953-58; advt. account exec. Batton, Barton, Durstine & Osborn, N.Y.C., 1958-59; advt. mgr. Am. Cyanamid Co., N.Y.C., 1959-64; dir. advt. Fiber div. FMC Corp., N.Y.C., 1964-84; v.p., dir. public relations and communications Avtex Fibers Inc., N.Y.C., 1976—; bd. dirs. Kelhan Ltd. Cath. co-chmn. Peekskill area NCCJ, 1961-64, bd. dirs. Westchester County, 1969-79, nat. bd. dirs., 1969-87; trustee Mercy Coll., Dobbs Ferry, N.Y., 1965-69; trustee emeritus St. Peter's Coll.; councilman Town of Cortlandt (N.Y.), 1962-66, mem. Simon Wiesenthal Ctr., Am. Conf. for Irish Studies, Zoning Bd., 1971-74, mem. Bd. Ethics, 1975-79; mem. Cardinal's Com. of Laity, 1961-71; mem. Greater N.Y. Area council Boy Scouts Am., 1971-79. Mem. Public Relations Soc. Am., Assn. Nat. Advertisers, Public Relations Club N.Y., Am. Fiber Mfr. Assn. (chmn. pub. relations com., edn. and pub. relations subcoms.), Bd. Trade N.Y. (textile sect., v.p. 1954-60), Am. Israel Friendship League, Am. Irish Hist. Soc., Internat. Platform Assn., St. Peter's Coll. Alumni Assn. (bd. dirs. 1959-65), Hudson Valley Gaelic Soc. Democrat. Roman Catholic. Clubs: The Univ., Garrison Golf. Home: 21 Furnace Woods Rd Cortlandt NY 10566 Office: Avtex Fibers Inc 1185 Ave of the Americas New York NY 10036

KELLY, PAUL KNOX, investment banker; b. Boston, Feb. 18, 1940; s. Thomas Joseph and Rita Patricia Kelly; m. Nancy Lee Belden, July 17, 1978; 1 child, 3 stepchildren. A.B. in English, U. Pa., 1962; M.B.A. in Fin, Wharton Sch., 1964. Investment analyst bond dept. Prudential Ins. Co. Am., 1964-65; asst. treas. Comml. Credit Co., 1965-68; v.p. First Boston Corp., N.Y.C., 1968-75; ptnr., mem. mgmt. com., dir. Prescott, Ball & Turben, Cleve., 1975-77; sr. v.p., dir. Butcher & Singer, Inc., 1977-78; exec. v.p., mem. exec. com., dir. Blyth Eastman Dillon & Co., N.Y.C., 1978-80; mng. dir. Merrill Lynch White Weld Capital Markets Group, N.Y.C., 1980-82; exec. v.p., dir. Dean Witter Reynolds, Inc., 1982-84; pres., dir. Quadrex Securities Corp., 1984-85, Peers & Co., 1985—; bd. dirs. THT, Inc., Hydrox Corp., Ltd. (N.Z.). Clubs: Union (Cleve.); Chagrin Valley Hunt; Princeton (N.Y.C.). Home: 16 Edgemarth Hill Rd Westport CT 06880 Office: Peers & Co 1133 Ave of the Americas New York NY 10036

KELLY, ROBERT LYNN, advertising agency executive; b. Chgo., Oct. 25, 1939; s. Carl Robert and Annabel Pauline (Lindsay) K.; m. Maria Graciela Gonzalez, Oct. 26, 1963; children: Albert E., Elizabeth A. BA, Gettysburg Coll., 1961. Dir. pub. info. Oxnard AFB, Calif., 1961-64; with Armstrong Cork Co., Lancaster, Pa., 1964-67; owner Bob Kelly Advt., Quito, Ecuador, 1967-70; partner, writer, account exec., mgr. Ibold & Kelly Advt., Lancaster, 1970-72; founder, pres. Kelly Advt., Inc., Lancaster, 1972-84; pres. Kelly Michener Inc., Lancaster, Pa., 1984—; guest lectr. F & M Coll., and Millersville U., 1971—; lectr. Lancaster Community Gallery, 1977 . Active various civic orgns.; bd. dirs. Lancaster Community Gallery, 1978—, v.p., 1983—; mem. campaign coms., Lancaster County Rep. orgns., 1973-75; bd. dirs. Rockford Plantation, 1979—, v.p., 1988—; v.p. Let's Lifebelt Lancaster, 1984-85. Served with USAF, 1961-64. Mem. Nat. Advt. Agy. Network (nat. chmn. 1984), Am. Assn. Advt. Agys. (chmn.regional bd. govs. 1988—), Lancaster Advt. Agy. Council (sec. 1987—). N.G. Assn. U.S., Sales and Mktg. Execs. Episcopalian. Clubs: Hamilton; Lancaster Tennis and Yacht (bd. dirs., v.p. 1986-87, commodore 1988). Contbr. articles to profl. jours. Home: 1112 Wheatland Ave Lancaster PA 17603 Office: Kelly Michener Inc 416 W Marion St Lancaster PA 17603

KELLY, ROBERT VINCENT, JR., metal company executive; b. Phila., Sept. 29, 1938; s. Robert Vincent and Catherine Mary (Hanley) K.; m. Margaret Cecilia Taylor, Feb. 11, 1961; children: Robert V. III, Christopher T., Michael J., Tasha Marie. BS in Indsl. Mgmt., St. Joseph's U., Phila., 1960; postgrad., Roosevelt U., 1965-66. Gen. foreman prodn. Republic Steel Corp., Chgo., 1963-68; supt. prodn. Phoenix Steel Corp., Phoenixville, Pa., 1969-73; gen. supt. ops. Continental Steel Corp., Kokomo, Ind., 1973-77; gen. mgr. Mac Steel div. Quanex Corp., Jackson, Mich., 1977-81; corp. v.p. Quanex Corp., Houston, 1979—; pres. steel and bar group Quanex Corp., Jackson, 1982—; pres. La Salle Steel Co., Hammond, Ind., 1985-87, Arbuckle Corp., Jackson, 1984-88. Leader, com. mem. Boy Scouts Am., Jackson. Lt. USN, 1960-63. Mem. Am. Mgmt. Assn. (pres.), Inst. Indsl. Engrs., Assn. Iron and Steel Engrs., Am. Soc. for Metals, USN Inst., Jackson C. of C. Clubs: Jackson Country. Home: 1734 Metzmont Dr Jackson MI 49203 Office: Quanex Corp Steel and Bar Group 1 Jackson Sq Jackson MI 49201

KELLY, ROBERT VINCENT, III, railroad executive; b. Sheboygan, Wis., May 22, 1962; s. Robert Vincent Jr. and Margaret Cecilia (Taylor) K. BSE, U. Mich., 1984; MBA, Case Western Res. U., 1986. Ops. analyst Burlington No. R.R., Chgo., 1986-87, mgr. ops. analysis, 1987-88; asst. market mgr. intermodal mktg. Burlington No. R.R., Ft. Worth, 1988—. Vol. Tarrant County Spl. Olympics, Ft. Worth, 1988. Mem. Inst. Indsl. Engrs., Am. Mgmt. Assn., Alpha Tau Omega, U. Mich. Alumni Club. Home: 7658 Blue Carriage Ct Fort Worth TX 76112 Office: Burlington No RR 777 S Main St Fort Worth TX 76110

KELLY, STEPHEN ROBERT, real estate broker; b. Mineola, N.Y., July 5, 1953; s. James Barton and Eileen Mary (Redling) K.; m. Allison Jean Levy, May 7, 1983; 1 child, Jonathan Lightner. BS, U. Vt., 1975. Asst. scheduler Gt. No. Paper Co., Stamford, Conn., 1975-78; scheduler Riviere du Loup Paper Co., Greenwich, Conn., 1978-81; sales service mgr. Bear Island Paper Co., Boswell, Va., 1981-83; residential salesman Realtech Realtors, New Canaan, Conn., 1983-85; comml. salesman Helmsley Spear Co., Stamford, 1985; comml. broker Cross and Brown Co., Stamford, 1985-87, Re-Max Jax South, Inc., Jacksonville, Fla., 1987-88, So. Appraisal Corp., Ormond Beach, Fla., 1988—. Home: 17A Lisbon St Saint Augustine FL 32084

KELLY, THOMAS BROOKE, accounting and consulting firm executive; b. Topeka, Feb. 12, 1943; s. Edward Arnold and Sarah Elizabeth (Brooke) K.; m. Deborah Ellen Gooch, Nov. 27, 1965; children: Timothy M., Cary A., Ellen B. BA, Washburn U., 1965; MBA, U. Kans., 1967. Cons. ptnr. Arthur Andersen & Co., Sao Paulo, Brazil, 1974-77, Dallas, 1977-80, Australia, 1980-84; mng. ptnr. Arthur Andersen & Co., Chgo., 1984—. Advisor Shelter for Battered Women, Evanston, Ill., 1988; alt. dir. Fulbright Found., Sao Paulo, 1977; founder, assoc. dir. Info. Industry Council, Chgo., 1985-87; v.p. Inst. Mgmt. Sci., Milw., 1971-73; trustee North Shore Country Day Sch., Winnetka, Ill., 1987—; bd. dirs. Jaycees, Milw., 1977, Am. C. of C., Sao Paulo, 1976-77. Mem. Mid-Am. Club, T-Bar M Club. Episcopalian. Office: Arthur Andersen & Co 69 W Washington St Chicago IL 60602

KELLY, THOMAS DAWSON, aerospace industry executive; b. Washington, D.C., July 13, 1929; s. Edward James and Blanche May (Dawson) K.; m. Norma Lee Hannas, Nov. 27, 1952; 1 child, Susan Ann. B.A., Va. Mil. Inst., 1950; M.B.A., Harvard U., 1954. V.p. fin. E-Systems Inc., Falls Church, Va., 1958-78; v.p., controller corp. hdqrs. E-Systems Inc., Dallas, 1978-80; v.p. fin., adminstr. ECI div. E-Systems Inc., St. Petersburg, Fla., 1980-81, v.p. fin., adminstr. Fla. operations, 1981-83; v.p. fin., chief fin. officer corp. hdqrs. E-Systems Inc., Dallas, 1983—. Served to 1st lt. U.S. Army, 1950-52. Mem. Aerospace Industries Assn., Machinery and Applied Products Inst. Republican. Roman Catholic. Clubs: Bent Tree Country (Dallas); St. Petersburg Yacht. Office: E-Systems Inc PO Box 660248 Dallas TX 75266

KELLY, THOMAS JOSEPH, information systems director; b. Waterbury, Conn., Sept. 15, 1956; s. Thomas Joseph Jr. and Elsa Ann (Mrazik) K. Grad. high sch., Southington, Conn.; cert. in programming, Computer Processing Inst., East Hartford, Conn., 1978. Bus. systems analyst Choice-Vend, Inc., Windsor Locks, Conn., 1976-80; project leader Digital Equipment Corp., Windsor Locks, Conn., 1976-80, Maynard, Mass., 1980-82; project mgr. Farm Credit Banks of Springfield, Agawam, Mass., 1982-85; mgr. application devel. Berkshire Med. Ctr., Pittsfield, Mass., 1985-88, info. systems dir., 1988—; prin. Thomas Kelly Cons., Windsor Locks, 1980-85. Named Mr. Future Bus. Leader Am. Future Bus. Leaders Am., 1974, Pres. of Yr. Conn. Jr. Achievement, 1974. Mem. Assn. Computing Machinery, Digital Equipment Computer Users Soc. Republican. Home: 26 Highfield Dr Lee MA 01238 Office: Berkshire Med Ctr 725 North St Pittsfield MA 01201

KELLY, WILLIAM R., employment agency executive; b. 1905; married. Grad., U. Pitts., 1925. With Kelly Services, Inc., 1946—; chmn. Kelly Svcs., Inc., Troy, Mich., 1965—, also bd. dirs. Office: Kelly Svcs Inc 999 W Big Beaver Rd Troy MI 48084 *

KELLY LENTINI, PATRICIA MARY, financial analyst; b. Pitts., Dec. 27, 1959; d. James Joseph and Patricia Mary (Johnson) K.; m. David Peter Lentini, Oct. 10, 1987. BA in Econs., U. Calif., Sant Cruz, 1982; MBA, Harvard U., 1987. Fin. analyst First Deposit Corp., San Francisco, 1982-83, Dean Witter Reynolds, San Francisco, 1983-84, Kidder Peabody & Co., N.Y.C., 1984-85; v.p. portfolio mgmt. Ivy Funds, Boston, 1987—; fin. cons. San Francisco and Boston, 1985-88. Mem. Boston Computer Soc., NOW. Office: Ivy Funds 40 Industrial Park Rd Hingham MA 02043

KELMENSON, LEO-ARTHUR, advertising executive; b. N.Y.C., Jan. 3, 1927; s. Joseph A. and Ruth (Rothberg) K.; divorced; children: Todd-Arthur, Joel Adam. B.S., Columbia U., 1951; postgrad., Grad. Sch. Bus., 1952. From TV prodn. to sr. v.p., asst. to pres. Lennen & Newell, 1951-65; exec. v.p., mem. exec. com. Norman Craig & Kummel, 1965-66; sr. v.p., dir., mem. exec. com. Kenyon & Eckhardt, 1967-68, chmn., chief exec. officer, 1968-86; chmn. exec. com. Bozell, Jacobs, Kenyon & Eckhardt, 1986-88; chmn. bd. advisors, chmn. devel. com. Tisch Sch of Arts NYU, 1988—; pres. Kelmenson Funds Ltd.; dir. Lorimar, Locations Unltd., On-Line Software Internat.; bd. trustees Am. Cinematheque; lectr. New Sch. Social Research.; Adviser communications office U.S. Atty. Gen., 1960-63; spl. project officer Dept. State, 1952-64; v.p., dir. African Med. and Research Found., 1957—. Author: poetry Epilogue, 1964; also short stories. Mem. pub. relations com. Nat. Cancer Found., 1958—; adv. com. Nat. Cultural Center, 1962; pres. Shoes for Little Souls, 1960, Remsenburg Assn., 1968; bd. dirs. ASPCA; mem. pres.'s adv. council Am. Diabetes Assn., 1977-78. Served with USMCR, World War II. Recipient Theodore Roosevelt Man of Year award, 1955; Silver Quill Poetry award, 1955; Res. Officers Assn. award, 1965; Guggenheim World Peace award, 1951; Am. Jewish Com. Humanitarian award; Humanitarian award St. Frances Cabrini. Mem. U.S. Olympic Com., N.Y. Advt. Club, Soc. Am. Businessmen Club, Sigma Phi Epsilon. Clubs: Sands Point, Ocean Reef, Key Largo, Sands Point Yacht, L.I. Polo, U.S. Yacht Racing Assn. (N.Y.). Office: Tisch Sch Arts NYU New York NY

KELSAY, ROYAL EDWARD, II, oil company executive; b. Ft. Worth, May 6, 1930; s. Royal Edward I and Carmen Azlee (Isaacks) K.; m. Josephine Hess, Mar. 11, 1950; children: Royal Edward III, Douglas M., James M., Janet Elaine. Student, U. Denver, 1947-48. Br. mgr., fin. mgr. Am. Motors Co., Detroit, 1954-58; div. mgr. Whirlpool Fin. subs RCA, Benton Harbor, Mich., 1958-60; owner, operator La Jolla (Calif.) Acceptance Co., 1961-67, R.E. Kelsay & Co., La Jolla, 1968-71; semi-ret. San Jose, Costa Rica, 1972-74; oil investor Jacksboro, Tex., 1975-77; with Circle Seven Oil and Gas Inc., Jacksboro, 1978—, pres., chief exec. officer, 1988; bd. dirs. in charge oil and gas activities Canadex Resources Ltd., Toronto, 1987—. Author: An Insider's View of the Drilling Funds, 1981. Home: PO Box 670 Jacksboro TX 76056 Office: Circle Seven Oil and Gas Co PO Box 867 Jacksboro TX 76056

KELSEY, HARRY FRANKLIN, JR., academic administrator; b. Ft. Wayne, Ind., July 16, 1926; s. Harry Franklin Sr. and Mabel Ida (Dunkle) K.; m. Lyn Rose Thomas, Aug. 24, 1970 (div. 1972). MBA, Ind. U., 1975, Din Bus. Adminstrn., 1976. Pres. Kelsey Enterprises, Los Angeles, 1960-64; exec. Bonsib Pub. Relations, Ft. Wayne, Ind., 1964-66; pres. Ren, Inc., Indpls., 1966-73; dir. Babcock Ctr. Wake Forest U., Winston-Salem, N.C., 1976-79; dean Coll. of Bus. Jacksonville (Fla.) U., 1979-83; dean Sch. of Bus. Calif. State U., Bakersfield, 1983—; chmn. bd. dirs. Kern Econ. Devel. Corp., Bakersfield, 1987—. Served to capt. USAF, 1958-62. Mem. Kegley Inst. Ethics (bd. dirs. Bakersfield chpt. 1987—), Dorian Soc. (bd. dirs. Bakersfield chpt. 1984—), Pub. Relations Soc. Am. (cert.), Beta Gamma Sigma, Sigma Iota Epsilon. Republican. Presbyterian.

KELSO, LOUIS ORTH, investment banker, economist; b. Denver, Dec. 4, 1913; s. Oren S. and Nettie (Wolfe) K.; m. Betty Hawley (div.); children: Martha Jennifer Kelso Brookman, Katherine Elizabeth Balestreri; m. Patricia Hetter. BS cum laude, U. Colo., 1937, LLB, 1938; DSc, Araneta U., Manila, 1962; LLD, Tusculum Coll., Tenn., 1986. Bar: Colo. 1938, Calif. 1946. Assoc. Pershing Bosworth, Dick & Dawson, 1938-42; ptnr. Brobeck, Phleger & Harrison, 1946-58; sr. ptnr. Kelso, Cotton, Seligman & Ray, 1958-70; mng. dir. Louis O. Kelso, Inc., San Francisco, 1970-75; chmn. Kelso & Co., Inc. (mcht. bankers), San Francisco, Newport Beach and N.Y.C., 1975—; also dir. Kelso & Co., Inc. (mcht. bankers), San Francisco; assoc. prof. law U. Colo., 1946; pres. Kelso Inst. Study Econ. Systems, San Francisco; econ. policy advisor ESOP Assn. Am., Washington, 1983—. Author: (with Mortimer J. Adler) The Capitalist Manifesto, 1958, The New Capitalists, 1961, (with Patricia Hetter) Two-Factor Theory: The Economics of Reality, 1967, (with Patricia Hetter Kelso) Democracy and Economic Power: Extending the ESOP Revolution, 1986. editor-in-chief Rocky Mountain Law Rev, 1938; contbr. articles to profl. jours. Bd. dirs. Inst. Philos. Research, Chgo.; founding trustee Crystal Springs Sch. Girls, Hillsborough, Calif. Served to lt. USNR, 1942-46. Mem. ABA, Calif. Bar Assn., San Francisco Bar Assn., San Francisco Com. Fgn. Relations. Clubs: Pacific-Union, Bohemian, Villa Taverna (San Francisco); Chicago. Address: 505 Sansome St Ste 1005 San Francisco CA 94111

KELSON, IRWIN STUART, computer and software consultant; b. Perth Amboy, N.J., Feb. 28, 1932; B.S. in Indsl. Engring., Johns Hopkins U., 1954; M.Indsl. Engring., U. So. Calif., 1961. With IBM, 1962-78, sr. program mgr. data processing div., 1976-78; pres., chief operating officer Ins. Inst. for Research, White Plains, N.Y., 1978-81; pres. Northeast Cons. Group, N.Y.C., 1981—; computer cons. software devel., N.Y.C., 1981—. Mem. Soc. Ins. Research, Assn. Computing Machinery, Am. Inst. Indsl. Engrs., Am. Soc. Assn. Execs., Am. Mgmt. Assn. Home: 4 Dorado Dr Purchase NY 10577 Office: 6 E 39th St New York NY 10016

KEMBLE, MIMI MADDOCK, interior designer; b. Palm Beach, Fla., Sept. 25, 1947; d. Paul Lacoste and Ruth (Quigley) Maddock Fleitas; m. William Tyson Kemble, Jr., Apr. 10, 1971; children: Cecilia Lacoste, Phoebe Powers. AA, Briar Cliff Coll., 1969. Designer Smith Knudson, Palm Beach, 1975-77, Jessup Inc., Palm Beach, 1977-87; pres., owner Kemble Interiors, Inc., Palm Beach, 1987—. Contbr. articles to profl. jours. Mem. Garden Club (chmn. 1988), Bath and Tennis Club (bd. dirs. 1985—), Everglades Club. Republican. Episcopalian. Office: Kemble Interiors 232 Royal Palm Way Palm Beach FL 33480

KEMERLING, JAMES LEE, paper company executive; b. Battle Creek, Mich., 1939. BA, Mich. State U., 1961, MBA. Asst. to v.p. mktg. Mosinee (Wis.) Paper Co., 1968-69, gen. sales mgr., 1969-70, v.p. mktg., 1970-72, asst. gen. mgr pulp and paper, 1972-74, gen. mgr. pulp and paper, 1974-81, pres., chief operating officer, 1981-83, pres., chief exec. officer, 1984-88, also bd. dirs.; bd. dirs. Specialty Packaging Group, Inc., Wausau, Wis. Valley Trust Co., M&I First Am. Nat. Bank, Wausau. Bd. dirs. Wis. Valley Improveemnt Co., Community Health Care, Inc., Wausau, Wausau Hosp. Ctr., Wausau Child Care Found., YMCA Found. Wausau, United Way of Marathon County, Paper Sci. Found. of U. Wis.-Stevens Point. Office: Shade Info Systems PO Box 19730 Green Bay WI 54307-9730

KEMMER, RICHARD JULIUS, investment banker; b. Feb. 10, 1945; s. Julius George and Josephine (Sailer) K.; children: Michael, Tara. BA in English, Canisius Coll., 1966; MA in Philosophy, CUNY, 1971; MBA, U. Chgo., 1974. Systems analyst, programmer Standard Oil Co. Inc., Chgo., 1971-72; securities sales rep. Continental Ill. Bank, Chgo., 1972-73; account mgr. Citibank N.C., N.Y.C., 1974-77; treas. F&M Shaefer Corp., N.Y.C., 1977-78; v.p. Westdeutsche Landesbank, N.Y.C., 1978-84, Dusseldorf, Fed. Republic of Germany, 1984-85; v.p., mgr. capital markets group Westdeutsche Landesbank, N.Y.C., 1985-88, v.p. project fin., 1989—. With USMC, 1966-71. Roman Catholic. Home: 363 76th St New York NY 10021 Office: Westdeutsche Landesbank 450 Park Ave New York NY 10022-2605

KEMMERER, PETER REAM, financial executive; b. N.Y.C., Dec. 20, 1942; s. Mahlon Sistie and Colette Noel (Fitch) K. BBA, Georgetown U., 1966; MBA, Am. U., 1970; MA, New Sch., 1975. Analyst corp. planning Otis Elevator Co., N.Y.C., 1971-74; mgr. fin. and adminstrn. bus. equipment div. SCM Corp., N.Y.C., 1975-80; pres. Mesa Verde, Inc., N.Y.C., 1980—; mng. ptnr. Jezel-Bezel Ptnrs., N.Y.C., 1980—; bd. dirs., treas. Stuart-Hall, Inc., N.Y.C., Spencer-Bezel, Inc., N.Y.C.; bd. dirs. Mesa Verde, Inc., N.Y.C. Roman Catholic. Club: Princeton (N.Y.C.). Office: Mesa Verde Inc 516 5th Ave New York NY 10036

KEMP, FRANCIS BOLLING, III, banker; b. Greensboro, N.C., Sept. 10, 1940; s. Francis B. and Billie (Stocks) K.; m. Virginia Wadsworth Millner, Aug. 15, 1964; children: Francis Bolling IV, Elizabeth R. A.B. cum laude, Davidson Coll., 1963; M.B.A., Harvard U., 1967. V.p. NCNB Nat. Bank of N.C., 1971-72, sr. v.p., 1972-75, exec. v.p., 1975-83, corp. banking group exec., 1975-77, N.C. banking group exec., 1977-85, pres., 1983-88; corp. exec. v.p. NCNB Corp., 1983-85, pres., 1985—; chmn. NCNB Tex., Dallas,

1988—; bd. dirs. VISA U.S.A. Inc., VISA Internat. Inc.; chmn. VISA U.S.A., 1988—. Mem. bd. visitors Davidson Coll., 1978-81, trustee, 1988—, bd. dirs.; trustee N.C. Symphony, 1978-84, pres., 1979-80, vice chmn., 1980-81; bd. dirs. Spirit Sq. Performing Arts Center, 1980-85, pres., 1982-83; bd. dirs. Charlotte Uptown Devel. Corp., 1987-88; pres. Arts and Scis. Council, 1983-84; bd. dirs., exec. com. Arts and Scis. Council of Charlotte-Mecklenburg, Inc., 1981-85; bd. dirs. Gov.'s Council on Arts and Humanities, 1983-88, Univ. Research Park, 1983-88, Greater Dallas C. of C., 1988—, Citizens' Coun. Dallas, 1988—; trustee Charlotte Country Day Sch., 1983-85; bd. dirs., mem. exec. com. United Way Cen. Carolinas, Inc. Served to 1st. lt. U.S. Army, 1963-65. Mem. Charlotte C. of C. (chmn. 1986), Greater Dallas C. of C. (bd. dirs. 1988—), Robert Morris Assocs., Assn. Res. City Bankers, N.C. Bankers Assn. (pres. 1985-86), N.C. Citizens Bus. and Industry, Phi Beta Kappa, Beta Theta Pi. Republican. Presbyterian. Clubs: Charlotte City, Country of N.C, Quail Hollow Country. Office: NCNB Tex PO Box 83100 Dallas TX 75283

KEMP, KAREN L., banker; b. Salamanca, N.Y., Jan. 30, 1951; d. John Philo and Mary (Jones) K. Fin. analyst New Eng. Elec. Co., Westboro, Mass., 1982-83; dir. fin. planning Goldome Bank, Buffalo, 1983-87, dir. corp. compensation, 1987—. Mem. allocations com. United Way, Buffalo, 1986—. Mem. Nat. Assn. Accts., Am. Compensation Assn., Am. Soc. Personnel Adminstrs. Republican. Roman Catholic. Office: Goldome Bank One Fountain Pla Buffalo NY 14203

KEMP, RALPH GENE, JR., construction executive; b. Tyler, Tex., May 18, 1944; s. Ralph G. and Willie L. (Capes) K.; m. Felicity A. Brandon, June 24, 1978; children: Matthew, Jennifer, Michael. Student, U. Tex.; BBA, So. Meth. U., postgrad. Staff auditor Ernst & Whinney, Dallas, 1967-68; acctg. mgr. Frito-Lay, Inc., Dallas, 1971-74; group controller Internat. Systems, Houston, 1974-77; controller Wallace Internat., Dallas, 1978-82; v.p. C.T. Main Corp., Boston, 1982-85; chief fin. officer George A. Fuller Co., N.Y.C., 1986—. Contbr. articles to profl. jours. 1st Lt. U.S. Army, 1968-71. Mem. Constrn. Fin. Mgmt. Assn. N.Y. (pres. 1987—), Nat. Constrn. Fin. Mgmt. Assn. (dir. 1985-86), Fin. Exec. Inst. Republican. Methodist. Home: 45 Halsey Dr Old Greenwich CT 06870 Office: George A Fuller Co 919 3rd Ave New York NY 10022

KEMPE, ROBERT ARON, venture management executive; b. Mpls., Mar. 6, 1922; s. Walter A. and Madge (Stoker) K.; m. Virginia Lou Wiseman, June 21, 1946; children: Mark A., Katherine A. BS in Chem. Engring., U. Minn., 1943; postgrad. metallurgy, bus. adminstrn., Case Western Res. U., 1946-49. Various positions TRW, Inc., Cleve., 1943-53, div. sales mgr., 1953; v.p. Metalphoto Corp., Cleve., 1954-63, pres., 1963-71, pres. Allied Decals, Inc., affiliate, Cleve., 1963-68; v.p., treas. Horizons Rsch. Inc., 1970-71; pres. Reuter-Stokes, Inc. (subs. of GE Corp.), 1971-87; pres. Kempe Everest Co., Hudson, Ohio, 1987—; assoc. Paul Williams & Assocs., Medina, Ohio, 1987—; mem. adv. bd. Horizons Inc.; mem. commercialization com. Edison BioTech. Ctr, Cleve.; bd. dirs. Bicron Corp., TGM Detectors, Inc. Lt. (j.g.) USNR, 1944-46, PTO. Mem. Am. Nuclear Soc. (chmn. No. Ohio sect.), Am. Soc. Metals. Sigma Chi. Club: Chemists (N.Y.C.); Country of Hudson (Ohio). Contbr. articles to profl. jours. Patentee in field. Home: 242 E Streetsboro St Hudson OH 44236 Office: Kempe Everest Co 10 W Streetsboro St Hudson OH 44236

KEMPER, CASEY RANDOLPH, real estate investment banker; b. Centralia, Ill., Nov. 21, 1947; s. Edward Charles and Mary Louise (Green) K.; m. Mary Dianne Bowers, Sept. 14, 1968; children: Michelle, Carin, Courtney. BS, So. Ill. U., 1969; MBA, Babson Coll., 1979. CLU; chartered fin. cons. Mgr. Equitable Life Assurance, N.Y.C., 1969-76; v.p., treas. Equitable Life Mortgage and Realty Investors, Boston, 1976-83; treas. Consol. Capital, Emeryville, Calif., 1983-84; sr. v.p. Equitable Real Estate Group, N.Y.C., 1984-87, Deutsche Bank Capital Corp., N.Y.C., 1987—; advisor Am. Real Estate Investment Co., N.Y.C., 1987—. Coord. Bus. Exec. for Nat. Security, Westchester, N.Y., 1985—; mem. Parent's Fund Com. UVM, 1988, Habitat for Humanity Westchester County. With USAR, 1970-76. Ill. State scholar, 1965. Mem. Nat. Assn. Real Estate Investment Trusts, Urban Land Inst., KC (social chmn. 1974-75). Democrat. Roman Catholic. Home: 119 Brewster Rd Scarsdale NY 10583 Office: Deutsche Bank Capital Corp 31 W 52d St New York NY 10019

KEMPER, DAVID WOODS, II, banker; b. Kansas City, Mo., Nov. 20, 1950; s. James Madison and Mildred (Lane) K.; m. Dorothy Ann Jannarone, Sept. 6, 1975; children: John W., Elizabeth C., Catherine B., William L., Silliam L. B.A. cum laude, Harvard U., 1972; M.A. in English Lit., Oxford, Worcester Coll., 1974; M.B.A., Stanford U., 1976. With Morgan Guaranty Trust Co., N.Y.C., 1975-78; v.p. Commerce Bank of Kansas City, Mo., 1978-79; sr. v.p. Commerce Bank of Kansas City, 1980-81; pres. Commerce Bancshares, Inc., 1982-86, pres. and chief exec. officer, 1986—, also dir.; chmn. Commerce Bank of St. Louis, 1985—; bd dirs. BMA, Kansas City, Mo., Fed. Res. Bank of St. Louis, Tower Properties, Kansas City. Contbr. articles on banking to profl. jours. Bd. dirs. Mo. Botanical Garden, St. Louis Symphony Orch. Mem. Assn. Res. City Bankers. Clubs: Kansas City Country, University, River (Kansas City); St. Louis, Racquet (St. Louis). Office: Commerce Bancshares Inc 1000 Walnut St PO Box 13686 Kansas City MO 64199 also: Commerce Bancshares Inc Commerce Bank Bldg 8000 Forsyth Clayton MO 63105 also: Commerce Bank of St Louis NA 8000 Forsyth Saint Louis MO 63105

KEMPER, JAMES MADISON, JR., banker; b. Kansas City, Mo., Oct. 10, 1921; s. James M. and Gladys (Grissom) K.; m. Mildred Lane, Mar. 30, 1948 (dec. Dec. 1986); children: Laura Lane, David Woods, Jonathan McBride, Julie Ann; m. Susanne Shutz Curry, Aug. 1, 1987. B.A., Yale U., 1943. With Commerce Trust Co. (now Commerce Bank of Kansas City), Kansas City, 1946—; asst. cashier Commerce Trust Co. (now Commerce Bank of Kansas City), 1946-49, v.p., dir., 1949-55, exec. v.p., 1955, pres., 1955-64, chmn., 1964; chmn. bd., pres. Commerce Bank of Kansas City, 1964-66, chmn. bd., 1966-83, dir., 1983—; chmn., pres. Commerce Bancshares, Inc., Kansas City, Mo., 1966-86, chmn., chief exec. officer, 1986—, chmn. bd., 1986—; pres., chmn. Tower Properties, Inc.; dir. Commerce Bank, St. Joseph, 1987—, Springfield, 1987—, Columbia, 1988—. Office: Commerce Bancshares Inc 1000 Walnut St PO Box 13686 Kansas City MO 64199-3686

KEMPF, MARTINE, voice control device manufacturing company executive; b. Strasbourg, France, Dec. 9, 1958; came to U.S., 1985; d. Jean-Pierre and Brigitte Marguerite (Klockenbring) K. Student in Astronomy, Friedrich Wilhelm U., Bonn, Fed. Republic of Germany, 1981-83. Owner, mgr. Kempf, Sunnyvale, Calif., 1985—. Inventor Comeldir Multiplex Handicapped Driving Systems (Goldenes Lenkrad Axel Springer Verlag 1981), Katalavox speech recognition control system (Oscar, World Almanac Inventions 1984, Prix Grand Siecle, Comite Couronne Francaise 1985). Recipient Medal for Service to Humanity Spinal Cord Soc., 1986; street named in honor in Dossenheim-Kochersberg, Alsace, France, 1987; named Citizen of Honor City of Dossenheim-Kochersberg, 1985. Home: 730 E Evelyn Sunnyvale CA 94086 Office: Kempf 1080 E Duane Ave Ste E Sunnyvale CA 94086

KEMPNER, ISAAC HERBERT, III, sugar company executive; b. Houston, Aug. 28, 1932; s. Isaac Herbert and Mary (Carroll) K.; m. Helen Hill, July 1, 1967. Grad., Choate Sch., 1951; B.A., Stanford U., 1955, M.B.A., 1959. Asst. v.p. Tex. Nat. Bank, Houston, 1959-64; v.p., sec.-treas., mgr. raw sugar Imperial Holly Corp (formerly Imperial Sugar Co.), Sugarland, Tex., 1964-71, chmn. bd., 1971—; chmn. bd. SLT Communication Inc.; pres. Foster Farms Inc. Trustee H. Kempner Trust Assn., Meth. Hosp., Houston, Houston Mcpl. Arts Commn. Served to 1st lt. USMCR, 1955-57. Mem. U.S. Cane Sugar Refiners Assn. (chmn.). Clubs: Tejas, Bayou, Houston Country (Houston); Camden Ale and Quail (Tex.). Office: Imperial Holly Corp One Imperial Sq Sugar Land TX 77478

KENDALL, DONALD MCINTOSH, food products company executive; b. Sequim, Wash., Mar. 16, 1921; s. Carroll C. and Charlotte (McIntosh) K.; student Western Ky. State Coll., 1941-42; LL.D., Stetson U., 1971; m. Sigrid Ruedt von Collenberg, Dec. 22, 1965; children—Donna Lee Kendall Warren, Edward McDonnell, Donald McIntosh, Kent Collenberg. Spl. field rep. Pepsi-Cola Co., 1947-48, mgr. fountain sales, 1948-49, br. plant mgr. fountain sales, 1949-50, spl. rep., 1950-52, v.p. nat. accounts fountain sales, 1952-57, pres. Pepsi Cola Internat., 1953-63, pres. Pepsi-Cola Co., 1963-65 (merger with Frito-Lay 1965), PepsiCo, Inc., 1965—, pres., chief exec. officer, 1965-71, chmn. bd., chief exec. officer, 1971-86, also bd. dirs., dir., chmn. exec. com., 1986—; dir. Pan Am. Airways, Atlantic Richfield, Investors Diversified Services Mut. Fund Group. Chmn., NOVA Pharm., Lorimar-Telepictures, Nat. Alliance Businessmen, 1969-70, dir., 1970-78. Chmn., Nat. Center for Resource Recovery, Inc. 1970-76, dir., from 1976—; chmn. Emergency Com. for Am. Trade, 1969-76, mem., 1976—; dir. U.S.-USSR Trade and Econ. Council. Chmn., Am. Ballet Theatre Found., 1973-77, chmn. exec. com., 1977-83. Served to lt. AC, USNR, 1942-47. Mem. Internat. C. of C. (trustee council), C. of C. U.S. (dir., vice-chmn. 1980-81, chmn. 1981-82). Clubs: Blind Brook, Links, Lyford Cay, River, Round Hill. Office: Pepsico Inc Office of Pres Purchase NY 10577 *

KENDALL, GEORGE JASON, public accountant, computer consultant; b. New Castle, Pa., Aug. 20, 1937; s. George J. and Ester (Belknap) K.; m. Carole J. Stewart, May 5, 1956 (div. Dec. 1985); m. Elaine A. Russell, May 10, 1986; children: Deborah, Penny, Laurie. AA, New Castle Bus. Coll., 1964. CPA, Pa. Payroll clk. Internat. Staple, Butler, Pa., 1964; jr. acct. Bachman, Marsch & Co., Butler, 1964-66; mgr. Lamb, Marsch & Co., Butler, 1967-75; ptnr. Kendall, Marsch & Co., Butler, 1975-84, owner, 1984-87; ptnr. Kendal, Metz & Co., Butler, 1988—; v.p. Villa Arena, Inc., Farrell, Pa., 1988—; cons. in field, 1983—. Mem. Nat. Assn. Accts., Pa. Soc. PA's. Republican. Methodist. Office: Kendall Metz & Co 308 N Washington St PO Box 1856 Butler PA 16003

KENDALL, GEORGE PRESTON, SR., retired insurance company executive; b. Seattle, Aug. 11, 1909; s. George R. and Edna (Woods) K.; m. Helen A. Hilliard, Sept. 30, 1933; children: George Preston, Thomas C., Helen R. BS, U. Ill., 1931. With Washington Nat. Ins. Co., Evanston, Ill., 1931-75; sec. Washington Nat. Ins. Co., Evanston, 1950-56, exec. v.p., 1956-68, dir., 1948—, pres., 1962-67, chmn. bd., chief exec. officer, 1968-75; chmn. bd. Washington Nat. Corp., 1968-82, dir., 1968—; bd. dirs. NBD Bank Evanston. 1st lt., inf. AUS, 1942-45. Decorated Purple Heart. Mem. Westmoreland Country Club, Masons, K.T., Shriners, Theta Chi. Office: Washington Nat Ins Co 1630 Chicago Ave Evanston IL 60201

KENDERDINE, ROBERT LEONARD, JR., savings and loan executive; b. Ft. Worth, Jan. 20, 1917; s. Robert Leonard and Caroline Pauline (Raab) K.; B.S. in Bus. Adminstrn., Ind. U., 1938; m. Daphne Dunning, May 25, 1940; children—Robert C., Stewart M., Claire, Kay. Spl. agt. Aetna Life & Casualty Co., Dallas, 1938-42, bond supt., Rochester, N.Y., 1942-43; partner Keller, Kenderdine & Keller, ins., 1946-56; pres. Palestine Savs. & Loan Assn. (Tex.), 1956-82, also dir.; chmn. Superior Savs. Assn. (merger), 1982—; pres. Kenderdine Agy. Inc., Palestine, 1956—; dir. East Tex. Nat. Bank, KER Properties Inc. Pres., Palestine Indsl. Found., 1977-79; trustee Palestine Ind. Sch. Dist., 1959-61. Served to lt. (j.g.) USN, 1943-46; PTO. Mem. Ind. Ins. Agts. Am., Ind. Ins. Agts. Tex. (pres. 1964), Palestine C. of C. (pres.). Episcopalian. Club: Rotary (dist. gov. 1959-60). Home: 1001 E Angelina St Palestine TX 75801 Office: PO Box C 103 E Oak St Palestine TX 75801

KENDRICK, JAMES EARL, computer consulting company executive; b. Indpls., Sept. 12, 1940; s. John William and Mable E. (Colman) K.; B.A., Butler U., 1963; m. Carrie L. Fair, July 19, 1969; children: Carrie F., Leslie F., John F. Exec. dir. Knox County Econ. Opportunity Council, Barbourville, Ky., 1965-66; research scientist N.Y. U., 1967-68; mgr. Volt Info. Scis., Washington, 1968-71, Nat. Urban Coalition, 1972-74; pres. Kendrick & Co., Washington, 1974—. Recipient Rural Service award OEO, 1968; citation Washington chpt. Am. Soc. Tng. and Devel., 1971. Mem. Inst. Mgmt. Consultants (bd. dirs. Washington chpt.), CEO Club, Air Traffic Controllers Assn., Soc. Profl. Mgmt. Cons., Met. Washington Bd. Trade, Sigma Delta Chi. Author: Community Energy Workbook, 1974; National Urban Agenda Survey, 1974; (video) Americans on the Move, 1984; (software) Help for PC DOS, 1985; contbr. articles to profl. jours. Presbyterian. Home: 1412 Dale Dr Silver Spring MD 20910 Office: Kendrick & Co 1025 Connecticut Ave NW Washington DC 20036

KENDRICK, MARK C., real estate executive; b. Augsburg, Germany, Dec. 30, 1957; (parents Am. citizens); s. Chester Delmon and Eva Anna (Mitterndorfer) K. AA in Emergency Medicine, Fayetteville Community Coll., 1977, AA in Law Enforcement, 1982; BA in Social Work, Methodist Coll., Fayetteville, N.C., 1983; M in Bus., Campbell U., Ft. Bragg, N.C., 1985—; M in Guidance, Century U. Emergency response team Moore Meml. Hosp., Pinehurst, N.C., 1975-76; mgr. Fleishman's, Fayetteville, N.C., 1977-78; mgr. furnishings Nowell's, Fayetteville, 1978-79; deputy Cumberland Co. Sheriff's Dept., Fayetteville, 1982-83; ptnr. Kendrick Real Estate, Fayetteville, 1983—. Researcher in field. Vol. N.C. Dept. of Corrections, 1981-82, intern 1980; spl. deputy, Cumberland County Sheriff's Dept., 1982—; sec. Myrover-Reese Fellowship House, 1982-84; comptroller Cape Fear Fair Assn., 1985—; v.p. Cumberland County Heart Assn., 1984-85; sub-sgt. Cumberland County Rescue Squad, 1979-82; adv. commn. Fayetteville Parks & Recreation, 1982-86; bd. dirs. Meth. Coll. Recruitment, 1984-85, Meth. Coll. Alumni, 1985—, Fayetteville Sr. Citizens Service Ctr., 1983-86, Fayetteville Parks & Recreation Five Yr. Study Commn., 1984-86; Fayetteville City councilman, 1986—; mem. Fayetteville Revitalization commn., 1986—, County Liaison com., 1986—, City Bldgs. and Grounds com., 1986—, City-County Fire Liaison com., 1986—, Am. Red Cross Disaster Team, 1984—, Young Dem. Club, N.C. Transp. Adv. Com.; chmn. City Streets-Sidewalks and Transp. Com., City-County Liaison. Named to Eagle Scouts Boy Scouts Am., 1972, 1st 10th Degree Jaycee U.S. Jaycees, 1985, one of Five Outstanding Young Men in N.C. Farm Bur., 1985, Outstanding Young Person in Govt., 1986; recipient Disting. Svc. award, 1985; recipient Charles Kulp Jr. Meml. award U.S. Jaycees, 1986, Larry Bowers award, 1986, N.C. Thomas Jefferson award Sta. WTVD-TV, 1985. Mem. Fayetteville Jaycees (pres. 1984-85, treas. 1985—, sec. 1982-84), N.C. Jaycees (regional dir. 1985-86, awards chmn. 1986—, Freedom Guard award 1984, Linn D. Garibaldi award 1985), Lambda Chi Alpha. Democrat. Baptist. Lodges: KP, Toastmasters (N.C. state speaker, 1984). Home: 2618 Dartmouth Dr Fayetteville NC 28304 Office: Kendrick Real Estate PO Box 40841 Fayetteville NC 28309

KENEN, DR. PETER BAIN, economist, educator; b. Cleve., Nov. 30, 1932; s. Isaiah Leo and Beatrice (Bain) K.; m. Regina Horowitz, Aug. 21, 1955; children: Joanne Lisa, Marc David, Stephanie Hope, Judith Rebecca. AB, Columbia U., 1954; MA, Harvard U., 1956, PhD, 1958. Mem. faculty Columbia U., 1957-71, prof. econs., 1964-71, chmn. dept., 1967-69, provost univ., 1969-70, adviser to pres., 1970-71; prof. econs. and internat. finance, dir. internat. finance sect. Princeton (N.J.) U., 1971—; Ford research prof. U. Calif., Berkeley, 1979-80; Res. Bank Australia professorial fellow Australian Nat. U., 1983-84; research on econ. basis for internat. trade, internat. monetary theory and policy; cons. Council Econ. Advisers, 1961, U.S. Treasury, 1962-68, 77-80, Bur. Budget, 1964-68. Author: British Monetary Policy and the Balance of Payments (1951-57), 1960, Giant Among Nations, 1960, (with A.G. Hart and A. Entine) Money, Debt and Economic Activity, 4th edit., 1969, (with R. Lubitz) International Economics, 3d edit, 1971, A Model of the U.S. Balance of Payments, 1978, (with P.R. Allen) Asset Markets, Exchange Rates, and Economic Integration, 1980, Essays in International Economics, 1980, The International Economy, 1985, 2d edit., 1989, Managing Exchange Rates, 1988, Exchange Rates and Policy Coordination, 1989; editor: International Trade and Finance, Frontiers for Research, 1975, (with R. Lawrence) The Open Economy, 1968, (with others) The International Monetary System under Flexible Exchange Rates, 1982, (with R.W. Jones) Handbook of International Economics, 1984, (with others) The Global Repercussions of U.S. Monetary and Fiscal Policy, 1984; contbr. articles to profl. jours. Recipient David A. Wells prize Harvard U., 1958-59, Univ. medal Columbia U., 1977; fellow Ctr. Advanced Study Behavioral Scis., 1971-72, John Simon Guggenheim Found., 1975-76, Royal Inst. Internat. Affairs, 1987-88, German Marshall Fund, 1987-88. Mem. Am. Econ. Assn., Royal Econ. Soc., Council Fgn. Relations, Group of Thirty. Home: 15 Forester Dr Princeton NJ 08540 Office: Princeton U Internat Fin Sect Dickinson Hall Princeton NJ 08544

KENKEL, ROBERT AUGUST, manufacturing company executive; b. Defiance, Iowa, Aug. 20, 1934; s. Nicholas and Mary (Eckermann) K.; m. Bernice A. Donohue, June 15, 1957; children: Gregory, Kurt, Matthew, Therese, Karen, Vincent, Amy, Robert. BSME, Iowa State U., 1956. Pres. Gravely div. McGraw-Edison, Winston-Salem, N.C., 1975-80, Internat. Metal Products div. McGraw-Edison, Phoenix, 1980-82; pres. Wagner div. McGraw-Edison, Parsippany, N.J., 1982-84; exec. v.p. McGraw-Edison, 1984-85; pres., chief operating officer FL Industries, Livingston, N.J., 1985-88; pres., chief exec. officer Pullman Co., Princeton, N.J., 1988—. With AUS, 1957. Republican. Roman Catholic. Home: 1 Indian Ln Florham Park NJ 07932 Office: Pullman Co 182 Nassau St Princeton NJ 08540

KENLEY, ELIZABETH SUE, oil company official; b. Kansas City, Mo., Oct. 4, 1945; d. Ralph Raymond and Josephine Allen (Wells) Cummins. B.S., Kans. U., 1968, M.P.A., 1972. Asst. city mgr. Winfield (Kans.), 1968-70; adminstrv. asst. Kansas City (Mo.) Police Dept., 1970; cons., 1973; with E.I. DuPont Co., Kingwood, Tex., 1974—, regional tech. buyer, 1977-79, cons., plant start up, 1979, regional tech. buyer, 1980-82; internat. project buyer Aramco, Houston, 1982-86, quality assurance liaison, supr. refinery no. area projects unit, 1986—, owner, pres. Internat. Commerce & Transp., Houston, 1989—. Mem. Houston C. of C., Am. Mgmt. Assn. Home: 9632 Briarforest Houston TX 77063 Office: 2215 Harbor Blvd Houston TX 77020

KENLY, GRANGER FARWELL, marketing consultant, college official; b. Portland, Oreg., Feb. 15, 1919; s. F. Corning and Ruth (Farwell) K.; m. Suzanne Warner, Feb. 7, 1948 (div. Nov. 1977); children: Margaret F. Kenly Narver, Granger Farwell Jr.; m. Stella B. Angevin, Oct. 8, 1978. A.B. cum laude, Harvard U., 1941. Adminstrv. asst. to v.p. Poole Bros., Inc., Chgo., 1941-42; asst. advt. mgr. Sunset Mag., San Francisco, 1946-47; pub. relations, sales promotion mgr. Pabco Products, Inc., San Francisco, 1947-51; v.p. mgmt., supr. Needham, Louis & Brorby, Inc., Chgo., 1951-60; mgr. mktg. plans dept. Pure Oil Co., Palatine, Ill., 1961-62; v.p. pub. relations, personnel Pure Oil Co., 1962-66; v.p. pub. affairs Abbott Labs., North Chicago, Ill., 1966-71; v.p. corporate and investor relations IC Industries, Inc., Chgo., 1972-83; exec. dir. career planning and placement Lake Forest Coll., Ill., 1984—; chmn., exec. bd. Keystone-Garrett Properties, Houston, 1984—; Mem. 22d Ann. Global Strategy Conf. U.S. Naval War Coll., 1970; mem. pub. affairs council Am. Productivity Ctr., 1980-85. Bd. dirs. Evanston Hosp., 1963-82; trustee Ill. Soc. Prevention Blindness, 1958-64, Lawson YMCA, Chgo., 1972-83, Off the Street Boys Club, Chgo., 1978—; mem. Exec. Service Corps Chgo., 1984—. Served to maj. USAAF, 1942-46, ETO. Mem. Pub. Relations Soc. Am., Pub. Relations Seminar, Chgo. Assn. Commerce, Newcomen Soc. N.Am. Republican. Episcopalian. Clubs: Chicago (Chgo.), University (Chgo.), Economic (Chgo.); Onwentsia (Lake Forest, Ill.); Edgartown Yacht, The Reading Room (Edgartown, Mass.); Hole-in-the-Wall Golf (Naples, Fla.). Home: 1160 N Sheridan Rd Lake Forest IL 60045 Office: Lake Forest College Sheridan and College Rds Lake Forest IL 60045

KENNAN, CHRISTOPHER JAMES, investment executive, fundraiser; b. Washington, Nov. 24, 1949; s. George Frost and Annelise (Sorensen) K.; m. Domitilla Elena Enders, Apr. 24, 1982. BA, Yale U., 1975. Legis. liaison State of N.J., Trenton, 1975-78; dir. econ. devel. Mercer County, Trenton, 1978-80; sales rep. A.G. Becker Inc., N.Y.C., 1981-82; assoc. to David Rockefeller, Rockefeller Family & Assocs., N.Y.C., 1982—; assoc. Rockefeller & Co., N.Y.C., 1987—; trustee Accion, Inc. Mem. Council on Fgn. Relations, Wilson Council. Democrat. Episcopalian. Club: Yale (N.Y.C.). Office: Rockefeller Family & Assocs 30 Rockefeller Pla #5600 New York NY 10112

KENNEDY, AARON EMSLEY, III, financial planner; b. Fayetteville, N.C., Nov. 16, 1948; s. Aron E. Jr. and Evelyn (Crumpler) K.; m. Marie Whitfield, Aug. 29, 1969 (div. 1982); m. Sandra Cone, Sept. 11, 1982; children: Paige, Ryann. BS, Campbell Coll., Buies Creek, N.C., 1970; MBA, Wake Forest U., 1979. Cert. fin. planner. Pres. K&K Dimensions, Clinton, N.C., 1974-79, Kennedy & Assocs., Cary, N.C., 1986-88, Kennedy Fin. Svcs., Cary, 1988—; v.p. Dean Witter Reynolds, Raleigh, 1979-81; 1st v.p. Interstate Securities Corp., Cary, 1981-86. Mem. Inst. Cert. Fin. Planners, Internat. Assn. Fin. Planning. Home: 106 E Wind Ln Cary NC 27511 Office: Kennedy Fin Svcs 4601 Six Forks Rd Ste 500 Raleigh NC 27609

KENNEDY, BERNARD JOSEPH, utility executive; b. Niagara Falls, N.Y., Aug. 16, 1931; s. Edward J. and Frances (Coyle) K.; m. Geraldine Drexelius, Sept. 20, 1958; children: Mary Kathleen, Maureen Jean, Patricia, Colleen, Joseph B. B.A., Niagara U., 1953; LL.B., U. Mich., 1958. Bar: N.Y. 1960. Legal asst. Nat. Fuel Gas Distbn. Corp., Buffalo, 1958-63, gen. atty., 1963-67, sec., gen. counsel, 1967—, v.p., gen. counsel, 1975-77, sr. v.p., 1977-87; pres., chief exec. officer Nat. Fuel Gas Co., Buffalo, 1988—, chmn. bd., 1989—; pres. Nat. Fuel Gas Supply Corp., 1978—, Penn-York Energy Corp., 1978—, Seneca Resources Corp., 1978—, Empire Exploration, 1983—; dir. Associated Electric & Gas Ins. Service Ltd., Marine Midland Bank, N.A. Western Regional, Mchts. Mut. Ins. Co., Am. Precision Industries, Inc., The Bus. Council N.Y. State, Inc. Past chmn. bd. advisers Erie County Dept. Social Welfare; past chmn. council Bus. Sch., Canisius Coll. (chmn. bd. regents), also trustee; bd. dirs. Erie County chpt. ARC; chmn. Cath. Charities Appeal, 1981; trustee Niagara (N.Y.) U. Served to 1st lt. AUS, 1953-55. Mem. ABA (vice chmn. gas com.), Erie County Bar Assn., N.Y. Bar Assn. (chmn. pub. utilities com. 1973), Fed. Energy Bar Assn., Am. Gas Assn. Club: Buffalo; Buffalo Canoe, Sitzmarker Ski. Home: 33 Ruskin Rd Eggertsville NY 14226 Office: Nat Fuel Gas Co 10 Lafayette Sq Buffalo NY 14203

KENNEDY, BETH BLUMENREICH, film studio executive; b. Detroit, Mar. 11, 1950; d. Leonard and Bernice Blumenreich; m. Michael F. Kennedy; 1 child, Joshua Hayes. BA, U. Mich., 1971; MA, UCLA, 1974; JD, Southwestern U., 1984. Mgr. sensurround dept. Universal Studios, Universal City, Calif., 1975; asst. to studio mgr. Universal Studios, Universal City, 1977, adminstr. transp. dept., 1978, dir. infor systems TV & UP, 1980, dir. corp. int. mgmt., 1982-86, v.p. planning and adminstrn., 1987-89, sr. v.p. planning and adminstrn., 1989—. Contbr. articles to profl. jour. Mem. legal com. The Nurtury, Sherman Oaks, Calif., 1988—. Named one of Outstanding Young Women of Am., Outstanding Young Women of Am. awards program, 1980. Mem. ABA, Women in Bus. (mem. com. 1985-88), Orgn. of Women Execs. (chair membership com. 1989, bd. dirs.), NAFE, Women's Referral Svc., Inc, Women in Film, Beverly Hills Bar Assn., L.A. County Bar Assn. Office: Universal City Studios 100 Universal City Pla Universal City CA 91608

KENNEDY, BRIAN JAMES, transportation company executive; b. N.Y.C., Nov. 7, 1941; s. James and Una K.; m. Donna Lee Rugendorf, Dec. 7, 1968; children: Kerry, Kelly. BS in Fgn. Service, Georgetown U., 1963; grad. Japanese lang., Def. Lang. Inst., 1965; postgrad., NYU, Monterey Inst. Fgn. Studies. Various positions, then v.p. advt. and sales TWA, N.Y.C., 1967-83; sr. v.p. mktg. The Hertz Corp., N.Y.C., 1983-87, exec. v.p., 1987—; pres. Duneview Devel. (real estate) Corp., Wainscott, N.Y. Home: Bay Ln Water Mill NY 11976 Office: The Hertz Co 225 Brae Blvd Park Ridge NJ 07656

KENNEDY, DEBORAH CHRISTINE, senior financial analyst; b. Valparaiso, Fla.. BS in Acctg., Villanova U., 1983. CPA. Sr. auditor Alco Standard Corp., Valley Forge, Pa., 1983-86; sr. financial analyst Alco Office Products, Valley Forge, 1986-87, mgr. fin. planning, 1987—; treas. Archival Cons. Inc., Houston. Mem. AICPA, Inst. Internal Auditors, Pa. Inst. CPAs, Villanova Alumni Assn.

KENNEDY, DONALD ALEXANDER, management consultant executive; b. Littleton, N.H., July 24, 1929; s. Donald Snow Kennedy and Dorothy Patricia (Bodwell) Nichols; m. Mary Welles Rast, Oct. 3, 1951; children: Douglas Robert, Karen Elizabeth, Stuart Campbell, Deborah Snow, Craig Welles. AB cum laude, Harvard U., 1951; PhD, Cornell U., 1959. Sr. instr. Tufts Med. Sch., Boston, 1965-66, asst. prof., 1966-68; lectr. Harvard Sch. Pub. Health, Boston, 1968-73; assoc. prof. Pa. State Med. Sch., Hershey, 1973-77; prof., asst. dean U. Wyo. Med. Sch., Laramie, 1977-83; v.p. rsch. Xicom, Inc., Tuxedo, N.Y., 1983-88; pres. Wind River Assocs., Warwick, N.Y., 1988—; asst. dir. Harvard Med. Sch., Ctr. Community Health & Med. Care, 1968-71; faculty mem. Harvard Bus. Sch. Health System Mgnt., 1972-73. Author: (with others) Medical Education and the Behavioral Sciences, 1983, (multimedia program) Face to Face Communication, 1985; research, adv. editor soc. sci. and med. internat. jour. Mem. sch. com., Littleton,

1966-71; pres. Mental Health Assn. N. Cen. Mass., Fitchburg, 1966-67, behaviorial sic. test com. Nat. Bd. Med. Examiners, 1969-75; trustee Nashoba Community Hosp., Ayer, Mass., 1964-69. Served as cpl. U.S. Army, 1951-53. Fellow Soc. Applied Anthrop.; mem. AAAS, Assn. for Behavioral Sci. and Med. Edn. (cert., sec., treas. 1970-80, pres. 1981-82), Am. Anthrop. Assn. Democrat. Congregationalist. Office: Wind River Assocs 158 Hwy 17A Warwick NY 10990

KENNEDY, FRANCIS KENNETH, finance executive; b. Bklyn., July 11, 1936; s. James Joseph and Mary (Riccigliano) K.; m. Eleanor Mary Bouchard, Oct. 2, 1955; children: Kenneth, Catherine, Michael, Patricia, James. AAS in Acctg., SUNY, Farmingdale, 1966; BS in Acctg., N.Y. Inst. Tech., 1973, postgrad., 1978-79. Acct. Sperry Gyroscope, Great Neck, N.Y., 1955-62, chief cost acct., 1962-66; mgr. cost control, estimating and adminstrn. Sperry Def. Electronics, Great Neck, 1966-79; mgr. fin. adminstrn. and control Sperry Microwave Electronics, Clearwater, Fla., 1979-80, controller, 1980-86; controller Hercules Def. Elec. Systems, Clearwater, 1986-87, dir. fin., bus. adminstrn., 1987-88, v.p. fin., bus. adminstrn., 1988—. Pres., v.p. St. Pius X Youth Council, Plainview, N.Y., 1973-77. Mem. Nat. Contract Mgmt. Assn. Republican. Roman Catholic. Club: Feathersound Country. Home: 14521 Teal Ct Clearwater FL 34622 Office: Hercules Def Electronics Systems 13133 34th St N Clearwater FL 34618

KENNEDY, GEORGE D., chemical company executive; b. Pitts., May 30, 1926; s. Thomas Reed and Lois (Smith) K.; m. Valerie Putis; children: Charles Reed, Jamey Kathleen, Susan Patton, Timothy Christian. BA, Williams Coll., 1948. With Scott Paper Co., 1947-52, Champion Paper Co., 1952-65; pres. Brown Co., 1965-71; exec. v.p. Internat. Minerals & Chem. Corp., Northbrook, Ill., 1971-78, pres., 1978-86, chmn., 1986—, chief exec. officer, 1983—, also bd. dirs.; com. mem., bd. dirs. Brunswick Corp.; bd. dirs., mem. exec. com. Kemper Corp.; bd. dirs. Ill. Tool Works. Chmn. Children's Meml. Hosp.; bd. dirs. McGaw Med. Ctr. Northwestern U.; trustee Chgo. Symphony; mem. Chgo. Com., Mid-Am. Com., Com. for Econ. Devel.; mem. bus. adv. council Carnegie-Mellon U. Grad. Sch. Indsl. Adminstrn.; trustee Nat. Com. Against Drunk Driving; chmn. Jr. Achievement Chgo., 1988-89. Mem. Chgo. Assn. Commerce and Industry (bd. dirs.), Chgo. Council Fgn. Relations (bd. dirs.), Board Room Club, N.Y. Athletic Club, Larchmont Yacht Club, Sleepy Hollow Country Club, Skokie Country Club, Comml. Club. Office: Internat Minerals & Chem Corp 2315 Sanders Rd Northbrook IL 60062

KENNEDY, HAROLD EDWARD, lawyer; b. Pottstown, Pa., Oct. 18, 1927; s. Freeman S. and Alice (Brehm) K.; m. Eleanor Henry, Jan. 9, 1960; children: Kathleen, Nancy, Harold, Robert, Ellen, Anne, Susan. Student, Colgate U., 1945-47; LLB, Syracuse U., 1952. Bar: N.Y. 1952, U.S. Dist. Ct. (no. dist.) N.Y. 1954, U.S. Supreme Ct. 1956, U.S. Dist. Ct. (so. dist.) N.Y. 1962. Ptnr. Taylor & Kennedy, Amsterdam, N.Y., 1952-59; sr. assoc. Kissam & Halpin, N.Y.C., 1959-60; vice chmn., gen. counsel Foster Wheeler Corp., Clinton, N.J., 1960—, also bd. dirs.; trustee Compass Group Mut. Funds. Trustee First Presbyn. Ch., Orange, N.J., 1973-76, St. Barnabas Med. Ctr., 1986—, Kessler Inst. for Rehab., 1987—; bd. visitors Syracuse U. Coll. of Law, 1987—; bd. dirs. N.J. Alliance for Action, 1986—. Served with USAAF, 1945-47. Mem. ABA, Machinery and Allied Products Inst., Order of Coif, Baltusol Golf Club. Office: Foster Wheeler Corp Perryville Corporate Pk Clinton NJ 08809-4000

KENNEDY, JAMES ANTHONY, lawyer; b. Yonkers, N.Y., Oct. 26, 1958; s. John James Kennedy and Jean Marie (Baldassare) Jarusinsky. BS, U. Conn., 1980; JD, U. Pitts., 1983; LLM, So. Meth. U., 1987. Bar: Pa. 1983, U.S. Tax Ct. 1984, U.S. Supreme Ct. 1987. Lawyer U.S. Dept. Labor, Pitts., 1984-85; tax atty. USX Corp., Pitts., 1985-86, 87—, Dallas, 1985-87. Solicitor United Way, Pitts., 1987, The Carnegie, Pitts., 1988, Juvenile Diabetes Found., Pitts., 1989. Mem. ABA (sect. of taxation, mem. employee benefits com. 1986—). Mem. Christian Ch. Office: USX Corp 600 Grant St Rm 2477 Pittsburgh PA 15230

KENNEDY, JAMES HARRINGTON, editor, publisher; b. Lawrence, Mass., Feb. 20, 1924; s. James H. and Margaret Helen (Hyde) K.; m. Sheila Conway, July 1, 1950; children: Kathleen, Brian, Kevin, Gail, Patricia, Maureen, Constance. BS, Lowell Textile Inst., 1948; MS, MIT, 1950. Mgmt. trainee Chicopee Mfg. Corp., Manchester, N.H., 1950-51; mng. editor Textile World McGraw Hill Pub. Co., Greenville, S.C., 1951-54; dir. communications Bruce Payne & Assocs., Westport, Conn., 1954-58; pres. James H. Kennedy & Co., Westport, 1958-70; editor, pub. Cons. News, Fitzwilliam, N.H., 1970—, Exec. Recruiter News, 1980—. Founder Fitzwilliam Conservation Corp., pres., 1970-72; chmn. Fitzwilliam Sq. Dances, 1970—; mem. Fitzwilliam Planning Bd., 1970-72; trustee Am. Liquid Trust, Greenwich, Conn., 1975-78. Served to capt., inf. AUS, 1942-46. Mem. Fitzwilliam Hist. Soc., Acad. Mgmt., N.Y. Bus. Press Editors, Phi Psi. Republican. Roman Catholic. Clubs: Fitzwilliam Swimming (pres. 1978-84), Nat. Press. Address: Templeton Turnpike Fitzwilliam NH 03447

KENNEDY, JANICE MARIE, accountant; b. Wichita, Kans., Jan. 4, 1943; d. Oren L. and Jean H. (Harrison) Shelley; m. David W. Kennedy, Aug. 29, 1964; children: Christopher L., Drue D. BS in Bus. Adminstrn., U. Kans., 1964; MS in Acctg., Wichita State U., 1981. CPA, Kans. Staff acct. Kennedy and Coe, CPAs, Wichita, 1981-84; pvt. practice acctg. Wichita, 1984—. Adv. bd. Kans. Children's Service League, Wichita, 1984—; treas., bd. dirs. Literacy Vols. of Am., Wichita, 1986—. Mem. Nat. Assn. Accts. (treas., pres. 1981—), Am. Inst. CPA's, Kans. Soc. CPA's (com. mem.), Am. Soc. Women Accts. (bd. dirs., v.p. 1982-83). Republican. Episcopalian. Home: 6211 Beachy Wichita KS 67208 Office: 4930 E Lincoln Wichita KS 67218

KENNEDY, JOE ARTHUR, product manager; b. Muncie, Ind., Feb. 3, 1957; s. Don W. and Ruby K. (Harris) K. BS, Ball State U., 1981. Account mgr. Anaconda Ericsson, Greenwich, Conn., 1981-83; product mgr. Baker div. Sonoco Products Co., Hartselle, Ala., 1983-88; mkt. mgr. Sonoco Products Co., Hartselle, 1988—. Mem. Wire Assn. Internat. (mem. mkt. info. com. 1986—), Decatur (Ala.) Jaycees. Home: 884 Ivanhoe Dr Florence SC 29501 Office: Sonoco Products PO Box 160 Hartsville SC 29550

KENNEDY, JOHN B., data processing executive; b. Evanston, Ill., Feb. 17, 1951; s. John A. and Mary Ann (Bremmer) K.; m. Carol J. Hammerman, Aug. 21, 1985; children: Brendan, Charlie. BS, Georgetown U., 1973; Masters in Mgmt., Northwestern U., 1977. Tchr. physics The Abby Sch., Canon City, Colo., 1973-74; with Goulds Pumps, Chgo., 1974-76; cons. Mgmt. Analysis Ctr., Chgo., 1976; staff corp. planning Brunswick Corp., Chgo., 1976-79; pres. Kennedy Cons., Chgo., 1979-81, Mktg. Info. Systems, Evanston, Ill., 1981—. Bd. dirs. United Way, Chgo., 1982-83, Jane Adams Resource Ctr., Chgo., 1986—. Mem. Chgo. Athletic Assn. Office: Marketing Info System 906 University Pl Evanston IL 60201

KENNEDY, JOHN JOSEPH, bank controller; b. Bkyln., Jan. 28, 1948; s. John J. and Doris M. (Maguire) K.; m. Linda Graham, Sept. 27, 1969; children: John, Richard, Graham. BS, Fordham U., 1969. CPA, N.Y. Acct. Peat, Marwick, Mitchell & Co., N.Y.C., 1971-83; v.p. controller Generale Bank, N.Y.C., 1984—. Served to 1st lt. U.S. Army, 1969-71. Mem. Am. Inst. CPA's N.Y. State Soc. CPA;s, Nat. Assn. Accts., Fin. Execs. Inst. Roman Catholic. Home: 29 Rockwell Circle Marlboro NJ 07746 Office: Generale Bank 12 E 49th St 22d Fl New York NY 10017

KENNEDY, JOHN R., JR., paper manufacturing company executive; b. 1930; married. BA, Georgetown U., 1952. With Fed. Paper Bd. Co. Inc., Montvale, N.J., 1952—, v.p., 1959-61, sr. v.p., 1961-65, pres., 1965-75, pres., chief exec. officer, 1975—, also bd. dirs. Office: Fed Paper Bd Co Inc 75 Chestnut Ridge Rd Montvale NJ 07645 *

KENNEDY, KAEL BEHAN, lawyer; b. Chgo., Sept. 1, 1941; s. W. McNeil and Dot (Behan) K.; m. Pam Wilt, Aug. 29, 1964; 1 child, Mark Wilt. BS, Loyola U., 1963; JD, U. Iowa, 1966. Bar: Iowa 1966, Ill. 1967, U.S. Dist. Ct. (no. dist.) Ill. 1967, (we. dist.) Mo. 1971, (ea. dist.) Mo. 1975, (so. dist.) Tex. 1977, (so. dist.) N.Y. 1978, Dist. S.C. 1982, U.S. Ct. Apls. (7th cir.) 1967, (8th cir.) 1973, (5th cir.) 1980, Mich. 1987, U.S. Dist. Ct. (ea. and we. dists.) Mich. 1987, U.S. Ct. Appeals (6th cir.) 1986. Assoc. Pope, Ballard, Shepard & Fowle, Chgo., 1966-73; ptnr. Pope, Ballard, Shepard & Fowle, Chgo., 1973-79, Katten, Muchin, Zavis, Pearl & Galler, Chgo., 1979-85, Varnum, Riddering, Schmidt & Howlett, Grand Rapids, 1986-88, Matkov, Salzman, Madoff & Gunn, Chgo., 1988—; lectr. in field; instr. Arthur Andersen & Co., St. Charles, Ill., 1983, Ill. Inst. Continuing Legal Edn., Chgo., 1983, 84, Nat. Inst. Trial Adv., Chgo., 1986, 87, 88, 89, Mich. Bar Assn., 1987. Co-author: Antitrust Consent Decree Manual, 1978, Expediting Pretrials and Trials of Antitrust Cases, 1979, Antitrust Law and Mcpl. Govt., 1988. Editorial staff CCH Corp. Law Guide, 1963, 64; mem. U. Iowa Law Rev., 1965, 66. Bd. dirs. Lawyers Com. for Civil Rights Under Law, Chgo., 1983, 84; committeeman Deerfield Twp. Rep. Com., Highland Park, Ill., 1982-84; cooperating counsel ACLU, Chgo., 1967-72. Mem. ABA, Ill. Bar Assn. (council Antitrust Law sect.), Mich. Bar Assn. (council antitrust law sect.), Chgo. Bar Assn., Am. Soc. of Assn. Execs. Clubs: University, Legal, Nat. Lawyers, Chgo., Macatawa Bay Yacht. Home: 3920 N Lake Shore Dr Chicago IL 60613 Office: Matkov Salzman Madoff & Gunn 100 W Monroe St #1500 Chicago IL 60603

KENNEDY, KEITH SANFORD, oil executive, lawyer; b. Welland, Ont., Can., Jan. 18, 1945; s. Frank Mettler and Marion Louise (Thornton) K.; m. Joan Margaret Finke, Aug. 20, 1966; children: David Michael, Scott Alan. BSBA, W.Va. U., 1966; JD, Duquesne U., 1970. Bar: Pa. 1971. Personnel trainee Crucible Steel Co., Pitts., 1966-67; personnel adminstr. Westinghouse Electric Corp., 1967-71; atty. Allegheny Power System, N.Y.C., 1971-76; asst. gen. counsel Chase Brass & Copper Co., Inc., Cleve., 1976-79, gen. counsel, 1979-81; sr. counsel Standard Oil Co., 1981-85; asst. treas., dir. ins. BP Am., Inc. and predecessor firms, 1985—. Mem. editorial bd. mags. Risk and Benefits Mgmt., 1987—. Mem. Risk and Ins. Mgmt. Soc., Oil Ins. Ltd. (bd. dirs., exec. com. 1986—), Oil Casualty Ins. Ltd. (bd. dirs., exec. com. 1987—), Am. Steamship Owners Mut. (bd. dirs., fin. com. 1986—), P & I Assn., Corp. Officers and Dirs. Assurance Ltd. (bd. dirs. 1986—). Presbyterian. Home: 17950 Birch Hill Dr Chagrin Falls OH 44022 Office: BP Am Inc 200 Public Sq 11-3556D Cleveland OH 44114-2375

KENNEDY, MARC J., lawyer; b. Newburgh, N.Y., Mar. 2, 1945; s. Warren G. K. and Frances F. (Levinson) K.; m. Debra L. Shaw, Apr. 19, 1986; 1 child, Michael L. BA cum laude, Syracuse U., 1967; JD, U. Mich., 1970. Bar: N.Y. 1971. Assoc. Davies, Hardy, Ives & Lawther, N.Y.C., 1971-72, London, Buttenweiser & Chalif, N.Y.C., 1972-73, Silberfeld, Danziger & Bangser, N.Y.C., 1973; counsel Occidental Crude Sales, Inc., N.Y.C., 1974-75; v.p., gen. counsel Internat. Ore & Fertilizer Corp., N.Y.C., 1975-82; asst. gen. counsel Internat. Ore & Fertilizer Corp., Houston, 1982; v.p., gen. counsel Occidental Chem. Agrl. Products Inc., Tampa, Fla., 1982-87; v.p., gen counsel agrl. products group Occidental Chem. Corp., Tampa, 1987—; faculty mentor Columbia Pacific U., Mill Valley, Calif., 1981—. Trustee Bar Harbor Festival Corp., N.Y.C., 1974-87; bd. dirs. Am. Opera Repertory Co., 1982-85; mem. com. planned giving N.Y. Foundling Hosp., 1977—; Explorer post advisor Boy Scouts Am., 1976-78. Mem. ABA (vice-chmn. com. internat. law, liaison young lawyers sect. 1974-75, chmn. sub-com. proposed trade barriers to the importation of products into U.S. 1985-88), Am. Corp. Counsel Assn., Internat. Bar Assn., Maritime Law Assn., N.Y. State Bar Assn., Assn. of Bar of City of N.Y. (admiralty law com. 1982-83), Clearwater Yacht Club. Home: 240 Windward Passage #803 Clearwater FL 34630 Office: Occidental Chem Corp Agrl Products Group 4830 W Kennedy Blvd Tampa FL 33609

KENNEDY, QUENTIN J., SR., paper company executive; b. N.Y.C., May 27, 1933; married. BS, Georgetown U., 1955, LLB, 1957. With Fed. Paper Bd Co., Inc., Montvale, N.J., 1959—, sec., 1963-70, v.p. sec., 1970-75, v.p. sec.-treas., 1975-83, exec. v.p. sec., 1983—, also bd. dirs. Office: Fed Paper Bd Co Inc 75 Chestnut Ridge Rd Montvale NJ 07645

KENNEDY, ROBERT DELMONT, petrochemical company executive; b. Pitts., Nov. 8, 1932; s. Thomas Reed and Lois (Smith) K.; m. Sally Duff, Jan. 28, 1956; children: Robert Boyd, Kathleen Tyson, Thomas Alexander, Melissa Kristine. B of Mech. Engring., Cornell U., 1955. With Union Carbide Corp., 1955—, indsl. engr. Nat. Carbon Div., Dayton and Cleve., 1955-59, sales mgr., product mgr., Chgo., 1959-66, mgr. mktg., N.Y.C., dir. internat. mktg., 1964-71, dir. mktg., Europe, 1971-75, sr. v.p., 1975-77, pres. Linde Div., N.Y.C., 1977-81, corp. exec. v.p., 1982-85, pres., chief operating officer chemicals and plastics, 1985-86, chmn., pres., chief exec. officer, 1986—. Chmn. bd. trustees, New Hampton Sch.; moderator Aspen Inst. Program Humanistic Studies, 1979—. Mem. Chem. Mfrs. Assn. (chmn., exec. com.). Republican. Avocations: golf, fishing, boating. Office: Union Carbide Corp 39 Old Ridgebury Rd Danbury CT 06840

KENNEDY, ROBERT EUGENE, advertising agency executive; b. N.Y.C., June 2, 1942; s. John David and Katherine Patricia K.; m. Roseanne C. McNeill, June 26, 1965; children—Noelle, Stephen, Elizabeth, Kristen. Student, Iona Coll., 1961-68. With Dancer-Fitzgerald-Sample Inc., N.Y.C., 1961-66, asst. controller, 1969-72, v.p., controller, 1972-76, sr. v.p., 1976-78, treas., 1977-86, vice chmn., chief fin. officer, 1979-86; also chmn. subs. Program Syndicated Services, Inc., 1979—; vice chmn. DFS Internat., Inc., 1981-86; vice chmn., chief fin. officer DFS Holdings Inc., 1982-86; sr. exec. v.p., chief fin. officer, treas. DFS Dorland Worldwide Inc., 1986-87; vice chmn., chief fin. officer, treas. Saatchi and Saatchi DFS, Inc., 1987—. Served with USMC, 1965. Mem. Advt. agy. Fin. Mgmt. Group, Fin. Execs. Inst., Pascack Valley Hosp. Assn. Clubs: Arcola Country (Paramus, N.J.); Pinnacle (N.Y.C.), Union League, N.Y. Athletic. Office: Saatchi & Saatchi Advt Worldwide 375 Hudson St New York NY 10014

KENNEDY, ROBERT JOHN, banker, engineer; b. Phila., Oct. 11, 1913; s. William J. and Bertha (Vurpillot) K.; m. Elelyn M. Anderson, Sept. 3, 1939; children: Jan B., Kit C. BSME, U. Pa., 1935; LLB, Temple U., 1940. Chmn. bd. Hammond Kennedy and Co., N.Y.C., 1944—; v.p. Kessler Rsch. Found., West Orange, N.J., 1986—. Mem. Forest Farmers Assn., Sky Club, Canoebrook Country, N.Y. Yacht Club. Republican. Home: 1 Warwick Circle Springfield NJ 07081 Office: Hammond Kennedy and Co 230 Park Ave New York NY 10169

KENNEDY, SAM DELK, newspaper executive, lawyer; b. Hampshire, Tenn., Dec. 9, 1926; s. Henry Grady and Annie Porter (Delk) K.; m. Elizabeth Ridley Finney, Nov. 6, 1954; children: Sam Delk Jr., Elizabeth Blackstone. Student, David Lipscomb Coll., 1943-44, N.C. State U., 1944-45; LLB, Cumberland U., 1950, JD, 1966. Bar: Tenn., U.S. Supreme Ct. Judge gen. sessions State Judiciary, Columbia, Tenn., 1952-54; asst. atty. gen. Tenn. Dist. Ct. (11th dist.), Columbia, 1958-62, dist. atty. gen., 1962-65; editor, pub. Daily Herald, Columbia, 1965-83; pres. Kennedy Newspaper Co., Columbia, 1983—; ptnr. Kennedy & Kennedy, Columbia, 1987—; bd. dirs. 1st Farmers and Merchant Bank, Columbia. Past bd. dirs. Audit Bur. Circulation. Sgt. U.S. Army, 1945-47. Mem. ABA, Tenn. Bar Assn. (pres. 1978-79), Tenn. Press Assn. (chmn. legis. com. 1967—). DemocrT. Presbyterian. Lodge: Kiwanis. Home: Rte 5 Box 405 Columbia TN 38401 Office: Kennedy & Kennedy 805 S Garden St Columbia TN 38402

KENNEDY, THOMAS EDGAR, information systems executive; b. Stockton, Calif., Aug. 16, 1958; s. Thomas Jefferson and Evelyn Marie (Bodimer) K.; m. Susan Grace Harris Kennedy, May 4, 1986. BS, U. Pacific, 1980; MBA, Claremont Grad. Sch., 1981. Internal cons. Foster Farms, Livingston, Calif., 1982; acquisitions analyst Cal Gas, Sacramento, Calif., 1982-83, mgr. market planning, 1983-84; turnaround specialist Williams Assocs., Walnut Creek, Calif., 1984-85; chief exec. officer ICSG Info. Systems, Stockton, Calif., 1985-88, Integrative Svcs. Group, Stockton, 1988—; mktg. cons. Harris Health Ins. Adminstrn., Stockton, Calif., 1985—. Alt. mem. Rep. Cen. Com., Stockton, Calif., 1985. Outstanding Young Man of Am., 1983. Phi Kappa Phi. Republican. Baptist. Office: Integrative Svcs Group 1151 W Robinhood Ste 12B Stockton CA 95207

KENNEDY, THOMAS PATRICK, communications consultant, financial executive; b. N.Y.C., Oct. 13, 1932; s. Andrew Francis and Marie P. (Scullen) K.; BS, St. Peter's Coll., 1958; postgrad. Seton Hall U., 1959; m. Mary P. Drennan, Jan. 14, 1956 (dec.); children—Thomas Patrick, Kevin M., Michael J., Mary P., Deborah A. Accountant, Haskins & Sells, CPA's, N.Y.C., 1953-54, 55-57; staff Emerson Radio & TV, N.Y.C., 1957-58; various exec. positions CBS, N.Y.C., 1958-67; with Ford Found., N.Y.C., 1967; dir. fin. Pub. Broadcasting Lab., N.Y.C., 1967-69; with Children's TV Workshop Sesame St., N.Y.C., 1969-80, v.p. fin. and adminstrn., 1969-78, treas. 1969-78, sr. v.p., 1978-80; pres. Tomken Mgmt., Ltd., 1980—, chmn. bd., 1983—; chmn. bd., chief exec. officer Effie Techs. Inc., 1984—; v.p., corp. fin. Jersey Capital Mkts Group, Inc., 1987-88; chief exec. officer, chmn. bd. Corp. Strategies Group, Inc., 1988—; cons. in field. Bd. advisers Franciscan Communication Ctr.; bd. dirs. Home Monitor Inc., Cleat Capitol Resources, Inc., Home Energy Savings, Inc.; bd. dirs., exec. dir. Ctr. for Non-Broadcast TV. Served with C.E., U.S. Army, 1954-55. Mem. Fin. Exec. Inst., Internat. Radio and TV Soc., Inst. Broadcast Fin. Mgmt., Nat. Assn. Accountants, Internat. Broadcast Inst., Internat. Inst. Communication, Internat. Assn. Fin. Execs., Am. Assn. Ind. Investors. Roman Catholic. Home: 40 Leonardville Rd Belford NJ 07718 also: Riverview Hist Pla 45 Newark St Hoboken NJ 07030

KENNEWAY, ERNEST KEATING, JR., filtration and separations equipment company executive; b. Worcester, Mass., May 12, 1938; s. Ernest Keating and Pauline J. (Menzenski) K.; B.S. in Bus. Adminstrn., Clark U., 1961; postgrad. Sch. Indsl. Mgmt., Worcester Poly. Inst., 1969; m. Marlene Toloczko, Sept. 11, 1966; children—Melissa, Matthew. Asst. purchasing agt. Hobbs Mfg. Co., Worcester, 1963-65, prodn. control supr., 1965-66; inventory mgr. George Meyer Mfg. Co., Worcester, 1966; materials mgr. Leland-Gifford Co., Worcester, 1966-69, controller, 1969-71; v.p. fin. Americold Compressor Co., Cullman, Ala., 1971-74; pres., gen. mgr. R-P&C Valve, Inc., Fairview, Pa., 1974-81; pres., gen. mgr. Wolverine Brass Works, Grand Rapids, Mich., 1981-83; pres., chief operating officer Separations Tech. Inc., Kentwood, Mich., 1983-87; pres., chief exec. officer MEK Industries Inc., Grand Rapids, Mich., 1987—. Served with U.S. Army, 1962. Mem. Mich. Mfg. Assn., Filtration Soc., U.S. C. of C. Home: 7037 Bridgewater St SE Grand Rapids MI 49506 Office: 470 Market Ave SW Grand Rapids MI 49503

KENNEY, F. DONALD, investment banker; b. Olean, N.Y., Mar. 9, 1918; s. John P. and Winifred (Shortell) K.; BA, Coll. of Holy Cross, 1939; MA, Harvard U., 1941, MBA, 1951; postgrad. Oxford (Eng.) U., 1948. Teaching fellow in English, Harvard U., 1947-51; with Harriman Ripley & Co., Inc., 1951-70 asst. v.p., 1958-61, v.p., dir., 1961-70; pres., dir. Harriman Ripley (Can.) Ltd., Toronto, Ont., 1960-70; chmn. Harriman Ripley Internat. S.A-R.L., Luxembourg, 1964-70; vice chmn. Merrill Lynch, Pierce, Fenner & Smith Securities Underwriter Ltd., 1970-74, chmn., 1974-76; co-chmn. bd. Goldman Sachs Internat. Corp., 1976—; treas., dir. 785 Park Ave. Corp., 1969—; bd. dirs. United Reins. Corp. of N.Y., Pohjola Reins. Corp. Am. Trustee, Suomi Coll., 1974—, Am. Scandinavian Found.; mem. president's council St. Bonaventure U., 1980—; fellow Met. Mus.; bd. dirs. Internat. Council Mus. Found., 1977—; chmn. F. Donald Kenney Found., Ireland Am. Arts Exchange; bd. dirs., v.p. Ireland-U.S. Council; Internat. dir. ROSC. Lt. commdr., USNR, 1942-46. Decorated comdr. Order of Lion, Finland, 1963; comdr. Order Merit, Luxembourg, 1971; knight comdr. Royal Norwegian Order of St. Olaf; Knight of Malta, recipient Silver Medal City of Helsinki. Mem. Finnish Am. Assn. (dir. 1967—, v.p. 1968-70, 88—, pres. 1970-71), Norweigian C. of C., Am. C. of C., Council Fgn. Relations, Pilgrims. Clubs: Harvard (N.Y.C., Boston); Knickerbocker, Downtown Assn. (N.Y.C.). Home: 785 Park Ave New York NY 10021 Office: 85 Broad St New York NY 10004

KENNEY, SCOTT ROBERT, service executive, accountant; b. Manistique, Mich., Nov. 2, 1956; s. Robert Jack kenney and Anita Marie (Smithson) Stockham; m. Nancy Aileen Nyholm, Aug. 15, 1976; children: Christina, Robert. BS in Acctg, Ferris State Coll., 1977. CPA, Mich. Staff acct. Fleury, Singler & Co., P.C., Iron Mountain, Mich., 1977-80; ptnr. Andrew F. Davis & Co., P.C., Iron River, Mich., 1980-81; asst. adminstr. Crystal Falls (Mich.) Community Hosp., 1981-87; contr. Dickinson County Hosps., Iron Mountain, 1987, v.p. fin., 1987—; mem. adj. faculty Gogebic Community Coll., Ironwood, Mich., 1981-87; cons. computers Crystal Falls Community Hosp., 1987—. Chmn. parent adv. com. Forest Park Bd. Edn., Crystal Falls, 1986. Mem. Healthcare Fin. Mgmt. Assn. (No. Great Lakes chpt., pres. 1988-89), Mich. Assn. CPAs, Masons (Worshipful Master 1987). Lutheran. Home: N5011 Bass Lake Rd 607 Iron Mountain MI 49801 Office: Dickinson County Hosps 400 Woodward Ave Iron Mountain MI 49801

KENNEY, WILLIAM FITZGERALD, lawyer; b. San Francisco, Nov. 4, 1935; s. Lionel Fitzgerald and Ethel Constance (Brennan) K.; m. Susan Elizabeth Langfitt, May 5, 1962; children—Anne, Carol, James. BA, U. Calif.-Berkeley, 1957, JD, 1960. Bar: Calif. 1961. Assoc. Miller, Osborne Miller & Bartlett, San Mateo, Calif., 1962-64; ptnr. Tormey, Kenney & Cotchett, San Mateo, 1965-67; pres. William F. Kenney, Inc., San Mateo, 1968—; gen. ptnr. All-Am. Self Storage, 1985—. Trustee San Mateo City Sch. Dist., 1971-79, pres., 1972-74; pres. March of Dimes, 1972-73; bd. dirs. Boys Club of San Mateo, 1972—. With U.S. Army, 1960-62. Mem. State Bar of Calif. (taxation com. 1973-76), San Mateo County Bar Assn. (bd. dir. 1973-75), Calif. Assn. Realtors (legal affairs com. 1978—), San Mateo C. of C. (bd. dirs. 1987—), Self Svc. Storage Assn. (bd. dirs. western region 1987—, pres. 1989—). Republican. Roman Catholic. Club: Rotary (pres. 1978-79). Lodge: Elks (exalted ruler 1974-75). Home: 221 Clark Dr San Mateo CA 94402 Office: William F Kenney Inc 120 N El Camino Real San Mateo CA 94401

KENNING, BRIAN G., corporation executive; b. 1949. BA in Econs., Queen's U., Kingston, 1971, MBA, 1973. Project mgr. Marathon Realty, 1973-75; br. mgr. Coronation Credit Corp. Ltd., 1975-76, v.p., 1976-80; mgr. corp. planning Versatile Corp., Vancouver, B.C., 1980-84, asst. v.p. corp. planning, 1984-87; pres., mng. ptnr. B.C. Pacific Capital, Vancouver, B.C., 1987—; bd. dirs. Bralorne Resources Ltd., Varitech Investors Corp., Council for Canadian Unity. Gov. Brentwood Coll. Home: 3865 W 36th Ave, Vancouver, BC Canada V6N 2S5 Office: BC Pacific Capital Corp, 1055 W Georgia St Ste 1632, PO Box 11179 Royal Ctr, Vancouver, BC Canada V6E 3R5

KENNY, JOHN EDWARD, computer analyst; b. Buffalo, Oct. 28, 1945; s. Thomas Edmund and Dorothy Elizabeth (Krull) K.; AAS, Erie Community Coll., 1972. Systems analyst Nat. Fuel Gas, Buffalo, 1969-70; programmer Westwood Pharm., Buffalo, 1972-73; programmer Sevc. Systems Corp., Clarence, N.Y., 1974-77, Carborundum, Niagara Falls, N.Y., 1973-74; analyst, programmer A, Marine Midland Bank N.A., Buffalo, 1977-83; sr. analyst, programmer, project leader Empire of Am., FSA, Buffalo, 1983-85, applications project supr., 1985—; tchr. programming langs. Advanced Tng. Ctr., Buffalo. Mem. Rep. Presdl. Task Force; mem. Town of Tonawanda Conservative Com., 1980—; vice chmn. Town of Tonawanda Conservative Com. Mem. Erie County Conservative Com. Exec. Com., U.S. Jr. C. of C., Am. Inst. Banking, Assn. Systems Mgmt., Kenton Jr. C. of C., Kenmore C. of C., Internat. Platform Assn., Smithsonian Assn., Assn. Computing Machinery, Nat. Geographic Soc., U.S. Golf Assn. (assoc.), Tonawanda Chmn. Men's Club, Glen Oak Golf Club, KC, Lions, Internat. Order Alhambra. Roman Catholic. Home: 212 McKinley Ave Kenmore NY 14217 Office: 626 Commerce Dr Amherst NY 14150

KENNY, ROGER MICHAEL, executive search consultant; b. N.Y.C., Oct. 3, 1938; s. Michael F. and Mary T. (Glynn) K.; m. Carole Ann Smith, Oct. 3, 1959; children: Glynn Scott, Lynn Marie. BBA, Manhattan Coll., 1959; MBA, N.Y. U., 1961. With Port Authority of N.Y. and N.J., 1959-67, mgr. bus. ops., 1965-67; assoc. Spencer Stuart & Assos., N.Y.C., 1967-70, v.p. West Coast ops., 1970-77; sr. v.p., ptnr. Spencer Stuart & Assocs., 1977-82, Kenny, Kindler, Hunt & Howe, N.Y.C., 1982—; mng. dir. Boardroom Cons., Inc. Contbr. articles to profl. jours. Served with U.S. Army, 1961-63. Mem. Nat. Assn. Corp. and Profl. Recruiters, Am. Soc. Public Adminstrs., Assn. Exec. Search Cons. (bd. dirs.), Board Room Club, Econ. Club, Westchester Country Club. Home: 33 Mount Holly Dr Rye NY 10580 Office: Kenny Kindler Hunt & Howe 780 3d Ave New York NY 10017

KENRICH, JOHN LEWIS, lawyer; b. Lima, Ohio, Oct. 17, 1929; s. Clarence E. and Rowena (Stroh) Katterheinrich; m. Betty Jane Roehll, May 26, 1951; children: John David, Mary Jane, Kathryn Ann, Thomas Roehll, Walter Clarence. B.S., Miami U., Oxford, Ohio, 1951; LL.B., U. Cin., 1953. Bar: Ohio 1953, Mass. 1969. Asst. counsel B.F. Goodrich Co., Akron, Ohio, 1956-65; asst. sec., counsel W.R. Grace & Co., Cin., 1965-68; corp. counsel, sec. Standex Internat. Corp., Andover, Mass., 1969-70; v.p. Splty. Products Group div. W.R. Grace & Co., Cin., 1970-71; v.p., sec. Chemed Corp., Cin., 1971-82; sr. v.p., gen. counsel Chemed Corp., 1982-86, exec. v.p., chief adminstrv. officer, 1986—; bd. dirs. Chemed Corp., Nat. Sanitary Supply Co., Roto-Rooter Inc., Omnicare, Inc., Dubois Chemie GmbH, Germany, DuBois Chemicalien BV, Netherlands. Trustee Better Bus. Bur. Cin., 1981—; mem. bus. adv. council Miami U., 1986-88; mem. City Planning Commn., Akron, 1961-62; mem. bd. visitors Coll. Law U. Cin., 1988—. 1st lt. JAGC AUS, 1954-56. Mem. Am., Ohio, N.Y. Bar Assns., Queen City Club, Bankers Club, Beta Theta Pi, Omicron Delta Kappa, Delta Sigma Pi, Phi Eta Sigma. Republican. Presbyterian. Home: 3516 Forest Oak Ct Cincinnati OH 45208 Office: Chemed Corp 1200 DuBois Tower Cincinnati OH 45202

KENT, RICHARD EDMUND, lawyer; b. Detroit, Oct. 20, 1928; s. Philip J. Kent and Katherine E. Manning; m. Laura T. Thorne; children: Kerry E., Patricia A., Peter D., Jack L. BS, Cornell U., Ithaca, 1950; JD, U. Mich., 1955. Bar: Mich. 1955, Oreg. 1969. Ptnr. Hill, Lewis, et. al., Detroit, 1955-69; v.p., sec. and gen. counsel Evans Products Co., Portland, 1969-84; ptnr. Weiss, Des Camp & Botteri, Portland, Oreg., 1984-86; v.p., sec. and gen. counsel Grossman's, Inc., Boston, 1986—; Bd. dirs. Biotag Inc., Milbrook, N.Y., 1987—. Democrat. Episcopalian. Office: Grossmans Inc 200 Union St Braintree MA 02184

KENT, ROBERT WARREN, lawyer; b. Oceanside, N.Y., July 8, 1935; s. Meredith L. and Ruth W. K.; m. Sally Anne Macnair, Aug. 24, 1957; children: Robert W., William M., Richard M., Deborah K. A.B., Princeton U., 1957; J.D., Harvard U., 1960; postgrad., Advanced Mgmt. Program. Asso. firm Breed, Abbott & Morgan, N.Y.C., 1960-67; asso. counsel Armco Inc., Middletown, Ohio, 1967-69; asst. counsel Armco Inc., 1969-73, counsel, 1973-78, asst. gen. counsel, 1978-81, corp. v.p. law, gen. counsel, sec., 1981—. Pres. Moundbuilders Area council Boy Scouts Am., 1980-81. Mem. Ohio Mfrs. Assn. (chmn. bd. dirs. 1983-85), Am. Bar Assn. Episcopalian. Office: Armco Inc 300 Interpace Pkwy Parsippany NJ 07054-0324

KENT, ROMAN ROBERT, management consultant; b. Lodz, Poland, Apr. 18, 1929; came to U.S., 1946; s. Emanuel and Sonia (Lifshitz) Kniker; m. Hannah Starkman, Apr. 7, 1957; children: Susan Irene, Jeffrey Edward. Student, Emory U. V.p. Stafford Internat., N.Y.C.; pres. Namor Internat. Corp., N.Y.C. Producer: Children of the Holocaust (Internat. Film Festival award 1980). chmn. Am. Gathering Jewish Holocaust Survivors, N.Y.C.; bd. dirs. Tel Aviv U., N.Y.C.; mem. internat. com. Anti-Defamation League, N.Y.C.; treas. Friends of Israeli Def. Forces, N.Y.C. Office: 836 Fifth Ave Ste 711 New York NY 10001

KENWORTHY, HARRY WILLIAM, company executive; b. Utica, N.Y., Nov. 15, 1947; s. Robert Wild and Marcina Agnes (Suraske) K.; m. Elaine Fedor, July 17, 1971; children: Rebekah, Amanda. BS in Materials Engring., Rensselaer Poly. Inst., 1969; MBA in Fin., Syracuse U., 1973. Registered profl. engr., Conn.; cer. quality engr. Process engr. Revere Copper & Brass, Rome, N.Y., 1969-70, supr., 1970-72; ops. mgr. BZ industries, Little Falls, N.Y., 1973-74; asst. plant mgr. Die Molding Corp., Canastota, N.Y., 1974-75, plant mgr., 1975-78; ops. mgr. Rogers Corp., Willimantic div., South Windham, Conn., 1978-83, div. mgr., 1983—. With USNG, 1969-75. Mem. Am. Soc. Quality Control (adv. com., quality improvement award), Assn. Mfg. Excellence, Am. Quality and Productivity Inst., Willimantic C. of C., Norwich C. of C., Minnechaug Swim and Tennis Club (Glastonbury, Conn., pres. 1986-87). Republican. Roman Catholic. Office: Rogers Corp 230 Norwich Rd South Windham CT 06266

KENYON, BRUCE DAVIS, utilities executive; b. Middletown, Ohio, Mar. 8, 1943; s. Lawrence Hughes Kenyon and Mildred Anita (Davis) Waligurski; m. Barbara Ryan, Dec. 23, 1966; children: Erin, Thomas, Robert. BA in Math., Miami U., Oxford, Ohio, 1965. Various mgmt. positions Northeast Utilities, Waterford, Conn., 1970-76; mgr. nuclear support Pa. Power and Light Co., Allentown, 1976-78, constrn. mgr., 1978-79, v.p. nuclear ops., 1980-84, sr. v.p. nuclear ops., 1984-88, sr. v.p. div. ops., 1988—; chmn. tech. issues, chmn. working group on security Nuclear Utility Mgmt. and Resource Council Priority Working Group, Washington; mem. Atomic Indsl. Forum Nat. Environment Studies Group, Washington; mem. evaluation and assistance industry rev. group Inst. Nuclear Power Ops., Atlanta. Served as lt. nuclear submarine program USN, 1965-70. Mem. No. Pa. chpt. Am. Nuclear Soc. (bd. dirs. 1985—). Methodist. Office: Pa Power & Light Co 2 N Ninth St Allentown PA 18101

KEOGH, KEVIN, investment executive; b. Rochester, N.Y., Nov. 12, 1935; s. Francis John and Madeline Inez (MacNamara) K.; m. Joan Lee Spencer, Aug. 7, 1965; children: Sean, Maura, Kyle. AB in Math., Hamilton Coll., 1957; MBA, Harvard U., 1961. Security analyst Laird & Co., N.Y.C., 1961-65; investment analyst Ford Found., N.Y.C., 1965-69; investment officer U. Rochester, N.Y., 1969-71, 72-81; asst. v.p. Mellon Bank, Pitts., 1971-72; pres. Univ. Ventures, Pittsford, N.Y., 1981-83; prin. Horsley, Keogh & Assocs., Pittsford, 1983—; gen. ptnr. Horsley Keogh Venture Fund, Pittsford, 1985—; adviser Minor Fund Hamilton Coll., Clinton, N.Y., 1984—. Pres. Pittsford Sch. Bd. Edn., 1975-80; mem. alumni council Hamilton Coll., 1987—. Mem. Am. Soc. Chartered Fin. Analysts, Pittsford Sch. Bd. Edn., N.Y. Athletic Club. Democrat. Roman Catholic. Home: 37 Charter Oaks Dr Pittsford NY 14534 Office: Horsley Keogh & Assocs 11 Tobey Office Pk Pittsford NY 14534

KEOUGH, DONALD RAYMOND, beverage and entertainment company executive; b. Maurice, Iowa, Sept. 4, 1926; s. Leo H. and Veronica (Henkels) K.; m. Marilyn Mulhall, Sept. 10, 1949; children: Kathleen Anne, Mary Shayla, Michael Leo, Patrick John, Eileen Tracy, Clarke Robert. BS, Creighton U., 1949, LLD (hon.), 1982; LLD (hon.), U. Notre Dame, 1985. With Butter-Nut Foods Co., Omaha, 1950-61; with Duncan Foods Co., Houston, 1961-67; v.p., dir. mktg. foods div. The Coca-Cola Co., Atlanta, 1967-71, pres. div., 1971-73; exec. v.p. Coca-Cola USA, Atlanta, 1973-74; pres. Coca-Cola USA, 1974-76; exec. v.p. The Coca-Cola Co., Atlanta, 1976-79, sr. exec. v.p., 1980-81, pres., chief operating officer, dir., 1981—; chmn. bd. dirs. Coca-Cola Enterprises Inc., Atlanta, 1986—, Columbia Pictures Entertainment Inc., 1988—; bd. dirs. Nat. Service Industries, Inc. Mem. pres.'s council Creighton U.; trustee Spelman Coll., The Lovett Sch., Agnes Scott Coll.; chmn. bd. trustees U. Notre Dame. Served with USNR, 1944-46. Clubs: Capital City, Piedmont Driving, Commerce. Office: Coca-Cola Co One Coca-Cola Pla NW Atlanta GA 30313

KEPPLER, WILLIAM EDMUND, multi-national company executive; b. N.Y.C., June 12, 1922; s. Louis and Amelia (Koszut) K.; m. Natalie E. Lang, July 15, 1944; children: Gail, William Edmund, Jean. B.S. in Chem. Engring, Pratt Inst., 1943; M.S. in Chem. Engring, N.Y. U., 1944. Vice pres. Merck Sharp & Dohme, West Point, Pa., 1965-71; Vice pres. Squibb Corp., Holmdel, N.J., 1971-73; pres. Bell Mgmt., Blue Bell, Pa., 1973-74, Engel Industries, St. Louis, 1974-75; sr. v.p. tech. ops./mgmt. systems Schering-Plough Corp., Kenilworth, N.J., 1975-87; pres. Bell Mgmt., Inc., 1987—; tchr. chem. engring. Cooper Union, N.Y. U., U. Bd. dirs. Phila. chpt. Am. Cancer Soc., 1979; pres. Montour County (Pa.) Cerebral Palsy, 1953-57. Fellow Am. Inst. Chem. Engrs.; mem. Am. Mgmt. Assn. Episcopalian. Club: Whitemarsh Valley Country (Lafayette, Pa.). Home: 773 Midway Ln Blue Bell PA 19422

KERLEY, JANICE JOHNSON, personnel executive; b. Coral Gables, Fla., Nov. 28, 1939; d. Howard Love and Lois Dean (Austin) Johnson; m. Bobby Joe Kerley, May 16, 1959; children: Janice Elisabeth Kerley Vela, Meredith Ann Kerley Tucker. AA, Stephens Coll., 1958; B in Music Edn., U. Miami, Fla., 1960. Tchr. Dade County Pub. Schs., Miami, 1960-69; asst. to v.p. engr. Racal-Milgo, Inc., Miami, 1972-80; dir. sales and mktg. B. Joe Kerley, Realtor, Miami, 1980-83; dir. customer service, ops. mgr. Modern-Age Furniture Co., Miami, 1983-85; chief exec. officer Adia Personnel Services, Greensboro, Winston-Salem, N.C., 1985—. Named Small Businessperson of Yr. Greensboro Area C. of C., 1988. Mem. Am. Bus. Women's Assn. (nat. bd. dirs. 1978-79, trustee nat. scholarship fund 1978-79, named one of top ten businesswomen, 1988). Office: Adia Personnel Services 315-B Pomona Dr Greensboro NC 27407 also: 4300 Indiana Ave Ste 35 Winston-Salem NC 27106

KERN, EDNA RUTH, insurance executive; b. Rochester, N.Y., Dec. 31, 1945; d. Carl H. and Mildred B. (Fronk) McRorie; m. Charles E. Kern, Nov. 1, 1968 (div. July 1975); 1 child, Barbara Renee. BBA summa cum laude, Tex. Wesleyan Coll., 1978. CLU; chartered fin. cons., registered health underwriter. Pvt. detective Statewide Detective Agy., Orlando, Fla., 1968-78; agt. Pacific Mut. Ins., Ft. Worth, 1978-79, Conn. Mut. Ins., Ft. Worth, 1979-83; gen. agt. Gen. Am. Life Ins., Ft. Worth, 1983-85; ins. owner Kern & Assocs., Ft. Worth, 1985—. Pres. All Saints Hosp. Execs. Forum, Ft. Worth, 1986-87; bd. dirs. YWCA, 1984-85. Mem. Ft. Worth Assn. Life Underwriters (bd. dirs. 1986—, moderator 1984-86, chmn. health com., chmn. edn. com. 1986—), Tarrant County Assn. Health Underwriters (pres. 1986-87), Sales and Mktg. Exec. Club (bd. dirs. 1985-87, v.p. 1986-87), Tex. Assn. Health Underwriters (state sec., bd. dirs. 1987-88, pres. 1988—), Mensa. Republican. Office: Kern & Assocs PO Box 331296 Fort Worth TX 76163

KERN, EUGENE FRANCIS, corporation executive; b. San Francisco, July 23, 1919; s. Eugene F. and Dorothy (Danforth) K.; m. Paula Stevenson, Oct. 3, 1942; children: Eugene, Tay, Kathy S.; m. 2d. Vida Del Fiorentino, June 10, 1964. AB, Stanford U., 1942. Wholesaleman, price clk. Tay Holbrook, Inc., Fresno, Calif., 1946-47, salesman, 1947-49; indsl. sales Tay Holdbrook, Inc., San Francisco, 1949-51, dir., 1951-64, asst. purchasing agt., 1951-57, corp. sec., 1952-64, mgr., 1957-60, gen. sales mgr., 1960-62, exec. v.p., 1961-62, dir. purchases, 1962-63, exec. v.p. sales, 1963-64; pres., dir. Par-Kern Supply, Inc., San Leandro, Calif., 1964—. Dir. San Francisco Employers Council, 1959-66. Served from 2d lt. to maj. AUS, 1942-45. Decorated Bronze Star. Mem. Western Suppliers Assn., No. Calif. Suppliers Assn. (treas. 1961-62, dir. 1961-63), Am. Arbitration Assn. (nat. panel arbitrators), Internat. Platform Assn., Nat. Assn. Wholesalers, Stanford Alumni Assn. Clubs: Olympic, Commonwealth, Stanford Buck. Home: 743 Parkway South San Francisco CA 94080 Office: 888 Carden St San Leandro CA 94577

KERN, FRANK NORTON, lawyer; b. Waymansville, Ind., Feb. 19, 1920; s. Frank W. and Irene (Everdon) K.; m. Minnetta Louise Wooden, Apr. 9, 1944; children—Cynthia Jennifer, Candace. B.A., Ohio Wesleyan U., 1941; M.B.A., Harvard, 1943, LL.B. cum laude, 1948. Admitted to Ohio bar, 1948, Pa. bar, 1953, N.Y. bar, 1956, D.C. bar, 1970; practiced in Cleve., 1948-51, N.Y.C., 1956—; asso. firm Squire, Sanders & Dempsey, Cleve., 1948-51; tax atty. U.S. Steel Corp., Pitts., 1951-54; partner charge tax dept. Reid & Priest, N.Y.C., 1955-80. Mem. Ohio Wesleyan U. Assos. and Investment Com., 1962—. Sr. warden Christ's Ch., Rye, N.Y., 1986—. Served to lt. with USNR, 1943-46. Mem. Am., Inter-Am. bar assns., Phi Beta Kappa. Republican. Episcopalian. Clubs: Metropolitan (Washington); Apawamis (Rye); Sky, Recess (N.Y.). Contbr. articles to profl. jours. Home: Puritan Rd Rye NY 10580 Office: 40 Wall St New York NY 10005

KERN, MARTIN H(AROLD), supermarket chain executive; b. Jersey City, Apr. 3, 1941; s. William and Harriett (Arendt) K. Student, Rutgers U. Vice pres. frozen food T-A Shop Rite Supermarkets div. Wakefern Food Corp., Elizabeth, N.J., 1959-65, v.p. dairy-deli, 1965-70; sr. v.p. mktg. Wakefern Food Corp., Elizabeth, N.J., 1970-80; pres., chief exec. officer Jetro Holdings, N.Y.C., 1980-82; exec. v.p. Gt. Atlantic & Pacific Tea Co., Montvale, N.J., 1982-88; pres. Diversified Resources, Inc., N.Y.C., 1988—; asst. prof. Kingsboro Community Coll.; pres. Supermarket Dist., Inc.; chmn. Supermarket Services, Inc.; bd. dirs. Memory Metals Inc., NASdAQ-MRMT, Diversified Foods Corp NASdAQ; chmn. Nat. Car Care, Inc. Contbr. numerous articles on food mktg. and distbn. to profl. jours. Active Park East Synagogue, N.Y.C., Israel Bonds Assn., Anti Defamation League, N.Y.C.; mem. Deborah Hosp.; pres. Mercox Landing Assn., Water Mill, N.Y. Served with USAFR, 1959-65. Recipient awards from trade assns., schs. Mem. Young Pres. Orgn. (bd.dirs.), Eastern Daily Deli Assn. (bd. dirs. 1970—, pres.), Eastern Frozen Food Assn. (dir. 1963-71), les Amis de Escoffier Soc. Home: 60 Sutton Pl S New York NY 10022 Office: Diversified Resources Inc New York NY 10022

KERN, RICHARD DAVIS, automobile executive, industrial engineer, real estate executive; b. Chester, Pa., Jan. 17, 1920; s. Henry Presley and Anna Violet Smith; m. Alison Louise Cooper, Aug 8, 1942 (dec. June 1955); children: Anne Kern Graham, Alison Kern Kaval, Richard Davis Jr.; m. Gertrude Deanmont Golightly, Aug. 15, 1958; 1 child, Todd Jeffery. Cert. in Indsl. Engring., Va. Poly. Inst., 1942. Registered profl. engr., Va. Indsl. engr. Am. Viscose, Frout Royal, Va., 1946; pres., chmn. bd. Kern Motor Co., Winchester, Va., 1946—, Shenandoah Pools, Inc., Winchester, 1958—, Kern Bros., Inc., Winchester, 1960—; bd. dirs. Commonwealth Dealers Ins., Fairfax, Va. Vice mayor, mem. council City of Winchester, 1977—. Maj. inf. U.S. Army, 1942-45. Mem. Nat. Auto Dealers Assn., Va. Auto Dealers Assn. (bd. dirs. 1985—), Winchester Auto Dealers Assn. (pres. 1963-85). Republican. Lutheran. Office: Kern Motor Co 2110 Valley Ave Winchester VA 22601

KERNER, FRED, book publisher, writer; b. Montreal, Can., Feb. 15, 1921; s. Sam and Vera (Goldman) K.; m. Jean Elizabeth Somerville, July 17, 1945 (div. Apr. 1951); 1 son, Jon Fredrik; m. Sally Dee Stouten, May 18, 1959; children: David, Diane. BA, Sir George Williams U., Montreal, 1942. Asst. sports editor Montreal Gazette, 1942-44; news editor Can. Press, Montreal, Toronto, N.Y.C., 1944-50; asst. night city editor A.P., N.Y.C., 1950-57; editor Hawthorn Books, Inc., N.Y.C., 1957-58, pres., 1965-68; exec. editor Crest-Premier Books, Fawcett World Libr., N.Y.C., 1958-63, editor-in-chief, 1963-65; pres. Centaur House, Inc. (pubs.), 1964-80, Paramount Securities Corp., 1965-67, Veritas Internat. Pubs., 1976—, Publishing Projects, Inc., 1967—; editorial dir. book and ednl. divs. Reader's Digest, Can., 1969-75; v.p., pub. dir. Harlequin Enterprises Ltd., 1975-83, editor emeritus, sr. cons. editor, 1984—; v.p. Publitex Internat. Corp. (pubs.), 1968-75; pres. Athabaska House, 1975-77; dir. Nat. Mint, Inc.; panelist various profl. confs.; chmn. Internat. Affairs Conf. Coll. Editors, 1965. Author: (with Leonid Kotkin) Eat, Think and be Slender, 1954, (with Walter M. Germain) The Magic Power of Your Mind, 1956, (with Joyce Brothers) Ten Days to a Successful Memory, 1957, Stress and Your Heart, 1961; pseudonym Frederick Kerr: Watch Your Weight Go Down, 1962, (with Walter M. Germain) Secrets of Your Supraconscious, 1965, (with David Goodman) What's Best for Your Child and You, 1966, (with Jesse Reid) Buy High, Sell Higher, 1966; (pseudonym M.H. Thaler) It's Fun to Fondue, 1968, (with Ion Grumeza) Nadia, 1977, Mad About Fondue, 1986, (with Andrew Willman) Prospering in the Coming Great Depression, 1988; contbg. author: Successful Writers and How They Work, 1958, Words on Paper, 1960, Overseas Press Club Cookbook, 1964, The Seniors' Guide to Life in the Slow Lane, 1986, Chambers's Ency.; books transl. into French, German, Japanese, Portuguese, Spanish and Italian; editor: Love is a Man's Affair, 1958, Treasury of Lincoln Quotations, 1965, The Canadian Writer's Guide, 9th edit., 1985, 10th edit., 1988; chmn. editorial adv. com. Can. Author & Bookman, 1978—, pub., 1986—. Mem. local sch. bd., N.Y.C., 1968-69; chmn. sch. com. Westmount High Sch., 1970-72; mem. sch. com. Roslyn Sch., 1973; chmn. pubs. com. Edward R. Murrow Meml. Fund; judge Dr. William Henry Drummond Nat. Poetry Contest; trustee Gibson Lit. Awards, C.A.A. Lit. awards, Benson & Hedges Lit. awards, CA&B Student Creative Writing awards; bd. govs. Concordia U., 1975-79; hon. life mem. Can. Book Pubs. Council; mem. exec. com. Pub. Lending Rights Commn., 1986-89, vice-chmn., 1988—; founding chmn. C.A.A. Fund to Develop Can. Writers, 1983-89. Fellow Can. Copyright Inst. (vice chmn.), Acad. Can. Writers (vice chmn., bd. govs. 1986—); mem. Orgn. Can. Authors and Pubs. (founding dir.), Can. Authors Assn. (v.p. 1972-80, founding dir. Lit. Luncheons, pres. Montreal br. 1974-75, nat. pres. 1982-83, hon. life), Periodical Writers' Assn. Can., Can. Writers' Found. (bd. govs. 1982—), Mystery Writers Am., Writers' Union Can. (grievance com.), Can. Soc. Profl. Journalists, Nat. Speakers Assn., Authors Guild, Authors League Am., Internat. P.E.N., Nat. Speakers Assn., Am. Acad. Polit. and Social Sci., Can. Assn. Restoration of Lost Positives (pres.), Can. Soc. for the Preservation of the Natural Bowtie (pres.), Sir George Williams U. Alumni Assn. (exec. com. 1970-75, pres. 1971-73), Sigma Delta Chi. Clubs: Advt., Deadline, Overseas Press, Dutch Treat (N.Y.C.); Toronto Men's Press; Author's (London). Home: 25 Farmview Crescent, Willowdale, ON Canada M2J 1G5 Office: PO Box 952, Station B, Willowdale, ON Canada M2K 2T5

KERR, DONALD MACLEAN, JR., physicist; b. Phila., Apr. 8, 1939; s. Donald MacLean and Harriet (Fell) K.; m. Alison Richards Kyle, June 10, 1961; 1 dau., Margot Kyle. B.E.E. (Nat. Merit scholar), Cornell U., 1963, M.S., 1964, Ph.D. (Ford Found. fellow, 1964-65, James Clerk Maxwell fellow 1965-66), 1966. Staff Los Alamos Nat. Lab., 1966-76, group leader, 1971-72, asst. div. leader, 1972-73, asst. to dir., 1973-75, alt. div. leader, 1975-76; dep. mgr. Nev. ops. office Dept. Energy, Las Vegas, 1976-77; acting asst. sec. def. programs Dept. Energy, Washington, 1978; dep. asst. sec. def. programs Dept. Energy, 1977-79, dep. asst. sec. energy tech., 1979; dir Los Alamos Nat. Lab., 1979-85; sr. v.p. EG&G, Inc., Wellesley, Mass., 1985-88, exec. v.p., 1988-89, pres., 1989—; mem. Navajo Sci. Com., 1974-77; mem. sci. adv. panel U.S. Army, 1975-78; mem. engring. advs. bd. U. Nev.-Las Vegas, 1976-78; chmn. com. research and devel. Internat. Energy Agy., 1979-85; mem. nat. security adv. council SRI Internat., 1980—; mem. adv. bd. U. Alaska Geophys. Inst., 1980-85; mem. sci. adv. group Joint Strategic Planning Staff, 1981—; mem. Naval Research Adv. Com., 1982-85; adv. bd. Georgetown U. Center Strategic and Internat. Studies, 1981-87; mem. corp. Charles Stark Draper Lab., 1982—; bd. dirs. Mirase Systems, Sunnyvale, Calif., 1988—. Published research on plasma physics, microwave electronics, ionospheric physics, energy and nat. security. Trustee New Eng. Aquarium, 1989—. Fellow AAAS; mem. Am. Phys. Soc., Am. Geophys. Union, Nat. Assn. Mfrs. (bd. dirs. 1986—), Southwestern Assn. Indian Affairs, World Affairs Coun. Boston (bd. dirs. 1988—), Sigma Xi, Tau Beta Pi, Eta Kappa Nu. Club: Cosmos (Washington). Office: EG&G Inc 45 William St Wellesley MA 02181

KERR, JOHN WARD, JR., public accountant; b. Fort Monroe, Va., July 30, 1937; s. John Ward and Florence (Bricker) K.; B.B.A., Old Dominion U., 1960; J.D., George Washington U., 1965; m. Carole Anne Alexander, Jan. 18, 1958; children—Katherine Lynne, John Ward III, Elizabeth Carole. CPA. Appellate conferee and field agt. IRS, Washington, 1960-65; tax mgr. Coopers & Lybrand, Richmond, 1965-69; tax mgr. Peat, Marwick, Mitchell & Co., Richmond, 1969-72; tax coord. J.K. Lasser & Co., Jacksonville, Fla., 1972-73; tax ptnr. Goodman & Co., Norfolk, Va., 1973-88 ; past mem. Va. State Bd. Accountancy; prof. taxation Old Dominion U., Norfolk, exec. in residence, Old Dominion U, 1988—, U. Va.; prof. real estate taxation U. Va. C.P.A., Va., Fla. Mem. Am. Inst. C.P.A.'s, Va. Soc. C.P.A.'s (past tax com. chmn.), Am., Va. bar assns., Nat. Assn. Accountants, Fed. Govt. Accountants Assn., Alpha Kappa Psi, Pi Kappa Alpha, Phi Alpha Delta. Presbyterian. Clubs: Harbor (Norfolk); Town Point; Kiwanis; Bull and Bear (Richmond). Home: 1160 Revere Point Rd Virginia Beach VA 23455 Office: Goodman & Co CPAs 234 Monticello Ave Ste 1100 Norfolk VA 23514

KERR, ROBERT WILLIAM, pipe fitting company executive; b. Corpus Christi, Tex., Feb. 10, 1945; s. Alfred Thomas and Lillian (Hester) K.; m. Paula Treff, Dec. 19, 1944; children: David, Lindsay. BA, Vanderbilt U., 1967. Salesman A.J. Smith Co., Nashville, 1969-74, Consol. Pipe and Supply Co. Inc., Nashville, 1974-75; br. mgr. Consol. Pipe and Supply Co. Inc., Houston, 1975-83; exec. v.p. Consol. Pipe and Supply Co. Inc., Birmingham, Ala., 1983—. Served as 1st lt. U.S. Army, 1967-69. Republican. Episcopalian. Clubs: Country Club Birmingham, Monday Morning Quarterback. Office: Consol Pipe & Supply Co Inc 1205 Hilltop Pkwy Birmingham AL 35204

KERR, WILLIAM STERLING, III, financial planner, investment advisor; b. Groveton, N.H., Aug. 26, 1939; s. William S. Kerr II and Hope (Houghton) Durow; m. Maria J. Sabino, Aug. 21, 1959; children: William IV, Mark, Scott. BEd, Plymouth State Coll., 1964; MA, U. Okla., 1966, PhD, 1970. Asst. prof. U. West Fla., Pensacola, 1970-74; salesperson Northwestern Mutual Life, Pensacola, 1974-75; adminstr. Travelers Ins. Co., Pensacola, 1975-78; planner fin. and sales E.F. Hutton Fin. Services, Pensacola, 1978-82, Granada Fin. Services, Houston, 1982-85; planner fin. and sales Sterling Kerr & Assocs., Houston, 1985-88, Sarasota, Fla., 1988—; cons. Shell Oil Co., Houston, 1983—, Dow Chem. Co., 1984-87. Author, nat. and internat. lectr. (workshop) Retirement Planning, 1985, (seminar) Investing Aging America, 1987; host weekly TV talk show, Sarasota; contbr. articles to profl. jours. and newsletters. Mem. endowment com. Sarasota Meml. Hosp. Found.; mem. Better Bus. Br., Houston, 1988. Served with USN, 1960-64. Gamma Theta Upsilon scholar U. Okla., 1969. Mem. Internat. Assn. Fin. Planning, Nat. Assn. Securities Dealers, Am. Men and Women of Sci., Inst. Cert. Fin. Planners, Registered Investment Advisors, Houston C. of C., Siesta Kay C. of C., Sigma Xi. Republican. Club: Hamilton (Houston).

KERRIGAN, WALTER W., II, financial planner; b. Pitts., May 6, 1953; s. Walter W. and Doris E. (Ward) K.; m. Susan F. Jagniszak, Apr. 8, 1978; 1 child, Kelly F. BA, U. Pitts., 1978. Cert. fin. planner. Chief exec. officer Inst. Fin. Planning, Dearborn, Mich., 1981—. Mem. Internat. Assn. Fin. Planners (bd. dirs. Southeast Mich. chpt. 1984-86, co-founder, pres., chmn. bd. dirs. Metro Detroit Soc. chpt. 1985-86), Nat. Assn. Personal Fin. Advisors, Inst. Cert. Fin. Planners, Am. Arbitration Assn. (comml. panel arbitrators). Republican. Presbyterian. Office: Inst Fin Planning Inc The Financial Pla 400 Town Center Dr Dearborn MI 48126

KERSCHNER, BARBARA BUCKLEY, real estate developer; b. Gainesville, Fla., Aug. 28, 1926; d. Rolf Kennard and Margaret Mabel (Crawford) Buckley; m. Nolan Kellerman Kerschner, Mar. 2, 1945; children: Steven Nolan, Amy Margaret, Andrew Buckley, Sarah Ivy. BS, Sacred Heart U., Conn., 1978. Treas. Nolan K. Kerschner Co. Inc., Norwalk, Conn., 1964—. Treas. Arts Coun. Norwalk, 1978-82, bd. dirs.; chmn. dist. E Dem. Com., 1983-87; mem. Norwalk Bd. Estimate and Taxation, 1984—; vice-chmn. Norwalk Dem. Town Com., 1988—, treas. 1984-88; bd. dirs. Norwalk Econ. Opportunity Now, Inc. Congregationalist. Home: 23 Split Rock Rd Norwalk CT 06854 Office: Kerschner Cos 5 Eversley Ave Norwalk CT 06851

KERSHAW, SHIRLEY ANN, financial analyst; b. Vallejo, Calif., Oct. 2, 1960; d. Dale and LaVon Mae (Case) K. AA, Edmonds Community Coll., 1982; BS, Brigham Young U., 1984. CPA. Pvt. practice Wash.; clk. accounts payable Contel of the Northwest, Bellevue, Wash., 1985-86; budget analyst Contel of the Northwest, Bellevue, 1986—. Mem. AICPA, Wash. Soc. CPA's, Brigham Young Univ. Mgmt. Soc., Lamda Delta Sigma. Mem. Ch. of Jesus Christ of Latter-Day Saints. Home: 18714 24th Ave SE Bothell WA 98012 Office: Contel of the Northwest 1745 114th Ave SE Ste 200 Bellevue WA 98004

KERSHAW, THOMAS ABBOTT, restaurant company executive; b. Phila., Dec. 1, 1938; s. Melville Gartside and Florence Frieda (Yackle) K.; B.S. in Mech. Engring., Swarthmore Coll., 1960; M.B.A., Harvard U., 1962. Mem. market devel. staff E.I. duPont de Nemours, Wilmington, Del., 1962-64; production mgr. Data Packaging Corp., Cambridge, Mass., 1964-65; owner Primus Assos., Warren, Vt., 1965-66; market devel. mgr. Bolt Beramek & Newman, Cambridge, 1966-69; pres. Exec. Townhouse Corp., Boston, 1969-81; pres. Hampshire House Corp., 1969—, Bull Finch Pub on Pickering Wharf, 1984—, Bull Finch Enterprises, 1985—. Pres., Beacon Hill Bus. Assn., 1979-84; bd. dirs. Beacon Hill Civic Assn.; Rep. ward chmn., vice chmn. city com., Eagle. Named Restauranteur of Year, Mass. Restaurant Assn., 1984.Chmn. bd. Greater Boston Conv. and Visitors Bur. Mem. Theater Dist. Assn., Harvard Bus. Sch. Assn., Nat. Restaurant Assn. (bd. dirs., chmn. polit. action com.), Mass. Restaurant Assn. (v.p.), Boston C. of C. Presbyterian. Clubs: Harvard (Boston, N.Y.C.); Union Boat, Corinthian Yacht. Home: 84 Beacon St Boston MA 02108

KERSTETTER, MICHAEL JAMES, manufacturing company executive; b. Spokane, Wash., Sept. 3, 1936; s. James B. and Ruth (Marquardt) K.; m. Eileen Virginia Behm, June 26, 1955; children: Michael Stuart, Steven Douglas. AA, Long Beach (Calif.) City Coll., 1957; BSCE, Calif. State U., Long Beach, 1962, MSCE, 1968. Registered structural engr., Ca., civil engr., Ca. Process engr. Aerojet-Gen., Downey, Calif., 1955-62; design engr.Aetron div. Aerojet-Gen., Covina, Calif., 1962-64; structural engr. C.F. Braun & Co., Alhambra, Calif., 1964-69, structural engr. section head, 1969-70; engr. Conrock Co., Los Angeles, 1970-72, asst. prodn. mgr., 1972-75, ops. mgr., 1975-79, v.p., 1979-84; exec. v.p., gen. mgr. ConAgg div. CalMat Co. (formerly Conrock Co.), Los Angeles, 1984—. Pack master Cub Scouts Am., West Covina, Calif., 1976; steering com. Boy Scouts Am. Troop 443, West Covina, 1977-79. Fellow Am. Concrete Inst. (pres. So. Calif. chpt. 1984-85), Inst. Advancement Engring.; mem. Structural Engrs. Assn. So. Calif. (sec. 1979-80), Nat. Ready Mixed Concrete Assn. (bd. dirs. 1985—), So. Calif. Rock Products Assn. (chmn. 1987—). Clubs: Jonathan (Los

Angeles); Glendora (Calif.) Country. Office: CalMat Co 3200 San Fernando Rd Los Angeles CA 90065

KERWIN, THOMAS HUGH, transportation company executive; b. Cleve., Oct. 8, 1930; s. Myron Louis and Gertrude Lillian (Schultz) K.; m. Idaclaire Herbst, Oct. 29, 1954; children: Charles Hugh, Michael Thomas. BS in Bus. Adminstrn., Kent State U., 1956; MBA, Case Western Res. U., 1964. Sr. fin. analyst Chesapeake & Ohio Ry. Co., Balt., 1964-68; mgr. fin. planning So. Ry. Co., Washington, 1970-72, dir. fin. planning, 1972-78, asst. v.p. fin. planning, 1978-81, v.p. fin., 1981-82; v.p., treas. Norfolk (Va.) So. Corp., 1982—; bd. dirs. Norfolk & Portsmouth Belt Line R.R. Co., R.R. Assn. Ins. Ltd., Hamilton, Bermuda, Advanced Telecommunications Corp., Transp. and R.R. Assurance Co. Ltd., Hamilton. Served with USN, 1953-55. Mem. Washington Soc. Security Analysts, Soc. for Indsl. Archaeology, Fin. Execs. Inst., Feldman Chamber Mus. Soc. Lodge: Rotary. Office: Norfolk So Corp 3 Commercial Pl Norfolk VA 23510-2191

KERWOOD, LEWIS O., trade associaton administrator; b. Warrensburg, Ill., Aug. 9, 1917; m. Frances Marie Jarrett, June 15, 1940; children: Susan Alane, Ronald, Joan, Jeffry. BEd in Commerce, Ill. State U., 1939; MS in Edn. Adminstrn., U. Ill., 1953. Tchr. adminstr. various Ill. high schs., 1939-42; asst. to gen. mgr. Allen & Kelley, V. Jobst & Sons, Decatur, Ill., 1942-43; dir. admissions, registrar U. Ill., Galesburg, 1946-50; dir. acad. evaluation U. Ill., Urbana, 1950-51, asst. dean faculty bus., 1951-54; dir. edn. and research Mortgage Bankers Assn. Am., Chgo., 1954-68; sr. dir., edn. mgr. Mortgage Bankers Assn. Am., Washington, 1968-78; exec. v.p. Nat. Soc. for Real Estate Fin., Washington, 1978—; cons. various cos., 1978—; exec. v.p. Nat. Consortium on Testing, 1982; adv. bd. Southern Meth. U., 1972-75, Internat. Real Estate Mktg. Info. Network, 1987—; vice-chmn. Dobson & Johnson, Nashville, Tenn., 1980—, vice-chmn. Author: Processing the Loan, Mortgage Loan Origination, Mortgage Loan Collections; editor: Mortgage Banking, 1965, Financing Income-Producing Real Estate, 1977. Pres. PTA, Villa Park, Ill., 1964-65; scoutmaster Sullivan Ill. troop Boy Scouts Am., 1940-42; bd. dirs. YMCA, Elmhurst, Ill. Lt. (j.g.) USN, 1943-46. Named Ky. Col., Gov. Ky. Mem. Nat. Soc. Real Estate Fin. (disting. fellow 1979, cert. real estate financier 1982), Rho Epsilon, Lambda Alpha. Office: Nat Soc Real Estate Fin 2300 M St Suite 800 Washington DC 20037

KESHIAN, RICHARD, lawyer; b. Arlington, Mass., Aug. 11, 1934; s. Hamayak and Takuhe (Malkesian) K.; m. Jacqueline C. Cannilla, Sept 11, 1965; children—Carolyn D., Richard M.. BS in Bus. Adminstrn., Boston U., 1956, JD, 1958. Bar: Mass. 1958. Pvt. practice law, Arlington, Mass., 1964-71; ptnr. Keshian & Reynolds, P.C., Arlington, 1971—; instr. law George Washington U., 1961-63; instr. real estate law Inst. Fin. Edn., 1976-80; instr. bus law George Washington U., Washington, 1961-63; mem. adv. bd. Coop. Bank Concord, Arlington, 1983-86; corporator Bank Five for Savs., Arlington, 1984—; bd. dirs., gen. counsel Arlington Coop. Bank, 1978-83. Chmn. Arlington Zoning Bd. Appeals, 1972-76; pres. Arlington C. of C., 1976; v.p. Mass. Fedn. Planning Bds., 1978-85; mem. Arlington Contributory Retirement Bd., 1984—. With USMC, 1958-64; maj. Res. ret. Mem. ABA, Mass. Bar Assn., Mass. Conveyancers Assn. (title standards com.), Mass. Assn. Bank Counsel, Middlesex County Bar Assn. Democrat. Congregationalist. Home: 93 Falmouth Rd W Arlington MA 02174 Office: 1040 Massachusetts Ave PO Box 440 Arlington MA 02174

KESISOGLU, GARBIS, publishing company executive; b. Istanbul, Turkey, June 27, 1936; came to Fed. Republic Germany, 1955; s. Serkis and Varvar (Norhadian) K.; m. Mari Demirhekim, Jan. 7, 1977. M.Sc., Tech. U. Munich, Fed. Republic Germany, 1960. Engr. A Kunz & Co., Munich, 1960-64, 1966-68; corr. Hurriyet Newspaper, Frankfurt, Fed. Republic Germany, 1968-71; mng. dir. Ege-Pub. Ltd., Frankfort, 1971-83, Ter-Pub. Ltd., Frankfurt, 1983-89; mng. dir. A.N.G. Ltd., Fed. Republic Germany, 1989—; bd. dirs. Media Print Co., Istanbul, Turkey. Served to lt. Turkish Army, 1964-66. Mem. Bavarian Journalists, Internat. Airline Passenges Assn. Dallas, Internat. Circulation Mfrs. Assn. Clubs: Press (Munich); Clipper, TWA Ambassador, Six Continents, Brit. Airways Exec. Home: Jakob Latscha Strasse 29, 6072 Dreieich 3 Federal Republic of Germany Office: ANG Print und Mktg GmbH, Admiral Rosendahl Str 3B, 6078 Neulsenburg 4 Federal Republic of Germany

KESSELER, ROGER LOUIS, controller, financial executive; b. Grayling, Mich., Sept. 27, 1936; s. George Jerome and Loretta Helena (Sorenson) K.; m. Phyllis Joan Ziebell, Aug. 10, 1957; children: Lisa Ann, Lori Ann, Michael Louis, Maureen Kay. BBA, Cen. Mich. U., 1958. Acct. The Dow Chem. Co., Midland, Mich., 1958-71; div. controller, mgr. employee relations The Dow Chem. Co., Freeport, Tex., 1971-79; mgr. corp. reporting The Dow Chem. Co., Midland, 1979-81, corp. controller, 1981—. Fin. chmn. Midland County Rep. Orgn., 1980-88; bd. dirs. Midland County Cancer Soc., 1982-88, Midland Hosp. Assn., 1984-88, Cen. Mich. U. Devel. Fund, Mt. Pleasant, Mich., 1985-88. Served as capt. USAR, 1958-66. Recipient Alumni Recognition award Alumni Assn. Cen. Mich. U., 1982; named Outstanding Alumni, Cen. Mich. U. Acctg. Soc., 1984. Mem. Nat. Assn. Accts. Roman Catholic. Office: Dow Chem Co 2030 Willard H Dow Ctr Midland MI 48674

KESSELMAN, THEODORE LEONARD, retired banker; b. Youngstown, Ohio, May 1, 1932; s. Leonard and Clara (Brailovsky) K.; m. Shirley Hope Cohen, June 14, 1953; children: Suzanne Lynn, Stuart Jonathan. AB magna cum laude, Harvard U., 1954, LLB, 1957. With Bankers Trust Co., N.Y.C., 1957-88; head adminstrv. services banking ops. Bankers Trust Co., 1965-66, v.p. in charge securities ops., 1966-68, asst. to exec. v.p., 1969-70, asst. to office of chmn., 1970-72, v.p., head strategic analysis div., 1972-73, 1st v.p., head corp. devel. dept., 1973-74, sr. v.p., 1974-79, exec. v.p., 1979-88; mem. panel arbitrators N.Y. Stock Exchange, N.Y. Futures Exchange. Bd. dirs., mem. exec. com. Arts and Bus. Council; trustee, mem. exec. com. Mus. Am. Folk Art; trustee, pres. N.Y. Youth Symphony; trustee Vineyard Theatre. Mem. ACLU, Harvard Law Sch. Assn., Phi Beta Kappa. Club: Harvard of N.Y.C. Jewish. Home: 193-40 McLaughlin Ave Holliswood NY 11423

KESSLER, A. D., business, financial, investment and real estate advisor, consultant, educator, lecturer, author; b. N.Y.C., May 1, 1923; s. Morris William and Belle Miriam (Pastor) K.; m. Ruth Schwartz, Nov. 20, 1944; children: Brian Lloyd, Judd Stuart, Earl Vaughn. Student U. Newark, 1940-41, Rutgers U., 1941-42, 46, Albright Coll., 1942, Newark Coll. Engring., 1946; MBA, Kensington U., 1976, PhD in Mgmt. and Behavioral Psychology, 1977. Sr. cert. rev. appraiser (CRA), cert. exchangor (CE); registered mortgage underwriter (RMU); registered investment advisor (RIA). Pvt. practice real estate, ins. and bus. brokerage, N.J., Pa., Fla., N.Y., Nev., Calif., Hong Kong, 1946—; pres. Armor Corp. , 1947-68; pres. Folding Carton Corp., Am., N.Y.C., 1958-68; exec. v.p. Henry Schindall Assocs., N.Y.C., 1966-67; tax rep. Calif. State Bd. Equalization, 1968-69; aviation cons. transp. div. Calif., Dept. Aeros., also pub. info. officer; 1969-71; FAA Gen. Aviation Safety Counselor; broker, mgr. La Costa (Calif.) Sales Corp., 1971-75; chmn. bd. Profl. Ednl. Found., 1975—, Timeshare Resorts Internat., 1975—, Interex, Leucadia, Calif., 1975-82, The Kessler Orgn., Rancho Santa Fe, Calif., 1975—, The Kessler Fin. Group, Fin. Ind. Inst., 1977—; pres. Ednl. Video Inst., 1978—, Fin. Planning Inst., 1975—, Rancho Santa Fe Real Estate & Land, Inc., 1975—; treas., exec. bd. dirs. Nat. Challenge Com. on Disability, 1983—; dir. Practice Mgmt. Cons. Abacus Data Systems, 1984—; broker mgr. Rancho Sante Fe Acreage & Homes, Inc., 1987—; mktg. dir. Commercial Real Estate Services, Rancho Sante Fe, 1987—; cons. broker Glenct. Properties Ptnrs., 1989—; publisher, editor in chief Creative Real Estate Mag., 1975—; publisher Creative Real Estate Mag. of Australia and New Zealand; founder, editor Moderator of Tape of the Month Club; founder, producer, chmn. Internat. Real Estate Expo; chmn. bd. The Brain Trust, Rancho Santa Fe, Calif., 1977—; fin. lectr. for Internat. Cruise Ships, Cunard Line, Norwegian Am. Cruises, others; lectr. life enrichment and stress mgmt. Internat. Cruise Ships; Calif. adj. faculty, prof. fin. Clayton U., St. Louis. Scoutmaster Orange Mountain council Boy Scouts Am., 1955-62; harbor master N.J. Marine Patrol, 1958-67; dep. sheriff, Essex County, N.J., 1951-65. Served with USAF, 1942-45. Decorated D.F.C., Air medal, Purple Heart; named to French Legion of Honor, Order of Lafayette. Mem. Am. Soc. Editors and Publishers, Author's Guild, Internat. Platform Assn., Nat. Speakers Assn., Nat. Press Photographers Assn., Guild Assn. Airport Execs., Aviation and Space Writers Assn., Nat. Assn. of Real Estate Editors (NAAREE), Internat. Exchangors Assn. (founder), Nat. Press Club, Overseas Press Club. Clubs: La Costa Country, Cuyamaca, Rancho Santa Fe Country, Passport. Lodges: Masons, Shriners. Author: A Fortune At Your Feet, 1981, How You Can Get Rich, Stay Rich and Enjoy Being Rich, 1981, Financial Independence, 1987, The Profit, 1987; author and inst. "Your Key to Success" seminar, 1988; editor: The Real Estate News Observer, 1975—; fin. editor API, 1978—; fin. columnist Money Matters, 1986—; syndicated columnist, radio and tv host of "Money Making Ideas," 1977—; songwriter: Only You, 1939, If I'm Not Home For Christmas, 1940, Franny, 1940, Flajaloppa, 1940, They've Nothing More Dear Only They've Got It Here, 1941, The Summer of Life, 1956; producer (movies) The Flight of the Cobra, Rena, We Have Your Daughters, Music Row; speaker for radio and TV as The Real Estate Answerman, 1975—; host (radio and TV show) Ask Mr. Money. Inventor swivel seat, siptop, inflatumbrella. Home: Box 1144 Rancho Santa Fe CA 92067

KESSLER, BRUCE ALLEN, marketing executive. BA in Econs., U. Kans., 1973, MBA, 1976. Sales mgr. Oppenheimer Industries, Inc., Kansas City, Mo., 1976-78; investment cons. Coldwell Banker Comml. Brokerage, Kansas City, 1978-80; v.p., mgr. B.C. Christopher Securities Co., Kansas City, 1980-84; v.p. mktg. U.S. Shelter Corp., Dallas, 1985; nat. sales mgr. Available Self-Storage Corp., Dallas, 1986; asst. v.p. Stern Bros., Kansas City, 1987; Western Plains States regional mktg. dir. V.J. McGuinness & Assocs., Corona del Mar, Calif., 1987—. Home and Office: 9222 W 73d #201 Merriam KS 66204

KESSLER, JUDD STUART, financial executive; b. Orange, N.J., Dec. 17, 1952; s. A.D. and Ruth (Schwartz) K.; m. Andrea Carol Welch, Feb. 14, 1982; 1 child, Alexander Judson. BA, U. Calif., San Diego, 1972. Cert. fin. planner. Real estate broker Calif., 1972—; pres. Space Bldg. Assn., Carlsbad, Calif., 1972-75; dir. mktg. Profl. Ednl. Found., Carlsbad, 1976-80; pres. Timeshares Resorts Internat., Carlsbad, 1980-82, Abacus Data Systems, Inc., Del Mar, Calif., 1983—, Kessler Fin. Group, Del Mar, Calif., 1987—. Patentee computer software. Recipient Commendation award Fin. Products Standards Bd., 1986. Mem. Internat. Assn. Fin. Planning, Inst. Cert. Fin. Planners (fin. writer's award 1984). Republican. Home: Box 8873 Rancho Santa Fe CA 92067 Office: 2775 Via De La Valle Ste 101 Del Mar CA 92014

KESSLER, LAURENCE, chain restaurant executive; b. N.Y.C., Oct. 25, 1942; s. David and Mollie (Havio) K.; m. Judith Lenore Lesk, Dec. 25, 1966; children: Reeca, Jonathan. BA, Adelphi U., 1965. V.p. Thompson McKinnon, 1973-74; pres. Kessler Group, Inc. (17 Burger King franchises), Rochester, N.Y., 1975—; mem. Bus. and Mktg. Planning Council, Burger King Corp., Miami, Fla. Bd. dirs. Jewish Community Ctr., Rochester, 1986, Jewish Family Service, Rochester, 1986, Hillel Found., Rochester, 1986, Kidney Found. Upstate N.Y., 1986; treas. com. Jewish Community Fedn., Rochester, 1986-87, bd. dirs., ARC Rochester region. Office: Kessler Group Inc 410 White Spruce Blvd Rochester NY 14623

KESSLER, LAWRENCE W., scientist, scientific instrument company executive; b. Chgo., Sept. 26, 1942; s. Michael C. and Sue (Sniader) K.; m. Francesca Agramonte, Nov. 30, 1985; children: Jeffrey, Brett, Corey, Brandy, Lindsay. BSEE, Purdue U., 1964; MS, U. Ill., 1966, PhD, 1968. Mem. rsch. staff Zenith Radio Corp., Chgo., 1968-74; pres. Sonoscan, Inc., Bensenville, Ill., 1975—; adj. prof. info. engring., U. Ill., Chgo., 1978-81; organizer 7th Internat. Symposium Acoustical Imaging and Holography, 1976, 16th Internat. Symposium on Acoustical Imaging, June 1987; mem. statutory adv. com. FDA, 1973-75. Editor: Procs. Ultrasonics Symposium, IEEE, Inc. 1970; Acoustical Holography, Vol. 7, 1977, Vol. 16, 1988; contbr. articles to tech. jours. Patentee acoustical microscopy, Bragg diffraction imaging, also liquid crystal device. Fellow Acoustical Soc. Am.; sr. mem. IEEE (sec.-treas. sonics and utrasonics div. 1969-71, pres. div. 1971-73, nat. lectr. 1981-82); mem. Am. Inst. Ultrasound in Medicine, Am. Soc. Non-destructive Testing, Sigma Xi, Eta Kappa Nu. Home: 543 Rutgers Ln Elk Grove Village IL 60007 Office: Sonoscan Inc 530 E Green St Bensenville IL 60106

KESSLER, MILTON, manufacturing executive; b. E. Pitts., Nov. 2, 1917; s. Harry and Rose (Hirsch) K.; m. Justine Levy, Nov. 16, 1947; children—Ronald N., Kathyann, Wendy, Brian. Pres., Kessler Products Co., Inc., Youngstown, Ohio, 1940—, Kessler Inc., Youngstown, 1955—, Dover Molded Products (Ohio), 1958—, Youngstown Kitchens, 1975—, Anderson (S.C.) Textile, 1974—; chmn. bd. Space Links, Youngstown, 1975—, Youngstown Thermal Inc., 1981—, Thermal Resources Ohio, Thermal Resources St. Louis, Thermal Resources Balt. Bd. dirs. Heritage Manor, Youngstown, 1960. Mem. Am. Mgmt. Assn., Young Pres. Orgn., Youngstown C. of C., Soc. Plastics Industry, Soc. Plastics Engrs. Republican. Jewish. Clubs: Squaw Creek Country (dir. 1977), B'nai B'rith, Masons (32d degree). Inventor in field. Home: 6690 Harrington St Boardman OH 44512 Office: 302 McClurg Rd Youngstown OH 44512

KESSLER-HODGSON, LEE GWENDOLYN, actress; b. Wellsville, N.Y., Jan. 16, 1947; d. James Hewitt and Reba Gwendolyn (Adsit) Kessler; m. Bruce Gridley, June 22, 1969 (div. Dec. 1979); m. Jeffrey Craig Hodgson, Oct. 31, 1987. BA, Grove City Coll., 1968; MA, U. Wis., 1969. Prof. Sangamon State U., Springfield, Ill., 1969-70; personnel exec. Bullock's, Los Angeles, 1971-74; owner Brunnen Enterprises, Los Angeles, 1982—. Author: A Child of Arthur, 1981; producer, writer play including Anais Nin: The Paris Years, 1986; actress appearing in TV movies, mini-series including Roots, 1978, Backstairs at The White House, 1979, Blind Ambition, 1980, Hill Street Blues, 1984-87, Murder By Reason of Insanity, 1985, Hoover, 1986, Creator, 1987, Our House, 1988, Favorite Son, 1988, Lou Grant 1983, 84, Barney Miller, 1979, 80, numerous others. Knapp Prize fellow U. Wis., 1969. Mem. Screen Actors Guild, Actors Equity Assn., AFTRA. Republican. Mem. Ch. Scientology. Home: 1527 Adele Pl Thousand Oaks CA 91366

KESTLER, JOSEPH ALLEN, business owner; b. Washington, Aug. 12, 1945; s. Joseph Adam and Alma Rita (McGuire) K. Grad. high sch. Apprentice jewelry engraver I.B. Goodman Mfg. Co., Cin., 1964-65; postal carrier U.S. Postal Svc., Groesbeck, Ohio, 1966-68; owner Kestler's Grooming, Cin., 1968—. Tchr. St. Aloysius Council Christian Doctrine, Bridgetown, Ohio, 1987—; mem. econ. devel. council Western Hamilton County; advocate Hamilton County Park Dist., 1987-88. Mem. Nat. Dog Grooming Assn., Am. Theatre Organ Soc., Ancient Order of Hibernians (chmn. cath. action, treas., chmn. missions 1975-88). Democrat. Mem. United Ch. of Christ. Home: 3631 Puhlman Ave Cheviot OH 45211 Office: Kestlers Grooming 5530 Bridgetown Rd Cincinnati OH 45248

KESTLER, MAXIMILIANO, television company executive, lawyer, educator; b. San Felipe, Guatemala, June 6, 1919; s. Maximiliano and Silda (Farnes) K.; m. Maria Teresa Amparo Morán, June 25, 1955; children: Maximiliano, Eduardo Cristián. Atty. and Notary, U. San Carlos, Guatemala, 1950; cert. internat. law, Internat. Tng. Centre, Strasbourg, France, 1975. Prof. law and social sci. U. San Carlos, 1952-56, U. Rafael Landivar, 1961-64, U. Francisco, Marroquín, Guatemala, 1966-79; vice-minister fgn. affairs Guatemala, 1961-66; pres. Radiotelevisión Guatemala-Channel 3, Guatemala City, 1981—; advisor various Guatemalan fin. instns.; rep., chief ambassador Mission of Guatemala to UN, 1966; dir. Sch. Internat. Relations Guatemala Ministry Fgn. Affairs, 1974—. Author: Introduction to Guatemalan Constitutional Law, 1950 (Gold Medal 1951). Mem. Com. to Eradicate Illiteracy in Guatemala. Recipient Civil Order Merit Govt. of Spain, 1962, Grand Cross Republic of Chile, 1963, Estrella Brillante Republic of China, 1961, Grand Cross of Disting. Service Govt. Peru, 1965, Order Aztec Eagle, Govt. Mexico, 1966, Order San Silvestre Pope John Paul II, 1981, Grand Cross Honor al Mérito Antonio José de Irisarri Republic of Guatemala, 1988. Mem. Guatemalan Assn. Internat. Law (exec. dir. 1964—), Phi Delta Phi. Home: Fourth Ave 20-44, Zone 14, Guatemala City Guatemala Office: Canal 3-Radio-TV Guatemala, 30 Avenida 3-40, Zona 11 Apartado 1376, Guatemala City Guatemala

KESTLER, THOMAS RICHARD, financial planner; b. Avalon, N.J., Jan. 25, 1952; s. T. Richard and Jeanne (Holmes) K.; m. Deborah Henley, Dec. 10, 1972 (div. Dec. 1978); 1 child, Jason Andrew; m. Lesa Hockersmith; children: Kevin Thomas, Jacqueline Christine. BA, Millersville U., 1973. Sales mgr. Penncorp Fin. Inc., Silver Spring, Md., 1977-80, IMS Svcs. Corp., Falls Church, Va., 1980-81; pres. Asset Mgmt., Inc., Mechanicsburg, Pa., 1981—; dir. agys. Consumers Life Ins. Co., Camp Hill, Pa., 1984-86; adj. instr. Wilson Coll., Chambersburg, Pa., 1988, Coll. Fin. Planning, Denver, 1988. Mem. Internat. Brotherhood Cert. Fin. Planners, Internat. Assn. Fin. Planning, Internat. Assn. Registered Fin. Planners. Home: 6350 S Powderhorn Rd Mechanicsburg PA 17055 Office: Asset Mgmt Inc 5170 E Trindle Rd Ste 101 Mechanicsburg PA 17055

KETCHA, NICHOLAS JOSEPH, JR., financial executive; b. Peckville, Pa., May 12, 1943; s. Nicholas and Emma Rose (Sanchini) K.; B.S. in Bus. Mgmt. cum laude, U. Scranton, 1965; grad. Stonier Grad. Sch. Banking, Rutgers U., 1978; m. Marianne Regina Farrell, July 27, 1968; children—Romayne, Jeanne Marie. Bank examiner FDIC, N.Y.C., 1965-67, sr. asst. bank examiner, 1969, bank examiner, 1970-72, sr. bank examiner, 1972-74, head bank examiner, 1974-77, sr. head bank examiner, 1977-78, review examiner EDP, 1978-79, 80-82, acting asst. regional dir. N.Y. region, 1982-83, asst. regional dir., 1983-84, spl. asst. to dir. acctg. and corp. services, 1984-86, assoc. dir. fin. services br., 1986-88, dir. N.Y. region, N.Y.C., 1988—; project cons. electronic data processing audit Tenneco, Inc., Houston, 1979-80; instr. FDIC Tng. Ctr., Rosslyn, Va., 1971-79, Inst. Internal Auditors, 1980; mem. faculty Stonier Grad. Sch. Banking, Rutgers U., 1979-83, Nat. Sch. Savs. Banking, Fairfield U., 1981-82; participant President's Exec. Exchange Program, 1979-80. Served with USN, 1967-68. Cert. info. systems auditor. Republican. Roman Catholic. Home: 12507 Chasbarb Terr Fox Mill Estates Herndon VA 22071 Office: FDIC 452 Fifth Ave New York NY 10018

KETCHAM, ALLEN FRANCIS, managememt consultant; b. Kalamazoo, Mich., Dec. 6, 1945; s. Allen D. and Frances I. Ketcham; BS, Ind. U., 1973; MEd, U. Ariz., 1975, PhD, 1982; MBA, Corpus Christi State U., 1983, MA Tex. A&I U., 1989; nat. fellow, Hoover Instn., Stanford U., 1985-86; m. Gale S. Stuart, May 3, 1980; children—Damian, Thane. Dir., Modal Analytics Co., Tucson, 1977-81; dir. Ketcham & Assocs., Inc., Corpus Christi, Tex., 1981—, asst. prof. bus., Tex. Agrl. & Indsl. U., Kingsville, 1986-87. assoc. faculty psychology Pima Coll., Tucson, 1976-79. Vice-chmn. transp. com. Coastal Bend Council Govts., 1979-81; mem. adv. council Coastal Bend Area Agy. on Aging, 1982; mem. profl. adv. bd. Concepts of Care, Inc., 1983—. Mem. Nueces Psychol. Assn., Comparative and Internat. Edn. Soc., Am. Mktg. Assn., S.W. Mktg. Assn. Republican. Episcopalian. Contbg. author Hoover Instn. on War, Revolution and Peace; contbr. articles to profl. jours.; author geometric content analysis method for markets. Office: CBA Tex A&I U PO Box 187 Kingsville TX 78363

KETCHERSID, WAYNE LESTER, JR., hospital laboratory administrator, chemist, consultant; b. Seattle, Oct. 16, 1946; s. Wayne Lester and Hazel May (Greene) K.; m. Wilette LaVerne Mautz, Oct. 6, 1972; 1 son, William Les. BS in Biology Pacific Luth. U., 1976, BS in Med. Tech. , 1978, MS in Adminstrn. Cen. Mich. U., 1989. Cert. clin. lab. scientist. Staff technologist Tacoma Gen. Hosp., 1978-79, chemistry supr., 1979-81, head chemistry, 1981-83; head chemistry Multicare Med. Ctr., 1984-86, mgr., 1986—. Mem. Nat. Rep. Com. Served with U.S. Army, 1966-68. William E. Slaughter Found. scholar, 1975-76. Mem. Am. Assn. Clin. Chemistry, Am. Hosp. Assn., Am. Soc. Med. Tech. (cert.; chmn. region IX adminstrn. 1984—, nat. del. 1984—), Wash. State Soc. Med. Tech. (chmn. biochemistry sect. 1983-86 dist. pres. 1986—, cert. merit 1983, 84, 86, 88, pres.-elect 1988-89, pres. 1989—), Am. Soc. Clin. Pathologists (med. technolgist), N.W. Med. lab. Symposium (chmn. 1986-88, 90), Internat. Platform Assn. Lutheran. Contbr. articles to profl. jours. Office: Multicare Med Ctr 315 S K St Tacoma WA 98405

KETELSEN, JAMES LEE, diversified industry executive; b. Davenport, Ia., Nov. 14, 1930; s. Ernest Henry and Helen (Schumann) K.; children: James V., Lee. B.S., Northwestern U., 1952. C.P.A., Tex., Ill. Accountant Price Waterhouse & Co. (C.P.A.s), Chgo., 1955-59; v.p. finance, treas. J.I. Case Co., Racine, Wis., 1962-68; pres., chief exec. officer J.I. Case Co., 1968-72; exec. v.p. Tenneco Inc., Houston, 1972—; chmn. bd., chief exec. officer Tenneco Inc., 1978—, also dir.; dir. J.P. Morgan & Co., Sara Lee Corp., GTE Corp., Alliance for Free Enterprise, Houston C. of C., Exec. Council on Fgn. Diplomats. Mem. Pres.' Bd. of Advisors on Pvt. Sector Initiatives, Com. for Econ. Devel.; bd. dirs. Am. Petroleum Inst.; trustee Northwestern U., Conf. Bd. Served to lt. USNR, 1952-55. Mem. Nat. Petroleum Council, Bus. Roundtable, Chi Psi. Clubs: River Oaks Country (Houston), Petroleum (Houston). Office: Tenneco Inc 1010 Milam St PO Box 2511 Houston TX 77002 also: Monroe Auto Equipment Co 1 International Dr Monroe MI 48161

KETNER, RALPH WRIGHT, retail food company executive; b. Salisbury, N.C., Sept. 20, 1920; s. George Robert and Effie Viola (Yost) K.; m. Ruth Jones, Aug. 1, 1947; children: Linda, Robert; m. Anne Blizzard, Mar. 22, 1980. BS in Bus., Tri-State Coll., 1939; D (hon.), Tri-State U., 1984, Catawba Coll., 1983. Auditor Cannon Mills Co., Kannapolis, N.C., 1939-42; gen. mgr. Excel Grocery, Salisbury, 1950-56; head grocery buyer Winn Dixie Co., Raleigh, N.C., 1956-57; pres., treas. Food Town Stores Inc., Salisbury, 1957-81; chmn. bd., chief exec. officer, treas. Food Town Stores Inc. (now Food Lion, Inc.), Salisbury, 1981-86, chmn. bd., 1986—; v.p. Save-Rite, Inc., 1986; bd. dirs. Security Bank and Trust Co., Rose's Inc., N.C. Transp. History Corp.; exec.-in-residence Catawba Coll., Salisbury. Holder copyright on inventory form. Mem. adv. bd. Salvation Army; N.C. Job Tng. Coordinating Coun.; past bd. dirs. Rowan County (N.C.) Vocat. Rehab., mem. adv. com. distbrv. edn., N.C., mem. N.C. adv. bd.; hon. life mem. DECA; trustee N.C. Devel. Fund, 4-H Clubs, Catawba Coll.; bd. dir. N.C. Crime Prevention; bd. dirs. Nat. 4H Coun., 4H Devel. Bd.; bd. mgrs. Nazareth Children's Home. With U.S. Army, 1942-47. Recipient N.C. Grocery of Yr. award, 1972-73, Chief Exec. Officer Gold award Wall St. Transcript; named N.C. Retailer of Yr., 1977; Paul Harris fellow. Mem. VFW, Salisbury-Rowan C. of C. (past dir.), Nat. Grocers Assn. (bd. dirs. 1985—), N.C. Food Dealers (past pres., dir.), Mchts. Assn. (past pres.), Am. Legion, Spencer Hist. Assn. (bd. dirs.). Presbyterian (elder). Club: Asparagus. Lodges: Rotary (bd. dirs. local chpt. 1980-83), Lions (hon. 1984—, Named Man of Yr. 1985), Elks, Moose. Home: 936 Confederate Ave Salisbury NC 28144 Office: Food Lion Inc PO Box 1330 Harrison Rd Salisbury NC 28145-1330

KETOVER, PHILIP STEVEN, publisher, fundraiser; b. Bklyn., Sept. 20, 1952; s. Lawrence Robert and Irene (Varcoe) K.; m. Janet Lee Martz, Sept. 23, 1977; children: Fame Justin, Rheannon Dian-Joy. BS in Psychology and Zoology, Colo. State U., 1978. Dir. WorldWide Animal Import, Calif. and N.Y., 1970-75; cons. Saleh Industries, Mombasa, Kenya, 1980-82; pvt. practice research ethologist Colo. and Kenya, 1977-82; dir. The Bush Art Gallery, Marco Island, Fla., 1982-84; pub. Sun-News, Marco Island, 1983—; exec. dir. Serving For Hunger, Marco Island, 1984—; pres. Woldwide Animal Relief, Naples, Fla., 1986—; pres., chief exec. officer Sweet Annie's Ice Cream, 1986—, Starburgers, 1988—. Author: Going Home for the First Time, 1988; producer Amazing Marco Post Card Video, 1987; TV producer, Fla. Rev., 1986; contbr. articles to AP, various pubs. U.S.A., Europe, Africa. Mem. Marco Island Merchants Assn. (pres. 1986), Nat. Wildlife Fedn., Animal Relief Group, U.S. Pro Tennis Assn., Internat. Platform Assn., Fla. Tennis Assn., Hideaway Beach Assn., East African Wildlife Assn. Jewish. Office: Sun-Daze Prodns Inc 692 Bald Eagle Dr Marco Island FL 33937

KETT, HERBERT JOSEPH, drug store chain executive; b. Queens Village, N.Y., Apr. 3, 1933; s. Herbert and Rose A. (Coyle) K.; m. Patricia M. Campbell, Aug. 29, 1953; children: Kathleen, Kevin, Eileen. BS in Pharmacy, St. John's U., 1954, D in Comml. Sci. (hon.), 1979; MBA, N.Y. Inst. Tech., 1975. Registered pharmacist N.Y., Conn., Mass.; lic. real estate broker, N.Y. From pharmacist to sr. v.p. Genovese Drug Stores, Inc., Melville, N.Y., 1953—, also bd. dirs.; adj. prof. Coll. Pharmacy and Allied Health Professions Grad. div. St. John's U., 1976-78, 83—; mem. N.Y. State Bd. Pharmacy, 1975—, chmn. 1983-84, hearing and discipline officer, 1985; mem. com. for profl. assistance N.Y. State Dept. Edn., 1983—; adv. council chain drug stores Roche Labs., 1975—; pharm. adv. council E.R. Squibb, Inc., 1985—; pharmex adv. bd. Automatic Bus. Products Co., 1979-81; chain store rep. pharmacy adv. com. N.Y. State Dept. Social Services, 1975-80; adv. bd. Empire Am. Fed. Savs. Bank, 1986-87. Trustee L.I. div. Arthritis Found., 1982—; chmn. bd. trustees L.I. div. Medic Alert Found. Internat., 1982-83. Recipient John Collier award Bus. and Fin., 1972, Pietas award St. John's U., 1978, Upjohn award, 1980, Harold W. Pratt award, 1987 Nat.

Assn. Chain Drug Stores, 1980. Mem. N.Y. Acad. Pharmacy (trustee), Pharm. Soc. State N.Y. (impaired pharmacist adv. bd. 1986—), Am. Pharm. Assn., Nat. Cath. Pharmacists Guild, Delta Mu Delta. Lodge: Knights of Malta. Office: Genovese Drug Stores Inc 80 Marcus Dr Melville NY 11747

KETTERER, KENNETH CHARLES, human resources executive; b. Pitts., Oct. 27, 1929; s. Edward T. and Julia P. (Booth) K. BBA, U. Pitts., 1961; postgrad., Marquette U., 1970-71, U. Wis., 1977. Various positions PPG Industries, Inc., Pitts., Milw., Houston, and Oak Creek, Wis., 1966-80; dir. personnel Doerr Electric Corp. mfg. group W.W. Grainger Co., 1980-83; v.p. human resources Wackenhut Corp., Coral Gables, Fla., 1983—. Capt USAF, 1961-66. Home: 14005 SW 72d Ct Coral Gables FL 33158 Office: Wackenhut Corp 1500 Sam Remo Ave Coral Gables FL 33146

KETTERINGHAM, JOHN M., corporate executive; b. Bournemouth, Dorset, Eng., Mar. 9, 1940; arrived in U.S., 1964; s. Albert James and Margaret Lilian (Grimshaw) K.; m. Susan M. Pattisson, Aug. 4, 1964; children: Emma, Caryn, Michael. BA, Oxford U., Eng., 1961, MA, 1964, PhD, 1964. Profl. staff Arthur D. Little Inc., Cambridge, Mass., 1964-76, v.p., 1976-86, sr. v.p., 1986—; bd. dirs. Cambridge Cons. Ltd., Eng., Opinion Research Corp., Princeton, N.J. Author: Breakthroughs, 1986; contbr. chpt. Competitive Strategic Mgmt., 1984, Artificial Lungs, 1978. Mem. AAAS, Am. Mgmt. Assn., Am. Soc. Artificial Internal Organs. Republican. Club: Parkstone Yacht (Poole, Eng.). Office: Arthur D Little Inc 25 Acorn Pk Cambridge MA 02140

KEUCK, LEROY LYLE, personnel executive; b. Moville, Iowa, Feb. 1, 1937; s. Frederick Christian Albert and Juanita Audrey (Dragoo) K.; m. Diane Dale Hanlen, June 16, 1973; children: Toni Marie Crutchfield, Nikki Leigh, Jodi Lynn. BS, U. Wyo., 1965; MBA, Baldwin-Wallace Coll., 1982. Programming supr. Wyo. Hwy. Dept., Cheyenne, 1964-65; mathematician RCA Corp., Cape Kennedy, Fla., 1965-66; programmer, analyst Firestone Tire and Rubber Corp., Akron, Ohio, 1966-70; mgr. mgmt. info. systems Babcock & Wilcox, Barbeton, Ohio, 1970-83; dir. mgmt. info. svcs. Brockway Inc., Jacksonville, Fla., 1983-88; pres. Dunhill Search of Jacksonville, 1988—; bd. dirs. Info. Mgmt. Inst. of Jacksonville. Mem. adv. com. U. N. Fla., Jacksonville, 1987—. Republican. Lutheran. Home: 455 20th St Atlantic Beach FL 32233 Office: Dunhill Search of Jacksonville 645 Mayport Rd Ste 3D Atlantic Beach FL 32233

KEULER, ROLAND LEO, shoe company executive; b. Kiel, Wis., Aug. 28, 1933; s. Joseph N. and Christina (Woelfel) K.; m. Shirley Ann Johst, June 22, 1957; children: Suzanne Marie, Catherine Ann, David Richard, Carolyn Marie, Brian John and Barbara Jean (twins). BS in Acctg., Marquette U., 1959. CPA, Wis. Acct. Arthur Andersen & Co., Milw., 1959-65; sec.-treas. Napco Graphic Arts, Inc., Milw., 1965-70; controller Weyenberg Shoe Mfg. Co., Milw., 1970-72, treas., 1972—, sec., 1986—; cons. Project Bus., Milw., 1977-84. Served with U.S. Army, 1954-56. Mem. Am. Inst. CPA's, Wis. Inst. CPA's, Beta Gamma Sigma, Beta Alpha Psi. Roman Catholic. Home: 720 W Fairfield Ct Glendale WI 53217 Office: Weyenberg Shoe Mfg Co 234 E Reservoir Ave PO Box 1188 Milwaukee WI 53201

KEY, DAVID MCKENDREE, investment banker, agricultural economist; b. Washington, Jan. 10, 1954; s. Albert Lenoir and Julia (Browdoin) K.; m. Robin Mack, Jan. 8, 1977; children: Mckendree, Lindsay, Ely. BS, U. Vt., 1977; MS, Cornell U., 1984. County agrl. agt. USDA extension, U. Vt., Brattleboro, 1976-80; asst. v.p. Farm Credit Banks Funding Corp., N.Y.C., 1982-85; v.p. Agricapital Corp., N.Y.C., 1985—. Contbr. articles on dairy prodn. and mktg. activities to numerous publs. Mem. Am. Soc. Farm Mgrs. and Rural Appraisers. Republican. Home: 64 Jane St New York NY 10014 Office: Agricapital Corp 420 Lexington Ave Ste 1925 New York NY 10170

KEY, STEPHEN LEWIS, financial services company executive; b. N.Y.C., June 26, 1943; s. Theodore and Anne Elizabeth (Wilkinson) K.; m. Marie S. Sommer, Aug. 10, 1968; children: Samantha, Alex, Spencer. AB, Dartmouth Coll., 1966; MBA, Cornell U., 1968. Mgr. Arthur Young & Co., N.Y.C., 1972-75, prin., 1975-77, ptnr., 1977—, dir. fin. svcs., 1983-88, mng. ptnr., 1988—. Editor Arthur Young Mergers and Acquisitions Newsletter, 1985. Mem. AICPA, N.Y. Soc. CPAs. Office: Arthur Young & Co 277 Park Ave New York NY 10172

KEYES, JAMES HENRY, manufacturing company executive; b. LaCrosse, Wis., Sept. 2, 1940; s. Donald M. and Mary M. (Nodolf) K.; m. Judith Ann Carney, Nov. 21, 1964; children: James Patrick, Kevin, Timothy. BS, Marquette U., 1962; MBA, Northwestern U., 1963. Instr. Marquette U., Milw., 1963-65; CPA Peat, Marwick & Mitchell, Milw., 1965-66; with Johnson Controls, Inc., Milw., 1967—, mgr. systems dept., 1967-71, div. controller, 1971-73, corp. controller, treas., 1973-77, v.p., chief fin. officer, 1977-85, exec. v.p., 1985-86, pres., 1986—, chief operating officer, 1986-88, chief exec. officer, 1988—. Active Milw. Symphony Orch., 1980—. Mem. Fin. Execs. Inst., Am. Inst. CPA's, Wis. Inst. CPA's. Office: Johnson Controls Inc 5757 N Green Bay Ave Box 591 Milwaukee WI 53201 *

KEYKO, GEORGE JOHN, watch electronics company executive; b. New Britain, Conn., May 6, 1924; s. John Simonovich and Nellie Ivanovna (Gretcha) K.; B.S., Yale, 1949; m. Anne Romanchuk, Jan. 31, 1948; children—David, Mark. Spl. rep. Lederle Labs., Conn. and N.Y., 1949-52; pres. Teacher Toys, Inc., Conn., 1952-56; sales mgr. Washington Forge, N.J., 1956-60; sales mgr. shaver div. Ronson Corp., Woodbridge, N.J., 1960-63; sales mgr. Caravelle and BEP div. Bulova Watch Co., N.Y.C., 1963-66; v.p. mktg. Technipower div. Benrus Watch Co., Ridgefield, Conn., 1966-68; exec. v.p. Heuer Time & Electronics Corp., Springfield, N.J., 1969, pres., 1970-75; now pres. Lumisphere Inc.; dir. New Products Devel. Assocs, Etilmech, Inc., Novato, calif., Chemical Device Corp., Yorktown Heights, N.Y., Century Mktg., Republic of China, Wet-Lite Corp. Chief timer internat. Ski Racers Assn., 1970-72; vestryman St. Paul's Ch., Westfield, N.J.; Founder Life-Link Assn. Recipient Spl. award from INTREPID 22 - 12 Meter Yacht America's Cup, 1970. Mem. Am. Watch Mfg. Assn., Sports Car Club Am., N.Y. Sales Exec. Club. Republican. Episcopalian. Club: Echo Lake Country (Westfield, N.J.). Home: 931 Kimball Ave Westfield NJ 07090

KEYSER, MARTHA FLORENCE, public relations executive; b. Salt Lake City, Feb. 8, 1943; d. James Farrington and Margaret (Ballard) K. Cert., U. Geneva, 1964; BA, U. Utah, 1965; MBA Studies, U. Colo., 1975. Mgr. mktg. communications Owens-Corning Fiberglass, Toledo, Ohio, 1974-79; mgr. communications Champion, Stamford, Conn., 1979-82; pres. Keyser Assocs., Rowayton, Conn., 1982-85; mgr. pub. affairs Savin Corp, Stamford, 1985-87; v.p. corporate communications Madison Sq. Garden, N.Y.C., 1988—. Bd. dirs. Bell Island, Rowayton, 1985—, Family Recovery Ctr., New Canaan, Conn., 1987—. Mem. Women in Communications, Pub. Relations Soc. Am., Women in Mgmt. Republican. Episcopalian. Home: 12 E Beach Dr Rowayton CT 06853 Office: Madison Square Garden 2 Pennsylvania Pla New York NY 10121

KHALSA, HARI NAM SINGH, financial planner, lawyer; b. Bklyn., Mar. 14, 1952; d. Max and Helene (Fidelman) Perlman; m. Nav Jiwan Kaur Khalsa. BA, U. Md., 1974; JD, St. John's U., 1977; postgrad., Coll. for Fin. Planning, 1986; LLM in Taxation, U. San Diego, 1985. Cert. fin. planner; Bar: N.Y. 1978, Oreg. 1979, U.S. Ct. Appeals (9th cir.) 1980. Staff atty. VISTA, Portland, Oreg., 1978-79; sole practice Portland, 1980—; pres. Smart Money, Portland, 1986—. Mem. N.Y. State Bar Assn., Oreg. Bar Assn., Fed Bar Assn., Internat. Assn. Fin. Planning., Campaigners Club, Toastmasters. Democrat. Home: 221 SW Palatine Hill Rd Portland OR 97219 Office: Smart Money Inc 621 SW Alder 680 Portland OR 97205

KHAMISA, AZIM NOORDIN, financial consultant; b. Kisumu, Nyanza, Kenya, Feb. 10, 1949; came to U.S., 1974; s. Noordin Hasham and Rahemat (Ahmed) K.; m. Almas B. Hasham, May 8, 1971 (div. Nov. 1980); children: Tasreen, Tariq. Student, Medway Sch. Advanced Tech., Kent, Eng., 1965-66, Loughborough Coll. Advanced Tech., Midland, Eng., 1966-67; BS in Math., U. Nairobi, Kenya, 1968; grad. degree in acctg., Southwest London Coll., 1970. Mng. dir. Rainbow Group Cos., Kenya, 1970-74; v.p. Combined Enterprises, Inc., Can., 1974-78; from v.p. to pres. Readco, San Diego, 1978-81, Islandco, Vancouver, Colo., 1978-81; cons. mergers and acquisitions Atlanta, 1982—; participant various confs. and seminars. Bd. dirs. Gaslamp Theatre Co., San Diego. Mem. Atlanta Venture Forum, Atlanta C. of C., Aga Kahn Found. (spl. coordinator), Aga Khan Bus. Council, Internat. Bus. Council, M & A Assn., Hospitality Assn., Exec. Com., Brit. Am. Bus. Group, Nat. Assn. Hotels and Motels, Profl. Cons. Assn. Lodge: Masons. Office: 8008 Girard Ave #320 La Jolla CA 92037

KHAN, GORDON SIMEON, financial executive; b. New Amsterdam, Berbice, Guyana, Sept. 24, 1943; came to U.S., 1983; s. Walter Simeon and Beryl Amelia (Rohlehr) K.; m. Barbara Elizabeth Dykstra, Nov. 20, 1971; children: Jason, Julianne. BBA with honors, Waterloo (Ont., Can.) U., 1971. Staff auditor Arthur Andersen & Co., Toronto, Ont., 1971-74, audit mgr., 1975-77; controller mktg. Kendall Can., Toronto, 1977-80, v.p. finance, 1980-83; dir. budgets/planning Kendall Co., Boston, 1983-84, asst. controller, 1984-85, v.p. fin. and adminstrn., 1985-88, sr. v.p. adminstrn., chief fin. officer, 1988—. Mem. Can. Inst. Chartered Accts., Boston C. of C. Lutheran. Office: Kendall Co 1 Federal St Boston MA 02101

KHAN, MUZAFFAR ALI, oil company executive; b. Umraoti, India, July 5, 1938; s. Mahboob Ali Khan and Abida Begum; m. Fauzia Khan, Mar. 21, 1973; 1 dau., Zainab. BE Commerce, U. Karachi, (Pakistan), 1959; PhD (hon.) Marquis Scicluna Internat. U. Found. Experience Acctg. clk. Burmah Oil Co., Karachi, Pakistan, 1955-61; acctg. asst. Pakistan Internat. Airlines Co., Karachi, 1961-63; asst. cost acct. Colony Textile Mills, Multon, Pakistan, 1964-65; accounts officer Mitchells' Fruit Farms, Renala, Khurd, 1965-69; mgr. Shishmahal Hosiery Co., Lahore, Pakistan, 1969-70; comptroller Petrolube, Jeddah, Saudi Arabia, 1971—. Contbr. articles to profl. acctg. jours. Fellow Inst. Cost and Mgmt. Accts. of Pakistan, Chartered Inst. Secs. and Adminstrs. (London); mem. Assn. Bus. Execs., Brit. Inst. Mgmt., Am. Mgmt. Assn. (internat.), Inst. Petroleum, European Econ. Assn. (founder), Am. Enterpreneur Assn., Inst. Mktg. Mgmt. Pakistan (assoc.), Nat. Alliance Fin. Cons., Inst. Corp. Secs. Pakistan (assoc.), Oxford Club (life, Washington). Home: 40th St Alazizyah, Jeddah Saudi Arabia Office: Petromin Lubricating Oil Co, PO Box 1432, Jeddah Saudi Arabia

KHANNA, KAILASH CHAND, information systems executive; b. India, Sept. 15, 1938; came to U.S., 1959; s. Ram Chand and Lalo Devi K.; m. Lee Cullen, Aug. 29, 1965; children: Melanie Jean, Kevin James. BE, Delhi U., 1959; MS, Columbia U., 1961, D in Engrng. Sci., 1969. Mgr. ops. rsch. Trans World Airlines, Inc., N.Y.C., 1964-70; sr. dir. co. and com. services Am. Airlines Inc., N.Y.C., 1970-79; v.p. corp. systems and tech. Am. Express Co., N.Y.C., 1979-88; sr. v.p. systems and tech. CIT Group Inc./Mfrs. Hanover Bank., Livingston, N.J., 1988—; bd. dirs. Complete Bus. Solutions Inc., Detroit. Contbr. articles to profl. jours. Mem. Am. Mgmt. Assn. (mem. tech. council). Office: CIT Group/Mfrs Hanover 650 CIT Dr Livingston NJ 07039

KHASAT, NAMITA, chief financial officer; b. Hyderabad, India, May 11, 1960; came to U.S., 1981; d. Satish and Vijay Jaiswal; m. Nitya Prakash Khasat, Jan. 14, 1981; children: Vikram, Vivek. BA, St. Francis Coll., Hyderabad, 1978; MA, Osmania U., Hyderabad, 1980; MPA in Fin. and Computers, U. Del., 1983. Mgmt. analyst Del. Dept. Labor, Wilmington, 1983-84; budget analyst, bus. svcs. mgr. div. revenue Del. Dept. Fin., 1984-85; chief fin. officer Del. YMCA, 1985-88. Recipient Acad. Gold Medal Osmania U., 1980, Athletic Individual Championship award, 1980. Mem. Nat. Assn. Female Execs., Nat. Assn. Accts., Am. Mgmt. Assn. (assoc.), Assn. YMCA Profl. Dirs., Urban Group YMCA Assn. (chief fin. officer). Home: 67 Willow Creek Ln Newark DE 19711

KHAYAT, FADY HEKMAT, marketing professional; b. Beirut, Lebanon, July 27, 1957; s. George Sami and Marie (Debai) K.; m. Ann Louise Erickson, Dec. 27, 1980; children: Stephany, Mark. BS in Chem., Purdue U., 1980; MBA, St. Edwards U., 1981. Mgr. Middle East Searle Pharm. Co., Chgo., 1982-87; mktg. mgr. Middle East region Cilag Ag. Products (Johnson & Johnson), Switzerland, 1987—. Mem. Am. Chem. Soc. Home: 1409 N Salisbury St West Lafayette IN 47906 Office: Cilag Agr Products, Industriestrasse 24, ZUG 6300 Switzerland Switzerland

KHOURY, RIAD PHILIP, corporation executive, financial consultant; b. Beirut, May 25, 1935; came to U.S., 1979; s. Philip Mitri and Efrocine (Moujaes) K.; m. Samira Saade, Apr. 24, 1964; children: Philip, Marc, Serge. Graduate studies in fin. and mgmt. Ind. fin. cons. Baghdad, Iraq, 1955-58; ind. fin. investment adviser Jeddah, Saudi Arabia, 1959-61; mgr. Eastern Comml. Bank, Beirut, 1962-65; chief exec. officer United Bank of Lebanon and Pakistan, Beirut, 1965-70; vice chmn., chief exec. officer ADCOM Bank, Beirut, 1971-74; pres. Khoury Assocs. Internat., Annandale, Va., 1980—; banking and fin. cons. Lebanese Ministry Fin., Beirut, 1978-79. Recipient Officier Scientifique De L'ordre Du Merite award Le Merite, Paris, 1964, Cravate D'Honneur award Groupment Philantropique, Brussels, 1965. Home and Office: 6320 Wendy Ann Ct Fairfax Station VA 22039

KHUU, MAI H., accountant; b. Vietnam, July 28, 1955; came to U.S., 1975; d. Bao and Ngo Nguyen; m. David X. Khuu, May 15, 1976; 1 child, Krystal K. BS in Acctg. and Fin., Metro Coll., 1980. Acctg. officer Colo. State Bank, Denver, 1978—. Mem. Nat. Acctg. Assn. Office: Colo State Bank 1600 Broadway Denver CO 80202

KIBBE, JAMES WILLIAM, real estate broker; b. Bound Brook, N.J., Oct. 5, 1926; s. Orlando A. and Anna Rose (Tomb) K.; B.S., U. Md., 1951; m. Bettie Brooks Dailey, June 11, 1949; children—James William Jr., Linda Jean. Real Estate salesman Eig & Mc Keever, Silver Spring, Md., 1955-57, Weaver Bros, Inc., Chevy Chase Bldg. (Md.), 1957-70, asst. v.p. sales, leasing dept., 1970-72, sales mgr., 1972-73, v.p. sales mgr., 1973-82, sr. v.p., sales mgr., 1983—; lectr, in field; chmn. Brokers and Salesmen's council, 1968-69. Served with USNR, 1944-46. Mem. Soc. Indsl. and Office Realtors (pres. Md. and D.C. chpt. 1985-86, nat. bd. dirs. 1988—), Nat. Assn. Realtors, D.C. Assn. Realtors, Montgomery County Bd. Realtors, Md. Assn. Realtors, Washington Bd. Trade, Washington Builders Assn., Nat. Assn. Indsl. and Office Parks (bd. dirs. 1987), Nat. Inst. Real Estate Brokers (state chmn. 1968-70), New Am. Network (adv. bd. dirs. 1986—). Republican. Methodist. Club: Sandy Spring Lions (pres. 1965-66). Home: 1000 Ashland Dr Ashton MD 20861 Office: 5530 Wisconsin Ave Chevy Chase MD 20815

KICK, FRANCIS RAYMOND, JR., music educator, consultant; b. Buffalo, Dec. 6, 1965; s. Francis Raymond and Patricia Valerie (Joslyn) K. Student, Bowling Green State U., 1984-85; MusB, Wright State U., 1987. Cert. tchr. music edn., Ohio. Coordinator, founder Instrn. and Design Concepts, Spring Valley, Ohio, 1985—; cons., band dir. Centerville (Ohio) High Sch., 1989—; band dir. Xenia (Ohio) High Sch., 1988. Mem. Nat. Band Assn., Ohio Judges Assn. (v.p. 1986-87, publicity dir. 1985-86, editor 1985-87), Am. Soc. Tng. and Devel. Roman Catholic. Home and Office: Instrn and Design Concepts 9426 Ash Hollow Ln Spring Valley OH 45370

KICKEL, JAMES ROBERT, financial executive; b. Cleve., Mar. 18, 1949; s. John W. and Olga M. (Schauer) K.; m. Jacqueline M. Tegowski, June 13, 1971 (div. 1976); children: Jennifer Ann, James John. BA, Kent State U., 1971; Cert., Coll. Fin. Planning, 1986. Sales rep., mgr. Met. Life Ins. Co., Cleve., 1972-77; dist. agt. Nat. Life of Vt., Cleve., 1977-79; gen. mgr. Paul Revere Ins. Group, Independence, Ohio, 1979—; v.p. Wall St. Money Mgrs. Inc., Independence, Ohio, 1986—. Mem. F.A.I.R. Nat. Fathers Orgn., Del., 1987. Mem. Pres. Club, Nat. Life Vt., 1977-78. Mem. Nat. Assn. Health Underwriters (Nat. Sales Achievement award 1973), Internat. Assn. Fin. Planners, Inst. Cert. Fin. Planners. Home: 10076 Highland Dr Brecksville OH 44141 Office: Wallstreet Money Mgrs Inc 4141 Rockside Rd Ste 220 Seven Hills OH 44131

KIDD, DEBRA JEAN, communications executive; b. Chgo., May 13, 1956; d. Fred A. and Jean (Pezzopane) Winchar; m. Kim Joseph Kidd, July 22, 1978; children: Jennifer Marie, Michele Jean. AA in Bus. with high honors, Wright Jr. Coll., 1977. Legal sec. Sidley & Austin, Chgo., 1977-80; investment adminstr. Golder, Thoma & Co., Chgo., 1980-81, exec. asst., 1981-84; sales rep. Dataspeed, Inc., Chgo., 1984, midwestern regional mgr. Dataspeed, Inc., Chgo., 1985; communications cons. Chgo. Communications, Inc., Chgo., 1986—; owner, founder Captain Kidd's Video, Niles, 1981-84. Vol. Am. Lung Assn., Chgo., 1979; vol. tchr. CCD Our Lady Mother of Ch., Norridge, Ill., 1981-83; vol. Parents Who Care, 1988—. Mem. NAFE, Nat. Assn. Bus. Women, Nat. Assn. Profl. Saleswomen, Nat. Network of Women in Sales, Bus. and Profl. Women's Club, Phi Theta Kappa. Roman Catholic. Avocations: camping; snow and water skiing; horseback riding; sailing; reading; needlepoint.

KIDD, ROBERT HUGH, financial executive, accountant; b. Toronto, Ont., Can., June 1, 1944; s. Donald Alexander and Mary Isabelle (Sutton) K.; m. Elizabeth M. Warner; children: Donald, Scott, Suzanne. B in Commerce, U. Toronto, 1966; MBA, York U., Toronto, 1973. Chartered Acct. Acct. Thorne Ernst & Whinney, Toronto, 1966-72, ptnr., 1973-81; chief fin. officer, sr. v.p. George Weston Ltd., Toronto, 1981—, also bd. dirs.; bd. dirs. Loblaw Cos., Ltd., Toronto, Credit Suisse Can., Toronto, B.C. Packers, Vancouver, Can. Author: Earnings Forecast, 1976; co-author: Terminology for Accountants, 1976. Recipient Victoria Coll. Gold medal U. Toronto, 1966, Gov. Gen.'s Gold medal Can. Inst. Chartered Accts., 1968. Mem. Inst. Chartered Accts. Ont., Can. Tax Found. Office: George Weston Ltd, 22 St Clair Ave E #1901, Toronto, ON Canada M4T 2S7

KIDDE, JOHN LYON, investment manager; b. June 5, 1934. BA, Princeton U., 1959; postgrad., Columbia U., 1955-56. Indsl. research analyst Federated Employers San Francisco, 1956-57; fin. dir. Walter Kidde S.A. do Brasil, Rio De Janeiro, 1959-60; European mgr. Walter Kidde Co., Inc., Paris, 1962-66; joint mng. dir. Walter Kidde Co., Ltd., Northolt, Eng., corp. European mgr., 1966-67; dir. internat. ops. Kidde, Inc., U.S.A., Saddle Brook, N.J., 1967-68, v.p., dir. internat. ops., 1968-88; currently pres. KDM Devel., Upper Montclair, N.J., Can. Am. Investment Mgmt. Ltd., Halifax, N.S. & The Mac Donald Co. Ltd., Cayman Islands; gen. ptnr. Claflin Capital I, II, III, & IV, Boston, The Opportunity Fund, Boston.; bd. dirs. Celtic Trust Co. Ltd., Tortola, British Virgin Islands, Metalbanc, Inc., Miami, Fla., Interfin. Inc., N.Y.C., U.S. Investment Pub., N.Y.C. The Futures Group, Glastonbury, Conn., Internat. Resource Group, Inc., Setauket, N.Y., Pasco Internat., Saddle brook, Md., Metalbanc Inc., Constrn. Specialties, Cranford, N.J., Australasia, Inc., Cayman Island, Guaranty Fed. Savs. Bank, Fayetteville, N.C. Essex Life Ins. Co., Inc., West Orange, N.J., Internat. AgriTech Resources, Inc., N.Y.C. Trustee Pace U., Clara Maass Med. Ctr., Belleville, N.J., Internat. Coll. Cayman Island, Grand Cayman, Charles Hayden Found., N.Y.C., Stevens Inst. Tech., Hoboken, N.J.; pres. Community Found. N.J., Morristown, Albert Payson Terhune Found., Pompton Lakes, N.J.; chmn. bd. trustees Assist Inc., Peterborough, N.H.; mem. adv. bd. Midlantic Nat. Bank/North, West Patterson, N.J. Served with U.S. Army. Home: 154 Oldchester Rd Essex Fells NJ 07021 Office: Kidde Inc Park 80 West-Plaza Two Box 5555 Saddle Brook NJ 07662

KIDO, KAZUAKI, banker; b. Tokyo, Sept. 26, 1951; s. Kanetsugu and Rumie (Yano) K.; m. Tomoko Dai, Jan. 27, 1985; 1 child, Kentaro. LLB, U. Tokyo, 1975; MBA, Stanford U., 1982. Asst. mgr. Kichijoji Br. Mitsubishi Trust and Banking Corp., Tokyo, 1975-77; mgr. securities dept. Mitsubishi Trust and Banking Corp., 1977-80, mgr. internat. banking group, 1982-84, v.p. N.Y.C. br., 1986—; rep. to N.Y.C. office Ryoshin Leasing Corp. (div. Mitsubishi Trust and Banking Corp.), 1984-86; founding mem. Shotosha Internat., N.Y.C., 1980—. Buddhist. Office: Mitsubishi Trust & Banking Corp 520 Madison Ave New York NY 10022

KIEFER, ROBERT JOHN, mechanical engineer; b. Cleve., Dec. 7, 1936; s. Paul Everette and Beulah Elizabeth (Moore) K.; m. Barbara Gayle Niemiec, June 14, 1958 (div. Aug., 1981); children: Kelly Jane Pace, Paul Joseph; m. Aura Ann Khosby, Sept. 4, 1982; children: Kimberly Fenske, Kerri Fenske. BSME, MSME, Ohio State U., 1959. Registered profl. engr., mechanical, nuclear, Ohio, Calif. Project officer Air Force Weapons Lab, Albuquerque, N.Mex., 1959-62; mgr., fuel applications engring. Gen. Atomic Co., San Diego, Calif., 1962-76; mgr. tech. tng. Scientific Atlanta, San Diego, 1976—; staff cons. Air Force Space Div., L.A., 1976-87. Contbr. articles to profl. jours. Lt. col. USAFR, 1959-87. Mem. Soc. Am. Mil. Engrs. (gold medal, 1959), Sigma Xi, Pi Tau Sigma, Tau Beta Pi, Am. Soc. Mechanical Engrs., Inst. Environ. Scis., NSPE. Republican. Baptist. Home: 10215 Saunders Dr San Diego CA 92131 Office: Scientific Atlanta 4141 Ruffin Rd San Diego CA 92123

KIEHNE, ANNA MARIE, accountant, educator, systems analyst; b. Preston, Minn., Dec. 15, 1947; d. Alvin H. and Anna M. (Goldsmith) K. B.B.A., Winona State U.; postgrad. Calif. State U.-Los Angeles, 1974-78; cert. in systems analysis UCLA, 1984. Acct. Murray Howard Realty, L.A., 1974-78; staff acct. Bowest Corp., La Jolla, Calif., 1978-79; acctg. supr. Majestic Investment, Denver, 1979-81; adminstrv. acct. ECA/Intercomp. systems analyst Home Savs., 1983-88; Fin. Systems Analyst Cray Rsch., Inc., 1988—; tchr. adult edn. Election judge, Denver; del. to primary, county, state Dem. convs., 1980, 82, Sister City Internat., City of Richfield Commn., 1989. Mem. Nat. Assn. Accts. (cert. in flexible budgeting and performance reporting), Internat. Platform Assn. Lutheran. also: Cray Rsch Inc 608 Second Ave S Minneapolis MN 55402

KIELY, DAN RAY, banking and real estate development executive; b. Ft. Sill, Okla., Jan. 2, 1944; s. William Robert and Leona Maxine (Ross) K.; BA in Psychology, U. Colo., 1966, JD, Stanford U., 1969; m. Lucianne Holt, June 11, 1966; children: Jefferson Ray, Matthew Ray. Bar: Colo 1969, D.C. 1970, Va. 1973. Assoc. firm Holme, Roberts and Owen, Denver, 1969-70; pres. DeRand Equity Group, Arlington, Va., 1973—; pres., chmn. bd. Bankwest Corp. and related banks, Denver.; pres., dir. United Gibraltar Corp. Del., Inc., 1987—; dir. DeRand Corp. and affiliates; trustee DeRand Real Estate Investment Trust; speaker, lectr. in field. Deacon, McLean (Va.) Baptist Ch., 1977-80. Served as officer, USAR, 1969-73. Decorated Legion of Merit; cert. property mgr. Mem. Nat. Bd. Realtors, Inst. Real Estate Mgmt., Nat. Assn. Rev. Appraisers, Internat. Council Shopping Centers, Nat. Assn. Real Estate Investment Trusts, Am. Bar Assn., Colo. Bar Assn., D.C. Bar Assn. Colo. Indsl. Bankers Assn. (bd. dirs.), The Internat. Inst (cert. valuer). Home: 501 E Causeway Vero Beach FL 32963 Office: 2201 Wilson Blvd Arlington VA 22201

KIENEL, FREDERICK EDWARD, financial executive; b. Marietta, Ga., July 29, 1938; s. Frederick Bernard and Louise (Gantt) K.; m. Norma Breazeale, Junly 24, 1965; children: Frederick Dowell, Meredith Paige, Jennifer Anne. BS in Indsl. Mgmt., Ga. Inst. Tech., 1962; postgrad., U. Richmond, 1966-69; postgred., Wharton Sch., 1985-87. Prodn. control engr. Allied Chem. Corp., Hopewell, Va., 1965-67; staff indsl. engr. Reynolds Metals Co., Richmond, 1967-68; acct. exec. Merrill Lynch, Richmond, 1968-73, instnl. acct. exec., 1973-78; sr. v.p., mgr. Dean Witter Reynolds, Inc., Richmond, 1978—; sr. mgmt. adv. mem. Dean Witter Reynolds, Inc., N.Y.C., 1981-82. Trustee Trinity Episcopal Sch., Richmond, 1987; mil. aide de camp to gov. State Va., 1982-86. 1st lt. USMC, 1962-65, lt. col. Res. 1965-82. Mem. Richmond Soc. Fin. Analysts, Nat. Assn. Securities Dealers (arbitration com. 1985—), NYSE (arbitration com. 1985—), Richmond C. of C., Va. C. of C., Ga. Tech. Alumni Assn. (pres. 1977-78), Bull and Bear Club. Republican. Roman Catholic. Office: Dean Witter Reynolds Inc 700 E Main St Richmond VA 23219

KIERKUT, ALAN, travel company executive; b. London, May 17, 1935; came to U.S., 1963; s. Lejzor Jonas and Flora Kierkut; m. Esther Yochai, Aug. 14, 1968; children: Galit, Liorra. Ed. in Eng. Tour escort Global of London, 1961-63; sales rep. El Al Israel Airlines, Phila., 1964-66; group travel cons. Garber Travel, Boston, 1966-68; tour operator Peltours Ltd., Tel Aviv, 1968-71; ops. mgr. Peltours Ltd., N.Y.C., 1971-72; v.p. ops. Tower Travel Corp., N.Y.C., 1972-74; dir. ops. Hawaiian Holidays, Inc., N.Y.C., 1974-77; mgr. tour product devel. Holiday Inns, Inc., Memphis, 1977-80; pres. Tourcheck Am., Inc., N.Y.C., 1980—. Contbr. articles on travel to various publs. Mem. Travel Industry Assn. Am. Jewish. Office: Tourcheck Am Inc 56 Harrison St Ste 404 New Rochelle NY 10801

KIERNAN, TERENCE JAMES, hospital executive; b. Chgo., June 29, 1949; s. James Walter and Ethelda (Tatterson) K.; m. Joan P. Poyser, Sept. 4, 1971; children: Colleen, Terence J. Jr., Meghan. BBA, U. Miss., 1971. Gen. acctg. supr. Alltel Telephone Corp. (formerly Mid-Continent Telephone Corp.), Rantoul, Ill., 1971-74; mgr. acctg. Louis A. Weiss Meml. Hosp., Chgo., 1974-76, assoc. dir. fin., 1976-80, dir. fin., 1980-81, v.p. fin., 1981—. Tchr. Sts. Faith, Hope and Charity Ch., Winnetka, Ill., 1984-87; den leader Cub Scouts, Boy Scouts Am., Wilmette, Ill., 1987—. Mem. Healthcare Fin.

Mgmt. Assn. (advanced). Republican. Office: Louis A Weiss Meml Hosp 4646 N Marine Dr Chicago IL 60640

KIESCHNIK, RONALD CARL, financial planner; b. Houston, July 9, 1956; s. Elton Carl and Mary Rose (Theiss) K.; m. Anne Louise Pheiffer, Dec. 16, 1978. BBA, U. Tex., 1978. Assoc. Assocs. in Fin. Planning, Houston, 1978-80; v.p. J.R. Ringnald & Assocs., Inc., Houston, 1981-82; pres. Kieschnik & Assocs., Inc., Houston, 1983—. Bd. dirs. Mcpl. Utility Dist. #10, Harris County, Tex., 1987, 88; del. Rep. Senatorial Dist. Conv., Harris County, 1988, Rep. State Conv., Houston, 1988. Mem. SEC, Nat. Assn. Securities Dealers, Inner Loop Bkft. (pres. 1986-87, sec. 1987—). Lutheran. Office: Kieschnik & Assocs Inc 550 Westcott Ste 340 Houston TX 77007

KIESEWETTER, THEODORE CAMBIER, importer; b. Seattle, May 21, 1937; s. E. and Wilhelmina L. (Cambier) K.; m. Barbara L. Souza, Dec. 21, 1958 (div. 1988); children: Jacqueline, Anita. BS, San Francisco State Coll., 1961; internat. relations diploma, U. Lausanne, Switzerland, 1962; postgrad., NYU, Lieden, Holland, 1962. Regional mgr. Dmark Ind. Inc., Amsterdam, Holland, 1962-67; pres. Internat. Playthings, Inc., Bloomfield, N.J., 1967—. Served with USN, 1955-57. Office: Internat Playthings 120 Riverdale Rd Riverdale NJ 07457

KIESOW, LINDA F., data processing executive; b. Rock Island, Ill., July 5, 1953; d. Oscar Ray and Helen F. (Junk) McElroy; m. James Thomas Kiesow, May 26, 1973. BA in Acctg., Western Ill. U., 1979; MBA, U. Iowa, 1985. Cert. data processor. Produce mgr. Carthage (Ill.) Super Valu, 1974-75; aggregate sample analyst Valley Quarry, St. Augustine, Ill., 1975-76; data processing mgr. Moline (ILL.) Consumers Co., 1979-87; ops. supr. Alcoa, Davenport, Iowa, 1987—. Fulbright scholar Western Ill. U., Macomb, 1977; Coll. Bus. Scholar, Western Ill. U., 1978; Acctg. Dept. scholar Western Ill. U., 1978. Mem. Acctg. Soc. (mem. banquet com. chmn., v.p. 1977-78), Nat. Assn. Female Execs., Data Processing Mgmt. Assn., Assn. of Inst. for Cert. of Computer Profls., Alpha Lambda Delta, Phi Kappa Phi. Republican. Baptist. Avocations: reading; sports. Home: 4907 48th Ave Moline IL 61265 Office: Alcoa-Davenport Works Box 3567 Davenport IA 52808

KIGIN, THOMAS JOHN, lawyer, broadcast executive; b. St. Cloud, Minn., Sept. 29, 1948; s. Jerome Joseph and Marjorie Marie (Bellig) K.; m. Donna Louise Avery, Sept. 6, 1980; children: Mackenzie Louise, Elizabeth Hannah. BA cum laude, St. John's U., 1970; JD cum laude, U. Minn., 1977. Bar: Minn. 1977. V.p., gen. counsel Minn. Pub. Radio, St. Paul, 1977—; bd. dirs., mem. Distbn. Interconnection com., Nat. Pub. Radio, Washington; v.p., gen. counsel Minn. Communications Group; treas., bd. dirs. The World Theater Corp.; sec. treas. Greenspring Corp., Minn. Monthly Publs. Inc., The MNN Radio Networks Inc., Rivertown Trading Corp., St. Paul. Served to 1st lt. USMC, 1970-73. Mem. ABA, Univ. Club, St. Paul Athletic Club. Office: Minn Pub Radio 45 E Seventh St Saint Paul MN 55101

KIJEWSKI, GLENN JAY, data processing executive; b. Buffalo, May 2, 1961; s. William and Beverly (Hill) K.; m. Carolyn Badhorn, Mar. 19, 1983; children: Stephanie, Sarah. Grad. high sch., Buffalo. Tech. clk. Barrister Info. Systems Corp., Buffalo, 1980-81, with tech. support, 1981-82, systems test engr., 1982-83, with nat. tech. support, 1983-84, western area mgr., 1985-86, mgr. nat. field svc. ops., 1986—. Mem. Am. Mgmt. Assn., Am. Field Svc. Mgmt. Assn. Office: Barrister Info Systems Corp 45 Oak St Buffalo NY 14203

KILANOWSKI, MICHAEL CHARLES, JR., oil, natural gas, minerals exploration company executive, lawyer; b. Youngstown, Ohio, May 14, 1948; s. Michael Charles and Eleanore Rita (Kollar) K.; m. Mary Ellen Richards, Oct. 7, 1978; Dawn, Meridith, Melissa; 1 stepchild, William. BBA, Kent State U., 1970; JD, U. Akron, 1975; MBA, Ohio U., 1979. Bar: Ohio, 1975. Sales rep. Lincoln Nat. Life Ins. Co., Youngstown, 1970-71; mgr. retail sect. Phillips Petroleum Co., Akron, Ohio, 1971-73; contract analyst Babcock & Wilcox Co., North Canton, Ohio, 1973-75, atty., 1975-76, mgr. contracts-legal, 1976-79, mgr. market data and forecasting, 1979-81; atty. McDermott Internat. Inc., New Orleans, 1981-86; sr. atty. Freeport-McMoRan Inc., New Orleans, 1986, corp. sec., 1986—; instr. Kent (Ohio) State U., 1979-81. Mem. Little Oak PTA, Slidell, La., 1986—. Mem. ABA, Am. Soc. Corp. Secs. (co-chmn. New Orleans chpt. 1987, pres. 1988, adj. faculty seminars 1988-89). Roman Catholic. Home: 397 Cross Gates Blvd Slidell LA 70461 Office: Freeport-McMoran Inc 1615 Poydras St New Orleans LA 70112

KILBORNE, GEORGE BRIGGS, investment company executive; b. N.Y.C., Oct. 7, 1930; s. Robert Stewart and Barbara Briggs Kilborne; B.A., Yale U., 1952; m. Lucie Wheeler Peck, Nov. 12, 1960 (div. 1978); children—George Briggs, Kim McNeil, Sarah Skinner. Vice pres. William Skinner & Sons, N.Y.C., 1955-60; pres. Bus. Research Co., Birmingham, Mich., 1961-74, Creative Capital of Mich., Inc., Birmingham, 1962-70; partner Comac Co., 1968-70; chmn., pres. First Citizen Bank, Troy, Mich., 1970-74; engaged in real estate investing and cons., Palm Beach, Fla., 1975-79; mng. dir. corp. acquisitions Bessemer Securities Corp., N.Y.C., 1980-84; pres. Bay Street Corp., Palm Beach, 1984—; pres. Pon Capital Corp., Braintree, Mass., 1987—; chmn. State Bank of Mich., Coopersville, 1966-67, Muskegon (Mich.) Bank & Trust, 1967-68, Bank of Lansing (Mich.), 1968-69; vice chmn. Creative Capital Corp., N.Y.C., 1968-70, Hockey Club of Pitts., 1968-70; dir. Watts Industries, Inc., N. Andover, Mass., 1981-84, Roller Bearing Corp. of Am., West Trenton, N.J., 1987—, Diversified Communications, Portland, Maine, 1982—. Bd. dirs. Oakland (Mich.) unit. Am. Cancer Soc., 1973-74; mem. Republican Com., Dist. 13, Palm Beach County, Fla., 1976-80; mem. Palm Beach County Rep. Exec. Com., 1976-80; bd. dirs. Palm Beach Rep. Club, 1977-80. Served to lt. (j.g.) USN, 1953-55. Recipient Disting. Service award First Citizen Bank, Troy, 1974, Midwest Assn. Small Bus. Investment Cos., 1970. Mem. Nat. Assn. Small Bus. Investment Cos. (gov. 1967-70, mem. exec. com. 1967, pres. Midwest assn. 1970). Clubs: Yale of the Palm Beaches (pres. 1979-80), Bath and Tennis (Palm Beach, Fla.); Wianno (Mass.) Yacht, Wianno; Univ. (N.Y.C.).

KILBURN, H(ENRY) T(HOMAS), JR., investment banker; b. N.Y.C., Aug. 1, 1931; s. Henry Thomas and Florence (Cross) K. A.B., Princeton U., 1953; J.D., Columbia U., 1959. Bar: N.Y. 1959. Exec. trainee Bankers Trust Co., N.Y.C., 1953-54; assoc. Kelley Drye Newhall & Maginnes, N.Y.C., 1959-66; v.p. fin., gen. counsel W.E. Parfitt & Assocs. N.Y.C., 1967-71; assoc., then 1st v.p., sr. v.p., dir. Blyth Eastman Dillon, N.Y.C., 1972-78; exec. v.p. Blyth Eastman PW Inc., N.Y.C., 1978-80; mng. dir. PaineWebber, Inc., N.Y.C., 1980-88, adv. dir., 1988—; dir. PaineWebber Leasing Corp. Served to 1st lt. U.S. Army, 1954-56. Mem. N.Y. Bar Assn., Securities Industry Assn. (chmn. regulated industries com. 1980-81). Republican. Episcopalian. Clubs: Links, Princeton (N.Y.C.). Home: 48 Walsh Ln Greenwich CT 06830 Office: Paine Webber Inc 1285 Ave of Americas New York NY 10019

KILEY, DANIEL CORCORAN, financial services executive; b. South Bend, Ind., July 6, 1959; s. Thomas Michael and Mary Lane (Storen) K.; m. Marilee Beth Zinsmeister, June 9, 1984. BA in Gen. Studies cum laude, Harvard U., 1981. Cert. fin. planner. With Intermark Realty, Houston, 1981-83; investment adviser, ptnr. Kiley and Assocs., Cin., 1983-87; pres. Fin. Care Corp., Cin., 1987-88, pres. retirement planning, 1989—. Mem. Cin. Bicentennial Commn., 1988. Mem. Internat. Assn. Fin. Planners, Investment Co. Inst. (registered investment advisor com. 1987). Republican. Roman Catholic. Office: Fin Care Corp 4555 Lake Forest Dr Ste 194 Cincinnati OH 45242

KILGORE, ROBERT MARTIN, lawyer; b. Beckley, W.Va., Jan. 3, 1924; s. Harley Martin and Lois (Lilly) K.; B.S. in Physics, Georgetown U., 1947; postgrad. Columbia, 1947-49; J.D., George Washington U., 1952; m. Helen Hogan, Dec. 14, 1974. Admitted to D.C. bar, 1952, W.Va. bar, 1953; patent examiner U.S. Patent Office, Washington 1951-55, 68-85; counsel Com. on Judiciary, U.S. Senate, 1955-58; asso. firm Powell, Dorsey & Blum, Washington, 1959-61; pvt. practice, Washington, 1961-80; legal cons. Bd. Vet. Appeals, VA, 1966-67. CD dir. Forest Heights, Md., 1956-58; instr. first aid ARC, 1955-76, first aid chmn. D.C. chpt., 1971-75, instr. sailing, 1972-76; pres. 2d Homeowners Assn., 1973-76, P.T.O. Credit Union, 1980. Served from pvt. to lt. AUS, 1943-46. Registered parliamentarian. Mem. Am., Fed., W.Va., D.C. bar assns., DAV, W.Va. State Soc. (v.p. 1956-58), SAR, Patent Office Soc. (exec. com. 1972-80, pres. 1975-77, chmn. bd. govs. jour. 1977-83, Outstanding Service award 1981), Am. Camillia Soc., Nat. Assn. Parliamentarians (unit pres. 1976-78, state treas.), Am. Inst. Parliamentarians (nat. dir. 1974-75, pres. D.C. chpt. 1974-76), Am. Legion, Am. Judicature Soc., Washington Area Intergroup Assn. (chmn. 1971). Democrat. Baptist. Clubs: George Washington U.; Toastmaster (dist. lt. gov. 1972-74). Home: 14827 N Anderson Ct Woodbridge VA 22193

KILIAN, MARK KENNETH, electronic engineer, computer consultant; b. Des Plaines, Ill., Aug. 3, 1961; s. Kenneth Edward and Suzanne Marie (Larsen) K. AS in Avionics Systems, Embry-Riddle Aero. U., Daytona Beach, Fla., 1982, B in Aviation Tech. cum laude, 1984. Registered profl. engr., Ill. Aircraft engr. United Tech./Sikorsky Aircraft, Palm Beach, Fla., 1984-86; test systems engr. Electro Dynamics, Inc., Rolling Meadows, Ill., 1986-88, Gandalf Data, Inc., Wheeling, Ill., 1988-89; sr. systems engr. Motorola, Inc., Arlington Heights, Ill., 1989—; part-time computer system cons., 1988—. Office: Motorola Inc 1501 Shure Dr Arlington Heights IL 60004 also: 814 Braeburn Rd Inverness IL 60067

KILLEN, CARROLL GORDEN, electronics company executive; b. Provencal, La., Mar. 22, 1919; s. Carroll Graves and Ella (Crowder) K.; m. Clara Donald Butler, Aug. 15, 1941; children: Carroll Gorden III, Margaret Karen, Lloyd Butler, Sara Elizabeth. Grad., La. State U.; B.S., La. Northwestern State Coll. Electronics engr. Magnolia Petroleum Co., Dallas, 1940-42; electronics engr. Watson Labs., Red Bank, N.J., 1942-45; chief application engr. Sprague Electric Co., North Adams, Mass., 1947-55, mgr. field engring., 1955-60, v.p. mktg. and sales, 1960-73, sr. v.p. mktg. and sales, 1973-85; v.p., gen. mgr. Tansitor Electronics, Inc., Bennington, Vt., 1985—, also dir.; dir. Cera-Mite Corp., Grafton, Wis.; cons. U.S. Dept. Def., Washington, 1949-73, U.S. Dept. Commerce, 1984—; dir. Tantalum International. Study Ctr., Brussels, Belgium, 1983-85, mem. exec. com., 1983—; pres. T.I.C., 1984-85. Author: Factors Influencing Capacitor Reliability, 1955. Served to 1st lt. USAF, 1945-47, PTO. Mem. IEEE (chmn. conf. bd. 1971-74, chmn. electro conf. 1976-79), Electronic Industries Assn. (gov. 1976—), Am. Ordnance Assn., Newcomer Soc., Nat. Security Indsl. Assn. (trustee 1980-85), Am. Mgmt. Assn. Republican. Baptist. Club: Sales Execs. Lodge: Masons. Home: 511 Gage St Bennington VT 05201 Office: Tansitor Electronics Inc West Rd PO Box 230 Bennington VT 05201

KILLGORE, KENNETH WAYNE, municipal official; b. Birmingham, Ala., Feb. 27, 1948; s. Travis Ellis and Mae Drue (Campbell) K. BS, U. S.Fla., 1972; MBA, Nova U., 1982. Asst. fin. dir. Met. Devel. Agy., Tampa, 1971-74, City of Cocoa, Fla., 1974-77; fin. dir. Dity of St. Cloud, Fla., 1977-81, City of Cocoa Beach, Fla., 1981-82; fin. dir. City of Cocoa, 1982-84, city mgr., 1984-86; assoc. Travis E. Killgore Realty, Winter Pk., Fla., 1986-87; dir. fin. City of Kissimmee, Fla., 1987—. Mem. Gov. Fin. Officers Assn. Office: City of Kissimmee 101 N Church St Kissimmee FL 32741 Home: 2684 Horeshoe Bay Dr Kissimmee FL 32741

KILLINGBECK, LINDA ANN, financial analyst; b. New Haven, Conn., Feb. 7, 1961; d. Rowland R. and Ethel M. (Belfanc) K. BA, Yale U, 1982; MBA, Pace U., 1987. Asst. controller Mech. Plastics Corp., Pleasantville, N.Y., 1982-87; fin. analyst Zierick Mfg. Corp., Mt. Kisco, N.Y., 1987-88; cost analyst Ciba-Geigy Corp., Ardsley, N.Y., 1988—; computer cons. C.W. Brown Inc., White Plains, N.Y., 1988. Mem. NAFE, Yale Women's Lacrosse Assn. (bd. dirs. 1988—), Yale Women's Basketball Assn. (bd. dirs. 1983-85). Avocations: skiing, travling, computers. Home: 802 Williamsburg Dr Mahopac NY 10541 Office: Ciba-Geigy Corp 444 Saw Mill River Rd Ardsley NY 10502

KILLINGSWORTH, WILLIAM DAVID, recycling company administrator; b. Dublin, Ga., Feb. 5, 1959; s. Robert David and Emily (Standard) K.; m. Alexia Neighbors, June 30, 1985. Student, Valdosta State Coll., 1977-78; deg. in Biblical Studies, Salvation Coll., San Diego, 1978-82; PhD, Universal Life Coll., 1987. Engr. So. Bell Tel. Co., Vidalia, Ga., 1978-81; gen. mgr. Southeast Recycling Corp., Daytona Beach, Fla., 1981-86; div. mgr. Southeast Recycling Corp., Montgomery, Ala., 1986—. Mem. com. Keep Am. Beautiful, Montgomery, 1987—; mem. steering com. Montgomery Clean City Commn., 1987—. Mem. Montgomery C. of C., Govtl. Refuse and Collection Disposal Assn., Nat. Assn. Recycling Industries, Assn. Retarded Citizens. Republican. Baptist. Home: 3528 Cambridge St Montgomery AL 36111 Office: SE Recycling Corp 110 Pollard St Montgomery AL 36104

KILLION, CAROL ANN, business educator; b. Jonesboro, Ark., Nov. 20, 1942; d. William Millard and Miriam (Rickman) Bailey; m. Ulys Grant Killion, Aug. 12, 1962; children: Deborah Lynne, Brenda Dianne. Student, Harding U., 1959-62; BE, Ark. State U., 1974, MEd, 1987. Cert. bus. edn. tchr. Tchr. Dalton (Ark.) High Sch., 1962-63, Ravenden Springs (Ark.) High Sch., 1970-71; instr. bus. Black River Vocat. Tech. Sch., Pocahontas, Ark., 1975—; adviser bus. edn. dept. Oak Ridge Cen. Sch., Ravenden Springs, 1985—. Mem. Am. Vocat. Assn., Ark. Vocat. Assn., Nat. Bus. Edn. Assn., Ark. Bus. Edn. Assn., So. Bus. Edn. Assn., Assn. Supervision and Curriculum Devel., Phi Beta Lamda, Beta Gamma Sigma, Delta Pi Epsilon, Pocahontas Woman's Club (sec. 1985-86, chmn. edn. com. 1987-88), Northeast Ark. Chorale. Democrat. Mem. Ch. of Christ. Home: 1705 Thomasville Rd Pocahontas AR 72455 Office: Black River Vocat-Tech PO Box 468 Pocahontas AR 72455

KILLOUGH, JACK CHRISTOPHER, security company executive, police officer; b. San Antonio, Tex., Sept. 8, 1948; s. Joe and Mary Dixon (Henry) K.; m. Caroline Parmelee, Apr. 12, 1964. BA, Lone Mountain Coll., 1974; postgrad., Sonoma Coll., 1976-77, Golden Gate U., 1978-80. Asst. to pres. John F. Kennedy Univ., Orinda, Calif., 1974-76; reserve dep. sheriff Contra Costa County Sheriff's Dept., Martinez, Calif., 1975-78; correctional officer San Quentin (Calif.) State Prison, 1977-80; chief exec. officer Phoenix Ops. Inc., San Francisco, 1986—; police officer San Francisco Police Dept., 1980—. Mem. Martinez Human Relations Commn.; active World Affairs Council San Francisco. Named one of Outstanding Young Men Am. U.S. Jaycees, 1975; recipient Proclamation Mayor Dianne Feinstein of San Francisco, 1985, Outstanding Police Work Commendation San Francisco Police Commn., 1985. Mem. Calif. Assn. Lic. Investigators, Scottish Assn., San Francisco C. of C. Club: Commonwealth. Lodge: Oriental.

KILLOUGH, RAY BERNARD, oil and gas mining executive; b. Charlotte, N.C., July 12, 1948; s. Ray Winford and Hattie Lucille (Privette) K.; m. Judith Carolyn Griffin, July 31, 1971; children: Mary Winn, Lauren Elizabeth. BS in Engring., N.C. State U., 1970. Supr. LNG plant Piedmont Natural Gas Co., Charlotte, 1973-77, successively design engr., mgr. design and constrn., mgr. engring., dir. engring., 1977-86, v.p. engring., 1986—; pres. Utilities Locating Co., Greensboro, N.C. Patentee in field. Chmn. deacons Pleasant Plains Bapt. Ch., Matthews, N.C., 1987—; mem. Mecklenburg Council for Children, Charlotte, 1985-86; co-pres. Indian Trail Elem. Sch. PTO, 1988—. With U.S. Army, 1971-73. Mem. NSPE, ASHRAE, Profl. Engrs. N.C., Am. Soc. Agrl. Engrs., Am. Gas Assn (com. chmn. 1987—), Toastmasters Club (sgt. at arms). Democrat. Home: 5025 Old Monroe Rd Matthews NC 28105 Office: Piedmont Natural Gas Co 1915 Rexford Rd Charlotte NC 28233

KILLPACK, JAMES ROBERT, bank holding company executive; b. Persia, Iowa, Aug. 11, 1922; s. James Marion and Dorothy (Divelbess) K.; m. Norma Hewett, June 11, 1949; children—James, John, Steven. BS, Miami U., Oxford, Ohio, 1946. CPA, Ohio. With Peat, Marwick, Mitchell & Co., Cleve., 1946-58; treas. Ferro Corp., Cleve., 1958-66; fin. v.p. Island Creek Coal Co., Cleve., 1966-68; dir.corp. planning Eaton Corp. (formerly Eaton Yale & Towne Inc.), Cleve., 1968-69; v.p. corp planning Eaton Corp. (formerly Eaton Yale & Towne Inc.), 1969, v.p. adminstrn., 1970, v.p. fin., 1970-78, exec. v.p. fin. and adminstrn., 1978-79; dir. Nat. City Bank, Cleve., from 1979, vice chmn., 1979, pres., 1979-84; dir. Nat. City Corp., Cleve., 1979—, vice chmn., 1979-80, pres., 1981-86, chmn., chief exec. officer, 1986-87, ret.; bd. dirs. Sherwin-Williams Co., Weatherhead Industries, Nat. City Corp., LDI Corp., Nat. City Bank. With AUS, 1942-45. Mem. Fin. Execs. Inst. (dir. Cleve. chpt., pres. 1970-71), Am. Inst. CPA's. Mem. Christian Ch. Clubs: Tavern (Cleve.), Union (Cleve.), Pepper Pike Country, The Country; Shaker Country (Shaker Heights, Ohio); John's Island (Fla.). Home: 13515 Shaker Blvd Ste 8-B Cleveland OH 44120 Office: Nat City Corp PO Box 5756 Cleveland OH 44101 also: 281 John's Island Dr Vero Beach FL 32961

KILMANN, RALPH HERMAN, business educator; b. N.Y.C., Oct. 5, 1946; s. Martin Herbert and Lilli (Loeb) K.; m. Ines Colon, May 28, 1988; children : Catherine Mary, Christopher Martin, Arlette. B.S., Carnegie-Mellon U., 1970, M.S., 1970; Ph.D., UCLA, 1972. Instr. Grad. Sch. Bus., U. Pitts., 1972, asst. prof., 1972-75, assoc. prof., 1975-79, prof., 1979—, coordinator organizational studies group, 1981-84, 86-89, dir. program in corp. culture, 1983—; pres. Organizational Design Cons., Pitts., 1975—. Author: Social Systems Design: Normative Theory and the MAPS Design Technology, 1977, Beyond the Quick Fix: Managing Five Tracks to Organizational Success, 1984, Managing Beyond the Quick Fix: A Completely Integrated Program for Creating and Maintaining Organizational Success, 1989; co-author: Methodological Approaches to Social Science: Integrating Divergent Concepts and Theories, 1978, Corporate Tragedies: Product Tampering, Sabotage and Other Catastrophes, 1984, The Management of Organization Design: Vols. I and II, 1976, Producing Useful Knowledge for Organizations, 1983, Gaining Control of the Corporate Culture, 1985, Corporate Transformation: Revitalizing Organizations for a Competitive World, 1988; mem. editorial bd. Jour. Mgmt., 1983-86, Acad. Mgmt. Exec., 1987—, Jour. Organizational Change Mgmt., 1988—; developed Kilmann Insight Test, Learning Climate Questionnaire, Thomas-Kilmann Conflict-Mode Instrument in Ednl. Testing Svc., MAPS Design Tech. for Social Systems Design, Kilmann-Saxton Culture-Gap Survey; contbr. chpts. to books, articles to profl. jours. Mem. Eastern Acad. Mgmt. (treas. 1975-76, dir. 1983-86), Am. Psychol. Assn., Inst. Mgmt. Scis. (1st prize Nat. Coll. Planning competition 1976), Beta Gamma Sigma. Home: 165 Millview Dr Pittsburgh PA 15238 Office: U Pitts Jos M Katz Grad Sch Bus Roberto Clemente Dr Pittsburgh PA 15260

KILMARTIN, JOSEPH FRANCIS, JR., business executive, consultant; b. New Haven, Mar. 11, 1924; s. Joseph Francis and Lauretta M. (Collins) K.; student St. Thomas Sem., 1944; B.A., Holy Cross Coll., 1947; m. Gloria M. Schaffer, June 26, 1954; children—Joanne, Diane. Prodn. mgr. A.C. Gilbert Co., New Haven, 1947-49; profl. performer Broadway show Small Wonder, also TV shows Your Hit Parade, Philco Playhouse, Armstrong Circle Theatre, 1949-50; producer NBC-TV, N.Y.C., 1950-53; v.p. sales Cellomatic Corp., N.Y.C., 1953-59; sr. v.p. Transfilm Inc., N.Y.C., 1959-62, MPO Videotronics, N.Y.C., 1962-66; pres. Bus. Programs Inc., Larchmont, N.Y., 1966-75, Greenwich, Conn., 1975—; lectr. in field, cons. Mexican Dept. Agrarian Affairs and Colonization, 1974—. Active fund-raising Community Chest, 1947-49, ARC, 1947-49, Boy Scouts Am., 1958-66, United Fund, 1970-73; mem. Congl. Adv. Bd., Presdl. Task Force, Atlantic Council, Conn. Venture Group. Recipient medal of excellence Mexican Agrarian Affairs and Colonization Dept., 1976; Golden Medallion award in bus. communication Miami Internat. Film Festival, 1978. Mem. Am. Mgmt. Assn., N.Y. Sales Exec. Club, TV Execs. Soc., Pres.'s Assn., Five Hundred Club. Republican. Roman Catholic. Clubs: Larchmont (N.Y.) Yacht; Bonnie Brair Country (bd. govs. 1970-72); Westchester Country; University (N.Y.C.) Home: 30 Bowman Dr S Greenwich CT 06830 Office: 87 Greenwich Ave Greenwich CT 06830

KILMER, JOYCE CARL, real estate company executive; b. Malmo, Minn., Aug. 29, 1924; s. Carl William and Anna Christine (Ostermann) K.; m. Ione Bernice Hust, Jan. 3, 1953; children—Jeffrey K., Jana Lee Kilmer Wallace. Student, U. Minn., 1944-45, Colo. U., 1967-68; cert. in real estate sales Regis Coll., 1981. Lineman Mountain Bell Telephone Co., Denver, 1947-50, recordman, 1950-53, right-of-way engr., Denver, 1953-55, right-of-way agent, 1955-83; field supr. U.S. Telecommunications, Kansas City, Kans., 1985-86; project supt. acquisitions, Williams Telecommunications Co., Tulsa, 1986—; real estate cons., Livingston, Mont., 1983-84, GTE-Sprint, Orlando, Fla., 1984—, Mountain Bell Telephone Co., Grand Junction, Colo., 1984—, City of Grand Junction, 1984—, Butler Service Group, Durango, Colo. and Orlando, Fla., 1983-84; right-of-way cons. U.S. Telecom, Inc., 1985-86, Wiltel, Inc., 1986; cons. and supr. United Telephone Co. of Ohio, 1986; right-of-way sr. project engr. Ill. Bell Telphone Co., Peoria, 1988. Active Boy Scouts Am., Denver, 1954, 61-78; vice commdr. USCG Aux., Grand Junction, 1975-76, flotilla commdr., 1976-78. Served with U.S. Army, 1943-43. Sr. mem. Internat. Right-of-Way Assn. (pres. Colo. West chpt. 70, 1978, dir. Rocky Mountain region 1982, Profl. of Yr. 1982, 83, Frank C. Balfour award finalist, 1983, 85); mem. Nat. Assn. Ind. Appraisers, Am. Legion. Republican. Methodist.

KILPATRICK, FRANK STANTON, investment banker, management consultant; b. San Jose, Calif., Dec. 2, 1950; s. Frank George and Marian (Polk) K.; AB in Polit. Sci., U. Calif., Berkeley, 1975, postgrad., 1976; student U. Wis., 1968-71, Stanford U. Grad. Sch. Bus., 1981. Successively writer, advt. sales rep., Midwest regional mgr., Western mktg. mgr. 13-30 Corp., Whittle Communications, 1970-74; with Grey Advt., 1977; mktg. mgr. East/West Network, 1978-79; mktg. dir. Calif. Bus. mag., Los Angeles, 1979-81; v.p. mktg. Laufer Co. div. Harlequin Enterprises, 1981; gen. mgr. new venture devel. Knapp Communications Corp. (pub. Archtl. Digest, Bon Appétit, GEO and Home mags.), 1981-84; gen. ptnr. Pacific Cellular, 1982-86; gen. ptnr. Calif. Coast Communications, 1981-84; dir. Pasadena Media Inc., 1984-85, pres. 1984-85; investment banker/mgmt. cons. Frank S. Kilpatrick & Assocs., Los Angeles, 1984—; lectr. entrepreneur program U. So. Calif. Sch. Bus. Adminstrn., 1984-85; venture capital/investment banking; pres. Capital Equity Group, 1986-87. Vol. counselor 1736 Teen Crisis Ctr., Hermosa Beach, Calif. Mem. Los Angeles Advt. Club (Belding award 1980), Direct Mktg. Club So. Calif., Western Publs. Assn., Town Hall Calif., U. Calif. Alumni Assn., Stanford Grad. Sch. Bus. Alumni Assn. (sec. 1985-86, v.p. events 1986-87, dir. 1987—, coordinator entrepreneurial forum 1987-88), Los Angeles Venture Assn. (charter mem. 1985—). Home and Office: 2007 Highland Ave Manhattan Beach CA 90266-4619

KILPATRICK, ROBERT DONALD, insurance company executive; b. Fairbanks, La., Feb. 5, 1924; s. Thomas David and Lula Mae (Crowell) K.; m. Faye Hines, May 29, 1948; children: Robert Donald, Kathleen Spencer, Lauren Douglas Petrovits, Tracy Crowell, Thomas David. B.A., U. Richmond, 1948; postgrad., Harvard U. Grad. Sch. Bus., 1973; received honorary degrees from, Univ. Hartford, Univ. Richmond (Va.), Trinity Coll. (Conn.). With Conn. Gen. Life Ins. Co. (subs. CIGNA Corp.), Hartford, 1954-82, pres., chief exec. officer; also bd. dirs., 1976-82; pres. CIGNA Corp., 1982-85, co-chief exec. officer, 1982-83, chmn., chief exec. officer, 1983—; dir. Allied Signal Inc.; trustee The Conf. Bd., Com. for Econ. Devel. Trustee, vice rector U. Richmond; bd. dirs. Nat. Sci. Ctr. for Communications and Electronics, Com. for a Responsible Fed. Budget; sponsors trustee Colgate Darden Grad. Sch. U. Va.; bd. dirs. Assocs. of Harvard U. Grad. Sch. Bus. Adminstrn.; mem. Phila. World Affairs Council; chmn. Corp. Council Winterthur Mus., Phila. Mem. Bus. Roundtable (exec. com., chmn. com. on fed. budget, policy com.). Office: Cigna Corp 1 Logan Sq Philadelphia PA 19103

KIM, ANDREW BYONG-SOO, portfolio manager; b. Seoul, Korea, Sept. 12, 1936; came to U.S., 1956, naturalized, 1977; s. Yong Choon and Yong Ku (Lee) K.; m. Wan Ryun Rha, June 10, 1961; children: Gene Yong, Ty Yong. Grad. Seoul Nat. U., Korea, 1955; postgrad. Columbia U., 1960-61; MBA, Cornell U., 1963. Analyst, E.I. DuPont Corp., N.Y.C., 1963-65; exec. v.p. Eberstadt Fleming Inc., N.Y.C., 1965-89, also, bd. dirs.; pres. Sit/Kim Internat. Investment Assocs., N.Y.C., 1989—; chmn. investment policy com. Mem. N.Y. Airline Analysts (pres. 1978), N.Y. Soc. Security Analysts, Chartered Fin. Analysts, AIAA. Club: Downtown Athletic (N.Y.C.), World Trade Ctr. Home: 22 E 94th St New York NY 10128 Office: Two World Trade Ctr New York NY 10048

KIM, HACK HYUN, telecommunications executive; b. Republic of Korea, Jan. 8, 1942; m. Myungja Mindy Lee, Jan. 22, 1972; children: Stanley, Sharon. BSEE, Seoul Nat. U., 1964; MSEE, Columbia U., 1975; postgrad., Harvard U., 1987. Sr. field engr. Harris Data Communication, N.J., 1972-76; sr. v.p. MCI Telecommunications, Washington, 1976—. Office: MCI Telecommunications 8283 Greensboro Dr McLean VA 22102 also: MCI Telecommunications Corp 1133 19th St NW Washington DC 20036

KIM, YOUNG SOO, machinery manufacturing company executive; b. Seoul, Korea, Dec. 10, 1940; s. Suk Joo and Soon Keum K.; m. Son Sun Za.; children—Maeng Zoon, Zung A., Kyung A. B.A., Hankuk U. fgn. studies, Seoul, Korea, 1967. Gen. mgr. Hyundai Constrn. Co., Bangkok, Thailand, 1972-75; gen. mgr. Hyundai Am. Corp., Agana, Guam, 1975-78; sr. dir. Hyunda Internat. Inc., Seoul, 1978-79; exec. dir. Korea Heavy Industries and Constrn. Co. Ltd., Seoul, 1979—; exec. dir. Perak Hanjoon Simen, Ipoh, 1980—. Avocations: reading; golf. Home: 1 Tiger Close, Ipoh, Perak Malaysia also: 187-40 Yunhi-Dong, Sudaemun-Ku, Seoul Korea

KIMBALL, ELDEN ALLEN, banker, accountant; b. Waterloo, Iowa, Oct. 20, 1931; s. Merrill L. and Genevie J. (Dillinghan) K.; m. Elizabeth Caroll O'Dell, Aug. 23, 1959; children: Toni A., Donita B. BA, Cen. Mo. State U., 1958; MBA, U. Mo., 1963; postgrad., U. Wis., 1966-69. Asst. examiner FDIC, St. Louis, 1958-62; asst. v.p., cashier 1st Nat. Bank, Independence, Mo., 1963-66; asst. comptroller United Mo. Bank, Kansas City, 1966-70; pres. Bankers Auditing Corp., Kansas City, 1970-80; sr. v.p. Stadium Bank, Kansas City, 1980-85, Concordia (Mo.) Bank, 1985—. Served as sgt. USMC, 1952-55, including Korea. Mem. Mo. Bankers Assn. (conv. com. 1988—), Tax Execs. Inst. Republican. Club: Lions (Concordia). Office: Concordia Bank 547 Main Concordia MO 64020

KIMBALL, JAMES N., corporate media executive; b. LaVerkin, Utah, Oct. 27, 1934; s. Abram Noble and Louise (James) K.; m. Joan C. Kimball, Dec. 28, 1959; children: Ted, John, Amy. BS, U. Utah, 1959, MS, 1961. V.p. Terracor, Salt Lake City, 1969-73, Ivory & Co., Salt Lake City, 1978-80, Boyer Co., Salt Lake City, 1980-84, Morris/Ask Mr. Foster, Salt Lake City, 1986-89; pres. Kimbal Travel Cons., Salt Lake City, 1971-86, Kimbal Incentives, Salt Lake City, 1986-89; dir. media rels. Huntsman Chem. Corp., Salt Lake City, 1989—; dir. Phlcorp, Inc., Phila. Columnist Deseret News, Utah Holiday mag. Mem. Dem. State Cen. Com., Salt Lake City, 1965-70; dep. dir. dept. devel. services of Utah, Salt Lake City, 1966-68; mem. instnl. council Dixie Coll., St. George, Utah, 1972-74; commr. Utah State Pub. Service Commn., Salt Lake City, 1978-80. Mem. Soc. Incentive Travel Execs., Meeting Planners Internat. Mormon. Home: 1509 Military Way Salt Lake City UT 84103

KIMBALL, ROBERT DAVERN, lawyer; b. San Diego, Apr. 20, 1956; s. George William and Martha Washington (Davis) K.; m. Sharon Elaine Readhimer, Mar. 20, 1982; children: Michael J., Brian P. AB cum laude, Yale U., 1977, JD, 1980. Bar: N.Y. 1981, Tex. 1984, U.S. Dist. Ct. (so. dist.) N.Y. 1981, U.S. Dist. Ct. (no. dist.) Tex. 1984, U.S. Ct. Appeals (9th cir.) 1982, U.S. Ct. Appeals (5th cir.) 1984. Assoc. Davis Polk & Wardwell, N.Y.C., 1980-84, Gibson, Ochsner & Adkins, Amarillo, Tex., 1984-87; ptnr. Gibson, Ochsner & Adkins, Amarillo, 1988—. Bd. dirs. Amarillo Little Theatre, 1985-87; mem. scholarship com. St. Thomas the Apostle Parish, Amarillo, 1986-87; mem. com. Amarillo United Way, 1985. Mem. Assn. of Bar of City of N.Y., State Bar Tex., Amarillo Bar Assn., Manuscript Soc. (admissions com. 1977-79), Yale Club Amarillo (alumni schs. com. 1986—). Republican. Roman Catholic. Office: Gibson Ochsner & Adkins Eighth Ave & Taylor St Amarillo TX 79101-2499

KIMBERLY, WILLIAM ESSICK, investment banker; b. Neenah, Wis., Mar. 19, 1933; s. John Robbins and Elizabeth McFarland (Essick) K.; m. Elena Guajardo, Nov. 27, 1965; children: Essicka Amelia, Ariadne Elena, Dagny Maria. Student U. Wis., 1953-54. Sr v.p. Kimberly-Clark Corp, Neenah, Wis., 1959-83; prin. W.E. Kimberly Investments, Neenah, 1983-85; pres. Kimberly, Brunell, & Lehmann, Inc., Washington, 1986—; bd. dir. Capitol Video Corp., Washington, Systems Impact Inc., Kimberly Gallery of Art Inc., Washington, Emergency Aid Systems, Inc. With USNR, 1956-58. Republican. Episcopalian. Club: Met. (Washington). Avocations: auto racing, music, art, movies. Home: 4082 Ridgeview Circle Arlington VA 22207 Office: Kimberly Brunell & Lehmann Inc 2828 Pennsylvania Ave NW Ste 301 Washington DC 20007

KIMBROUGH, RALPH BRADLEY, JR., accountant, educator; b. Bluefield, W.Va., Apr. 8, 1954; s. Ralph Bradley Sr. and Gladys (King) K. BSBA with honors, U. Fla., 1976, MS in Acctg., 1980. CPA, Fla. Staff acct. Ernst & Whinney, Orlando, Fla., 1976-77, Hentschel, Crawford, Hopkins & Thompson, CPA's, Melbourne, Fla., 1977-78; bus. cons. & supr. sponsored research div. U. Fla., Gainsville, 1980; mgmt. auditor Associated Coca-Cola Bottling Co., Daytona Beach, Fla., 1980-82; pvt. practice acctg. Daytona Beach, Fla., 1982-88; asst. prof. aviation bus. adminstrn. Embry-Riddle Aero. U., Daytona Beach, 1982-88, chmn., mem. various coms.; internal auditor U. Fla., Gainesville, 1988—. Contbr. papers to profl. publs. Faculty rep. Daytona Beach United Way Campaign, 1985-86. Mem. Am. Inst. CPA's, Fla. Inst. CPA's, Nat. Assn. Accts., Acctg. Research Assn., Phi Kappa Phi, Phi Eta Sigma. Lodge: Optimists (chmn. oratorical contest 1983-85).

KIMMEL, GEORGE STUART, engineering and process technology executive; b. Rochester, N.Y., Aug. 22, 1934; s. George N. and Marcella M. (Rogers) K.; married; children: Frederick, Marcella, Patricia. BBA, Clarkson U., 1957. CPA, N.Y., La. Mgr. Peat Marwick Mitchell & Co., Rochester, N.Y., 1957-68; asst. treas. G. W. Murphy Industries, Inc., Houston, 1968-69; mgr. Peat Marwick Mitchell & Co., Houston, 1969-70; v.p., chief fin. officer Lykes Corp., New Orleans, 1970-79; v.p. fin., chief fin. officer Combustion Engring., Inc., Stamford, Conn., 1979-84, exec. v.p., chief fin. officer, 1985-87, exec. v.p. ops., 1987-88; pres., chief oper. officer Combustion Engring., Inc., Stamford, 1988—; also bd. dirs. Combustion Engring., Inc., Stamford, Conn. Trustee Clarkson U., Potsdam, N.Y. Served with U.S. Army, 1958-60. Office: Combustion Engring Inc 900 Long Ridge Rd PO Box 9308 Stamford CT 06904

KIMMEL, MARK, venture capital company executive; b. Denver, Feb. 15, 1940; s. Earl Henry and Gerry Claire Kimmel; m. Gloria J. Danielewicz, Jan. 29, 1966 (div.); children: Kenton, Kristopher; m. Lucy Beale, Mar. 21, 1987 (div.). BS in Elec. Engring., U. Colo., 1963, BS in Mktg., 1963; MBA in Fin., U. So. Calif., 1966. Sales engr., market research analyst 3M Co., Calif. and Minn., 1963-70; mktg. mgr. Am. Computer and Communications, Calif., 1970-71; mgr. new bus. devel. Motorola, Inc., Schaumburg, Ill., 1971-76; v.p. corp. devel. Nat. City Lines, Denver, 1976-77; pres. Enervest, Inc., Denver, 1977-84; gen. ptnr. Columbine Venture Fund Ltd., Columbine Venture Fund II, Columbine Venture Mgmt. II; pres. Columbine Venture Mgmt. Inc., now gen. ptnr.; bd. dirs. Athens Inc., Krysalis Corp., Innovus Inc. Mem. Nat. Assn. Small Bus. Investment Cos. (past bd. govs.), Venture Capital Assn. Colo. (past chmn.). Republican. Home: 7500 E Dartmouth Ave #20 Denver CO 80231 Office: 6312 Fiddler Green Circle #260 N Englewood CO 80111

KIMMEL, ROBERT O., marketing executive; b. Bklyn., Aug. 31, 1928; s. Philip Murray and Katherine (Mittleman) K.; BEE cum laude, Bklyn. Poly. Inst., 1951; children by previous marriage: Kenneth, Jeanne; m. Barbara Gajdik, Oct. 12, 1969; children: Katherine Nicole, Todd Philip. Field engr. Gen. Electric Co., 1951-53; sales engr. Raytheon Co., Los Angeles, 1953-60; regional mktg. mgr. Hughes Aircraft Co., Torrance, Calif., 1960-69; v.p. ABC Electronic Sales, Inc., Williston Park, N.Y., 1969-84; pres. R. O. Kimmel Assocs., Inc.; dir. Acro-Com, KW Internat. Corp.; dir. Pacific Rim Interface Member Enterprises, N.Y.C., mktg. hdqrs., San Diego. Mem. IEEE, Tau Beta Pi, Eta Kappa Nu.

KIMMELL, LEE H., investment banker; b. Fort Worth, Jan. 21, 1950; s. Sam and Rowena (Ginsburg) K.; m. Barbara Marcus Kimmell, Aug. 16, 1975; children: David Marcus, Barbara Elizabeth. B.S. in Econs., U. Pa., 1972, M.B.A., 1974. Assoc. Smith, Barney & Co., N.Y.C., 1974-75; assoc. Salomon Brothers Inc, N.Y.C., 1976, v.p., 1978, mng. dir., 1982—, bd. dirs., 1988—. Bd. dirs. N.Y. Service for Handicapped, N.Y.C., 1982—, Jackie Robinson Found., 1988—. Jewish. Office: Salomon Bros Inc 1 New York Pla New York NY 10004

KIMMELMAN, DAVID H., financial industry specialist; b. N.Y.C., May 13, 1955; s. Morris and Rosalind (Engel) K.; m. Lee A. Hawley, Aug. 10, 1985. BBA in Acctg., Pace U., 1977. Chartered bank auditor. Auditor Irving Bank Corp., N.Y.C., 1978-81; audit supr. Barclay's Bank N.Y., Scarsdale, 1981-84, v.p. and dep. controller, 1984-86; treas., mng. dir. Res. Mgmt. Corp., N.Y.C., 1986—. Democrat. Jewish. Office: Res Mgmt Corp 810 Seventh Ave New York NY 10019

KIMSEY, JIMMY R., banker; b. Geraldine, Ala., Nov. 11, 1939; s. Garland L. and Audie (Rucks) K.; m. Judy S. Hall, May 12, 1961 (dec. May 1987); children: Carla Kimsey Vinson, Jonathan B. Student, Snead Coll., 1960, U. Ala., 1961; cert., Sch. of Banking, South Baton Rouge, La., 1974, Nat. Grad. Comml. Lending Sch., Norman, Okla., 1976. Chartered bank auditor; cert. comml. lender. Clk. Peoples Bank, Collinsville, Ala., 1959-60, 1st Nat. Bank, Gadsen, Ala., 1960-61, Ala. City Bank, Gadsen, 1961-62; bank examiner Fed. Deposit Ins. Corp., Atlanta, 1962-66; exec. v.p. Bank of Moulton, Ala., 1966-78; pres. The Home Bank, Guntersville, Ala., 1978—; also bd. dirs. The Home Bank; chmn. bd. Bank of Albertville, Ala., 1987—; bd. dirs. HomeBanc Corp., Guntersville, pres., 1978—; bd. dirs. TAB Fin. Systems, Inc., Guntersville, Comptronix Corp. Author computer program INSTALOAN, 1985. Mem. Ind. Community Bankers of Ala. (bd. dirs. 197), Ala. Bankers Assn. (group chmn. 1983), Rotary (pres. 1987). Office: The Home Bank 3433 Creek Cir Guntersville AL 35976

KIMURA, TSUTO, architectural design company executive; b. Tokyo, Okubo Shinjuku-ku, Japan, Aug. 15, 1933; s. Norio Honda and Chyo (Kimura) K.; m. Sachiko Sekine, Nov. 10, 1961; children: Takeshi, Sigeru, Shuzo. BS in Architecture, Waseda U., 1958; MArch, U. Ill., 1967. Asst. Waseda U., Tokyo, 1958-60; architect Sta. NHK-TV Broadcasting Ctr., Tokyo, 1960-65; pres. Tsuto Kimura Architects & Assocs., Tokyo, 1968—; research and teaching asst. U. Ill., 1965-67, Waseda U., Tokyo, 1968-77. Prin. works include NHK-TV Broadcasting Complex Bldg., Kamakura Rojuman. Recipient Murano prize Waseda U. Archtl. Dept., 1958, 1st prize Internat. Design Competition, Perugia, Italy, 1971, 3d prize Internat. Design Competition, Vienna, Austria, 1971. Mem. Machida City Planning Deliveration, Koganei City Planning Deliveration, Japan Inst. Architecture, Archtl. Inst. Japan. Office: Tsuto Kimura Architect & Assocs, 6F Plaza Shinoju, 168 Shinjuku Japan also: Mauna Lani Resort Point Condo F-201 Kohala Coast HI 96743

KINCADE, CHRISTOPHER LEE, financial planner, insurance agent, stock broker; b. Cleve., Oct. 19, 1940; s. Gerard M. and Hildegarde (Hadley) K.; m. Joan Patt, Aug. 23, 1963; children: Laura L., Christopher L. Jr., Andrew H. BA, Yale U., 1964. CLU; chartered fin. cons. Reporter N.Y. World-Telegram & Sun, N.Y.C., 1964-65; writer, news editor AP, Detroit, 1966-71; asst. chief bur. AP, Dallas, 1972-72; chief bur. AP, Louisville, 1972-75; editor, pub. The Reporter, Louisville, 1976-78; agt. Nat. States Ins. Co., Louisville, 1978, Mut. Benefit Life Ins. Co., Louisville, 1981—; pvt. practice fin. planning Louisville, 1986—; reporter Detroit News, summer 1963. Chmn. bd. Louisville Swim Assn., 1976-77, City of Brownboro Farm, Louisville, 1976-77, Walden Theatre, Louisville, 1984-86; sec. Yale in Ky., Inc., Louisville, 1981—. Mem. Am. Soc. CLU's and Chartered Fin. Cons., Nat. Assn. Life Underwriters. Democrat. Episcopalian. Home: 3707 Old Brownsboro Hill Rd Louisville KY 40141 Office: 100 E Liberty St PO Box 70289 Louisville KY 40270

KINDER, RICHARD DAN, natural gas pipeline, oil and gas company executive; b. Cape Girardeau, Mo., Oct. 19, 1944; s. Luke Frazelle and Edna (Corbin) K.; m. Anne Lamkin; 1 child, Kara. BA, U. Mo., 1966, JD, 1968. Sole practice, Cape Girardeau, Mo., 1972-80; sr. atty. Continental Resources/Fla. Gas Cos., Winter Park, 1981-82, v.p., gen. counsel, 1982-84; sr. v.p., gen. counsel Houston Natural Gas Corp., 1985, HNG/InterNorth Inc., Houston, 1985-86; exec. v.p. law and corp. devel. Enron Corp., Houston, 1986-87, exec. v.p., chief of staff, 1987—. Bd. dirs. Soc. Performing Arts, Houston, 1986—, Mus. Fine Arts, Houston, 1987—. Served to capt. U.S. Army, 1968-72. Mem. ABA, Mo. Bar Assn., Houston Bar Assn. Methodist. Clubs: Houston Racquet; Petroleum. Office: Enron Corp 1400 Smith PO Box 1188 Houston TX 77002-1188

KINDLEBERGER, CHARLES P., II, economist, emeritus educator; b. N.Y.C., Oct. 12, 1910; s. E. Crosby and Elizabeth Randall (McIlvaine) K.; m. Sarah Bache Miles, May 1, 1937; children: Charles P., Richard S., Sarah, E. Randall. AB, U. Pa., 1932, DS (hon.), 1984; AM, Columbia U., 1934, PhD, 1937; Dr. h.c., U. Paris, 1966, U. Ghent, 1975, U. Pa., 1984. Research in internat. trade and fin. Fed. Res. Bank N.Y., 1936-39, Bank Internat. Settlements, 1939-40, Bd. Govs. FRS, 1940-42; Am. sec. Joint Econ. Com. U.S. and Can., 1941-42; served with OSS, Washington, 1942-44, 45; chief div. German and Austrian Econ. Affairs, Dept. State, Washington, 1945-48; assoc. prof. econs. MIT, 1948-51, prof., 1951-76, prof. emeritus, 1976—, chmn. faculty, 1965-67; vis. prof. econs. Brandeis U., 1983-87. Author: International Short-Term Capital Movements, 1937, The Dollar Shortage, 1950, International Economics, 1953, rev. edits., 1973, 78, The Terms of Trade, 1956, Economic Development, 1958, rev. edits., 1965, 77, Foreign Trade and the National Economy, 1962, Economic Growth of France and Britain, 1851-1950, 1964, Europe and the Dollar, 1966, Postwar European Growth, 1967, American Business Abroad, 1969, Power and Money, 1970; editor: The International Corporation, 1970, The World in Depression, 1929-39, 1973, rev. edit., 1986, Economic Response, 1978, Manias, Panics and Crashes, 1978, International Money, 1981, A Financial History of Western Europe, 1984, Multinational Excursions, 1984, Keynesianism vs Monetarism, 1985, Marshall Plan Days, 1987, International Capital Movements, 1987, International Economic Order, 1988. Internat. Econ. Order, 1988; Intelligence officer 12th Army Group, 1944-45; disch. rank of maj., Gen. Staff Corps. Decorated Legion of Merit, Bronze Star; recipient Harms prize Institut für Weltwirtschaft, Kiel, 1978. Fellow Am. Philos. Soc., Am. Econ. Assn. (Disting. fellow, v.p. 1966, pres. 1985); mem. Am. Acad. Arts and Scis., Phi Beta Kappa, Delta Psi. Episcopalian. Home: Bedford Rd Lincoln MA 01773

KING, ALFRED MEEHAN, professional association executive; b. Boston, Oct. 31, 1933; s. Lester S. and Marjorie C. (Meehan) K.; A.B. magna cum laude, Harvard Coll., 1954, M.B.A., 1959; m. Mary Jane Oliver, Dec. 19, 1976; 1 son, Thomas A. Acctg. supr. Gen. Motors Co., LaGrange, Ill., 1959-64; asst. controller J.I. Case Co., Racine, Wis., 1964-69; v.p. fin. Am. Appraisal Co., Milw., 1969-77; sr. v.p. fin. Valuation Research Corp., Milw., 1978-81; mng. dir. Nat. Assn. Accts., Montvale, N.J., 1981—; adj. asst. prof. U. Wis.-Parkside, Kenosha, 1978-81. Treas., Village of North Bay, Wis., 1972-76, Racine Symphony Orch., 1979-81. Mem. Inst. Mgmt. Acctg. (regent 1978-81), Fin. Execs. Inst. Republican. Congregationalist. Author: Increasing the Productivity of Company Cash, 1969. Home: 14 Fox Hedge Rd Saddle River NJ 07458 Office: Nat Assn Accts Paragon Dr Montvale NJ 07645

KING, BETTY BLAKE, accountant; b. Pinehurst, N.C., Jan. 29, 1957; d. Jesse William and Grace Alice (Burr) B; m. Robin Aycock King, Oct. 13, 1979; children: Aaron Keith, Katherine M. AA, Sandhills Community Coll., Southern Pines, N.C., 1984. CPA, N.C. Acct. Dixon, Odom & Co., CPA's, Southern Pines, 1984—. Mem. Am. Inst. CPA's, N.C. Assn. CPA's.

KING, BRIAN A., financial executive; b. Evanston, Ill., Dec. 2, 1958; s. Roy Howard and Nadine Lorraine (Hadley) K.; m. Diane Whiting, May 23, 1987; 1 child. BA in Acctg., Morehouse Coll., 1980; MBA in Fin., U. Pa., 1982. Comml. loan officer Chem. Bank, N.Y.C., Houston, 1982-85; v.p., comml. loan officer Harris Bank, Chgo., 1985; chief fin. officer City & Suburban Distbrs., Chgo., 1985—; real estate cons. King & Assocs., Evanston, 1985—. Cons. Evanston Housing Commn, 1987. Home: 1017 Garnett Pl Evanston IL 60201 Office: City and Suburban Distbrs 820 N Franklin Ste 400 Chicago IL 60610

KING, CARL B., tool company executive; b. 1942; married. B.A., U. Tex., 1965, LL.B., 1966; M.B.A., Wharton Sch. Bus., U. Pa., 1968. Counsel corp. planning Exxon Corp., 1968-74; counsel Cameron Iron Works, Inc., Houston, 1974-75, v.p. corp. services, 1975-81, sr. v.p., sec., 1981-83, sr. v.p., gen. mgr. oil tool div., 1984—. Office: Cameron Iron Works Inc Oil Tool Div 13013 Northwest Freeway Box 1212 Houston TX 77251-1212

KING, CARL EDWARD, employee screening executive; b. Pine Bluff, Ark., June 19, 1940; s. Carl B. King and Claudia Marie (Fulbright) Ingham; m. Jonna Sue DeWeese, Mar., 1964 (div. Nov. 1974); 1 child, Grant Edward; m. Paula Honor Finnell, Mar. 6, 1975. LLB, U. Chgo., 1971; BS in Criminal Justice, U. Nebr., 1978; Masters in Bus. Mgmt., Cen. Mich. U., 1979. Enlisted USMC, 1957, commd. 2d lt., 1969, advanced through grades to maj., 1981; ops. officer, co. commdr. Mil. Police Co., Okinawa, Japan, 1973-74; asst. provost marshal USMC, Barstow, Calif., 1975; provost marshal USMC, Beaufort, S.C., 1975-77, Kaneohe Bay, Hawaii, 1978-81; ret. USMC, 1981; salesman Smith Protective Services, Houston, 1981-82, mgr. investigations div., sales mgr., 1982-83, v.p. mktg., 1983-84; co-founder, chief exec. officer Team Bldg. Systems, Houston, 1984—. Mem. loss prevention adv. bd. U. Houston, 1986—. Decorated Bronze Star, Purple Heart with oak leaf cluster. Mem. FBI Nat. Acad., Internat. Assn. Chiefs of Police, Am. Soc. Indsl. Security, Nat. Order Battlefield Commns., Marine Mustang Assn. Republican. Methodist. Home: 16 Diamond Oak Ct The Woodlands TX 77381 Office: Team Bldg Systems 363 N Belt Ste 990 Houston TX 77060

KING, CLARK ELMER, utilities executive; b. Sunderland, Iowa, July 24, 1934; s. Elmer E. and Willma (Clark) K.; m. Margaret Thompson, Dec. 2, 1960; children: Ronald Clark, Kathy Kay. BSEE, Finlay Engring. Coll., Kansas City, 1954. Engr. trainee/service engr. Pub. Service Co. of Okla., Tulsa, 1954-65, project. engr., 1965-67, sales supr., 1967-73, dir. area devel., 1973-74, div. asst. mgr., 1974-76; dist. mgr. Pub. Service Co. of Okla., Lawton, 1976-78; mgr. rates Pub. Service Co. of Okla., Tulsa, 1978-81; div. mgr. Pub. Service Co. of Okla., McAlester, 1981-83; v.p. mktg. ops. Pub. Service Co. of Okla., Tulsa, 1983—; dir. Ark. Basin Devel. Auth., Tulsa, 1986—. With U.S. Army, 1957-59. Office: Pub Svc Co of Okla 212 E Sixth St Tulsa OK 74119

KING, DANIEL PATRICK, communications executive; b. Wauwatosa, Wis., Feb. 23, 1942; s. Daniel Joseph and Margaret Ruth (McGowan) K.; m. Guadalupe Vasquez, Dec. 11, 1971. BS, U. Wis., 1965; MA, Marquette U., 1979. Freelance writer, editor 1965-74; pres. Daniel P. King Assocs, Whitefish Bay, Wis., 1974—; lectr. U. Wis., Madison, 1978; instr. Milw. Area Tech. Coll., 1974—. Author: Twentieth Century Crime & Mystery Writers, 1980, 86; book reviewer: World Literature Today, 1976—; contbr. articles and essays to profl. jours. Del. Wis. Rep. Conv., 1980—. Fellow Royal Soc. Arts; mem. Crime Writers Assn., Assn. Authors, Assn. Former Intelligence Officers. Home: 5125 N Cumberland Blvd Whitefish Bay WI 53217 Office: Daniel P King Assocs PO Box 11888 Milwaukee WI 53211

KING, DAVID ALDERSON, banker, lawyer; b. Charleston, W.Va., Aug. 8, 1936; s. George Washington and Alice Carroll (Alderson) K.; m. Georgiana Schoolfield Bailey, Sept. 19, 1958; children: Georgiana, Alice. BA, W.Va. U., 1958, JD, 1961. Bar: W.Va. 1961. Pvt. practice Charleston, 1961-66; rep. Bache & Co., Charleston, 1967; v.p. One Valley Bank, N.A., Charleston, 1967-76, sr. v.p., 1976-86, exec. v.p., 1986—; also bd. dirs. One Valley Bank, N.A., Huntington, W.Va. Bd. dirs. Salvation Army, Charleston, 1986—. Mem. Englewood Club, Masons, Shriners. Office: One Valley Bank Box 1793 Charleston WV 25325

KING, EMMETT ALONZO, III, business executive, insurance consultant; b. Norfolk, Va., June 9, 1942; s. Emmett S. and Mary Lee (Sutton) K.; m. Yvonne J. Bullock, Apr. 5, 1965 (div. 1979); children: Andre, Jacqueline; m. Yvonne Levelle Kier, Oct. 19, 1980; stepchildren: Richard, Roland. Student, Mary-Hardin-Baylor Coll., 1967, Coll. of Ins., 1971. Benefits rep. EBS Mgmt. Cons., Inc., N.Y.C., 1968; sr. group adminstr. group ins. sales office Conn. Gen. Life Ins. Co., N.Y.C., 1968-70; successively group adminstr., account exec., asst. v.p., v.p., mgr. employee benefits dept. Bayly, Martin & Fay, Inc., N.Y.C., 1971-83; sr. cons., nat. account exec. Graycliffe Associates, Inc., N.Y.C., 1983-84; account exec. Hartford Ins. Cos., N.Y.C., 1984-86; nat. account exec., sr. cons. GAB Bus. Services, Inc., Parsippany, 1986-88; dir. mktg. Total Plan Adminstrs., Inc. (subs. Blue Cross and Blue Shield N.J. Inc.), Cranford, N.J., 1988—; vis. lectr. Princeton U.; 3-time judge Ala. Jr. Miss. Program; hon. trooper Ala. State. Charter mem. Tri-W Black Families, Inc., 1979—. Served with U.S. Army 1961-67. Mem. Nat. Ins. Industry Assn. (charter), 100 Black Men Inc., Am. Spl. Risks Assn., Group Ins. Assn. Greater N.Y., Self Ins. Inst. Am., N.Y.C. C. of C., Tri-West Black Families Inc. (charter mem. 1979-82), First Tuesday Group (founder 1982—). Office: Total Plan Adminstrs Inc 14 Commerce Dr Cranford NJ 07016

KING, GEORGE RALEIGH, manufacturing company executive; b. Benton Harbor, Mich., May 13, 1931; s. Maurice Peter and Opal Ruth (Hart) King; m. Phyllis Stratton, Apr. 10, 1950; children—Paula King Zang, Angela King Moleski, Philip. Student Adrian Coll., 1950-51. Cert. purchasing profl. exec. status. With Kirsch Co., Sturgis, Mich., 1951—, data processing trainee, 1951-53, data processing mgr., 1953-59, asst. purchasing agt., 1959-62, purchasing agt., 1962-68, asst. dir. purchasing, 1968-71, dir. purchasing, 1971—. Author: Rods & Rings, 1972. Elder, 1st Presbyterian Ch., Sturgis, 1970; pres. Sturgis Civic Players, 1972. Recipient citation Boy Scouts Am., 1966, Jr. Achievement, 1967; nominated candidate for adminstr. Fed. Procurement Policy, Reagan Adminstrn., Washington, 1980. Mem. Am. Purchasing Soc. (pres. 1979-81), Nat. Assn. Purchasing Mgmt., Southwestern Purchasing Assn. Clubs: Klinger Lake Country, Exchange (pres. Sturgis 1959, dist. gov. dist and nat. clubs 1961). Masons, Elks. Home: 906 S Lakeview Sturgis MI 49091 Office: Kirsch Co 309 N Prospect St Sturgis MI 49091

KING, JEFFREY ALLEN, systems engineer; b. York, Pa., July 16, 1963; s. Wayne Roy and Fern Anna May (Hull) K. AS, Pa. State U., York, 1983; BS, Pa. State U., Middletown, 1985. Technical staff systems engr. Hughes Aircraft Co., Fullerton, Calif., 1985—. Mem. Pa. State U. Alumni of Orange County. Republican. Home: 1016 Steele Dr Brea CA 92621 Office: Hughes Aircraft Co Ground Systems Group Bldg 676 Mail Sta F319 PO Box 3310 Fullerton CA 92634

KING, JOHN JOSEPH, manufacturing company executive; b. Toledo, Jan. 12, 1924; s. Walter and Frances (Gwozd) Kawecka; m. Joy G. Mohler, Jan. 28, 1950; children: Catherine M., Carolyn S., David J., Michael R., Mark A.R. BSME magna cum laude, U. Toledo, 1957, MS in Indsl. Engring., 1961. Registered profl. engr., Ohio. Draftsman, Tecumseh Products Co., 1941-42; die designer Bingham Stamping Co., 1942-46; tool designer Spicer Mfg. Co., 1946-47; product designer Am. Floor Surfacing Co., 1947-50; founder, mgr. engr. Kent Industries, 1950-52; mech. engr. Owens Ill. Inc., Toledo, 1953-63; mgr. rsch. and devel. Permaglass Inc., Genoa, Ohio, 1963-69; founder, pres. Ashur Inc., Rossford, Ohio, 1969—, also chmn. bd. dirs. Patentee in field. Mem. Am. Ceramic Soc., Soc. Mfg. Engrs., Phi Kappa Phi, Tau Beta Pi. Republican. Roman Catholic. Clubs: Devils Lake Yacht, Ukranian Am. Citizens. Lodges: KC, Eagles. Home: 1111 W Elm Tree Rd Rossford OH 43460 Office: Ashur Inc 1117 Elm Tree Rd Rossford OH 43460

KING, LAWRENCE DAVID, manufacturing company executive; b. Vermillion, S.D., July 1, 1938; s. George Harold and Lucille Madeline (Lindsay) K.; (div. 1964); children: Dawn Suzanne, Laura Jo. Student, U. S.D., 1957, Wash. U., Mo., 1964-68. Registered profl. engr. Calif. Tech. rep. Douglas Aircraft Co., various cities, Calif., Mo., 1958-73; mgr. quality assurance Defense Systems Div. Am. Air Filter Co., St. Louis, 1973-82; mgr. quality assurance Engineered Air Systems Inc., St. Louis, 1982-83, v.p. quality assurance, 1984-86, v.p. planning and material control, 1986-87, v.p. mgmt. systems, 1987-88, mgr. engring. adminstrn., 1988—. Recipient citizen ship award Am. Legion, 1956. Home: 2024 Silent Spring Dr Saint Louis MO 63043 Office: Engineered Air Systems Inc 1270 N Price Rd Saint Louis MO 63132

KING, L(EONARD) RICHARD, grocery chain executive; b. Astoria, Oreg., Aug. 15, 1928; s. Leonard and Phyllis (Piper) K.; m. Ann Marie Ayres, June 27, 1953; children: Gail Ann King Yockey, Ronald Scott. BBA, Wash. State U., 1951. Warehouseman U.R.M. Stores, Inc., Spokane, Wash., 1951-52, field rep., 1952-54, buyer, 1954-64, asst. gen. mgr., 1964-70, pres., chief operating officer, 1970-78, pres., chief exec. officer, 1978—, also chmn. bd.; chmn. Western Family Foods, Inc., Portland, Oreg., 1974-85. Pres. Spokane Jr. Achievement, 1972-74; bd. dirs. Spokane Area Devel. Council, 1976-80. Mem. Spokane C. of C. (bd. dirs. 1976-78), Nat. Am. Wholesale Grocers Assn. (bd. dirs. 1984—), Nat. Grocers Assn. (chmn. 1979-81). Republican. Club: Manito Golf and Country (Spokane) (pres. 1969). Office: URM Stores Inc N 7511 Freya PO Box 3365 Spokane WA 99220

KING, LLEWELLYN JOSEPH, JR., financial executive; b. N.Y.C.; s. Llewellyn Joseph Sr. and Estella Mary (Willman) K.; children: Geraldine Juanita, Daniel Joseph. BBA, Pace U., 1973; MBA, NYU, 1979. Mgr. fin. planning Nabisco Brands, Inc., Parsippany, N.J., 1978-80; mktg. controller Sandvik, Inc., Fair Lawn, N.J., 1980-82, Pepsi-Cola, USA, Purchase, N.Y., 1982-86; v.p., chief fin. officer Phila. Coca-Cola Bottling Co., 1986—; bd. dirs. Liberty Advt., Phila. Airport Adv. Bd. Bd. dirs. Urban League of Phila.

KING, PETER JOSEPH, JR., retired gas company executive; b. Concord, N.H., Aug. 5, 1921; s. Peter Joseph and Helen (Hallinan) K.; m. Louise L. Lynch, Sept. 11, 1948; children: Anne, Peter. B.S., Georgetown U., 1942; LL.B., Harvard U., 1948, postgrad. Advanced Mgmt. Program, 1966. Bar: N.H. 1949, Mass. 1950, Colo. 1963. Practice law N.H., 1948-51; with AEC, 1952-53; with Colo. Interstate Gas Co., Colorado Springs, 1953-86, pres., chief operating officer, dir., 1977-85; vice chmn. Colo. Interstate Gas Co., 1985-86; bd. dirs. Colo. Instate Gas Co. Bd. dirs. Myron Stratton Home, Colorado Springs, 1974—, Pikes Peak Library Dist., 1987—; commr. Colo. Hwy. Commn., 1987—. Served to 1st lt. AUS, 1942-45, 51-52. Roman Catholic. Clubs: Garden of the Gods, El Paso, Broadmoor Golf. Home: 7 Chase Ln Colorado Springs CO 80906

KING, ROBERT LEONARD, warehousing executive; b. Seattle, Feb. 20, 1938; s. Robert Leonard and Phoebe Easley (Edmunds) K.; m. Helen Blair Lewis, Sept. 11, 1959; children: Robert E., David B., Elizabeth S., Victoria R. BA, Dartmouth coll., 1959, MBA, 1960; LLB, LaSalle coll., 1964. CPA, Wash. Acct. Haskins & Sells, Seattle, 1960-63; trader Marshall & Meyer, Seattle, 1963-64; pres. Herron Northwest, Inc., Seattle, 1964-73; v.p. Piper Jaffray & Hopwood, Mpls., 1973-74; pres. Klamath Fin. Services, Klamath Falls, Oreg., 1974-76, Seafirst Investment Advs., Seattle, 1975-80; v.p. Pruvential Bache Securities, Seattle, 1980-85; pres. Rainier Cold Storage & Ice, Seattle, 1985—. Trustee, treas. Lakeside Sch., Seattle, 1966-82, Va. Mason Med. Found., 1976-81; trustee, pres. St. Thomas Day Sch., Bellevue, 1976-81; trustee, pres., chmn. Seattle Repertory Theater, Seattle. Mem. Am. Inst. CPA's, Wash. Soc. CPA's, Internat. Assn. Refrigerated Warehouses, Nat. Fisheries Inst. Clubs: Univesity, Seattle Tennis. Office: Rainier Cold Storage & Ice 6004 Airport Way S Seattle WA 98108

KING, RUTH ALLEN, management consultant; b. Providence, Oct. 8, 1910; d. Arthur S. and Wilhelmina H. (Harmon) Allen; grad. Tefft Bus. Inst., Providence, 1929; 1 dau., Phyllis King Dunham. Sec. to atty., Providence, 1929; stenographer N.Y. Urban League, N.Y.C., 1929; sec. adminstrn., adminstrv. asst., placement officer, asst. dir. Nat. Urban League Skills Bank, 1929-75; founder/sec. The Edges Group, Inc., 1969—; minority relations cons., Hazeltine Corp., Greenlawn, N.Y., 1976—; cons. to exec. v.p. Sony Corp. Am., Park Ridge, N.Y., 1980—; Named Affirmative Action Pioneer, Met. N.Y. Project Equality, 1975; Ruth Allen King Scholarship Fund established, 1970; EDGES Ruth Allen King Ann. Excalibur award established, 1978; recipient Ann Tanneyhill award for commitment to Urban League Movement, 1975; Recognition award NCCJ, 1975; spl. citation Gov. of R.I. and Providence Plantations, 1981; Ruth Allen King Appreciation Day proclaimed in her honor, Providence, Mar. 9, 1981, N.Y.C., 1975; citation R.I. Ho. of Reps., 1981; plaque Urban League R.I., 1981; Woman of Yr. award Suffolk (N.Y.) chpt. Jack and Jill of Am., 1982; numerous others. Mem. N.Y. Personnel Mgmt. Assn., Council Concerned Black Execs., Julius A. Thomas Soc. (charter), NAACP (life). Home and Office: 185 Hall St Apt 1715 Brooklyn NY 11205

KING, SAMUEL, security professional, publisher, leasing executive; b. Steubenville, Ohio, June 10, 1948; s. Cassie Mae (Mohone) King; m. Wendy Lou Mason, Jan. 15, 1969; children: Samuel III, Angela Denise. Student, U. Steubenville, 1970-72, West Va. No. Coll., 1972-73, Wheeling (W. Va.) Coll., 1973-74; AA in Criminal Justice, Jefferson Coll., Steubenville, 1975. Chief exec. officer Centurion Security Agy., Lakewood, Calif., 1976—, King's Pub. Co., Lakewood, 1986—; pres. Universal Leasing & Fin., Lakewood, 1985—; cons. various orgs., Steubenville, 1970-81. Arthur: Real Estate, 1986; author, editor: Home Business Directory, 1986. Sgt. USAF, 1967-71. Democrat. Baptist. Office: 1030 Dublin Rd Ste 203 Columbus OH 43215

KING, THOMAS ALLEN, association executive; b. Indpls., Mar. 6, 1942; s. Ben Allen and Mildred Ruth (Waters) K.; m. Verletta Sue Jackson, July 3, 1965; children: Brian, Scott, Greg. B.A., Butler U., 1966. Public relations asst. Indpls. Newspapers, Inc., 1963-66; with Indpls. C. of C., 1970—, pres., 1979—; bd. dirs. Butler U., Indpls. Bd. dirs. Big Bros. Indpls., Indpls. Area Red Cross, Goodwill Industries Indpls., '500' Festival Assocs. Served with USAF, 1966-70. Mem. Am. C. of C. Execs. Assn. Republican. Methodist. Club: Indpls. Athletic. Home: 7850 Holly Creek Ln Indianapolis IN 46240 Office: Indpls C of C 320 N Meridian St #923 Indianapolis IN 46204

KINGCADE, ALVIN, insurance company officer; b. Phila., June 26, 1950; s. Marvin and Elizabeth (Dawkins) K.; m. Annie Rose Brown, Sept. 18, 1971; children: Alvin, Alicia, Alison. AAS, Community Coll. of Phila., 1970; BS in Econs., U. Pa., 1972. Pension design specialist Penn Mutual Life Ins. Co., Phila., 1972-78, dist. pension sales mgr., 1978-82, pension mktg. mgr., 1982-84, mgr. pension tng., 1984-86, mgr. agt. tng., 1986-87, mgr. fin. planning, 1987-88, dir. pension sales, Mass. Mutual Life Ins. Co., 1988—. Contbr. articles to profl. jours. including Best Rev. V.p., sec. Wayland Temple Youth Assn., 1970—; mem. com. for voting registration Penrose Park, 1980—. Recipient Am. Mgmt. Soc. award, 1970, Good Citizen of Yr. award, Crispus Attucks Bus. award, 1967. Mem. Wharton Grad. Assn., Nat. Assn. Securities Dealers, Life and Health Ins. Home: 7911 Pompey Pl Philadelphia PA 19153 Office: Mass Mut Life 1845 Walnut Philadelphia PA 19103 Office: Penn Mut Life Sixth and Walnut Philadelphia PA 19172

KINGMAN, ALTON (HAYWARD), JR., banker; b. Brockton, Mass., May 6, 1922; s. Alton Hayward and Ethel (Wales) K.; m. Mary Ellen Stavely, Oct. 7, 1945; children: Joan, Dan, Mary Lou. Student, Lehigh U., 1940-43; grad., Pacific Coast Banking Sch., U. Wash., 1969. With First Interstate Bank of Calif., San Francisco, 1949-89; sr. v.p. br. adminstrn. First Interstate Bank of Calif., 1971-74, sr. v.p., mgr. personal bank, 1974-76, exec. v.p. and sr. adminstrv. officer No. Calif., 1976—. Past pres., bd. dirs. Ind. Colls. No. Calif.; bd. dirs., mem. adv. bd. Jr. Achievement of Bay Area Inc.; bd. dirs. Marshall Hale Meml. Hosp., YMCA, United Way, Bay Area, Bay Area Council; mem. exec. bd. San Francisco Bay Area council Boy Scouts Am; trustee U. San Francisco. Served to 1st lt. USAAF, 1942-45. Mem. Western States Bankcard Assn. (chmn. exec. com.), Robert Morris Assos., San Francisco Conv. and Visitors Bur. (dir.). Clubs: Bankers (San Francisco); Sequoyah Country, Pacific Union, Villa Taverna. Home: 81 Graeagle Oakland CA 94605 Office: 1st Interstate Bank Calif 707 Wilshire Blvd Los Angeles CA 90017

KINGMAN, DONG, JR., communications executive; b. San Francisco, June 15, 1936; s. Dong and Janice (Wong) Kingman; m. Elaine Soong, June 22, 1969; children: Melissa, Jonathan. Student, Trinity Coll., Hartford, Conn., 1959. Journalist Hong Kong Standard, 1963-66; corp. editor The Equitable, N.Y.C., 1967-71, CBS, Inc., N.Y.C., 1972-73; corp. editor Marsh & McLennan Cos., Inc., N.Y.C., 1973-76, mgr. publs., 1977-79, dir. pub. rels., 1979-81, mgr. corp. communications, 1981—; artist, cons. Brit. Am. Tobacco Co., 1965; artist, asst. N.Y. Hilton Hotel, 1967, artist, designer Cue mag., 1968, Composers Recs., 1968-70. With Army Security Agy., U.S. Army, 1959-62. Recipient silver, 3 bronze, best ann. report in industry awards Fin. World mag., 1975-86. Mem. Internat. Assn. Bus. Communicators (8 regional awards of excellence, 12 merit awards, 8 Gold Quill awards 1975—), Coun. Communication Mgrs., N.Y. Hist. Soc., N.Y. Lawn Bowling Club (pres. 1988—), Dutch Treat Club. Democrat. Episcopalian. Office: Marsh & McLennan Cos Inc 1221 Ave of the Americas New York NY 10020

KINGSFORD, WILLIAM CHARLES, retail executive; b. Providence, Sept. 18, 1946; s. Arthur Ashley and Muriel Maddox (Gemmell) K.; m. Rosemary Veronica Durans, Sept. 20, 1968 (div. May 1979); children: William, Kinberly, Brian; m. Paulette Francis Nicolaides, Nov. 8, 1980; 1 child, Ashley. BBA, Bryand Coll., 1969. CPA, R.I. Audit mgr. Peat, Marwick, Main & Co., Providence, R.I., 1969-79; v.p., controller corp. Melville Corp., Harrison, N.Y., 1979—. Mem. Retail Fin. Execs. Republican. Episcopalian. Home: PO Box 79 Briarcliff Manor NY 10510 Office: Melville Corp 3000 Westchester Ave Harrison NY 10528

KINGSLEY, OLIVER DOWLING, JR., energy company executive; b. Ozark, Ala., Dec. 3, 1942; s. Oliver Dowling and Frances (Parker) K.; m. Sally H. Yeaman, Oct. 8, 1967; children: Amy, Betsey, Abby, Benjamin. Sr. engr. Ala. Power Co., Birmingham, 1971-72, asst. mgr. Farley Nuclear Plant, 1971-77, mgr. Farley Nuclear Plant, 1977-78, asst. mgr. nuclear generation, 1978-80, mgr. nuclear engring. and tech. support, 1980-84; dir. nuclear plant support So. Co., Birmingham, 1984-85; v.p. nuclear ops. Miss. Power and Light, Jackson, 1985-86, System Energy Resources, Inc., Jackson, 1986—; bd. dirs. INPO's Nat. Nuclear Accreditation Bd., Atlanta, Am. Tech. Inst., Memphis. Mem. regional adv. council Boy Scouts Am., Dothan, Ala., 1978-79. Lt. USN, 1966-71. Mem. Am. Nuclear Soc., Jackson C. of C. Republican. Methodist. Clubs: Riverchase Country (Birmingham) (bd. dirs. 1984-85); Jackson Country. Office: System Energy Resources Inc 5360 I-55 N Jackson MS 39211

KINNEAR, GEORGE E. R., II, university executive; b. Mounds, Okla., Jan. 12, 1928; s. Neil Tilman and Mary Miller (Bancroft) K.; m. Beverley Bell, Dec. 30, 1948 (div. Aug. 1984); children: George III, D. Kevin, Kandace M., P. Kimberley, Holley A., Douglas A.; m. Mary Edwina Cundari, Sept. 15, 1984; stepchildren: Stephen Cundari, Christina Cundari, David Cundari. BA, MA, George Washington U., 1957; MS, PhD, Stanford U., 1966. Commd. ensign USN, 1945, advanced through grades to adm., 1981; asst. chief navy personnel USN, Washington, 1972-74; comdr. carrier group 1 USN, San Diego, 1974-75; chief legis. affairs USN, Washington, 1975-78; commdr. naval air force USN, Norfolk, Va., 1978-81; U.S. mil. rep. to NATO USN, Brussels, 1981-82; ret. USN, 1982; v.p. Grumman Internat., Arlington, Va., 1982-85; v.p. Grumman Corp., Arlington, 1985-86, sr. v.p., 1986-88; exec. v.p., chief fin. officer U. N.H., Durham, 1988—; bd. dirs. Compaq Co., Houston. Mem. bd. visitors Sch. Bus. U. So. Calif.; bd. dirs. Navy Meml., Washington, 1982-88, Yorktown Mus., Charleston, S.C., 1985-88; bd. dirs. Study for Ctr. Study of the Presidency, N.Y.C., 1982-88, Nat. Contract Mgmt. Assn., Washington, 1978-88. Decorated D.S.M. with oak leaf cluster, Legion of Merit with 3 oak leaf clusters, D.F.C. with 3 oak leaf clusters. Mem. Cosmos Club, Army-Navy Club. Republican. Episcopalian. Office: Grumman Corp 1111 Stewart Ave Bethpage NY 11714

KINNEAR, JAMES WESLEY, III, petroleum company executive; b. Pitts., Mar. 21, 1928; s. James Wesley and Susan (Jenkins) K.; m. Mary Tullis, June 17, 1950; children: Robin Wood (Mrs. David Bruce Anderson), Susan, James Wesley IV, William M. BS with distinction, U.S. Naval Acad., 1950. With Texaco Inc., 1954—; sales mgr. Texaco Inc., Hawaii, 1959-63; div. sales mgr. Texaco Inc., Los Angeles, 1963-64; asst. to vice chmn. bd. dirs. Texaco Inc., N.Y.C., 1964-65, asst. to chmn. bd. dirs., gen. mgr. marine dept., 1965, v.p. supply and distbn., 1966-70, sr. v.p. strategic planning, 1970-71, sr. v.p. worldwide refining, petrochems., supply and distbn., 1971-72, sr. v.p. world wide mktg., also in charge internat. marine ops. and petrochems., 1972-76, sr. v.p. internat. marine and aviation sales petrochem. dept., marine dept., mktg. and refining in Europe, 1976-78, exec. v.p., 1978-83, also bd. dirs.; pres. Texaco U.S.A., 1982-84; vice chmn. bd. dirs. Texaco Inc., N.Y.C., 1983-86, pres., chief exec. officer, 1987—; bd. dirs., mem. Am. Petroleum Inst., Nat. Petroleum Council, Corning Glass Works, Bus. Council of N.Y.; mem. Bus. Round Table. Pres. bd. trustees St. Paul's Sch., Concord, N.H. Served to lt. comdr. USNR, 1950-54. Mem. U.S. Naval Inst. Episcopalian. Clubs: Round Hill (Greenwich, Conn.); Verbank Hunting, Brook (N.Y.C.); Iron City Fishing (Parry Sound, Ont.); Augusta (Ga.) Nat. Golf. Home: 149 Taconic Rd Greenwich CT 06830 Office: Texaco Inc 2000 Westchester Ave White Plains NY 10650

KINNEBREW, GUY FORREST, health care executive; b. Shreveport, La., Nov. 16, 1949; s. Collier A. and Doris (Jacoby) K.; m. Glenda Sue Blaney, Nov. 22, 1980; 1 child, Bryan Collier. Student, La. Tech. U., 1967-70; BS, La. State U., 1974. Regional rep. Blue Cross La., Shreveport, 1974-78; exec. dir. Coordinated Health Plan, Shreveport, 1978-80; dir. Blue Cross Blue Shield Miss., Jackson, 1980-85; v.p. Willis-Knighton Health System, Shreveport, 1986—; exec. dir. Willis-Knighton Health Plan, Shreveport, 1986—, also bd. dirs. Mem. Sales and Mktg. Execs. (bd. dirs. 1987—), Shreveport C. of C., La. Hosp. Assn., Healthcare Fin. Mgmt. Assn., La. State U. Alumni Assn., Kappa Sigma. Baptist. Home: 520 Turtlecreek Dr Shreveport LA 71115 Office: Willis-Knighton Health System 2708 Greenwood Rd Shreveport LA 71109

KINNEY, ABBOTT FORD, radio broadcasting executive; b. Los Angeles, Nov. 11, 1909; s. Gilbert Earle and Mabel (Ford) K.; student Ark. Coll., 1923, 26, 27; m. Dorothy Lucille Jeffers, Sept. 19, 1943 (dec. Jan. 1986); children—Colleen, Joyce, Rosemary. Editor Dermott News, 1934-39; partner Delta Drug Co., 1940-49; pres., gen. mgr. S.E. Ark. Broadcasters, Inc., Dermott and McGehee, 1951—; corr. Comml. Appeal, Memphis, Ark. Gazette, Little Rock, 1935-53; research early aeros. Inst. Aero. Scis., 1941, castor bean prodn., 1941-42. Mem. Ark. Geol. and Conservation Commn., 1959-63; chmn. Ark. Planning Commn.; mem. Mississippi River Pkwy. Commn., Park Commn. Past pres., mem. exec. bd. DeSoto Area council Boy Scouts Am.; chmn. County Library Bd.; mem. past pres. Hosp. Adv. Bd.; mem. bd. McGehee-Dermott Indsl. Devel. Corp., Chicot Fair Assn., Christian Rural Overseas Program. Recipient Silver Beaver award Boy Scouts Am.; honored with Abbott Kinney Day by civic orgns. and schs. S.E. Ark., 1955; named one of Ark.'s 10 Outstanding Community Leaders, 1969. Mem. AIM, Nat. Assn. Radio and TV Broadcasters, Ark. Broadcasters Assn., Ark., S.E. Ark. chambers commerce, Internat. Broadcasters Soc. (editorial adv. bd.), Ark. Hist. Assn., Am. Numis. Assn. Club: Rotary. Home: Dermott AR 71638 Office: SE Ark Broadcasters Inc Dermott AR 71638

KINNEY, EARL ROBERT, mutual funds company executive; b. Burnham, Maine, Apr. 12, 1917; s. Harry E. and Ethel (Vose) K.; m. Margaret Velie Thatcher, Apr. 23, 1977; children: Jeanie Elizabeth, Earl Robert, Isabella Alice. A.B., Bates Coll., 1939; postgrad., Harvard U. Grad. Sch., 1940. Founder, North Atlantic Pack Co., Bar Harbor, Maine, 1941; pres. North Atlantic Pack Co., 1941-42, treas., dir., 1941-64; with Gorton Corp. (became subs. Gen. Mills, Inc. 1968), 1954-68, pres., 1958-68; v.p. Gen. Mills, Inc., 1968-69, exec. v.p., 1969-73, chief fin. officer, 1970-73, pres., chief operating officer, 1973-77, chmn. bd., 1977-81; pres., chief exec. officer IDS Mut. Fund Group, Mpls., 1982—; dir. Nashua Corp., Deluxe Check Printers, Inc., Crystal Brands, Inc., Hannaford Bros. Co., Portland, Maine, Union Mut. Life Ins. Co., Portland Jackson Lab. Trustee Bates Coll., also chmn. alumni drives, 1960-64. Office: IDS Bond Fund Inc 1000 Roanoke Bldg Minneapolis MN 55474

KINNUNE, WILLIAM P., forest products executive; b. 1939. Grad., U. Wash., 1961. With Willamette Industries, Inc., Portland, Oreg., 1961—, various sales and mgmt. positions, 1961-75, v.p., 1975-77, sr. v.p., from 1977, now exec. v.p. Office: Willamette Industries Inc 1300 SW Fifth Ave Portland OR 97201

KINSER, DIANNE LEE, typography service executive; b. Wichita Falls, Tex., Jan. 28, 1944; d. Wayne Dee and Sara Ruth (Foster) Schall; m. Ralph E. Kinser, Dec. 30, 1964 (div. Nov. 1972); 1 child, Wayne. Student, U. Minn., 1961-62; AA in Edn., Palm Beach Jr. Coll., 1966; student, Fla. Atlantic U., 1967-70. Asst. advt. mgr. Stevenson's, Mpls., 1961-63; advt. mgr. Belk's, West Palm Beach, Fla., 1963-67; advt. asst. Palm Beach Newspapers, West Palm Beach, 1967-70; prodn. mgr. Artype, West Palm Beach, 1972-75; mng. ptnr. The Type House, West Palm Beach, 1975—; instr. Palm Beach Jr. Coll., Lake Worth, Fla., 1985—; steering com. bd. advisors Fla. Atlantic U., Fla. Internat. U., Small Bus. Devel. Ctr., Internat. Trade Ctr.; instr., bd. advisors and instr. City West Palm Beach Small Bus. Devel. Edn. Program and Program Design Group. Del. White House Conf. on Small Bus., 1986; mem. selection com. county airport concessions, mem. county small bus. leadership commn. Palm Beach County. Named one of Women in Bus. Adv. of Yr., Fla. SBA, 1989. Mem. Am. Advt. Fedn., Greater Palm Beach C. of C., (small bus. and govt. coms.), Nat. Assn. Women Bus. Owners (local pres. 1986-87, nat. dir. 1987-88), Advt. Club of the Palm Beaches, Palm Beach County Women in Bus. (leadership coun.), Palm Beach County Small Bus. Leadership Commn. Home: PO Box 6463 Lake Worth FL 33466-6463 Office: The Type House 2833 Exchange Ct West Palm Beach FL 33409

KINSER, RICHARD EDWARD, management consultant; b. Los Angeles, May 14, 1936; s. Edward Lee and M. Yvonne (Withes) K.; m. Suzanne Carol Logan, Mar. 22, 1958. BA in Econs., Stanford U., 1958. Mgr. U.S. Steel Corp., San Francisco, 1958-65; v.p. Booz-Allen & Hamilton, Inc., San Francisco, 1965-78, Washington, 1971-73; sr. v.p., bd. dirs. William H. Clark Assocs., Inc., San Francisco, 1979-81; dep. dir. presdl. personnel The White House, Washington, 1981-83; mng. ptnr. Gould & McCoy, Inc., 1983-86; pres. Kinser & Assoc., N.Y.C., 1986—; bd. dirs. Measurmatic, Inc., San Francisco, Pure Water, Inc., Lincoln, Nebr.; lectr. in field. Bd. dirs. San Francisco Bicentenial Com., 1976, Americans for Oxford; mem. vice-chancellor's advisor Oxford U. Fellow Aspen Inst.; mem. World Affairs Council, White House Fellows Commn. (commr.). Republican. Clubs: Bankers, Commonwealth, Economics, Mid-Atlantic. Home: 415 E 54th St New York NY 10022 Office: 405 Lexington Ave #4515 New York NY 10174

KINTIGH, ALLEN E., public utility executive; b. Oronoque, Kans., Dec. 30, 1924; s. Ellis E. and Anna M. (Abernathy) K.; m. Joanne Pratt, Jan. 9, 1953; children—Carol, David, Eric. B.S. in M.E., B.S. in E.E., U. Colo., 1947. Registered profl. engr., N.Y., Pa. Area ops. supt. N.Y. State Electric & Gas Corp., Brewster, 1957-66, gen. ops. supt., Binghamton, 1966-73, asst. v.p. ops., 1973-76, v.p. ops., 1975-76, v.p. generation, 1976-83, sr. v.p. generation, 1983-87, exec. v.p., 1987-88; pres., chief operating officer, 1988—. Mem. IEEE, Soc. Profl. Engrs. Republican. Presbyterian. Home: 3605 Scribner Dr Endwell NY 13760 Office: NY State Electric & Gas Corp 4500 Vestal Pkwy E Binghamton NY 13903

KIPP, JERRY STEVEN, civil engineer; b. L.A., Mar. 9, 1952; s. Raymond Joseph and Margaret D. (Bradley) K.; m. Lee Ann Phillips, July 19, 1986; 1 child, Katharine E. BSCE, Marquette U., 1976, MSCE, 1987. Registered profl. engr., Wis. Mgr. engring. svcs. Donohue & Assocs., Inc., Waukesha, Wis., 1975-87; sr. project adminstr. Milw. Met. Sewage Dist., 1987-88; sr. product mgr. Metcalf & Eddy Svcs., Inc., Milw., 1988—; instr. seminar extension program U. Wis., Madison, 1984-85. Contbr. articles to profl. jours. Mem. Am. Pub. Works Assn., Am. Water Works Assn., Am. Soc. Civil Eng., Water Pollution Control Fedn., Smithsonian Instn. Home: 3130 Old Lantern Dr Brookfield WI 53005

KIPPEN, RICHARD MARLIN, wine and spirits company executive; b. Grand Rapids, Mich., May 1, 1932; s. John and Norine (Bragg) K.; m. Eileen Louise Gassert; children: Collette, Richard Marc. BA, Valparaiso U., 1954, JD, 1956. Ins. adjustor Western Adjustment Inspection Co., Detroit, 1956-57; pvt. practice Grand Rapids, Mich., 1958-59; atty. Grand Trunk R.R. Co., Detroit, 1960-63; resident counsel Hiram Walker & Sons Inc., Detroit; resident counsel Hiram Walker-Gooderham & Worts Ltd., Windsor, Ont., Can., asst. sec., 1967-77, corp. sec., 1977—, v.p., gen. counsel, 1984-88, exec. v.p., 1988—. Recipient Outstanding Alumnus award Valparaiso U., 1986. Mem. ABA, Fla. Bar Assn., Mich. Bar Assn., Am. Soc. Corp. Secs. (pres. Detroit regional group 1977), U.S. Trademark Assn., Nat. Assn. Beverage Importers Inc. (mem. exec. com. 1981, 89, treas. 1987, vice-chmn. 1989), Distilled Spirits Coun. U.S. Inc. (co-chmn. 1989, exec. com.), Detroit Athletic Club. Republican. Lutheran. Home: 320 W Dawson Rd Milford MI 48042 Office: Hiram Walker-Gooderham & Worts Ltd, 2072 Riverside Dr E, Windsor, ON Canada N8Y 4S5

KIPPING, VERNON LOUIS, film consultant, marine scientist; b. Cape Girardeau, Mo., Oct. 19, 1921; s. Theodore Frederick and Augusta (Meyer) K.; m. Anna Ruth Uelsmann, Mar. 26, 1944; children: Theodore Paul, John Louis, Douglas Kim. Student, S.E. Mo. State U., 1940-41; AA, Multnomah Coll., 1948; JD, U. San Francisco, 1951. Fingerprint examiner FBI, Washington, 1941-43; with radio communications FBI, Portland, Oreg., 1943-44; spl. employee FBI, Portland, 1946-48; spl. employee San Francisco, 1948-71, 72-76, Chgo., 1971-72; freelance film cons. San Francisco, 1976—; testified as expert witness Patricia Hearst trial. Owner 19 U.S. and fgn. patents motion picture tech., marine sci.; invented means to convert still photos of Patricia Hearsts bank robbery into motion picture for use at trial. Expert witness at Patricia Hearst trial. Served as sgt. USAAF, 1944-46, PTO. Recipient Spl. prize San Francisco Film Festival, 1957. Mem. Soc. Motion Picture and TV Engrs. (program chmn. 1977-79, mgr. 1979-81, membership chmn. 1981-85, spl. events chmn. 1985-88, sec./treas. 1988—, past audio-visual conf. chmn., Citation for Outstanding Service 1986). Republican. Club: No. Calif. Imperial Owners (San Francisco) (v.p. 1979-83, pres. 1983-87). Home and Office: 540 Melrode Ave San Francisco CA 94127

KIRBAN, LLOYD, marketing research executive; b. N.Y.C., June 17, 1931; s. Bernard Kirban and Toby Tischler; m. Annette Sylvia Handelman, Oct. 10, 1953; children: Susan Holis, Elise Edith. BA, CUNY, 1952; MA, NYU, 1957, PhD, 1965; MBA, Rutgers U., 1959. Head consumer research PepsiCola Co., N.Y.C., 1959-61; rsearch dir. Opinion Research Corp., Princeton, N.Y., 1961-65; dir. survey services Mkt. Research Corp. Am., N.Y.C., 1965-69; assoc. dir. survey div. Audits and Surveys Inc., N.Y.C., 1969-79; dir. research Burson-Marsteller, N.Y.C., 1979—; adj. assoc. prof. Grad. Sch. Bus. Rider Coll., Trenton, N.J., 1968-75, Grad. Sch. Bus. Pace U., N.Y.C., 1980-84. Contbr. articles to profl. jour. Served to lt. (j.g.) USNR, 1952-57. Mem. Am. Mktg. Assn., Am. Assn. Pub. Opinion Research, Am. Psychol. Assn. Democrat. Jewish. Office: Burson-Marsteller 230 Park Ave S New York NY 10003

KIRBY, BRUCE RAYMOND, accountant; b. Balt., June 2, 1955; s. Raymond Jacob and Marie Elizabeth (Detress) K.; m. Susan Carol Brashears, Sept. 17, 1977; children: Anthony Raymond, Amy Lee, Christopher Charles. BS, Towson State U., 1977, U. Md., 1975. CPA, Md. Internal auditor Sears, Roebuck & Co., Balt., 1976-77; staff acct. Monumental Life Ins. Co., Balt., 1977-79, sr. acct., 1979-82; mgr. fin. control Monumental Gen. Ins. Co., Balt., 1982-83, dir. acctg. systems, 1984-86, asst. controller, 1987—; treas. abc steering com., Info. Systems Am., Atlanta, 1987—. Mem. Am. Assn. CPAs, Md. Soc. CPAs. Republican. Lutheran. Home: 6428 Wilben Rd Linthicum MD 21090 Office: Monumental Gen Ins Co 1111 N Charels St Baltimore MD 21201

KIRBY, FRED MORGAN, II, corporation executive; b. Wilkes Barre, Pa., Nov. 23, 1919; s. Allan P. and Marian G. (Sutherl) K.; m. A. Walker Dillard, Apr. 30, 1949; children: Alice Kirby Horton, Fred Morgan III, Dillard, Jefferson. Grad., Lawrenceville Sch., 1938; A.B., Lafayette Coll., Easton, Pa., 1942; postgrad., Harvard Grad. Sch. Bus. Adminstrn., 1947. From v.p. to pres., bd. dirs. Allan Corp., 1953-75; pres., chmn. bd. dirs. Filtration Engrs., Inc., 1951-56; dir. Alleghany Corp., 1958-61, 63—, v.p., 1961, exec. v.p., 1963-67, chmn. bd., 1967—, pres., 1968-77, mem. exec. com., 1968—; bd. dirs., mem. exec. com. Cyclops Industries, Inc., Pittston Co., F.W. Woolworth Co.; bd. dirs. Am. Express Co., Chgo. Title and Trust Co., Chgo. Title Ins. Co., Shelby Ins. Co., Shelby Life Ins. Co., Shelby Fin. Corp., Affirmative Ins. Co., Insura Property & Casualty Ins. Co. Pres., dir. F.M. Kirby Found., Inc. Served to lt. (s.g.) USNR, 1942-46. Mem. Zeta Psi. Clubs: Westmoreland (Wilkes Barre, Pa.); Racquet and Tennis, World Trade (N.Y.C.); Spring Valley (N.J.) Hounds. Office: 17 DeHart St PO Box 151 Morristown NJ 07963-0151

KIRBY, RITA MAYE KNOWLES (MRS. CARLTON BEDFORD WATTS), real estate management company executive; b. Dalhart, Tex., Sept. 10, 1941; cert. apt. mgr.; cert. property mgr.; cert. apt. property supr. d. Luby F. and Jonnie Reta Knowles; student Frank Phillips Jr. Coll., Borger, Tex.; m. Jerry W. Kirby, May 6, 1961 (div. 1976); children: Michael, Daniel; m. Carlton Bedford Watts, Aug. 12, 1983. Property mgr. Villa France Apts., Irving, Tex., 1971-72; mgmt. v.p. First Property Mgmt. Corp., Chgo. and Dallas, 1972-80; v.p. ops. S&S Properties, Inc., Dallas, 1980—; exec. v.p., partner Capital Concept Mgmt. Corp., Dallas, 1980-84, pres., mng. ptnr., 1984-87; pres. 1st Capital Mgmt. Corp., 1988, CentreFirst Mgmt. Corp., 1989—. Named Cert. Apt. Mgr. of Yr., 1984. Mem. Dallas Apt. Assn. (dir. 1979—, sec.-treas. 1981-82, 1st v.p. 1982-83, pres. 1983-84), Tex. Apt. Assn. (dir. 1979—, chmn. edn. com. 1981), Nat. Apt. Assn. (dir. 1978—, chmn. edn. com. 1980-81, chmn. Nat. Apt. Mgmt. Accreditation Bd. 1980, 85, regional v.p. 1983), Inst. Real Estate Mgmt. (govt. coun. 1988, v.p. pub. rels., 1988, v.p. edn., 1989). Baptist. Author: Community Directors Guide, 1975; co-author: Property Evaluation and Takeover, 1982. Home: 1606 W Shady Grove Irving TX 75060 Office: 4825 LBJ Fwy Ste 140 Dallas TX 75244

KIRCHNER, ALFRED F., JR., marketing executive; b. Bklyn., July 18, 1930; s. Alfred. F. and Mary C. (Hurtado) K.; m. Joan M. Gruet; children: Robert J., Steven A., Janet A. BA, Hofstra U., 1956; cert. in mgmt., Harvard U., 1962; cert. in chemistry, Duke U., 1978. Sales and ops. mgr. Esso Standard S.A. Ltd., various Latin Am. countries, 1956-65; mktg. ops. mgr. Internat. Petroleum Co., Lima, Peru, 1965-68; sr. sales rep. Esso Internat., N.Y.C., 1968-70; v.p. mktg./mfg. Amoco Internat. Oil Co., Chgo., 1971-76; a.p. internat. bus. ventures Amoco Chem. Co., Chgo., 1977-78, v.p., sr. v.p. mktg., 1978—. Pres. United Ch. in Peru, Lima, 1965; bd. mem. Roosevelt Sch., Lima, 1966; bd. dirs. Child-Family Services, Chgo., 1979. Served as sgt. USMC, 1949-52. Mem. Am. Petroleum Inst., Soc. Chem. Inds., Chem. Manufacturer's Assn., Nat. Petroleum Refiners Assn., Synthetic Organic Chem. Manufacturer's Assn. (bd. govs.). Republican. Methodist. Club: Sunset Ridge Country (Northbrook, Ill.). Office: Amoco Chem Co 200 E Randolph Dr Chicago IL 60601

KIRK, CARMEN ZETLER, data processing executive; b. Altoona, Pa., May 22, 1941; d. Paul Alan and Mary Evelyn (Pearce) Zetler. BA, Pa. State U., 1959-63; MBA, St. Mary's Coll. Calif., 1977. Cert. in data processing. Pub. sch. tchr. State Ga., 1965-66; systems analyst U.S. Govt. Dept. Army, Oakland, Calif., 1967-70; programmer analyst Contra Costa County, Martinez, Calif., 1970-76; applications mgr. Stanford (Calif.) U., 1976-79; pres. Zetler Assocs., Inc., Palo Alto, Calif., 1979—; cons. State Calif., Sacramento, 1985—. Author: (tech. manuals) Comparex, 1982-83. Vol. Stanford Med. Ctr. Aux., 1985—. Office: Zetler Assocs Inc PO Box 50395 Palo Alto CA 94303

KIRK, CASSIUS LAMB, JR., lawyer, investor; b. Bozeman, Mont., June 8, 1929; s. Cassius Lamb and Gertrude Violet (McCarthy) K.; A.B., Stanford U., 1951; J.D., U. Calif., Berkeley, 1954. Bar: Calif. 1955; lic. real estate broker. Assoc. firm Cooley, Godward, Castro, Huddleson & Tatum, San Francisco, 1956-60; staff counsel for bus. affairs Stanford U., 1960-78; chief bus. officer, staff counsel Menlo Sch. and Coll., Redwood City, Calif., 1978-81; pres. Eberli-Kirk Properties, Inc., Menlo Park, 1981—; mem. faculty Coll. Bus. Adminstrn. U. Calif., Santa Barbara, 1967-73; bd. dirs. Just Closets, Inc., San Rafael, Calif.; bd. dirs. San Francisco Pocket Opera; mem. adv. bd. Allied Arts Guild, Menlo Park. With U.S. Army, 1954-56. Mem. Calif. Bar Assn., Stanford Assocs., Order of Coif, Phi Alpha Delta. Republican. Club: Stanford Faculty. Home: 1330 University Dr Apt 52 Menlo Park CA 94025 Office: 3551-N Haven Ave Menlo Park CA 94025

KIRK, DONALD JAMES, accountant, educator; b. Cleve., Nov. 28, 1932; s. John James and Helen Anna (Pilskaln) K.; m. Tara Collins, May 30, 1975; children: J. Alexander, Bruce D.; stepchildren: John Needham, Elizabeth Needham. B.A., Yale U., 1959; M.B.A., NYU, 1961; LL.D. (hon.), Lycoming Coll., 1979. Acct., Price Waterhouse & Co., N.Y.C., London and Washington, 1959-73; partner Price Waterhouse & Co., 1967-73; mem. Fin. Acctg. Standards Bd., Stamford, Conn., 1973-77, chmn., 1978-86; prof. acctg. Columbia U. Grad. Sch. of Bus., 1987—; dir. Gen. Re Corp., 1987—; trustee Fidelity Group Mut. Funds, 1987—;. Officer, bd. dirs. Urban League of Southwestern Fairfield County, Conn., 1971-77; mem. Greenwich (Conn.) Rep. Town Meeting, 1971-77, Greenwich Bd. of Estimate and Taxation, 1977—; bd. dirs. Nat. Arts Stabilization Fund, 1983—; bd. overseers NYU Schs. Bus., 1985—. Served as aviator USN, 1953-57. Recipient Alumni Achievement award NYU Grad. Sch. Bus. Adminstrn., 1980. Mem. Am. Inst. CPA's (mem. governing council, Gold Medal award for disting. service 1986), Am. Acctg. Assn., Govt. Fin. Officers Assn., Stanwich Club (dir.). Office: Columbia U Grad Sch Bus 602 Uris Hall New York NY 10027

KIRK, JAMES ROBERT, research and development executive; b. DuBois, Pa., Oct. 30, 1941; s. Joseph James and Vinetta Helen (Fromm) K.; m. Elaine Gralton, Jan. 5, 1963 (div. July 1985); children—Leanne, James Joseph, John Daniel; m. Paulette DeJong, Sept. 15, 1985. B.S. in Biology, Holy Cross Coll., 1964; M.S. in Food Sci., Mich. State U., 1966, Ph.D., 1971. Asst. prof. Mich. State U., East Lansing, 1971-74; assoc. prof. Mich. State U., 1974-78, prof., 1978; prof., chmn. dept. food sci. and human nutrition U. Fla., Gainesville, 1978-83; corp. v.p. research and devel. Campbell Soup Co., Camden, N.J., 1983—; exec. v.p. Campbell Inst. Research and Tech., Camden, 1983-88, pres., 1988—; dir. Nat. Nutrition Consortium, 1979-83; chmn. food and nutrition conf. Gordon Rsch. Conf., 1982; mem. food nutrition bd. Nat. Acad. Scis., 1982-87; mem. food and nutrition bd. NRC, 1982—; dir. DNA Plant Tech. Corp., 1987—. Contbr. over 100 articles to profl. jours. Recipient Future Leader award Nutrition Found., 1977. Fellow Inst. Food Technologists (Babcock Hart award 1983; exec. com. 1983-86); mem. Am. Soc. Agrl. Engrs., Research and Devel. Assn., Am. Chem. Soc. Office: Campbell Soup Co Campbell Pl Camden NJ 08101

KIRK, RICHARD AUGUSTUS, banker; b. Morristown, N.J., Oct. 19, 1930; s. William T. and Edith (Ely) K.; m. Gladys Nicholson, June 4, 1955 (dec.); children—Laura Kirk, Pamela Kirk Magill, Elizabeth Ely Kirk Potter; m. Susan Cosgriff Mueller, Sept. 7, 1985. BA, Haverford Coll., 1952; postgrad., Stonier Grad. Sch. Advanced Mgmt., Rutgers, N.Y., 1965-67, Harvard U., 1972-73. Mgmt. trainee, ofcl. asst. 1st Nat. City Bank, N.Y.C., 1955-57; systems analyst Warner Pharm. Co., 1957; from bus. devel. asst. to chmn. United Bank of Denver, Denver, 1958—; also dir. United Bank of Denver; vice chmn., dir. United Banks of Colo.; bd. dir. Allied Bank Internat., Greater Denver Corp., Downtown Denver, Inc. Mem. Gov.'s Econ. Devel. Action Coun., Pub. Edn. Coalition, Nat. Western Stockshow, Colo. Alliance Bus.; trustee Denver Bot. Gardens. Mem. Am. Bankers Assn., Assn. Res. City Bankers, Denver C. of C. (bd. dir.). Republican. Episcopalian. Clubs: Denver Country, Castle Pines Golf, Garden of the Gods, Univ. Lodges: Rotary, Confrerie des Chevaliers du Tastevin-Argentier. Office: United Bank One United Bank Ctr 1700 Broadway Ste 3100 Denver CO 80274

KIRKLAND, BERTHA THERESA (MRS. THORNTON CROWNS KIRKLAND, JR.), engineer; b. San Francisco, May 16, 1916; d. Lawrence and Theresa (Kanzler) Schmelzer; m. Thornton Crowns Kirkland, Jr., Dec. 27, 1937 (dec. July 1971); children: Kathryn Elizabeth, Francis Charles. Supr. hosp. ops. Am. Potash & Chem. Corp., Trona, Calif., 1953-54; office mgr., T.C. Kirkland, elec. contractor, 1954-56; sec.-treas., bd. dirs. T.C. Kirkland, Inc., San Bernardino, Calif., 1958-74; design-install estimator Add-M Electric, Inc., 1972-82, v.p., 1974-82; estimator, engr. Corona Indsl. Electric, Inc. (Calif.), 1982-83; asst. project engr. Fischbach and Moore, Inc., Los Angeles, 1984—. Episcopalian. Club: Arrowhead Country (San Bernardino). Home: 526 E Sonora St San Bernardino CA 92404 Office: Fischbach and Moore Inc 4632 Worth St Los Angeles CA 90063

KIRKLAND, JAMES ALAN, financial planner; b. Warren, Ohio, Nov. 15, 1957; s. Robert Kirkland and Shirley (Boger) K.; m. Virginia A. Stone, Nov. 4, 1978; children: Robert Riley, Melissa Marie. Student in bus., St. Mary U., Nova Scotia, Can., 1975-77, Kent State U., 1977-78. Cert. estate and bus. analyst, 1984; cert. fin. planner, 1987. Ins. agt. Lincoln Nat. Life Ins. Co., Troy, Mich., 1978-81, estate planner, 1981-82, fin. planner, 1982-84; fin. planner Diversified Fin. Cons. Co., Troy, Mich., 1984—, pres. bd. dirs.; registered rep. SEC, Washington, 1986—, registered investment adv., 1986—. Author, editor investment and fin. newsletter, 1986—. Instr. Pub. Schs. Adult Edn. program on fin. and money mgmt., Oakland County, Mich., 1988—. Mem. Internat. Assn. Fin. Planners, Soc. Cert. Fin. Planners, Oakland County C. of C. (chmn., founder Crime Prevention com. 1983, Ambassador Club 1984), Registry Fin. Planners. Republican. Presbyterian. Office: Diversified Fin Cons Co 2690 Crooks Rd Suite 409 Troy MI 48084

KIRKORIAN, ROY, telecommunications executive; b. Fresno, Calif., Aug. 5, 1945; s. Berge and Jessie Elizabeth (Koesheyan) K.; m. Gayle Jacquelyn Jones, Mar. 27, 1971; children: Nicole, Gina, Adam. Student, U. Uppsala, Sweden, 1965-66; B.S., Calif. State Poly. Coll., 1967; J.D., U. Calif. Hasting Coll. Law, San Francisco, 1970. Bar: Calif. 1970. With firm Conron, Heard & James, Bakersfield, Calif., 1971-74, Cahill Gordon & Reindel, N.Y.C., 1974-75; asst. v.p. legal Continental Telephone Corp., Atlanta, 1975-78; v.p. legal and sec. Continental Telecom Inc., Atlanta, 1978-83; pres. Contel Texocom, Atlanta, 1983-86; pres., chief operating officer CP Nat. Corp., 1987—. Bd. dirs. Metro Arts, Atlanta, 1983. Mem. ABA, Calif. Bar Assn. Club: Capital City, Georgia (Atlanta); Crow Canyon Country (San Ramon, Calif.). also: CP Nat Corp PO Box 8192 Walnut Creek CA 94596

KIRKPATRICK, ESMERELDA GRACE, human resources executive; b. Phila., Sept. 13, 1942; d. George Washington Royer and Esmarelda (Dougherty) K. BSBA, Pa. State U., 1964. Indsl. spy Gen. Mercantile Industries, N.Y.C., 1964-65; adminstrv. asst. trust Phila. Nat. Bank, 1965-70; actuarial asst. thru account exec. Johnson & Higgins of Pa., Inc., Phila., 1970-75; pension trust officer thru head adminstrn. Girard Bank, Phila., 1975-79; mgr. trust fund adminstrn. Communications Satellite Corp., Washington, 1979—, dir. human resources corp. staff, 1987—. Mem. Am. Soc. Personnel Adminstrs.

KIRKPATRICK, FORREST HUNTER, management consultant; b. Galion, Ohio, Sept. 4, 1905; s. Arch M. and Mildred (Hunter) K. Student, U. Dijon, 1926; A.B., Bethany Coll., 1927, LL.D., 1949; A.M., Columbia U., 1931, profl. diploma, 1934, 36; postgrad., U. London, U. Pitts., U. Pa., U. Cambridge, U. Oxford; LL.D., Coll. Steubenville, 1958, Drury Coll., 1968; Hum.D., Wheeling Coll., 1981. Dean, prof. Bethany Coll., 1927-40, 46-52; gen. mgr. personnel adminstrn. RCA, 1941-46, edn. cons., 1946-60; vis. prof. or lectr. N.Y. U., U. Pitts., Columbia U., U. Akron, U. Wis., Cornell U., 1938-54; asst. to chmn. Wheeling-Pitts. Steel Corp., 1952-64, v.p., 1964-70; vis. prof. W.Va. U., 1970-80; adj. prof. Bethany Coll., 1970-87; dir. Sharon Tube Co., Banner Fibreboard Co. Cons. Am. Council on Edn., 1938-45, War Manpower Com., 1942-44, Dept. State, 1944, U.S. Civil Service, 1945, Post Office Dept., 1953, HEW, 1970; mem. ednl. program com. USAF, 1948-51; mem. mission to Sweden Dept. Labor, 1962, mem. manpower adv. com., 1963-68; dir. Blue Cross & Blue Shield of W.Va., 1955-85. Mem. W.Va. Commn. Higher Edn., 1964-70, Edn. Com. of the States, 1973-77, Humanities Found. of W.Va., 1972-77, W.Va. Water Resources Bd., 1975-83, State Bldg. Commn., 1983—; bd. govs. W.Va. U., 1957-69; bd. dirs. Wheeling Symphony Soc., Inc., 1950-81, Wheeling Country Day Sch., 1953-64, 70-73, Northern Panhandle Behavioral Health Center, 1974-84; trustee Ohio Valley Med. Center, Inc., Wheeling, 1954-89. Mem. Indsl. Relations Research Assn. (life), Nat. Assn. Mfrs. (dir. 1965-70), Acad. Polit. Sci. (life), Am. Personnel and Guidance Assn. (life), NEA (life), AAUP (emeritus), Am. Mgmt. Assn. (emeritus), Nat. Vocat. Guidance Assn., Nat. Alliance Businessmen (met. chmn. 1971-72), Beta Gamma Sigma, Beta Theta Pi, Alpha Kappa Psi, Kappa Delta Pi, Phi Delta Kappa. Clubs: University (N.Y.C. and Pitts.); Fort Henry, Wheeling Country (Wheeling); Duquesne (Pitts.); Soc. Friends of St. George (Windsor Castle). Home: Tally Ho Apts 931 National Rd Wheeling WV 26003 Office: PO 268 Wheeling WV 26003

KIRKWOOD, WILLIAM THOMAS, corporate professional; b. Marion, Ohio, Aug. 19, 1948; s. Hugh E. and Mildred M. (Schaeffer) K. Jr.; m. Deborah Hedges, Jan. 4, 1967 (div. Aug. 1980); children: Krista, Konni, Bobby; m. Beth C. Mitchell, May 30, 1981 (div. Aug. 1988). BS in Acctg., Franklin U., 1976. CPA. Acct. Worthington (Ohio) Foods, Inc., 1970-75, cost. supr., 1975-78, acctg. mgr., 1978-82, controller, 1982-86, asst. treas., 1986—. Office: Worthington Foods Inc 900 Proprietors Rd Worthington OH 43085

KIRSCH, RALPH M., oil company executive; b. Burton, Nebr., Nov. 15, 1928; s. George J. Kirsch and Gladys Hudson; m. Delores M. Birkel, Feb. 3, 1952; children: Michael, Alan. BS in Edn., U. Nebr.-Lincoln, 1953; JD, U. Wyo., 1956. Bar: Wyo. 1956, Utah 1961. Spl. asst. to atty. gen. State of Wyo., Cheyenne, 1957-59; legal dept. Mountain Fuel Supply, Salt Lake City, 1959-74, mgr. contracts, lands, 1974-79; exec. v.p. Wexpro Co., Salt Lake City, 1977-80, pres., chief exec. officer, 1980—; pres., chief exec. officer Celsius Energy Co., Salt Lake City, 1982—, also dir., 1982—; dir. Entrada Industries, Inc., Salt Lake City, 1982—, Wexpro Co., 1976—; pres., chief exec. officer Universal Resources Corp., 1988—. Served with USN, 1945-47, 50-51, PTO. Mem. Ind. Petroleum Assn. Am., Rocky Mountain Oil and Gas Assn., Rocky Mountain Mineral Law Found., Utah Petroleum Assn., Domestic Petroleum Council, Utah State Bar Assn., Wyo. State Bar Assn. Office: Wexpro Co 79 S State St Salt Lake City UT 84111

KIRSCHENBAUM, PAULENNE ROESKE, brokerage house executive.; b. Port Chester, N.Y., June 5, 1936; d. Paul John and Gertrude Frieda (Haefele) Roeske; AAS, Fashion Inst. Tech., 1956; student N.Y. Inst. Fin., 1960-61; m. J. Michael Kirschenbaum, May 17, 1968; children—Lisa L., Nina Sue, Jill M. Stockbroker Bache & Co., N.Y.C., 1964-67; stockbroker, br. mgr., gen. ptnr. Bruns-Nordeman, N.Y.C., 1967-71; stockbroker, investment banker Adams & Peck, N.Y.C., 1972-73; registered investment adviser, Washington, 1974—; pres. Energystics, Inc., Bernardsville, N.J., 1975-85; sr. v.p. investment Prudential Backe Securites, 1985—. Bd. dirs. Westmont Sch., Chester, N.J., 1977-79, Garden State Orch. Mem. Women's Stockbrokers Assn. (dir. 1968-69), Internat. Platform Assn., N.Y. Acad. Scis., Roxiticus Country Club.

KIRSCHENBAUM, WILLIAM, corporate executive; b. N.Y.C., Dec. 12, 1944; s. Benjamin and Fannie (Mintzer) K.; m. Clarissa Wald, June 17, 1979; 1 child, Benjamin. BA, CCNY, 1965; postgrad. CUNY, 1969. Asst. to sr. v.p. Ogden Corp., N.Y.C., 1968-70; ptnr. Palm State Properties, Ft. Lauderdale, Fla., 1970-74; mgr. ea. region Booz Allen Acquisition Services, N.Y.C., 1974-78; mng. dir. corp. fin. Neuberger & Berman, N.Y.C., 1978-82; pres. Unicorp Am. Corp., N.Y.C., 1982-83, also bd. dirs.; chmn. bd. dirs. Hamilton Savs. Bank, 1984—, Hamilton, Carter, Smith, Inc., Bankers and Shoppers Ins. Co. subs. Travellers Ins. Co.; mem. exec. com. of bd. dirs. Bankers & Shippers Ins. Co. Bd. dirs. Am. Jewish Congress, 1972-83, Com. for Present Danger, 1978—, Jewish Conciliation Bd. Am., 1979—; mem. nat. young leadership cabinet United Jewish Appeal, 1978-80; bd. dirs. Com. for Econ. Growth of Israel, 1977—, Nat. Jewish Coalition, 1985-88, Associated Builders and Owners of Greater N.Y., 1986—; chmn. bd. N.Y. Adv. Bd. Starlight Found., 1986-87. Mem. N.Am. Soc. Corp. Planning (N.Y. dir. 1977-80), Assn. Corp. Growth, Blue Key, Pi Sigma Alpha. Club: City Athletic. Home: 1020 Park Ave New York NY 10028

KIRSCHNER, JAY LARRY, marketing executive; b. N.Y.C., June 6, 1955; s. Seymour and Thelma Joy (Fuchs) K.; m. Laurie Taryn Metz, Oct. 28, 1979; children: Tracy, Jamie. BS in Math., SUNY, Cortland, 1977. Sales/market analyst Nabisco Brands Inc., N.Y.C., 1977-79; dir. product research Children's TV Workshop, N.Y.C., 1979-85; mgr. mktg. research Argo Communications corp., New Rochelle, N.Y., 1986; dir. mktg. and sales UA-Columbia Cablevision, Oakland, N.J., 1986; officer Metro Cable Coop., Teaneck, N.J., 1987—. Recipient Chair of Distinction award Englewood (N.J.) Hosp., 1987. Mem. Cable TV Adminstrn. and Mktg. Soc. Office: UA Columbia Cablevision 7 Fir Ct Oakland NJ 07436

KIRSCHNER, SIDNEY, diversified services company executive; b. 1934, Ottawa, Ont., Can.; married. BSME, New Mexico Inst. Mining and Tech., 1956. Engr. Aerojet-Gen. Corp., 1956-60; dir. engring. Aerospace Corp., 1960-63; asst. to pres. Curtiss-Wright Corp., 1963-67; pres. Gen. Dynamics div. Electro Dynamic, 1967-73; group v.p. Nat. Service Industries, Inc., Atlanta, 1973-77, exec. v.p., 1977-79, chief operating officer, 1977—, pres., 1979—, chief exec. officer, 1987—, also bd. dirs. Office: Nat Svc Industries Inc 1180 Peachtree St NE Atlanta GA 30309 *

KIRSHBAUM, RONALD MICHAEL, business executive; b. Chgo., Apr. 20, 1938; s. Charles C. and Frances (Walker) K.; m. Adrienne C. Kaufman, Aug. 22, 1965; children—Benjamin, Jonathan, Sarah, Daniel. B.A. cum laude, Northwestern U., 1960; M.S. in Indsl. Mgmt., MIT, 1962. Mktg. research analyst Swift & Co., Chgo., 1962-64; asst. product mgr. Alberto Culver Co., Melrose Park, Ill., 1964-65, product mgr., 1965-67, group product mgr., 1967-69, dir. mktg., 1969-73, gen. mgr. Household/Grocery div., 1973-77, v.p., gen. mgr. Food Service div., 1977-84, v.p., gen. mgr. Food Service and Splty. Products div., 1984—; bus. cons. Served with U.S. Army, 1962-68. Jewish. Home: 154 Green Bay Rd Highland Park IL 60035 Office: Alberto Culver Co 2525 Armitage Ave Melrose Park IL 60160

KIRWAN, KERRY BRIAN, business executive; b. Stockton, Calif., Mar. 1, 1960; s. Dennis Daniel amd Sophia Paulina (Kubas) K.; m. karen Ann Lariciere, Sept. 19, 1987. BA, UCLA, 1983. Account exec., import supr. George S. Bush & Co., Inc., Los Angeles, 1984—. Mem. Phi Kappa Sigma. Democrat. Roman Catholic. Home: 7607 St Bernard St Apt 6 Playa Del Rey CA 90293 Office: George S Bush & Co Inc 417 Hill St Suite 590 Los Angeles CA 90013

KIRWAN-TAYLOR, PETER ROBIN, investment banker; b. Virginia Water, Surrey, England, Jan. 18, 1930; came to U.S., 1981; s. William John Kirwan-Taylor and Hélène Charlotte (de Berqueley Grant Richards) Kemble; m. Julia Ogden, 1952 (div. 1965); children: Antonia, Charles, Laura; m. Michele Eads Clarke, 1966 (div. 1970); 1 child, Hélène; m. Nancy Ann Norman, Oct. 1, 1970; 1 child, John. Student, Trinity Coll., Cambridge, Eng., 1950-51. Mgr. Peat Marwick Mitchell & Co., London, 1951-59; dir. Hill Samuel & Co., London, 1960-70, English Property Corp., London and N.Y. C., 1970-76; pres. Maxwell Cummings & Sons, Montreal, Can., 1976-81; vice chmn. Danville Resources Inc., N.Y.C., 1981-85; bd. dirs. The Prospect Group, Inc., N.Y.C., 1983—; bd. dirs. Adobe Resources, N.Y.C., Adacorp, Inc., Dallas, Landmark Land Co., Inc., Carmel, Calif., London United Investments PLC, Abermin Corp., Vancouver, B.C.; chmn. Am. Gold Resources, Denver. Fellow Inst. Chartered Accts. Home: 160 E 72d St New York NY 10021 Office: The Prospect Group Inc 667 Madison Ave New York NY 10021

KISEDA, JAMES ROBERT, electrical engineer, researcher; b. Monessen, Pa., Dec. 7, 1924; s. George and Rose Theresa (Komorosky) K.; m. Virginia Helen Pataky, Sept. 11, 1954; children: Susan D., James J. BSEE, U. Pitts., 1956, MSEE, 1957. Mem. rsch. staff, rsch. cons. to various divs. on spl. projects IBM, Yorktown Heights, N.Y., 1957-64, devel. engr., 1964-88. Contbr. articles to profl. jours.; patentee on computer systems/circuits. With U.S. Army, 1949-52. Owens fellow U. Pitts., 1956. Mem. IEEE. Republican. Roman Catholic. Home: 22 Pleasant Hill Rd Hopewell Junction NY 12533

KISH, KATHERINE MARIA, management consultant company executive; b. Hattiesburg, Miss., May 26, 1943; d. Louis S. and Maria (Rusynyk) K.; m. William D. Kraft, May 11, 1985; 1 stepchild, William D. Kraft III. BA, Allegheny Coll., 1965; M in Teaching, Antioch U., 1969. Coordinator, tchr. Lakewood (Ohio) Bd. Edn., 1965-68; cons. Fgn. Policy Assn., Pathe Newsfilm, Internat. Film Found., 1968-69; mktg. coordinator NBC Ednl. Enterprise, N.Y.C., 1969-74; dir. mktg. and spl. projects Harcourt Brace Jovanovich, Inc., N.Y.C., 1974-78; v.p. planning The Singer Co., Stamford, Conn., 1978-81; v.p. mktg. and sales Faxon Co., Westwood, Mass., 1981-82; pres. Market Entry, Inc., Cranbury, N.J., 1982—. Contbr. chpt. to book. Williams Coll. fellow, 1967, U. Hawaii fellow, 1968. Mem. Assn. Media Producers (bd. dirs., officer 1976-81), Planning and Devel. Forum., Am. Soc. Tng. and Devel., Nat. Assn. Women Bus. Owners (N.J. program chmn., bd. dirs., v.p., pres.-elect), N.J. Assn. Women Bus. Owners, Princeton Area C. of C. Democrat. Mem. Eastern Orthodox Ch. Office: Market Entry Inc 18 George Davison Rd RD 3 Cranbury NJ 08512

KISHIMOTO, YUJI, architect, educator; b. Tokyo, Nov. 6, 1938; s. Hideo and Miyo (Anesaki) K.; m. Toshiko Mitsumori, Oct. 22, 1970; 1 child, Kyo. BArch, Waseda U., 1963; MArch, Harvard U., 1965; EdM, U. Mass., 1976. Registered architect. Designer Vincent G. Kling Assocs., Phila., 1966-67; design critic Boston Archtl. Ctr., 1966-69; instr. R.I. Sch. of Design, Providence, 1966-70; ptnr. Design Collaboratives, Boston, 1967-71; instr. Deerfield (Mass.) Acad., 1971-76; asst. prof. U. Hawaii, Honolulu, 1976-78; assoc. prof. Va. Poly. Inst. and State U., Blacksburg, 1978-80; assoc. prof. Clemson (S.C.) U., 1980-87, prof., 1987—; with Kishimoto and Assocs., Clemson, 1988—; urban design cons. Boston Redevel. Authority, 1966-67; design cons. Commonwealth Architects, Boston, 1966-68, Hawaii Group Architects, Honolulu, 1978. Oil and acrylic paintings exhbtd. George Walter Vincent Smith Art Mus., Springfield, Mass., 1974 (Springfield Art League award), one-man show Hilson Gallery Deerfield (Mass.) Acad., 1972 and 3-man show, 1971; contbr. articles to profl. jours. V.p. Clemson Area Internat. Friendship, Clemson, 1985—. Harvard Univ. fellow, 1964; travel grantee Asia Found., 1964, Deerfield Acad., 1972, 74; research grantee Va. Poly. Inst. and State U., 1979, Clemson U., 1981, Clemson U. Provost, 1982. Mem. AIA, Archtl. Inst. of Japan, S.C. Am. Inst. Architects, The Ednl. Arts Assn. and Adv. for Open Edn., Japan Inst. Architects, Japan Am. Assn. of Western S.C. (pres. 1988). Lodge: Sertoma (v.p. Clemson club 1986-87). Home: 216 Crestwood Dr Clemson SC 29631 Office: Clemson Coll Architecture Lee Hall Clemson SC 29634-0503

KISHPAUGH, ALLAN RICHARD, mechanical engineer; b. Dover, N.J., Aug. 31, 1937; B.S. in Mech. Engring., N.J. Inst. Tech., 1967; m. Maryann M. Bizub, July 31, 1965. Engring. technician Stapling Machines Co., Rockaway, N.J., 1956-65; design engr. Airoyal Engring. Co., Livingston, N.J., 1965-66; project engr. Simautics Co., Fairfield, N.J., 1966-67; design engr. Pyrofilm Resistor Mfg. Co., Cedar Knolls, N.J., 1967-68; sr. engr., project mgr. Packaging Systems div. Standard Packaging Corp., Clifton, N.J., 1968-77; sr. machine design engr. Travenol Labs., Round Lake, Ill., 1977-79; dir. engring. TEC, Inc., Alsip, Ill., 1979-80; mgmt. cons., machine developer, Palos Heights, Ill., 1980—; owner Ark Internat., 1981—. Mem. food, drug and beverage equipment com. Nat. Sanitation Found., 1988—; councilman, Borough of Victory Gardens (N.J.), 1969-71, council pres., 1971, police commnr., 1970-70, chmn. fin. com., 1970; pres. Pompton River Assn., Wayne, N.J., 1976-77; mem. Wayne Flood Control Commn., 1976-77; past deacon, elder, Sunday sch. tchr. and supt. local Presbyn. chs. Served with Air N.G., 1960-61, 62-65, with USAF, 1961-62. Registered profl. engr., N.J., Ill. Mem. ASME (vice chmn. N.J. sect. 1973-74, numerous other regional offices, food, drug and beverage equipment com. 1983-88), Nat. Soc. Profl. Engrs., Midwest Soc. Profl. Cons. (bd. dirs. 1986, 87), Ill. Soc. Profl. Engrs. (chpt. officer 1984—), Chgo. Assn. Commerce and Industry, Nat. Sanitation Found. (food, drug and beverage equipment com. 1988—). Patentee mechanism for feeding binding wire, wirebound box-making machine, method packaging granular materials, others in field. Address: 6118 W 123d St Palos Heights IL 60463

KISOR, MANOWN, JR., banker; b. Flushing, N.Y., May 23, 1936; s. Manown and Judith (Dubois) K.; m. Margaret Ayres Leonard, Sept. 5, 1960; children: Anne, Judith, William. B.A. cum laude, Trinity Coll., 1958; postgrad., Northwestern U., 1958-60; M.B.A., NYU, 1963. Asst. sec. Bank of N.Y., 1960-64; v.p. Standard Stats. Co., 1965-66; sr. v.p. Paine Webber Jackson & Curtis, 1967-77; exec. v.p. Comerica Bank-Detroit, 1977—, officer in charge trust investments, 1977—. Woodrow Wilson fellow, 1958-59. Mem. Am. Fin. Assn., Nat. Assn. Bus. Economists, N.Y. Soc. Security Analysts., Fin. Analysts Soc. Detroit. Clubs: Detroit, Metamora, Metamora Hunt. Office: Comerica Bank 211 W Fort St Detroit MI 48275-1032

KISSLING, FRED RALPH, JR., insurance agency executive; b. Nashville, Feb. 10, 1930; s. Fred Ralph and Sarah Elizabeth (FitzGerald) K.; m. Mary Jane Gallaher; children: Sarah FitzGerald, Jayne Kirkpatrick. BA, Vanderbilt U., 1952, MA, 1958. Spl. agt. Northwestern Mut. Life Ins. Co., Nashville, 1953-58, gen. agt., Lexington, Ky., 1962-80; gen. agt. New Eng. Mut. Life Ins. Co., 1981-87; mgr. life dept. Bennett & Edwards, Kingsport, Tenn., 1958-62; pres. Employee Benefit Cons., Inc., Lexington, 1961—; ptnr. Kennington Assocs., 1967—; pub. Leader's mag., 1973—, editor, 1981—. Author: Sell and Grow Rich, 1966; editor: Questionnaire in Pension Planning, 1971, Questionnaire in Estate Planning, 1971. Adv. bd. Salvation Army, Lexington, 1971—, chmn., 1988—; gen. chmn. United Way of Blue Grass, 1975, bd. dirs., 1975-78, 80-83; trustee, chmn. bd. Lexington Children's Theatre, 1979-81, pres., 1981-83. Mem. Am. Soc. CLU's (chpt. pres. 1969-70, 80-81, regional v.p. 1971-73), Ky. Gen. Agts. and Mgrs. Assn. (pres. 1965-66), Million Dollar Round Table (life mem., v.p., program chmn. 1976), Assn. for Advanced Underwriting (bd. dirs. 1976-84, sec.-treas. 1979-80, v.p. 1980-81, pres. 1982-83), Am. Soc. Pension Actuaries (bd. dirs. 1971-78, pres. 1974), Nat. Assn. of Estate Planning Councils (bd. dirs. 1986—, v.p. 1988-89), Sigma Chi (national sec., treas. 1987-88), Lexington Club, Iroquois Hunt Club, Masons, Shriners. Office: 98 Dennis Dr Lexington KY 40503

KITAYAMA, TAKAO, development planning and project management company executive; b. Kobe, Hyogo, Japan, Sept. 13, 1941; s. Mitsugu and Asako (Ando) K.; m. Keiko Kitayama, Apr. 17, 1950; children: Tetsuko, Shin. Exec. v.p. Hamano Inst., Tokyo; cons. Issey Miyake Design Studio, Tokyo, 1984—, Todao Ando Archtl. Assocs., Osaka, 1980—, Shiro Kuramata Design Office, Tokyo, 1980—, Toshiyuki Kita Design Office, Osaka, 1983—, Cassina Japan, Tokyo, 1982—. Projects include: From 1st Bldg. (Japan Archtl. Acad. award), Axis Bldg. (Mainichi Newspaper Design award), Rose Garden Bldg., Kobe, Step Bldg., Takamatsu, Japan, Festival Bldg., Okinawa, Japan, PortoPia '81 Fashion Live Theater, Collezione Bldg., numerous others. Home: 1 25 12 Seta, Setagayaku Tokyo 158, Japan Office: Hamano Inst, 1 9 7 Nishi Azabu Minatoku, Tokyo 106, Japan

KITCHEN, LAWRENCE OSCAR, aircraft/aerospace corporation executive; b. Ft. Mill, S.C., June 8, 1923; s. Samuel Sumpter and Ruby Azalee (Grigg) K.; m. Brenda Lenhart, Nov. 25, 1978; children by previous marriage: Brenda, Alan, Janet. Ed., Foothill Coll. Aero. engr. U.S. Navy Bur. Aeronautics, Washington, 1946-58; staff asst. to asst. chief bur. U.S. Navy Bur. Aeronautics, 1958; with Lockheed Missiles & Space Co., Sunnyvale, Calif., 1958-70; mgr. product support logistics Lockheed Missiles & Space Co., 1964-68, dir. fin. controls, 1968-70; v.p.-fin. Lockheed-Ga. Co., Marietta, 1970-71; pres. Lockheed-Ga. Co., 1971-75; pres. Lockheed Corp., Burbank, Calif., 1975-76, pres., chief operating officer, 1976-85, chmn. bd. dirs., chief exec. officer, 1986-88, chmn. exec. com., also bd. dirs., 1989—; bd. dirs. Security Pacific Nat. Bank, Security Pacific Corp. Mem. nominating com. Aviation Hall of Fame. With USMC, 1942-46. Mem. Nat. Def. Transp. Assn., AIAA, Navy League, Soc. Logistics Engrs., Air Force Assn., Assn. U.S. Army. Clubs: North Ranch, Lakeside Golf. Office: Lockheed Corp 4500 Park Granada Blvd Calabasas CA 91399

KITCHENS, FREDERICK LYNTON, JR., insurance company executive; b. Detroit, Sept. 30, 1940; s. Frederick Lynton and Madeline Dorothy (Jacobs) K.; m. Carol Ann Crane, Dec. 22, 1961; children: Frederick Lynton, Anne LeBarron, Susan Elizabeth. BA, Mich. State U., 1962. CPCU. Mgr. underwriting Royal Ins. Co., N.Y.C., 1968-70; asst. to pres. Grow, Keller, Englebert & Freese, Detroit, 1970-71; v.p. Dobson McOmber, Inc., Ann Arbor, Mich., 1971-73; exec. v.p. Hylant MacLean, Inc., Toledo, 1973-83; chmn., chief exec. officer Cherokee Ins. Co., Nashville, 1983-84; chmn. Coastal Plains Ins., Jacksonville, Fla., 1984—; instr. Coll. Ins., N.Y.C., 1969-70. Trustee Hope Haven Childrens Clinic, 1988—, Jacksonville Country Day Sch., 1985—; mem. C. of C. Community Devel. Bd., Jacksonville, 1986. Capt. U.S. Army, 1962-67, Vietnam. Decorated Bronze Star; recipient Commendation medal NATO, 1965. Mem. Lloyd's of London, Jacksonville Commodores League, L.A. Yacht Club (commodore 1989—). Republican. Presbyterian. Clubs: Fla. Yacht, Meninak, Deerwood Country, River (Jacksonville), University. Lodge: Rotary. Office: Coastal Plains Ins 121 W Forsyth St PO Box 52897 Jacksonville FL 32201

KITO, TERUO, international trading company executive; b. Nagoya, Japan, Jan. 27, 1932; came to U.S., 1963; s. Otomaro and Hatsu (Mizuno) K.; m. Eiko Kito, Mar. 3, 1966; 1 child, Teruyo. M of Econs., Hitoshubashi U., 1954. With Mitsui & Co. Ltd., Tokyo, 1954-63, gen. mgr., 1966-73, sr. gen. mgr., 1979-83; asst. gen. mgr. Mitsui & Co. (USA), Inc., N.Y.C., 1963-66; sr. gen. mgr. Mitsui & Co. (USA), Inc., L.A., 1973-79; v.p., regional gen. mgr. Mitsui & Co. (USA), Inc., Seattle, 1983-85; sr. v.p., chief operating officer Mitsui & Co. (USA), Inc., N.Y.C., 1985—. Mem. Scarsdale Country Club, Nippon Club, Sky Club. Office: Mitsui & Co USA Inc 200 Park Ave New York NY 10166

KITTLE, BERNARD WAYNE, aerospace industry executive; b. Hayes Ctr., Nebr., Mar. 24, 1931; s. George Andrew and Elva C. (Birchall) K.; m. Lodema Joy Housman, Dec. 23, 1950; children: Douglas, Daniel, Randall. BSME, U. Nebr., 1953. Project engr. Sundstrand Corp., Rockford, Ill., 1955-58, group engr., 1958-63, sect. engr., 1963-65, chief project engr., 1965-68, v.p. engring., 1968-70, v.p., gen. mgr. aircraft equipment div., 1970-72, v.p. mech. and fluid pumping sect., 1972-73, v.p., gen. mgr. aviation mech., 1973-77, group v.p. advanced tech., 1977—. 3 patented engine starters. Served to 1st lt. USAF, 1953-55. Mem. Aerospace Industries Assn., Soc. Mfg. Engrs. Republican. Office: Sundstrand Corp PO Box 7002 Rockford IL 61125

KITTLESON, HENRY MARSHALL, lawyer; b. Tampa, Fla., May 13, 1929; s. Edgar O. and Ardath (Ayers) K.; m. Barbara Clark, Mar. 20, 1954; 1 dau., Laura Helen. B.S. with high honors, U. Fla., 1951, J.D. with high honors, 1953. Bar: Fla. 1953. Partner Holland & Knight, Lakeland and Bartow, Fla., 1955—; mem. adv. bd. Fla. Fed. Savs. & Loan Assn., 1974-86; mem. Fla. Law Revision Commn., 1967-76, vice chmn., 1969-71; mem. Gov.'s Property Rights Study Commn., 1974-75, Nat. Conf. Commrs. Uniform State Laws, 1982—. Mem. council U. Fla. Law Center, 1974-77. Served to maj. USAF, 1953-55. Fellow Am. Bar Found.; mem. ABA (chmn. standing com. on ethic and profl. responsibility 1980-81), Am. Law Inst., Am. Coll. Real Estate Lawyers, Fla. Bar (chmn. standing com. profl. ethics 1965-66, tort litigation rev. commn. 1983-84), Blue Key, Sigma Phi Epsilon, Phi Delta Phi, Phi Kappa Phi, Beta Gamma Sigma. Democrat. Presbyterian. Clubs: Lakeland Yacht and Country, Tampa. Home: 5334 Woodhaven Ln Lakeland FL 33813 Office: 92 Lake Wire Dr Lakeland FL 33802 also: PO Box 32092 Lakeland FL 33802

KITTNER, EDWIN HENRY, gypsum industrial products manufacturing company executive; b. Utica, N.Y., Mar. 7, 1925; s. Emanuel Joseph and Genevieve Victoria (Rybicki) K.; B.S., Kans. State U., 1950; m. Mary Elizabeth Totten, Oct. 20, 1950; children—Jane Elizabeth, Katherine Ann, Joseph Andrew, John David. Plant engr. Certain-Teed Products Co., Blue Rapids, Kans., 1950-57; chief project engr. Bestwall Gypsum Co., Blue Rapids, Kans., 1957-61, project engr. central engring. dept., Paoli, Pa., 1961-63; with Georgia-Pacific Corp., Blue Rapids, Kans., 1963—, maintenance and engring. supt., 1963—; condr. seminars. Mem. Blue Rapids (Kans.) Bd. of Edn., 1963-72; mem. Jayhawk Council Exec. Bd., Boy Scouts Am., 1963—; mayor and councilman City of Blue Rapids, 1954-61, 74—. Served with U.S. Army, 1943-46; ETO. Decorated Purple Heart. Recipient Silver Beaver award Boy Scouts Am., 1969; registered profl. engr., Kans. Mem. Nat. Soc. Profl. Engrs., Kans. Engring. Soc. (dir. 1982—), Tri-Valley Engring. Soc. (pres. 1980), Am. Legion, VFW. Republican. Roman Catholic. Club: Lions (pres., zone chmn. 1955-65). Contbr. articles in field to profl., jours., also profl. handbooks. Home: 604 East Ave Blue Rapids KS 66411 Office: Box 187 Blue Rapids KS 66411

KITTREDGE, JOHN KENDALL, retired insurance company executive; b. Pitts., July 7, 1927; s. Richard Carlyle and Velma (Null) K.; m. Elizabeth Delo, May 26, 1951; children—Amy, Carol. B.A., Williams Coll., 1948. With Prudential Ins. Co. Am., 1948-88, v.p., 1965-73, sr. v.p., 1973-77, exec. v.p., 1977-88; chmn. Prudential Real Estate Affiliates, 1987, Prudential Property and Casualty Co., 1978-82, Prudential Reins. Co., 1978-87. Mem. N.J. Bd. Higher Edn., 1971-73; bd. dirs. Mental Health Assn., Essex County, 1968-72; trustee Coll. Medicine and Dentistry N.J., 1970-79, chmn., 1971-78; trustee Employee Benefit Rsch. Inst., chmn., 1986-87 ; mem. bd. overseers U. Pa. Sch. Nursing, 1982—; mem. Fed. coun. on Grad. Med. Edn., 1986-88, bd. Am. Acad. Actaries, 1989—. Fellow Soc. Actuaries; mem. Am. Acad. Actuaries, Inst. of Medicine, Phi Beta Kappa. Home: 878 Pinehurst Dr Chapel Hill NJ 27514

KITZMAN, TIMOTHY LEE, city manager; b. Janesville, Wis., Oct. 3, 1955; m. Valarie Lynn Kuehl. BA, U. Wis., Whitewater, 1977. Treas., fin. dir. City of Portage, Wis., 1986—. Mem. Mcpl. Treas.' Assn. of U.S. and Can., Wis. Mcpl. Fin. Officers Assn. Lodge: Elks. Office: City of Portage 115 W Pleasant St Portage WI 53901

KLAASSE, GEORGE EDWIN, oil and gas company executive; b. Lancaster, Wis., Jan. 20, 1936; s. Leonard S. and Lulu L. K.; m. Deanna L. Smith, June 14, 1958; children: Scott, Staci, Steven. BSBA in Acctg., Cen. Mich. U., 1969, MBA in Fin., 1975. Acct. Redman Industries, Dallas, 1960-67, DMH Co., St. Louis, 1967-79; controller All Products Co., Farwell, Mich., 1979-82; div. controller Indril, Mt. Pleasant, Mich., 1982—. Mem. Nat. Assn., Elks. Home: 934 Iowa St Alma MI 48801

KLAFFKE, STEPHAN JOSEPH, financial analyst; b. Ft. Wayne, Ind., Mar. 19, 1958; s. Johannes Georg and Marianne (Niederholtmeyer) K.; m. Barbara Ann Rhoda, Dec. 7, 1985; children: Lauren Elizabeth, Johannes Heinrich. BS, Ind. U., 1981; MBA, Tex. Christian U., 1984. Fin. analyst Ekstrom Enterprises, Ft. Worth, 1984-87; v.p. JKE Equity Research, Ft. Worth, 1987—. Fellow Dallas Inst. Investment Analysts; mem. Inst. Chartered Fin. Analysts, Beta Gamma Sigma. Republican. Roman Catholic. Home: 4104 Shannon Dr Fort Worth TX 76116 Office: JKE Equity Rsch 6500 W Fwy Fort Worth TX 76116

KLAGES, WILLIAM A., JR., sales executive; b. Bronx, N.Y., Feb. 15, 1952; m. Catherine, May 27, 1979; children: Jacqueline, Colleen. BSME, Manhattan Coll., 1973; MA, CUNY, 1975. Tchr. Ardsley (N.Y.) Middle Sch., 1975-77; salesman Cerrone Real Estate, Ardsley, N.Y., 1977-78; engr. sales Nash Engring., Norwalk, Conn. 1978-79, Downers Grove, Ill., 1979-83; specialist product Knotts Co., Berkley Heights, N.J., 1983; mgr. dist. Leybold Inc., Mt. Laurel, N.Y., 1983-85; mgr. region Leybold Inc., Brewster, N.Y., 1985—. Office: Leybold Inc Rte 22 Mount Ebo Corporate Ctr Brewster NY 10509

KLAGSBRUNN, HANS ALEXANDER, lawyer; b. Vienna, Austria, Apr. 28, 1909; came to U.S., 1912; s. Hugo and Lili (Brandt) K.; m. Elizabeth Mapelsden Ramsey, Jan. 27, 1934. Student, Vienna Gymnasium, 1922-25; B.A., Yale U., 1929, LL.B., 1932; postgrad., Harvard U. Law Sch., 1932-33. Bar: D.C., U.S. Supreme Ct 1935. Asso. RFC (and affiliates), 1933-45; exec. v.p., gen. counsel, dir. and mem. exec. com. Def. Plant Corp.; surplus property dir. and asst. gen. counsel RFC; RFC mem. Hancock Contract Settlement Bd. and Clayton Surplus Property Bd. in Office War Mblzn.; dep. dir. Office War Mblzn. and Reconversion, The White House, 1945-46; mem. Army Chem. Corps Reorgn. Com., 1955-56; sr. mem. Klagsbrunn & Hanes (attys.), 1946-68; counsel to successor firm 1969-83; Mem. Jud. Conf. D.C. Circuit, 1964-66; chmn. com. criminal indigents; mem. U.S. Ct. Appeals Com. on Admissions and Grievances, 1967-74, chmn., 1972-74; mem. task force on U.S. energy policy Twentieth Century Fund, 1976-77; Mem. Health and Welfare Council, bd. dirs., 1958-73, pres., 1961-63; mem. Loudoun County Sanitation Authority, 1959-68, vice chmn., 1965-68; mem. Piedmont (Va.) Environ. Council, 1975-76. Bd. dirs. Friendship House, 1957-68, pres., 1959-68; bd. dirs. Columbia Hosp. for Women, 1964-74, sec., 1966-67, 1st v.p., 1967-68. Recipient Health and Welfare Council Community Service awards, 1961, 63. Mem. Am. Bar Found., Fed. Bar Assn., Am. Arbitration Assn. (nat. panel), Bar Assn. D.C. (chmn. U.S. Ct. Appeals com. 1966-67), ABA (past chmn. coms.), Nat. Planning Assn., A.I.M., Am. Judicature Soc., Newcomen Soc., Phi Beta Kappa, Order of Coif, Phi Beta Kappa Assos., Nat. Symphony Orch. Assn. Clubs: Metropolitan, Yale, Nat. Press, City Tavern; Mory's (New Haven, Ct.). Home: 3420 Q St NW Washington DC 20007 also: Salem Farm RFD 1 Purcellville VA 22132 Office: 3420 Q St NW Washington DC 20007

KLAISS, DONALD EDWARD, computer software company executive; b. Bergenfield, N.J., June 22, 1951; s. Edward A. Jr. and Edith (Bott) K. BSE, Rutgers U., 1973; MEE, Stanford U., 1976; postgrad., Santa Clara U., 1976-78. Mgr. engring. Hewlett Packard Co., Palo Alto, Calif., 1973-82; v.p. engring. Covalent Systems Corp., Sunnyvale, Calif., 1982-85; v.p. rsch. and devel. NCA Corp., Santa Clara, Calif., 1986-87; v.p. engring. ASK Computer Systems Inc., Mountain View, Calif., 1987—. Mem. Am. Electronics Assn., IEEE, Soc. Mech. Engring., Stanford U. Alumni Assn. (bd. dirs.). Home: 22865 Poplar Grove Cupertino CA 95014 Office: 2440 W El Camino Real PO Box 7640 Mountain View CA 94039-7640

KLAMMER, JOSEPH FRANCIS, management consultant; b. Omaha, Mar. 25, 1925; s. Aloys Arcadius and Sophie (Nadolny) K.; B.S., Creighton U., 1948; M.B.A., Stanford, 1950; cert. in polit. econs. Grad. Inst. Internat. Studies, U. Geneva, 1951. Adminstrv. analyst Chevron Corp. (formerly Standard Oil Co. Calif.), San Francisco, 1952-53; staff asst. Enron Corp. (formerly Internorth, Inc.), Omaha, 1953-57; mgmt. cons. Cresap, McCormick and Paget, Inc., San Francisco, 1957-75, v.p., mgr. San Francisco office; mgmt. cons., prin. J.F. Klammer Assocs., San Francisco, 1975—. Served to 1st lt. USAAF, 1943-46; lt. col. USAFR (ret.). Rotary Found. fellow, 1950-51. Republican. Roman Catholic. Clubs: Univ. Home: 1998 Broadway San Francisco CA 94109 Office: 1 Market Pla San Francisco CA 94105

KLAMON, LAWRENCE PAINE, diversified company executive; b. St. Louis, Mar. 17, 1937; s. Joseph Martin and Rose (Schimel) K.; m. Jo Ann Karen Beatty, Nov. 1957 (div. Feb. 1974); children: Stephen Robert, Karen Jean, Lawrence Paine; m. Frances Ann Estes, Mar. 1980. A.B., Washington U., St. Louis, 1958; J.D., Yale U., 1961. Bar: N.Y. bar 1964. Confidential asst. Office Sec. Def., Washington, 1961-62; spl. asst. to gen. counsel Office Sec. Def., 1962-63; asso. Cravath, Swaine & Moore, N.Y.C., 1963-67; v.p., gen. counsel Fuqua Industries, Inc., Atlanta, 1967-73; sr. v.p. fin. and adminstrn. Fuqua Industries, Inc., 1971-81, pres., 1981-89, chief exec. officer, 1989—; dir. Fuqua Industries Inc., Pier 1 Inc., Advanced Telecommunications Inc. Bd. editors: Yale Law Jour, 1959-61. Mem. ABA, Assn. Bar City N.Y., Phi Beta Kappa, Order of Coif, Omicron Delta Kappa. Home: 2665 Dellwood Dr NW Atlanta GA 30305 Office: Fuqua Industries Inc 4900 Georgia-Pacific Ctr Atlanta GA 30303

KLAPPER, HARRIET THELMA, accountant; b. N.Y.C., May 20, 1929; d. Norbert and Steffie (Weinberger) Salzinger; m. Martin Klapper, Apr. 4, 1948; children: Iris, Norman. AAS, Sullivan County Community Coll., Loch Sheldrake, N.Y., 1967; BS magna cum laude, Fairleigh Dickinson U., 1973, MBA with honors, 1976. CPA, N.Y. Controller Sullivan County Community Coll., 1970-78; assoc prof. acctg. SUNY, New Paltz, N.Y., 1978-82; co-owner Wilen & Klapper, Poughkeepsie, N.Y., 1982—. Mem. AICPA, N.Y. State Soc. CPA's, Assn. Women CPA's. Office: Wilen & Klapper 11 Market St Poughkeepsie NY 12601

KLARMAN, DOUGLAS FRANK, sales executive; b. Cassville, Wis., July 19, 1934; s. Charles Franklin and Retha Luceil (Cardey) K.; m. Georgia Frances Barr, June 1, 1956; children: Dawn Marie, Jeffrey Alan. BS, U. Wis., Platteville, 1956. Materials mgr. Barber-Colman, Rockford, Ill., 1957-78; owner, pres. Spec-Cast, Inc., Rockford, 1978-80; prodn. control mgr. Halsey-Taylor/Structo, Freeport, Ill., 1980-82; sales mgr. V-Tip, Inc., Rockford, 1982—. Mem. PTA, Rockford, 1967-79; active Navy Jr. ROTC Paretn Assn., Rockford, 1976-78. Mem. Nat. Soc. Tng. and Devel., Nat. Soc. for Performance and Instrn. Republican. Club: Am. Bus. Men's. Office: V-Tip Inc 407 Green St Rockford IL 61102

KLASNIC, JOHN CHARLES (JACK), graphic arts company executive; b. McKeesport, Pa., Nov. 11, 1939; s. Stephen Andrew and Helen Lucille (Domarski) K.; m. Kathleen Frances Carroll, June 24, 1967; 1 child, Kathleen Jackie. BS in Printing Mgmt., Carnegie-Mellon U., 1962; Acctg. cert. U. Balt., 1976. Chief estimator King Brothers, Balt., 1963-66; branch mgr. Am. Bank, Norfolk, Va., 1966-67; plant mgr. Waverly Press, Balt., 1967-73; asst. v.p. mfg., Port City Press, Pikesville, Md., 1973-76; pres. Klasnic and Assocs., Inc., White Hall, Md., 1976—; instr. Catonsville (Md.) Community Coll., 1977—; instr. Printing Industries Md., Balt., 1979—, Printing Industries, P.C., Washington, 1981-86. Author: In Plant Printing Handbook, 1981, Printing Handbook, 1984, How to Kill an Inplant, 1986; contbr. over 750 articles to profl. jours., lectr. to profl. seminars. Fund raiser numerous charities, Balt. County, 1968—; adviser Md. Penitentiary Rehab. Program, Balt., 1979—; mem. PTA Hereford Mid. Sch., Hereford, Md., 1980-86 . Served with U.S. Army, 1962-63. Named In-Plant Reprodns. and Electronic Pub. 1987 Industry Leader of Yr.; named Dean of In-Plant Cons.; recipient numerous awards for excellence in graphic arts. Fellow In-Plant Mgmt. Assn.; mem. Assn. Graphic Arts Cons. (pres. 1983-85), Printing Industry Am., Graphic Arts Tech Found., Nat. Assn. Printers and Lithographers, Am. Legion Democrat. Roman Catholic. Home: 18925 Vernon Rd White Hall MD 21161

KLATELL, ROBERT EDWARD, lawyer, electronics company executive; b. Tampa, Fla., Dec. 11, 1945; s. Jack S. and Arla M. (Bragin) K.; m. Penelope E. Manegan, June 14, 1970; children—Christopher J., James M., Jeremy N. B.A., Williams Coll., 1968; J.D., NYU, 1971. Bar: N.Y. 1972. Asso. Kramer, Lowenstein, Nessen, Kamin & Soll, N.Y.C., 1970-76; gen. counsel Arrow Electronics, Inc., N.Y.C., 1976—; v.p. Arrow Electronics, Inc., 1979-88, sr. v.p., 1988—. Mem. ABA, Assn. Bar City N.Y., Westchester-Fairfield County Corp. Counsels Assn. Office: Arrow Electronics Inc 25 Hub Dr Melville NY 11747

KLATSKY, BRUCE J., apparel company executive; b. N.Y.C., July 14, 1948; s. Herbert W. and Pearl (Starkman) K.; m. Iris Ann Gussow, Aug. 15, 1970; 1 child, Peter. B.S., Western Res. U., 1970; postgrad., Georgetown U., 1970-71. Chmn. bd., chief exec. officer Van Heusen Group, Phillips-Van Heusen Corp., N.Y.C., 1971—; pres., chief operating officer Phillips-Van Heusen Corp. (parent), N.Y.C., 1987—. Office: Phillips-Van Heusen Corp 1290 Ave of the Americas New York NY 10104 *

KLAUSER, ARTHUR EBBERT, lawyer, general trading company executive; b. Toledo, Apr. 26, 1923; s. Arthur O. and Georgia (Ebbert) K.; m. Dec. 28, 1960 (dec.). Student DePauw U., 1941-43; cert. in Japanese, U. Chgo., 1944; A.B., U. Mich., 1945, M.A., 1948; J.D., Yale U., 1958; grad. Advanced Mgmt. Program, Harvard U., 1974, Sr. Mgrs. in Govt., 1977. Bar: N.Y. 1959, D.C. 1978. Atty. Vicks Chem. Co., N.Y.C., 1957-59, Richardson Found., N.Y.C., 1959-60; v.p. Royal Crown Internat., Coral Gables, Fla., 1960-62; dir. licensing/planning AMF Internat., Geneva and London, 1962-65; gen. mgr. consumer products Pfizer Internat., Tokyo, 1965-67; with Dow Corning Corp., 1967-79, v.p. internat., mgr. Tokyo Office, 1967-73 dir. corp. communications, 1973-76, v.p., dir. govt. relations and pub. affairs, Washington, 1976-78, asst. sec. corp., 1979; sr. v.p., exec. asst. to pres., dir. govt. relations and pub. affairs, Mitsui & Co. (U.S.A.), Inc., Washington, 1979—; lectr. on Japanese bus. to univs., profl. groups. Contbr. articles on bus. in Japan to profl. trade jours.; translator (into Japanese): The Young Lions (Irwin Shaw), 1951. Bd. trustees DePauw U. Served to lt. U.S. Army, 1943-47. Mem. ABA, N.Y. State Bar Assn., D.C. Bar Assn., Assn. Bar City N.Y., Am. C. of C., Tokyo Arbitration Assn., Asiatic Soc., Am.-Japan Soc. (trustee), Washington Japan Am. Soc., Washington Export Council, Washington Internat. Bus. Council, Micdland Symphony Orch. Soc., Pub. Affairs Council (dir.). Episcopalian. Clubs: Yale of N.Y.; Internat., Univ., Harvard, Yale, Nat. Democratic, Capitol Hill (Washington).

KLAUSNER, MORLEY, film company executive; b. Miami, Fla., Mar. 23, 1948; d. Walter Albert and Ann (Getzug) Lavigne; divorced; 1 child, Erica Rosenfeld; m. Peter L. Klausner, Dec. 23, 1987. BA, Western Coll. for Women, 1968; postgrad., UCLA, 1971. Adminstr. State St. Bank & Trust Co., Boston, 1968-69, Capital Rsch. & Mgmt., L.A., 1969-70; asst. to pres. Seabord Corp., L.A., 1970-71; buyer Burdines, Inc. div. Federated Stores, Miami, 1971-73; owner, ptnr. Johnar Film Prodns., L.A., 1973-81; v.p. bus. affairs Edward R. Pressman Film Co., L.A. and N.Y.C., 1982-88, Hollywood Pictures, Inc., L.A. and N.Y.C., 1982-88; sr. v.p. Aaron Russo Films, Inc., N.Y.C., 1988—. Democrat. Jewish. Office: Aaron Russo Films Inc 601 W 50th St New York NY 10019

KLEE, KARL HEINZ, lawyer; b. Innsbruck, Austria, June 9; s. Ernst and Anna Barbara (Richter) K.; LL.D., U. Innsbruck, 1953; m. Charlotte Haslwanter, Jan. 19, 1961; 1 dau., Katharina. Admitted to bar, 1960, since practiced in Innsbruck; dir. organizing com. Alpine Ski World Championships; pres. Alpbacher Bergbahn Gesellschaft. Mem. Austrian Olympic Com., 1965, v.p., 1969, hon. mem., 1977; pres. Austrian Ski Fedn., 1966, Austrian Ski Pool, 1971; sec. gen. XII Olympic Winters Games, Innsbruck, 1973-78. Recipient Golden Badge of Honor, Republic of Austria and Land of Styria; hon. ring City of Innsbruck; Coubertin medal; decorated knight Royal Swedish Order Polar Star; comdr. Order Nat. duMerite (France). Mem. Tyrolean Bar Chamber (v.p.), Internat. Ski Assn. Club: Innsbruck Panathlon (pres.). Home: 16 Gartenweg, A6064 Rum Austria Office: 38 Maria Theresienstrasse, A6020 Innsbruck Austria

KLEGON, KENNETH LOUIS, financial adviser; b. Detroit, Sept. 7, 1951; s. Robert S. and Gail (Leeman) K.; m. Karen Lee Barnes, July 12, 1984; children: Benjamin, Samuel. BA, Mich. State U., 1973; BS, Mercy Coll., Detroit, 1975. Cert. fin. planner. Exec. dir. Mich. Pub. Health Assn., East Lansing, Mich., 1979-83; pres. Fin. Mgmt. Assocs., Lansing, Mich., 1983—; personal fin. affairs advisor, fin. com. Lansing State Jour., 1985—, Am. Lung Assn., Lansing, 1985—. Bd. dirs. Averill Elem. PTA, Lansing, 1985—, pres., 1986—; bd. mgrs. Mich. PTA, Lansing, 1987—. Mem. Internat. Assn. Fin. Planning (bd. dirs. mid-Mich. chpt. 1984—, pres. 1987—), inst. Cert. Fin. Planners. Office: Fin Mgmt Assocs 1010 Washington Sq Bldg Lansing MI 48933

KLEIMAN, BERNARD, lawyer; b. Chgo., Jan. 26, 1928; s. Isadore and Pearl (Wikoff) K.; m. Gloria Baime, Nov. 15, 1986; children—Leslie, David. B.S., Purdue U., 1951; J.D., Northwestern U., 1954. Bar: Ill. bar 1954. Practice law in assn. with Abraham W. Brussell, 1957-60; dist. counsel United Steel Workers Am., 1960-65, gen. counsel, 1965—; partner Kleiman, Cornfield & Feldman, Chgo., 1960-75; prin. B. Kleiman (P.C.), 1976-77, Kleiman, Whitney, Wolfe & Gore, P.C., 1978—; Mem. collective bargaining coms. for nat. labor negotiations in basic steel, aluminum and can mfg. industries. Contbr. articles to legal jours. Served with U.S. Army, 1946-48. Mem. Am., Ill., Chgo., Allegheny County bar assns. Office: 1 E Wacker Dr Chicago IL 60601 also: 5 Gateway Ctr Pittsburgh PA 15222

KLEIMAN, GARY HOWARD, radio station executive, consultant; b. Phila., Jan. 24, 1952; s. Leon and Martha (Rubin) K.; m. Annette Suzanne Vranich, Sept. 23, 1978; children: Aaron Jay, Jared Adam. Diploma Am. Acad. Broadcasting, Phila., 1969, Pa. State Fire Sch., Media, 1969; BS, Temple U., 1972. Cert. radio mktg. cons. Gen. mgr. Sta. WFEC, Harrisburg, Pa., 1974-75; local sales mgr. Sta. WYSP-FM, Phila., 1976-79; pres. A.S.K. Advt., King of Prussia, Pa., 1976-80; v.p., gen. mgr. Sta. WGLU-FM, Johnstown, 1980-82, Sta. WAJE, Edensburg, Pa., 1982-84, Sta. WSBY-WQHQ-AM-FM, Salisbury, Md., 1984-86; mgr. Sta. WJDY, Salisbury, 1986-87; pres. Ideas Unltd. Mktg. and Advt. Co., Salisbury, 1986—; gen. mgr. Sta. WACS-FM, Schenectady, N.Y., 1988-89; v.p., gen. mgr. WDLE-FM, Federalsburg, Md., 1989—; media cons., Sta. WMDT TV, Salisbury, Md., 1988; dir., tchr. Am. Acad. Broadcasting, Phila., 1976-79. Contbr. articles to profl. publs. Active campaigner Cambria County Democratic Com., 1982-84; com. chmn. Salisbury Revitalization, 1984—; bd. dirs. Salisbury Regional Urban Design Action Team, 1984—, Deers Head Hosp. Found., 1987—; co-sponsor projects Lower Shore Easter Seals, Salisbury, 1985, Am. Cancer Soc., 1984-85, Kidney Found., 1985, Epilepsy Assn., 1985; promotion coord. Salisbury Festival com., 1985, 87, 88, vice-chmn., 1985-89; mem. exec. com. Lower Shore chpt. March of Dimes, 1984—; bd. dirs. Am. Heart Assn., 1987-89, Johnstown Area Regional Industries, 1981-84. Recipient numerous awards from local civic orgns., 1981—. Mem. Downtown Salisbury Assn., Salisbury Area C. of C., Salisbury Jaycees (Jaycee Springboard award 1985), Johnstown Jaycees. Democrat. Jewish. Club: Salisbury State Coll. Athletic. Avocations: photography, camping, skiing, softball, volleyball. Home: 115 Tall Timber Dr Fruitland MD 21826 Office: Sta WDLE FM Broadcast Ctr Federalsburg MD 20632

KLEIN, BERNARD, publishing company executive; b. N.Y.C., Sept. 20, 1921; s. Joseph J. and Anna (Wolfe) K.; m. Betty Stecher, Feb. 17, 1946; children: Cheryl Rona, Barry Todd, Cindy Ann. B.A., CCNY, 1942. Founder, pres. U.S. List Co., N.Y.C., 1946—; founder, pres., chief editor B. Klein Publs., Inc., Coral Springs, Fla. and Rye, N.Y., 1953—; cons. direct mail advt. and reference book pub. to pubs., industry, 1950—. Author: all biennials Ency. of American Indian, 1954—; Guide to American Directories. Served with AUS, 1942-45, ETO. Mem. Direct Mail Advt. Assn. Lodge: Masons.

KLEIN, CHARLES DAVID, financial advisor; b. Phila., May 26, 1938; m. Jane Parsons; children: Andrew, Elizabeth. BA, Bard Coll., 1960; LLB, NYU, 1963. Fin. adviser William Rosenwald and Family, N.Y.C., 1978—; bd. dirs. Reading, Phila., Ametek Inc., N.Y.C., Am. Securities Corp., N.Y.C., Ketema Inc., Bensalem, Pa. Trustee Columbia Grammar Learning Ctr., 1987. Served with USAR, 1963-69. Clubs: Apawamis (Rye, N.Y.); Sky (N.Y.C.).

KLEIN, CHARLES HENLE, lithographing company executive; b. Cin., Oct. 5, 1908; s. Benjamin Franklin and Flora (Henle) K.; student Purdue U., 1926-27, U. Cin., 1927-28; m. Ruth Becker, Sept. 23, 1938; children—Betsy (Mrs. Marvin H. Schwartz), Charles H., Carla (Mrs. George Fee III). Pres., Progress Lithographing Co., Cin., 1934-59, Novelart Mfg. Co., Cin., 1960—; dir. R.A. Taylor Corp. Founding mem. Chief Execs. Orgn., Losantiville Country Club, Queen City Club, Bankers Club. Home: 6754 Fairoaks Dr Amberley Village Cincinnati OH 45237 Office: 2121 Section Rd Amberley Village Cincinnati OH 45237

KLEIN, FREDERICK TIMOTHY, marketing professional; b. N.Y.C., Apr. 19, 1940; s. Ernest Donald and Demetria Ann (Aaglan) K.; m. Mary Kay Casey, Oct. 3., 1964; children: Christine, Cecilia. Student, NYU, 1957-58,

U. Colo., 1958-61; grad. summa cum laude, U.S. Army Intelligence Sch., 1962; BA in Human Behavior, Newport U., 1988. Machine acct. Haskins & Sells, N.Y.C., 1957-65; methods analyst Ford Motor Co., Newark, 1965-68; div. supr. Thiokol Chem. Co., Trenton, N.J., 1968-72; br. mgr. McDonnell Douglas Automation Co., Denver, 1972-79; dist. mgr. United Info. Systems, Englewood, Colo., 1979-81; pres. Nat. Resources Cos., Englewood, Colo., 1981-83; mktg. mgr. Analysts Internat. Corp., Englewood, 1983—; publ. critic computer scis. dept. U. Minn., 1986-88. Author: (manual) Div. Policy and Procedures, 1971. Chmn. Littleton (Colo.) Leadership Retreat, 1986-88; com. chmn. Colo. Centennial Conf., Denver, 1987-88; precinct capt. Colo. Operation ID, Littleton, 1983—; mem. Statue of Liberty Found., N.Y.C., 1985—, U.S. Olympic Com., 1968. Served in U.S. Army, 1962-64. Recipient Humanitarian award N.J. Sch. for the Deaf, 1971, Outstanding Service award Nat. Security Agy., 1964. Mem. Am. Mgmt. Assn. (mem. com. 1968-72), Soc. for Info. Mgmt. (chmn. 1985-86, Outstanding Mem. 1984), Data Processing Mgmt. Assn. (program chmn. 1971). Roman Catholic. Clubs: Summit (pres. 1988), Highline Athletic (Littleton), Pres.' (Denver). Home: 7139 S Curtice Littleton CO 80120 Office: Analysts Internat Corp 14 Inverness Dr E Englewood CO 80112

KLEIN, GEORGE, manufacturing company executive, microcomputer system and engineering consultant; b. Budapest, Hungary, Aug. 4, 1934; came to U.S., 1950; s. Louis and Sue (Fleiner) K.; m. Marcella E. Baum, Aug. 23, 1964; children: Diane L., Elliot C., Louis H., David A. BEE, CUNY, 1964; MBA, Hofstra U., 1971. Registered profl. engr., N.Y. Project dir. Alphanumerics, Inc., Lake Success, N.Y., 1967-70; founder, officer, dir. Catoptrics, Inc., New Hyde Park, N.Y., 1970-72; consulting engr. G. Klein & Assocs., New Hyde Park, 1972-77, 78-81; dir. engring. Codata Corp., Larchmont, N.Y., 1977-78; founder, sr. v.p. DCS Controls Corp., Great Neck, N.Y., 1981-86; founder, pres., dir. Landmark Systems, Inc., N.Y.C., 1986—; prin. Stack, Klein and Labiak Fin. and Mgmt. Cons.; founder, pres., dir. GPK Technologies Corp., New Hyde Park, N.Y., 1986—; prin. Stack, Klein and Labiak Fin. and Mgmt. Cons. Contbr. articles to profl. jours. Patentee signal measurement system, 1972, communications network, 1979, universal input/output device, 1983. Served with U.S. Army, 1957-59. Mem. IEEE, ASHRAE, Am. Energy Engrs. Avocations: weight lifting, racquetball, squash, reading. Home: 159 Robby Ln Manhasset Hills NY 11040 Office: Stack Klein & Labiak Inc Garden City NY 11530

KLEIN, HARRY, corporation executive; b. Ecuador, Oct. 14, 1921; s. Isaac Robert and Augusta (Mann) K.; m. Judy Murelman, Apr. 15, 1967 (dec. 1987); children: Roberto, Martin, Andros, Daniel, Fredy; m. Sonja Zuckerman, Apr. 1, 1988. Student, Iowa State Coll.; M in Agrononmy, U. Latin Am., Buenos Aires. Consul gen. Ecuadorian Embassy, Marseille, France, 1953-68; pres. Omega-Tuboplat, Quito, Ecuador, 1969-86, Paco Internat., Quito, 1971—, Ingasa-Omega Industries, Quito, 1972—, Fadesa Group, Quito, 1972—, Eternit Group, Quito, 1973—, Barker & Pronaca Group, Quito, 1974—, Indaves Group, Quito, 1974—, Panoceanica Group, Quito, 1987—. Del. UNESCO, Paris, UN, 1955-68, Geneva, 1955-68; amb. People to People to China U. Calif., 1988. Col. Ecuador armed forces res. Decorated Legion of Merit (Ecuador), Legion of Merit (France). other: Colon 1480, Quito Ecuador Office: Lasso 161 Casilla, 230 Quito Ecuador

KLEIN, IRMA FRANCES, career development educator, consultant; b. New Orleans, Jan. 5, 1936; d. Harry Joseph and Gesina Frances (Bauer) Molligan; m. John Vincent Chelena (dec. 1963); 1 child, Joseph William; m. Chris George Klein, Aug. 14, 1965; 1 stepchild, Arnold Conrad. BS in Bus. Augustine Coll., postgrad. Mktg. Inst., Chgo., Loyola U., Chgo., Realtors Inst., Baton Rouge. Mgr. Stan Weber & Assocs., Metairie, La., 1971-75; tng. dir., 1975-81; cons. Coldwell Banker Comml. Co., New Orleans, 1981; dir. career devel. Coldwell Banker Residential Co., New Orleans, 1982-85. Instr. U. New Orleans, Bonnabel High Sch., Realtors Inst., La. Real Estate Commn. Author: Career Development, 1982; Training Manual, 1978, Obtaining Listings, 1986, Participative Marketing, 1986, Marketing & Servicing Listings, 1987, Designing Training Curriculum, 1987. Active Friends of Longue Vue Gardens, La. Hist. Assn. Meml. Hall Found. Mem. La. Realtors Assn. (bd. dirs. 1973-74, grad. Realtors Inst. 1976), Jefferson Bd. Realtors (v.p. 1984), Edn. and Resources (cert., pres. La. chpt.), Research Club of New Orleans (pres. 1984-85), Realtors Nat. Mktg. Inst. (ambassador Tex. and La. 1985—, Outstanding Achievement award 1985, cert. broker 1980, residential specialist 1977), Nat. Assn. Realtors (nat. conv. speaker 1986), CRB (pres. La. chpt. 1982-83, chmn. edn.), CRS (pres. La. chpt. 1988—), Forty Scholars Soc., Am. Dental Assts. Assn. Republican. Roman Catholic. Clubs: Antique Study Group of New Orleans, Confederate Lit. (New Orleans) (pres.), Research (New Orleans). Avocation: antiques.

KLEIN, LAWRENCE ROBERT, economist, educator; b. Omaha, Sept. 14, 1920; s. Leo Byron and Blanche (Monheit) K.; m. Sonia Adelson, Feb. 15, 1947; children: Hannah, Rebecca, Rachel, Jonathan. B.A., U. Calif.-Berkeley, 1942; Ph.D., MIT, 1944; M.A., Lincoln Coll., Oxford U., 1957; LL.D. (hon.), U. Mich., 1977, Dickinson Coll., 1981; Sc.D. (hon.), Widener Coll., 1977, Elizabethtown Coll., 1981, Ball State U., 1982, Technion, 1982, U. Nebr., 1983; Dr. honoris causa, U. Vienna, 1977; Dr.Ed., Villanova U., 1978; Dr. (h.c.), Bonn U., 1974, Free U. Brussels, 1979, U. Paris, 1979, U. Madrid, 1980. Faculty U. Chgo., 1944-47; research assoc. Nat. Bur. Econ. Research, 1948-50; faculty U. Mich., 1949-54; research assoc. Survey Research Center, 1949-54, Oxford Inst. Stats., 1954-58; faculty U. Pa., Phila., 1958—, prof., 1958—, Univ. prof., 1964—, Benjamin Franklin prof., 1968—; vis. prof. Osaka U., Japan, 1960, U. Colo., 1962, CUNY, 1962-63, 82, Hebrew U., 1964, Princeton U., 1966, Stanford U., summer 1968, U. Copenhagen, 1974; Ford vis. prof. U. Calif. at Berkeley, 1968, Inst. for Advanced Studies, Vienna, 1970, 74; cons. Canadian Govt., 1947, UNCTAD, 1966, 67, 75, 77, 80, McMillan Co., 1965-74, E.I. du Pont de Nemours, 1966-68, State of N.Y., 1969, AT&T, 1969, Fed. Res. Bd., 1973, UNIDO, 1973-75, Congl. Budget Office, 1977—, Council Econ. Advisers, 1977-80; chmn. bd. trustees Wharton Econometric Forecasting Assocs., Inc., 1969-80, chmn. profl. bd., 1980—; trustee Maurice Falk Inst. for Econ. Research, Israel, 1969-75; adv. council Inst. Advanced Studies, Vienna, 1977—; chmn. econ. adv. com. Gov. of Pa., 1976-78; mem. com. on prices Fed. Res. Bd., 1968-70; prin. investigator econometric model project Brookings Instn., 1963-72, Project LINK, 1968—; sr. adviser Brookings Panel on Econ. Activity, 1970—; mem. adv. com. Inst. Internat. Econs., 1983; coordinator Jimmy Carter's Econ. Task Force, 1976; mem. adv. bd. Strategic Studies Center, Stanford Research Inst., 1974-76. Author: The Keynesian Revolution, 1947, Textbook of Econometrics, 1953, An Econometric Model of the United States, 1929-1952, 1955, Wharton Econometric Forecasting Model, 1967, Essay on the Theory of Economic Prediction, 1968, An Introduction to Econometric Forecasting and Forecasting Models, 1980; Author-editor: Brookings Quar. Econometric Model of U.S.; Ecometric Model Performance, 1976, Lectures in Econometrics, 1983; Editor: Internat. Econ. Rev, 1959-65; asso. editor, 1965—; Editorial bd.: Empirical Econs, 1976—. Recipient William F. Butler award N.Y. Assn. Bus. Economists, 1975; Golden Slipper Club award, 1977; Pres.'s medal U. Pa., 1980; Alfred Nobel Meml. prize in econs., 1980. Fellow Econometric Soc. (past pres.), Am. Acad. Arts and Scis., Nat. Assn. Bus. Economists; mem. Am. Philos. Soc., Nat. Acad. Scis., Social Sci. Research Council (fellow 1945-46, 47-48, com. econ. stability, dir. 1971-76), Am. Econ. Assn. (John Bates Clark medalist 1959, exec. com. 1966-68, pres. 1977), Eastern Econ. Assn. (pres. 1974-76). Office: U Pa Dept Econs and Fin Philadelphia PA 19104 *

KLEIN, LOUIS EDWARD, business consultant; b. Richard City, Tenn., Sept. 20, 1920; s. William Henry and Jesse Cresswell (Booker) K.; m. Allie Crockett Leslie, Feb. 3, 1950 (div.); children: Susan W., William E., Jane C.; m. Carol Bick, Feb. 18, 1981. BS in Chem. Engring., Lehigh U., 1942; MS in Chem. Engring., Calif. Inst. Tech., 1947. Shift supr. Ky. Ordnance Works, Atlas Powder, Paducah, 1942-43; project specialist organic div. Monsanton Co., St. Louis, 1947-66, asst. dept. dir., dir. new bus. devel., asst. gen. mgr. organic div., 1947-66, asst. gen. mgr. internat. div., 1966-67, dir. bus. devel. new enterprise div., 1967-71, corp. dir. licensing, 1971-77, dir. new ventures, 1977-83; pres. Klein Assocs., St. Louis, 1983—; sr. assoc. Strategic Planning Inst., Cambridge, Mass., 1984—; gen. ptnr. Baring Bros., Hambrecht & Quist, London, 1984—; cons. Venture Econs., Inc., Wellesley Hills, Mass., 1984—; guest lectr. Wharton Sch., U. Pa., Phila., 1986—. Patentee in field. Mem. Clayton (Mo.) Library Bd., 1962-64; mem. Parks and Recreation Commn., Clayton, 1964-66; mem. Clayton Bd. Edn., 1963-65; mem. Sci. and Engring Commn., Regional Commn. and Growth Assn., St. Louis, 1980—. Lt. (j.g.) USN, 1943-46, WWII. Fellow Royal Soc. Arts, Mfg. and Community; mem. Am. Chem. Soc., AAAs, Comml. Devel. Assn., Licensing Execs. Soc. Home: 1100 S Spoede Rd Saint Louis MO 63131 Office: L Edward Klein Assocs Inc PO Box 12491 Saint Louis MO 63132

KLEIN, PETER MARTIN, lawyer, transportation company executive; b. N.Y.C., June 2, 1934; s. Saul and Esther (Goldstein) K.; m. Ellen Judith Matlick, June 18, 1961; children: Amy Lynn, Steven Ezra. A.B., Columbia U., 1956, J.D., 1962. Bar: N.Y. 1962, D.C. 1964, U.S. Supreme Ct. bar 1966. Asst. proctor Columbia U., 1959-62; asst. counsel Mil. Sea Transp. Service, Office Gen. Counsel, Dept. Navy, Washington, 1962-65; trial atty. civil div. U.S. Dept. Justice, N.Y.C., 1966-69; gen. atty. Sea-Land Service, Inc., Menlo Park, N.J., 1969-76; v.p., gen. counsel, sec. Sea-Land Service, Inc., 1976-79, Sea-Land Industries, Inc., Menlo Park, 1979-84; asso. gen. counsel R.J. Reynolds Industries, Inc., Winston-Salem, N.C., 1978-84; sr. v.p., gen. counsel, sec. Sea-Land Svc., Inc. (formerly Sea-Land Corp.), Iselin, N.J., 1984—, also bd. dirs.; mem. adv. com. on pvt. internat. law Dept. State, 1974—; mem. U.S. delegation UN Conf. on Trade and Devel., UN Commn. on Internat. Trade Law, 1975-76, trade regulation adv. bd. Bur. Nat. Affairs, 1986-88. Trustee Jewish Edn. Assn. Met. N.J., 1973-76; trustee Temple B'nai Abraham of Essex County, N.J., 1973—, v.p., 1976-81, pres., 1981-83; mem. Essex County Dems. Com., 1986-88. Served with USN, 1956-59, Antarctica. Mem. Am. Maritime Assn. (dir., chmn. coms. on law and legis. 1974-78), Am. Polar Soc., ABA, Navy League U.S. (life mem.), Fed. Bar Assn., N.Y. State Bar Assn., D.C. Bar Assn., Internat. Bar Assn., Maritime Law Assn., U.S. Club, Nat. Press. Home: 22 Sandalwood Dr Livingston NJ 07039 Office: Sea-Land Svc Inc PO Box 800 Iselin NJ 08830

KLEIN, PETER WILLIAM, lawyer, corporate secretary, finance company executive; b. Lorain, Ohio, Sept. 22, 1955; s. Warren Martin Klein and Barbara (Lesser) Pomeroy; m. Jennifer Lynn Ungers, Aug. 3, 1984. Student, U. Sussex, 1975-76; BA, Albion Coll., 1976; JD, Cleve. Marshall Coll. Law, 1981; LLM, NYU, 1982. Bar: Ohio 1981, Ill. 1984. Assoc. Guren, Merritt, Feibel, Sogg & Cohen, Cleve., 1982-84, Siegan, Barbakoff, Gomberg & Gordon, Ltd., Chgo., 1984-86; v.p., sec., gen. counsel Trivest Inc. and affiliated cos., Miami, Fla., 1986—. Mem. ABA (taxation sect., corp. sect., banking and bus. law), Am. Soc. Corp. Secs. Home: 3618 Palmetto Ave Coconut Grove FL 33133 Office: Trivest Inc 2665 S Bayshore Dr Ste 801 Miami FL 33133

KLEIN, RICHARD DEAN, banker; b. Elkhart, Ind., Mar. 11, 1932; s. Wilbert Joseph and Mary Katherine (Elsasser) K.; m. Marian Garfield, Aug. 2, 1958; children—James Garfield, Allen Harwood, Robert Howlett. B.A., Kalamazoo Coll.; postgrad., Mich. State U., 1954; postgrad. Grad. Sch. Banking, U. Wis., 1958. Vice chmn. First of Am. Bank Corp., Kalamazoo; dir. numerous banks in Mich., Ill., Ind. Chmn. Mich. Higher Edn. Commn., 1973-77, Mich. Higher Edn. Facilities Commn., 1973-77. Mem. Am. Bankers Assn., Mich. Bankers Assn. Republican. Presbyterian. Clubs: Kalamazoo Country, Park (Kalamazoo), Chgo. Office: 1st Am Bank Corp 108 E Michigan Ave Kalamazoo MI 49007

KLEIN, RICHARD LEE, wholesale pharmaceutical executive; b. Oak Park, Ill., May 10, 1933; s. Albert N. and Ruth E. (Titus) K.; m. Merilynn Pat Oelkers, Sept. 4, 1965; children: Stephen, Deborah. BS in Acctg., U. Ill., 1957; MBA in Fin., U. Chgo., 1973. CPA, Ill. Controller ITW, Chgo., 1965-71; corp. controller Scott, Foresman, Glenview, Ill., 1971-75; v.p., corp. controller Tonka, Mpls., 1975-78; v.p., chief fin. officer Barry Wehmiller, St. Louis, 1978-84, Healthdyne, Atlanta, 1984-85; sr. v.p., chief fin. officer Durr-Fillauer Med., Montgomery, Ala., 1986—; bd. dirs. Mich. Gen. Corp., Dallas. Mem. Fin. Execs. Inst. Home: 8013 Lakeridge Dr Montgomery AL 36117 Office: Durr-Fillauer Med Inc 218 Commerce St Montgomery AL 36104

KLEIN, ROBERT EDWARD, publishing company executive; b. Cin., Dec. 27, 1926; s. Albert and Elisabeth (Muschnau) K.; m. Nancy Minter, May 28, 1958; children: Robert Schuyler, Elisabeth Susan. AB, Kenyon Coll., 1950; MBA, Cornell U., 1952; AM, U. Chgo., 1969, PhD, 1983. With Sealy Inc., Chgo., 1964-66; chief exec. officer Market Power, Inc., Chgo., 1966-69; dist. mgr. McGraw Hill Co., Chgo., 1971-87, Housing mag., 1980, v.p. sales Plastics Today, 1987—; Modern Plastics Internat. mag.; cons. U.S. Dept. Justice, 1967-71, Time/Life Books, 1980; lectr. in Soviet history Barat Coll., 1970-72; lectr. in history Mallinckrodt Coll., 1983-85; assoc. dept. history Northwestern U., Evanston, Ill., 1986—. Author: J.F.C. Fuller and The Tank, 1983, Christian Opposition to Hitler, The Underground Christian Church in The Soviet Union. Served with U.S. Army, 1944-46, PTO. Grolier scholar, 1952. Mem. Am. Legion, Am. Hist. Assn., Beta Theta Pi. Republican. Episcopalian. Clubs: Westmoreland Country (Wilmette, Ill.); Cornell. Lodge: Masons. Avocations: writing, lecturing. Home: 633 Park Dr Kenilworth IL 60043 Office: McGraw Hill Co 645 N Michigan Ave Chicago IL 60611

KLEIN, STEVE A., small business owner; b. Chgo., Nov. 28, 1951; s. S. Robert and Phyllis (Groner) K.; m. Roberta Ann Prueter, July 7, 1950; children: Erik Daniel, Douglas Ryan. BA, No. Ill. U., 1974. News dir., promotion dir. Sta. KHAS, Hastings, Nebr., 1974-76; salesman Sta. KSAL, Salina, Kans., 1976-78, Sta. KLIF, Dallas, 1978-79, Internat. Monetary Group, Dallas, 1980, Sta. WRR, Dallas, 1980; owner Profl. Devel. Ctr., Richardson, Tex., 1980—; Cert. radio mktg. cons. Mem. Sales and Mktg. Execs. Dallas (officer 1986-89), Dallas C. of C. (team capt. Lasso club 1983-86, Adopt-a-Sch. Vol. of Yr. 1985, capt. 1985), Success Motivation Inst. (Rookie of Yr. 1981, World Sales Leader of Yr. 1982, Distbr. of Yr. 1982-87, Sales Leader of Yr. 1984, World Motivator of Yr. 1985, 88). Office: Profl Devel Ctr 845 E Arapaho #108 Richardson TX 75081

KLEIN, WALTER CHARLES, agricultural products company executive; b. N.Y.C., May 11, 1918; s. Joseph Charles and Charlotte K.; m. Mary Kennard Eddy, Apr. 5, 1941; children: Walter Charles, John E., Margaret K. A.B., Harvard U., 1939. Asst. v.p. Bunge Corp., N.Y.C., 1947-52, v.p., 1952-59, dir., 1955—, pres., chief exec. officer, 1959-85, chmn., 1985—; adv. bd. Chem. Bank. Overseer Exec. Council Fgn. Diplomats, Washington; bd. dirs. U.S.-USSR Trade and Econ. Council; exec. council Found. Commemoration U.S. Constitution. Republican. Congregationalist. Clubs: Orange Lawn Tennis (South Orange, N.J.) (gov. 1959-62); Short Hills (N.J.) (bd. dirs., pres. 1984, 86); Knickerbocker (N.Y.C., bd. dirs.), India House (N.Y.C.), Downtown Assn. (N.Y.C.); Baltusrol Golf (Springfield, N.J.). Office: Bunge Corp One Chase Manhattan Pla New York NY 10005

KLEINER, AARON, corporate professional; b. Munich, May 10, 1947; came to U.S., 1948; B in Mgmt., MIT, 1970, Masters, 1970. Tng. adminstrv. Citibank, 1970-72; sr. tng. adminstrv. Johnson & Johnson, 1972-74; co-founder, exec. v.p. subs. Xerox Kurzweil Computer Products, Cambridge, Mass., 1974-82; co-founder, vice chmn. Kurzweil Applied Intelligence, Waltham, Mass., 1982—, Kurzweil Music Systems Inc., Waltham, 1982—. Chmn. enterprise forum MIT, 1988—. Mem. Technion Entrepreneural Assn. (co-chmn. 1987—). Office: Kurzweil Music Systems Inc 411 Waverly Oaks Rd Waltham MA 02154

KLEINER, BRIAN, industrial center executive, consultant; b. Bklyn., Nov. 16, 1959; s. Irving N. and Lee (Auerbach) K.; m. Deborah Jo Thomas, June 15, 1985; 1 child, Heidi Rebekah. BA, SUNY, Cortland, 1981; MS, U. Buffalo, 1983, postgrad., 1983—. Teaching asst. dept. indsl. engring. U. Buffalo, 1981-83, rsch. asst., 1981-83, project coordinator, 1985-87, dir. Ctr. for Indsl. Effectiveness, 1987—; mfg. cons., Buffalo, 1983—; cons. Applied Ergonomics Group, Buffalo, 1985—. Contbr. articles to profl. jours. Mem. Inst. Indsl. Engrs., Human Factors Soc., Sigma Xi. Home: 87 Dalton Dr Buffalo NY 14223 Office: U Buffalo Ctr Indsl Effectiveness 433 Bell Hall Buffalo NY 14260

KLEINLEIN, KATHY LYNN, training and development executive; b. S.I., N.Y., May 2, 1950; d. Thomas and Helen Mary (O'Reilly) Perricone; m. Kenneth Robert Kleinlein, Oct. 30, 1983. BA, Wagner Coll., 1971, MA, 1974; MBA, Rutgers U., 1984. Cert. secondary tchr., N.Y., N.J., Fla. Tchr. English, N.Y.C. Bd. Edn., S.I., 1971-74; Matawan (N.J.) Bd. Edn., 1974-79; instr. English, Middlesex County Coll., Edison, N.J., 1978-81; med. sales rep. Pfizer/Roerig, Bklyn., 1979-81, mgr. tng. ops., N.Y.C., 1981-87; dir. sales tng. Winthrop Pharms. div. Sterling Drug, N.Y.C., 1987-88, Reuters Info. Systems, N.Y.C., 1988—; pres. dir. sales tng., Women in Transition, career counseling firm; personnel mgmt. officer U.S. Army Res., N.J., 1981-86; dir. sales tng. and devel. Sterling Drug, Inc. div. Winthrop Pharms., N.Y.C.; cons. Concepts & Producers, N.Y.C., 1981-85. Trainer United Way, 1982-83, mem. polit. action com., 1982—; mem. Rep. Presdl. Task Force, Washington, 1983—. Capt. U.S. Army, 1974-78. First woman in N.Y. N.G., 1974; first woman instr. Empire State Mil. Acad., Peekskill, N.Y., 1976. Mem. Nat. Soc. Pharm. Sales Trainers, Sales and Mktg. Execs., Am. Soc. Tng. and Devel., N.J. Assn. Women Bus. Owners, LWV, Matawan C. of C., Alpha Omicron Pi. Republican. Roman Catholic. Club: Atlantis Divers (N.Y.C.). Home: 93 Idolstone Ln Matawan NJ 07747 Office: Reuters Info Systems 1700 Broadway St New York NY 10019

KLEINMAN, GEORGE, commodities executive; b. Bklyn., Aug. 10, 1951; s. Herman and Helen Kleinman; m. Sherri Ellen Meadow; children: Kevin, Craig. BS in Bus., Ohio State U., 1973; MBA in Fin., Hofstra U., 1975. Product mgr. Mead Johnson Labs., Evansville, Ind., 1974-77; sr. v.p. commodities Merrill Lynch, Mpls., 1977-83; pres. Commodity Resource Corp., Mpls., 1983—; owner CRC Cow/Calf Co., Red Wing, Minn., 1986—; bd. dirs. K&W Cattle Co., Ainsworth, Nebr. Columnist Am. Trans Air Sun Country mag., 1986—. Referee Nat. Youth Soccer Assn., Mpls., 1983—. Mem. Mpls. Grain Exch. (bd. dirs.), Nat. Futures Assn., Entrepreneur's Network, Grain Shippers Assn., Nat. Cattlemen's Assn., Delta Sigma Pi. Office: Commodity Resource Corp Minneapolis Grain Exchange Bldg Minneapolis MN 55415

KLEINMAN, LAURENCE VICTOR, utilities executive; b. N.Y.C., Dec. 7, 1942; s. Sigmund and Gertrude (Rossoff) K.; m. Linda Kern, Jan. 8, 1967; 1 child, Laura. BA, Clark U., 1964. Reporter, editor Worcester (Mass.) Telegram & Gazette, 1966-67; corr. AP, Springfield, Mass., 1967-68; reporter Suffolk Sun, Deer Park, N.Y., 1968; reporter, editor New York Post, 1968-78; account exec. Carl Byoir & Assocs., N.Y.C., 1979; dir. pub. info. Consol. Edison, N.Y.C., 1980-86, v.p. corp. communications and pub. info., 1986—. Cons. Fedn. Jewish Philanthropics, N.Y.C., 1986—; bd. dirs. Blythedale Children's Hosp., Valhalla, N.Y., 1986—. Recipient cert. of merit ABA, 1972. Office: Consol Edison 4 Irving Pl New York NY 10003

KLEMENT, KENNETH RAYMOND, manufacturing executive; b. Milw., Apr. 23, 1951; s. Frank L. and Laurel M. (Fosnot) K.; m. Deborah M. Nehls, Apr. 16, 1983. BSBA cum laude, Marquette U., 1973. CPA, Wis. Fin. trainee Rexnord, Inc., Milw., 1973-74; staff acct. Rexnord, Nordberg Machinery Group, Milw., 1974-79; supr. gen. acctg. Rexnord, process machinery div., Milw., 1980-82; project mgr. fin. systems Rexnord Inc., Milw., 1982-83; controller Rexnord Ry. Equipment div., Milw., 1983-87; controller, treas. Ry. Maintenance Equipment Co., Milw., 1987; v.p. fin., controller Nordco Inc. (formerly Ry. Maintenance Equipment Co.), Milw., 1988—. Fellow Wis. Inst. CPAs. Avocations: golf, fishing, racquetball. Home: 4906L S 19th St Milwaukee WI 53221 Office: Nordco Inc 182 W Oklahoma Ave Milwaukee WI 53207

KLEMM, RICHARD HENRY, investment manager; b. N.Y.C., Aug. 10, 1931; s. Richard F. and Sophie (Leymann) K.; m. June Christ, Feb. 21, 1954; children: Janet, Lynda, Richard. BSCE, Bucknell U., 1953; MBA in Econs., NYU, 1964. Registered profl. engr., N.Y. Fin. planner N.Y. Telephone, N.Y.C., 1956-65; div. mgr. AT&T Corp., N.Y.C., 1965-81; v.p. GTE Investment Mgmt. Corp., Stamford, Conn., 1981-85; sr. v.p. Warburg, Pincus Counsellors, N.Y.C., 1985—; prin. ExecuServ, Bernardsville, N.J., 1985—; dir. Ridge Oak, Inc., Basking Ridge, N.J. Bd. dirs. Family Counselling Somerset County, Bound Brook, N.J., 1976-81, 85-87. Fellow Fin. Analysts Fedn.; mem. N.Y. Soc. Security Analysts, Inst. Cert. Fin. Planners. Republican. Episcopalian. Office: Warburg Pincus Counsellors Inc 466 Lexington Ave New York NY 10017

KLEMME, CARL WILLIAM, banker; b. Ft. Wayne, Ind., Sept. 11, 1928; s. Ludwig and Marianne (Rupil) K.; m. Ann Elise Wichman, Sept. 11, 1954; children: Ellen Elise Taylor, Sarah Ann Venizelos, Carl Andrew. BS, Yale U., 1950; MBA, NYU, 1956; postgrad. mgmt., Harvard U., 1971. With Morgan Guaranty Trust Co., N.Y.C., 1950-80, v.p., 1961-70, sr. v.p., 1970-72, exec. v.p., 1972-80; exec. v.p. Russell Reynolds Assocs., Inc., N.Y.C., 1981-82, Nat. Westminster Bank U.S.A., N.Y.C., 1982—. Mem. Millburn Bd. Edn., 1967-73; trustee Howard U., 1975—, Millburn (N.J.) Pub. Library, 1979-84, Wittenberg U., 1983—, New Eyes for the Needy, 1980-86; bd. dirs. Downtown-Lower Manhattan Assn., 1972-80; bd. dirs. Bank Adminstrn. Inst., 1975-81, chmn., 1979-80. Served with U.S. Army, 1950-52. Mem. Phi Beta Kappa. Republican. Episcopalian. Home: 35 Woodfield Dr Short Hills NJ 07078 Office: Nat Westminster Bank USA 175 Water St New York NY 10038

KLEMPEL, JOANNE NANCY, accountant; b. Huntington, N.Y., Dec. 31, 1962; d. Rudi and Hilde (Schmeisser) K. BA, Muhlenberg Coll., 1984. CPA, Pa. Internal auditor Times Mirror Mag., Inc., N.Y.C., 1984; acct. Bruce Mina & Co., CPA, Huntington, 1985-88, Wolpert & Buss, CPAs, New Hyde Park, N.Y., 1988—. Treas. Gloria Del Luth. Ch., Huntington, 1985-88. Mem. NAFE. Republican. Home: 10 Lafayette St Huntington NY 11743 Office: Wolpert & Buss CPAs 1700 Jericho Turnpike New Hyde Park NY 11040

KLERKX, MARTIN ALAN, information management executive; b. Detroit, Dec. 1, 1942; s. Walter Martin and Sylvia Imogene (Greene) K.; B.S., Mich. State U., 1964; m. Cheryl Kay McCubbin, Apr. 14, 1989; children by previous marriage: Gregory William, David Walter; m. Cheryl Kay Mc Cubbin, apr. 14, 1989. Staff systems analyst Mich. Consol. Gas Co., Detroit, 1968-69; systems cons. Univ. Computing Co., Detroit, 1969-72; mgmt. cons. Ernst & Whinney, 1972-73; info. systems dir. Mich. Judicial Data Center, 1973-81; mgmt. cons. Peat Marwick Mitchell & Co., 1981-82; gen. mgr. Info. Systems div. TIC Internat., Indpls., 1982-83; dir. info. services agy. City of Indpls. and Marion County, 1984-86; project supr. Guardian Industries Corp., Northville, Mich., 1986—. Served with USN, 1964-68. Mem. Am. Mgmt. Assn., Soc. Mgmt. Info. Systems, Naval Inst. Methodist. Home: 14384 Mercedes Redford MI 48239 Office: Guardian Industries Corp 43043 W Nine Mile Rd Northville MI 48167

KLEVANA, LEIGHTON QUENTIN JOSEPH, lawyer; b. Czechoslovakia, Oct. 7, 1934 (born Am. citizen); s. Joseph V. and Bellina N. (Karlovsky) K.; B.A., Cornell U., 1957; postgrad. U. Paris, The Sorbonne, 1958; J.D., U. Va., 1961. Admitted to N.Y. bar, 1963, Vt. bar, 1971; assoc. atty. Meyer, Kissell, Matz & Seward, N.Y.C., 1961-63, Olwine, Connelly, Chase, O'Donnell & Weyher, 1963-67; sec. Helme Products, Inc., N.Y.C., 1967, sec., gen. counsel, 1967-70; v.p., sec., dir. Transit Air Freight, Inc., 1966-75; partner law firm Mahady & Klevana, 1973-76, Klevana & Rounds, P.C., 1977-79; pres., dir. Windsor County Properties, Inc., 1974-76, Practicing Real Estate Inst., Inc., 1974—, Klevana Inst. Inc., 1984—, Klevana Group, Inc., 1987—, Connecticut River Valley Properties, Inc., 1976-79; assoc. Norwood Group Realty, Inc., 1981-87. Asst. atty. gen., Vt., 1970-73. Home: 115 N Adams St Manchester NH 03104 Office: 77 Lowell St Manchester NH 03104 also: 468 Chestnut St Manchester MH 03104

KLIEM, PETER OTTO, photographic equipment company executive; b. Berlin, May 13, 1938; s. Carl and Berta (Daniel) K.; m. Erika Hanloser, July 7, 1962; children: Peter Carl, Eric Alexander, John Curtis. BS in Chemistry, Bates Coll., 1960; MS in Chemistry, Northeastern U., 1965. Scientist Polaroid Corp., Waltham, Mass., 1960-67, mgr., 1967-72, sr. engring. mgr., 1972-75, div. v.p., 1975-77, asst. v.p., 1977-80, v.p., 1980-82; sr. v.p., asst. research dir. Polaroid Corp., Cambridge, Mass., 1982-85, sr. v.p., dir. research, 1985-86, sr. v.p., dir. research and engring., 1986—; chmn. PBDS Inc., Westwood, Mass., 1985—. Trustee Waltham-Weston Med. Ctr., 1984-86. Mem. Am. Chem. Soc., Soc. Photographic Scientists and Engrs., Indsl. Research Inst., Nat. Acad. Sci. (acad. industry program adv. com.). Office: Polaroid Corp 549 Technology Sq Cambridge MA 02139

KLIMBACK, ELIZABETH MARTON, public relations executive, promoter; b. Bodrogolaszi, Hungary, Jan. 12, 1949; came to U.S., 1957; d. Joseph and Elizabeth (Árvai) Marton; m. Thomas John Klimback, Sept. 22, 1972. BA in English and Secondary Edn., Caldwell Coll., 1972; postgrad., Seton Hall U., 1975-79. Tchr. English West Essex Bd. Edn., North

Caldwell, N.J., 1972-81; prodn. asst., project and mktg. coordinator Ga. Pub. Telecommunications, Atlanta, 1981-83; dir. pub. info., promotions Alamo Pub. Telecommunications Council, San Antonio, 1983—; dir. promotions Sta. KLRN, San Antonio, 1983-86, Sta. KLRU, Austin, Tex., 1983-86. Author, editor: (program guide) Promotions Director, 1983—, various nat. press kits, 1983—, various local, regional nat. program promotions, 1983—. mem. bd. for higher edn. St. Mary's U., San Antonio, 1983-85; exec. mem. Rely on San Antonio, 1983—. Mem. Broadcast Promotions and Mktg. Execs., Nat. Assn. Pub. TV Stas. Home: 2318 Cripple Creek Arlington TX 76014 Office: Sta KLRN-TV Alamo Pub Telecommunications Coun 801 S Bowie San Antonio TX 78205

KLINE, FRANK ROBERT, JR., computer company executive; b. Mahanoy City, Pa., Sept. 5, 1950; s. Frank Robert Sr. and Agnes (Hawkes) K.; m. Shelly Lipkin, Aug. 27, 1972; 1 child, Frank-Robert III. BS in Commerce, Rider Coll., 1972; MSBA, U. Mass., 1974. Research analyst Echlin Mfg., Branford, Conn., 1974-75; analyst Internat. Data Corp., Waltham, Mass., 1975-79; v.p. research Drexel Burnham Lambert, N.Y.C., 1979-81, v.p. corp. fin., 1981-84; pres. Pacific tech. Venture Fund, San Francisco and Tokyo, 1984—; gen. ptnr. Lambda Lambda Funds, Drexel Burnham Lambert, N.Y.C.; bd. dirs. Carlyle Systems, Berkeley, Calif., 1045 Fifth Owners Corp., N.Y.C., SuperShuttle Internat., Los Angeles, Basic Measuring Instruments, Foster City, Calif. Mem. Nat. Venture Capital Assn., Western Assn. Venture Capitalist, Assn. Computing Machinery, So Cal Ten. Home: 1045 Fifth Ave New York NY 10028 Office: Drexel Burnham Lambert 60 Broad St New York NY 10004

KLINE, GEORGE WILLIAM, II, television producer; b. San Antonio, July 5, 1949; s. Robert Walter and Adelaide McCall (Carter) K.; m. Kristin Scheffey, Mar. 5, 1977; children: Amanda Dupree, George William III, Luke Carter. BA, Austin Coll., 1971. Road mgr. Kris Kristofferson, N.Y.C., 1971-73; producer Sta. KERA-TV (PBS affiliate), Dallas, 1973-75; ind. producer Strongbow Prodns., Los Angeles, 1975-77; producer Bill Stokes Assocs., Dallas, 1977-78; exec. producer TannebringRose Assocs., Dallas, 1978-82; pres. Geo. Kline Co., Inc., Dallas, 1982—; bd. dirs., v.p. Motion Picture Producers Tex. Chmn. bd. Addison (Tex.) Airport, 1986; mem. adv. com. N. Tex. Film Commn.; bd. dirs. U.S.A. Film Festival, 1986—. Named a Southwest Creative All-Star, Adweek Mag., 1984, 87; recipient Gold award Internat. Film & TV Festival, N.Y., 1983, 87-88, Dallas Advt. League Gold Award, Best 30 Second Commercial, 1986, Matrix award Women in Communications, 1987, Silver Internat. Film & TV Festival, N.Y., 1987, 3 gold Addys, 2 silver Addys Dallas Advtg. League, 1987, Best of Show award 10th Dist. Addys, 1988, Gold award Houston Internat. Film Festival; also awards from Art Dirs. Club, N.Y., 1983, Communication Arts mag., Palo Alto, 1982. Mem. Motion Picture Producers of Tex. (v.p.), Assn. Ind. Comml. Producers, Highland Pk. League. Episcopalian. Clubs: Steeplechase (Ft. Worth); Balboa de Mazatlan S.A. (Mex.); Hackberry Creek Country (Dallas). Home: 4604 Fairfax Dallas TX 75209 Office: 3009 Maple Ave Dallas TX 75201

KLINE, LINDA, employment consultant; b. Boston, Aug. 8, 1940; d. George and Eva (Weiner) Kline; B.A. in Biology, Boston U., 1962. Personnel dir. Block Engring. Inc., Cambridge, Mass., 1964-66; brokerage mgr. Eastern Life Ins. Co. N.Y., Boston, 1966-68; mgr. direct placement Lendman Assos., N.Y.C., 1968-72; dir. women-in-mgmt. div. Roberts-Lund, Ltd., N.Y.C., 1972-77; pres. Kline-McKay, Inc., Exec. Search and Outplacement Cons., Maximus Cons., Inc., N.Y.C., 1978—; exec. dir. Majority Money, women's network, 1976-79; tchr. fin. planning for women Marymount-Manhattan Coll., 1977; lectr. and/or cons. women's programs at several colls. and univs. and corps. Co-author: Career Changing: The Worry-Free Guide, 1982. Bd. dirs. Women Bus. Owners Edn. Fund, 1982-86 , Mom's Amazing, 1985-88; community bd. dirs. Mt. Sinai Med. Ctr., 1984—. Mem. Women Bus. Owners N.Y. (bd. dirs. 1978-84), Nat. Coalition Women's Enterprise (adv. bd. 1988—). Address: 3 E 48th St #6 New York NY 10017

KLINE, MARVIN I., investment banker; b. Canton, Ohio, Jan. 19, 1952; s. Maurice and Edith J. (Gilbert) K.; m. Abby J. Rubin, May 3, 1980; children: Daniel, David. BS, Case-Western Res. U., 1974; MBA, U. Pa., 1976. Analyst Mich. Consol. Gas Co., Detroit, 1976-77; assoc. Phila. Capital Advisors, 1977-79, asst. v.p., 1980-83, v.p., 1983-85, sr. v.p., 1985—. Contbr. articles to profl. publs. Mem. Phila. Analysts Soc., Tau Beta Pi, Beta Gamma Sigma. Home: 801 Lombard St Philadelphia PA 19147 Office: Phila Capital Advisors PNB Bldg Broad and Chestnut Sts Philadelphia PA 19107

KLING, PETER HELMAR, advertising executive, marketing consultant; b. Rockford, Ill., Feb. 5, 1931; s. Helmar G. and Orpha (Halleen) K.; m. Marlene D., Sept. 19, 1952 (div. May 1984); children: Steven, David, Timothy, Pamela; m. Delores Jones, May 15, 1987. BS, U. So. Calif., 1955. Sales mgr. Wylde & Sons Printing, Maywood, Calif., 1958-61; pres. Media IV Advt., Long Beach, Calif., 1961-76, Trimagination Creative, Santa Ana, Calif., 1976-82, Custom Bus. Systems, Santa Ana, 1980-82; v.p. Smith & Myers Advt., Santa Ana, 1982-87; pres. Hernandez and Kling Advt., Garden Grove, Calif., 1987—. Contbr. indsl. publs. and films. Cpl. U.S. Army, 1952-54. Mem. Bus. and Profl. Advt. Assn. (cert. bus. communicator 1985), Sales & Mktg. Club (L.A., bd. dirs. 1960-62). Republican. Mem. Evang. Free Ch. of Am.

KLING, RICHARD WILLIAM, insurance executive, actuary; b. St. Paul, May 23, 1940; s. William C. and Helen A. Kling; m. Betty Kling; children: Jeffrey, David. BA, St. Thomas Coll., St. Paul, 1962; grad., Coll. Fin. Planning, 1987. Cert. fin. planner. Actuary various positions with IDS Life Ins. Co., 1962-82, exec. v.p., 1982—; v.p. ins. mktg. products IDS Fin. Services Inc. (formerly Investors Diversified Services Inc., IDS/Am. Express Inc.), 1984—; pres., chief exec. officer Am. Enterprise Life Ins. Co., 1986-87; also bd. dirs. IDS Life N.Y.; exec. v.p. IDS Ins. Agys., Inc., Ohio, Wyo., Mass., N.Mex., N.C., Ark., Ala., 1985—;mem. IDSL Series Funds, Variable Annuity Separate Accounts Bd. Mgrs. Fellow Soc. Actuaries; mem. Am. Acad. Actuaries. Club: Twin Cities Actuarial. Office: IDS Life Ins Co 800 IDS Tower 10 80 S Eighth St Minneapolis MN 55474

KLINGENSMITH, RITCHEL GEORGE, computer scientist; b. Armstrong County, Pa., Jan. 4, 1942; s. Ritchel George and Cecile Ida (Bowser) K.; student Montgomery Jr. Coll., 1965, in bus. adminstrn. Ind. U., 1965-67, State U. N.Y., 1978—; m. Arlene Ruth Mauthe, Aug. 3, 1963; children—Debra Kristine, Kenneth Floyd. Staff asst. Virto Lab., Silver Spring, Md., 1962-65; sr. staff specialist Automation Industries, Silver Spring, 1967-76; computer analyst HEW, Washington, 1976—; computer analyst/cons. Leader Lutheran Youth Activities, Woodbine, Md., 1974-76; v.p. Mt. Airy (Md.) PTA, 1975-76, treas., 1976-78, v.p., 1978-79. Served with USN, 1959-62. Mem. Washington Mark IV Users Exchange, Airplane Owners and Pilots Assn. Republican. Lutheran. Club: Seneca. Home: 4828 Ridge Rd Mount Airy MD 21771 Office: Ritchel K Inc Baltimore MD 21207

KLINGERMAN, ROBERT HARVEY, manufacturing company executive; b. Freeland, Pa., Nov. 10, 1939; s. Thomas Van and Emma Yeager (Hoffman) K.; m. Eleanor Jean Deemer, Aug. 31, 1963; children: Jeffrey Allen, Timothy Scott. BS in Chem. Engring., Lehigh U., 1961. Sr. applications engr. Elliott Co. div. Carrier Corp., Jeannette, Pa., 1961-66; project mgr. Stokes div. Pennwalt Corp., Phila., 1966-70, Cragmet Corp., Rancocas, N.J., 1970-74; v.p. engring. Cheston Co. (now Consarc Corp.), Rancocas, 1974-78; dir. ops. Inducto Heat, Madison Heights, Mich., 1978-82; pres. W.J. Savage Co., Knoxville, Tenn., 1982—, also bd. dirs.; bd. dirs. Metl-Saw, Inc., Benecia, Calif. Patentee in field. Mem. Abrasive Engring. Soc., Am. Soc. Metals, Nat. Machine Tool Builders, Bldg. Stone Inst., Marble Inst. Am. Republican. Methodist. Home: 700 Chateaugay Knoxville TN 37923 also: WJ Savage Co 1 Hopkins St Knoxville TN 37921

KLINSKY, ARNOLD, communications executive; b. Chgo., Jan. 12, 1944; s. Nathan and Ruth (Fensin) K.; m. Hisako Tomisato, Dec. 8, 1970; children: Kevin, Ami. BS, U. Ill., 1966. News dir. and anchor Sta. WICD-TV, Champaign, Ill., 1968; dir. pub. affairs, reporter Sta. WOC AM-FM/TV, Davenport, Iowa, 1968-73; mng. editor news Sta. KTVI-TV, St. Louis, 1973-78; dir. news Sta. WVIT-TV, West Hartford, Conn., 1978-82; v.p. ops. Sta. WVIT-TV, 1982-83; v.p., gen. mgr. Sta. WHEC-TV 10, Rochester, N.Y., 1983—. Mem. com. Martin Luther King Festival, Rochester, 1987-88; chmn. Urban League, Rochester, 1987—; treas. Arts for Greater Rochester, 1988—; bd. dirs. Community Ptnrs. for Youth, 1988—. Mem. N.Y. State Broadcasting Assn. Jewish. Home: 19 Barrington Hills Pittsford NY 14534 Office: Sta WHEC-TV 191 East Ave Rochester NY 14604

KLODZINSKI, JOSEPH ANTHONY, data communications executive, consultant; b. Chgo., Aug. 19, 1942; s. Joseph Fabian and Haline Ann (Bieganski) K.; m. Mary Margaret Osten, Nov. 19, 1966; children: Joseph II, Catherine Ann, Patricia Ann. BBA, Loyola U., Chgo., 1964; MEd, Boston U., 1968; MBA, Northwestern U., 1971. Packaging engr. Westvaco, Chgo., 1969-72; regional mgr. MacMillan, Chgo., 1972-74; fin. applications cons. IC Systems Corp., Schaumburg, Ill., 1974-77; mgmt. info. systems salesman Honeywell, Chgo., 1977-80; mgmt. info. systems and communications cons. Intertel, Chgo., 1980-82; distbr. sales mgr. UDS/Motorola, Chgo., 1982-89; nat. sales and mktg. mgr. Incom Data Systems, Chgo., 1989—. Contbr. articles to profl. jours. Mem. parish council Ch. of Holy Spirit, Schaumburg, 1980-85. Capt. U.S. Army, 1965-69, Vietnam. Decorated Bronze Star; named Pacesetter, Honeywell Mktg. Mgmt., 1978, Top Sales Mgr., IC Systems Corp., 1975-76, Top Sales Mgr., MacMillan, 1974; fellow Lions Clubs Internat. Found., 1984. Mem. Am. Numismatic Assn. (life), co-founder Australian Numismatic Assn. (Sydney), Oceanic Navigation Research Soc. Roman Catholic. Lodges: K.C., Elks, Lions (pres. Schaumburg 1980-82, DG cabinet No. Ill. zone chmn. 1982-86, dep. dist. gov. 1986—, DG awards 1983-88). Home: 1419 Chalfont Dr Schaumburg IL 60194 Office: Incom Data Systems Wheeling IL 60090

KLOPFENSTEIN, E. JAY, securties executive; b. Gridley, Ill., Feb. 19, 1925; s. Elmer J. and Anna (Gramm) K.; B.A., Ill. Wesleyan U., Bloomington, 1949; m. Ruth Vortman, Oct. 13, 1951; children—Linda, Bruce. Stockbroker, Hornblower & Weeks, Chgo., 1957-70; v.p. Heinold Commodities, Inc., Chgo., 1970-77; pres. Norwood Securities, Chgo., 1977—. Served with USNR, 1943-46. Lic. gen. securities broker and dealer, investment adv.; registered options prin. Mem. Sigma Chi. Clubs: Germania, Big Foot Country. Pub. Norwood Index. Office: 6134 N Milwaukee Ave Chicago IL 60646

KLOPFENSTEIN, GARY CARLTON, securities broker; b. Normal, Ill., Dec. 10, 1961; s. Carlton Joseph and Betty Jane (Koehl) K.; m. Candice J. Knochel, June 22, 1986, Livonia, Mich. BA summa cum laude, Ill. Wesleyan U., 1985. Pres. Roth Honegger Co., Bloomington, Ill., 1981-83; br. mgr. Norwood Securities, Bloomington, Ill., 1984—; pres. G K Capital Mgmt., Inc., 1986—; commodity pool operator and trading advisor. Author: Structural Analysis of Securities Brokerage Industry, 1985. Recipient Wall Street Jour. Achievement award, 1985. Mem. Phi Kappa Phi. Republican. Home: 902 S Mercer Ave Bloomington IL 61701 Office: Norwood Securities 102 S East St Bloomington IL 61701

KLOSKA, RONALD FRANK, manufacturing company executive; b. Grand Rapids, Mich., Oct. 24, 1933; s. Frank B. and Catherine (Hilaski) K.; m. Mary F. Minick, Sept. 7, 1957; children—Kathleen Ann, Elizabeth Marie, Ronald Francis, Mary Josephine, Carolyn Louise. Student, St. Joseph Sem., Grand Rapids, Mich., 1947-53; Ph.B., U. Montreal, Que., Can., 1955; M.B.A., U. Mich., 1957. Staff accountant Coopers & Lybrand, Niles, Mich., 1957; staff to sr. accountant Coopers & Lybrand, 1960-63; treas. Skyline Corp., Elkhart, Ind., 1963, v.p., treas., 1964-67, exec. v.p. finance, 1967-74, pres., 1974-85, pres., chief oper. officer, 1985—; dir. Midwest Commerce Banking Co., Elkhart. Served with U.S. Army, 1957-60. Mem. AICPA, Mich. Soc. CPAs, Ind. Soc. CPAs. Roman Catholic. Club: South Bend Country. Home: 1329 E Woodside St South Bend IN 46614 Office: Skyline Corp 2520 By Pass Rd Elkhart IN 46514

KLOSTER, BURTON JOHN, JR., financial corporation executive, lawyer; b. Hackensack, N.J., Oct. 27, 1931; s. Burton John and Myra C. (Young) K.; m. Hildegard Sobek, July 6, 1957; children: Doris, John. BA, Cornell U., 1953, LLB, 1957. Bar: N.Y. 1958, Ky. 1961. Mem. legal staff Gen. Electric Co., 1957-76; v.p., gen. counsel, sec. Gen. Electric Capital Corp., Stamford, Conn., 1976-84, sr. v.p., sec., gen. counsel, 1984—. Served to 1st lt. QMC U.S. Army, 1954-56. Mem. ABA, N.Y. State Bar Assn., Ky. Bar Assn. Republican. Congregationalist. Home: 30 Quail Ridge Rd Wilton CT 06897 Office: GE Capital Corp 260 Long Ridge Rd Stamford CT 06902

KLOSTERMAN, ROBERT JOHN, financial planner; b. Sibley, Iowa, Apr. 8, 1951; s. Donald Anthony and Shirley Lynn (Mayer) K.; m. Muriel Jean Studer, July 2, 1971; children: Kelly Lynn, Michael John, Adam Anthony. Assoc. in Applied Sci., Iowa Lakes Community Coll., 1971. CLU, Chartered Fin. Cons. Office mgr. Community Credit Co., Edina, Minn., 1971-75; registered rep. Investors Diversified Services, Mpls., 1975-78; owner Klosterman and Co., Maple Grove, Minn., 1978-83; pres. Synergistic Planning Group, Mpls., 1983-86; founder R.J. Klosterman & Co., Mpls., 1986—. Chairperson 9th precinct Maple Grove Ind. Rep. Party., state del., 1980; mem. bd. mgmt. N.W. YMCA. Mem. Internat. Assn. Fin. Planners, Am. Soc. CLU's (past pres. Mpls. chpt.), Registry Fin. Planning Practitioners, Mpls. C. of C., Twin West C. of C. Roman Catholic. Office: 1005 Interchange Tower 600 S Hwy 169 Minneapolis MN 55416

KLOTT, DAVID LEE, lawyer; b. Vicksburg, Miss., Dec. 10, 1941; s. Isadore and Dorothy (Lipson) K.; m. Maren J. Randrup, May 25, 1975. BBA summa cum laude, Northwestern U., 1963; JD cum laude, Harvard U., 1966. Bar: Calif. 1966, U.S. Ct. Claims. 1968, U.S. Supreme Ct. 1971, U.S. Tax Ct. 1973, U.S. Ct. Appeals (Fed. cir.) 1982. Ptnr. Pillsbury, Madison & Sutro, San Francisco, 1966—; mem. tax adv. group to subchpt. C J and K., Am. Law Inst.; tchr. Calif. Continuing Edn. of Bar, Practising Law Inst., Hastings Law Sch., San Francisco. Commentator Calif. Nonprofit Corp. Law. Served with USAR, 1967. Mem. ABA (tax exempt financing com.), Calif. State Bar Assn., San Francisco Bar Assn., Am.-Korean Taekwondo Friendship Assn. (1st dan-black belt), Beta Gamma Sigma, Beta Alpha Psi (pres. local chpt.). Clubs: Harvard (San Francisco), Northwestern (San Francisco), Olympic, City Club of San Francisco (founding mem.). Office: Pillsbury Madison & Sutro 225 Bush St San Francisco CA 94104-2105

KLOTTER, RONALD LAWRENCE, pension consultant; b. Louisville, Sept. 27, 1960; s. John Charles and Susan Jane (Riddle) K.; m. Julie Marie Englehart, May 28, 1983. BS in Fin., Miami U., Oxford, Ohio, 1982; MBA, Northwestern U., Evanston, Ill., 1984. V.p. E.F. Hutton & Co., Inc., Chgo., 1984-88; cons. Hewitt Assocs., Lincolnshire, Ill., 1989—. Mem. Beta Gamma Sigma. Club: Hinsdale Racquet. Home: 110 N Adams St Hinsdale IL 60521 Office: Hewitt Assocs Lincolnshire IL 60015

KLOTZ, CHARLES RODGER, chemical company executive; b. Englewood, N.J., Apr. 14, 1942; s. George Edward and Beryl Edith (Cullingford) K.; m. Deborah Goodwin, June 25, 1966; children: Christine, Suzanne. BS, Trinity Coll., Hartford, Conn., 1964; MBA, Dartmouth Coll., 1966. Officer Bank of Boston Corp., 1969-85; pres., chief exec. officer Gulf Resources & Chem. Corp., Boston, 1985-89; also bd. dirs. Gulf Resources & Chem. Corp.; with Bingham, Dana & Gould, Boston, 1989—; chief exec. officer, chmn. bd. Gotaas Larsen Shipping Corp., 1988—, also bd. dirs. Lt. USCG, 1966-69. Office: Bingham Dana & Gould 150 Federal St Boston MA 02110

KLOTZBACH, JAMES KENT, food packaging executive, engineer; b. Quincy, Ill., Jan. 17, 1936; s. John Roy and Vera C. (Huseman) K.; m. Carolyn A. Thompson, June 24, 1977. Grad. high sch., Keokuk, Iowa. Indsl. electrician Quaker Oats, Cedar Rapids, Iowa, 1968-70; electrician, mechanic Union Carbide, Keokuk, 1970; supr. maintenance Armour-Dial, Inc., Ft. Madison, Iowa, 1972-77, Miller Brewing Co., Ft. Worth, 1977-84; mgr. maintenance McCormick & Co. Inc., Lewisville, Tex., 1984—; labeling specialist Miller Brewing Co., Ft. Worth, 1973-77; with tng. Krones, Regensburg, Fed. Republic Germany, 1973-77. With USN, 1954-58. Home: 637 Abilene Dr Lewisville TX 75067 Office: McCormick Co Inc 1137 N Kealy Lewisville TX 75067

KLUG, RICHARD PAUL, financial executive; b. Milw., Sept. 13, 1934; s. Aaron and Theodora Maria (Wendt) K.; m. Arleen JoAnn Wittig, Apr. 19, 1958; children: Jeffrey Richard, Jannifer JoAnn. BA, Elmhurst (Ill.) Coll.; postgrad., U. Wis., 1966; ciploma in comml. lending, U. Okla., 1971. Mgr. Household Fin. Corp., Milw., 1956-60; from compliance officer, exec. v.p./chief operating officer, sr. v.p./chief lending officer to chmn./chief exec. officer F&M Bank, Menomonee Falls, Wis., 1960—, also bd. dirs., mem. exec. com.; chmn., pres., chief exec. officer F&M Fin. Svcs. Corp., Menomonee Falls, 1982—, also bd. dirs., mem. exec. com.; owner Kildeer Orchards; ptnr. Klug's Photo World; chmn., bd. dirs. F&M Trust Co. Inc.; mem. Robert Morris Assocs. Contbr. articles to profl. jours.; speaker various groups, clubs, orgns. Chmn. Greater Menomonee Falls Com., 1983—; past chmn. Police and Fire Commn., Monomonee Falls, mem. 1962-84; mem. exec. bd. Met. YMCA, Milw., 1988—, bd. dirs. 1970-83, mem. bldg. com.; active Tri-County YMCA, Monomonee Falls, bd. dirs. 1959-85, former youth sports coach, mem. Friar's Com., chmn. 1970-73; treas. Am. Can Soc. Wis. Div., 1982, bd. dirs. Waukesha North unit 1980-86; gen. chmn. Monomonee Falls Diamond Jubilee; chmn. suburban unit Greater Milw. United Way, 1986, chmn. Metro North Gen. Bus., 1983, bd. dirs. 1985—; active Rep. polit. campaigns, mem. gov.'s task force on Rural Devel.; mem. Waukesha County Criminal Justice Coun.; bd. dirs. Waukesha Found. U. Wis., 1986—, Community Meml. Hosp., Monomonee Falls, 1984—, Cedar Lake (Wis.) Home, 1984—. With U.S. Army, 1953-55. Recipient various awards for civic work including Friar's award YMCA, Tri-County Disting. Citizen award Potowatomi Area Coun. Boy Scouts Am., 1987; named Boss of Yr. Am. Businesswomen's Assn., 1982. Mem. Am. Bankers Assn. (com. bank leadership 1986—, task force payment systems laws 1987—), Am. Inst. Banking, Am. Mgmt. Assn., Wis. Installment Bankers Assn. (state pres. 1972, bd. dirs.), Wis. Bankers Assn. (exec. coun. 1983—, chmn. 1987-88), Monomonee Falls C. of C. (Man of Yr. 1970, legis. com., pres. 1962), North Hills Country Club, Rotary (corp. bd. dirs. 1983—, pres. 1988—), Kiwanis, Masons. Mem. Ch. Christ. Home: 4230 Hwy 167 Hubertus WI 53033 Office: F&M Fin Svcs Corp N88 W16554 Main St Menomonee Falls WI 53051

KLUTZNICK, PHILIP M., lawyer, former government official; b. Kansas City, Mo., July 9, 1907; s. Morris and Minnie (Spindler) K.; m. Ethel Riekes, June 8, 1930; children: Bettylu, Richard (dec.), Thomas Joseph, James Benjamin, Robert, Samuel. Student, U. Kans., 1924-25, U. Nebr., 1925-26; JD, Creighton U., Omaha, 1929, LLD (hon.), 1957; DHL (hon.), Dropsie Coll., 1954, Hebrew Union Coll.-Jewish Inst. Religion, 1957, Coll. Jewish Studies, 1968; LLD (hon.), Wilberforce (Ohio) U., 1959, Chgo. Med. Sch., 1968, Yeshiva U., 1974, Brandeis U., 1974, Roosevelt U., 1981, U. Ill.-Chgo., 1983; LHD (hon.), Governor's State U., 1983; LLD (hon.), Northwestern U., 1984, DePaul U., 1984. Admitted to bar, 1930. U.S. commr. Fed. Pub. Housing Authority, 1944-46; mem. U.S. dels. to UN, 1957, 61, 62; U.S. rep., rank of ambassador, to ECOSOC, 1961-63; mem. President's Adv. Com. on Indo-Chinese Refugees; sec. commerce Washington, 1980-81. Bd. dirs. Nat. Jewish Welfare Bd., Exec. Service Corps; founder Inst. Jewish Policy Planning; nat. council Boy Scouts Am.; chmn. exec. com. Dearborn Park; trustee Gen. Marshall Found.; hon. bd. dirs. Creighton U., Roosevelt U., Lyric Opera Chgo.; trustee Com. Econ. Devel.; pres. emeritus World Jewish Congress, 1977— ; bd. govs. Chgo. Symphony. Recipient Ralph Bunche peace award, 1981; named to Chgo. Bus. Hall of Fame, 1985. Mem. UN Assn. U.S.A. (gov.; sr. dir.), Chgo. Assn. Commerce and Industry (adv. com.), Lambda Alpha, Zeta Beta Tau (hon.), B'nai B'rith (hon. internat. pres.). Clubs: Cosmos, Army-Navy (Washington); Standard, Carlton, Commercial, (Chgo.). Office: 737 N Michigan Ave Ste 920 Chicago IL 60611

KNAPP, DENNIS LEROY, healthcare administrator; b. Auburn, Ind., Nov. 13, 1945; s. Dale I. and Ruth I. (Smith) K.; m. Karen J. Jasonka, Feb. 14, 1985; children: Jason, Erika. AS, Jackson Coll., 1973; cert., Nuclear Med. Inst., Cleve., 1974; BBA, Eastern Mich. U., 1981; MBA, U. Notre Dame, 1986. Dir. nuclear medicine dept. W.A. Foote Hosp., Jackson, Mich., 1975-78, adminstr. radiation medicine dept., 1978-83; asst. adminstr., chief fin. officer Cameron Hosp., Angola, Ind., 1983-86; chief fin. officer DeKalb Meml. Hosp., Auburn, 1987-88; chief exec. officer Dr.'s Hosp., Jackson, 1988—; cons. clin. program Nuclear Med. Inst., 1976, nuclear medicine Hillsdale (Mich.) Hosp., 1976-78. Mem. fin. Midwest Health Network, Columbia City, Ind., 1984; rep. Rural Hosp. Legis. Group., Washington, 1984. Served with U.S. Army, 1966-68. Mem. Healthcare Financing Mgrs. Assn, Am. Coll. Healthcare Execs. Lodge: Rotary (v.p. 1986—, Angola club 1975—). Home: RR2 PO Box 212 Angola IN 46703 Office: Dr's Hosp 110 N Elm St Jackson MI 49202

KNAPP, GARY BURTON, investment banker; b. Fergus Falls, Minn., Oct. 24, 1943; s. Charles Harry and Gertrude Thelma (Duenow) K.; m. Kay Ann, Mar. 1967 (div. 1973); 1 child, Jessica Marie. AS, N.D. State Sch. of Sci., 1963; BA, Moorhead State Coll., 1965; MA, Mankato (Minn.) State Coll., 1967; DBA, U. Ky., 1977. Registered principal, registered rep. Outside rep. Northwestern Bell Telephone, Fargo, N.D., 1965; instr. mktg., mktg. research Stephen F. Austin State U., Nacogdoches, Tex., 1967-69; instr. Mankato (Minn.) State U., 1969-72; asst. budget dir. U. Ky., Lexington, 1975-77; assoc. prof. mktg. research and strategies U. Houston, 1977-82; pres. Knapp & Assocs., Houston, 1982-87, Knapp Securities, Inc., Houston, 1987—; cons. Sakowitz Dept. Stores, Houston, 1979, Nat. Assn. Home Builders, Washington, 1982. Chmn., pres. Mariner Village Townhouse Assn., Inc., Seabrook, Tex., 1979. Mem. Nat. Assn. Securities Dealers, Am. Mktg. Assn., Clear Lake C. of C. (chmn. research div. 1979-80). Lutheran. Club: Houstonian, Houston Polo. Office: 2525 Bay Area Blvd Houston TX 77058

KNAPP, HARRY EMIL, JR., investment executive, actuary; b. Bronx, N.Y., Feb. 2, 1954; s. Harry Emil and Janet (Weyrauch) K.; m. Joanne Sabestinas, June 12, 1976; 1 child, Kimberly Elise. AB, Princeton U., 1976; cert. program for mgmt. devel., Harvard U., 1984. CLU, CFA. Various actuarial positions Prudential Ins. Co. Am., Newark and L.A., 1976-84; v.p. Prudential Mortgage Capital Co. subs. Prudential Ins. Co. Am., Newark, 1984-88, mng. dir. corp. fin., 1988—. Fellow Soc. Actuaries; mem. Huguenot Yacht Club (New Rochelle, N.Y.), Princeton Club, Dial Lodge, Phi Beta Kappa. Republican. Methodist. Home: 78 Poplar Dr Morris Plains NJ 07950 Office: Prudential Ins Co Am Four Gateway Ctr Newark NJ 07102

KNAUSS, DALTON LEVERN, electronic components manufacturing company executive; b. Imboden, Ark., May 18, 1928; s. Charles E. and Greta Lou (Lawrence) K.; m. Elaine V. Nybakken, June 16, 1951; children: Cynthia L. Diaz, William C. Grad., DeVry Coll., 1951; Student, Ill. Inst. Tech., 1956. V.p. co-founder Dickson Electronics, Tempe, Ariz., 1960-67; pres., founder Gen. Semiconductor Industries, Tempe, 1968-81, pres., 1982; pres. advanced tech. group, v.p. corp. devel. and tech. Sq. D Co., Palatine, Ill., 1982-83, vice chmn., chief exec. officer, 1983-84, chmn., pres., chief exec. officer, 1984-86, chief exec. officer, 1986—, also chmn. bd. dirs.; bd. dirs. Kemper Corp., Long Grove, Ill., 1984—. Patentee in field. Bd. sponsors Good Shepherd Hosp., Barrington, Ill., 1984—; campaign chmn. Jr. Achievement, Chgo., 1987—. With USN, 1945-49. Mem. Nat. Elec. Mfrs. Assn. (bd. govs. 1984—), Elec. Mfrs. Club (bd. govs. 1987—), Barrington Hills Club, Desert Forest Club. Republican. Mem. Ch. Nazarene. Home: PO Box 2173 Carefree AZ 85377 Office: Square D Co 1415 S Roselle Rd Palatine IL 60067

KNECHT, GEORGE BRUCE, development officer; b. Morristown, N.J., Mar. 9, 1958; s. George B. and Barbara Ann (Freeston) K. BA, Cogate U., 1980; MBA, Harvard U., 1986. Asst. editor Bus. Month, N.Y.C., 1981-83; sr. fin. writer Los Angeles Herald Examiner, 1983-84; assoc. Tishman Speyer Properties, N.Y.C., 1986-87; devel. officer Lincoln Property Co., Roseland, N.J., 1987—. Mem. N.Y. Real Estate Bd., Harvard Club of N.Y. Office: Lincoln Property Co 103 Eisenhower Pky Roseland NJ 07068

KNEDLIK, RONALD W., food wholesale and retail executive; b. Charlotte, N.C., Feb. 20, 1949; m. Anita T. Knedlik; children: Courtney, Nathan. BS in Acctg., U. N.C., 1971; MBA, Wake Forest U., 1982. Staff acct. Strand, Skees, Jomes & Co., Greensboro, N.C., 1971-74; controller Mchts. Distbrs., Inc., Hickory, N.C., 1974-80; v.p. fin. Mchts. Distbrs., Inc., 1980-87, sr. v.p. fin., adminstrn., 1987—; bd. dirs. Instn. Food House, Inc., Hickory, Lowe's Food Stores, Inc., Wilkesboro, N.C.; pres., bd. dirs. Mchts. Distbrs. Inc. Employees Fed. Credit Union, Hickory, 1980—. Mem. Am. Inst. CPA's, N.C. Assn. CPA's, N.C. Real Estate Brokers, Hickory C. of C. (bd. dirs. 1988—), Catanba County C. of C. (bd. dirs. 1988—), Rotary (treas. Hickory chpt. 1987—). Office: Mchts Distbrs Inc 543 12th St Dr NW Hickory NC 28601

KNEELAND, BRUCE FRANKLIN, pharmaceutical executive; b. Needles, Calif., Sept. 2, 1947; s. Floyd Cassius and Lillian (Wareham) K.; m. Donna Liane Bates, Dec. 18, 1971; children: Robyn, Christopher, Jillyn, Linda, Kelly. BA in Communications, Brigham Young U., 1973; Student, Webster (Mo.) Coll. Sales rep. Roerig div. Pfizer Pharms., Fargo, N.D., 1973-76; hosp. rep. Pfizer Pharms., St. Louis, 1976-77; dist. mgr. Medicine Shoppe Internat., St. Louis, 1977-80, regional mgr., 1982-84; sales rep. PharAssist, Inc., St. Louis, 1980-81, Generix Drug, Inc., St. Louis, 1981-82; dir. profl. svcs. Health Mart, Inc., Dallas, 1984-86, v.p. profl. svcs., 1986-87, v.p. franchise sales, 1987—; asst. instr. Dale Carnegie, St. Louis, 1980-82. Unit leader Boy Scouts Am., Dallas, 1987—. With U.S. Army, 1968-70, Vietnam. Mem. Internat. Franchise Assn., Am. Pharm. Assn. (presenter 1987). Republican. Mormon. Home: 4921 Wolf Creek Trail Flower Mound TX 75028 Office: Health Mart Inc 1220 Senlac Rd Carrollton TX 75006

KNEEN, JAMES RUSSELL, health care administrator; b. Kalamazoo, Dec. 16, 1955; s. Russell Packard and Joyce Elaine (Knapper) K.; m. Peggy Jo Howard, Aug. 4, 1979; children: Benjamin Russell, Katherine Elaine. BA, Alma Coll., 1978; MHA, U. Mo., 1982. Systems analyst Bronson Meth. Hosp., Kalamazoo, 1976-79; cons. U. Mo., Columbia, 1979-81; adminstrv. resident Meth. Hosp. Ind., Indpls., 1981-82; div. dir. psychiat. care svcs. Parkview Meml. Hosp., Ft. Wayne, Ind., 1982-88; exec. v.p. Meml. Hosp.at Ocomonowoc (Wis.), 1988—. Bd. dirs. Washington House Alcoholism Treatment Ctr.; bd. dirs., sec.-treas. Parkview Regional Outreach, 1985-88. Mem. Allen County Mental Health Assn., Am. Coll. Healthcare Execs., Am. Hosp. Assn. Office: Meml Hosp Oconomowoc 791 E Summit Ave Oconomowoc WI 53066

KNEPPER, EUGENE ARTHUR, realtor; b. Sioux Falls, S.D., Oct. 8, 1926; s. Arlie John and May (Crone) K.; B.S.C. in Acctg., Drake U., Des Moines, 1951; m. LaNel Strong, May 7, 1948; children—Kenton Todd, Kristin Rene. Acct., G.L. Yager, pub. acct., Estherville, Iowa, 1951-52; auditor R.L. Meriwether, C.P.A., Des Moines, 1952-53; acct. govt. renegotiation dept. Collins Radio Co., Cedar Rapids, Iowa, 1953-54; head acctg. dept. Hawkeye Rubber Mfg. Co., Cedar Rapids, 1954-56; asst. controller United Fire & Casualty Ins. Co., Cedar Rapids, 1956-58; sales assoc. Equitable Life Assurance Soc. U.S., Cedar Rapids, 1958-59; controller Gaddis Enterprises, Inc., Cedar Rapids, 1959-61; owner Estherville Laundry Co., 1959-64; sales assoc., comml. investment div. mgr. Tommy Tucker Realty Co., Cedar Rapids, 1961-74; owner Real Estate Investment Planning Assocs., Cedar Rapids, 1974—; controlling ptnr. numerous real estate syndicates; cons. in field, fin. speaker; guest lectr. Kirkwood Community Coll., Cedar Rapids, Mt. Mercy Coll., Cedar Rapids, Cornell Coll., Mt. Vernon; creative financing instr. Iowa Real Estate Commn.-Iowa Assn. Realtors. Patron Cedar Rapids Symphony, 1983—, treas., mem. exec. com., bd. dirs.; bd. dirs. Oak Hill-Jackson Outreach Fund, 1970-83, pres., 1973-74; bd. dirs. Consumer Credit Counseling Service Cedar Rapids-Marion Area, 1974-80, pres., 1974-80. Served with USNR, 1945-46. Recipient Storm Manuscript award, 1976. Mem. Nat. Assn. Realtors (state mcpl. legis. com., subcom. on multi-family housing), Iowa Assn. Realtors (pres. comml. investment div. 1973, 80, named life mem.; state legis. com., savs. and loan formation feasibility com., mcpl. and county legis. com.),Nat. Assn. Accountants, Nat. Inst. Real Estate Brokers (membership chmn. Iowa 1972-73, regional v.p.), Real Estate Securities and Syndication Inst. (small group investment council, steering com. 1985, vice chmn. regional officers and state officers devel. com.; gov. Iowa div.), Cedar Rapids Bd. Realtors, Internat. Platform Assn., Internat. Inst. Valuers. Methodist. Clubs: Cedar Rapids Optimist (past chmn. boys work com.); Eastern Iowa Execs. (dir., pres. 1981-82). Contbr. articles to profl. jours. Home: 283 Tomahawk Trail SE Cedar Rapids IA 52403 Office: 1808 IE Tower Cedar Rapids IA 52401

KNERLY, MARY JOHNSON, service company executive, business seminar developer; b. Cleve., Feb. 5, 1925; d. Lawrence Redfield and Margaret (Geltz) Johnson; m. Stephen J. Knerly, Sept. 20, 1944 (div. Dec. 1974); children: Margit Anne Knerly Daley, Stephen J. Jr., Mary Ellen Knerly Kosicki. Student, Lake Erie Coll., Painesville, Ohio, 1942-44; BA, Case Western Res. U., 1946, postgrad., 1948-49. Nursery sch. tchr. Bingham Day Nursery, Cleve., 1945-46; book reviewer Cleve. Press newspaper, 1946-62; ednl. cons. The Lakewood (Ohio) Found., 1957-65; v.p. The Fairmount Theatre of the Deaf, Cleve., 1978-81, pres., 1981-84; pres. Service Service Inc., Cleve., 1984—; owner Beaconhill Ltd., Cleve., 1984-87; part-time counselor Service Corps of Retired Execs., Cleve., 1987—. Columnist The Business Score, Sun Newspapers, Cleve., 1987. Pres. Cleve. Gallery Group, 1960-70; bd. dirs. Cleve. Music Sch. Settlement, 1961-87, Cleve. Ballet, 1977-84; exec. com. The Singing Angels, Cleve., 1967-87. Mem. Am. Womens' Econ. Devel. Corps, Nat. Assn. Female Execs., Women Bus. Owners Assn., Western Res. Archtl. Historians (pres. 1981-83). Republican. Clubs: City, Twentieth Century, Mid-Day. Office: Service Service Inc 11428 Cedar Ave Rm C-1 Cleveland OH 44106

KNETTEL, MICHAEL G., structural designer, civil engineer; b. Freeport, N.Y., July 10, 1955; s. Gerald F. and Barbara (Bostick) K.; divorced; children: Michael Jr., Kyla Nicole, Kelley Erin, Jacqueline Francis; m. Cynthia Ann Slough, Jan 1, 1983. BSC, Sussex (Eng.) Coll., 1978. Dir. engring. specialty metals div. Daly Aluminum, Palm Harbor, Fla., 1979-82; dir., v.p. R & D Lifeguard Corp., Clearwater, Fla., 1982-83; contract adminstr., engr. Smith, Korach, Hayet, Haynie, St. Petersburg, Fla., 1983—; v.p. C.A.K. Inc., St. Petersburg, Fla., 1987—. Author: Construction Marketing, 1988. Campaign chmn. re-election com. City Coun. St. Petersburg, 1982, 86; active Big Bros. Pinellas; dir., coord. Christmas Toy Workshop. Named Outstanding Mem. Big Bros. Pinellas, 1977. Mem. Am. Concrete Inst., Kiwanis (chmn. bus. and pub. affairs). Republican. Roman Catholic. Home: 876 44th Ave N Saint Petersburg FL 33703

KNICELY, HOWARD V., human resource executive; b. Parkersburg, W.Va., Mar. 2, 1936; s. Howard V. and Edith H. (White) K.; m. Peggy Ann Thorne, Aug. 31, 1958 (dec.); children: Cynthia, Michael. BA, Marietta Coll., 1959; MS, W.Va. U., 1960. Mgr. indsl. relations chem. div., FMC Corp., Charleston, W.Va., 1961-68; regional employee relations mgr. chem. div. Mobil Oil Corp., Edison, N.J., 1969, dir. employee and labor relations, N.Y.C., 1970-74; v.p. personnel Admiral Group, Rockwell Internat., Chgo., 1974-75, v.p. personnel Consumer Ops., 1975-77; v.p. human resources Hart, Schaffner & Marx, Chgo., 1977-79; v.p. human relations TRW, Inc., Cleve., 1980—; instr. personnel and mgmt. scis. Morris Harvey Coll., Charleston, W.Va., 1964-66; lectr. MIT, Purdue U., U. Pa.; past chmn. Ohio State Jobs Council; trustee Nat. Ctr. Occupational Readjustment. Trustee Inroads, Cleve. Ballet, Greater Cleve. Roundtable. Mem. Am. Soc. Personnel Adminstrn., Bus. Roundtable (past vice chmn. employee relations com.), Conf. Bd. (personnel adv. com.), Labor Policy Assn. (mem. exec. com.), Am. Mgmt. Assn., Human Resource Assn. Chgo. (past pres.). Home: 32131 Meadowlark Way Pepper Pike OH 44124 Office: 23555 Euclid Ave Cleveland OH 44117

KNICELY, JAMES JEFFREY, lawyer; b. Lincoln, Nebr., Sept. 1, 1946; s. Jack R. and Betty M. (Klingel) K.; m. K. Leslie Scent, Sept. 26, 1981; children: Rebecca, Esther, Sara Kay. BA with distinction, George Washington U., 1969; JD, Harvard U., 1972. Bar: Nebr. 1973, Va. 1980, U.S. Ct. Appeals (D.C. cir.), 1973, U.S. Supreme Ct. 1974. Assoc. then ptnr. Kutak, Rock & Huie, Omaha, Nebr., 1977-79; assoc. Hunton & Williams, Richmond, Va., 1980-84; prin. Graber, Knicely & Cotorceanu P.C., Williamsburg, Va., 1984—; bd. dirs., sec. Rutherford Inst., Manassas, Va. Contbr. to Miss. Law Jour. Mem. exec. com. York County Rep. Com., 1985-86; bd. dirs. Festival Williamsburg, 1986. Lt. JAGC, USNR, 1974-77. Mem. Va. Bar Assn., Nat. Assn. Bond Lawyers. Office: Graber & Knicely PC 487 McLaws Circle Ste 2 Williamsburg VA 23185

KNIGHT, CHARLES FIELD, electrical equipment manufacturing company executive; b. Lake Forest, Ill., Jan. 20, 1936; s. Lester Benjamin and Elizabeth Anne (Field) K.; m. Joanne Parrish, June 22, 1957; children: Lester Benjamin III, Anne Field, Steven P., Jennifer Lee. B.S. in Mech. Engring., Cronell U., 1958; M.B.A., Cornell U., 1959. Mgmt. trainee Goetzewerke A.G., Burscheid, W. Ger., 1959-61; pres. Lester B. Knight Internat. Corp., 1961-63; exec. v.p. Lester B. Knight & Assocs., Inc., Chgo., 1963-67; pres. Lester B. Knight & Assocs., Inc., 1967-69, pres., chief exec. officer, 1969-73; vice chmn. bd. Emerson Electric, St. Louis, 1973; sr. vice chmn. bd., corp. exec. officer Emerson Electric Co., 1973, vice chmn. bd., 1973-74, chmn. bd., 1974—, chief exec. officer, 1973—, pres., 1987—, dir.; dir. Southwestern Bell Telephone Co., Mo. Pacific Corp., Ralston Purina Co., First Union Bancorp., Trans. World Corp. Mem. Civic Progress, 1973; bd. dirs. United Way Greater St. Louis; bd. dirs. Arts and Edn. Council; bd. dirs. Barnes Hosp.; trustee Washington U., St. Louis. Mem. Sigma Phi. Clubs: St. Louis Country; Log Cabin (St. Louis), Racquet (St. Louis); Glen View Golf (Ill.); Chicago. Office: Emerson Electric Co 8000 W Florissant Ave Saint Louis MO 63136 *

KNIGHT, DOUGLAS MAITLAND, educational administrator, corporate executive; b. Cambridge, Mass., June 8, 1921; s. Claude Rupert and Fanny Sarah Douglas (Brown) K.; m. Grace Wallace Nichols, Oct. 31, 1942; children: Christopher, Douglas Maitland, Thomas, Stephen. A.B., Yale U., 1942, M.A., 1944, Ph.D., 1946; LL.D. (hon.), Ripon Coll., Knox Coll., Davidson Coll., 1963, U. N.C., 1965, Emory U., 1965, Ohio Wesleyan U., 1970, Center Coll., 1973; L.H.D. (hon.), Lawrence U., 1964, Carleton Coll., 1966; Litt.D. (hon.), St. Norbert Coll., Wake Forest Coll., 1964. Instr. English, Yale U., 1946-47, asst. prof., 1947-53; vis. asst. prof. English, U. Calif.-Berkeley, summer 1949; Morse Research fellow 1951-52; pres. Lawrence Coll., Appleton, Wis., 1954-63, Duke U., Durham, N.C., 1963-69; div. v.p. ednl. devel. RCA, N.Y.C., 1969-71; div. v.p. edn. services RCA, 1971-72, staff v.p. edn. and community relations, 1972-73, cons., 1973-75, pres. RCA Iran, 1971-72, dir., 1971-73; pres. Social Econ. and Ednl. Devel., Inc., 1973—, Questar Corp., 1976—; U.S. del. SEATO Conf. Asian Univ. Pres., Pakistan, 1961; nat. commn. UNESCO, 1965-67; chmn. Nat. Adv. Commn. Libraries, 1966-68; adviser Imperial Orgn. for Social Service of Govt. Iran. Author: Pope and the Heroic Tradition, 1951, (poetry) The Dark Gate, 1971; editor, contbr. The Federal Government and Higher Education, 1960, Iliad and Odyssey, Twickenham edit., 1967, Medical Ventures and the University, 1967, Libraries at Large, Tradition, Innovation and the National Interest, 1970, Street of Dreams: The Nature and Legacy of the 1960's, 1989. Former mem. corp. MIT; bd. dirs., chmn. Woodrow Wilson Nat. Fellowship Found.; bd. dirs. Catalyst, 1961-73, Near East Found., 1975-84, Internat. Schs. Services, 1976-82, Solebury Sch., 1975-83; trustee Questar Library of Sci. and Art, 1982—. Mem. Am. Assn. Advancement of Humanities (dir. 1979-83), Phi Beta Kappa. Clubs: Grolier, Century Assn. (N.Y.C.); Cosmos (Washington); Elizabethan, Berzelius (New Haven). Home: RFD 3 Box 278 Stockton NJ 08559 Office: Questar Corp PO Box 59 New Hope PA 18938

KNIGHT, HAROLD EDWIN HOLM, JR., utility company executive; b. Bklyn., Mar. 23, 1930; s. Harold Edwin Holm and Dorothy (Brown) K.; m. Janet Luft, Feb. 16, 1953. B.S., Yale U., 1952. Test engr. Gen. Electric Co., Pittsfield, Mass., 1952; with Bklyn. Union Gas, 1954—, dir. ins., 1971-74, asst. sec., asst. treas., 1974-78, sec., 1978-84, v.p., sec., 1984—. Pres. Bklyn. council Boy Scouts Am.; past pres. Estates Property Owners Assn., Garden City, N.Y., Garden City Community Fund. Served to capt. USAF, 1952-54. Mem. Brooklyn Club (bd. dirs., pres. 1989—). Home: Calves Neck Rd Southold NY 11971

KNIGHT, HARRY W., management and financial consultant; b. Sedalia, Mo., Apr. 20, 1909; s. Harry William and Florence (Lay) K.; m. Agnes Berger, Sept. 15, 1934; children: Kirk Lay, Harry William. AB, Amherst Coll., 1931; postgrad., Harvard U. Grad. Sch. Bus. Adminstrn., 1931-32; MA, Northwestern U., 1940. With Harris Trust Co., Chgo., 1932-33; sales adminstr. Bauer & Black, 1934-36; fin. dir. City of Winnetka, Ill., 1937-40; city mgr. Two Rivers, Wis., 1941; chief budget sect. War Prodn. Bd., Washington, 1942; asst. chief program control div., munitions assignment bd. Combined Chiefs of Staff, Washington, 1942-45; fin. dir. UNRRA, 1945; sec. fin. com. 3d Council Meeting UNRRA, London, 1945; v.p. Booz, Allen & Hamilton, Inc., 1945-66; chmn. bd. Knight, Gladieux & Smith, 1966-73, Hillsboro Assocs., Inc., N.Y., 1973—, Cigna/Licony, N.Y.; bd. dirs. Shearson Lehman Appreciation Fund and Shearson Lehman Managed Govt. Fund, Cigna/Licony, N.Y.; past bd. dirs. Burlington Industries, Waldorf Astoria, Foxboro and Menlo Venture Capital Fund, Bancroft Racquet Co., other corp. bds. Chmn. Darien Community Fund Dr., 1954; chmn. career conf. Amherst Coll., 1951-54, nat. chmn. capital program, 1962-65, trustee, 1964-81, trustee emeritus, 1981—; pres. Harvard Bus. Sch. Assn., 1960, chmn. golden anniversary, 1958; chmn. adv. council Sch. Internat. Affairs, Columbia U., 1975-82; chmn. Rep. fin. campaign, Darien, 1952; trustee Com. Econ. Devel., 1968—, Hampshire Coll., 1968-76, Hudson Inst., 1973-78. Lt. USNR, 1942-45. Recipient Eminent Service medal Amherst Coll. Mem. Fgn. Policy Assn. (bd. dirs. 1955-70), UN Assn. (past treas., gov., now vice chmn.), Delta Kappa Epsilon. Presbyterian. Clubs: Harvard Bus. Sch. (pres. 1970-71), Univ., Sky (N.Y.C.); Wee Burn Country (Darien, Conn.); Jupiter Island; John's Island Country (Fla.); Pine Valley Golf (N.J.); Sharon Park Country (Menlo Park, Calif.). Home: 110 E 57th St Suite 11-H New York NY 10022 Home (also): 1230 Sharon Park Dr Apt 57 Menlo Park CA 94025 also: 400 Beach Rd Vero Beach FL 32960 Office: Hillsboro Assocs 110 E 57th St Ste 11H New York NY 10022

KNIGHT, PHILIP H(AMPSON), shoe manufacturing company executive; b. Portland, Oreg., Feb. 24, 1938; s. William W. and Lota (Hatfield) K.; m. Penelope Parks, Sept. 13, 1968; children: Matthew, Travis. B.B.A., U. Oreg.; M.B.A., Stanford U. C.P.A., Oreg. Chmn., pres., chief exec. officer Nike, Inc., Beaverton, Oreg., 1967—; dir. Metheus Corp. Trustee Reed Coll., Portland; mem. adv. council Stanford U. Grad. Sch.; bd. dirs. U.S.-Asian Bus. Council, Washington. Served to 1st lt. AUS, 1959-60. Named Oreg. Businessman of Yr., 1982. Mem. Am. Inst. C.P.A.s. Republican. Episcopalian. Office: Nike Inc 3900 SW Murray Blvd Beaverton OR 97005 *

KNIGHT, ROBERT ALLEN, JR., accountant, management consultant; b. Lebanon, Mo., July 15, 1956; s. Robert Allen and Dorothy Joan (Fulbright) K.; m. Caren Mae Rash, Oct. 17, 1987; 1 child, Alexandra Noelle. BSBA in Acctg., U. Mo., 1978. Staff acct. D.L. Salveter, CPA, Waynesville, Mo., 1978-80; staff acct. Ralph C. Johnson & Co., CPAs, Kansas City, Kans., 1980-83, audit mgr., 1983-87; ptnr. Nossaman Knight & Assocs., Prairie Village, Kans., 1987—. Mem. Johnson County Rep. Cen. Com., Overland Park, Kans., 1987-88; active Shawnee Tomorrow Leadership Program. Mem. AICPA, Mo. Soc. CPA's, Kans. Soc. CPA's, U. Mo. Bus. Sch. Alumni Assn., Greater Kansas City C. of C. (small bus. com. 1986-87), Shawnee C. of C. (econ. devel. com. 1988), Kansas City Soc. Assn. Execs. Republican. Methodist. Home: 12414 W 69th St Shawnee KS 66216 Office: Nossaman Knight & Assocs PO Box 8413 Prairie Village KS 66208

KNIGHT, ROBERT EDWARD, banker; b. Alliance, Nebr., Nov. 27, 1941; s. Edward McKean and Ruth (McDuffee) K.; BA, Yale U., 1963; MA, Harvard U., 1965, PhD, 1968; m. Eva Sophia Youngstrom, Aug. 12, 1966; Asst. prof. U.S. Naval Acad., Annapolis, Md., 1966-68; lectr. U. Md., 1967-68; fin. economist Fed. Res. Bank of Kansas City (Mo.), 1968-70, research officer, economist, 1971-76, asst. v.p., sec., 1977, v.p., sec., 1978-79; pres. Alliance (Nebr.) Nat. Bank, 1979—, now also chmn.; pres. Robert Knight Assocs., banking and econ. cons., Alliance, 1979—; vis. prof., chair banking and fin. E. Tenn. State U., Johnson City, 1988; mem. faculty Stonier Grad. Sch. Banking, 1972—, Colo. Grad. Sch. Banking, 1975-82, Am. Inst. Banking, U. Mo., Kansas City, 1971-79, Prochnow Grad. Sch. Banking, U. Wis. Trustee, 1984-85, Knox Presbyn. Ch., Overland Park, Kans., 1965-69; bd. regents Nat. Comml. Lending Sch., 1980-83; chmn. Downtown Improvement Com., Alliance, 1981-84; trustee U. Nebr. Found.; bd. dirs. Stonier Grad. Sch. Banking, Box Butte County Devel. Commn., Nebr. Com. for Humanities, 1986—; mem. fin. com. United Meth. Ch., Alliance, 1982-85, mem. adminstrv. bd., 1987—; Box Butte County Industrial Devel. Bd., 1987—; mem. Nebr. Com. for the Humanities, 1986—; ambassador Nebr. Diplomats. Woodrow Wilson fellow, 1963-64. Mem. Am. Econ. Assn., Am. Fin. Assn., So. Econ. Assn., Nebr. Bankers Assn. (com. state legis. 1980-81, com. comml. loans and investments 1986-87), Am. Inst. Banking (state com. for Nebr. 1980—), Am. Bankers Assn. (econ. adv. com. 1980-83, community bank leadership council), Western Econ. Assn., Econometric Soc., Rotary, Masons. Contbr. articles to profl. jours. Home: Drawer E Alliance NE 69301 Office: Alliance Nat Bank Alliance NE 69301

KNIGHT, ROBERT VERNON, JR., financial company executive; b. Tarboro, N.C., Oct. 27, 1928; s. Robert Vernon and Ruth Sydnor (Dedmon) K.; m. Betsy Rue Knott, May 9, 1952 (dec. Nov. 1979); children: John Ruffin, Ruth Sydnor Knight Gammon. BS, Davidson Coll., 1949. With exec. tng. program Wachovia Bank & Trust Co., Winston-Salem, N.C., 1953-55; asst. to regional v.p. Wachovia Bank & Trust Co., Raleigh, N.C., 1955-58; with Barclays Am. Corp. (and predecessor cos. Home Fin. Corp. and Am. Credit Corp.), Charlotte, N.C., 1958-60, organizer, head dept. advt., 1960-65, sr. v.p. adminstrv. functions, 1965-86, dir. corp. and govtl. affairs, 1986—; bd. dirs. various cos. Pres. Arts and Sci. Council, Charlotte, 1971; Pres.'s div. campaign chmn. United Way, Charlotte, 1976, campaign chmn. comml. div., 1972; treas., founder, trustee Charlotte Latin Sch., 1970-86; pres. Friends U. N.C., Charlotte, 1980-81; active Spirit Sq. Devel. Group, 1975-76; past mem.-at-large Mecklenburg County Council Boy Scouts Am.; campaign chmn. capital funds drive Jr. Achievement, Charlotte, 1978; bd. dirs. 1983-85; bd. dirs. Cen. Charlotte Assn., 1981,84, Hapdicapped Organized Women. Capt. USAF, 1951-53. Mem. Fla. Consumer Fin. Assn., Ga. Consumer Fin. Assn., Miss. Consumer Fin. Assn., N.Y. Consumer Fin. Assn., N.C. Consumer Assn., Ohio Consumer Fin. Assn., Tenn. Consumer Fin. Assn., Tex. Consumer Fin. Assn., W.Va. Consumer Fin. Assn., Charlotte Mchts. Assn. (bd. dirs. 1980-87), Mint Mus., Collectors Circle, Charlotte Country Club, Charlotte City Club, Capital City Club (Raleigh). Democrat. Presbyterian. Home: 326 Colville Rd Charlotte NC 28207 Office: Barclays Am Corp 201 S Tryon St PO Box 31488 Charlotte NC 28231

KNIGHT, VIRGINIA CORK, investment banker; b. Washington, Nov. 18, 1952; d. Malcolm F. and Virginia (Cork) K. BA in Intenat. Studies, Va. Poly. Inst. and State U., 1975; Degree in Common Market Econs., Coll. Europe, Bruges, Belgium, 1977. Dir. program devel. Nat. Demonstration Water Project, Washington, 1978-80; pres. Med Data Services, Alexandria, Va., 1981-83; v.p., co-mgr. corp. fin. Ferris and Co., Washington, 1984-88; v.p., co-mgr.corp. fin. The Savoy Group, Washington, 1989—. Mem. MIT Enterprise Forum Washington-Balt. (bd. dirs. 1984—, chmn. 1986-87), Balt.-Washington Venture Group (bd. dirs. 1988—), LWV (bd. dirs. Alexandria chpt. 1983-86). Home: 1415 Mount Vernon Ave Alexandria VA 22301 Office: The Savoy Group 2000 Pennsylvania Ave Washington DC 20006

KNIGHT, WILLIAM HENRY, III, insurance company executive; b. Ft. Bragg, N.C., May 16, 1956; s. William Henry Jr. and Catherine (Fulton) K. BA in Biology, Boston U., 1977. Underwriting trainee Liberty Mut. Ins. Co., Boston, 1977-78; underwriter Eagle Star Ins. Co. U.S., N.Y.C., 1979-80; reins. coordinator auto dept. AIU div. Am. Internat., N.Y.C., 1980-81, tng. supr., lectr., 1981—, auto mgr., 1982-87, regional auto mgr., 1984-86, personal lines regional mgr., 1986—, personal lines system mgr., 1987—. Mentor AIG Brandeis High Sch., N.Y.C., 1986—. Mem. Am. Mgmt. Assn., Nat. Ins. Industry Assn. Democrat. Episcopalian. Club: PCA. Office: AIU 70 Pine St New York NY 10270

KNIPP, RICHARD HENRY, building contractor; b. Tipton, Mo., Nov. 14, 1914; s. Carl Henry and Rosa Elizabeth (Hartmen) K. Owner Knipp Constrn. Co., Columbia, Mo., 1940—; v.p. Cen. Mo. Abstact and Title Co.; v.p. Glenview Drug Co., Columbia, 1965; trustee Mo-Kan Teamsters Pension Trust Fund, 1971—. Mem. Columbia City Council, 1963-73, 79-81, Columbia Planning and Zoning Commn., 1981-89. Mem. Kansas City Builders Assn., Assoc. Gen. Contractors Am. Roman Catholic. Club: Country of Mo., Columbia Country. Lodges: Lions, Elks, KC. Home: 210 W Forest Ave Columbia MO 65203 Office: Richard Knipp Assocs 1204 Pannell St Columbia MO 65201

KNISEL, RUSSELL H., banker; b. Englewood, N.J., June 18, 1933; s. Adolph C. and Elsie (Vieght) K.; m. Diane Taylor, June 18, 1955; children: Susan, Kimberly, Sally, Russell H. B.A., Wesleyan U., Middletown, Conn., 1955; postgrad., Harvard Grad. Sch. Bus., 1963. Pension mgr. Conn. Gen. Life Ins. Co., 1955-58; with Marine Midland Bank, N.Y.C., 1958-78; sr. v.p. Marine Midland Bank, 1968-74, exec. v.p., 1974-76, group exec. v.p., 1976-78; vice chmn. Conn. Nat. Bank, 1978—; dir. Miller Co., Chase Packaging Corp. Trustee Conn. Trust Historic Preservation, Stamford Health Corp. Mem. Assn. Res. City Bankers, Wesleyan Alumni Assn., Southwestern Area Commerce Assn. (dir.). Clubs: Wee Burn Country (Darien) (dir.); Landmark (dir.); Hartford. Home: Garden Gate 2265 Boston Post Rd Darien CT 06820 Office: Conn Nat Bank 777 Main St Hartford CT 06115

KNISELY, DOUGLAS CHARLES, accountant; b. Cleve., May 7, 1948; s. Victor D. and Lydia (Sichau) K.; m. Ruth Hedges, Dec. 24, 1971; children: Brent, Megan, Amanda. BS, Ohio State U., 1971; MBA, Capital U., 1981. CPA, cert. fin. planner, Ohio. Draftsman A.H. Sichau, Architect, Brook Park, Ohio, 1971-73; auditor E.C. Redman, CPA, Columbus, Ohio, 1973-76; ptnr. Bolon, Hart & Turley, Columbus, 1976-80; prin. Bolon, Hart & Buehler, Columbus, 1980—; trustee Gamma Tau Corp., Columbus, 1974. Mem. St. John's Evang. Luth. Ch.; bd. dirs., treas. Luth. Sr. City, 1986—; mission interpreter Am. Luth. Ch., Mpls., 1985-87. Named one of Outstanding Young Men of Am., 1978. Mem. Am. Inst. CPA's, Ohio Soc. CPA's, Am. Mgmt. Assn., Internat. Assn. Fin. Planners, Lambda Chi Alpha. Club: Toastmasters (pres. Midday chpt. 1980-81, Outstanding Area Gov. 1982). Home: 5875 Grove City Rd Grove City OH 43123 Office: Bolon Hart & Buehler Inc CPAs 65 E State St Columbus OH 43215

KNOELL, WILLIAM H., steel company executive; b. Pitts., Aug. 1, 1924; s. William F. and Hazel (Holverstott) K.; m. E. Anne Kirkland, Jan. 26, 1952; children—Kristin Anne, Susan Elizabeth, Amy Lynn, Gretchen. Student, Cornell U., 1942; BS in Mech. Engring, Carnegie Mellon U., 1947; JD, U. Pitts., 1950. Assoc. Shoemaker-Knoell, 1949-50; asst. to exec. v.p. Pitts. Corning Corp., 1950-55; asst. sec. Crucible Steel Co. Am., 1955-57, sec., 1957-63, v.p., 1963-67; v.p., asst. to pres. Cyclops Corp., 1967-68, exec. v.p., 1968-72, pres., 1972-87, chief exec. officer, 1973—, chmn., 1987—; bd. dirs. Duquesne Light Co. Bd. dirs. St. Clair Meml. Hosp.; trustee, mem. exec. com., Carnegie-Mellon U. Served with USAAF, 1943-45. Mem. ABA, Pi Tau Sigma, Theta Tau, Beta Theta Pi, Phi Alpha Delta. Clubs: University (dir.), Duquesne (dir.); St. Clair Country (Pitts.); Laurel Valley Golf, Rolling Rock. Office: Cyclops Industries Inc 650 Washington Rd Pittsburgh PA 15228

KNOLL, PEM CARLTON, real estate development executive; b. Columbus, Ohio, Aug. 31, 1954; s. Milton and Nora Jean (Marvin) K. BS in Acctg., La. State U., 1977; MBA, U. Tex., 1980. CPA, La. Acct. L. A. Champagne & Co., Baton Rouge, 1978, Touche Ross & Co., New Orleans, 1978-79; v.p. The Knoll Group, Newark, Ohio, 1980-83; pres. Carolina Summit Properties, Inc., Hilton Head, S.C., 1983-87, P. Carlton Knoll Interests, Inc., Hilton Head, 1987—; instr. U. S.C., 1985—. Mem. La. Bd. CPA's, Hilton Head Homebuilders Assn. (exec. officer award), Hilton Head C. of C. Republican. Presbyterian. Office: P Carlton Knoll Interests Inc 147 Spanish Wells Rd Ste 2-G Hilton Head Island SC 29928

KNOLL, RICHARD, JR., manufacturing executive; b. Senden, Bavaria, West Germany, Apr. 10, 1928; came to U.S., 1967; s. Richard and Maria (Grillhiesl) K.; m. Sabine Dressel, June 3, 1949; 1 child, Harald Richard. Engring. diploma, Polytechnikum, Munich, 1955; postgrad., U. Pitts., 1967-69, Hamilton Inst., N.Y.C., 1970-73. Registered profl. engr., Fla. Design engr. Wieland Werke, Ulm, Fed. Republic Germany, 1948-67; project engr. Aetna Standard Co., Pitts., 1967-70; v.p. engring. Penn Brass & Copper Mills, Erie, Pa., 1970-75; gen. mgr. Norsk Hydro Aluminum, Tonder, Denmark, 1975-78; gen. mgr. Norsk Hydro Aluminum, Rockledge, Fla., 1978-82, chmn. bd., 1982-84; pres. Norsk Hydro Aluminum Automotive, Cocoa, Fla., 1985—, bd. dirs.; dir. advanced automotive concepts Hydro Aluminum Extrusion Group, Cocoa, 1988—; adj. prof. Brevard Community Coll., Cocoa, 1981; bd. dirs. Aluminum Extruder Council, Chgo.; lectr., speaker various industry convs., confs. Patentee in field. Recipient Bronze Medal Internat. Inventors Congress, Nurnberg, Fed. Republic Germany, 1961. Mem. Aluminum Assn., Am. Soc. for Metals, Soc. Automotive Engrs., Automotive Industry Action Group. Republican. Roman Catholic. Clubs: Overseas Press Am. (N.Y.C.); Suntree Country (Melbourne). Home: PO Box 320127 Cocoa Beach FL 32932 Office: Hydro Aluminum Extrusion Group 96 Willard St 306 Mariner Square Cocoa FL 32922

KNOPFELMACHER, GRACE ROSE WYNN, insurance consultant, b. Milw., Feb. 7, 1937; d. Joseph Frank and Evelyn Valerie Wysocki. Student U. Wis., Milw., 1961-63. Office mgr. A.R. Korbel, C.L.U., Milw., 1961-65; sales asst. Korbel Corp., Milw., 1961-68; ins. agt. Central Life Assurance Co., Milw., 1968—; agt., partner Wynn & Mottl, C.L.U.s, Milw., 1968-83; owner G.R. Wynn, C.L.U. & Assocs., Milw., 1983-87; prin. Regency Fin. Services Co., Milw., 1987—. Recipient Nat. Sales Achievement awards Nat. Assn. Life Underwriters, 1972—, Nat. Quality awards, 1971—; Mem. Assn. Life Underwriters (past dir.), Million Dollar Round Table (life, qualifying), Women's Leader Round Table (life, qualifying), Central Life Ins. Agts. Adv. Council (pres. 1979-85, pres.' cabinet 1972—), Life Underwriter Tng. Council (moderator 1984), Estate Counselors Forum, Milw. Chpt. C.L.U.'s, Wis. Women's Entrepreneurs (dir. 1986—). Republican. Roman Catholic. Home: 929 N Astor St Milwaukee WI 53202 Office: Regency Fin Services Co 400 N Broadway Milwaukee WI 53202

KNOPSNYDER, DONALD DWAYNE, home builder; b. Somerset, Pa., Aug. 16, 1953; s. Richard Ernest and Arlene Velma (Pletcher) K. BA, U. Pitts., 1975. Asst. mgr., sales rep. Johnstown Paint & Glass Co. div. Watson-Standard Co., Pitts., 1975-85; sales rep. Marhefka Chevrolet, Windber, Pa., 1985-87, Pa. Wines & Spirits, West Mifflin, Pa., 1987; sales mgr. Hughes-Patwil Homes, Inc., Johnstown, Pa., 1987—. Sustaining mem. Repiblican Nat. Com., 1985—, mem. Rep. Presdl. Task Force, 1985—. Mem. VFW, Am. Legion, Home Builders Assn. Office: Hughes-Patwil Homes Inc RD 6 Box 56 Indiana PA 15701

KNOTT, WILEY EUGENE, customer support manager; b. Muncie, Ind., Mar. 18, 1938; s. Joseph Wiley and Mildred Viola (Haxton) K.; BS in Elec. Engring., Tri-State U., 1963; postgrad. Union Coll., 1970-73, Ga. Coll., 1987. 1 child, Brian Evan. Assoc. aircraft engr. Lockheed-Ga. Co., Marietta, 1963-65; tech. publs. engr. Gen. Electric Co., Pittsfield Mass., 1965-77, sr. publs. engr., 1977-79, group leader, 1967-79; specialist engr. Boeing Mil. Airplane Co., Wichita, Kans., 1979-81, sr. specialist engr., 1981-84, logistics mgr., 1984-85, customer support mgr., 1985—; part-time bus. cons., 1972—. Active Jr. Achievement, 1978-79, Am. Security Council, 1975—, Nat. Rep. Senatorial Com., 1979-86 , Nat. Rep. Congl. Com., 1979-87, Rep. Nat. Com., 1979-87 , Rep. Presdl. Task Force, 1981-86, Joint Presdl./Congl. Steering Com., 1982-86, Rep. Polit. Action Com., 1979-86, Mus. of Aviation, 1987—; state advisor U.S. Congl. Adv. Bd., 1981-86; adviser Jr. Achievement, 1978-79. With AUS, 1956-59. Mem. Am. Def. Preparedness Assn. (life), Am. Mgmt. Assn., Soc. Logistics Engrs., U.S. Golf Assn., Fraternal Order Police (assoc.), Am. Fedn. Police, Am. Assn. Retired Persons, Air Force Assn. (life), Assn. Old Crows, Boeing Mgmt. Club, Nat. Audubon Soc. Methodist.

KNOUSE, RICHARD EDMUND, software executive; b. Summit, N.J., May 12, 1948; s. Wayne Edmund Knouse and Ellen Broughton (Tall) Cole; m. Lise Van Cortlandt Greer, Dec. 15, 1983; children: Jennifer, Arthur. BA in Maths., Fairleigh Dickinson U., 1975. Project leader Republic Nat. Bank, N.Y.C., 1976-77; tech. mgr. Data Methods, Inc., Secaucus, N.J., 1978; cons. N.Y.C., 1978-86; owner Edmund Internat., 1987—. Author: Tancalc Software, 1984, Brokers Tool Software, 1987. With U.S. Army, 1969-72, Vietnam. Recipient Maharishi award, 1980. Mem. Ind. Computer Cons. Assn., Vietnam Vets Am. (bd. dirs. Manhattan chpt. 1987—). Republican. Office: Edmund Internat 666 West End Ave #20R New York NY 10025

KNOWLES, CLIFFORD L., manufacturing executive, consultant; b. Ft. Knox, Ky., Nov. 29, 1954; s. Dell Gene and Elnora Ruth (Loesch); m. E. Doniece Ross, June 26, 1976; children: Christopher, Chelsea, Stephen. BBA in Acctg., U. Tex., Arlington, 1977. CPA, Tex. Staff acct. Pool Cos., Dallas, 1977-78; gen. acctg. mgr. Pool Offshore, Harvey, La., 1978-80; ops. acctg. mgr. Carroll Co., Garland, Tex., 1980-83; v.p. fin. & adminstrn. Circle T Foods, Dallas, 1983—. Republican. Baptist. Home: 418 Cardinal Creek Duncanville TX 75137 Office: Circle T Foods 4560 Leston Dallas TX 75247

KNOWLES, JAMES H., JR., finance company executive; b. Pitts., Sept. 2, 1940; s. James H. and Gretchen Elizabeth (Rose) K.; m. Sherin Hetherington, Apr. 28, 1961; children: Janet H., Pack A., Sherin W. BA, Yale U., 1962; MBA, Harvard U., 1964. Loan officer, v.p., dept. mgr. comml. loans, internat. and venture capital Pitts. Nat. Bank, 1964-83; gen. ptnr. Loyalhanna Venture Fund, Ligonier, Pa., 1983—, Loyalhanna Commonwealth Fund, Ligonier, 1987—. Trustee Eye & Ear Hosp. of Pitts., 1971—, chmn. bd. trustees, 1983-85; trustee The Eye & Ear Inst., 1985—, chmn. bd. trustees, 1985-87.

KNOWLES, WILLIAM TOWNSEND, banker; b. Orange, N.J., Jan. 24, 1935; s. Alan C. and Elinor (Townsend) K.; m. Elizabeth Lunt; 1 child, Katy. B.A., Colgate U., 1957. Exec. v.p. Bankers Trust Co., N.Y.C., 1957-81; pres., chief ops. officer Nat. Westminster Bank USA, N.Y.C., 1981—, pres., chief exec. officer, dir., 1982-85, chmn., chief exec. officer, dir., 1985—; chmn., chief exec. officer, dir. Nat. Westminster Bancorp Inc., N.Y.C., 1988—. Bd. dirs. Montclair (N.J.) chpt. ARC, regional plan assn. United Way of N.Y.C.; trustee Carnegie Hall, Colgate U., Mountainside Hosp.; mem. Montclair Bd. Adjustment; mem. governing bd. Union Congrl. Ch., Upper Montclair. Served with AUS, 1958. Office: Nat Westminster Bank USA 175 Water St New York NY 10038

KNOWLTON, RICHARD L., food and meat packing company executive; b. 1932; married. B.A., U. Colo., 1954. With George A. Hormel & Co., Austin, MInn., 1948—; mgr. meat products div. and route car sales George A. Hormel & Co., Austin, Minn., 1967-69; asst. mgr. George A. Hormel & Co. (Austin plant), 1969; gen. mgr. George A. Hormel & Co., Austin, 1974, v.p. ops., 1974, group v.p. ops., 1975-79; pres., chief operating officer George A Hormel & Co., Austin, 1979; chmn., pres., chief exec. officer George A. Hormel & Co., Austin, 1981—, dir.; bd. dirs. Hormel Found. Bd., First Nat. Bank of Austin, First Bank Mpls., Northwestern Nat. Life Ins. Co. Bd. dirs. Mayo Found., U. Colo. Found. Mem. Am. Meat Inst. (dir.), Minn. Bus. Partnership (dir.). Office: George A Hormel & Co 501 16th Ave NE Austin MN 55912

KNOWLTON, TIMOTHY, investment banker; b. Hanover, N.H., July 29, 1944; s. William Richardson and Louise (Wilcox) K.; m. Lynn Lockwood Flanders, Jan. 25, 1969; children: Thomas F., Samuel W., Benjamin L. BA, U. N.C., 1970. From asst. mgr. mcpl. bonds to asst. mgr. Eurocurrencies Chem. Bank, N.Y.C., 1971-77; Eurocurrency arbitrage mgr. Union Discount Co., N.Y.C., 1977-79; chief trader, portfolio mgr. Texaco, Inc., White Plains, N.Y., 1980-81; fixed income mgr. Century Capital Assocs., N.Y.C., 1981-84; sr. investment officer Creditanstalt Bankverein, N.Y.C., 1985—; pres. Creditanstalt Asset Mgmt., Hamilton, Bermuda, 1987—, also bd. dirs. Sgt. USMC, 1963-68. Republican. Episcopalian. Office: Creditanstalt 245 Park Ave New York NY 10167

KNOX, BETTY AGEE, art dealer; b. Corpus Christi, Tex., Nov. 25, 1936; d. John Wesley and Shirley Margaret (Fugate) Agee; m. Seymour Horace Knox, June 15, 1979. BA, U. Tex., 1958. Art cons. Buffalo Fine Arts Acad., 1959-82; pres. Betty Knox Gallery, Inc., N.Y.C., 1984—; hon. chmn. Marine Midland Bank, Inc. Chmn. Guide Dog Found. for the Blind Benefit, N.Y.C., 1985; fellow Met. Mus. Art, N.Y.C., Met. Opera Assn., Golden Horseshoe, Huntington Art Gallery at U. Tex.; mem. Pres.' Circle Nat. Gallery Art, Washington, Nat. Rep. Com., Washington, Ellis Island Found., 1988, Studio Arena Theater, Buffalo, 1979-87; mem. annual fund Mus. Modern Art, 1979—; friend Whitney Mus. Art Circle, Saratoga Performing Arts Ctr., Yale U. Art Gallery; life mem. Albright-Knox Art Gallery, Buffalo, N.Y. Geneal. and Biog. Soc. Library; internat. mem. Guggenheim Mus., 1986-87. Named to Ellis Island Wall of Honor. Mem. AAUW, Nat. English Speaking Union, Nat. Acad. TV Arts and Scis., Art Dealers' Assn., Smithsonian Assocs., U. Tex. Ex-Students Assn. (mem. history marker), Am. Horse Show Assn. (life), Nat. Horse Show Found. (life), Yale Club of N.Y.C., Capitol Hill Club. Episcopalian. Office: 515 E 72d St New York NY 10021

KNOX, GEORGE L(EVI), III, corporate executive; b. Indpls., Sept. 6, 1943; s. George L. II and Yvonne M. (Wright) K.; m. B. Gail Reed, Jan. 1, 1979; children: Reed H.W., Gillian S.G. BS in Polit. Sci., Tuskegee U., 1967; MBA, Harvard U., 1975. Fgn. service officer Dept. State, Washington and Tokyo, 1968-73; assoc. McKinsey & Co., N.Y.C. and Tokyo, 1975-77; mgr. internal cons. Philip Morris Inc., N.Y.C., 1977-79, mgr. fin. relations, 1979-83, dir. fin. relations and adminstrn., 1983-85; dir. communications Philip Morris Mgmt. Corp., N.Y.C., 1985-87; staff v.p. pub. affairs Philip Morris Cos. Inc., N.Y.C., 1987—. Mem. Civilian Pub. Affairs Com. U.S. Mil. Acad., West Point, N.Y., 1988; trustee Studio Mus. in Harlem, N.Y.C., 1979; bd. dirs. Arts and Bus. Council, N.Y.C., 1988, Ind. Coll. Fund N.Y., N.Y.C., 1987—. Mem. Nat. Investor Relations Inst. Democrat. Episcopal. Office: Philip Morris Cos Inc 120 Park Ave New York NY 10017

KNOX, JAMES EDWIN, lawyer; b. Evanston, Ill., July 2, 1937; s. James Edwin and Marjorie Eleanor (Williams) K.; m. Rita Lucille Torres, June 30, 1973; children—James Edwin III, Kirsten M., Katherine E., Miranda G. B.A. in Polit. Sci., State U. Iowa, 1959; J.D., Drake U., 1961. Bar: Iowa 1961, Ill. 1962, Tex. 1982. Law clk. to Justice Tom C. Clark, U.S. Supreme Ct., 1961-62; assoc., then ptnr. Isham, Lincoln & Beale, Chgo., 1962-70; v.p. law Northwest Industries, Inc., Chgo., 1970-80; exec. v.p., gen. counsel Lone Star Steel Co., Dallas, 1980-86, sr. v.p., gen. counsel Itel Corp., Chgo., 1986—; instr. contracts and labor law Chgo. Kent Coll. Law 1964-69; arbitrator Nat. Ry. Adjustment Bd., 1967-68. Mem. ABA, Ill. Bar Assn., Phi Beta Kappa, Order of Coif, Phi Eta Sigma. Office: Itel Corp 2 N Riverside Pla Chicago IL 60606

KNUDSEN, CONRAD CALVERT, lumber/allied products company executive; b. Tacoma, Oct. 3, 1923; s. Conrad and Annabelle (Callison) K.; LL.B., U. Wash., 1950; Univ. fellow in law, Columbia U., 1951; m. Nov. 22, 1950; children—Conrad Calvert, Elizabeth Page, Colin Roderick, David Callison. Bar: Wash. 1950. Assoc. firm Bogle, Bogle & Gates, Seattle, 1951-61; exec. v.p., dir. Aberdeen Plywood & Veneer Co. (Wash.) 1961-63; exec. v.p., pres., chief adminstrv. officer, vice chmn. Evans Products Co., Portland, Oreg., 1963-68; sr. v.p. Weyerhaeuser Co., Tacoma, 1969-76; chmn., chief exec. officer MacMillan Bloedel, Ltd., Vancouver, B. C., Can., 1976-83, vice chmn., 1983—, also bd. dirs.; dir. Rainier Bancorp., Rainer Nat. Bank, Cascade Corp., Penwest Ltd., Portland Gen. Electric, Safeco Corp., West Fraser Timber Co. Ltd., Security Pacific Corp., Los Angeles; dir. emeritus Can. Imperial Bank of Commerce; chmn. bd. trustees Seattle Art Mus; owner Knudsen Vineyards. Served with U. S. Army, 1942-46. Mem. Am. Bar Assn., Wash. Bar Assn. Clubs: Rainier, University, Seattle Tennis (Seattle); Multnomah Athletic (Portland); Arlington. Office: MacMillan Bloedel Ltd, 1075 W Georgia St, Vancouver, BC Canada V6E 3R9

KNUDSEN, DAG INGE, corporate executive, consultant; b. Oslo, Norway, Sept. 9, 1940; came to U.S., 1964; s. Finn Brun; m. Karen J. VanHise, Nov. 25, 1965 (div. Mar. 1989); children: Jan, Kurt, Kristian. BSEE, Oreg. State U., 1966. Registered profl. engr., Minn., Ohio, Md. Sales engr. Leeds & Northrup Co., L.A., 1966-72; br. mgr. Leeds & Northrup Co., Mpls., 1972-73, area mgr., 1973-76; sr. v.p. EMA, Inc., St. Paul, 1976-86; pres. Dag I. Knudsen & Assocs., Inc., St. Paul, 1986—; bd. dirs. EMA, Inc., St. Paul. Author: (with others) Managers Guide to Computer Systems Design, 1983; editor book Process Instrumentation, 1984; contbr. articles to profl. jours. Bd. dirs., sec. LYRA Baroque Orch., St. Paul, 1987—. Cpl. Norwegian Army, 1960-62. Mem. IEEE (sr.), Instrument Soc. Am. (sr., div. dir. 1980-82), Nat. Speaker Assn. (bd. dirs. Minn. chpt. 1987-88), Cons. Engrs. Coun. Minn. (bd. dirs.), Toastmasters. Republican. Office: 6950 France Ave S Minneapolis MN 55435

KNUDSON, MARK BRADLEY, medical corporation executive; b. Libby, Mont., Sept. 24, 1948; s. Melvin R. and Melba Irene (Joice) K.; m. Susan Jean Voorhees, Sept. 12, 1970; children: Kirstin Sue, Amy Lynn. BS, Pacific Luth. U., 1970; PhD, Wash. State U., 1974. Lectr. Wash. State U., Pullman, 1973-75; research assoc., U. Wash., Seattle, 1976-78, asst. prof., 1976-79; physiologist Cardiac Pacemakers, Inc., St. Paul, 1979-80, mgr. research, 1980-82, dir. applied research, 1979-83; pres., chmn. bd. SenTech Med. Corp., St. Paul, 1983-86; pres. Arden Med. Systems Inc. subs. Johnson & Johnson, 1986—, pres., dir. Johnson and Johnson Profl. Diagnostics, Inc., Rariton, N.J., 1988—; lectr. in field. Bd. dirs. St. Paul YMCA, 1987—; active Am. Heart Assn. NIH fellow Wash. State U., 1974-75, U. Wash. 1975-76. Mem. AAAS, Am. Assn. Veterinary Physiologists and Pharmacologists, Am. Assn. Clin. Chemistry, Am. Coll. Sports Medicine, Sigma Xi. Republican. Lutheran. Contbr. articles to profl. jours.; patentee in field. Office: Arden Med Systems Inc 2675 Long Lake Rd Roseville MN 55113

KNUETTEL, FRANCIS PAUL, brokerage executive; b. Phila., July 30, 1941; s. Frank Denys and Sophie (Frenzel) K.; m. Marie Alice Frank; children: Francis Paul II, Timothy Drew, Gregory Scott. BS, LaSalle U., 1963; MBA, St. John's U., 1969. Jr. analyst Hayden Stone, N.Y.C., 1966-71; sr. portfolio mgr. Petoleum and Resource, Balt., 1971-83; ptnr. Gintel Equities, Greenwich, Conn., 1983-85; sr. energy analyst Prudential-Bache Securities, N.Y.C., 1985—. Mem. Old Bridge (N.J.) Sch. Bd., 1980-83, pres., 1983. Served to 1st lt. U.S. Army, 1963-65. Mem. Nat. Assn. Petroleum Investment Analysts (sec. 1983-84, v.p. 1985, pres. 1986), N.Y. Soc. Security Analysts (chmn. energy com. 1987—), Am. Petroleum Inst. Office: Prudential-Bache Securities 1 Seaport Pla New York NY 10292

KNUP, STEPHEN CHARLES, mining company executive; b. New Haven, May 12, 1942; s. Charles Stephen Knup and Olga Poperaden. BBA, U. Notre Dame, 1963; MBA, NYU, 1969. CPA, N.Y. Staff acct. Coopers & Lybrand, N.Y.C., 1966-77, ptnr., 1977-88; sr. v.p., chief fin. officer Amax Inc., N.Y.C., 1988—. Treas., bd. dirs. Newtown (Conn.) Montessori Sch., 1987-89. Mem. AICPA, N.Y. State Soc. CPA's, Am. Mining Congress (fin. execs. adv. com., 1986—), Soc. Mining Engrs. of AIME, Ridgewood Country Club (Danbury, Conn.). Roman Catholic. Office: Amax Inc 200 Park Ave New York NY 10166

KNUTSON, WILLIAM JAMES, communications company executive; b. Joliet, Ill., Oct. 20, 1941; s. Orvin Leroy and Pearle Ruby (Woodhouse) K.; m. Willa Jean Blood, Dec. 1963; children: Kevin, Daniel. BSEE, U. Ill., 1967. Registered profl. engr., Ill., Fla. Electrical engr. Motorola, Inc., Chgo., 1967-71, group leader, 1971-74; section mgr. Motorola, Inc., Plantation, Fla., 1974-77; engring. mgr. Motorola, Inc., Plantation, 1977-80, product mgr., 1980-85, sr. product mgr., 1985—. Patentee in field. Mem. Gideons (scripture sec. 1987-88), Tau Beta Pi. Republican. Presbyterian. Office: Motorola Inc 8000 W Sunrise Blvd Plantation FL 33322

KO, WALTER WAH-OY, trading company executive; b. Canton, Republic of China, Oct. 29, 1949; came to U.S., 1973; s. Kow Kin and Jean Sok Wah (Seit) K.; m. Lily Lai-Lai Leung, Aug. 6, 1978; children: Lissan, Vinfung. AA, Forest Pk. Community Coll., 1979; BS, U. Mo., 1982; MS, Cen. Mo. State U., 1984. Pres. Style Trading Co., St. Louis, 1984—. Mem. Better Vision Inst.

KOBAK, JAMES BENEDICT, management consultant; b. St. Louis, Mar. 4, 1921; s. Edgar and Evelyn (Hubert) K.; m. Hope McEldowney, June 13, 1942; children—James Benedict, John D. (dec.), Thomas M. B.S., Harvard U., 1942; postgrad. in accounting, Pace Coll., 1946-49. C.P.A., N.Y., La., Union S.Africa. Assoc. J.K. Lasser & Co., N.Y.C., 1946-71; partner J.K. Lasser & Co., 1954-64, adminstrv. partner, 1964-71; internat. adminstrv. partner Lasser, Harmood Banner, Dunwoody, N.Y.C., 1964-71; pres. James B. Kobak & Co., Darien, Conn., 1971—; owner Kirkus Revs.; partner James B. Kobak Bus. Models Co., 1972-82; founder Kobak Open; Electronics Pub. Systems, Triad Publs., Gifted and Talented, Human Resource Services Inc., Oceans Mag., Kick Enterprises. Contbr. articles to profl. publs. Chmn. mag. com., mem. bus. com. Nat. council Boy Scouts Am.; co-founder, sec.-treas. John D. Kobak Appalachian Edn. Found., Darien; trustee Hill Sch., Pottstown, Pa. Served to capt., F.A. AUS, 1942-46. Mem. Am. Inst. C.P.A.s, N.Y. State Soc. C.P.A.s, Transvall Soc. Accountants. Presbyterian. Clubs: Harvard (N.Y.C.); Wee Burn Country (Darien); Univ. (Chgo.). Home and Office: 774 Hollow Tree Ridge Rd Darien CT 06820

KOBAYASHI, ATSUMOTO, manufacturing executive, consultant; b. Tochigi, Japan, Mar. 9, 1934; s. Shoji and Hanako (Kobayashi) K.; m. Yoko Gonoi, Dec. 23, 1962; children: Rumi, Masatomo. B in Engring., Tohoku U., Sendai, Japan, 1956. Cert. in engring., safety. Engr. automobile div. Nissan Motor Co., Ltd., Tokyo, 1956-68, mgr. automotive div., 1969-79, mgr. marine div., 1980-83, dep. gen. mgr. textile machinery div., 1984—, leader mgmt. analysis, 1987—; engring. cons., 1965—; safety cons., 1987—; sr. cons. Global Brain Corp., 1989—. Patentee in field. Mem. Japan Cons. Engrs. Assn., Japan Safety and Health Cons. Assn. Avocation: Shogi (Japanese chess), personal computers. Home and Office: Ogikubo 5-30-17-608, Suginami-ku, Tokyo 167, Japan

KOBAYASHI, SUSUMU, data processing executive; b. Kumamoto, Japan, Apr. 3, 1939; s. Senkichiro and Michiko Kobayashi. BS, Tokyo Inst. Tech., 1963. Programmer Osaka (Japan) Gas Co., Ltd., 1963-65, C. Itoh Computing Services Co., Ltd., Tokyo, 1965-67; applications analyst, systems engr. Control Data Far East, Inc., Tokyo, 1967-75; asst. gen. mgr. systems dept. JMA Systems, Inc., Tokyo, 1975-79; dir. Nuclear Data Corp., Tokyo, 1979-89, Supertek Computers Japan, Inc., Tokyo, 1989—. Translator and editor: Fortran 4 (D.D. McCracken), 1968, Lisp 1.5 Primer (C. Weissman), 1970; contbr. articles to electronics mags. Mem. Assn. Computing Machinery, IEEE, Inc., Japan Math. Soc., Japan Info. Processing Soc. Home: 85-2-206 Migawa 2-chome, Mito-shi, Ibaraki-ken 310, Japan Office: Supertek Computers Japan Inc, Tsunekura Bldg, 2-20 Kandajimbocho, Chiyuda-ky, Tokyo 101, Japan

KOBLENZ, MICHAEL ROBERT, lawyer; b. Newark, Apr. 9, 1948; s. Herman and Esther (Weisman) K.; m. Bonnie Jane Berman, Dec. 22, 1973; children—Adam, Alexander. B.A., George Washington U., 1969, LL.M., 1974; J.D., Am. U., 1972. Bar: N.J. 1972, D.C. 1973, N.Y. 1980, U.S. Dist. Ct. N.J. 1972, U.S. Dist. Ct. D.C. 1973, U.S. Dist. Ct. (so. dist.) N.Y. 1980, U.S. Ct. Appeals (7th cir.) 1976, U.S. Ct. Claims 1973, U.S. Tax Ct. 1973, U.S. Mil. Ct. Appeals 1974. Atty., U.S. Dept. Justice, Washington, 1972-75; lectr. Am. U., 1975-78; spl. asst. U.S. atty. Office of U.S. Atty., Chgo., 1976-78; atty. Commodity Futures Trading Commn., Washington, 1975-77; spl. counsel, 1977, asst. dir., 1977-78; regional counsel, N.Y.C., 1978-80; assoc. Rein, Mound & Cotton, N.Y.C., 1980-82, ptnr., Mound, Cotton & Wollan (and predecessor firms), 1983—. Contbr. articles to legal jours. Mem. bd. appeals Village of Flower Hill, Manhasset, N.Y., 1983-84, trustee, 1984-86; trustee Village of East Hills, 1988—. Recipient Cert. of Appreciation for Outstanding Service U.S. Commodity Futures Trading Commn., 1977. Home: 20 Hemlock Dr East Hills Roslyn NY 11576 Office: Mound Cotton & Wollan 125 Maiden Ln New York NY 10038

KOBLITZ, MICHAEL JAY, investment banker; b. Cleve., Aug. 18, 1949; s. Maurice Joseph Koblitz and Dorothy (Katz) Colbert; m. Ellen Bollen, May 21, 1978; children: Lauren J., Marcus Jasper. BS, Bradley U., 1971; MBA, Case-Western Res. U., 1977. Account exec. Murch & Co., Inc., Cleve., 1971-74; investment broker, prin. Joseph Miller & Russell, Inc., Cleve., 1974-78; v.p. Butcher & Singer, Inc., Cleve., 1978-80; mng. dir. Gruntal & Co., Inc., N.Y.C., 1983—; asst. v.p. Warburg, Paribas, Becker, Inc., N.Y.C., 1980-83. Mem. Am. Fin. Assn., Am. Bankruptcy Inst. Office: Gruntal & Co Inc 14 Wall St New York NY 10005

KOCAOGLU, DUNDAR F., engineering management educator, consultant, researcher; b. Turkey, June 1, 1939; came to U.S., 1960; s. Irfan and Meliha (Uzay) K.; m. Alev Baysak, Oct. 17, 1968; 1 child, Timur. BSCE, Robert Coll., Istanbul, Turkey, 1960; MSCE, Lehigh U., 1962; MS in Indsl. Engring., U. Pitts., 1972, PhD in Ops. Research, 1976. Registered profl. engr., Pa., Oreg. Design engr. Modjeski & Masters, Harrisburg, Pa., 1962-64; ptnr. TEKSER Engring. Co., Istanbul, 1966-69; project engr. United Engrs., Phila., 1964-71; research asst. U. Pitts., 1972-74, vis. asst. prof., 1974-76, assoc. prof. indsl. engring., dir. engring. mgmt., 1976-87; prof., dir. engring. mgmt. program, Portland State U., 1987—; pres. TMA-Tech. Mgmt. Assocs., Portland, Oreg., 1973—. Author: Engineering Management, 1981, Management of R&D and Engineering, 1989, Handbook of Technology Management, 1989; series editor Wiley Series in Engring. Mgmt.; editor-in-chief IEEE Transactions on Engring. Mgmt.; contbr. articles on tech. mgmt. to profl. jours. Served to lt. C.E., Turkish Army, 1966-68. Recipient Centennial medal IEEE, 1984. Mem. Inst., Mgmt. Scis. (pres. Coll. Engring. Mgmt. 1979-81), Am. Soc. Engring. Edn. (chmn. engring. mgmt. div. 1982-83), IEEE Engring. Mgmt. Soc. (sr.; publs. dir. 1982-85), ASCE (mem. engring. mgmt. adminstrv. coun. 1988—), MIM Soc. Turkish Engrs. and Scientists, Am. Soc. Engring. Mgmt. (dir. 1981-86), Omega Rho (pres. 1984-86).

KOCH, ALBERT ACHESON, corporate executive; b. Atlanta, May 16, 1942; s. Albert H. and Harriet M. (Acheson) K.; BS cum laude, Elizabethtown Coll., 1964; m. Bonnie Royce, June 6, 1964; children—Bradford Allen, David Albert, Robert Acheson, Donald Leonard. With Ernst & Whinney, 1964-88, nat. dir. client services nat. office, Cleve., 1977-81, mng. ptnr. Detroit office, 1981-88; mng. dir. Equity Ptnrs. Am., Troy, Mich., 1988—; mem. adv. com. on replacement cost implementation SEC, 1976. Bd. dirs. Harper-Grace Hosps., 1982—, DMC Health Care Ctrs., 1984—, New Detroit, 1986-87, Elizabethtown Coll., 1981—, Met. Detroit YMCA, 1982—, Mich. Colls. Found., 1981-87, Detroit Symphony Orch., 1983-88, Detroit Receiving Hosp. Univ. Clinic, 1988—. Served to 1st lt. Fin. Corps, USAR, 1966-72. Recipient Elijah Watt Sells Gold Medal award Am. Inst. CPA's, 1965, Educate for Service award Elizabethtown Coll., 1966. Fellow Life Mgmt. Inst.; mem. Am. Inst. CPA's, Mich. Assn. CPA's. Clubs: Bloomfield Hills Country, Orchard Lake Country. Co-author: SEC Replacement Cost Requirements and Implementation Manual, 1976. Office: Equity Ptnrs Am 1850 Ring Dr Troy MI 48084

KOCH, CARL G., telecommunications executive; b. Milw., Sept. 24, 1931; s. Carl F. and Viola J. (Angerstein) K.; m. Patricia B. Perock, Nov. 6, 1954; children: Kathy Sue Koch Mallory, Karyl Lynn Koch Winch, Carl F., Kim P. BS in Philosophy and Math. magna cum laude, Marquette U., 1953; MBA with distinction, Northwestern U., 1960. Mem. acctg. staff Ill. Bell Telephone Co., Chgo., 1953-59; acct., statistician various depts. Wis. Bell, Inc., Milw., 1959-68, dir. fin. planning, asst. v.p., 1973-83, v.p. revenue, 1983; fin. staff mgr., dir. required earnings AT&T, N.Y.C., 1968-73; v.p., treas.-designate Regional Holding Co., Chgo., 1983-84; v.p., treas. Ameritech, Chgo., 1984—. Past chmn., treas. and clk. New Berlin (Wis.) Bd. Edn. Served with U.S. Army, 1954-56. Named Treas. of Yr. for Large Corps., Cashflow mag., 1985. Mem. Fin. Execs. Inst., Fin. Mgmt. Assn. (instl. dir. 1986—), Nat. Soc. Rate Return. Republican. Lodge: Lions (pres. New Berlin, Wis. 1965-66). Home: 25274 W Elm Grove Dr Barrington IL 60010 Office: Ameritech 30 S Wacker Dr Ste 3800 Chicago IL 60606

KOCH, CRAIG R., automobile rental and leasing company executive; b. 1946; married. BS, Lehigh U., 1968, MBA, 1971. Mktg. assoc. RCA Corp., 1971-72; mgr. fleet planning Hertz Corp., 1972-73, mgr. fleet ops. adminstrn., 1973-77, div. v.p. fleet ops. adminstrn., 1977-78; div. v.p. Hertz Europe Ltd., 1978-80; v.p. Rent-A-Car div. Hertz Corp., 1980-83, exec. v.p. Rent-A-Car div., 1983-87, pres., chief operating officer, 1987—. Office: Hertz Corp 660 Madison Ave New York NY 10021 *

KOCH, DONALD GEOFFREY, accountant, lawyer; b. Bklyn., May 18, 1944; s. Mack and Tiby (Cantor) K.; m. Irene B. Schuchman, July 15, 1987; 1 child, Matthew; m. Sheila F. Cohen, Dec. 1979 (div.); children: Leigh, Alyssa, Michael. BS in Acctg., Temple U., 1965; MBA in Acctg., NYU, 1967, LLM in Taxation, 1975; JD, Bklyn. Law Sch., 1971. Bar: N.Y. 1972, N.J. 1973, Fla. 1971, U.S. Ct. Claims 1971, U.S. Tax Ct. 1972, U.S. Supreme Ct. 1978; CPA, N.Y., N.J. Tax assoc. Burke & Burke Esquires, N.Y.C., 1971-74, S. Walter Kaufman & Co., CPA's, N.Y.C., 1974-76, Jones, Cuccio & Klinger, Hackensack, N.J., 1976-79; ptnr. S.W. Azrilant, P.C., N.Y.C., 1979-83; dir. tax rsch. Jacobs, Evall, Hirson & Blumenfeld, CPA's, N.Y.C., 1983-85; pvt. practice N.Y.C., 1983-85; tax ptnr. Bachmann, Schwartz & Abramson, CPA's, N.Y.C., 1985-88; dir. taxes McGladrey & Pullen, CPA's, N.Y.C., 1989—; lectr. acctg. N.Y. Inst. Tech., 1966-69; instr. acctg. CUNY, 1969-71; adjunct prof. taxation Pace U., 1978-80; lectr. profl. meetings. Contbr. articles to profl. jours. Mem. ABA, Am. Inst. CPA's (personal fin. planning div. tax div.), N.Y. State Bar Assn., N.Y. State Soc. CPA's (tax practice adminstrn. com.), N.J. Soc. CPA's, Tax Soc. NYU. Republican. Jewish. Office: McGladery & Pullen CPAs 1133 Ave of the Americas New York NY 10036

KOCH, EDWARD RICHARD, lawyer, banker; b. Teaneck, N.J., Mar. 25, 1953; s. Edward J. and Adelaide M. (Wunner) K. BS in Econs. magna cum laude, U. Pa., 1975; JD, U. Va., 1980; LLM in Taxation, NYU, 1986. Bar:

N.J. 1980, U.S. Dist. Ct. N.J. 1980, U.S. Tax Ct. 1981, U.S. Ct. Claims 1981. Staff acct. Touche Ross & Co., Newark, 1975-77; assoc. Winne, Banta & Rizzi, Hackensack, N.J., 1980-82; tax atty. Allied Corp. (name now Allied-Signal, Inc.), Morristown, 1982-87; asst. v.p. Chem. Bank, N.Y.C., 1987—. Vice chmn. law and legis. com. Athletics Congress, Indpls., 1985—, chmn., 1989—, chmn. ins. com., 1984-88, bd. dirs., 1989—; pres. N.J. Athletics Congress, Red Bank, 1986—. Mem. ABA, N.J. State Bar Assn., AICPAs, N.J. Soc. CPAs, Am. Assn. Attys.-CPAs, N.J. Striders Track Club (chmn. 1981—). Republican. Roman Catholic. Home: 47 Brandywyne Dr Florham Park NJ 07932 Office: Chem Bank Tax Dept 380 Madison Ave 11th Fl New York NY 10017

KOCH, RICHARD JOSEPH, lawyer, publishing company executive; b. N.Y.C., Feb. 2, 1947; s. Joseph John and Mary Virginia (Nolan) K.; m. Kathleen Jean Leahy, Mar. 13, 1971; children: Rosemary, Daniel, Patrick, Catherine, Joseph, Kevin. BS in Econs., Siena Coll., 1969; JD, U. Mo., 1976. Bar: Mo. 1976; CPA, Mo. Tax acct. Arthur Andersen & Co., Kansas City, Mo., 1976-77; head tax dept. Fox & Co., Kansas City, 1977-80; gen. counsel Russell Worley & Co., Kansas City, 1980-83; sr. v.p., gen. counsel, sec. Am. City Bus. Jours., Kansas City, 1983—; bd. dirs. Operation Breakthrough, Inc., Kansas City. Chmn. troop 25 Boy Scouts Am., Kansas City, 1987. Mem. ABA, Mo. Bar Assn., AICPA, Mo. Soc. CPA's. Home: 11908 Mohawk Rd Leawood KS 66209 Office: Am City Bus Jours 3535 Broadway Kansas City MO 64111

KOCH, ROBERT CHARLES, technology consultant; b. Reddick, Ill., June 22, 1922; s. Charles Robert and Lillian Rose (Tanner) K.; m. Addie Pelfrey, Aug. 13, 1960 (div. Feb. 1974); children: Melinda Ann, Robert Michael. AS, Blackburn Coll., 1941; BS, U. Ill., 1943; postgrad., U. Akron. Mgr. tire & rubber tech. Firestone Tire & Rubber Co., Akron, Ohio, 1943-44, 46-50, 50-83; pvt. cons. practice Akron, 1983—. Holder of 14 patents in tire and rubber tech. Mem. Rep. Nat. Com. Served to lt. USN, 1944-46, PTO; with res., 1950-52. Mem. Am. Chem. Soc., Akron Rubber Group. Home and Office: 1121 Merriman Rd Akron OH 44313

KOCH, ROBERT LAWRENCE, retail executive; b. Perth Amboy, N.J., Apr. 13, 1930; s. Morris and Agnes (George) K.; m. Linda J. BA magna cum laude, Rutgers U., 1972. Personnel dir. A.S. Beck Shoe Corp., N.Y.C., 1962-67; intern recruiting, employment USN Resale System, N.Y.C., 1967-72; exec. dir. Nat. Commn. Productivity, Washington, 1973-74; personnel dir. Lane Bryant Inc., N.Y.C., 1974-79; v.p., human resources Felsway Corp., Totowa, N.J., 1979-82, Bally of Switzerland, New Rochelle, N.Y., 1982—; cons. Am. Airlines, Mt. Sinai Hosp., N.Y.C., Nathan's Famous Etc. Food Service, 1973-74, Chrysler Corp., 1988; panel mem. Pub. Employment Dispute Settlement Am. Arbitration Assn.; adj. prof. mgmt. NYU Sch. of Bus., Inst. Retail Mgmt.; lectr. to mgmt. groups and univs. Contbr. articles to profl. jours. Mem. CIS Adv. Commn., New Rochelle, 1988, CIS Bus. Community Com., 1988, Distributive Edn. Adv. Commn, N.Y.C. Bd. Edn., 1965-74. Served with U.S. Army, 1948-49. Mem. N.Y. C. of C. (chmn. labor law sub-com. 1970), Alpha Sigma Lambda. Home: 116 Central Park S New York NY 10019 Office: Bally of Switzerland One Bally Pl New Rochelle NY 10801

KOCH, ROBERT LOUIS, II, manufacturing company executive, mechanical engineer; b. Evansville, Ind., Jan. 6, 1939; s. Robert Louis and Mary L. (Bray) K.; m. Cynthia Ross, Oct. 17, 1964; children: David, Kevin, Kristen, Jennifer. BSME, U. Notre Dame, 1960; MBA, U. Pitts., 1962. Registered profl. engr., Ind. V.p. Ashdee Corp., Evansville, 1962-68, pres., 1968-82; ptnr. Fesk Partnership, Evansville, 1964—; v.p., dir. Gibbs Aluminum Die Casting Corp., Henderson, Ky., 1976—; pres., dir. George Koch Sons, Inc., Evansville, 1982—; v.p., dir. Nat. Sealants and Adhesive Co., Evansville, 1984—, Brake Supply Co., Evansville, 1986—; exec. in residence U. So. Ind., Evansville, 1987; bd. dirs. CNB Bancshares, Inc., Evansville, So. Ind. Gas & Electric Co., Evansville, Bindley Western Industries, Indpls., Uniseal Rubber Products, Inc., St. Louis. Inventor, patentee water purifier, drying oven, powder coating booth, electro painting system. Controller, dep. mayor City of Evansville, 1976-80; mem. Gov.'s Fiscal Policy Adv. Com., Indpls., 1978—; trustee U. Evansville, 1985—, Evansville Mus. Arts and Scis., 1982-88; bd. dirs. SW Ind. Pub. Broadcasting, 1985—, Pub. Edn. Found., Evansville, 1986-88; treas. Vanderburgh County Rep. Com., Evansville, 1984-88; pres. Cath. Edn. Found., Evansville, 1978-82; parents exec. com. Purdue U., West Lafayette, 1985-88; mem. Sch. Bd. nominating com., 19887—. 1st lt. USAR, 1961-67. Recipient Challenger award Nat. Assn. Woodworking Machinery Mfrs., Louisville, 1980; named Exec. of Yr. Profl. Secs. Assn., 1984. Mem. Young Pres. Assn., Metro. Evansville C. of C. (bd. dirs. 1985—, chmn. bd. 1987—), Ind. C. of C. (bd. dirs.). Clubs: Evansville Country, Tri State Racquet (Evansville). Lodge: KC. Home: 4120 Mulberry Pl Evansville IN 47715-4074 Office: George Koch Sons Inc 10 S 11th Ave Evansville IN 47744

KOCH, SIDNEY, investment banker; b. N.Y.C., Apr. 22, 1935; s. Harry and Charlotte (Lind) K.; m. Sheila Nevins, July 16, 1972; 1 son, David. B.S. in Econs., U. Pa., 1956; M.B.A., NYU, 1962. Fin. v.p. CHK Corp., N.Y.C., 1957-62; v.p. Drexel Burnham Lambert, N.Y.C., 1962-75; sr. v.p. ABD Securities Corp., 1975-86; sr. v.p., head mergers acquisitions & pvt. placements Daiwa Securities Am. Inc., N.Y.C., 1986—; dir. Lamont & Getrag Gear Corp., Norristown, Pa., 1981—. Served with U.S. Army, 1957. Mem. Internat. Mgmt. and Devel. Inst., Econ. Club N.Y. Club: India House (N.Y.C.). Office: Daiwa Securities Am Inc One World Finance Ctr 200 Liberty St New York NY 10281

KOCH, WILLIAM JOSEPH, corporate public relations executive; b. Celina, Ohio, June 6, 1949; s. George Albert and Helen Marie (McKovich) K.; B.A., U. Akron, 1974; m. Susan Margaret Griffith, June 14, 1969; children—Brian William, Dana Marie. Draftsman, Summit County Engr.'s Office, Akron, Ohio, 1968-72; public info. officer Ohio Dept. Transp., Ravenna, 1972-75; asst. dir. mktg. and public relations Metro Regional Transit Authority, Akron, 1975-78; sr. account exec. Meeker-Mayer Agy., Akron, 1978-83; v.p. Meeker-Mayer Pub. Relations, 1983-84; exec. v.p., chief exec. officer, David A. Meeker & Assocs., Inc./Pub. Relations, 1984-87, mgr. pub. affairs Tricil, Inc., Akron, 1987—. Trustee All-Am. Soap Box Derby, Inc., 1978—; profl. advisor Kent State U. Pub. Relations Student Soc. Am. Co-author No Surprises: The Crisis Communications Management System, 1988. Mem. Pub. Relations Soc. Am. (bd. dirs. Akron chpt.), Inst. for Chem. Waste Mgmt. (mem. pub. affairs com.); Nat. Solid Wastes Mgmt. Assn. Democrat. Roman Catholic. Clubs: Jaycees (senator, Disting. Service award 1983), Akron Press. Home: 3325 Bancroft Rd Akron OH 44313 Office: 1640 Akron-Peninsula Rd Akron OH 44313

KOCI, DOUGLAS GRANT, financial planner; b. Berwyn, Ill., June 8, 1956; s. Richard Irwin and Donna Faye (Brown) K.; m. Martha Iris Fernandez, July 7, 1978; children: Emily Raquel, Richard Douglas, Bonnie Faye. BS in Fin., Brigham Young U., 1980; cert. in fin. planning, Coll. for Fin. Planning, 1983. Fin. planner Hamilton Gregg & Co., Falls Village, Conn., 1980-83, Mason Assocs., Inc., Herndon, Va., 1983—. Scouting coordinator Boy Scouts Am. Troop 878, Herndon, Va., 1987; varsity scout coach BSA, Sterling, Va., 1988. Mem. Inst. Cert. Fin. Planners (cert.), Internat. Assn. for Fin. Planning (pres. No. Va. chpt. 1986-87, chmn. 1987-88). Mormon. Home: 351 Hillwood Ct Herndon VA 22070 Office: Mason Assocs Inc 607 Herndon Pkwy Ste 105 Herndon VA 22070

KOCI, LUDVIK FRANK, manufacturing company executive; b. Chgo., May 3, 1936; s. Ludvik Joseph and Elsie (Prucha) K.; m. Carlotta Trevette Walker, May 4, 1957; children: Charles L. (dec.), Christine G. Berkheiser, Carla T., Cynthia J., Carl A., Carol A. BSMechE, Gen. Motors Inst, Flint, Mich., 1959; M.S. in Theoretical and Applied Mechanics, Mich. State U., Lansing, 1960; Mgmt. Devel. Program, U. Ill., Chgo., 1963-66; Exec. Program, Stanford U., Calif., 1978. Sr. project engr. Electro-Motive div. Gen. Motors, La Grange, Ill., 1961-63, supr. product engring., 1963-70, chief locomotive devel. engr., 1970-72, asst. chief engr., 1972-79; dir. engring. Detroit Diesel Allison div. Gen. Motors, 1979-81, gen. dir. engring., 1981-82, v.p., gen. mgr., 1982-87; dir. Moto Diesel Mexicana, Aguascalientes, Mexico, 1982-87; exec. v.p. Detroit Diesel Corp., 1988—, also bd. dirs.; bd. dirs. Diesel Tech. Corp. Mem. Western Hwy. Inst. (exec. com. 1983—), Assn. U.S. Army, Soc. Automotive Engrs. Republican. Club: Pine Lake Country (West Bloomfield, Mich.). Office: Detroit Diesel Corp 13400 W Outer Dr Detroit MI 48239-4001

KOCK, VIRGINIA STEWART, financial planner; b. New Orleans, Jan. 12, 1960; d. Edouard James and Mary (Foster) K. BA, U. Va., 1982. Cert. fin. planner. Sales asst. Merrill, Lynch, Pierce, Fenner & Smith, New Orleans, 1982-84; investment assoc. Wheat, First Securities, Richmond, Va., 1984-87; mgr. fin. planning dept. Howard, Weil, Labouisse, Friedrichs, Inc., New Orleans, 1987-88. Mem. Inst. Cert. Fin. Planners, Internat. Assn. Fin. Planning, U. Va. Alumnae Assn., Jefferson Scholars Schs. Com. Republican. Roman Catholic. Home: 910 S Carrollton Ave Apt N New Orleans LA 70118

KODIS, MARY CAROLINE, marketing consultant; b. Chgo., Dec. 17, 1927; d. Anthony John and Callis Ferebee (Old) K.; student San Diego State Coll., 1945-47, Latin Am. Inst., 1948. Controller, div. adminstrv. mgr. Fed. Mart Stores, 1957-65; controller, adminstrv. mgr. Gulf Mart Stores, 1965-67; budget dir., adminstrv. mgr. Diana Stores, 1967-68; founder, treas., controller Handy Dan Stores, 1968-72; founder, v.p., treas. Handy City Stores, 1972-76; sr. v.p., treas. Handy City div. W.R. Grace & Co., Atlanta, 1976-79; founder, pres. Hal's Hardware and Lumber Stores, 1982-84; retail and restaurant cons., 1979—. Treas., bd. dirs. YWCA Watsonville,1981-84, 85-87; mem. Santa Cruz County Grand Jury, 1984-85. Recipient 1st Tribute to Women in Internat. Industry, 1978; named Woman of the Yr., 1986. Mem. Ducks Unltd. (treas. Watsonville chpt. 1981—). Republican. Home and Office: 302 Wheelock Rd Watsonville CA 95076

KOEHL, STUART LAURENCE, military systems analyst; b. Bklyn., Apr. 24, 1956; s. Howard V. and Judith Ann (Greenberg) K.; m. Greta Madeline Brinlee, Oct. 16, 1982. Student, Bklyn. Coll., 1972; BS in Fgn. Svc., Georgetown U., 1979. Mil. analyst C & L Assocs., Potomac, Md., 1979-83, Univ. Rsch. Corp., Bethesda, Md., 1983-84; strategic analyst Applied Tech. Assocs., Alexandria, Va., 1984-88; cons. in field. Author: Dictionary of Modern War, 1989; contbr. articles to profl. jours. Mem. Sci. and Engring. Com. for Free World, Washington, 1987—. Mem. U.S. Naval Inst., Navy League, Air Force Assn., Am. Astronautical Soc. Republican.

KOEHLE, WILLIAM JOSEPH, manufacturing company official; b. Kankakee, Ill., Nov. 29, 1950; s. Rudy Chester and Rosemary (Joyce) K.; m. Patricia Eileen McGhee, Nov. 6, 1976; children: Elspeth, Nathaniel, Andrew. BA, U. Pitts., 1971. Constrn. mgr. Multi-Svcs., Inc., Erie, Pa., 1974-78; asst. mgr. P&IC Zurn Industries, Inc., MDD, Erie, Pa., 1978—. Precinct committeeman Erie Rep. Com., 1984-86. Served with USMC, 1972-74, maj. USMCR. Mem. Am. Prodn. and Inventory Control Assn. (cert., treas. 1986-88, exec. v.p. 1988—), Marine Corps Res. Officers Assn., Marine Corps Assn., Am. Legion, Marine Corps League, Erie Maennerchor. Home: 1203 W 27th St Erie PA 16508 Office: Zurn Industries Inc MDD 1801 Pittsburgh Ave Erie PA 16514

KOEHLER, JERRY WILLIAM, management educator, consultant, researcher; b. Henry, Ill., June 16, 1941; s. George Clarence Koehler and Louise Hoscheit; m. Noreen Koehler; children: Ellen, Laura. BS in Speech, Western Ill. U., Macomb, 1963, MA in Speech, 1965; EdD, Pa. State U., 1968. Asst. to the chief exec. officers Tchrs. Mgmt. & Investment Co., Newport Beach, Calif., 1969-71; regional rep. Am. Express Investment Co., Los Angeles, 1971-72; dir. UCI exec. program Grad. Sch. Adminstrn. U. Calif., Irvine, 1972-76; assoc. prof. communication dept. U. So. Fla., Tampa, 1976-78, asst. to pres., 1978-79, dean sch. continuing edu., 1979-85, chmn., assoc. prof. dept. mgmt., 1985-88, assoc. prof., 1988—; cons. Smiths Industries, Clearwater, Fla., 1986—, Laventhol and Horwath, Tampa, 1986—, U. Hosp., Tampa, 1987—. Author: The Corporation Game, 1975; co-author: Organizational Communications, 1976, Public Communications, 1978, Business Communications, 1980, Quality Presentations, 1989. Chmn. Leadership, Tampa, 1985-86. Mem. Acad. of Mgmt., Internat. Communicaiton Assn., Am. Bus. Communications Assn. Democrat. Roman Catholic. Club: Tampa Palms. Lodge: Civitan. Office: U So Fla Fowler Ave Tampa FL 33618

KOEHLER, JOHN EDGET, aerospace company executive; b. Olympia, Wash., June 8, 1941; s. Herman Richard and Frances (Schwartz) K.; m. Jane R. Wiedlea, Aug. 24, 1963; 1 child, Andrew C. BA, Yale U., 1963, MA, 1965, PhD, 1968; postgrad., MIT, 1963-64. Economist, assoc. dept. head Rand Corp., Santa Monica, Calif., 1967-75; asst. dir. Congl. Budget Office, Washington, 1975-78; dep. to dir. cen. intelligence resource mgmt. Intelligence Community Staff, Washington, 1978-81, dir., 1981-82; dir. resource planning Hughes Aircraft Co., El Segundo, Calif., 1982-84, exec. v.p. Hughes Communications, 1984-86, pres., chief exec. officer, 1986-87; v.p. internat. Hughes Aircraft Co., L.A., 1987-88; corp. v.p. Hughes Aircraft Co., Los Angeles, 1988—. Co-author The Matrix Policy in the Philippines, 1971; contbr. articles on internat. econs. and nat. security to profl. jours. Recipient Nat. Intelligence Disting. Svc. medal Nat. Fgn. Intelligence Bd., 1981. Mem. Internat. Inst. for Strategic Studies. Office: Huges Aircraft Co PO Box 92919 Building S41/B340 Los Angeles CA 90009

KOELLE, PETER O(TTO), bank executive; b. Wolnzach, Federal Republic Germany, Apr. 26, 1945; came to U.S., 1981.; s. Otto and Walburga (Schmid) K.; m. Veronika Berg, May 27, 1971; children: Alexandra, Katharina, Helena. MA in Polit. Sci, U. Munich, 1969; MS, Union Coll., Schenectady, N.Y., 1970; MBA, INSEAD, Fontainebleau, France, 1971. Dist. head corp. banking Morgan Guaranty Trust Co. N.Y., Frankfurt, Fed. Republic Germany, 1971-77; gen. mgr. Bayerische Vereinsbank, Tokyo, 1977-81; gen. mgr. N.Am. offices Bayerische Vereinsbank, N.Y.C., 1981—; dir. Remaco, Inc., Northvale, N.J. Mem. Econ. Club N.Y. Roman Catholic. Club: Deutscher Verein (N.Y.C.). Lodge: Rotary. Home: 7 Dunham Rd Scarsdale NY 10583 Office: Bayerische Vereinsbank AG 335 Madison Ave New York NY 10017

KOELLING, HERBERT LEE, printing company executive; b. Perdido Beach, Ala., Feb. 19, 1932; s. Herbert Jessen and Dallas Allison (Lee) K.; m. Carroll Cameron, Sept. 13, 1952; children: Kendall Scott, Peter Michael, David Cameron. BS, U. Ill., 1953. Prodn. mgmt. trainee Uarco Inc., Chgo., 1955-59; prodn. assignmnts Uarco Inc., Watseka, Ill., 1959-66; mgr. Cleve. plant Uarco Inc., 1966-69, mgr. Deep River (Conn.) plant, 1969-71; mgr. so. div. Uarco Inc., Paris, Tex., 1971-76; mgr. western div. Uarco Inc., Riverside, Calif., 1976-78; v.p. prodn. Uarco Inc., Barrington, Ill., 1978-83, exec. v.p. ops., 1983-86, chmn., chief exec. officer, 1986—. Served to 1st lt. U.S. Army, 1953-55. Mem. Phi Beta Kappa. Republican. Episcopalian. Clubs: Barrington Hills Country; Meadow (Rolling Meadows, Ill.). Office: UARCO Inc W County Line Rd Barrington IL 60010

KOELLING, WOODROW WILLIAM, banker; b. Centralia, Ill., Dec. 23, 1918; s. Louis Christ and Bertha (Lehde) K.; m. Elizabeth Gaye Ober, Feb. 2, 1946; children: Richard, Nancy G. Peterson, Betsy K. Ross. BS, U. Ill., 1941. Owner 20th Century Sporting Goods, Centralia, 1947-57, Melody Shop, Centralia, 1950-83; pres. 1st Banc Group Inc., Centralia, 1983-87; ptnr. Koelling Enterprises, Centralia, 1986—; bd. dirs. 1st Nat. Bank, Centralia, Hoyleton State and Savs. Bank, Hoyleton, Ill., Magna Bank, Centralia; vice-chmn. bd. 1st Nat. Bank, Centralia. Bd. dirs., bd. counselors Mitchell Mus., Mt. Vernon, Ill., 1982-87; bd. dirs. Big Bros. and Sisters of Marion County, Ill., 1982-87, Ill. Arts Alliance, Chgo., 1972, Okaw Valley Council Boy Scouts Am., 1983—, Ill. Polit. Action Com., Springfield; bd. dirs., United Cerebral Palsy of Ill., Springfield, 1976—, treas. 1988—; v.p. So. Ill. Arts; chmn. pub. relations and devel. council St. Mary's Hosp., 1983—. Served with USAAF, 1941-45, PTO and Australia. Mem. Centralia C. of C. (pres. retail div.), U. of Ill. Alumni Assn., Ill. State C. of C. (bd. dirs. 1983—), Beta Sigma Psi. Mem. Centralia C. of C. (pres. retail div.), U. Ill. Alumni Assn., Ill. State C. of C. (bd. dirs. 1983—), Beta Sigma Psi, Rotary (pres. Centralia chpt. 1988—). Lodge: Rotary. Home: 7 Lilac Ln Centralia IL 62801 Office: Koelling Enterprises 502 First National Bank Bldg Centralia IL 62801

KOELMEL, LORNA LEE, data processing executive; b. Denver, May 15, 1936; d. George Bannister and Gladys Lee (Henshall) Steuart; m. Herbert Howard Nelson, Sept. 9, 1956 (div. Mar. 1967); children: Karen Dianne, Phillip Dean, Lois Lynn; m. Robert Darrel Koelmel, May 12, 1981; stepchildren: Kim, Cheryl, Dawn, Debbie. BA in English, U. Colo., 1967. Cert. secondary English tchr. Substitute English tchr. Jefferson County Schs., Lakewood, Colo., 1967-68; sec. specialist IBM Corp., Denver, 1968-75, personnel administr., 1975-82, asst. ctr. coordinator, 1982-85, office systems specialist, 1985-87, backup computer operator, 1987—; computer instr. Barnes Bus. Coll., Denver, 1987—; owner, mgr. Lorna's Precision Word Processing and Desktop Pub., Denver, 1987—. Organist Christian Sci. Soc., Buena Vista, Colo., 1963-66, chmn. bd. dirs.,Thornton, Colo., 1979-80. Mem. NAFE, Nat. Secs. Assn. (retirement ctr. chair 1977-78, newsletter chair 1979-80, v.p. 1980-81), U. Colo. Alumni Assn., Alpha Chi Omega (publicity com. 1986-88). Republican. Club: Nat. Writers. Lodge: Job's Daus. (recorder 1953-54).

KOENIG, CAROLYN DEWITT, magazine editor; b. Kingston, N.Y., Jan. 24, 1938; d. John Warren and Mildred Crawford (Goodnow) DeWitt; m. Robert Francis Koenig, Aug. 20, 1977. BJ, U. Minn., 1959. Desk editor Nat. Petroleum News/McGraw-Hill Publs., N.Y.C., 1959-65, copy editor, 1973-76, mng. editor, 1976-81; editor-in-chief Harris Pub. Co., N.Y.C., 1965-67; copy editor Women's Wear Daily, N.Y.C., 1967-69; editor-in-chief Haire Pub. Co., N.Y.C., 1970-73; mng. editor Graduating Engineer mag./ McGraw-Hill, N.Y.C., 1981-85, Architectural Record/McGraw-Hill, N.Y.C., 1985—. Recipient Jesse Neal award, 1974, 80. Democrat. Episcopalian. Home: 327 W 76th St New York NY 10023 Office: McGraw-Hill Inc 1221 Ave of the Americas New York NY 10020

KOENIG, JOHN L., management leadership consultant; b. Manchester, N.H., Jan. 10, 1938; s. Otto G. and Margaret (Lord) K. BA, Elon Coll., 1961; MA, Villanova U. Past pres. Nat. Energy Cons., Bryn Mawr, Pa.; former congl. aide U.S. Congress House Select Com. on Crime; ptnr. Koenig-Becker and Assocs., Bryn Mawr, 1987—; cons. to dir. Bd. Pub. Safety, Indpls., Crime Deterrent Programs, Dept. Human Resources, Washington; cons. Md. Bicentennial Program; pres. Nat. Adv. Counicl on Leadership for Am.'s Future. Hon. nat. rep. Johnny Horizon '76 program U.S. Dept. Interior; trustee Pop Warner Little Scholars, Inc., Phila. Served as officer USMC. Nominee for Nobel Peace prize, 1981. Mem. Res. Officers Assn. U.S. (life), Navy League U.S. (life), St. Andrew's Soc. Phila. (life), Chapel of Four Chaplains (life, Phila.), Soc. of the Friendly Sons of St. Patrick (life), SAR (life), Nat. Assn. Steeplechase and Hunt Assn., Masons, Shriners, Rotary. Office: PO Box 1343 Bryn Mawr PA 19010

KOEPCKE, F. KRISTEN, lawyer; b. Madison, Wis., July 30, 1935; s. Kenneth A. and Esther D. (Nybroten) K.; m. Kayleen Vinton, Jan. 29, 1956 (div.); children: Kristeen, Kendra; m. Shirley Peraino, Oct. 13, 1973. B.S., U. Wis., 1957, LL.B., 1964. Bar: Wis. 1964, Ind. 1972, U.S. Patent Office 1967, U.S. Supreme Ct. 1972. Assoc. Bast & Sendik, Milw., 1964-66; sr. atty. Koehring Co., Milw., 1966-72; v.p., gen. counsel, sec. Hillenbrand Industries, Batesville, Ind., 1972—. Served to capt. U.S. Army, 1958-61. Mem. U.S. Patent Law Assn., ABA, Nat. Soc. Corp. Secs. Episcopalian. Club: Hillcrest Country (pres. 1978-81). Home: Rte 2 Box 376D Batesville IN 47006 Office: Hillenbrand Industries Inc Rte 46 Batesville IN 47006

KOEPKE, DON LORENZ, manufacturing company executive; b. Rice Lake, Wis., Apr. 27, 1938; s. Lawrence Herman and Genevieve Marie (Kavanaugh) K.; m. Marion Ruth Zordel, Nov. 21, 1959; children: Julie Ann, Susan Lee, Douglas Lorenz. Student, Monmouth (Ill.) Coll., 1958. V.p. Koepke Sand and Gravel Co., Appleton, Wis., 1954-60; pres. Concrete Pipe Corp., Appleton, 1960-82, Visions Unlimited of Am., Inc., Appleton, 1983—; bd. dirs. Valley Nat. Bank, Appleton. Mem. Mayor's Citizens Adv. Commn., Appleton; telethon chmn. Rawhide Boy's Ranch, New London, Wis.; bd. dirs. United Cerebral Palsy, Oshkosh, Wis. Served to 2d lt. U.S. Army. Mem. Concrete Pipe Assn. Wis. (pres. 1972), Wis. Assn. Tng. and Devel., Wis. Profl. Speakers Assn. Lodges: Rotary, Elks. Home and Office: Rte #2 Broadway Dr Appleton WI 54915

KOERTING, RICHARD J., health care products company executive; b. Elkhart, Ind., Jan. 26, 1937; s. William E. and Helen M. Koerting; m. Gretchen Wambaugh, 1961; children: Richard, Walter, David. BA, Stanford U., 1958; MBA, Northwestern U., 1962. With Hewlett-Packard Co., Palo Alto, Calif., 1962-63, FMC Corp., San Jose, Calif., 1963-66; with Miles Inc., Elkhart, 1966—, staff v.p. planning, pub. rels. and communication, 1985—. Chmn. bd. dirs. Oaklawn Psychiat. and Community Mental Health Ctr. Inc., Goshen, Inc., 1987—. With U.S. Army, 1958-60. Mem. Nat. Assn. Bus. Economists, Internat. Soc. for Planning and Strategic Mgmt. Office: Miles Inc 1127 Myrtle St Elkhart IN 46514

KOESTER, BERTHOLD KARL, lawyer, honorary consul Federal Republic of Germany; b. Aachen, Germany, June 30, 1931; s. Wilhelm P. and Margarethe A. (Witteler) K.; m. Hildegard Maria Buettner, June 30, 1961; children: Georg W., Wolfgang J., Reinhard B. JD, U. Muenster, Fed. Republic Germany, 1957. Cert. Real Estate Agt., Ariz. Asst. prof. civil and internat. law U. Muenster, 1957-60; atty. Cts. of Duesseldorf, Fed. Republic Germany, 1960-82; v.p. Bank J. H. Vogeler & Co., Duesseldorf, 1960-64; pres. Bremer Tank-u. Kuehlschifahrts Gesellschaft, Bremen, Fed. Republic Germany, 1964-72; atty., trustee internat. corps., Duesseldorf and Phoenix, 1973-82, Phoenix, 1983—; of counsel Tancer Law Offices, Phoenix, 1978-86; prof. internat. bus. law Am. Grad. Sch. Internat. Mgmt., Glendale, Ariz., 1978-81; with Applewhite, Laflin & Lewis, Real Estate Investments, Phoenix, 1981-86, ptnr., 1982-86, Beucler Real Estate Investments, 1986-88, Scottsdale, Ariz.; hon. consul Fed. Republic of Germany for Ariz., 1982—; chmn., chief exec. officer Arimpex Hi-Tec, Inc., Phoenix, 1981—. Contbr. articles to profl. jours. Pres. Parents Assn. Humboldt Gymnasium, Duesseldorf, 1971-78; active German Red Cross, from 1977. Mem. Duesseldorf Chamber of Lawyers, Bochum (Fed. Republic Germany) Assn. Tax Lawyers, Bonn German-Saudi Arabian Assn. (pres. 1976-79), Bonn German-Korean Assn., Assn. for German-Korean Econ. Devel. (pres. 1974-78), Ariz. Consular Corps, German-Am. C. of C., Phoenix Met. C. of C. Club: Rotary (Scottsdale, Ariz.). Home: 6201 E Cactus Rd Scottsdale AZ 85254

KOESTER, CHARLES WILLIAM, JR., greeting card company executive; b. Raleigh, N.C., Apr. 17, 1945; s. Charles William and Sarah Ellen (Snipes) K.; m. Constance Sue Smith, Aug. 12, 1967; children: Charles W. III, S. Matthew. BBA, Northwestern U., 1967; MBA, U. Pa., 1969. Various fin. positions Hallmark Cards, Inc., Kansas City, Mo., 1971-79, mgr. internal audit, 1979-81, asst. controller, 1981-84, asst. to exec. v.p., 1984-85, corp. controller, 1985-86, v.p. fin., 1986-89, group v.p. adminstrn., 1989—; bd. dirs. Ace Ltd., Cayman Island, B.W.I., Univision Holdings Inc., N.Y.C., Binney & Smith, Inc.; adv. bd. dirs. Allendale Mut. Ins. Co., Providence, R.I. Chmn. Hallmark Corp. Polit Action com., 1987—. Served to 1st lt. U.S. Army, 1969-71. Episcopalian. Home: 1901 Brookwood Rd Shawnee Mission KS 66208-1222 Office: Hallmark Cards Inc #332 2501 McGee PO Box 419580 Kansas City MO 64141

KOFFMAN, MILTON AARON, corporate executive; b. Binghamton, N.Y., Sept. 10, 1923; s. Bernard and Eva (Lipman) K.; m. Barbara Elaine Smith, Aug. 3, 1947; children: Jack Schuyler, Janice Schulyer Koffman. BS, Ohio State U., Columbus, 1945. V.p. Pub. Loan Co., Inc., Binghamton, 1963—; exec. v.p. Great Am. Industries, Inc., Binghamton, 1972—, also bd. dirs.; chmn. Chemold Corp., Binghamton, 1967—, Jayark Corp., Binghamton, 1977—, Centuri, Inc., Binghamton, 1978—, chmn. Poloron Products, Binghamton, 1973—; vice chmn. I.E.C. Corp., Newark, N.Y., 1986—; bd. dirs. Gruen Mktg. Corp., Secaucus, N.J., First Women's Bank, N.Y.C., Internat. Seaway, Cleve. Bd. dirs. Binghamton Symphony, 1982—; lifetime trustee Temple Israel, Binghamton; Served with U.S. Army, 1943-45. Jewish. Club: Binghamton. Lodge: Masons. Home: 16 Ivanhoe Rd Binghamton NY 13903 Office: Great Am Industries Inc 300 Plaza Dr Binghamton NY 13903

KOFMEHL, PAUL JACOB, retired business machines company executive; b. Cin., June 3, 1928; s. Paul and Emma (Zingg) K.; m. Dorothy Frickman, June 14, 1952 (dec. Feb. 1970); children: Sharon Leslie, Sandra Lynne; m. Linda De Stefanis, Feb. 24, 1971. BS, MA, U. Cin.; postgrad. in mgmt. Harvard U.; LL.D. (hon.), Lincoln U., 1984; HHD (hon.) Mo. Western State Coll., 1987. Economist Cin. Gas & Electric Co., 1950-55; various mgmt. positions IBM, Armonk, N.Y., 1955-88, including v.p. and group exec., IBM World Trade Ams. Group; bd. dirs. Howe Richardson, Soc., Am. Coll. in Paris Found., 1983—; mem. exec. com. Bus. Council Internat. Understanding; exec. dir. Mayor's Pvt. Sector Survey, N.Y.C. Home: Greenwich CT 06830 Office: IBM World Trade Ams Group Rockwood Rd North Tarrytown NY 10591

KOGAN, RICHARD JAY, pharmaceutical company executive; b. N.Y.C., June 6, 1941; s. Benjamin and Ida K.; m. Susan Linda Scher, Aug. 29, 1965. B.A., CCNY, 1963; M.B.A., NYU, 1968. Dir. planning and adminstrn. Ciba Corp., Summit, N.J., 1968-69; v.p. planning, pharm. div. Ciba-Geigy Corp., Summit, 1970-76; pres. Can. pharm. div. Ciba-Geigy Corp., Can., 1976-79; pres. U.S. pharm. div. Ciba-Geigy Corp., Summit, 1979-82; exec. v.p. pharm. ops. Schering-Plough Corp., Madison, N.J., 1982-86; pres., chief operating officer Schering-Plough Corp., Kenilworth, N.J., 1986—, also dir.; bd. dirs. Nat. Westminster Bank U.S.A., Rite Aid Corp.; b. overseers sch. bus. NYU. Trustee St. Barnabas Med. Ctr., Livingston N.J., 1981—, Food and Drug Law Inst. Office: Schering-Plough Corp 1 Giraldi Farms Madison NJ 07940

KOGUT, JOHN ANTHONY, retail executive, pharmacist; b. Lackawanna, N.Y., Dec. 8, 1942; s. John J. and Rose J. (Gaj) K.; m. Carol A. Lowden; children—David J., Robert J., Katherine A. B.S. in Pharmacy, U. Buffalo, 1965; M.B.A., Syracuse U., 1978. Pharmacist, mgr. Fay's Drug Co., Liverpool, N.Y., 1969-75, v.p., 1975-79, sr. v.p., 1979-89, pres., 1989—, also bd. dirs.; mem. N.Y. State Bd. Pharmacy, 1987—. Served to capt. U.S. Army, 1966-69. Mem. Am. Pharm. Assn., Pharm. Soc. of State N.Y., Am. Mgmt. Assn., Nat. Assn. Chain Drug Stores (pharmacy affairs com. chmn. 1982-83), N.Y. State Bd. Pharmacy. Republican. Roman Catholic. Office: Fay's Drug Co 7245 Henry Clay Blvd Liverpool NY 13088

KOHLBERG, JEROME, JR., lawyer, business executive; b. N.Y.C., 1925. Grad., Swarthmore Coll., 1946; JD, Columbia U., 1950. Bar: N.Y. Sr. ptnr. Kohlberg, Kravis, Roberts & Co., N.Y.C.; chmn. Houdaille Industries, Inc., Fort Lauderdale, Fla., chmn. exec. com.; now chmn. Kohlberg and Co., N.Y.C.; bd. dirs. Sterndent Corp. Office: Kohlberg and Co care Jennifer Magnone 20 W 55th St New York NY 10019 *

KOHLENBERG, STANLEY, mktg. exec.; b. Bklyn., Aug. 19, 1932; s. Max and Minnie (Roth) K.; BS, Columbia U., 1953; postgrad. N.Y. U., 1956-58; m. Ruth Barbara Itkin, Dec. 11, 1955; children: Robin Sue, Mark Stuart, Howard Scott. Account supr. L.W. Frohlich, N.Y.C., 1959-62; advt. mgr. Pfizer Lab., N.Y.C., 1962-63; mktg. dir. Tussy Cosmetics, N.Y.C., 1964; sr. v.p., dir. client service Sudler & Hennessey, N.Y.C., 1964-66; pub. Cosmetics Fair mag., N.Y.C., 1966-68; exec. v.p. Spectrum Cosmetics, 1968-70; pres. Coty Inc., 1970-72; exec. v.p. Revlon Inc., N.Y.C., 1972-76; pres. Calvin Klein Cosmetics, Inc., N.Y.C., 1977-79; pres. CFT Mktg., Inc., N.Y.C., 1980-84; pres. Sanofi Beauty Poducts, Inc., N.Y.C., 1984—; cons., advt. and sales promotion. Served with M.D., AUS, 1953-55. Home: Shad Rd W Pound Ridge NY 10576 Office: Sanofi Beauty Products Inc 40 E 52d St New York NY 10022

KOHLER, FRED CHRISTOPHER, financial reporting manager; b. Cleve., Oct. 21, 1946; s. Fred Russell and Ruth Mary (Harris) K.; B.S. (Austin scholar), Northwestern U., 1968; M.B.A. (Faville fellow), Stanford, 1970. Sr. analyst adminstrv. services div. Arthur Andersen & Co., San Francisco, 1970-75, financial systems analyst, sr. cost accountant Hewlett Packard Co., Palo Alto, Calif., 1975-77, internat. mktg. systems adminstr., 1977-80, sr. planning and reporting analyst corp. hdqrs., 1980-86, legal planning and reporting mgr., 1986—. Mem. World Affairs Council No. Calif., Internat. Forum, Northwestern U. Alumni Club No. Calif. (dir.), Stanford Alumni Assn., Beta Gamma Sigma. Home: 1736 Oak Creek Dr Palo Alto CA 94304 Office: 3000 Hanover St Palo Alto CA 94304

KOHLER, RICHARD ALLEN, marketing executive, management consultant; b. Chgo., July 10, 1950; s. Jerry Frank and Virginia Josephine (Powell) K.; m. Arlene Ruth Koeppl, May 4, 1974; 1 child, Tiffany Alexandra. BSME, So. Ill. U., 1973; MBA in Mktg., U. Chgo., 1978. Mgr. mfg. Jet Die Casting Corp., Elk Grove Village, Ill., 1973-78; product specialist Nalco Chem. Co., Oak Brook, Ill., 1979-80; mgmt. cons. Mitchell Watkins & Assocs., Chgo., 1980-83; bus. devel. mgr. Astronautics Corp. of Am., Milw., 1983-86; product mgr. Badger Meter, Inc., Milw., 1986-88; mgr. program devel. Eaton Corp., Milw., 1988—; cons. Mgmt. Resource Group, Brookfield, Wis., 1987—. Mem. Sales and Mktg. Execs. Milw. Republican. Lutheran. Home: 13505 Keefe Ave Brookfield WI 53005 Office: Eaton Corp 4201 N 27th St Milwaukee WI 53216

KOHLHEPP, EDWARD JOHN, consultant; b. Phila., Aug. 11, 1943; s. Edward H. and Helen Kathleen (Egan) K.; BS in Acctg., LaSalle U., 1967; MBA in Mgmt., Temple U., 1969; m. Elizabeth A. Bretschneider, June 21, 1969; children: Edward Joseph, Karen Ann, Mary Beth. Instr., Bucks County Community Coll., Newtown, Pa., 1969-72, asst. prof., 1976-79, assoc. prof., 1979-83, sr. assoc. prof., 1983-86; sec./treas. Lincoln Investment Planning, Inc., Jenkintown, Pa., 1972-75; cons. Neil G. Kyde, Inc., Yardley, Pa., 1975-79; v.p. William L. Marshall Assos., Inc., Doylestown, Pa., 1979-80; pvt. practice fin. planner, 1980-87; pres. Van Buren & Kohlhepp, Ltd., 1987—. Cert. pension cons.; CLU; cert. fin. planner; registered prin. N.A.S.D.; chartered fin. cons. Mem. Internat. Assn. Fin. Planning, Inst. Cert. Fin. Planners, Am. Acad. Actuaries, Am. Soc. Pension Actuaries, Bucks County Estate Planning Coun., Registry Fin. Planning Practitioners (admitted), Beta Gamma Sigma, Beta Alpha. Home: 29 Woods End Dr Doylestown PA 18901 Office: 140 Terry Dr Ste 102 Newtown PA 18940

KOHLOSS, FREDERICK HENRY, consulting engineer; b. Ft. Sam Houston, Tex., Dec. 4, 1922; s. Fabius Henry and Rowena May (Smith) K.; m. Margaret Mary Grunwell, Sept. 9, 1944; children: Margaret Ralston, Charlotte Todesco, Eleanor. B.S. in Mech. Engring, U. Md., 1943; M.Mech. Engring., U. Del., 1951; J.D., George Washington U., 1949. Mem. engring. faculty George Washington U., Washington, 1946-50; devel. and standards engr. Dept. Def., 1950-51; chief engr. for mech. contractors Washington, 1951-54, Cleve., 1954-55; chief engr. for mech. contractors Honolulu, 1955-56, cons. engr., 1956-61; pres. Frederick H. Kohloss & Assocs., Inc., Cons. Engrs., Honolulu, Tucson, Denver, 1961—. Contbr. to publs. in field. Served with U.S. Army, 1943-46. Fellow ASME, ASHRAE, Am. Cons. Engrs. Council, Chartered Inst. Bldg. Services Engrs., Instn. Engrs. Australia, Soc. Mil. Engrs.; mem. IEEE (sr.), Nat. Soc. Profl. Engrs., Illuminating Engring. Soc. Clubs: Oahu Country (Honolulu). Home: 1645 Ala Wai Blvd Penthouse 1 Honolulu HI 96815 Office: 1001 Bishop St Pauahi Tower Ste 390 Honolulu HI 96813

KOHN, DAWN RUTH, municipal official; b. Wausau, Wis., Nov. 2, 1932; d. Jerry Edward and Amelia (Abraham) Witter; m. Joseph Marvin Kohn, Aug. 30, 1952; children: Barbara Kohn Rausch, Lynn Kohn Klinkert. Student, U. Wis., Wausau, 1964-70. Sec., bookkeeper Wausau Bd. Edn., 1953-63; acct. City of Wausau, 1963-66, supr. data processing, 1967-69, office mgr. fin. dept., 1969, dep. fin. dir., city treas., 1970—. Chmn. govt. sector United Way Wausau, 1982-83, vice chmn., 1984-85. Mem. Govt. Fin. Officers U.S. and Can., Wis. Govt. Fin. Officers Assn., Mcpl. Treas. Assn. U.S. and Can., Mcpl. Treas. Assn. Wis., Wis. Clks., Treas. and Fin. Officers Assn., LWV. Home: 406 N 28th Ave Wausau WI 54401 Office: City of Wausau 407 Grant St Wausau WI 55401

KOHN, HAROLD ELIAS, lawyer; b. Phila., Apr. 5, 1914; s. Joseph C. and Mayme (Rumm) K.; m. Edith Anderson, Dec. 30, 1946; children: Amy, Ellen, Joseph Carl. A.B., U. Pa., 1934, LL.B., 1937. Bar: Pa. 1938. Pres. Kohn, Savett, Klein & Graf, P.C., Phila.; spl. counsel transit matters City of Phila., 1952-53, 56-62; counsel to gov. State of Pa., 1972; mem. bd. Southeastern Pa. Transp. Authority, 1972-77; mem. Pa. Jud. Inquiry and Rev. Bd., 1973-77; bd. consultors Villanova U. Law Sch. Sec., treas., bd. dirs. Kohn Found.; pres., bd. dirs. Arronson Found., Lavine Found.; bd. dirs. Moss Rehab. Hosp., Phila. Geriatric Ctr.; trustee, mem. exec. com. Phila. Fedn. Jewish Agys.; trustee Temple U., U. of the Arts; past mem. exec. com. United Jewish Appeal; past mem. bd. dirs. Phila. Psychiat. Ctr.; past v.p., bd. dirs. Phila. chpt. ACLU. Mem. ABA, Pa., Phila., D.C. Bar Assns., Internat. Acad. Trial Lawyers, Jud. Conf. 3d Circuit, Am. Law Inst., Order of Coif, Phi Beta Kappa. Home: Philadelphia PA 19106 Office: 1101 Market St Philadelphia PA 19107

KOHN, ROBERT SAMUEL, JR., real estate investment consultant; b. Denver, Jan. 7, 1949; s. Robert Samuel and Miriam Lackner (Neusteter) K.; BS, U. Ariz., 1971; m., Eleanor B. Kohn; children: Joseph Robert, Randall Stanton, Andrea Rene. Asst. buyer Robinson's Dept. Store, L.A., 1971; agt. Neusteter Realty Co., Denver, 1972-73, exec. v.p., 1973-76; pres. Project Devel. Svcs., Denver, 1976-78, pres., chief exec. officer, 1978-83; pres. Kohn and Assos., Inc., 1979-83, The Burke Co., Inc., Irvine, Calif., 1983-84, ptnr. 1984—. Mem. Bldg. Owners and Mgrs. Assn. (pres. 1977-78, dir. 1972-78, dir. S.W. Conf. Bd. 1977-78), Denver Art Mus., Denver U. Library Assn., Central City Opera House Assn., Inst. Real Estate Mgmt., Newport Beach Tennis Club. Republican. Jewish. Home: 10 Skysail Dr Corona Del Mar CA 92625 Office: The Burke Co Inc 2111 Business Center Dr Irvine CA 92715

KOHN, STEPHEN JEROME, accounting company executive; b. N.Y.C., July 16, 1939; s. Louis and Belle (Buchsbaum) K.; children from previous marriage: Felicia Suzanne, Jennifer Lynn; m. Margaret Wolf, Mar. 2, 1986. BA, Queens Coll., 1962; ABD, CUNY, 1970. Lectr. Queens Coll., Flushing, N.Y., 1964-66; v.p. Akron (Ohio) Nat. Bank, 1966-72; supt. of banks State of Ohio, Columbus, 1972-74; v.p. Union Commerce Bank, Cleve., 1974-75; dir. fin. svcs. cons. Ernst & Whinney, N.Y.C., 1974-84, nat. dir. fin. svcs. industry, 1985-87, nat. dir. fin., 1987-89, co-chmn. U.S. and internat. banking practices, 1989—; sr. mgr. Ernst & Whinney, Cleve., 1976-79; v.p. Booz, Allen & Hamilton, N.Y.C., 1984-85; bd. dirs. N.Y. Forum on Internat. Bus. Contbr. articles to profl. jours. Mem. Nat. Def. Rose Edn. Act fellow Dept. Def., 1962-64. Mem. Rockefeller Ctr. Club. Office: Ernst & Whinney 787 Seventh Ave New York NY 10019

KOHNE, RICHARD EDWARD, consulting engineering and construction company executive; b. Tientsin, China, May 16, 1924; s. Ernest E. and Elizabeth I. (Antonenko) K.; m. Gabrielle H. Vernaudon; children—Robert, Phillip, Daniel, Paul, Renee. B.S., U. Calif., Berkeley, 1948. Structural engr. hydro projects Pacific Gas & Electric Co., San Francisco, 1948-55; with Morrison-Knudsen Engrs., Inc., San Francisco, 1955—, regional mgr. for Latin Am., then v.p., 1965-71, exec. v.p. world-wide ops. in engring. and project mgmt., 1971-79, pres., 1979-87, chmn., chief exec. officer, 1987—, also dir.; pres., dir. Cia. Int. de Ingenieria; pres. Morrison-Knudsen Internat. West Inc. Decorated Chevalier Nat. Order of Leopold (Zaire). Mem. ASCE, U.S. Com. Large Dams, Am. Inst. Mining Engrs., Soc. Am. Mil. Engrs., Am. Mgmt. Assn., Am. Nuclear Soc., Assn. U.S. Army, Am. Cons. Engring. Council, Cons. Engrs. Assn. Calif. Democrat. Roman Catholic. Clubs: World Trade (San Francisco), Engineers (San Francisco), Bankers (San Francisco). Home: 1827 Doris Dr Menlo Park CA 94025 Office: Morrison-Knudsen Engrs Inc 180 Howard St San Francisco CA 94105

KOHRING, DAGMAR LUZIA, fundraiser, consultant; b. Lage, Fed. Republic Germany, Mar. 8, 1951; came to U.S., 1966; d. Wilfried and Luzia W. (Knichel) K.; m. Arthur Gingrande Jr., Dec. 29, 1976 (div. June 1982). BA, Am. U., 1972, MA, 1974. Cert. fundraising exec. Asst. dir. devel. Harvard Art Mus., Cambridge, 1981-83; campaign officer Harvard U., Cambridge, 1983-85; sr. cons., campaign dir. C.H. Benz Assocs., Westfield, N.J., 1985-88; v.p. Brakeley, John Price Jones Inc., Stamford, Conn., 1988—. Nat. Endowment for the Arts fellow, 1983. Mem. Nat. Soc. Fundraising Execs. Club: Harvard (N.Y.C.). Home: 36 Hancock St Apt 7A Boston MA 02114 Office: Brakeley John Price Jones Inc 1600 Summer St Stamford CT 06905

KOHRS, LLOYD FREDERICK, electrical engineer; b. St. Charles, Mo., Sept. 6, 1927; s. William August and Lolita Kathrine (Nolle) K.; m. Diana Joyce Button, Mar. 14, 1960; 1 stepchild, Randall Grant Pemberton; 1 child, Charmaine Lynette Kohrs Seavy. BSEE, Washington U., 1950. Test conductor McDonnell Aircraft, St. Louis, 1950-55; mgr. space propulsion Aerojet Gen. Corp., Sacramento, Calif., 1955-67; mgr. propulsion Hughes Aircraft, El Segundo, Calif., 1967-69; chief propulsion engr. McDonnell Douglas Astronautics, St. Louis, Mo., 1969-73; mgr. space shuttle program McDonnell Douglas Astronautics, St. Louis, 1973-83, mgr. DSP Laser Crosslink program, 1983—. Served with U.S. Army, 1945-46. Recipient Disting. Pub. Service medal NASA, 1982. Mem. Am. Inst. Aeronautics and Astronautics (Wyld Propulsion award 1982). Democrat. Home: 3 Pretoria Ct Saint Charles MO 63303 Office: McDonnell Douglas Astronautics Co PO Box 516 Saint Louis MO 63166

KOHUT, JOHN WALTER, merchant banker; b. N.Y.C., Nov. 13, 1946; s. Walter and Stelle (Dudar) K.; m. Linda Susan Ram, Jan. 3, 1987. Mgmt. trainee Bankers Trust Co., N.Y.C., 1969-73, asst. treas. in comml. banking, 1973-76, asst. v.p. spl. loans, 1976-79; v.p. European Energy Bankers Trust Co., London, 1979-82, v.p. Global Aerospace, 1982-85, mng. dir. Pvt. Equity, 1985—; bd. dirs. The Recreation Co., Warminster, Pa., Automotive Holdings, Inc., Washington; v.p. Pyramid Investors, N.Y.C., 1988—. Bd. dirs. 309 E. 49th St. C.A., N.Y.C., 1985—; elected committeman Rep. County, Somerset, N.J., 1976-79. Mem. AIAA (bd. dirs. 1987—), Tau Kappa Epsilon. Roman Catholic. Home: 309 E 49th St New York NY 10017 Office: Bankers Trust Co 280 Park Ave New York NY 10017

KOHUT, WILLIAM, real estate executive; b. Bethlehem, Pa., Nov. 14, 1938; s. Joseph and Sophia (Chemy) K.; m. Joann C. Kospian, June 18, 1960; children: William Jr., Christine M. BS in Chem. Engring., Lehigh U., 1960; MBA, Duquesne U., 1967. Prodn. engr. J & L Steel Co., Pitts., 1960-64, Am. Cyanamid Co., Wallingford, Conn., 1964-67; v.p. real estate and store constrn. Sherwin-Williams Co., Cleve., 1967-85; pres. Figgie Properties Inc., Richmond, Va., 1985—. Served with U.S. Army, 1964. Mem. NACORE (pres. Richmond chpt. 1987-88), ICSC, NAIOP, AICAM. Club: Hermitage Country. Office: Figgie Properties Inc Box C 32064 Richmond VA 23060

KOIDE, MORIHIKO, electronics company executive; b. Tokyo, Sept. 9, 1935; s. Shogo and Shuzuko K.; m. Tomoko Aono, Apr. 22, 1961; children: Mikihiko, Mikako. BSc, Waseda U., 1960. With Hitachi Ltd., Yokohama, Japan, 1960—; exec. v.p., gen. mgr. Hitachi Sales Corp. Can., after 1974; gen. mgr. Hitachi Consumer Products Am., after 1979, exec. v.p., 1982-86; pres. Hitachi Consumer Products de Mex., 1986—. Mem. IEEE, Am. Mgmt. Assn., Japanese Inst. TV Engring. Home: 96 Montego Ct Coronado CA 92118 Office: 901 E South St Anaheim CA 92805

KOK, HANS GEBHARD, consulting engineer; b. Potshausen, Germany, Apr. 5, 1923; s. George J. and Antina K. (Janssen) K.; student Suderburg (Germany) Engring. Coll., 1940-42, Hamburg Engring. Coll., 1945-46; Dipl. Ing., Technische Hochschule, Aachen, 1950; m. Roselle V. Venier, June 22, 1960; children—George H., Karen R. Came to U.S., 1951, naturalized, 1959. Design engr. Lummus Co., N.Y.C., 1951-53; structural engr. M. H. Treadwell Co., N.Y.C., 1953-56, head structural engring. sect., 1956-62, chief structural engr., 1962-63; mgr. plant design div. Treadwell Corp., N.Y.C., 1963-69, asst. v.p. engring., 1969-73, v.p. engring., 1973-83; pres. Treadwell Corp. Mich. Inc., 1974-83; cons. engr., 1983—; dir. Basset Miller Treadwell Pty. Ltd. 1983—consulting Engineer Chmn. exec. com. Council Engring. Laws, 1976. Recipient 1st award James F. Lincoln Arc Welding Found., 1966. Registered profl. engr., N.Y., Pa., Ill., Mich., Mo., Minn., Ohio, W. Va., Utah, Tex., La., N.M., Ariz., Md., Mass., Tenn. Fellow ASCE, mem. Nat., N.Y. State socs. profl. engrs., Am. Inst. Mining, Metall. and Petroleum Engrs. (chmn. materials handling com.), Am. Mining Congress, Am. Mgmt. Assn. Contbr. to profl. jours. Home: 15 Alpine Dr Lake Hopatcong NJ 07849 Office: 28 W 95th St New York NY 10025

KOKOLA, MELODY BACSKO, library director; b. New Brunswick, N.J., Dec. 1, 1947; d. Albert B. and Helen Geczy Bacsko; m. Walter Alexander Kokola, Jan. 19, 1969; children: John Christopher, Carolee Alison. BA, Rutgers U., 1970; MS, Grad. Sch. Library Service, Columbia U., 1977. Librarian Bayonne (N.J.) Pub. Library, 1977-86; library dir. Metuchen (N.J.) Pub. Library, 1986—; treas. Libraries of Middlesex County, N.J., 1987—, N.J. Library Compact Disc Cir., Woodbridge, 1987—l v.p. Libraries of Middlesex Automation Consortium, 1988—. Sec. Meml. Park Commn., Metuchen, 1987—, Cable TV Adv. Commn., Metuchen. Mem. ALA, N.J. Library Assn., Pub. Library Assn., Columbia U. Library Sch. Alumni Assn. (mem. Alumni bd. dir. 1988—), Kiwanis (publicist 1987—, 1st v.p. Metuchen chpt. 1988—). Mem. Reformed Ch. Am. Home: 27 Magnolia Rd Somerset NJ 08873 Office: Metuchen Pub Libr 480 Middlesex Ave Metuchen NJ 08840

KOLANOSKI, THOMAS EDWIN, financial company executive; b. San Francisco, Mar. 1, 1937; s. Theodore Thaddeus and Mary J. (Luczynski) K.; m. Sheila O'Brien, Dec. 26, 1960; children: Kenneth John, Thomas Patrick, Michael Sean. BS, U. San Francisco, 1959, MA, 1965. Cert. fin. planner. Educator, counselor, adminstr. San Francisco Unified Sch. Dist., 1960-79; adminstr. Huntington Beach (Calif.) Union, 1969-79; v.p. fin. svcs. Waddell & Reed, Inc., Ariz., Nev., Utah, So. Calif., 1969—. Fellow NDEA, 1965. Mem. Nat. Assn. Secondary Sch. Prins., Internat. Assn. of Fin. Planners, Nat. Assn. Securities Dealers. Republican. Roman Catholic. Home: 1783 Panay Circle Costa Mesa CA 92626 also: 10218 N Central Phoenix AZ 85021

KOLB, JERRY WILBERT, accountant; b. Chgo., Dec. 22, 1935; s. Herman and Myrtle (Richter) K.; m. Marlene Joyce Tipp, Feb. 3, 1957 (div. July 1986); children—Bradley, Steven, Lisa; m. Carol Ann Fleming, Dec. 14, 1986. B.S. in Acct. with highest honors, U. Ill., 1957; M.B.A., DePaul U., 1962. C.P.A., Ill., N.Y., Iowa. Acct. Deloitte Haskins & Sells C.P.A.s, Chgo., 1957-68, ptnr., 1968-76, ptnr.-in-charge Chgo. Office, 1976-83; ptnr.-in-charge profl. services Deloitte Haskins & Sells C.P.A.s, N.Y.C., 1983-86, mem. policy com., 1979-85, vice chmn., chief fin. and adminstrv. officer, 1986—; lectr. DePaul U., Chgo., 1962-76, mem. adv. council dept. acctg., 1981-83; mem. profl. adv. bd. dept. accountancy U. Ill., Urbana, 1979-82; mem. adv. council Sch. Accountancy, Northwestern U., Evanston, 1980-83. Recipient Disting. Alumni award DePaul U., 1970. Mem. AICPA, Ill. CPA Soc. (bd. dirs. 1973-77, v.p. 1976-77, Sells Gold Medal award 1957), Am. Acctg. Assn. Clubs: Chicago, Standard, Mid-America (dir. 1982-83) (Chgo.); Board Room (N.Y.C.). Home: 308 W Lyon Farm Dr Greenwich CT 06831 Office: Deloitte Haskins & Sells 1114 Ave of the Americas New York NY 10036

KOLBERT, KATHRYN, lawyer; b. Detroit, Apr. 8, 1952; d. Melvin and Rosalie Betty (Frank) K.; children: Samuel Kolbert-Hyle, Kat Kolbert Hyle. BA, Cornell U., 1974; JD, Temple U., 1977. Bar: Pa. 1977, U.S. Dist. Ct. (ea. dist.) Pa. 1972, U.S. Ct. Appeals (3d cir.) 1977, U.S. Supreme Ct. 1985. Atty. Community Legal Svcs., Phila., 1977-79, Women's Law Project, Phila., 1979-88; co-founder, dir. policy Women's Agenda, Phila., 1984-88; cons. Planned Parenthood Fedn., Phila., 1988—; lectr. dept. women's studies U. Pa., 1978-86; cons. reproductive freedom project ACLU, N.Y.C, 1988—, Nat. Abortion Rights Action League, Washington, 1987. Contbr. chpts. to books. Founder, Commn. to Elect Women Judges, Women Judges Pac, Phila, 1984; bd. dirs. Com. to Elect the Cosey 5, Phila. Recipient Dedicated Advocacy award Nat. Abortion Rights Action League Pa., 1986, Pa. Coalition Against Domestic Violence, 1986, Luth. Settlement House Women's Program, 1987, Am. Dem. Action award, 1989. Democrat. Jewish.

KOLDE, RICHARD ARTHUR, insurance company executive, consultant; b. Pomona, Calif., Jan. 25, 1944; s. Arthur and Rosemary (Decker) K.; m. Lark Holly Kolde, Apr. 30, 1988; children: Nicole Rochelle, Eric Christian. AA, Mt. San Antonio Coll., 1963; BS, U. So. Calif., 1965; AS, Mira Costa Coll., 1979. Asst. mgr., mgr. Lord Rebel Ind., Montclair, Costa Mesa and Carlsbad, Calif., 1971-74; agt. Conn. Mut. Life Ins. Co., San Diego and Carlsbad, 1974-77; pres., owner Investment Assocs., Carlsbad, 1977-82; mng. gen. agt. E.F. Hutton Life Ins. Co., San Diego, 1982—; cons. Hansch Fin. Group, Laguna Hills, Calif., 1984. Bd. dirs. Boys Club Am., Carlsbad, 1980-84, adv. bd., 1984—; bd. dirs. YMCA, Pomona, 1960-64. Served with USAF, 1966-71. Decorated Outstanding Unit award, Small Arms Expert award, Security 1 & 2 Protection of Pres. U.S. award; named Largest Producing Mng. Gen. Agt. in Nation, E.F. Hutton Life Co., 1982, 83. Mem. Nat. Assn. Life Underwriters (legis. officer 1974—), Calif. Assn. Life Underwriters, Internat. Assn. Fin. Planners (Mem. of Yr. award 1977), U.S. Gymnastics Fedn. (coaching credentials, ofcl. judge collegiate level), VFW, Phi Sigma Beta. Republican. Lodge: Rotary.

KOLF, JAMES, home health care executive; b. Detroit, July 22, 1948; s. John A. and Mary M. (Whalen) K.; m. Marie Anne Mace, Nov. 25, 1970; children: Heather Anne, Rebecca Lynn, Kelly Marie. BS, Wayne State U., 1970, postgrad., 1972-73. Cert. tchr., Mich. Tchr. St. Raymond Sch., Detroit, 1970-73; pharm. sales Eaton Labs., Norwich, N.Y., 1973-74; ter. mgr. Baxter Travenol Labs., Deerfield, Ill., 1974-75, field tng., 1976-81; med. edn. coord. Mt. Carmel Hosp., Detroit, 1975-76; gen. mgr./antibiotic/TPN specialist Home Health Care Am., Newport Beach, Calif., 1981—; gen. mgr. New Eng. Critical Care, 1987—; mem Home Therapy Task Force, Grand Rapids, Mich., 1987. Mem. adminstrn. com. St. Paul of Tarsus, 1988—, Negotiating Skills, Boston Coll., 1988, Leadership Devel. Conf., Eckerd Coll., 1988, Mgmt. Devel. Program Sterling Inst., 1989. PTO grantee, 1971. Mem. Assn. Hosp. Med. Edn., Sigma Pi (sec. 1967-68), 200 Club, 400 Club. Republican. Roman Catholic.

KOLLAT, DAVID TRUMAN, management consultant; b. Elkhart, Ind., July 7, 1938; s. Walter A. and Mildred E. (Good) K.; children: Lisa, Andra. BBA, Western Mich. U., 1960, MBA, 1962; D of Bus. Adminstrn., Ind. U., 1966. Mem. faculty Ohio State U., Columbus, 1965-72; v.p., then exec. v.p., dir. rsch. Mgmt. Horizons, Columbus, 1972-76; v.p. The Limited Stores, Inc., Columbus, 1976-77; exec. v.p. The Limited Stores, Inc., 1977-84; exec. v.p. mktg. The Limited Inc., 1984-87, also bd. dirs.; mgmt. cons. Worthington, Ohio, 1987—; bd. dirs. Cooker Restaurant Corp. Co-author: Strategic Marketing, 1972, Consumer Behavior, 1978. Served with AUS, 1960-68. Mem. Am. Mktg. Assn. (v.p. 1979-80), Assn. Consumer Rsch., Beta Gamma Sigma, Omicron Delta Kappa. Home: 6064 Olentangy River Rd Worthington OH 43085

KOLMER, JOHN H., JR., banker; b. Mar. 2, 1945; s. John H. and Gertrude B. (McAllister) K.; m. Nora Dillon, July 19, 1968; 1 child, John H. III. AB in Sociology, Villanova (Pa.) U., 1967. Trader Elkins Morris Stroud & Co., Phila., 1967-75; mgr. and trader corp. bonds First Boston Corp., N.Y.C., 1975-83, mng. dir., head high yield securities, 1983—. Fellow Corp. Bond Traders Assn., Bond Club N.Y.; mem. Villanova Fin. Club (cofounder N.Y. chpt.), N.Y. Athletic Club, Navesink (N.J.) Country Club, Club at Pelican Bay (Fla.). Home: 39 Howland Rd Middletown NJ 07748 Office: 1st Boston Corp 55 E 52nd St 6th Fl New York NY 10055

KOLSKY, ALLAN, real estate development company executive; b. Bklyn., June 30, 1932; s. Jack R. and Lee (Wolf) K.; m. Phyllis Lillian South, Jan. 17, 1970; children—Bruce, Mark, Diane. Student pub. schs., New Brunswick, N.J. Lic. real estate broker, N.Y. Real estate and home builder, Sunrise Estates, Nanuet, N.Y., 1955-59; self employed in real estate and comml. devel., New Brunswick, N.J., 1960-69; v.p. real estate and real estate dir. Lionel Leisure, Phila., Fla., Ga., N.Y., N.J., 1970-74; exec. v.p., Wolf Corp., N.Y.C., 1975-78; pres. Redevco Corp., Ft. Lauderdale, Fla., 1978—; pres., dir. Redevco Mgmt. Corp., Redevco Devel. Corp.; mng. ptnr. Redevco Assocs., 1985—; pres., dir. Redevco I, Inc., Redevco II, Inc., Tamiami Plaza, Inc.; mng. ptnr. Plaza South Assocs., Las Tiendas Assocs., Trail Plaza Assocs., Shadowood Sq. Assocs., 1988—, Flagler & 82d Ltd., Tri-County Assocs. Ltd.; pres. Commpact II, Inc., 1987, S & K Assocs., Inc., Tri-County Sq., Inc. Hon. dir. Assn. Advancement of Mentally Handicapped, Miami, Fla., 1983-; nat. adv. bd. Research and Devel. Inst. for Nat. Assn. Retarded Citizens, Dallas, 1983—; pres. Ctr. for Curative Research, Inc.; state dir.-at-large Fla. Assn. Retarded Citizens. Served with USAF, 1952-53. Mem. C. of C., Better Bus. Bur., Internat. Council Shopping Centers, Am. Soc. Notaries, Nat. Rifle Assn. Clubs: U.S. Senatorial; Turnberry Yacht and Racquet (Miami). Office: Redevco Corp 2000 W Commercial Blvd Suite 232 Fort Lauderdale FL 33309

KOLTAI, STEPHEN MIKLOS, mechanical engineer, consultant, economist; b. Ujpest, Hungary, Nov. 5, 1922; came to U.S., 1963; s. Maximilian and Elisabeth (Rado) K.; m. Franciska Gabor, Sept. 14, 1948; children: Eva, Susy. MS in Mech. Engring., U. Budapest, Hungary, 1948, MS in Econs., MS, BA, 1955. Engr. Hungarian Govt., 1943-49; cons. engr. and diplomatic service various European countries, 1950-62; cons. engr. Pan Bus. Cons. Corp., Switzerland and U.S., 1963-77, Palm Springs, Calif., 1977—. Patentee in field. Charter mem. Rep. Presdl. task force, Washington, 1984—.

KOLTERJAHN, PAUL HENRY, banker; b. Hackensack, N.J., May 2, 1924; s. Paul Henry and Ida Linnea (Nelson) K.; m. Marilyn Jean Hammer, Sept. 3, 1949; children—Paul Howard, Donald Scott. B.B.A., Westminster

Coll., 1949; postgrad. Progam for Mgmt. Devel., Harvard U., 1961. Asst. cashier Citibank, N.A., N.Y.C., 1949-59, v.p. research and devel., 1959-66, v.p. met. div. ops, 1966-70, sr. v.p. N.Y. banking, 1970-83; sr. v.p. sec. Citicorp, N.Y.C., 1983-87; dir. Citibank, N.A., N.Y.C., 1983-86; chmn. Citiflight, 1984—. Office Citicorp 399 Park Ave New York NY 10043. Trustee Westminster Coll., New Wilmington, Pa.; pres. bd. trustees Westfield Meml. Library, N.J. Served to capt. U.S. Army, 1942-46; ETO. Mem. Am. Soc. Corp. Secs. Republican. Presbyterian. Club: Latrobe Country (Pa.). Home: 644 Shackamaxon Dr Westfield NJ 07090 Office: Citicorp 399 Park Ave New York NY 10043

KOLTS, HARVEY SEELEY, manufacturers representative; b. Kingston, N.Y., May 7, 1927; s. Harvey Seeley and Edna N. K.; m. Phyllis Louise Decker, Mar. 22, 1952 (dec. 1970); children: Barry H., Dean R., Alan. J., Vicki Lee. Student, Alfred U., 1947-48. Mgr. Kolts Electric Supply Co., Kingston, 1949-54; ptnr. Diversified Lighting System, Syracuse, N.Y., 1970—. Active Eye Bank Lions Club, 1950-54. Mem. Illuminating Engr. Soc. Mem. Dutch Reform Ch. Home: 404 Melrose Ave Syracuse NY 13206

KOMDAT, JOHN RAYMOND, data processing consultant; b. Brownsville, Tex., Apr. 29, 1943; s. John William and Sara Grace (Williams) K.; m. Linda Jean Garrette, Aug. 26, 1965 (div.); m. Barbara Milroy O'Cain, Sept. 27, 1986; 1 child, Philip August. Student U. Tex., 1961-65. Sr. systems analyst Mass. Blue Cross, Boston, 1970-74; pvt. practice data processing cons., San Francisco, 1974-80, Denver, 1981—; prin. systems analyst mgmt. info. services div. Dept. of Revenue, State of Colo., 1986-89; prin. systems analyst Dept. Adminstrn. State Colo., 1989—; mem. CODASYL End User Facilities Com., 1974-76, allocation com. Mile High United Way. Served with U.S. Army, 1966-70. Mem. AAAS, Assn. Computing Machinery, Denver Downtown Dem. Forum (mem. exec. com.), Mus. Modern Art, Denver Art Mus., Friend of Pub. Radio, Friend of Denver Pub. Library, Colo. State Mgrs. Assn. Democrat. Office: PO Box 10666 Denver CO 80210

KOMUREK, CHARLES FRANCIS, health care facility executive; b. Utica, N.Y., May 11, 1947; s. John and Gladys (Szczygiel) K.; m. Johann Cerminaro, June 14, 1969; Kathianne, David Charles. BS in Acctg., Syracuse U., 1969. Lic. nursing home adminstr. Sr. staff acct. Coopers & Lybrand, Syracuse, N.Y., 1969-73; dir. fin. Loretto Geriatric Ctr., Syracuse, 1973-81; sr. v.p. fin. Presbyn. Homes Western N.Y., Inc., Buffalo, 1981-88; chief fin. officer Rosa Coplon Jewish Home, Buffalo, 1988—. Mem. Health Care Fin. Mgmt. Assn. (bd. dirs. 1977-79, sec. 1978-79, William Follmer award 1979), Am. Coll. Health Care Adminstrs. Republican. Roman Catholic. Lodges: KC (pursor 1978-80). Home: 224 Cimarand Ct Getzville NY 14068 Office: Rosa Coplon Jewish Home 10 Symphony Circle Buffalo NY 14201

KONDAS, NICHOLAS FRANK, shipping executive; b. Eger, Hungary, Sept. 26, 1929; came to U.S., 1957.; s. Miklos and Ilona (Racz) K.; m. Elfriede O. Strauss; children: Walter, Nicolette. MA in Econs., Karl Marx U., Budapest, Hungary, 1952. Mgr. Szovosz Cent., Budadpest, Hungary, 1952-56; assembler S. Goldberg Inc., Hackensack, N.J., 1957-67; supr. Alfred Industries, Richfield Park, N.J., 1967-68; mgr. C.R. Bard, New Providence, N.J., 1968-69; v.p. Seatrain Lines Inc., N.Y.C., 1969-81; gen. mgr. Harper Robinson Co., San Francisco, 1981-82; v.p. Farrell Lines Inc., N.Y.C., 1982—; v.p. Transp. Systems Internat., Washington, 1980—. Served to lt. Hungary Army Res., 1952-56. Mem. Nat. Def. Transp. Assn., 1982—. Office: Farrell Lines Inc 1 Whitehall St New York NY 10004

KONDO, MASATOSHI STEPHAN, pharmaceutical executive, educator; b. Asahikawa, Hokkaido, Japan, Feb. 8, 1940; came to U.S, 1984; s. Saburo Mikame and Hanae Kondo; m. Barbara Renate Bunk, Aug. 5, 1964 (div.); 1 child, Mika Naomi. BS, Tokyo U., 1962; PhD, U. Ill., Urbana, 1967; DSc, U. Antwerp, Belgium, 1976. Asst. prof. U. Zurich, Switzerland, 1970-72; prof. U. Antwerp, 1972-82; dir. Yamanouchi Pharm. Co., Tokyo, 1982-84, Bristol-Myers Co., Wallingford, Conn., 1984-88; pres. Strategic Informatica Internat., Wallingford, Conn., 1988—; prof. Yale U., New Haven, Conn., 1985—, U. Conn., Storrs, Conn., 1986—. Author: Microbiology (in Dutch), 1975. Fellow Internat. Agy. for Research on Cancer, WHO, 1976, sr. NATO, 1981; named Leopold II Knight , Kingdom of Belgium, 1980. Mem. AAAS, German Biochem. Soc., Belgian Biochem. Soc., Austrian Biochem. Soc.

KONE, ALLEN JAY, investment banker, lawyer; b. New Haven, Oct. 24, 1942; s. Eugene Harold and Estelle Lenore (Alpert) K.; m. Ann Berry Scott, June 30, 1968; children—Johannah Berry, Justina Bennett. B.A., Yale U., 1966; postgrad. in bus. adminstrn. Columbia U. Grad. Sch., 1966-67, U. Mich. Sch. Bus. Adminstrn. Pub. Fin. Inst., 1986; J.D., Bklyn. Law Sch., 1976. Bar: N.Y. 1977, U.S. Dist. Cts. (so. and ea. dists.) N.Y. 1978. Asst. to cashier Second Nat. Bank of New Haven, 1967; asst. treas. Bankers Trust Co., N.Y.C. and London, 1967-73; dir. Office of N.Y. Fin., U.S. Dept. Treasury, 1976-82; co-mgr. mcpl. fin. Lebenthal & Co., Inc., N.Y.C., 1982-84; v.p. Matthews & Wright, Inc., N.Y.C., 1984-85, mng. first v.p., dep. mgr. pub. fin. dept., 1986—; cons. Dept. Treasury, Washington, 1982; sec., gen. counsel Orngl. Resources Group, Inc., Purdys, N.Y., 1982—; sec. 133 Pacific St. Housing Corp., Bklyn., 1973—. Co-author research study: An Analysis of the Brooklyn Law School Curriculum, 1976. Contbr. articles to mag. Vice pres. Cobble Hill Assn., Inc., Bklyn., 1972, gen. counsel, bd. dirs., 1979—; pres. P.S.B.A. of Cobble Hill, Inc., 1971-81; v.p. Morgan 3/4 Group, Ltd., N.Y.C., 1979, gen. counsel, 1980—. Mem. ABA, New York County Lawyers Assn. Home: 19 Strong Pl Brooklyn NY 11231 also: Dugway Rd Salisbury CT 06031 Office: Matthews & Wright Inc 100 Broadway 17th Fl New York NY 10005

KONES, RICHARD J., cardiologist, medical service company executive; b. N.Y.C., May 8, 1950; s. Joseph Irwin and Ruth (Winkler) K.; m. Sandra Lee Morrissey, Dec. 26, 1969 (div.); children: Kimberly Susan, Robin Melissa (dec.), Melanie Ann, Sabrina Lee. BS in Chem. Engring., NYU, 1960, MD, 1964; DSc, Somerset U., Eng., 1988. Diplomate Am. Bd. Internal Medicine. Intern Kings County Hosp., Bklyn., 1964-65; resident in surgery Bronx Mcpl. Hosp., N.Y.C., 1965-66; resident in medicine Lenox Hill Hospital, N.Y.C., 1966-68; fellow in cardiology, physician in charge ICU Arthur Logan Hosp., N.Y.C., 1968-69; USPHS-NIH fellow in cardiology, chief resident Tulane U. Sch. Medicine, New Orleans, 1969-71; asst. prof. cardiology N.Y. Med. Coll., N.Y.C., 1971, chief coronary care unit (CCU), 1971-75; cons. and chief CCU Community Hosp., Flatbush Gen. Hosp. and others, N.Y.C., 1971-79; asst. physician, dir., ECG conf. coord. No. Westchester Hosp., Cornell Med. Ctr., Mount Kisco, N.Y., 1972-75; chief exec. officer Community Med. Offices, Inc., Houston and N.Y.C., 1974—; asst. physician, dir., ECG conf. coord. Park City Hosp., Bridgeport, Conn., 1975-78; physician and cons. in cardiology Westchester County Med. Ctr., Valhalla, N.Y., 1978-80; instr. medicine Tulane U., 1969-71, vis. physician sect. cardiology, 1972—; lectr. medicine U. Tex., Houston, 1979—; asst. prof. then assoc. prof. medicine N.Y. Med. Coll., 1971—; pres. Nutrition, Sportsfitness and Preventive Wellness Med. Ctr. and Found., Houston; owner, operator Am. Health Industries, Inc., Houston; lectr. medicine and cardiology U. Tex. Health Sci. Ctr., Houston Med. Ctr., Baylor Coll. Medicine, 1979—. Author, editor books on biochemistry, physiology, cardiology, metabolism and sports medicine; contbr. research papers to profl. pubs. Fellow Am. Coll. Chest Physicians, Royal Soc. Medicine, Am. Coll. Sportsmedicine, Am. Assn. Nutritional Cons., Inst. Advancement of Health; mem. Am. Running and Fitness Assn., Nutritional Rsch. Council, Nat. Strength and Conditioning Assn., Am. Coll. Clin. Nutrition, Internat. Acad. Bariatric Medicine, Am. Med. Athletic Assn., Am. Dietetic Assn., Am. Diabetes Assn., Am. Heart Assn., Am. Pub. Health Assn., Southern Med. Assn., Soc. for Nutrition Edn, Am. Physiol. Soc., Am. Coll. Cardiology and others. Home and Office: 7443 Tunbury Ln Houston TX 77095-3503

KONEZNY, LORETTE M. SOBOL, publishing executive; b. N.Y.C., Sept. 5, 1948; d. Jack and Florence (Silver) Sobol; m. Gerald Walter Konezny, June 4, 1972 (div. 1988); 1 child, Scott David. BS, U. Bridgeport, 1971; postgrad. Adelphi U., 1972-73, Parsons Sch. Design, 1977. Instr., Middle Sch., Malverne, N.Y., 1971-72; pvt. instr. art, L.I., 1972-76; instr. art, adult art end. programs, Rockville Centre, Oceanside and Lawrence, N.Y., 1976-79; pres. Pen Notes, Inc., Freeport, N.Y., 1979—; art cons. Rockville Centre High Sch., 1976-77; exhibited in group shows Adelphi U., 1973, Hewlett East Rockway Temple, 1976, Moscow Internat. Book Fair, 1987; represented in permanent collection Yeshiva U., L.A.; bus. cons. Baldwin C. of C., 1986. Author, pub.: Learning to To Tell Time, 1982, Learning to Print, 1984, Learn Handwriting, 1986, Learn to Write Numbers, 1987; patentee in field; pub. Aprendiendo A Escrbir Las Letras, 1989 exhibited at Moscow Internat. Book Fair, 1987. Mem. L.I. Networking Entrepreneurs (founding pres. 1984-85), Soc. Scribes. Office: 134 Westside Ave Freeport NY 11520

KONHEIM, HARVEY, management consultant; b. N.Y.C., July 2, 1902; s. Gustave A. and Ida (Leavy) K.; student Coll. City N.Y., 1920-23; m. Beatrice S. Goldstein, Nov. 29, 1933; children—Susan (Mrs. Burton Sobel), Jon. Product and mfg. engr. Viscosity Devices Corp., N.Y.C., 1928-34, Gen. Electric Co., Bridgeport, Conn., 1942-44, Western Electric Co., Kearny, N.J., 1944-49, W.L. Maxson Corp., N.Y.C., 1950-54; exec. staff Remington Rand Univac div. Sperry Rand Corp., N.Y.C., 1956-60, mgr. mfg. Univac, Phila., 1960-67; mgmt. cons., N.Y.C., 1968—; mem. Exec. Vol. Corps, N.Y.C. Econ. Devel. Adminstrn., 1968-75. Active in conservation as mem. Adirondack Mountain Club, Sierra Club; dir. Sr. Action Line ombudsman unit N.Y.C. Council Pres.'s Office, 1979—. Mem. ASME (life; nat. interest com. 1982—, chmn. manpower utilization and planning 1984—), Am. Soc. Tool Engrs. (life). Office: 500 E 77th St New York NY 10021

KONNEY, PAUL EDWARD, consumer products company executive, lawyer; b. Hartford, Conn., June 24, 1944; s. William Frederick and Dorothy (Dittmer) K.; m. Barbara Jean Greaves, June 2, 1979; children: Gretchen Blair, Tyler Wingard. BA cum laude, Harvard U., 1966; LLB, U. Pa., 1969. Bar: N.Y. 1973. Law clk. to presiding judge U.S. Ct. Appeals, Phila., 1969-70; assoc. Debevoise & Plimpton, N.Y.C., 1971-81; v.p., gen. counsel Tambrands Inc., Lake Success, N.Y., 1982-83, v.p., gen. counsel, sec., 1983-89, sr. v.p., gen. counsel, sec., 1989—; bd. dirs. Taylor & Dodge Inc., N.Y.C.; mem. U.S. del. to 1st U.S.-USSR legal seminar. Article and book rev. editor U. Pa. Law Rev., 1968-69. Mem. U.S. delegation to 1st U.S.-USSR legal seminar. Mem. ABA, Am. Soc. Corp. Secs., NYU Corp. Real Estate Forum (v.p.), U.S. C. of C. (internat. policy com.). Episcopalian. Clubs: Harvard (N.Y.C.) (bd. mgrs., past dir. found.), Southampton Bath and Tennis. Home: 220 E 65th St New York NY 10021 Office: Tambrands Inc 1 Marcus Ave Lake Success NY 11042

KONOWITZ, HERBERT HENRY, textile company executive; b. Brookline, Mass., Feb. 13, 1937; s. Robert Isaac and Sarah (Freedman) K.; m. Linda Phyllis Swartzman, Dec. 20, 1958; children: Cindy Lee, Jeffrey Scott. BSBA, Babson Coll., 1958. V.p. Vita Rest Sales Co., N.Y.C., 1958-63, Lady Linda Covers Inc., N.Y.C., 1963—; pres. Milford Stitching Co. (Del.), 1968—; v.p. Comml. Drapery Contractors, Inc., Silver Springs, Md., 1976-81; dir. Greater Del. Corp., Dover, Del. Nat. Life, Yankee Land, Inc., Reclamation Center, Inc., 1972-75, G.L.K., Inc. Mem. Gov. Del. Council Consumer Affairs, 1971-76; commr. State Lottery Commn., 1978-81; bd. dirs. Job for Del. Grads., Inc., 1979, Health Plan of Del. Chmn. Local Republican Dist. Com., 1971-75; dir. Del. Dept. of Tourism, 1988—; mem. Del. Rep. Central Com., 1971—; vice chmn. Kent County Rep. Com., 1975-79, chmn., 1979-81; v.p. Kent County chpt. Am. Heart Assn., 1974-75, pres., 1975-76; mem. State Council Tourism, 1988; trustee Broadmeadow Sch., 1980-84, Congregation Beth Sholom, 1980-86; mem. parent's council Northfield-Mt. Hermon Sch., 1984-86; county chmn. Gov.'s Election Com., 1984; mem. adv. council Goldey Beacon Coll., 1987. Lodges: Masons, Elks. Home: 55 Beloit Ave Dover DE 19901 Office: Milford Stitching Co S Marshall St Milford DE 19963

KONTNY, VINCENT LAWRENCE, engineering and construction company executive; b. Chappell, Nebr., July 19, 1937; s. Edward James and Ruth Regina (Schumann) K.; m. Joan Dashwood FitzGibbon, Feb. 20, 1970; children: Natascha Marie, Michael Christian, Amber Brooke. BSCE, U. Colo., 1958. Operator heavy equipment, grade foreman Peter Kiewit Son's Co., Denver, 1958-59; project mgr. Utah Constrn. and Mining Co., Western Australia, 1965-69, Fluor Australia, Queensland, Australia, 1969-72; sr. project mgr. Fluor Utah, San Mateo, Calif., 1972-73; sr. v.p. Holmes & Narver, Inc., Orange, Calif., 1973-79; mng. dir. Fluor Australia, Melbourne, 1979-82; group v.p. Fluor Engrs., Inc., Irvine, Calif., 1982-85, pres., chief exec. officer, 1985-87; group pres. Fluor Daniel, Irvine, Calif., 1987-88, pres., chief exec. officer, 1988—. Contbr. articles to profl. jours. Mem. engring. devel. council, U. Colo. Lt. USN, 1959-65. Mem. AIME (soc. mining engrs.), Am. Assn. Cost Engrs., Australian Assn. Engrs., Am. Petroleum Inst. Republican. Roman Catholic. Club: Cet. (Costa Mesa, Calif.). Home: 10255 Overhill Dr Santa Ana CA 92705 Office: Fluor Corp 3333 Michelson Dr Irvine CA 92730

KONWIN, THOR WARNER, financial executive; b. Berwyn, Ill., Aug. 17, 1943; s. Frank and Alice S. (Johnson) K.; m. Carol A. Svitak, Aug. 2, 1967; 1 child, Christoper Vernon. AA, Morton Jr. Coll., 1966; BS, No. Ill. U., 1967; MS, Roosevelt U., 1971. Acct. Beckerman & Terrill, CPA's, Chgo., 1967-68; cost acct. Sunbeam Corp., Chgo., 1968-72; controller Gen. Molded Products, Inc., Chgo., 1972-75, Sunbeam Appliance Co., Chgo., 1975-81; chief fin. officer Bear Med. System, Inc., Riverside, Calif., 1981-84, Bird Products Corp., Palm Springs, Calif., 1984—; gen. ptnr., mng. ptnr. Tucko Rental, Ltd., Riverside, 1985—; pres. B&B Ventures Ltd., Riverside, 1987—; dir. BP Holdings, Inc., Palm Springs, Calif., Bird Products Corp., Palm Springs, Bird Internat., Inc., Riverside, B&B Ventures, Inc., Riverside. Served with U.S. Army, 1969-71. Home: 3254 Pachappa Hill Riverside CA 92506 Office: Bird Products Corp 3101 E Alejo Rd Palm Springs CA 92263

KOOKEN, JOHN FREDERICK, bank holding company executive; b. Denver, Nov. 1, 1931; s. Duff A. and Frances C. K.; m. Emily Howe, Sept. 18, 1954; children: Diane, Carolyn. M.S., Stanford U., 1954, Ph.D., 1961. With Security Pacific Nat. Bank-Security Pacific Corp., Los Angeles, 1960—; exec. v.p. Security Pacific Corp., Los Angeles, 1981-87, chief fin. officer, 1984—, vice chmn., 1987—; bd. dirs. U.S. Facilities Corp.; lectr. Grad. Sch. Bus., U. So. Calif., 1962-67. Pres. bd. dirs. Children's Bur. Los Angeles, 1981-84; bd. dirs. United Way Los Angeles, 1982—, Huntington Meml. Hosp., Pasadena, 1985—. Served to lt. (j.g.) USNR, 1954-57. Mem. Fin. Execs. Inst. (pres. Los Angeles chpt. 1979-80, dir. 1981-84). Office: Security Pacific Corp 333 S Hope St Los Angeles CA 90071

KOONTZ, RICHARD HARVEY, financial printing company executive; b. Bedford, Pa., May 10, 1940; s. Ray S. and Rose (Imler) K.; m. Ann A. Mirche, Apr. 18, 1970; children: Carisa R., Clifton R. BS in Acctg., Pa. State U., 1962. CPA, N.Y.C. Acct. Ernst & Whinney, N.Y.C., 1962-73; corp. contr. Bowne & Co., Inc., N.Y.C., 1973-79; v.p. Bowne & Co., Inc., 1980-82, exec. v.p., chief operating officer, 1983-85, pres., chief operating officer, 1986-87, pres., chief exec. officer, 1988—. Home: 282 Gardner Rd Ridgewood NJ 07450 Office: Bowne & Co Inc 345 Hudson St New York NY 10014

KOOP, DAVID ANDREW, legal services executive; b. Fresno, Calif., Dec. 6, 1958; s. Thomas Abraham and Jenny (Hatch) K. Forest mgmt. technician Interstate Reforesters, Bend, Oreg., 1976-78; pres. High Desert Reforestation, Bend, 1978—; sales dir. We Care America, St. Louis, 1980-81; pres., chief exec. officer Nat. Legal Shield, Denver, 1981—; founder, pres. Diversified Admin Diversified Adminstrs., Inc., 1985—. Author: Everything You Wanted to Know About Selling Christmas Trees (But Didn't Know Who To Ask), 1979, Understanding Prepaid Legal Plans, 1986. Recipient award for outstanding support of minority bus. Calif. Package Liquor and Tavern Owners Assn., 1985. Mem. Am. Prepaid Legal Services (program and legis. coms. 1983—), Nat. Resource Ctr. for Consumers, Colo. Bar Assn.'s Continuing Legal Edn. Div. (faculty 1986). Avocations: sailboat racing, snow skiing, golf. Office: Nat Legal Shield 390 Union Blvd Ste 110 Lakewood CO 80228

KOOPERSMITH, JEFFREY MACARTHUR, fuels trading company executive, consultant; b. Chgo., Oct. 8, 1948; s. Theodore Benjamin and Sylvia (Reese) K.; m. Clare Bronowski, Dec. 29, 1979 (Jan. 1985); children: Theodore Benjamin II. BA, Calif. State U., Northridge, 1971; postgrad., Southwestern Sch. Law, 1971-75, U. So. Calif. V.p. CT Engring., Lawndale, Calif., 1978-81; pres. Eliott Curson Advt., Beverly Hills, Calif., 1981-84; cons. J.M. Koopersmith, Inc., N.Y.C., 1984—; chief exec. officer Mandarin Fuels, Inc., 1984—, Impetus Group, D.C.; pres., founder, Am. Legis. Cons. Assn., Los Angeles, 1978-80, bd. dirs.; guest lectr. Tokyo Waseda U., 1982. Author: The California Medfly Cookbook, 1982; pub. Radon Week; exec. producer documentary film On Any Street, 1981 (Cine Golden Eagle award 1982). Mem. policy com. Dem. Fin. and Bus. Councils, Washington, 1984; founder Dem. Nat. Com. Hdqrs., Washington, 1983. Clubs: University (Washington); L.A. Athletic (Los Angeles). Home: 145 W 58th St New York NY 10019 Office: JM Koopersmith 1377 K St NW Washington DC 20005

KOOPMANN PARRISH, RETA COLLENE, retail executive; b. Oklahoma City, Feb. 27, 1944; d. Henry William and Hazel (Rollins) Singleton; m. Fred Koopman, June 1, 1963 (div. 1974); 1 child, Rebecca Dawn; m. Walter J. Parrish, Jan 3, 1987. BS, Calif. Coast U., 1987, postgrad. in bus. adminstrn., 1987—. Front end mgr. Kroger Co., Cleve., 1969-72; with acctg. dept. Johns Manville, Denison, Tex., 1972-74; bakery/deli merchandiser Kroger Co., Columbia, S.C., 1974-83; v.p. bakery, deli Kash & Karry div. Lucky's Inc., Tampa, Fla., 1983-88; v.p. Kash & Karry Food Stores Inc., Tampa, 1988—, Ibo, bd. mem.; bd. trustees James Borck Deli-Bakery Ednl. Found., Inc., 1988. Authro tng. manuals, 1984, 86, 87. Vol. Spl. Olympics, Tampa, 1986, 87, 88. Mem. Internat. Deli/Bakery Assn. (exec. bd.), NAFE., Internat. Platform Assn. Republican. Mem. Ch. Christ. Lodge: Eagles. Home: 505 Rooks Rd Seffner FL 33584 Office: Kash & Karry Food Stores Inc 6422 Harney Rd Tampa FL 33810

KOPCYCH, ANTHONY, JR., electronics company executive; b. Bridgewater, Mass., June 12, 1971; s. Anthony and Bertha (Smith) K.; m. Shirley A. Lawton, June 12, 1971; children: Karissa, Anthony III. BSA, U. Hawaii, 1969. Mgr. mgmt. info. svcs. Ampex Corp., Redwood City, Calif., 1971-75; dir. mgmt. info. svcs. Nat. Semiconductor Co., Santa Clara, Calif., 1976-82, Veld Bind Inc., Sunnyvale, Calif., 1982-83, Altos Computer Systems, San Jose, Calif., 1984-88, Solitec Inc., San Jose, Calif., 1988—; founder, owner Valley Software, Cupertino, Calif., 1984—; bd. dirs. Replico Technologies Inc., San Jose. Author computer software. With USN, 1962-66. Republican. Home: 1028 Tuscany Pl Cupertino CA 95014 Office: Valley Software PO Box 710233 San Jose CA 95171

KOPPEL, AUDREY FEILER, electrologist, educator; b. N.Y.C., Sept. 25, 1944; d. Jules Eugene and Lee (Gibel) Feiler; m. Mark Alyn Koppel, May 28, 1967; children—Jason, Seth. B.A., Bklyn. Coll., 1972; diploma in electrolysis Hoffman Inst., 1975; postgrad. George Washington U., 1984, Essex Community Coll., 1984, Kree Inst., 1980. Electrologist, Bklyn., 1976, Glemby Internat., N.Y.C., 1976-78, Island Electrolysis, Manhasset, N.Y., 1982-84; registrar, supervising instr. Kree Inst., N.Y.C., 1978-82; pres. North Shore Electrolysis, Manhasset, 1982-84; dir., electrologist Bklyn. Studio, 1982—; pres. Ray Internat., 1986—. Editor, author pamphlet Glossary for Electrolysis, 1985; contbr. articles to profl. jours. Active Greater N.Y. council Boy Scouts Am., 1977-84; flag lt. Bklyn. Power Squadron. Mem. Am. Electrology Assn. (v.p. 1984—, edn. chmn. 1984—, continuing edn. coordinator 1985, chmn. pub. rels. com. 1989—), N.Y. Electrolysis Assn. (corr. sec. 1983-85, pres. 1985—), Internat. Guild of Electrologists (merit award 1978). Democrat. Jewish. Clubs: U.S. Power Squadron, Bklyn. Yacht. Avocations: boating; swimming; music. Office: Bklyn Studio of Electrolysis 2376 E 16th St Suite 1 Brooklyn NY 11229

KOPPELMAN, KIM ARDEN, advertising executive, public relations consultant; b. Breckenridge, Minn., Oct. 16, 1956; s. Ewald Fredrick and Renata Marie K.; m. Torey Antoinette Schuler, Sept. 16, 1978; children: Benjamin Kim, Rebekah Joy, Paul Andrew. Student, N.D. State Coll., Wahpeton, 1974-76. Dir. instrumental music North Sargent Pub. Schs., Gwinner, N.D., 1975; owner Koppelman Enterprises, Lidgerwood and West Fargo, N.D., 1973-79; mktg. field rep. U.S. C. of C., Washington, 1979-80; editor West Fargo Pioneer, 1980-81; account exec. G.L. Ness Advt. Agy., Fargo, 1981; dir. advt., mktg. and pub. relations Classic Roadsters, Ltd., Fargo, 1982-84; pres. Kim Koppelman & Assocs., Fargo, 1984—. Contbr. articles to profl jours.. Alderman Riverside City Council, 1982-86; Rep. precinct chmn. Riverside Dist. 13, 1988, del. N.D., Bismarck, 1988. Mem. Fargo-Moorhead Advt. Fedn. (bd. dirs. 1984-86, Addy award 1983, 84, 85), Fargo C. of C. (bd. dirs. 1982-85), Am. Advt. Fedn. (Addy award 1984), West Fargo Jaycees (numerous offices 1978-84), Fargo-Moorhead Christian Businessmen's Assn., Sigma Delta Chi. Republican. Mem. Evangelical Free Ch. Office: Kim Koppelman & Assocs 808 3d Ave S Ste 201 Fargo ND 58103

KOPPUS, BETTY JANE, retired savings and loan association executive; b. Toledo, June 14, 1922; d. Carl Emerson and Hilda Sarah (Semlow) K.; student pub. schs. With United Savs. and Loan Assn. (now United Home Fed.), Toledo, 1940—, asst. sec., 1943, treas., 1943-73, sec., 1973-78, v.p. 1978-84. Former trustee, sec. Lutheran Social Service Northwestern Ohio; mem. St. Mark's Luth. Ch. Mem. Toledo C. of C. (past treas., trustee), Toledo Area Govt. Research Assn. (past treas., dir.), Twin Mgmt. Forum, Beta Sigma Phi. Clubs: Zonta (Toledo I), Brandywine Country, River Road Garden. Address: 5709 Chardonnay Dr Toledo OH 43615

KORANDA, DAVID EDWARD, advertising executive; b. Fort Wayne, Ind., June 17, 1947; s. Leroy Fredrick and Jean Ester (Weil) K.; m. Laura Jo Golden, Mar. 18, 1978; 1 child, Julianne Yumiko. BA in Bus., Wilkes Coll., 1970; BS in Journalism, U. Oreg., 1978. Media buyer Jim Cox Advt., Eugene, Oreg., 1978-80; media dir. Advt. Svcs. Cappelli Miles & Wiltz, Eugene, 1980-84; media dir., pres. Koranda Communications, Eugene, 1984—; media dir., v.p. Baden & Co., Eugene, 1984—; vice-chmn. adv. bd. KLCC, Eugene, 1985-89, chair, 1989—; cons. Sta. KUGN Radio, Eugene, 1985—, U. Oreg. admissions, Eugene, 1985—. Pub. rels., bd. dirs. Boy Scouts Am. (Cub Scouts), Eugene, 1983; bd. dirs. Easter Seals, Eugene, 1983-84; adv. bd. YMCA, Eugene, 1984-85. Mem. Mid-Oreg. Ad Club (excellence award 1988). Democrat. Buddhist. Office: Baden & Co/ Koranda Communications 296 E Fifth NBU 9-4 Eugene OR 97401

KORB, KENNETH A., lawyer; b. Boston, Oct. 11, 1932; s. Allan and Mynue (Herbert) K.; m. Jaclyn C. Patricof, June 30, 1962; 1 son, Jason B. BA magna cum laude, Harvard Coll., 1953, JD cum laude, 1956. Bar: Mass. 1956. Law clk. Supreme Jud. Ct. Mass., 1956-57; assoc. Hutchins & Wheeler, Boston, 1957-60; assoc. Kargman & Kargman, Boston, 1960-63; sr. ptnr. Brown, Rudnick, Freed & Gesmer, Boston, 1963—; lectr. Mass. Continuing Legal Edn., 2d Nat. Coun. Savs. Instns.; sec., dir., gen. counsel Safety Ins.Co., 1980—; underwriting mem. Lloyd's of London, 1984—. Internat. pres. Soc. Israel Philatelists, 1974-76, bd. dirs. 1976-80; bd. dirs. Watergate East Condominium U.S.V.I., 1989—. Served with USAR, 1956-62. Mem. ABA, Mass. Bar Assn., Boston Bar Assn. Democrat. Contbr. articles to profl. jours. Home: 24 Helene Rd Waban MA 02168 Office: One Financial Pl Boston MA 02110

KORDICK, LEO MATHIAS, insurance agent; b. Winterset, Iowa, Feb. 4, 1934; s. Leo Joseph and Anna Cecilia (Schreiner) K.; m. Mary Janelle Finnegan, Oct. 20, 1956; children: Karen K., Loretta Ann, Dorothy E., Daniel E., Janelle M., Patricia L. Grad. high sch., Granger, Iowa. With parts control dept. Solar Aircraft Co., Des Moines, 1955-57; owner, operator Kordick Ins. Agy., West Des Moines, 1957—. Mem. Des Moines Astron. Soc., The Planetary Soc., Des Moines Choral Soc. Served with U.S. Army, 1953-55. Mem. The Planetary Soc., Izaak Walton League. Democrat. Roman Catholic. Home and Office: 1046 20th St West Des Moines IA 50265

KORDONS, ULDIS, lawyer; b. Riga, Latvia, July 9, 1941; came to U.S., 1949; s. Evalds and Zenta Alide (Apenits) K.; m. Virginia Lee Knowles, July 16, 1966. AB, Princeton U., 1963; JD, Georgetown U., 1970. Bar: N.Y. 1970, Ohio 1977. Assoc. Whitman & Ransom, N.Y.C., 1970-77, Anderson, Mori & Rabinowitz, Tokyo, 1973-75; counsel Armco Inc., Parsippany, N.J., 1977-84; v.p., gen. counsel, sec. Sybron Corp., Saddle Brook, N.J., 1984-88, Hillenbrand Industries, Batesville, Ind., 1989—; bd. dirs. Brinkmann Instruments Inc., Westbury, N.Y. Mem. nat. com. Boy Scouts Am., 1982—. Served to lt. USN, 1963-67, Vietnam. Mem. N.Y. Bar Assn., Ohio Bar Assn. Republican. Home: 13 Timberline Rd Ho Ho Kus NJ 07423 Office: Hillenbrand Industries Inc Batesville IN 47006-9166

KORFF, IRA A., lawyer; b. Boston, Aug. 30, 1949; s. Nathan and Helen (Pfeffer) K.; m. Shari E. Redstone, May 25, 1980; children: Kimberlee A., Brandon J., Tyler J. BJE, Hebrew Coll., 1968; BA, Columbia U., 1969; DD, Rabbinical Acad., 1971; JD, Bklyn. Law Sch., 1972; MA in Internat. Rels.,

Tufts U., 1973, MA in Law and Diplomacy, 1975, PhD in Internat. Law, 1976; grad. resident Divinity Sch., Harvard U., 1975; LLM, Boston U., 1980. Bar: Mass. 1974, U.S. Dist. Ct. Mass. 1975, U.S. Tax Ct. 1976, U.S. Ct. Appeals (1st cir.) 1976, U.S. Supreme Ct. 1978, D.C. 1980. Ptnr. Lewenberg & Korff, Boston, 1974—; spl. cons. to dist. atty. Norfolk County, Mass., 1975-85; spl. asst. to atty. gen. Commonwealth of Mass., Boston, 1977-85; mem. Rabbinical Ct. Justice, Boston, 1975—; hon. consul Austrian Consulate, Boston, 1987—; sr. v.p., bd. dirs. Viacom, Inc., N.Y.C., 1987—, Viacom, Internat., N.Y.C., 1987—; pres. Nat. Amusements Inc., Dedham, 1988—, pres., mng. dir. Nat. Amusements (UK) Ltd., Dedham, 1987—; bd. dirs. Council on Religion and Law, Boston, 1978-84. Mem. Friends of Fletcher Sch. Law and Diplomacy, Boston, 1974—, Boston Consumers Council, 1975-80. Mem. Internat. Bar Assn., ABA, Mass. Bar Ass., Boston Bar Assn., Internat. Law Assn., Am. Soc. for Internat. Law, Am. Arbitration Assn., Harvard U. Club (Boston and N.Y.), St. James Club (London). Office: Lewenberg & Korff 211 Congress St Boston MA 02110

KORMES, JOHN WINSTON, lawyer; b. N.Y.C., May 4, 1935; s. Mark and Joanna P. Kormes; m. Frances W. Kormes, Aug. 19, 1978; 1 child, Mark Vincent. B.A. in Econs., U. Mich., 1955, J.D., 1959. Bar: Pa. 1961, D.C. 1961, U.S. Sup. Ct. 1968. With License and Inspection Rev. Bd. Phila., 1972-73; asst. dist. atty. City of Phila., 1973-74, asst. city solicitor, 1974-80; pvt. practice, Phila., 1961—; moot ct. advisor. Mem. staff Re-Elect the Pres. Com., 1972, Rizzo for Mayor Com., 1971, 75, Phila. Flag Day Assn., 1965—. Served with USAF, 1956-57. Recipient N.Y. Intercoll. Legis. Assembly award, 1954; R.I. Model Congress award, 1954, Queens Coll. Speech Guild award. Fellow Lawyers in Mensa (charter), Internat. Soc. Philos. Enquiry (sr., pub. Best Telicom. 1986, 87); mem. Phila. Bar Assn., Phila. Trial Lawyers Assn., N.Y. State Trial Lawyers Assn., Am. Arbitration Assn., Fed. Bar Assn., Pitts. Inst. Legal Medicine, Assn. Trial Lawyers Am., Intertel, Internat. Platform Assn., Internat. Soc. Philos. Enquiry (legal officer 1986—, mgr. new mem. welcome program 1988—), Cincinnatus Soc., Delta Sigma Rho. Republican. Clubs: Masons, Shriners, KP, Lions. Home: 1070 Edison Ave Philadelphia PA 19116 Office: 2840 PSFS Bldg 12 S 12th St Philadelphia PA 19107

KORN, BARRY PAUL, equipment leasing company executive; b. N.Y.C., May 27, 1944; s. Nat and Judith (Safro) K.; m. Judith Ann Kron, Aug. 2, 1969; children: Lisa Michele, Suzanne Leslie, Amy Beth. BBA in Acctg., CCNY, 1966; MBA in Fin., CUNY, 1969. Assoc. E.M. Warburg, Pincus & Co., Inc., N.Y.C., 1964-70; treas., sec. Interstate Brands (formerly DPF Inc.), Hartsdale, N.Y., 1970-75; pres. Barrett Capital & Leasing Corp., Mamaroneck, N.Y., 1975—; bd. dirs. N.Y. area unit Better Bus. Bur., 1983-88. Mem. Supt. Schs. Adv. Council, White Plains, 1975-78. Mem. Am. Assn. Equipment Lessors (bd. dirs. 1974-77), Fin. Execs. Instr. (pres. Westchester chpt. 1976-77), Computer Dealers and Lessors Assn. (treas. 1971-72, bd. dirs. 1979-84, chmn. industry practices com. 1979-82, v.p. 1982-84), Mamaroneck C. of C. (bd. dirs., chmn. indsl. div.). Office: 930 Mamaroneck Ave Mamaroneck NY 10543

KORN, LAWRENCE, financial planning executive; b. Jersey City, Aug. 13, 1937; s. Harry and Helen (Feldman) K.; m. Ruth H. Tischler, June 11, 1960; children: Deborah L., Sharon L. BA, Rutgers U., 1959; JD, NYU, 1963. CLU; cert. fin. planner; admitted Registry Fin. Planning Practitioners. Dir. advanced underwriting and pensions Fidelity Mut. Life Ins. Co., Radnor, Pa., 1965-70; pres. Deferred Benefits Corp. and DB Asset Planning Corp., Springfield, N.J., 1970-87, Econ. Benefits Corp., Springfield, 1987-88, EB Adv. Corp., Springfield, N.J., 1987-88; v.p. Schechner, Lifson, Ackerman, Chodorcoff Inc., Milburn, N.J., 1988—. Mem. Internat. Assn. for Fin. Planning (bd. dirs. Cen. N.J. 1986—), Inst. Cert. Fin. Planners, Nat. Assn. Life Underwriters, Am. Soc. CLUs and Chartered Fin. Cons. Jewish. Office: Schechner Lifson Ackerman Chodorcoff Inc 225 Millburn Ave Ste 303 Millburn NJ 07041

KORN, LESTER BERNARD, business executive, ambassador; b. N.Y.C., Jan. 11, 1936. BS with honors, UCLA, 1959, MBA, 1960; postgrad., Harvard Bus. Sch., 1961. Mgmt. cons. Peat, Marwick, Mitchell & Co., Los Angeles, 1961-66, ptnr., 1966-69; pres., co-founder Korn/Ferry Internat., Los Angeles, 1969, chmn. bd., 1980; ambassador and U.S. rep. Econ. and Social Council UN, 1987-88; alt. rep. 42d UN Gen. Assembly, until 1988; chmn., chief exec. officer Korn/Ferry Internat., L.A., 1988—; bd. dirs. Continental Am. Properties, Leisure & Tech. Corp., Josephson Internat., Inc., Music Ctr. Operating Co., Curb Communications Inc., Musifilm Ltd. Bd. dirs. NCCJ; trustee UCLA Found., City of Hope Med. Center; bd. overseers Grad. Sch. Mgmt., UCLA; trustee, founding mem. Dean's Council UCLA; bd. govs. Cedars-Sinai Med. Center; bd. councilors Grad. and Undergrad. Schs. Bus. Adminstrn. and Sch. Bus., U. So. Calif.; spl. advisor, del. UNESCO Inter-gov. Conf. on Edn. for Internat. Understanding, Coop., Peace, 1983; adv. bd. Women in Film Found., 1983-84; chmn. Commn. on Citizen Participation in Govt., State of Calif., 1979-82; bd. dirs. John Douglas French Found. for Alzheimer's Disease; mem. Republican Nat. Exec. Fin. Com., 1985; mem. Pres.'s Commn. White House Fellowships; hon. chairperson 50th Am. Presdl. Inaugural, 1985; co-chmn. So. Calif. region NCCJ; trustee Acad. for Advancement Corp. Governance, Fordham U. Grad. Sch. Bus. Adminstrn. Recipient UCLA Alumni Profl. Achievement award, 1984. Mem. Am. Bus. Conf. (founding mem.), Am. Inst. CPA's, Calif. Soc. CPA's. Clubs: Hillcrest Country, Los Angeles Athletic, Regency (Calif.); Board Room (N.Y.C.). Office: 237 Park Ave New York NY 10017 also: Korn/Ferry Internat 1800 Century Pk E Ste 900 Los Angeles CA 90067

KORN, STEPHEN, lawyer; b. Vineland, N.J., Sept. 18, 1945; s. Harry P. and Etta (Deutchman) K.; m. Susan W. Relin, Nov. 22, 1969; children: Peter D., Brian D. BA, Brandeis U., 1967; MA, Columbia U., 1968; JD, Harvard U., 1974. Bar: Mass. 1974, U.S. Dist. Ct. Mass. Assoc. Widett, Slater & Goldman, Boston, 1974-80, ptnr., 1980-86; chmn. corp. dept. Widett, Slater & Goldnan, Boston, 1985-86; v.p., gen. counsel, sec. Symbolics Inc., Burlington, Mass., 1986—. With USPHS, 1969-71. Mem. Nat. Assn. Securities Dealers (bd. arbitrators), Am. Arbitration Assn. (panel of arbitrators), Am. Mgmt. Assn., Mass. Bar Assn., Boston Bar Assn., Phi Beta Kappa. Home: 259 Ward St Newton MA 02159 Office: Symbolics Inc 8 New England Executive Park Burlington MA 01803

KORNBLATT, DAVID WOLFE, real estate developer; b. Balt., June 30, 1927; m. Barbara Rudbell, Apr. 1, 1951; children: Rebecca, Sondra, Henry, Anne. BBA, U. Md., 1950. Pres. David Kornblatt Co., Balt., 1958—. Bd. dirs. Charles Street Mgmt., Balt., 1978-88. Served with USCG, 1945-46. Mem. Am. Soc. Real Estate Counselor (greater com. Balt. chpt.). Democrat. Office: David Kornblatt Co 25 S Charles St Baltimore MD 21201

KORNBLUTH, SANDRA JOAN, transportation company administrator; b. N.Y.C., Oct. 27, 1951; d. Louis and Rose (Rosansky) K. BA magna cum laude, Queens Coll., 1973; MA in Romance Langs., Princeton U., 1975. Instr. French lang. Princeton (N.J.) U., 1973-77; mgr. cargo tariffs Air France, N.Y.C., 1977-82; mgr. internat. pricing Emery Worldwide, Wilton, Conn., 1982-86, dir. pricing, 1986—; mem. adv. bd. Cargo Rate Services, Miami, Fla., 1984—. Bd. dirs. Literacy Vols. Greater Norwalk, 1987. Fullbright-Hayes scholar, 1973. Office: Emery Worldwide Old Danbury Rd Wilton CT 06896

KORNFELD, ALLAN A., manufacturing company executive; b. Bklyn., Sept. 19, 1937; s. Samuel and Shirley (Schiff) K.; m. Gail Kowit, Aug. 20, 1967; children: Leslie Sue, Sheryl Beth. BS in Econs., U. Pa., 1959; LLB, NYU, 1964. Bar N.Y. 1964; CPA. Ptnr. Arthur Young & Co., N.Y.C., 1960-75; from comptroller to sr. v.p., chief fin. officer Ametek, Inc., Paoli, Pa., 1975—; mem. replacement adv. com. to SEC, Washington, 1976-77. Served with USAF, 1959, 62. Mem. Am. Inst. CPA's (task force on LIFO acctg.), N.Y. State Soc. CPA's, ABA, Fin. Execs. Inst. (pres. Phila. chpt. 1986-87, com. on corp. reporting), Machinery and Allied Products Inst. (fin. coun. III), Beta Gamma Sigma, Beta Alpha Psi. Home: 5 Patterson Pl Newtown Square PA 19073 Office: Ametek Inc 2 Station Sq Paoli PA 19301

KORNSTEIN, EDWARD, manufacturing executive; b. N.Y.C., Sept. 7, 1929; s. Max and Margit (Stahl) K.; m. Marion Beatrice Stein, Dec. 20, 1958; children: Sandra P., Martin R. BA, NYU, 1951; MA, Drexel U., 1954; postgrad., Boston U., 1957-59. Optics engr. RCA, Camden, N.J., 1951-57; group leader optical physics RCA, Burlington, Mass., 1966-70; mgr. optical physics group RCA, Burlington, 1970-72; cons. physical research lab. Boston U., 1958-60; v.p. Optel Corp., Princeton, N.J., 1970-72; pres. Kortron Cons., Princeton, 1972-78; v.p. Object Recognition Systems, Inc., Princeton, 1978-87; pres. ORS Automation, Inc., Princeton, 1987—; cons. Holographix, Inc., Burlington, 1986—, Waltham/Elgin Watch Co., Chgo., 1973-80, Ricoh Watch Co., Nagoya, Japan, 1974-78, Cosmo, Tokyo, 1978-80. 3 patents in field; contbr. articles to profl. jours. Com. mem. Boy Scouts Am., West Windsor, N.J., 1973-85; mem. West Windsor Econ. Devel. com., 1972-78. Grantee Nat. Sci. Found., 1959. Mem. Optical Soc. Am. (travel grantee 1959), Soc. Info. Display, IEEE, Soc. Motion Picture and TV Engrs. (chmn. Boston area 1966-67), Princeton C. of C. Home: 10 Channing Way Cranbury NJ 08152 Office: ORS Automation Inc 402 Wall St Princeton NJ 08540

KORS, R. PAUL, executive search company executive; b. Pontiac, Mich., June 12, 1935; s. Ralph Dewey and Lydia Elizabeth (Shavlik) K.; m. Carol Jayne Kullick, July 17, 1966; children: Kristen Patricia, Shannon Elizabeth. BBA, U. Mich., 1958; MBA, U. So. Calif., 1965. Salesman Nalco Chem. Co., Los Angeles, 1958-56; investment mgr. Dean Witter & Co., Los Angeles, 1966-73; sr. assoc. Korn Ferry Internat., Los Angeles, 1973-74; v.p. Korn Ferry Internat., Houston, 1974-77, v.p., mgr., 1977-78; founder, pres., chief exec. officer Kors, Marlar, Savage & Assocs., Houston, 1978—. Served to 1st lt. U.S. Army, 1958. Mem. World Tech. Exec. Network (bd. dirs. 1985—). Republican. Clubs: Houston Racket, University. Home: 14306 Heatherfield Houston TX 77079 Office: Kors Marlar Savage & Assocs 1980 S Post Oak Blvd Houston TX 77056

KORSCHOT, BENJAMIN CALVIN, financial executive; b. LaFayette, Ind., Mar. 22, 1921; s. Benjamin G. and Myrtle P. (Goodman) K.; m. Marian Marie Schelle, Oct. 31, 1941; children—Barbara E. Korschot Haehlen, Lynne D. Korschot Gooding, John Calvin. B.S., Purdue U., 1942; M.B.A., U. Chgo., 1947. Vice pres. No. Trust Co., Chgo., 1947-64; sr. v.p. St. Louis Union Trust Co., 1964-73; exec. v.p. Waddell and Reed Co., Kansas City, Mo., 1973-74; pres. Waddell and Reed Co., 1974-79, vice-chmn. bd., 1979-85; pres. Waddell & Reed Investment Mgmt. Co., 1985-86; chmn. bd. Waddell & Reed Asset Mgmt. Co., 1973-86; pres. United Group of Mut. Funds, Inc., Kansas City, Mo., 1974-85, chmn., 1985-86 ; vice chmn. Roosevelt Fin. Group, St. Louis.1968—; chmn. bd. govs. Investment Co. Inst., 1980-82; chmn. bd. Fin. Analyst Fedn., 1978-79. Contbr. articles on investment fin. to profl. publs. Mem. Civic Council Greater Kansas City, Mo., 1974-85; chmn. fin. com. ARC Retirement System, 1986-87. Served with USN, 1942-45, 50-52. Mem. Inst. Chartered Fin. Analysts, Fin. Execs. Inst., Kansas City Soc. Fin. Analysts. Republican. Clubs: Kansas City, Indian Hills Country. Home: 101 Hackberry Lee's Summit MO 64063 Office: United Income Funds Inc PO Box 1343 Kansas City MO 64141

KORT, ERNEST GEORGE, mechanical engineer; b. Marmarath, N.D., Nov. 13, 1910; s. Adolph George and Jessie Johnstone (Milne) K.; B.S. in Elec. Engring., Northwestern U., 1932; 1 child, Carol K. West. Chief engr. mfg. products div. Alcoa, New Kensington, Pa., 1942-52, asst. works mgr. cooking utensils div., 1952-58, works mgr., New Kensington Works, 1958-67, div. mgr. joining div. Alcoa Labs., Alcoa Center, Pa., 1967-74, ret., 1974; consulting engr., Conneaut Lake, Pa., 1975—. Registered profl. engr., Pa. Mem. SBA Service Core of Retired Execs.; citizen ambass. People to People program; mem. nat. panel consumer arbitrators Better Bus. Bur. Mem. ASME, Soc. Mfg. Engrs. (life cert. mfg. engr.), Internat. Exec. Service Corps, Sigma Xi, Pi Kappa Alpha. Republican. Presbyterian. Clubs: Iroquois (Conneaut Lake); Taylor Hose (Meadville, Pa.). Home and Office: RD 1 Box 136 Conneaut Lake PA 16316-8919

KORTEN, THEODORE FREDERICK (TED), retail executive; b. Chgo., Apr. 9, 1910; s. Charles A. and Lydia B. (Boehl) K.; student Wash. State U., 1928-29; m. Margaret R. Heltzel, June 20, 1934; children—David Craig, Robert Philip. With Kortens, Inc., Longview, Wash., 1927—, chmn. bd., chief exec. officer, 1978—; v.p., dir. First Fed. Savs. and Loan of Longview, 1962-81, dir. emeritus, 1981—; pres., dir., Longview Meml. Park, 1971-85; v.p., dir. Cascade Music Co., Portland, Oreg., 1962—; dir. Brudi Equipment Co., Kelso, Wash., Wayron Corp., Longview, Air Sensors Inc., Seattle, Bodyscan Corp., Seattle. Pres., ARC, Longview, 1950-51; bd. dirs. Monticel Med. Center, 1967-78; mem. Wash. Retail Council, 1960—, pres., 1970-72; active Boy Scouts Am., 1944-45. Mem. Longview C. of C. (pres. 1953), Nat. Assn. Music Mchts. (dir. 1948-63, pres. 1961-63), Am. Music Conf. (pres. 1970-72), Assn. Wash. Bus. (dir. 1962-86), Nat. Assn. Retail Dealers, Phi Mu Alpha (life). Republican. Methodist. Clubs: Kiwanis (pres. 1942, lt. gov. 1946), Longview Country, Elks. Home: 2327 Cascade Way Longview WA 98632 Office: 1400 Commerce Ave Longview WA 98632

KOSCHINSKA, GREGORY DON, accountant; b. Mpls., Nov. 1, 1945; s. Don W. and Harriet (Hennen) K.; m. Coralyn Jane Roy, June 22, 1968; children: Sarah Ann, Emily Jane, Timothy Greg. BS in Bus. Acctg., U. Minn., 1967. CPA. Account supr. Ernst & Whinney, Mpls., 1967-71; controller Target Stores, Mpls., 1971-73; founding ptr. Hansen, Koschinska & Co., Mpls., 1973-81; ptnr. in charge adminstrn. Larson, Allen, Weishair & Co., Mpls., 1981-87, ptnr. in charge of Mpls. office, 1987—. Pres. Episc. Community Service, Mpls.; tres., bd. dirs. Eden Prairie Rotary, Minn., 1982-83; sr. warden St. Alban's Episc. Ch., Edina, Minn., 1983-85. Recipient Appreciation award Bloomington C. of C., 1980. Mem. Am. Inst. CPAs, Minn. Soc. CPAs (chmn. 1983-84, named outstanding, 1983-84), Mpls. Athletic Club, Flagship Athletic Club. Home: 11093 Branching Horn Eden Prairie MN 55437 Office: Larson Allen Weishair & Co 920 Second Ave S Suite 650 Minneapolis MN 55402

KOSHEFF, MARTIN JOEL, financial executive, consultant; b. Queens, N.Y., Feb. 17, 1938; s. Nathan and Lilyan (Morgan) K.; student MIT, 1954-55; BS, U. Pa., 1958; m. Janet Livingstone Haley, June 14, 1958; children: Jonathan, Andrew, Elizabeth, Charles. Staff. cons. Scovell, Wellington & Co., Boston, 1958-61; financial v.p. Adv. Devel. Labs., Nashua, N.H., 1961-65; exec. v.p., dir. Sanders Assocs., Inc., Nashua; pres. Calif. Computer Products, Inc., Anaheim, 1980-84; sr. v.p. Sci. Applications Internat. Corp., La Jolla, Calif., 1984-87; exec. v.p. M/A-COM, Inc., Burlington, Mass., 1987-89; pres. M.J. Kosheff Assocs., Charlestown, Mass., 1989—. Mem. Fin. Execs. Inst., Am. Inst. CPAs, Mass. Soc. CPAs.

KOSKELLA, WILFRED IRVING, retired industrial engineer; b. Republic, Mich., May 1, 1909; s. Jacob and Mary Sofia (Antilla) K.; m. Elsie Ovedia Best, June 9, 1932; children: Wilfred J., Karyn E., Don A. Student, Mich. Coll. Mines, Houghton. Engring. draftsman Ford Motor Corp., Iron Mt., Mich., 1927-37; structural engr. H.E. Byster Corp., Detroit, 1937-41; v.p., dir. foundry engring. Giffes Assocs., Inc., Detroit, 1941-75, ret., 1975; lectr. in field. Contbr. articles to profl. jours. Mem. Foundry Equipment Mfrs. Assn. (bd. dirs. 1968-70), Western Golf and Country Club, Masons. Home: 301 E Brook Hollow Dr Phoenix AZ 85022

KOSKINAS, STEPHAN ARISTOTLE, manufacturing company executive; b. Teaneck, N.J., Jan. 23, 1946; s. Thomas and Mary (Dervos) K.; m. Francine C. Grimaldi, Nov. 24, 1973; children: Gregory, Caroline. BA, Rutgers U., 1968; MBA, Columbia U., 1970. Internat. banker Irving Trust Co., N.Y.C., 1970-71; internat. treas. Wheelabrator-Frye Inc., Hampton, N.H., 1972-79; chief fin. officer, sr. v.p. Schlegel Corp., Rochester, N.Y., 1980—; bd. dirs. Marine Midland Bank, Rochester, Genesee Valley Arts Found., Inc., 1988—. Mem. Nat. Assn. Corp. Treas., Assn. Corp. Growth, Fin. Execs. Inst. Clubs: Genesee, University (Rochester); Hunt Hollow (Naples, N.Y.) (bd. dirs. 1987—). Home: 30 Trevor Ct Rd Rochester NY 14610 Office: Schlegel Corp 400 East Ave PO Box 23113 Rochester NY 14692

KOSKINEN, JOHN ANDREW, asset management executive; b. Cleve., June 30, 1939; s. Yrjo Alfred and Irja (Danska) K.; m. Patricia Salz, June 15, 1963; children: Jeffrey, Cheryl. BA magna cum laude, Duke U., 1961; JD cum laud, Yale U., 1964; postgrad., Cambridge U., Eng., 1964-65. Bar: Calif., Conn. Clk. to presiding justice U.S. Ct. Appeals, Washington, 1965-66; lawyer Gibson, Dunn & Crutcher, Los Angeles, 1966-67; spl. asst. to dep. exec. dir. Nat. Adv. Commn. Civil Disorders (also called Kerner Commn.), Washington, 1967-68; legis. asst. to Mayor John Lindsay N.Y.C., 1968-69; adminstrv. aast. to Senator Abraham Ribicoff Conn., 1969-73; v.p. Palmieri Co., Washington, 1973-77, pres., chief operating officer, 1977-79, pres., chief exec. officer, 1979—. Mem. Pres.'s Mgmt. Improvement Council, 1979-80; mem. bd. dirs. Nat. Captioning Inst., 1979—, chmn. 1986-87; vice chmn. 1979-86; trustee Coop. Assistance Fund, 1982—, Duke U., 1985—; vice chmn. Am. Soccer League, 1987—. Mem. Duke U. Gen. Alumni Assn. (pres. 1980-81), Pension Real Estate Assn. (bd. dirs. 1983-86), Phi Beta Kappa. Office: The Palmieri Co 2000 L St NW Ste 407 Washington DC 20036

KOSTAS, EVANS, manufacturing executive; b. Chgo., Jan. 13, 1935; s. James Christopher and Christina (Tavoulare) K.; m. Janet Leah Fontana, Apr. 7, 1962; children: Lauren, Ellen, James, Karen, John, Andrew. BS in Engring., Ill. Inst. Tech., 1970; MBA, U. Chgo., 1974. With Rockwell Internat., Chgo., 1953-75; sr. engring. exec. Rockwell Internat., Pitts., 1975-79; v.p. tech. Nordson Corp., Amhest, Ohio, 1979-84; also chief exec. officer, pres. Pubs. Equipment Corp., Dallas, 1984—, chmn. bd. dirs.; bd. dirs. King Press, Joplin, Mo., Tex. Wet Inc., Dallas, Dunwell Corp., Rockford, Ill. Inventor in field. Mem. vis. com. Case Inst Tech., Cleve., 1981, bd. overseers Case Western Reserve U., Cleve., 1982. Served as sgt. U.S. Army, 1956-58. Mem. Am. Mgmt. Assn., Indsl. Research Inst. Greek Orthodox. Home: 5821 Watertree Ln Plano TX 75093 Office: Pub Equipment Corp 16660 Dallas Pkwy Dallas TX 75248

KOSTECKE, B. WILLIAM, utilities executive; b. Caro, Mich., Aug. 1, 1925; s. Steve and Stella (Telewiek) K.; m. Lo Rayne M. Smith, Mar. 25, 1950; children: Diane, Keith. B.S., U.S. Mcht. Marine Acad., 1947, Mich. State U., 1951. Controller Miller Brewing Co., Milw., 1963-66, treas., chief financial officer, 1966-70, pres., 1970-72; v.p., treas., dir. Wis. Gas Co., Milw., 1972-88; v.p., treas., sec., dir. WICOR, Inc., Milw., 1972-88. Gen. chmn. Milw. Nat. Alliance Businessmen, 1972; bd. dirs. Milw. County Coun. Boy Scouts Am., Wis. Coun. on Econ. Edn. Recipient Dean Mellencamp award U. Wis., Milw., 1967, Outstanding Profl. Achievement award Kings Point Alumni Assn., 1972. Mem. Financial Execs. Inst. Clubs: Blue Mound Golf and Country; University (Milw.). Home: 10708 N Fairway Circle Mequon WI 53092 Office: Wicor Inc 777 E Wisconsin Ave Milwaukee WI 53201

KOSTOULAS, IOANNIS GEORGIOU, physicist; b. Petra, Pierias, Greece, Sept. 12, 1936; came to U.S., 1965, naturalized, 1984; s. Georgios Ioannou and Panagiota (Zarogiannis) K.; m. Katina Sioras Kay, June 23, 1979; 1 child, Alexandra. Diploma in Physics U. Thessoloniki, Greece, 1963; MA, U. Rochester, 1969, PhD, 1972; MS, U. Ala., 1977, Instr. U. Thessaloniki, 1963-65; teaching asst. U. Ala., 1966-67, U. Rochester, 1967-68; guest jr. research assoc. Brookhaven Nat. Lab., Upton, N.Y., 1968-72; research physicist, lectr. UCLA, U. Calif.-San Diego, 1972-76; sr. research assoc. Mich. State U., East Lansing, 1976-78, Fermi Nat. Accelerator Lab., Betavia, Ill., 1976-78; research staff mem. MIT, Cambridge, 1978-80; sr. system engr., physicist Hughes Aircraft Co., El Segundo, Calif., 1980-86; sr. physicist electro-optics and space sensors Rockwell Internat. Corp., Downey, Calif., 1986—. Contbr. articles to profl. jours. Served with Greek Army, 1961-63. Research grantee U. Rochester, 1968-72. Mem. Am. Phys. Soc., Los Alamos Sci. Lab. Exptl. Users Group, Fermi Nat. Accelerator Lab. Users Group, High Energy Discussion Group of Brookhaven Nat. Lab., Pan Macedonian Assn., Save Cyprus Council Los Angeles, Sigma Pi Sigma. Club: Hellenic U. Lodge: Ahepa. Home: 2404 Marshall Field Ln #B Redondo Beach CA 90278 Office: Rockwell Internat Co MC EA20 Space Transp System Div 12214 Lakewood Blvd Downey CA 90241

KOSTREWSKI, GARY STEVEN, real estate developer; b. Aug. 30, 1954; s. Michael Francis and Mabel Louise (Darde) K.; m. Catharine J. King, May 22, 1980 (div. Aug. 1987). Student, Suffolk Community Coll., 1973-74. Gen. mgr. Windowrama Corp., Deer Park, N.Y., 1975-78; owner Westbridge Constrn., Rocky Point, N.Y., 1978-82; project mgr. Route 347 Realty Corp., Port Jefferson, N.Y., 1982-85; project dir. Lizda Realty Ltd., Southold, N.Y., 1985—; dir. Founders Village Homeowners Assn., Southold, N.Y., 1985—, Founders Village Condominiums, Southold, N.Y., 1985—. Mem. Const. Specifications Inst., Nat. Assn. Home Builders, Greenport C. of C., Peconic Lodge (past master, past officer Sithra chpt.). Republican. Episcopalian. Home: 6 Oyster Point Box 348 Greenport NY 11944 Office: 2555 Youngs Ave Southold NY 11971

KOTCHER, SHIRLEY J. W., lawyer; b. Bklyn.; d. Irving and Violet (Miller) Weinberg; m. Harry A. Kotcher; children: Leslie Susan, Dana Anne. BA, NYU; JD, Columbia U. Bar: N.Y. In-house counsel Booth Meml. Med. Ctr., Flushing, N.Y., 1975-83, gen. counsel, 1983—; advisor health care Borough Pres. Queens, N.Y., 1978. Author: Hidden Gold and Pitfalls in New Tax Law, 1970. Mem. ABA (health law forum com.), Nat. Health Lawyers Assn., Am. Acad. Hosp. Attys., Nassau County Bar Assn., Am. Soc. Law and Medicine, Am. Soc. Health Care Risk Mgmt., Assn. for Hosp. Risk Mgmt. N.Y., Greater N.Y. Hosp. Assn. (legal adv. com. 1976—). Office: Booth Meml Med Ctr Main St Flushing NY 11355

KOTEN, JOHN ALFRED, communications executive; b. Indpls., May 21, 1929; s. Roy Y. and Margaret (Neerman) K.; m. Catherine M. Hruska, Nov. 22, 1952; children: John, Mark, Sarah. BA, North Cen. Coll., Naperville, Ill., 1951; postgrad., Northwestern U., 1953. Supr. field advt. Montgomery Ward, Chgo., 1951-52; asst. dir. pub. relations Am. Osteo. Assn., Chgo., 1952-53; editorial asst. Ill. Bell Telephone Co., Chgo., 1955-56, editor Telebriefs newsletter, 1956-57, supr. info., 1957-59, supr. comml. staff, 1959-60; supr. news service and advt. Ill. Bell Telephone Co., Springfield, 1960-62, dist. comml. mgr., 1962-63; supr. pub. info. AT&T, N.Y.C., 1963, supr. customer relations, 1963-64, supr. film project and planning, 1964-65; mgr. div. traffic Ill. Bell Telephone Co., Chgo., 1965-66, mgr. pub. relations, 1966-68, asst. v.p. civic affairs, 1968-69, asst. v.p. Chgo. ops., 1969-70; gen. mgr. upstate area Ill. Bell Telephone Co., Joliet, 1970-71; dir. state regulatory matters AT&T, Lisle, Ill., 1971-72; asst. v.p. pub. relations Ill. Bell Telephone Co., Joliet, 1972-74; dir. pub. relations AT&T, N.Y.C., 1974-75; v.p. pub. relations N.J. Bell Telephone Co., Newark, 1975-77; v.p. pub. relations Ill. Bell Telephone Co., Chgo., 1977-80, v.p. corp. communications, 1980-87; sr. v.p. corp. communications Ameritech Corp., Chgo., 1987—; mem. bd. vis. Northwestern U. Medill Sch. Jour., 1988—. Trustee Chgo. Symphony Orch., 1985—, Joint Coun. on Econ. Edn., N.Y.C., 1987—; pres. Arthur W. Page Soc., 1985-87, Ameritech Found., Chgo., 1987—; vice chmn. Ill. Arts Alliance, Chgo., 1986—; bd. dirs. Am. Symphony Orch. League, Washington, 1982—, Am. Arts Alliance, Washington, 1983—; v.p. Associated Colls. Ill., Chgo., 1986—; assoc. trustee Wordsworth Trust, England, 1988; mem. svcs. industry coun. U.S. C. of C., 1987; corp. coun. Bus. Com. for the Arts, 1988. Served with U.S. Army, 1953-55. Mem. Pub. Relations Soc. Am., Nat. Assn. Mfrs. Pub. Relations Council, Chgo. Advt. Club (bd. dirs. 1978-82), Pub. Affairs Council, Assn. Governing Bds. Univs. and Colls., Brookings Council, Ameritech Found. (pres. Chgo. 1987—). Clubs: Chgo., Tavern, Econ. (Chgo.), Chgo. Advt. (bd. dirs. 1978-82). Home: 271 Otis Rd Barrington Hills IL 60010 Office: Ameritech Corp 30 S Wacker Dr Chicago IL 60606

KOTHARI, BIJAY SINGH, accountant; b. Sept. 2, 1928; m. Smt. Puspa, Feb. 16, 1951; 1 child, Amitav. B in Commerce, Calcutta (India) U., 1948, MA, 1951. Chartered acct., India. Sr. ptnr. Kothari & Co., Chartered Accts., Calcutta and Bombay, 1951—; lectr. internat. confs.. Author numerous pamphlets and booklets on acctg.; mem. editorial bd. Chartered Accts. and Fin. and Commerce; contbr. articles to profl. jours. Justice of Peace, India; port commr. West Bengal (India) adv. com.; mem. Telephone adv. com., Calcutta Electric Supply consultative com.; trustee Kothari Lok Kalyan Trust. Mem. Inst. Chartered Accts. (cen. council, 1967-71), Consumer's Assn. (pres.), Assn. Co. Secs., Execs. and Advisers Calcutta (pres. 1967-68), Merchants C. of C. (pres. 1968-70, trustee). Clubs: Calcutta, India Internat. Ctr., New Delhi, Bengal Rowing, All Nations, Sangit Kala Mandir. Lodge: Lions (pres. Calcutta chpt. 1968-69, life). Address: 8-E Neelkanth Apts 26-B, Camac St, Calcutta 700016, India

KOTKINS, HENRY LOUIS, JR., luggage company executive; b. Seattle, Sept. 11, 1948; s. Henry L. and Marion F. (Friedman) K.; m. Jacqueline A. Levin, Nov. 20, 1976; children: Katherine M., Joseph H. AB in Am. Civilization, Williams Coll., 1970; MBA, Harvard U., 1972. Dir. planning Skyway Luggage Co., Seattle, 1971-74, v.p., 1974-80, pres., 1980—; mem. dist. export council U.S. Dept. Commerce, Seattle, 1984-85; bd. dirs. Security

Pacific Bank Wash., Seattle, Security Pacific Northwest Bancorp. Patentee in field. Pres. Seattle Repertory Theater, 1986-88, chmn., 1988—; bd. dirs., v.p. Big Bros. of Seattle/King County, 1976-82; bd. dirs. Ctr. for Retail and Distbn. Mgmt., U. Wash. Sch. Bus., Seattle, 1986—. 1st lt. USNG, 1970-76. Named to 100 Newsmakers of Tomorrow, Time mag., 1978. Mem. Luggage and Leathergoods Mfrs. Am. (bd. dirs. 1979-82, 84-86), Harvard Bus. Sch. Assn., Seattle C. of C. (bd. dirs. 1981-84). Office: Skyway Luggage Co 10 Wall St Seattle WA 98121

KOTLER, STEVEN, investment banker; b. N.Y.C., Jan. 9, 1947; s. Louis and Etta (Smeltzer) K.; B.B.A., CCNY, 1967; m. Carolyn Miller, Sept. 26, 1973; children—William, Thomas. Vice pres. N.Y. Hanseatic Corp., N.Y.C., 1967-74; with Wertheim Schroder & Co. Inc., N.Y.C., 1974—, gen. partner, 1979—, mng. dir., 1981—, pres. 1987—; chmn. exec. com., dir. Moore Med. Corp., Oak Hill Sportswear, Inc., Del Labs., Inc. Served with USAR, 1967-72.

KOTTKE, FREDERICK EDWARD, economics educator; b. Menominee, Mich., Sept. 6, 1926; s. Edward Frederick and M. Marie (Braun) K.; B.S., Pepperdine U., 1950; postgrad. U. Wis., 1950-52; M.A., U. So. Calif., 1957, Ph.D., 1960; m. Lillian Dorathy Larson, Aug. 27, 1950; children—Karin Lee, Kurt Edward. Lectr., Pepperdine U., 1952-53; asst. prof. U. So. Calif., 1956-63; assoc. prof. econs., chmn. dept., speaker of gen. faculty Stanislaus State Coll., Turlock, Calif., 1963-68, prof., also chmn. div. arts and scis., 1968—; pres. KK Economic Consultants, Inc.; independent tax adviser, managerial adviser, 1960—. Chmn., Stanislaus County United Crusade, 1964-65; pres., Stanislaus State Coll. Found., 1972; trustee Emanuel Med. Center, 1974—; v.p. Good Shepherd Lutheran Ch. Served with USNR. 1943-46. Recipient Pologrammatic award Pepperdine Coll., 1952, Outstanding Prof. award Calif. State U., Stanislaus, 1987-88. Haynes Found. Postgrad. Research award U. So. Calif., 1959. Mem. Am., Western econ. assns., Nat. Tax Assn., Am. Finance Assn., C. of C., Omicron Delta Epsilon. Lodge: Kiwanis. Author: An Economic Analysis of Toll-Highway Finance, 1956, An Economic Analysis of Financing an Interstate Highway System, 1959. Home: 1890 N Denair Ave Turlock CA 95380 Office: Calif State Coll Stanislaus 801 W Monte Vista Ave Turlock CA 95380

KOURAKOS, TINA, financial service company executive; b. Phila., May 7, 1955; d. Paschal James and Mary (Petrillo) Centrella; m. Stanley Christie Kourakos, Nov. 15, 1955; children: Alexander John, Kimberly Lynn. BSBA, Pa. State U., 1977; MBA, St. Joseph's U., 1988. Asst. contract adminstr. Betz Environ. Engrs., Plymouth Meeting, Pa., 1978-80; sr. fin. analyst Formation, Inc., Mt. Laurel, N.J., 1980-83; asst. dir. CIGNA Corp., Phila., 1983—. Home: 435 Leah Dr Fort Washington PA 19034 Office: CIGNA Corp 1600 Arch St Ste 10T Philadelphia PA 19103

KOURIS, PAUL ANDREW, lawyer, accountant; b. Chgo., Mar. 24, 1949; s. Paul Kouris and Mary Brown. AA, Wright City Coll., 1968; BS, U. Ill., 1970, MS, 1972; JD, Ill. Inst. Tech., 1975. CPA. Trial atty. SEC, Chgo., 1975-77; atty. Nat. Assn. Securities Dealers, Los Angeles, 1978-79; sr. atty. Beckman Instrument, Inc., Fullerton, Calif., 1979-86; v.p., gen. counsel Sci. Applications Internat. Corp., San Diego, 1986—. Bd. dirs. Leukemia Soc. Am., Orange County, Calif., 1984-86. Mem. San Diego Bar Assn. Office: Sci Applications Internat Corp 10260 Campus Point Dr San Diego CA 92121

KOUTROS, STEPHEN ANTHONY, business executive, computer consultant; b. Rockville Center, N.Y., Oct. 25, 1955; s. Anthony Sarandos and Anna Mae (Mylonas) K.; m. Ingrid Adriana Maria Kuijpers, Aug. 11, 1983. BA in Polit. Sci., Emory U., 1977; MBA in Acctg., St. John's U., Jamaica, N.Y., 1981. With Mobil Oil Corp., N.Y.C., 1978-81; planning analyst Mobil Overseas Service, London and The Netherlands, 1981-83; sr. cons. acct. Mobil Oil Corp., Houston, 1983-85; pres. The TAFT Co., New Rochelle, N.Y., 1985—. Sponsor Nat. Rep. Com., N.Y., 1978-86. Named Man of Yr., YMCA, 1981. Mem. Nat. Assn. Accts. (bd. dirs. 1986—), Data Processing Mgmt. Assn., Computer Cons. Assn., Westchester C. of C. (bd. dirs. 1985—), Alpha Epsilon Pi. Greek Orthodox. Home: 485 Pelham Rd Apt B-29 New Rochelle NY 10805 Office: The Taft Co 640 Pelham Rd Ste 5D New Rochelle NY 10805

KOUYOUMJIAN, CHARLES H., financial services, investment company executive; b. Cambridge, Mass., Nov. 20, 1940; s. Housep J. and Victoria M. (Madenjian) K.; B.S. in Bus. Adminstrn., Boston U., 1963; postgrad. Boston Coll., 1969-71; m. Karen L. Dennison, June 19, 1965; children—Joseph, Charles. Dir. purchasing Allis Chalmers Mfg. Co., Boston, 1968; investment broker Hornblower & Weeks Hemphill Noyes Inc., Boston, 1969-71, v.p., resident mgr., Springfield, Mass., 1971-76, regional hdqrs., Boston, 1976-77; v.p., resident mgr. Paine Webber, Inc., Boston, 1977-79, regional sales mgr. Fla. div., 1980-81, dir. Asset Mgmt. Group, nat. hdqrs., N.Y.C., 1982-83, v.p. spl. accounts dept. Boston, 1983-85; pres., chief exec. officer, Empire Nat. Securities, Buffalo, 1985-88, Charles Assocs., 1988—. Mem. camp com. Springfield YMCA, 1973-76; bd. dirs. Health Care Found. Western Mass., 1973-74. Served to capt. USAF, 1963-67. Mem. Boston Options Soc. (chmn.), Springfield C. of C. (dir. 1973-75), Nat. Assn. Securities Dealers (mem. quotation com. 1975-76), Boston Fin. Research Assos., Boston Investment Club, Boston Stockbrokers Club, Securities Industry Assn., Newcomen Soc. U.S. and Gt. Britain, Internat. Assn. Fin. Planning. Clubs: Bond of Boston, Bond of Buffalo. Home: 16 Greenridge Rd Weston MA 02193 Office: Charles Assocs 30 Clematis Ave Waltham MA 02154

KOVACH, ANDREW LOUIS, marketing executive; b. Greensboro, Pa., Feb. 4, 1948; s. Andrew and Pauline (Nassar) K.; m. Cindy Juliani, Nov. 28, 1970; 1 child: Courtney. BS in Indsl. Engineering, W.Va. U., 1969. Engr. DuPont, Marinsville, Va., 1970-73; supt. engr. Allied Corp., Syracuse, N.Y., 1973-75; mgr. employee relations Allied Corp., Morristown, N.J., 1976-80, mgr. orgnl. devel., 1980; dir. human resources Allied Corp., N.Y.C., 1981-82, dir. comml. devel., 1983-87; ptnr. Thomas Andrew Assoc., Morristown, N.J., 1987—; v.p. human resources Morristown Meml. Hosp., 1988—. Mem. Indsl. Engring. Adv. Orgn., Morristown Club. Presbyterian. Office: Morristown Meml Hosp 100 Madison Ave Ste C Morristown NJ 07960

KOVACH, WILLIAM DAVID, accountant, utility company executive; b. Youngstown, Ohio, July 17, 1952; s. Joseph and Virginia (Gayetsky) K.; m. Sheryl Lynn Rish; children: Amy Catherine, Matthew Aaron, Megan Elizabeth. BBA, U. Cin., 1974. CPA, Tex., Mich., Ohio. Auditor Coopers & Lybrand, Dayton, Ohio, 1974-76; controller The Luth. Retirement Ctr., Ann Arbor, Mich., 1976-77; audit mgr. Earl's Taylor & Co. CPA's, Ann Arbor, 1977-78; auditor Gen. Motors Corp., Ypsilanti, Mich., 1978-80; auditor Houston Lighting and Power Co., 1980, controller STP, 1981-87, dir. nuclear acctg., 1987-88, mgr. nuclear acctg. and fin., 1988—. Mem. AICPA, Tex. Soc. CPAs, Am. Nuclear Soc. Republican. Methodist. Home: 814 Donald El Campo TX 77437 Office: Houston Lighting & Power Co PO Box 547 Wadsworth TX 77483

KOVACIK, NEAL STEPHEN, hotel and restaurant executive; b. Toledo, Mar. 2, 1952; s. Albert Joseph and Phyllis (Lesinski) K.; m. Denise Reichert, Apr. 20, 1974 (div. June 1976). Student, Bowling Green State U., 1971-72, U. Toledo, 1973-74, Owens Tech. Coll., 1975. Dir. food and beverages Motor Inn of Perrysburg, Ohio, 1976-78; v.p. food and beverage ops. Bennett Enterprises, Perrysburg, 1978-82, v.p. hotel and restaurant ops., 1982—. Recipient Food and Beverage Dir. of Yr. award Holiday Inns. Inc. and Internat. Assn. Holiday Inns, 1976. Mem. Northwestern Ohio Restaurant Assn. (bd. dirs. 1980-84), Toledo Hotel and Motel Assn. Democrat. Roman Catholic. Home: 9640 Monclova Rd Monclova OH 43542 Office: Bennett Enterprises Corp 27476 Holiday Ln Perrysburg OH 43551

KOVACS, CHARLES JOSEPH LESLIE THOMAS, bank executive; b. Budapest, Hungary, July 11, 1945; s. Joseph Charles and Eva Evelyne (Neuman) K.; m. Catherine Irene Francoise Negrerie, July 16, 1973; one daughter. BA, Clark U., 1969; MA, Fletcher Sch. Law and Diplomacy, 1970; MA in Law and Diplomacy, Fletcher Sch. Diplomacy, 1971. Various lending & credit assignments Chase Manhattan Bank, Singapore, Beirut, Athens and London, 1973-81; mgr. strategic projects middle east area Chase Manhattan Bank, London, 1982-83; mgr. internat. fin. programs Chase Manhattan Bank, N.Y.C., 1987—; chmn. task force LDC Debt & Investment, U.S. Coun. Internat. Bus., 1988. Author: The Competitive Challenges Facing US Banks, 1987. Bd. dirs. The Netherlands-Am. Amity Trust, 1988—. Staff sgt. U.S. Army, 1965-68. Mem. Royal United Services Inst. (assoc.), U.S. Naval Inst. (assoc.), Navy League. Office: Chase Manhattan Bank One Chase Manhattan Pla 16th Fl New York NY 10081

KOVACS, ELIZABETH ANN, public relations executive, professional society administrator; b. N.Y.C., July 25, 1944; d. Henry Philipp and Toni (Selby) Leitner; children: Tobin Philipp, Kathryn Ena Michel. B.A., Conn. Coll., 1965; M.A.T., Yale U., 1967. Cert. assn. exec. Exec. dir. Assn. for Advancement of Behavior Therapy, N.Y.C., 1971-80, Soc. Behavioral Medicine, N.Y.C., 1978-80; exec. v.p. Pub. Relations Soc. Am., N.Y.C., 1980—; tchr. assn. mgmt. Fellow Am. Soc. Assn. Execs. (evaluation com.); mem. N.Y. Soc. Assn. Execs., Found. Am. Soc. Assn. Execs. (bd. dirs.), Melodious Accord (bd. dirs.). Home: 201 W 89th St New York NY 10024 Office: Pub Rels Soc Am 33 Irving Pl New York NY 10003

KOVAL, CHARLES TERRANCE, oil and gas company executive; b. Canonsburg, Pa., Dec. 3, 1933; s. Charles William and Mary Elizabeth (Mickledge) K.; m. Joan Mueller, Nov. 2, 1958 (div. Oct. 1980); children: Charles Raphael, Dannielle Marie, Eric Damian, Carly Lee, Alicia Lynn; m. Karen Ann Girardot, Nov. 13, 1980. Student, Naval Aviation Flight Sch., Pensacola, Fla., 1957; BS, Pa. State U. Sales mgr. Federated Investors, Pitts., 1960-64; pres., owner Allegheny Planned Income, Inc., Pitts., 1964-71; chmn. bd. Atlas Energy Group, Inc., Coraopolis, Pa., 1971—; bd. dirs. Imperial Harbor, Inc., Bonita Springs, Fla. Mem. Presdl. Bank Rev. Bd., Phila., 1982. Served to capt. USMC, 1955-60. Mem. Pa. Natural Gas Assn., Ohio Oil and Gas Assn., Mich. Oil and Gas Assn., Pa. Soc., Mt. Nittany Soc., Pa. Wildlife Fedn. (bd. dirs., vice chmn. 1981—). Roman Catholic. Clubs: Montour Heights (Coraopolis); Toftrees (State College); Sewickley (Pa.) Heights Country. Office: Atlas Energy Group Inc 311 Rouser Rd Coraopolis PA 15108

KOVAR, LESTER J., advertising executive; b. N.Y.C., Mar. 29, 1916; s. Louis Jacob Kovar and Anna Leiken; m. Mariann Diane Pomerantz, Oct. 21, 1944; children: Shelley Kovar Becker, Lance J. BS, CCNY, 1937; postgrad., U.S. Naval Acad. Tchr. James Monroe High Sch., 1937; dist. mgr. Liebel-Flarsheim, Mich. and Ohio, 1945-52; owner Beltone, N.Y.C., 1952-54; salesman Goodren Products Corp., Englewood, N.J., 1954—; now v.p. sales Goodren Products Sales, Englewood, N.J. Pres. Riverdale Temple, 1973-75, Riverdale Community Assn., 1975; chmn. Reformed Jewish Appeal, Riverdale, 1972. Lt. comdr. USNR, 1942-45. Decorated 11 Battle Stars. Mem. Am. Arbitration Assn. (arbitrator), Point of Purchase Advt. Inst., Mass. Retailing, Sales Execs. Club, Fountains of Palm Beach Country Club. Democrat. Jewish. Home: 600 W 246th St Riverdale NY 10471 Office: Goodren Products Corp 101 W Forest Ave Englewood NJ 07631

KOWALESKI, JANE ELIZABETH, real estate executive; b. Stamford, Conn., Nov. 7, 1948; d. Stanley Francis and Sally Sophie (Wolak) K. AA, Norwalk Community Coll., 1969; AS in Fashion Merchandising, U. Bridgeport, 1985. Retail mgr. and buyer Bob's Sports Inc., Stamford, 1966-84; realtor G. Stanton Properties, Stamford, 1984—. Mem. Nat. Bd. Realtors, Conn. Bd. Realtors, Stamford Bd. Realtors, Real Estate Inst. (grad., v.p. bus. brokerage div.). Home: 24 Benstone St Stamford CT 06905 Office: G Stanton Properties 1074 Hope St Stamford CT 06907

KOWALSKI, NEAL ANTHONY, transportation executive; b. Cleve., Nov. 30, 1945; s. John Michael and Sally Therese (Maceijewski) K. BA, Cleve. State U., 1971. V.p. Century Lines Inc., Cleve., 1973-88, chief exec. officer, 1988—; v.p. Kealy Trucking Co., Cleve., 1985—, Century Transp. Inc., Cleve., 1986—. Mem. Cleve. Trucking Assn. Roman Catholic. Club: Traffic (Cleve.). Home: 6924 Ottawa Rd Cleveland OH 44105 Office: Century Lines Inc 3725 Lakeside Ave Cleveland OH 44114

KOWALSKY, WILLIAM ALLEN, communications company executive; b. Rockville Centre, N.Y., Oct. 19, 1946; s. William and Hazel (Kowalski) K.; m. Virginia April Christensen. BA in Internat. Relations, Brown U., 1968; MBA in Fin., Cornell U., 1971. Fin. adminstr. Sperry Corp., N.Y.C., 1972-74; controller Can. ops. SCM (Canada), Toronto, Ont., 1974-77; group controller SCM (Consumer Product Direct Response Group), N.Y.C., 1978-82; v.p. fin. and planning, chief fin. officer ACB, Inc., N.Y.C., 1983—. Mem. Nat. Assn. Accts., Bus. Planning and Controllers Council, Internat. Newspaper Fin. Execs., Electronic Banking Econs. Soc. Office: ACB Inc 500 Fifth Ave New York NY 10110

KOYANO, KEIICHIROU, gas company executive; b. Tokyo, Jan. 21, 1953; s. Takaji and Michiyo (Shimizu) K. Student, Nihon U., Tokyo, 1973-77. V.p. Fuji Tubame Co. Ltd., Shizuoka, Japan, 1983—. Home: Ryogaecho 1-4-1, Shizuoka Japan Office: Tubame Co Ltd, Gofukucho 1-4-5, Shizuoka Japan

KOZA, RICHARD ALAN, insurance agency owner; b. Portsmouth, Va., June 15, 1951; s. Eugene R. and Juanita K.; m. Kristin L. Scheopner, May 19, 1973; children: Russ, Kelly, Jenny. BS, Chadron State Coll., 1973, MS, 1981. Educator pub. schs., Ogallala, Nebr., 1973-78; owner Midwest Mgmt. Co., Chadron, Nebr., 1978—; instr. Chadron State Coll., 1978—; owner franchise Valentinos Am. Restaurant. Chmn. City Planning com. Chadron, 1985; scoutmaster Chadron troop Boy Scouts Am., 1985-88; mem. Chadron Econ. Devel. Corp. Named Outstanding Young Educator, Ogallala Jr. C. of C., 1978; mem. Great Navy of Nebr., Gov. Nebr. 1986. Mem. Cert. Real Estate Appraisers. Republican. Roman Catholic. Lodges: Kiwanis (Chadron) (pres. 1986-87, Kiwanian of Yr. 1986), Elks. Office: Midwest Mgmt Co PO Box 230 Chadron NE 69337

KOZBERG, DONNA WALTERS, rehabilitation adminstration executive; b. Milford, Del., Jan. 1, 1952; d. Robert Glyndwr and Gailey Ruth (Bedorf) Walters; m. Ronald Paul Kozberg, June 8, 1974. BA, U. Fla., 1973, M in Rehab. Counseling, 1974; MFA, CUNY, 1979; MBA, Rutgers U., 1986. Cert. rehab. counselor. Rehab. counselor Office Vocat. Rehab., N.Y.C., 1975-81; area dir. Lift, Inc., Staten Island, N.Y., 1981-83; ea. region dir. pub. relations, advt. Lift, Inc., Mountainside, N.J., 1983-85, v.p., 1985—; self-employed writer, editor 1975—. Contbr. articles to profl. jours.; assoc. editor Parachute mag., 1978; editor-in-chief (newsletter) Counselor Adv, 1980. Mem. Nat. Rehab. Assn. (Spl. citation 1974, grantee 1973), Nat. Rehab. Adminstrs. Assn., Nat. Rehab. Counselors Assn., Poets and Writers, Nat. Assn. Female Execs. Home: 714 Woodland Ave Westfield NJ 07090 Office: Lift Inc PO Box 1072 Mountainside NJ 07092

KOZHUHAROV, CHRISTOPHOR, physicist; b. Plovdiv, Bulgaria, Jan. 7, 1946; arrived in Fed. Republic Germany, 1970.; s. Vassil and Nadejda (Aceva) Kojouharov; m. Molly Sue Affleck, Aug. 5, 1983. Mgr inz., Politechnika Slaska, Gliwice, Poland, 1969; Dr. rer. nat., Technische U., Munich, 1974. With Technische U., Munich, 1974-78, GSI, Darmstadt, Fed. Republic Germany, 1979—. Home: Kohlweg 19, 6101 Messel Federal Republic of Germany Office: GSI, Planckstr, 6100 Darmstadt Federal Republic of Germany

KOZIAR, STEPHEN FRANCIS, JR., lawyer, power company executive; b. Webster, Mass., July 27, 1944; s. Stephen Francis and Stasia Barbara (Danilowicz) K.; m. Patricia Rose Forehly; 1 child, Stephanie Lynn. B.S., U. Dayton, 1967; J.D., No. Ky. U., 1971. Elec. engr. Dayton Power & Light Co., 1966-71, atty., 1971-79, asst. gen. counsel, 1979-81, counsel and sec., 1981-86, v.p., gen. counsel, 1986-87, group v.p., gen. counsel, 1987—. Served to capt. U.S. Army, 1971. Mem. ABA, Ohio Bar Assn., Dayton Bar Assn. Office: DPL Inc Courthouse Pla SW Box 1247 Dayton OH 45402

KOZLOWSKI, JANIECE RAE, accountant; b. Dayton, Ohio, June 25, 1959; d. Gerald Rae and Joann (Davis) Moore; m. Richard Ernest Kozlowski, May 23, 1981; 1 child, Kristen Rae. BS in Bus. and Acctg., Wright State U., Fairborn, Ohio, 1981. CPA, Ohio. Gen. acct. Ledex, Inc., Vandalia, Ohio, 1982-85, asst. to acct., 1986-88, acctg. specialist, 1988—. Mem. Miami Valley Mgmt. Assn. Home: 442 Deeds Ave Dayton OH 45404

KOZLOWSKI, L. DENNIS, manufacturing company executive; b. Irvington, N.J., Nov. 16, 1946; s. Leo Kelly and Agnes (Kozell) K.; B.S., Seton Hall U., 1968; M.B.A., Rivier Coll., 1976; m. Angie Suarez, Mar. 13, 1971; children—Cheryl Marie, Sandra Lisa. V.p. fin. Grinnell Fire Protection Systems div., Providence, 1976-81; v.p., chief fin. officer Ludlow Corp., subs. Tyco Labs., Needham, Mass., 1981-82, pres., chief exec. officer, Grinnell Corp., 1982—; bd. dirs. Whitman and Howard Cons. Engrs., Tyco Labs., Inc., Atlantic Bank and Trust Co.; Better Bus. Bur. of R.I. (chmn., dir.). Home: Runnymede Dr North Hampton NH 03862 Office: Grinnell Corp 3 Tyco Pk Exeter NH 03833

KRACH, MITCHELL PETER, financial executive; b. Westfield, Mass., Nov. 2, 1924; s. John Joseph and Sophie Mary (Swiatlowski) K.; cert. Mass. Extension U., 1944, Harvard U. Grad. Sch. Bus. Admnstrn., 1966; m. Theresa Florence Sanczuk, May 29, 1957; children—Susan, Gregory, Mitchell, Jonathan, Matthew. Auditor, H.F. Lynch Lumber Co., West Springfield, Mass., 1946-51, dir., 1951-79, sec. bd. dirs., 1951-79, mgr. purchasing, 1951-61, central mgr. purchasing, 1961-71, v.p. purchasing, 1971-76, v.p. purchasing and fin., 1976-79, treas. bd. dirs. 1976-79; treas., chmn. bd. dirs. Nat. Res. Corp., Longmeadow, Mass., 1957—; legal arbitrator bldg. materials. Exec. mem., vice-chmn. bd. govs. Shriners Hosp. for Crippled Children, Springfield, 1980. Cert. purchasing mgr.; notary public; registered and bonded real estate broker, Mass. Mem. Nat. Fedn. Ind. Bus. (nat. adv. council 1978), Nat. Assn. Purchasing Mgmt. (dir. nat. affairs 1965, nat. lumber chmn. 1970-80), Am. Soc. Notaries, Purchasing Mgmt. Assn. W. New Eng. (pres. 1963-64), Purchasing Mgmt. Assn. Worcester, Mfrs. Agts. Nat. Assn. Democrat. Roman Catholic. Clubs: Valley Press, 100 of Mass., Am. Turners, Elks (chmn. bd. trustees), Melha Temple, Masons, Shriners, K.T. Contbr. numerous articles to profl. jours. Home: 33 Forest Glen Rd Longmeadow MA 01106 Office: 1105 Main St W Springfield MA 01089

KRAEMER, LILLIAN ELIZABETH, lawyer; b. N.Y.C., Apr. 18, 1940; d. Frederick Joseph and Edmee Elizabeth (de Watteville) K.; m. John W. Vincent, June 22, 1962 (div. 1964). BA, Swarthmore Coll., 1961; JD, U. Chgo., 1964. Bar: N.Y. 1965, U.S. Dist. Ct. (so. dist.) N.Y. 1967, U.S. Dist. Ct. (ea. dist.) N.Y. 1971. Assoc. Cleary, Gottlieb, Steen & Hamilton, N.Y.C., 1964-71; assoc. Simpson, Thacher & Bartlett, N.Y.C., 1971-74, ptnr., 1974—; mem. vis. com. U. Chgo. Law Sch., 1988—; chmn. ea. region capitol fund drive U. Chgo. Law Sch., 1983-86; co-chmn. major gifts annual fund, 1988—. Mem. ABA, Assn. Bar City of N.Y. (various coms.) Council Fgn. Relations, N.Y. State Bar Assn., Union Internat. des Avocats, Order of Coif, Phi Beta Kappa. Democrat. Episcopalian. Home: 2 Beekman Pl New York NY 10022 Office: Simpson Thacher & Bartlett 425 Lexington New York NY 10017

KRAEMER, PHILIPP, mfg. co. exec., inventor; b. Hahn, Ger., Jan. 17, 1931; s. George Heinrich and Anna Erna K.; student vocat. sch., Darmstadt, Ger.; m. Rosemarie Sandner, June 2, 1956; children—Lynda, Irene, Sandra. Tool and die maker, 1956-61; tool maker Quality Tool & Massey Ferguson, 1961-64; founder Kraemer Tool & Mfg. Co., Ltd., Weston, Ont., Can., 1964, since pres., gen. mgr. Mem. Pollution Control Assn., Can. Mfg. Assn. Lutheran. Patentee oil-sand separator, others (8). Home: 34 Kendleton Dr, Rexdale, ON Canada M9V 1V4 Office: Devon Rd, Brampton, ON Canada L6V 2K6

KRAFCISIN, MICHAEL HARRY, radio station manager; b. Chgo., Mar. 4, 1958; s. Michael John and Josephine Lucy (Szela) K. Student, Loyola U., Chgo., 1976-77. Ops. mgr., programmng cons., rec. engr. The FM 100 Plan, Chgo., 1976-81; ops. mgr., programmng cons. Bonneville Broadcasting System, Palatine, Ill., 1981-84; dir. client services Bonneville Broadcasting System, Northbrook, Ill., 1984-85; gen. mgr. Stas. WSEX/WCBR-FM, Chgo. and Arlington Heights, Ill., 1986-89; dir. client svcs. Bonneville Broadcasting System, Northbrook, Ill., 1989—. Ill. State scholar, 1976. Roman Catholic. Home: PO Box 847 Barrington IL 60011-0847 Office: Bonneville Broadcasting System 4080 Commercial Ave Northbrook IL 60062-1892

KRAFT, BAYARD RANDOLPH, III, financial executive; b. Mt. Holly, N.J., Apr. 20, 1951; s. Bayard Randolph, Jr. and Ann Beverly (Phelps) K.; m. Pamela Jeanne Thomas, Sept. 27, 1986. Student, Stetson U., 1969-70, U. Vt., 1974-76. Sec., dir. Randolph Assocs., Inc., Stowe, Vt., 1980-85; sr. acct. Van Blarcom and Harrison, CPA's, Stowe, Vt., 1976-85; asst. sec. Environ. Power Corp., Boston, 1985—, controller, 1986—, treas., 1987—. Trustee Stowe Winter Carnival Assn., 1979-85. Mem. Am. Mgmt. Assn., Mass Bar Assn. Presbyterian. Office: Environ Power Corp PO Box 45 109 Union St Manchester VT 05254

KRAFT, BURNELL D., agricultural products company executive; b. Chester, Ill., July 24, 1931; s. Herman F. and Ella Kraft; m. Shirley Ann Huch, Dec. 30, 1950; children: Jon B., Julie Ann Kraft Schwalbe. BS, So. Ill. U., 1956. Acct., mcht. Tabor and Co., Decatur, Ill., 1956-59, v.p., 1959-61, exec. v.p., 1961-70, pres., 1970-75; with Archer Daniels Midland Co. (merged with Tabor and Co.), Decatur, 1975-84, corp. v.p., 1984—, pres. ADM/GROWMARK River System div., 1985—. Trustee Millikin U., Decatur, 1983—; bd. dirs. Decatur Meml. Hosp., 1970-80. Served with U.S. Army, 1951-52, Korea. Mem. N.Am. Export Grain Assn., Nat. Feed Grains Council, Nat. Grain and Feed Assn., Mpls. Grain, St. Louis Mchts. Exchange, Chgo. Bd. Trade, Decatur C. of C. (past bd. dirs.), Phi Kappa Phi, Beta Gamma Sigma. Republican. Lutheran. Clubs: Decatur, Country Club Decatur (bd. dirs. 1974-78). Office: Archer Daniels Midland Co 4666 Faries Pkwy PO Box 1470 Decatur IL 62526

KRAFT, KENNETH HOUSTON, JR., insurance agency executive; b. Chgo., Apr. 2, 1934; s. Kenneth Houston and Elizabeth (Preston) K.; m. Ruth Neely, Aug. 11, 1956 (div. Sept. 1979); children: Katherine Elizabeth, Carolyn Ruth, Kenneth Houston III; m. Kathleen Hartung, Mar. 16, 1985. BS in Fin., Purdue U., 1956. Pres., chmn. bd. Kraft Ins. Agy., Inc., Winter Park, Fla., 1960—, KHK Fin. Corp., Winter Park, 1974—; chmn. bd. Echo Pub. Co., Sulfur Springs, Tex., 1970—; sr. mem. bd. dirs., mem. exec., fin., consumer loan, audit and examining coms. Barnett Bank Cen. Fla., Orlando; bd. dirs. Goodings Groceries of Fla., Altamonte Springs, Fla., Schwartz Electro-Optics, Orlando, Princeton Fin. Corp. Bd. dirs. Winter Park C. of C., 1965-70, Orange County chpt. ARC, Orlando, 1963-65, Orange County chpt. United Way, Winter Park, 1970-72, Winter Park YMCA, 1972-75; mem. Fla. Citrus Mut., Lakeland, 1966—, Com. of 100 of Orange County, Inc., Orlando, 1983—; sec. bd. trustees Winter Park Hosp., 1969-88, also exec. com., compensation com., chmn. long range planning com.; chmn. Winter Park Community Trust Fund, 1981—; mem. grievance com. 9th Jud. Cir., 1987—. Served to lt. (j.g.) USNR, 1956-58. Named Outstanding Young Man of Winter Park, Winter Park Jaycees, 1970. Mem. Cen. Fla. Assn. Ins. Agts. (pres. 1963-64), Fla. Assn. Ins. Agts., Nat. Assn. Ins. Agts., Purdue Alumni Assn. Republican. Presbyterian. Clubs: Orlando Country, University, Citrus, Captiva Island Yacht. Lodges: Masons, Rotary (bd. dirs. Winter Park club). Home: 231 Chelton Circle Winter Park FL 32789 Office: Kraft Ins Agy Inc PO Box 939 Winter Park FL 32790

KRAFT, WALTER HANS, transportation executive; b. Newark, Dec. 31, 1938; s. Hans Christopher and Emma Maria (Adam) K.; m. Margaret Pauline Meidlein, June 20, 1959; children: Robin, Karen, Lynda. BSCE, Newark Coll. Engring., 1962, MSCE, 1965; D in Engring. Sci., N.J. Inst. Tech., 1975. Registered profl. engr. N.J., N.Y., Pa., Ky., Calif., Ohio, Conn., Del., Tex., Minn., profl. planner N.J. Asst engr. Edwards & Kelcey, Inc., Livingston, N.J., 1962—, assoc., 1971-73, asst. v.p., 1973-75, v.p. chief traffic and transp. div., 1975-77, v.p., 1977-84, sr. v.p. chief traffic and transp., 1984—; adj. prof. N.J. Inst. Tech., Poly. Inst. N.Y.; lectr. Carnegie-Mellon U., St. John's U., Staten Island; lectr. in field. contbr. numerous articles to profl. jours. Mem. So. N.J. Devel. Coun., trustee, 1984; mem. Twp. of Irvington Econ. Devel. Com., 1984-88, other. Fellow ASCE (local pres. 1978-79, chmn. various coms., Robert Ridgeway award 1962, Frank Masters award 1982), Inst. Transp. Engrs., Disting. Svc. award 1986, Ivor S. Wisepart Transp. Engr. award 1986; del. 1975, local treas. 1976, sec. 1977, com. v.p. 1978, pres. 1978-79, chair 1979, internat. v.p. 1986, internat. pres. 1987); mem. Soc. Computer Simulation, Am. Soc. Hwy. Engrs., Nat. Soc. Profl. Engrs., Am. Mgmt. Assn., Chi Epsilon, Tau Beta Pi, Gauverband Nordamerika Club (sec.), Bayern Verein Newark Club. Democrat. Lutheran. Office: Edwards and Kelcey Inc 70 S Orange Ave Livingston NJ 07039

KRAFTSON, RAYMOND H., corporate executive, lawyer; b. DelawareCounty, Pa., June 20, 1940; s. Harry A. and Elisabeth (Hallstrom) k.; m. Marguerite Knewstub; children: Donald W., Marguerite O., Audrey E., Michele S. BA, U. Pa., 1962; JD, Coll. of William and Mary, 1967. Trial atty. SEC, Washington, 1967-68; counsel Ringe, Peet & Mason, Phila., 1968-70, Monsanto Co., St. Louis, 1970-71; sr. v.p., gen. counsel Life of Pa. Fin. Corp., Phila., 1972-78; sr. staff counsel INA Corp., Phila., 1978-80; v.p., gen. counsel Safeguard Scientifics, Inc., King of Prussia, Pa., 1980—; bd. dirs. Ailes Communications, Inc., N.Y.C., Hoffman Surgical Equipment Co., Conshohocken, Pa., Tangram Systems, Inc., Raleigh, N.C., Premier Systems, Inc., Wayne, Pa. Mng. editor William and Mary Law Rev., 1966-67. Pres. Gladwyne Montessori Sch., 1986-88; v.p., trustee The Baldwin Sch., Bryn Mawr, 1987—; vestry mem. St. David's Ch., 1988—. Mem. ABA, Montgomery Bar Assn., Phila. Bar. Assn., Nat. Assn. Corp. Dirs., Am. Soc. of Corp. Secs., Merion Cricket Club (Haverford), The Racquet Club (Phila.). Republican. Episcopalian. Office: Safeguard Scientifics Inc 630 Park Ave King of Prussia PA 19406

KRAFVE, ALLEN HORTON, management consultant; b. Superior, Wis., Jan. 26, 1937; s. Richard Ernest and Frances Virginia (Horton) K.; m. Lois Anne Reed, Aug. 15, 1959; children—Bruce Allen, Anne Marie, Carol Elizabeth. B.S. in Mech. Engring., U. Mich., 1958, M.B.A., 1960, M.S. in Mech. Engring., 1961. Asst. prof. mech. engring. San Jose State U. (Calif.), 1961-65; various positions including quality control mgr. Ford Motor Co., Dearborn, Mich., 1965-77; engring. mgr. Kysor/Cadillac, Cadillac, Mich., 1977-82; mgmt. cons., Lake City, Mich., 1982—; bd. dirs. NOC Industries, Cadillac; pres. Lark Homes, Inc., 1979—. Co-author: Reliability Considerations in Design, 1962, internat. conf. paper, 1961. Bd. dirs. Crooked Tree council Girl Scouts U.S.A., Traverse City, Mich., 1983. Mem. ASME, Soc. Automotive Engrs., Am. Soc. Quality Control, Am. Soc. Engring. Edn. Republican. Methodist. Home: 145 Duck Point Dr Lake City MI 49651 Office: Allen H Krafve Cons 2604 Sunnyside Dr Cadillac MI 49601

KRAHEL, THOMAS STEPHEN, account executive; b. Bklyn., Oct. 4, 1947; s. John Frank and Anna (Trusz) K.; m. Jill Susan Friedl, June 12, 1969; children: Bryan Thomas, Audrey Gerda, Leah Ann. PhB, Bklyn. Coll., 1970; MA in Banking and Mgmt. with honors, Adelphi U., 1980. Asst. treas. Chase Manhattan Bank, N.Y.C., 1970-82; sales mgr. Glossit Mfg., Northport, N.Y., 1982-84; mktg. rep. Executone of L.I., Hauppauge, N.Y., 1984-85; account exec. Fin. Mktg. Corp., N.Y.C., 1985-86; acct. exec. UARCO, Inc., N.Y., 1986—; Instr. Dale Carnegie Courses. Co-founder, treas. Tuscany Gardens Assn., Great Neck, N.Y., 1970-80; counselor L.I. Youth Guidance Program; elder 1st Presbyn. Ch. Northport, N.Y. Mem. Mensa, Delta Mu Delta. Republican. Presbyterian. Club: Couples (Greatneck) (pres. 1976-77). Home: 16 West St Northport NY 11768

KRAKOW, AMY GINZIG, advertising agency executive; b. Bklyn., Feb. 25, 1950; d. Nathan and Iris (Minkowitz) Ginzig; m. Gary Scott Krakow, Nov. 7, 1976. BA in Speech and Theatre, Bklyn. Coll., 1971, postgrad. in TV prodn. Promotion mgr. Popular Mechanics, N.Y.C., 1976-77; N.Y. copy mgr. U.S. News and World Report, N.Y.C., 1977-80; promotion mgr. Sta. WINS-Radio, N.Y.C., 1980-82, creator, supervising exec. advt. campaign, , 1981-82; promotion dir. CBS Mags., N.Y.C., 1982-84, The Village Voice, N.Y.C., 1984-85, New York Woman (Am. Express Pub.), 1987—; cons. Silverman Collection, Santa Fe, 1985—; sem. leader Radcliffe Pub. Workshop, 1987, 88; producer Festival of Street Entertainers, N.Y.C., 1984, 85, 87, 88, Albuquerque, 1986. Contbr. articles to consumer and trade mags. including New York, Family Circle, Working Woman, others; producer, artistic dir. Ann. Coney Island Tattoo Festival, 1986, 87, 88, The Psychedelic Festival, 1988. Bd. dirs. Sideshows by the Seashore, Coney Island, U.S.A., Bklyn., 1985—, Bond Street Theater Coalition, 1985—, City Lore, N.Y.C., 1987—. Creator, producer artistic dir. Annual Coney Island Tattoo Festival 1986, 87, 88, The Psychedelic Festival, 1988. Recipient Addy award, 1995, BPA award, 1981. Mem. Advt. Women N.Y., Delta Phi Epsilon (exec. bd. 1984-85). Home and Office: 57 Warren St New York NY 10007

KRAKOWER, BERNARD HYMAN, management consultant; b. N.Y.C., May 11, 1935; s. David and Bertha (Glassman) K.; m. Sondra Joan Fishbein, Apr. 14, 1968; children: Lorna, Victoria, Ariela Shauna. BA in Advt., UCLA, 1959, cert. in real estate, 1966, cert. in indsl. relations, 1972; MBA, Pepperdine U., 1979. Loan officer Lytton Fin. Corp., Los Angeles, 1961-65; mgmt. cons. James R. Colvin & Assocs., Los Angeles, 1965-67; sr. indsl. relations rep. Sci. Data Systems (Xerox), 1967-68; dir. ops. Tratec, Inc., Los Angeles, 1968-70; chmn. Krakower/Brucker Internat., Inc., Los Angeles, 1970-88; sr. ptnr. Krakower Finnegan Assocs., Los Angeles, 1988—. Mem. citizens liaison com. Los Angeles Dept. Recreation and Parks, 1973; apptd. commr. L.A. Countwide Citizens Planning Coun. by L.A. County Bd. Suprs., 1988—; pres., bd. dirs. Western Los Angeles Chamber Found. Recipient cert. of Appreciation City of Los Angeles, 1974, 77-79. Mem. Los Angeles West C. of C. (treas. 1983, v.p. 1984, v.p. corp. fin. 1986, vice chmn. 1987-88, chmn. bd. bus. council 1988—), UCLA Alumni Assn., Pepperdine U. Alumni Assocs., Calif. Exec. Recruiters Assn., Sierra Club (exec. com. West Los Angeles 1971-72). Office: 6033 W Century Blvd Ste 800 Los Angeles CA 90045

KRALICK, CHARLES, financial executive, accountant; b. N.Y.C., Jan. 2, 1953; s. Edward G. and Frances B. (Korvas) K.; m. Sharon Coffey Kralick, May 29, 1977; children: Adrienne J., Jonathan E. BS in Acctg., NYU, 1974. CPA, N.Y., N.C. Mem. audit staff Touche Ross & Co., N.Y.C., 1974-82; audit mgr. Touche Ross & Co., Raleigh, N.C., 1982-87; v.p., chief fin. officer Rocky Mount (N.C.) Undergarment Co., Inc., 1987—. Advancement chmn. Occoneechee Council Boy Scouts Am., Raleigh, 1987. Mem. N.Y. State Soc. CPA's, N.C. Assn. CPA's, N.C. World Trade Assn., Rotary. Baptist. Office: Rocky Mount Undergarment Co Inc PO Box 1280 Rocky Mount NC 27802

KRALOVEC, PAUL DOUGLAS, SR., pharmaceutical company executive; b. Appleton, Wis., Oct. 3, 1951; s. Earl Arthur and Marie Ann (De Keyser) K.; m. Nance Lee Gutzwiller, Jan. 3, 1976; children: Angela, Paul II, Daniel. BS in Acctg., Mankatao State U., 1979; MBA, U. Minn., 1985. CPA, Minn.; cert. prodn. and inventory control mgr. Leadman, tester Kato Engring. Co., Mankato, Minn., 1974-79; staff auditor Deloitte, Haskins & Sells, Mpls., 1979-80; staff acct. Northrup King Co., Mpls., 1980-81, sr. fin. analyst, 1981-83, supr. cost acctg. dept., 1983-84; mgr. acctg. dept. Upsher-Smith Labs., Plymouth, Minn., 1984-86; controller Upsher-Smith Labs., Plymouth, 1986-87, dir. fin., 1987—. Mem. Am. Prodn. and Inventory Control Soc., Soc. Risk & Ins. Mgmt., Minn. Soc. CPAs. Republican. Roman Catholic. Office: Upsher-Smith Labs Inc 14905 23d Ave N Plymouth MN 55447

KRAMER, ALEX, information systems executive; b. Budapest, Hungary, Sept. 25, 1947; came to U.S., 1949; s. Leo L. Kramer and Irene (Schreter) Kramer Abrams; m. Shana Kellner, June 16, 1968; children: Malka, Armin, Ben, Sarah, Kay, Rebecca. BA, Johns Hopkins U., 1968; MA, Ner Israel Coll., Balt., 1970; postgrad., St. Louis U., 1971-73. Adminstr. Evergreen Nursing Home, St. Louis, 1970-73; pres. AccuComp, Inc., 1973-75; v.p. ADP, Roseland, N.J., 1975-85, IMS, Totowa, N.J., 1985—. Mem. Gov.'s Com. State of Mo., 1973. Office: IMS 100 Campus Rd Totowa NJ 07512

KRAMER, JOEL ABRAHAM, electronics executive; b. N.Y.C.. BEE, Fairleigh Dickinson U., 1960. Engr. Lockheed Electronics Co., Plainfield, N.J., 1960-61, Computer Systems, Inc., Monmouth Junction, N.J., 1961, Lundy Electronics, Glen Head, N.Y., 1961-62; project engr. EMR Co., Sarasota, Fla., 1962-65; applications engr. EMR Co., Silver Springs, Md., 1965-66; assoc. engr. EMR Co., College Park, Md., 1966-67; systems engr. NASA, Greenbelt, Md., 1967-68; v.p. engring. Computer Entry Systems, Silver Spring, 1968-73; v.p. N. Atlantic Industries, Hauppauge, N.Y., 1973-82; pres. Qantex div., Hauppauge, N.Y., 1973-82; pres., chief exec. officer Telebyte Tech., Inc., Greenlawn, N.Y., 1982—. Home: 4 Sycamore Dr Woodbury NY 11797 Office: Telebyte Tech Inc 270 E Pulaski Rd Greenlawn NY 11740

KRAMER, JUDITH HAHN, retail executive; b. Phila., June 27, 1942; d. Frank Eugene Jr. and Margaret (Berg) Hahn; m. Mitchell A. Kramer, July 5, 1963; children: Barbara H., Mitchell F. BA, U. Pa., 1964; cert., Inst. Paralegal Tng., Phila., 1976. Paralegal Mitchell A. Kramer & Assocs., Phila., 1976-81; saleswoman Global Books, Trevose, Pa., 1981-84; owner, mgr. Books & Co., Phila., 1984—. Committeewoman Abington/Rockledge (Pa.) Dem. Com., 1975—; hon. pres. Camp Coun. Inc., Phila., 1980—. Mem. Am. Booksellers Assn., Mid. Atlantic Booksellers Assn., Rydal Country Club (bd. dirs.). Jewish. Home: 211 Meetinghouse Rd Jenkintown PA 19046

KRAMER, KENNETH STEVEN, investment banker; b. Bklyn., Dec. 5, 1938; s. Irving W. and Ruth J. (Eisenberg) K.; m. Bonita S. Walton, Dec. 1, 1963; children: Kim, Jodie, Carrie. BA, U. Pa., 1960; postgrad., NYU Sch. Bus., 1960-62, New Sch. for Social Research, 1960-63. Purchasing coord. Orange Pulp and Paper Mills div. Equitable Bag Co., L.I. City, N.Y., 1960-65; account exec. Blair & Co., Mineola, N.Y., 1966-69; v.p E.F. Hutton & Co., Jericho, N.Y., 1970-87, Shearson Lehman Hutton, Jericho, 1987—. Mem. Old Brookville (N.Y.) Aux. Police Dept., sgt., Glen Head, N.Y.; mem. Muttontown (N.Y.) Village Planning Bd., L.I. div. Am. Cancer Soc., past bd. dir.; mem. Nat Ski Patrol System;. Mem. U. Pa. Club (Long Island). Republican. Jewish. Office: Shearson Lehman Hutton 1 Jericho Pla Main Fl Lobby Jericho NY 11753

KRAMER, PAUL CLETUS, corporate professional; b. Harpers Ferry, Iowa, Jan. 28, 1931; s. Emil C. and Olive T. (Goerdt) K.; m. Barbara A. Valdes, Apr. 18, 1959; childre: John, Judy, James. BS in Commerce with honors, State U. Iowa, 1958. CPA, Ill. Sr. auditor Arthur Andersen & Co., Chgo., 1958-61; copr. mgr. cost acctg. Abbott Labs, North Chicago, Ill., 1961-65; plant controller Reynolds Metals, McCook, Ill., 1966-69; corp. treas. W.F. Hall Printing, Chgo., 1969-78; chief fin. officer Lands' End, Inc., Dodgeville, Wis., 1978—; bd. dirs. M & I Bank of Madison, Wis., Wis. Mfgrs. & Commerce, Madison. With USN, 1951-54. Mem. Beta Gamma Sigma. Republican. Roman Catholic. Office: Lands End Inc Lands End Ln Dodgeville WI 53595

KRAMER, RUTH, accountant; b. N.Y.C., June 20, 1925; d. Isidore and Sarah (Heller) Kleiner; m. Paul Kramer, Oct. 27, 1946; children: Stephen David, Lynne Adair. BA, Bklyn. Coll., 1946. Registered pub. acct., N.Y. Tchr. elem. sch. N.Y.C. Bd. Edn., 1946-50; acct. Lichtenstein & Kramer, N.Y.C., Lynbrook, N.Y., 1954; jr. ptnr. Paul Kramer & Co., Lynbrook, 1954-56, ptnr., 1956-65, mng. ptnr., 1965—; cons. Nassau County (N.Y.) Dist. Attys. Office, 1956-65; expert witness acctg. matters Nassau County Grand Juries, 1956-65; mem. IRS liaison com. Bklyn. Dist., 1965-76; mem. N.Y. State Bd. for Pub. Accountancy, 1982—. Troop leader Girl Scouts U.S., 1947-48; chmn. Tri-Town sect. Anti Defamation League, 1952-53; active Heart Fund; pres. Lynbrook Women's Rep. Club, 1956-58; treas. Assembly Candidates Campaign Com., 1964; mem. Nassau County Fedn. Rep. Women, Syosset Woodbury Rep. Club. Named Woman in Acctg., local TV channel, 1974. Mem. Nat. Soc. Pub. Accts. (del.), Empire State Assn. Pub. Accts. (Meritorious Service award, 2d v.p., 1975-76, 1st v.p. 1977-78, pres. 1978-79, Pres.'s award, 2d past pres. exec. bd. 1979-80, 1st past pres. exec. bd. 1981-82, pres. Nassau County chpt. 1962-63, 75-76, state bd. dirs. 1980—, Woman of Yr. award 1982), Tax Inst. C.W. Post Coll., Acctg. Inst. C.W. Post Coll. Clubs: Sisterhood North Shore Synagogue; Am. Jewish Congress, Lynbrook Pythian Sisters (past chief). Home and Office: 23 Hilltop Dr Syosset NY 11791

KRAMER, SANDRA, broadcast communications executive; b. Chgo., Nov. 10, 1943; d. Mortimer Stanton and Ida (Dewoskin) Gold; divorced; children: Kimberly, Kelly, Scott. Acct. exec. Coordinators, Chgo., 1975-77; gen. mgr. Sta. WEEF, Highland Park, Ill., 1977-80; v.p., exec. producer Pub. Interest Affiliates, Chgo., 1980—; v.p., bd. dirs. Chgo. Antique Radio Corp., Inc., 1987—; v.p., sec. Petro Products, Inc., Chgo., 1978—. Exec. producer: (radio div.) Northwestern Reviewing Stand, 1985—, Campbell Playhouse with Helen Hayes, 1986-88, Campbell Souper Stars with Kathy O'Malley, 1988—, Eddie Albert's Medscan, 1985-86, Crain's Bus. Report, 1987—, (radio spl.) Pete Townshend-My Generation, 1985, The JFK Conflict with Edwin Newman, 1988, (audio books) James Burke, 1989; nat. syndicated host (radio series and inflight audio programing) Am. Airlines, Pan Am., United Airlines. Mem. Star Light Found., Broadcast Promotion and Mktg. Execs., Nat. Assn. Broadcasters, New Chgo. Coalition, Jewish United Fund, Anti-Cruelty Soc. Club: East Bank (Chgo.). Office: Pub Interest Affiliates 666 N Lake Shore Dr Ste 800 Chicago IL 60611

KRAMER, WILLARD GEORGE, JR., accountant; b. Pitts., Oct. 2, 1929; s. Willard George Sr. and Olive Francis (McVey) K.; m. Nora Mae Martin, June 26, 1951; children: Bradley, Patricia. BS in Commerce, Grove City Coll., 1952. CPA, Pa., Mich. Staff acct. Price Waterhouse, Pitts., 1952-56, audit sr., 1956-59, audit mgr., 1959-65; audit ptnr. Price Waterhouse, Detroit, 1965-76, mng. ptnr., 1976-88, group mng. ptnr., 1988—. Chmn. Bon Secours of Mich. Healthcare, Grosse Pointe, 1982—, Civic, Inc., 1982—, St. Paul Evang. Luth. Ch., Grosse Pointe Farms, Mich., 1969-75. Sgt. Security Agy. U.S. Army, 1947-48. Mem. AICPA, Pa. Inst. CPA's, Mich. Assn. CPA's, Detroit Athletic Club, Lochmoor Club (pres., treas. Grosse Pointe Woods, Mich. 1971-79). Republican. Office: Price Waterhouse 200 Renaissance Ctr Ste 3900 Detroit MI 48243

KRAMER, WORTH ALAN (LANCE), industrial products company executive; b. Cleve., Sept. 9, 1941; s. Worth Hollis and Alice Farnhum (Hogue) Funk; m. Laura Ann Root, May 25, 1974; children: Courtney, Andrew. BA, Hillsdale Coll., 1966; MBA, So. Ill. U., 1972. Accounts receivable mgr. Monsanto Co., St. Louis, 1972-74; contr. Interface Tech., St. Louis, 1974, exec. v.p., 1974-75, pres., 1975-79; v.p. fin. and adminstrn. Smith-Scharff, St. Louis, 1979-82; sec., treas. Watlow Electric Mfg. Co., St. Louis, 1982-88, v.p. fin. and adminstrn., 1988—; mem. small bus. adv. com. Regional Commerce and Growth Assn., St. Louis, 1977-82. trustee Robinwood West Improvement Assn., St. Louis, 1979-82; vestry mem. St. Timothy Episcopal Ch., St. Louis, 1985-86, sr. warden, 1986; bd. dirs. St. Louis Hearing and Speech Ctrs., 1987—; active fin. com. Episcopal Diocese of Mission, 1989—. Lt. USNR, 1966-71, Vietnam. Decorated Purple Heart, 1968, Bronze Star with Navy Air medal, 1969. Mem. Fin. Exec. Inst., Internat. Execs. Roundtable, Chief Execs. Roundtable (chmn. 1979-80), Fin. Exec. Roundtable (chmn. 1983-84), Alpha Tau Omega. Republican. Club: Greenbriar Hills Country (St. Louis). Home: 2536 Oak Springs Ln Town and Country MO 63131 Office: Watlow Electric Mfg Co 12001 Lackland Rd Saint Louis MO 63146

KRAMM, DEBORAH ANN, data processing executive; b. Pasadena, June 24, 1949; d. Donald F. and Mary (Roach) Coonan; m. Kenneth R. Kramm, Dec. 20, 1969; children: Deidre Lyn, Jonathan Russel. BA, U. Calif.-Irvine, 1971; MS, Mich. Tech. U., 1981. Math. asst. NASA-Jet Propulsion Lab., Pasadena, 1967-70; library asst. U. Calif. Irvine Libr., 1967-71; rsch. assoc. animal behavior lab. Mich. Tech. U. , Houghton, 1971-80; programmer/analyst Shell Oil Co., Houston, 1981-85, corp. auditor EDP, 1985-87, team leader systems analyst, 1987-88, group leader SLA, 1988—; chmn. bd. MMARK, Houston, 1983-85. Contbr. articles to profl. jours.; Designer (program application software) Shell Point-of-Sale Terminal, 1982-85. Treas. KFHS Orch., 1986-88; co-leader Boy Scouts Am., Houston, 1981-83. AAUW scholar, 1980, Calif. State scholar, 1967-71. Mem. NAFE, AAUW (pres. br. 1975-81). Club: Shell Data Processors. Home: 5814 Pinewilde Houston TX 77066 Office: Shell Oil Info Ctr 1500 Old Spanish Trail Houston TX 77054

KRANENDONK, CARL JOHN, marketing educator; b. Sheboygan, Wis., Apr. 29, 1930; s. Henry and Elizabeth (TeSelle) K.; m. Phyllis Dorothy Wangerin, June 16, 1951 (div. Mar. 1975); children: Linda, Debra, Diane; m. Judith Karen Wilcox, June 30, 1976. BBA, U. Wis., 1952; MBA, U. Tulsa, 1969. With retailing and sales Firestone Tire and Rubber Co., Milw., 1952-56; acctg. and systems analyst Shell Oil Co., Chgo., 1956-64; mgr. mktg. planning and research Sunray DX Oil Co., Tulsa, 1964-70; v.p. mktg. Lum's Inc., Miami, Fla., 1970-73; pres. Computer Mkt. Analysis Inc., Miami, 1973-77; adj. prof. Fla. Internat. U., Miami, 1976-81, lectr., 1982—; cons. Tecton Inc., Miami, 1986-88, Fed. Savs. & Loan Ins. Corp., Miami, 1987, Fed. Asset Disposition Assn., Miami, 1987. Contbr. articles to profl. jours. Pres. jr. high sch. PTA, Tulsa, 1969; exec. com. elem. sch. PTA, Tulsa, 1967; com. mem. United Way Fund Raising Com., Tulsa, 1968. Mem. Am. Mktg. Assn. (Miami chpt. pres. 1985-86, v.p. 1981-84; Tulsa chpt. pres. 1966-67, v.p. 1964-66; nat. chmn. 1968-69). Republican. Presbyterian. Office: Fla Internat U Coll Bus North Miami FL 33181

KRASKO, MICHAEL JOHN, investment banker; b. Jersey City, Jan. 27, 1943; s. Michael Joseph and Ann (Kushneruk) K.; m. Carol Lee Jouaneau, Apr. 24, 1965; children: Kimberlee, Kristen, Courtney. BS in Econs., St. Peters Coll., 1965; MBA, Pace U., 1969. V.p., analyst Oppenheimer, N.Y.C., 1976-78; v.p., sr. analyst group mgr. Merrill Lynch, N.Y.C., 1978-83; mng. dir. tech. research dir. L.F. Rothschild, Unterberg, Towbin, N.Y.C., 1983-88; mng. dir. Prudential-Bache Securities, Inc., N.Y.C., 1988—, co-head tech. banking group; lectr. in field. Contbr. articles to profl. jours. Vice chmn. planning bd. Town of Allenhurst, 1985, chmn. 1987; pres. Home Owners Assn., 1978-80. Served with U.S. Army, 1967-72. Fellow N.Y. Soc. Security Analysts; mem. Electronic Analysts Soc. (pres. 1984-85), IEEE, Deal Golf and Country Club, Gov.'s Club N.J. Republican. Roman Catholic. Office: Prudential Bache Securities Inc 199 Water St 30th Fl New York NY 10292

KRASNOFF, ABRAHAM, business executive; b. Newark. Grad. magna cum laude, NYU, post grad.; LHD (hon.), Long Island U., 1985. CPA, N.Y. From controller to treas. to v.p. to exec. v.p. Pall Corp., Glen Cove, N.Y., 1951-69, pres., vice chmn., chief exec. officer, 1969—. Past. bd. overseers sch. bus. NYU, past chmn. exec. council conf. bd.; past chmn. Glen Cove Planning Bd.; trustee, past chmn. bd. dirs. Long Island U.; bd. dirs. Glen Cove Community Hosp., Neighborhood Assn. Recipient Madden award NYU, 1982. Mem. Am. Bus. Conf. (founding). Office: Pall Corp 30 Sea Cliff Ave Glen Cove NY 11542

KRASNOFF, MARY ROBSHAW, marketing executive; b. Dublin, Ireland, Aug. 14, 1954; came to U.S., 1975; d. Ray and Maureen (Gildea) Robshaw; m. Richard I. Krasnoff, Aug. 17, 1985. BA in English, Univ. Coll. Dublin, 1975; postgrad., Boston U., 1982-83. Asst. office mgr. Simpson Gumpertz & Heger Inc., Cambridge, Mass., 1975-82; tng. developer Wang Labs., Burlington, Mass., 1983-84; mktg. specialist Compudas Corp., Ithaca, N.Y., 1984-87, Nat. Planning Data Corp., Ithaca, 1987—. Author: Lex Word-processing on DEC PDP-ll, 1982. Fundraiser Planned Parenthood Tompkins County, Ithaca, 1988. Mem. Am. Mktg. Assn., Fingerlakes Graphics Assn., Nat. Trust for Historic Preservation, Dewitt Hist. Soc. Democrat. Roman Catholic. Office: Nat Planning Data Corp 20 Terrace Hill Ithaca NY 14851

KRASTS, AIVARS, oil company executive; b. Riga, Latvia, Apr. 8, 1938; came to U.S., 1948, naturalized, 1956; s. Janis and Milda Lusis K.; m. Linda Compton Reich, Aug. 10, 1962; children: Evan Compton, Kerry Elizabeth. AB, Middlebury Coll., 1960; MBA, U. Chgo., 1962. Project coordinator, new projects Conoco Inc., N.Y.C., 1962-70, dir. coordinating and planning, 1970-78; gen. mgr. coordinating and planning Conoco Inc., Stamford, Conn., 1978-80; v.p. coordinating and planning Conoco Inc., Stamford and Wilmington, Del., 1980-87; v.p. planning and analysis Conoco Inc., Houston, 1987—. Contbr. articles to profl. jours. Served with Med. Service Corps USAR, 1960-68. Mem. Planning Forum, Assn. Corp. Growth. Clubs: Greenville Country (Wilmington); Houston Racquet. Office: Conoco Inc 600 N Dairy Ashford Rd Houston TX 77079

KRAT, GARY WALDEN, financial services company executive; b. Rockville Centre, N.Y., Aug. 22, 1947; s. Irving and Pearl (Walden) K.; m. Leslie Muney, Oct. 26, 1969; children: Jaime Beth, Joshua Evan. BA, U. Pitts., 1969; JD, Fordham U. Sch. Law, 1973. Bar: N.Y. 1974, U.S. Cir. Ct. (2nd cir.) N.Y. 1974. Assoc. Proskauer Rose Goetz & Mendelsohn, N.Y.C., 1973-77; exec. Integrated Resources, Inc., N.Y.C., 1977-79, v.p., 1979-81, sr. v.p., 1981-83, exec v.p., 1983—; pres. Integrated Resources Equity Corp., N.Y.C., 1986—; bd. dirs. Hanifen Imhoff, Inc., Denver, 1987. Mem. N.Y.C. Bar Assn., Internat. Assn. Fin. Planners. Jewish. Office: Integrated Resources Equity Corp 10 Union Sq E New York NY 10003

KRATZ, JANET CONROY, investment advisor; b. Chgo., Dec. 9, 1952; d. Ambrose Francis and Janet Elizabeth (McCann) Conroy; m. Richard Ivan Kratz, Mar. 27, 1982; children: Joseph Ambrose, Patrick Howard. BFA, Western Ill. U., 1975. Book mfg. sales Rand McNally, Skokie, 1975-77; sales administr. Conn. Gen. Life Ins., Chgo., 1977-81; registered rep. Kidder Peabody & Co., Milw., 1981-84; investment advisor Janco Investment Counsel, Milw., 1985—. Mem. Profl. Dimensions. Republican. Roman Catholic.

KRAUS, HARRY ARNOLD, marketing communications company executive; b. N.Y.C., Aug. 11, 1936; s. Harry A. and Rosalie Kraus; student Pace Coll., 1954-58, N.Y. U., 1963-65, New Sch., 1966-69; m. Diana Izzi, Apr. 18, 1971; 1 dau., Juliana Margaret; children by previous marriage—Ellen Beth, David Joseph. Vice pres. LHO Inc., N.Y.C., 1969-72; dir. market services Nat. Union Electric Corp., Stamford, Conn., 1962-69; dir. advt. and sales promotion Fedders Corp., Edison, N.J., 1958-62; pres. Modular Mktg. Inc., N.Y.C., 1972—; faculty mem. Inst. Advt. Mgmt.; lectr. and writer in field. Mem. Queens County Republican Com., 1963-65; bd. dirs. Queens Symphony Orch., Alcoholism Council Greater N.Y., Assn. for Classical Music. Recipient Boli awards 1975, 76, 77, 79, Andy awards 1976, 77, 78, 79, John Caples award, 1987. Mem. Direct Mail Mktg. Assn. (Echo award 1980, 81), Council of Sales Promotion Agys., Direct Mktg. Assn. Clubs: Atrium, Friars. Home: 125 W 76th St New York NY 10023 Office: Modular Mktg Inc 1841 Broadway New York NY 10023

KRAUS, JACK CHARLES, real estate corporation executive; b. La Porte, Ind., June 16, 1947; s. Charles Frederich and Rose (Conforti) K.; children: Jennifer Louise, Ryan Christopher. AA in Applied Sci., Purdue U., 1978, BS in Tech. with distinction, 1985. Constrn. worker No. Ind. Pub. Service Co., Gary, 1970-72; electrician No. Ind. Pub. Service Co., Bailey, 1972-77; instr., tng. dept. No. Ind. Pub. Service Co., La Porte, 1977-82, head tng. dept., 1982-84; mgr. No. Ind. Pub. Service Co., Hammond, 1985-88; pres. Real Property Rebates, Inc., La Porte, 1988—; instr. Purdue U., Westville, Ind., 1985—. Bd. dirs. Lake County Council on Sustance Abuse; coordinator NIPSO Employee Assistance Program. Served as sgt. USMC, 1966-69, Vietnam. Mem. Associated Mgmt. Inst., Purdue Alumni Assn., IEEE, Nat Palm Soc. for No. Ind. Clubs: Cougars (Des Plaines, Ill.). Lodge: Moose. Home and Office: 202 Orchard Bluff La Porte IN 46350

KRAUS, JEAN ELIZABETH GRAU, insurance agent; b. New Orleans, June 8, 1932; d. Adolph Eugene and Katherine Caroline (O'Nion) Grau; divorced; children: Steven, Marilyn, Laurence, Lorraine. BEd, Loyola U. of New Orleans, 1953, MS, 1972. Cert. tchr., La. Tchr. French and English Notre Dame Acad., Washington, 1954-55; tchr. French Orleans Parish Pub. Sch. Dist., New Orleans, 1953-54, 72-86; pvt. practice insurance New Orleans, 1980—; tchr. gifted students Plaquemines Parish Pub. Schs., 1987—. Author numerous poems, contbr. poetry to Scimitar and Song, Yearbook Modern Poetry, others. Pres. Aurora-Hyman-Kabel Civic Orgn., New Orleans, 1982—, del. Pres.' Council of Civic Orgns., 1984—; adv. bd. Algiers Community Network, 1985—; active Algiers Priorities Conv., 1986—, Non-Pack Police Support Group, West Bank Action Com. Mem. AAUW (past pres. Crescent City chpt.), Codofil, France-Amérique, Am. Assn. Tchrs. French, La. Edn. Assn., L'Athénée Louisinais, Internat. Platform Assn., Kappa Kappa Iota, Delta Epsilon Sigma, Kappa Delta Pi. Republican. Roman Catholic. Home and Office: 1601 Kabel Dr New Orleans LA 70131

KRAUS, NORMA JEAN, business executive; b. Pitts., Feb. 11, 1931; d. Edward Karl and Alli Alexandra (Hermanson) K. B.A., U. Pitts., 1954; postgrad. NYU Grad. Sch. Bus. Adminstrn., 1959-61, Cornell U. Grad. Sch. Labor Relations, 1969-70. Personnel mgr. for several cos., 1957-70; corp. dir. personnel TelePrompter Corp., N.Y.C., 1970-73; exec. asst., speech writer to lt. gov. N.Y. State, Office Lt. Gov., Albany, 1974-79; v.p. human resources, labor relations and stockholder relations Volt Info. Scis., Inc., N.Y.C., 1979—. Co-founder, Manhattan Women's Polit. Caucus, 1971, N.Y. State Women's Polit. Caucus, 1972, vice chair N.Y. State Women's Polit. Caucus, 1978; bd. dirs. Ctr. for Women in Govt., 1977-79. Served to lt. (s.g.) USNR, 1954-57. Pa. State Senatorial scholar, 1950-54. Mem. Women's Econ. Roundtable, Indsl. Relations Research Assn., Employment Mgmt. Assn., Am. Compensation Assn. Democrat. Avocations: politics, women's rights, breeding Persian cats. Office: Volt Info Scis Inc 101 Park Ave New York NY 10178

KRAUS, PANSY DAEGLING, gemology consultant, editor; b. Santa Paula, Calif., Sept. 21, 1916; d. Arthur David and Elsie (Pardee) Daegling; m.

Charles Frederick Kraus, Mar. 1, 1941 (div. Nov. 1961). AA, San Bernardino Valley Jr. Coll., 1938; student Longmeyer's Bus. Coll., 1940; grad. gemologist diploma Gemological Assn. Gt. Britain, 1960, Gemological Inst. Am., 1966. Clk. Convair, San Diego, 1943-48; clk. San Diego County Schs. Publs., 1948-57; mgr. Rogers and Boblet Art-Craft, San Diego, 1958-64; part-time editorial asst. Lapidary Jour., San Diego, 1963-64, assoc. editor, 1964-69, editor, 1970—, sr. editor, 1984-85; pvt. practice cons., San Diego, 1985—; lectr. gems, gemology local gem, mineral groups; gem & mineral club bull. editor groups. Mem. San Diego Mineral & Gem Soc., Gemol. Soc. San Diego, Gemol. Assn. Great Britain, Mineral. Soc. Am., Epsilon Sigma Alpha. Author: Introduction to Lapidary, 1987; editor, layout dir.: Gem. Cutting Shop Helps, 1964, The Fundamentals of Gemstone Carving, 1967, Appalachian Mineral and Gem Trails, 1968, Practical Gem Knowledge for the Amateur, 1969, Southwest Mineral and Gem Trails, 1972, revision editor Gemcraft (Quick and Leiper), 1977; contbr. articles to Lapidary jour., Keystone Mktg. catalog. Home and Office: PO Box 20908 San Diego CA 92120

KRAUSE, DAVID JAMES, accountant, retail company executive; b. Detroit, Apr. 19, 1953; s. Loran F. and Mary (Smellie) K.; m. Betty Lynn Rapp, June 19, 1976; children—Melissa Ann, Rebecca Lynn. BA in Econs., Bus. Adminstrn., Adrian Coll., 1975; MBA, U. Pitts., 1983. CPA, Pa. Mem. audit staff, Coopers & Lybrand, Pitts., 1975-78; asst. controller G.C. Murphy Co., McKeesport, Pa., 1978-79, corp. controller, 1979-85, v.p. fin., Family Dollar Stores, Inc., Charlotte, N.C., 1985-88; sr. v.p. fin. Family Dollar Stores, Inc., 1988, v.p., corp. controller Revco D.S. Inc., Twinsburg, Ohio, 1988—. Mem. Am. Inst. CPA's, Pa. Inst. CPA's. Republican. Avocations: golf, reading, landscaping. Home: 16 Pitkin Cir Hudson OH 44236 Office: Revco D S Inc 1925 Enterprise Pkwy Twinsburg OH 44087

KRAUSE, RICHARD ARTHUR, finance company executive; b. Detroit, Dec. 12, 1939; s. Arthur Walter and Crystal Marie (Carnes) K.; m. Margaret Elizabeth Gormly, Sept. 1, 1961; children: Robert A., Nicole L., Deidre L., Kimberly A. and Kelly E. (twins), Ashlei S. BA, Stetson U., 1962, MA, 1963. Exec. v.p. finance, treas. Rinker Materials Corp., West Palm Beach, Fla., 1963—; bd. dirs. Barnett Bank Palm Beach County, West Palm Beach; chmn. fin. com., trustee Palm Beach Atlantic Coll., West Palm Beach, 1986—. Mem. Nat. Corp. Cash Mgmt. Assn. Reublican. Baptist. Lodge: Kiwanis. Home: 1520 Mediterranean Rd West Palm Beach FL 33406 Office: Rinker Materials Corp 310 Okeechobee Blvd West Palm Beach FL 33401

KRAUSS, GARY LEE, accountant; b. Belleville, Ill., June 22, 1945; s. Robert H. and Laverna K. (Obst) K.; m. Terrie P. Cange, July 14, 1972; children: Melissa, Brandon, Jennifer. BS in Acctg., Washington U., St. Louis, 1969; MS in Fin., St. Louis U., 1974. CPA, Mo., Ill. Staff acct. Lopata, Lopata & Dubinsky, Clayton, Mo., 1969-76; pvt. practice Belleville, Ill., 1976—; instr. So. Ill. U., Edwardsville, 1976-82. Mem. Am. Inst. CPA's, Ill. CPA Soc.. Republican. Lutheran. Club: Oak Hill Bath (Belleville). Lodges: Masons, Optimists (sec. Belleville chpt. 1986-88). Office: 5320 W Main St Belleville IL 62221

KRAUSS, JOHN EDWARD, radio station administrator; b. Bklyn., Apr. 12, 1949; s. J. Edward and Jeannette (Taggart) K.; m. Judy I. Brown, May 7, 1983. BS, SUNY, Oswego, 1973, postgrad., 1987—. With Sta. WRVO-FM, Oswego, 1973—, dir. devel., 1977-84, asst. sta. mgr., 1984—; owner Lakeshore Communications Rsch., 1980—. Treas. Grace Luth. Ch., Oswego. Mem. Masons. Office: Sta WRVO FM Oswego NY 13126

KRAUT, GERALD ANTHONY, data processing services company executive; b. St. Paul, Oct. 21, 1951; s. Eugene Arthur and Laurine Antoinette (LaScotte) K.; m. Marcia Mae Mittelstadt, July 21, 1979; 1 child, Elizabeth Ann. B.S., U. Minn., Mpls., 1973, M.B.A., 1975. Asst. v.p. First Bank, Mpls., 1977-78, v.p., 1978-83, sr. v.p., 1983-84; exec. v.p. First Bank System, Mpls., 1984-88; pres., chief oper. officer Warrington Fin. Systems, Inc., Hopkins, Minn., 1988—. Contbr. article to mag. Recipient High Distinction award U. Minn., 1973; Grad. fellow Minn. Bankers Assn., 1975. Mem. Minn. Bankers Funds Mgmt. Com., Beta Gamma Sigma. Republican. Roman Catholic. Club: Minn. Soaring (Stanton). Home: 5864 Oxford St Shoreview MN 55126 Office: Warrington Fin Systems Inc 601 2nd Ave S Hopkins MN 55343

KRAVCHUK, ROBERT SACHA, management educator, consultant; b. Stamford, Conn., July 4, 1955; s. Sacha and Estelle Helen (Wachowski) K.; m. Natalie Maria Kuzma, June 24, 1978; 1 child, Elisabeth Aasta. BA, BS cum laude, U. Conn., 1977; MPA, U. Hartford, 1979; MBA, Columbia U., 1980, MA Syracuse U., 1987, PhD, 1989. Cert. internal auditor, mgmt. acct. Group ins. underwriter Conn. Gen. Life Ins. Co., Hartford, 1977-79; adj. prof. William Paterson Coll., Wayne, N.J., 1980; sr. control analyst Conn. Gen. Life Ins. Co., Hartford, 1981-82, cash flow product mgr., 1982-83; assoc. Booz, Allen & Hamilton, N.Y.C., 1984-86; doctoral fellow, Maxwell Sch. Citizenship and Pub. Affairs, Syracuse (N.Y.) U., 1986—; adj. instr., Le Moyne Coll., Syracuse, 1986-88; instr., 1988—. Fellow Life Mgmt. Inst.; mem. Am. Soc. Public Adminstrn., Am. Polit. Sci. Assn. Republican. Roman Catholic. Home: 5696 Thompson Rd DeWitt NY 13214 Office: Le Moyne Coll Syracuse NY 13214

KRAW, GEORGE MARTIN, lawyer; b. Oakland, Calif., June 17, 1949; s. George and Pauline Dorothy (Herceg) K.; m. Sarah Lee Kenyon, Sept. 3, 1983. BA, U. Calif.-Santa Cruz, 1971; student, Lenin Inst., Moscow, 1971; MA, U. Calif.-Berkeley, 1974, JD, 1976. Bar: Calif. 1976, U.S. Dist. Ct. (no. dist.) Calif. 1976, U.S. Supreme Ct. 1980. Assoc. Bachan, Skillicorn, Watsonville, Calif., 1976-79, Trepel & Clark, San Jose, Calif., 1979-81; ptnr. Mount, Kraw & Stoelker, San Jose, 1981-88, Kraw & Kraw, San Jose, 1988—; asst. sec. Sysgen, Inc., Fremont, Calif., 1982—. Mem. ABA, Inter-Am. Bar Assn. Clubs: Metropolitan, University (San Jose). Office: Kraw & Kraw 333 W San Carlos Ste 1050 San Jose CA 95110

KREAGER, EILEEN DAVIS, bursar; b. Caldwell, Ohio, Mar. 2, 1924; d. Fred Raymond and Esther (Farson) Davis. B.B.A., Ohio State U., 1945. With accounts receivable dept. M & R Dietetic, Columbus, Ohio, 1945-50; complete charge bookkeeper Magic Seal Paper Products, Columbus, 1950-53, A. Walt Runglin Co., Los Angeles, 1953-54; office mgr. Roy C. Haddox and Son, Columbus, 1954-60; bursar Meth. Theol. Sch. Ohio, Delaware, 1961-86; adminstrv. cons. Fin. Ltd., 1986—; ptnr. Coll. Administrv. Sci., Ohio State U., 1975-80; seminar participant Paperwork Systems and Computer Sci., 1965, Computer Systems, 1964, Griffith Found. Seminar Working Women, 1975; pres. Altrusa Club of Delaware, Ohio, 1972-73. Del. Altrusa Internat., Montreal, 1972, Altrusa Regional, Greenbrier, 1973. Mem. AAUW Assoc. Am. Inst. Mgmt. (exec. council of Inst., 1979); Am. Soc. Profl. Cons., Internat. Platform Assn., Ohio State U. Alumna Assn., Columbus Computer Soc., Kappa Delta. Methodist. Clubs: Ohio State U. Faculty, Delaware Country. Home: PO Box 214 Worthington OH 43085

KREBS, ROBERT DUNCAN, transportation company executive; b. Sacramento, May 2, 1942; s. Ward Carl and Eleanor Blauth (Duncan) K.; m. Anne Lindstrom, Sept. 11, 1971; children: Robert Ward, Elisabeth Lindstrom, Duncan Lindstrom. B.A., Stanford U., 1964; M.B.A., Harvard U., 1966. Asst. gen. mgr. So. Pacific Transp. Co., Houston, 1974-75; asst. regional ops. mgr. So. Pacific Transp. Co., 1975-76; asst. v.p. So. Pacific Transp. Co., San Francisco, 1976-77; asst. to pres. So. Pacific Transp. Co., 1977-79, gen. mgr., 1979, v.p. transp., 1979-80, v.p. ops., 1980-82, pres., 1982-83, also dir.; pres., chief operating officer Santa Fe So. Pacific Corp., 1983-88, pres., chief exec. officer, chmn. bd., 1988—, also bd. dirs. Trustee Glenwood Sch. for Boys, John G. Shedd Aquarium, Northwestern Meml. Hosp., Chgo., Sta. WTTW-TV, Ravinia; mem. Northwestern U. Assocs., bd. dirs. Phelps Dodge Corp. Mem. Stanford U. Alumni Assn., Phi Beta Kappa, Kappa Sigma. Republican. Episcopalian. Clubs: Onwentsia (Lake Forest, Ill.); Pacific Union, World Trade, Bohemian, Chicago. Office: Santa Fe So Pacific Corp 224 S Michigan Ave Chicago IL 60604

KREER, IRENE OVERMAN, meeting management executive; b. McGrawsville, Ind., Nov. 11, 1926; d. Ralph and Laura Edith (Sharp) Overman; m. Henry Blackstone Kreer, Dec. 22, 1946; children: Laurene (dec.), Linda Kreer Witt. BS in Speech Pathology, Northwestern U., 1948. Speech pathologist pub. schs. Chgo., 1947-49; staff asst., lectr. Art Inst. Chgo., 1962—; pres. Irene Overman Kreer & Assocs., Inc., Chgo., 1962—; bd. dirs., officer SKK Inc., Chgo., 1962—; frequent lectr. on art, architecture Chgo. area; TV appearances representing Art Inst. edn. programs. Formerly bd. dirs. Glenview (Ill.) Pub. Library; mem. Glenview Community Ch. Mem. Field Mus., Chgo. Architecture Found., Smithsonian Assocs., Nat. Trust for Hist. Preservation, Assoc. Alumnae Northwestern U. (bd. dirs. 1975—), Delta Delta Delta. Republican.

KREHBIEL, FREDERICK AUGUST, electronics company executive; b. Chgo., June 2, 1941; s. John Hammond and Margaret Ann (Veeck) K.; m. Kay Kirby, Dec. 20, 1974; children—William Veeck, Jay Frederick. B.A., Lake Forest Coll., 1963; postgrad., Georgetown U., U. Leicester, Eng. Export mgr., then v.p. internat. Molex Inc., Lisle, Ill., 1970-75, exec. v.p., dir., 1976—; pres. Molex Internat. Co., 1976-89, vice chmn. and chief exec. officer, 1988—; dir. Tellabs Inc., Molex, Inc., No. Trust Bank, A.M. Castle & Co. Trustee Inst. Internat. Edn., Chgo., Rush Med. Ctr., Chgo., Lake Forest Coll., Chgo. Zool. Soc.; dir. Sch. Art Inst. Chgo. Mem Hinsdale (Ill.) Golf Club, Chgo. Club, Chgo. Yacht Club, Racquet Club Chgo. Home: 1260 N Lake Shore Dr Chicago IL 60610 Office: Molex Inc 2222 Wellington Ct Lisle IL 60532

KREIDER, LEONARD EMIL, economics educator; b. Newton, Kans., Feb. 25, 1938; s. Leonard C. and Rachel (Weaver) K.; m. Louise Ann Pankratz, June 10, 1963; children: Brent Emil, Todd Alan, Ryan Eric. Student, Bluffton Coll., 1956-58; BA, Bethel Coll., 1960; student, Princeton U., 1960-61; MA, Ohio State U., 1962, PhD, 1968. Economist So. Ill. U., Carbondale, 1965-70; asst. prof. Beloit (Wis.) Coll., 1970—, prof., 1978, chmn. Dept. Econs. & Mgmt., 1984—, acting v.p. acad. affairs, 1987-88; chief of party, Devel. Assocs., Asuncion, Paraguay, 1970; economist Deere and Co., 1973, Castle and Cooke, San Francisco, 1975-76, AmCore, Rockford, Ill., 1984; cons. corps. and attys. Author: Development and Utilization of Managerial Talent, 1968; contbr. numerous articles, reports to profl. jours. Mem. Nat. Assn. Bus. Economists, Am. Econs. Assn., Am. Assn. Higher Edn., Soc. Internat. Devel. (pres. So. Ill. chpt. 1969), Indsl. Relations Research Assn. (elections com. 1974). Presbyterian. Home: 820 Milwaukee Rd Beloit WI 53511 Office: Beloit Coll Dept Econ Mgmt Beloit WI 53511

KREISBERG, NEIL IVAN, advertising executive; b. N.Y.C., Feb. 1, 1945; s. Leo and Lucille (Levy) K.; children: Andrew Jay, Tracy, Michelle; m. Linda Gering, Sept. 24, 1986; 1 child, William Gering. BSBA, Rider Coll., Trenton, N.J., 1966. With Grey Advt. Inc., N.Y.C., 1966—; v.p., mgmt. supr. Grey Advt. Inc., 1974-79, sr. v.p., account mgmt., 1979-85, exec. v.p., 1985—. Jewish. Office: Grey Advt Inc 777 3rd Ave New York NY 10017

KREMER, HONOR FRANCES (NOREEN), business executive; b. Ireland, Aug. 9, 1939; came to U.S., 1961; m. Manny Kremer, May 17, 1963; 1 child, Patrick David. BS, CUNY; MS, Baruch Coll. Group sec. Bentalls, Ltd., Kingston-On-Thames, Surrey, Eng., 1954-58, Cen. Secondary Sch., Hamilton, Ont., Can., 1959-61; office mgr. Aschner Assocs., N.Y.C., 1961-63; pub. relations asst. McMaster U., Hamilton, 1963-64; office mgr. Packaging Components, N.Y.C., 1965-67; head acctg. Shaller Rubin Assocs., N.Y.C., 1967-72, v.p. fin. and adminstrn., 1972-79, sr. v.p., 1979-82, sr. v.p., mem. exec. com., 1982—, sec.-treas. multi-media div., 1972-75; pvt. practice bus. cons., 1986-88; sr. v.p., chief exec. officer Gace Med. Advt., N.Y.C., 1988—; fin. officer Lewis & Gace Med. Advt., N.Y.C., 1989—. Mem. Nat. Fedn. Bus. and Profl. Women (bd. dirs., v.p.), Advt. Fin. Mgmt. Group. Roman Catholic. Office: 82 Riverside Dr New York NY 10024

KREMER, JOHN FREDERICK, publisher, writer, consultant; b. Perham, Minn., Jan. 16, 1949; s. Frank Matthew and Lucille Ernee (Nester) K. BA, Macalester Coll., 1971; MA, Maharishi Internat. U., 1975. Writer Mpls., 1971-73; tchr. Internat. Meditation Soc., Mpls., 1973-75; instr. writing Maharishi Internat. U., Fairfield, Iowa, 1974-77; dir., adminstr. Transcendental Meditation Ctr., St. Paul, 1977-80; dir. rshc. and devel. First Impressions, Fairfield, 1981-83; pub. Ad-Lib Pubs., Fairfield, 1983—; bd. advisers Am. Book Coun., Scranton, Pa., 1986-88, Info. Mktg. Newsletter, Davis, Calif., 1985-87. Author: 1001 Ways to Market Your Book, 1989, Book Marketing Made Easier, 1986, Mail Order Made Easy, 1983, Book Market Opportunities, 1986, Tinseltowns USA, 1988; editor: (newsletter) Book Marketing Update, 1986—. Mem. Pub. Mktg. Assn, Mid-Am. Pub. Assn. (vice chmn. 1987—), Am. Booksellers Assn., Upper Midwest Booksellers Assn., Am. Book Coun. (bd. advisors 1986-88), Am. Film Inst., Com. Small Mag. Editors and Pubs. (bd. dirs. 1985-89). Roman Catholic. Home: 51 N Fifth St Fairfield IA 52556 Office: Ad Lib Publs PO Box 1102 Fairfield IA 52556-1102

KREMSDORF, JULIAN, stationery manufacturing company executive; b. N.Y.C., June 13, 1920; s. Irving and Mary (Jukofsky) K.; m. Sylvia Estelle Baum, Aug. 16, 1942; children—Arlene Thomashow, Joel, Wendy. B.S., NYU, 1940. With Lessco Sales Inc., Los Angeles, 1963-83, v.p., dir., 1963, pres. 1966; with Gussco Mfg. Inc., Bklyn., 1940ú85,ret., 1985; sec., 1951, v.p., 1956, dir., 1963, pres., 1965. Served to sgt. Q.M.C., U.S. Army, 1941-45.

KRENGEL, THEODORE H., diversified metal manufacturing company executive; b. 1928; married. BS MetE, Purdue U., 1949. With Internat. Mills, 1949-55, Westmoreland Metal Mfrs. Co., 1955-59, Allied Tube and Conduit Corp., 1959—; now also chmn., pres., chief exec. officer, dir. Atcor Inc., Harvey, Ill. Office: Atcor Inc 16100 S Lathrop Ave Harvey IL 60426 *

KREPS, JUANITA MORRIS, former secretary of commerce; b. Lynch, Ky., Jan. 11, 1921; d. Elmer M. and Cenia (Blair) Morris; m. Clifton H. Kreps, Jr., Aug. 11, 1944; children: Sarah, Laura, Clifton. A.B., Berea Coll., 1942; M.A., Duke U., 1944; Ph.D., 1948; hon. degrees, Bryant Coll., 1972, U. N.C. at Chapel Hill, 1973, Denison U., 1973, Cornell Coll., 1973, U. Ky., 1975, Queens Coll., 1975, St. Lawrence U., 1975, Wheaton Coll., 1976, Claremont Grad. Sch., 1979, Berea Coll., 1979, Tulane U., 1980, Colgate U., 1980, Trinity Coll., 1981, U. Rochester, 1984. Instr. econs. Denison U., 1945-46, asst. prof., 1948-50; mem. faculty Duke U., 1955-77, assoc. prof., 1962-68, prof. econs., 1968-77; James B. Duke prof. Duke, 1972-77; asst. provost Duke U., 1969-72, v.p., 1973-77; U.S. sec. commerce 1977-79; bd. dirs. N.Y. Stock Exchange, 1972-77; dir. Eastman Kodak Co., ARMCO, UAL Corp., J.C. Penney, AT&T, Deere & Co., Zurn Industries, Inc., Chrysler Corp.; Trustee Berea Coll., Duke Endowment, Nat. Humanities Center, 1983-86, HumRRO, 1980-83, Council on Fgn. Relations, 1983—; trustee Tchrs. Ins. and Annuity Assn. Stock; mem. Coll. Retirement Equities Fund, 1985—; bd. dirs. Nat. Merit Scholarship Corp., 1972-77, Ednl. Testing Service, 1971-77; mem. Nat. Manpower Policy Task Force. Author: (with C.E. Ferguson) Principles of Economics, 2d rev. edit, 1965, Lifetime Allocation of Work and Income, 1971, Sex in the Marketplace: American Women at Work, 1971, Women and the American Economy, 1976; co-author: (with C.E. Ferguson) Contemporary Labor Economics, 1973; Editor: (with C.E. Ferguson) Employment, Income and Retirement Problems of the Aged, 1963, Technology, Manpower and Retirement Policy, 1966, Sex, Age and Work, 1975. named to Presdl. Commn. on Nat. Agenda for the 80's, 1979; recipient N.C. Pub. Service award, 1976; Stephen Wise award, 1978, Woman of Yr. award Ladies Home Jour., 1978, Duke U. Alumni award, 1983, Haskins award Coll. Bus. and Pub. Adminstrn., NYU, 1984, first Corp. Governance award Nat. Assn. Corp. Dirs., 1987, Dir.'s Choice Leadership award Nat. Women's Econ. Alliance Found., 1987, Disitng. Meritorious Service medal Duke U. Alumni, 1987. Fellow Gerontol. Soc. (v.p. 1971-72), Am. Acad. Arts and Scis.; mem. Am. Econ. Assn. (v.p. 1983-84), So. Econ. Assn. (pres. 1975-76), AAUP, AAUW (Achievement award 1981), Indsl. Relations Research Assn. (exec. com.). Office: Duke U 115 E Duke Bldg Durham NC 27708

KRESA, KENT, aerospace executive; b. N.Y.C., Mar. 24, 1938; s. Helmy and Marjorie (Boutelle) K.; m. Joyce Anne McBride, Nov. 4, 1961; 1 child, Kiren. B.S.A.A., MIT, 1959, M.S.A.A., 1961, E.A.A., 1966. Sr. scientist research and advanced devel. div. AVCO, Wilmington, Mass., 1959-61; staff mem. MIT Lincoln Lab., Lexington, Mass., 1961-68; dep. dir. strategic tech. office Def. Advanced Research Projects Agy., Washington, 1968-73; dir. tactical tech. office Def. Advanced Research Project Agy., Washington, 1973-75; v.p., mgr. Research & Tech. Ctr. Northrop Corp., Hawthorne, Calif., 1975-76; v.p., gen. mgr. Ventura div. Northrop Corp., Newbury Park, Calif., 1976-82; group v.p. Aircraft Group Northrop Corp., Los Angeles, 1982-86, sr. v.p. tech. devel. and planning, 1986-87, pres., chief operating officer, 1987—; bd. dirs. John Tracy Clinic.; mem. Chief of Naval Ops. exec. panel Washington, Def. Sci. Bd., Washington, DNA New Alternatives Working Group, Los Angeles, Dept. Aeronautics and Astronautics Corp. Vis. Com. MIT. Recipient Henry Webb Salsbury award MIT, 1959, Arthur D. Flemming award, 1975; Sec. of Def. Meritorious Civilian Service medal, 1975, USN Meritorious Pub. Service citation, 1975, Exceptional Civilian Service award USAF, 1987. Fellow AIAA; mem. Naval Aviation Mus. Found., Navy League U.S., Soc. Flight Test Engrs., Assn. of U.S. Army, Nat. Space Club, Am. Def. Preparedness Assn. Club: Mountaingate Country. Office: Northrop Corp 1840 Century Park E Los Angeles CA 90067

KRESCH, SANDRA DARYL, newsmagazine development director; b. N.Y.C., Sept. 13, 1945; d. Howard and Jean Gleich; m. Samuel H. Hagler. BS in Physiol. Psychology, U. Penn, 1966. Research assoc. Simat, Helliensen & Eichner, Inc., N.Y.C., 1966-67; study dir. Nat. Analysts, Inc., Phila., 1968-69; pres. Sandra D. Kresch Consulting Services, Atherton, Calif., 1969-70; mgr. market research v.p. Booz, Allen & Hamilton, N.Y.C., 1970-75; v.p. Booz, Allen Venture Mgmt., Inc., N.Y.C., 1976-78; corp. devel. v.p. Booz, Allen & Hamilton, Inc., N.Y.C., 1978-80, mgmt. cons. practice v.p., 1980-82; mkgt. sr. v.p. devel. and info. services div. Time Inc., N.Y.C., 1983-84, dir. strategic planning Magazine Group, 1984-86, worldwide devel. dir., 1986-89; pres., cons. assoc. 1989—; bd. dirs. Pub. Investors Am., AMA/Am. Assn. Advertising Agys. Joint Research Com. on Children's Advertising, Vol. Cons. Group. Presenter numerous career-related speeches. Pres. Jose Limon Dance Found., Inc.; chmn. exec. and nominating com.; bd. dirs. Spence-Chapin Services to Families & Children; mem. exec., and fin. com.; bd. dirs. YWCA of N.Y., devel. com.; mem. personnel and program com.; chmn. Long Range Planning Com. Recipient Tribute to Women in Internat. Ind. award YWCA, 1978. Home: 14 E 75th St New York NY 10021

KRESESKI, MARY LEE, financial company manager; b. Santa Clara, Calif., Apr. 8, 1959; d. Wayne Lawrence and Vera Mable (Brantley) Slinker; m. Frank Edward Kreseski, June 18, 1982; 1 child, Dean Edward. Grad. high sch., Santa Clara. With Am. Express, Greensboro, N.C., 1981—. Mem. NAFE. Office: Am Express 6522 Airport Pkwy Greensboro NC 27000

KRESS, GEORGE F., packaging company executive; b. Green Bay, Wis., Sept. 15, 1903; s. Frank F. and Louise (Schmidt) K.; m. Marguerite Christensen, Nov. 10, 1926; children—James, Marilyn Kress Swanson, Donald. B.A., U. Wis., 1925. With Green Bay Packaging Inc., 1933—, chmn. bd., 1963—. Trustee Charitable, Ednl. and Sci. Found. of Wis. Med. Soc.; pres., chmn. bd. Green Bay affiliate Am. Found. Counseling Services, Inc.; mem. Brown County Republican Com. Mem. Ch. of Christ. Clubs: N.Y. Yacht, Great Lakes Cruising, Mackinac Island Yacht, Sun Valley Ski, Elks. Home: 2376 Du Charme Ln Green Bay WI 54301 Office: Green Bay Packaging Inc PO Box 19017 Green Bay WI 54307 also: Green Bay Packaging Inc 1700 N Webster Ave Green Bay WI 54302

KRESS, THOMAS GEORGE, manufacturing company executive; b. Dubuque, Iowa, May 11, 1931; s. Henry L. and Jane (Schadle) K.; m. Lou Ann Kuehnle, Sept. 6, 1952; children—Kristine, Elizabeth, Kathleen, Susan, Thomas George, Andrew, Julianna, Matthew, Michael. B.A., Loras Coll., 1953; M.B.A., Northwestern U., 1961; grad., Advanced Mgmt. Program, Harvard, 1971. Cost analyst Gen. Electric Co., Chgo., 1956-62; div. controller Sheller Mfg. Corp., Keokuk, Ia., 1962-64; asst. corp. controller Sheller Mfg. Corp., Detroit, 1964-66; corp. controller Sheller Globe Corp., Toledo, 1967-72, treas., 1972-74, v.p. treasury, 1974-84, v.p. mgmt. info. and telecommunications systems, 1984-85, v.p. finance, 1986; v.p., gen. mgr. indsl./comml. div. The DeVilbiss Co., Toledo, 1986—; v.p., chief fin. officer Champion Spark Plug Co., Toledo, 1987—. Served with U.S. Army, 1953-55. Mem. Financial Execs. Inst., Nat. Assn. Accountants. Clubs: Toledo, Inverness. Home: 4731 Rose Glenn St Toledo OH 43615 Office: Champion Spark Plug Co PO Box 910 Toledo OH 43661

KRESSLER, JAMES PHILLIP, investment and operations company executive; b. Trenton, N.J., Sept. 22, 1931; s. Earl James and Ruth Emily (Jacoby) K.; m. Nancy Carolyn Loux, Aug. 28, 1954; children: David, Robert, Nancy. B.S., Lehigh U., 1953; M.B.A., Harvard U., 1955. Asst. controller Itek Corp., Lexington, Mass., 1958-62, 65-70; v.p., treas., controller Radiation Counter Labs., Inc., Skokie, Ill., 1962-65; sr. v.p., controller Macmillan, Inc., N.Y.C., 1970-80; v.p., chief fin. officer U.S. Filter Corp., N.Y.C., 1980-82; sr. v.p. fin., chief fin. officer Ashland Tech. Inc., N.Y.C., 1982-85; gen. ptnr. J.B. Poindexter & Co., N.Y.C., 1986—; chief fin. officer Traxxon Inc., 1986—; chief fin. officer Leer Holdings, Inc., 1987—, also bd. dirs.; bd. dirs. EFP Corp., Nat. Steel Service Ctrs. Inc., Leer Holding, Inc. Chmn. bd. auditors Lower Makefield Twp. Served to lt. USNR, 1955-58. Mem. Financial Execs. Inst., Nat. Indsl. Security Assn. (v.p. 1969-70), Nat. Soc. Bus. Budgeting (v.p. 1962), Sigma Phi, Alpha Kappa Psi, Pi Gamma Mu. Lodge: Masons. Home: 908 Sensor Rd Yardley PA 19067 Office: 1719-A Rte 10 Parsippany NJ 07054

KREUTZ, EDWARD C., real estate developer; b. Clayton, Mo., Dec. 27, 1926; s. Edward W. and Florence (Enke) K.; m. Clarice m. Petersen, Sept. 27, 1952; children: Roger, Richard, Robert, Edward jr., Christopher. BBA, U. Miami, Fla., 1949. V.p. Chesterfield Bank, Mo., 1952-59; real estate devel. St. Louis and St. Charles counties, 1959-71; owner Viking Hotel, St. Louis, 1971, Imperial Baking Co., St. Louis, 1983—; adv. dir. Liberty Mus. Ins., Boston, C.T. Supply Co., St. Louis. With U.S. Army, 1944-45. Mem. Rotary (pres. 1969). Republican. Roman Catholic. Home: 62 Portland Dr Frontenac MO 63127 Office: Holiday Inn St Louis SW/Viking 10709 Hwy 366 Saint Louis MO 63127

KRIEGER, BENJAMIN WILLIAM, paper company executive; b. Cin., July 7, 1937; s. William Anthony and Catherine Regina (McDevitt) K.; A.A., U. Cin., 1965; grad. Advanced Mgmt. Program, Harvard U., 1980; m. Rosemary George, Apr. 12, 1958; children—Gregory, Kenneth, Catherine. Sales and asst. sales mgr. Chatfield Paper Corp., Cin., 1956-67; gen. sales mgr. Union Paper & Twine Co. div. Mead Corp., Cleve., 1967-69, v.p., 1969-75, gen. mgr. and pres., 1975-78, pres., Mich. area mgr. Beecher Peck & Lewis Co. div., Detroit, 1978-81; v.p. Dixon Paper Co., Denver, from 1981; pres., chief exec. officer Ris Paper Co., 1984—; pres. Cleve. Graphic Arts Council, 1975; mem. nat. adv. bd. Mead Papers, 1971-73, adv. council Mead Merchants, 1987; chmn. nat. adv. bd. Gilbert Paper Co., 1973-75; chmn. Weyerhauser adv. council, 1987; mem. packaging div. adv. council Reynolds Metals; mem. distbr. council 3M Co. Trustee, pres. North Hills Assn., 1974-75; active United Appeal Fund drive, Jr. Achievement, Greater Cleve. Growth Assn. Mem. Wholesale Distbrs. Assn., Paper Distbn. Council, Nat. Paper Trade Assn., Newcomen Soc., Buckeye Paper Trade Assn., Craftsman Internat., Sales and Mktg. Execs., Cleve. Advt. Club, Cleve. Graphic Arts Assn., Advt. Prodn. Club, Jr. C. of C., Hon. Order Ky. Cols., Assn. Ohio Commodores. Republican. Roman Catholic. Clubs: K.C., Pine Lake Country, Renaissance, Fairlane, Hiwan Country, Boca Teeca Country. Home: 18 Sherwood Dr Oyster Bay CO 11771 Office: Ris Paper Co 1225 Franklin Ave Garden City NY 11530

KRIEGER, PAUL EDWARD, lawyer; b. Fairmont, W.Va., Mar. 30, 1942; s. Paul Julius Krieger and Martha Frances (Graham) Ralph; m. Elizabeth N. Krieger, July 2, 1965; children: Andrew, Thomas. BS in Mining Engring., U. Pitts., 1964; postgrad. Pa. State U., 1964-65; LLB, U. Md., 1968; LLM, George Washington U., 1971. Bar: Md. 1968, D.C. 1973, Tex. 1979, U.S. Patent and Trademark Office, 1970. Faculty research asst. U. Md., 1967-70; assoc. Brumbaugh, Graves, Donohue & Raymond, N.Y.C., 1970-71; ptnr. Lane, Aitken, Dunner & Ziems, Washington, 1971-78; sr. pat. atty. Dresser Industries Inc., Dallas, 1978-79; ptnr. Pravel, Gambrell, Hewitt, Kimball & Krieger, Houston, 1979—; adj. prof. U. Houston Law Ctr., 1985—. Mem. ABA, Am. Pat. Law Assn., Tex. Bar Assn., Houston Pat. Law Assn., N.Y. Pat. Law Assn., U.S. Trademark Assn., Lic. Exec. Soc. Home: 11 Sandalwood Houston TX 77024 Office: 1177 W Loop S Suite 1010 Houston TX 77027

KRIEGER, ROBERT LEE, JR., management consultant, educator; b. Louisville, Nov. 13, 1946; s. Robert Lee and June Elise (Waters) K. B.B.A.,

Memphis State U., 1968, M.B.A., 1969. Adminstrv. asst. to mayor City of Memphis, 1969-72; dir. devel. programs Memphis State U., 1972-74; cons. pvt. practice, Memphis, 1974-76; exec. v.p. Randall Howard & Assocs., Memphis, 1976—; faculty Memphis State U. Coll. Bus., 1984—; speaker numerous profl. groups. Trustee Republican Presdl. Task Force, Washington, 1980—; mem. Rep. Nat. Adv. Com., Washington, 1972—; mem. U.S. Olympic Soc., Boulder, Colo., 1968—. Recipient U.S. Treasury award U.S. Dept. Treasury, 1971; Nat. Presdl. medal of Merit, Rep. Presdl. Task Force, 1984; Pres.'s award Memphis Cotton Carnival Assn., 1968—. Mem. Data Processing Mgmt. Assn., Am. Mgmt. Assn., Am. Film Guild, Met. Opera Guild, Nat. Wildlife Fedn., Alpha Delta Sigma, Sigma Delta Chi. Episcopalian. Clubs: Mensa, Memphis State Alumni. Avocations: writing; bowling; movies and photography; travel; public speaking. Home: 2948 Dalebrook St Memphis TN 38127 Office: Randall Howard & Assocs Inc 5353 Flowering Peach Memphis TN 38115

KRIEGER, WALTER LESLIE, clothing company executive; b. N.Y.C.; s. Irving and Mae (Blaustein) K.; m. Alice Ann Weisberg, Feb. 11, 1962; children—Robert, Carolyn; BBA, CCNY, 1957. With Clarence Rainess & Co., C.P.A.'s, 1957-64; asst. controller McGregor Doniger, Inc., N.Y.C., 1964-65, Jonathan Logan, Inc., N.Y.C., 1965-77, controller, corp. sec., 1977—; v.p. fin. ops. Liz Claibourne, Inc., 1984—; bd. dirs. Garment Ctr. Congregation, 1973—; treas. Men's Club, Congregation B'nai Israel, 1977—. C.P.A., N.Y. Mem. Am. Inst. C.P.A.'s, N.Y. State Soc. C.P.A.'s, Am. Apparel Mfgs. Assn. (fin. mgmt. com. 1986—). Home: Karen Ln Emelson NJ 07630 Office: Liz Claiborne Inc 1 Claiborne Ave North Bergen NJ 07047

KRIENKE, CAROL BELLE MANIKOWSKE (MRS. OLIVER KENNETH KRIENKE), realtor, appraiser; b. Oakland, Calif., June 19, 1917; d. George and Ethel (Purdon) Manikowske; student U. Mo., 1937; B.S., U. Minn., 1940; postgrad. UCLA, 1949; m. Oliver Kenneth Krienke, June 4, 1941; children—Diane (Mrs. Robert Denny), Judith (Mrs. Kenneth A. Giss), Debra Louise (Mrs. Ed Paul Davalos). Demonstrator, Gen. Foods Corp., Mpls., 1940; youth leadership State of Minn. Congl. Conf., U. Minn., Mpls. 1940-41; war prodn. worker Airesearch Mfg. Co., Los Angeles, 1944; tchr. Los Angeles City Schs., 1945-49; realtor DBA Ethel Purdon, Manhattan Beach, Calif., 1949; buyer Purdon Furniture & Appliances, Manhattan Beach, 1950-58; realtor O.K. Krienke Realty, Manhattan Beach, 1958—. Manhattan Beach bd. rep. Community Chest for Girl Scouts U.S., 1957; bd. dirs. South Bay council Girl Scouts U.S.A., 1957-62, mem. Manhattan Beach Coordinating Council, 1956-68; mem. Long Beach Area Childrens Home Soc. (v.p., 1967-68, pres. 1979; charter mem. Beach Pixies, 1957—, pres. 1967; chmn. United Way, 1967); sponsor Beach Cities Symphony, 1953—. Mem. DAR (life, citizenship chmn. 1972-73, v.p. 1979, 83—), Colonial Dames XVII Century (charter mem. Jared Eliot chpt. 1977, v.p., pres. 1979-81, 83-84), Friends of Library, Torrance Lomita Bd. of Realtors, South Bay Bd. Realtors, Nat. Soc. New England Women (life, Calif. Poppy Colony), Internat. Platform Assn., Soc. Descs. of Founders of Hartford (life), Friends of Banning Mus., Manhattan Beach Hist. Soc., Manhattan Beach C. of C. (Rose and Scroll award 1985), U. Minn. Alumni (life). Republican. Mem. Community Ch. (pres. Women's Fellowship 1970-71). Home: 924 Highview St Manhattan Beach CA 90266 Office: OK Krienke Realty 1716 Manhattan Beach Blvd Manhattan Beach CA 90266

KRIER, JOSEPH R., city official. m. Cyndi Taylor. BA, U. Tex., 1968, JD, 1971. Assoc. real estate sect. Bracewell & Patterson, Houston; ptnr., mem. corp. and comml. litigation sect., legal pers. com., chmn. client rels. com. Groce, Locke & Hebdon; assoc. Grieshaber & Roberts, San Antonio; pres., chief exec. officer Greater San Antonio C. of C., 1987—; head JK & Assocs. Mem. centennial commn. U. Tex.; coordinating chmn. task force Target '90: Goals for San Antonio project; past pres., bd. dirs. San Antonio Amateur Sports Found.; past chmn., bd. dirs. Arts Coun. San Antonio; founder, bd. dirs. San Antonio Winston Sch.; bd. dirs. Ctr. for Multiple Handicapped Children, Tex. Soc. for the Prevention of Blindness, San Antonio Community Radio Corp., San Antonio chpt. Tex. Exes, Tex. Bus. Hall of Fame; bd. visitors M.D. Anderson Cancer Clinic, co-chmn. Annual Gift Campaign South Tex., 1987; mem. adv. bd. Tex. Lyceum. Fellow Tex. Bar Assn.; mem. San Antonio Bar Assn., Greater San Antonio C. of C. (chmn. criminal justice task force), Omicron Delta Kappa. Office: Greater San Antonio C of C 602 E Commerce PO Box 1628 San Antonio TX 78296

KRINSLY, STUART Z., lawyer, manufacturing company executive; b. N.Y.C., May 19, 1917; m. Charlotte Wolf, Aug. 18, 1944; children—Ellinjane, Joan Susan. B.A., Princeton U., 1938; LL.B., Harvard U., 1941. Bar: N.Y. Asst. U.S. atty. So. Dist. N.Y., 1942-45; mem. firm Schlesinger & Krinsly, 1945-57; sec. Sun Chem. Corp., N.Y.C., 1957-65, v.p., gen. counsel, 1965-76, sr. v.p., gen. counsel, 1976-78, exec. v.p., gen. counsel, 1978-82, also bd. dirs.; sr. exec. v.p., gen. counsel Sequa Corp., N.Y.C., 1982—; also bd. dirs.; bd. dirs. Ketchum & Co.; ptnr. firm Rich, Lillienstein, Krinsly, Dorman & Hochhauser. Clubs: Beach Point, Princeton of N.Y. Home: 1135 Greacen Point Road Mamaroneck NY 10543 Office: Sequa Corp 200 Park Ave New York NY 10166

KRISHER, PATTERSON HOWARD, management consultant; b. Oklahoma City, Sept. 14, 1933; s. Sherman and Gladys (Patterson) K.; m. Mary Anne Howard, Nov. 21, 1973; children: Sherman H., Bryan P. B.S. in Indsl. Engring., Okla. State U., 1956; A.M.P., Harvard U., 1971. Cert. mgmt. cons. Plant indsl. engr. Procter & Gamble Mfg. Co., Dallas, 1959-60; mktg. rep. IBM, Dalls, 1960-61; mgmt. cons. Arthur Young & Co., San Francisco, Los Angeles and Dallas, 1961-77; nat. dir. mgmt. services Arthur Young & Co., 1977-83, dir. mgmt. services N.Y.C. Office, 1983-86; gen. ptnr. Leep Assocs., Stamford, Conn., 1986—; pres. LP of Fairfield Co. Inc., 1986—; treas. Inst. Mgmt. Cons., 1984-86; guest instr. U. Tex., Ohio State U.; bd. dirs. Control Mgmt. Systems, Colorado Springs, Colo., Integrity Systems Inc., St. Louis. Contbr. to: Handbook of Business Problem Solving, 1980; mem. editorial bd.: Jour. Mgmt. Cons., 1983-86, Boardroom Reports, 1984—. Chmn. Arthur Young Polit. Action Com., 1978-86; bd. dirs. Homeowners Assn.; mem. vis. com. indsl. engring. dept. Lehigh U., 1984—. Served with USAF, 1956-59. Congregationalist. Clubs: Island Country (Marco Island, Fla.); Sky (N.Y.C.); Burning Tree Country (Greenwich, Conn.) (dir. 1981—). Office: 277 Park Ave New York NY 10172

KRIST, MARTIN ALLAN, auditor; b. Pitts., June 13, 1961; s. Ronald Allan and Celia S. (Dolata) K.; m. Karen Jane Leopold, Aug. 23, 1986. BA, Case Western Reserve U., 1983, M in Acctg., 1985. CPA, Ohio. Sr. computer auditor Ernst and Whinney, Cleve., 1984-86; electronic data processing auditor Lubizol Corp., Wickliffe, Ohio, 1986—. Contbr. articles to profl. jours. Treas. DanceCleveland, 1984—. Mem. EDP Auditors Assn., AICPA. Home: 3927 Bridge Ave Cleveland OH 44113 Office: Lubrizol Corp 29400 Lakeland Blvd Wickliffe OH 44092

KRIST, PETER CHRISTOPHER, former petroleum company executive; b. Ansonia, Conn., Aug. 23, 1919; s. Nicholas and Mary (Vasil) K.; m. Vede Makarion, Nov. 3, 1946; children—David P., Robert P. A.B. magna cum laude in Psychology, Dartmouth Coll., 1942. Dir. Wage and salary adminstrn. Am. Overseas Airlines, N.Y.C., 1946-47; dir. labor relations Wage and salary adminstrn. Am. Overseas Airlines, 1947-48; labor relations rep. Am. Airlines, Inc., N.Y.C., 1948-51; asst. to v.p. indsl. relations Bendix Corp., N.Y.C., 1951-52; mgr. personnel adminstrn. Bendix Corp., 1952-53; dir. wage and salary adminstrn. Ry. Express Agy. Inc., N.Y.C., 1953-55; dir. personnel adminstrn. Ry. Express Agy. Inc., 1955-60; mgr. employee communications, corp. employee relations dept. Mobil Oil Corp., N.Y.C., 1960-61; employee relations adviser Mobil North and Southeast Europe (Internat. Div.), London, 1961-66; gen. mgr. corp. employee relations dept. Mobil North and Southeast Europe (Internat. Div.), N.Y.C., 1966-69; v.p. employee relations Mobil North and Southeast Europe (Internat. Div.), 1969-77, sr. v.p. employee relations, 1977-84, also dir.; prin. Krist Assocs., 1984—. Bd. dirs. Westport-Weston United Way; bd. dirs. at large-ptnr. relations com. United Way of Tri-State, 1960-65; mem. bus. adv. council NAACP Spl. Contbn. Fund, 1971—; mem. commerce and industry council Nat. Urban League, Inc., 1973—; mem. labor mgmt. com. Nat. Council on Alcoholism, 1974—; former bd. dirs. Unemployment Benefits Adv.; bd. dirs., mem. coms. Nat. Soc. to Prevent Blindness; bd. dirs., treas. Citizens Crime Commn. N.Y.C.; Trustee John E. Gray Inst.; Bd. dirs. Regional Plan Assn. Served to maj. AUS, 1942-46. Clubs: Marco Polo, Dartmouth (N.Y.), Yale. Office: Krist Assocs 1221 Post Rd E Westport CT 06880

KRISTENSEN, STEVEN ARTHUR, accountant; b. Rice Lake, Wis., Apr. 18, 1958; s. Lowell A. and Shirley (Ries) K. BBA in Acctg., U. Wis., 1981. CPA, Colo., Wis. Internship Brown, Clark, Cingoranelli & Koehler, CPAs, Pueblo, Colo., 1982; economy and efficiency reviewer Rodriguez, Roach & Assoc., Denver, 1982-84; pvt. practice acctg. Denver, 1984-88, Rice Lake, Wis., 1988—; bd. dirs. Sage Advt. Inc. Denver; fraud auditor, FBI, Cut Bank, Mont., 1983. Bd. regents Citizens Against Govt. Waste, Washington, 1983-84. Mem. Colo. Soc. CPAs (com. continuing edn. 1985), Am. Inst. CPAs. Republican. Clubs: Soc. Micro Users Group, Denver, Toastmasters (award, 1986). Office: 1020 Lake Shore Dr Rice Lake WI 54868

KRISTIAN, KATHLEEN ANNE, accountant; b. Balt., Dec. 26, 1964; d. John and Dale Margaret (Jones) K. BS in Acctg., Towson State U., Balt., 1986; postgrad., Loyola Coll., 1986—. CPA, Md. Staff acct. Clifton Gunderson & Co., Balt., 1986; tax acct. Black & Decker Corp., Balt., 1986-88, analyst group consolidations internat., 1988—. Mem. fin. com. Sheltered Workshop Anne Arundel County, 1987, bd. dirs., 1988. Mem. Md. Assn. CPA's. Democrat. Roman Catholic. Home: 9264 Throgmorton Rd Carney MD 21234 Office: Black & Decker Corp 701 E Joppa Rd Towson MD 21204

KRISTICK, K. RANDOLPH, marketing executive; b. Walnut Creek, Calif., Mar. 27, 1957; s. David A. and Marilyn C. (Podva) K.; m. Karie L. Benson, Aug., 1979; children: Kyle Lemay, Keaton Charles. Student, No. Ill. U., 1979-81; BS, Elmhurst Coll., 1984. U.S. sales agt. Air Can., Chgo., 1978-84; regional sales rep. Profit Freight Systems, Inc., Chgo., 1984-85; mktg. mgr. Transamerica Corp., Chgo., 1985—; mktg. exec. for lease sales Transamerica, Lombard, Ill., 1987—. Mem. Am. Assn. Equipment Lessors, Am. Mgmt. Assn., Internat. Transp. Assn., Nat. Railroad Intermodal Assn. Office: Transam Rail Leasing 1 E 22d St Suite 410 Lombard IL 60148

KRISTOF, MARK BENEDICT, corporation executive; b. Chgo., July 6, 1950; s. Eugene Gabriel and Mary Kay (Moeller) K.; m. Beth Victoria Ward, Oct. 10, 1987. BME, Gen. Motors Inst., 1973; MBA, Carnegie-Mellon U., 1974. Fin. analyst Skelly Oil Co., Tulsa, 1974-77; asst. treas. Getty Refining and Mktg. Co., Tulsa, 1977-79, Getty Oil Co., Los Angeles, 1979-84; treas. Care Enterprises Inc., Tustin, Calif., 1985—. Mem. Los Angeles Treas. Club. Home: 424 30th St Manhattan Beach CA 90266

KRISTY, JAMES E(UGENE), financial management consultant; b. Kenosha, Wis., Sept. 3, 1929; s. Eugene H. and Ann T. Kristy; BS in Econs., U. Wis., 1951; MBA in Fin., U. So. Calif., 1964; postgrad. Claremont (Calif.) Grad. Sch.; PhD in Mgmt. and Edn., Columbia-Pacific U., 1981; m. Edith L. Reid, Feb. 19, 1955; children—James R., Ann E., Robert E. Vice-pres., Lloyds Bank Calif., L.A., 1969-71; chief treasury officer Computer Machinery Corp., L.A., 1971-75; sr. v.p., chief fin. officer Century Bank, L.A., 1979; self-employed cons., writer, and lectr., Buena Park, Calif., 1975-78, 80—; mem. faculty Redlands (Calif.) U., Golden Gate U., L.A., at U. Calif., Berkeley, Santa Cruz, Irvine and Riverside, U. So. Calif.; vice-chmn. City of Buena Park Fin. Com., 1986—; past dir. Grycner Motors Corp., Madera Mfg. Co. 1st lt. U.S. Army, 1951-53; Korea. Recipient Pub. Svc. award SBA, 1971. Author: Analyzing Financial Statements: Quick and Clean, 4th edit., 1984; Price Deflator Software, 1986; Handbook of Budgeting, 1981; (with others) Finance Without Fear, 1983; Analyzing Financial Statements with Electronic Spreadsheets, 1984, Commercial Credit Matrix Software, 1989. Address: PO Box 113 Buena Park CA 90621

KRIT, ROBERT LEE, development executive; b. Chgo., Apr. 6, 1920; s. Jacob and Tania (Etzkowitz) K.; B.S. in Commerce, DePaul U., 1946; A.B.A., N. Park Coll., 1939; children—Melissa, Margaret, Justin. Dir. Chgo. Herald Am. Mercy Fleet charity drives, 1940-41; asst. exec. dir. cancer research found. U. Chgo., 1947-48; state campaign dir. Am. Cancer Soc., Inc., Chgo., 1948-63; dir. med. devel. U. Chgo., 1963-67; v.p. devel. U. Health Scis./Chgo. Med. Sch. (formerly Chgo. Med. Sch.), 1967—. Moderator, NBC-TV series Tension in Modern Living, Drug Abuse, Aging and Retirement, Health and Devel. Children, Cancer, Bridge For Tomorrow, Healthy Life Style, NBC Ednl. Exchange; host producer TV series Med. Looking Glass, Relevant Issues in Health and Medicine, Coping, Su Salud, Spanish TV series, Chgo. Med. Sch. Reports, radio series; chmn. Ill. Comm. for Nat. Health Agys. Fed. Service Campaigns; mem. adv. bd. Central States Inst. for Addiction Services; v.p. Drug Abuse Council of Ill.; bd. dirs. Lawson YMCA, United Way Lake County, Ill. Found. Dentistry for the Handicapped; vice chmn. North Chgo. Citizens Against Drug & Alcohol Abuse. Served to 1st lt. USAAF, 1942-46. Fellow Inst. Medicine Chgo. (co-chmn. com. on public info., editorial bd. Procs.; Disting. Service award); mem. Chgo. Soc. Fund Raising Execs. (pres. 1964-65), Chgo. Assn. Commerce and Industry (health-in-industry com.), Nat. Acad. TV Arts and Scis. Office: 200 E Randolph Dr Ste 7938 Chicago IL 60601

KRITZER, PAUL ERIC, newspaper executive, communications lawyer; b. Buffalo, May 5, 1942; s. James Cyril and Bessie May (Biddlecombe) K.; m. Frances Jean McCallum, June 20, 1970; children: Caroline Frances, Erica Hopkins. BA, Williams Coll., 1964; MS in Journalism, Columbia U., 1965; JD, Georgetown U., 1972. Bar: D.C. 1973, Iowa 1977, U.S. Supreme Ct. 1978, Wis. 1980. Reporter, copy editor Buffalo Evening News, 1964, 69, 70; instr. English Augusta (Ga.) Coll., 1968-69; law clk. Office of FCC Commr., Washington, 1971, MCI, Washington, 1972; counsel U.S. Ho. of Reps., Washington, 1972-77; assoc. counsel Des Moines Register & Tribune, 1977-80; editor, pub. Waukesha (Wis.) Freeman, 1980-83; asst. sec., gen. counsel Jour. Communications Inc., Milw., 1983—; bd. dirs. Jour./Sentinel Inc., Milw., 1986—. Trustee Carroll Coll., Waukesha, 1981—; producer Waukesha Film Festival, 1982; bd. dirs. Des Moines Metro Opera Inc., 1979-80. With U.S. Army, 1965-68. Republican. Presbyterian. Home: 211 Oxford Rd Waukesha WI 53186 Office: Jour Communications Inc 333 W State St PO Box 661 Milwaukee WI 53201

KRIVO, DAVID ALAN, industrial supply company executive; b. Chgo., June 23, 1950; s. Albert A. and Marcia (Goldberg) K.; m. Patti E. Tyser, June 15, 1974; children: Ariel Sara, Eliza Florence, Sydney Ava. Chief exec. officer Krivo Indsl. Supply Co., Chgo., 1972—, corp. v.p., 1977-86, exec. v.p., 1986—. Active Jewish United Fund. Mem. Nat. Indsl. Distbrs. Assn., Cen. States Indsl. Distbrs. Assn., Ill. Indsl. Distbrs. Assn. Democrat. Home: 4410 Bobolink Terr Skokie IL 60076 Office: Krivo Indsl Supply Co 1618 W Fullerton St Chicago IL 60614

KRIZSA, THOMAS FREDERICK, controller; b. Cin., June 26, 1948; s. Louis John and Marion Elizabeth (Speckert) K.; m. Kathleen Ann Heider, Aug. 16, 1969; children: Thomas F. Jr., Angela Marie, Stephanie Rose. B in Math., Bellarmine Coll., 1970; postgrad. studies in edn., Northern Ky. U., 1971-73; postgrad. studies in acctg., Franklin U., 1976-78. CPA, Ohio. Gen. acctg. supr. Revlon-Realistic, Cin., 1981-83, controller, 1983-84; asst. controller Revlon Profl. Products, Jacksonville, 1984-85; corp. controller Cornerstone Mfg., Orange Park, Fla., 1985-86; bd. dirs. Pulstar Corp. Gainesville, Fla.; instr. Becker CPA Rev., Jacksonville, Fla., 1985-86. Mem. Ch. Athletic Group for Kids, Cin., 1980-83, soccer and basketball coordinator, v.p., 1982, pres. 1983. Mem. Fla. Inst. CPA's (industry govt. edn. com.), Ohio Soc. CPA's, Am. Inst. CPA's. Roman Catholic. Home: 6250 Kingoak Dr Cincinnati OH 45248 Office: Xetron Corp 40 W Crescentville Rd Cincinnati OH 45246

KROENER, WILLIAM FREDERICK, III, lawyer; b. N.Y.C., Aug. 27, 1945; s William Frederick Jr. and Barbara (Mitchell) K.; m. Evelyn Somerville Bibb, Sept. 3, 1966; children—Mary Elizabeth, Evangeline Alberta, James Mitchell. AB, Yale Coll., 1967; MBA, Stanford U., 1971, JD, 1971. Bar: Calif. 1972, N.Y. 1979, D.C. 1983. Assoc. Davis Polk & Wardwell, N.Y.C. and London, 1971-79, ptnr., N.Y.C., 1979-82, Washington and N.Y.C., 1982—; bd. dirs. Indosuez & Ptnrs. N.Am. III N.V., Mitsubishi Bank Trust Co. N.Y., Mitsubishi Capital Inc. Mng. editor Stanford Law Rev., 1970-71. Mem. bd. visitors Stanford U. Law Sch., 1983—. Mem. ABA, N.Y. State Bar Assn., Assn. of Bar of City of N.Y., Fed. Bar Assn., N.Y. Law Inst., Yale Club, Wall St. CLub, Univ.Club, Kenwood Golf Club. Republican. Episcopalian. Home: 6412 Brookside Dr Chevy Chase MD 20815 also: 404 E 79th St Apt 28-E New York NY 10021 Office: Davis Polk & Wardwell 1575 Eye St NW Ste 400 Washington DC 20005 also: Davis Polk & Wardwell 1 Chase Manhattan Pla New York NY 10005

KROGH, HARRY M., consumer products company executive; b. 1929. Student, McCook Jr. Coll., 1949, Nebr. Wesleyan U., 1951, U. Denver, 1954. Mgr. adminstrv. services Arthur Andersen & Co., Chgo., 1954-68; mgr. mfg. controls Peat Marwick Mitchell & Co., 1968-70; dir. fin. and adminstrn. Boise (Idaho) Cascade Corp., 1970-72; v.p. fin. Bendix Home Systems, Boise, 1973-74; with Interco Inc., St. Louis, 1974—, v.p. fin. Florsheim Shoe div., 1974-80, pres. Florsheim Shoe div., 1980-85, pres., 1985—. Served with USAF, 1951-53. Office: Interco Inc 101 S Hanley Rd Saint Louis MO 63105

KROGIUS, TRISTAN ERNST GUNNAR, business executive; b. Tammerfors, Finland, Apr. 13, 1933; came to U.S., 1939; s. Helge Lorenz and Valborg Isolde (Antell) K.; m. Barbara Jane Brophy, Aug. 29, 1952; children—Ferril Anne, Lars Anthony, Karin Therese, Eric Lorenz, Marian Elaine, Rebecca Kristina. B.A., U. N.Mex., 1954; M.A., Calif. State U.-Los Angeles, 1962; grad. Advanced Mgmt. Program, Harvard U., 1980. With Scott Paper Co., Phila., 1960-65, Hunt-Wesson Foods, Fullerton, Calif., 1965-75; pres. Hunt-Wesson Foods Can., Ltd., Toronto, Ont., 1969-71, pres. frozen and refrigerated foods div., 1971-75; pres., chief exec. officer Dalgety Foods, Salinas, Calif., 1975-78; v.p., gen. mgr. food div. Tenneco West, Inc., Bakersfield, Calif., 1978-80, pres., chief exec. officer, 1981-87; pres. Landmark Mgmt., Inc., 1987-88; ptnr. The Cons. Co., South Laguna, 1988—. Bd. dirs. South Coast Med. Ctr., Laguna Beach, Calif., 1969-74, pres., chief exec. officer, 1974; bd. dirs. South Sierra council Boy Scouts Am., 1981-87, Calif. State Coll. Found., Bakersfield, 1983-87, Found. for 21st Century, 1987—. Served to capt. USMC, 1954-60. Recipient World Food award Ariz. State U., Tempe, 1982. Republican. Episcopalian. Office: The Consulting Co 31706 Coast Hwy Ste 401 South Laguna CA 92677

KROL, JOSEPH, mechanical and industrial engineer, emeritus educator, underwriter; b. Warsaw, Poland, Jan. 14, 1911; came to U.S., 1956, naturalized, 1962; s. Kazimierz and Feliksa (Tokarzewski) K.; m. Evelyn Swingland, Apr. 15, 1952. MS, Warsaw Inst. Tech., 1937; PhD U. London, 1947. Registered profl. engr., Ga. Tech. officer with directorate ammunition prodn. Brit. Ministry of Supply, London, 1941-45; research scientist U. London, 1946-47; cons. engr., Montreal, Que., Can., 1948-51; assoc. prof. mech. engring. U. Manitoba (Can.), 1951-56; prof. indsl. engring. Ga. Inst. Tech., Atlanta, 1956-79, prof. emeritus indsl. and systems engring., 1980—; underwriting mem. Lloyd's of London, 1985—. Contbr. articles on engring. and mgmt. to profl. jours. Recipient George Stephenson prize, 1951, Centennial medallion Ga. Inst. Tech., 1987. Fellow Inst. Mech. Engrs.; mem. ASME, Engring. Inst. Can., Corp. Profl. Engrs. Que., Am. Econ. Assn., Instrument Soc. Am., AAAS, Am. Statis. Assn., Econometric Soc., Inst. Mgmt. Scis., AAUP, N.Y. Acad. Scis., U.S. Naval Inst., Sigma Xi. Club: Royal Over-Seas League (London). Home: 311 10th St NW Atlanta GA 30318 also: Maison Grande Condominium 6039 Collins Ave Miami Beach FL 33140

KROLCZYK, JOSEPH FRANCIS, investment analyst; b. Balt., July 16, 1961; s. Melvin Daniel and Teresa Ann (Sandvick) K.; m. Elizabeth Emanuel, Sept. 1, 1962. BS, Lebanon Valley Coll., 1983; MS in Indsl. Adminstrn., Carnegie-Mellon U., Pitts., 1986. CPA, Md. Staff acct. Zimmermen & Miller CPA's, Balt., 1983-84; strategic planner AT&T Technologies, Holmdel, Holmdel, N.J., 1985; assoc. investment analyst Ford Motor Credit Co., Dearborn, Mich., 1986-88; treas. fin. analyst Ford Motor Credit Co., Dearborn, 1988—; ptnr. Krolczyk & Krolczyk Enterprises, Balt., 1984—. Mem. Carnegie-Mellon Alumni Assn. (vice-chmn. 1987—). Republican. Home: 30611 Crest Forest Farmington Hills MI 48331 Office: Ford Motor Credit Co The American Rd Dearborn MI 48021

KROLL, ARNOLD HOWARD, investment banker; b. N.Y.C., Jan. 20, 1935; s. Henry and Jean (Brecker) K.; m. Lois Ann Montana, Aug. 11, 1965; children: Alison Cordelia, Luisa Clayton, Heather Todd. BA, Dartmouth Coll., 1956; LLB, Harvard U., 1959. Bar: N.Y. Assoc. Lehman Bros., N.Y.C., 1960-70; 1st v.p. Dean Witter & Co., N.Y.C., 1970-72; adminstrv. mng. dir. L.F. Rothschild & Co., N.Y.C., 1972-88; mng. dir. Wertheim Schroder & Co., Inc., N.Y.C., 1988—; bd. dirs. Am. West Airlines, Phoenix. 1st lt. U.S. Army, 1959-65. Mem. Univ. Club, Century Country Club. Home: 4 E 72d St New York NY 10021 Office: Wertheim Schroder & Co Inc 787 7th Ave New York NY 10019

KROMBERG, WILLIAM A., air freight company executive; b. N.Y.C., Apr. 1, 1945; s. Herman L. and Lillian (Rosenshein) K.; m. Marian Perlman, Dec. 1, 1973; children: Jonathan, Elizabeth. BBA, Adelphi U., 1969; MBA, Iona Coll., 1976. CPA, N.Y. Sr. tax acct. Arthur Andersen & Co., N.Y.C., 1969-73; tax analyst Pfizer, Inc., N.Y.C., 1973-76; mgr. tax planning Norton Simon Inc., N.Y.C., 1976-82; dir. taxes Emery Air Freight Corp., Wilton, Conn., 1982-86, v.p. taxes, 1986—. Mem. N.Y. State Adv. Com., 1974. Mem. Am. Inst. CPA's, N.Y. State Soc. CPA's, Tax Execs. Inst. Office: Emery Air Freight Corp Old Danbury Rd Wilton CT 06897

KROMM, DAVID VALENTINE, architect; b. St. Louis, Apr. 24, 1947; s. Walter Benjamin and Mary Catherine (Dorlac) K.; m. Young-Hie Nahm, June 29, 1973; children: Jonathan, Virginia. MArch, Washington U., St. Louis, 1971. Architect The Engrs. Collaborative, Chgo., 1972, Louis Sauer & Asocs., Phila., 1972-73, Caudill, Rowlett & Scott, Houston, 1973-74, Kromm Rikimaru & Johansen, St. Louis, 1974-87; pres. Kromm Rikimaru & Johansen, 1987—. Contbr. articles to profl. jours. Bd. govs. Washington U., St. Louis. Mem. AIA, Mo. Council Architects, Am. Value Engrs., Constrn. Specifications Inst. Roman Catholic. Office: Kromm Rikimaru & Johansen Inc 112 S Hanley Rd Saint Louis MO 63105

KRONEN, ERIC SCOTT, broadcast executive; b. Washington, June 8, 1943. BA, Middlebury Coll., 1965; MBA, Cornell U., 1970. V.p., gen. mgr. Viacom Cable, Everett, Wash., 1983—; chmn. N.Y. State Cable TV Assn., Albany, 1987—. Served with U.S. Army, 1965-68, Vietnam. Office: Viacom Cable 900 132d St Everett WA 98204

KROWE, ALLEN JULIAN, computer company executive; b. Deltaville, Va., June 17, 1932; s. Julian and Margaret Ruth (Weston) K.; m. Frances Altha Morrette, Sept. 4, 1953; children: Vivian, Valerie. B.S., U. Md., 1954. With IBM, Armonk, N.Y.; bd. dirs. mgmt. com. and corp. mgmt. bd. IBM; dir. PPG Industries;. Bd. dirs. Westchester-Putnam council Boy Scouts Am., 1970—, St. Agnes Hosp., 1975—, U. Md. Found. Served with USAF, 1955-58. Mem. Fin. Execs. Inst., Am. Inst. C.P.A.'s, U.S. C. of C. (bd. dirs. 1987—). Club: Whippoorwill Country. Office: Texaco Inc 2000 Westchester Ave White Plains NY 10650

KRUCKS, WILLIAM, electronics manufacturing executive; b. Chgo., Dec. 26, 1918; s. William and Florence (Olson) K.; m. Lorraine C. Rauland, Oct. 23, 1947; children: William Norman, Kenneth Rauland. BS, Northwestern U., 1940; postgrad., Loyola U., Chgo., 1941-42. Auditor Benefit Trust Life Ins. Co., Chgo., 1940-42; chief tax acct., asst. to comptroller C.M., St.P.&P. R.R., Chgo., 1942-56; asst. comptroller, dir. taxation, asst. treas. C. & N.W. Ry., Chgo., 1956-58, treas., 1968-75; asst. treas. N.W. Industries, Inc., 1968-72; chmn. bd., chief exec. officer, pres. Rauland-Borg Corp., Skokie, Ill.; chmn. bd., pres. Rauland-Borg (Can.) Inc., Skokie; bd. dirs. ATR Mfg. Ltd., Kowloon, Hong Kong, Accura Molding Ltd., Kowloon. Bd. dirs. Civic Fedn. Chgo. Mem. Nat. Tax Assn., Tax Execs. Inst., Ill. C. of C., Internat. Bus. Coun. Mid Am., Tower Club, Exec. Club, Union League Club, Internat. Trade Club. Republican. Congregationalist. Home: 21 Indian Hill Rd Winnetka IL 60093 Office: Rauland-Borg Corp 3450 W Oakton St Skokie IL 60076-2951

KRUEGER, ALAN DOUGLAS, communications company executive; b. Little Rock, Dec. 24, 1937; s. Herbert C. and Estelle B. Krueger; m. Betty Burns, Apr. 4, 1975; children: (by previous marriage) Scott Alan, Dane Kieth, Kip Douglas, Bryan Lee. Student, U. Ill., 1956, Wright Coll., 1957-58. Project engr. Motorla, Inc., Chgo., 1956-64; service mgr., field tech. rep. Motorla, Inc., Indpls., 1964-67; pres. Communications Maintenance, Inc., Indpls., 1967-68, Communications Unlimited, Inc., Indpls., 1968—. Methodist. Club: Elks. Home: RR 2 Box 119 Franklin IN 46131 Office: Communications Unlimited Inc 4032 Southeastern Ave Indianapolis IN 46203

KRUEGER, ARTUR W. G., international business consultant; b. Neuendorf, Ger., Jan. 16, 1940; came to U.S., 1975; s. Werner Georg and Charlotte (Klein) K.; Betriebswirt grad., Wirtschafts-Akademie, Bremen, Ger., 1968; MS in Bus. Policy, Columbia U., 1978. Mktg. exec., gen. mgr., Rosenthal A.G. Subsidaries in Spain, Scandinavia and U.S., 1970-79; pres. Am. European Cons. Co. Inc., Houston, 1980—; lectr. in field. Mem. Am. Mgmt. Assn., Space Found., Columbia Bus. Assocs., Internat. Bus. Council, Marine Tech. Soc., Instrument Soc. Am., U.S. C. of C., Houston C. of C., German Am. C. of C., Swiss Am. C. of C., French Am. C. of C. Office: Am European Cons Co Inc PO Box 20147 Houston TX 77225

KRUEGER, BETTY JANE, telecommunication company executive; b. Indpls., Oct. 4, 1923; d. Forrest Glen and Hazel Luellen (Taylor) Burns; student Butler U., 1948-49; m. Alan Douglas Krueger, Apr. 4, 1975; 1 son by previous marriage—Michael J. Vornehm. Supr., instr. Ind. Bell Telephone Co., Indpls., 1941-54; supr. communications Jones & Laughlin Steel Co., Indpls., 1954-56, Ford Motor Co., Indpls., 1956-64, U.S. Govt., Camp Atterbury, Ind., 1964-66; dir. communications Meth. Hosp. of Ind., Indpls., 1966-79; pres. owner Rent-A-Radio, Inc. of Ind., Indpls., after 1979; sec.-treas. Communications Unltd., Inc. Former pres. Am. Legion Aux.; chmn. for Ind., Girls State U.S.A., 1972-77; probation officer vol., 1973-74; suicide prevention counselor, 1972-73. Recipient award for outstanding community service Ford Motor Co., 1961. Mem. Am. Soc. Hosp. Engring., Am. Hosp. Assn., Nat. Assn. Bus. and Ednl. Radio, Inc., Internat. Teletypewriters for the Deaf, Asso. Public Safety Communications Officers, Inc., Am. Bus. Women. Methodist. Home: RR 2 Box 119 Franklin IN 46131 Office: 4032 Southeastern Ave Indianapolis IN 46203

KRUEGER, DONALD MARC, equity company executive; b. Newark, Apr. 26, 1952; s. Jerome and Esther (Siegel) K.: divorced, children: Gwendolyn Brooke, Jacob Michael; m. Micki Krueger. BA, U. Rochester, 1974; MBA, Harvard U., 1978. V.p. Capital Research Co., Los Angeles, 1978-86; v.p. rsch. Wertheim Schroder Co., N.Y.C., 1986-88; sr. v.p., dir. Japanese rsch. Sanyo Securities Am., N.Y.C., 1988—. Bd. dirs. Internat. Assn. Mgmt. and Econs. Students Congress, 1988. Named One of Top Ten Buy Side Analysts in U.S., Instnl. Investment Mag., 1986. Mem. Inst. Chartered Fin. Analysts. Democrat. Jewish. Office: Sanyo Securities Am 45 Broadway New York NY 10006

KRUEGER, JOHN CHARLES, financial planner, investment advisor; b. St. Louis, Oct. 5, 1951; s. Edward Rice and Frances (Lingel) K.; m. Mary Jo Holtz, Apr. 20, 1979; children: Kimberly Ann, Eric John. BS in Bus., U. Miss., 1974; MBA, U. Phoenix, 1987. CLU; cert. fin. planner; chartered fin. cons.; registered investment advisor. With Aetna Life Ins., Phoenix, 1975-76; fin. planner, investments advisor Krueger Fin. Services Inc., Phoenix, 1976—; guest instr. Ariz State U., 1983-86; lectr. and coordinator cable TV programs on fin., Ariz., 1983, 84; adj. faculty mem. Coll Fin. Planning, Denver, 1984—. Guest instr. in fin. planning. City of Phoenix Retirement Ctr., 1984—, City of Mesa (Ariz.) Retirement Ctr., 1984, City of Tempe (Ariz.) Retirement Ctr., 1984-85. Mem. Internat. Assn. Fin. Planning, Inst. Cert. Fin. Planners (past pres. greater Phoenix Chpt.), Am. Soc. CLU's. Republican. Presbyterian. Club: Ariz. Athletic (Tempe). Home: 2940 N Ellis Chandler AZ 85224 Office: Krueger Fin Svcs 3033 N 44th St #360 Phoenix AZ 85018

KRUEGER, THOMAS C., building company executive; b. Milw., Dec. 18, 1939; s. Otto J. and Irene (Michalak) K.; m. Diane L. Hahs, June 30, 1969; children: Gregory, Amy. BS, U. Wis., Milw., 1967; postgrad., F.E. Seidmen Grad. Sch. Bus. Adminstrn., 1979-81. Office mgr. Gen. Telephone & Electronics Co., Portage, Wis., 1967-71; cost and valuation engr. Gen. Telephone & Electronics Co., Sun Prairie, Wis., 1971-76, budget mgr., 1976-79; asst. sec., asst. treas. Gen. Telephone & Electronics Co., Muskegon, Mich., 1979-81; asst. treas., risk mgr. Champion Enterprises, Inc., Dryden, Mich., 1981—. Fundraiser YMCA, Rochester, Mich., 1981-85. Recipient Community Service award Gen. Telephone & Electronics, 1970, 71. Mem. Detroit Corp. Cash Mgmt. Assn. (pres. 1985, trustee), Risk Ins. Mgmt. Soc., Nat. Assn. Individual Investors. Republican. Roman Catholic. Club: Brookwood (Rochester). Office: Champion Enterprises Inc 5573 North St Dryden MI 48428

KRUGUER, IGNACIO, international consultant; b. Buenoa Aires, Apr. 5, 1939; s. Jose and Catalina (Lutvak) K. B in Bus. Adminstrn., U. So. Calif., Los Angeles, 1966; MBA, U. So. Calif., 1968. Instr. Los Angeles Bd. Edn., 1967-68; internal auditor Gulf Oil U.S., Los Angeles, 1968-69; mgr. planning Gulf Oil Latin Am., Coral Gables, Fla., 1969-73; v.p. Gulf Oil Latin Am., Coral Gables, 1973-76, Gulf Oil, Houston, 1976-81; pres. Mac Sudamerica S.A., Buenos Aires, 1981—; bd. dirs. Crown Products, Buenos Aires, 1986—, Dapetrol, Buenos Aires, 1984—; dir. UN Devel. Program, Panama, 1985-87. Office: Mac Sudamerica SA, L N Alem 1002 14th floor, 1002 Buenos Aires Argentina

KRUIDENIER, DAVID, newspaper executive; b. Des Moines, July 18, 1921; s. David S. and Florence (Cowles) K.; m. Elizabeth Stuart, Dec. 29, 1948; 1 child, Lisa. B.A., Yale U., 1946; M.B.A., Harvard U., 1948; LL.D., Buena Vista Coll., 1960, Simpson Coll., 1963. With Mpls. Star and Tribune, 1948-52; with Des Moines Register and Tribune, 1952-85, pres., pub., 1971-78, chief exec. officer, 1971-85, chmn., chief exec. officer, 1982-85, chief exec. officer, 1983-86, chmn., 1985—. Pres. Gardner and Florence Call Cowles Found.; trustee Drake U., Menninger Found., Des Moines Art Ctr., Walker Art Ctr., Grinnell Coll., Civic Ctr. Greater Des Moines, 1975-88. Served with USAAF, 1942-45. Decorated Air medal with three clusters, D.F.C. Mem. Am. Newspaper Pubs. Assn., Council on Fgn. Relations, Newspaper Advt. Bur. (bd. dirs. 1983—), Des Moines Club, Mpls. Club, Sigma Delta Chi, Beta Theta Pi, Beta Gamma Sigma. Home: 3409 Southern Hills Dr Des Moines IA 50321 Office: Cowles Media Co 329 Portland Ave Minneapolis MN 55415 also: 715 Locust St Des Moines IA 50309

KRUIZENGA, RICHARD JOHN, energy company executive; b. Spring Lake, Mich., Sept. 25, 1930; s. Richard James and Kathryn Ella K.; m. Margaret Helene Feldmann, Sept. 6, 1952; children—Derek Diedrich, Meg Mulder. B.A. in Econs, Hope Coll., 1952; Ph.D. in Econs, M.I.T., 1956. Chief economist Exxon Corp., 1966-69; logistics mgr. Esso Eastern, 1969-71; v.p. Esso Sekiyu, Tokyo, 1971-72; chmn. Esso Australia, 1972-77, Esso Prodn. Malaysia, Inc., 1977-80; v.p. corp. planning Exxon Corp., N.Y.C., 1981—. Trustee Hope Coll.; bd. govs. MIT Alumni Ctr. of N.Y.; bd. dirs. Bus. Council for Internat. Understanding. Mem. Council Planning Execs., Conf. Bd., Nat. Planning Assn. (com. on new Am. realities). Office: Exxon Corp 1251 Ave of the Americas New York NY 10020

KRUMAN, MARK STEVEN, insurance sales representative; b. Phila., Feb. 3, 1953; s. Jerome Kenneth and Marjorie Jean (Conner) K.; m. Jodi Lynn McGahee, May 29, 1984; 2 children. BS magna cum laude, Duke U., 1975; MBA, Brigham Young U., 1981. Group ins. underwriter The Prudential, Parsippany, N.J., 1981-82; spl. agt., group ins. sales rep. The Prudential, Morristown, N.J., 1982-83, Princeton, N.J., 1983—. Missionary zone leader Mormons, Albuquerque, 1975-77; award coordinator Arthritis Found. Walkathon, Provo, 1981; mem. Randolph Twp. Environ. Commn., 1982, chmn., 1983; com. mem Bucks County Rep. Party, 1988—. Mem. Nat. Assn. Life Underwriters (nat. sales achievement award 1987, 88), Greater Trenton Assn. Life Underwriters, Million Dollar Round Table. Office: The Prudential 100 Nassau Park Blvd Ste 102 Princeton NJ 08540

KRUMINS, GIRTS, lawyer; b. Latvia, May 7, 1932; came to U.S., 1951, naturalized, 1957; s. Janis and Zelma (Zupe) K.; m. Carol Ann Curran, Apr. 15, 1988. BSBA, U. Denver, 1959, LLB, 1964. Bar: Colo. 1964. Dir. legal svcs. Colo.-Ute Electric Assn., Montrose, 1973-75, v.p., gen. counsel, 1975-80, exec. v.p., 1980-81, pres., chief exec. officer, 1981-88, ret., 1989, pres. emeritus, 1989—; of counsel Carol A. Curran Law Offices, Montrose; counsel Pub. Utilities Commn. Colo., 1970-73. Mem. Colo. Bar Assn., 7th Jud. Bar Assn., Montrose County C. of C. (pres. 1985), Colo. Assn. Commerce and Industry (vice-chmn. 1986-87, chmn. 1989), Econ. Club of Colo. Republican. Office: 16655 6250 Rd Montrose CO 81401

KRUMM, DANIEL JOHN, manufacturing company executive; b. Sioux City, Iowa, Oct. 15, 1926; s. Walter A. and Anna K. (Helmke) K.; m. Ann L. Klingner, Feb. 28, 1953; children: David Jonathan, Timothy John. B.A. in Commerce, U. Iowa, 1950; postgrad., U. Mich., 1955; D.B.A. (hon.), Westmar Coll., Le Mars, Iowa, 1981; D. Comml. Sci. (hon.), Luther Coll., Decorah, Iowa, 1983. With Globe Office Furniture Co., Mpls., 1950-52; with Maytag Co., Newton, Iowa, 1952-86, v.p., 1970-71, exec. v.p., 1971-72, pres., treas., 1972-74, chief exec. officer, 1974-86; pres., chief exec. officer Maytag Co. Ltd., Toronto, Ont., Can., 1970—; chmn., chief exec. officer Maytag Corp., Newton, 1986—; bd. dirs. Centel Corp., Chgo., Snap-On-Tools Corp., Kenosha, Prin. Fin. Group, Des Moines. Mem. bd. of visitors U. Iowa Coll. Bus. Adminstrn.; mem. steering com. for Iowa Endowment 2000 campaign; past chmn. Iowa Natural Heritage Found.; bd. govs. Iowa Coll. Found.; chmn. bd. dirs. Grand View Coll., Des Moines; bd. dirs. Des Moines Symphony Assn., U. Iowa Found., Vocat. Rehab. Workshop for Handicapped Citizens of Jasper County, Iowa, NAM; vice chmn. Iowa Venture Capital Fund, Iowa Bus. Council; mem. com. for econ. devel. Iowa Peace Inst.; trustee FINE Edn. Research Found., 1987—. Served with USNR, 1944-46. Recipient Oscar C. Schmidt Iowa Bus. Leadership award, 1983; Disting. Achievement award U. Iowa Alumni Assn; named Iowa Bus. Leader of the Yr., 1986. Mem. Am. Mktg. Assn. (past pres. Iowa), Elec. Mfrs. Club, Newton C. of C. (community service award 1980), Maytag Mgmt. Club. Republican. Lutheran. Club: Newton Country. Office: Maytag Corp 403 W Fourth St N Newton IA 50208 *

KRUMSKE, WILLIAM FREDERICK, JR., marketing educator, business consultant; b. Chgo., Dec. 17, 1952; s. William Frederick and Harriet Marie (Piwowarczyk) K.; BS, Ill. Inst. Tech., 1974; MS in Bus. Adminstrn., No. Ill. U., 1978; PhD in Mktg., U. Ill., 1987. Salesman, warehouse mgr. Lus-Ter-Oil Beauty Products, Palos Heights, Ill., 1972-74; pub. relations dir. Crouching Lion Inn, Alsip, Ill., 1974; mgr. food and beverage Inn Devel. & Mgmt., Chicago Heights, Ill., 1974-75; v.p., dir. mktg. DeKalb (Ill.) Savs. and Loan Assn., 1975-81; sr. v.p. mktg. Regency Fed. Savs. and Loan Assn., Naperville, Ill., 1981-83; mktg. and research cons., Champaign, Ill., 1983-87; asst. prof. mktg. DePaul U., Chgo., 1987-89, Ill. Inst. Tech., Chgo., 1989—; cons. in field Oakbrook Terrace, Ill., 1987—; dir. Rock Valley Network, Inc., Rockford, Ill., 1981-82; instr. Coll. Bus., No. Ill. U., 1978-83; mktg. mgr. Jordan Gallagher for State's Atty. campaign, 1976. AMA Doctoral Consortium fellow, 1986, Walter H. Stellner fellow in Mktg., 1985-87; recipient David Kinley Grad. Fellowship award, 1986, William J. Hendrickson award, 1980. Mem. Am. Mktg. Assn., Ill. Savs. and Loan League (mktg. com. 1977-81, chmn. 1979-80), Savs. Instns. Mktg. Soc. Am. 1976-83, Quill and Scroll, Beta Gamma Sigma. Lutheran. Contbr. articles to profl. and scholarly jours. Home: 17 W 710 Butterfield Rd Apt 201 Oakbrook Terrace IL 60181 Office: Ill Inst Tech Stuart Sch Bus Adminstrn IIT Center Chicago IL 60616

KRUPKA, ROBERT GEORGE, lawyer; b. Rochester, N.Y., Oct. 21, 1949; s. Joseph Anton and Marjorie Clara (Meteyer) K.; m. Paula Kelly Leist, Sept. 15, 1973; children: Kristin Nicole, Kerry Melissa. BS, Georgetown U., 1971; JD, U. Chgo., 1974. Bar: Ill. 1974, U.S. Dist. Ct. (no. dist.) Ill. 1974, U.S. Dist. Ct. (ea. dist.) Wis. 1974, U.S. Ct. Appeals (7th cir.) 1976, U.S. Supreme Ct. 1978, U.S. Dist. Ct. (cen. dist.) Ill. 1980, U.S. Dist. Ct. (no. dist.) Calif. 1980, U.S. Ct. Appeals (4th and fed. cirs.) 1982, U.S. Ct. Appeals (6th cir.) 1985. Assoc. Kirkland & Ellis, Chgo., 1974-79, ptnr., 1979—. Author: Infringement Litigation Computer Software and Database, 1984, Computer Software, Semiconductor Design, Video Game and Database Protection and Enforcement, 1984. Mem. ABA (chmn. sect. com. 1982-88, chmn. div. 1988—), Computer Law Assn., U.S. Patent Quar. Adv. Bd., Am. Intellectual Property Law Assn. (subcom chmn. 1988—), Chgo. Athletic Assn., Mid-America Club, Chicago Club. Roman Catholic. Club: Mid-Am., Chicago. Office: Kirkland & Ellis 200 E Randolph Dr Chicago IL 60601

KRUPNIK, VEE M., business executive; b. Chgo.; d. Phillip and Jane (Glickman) K.; m. Melvin Drury, Sept. 24, 1978. B.S., Northwestern U., C.P.A., cert. fin. planner, real estate broker, ins. broker, Ill. Assoc. dir. corp. fin. Weis, Voisin, Cannon, Chgo., 1967-68; pres. PEC Industries Inc., Ft. Lauderdale, Fla., 1969-71; acct., real estate and ins. broker Vee M. Krupnik & Co., Chgo., 1971-73; sales cons. Baird & Warner Inc., Chgo., 1973-81, asst. v.p. comml.-investment div., 1981-85, v.p. corp. group, 1985—. Mem. Internat. Assn. Fin. Planning (bd. dirs. 1985-87), Internat. Council Shopping Ctrs., Nat. Assn. Corp. Real Estate Execs., Nat. Assn. Securities Dealers, Women's Exec. Network, Nat. Assn. Realtors (bd. dirs. 1983-84, comml. investment council), Cert. Comml. Investment Mems. (pres. Ill. chpt. 1983-84), Ill. Assn. Realtors (bd. dirs. 1983-84), Chgo. Bd. Realtors (bd. dirs. 1982-85, 88—), Chgo. Assn. Commerce and Industry, Comml. Investment Multiple Listing Service (pres. 1982-84), Comml. Real Estate Orgn., Network of Women Entrepreneurs, Chgo. Real Estate Exec. Women. Home: 5757 N Sheridan Rd Chicago IL 60660 Office: Baird & Warner Inc 200 W Madison St #2500 Chicago IL 60606

KRUSE, DENNIS WAYNE, hospital finance executive; b. Red Bud, Ill., Sept. 8, 1943; s. Alfons and Bernadine (Rieke) K.; m. Joyce N. Hahn, Jan. 4, 1964; children: DeeAnn, Brent W. AS, Belleville (Ill.) Area Coll., 1970; BS, So. Ill. U., 1974, MBA, 1977. Supr. trainee McQuay Norris Mfg. Co., St. Louis, 1962-65; acctg. clk. Midwest Cons., St. Louis, 1965-66; bus. mgr. Chester (Ill.) Meml. Hosp., 1966-68; asst. controller Deaconess Hosp., St. Louis, 1969-75, controller, 1975-79, v.p. fin., 1979—; treas. Deaconess Manor, St. Louis, 1987—, Brandenburg Press, St. Louis, 1987—. Alderman City of Red Bud, 1977—; bd. dirs. Fairview Heights Med. Ctr. With U.S. Army, 1961-69. Mem. Healthcare Fin. Mgmt. Assn. (bd. dirs. 1980-82, sec., treas., pres. 1975-76, William G. Follmer Merit award 1975, Robert H. Reeves Merit award 1980, Muncie Gold Merit award 1987), Fin. Execs. Inst., No. County Country Club (treas. 1981—). Home: 314 Summit St Red Bud IL 62278 Office: Deaconess Hosp 6150 Oakland Ave Saint Louis MO 63139

KRUTECK, LAURENCE R., lawyer, consultant; b. N.Y.C., Dec. 11, 1941; s. Alan R. and Sylvia (Stekler) K.; m. Laura Branigan, Dec. 10, 1980; children—Michael, Sally. B.A., Dartmouth Coll., J.D., U. Va.; grad. U.S. Army Command and Gen. Staff Coll. Bar: Va. 1966, N.Y. 1967. Ptnr. Kruteck & Leaness, N.Y.C.; mgr., atty. Laura Branigan, Iran Barkley, Lonnie Lista Smith, Tori Read, Rockland, Pulace & Don Mattingly; formerly dir., v.p. and gen. counsel Shenandoah Corp., Washington Diplomats Soccer Team, SJR Communications, Inc. Served to col. USAR. Mem. ABA, N.Y. State Bar Assn., Assn. Bar N.Y.C., Va. Bar Assn., Judge Advs. Assn., Res. Officers Assn. Club: Princeton (N.Y.C.). Office: 509 Madison Ave New York NY 10022

KRYDER, PHILLIP VERNE, accountant; b. South Bend, Ind., Aug. 4, 1962; s. Verne LeRoy and Mary Lou (Barnes) K.; m. Cynthia Renée Hoon, Apr. 12, 1986. BS in Bus. magna cum laude, Ind. U., 1984. CPA, Ind. Sr. acct. Price Waterhouse, Indpls., 1984—. Mem. Order of the Arrow Boy Scouts of Am. Recipient Eagle Scout award Boy Scouts Am., South Bend, Ind., 1978; Am. Electrical Power Scholar, 1981-83, Hoosier scholar, 1980. Mem. Ind. State Soc. CPA's, Am. Inst. of CPA's, Ind. U. Acctg. Club (pres. 1984), Order of Arrows, Beta Alpha Psi (internal sec. Beta Alpha chpt.). Republican. Home: 3859 New Jersey Indianapolis IN 46205

KRYN, RANDALL LEE, public relations executive; b. Chgo., Oct. 12, 1949; s. Chester N. and Beatrice K. Kryn. AA, Morton Coll., 1970; BS in Journalism, No. Ill. U., 1973. Writer and researcher William M. Young & Assocs., Oak Park, Ill., 1977; asst. public relations dir. Oak Park Festival, 1978; founder Oak Park Ctr. of Creativity, 1978, pres., 1978—; founder, dir. Reality Communication, Oak Park, 1976—. Legis. aide to rep. 21st dist. Ill. Gen. Assembly, 1980-83; Rep. candidate for Ill. State Senate, 1982; chmn. 7th Congl. Rep. Council, 1986—; 7th Congl. Dist. Ill. Young Reps., 1982-86; mem. Ill. Rep. Platform Com., 1986—. Recipient Golden Trumpet award Publicity Club of Chgo., 1979; named One of 48 Outstanding Young Men of Am. from Ill., Ill. Jaycees, 1980; ambassador for Canberra, Australia, 1982. Mem. Public Relations Soc. Am., Seward Gunderson Soc. (co-founder 1978), Ill. Soc. for Psychic Rsch. (bd. dirs. 1975-76, v.p. 1977-79, pres. 1980), Mensa. Author: James Bevel, The Strategist of the 1960s Civil Rights Movement. Home and Office: 1030 Wenonah St Oak Park IL 60304

KRZESINSKI, THOMAS STEVEN, financial company executive; b. Hamtramck, Mich., Dec. 21, 1947; s. Alfons L. Krzesinski; m. Sharon I. McDermott, July 1969; children: Heather, Mathew. BS, Mich. State U., 1969; MBA, Ea. Mich. U., 1974. Systems analyst Hydra-Matic div. Gen. Motors, Ann Arbor, Mich., 1969-70; fin. dir. Gen. Motors, Detroit, 1973-77; chief fin. officer Gen. Motors Trading, Detroit, 1980-81; dir. mergers and acquisitions Figgie Internat., Richmond, Va., 1982-83; v.p. planning and devel. Fla. Progress Corp., St. Petersburg, 1984-86, group v.p. fin. svcs., 1987—; adv. in field; bd. dirs. Mid-Continent Life Ins., Oklahoma City, Progress Fin. Svcs., St. Petersburg, Progress Leasing Corp., Stamford, Conn., Fla. Investment Assocs. Inc., Money Mgmt., Tampa, Fla., Advanced Separation Techs., Lakeland, Fla., Progress-Potomac Capital Ventures, Washington, Fla. Fed. Savs. Bank, St. Petersburg. Baseball organizer Fla. Suncoast Domed Stadium, St. Petersburg, 1986—; with pub. affairs Pinellas County Basketball (high schs.), Fla., 1988—; bd. dirs. Northeast Youth Recreation Program, 1987—, Fossil Park Youth Baseball, St. Petersburg, 1986—; state dir. Fla. Little Maj. League State Assn., 1988—. Mem. Nat. Assn. Accts., Beta Gamma Sigma. Club: President's. Office: Fla Progress Corp 270 First Ave S Saint Petersburg FL 33733

KRZYZANOWSKI, RICHARD LUCIEN, lawyer, corporate executive; b. Warsaw, Poland, Mar. 25, 1932; came to U.S., 1967, naturalized, 1972; s. Andrew K. and Mary (Krzyzanowski); children: Suzanne, Peter. B.A., U. Warsaw, 1956; M.Law, U. Pa., 1960; Ph.D., U. Paris, 1962. Bar: Pa. With Crown Cork & Seal Co., Inc., Phila., 1967—, now dir., v.p. gen. counsel. Office: Crown Cork & Seal Co Inc 9300 Ashton Rd Philadelphia PA 19136

KSANSNAK, JAMES E., service management company executive; b. Hazleton, Pa., Mar. 13, 1940; s. Edward J. and Helen (Holodick) K.; m. Valerie M. Anderson, June 9, 1962 (div. 1986); children—Keith, Janet, Linda; m. Suzanne M. Teefy, Feb. 21, 1987. B.S. magna cum laude in Acctg., St. Joseph's U., Phila., 1962. C.P.A. With Arthur Andersen & Co., Phila., 1962—; sr. mem. staff Arthur Andersen & Co., 1964-67, mgr., 1967-71, ptnr., 1971-79, mng. ptnr., 1979-86; sr. v.p. ARA Services, Inc., Phila., 1986—, chief fin. officer, 1988—. Contbr. articles to profl. jours. Mem. Community Leadership Seminar, 1972, trustee, bd. dirs., 1984; treas., bd. dirs. Ambler (Pa.) Youth Services, 1974-79; bd. dirs., mem. exec. com. Phila. YMCA, 1974—, chmn. fin. com., chmn. ann. meeting, city fund raising chmn., 1974-83, maj. gifts chmn., 1984-87, chmn., 1987—; treas. St. Joseph's Bldg. Fund, Ambler, 1976-79; mem. exec. com. Phila. Urban Affairs Partnership, 1978—; bd. dirs. Greater Phila. Internat. Network, 1980-86 , INROADS-Phila., Inc., 1981—; mem. Mayor's Tax. Rev. Com., Phila., 1980-82, Mayor's Econ. Roundtable, Phila., 1983-85 , Mayor's Com. on Literacy, Phila., 1984-85; mem. fin. com., exec. com. Presbyn.-U. Pa. Med. Ctr., 1981—, chmn. found., 1986; vice chmn. United Way, 1982; trustee Coll. Bus., St. Joseph's U., 1982-85. Recipient alumni award St. Joseph's U., 1980; named Profl. of Yr., Phi Chi Theta, 1981. Mem. Am. Inst. C.P.A.s, Pa. Inst. C.P.A.s (chmn. tech. meetings 1970, chmn. coop. with attys. 1972, exec. com. Phila. chpt. 1980-82), Planning Execs. Inst. (chmn. bd. 1981, Neil Denen award 1984). Republican. Roman Catholic. Clubs: Cedarbrook Country (Blue Bell, Pa.); Union League, Downtown (Phila.); Sunnybrook Golf. Lodge: Knights of Malta. Home: 3102 Hopkinson House Washington Sq Philadelphia PA 19106 Office: ARA Svcs Inc 1101 Market St Philadelphia PA 19107

KU, CATHERINE KA-LAI, accountant; b. Hong Kong, Feb. 16, 1958; came to U.S., 1976; d. Hing-Ken and Gen-You Leung Koe; 1 child, Christopher Y. Yee. BS, Calif. State U., L.A., 1980. Jr. acct. Glendale (Calif.) Newspapers, Inc., 1984-86, payroll and accounts payable asst., 1986-87, staff acct., 1987-88, sr. acct., 1988—. Home: 537 S Orange Ave Monterey Park CA 91754 Office: Glendale Newspapers Inc 111 N Isabel St Glendale CA 91206

KU, CHIA-SOON, engineer; b. Nanking, Republic of China, Apr. 15, 1946; came to U.S., 1969; s. Cheng Kang and May (Wang) K.; m. Yueh Li, Nov. 14, 1984; 1 child, Philip Y. BS, Nat. Taiwan U., 1968; MS, Worcester (Mass.) Poly. Inst., 1971; PhD, Pa. State U., 1977. Registered profl. engr., Md., Va., Pa. Research asst. Worcester Poly. Inst., 1969-71, Pa. State U., 1971-77; asst. prof. chem. engring. Lafayette Coll., Easton, Pa., 1977-78; sr. chem. engr. Versar, Inc., Springfield, Va., 1978-79; sr. engr. Nat. Bur. Standards (now Nat. Inst. Standards and Tech.), Gaithersburg, Md., 1979—; Bd. dirs. Washington-China Post, pres., 1986. Contbr. numerous articles to profl. jours. Decorated Bronze Star. Mem. ASTM, Soc. Automotive Engrs., Soc. Tribology and Lubrication Engrs. Office: Nat Inst Standards and Tech A-215 Bldg 220 Gaithersburg MD 20899

KU, Y. H., engineering educator; b. Wusih, Kiangsu, China, Dec. 24, 1902; came to U.S., 1950; s. Ken Ming Ku and Ching-Su Wang; m. Wei-zing Wang, Apr. 1, 1929; children: Wei-Lien, Wei-Ching, Wei-Wen (Mrs. Chi-Liang Hsieh), Walter, John, Victor, Anna (Mrs. Yuk-Kai Lau). S.B., MIT, 1925, S.M., 1926, Sc.D., 1928; M.A., LL.D., U. Pa., 1972. Prof. elec. engring., head dept. Chekiang U., China, 1929-30; dean engring. Cen. U., China, 1931-32; pres. Central U., 1944-45; dean engring. Tsing Hua U., China, 1932-37; vice minister Ministry Edn., Republic of China, 1938-44; edn. commr. Shanghai, 1945-47; pres. Nat. Chengchi U., Nanking, 1947-49; vis. prof. MIT, 1950-52; prof. U. Pa., 1952-71, prof. emeritus, 1972—; hon. prof. Jiao-Tong U., Shanghai, 1979—, Xi'an, Southwestern and Northern, 1985—, Northeastern U. Tech. and NW Inst. Telecommunications, 1986—, S.E. U. Nanjing, 1988—; cons. Gen. Electric Co., Univac, RCA. Author: Analysis and Control of Nonlinear Systems, 1958, Electric Energy Conversion, 1959, Transient Circuit Analysis, 1961, Analysis and Control of Linear Systems, 1962, Collected Scientific Papers, 1971; poems, plays, novels, essays in Chinese Collected Works, 1961; Woodcutter's Song, 1963, Pine Wind, 1964, Lotus Song, 1966, Lofty Mountains, 1968, The Liang River, 1970, The Hui Spring, 1971, The Si Mountain, 1972, 500 Irregular Poems, 1972, The Great Lake, 1973, 1000 Regular Poems, 1973, 360 Recent Poems, 1976, The Tide Sound, 1980, History of Chan (Zen) Masters, 1976, History of Japanese Zen Masters, 1977, History of Zen (in English), 1979, The Long Life, 1981, One Family-Two Worlds (in English), 1982, Poems after Chin Kuan, 1983, Poems after Tao Chien, 1984, 303 Poems after Tang Poets, 1986, Flying Clouds and Flowing Water, 1987, Poems After Wu Wen-Ying, 1988. Recipient Gold medal Ministry Edn., Republic of China; Pro Mundi Beneficio Gold medal Brazilian Acad. Humanities, 1975; Gold medal Chinese Inst. Elec. Engrs., 1972. Fellow Academia Sinica, IEEE (Lamme medal 1972), Instn. Elec. Engrs. (London); mem. Am. Soc. Engring. Edn., Internat. Union Theoretical and Applied Mechanics (mem. gen. assembly), U.S. Nat. Com. on Theoretical and Applied Mechanics, Sigma Xi, Eta Kappa Nu, Phi Tau Phi. Home: 1420 Locust St 22G Philadelphia PA 19102 Office: 200 S 33d St Philadelphia PA 19104

KUBA, DEBORAH IRENE, sales director; b. Bridgeport, Conn., Mar. 26, 1955; d. Richard Wallace and Doris Irene (Feher) K. BS in Math., Fairfield U., 1977, Georgetown U., 1977; MBA in Fin., Am. U., 1985. Account mgr. Aztech Corp., Washington, 1977-79, Audyxx Corp., Washington, 1979-82; dir. sales Martin Marietta Corp., Bethesda, Md., 1982-87, Western Union, McLean, Va., 1987-89; v.p. sales and mktg. Centel Corp., Reston, Va., 1989—; v.p. Broadview Estates, Annapolis, Md., 1986-88. Mem. SOS Sailing Club. Home: 2806 Broadview Terr Annapolis MD 21401 Office: Centel Corp 11400 Commerce Park Dr Reston VA 22091

KUBE, HAROLD DEMING, retired financial executive; b. Buffalo, June 16, 1910; s. Carl Christen and Inez (Mather) K.; m. Shirley Smith; children: Robert Ford, Thomas Smith. BS, U. Nebr., 1932; MBA, Harvard U., 1934. Owner Beef Cattle Farm, Warrenton, Va., 1950-80; co-owner Resources Devel. Assocs., 1965-80; dir. emeritus Jefferson Savs. and Loan Assn., Warrenton, 1980—, Greater Washington Investors, Inc., 1987—; bd. dirs. Ark Land and Cattle Corp., Warrenton. Co-author: Manufacturing Distribution in U.S., 1938. With USN, 1944-46. Mem. Am. Econ. Assn. Episcopalian. Home and Office: RFD 1 Box 68 Broad Run VA 22014

KUBIDA, WILLIAM JOSEPH, patent lawyer; b. Newark, Apr. 3, 1949; s. William and Catherine (Gilchrist) K.; m. Mary Jane Hamilton, Feb. 4, 1984. B.S.E.E., U.S. Air Force Acad., 1971; J.D., Wake Forest U., 1979. Bar: N.C. 1979, U.S. Patent Office 1979, Ind. 1980, U.S. Dist. Ct. (no. dist.) Ind. 1980, U.S. Dist. Ct. (so. dist.) Ind. 1980, U.S. Ct. Appeals (7th cir.) 1981, U.S. Dist. Ct. (Ariz.) 1982, U.S. Ct. Appeals (9th cirs. and fed.) 1982, Ariz. 1982. Patent and trademark lawyer Lundy and Assocs., Ft. Wayne, Ind., 1979-81; patent atty. Motorola, Inc., Phoenix, 1981-85; Intellectual Property Counsel Nippon Motorola, Ltd., Tokyo, 1985-87; ptnr., Lisa & Kubida, P.C., Phoenix, 1987—. Served to 1st lt. USAF, 1971-76. Mem. ABA (patent/

trademark/copyright sect., litigation sect.), Am. Intellectual Property Law Assn., Am. C. of C. (patents, trademarks and lic. sect., Japan), Maricopa County Bar Assn., Mensa. Republican. Presbyterian. Club: Tokyo Am. Home: 8110 N 18th Pl Phoenix AZ 85020

KUBILUS, JOHN VITO, construction management executive; b. Yonkers, N.Y., May 6, 1947; s. Vito John and Joanna Bernise Kubilus; m. Janice Florence Haefner, Nov. 25, 1978; children: Danielle, Michelle. BBA, Iona Coll., 1969. Auditor Peat, Marwick, Main and Co., White Plains, N.Y., 1969-72; asst. to corp. controller Simmonds Precision Products, Inc., Tarrytown, N.Y., 1972-75; asst. controller, motion controls div. Simmonds Precision Products, Inc., Cedar Knolls, N.J., 1975-78; v.p. and controller, product support div. Simmonds Precision Products, Inc., Miami, 1978-84; v.p., instrument sys. div. Simmonds Precision Products, Inc., Vergennes, Vt., 1984-86; v.p., controller Lehrer McGovern Bovis, Inc., N.Y.C., 1986-88, treas., 1988—. Mem. Constrn. Fin. Mgrs. Assn. Republican. Roman Catholic. Home: 247 Conger Rd New City NY 10956 Office: Lehrer McGovern Bovis Inc 387 Park Ave S New York NY 10016

KUBILUS, NORBERT JOHN, management executive; b. Newark, Oct. 6, 1948; s. Vity Leo and Ursula Eva (Yarusavage) K.; m. Linda J. Ferri, July 23, 1988; 1 child from previous marriage, Jessica Leigh; 1 stepchild, James M. Feigert. ScB cum laude, Seton Hall U., 1970; MS (NSF trainee) Rensselaer Poly. Inst., 1972. Research asst. Rensselaer Poly. Inst., Troy, N.Y., 1971-72; systems programmer, analyst RAPIDATA, Fairfield, N.J., 1972-76, mgr. quality assurance, 1976-78, mgr. corp. support services, 1978-79, mgr. data mgmt. software devel., 1979-80, asst. v.p. ops. adminstrn., 1980-81; v.p. systems devel. and ops. RAPIDATA div. NDC, Fairfield, 1981-83; v.p. info. systems and tech. Ednl. Testing Service, Princeton, N.J., 1983-86, mng. ptnr., Norda Group, Yardley, Pa., 1986—; v.p. mgmt. services Optimal Solutions, Inc., Hoboken, N.J., 1988—; reviewer Reston Pub. Co. (Va.); adj. grad. faculty N.J. Inst. Tech., 1976-84; nat. lectr. Assn. Computing Machinery, 1976-80. Author: Developing Computer-Based Accounts Receivable, 1981, Manager's Guide to Distributed Data Processing, 1982, How to Implement Management Information Systems, 1983, How to Select Small Business Computer Software, 1984; contbr. articles to profl. jours. Treas. Cedar Grove (N.J.) Jaycees, 1977; bd. dirs. Gathering Internat. Families Together, 1983-86. Recipient Physics medal Seton Hall U., 1970, Medal of Honor Am. Biographical Inst., 1986. Mem. Assn. Computing Machinery, Digital Equipment Computer Users Soc. (U.S. exec. bd. 1977-81), Data Processing Mgmt. Assn. (legis. network 1985—, bd. dirs. 1988—, Individual Performance award 1987), Planning Forum, Inst. Cert. Computer Profls. (life, cert. data processor, cert. systems profl., cert. ambassador 1980-82, N.J. state dir. 1989—), Am. Mgmt. Assn. (info. systems & tech. council 1985—), Internat. Platform Assn., Sigma Pi Sigma, Upsilon Pi Epsilon. Office: Optimal Solutions Inc 80 River St Hoboken NJ 07030

KUBO, KAORU, banker; b. Yokohama, Japan, Sept. 10, 1953; came to U.S., 1985; s. Kiyonari and Sadako (Yokomizo) K.; m. Hiromi Takamura, Oct. 13, 1984; children: Marie Ann, Satoru Arthur. BA in Commerce, Keio Gijuku U., Tokyo, 1976. With Bank of Yokohama, Ltd., 1976—; asst. mgr. internat. dept. Bank of Yokohama, Ltd., Tokyo, 1981-85; asst. gen. mgr. N.Y. br. Bank of Yokohama, Ltd., N.Y.C., 1985—. Office: Bank of Yokohama Ltd One World Trade Ctr Ste 8067 New York NY 10048

KUBY, EDWARD RAYMOND, insurance company executive; b. Toronto, Ont., Can., Feb. 15, 1938; s. Paul and Ann (Sawchuk) K.; m. Judith Carolyn Jones, Aug. 24, 1963; children: Kevin, Kimberly. BS, Gen. Motors Inst., 1962. Asst. budget dir. Allstate Ins. Co., Northbrook, Ill., 1971-73, zone controller, 1973-75; zone controller Allstate Ins. Co., Atlanta, 1975-77; asst. regional mgr. Allstate Ins. Co., Charlotte, N.C., 1977-79; asst. v.p., regional mgr. Allstate Ins. Co., Basking Ridge, N.J., 1979-81; dir. corp. planning Sears Roebuck, Chgo., 1981-83; asst. v.p. Allstate Ins. Co., Northbrook, 1983-85, v.p. mktg., 1985—. Bd. dirs. Jr. Achievement, Charlotte, 1977-79, Brunswick, N.J., 1980-82, Chgo., 1984—. Home: 679 Plum Tree Barrington IL 60010 Office: Allstate Ins Co Allstate Plaza Northbrook IL 60062

KUCHARSKI, JOHN MICHAEL, scientific instruments manufacturing company executive; b. Milw., Feb. 10, 1936; s. Harry Raymond and Hedwig (Kopecki) K.; m. Marilyn Kay Chovanec, Nov. 28, 1957; children: Mary, Janet, Michalanne, Norah. BSEE, Marquette U., 1958; LLB, George Washington U., 1965. Bar: D.C. 1966. Engr. AC Electronics, Milw., 1958-61; dir. engring. Howard Research Co., Arlington, Va., 1961-65; pres. Challenger Research, Rockville, Md., 1965-72; with EG&G Inc., Wellesley, Mass., 1972—, v.p., 1979-81, group v.p., 1981-82, sr. v.p., 1982-85, exec. v.p., 1985-86, pres., dir., 1986—, chief operating officer, 1987, chief exec. officer, 1987—, chmn.; pres., gen. mgr. Washington Analytical Services Ctr. (subs.), 1972-81. Mem. Nat. Indsl. Security Assn. (trustee 1980—), Marine Engring. Soc.; dir. Bank of New England, N.A. Office: EG&G Inc 45 William St Wellesley MA 02181 *

KUCHARSKI, ROBERT JOSEPH, finance executive; b. Milw., Nov. 5, 1932; s. Casimir and Angeline Kucharski; m. Caroline L. Garlock, May 5, 1962; children: Kathryn Mary, Michael Robert, David John, Mark Joseph. B.B.A., U. Wis., Milw., 1959. C.P.A. Acct., Price Waterhouse & Co., Milw., 1959-72; fin. v.p. A.L. Grootemaat & Sons, Inc., Milw., 1972-74; v.p. treas. IE Industries Inc., Iowa Elec. Light & Power Co., Cedar Rapids, 1974—; treas., dir. Cedar Rapids & Iowa City Ry.; dir. Mid-Am. Tax Exempt Bond Fund Inc., Mid-Am. High Yield Bond Fund Inc., Mid-Am. Mut. Fund Inc., Mid-Am. High Growth Fund Inc.; v.p., treas. Indsl. Energy Applications Inc.; chmn. bd. EnDyna Power Corp. Chmn. bd. Cedar Rapids Jr. Achievement; chmn. fin. com. All Saints Parish; bd. dirs. United Way East Central Iowa, Big Bros./Big Sisters, Iowa Bud. Devel. Credit Corp. Served with U.S. Army, 1953-55. Mem. Am. Inst. C.P.A.s, Iowa Soc. C.P.A.s, Nat. Assn. Accts., Edison Elec. Inst., Mo. Valley Elec. Assn., Midwest Gas Assn. Roman Catholic. Home: 3221 Parkview Ct SE Cedar Rapids IA 52403 Office: Iowa Electric Light & Power Co PO Box 351 Cedar Rapids IA 52406

KUCHOVA, ROBBIN CALVERT, marketing professional; b. Doylestown, Pa., July 15, 1952; d. Burton Clair and Marilynn (Wardwell) Calvert; m. Nicholas Randal Kuchova, July 28, 1973. Student, U. Bridgeport, 1970-71; AA, Berkely Bus. & Fashion Inst., 1972. Dept. mgr. Hombergers, Atlantic City, 1975-76; co-mgr. Fla., San Francisco operation Reese Palley, Inc., Atlantic City, 1976-78; dir. mktg., coordinator pub. relations Avalon (N.J.) Furniture, 1978-79; dist. mktg. mgr. Teleprompter Corp., Ocean City, N.J., 1979-81; pres. Circle R Group, Absecon, N.J., 1981-82, QDT Group Services, Inc., Pleasantville, N.J., 1983-86; v.p. Gambol Air, Inc., Pleasantville, 1983-85; pres. Queen of Diamonds Tours, Inc., Pleasantville, 1982-86; group charter mktg. coordinator So. Jersey Airways, Inc., Atlantic City, 1986-88; dir. mktg. Emerald Airlines, Inc., Atlantic City, 1988—; cons. Dardanel/Destek Trading, Istanbul, Turkey, 1987—. Editor: Neighbor to Neighbor Super Saver Coupon Book, 1985-86, The Bus Buzz, 1982-86; co-host Sneak Preview telethon, 1979-81. Cons. Nicholas Kuchova polit. campaign, Atlantic County, N.J., 1974-76. Named one of People to Watch Atlantic City Mag., 1985. Mem. Travel Industry Sales and Mktg., Inc., Atlantic City Hotel Motel Assn., Atlantic City Hotel Sales and Mktg. Assn., So. Jersey Regional Council, Greater Mainland C. of C., Atlantic City Women's Chamber (dir. pub. relations 1978-79). Republican. Home: 203 Tremont Ave Absecon NJ 08201 Office: Robbin Kuchova QDT Group Svc Inc PO Box 638 Northfield NJ 08225

KUCZEK, CHRISTOPHER STANLEY, chemical company executive; b. Cleve., Dec. 19, 1954; s. Stanley Walter and Helen June (Henrich) K.; m. Sharon Ann Jenne, Apr. 13, 1985; 1 child, Mitchell William. BBA, Miami U., 1976. Owner Exterior Painters Co., Aurora, Ohio, 1973-78; auditor, cons. Mead Corp., Dayton, Ohio, 1977-79; adminstrv. mgr. Mead Corp., Chgo., 1979-81; group controller Hilton-Davis Chem. Co., Cin., 1981-84, dir. fin., 1984-86, v.p. fin., chief fin. officer, 1987—; mem., chmn. adv. com. Scarlet Oaks Vocat. Sch. Bus., Cin., 1983—. Mem. Fin. Execs. Inst., Delta Sigma Pi. Roman Catholic. Home: 6366 Derbyshire Ln Loveland OH 45140 Office: Hilton-Davis Chem Co 2235 Langdon Farm Rd Cincinnati OH 45237

KUCZYNSKI, PEDRO-PABLO, investment banker; b. Lima, Peru, Oct. 3, 1938; s. Maxime and Madeleine Louise (Godard) K.; m. Jane Casey, June 29, 1962; children: Carolina, Alexandra, John-Michael. B.A. (Coll. scholar), Exeter Coll., Oxford (Eng.) U., 1959; M.P.A. (John Parker Compton fellow), Princeton U., 1961. Economist World Bank, 1961-67, sr. economist, 1971-73; dep. dir.-gen. Central Res. Bank Peru, 1967-69; sr. economist Internat. Monetary Fund, Washington, 1969-71; v.p., partner Kuhn, Loeb & Co. Internat., N.Y.C., 1973-75; dir. dept. econs. Internat. Finance Corp., Washington, 1975-77; pres., chief exec. officer Halco Mining Inc., Pitts., 1977-80; minister of energy and mines Peru, 1980-82; chmn. First Boston Internat. Co., N.Y.C., 1982—, 1988—; mng. dir. First Boston Corp., N.Y.C., 1982—; bd. dirs. ROC Taiwan Fund. Author: Peruvian Democracy under Economic Stress: an Account of the Belaunde Administration, 1963-68, 1977, The Latin American Debt Question, 1988. Mem. Am. Econ. Assn. Clubs: Univ. (Washington); Pitts. Golf, Princeton of N.Y.C, Chevy Chase, Racquet & Tennis. Home: 3731 48th St NW Washington DC 20016 Office: 1st Boston Corp Park Avenue Pla 55 E 52nd St New York NY 10055

KUDESH, STEPHEN BERNARD, management consultant executive; b. N.Y.C., Jan. 19, 1944; s. Sidney F. and Stefanie (Stern) K.; B.S., St. Lawrence U., 1964; M.B.A., St. John's U., 1971; m. Enid Zucker, Sept. 27, 1969; children—Michelle, Jeremy. Systems analyst Sperry Univac, N.Y.C., 1967-69; sr. mktg. rep. Computer Scis. Corp., N.Y.C., 1969-72; nat. account rep. Honeywell Info. Systems, N.Y.C., 1972-74, nat. account mgr., 1974-76; asso. dir. Source EDP, Union, N.J., 1976-79; v.p., dir. ops. Cornell Computer Corp., Edison, N.J., 1979-83, v.p., mng. dir., 1983-87, corp. v.p., 1987—, also dir. Chmn. corp. gifts Middlesex County Jewish Community Center Capital Fundraising Campaign; coach Metuchen-Edison Youth Soccer League. Mem. Am. Mktg. Assn., Assn. Systems Mgmt., Data Processing Mgmt. Assn., Middlesex County Jr. C. of C. (dir., v.p. 1987—). Avocations: skiing, swimming. Home: 37 Walker Ave Edison NJ 08820 Office: Cornell Computer 100 Menlo Park Edison NJ 08837

KUEBLER, DAVID WAYNE, insurance company executive; b. New Orleans, Apr. 18, 1947; s. Royce Matthew and Rosemary (West) K.; m. Alida Anderson, Dec. 10, 1965; children: Kendra Leigh, Krystal Lynn, Kira Louise. B. in Bus. Mgmt., Loyola U., New Orleans, 1969. Lic. ins. broker, investment mgr., CLU. Asst. mgr. Winn-Dixie, Inc., New Orleans, 1962-69; account exec. Travelers Ins. Co., St. Louis, 1969-74; sr. account exec. Gen. Am. Life., St. Louis, 1974-76; dist. mgr. Guardian Life Ins., New Orleans, 1976-81; pres. Profl. Planners, Inc., Kenner, La., 1981—; br. chief 377 Taacom, New Orleans, 1987. Coach girls athletics, Metairie, La., 1987. Served to lt. col. USAR, 1965—. Mem. Internat. Assn. Fin. Planners, Nat. Assn. Life Underwriters, New Orleans Assn. Life Underwriters, Million Dollar Round Table, Met Plus Group Millionaires. Democrat. Roman Catholic. Home: 29 Chateau Haut Brion Kenner LA 70065 Office: Profl Planners Inc Box 640298 Kenner LA 70064

KUEHL, HAL C., retired banker; b. Davenport, Iowa, Mar. 21, 1923; s. Donald J. and Martha A. (Sierk) K.; m. Joyce M. Helms, May 20, 1950; children: Cynthia Ann, David Charles. BBA, U. Wis., 1947, MBA, 1954; postgrad., Grad. Sch. Banking, 1953. CPA, Wis. V.p. First Wis. Nat. Bank, Milw., 1968-71, exec. v.p., 1971-77, pres., chief adminstrv. officer, 1977-78, pres., chief exec. officer, 1978-86, chmn., chief exec. officer, 1986-88; also bd. dirs. First Wis. Nat. Bank; bd. dirs. First Wis. Trust Co., Ameritech, Venture Capital Fund, Inc. Bd. dirs. Vis. Nurse Found.; trustee Kohler Trust for Arts & Edn.; trustee, mem. fin. com., exec. com. Marquette U.; mem. Sch. Bus. Bd. Visitors U. Wis. Served with USNR, 1943-45. Mem. Met. Milw. Assn. Commerce (mem. exec. com., bd. dirs.), Milw. Club., Bent Pine Club, Milw. Country Club (bd. dirs.), Navy League U.S., Sigma Chi. Episcopalian. Office: 777 E Wisconsin Ave Suite 3375 Milwaukee WI 53202

KUEHL, NANCY LOUISE, shorthand agency executive; b. Lufkin, Tex., May 22, 1947; d. Vance DeVille Ethridge and Sally Viola (Seale) Loggins; m. Jack B. Ely, Mar. 13, 1966 (div. 1967); 1 child, Robert Sterling; m. William Albert Kuehl Jr., Sept. 23, 1972 (div. 1989); children: Kristofer Jason, Kerry Elissa. BA, Stephen F. Austin State U., 1981. Paralegal asst. Harvill & Hardy, Houston, 1976-77; litigation supr. Fenley & Bate, Lufkin, 1976-77; legal asst. Forrest G. Braselton, Nacogdoches, Tex., 1977-78; owner, prin. Letter-Perfect, Nacogdoches, 1980-85, Kuehl Reporting Service Inc., Bryan, Tex., 1987—; ct. reporter Hill & Mace, Nacogdoches, 1982-87. Author: How to Set Up a Successful Typing Service, 1982, The Glass Staircase, 1982, A Seale Anthology, Vols. 1 and 2, 1985, Henry Seale, The King's Bookseller, 1989. Mem. Nat. Assn. Legal Secs., Tex. Assn. Legal Secs., Houston Assn. Legal Secs., Nat. Shorthand Reporters Assn., Tex. Shorthand Reporters Assn., Nacogdoches Writer's Group, Nat. Stenomask Verbatim Reporters Assn., Internat. Platform Assn., Phi Alpha Theta, Pi Sigma Alpha, Sigma Tau Delta. Democrat. Mem. Christian Church (Disciples of Christ). Office: Kuehl Reporting Svc PO Box 4165 Bryan TX 77805-4165

KUEHLER, JACK DWYER, manufacturing company executive; b. Grand Island, Nebr., Aug. 29, 1932; s. August C. and Theresa (Dwyer) K.; m. Carmen Ann Kubas, July 16, 1955; children—Cynthia Marie, Daniel Scott, Christina L., David D., Michael P. BSME, U. Santa Clara. Design engr. jet engines dept. Gen. Electric Co., Evandale, Ohio, 1954-55; with IBM Corp., 1958—; dir. IBM Raleigh Comunications Lab., 1967-70, IBM San Jose and Menlo Park Labs., 1970-72; v.p. devel. gen. products div. Ibm Corp., 1972-77, asst. group exec. data processing product group, 1977-78, pres. system products div., 1978-80, v.p. IBM Corp., from 1980; pres. gen. tech. div. Ibm Corp., White Plains, N.Y., 1980-81, info. systems and tech. group exec., 1981-82, sr. v.p., 1982-88, now vice chmn., 1982-88. Patentee in field. Trustee U. Santa Clara (Calif.). Served as 1st lt. U.S. Army, 1955-57. Mem. IEEE (sr.), Nat. Acad. Engring., Am. Electronics Assn. Office: IBM Corp Old Orchard Rd Armonk NY 10504 also: IBM Corp Info Systems & Tech Group 1000 Westchester Ave White Plains NY 10604 *

KUEHN, RONALD L., JR., natural resources company executive; b. Bklyn., Apr. 6, 1935; m. Allison Spencer, June 7, 1986; children: Kathleen, Kelly, Erin, Coleen, Shannon. B.S., Fordham U., 1957, LL.B., 1964. Bar: N.Y. 1964. Assoc. Hughes, Hubbard & Reed, N.Y.C., 1964-68; exec. v.p., gen. counsel Allied Artists Pictures, N.Y.C., 1968-70; v.p., gen. counsel, sec. So. Natural Resources, Inc., Birmingham, Ala., 1970-79, exec. v.p., 1979-81; pres., chief operating officer Sonat Inc., 1982-83, pres., 1982—, chief exec. officer, 1983—, chmn., 1986—, also bd. dirs.; dir. Sonat Offshore Drilling Inc., Sonat Exploration Co., Teleco Oilfield Services Inc., So. Natural Gas Co., Union Carbide Corp., AmSouth Bancorp. Trustee Boys Club Am., Birmingham-So. Coll.; bd. dirs. area council Boy Scouts Am.; mem. pres.'s council U. Ala.-Birmingham. 1st lt. U.S. Army, 1958-59. Mem. Newcomen Soc. of U.S., Bretton Woods Com., ABA, N.Y. State Bar Assn., Fed. Energy Bar Assn., Am. Gas Assn. (bd. dirs.), Gas Research Inst. (bd. dirs.), Interstate Natural Gas Assn. (bd. dirs.), Nat. Petroleum Council, Assn. Bar N.Y.C. Roman Catholic. Office: Sonat Inc 1900 Fifth Ave N Birmingham AL 35203

KUEHNLE, CHRISTOPHER CHARLES, real estate firm executive; b. Chgo., Mar. 3, 1944; s. Walter R. and Mary Alice (Ferris) K.; m. Ann Foster, Feb. 15, 1986. BS, U. Ariz., 1967; MS, DePaul U., 1971. With Walter R. Kuehnle & Co., Chgo., 1968—, dir. appraisal and counseling, 1974-76, v.p., 1976-80, exec. v.p., 1981-86, sr. prin., chief operating officer, 1987—; cons. in field. Editor: The Appraisal of Real Estate, 1977; contbr. articles to profl. publs. Pres., chmn. bd. dirs. Newgard Condo Assn., Chgo., 1976-87; vol. counselor Chem. Abuse-Family Program, Northwestern Hosp., Chgo., 1982—. Mem. Am. Soc. Appraisers (pres. Chgo. chpt. 1983-84; Outstanding Service award 1985), Chgo. Bd. Realtors (chmn. 1982—), Am. Inst. Real Estate Appraisers, Am. Soc. Real Estate Counselors, Ill. Cert. Real Estate Appraisers, Art Inst. Chgo., Alpha Tau Omega. Republican. Presbyterian. Clubs: Chgo. Athletic, Chgo. Yacht. Home: Harbor Point Chicago IL 60601 Office: Walter R Kuehnle & Co 155 N Harbor Dr Chicago IL 60601-7328

KUETHER, RONALD CLARENCE, utility company executive; b. Sheboygan, Wis., June 1, 1934; s. Clarence Edwin and Eleanora Emma (Haas) K.; m. Orlanda Diana, Sept. 24, 1954; children: Kim, Craig, Todd. B.S.M.E., U. Wis., 1959. Registered profl. engr., Fla., Utah, Kans., Colo. Unit supr. Wis. Electric Co., Milw., 1959-67; project engr., mgr. Stearns-Roger, Denver, 1967-70; assoc. mng. dir. Jacksonville Electric Authority (Fla.), 1971-77; exec. mgr. electric ops. Kans. Power and Light Co., Topeka, 1977, v.p. power prodn. systems ops., 1977-80, sr. v.p. electric ops., 1980—. Served with AUS, 1954-56. Mem. ASME. Home: 3940 Worwick Town Rd Topeka KS 66610 Office: Kans Power & Light Co 818 Kansas Ave Topeka KS 66612

KUGLE, J. ALAN, food company executive; b. Marietta, Pa., Oct. 26, 1937; s. John H. and Laura (McCune) K.; m. Lynn Virginia Eckert, Aug. 25, 1962; children: Gregory, Scott. BA in History, Franklin & MArshall Coll., 1959; LLD, NYU, 1962. Bar: Pa. 1962, U.S. Dist. Ct. 1962, U.S. Ct. Appeals (3d cir.) 1962. Ptnr. Drinker, Biddle & Reath, Phila., 1962-69; exec. v.p., gen. counsel Gino's Inc., King of Prussia, Pa., 1969-76, C. Brewer & Co. Ltd., Honolulu, 1976—; bd. dirs. C&H Sugar Co., San Francisco, Mauna Loa Resources Inc., Honolulu, Hawaii, Hilo Coast Processing Co.; chmn., pres. Mauna Loa Macademia Nut Corp., Honolulu, 1983—; chmn. Kilavea Agronomics Inc., HT&T Inc. Mem. exec. bd. dirs. Aloha Boy Scouts Am., Honolulu, 1980—; trustee Palawa Settlement, Honolulu, 1985, Am. Diabetes Assn. Served with U.S. Army, 1963-69. Mem. ABA, Pa. Bar Assn., Phila. Bar Assn., Hawaii Bar Assn., Plaza Club. Republican. Office: C Brewer & Co Ltd PO Box 1826 Honolulu HI 96805

KUGLER, E(RNEST) RICHARD, management consultant; b. Providence, June 25, 1932; s. Edward Herman and Aimee Louise (Paquette) K.; A.B. in Philosophy (NROTC scholar), Brown U., 1956; m. Elaine Clara Rattey, June 9, 1956; children—Ernest Richard, David Rattey, Gail Anne, Cheryl Gertrude, Eric Edward. Pres., founder Kugler Konstruction, Johnston, R.I., 1960-66; sr. asso. program analyst IBM, Kingston, N.Y., 1966-70; chief of installations Alexander Proudfoot Co., Chgo., 1970-71; founder, pres. Kfoury, Kugler & Assos., Inc., Kingston, 1971-73, E. Richard Kugler Mgmt. Counsel, Inc., Woodstock, N.Y., 1973-80, I/O Systems, Inc., Woodstock, Rochester, N.Y., 1977—; bd. dirs. The Gardner Group Inc., Princeton, N.J., Gunthrop-Warren Printing Co., Chgo.; cons. strategic bus. planning and info. systems to industry, assns., 1970—; nat. speaker Business Week mag. seminar, How to Construct a Winning Business Plan, 1984—. Founder, pres. Johnston (R.I.) Citizens Com. for Better Edn., 1965; founder, treas. Onteora Sch. Dist. Citizen's Com., 1976—. Served to capt. USMC, 1956-60. Mem. Am. Prodn. and Inventory Control Soc., Assn. Computing Machinery, Bricklayer's, Mason's and Plasterer's Internat. Union. Home and Office: Byrdcliffe Woodstock NY 12498

KUHAR, JUNE CAROLYNN, retired fiberglass manufacturing company executive; b. Chgo., Sept. 20, 1935; d. Kurt Ludwig and Dorothy Julia (Lewand) Stier; m. G. James Kuhar, Feb. 5, 1953; children: Kathleen Lee, Debra Suzanne. Student William Rainey Harper Coll., Chgo. Engaged in fiberglass mfg., 1970—; sec.-treas. Q-R Fiber Glass Industries Inc., Rolling Meadows, Ill., 1970—. Mem. Multiple Sclerosis Soc., Nat. Fedn. Ileitis and Colitis, Bus. and Profl. Women N.W., Bus. and Profl. Woman's Club (pres. 1984—), Women in the Arts (charter). Home: 2303 Meadow Dr Rolling Meadows IL 60008

KUHN, CHARLES, industrial executive; b. Cin., Nov. 29, 1919; s. Leo and Vivian (Van Hallenger) K.; student Purdue U., 1938-39; m. Elna Jane Smith, Nov. 17, 1944 (div. 1975); children—James Roland, Karen Jo Ann; m. 2d, Patricia L. McVicar, Nov. 27, 1976 (div. 1980). Vice pres. Fansteel Metall. Corp., 1950-55, Hills McCanna Co., 1955-58; v.p. Dresser Mfg. div. Dresser Industries, Inc., 1958-60, pres., 1960-64, group v.p., dir. parent co., 1964-65; exec. v.p., 1965-68, pres., 1968-70, also chief ops. officer, dir. subs. cos.; pres., dir. Wylain Inc., Dallas, chief exec. officer, 1970-72, chmn. bd., chief exec. officer, 1972-80; chmn. bd., dir. Mich. Gen. Corp., Dallas, 1983—; dir. Lafarge Corp., Dallas, Bay Beer Distbrs., Redondo Beach, Calif. Served with USNR, 1940-42. Mem. Am. Gas Assn., Newcomen Soc. N.Am., Am. Water Works Assn., Pa. Soc., Canadian Gas Assn., Tex. Mid-Continent Oil & Gas Assn. Home: 96 Linda Isle Newport Beach CA 92660 Office: PO Box 400443 Dallas TX 75240

KUHN, JAMES PAUL, management consultant; b. Milw., July 11, 1937; s. Clarence George and Genevieve Mary (Fenlon) K.; B.M.E., Marquette U., 1961; M.B.A., U. Chgo., 1972; m. Josephine M. Keller, Dec. 27, 1958; children—Christine, Cynthia, George. Mfg. mgr. Gen. Electric Co., Fairfield, Conn., 1961-65; prin. A.T. Kearney Inc., Chgo., 1966-74; v.p. Booz Allen & Hamilton, Inc., N.Y.C., 1975-77; pres. Case Mfg. Services, Inc., Chgo., 1978-83; dir. Case & Co., Inc., N.Y.C., 1980-83; v.p. A.T. Kearney, Inc., Chgo., 1984—; chmn. bd. Timeless Designs, Inc., 1984—. Mem. Art Inst. Chgo., Inst. Mgmt. Cons. (dir. N.Y. region 1976-77), Chgo. Exec. Program Club, Pi Tau Sigma. Clubs: Metropolitan, Marco Island Country. Contbr. articles to profl. jours.

KUHRMEYER, CARL ALBERT, manufacturing company executive; b. St. Paul, May 12, 1928; s. Carl and Irma Luella (Lindeke) K.; m. Janet E. Pedersen, Oct. 31, 1953; children: Karen Graden, John, Paul. BSME, U. Minn., 1949. Registered profl. engr., Minn. Design engr. Magney, Tusler & Setter, St. Paul, 1950-51; with 3M Co., St. Paul, 1951—, successively product devel. engr., machine devel. engr., project leader, copy machine prodn. supr., process engring. and contracting supr., process engring. mgr., project mgr., until 1964, tech. dir., 1964-66, div. v.p., 1967-70, corp. group v.p., 1970-80, corp. v.p., 1980—; bd. dirs. Bio-Genetic Rsch. Inc., Mpls., SPH Hotel Co., St. Paul, COM Squared Systems Inc., St. Paul. Patentee in field. Mem. nat. adv. coun. Nat. Multiple Sclerosis Soc., 1973—; trustee United Theol. Sem., St. Paul, 1986—; bd. dirs. Minn. Protestant Found., St. Paul, 1987—, Minn. Pvt. Coll. Fund, St. Paul, 1986—, St. Paul Winter Carnival Assn., 1987—. Mem. St. Paul C. of C. (dir. 1988), Univ. Minn. Computer Sci. Assocs., St. Paul Athletic CLub (bd. dirs. 1971-73), White Bear Yacht Club, North Oaks Country Club (bd. dirs. 1981-83, pres. 1983), Osman Temple. Mem. United Church of Christ. Office: 3M Co 3M Center Saint Paul MN 55144

KUKLA, WALTER JOSEPH, retired data processing executive; b. Chgo., July 5, 1933; s. Walter and Jane (Piwkiewicz) K.; m. Jacquelyn Joan Miller, Feb. 28, 1953; children: Faye, Walter Jr., Thomas, John, Christopher. Systems analyst RCA, Chgo., 1963-65; asst. cashier Cen. Nat. Bank, Chgo., 1965-68; v.p., loan officer Tri State Bank, Markham, Ill., 1968-70; v.p., cashier Woodfield Bank, Schaumburg, Ill., 1970-73; v.p. No. Mich. Bank, Marquette, 1973-74; exec. v.p., gen. mgr. Lasco Devel. Corp., Marquette, 1974-87, ret., 1987; chmn. grievance com. Mastercard, Inc., Chgo., 1966-68. Elected trustee Village of Tinley Pk., Ill., 1964-68; pres. Schaumburg C. of C., 1972-73. Named Jaycee of Yr., Tinley Pk., 1964, Outstanding Pres. in State of Ill, Jaycees, 1965. Mem. Data Processing Mgmt. Assn. (mem. chmn.), Mich. Bankers Assn., Bank Admintrn. Inst., Marquette C. of C. Republican. Roman Catholic. Clubs: Economic, Marquette (pres. 1982-83). Lodges: Kiwanis (pres. 1982-83). Home: 4043 Sunset Ln Michigan City IN 46360

KULBIN, VELLO, publisher, writer; b. Valga, Karula, Estonia, May 8, 1937; came to U.S., 1949, naturalized, 1956; s. Jaan and Emilie (Sona) K.; m. Juta Meius, 1967; children: Kalev Mark, Lembit Jaan. Student U. Ill., 1956-59, Ambassador Coll., 1969-70, Valley Coll., 1976—. Pres. Western Mktg. Assn., Pasadena, Calif., 1972-78, Penny Stocks Newsletter, Redlands, Calif., 1978—; pub. Vello Kulbin's Investments Newsletter, 1981—, Vello Kulbin's Commentary, 1984—. Author: Your Resume and Job Campaign, 1973. Mem. Alpha Delta Phi. Mem. Worldwide Ch. of God. Club: Spokesman (past pres.) (Yucaipa, Calif.). Office: Penny Stocks Newsletter 31731 Outer Hwy 10 Redlands CA 92373

KULCZYCKI, MICHAEL TERRY, marketing professional; b. Chgo., May 29, 1952; s. Michael C. and Diane K. Kulczycki; m. Susan A. Richards, June 15, 1974; children: David M., Julie K. AB in Communications, U. Notre Dame, 1974; M in Mgmt., Northwestern U., 1987. Asst. pub. relations Weiss Meml. Hosp., Chgo., 1974-76; asst. dir. pub. relations Augustana Hosp., Chgo., 1976-80; dir. communications Hosp. Research and Ednl. Trust, Chgo., 1980-85; dir. mktg. Healthcare Fin. Mgmt. Assn., Oak Brook, Ill., 1985—. Editor: The Hospital's Role in Caring for the Elderly: Leadership Issues, 1983; contbr. chpt. to book. Mem. Internat. Assn. Bus. Communicators (Spectra award 1983, 85, 88), Am. Mktg. Assn. (planning com. Kotler awards 1984-85, publ. rev. com., 1988-89, judge Acad. Awards 1988, publs. rev. com. 1988-89), Acad. Hosp. Pub. Relations (McEachern award 1979), Soc. Tech. Communications (Merit award Chgo. chpt., Cert. Achievement, Disting. Tech. Communication award 1984), Chgo. Hosp. Pub. Relations Soc. (sec. 1976-77), Welfare Pub. Relations Forum (Helen Cody Baker award), Chgo. Jaycees, Am. Soc. Assn. Execs. (membership sect.

council 1988-89, cert. exec. 1988, conf. adv. com. 1988, cert. exec. 1988, Gold Circle award 1987, Excellence in Edn. award 1987, 88), Notre Dame Club (Chgo.), Kellogg Alumni Club. Roman Catholic. Home: 1100 S Grove Oak Park IL 60304 Office: Healthcare Fin Mgmt Assn 2 Westbrook Corporate Ctr Ste 700 Westchester IL 60154

KULESH, WILLIAM ADAM, insurance executive; b. Bronx, N.Y., Sept. 13, 1929; s. William Adam and Sophia Annastatia (Kurtz) K.; student pub. schs., Bklyn.; m. Catherine Marie Bechler, May 25, 1957; children—Claudia Elizabeth, Christopher John, Terence William. Field underwriter Mchts. Fire Assurance Corp. N.Y., N.Y.C., 46-57; dist. mgr. Kemper Ins. Group, Garden City, N.Y., 1957-59; mgr. Frank E. Wright & Sons Agy., Inc., West Hempstead, N.Y., 1959-64; founder, pres., chief exec. officer Nat. Coverage Corp., Seaford, N.Y., 1964—; mem. Lloyds' of London. Lord of Brampton, Huntingdon, Cambridgeshire. Served with U.S. Army, 1951-53. Mem. Nat. Small Bus. Assn., L.I. Assn., Internat. Platform Assn., Ind. Ins. Agts. Assn. Russian Orthodox. Clubs: Cherry Valley Country, New Hyde Park Elks. Home: 62 First St Garden City NY 11530

KULESHA, KEVIN JOHN, investment banker; b. Englewood, N.J., May 15, 1956; s. Kasmier J. and Florence L. (Anguissola) K.; BSBA, Georgetown U., 1976; MSIA, Carnegie Mellon U., 1979. Field dir. Bradley for Senate Com., Bethesda, Md., 1975-76; commodity trader, Chgo., 1977; assoc. Morgan Stanley & Co., N.Y.C., 1979-83; v.p. Lazard Frères & Co., N.Y.C., 1983-86; Furman Selz Mager Dietz & Birney, 1986-87; v.p. Merrill Lynch Capital Markets, N.Y.C., 1987-88, bd. dir., 1989—. Mem. Jumby Bay Club.

KULLBERG, DUANE REUBEN, accounting firm executive; b. Red Wing, Minn., Oct. 6, 1932; s. Carl Reuben and Hazel Norma (Swanson) K.; m. Sina Nell Turner, Oct. 19, 1958; children: Malissa Cox, Caroline Turner. BBA, U. Minn., 1954. CPA, Minn., Ill., Mich., Iowa. With Arthur Andersen & Co., CPAs, 1954—, ptnr., 1967—; mng. ptnr. Arthur Andersen & Co., CPAs, Mpls., 1970-74; dep. mng. ptnr. Arthur Andersen & Co., CPAs, Chgo., 1975-78, vice chmn. acctg. and audit practice, 1978-80, mng. ptnr., chief exec. officer, 1980-89; mem. services policy adv. com. Office U.S. Trade Rep. Trustee Northwestern U., Fin. Acctg. Found., Tax Found. Inc., U. Minn. Found., Art Inst. Chgo.; bd. dirs. Chgo. Council Fgn. Relations, Chgo. Cen. Area Com., Japan-U.S. Bus. Council. Served with AUS, 1956-58. Mem. Am. Inst. CPA's, Ill. Soc. CPA's, Minn. Soc. CPA's, Beta Gamma Sigma (dir.'s table). Republican. Clubs: Chicago, Mid-Am., Attic, Monroe, Commercial (Chgo.); Minneapolis. Home: 2750 Sheridan Rd Evanston IL 60201 also: 12 Gustave-Ador, Geneva Switzerland also: 6444 N 79th St Scottsdale AZ 85253 Office: Arthur Andersen & Co SC 69 W Washington St Chicago IL 60602 also: 18 Quai General Guisan, 1211 Geneva 3 Switzerland

KULOK, WILLIAM ALLAN, entrepreneur; b. Mt. Vernon, N.Y., July 24, 1940; s. Sidney Alexander and Bertha (Lembeck) K.; B.S. in Econs., Wharton Sch., U. Pa., 1962; m. Susan B. Glick, June 26, 1965; children—Jonathan, Brian, Stephanie. CPA, N.Y. Acct., David Kulok Co., N.Y.C., 1962-67; asst. to pres. Syndicate Mags., N.Y.C., 1967-70; founder, 1970, since pres. Kulok Capital Inc., N.Y.C.; dir. Listcomp Corp., Mail Mgmt. Corp., Mag. Devel. Fund, Lazard Spl. Equities Fund, N.Y. Import/Export Ctr., Inc., Ctr. for Exec. Edn., Arts & Events, Inc., Sax and Co., Art Horizons Internat.; lectr. Wharton Sch., U. Chgo., N.Y.U. Pres. N.Y. Soc. Ethical Culture, 1978-80; vice chmn. bd. Ethical Culture Schs., 1979, chmn., 1982-86. Mem. Am. Inst. CPA's. Clubs: Rockaway River Country, Sleepy Hollow Country; Tryall Golf and Beach (Jamaica, W.I.). Home: 40 E 84th St New York NY 10028 Office: Waldorf Astoria 301 Park Ave Ste 1855 New York NY 10022

KULP, J. ROBERT, metal company executive; b. Buffalo, June 23, 1935; s. Joseph Francis Kulp and Mary Gertrude (O'Brian) Kulp O'Hearn; m. Suzanne Frances Schultz, Jan. 26, 1957; children: J. Robert Jr., Kaaren S., Kevin E., Kenneth C. BS in Bus., U. Buffalo, 1967; MBA, Canisius Coll., 1972. Sales Reynolds Metals Supply Co., Miami, Fla., 1957-58, Ryerson Steel Co., Buffalo, 1958-72; ptnr., v.p. Oehler Industries Inc., Buffalo, 1972—; ptnr., pres. Machines for Industry, Buffalo, 1983—, Denler Metal Products, Buffalo, 1984—; bd. dirs. Erie County Industry Devel. Agy., Buffalo, 1980-86. Pres. Episcopal Charities Bd., Buffalo, 1979-83; mem. bd. regents Canisius Coll., Buffalo, 1980-84; mem. pres.'s Adv. Council D'Youville Coll., Buffalo, 1987—. Recipient Bernard J. Martin Outstanding M.B.A. award Canisius Coll., 1979. Mem. Am. Soc. Metals, Engring. Soc. Buffalo (bd. dirs. 1982-85), Frontier Metal Trades Assn. (pres. 1984-86), Canisius Coll. Alumni Assn. (pres. 1985, v.p. 1984), MBA Alumni Assn. (pres. 1979), Buffalo C. of C. (chmn. existing industries com. 1978-79), Beta Gamma Sigma. Republican. Roman Catholic. Clubs: Orchard Park Country (N.Y.) (bd. dirs., sec. 1988—); Saturn (Buffalo). Lodge: Shrine. Home: 12 Briar Hill Rd Orchard NY 14127 Office: Oehler Industries Elk Smith St Buffalo NY 14210

KUMAGAI, TAKENOBU, quantity surveyoring executive; b. Morioka, Iwate, Japan, Jan. 11, 1937; s. Gosuke and Miyuki (Omura) K.; m. Masako Higuchi, Mar. 27, 1963; children: Naoki, Mariko, Seiyu. Grad., Morioka Engring. Sch., 1956. With staff Taisei Constrn. Ltd., Sapporo, Japan, 1956-69; pres. Sekisan Cons. Ltd., Sapporo, 1969—. Mem. Bldg. Surveyors' Inst. Japan (bd. dirs. Hokkaido 1982—), Japan Inst. Architects, Assn. Bank Users (bd. dirs. 1985), Assn. Goodwill Tax Payers (bd. dirs. 1986—). Lodge: Rotary.

KUMAR, KAPLESH, materials scientist; b. Lucknow, India, Nov. 9, 1947; came to U.S., 1970; s. Shiam and Vidya (Devi) Sunder; m. Savinder Kaur, May 27, 1974; children—Priyadarshini, Ruchira. B.Tech., Indian Inst. Tech., 1969; M.S., Stevens Inst. Tech., 1971; Sc.D., MIT, 1975. Mem. tech. staff Charles Stark Draper Lab., Inc., Cambridge, Mass., 1975-80, chief materials devel. sect., 1980-88, chief materials sci. & tech. sect., 1988—. Patentee in materials processing. Contbr. articles to profl. publs. Recipient Patent award Charles Stark Draper Lab., Inc., 1982, Invention Disclosure award NASA, 1983. Mem. MIT Sangam Club for India Affairs (pres. 1972-73). Current work: Permanent and soft magnetic materials; structural materials; friction and wear in sliding contacts and surfaces; high temperature superconductors. Subspecialties: Materials; Ceramics.

KUMAR, KRISHAN, management consultant company executive; b. Patiala, India, Aug. 17, 1944; s. Sewa Ram and Savitri (Devi) Aggarwal; B.S.M.E. (Merit scholar), Birla Inst. Tech. and Sci., India, 1966; M.S.I.E., N.J. Inst. Tech., 1975; m. Saroj, July 23, 1969; children—Anuj, Amit. Engring. positions in U.S. and India, 1966-73; indsl. engr., then sr. indsl. engr. Berkey Photo, Inc., Clifton, N.J., 1973-76; assoc. Walter Frederick Friedman & Co., West Orange, N.J., 1977—, v.p., 1981-85; pres. Eskay Cons. Group, Edison, N.J., 1985—. Mem. Am. Inst. Indsl. Engrs. (sr.), Inst. Mgmt. Cons. (cert.), Nat. Council Phys. Distbn., Am. Arbitration Assn. (panelist). Contbr. articles to profl. jours. Home and Office: 11 Whittier St Edison NJ 08820

KUMAR, SUBODH, investment banker; b. New Delhi, India, Jan. 1, 1953; came to Can., 1968; s. Satyaindar and Savitri Devi K. Sudan Sch. Cert., Comboni Coll., 1968; postgrad. St. Michael's Coll., Toronto, 1969; B.A.Sc. with honors in Chem. Engring., U. Toronto, 1973, M.B.A., 1976. Chartered fin. analyst. Chem. design engr. Imperial Oil, Sarnia, 1973-74; research analyst Wood Gundy, Toronto, Ont., 1976—, asst. v.p., 1981-85, v.p. 1985-88, dir. 1988—. J.P. Bickell Found. scholar, 1970; U. Toronto masters fellow, 1974. Fellow Inst. Chartered Fin. Analysts; mem. Fin. Analysts Fedn. Office: Wood Gundy Inc, PO Box 274, Toronto Dominion Centre, Toronto, ON Canada M5K 1M7

KUMM, WILLIAM HOWARD, energy products company executive; b. Bahia, Brazil, Feb. 6, 1931; s. Henry William and A. Joyce (Beale) K.; brought to U.S., 1938, naturalized, 1949; B.A., Amherst Coll., 1952; cert. bus. adminstrn. McCoy Coll., Johns Hopkins U., 1959; m. Anne K. Gibson, July 11, 1953; children—John H., Elizabeth A., Katharine L. With Westinghouse Electric Corp., 1952-78, student, Pitts., 1952-53, jr. engr. AirArm div., Balt., 1953-54, sr. engr., 1955-60, supervisory engr. Westinghouse Surface div., Balt., 1961-62, supervisory engr. Systems Ops. div., 1962-65, mgr. advanced concept engring. sect. Westinghouse Ocean Research & Engring. Center, Annapolis, Md., 1965-69, subdiv. mgr., 1969-71; presdl. interchange exec. Pres.'s Commn. on Personnel Interchange, assigned NOAA, 1971-72; staff Nat. Adv. Com. on Oceans and Atmosphere, Washington, 1972; program mgr. submarine transp. project U.S. Maritime Adminstrn., 1972-73; mgr. marine programs Westinghouse Oceanic Div., 1973-78; pres., chief exec. officer Arctic Enterprises, Inc., 1978—, Arctic Energies Ltd., Trans Polar Shipping Co., Inc., Ottawa, Ont., Can., 1981—; participant joint Nat. Acad. Scis.-Nat. Acad. Engring. planning effort on Internat. Decade Ocean Exploration for Nat. Council on Marine Resources and Engring., 1968-69. Mem. Rural Area Devel. Bd., Carroll County, N.H., 1964-65; mem. Citizens Adv. Council on Edn., 1970-72; del. County Council PTAs, 1970, 71, treas. Cub Scout pack 332, Boy Scouts Am., Catonsville, Md., 1963-65; participant congl. office of Tech. Assessment Study of Marine Applications for Fuel Cell Tech., 1985. Registered profl. engr., Md. Mem. Naval Submarine League, Presdl. Interchange Exec. Assn. Participant Nat. Sci. Found., 1987. Patentee in field. Contbr. chpt. to Man Beneath the Sea, 1972. Home: 511 Heavitree Ln Severna Park MD 21146 Office: 511 Heavitree Ln Severna Park MD 21146

KUMMER, GLENN F., mobile home company executive; b. Park City, Utah, 1933; married. B.S., U. Utah, 1961. Sr. acct. Ernst & Ernst, 1961-65; trainee Fleetwood Enterprises Inc., Riverside, Calif., 1965-67, purchasing mgr., 1967-68, plant mgr., 1968-70, gen. mgr. recreational vehicle div., 1970-71, asst. v.p. ops. to v.p. ops., 1971-72, sr. v.p. ops., 1972-77, exec. v.p. ops., 1977-82, pres., 1982—, dir. Office: Fleetwood Enterprises Inc 3125 Myers St Box 7638 Riverside CA 92523 also: Fleetwood Motor Homes of Calif 5300 Via Ricardo Riverside CA 92502 *

KUMP, PETER CLARK, cooking school adminstrator; b. L.A., Oct. 22, 1937; s. Ernest Joseph and Josephine Clark (Miller) K.; m. Carolyn Curme Davis, May 7, 1960 (div. 1967); 1 child, Christopher. BA in Speech and Drama, Stanford U., 1961; MFA, Carnegie-Mellon U., 1969. Cert. culinary profl. Exec. producer Comedia Repertory Co., Palo Alto, Calif., 1957-66; dir. Evelyn Wood Reading Dynamics, Pitts., 1967-69; nat. dir. edn. Diversified Edn. and Rsch. Corp., N.Y.C., 1970-74; pres. Breakthrough Rapid Reading, N.Y.C., 1974-81, Peter Kump's N.Y. Cooking Sch., N.Y.C., 1974—; cons. Stanley H. Kaplan, Ltd., N.Y.C., 1982—. Author: Quiche and Pate, 1982, (syndicated column) The Practical Cook, 1985—. Mem. Internat. Assn. Cooking Profls. (pres. 1987-88, Tastemaker award, 1983), N.Y. Assn. Cooking Tchrs. (pres.), Am. Inst. Wine and Food, San Francisco Profl. Food Soc., The James Beard Found. (pres. 1985—). Republican. Episcopalian. Office: Peter Kump's NY Cooking Sch 307 E 92d St New York NY 10128

KUMURA, JAMES YUTAKA, accountant; b. Harbor City, Calif., Mar. 3, 1962; s. Shigeru Roy and Kiyoko Jane (Kuramoto) K. BA, Calif. State U., 1986. Support specialist FBI, Los Angeles, 1982-87; acct. Neilson, Elggren, Durkin & Co., Century City, Calif., 1987—. Active Nat. Eagle Scouts Assn., Los Angeles, 1986—. Home: PO Box 24775 Los Angeles CA 90024 Office: Neilson Elggren Durkin & Co 10100 Santa Monica Blvd Ste 1110 Century City CA 90067

KUNDAHL, GEORGE GUSTAVUS, government official; b. Washington, July 7, 1940; s. George G. and Adelaide (Wampler) K.; m. Janette Adcox, Feb. 10, 1962; children: Gustavus George, Griffith Allen; m. Joy Carol Wons, June 28, 1975. B.A., Davidson Coll., 1962; M.A., U. Ala., 1964, Ph.D., 1967. Instr. U. Ala., Tuscaloosa, 1965-66; budget examiner Office Mgmt. and Budget, Washington, 1968-77; dep. exec. dir. SEC, Washington, 1977-81, exec. dir., 1981—. Served to capt. U.S. Army, 1966-68, col. Res., 1969—. Home: 1377 N Pegram St Alexandria VA 22304 Office: SEC 450 Fifth St NW Washington DC 20549

KUNG, PATRICK CHUNG-SHU, biotechnology executive; b. Nanjing, Republic of China, July 10, 1947; came to U.S., 1969; s. Tao and Yuing (Li) K.; m. Rita Wu, Feb. 11, 1980; children: Julia, Calvin. BS, FuJen U., Republic China, 1968; PhD, U. Calif., Berkeley, 1974. Research fellow MIT, Cambridge, 1974-77; sr. research fellow Ortho Pharm. Co., Raritan, N.J., 1978-81; v.p. research Centocor Inc., Malvern, Pa., 1982-83; co-founder, exec. v.p. T Cell Scis., Inc., Cambridge, 1984-88; vice chmn. bd. T-Cell Scis., Inc., Cambridge, 1989—; vis. prof. Columbia U., N.Y.C., 1981—; mem. exec. bd. Coll. Letters & Scis. U. Calif., Berkeley, 1989—. Contbr. articles to profl. jours. Recipient Philip Hoffman award Johnson & Johnson Co., 1979, Achievement award Chinese Inst. Engrs., 1988. Mem. Am. Assn. Immunologists, N.Y. Acad. Scis., Sigma Xi. Roman Catholic. Office: T Cell Scis Inc 38 Sidney St Cambridge MA 02139-4135

KUNISCH, ROBERT DIEDRICH, business services company executive; b. Norwalk, Conn., July 7, 1941; s Irving William and Margaret (Diedrich) K.; m. Alicia Stephenson, Aug. 22, 1964; children: Alicia Mary, Robert D. BS, NYU, 1963. Regional mgr. residential sales Homequity, Wilton, Conn., 1966-68, dir., 1968-69, dir. corp. mktg., 1969-71, sr. v.p. mktg. and services, 1971-76, pres., 1976-84; exec. v.p. PHH Corp., Inc., Hunt Valley, Md., 1981-84, pres., chief operating officer, 1984-88, pres. chief exec. officer, dir., 1988—; dir. Corp., Merc. Bankshares Corp., Balt., Merc. Safe Deposit & Trust Co., Balt. Bd. dirs. Ctr. Stage, Balt., 1984, Noxell Corp., Alex Brown, Inc., Preston Corp., Blue Cross & Blue Shield Md., Inc. Mem. Balt. Leadership Devel. Program, 1984; trustee Am. Shakespearean Theatre; mem. devel. com. John F. Kennedy Inst., Balt., 1984. Democrat. Roman Catholic. Office: PHH Corp 11333 McCormick Rd Hunt Valley MD 21031

KUNKEL, RUSSELL JEFFREY, bank holding company executive; b. Reading, Pa., Aug. 18, 1942; s. Russell C. and Doris J. (Evans) K.; children: Michael D., Kathy C., Steven P. BS in Econs., Albright Coll., 1964. Premium auditor CNA Ins., Chgo., 1964-67; with Meridian Bank (formerly Am. Bank & Trust Co. Pa.), Reading, 1967—; vice chmn. loan adminstrn. and ops. areas Meridian Bancorp, Inc. (holding co. Meridian Bank), Reading, 1983—; bd. dirs. Meridian Mortgage Corp., Wayne, Pa. Trustee, fin. chmn. Community Gen. Hosp., Reading, 1982—; trustee Berkshire Health Systems, Inc., Reading, 1985—; v.p., bd. dirs. Hawk Mountain Council Boy Scouts Am., Reading, 1982—. Mem. Robert Morris Assocs. (dir. local chpt. 1980-81). Republican. Mem. United Ch. of Christ. Office: Meridian Bancorp Inc 35 N Sixth St PO Box 1102 Reading PA 19603

KUNKLE, SANDRA LEE, brokerage house executive, sales executive; b. Park Ridge, Ill., June 20, 1960; d. Arland Blaine Kunkle and Judith (Spyrison) Carpenter. BS in Fin., U. Ky., 1982. Cert. fin. planner. Acct. exec. Paine Webber and Co., Chgo., 1982-84; v.p., mut. fund coordinator Bear Stearns and Co., Chgo., 1984—; sales mgr. Gruntal & Co.; instr. "Successful Investing" Chgo. Bar Assn., 1985—. Contbr. articles to women's mags., 1985. Mgr. campaign Rep. com., Chgo., 1985-87. Mem. Am. Horse Show Assn. (Chgo. and Ky. chpts.). Home: 145 W Burton Pl Chicago IL 60610 Office: 135 S LaSalle Ste 4200 Chicago IL 60603

KUNTZ, EARL JEREMY, telephone communications co. exec.; b. Chgo., July 21, 1929; s. S. Emil and G. Ruth (Beitscher) K.; student Northwestern U., 1948-50; m. Mary M. Kohls, July 28, 1957; children—Karen A., Bradford G. Salesman sales display advt. Chgo. Fgn. Newspapers, Chgo., 1948-50; partner Gen. Bus. Svc., Chgo., 1951-59; pres. Gen. Telephone Answering Svc., Chgo., 1960—; owner Chgo. Office Forms Co., 1957—; pres. Partimers, Inc., 1970—; founder Gen. Tele-Communications, 1968—, Gen. Tele-Distbrs., 1976—; mktg. cons., v.p. Phone Aide Co., Inc. div. Wells Gardner Electronics, 1972-76; pres. Telephone Answering Svcs. of Ill., Inc., 1972-74. Trustee Communications Rsch. Found., Sausalito, Calif., 1976-82. Mem. Assn. Telephone Answering Exchs. (dir.), Nat. Assn. Electronic Video Exchs. Owners, Execs. Club, Monroe Club (Chgo.). Inventor telephone related devices to improve and simplify communication in telephone answering industry. Office: 30 W Washington St Chicago IL 60602

KUNTZ, HAL GOGGAN, petroleum exploration company executive; b. San Antonio, Dec. 29, 1937; s. Peter A. and Jean M. (Goggan) K.; children: Hal Goggan, Peter, Michael B. BS in Engring., Princeton U., 1968; MBA, Oklahoma City U., 1972. Line, staff positions Mobil Oil Corp., Dallas, Oklahoma City, New Orleans, 1963-74; co-founder, pres. CLK Corp., New Orleans, Houston, 1974—, IPEX Co., New Orleans, 1975—; pres. Gulf Coast Exploration Co., New Orleans, 1979—, pres. CLK Investments I, II, III and IV, 1979—, CLK Producing, CLK Oil and Gas Co., CLK Exploration Co., 1980—; Mem. Mus. Fine Arts, Houston, 1978—; mem. condrs. circle Houston Symphony, 1980; governing bd. Houston Opera. Served with AUS, 1960-63. Mem. Am. Mgmt. Assn., Nat. Small Bus. Assn., Inter-Am. Soc., Soc. Exploration Geophysics, Am. Assn. Petroleum Geologists, Aircraft Owners and Pilots Assn. Republican. Roman Catholic. Clubs: Petroleum of Houston, University of Houston; Argyle, Order of Alamo (San Antonio), Brae-Burn Country. Avocations: golf, skiing, birdshooting. Office: Gulf Coast Exploration 1001 Fannin Ave Ste 100 Houston TX 77002

KUNTZ, JAMES THOMAS, manufacturing executive; b. Waynesville, Ohio, Aug. 4, 1938; s. James Paul and Virginia Majorie (Florence) K.; m. Patsy Ann Mitchell, Dec. 19, 1958; children: Melody Ann, Scott Thomas. BS, Calif. State U., 1979, MBA, 1981; PhD, Pepperdine U., 1987. Material supr. guidance and control div. Litton, Woodland Hills, Calif., 1962-64; gen. supr. materials TRW Inc., L.A., 1964-69; mgr. material and prodn. ops. Litton Environ. System, Camarillo, Calif., 1969-71; mgr. material ops. Interdata Inc., Oceanport, N.J., 1971-72; mfg. controls/systems mgr. Curtiss-Wright Corp., Caldwell, N.J., 1972-73; mgr. group purchasing TRW Electronics and Def., L.A., 1973-85; dir. purchasing TRW Corp., Cleve., 1985-86; v.p. ops. Am. Gen./LTV, South Bend, Ind., 1986—. With USAF, 1957-61. Mem. Machinery and Allied Products Inst., Am. Prodn. and Inventory Control Soc., Masons (sr. deacon 1964-68). Republican. Baptist. Home: 51300 Pebble Beach Granger IN 46530

KUNZ, LAWRENCE JOSEPH, lock manufacturing company executive; b. N.Y.C.; s. Anthony Joseph and Margaret (Moloney) K.; m. Catherine P. Lambe. BBA, St. John's U., 1963, MBA, 1977. Bus. analyst Atlantic Richfield Oil Co., N.Y.C., 1967-70; contr. Arrow Lock Corp., N.Y.C., 1970-71; v.p. fin., chief operating officer Arrow Lock Mfg. Co., N.Y.C., 1971—. Co-chmn. fund raising Brookdale Hosp., Bklyn., 1986-87. With USAR, 1959-65. Mem. Am. Prodn. and Inventory Control Soc. (cert.). Office: Arrow Lock Mfg Co 103-00 Foster Ave Brooklyn NY 11236

KUO, MAVIS MAI-HUA, jewelry corporation executive; b. Taipei, Taiwan, Dec. 11, 1950; came to U.S., 1971, naturalized, 1983; d. Richard Wu-Chiao and Cheng Hua (Chan) Kuo; m. Wey Chaung Kuo, Apr. 12, 1975; children—Anne, Andrew. A.A., San Francisco Community Coll., 1975. Waitress January restaurant, San Francisco, 1971-73; bookkeeper, sec. George Oshima, C.P.A., San Francisco, 1973-75; pres. Kuo W.M. Co., Troy, Mich., 1975—. Office: 2959 Crooks Rd #8 Troy MI 48084

KUPOR, ROBERT, biotechnologist; b. N.Y.C., Mar. 14, 1946; s. Max and Gertrude (Stein) K.; m. Sandy Kay Ross, June 27, 1971; children: Devra, Elana, Daniella. BA in Biology, Bklyn. Coll., 1966; PhD in Microbiology, Harvard U., 1971; MBA in Fin., U. Washington, 1981; postdoctoral, U. Calif., San Francisco, 1971-74. Asst. prof. biology U. Tenn., Chattanooga, 1974-80; supr. med. affairs Advanced Tech Labs., Bothell, Wash., 1982-83; biotech. stock analyst Cable, Howse & Ragen, Seattle, 1983-88, Kidder, Peabody & Co., N.Y.C., 1988—. Named Indsl. Investor All Am. Analyst Instnl. Investor Mag., 1987. Office: Kidder Peabody & Co 10 Hanover Sq New York NY 10005

KUPROWICZ, REBECCA JANE, marketing professional, researcher, information specialist; b. Martins Ferry, Ohio, Jan. 31, 1958; d. John and Elizabeth jean (Pazzoni) K. BBA in Mktg., Kent (Ohio) State U., 1980; postgrad., Duke U., 1988—. With retail sales The Gap, Akron, Ohio, 1980; with sales svcs. Sta. WTRF-TV, Wheeling, W.Va., 1981-82; profl. rep. Burroughs Wellcome, St. Clairsville, Ohio, 1982-85, profl. tng. rep., 1985-87; sr. sales info. analyst Burroughs Wellcome, Research Triangle Park, N.C., 1988—. Vol. Big Bros./Big Sisters, Kent, 1980. Mem. Am. Mktg. Assn., Nat. Assn. Coll. Women, Delta Sigma Pi (chancellor, v.p. profl. rels. 1979—), Pilot Club (del. 1981-82). Roman Catholic. Office: Burroughs Wellcome Co 3030 Cornwallis Rd Research Triangle Park NC 27709

KURFEHS, HAROLD CHARLES, real estate executive; b. Jersey City, Dec. 10, 1939; s. Harold Charles and Matilda Gertrude (Ruschman) K.; B.S. (Oaklawn Found. scholar), St. Peter's Coll., 1962; M.B.A., Wharton Sch., U. Pa., 1964; m. Linda Roberta Lepis, Aug. 1, 1964; children—Harold Charles III, Diane E., Robert C. Product mgr. Am. Brands, Inc., N.Y.C., 1958-62, 64-66; account exec. Benton & Bowles, N.Y.C., 1966-68; account mgr. Wells, Rich, Greene, Inc., N.Y.C., 1968-69; v.p., dir. marketing Meta-Language Products, Inc., N.Y.C., 1969-70; sr. account exec. McCaffrey & McCall, Inc., N.Y.C., 1970-71; dir. advt. Ethan Allen, Inc., N.Y.C., 1972-75; v.p., gen. mgr. retail/franchise div. N.Am. ops. Reed Ltd., Toronto, Ont., Can., 1975-76, also v.p., gen. mgr. fabric div. Reed Nat. Drapery Co., Sanderson, Can., 1975-76; pres. Fairfield Book Co. Inc., Brookfield, Conn., 1977-83, dir. advt. and pub. relations, bd. dirs., mem. mktg. planning bd. Ethan Allen, Inc., Danbury, Conn., 1983-85; comml. investment realtor William Raveis Comml. Investment Real Estate, Danbury, Conn., 1985—; lectr. Western Conn. State U., 1985—. Mem. Co. Mil. Historians, Wharton Grad. Club N.Y., U.S. Naval Inst., Nat. Def. Preparedness Assn., Nat. Rifle Assn. (life), Pi Sigma Phi. Home: 42 Obtuse Rd N Brookfield Center CT 06805 Office: 48 Mill Plain Rd Danbury CT 06811

KURITA, DEBRA LYNN, city official; b. Salt Lake City; d. Ikuya and Rosemary (Baer) K.; m. Keene N. Wilson, Oct. 1, 1983; 1 child, Skyler E. Ba in Polit. Sci., U. Calif., Davis, 1976; MPA, U. So. Calif., 1981. Adminstrv. intern small bus. L.A. Mayor's Office, 1979-80; with mcpl. svcs. dept. City of Lawndale, Calif., 1980-81; adminstrv. specialist fin. dept. City of Torrance, Calif., 1981-84; adminstrv. asst. I and II community devel. agy City of Santa Ana, Calif., 1984-86, mgr. adminstrv. svcs., 1986—. Mem. Am. Soc. Pub. Adminstrn., Mcpl. Mgmt. Assts. So. Calif. (treas. 1984-85). Office: City of Santa Ana 20 Civic Ctr Pla M25 Santa Ana CA 92701

KURNIAWAN, DEWANTO, corporate executive; b. Palembang, Indonesia, Nov. 15, 1942; s. Soetarto and Maria Kurniawan; student Indonesian schs.; m. Gracie Tasman, Sept. 7, 1963; children—Michael, Florence, Charles, Richard. Pres., dir. P.T. Green ville Real Estate, 1973—, P.T. Galena Tambang, 1975—, P.T. Dewanata Coy Ltd., 1975—, P.T. Dewanta Karsa Internat. Corp., 1975—, P.T. Villa Sari Mas, 1976—, P.T. Tri Karsa Dewantara Corp., 1976—, Dewantara Richwood Indonesia, 1977—, P.T. Pasar Baru Indah Dept. Store (all Jakarta), 1977—, P.T. Wahyu Waruna Watan, P.T. Bluendo Groto; chmn. Lindtan Internat. Corp. Singapore, 1976—; pres., supr. P.T. Brazindon, 1976—; supr. P.T. Bank Indonesia Raya, 1975—; dir. P.T. Sarang Sapta Putra, C.V. Indonesia Jaya Raya, P.T. Grawisa Contractors, P.T. Taman Lina Permai, P.T. Green Garden Ltd., P.T. Cakung Remaja Indah Jaya Housing, P.T. Taman Kedoya Barat Indah, P.T. Star Parama Purnama, P.T. Star Parama Cakrawala, P.T. Delta Samudra, P.T. Manggala Putra Kaloka Manado, P.T. Taman Kota; mem. commissary P.T. Tanjung Sedari Abadi. Home: Blok Y/13 Kepa Duri, Tomang Barat, Jakarta Indonesia Office: PT Greenville Real Estate, Block C3/No 1 J1, Tanjung Duren Barat Complex, Tomang Barat Jakarta, Indonesia

KURRY, JOSEPH RICHARD, finance executive; b. Chgo., May 2, 1950; s. Joseph Richard and Dorothy M. (Buoscio) K.; m. Libby Ann Heskin, Apr. 23, 1977; children: Mary Elizabeth, Delia Rose, Joseph Edmund. BS in Bus. Adminstrn., Georgetown U., 1972. Acct. Arthur Anderson and Co., Chgo., 1972-75; audit mgr. Arthur Anderson and Co., Washington, 1975-79; controller ManTech Internat. Corp., Alexandria, Va., 1979-85; chief fin. officer, treas. Essex Corp., Alexandria, 1985—. Mem. Am. Inst. CPA's, Grant Thornton Bus. Roundtable (govt. contractors sect.), Georgetown U. Alumni Assn. Democrat. Roman Catholic. Lodge: Civitan (v.p. Washington chpt. 1977-83, Outstanding Service award 1979). Office: Essex Corp 333 N Fairfax St Alexandria VA 22314

KURSEWICZ, LEE Z., marketing consultant; b. Chgo., Oct. 26, 1916; s. Antoni and Henryka (Sulkowska) K.; ed. Chgo. and Bata ind. schs.; m. Ruth Elizabeth Venzke, Jan. 31, 1940; 1 son, Dennis. With Bata Shoe Co., Inc., 1936-78, plant mgr., Salem, Ind., 1963-65, v.p., mng. dir., Batawa, Ont., Can., 1965-71; v.p., dir. Bata Industries, Batawa, 1965-71, plant mgr., Salem, 1971-76; pres. Bata Shoe Co., Inc., Belcamp, Md., 1976-77, sr. v.p., dir., 1977-79; gen. mgr. Harford Insulated Panel Systems div. Hazleton Industries, 1981-82. City mgr. City of Batawa, 1965-71; vice chmn. Trenton (Ont.) Meml. Hosp., 1970-71; pres. Priestford Hills Community Assn., 1979-80;

chmn. adv. bd. Phoenix Festival Theatre, Hartford County Community Coll., 81; vice chmn. Harford County chpt. ARC, 1980-81, chmn., 1982-83; chmn. Harford County Econ. Devel. Adv. Bd., 1983-85; mem. Susquehanna Region Pvt. Industry Council, 1983-85. Mem. Am. Mgmt. Assn. Clubs: Rotary, Bush River Yacht (commodore 1956), Bush River Power Squadron (comdr. 1957), Western Hills Country of Salem (pres. 1975), Trenton Country (pres. 1968-69), Md. Country. Home and Office: 29707A Niguel Rd Laguna Niguel CA 92677

KURTZ, JOEL BARRY, finance director; b. Bklyn., Aug. 2, 1944; s. Milton and Claire (Diamond) K.; B.B.A., Pace U., 1970; M.B.A., C.W. Post Coll., 1981; m. Judith M. Austin, Aug. 11, 1968; children—Brian, Steven, Stacey. Staff acct. Arthur Andersen & Co., Melville, N.Y., 1970-73; div. controller Elec. Comp. div., Gould Inc., Farmingdale, N.Y., 1973-78; controller CBS-Holt, Rinehart & Winston, N.Y.C., 1979-80; controller Siemens Data Switching Systems, formely Databit Inc., Hauppauge, N.Y., 1981-87; dir. fin. Linotype Co., Hauppauge, N.Y., 1987—. Active L.I. Assn., 1981—. Served with U.S. Army, 1966-68. C.P.A., N.Y. Mem. Nat. Assn. Accts. (chpt. pres. 1976-77), N.Y. Soc. C.P.A.s, Am. Inst. C.P.A.s, Am. Mgmt. Assn. Home: 84 Vera Ln Commack NY 11725 Office: 425 Oser Ave Hauppauge NY 11788

KURTZ, ROBERT ARTHUR, finance company executive; b. Holyoke, Mass., June 16, 1943; m. Peggy Dean, Apr. 5, 1986. BS in Fin., Am. Internat. Coll., Springfield, Mass., 1967; MBA in Fin., U. Okla., 1969. Sr. fin. analyst corp. treas. office Gulf Oil Internat., Pitts., 1969-71; with corp. fin. staff Humble Oil div. Exxon, Houston, 1971-73; account exec. Merrill Lynch, Atlanta, 1973-75; personal and corp. fin. advisor Atlanta, 1975-77; pres., founder Internat. Trade and Mktg. Corp., Atlanta, 1977-84; chmn. Kray Fin. Corp., Atlanta, 1984—. Mem. Soc. Neuro-Linguistic Programming, Am. Assn. for Counseling and Devel. Lutheran. Home: 2705 Kozy Ct Marietta GA 30066

KURTZIG, SANDRA L., software company executive; b. Chgo., Oct. 21, 1946; d. Barney and Marian (Boruck) Brody; children: Andrew Paul, Kenneth Alan; B.S. in Math., UCLA, 1967; M.S.in aeronaut. engring., Stanford U., 1968. Math analyst TRW Systems, 1967-68; mktg. rep., Gen. Electric Co., 1969-72; chmn. bd., chief exec. officer, pres. ASK Computer Systems, Mountain View, Calif., 1972-85, chmn. bd., 1986-89. Cited one of 50 most influential bus. people in Am., Bus. Week, 1985. Office: ASK Computer Systems Inc 2440 W El Camino Real Mountain View CA 94039-7640

KURYK, DAVID NEAL, lawyer; b. Balt., Aug. 24, 1947; s. Leon and Bernice G. (Fox) K.; m. Alice T. Lehman, July 8, 1971; children—Richard M., Robert M., Benjamin A. B.A., U. Md., 1969; J.D., U. Balt., 1972. Bar: Md. 1972, U.S. Dist. Ct. Md. 1973, U.S. Ct. Mil. Appeals 1973, D.C. 1974, U.S. Ct. Appeals (4th cir.) 1974, U.S. Supreme Ct. 1976, U.S. Ct. Appeals (Fed. cir.) 1982. Assoc. Harold Buchman, Esq., Balt., 1970-76; sole practice, Balt., 1976—. Served to sgt. USAF, 1967-73. Mem. ABA (products, gen. liability and consumer law com. 1976—, com. auto law 1977), Md. State Bar Assn., Bar Assn. Balt. City, Assn. Trial Lawyers Am., U. Balt. Alumni Assn., Zeta Beta Tau. Democrat. Jewish. Mem. bd. editors Md. Bar Jour., 1973-76. Home: 11200 Five Spring Rd Lutherville MD 21093 Office: 5 Light St Suite 950 Baltimore MD 21202

KURZ, GERHARD EUGEN, oil company executive; b. Stuttgart, Germany, Aug. 25, 1939; s. Eugen and Martha (Fried) K.; came to U.S., 1965, naturalized, 1973; BA with honors, U. Wales, 1964; MBA, N.Y. U., 1971; m. Emma Margaretha E. Olving, Oct. 2, 1964; children—Thomas, Christopher, Annika, Christina. With Mobil Shipping Co., 1964—, mgr. industry studies, N.Y.C., 1972-75, mgr. joint ventures, 1976-79, mgr. fin. planning, analysis, and controls, 1980-81, v.p. Middle East and marine planning, 1982-88; pres. Mobil Shipping and Transp. Co., 1988—. Mem. North Am. Soc. for Corp. Planning, Planning Execs. Inst. (bd. dirs. Tovalop), Westfield Jr. C. of C. (treas., bd. dir. 1973-74), Am. Mgmt. Assn., Transp. Rsch. Forum. Presbyterian. Club: Echo Lake Country (Westfield, N.J.). Home: 320 Woodland Ave Westfield NJ 07090 Office: 150 E 42nd St New York NY 10017

KUSE, JAMES RUSSELL, chemical company executive; b. Lincoln, Nebr., Aug. 20, 1930; s. Walter Herman and Gladys Katherine (Graham) K.; m. Shirley Rae Ernst, Sept. 27, 1953; children: Lynn, Carol Kuse Ehlen, Michael. B.S.Ch.E., Oreg. State U., 1955. Indsl. chems. salesman Ga.-Pacific Corp., Atlanta, 1967-68, mgr. splty. chem. div., 1968-70, mgr. chem. sales, 1970-74, mgr. comml. chems., 1974-76, v.p. chem. div., 1976-78, sr. v.p. chem. div., 1978-84; chmn., pres., chief exec. officer Ga. Gulf Corp., 1985—. Bd. dirs. Clark Coll., Atlanta, 1983. Served to cpl. U.S. Army, 1953-55. Mem. Nat. Petroleum Refiners Assn. (dir.), Am. Inst. Chem. Engrs., Chem. Mfrs. Assn., Am. Chem. Soc. Republican. Lutheran. Club: Capital City (Atlanta). Office: Ga Gulf Corp 400 Perimeter Center Terr Ste 595 Atlanta GA 30346

KUSHEL, GLENN ELLIOT, lawyer; b. Bklyn., May 5, 1945. BME, CUNY, 1968; MSME, Columbia U., 1970; JD, Seton Hall U., 1974; LLM, NYU, 1978; cert., Coll. Fin. Planning, 1987. Bar: N.J. 1974, N.Y. 1977, U.S. Supreme Ct. 1978. Mem. tech. staff Bell Telephone Labs., Whippany, N.J., 1968-71; cost engr. Exxon Resource and Engr. Co., Florham Park, N.J., 1971-72; dep. atty. gen. State of N.J., Trenton, 1974-76; assoc. Rosenman and Colin, N.Y.C., 1976-81; sole practice Bklyn., 1981—. assoc. mem. malpractice panel N.Y. State Supreme Ct., Kings County, 1986—. Atomic Energy Commn. fellowship, 1968. Mem. ABA, Bklyn. Bar Assn., N.Y. State Trial Lawyers Assn., Pi Tau Sigma, Tau Beta Pi. Office: 32 Court St Brooklyn NY 11201

KUSHEN, ALLAN STANFORD, lawyer; b. Chgo., Oct. 5, 1929; s. Barney and Ethel (Friedman) K.; m. Betty Cohen, Sept. 2, 1951; children: Annette Joyce, Robert Allan. BBA cum laude, U. Miami, Fla., 1952, LLB cum laude, 1952; LLM (Food and Drug Law Inst. fellow), NYU Sch. Law, 1955. Bar: Fla. 1952, N.Y. State 1956. Atty. Schering Corp., Bloomfield, N.J., 1955-67, Schering Corp. (counsel labs. div.), Bloomfield, 1967-69, Schering Corp. (domestic ops. div.), Bloomfield, 1969-73; v.p., gen. counsel Schering-Plough Corp., Kenilworth, N.J., 1973-80; sr. v.p. pub. affairs Schering-Plough Corp., Madison, N.J., 1980—; mem. N.Y. adv. com. Allendale Ins. Co.; lectr. in field. Trustee Food and Drug Law Inst., Newark Mus.; trustee, pres. Arts Coun. of Morris Area; chmn. Morris Area Performing Arts Ctr. Corp.; bd. visitors Yale Law Sch. Civil Liability Project; pres. Schering-Plough Found.; bd. dirs. Pub. Affairs Coun.. 1st lt. JAG AUS, 1952-54. Mem. ABA, N.Y. State Bar Assn., N.J. Bar Assn. (asso.), Fla. Bar, Am. Coll. Legal Medicine (asso. in law), Phi Delta Phi. Home: 1 Raynor Rd West Orange NJ 07052 Office: Schering-Plough Corp 1 Giralda Farms Madison NJ 07940

KUSHNER, JEFFREY L., manufacturing company executive; b. Wilmington, Del., Apr. 7, 1948; s. William and Selma (Kreger) K.; m. Carolyn Patricia Hypes, May 2, 1975; children: Tawnya Lynne. BBA summa cum laude, U. Hawaii, 1970; MBA, Columbia U., 1972. Sr. fin. analyst Black & Decker, Towson, Md., 1972-73; div. controller Black & Decker, Solon, Ohio, 1973-74; asst. div. controller Rockwell Internat., Pitts., 1974-75; div. controller Carborundum Corp., Niagara Falls, N.Y., 1975-77; mgr. fin. planning United Techs. Corp., Hartford, Conn., 1977-80, corp. v.p. fin. planning, 1986—; asst. controller Sikorsky Aircraft, Stratford, Conn., 1980-82, div. controller, 1982-83, v.p. fin., chief fin. officer, 1983-85. Bd. dirs. ACR, Hartford. 1987. Recipient Brotherhood Fund. fellowship, 1970. Mem. Conf. Bd. (council mem. 1987—). Home: 40 Westcliff Dr West Hartford CT 06117 Office: United Techs Corp One Financial Pla Hartford CT 06101

KUSHNER, ROBERT ARNOLD, steel company executive; b. N.Y.C., Dec. 11, 1935; s. Sidney and Doris Gloria (Kaplowitz) K.; m. Alice Fried, June 8, 1957; children: Audrey, Donald. B.S., NYU, 1957, J.D. cum laude, 1960. Bar: N.Y. 1960, Pa. 1977. Atty.-adviser FTC, 1960-61; asso. firm Parker, Chapin, Flattau and Klimpl, N.Y.C., 1961-67; v.p. legal, sec. Ward Foods, Inc., N.Y.C., 1967-72; asst. gen. counsel Pan Am. Airways, N.Y.C., 1972-76; v.p., sec., gen. counsel Cyclops Industries, Pitts., 1976—. Bd. dirs. Pitts. Dance Council, Pitts. Opera, Am. Jewish Com. Mem. ABA, Am. Corp. Counsel Assn. (past pres., bd. dirs Western Pa. chpt.), Mid-Atlantic Legal Found. (legal adv. counsel), Order of Coif. Clubs: Rolling Hills Country, Duquesne. Home: 30 Vernon Dr Pittsburgh PA 15228 Office: Cyclops Industries Inc 650 Washington Rd Pittsburgh PA 15228

KUTASI, KATALIN ERZSEBET, banker; b. Ann Arbor, Mich., Sept. 7, 1956; d. Karoly and Margaret (Vidonyi) K. BA in Acctg., Mich. State U., East Lansing, 1978; MBA in Fin., DePaul U., 1983. Cost acct. Continental Ill. Nat. Bank and Trust Co. of Chgo., 1978-80, banking officer trade fin., 1980-85, 2d v.p., 1985-88, v.p., 1988; workout specialist FDIC, Chgo., 1989—. Active Chgo. Council on Fgn. Relations, 1984-85. Mem. Am. Council for the Arts, Mich. State U. Alumni Assn. (bd. dirs. 1978-85), Gamma Phi Beta. Republican. Roman Catholic.

KUTCHER, FRANK EDWARD, JR., printing company executive; b. Teaneck, N.J., Dec. 20, 1927; s. Frank Edward Sr. and Helen Marie (Crowley) K.; m. Elizabeth Vespaziani, Jan. 19, 1952; children—Kenneth, Karen, Kristin. B.S. cum laude, Fairleigh Dickinson U., 1953. Mgmt. cons. Peat, Marwick, Mitchell & Co., Inc., 1961-63; controller Celanese Plastics Co., 1963-65, Pfister Chem. Co., Ridgefield, N.J., 1965-67; v.p. fin. Litton Industries, N.Y.C., 1967-70; v.p., controller McCall Pub. Co.-Norton Simon, Inc., N.Y.C., 1970-73; pres. Foote & Davies-Lincoln, Nebr., 1978—; chmn., pres., chief exec. officer FDI Holdings, Inc., Doraville, 1985—. Served with USN, 1945-46. Mem. Graphics Arts Tech. Found. (bd. dirs. 1982—), Fin. Execs. Inst., Nat. Assn. Accts., Mensa. Clubs: Atlanta Athletic, Commerce (Atlanta); Atrium (N.Y.C.). Office: Foote & Davies Inc 3101 McCall Dr Doraville GA 30340

KUTEMEYER, PETER MARTIN, industrial engineering executive; b. Freiburg, W. Germany, Nov. 19, 1938; s. Martin Henry and Gertrude Barbara (Buechel) K.; came to U.S., 1954, naturalized, 1956; B.M.E. with distinction, Ariz. State U., 1968, M.S. in Engring. Mechanics, 1969; M.B.A., U. Utah, 1977; m. Fresquez, June 25, 1961 (div. Aug. 1986); children—Michael, Kristina. Enlisted USAF, 1958, commd. 2d. lt. 1967, advanced through grades to capt., 1970; aero. engr., 1969-71, systems devel. engr., 1971-74, tech. liaison officer to W. German Fed. Govt., 1974-78; ret., 1978; indsl. mgr. Mining Progress, Inc., Highland Mills, N.Y., 1978-79, prodn. mgr., 1979-81; gen. mgr. Bischoff Environ. Systems div. Intertech Inc., Highland Mills, 1981—. Mem. ASME, AIAA, Assn. Iron and Steel Engrs., Air Pollution Control Assn., TAPPI (asso.), Am. Soc. Metals, AIME. Home: 71 6th St #40 Shalimer FL 32579 Office: Bischoff Environ Systems div Intertech Inc 135 Cumberland Rd Pittsburgh PA 15237

KUWAHARA, MITSUNORI, judicial scrivener and consultant; b. Saseho, Nagasaki, Kyushu, Japan, Sept. 25, 1936; s. Ryoichi and Shizuko Iida K.; m. Kimie Haibara, June 12, 1964; children: Mamie, Koichiro. LLB, Chuo U., Tokyo, 1966. Gen. mgr. law dept. Japan High-rising Housing Co. Ltd., Tokyo, 1967-70; pres. Techunorand Co, Ltd., Tokyo, 1970—; chmn. Kuwahara Firm, Tokyo, 1968—. Mem. Tokyo Jud. Scrivener Assn., Tokyo Cons. on Adminstrv. Papers Assn. Liberal Democrat. Clubs: Do Sports Plaza (Shinjuku, Tokyo); Hayama Mariner (Kanagawa). Home: 1-36-7 Wakamiya, Nakano-ku, Tokyo Japan Office: Kuwahara Firm, Shinjuku Nomura Bldg 9th Floor, 1-26-2 Nishishinjuku, Shinjuku-ku, Tokyo 163, Japan

KUZINA, JAN CELESTE, aeronautical engineer; b. Winnipeg, Man., Can., Oct. 30, 1956; d. John and Iris Alice (Huziak) K. BSC in physics with honors, U. Manitoba, 1982; M in Aero. Engring., Carleton U., 1985. Flight instr. Winnipeg Flying Club, 1975-77; charter pilot Aero Trades Western Ltd., Winnipeg, 1977; research officer Nat. Research Council Can., Ottawa, Ont., Can., 1981, Low Speed Aerodyns. Lab., Ottawa, Ont., Can., 1982-83, Nat. Research Council Can. Unsteady Aerodyns. Lab., Ottawa, Ont., 1984-85; aerodyn. flight test coordinator de Havilland div. Boeing Aircraft Co., Toronto, Ont., 1986—; speaker in field. Contbr. articles to profl. jours. Recipient Female Pvt. Pilot of Yr. award Royal Can. Flying Clubs Assn., 1973, Allister R. Gillespie Meml. award, 1975; S.F. Kay scholar in sci., 1980; Amelia Earhart fellowship Zonta Internat., 1984. Mem. Canadian Aeros. and Space Inst., Fedn. Engring. and Scientific Assns. Office: Boeing Aircraft Co, de Havilland Aircraft div, Garratt Blvd, Toronto, ON Canada M3K 1Y5

KUZMA, DAVID RICHARD, natural gas company executive; b. Pitts., Nov. 1, 1945; s. Joseph R. and Stella C. (Kicinski) K.; m. Marianne K. Best, Feb. 24, 1973; children: Heather, Eric. BA, Duquesne U., 1968, MA, 1974. Auditor Price Waterhouse & Co., Pitts., 1968-71; staff auditor Consol. Natural Gas Co., Pitts., 1971-73, fin. analyst, 1973-76, mgr. fin., 1976-78, dir. internal auditing, 1978-81, asst. treas., 1981-84, treas., 1984-88, v.p. spl. project financing, 1988—. Bd. dirs., treas. Pitts. Ctr. for Arts, 1987—. Served to 1st lt. USAR, 1968-70. Mem. Am. Inst. CPAs, Pa. Inst. CPAs, River Club, Gateway Ctr. Republican. Roman Catholic. Office: Consol Natural Gas Co CNG Tower 625 Liberty Ave Pittsburgh PA 15222

KVENVOLD, TONY MARK, electronics executive, consultant; b. Madison, S.D., Oct. 28, 1956; s. Alden Theodor Kvenvold and Dorothy Clara (Verhay) Johnson; m. Wynne Whiting Treanor, June 23, 1979; children: Kristopher, Allyssa. AA, Rochester Community Coll., 1980; BS, Winona State U., 1983. Electronic design engr. Watlow Co., Winona, Minn., 1980-86; pres. Finch Systems, Winona, 1983—; sr. design engr. Quantem Corp., Trenton, N.J., 1986—; Inventor electronic computer chip, 1985. Office: Quantem Corp Box 7599 Trenton NJ 08628

KWASHA, H. CHARLES, consultant actuary; b. Providence, Dec. 2, 1906; s. Barnard and Lena (Lisker) K.; A.B., Brown U., 1928; m. Sylvia I. Herman, Aug. 20, 1939; children—Linda Dianne, Bruce Charles, Robert Dexter. Mem. faculty Brown U., 1929, actuary Travelers Ins. Co., 1929-37; head pension dept. Marsh and McLennan, Inc., 1937-44; organized firm, cons. actuarial work H. Charles Kwasha, cons. actuary, 1944; partner Kwasha Lipton, 1947—. Mem. Soc. Actuaries, Sigma Xi, Phi Beta Kappa. Author articles on employee retirement, employee benefit programs. Home: Jockey Club Apt 2204 Miami FL 33161 Office: 10800 Biscayne Blvd Ste 735 Miami FL 33161

KWASNICK, PAUL J., retail executive; b. N.Y.C., Apr. 8, 1925; s. Joseph and Dorothy (Ginsberg) K.; m. Selma Marcus, Sept. 7, 1947; children: Raymond, Diane, Robert. BBA, CCNY, 1947, MBA, 1957. Fin. exec. M.H. Fishman Co., Inc., N.Y.C., 1947-61; asst. sec.-treas. Zayre Corp., Natick, Mass., 1961-66; v.p., asst. sec.-treas. Zayre Corp., 1966-68, v.p., treas., 1968-72, sr. v.p., treas., 1972-73; exec. v.p., gen. mgr. Kings Dept. Stores, Inc., Newton, Mass., 1973-75; pres., chief operating officer Kings Dept. Stores, Inc., 1975-78, pres. retail div., chief operating officer, dir., mem. exec. com., 1981; chmn., pres., chief exec. officer, dir., mem. exec. com. Mars Stores, Inc., North Dighton, Mass., 1982—; pres., chief exec. officer, chmn. Data Printer Corp., Malden, Mass., 1978-80, bd. dirs., 1967-83; regional dir., bd. dirs. Shawmut Community Bank, Framingham, Mass. Bd. dirs., asst. treas. Mass. Easter Seal Soc., 1986—; trustee Combined Jewish Philanthropies of Greater Boston, 1977—, The West Suburban YMCA, Newton, 1984—. Served with AUS, 1943-46. Mem. Internat. Mass Retail Assn. (bd. dris. 1981—, treas. 1986—). Jewish. Office: Mars Stores Inc 680 Spring St North Dighton MA 02764

KWATERSKI, EDMUND ALBERT, JR, manufacturing company executive; b. Green Bay, Wis., Aug. 3, 1948; s. Edmund Albert and Agatha Garnet (Schott) K.; m. Sally Maahs, Feb. 12, 1972; children: Scott Gregory, Stephen Wade. BBA, U. Wis., Whitewater, 1971; postgrad., Dartmouth Coll., 1979. Asst. store mgr. F.W. Woolworth Co., Milw., 1971-72; dist. rep. Dun & Bradstreet, Milw., 1972-74; credit mgr. Heil Co., Milw., 1974-85; credit and cash mgr. Ortho Kinetics, Waukesha, Wis., 1985-86; corp. credit, cash mgr. Schreiber Foods, Inc., Green Bay, 1986-88; dir. corp. credit Fort Howard Corp., Green Bay, 1988—. Chmn. Nat. Truck Equip. Credit Assn., Chgo., 1978-79, 83-84; cons. Project Bus., Jr. Achievement, 1980-81; CPR instr. ARC, Milw. and Green Bay, 1980— (cert. merit 1981).. Recipient Exec. award Credit Rsch. Found., 1979. Mem. Nat. Food Mfg. Credit Assn., Nat. Food Svc. Mfg. Credit Assn., Nat. Paper Plastics Credit Assn. Republican. Roman Catholic. Home: 540 Rolling Green Dr Green Bay WI 54313 Office: Fort Howard Corp 1919 S Broadway Green Bay WI 54307

KYLE, ALASTAIR (BOYD) (ALECSANDR CUIL DE STRATCLUT), merchant banker; b. London, Mar. 12, 1931; s. Allan Granger and Dora Jessie Ellen (Taylor) Kyle; m. Corinne Lois Silverman, Aug. 28, 1959; children: Joshua Reis, Peredur Thomas, Julia Dora; m. 2d, Mary Carmela Giarrizzo, Mar. 3, 1969; children: Allan Salvatore, Kentigern Sigvard. Student, St. John's Coll., 1947-49; AB, U. Michoacán, 1951; postgrad., U. Havana, 1951-52, U. Chgo., 1959. Child actor radio, stage and TV 1940-44; radio dir. Clyde de Mex. S.A., Acapulco, 1950; salesman Radiovision Internacional, Mexico City, 1951; with Atlantic Union Com., N.Y.C., 1953-54; with investment dept. Grace Internat. Devel. Co., N.Y.C., 1955-56; v.p., bd. dirs. Index & Retrieval Systems, Inc., N.Y.C. and Woodstock, Vt., 1957-62; prin. Alec Kyle & Co., N.Y.C., 1962-66; pres. Inst. Computer Assisted Instrn., Inc., Doylestown, Pa., 1967-70; mng. ptnr. Corp. Fin. Cons., Phila. and Princeton, N.J., 1971-82; prin. Cromwell & Kyle, Fountainville, Pa. and Fairfield, Conn., 1982-85, Kyle & Hayes-Morrison, Frazer, Pa. and Jamestown, R.I., 1986—; trustee Ymddiriedolaeth Llinach Brenhiniaeth y Cwmbriaid, 1963—; chmn. Strathclyde Corp., Phila.; seminar leader and lectr. in field. Co-founder, bd. dirs. Am. Council on NATO, 1954-57; sec. dir. No. New England passenger R.R. Conf., 1960-62; co-founder, sec. Fountainville Hist. Farm Assn., Bucks County, Pa., 1972—; cons. preservation agrl. land Buckingham (Pa.) Twp., 1978-79; pres. New Britain (Pa.) Twp. Democratic Orgn., 1974-78; mem. exec. bd. Bucks County Dem. Com., 1974-78; chmn. Nat. Task Force on Religion and Animal Rights, 1981-85; bd. dirs. Pa. Soc. Prevention of Cruelty to Animals, 1987—; chmn. Internat. Network for Religion and Animals, 1985-87, treas. 1987—; lay reader, dep. convs., mem. coms. Episcopal Diocese Pa.; vestryman St. Paul's Ch., Doylestown, Pa., Anglican Ch. of the Incarnation, Telford, Pa., Holy Sacraments' Anglican Ch., King of Prussia, Pa. Recipient Suprs. commendation Buckingham Twp., 1979. Mem. Newcomen Soc., Inst. Effective Mgmt. (v.p. 1978—), Assn. Corp. Growth, Am. Mgmt. Assn. (cons.), Family Assn. Cumbrian Dynasty (convenor), Welsh Soc. Phila. (steward 1982-84, 2d v.p. 1984-86, v.p. 1986—), Royal Stuart Soc., Cymdeithas Madog, Celtic League, Internat. Com. for the Def. of the Breton Lang. (bd. dirs. Am. br., 1984—), Mensa, Phila. Vegetarian Soc. Clubs: St. Andrew's, Atheneum (Phila.), St. Andrew's (Mexico City), Cercle des Princes (Paris), Sloane (London). also: Garden End Belvoir, Grantham Lincs England Office: 7 Frame Ave PO Box 925 Frazer PA 19355

KYLE, CORINNE SILVERMAN, management consultant; b. N.Y.C., Jan. 4, 1930; d. Nathan and Janno (Harra) Silverman; m. Alec Kyle, Aug. 29, 1959 (div. Feb. 1969); children: Joshua, Perry (dec.), Julia. BA, Bennington Coll., 1950; MA, Harvard U., 1953. Assoc. editor Inter-Univ. Case Program, N.Y.C., 1956-60; co-founder, chief editor Financial Index, N.Y.C., 1960-63; research analyst McKinsey & Co., N.Y.C., 1963-64; sr. research asso. Mktg. Sci. Inst., Phila., 1964-67; founding partner Phila. Group, 1967-70; sr. asso. Govt. Studies and Systems, Phila., 1970-72, cons. program planning and control, Phila., 1972—, sr. asso. Periodical Studies Service, 1978—; v.p., dir. research Total Research Corp., Princeton, N.J., 1981-82; mgr. social research The Gallup Orgn., Princeton, 1982-86; v.p., Response Analysis Corp., 1986—; lectr. research methods Temple U., 1981—; dir. Verbena Corp., N.Y.C. Contbr. numerous articles to profl. publs. Mem. adv. council to 8th Dist. city councilman, Phila., 1971-79; mem. 22d Ward Democratic Exec. Com., 1971-78, State Dem. Com., 1974-76; mem. Pa. Gov.'s Council on Nutrition, 1974-76; v.p. Miquon Upper Sch. Bd., Phila., 1977-78; trustee Princeton Regional Scholarship Found., 1982—, pres., 1984-85; mem. bd. edn. Princeton Regional Sch. Dist., 1984—, pres. 1987—. Mem. Am. Polit. Sci. Assn., Am. Assn. for Pub. Opinion Research. Home: 156-A Spruce St Princeton NJ 08540

KYLE, FREDERICK W., pharmaceutical company executive; b. 1932. Student, Swarthmore Coll., Harvard U. With Smithkline Beckman Corp., 1981—; v.p. Latin Am. Smithkline and French Labs., v.p. Africa, Asia, Oceania, 1983-85; v.p. corp. planning Smithkline Beckman Corp., 1985-86; pres. Smithkline Beckman, Japan, 1986-88; v.p. Smithkline Beckman Corp., 1988—; pres. Smithkline and French Labs., U.S., 1988—. Office: Smith Kline & French Labs 1500 Spring Garden St PO Box 7929 Philadelphia PA 19101 *

KYLE, HENRY CARPER, lawyer; b. Houston, Oct. 17, 1909; s. Henry Carper and Medie Pitts (Rylander) K.; m. Marain Morris Camp, Sept. 6, 1936; children: Henry Carper III, Elizabeth Pitts Kyle Winn. BS, S.W. Tex. State U., 1931; LLB, Cumberland U., 1932. Bar: Tex., 1932. Mem. Tex. Ho. Reps., Austin, 1933-34; county atty. Hays County, San Marcos, Tex., 1936-46; sole practice San Marcos, 1932—; pres. Guaranty Title & Abstract Co., San Marcos, 1951—; bd. dirs. First Nat. Bank, San Marcos. Mem. ABA, Tex. State Bar. Republican. Methodist. Lodge: Kiwanis (pres. 1939-40).

KYLE, JOHN DEAN, banker; b. Newark, June 6, 1935; s. Gordon I. and Amy (Turner) K.; children: Amy, Susan, Barbara. B.A., Princeton U., 1957; grad. Advanced Mgmt. Program,, Harvard U., 1979. With Chem. Bank, N.Y.C., 1963—; v.p., then sr. v.p. real estate div. Chem. Bank, 1968-77, exec. v.p., 1980—; dir. Kerr Glass Mfg. Corp.; mem. N.Y. adv. bd. Chgo. Title Ins. Co. Bd. dirs. N.Y.C. Community Preservation Corp., Instl. Owners div. Real Estate Bd. N.Y., Regional Plan Assn.; mem. president's council Brandeis U.; mem. Can.-Am. Com. Clubs: Princeton (N.Y.C.); Princeton Charter (gov.), Sleepy Hollow Country. Office: Chem Bank 277 Park Ave New York NY 10172

KYLE, ROBERT CAMPBELL, II, publishing executive; b. Cleve., Jan. 6, 1935; s. Charles Donald and Mary Alice (King) K.; m. Barbara Ann Battey, June 8, 1957; children: Peter F., Christopher C., Scott G. BS, U. Colo., 1956; MA, Case Western Res. U., 1958; MBA, Harvard U., 1963, DBA, 1966. Ptnr. McLagan & Co., Chgo., 1966-67; founder, pres. Devel. Systems Corp. (now subs. Longman Group USA), 1967-82, pres. Longman Group USA, Chgo., 1982—; bd. dirs. Grubb & Ellis Co., San Francisco, Addison-Wesley-Longman Group Ltd., London. Author: Property Management, 1979, Profits in Real Estate, 1987; co-author: Modern Real Estate Practice, 1967, How to Profit From Real Estate, 1988. Mem. Real Estate Educators Assn. (pres. 1981), Internat. Assn. Fin. Planning, Real Estate Securities and Syndication Inst., Chgo. Book Clinic (dir.), Harvard Club of N.Y., Econs. Club, Chgo. Yacht Club, San Diego Yacht Club. Avocations: yacht racing, tennis. Home: 935 Private Rd Winnetka IL 60093 Office: Longman Group USA Inc 520 N Dearborn St Chicago IL 60610

KYMAN, ALEXANDER LEON, banker; b. N.Y.C., Nov. 8, 1929; s. Jack H. and Fannie (Senauke) K.; m. Jean Poffenberger, Apr. 13, 1951; children: Lynn, David, Miriam, Rebecca. B.A., So. Meth. U., 1950; LL.B., Harvard, 1953. Asst. treas. Chase Nat. Bank., N.Y.C., 1953-62; asst. v.p. Sterling Nat. Bank, N.Y.C., 1962-64; v.p. Union Bank, Los Angeles, 1964-66; sr. v.p. City Nat. Bank, Los Angeles, 1966-77; exec. v.p. City Nat. Bank, 1977-83, pres., 1984—, also bd. dirs.; bd dirs. CNB Mortgage Corp., City Ventures, Inc., City Nat. Fin. Services Corp.; pres., bd. dirs. City Nat. Corp.; dir. Calif. Bankers Assn., Calif. Bankers Clearing House Assn. Mem. Los Angeles Jewish Fedn. Council, 1967—, Nat. Commn. Anti-Defamation League, Anti-Defamation League; bd. dirs. United Way Greater Los Angeles. Mem. Harvard Law Sch. Assn., Am. Bankers Assn. Clubs: Harvard So. Calif, El Caballero Country. Office: City Nat Bank 400 N Roxbury Dr Beverly Hills CA 90210

LAB, RICHARD CRAIG, brokerage executive; b. Canton, Ohio, Aug. 12, 1949; s. Richard Cletus adn Rosemary C. (Paul) L.; divorced. AA, Kent State U., 1975, BBA in Acctg., 1976, MBA, 1981. Elec. tester Hoover Co., North Canton, Ohio, 1968-75; quality control supr. Hoover Co., 1975-81, systems analyst, 1981-83; account exec. Dean Witter Reynolds, Inc., Akron, Ohio, 1984-86; assoc. v.p. investments Dean Witter Reynolds, Inc., Fairlawn, Ohio, 1986—; instr. seminars Cuyahoga Community Coll., Cleve., Notre Dame U. of Ohio, Cleve., Akron U., 1985—. Mem. Medina Young Rep. Mem. Soc. Sales and Mktg. Execs. (treas. 1986-87), Kent State U. Alumni Assn. (charter mem. dean's coun.), K.C. Roman Catholic. Home: 5030 Hills and Dales Rd NW Canton OH 44708 Office: Dean Witter Reynolds Inc 3560 W Market St Fairlawn OH 44313

LABARRE, JEROME EDWARD, lawyer; b. Mpls., May 6, 1942; s. Roy George and Mary Ann (Kennefic) LaB.; m. Mary R. Connelly, Feb. 17, 1968; children: Paul, Katherine, Sarah. BS, U. Oreg., 1964; JD, Georgetown

U., 1969. Bar: Oreg. 1969, D.C. 1969, U.S. Supreme Ct. 1972, U.S. Ct. Appeals (9th cir.). Dep. dist. atty. Multnomah County, Portland, 1969-72; assoc. Carey & Stoll, Portland, 1972-74; sole practice Portland, 1974-79; ptnr. Glasgow, LaBarre & Kelly, Portland, 1980-82, LaBarre & Assocs., Portland, 1982—; asst. prof. Lewis & Clark Northwestern Coll. Law, Portland; instr. Portland Community Coll. Founder Cath. Lawyers for Social Justice, 1983; mem. Multnomah County Bar Assn. Legal Aid Service, 1971-74. Mem. ABA, Multnomah Bar Assn. (treas. 1981, sec. 1982, 3d v.p. 1983, 2d v.p. 1984, 1st v.p./pres.-elect 1985, pres. 1986, award of Merit 1976, Spl. award for Dedicated Service to Pub., Bench and Bar 1978, chmn. corrections com. 1974-77), Oreg. Trial Lawyers Assn., Assn. Trial Lawyers Am., Internat. Bar Assn., ACLU, Am. Inn of Ct. XXVIII (pres. 1987-88). Democrat. Roman Catholic. Club: Portland City. Office: LaBarre & Assocs PC 900 SW Fifth Ave Ste 1212 Portland OR 97204-1268

LABINER, PAUL STEVEN, financial executive; b. Bronx, N.Y., Oct. 25, 1954; s. Eugene and Ruth (Gottlieb) L.; m. Adria Amy Mazarsky, June 12, 1983. BA, U. Md., 1976; JD, Cardozo Sch. Law, 1979. Cert. life underwriter. Assoc Entin, Rosenthal & Daniels, Levittown, N.Y., 1979-80; fin. counselor, staff counsel Capital Analyst, N.Y.C., 1980-82; fin. counselor Cigna Individual Fin. Svcs., N.Y.C, 1982-84; v.p. Kornreich Fin. Svcs., Inc., N.Y.C, 1984-86; pres. Goldberg/Labiner Adv. Group, Suffern, N.Y., 1986—. Chmn. United Jewish Community, Rockland, N.Y., 1987—. Fellow Internat. Assn. Fin. Planning; mem. Estate Planning Coun., Life Underwriters Assn., Am. Soc. Chartered Fin. Planners, Rotary. Home: 28 Dakota Ct Suffern NY 10901 Office: Goldberg Labiner Adv Group 75 Montebello Rd Suffern NY 10901

LA BLANC, CHARLES WESLEY, JR., financial consultant; b. Bayshore, L.I., N.Y., June 4, 1925; s. Charles Wesley and Anne (Dobson) LaB.; m. Marie Dolan, Oct. 26, 1963 (dec. Jan. 1985); children—Charles Wesley III, Gregory, Suzanne. B.S., Tufts Coll., 1949; M.B.A., N.Y.U., 1952, Ph.D., 1956. Securities portfolio mgr. Manhattan Life Ins. Co., N.Y.C., 1952-57; asst. to pres. Magnavox Co., Ft. Wayne, Ind., 1957-60; security analyst C.W. LaBlanc & Assos., N.Y.C., 1960-62; treas. Macke Co., Cheverly, Md., 1962-72, dir., 1974-80; exec. v.p., sec.-treas., dir. After Six, Inc., Phila., 1972-83; pres. Bert Paley Ltd., Inc. subs., 1976-77; chmn. bd. Cymaticolor, 1983-84; chief fin. officer and dir. Standard Telecommunications Systems Inc., South Hackensack, N.J., 1983-87; bd. dirs. Robert Bruce Industries Inc., Modern Chem. Techs. Inc., Standard Profit Sharing Fund, pres. investments Standard Profit Sharing Fund, 1987—. Pres. Queens County Young Reps., 1955-57; bd. dirs. adv. council Temple U. Served with AC USNR, 1943-46. Fellow N.Y. Soc. Security Analysts; mem. Washington Soc. Investment Analysts, Financial Analysts Phila., Financial Execs. Inst., Am. Accounting Assn., Am. Soc. Ins. Mgmt., Pub. Relations Soc. Am., Nat. Assn. Bus. Economists, Nat. Investor Relations Inst., Nat. Assn. Corp. Dirs., Phila. Securities Assn., Am. Stock Exchange Club. Club: The Bond (Phila.), Union League (Phila.). Home: 370 Aubrey Rd Wynnewood PA 19096 also: 111 N Pompano Beach Blvd Apt 1910 Pompano Beach FL 33062

LA BONTÉ, C(LARENCE) JOSEPH, apparel company executive; b. Salem, Mass., Sept. 23, 1939; s. Arthur and Alice Bella (Lecombe) LaB.; m. Donna Marie Chiaradonna, Aug. 2, 1959; children: Linda Jean, Joseph Michael. B.S., Northeastern U., 1966, A.M.E., 1968; M.B.A. with distinction (Baker scholar), Harvard U., 1969. With H.P. Hood & Sons, Boston, 1958-63; project engr., mktg. coordinator Market Forge Co., Everett, Mass., 1963-67; with ARA Services, Inc., Phila., 1969-79, exec. asst. to pres., 1969-71, v.p., 1971-72, exec. v.p., 1976-79; pres. Western Co., Los Angeles, 1972-76; pres., chief operating officer Twentieth Century-Fox Film Corp., Beverly Hills, Calif., 1979-83; chmn., chief exec. officer The Vantage Group Inc., 1983-87, Il Fornaio, Am. Corp., 1983—; pres., chief operating officer Reebok Internat., Canton, Mass., 1987—, also bd. dirs. Nat. bd. dirs. Big Bros. Am., 1970-74; v.p., bd. dirs. Los Angeles Philharm. Assn., 1980—; vis. bd. dirs. Northeastern U., 1974—; mem. Harvard U. Bus. Sch. Fund, 1971—; trustee Orthopaedic Hosp., Los Angeles. Recipient Brown award Harvard U. Bus. Sch. Mem. Harvard U. Bus. Sch. Assn. (dir. So. Calif. chpt.), 100 Club, Husky Assos. Northeastern U. Clubs: Philadelphia Country, Down Town, Vesper; Bankers (San Francisco); 100 of Los Angeles. Office: Reebok Internat Ltd 150 Royal St Canton MA 02021

LABOON, LAWRENCE JOSEPH, personnel consultant; b. St. Louis, Aug. 4, 1938; s. Joseph Warren and Ruth (Aab) LaB.; divorced; children: Lindsey Beth, Allison Ruth. BS magna cum laude, Tex. Wesleyan Coll., 1962. Operating mgr. Firestone Tire & Rubber Co., Akron, Ohio, 1962-66; pres. Met. Personnel, Inc., Phila., 1966—, Metro Tech, Valley Forge, Pa., 1977—Metro Temps, Valley Forge, 1978—; dir. Alpha-Indian Rock Savs. and Loan Assn., chmn. compensation com., 1986—; chmn. pvt. employment agy. adv. coun. Pa. Dept. Labor and Industry, 1973—; guest lectr. Drexel U., 1976—. Served with USAF, 1954-60. Cert. personnel cons. Mem. Nat. Employment Assn. (state certification bd. chmn. 1969-71, dir. 1972-74, chmn. bd. regents 1973), Pa. Assn. Personnel Services (pres. 1971-72, Blanchet Meml. award 1973), Nat. Assn. Personnel Cons., Am. Soc. Personnel Adminstrn., Mid-Atlantic Assn. Temporary Services (pres. 1983-84), TEMPNET (dir. 1986-88), Exec. Riders Ltd. (pres. 1986-88), Glenhardie Condominium Assn. (non-resident exec. bd. mem. 1989), Alpha Chi. Republican. Methodist. Home: 205 Brighton Circle Devon PA 19333 Office: 565 Swedesford Rd Ste 220 Wayne PA 19087

LABOON, ROBERT BRUCE, lawyer; b. St. Louis, June 14, 1941; s. Joseph Warren LaBoon and Ruth (Aab) LaBoon Freling; m. Ramona Ann Hudgins, Aug. 24, 1963; children—John Andrew, Robert Steven. B.S.C., Tex. Christian U., 1963; LL.B. cum laude, So. Meth. U., 1965. Bar: Tex. 1965. Ptnr. Liddell, Sapp, Zivley, Hill & LaBoon, Houston, 1965-86, 88—; vice chmn. and gen. counsel Tex. Commerce Bancshares, Inc., 1986-88; dir. Big Three Industries, Inc., Houston, 1975—; dir. Tex. Commerce Bankshares, Retina Rsch. Found, Houston Symphony Soc., Soc. for the Performing Arts, Da Camera Soc.; pres. The Houston Internat. Festival, 1988-89, Houston Estate and Fin. Forum, 1976; mem. Republican Senatorial Trust Com., Washington, 1978—; bd. dirs. Lighthouse of Houston, 1983-86; trustee Tex. Med. Ctr., Houston, 1984—, Tex. Christian U. Fellow Am. Coll. Probate Counsel, mem. ABA, Houston Bar Assn., State Bar Tex. Presbyterian. Office: Liddell Sapp Zivley Hill & LaBoon 3500 Tex Commerce Tower Houston TX 77002

LABRECHE, ANTHONY WAYNE, chamber of commerce executive; b. Menominee, Mich., June 17, 1936; s. Anthony Loyd and Elaine (Weber) L.; children—Scott Anthony, Kay Marie. Grad. high sch., Milw. Mgr., Woolworth Co., St. Paul, Minn., 1962-63, Atlantic, Iowa, 1963-68, Corn Palace Co., Mitchell, S.D., 1970-79; div. mgr. Woolco Co., Charlotte, N.C., 1968-69, asst. gen. mgr., 1969-70; exec. dir. Mitchell C. of C., S.D., 1979-81; pres. Hastings (Nebr.) C. of C., 1981-85; exec. v.p. Chino Valley (Calif.) C. of C., 1985—. Advisor on local booklets. Mem. Nebr. C. of C. Execs.(communication coun., v.p. 1984-85, pres. 1985), Nebr. Assn. Commerce and Industry (bd. dirs.), Black Hills Badlands and Lakes Assn. (chmn. bd. 1980-81, Plaque award 1981) . Lodges: Rotary, Elks (house com. 1980-81), Lions (bd. dirs. 1983—). Office: Chino Valley C of C 13134 Central St Chino CA 91710

LABRECQUE, THOMAS G., banker; b. Long Branch, N.J., Sept. 17, 1938; s. Theodore Joseph and Marjorie (Uprichard) L.; m. Sheila English Cardone, June 16, 1962; children: Thomas, Douglas, Karen, Barbara. B.A., Villanova U., 1960; postgrad., Am. U., 1962-64, N.Y. U., 1965. Asst. treas. corporate portfolio adv. group Chase Manhattan Bank (N.A.), N.Y.C., 1966-67, 2d v.p., 1967-69, v.p., mgr. corp. bank portfolio adv. dept., 1969-70, mgr. customer adv. div., 1970-71, asso. planning sec. to corp. exec. office, 1970-71, sr. v.p. bank portfolio group, 1971-74; exec. v.p. treas. dept. and treas. Chase Manhattan Bank, N.Y.C., 1974-80, vice chmn., chief operating officer, 1980-81, pres., 1981—; dir. AMAX, Inc. Trustee Cen. Park Conservancy; chmn. United Way N.Y.C.; bd. visitors Fuqua Sch. Bus.; mem. research devel. council Cystic Fibrosis Found.; mem. Bus.-Higher Edn. Forum. Served to lt. USNR, 1960-64. Office: Chase Manhattan Corp One Chase Manhattan Pla New York NY 10081

LABUDDE, ROY CHRISTIAN, lawyer; b. Milw., July 21, 1921; s. Roy Lewis and Thea (Otteson) LaB.; m. Anne P. Held, June 7, 1952; children—Jack, Peter, Michael, Susan, Sarah. A.B., Carleton Coll., 1943; J.D., Harvard U., 1949. Bar; Wis. 1949, U.S. Dist. Cts. (ea. and we. dists.) Wis. 1950, U.S. Ct. Appeals (7th cir.) 1950, U.S. Supreme Ct. 1957. Assoc., Michael, Best & Friedrich, Milw., 1949-57, ptnr., 1958—; dir. DEC-Inter, Inc., Milw. Western Bank, Western Bancshares, Inc., Superior Die Set Corp., Aunt Nellie's Farm Kitchens, Inc., Wis. Hist. Soc. Found.; Chmn., bd. dirs. Milw. div. Am. Cancer Soc. Served to lt. j.g. USNR, 1943-46. Mem. Milw. Estate Planning Counsel (past pres.), Wis. Bar Assn., Wis. State Bar Attys. (chmn. tax sch., bd. dirs. taxation sect.). Republican. Episcopalian. Clubs: University, Milw., Milw. Country (Milw.); Mason, Shriners. Home: 9000 N Bayside Dr Milwaukee WI 53217 Office: 250 E Wisconsin Ave Rm 2000 Milwaukee WI 53202

LAC, MING Q., data processing and electronics executive; b. Canton, Peoples Republic China, Sept. 14, 1948; came to U.S., 1971; s. N.V. Lac and Hang-Yung Chung; m. Sally W.F. Shih, July 14, 1973; children: Daisy Nice, Anne F., Larry M. BSEE, Nat. Taiwan U., Taipei, 1971; MS, Ohio State U., 1973, postgrad., 1975. Research assoc. Ohio State U., Columbus, Ohio, 1971-74, programmer, 1974-76; mgr., firmware engr. MI Square Corp., Columbus, 1976-78; sr. engr. Diebold Inc., Hebron, Ohio, 1978-81; v.p. products ID Systems Corp., Dublin, Ohio, 1981-84; v.p., engring. GTECH Corp., Providence, R.I., 1984—. Mem. IEEE, R.I. Council Tech. (tech. com.). Home: 360 Spring Valley Dr East Greenwich RI 02818 Office: GTECH Corp 30 Planway Warwick RI 02886

LACER, KATHRYN LORENE, corporate assistant secretary; b. Cromwell, Okla., Oct. 20, 1930; d. William Alfred and Beulah Addie (Hankins) Hopkins; m. Orland G. Lacer, May 27, 1951. Student, Amarillo Coll., 1983-85. Sec. Mansur-Campbell Ins. Agy., Wewoka, Okla., 1948-51, Phillips Petroleum Co., Borger, Tex., 1951-52; with Southwestern Pub. Svc. Co., Amarillo, Tex., 1952—, corp. asst. sec., 1983—. Participant Leadership Amarillo, 1984, regional chair., 1987-89, Leadership Tex., 1984; chmn. Civic Beautification Com. C. of C., 1987-88. Recipient Achievement award Amarillo Women's Network, 1984; named Woman of Yr. Am. Bus. Women's Assn., 1969. Mem. Amarillo C. of C. (chmn. com., women's coun.), Nat. Investor Rels. Inst., S.W. Securities Transfer Assn., Leadership Amarillo Alumni Assn. (bd. dirs. 1988-89), Amarillo Club, Tascosa Country Club. Office: Southwestern Pub Svc Co Tyler at Sixth Amarillo TX 79170

LACH, DONNA M., financial executive; b. Salem, Mass., Jan. 18, 1954; d. Leonard Joseph and June Dorothy (Roberts) Gravel; m. William T. Lach, July 7, 1973; children: Kelly Theresa, Erik William. Student, U. Mass., 1971-72. Rep. savs./sales Salem 5 Cents Savs. Bank, 1972-77; supr. credit Lechmere Sales, Danvers, Mass., 1977-80; with Salem Sch. Dept., 1984-87, Salem 5 Cents Savs. Bank, 1987—. Pres. PTA-Witchraft Heights Sch., Salem, 1984-86; troop leader Girl Scouts USA, Salem, 1983; coach Peanuts Soccer Team Salem Youth Soccer, 1981-83; mem. sch. improvement council Mass. Bd. Edn., 1986, United Parents Salem, 1986. Mem. YMCA. Roman Catholic. Home: 17 Belleview Ave Salem MA 01970 Office: Salem 5 Cents Savs Bank 210 Essex St Salem MA 01970

LACHANCE, PAUL ALBERT, food science educator, clergyman; b. St. Johnsbury, Vt., June 5, 1933; s. Raymond John and Lucienne (Landry) L.; m. Therese Cecile Cote; children: Michael P., Peter A., M.-Andre, Susan A. B.S., St. Michael's Coll., 1955; postgrad., U. Vt., 1955-57; Ph.D., U. Ottawa, 1960; D.Sc. (hon.), St. Michael's Coll., 1982. Ordained deacon Roman Cath. Ch., 1977. Aerospace biologist Aeromed. Research Labs., Wright-Patterson AFB, Ohio, 1960-63; lectr. dept. biology U. Dayton, Ohio, 1963; flight food and nutrition coordinator NASA Manned Spacecraft Center, Houston, 1963-67; assoc. prof. dept. food sci. Rutgers U., New Brunswick, N.J., 1967-72; prof. Rutgers U., 1972—, dir. grad. program food sci., 1988—, dir. Sch. Feeding effectiveness research project, 1969-72; assigned to St. Paul's Ch., Princeton, N.J.; cons. nutritional aspects of food processing; mem. sci. adv. bd. Roche Chem. div. Hoffmann LaRoche Co.; mem. nutrition policy com. Beatrice Foods Co., 1979-86; mem. religious ministries com. Princeton Med. Center. Mem. editorial adv. bd., Sch. Food Service Research Rev., 1977-82, Jour. Am. Coll. Nutrition, 1986—, Jour. Med. Consultation, 1985—, Nutrition Reports Internat., 1963-83, Profl. Nutritionist, 1977-80; contbr. articles to profl. jours. Served to capt. USAF, 1960-63. Fellow Inst. Food Technologists, Am. Coll. Nutrition; mem. Am. Assn. Cereal Chemists, AAAS, Am. Inst. Nutrition, N.Y. Inst. Food Technologists (chmn. 1977-78), Am. Soc. Clin. Nutrition, N.Y. Acad. Sci., Am. Dietetic Assn., Soc. Nutrition Edn., Am. Public Health Assn., Nat. Assn. Cath. Chaplains, Sociedad Latino Americano de Nutricion, Sigma Xi, Delta Epsilon Sigma. Home: 34 Taylor Rd RD 4 Princeton NJ 08540 Office: Rutgers U PO Box 231 New Brunswick NJ 08903

LACHAPELLE, FRANK J(OSEPH), data processing executive; b. San Francisco, May 31, 1940; m. Ann Lindstrom Scott, Jan. 19, 1962 (div. Mar. 1972); m. Carole Key Crane, Oct. 11, 1975; stepchildren: Steven Scott Crane, Shawn Marie Crane. BS in Math., U. Wash., 1961. Assoc engr. Boeing Aircraft Co., Seattle, 1962; programmer, analyst System Devel. Corp., Santa Monica, Calif., 1962-66; sr. programmer Bunker-Ramo, Heidelberg, Germany, 1966-69; group head System Devel. Corp., Santa Monica, 1969-71; designer, developer, researcher Abacus Programming Corp., Santa Monica, 1971-73; v.p. Interscience Systems, Inc., Canoga Park, Calif., 1973-83; pres., owner Interscience Computer Corp., Agoura Hills, Calif., 1983—. Mem. IEEE, Nat. Computer Svc. Network, Computer Dealers & Lessors Assn., Assn. Computing Machinery, Las Virgenes C. of C., Malibu C. of C., Chief Exec. Officers Club, North Ranch Country Club (Westlake Village, Calif.). Republican. Office: Intersci Computer Corp 5171 Clareton Dr Agoura Hills CA 91301

LACHER, EGON LEONHARDT, plastic manufacturing company executive; b. Cologne, Fed. Republic Germany, Nov. 27, 1950; came to U.S., 1985; s. Johann and Wilhelmine (Marx) L.; m. Maria Victoria De La Flor, Jan. 25, 1974; 1 child, Eric Michael. Student, Vocat. Acad., Wilhelmshaven, Fed. Republic Germany, 1969; Diploma in Engring., Univ. Coll., Munich, 1973; Degree in Govt. Engring., Tech. U., Berlin, 1981; Almerito in Engring. (hon.), Nat. U., Trujillo, Peru, 1976. Design engr. Olympia Werke AG, Wilhelmshaven, 1969-70; vis. prof. engring. Nat. U., Trujillo, 1973-76; product mgr. Mannesmann Seiffert GmbH, Berlin, 1982-83, ops. mgr., 1984-85; nat. sales mgr. Bachmann Industries, Inc., Lewiston, Maine, 1985-87; gen. mgr. European ops. Fluoroware, Inc., Chaska, Minn., 1987—; also chmn., mng. dir. Fluoroware, GmbH., Badrappenau, Fed. Republic Germany. Authors: Industrial Design I, UNT, 1973, Industrial Design II UNT, 1974, Design of Mechanical Elements UNT, 1975. Mem. Verein Deutscher Ingenieure. Home: 8041 Erie Ave Chanhassen MN 55317 Office: Fluoroware Inc 102 Jonathan Blvd Chaska MN 55318

LACKEY, LARRY ALTON, SR., lawyer, real estate developer; b. Galax, Va., Aug. 24, 1941; s. Alton and Reba Mae (Phipps) L.; B.S. in Accountancy, Southeastern U., 1962, postgrad. in Bus. Adminstrn., 1962; LL.D., (hon.), Midwestern U., 1963; diploma in advanced accountancy La Salle U., Chgo., 1965, LL.B., 1965; Ph.D. in Bus. Adminstrn., Calif. Pacific U., 1977; m. Ilene Jane Minhinnett, June 7, 1963; children—Larry Alton, Teresa Ann, Lisa Marie. Asst. proof dept. Riggs Nat. Bank, Washington, 1958-59, bookkeeper corp. accounts, also comml. accounts teller, 1959, asst. head teller, 1959-60; asst. head teller, then head teller and head note teller, also br. asst. Old Dominion Bank, Arlington, Va., 1960-61; pub. acct., bus. mgmt. analyst, Washington, 1961-68; dir. accounting, treas. W.W. Chambers Co. Inc., undertaking, Washington, 1968-69; exec. v.p., gen. mgr. Old Dominion Casket Co. Inc., Washington, 1969-70; sr. ops. analyst Macke Corp., vending and food service, Washington, 1970-71, asst. dir. corp. taxes, 1970-71; bd. dirs. Hamilton Bank & Trust Co., 1973-75; pub. acct., tax analyst, bus. mgmt. counselor, efficiency analyst firm Mervin G. Hall Co., Oakton, Va., 1971, founder Bus. Mgmt. Services div., fin. analysis, 1971; chmn. bd. dirs. Internat. Moving & Storage Co. Inc.; pres., chmn. bd. dirs. Key Investment Corp.; sec., dir., founder, ALA Corp., nat. automotive system chain, 1975; founder, pres. Bus. Mgmt. Prodns. Inc., 1985—, Westshore Corp., 1985—, Minute Mart Stores Inc., 1986—; founder, ptnr. DeSoto CableVision Inc., 1988—; Instr. Boyd Sch. of Bus., 1969-71, also trustee; spl. lectr. pub. high schs., Arlington County, Va., 1970-72; spl. cons. Commonwealth Doctors Hosp., Fairfax, Va., 1973—; founder, pres. Bus. Mgmt. Inst., 1978—. Treas., v.p. Camp Springs (Md.) Civic Assn., 1971-73; sec.-treas. Camp Springs Boys Club, 1971-73; baseball asst. Little League, Annandale, Va., 1974-76; trustee Calif. Pacific U., 1977—. Mem. Am. Soc. Internat. Law, Internat. Bar Assn., Nat. Bar Assn., Nat. Lawyers Club, Asia Pacific Lawyers Assn., Am. Soc. Univ. Profs., Annandale Jaycees, Arcadia Village Country Club, Spanish Village Country Club. Republican. Roman Catholic. Author: How To Start A Small Business, 1971, Greater Achievements Through Greater Knowledge, The People Business...We're In It, Birth of a Small Business—Its Nature and Scope, Recordkeeping for a Small Business, Establishing Its Value and Selling Your Business. Office: PO Box 552 Sarasota FL 33578

LACKEY, ROBERT SHIELDS, insurance executive; b. Bryn Mawr, Pa., Nov. 4, 1936; s. Homer C. and Elizabeth L. L.; m. Sandra Frerichs, June 4, 1960; children: Courtney, Elise, Sara; m. Carolyn Phelps, Apr. 1, 1981; stepchildren: Heidi, Jennifer, Misty. B.S., U.S. Naval Acad., 1958; M.B.A., Harvard U., 1964. Cons. McKinsey & Co., Inc., San Francisco, 1964-66, London, 1966-68; pres., chief exec. officer Atlantic Microfilm Corp., Spring Valley, N.Y., 1968-72, Mohwak Recreation Products, Ramsey, N.J., 1972-74; exec. v.p. Fidelity Union Life Ins. Co., Dallas, 1975-80; pres. Beneficial Standard Life Ins. Co., Los Angeles, 1981-83; v.p. Trilon Fin. Corp., Toronto, Ont., Can., 1983-88; v.p. corp. devel. London Life Ins. Co. (Ont.), 1983-88; pres., chief exec. officer Hartford Life Ins. Cos., Simsbury, Conn., 1983—; dir. WFS Fin. Svcs. and Wheat First Securities Inc., Richmond, Va., 1988—, Abbey Life Ins. Co., Burlington, Ont., Can., 1988—, ITT Life Ins. Co., Mpls., 1988—, Hartford (Conn.) Fire Ins. Co., 1988—. Served with USAF, 1958-62. Office: Hartford Life Ins Cos 200 Hopmeadow St Simsbury CT 06089

LACROCE, JOSEPH RODNEY, communications executive; b. Derby, Conn., Dec. 29, 1964; s. Louis Joseph and Jeannine (Mohera) LaC.; m. Teresa Marie Bertram, June 27, 1987. BS in Bus., Fairfield U., 1986. Jr. application developer AT&T, White Plains, N.Y., 1986-87; sr. application developer AT&T, White Plains, 1987—. Mem. Future Telephone Pioneers Am. (chmn. White Plains chpt. 1987—). Republican. Roman Catholic. Office: AT&T 1 N Lexington Ave White Plains NY 10601

LACY, ALAN JASPER, fragrance company executive; b. Cleveland, Tenn., Oct. 19, 1953; s. William J. and Mary (Leigh) L.; m. Caron Ann Cap, May 16, 1981; children: Daniel Alan, Brian Matthew. BSIM, Ga. Inst. Tech., 1975; MBA, Emory U., 1977. Chartered fin. analyst., 1982; fin. analyst Holiday Inns, Inc., Memphis, 1977-79; mgr. investor relations Tiger Internat., Los Angeles, 1979-80, Dart Industries, Los Angeles, 1980-81; dir. corp. fin. Dart & Kraft, Northbrook, Ill., 1981-82, asst. treas., 1982-83, treas., v.p., 1984-86, v.p. fin. and adminstrn. internat., 1987-88; v.p., treas., chief fin. officer Minnetonka Corp., Bloomington, Minn., 1988—. Mem. Fin. Analysts Fedn., Inst. Chartered Fin. Analysts, Economic Club (Chgo.). Office: Minnetonka Corp 8400 Normandale Blvd Bloomington MN 55437

LADD, ALAN WALBRIDGE, JR., motion picture company executive; b. Los Angeles, Oct. 22, 1937; s. Alan Walbridge and Marjorie Jane (Harrold) L.; m. Patricia Ann Beazley, Aug. 30, 1959 (div. 1983); children: Kelliann, Tracy Elizabeth, Amanda Sue; m. Cindra Kay, July 13, 1985. Motion picture agt. Creative Mgmt., Los Angeles, 1963-69; v.p. prodn. 20th Century-Fox Film Corp., Los Angeles, 1973-74; sr. v.p. 20th Century-Fox Film Corp. (Worldwide Prodns. div.), Beverly Hills, Calif., 1974-76; pres. 20th Century-Fox Pictures, 1976-79, Ladd Co., Burbank, Calif., 1979-83; pres., chief operating officer MGM/UA Entertainment Co, 1983-86, chief exec. officer, from 1986, also chmn. bd. dirs.; chmn., chief exec. officer Metro-Goldwyn-Mayer Pictures, Inc., Culver City, Calif., until 1988; pres. Am. Pathe Entertainment, Los Angeles, 1989—. Producer: (films) Walking Stick, 1969, A Severed Head, 1969, TamLin, 1970, Villian Zee and Co, 1971, Fear is the Key, 1973; exec. producer: (films) Nightcomers, 1971, Vice Versa, 1988. Served with USAF, 1961-63. Office: Am Pathe Entertainment 640 S San Vicente Blvd Los Angeles CA 90048

LADD, ELDON CLINTON, medical diagnostics equipment executive; b. Lima, Ohio, Oct. 6, 1942; s. Harold Franklin and Martha Elizabeth (Peters) L.; m. Marilyn Ann Hopkins, Oct. 31, 1964; children: Shelley Ann, Darin Alan. AA, Ventura Coll., 1968; BS in Acctg., San Jose State U., 1971. Sr. auditor Ampex Corp., Redwood City, Calif., 1971-73; acctg. mgr. Systems Control, Inc., Palo Alto, Calif., 1973-74; resident auditor Ampex Corp., Colorado Springs, Colo., 1975-76; controller Wilkerson Corp., Englewood, Colo., 1976-80, v.p. fin., treas., 1980-84; dir. fin. and adminstrn. Data Design Assocs., Sunnyvale, Calif., 1984-87; chief operating officer Cadwell Labs. Inc., Kennewick, Wash., 1987-88, 1988—; acctg. instr. Arapahoe Community Coll., 1978-84. Mem. Fin. Exec. Inst. Republican. Home: 2341 Snohomish Ave Richland WA 99352 Office: Cadwell Labs Inc Kennewick WA 99336

LADD, JOSEPH CARROLL, insurance company executive; b. Chgo., Jan. 26, 1927; s. Stephen C. and Laura (McBride) L.; m. Barbara Virginia Carter, June 5, 1965; children: Carroll, Joseph Carroll, Barbara, Virginia, William. BA, Ohio Wesleyan U., 1950; CLU, Am. Coll., Bryn Mawr; D in Bus. Adminstrn. (hon.), Spring Garden Coll., 1985. Agt. Conn. Gen. Life Ins. Co., Chgo., 1950-53; staff asst. Conn. Gen. Life Ins. Co., 1953-54, mgr. Evanston (Ill.) br. office, 1954-60, dir. agys., 1960-62, mgr. Los Angeles br. office, 1963; v.p. sales Fidelity Mut. Life Ins. Co., Phila., 1964-67; sr. v.p. sales Fidelity Mut. Life Ins. Co., 1968, exec. v.p., 1969-71, pres., chief exec. officer, dir., 1971-84, chmn., chief exec. officer, dir., 1984—; bd. dirs. Rorer Group Inc., 1st Pa. Corp., Phila. Suburban Corp., Phila. Electric Co., 1st Pa. Bank, Greater Phila. 1st Corp. Trustee Bryn Mawr Hosp.; trustee United Way of S.E. Pa.; trustee Phila. United Way, also gen. chmn. 1978 campaign; bd. dirs. Phila. YMCA. Served with USNR, 1945-46. Recipient Civic Achievement award Am. Jewish Com., 1978, Achiever's award WHEELS Med. and Specialized Transp., 1978, Ohio Wesleyan U. Life Achievement award Delta Tau Delta, 1982, William Penn award, Greater Phila. C. ofC. and PENJERDEL Coun., 1988, Robert Morris Citizenship award Valley Forge Coun. Boy Scouts Am., 1988; named YMCA Man of Yr., 1979, William Penn Found. Disting. Pennsylvanian, 1980. Mem. Life Office Mgmt. Assn. (bd. dirs.), Greater Phila. C. of C. (dir., chmn. 1979, 83-84), Phila. Country Club, Union League Club (Phila.), Summer Beach (Fla.) Country Club. Office: Fidelity Mut Life Ins Co 250 King of Prussia Rd Fidelity Mut Life Bldg Radnor PA 19087

LADD-RADISKE, LOUISE ELIZABETH, investment broker, financial planner; b. Waco, Tex., Sept. 17, 1950; d. Ludwig Nitter and Rae (Skibrek) Ladd; m. Douglas Robert Radiske, July 11, 1981. BA, U. Wis., 1972; cert. fin. planner, Coll. Fin. Planning, Denver, 1985. Mgr. BankAmericard div. Marine Bank Madison, Wis., 1972-73; rep. corp. mktg. Marine Bank Corp. Hdqrs., Milw., 1973; sales rep., mgr. Xerox Corp., Milw., 1974-78; investment broker, v.p. investments Dean Witter Reynolds, Wauwatosa, Wis., 1978-82, asst. v.p., 1982-85, v.p., 1985—, coordinator tax adv. investments, 1984—. Bd. dirs. Profl. Dimensions, Milw., 1982-83, 85-86, Music Under The Stars, Milw., 1984—, Pachyderms, Milw., 1985—. Mem. Inst. Cert. Fin. Planners. Republican. Lutheran. Club: Vagabond Ski (Milw.). Office: Dean Witter Reynolds 2500 N Mayfair Rd Ste 600 Wauwatosa WI 53226

LADE, DAVID ALAN, controller; b. Parma, Ohio, June 29, 1955; s. Lawrence Carl and Ruth Helen (Vogler) L.; m. Sharon Dehn Arzt, Nov. 16, 1974; 1 child, Timothy David. BA, Dayton (Ohio) Bible Coll., 1978; M in Divinity, United Theol. Sem., Dayton, 1981; MBA, Wright State U., 1983. CPA, Ohio. Acctg. supr. Gen. Cinema Corp., Pepsi-Cola Bottling Co., Dayton, 1981-83; audit sr. Arthur Andersen & Co., Cleve., 1983-87; controller AGA Gas Cen., Inc., Hammond, Ind., 1987—. Cubmaster Boy Scouts Am., North Olmsted, Ohio, 1984-87. Recipient Outstanding MBA award Wright State U., 1983. Mem. Nat. Assn. Accts. Home: 3209 Knollwood Ln Homewood IL 60430 Office: AGA Gas Cen Inc 3930 Michigan St Hammond IN 46323

LADEHOFF, LEO WILLIAM, metal products manufacturing executive; b. Gladbrook, Iowa, May 4, 1932; s. Wendell Leo and Lillian A. L.; m. Beverly Joan Dreessen, Aug. 1, 1951; children: Debra K., Lance A. B.S., U. Iowa, 1957. Supt. ops. Square D Co., 1957-61; mfg. mgr. Fed. Pacific Electric Co., 1961; v.p. ops. Avis Indsl. Corp., 1961-67; pres. energy products Group Gulf & Western Industries, Inc., 1967-78; chmn. bd., pres., chief exec. officer, dir. Amcast Indsl. Corp., Ohio, 1978—; bd. dirs. Krug Internat., Inc., GF Bus. Equipment Co., Soc. Bank N.A., Hobart Bros., Troy, Ohio, Soc. Corp. of Cleve. Mem. Dayton Area Progress Council. Served with USAF, 1951-54, Korea. Mem. Am. Foundrymen's Soc., Soc. Automotive Engrs., Iron Castings Soc., Dayton Area C. of C., Dayton One Hundred Club, Newcomen Soc., U. Alumni Alumni Assn., Alpha Kappa Psi. Republican. Clubs:

Moraine Country, Dayton Racquet. Home: 4501 Troon Trail Dayton OH 45429 Office: Amcast Indsl Corp 3931 S Dixie Ave Kettering OH 45439

LADEHOFF, VIOLET IRENE, sales administrator; b. Pleasanton, Kans., Jan. 17, 1941; d. Claude Wiliam and Grace Irene (Wheeler) Sturm; m. John Edward Jackson II, Mar. 19, 1960 (dec. 1977); children: Scarlet LeeAnn Jackson Butts, Teresa Marie Jackson Honn, John Edward III; m. Harvey Edward Ladehoff, Oct. 7, 1978; stepchildren: Paul Harvey, Susan Kay. Grad. high sch., Butler, Mo. Sec. Henry Radio Co., Butler, 1962-73; with Pace Products, Inc., 1973—; sales mgr. Pace Products, Inc., Kansas City, 1977—. Mem. Am. Bus. Women's Assn. (pres. 1985-86, Woman of Yr. award 1987). Lutheran. Lodge: Elkettes (pres. 1983). Home: Rte 3 Box 228 Cameron MO 64429

LADIN, EUGENE, communications company executive; b. N.Y.C., Oct. 26, 1927; s. Nat and Mae (Cohen) L.; m. Millicent Dolly Frankel, June 27, 1948; children: Leslie Hope, Stephanie Joy. B.B.A., Pace U., 1956; M.B.A., Air Force Inst. Tech., 1959; postgrad., George Washington U., 1966-69. Cost engr. Rand Corp., Santa Monica, Calif., 1960-62; mgr. cost and econ. analysis Northrop Corp., Hawthorne, Calif., 1962-66; dir. financial planning Communications Satellite Corp., Washington, 1966-70; treas., chief fin. and adminstrv. officer Landis & Gyr, Inc., Elmsford, N.Y., 1970-76; v.p., treas., comptroller P.R. Telephone Co., San Juan, 1976-77; v.p. fin. Comtech Telecommunications Corp., Smithtown, N.Y., 1977—; acting pres. Comtech Antenna Corp., St. Cloud, Fla., 1978-80; chmn., chief exec. officer Telephone Interconnect Enterprises/Sunshine Telephone Co., Balt., Md. and Orlando, Fla., 1980-82; pres. Ladin and Assocs., Cons. and Commodity Traders, Maitland, Fla., 1982-84; pres., chief fin. officer Braintech Inc., South Plainfield, N.J., 1984; sr. v.p. fin., chief fin. officer Teltec Savs. Communications Co., Miami, Fla., 1984—; assoc. prof. acctg. So. Ill. U., East St. Louis, 1960; asso. prof. bus. U. Md., 1969-70; adj. prof. George Washington U., 1969-70; vis. prof. acctg. Pace U., 1970. Served to capt. USAF, 1951-60. Decorated Air Force Commendation medal; recipient Air Force Outstanding Unit award. Mem. Nat. Assn. Accts., Fin. Exec. Inst. Democrat. Jewish. Club: Bankers (Miami), Williams Island Country, Turnberry Yacht and Country. Home: 20355 NE 34th Del Vista Ct North Miami Beach FL 33180

LADJEVARDI, HAMID, investment manager; b. Tehran, Iran, June 11, 1948; came to U.S., 1948; s. Ahmad and Banoo (Barzin) L.; m. Manijeh Mirdamad, July 19, 1978; children: Adella, Lilly. BA in Econs., BA in Polit. Sci., U. Calif., Berkeley, 1971; MBA, Harvard U., 1973. Dep. mng. dir., vice chmn. Behshahr Indsl. Group, Tehran, 1974-79; vice chmn., fin. dir. Akam Group of Cos., Tehran, 1975-79; investment mgr., v.p. Morgan Stanley & Co., N.Y.C., 1980—; instr. Fairleigh Dickinson U., Rutherford, N.J., 1984. Mem. Polit. Risk Analysts Assn., Fgn. Policy Assn., Carnegie Council on Ethics and Internat. Affairs, U.S. Senatorial Club. Club: Harvard (N.Y.C.). Home: 66 Brite Ave Scarsdale NY 10583 Office: Morgan Stanley & Co 1251 Ave of the Americas New York NY 10020

LADLY, FREDERICK BERNARD, health services company executive; b. Toronto, Ont., Can., July 14, 1930; s. John Bernard and Olivia Montgomery (Fenimore) L.; m. Sharon Mary Davidson; children: Patricia, Elizabeth, Katherine, Martha, Sarah, Meghan. B.A., U. Toronto, 1951. Gen. mgr. internat. ops. Can. Packers Inc., Toronto, 1973, v.p., 1974-78, dir., 1975-84, exec. v.p., 1978-84; pres., chief exec. officer Extendicare Health Svcs. Inc., Toronto, 1984—; chmn., chief exec. officer United Health, Inc., Milw., 1984—; bd. dirs. Crownx Inc., Toronto, 1986—; chmn. Internat. Care Svcs. (U.K.), 1986—. Mem. Toronto Lawn Tennis Club, Beaver Valley Ski Club.

LADNER, CHARLES LEON, diversified utility company executive; b. Orange, N.J., Feb. 13, 1938; s. George R. and Jeanette (Gross) L.; m. Diane Cecelia Paul, Jan. 27, 1962; children: John, Gregory, Paul, Ellen. BA, U. Notre Dame, 1960; MBA, Columbia U., 1961. Mgr. budgets ITT, Pa., 1968-69; v.p. fin., controller Valley Forge Corp., Pa., 1968-71; v.p. fin. UGI Corp., Valley Forge, Pa., 1971-73, v.p. fin., treas., 1973-78, sr. v.p. fin., chief fin. officer, 1978—; bd. dirs. EnergyNorth Inc., Manchester, N.H., Sovereign Investors Inc., Phila. Trustee Rosemont (Pa.) Sch., 1977-87. Served to 1st lt. U.S. Army, 1962-64. Mem. Am. Gas Assn. (chmn. pension com., fin. com.), Fin. Execs. Inst. Clubs: Aronimink Golf (Newtown Sq., Pa.); Miles River Yacht (St. Michael's, Md.); Sunday Breakfast (Phila.). Office: UGI Corp PO Box 858 Valley Forge PA 19482

LAFAIR, THEODORE, investment company executive, financial consultant; b. Phila., Aug. 31, 1927; s. Isadore and Clara (Gerber) L.; m. Sally R. Somerson, Aug. 11, 1957; children: Laurie J., Michael S. BS in Econs., U. Pa., 1951. Exec. dir. Atlantic City Centennial Assn., 1952-54; gen. mgr. Lafair & Sons, Inc., Phila., 1954-62; pres. Capri Internat. Inc., Pennsauken, N.J., 1962-68; sr. v.p. Shearson Lehman Hutton, Inc., Bala Cynwyd, Pa., 1969—. Investment com. Fedn. Allied Jewish Appeal, Phila., 1975—, Golden Slipper Club Charities, Phila., 1983—; bd. dirs. Am. Assocs. Ben Gurion U. Mid-Atlantic Area, Phila., 1984—. Served with USN, 1945-46. Republican. Office: Shearson Lehman Hutton Inc 3 Bala Pla E Bala-Cynwyd PA 19004

LAFER, FRED SEYMOUR, data processing company executive; b. Passaic, N.J., Mar. 17, 1929; s. Abraham David and Pauline (Braer) L.; m. Barbara Bernstein, Apr. 4, 1954; children: Deborah, Gordon, Diana. B.I.E., NYU, 1950, J.D., 1961. Bar: N.J. 1961. Sec. to Justice Hayden Proector, N.J. Supreme Ct., 1961-62; partner firm Hoffman Humphreys Lafer, Wayne, N.J., 1962-67; sec., gen. counsel Automatic Data Processing, Inc., Clifton, N.J., 1967—; v.p. Automatic Data Processing, Inc., 1968-81, sr. v.p., 1981—; pres. N.J. Nets Profl. Basketball Team, 1984. Chmn. United Jewish Appeal Fedn. North Jersey, 1973-74; pres. Jewish Fedn. North Jersey, 1976-77; v.p. N.J. Bd. Edn., 1967-68; bd. dirs. Chilton Meml. Hosp., Pompton Plains, N.J., 1970-72; trustee William Paterson Coll., 1974—, vice-chmn. bd., 1977, chmn. bd., 1978-80; pres. Am. Friends of Hebrew U., 1985—. Served to lt. USAF, 1951-52. Mem. Computer Law Assn. (pres. 1972-74), Assn. Data Processing Service Orgns. (chmn. 1983), ABA. Office: ADP Inc 1 ADP Blvd Roseland NJ 07068

LAFFERTY, CHARLES DOUGLAS JOSEPH, advertising company executive; b. Rochester, Pa., Mar. 27, 1930; s. William Charles and Kathryn (Devine) L.; m. Inger Antionette Sorum, Nov. 17, 1967. BA, U. Pitts., 1956. Mgr. sales devel. Maloney Regan & Schmitt, N.Y.C., 1956-69; dir. mktg. exec. v.p. planning, corp. treas. Branham, Inc., N.Y.C., 1969-82, vice chmn. bd., 1982-83, chmn. bd., chief exec. officer, 1983—. Recipient The Sid Goldish award, Internat. Newspaper Promotion Assn. 1982. Mem. Marco Polo, Employee Stock Ownership Plan Assn. (bd. dirs. 1987—), Internat. Newspaper Advt., (com. mem.), Exec. Assn. Home: 58 Redcoat Rd Westport CT 06880 Office: Branham Newspaper Sales 733 Third Ave New York NY 10017

LAFONTANT, JEWEL STRADFORD, lawyer; b. Chgo., Apr. 28, 1922; d. Cornelius Francis and Aida Arabella (Carter) Stradford; 1 son, John W. Rogers III. AB, Oberlin Coll., 1943; JD, U. Chgo., 1946; LLD (hon.), Cedar Crest Coll., 1973; D Humanitarian Svc. (hon.), Providence Coll., 1973; LLD (hon.), Ea. Mich. U., 1973; LHD (hon.), Howard U., 1974; LLD (hon.), Heidelberg Coll., 1975, Lake Forest Coll., 1977, Marymount Manhattan Coll., 1978, Oberlin Coll., 1979; LHD (hon.), Governor's State U., 1980, LLD (hon.), 1980; citation for pub. svc., U. Chgo., 1980; LLD (hon.), Chgo. Med. Sch., 1982, Loyola U. of Chgo., 1982. Bar: Ill. bar 1947. Asst. U.S. atty. 1955-58; sr. ptnr. Vedder, Price, Kaufman & Kammholz, Chgo., 1983-89; dep. solicitor gen. U.S. Washington, 1972-75; dir. Midway Airlines, Chgo., 1988-89; ambassador-at-large, U.S. Coord. for Refugee Affairs 1989—; bd. dirs. Mobil Corp., Continental Bank, Foote, Cone & Belding, Equitable Life Assurance Soc. U.S., Trans World Corp., Revlon, Inc., Ariel-Capital Mgmt., Harte-Hanks Communications, Inc., Pantry Pride, Inc., Revlon Group, Howard U.; past dir. Jewel Cos., Inc., TWA, Hanes Corp.; past mem. U.S. Adv. Commn. Internat. Edn. and Cultural Affairs, Nat. Coun. Minority Bus. Enterprises, Nat. Coun. on Ednl. Rsch.; past chmn. adv. bd. Civil Rights Commn.; mem. Pres.'s Pvt. Sector Survey Cost Control; pres. Exec. Exchange; past U.S. rep. to UN. Bd. editors: Am. Bar Assn. Jour. Former trustee Lake Forest (Ill.) Coll., Oberlin Coll., Howard U., Tuskegee Inst.; bd. govs. Ronald Reagan Presdl. Found.; mem. Martin Luther King, Jr., Fed. Holiday Commn.; dir. Project Hope. Fellow Internat. Acad. Trial Lawyers; mem. Chgo. Bar Assn. (bd. govs.). Home: 2700 Virginia Ave NW Apt 4004 Washington DC 20037 Office: US Dept State Washington DC 20525 also: Mobil Corp 150 E 42d St New York NY 10017

LA FORCE, JAMES CLAYBURN, JR., economist, educator; b. San Diego, Dec. 28, 1928; s. James Clayburn and Beatrice Maureen (Boyd) La F.; m. Barbara Lea Latham, Sept. 23, 1952; children: Jessica, Allison, Joseph. B.A., San Diego State Coll., 1951; M.A., UCLA, 1958, Ph.D., 1962. Asst. prof. econs. UCLA, 1962-66, assoc. prof., 1967-70, prof., 1971—, chmn. dept. econs., 1969-78, dean Anderson Sch. Mgmt., 1978—; dir. Nat. Intergroup Inc., Rockwell Internat., Eli Lilly & Co., Jacobs Engring. Group Inc., Transport Indemnity, Inc., 1976-81 Cypress Mines. Inc., 1978-79, Getty Oil Co., 1983-84, First Nationwide Fin. Corp., First Nationwide Savs., Indsl. Indemity Co., E.F. Hutton V.I.P. Separate Account; chmn. adv. com. Calif. Workmen's Compensation, 1974-75. Author: The Development of the Spanish Textile Industry 1750-1800, 1965, (with Warren C. Scoville) The Economic Development of Western Europe, vols. 1-5, 1969-70. Bd. dirs. Nat. Bur. Econ. Research, 1975—; trustee Inst. Contemporary Studies, 1974—; trustee Found. for Research in Econs. and Edn., 1970—, chmn., 1977—; trustee Pacific Legal Found., 1981-86; bd. overseers Hoover Inst. War, Revolution and Peace, 1979-85, 86—; mem. nat. council on humanities NEH, 1981—; chmn. President's Task Force on Food Assistance, 1983-84; bd. dirs. Found. Francisco Marroquin. Social Sci. Research Council research tng. fellow, 1958-60; Fulbright sr. research grantee, 1965-66; Am. Philos. Soc. grantee, 1965-66. Mem. Econ. History Assn., Mont Pelerin Soc., Phi Beta Kappa. Office: UCLA Grad Sch Mgmt 405 Hilgard Ave Los Angeles CA 90024

LAFRANKIE, JAMES V., water utility holding company executive; b. Elizabeth, Pa., Mar. 26, 1927; s. John Lewis and Susan Marie (Heidrick) L.; m. Nancy Louise Wiegel, June 12, 1954; children—Terence, James Jr., Jane, Donna, Kenneth, Mark, William. B.S. in Mgmt., Georgetown U., 1964. Office clk. Am. Water Works Co. Inc., Elizabeth, from 1948, now pres.; dir., exec. com. Am. Water Works Co. Inc., Wilmington, Del. Mem. Am. Water Works Assn. (Fuller award, hon. mem.), Nat. Assn. Water Cos. (past chmn. bd.). Republican. Roman Catholic. Home: 120 W Walnut Ave Moorestown NJ 08057 Office: Am Water Works Co Inc 1025 Laurel Oak Rd PO Box 1770 Voorhees NJ 08043

LAGANGA, DONNA BRANDEIS, publishing company sales executive; b. Bklyn., June 27, 1949; d. Sidney L. and Sylvia (Herman) Brandeis; B.S. in Bus. Edn., Central Conn. State Coll., New Britain, 1972, M.S., 1975; m. Thomas LaGanga, Aug. 11, 1974. Various secretarial positions, 1969-72; tchr. bus. Lewis S. Mills Regional High Sch., Burlington, Conn., 1972-78; cons. Southwestern Pub. Co., Pelham Manor, N.Y., 1978-84, dist. sales mgr., 1984—; co-owner Colonial Welding Service; seminar condr., 1980—. Adv. bd. secretarial sci. dept. LaGuardia Community Coll., Long Island City, N.Y., 1982—; adv. bd. Krissler Bus. Inst. EDPA grantee, 1973; mem. nonpartisan ednl. reform task force Pres. George Bush; cert. profl. sec. Mem. Nat. Assn. Female Execs., Assn. Info./Systems Profls., Am. Mgmt. Assn., Nat. Bus. Edn. Assn., Profl. Secs. Internat., Eastern Bus. Edn. Assn., Conn. Bus. Edn. Assn., New Eng. Bus. Edn. Assn., Profl. Secs. Assn. N.Y., Nat. Assn. Cert. Profl. Secs., U.S. Golf Assn., Delta Pi Epsilon. Avocations: knitting, sewing, reading, bicycling, golfing. Home: 612 S Main St Torrington CT 06790 Office: South Western Pub Co 5101 Madison Rd Cincinnati OH 45227

LAGARDE, MARY ELIZABETH, corporate professional; b. Providence, Feb. 11, 1957; d. Albert Louis and Lorraine Gladys (Bilodeau) L.; 1 child, Matthew LaGarde Manco. BA, U. R.I., 1979. Cert. elem. tchr. Tchr. Newfield (N.Y.) Elem. Sch., 1980-82; registered rep. Balt. Fed., 1982-85; adminstrn. officer Old Stone Trust Co., Providence, 1985—. Mem. Internat. Assn. for Fin. Planners, Inst. Cert. Fin. Planners. Democrat. Roman Catholic. Home: 60 Revere Ave West Warwick RI 02893 Office: Old Stone Trust Co 180 S Main St Providence RI 02903

LAGOWSKI, THOMAS JOHN, construction executive; b. Easthampton, Mass., Oct. 6, 1954; s. Fred J. and Eleanor (Dorunda) L.; m. Jane E. Wells, Oct. 16, 1976; children: Jill Marie, Ann Marie, Matthew Thomas. BSBA, Western New Eng. Coll., 1976. Sr. acct. Peat, Marwick & Mitchell, Hartford, Conn., 1976-77, White Plains, N.Y., 1977-78; sr. acct. consol. fin. reporting. Good Hope Industries, Springfield, Mass., 1978; controller Fontaine Bros., Inc., Springfield, Mass., 1978-88, treas., 1988—; bd. dirs. Magna House Corp., Springfield, Shadowfax Devel., East Longmeadow, Mass., Tinkham Mgmt. Corp., Springfield, also v.p. Bd. dirs. Magna House Condo Assn., Northampton, Mass., 1986-87. Roman Catholic. Home: 48 Hannum Brook Dr Easthampton MA 01027 Office: Fontaine Bros 66 Industry Ave Springfield MA 01104

LAHAYE, PAM MATERA, infosystems company executive; b. San Antonio, Nov. 19, 1955; d. William A. and Esther V. (Granizo) Matera; m. Philip A. LaHaye, Mar. 1, 1980. BS cum laude, Trinity U., 1977. Mfg. mgr. Johnson & Johnson, Sherman, Tex., 1977-79, Vicra div. Baxter Travel, Dallas, 1979-80; cost. acct. Gen. Portland, Inc., Dallas, 1980; mgr. sales, fin. Ionicron/Hydronics, Dallas, 1980-83; v.p. leasing Delta Bus. Systems, Orlando, Fla., 1983—; bd. dirs. Pure Water Systems, Orlando, Fla. Scholar Trinity U., 1973-77. Mem. Sunshine Club. Republican. Episcopalian. Home: 732 Summerland Dr Winter Springs FL 32708 Office: Delta Bus Systems 4150 John Young Pkwy Orlando FL 32804

LAHEY, BARBARA GIBSON, building materials company executive; b. Burlington, N.C., Apr. 6, 1963; d. Gordon Cyril and Barbara Ann (Zemlonsky) L. BA in Bus. Mgmt., N.C. State U., 1985. Sales rep. Owens-Corning Fiberglas Corp., Grand Rapids, Mich., 1985-87; ter. sales rep. Owens-Corning Fiberglas Corp., Atlanta, 1987-88; sales engr. Gates Energy Products, Norcross, Ga., 1988—. Mem. Insulation Contractors Assn. Am., N.C. State U. Alumni Assn., High Mus., Young Careers Club. Republican. Methodist. Office: Gates Energy Products 5555 Triangle Pkwy Ste 330 Norcross GA 30092

LAHEY, EDWARD VINCENT, JR., soft drink company executive; b. Boston, Mar. 11, 1939; s. Edward Vincent and Margery Tharsilla (Mehegan) L.; m. Joan M. McCafferty, Sept. 26, 1964; children—Sheila, Edward Vincent III, Matthew. A.B., Holy Cross Coll., 1960; J.D., Georgetown U., 1964; postgrad., Bus. Sch. Columbia, 1969-70. Bar: D.C. bar 1964, N.Y. bar 1966. Mem. firm Hester, Owen & Crowder, Washington, 1964-65; atty. PepsiCo, Inc., Purchase, N.Y., 1965-68, asst. gen. counsel, 1969-73, sec., 1970—, v.p., gen. counsel, 1973-86, sr. v.p., 1986—; bd. dirs. Westchester Fairfield Corp. Counsel Assn. Trustee Village of Tuckahoe, N.Y., 1970, Mus. Art, Sci. and Industry, 1987—. Served to lt. USNR, 1960-62. Mem. Am., D.C. bar assns., Am. Soc. Corporate Secs., Am. Law Inst. Office: Pepsico Inc Anderson Hill Rd Purchase NY 10577

LAHEY, REGIS HENRY, trust and investment officer; b. Pitts., July 15, 1948; s. Michael Patrick and Henrietta (Szczesny) L. Diploma in Indsl. Mgmt., Ednl. Inst. Pitts., 1968; BS, Robert Morris Coll., Pitts., 1981. Corp. trustee Union Nat. Bank, Pitts., 1968-70; asst. supr. Mellon Bank N.A., Pitts., 1978-80, supr., 1980-83, unit mgr., 1983-84, asst. ops. officer, 1984-86, ops. officer, 1986-87, trust and investment officer, 1987—; instr. cash mgmt. Master Trust U., Pitts., 1987—. Mem. Am. Mgmt. Assn. Republican. Roman Catholic. Office: Mellon Bank One Mellon Ctr Pittsburgh PA 15258-0001

LAHOURCADE, JOHN BROSIUS, service company executive; b. San Antonio, Tex., Nov. 18, 1924; s. Frederic Eugene and Hildagarde (Brosius) L.; m. Mary Lou Williamson, Sept. 6, 1947; children: Lynne Breuer, Lee A., Lance. BBA, U. Tex., 1948. CPA, Tex. Staff acct. Stanolind Oil & Gas Co., Brownfield, Tex., 1948-51, Carneiro Chumney CPA's, San Antonio, 1951-55; ptnr. Bielstein, Lahourcade & Lewis CPA's, San Antonio, 1955-69; v.p. Luby's Cafeterias Inc., San Antonio, 1969-74, sr. v.p. fin., 1974-79, exec. v.p., 1979-82, pres., chief exec. officer, 1982-88, chmn., chief exec. officer, 1988—; bd. dirs. First RepublicBank San Antonio, 1982-88. Trustee S.W. Tex. Meth. Hosp., San Antonio, 1974-83; adv. council U. Tex. Sch. Bus. Adminstrn. Found., Austin, 1986—; bd. dirs. San Antonio Econ. Devel. Found., 1984—. Mem. Tex. Soc. CPA's (bd. dirs. 1965-68), San Antonio CPA's (pres. 1965). Office: Luby's Cafeterias Inc PO Box 33069 San Antonio TX 78265

LAI, SHIH-TSE JASON, chemistry researcher, educator; b. Chia-yi, Republic of China, Oct. 29, 1951; came to U.S., 1977, naturalized, 1985; s. Chi-Kuei and Yu-Lien (Kao) L.; m. Wei Bamboo Lee, June 25, 1980; 1 child, Jeffrey. BS, Nat. Chung-Hsing U., Taichung, Republic of China, 1974; PhD, CUNY, 1983; postgrad., West Coast U. Adminstrn. asst. Tunghai U., Taichung, 1976-77; adjunct lectr. CUNY, Bklyn., 1977-78; research fellow CUNY, Flushing, 1978-83; sr. chemist semicondtr. products div. Rockwell Internat., Newport Beach, Calif., 1983-85; head mass spectrometry lab., sr. staff scientist, project scientist Tech. & Ventures div. Baxter Healthcare Corp., Irvine, Calif., 1985-89, head gas, liquid chromatography, mass spectrometry lab., 1989—; vis. assoc. prof. Ta-Hwa Inst. Tech., Hsinchu, Republic of China, 1986, 87; instr. tech. workshops Analytical Svc. Ctr. Tech. & Ventures div. Baxter Healthcare Corp., Irvine, 1985—; seminar speaker Union Chem. Labs., Cen. Police Acad., Nat. Sun Yat-Sen U., Nat. Chung-Hsing U., Republic of China, 1987, mem. planning com., Pacific Conf. on Chemistry & Spectroscopy, 1989. Contbr. numerous articles to profl. jours. Coach Tunghai U. Rugby Team, 1976-77; patron Laguna Moulton Playhouse, Laguna Beach, Calif., 1986-87; mem. Orange County Sheriff's Adv. Bd. University fellow, CUNY, 1977; recipient Fellow A scholarship CUNY, 1978-83. Fellow Am. Inst. Chemists; mem. AAAS, N.Y. Acad. Scis., Am. Chem. Soc. (mem. program com. Orange County chpt. 1985-87), Chinese Culture Assn. (pres. CUNY chpt. 1978-80), Friends Orange County Performing Art Ctr., Nat. Chung-Hsing U. Alumni Assn. (v.p. So. Calif. chpt. 1986-88, pres. 1989—), Taiwan Benevolent Assn. (nat. advisor 1985—, adv. So. Calif. chpt. 1986—, v.p., dir. 1984-86), Asian Am. Alliance Calif. (co-founder, co-chmn.), Am. Soc. Mass Spectrometry, So. Calif. Mass Spectrometry (chmn. program com. 1988—), Fedn. Chinese Student Assn. in USA (bd. dirs. 1978-80), Joint Chinese U. Alumni Assn. So. Calif. (bd. dirs. 1988—), Sigma Xi.

LAIDIG, WILLIAM RUPERT, paper company executive; b. Sterling, Ill., Feb. 3, 1927; s. George and Margaret Anne (Gnewuch) L.; m. Lorraine Mae Grom, Jan. 2, 1952; children: Ann Marie, Mary Katherine, Margaret Anne, William Andrew. B.S.M.E., Marquette U., 1949. Registered profl. engr., Ga., Ala., Wis., Ark. Engr. Inland Steel Products, 1949-50; engr. Nekoosa Papers Inc., Port Edwards, Wis., 1950-62, mgr., 1962-66; mgr. Nekoosa Papers Inc., Ashdown, Ark., 1966-72; mill mgr. Nekoosa Papers Inc., Port Edwards, Wis., 1972-75; v.p., resident mgr. Gt. So. Paper Co., Cedar Springs., Ga., 1975-80, sr. v.p., 1979-80, pres., 1980-84; exec. v.p. Gt. No. Nekoosa, Stamford, Conn., 1980-84, pres., chief exec. officer, chmn., dir., 1984—; dir. Bank of N.Y. Co. Pres. Village of Port Edwards, (Wis.), 1966-67; trustee Marquette U., Milw. Served to lt. USN, 1952-53. Mem. Am. Paper Inst. (dir.), Nat. Coun. of the Paper Industry for Air and Stream Improvement, Inc., Tech. Assn. of the Pulp and Paper Industry. Roman Catholic. Club: Dothan Country (Ala.). Lodges: K.C; Elks. Home: 320 Hurlbutt St Wilton CT 06897 Office: 40 Merritt 7 PO Box 5120 Norwalk CT 06856-5120

LAIDLAW, WILLIAM SAMUEL HUGH, oil company executive; b. London, Jan. 3, 1956; s. Christopher Charles Fraser and Nina Laidlaw. MA, Cambridge U., 1977; MBA, Insead, France, 1981. Solicitor Macfarlanes, London, 1977-79; corp. planner Société Françaises Pétroles B.P., Paris, 1979-80; mgr. corp. planning Amerada Hess Corp., N.Y.C., 1981-83; v.p. Amerada Hess Corp., London, 1983-85; sr. v.p. Amerada Hess Corp., N.Y.C., 1986—; mng. dir. Amerada Hess Ltd., London, 1986—. Mem. Inst. Petroleum. Home: 2 Stephen St, London WI, England Office: Amerada Hess Corp 1185 Ave of the Americas New York NY 10036

LAINO, LEE, financial public relations executive; b. N.Y.C., July 3, 1940; s. Leon Eugene and Jean Dorothy L.; BA, St. John's U., 1963; spl. postgrad., UCLA, 1960-61; degré supérieur, U. Paris, 1964; m. Kathryn M. Augustine, 1968; 1 child, Stephen Michael. Mgr. press relations sta. WCBS-TV, N.Y.C., 1966-68; dir. pub. relations Am. Express Co., N.Y.C., 1968-70, Am. Airlines Flagship Hotels & Sky Chefs subs., N.Y.C., 1970-72; dir. corp. and fin. relations Liggett Group, N.Y.C., 1972-75; group. v.p. Edward Gottlieb & Assocs., N.Y.C., 1976-77; sr. v.p. Carl Byoir & Assocs., N.Y.C., 1977-84; sr. v.p., gen. mgr. Needham Porter Novelli, N.Y.C., 1984-86; prin. Lee Laino Assocs., Inc. Pub. Relations and Advt., N.Y.C., 1986—; mem. exec. com. N.Am. ops. Drake and Raleigh. Served with U.S. Army, 1964-66. Mem. Nat. Investor Relations Inst., Aviation/Space Writers Assn., Sci. Exploration Soc. of Gt. Brit. Clubs: N.Y. Athletic, Westchester Country. Home: 25 E 83d St New York NY 10028 Office: 1180 Ave of the Americas New York NY 10036

LAIRD, JOHN ROBERT, financial company executive; b. Erie, Pa., June 21, 1942; s. James Harris and Greta Doris (Campbell) L.; m. Ruth Jane Young, Jan. 30, 1965; children: James, Nancy, David. BS, Syracuse U., 1964, MBA, 1965; cert. Advanced Mgmt., Harvard U., 1983. With internat. fin. mktg. Gould Inc., Chgo., 1968-77; sr. v.p., treas. Am. Express Co., N.Y.C., 1977—. Active Internat. Multiple Sclerosis Socs., New Canaan, Conn. Lt. U.S. Army, 1966-68. Mem. Fin. Execs. Inst., Nat. Assn. Corp. Treasurers.

LAIRD, MARY See WOOD, LARRY

LAIRD, WALTER JONES, JR., investment professional; b. Phila., June 15, 1926; s. Walter Jones and Rebecca (Sedberry) L.; m. Antonia Valerie Bissell, Nov. 24, 1951; children: David E., William Ian, Philip L., Walter J. III, Emily B., Stephen. BS, Princeton U., 1948; MSCE, M.I.T., 1950. Mgr. bldg. product sales E.I. duPont de Nemours, Wilmington, Del., 1951-68; exec. v.p. Laird, Bissell and Meeds, Wilmington, Del., 1968-73; sr. v.p. Dean Witter Reynolds, Wilmington, Del., 1973—; bd. dirs. Delaware Trust Co., Wilmington. Chmn., bd. trustees Winterthur Mus. & Gardens, Wilmington, 1969—; trustee St. Andrews Sch., Middletown, Del., 1967—. Mem. Fin. Analysts Fedn. Clubs: Wilmington (gov. 1978—), Wilmington Country. Lodge: Chevaliers du Tastevin Grand Senechal. Home: 1202 Stockford Rd Chadds Ford PA 19317 Office: Dean Witter Reynolds Inc PO Box 749 Wilmington DE 19899

LAITY, DAVID GEORGE, corporate executive; b. Detroit, Apr. 29, 1948; s. William G. and Betty E. (Davey) L.; m. Susan M. Vennix, Mar. 3, 1973; children: Kristin M., Sarah S. Student, Henry Ford Community Coll., 1966-68; BS, Mich. State U., 1971; postgrad., Saginaw Valley Coll., 1972. Field engr. Townsend and Bottum, Inc., Bay City, Mich., 1971-75; procurement supr. Townsend and Bottum, Inc., Ann Arbor, Mich., 1975-83, mgr. equipment dept., 1983-87, dir. procurement, 1987—. Chmn. South Lyon (Mich.) Planning Commn., 1983-86, sec., 1980-83. Mem. Phi Gamma Delta (pres.). Office: Townsend & Bottum Inc 2245 S State St Ann Arbor MI 48104

LAKA, EUGENE JOHN, international management and finance writer, consultant; b. Dobrocyn, Ukraine, Oct. 15, 1942; s. Ivan Mikitovich and Irena (Martyn) L. AB, Dartmouth Coll., 1964; MBA, Columbia U., 1967. With ops. research and systems devel. Citibank, N.Y.C., 1971-75, v.p., chief of staff N.Y. State expansion project, 1975-76, v.p. exec. devel. div., 1976-78, v.p. strategic planning, dep. to exec. v.p. in charge of Ten Yr. Plan Task Force, 1978-81; free lance writer, pvt. practice cons. N.Y.C., 1981—. Served with USCG, 1968-71. Home and Office: 245 E 63d St New York NY 10021

LAKE, CHARLES WILLIAM, JR., retired printing company executive; b. LaPorte, Ind., June 21, 1918; s. Charles William and Jessie Mae (Lyon) L.; m. Louise Safford Sprague, July 4, 1946; children: Charles William III, Elizabeth L. Dolan. Student, U. Wis., 1936-37; BS, Cornell U., 1941; MBA, U. Chgo., 1949. With R.R. Donnelley & Sons Co., Chgo., 1946—, successively asst. to treas., mgr. mgmt. studies, dir. indsl. engring., 1947-56, dir. engring. rsch. and devel., 1956-58, dir. operating, 1958-59, dir. Chgo. mfg. div., 1959-62, dir. sales div., 1963-64, v.p. co., 1953-63, sr. v.p., 1963-64, pres., 1964-83, chmn. exec. com., 1983—, chmn. bd., 1975-83, also dir. Mem. vis. com. Div. Sch., Grad. Sch. Bus., U. Chgo.; mem. citizens bd. U. Chgo., vis. com. to library; mem. Cornell U. devel. adv. com., chmn. emeritus, engring. coun. mem., Cornell Coun. of Chgo.; emeritus trustee, presdl. councillor, mem. univ. coun. Cornell U.; bd. dirs. Protestant Found. Greater

Chgo., mem. Northwestern U. Assocs.; mem. Library Coun. U. Chgo.; bd. dirs. Exec. Svc. Corps; bd. dirs. Nat. Merit Scholarship Assn.; bd. govs. Shedd Aquarium; life trustee Mus. Sci. and Industry; dir. John Crerar Library Found. Capt., ordnance AUS, 1941-46. Named Grad. Sch. of Bus. Disting. Alumnus, U. Chgo., 1983. Mem. Univ. Club, Sunday Evening Club (trustee), Comml. Club, Chgo. Club, Cornell Club, Hinsdale Golf Club, Old Elm Club, Links Club, Blind Brook Golf Club, Royal Poinciana Golf Club, Hole in the Wall Golf Club, Naples Yacht Club, Masons, Tau Beta Pi, Beta Gamma Sigma. Congregationalist. Office: R R Donnelley & Son Co 2223 Martin Luther King Dr Chicago IL 60616

LAKHANI, HUSSAIN GULAMHUSAIN, financial planner, hotel executive; b. Bombay, India, Mar. 21, 1946; came to U.S., 1965; s. Gulam Husain Bhanji and Khadija (Hirji) L.; m. Mumtaz Lakhani; children: Azeem, Sharmeen, Zulfiqar. BS, MIT, 1968, MS, 1969; MBA, Clark U., 1971. Engring. supr. Norton Co., Worcester, Mass., 1968-72; asst. prof. engring. Cen. New England Coll., Worcester, 1976-83; propr. Shalamar Enterprises, Holden, Mass., 1984-88; pres., owner Shalamar Inns, Lakeland, Fla., 1988—; sec. Vista Inns, Jacksonville, Fla., 1987—. Patentee in field. Club: Nizari Investment (Boston) (pres. 1985-86). Home: 1042 N Vermont St Lakeland FL 33801 Office: Shalamar Inns Inc 508 E Memorial Blvd Lakeland FL 33801

LAKSHMI-RATAN, RAMNATH AYYAN, marketing professional; b. Bombay, India, Apr. 10, 1953; came to U.S., 1971; s. Subramania Ayyan and Jayalakshmi (Iyer) L-R; m. Olga Chandra Ratan, June 7, 1981 (div. 1988); 1 child, Rabindra Ayyan. Student, Ripon Coll., 1971-73; BS, U. Poona (India), 1976; MMS, U. Bombay, 1978; PhD, U. Pitts., 1984. Tech. supr. Green Giant Co., Ripon, 1971-72; probationary mgr. ops. Associated Cement Co. of India, Ltd., Bombay, 1977; mgr. new products devel. appliances div. Voltas, Ltd., Bombay, 1978-79; cons. mktg. sci. U. Pitts., 1979-82, instr. mktg. grad. sch. bus., 1982-84; mgr., primary researcher Bur. Bus. Rsch., Pitts., 1980-82; asst. prof. mktg. U. Wis., Madison, 1984-86; mem. tech. staff AT&T Bell Labs., Murray Hill, N.J., 1986—; cons. Pullman-Swindell, Pitts., 1980, Elger Plumbing Ware, Pitts., 1981, Presbyn. U. Hosp., Pitts., 1982, Wis. Milk Mktg. Bd., Madison, 1985; speaker in field; adj. prof. Rutgers U., 1988—. Recipient award The India Found., 1971, Mu Kappa Tau Outstanding Educator award U. Wis., 1985. Mem. Am. Mktg. Assn., Am. Stats. Assn., Assn. Consumer Rsch., Inst. for Mgmt. Sci., Psychometric Soc. Office: AT&T Bell Labs 600 Mountain Ave Murray Hill NJ 07974

LALAMA, DOUGLAS JOSEPH, human resouces director; b. Rochester, Pa., June 16, 1955; s. Guy Joseph and Elizabeth (Pcsolyar) L.; m. Michelle Hope Haynes, Oct. 19, 1985; children: Douglas Jordan, Elise Kristine. BA, Pa. State U., 1977; MA, Wayne State U., 1982. Labor relations asst. Hoskins Mfg. Co., Detroit, 1979-80; supr. labor relations Koskins Mfg. Co., Detroit, 1980-82, mgr. employee relations, 1983-85; dir. human resources J.P. Industries Inc., Ann Arbor, Mich., 1985—. Trustee Ars Musica, Ann Arbor, 1987-88. Mem. Am. Soc. Employers, Am. Soc. Personnel Adminstrs., Am. Soc. Quality and Participation (midwest pension conf.). Office: JP Industries Inc 325 E Eisenhower Ann Arbor MI 48109

LALLY, WILLIAM JOSEPH, financial planner; b. N.Y.C., Sept. 28, 1937; s. William Joseph and Madeline (Bradley) L.; m. Janet Lou Miars, July 30, 1960; children: Catherine Mary, Elizabeth Ann, Maureen Susan, Monica Eileen, Patricia Jude. AB in Econs., Coll. Holy Cross, 1959; MBA, Rutgers U., 1961. CPA, Conn., N.Y., N.J. Mgr. Peat, Marwick, Mitchell & Co., Newark, 1960-70; ptnr. Peat, Marwick, Mitchell & Co., White Plains, N.Y., 1970-76; sr. v.p. Gregg Group, Inc., Falls Village, Conn., 1977-83; pres. Hamilton Gregg Fin. Services, Falls Village, 1983-84, Lally & Assocs., Inc., Stamford, Conn., 1984—; adv. bd. Inst. Fin. Planning Quinnipiac Coll., Hamden, Conn., 1986—, lectr. Adv. bd. Cath. Family Svcs., Stamford, Conn. Mem. Am. Inst. CPA's, Conn. Soc. CPA's, N.Y. Soc. CPA's, N.J. Soc. CPA's, Southern Conn. Chpt. Internat. Fin. Planning Assn. (trustee), Registry of Fin. Planning Practitioners. Republican. Roman Catholic. Clubs: Landmark (Stamford); Chemists (N.Y.C.). Office: Lally & Assocs Inc 1150 Bedford St Stamford CT 06905

LALONDE, JOHN STEPHEN, SR., financial planning executive; b. Berwyn, Ill., June 27, 1948; m. Shellie Debra Warman, Jan. 12, 1977; 1 child, John Stephen Jr. BS, No. Ill. U., 1971; cert., Coll. for Fin. Planning, Denver, 1985; cert. in computer sci., DePaul U., 1985. With sales and mgmt. depts. Physicians Planning Svc., Chgo., 1972-76; pres., chief exec. officer Fin. Exch., Des Plaines, Ill., 1976—, also bd. dirs.; bd. dirs. First Benefit Adminstrv. Svcs., Des Plaines. Author: (manual) Capital Accumulation Transfer, 1981. Mem. Senatorial Inner Circle, Washington, 1984—. Mem. Internat. Assn. for Fin. Planning, Inst. Cert. Fin. Planners. Republican. Clubs: Inverrary Country, Environ Men's (Lauderhill, Fla.). Office: Fin Exch 2604 E Dempster Ave Ste 404 Des Plaines IL 60016

LAM, BILLY, finance company executive; b. Hong Kong, Feb. 27, 1960; s. Muk Kwong and Pui Ha (Wong) L. BS, Queen Mary Coll., London, 1982; MS, London Sch. Econs., 1984. Dir. Shing Fung Fin. Co., Ltd., Hong Kong, 1983—; asst. mgr. Tai Sun Co., Hong Kong, 1983—. Home: 3 Cassia Rd Ground Fl, Yau Yat Chuen Kowloon Hong Kong Office: Tai Sun Co, 1301 Fin Bldg, 254/256 Des Voeux Rd, Hong Kong Hong Kong

LAMACCHIA, JOHN THOMAS, telecommunications executive; b. Washington, Sept. 19, 1941; s. Philip J. and Emma H. (Wuterich) LaM.; m. Elizabeth Hamilton, Dec. 28, 1964; children: John Philip, Thomas Frederick, Charles Robert, Elizabeth Emeline, Mary Elena. BEE, Cath. U., 1963, PhD in Physics, 1966; JD, Ind. U., Indpls., 1976. Bar: N.J. 1977, Ohio 1985. Mem. tech. staff solid state device lab. Bell Labs., Murray Hill, N.J, 1966-68; supr. optical interactions group, dept. head continuing edn. Bell Labs., Holmdel, N.J, 1968-72; dept. head telephone systems dept. Bell Labs., Indpls., 1972-76; dept. head network measurements dept. Bell Labs., Holmdel, 1976-79; mgr. strategic planning div. AT&T, N.Y.C, 1979-80; dir. strategic planning div. AT&T, Basking Ridge, N.J., 1980-83; pres. Cin. Bell Info. Systems Inc., 1983-87, exec. v.p., 1986-87, also bd. dirs.; pres., chief operating officer Cin. Bell Inc., 1988—. Contbr. articles to profl. jours.; patentee in field. Trustee U. Cin. Found., 1985—, St. Joseph Infant & Maternity Home, Cin., 1985—; dep. mayor, police commr. Berkeley Heights, N.J., 1970-72; mem. twp. com. Twp. of Berkeley Heights, 1970-72. Named Outstanding Young Electrical Engr., Eta Kappa Nu, 1973; fellow NSF, 1963, NASA, 1964-66. Mem. IEEE, ABA. Clubs: Queen City, Bankers, Kenwood Country (Cin.), Commonwealth, Cin. Home: 7800 Deer Crossing Cincinnati OH 45243 Office: Cin Bell Inc PO Box 2301 Cincinnati OH 45201

LAMALIE, ROBERT EUGENE, executive search company executive; b. Fremont, Ohio, June 3, 1931; s. Glennis and Mildred M. (Hetrick) L.; m. Dorothy M. Zilles, June 20, 1953; children: Deborah, Dawn, Elaine. BA, Capital U., Columbus, Ohio, 1954; postgrad., Case Western Res. U. Asst. dir. recruiting Xerox Corp., 1959-62; mgr. orgn. planning and profl. recruiting Glidden Co., 1962-65; search cons. Booz, Allen & Hamilton, Inc., Cleve., 1965-67; pres., chief exec. officer Lamalie Assocs., Inc., Tampa, Fla., 1967-84, chmn. bd. dirs., chief exec. officer, 1984-87, chmn. bd. dirs., 1987-88; pres. Robert Lamalie, Inc., Marco Island, Fla., 1988—. Served with U.S. Army, 1954-56, Korea. Office: 317 N Collier Blvd Marco Island FL 33937

LAMANTIA, CHARLES ROBERT, management consultant, industrial research company executive; b. N.Y.C., June 12, 1939; s. Joseph Ferdinand and Catherine (Perniciaro) LaM.; m. Ann Christine Carmody, Sept. 16, 1961; children: Elise, Matthew. BA, Columbia U., 1960, BS, 1961, MS, 1962, ScD, 1965; grad. advanced mgmt. program, Harvard Bus. Sch., 1979. Cons. staff Arthur D. Little, Inc., Cambridge, Mass., 1967-77, v.p., 1977-81, pres., chief oper. officer, 1987-88, pres., chief exec. officer, 1988—, also bd. dirs.; pres., chief exec. officer Koch Process Systems, Westboro, Mass., 1981-86; bd. dirs. CFS, Inc.; mem. engr. coun. Columbia U.; mem. bd. overseers New England Med. Ctr.; trustee Meml. Dr. Trust, 1989. Corp. mem. Mus. Sci., Boston, 1986—. Served to lt. USN, 1965-67. NSF fellow, 1965; Sloan Found. fellow, 1962. Mem. Am. Inst. Chem. Engrs. Office: Arthur D Little Inc 25 Acorn Pk Cambridge MA 02140

LAMARRE, BERNARD C., engineering, contracting and manufacturing company executive; b. Chicoutimi, Que., Can., Aug. 6, 1931; s. Emile J. and Blanche M. (Gagnon) L.; m. Louise Lalonde, Aug. 30, 1952; children: Jean, Christine, Lucie, Monique, Michele, Philippe, Mireille. BASc, Ecole Poly., Montreal, 1952; MSc, Imperial Coll., U. London, 1955; LLD, St. Francis Xavier U., N.S., Can., 1980; D in Engring. (hon.), U. Waterloo, Can., 1984; LLD (hon.), U. Concordia, Montreal, 1985; D in Engring. (hon.), U. Montreal, 1985; D in Applied Sci. (hon.), U. Sherbrooke, Can., 1986; D in Sci. (hon.), Queen's U., Kingston, Ont., 1987; D in Bus. Adminstrn. (hon.), U. Quebec, Chicoutimi, 1987; D in Engring. (hon.), U. Ottawa, Can., 1988. Structural and founds. engr. Lalonde-Valois, Montreal, Que., 1955-58, chief engr., 1958-63; ptnr. Lalonde-Valois, Lamarre Valois, Montreal, 1962-72; chmn., chief exec. officer Lavalin Group, Montreal, 1972—; bd. dirs. La Laurentienne Générale Ins. Co., Can. Gen. Electric, Nat. Bank Can.; former chmn. Can. Devel. Investment Corp. Contbr. articles to profl. jours. Bd. dirs. Royal Victoria Hosp., Montreal, 1980—; bd. dirs. Montreal Fine Arts Mus., 1979—, chmn. bd., 1982—; mem. corp. Coll. Marie de France, Montreal, 1975—, Coll. Stanislas, 1976—. Decorated officer Order of Can., Order of Que., 1985; recipient Gold medal Nat. Council Engrs. Can., 1986; Athlone scholar, 1952. Fellow Engring. Inst. Can.; hon. fellow Royal Can. Inst. Architects; Mem. Order of Engrs. of Que., ASCE, Prestressed Concrete Inst., ASCE. Roman Catholic. Clubs: Mont-Royal (Montreal), St. Denis (Montreal), Laval Golf (Montreal). Home: 4850 Cedar Crescent, Montreal, PQ Canada H3W 2H9 Office: 1100 Blvd Rene Levesque W, Montreal, PQ Canada H3B 4P3

LAMB, FREDERIC DAVIS, lawyer; b. Oak Park, Ill., Nov. 23, 1931; s. Frederic Horace and Alice Emily (Davis) L.; m. Barbara Ann Bullard, Apr. 6, 1954; children: Deborah Ann Lamb Dunn, Jeffrey Davis. BA, Wabash Coll.; JD, U. Mich. Bar: Ohio. Atty. Vick Chem. Co., N.Y.C. and Cin., 1956-63; v.p., counsel Merrell div. Richardson-Merrell Inc., Cin., 1964-80; asst. gen. counsel Richardson-Vicks Inc., Wilton, Conn., 1981-83, v.p., gen. counsel, sec., 1984—. Mayor, councilman City of Forest Park, Ohio, 1971-75; chmn. Forest Park Charter Commn., 1969-70, bd. trustees Food Drug Law Inst. (scholarship com. 1985—). Mem. ABA, Ohio Bar Assn., Westchester-Fairfield Corp. Counsel Assn., Am. Soc. Corp. Secs., Silver Spring Country Club (pres. 1989—). Republican. Home: 30 Keelers Ridge Rd Wilton CT 06897 Office: Richardson-Vicks Inc 10 Westport Rd Wilton CT 06897

LAMB, J(OHN) WYMAN, utilities executive; b. Augusta, Ga., May 31, 1935; s. John Clover and Willie (Cartledge) L.; m. Judith Blackmon, July 16, 1955; children: Mark, Tracie, Todd. B in Indsl. Engring., Ga. Inst. Tech., 1958; JD, Emory U., 1968. Bar: Ga. 1967, U.S. Supreme Ct. 1968. With Ga. Power Co., Atlanta, 1953—, v.p. risk mgmt., 1976—; mem. faculty U. Pa. Sch. of Medicine. Trustee Bus. Council Ga. Group Benefit Trust, 1981—; bd. counselors Ga. State U. Gerontology Ctr., 1986—; vice-chmn. adv. bd. Burn Ctr. Excellence, Human Hosp., 1983—; chmn. com. radiation compensation litigation U.S. Council Energy Awareness. Mem. ABA, Ga. Bar Assn., Corp. Counsel Assn. Atlanta, Atlanta Bar Assn., Atlanta Claims Assn., Alpha Pi Mu, Chi Phi. Democrat. Baptist. Home: 4946 Chedworth Dr Stone Mountain GA 30087 Office: Ga Power Co PO Box 4545 Atlanta GA 30302

LAMB, ROBERT LEWIS, electric utility executive; b. Goodland, Kans., Mar. 29, 1932; s. Perl and Josephine (Cullins) L.; m. Patricia Jean Kanuch, Sept. 6, 1953; children: Nancy Jo, David Lewis. B.S.E.E., U. Kans., 1955. Engr. The Empire Dist. Electric Co., Joplin, Mo., 1958-67, distbn. engr., 1967-69; supt. engring. The Empire Electric Co., Joplin, 1969-74; v.p. customer services The Empire Dist. Electric Co., Joplin, 1974-78, exec. v.p., 1978-82, pres., chief exec. officer, 1982—, dir., 1978—; chmn. Mokan Power Pool, 1986-87, S.W. Power Pool, 1989—. Pres. Joplin United Way, 1981; v.p. Joplin Indsl. Devel. Authority, 1980-88; v.p., dir. Joplin So. Corp., 1974—; bd. dirs. St. John's Regional Med. Ctr., Joplin, 1981—, chmn. bd., 1982-84, 1988—; bd. dirs. Mo. So. State Coll. Found., 1986—. Served to capt. USAF, 1955-58. Mem. Joplin C. of C. (pres. 1979-80). Republican. Lutheran. Clubs: Twin Hills Country (Joplin); Kansas City (Mo.). Office: Empire Dist Electric Co 602 Joplin St PO Box 127 Joplin MO 64801

LAMBERSON, JOHN ROGER, insurance company executive; b. Aurora, Mo., Aug. 16, 1933; s. John Oral Lamberson and Golda May (Caldwell) Tidwell; m. Virginia Lee, Aug. 10, 1957; 1 child, John Clinton. BA, U. Calif., Berkeley, 1954. Coach, tchr. Thousand Palms (Calif.) Sch., 1954-55; underwriter trainee Fireman's Fund Ins. Co., San Francisco, 1955; surety mgr. Safeco Ins. Co. (formerly Gen. Ins. Co.), San Francisco and Sacramento, Calif., 1957-61; exec. v.p., chief operating officer Corroon & Black Corp., N.Y.C., 1961—, also bd. dirs., chmn. constrn. industry div., mem. exec. com., aquisition com.; guest lectr. Grad. Sch. Engring. Stanford U., Fails Mgmt. Inst., participant numerous sems. and forums. Mem. Nat. Assn. Heavy Engring. Constructors (bd. dirs. 1985—), Constrn. Fin. Mgmt. Assn. (bd. dirs. 1987—, exec. com.), Assoc. Gen. Contractors Am. (membership devel. com., past chmn. bd. dirs. nat. assoc. mems. council), Assoc. Gen. Contractors Calif. (bd. dirs. 1976, various past coms.), Nat. Assn. Surety Bond Producers (past nat. pres., regional v.p.), Am. Inst. Contractors, Soc. Am. Mil. Engrs., Young Pres.' Orgn. (sem. leader). Clubs: Bankers (San Francisco); Sharon Heights Golf and Country (Menlo Pk., Calif.). Home: 85 Greenoaks Dr Atherton CA 94025 Office: Corroon & Black Corp Wall St Plaza New York NY 10005

LAMBERT, ALLEN THOMAS, banker; b. Regina, Sask., Can., Dec. 28, 1911; s. Willison Andrew and Sarah (Barber) L.; m. Marion Grace Kotchapaw, May 20, 1950; children: William Allen, Anne Barber. Ed. Victoria pub. high schs. With Toronto Dominion Bank, 1927-78, asst. gen. mgr., 1953-56, gen. mgr., 1956, v.p., bd. dirs., 1956-60, pres., 1960-72, chmn. bd. dirs., 1961-72, chmn. bd. dirs., chief exec. officer, 1972-78; chmn. fin. services group Edper-Brascan Group; bd. dirs. Great Lakes Group Inc., Hees Internat. Corp., Brascan Ltd., Atico Fin. corp., R. Angus Alta., Ltd., Western Internat., Raritan River Steel Co., Royal Trustco, Ltd., Rolls-Royce Industries Can., Ltd., Falconbridge Ltd., Inspiration Resources Corp., Royal LePage Ltd., The Holden Group, Trilon Fin. Corp., Lonvest Corpl.;chmn. bd. dirs. Hudson Bay Mining and Smelting Co., Ltd. Served with Royal Canadian Navy, 1943-45. Mem. United Ch. Can. Clubs: Toronto, Toronto Golf, Toronto Hunt, Granite, York (Toronto). Office: Trilon Fin Corp, Box 86, Toronto-Dominion Ctr, Toronto, ON Canada M5K 1G8

LAMBERT, HENRY RAYMOND, food company executive; b. Wilmington, Del., Aug. 12, 1951; s. William Harrison and Elinor (Reppe) L.; m. Deborah Ann Dodd, Sept. 11, 1976; children: William, Christopher, Ann. BA, Union Coll., Schenectady, 1973; MBA, U. Chgo., 1975. Fgn. currency cons. Harris Bank, Chgo., 1975-78; mgr. internat. treasury Heublein, Inc., Farmington, Conn., 1978-80, dir., 1980-82; dir. European treasury R.J. Reynolds Industries, Inc., London, 1982-83; mng. dir. RJR Industries (U.K.) Ltd., London, 1983-85; v.p. RJR-Nabisco, Inc., Winston-Salem, N.C., 1985-87; v.p. planning and bus. devel. Nabisco Brands, Inc., East Hanover, N.J., 1987—. Trustee N.C. Sch. Arts, Winston-Salem, 1986-87; mem. Leadership Greater Hartford, 1982-83. Mem. Planning Forum, Omicron Delta Epsilon. Republican. Roman Catholic. Club: Noe Pond (Madison, N.J.). Home: 54 Union Hill Rd Madison NJ 07940 Office: Nabisco Brands Inc 7 Sylvan Way PO Box 304 Parsippany NJ 07054

LAMBERT, JOSEPH CALVIN, JR., liquor company executive; b. Columbus, Ga., Feb. 26, 1945; s. Joe Calvin and Dora McGehee L.; m. Shirley Anne Best, Apr. 27, 1968 (div. Feb. 1986); children: Joseph Calvin III, James Edward, Kristin Carole. SB, MIT, 1966; MBA, Harvard U., 1972. Engr., group leader C.S. Draper Lab., MIT, Cambridge, Mass., 1965-69; asst. treas. Whitehall Co. Ltd., Norwood, Mass., 1972-81; v.p., chief fin. officer Beverage Distbrs. Co. div. Devon Group, Inc., Aurora, Colo., 1981—. Mem. Colo. Rep. Fin. Com., Denver; v.p., bd. dirs. Am. Contract Bridge League unit 108, Boston, 1979-81. Served with USN, 1969, with Res. 1970-79. Republican. Episcopalian. Club: University (Denver). Office: Beverage Distbrs Co 14200 E Moncrieff Pl Aurora CO 80011

LAMBERT, THOMAS WAYNE, electronics company executive; b. Milw., Feb. 13, 1943; s. Thomas Joseph and Viola Hildegard (Gehrke) L.; m. Rosemary Josephine Wagner, Nov. 7, 1977; 1 child, Melissa Ann. BS in Physics, U. Wis., 1966. With Gen. Elec. Med. Systems, Milw., 1966-86, spl. prodn. engring. mgr., 1975-76, computed tomography elec. engring. mgr., 1976-78, elec. engring. mgr., 1978-80, digital radiography engring. mgr., 1980-83, x-ray products engring. mgr., 1983-86; pres. Camtronics Ltd., Delafield, Wis., 1986—; also dir. Contbr. articles to profl. jours.; patentee in field. Recipient IR100 award Indsl. Rsch. & Devel., 1982; Wis. Gov.'s New Product award Wis. Soc. Profl. Engrs., 1982, 83, 87. Mem. Am. Inst. Ultrasound in Medicine, Soc. Motion Picture and TV Engrs. Home: N8W29582 Thames Ct Waukesha WI 53188 Office: Camtronics Ltd PO Box 307 Delafield WI 53018

LAMBLY, SHARON ANN, computer company executive; b. Colville, Wash., June 4, 1940; d. Charles Albert and Helen Louise (Oswald) L. B.S. in Civil Engring., Bucknell U., 1962. Br. mgr. IBM, Syracuse, 1974-77, program dir., Armonk, N.Y., 1977-79, mgr. mgmt. services, Manassas, Va., 1979-82, dir. personnel, Bethesda, Md., 1982-84, v.p. mgmt. svcs., 1984-85, dir. corp. personnel, 1986-87, U.S. personnel programs dir., 1987-88; v.p. human resources Hershey (Pa.) Foods Corp., 1988—; pres. Shel of K.W. Inc., Key West, Fla., 1982—; dir. Bucknell Engring., Lewisburg, Pa. Mem. exec. com. Jr. Achievement, Bethesda, 1983-85; bd. dirs. Children's Hosp., Washington, 1985-87; dir. adv. com. Urban League Tng. Ctr., Washington, 1983-85; trustee Hood Coll., Frederick, Md., 1985-86. Republican. Presbyterian. Avocations: sculling; racquetball; cycling; photography. Home: 880 Zermatt Dr Hommelstown PA 17036 Office: Hershey Foods Corp 100 Monsier Rd Hershey PA 17033

LAMB-MAYS, SHEILA, retail executive; b. Greensboro, N.C., Feb. 22, 1955; d. Dwight Lee and Evelyn (Durham) Welborn; m. K. Eugene Lamb, June 9, 1973 (div. Apr. 1984); 1 child, Ivey Nicole; m. Charles Ray Mays, Nov. 16, 1984. Grad. in fashion merchandising, U. N.C., 1987; A in life office mgmt., Jefferson Standard, Greensboro, N.C. Clk. First Union Nat. Bank, Raleigh, N.C., 1973-74; clk. Guardian Life Ins. Co., Greensboro, 1974-77, office mgr., 1977-83; v.p., co-owner Sportline of Hilton Head, Greensboro, 1983-87; exec. buyer Sportline of Hilton Head, Ltd., Greensboro, 1987—. Mem. Greensboro C. of C., Greensboro Merchants Assn., Winston-Salem Merchants Assn., Friendly Ctr. Merchants Assn. (bd. dirs.). Home: 3019 Lake Forest Dr Greensboro NC 27408 Office: Sportline of Hilton Head Ltd 816 Friendly Ctr Greensboro NC 27408

LAMEIRO, GERARD FRANCIS, computer network consultant, columnist; b. Paterson, N.J., Oct. 3, 1949; s. Frank Raymond and Beatrice Cecilia (Donley) L.; BS, Colo. State U., 1971, MS, 1973, PhD, 1977. Sr. scientist Solar Energy Research Inst., Golden, Colo., 1977-78; asst. prof. mgmt. sci. and info. systems Colo. State U., Fort Collins, 1978-82, lectr. dept. computer sci., 1983, lectr. dept. mgmt., 1983; pres. Successful Automated Office Systems, Inc., Fort Collins, 1982-84; product mgr. Hewlett Packard, 1984-88; computer networking cons., 1988—, Ft. Collins.; columnist The HP Chronicle, 1988—. Mem. Presdl. Electoral Coll., 1980. Recipient nat. disting. Service award Assn. Energy Engrs., 1981. Colo. Energy Research Inst. fellow 1976; NSF fellow 1978. Mem. Assn. for Computing Machinery. Roman Catholic. Contbr. articles in mgmt. and tech. areas to profl. jours. Home: PO Box 9580 Fort Collins CO 80525 Address: 3313 Downing St Fort Collins CO 80526 Office: Hewlett Packard Co 3313 Downing Ct Fort Collins CO 80526

LAMEY, WILLIAM LAWRENCE, JR., manufacturing company executive; b. Evanston, Ill., June 19, 1938; s. William Lawrence and Dorothy Matilda (Mann) L.; m. Barbara Mary Matulewicz, Oct. 7, 1961; children: William Lawrence III, Patricia, Elizabeth. B.S. in Bus. Adminstrn, Xavier U., 1960. C.P.A., Ill. Staff auditor Haskins & Sells, Chgo., 1960, 62-63, Celanese Corp., Charlotte, N.C., 1963-64; with DeSoto, Inc., Des Plaines, Ill., 1964—; treas. DeSoto, Inc., 1970-71, controller, 1971-73, asst. v.p. finance, 1973-74, v.p. fin., 1975—, dir., 1976—; dir. De Soto Titanine Plc, 1986—. Served with AUS, 1961-62. Mem. Am. Inst. C.P.A.s, Ill. C.P.A. Soc., Financial Execs. Inst., Chgo. Zool. Soc. Home: 1520 Chapel Ct Deerfield IL 60015 Office: De Soto Inc 1700 S Mt Prospect Rd Box 5030 Des Plaines IL 60017

LAMIA, THOMAS ROGER, lawyer; b. Santa Monica, Calif., May 31, 1938; s. Vincent Robert, II, and Maureen (Green) L.; m. Susan Elena Brown, Jan. 10, 1969; children: Nicholas, Katja, Jenna, Tatiana, Carlyn, Mignon. Student U. So. Calif., 1956, BS, 1961; student U. Miss., 1957-58; JD, Harvard U., 1964. Bar: Calif. 1965, U.S. Dist Ct. (cen. dist.) Calif. 1965, D.C. 1980, U.S. Dist. Ct. D.C. 1980, U.S. Ct. Appeals (D.C. cir.) 1980, U.S. Tax Ct. 1982. Assoc. McCutchen, Black, Verleger & Shea, Los Angeles, 1964-66; lectr. in law U. Ife, Ile-Ife, Nigeria, 1966-67, U. Zambia, Lusaka, 1967-68; assoc. Paul Hastings, Janofsky & Walker, L.A., 1968-72, ptnr., 1972-80, Washington, 1980-87, N.Y., 1987—, mng. ptnr. Washington office, 1980-83; bd. dirs. Acme Rents Inc. Mem. ABA (bus., banking, fed. regulation of securities com., SEC adminstrn., budget and legislation subcom., internat. law com., African law and extraterritorial application of U.S. law subcoms.), Internat. Bar Assn. (product liability, false advt. and consumer protection com.), Harvard Law Sch. Assn., Nat. Aquarium Soc. (bd. dirs. 1982—). Office: Paul Hastings Janofsky Walker 9 W 57th St New York NY 10019

LAMM, HARVEY H., foreign car and parts importer; b. Phila., Nov. 10, 1935; s. Edward S. and Rosalie Lamm; m. Sandra Budilov, May 3, 1964; children: Marla, Davin. Student, Pa. State U., Drexel U. Exec. v.p. Subaru of Am., Inc., Pennsauken, N.J., 1967-70, chief operating officer, vice chmn. bd., 1970-75, chief exec. officer, dir., 1975—, pres., 1975-86, chmn., 1986—, also bd. dirs. Mem. Young Pres. Orgn. Office: Subaru Am Inc Subaru Pla 2235 Rte 70 W Cherry Hill NJ 08002 *

LAMME, RICHARD, executive search consultant; b. N.Y.C., Dec. 28, 1953; s. John and Peggy Genes. Student Fairleigh Dickinson U., 1971, Pace U., 1972-77; divorced; 1 child, Jennifer Ann. Sr. fin. analyst RCA/Div. Random House, N.Y.C., 1972-74; employment mgr. Robert Half Personnel, N.Y.C., 1974-76; sr. assoc. Foster McKay Group, N.Y.C., 1976-78; mgr. Key Industries, Inc., N.Y.C., 1978-80; pres. Richard Lamme Assocs., Inc., Bridgeport, Conn., 1980—; Richard Lamme Assocs., Inc. of N.J., Hackettstown, 1987—. Office: PO Box 341 Trumbull CT 06611

LAMON, HARRY VINCENT, JR., lawyer; b. Macon, Ga., Sept. 29, 1932; s. Harry Vincent and Helen (Bewley) L.; m. Ada Healey Morris, June 17, 1954; children: Hollis Morris, Helen Kathryn. BS cum laude, Davidson Coll., 1954; JD with distinction, Emory U., 1958. Bar: Ga. 1958, D.C. 1965. Sr. ptnr. Hurt, Richardson, Garner, Todd & Cadenhead, Atlanta, 1984—; adj. prof. law Emory U., 1960—. Contbr. articles to profl. jours. Mem. adv. bd. Salvation Army, 1963—, chmn., 1975-79, mem. nat. adv. bd., 1976—; mem. Adv. Coun. on Employee Welfare and Pension Benefit Plans, 1975-79; mem. Pension Reporter adv. bd. Bur. Nat. Affairs; bd. visitors Davidson Coll.; trustee, past pres. So. Fed. Tax Inst. Inc.; trustee Inst. Continuing Legal Edn. in Ga., 1976—, Embry-Riddle Aero. U., 1989—, Cathedral of St. Philip, Atlanta. 1st lt. AUS, 1954-56. Recipient Others award Salvation Army, 1979. Fellow Am. Coll. Probate Counsel, Am. Coll. Tax Counsel, Internat. Acad. Estate and Trust Law; mem. ABA, Fed. Bar Assn., Atlanta Bar Assn., Am. Law Inst., Am. Pension Conf., So. Pension Conf. (pres. 1972), State Bar Ga. (chmn. sect. taxation 1969-70, vice chmn. commn. on continuing lawyer competency 1982—), Am. Judicature Soc., Atlanta Tax Forum, Lawyers Club of Atlanta, Nat. Emory U. Law Sch. Alumni Assn. (pres. 1967), Practicing Law Inst., ALI-ABA Inst., CLUs Inst., Kiwanis Club (pres. 1973-74), Breadfast Club, Peachtree Racket Club (pres. 1986-87), Capital City Club, Commerce Club, Univ. Club., Phi Beta Kappa, Omicron Delta Kappa, Phi Delta Phi, Phi Delta Theta (chmn. community svc. day 1969-72, legal commr. 1973-76). Episcopalian. Home: 3375 Valley Rd NW Atlanta GA 30305 Office: Hurt Richardson Garner Todd & Cadenhead 999 Peachtree St NE Ste 1400 Atlanta GA 30309-3999

LAMONA, THOMAS ADRIAN, consulting engineer; b. Los Angeles, Aug. 19, 1925; s. Thomas Adrian and Joy A. (Kirkman) L.; m. Jeanne Muse, May 21, 1953 (div. 1958); m. Joyce Maurer, Dec. 12, 1971. Student San Fernando Valley Jr. Coll., 1945-46, UCLA, 1948, U. So. Calif., 1955. Various positions 1943-54; sales engr. Everlube Corp., North Hollywood, Calif., 1954-57; cons. engring., Newport Beach, Calif., 1957-67, 1973—; sales engr. Lubeco, Compton, Calif., 1967-73; pres. Thomas A. Lamona & Assocs. Inc., Newport Beach, 1979—; v.p., bd. dirs. Coating Tech. Corp., Glen Ellyn, Ill., 1986-88. With U.S. Army, 1951. Recipient Spl. Svc. citation Soc. Mfg. Engrs., region VII, 1979. Mem. Standards Engring. Soc. (Los Angeles sect., mem. chmn. 1975-77, program dir. 1977-78, treas. 1978-81, chmn. 1981-82,

Spl. Service citation 1978, cert. in standards engring. 1979, Outstanding Sect. Mem. 1984), Porsche Owner's Club, Calif. Sports Car Club Am. (Los Angeles) (press relations com. 1955-63). Home and Office: PO Box 2195 Newport Beach CA 92663

LAMONICA, WILLIAM JOSEPH, conglomerate executive; b. N.Y.C., Aug. 19, 1939; s. Philip and Phyllis (Makowski) LaM.; m. Pamela Marie Vinciquerra, Oct. 5, 1963; children: Suzette, Danielle. BS, Fordham U., 1961. Auditor J.K. Lasser & Co., N.Y.C., 1961-66; controller Gotham Ednl. Equipment Co., Inc., New Rochelle, N.Y., 1966-72; v.p. fin. Data-Plex Systems Inc., Greenwich, Conn., 1972-74; v.p. fin. and adminstrn. Telepro Industries, Inc., Cherry Hill, N.J., 1974-80; 2d v.p. Chase Comml. Corp. div. Chase Manhattan Bank, N.Y.C., 1980-82; exec. v.p. Jordan Group, Kearny, N.J., 1982-84, SGI Industries, Inc., East Rutherford, N.J., 1985—; bd. dirs. Star-Glo Industries, Inc., East Rutherford, N.J., Detroit Body Products Inc., Wixom, Mich., Butler Industries, Valencia, Calif.; cons. WJL Assocs. Inc., Medford Lakes, N.J., 1984—. Mem. Nat. Assn. Accounts, U.S. C. of C. Club: Medford Lakes Colony (bd. dirs. 1977-83). Office: SGI Industries Inc 2 Carlton Ave East Rutherford NJ 07073

LAMOTHE, WILLIAM EDWARD, food company executive; b. Bklyn., Oct. 23, 1926; s. William John and Gertrude (Ryan) LaM.; A.B., Fordham U., 1950; m. Patricia Alexander, June 24, 1950; 6 children. With Kellogg Sales Co., 1950-60, product devel. coordinator, 1958-60; asst. to pres. Kellogg Co., Battle Creek, Mich., 1960-65, v.p., 1962-70, v.p., corporate devel., 1965-70, sr. v.p. corporate devel., 1970-72, exec. v.p., 1972, pres., chief operating officer, 1973-80, pres., chief exec. officer, 1979-80, chmn. bd., chief exec. officer, 1980—, also dir.; bd. dirs. Burroughs Corp., Kimberly-Clark Corp., Upjohn Co.; bd. dirs. Grocery Mfrs. Am., chmn., 1986—. Office: Kellogg Co 1 Kellogg Sq PO Box 3599 Battle Creek MI 49016-3599 *

LAMOTTE, WILLIAM MITCHELL, insurance brokerage company executive; b. Phila., Sept. 3, 1938; s. Ferdinand and June (Mitchell) LaM.; B.A., Princeton U., 1961; m. Elizabeth Ewing, Sept. 16, 1961; children—William Mitchell, Anne Hilliard, Nicole. Underwriter, Chubb & Son, N.Y.C., 1961-62; various assignments Johnson & Higgins Pa., Inc., Phila., 1962-69, pres. Johnson & Higgins Wilmington, Del., 1969-75, pres. Johnson & Higgins Mo. Inc., St. Louis, 1975-77, Johnson & Higgins Ill. Inc., Chgo., 1977—, dir. parent firm. Vice pres. Boys Clubs Wilmington, 1974-75; bd. dirs. St. Louis Zoo Friends Assn., 1976-77, Lincoln Park Zool. Soc., 1981—; bd. dirs. Chgo. Boys and Girls Clubs, 1983—, pres., 1984. Clubs: Corinthian Yacht (Phila.); Chicago, Chgo. Yacht, Indian Hill. Home: 109 Greenbay Rd Hubbard Woods IL 60093 Office: Johnson & Higgins Ill Inc 500 W Madison St Chicago IL 60606

LAMPE, HENRY O., stockbroker; b. Bremen, Germany, Apr. 8, 1927 (parents U.S. citizens); s. Henry D. and Dorothea C. (Gatje) L.; m. Virginia Harvey, July 18, 1953 (dec. 1984). BS with honors, Am. U., 1952. Investigator pub. safety Office Mil. Govt., Berlin, 1947-49; methods examiner Bur. Consular Affairs, Dept. State, 1952-53; investigator USIA, Office of Security, 1953-55; budget examiner Resources and Civil Works div. Bur. Budget, Washington, 1955-58; v.p., br. mgr. Birely & Co., Washington and Arlington, Va., 1959-66; v.p. Thomson McKinnon Securities Inc., Arlington, 1967—; dir. Home Health Equipment Co., Med.-Tech, Inc.; cons., lectr. in field. Co-author: Faculty Handbook, George Mason U., 1985. Mem., past chmn. Arlington Com. of 100, 1963—; mem. Va. Legislature, 1970-72; trustee Arlington Hosp. Assn., 1976-86, chmn. 1982-85; bd. trustees Arlington Hosp. Found., 1986—, sec., treas., 1988—; bd. visitors George Mason U., 1980-88; vice chmn. Home Health Services Co. Va., 1984-86. Served with USN, 1945-46. Recipient merit citation U.S. Office Mil. Govt., Berlin, 1949, Lifetime Achievement award Am. Univ., 1987; named Arlington County Man of Yr., 1985. Mem. Arlington C. of C. (bd. dirs. 1985, exec. com. 1986—), Bond Club of Washington. Republican. lican. Lutheran. Clubs: Bull and Bear (Richmond); Lions (Arlington). Avocation: gardening. Home: 2914 N Greencastle St Arlington VA 22207 Office: Thomson McKinnon Securities Inc 3030 Clarendon Blvd Arlington VA 22201

LAMPE, SETH RICHMOND, public relations executive; b. Detroit, Mar. 26, 1938; s. William Seth and Harriett Colwell (Richmond) L.; m. Patricia Joan O'Malley, Aug. 7, 1965; children: Christopher Seth (dec.), Kerstin Joan, Carin Elizabeth. BS in Bus. Mgmt., Pa. State U., 1960. Account exec. B.T. Salisbury & Co., Detroit, 1960-63; state editor Argus Press, Owosso, Mich., 1963-65; reporter Citizen Patriot, Jackson, Mich., 1965-67; editor Florist Transworld Delivery, Detroit, 1968-69; dir. pub. relations Jervis B. Webb Co., Detroit, 1969-76; dir. community relations Greater Detroit Area Hosp. Council, 1976-79; pres. Lampe Communications, Inc., Pontiac, Mich., 1976—. Editor: Trustees Guide, 1978; editor Directory of News Media, 1977, newsletter Together, 1981, newsletter Future Factory News, 1983—. Mem. Mich. Tech. Council, 1986—; com. chmn. Clinton Valley council Boy Scouts Am., Pontiac, 1978-84; founder SE Mich. Info. and Referral Alliance, Detroit, 1978; bd. dirs. SEM chpt. ARC, Detroit, 1980—; chmn. Cen. Scholarship Funds, Orchard Lake, Mich., 1981—, Pontiac Oakland Vis. Nurse Assn., 1987—; bd. dirs. Vietnam Vets. Leadership Program, Pontiac, 1984-86. Served with U.S. Army, 1961-63. Recipient Recognition award for community svc., State of Mich., 1988. Mem. Pub. Relations Soc. Am. (former accreditation chmn.), Mich. Hosp. Pub. Relations Assn. (hon., spl. award 1978), Detroit Auto Writers Group, Bloomfield City Club (bd. dirs.), Oakland County Boat Club, Ad Craft Club, Elks. Republican. Home: 3095 Westacres Blvd Orchard Lake MI 48033 Office: Lampe Communications Inc 902 Riker Bldg Pontiac MI 48058

LAMPERT, ELEANOR VERNA, employment development specialist; b. Porterville, Calif., Mar. 23; d. Ernest Samuel and Violet Edna (Watkins) Wilson; student in bus., fin. Porterville Jr. Coll., 1977-78; grad. Anthony Real Estate Sch., 1971; student Laguna Sch. of Art, 1972, U. Calif.-Santa Cruz, 1981; m. Robert Mathew Lampert, Aug. 21, 1935; children—Sally Lu Winton, Lary Lampert, Carol R. John. Bookkeeper, Porterville (Calif.) Hosp., 1956-71; real estate sales staff Ray Realty, Porterville, 1973; sec. Employment Devel. Dept., State of Calif., Porterville, 1973-83, orientation and tng. specialist CETA employees, 1976-80. Author: Black Bloomers and Han-Ga-Ber, 1986. Sec., Employer Adv. Group, 1973-80, 81—; mem. U.S. Senatorial Bus. Adv. Bd., 1981-84; charter mem. Presdl. Republican Task Force, 1981—; mem. Rep. Nat. Congl. Com., 1982-88; pres. Sierra View Hosp. Vol. League, 1988-89 ; vol. Calif. Hosp. Assn., 1983-86, Calif. Spl. Olympics Spirit Team. Recipient Merit Cert., Gov. Pat Brown, State of Calif., 1968. Mem. Lindsay Olive Growers, Sunkist Orange Growers, Am. Kennel Club, Internat. Assn. Personnel in Employment Security, Calif. State Employees Assn. (emeritus Nat. Wildlife Fedn., NRA, Friends of Porterville Library, Heritage Found., DAR (Kaweah chpt. rec. sec. 1988—), Internat. Platform Assn., Dist. Fedn. Women's Clubs (recording sec. Calif. chpt. 1988—), Ky. Hist. Soc., Porterville Women's Club (pres. 1988—, dist. rec. sec. 1988—), Internat. Sporting and Leisure Club.

LAMPROS, JACK DIMITRIOS, bank executive; b. Ocala, Fla., Sept. 15, 1926; s. James Dimitrios and Rose Lee (Laney) L.; m. Betty Jean Hess, July 25, 1947; children: Athena, Gregory, Jacklyn, Jamie. BBA, U. Fla., 1949; postgrad., U. Wash. Grad. Sch. Banking, 1963-65; HHD (hon.), Weber State Coll., Ogden, Utah, 1988. V.p., trust officer and mgr. First Security Bank of Utah, N.A., Ogden, 1951—. Mem. Utah State Univ. Pres.'s Nat. Adv. Bd.; bd. dirs. (hon.) Weber State Coll. Found.; trustee Roland Hall-St. Marks Sch., 1980-82; pres. ARC, Ogden, 1971-73, McKay-Dee Found., Ogden, 1975-77; trustee McKay-Dee Hosp. Governing Bd.; advisor Utah Symphony Assn. Served with USN, 1944-46. Recipient Disting. Service award Utah State U., 1982, Disting. Exec. award Utah State U., 1982, Presdl. citation Weber State Coll., Ogden, 1982, Disting. Service award Weber State Coll., 1986, Disting. Service award Dixie Coll., 1987. Democrat. Mormon. Lodge: Rotary (pres. local club 1981-82). Home: 1802 Whispering Oaks Dr Ogden UT 84403 Office: First Security Bank Utah NA 2404 Washington Blvd Ogden UT 84401

LAMSON, EVONNE VIOLA, computer software company executive, computer consultant; b. Ithaca, Mich., July 8, 1946; d. Donald and Mildred (Perdew) Guild; m. James E. Lamson, Nov. 2, 1968; 1 child, Lillie D. Assoc. in Math., Washtenaw Community Coll., Ypsilanti, Mich., 1977; student Eastern Mich. U., 1977—. Data base mgr. ERIM, Ann Arbor, Mich., 1978-81; mgr. product services Comshare, Ann Arbor, 1981—; founder, pres. G & L Consultants, Brighton, Mich., 1982—. Study leader Brighton Wesleyan Ch., 1981—; program dir. Wesleyan Womens Assn. of Brighton, 1983—. Mem. Am. Mgmt. Assn., Nat. Assn. Female Execs., Fairbanks Family of Am., Internat. Platform Assn. Avocations: skiing, motivational speaking, reading. Home: 9585 Portage Lake Dr Pinckney MI 48169 Office: Comshare 3001 S State St Ann Arbor MI 48104

LANC, JOHN JAN, civil and geodetic engineer, land surveyor; b. Prague, Czechoslovakia, Sept. 6, 1941; came to U.S., 1969; s. Frantisek Lanc and Marie (Bouchner) Kaderabek; 1 child, Jan R. Engring. diploma, Czechoslovakia Tech. U., 1963. Registered profl. engr. N.Y., N.J., Pa., Conn., Tex.; cert. profl. land surveyor N.Y., N.J., Pa., Conn.; cert. profl. planner N.J. Geodetic and civil engr. Konstruktiva, Prague, 1964-68; land surveyor Eustance & Horowitz, P.C., Circleville, N.Y., 1969-71, proj. engr., land surveyor, 1972-73, v.p., prin. engr., 1973-85; pres., prin. engr. Lanc & Tully Engring. and Surveying, P.C., Goshen, N.Y., 1985—; cons. engr. various villages, towns, cities N.Y. state, 1973—. Active Nat. Ski Patrol, N.Y., 1985—. Fellow Am. Congress on Surveying & Mapping; mem. ASCE, NSPE, Orange County & Sullivan Counties chpt. NSPE (pres. 1981-82), Profl. Engrs. in Pvt. Practice. Home: 53 Vincent Dr Middletown NY 10940 Office: Lanc & Tully PO Box 687 Rte 207 Goshen NY 10924

LANCASTER, BARBARA M., management consulting company executive; b. Stafford Springs, Conn., Feb. 18, 1930; d. Harold D. and Ruth (Bristol) Stebbins; m. Colin T. Lancaster, June 5, 1948 (div. July 1979); children: Wayne, Sharon, Kevin, Karen, Kim. BS in Commerce, Rider Coll., 1981, MBA, 1984. CPA, N.J.; cert. fin. planner, chartered life underwriter, fin. cons. Acct. Electro Mech. Research, Princeton Junction, N.J., 1963-70; treas. Raritan Valley Ceilings, Inc., Monmouth Junction, N.J., 1970-78; adminstrv. asst. Total Enterprises, Princeton, N.J., 1979-81; pres. Lancaster Mgmt., Inc., Monmouth Junction, 1981—; tchr. Adult Sch., South Brunswick, N.J., 1986—; speaker Mercer County Coll., Trenton, N.J., 1986—, Women Life Underwriters, Freeport, Bahamas, 1988. Mem. small bus. adv. Princeton C. of C., 1984—; mem. adv. bd. Small Bus. Devel. Ctr., Newark, 1986—. Named Advocate of Yr., U.S. SBA, N.J., 1987. Mem. Nat. Assn. Women Bus. Owners (treas. N.J. chpt. 1987—), N.J. Assn. Women Bus. Owners (pres. 1986-88), Women Life Underwriters Conf. (pres. 1987-88, nat. treas.), Bus. and Profl. Women, Mid-Atlantic Venture Capital (v.p. 1988). Democrat. Home: 112 Appletree Ct Monmouth Junction NJ 08852

LANCHNER, BERTRAND MARTIN, lawyer, advertising executive; b. Boston, Oct. 3, 1929; s. Abraham Joseph and Mina (Grossman) L.; m. Nancy Nelson, Apr. 26, 1979; 1 son by previous marriage, David; 1 stepdau., Renate. B.A., Stanford U., 1951; postgrad., Columbia U. Grad. Sch. Bus., 1951-52, U. Vienna, Austria, summer 1955; J.D., Harvard U., 1955. Bar: N.Y. bar 1956. Asso. firm Sage, Gray, Todd & Sims, N.Y.C., 1955-57; atty. Warner Bros. Pictures, N.Y.C., 1957-59; asst. gen. counsel Dancer-Fitzgerald-Sample, N.Y.C., 1959-62; gen. counsel Lawrence C. Gumbinner Advt. Agy., N.Y.C., 1962-63; dir. bus. affairs and sports contract negotiations CBS-TV, N.Y.C., 1963-69; gen. counsel, exec. v.p. Videorecord Corp. Am., Westport, Conn., 1969-73; sr. v.p., sec., gen. counsel N.W. Ayer, Inc., N.Y.C., 1973—, also bd. dirs.; bd. dirs. 170 E. 79th St. Corp., Advt. Info. Services Inc., N.Y.C.; guest lectr. Yale U. Law Sch. Mem. adv. bd.: Communications and the Law. Mem. Am. Bar Assn., N.Y. State Bar Assn., Assn. of Bar of N.Y.C. (chmn. subcom. advt. agy. 1981-83), Copyright Soc. U.S., Am. Assn. Advt. Agys. (chmn. legal com. 1986—), Harvard N.Y.C. Club, Bridgehampton Tennis and Surf. Clubs: Harvard of N.Y.C, Bridgehampton Racquet and Surf, Tennisport, Uptown Racquet. Office: NW Ayer Inc 1345 Ave of the Americas New York NY 10105

LAND, KENNETH DEAN, test and balance agency executive, energy and environmental consultant; b. Central City, Nebr., Oct. 5, 1931; s. Andrew Kenneth Land and Marie Eveline (Weaver) Gehrke; m. Christa Cawthern. AAME, El Camino Coll., 1957; student, Long Beach City Coll., 1958, Calif. State Coll., 1959. Cert. test and balance engr. Gen. mgr. Air Heat Engrs., Inc., Santa Fe Springs, Calif., 1956-61; sales and estimating engr. Thermodyne Corp., Los Alamitos, Calif., 1962-64; pres., founder Air Check Co., Inc., Santa Ana, Calif., 1964-69; engring. technician Nat. Air Balance Co., Los Angeles, 1969-73; gen. mgr. B&M Air Balance Co., South El Monte, Calif., 1973-78; chief exec. officer, founder Land Air Balance Tech. (LABTECH), Las Vegas, Nev., 1978—; bd. dirs. Energy Resources and Mgmt., Inc., 1980—, San-I-Pac, Internat., Inc., 1980—, Energy Equities Corp., 1980—. Mem. Las Vegas Founders Club/Las Vegas Internat. PGA Pro-Am Tournament, 1983—; trustee Associated Air Balance Council/Sheet Metal Workers Internat. Apprenticeship Tng. Fund. Mem. ASHRAE (pres. so. Nev. chpt. 1983-84, editor chpt. bull. 1979—), CSI (co-founder Las Vegas chpt., pres. 1989—, editor, founder chpt. bull., 1988—) Assn. Energy Engrs., Am. Soc. Profl. Cons., Associated Air Balance Council (cert. test and balance engr. 1965—, pres. 1988—, bd. mem. 1982—, mem. many coms.), Sheet Metal Workers Internat. Tng. Fund, Internat. Conf. Bldg. Officials Assn., Constrn. Specifications Inst. (Las Vegas chpt., pres., v.p., co-founder 1987—), Nat. Fedn. Ind. Businessmen, Rotary (editor So. Elmonte, Calif. chpt. Bulletin 1977-78, Las Vegas SW club 1979—, bd. dirs. 1984-85, photographer 1987—), Rotary Internat. (4 Paul Harris fellows), Citizens for Pvt. Enterprise, Nev. TaxpayersAssn., Univ. Nev. Las Vegas Golf Found., Desert Inn Country Club. Office: Land Air Balance Tech Inc PO Box 26389 Las Vegas NV 89126-0389

LAND, RICHARD ROBERT, accountant; b. Milw., Aug. 17, 1949; s. Robert Warren and Ethel Elfrieda (Last) L. BBA, U. Wis., 1971, MBA, 1972. CPA. Mem. staff Price Waterhouse, Milw., 1972-79, Curacao, Netherlands Antilles, 1979-88; ptnr. in charge Price Waterhouse, Riyadh, Saudi Arabia, 1988—. Bd. dirs. Assn. Continuing Edn. Bus., U. Wis. Mem. Am. Inst. CPAs, Wis. Inst. CPAs, Fla. Inst. CPAs, Nat. Assn. Accts. (bd. dirs. 1975-79), Internat. Tax Planners Assn., Internat. Fiscal Assn., U. Wis. Alumni Assn., Curacao Yacht Club, Curacao Golf and Squash Club, Larousse Dinner Club, Zeelandia Bus. Ctr. Club (founding mem.). Lutheran. Home: 3000 Southeast Fin Ctr Miami FL 33131-2330 Office: Price Waterhouse, PO Box 86940, Riyadh 11632, Saudi Arabia

LANDA, ALFONSO BEAUMONT, II, financial executive; b. Palm Beach, Fla., Feb. 3, 1961; s. Alfonso Beaumont and Alexandra Francesca (Stephanopoulos) de Landa y Escandon. Grad, Choate Sch., Wallingford, Conn., 1979; BA, Stanford U., 1984. Pres. Landa Ednl. Found., West Palm Beach, 1984—. Mem. Alpha Phi Omega, Bath and Tennis Club, Everglades Club, Knights of Malta. Roman Catholic. Home: 10590 Wilshire Blvd Los Angeles CA 90024 Office: Landa Ednl Found 105 S Narcissus St West Palm Beach FL 33401

LANDAU, ABRAHAM JOSEPH, publishing executive; b. N.Y.C., Aug. 20, 1920; s. Harry and Fannie (Lev) Lipkowitz; m. Josephine Seaman, Aug. 21, 1949; children: Lynn, Pauline. BS in Social Sci., CCNY, 1942; MBA, Baruch Sch. Bus. Adminstrn., 1963. Media dir. Byrde, Richard & Pound Advt. Agy., N.Y.C., 1946-52; v.p. Playbill Mag., N.Y.C., 1952-71; pres. A.J. Landau, Inc., N.Y.C., 1971-84; sr. v.p. Performing Arts Network, L.A., N.Y.C., 1984-89; pres. A.J. Landau Assocs., White Plains, N.Y., 1989—; adj. assoc. prof. mktg. NYU Sch. Continuing Edn., N.Y.C., 1970—; mem. rsch. com. Sales Forecasting, 1984. Mem. Yale Club, Sales Exec. Club N.Y.

LANDAU, DAVID IAN, insurance executive; b. Cape Town, Cape Province, S. Africa, Aug. 10, 1951; came to U.S., 1976; s. Arthur and Queenie (East) L. B in Bus. Sci. with honors, U. Cape Town, 1973; MBA, Northwestern U., 1978. Investment analyst Syfrets Trust Co., Cape Town, 1974-76; investment analyst Equitable Life Assurance Soc. of U.S., N.Y.C., 1978-82, sr. investment analyst, 1982-84, investment mgr., 1984-85, sr. investment mgr., 1985—. Com. mem. MIT Enterprise Forum, 1986—. Jewish. Home: 177 E Hartsdale Ave Hartsdale NY 10530 Office: Equitable Capital Mgmt Corp 1285 Ave of the Americas New York NY 10019

LANDAU, ELLIS, hotel company executive; b. Phila., Feb. 24, 1944; s. Manfred and Ruth (Fischer) L.; m. Kathy Suzanne Thomas, May 19, 1968; children—Rachel, David. B.A. in Econs, Brandeis U., 1965; M.B.A., Columbia U., 1967. Fin. analyst SEC, Washington, 1968-69; asst. treas. U-Haul Internat., Phoenix, 1969-71; v.p., treas. Ramada, Inc., Phoenix, 1971—. Home: 4644 E Indian Bend Rd Paradise Valley AZ 85253 Office: Ramada Inc 2390 E Camelback Rd Phoenix AZ 85016

LANDAU, LAURI BETH, accountant, tax consultant; b. Bklyn., July 21, 1952; d. Jack and Audrey Carolyn (Zuckernick) L. BA, Skidmore Coll., 1973; postgrad., Pace. U., 1977-79. CPA, Oreg. Mem. staff Audrey Z. Landau, CPA, Suffern, N.Y., 1976-78; mem. staff Ernst & Whinney, N.Y.C., 1979-80, mem. sr. staff, 1980-82, supr., 1982-84; mgr. Arthur Young & Co., N.Y.C., 1984-87, prin., 1987—; speaker World Trade Inst., N.Y.C., 1987—. Composer songs. Career counselor Skidmore Coll., Saratoga Springs, N.Y., 1977—, mem. leadership com. Class of 1973, 1983-85, pres., 1985—, fund chmn., 1987—. N.Y. State Regents scholar, 1970. Mem. Am. Inst. CPA's, N.Y. State Soc. CPA's. Democrat. Clubs: Skidmore Alumni (N.Y.C.); German Shepherd Dog Am. Office: Arthur Young & Co 277 Park Ave New York NY 10172

LANDEFELD, EDWARD KENT, insurance company executive; b. South Connellsville, Pa., Nov. 19, 1933; s. Edward L. and Irene M. (Michaels) L.; m. Annetta Rose Goen, Dec 20, 1954; children: Kent E., Schuyler D., Garth M., Clete E. BS in Bus. Adminstrn., Ind. U., 1955. CPCU. Underwriter Hartford Fire Ins. Co., Chgo., 1955-56; underwriter Continental Casualty Co., Chgo., 1956; sec.-treas. Barner Hood & Van Watta, Inc., Connellsville, Pa., 1956-61; spl. agt. Comml. Union Ins. Group, Pitts., 1961-64; asst. br. mgr. Comml. Union Ins. Group, Washington, 1964-65; br. mgr. Comml. Union Ins. Group, Buffalo, 1965-69; v.p. Moss & Sullivan, Inc., Buffalo, 1969-78; v.p. Mid-Continent Ins. Co., Somerset, Pa., 1978-79, pres., 1979—; instr. CPCU Course Part I, Buffalo, 1977-78. Mem. Soc. Chartered Property and Casualty Underwriters. Republican. Methodist. Lodge: Odd Fellows.

LANDEGGER, CARL CLEMENT, machinery and pulp manufacturing executive; b. Vienna, Austria, Sept. 20, 1930; s. Karl F. and Helena (Berger) L.; came to U.S., 1937, naturalized, 1947; B. Social Sci., Georgetown U., 1951; children—Christine, Carl, Claudia, Cary, Celia, Gregory. Chmn., Parsons and Whittemore, Inc., N.Y.C., 1953—; with Black Clawson Co., N.Y.C., 1956—, exec. v.p., 1959-65, pres., 1965—, chmn., 1967—; chmn. St. Anne Nackawic Pulp & Paper Co., Ala. River Pulp Co., Monroeville, Ala.; dir. Downingtown Mfg. Co., N.Y.C. Treas. Landegger Found.; bd. dirs. Georgetown U.; trustee N.Y. Hist. Soc. 1st lt. USAF, 1951-53. Mem. Explorers Club, Road Runners Club (bd. dirs.). Office: Black Clawson Co 666 3d Ave New York NY 10017

LANDERS, DERRICK, small business consultant; b. Phila., June 24, 1963; s. Eugene Kenneth and Clara Ann (Washington) L. Cert. of achievement coll. of engring., Villanova U., 1980; student in bus. adminstrn., Pa. State U., 1984. Cons. Lancers, Smith & Simmons, Phila., 1985-88, sr. ptnr., 1988—; assoc. Anchor Assocs., Inc., Port Washington, N.Y., 1986—. Designer car entry system, revolving two story garage. Mem. Internat. Soc. Financiers, World of Info., Put and Call Club. Republican. Home: 1316 S Chadwick St Philadelphia PA 19146 Office: BCP Inc 4824 N Carlisle St Philadelphia PA 19140

LANDES, ROBERT ALTON, pharmacist, management consultant; b. Inglewood, Calif., Aug. 31, 1942; s. Glen Alton and Edith Irene (Demmon) L.; m. Cara Lou Hutchinson, Aug. 13, 1966 (div. July 1978). AA, Compton Coll., 1962; PharmD, UCLA, 1966, postgrad., 1974-75, 81-83; MBA, Calif. State U., Los Angeles, 1989. Registered pharmacist Calif., Nev. Staff Pharmacist Titus Pharmacy, Santa Ana, CAlif., 1966-69; clin. pharmacist St. Francis Med. Ctr., Lynwood, Calif., 1968-88, Torrance Meml. Hosp. Med. Ctr., Lynwood, 1988—; owner, pres. Robert's Reports, Torrance, Calif., 1983—; ptnr., cons. Grier, Landes and Assocs, Marina Del Rey, Calif., 1987—. Contbr. articles to profl. jours. Tchr. Sunday Sch. Grace Missionary Bapt. Ch., Redondo Beach, Calif., 1983-84. Mem. Orange County Soc. Hosp. Pharmacists (chmn. clin. services com. 1979-80), Am. Mgmt. Assn., Soc. Advancement Mgmt. (pres. 1984, editor newsletter 1985), AAAS, Am. Soc. Hosp. Pharmacists, Los Angeles C. of C. (chmn.), Phi Delta Chi, Rho Chi. Clubs: Bikecentennial (Missoula, Mont.), SportsConnection (Torrance). Home: 21321 Marjorie Ave Torrance CA 90503-5443 Office: Grier Landes and Assocs 2554 Lincoln Blvd #141 Marina Del Rey CA 90291

LANDINO, RICHARD EARL, accountant; b. Derby, Conn., Apr. 3, 1959; s. Richard Alan Paul and Helen Evelyn (Butler) L. BS in Acctg., Quinnipiac Coll., 1981. CPA, Conn. Staff acct. DeLeo and Co., P.C., New Milford, Conn., 1981, Ritch, Greenberg & Hassan, P.C., Shelton, Conn., 1982-85; sr. staff acct. Seward and Monde, CPA's, North Haven, Conn., 1985—. Mem. Am. Inst. CPA's, Conn. Soc. CPA's. Republican. Home: 210 Derby Ave Derby CT 06418 Office: Seward and Monde CPAs 296 State St North Haven CT 06473

LANDIS, EDGAR DAVID, services business company executive; b. Myerstown, Pa., Jan. 7, 1932; s. Edgar Michael and Anna Irene (Dubble) L.; m. Patrecia Ann Leininger, June 13, 1953; children—Susan Pauline, Jean Ann. B.S., Lebanon Valley Coll., 1953; M.B.A., U. Pa., 1957. C.P.A. Acct., audit supr. Peat, Marwick, Mitchell & Co., Phila., 1957-64; corp. controller, div. exec. v.p. Carlisle Corp., Pa., 1964-73; v.p., sr. v.p., now exec. v.p. CDI Corp., Phila., 1973—, also dir.; dir. affiliates in U.S. and Europe. Bd. dirs. Carlisle Sch. Dist., 1967-71, Carlisle City Airport, 1968-71, YMCA, Ardmore, Pa, 1981-87, chmn., 1984-86, YMCA, Phila., 1988—. Served with U.S. Army, 1954-56, Japan. Mem. Lebanon Valley Coll. Alumni Assocs. (regional chmn. 1977-82). Republican. Methodist. Home: 222 Church Rd Ardmore PA 19003 Office: CDI Corp 10 Pennsylvania Ctr Philadelphia PA 19103

LANDIS, ROGER ALAN, banker, financial and estate planner; b. Rochester, Ind., June 29, 1951; s. Richard Eugene and Joan Eloise (Dillman) L.; m. Cynthia Ann Price, Dec. 20, 1970; children: Melanie Lynn, Tyler Scott, Erika Ann. BS, U. Ariz., 1973. Cert. fin. planner. Tchr. Tanque Verde Sch. Dist., Tucson, 1973-75; spl. agt. Northwestern Mut. Life Ins. Co., Tucson, 1975-81; gen. agt. Guardian Life Ins. Co., Tucson, 1981-83; asst. v.p., trust officer Valley Nat. Bank Ariz., Tucson, 1983—. Mem. exec. bd. Catalina coun. Boy Scouts Am., 1986; bd. mgrs. H.L. Ott YMCA, Tucson, 1988. Mem. Internat. Assn. Fin. Planners (treas. so. Ariz. chpt.), So. Ariz. Estate Planning Coun. Republican. Office: Valley Nat Bank Ariz 5210 Williams Circle Ste 260 Tucson AZ 85711

LANDO, ROBERT N., franchise company executive; b. Pitts., Nov. 5, 1915; m. Patti B. Lando, Dec. 19, 1946; children—Sandi, Mark. B. in Journalism, U.Mo., 1938. Pres. Lando Advt. Agy., Inc., Pitts., 1946-75; chmn. bd. Athlete's Foot Mktg. Assocs., Inc., Atlanta, 1975—. Home: 5045 Fifth Ave Pittsburgh PA 15232 Office: Athlete's Foot Mktg Assocs Inc 3735 Atlanta Industrial Pkwy Atlanta GA 30331

LANDON, DONALD R., treasurer; b. Detroit, Oct. 20, 1945; s. John M. and Mary (Cassidy) L. BS, Ferris State Coll., 1968. Auditor State of Mich., Lansing, 1968-69, Nat. Bank Detroit, 1969-70; audit mgr. Victor Comptometer Corp., Chgo., 1970-77; dir. consolidations Victor United, Chgo., 1977-84; v.p. fin. Jed Enterprises, Moscow, Idaho, 1984-86; treas. Fay Electric Wire Corp., Chgo., 1986—. Office: Fay Electric Wire Corp 3900 N Elston Ave Chicago IL 60618

LANDRUM, LARRY JAMES, computer engineer; b. Santa Rita, N.Mex., May 29, 1943; s. Floyd Joseph and Jewel Helen (Andreska) L.; m. Ann Marie Hartman, Aug. 25, 1963 (div.); children—Larry James, David Wayne, Andrei Mikhail, Donal Wymore; m. 2d, Mary Kathleen Turner, July 27, 1980. Student N.Mex. Inst. Mining and Tech., 1961-62, N. Mex. State U., 1963-65: A.A. in Data Processing, Eastern Ariz. Coll., 1971; B.A. in Computer Sci., U. Tex., 1978. Tech. svc. rep. Nat. Cash Register, 1966-73; with ASC super-computer project Tex. Instruments, Austin, 1973-80, computer technician, 1973-75, tech. instr., 1975-76, product engr., 1976-78, operating system programmer, 1978-80; computer engr. Ariz. Pub. Svc., Phoenix, 1980-84, sr. computer engr., 1984-87, lead computer engr., 1987-88, sr. computer engr., 1988—; instr. computer fundamentals Eastern Ariz. Coll., 1972-73, Rio Salado Community Coll., Phoenix, 1985-86; chmn. bd. dirs. Epworth United Meth. Ch., 1989; community devel. adv. com. City of Glendale (Ariz.), 1988—; local arrangements chmn. Conf. on Software Maintenance, 1988. Mem. Assn. Computing Machinery, Mensa, Phi Kappa Phi.

Methodist. Home: 6025 W Medlock Dr Glendale AZ 85301 Office: Ariz Nuclear Power Project PO Box 52034 Phoenix AZ 85072-2034

LANDRY, MICHAEL GERARD, investmemt company executive; b. Ottawa, Ont., Can., July 20, 1946; came to U.S., 1982; s. Edmund Oscar and Clarice (St. Germain) L.; m. Nancy Margaret Kehoe, Oct. 19, 1968; children: Noel Michael, Adam Jonah. BA in Arts and Econ., Carleton U., 1969. V.p. MD Mgmt. Ltd., Ottawa, 1977-82, Templeton, Galbraith, Hansberger, Ft. Lauderdale, Fla., 1982-86; sr. v.p. Templeton Investment Counsel, Ft. Lauderdale, 1986-87; pres., chief exec. officer Mackenzie Investment Mgmt. Inc., Boca Raton, Fla., 1987—. Mem. Internat. Soc. Fin. Analysts (bd. dirs.), Assn. Can. Pension Mgmt. (bd. dirs. 1986—), Fin. Analysts Fedn. Roman Catholic. Office: Mackenzie Investment Mgmt Inc 1200 Federal Hwy Ste 200 Boca Raton FL 33432

LANDRY, PATIENCE DETURK, marketing professional; b. Springfield, Mass., Aug. 13, 1944; d. Ralph E. DeTurk and Beverly A. (Monroe) MacKay; m. Richard E. Landry, Apr. 12, 1965 (dec.); 1 child, Richard E. AA, Mass. Bay Community Coll., 1972-74; BA in Econs., Brandeis U., 1974-76. Lab. technician Waltham (Mass.) Hosp., 1962-66; mgr. service and software research Internat. Data Corp., Framingham, Mass., 1976-80; dir. bus. planning Software and Services Group div. Dun & Bradstreet, Wilton, Conn., 1980-85; pres. Specifics, Inc., Westport, Conn., 1985—. Author: Processing Service Section, Encyclopedia of Computer Science, 1981; also numerous market research studies. Campaign mgr., vol. worker Democratic candidates, Waltham, 1966-76. Mem. Assn. Data Processing Service Orgns. (chmn. research and stats. com. 1981-85, mem. pub. relations com. 1985—). Democrat. Office: Specifics Inc 117 Post Rd W Westport CT 06880

LANDRY, STEPHEN ANTHONY, banker; b. San Francisco, May 24, 1960; s. Edgar Peter and Karen Ann (Lecompte) L.; m. Maria Begoña, July 20, 1985; 1 child, Melissa Marie. BS, La. State U., 1985. Credit analyst First Republicbank Corp., Dallas, 1983-84; loan rep. First Republicbank Corp., Houston, 1984-85, banking officer, 1985-86; asst. v.p. First Republicbank Corp., New Orleans, 1986-88; v.p., mgr. NCNB Tex. Nat. Bank (formerly First Republicbank Corp.), New Orleans, 1988—. Mem. speakers bur. La. Council for Fiscal Reform, New Orleans, 1988; pres. Jr. Cath. Charities Assn. New Orleans, 1987-88. Republican. Roman Catholic. Lodge: Kiwanis (bd. dirs. Baton Rouge chpt. 1983).

LANE, CHARLES STUART, publisher, editor; b. Newton, Mass., Feb. 13, 1924. A.A., Boston U., 1949, B.A., 1952, M.A., 1958, doctoral student, Sch. Edn., 1968-69. English tchr. in pub. and pvt. secondary schs. and colls., 25 yrs.; headmaster Dunbarton Acad., Meredith, N.H., 1959-68; curriculum coordinator of English, Winthrop, Mass. 1970-81; pub.-editor, Jour. Print World, Meredith, N.H., 1978—; dir. Old Print Barn, Meredith, 1975—. Photographer nature photos, panoramas. Served with U.S. Army, 1943-46, PTO. Mem. Bostonian Soc., Am. Legion, VFW, Phi Delta Kappa. Subject of Pub. Broadcasting Service Interview, 1982, 84. Home: RFD 2 Box 1008 Meredith NH 03253 Office: Jour Print World 1000 Winona Rd Meredith NH 03253-9599

LANE, CHRISTOPHER THOMAS, international finance professional; b. N.Y.C., Mar. 25, 1941; s. Thomas Henry and Virginia (Chalmers) L.; m. Peggy Offutt, July 8, 1967 (div. 1979); children: Heather, Chris. BA, Dartmouth Coll., 1962; MBA in Internat. Fin., Harvard U., 1965. CPA; cert. mgmt. cons. Investment banking assoc. White Weld & Co., N.Y.C., 1965-67; fund mgr. Graham Loving & Co., N.Y.C., 1968-70; mng. officer Montrose Securities, Inc., N.Y.C., 1971-73; chief fin. officer Interbrew USA, Ltd., N.Y.C., 1972-74; chmn. Welling & Woodard, Inc., San Francisco, 1974—; dir. fin. Comml. Sci. Corp., Palo Alto, Calif., 1985-87; pres. Interchange Internat., Inc., San Francisco, 1984—; mem. internat. adv. coun. ACME, Inc. Mem. Inst. Mgmt. Cons. Republican. Episcopalian. Office: Welling & Woodard 1067 Broadway San Francisco CA 94133

LANE, DAVID ALAN, venture capital company executive; b. Los Angeles, Aug. 12, 1958. BSEE, U. So. Calif., 1981; MBA, Harvard U., 1987. Salesman IBM, Los Angeles, 1981-85; assoc. Harvard Mgmt. Co., Boston, 1987—. Mem. IEEE. Office: Harvard Mgmt Co 600 Atlantic Ave 15th Fl Boston MA 02210

LANE, EDWARD ALPHONSO RICHARD, systems analyst; b. Washington, June 13, 1953; s. Edward Kenneth and Lucile (Ellison) L. BS in Econs., U. Bridgeport, 1975; MBA, Columbia U., 1979. Cert. data processor, info. systems auditor. Fin. mgmt. trainee Gen. Electric Credit, Stamford, Conn., 1975-76; computer programmer So. New Eng. Tel., New Haven, 1976-77; systems analyst Nat. Cash Register, Dayton, Ohio, 1979; project contr. H.J. Wilson Co., Baton Rouge, 1979-81; fin. analyst Celanese Chem. Co., Bishop, Tex., 1981-83; EDP auditor Fidelity and Deposit Co. of Md., Balt., 1983-87, systems analyst, 1987-88, sr. aimplementation analyst, 1988—. Mem. EDP Auditors' Assn., Omega Psi Phi, Inc. (com. chmn. 1983-86, asst. treas. 1987-88). Roman Catholic. Home: 2541 Eastern Ave Baltimore MD 21224 Office: Fidelity and Deposit Co Md 210 North Charles St Baltimore MD 21224

LANE, GARY, legal educator; b. N.Y.C., Jan. 2, 1946; s. Jack Roger and Ruth (Lehrer) L. m. Rebecca Denise Stroud, Oct. 17, 1984; 1 child, Douglas. BA, CUNY, 1966; JD, U. San Diego, 1969; LLM, George Washington U., 1970; MA, U. So. Calif., 1972; LLM, NYU, 1974. Bar: Calif. 1972, D.C. 1974, N.Y. 1977, U.S. Dist. Ct. (cen. dist.) Calif. 1972, U.S. Ct. Appeals (2d, 9th, D.C. cirs.), U.S. Supreme Ct., U.S. Ct. Mil. Appeals, 1973, U.S. Dist. Ct. (ea. and so. dists.) N.Y. 1977. Pvt. practice, L.A., 1972-74, Washington, 1975-76, N.Y.C. and Washington, 1977-78, L.A. and Washington, 1979-81; pres. Govt. Affairs Consulting Co., L.A., Washington and N.Y.C., 1972—; asst. prof. law Del. Law Sch., Wilmington, 1976-77; gen. counsel, exec. asst. to the pres. Major Properties, L.A., 1981; corp. atty. Luth. Hosp. Soc. So. Calif., L.A., 1982; assoc. Overton, Lyman and Prince, L.A., 1983; prof. bus. adminstrn. Pepperdine U. Grad. Sch., 1982-83, 89; assoc. prof. law O.W. Coburn Sch. Law, Tulsa, 1983-86; supervising atty. Asbestos and Health Litigation dept. Simke, Chodos, Silberfeld & Anteau, Beverly Hills, Calif., 1986-87; adj. prof. Southwestern U., Sch. of Law, L.A., 1986-87; corp. counsel Meml. Health Svcs., Long Beach, Calif., 1987—; reserve exec. counsel Fed. Emergency Mgmt. Agy., 1983—. Author: Congress and Subversion, 1970, The President vs. the Congress, 1971, The UN in the Congo, 1972, Judicial Screening Processes, 1973, Joint Degree Programs and Law School, 1973. Mem. L.A. County Republican Central Com., 1971-73; campaign mgr. Luster for Mayor, L.A., 1982; mem. lawyers com. Calif. for Reagan for Pres., 1980, Okla., 1984. Mem. ABA (past chmn. subcom. internal security legislation sect. individual rights 1976), Fed. Bar Assn., Mensa. Office: Meml Health Services 2801 Atlantic Ave Long Beach CA 90801

LANE, JEFFREY BRUCE, financial services company executive; b. Bklyn., June 25, 1942; s. Murray and Arlene (Avram) L.; m. Nancy Stern, June 24, 1982. BA, NYU, 1964; MBA, Columbia U., 1970. With Shearson Lehman Hutton, N.Y.C., chief fin. officer, vice chmn., 1983-84, chief operating officer, 1984-87, pres., 1987—; vice chmn. bd. of govs. Am. Stock Exchange;. Bd. dirs. Woodmere Acad., N.Y., L.I. Jewish Hosp. Served to 1st lt. U.S. Army, 1966-68. Republican. Jewish. Office: Shearson Lehman Hutton Bros Inc Am Express Tower World Financial Ctr New York NY 10285-1900

LANE, MARVIN MASKALL, JR., electronics company executive; b. Oak Park, Ill., Apr. 25, 1934; s. Marvin Maskall and Lucille Ernestine (Fischer) L.; m. Joan Agar Wheeler, June 28, 1958; children—Elizabeth Agar, Marlene Celia. B.S. in Elec. Engring, U. Wis., 1956, M.B.A. in Indsl. Mgmt, 1957. With Texas Instruments Inc., Dallas, 1958—; asst. v.p. Texas Instruments Inc., 1978-80, v.p., treas., 1980-82, v.p., controller, 1982—. Trustee, v.p. fin.; chmn. Tejas Girl Scouts Council, 1981; bd. dirs. United Way Metro. Dallas, 1984—, Dallas Area Rapid Transit, 1986—. Mem. Fin. Execs. Inst. Presbyterian. Office: Tex Instruments Inc PO Box 655474 Dallas TX 75265

LANE, STEPHEN L., electronic equipment company executive; b. 1935; married. BA, U. Miami, 1957. With Kasselman and Co., N.Y.C., 1960-63, Emerson Radio Corp., No. Bergen, N.J., 1957-60; pres. Emerson Radio Corp., No. Bergen, 1963—, also bd. dirs. Office: Emerson Radio Corp 1 Emerson Ln North Bergen NJ 07047 *

LANE, WILLIAM W., automobile company executive; b. 1928. With GM, 1953—, dist. mgr. Oldsmobile div., 1953-55, office mgr. car distbn., 1955-56, dist. mgr. Milw. Oldsmobile div., 1956-59, mgr. bus. mgmt., 1959-60, asst. zone mgr. Omaha div., 1960-63, asst. zone mgr. Indpls. div., 1963-66, asst. zone mgr. Milw. div., 1967-69, zone mgr. Atlanta div., 1969-72, zone mgr. Detroit div., 1972-73, regional mgr. SW div., 1973-77, asst. gen. sales mgr. Oldsmobile div., 1978-80, asst. gen. sales mgr. ea. div., 1980-81, gen. sales mgr. Pontiac Motor div., 1981-84, gen. sales and service mgr. Pontiac Motor div., 1984-85, v.p., gen. mgr. Oldsmobile div., 1985—. Served with USAF, 1951-53. Office: GM Oldsmobile Div 920 Townsend St Lansing MI 48921

LANE, WILLIAM W., electronics executive; b. Roanoke, Va., Feb. 25, 1934; s. Melvin V. and Cecile (Lane); m. Ronnie G Lane, Sept. 14, 1978; 1 son, Jonathan D. B.A., Bklyn. Coll., 1956; M.B.A., Cornell U., 1958. Vice pres. Major Electronics Corp., 1959-70, chmn., dir., 1970; v.p., dir. Internat. Transistor Corp., Burbank, Calif., 1971-73; vice chmn., dir. Internat. Chia Hsin, Taipai, Taiwan, 1973-76; chmn., dir. Emerson (H.K. Ltd.), Hong Kong, from 1976, Emerson Radio Corp., North Bergen, N.J., 1974—; pres. Majorette Enterprises, from 1961; chmn. MAJ EXCO Imports Inc., 1977-85; dir. H.H. Scott, Inc. Cardiac Resusitator Corp., Portland, Oreg. Served with AUS, 1958-59. Mem. bus. adv. bd. U.S. Senate. Office: Emerson Radio Corp 1 Emerson Ln North Bergen NJ 07047 *

LANE-RETICKER, EDWARD, lawyer, banker; b. Chgo., Mar. 7, 1926; s. Edward and Jane Mary Reticker; m. Laura Ruth Lane, Aug. 9, 1947; children: Alison, Stoddard, Lydia. A.B., Dartmouth Coll., 1947; LL.B., Harvard U., 1952, grad. Advanced Mgmt. Program, 1979. Bar: N.C. 1954, Conn. 1960. Instr. Punahou Sch., Honolulu, 1947-49; mem. faculty U. N.C., Chapel Hill, 1952-56; assoc. prof. public law and govt. U. N.C., 1955-56; sr. researcher, then dir. research Conn. Public Expenditure Council, Hartford, 1956-60; with Conn. Bank & Trust Co., Hartford, 1960-85; asst. v.p. Conn. Bank & Trust Co., 1963-66, sec., 1966-85, gen. counsel, 1970-85, also dir., officer subsidiaries; gen. counsel, sec. Bank of New Eng. Corp., 1985—; lectr. U. Conn. Law Sch., Trinity Coll.; pres. Mark Twain Meml., Hartford, 1975-78, Hartford Stage Co., 1980-82, Sea Point Land Co., Brunswick, Maine, 1979-82, dir. New Eng. Legal Found., 1988—. Served to ensign USNR, 1943-46; capt. Res. ret. Mem. ABA, Am. Soc. Corp. Secs. (pres. Hartford chpt. 1977-78), Conf. State Bank Suprs. (chmn. adv. council 1977), Am. Bankers Assn., N.C. Bar Assn., Conn. Bar Assn. (chmn. corp. counsel sect. 1979-82), Conn. Bankers Assn. (exec. com. 1981), Hartford County Bar Assn., Tax Club Hartford (pres. 1964-65), Zeta Psi. Republican. Clubs: Hartford (Hartford), University (Hartford). Home: 161 Four Mile Rd West Hartford CT 06107 Office: Bank New Eng Corp 28 State St Boston MA 02109 also: 1 Constitution Pla Hartford CT 06115

LANESE, JILL RENEE, computer and management consultant; b. Neptune, N.J., June 3, 1952; d. William Herman and Blossom Roslyn (Feldman) Epstein; m. Louis Lanese, June 10, 1984. BA, C.W. Post Coll., 1974. Word processing specialist Nat. Produce Co., Inc., Neptune, 1974-78; systems mgr. AT&T, Basking Ridge, N.J., 1978-81; sr. systems mgr. ITT, N.Y.C., 1981-84; info. systems mgr. Breed, Abbott & Morgan, N.Y.C., 1984-86; word processing/data processing dir., advisor Compu-group, N.Y.C., 1985-88; automation cons, Jill Lanese Computer Cons., N.Y.C., 1986-88, pres. ComputerForce Inc., N.Y.C., 1988—. adv., bd. dirs. ComputerPro,N.Y.C., 1987—. Contbr. articles to newspapers, jours., mags. Bd. dirs., pres. Am. Found. for Animals, West End, N.J., 1982—, dir. fundraiser, 1985-88. Mem. Internat. Platform Assn., Doris Day Animal League, Ind. Computer Cons. Assn., Assn. Info. Systems Profls., Assn. for Women in Computing, Nat. Assn. Female Execs, World Wildlife Fund, Greenpeace, Jacques Cousteau Soc., Humane Soc. U.S., Fund for Ethical Treatment to Animals, Internat. Platform Assn. Republican. Avocations: writing, floral and interior design, nutrition, dogs, photography, travel. Home: 8874 24th Ave Brooklyn NY 11214 Office: ComputerForce Inc 298 Fifth Ave New York NY 10001

LANEY, SANDRA EILEEN, chemical company executive; b. Cin., Sept. 17, 1943; d. Raymond Oliver and Henrietta Rose (Huber) H.; m. Dennis Michael Laney, Sept. 30, 1968; children: Geoffrey Michael, Melissa Ann. AS in Bus. Adminstrn., Thomas More Coll., 1988. Adminstrv. asst. to chief exec. officer Chemed Corp., Cin., 1982, asst. v.p., 1982-84, v.p., 1984—, bd. dirs., 1986—; bd. dirs. Roto-Rooter, Cin., Nat. San. Supply Co., L.A., Omnicare, Inc., Cin. Mem. Cin. Club. Roman Catholic. Office: Chemed Corp 1200 DuBois Tower Cincinnati OH 45202

LANG, DAVID PAUL, medical products executive; b. St. Paul, Feb. 21, 1946; s. Mathias Aloysius and Katherine Anne (Condon) L.; m. Mary Kay Casserly, Nov. 22, 1968; children: John David, David Michael. BA in Econs., Harvard U., 1968. Mgr. internat. planning Medtronic, Inc., Mpls., 1970-74; mktg. dir. Medtronic Europe SA, Paris, 1974-75; ops. dir. Med. Europe GmbH, Munich, 1975-77; dir. sales and mktg. Med., Inc., St. Paul, 1977-79; pres. Cyberex Corp., Mpls., 1979-82; exec. v.p. Cardio-Pace Med., Inc. (subs. Novacon Corp.), Mpls., 1982-86; pres. Novacon Corp., Mpls., 1986—, bd. chmn.; vice-chmn. Oinming Med. Co., Baoji, People's Republic China, 1985—; bd. dirs. Midwest China Ctr., St. Paul, 1986—. Mem. Big Bros./Big Sisters, St. Paul, 1984-86; commr. Lake Elmo (Minn.) Planning Commn., 1985-86. Capt. U.S. Army, 1968-70. Mem. Am. Mktg. Assn., Harvard Club Minn. Roman Catholic. Office: Novacon Corp 8990 Springbrook Dr #100 Minneapolis MN 55433

LANG, FRANCIS HAROVER, lawyer; b. Manchester, Ohio, June 4, 1907; s. James Walter and Mary (Harover) L.; m. Rachel Boyce, Oct. 20, 1934; children: Mary Sue, Charles Boyce, James Richard. A.B., Ohio Wesleyan U., 1929; J.D., Ohio State U., 1932. Bar: Ohio 1932. Practice in East Liverpool, Ohio, 1932-42, 45—; with War Dept., 1942-45; chmn. bd. First Fed. Savs. & Loan Assn., East Liverpool, 1959-82; former pres., bd. dirs. Walter Lang companies.; hon. bd. dirs. First Nat. Community Bank East Liverpool, Ohio. Past bd. dirs. YMCA, Mary Patterson Meml.; past pres. Columbiana council Boy Scouts Am. regional com., E. Central region; mem. at large Nat. council, 1968—; bd. dirs. Bd. Global Ministries of United Methodist Ch., 1968-76. Mem. E. Liverpool C. of C. (past pres.), Columbiana County Bar Assn. (past pres.), Ohio State Bar Assn. Methodist. Clubs: Rotarian (past dist. gov.), E. Liverpool Country, Masons (33d degree). Home: Highland Colony East Liverpool OH 43920 Office: Potters Savs and Loan Bldg East Liverpool OH 43920

LANG, JAMES RICHARD, international trading company executive; b. Cleve., Feb. 7, 1945; s. Francis H. and Rachel L. (Boyce) L.; m. Marilyn F. Hosken, July 1, 1967; children: Christopher Charles, James Walter. Salesman Stas. WDHI-AM/WRTS-FM, East Liverpool, Ohio, 1967-68; gen. mgr. Sta. WEIR-AM, Weirion, W.Va., 1969-76; v.p. sales Paperwork Systems, Inc., Bellingham, Wash., 1976-78; v.p. market devel. Sta. Bus. Systems div. Control Date Corp., Greenwich, Conn., 1978-85; mgr. Eaglestone div. Siber Hegner N.Am., Inc., Milford, Conn., 1986—. Served with USN, 1968-69. Recipient Outstanding Service to Community award Italian Sons and Dads Am., 1970. Mem. Instrument Soc. Am., Direct Mktg. Assn., Jaycees (Community Service award 1975), Internat. Fellowship Magicians. Methodist. Lodge: Rotary (Man of Yr. 1975). Home: 24 Primrose Dr Trumbull CT 06611 Office: 84 Research Dr Milford CT 06460

LANG, ROBERT B., investment company executive; b. Phila., Aug. 11, 1934; s. Frederich Robert and Harriet (Caldwell) L.; m. Marjorie Schumacher, June 7, 1958; children: Robert C., Julie A., Jenny B. BA, Rutgers U., 1957. Chartered fin. analyst, investment counselor; cert. fin. planner, Ga. V.p. Thorndike Doran, Atlanta, 1970-79, Montag & Caldwell, Atlanta, 1979-80; pres. Farmer & Lang Inc, Atlanta, 1980—. Served to 1st lt. U.S. Army, 1957-59. Mem. Atlanta Soc. Fin. Analysts. Republican. Presbyterian. Home: 520 Forest Valley Rd Atlanta GA 30342 Office: Farmer and Lang Inc 8735 Dunwoody Pl Ste One Atlanta GA 30350

LANG, RONALD ANTHONY, trade association executive; b. Bklyn., May 12, 1936; s. Andrew C. and Margaret (Peculis) L.; m. Diane A. Nemeth, June 6, 1961 (div. 1971); children: David, Christopher, Keri Ann; m. Sharon Y. Diehl, Feb. 12, 1982. BS in Maths., Fordham U., 1958. Writer, columnist Newsday, Garden City, N.J., 1952-58; editor New Hyde Park (N.Y.) Courier, 1954-58; asst. to pres. Industry Svc. Burs., Inc., N.Y.C., 1958-64; pres. Synthetic Organic Chem. Mfrs. Assn., Washington, 1964—; dir. Am. Indsl. Health Coun., Washington, 1977—; free-lance writer 1954—; chmn. Coun. Chem. Assns., Washington, 1976-82. Mem. editorial bd. Toxic Substances Jour., 1981-85, Environ. Econs. Jour., 1982-85. Mentor Gifted Students' Program Rachael Carson Intermediate Sch., Queens, N.Y., 1981-85. Recipient Award of Merit, Chem. Industry Assn., 1980. Mem. Am. Soc. Assn. Execs., NAM (mem. assns. coun., bd. dirs. 1983-85), Societe de Chimie Industrielle, Chemists' Club (trustee 1979-81), LWV, Mensa, Skyline Racquet Club, Fordham U. Club, Overseas Press Club Am., Internat. Club of Washington. Republican. Roman Catholic. Home: 4717 Brookside Dr Alexandria VA 22312 Office: Synthetic Organic Chem Mfrs Assn 1330 Connecticut Ave NW Ste 300 Washington DC 20036

LANGAS, ASPASIA, financial executive; b. Worcester, Mass., Nov. 22, 1940; d. William J. and Efterpi Langas. BS summa cum laude, Boston U., 1980. Dir. Boston U., 1970-80; registered rep. Lincoln Nat. Life Ins. Co., Worcester, 1980-87; treas. Cultural Assembly Greater Worcester, 1987—. Bd. dirs., chmn. Capital Campaign-Faith, Inc., Worcester; allocations com. United Way Cen. New Eng., Worcester, Sec. Worcester Women's Network. Mem. Inst. Cert. Fin. Planners, Internat. Assn. Fin. Planners, Nat. Assn. Life Underwriters, Daughters of Penelope. Home: 1201 Grafton St Worcester MA 01604 Office: Lincoln Fin Svcs 316 Main St Worcester MA 01608

LANGDALE, JOHN WESLEY, timber executive; b. Valdosta, Ga., Feb. 8, 1917; s. Harley and Thalia (Lee) L.; m. Margaret Irene Jones, Dec. 19, 1946; children: Lee Dollens, John W., Margaret Perryman. AB in Econs., U. Ga., 1939, JD, 1940. Mem. Ga. Ho. of Reps., Atlanta, 1949-52, Ga. State Senate, Atlanta, 1957-58; pres. The Langdale Co., Valdosta, 1976-82, vice chmn., 1983—; vice chmn. Langdale Industries Inc., 1986—; chmn. bd. dirs. Valdosta Fed. Savs. and Loan Assn., 1957—. Chmn. U. Ga. Bd. Regents, 1967-69. Served to lt. comdr. USNR, 1941-46, PTO. Decorated Bronze Star. Mem. Ga. Bar Assn. Republican. Baptist. Lodge: Rotary (pres. local chpt. 1948-49, dist. gov. 1967-68).

LANGDON, CATHERINE ANNE, buyer; b. Toronto, Ont., Can., Nov. 23, 1960; d. Edwin Salter and Muriel Anne Catherine (Rose) L. Student, Queen's U., Kingston, Ont., 1980-82; diploma, St. Lawrence Coll., Kingston, Ont., 1985. Area mgr. Can.'s Wonderland Ltd., Toronto, 1982-85; fl. supr. Sporting Life Inc., Toronto, 1985-86; buyer Clark Group Ltd., Toronto, 1986-88, Old Firehall Sports Ltd., Unionville and Toronto, 1988—. Office: Firehall Sports Ltd, 50 Mural St Unit 8, Richmond Hill, ON Canada L4B 1E4

LANGDON, JOHN EDMUND, entrepreneur; b. San Francisco, Oct. 23, 1944; s. Jack M. and Dora Lee (Byars) L.; divorced; children: Clay, Kendall. BBA, Tex. Christian U., 1969; JD, S. Tex. Coll. Law, 1972. Bar: Tex. 1972. Asst. dist. atty. County of Tarrant, Ft. Worth, 1972-73; founder, acquisition of motion picture rights to various lit. properties Bumbershoot Prodns., Ft. Worth and Hollywood, Calif., 1974, pres., 1980—; founder, researcher Bioxy Internat., Ft. Worth, 1972-81, chmn. bd., 1981—; founder, pres., researcher World Energy Systems, Inc., Ft. Worth and Roanoke, Va., 1974; mng. gen. ptnr World Energy Systems, Inc., Ft. Worth, 1974—; pres. J.E.L. Mgmt. Corp, Ft. Worth, 1974—; founder, researcher Power Generating, Inc., Ft. Worth, 1976; founder Spacecom Corp., 1978; chmn. bd. Power Generating, Inc., Ft. Worth, 1982—; founder BSD Med. Corp., Ft. Worth and Salt Lake City, 1980—, bd. dirs., 1980-88, chmn. bd., 1982—. Served as sgt. USAF, 1965-73. Recipient athletic scholarship Tex. Christian U., 1963. Mem. ABA (natural resources law, sci. and tech. sects., Am. Jurisprudence award 1970, 71), Tex. Bar Assn., Phi Alpha Delta, Kappa Sigma. Office: 1407 Texas St Fort Worth TX 76102

LANGE, ARTHUR LESLIE, geophysicist; b. Plainfield, N.J., Mar. 25, 1926; s. Moritz and Margaret (Schutte) L.; m. Judith Marian Hayford, Mar. 19, 1966; children: Vreli Rebecca, Gerda Lorena. BS, Stanford U., 1950. Registered geophysicist, Calif. Data analyst Office Naval Rsch., Stanford, Calif., 1949-51; speleologist Western Speleogical Survey, Santa Barbara, Calif., 1951-55; geophys. engr. Newmont Exploration Ltd., Danbury, Conn., 1956-58; geophysicist SRI Internat., Menlo Park, Calif., 1959-71; chief geophysicist AMAX Geothermal, Denver, 1971-81; geophysicist, v.p. Mincomp Corp., Denver, 1981-82; gen. ptnr. Albireo Ltd., Denver, 1983-85, owner, mgr., 1985—; mgr. ops. The Geophysics Group, Denver, 1986—. Editor Jour. Caves & Karst, 1960-72; contbr. articles to profl. jours. With USNR, 1944-46. Mem. Soc. Exploration Geophysicists, European Assn. Exploration Geophysicists, Geothermal Resources Coun., Am. Geophys. Union, Am. Cave Conservation Assn. Lutheran. Home: 257 Alpine Ave Golden CO 80401 Office: The Geophysics Group 3798 Marshall St Wheat Ridge CO 80033

LANGENBERG, FREDERICK CHARLES, business executive; b. N.Y.C., July 1, 1927; s. Frederick C. and Margaret (McLaughlin) L.; m. Jane Anderson Bartholomew, May 16, 1953; children: Frederick C., Susan Jane. BS, Lehigh U., 1950, MS, 1951; PhD, Pa. State U., 1955; postgrad. execs. program, Carnegie-Mellon U., 1962. With U.S. Steel Corp., 1951-53; vis. fellow MIT, 1955-56; with Crucible Steel Corp., Pitts., 1956-68, v.p. research and engring., 1966-68; pres. Trent Tube div. Colt Industries, Milw., 1968-70; exec. v.p. Jessop Steel Co., Washington, Pa., 1970, pres., 1970-75, also bd. dirs.; pres., bd. dirs. Am. Iron and Steel Inst., Washington, 1975-78; pres. Interlake Corp., Oak Brook, Ill., 1979-81, pres., chmn, chief exec. officer, 1981—, also bd. dirs.; bd. dirs. Carpenter Tech., Reading, Pa., CNW Corp., Chgo. and Northwestern Transp. Co., Peoples Energy Corp. Contbr. articles to tech. jours.; patentee in field. Served with USNR, 1944-45. Named Oak Brook Bus. Leader of Yr., 1986, Disting. Bus. Leader DuPage County, 1988; Alumni fellow Pa. State U., 1977. Fellow Am. Soc. Metals (disting. life mem. 1982, trustee, Pitts. Nite lectr. 1970, Andrew Carnegie lectr. 1976; David Ford McFarland award Penn State chpt. 1973); mem. AIME, Assn. Iron and Steel Engrs., Metals Powder Industry Fedn., Phi Beta Kappa, Sigma Xi, Tau Beta Pi. Clubs: Duquesne, St. Clair Country (Pitts.); Univ., Congl., Burning Tree, Carlton (Washington); Chgo. Golf, Chgo., Butler Nat. Golf, Commercial (Chgo.); Laurel Valley, Rolling Rock (Ligonier, Pa.).

LANGENHEIM, ROGER ALLEN, lawyer; b. Seward, Neb., Feb. 21, 1935; s. Elmer L. and Esther L. (Gerkensmeyer) L.; B.S., U. Nebr., 1957, LL.B., 1960; m. Susan C. McMichael, Aug. 31, 1963; children—Ann Elizabeth, Mark Allen, Sara Ann. Admitted to Nebr. bar, 1960, Mo. bar, 1960; asso. firm Stinson, Mag, Thomson, McEvers & Fizzell, Kansas City, Mo., 1960-66; v.p., gen. counsel Black, Sivalls & Bryson, Inc., Kansas City, Mo., 1966-70; internat. atty. Dresser Industries, Inc., Dallas, 1970-71; group counsel Petroleum & Mineral Group, Houston, 1971-75; v.p., gen. counsel Oilfield Products Group, Houston, 1975-80; v.p., gen. counsel Magcobar Group, Houston, 1980-85; assoc. gen. counsel Dresser Industries Inc., Houston, 1985-87, sr. assoc. gen. counsel, 1987—. Mem. ABA, Nebr. Bar Assn., Mo. Bar Assn., Order of Coif. Republican. Roman Catholic. Clubs: Houston Petroleum, Elks. Editor U. Neb. Law Rev., 1958-59. Home: 6408 Wickerwood Dallas TX 75248 Office: 1600 Pacific Dallas TX 75201

LANGER, WILLIAM RICHARD, financial services executive, investment consultant; b. South Bend, Wash., Feb. 18, 1940; s. Otto Frank and Josephine (Randal) L.; m. Karren Lynn Nov. 7, 1964; children: Shelby Lynn, Brett Richard. AD in Acctg., Oreg. Inst. Tech., 1963; BS in Fin., Ariz. State U., 1977. Internal audit mgr. Arcoa Internat., Phoenix, 1963-67, controller, 1967-73, pres., 1973-77; office mgr. Wilhelm Trucking Co., Portland, 1977-81; dist. mgr. Waddell & Reed, Inc., Portland, 1981-85; div. mgr., Portland, 1985— . Bd. dirs. Williamette Tariff Bur., Portland, 1978-80; treas. U-Haul Fed. Credit Union, Phoenix, 1963-68, pres., 1968-73. Mem. Am. Assn. Individual Investors, Internat. Platform Assn., Inst. Internal Auditors, Am. Mgmt. Assn. Democrat. Home: 285 NW 87th Ave Portland OR 97229 Office: Waddell & Reed Inc 8625 SW Cascade Ave Ste 290 Beaverton OR 97005

LANGFIELD, RAYMOND LEE, real estate developer; b. Houtzdale, Pa., Jan. 31, 1921; s. Arthur A. and Sadie L. (Morris) L.; m. Helen Deborah Elion, Oct. 15, 1952; 1 child, Joanna Langfield Rose. BS in Indsl. Engring.,

Pa. State U., 1942. Registered profl. engr., Conn. Chief mgmt. engr. CIT Fin. Corp., N.Y.C., 1947-50; v.p. Mosler Safe Co., N.Y.C., 1950-60; pres. Spicer Fuel Co., Groton, Conn., 1960-86, United Fuel Corp., Groton, Conn., 1962-86, Spicer Gas Co., Groton, Conn., 1962-86, Conn. Hotel Corp., New London, Conn., 1980-84; bd. dirs. New London (Conn.) Fed. Savs. and Loan, Bank of Mystic (Conn.). Mem. Conn. Energy Adv. Bd., Hartford, 1985-87; pres. Garde Arts Ctr., New London, 1985-87. Mem. Southeast Conn. C. of C. (bd. dirs., chmn. bd. 1978-80), Ind. Conn. Petroleum Assn. (chmn. bd. 1973-74, Oil Man of Yr., 1975), New Eng. Fuel Inst. (bd. dirs. 1972-84), Navy League Conn. (bd. dirs. 1985-87). Democrat. Jewish. Home: 7594 Elmridge Dr Boca Raton FL 33433 Office: Conn Hotel Corp 300 Captain's Walk New London CT 06320

LANGFORD, DEAN TED, electrical products company executive; b. Princeton, Ill., June 19, 1939; s. Claude Robert and Dorothy Aeileen (Tuckerman) L.; m. Nancy Hirsch; 1 child, Douglas T. B.S. in Math. and Aero. Engring., U. Ill., 1962. Regional sales mgr. IBM-N.E. Region, Westport, Conn., 1980-81, corp. dir. mgmt. devel., Armonk, N.Y., 1981-82, group dir., communications, Ryebrook, N.Y., 1982-83; v.p. mktg. GTE Communications Systems, Stamford, Conn., 1983-84; pres. GTE Elec. Products, Danvers, Mass., 1984—. Mem. bd. advisers Sch. Engring., U. Ill.-Chgo., 1984—; mem. adv. bd. Northeastern U., 1984; trustee Civic Edn. Found. Lincoln-Filene Ctr., Tufts U. Mem. U. Ill. Alumni Assn. (bd. dirs.) Club: Salem Country. Avocations: biking, golf, racquetball, squash, skiing. Home: 29 Fairfield Boston MA 02116 Office: GTE Products Corp 100 Endicott St Danvers MA 01923

LANGFORD, GERALD TALMADGE, oil company executive; b. Kilgore, Tex., Jan. 13, 1935; s. DeWitt Talmadge and Lillian (Easterling) L.; m. Ora Kay Hess; children: Cheryl Kay, Randall DeWitt, Robin Leigh, David Larkin, Matthew Talmadge, Mary Camille. Student, Southwestern U., Georgetown, Tex., 1952-53; BS in Geology, U. Tex., 1957. Pres. Tex-L Exploration Corp., Longview, Tex., 1958-63, Cal-L Exploration Corp., Santa Barbara, Calif., 1964-69, Sabre Exploration Corp., Dallas, 1969-80, Condor Energy Corp., Dallas, 1981-82, DH&L Exploration Corp., Houston, 1982-83; cons. Sunbelt Energy Co., Dallas, 1983—; also bd. dirs. Seabelt Energy Co., Dallas; cons. various other cos., Dallas; bd. dirs. Solar Corp., Norco, La. Contbr. articles to profl. jours. Home and Office: 13900 Hillcrest Rd Dallas TX 75240

LANGFORD, JOHN WILLIAM, logistics and systems engineer, educator; b. Carrollton, Ky., Dec. 9, 1932; s. Audley Delbert and Marguerite Bland (Campbell) L.; m. Margery Ann Staley, Jan. 24, 1955; children—Mary Elizabeth, Margaret Carole, Dirk William. B.S. in Indsl. Engring., Ga. Inst. Tech., 1954; M.S. in Logistics Mgmt., Air Force Inst. Tech., Dayton, Ohio, 1965. Cert. profl. logistician, engr., Va. Commd. lt. U.S. Air Force, 1955, advanced through grades to lt. col., 1980; planning officer U.S. So. Command, Panama Canal Zone, 1968-71; asst. for logistics Hdqrs., U.S. Air Force, Pentagon, 1973-75; advisor to Shah of Iran, Imperial Command Staff, Tehran, 1976-78; ret., 1980; cons. in mgmt., Dept. Energy, Washington, 1980-82; mgr. marine services U.S. Navy, ERC Internat., Vienna, Va., 1982—; cons. edn. Dept. Def., Washington, 1983—; sr. assoc. Bus. Mgmt. Research, Arlington, Va., 1980—; prof. logistics engring. Fla. Inst. Tech., Melbourne, 1983—, George Mason U., Fairfax, Va., 1983—. Author: Air University Report: Defense Contract Profits, 1965; Air War College Report: Brazil Air Force Logistics, 1975; Author, editor series on logistics and systems engring. Soc. of Logistics Engrs. newsletter, 1983—; author, seminar Compendium of Quantitative Logistics Mathematical Methodologies, Third Internat. Logistics Congress, Florence, Italy, 1987, Fifth Internat. Logistics Congress, London, 1989, tutorial workshop compendium on Reliability, Maintainability, Availability, Fifth Internat. Logistics Engring. Congress, London, 1989. Decorated Air Force Commendation medal, Joint Service Commendation medal Dept. Def., Meritorious Service medal. Mem. Smithsonian Instn. (assoc.), Nat. Trust Hist. Preservation (Capital region assoc.), Am. Film Inst., Nat. Contract Mgmt. Assn., Royal Oak Found. (British Nat. Trust), Ky. Historical Soc., Inst. Indsl. Engrs., Soc. Logistics Engrs. (Forrest Waller award, tech. vice-chmn. 1987—), Ret. Officers Assn., U.S. Naval Inst., Ky. Hist. Soc., Royal Oak Found. Republican. Club: Westwood Country (Vienna) Lodges: Masons, Scottish Rites. Avocations: numismatics, military history, foreign languages, golf, woodworking. Home: 1900 Alto Ct Vienna VA 22182 Office: Evaluation Rsch Corp Internat 1725 Jefferson Davis Hwy Crystal Sq 2 Ste 300 Arlington VA 22202

LANGLEY, ELLIS BRADFORD, retired utility company executive; b. Denver, Aug. 10, 1923; s. Ellis Bradford and Margaret M. (McElroy) L.; m. Lee Ann Ballantyne, Sept. 15, 1945; children: Terrance, Susan, David and Thomas (twins). AA in Acctg., Hartnell Coll., Salinas, Calif.; MBA, St. Mary's Coll., Moraga, Calif., 1979. Comml. mgr. Pacific Gas & Electric Co., Eureka, Calif., 1961-64; sales mgr. Pacific Gas & Electric Co., San Rafael, Calif., 1964-65; div. mgr. Pacific Gas & Electric Co., Chico, Calif., 1965-67, San Jose, Calif., 1967-72; v.p. div. ops. Pacific Gas & Electric Co., San Francisco, 1972-79, sr. v.p. ops., 1979-88, exec. v.p., pres., gen. mgr. distbn., 1988. Mem. exec. bd. dirs. San Francisco Bay area council Boy Scouts Am. Served to capt. USAAF, 1942-45. Mem. Pacific Coast Electrical Assn. (pres. 1987-88, bd. dirs.), Pacific Coast Gas Assn., Engrs. Club San Francisco (bd. dirs.). Home: 137 Derby Ln Moraga CA 94129 Office: Pacific Gas & Electric Co 245 Market St San Francisco CA 94106

LANGLEY, EUGENE LOYLE, telecommunications company executive; b. Beaver, Okla., Aug. 23, 1924; s. Frank and Mable L.; m. Alena D. Jones; children: Larry, Danny F. Student, U. Wyo., 1943, U. Kans., 1963, NYU, 1968, Columbia U., 1973. With GTE Southwest, Inc., San Angelo, Tex., 1946-61, pres., 1981—; gen. plant mgr. Gen. Telephone Co. of Pa., Erie, 1961-65; v.p. ops. Gen. Telephone Co. of Fla., Tampa, 1965-74; pres. Gen. Telephone Co. of Ky., Lexington, 1974-78, Gen. Telephone Co. of S.E., Durham, N.C., 1978-81; bd. dirs. Tex. Commerce Bank, San Angelo, GTE Data Services Inc.; chmn. bd. Tex. Telephone Assn., Austin. Bd. visitors Duke U., 1979-85; mem. Dallas Citizens Council, 1983—; mem. exec. bd. Circle Ten council Boy Scouts Am., 1983, sustaning membership chmn. 1987; bd. dirs. United Way of Met. Dallas, 1988—; mem. nominating com. Tex. Research League; mem. regional high tech. programs com., chmn. bd. dirs. North Tex. Commn., 1987-88; chmn. Water for Tex. Future Task Force, 1985. Served with Signal Corps U.S. Army, 1942-46. Recipient Silver Beaver award Boy Scouts Am., 1971. Mem. Tex. Acad. of Math. and Sci. Adv. Bd. Republican. Presbyterian. Clubs: Country (San Angelo), Bentwood Country (San Angelo); Las Colinas Country, La Cima (Irving, Tex.); Pinnacle (Dallas). Lodge: Masons. Office: GTE SW Inc 2701 S Johnson St San Angelo TX 76904

LANGLINAIS, CHARLES EDWARD, land resources consultant; b. Lafayette, La., Aug. 14, 1949; s. Charles K. and Sylvia (LeBlanc) L.; m. Carolyn Gondron, June 15, 1981; children: David C., Margaret. Student, U. Southwestern La., 1967-74. Cons. Broussard, La., 1976—; co-owner Allied Svcs. Lafayette, Cajun Express, Cypress Land Devel. Co., J.G.L. Inc., L.C. Gauthier Estate Inc.; agt./mgr. Langlinais Properties, Ivy Properties. cons. on minerals Broussard City Council; co-chmn. project Beausoleil; spl. agt. La. Dept. Wildlife and Fisheries; aux. policeman Town of Broussard; cert. peace officer; chmn. citizens adv. com. Enterprise Zone Program, Econs. Devel., Broussard Mineral Com., Broussard Land Use Com.; mem. Broussard Town Council, 1987—. With USNR, 1969-71. Home and Office: 612 W Main St Broussard LA 70518

LANGLOIS, MICHAEL A(RTHUR), brokerage house executive; b. Springfield, Mass., July 4, 1956; s. Arthur Edward and Maria (Duchesneau) L.; m. Sandra R. Almonte May 19, 1979; children: Michelle, Jeffrey. BBA, Bryant Coll., 1978, MBA, 1982. Mfg. supr. Browne & Sharpe, Inc., North Kingstown, R.I., 1978-81; gen. mgr. N.H. Ball Bearing Inc., Peterborough, 1981-84; registered rep. Waddell & Reed, Inc., Cranston, R.I., 1982-86, dist. mgr., 1986-88; devel. mgr. Monarch Fin. Group, Providence, 1988—; pres. Langlois & Assoc., Cranston, 1988—; lectr. N.H. Coll. Personal Fin., Bryant Coll. Contbr. articles on personal fin. and retirement planning to profl. jours. Mem. Nat. Assn. Securities Dealers, Nat. Assn. Life Underwriters, Am. Arbitration Assn. (arbitrator), Am. Assn. Individual Investors, Internat. Assn. Fin. Planning, Internat. Assn. Registered Fin. Planners, Internat. Bd. Cert. Fin. Planners, Nat. Assn. Estate Planners. Republican. Roman Catholic. Home: 93 Hope Hill Terr Cranston RI 02921 Office: Langlois & Assocs Fin 121 Phenix Ave Cranston RI 02920

LANHAM, LOGAN EVERETT, electric utility executive; b. Ashland, Nebr., Aug. 23, 1926; s. Logan Everett and Rhetta Edna (Armstrong) L.; m. Mary Evelyn Hixson, Sept. 24, 1950; children: Carl Everett, Cynthia Jo, Lisa Marie. BA in Econs., Coll. Idaho, 1952. With Idaho Power Co., 1945—; successively groundman and journeyman lineman Idaho Power Co., Payette; comml. and indsl. sales Idaho Power Co., Ontario, Oreg.; dir. pub. affairs Idaho Power Co., Boise, 1963-74, v.p. pub. affairs, 1974-83, sr. v.p. pub. affairs, 1983—; mem. adv. bd. Bur. Land Mgmt., Boise, 1985; chmn. Idaho Hwy. Users, Boise, 1987. Mem. Pacific N.W. Waterways Assn. (pres. 1982-84), N.W. Electric Light and Power Assn. (chmn. pub. relations 1987), Boise C. of C., Ontario Golf Assn. (pres. 1960-62). Republican. Clubs: Hillcrest Country, Arid (Boise). Lodges: Masons (master 1961, grand high priest, Outstanding Royal Arch Mason Oreg. 1962), KT. Office: Idaho Power Co 1220 W Idaho St Boise ID 83707

LANIAK, DAVID KONSTANTYN, utility company executive; b. Rochester, N.Y., Sept. 10, 1935; s. Konstantyn and Anastasia (Andrieve) L.; m. Carol Hammond, Sept. 19, 1959; children: Mark, Todd. BEE, Rochester Inst. Tech., 1958; MBA, U. Rochester, 1985. Elec. engr. Rochester Gas and Electric Corp., 1959-75, supt. meter dept., 1975-78, div. supt., 1978-80, v.p. electric system planning, operation, 1980-82, v.p. corp. planning, 1982-87, sr. v.p. gas, electric distbn., corp. planning, 1988—; bd. dirs. Empire State Energy Rsch. Corp., Telog Instruments, INc., Paralogix Corp. ACC Corp. Mem. IEEE, Rochester Engring. Soc. Republican. Club: Chemists (N.Y.C.). Home: 10 Harvest Ln Rush NY 14543 Office: Rochester Gas & Electric Corp 89 East Ave Rochester NY 14649

LANIER, ANTHONY MUSGRAVE, financial executive; b. Rio de Janeiro, Jan. 21, 1952; s. Berwick Bruce and Sonja Marie (Ethoffen) L.; m. Isabel Marie Perera Dos Santos, Mar. 15, 1974; children: Nadine Isa Maria, Philippe Miguel. Econs. degree, U. Vienna, 1975. Jr. ptnr. Interpool KG, Vienna, Austria, 1976-80; v.p. internat. DRG Internat. 2 Inc., London, 1980-82; v.p. comml. loans DRG Fin. Corp., Washington, 1982-87; prin. Eastbanc Inc., Washington, 1988—; bd. dirs. Whittington Am., Inc., Del. Mem. Mortgage Bankers Assn., Royal Automobile Club (London), Pall Mall Club (LLondon). Roman Catholic. Office: Eastbanc Inc 915 15th St NW Washington DC 20007

LANIER, CHARLES BEDINGFIELD, JR., district manager; b. Athens, Ga., Oct. 8, 1948; s. Charles B. and Daphne (Smith) L.; m. Susan Warwick, June 6, 1971; children: Elizabeth W., Charles B. III. BBA, U. Ga., 1971; MBA, Augusta Coll., 1979. Cert. fin. planner. Asst. v.p. Citizens and So. Nat. Bank, Augusta, Ga., 1975-85; fin. planner Richard Young Assocs. Ltd., Augusta, 1985-86, The New Eng., Augusta, 1986—. Cubmaster Boy Scouts Am., Augusta, 1986-89; bd. dirs. Jr. Achievement, 1982-86, Augusta Ballet, Inc., 1987-88. 1st lt. U.S. Army, 1972-75, maj. USAR, 1975—. Mem. Internat. Assn. Fin. Planning (chpt. pres. 1986-87, S.E. regional council rep. 1987-88), Inst. Cert. Fin. Planners, Res. Officers Assn. (treas. 1982-86, Outstanding Jr. Officer State of Ga. 1984), Pinnacle, Kiwanis. Republican. Methodist. Home: 3109 Exeter Rd Augusta GA 30909 Office: The New Eng 614 Wheeler Executive Ctr Augusta GA 30909

LANIER, JAMES OLANDA, lawyer, banker, state legislator; b. Newbern, Tenn., Sept. 8, 1931; s. James P. and Robbye S. L.; m. Carolyn Holland, June 1, 1950; children: James E., Kay Lanier Berkley, Amy Lanier Whitnel. BS, Memphis State U., 1955, JD, 1969. Bar: Tenn. 1969, U.S. Ct. Appeals (6th cir.) 1969, U.S. Supreme Ct. 1975. Prin., James O. Lanier & Assocs., Dyersburg, Tenn., 1969—; apptd. dist. pub. defender 29th Jud. Dist. Tenn., 1987—; pres. Freightmasters, Inc., Union City, Tenn., Dyer County atty., 1973-79, 83—; pres., chmn. bd. Dukedom Bank, Dukedom, Tenn., 1979-82; pub. defender 29th Judicial Dist. of State of Tenn., 1987—; chmn., hearing officer Tenn. Malpractice Rev. Bd. Commr. Dyer County Levee and Drainage Dist., Dyersburg; chief referee Dyer County Juvenile Ct., 1984—; mem. Tenn. Ho. of Reps., 1959-63, 69-81, Ho. of Dels., 1983—; chmn. Com. on Legis., 1985—, Tenn. Tollway Authority, 1975-79; statewide campaign coordinator Gov. Lamar Alexander, 1978; chmn. 8th Congl. Dist. Dem. Convention, 1972; dir. Memphis State U. Nat. Alumni Assn., 1976-80; appointed dist. pub. defender 29th Jud. Dist., State of Tenn., 1987—. Mem. Dyer County Bar Assn., Tenn. Bar Assn. (del.), ABA, Am. Trial Lawyers Assn., Tenn. Trial Lawyers Assn., Tenn. Assn. of Criminal Def. Lawyers, Dyer County C. of C., Sigma Delta Kappa, Kappa Sigma. Methodist. Clubs: Dyersburg Country, Moose. Home: Rte 4 Box 349 Dyersburg TN 38024-0742 Office: 208 N Mill Ave PO Box 742 Dyersburg TN 38024

LANIER, JOSEPH LAMAR, JR., textile company executive; b. Lanett, Ala., Feb. 9, 1932; s. Joseph Lamar and Lura Brown (Fowlkes) L.; m. Ann Morgan, Aug. 21, 1954; children: Joseph Lamar III, Ann M. B.S., Washington and Lee U., 1954; student, Harvard Grad. Sch. Bus., 1954-55. Asst. mgr. Fairfax Mill West Point-Pepperell, Inc., 1958-62, corp. v.p., 1962-64, v.p. new product planning devel. ops., 1964-66, v.p. mfg. indsl. fabrics div., 1966-68, pres. indsl. fabrics div., dir., 1968-70, corporate exec. v.p., 1970-74, pres., 1974-79, pres., chief operating officer, 1975-79, chmn. bd., chief exec. officer, dir., 1979-89; dir. Textile Hall Corp., Flower Industries, Inc., Trust Co. Ga. (now Suntrust Banks), Torchmark Corp. Trustee LaGrange Coll. Served to 1st lt. U.S. Army, 1955-57. Mem. Am. Textile Mfrs. Inst. (bd. dirs.). Address: PO Box 610 802 3d Ave West Point GA 31833 *

LANIER, THOMAS, chemical and export company executive; b. Cienfuegos, Cuba, Sept. 18, 1923; came to U.S., 1938; s. Joseph and Irene (Medina) L.; m. Anne Marie Maillot, Apr. 1, 1973 (div. Feb. 1978); children: Margie, Robert, George, Thomas Emil. Student, Bowens Bus. Coll., 1939-40, Latin Am. Inst., 1940-41; BBA, Havana U., 1948; postgrad., St. Mary's U., San Antonio, 1955. Mgr. sales Joskes of Tex., San Antonio, 1949-51; mgr. office investment corp. San Antonio, 1951-55; v.p. internat. sales Sun-X Internat. Export Corp., San Antonio, 1955-59; pres. Sun-X Internat. Ltd., Houston, 1963-66; pres., mgr. Tri-X Internat. Co., North Bergen, 1963—; pres., chief exec. officer Lanier Shipping Co., Inc., North Bergen, N.J., 1966-87; internat. trade cons. Falor Assocs. Inc., North Bergen, 1987—, Factory Assocs. & Exporters, East Hanover, N.J., 1987—. Served with USAF, 1943-45. Recipient E award U.S. Govt., 1963. Mem. Am. Soc. Internat. Execs., C. of C. of Shipping (pres. North Bergen 1982-88), Bogota (N.J.) Tenants Assn., Am. Radio Relay League. Democrat. Roman Catholic. Office: Tri-X Internat Co 7500 Bergenline Ave North Bergen NJ 07047

LANIGAN, KEVIN JOHN, vitamin manufacturing executive; b. N.Y.C., Nov. 6, 1946; s. John Joseph and Anne Veronica (Keneally) L.; m. Peggy Ann Rebak, Dec. 28, 1968; children: Brian Michael, Kerry Colleen. BS in Engring., Cath. U. Am., 1968; MS in Computer Sci., U. So. Calif., 1970, MBA, 1973. Sr. engr. Rockwell Internat., Los Angeles, 1968-70; systems analyst Litton Systems, Data Systems, Van Nuys, Calif., 1970-73; product mgr. P. Leiner & Sons, Compton, Calif., 1973-75; dir. ops. P. Leiner & Sons, Torrance, Calif., 1975-79; v.p. ops. P. Leiner Nutritional Products, Torrance, 1979-86, sr. v.p. ops. planning, 1986—. Mem. Assn. Prodn. and Inventory Control. Republican. Roman Catholic. Clubs: San Pedro YMCA (Calif.); Palos Verdes High Sch. Booster (Calif.) (trustee). Office: P Leiner Nutritional Products 1845 W 205th St Torrance CA 90501

LANIGAN, ROBERT J., packaging company executive; b. Bklyn., Apr. 26, 1928; s. John F. and Katherine (Sheehy) L.; m. Mary Elizabeth McCormick, Dec. 30, 1950; children—J. Kenneth, Betty Jane Lanigan Snavely, Kathryn Ann Lanigan Pilewskie, Jeanne Marie Lanigan Schafer, Suzanne Marie Lanigan Georgetti. A.B. in Econs., St. Francis Coll., N.Y.C., 1950; B.A. (hon.), Nathaniel Hawthorne Coll., Antrim, N.H., 1979. Pres. domestic ops. Owens-Ill., Inc., Toledo, 1976-79, pres. internat. ops., 1979-82, pres., 1982-86, chief operating officer, 1982-84, chmn. bd., chief exec. officer, 1984—; dir. Chrysler Corp., Detroit, Toledo Trust Co., Sonat, Inc., Birmingham, Ala., Dun & Bradstreet Corp., N.Y.C. Trustee Toledo Symphony Orch., Toledo Mus. Art; bd. dirs. United Way Greater Toledo. Recipient achievement award St. Francis Coll. Alumni Assn., 1980. Mem. Beer Inst. (assoc. dir.). Roman Catholic. Clubs: Muirfield Village (Dublin, Ohio); Burning Tree (Bethesda, Md.). Home: 6206 Valley Park Dr Toledo OH 43623 Office: Owens-Ill Inc 1 Seagate Toledo OH 43666

LANIS, VIOLET ANN, business educator; b. Gary, Ind., Sept. 10, 1948; d. Steve and Danica (Arbutina) Bayus; m. Barry S. Lanis, Dec. 1, 1973. BS, Ball State U., 1970, MEd, 1972. Tchr. Thornton Twp High Schs., Harvey, Ill., 1970-73; lectr. Katharine Gibbs Secretarial Sch., Norwalk, Conn., 1974-78, Sacred Heart U., Bridgeport, Conn., 1974-79; adj. asst. prof. U. Bridgeport, 1974-81; tchr. Darien (Conn.) Pub. Schs., 1981-83; instr. Norwalk Community Coll., 1983-87, Dekalb Coll., Dunwoody, Ga., 1988—. Author secretarial procedures manual, 1979. Mem. NEA, Norwalk J. Women's Club (v.p. 1980-81), Delta Pi Epsilon. Roman Catholic. Home: 2605 Holcomb Springs Dr Alpharetta GA 30201 Office: Dekalb Coll 2101 Womack Rd Dunwoody GA 30338

LANKFORD, MARIE JO-ANN (MARIE JO-ANN PURTLE), insurance executive; b. Tampa, Fla., Aug. 18, 1938; d. Charles C. and Jennie (Boromei) Mirabella; m. William D. Lankford, Aug. 9, 1958 (div. 1973); children—William D., John Anthony, Billy Andrew; m. Glynn Ray Purtle, Dec. 3, 1983. B.S. summa cum laude, U. Tampa, 1958; cert. Educable Mentally Retarded Edn., U. Ky., 1969; M.S., E. Tex. State U., 1973, postgrad., 1972-73; postgrad. Midwestern State U., 1971-72. Lic. ins. agt.; cert. securities dealer. Tchr. Washington, Germany, Tampa, Lexington, Ky., 1958-70; tchr. spl. edn. Wichita Falls, Tex., 1970-77; tchr. adult basic edn., Wichita Falls, 1977-79; gen. agt. State Mut. Life Assurance Co. Am., Wichita Falls, 1981—; prin. Marie Lankford & Assocs., Wichita Falls, 1981—; assoc. Professional Ins., Wichita Falls, 1986—. Author articles, monograph on spl. edn. Dir. rehab. Beacon Lighthouse for the Blind, 1977-79, co-founder evaluation and tng. procedures; v.p. Wichital Falls chpt. Kidney Found. Mem. Lone Star Leaders; fed. govt. scholar, 1971-73; Wichita Falls City Council of PTAs scholar, 1973-74; named Outstanding Educator in Tex., 1974; recipient Pioneer award, State Mut. Life Assurance Co., 1982; mem. Inner Circle Club, 1983-85; recipient Nat. Quality award, 1985, Health Ins. Quality award, 1985, Nat. Sales Achievement award, 1985. Mem. Nat. Assn. Life Underwriters, Nat. Women's Life Underwriters, Am. Profl. Bus. Women, Wichita Falls Assn. Life I Underwriters (pres. 1983-84), Life Underwriters Assn. (bd. dirs.), University Club (exec. bd.), Sr.-Jr. Woman's Symphony. Methodist. Office: Advanced Security Planning 1401 Holliday Ste 216 Wichita Falls TX 76301

LANNA, ROBERT ARTHUR, insurance executive; b. Yonkers, N.Y., Sept. 22, 1934; s. Ettore and Clelia F. (Fornelli) L.; B.S., Hartwick Coll., 1958; postgrad. Sacred Heart U., 1979—; m. Catherine F. Russo, June 15, 1957; children—Christopher Joseph, Susan Mary, John Anthony. With Glens Falls Ins. Co. (N.Y.), 1958-65, agy. supt., 1961-62, mgr., 1962-65; v.p. Dowler Agy. Inc., Hempstead and Rockville Centre, N.Y., 1965-74, pres., 1974-77; v.p. Rollins, Burdick, Hunter of N.Y., Inc., Rockville Centre, 1977-79, sr. v.p., 1979-80, sr. v.p., sr. account adv., N.Y.C., 1980—, dir., 1979—; v.p. mktg. Home Ins. Co., 1981-85; pres. Personal Fin. Services Inc., 1985—; regional v.p. N/E ISU/Insuror Group.; underwriting mem. Lloyds of London. Commr., City-wide Little League Baseball, Nashville, 1963; pres. Hempstead (N.Y.) Community Chest, 1971; bd. dirs. N.E. Nassau Psychiat. Hosp., 1974; bd. dirs., v.p. ABC Inc. of New Canaan ; founder, pres. Concerned Citizens Party of Rockville Centre, 1972-74; chmn. bd. Coalition of Voluntary Community Mental Health Agys. Nassau County Inc., 1975; pres. Mental Health Assn. Nassau County, Inc., 1976-80; nat. chmn. ann. alumni fund Hartwick Coll., Oneonta, N.Y., 1979-80; trustee St. Michael's Coll., Winooski, Vt., 1983—. Served with U.S. Army, 1952-54; Korea. Recipient Community Service award Nashville Jaycees, 1963; Brotherhood award Hempstead service clubs, 1971; Man of Yr. award Mental Health Assn. Nassau County, 1980. Mem. Internat. Platform Assn. Republican. Roman Catholic. Club: Lake (New Canaan, Conn.). Home: 737 Carter St New Canaan CT 06840 Office: 65 Locust Ave New Canaan CT 06840

LANNAMANN, RICHARD STUART, executive recruiting consultant; b. Cin., Sept. 4, 1947; s. Frank E. and Grace I. (Tomlinson) L.; A.B. in Econs., Yale U., 1969; M.B.A., Harvard U., 1973; m. Margaret Appleton Payne, June 21, 1969; children—Thomas Cleveland, Edward Payne, John Stewart. Investment analyst U.S. Trust Co. N.Y., N.Y.C., 1969-71; research analyst Smith, Barney & Co., N.Y.C., 1973-75, 2d v.p., 1975-77, v.p. successor firm research div. Smith Barney Harris Upham & Co., 1977-78; v.p. Russell Reynolds Assocs., Inc., N.Y.C., 1978-83, mng. dir. 1983-86, 87—; sr. v.p. Mgmt. Asset Corp., Westport, Conn., 1986-87. Mem. N.Y. Soc. Security Analysts, Fin. Analysts Fedn., Inst. Chartered Fin. Analysts. Clubs: Riverside (Conn.) Yacht; Links, Yale (N.Y.C.). Home: 25 Cathlow Dr Riverside CT 06878 Office: 200 Park Ave New York NY 10166

LANNERT, ROBERT CORNELIUS, manufacturing company executive; b. Chgo., Mar. 14, 1940; s. Robert Carl and Anna Martha (Cornelius) L.; m. Kathleen A. O'Toole, July 10, 1965; children: Jacqueline, Krista, Kevin, Meredith. B.S. in Indsl. Mgmt., Purdue U., 1963; M.B.A., Northwestern U., 1967; grad. Advanced Mgmt. Program, Harvard U., 1978. With Navistar Internat. Transp. Corp. (formerly Internat. Harvester), Chgo., 1963—, staff asst. overseas fin., 1967-70; asst. mgr., treas. and controller IH Finanz AG Navistar Internat. Transp. Corp., Zurich, Switzerland, 1970-72; mgr. overseas fin. corp. hdqrs. Navistar Internat. Transp. Corp., Chgo., 1972-76, asst. treas., 1976-79; v.p., treas. Navistar Internat. Corp., Chgo., 1979—; also v.p., treas. and bd. dirs. Navistar Internat. Transp. Corp., Chgo.; v.p., bd. dirs. Harbour Assurance Co., Bermuda; bd. dirs. Harbour Assurance, London, Navistar Fin. Corp., Chgo. Mem. Fin. Mgrs. Assn. Chgo. (vice chmn.), Fin. Execs. Inst. Home: 130 N Grant Hinsdale IL 60521 Office: Navistar Internat Corp 401 N Michigan Ave Chicago IL 60611

LANNI, JOSEPH TERRENCE, hotel corporation executive; b. Los Angeles, Mar. 14, 1943; s. Anthony Warren and Mary Lucille (Leahy) L. B.S., U. So. Calif., 1965, M.B.A., 1967. Vice pres. Intervest, Inc., Los Angeles, 1967-69; treas. Republic Corp., Los Angeles, 1969-76; chief fin. officer C.W.I., Inc., Los Angeles, from 1977; now pres., chief operating officer Caesars N.J., Inc. subs. Caesars World, Inc., Atlantic City; pres., chief operating officer Caesars World, Inc., Los Angeles, 1981—; dir. OnLine Distributed Processing Co. Author: Anthology of Poetry, 1965. Bd. dirs. Holy Family Services Counseling and Adoption Agy.; bd. regents Loyola Marymount U.; active So. Calif. Civic Light Opera Assocs. Mem. Los Angeles Jr. C. of C. (dir. Century City region), Am. Mgmt. Assn., Commerce Assocs. Clubs: Bachelors; Crockfords (London), Beach (London). Office: Caesars World Inc 1801 Century Park E Ste 2600 Los Angeles CA 90067 *

LANNON, JOHN JOSEPH, energy holding company executive; b. Springfield, Ill., Apr. 8, 1937; s. Richard James and Anne (Malone) L.; m. Arlene Joan Mularski, Sept. 2, 1976; children—John Joseph, Susan Kay, Laura Colleen; stepchildren—Kurt Henry, Karen Joan, Lynne Eileen. B.S., U. Ill., 1961; M.B.A., U. Chgo., 1970. C.P.A., Ill. Tax and audit sr. Arthur Andersen & Co., Chgo., 1961-66; with No. Ill. Gas Co., 1966-84, treas., 1973-75, v.p., controller, 1975-77, v.p. central div., 1977-78, v.p., controller, 1978-83, v.p., 1983-84; v.p., controller NICOR Inc., Naperville, Ill., 1978-83, v.p., 1983-84, v.p. fin., 1984-87, sr. v.p., chief fin. officer, 1988—; dir. Chgo. Community Ventures, Inc., 1975-85, sec., 1976-85; dir. State Bank Saunemin, Ill., NICOR Oil and Gas Exploration, NICOR Marine Inc. Bd. dirs. Naperville YMCA, 1973-79, pres., 1978-79; bd. dirs. Taxpayers Fedn. Ill., 1979—, chmn., 1988—; bd. dirs. Ill. Tax Found., 1982—, chmn., 1982-84. Served with U.S. Army, 1956-58. Mem. Acctg. Rsch. Assn., Am. Gas Assn. (chmn. application acctg. prins. com. 1974-75, mem. acctg. adv. council 1982—, chmn. 1982-83), Fin. Execs. Inst., Midwest Gas Assn. (chmn. acctg. and fin. sect. 1974-75), Ill. Soc. C.P.A.'s, U. Ill. Coll. Commerce Alumni Assn. (pres. 1977-78), Chgo. Assn. Commerce and Industry, Econ. Club Chgo. Roman Catholic. Office: NICOR Inc 1700 W Ferry Rd Naperville IL 60566

LANSELLE, LEE PENN, leisure industry executive; b. Los Angeles, May 22, 1954; s. Claude Georges and Ann (Blind) L.; m. Masako Kuroda, Mar. 8, 1977; 1 child, Erika Penn. BA, Yale U., 1975; MBA, U. Mich., 1978. Mktg. research analyst Am. Hosp. Supply-Heyer Schulte, Goleta, Calif., 1978-79; asst. mgr. Tokyo Disneyland project WED Enterprises, Glendale, Calif., 1979-82; mgr. project adminstrn. Walt Disney Prodns. Japan Ltd., Tokyo, 1982-83, dir. bus. and legal affairs, 1983-85; dir. bus. affairs Disneyland Internat., Anaheim, Calif., 1985-87; v.p. adminstrn. Euro Disneyland Corp., Glendale, 1987—; sec. gen. Euro Disneyland Sarl, Paris, 1987—. Fulbright English fellow U.S.-Japan Ednl. Commn. Toyama, 1975-76. Mem.

Am. C. of C. in France. Club: Yale (Paris). Office: Euro Disneyland Sarl, 22 place de la Madeleine, 75008 Paris France

LANTZ, PHILLIP EDWARD, management consultant; b. Laramie, Wyo., Sept. 21, 1938; s. Everett Delmer and Elizabeth Mary (Stratton) L.; m. Paula Bogel, June 16, 1962; children: Kirk Edward, Eric William. BA in Math., U. Colo., 1960; MA in Math., U. Wyo., 1966; MS in Ops. Rsch., Johns Hopkins U., 1972. Grad. teaching asst. U. Wyo., Laramie, 1964-65; sr. engr. lab. applied physics Johns Hopkins U., Silver Spring, Md., 1965-70; v.p. Ops. Rsch. Inc., Silver Spring, Md., 1970-72; dir. Tetra Tech. Inc., Arlington, Va., 1972-74; pres. Systems Planning and Analysis Inc., Falls Church, Va., 1974—, also bd. dirs. Lt. USN, 1960-64. Home: 10421 Logan Dr Potomac MD 20854 Office: Systems Planning & Analysis Inc 5111 Leesburg Pike Ste 200 Falls Church VA 22041

LANYI, ALEXANDER SANDOR, rail transportation executive; b. Budapest, Hungary, Jan. 30, 1937; arrived in Can., 1957; s. Imre and Ilona (Balla) L.; m. Aniko Friedman, Aug. 16, 1964; children: Thomas, Peter, Susan. BS, Sir George Williams U., Montreal, Que., Can., 1963. Rsch. analyst CP Ltd., Montreal, 1967-69, asst. statistician, 1969-72, sr. statistician, 1972-73, mgr. costs and oper. stats., 1973-74; mgr. profit analysis CP Rail, Montreal, 1974-78, asst. dir. acctg., 1978-79, dir. profit analysis and devel., 1979-80, asst. contr. devel., 1980-81, contr., 1981—, v.p., 1985—; bd. dirs. Toronto (Ont., Can.) Terminals Ry. Co., Shawinigan (Ont.) Ry. Co. Mem. Assn. Am. R.R.s (chmn. acctg. div. 1987). Office: CP Rail, PO Box 6042, Sta A, Montreal, PQ Canada H3C 3E4

LANZ, ROBERT FRANCIS, corporate financial officer; b. Greenwich, Conn., Oct. 30, 1942; s. John Edwin and Katheryn Loretto (Jerman) L.; m. Elizabeth Kienlen, Nov. 11, 1967; children—Christopher, Jennifer. B.A., LaSalle Coll., Phila., 1964; postgrad., Law Sch., Fordham U., 1966-67; M.B.A., U. Conn., 1975. Corp. trust officer Chase Manhattan Bank, N.Y.C., 1966-71; cons. Stone & Webster, N.Y.C., 1971; sr. cons. EBASCO Services, N.Y.C., 1971-73; v.p., treas. Pacific/Corp., Inc., Portland, Oreg., 1973—; treas. Pacific/Corp., Inc., 1985—; sr. v.p. Pacific/Corp. Credit, Inc., Portland, Oreg., 1986—; pres. Willamette Devel. Corp. Mem. legal budget com. City of Lake Oswego, Oreg., 1975-80. Served with U.S. Army, 1964-66. Mem. Edison electric Inst. (fin. com. 1980-85), Northwest Electric Light and Power Assn. Democrat. Roman Catholic. Home: 17351 Canyon Dr Lake Oswego OR 97034 Office: Pacificorp 851 SW 6th Ave Portland OR 97204

LANZA, FRANK C., electronics executive; b. 1931. BS, Heralds Engring. Coll., 1956. Project engr. Philco Western Devel. Labs., 1957-59; v.p. Textron Corp., Providence, 1960-72; with Loral Corp., N.Y.C., 1972—, v.p., 1973-79, exec. v.p., 1979-81, corp. pres., chief operating officer, 1981—, also bd. dirs. Served with USCG, 1953-55. Office: Loral Corp 600 Third Ave 36th Fl New York NY 10016 *

LANZAFAME, SAMUEL JAMES, manufacturing company executive; b. Canastota, N.Y., Oct. 9, 1950; s. James Charles and Sarah Ann (Aiello) L.; m. Janet Mangan, Nov. 23, 1974; children: Bethany, Erin, John. BA, Holy Cross U., 1972; MBA magna cum laude, Notre Dame U., 1974. Project coordinator Oneida (N.Y.) Ltd., 1975-76, mgr. mktg. research and bus. devel., 1977-78, corp. mgr. spl. projects, 1979-80, br. mgr. No. Ireland subsidiary, 1980-82, sr. v.p. Camden Wire subsidiary, 1983-84, pres. Camden Wire subsidiary, 1985-86, pres. corp., 1986—. Office: Oneida Ltd Adminstrn Bldg Kenwood Ave Oneida NY 13421

LANZALONE, CHARLES J(AMES), financial planner; b. Phila., May 25, 1952; s. Jerry John and Marion Louise (Walking) L.; m. Roberta Mary Ann Jordan, Oct. 14, 1978; 1 child, David Charles. CLU; chartered fin. cons.; cert. fin. planner. Sr. teller Phila. Savs. Fund Soc., 1974-79; agt. John Hancock Mut. Life, Phila., 1979-80; sales supr. John Hancock Mut. Life, Cherry Hill, N.J., 1980-83; v.p. RTD Fin. Advs., Inc., Phila., 1983—. Treas., Barclay Area Civic Assn., Cherry Hill, 1985, v.p. 1986, chmn. 1987; fellow mem. Mayor's Croft Farm Devel. Com., 1985. Mem. Internat. Assn. Fin. Planning (regional rep. 1988-89, pres. Del. Valley chpt. 1987-88, chmn. bd. 1988-89), Am. Soc. Chartered Life Underwriters (bd. dirs. South Jersey chpt. 1987), Inst. Cert. Fin. Planners. Republican. Methodist. Clubs: PC of South Jersey, Tang Soo Do Karate Acad. Home: 111 Brace Rd Cherry Hill NJ 08034 Office: RTD Fin Advisors Inc 1500 Walnut St Ste 501 Philadelphia PA 19102

LANZANO, RALPH EUGENE, civil engineer; b. N.Y.C., Dec. 26, 1926; s. Ralph and Frances (Giuliano) L.; B.C.E., NYU, 1959. Engring. aide Seelye, Stevenson, Value, Knecht, N.Y.C., 1957-58; jr. civil engr. N.Y.C. Dept. Public Works (name changed to N.Y.C. Dept. Water Resources), 1960-63, asst. civil engr., 1963-68; civil engr., 1968-71; sr. san. engr. Parsons, Brinckerhoff, Quade & Douglas, N.Y.C., 1971-72; civil engr. N.Y.C. Dept. Water Resources, 1972-77, N.Y.C. Dept. Environ. Protection, 1978—. Registered profl. engr., N.Y. Mem. ASCE, ASTM, Nat., N.Y. socs. profl. engrs., Water Pollution Control Fedn., Am. Water Works Assn., Am. Public Health Assn., Am. Fedn. Arts (sustaining), U.S. Inst. Theatre Tech., NYU Alumni Assn., Am. Nat. Theatre and Acad., Lincoln Center Performing Arts (asso.), Am. Film Inst., Nat. Rifle Assn. (life), U.S. Lawn Tennis Assn. (life), Nat., Internat. wildlife fedns., Nat. Parks and Conservation Assn., Nat. Geog. Soc., Nat. Audubon Soc., Am. Automobile Assn., Bklyn. Bot. Garden, Am. Mus. Natural History, Chi Epsilon. Home: 17 Cottage Ct Huntington Station NY 11746 Office: 40 Worth St New York NY 10013

LANZKRON, ROLF WOLFGANG, manufacturing company executive; b. Hamburg, Germany, Dec. 9, 1929; s. Aron Artur and Hanna (Farbstein) L.; came to U.S., 1951, naturalized, 1961; B.S., Milw. Sch. Engring., 1953; M.S., U. Wis., 1955, Ph.D., 1956; m. Amy Virginia Yarri, Mar. 5, 1961; children—Paul Joshua, Sophie Miriam, Lisa Rachel. Registered profl. engr. Calif. Computer designer Univac Sperry Rand, St. Paul, 1956-58; guidance and control systems integrations staff Martin Marietta, Orlando, Fla., 1958-61, systems engr., Balt. 1961-68; became chief command and service module flight project div. NASA Manned Spacecraft Center, Apollo Program, Houston, 1963; graphic ops. mgr. Raytheon Co., Sudbury, Mass., 1968-82, dep. dir. air traffic control, 1982—. Served with Israeli Army, 1948-51. Recipient NASA Outstanding Achievement award, 1964, Spl. Service award, 1966; registered profl. engr., Calif. Mem. AIAA, Am. Math. Soc., IEEE, Am. Mgmt. Assn., Sigma Xi. Home: 8 Hickory Dr Medfield MA 02052 Office: Raytheon Co Equipment Div 528 Boston Post Rd Sudbury MA 01776

LAPHAM, LEWIS ABBOT, retired banker; b. N.Y.C., Mar. 7, 1909; s. Roger Dearborn and Helen Barbara (Abbot) L.; m. Jane Aldyth Foster, Sept. 14, 1932; children: Lewis Henry, Anthony Abbot. BA, Yale U. Pres. Am. Hawaiian S.S. Co., N.Y.C., 1947-53; pres. The Grace Line, N.Y.C., 1953-59, Bankers Trust New York Co., N.Y.C., 1960-74; bd. dirs. Macmillan, Inc., N.Y.C., Tri-Continental Corp., N.Y.C., Medusa Corp., N.Y.C. Decorated Knight Order of Orange-Nassau, The Netherlands, 1983. Clubs: Links, India House (N.Y.C.); Blind Brook (Purchase, N.Y.); Cypress Point (Pebble Beach, Calif.). Home: 170 John St Greenwich CT 06830 Office: 150 E 42d St New York NY 10017 *

LAPIDUS, NORMAN ISRAEL, food broker; b. N.Y.C., July 20, 1930; s. Rueben and Laurette (Goldsmith) L.; BBA, CCNY, 1952; m. Myrna Sue Cohen, Nov. 20, 1960; children: Robin Anne, Jody Beth. Candidate M.Internat. Relations, 1956; postgrad. NYU, 1957-60. Salesman, Rueben Lapidus Co., N.Y.C., 1954-56, pres., 1960—; sales trainee Cohn-Hall-Marx, N.Y.C., 1955; salesman to v.p. Julius Levy Co., Millburn, N.J., 1964-66, pres., 1966—; salesman Harry W. Freedman Co., 1975-76, v.p., treas., 1976-84, pres., 1984—; pres. Julius Levy/Rueben Lapidus and Harry W. Freedman Cos. div. Pezrow Corp., 1985-86; pres. L&H Food Brokers, 1986-87. Recipient Leadership Medallion United Jewish Appeal, 1970, 84. Mem. Maplewood (N.J.) Bd. Adjustment, 1975-82; gen. chmn. Maplewood Citizens Budget Adv. Com., 1977-79, chmn. Maplewood United Jewish Appeal Drive, 1975-76, 83-84; vice-chmn. Maplewood First Aid Squad Bldg. Fund Dr., 1978-79; co-founder Citizens for Charter Change in Essex County (N.J.), 1974, mem. exec. bd., 1974—, treas., 1983-84; founder, chmn. Music Theatre of Maplewood; pres. Maplewood Civic Assn., 1983-85; bd. mgrs. Essex County unit Am. Cancer Soc., v.p., 1984-87; mem. adv. bd. Essex County Coll., West Essex, N.J. Served with U.S. Army, 1952-54, Korea. Mem. Nat. Food Brokers Assn. (regional dir., recipient cert. exceptionally meritorious service), Nat. Food Service Sales Com., Met. Food Brokers Assn. (chmn. 1982—), Assn. Food Industries (bd. dirs.), Nat. Food Processors Assn., Young Guard Soc., Old Guard Soc., CCNY Alumni Assn., U.S. Navy Inst., Acad. Polit. Sci., Archeol. Inst. Am., Nat. Trust for Historic Preservation, Assn. Food Distbrs., Am. Legion, LWV. Republican. Jewish. Clubs: Lions (bd. dirs.), B'nai B'rith. Active local theatricals. Home: 21 Lewis Dr Maplewood NJ 07040 Office: 11 Dunbar Rd Springfield NJ 07081

LAPIDUS, STANLEY N., high technology company executive; b. N.Y.C., Apr. 24, 2949; s. M. and F. (Pergament) L.; m. Ruth Ben-Dov, Oct. 5, 1976; children: David Joel. BEE, Cooper Union, 1970. Engr. Elscint Ltd., Haifa, Israel, 1971-76; engring. mgr. Raytheon Co., Stamford, Conn., 1976-78; pres. Gentech Systems, Inc., Merrimack, N.H., 1979-82; chmn. Itran Corp., Manchester, N.H., 1982—; bd. dirs., chmn. Automated Vision Assn., Ann Arbor, Mich. Contbr. articles to tech. pubs.; patentee image processing field. Mem. IEEE, Am. Electronics Assn. (bd. dirs. New Eng. coun. 1987-88). Republican. Jewish. Office: Itran Corp 670 N Commercial St Manchester NH 03101

LA PIERRE, PHILIPE STEPHEN, motion picture distributing company executive; b. Grenada, Oct. 16, 1938; came to U.S., 1979; s. Valantine Stephen and Veronica (Cummings) La P.; BS, Poly. of London, 1961; m. Margaret Mary Lee, Apr. 2, 1959; children: Stephen Philipe, Linda Mary. Sr. electronics engr. Rediffusion, London, Eng., 1950-76; internat. system mgr. Speywood Electronics, Wembley, Eng., 1976-79; dir. research and devel. Carib Electronics, Cocoa, Fla., 1979-80; dir. research and devel. Inflight Motion Pictures, Jamaica, N.Y., 1980—; dir. engring. Video Technology Enterprises, 1987—. Fellow Cable Engrs. U.K.; mem. Cable Engrs. U.S. Home: 330 Pennsylvania Ave Freeport NY 11520 Office: 485 Madison Ave New York NY 10022

LA PINE, ANTHONY NELSON, electrical engineer; b. Blue Island, Ill., July 8, 1942; s. Ralph and Velma (Nelson) La P.; m. Mary Pratico, Sept. 1, 1962 (div. 1980); children: Ray, Lisa, Tanya; m. Pamela Bradley, Sept. 19, 1982; children: Michael, Amy. BEE, Calif. State U., 1965; MEE, Santa Clara U., 1971; MBA, U. San Francisco, 1986. Staff engr. IBM Corp., San Jose, Calif., 1964-69; v.p., gen. mgr. Memorex Corp., Santa Clara, Calif., 1969-81; chief operating officer Irwin Magnetic Systems, Ann Arbor, Mich., 1981-83; founder, chief exec. officer LaPine Inc., Milpitas, Calif., 1983-87, Los Gatos, Calif., 1987—. Patentee in storage and retrieval technology; contbr. articles to profl. jours.; guest TV programs. Bd. dirs. Jr. Achievement. Mem. Radio Relay League. Republican. Lutheran. Office: La Pine Inc 17420 High St Los Gatos CA 95032

LAPINSKI, RICHARD ALLEN, chief financial officer; b. Sewickley, Pa., May 12, 1953; s. Stanley Joseph and Ethel Mae (Stout) L.; m. Carol Lee Snider, July 30, 1983; children: Adam, Christopher, Heather. BS in Acctg., Gannon U., 1975. Cons. Universal Scheduling Co., Bala Cynwyd, Pa., 1975; internal auditor Wood div. Scripps Howard, Monogahela, Pa., 1976-77; asst. controller Cox Broadcasting Corp./WPXI TV, Pitts., 1977-83; corp. controller Sheridan Broadcasting Corp., Pitts., 1983—, asst. sec., 1987—; bd. dirs. Sheridan Broadcasting Network. Chmn. Fellowship Christian Athletes, 1970. Mem. Nat. Assn. Accts. (treas. 1981), Nat. Assn. Broadcasters. Democrat. Roman Catholic. Clubs: Chess; YMCA. Home: 10 2 Crest Dr Monaca PA 15061 Office: Sheridan Broadcasting Corp 411 Seventh Ave Ste 1500 Pittsburgh PA 15219

LAPLANTE, CONNIE AYRES, savings and loan executive; b. Zanesville, Ohio, July 25, 1956; d. Donald Ray and Delores Eileen (Kronenbitter) Ayres; m. Peter Ellsworth LaPlante, June 27, 1979. BA in Acctg., Muskingum Coll., 1978. CPA, Ohio. With First Fed. Savs. & Loan, Zanesville, 1978—, sr. v.p., treas., 1988—. Bd. dirs. Muskingum chpt. ARC, 1984. Mem. Am. Bus. Women's Assn., AICPA, Ohio Soc. CPAs, Authors Club, Rotary. Republican. Methodist. Office: First Fed Savs & Loan Fifth & Market Sts Zanesville OH 43701

LAPLANTE, LARRY EMILE, public utility executive; b. Waterville, Maine, Apr. 4, 1951; s. Emile J. and Lucille Y. (Thebarge) LaP.; m. Annette M. Kelley, June 21, 1980; children: Jennifer, Stephen, Andrew. BS, U. Maine, 1973. CPA, Maine. Staff Chester M. Kearney & Co., Presque Isle, Maine, 1974-77; ptnr. Felch and LaPlante, Caribou, Maine, 1977-83; controller, asst. treas. sec. Maine Pub. Svc. Co., Presque Isle, 1983—; instr. Husson Coll, 1976-78, U. Maine Presque Isle, 1984. served to 1st lt. USAR 1979-81. Mem. Am. Instit. of CPA's, Maine Instit. CPA's. Independent. Roman Catholic. Lodge: Rotary (sec. Presque Isle chpt.). Home: 95 Hardy St Presque Isle ME 04769 Office: Maine Pub Svc Co 209 State St Presque Isle ME 04769

LAPMAN, MARK CHARLES, investment executive; b. Irvington, N.J., Mar. 15, 1950; s. Horace Raymond and Phylis Ruth (Gottlieb) L.; m. Helene Gale Schechner, Sept. 16, 1973; children: Peter Grant, Lisa Brooke, Beth Stacey. BA, U. Md., 1972; MA, Harvard U., 1974, PhD, 1982. Teaching fellow Harvard U., Cambridge, Mass., 1976-80; rsch. analyst Independence Investment Assocs., Boston, 1979-84, v.p., 1984-87, sr. v.p., prin., 1987—. Author: Political Denunciations in Muscovy, 1982. Mem. Fin. Analysts Fedn., Boston Security Analysts Soc., Inst. Chartered Fin. Analysts, Nat. Council on Tchr. Retirement (assoc.), Nat. Council Pub. Employee Retirement Systems. Home: 54 Clubhouse Ln Wayland MA 01778 Office: Ind Investment Assocs 1 Liberty Sq Boston MA 02109

LAPORTE, CLOYD, JR., manufacturing company executive, lawyer; b. N.Y.C., June 8, 1925; s. Cloyd and Marguerite (Raeder) L.; m. Caroline E. Berry, Jan. 22, 1949; children—Elizabeth, Marguerite, Cloyd III. A.B., Harvard, 1946, J.D., 1949. Bar: N.Y. State bar 1949. Assoc. mem. firm Cravath, Swaine & Moore, N.Y.C., 1949-56; dir. adminstrn. Metals div. Olin Corp., N.Y.C., 1957-66; legal counsel Dover Corp., N.Y.C., 1966—, sec., 1971—. Served to 2d lt. A.C. AUS, World War II. Mem. ABA., N.Y. State Bar Assn., Assn. Bar City N.Y. Clubs: Harvard (N.Y.C.); Gipsy Trail (Carmel, N.Y.). Home: 108 E 82d St New York NY 10028 Office: Dover Corp 277 Park Ave New York NY 10172

LAPORTE, ROBERT PAUL, JR., real estate executive; b. Lowell, Mass., Apr. 3, 1947; s. Robert P. and Arlene (Russell) LaP.; m. Cynthia Rae Johnson, July 30, 1978; 1 child, Joseph R. BA, St. Anselm Coll., 1969. Owner, pres. Foster Appraisal & Cons., Fitchburg, Mass., 1969-82; sr. v.p. Meredith & Grew, Boston, 1982—. Author: (with others) Appraising the Single Family Residence, 1978. Past chmn. Chemsford Hist. Dist., Mass. With U.S. Army, 1969, 71, Vietnam. Named Outstanding Young Man Am. U.S. Jaycees, 1982. Mem. Am. Inst. Real Estate Appraisers (past pres. New England chpt. 1982-83, Soc. Real Estate Appraisers, Mass. Assn. of Realtors (pub. policy com.). Home: 12 New Towne Way Chelmsford MA 01824 Office: Meredith & Gres 106 Federal St Boston MA 02110

LAQUINTA, FRED JOHN, aerospace and chemicals company executive; b. Pitts., Nov. 30, 1949; s. John Anthony and Rose Marie (Marino) L.; m. Irene B. Jaszczun, Aug. 12, 1972; children: Diana Rose, Christa Maria. BA in Econs., U. Pitts., 1971, MBA, 1972. Mgr. benefits adminstrn. Air Products and Chems., Allentown, Pa., 1972-80; benefits planner Exxon Co. U.S.A., Houston, 1980-82; dir. domestic and internat. benefits Hercules, Inc., Wilmington, Del., 1982—. Founder, past chmn. Del. Health Care Coalition, Wilmington, 1983-86; bd. dirs. Rockford Psychiatric Hosp., Wilmington, 1985-86; mem. Gov.'s Health Care Commn., Dover, Del., 1986. Served to capt. USAR, 1972-76. Mem. Council on Employee Benefits, Pen Jer Del Employee Benefit Assn. (speaker). Democrat. Roman Catholic. Home: 1027 Squires Dr West Chester PA 19382 Office: Hercules Inc Hercules Pla Wilmington DE 19894

LAREAU, RICHARD GEORGE, lawyer; b. Woonsocket, R.I., June 11, 1928; s. Hector R. and Agnes P. (Valley) L.; m. Thelma Johnson, Aug. 11, 1970; 1 son, Alan Hartland; 1 son by previous marriage, William Wheeler Mohn. BA, St. Michael's Coll., Winooski Park, Vt., 1949; JD, U. Minn., 1952. Bar: Minn. 1952. Ptnr. Oppenheimer, Wolff & Donnelly, St. Paul, Mpls., 1956—; bd. dirs. Control Data Corp., Bloomington, Minn., Nash Finch Co.; sec., bd. dirs. Merrill Corp., St. Paul 1981—, Bio-Medicus, Inc., Eden Prairie, Minn., 1982—. Sec. Minn. Cooperation Office for Small Bus. and Job Creation, Mpls.; bd. dirs. Minn. Project on Corp. Responsibility, Mpls. 1st lt. USAF, 1952-56. Mem. ABA, Mich. Bar Assn., Hennepin County Bar Assn., Mpls. Club. Home: 20750 Linwood Rd Excelsior MN 55331 Office: Oppenheimer Wolff & Donnelly 45 S 7th St Minneapolis MN 55402

LARESE, JAMES, personnel executive; b. Detroit, Aug. 4, 1955; s. Bruno and Jacqueline Ann (Conflitti) L.; m. Marilyn Jean Freda, Nov. 11, 1977; children: Andrea, James. BBA, Cen. Mich. U., 1977, MA in Indsl. Mgmt., 1979. With div. casting Ford Motor Co., Flat Rock, Mich., 1977-79, rep. labor relations Mich. Casting Ctr., 1979-80; rep. labor relations elec. and electronics div. Rawsonville, Mich., 1980-82; rep. employee relations div. car product devel. Dearborn, Mich., 1982-84, specialist compensation div. body and chassis engring., 1984-85, staff cons. employee devel. world hdqrs., 1985-87; supr. salary and fgn. services adminstrn. Ford Motor Credit Co., Dearborn, 1987-88, orgn. and personnel planner, fin. and employee rels., truck ops., 1989—. Co-author: Performance and Career Management, 1986. Mem. Am. Soc. Personnel Adminstrn., Am. Foundrymen's Soc. Republican. Roman Catholic. Office: Ford Motor Credit Co Truck Ops 22000 Oakwood Bldg 1 Dearborn MI 48121

LARGE, EDWARD W., lawyer, business executive; b. Collingswood, N.J., Mar. 9, 1930; s. Edward W. and Kathryn (Baseler) L.; m. Madeleine Sophie Redditt, Oct. 27, 1956; children—Edward, Christopher, Gregory, Gustavus, Jennifer. B.A. in Polit. Sci., Marshall U., 1953; LL.B., U. Va., 1955. Assoc. Shearman & Sterling, N.Y.C., 1955-60; staff atty. United Techs. Corp., Hartford, Conn., 1960-64, asst. corp. counsel, 1964-69, gen. counsel, 1969-70, v.p., gen. counsel, 1970-79, sr. v.p., gen. counsel, 1979-81, exec. v.p. legal and corp. affairs, 1981-86, exec. v.p. corp. devel., 1986-89; exec. v.p., spl. advisor to chmn. United Techs. Corp., Hartford, 1989—; also bd. dirs. United Techs. Corp., Hartford, Conn.; bd. dirs. United Tech. Corp., Elliott Holdings Inc., Sheller-Globe Corp. Mem. ABA, Conn. Bar Assn., Soc. for Savs., (bd. dirs. Hartford), Greater Hartford C. of C. (bd. dirs.). Home: 170 Scarborough St Hartford CT 06105 Office: United Techs Corp United Techs Bldg Hartford CT 06101

LARGE, TIMOTHY WALLACE, religious organization administrator; b. Palo Alto, Calif., Feb. 23, 1942; s. Charles Delano Henry and Jean Eleanor (Parker) L.; m. Vickie Lee Olson, Aug. 6, 1978; children: Jonathan Jeffrey, Sarah Jean. BSBA, Menlo Coll., 1964; MBA, U. Santa Clara, 1966; cert., Multnomah Sch. Bible, Portland, Oreg., 1973; M of Div., Talbot Theol. Sem., La Mirada, Calif., 1978. CPA, Calif. Acct. Bramer Accountancy Corp., Santa Fe Springs, Calif., 1974-76; instr. Biola Coll., La Mirada, Calif., 1978; acct. Conservative Bapt. Assn. So. Calif., Anaheim, 1978-83; CPA H. Canaday, P.A., Santa Fe Springs, 1983—; adminstr. Temple Baptist Ch., Perris, Calif., 1985-87; treas. Inst. Evangelico, La Puenta, Calif., 1987—; cons. Exec. Leasing, La Mirada, 1976—. Treas. Founders chpt. Kidney Found. So. Calif., Orange County, 1974-76; chaplain Christian Hosp. Med. Ctr., Perris, 1985—. Served with U.S. Army, 1965-69. Fellow Nat. Assn. Ch. Bus. Adminstrs.; mem. AICPA, Am. Mgt. Assn., Christian Ministries Mgt. Assn. Republican. Baptist. Home: 26928 Potomac Dr Sun City CA 92381 Office: 14864 Valley Blvd La Puente CA 91744

LARGENT, PARKE HOLT, program director, pharmacist; b. Tipton, Okla., Oct. 25, 1938; s. Paul and Martha Ann (Ammons) L.; m. Glenda Ann Knight, June 20, 1960; 1 child, Piper Anne. BS in Pharmacy, U. Okla., 1961, MBA, 1978. Registered pharmacist. Pharmacist Conrad-Marr Drug, Oklahoma City, 1964-68; owner Largent Drug, Oklahoma City, 1968-71; mgr. Greene's Pharmacy Norman, Okla., 1972-76, The Medicine Shoppe, Okla., 1976-78; alumni relations dir. U. Okla. Coll. of Pharmacy, Oklahoma City, 1978-80, student affairs dir., 1980-81, bus. mgr., 1981—; with Okla. Bus. Network, Oklahoma City, 1987—. Mem. adv. bd. Okla. Pharmacy Heritage Found. Lt. USAF, 1961-64. Mem. Okla. Pharm. Assn. (continuing edn. seminar 1985-87), Pharmacy Alumni Assn. (sec., treas. 1987—), Am. Soc. Pharmacy Law, Am. Inst. Hist. Pharmacy, Masons, Phi Delta Chi. Republican. Baptist. Home: 2565 Hollywood Ave Norman OK 73072 Office: U Okla Coll Pharmacy PO Box 26901 1110 N Stonewall Oklahoma City OK 73190-5040

LARIME, MICHAEL WALL, manufacturing executive; b. Pontiac, Mich., Aug. 24, 1943; s. Carl M. and Jean Elizabeth (Wall) L.; m. Barbara Swartzloff, Aug. 14, 1965; children: Christopher, Matthew. Student, U. Mich., 1961-65; BS in Chemistry, Ea. Mich. U., 1967; cert., Harvard U., 1986, George Washington U., 1974, Stanford U., 1988. Chemist Tecumseh Products Co., Ann Arbor, Mich., 1965-72; rsch. chemist Chem-Trend, Inc., Howell, Mich., 1972-76; chem. engr. Thetford Corp., Ann Arbor, 1976-77, mgr. chem. and prodn. engring., 1977-78, sr. staff engr., 1979-84, gen. mgr. sales and mktg., 1985-86, v.p. sales and mktg., 1986—. Mem. Nat. Marine Mfrs. Soc., Am. Mgmt. Assn., Recreational Vehicle Industry Assn. (mem. show com. 1988—), Am. Chem. Soc., Warehouse Distbrs. Assn. Office: Thetford Corp PO Box 1285 Ann Arbor MI 48106

LARIMER, THOMAS RAYMOND, paper company executive; b. Latrobe, Pa., Apr. 13, 1930; s. S. Raymond and Mae (Stickle) L.; married, 1960 (div. Mar. 1976); children: Peter M., Jane E.; m. Angela McDonnell, 1979. BA in Bus., Pa. State U., 1953; MBA, Xavier U., 1965. Salesman Armstrong Cork Co., Lancaster, Pa., 1954-70; product mgr. Philip Carey Co., Cin., 1970-72; group product mgr. Jim Walter Corp., Tampa, Fla., 1972-80; v.p. sales CPM Inc., Claremont, N.H., 1981-85, v.p. mktg. and planning, 1985-88; v.p. sales, mktg. The Sorg Paper Co., Middletown, Ohio, 1988—; bd. dirs. Kraft and Packaging Papers div. Am. Paper Inst., N.Y.C. Served with U.S. Army, 1950-52. Mem. TAPPI. Republican. Office: The Sorg Paper Co Middletown OH 45042

LARKAN, ROBERT PEARCE, instrumentation engineer; b. Monroe, La., May 14, 1942; s. James Michael L. Jr. and Margarette Ruth (Pearce) Berner; m. Starr Linda Hamilton, Apr. 1, 1967; children: Robert Pearce Jr., Linda Ann. BEE, La. Tech. U., 1964, MEE, 1966. Registered profl. engr., La. Start-up engr. Leeds and Northrup, North Wales, Pa., 1966-67; instrumentation engr. Houston Lighting and Power Co., 1971-74; sr. elec. engr. Ford, Bacon and Davis Inc., Monroe, 1974-81, mgr. instrumentation sect., 1984—; engring. mgr. Sunbelt Engring. Inc., West Monroe, La., 1981-82; cons. engr. Rob Larkan Co., West Monroe, La., 1982; field engr. S&W Tech. Svcs., Zachary, La., 1983-84. Lt. USN, 1967-71. Mem. IEEE, Instrument Soc. Am. (mem. nat. standards com.), La. Engring. Soc. (program chmn. 1979-80), Eta Kappa Nu, Tau Beta Pi, Kappa Alpha. Republican. Baptist. Home: 114 Wall Williams Rd West Monroe LA 71291-4754 Office: Ford Bacon and Davis Inc 4001 Jackson St Monroe LA 71202

LARKIN, STEPHEN J., transportation executive; b. N.Y.C., Aug. 20, 1949; s. Thomas G. and Helen V. (McNulty) L. (div. Nov. 1984); children: Brian, Peter. BA in Bus., Marist Coll., 1970. Account exec. Xerox Corp., N.Y.C., 1971-73; v.p. airline mktg., v.p. franchise ops. Hertz Corp., N.Y.C., 1973-80; v.p. mktg. ops. First Internat. Services Corp., Darien, Conn., 1980-82; v.p. mktg. Assocs. Comml. Corp., Chgo., 1982—. Fellow Nat. Assn. Fleet Adminstrs., Am. Automotive Leasing Assn., Truck & Trailer Renting and Leasing Assn.; mem. Cystic Fibrosis Found. Roman Catholic. Office: Assocs Comml Corp 150 N Michigan Ave Chicago IL 60601

LARKIN, THOMAS ERNEST, JR., investment management company executive; b. Wilkes-Barre, Pa., Sept. 29, 1939; s. Thomas Ernest and Margaret (Gorman) L.; BA in Econs., U. Notre Dame (Ind.), 1961; postgrad. Grad. Sch. Bus., NYU, 1962-66; m. Margaret Givan, Nov. 2, 1979; 1 son, Thomas Ernest, III. New bus. rep. Mfrs. Hanover Trust Co., 1963-66; mgr. pension dept. Eastman Dillon, Union Securities, 1966-69; v.p. Shearson Hayden Stone, Inc., N.Y.C., sr. v.p. Bernstein Macaulay Inc., N.Y.C., 1969-75; sr. v.p. Crocker Investment Mgmt. Corp., San Francisco, 1975-77, Trust Co. of the West, Los Angeles, 1977, mng. dir., 1982—, pres., chief oper. officer, 1989—, TCW Asset Mgmt. Co., L.A., 1984—. Active Calif. Pediatric Center Aux., Hancock Park Hist. Soc.; mem. adv. bd. Coll. Bus. Adminstrn. U. Notre Dame. Served with U.S. Army, 1961-63. Mem. Assn. of Investment Mgmt. Sales Execs., Internat. Fedn. Employee Benefit Plans, Investment Counsel Assn. Am. Republican. Roman Catholic. Clubs: Calif., Jonathan,

Wilshire Country, Bel Air Bay, Regency, Los Angeles Tennis, Olympic (San Francisco), N.Y. Athletic, Westchester Country. Office: 400 S Hope St Los Angeles CA 90071

LA ROCHE, MARIE-ELAINE, banking executive; b. N.Y.C., Aug. 17, 1949; d. Andre and Madeleine (Hanin) LaR. BS in Internat. Affairs, Georgetown U., 1971; MBA, Am. U., 1978. With equity sales dept. Morgan Stanely Investment Banking Co., N.Y.C., 1978-81, v.p. investment banking, 1981-84; v.p. investment banking Morgan Stanely Investment Banking Co., London, 1984-85; prin. mktg. dir. fixed income div. Morgan Stanely Investment Banking Co., N.Y.C., 1985-86, mng. dir. fixed income div., 1986—. Bd. dirs. Hosp. Chaplancy, N.Y.C. Named to YWCA Acad. Women Achievers, 1983. Mem. Forum for Women Dirs., Fin. Womens Assn. of N.Y. Republican. Roman Catholic. Office: Morgan Stanley & Co Inc 1221 Ave of the Americas New York NY 10020

LARR, PETER, banker; b. Indpls., Jan. 17, 1939; s. David and Marjorie Kathleen (Hearne) L.; m. Rosamond Holmes Woodfield, July 7, 1962; children—Alexia Aisha, Diana Kirsten, David Hearne. B.A., Princeton U., 1960. Asst. mgr. London and Beirut brs. Chase Manhattan Bank, 1961-67, v.p., div. exec. land transp., 1976-78, v.p., group exec. credit tng. and devel., 1978-80, v.p., div. exec. commodity fin., 1980-83; sr. v.p., bus. exec. nat. corr. banking Chase Manhattan Bank, N.Y.C., 1983-85; sr. v.p., exec. domestic instl. banking Chase Manhattan Bank, 1985—; assoc. Res. City Bankers, 1986. Assoc. vestry Christ Ch., Rye, N.Y., 1983-85. Mem. Assn. Res. City Bankers (bank pay systems com.), Princeton Club., Am. Yacht Club, Apawamis Club. Office: Chase Manhattan Corp 1 Chase Manhattan Pla New York NY 10081

LARSEN, PER ARNE, electronics executive, engineer; b. Bergen, Norway, Dec. 29, 1944; came to U.S., 1976; s. Sverre M. and Ingrid (Mortensen) L.; m. Ellen Zirkle, Dec. 26, 1969; children: Camilla, Siri, Julianne. BS, Bergen Tech. Coll., 1969. Prodn. mgr. Giertsen Plastikkindusti, Bergen, 1970-72, Roza Plastindustri, Bergen, 1972-74; pres. Signa Plastindustri, Bergen, 1974-76; dept. supr. Keytronic Corp., Spokane, Wash., 1976-78; mgr. tooling Keytronic Corp., Spokane, 1978-80, dir. plastic, 1980-83; v.p. offshore ops. Keytronic Corp., Rep. of China and Ireland, 1983-85; v.p. ops. Keytronic Corp., Spokane, 1986—; bd. dirs. Keytronic Europe, Ireland, Keytronic Taiwan Corp., TAipei, Rep. of China; chmn. bd. Signa Plast, Bergen. Mem. Soc. Mfg. Engrs., Soc. Plastic Engring., Norwegian-Am. C. of C., Sons of Norway. Office: Keytronic Corp N4424 Sullivan Rd Spokane WA 99216

LARSEN, RICHARD GARY, accountant; b. Tampa, Fla., Nov. 28, 1948; s. Dagfinn T. Larsen and Elizabeth M. (Koch) Thompson; m. Harriet Taylor Jones, Dec. 19, 1970; children—Jonathan Daniel, Alice Taylor. B.B.A. in Acctg., George Washington U., 1971, J.D., 1974. Bar: Va. 1974; C.P.A., Conn. Mem. staff U.S. Senate, Washington, 1967-73; ptnr. Ernst & Whinney, Washington, 1973—; adj. prof. U. Md., College Park, 1976-78, Am. U., Washington, 1977-78. Mem. Am. Inst. CPA's, ABA, Conn. Soc. CPA's, Va. Bar Assn. Clubs: City (Washington). Home: 8510 Longfellow Pl Chevy Chase MD 20815 Office: Ernst & Whinney 1225 Connecticut Ave Washington DC 20036

LARSEN, TERRANCE A., bank holding company executive. BA, U. Dallas, 1968; PhD, Tex. A&M U., 1971. With Phila. Nat. Bank, from 1977, sr. v.p., 1980-83, exec. v.p., from 1983; exec. v.p. Corestates Fin. Corp. (parent), Phila., 1983-86, pres., 1986—, chief operating officer, 1986-87, chmn., chief exec. officer, 1988—, also bd. dirs. Office: Core States Fin Corp PO Box 7618 NE Corner Broad & Chestnut Sts Philadelphia PA 19107

LARSEN, TULINDA DEEGAN, aviation economist; b. Glen Cove, N.Y., Aug. 31, 1954; d. George and Janice (Shaddock) Deegan; m. Carl B. Larsen, Sept. 25, 1982; children: Bryce, Jenny. BA in Polit. Sci. and Econs., George Washington U., 1976, MA in Econs., 1979. Economist Dept. Transp., Washington, 1975-77, Nat. Transp. Study Commn., 1977; v.p. govt. rels. Regional Airline Assn., Washington, 1977-80; pres. Alaska Air Carriers Assn., Anchorage, 1980-82; v.p. econ. analysis Airline Econs., Inc., Washington, 1987—; founder, producer Airline Video, Sterling, Va., 1988—; bd. dirs. Scheduled Airline Traffic Offices, Inc. Recipient spl. recognition Aviation Week and Space Tech., 1986, spl. commendation, FAA, 1981, cert. of appreciation, 1984. Office: Airline Econs Inc 1350 Connecticut Ave Washington DC 20036

LARSON, CHARLES FRED, association executive; b. Gary, Ind., Nov. 27, 1936; s. Charles F. and Margaret J. (Taylor) L.; m. Joan Ruth Grupe, Aug. 22, 1959; children—Gregory Paul, Laura Ann. B.S.M.E., Purdue U., 1958; M.B.A. summa cum laude, Fairleigh Dickinson U., 1973. Registered profl. engr., N.J. Project engr. Combustion Engring., Inc., East Chicago, Ind., 1958-60; sec. Welding Research Council, N.Y.C., 1960-70, asst. dir., 1970-75; editor bulls. Welding Research Abroad, 1960-75; exec. dir. Indsl. Research Inst., Inc., N.Y.C., 1975—; sec. I.R.I. Research Corp. Assoc. editor: Jour. Pressure Vessel Tech, 1973-75. Mem. Wyckoff (N.J.) Bd. Edn., 1973-78, pres., 1976-77; reader In Touch Networks, Inc., N.Y.C., 1979—; bd. dirs. Materials Properties Council. Served with U.S. Army, 1959. Fellow AAAS; mem. Am. Soc. Assn. Execs., ASME, NSPE., Assn. Research Dirs., Council Engring. and Sci. Soc. Execs., Soc. Research Adminstrs. Republican. Methodist. Clubs: North Jersey Country, 60 East, Masons. Office: Indsl Rsch Inst Inc 1550 M St NW Washington DC 20036

LARSON, ELWIN S., natural gas distribution company executive; b. Bay Shore, N.Y., May 20, 1926; married. B.S., Rensselaer Poly. Inst., 1946. With Bklyn. Union Gas Co., 1947—, gen. supt. holder distbn., 1962-63, asst. energy distbn., 1963-66, asst. v.p., 1966-69, v.p., 1969-71, sr. v.p., 1971-76, exec. v.p., 1976-84, chief operating officer, 1976-86, pres., 1984—, chief exec. officer, 1986—, dir.; dir. Gas Energy Inc., Fuel Resources Inc., Methane Devel. Corp., Star Gas Co.; trustee Crossland Savs. Served with USN, 1944-46. Office: Bklyn Union Gas Co 195 Montague Brooklyn NY 11201

LARSON, GLORIA ANN CORDES, lawyer; b. Rosewell, N.Mex., Apr. 15, 1950; d. Harry N. and Rogene (Corn) Cordes; m. Daniel W. Macklin, Nov. 8, 1975 (div. 1982); m. Allen R. Larson, Dec. 20, 1987. Student, Trinity Coll., 1970-71; BA, Vassar Coll., 1968-72; JD, U. Va., 1977. Bar: Va. 1978, Mass. 1989. Dir. statewide legal svcs. for elderly Legal Svcs. Corp., Richmond, Va., 1977-79; program advisor funeral rule FTC, Washington, 1979-81, legal counsel to commr., 1981-88; ptnr. Larson, Curry & Larson, Hyannis, Mass., 1988—; bd. dirs. mental health law project T.C. Williams Law Sch., Richmond, 1978-80. Contbr. articles to profl. jours. Bd. dirs. Arts Found. Cape Cod, Hyannis, 1988—, Mass. Soc. Prevention Cruelty to Children, 1988—. Named One of Outstanding Young Women in Am., 1979. Mem. ABA, Va. Bar Assn. (chmn. com. on legal needs of elderly 1978-82), Mass. Bar Assn., U. Va. Law Women Club. (pres. 1976-77). Republican. Home: 30 Hallet St Yarmouth Port MA 02675 Office: Larson Curry & Larson 297 North St Hyannis MA 02601

LARSON, JULIA LOUISE FINK, land use planner; b. Bethesda, Md., July 11, 1950; d. James A. and Helen J. (Grubb) Fink; m. Louis C. Larson, May 27, 1978 (div. Dec. 1981). BS, Radford Coll., 1972; MS, Oreg. State U., 1975; postgrad., Ga. State U., 1986-88. Geography tchr. Rappahannock County High Sch., Washington, Va., 1972-73; research asst./sec. Oreg. Natural Area Preserves Adv. Com., 1974-75; energy conservation specialist Oreg. Dept. Energy, Salem, 1976-77; mem. Oreg. Fire Protection Master Planning Com., 1978-79, Oreg. State Environ. Edn. Adv. Com., 1977-80; growth mgmt. planner Salem Fire Dept., 1978-79; land use planner Salem Dept. Community Devel., 1979-83; field rep. Data Research & Applications, Inc., Atlanta, 1983-84; land use coordinator Ga. Mfd. Housing Assn., Atlanta, 1984-86; owner, The Planning Edge, Atlanta, 1986-87; project mgr., land use planner, EDAW, Inc., Atlanta, 1987—; editor: Summary of 1987 Energy and Environ. Legis., So. States Energy Bd.; cons. contbg. editor: 1979 Sun Calendar; co-editor: 1976 Energy Calendar. Co-author: Regulating Mobile Home Placement, 1988. Vice-pres. Liberty Jaycee Women, Salem, 1981; land use adv. Northside Neighbors, Salem, 1979. Recipient cert. of appreciation City of Salem, 1983. Mem. Am. Inst. Cert. Planners, Ga. Planning Assn. (editor Ga. Planner, 1986-87), Am. Mgmt. Assn., AAUW (group leader 1987-88, newsletter editor 1987—, bd. dirs. 1987—), Am. Assn. Geographers, Am. Bar Assn. (student mem.), Am. Assn. Women Law Students, Ga. Assn. Zoning Adminstrs. and Bldg. Ofcls. (editor newsletter 1989—), High Mus. Art, Smithsonian Assocs., Ga. Conservancy, Delta Theta Phi. Avocations: backpacking; writing; wine tasting. Home: 3236 Mercer University Dr #309 Chamblee GA 30341

LARSON, MARK EDWARD, JR., lawyer; b. Oak Park, Ill., Dec. 16, 1947; s. Mark Edward and Lois Vivian (Benson) L.; m. Patricia Jo Jekerle, Apr. 14, 1973; children: Adam Douglas, Peter Joseph, Alex Edward. B.S. in Acctg., U. Ill., 1969; J.D., Northwestern U., 1972; LL.M. in Taxation, NYU, 1977. Bar: Ill. 1973, U.S. Dist. Ct. (no. dist.) Ill. 1973, N.Y. 1975, U.S. Dist. Ct. (so. dist.) N.Y. 1975, U.S. Ct. Appeals (2d cir.) 1975, D.C. 1976, U.S. Ct. Appeals (7th cir.) 1976, U.S. Tax Ct. 1976, U.S. Supreme Ct. 1976, U.S. Dist. Ct. D.C. 1977, U.S. Ct. Appeals (D.C. cir.) 1977, U.S. Dist. Ct. Minn. 1982, U.S. Ct. Appeals (8th cir.) 1982, Minn. 1982, Tex. 1984; CPA, N.Y. acct. Deloitte Haskins & Sells, N.Y.C., 1973-75, Chgo., 1978-81; atty. Lindquist & Vennum, Mpls., 1981-83; ptnr. of counsel Hollrah, Lange & Thoma and predecessor firms, Houston, 1983—; prin., dir., gen. counsel Unitech Fin. Group Inc., Austin, Tex., 1986—; adj. prof. U. Minn., Mpls., 1982-83. Contbr. articles to profl. publs. Mem. AICPA, ABA, Am. Assn. Atty.-CPA's, Nat. Assn. Bond Lawyers, Houston Internat. Tax Forum.

LARSON, MICHAEL LEN, newspaper editor; b. St. James, Minn., Feb. 3, 1944; s. Leonard O. and Lois O. (Holte) L.; m. Kay M. Monahan, June 18, 1966; children: Christopher, David, Molly. BA, U. Minn., 1966; MBA, Mankato State U., 1986. Mng. editor Paddock Circle Inc., Libertyville, Ill., 1972-74, New Ulm (Minn.) Journal, 1974-76, Republican-Eagle, Red Wing, Minn., 1976-79; editor Mankato (Minn.) Free Press, 1979—. Bd. mem. Valley Indsl. Devel. Corp., Mankato, 1985—, treas. Served with U.S. Army, 1966-68, Vietnam. Recipient five First Place awards for investigative reporting Minn. Newspaper Assn., 1969, 71, 72, 76, 78, First Place award for feature writing, Suburban Newspapers Am., 1974. Mem. Adminstrv. Mgmt. Soc. (bd. dirs. St. Peter, Minn. chpt. 1983—), Minn. AP (pres. 1988—). Roman Catholic. Lodge: Kiwanis. Home: 109 W Glencrest Dr Mankato MN 56001 Office: Mankato Free Press 418 S 2d St Mankato MN 56001

LARSON, ROBERT WAYNE, communications executive; b. Myrtle Creek, Oreg., Sept. 17, 1957; s. Frank A. and Dorothy I. (Martin) L. Grad. high sch., Myrtle Creek. 3d class permit, FCC. Asst. mgr., projectionist Tri-City (Oreg.) Drive In, 1972-79, Starlite Theater Inc., Roseburg, 1972-79, Pine Drive In Inc., Roseburg, Oreg., 1975-79; announcer Sta. KRNR-Douglas Broadcasters Inc., Roseburg, 1977-83; asst. mgr. Tom Moyer Theaters, Roseburg, 1979-84; pres., bd. dirs. Cascade Pacific TV Assn. Inc., Myrtle Creek, 1979-84; pres., chief exec. officer Cascade Pacific Communications, Myrtle Creek, 1983—, Sta. KRGL-Gee Jay Broadcasting, Myrtle Creek, 1985—, Cinema West, Myrtle Creek, 1986—; mgr., projectionist Garden Valley Cinema, Roseburg, 1972-79; chief engr. Sta. KYES, Roseburg, 1972-79, Beterview Cable TV, Myrtle Creek, 1975-78; projectionist Rio Theatre, Myrtle Creek, 1972-75; owner Sta. KLRQ-FM, Tri City, Oreg., 1988—. Sponsor, TV studio time Jerry Lewis Telethon, Roseburg, 1983. Served with USAF, 1985—. Mem. Air Force Assn. Democrat. Club: Aereo. Home: 916 Douglas St Myrtle Creek OR 97457 Office: Gee Jay Broadcasting Inc PO Box 1555 Myrtle Creek OR 97457

LARSON, RONALD DALE, lawyer; b. Chgo., June 1, 1935; s. Harold W. and Marie (Doughty) L.; m. Pauline Bradley Paddock, Dec. 30, 1967; children: Paul B., David P., Elizabeth M. BA, Knox Coll., 1957; JD, Northwestern U., 1962; cert., Coll. Fin. Planning, Denver, 1985. Bar: Ill. 1962, D.C. 1971. Trust officer Continental Ill. Nat. Bank, Chgo., 1963-71; asst. v.p. Am. Security Bank, Washington, 1971-74, v.p., trust officer, 1974-80, v.p., sr. trust officer, 1980-87, v.p., gen. counsel, 1987-89; sr. v.p., chief trust officer Chevy Chase (Md.) Fed. Savs. Bank, 1989—; adjunct prof. law in estate planning Georgetown U., 1976-82; bd. dirs. Therapeutic Riding and Recreation Ctr. Contbr. articles on estate planning to profl. jours. Served to Capt. U.S. Army, 1957-59. Mem. D.C. Bar Assn., D.C. Estate Planning Council (bd. dirs. 1986—), Internat. Assn. Cert. Fin. Planners. Republican. Episcopalian. Clubs: University (Washington) (bd. admissions 1981-87), Kenwood Golf and Country (Bethesda, Md.). Lodges: Rotary, Masons.

LA RUE, CARL FORMAN, lawyer; b. Ann Arbor, Mich., Aug. 4, 1929; s. Carl D. and Evelina F. LaR.; m. Ann Williams Lindbloom, June 28, 1971; children—Steven, Edward; stepchildren—Eric, Sarah Relyea. A.B., Harvard U., 1952; LL.B., U. Mich., 1957. Bar: Ohio 1957, Ill. 1964, Calif. 1969. Assoc. firm Fuller, Henry, Hodge & Snyder, Toledo, 1957-59; asst. U.S. atty. for Northwestern Ohio, Dept. Justice, 1959-61; staff atty. Trinova Corp., Toledo, 1961-64, v.p., gen. counsel, sec., 1978-87; ptnr. Marshall & Melhorn, Toledo, 1988-89, counsel, 1989—; sr. atty. Armour and Co., Chgo., 1964-68; asst. gen. counsel Rockwell Internat., Los Angeles, 1968-78. With U.S. Army, 1952-54. Mem. ABA, Ohio Bar Assn., Toledo Bar Assn., Toledo Club, Toledo Tennis Club. Home: 3553 Brookside Rd Toledo OH 43606 Office: Marshall & Melhorn 4 Seagate Toledo OH 43604

LARUSSO, ANTHONY CARL, operations and planning executive, educator; b. Port Chester, N.Y., May 5, 1949; s. Nicholas and Rose (Ruspini) LaR.; m. Marianne Elizabeth Baviello, Apr. 4, 1971; children: Anne, Tony. BA, Fordham U., 1971; MBA, NYU, 1972. Cert. mgmt. acct. Sr. project mgr. Office Mgmt. and Control, N.Y.C. Dept. Human Resources, 1972-73; mgr. econ. planning Trans World Airlines, N.Y.C., 1973-76; mgr. planning and analysis AMAX, Inc., Greenwich, Conn., 1976-81, mgr. corp. devel., 1981-84, v.p. planning and mktg. metals, 1984-86, v.p. metal refining ops., 1986-87, pres. metal refining ops. 1987—; adj. assoc. prof. mgmt. Pace U., 1975—; author. Chmn. local homeowners assn., Mahopac, N.Y., 1982-83; asst. to chmn. ann. cookie sale Girl Scouts USA, Shrub Oak, N.Y., 1984; coach/safety dir. Am. Youth Soccer Orgn., Yorktown, N.Y., 1984-85. Mem. Acad. Mgmt., Inst. Mgmt. Acctg., Orgn. Devel. Inst., Soc. Mining Engrs., Strategic Mgmt. Soc. Republican. Roman Catholic. Avocations: racquetball, swimming, fishing. Home: Carey St Mahopac NY 10541 Office: AMAX Ctr Greenwich CT 06836

LASATER, DONALD E., banker; b. St. Louis, Dec. 8, 1925; s. Jacques and Kathryne (Haessel) L.; m. Mary E. McGinnis, Apr. 4, 1951; children—Kevin Michael, Timothy Patrick, Thomas Brady, Laura Clark, John Robert. Student, S.E. Mo. State Coll., 1942-43, U. Iowa, 1943; LL.B., U. So. Calif., 1948; student, Nat. Trust Sch., 1960. Bar: Mo. bar. Practice law St. Louis, 1949-54; asst. pros. atty. St. Louis County, 1955-56; counselor 1957-58; with Merc. Trust Co., St. Louis, 1959—; v.p. trust dept. Merc. Trust Co., 1965-67, dir., pres., 1967-70, chmn. bd., 1970—; dir. Ill. Power Co., Gen. Am. Life Ins. Co., St. Louis, Interco Inc. Mem. exec. com. St. Louis Area council Boy Scouts Am.; Bd. dirs. Barnes Hosp., St. Louis, Jr. Achievement Miss. Valley; trustee Washington U., St. Louis. Served with USNR, 1943-45. Mem. Mo. Bar Assn., Bar Assn. St. Louis, Am. Bankers Assn. (legis. council). Republican. Roman Catholic. Clubs: Noonday, St. Louis, Bogey, Old Warson Country. Home: 751 Cella Rd Ladue MO 63124 Office: Merc Bancorp Inc Merc Tower PO Box 524 Saint Louis MO 63166

LASCALA, ANTHONY CHARLES, financial company executive; b. Pittston, Pa., June 30, 1924; s. Anthony Dominic and Margaret (Mazzitelli) LaS.; m. Deborah Sherwood, Apr. 25, 1980; 1 child, Linda Andrews. Major appliance buyer Montgomery Ward, 1946-54; hard goods merchandiser Federated Dept. Stores, Los Angeles, 1954-56; v.p. mktg. Tappan O'Keefe & Merritt Co., Mansfield, Ohio, 1956-72; sr. v.p. Citizens Savs. & Loan, San Francisco, 1973-75; exec. v.p. Great Western Fin. Corp., Beverly Hills, Calif., 1975—, pres. retail banking and customer services div., 1981—; with Great Western Savs. & Loan, Beverly Hills, Calif., 1975-81; chmn., pres., chief exec. officer Great Western Bank, White Plains, N.Y., 1987—; bd. dirs. Great Western Brokerage, Beverly Hills, Calif.; chmn., dir. GW Fin. Direct Mktg. Co., Beverly Hills. Exec. v.p. Big Bros. Greater Los Angeles, 1979-80, pres., 1981-82, bd. dirs., 1976—; chmn. bd. Young Musicians Found., Los Angeles, 1984-85. Recipient Belding awards Advt. Club Los Angeles, 1977, 78. Club: Bel Air Country (Los Angeles). Office: Gt Western Fin Corp 8484 Wilshire Blvd Beverly Hills CA 90211

LASER, CHARLES, JR., oil company executive; b. Redford Twp., Mich., July 8, 1933; s. J.C. and Gertrude L.; student Mich. Tech. U., 1952-54, Central Mich. U., 1959-60; m. Glenda Johnson, Sept. 30, 1972; 1 dau., Susan Faye. With Retail Credit Co., 1958-60; exec. dir. Saginaw County Republican Com., 1960-65; exec. dir. Rep. Com. D.C., 1967; fin. dir. San Joaquin Republican Party, Stockton, Calif., 1968; owner Laser Advt., Bay City, Mich., 1969-75; exec. v.p. Vindell Petroleum, Inc., Midland, Mich., 1972-75, Geo Spectra Corp., Ann Arbor, Mich., 1977-86; pres. Laser Exploration Inc., Deerfield Beach, Fla. Chmn. Genesee County Republican Com., 1981-82, mem. Broward County Rep. Exec. Com., 1987-88; adv. com. Tall Pines council Boy Scouts Am.; mem. prevention adv. com. Juvenile Justice Delinquency, Fla., 1988—. Served with U.S. Army, 1954-58. Mem. Deerfield Beach C. of C. (v.p.), World Trade Council (Palm Beach, Fla. chpt.). Clubs: Detroit Econ., Bankers (Boca Raton), Rep. Men's (v.p. Boca Raton chpt.), Gold Coast Venture Capital (Delray Beach chpt.). Lodge: Rotary, Elks. Home: 1523 E Hillsboro St Apt 131 PO Box 8604 Deerfield Beach FL 33441

LASHWAY, TOD DANIEL, financial planner; b. Schenectady, N.Y., Dec. 12, 1956; s. John I. and Janet I. (Bissett) L.; m. Sally A. Knee, Apr. 12, 1980; children: Sharon Lynn, Jessica Ann. BS, Ariz. State U., 1980. Cert. fin. planner. Store mgr. Goodyear Tire and Rubber Co., Phoenix, 1979-82; dist. rep., assoc. gen. agt. tng. and devel. Luth. Brotherhood Tng. and Devel., Phoenix, 1983—. Fellow Life Underwriters Tng. Coun. (moderator 1985-87); mem. Nat. Assn. Life Underwriters (bd. dirs. 1985—, quality svc. award 1988), Internat. Assn. Fin. Planning, Inst. Cert. Fin. Planners, Nat. Assn. Frat. Ins. Counselors (local pres. 1987, quality svc. awards 1986-88), West Valley Assn. Life Underwriters, Ariz./N.Mex. Frat. Ins. Counselors (pres. 1987). Democrat. Lutheran. Office: Luth Brotherhood 4643 N 24th St Phoenix AZ 85016

LASKER, MARTIN, hospital learning center executive; b. Winnipeg, Man., Can., June 17, 1946; came to U.S., 1952; s. Saul and Tillie (Shenkarow) L.; m. Jill Ellyn Abelson, Jan. 25, 1970; children: Jodi Claire, Zachary Adam. BS, UCLA, 1968; MPA, U. So. Calif., 1973. Asst. adminstr. Century Med., Inc., Los Angeles, 1971-73, Cedars Sinai Med. Ctr., Los Angeles, 1973-77; adminstr. Hyatt Med. Enterprises, Los Angeles, 1977-78; exec. v.p. Hosp. Learning Ctrs., Los Angeles, 1978-85, pres., 1985—. Author: (seminar) Making Performance Evaluations Really Work, 1983; editor numerous seminar workbooks, 1985—. Bd. dirs. Adat Ari El, North Hollywood, Calif., 1973-87. Mem. Am. Soc. for Healthcare Edn. and Tng. (chmn. nominating com., merit award Greater Los Angeles chpt. 1987). Democrat. Jewish. Home: 5155 Teesdale Ave North Hollywood CA 91607 Office: Hosp Learning Ctrs Inc 6320 Van Nuys Blvd Ste 202 Van Nuys CA 91401

LASSEN, JOHN R., electric utility company executive; b. Tempe, Ariz., 1922. Grad., Phoenix Coll. Pres. Salt River Project Agrl. Improvement and Power Dist., Phoenix; dir. Citibank of Ariz. Mason. Office: Salt River Project Agrl Improvement & Power Dist PO Box 52025 Phoenix AZ 85072

LASSER, ROBERT PAUL, management; b. Detroit, Sept. 17, 1948; s. Joseph Paul and Alice Marie (Seger) L.; m. Judie Ann Fall, Mar. 21, 1970; children: Yvonne, Theodore. Student, Mich. State U., 1966-68; BS, Wayne State U., 1970-73. CPA, Mich. Audit supr. Coopers & Lybrand, Detroit, 1973-77; v.p. fin. Arbor Drugs, Inc., Troy, Mich., 1977-83; regional pres. Inacomp Computer Ctrs., Inc., Troy, 1983-86; chief fin. officer Hunter Environ. Services, Canton, Ohio, 1986-88; pres. Mgmt. Reports, Inc., Cleve., 1988—. Served to sgt. U.S. Army, 1968-70, Vietnam. Mem. Am. Inst. of CPA's, Mich. Assn. of CPA's. Office: Mgmt Reports Inc 23945 Mercantile Rd Cleveland OH 44122

LASSETER, CHARLES ERWIN, energy company executive; b. Freeport, Tex., Sept. 11, 1932; s. Charles Roy and Mary (Erwin) L.; m. Dorothy Jean Fausullo, Nov. 24, 1957; 1 child, Michael C. B.B.A. in Acctg., U. Tex., 1954. C.P.A. Acct., Harrell Drilling Co., Houston, 1958-62; dir. acctg. Union Tex. Petroleum, Houston, 1962-70; v.p., sec., controller ADA Resources, Houston, 1970-74; v.p., controller Anadarko Prodn. Co., Houston, 1974-79; v.p., controller Panhandle Eastern Pipe Line Co., Kansas City, Mo., 1979-83; sr. v.p., controller Panhandle Eastern Corp., Houston, 1983-88—, group v.p., controller, Panhandle Eastern Corp., 1988— . Treas. St. Michael's Episcopal Ch., Houston, 1969. Served with U.S. Army, 1954-56; Korea. Mem. Fin. Execs. Inst., Petroleum Acctg. Soc. (pres. Houston 1970-71), Am. Inst. C.P.A.s, Tex. Soc. C.P.A.s. Republican. Episcopal. Clubs: Warwick, Houston City, Yorkwood Civic (pres. 1970). Home: 10815 Creektree Houston TX 77070 Office: Panhandle Ea Corp 5400 Westheimer Ct Box 1642 Houston TX 77251

LASSITER, JAMES MORRIS, JR., real estate investment executive; b. Norfolk, Va., July 8, 1941; s. James Morris Sr. and Louise (Gompf) L.; m. Patricia Edwards, Jan. 21, 1961 (div. May 1978); m. Mary Stahl, Sept. 11, 1985; children: Cynthia Louise, James Morris III. Student, Va. Mil. Inst., 1959-60, Old Dominion U., 1960-62. Agt. Prudential Ins. Co., Norfolk, Va., 1962-67; asst. dir. agys. Richmond (Va.) Life Ins. Co., 1967-68; mgr. United Mortgagee, Norfolk and Houston, 1968-71; account exec. Houston Land Investment, 1971-74; ptnr. So. Gen. Land Co., Houston, 1974—, Olex Energy Co., Houston, 1987—; v.p., ptnr. So. Gen. Fin. Assocs. Bd. dirs. Norfolk Jr. C. of C., 1964-68. Mem. U.S. C. of C., Houston C. of C. Methodist. Lodges: Masons, Shriners. Office: So Gen Land Co 8323 Southwest Frwy #510 Houston TX 77074

LASSITER, RONALD CORBETT, oil company executive; b. Houston, Aug. 2, 1932; s. Mance and Pauline Marie (Lloyd) L.; m. Ella Lee Moechel, Dec. 26, 1951; children: Rona Lee, James Mance, Jennifer Lynn, Lynda Fay. B.A., Rice U., 1955; M.B.A., Harvard U., 1964. Sr. v.p. corp. devel. Zapata Corp., Houston, 1970-71, exec. v.p. natural resources, 1971-74, chief operating officer natural resources products, 1974-77, sr. exec. v.p. natural resource products, 1977-78, pres., chief operating officer, 1978-83, chief exec. officer, 1983, chief exec. officer, chmn. bd., 1986—, also dir.; bd. dirs. Zapata Off-Shore Co., Zapata Haynie Corp., Pesquera Zapata, Zapata Gulf Marine, Zapata Exploration Co., Daniel Industries, Inc.; exec. com. Nat. Ocean Industries, Inc. Mem. editorial bd. Offshore mag. Mem. dean's exec. council Coll. Bus. Adminstrn. U. Houston. Mem. Soc. Mining Engrs., AIME, Houston C. of C. (bd. dirs.). Club: Petroleum of Houston. Office: Zapata Corp Zapata Tower PO Box 4240 Houston TX 77210-4240

LASSWELL, DAVID CHARLES, software company executive; b. Springfield, Ill., Apr. 1, 1951; s. Charles E. and Margaret A. (Brown) L.; m. Shirley J. Howard, July 29, 1972; children: Jonathan, Michael. BS, U. Ill., 1974. Office mgr. Life for Laymen Co., Denver, 1976-79; programmer Escom Co., Denver, 1979-80, The Software Group, Denver, 1980-83; pres. D. Charles and Co., Littleton, Colo., 1983—; bd. dirs. Rocky West Mining Corp., Denver. Author software: Member/Donor Management System, 1982. Mem. Christian Ministries Mgmt. Assn. Office: D Charles and Co 2001 E Easter St #202 Littleton CO 80122

LATEF, JAVED ANVER, financial executive; b. Lyallpur, Punjab, Pakistan, July 11, 1943; came to U.S., 1984; s. Mohammed Anver and Mumtaz L.; m. Nasira, Dec. 26, 1978; children: Zafer, Nauf. BA, Punjab U., 1962, MA in Econs., 1965; MS in Bus., U. Edinburg (Scotland), 1976. chartered acct., Eng.; licensed acct., Tex. Auditor Tansley Witt & Co., Newcastle Upon Tyne, Eng., 1966-71, Ernst & Whinney, Newcastle Upon Tyne, 1971-75; head cost and mgmt. accounts Kuwait Nat. Petroleum Co., Newcastle Upon Tyne, 1977-84; controller Nas-Sak, Inc., Houston, 1984-85; sr. v.p. Roosevelt Hotel Corp., N.Y.C., 1986—; mng. dir. Logical Gen., Ltd., Middlesbrough, Eng. Fellow Inst. Chartered Accts. Eng. and Wales. Muslim. Office: Roosevelt Hotel Corp 45 E 45th St Ste 1900 New York NY 10017

LATH, PRADEEP KAILASH CHANDRA, accountant; b. Bombay, Maharashtra, India, Nov. 15, 1959; s. Kailash Chandra and Gayatri Devi (Bachuka) L.; m. Bela Kyal. B. Commerce, U. Bombay, 1980, M. Commerce, 1982. Cert. cost acct., India. Acct. Sunil Textile Mills, Bombay, 1978-80; jr. acct. Manjeet Transport Co., Bombay, 1980-82; cost acct. Larson & Toubro Ltd., Bombay, 1982-84, Hempel's Marine Paints (SA) WLL, Dammam, Saudi Arabia, 1984—. Mem. Inst. Costs and Works Accts. India. (assoc.). Mem. Bhartiya Janta Party. Hindu. Home: Flat #10, Walchand Apt, Cross Garden Bhayander (West) Maharashtra 401101, India Office: Hempel's Marine Paints (SA) WLL, PO Box 1077, Dammam 31431, Saudi Arabia

LATHAM, ARTHUR RUSSELL, chemical company executive; b. Moose Jaw, Sask., Can., Apr. 16, 1927; s. Arthur and Beulah (Hogarth) L.; m. Anne Katherine Peers, Aug. 18, 1950; children: Jane, Brant, Garth, Brenda, Ian. BS in Chem. Engring., U. B.C., 1950; MBA, Stanford U., 1952. Tech. asst. Can. Industries Ltd., 1952-54; exec. asst. Brunner Mond Can. Sales Ltd., 1954-58; asst. sales dir. Allied Chem. Can. Ltd., 1958, dir. sales, 1961-64, dir. mktg., 1964-67, v.p. mktg., 1967, pres., chief exec. officer, 1974, pres., 1974-77; exec. v.p. Indsl. Chem. div. Allied Corp., N.J., 1977-79; pres., chief exec. officer Allied Chem. Can. Ltd., 1980-82; pres. Allied Chem. div. Allied Can. Inc., 1982-85; pres., chief exec. officer Sherrit Gordon Mines Ltd., 1985—. Mem. Bus. Council on Nat. Issues, Can. Inst. Mining and Metallurgy, Metro Toronto Bd. Trade, Soc. Chem. Ind., Beta Theta Pi. Clubs: Mississauga Golf & Country; Ontario. Home: 2254 Shawanaga Trail, Mississauga CANADA L5H 3X8 Office: Sherritt Gordon Ltd, Commerce Ct W PO Box 28, Toronto, ON Canada M5L 1A1

LATHAM, RAYMOND R., JR., computer consultant; b. Gainesville, Fla., July 1, 1945; s. Raymond and Elizabeth (Isaly) L.; m. Croce Rizzo, Oct. 2, 1971; children: Thomas R., Daniel R. BS in Engring. and Bus., Ohio State U., 1968; postgrad., Syracuse U., 1970, Harvard U., 1978. Fin. mgmt. staff Gen. Electric, Syracuse, N.Y., 1968-70; cons., project leader Consultronics Inst., Columbia, S.C., 1970-71; project leader Celanese Corp., Charlotte, Louisville, 1971-76; mgr. systems Gen. Cable Corp., Greenwich, Conn., 1976-77; dir. mgmt. info. systems Sterndent Corp., Old Greenwich, Conn., 1977-81; pres. Latham & Assocs. Inc., Fairfield, Conn., 1981—. Asst. scoutmaster Boy Scouts Am., Fairfield, Conn., 1986—. Mem. Data Processing Mgmt. Assn. Office: 195 Tunxis Hill Rd Fairfield CT 06430

LATHAM, TOMMYE PAUL, financial analyst; b. Chgo., Apr. 19, 1945; s. William Edwin and Oneita (Hopper) L.; m. Kathy Crenshaw, Dec. 19, 1970; children: Andrew, Robin, Laura. BS, Union U., 1967; MBA, Memphis State U., 1986. Co-mgr. Kroger Co., Memphis, 1970-75; mgr. Highland Park Food Ctr., Jackson, Tenn., 1975-79; fin. analyst Porter Cable Corp., Jackson, 1979—. Asst. scoutmaster Boy Scouts Am., Jackson, 1984-88; mem. exec. com. and adv. bd. Salvation Army, Jackson, 1988; treas. Parkway Jr. High Sch. PTA, Jackson, 1988. 1st lt. USAR, 1967-70. Mem. Nat. Assn. Accts. Baptist. Home: 69 Vega Dr Jackson TN 38305 Office: Porter Cable Corp Hwy 45 at Young's Crossing Jackson TN 37302

LATIMER, PEYTON RANDOLPH, textile company executive; b. Washington, May 25, 1938; s. Samuel Edwin and Mary Kensett (Reese) L.; m. Diane Frances Dooley, Aug. 25, 1962; children—Bronwen Elizabeth, Jonathan Carroll. B.S., U.S. Naval Acad., 1960. Commd. ensign U.S. Navy, 1960, served to lt. comdr., resigned, 1968; asst. v.p. Chem. Bank, N.Y.C., 1969-72; mgr. acquisitions The Singer Co., 1973-75; treas. Singer Sewing Machine Co., N.Y.C., 1975-76; v.p., treas. Burlington Industries, Inc., N.Y.C., 1976—; bd. dirs. Corp. Officers and Dirs. Assurance Ltd. Bd. dirs. Soldier's, Sailor's and Airmen's Club. Republican. Episcopalian. Clubs: Army-Navy Country. Home: 330 Upper Mountain Ave Montclair NJ 07043 Office: Burlington Industries Inc 1345 Ave of the Americas New York NY 10105

LATIOLAIS, RENÉ LOUIS, natural resources company executive, chemical engineer; b. New Orleans, July 21, 1942; s. Lewis W. and Elise (Kernion) L.; m. Joan Filizola, Mar. 31, 1962; children: Renelle Latiolais Brame, Craig A., Christopher A. BChemE, La. State U., 1965; grad. mgmt. devel. program, Harvard U., 1978. Registered profl. engr. Chem. and prodn. engr. Freeport Sulphur Co., Port Sulphur, La., 1965-68, prodn. supt., 1968-74, ops. mgr., 1974-78; asst. to pres. Freeport Sulphur Co., New Orleans, 1978-79; asst. mgr. corp. devel. Freeport Minerals Co., N.Y.C., 1979, exec. v.p., 1984; pres. Nat. Potash Co. (sub. Freeport Minerals Co.), N.Y.C., 1979-84; v.p., dir. ops. rev. and investor relations Freeport Minerals Internat., N.Y.C., 1982; sr. v.p. Freeport-McMoRan Inc., New Orleans, 1986-88; pres., chief exec. officer Freeport-McMoRan Resource Ptnrs., New Orleans, 1988—. Patentee sulphur well sealing method, apparatus and method mining of subterranian sulphur. Mem. Am. Soc. Petroleum Engrs. Republican. Roman Catholic. Office: Freeport-McMoran Inc 1615 Poydras St New Orleans LA 70112

LATNO, ARTHUR CLEMENT, JR., telephone company executive; b. Ross, Calif., May 14, 1929; s. Arthur Clement and Marie (Carlin) L.; m. Dorothy Sheldon Guess, June 27, 1953; children—Jeannine Marie, Michele Claire, Arthur Clement III, Mary Suzanne, Patrice Anne. B.S., Santa Clara U., 1951. With Pacific Tel. & Tel. Co., San Francisco, 1952—; v.p. Pacific Tel. & Tel. Co., 1972-78, exec. v.p., 1978—; also dir. PacTel Corp.; dir. Nev. Bell, Marin Health System; WestAm. Bank, WestAm. Bancorp. v.p., dir. Pacific Coast Elec. Assocs., Inc. Bd. dirs. San Francisco Fine Arts Mus., Alamany Scholarship Fund.; chmn. San Francisco Econ. Devel. Corp.; chmn. adv. bd. Berkeley Program in Bus. and Social Policy, U. Calif.; mem. exec. com. San Francisco Host Com.; bd. dirs. Fromm Inst. Lifelong Learning; chmn. bd. trustees St. Mary's Coll. Calif.; trustee Marin Gen. Hosp. Found.; former U.S. Ambassador, chmn. U.S. Delegation, WATTC 1988 Treaty Conf. Mem. Knights of Malta (vice chancellor, bd. dirs.), San Francisco C. of C. (chmn. port com.), Alpha Sigma Nu. Club: Meadow. Home: 67 Convent Ct San Rafael CA 94901 Office: Pacific Telesis Group 130 Kearny St San Francisco CA 94108

LATORRE, LOUIS, sales executive; b. N.Y.C., Nov. 30, 1953; s. Sal and Mary (Caliendo) LaT.; m. Beth Cheryll Javorsky; children: Jason Stefan, Justin Scott. BBA, CCNY, 1975. Media planner Grey Advt., N.Y.C., 1975-76; rsch. mgr. RKO TV, N.Y.C., 1976-77; account exec. RTVR RKO Div., N.Y.C., 1977-78, MMT Sales Co., N.Y.C., 1979-80; mgr. local sales Sta. WTBS Turner TV, N.Y.C., 1980-81; sr. account mgr. WTBS Superstation Div., N.Y.C., 1982-84, v.p. N.Y. sales, 1985-86, sr. v.p., dir. nat. sales, 1987—. Mem. N.Y. Athletic Club, Elmwood Country Club. Home: 11 Devonshire Dr White Plains NY 10605 Office: Turner Broadcasting 6 E 43d St New York NY 10017

LATORTUE, GERARD RENE, minister foreign affairs Republic of Haiti; b. Haiti, June 19, 1934; s. Rene A. and Francoise A. (Dupuy) L.; LL.B., U. Haiti, 1955, LL.M., 1956; Degree in Econ. Devel., U. Paris (France), 1960; m. Marlene Zephirin, Sept. 3, 1966; children: Gaielle, Stephanie, Alexia. Economist, Labor Dept., Port-au-Prince, Haiti, 1960-62; prof. econs. U. Haiti, Port-au-Prince, 1961-63; co-founder, co-dir. Institut de Hautes Etudes Commerciales et Economiques, Port-au-Prince, 1961-63; prof. econs. Inter-Am. U. of P.R., San German, 1963-72, chmn. dept. econs. and bus. adminstrn., 1968-72; project mgr. assistance to small-scale industries in Togo, UN Indsl. Devel. Orgn., 1972-74, chief tech. adviser, 1974-77, chief tech. adviser, Ivory Coast, 1977-82, head indsl. planning sect., indsl. ops. div., Vienna, 1982-84; head negotiations br. Policy Coordination div. UNIDO, Vienna, 1984-86; dir. Systems of Consultations div., UN Indsl. Devel. Orgn., from 1986-88, dir. project rev. and appraisal div. UN Indsl. Devel. Orgn., Vienna, 1988—; minister worship, Republic of Haiti, 1987, minister fgn. affairs, 1987-88, minister internat. cooperation and fgn. affairs, 1988. Decorated Ordre Nat. Honneur et Mérite, Grand Croix (Haiti), Ordre de l'Etoile Brillante, Grand Cordon (Taiwan, Republic of China), officer Nat. Labor Order (Haiti). Mem. Am. Econ. Assn., Soc. for Internat. Devel., Am. Mktg. Assn., Nat. Planning Assn. Club: Lions. Contbr. chpts. to books. Home: Scheibelreitergasse 8/3, 1190 Vienna Austria Office: Ministry Fgn Affairs, Port-au-Prince Haiti

LATOS, ERIC B., credit card company executive; b. Detroit, Aug. 20, 1947; s. George and Gloria (Dobbelstine) L.; m. Susan Paris Rath, Jan. 13, 1979; 1 child, Christopher B. BS, Mich. State U., 1969. V.p. Am. Express, N.Y.C., 1970—. Mem. Knickerbocker, Sunnybrook Golf Club (Plymouth Meeting, Pa.), Litchfield (Conn.) Country Club. Home: 1158 Fifth Ave Apt 3D New York NY 10029 Office: Am Express 200 Vesey St New York NY 10285

LA TOUF, LARRY, cotton marketing executive; b. Austin, Tex., Feb. 11, 1939; s. John Edward and Helen Maxine (Abney) La T.; children: Blake, Kelsey, Kip. B.S., Southwest Tex. State U., 1961; A.M.P., Harvard U., 1981. Cotton weighter to exec. v.p. Calcot, Ltd., Bakersfield, Calif., 1961—; bd. dirs. Cotton Council Internat., Washington, 1985-89, pres. 1989; del. Nat. Cotton Council, Memphis, 1975—. Mem. Fgn. Ops. Com. Nat. Cotton Council. Home: 8101 Camino Media #11 Bakersfield CA 93311 Office: Calcot Ltd 1601 E Brundage Ln Bakersfield CA 93307

LATTA, JEAN CAROLYN, financial analyst, chemist; b. Chgo., Oct. 11, 1943; d. John Oscar and Katherine Helen (Schnitzer) Latta. BS in Chemistry, U. Ill., 1966; MS in Chemistry, IIT, 1970; MBA, U. Chgo., 1976. chemist, Gillette Co., Chgo., 1966-67; asst. research chemist, 1969-73; product designer Bunker-Ramo Corp., Chgo., 1973-75; staff exec. George S. May Internat. Co., Park Ridge, Ill., 1977; controller, ind. cons. Bayou City Service Co., Houston, 1978; staff acct. Chemtrust Industries, Franklin Park, Ill., 1979; fin. analyst U. Chgo., 1979-84; sr. price/cost analyst Northrop Corp., Pico Rivera, Calif., 1984-85. Patentee in electronic field. Democrat. Roman Catholic. Home: 17821 Heidi Cir Yorba Linda CA 92686

LATTERELL, PATRICK FRANCIS, venture capitalist; b. Cottage Grove, Oreg., Apr. 16, 1958; s. Cecil Arthur and Eleanor P. (Wolf) L. BS in Econs. and in Molecular Biology, MIT, 1980; MBA, Stanford U., 1983. Cons. Putnam, Hayes and Bartlett, Cambridge, Mass., 1980-81; mgr. corp. devel. Syntex Pharms., Palo Alto, Calif., 1983-85; gen. ptnr. Rothschild Ventures, Inc., N.Y.C., 1985—; pres., dir. Immulogic Pharms., Cambridge; dir. numerous healthcare and biotech. cos. Mem. Stanford Bus. Sch. Club N.Y., Stanford U. Alumni Assn., MIT Alumni Assn., Nat. Venture Capital Assn., Venture Capital Club N.Y., Phi Beta Kappa. Republican. Roman Catholic. Office: Rothschild Ventures Inc 1 Rockefeller Pla New York NY 10020

LATUSKY, WILLIAM JOHN, investment banker; b. Spokane, Wash., Jan. 12, 1943; s. William Eric and Alvina M. (Heinen) L.; m. Christine Janick, Oct. 25, 1969. BA in Econs., St. Mary's Coll., 1966; student, U. Minn., 1966-67. Fed. funds trader, bond portfolio acct. First Nat. Bank St. Paul, 1967-71, div. asst. bond. portfolio, 1971-74, bond portfolio officer, 1974-77; v.p. investments portfolio, chief investment officer First Western Savs. Assn., Las Vegas, Nev., 1977—; mem. investment adv. com. Bd. of Regents U. Nev., Carson City, 1983. Active United Way, St. Paul, 1975-76; bd. dirs. Am. Cancer Soc., 1976-77. Mem. Fin. Mgrs. Soc. for Savs. and Loans, Nat. Corp. Cash Mgmt. Assn., Toastmasters, Kiwanis (treas. 1981-85, bd. dirs. 1985-87, edn. chmn. Calif.-Nev. Hawaii dists. 1983-84). Republican. Roman Catholic. Home: 3155 E Rochelle Ave Las Vegas NV 89121 Office: First Western Savs Assn 2700 W Sahara Ave Las Vegas NV 89102

LATZ, WILLIAM JOHN, electronics executive, engineer; b. Milw., Dec. 18, 1943; s. Robert Edwin and Beulah Laura (Prudhomme) L.; m. Joan Mary Pfeifer, Apr. 20, 1968; children: Theresa, Jennifer, Robert. BSEE, U. Wis., 1972. Registered profl. engr., Wis. Technican AC Electronics, div. GM, Oak Creek, Wis., 1968-70; engr. Wis. Electric Power Co., Milw., 1972; evaluation engr. Johnson Controls, Milw., 1972-74; sr. project engr. Square D. Co., Milw., 1974-80; pres., chmn. bd., founder Adaptive Micro System, Inc., Milw., 1980—; chmn. bd. Adaptive Micro Systems, Inc., Milw., 1978—. Served as cpl. USMC, 1963-66. Mem. Wis. Soc. of Profl. Engrs. (exec. com.). Roman Catholic. Office: Adaptive Micro Systems Inc 7840 N 86th St Milwaukee WI 53224

LAU, DANNY DIN, leasing company executive; b. Plainfield, N.J., Apr. 12, 1956; s. Din Yik and Sue Fung (Eng) L.; m. Dana Louise Kapner, June 14, 1987. AA, Somerset County (N.J.) Coll., 1976; BA, Kean Coll., 1978. Account exec. Gen. Electric Credit Corp., Roseland, N.J., 1978-81; v.p. Vanguard Comml. Leasing Corp., Great Neck, N.Y., 1981-87, Danton Motor Car, North Plainfield, N.J., 1986-87; pres. Danton Motor Car, North Plainfield, 1987—, Lau Funding Group, Inc., High Bridge, N.J., 1987-88. Home: 18 Fine Rd High Bridge NJ 08829 Office: Lau Funding Group Inc 18 Fine Rd High Bridge NJ 08829

LAU, JOHN TAI-KONG, financial executive; b. Hong Kong, Apr. 5, 1947; came to U.S., 1970; s. Shai-tat and C.H. (Yu) Liu. BS in Agrl. Chemistry, Nat. Taiwan U., Taipei, Republic of China, 1969; MS in Chemistry, U. Calif., Davis, 1974; MBA, U. Santa Clara, 1976. CPA, Calif. Acting acct. mgr. TV Assocs. Inc., Mountain View, Calif., 1977-78; owner, mgr. Cosmos Trading Co., Milpitas, Calif., 1978-80; staff acct. Frank A. Russo, San Jose, Calif., 1980-81; asst. mgr. T.N. Soong & Co., Taipei, 1981-83; v.p. Wai Cheng Garment Mfg. co., Taipei, 1983-85; controller Link Techs. Inc., Fremont, Calif., 1985-86; dir. fin. Acer Techs. Corp., San Jose, 1986-88; v.p. fin. ops. Genesis Tech. Inc., Hayward, Calif., 1988—. Office: Genesis Tech Inc 30963 San Benito Ct Hayward CA 94544

LAU, JOHN TZE, communications executive; b. China, Aug. 19, 1948; came to U.S., 1963, naturalized, 1969; s. Hon Hing and Kaok Yu (Leung) L.; B.S. in Physics, SUNY, Stony Brook, 1970, M.A., 1973; m. Betty Seto, Aug. 28, 1976. Mgr. data processing Dah Chong Hong Trading Corp., N.Y.C., 1973-76; mgr. data communications Citibank, N.A., N.Y.C., 1976-80; v.p. data communications, ops. and planning Shearson/Am. Express, Inc., N.Y.C., 1980-83; pres. Lautek Corp., 1983—. Bd. dirs. Chinatown Planning Council Inc., N.Y.C., 1974-82; N.Y. and N.J. Minority Purchasing Council. Recipient Outstanding Vol. award Citicorp, 1976, AMENY Corp. Minority Bus. of Yr. award, 1987, Outstanding Minority Bus. award Nat. Minority Bus. Council, Inc., 1988. Home: 1 Megan Ct Edison NJ 08820 Office: 50 Randolph Rd Somerset NJ 08873

LAU, LAWRENCE JUEN-YEE, economics educator, consultant; b. Guizhou, China, Dec. 12, 1944; came to U.S., 1961, naturalized, 1974; s. Shai-Tat and Chi-Hing (Yu) Liu; m. Tamara K. Jablonski, June 23, 1984. B.S. with gt. distinction, Stanford U., 1964; M.A., U. Calif.-Berkeley, 1966, Ph.D., 1969. Acting asst. prof. econs. Stanford U., Calif., 1966-67, asst. prof., 1967-73, assoc. prof., 1973-76, prof., 1976—; cons. The World Bank, Washington, 1976—; vice chmn. Bank of Canton of Calif. Bldg. Corp. 1981-85; dir. Bank of Canton of Calif., San Francisco, 1979-85; dir. Property Resources Equity Trust, Los Gatos, 1987-88; vice-chmn. Complete Computer Co. Far East Ltd., Hong Kong, 1981—. Author: (with D.T. Jamison) Farmer Education and Farm Efficiency, 1982, Models of Development: A Comparative Study of Economic Growth in South Korea and Taiwan, 1986; contbr. articles in field to profl. jours. Mem. adv. bd. Self-Help for the Elderly, San Francisco, 1982. John Simon Guggenheim Meml. fellow, 1973; fellow Ctr. for Advanced Study in Behavioral Scis., 1982; Overseas fellow Churchill Coll., Cambridge U., Eng., 1984. Fellow Econometric Soc.; mem. Academia Sinica, Conf. Research in Income and Wealth. Republican. Episcopalian. Office: Stanford U Dept Econs Stanford CA 94305

LAU, RODNEY THEODORE, management consultant; b. Honolulu, Sept. 20, 1952; s. Lawrence Bun Chan and Elaine (Ching) L.; m. May Ling Alice Chan, Dec. 30, 1976 (div. Oct. 1984). BA, Occidental Coll., 1974; MBA, Harvard U., 1979. Planning analyst Amfac Inc., Honolulu, 1979-81; dir. planning Amfac Hotels & Resort, San Francisco, 1982; dir. mktg. Island Holidays, Honolulu, 1982-84; v.p., mgr. Bancorp. Bus. Systems, Honolulu, 1984-85; owner Rodney T. Lau & Assocs., Honolulu, 1985—. Bd. dirs. Child & Family Service, Honolulu, 1981-82, Hawaii Soc. Corp. Planners, Honolulu, 1980-82. Mem. Harvard Bus. Sch. Club. Roman Catholic. Office: Rodney T Lau & Assocs 1188 Bishop St #3207 Honolulu HI 96813

LAUB, GEORGE COOLEY, lawyer; b. Easton, Pa., Jan. 16, 1912; s. Herbert F. and Hannah A. (Cooley) L.; m. Elizabeth Traill Green, Jan. 19, 1939 (dec. Jan. 1986); m. Josephine Ely Greer, June 6, 1987. A.B., Lafayette Coll., 1933, LL.D. (hon.), 1983; LL.B., U. Pa., 1936. Bar: Pa. 1936, since practiced in Easton; legal adviser, mem. men's adv. bd. Easton Home for Aged Women, 1940-80; past dir. City of Easton Authority, Easton Nat. Bank and Trust Co.; mem. Northampton County Bd. Benchers, 1970-72. Bd. dirs. Community Chest, 1943-45, 49-52, drive chmn., 1949, pres., 1951; life trustee Lafayette Coll., 1958—, chmn. wills and trusts program, 1963-76, sec. bd., 1959-82, counsel, 1965-87. Served to 1st lt., Judge Adv. Gen.'s Dept., AUS, 1945-47. Mem. ABA, Pa. Bar Assn., (exec. com. 1952-54), Northampton County Bar Assn. (pres. 1954-55), SAR, Northampton County Hist. Soc., Am. Judicature Soc., Nat. Assn. Coll. and U. Attys., Trout Unltd., Nat. Skeet Shooting Assn., Quail Unlimited, Phila. Aviation Country Club, Sunnybrook Golf Club, Pomfret Club, Skytop (Pa.) Club, Easton Anglers Club, The Mink Pond, Phi Delta Theta. Presbyterian. Home: Waverly Hts A-120 1400 Waverly Rd Gladwyne PA 19035 Office: Laub Seidel Cohen & Hof Easton Dollar Savs and Trust Co Bldg 8 Centre Sq Easton PA 18042

LAUB, WILLIAM MURRAY, utility executive; b. Ft. Mills, Corregidor, Philippines, July 20, 1924; s. Harold Goodspeed and Marjorie M. (Murray) L.; m. Mary McDonald, July 26, 1947; children: William, Andrew, Mary, David, John. B.S. in Bus. Adminstrn, U. Calif. at Berkeley, 1947, LL.B., 1950. Bar: Calif. 1951. Practice law Los Angeles, 1951-55; with Southwest Gas Corp., Las Vegas, Nev., 1948—; v.p., gen. counsel Southwest Gas Corp., 1958-60, exec. v.p., 1960-64, pres., chief exec. officer, 1964-82, chmn., chief exec. officer, 1982-88, pres., 1984-87; also dir. Pres. Boulder Dam Area council Boy Scouts Am., 1967-69, So. Nev. Indsl. Found., 1967-68, So. Nev. Meth. Found., 1967-74; chmn. Nev. Equal Rights Commn., 1966-68; Chmn. Clark County Republican Central Com., 1964-66; nat. committeeman Nev. Rep. Com., 1968-80; trustee Sch. Theology at Claremont, Calif., 1977—; trustee Inst. Gas Tech., 1983; nat. bd. advisors, coll. bus. and pub. adminstrn. The U. Ariz., 1985—; bd. dirs. Alliance for Acid Rain Control, 1985—. Served to lt. (j.g.) USNR, 1941-45. Mem. ABA, Am. Gas Assn. (bd. dirs., chmn. 1986-87), Pacific Coast Gas Assn. (chmn. 1983,), Calif. Bar Assn., Nat. Coal Council. Methodist (trustee). Clubs: Jonathan (Los Angeles); Pauma Valley (Calif.) Country; Spanish Trail Golf & Country (Nev.), Las Vegas Country. Office: SW Gas Corp 5241 Spring Mountain Rd Las Vegas NV 89102

LAUBACH, GERALD DAVID, pharmaceutical company executive; b. Bethlehem, Pa., Jan. 21, 1926; s. Steward Lovine and Bertha (Rader) L.; m. Winifred Isabel Taylor, Oct. 3, 1953 (dec. Oct. 1979); children: Stephen, Andrea, Hilary. Student, Mt. St. Mary's Coll., 1944-45; AB in Chemistry, U. Pa., 1947; PhD, MIT, 1950; DSc (hon.), Hofstra U., 1979; LHD (hon.), Conn. Coll., 1986, Mt. Sinai Sch. Medicine CUNY, 1988. With Pfizer, Inc., N.Y.C., 1950—, mgr. medicinal products research, 1958-61, dir. dept. medicinal chemistry, 1961-63, group dir. medicinal research, 1963-64, v.p. medicinal products research and devel., 1964-68, dir., 1968—, mem. exec. com., 1969—, pres. pharm. ops., 1969-71; exec. v.p. Pfizer Inc., N.Y.C., 1971-72, pres., 1972—; dir. CIGNA Corp. of Phila., PMA, Millipore Corp., Bedford, Mass. Patentee in field; contbr. articles to tech jours. Mem. Pres.'s Commn. on Indsl. Competitiveness, 1983-85; mem. exec. com. Council on Competitiveness, 1986—; mem. council on health care tech. Inst. Medicine, 1987—; mem. Rockefeller U. Council; trustee Carnegie Inst. Washington. With USNR, 1944-46. Recipient Internat. Palladium medal Am. sect. Soc. de Chemie Industrielle, 1985, Mayor's award for Sci. and Tech., N.Y.C., 1985, Lillian D. Wald award Vis. Nurse Svcs. N.Y., 1983. Mem. AAAS, Am. Chem. Soc., Nat. Acad. Engring., Soc. Chem. Industry, Am. Mgmt. Assn., N.Y. Acad. Scis., Nat. Acad. Engrs., Chemists Club N.Y. (dir. 1968—, exec. com. 1969—), Food and Drug Law Inst. (bd. dirs.). Home: Lyme CT 06371 Office: Pfizer Inc 235 E 42d St New York NY 10017

LAUBAUGH, FREDERICK, association executive, consultant; b. Wilkes-Barre, Pa., Feb. 24, 1926; s. Andrew and Mary (Schumacher) L.; widowed; 1 child, Sarah Jane Rommel (dec.). Student comml. art, Murray Art Sch., Wilkes-Barre; student, U. Buffalo Sch. Bus., Niagara U. Sch. Bus. With Nat. Carbon Co., Nat. Lead Co., Bell Aircraft Co., Niagara Falls, N.Y., 1952-56; pres. Lubri-Gas Mideastern, Niagara Falls, N.Y., 1956-59; pres., chmn. Lloyds Labs. of Am., Inc., Niagara Falls, N.Y., 1958-62; Mid-Atlantic sales mgr. Cling-Surface Co., Buffalo, 1962—; multi-mfrs. rep., prin. Laubaugh Assocs., Niagara Falls, N.Y., 1976—; chmn. Prog. Intelligent Grouping, Niagara Falls, N.Y., 1980—; writer, journalist, columnist (Insight) Media Feeder, 1987—; dir. pub. relations Perfetti Assocs. Ltd., 1987-88; cons., dir. pub. relations Native Am. Ctr., Niagara Falls, 1980-84; cons. Niagara Falls Family YMCA; mktg. exec. La Maison Descartes of Montreal, 1983—; publicist, seminar coordinator; dir. mktg. Perfetti Assocs. Ltd., 1987—. Weekly columnist on pub. affairs and govt., 1985-86. Cons. Unity Park Housing Complex, Niagara Falls, 1985—, Area I Minority Devel., 1986; active Rep. Presdl. Task Force, Washington, 1982—; chmn. Rep. Party dist. 9, Niagara Falls, 1984-85, dist. 2, 1986—; 2d v.p. Niagara Falls Philharm. Orch., 1983—; bd. dirs. Main St. Bus. Assn., 1985—; mem. Niagara Falls Auxiliary Police, 1986-88; media cons., vol. Niagara Falls Grand Prix Races. Served with USN, 1943-45, 1951. Recipient cert. of service recognition United Way of Niagara Falls, 1983, Human Rights Commn., 1983-84, Nat. Rep. Congl. Com., 1982-85. Mem. Niagara Falls C. of C., Internat. Mktg. Assn., Internat. Platform Assn., Kiawanis Club (v.p.). Republican. Mormon. Lodges: Kiwanis, Masons. Office: PO Drawer 260 Niagara Falls NY 14304

LAUBE, ROGER GUSTAV, financial consultant; b. Chgo., Aug. 11, 1921; s. William C. and Elsie (Drews) L.; m. Irene Mary Chadbourne, Mar. 30, 1946; children: David Roger, Philip Russell, Steven Richard. BA, Roosevelt U., 1942; postgrad., John Marshall Law Sch., 1942, 48-50; LLB, Northwestern U., 1960; postgrad., U. Wash., 1962-64. Cert. fin. cons. With Chgo. Title & Trust Co., Chgo., 1938-42, 48-50; With Nat. Bank Alaska, Anchorage, 1950-72; mgr. mortgage dept. Nat. Bank Alaska, 1950-56, v.p., trust officer, mgr. trust dept., 1956-72; v.p., trust officer, mktg. dir., mgr. estate and fin. planning div. Bishop Trust Co., Ltd., Honolulu, 1972-82; instr. estate planning U. Hawaii, Honolulu, 1978-82; exec. v.p. Design Capital Planning Group, Inc., Tucson, 1982-83; pres., sr. trust officer, registered investment adviser Advanced Capital Advisory, Inc. of Ariz., Tucson, 1983—; registered rep., pres. Advanced Capital Investments, Inc. of Ariz., Prescott, 1983—; pres., chief exec. officer Advanced Capital Devel., Inc. of Ariz., Prescott, 1983—; mng. exec. Integrated Resources Equity Corp., Prescott, 1983—; pres. Anchorage Estate Planning Coun., 1960-62, Charter mem., 1960-72; Charter mem. Hawaii Estate Planning Coun., 1972-82, v.p., 1979, pres., 1980, bd. dirs., 1981-82; charter mem. Prescott Estate Planning Coun., 1986—, pres. 1988. Charter mem. Anchorage Community Chorus, pres., 1950-60, bd. dirs., 1960-72; mem. Anchorage camp Gideons Internat., 1946-72, Honolulu camp, 1972-82, mem. Cen.camp, Tucson, 1982-85, Prescott, 1985—; mem. adv. bd. Faith Hosp., Glennallen, Alaska, 1960—, Cen. Alaska Mission of Far Ea. Gospel Crusade, 1960—; sec.-treas. Alaska Bapt. Found., 1955-72; bd. dirs. Bapt. Found. of Ariz., 1985—, mem. investment com.; mem. mainland adv. coun. Hawaii Bapt. Acad., Honolulu, 1982—; pres. Sabinovista Townhouse Assn., 1983-85; bd. advisers Salvation Army, Alaska, 1961-72, chmn., Anchorage, 1969-72, bd. advisers, Honolulu, 1972-82, chmn. bd. advisers, 1976-78; asst. staff judge adv. Alaskan Command, 1946-48; exec. com. Alaska Conv., 1959-61, dir. music Chgo., 1938-42, 48-50, Alaska, 1950-72, Hawaii, 1972-82, Tucson, 1982-85, 1st So. Bapt. Ch., Prescott Valley, 1985—; chmn. bd. trustees Hawaii, 1972-81, Prescott Valley, 1986—; worship leader Waikiki Ch., 1979-82. 1st lt., JAGD U.S. Army, 1942-48. Recipient Others award Salvation Army, 1972. Mem. Am. Inst. Banking (instr. trust div. 1961-72), Am. Bankers Assn. (legis. com., trust div. 1960-72), Nat. Assn. Life Underwriters (nat com. for No. Ariz.), Yavapai-Prescott Life Underwriters Assn. (charter), Anchorage C. OF C. (mem. awards com. 1969-71), Internat. Assn. Fin. Planners, Anchorage chpt. 1969-72, treas., exec. com. Honolulu chpt. 1972-82, Ariz. chpt. 1982—, Del. to World Congress Australia and New Zealand 1987, Am. Assn. Handbell Ringers. Baptist. Home: 649 Filaree Dr Prescott AZ 86301 Office: Sun Pine Exec Ctr 915 E Gurley Ste 303 Prescott AZ 86301

LAUBER, MIGNON DIANE, food processing company executive; b. Detroit, Dec. 21; d. Charles Edmond and Maud Lillian (Foster) Donaker; student Kelsey Jenny U., 1958, Brigham Young U., 1959; m. Richard Brian Lauber, Sept. 13, 1963; 1 dau., Leslie Viane (dec.). Owner, operator Alaska World Travel, Ketchikan, 1964-67; founder, owner, pres. Oosick Soup Co., Juneau, Alaska, 1969—. Treas., Pioneer Alaska Lobbyists Soc., Juneau, 1977—. Mem. Bus. and Profl. Women, Alaska C. of C. Libertarian. Club: Washington Athletic. Author: Down at the Water Works with Jesus, 1982; Failure Through Prayer, 1983. Home: 321 Highland Dr Juneau AK 99801 Office: PO Box 1625 Juneau AK 99802

LAUBERT, HELEN ROSSBACH, electric utility executive; b. Mays Landing, N.J., Apr. 7, 1927; d. Hugo and Theresa (Koenig) Rossbach; m. Joseph F. Laubert, Feb. 18, 1950 (div. 1973); children: Pamela Laubert Crawford, Lynn Laubert Foulke. Student, Atlantic Community Coll., 1973, Rutgers U., 1975, Stockton State Coll., 1977. Clk. agrl. cons. program Atlantic Co., Mays Landing, 1945-52; personnel clk. to personnel mgr. Pacemaker Corp., Egg Harbor, N.J., 1964-76; employee rep. to mgr. personnel Atlantic Electric (subs. Atlantic Energy), Pleasantville, N.J., 1976—. Mem. vol. South Jersey Symphony Orch. Com., Vineland, N.J., 1987-88; chmn. co. program United Way Atlantic County, Atlantic City. Recipient Walter Clark award United Way Atlantic County, 1973. Mem. N.J. Utility Assn. (scholarship chmn. 1986-87, sec. EEO com. 1987—), Edison Electric Inst., Atlantic Area Bus. and Profl. Women (treas. 1983-85, v.p. 1985-87), N.J. Bus. and Industry Council. Republican. Roman Catholic. Office: Atlantic Electric 1199 Black Hors Pike PO Box MLC Pleasantville NJ 08232

LAUDANO, PETER JAMES, data communications company executive; b. New Haven, Dec. 30, 1956; s. Andrew John and Dorothy Jane (McKiernan) L. BA, Tufts U., 1979; MBA, U. Mich., 1981. Fin. analyst Dun & Bradstreet Corp. DunsNet Div., Wilton, Conn., 1981-83; dir. bus. planning and analysis Dun & Bradstreet Corp. DunsNet Div., Wilton, 1987—; sr. fin. analyst Data Switch Corp., Shelton, Conn., 1983-85, mgr. fin. analysis, 1986, mgr. gen. acctg., dir. fin. planning and analysis, 1987. Bus. vol. New Haven Arts Coun., 1986-87; alumni interviewer Tufts U., Medford, Mass., 1987-89. Mem. Thorstein Veblen Soc. (pres. 1987-89), Am. Heart Assn. (corp. fundraiser 1988-89). Office: DunsNet Inc 187 Danbury Rd Wilton CT 06897

LAUDER, ESTEE, cosmetics company executive; b. N.Y.C.; m. Joseph Lauder; children: Leonard, Ronald. LLD (hon.), U. Pa., 1986. Chmn. bd. Estee Lauder Inc., 1946—. Author: Estee: A Success Story, 1985. Named One of 100 Women of Achievement Harpers Bazaar, 1967, Top Ten Outstanding Women in Business, 1970; recipient Neiman-Marcus Fashion award, 1962; Spirit of Achievement award Albert Einstein Coll. Medicine, 1968; Kaufmann's Fashion Fortnight award, 1969; Bamberger's Designer's award, 1969; Gimbel's Fashion Forum award, 1969; Internat. Achievement award Frost Bros., 1971; Pogue's Ann. Fashion award, 1975, Golda Meir 90th Anniversary Tribute award, 1988; decorated chevalier Legion of Honor France, 1978; medaille de Vermeil de la Ville de Paris, 9, 1979; 4th Ann. award for Humanitarian Service Girls' Club N.Y., 1979; 25th Anniversary award Greater N.Y. council Boy Scouts Am., 1979; L.S. Ayres award, 1981; Achievement award Girl Scouts U.S.A., 1983; Outstanding Mother award, 1984; Athena award, 1985; honored Lincoln Ctr., World of Style, 1986; 1988 Laureate Nat. Bus. Hall of Fame. Office: Estee Lauder Inc 767 Fifth Ave New York NY 10153

LAUDER, LEONARD ALAN, cosmetic and fragrance company executive; b. N.Y.C., Mar. 19, 1933; s. Joseph H. and Estee (Mentzer) L.; m. Evelyn Hausner, July 5, 1959; children: William Phillip, Gary Mark. B.S., Wharton Sch., U. Pa., 1954. With Estee Lauder, Inc., N.Y.C., 1958—, exec. v.p., 1962-72, pres., 1972-82, pres., chief exec. officer, 1982—; vice chmn. bd. CFTA, N.Y.C., 1976-79. Trustee Aspen Inst. for Humanistic Studies, 1978—; trustee U. Pa., Phila., 1977—, Whitney Mus. Am. Art, 1977—; bd. dirs. Adv. Commn. on Trade Negotiations, Washington, 1983—; bd. govs. Joseph H. Lauder Inst. Mgmt. and Internat. Studies, 1983—. Served to lt. USN, 1955-58. Recipient New Yorker for New York award Citizens Com. for N.Y.C., 1983; Wharton Exec. fellow, 1983; recipient Humanitarian award Children's Asthma Research Inst. and Hosp., 1972, Good Scout Award Boy Scouts Am., 1968. Mem. Chief Execs. Orgn., Fgn. Policy Assn., French-Am. C. of C. in U.S., Nat. Com. on Am. Fgn. Policy, World Bus. Council. Office: Estee Lauder Inc 767 Fifth Ave New York NY 10153 *

LAUDICINA, PAUL A., research company executive; b. Bklyn., Aug. 9, 1949; s. Thomas P. and Catherine (Caroniti) L.; m. Susan Sammartano, June 17, 1973; children: Christopher, Lee. BA, U. Chgo., 1970. Team leader UN, N.Y.C., 1970-71; assoc. fellow Overseas Devel. Council, Washington, 1971-74; sr. staff assoc. Mobil Corp., N.Y.C., 1974-77; legis. dir. U.S. Senate, Washington, 1977-82; dir. internat. policy ctr., 1982-86; exec. dir. policy div. SRI Internat., Arlington, Va., 1986-88, v.p. SRI-Washington, 1988—. Author: World Poverty and Development, 1973; (with others) An Assessment of Investment Promotion, 1984; Offshore Financial Sector, 1982. Mem. Am. Econ. Assn., Acad. Polit. Sci. Office: SRI Internat 1611 N Kent St Arlington VA 22209

LAUER, CLINTON DILLMAN, automotive executive; b. Joliet, Ill., Dec. 8, 1926; s. Thomas Ayscough and Francis (Dillman) L.; m. Lea Merrill, Dec. 9, 1950; children: Joanne L. Gunderson, John C. BS, U. Ill., 1948; MBA, U. Pa., 1950. Dist. mgr. procurement div. automotive assembly Ford Motor Co., Dearborn, Mich., 1971-76, dir. body and assembly and purchasing N.Am. automotive ops., 1976-83, exec. dir. prodn. purchasing, 1983-87, v.p. purchasing and supply, 1987—. Mem. exec. bd. Detroit Area coun. Boy Scouts Am., fin. com. Meadowbrook-Oakland U., Rochester, Mich.; bd. dirs. nat. and S.E. Mich. Jr. Achievement. With U.S. Army, 1944-46, 1st lt., 1950-52. Mem. Soc. Automotive Engrs., Oakland Hills Country Club, Bear Creek Golf Club. Republican. Episcopalian. Home: 4053 Hidden Woods Birmingham MI 48010 Office: Ford Motor Co The American Rd Detroit MI 48121-1899

LAUER, FRANK WILLIAM, real estate, business broker; b. Alliance, Ohio, Nov. 5, 1930; s. Laurence William and Leota Georgia (Little) L.; m. Barbara Ann Davis, May 2, 1952 (div. Aug., 1965); children: Linda Moore, Toni Richter, Michael; m. Marilyn Ann Waters, July 20, 1980. BA, Mt. Union Coll., 1955. Salesman Burroughs Corp., Detroit, 1955-58, Nat. Cash Register, Canton, Ohio, 1958-59; prin. Frank Lauer Co., La Mesa, Calif, 1960-66, 81—; prod. control mgr. Stouffer Foods Corp., Cleve., 1966-73; materials mgr. Indsl. Electron Rubber Co., Akron, Ohio, 1973-74; salesman Century 21, San Diego, 1974-75; sales mgr. Forsythe Mortgage Co., San Diego, 1975-81. Bd. dirs. Heartland House, Inc., San Diego, 1982—. 1st lt. U.S. Army, 1951-53. Mem. Calif. Real Estate Commissionable Bus. Brokers Adv. Com., Bus. Brokers Exchange of San Diego (pres. 1983-86). Republican. Home: 2157 Cuyamaca Ct Spring Valley CA 92078 Office: Frank Lauer & Co Inc 2245 San Diego Ave San Diego CA 92110

LAUER, PETER H., consulting company executive; b. Hamburg, Federal Republic of Germany, May 25, 1918; came to U.S., 1938, naturalized, 1941; s. Paul and Mathilde Lauer; m. Therese A. Paleczny, Feb. 26, 1974; children: Steven K., Linda A. MBA, U. Chgo., 1956. Controller Ill. Inst. Tech. Research Inst., Chgo., 1946-56; controller, treas. Flexonics Corp., Chgo., 1956-60; v.p. fin. Interstate United Corp., Chgo., 1960-65; v.p. fin., dir. Eugene Dietzgen Co., Chgo., 1965-69; ptnr. Cousins & Preble, Inc., Chgo., 1969-70; pres. Lauer, Sbarbaro Assocs., Inc., Chgo., 1970-88, chmn., 1988, pres. Lauer Cons. Svcs., 1989—; instr. Univ. Chgo. Grad. Sch. Bus., 1957-59, DePaul Grad. Sch. Bus., 1968-72. Mem. Am. Inst. CPA's, Ill. Soc. CPA's, Fin. Execs. Inst. Club: Union League (Chgo.). Home and Office: Lauer Cons Svcs 3180 N Lake Shore Dr #13A Chicago IL 60657

LAUGHLIN, CHRISTINE NELSON, manufacturing company executive; b. Erie, Pa., Aug. 10, 1942; d. John Aaron and Frances Louise (Bauschard) Nelson; m. John William Andrews, Sept. 1, 1960 (div. 1971); children: Lynne Andrews Bargar, Denise; m. Robert W.H. Laughlin, Dec. 24, 1983. Student, U. Md., 1963-64, Allegheny Coll., 1974-75. Cert. in prodn. and inventory mgmt. Master scheduling supr. Joy Mfg. Co., Franklin, Pa., 1977-82; materials mgr. Gerber Garment Tech., Tolland, Conn., 1984-86; chief master scheduler Thermos Co., Norwich, Conn., 1986-87; mfg. systems mgr. Rogers Corp., Manchester, Conn., 1987-88; mgr. prodn. planning Gerber Garment Tech., Tolland, Conn., 1988—. Vol. Erie Playhouse, 1970-72, Conn. Pub. Broadcasting, Hartford, 1985-86; cellist Allegheny Civic Symphony, Meadville, Pa., 1975-80, reader Recording for the Blind, Austin, Tex., 1982-83; former mem. managerial women's adv. bd. Behrend Coll. Mem. Am. Prodn. and Inventory Control Soc. Republican. Presbyterian. Office: Gerber Garment Tech 24 Industrial Park Rd W Tolland CT 06084

LAUGHLIN, JAMES RODNEY, health care company executive; b. Birmingham, Ala., Dec. 4, 1946; s. James Earl and Gwen (Campbell) L.; m. Gail Bruton, Aug. 6, 1971; children: Micah Garrick, James Matthew, Mary Elizabeth. BBA, Ga. State U., 1969, MBA, 1972. Mgr. acctg. So. Bell Telephone Co., Atlanta, 1969-74; assoc. cons. acct. Touche Ross and Co., Atlanta, 1974-75; exec. v.p. planning and devel. Charter Med. Corp., Macon, Ga., 1975—, also bd. dirs.; bd. dirs. 1st Macon Bank. Served with USAR, 1969-75. Mem. Fedn. Am. Hosps. (bd. govs. 1979—), Nat. Assn. Pvt. Psychiatric Hosps. (trustee 1988), Am. Lung Assn. (bd. dirs. 1986-87). Republican. Presbyterian. Club: Idle Hour Country (Macon, Ga.). Lodge: Rotary. Home: 1215 Woodcrest Dr Macon GA 31210 Office: Charter Med Corp 577 Mulberry St Macon GA 31201

LAUGHLIN, LOUIS GENE, economic analyst, consultant; b. Santa Barbara, Calif., Sept. 20, 1937; s. Eston A. and Cornelia Helen (Snively) L.; student Pomona Coll., 1955-58; BA, U. Calif.-Santa Barbara, 1960; postgrad. Claremont Grad. Sch., 1966-70, 85-86, Sch. Bank Mktg., U. Colo., 1974-75, Grad. Sch. Mgmt., U. Calif.-Irvine, 1983. Mgr., Wheeldex-L.A. Co., 1961-62; v.p. Warner/Walker Assos., Inc., L.A., 1962; cons. Spectra-Sound Corp., L.A., 1964-65; rep. A.C. Nielsen Co., Chgo., 1962-64; rsch. analyst Security Pacific Nat. Bank, L.A., 1964-67, asst. rsch. mgr., 1967-68, asst. v.p., 1968-72, v.p., mgr. market info. and research div., 1972-76, v.p. rsch. adminstrn., pub. affairs/rsch. dept., 1976-82, v.p. govt. rels. dept., 1982-85; dir. rsch. and devel. Applied Mgmt. Systems, South Pasadena, Calif., 1986; pres. L.G. Laughlin & Assoc., Houston, 1987—; prin. Courtyard Holdings, Houston, 1988—; pres. chief exec. officer, Mastodon Capital Corp., Houston, 1988—; mem. Nat. Conf. on Fin. Svcs., 1982-84, mem. policy coun., 1983-84; mem. policy coun. Nat. Conf. on Competition in Banking, 1978-79, 81. Sec. econs. Town Hall of Calif., 1966. Mem. Am. Econs. Assn., Western Econ. Assn., Nat. Assn. Bus. Economists, L.A. C. of C. (food and agr. adv. com. 1981). Office: 7035 Highway 6 South Ste 336 Houston TX 77083

LAUGHLIN, ROBERT ARTHUR, accountant; b. Towanda, Pa., Mar. 2, 1939; s. Robert Donald and Mary Ann (Lewis) L.; m. Judith Ann Jerico, Sept. 4, 1960 (div. 1973); children—Maryann, Susan, Robert J. BS, Bklyn. Coll., 1960. CPA, N.Y., Ill. Investment analyst Dupont & Co., N.Y.C., 1958-60; acct. S.P. Cooper & Co., CPA's, N.Y.C., 1960-69, sr. ptnr., 1969—; gen. ptnr. Cal III, Ltd., Fort Lee, N.J., 1981—; bd. dirs., treas. CYNWYD Corp., Del.,1988, Gilpin Pl., Inc., Wilmington, Del., 1986—, 1506 Delaware Ave. Corp.; fin. cons. Old Boston Sq. Assocs., L.A., 1981—. Mem. U. Wyo. Pres.'s Coun. With U.S. Army N.G., 1956-62. Mem. N.Y. State Soc. CPA's, Am. Inst. CPA's, Le Club, Non-Club (Paris), Players Club, N.Y. Athletic Club. Repulican. Roman Catholic. Avocations: sailing, tennis, darts, squash, hiking. Office: SP Cooper & Co CPAs 733 3d Ave New York NY 10017

LAUGHLIN, TERRY XAVIER, management consultant; b. Oskaloosa, Iowa, Dec. 7, 1936; s. John Dwight and Beryle Beatrice (Bible) L.; m. Marilyn Jean Bendig, May 14, 1966. B.B.A., U. Notre Dame, 1960; LL.B., Blackstone Sch. Law, 1967; Ps.D., Coll. Metaphysics, 1971. Registered investment adviser. Real estate broker, Ill., 1965-89; ins. broker, 1968-89; div. mgr. Britannica Schs., Chgo., 1966-68; pres. Laughlin Assocs., Inc., Roselle, Ill., 1968—. Mem. Am. Soc. Profl. Cons., Nat. Assn. Securities Dealers, N.W. Suburban Assn. Commerce and Industry. Republican. Roman Catholic. Clubs: Ventura 21 (Roselle, Ill.); KC; Toastmasters (v.p.). Home: 56 N Salt Creek Rd Roselle IL 60172

LAUINGER, FRANK THOMAS, investment banking executive; b. Tulsa, July 26, 1940; s. Philip C. and Mary Frances (Flaherty) L.; m. Ellen Williams, Dec. 30, 1967 (div. July 1982); children: Frank Thomas Jr., Julie E.; m. Kathleen Keith, May 25, 1985; children: Joseph K., George Christian. AB, Georgetown U., 1962; MBA, Columbia U., 1967. Advt. salesman PennWell Pub. Co., Tulsa, 1967-69, also bd. dirs.; 1st v.p. Blyth Eastman Dillon & Co., N.Y.C., 1969-79; v.p., mng. dir. Eppler, Guerin & Turner, Inc., Dallas, 1979-86, dir. corp. fin., 1986—. Bd. regents Georgetown U., 1985—. Served to lt. USNR, 1962-66. Republican. Roman Catholic. Home: 5311 Stonegate Rd Dallas TX 75209 Office: Eppler Guerin & Turner Inc The Fountain Pl 1445 Ross Ave Ste 2300 Dallas TX 75202

LAUNCH, ROBERT MICHAEL, JR., manufacturing executive; b. St. Louis, Mar. 29, 1955; s. Robert Michael and Anna Mae (Vemmer) L.; m. Sandra Jean Muehlenfeld, Oct. 10, 1987. BSBA, St. Louis U., 1977. CPA, Fla., Mo. Sr. acct. Deloitte, Haskins and Sells, St. Louis, 1977-79; controller Aero Tech. Services, Ft. Walton Beach, Fla., 1980-85; planning analyst Chromalloy Compressor Techs., Ft. Walton Beach, Fla., 1986-88, dir. planning and adminstrn., 1988—. Mem. Am. Inst. CPAs, Fla. Inst. CPAs, Mo. Inst. CPAs. Office: Chromalloy Compressor Tech 630 Anchor St Fort Walton Beach FL 32548

LAUNER, ROBERT DAVID, data processing executive; b. N.Y.C., May 10, 1951; s. Arthur and Eileen Ilona (Steingeisser) L.; m. Kris Vilma Launer, Sept. 27, 1985. BSEE., UCLA, 1973. Computer lab. instr. U. So. Calif., 1969-70; computer programmer I, Sch. Engring., UCLA, 1972-75; computer systems engr. Electronic Data Systems Corp., San Francisco, 1975-80; dir. data processing Summit Workshops, Inc., Redwood City, Calif., 1980-85; Dir. DP/MIS, Emeryville, Calif., 1983-87; computer bus. cons. RDL Enterprises, 1988—; tchr. computer programming L.A. Sch. Dist., 1988-89. L.A. Coun. of Engrs. and Scientists scholar, 1970-71, 71-72; recipient Men of Achievement award, Cambridge, Eng., 1982, 87. Inst. for Advancement of Engring. scholar, 1970-71. Mem. IEEE, Am. Soc. Engrs. and Architects, Am. Assn. for Artificial Intelligence, Engring. Soc. of UCLA, Data Processing Mgrs. Assn., Boston Computer Soc. Contbr. articles to profl. jours. Office: RDL Enterprises 160 Monterey Blvd Suite 19 San Francisco CA 94131

LAUREN, RALPH (RALPH LIFSCHITZ), fashion designer; b. Bronx, N.Y., Oct. 14, 1939; s. Frank and Frieda L.; m. Ricky Low Beer, Dec. 30, 1964; children: Andrew, David, Dylan. Student, CCNY; DFA, Pratt U., 1988. Salesperson Bloomingdale's, N.Y.C., Brooks Bros., N.Y.C.; asst. buyer Allied Stores, N.Y.C.; rep. Rivetz Necktie Mfrs., N.Y.C.; neckwear designer Polo div. Beau Brummel, N.Y.C., 1967-69; founder Polo Fashions, Inc., N.Y.C., 1969—; established Polo Men's Wear Co., N.Y.C., 1969—, Ralph Lauren for Women, N.Y.C., 1971—, Polo Leathergoods, N.Y.C., 1979—, Polo/Ralph Lauren Luggage, N.Y.C., 1982—; chmn. Polo Ralph Lauren Corp. Served in U.S. Army. Recipient Coty Am. Fashion awards, 1970, 73, 74, 76, 77, 81, 84, also Coty Hall of Fame award for Menswear and Womenswear, Tommy award Am. Printed Fabrics Council, 1971, Neiman Marcus Disting. Service award, 1973, Am. Fashion award, 1975, award Council of Fashion Designers of Am., 1981. Office: Polo Ralph Lauren Corp 40 W 55th St New York NY 10019

LAURENCE, MARILYN LIGON, retail company executive; b. Lampasas, Tex., Nov. 29; d. Luke and Alma (Willy) Ligon; m. Paul J. Laurence, June 2, 1956; children: Lisa Rene, Stuart Ligon. BFA, U. Tex., 1955. Asst. to regional sales mgr. Gulf Atlantic Life Ins. Co., Ft. Worth, 1971-76; adminstrv. asst. Tandycrafts Inc., Ft. Worth, 1976-80, dir. corp. services, 1980—. Democrat. Baptist. Office: Tandycrafts Inc 1400 Everman Pkwy Fort Worth TX 76140

LAURENZANO, ROBERT SALVATORE, dentist; b. Bklyn., Oct. 31, 1946; s. Salvatore F. and Hilda (Ricco) L.; m. Carol Buchholtz, May 15, 1971; children: Julia, Christian. BA, U. Pitts., 1968, D in Dental Medicine, 1972. Resident Cath. Med. Ctr., Queens, N.Y., 1972-73; practice dentistry, corp. pres. Bethlehem, Pa., 1974—; gen. ptnr. Gateway Profl. Ctr. Assocs., Bethlehem, 1983—; pres. Gateway Enterprises, Inc., Bethlehem, 1987—; dir. gen. practice residency Muhlenberg Hosp. Ctr., 1980-87; pres. Gateway Enterprises Inc., Center Valley, Pa., 1987—. Bd. dirs. Am. Diabetes Assn., Bethlehem, 1984-85. Fellow Acad. Gen. Dentistry; mem. ADA. Lodge: Rotary (Bethlehem) (chmn. internat. student exchange program, dist. 743 summer youth exchange). Office: 2045 Westgate Dr Bethlehem PA 18017

LAURIN, PIERRE, financial company executive; b. Charlemagne, Que., Can., Aug. 11, 1939. MBA, U. Montreal, 1963; D in Bus. Adminstrn., Harvard U., 1969; PhD (hon.), Concordia U., Montreal, 1983. Dean bus. sch. U. Montreal, 1975-82; v.p. planning and adminstrn. Alcan Co. of Can., 1982-87; sr. v.p., dir. gen., Que., Merrill Lynch Can. Inc., Montreal, 1987—; also chmn. Sidbec-Dosco Inc, Montreal. Author mgmt. textbook. Office: Merrill Lynch Can Inc, 1800 McGill College Ave, Ste 2500, Montreal, PQ Canada H3A 3J6

LAUTENBACH, TERRY ROBERT, information systems and communications executive; b. Cin., Aug. 10, 1938; s. Robert C. and Frances M. (Herbert) L.; m. Carole Wuest; children: Jennifer, Susan, Julie, Martha, Mary, Anne. B.Physics, Xavier U., 1959, Dr. Law (hon.), 1977. Pres. data processing div. IBM Corp., White Plains, N.Y., 1976-78; pres. World Trade Ams., Far East Corp. Mt. Pleasant, N.Y., 1978-83; v.p. mktg. Purchase, N.Y., 1984-85; pres. communication products div. White Plains, 1985-86, group exec., info. systems and communications group, 1986-88; sr. v.p., gen. mgr. IBM U.S., 1988—; bd. dirs. Arkwright Mut. Ins. Co., Xavier U. V.p. Darien Library, Conn., 1988. Clubs: Tokeneke, Wee Burn. Home: Shennamere Rd Darien CT 06820 Office: IBM Corp 2000 Purchase St Purchase NY 10577

LAUTER, JAMES DONALD, stock broker; b. L.A., Sept. 3, 1931; s. Richard Leo and Helen M. (Stern) L.; BS, UCLA, 1956; m. Neima Zwieli, Feb. 24, 1973; 1 child, Walter James (dec.); 1 stepson, Gary Myerberg. Market rsch. mgr. Germain's Inc., L.A., 61; 1st v.p., mgr. Dean Witter & Co. Inc., Pasadena, Calif., 1961—. With Armed Forces, 1954-56. Recipient Sammy award L.A. Sales Execs. Club, 1961. Mem. AARP, UCLA Alumni Assn. (life, Bruin Bench), Pasadena Bond Club, Bruin Athletic Club. Home: 17237 Sunburst St Northridge CA 91325 Office: Dean Witter & Co Inc 751 Cordova St Pasadena CA 91109

LAUTH, ROBERT EDWARD, geologist; b. St. Paul, Feb. 6, 1927; s. Joseph Louis and Gertrude (Stapleton) L.; student St. Thomas Coll., 1944; BA in Geology, U. Minn., 1952; m. Suzanne Janice Holmes, Apr. 21, 1947; children—Barbara Jo, Robert Edward II, Elizabeth Suzanne, Leslie Marie. Wellsite geologist Columbia Carbon Co., Houston, 1951-52; dist. geologist Witco Oil & Gas Corp., Amarillo, Tex., 1952-55; field geologist Reynolds Mining Co., Houston, 1955; cons. geologist, Durango, Colo., 1955—. Appraiser helium res. Lindley area Orange Free State, Republic of South Africa, 1988, remaining helium res. Odolanow Plant area Polish Lowlands, Poland, 1988. With USNR, 1944-45. Mem. N.Mex., Four Corners (treas., v.p., pres., symposium com.) geol. socs., Rocky Mountain Assn. Geologists, Am. Inst. Profl. Geologists, Am. Inst. Mining, Metall. and Petroleum Engrs., Am. Assn. Petroleum Geologists, Helium Soc., N.Y. Acad. Sci. Am. Assn. Petroleum Landman, Soc. Econ. Paleontologists and Mineralogists, The Explorers Club. Republican. Roman Catholic. K.C. Clubs: Durango Petroleum (dir.), Denver Petroleum, Elks. Author: Desert Creek Field, 1958; (with Silas C. Brown) Oil and Gas Potentialities of Northern Arizona, 1958, Northern Arizona Has Good Oil, Gas Prospects, 1960, Northeastern Arizona; Its Oil, Gas and Helium Prospects, 1961; contbr. papers on oil and gas fields to profl. symposia. Home: 2020 Crestview Dr PO Box 776 Durango CO 81302 Office: 555 S Camino Del Rio Durango CO 81301

LAUTIERI, ANTOINETTE SYLVIA, marketing professional, marketing educator; b. Warwick, R.I., July 6, 1955; d. Rosindo and Luigia (DiCarlo) L.; m. Tullio D. Pitassi, July 21, 1985. BA in Math. and Econs., R.I. Coll., 1977; MBA, Bryant Coll., 1984. Actuarial asst. Amica Mut. Ins. Co., Providence, 1977-79, actuarial analyst, 1979-83, mktg. analyst, 1983-85; dir. mktg. Telemarketing Systems, Inc., Quincy, Mass., 1985-86, Janson Publs., Inc., Providence, 1986-88, Bay Loan and Investment Bank, Providence, 1988—; part-time prof. Bryant Coll., Smithfield, R.I., 1985—. Designer various advertisements, catalogues, brochures. Vol. Alzheimer's Disease Crisis Intervention Ctr., R.I., 1988—. Mem. Am. Mktg. Assn., Am. Mgmt. Assn., Nat. Assn. Female Execs., Providence Bus. and Profl. Women (treas. 1982-83, 1st v.p. 1984-85, pres. 1983-85), Smithsonian Assocs., Pi Mu Epsilon, Delta Mu Delta. Home: 299 Legion Way Cranston RI 02910 Office: Bay Loan and Investment Bank 610 Manton Ave Providence RI 02909

LAUVA, INES KRISTINA, environmental consulting company executive, researcher; b. Essen, Fed. Republic of Germany, May 4, 1951; came to U.S., 1951; d. Janis Alfred and Hilja (Lenk) L. BA, Northwestern U., 1973; PhD, U. Iowa, 1981. NIH postdoctoral fellow Cleve. Clinic Found., 1981-82, Am. Heart Assn. postdoctoral fellow, 1982-84; vis. scholar Med. Sch. Temple U., Phila., 1984-85, rsch. asst. prof., 1985-87; dir. lab. svcs. Sea, Earth & Air Environ. Cons., Inc., Chgo., 1987—. Contbr. articles to profl. jours. Procter and Gamble fellow, 1974. Mem. Nat. Asbestos Council, Postdoctoral Fellows Assn. (pres. Cleve. chpt. 1983-84), Sigma Xi, Alpha Gamma Delta. Presbyterian. Office: Sea Earth & Air Environ Cons Inc 6021 N Ridge Ave Chicago IL 60660

LAVALLEE, LEO PIERRE, telecommunications executive; b. Providence, Dec. 24, 1959; s. Leo Pierre and Theresa Maria (Correra) L. BA, Ithaca Coll., 1981. Tchr. Eudwell (N.Y.) Sch. Dist., 1981-82, Sch. Dist. #14, Woodbury, Conn., 1982-83; sales rep. Nutmeg Utility and Geutum Service Co. Inc., Cheshire, Conn., 1983-84; sales supr. Nutmeg Utility and Geutum Service Co. Inc., Cheshire, 1984-85, v.p. mktg., 1985—; gen. mgr. GSCI Midwest. Religion tchr. St. Bridgetts Roman Cath. Ch., Cheshire, 1984—. Republican. Home: 1090 King Rd Cheshire CT 06410 Office: Geutum Svc Co Inc 1755 Highling Ave Cheshire CT 06410

LAVALLEE, RODERICK LEO, international sales company executive; b. Sutton, Mass., Aug. 10, 1936; s. Roderick L. and Florence (Gagne) LaV.; m. Janice Vivian LaMotte, Sept. 17, 1960; children: Michelle J., Roderick J. BS, U. Mass., 1958; MBA, Rutgers U., 1970. Constrn. mgr. Hill Constrn. Co., Millbury, Mass., 1960-63; mfg. mgr. Am. Can Co., N.Y.C., 1963-68; corp. audit mgr. Pfizer Corp., N.Y.C., 1968-73; corp. mgr. PIC, GTE Sylvania, Stamford, Conn., 1973-74; dir. materials GTE Internat., Burlington, Mass., 1974-80; corp. v.p. Peabody Internat. Corp., Stamford, 1980-84; pres. Peabody World Trade Corp., Stamford, 1984-85; pres., owner PWWT Corp., 1986—. Served to 1st lt. U.S. Army Res., 1959-62. Home: 36 Oak St New Canaan CT 06840 Office: PWWT Corp 84 W Park Pl Stamford CT 06901

LAVELLE, BRIAN FRANCIS DAVID, lawyer; b. Cleve., Aug. 16, 1941; s. Gerald John and Mary Josephine (O'Callaghan) L.; m. Sara Hill, Sept. 10, 1966; children: S. Elizabeth, B. Francis D., Catherine H. BA, U. Va., 1963; JD, Vanderbilt U., 1966; LLM in Taxation, N.Y.U., 1969. Bar: N.C. 1966, Ohio 1968. Assoc. VanWinkle Buck, Wall, Starnes & Davis, Asheville, N.C., 1968-74, ptnr., 1974—; lectr. continuing edn. N.C. Bar Found., Wake Forest U. Estate Planning Inst., Hartford Tax Inst., Duke U. Estate Planning Inst. Contbr. articles on law to profl. jours. Trustee Carolina Day Sch., 1981—, sec., 1982-85; vice-chmn. Buncombe County Indsl. Facilities and Pollution Control Authority, 1976-82; bd. dirs. Geodetic Internat., Inc. U.S. div., Western N.C. Community Found., 1986— (sec. 1987—); mem. Asheville Tax Study Group, 1981—, chmn., 1984; bd. advs. U.N.C. Annual Tax Inst., 1981—. Capt. Judge Adv. Gen. USAF, 1966-67. Mem. N.C. Bar Assn. (bd. govs. 1979-82, councillor tax sect. 1979-83, councillor estate planning law sect. 1982-85), ABA, Am. Coll. Probate Counsel (state chmn. 1982-85, regent 1984—, lectr. continuing edn.), N.C. State Bar (splty. com. on estate planning and probate law 1984—, vice-chmn. 1987—, cert. 1987). Episcopalian (clk. vestry All Souls Ch.). Clubs: Biltmore Forest Country. Lodge: Rotary (Asheville). Home: 45 Brookside Rd Asheville NC 28803 Office: 11 N Market St PO Box 7376 Asheville NC 28802

LAVELLE, ROBIN ANN, accountant; b. Tacoma, Wash., Nov. 27, 1959; d. Gregory Henry and Shirley Ann (Heggen) L.; m. Gordon L. Nichols, Aug. 20, 1983; 1 child, Angela Elizabeth. BBA cum laude, Pacific Luth. U., 1985. CPA, Wash. V.p. acctg. and fin. Sorrento Enterprises, Inc., Spanaway, Wash., 1980-85; accountant, sr. audit dept. Ernst & Whinney, Seattle, 1985—. Mem. AICPA, Wash. Soc. CPAs, Nat. Assn. Accts. (dir. mem. acquisition 1985-87, Outstanding Achievement Mem. Acquisition award 1985-86), Pacific Luth. U. Bus. Alumni Assn., Beta Alpha Psi (pres. Delta Rho chpt.). Home: 514 E 86th St Tacoma WA 98445 Office: Ernst & Whinney 999 Third Ave Ste 3300 Seattle WA 98104

LAVENTHOL, DAVID ABRAM, editor; b. Phila., July 15, 1933; s. Jesse and Clare (Horwald) L.; m. Esther Coons, Mar. 8, 1958; children: Peter, Sarah. A.B., Yale U., 1957; M.A., U. Minn., 1960; Litt.D., Dowling Coll., 1979; LLD, Hofstra U., 1986. Reporter, news editor St. Petersburg (Fla.) Times, 1957-62; asst. editor, city editor N.Y. Herald-Tribune, 1963-66; asst. mng. editor Washington Post, 1966-69; assoc. editor Newsday, L.I., N.Y., 1969, exec. editor, 1970, v.p., 1971-74, editor, 1970-78, pub., chief exec. officer, 1978-85, chmn., 1986—; group v.p. newspapers Times Mirror Co., 1981-85, sr. v.p., 1986-87, pres., 1987—; chmn., bd. dirs. Pulitzer Prize. Trustee Hartford-Courant Found., 1982—; bd. dirs. N.Y. Partnership, 1985-87, United Negro Coll. Fund, 1988, L.A. Times Post News Svc., Washington, 1988, Times Mirror Found., 1987; sec. Am. Com. Internat. Press Inst.; vice chmn. Internat. Press Inst. With Signal Corps AUS, 1953-55. Mem. Am. Soc. Newspaper Editors (treas. ASNE Found. 1980—, chmn. writing awards bd. 1980-83), Council Fgn. Relations. Club: Century. Home: 800 W First St Apt 3202 Los Angeles CA 90012 Office: The Times Mirror Co Times Mirror Sq Los Angeles CA 90053

LAVESON, DAVID ANDREW, controller; b. Phila., Sept. 29, 1959; s. Alan and Rae Lois (Brofsky) L.; m. Maria Theresa Curtin, Apr. 9, 1988. BS in Acctg., St. Joseph's U., Phila., 1981. Mgr. internal audit Golden Nugget Hotel-Casino, Atlantic City, 1981-83; controller Inteleplex Corp., Pleasantville, N.J., 1983-84, Children's Seashore House, Atlantic City, 1985—; acctg. mgr. Duralith Corp, Millville, N.J., 1984-85. Mem. Healthcare Fin. Mgmt., Am. Mgmt. Assn., Resorts Internat. Squash Club. Jewish.

Home: 301 N Cornwall Ave Ventnor NJ 08406 Office: Children's Seashore House 4100 Atlantic Ave Atlantic City NJ 08401

LAVIGNE, LOUIS JAMES, JR., biotechnology company executive; b. Cheboygan, Mich., Apr. 24, 1948; s. Louis James and Shirley (Lahaie) L.; m. Rachel Joy Winikur, June 21, 1969; children: Stephanie Lynn, Gordon Scott. BSBA, Babson Coll., 1969; MBA, Temple U., 1976. Mgr. sales acctg. Pennwalt Corp., Phila., 1971-73, mgr. acctg. systems, 1973-74, mgr. acctg. info., 1974-79, asst. controller, 1979-82; asst. controller Genentech Inc., So. San Francisco, 1982-83, controller, 1983-84, controller, officer, 1984-86, v.p., controller, 1986-87, v.p., chief fin. officer, 1988—. Mem. Fin. Exec. Inst. (mem. com. corp. reporting), Nat. Assn. Accts. Office: Genentech Inc 460 Point San Bruno Blvd South San Francisco CA 94080

LAVIN, BERNICE E., business executive; b. 1925; m. Leonard H. Lavin, Oct. 30, 1947; children—Scott Jay, Carol Marie, Karen Sue. Student, Northwestern U. Sec., v.p., treas. Alberto-Culver Co., 1961—, also dir.; sec.-treas., dir. Alberto-Culver Export, Inc., Leonard H. Lavin & Co., Milani Foods, Inc., Draper Daniels Media Svcs., Inc., Sally Beauty Co.; sec.-treas. Pay-Less Beauty Supply Co. Home: Glencoe IL 60022 Office: Alberto-Culver Co 2525 Armitage Ave Melrose Park IL 60160

LAVIN, LEONARD H., personal care products company executive; b. 1919, Chgo.; married. BA, U. Wash., 1940. With Lucien Lelong, 1940-46; v.p. sales, gen. mgr. Halgar, Inc., 1946-51; with Leonard H. Lavin Co., 1951-55; with Alberto-Culver Co., Melrose Park, Ill., 1955—, now. chmn., pres., chief exec. officer, also bd. dirs. Served to lt. commdr. USNR, 1941-45. Office: Alberto-Culver Co 2525 Armitage Ave Melrose Park IL 60160

LAVIN, THOMAS J. A., investment banker; b. N.Y.C., Nov. 2, 1949; s. Thomas and Kathleen (Monahan) L.; m. Elizabeth Hickey, Aug. 26, 1977; children: Thomas L., Katherine Elizabeth, Margaret Ann, John Patrick. BA, Wesleyan Coll., 1971; MBA, Harvard U., 1978. Assoc. to mng. dir. First Boston Corp., N.Y.C., 1985—. Office: 1st Boston Corp 12 E 49th St New York NY 10017

LAVIN, WILLIAM KANE, retail executive; b. Bklyn., Sept. 23, 1944; s. Thomas Vincent and Agnes Elizabeth (Kane) L.; m. Eileen Mary Jones, June 24, 1967; children: Maureen Anne, Jeanine Anne, Patricia Anne, William Kane, Maribeth Anne, James Thomas, Robert Vincent. B.B.A., St. John's U., 1965. C.P.A., N.Y.C. Audit mgr. Peat, Marwick, Mitchell & Co., N.Y.C., 1965-72; asst. to pres.-fin. Kennilworth Mgmt. Co., N.Y.C., 1972-73; mgr. fin. reporting J.C. Penney Co., Inc., N.Y.C., 1973-81; asst. controller F.W. Woolworth Co., N.Y.C., 1981-83, sr. v.p. fin., chief fin. officer, 1983-86, exec. v.p. fin., chief fin. officer, 1986—; bd. dirs. St. John's U., 1989—. Bd. dirs. Cath. Guardian Soc. Served with USNG, 1965-70. Recipient Humanitarian Cath. award Guardian Soc., 1982. Mem. Fin. Execs. Inst., Am. Inst. C.P.A.s, Am. Mgmt. Assn., Nat. Assn. Accts., N.Y. State Soc. C.P.A.s, Internat. Platform Assn. Republican. Roman Catholic. Club: Belle Harbor Yacht (N.Y.) (dir.). Office: F W Woolworth Co 233 Broadway New York NY 10279

LAVINE, HERBERT H., life insurance executive; b. Trenton, N.J., July 18, 1934; s. Herman and Frieda (Rabinowitz) L.; m. Harriet G. Miller, Sept. 16, 1962; children: Stephen C., David B. BS, U. Mich., 1956. Regional underwriter MONY, N.Y.C., 1956-65; 2d v.p. Congl. Life Ins. Co., N.Y.C., 1965-69; v.p. Eastern Life Ins. Co., N.Y.C., 1969-71; 2d v.p. Standard Security Co., N.Y.C., 1971-73; sr. v.p. Am. Mayflower and 1st Colony, N.Y.C., 1973-77; exec. v.p. Integrated Resources Life Ins. Co., Ft. Lee, N.J., 1977—, Capitol Life Ins. Co., Ft. Lee, N.J., 1977—; sec.-treas. Impaired Risk Underwriting Assocs., 1986-87, v.p., 1987-88, pres. 1988-89; bd. dirs. Integrated Resources Life Ins. Co., Des Moines, Capitol Life Ins. Co., Denver. Served with U.S. Army, 1957-59. Cavendish Club (N.Y.C.) (bd. dirs. 1987—). Jewish. Office: Integrated Resources Life Ins Co One Bridge Pla Fort Lee NJ 07024

LAVINE, KENNETH N., JR., banker; b. Washington, June 26, 1945; s. Kenneth N. and Mary Virginia (Dailey) LaV.; m. Angel M. Foley, June 21, 1969; children: Kenneth N. III, Christopher D. BA, Coll. of the Holy Cross, 1967; MBA, U. Va., 1969. With Chem. Bank, N.Y.C., 1969-83, chief fin. officer, 1983—. Bd. dirs. Vis. Nurse Service N.Y., 1985—. Office: Chem Bank 277 Park Ave New York NY 10172

LAVINGTON, MICHAEL RICHARD, jewelry company executive; b. Purley, Surrey, Eng., Feb. 21, 1943; came to U.S., 1972; s. Richard H. and Patricia (Young) L.; m. June Watford, Aug. 13, 1966; children: Susan, Victoria. B.A., Cambridge U., 1964; M.A., Columbia U., 1965; Ph.D., Lancaster U., (Eng.), 1968. Dir. Ralli Australia, 1969-71, Bowater America, N.Y.C., 1971-74; pres. Kay Jewelers Inc., Alexandria, Va., 1974—. Gov. St. Agnes Sch., Alexandria, 1981—. Office: Kay Jewelers Inc 320 King St Alexandria VA 22314

LA VITA, ROBERTO, art gallery director; b. Lecce, Apulia, Italy, July 23, 1950; came to U.S., 1979; s. Ugo and Jolanda (Romano) LaV.; m. Barbara Jameson, Dec. 23, 1975; children: Ananda, Giacomo. Degree in architecture, U. Florence, Italy, 1978. Prin. La Vita Products, Florence, Italy, 1975-78; ptnr. Secrest and La Vita, Inc., Bethesda, Md., 1979-83; prin. La Vita Fine Arts, Inc., Bethesda, Md., 1983-87, Unica Design, Bethesda, Md., 1984-87; dir. Washington Gallery of Fine Arts, 1987—; cons. in field. Mem. Am. Conservation Instit. also: Tuttufficio, Via S Margherita 51, 50047 Prato Florence Italy

LAVRICH, CAROL CELESTE, corporate development manager; b. Cin., July 5, 1955; d. James Howard and Kathryn (Defler) L. BS in Biol. Scis., Ohio State U., 1978; MBA, Duke U., 1988. Lab technologist Ohio State U. Hosps., Columbus, 1977-78; resch. asst. Ohio State U., Columbus, 1978-80; tech. resch. assoc. Consol. Biomed. Labs., Dublin, Ohio, 1980-82; tech. sales rep. Bioanalytical Systems, West Lafayette, Ind., 1982-84, Waters Assoc., San Diego, 1984-85; regional mgr. Amicon Corp., San Diego, 1985-86; summer intern, resch. assoc. N.C. Biotech. Ctr., Research Triangle Park, 1987; corp. devel. mgr. Life Tech. Inc., Gaithersburg, Md., 1988—; cons. Membrane Prodn. Tech., Raleigh, N.C., 1988. Democrat. Home: 19927 Sweetgum Circle #42 Germantown MD 20874 Office: Life Tech Inc 8717 Grovemont Circle Gaithersburg MD 20877

LAWARE, JOHN PATRICK, banker; b. Columbus, Wis., Feb. 20, 1928; s. John Henry and Ruth (Powles) L.; m. Margery Ann Ninabuck, Dec. 22, 1952; children—John Kevin, Margaret Ann. B.A., Harvard, 1950; grad., Advanced Mgmt. Program, 1975; M.A., U. Pa., 1951. Trainee Chem. Bank & Trust Co., N.Y.C., 1953-54, with credit dept., 1954-56, asst. sec., 1957-60, asst. v.p., 1960-62, v.p., 1962-65, v.p. in charge mktg. div., 1965-68, sr. v.p., 1968-72; sr. v.p. in charge holding co. ops. Chem. N.Y. Corp., from 1972; pres., dir. Shawmut Corp., 1978—, Shawmut Bank of Boston N.A., 1978-80, chmn., dir., 1980—; pres., dir. Shawmut Assn., Inc., 1978-80; chmn., chief exec. officer Shawmut Corp., 1980—; mem. bd. govs. Fed. Reserve System, Washington, 1988—; pres., dir. Devonshire Fin. Service Corp., 1978—; chmn., treas. Boston Clearing House Assn., Inc.; Shawmut Corp. subs.; mem. Internat. Fin. Conf.; trustee, chmn.-elect Children's Hosp. Med. Ctr. Served from pvt. to 2d lt. USAF, 1951-53. Mem. Assn. Bank Holding Cos. (dir.), Harvard Advanced Mgmt. Assn., Assn. Res. City Bankers, Mus. of Sci. Clubs: Harvard (N.Y.C.); Fox Meadow Tennis; Harvard, Algonquin, Comml., Union, Somerset (Boston); Country (Brookline, Mass.). Home: 11505 Skipwith Ln Potomac MD 20854 Office: Fed Res Bd 20th & Constitution Ave NW Washington DC 20551 also: Fed Res System 20th and C Sts NW Washington DC 20551

LAWATSCH, FRANK EMIL, JR., lawyer; b. Avenel, N.J., May 11, 1944; s. Frank Emil and Jessie Margaret L.; m. Deanna Conover, May 25, 1969; children: Amanda, Abigail, Frank. BA, Colgate U., 1966; JD, Cornell U., 1969. Bar: N.Y. 1969. Assoc. Shearman & Sterling, N.Y.C., 1969-78; sr. v.p., sec., gen. counsel Midlantic Corp., Edison, N.J., 1978—. Mem. ABA, N.J. Bar Assn., Bar Assn. City N.Y., Am. Soc. Corp. Secs. Episcopalian. Home: 185 Park St Montclair NJ 07042 Office: Midlantic Corp Metro Park Pla PO Box 600 Edison NJ 08818

LAWCH, MICHAEL JAY, financial company executive; b. N.Y.C., Mar. 24, 1950; s. Robert Carl and Audrey Lois (Levy) L.; m. Amy Joan Snyder, Feb. 12, 1971; 1 child, Joshua Neil. BS in Indsl. Engring., Northwestern U., 1972, MBA, 1974. Analyst Esso Eastern, Inc., Houston, 1974-77; asst. controller Aminoil USA, Inc., Houston, 1977-84, v.p., treas., 1984-85; v.p. fin., treas. Criterion Group, Inc., Houston, 1985—. Mem. Am. Inst. CPA's, Tex. Soc. CPA's. Office: Criterion Group Inc 1000 Louisiana Houston TX 77002

LAWHON, WILLIAM G., controller; b. Niagara Falls, N.Y., Apr. 24, 1952; s. William E. and Mary E. (Young) L.; m. Susan R. Wallace, Aug. 20, 1983. BBA, Fredonia (N.Y.) State U., 1974. Fin. coordinator Chautauqua Opportunities, Inc., Mayville, N.Y., 1974-78; asst. controller VAC Air Alloys Corp., Frewsburg, N.Y., 1978-82; controller Goodman Pipe Co., Bradford, Pa., 1982-83, Jamestown (N.Y.) Community Coll., 1983—. Mem. N.Y. State Community Coll. Bus. Officers Assn. (treas. 1987-88, v.p. 1988—), Exchange Club (fundraiser 1987-88), Moose LOdge, Vikings Lodge. Roman Catholic. Office: Jamestown Community Coll 525 Falconer St Jamestown NY 14701

LAWHORN, DONALD SAMUEL, insurance company executive; b. Indpls., Sept. 7, 1925; s. Roy D. and Angie (Blunt) L.; m. Juanita E. Freeland, June 15, 1947; children—Cynthia D., Deborah A., Bruce L. B.S., Ind. U., 1949. Investment analyst Am. United Life, Indpls., 1949-61; v.p., treas. Vol. State Life, Chattanooga, 1962-68; sr. v.p., chief investment officer Indpls. Life Ins. Co., Indpls. Life Pension and Ins. Co., Indpls., 1968—; pres., chief exec. officer Indpls. Life Investment Mgmt., Inc., 1985—, Indpls. Life Series Fund, Inc., 1985—. Served with USAAF, 1943-45, ETO. Mem. Indpls. Soc. Fin. Analysts Soc. (pres. 1960-61), Assn. Ind. Legal Res. Life Cos. (chmn. investment and value of assets com. 1976-77), Am. Council Life Ins. (chmn. subcom. investment aspects 1980-81), Masons, Beta Gamma Sigma. Republican. Methodist. Home: 1737 Timber Heights Dr Indianapolis IN 46280 Office: Indpls Life Ins Co 2960 N Meridian St Indianapolis IN 46208

LAWLER, NOEL FRANCIS, manufacturing and financial executive; b. Chgo., Dec. 25, 1944; s. Walter Francis and Margaret Florence (Henry) L.; m. Marilyn Bernice Tischer, Aug. 28, 1965; children: Michael Patrick, Kevin Walter. AA in Applied Sci., Richard J. Daley Jr. Coll., Chgo., 1975; BBA, Roosevelt U., 1977. Mgr. computer ops. Sunbeam Corp., Chgo., 1966-70, Canteen Corp. of Am., Chgo., 1970-72, Option Clearing Corp., Chgo., 1972-74; dir. data processing Heritage Bank Corp., Chgo., 1974-76; mgr. mgmt. cons. Consumer Systems Corp., Oak Brook, Ill., 1976-79; mgr. mgmt. info. systems Hollister, Inc., Libertyville, Ill., 1979-80; dir. bus. devel. CGA, Inc., Des Plaines, Ill., 1980-85; pres. Nomar, Inc., Worth, Ill., 1985—; Hon. appt. rsch. bd. advisors ABI. Named one of Men of Achievement, 1988; recipient Disting. Leadership award for svcs. to mgmt. info. and cons. industries. Mem. Am. Mgmt. Assn., Data Processing Mgmt. Assn., Internat. Platform Assn. Office: Nomar Inc 5146 W 115th St Worth IL 60482

LAWLER, THOMAS AQUIN, economist; b. Alexandria, Va., Mar. 11, 1953; s. Thomas Comerford and Patricia Ann (Fullerton) L.; m. Rosemary Margaret Stoffe; children: Stephen, Kevin. BA in Econs., U. Va., 1975, MA in Econs., 1979. Sr. research assoc. Fed. Res. Bank Richmond, Va., 1976-78; economist Chase Manhattan Bank, N.Y.C., 1978-82, v.p., 1982-84; economist Fed. Nat. Mortgage Assn., Washington, 1984-86, v.p., 1986—. Contbr. articles to profl. jours. Office: Fed Nat Mortgage Assn 3900 Wisconsin Ave NW Washington DC 20015

LAWLESS, ROBERT WILLIAM, airline company executive; b. Baytown, Tex., Feb. 13, 1937; s. James Milton and Belva Ambaline (Mode) L.; m. Marcella Jane Emmert; children: Christopher, Cheryl, Diana. B.S., U. Houston, 1964; Ph.D., Tex. A&M U., 1968. Instr., asst. prof. Tex. A&M U., College Station, 1967-69; prof., sr. vice chancellor U. Houston, 1969-82; v.p., chief fin. officer S.W. Airlines, Dallas, 1982-85; exec. v.p., chief operating officer S.W. Airlines, 1985—; cons. Tex. Hosp. Assn., Austin, 1966-82, banks, savs. and loans, 1970-72, NASA, 1970. Contbr. articles to profl. jours. Mem. formula adv. com. Tex. State Coordinating Bd., Austin, 1977—. Recipient Teaching Excellence award U. Houston, 1972, Disting. Faculty award Coll. Bus. Alumni, 1971, Disting. Alumni award Lee Coll., 1983. Mem. Am. Inst. Decision Sci., Am. Statis. Assn., Ops. Research Soc. Am., Inst. Mgmt. Sci. Office: SW Airlines Co PO Box 37611 Dallas TX 75235

LAWLESS, RONALD EDWARD, transportation executive; b. Toronto, Ont., Can., Apr. 28, 1924. Student, McGill U., Montreal, U. Toronto, Concordia U. Mem. express dept. Can. Nat. Rys., Toronto, 1941-43, numerous positions, 1946-61, officer employee relations, 1961-62, gen. supt.-express Great Lakes region, 1962-69; system mgr. container devel. Montreal, Que., 1969-70, gen. mgr. express and intermodal systems, 1970-72, v.p. freight sales, 1972-74, v.p. mktg., 1974-79; v.p. mktg. Can. Nat. Rys., from 1987; pres., chief exec. officer Montreal, Que., 1985-87, Can. Nat. Railways, Montreal, Que., 1987—; also bd. dirs. Montreal, Que.; pres. CN Rail, Montreal, 1979-82, pres., chief operating officer, 1982-85; bd. dirs. Can. Nat. Rys., Assn. Am. R.R.s, Grand Trunk Corp. (chmn.), Grand Trunk Western R.R. Co. (chmn.), Cen. Vt. Ry. Inc.(chmn.), Duluth, Winnipeg & Pacific R.R. Co. (chmn.), Concordia Bd. Govs. (1987-90), Dome Consortium Investments Inc., Ry. Assn. of Can. (chmn.), Can. Transp. Edn. Found. Bursary Bd., U. Manitoba Adv. Com. Bd. dirs. Old Brewery Mission, The Montreal Bd. of Trade, Heritage Found., Bishop's U. With RCAF, 1943-46. Decorated Knight Order of St. John; named Can.'s Transp. Man of Yr., 1986. Fellow Chartered Inst. Transport; mem. Can. Inst. Traffic and Transp. (hon.), Nat. Freight Transp. Assn., N.Y. Traffic Club, Toronto Ry. Club, Transp. Club of Toronto, Montreal Bd. Trade, Can. Ry. Club, Traffic Club of Montreal, Can. Club of N.Y., Can. Club of Montreal, McGill Assocs., Beaconsfield Golf Club, Mount Royal Club, St. James Club. Office: Can Nat Rys, PO Box 8100, Montreal, PQ Canada H3C 3N4 also: 935 Lagauchetiere St W, Montreal, PQ Canada H3B 2M9

LAWLEY, SUSAN MARC, investment banking company executive; b. N.Y.C., July 5, 1951; d. Romolo and Catherine (Giacalone) Marucci; m. Robert Lawley, Feb. 11, 1978; 1 child, Gregory. BA with honors, Herbert H. Lehman Coll., N.Y.C., 1972; MBA, Fairleigh Dickinson U., 1982. With AT&T, N.Y.C. and Bedminster, N.J., 1972-80; v.p., head adminstrn. investment banking dept. Bankers Trust Co., N.Y.C., 1980-87; v.p. head planning and adminstrn. mortgage securities dept. Goldman, Sachs & Co., N.Y.C., 1987—; cons. Camelot Cons. Group, Inc., N.Y. and N.J., 1987—. Bd. dirs. Katherine Gibb Scholarship Found., N.Y.C., 1986—; v.p. Edith Imre Found., N.Y.C., 1985—. Mem. Am. Mgmt. Soc., Am. Soc. Personnel Adminstrn., AWED, NAFE, Women's Club of Fairfield. Republican. Roman Catholic. Office: Goldman Sachs & Co 85 Broad St New York NY 10004

LAWLOR, ANDREW JAMES, financial executive, consultant; b. Bklyn., Jan. 21, 1939; s. Nicholas and Margaret E. (Comerford) L.; m. Rita Manning, July 22, 1967; children: David A., Kathleen E. BA, U. Notre Dame, 1961. Field adv. rep. Procter & Gamble, Cin., 1961-62; staff cons. Coopers & Lybrand, N.Y.C., 1966-72, prin., 1972—. Co-author: Non-Pension Benefits for Retired Employees, 1985, Employee Benefit Handbook, 1986. Mem. parish coun. St. Teresa's Roman Cath. Ch., Summit, N.J., 1987-88. Lt. USNR, 1962-66. Mem. Am. Compensation Assn., Am. Pension Conf., Univ. Club, Baltusrol Golf Club, Canoe Brook Country Club. Office: Coopers & Lybrand 1251 Ave of the Americas New York NY 10020

LAWRENCE, ALBERT WEAVER, insurance company executive; b. Newburgh, N.Y., Aug. 4, 1928; s. Claude D. and Janet (Weaver) L.; m. Barbara Corell, June 28, 1950; children: David, Janet, Elizabeth. BSAE in Engring., Cornell U., 1950; postgrad., Rensselaer Poly. Inst., 1975. Ins. agt., exec. 1953—; founder, chmn. A.W. Lawrence and Co. Inc., Schenectady, N.Y., 1954-82; chmn. bd. dirs. United Community Ins. Com., N.Y.C., N.Y., 1982—, Lawrence Agy. Corp., Albany, N.Y., 1982—, Lawrence Ins. Group Inc., Albany, N.Y., 1986—, Lawrence Group Inc., Schenetady, N.Y., 1986—, ADAPT, Inc., Schenectady, N.Y., 1989; chmn. adv. bd. Norstar Bank, Schenectady, 1984—; bus. adv. bd. Health Services Agy. N.Y., Albany, 1985—; bd. dirs. Hermitage Ins. Co., N.Y.C.; underwriting mem. Lloyds of London. Bd. overseers, grad. sch. of bus. Rensselaer Poly. Inst., Troy, N.Y.; past pres. Schenectady Girls Club, Family and Child Service Schenectady; bd. dirs. Ind. Living for Physically Disabled; past chmn. Schenectady United Fund drive, Jr. Achievement Capital Dist.; trustee Russell Sage Coll., Troy, N.Y., Sunnyview Hosp. and Rehab. Ctr., Schenectady, St. Clare's Hosp. Found.; bd. dirs. Proctors; founder (with wife) The Lawrence Inst. Served as corp. AUS, 1946-47. Recipient Sca-Nec-Ta-De Civic award, 1967. Mem. Nat. Assn. Ins. Brokers (bd. dirs.), Washington D.C. Hist. Soc. (trustee), Nat. Assn. Ins. Brokers (bd. dirs.), Schenectady C. of C. (past pres.). Republican. Mem. Dutch Reformed Ch. Clubs: Wall Street, Mohawk, Mohawk Golf, Curling, Univ., Ft. Orange (Albany); Cornell, N.Y. Athletic (N.Y.C.); No. Lake George Yacht (past commodore). Home: 1601 Baker Ave Schenectady NY 12309 Office: Lawrence Group Inc 108 Union St Schenectady NY 12305

LAWRENCE, GARY DALE, financial planning executive; b. Mpls., Jan. 13, 1947; s. Nelson Anthony Longerbone and Anne Marie (Gorshe) L.; m. Judy Ann Johnson, Sept. 6, 1969; children: Adam Matthew, Christina Marie. AA, U. Minn., 1968, BS, 1970, MEd, 1976. Tchr. econs. Robbinsdale (Minn.) Pub. Schs., 1970-80; assoc. planner Paul R. Kenworthy, Richfield, Minn., 1980-81; mktg. specialist IDS, Mpls., 1981-83, mgr. fin. planning, 1983-85; sr. mgr. IDS Fin. Svcs., Mpls., 1985-86, dir. strategy, 1986—. Pres. Minnetonka (Minn.) Environ. Group, 1973-74; mem. Minnetonka City Charter Commn., 1979-83, Minnetonka City Task Force, 1974. Mem. Internat. Assn. for Fin. Planning, Inst. Cert. Fin. Planners, Internat. Assn. for Fin. Planning Found. (bd. dirs. 1988—), Jaycees (v.p. Minnetonka chpt. 1974-75). Home: 12524 Creek Rd W Minnetonka MN 55343 Office: IDS Fin Svcs Inc IDS Tower 10 Minneapolis MN 55343

LAWRENCE, GERALD GRAHAM, management consultant; b. U.K., June 21, 1947; came to U.S., 1972; naturalized, 1977; s. Raymond Joseph and Barbara Virginia L.; 1 child, Ian Andrew. BA in Math., Northeastern U., 1970, MA in Econs., 1973; MBA, U. Pa., 1975. Optics rsch. technologist Polaroid Corp., Cambridge, Mass., 1968-70; intern Corning Glass Works, Inc., N.Y.C., 1974; asst. brand mgr. Procter and Gamble, Cin., 1975-76; assoc. Theodore Barry & Assocs., N.Y.C., 1976-79; dir. performance improvement systems Stone & Webster Mgmt. Cons., N.Y.C., 1979-84; mgr. utility MAS Deloitte Haskins & Sells, N.Y.C., 1984-86; pres. PMC Mgmt. Cons., Inc., Three Bridges, N.J., 1986—; con. internat. mgmt. N.J.; past bd. dir. Olympus, Inc.; speaker in field. Designer auditor system nuclear power plant constrn.; contbr. articles to profl. jours. Econs. fellow Northeastern U., 1973, adminstrv. fellow Wharton Sch. U. Pa., 1975. Home: 11 Thistle Ln Flemington NJ 08822 Office: PO Box 332 Three Bridges NJ 08887

LAWRENCE, MRS. HARDING See LAWRENCE, MARY GEORGENE WELLS

LAWRENCE, JOHN KIDDER, lawyer; b. Detroit, Nov. 18, 1949; s. Luther Ernest and Mary Anna (Kidder) L.; m. Jeanine Ann DeLay, June 20, 1981. AB, U. Mich., 1971; JD, Harvard U., 1974. Bar: Mich. 1974, U.S. Supreme, 1977, D.C. 1978. Assoc., Dickinson, Wright, McKean & Cudlip, Detroit, 1973-74; staff atty. Office of Judge Adv. Gen., Washington, 1975-78; assoc. Dickinson, Wright, McKean, Cudlip & Moon, Detroit, 1978-81; ptnr. Dickinson, Wright, Moon, VanDusen & Freeman, Detroit, 1981—. Exec. sec. Detroit Com. on Fgn. Rels., 1988—; patron Founders Soc. Detroit Inst. Arts, 1979—; mem. founds. com. Detroit Symphony Orch., 1983—. With USN, 1975-78. Mem. ABA, Fed. Bar Assn., State Bar Mich., D.C. Bar Assn., Am. Judicature Soc., Internat. Bar Assn., Am. Hist. Assn., Phi Eta Sigma, Phi Beta Kappa. Democrat. Episcopalian. Club: Detroit. Office: Dickinson Wright Moon VanDusen & Freeman 800 First National Bldg Detroit MI 48226

LAWRENCE, LOUIS JAMES, JR., automotive company executive; b. Nashville, Apr. 7, 1935; s. Louis J. and Mary H. (Bethel) L.; m. Kay L. Smitherman; children—Cathy, Louis III, Larry, Linda, Lisa, Lori, Lana. BS in Indsl. Engring., U. Tenn., 1959; MBA, Ea. Mich. U., 1970. Engr. Trane Co., La Crosse, Wis., 1959-63; with Ford Motor Co., Dearborn, Mich., 1963-77; vice pres., gen. mgr. Philco Ford Co., Toronto, Ont., Can., 1977-79; corp. v.p. prodn. ops. Bendix Corp., Southfield, Mich., 1979-82; pres., chief exec. officer Goetze Corp. of Am., Muskegon, Mich., 1982-86; sr. v.p. AMCA Internat. Ltd., Hanover, N.H., 1986—. Bd. cons. Ea. Mich. U., Ypsilanti, 1980—. Sr. research fellow U. Chgo., 1957. Mem. Soc. Automotive Engrs., Detroit Engring. Soc., Am. Mgmt. Assn. (v.p. mfg. council 1981—, trustee 1981—). Roman Catholic. Clubs: Plum Hollow Country (Southfield); Century (Muskegon); Spring Lake Country, Farmington Hunt (Mich.). Home: #8 The Courtyard Hanover NH 03755 Office: AMCA Internat Ltd Dartmouth Nat Bank Bldg Hanover NH 03755

LAWRENCE, MARGERY H(ULINGS), utilities executive; b. Harmarville, Pa., June 17, 1934; d. Richard Nuttall and Alva (Burns) Hulings; student Bethany Coll., 1951-52; B.S. in Mktg., Carnegie-Mellon U., 1955. Asst. mdse. buyer Joseph Horne Co., Pitts., 1955-57; home econs. editor Pitts. Group Cos. Columbia Gas System, Pitts., 1957-64, dir. home econs., 1968-72; home economist Columbia Gas Pa., Jeannette, 1964-68, dist. marketing mgr., 1972-87, div. mgr., 1987—. Bd. dirs. Ohio Valley Gen. Hosp. Mem. DAR, Am. Gas Assn. (Home Service Achievement award 1964), Pa. Gas Assn., Exec. Women's Council Pitts., Mfrs. Assn. of Tri-Counties (bd. dirs.). Presbyterian. Republican. Office: Columbia Gas Pa Inc 911 Fifth Ave New Brighton PA 15066

LAWRENCE, MARY GEORGENE WELLS (MRS. HARDING LAWRENCE), advertising executive; b. Youngstown, Ohio, May 25, 1928; d. Waldemar and Violet (Berg); m. Harding Lawrence, Nov. 25, 1967; children: James, State, Deborah, Kathryn, Pamela. Ed., Carnegie Inst. Tech., 1949; LL.D., Babson Coll., 1970. Copywriter McKelvey's Dept. Store, Youngstown, 1951-52; fashion advt. mgr. Macy's, N.Y.C., 1952-53; copy group head McCann-Erickson, N.Y.C., 1953-56; with Doyle, Dane, Bernbach, N.Y.C., 1957-64, v.p., assoc. copy chief, 1963-64; sr. ptnr., creative dir. Jack Tinker & Partners, N.Y.C., 1964-66; chmn. bd., chief exec. officer Wells, Rich, Greene, Inc., N.Y.C., 1966—. Named to Copywriters Hall of Fame Copy Club, 1969; named Mktg. Stateswoman of Year Sales Execs. Club N.Y., 1970, Advt. Woman of Year Am. Advt. Fedn., 1971. Mem. Dallas Advt. Club. Office: Wells Rich Greene Inc 9 W 57th St New York NY 10019 *

LAWRENCE, PELHAM BISSELL, poultry executive; b. N.Y.C., Oct. 31, 1945; s. David and Nancy (Wemple) B.; m. Virginia Marie Elsworth, July 4, 1969; children: Joseph Pelham, Michael Pelham, Ann Kathryn. A.A., Manatee Jr. Coll., 1966; B.A., U. Fla., 1968. C.P.A., Md. Asst. mgr. Chem. Bank, N.Y.C., 1971-74; dir. treasury Perdue Farms, Inc., Salisbury, Md., 1974-77; treas. Perdue Farms, Inc., 1977-80, treas., chief fin. officer, 1980-82, v.p. fin., 1982—. Served to 1st lt. U.S. Army, 1969-71. Decorated Army Commendation medal. Mem. Am. Inst. C.P.A.s, Fin. Execs. Inst., Phi Beta Kappa. Roman Catholic. Office: Perdue Farms Inc PO Box 1537 Salisbury MD 21801

LAWS, DAVID GARRARD, data processing executive; b. Maitland, N.S.W., Australia, Mar. 5, 1930; came to U.S., 1975; s. Reginald G. and Alicia M. (Jamieson) L.; m. Mary C. Steele, Jan. 26, 1956; children: Stephanie, Phillipa, Stuart. B.A. with honors, U. Sydney, Australia, 1950, diploma in Edn., 1951. Exec. asst. to chmn. NCR Corp., Dayton, Ohio, 1975-76, v.p. product mktg., 1976-78, v.p. product mgmt., 1978-83, v.p., officer; pres., chief exec. officer Applied Digital Data Systems, Inc. subs. NCR Corp., Hauppauge, N.Y., 1983—; bd. dirs. NCR Comten, St. Paul. Fellow Australian Inst. Mgmt. Republican. Presbyterian. Club: Nissequogue Golf (N.Y.). Office: Applied Digital Data Systems Inc 100 Marcus Blvd Hauppauge NY 11788

LAW-SMITH, DAVID JOHN, oil company executive; b. Nairobi, Kenya, Jan. 16, 1940; came to U.S., 1977; s. John Law-Smith and Patricia (Alexander) Moore; m. Delena Port, May 2, 1964; children: Craig, Kevin. Educated in, Eng. Cert. in fin. and acctg., corporate law. Pub. acct. Eng. and Kenya; various fin. positions Caltex Petroleum Corp., Africa, Asia, Australia, 1965-77; asst. treas., fin. planner Caltex Petroleum Corp., N.Y.C., 1977-86; treas. Caltex Petroleum Corp., Dallas, 1987—; bd. dirs., officer various subs. and affiliates worldwide Caltex Petroleum Corp. Fellow

Chartered Assn. Accts., Chartered Inst. Secs., Las Colinas Country Club (Irving, Tex.), Brookhaven Country Club (Dallas). Home: 11132 Rosser Ct Dallas TX 75229 Office: Caltex Petroleum Corp PO Box 619500 Dallas TX 75261

LAWSON, ANDREW LOWELL, JR., defense industry company executive; b. Macon, Ga., Jan. 16, 1938; s. Andrew Lowell and Valerie Ula (Brazzeal) L.; m. Carol Belle Few, Dec. 31, 1961; children: Andrew L. III, Steven Brian. Student, Mercer U., 1955; cert., Middle Ga. Coll., 1956-58; BS in Math, U. Ga., 1960. Contract price analyst WRAMA, Robins AFB, Ga., 1960-64; with E-Systems, Inc., Greenville, Tex., various fin. positions, 1964-70; v.p. fin., div. controller Huntington, Ind., 1970-73; corp. v.p., controller Dallas, 1973; corp. v.p., div. v.p. fin. & adminstrn. Greenville, 1973-78, corp. v.p., gen. mgr. Greenville div., 1978-83; sr. v.p., group exec. aircraft systems group Dallas, 1983-87, exec. v.p., 1987—, also bd. dirs. Deacon Ridgecrest Bapt. Ch., Greenville. Served with USNR, 1955-63. Mem. Aerospace Industries Assn., Am. Def. Preparedness Assn., Armed Force Communnications and Electronic Assn., Assn. U.S. Army, Air Force Assn., Navy League, Old Crows. Office: E-Systems Inc PO Box 660248 Dallas TX 75266 *

LAWSON, BARBARA ELLEN, accountant; b. Abington, Pa., May 12, 1963; d. Harry Elton and Elizabeth Estelle (Watson) L. BS in Acctg., Rutgers U., 1986. Fiber acctg. analyst Scott Paper Co., Phila., 1986-88, assoc. auditor internal audit dept., 1988—; coll. instr. computer programming, 1988. Mem. Am. Soc. Women Accts., Nat. Assn. Accts. (bd. dirs. S. Jersey chpt. 1987—). Republican. Episcopalian. Home: 8 Regent Rd Cherry Hill NJ 08003 Office: Scott Paper Co Internal Audit Pla I Philadelphia PA 19113

LAWSON, DONALD STUART, atomic energy company executive; b. Liverpool, Eng., Jan. 18, 1935; s. Allan Stuart and Jane (Horridge) L.; m. Rosanne Morton, Aug. 10, 1957; children—David, Nicholas, Hugh. B.Sc. in Engring. with honors, U. Bristol, Eng., 1956. With U.K. Ministry of Supply, London, 1956-58; engr. English Electric (GEC), 1958-77; chief engr., engring. mgr. Reactor Equipment Ltd. English Electric (GEC), Leicester, 1969-77; v.p. Sanderson and Porter, Inc.; pres. CANDU ops. Atomic Energy of Can. Ltd., Mississauga, Ont., 1978—; dir. Nuclear Project Mgrs., Montreal, Que., Can. Recipient James Clayton prize, 1969. Mem. Assn. Profl. Engrs. Ont., Can. Nuclear Soc. Home: 1272 Baldwin Dr, Oakville, ON Canada L6J 2W5 Office: Atomic Energy Can Ltd, CANDU Ops, Mississauga, ON Canada L5K 1B2

LAWSON, FRED RAULSTON, bank executive; b. Sevierville, Tenn., Mar. 26, 1936; s. Arville Raulston and Ila Mary (Lowe) L.; m. Sharon Sheets, Jan. 1, 1982; children: Terry Lee Lawson Akins, Laura Ann, Kristi Yvette. Student, U. Tenn., 1953-59, La. State U. Sch. Banking of South, 1965-68, Harvard Inst. Fin. Mgmt., 1968. From br. mgr. to exec. v.p. Blount Nat. Bank, Maryville, Tenn., 1958-68, pres., 1968—, also bd. dirs.; pres. Tenn. Nat. Bancshares, Inc., Maryville, 1971-86, Bank of East Tenn., Knoxville, 1986—; also bd. dirs. Tenn. Nat. Bancshares, Inc., Maryville; bd. dirs. Areawide Devel. Corp., Knoxville. Dir. Blount County Indsl. Devel. Bd., 1969—; chancellors assoc. U. Tenn., Knoxville, 1972-78; trustee Carson-Newman Coll., Jefferson City, 1984—; Harrison-Chilhowee Bapt. Acad., Seymour, Tenn., 1972-85; mem. adv. bd. Maryville Coll., 1979—; mem. U. Tenn. Meml. Research Ctr. and Hosp. Adv. Bd.; bd. regents Mid-South Sch. Banking, Memphis, 1982; bd. dirs Thompson Cancer Survival Ctr., Knoxville, 1987—. Served with USNR, 1956-57. Recipient Tenn. Indsl. Devel. Vol. award, 1977. Mem. Assn. Bank Holding Cos. (bd. dirs. 1979-82), Tenn. Bankers Assn. (chmn. state legis. com. 1980, chmn. banking practice com. 1983), Am. Bankers Assn. Republican. Baptist. Lodge: Masons. Home: 2101 Cochran Rd Maryville TN 37801

LAWSON, FREDERICK HEBEL, mining company executive; b. Rock Island, Ill., June 30, 1927; s. Clarence DeWitt and Anna Elizebeth (Hebel) L.; m. Margaret Lewis; children: Theodore Lewis, Thomas Ward. BS, U. Ill., 1952; diploma, Stanford Grad. Bus. Sch., 1963. Employee relations mgr. Kaiser Aluminum and Chem. Corp., Spokane, Wash., 1952-54; supt. indsl. relations Moss Landing, Calif., 1955-57, Pernamente, Calif., 1958-61; Stanford (Calif.)-Sloan fellow 1962-63; mgr. adminstrn. Gladstone, Australia, 1964-67; div. mgr. employee relations Oakland, Calif., 1968-72, mgr. indsl. relations, 1971-72, v.p., 1973-81; corp. dir. BHP-Utah Coal Ltd., Brisbane, Australia, 1982-88, Iron, Oreg., 1988—. Author: Management Manpower Planning, 1963. Chmn. bd. Stanford-Sloan Grad. Sch. Bus., 1972-75; mem. U.S. Army Res. Policy Bd., Washington, 1975-78; mem. Dept. Def. Res. Policy Bd., 1978-82; bd. dirs. Nat. Urban League, N.Y.C., 1978-80. Served to 1st lt. U.S. Army, 1945-48, ETO. Decorated D.S.M.; named to U.S. Army Hall of Fame, Ft. Benning, Ga., 1978; recipient Disting. Eagle Scout Boy Scouts Am., 1982, Silver Beaver award, 1980. Mem. Indsl. Relations Soc., Mercer County Hist. Soc., Res. Officers Assn. Democrat. Methodist. Office: BHP-Utah Iron One, 200 St Georges Ter, Perth Western 6000, Australia

LAWSON, JAMES EARL, osteopath; b. Detroit, June 4, 1945; s. Gerald James and Janet Virginia (Owen) L.; m. Lois Ann Levitt, June 29, 1968 (div. Sept. 1975); 1 child, Matthew Owen; m. Mary Ann Spencer, June 10, 1978 (div. Dec. 1982); 1 child, David James; m. Marian Judith Marcero, May 8, 1986. BS in Zoology, U. Mich., 1967; DO, Kirksville (Mo.) Coll. Osteo. Medicine, 1971. Cert. Am. Osteo. Bd. Internal Medicine. Chief exec. officer BioMed. Applications of Detroit, 1978—; med. dir. Inst. for Health Maintenance, Southfield, Mich., 1981-83; pres. Met. Nephrologists, Detroit, 1981—; mem. med. rev. bd. End Stage Renal Disease Network; asst. clin. prof. Osteo. Medicine Mich. State U. Coll. Osteo. Medicine, East Lansing, 1976—; clin. asst. prof. Dept. Internal Medicine Wayne State U. Sch. Medicine, Detroit, 1983—. Team mem. Youth at Risk, Detroit, 1986. Mem. Am. Osteo. Assn., Mich. Assn. Osteo. Physicians and Surgeons, Wayne County Osteo. Assn., Am. Coll. Osteo. Internists, Nat. Kidney Found., Am. Soc. Nephrology, Renal Physicians Assn., Am. Heart Assn., Physicians for Social Responsibility, Am. Med. Athletics Assn., Motor City Striders Club, Riverbend Striders. Office: Met Nephrologists PC 101 Hutzel Profl Bldg 4727 Saint Antoine Detroit MI 48201

LAWSON, RANDALL CLAYTON, II, service company executive; b. Wabash, Ind., June 20, 1948; s. Randall Clayton and Evelyn Beatrice (Wright) L.; m. Julie Ann Severin, June 30, 1973; children—Randall Clayton III, Erin Elizabeth. B.S., Butler U., 1970. C.P.A., Ind., Ohio. Jr. acct. Price Waterhouse, Indpls., 1970-73; sr. acct. Price Waterhouse, Indpls. and Cin., 1973-76; audit mgr. Price Waterhouse, Cin., 1976-79; unit devel. controller Ponderosa, Inc., Dayton, Ohio, 1979-81, asst. corp. controller, 1981-82, corp. controller, 1982-84, v.p., corp. controller, 1984-85, sr. v.p., chief acctg. officer, 1985-87, sr. v.p., chief fin. officer, 1987; v.p., chief fin. officer Tad Tech. Services Corp., Cambridge, Mass., 1988—; bus. cons. 1987—. Mem. agy. audit com. United Way Greater Cin., 1975; mem. fin. and resource allocation com. United Way Greater Dayton, 1985, mem. com. on agy. fins., 1986-87. Mem. AICPA, Mass. Soc. CPAs, Fin. Execs. Inst., Phi Kappa Psi. Republican. Presbyterian. Clubs: Queen City Assn. (bd. dirs. 1978) (Cin.), Dayton Racquet. Lodge: Elks. Home: 53 Wood Rd Marlborough MA 01752 Office: Tad Tech Svcs Corp 639 Massachusetts Ave Cambridge MA 02139

LAWSON, THOMAS CHENEY, security, information and credit bureau company executive; b. Pasadena, Calif., Sept. 21, 1955; s. William McDonald and Joan Bell (Jaffee) L.; m. Cathy Lee Taylor. Student Calif. State U., Sacramento, 1973-77. Pres., Tomatron Co., Pasadena, 1970-88, Tom's Tune Up & Detail, Pasadena, 1971-88, Tom's Pool Service, Sacramento, 1975-78, Tom Supply Co., 1975—; mgmt. trainee Permoid Process Co., Los Angeles, 1970-75; regional sales cons. Hoover Co., Burlingame, 1974-76; mktg. exec. River City Prodns., Sacramento, 1977-78; prof. automechanics Calif. State U., Sacramento, 1973-75; territorial rep. Globe div. Burlington House Furniture Co., 1978; So. Calif. territorial rep. Marge Carson Furniture, Inc., 1978-80; pres. Ted L. Gunderson & Assos., Inc., Westwood, Calif., 1980-81; pres., chief exec. officer Apscreen, Newport Beach, Calif., 1981—; chmn. bd. dirs. Creditbase Co., Newport Beach, Worldata Corp., Newport Beach. Calif. Rehab. scholar, 1974-77. Mem. Christian Businessmen's Com. Internat., Council Internat. Investigators, Am. Soc. Indsl. Security (cert., vice-chmn. Orange County chpt. 1989), Nat. Pub. Records Research Assn., Personnel and Indsl. Relations Assn. Office: 2043 Westcliff Dr Ste 300 Newport Beach CA 92660

LAWSON, WILLIAM DAVID, III, cotton company executive; b. Jackson, Miss., Oct. 30, 1924; s. William David, Jr. and Elizabeth Vaiden (Barksdale) L.; m. Elizabeth Coppridge Smith, June 9, 1948; children—Margaret Monroe Headrick, William David, IV, Susan Barksdale Grunke, Thomas Nelson. B.S., Davidson (N.C.) Coll., 1948; M.B.A., Wharton Sch., U. Pa., 1949. Trainee T.J. White and Co., Memphis, 1949-52; v.p. W.D. Lawson and Co., Gastonia, N.C., 1952-70, pres., 1971-81; pres. Lawson, Lewis & Peat, Gastonia, 1981-85, Lawson Cotton Co., Gastonia, 1985—; v.p. Hohenberg Bros. Co. div. Cargill Inc., Memphis, 1988—; dir. First Union Nat. Bank, Gastonia. Bd. dirs., Covenant Village. Served as 1st lt., inf. AUS, 1943-46. Named Cotton Man of Year Cotton Digest, 1969, 76. Mem. Nat. Cotton Council (pres. 1975-76), Am. Cotton Shippers Assn. (pres. 1968-69), Atlantic Cotton Assn. (pres. 1957-58), Cotton Council Internat. (pres. 1972-73), Am. Cotton Exporters Assn. (treas.), Newcomen Soc., Gaston County C. of C. (pres. 1972-73), Am. Legion, Kappa Sigma. Republican. Presbyterian (elder). Clubs: Gaston Country, Gastonia City. Lodge: Rotary (pres. 1964-65). Home: 2444 Armstrong Circle Gastonia NC 28054 Office: Lawson Cotton Co 509 East Main St Gastonia NC 28054

LAWSON-JOHNSTON, PETER ORMAN, foundation executive; b. N.Y.C., Feb. 8, 1927; s. John R. and Barbara (Guggenheim) L.; m. Dorothy Stevenson Hammond, Sept. 30, 1950; children: Wendy, Tania, Peter, Mary. Reporter, yachting editor Balt. Sun Papers, 1951-53; exec. dir. Md. Classified Employees Assn., Balt., 1953-54; pub. info. dir. Md. Civil Def. Agy., Pikesville, 1954-56; sales mgr. Feldspar Corp. subs. Zemex Corp. (formerly Pacific Tin Consol.), N.Y.C., 1956-60, v.p. sales, 1961-66, v.p., 1966-72, chmn., 1972-81, bd. dirs., 1959—; v.p. Zemex Corp., 1966-72, vice chmn. 1972-75, pres., 1975-76, chmn., 1975—, also bd. dirs.; chmn. Anglo Energy, Inc., 1973-86; trustee Solomon R. Guggenheim Found. (operating Guggenheim Mus., N.Y.C. and Peggy Guggenheim Collection, Venice, Italy), 1964—, v.p. bus. adminstrn., 1965-69, pres., 1969—; dir. Harry Frank Guggenheim Found., 1968—, chmn., 1971—; ptnr. Guggenheim Bros., 1962-70, sr. ptnr., 1971—; ltd. ptnr. emeritus Alex. Brown & Sons, Inc.; pres., bd. dirs. Elgerbar Corp.; bd. dirs. McGraw Hill Inc., Nat. Rev. Inc. Chmn. Jeffersonian Restoration Adv. Bd., U. Va.; trustee The Lawrenceville Sch., bd. dirs. Coun. for U.S. and Italy. Served with AUS, 1945-47. Mem. Pilgrims of U.S., Carolina Plantation Soc., U.S. Srs. Golf Assn., Edgartown Yacht Club, Edgartown Reading Room Club, Green Spring Valley Hunt Club, River Club, Century Assn., Links, Nassau Gun Club, Bedens Brook Club, Pretty Brook Tennis Club, Md. Club, Seminole Golf Club, Island Club. Republican. Episcopalian. Home: 215 Carter Rd Princeton NJ 08540 Office: Solomon R Guggenheim Found 527 Madison Ave New York NY 10022

LAWTON, GREGORY MOSS, marketing professional; b. Youngstown, Ohio, Jan. 10, 1958; s. Edward Rigby Lawton and Peggy (Egan) Lawton Albert. Student, U. Colo., 1977; BS in Fin., Ft. Lewis Coll., 1981; postgrad., Fordham U., 1984-85. Pres. San Juan Mountaineering, Telluride, Colo., 1977-82; dir. mktg. Western Ski Vacations, N.Y.C., 1982-83; nat. sales mgr. Citicorp. Devel. Div., N.Y.C., 1983-85; exec. v.p., dir. mktg. Stephenson and Co., Denver, 1985—; bd. dirs. Charter Bank and Trust, Englewood, Colo., Larson Heavy Industries, Denver. Chmn. Dam Patean Denver Art Mus., 1986—. Office: Stephenson and Co 100 Garfield St Ste 400 Denver CO 80206

LAWTON, JACQUELINE AGNES, retired communications company executive, management consultant; b. Bklyn., June 9, 1933; d. Thomas G. and Agnes R. (McLaughlin) Maguire; m. George W. Lawton, Feb. 14, 1954; children—George, Victoria, Thomas. With N.Y. Telephone, 1954-82, mktg. mgr. govt., edn. and med. Mid State, 1978-81, mktg. mgr. health care, N.Y.C., 1981-82; dist. field market mgr. health care and lodging; region 1 N.E. and Region 2 Mid Atlantic, AT&T-Am. Bell, N.Y.C., 1982-83; Eastern region mgr. personnel, mktg. and sales AT&T Info. Systems, Parsippany, N.J., 1983-86, pvt. practice mgmt. cons., Cornish Flat, N.H., 1986—. Mem. Nat. Assn. Female Execs. Republican. Roman Catholic. Home and Office: PO Box 163 Cornish Flat NH 03746

LAWTON, LORILEE ANN, pipeline supply company owner, accountant; b. Morrisville, Vt., July 17, 1947; d. Philip Wyman Sr. and Margaret Elaine (Ather) Noyes; m. Lee Henry Lawton, Dec. 6, 1969; children: Deborah Ann, Jeffrey Lee. BBA, U. Vt., 1969. Sr. acct., staff asst. IBM, Essex Junction, Vt., 1969-72; owner, treas. Red-Hed Supply Inc, Winooski, Vt., 1972—. Apptd. bd. dirs. Colchester (Vt.) Community Devel. Assn., 1987, also treas./sec., Baird Ctr., Burlington, Vt., Assoc. Gen. Contractors Vt.; v.p. Colchester Vt. Community Devel. Assn.; mem. Bus. Edn. Adv. Com. Colchester High Sch. Mem. Associated Gen. Contractors Am., Associated Gen. Contractors Vt. (bd. dirs.), Am. Water Works Assn., Vt. Waterworks Assn., New Eng. Waterworks Assn., No. Vt. Homebuilders Assn., Greater Burlington Computer Users Group, Water and Sewer Distbrs. Am., Associated Builders and Contractors N.H. and Vt. Republican. Home: 53 Middle Rd Colchester VT 05446

LAY, TERRY LYNN, apparel company executive; b. Herington, Kans., Dec. 2, 1947; s. William James and Jean Lea (Meyer) L.; m. Sandra Kay Yount, May 27, 1978; 1 child, Emily. BA in Econs., Pittsburg (Kans.) State U., 1969. Mgr. specifications Lee Co., Ottawa, Kans., 1974-76; plant indsl. engr. Lee Co., Sulphur Springs, Tex., 1976-78; from asst. v.p. mfg. to sr. v.p. bus. planning and devel. Lee Co., Merriam, Kans., 1980-88, v.p., gen. mgr. menswear, 1988-89; v.p. ops. Jantzen, Inc., Portland, Oreg., 1989—. Mem. Am. Apparal Mfrs. Assn. (tech. adv. com., 1984—). Republican. Baptist. Office: Jantzen Inc PO Box 3001 Portland OR 97208

LAYBOURN, HALE, insurance company executive; b. Cedar Rapids, Iowa, July 20, 1923; s. Harold Hale and Reba S. (Strudevant) L.; B.S.B.A., U. Wyo., 1949; m. Barbara G., Dec. 21, 1947; children—Lillian Louise Laybourn Casares, Constance Grace Laybourn Harb, Deborah Hayle Laybourn Davis, Paul James, Richard Tod, Dorothy M. Asst. bus. mgr. Cheyenne (Wyo.) Newspapers, Inc., 1949-50; fiscal and personnel officer, dir. hosp. facilities Wyo. Dept. Health, 1950-60; dir. internal ops. Blue Cross and Blue Shield, Cheyenne, Wyo., 1960-65; pres. Blue Cross N.D., Fargo, 1965-86; pres., chief exec. officer Dental Service Corp., Vision Service, Inc., 1976-86; Coordinated Ins. Service, 1982-86 ; chmn. bd. No. Plains Life Ins. Co., 1983-86, chmn. bd., pres., 1986-88; v.p. Care Plan HMO; bd. dirs. Nat. Blue Cross Assn., 1973-77; chmn. Dist. X Plan Pres's., 1970-73; dir. West Fargo State Bank. Pres., Fargo-Moorhead Civic Opera Co., 1968-81, chmn. bd., 1981—; chmn. United Fund, Fargo, 1972. Served with inf. U.S. Army, 1942-45. Mem. Fargo C. of C. (pres. 1977). Republican. Episcopalian. Clubs: Elks, Kiwanis. Office: 3002 Fiechther Dr Ste B Fargo ND 58103

LAYBOURNE, GEORGE THOMAS, scientist, quality control engineer; b. Springfield, Ohio, July 21, 1929; s. George T. and Grace Clara (Tossey) L.; m. Gail Audrey Niethamer, July 3, 1953; children: Neal Thomas, Ned Robert, Nan Louise. BA, Wittenberg U., 1955; MBA, Am. Internat. Coll., 1962. Registered profl. engr., Calif. Lab. asst., metalurgist Internat. Harvester Co., Springfield, 1947-55; chemist Monsanto Chem. Co., Columbus, Ohio, 1955-57; group leader Monsanto Chem. Co., Springfield, Mass., 1957-63; supr. lab. USI Film Products, Bridgeport, Conn., 1963-65; mgr. quality control Alamo (USIFP) Corp., Stratford, Conn., 1965-67; supr. research Chemplex Co., Rolling Meadows, Ill., 1967-85; sect. leader Norchem Co./Enron Co., Rolling Meadows, 1985-87; assoc. scientist USI Chem. Co., Rolling Meadows, 1987-88; sr. project leader Quantum-USI div., Rolling Meadows, 1988—; mem. adv. bd. Ferris State U., Big Rapids, Mich.; instr. Conn. Vocat. Inst., Bridgeport, 1965-67, Elgin (Ill.) Community Coll., 1976-85. Contbr. articles to profl. jours. Mem. Sch. Survey Bd., Hampden, Mass., 1958-59, Rep. Town Com., Trumbull, Conn., 1963-67, bd. govs. Timber-Lee Christian Camp, East Troy, Wis., 1982—; chmn. Bd. Assessors, Hampden, 1960-63; mem. adv. bd. N.W. Suburban Council, Springfield, Bridgeport and Arlington Heights, Ill., 1956—, Signal Hill Dist. Merit award, Ill., 1972, Silver Beaver award, 1974. Served with U.S. Army, 1951. Mem. Soc. Plastic Engrs. (sr., edn. chmn. 1978-84, bd. dirs. 1976-87), Am. Soc. Quality Control (sr., treas. 1957, sec. 1958-59, bd. dirs. 1981-85), Am. Soc. Testing and Materials (sec. 1972-78, group chmn. 1968-72, exec. com. 1972-78, task group chmn. 1980—). Mem. Evang. Ch. Lodge: Masons. Home: 145 E County Line Rd Barrington IL 60010 Office: USI Chem Co 3100 Golf Rd Rolling Meadows IL 60008

LAYFIELD, ARTHUR WAYNE, vending company executive; b. Salisbury, Md., Aug. 14, 1960; s. Arthur Stanley Layfield and Agusta Lee (Geoghegan) Norris; m. Elaine Dee Green, Aug. 19, 1979 (div. Sept. 1982); 1 child, Ashley Brooke; m. Donna Marie Hicken, Mar. 29, 1985 (div. Oct. 1988); m. Betty Ann Goodman, Dec. 3, 1988; 1 child, Victoria Erin. Grad. high sch., Centreville, Md., 1978. Asst. mgr. Dawkins Mktg. Inc., Easton, Md., 1978-79; mgr. Shore Pizza Hut, Inc., Grasonville, Md., 1979-86, cons., 1986-87; gen. mgr. Island Vending Co., Inc., Queenstown, Md., 1986—, dir. ops., 1987—. Mem. Smithsonian Instn. Mem. Preservation for Hist. Bldgs., Kent Island Jaycees (pres. 1987), Am. Film Inst., Amnesty Internat., Jacques Coustea Soc., Internat. Platform Assn. Republican. Methodist. Home: 1595 Secretariat Dr Annapolis MD 21401 Office: Island Vending Co Inc Rte 301 PO Box 250 Queenstown MD 21658

LAYSON, WILLIAM MCINTYRE, research consulting company executive; b. Lexington, Ky., Sept. 24, 1934; s. Zed Clark and Louise (McIntyre) L.; m. Robin Dale Fort, July 28, 1982. B.S., MIT, 1956, Ph.D., 1961; postgrad., U. Sydney, Australia, 1957-58. Research scientist European Ctr. Nuclear Research, Geneva, 1960-62; research scientist U. Calif.-Berkeley, 1962-64; mem. tech. staff Pan Am World Airways, Patrick AFB, Fla., 1964-67; research scientist Gen. Research Corp., Rosslyn, Va., 1967-70; dir. Sci. Applications Internat. Corp., McLean, Va., 1970—, sr. v.p., chmn. incentives com., coordinator def. nuclear programs, 1975—. Fulbright scholar U. Sydney, Australia, 1957-58. Mem. Am. Def. Preparedness Assn. Democrat. Presbyterian (elder). Home: 8301 Summerwood Dr McLean VA 22102 Office: Sci Applications Internat Corp 1710 Goodridge Dr McLean VA 22102

LAYTON, GARLAND MASON, lawyer; b. Boydton, Va., Aug. 20, 1925. LLB, Smith-Deal-Massey Coll. Law, 1952; LLD, Coll. of William and Mary, 1962. Bar: Va. 1951, U.S. Dist. Ct. (ea. dist.) Va. 1961, U.S. Supreme Ct. 1968. Sole practice Virginia Beach, Va., 1952—; of house counsel Tau Ceti, Inc., East Coast Automotive Svc., Inc. Served with USMC, 1940-45, PTO. Mem. ABA, Fed. Bar Assn., Nat. Lawyers Club, Va. Beach Bar Assn. Democrat. Methodist. Home: PO Box 5211 Bayside Sta Virginia Beach VA 23455 Office: 4809 Baybridge Ln PO Box 5211 Virginia Beach VA 23455

LAYTON, HARRY CHRISTOPHER, artist, lecturer; b. Safford, Ariz., Nov. 17, 1938; s. Christopher E. and Eurilda (Welker) L.; LHD, Sussex Coll., Eng., 1969; DFA (hon.), London Inst. Applied Research, 1972, DSc (hon), 1972; DD (hon.), St. Matthew U., Ohio, 1970, PhD (hon.), 1970; m. Karol Barbara Kendall, July 11, 1964 (div. Jan. 1989); children: Deborah, Christopher, Joseph, Elisabeth, Faith, Aaron, Gretchen, Benjamin, Justin, Matthew, Peter. Cert. clin. hypnotherapist. Lectr. ancient art Serra Cath. High Sch., 1963-64, Los Angeles Dept. Parks and Recreation, summer 1962, 63, 64; interior decorator Cities of Hawthorne, Lawndale, Compton, Gardena and Torrance (Calif.), 1960-68; one-man shows paintings; Nahas Dept. Stores, 1962, 64; group shows include: Gt. Western Savs. & Loan, Lawndale, Calif., 1962, Gardena (Calif.) Adult Sch., 1965, Serra Cath. High Sch., Gardena, 1963, Salon de Nations Paris, 1983; represented in permanent collections: Sussex Coll., Eng., Gardena Masonic Lodge, Culver City-Foshey Masonic Lodge, Gt. Western Savs. & Loan; paintings include: The Fairy Princess, 1975, Nocturnal Covenant, 1963, Blindas Name, 1962, Creation, 1962. Elder Ch. of Jesus Christ of Latter-day Saints, Santa Monica, Calif., 1963—. Recipient Golden Poet award, World of Poetry, 1986, 88. Mem. Am. Hypnotherapy Assn., Gardena Valley Art Assn., Centinella Valley Art Assn., Internat. Soc. Artists, Internat. Platform Assn., Am. Security Council, Soc. for Early Historic Archaeology, Am. Councilor's Soc. of Psychol. Counselors, Le Salon Des Nation Paris Geneva, Ctr. Internat. d'Art Contemporain, Am. Legion, Alpha Psi Omega. Republican. Clubs: Masons (32 deg.), Shriners, K.T. Home: 3658 Centinela Ave Ste 6 Mar Vista CA 90066 Office: Layton Studios Graphic Design P O Box 66849 Los Angeles CA 90066

LAZARA, VINCENT ANTHONY, brokerage house executive; b. Bklyn., Oct. 2, 1946; s. Vincent S. and Rosalind (Donadio) L.; m. Nancy E. Ash, Mar. 24, 1984. BA, NYU, 1968; MA, U. Ariz., 1971, PhD, 1973. Account exec. Blythe Eastman Dillon, Tucson, 1979, Paine Webber, Tucson, 1979-82; v.p. investments Prudential Bache Securities, Tucson, 1982—; adj. instr. Coll. Fin. Planning, 1980-85; cons. Nat. Ctr. Fin. Edn., 1984—, Dima Coll. Fin. Edn., 1987-88. Treas. Humane Soc. Tucson, 1982. Mem. Inst. Cert. Fin. Planners (pres. Tucson chpt.), Southwestern League Fine Arts (v.p. 1987-88, pres. 1988—). Office: Prudential Bache Securities 5255 E Williams Circle 205 Tucson AZ 85711

LAZARE, HOWARD TED, engineering executive; b. Chgo., Oct. 10, 1936; s. Henry and Jeanne (Sodakoff) LaZ.; m. Phyllis F. Carter, July 15, 1959; children: Adam, Kim. BSEE, West Coast U., Los Angeles, 1969, BSME, 1970. Registered profl. engr., Calif. V.p. engring. Consol. Film Industries, Hollywood, Calif., 1964-84; sr. v.p. engring. Deluxe Labs., Hollywood, 1984—. Patentee shutterless film projector. Fellow Soc. Motion Picture TV Engrs. (v.p. motion picture affairs 1982-83, editorial v.p. 1985-88, Class II Academy awards 1973, 82); mem. Acad. Motion Pictures Arts Scis., Am. Soc. Cinematographers (assoc.), IEEE (senior mem.), British Kinematograph Sound TV Engrs. (corp. mem.). Republican. Jewish. Home: 10825 Fullbright Ave Chatsworth CA 91311 Office: Deluxe Labs 1377 N Serrano Ave Hollywood CA 90027

LAZAROWICZ, JOHN FRANCIS, real estate developer; b. Coalport, Pa., Jan. 13, 1924; s. Walter Casper and Stella (Domino) L.; m. Virginia Beatrice Ditch, June 29, 1946; children: Janet, Beth Ann, Cindi. Student, Pa. State Extension, Indiana, Pa., 1946-48, Ind. State Coll., Indiana, Pa., 1948-49, Montgomery Tech. Inst., 1970. Surveyor Rochester & Pitts. Coal Co., Indiana, 1942-62; mgr. positions Realty Cos., Tenn., Ohio, and N.C., 1962-74; v.p. Pioneer Energy, Inc., Bluefield, West Va., 1975-76; constrn. mgr. Thurston Motor Lines, Charlotte, N.C., 1976-77; v.p. Mark Ten Properties, Charlotte, 1977-83; exec. v.p. Patten Realty Corp., Columbia, S.C., 1983-84; pres. Lazner Investment Corp., Charlotte, 1984—. Pres. Holy Name Soc., Homer City, Pa., 1955-56. Republican. Roman Catholic. Lodge: KC (Indiana, Pa.).

LAZARUS, ARLIE GARY, corporate executive; b. N.Y.C., Jan. 29, 1938; s. Leon and Celia L.; m. Gloria Hindman, Mar. 29, 1959; children—Mark, Lee, Lisa. B.S., Hunter Coll., 1959. Acct. Eisner & Lubin (C.P.A.'s), N.Y.C., 1959-64; controller Miracle Mart, Inc., N.Y.C., 1964-68; fin. v.p. Jamesway Corp., Secaucus, N.J., 1968-73; exec. v.p. Jamesway Corp., 1973-76, pres., 1977—; bd. dirs., mem. adv. bd. Discount Store News. Mem. Internat. Mass Retailing Assn. (bd. dirs.). Jewish. Office: Jamesway Corp 40 Hartz Way Secaucus NJ 07096-1526

LAZARUS, JONATHAN DONIEL, software company and publishing executive; b. Mar. 29, 1951; s. Earl and Lucille (Wallace) L.; m. Sharon Gibson, Oct. 13, 1979. BS, Temple U., 1973. Prin. QQF Ltd., N.Y.C., 1981-82; editor PC Mag., N.Y.C., 1983; editor-in-chief PC Week Mag., N.Y.C., 1983; editorial dir. Ziff-Davis Pub. Co., N.Y.C., 1983-84, v.p. editorial, 1984-85; pres. H. Roark & Assocs., N.Y.C., 1986—; editor and publisher Microsoft Systems Jour., N.Y.C., 1986—; dir. systems strategy Microsoft Corp., N.Y.C., 1987—; sr. cons. A.C. Nielson Co., N.Y., 1980-81. Office: Microsoft Corp 666 3rd Ave 16th Fl New York NY 10017

LAZENBY, FRED WIEHL, insurance company executive; b. Chattanooga, Jan. 13, 1932; s. John Wesley and Adela (Valenzuela) L.; m. Kathryn Woodard, Sept. 20, 1958; children: Kathryn Wesley, Grace Woodard. BA cum laude, Vanderbilt U., 1954. CLU. With Nat. Life & Accident Ins. Co., Nashville, 1956—, from agt. to pres., 1956-83; chmn. bd., chief exec. officer Southlife Holding Co., Nashville, 1983—, Pub. Savs. Life Ins. Co., Charleston, S.C., 1984—, Security Trust Life Ins. Co., Macon, Ga., 1987—; bd. dirs. Nashville Bank of Commerce. Trustee Life Underwriting Tng. Coun., 1978-82; mem. bd. advisors Massey Sch. 1st lt. U.S. Army, 1954-56. Mem. Life Ins. Mgmt. Rsch. Assn. (bd. dirs. 1985-88, past chmn. combination cos. exec. com.); vice-chmn. Life Ins. Conf. (exec. com.), Belle Meade Country Club, Carolina Yatch Club, Rotary. Republican. Methodist. Clubs:

Belle Meade Country, Nashville Cumberland, Carolina Yacht. Lodge: Rotary. Office: Southlife Holding Co Southlife Bldg 211 Seventh Ave W Nashville TN 37219 also: Pub Savs Life Ins Co 304 Meeting St PO Box 10020 Charleston SC 29411

LEA, ALBERT ROBERT, manufacturing executive; b. Melrose, Mass., May 27, 1921; s. Robert Wentworth and Lillian (Ryan) L.; m. Joyce Winona Padgett, May 17, 1943 (div.); children: Patricia, Jennifer, Anne, Melissa Lea; m. Helen Clay Jones, May 12, 1961; children: Albert Robert, Robbert Wentworth II. AB, Amherst Coll., 1943; student Harvard Grad. Sch. Bus. Adminstrn., 1943. Exec. v.p. Ashcraft Inc., Kansas City, 1957-67, 83-86, pres., 1967-83, also dir.; pres. The Lea Co., 1986—. Trustee Westminster Coll., Fulton, Mo., 1983-88. Lt. Supply Corps, USNR, 1943-46. Mem. Mission Hills Country Club, University Club, Met. Club, Phi Gamma Delta. Home: 625 W Meyer Blvd Kansas City MO 64113 Office: 605 W Meyer Blvd Kansas City MO 64113

LEA, LORENZO BATES, lawyer; b. St. Louis, Apr. 12, 1925; s. Lorenzo Bates and Ursula Agnes (Gibson) L.; m. Marcia Gwendolyn Wood, Mar. 21, 1953; children—Victoria, Jennifer, Christopher. B.S., M.I.T., 1946; J.D., U. Mich., 1949; grad. Advanced Mgmt. Program, Harvard U., 1964. Bar: Ill. bar 1950. With Amoco Corp. (formerly Standard Oil Co. Ind.), Chgo., 1949—, asst. gen. counsel, 1963-71, assoc. gen. counsel, 1971-72, gen. counsel, 1972-78, v.p., gen. counsel, 1978—. Trustee Village of Glenview (Ill.) Zoning Bd., 1961-63; bd. dirs. Chgo. Crime Commn., 1978—, Midwest Council for Internat. Econ. Policy, 1973—, Chgo. Bar Found., 1981—, Chgo. Area Found. for Legal Services, 1981—; bd. dirs. United Charities of Chgo., 1973—, chmn., 1985—. Served with USNR, 1943-46. Mem. Am. Bar Assn., Ill. Bar Assn., Chgo. Bar Assn., Am. Petroleum Inst., Assn. Gen. Counsel, Am. Arbitration Assn. (dir. 1980—), Order of Coif, Sigma Xi. Republican. Mem. United Ch. of Christ. Clubs: Law, Econs., Legal, Mid-Am. (Chgo.); Glen View. Office: Amoco Corp 200 E Randolph Dr Chicago IL 60601

LEA, PAMELA WARREN, real estate appraiser; b. South Charleston, W.Va., June 3, 1947; d. George Herbert Warren and Eileen Kathel (Ellis) Warren Hoflich; m. Ted Mann Lea, Aug. 21, 1971 (div. Nov. 1982); children: Lisa Dawn, Robert Christopher, Andrea Elizabeth. Student, U. N.C., Greensboro, 1965-67, 69-71, Ga. State U., Atlanta, 1984. Data entry operator Ticor Mortgage Ins. Co., Atlanta, 1983-84; underwriting asst. United Guaranty, Atlanta, 1984-85; real estate appraiser Arnold M. Schwartz & Assocs., Atlanta, 1985—. Baptist. Home: 2839 Arden Way Smyrna GA 30080

LEA, SCOTT CARTER, packaging company executive; b. New Orleans, Nov. 14, 1931; s. Leonard G. and Helen (Stoughton) L.; m. Marilyn Ruth Blair, Oct. 25, 1957; children—Scott, Nancy B., Mark S. B.A., Amherst Coll., 1954; M.B.A., U. Pa., 1959. Sales and mktg. positions Riegel Paper, 1959-66, sales mgr. folding carton dept. southeastern div., 1966-67, gen. sales mgr., 1967-69, v.p. folding carton dept., 1969-71; v.p. bd. conversion div. Rexham Corp., Charlotte, N.C., 1971-73; v.p. packaging group Rexham Corp., 1973-74, pres., 1974—; dir. Quantum Chem. Corp., Consol. Electronics Industries Corp. Trustee Johnson C. Smith U., Charlotte, N.C.; bd. dirs. Found. U.N.C.-Charlotte. Served with U.S. Army, 1954-57. Mem. Charlotte C. of C. (dir. 1977-78). Clubs: Carmel Country, Quail Hollow Country (Charlotte); Union League (N.Y.C.), Sky (N.Y.C.). Home: 3704 Stone Ct Charlotte NC 28226 Office: Rexham Corp 7315 Pineville-Matthews Rd Box 2528 Charlotte NC 28226

LEACH, DONALD PAUL, institute executive; b. Mount Vernon, N.Y., Mar. 17, 1945; s. Alfred Grahame and Anne Marie (Hantz) L.; m. Nancy Lynne Davis, Jan. 30, 1967; children: Donald Paul, Brian, Deborah. BS, Cedarville Coll., 1968; MBA, U. Dayton, 1974. Acct., mem. corp. staff Top Value Enterprises, Dayton, Ohio, 1969-72; tax analyst, corp. staff Philips Industries, Inc., Dayton, 1972-73; tax mgr. Danis Industries Corp., Dayton, 1973-76, asst. v.p., 1976-78, v.p., treas. constrn. products group, 1978-82; v.p., treas. Moody Bible Inst., Chgo., 1982-88, v.p., spl. asst. to pres. Moody Consumer Ministries, 1988—; instr. acctg. Sinclair Community Coll., Dayton, 1974-82. Mem. fin. com. Dayton Christian Schs., 1981-82; trustee Washington Hts. Bapt. Ch., Dayton, 1981-82, supt., 1977-80; deacon Faith Bapt. Ch., Winfield, Ill., 1984-87; treas. Alumni Council of Cedarville (Ohio) Coll., 1981-83, chmn., 1983-87; pres. Dayton Tax Club, 1977-78. Served with U.S. Army, 1967. Mem. Nat. Assn. Accountants, Inst. Internal Auditors, Christian Ministries Mgmt. Assn. Home: 1481 Fanchon St Wheaton IL 60187 Office: Moody Bible Inst 820 N La Salle St Chicago IL 60610

LEACH, JAMES HESS, finance company executive; b. Providence, Aug. 7, 1959; s. Oscar A. and Lenore (Hess) L. Student, Boston U., 1983-84; BA, Nasson Coll., 983. Treas. Indsl. Devel. Corp., Providence, 1983—; pres., chief exec. officer The Goodall Corp., Providence, 1985—; asst. sec. Norwood Chevrolet Co., Warwick, R.I., 1988—; bd. dirs. Page One Beepers, Inc., Atlanta, Modern Tractor & Truck Svc., Seekonk, Mass., Twenty Westminster St., Inc., Providence, Bayphar Corp., Providence, Chevrolet Mgmt. Corp., Providence. Mem. Boston TheatreDist. Assn., 1988—, Nat. Kidney Found. Mass., Boston, 1988—, Opera Soc. Boston, 1988—, City Planning Commn., Providence, 1989—; bd. dirs. Music Sch. Mem. Internat. Coun. Shopping Ctrs., R.I. Hist. Soc., Ledgemont Country Club, Turks Head Club, Aurora Club, Firefly Country Club (bd. dirs.). Home: 500 Blackstone Blvd Providence RI 02906 Office: The Goodall Cos 20 Westminster St Providence RI 02903

LEACH, JEFFREY ROBERT, investment banker; b. New Haven, Jan. 24, 1961; s. Benton Ray and Elizabeth (Cox) L.; m. Judith Buckingham, Oct. 11, 1986. BS in Econs., Bucknell U., 1983. Ptnr. Bleakley, Dwyer, Leach & Schwartz, Fairfield, N.J., 1984-88; mng. dir. Commonwealth Assocs., N.Y.C., 1988—; bd. dirs. Mediacom Communications, L.A., Health Advancement Systems, Tempe, Ariz. Recipient Bronze and Silver awards Northwestern Mut. Life, 1984, 85. Republican. Home: 96 Skyline Dr Morristown NJ 07960 Office: Commonwealth Assocs One Exchange Pla New York NY 10006

LEACH, RICHARD MAXWELL (MAX), JR., corporate professional; b. Chillicothe, Tex., June 14, 1934; s. Richard Maxwell and Lelia Booth (Page) L.; m. Wanda Gail Groves, Feb. 4, 1956; children: Richard Clifton, John Christopher, Sandra Gail, Kathy Lynn. BS in Acctg. magna cum laude, Abilene Christian U., 1955. Registered Fin. Planner., CLU. Asst. dir. agys. Am. Founders Ins. Co., Austin, Tex., 1960-62; owner A.F. Ins. Planning Assocs., Temple, Tex., 1962-65; v.p. sales Christian Fidelity Life Ins. Co., Waxahachie, Tex., 1966-67; exec. v.p. Acad. Computer Tech., Inc., Dallas, 1968-69; pres., chief exec. officer Inta-Search Internat., Inc., Dallas, 1969-71; prin., chief exec. officer, fin. cons. Leach and Assocs., Albuquerque, 1971—; chmn. bd. United Quest Inc., Albuquerque, Hosanna Inc., Albuquerque; real estate broker; commodity futures broker; exec. dir., bd. dirs. New Heart, Inc., Albuquerque, 1975-85; owner Insta-Copy, Albuquerque, 1973-76, Radio Sta. KYLE-FM, Temple, 1963-64. Editor, author Hosanna newspaper, 1973-74. Gen. dir. Here's Life, New Mexico, Albuquerque, 1976; exec. dir. Christians for Cambodia, Albuquerque, 1979-80. Served with U.S. Army, 1955-57. Home: 3308 June NE Albuquerque NM 87111 Office: 7200 Montgomery Blvd NE Albuquerque NM 87109

LEACH, RONALD JAMES, federal agency administrator; b. Athens, Ga., July 6, 1960; s. Richard William and Patricia Ann (Mauser) L. BS in Housing and Econs., U. Ga., 1985. Staff asst. Office Sec. U.S. Treasury, Washington, 1985-86; budget officer Fed. Retirement Thrift Investment Bd., Washington, 1986—. Mem. Council Consumer Interests, Athens, Ga., 1984-86; Ga. Trust, Atlanta, 1984-86, Nat. Trust Hist. Preservation, Washington, 1984—. Office: Fed Retirement Thrift Investment Bd 805 15th St NW Washington DC 20005

LEACH, RONALD LEE, manufacturing company executive; b. Athens, Ohio, Aug. 22, 1934; s. Ralph and Lelia Celesta (Woodruff) L.; m. Marilyn Rose Dreger, Sept. 3, 1956; children: Cynthia Diane, Mark Ronald, Douglas Ralph. B.S., Ohio U., 1958. With Ernst & Ernst, Cleve., 1960-70, mgr., 1967-70; asst. to v.p. and controller Eaton Corp., Cleve., 1970-72, asst. controller fin. acctg., 1972-77, corp. controller, 1977-78, v.p., controller, 1979-81, v.p. acctg., 1981—, dir., officer several subs. Mem. exec. adv. bd. bus. adminstrn. Ohio U., 1978—; treas. Lakeview Ch. of God, Parma, Ohio, 1968-84, trustee, 1969—, chmn. bd., 1984—; trustee, treas. Univ. for Young Ams., 1981—. Served with USAF, 1958-60. Mem. Fin. Execs. Inst. (dir. NE Ohio chpt. 1979-80, v.p. 1980-81, pres. 1981-82), Fin. Execs, Inst. (com. corp. reporting 1979—), Greater Cleve. Growth Assn., Am. Inst. C.P.A.s, Ohio Soc. C.P.A.s, Am. Acctg. Assn., Nat. Assn. Accts., Nat. Elec. Mfgrs. Assn., Beta Alpha Psi, Pi Gamma Mu, Beta Gamma Sigma. Republican. Club: Clevelander. Office: Eaton Corp Eaton Ctr Cleveland OH 44114

LEADABRAND, RAY L., research and development corporation executive; b. Pasadena, Calif., Oct. 12, 1927; s. Russell Lewis and Monica Laurel (Irwin) L.; m. Mildren Helen Armbruster, Apr. 2, 1955; 1 child, Paul Lewis. AA, Visalia Jr. Coll., 1948; BS, San Jose State U., 1950; MSEE, Stanford U., 1955. Project leader SRI Internat., Menlo Park, Calif., 1955-62, dir., 1962-69, exec. dir., 1969-77, v.p., 1977-79, sr. v.p., 1979-86; sr. v.p. Sci. Applications Internat. Corp., Los Altos, Calif., 1986—; chmn. Naval Studies Bd. Radio-Elec. Battle Mgmt. Panel, Washington, 1987-88; mem. com. Nat. Research Council, Washington, adv. com. Def. Intelligence Agy., Washington, 1983—, adv. panel Office Tech. Assessment, Washington, 1987—. Contbr. articles to profl. jours. Served with USN, 1945-46. Fellow IEEE; mem. AIAA, Am. Geophys. Union, Armed Forces Communication and Electronics Assn., Assn. Unmanned Vehicle Systems, Am. Bonanza Soc. (bd. dirs.), Assn. Old Crows. Club: Cosmos (Washington). Home: 80 Joaquin Rd Portola Valley CA 94025

LEAF, DOUGLASS, JR., retail executive; b. Staten Island, N.Y., Jan. 1, 1927; s. Douglass and Bessie (Bowers) L.; m. Barbara Ann Weissner, May 9, 1953; children: Cynthia Ann, Diana Jean. BA, Pa. State U., 1951. Trainee Brandis & Sons, Inc., Bklyn., 1951-53, salesman, 1953—, corp. sec., 1955—; pres., chief exec. officer Brandis & Sons, Inc., Bklyn. and Pleasantville (N.Y.), 1961—; pres. The Am. Surveyor's Pub. Co., Falls Church, Va., 1985. Served as sgt. USAAF, 1945-47. Mem. Am. Congress on Surveying and Mapping, Conn. Soc. Civil Engrs., N.Y. State Assn. Profl. Land Surveyors, Conn. Soc. Land Surveyors, N.J. Soc. Profl. Land Surveyors. Republican. Presbyterian. Club: Scarsdale Golf (Hartsdale, N.Y.) (v.p. 1984—). Lodge: Rotary. Office: Brandis & Sons Inc 62 Clinton Ave Pleasantville NY 10570

LEAHEY, MILES CARY, economist; b. Washington, Sept. 14, 1952; s. Thomas Francis and Eva Smith (Hardy) L. AB with high honors, Clark U., 1974; MA, U. Pa., 1977, PhD, 1978. Fiscal economist Office of Mgmt. and Budget, Washington, 1978-80; sr. economist DRI, Lexington, Mass., 1980-83; v.p., sr. economist Shearson Lehman Bros., N.Y.C., 1983-88; dir. econ. staff GM, 1988—; lectr. U. Pa., 1977, Swarthmore (Pa.) Coll., 1978, Boston U., 1983. Author: Government and Capital Formation, 1979; (journal) Bus. Econs., 1985, Jour. of Policy Modeling, 1985. Mem. Am. Econs. Assn., Nat. Assn. Bus. Economists. Democrat. Episcopalian. Club: Blue Hill Troupe (N.Y.C.). Home: 410 Riverside Dr #33 New York NY 10025 Office: GM 767 Fifth Ave 26th Fl New York NY 10153

LEAHIGH, ALAN KENT, public relations executive; b. Chgo., Dec. 25, 1944; s. Leland Jean and Rena Mathilda (Rodda) L.; m. Lorrie Lynn Johnson, Aug. 19, 1967; children: Matthew Alan, Nathan Andrew. BA, Ill. Wesleyan U., 1967; MA, U. Mo., 1971. Reporter, editor Daily Pantagraph, Bloomington, Ill., 1969-71; tchr. Joliet (Ill.) Pub. Sch. Dist., 1969-71; assoc. dir. pub. info. Am. Dental Assn., Chgo., 1971-75, dir. pub. edn., 1976-77, editor ADA News, 1978-80; v.p. Pub. Communications Inc., Chgo., 1981-83, sr. v.p., ptnr., 1983—; v.p. Living Learning Devel. Corp., Wheaton (Ill.), 1980—, Marion Park Inc., Wheaton, 1980—; lectr. workshops in field. Contbr. articles to profl. jours. Mem. Wheaton Hist. Preservation Soc., 1978—; chmn. Wheaton Community TV Cmmn., 1986—. Mem. Pub. Relations Soc. Am. (Silver Anvil award 1982, 85, 86), Soc. Profl. Journalists, Chgo. Publicity Club, Am. Hosp. Assn., Chgo. High Tech. Soc., Chgo. Headline Club, Masons. Presbyterian. Office: Pub Communications Inc 35 E Wacker Dr Chicago IL 60601

LEAHY, THOMAS FRANCIS, broadcasting executive; b. N.Y.C., June 30, 1937; m. Patricia B. Flanagan, May 5, 1962; children: Patricia Ann, Allison Marie, Thomas Francis, Kirsten Elizabeth, Caitlin Coxe. B.E.E., Manhattan Coll., 1959; D. Comml. Sci. (hon.), St. John's U., Jamaica, N.Y., 1983. With CBS-TV, N.Y.C., 1962—; group exec. v.p. CBS/Broadcast Group, N.Y.C., 1981-86; pres. CBS-TV Network, N.Y.C., 1987-88, Mktg. div. CBS, N.Y.C., 1988—. Past mem. exec. com. N.Y.'s Better Bus. Bur.; bd. dirs. Big Bros. N.Y., Red Cross of Greater N.Y.; past trustee Fordham Prep. Sch., Coll. Mt. St. Vincent, Stonehill Coll.; mem. Mayor's Mid-Town Com.; mem. Assn. for a Better N.Y.; founding dir. Youth Suicide Nat. Ctr., Washington; dir. The Just Say No Found., Walnut Creek, Calif. (exec. com.), Advt. Coun., Inc. Served with U.S. Army, 1959-65. Recipient Nat. Disting. Achievement in Communications award Am. Jewish Com., 1985, Joseph E. Connor Meml. award Phi Alpha Tau, Emerson Coll., Boston, 1986. Mem. Internat. Radio/TV Soc. (past dir.), Nat. Acad. TV Arts and Scis. (past pres. internat. coun.), Am. Irish Hist. Soc. (exec. coun.), Siwanoy Country Club, Met. Club. Office: CBS Mktg Div 51 W 52d St New York NY 10019

LEAKE, FRANK DUDLEY, business executive; b. Indpls., Aug. 24, 1948; s. Fred Henry and Ceffie (Evans) L.; 1 child, Charmaine. Grad. high sch. Pres., owner Leake Enterprises, Indpls. With U.S. Army, 1968-70, ETO. also: 1127 W Eugene Indianapolis IN 46208

LEAKE, VERNELL, intermediary for government, accountant; b. Durham, N.C., July 7, 1955; s. James Vester and Odelia (Upchurch) L. BA, Winston-Salem State U., 1977; postgrad., Duke U., 1986—. Mgr. Group Homes, Inc., Durham, 1978; tax preparer H&R Block, Inc., Durham, 1979; acct. Blue Cross-Blue Shield of N.C., Durham, 1980—; pvt. practice cons., Durham area, 1979—. Vol., chmn. youth com. ARC, Durham, 1985—. Mem. Nat. Geographic Soc., Pi Gamma Mu. Office: Blue Cross & Blue Shield of NC PO Box 2291 Durham NC 27702

LEAMAN, J. RICHARD, JR., paper company executive; b. Lancaster, Pa., Sept. 22, 1934; s. J. Richard and Margaret B. (Leaman); m. Helen Brown, June 15, 1957; children: Lynda B., J. Richard, III. BA, Dartmouth Coll., 1956, MBA, 1957; PhD (hon.), Widener U., 1988. With Scott Paper Co., Phila., 1960—, v.p. comml. products, 1975-78; exec. v.p. mktg. and sales Scott Paper Co., 1978—, pres. Packaged Products div., 1983—, dir., 1986; pres. Scott Worldwide, 1986; bd. dirs. Church & Dwight Co., Inc. Vice chmn. exec. com. and bd. trustees Widener U., 1987; bd. govs. Acad. Food Mktg. at St. Joseph's U.; trustee Tyler Arboretum. Served to capt. USAF, 1957-61. Recipient Disting. Performance in Mgmt. award Widener U. Mem. Am. Paper Inst. (internat. bus. com.), Grocery Mfrs. Am. (mem. Industry Productivity Com.). Republican. Episcopalian. Clubs: Dartmouth (Phila.); Rose Tree Media Optimists. Home: 317 Boot Rd Malvern PA 19355 Office: Scott Paper Co Scott Pla Philadelphia PA 19113

LEAR, FLOYD RAYMOND, III, entrepreneur; b. Easton, Pa., June 20, 1942; s. Floyd Raymond Jr. and Midred M. (Sterner) L.; m. Judith Marie Smith, Dec. 31, 1962 (div. Dec. 1973); children: Eric James, Michael Thomas. Grad., Blair Acad., 1960; attended, Rider Coll., 1961-62. Sales rep. Indsl. Engraving Co. Inc., Easton, 1965-73, v.p. adminstrn. and sales, 1973-82, pres., chief exec. officer, chmn. bd., 1982—; owner, operator Lear Publs., Inc., Easton, 1970-74; co-owner Travel With Carole, Inc., Bethlehem, Pa., 1985—, Silk Flower Shop, 1982—; owner King's Hill Antiques, Easton, 1986—; vice chmn. bd. Lafayette Trust Bank, Easton, 1987—. Officer Easton Area Jaycees, 1964-79; active Bethlehem, Easton United Way, 1967, ABE Airport Adv. Com., Allentown, Pa., 1983-85; charter mem., bd. dirs. Hist. Easton , 1974-79; mem. exec. com., dir. found. bd. Northampton Area Community Coll., Bethlehem, 1981—. Named Jaycee of Yr., Easton Area Jaycees, 1965; recipient several pres. awards and honor Easton Area Jaycees, Cornerstone Soc. award Northampton Area Community Coll., 1983. Mem. Allentown Art Mus., Northampton County (Pa.) Hist. Soc. Club: Rushlight (Wetherfield, Conn.). Office: Indsl Engraving Co Inc 1350 Sullivan Trail Easton PA 18042

LEARN, DORIS LYNN, school district purchasing director; b. Long Beach, Calif., May 11, 1949; d. Rowe Francis and Annie Mae (Tunstill) Christopher; m. Thomas Robert Learn, Oct. 17, 1987. Student Foothill Coll., 1966-67, DeAnza Coll., 1969-71. Cashier Navy Exchange, China Lake, Calif., 1965-66, Navy Exchange, Moffett Field, Calif., 1966-67; exec. sec. Varian Assocs., Palo Alto, Calif., 1967-75; salesperson Jorgensen Steel, Langhorne, Pa., 1976; exec. sec. Pennsbury Sch. Dist., Fallsington, Pa., 1976-82, dir. purchasing, 1982—. Mem. Pa. Assn. Sch. Bus. Ofcls. (Pa. registered sch. bus. specialist 1986, mem. conf. com. 1986), Assn. Sch. Bus. Ofcls., Pa. Sch. Bds. Assn., Nat. Assn. Female Execs., Govt. Fin. Officers Assn., Pennsbury Assn. Suprs. and Adminstrs., Nat. Purchasing Assn., Delaware Valley Assn. Sch. Bus. Officials. Republican. Presbyterian. Avocations: needlecrafts, golf, spectator sports. Home: 1365 Brook Ln Jamison PA 18929 Office: Pennsbury Sch Dist 134 Yardley Ave Box 338 Fallsington PA 19054

LEARY, NANCY JANE, marketing professional; b. Natick, Mass., Mar. 25, 1952; d. Norman Leslie and Dorothy (Holmquist) Pidgeon; m. Patrick J. Leary, Sept. 17, 1977 (div. May 1984). AA, Mass Bay Coll., Wellesley, Mass., 1979; BS, Lesley Coll., Cambridge, Mass., 1988. Sec. GTE Corp., Needham, Mass., 1973-78; coordinator edn. Cullinet Software Inc., Westwood, Mass., 1983-84, adminstrv. asst., 1984-85, mgr. adminstrn., 1985-86; specialist product mktg. Cullinet Co., Westwood, Mass., 1986-88; v.p. mktg. and adminstrn. Jonathan's Landscaping, Bradenton Beach, Fla., 1988-89; with tech. support staff/A plus Tax product group Arthur Andersen, Inc., Sarasota, Fla., 1989—. Mgr. Fla. Community Assn. Office: 2803 Fruitville Rd Sarasota FL 34239

LEASBURG, RONALD HENRY, utility holding company executive; b. Clarksburg, Va., Mar. 16, 1933; s. Henry Clarence and Catherine Awilda (Van Dover) L.; children: Laura Jean, Cara Lynn. BA in Chemistry, Youngstown State U., 1967. Chemist Duquesne Light Co., Pitts., 1956-58, reactor engr., 1958-62, operating engr., 1962-67; project mgr. Gen. Electric Co., Tsuruga, Japan, 1968-70, Zurich, Switzerland, 1972-79; project mgr. Brown & Root, Houston, 1980-81; v.p. nuclear ops. Va. Power Co., Richmond, 1981-82, v.p. constrn., 1982-84, sr. v.p. engring. and constrn., 1984-87, sr. v.p. power ops. and engring., 1988; sr. v.p. Dominion Resources, Richmond, 1988—; pres. Dominion Energy, Richmond, 1988, also bd. dirs.; mem. adv. council N.C. State Sch. Engring., Raleigh, 1984-87; bd. dirs. Dominion Capital. Served as cpl. U.S. Army, 1950-52, Korea. Recipient Community Service award Richmond Joint Engrs. Council, 1986. Mem. Richmond Engrs. Club (bd. dirs. 1986—). Republican. Club: Stonehenge Country (Richmond). Office: Dominion Resources PO Box 26532 Richmond VA 23261

LEATHER, RICHARD BRENK, mineral company executive; b. N.Y.C., Feb. 22, 1932; s. Basil Henry and Elizabeth Marie (Brenk) L.; m. Penelope Jessie Pope, May 28, 1960; children: Edward, Ann, Charles. B.A., Yale U., 1953; cert., U. Paris, 1952; LL.B., Harvard U., 1958. Bar: N.Y. 1959. Assoc. Chadbourne Parke Whiteside & Wolff, 1958-66, ptnr., 1966-70; atty. Newmont Mining Corp., N.Y.C., 1970-71, gen. counsel and sec., 1971-74, v.p., gen. counsel, 1975-78, sr. v.p., 1978-79, exec. v.p., 1979-88; vice-chmn. Newmont Mining Corp., Denver, 1988—, Newmont Gold Co., Denver, 1988—; chmn. bd. Foote Mineral Co., Exton, Pa., 1980-88; bd. dirs. Newmont Gold Co., So. Peru Copper Corp. Trustee L.W. Frohlich Found., N.Y.C.; mem. vis. com. Met. Mus. Art. Served with AUS, 1954-56. Mem. ABA, Copper Devel. Assn. (sec. 1972-83), Smelter Environ. Research Assn. (trustee 1974-80), Am. Bur. Metal Stats. (trustee 1974—). Clubs: Racquet and Tennis (N.Y.C.), N.Y. Yacht; Manhasset Bay Yacht (Port Washington, N.Y.); Metropolitan (Washington). Office: Newmont Mining Corp 1700 Lincoln St Denver CO 80203

LEATHERMAN, STEVEN EDWARD, investment banker; b. Denver, Mar. 5, 1947; s. Earl Dean and Maryellen (Fitzpatrick) L.; m. Kathleen Garrity, Nov. 21, 1971; children: Matthew, Aimee, Mark. BS, U. Colo., 1969, MBA, 1972. Comml. banker 1st Nat. Bank Chgo., 1973-75; v.p. corp. fin. dept. Dain Bosworth, Denver, 1977-84; v.p. Security Pacific Capital Markets Group, Denver, 1984-85; sr. v.p., mgr. mergers and acquisitions group Boettcher & Co. Inc., Denver, 1985—. Contbr. articles to profl. jours., newspapers. Candidate U.S. Senate, Colo., 1984; bd. dirs. Cath. Charities, Colo., 1981; chmn. Wilderness Experience Program, Colo., 1979. Served to 1st lt. inf. U.S. Army, 1969-71, Vietnam. Mem. Colo. Bus. and Economics Council (chmn. 1986—). Democrat. Roman Catholic. Home: 5162 S Holland St Littleton CO 80123 Office: Boettcher & Co Inc 828 17th St Denver CO 80201

LEATON, EDWARD K., actuarial and consulting company executive; b. Mt. Vernon, N.Y., Oct. 2, 1928; s. Lionel M. and Henrietta (Kline) L.; m. Janet Kemp; children: Edward M., Kenneth (dec. Mar. 1974), William (dec. Aug. 1972), Robert, Thomas, James, Richard. BS in Mech. Engring., Lehigh U., 1949; MBA, Yale U., 1950. Grad. instr. Yale U., 1949-50; from trainee to asst. supt. Gen. Motors Corp., 1950-54; asst. to exec. v.p. Rowe Mfg. Corp., Whippany, N.J., 1955-56, v.p., dir. mfg., 1956-57; cons. Lambert M. Huppeler Co., Inc., N.Y.C., 1957-69, exec. v.p., 1969-74, pres., chief exec. officer, 1974—, chmn., 1978—, also bd. dirs.; pres. Leaton & Huppeler Co., Inc., N.Y.C., 1967-78, vice chmn., 1978—, also bd. dirs.; gen. agt. Leaton-Burns Agy., N.Y.C.; pres. Exec. Programs, Inc. and Analytical Planning Services, Inc. (both N.Y.C.); pres., bd. dirs. G.A.M.C. Contbr. articles to profl. jours.; speaker before numerous internat., nat. and regional orgns.; inductee to Agy. Mgmt. Hall of Fame, 1987. Chmn. coordinating com. ERISA; sr. warden, lay reader St. Paul's Ch.; mem. leadership com. Community Fund. Trustee Gordon (Mass.) Coll., Trinity Sch. for Ministry, The Am. Coll. Mem. Am. Ordnance Assn. (pres. Lehigh Valley post 1948-49), Life Mgrs. Assn. N.Y. (pres., bd. dirs.), Life Underwriters Assn. N.Y.C. (chmn. bd.), Am. Soc. Pension Actuaries (v.p., bd. dirs.), Assn. Advanced Life Underwriters (bd. dirs.), Am. Soc. CLU's, MDRT Found. (pres., bd. dirs.), Am. Mgmt. Assn., Am. Pension Conf., Nat. Assn. Pension Cons. and Adminstrs. (pres., bd. dirs.), Small Bus. Council Am. (bd. dirs.). Clubs: Union League, Yale (N.Y.C.); Country of Darien (gov., trustee), Nutmeg Curling (Darien, Conn.); Mid-Ocean (Tucker's Town, Bermuda). Office: 101 Park Ave New York NY 10178

LEAVITT, DANA GIBSON, management consultant; b. Framingham, Mass., Dec. 4, 1925; s. Luther C. and Margaret (Gibson) L.; m. Frances Smith, Apr. 12, 1952; children: Margaret Gibson, Jonathan. B.A., Brown U., 1948; postgrad., Harvard U. Bus. Sch., 1954-55. Home office rep. Aetna Life Ins. Co., Boston, also Long Beach, Calif., 1949-54; v.p., sec.-treas., exec. v.p. N. Am. Title Ins. Co., Oakland, Calif., 1955-64; pres. Transam. Title Ins. Co., Oakland, 1964-72; v.p. Transam. Corp., 1969-71, group v.p., 1971-77, exec. v.p., 1977-81; bd. dirs. Syntex Corp., Napa Valley Bank, Napa Valley Bancorp, Chgo. Title and Trust Co., Chgo. Title Ins. Co. Bd. dirs. Children's Hosp. Med. Ctr. and Found., 1969-72; trustee Lewis and Clark Coll., Portland, Oreg., 1972-75, Queen of Valley Hosp., Napa, Calif., 1988—, Nat. Wildflower Rsch. Ctr., Austin, 1988—, Brown U., Providence, 1973-78, trustee emeritus, 1978—. Served with USMCR, World War II. Mem. World Bus. Council (bd. dirs. 1986), Delta Kappa Epsilon. Republican. Clubs: Brown U. of No. Calif, Harvard Bus. Sch. of No. Calif, Napa Valley Country; Bohemian (San Francisco), Pacific Union (San Francisco). Office: 1100 Union St San Francisco CA 94109

LEAVITT, HORACE MADISON, JR., former naval officer, communications company executive; b. Long Beach, Calif., Apr. 26, 1929; s. Horace Madison and Gertrude (Webb) L.; m. Nancy Dohring, July 16, 1955; children—Horace Madison III, Lisa Grace. B.S. in Naval Sci., U.S. Naval Acad., 1953; B.S.E.E. in Ordnance Engring., U.S. Naval Postgrad. Sch., Monterey, Calif., 1961. Commd. ensign U.S. Navy, 1953, advanced through grades to capt., 1973; comdg. officer USS Carbonero, 1965-67; mgr. Rewson Program, 1978-82, ret., 1982; sr. v.p. Western Union Corp., Upper Saddle River, N.J., 1983—; pres. Advanced Transmission Systems Div., Upper Saddle River, N.J., 1988—. Mem. IEEE, Old Crows (gold award 1981). Republican. Home: 3 Yeoman Dr Upper Saddle River NJ 07458 Office: Western Union Corp 1 Lake St Upper Saddle River NJ 07458

LEAVITT, MICHAEL OKERLUND, insurance executive; b. Cedar City, Utah, Feb. 11, 1951; s. Dixie and Anne (Okerlund) L.; m. Jacalyn Smith; children: Michael Smith, Taylor Smith, Anne Marie, Chase Smith. BA, So. Utah State Coll., 1978. Charted property casualty underwriter. Sales rep. Leavitt Group, Cedar City, 1972-74, account exec., 1974-76; mgr. underwriting Salt Lake City, 1976-82; chief operating officer 1982-84, pres., chief exec. officer, 1984—; bd. dirs. Pacificorp, Portland, Oreg., Utah Power and Light Co., Salt Lake City, Great Western Thrift and Loan, Salt Lake City. Chmn. instl. council So. Utah State Coll., Cedar City, 1985—; campaign chmn. U.S. Senator Orrin Hatch, 1982, 88, U.S. Senator Jake Gern, 1980, 86; cons. campaign Gov. Norman Bangerter, 1984; mem. staff Reagan-Bush '84. Served to 2d lt. USNG, 1969-77. Named Disting. Alumni So. Utah State Coll. Sch. Bus., 1986. Mem. Chartered Property Casualty Underwriters. Republican. Mormon. Office: Leavitt Group 1358 S Main St Salt Lake City UT 84115

LEBDA, WALTER ROBERT, marketing executive; b. Philipsburg, Pa., Nov. 28, 1944; s. Walter and Kathryn (Ribnikar) L.; m. Judith Ann Trutt; children: Douglas Robert, Melissa Anne. BS in English, Lock Haven (Pa.) U., 1966; MS in Ednl. Adminstrn., Bucknell U., 1970. Tchr., coach East Lycoming Sch. Dist., Hughesville, Pa., 1966-68, Shikellamy Sch. Dist., Sunbury, Pa., 1968-70; tchr., coach, adminstr. Lewisburg Area Schs., 1970-79; asst. to pres. Townecraft Inc., Glen Rock, N.J., 1979-80; owner, pres. Townecraft of Cen. Pa., Lewisburg, 1980—. Contbr. articles to profl. jours. Deacon 1st Presbyn. Ch., Lewisburg. Republican. Home: 49 Beth Ellen Dr Lewisburg PA 17837 Office: Townecraft of Cen Pa 118 Market Lewisburg PA 17837

LEBED, HARTZEL ZANGWILL, former insurance company executive, university president; b. Columbia, Pa., Mar. 1, 1928; m. Ann Kronick, June 12, 1956; children: Holly, Jay, Alex. B.S. in Commerce, U. N.C., 1950. With Conn. Gen. Life Ins. Co., Hartford, 1950—; v.p. group sales Conn. Gen. Life Ins. Co., 1971-73; sr. v.p. group pension ops. Conn. Gen. Life Ins. Co., Hartford, 1973-76, exec. v.p. group pension ops. and reinsurance ops., 1976-78, exec. v.p., chief investment officer, 1978-82; exec. v. p. CIGNA Corp., Hartford, 1982-85, pres., 1985-88; interim pres. U. Hartford, 1988-89; bd. dirs. Kaman Corp., Catalyst; chmn. bd. Visitors Greenberg Ctr. for Judaic Studies U. Hartford. Bd. dirs. Hartford Jewish Fedn.; campaign mem. Holocaust Mus., Washington; regent U. Hartford. Served with USN, 1945-47. Mem. Phi Beta Kappa. Home: 54 Kenmore Rd Bloomfield CT 06002 Office: Conn Gen Life Ins Co 900 Cottage Grove Rd Bloomfield CT 06002

LEBEDEFF, NICHOLAS BORIS, consulting executive; b. Hollywood, Calif., Apr. 16, 1944; s. Boris Paul and Alexandra Esidorovna (Koshell) L.; m. Judith Leah Moffett, Nov. 22, 1969 (div. Aug. 1985); children: Christina, Christopher. BBA, Loyola U., Los Angeles, 1967; MBA, U. So. Calif., 1970. Budget and adminstrv. analyst City of Los Angeles, 1967-73; mgr. budget and fiscal ops. Van de Kamp's Holland Dutch Bakers div. Gen. Host Corp., Los Angeles, 1973-74; mgr. fin. planning and analysis dept. U.S. Borax and Chem. Co., Los Angeles, 1974-75; pres. NBL Assocs., Los Angeles, 1976-85, Micro-Software, Inc., Los Angeles, 1977—, Planning Systems Group, Los Angeles, 1982-85, Forecasting and Fin. Planning Group, 1982—. Bd. dirs. Am. Med. and Ednl. Services in Africa. Mem. U. So. Calif. Alumni Assn., Commerce Assocs. Republican. Mem. Orthodox Ch. Am. Home: 17400 Flanders St Granada Hills CA 91344

LEBENSFELD, HARRY, manufacturing company executive; b. N.Y.C., Aug. 25, 1904; s. Samuel and Bertha (Wolfshaut) L.; m. Edith Goldman, Sept. 15, 1937; 1 dau., Lynne Pasculano. With UIS, Inc., N.Y.C., 1945—(formerly United Indsl. Syndicate, Inc.), now chief exec. officer, chmn. bd. Club: Harmony. Home: 980 Fifth Ave New York NY 10021 Office: UIS Inc 600 Fifth Ave New York NY 10020

LEBL, GIORA M., manufacturing and consulting executive; b. Subotica, Yugoslavia, July 31, 1931; s. Marcell S. and Clara J. (Frenkel) L.; children: Marc J., John A. BS, Columbia U., 1960; MBA, U. Pa., 1963. Account dir. McCann Erickson Advt. Agy., N.Y.C., 1962-67; mktg. mgr. for Latin Am. Revlon, Inc., N.Y.C., 1967-70; dir. for Europe Helene Curtis Industries, Chgo., 1970—; pres. Spalding Internat. div. Questor Co., Chicopee, Mass., 1971-74, J. Linmar Internat. Ltd., Woodbury, Conn., 1975—. Club: U. Pa. Alumni. Office: PO Box 944 Woodbury CT 06798

LEBLANC, JEFFREY IRWIN, telephone company executive; b. New Orleans, Nov. 1, 1951; s. Irwin Ernest and Martha (Boryczka) L.; m. Mary Carol Gamotis, Oct. 23, 1974 (div. Sep. 1982); 1 child, Karen Marie. BS in Mktg., U. South Ala., 1973, MBA, 1980. Dist. planner SouthCentral Bell, Mobile, Ala., 1973-82; mgmt. recruiter SouthCentral Bell, Birmingham, Ala., 1983-84, BellSouth Corp., Atlanta, 1985, BellSouth Services, Birmingham, 1986—. Mem. U. South Ala. Alumni Assn., Birmingham C. of C., Ala. Coll. Placement Assn. (bd. dirs. 1984), Am. Soc. Personnel Adminstrn., So. Coll. Placement Assn. (chmn. ethics and legal affairs com. 1987, conf. budget dir. 1987), Internat. Assn. Quality Circles, Personnel Assn. Birmingham and Atlanta Personnel Soc. Republican. Roman Catholic. Office: BellSouth Svcs 600 N 19th St 21st Fl Birmingham AL 35203

LEBLOND, MICHAEL HARRY, foundation administrator; b. Wichita, Kans., Oct. 20, 1950; s. Jack Donald and Francis Genevieve (Michael) LeB. Student U. Kans., 1968-71; MBA, U. Denver, 1984-85. Pres. Continental Air Industries, Denver, 1974-77; sales rep. Pitney Bowes, Denver, 1977-78; sales rep. Wang Labs., Denver, 1978-80, br. mgr., Dallas, 1980-82, sr. account exec., 1982-87; pres. Western Heritage Found., Inc., Englewood, Colo., 1986—; nat. acct. exec. Apple Computers, Englewood, 1988—. treas., bd. dirs. S.S.I. Cons. Inc., Denver, 1985-87; exec. dir. Denver Urban Tng. Inst., 1984-86. Vol. Denver Leadership Found., 1977—; bd. dirs. Denver Leadership, 1984—, Bridge, Denver, 1982-84; mem. adv. bd. Nat. Bd.-Urban Ministries, Young Life, Denver, 1984-85. Mem. Sales & Mktg. Execs. Denver (bd. dirs. 1978-79). Republican. Office: 6400 S Fiddlers Green Cir Ste 2000 Englewood CO 80111

LEBO, KEVIN JOSEPH, transportation company executive; b. Newton, Mass., Feb. 17, 1961; s. Joseph S. and Ramona Fay (Taylor) L. BBA in Mgmt., U. Mass., 1983. Asst. to adminstr. Brockton (Mass.) Area Transit Authority, 1982-83; project mgr. Pioneer Valley Transit Authority, Springfield, Mass., 1983-85, asst. fin. officer, 1985-86; controller, chief fin. officer Springfield Transit Mgmt. Inc., Springfield, 1986—; cons. TMS Group, Springfield, 1984-86; v.p. Masstrax, Springfield, 1988—. Mem. Am. Pub. Transit Assn., New Eng. Pub. Transit Assn., Greater Springfield C. of C., Wason/North Bus. Assn. Home: 164 Eddywood St Springfield MA 01118 Office: Springfield Transit Mgmt Inc 2840 Main St Springfield MA 01107

LEBRO, THEODORE PETER, property tax service exec.; b. Fulton, N.Y., Feb. 12, 1910; s. Peter and Mary (Karpala) L.; BS, Syracuse U., 1954; m. Wanda Saffranski, Oct. 16, 1932. Farmer nr. Fulton, 1935-76; various positions restaurants, grocery, Fulton, 1929-54; owner, operator Lebro Real Estate and Ins. Agency, Fulton, 1951—. Bd. dirs. Lee Meml. Hosp.; pres. Catholic Youth Orgn. Fulton, 1976—; dir. Cath. Charities. Served with 35th inf. U.S. Army, 1942-46; PTO. Certified property mgr. Mem. Soc. Real Estate Appraisers, Oswego County Bd. Realtors, N.Y. State Soc. Appraisers (gov.), Assn. County Dirs., V.F.W., Am. Legion, St. Michael's Soc. (pres. 1960—). Republican. Roman Catholic. Clubs: Beaver Meadow, Pathfinders Game and Fish (life). Lodges: KC, Elks. Home: RFD 1 Box 111 Rte 48S Phoenix NY 13135 Office: 316 W 1st St Fulton NY 13069

LECLERCQ, JACQUES JEAN, retail grocery exexcutive; b. Brussels, Aug. 15, 1929; came to U.S., 1981; s. Jean Louis and Marguerite (Francois) LeC.; m. Therese Blaton, Sept. 12, 1954 (div. 1983); 1 child, Sophie; m. Winnie Mae Chandler, Mar. 16, 1983; 1 child, Sophie. BSBA, U. Antwerp, 1951. With La Couverture, Alost, Belgium, 1954-57, Dehaize The Lion Am., Inc., Atlanta, 1957—; dir. Food Lion, Inc., Salisbury, N.C., 1974—, Johnson Wax/Belgium, Brussels, Le Lion/Belgium; pres. Delhaize/Am., Atlanta, 1981—; site cons. Wakefern Food Corp., Edison, N.J., 1987—. Res. lt. Belgian Army, 1952-54. Decorated Order of Merit French Govt., Order of Merit Belgian Govt., Order of Merit Italian Govt. Mem. Food Mktg. Inst., Internat. Assn. Chain Stores, World Trade Club, Tastevin Club, Cherokee Club. Republican. Roman Catholic. Home: 3224 Andrews Ct Atlanta GA 30305 Office: Delhaize The Lion Am Inc 950 E Paces Ferry Rd Ste 2160 Atlanta GA 30326

LECLERE, DAVID ANTHONY, lawyer; b. New Orleans, Sept. 5, 1954; s. Paul Richard and Rosalee (Cefalu) LeC.; m. Debra Jane Coltarp; children: Chris, David III. BA, La. State U., 1978, JD, 1979. Bar: La. 1979, U.S. Dist. Ct. (mid. dist.) La. 1979, U.S. DIst. Ct. (ea. dist.) 1982, U.S. Dist Ct. (we. dist.) 1983, U.S. Ct. Appeals (5th cir.) 1984. Assoc. Perrault & Uter, Baton Rouge, 1979-81, jr. ptnr., 1981-83; ptnr. Perrault, Uter & LeClere, Baton Rouge, 1983-87, Schwab & LeClere, Baton Rouge, 1987—. Assoc. chmn. East Baton Rouge Parish Notary Pub. Exam. Com., 1982. Mem. ABA, La. State Bar Assn., Comml. Law League of Am., Baton Rouge Bar Assn. Republican. Roman Catholic. Office: Schwab & LeClere PO Box 80491 10114 Jefferson Hwy Baton Rouge LA 70809

LECORNEC, MICHAEL THOMAS, financial consultant; b. Jersey City, June 4, 1954; s. Alfred George and Sylvia (Bolembach) LeC. BA, So. Conn. State U., 1976; MA, NYU, 1981; cert. fin. planner, Adelphi U., 1983. Cert. tchr., N.Y. Therapist S.I. Devel. Ctr., N.Y.C., 1976-77; sr. therapist South Beach Psychiat. Ctr., N.Y.C., 1977-81; registered rep. First Investors Corp., N.Y.C., 1981-82, Fitzgerald, DeArman & Roberts, Inc., N.Y.C., 1982-83, MONY Fin. Svcs., N.Y.C., 1983-85; v.p. McDermott Planning Assocs., N.Y.C., 1985-86; prin. LeCornec Fin. Svcs., N.Y.C., 1982—; adj. prof. Baruch Coll. CUNY, N.Y.C., 1985—; dir. Sch. Ins. Securities Tng. Corp., N.Y.C., 1987—; speaker in field., presenter seminars. Contbr. to profl. publs. Mem. Interna. Assn. Fin. Planning, Nat. Assn. Life Underwriters, Soc. Ins. Trainers and Educators, Inst. Cert. Fin. Planners, Ins. Soc. N.Y., Toastmasters Internat., Spokesman Club, NYU Grad. Club. Lodge: Lions. Home: 87 Dubois Ave Staten Island NY 10310 Office: Securities Tng Corp 17 Battery Pl New York NY 10004

LEDBETTER, WILLIAM JOE, manufacturing company executive, lawyer; b. Memphis, Jan. 24, 1927; s. Andrew F. and Jessie (Williams) L.; m. Shirley Ann Good, May 5, 1956; children—Gleghn Andrew, Sally Ann. Student, Memphis State Coll., 1944-45, 46-47, U. Neb., 1945-46; LL.B., Washington and Lee U., 1950. Bar: Tenn. bar 1949, N.Y. bar 1951, Minn. bar 1964. Assoc. firm Townsend & Lewis, N.Y.C., 1950-51, Cravath, Swaine & Moore, N.Y.C., 1951-57; atty., then assoc. corp. counsel Gen. Electric Co., 1957-64; corp. counsel Honeywell Inc., Mpls., 1964-65, sec., gen. counsel, 1965-69; v.p., sec., gen. counsel Magnavox Co., N.Y.C., 1969-71; sr. v.p. adminstrn. and finance Addressograph Multigraph Corp., Cleve., 1971-72, exec. v.p. internat. operations, dir., 1972-74; v.p. finance Textron Inc., Providence, 1974-78, sr. v.p. fin., 1978-79, exec. v.p. fin. and adminstrn., 1979-80, exec. v.p. fin. and planning, 1981-85, sr. exec. v.p. adminstrn. and planning, 1985—. Mem. Am. Bar Assn., Order of Coif, Phi Beta Kappa. Clubs: Turk's Head, Agawam Hunt, Acoaxet. Home: 141 Morris Ave Providence RI 02906 Office: Textron Inc 40 Westminster St Providence RI 02903

LEDBETTER-STRAIGHT, NORA KATHLEEN, insurance company executive; b. Gary, Ind., May 11, 1934; d. Jacob F. and Nora I. (Bollen) Moser; student U. Houston, 1954-58; m. Robert L. Straight, Aug. 9, 1975; 1 dau., Cindy Kathleen Ledbetter Baurax. Vice pres. Hindman Mortgage Co., Inc., Houston, 1960-70, also mng. partner Assocs. Ins. Agy.; corp. sec. N.Am. Mortgage Co., Houston, 1970—; mng. partner N.Am. Ins. Agy., 1970—, now also pres. and mng. officer; ins. counselor Houston Apt. Assn., 1978—, dir. product service council, 1981—; mem. adv. bd. for continuing edn., State Bd. Ins.; v.p., sec. Better Bodies of Tex., Inc. CPCU; cert. Ins. Inst. Am., Soc. Cert. Ins. Counselors. Mem. Ind. Ins. Agts. Am., Soc. Cert. Ins. Counselors, Soc. C.P.C.U.s, Community Assos. Inst. (dir. 1976-80), Ind. Ins. Agts. Tex., S.W. Assn. Affiliated Agts (v.p., bd. dirs.), Tex. Assn. Affiliated Agts. (v.p., bd. dirs.), Ind. Ins. Agts. Houston (dir. 1974-78). Republican. Methodist. Author curriculum materials in field. Office: 14825 St Mary's Ln Houston TX 77079

LEDDICOTTE, GEORGE COMER, relocation managment services executive, consultant; b. Oak Ridge, Tenn., May 28, 1947; s. George W. Leddicotte and Virginia (Comer) Leddicotte Stratton; m. Connie Laverne Sterrett, Jan. 25, 1969; 1 child, Matthew Sterrett. BA in Polit. Sci., U. Mo., 1970. Customer service supr. Crown Zellerbach, San Francisco, 1973-74; exec. recruiter Christopher & Long, St. Louis, 1974; regional ops. mgr. Curtin Matheson Scientific, Inc., Houston, 1974-80; regional mgr., mng. cons. Merrill Lynch Relocation Mgmt., White Plains, N.Y., 1980-82, regional v.p., nat. accounts, 1982-83, regional v.p. govt. svcs., 1983-84; dir. govt. svcs. Coldwell Banker Relocation Mgmt., Washington, 1984-85; dir. sales., account mgmt. Homequity, Wilton, Conn., 1985-87; v.p. nat. sales Premier Relocation Svcs., Inc., Irvine, Calif., 1987-88; v.p., sr. mng. cons. Premier Decision Mgmt., Irvine, 1988—; mng. dir. Feasiblility Inc., Brookfield, Conn., 1989—. First lt. U.S. Army, 1970-72, Korea. Mem. Am. Mktg. Assn., Am. Mgmt. Assn., Am. Soc. Personnel Adminstrn., Employee Relocation Council. Home: 9 Broadview Dr Brookfield CT 06804 Office: Feasibility Inc 9 Broadview Dr Brookfield CT 06804

LEDECKY, JONATHAN JOSEPH, venture capitalist; b. N.Y.C., Feb. 9, 1958; s. Jaromir and Berta Ruth (Greenwald) L. BA cum laude, Harvard U., 1979; MBA, Harvard U., Boston, 1983; postgrad., JFK Sch. Govt., Harvard U., 1982-83. Assoc. Kidder Peabody, N.Y.C., 1979-81, Morgan Stanley, N.Y.C., 1982; asst. v.p. Allied Capital Corp., Washington, 1983-85, v.p., 1985, sr. v.p., 1986-87; ptnr. Allied Venture Ptnrs., Washington, 1985-87, Adler & Co., N.Y.C., 1987—; teaching fellow Harvard U., Cambridge, 1983; dir. Media Materials, Inc., Balt., 1986-87, Environ. Control Group, 1987, Asbestoway Corp., U.S. Water Corp. Editor Harvard Summer Times, 1978-79. John Harvard scholar, 1978. Mem. Nat. Venture Capital Assn., Nat. Assn. Small Bus. Investment Cos., Harvard Class Secs. Assn. (mem. exec. com. 1985-89, sec. 1989—), Harvard Alumni Assn. (nat. committeman 1981-89, sec. 1989—). Club: Harvard Bus. Sch. (Washington) (v.p. 1986-87). Home: 1400 34th St NW Washington DC 20007 Office: Adler & Co 375 Park Ave #3303 New York NY 10152

LEDERMAN, IRA SETH, insurance executive, lawyer; b. N.Y.C., Apr. 25, 1953; m. Carol Susan Jupiter; children: Rachael, Aaron. Bar: N.Y. 1980. Assoc. Rein Mound and Cotton, N.Y.C., 1979-83; assoc. counsel W.R. Berkley Corp., Greenwich, Conn., 1983-86, v.p., ins. counsel, 1986—. Mem. ABA, N.Y. County Lawyers Assn., Westchester/Fairfield County Lawyers Assn. Office: WR Berkley Corp 165 Mason St Greenwich CT 06830

LEDERMAN, PETER (BERND), environmental consulting company executive; b. Weimar, Germany, Nov. 16, 1931; came to U.S., 1939, naturalized, 1945; s. Ernst M. and Irmgard R. (Heilbrunn) L.; B.S.E., U. Mich., 1953, M.S.E., 1961, Ph.D.; m. Susan Sturc, Aug. 25, 1957; children—Stuart M., Ellen L. Instr., U. Mich., 1959-61; research engr. Esso Research Labs., Baton Rouge, La., 1961-63; sr. engr. Esso Research & Engring. Co., Florham Park, N.J., 1963-66; asso. prof. chem. engring. Poly. Inst. Bklyn., 1966-72, adj. prof., 1972-75; dir. Ind. Waste Treatment Research Lab., EPA, Edison, N.J., 1972-75, dir. indsl. and extractive processes research, Washington, 1975-76; v.p. Cotrell Environ. Scis. Div., Research Cottrell, Bound Brook, N.J., 1976-80; v.p. hazard/toxic materials mgmt. Roy F. Weston, Inc., Summit, N.J., 1980—; mem. NRC-Nat. Acad. Sci. Rev. Panel, Office Recycled Tech., U.S. Bur. Standards, 1980-83. Mem. exec. bd. Watchung Area council Boy Scouts Am., 1970-86; mem. affirmative action adv. com. New Providence (N.J.) Bd. Edn., 1979-83. Served with AUS, 1953-55. Recipient Silver medal EPA, 1976. Fellow Am. Inst. Chem. Engrs. (chmn. profl. devel. com., chmn. N.J. sect., recipient Larry K. Cecil award 1987); mem. Am. Chem. Soc., AAAS, Am. Soc. Engring. Edn., Nat. Soc. Profl. Engrs., ASME, Am. Acad. Environ. Engrs., NAM, Sigma Xi, Phi Kappa Phi, Phi Lambda Upsilon. Contbr. numerous articles on environ. regulations, solid waste mgmt., hazardous waste mgmt., computer tech. to profl. jours. Home: 17 Pittsford Way New Providence NJ 07974 Office: PO Box 1333 Summit NJ 07901

LEDERMAN, SCOTT CHARLES, university treasurer; b. Colon, Panama, June 29, 1941; came to U.S., 1941; s. Milton David Lederman and Helen Jane (Beck) Banks; m. Abigail Frances Merriam, Sept. 8, 1973; children: Timothy, Matthew, Anne. BS, Rensselaer Poly. Inst., 1964; MBA, U. Pa., 1977. Chartered fin. analyst. Dir. planning Wharton Grad. Sch. U. Pa., Phila., 1969-72, exec. asst. v.p. for mgmt., 1972-75, dir. investments, 1982-87, treas., 1987—; v.p. Franklin Investment Co., Phila., 1975-82. Capt. U.S. Army, 1964-67, Vietnam. Democrat. Episcopalian. Office: Univ Pa 3451 Walnut St Philadelphia PA 19104

LEDINH, TONY, manufacturing executive, economist, lawyer; b. Hatinh, Socialist Republic of Vietnam, Feb. 4, 1941; s. Hue and Kiem-Quang Tran; m. Xuan-Ly Pham, Dec. 26, 1981; children: Tina, Lynn. BA in Econs., U. We. Australia, 1962; Licence en Droit, Saigon (Socialist Republic of Vietnam) Law Sch., 1971, Maitrise in Pub. Law, 1973. Economist Ministry of Economy, Saigon, 1965-68; economist, 1st lt. Joint Chiefs of Staff, Saigon, 1969-73; diplomat Ministry Fgn. Affairs, Saigon, 1973-75; mgr. export Gen. Irrigation Co., Carthage, Mo., 1975-80; gen. mgr. Mark Controls Corp., Singapore, 1981-85; v.p. strategic planning Mark Controls Corp., Evanston, Ill., 1985-86; v.p. internat. MCC Powers, Northbrook, Ill., 1986-87, Landis & Gyr Powers, Inc., Northbrook, 1987—; dir. Landis & Gyr Fareast, Hong Kong, 1986—, Powers France, Lyon, 1986—. Office: Landis & Gyr Powers Inc 1000 Deerfield Pkwy Northbrook IL 60015

LEDOUX, JACK, author, retired race track executive; b. Orlando, Fla., Oct. 4, 1928; s. Leonard K. and Louise (Downs) L.; m. Lenita C. Riles, Sept. 22, 1981; children: Michele, Lance, Stephen, Lola. BS in Journalism, U. Fla., 1950. Sportswriter, columnist Orlando Sentinel-Star, 1948-53; pub. relations dir. Sarasota, Daytona Beach (Fla.) Kennel Clubs, 1953-55; gen. mgr., corp. sec. Sanford-Orlando Kennel Club, 1955-72; gen. mgr., exec. v.p. Black Hills Kennel Club, Rapid City, S.D., 1964-71; pres., co-owner Exec. Travel, Winter Park, Fla., 1977—, Triex Enterprises, Inc., Winter Park, 1977—; ind. editorial columnist, free-lance writer, 1972—; dir. Ctr. Stage. Mem. Fla. Golf Assn. (chmn. adv. com. 1964-65, bd. dirs., pres.), Am. Greyhound Track Operators Assn. (publ. and supervisory com. Am. Greyhound Racing Ency., pub. 1963, nat. pres.), World Racing Fedn. (chmn.), World Greyhound Racing Fedn. (pres.), U. Fla. Alumni Assn. (past pres. Sarasota County chpt.), Sigma Delta Chi, Theta Chi. Democrat. Clubs: Univ., Country. Home: PO Box 2127 Winter Park FL 32790

LEDWIG, DONALD EUGENE, public broadcasting executive, former naval officer; b. Lubbock, Tex., Mar. 2, 1937; s. Paul Lawrence and Rose L.; m. Gail Wilcox, Jan. 30, 1965; children: Donald Eugene, David W. BS, Tex. Tech. U., 1959; MBA, George Washington U., 1973; Disting. Grad. Naval War Coll., 1977. Cert. profl. contracts mgr. Commd. ensign, U.S. Navy, 1959, advanced through grades to capt., 1980, ship's officer U.S. Pacific Fleet, 1959-65, 77-79, staff Adm. H.G. Rickover, Nuclear Propulsion Program, 1966-72, dir. contract policy Naval Material Command, Washington, 1979-81, dep. comdr. Naval Electronic Systems Command, Washington, 1981-84, ret. 1984; Washington rep. L.T.V. Aerospace Corp., 1984; v.p., treas. Corp. for Pub. Broadcasting, Washington, 1984-86, pres., chief exec. officer, 1987. Named Community Amb. to Finland City of Lubbock, Tex. C. of C., 1958; decorated Legion of Merit; recipient Barron Meml. award Hastings Coll. Law, 1989. Mem. Nat. Contract Mgmt. Assn., Nat. Press. Club, Army and Navy Club, Army/Navy Country Club. Office: Corp for Pub Broadcasting 1111 16th St NW Washington DC 22036

LEDZINSKI, STANLEY PAUL, training and development specialist; b. Warren, Ohio, June 22, 1959; s. Stanley Paul and Anna Marie (Minda) L. BS in Acctg., BS in Bus., Alliance Coll., 1980; MBA in Mktg., Gannon U., 1983; MEd, Duquesne U., 1988. Evenings mgr. Seven Oaks Country Club, Beaver, Pa., 1981-83; dir. The Midland (Pa.) Ctr., 1983—; chief exec. officer, pres., sec., treas. Beaver County Labor-Mgmt. Com., Midland, Pa., 1987—; bd. dirs. Corp. for Owner Operator Projects, Beaver,1984—, pres. 1984-85;bd. dirs. Nat. Youth Sports Pogram, Monaca, Pa., 1985-86; nat. presenter Nat. Alliance Bus., Detroit, 1984. Author: MCCD Title III, 1983, TARGET: Reentry, 1986. Mem. Am. Mgmt. Assn., Midland C. of C. (bd. dirs. 1984-85). Republican. Roman Catholic. Home: 5190 Tuscarawas Rd Beaver PA 15009 Office: The Midland Ctr 617 Midland Ave Midland PA 15059

LEE, ALAN FRANCIS, data processing executive; b. N.Y.C., Dec. 11, 1945; s. George and Irene Charlotte (Oertel) L.; m. Patricia June Ball, Apr. 7, 1970 (div. Apr. 1981); 1 child, Curtis Alan; m. Patricia Gene McGuire, Nov. 22, 1986. Pres. Utilis Computer, Dallas, 1971-75; acct. dir. Insyte Corp., Dallas, 1975-78; pres. MAGEC Software, McKinney, Tex., 1978—. Contbr. articles to tech. jours. Recipient Million Dollar award Internat. Computer Programs, Indpls., 1987. Republican. Office: MAGEC Software PO Box 260319 Plano TX 75026-0319

LEE, BERNARD Z., accountant. Chmn. Seidman and Seidman (now BDO Seidman), 1974-83, chmn. internat. exec. com., 1985-88; asst. to chmn. AICPA's, Washington, until 1988, dep. chmn. fed. affairs, 1988—. Office: AICPAs 1455 Pennsylvania Ave NW Washington DC 20004 Office: Seidman & Seidman 15 Columbus Cir New York NY 10023 *

LEE, BOK SIN See POWELL, JOY LEE

LEE, BRIAN THOMAS, trust company executive; b. Tuscola, Ill., Dec. 2, 1957; s. Raymond Lester and Billie Jean (Chrysler) L.; m. Cheryl Lynn White, Dec. 6, 1987; 1 child, Andrea Nicole. BS in Liberal Arts, Ill. Wesleyan U., 1980. Trust officer First Nat. Bank of Springfield (Ill.), 1980-83; trust adminstrv. officer Old Kent Bank and Trust Co., Grand Haven, Mich., 1984-87, asst. v.p., 1988—. Dist. chmn. West Mich. Shores council Boy Scouts Am., 1988, dist. fin. chmn., 1986-87. Mem. Internat. Assn. Fin. Planning, Inst. Cert. Fin. Planners (cert.), W. Mich. Estate Planning Coun., Grand Haven Jaycees. Republican. Methodist. Office: Old Kent Bank and Trust Co 233 Washington St Grand Haven MI 49417

LEE, CURTIS HOWARD, mechanical engineer, consultant; b. San Francisco, June 7, 1928; s. Lum Quong and Kum Ho (Lee) L.; B.S. with honor, Calif. State Poly. Coll., 1952; postgrad. McGeorge Coll. Law, 1964-67; m. Mildred Lee; children—Melinda, Roberta, Lorie, Sabrina, Kristina. Mech. engr. Buonaccorsi & Assos., cons. engrs., San Francisco, 1953-57, Eagleson Engrs., cons. engrs., San Francisco, 1957-59; 60-63; chief engr. C.S. Hardeman, San Francisco, 1959-60; spl. project engr. A.E. D'Ambly, cons. engrs., Phila., 1963-64; self-employed as cons. engr., Sacramento, 1964-67; chief engr. George W. Dunn & Assos., cons. engrs. San Diego, 1967-69; prin. Dunn-Lee-Smith-Klein & Assocs., San Diego, 1969-87, Curtis H. Lee Cons. Group, Chula Vista, 1987—. Mem. Accrediting Commn. of Assn. of Ind. Colls. and Schs., 1970-76; mem. adv. panel Calif. State Bldg. Standards Commn., 1971-76; mem. San Diego City Bd. Bldg. Appeals, 1974-79; mem. Chula Vista City Bd. Appeals, 1980-88—. Served with AUS, 1947-48. Registered profl. engr., Ariz., Calif., Colo., Fla., Ga., Wash., Nev., N.Mex., Ohio, Oreg., Pa., Tex. Fellow ASHRAE; mem. Am. Arbitration Assn. (mem. nat. panel 1969—, regional adv. bd. 1977—), Am. Acad. Forensic Scis., Nat. Soc. Profl. Engrs. (pres. San Diego chpt. 1972-73, state dir. 1973-74, nat. dir. 1974-76), ASME, Am. Soc. Plumbing Engrs. (charter pres. San Diego chpt. 1970, nat. 3d v.p. 1970-72), Constrn. Specifications Inst. (dir. San Diego chpt. 1974-75, pres. 1976-77, Inst. com. 1978—, named fellow 1983), Am. Soc. Profl. Estimators, Am. Soc. Quality Control, Instrument Soc. Am., Am. Soc. Testing and Materials, Internat. Assn. Plumbing and Mech. Ofcls., Nat. Fire Protection Assn. Office: 492 3rd Ave #101 Chula Vista CA 92010-4614

LEE, DANIEL RICHARD, securities analyst; b. Syracuse, N.Y., Oct. 18, 1956; s. Alfred Edward and Mary Jean (See) L. BS, Cornell U., 1977, MBA, 1980. Ops. analyst Hilton Internat., San Juan, P.R., 1977-79; research analyst Drexel Burnham Lambert, Inc., N.Y.C., 1980-81, v.p. research, 1981-85, corp. v.p., 1985-88, corp. 1st v.p., 1988—. Contbr. articles to hotel and restaurant jours. Mem. Cornell Soc. Hotelmen, Cornell Exec. Alumni Council, Cornell Real Estate Adv. Bd., N.Y. Soc. Security Analysts. Office: Drexel Burnham Lambert Inc 60 Broad St New York NY 10004

LEE, DEBRA NISON, advertising company executive; b. Sedan, Kans., Mar. 10, 1955; d. George Robert Lockett and Elise Sabbah (div.); 1 child, Sarah Elise. BS in Journalism, U. Kans., 1977. Advt. rep. Kans. Press Assn., Topeka, 1977-78, Topeka Capitol Jour., 1978-79; sales exec. Sta. KWCH-Channel 12, Wichita, Kans., 1979-83, Sta. KCTV-Channel 5, Kansas City, Kans., 1983-84; gen. mgr. Am Advt. Co., Topeka, 1984-85; pres., owner Am. Advt. Co., Wichita, 1985—. Recipient Best Retail Advertisement award, 1979; named to Outstanding Young Women Am., 1982. Mem. Topeka C.of C., Wichita C. of C. Office: Am Advt Distrbn 400 N Woodlawn Ste 5 Wichita KS 67208

LEE, DIANA BELINDA, banker; b. Florence, S.C., July 2, 1953; d. Henry Barker and J Jeannine (Berry) L. AB, Coker Coll., 1973; AA, Fashion Inst. Am., 1973; diploma retail banking Am. Inst. Banking, 1983; postgrad Coker Coll. Customer service rep. 1st Nat. Bank S.C., Columbia, 1974-79; with S.C. Nat. Bank, Florence and Columbia, 1979-82; with S.C. Fed., various locations, 1982-87, br. mgr., Columbia, 1983-85, asst. sec., br. mgr., Hartsville, 1985-87, br. mgr. Security Fed. Savs. & Loan Assn., Columbia, 1987—; br. mgr. Security Fed., 1986-89, asst. v.p., 1989—. Bd. dirs. Am. Cancer Soc., 1985—, chmn. regional edn. funds crusade, 1985—, regional dir., 1987-88; chmn. Hartscapades parade, 1986; co-chmn. Richland County First Lady Cookbooks. Mem. C. of C. Columbia, Forest Acres Area Council C. of C. (pres. 1985, bdr. dirs. 1987—), Nat. Assn. Bank Women, Am. Bus. Womens Assn. (chmn. fund raising 1984-85), Am. Inst. Banking. Republican. Presbyterian. Avocations: reading, sewing, dance, crafts, designing. Office: Security Fed 7001 Garners Ferry Rd Columbia SC 29209

LEE, DUANE EDWARD, banker; b. Harvey, Ill., Apr. 7, 1955; s. Duane Edward Lee and Laura Emily (Schmidt) Thometz; m. Susan K. Lynn, Oct. 6, 1984; 1 child, Christa Ann. B.S. in Fin., U. Ill., 1977; Assoc. Sci. in Real Estate, Triton Coll., 1981; M.B.A. in Fin., DePaul U., 1984. Cert. employee benefit specialist, chartered fin. planner. Nat. trust examiner U.S. Treasury, Chgo., 1977-82; sr. v.p. United Bank Ill., Rockford, 1982-85; adminstrv. v.p. Mfrs. and Traders Trust Co., Buffalo, 1985—; dir. Rockford Honda Motors, Rockford Honda Cycle. Lectr. Bank Adminstrn. Inst., Ill. Bankers Assn. Contbr. articles to profl. jours. Ill. state scholar, 1973. Mem. Rockford C. of C., Buffalo C. of C., Nat. Assn. Investment Clubs, Nat. Speakers Assn., Internat. Assn. Fin. Planners, Ill. Land Trust Council, No. Ill. Employee Benefit Assn., Am. Assn. Individual Investors. Republican. Lutheran. Home: 50 Chicory Ct East Amherst NY 14051 Office: M&T Bank 1 M&T Pla Buffalo NY 14240

LEE, EARL BROWN, nursing facility administrator; b. Coleman, N.C., Aug. 24, 1925; s. Ernest Cleveland and Eunice Earl (Brown) L.; m. Jane Alice Stewart, Apr. 7, 1956; children: Brian Stewart, Karen Brown. BBA, U. Richmond, 1950. Adminstr. James River Nursing Home, Newport News, Va., 1964-67; asst. adminstr. Portsmouth (Va.) Gen. Hosp., 1967-73; adminstr. Holly Manor Nursing Home, Farmville, Va., 1973—, also bd. dirs.; bd. dirs. Prince Edward Acad., Farmville. With USCG, 1943-46. Mem. Rotary (pres. Farmville chpt. 1980-81). Baptist. Home: Blemont Cir Farmville VA 23901 Office: Holly Manor Nursing Home 2003 Cobb St Farmville VA 23901

LEE, EARL VICTORY, utility co. exec.; b. Bay Minette, Ala., Sept. 28, 1929; s. Lathen and Lila (Catrett) L.; A.A., Pensacola Jr. Coll., 1955; B.S., Fla. State U., 1957, M.S., 1958; m. Janie Louise Cabler, Aug. 31, 1957; children—Janet Louise, David Earl. Bookkeeper, Pensacola Hardware Co., 1947-50; jr. acct. Baggett and Barfield, C.P.A.s, Pensacola, 1956, sr. acct., 1957; sr. acct. Allen & Allen, C.P.A.s, Tallahassee, 1956-58; spl. acct. Gulf Power Co., Pensacola, Fla., 1958-59, sr. acct., 1959-63, adminstrv. asst. to v.p., 1963-64, supr. audits, 1965-69, supr. audits, billing and computer services, 1969-71, supr. customer acctg., 1971-72, mgr. customer acctg., 1972-73, div. acctg. mgr., 1973-76, corp. sec., dir. corp. performance, 1976-80, controller, asst. treas., 1980—; instr. Pensacola Jr. Coll., 1961—, Fla. State U., 1966-67, U. West Fla., 1967-69. Trustee, Pensacola Sch. Bd., 1964-65; pres. Western div. Children's Home Soc., 1981-82, treas. 1982—. Served with USAF, 1950-54. C.P.A., Fla. Mem. Am. Inst. C.P.A.s, Edison Electric Inst., Southeastern Electric Exchange, Fla. Inst. C.P.A.s (pres. West Fla. chpt. 1963-65, chmn. ind. conf. state com.), Seminole Boosters, Fla. State Alumni Assn. Democrat. Mem. Ch. of Christ. Club: Executive. Home: 1810 N 58th Ave Pensacola FL 32506 Office: 500 Bayfront Pkwy Pensacola FL 32501

LEE, EDWARD BROOKE, JR., real estate executive, fund raiser; b. Silver Spring, Md., Oct. 25, 1917; s. E. Brooke Lee and Elizabeth (Wilson) Aspinwall; m. Camilla Edge, Apr. 15, 1944 (div. Feb. 1983); children: Camilla Lee Alexander, E. Brooke III, Kaiulani Lee Kimbrell, Katherine Blair Lee St. John, Richard Henry, Elizabeth Ashe Somerville; m. Deborah Roche, Apr. 30, 1983; children: Samuel Phillips II, Regina Blair. AB, Princeton U., 1940; student, The Infantry Sch., 1942; postgrad. bus. sch., Harvard U., 1957. Cert. real estate broker Md., D.C., Va. Various indsl. positions to nat. account mgr. Scott Paper Co., Phila., 1940-62; comml. broker Shannon and Luchs, Washington, 1962-83, Merrill Lynch Comml. Realty, Washington, 1983—; pres. E. Brooke Lee Properties, Inc., Montgomery County, Md., 1979—; fund raiser key gifts Nat. Found. for Cancer Research, Bethesda, Md., 1985—; v.p. Ga. Ave. Properties, Montgomery County, Ga.-Conn., Inc., Montgomery County, Conn. Aspen, Inc., Montgomery County, 1962—; sec.-treas. Brooke Lee Family, Inc., Montgomey County, 1962—. Author numerous sales articles for purchasing mags. Chmn. Drug Action Coalition, Inc., fin. v.p., bd. dirs., 1966-70; rep. candidate for Mayor of Washington, 1982, rep. primary candidate for U.S. Senate, State of Md., 1986. Served to capt. inf. U.S. Army, 1943-45, ETO. Named Realtor Assoc. of Yr., Washington Bd. of Realtors, 1984. Mem. Harvard Bus. Sch. Club (pres. 1962, exec. v.p. 1975), Princeton Club of Washington (sec., bd. dirs. 1970-75), Princeton Club of N.Y., Nat. Account Mktg. Assn. (pres. 1959-62). Republican. Episcopalian. Clubs: Met., Chevy Chase Country (Washington). Lodge: Kiwanis. Home: 208 Primrose St Chevy Chase MD 20815 Office: Nat Found Cancer Rsch 7315 Wisconsin Ave Bethesda MD 20814 also: Merrill Lynch Comml Realty 6701 Rockledge Dr Ste 390 Bethesda MD 20817

LEE, EMERY JAY, manufacturing executive; b. Ogallala, Nebr., Oct. 14, 1946; s. George Allen and Maysel (Wheeler) L.; m. Donna Jean Kudobe, July 1, 1972; 1 child, Nathaniel. BSBA, Black Hills State Coll., 1969. Cert. mgmt. acct. Internal auditor Mason & Hanger, Burlington, Iowa, 1969-73; asst. treas. DeLong Sportswear, Grinnell, Iowa, 1973-77; contr. Weigh-Tronix Inc., Fairmont, Minn., 1977—. Office: Weigh-Tronix Inc 1000 N Armstrong Dr Fairmont MN 56031

LEE, ERIC M., importing company executive; b. Swatow, Guangdong, China, Apr. 19, 1949; came to U.S., 1977; s. Cheuk-Wong and Yum-Ying (Chan) L.; m. Maria W.C. Ma, Oct. 1, 1975; children: Adora, Brenda, Joseph. BBA in Mktg., U. Puget Sound, 1975. Mgr. Master Garment Mfg. Co., Hong Kong, 1967-73, 75-77; pres. Chivan Internat. Inc., N.Y.C., 1978—, Popular Industries, Inc., N.Y.C., 1983—; cons. Direct Mktg. Day Conv., Nat. Assn. Textile and Apparel Distbrs. Conv. Mem. Am. Mgmt. Assn. Club: Holiday Spa Health. Home: 34 Edna Dr Syosset NY 11791 Office: Popular Industries Inc 47 W 34th St New York NY 10001

LEE, HAROLD PHILIP, electronics executive, consultant; b. Greenwich, Conn., June 22, 1944; s. Harold Joseph and Margaret Mary (Ward) L.; m. Georgiann M. Lee. BS in Acctg., U. Dayton, 1966; MBA, Iona Coll., 1985. Fin. analyst Picker Corp., N.Y.C., 1968-69, Singer Corp., N.Y.C., 1969-73, Celanese Corp., N.Y.C., 1974; mgr. budget reporting Timex Corp., Middlebury, Conn., 1974-77; chief fin. officer Far East region Timex, Manila, 1977-82; dir. fin. planning Timex, Middlebury, 1982-84; v.p. fin., adminstrn. Brian Alden, Inc., Clinton, Conn., 1984-85; chief fin. officer Firing Circuits, Inc., Norwalk, Conn., 1985—. Served with USCGR, 1967-73. Mem. Fin. Exec. Inst. Republican. Roman Catholic. Club: Exchange (Cheshire, Conn.) (pres. 87-88). Lodge: K.C. Home: 54 Currier Way Cheshire CT 06410 Office: Firing Cirs Inc Muller Ave PO Box 2007 Norwalk CT 06852

LEE, J. RICHARD, advtertising executive, clergyman; b. Indpls., Jan. 11, 1925; s. Edgar Lee and Laura (Hamm) Meischke; B.A., Anderson Coll. and Theol. Sem., 1946; Ph.D. in Communications, D.D., P.E. Univ., London, Eng., 1965; m. Dorothy Katherine Dyer, Apr. 10, 1960; 1 dau., Jane Allison. Announcer, Sta. WIRE, Indpls., 1944-45; nat. radio-TV dir. Ch. of God, Anderson, Ind., 1946-52; TV newscaster, religious dir. Sta. KKTV, prodn. mgr. Sta. KVOR, Colorado Springs, Colo., 1953-54; pres., chief exec. officer J. Richard Lee, Inc., Advt., Oceanside, Calif., and N.Y.C., 1954—; pres. Continental Radio Network, Hollywood, Calif., 1962—, Exxel Co., Los Angeles and Oceanside, Calif., 1977—. Ordained to ministry Ch. of God, 1946; minister Country Ch. of Hollywood, 1956-60, Christ's Ch., Los Angeles, 1961-70. Fellow Royal Geog. Soc. London (Eng.). Home: 1200 Harbor Dr N Oceanside CA 92054 Office: 700 First St Oceanside CA 92054 also: One Penn Plaza New York NY 10119

LEE, JAMES KING, technology corporation executive; b. Nashville, July 31, 1940; s. James Fitzhugh Lee and Lucille (Charlton) McGivney; m. Victoria Marie Marani, Sept. 4, 1971; children—Gina Victoria, Patrick Fitzhugh. B.S., Calif. State U.-Pomona, 1963; M.B.A., U. So. Calif., 1966. Engring. adminstr. Douglas MSSD, Santa Monica, Calif., 1965-67; mgr. mgmt. systems TRW Systems, Redondo Beach, Calif., 1967-68; v.p. corp. devel. DataStation Corp., Los Angeles, 1968-69; v.p., gen. mgr. Aved Systems Group, Los Angeles, 1969-70; mng. ptnr. Corp. Growth Cons., Los Angeles, 1970-81; chmn., pres. chief exec. officer Fail-Safe Tech. Corp., Los Angeles, 1981—. Author industry studies, 1973-79. Mem. Los Angeles Mayor's Community Adv. Com., 1962-72; asst. adminstr. SBA, Washington, 1974; vice chmn. Traffic Commn., Rancho Palos Verdes, Calif., 1975-78; chmn. Citizens for Property Tax Relief, Palos Verdes, 1976-80; mem. Town Hall Calif. Recipient Golden Scissors award Calif. Taxpayers' Congress, 1978. Mem. So. Calif. Tech. Execs. Network, Am. Electronics Assn. (chmn., L.A. coun. 1987-88, nat. bd. dirs. 1986-89), Nat. Security Industries Assn. Republican. Baptist. Home: 28874 Crestridge Rd Rancho Palos Verdes CA 90274-5063 Office: Fail-Safe Tech Corp 5757 W Century Blvd Ste 645 Los Angeles CA 90045-6407

LEE, JASON DAVIS, communications executive; b. Portland, Oreg., Oct. 25, 1949; s. Jason Dwight and Dorothy Bernadine (Davis) L.; m. Lauri Scheyer, May 28, 1972; children: Ryan, Rustin, Marit. BA, Reed Coll., 1972; MS in Indsl. Adminstrn., Carnegie-Mellon U., 1974. Sr. assoc. Booz, Allen & Hamilton, Chgo., 1974-79, prin., 1981-88; prin. Braxton Assocs., Boston, 1979-81; asst. v.p. investments and acquisitions Ameritech Devel. Corp., Chgo., 1988—. Co-chmn. Roycemore Sch. Charity Benefit, Evanston, Ill., 1988. Mem. Info. Industry Assn., Soc. Automotive Engrs. Republican. Jewish. Home: 1070 Meadow Rd Glencoe IL 60022 Office: Ameritech Devel Corp 10 S Wacker Dr Chicago IL 60606

LEE, JOHNNY EDWARD, sales director; b. Paris, Tex., Nov. 2, 1948; s. Dennis Raymond and Margie Evelyn (Bankhead) L.; m. Linda Darlene Sharp, June 27, 1970; children: Meredith Nicole, Jeffrey Alan. BBA in Banking and Fin., North Tex. State U., 1972. Sales rep. The Carnation Co., Dallas, 1972-74, G.D. Searle & Co., Dallas, 1975-78; supr. sales tng. G.D. Searle & Co., Chgo., 1978-79; mgr. dist. sales G.D. Searle & Co., Rochester, N.Y., 1979-82, cons. dist. sales mgr., 1982-83; product mgr. cardiovascular div. G.D. Searle & Co., Chgo., 1983-84; regional dir. sales G.D. Searle & Co., Dallas, 1985-88; sr. dir. field sales ops. G.D. Searle & Co., 1988—. Republican. Episcopalian. Office: GD Searle & Co 5200 Old Orchard Skokie IL 60077

LEE, JOHNSON Y., financial executive; b. Rangoon, Burma, June 10, 1955; came to U.S., 1968; s. Tat K. Lee and Thoy Lin (Ng); m. Lorraine Tran, June 29, 1981; children: Kent F., K. Ming. AA, City Coll., San Francisco, 1975; student, U. Calif., Berkeley, 1976. Cert. fin. planner. Agt. Prudential Ins. Co., Daly City, Calif., 1976-78; mgr. Prudential Ins. Co., Menlo Park, Calif., 1978-79; cons., pres. J.Y. Lee Pension Cons., L.A., 1979-83; broker Dean Witter, L.A., 1983-84; cons. Coast Cons., San Diego, 1987—; v.p. Triple S.W. Devel., Inc., Pasadena, Calif., 1987—, Tuan Investment Corp., Alhambra, Calif., 1988—; pres. Sun Cal Fin. Group, INc., Pasadena, 1986—; v.p. TransCapital, Alexandria, Va., 1984—; pres. Lone Hill Heights Corp., 1988—, Casadr Murirta Corp., 1988—, Palmdale Group Right Group, 1989—; gen. ptnr. H&W Resource, 1988—; cons. Glenn's Galleria, Inc., L.A., 1983—. Assoc. Friends of March Fund, L.A., 1984—; cons. Ming-Ye Buddhist Found. L.A., 1987—. Recipient Presdl. Citation Prudential Ins. Co., 1976-77. Mem. Inst. Cert. Fin. Planners. Home: 3004 Charlinda St West Covina CA 91791 Office: Transcapital 8150 Leesburg Pike Vienna VA 22180

LEE, JULIA TSAI, manufacturing company executive; came to U.S., 1949, naturalized, 1955; B.A., St. Johns U., Shanghai, 1948; M.A., Columbia U., 1950. Sec., China Inst., N.Y.C., 1953-54; mem. traffic staff WFAS Radio, Hartsdale, N.Y., 1965-69; export asst. Montclaire Electronic, New Rochelle, N.Y., 1969-71; asst. v.p. internat. Henningsen Foods, Inc., White Plains, N.Y., 1972—. Mem. Westconn Internat. Trade Assn. (dir.). Republican. Presbyterian. Office: 2 Corporate Park Dr White Plains NY 10604

LEE, KYO SEON, housing company executive; b. Icheon, Kyunggi, Republic Korea, June 10, 1935; s. Seon Kab and Bong Hee (Kim) L.; m. Young Sook Chang, Feb. 18, 1967; 1 child, Ho Chul, Jin Hee, Ho Chan. B of Econs., Korea U., 1961. Mgr. Daihan Coal Corp., Seoul, Republic Korea, 1976; v.p. Samchully Housing Co., Ltd., Seoul, 1985-86, pres., 1986—. Served to cpl. Korean Army, 1956-58. Office: Samchully Housing Co Ltd, Chunji Bldg 1022-7, Bangbae-Dong, Seocho-ku, Seoul 137-063, Republic of Korea

LEE, LAURENCE RAYMOND, retired pharmaceutical company executive; b. Chgo., Feb. 3, 1928; s. Victor L. and Evelyn (Plumhoff) L.; m. Barbara E. Rogers, Jan. 28, 1956; children: Justin, David. PhB, U. Chgo., 1946, JD, 1951. Bar: Ill. 1951. Assoc. Miller, Gorham, Wescott & Adams, Chgo., 1951-55; atty. Abbott Labs., North Chicago, Ill., 1955-63, gen. counsel, 1963-81, sr. v.p., sec., 1981-88. Trustee Village of Lake Bluff, Ill., 1989—. With U.S. Army, 1946-48.

LEE, LAURIE, mortgage company executive; b. Youngstown, Ohio, Nov. 2, 1950; d. Francis Howard and Jane Patricia (Halas) Reel; m. Ronald James Lee, Mar. 19, 1969; children: Shawn, Scott, Dustin. Grad. high sch., Boston. Owner Lee & Masters Ins. Agy., Cleve., 1982-85; asst. bank mgr. Security First Savs. Loan, Orlando, Fla., 1985-87; loan mgr. Citrus State Mortgage, Orlando, 1986-87; sr. loan processor Empire Am., Altoona Springs, Fla., 1986-87; mortgage banker Imperial Savs., Maitland, Fla., 1987, First Western Mortgage Corp., Maitland, 1987, GMAC Mortgage Corp., Maitland, 1988—. Room mother St. Bernadette Sch., Westlake, Ohio, 1978-85. Mem. Fla. Assn. Mortgage Brokers, Mortgage Bankers Am., Ins. Women Am. Democrat. Roman Catholic. Home: 1059 Chesterfield Circle Winter Springs FL 32708

LEE, LAWRENCE WINSTON, banker; b. Vicksburg, Miss., Nov. 3, 1938; m. Marcia M. Manning, Apr. 8, 1967; children: Susan W., Diane W. SB, U. Calif., Berkeley, 1962; MBA with distinction, Harvard U., 1969. V.p. Citibank, N.A., N.Y.C., 1962-87; exec. v.p. Irving Trust Co., N.Y.C., 1987—. 1st lt. U.S. Army, 1958-60. Office: Irving Trust Co 1 Wall St New York NY 10005

LEE, MICHAEL ERIC, lawyer; b. Greensboro, N.C., Oct. 16, 1945; s. John Kenneth and Nancy (Young) L.; m. Sandra Hampton; children: John Kenneth II, Michele Price, Michael E. Jr. BS, N.C. Agrl. and Tech. U., 1974; JD, N.C. U., 1975. Bar: N.C. 1975, U.S. Dist. Ct. (mid. dist.) N.C. 1975, U.S. Ct. Appeals (4th cir.) 1981. Research asst. N.C. Ct. Appeals, Raleigh, 1975-76; sr. ptnr. Lee, Johnson and Schmidly, P.A., Greensboro; then Lee, Johnson and Williams, P.A., Greensboro; now pvt. practice Greensboro; past bd. dirs. Vols. to Ct., Greensboro, Cen. Carolina Legal Svcs., Greensboro, 1979; mem. N.C. Jud. Planning Com., Raleigh, 1979, N.C. Medicaid Fraud Adv. Bd., Raleigh, 1979. Past mem. Guilford County Planning Com., U.S. Commn. Civil Rights-adv. commn. N.C. Recipient Outstanding Young Men of Am.award, 1980. Mem. ABA, N.C. Bar Assn., N.C. Black Lawyers Assn. (past pres.), N.C. Acad. Trial Lawyers, Guilford County Black Lawyers Assn. (past pres.), Guilford County Criminal Def. Lawyers (past pres.), Greensboro Bar Assn., Kappa Alpha Psi. Democrat. Presbyterian. Office: 3011 E Market St Greensboro NC 27405

LEE, OSCAR, strategic planning executive; b. Tegucigalpa, Honduras, Mar. 13, 1953; came to U.S., 1966; s. Oscar W. and Haydee (Chiu) L.; m. Rosa Wei-Chih Yuan, July 4, 1984. BS in Mgmt. Sci., Case Western Res. U., 1978; MBA, Baldwin-Wallace Coll., 1981. Programmer Gen. Electric Co., Cleve., 1976-79; asst. analyst Ohio Bell Co., Cleve., 1979-82; cons. internat. systems Alltel Corp., Hudson, Ohio, 1982-84; systems analyst Alltel Corp., Hudson, 1984-86, mgr. strategic planning, 1986-88, product mgr. data svcs., 1987-88, contingency planner, 1988—; systems cons. Saudi Arabian Royal Commn., Yanbu, Saudi Arabia, 1982-84, sr. cons. Mobile Telephone Systems, Co., Kuwait, 1986; dir. internat. trade devel. Mich. Trade Exchange Internat., Oak Pk., Mich. Chmn. social events Chinese Assn. Greater Cleve., 1985; active Cleve. Growth Assn.; mem. exec. council Baldwin-Wallace Coll. MBA Assn., Berea, Ohio. Mem. Am. Mgmt. Assn., Info. Group, Planning Forum, Orgn. Overseas Chinese, Orgn. Chinese Americans, On-Leong Benevolent Assn. Home: 1583 E 36th St Cleveland OH 44114 Office: Alltel Corp 2000 Highland Rd Twinsburg OH 44087

LEE, PAMELA ANNE, accountant; b. San Francisco, May 30, 1960; d. Larry D. and Alice Mary (Reece) L. BS in Bus., San Francisco State U., 1981. CPA, Calif. Typist, bookkeeper, tax acct. James G. Woo, CPA, San Francisco, 1979-85; tutor bus. math. and statistics San Francisco State U., 1979-80; teller to ops. officer Gibraltar Savs. and Loan, San Francisco, 1978-81; sr. acct. Price Waterhouse, San Francisco, 1981-86; corp. acctg. mgr. First Nationwide Bank, Daly City, Calif., 1986—; acctg. cons. New Performance Gallery, San Francisco, 1985, San Francisco Chamber Orch., 1986. Founding mem., chair bd. trustees Asian Acctg. Students Career Day, 1988—. Mem. Am. Inst. CPA's, Calif. Soc. CPA's, Nat. Assn. Female Execs., Nat. Assn. Asian-Am. CPA's (bd. dirs. 1986, news editor 1987, pres. 1988). Republican. Avocations: reading, music, travel, personal computing. Office: First Nationwide Bank 455 Hickey Blvd Daly City CA 94015

LEE, R(AYMOND) WILLIAM, JR., apparel company executive; b. Richmond, Va., Apr. 24, 1930; s. Raymond William and Sally (Beal) L.; m. Marianne Hollingsworth, June 21, 1952; children: Lelia, Carol, Raymond William, III, Sally. A.B., Duke U., 1951. With Oxford Industries, Inc., Atlanta, 1955—; v.p. men's wear Oxford Industries, Inc., 1970-77, v.p. fin. and adminstrn., 1977-86, exec. v.p. fin. and adminstrn., 1986—; adv. bd. Allendale Ins. Co.; bd. dirs. major leasing. Vice-chmn. Ga. Republican party, 1981-83; bd. dirs. Ga. Coop. Services for Blind, 1974—, pres., 1979-80. Served with USMCR, 1951-53. Mem. Am. Apparel Mfrs. Assn. (dir. 1964-70), Men's Fashion Assn. (dir. 1974-86), Father's Day Council (dir. 1975-85). Republican. Episcopalian. Clubs: Cherokee Town and Country (treas. 1977-78, dir. 1979-83, pres. 1982-83), Kiwanis. Home: 6265 Riverside Dr NW Atlanta GA 30328 Office: Oxford Industries Inc 222 Piedmont Ave NE Atlanta GA 30308

LEE, ROBERT ERICH, management and information systems director; b. Spokane, Wash., Dec. 26, 1955; s. Robert Edward Lee and Edith Freida (Klasen) Moore; m. Vicky Ann Rowland, Jan. 31, 1981; children: Erich Rowland, Christopher Rowlands. Student, Vanderbilt U., 1973-77, Corpus Christi (Tex.) State U., 1977, U. Tex., El Paso, 1980. Mgr., instr. Neptune Equipment Co., Nashville, 1976-77; customer engr. Hewlett-Packard Co., Los Angeles, 1977-82, dist. service mgr., 1982-85; region service adminstrn. mgr. Hewlett-Packard Co., North Hollywood, Calif., 1985-86; dir. mgmt. info. Tova Corp., Beverly Hills, Calif., 1986-87; dir. mgmt. info. staff Sequoia Supply, Inc., Irvine, Calif., 1987—. Mem. Town Hall Calif. Republican. Club: Magic Island. Home: 17 Alba W Irvine CA 92720 Office: Sequoia Supply Inc 1881 Langley Rd PO Box 19727 Irvine CA 92714

LEE, ROBERT HUGH, management executive; b. Honolulu, Jan. 3, 1950; s. Hugh Sebastian and Margaret Carol (Bennett) L.; m. Lois Ann Brown, Jan. 31, 1981. BA in Communications, Coll. St. Francis, 1972; MBA, No. Ill. U., 1977. Pres., owner Robert Hugh Lee Pub., Lockport, Ill., 1973-76; pres. Robert Hugh Lee, MBA and Assocs., DeKalb, Ill., 1978—; pres., chmn. bd. dirs., treas. Lee, Williams, Rogers & Assocs., Inc., Freeport, Ill., 1988—; lectr. , tchr. bus. strategy, mktg. and fin. at several univs. in Midwest. Dem. candidate Clk. of Cir. Ct., McLean County, Ill., 1980, Treas. DeKalb County, Ill., 1986, DeKalb County bd., 1988, Ill. Gen. Assembly, 1988; Dem. ward capt. cen. com., Blackhawk County, Iowa, 1982-85; trustee DeKalb County Regional Sch. Bd., 1987—. Mem. Internat. Sons of Norway. Home: 1512 Somonauk Rd #79 De Kalb IL 60115 Office: PO Box 801 De Kalb IL 60115

LEE, ROBERTO, chemical engineer; b. Shanghai, China, Jan. 10, 1937; came to U.S., 1954; s. Kin Wood and Yueh Chiu (Liu) L.; m. Alice Ong, Jan. 26, 1963; children—Vivienne, Denise. B.S., U. Ill., 1958; M.S., Purdue U., 1960, Ph.D., 1964. Registered profl. engr., Mo. Chem. engr. Corning Glass Works, N.Y., 1960; research engr. DuPont Co., Wilmington, Del., 1961; engring. group cons. Monsanto Co., St. Louis, 1963—. Patentee in field. Mem. Am. Chem. Soc., Am. Inst. Chem. Engrs. (nat. bd. dirs. 1985-87), Sigma Xi. Avocations: tennis; jogging; table tennis. Home: Saint Louis MO 63141 Office: Monsanto Co 800 N Lindbergh Blvd Saint Louis MO 63167

LEE, STEPHEN JAY, financial planner; b. Bethesda, Md., Jan. 26, 1951; s. John Edward and Rosa Esther (Pitta) L. BA, U. Md., 1973; M of Adminstrv. Sci., Johns Hopkins U., 1979; JD, U. Balt., 1982. Bar: Md. 1983. Account mgr. Burroughs Corp., Balt., 1974-80; law clk. Miles & Stockbridge, Balt., 1983; estate planner Farm Credit System, Balt., 1983; fin. planner The Copeland Cos., Columbia, Md., 1983-86; pres. Lee Fin. Group, Inc., Columbia, 1986—. Mem. Batl. Assn. Fin. Planners (bd. dirs. 1987-88, treas. 1988—), Inst. Cert. Fin. Planners, ABA, Md. Bar Assn. Office: Lee Fin Group Inc 4868 Greenbrier Rd Dayton MD 21036

LEE, STEPHEN MICHAEL, infosystems specialist; b. San Jose, Calif., Aug. 2, 1961; s. Stephen D. and Marsha A. (Boarts) L.; m. Stacee P. Cohn, Apr. 9, 1988. AA, Am. Coll. Switzerland, 1983; BA in Econs., UCLA, 1986. Salesman Sunset Realty Co., Santa Barbara, Calif., 1986, Wang Labs. Inc., Englewood, Colo., 1986—. Mem. UCLA Bus. Soc. (asst. dir. mktg. 1985-86). Home: 4150 Eutaw Dr Boulder CO 80303 Office: Wang Labs Inc 8505 E Orchard Rd Ste 1000 Englewood CO 80111

LEE, SUSAN PREVIANT, newspaper editor and writer; b. Milw., Aug. 7, 1948; d. David Spencer and Lois (Huebner) Previant; m. Kenneth R Weisshaar, Sept. 4, 1988; 1 child, Spencer. BA, Sarah Lawrence Coll., 1965; MA, Columbia U., 1972, PhD with distinction (John Jay fellow), 1975. Assoc. editor Fortune mag., N.Y.C., 1980-81; editorial bd. The Wall Street Jour., N.Y.C., 1981-83; sr. writer Bus. Week mag., N.Y.C., 1983-84; sr. editor, columnist Forbes mag., N.Y.C., 1984-88; dep. editor Op-Ed Page The N.Y. Times, N.Y.C., 1988—; adj. asst. prof. econs. Columbia U., N.Y.C., 1977-80, adj. prof., 1980-84; cons. Nightline TV program, 1987—; frequent TV guest Good Morning, America. Columnist Vogue mag., 1982-84; regular guest editor Ind. Network News "From the Editor's Desk", 1981-85; author: The Signet Book of Inexpensive Wine, 1977, 2d edit., 1979, The Cotton Economy: Perceptions and Realities, 1977, A New Economic View of American History, 1979, revised edit., 1987, Susan Lee's ABZ's of Economics, 1987, Susan Lee's ABZ's of Money and Finance, 1988; contbr. articles to mags., newspapers, profl. jours., including The New York Times, Barron's, The New Republic, The Washington Post. Bd. visitors U. Calif. Grad. Sch. Bus., Davis, 1985—. Recipient NCFE award in editorial writing for Wall Street Journal, 1982, Amos Tuck Communist award Dartmouth Coll., 1984.

LEE, THOMAS JOSEPH, JR., utility company executive, public affairs executive; b. Spring, Tex., July 20, 1921; s. Thomas Joseph and Annie Lela (Winslow) L.; m. Juanita Fern Boehm, June 18, 1947; children: Sandra Kay Lee Hebert, Thomas Joseph III. Student, Tex. A&M U., 1939-42; cert. mech. engring., NYU, 1944; M.B.A., Pepperdine U., 1978; Ph.D. in Mgmt., Columbia Pacific U., 1981. Jr. engr. Entex, Inc. and predecessor cos., Houston, 1947-49; various adminstrv. positions Entex, Inc. and Predecessor cos., Houston, 1950-79; sr. v.p. pub. affairs Entex, Inc. and predecessor cos., Houston, 1980-87; v.p. pub. and regulatory affairs United Tex. Transmission Co. subs. MidCon Corp., Houston, 1987—. Bd. dirs. Tex. Research League, Austin, 1983—; mem. exec. com. Tex. Council Econ. Edn., 1987—; chmn. bd. Tax Research Assn. of Houston and Harris County, 1982, 83; commr. Houston Clean City Commn., 1986—. Served to capt. Chem. Corps. U.S. Army, 1942-46, 51-53. Decorated Bronze Star; commd. adm. Tex. Navy. Mem. Am. Gas. Assn., So. Gas Assn. (govt. relations com.), Tex. Gas Assn. (chmn. govtl. affairs com.), Greater Lake Charles C. of C. (pres. 1968-69 I.M. George award), Houston C. of C., Nat. Assn. Mfrs., Tex. Assn. Bus. Presbyterian. Clubs: Houston Petroleum, Houston City; Headliners (Austin, Tex.); Lodges: Masons; Shriners. Home: 702 Center Hill Dr Houston TX 77079 Office: United Tex Transmission Co 3200 Southwest Frwy Houston TX 77210-4758

LEE, WILLIAM STATES, utility executive; b. Charlotte, N.C., June 23, 1929; s. William States and Sarah (Everett) L.; m. Janet Fleming Rumberger, Nov. 24, 1951; children—Lisa, States, Helen. B.S. in Engring. magna cum laude, Princeton U., 1951. Registered profl. engr., N.C., S.C. With Duke Power Co., Charlotte; 1955—, engring. mgr. Duke Power Co., 1962-65, v.p. engring., 1965-71, sr. v.p., 1971-75, exec. v.p., 1976-77, pres., chief operating officer, 1978-82, chmn., chief exec. officer, 1982—, also dir., mem. exec. and fin. coms.; mem. U.S. Com. on Large Dams, 1963—; dir. J.A. Jones Constrn. Co., Liberty Corp., J.P. Morgan Co., Morgan Guaranty Trust Co. Bd. dirs. United Community Services, Am. Nuclear Energy Council, Edison Electric Inst., Found. of the Carolinas; mem., chmn. N.C. Gov.'s Bus. Council, 1985—; chmn. trustees Queens Coll., U. N.C. Charlotte Found., Presbyn. Hosp. Found. Served with C.E. USNR, 1951-54. Named Outstanding Engr. N.C. Soc. Engrs., 1969. Fellow ASME (George Westinghouse gold medal 1972), ASCE; mem. Nat. Acad. Engring., Nat. Soc. Profl. Engrs. (Outstanding Engr. award 1980), Edison Electric Inst. (dir. econs. and fin. policy com., dir.), Charlotte C. of C. (chmn. 1979), Am. Nuclear Soc., Phi Beta Kappa, Tau Beta Pi. Presbyn. (ruling elder). Office: Duke Power Co 422 S Church St Charlotte NC 28242

LEE, YOUNG WOO, financial executive; b. Seoul, Republic of Korea, July 13, 1941; came to U.S., 1971; s. Jong J. and Boo S. (Kim) L.; m. Julie D. Cho, Sept. 23, 1973; children: Samuel S., Grace. BS in Acctg., Calif. State U., Hayward, 1974. CPA, Colo. Internal auditor, asst. treas., controller Am. Home Shield Corp., Santa Rosa, Calif., 1978-86, treas., v.p. fin., 1986—; treas. Am. Mortgage Service Inc., Compu Fund Inc., Dublin, Calif., 1982-85. Recipient Acad. award Korean and Am. Women's Club, 1974, Pres.'s award for Disting. Service, Am. Home Shield Corp., 1981. Mem. AICPA, Nat. Assn. Enrolled Agts. Home: 4676 Los Gatos Ct Santa Rosa CA 95403 Office: Am Home Shield Corp 90 South E St Santa Rosa CA 95404

LEECH, JAMES WILLIAM, diversified holding company executive; b. Boniface, Man., Can., June 12, 1947; s. George Clarence and Mary Elizabeth (Gibson) L.; m. Jacqueline Roberts; children: Jennifer Hilton, Joanna Marjorie, James Andrew Douglas. BS in Math. and Physics with hons., Royal Mil. Coll. Can., 1964; MBA, Queen's U., Can., 1973. Exec. asst. to pres. Commerce Capital Corp., Ltd., Montreal, Que., Can., 1973-74, v.p., 1974-75; exec. v.p. Commerce Capital Trust Co., Calgary, Alta., Can., 1976-78; sr. v.p. Eaton/Bay Fin. Services Ltd., Toronto, Ont., Can., 1979; pres., bd. dirs. Unicorp Can. Corp., Toronto, 1979—; also sr. v.p., bd. dirs. Unicorp Am. Corp. subs.; pres., dir. Union Enterprises, Ltd. subs. Unicorp Can. Corp., Toronto; vice chmn., dir. Union Gas Ltd., also bd. dirs.; chmn., dir. Unigas Corp.; mng. dir. and dir. Kingsbridge Capital Group, Inc.; bd. dirs. Harris Steel Group, Inc.; chmn., bd. dirs. Mark Resources Ltd. Vice chmn. adv. council Queen's U., 1979-83, mem. gen. council, 1978—, mem. investment com. bd. trustees, 1980—, trustee, 1984—, Queen's U. fund council, 1988—; bd. dirs., mem. exec. com., chmn. fundraising Can. Stage Co. Capt. Can. Armed Forces, 1968-71. D.I. McLeod scholar, 1971, 73; research fellow, Seagram, 1973, Samuel Bronfman Found. fellow, 1973, Transp. Devel. Agy. fellow, 1972. Mem. Young Pres. Orgn. (upper Can. chpt.), The Nat. Club, Ranchmen's Club, Calgary Club, Glencoe Club. United Ch. Can. Home: 70 Garfield Ave, Toronto, ON Canada M4T 1E9 Office: Unicorp Can Corp, 21 St Clair Ave E, Toronto, ON Canada M4T 2T7

LEEDOM, E. PAUL, banker; b. Havre de Grace, Md., June 11, 1925; s. Elridge L. and Beatrice L. (Brown) L.; B.S., U. Md., 1951; M.B.A., Adelphi U., 1967; m. Mildred E. Both, Oct. 21, 1978. Civilian tech. cons. Aberdeen Proving Ground, Md., 1953-57; various mgmt. postitions Ambac Industries, Inc., Carle Place, N.Y., 1957-68; pres. Digimatics Inc., Garden City, N.Y. 1968-74; 1st v.p. Anchor Savs. Bank, Northport, N.Y., 1974—. Active men's coms. troop 55 Boy Scouts Am.; dist. capt. United Community Fund; treas. L.I. United Campus Ministries; life mem. Republican Nat. Com. Served with USN, 1943-46, with Signal Corps U.S. Army, 1951-52. Named to corridor of disting. alumni Sch. Bus. Adminstrn. Adelphi U. Mem. Am. Mgmt. Assn., Internat. Assn. for Fin. Planning, Delta Mu Delta (hon.) Baptist. Home: 498 Weymouth Dr Wyckoff NJ 07481 Office: Anchor Savs Bank 1460 Valley Rd Wayne NJ 07470

LEEDS, RONALD P. E., financial corporation executive; b. N.Y.C., Nov. 14, 1939; s. George J. and Virginia (Jantzen) L.; m. Darcy M. Damgard, Feb. 22, 1983; 1 child, Natalie. BS, U. Pa., 1962. Commd. ensign U.S. Navy, 1962, advanced through grades to lt., 1966; naval attache, Lebanon, Jordan, Syria, Cyprus, 1966-68; ret., 1968; exec. dir. Exec. Services Internat. SARL, Beirut, 1969-73; pres. Exerv Corp. S.A., Switzerland, 1973—; chmn. Jesup & Lamont Asset Mgmt., Inc.; bd. dirs. Aiand Internat. Corp., Value Matrix Mgmt., Inc., The Jesup Group, U.S. Playing Card Corp., Congress Video Group, Inc., Global-Gucci S.A.M., Monaco. Mem. campaign com. Am. Cancer Soc., N.Y.C. div., 1978-79; dir., mem. fin. com. Damon Runyon-Walter Winchell Cancer Fund; mem. spl. projects com. Sloan Kettering; mem. nat. com. Rep. Party, Rep. Ground Floor Com., Presdl. Task Force; chmn. Reps. Abroad, Lebanon, regional chmn. Middle East and Africa, mem. exec. com. Mem. Naval Res. Assn. Roman Catholic. Clubs: Meadow, Bathing Corp. (Southampton); Sky, Union League (N.Y.C.); Annabel's (London); Golf de St. Cloud (Paris); St. Georges (Beirut); Zuoz (Switzerland). Office: care Jesup & Lamont Asset Mgmt 360 Madison Ave New York NY 10017 also: Exerv Corp, PO Box 11-7284, Beirut Lebanon

LEEK, JAY WILBUR, management consultation executive; b. Albany, N.Y., Apr. 24, 1928; s. Cecil and Hazel (Lindley) L.; m. Geneva Adams, June 30, 1968; children: Roderick Jay, Stacy LeAnn, Scott Lee, Timothy Lane, Debra Jan, Marilynn Sue, James Jay. BS in Indsl. Engring., Pacific Western, 1969, MS in Mgmt., 1976, D in Bus. Adminstrn., 1980. Registered profl. engr., Calif. Mgr. Nutone, Inc., Cin., 1951-53, Bulova Watch Co., N.Y.C., 1953-59, Martin Marietta Corp., Orlando, Fla., 1959-75; v.p. Northrop Corp., Los Angeles, 1975-80; pres., chief operating officer Philip Crosby Assocs., Winter Park, Fla., 1980-87, also bd. dirs.; prin. Leek/Internat., Winter Park, 1987—; bd. dirs. So. Bank, Longwood, Fla., Electro-World, Orlando. Author: Workmanship Standards, 1974; co-author: (with others) AMA Management Handbook, 1986, Quality Management Handbook, 1986. Trustee Orlando Sports, Inc., 1985-87, Fla. State Univ. Found., Tallahassee, 1986—; bd. dirs. Fla. Citrus Sports Assn., Orlando, 1984—. Served with USN, 1944-46. Recipient Academician award Internat. Acad. for Quality, Grobenzell, Fed. Republic Germany, 1985; Named to Wall of Fame, Am. Mgmt. Assn., 1979. Fellow Am. Soc. Quality Control (pres. 1980-81). Republican. Clubs: Fidlesticks Country (Ft. Myers, Fla.), Interlachen Country (Winter Park), Marshwood Country (Savannah, Ga.). Lodges: Masons, Shriners. Home: 2427 Gallery View Dr Winter Park FL 32792 Office: 15820 Kilmarnock Dr Fort Myers FL 33912

LEEKLEY, JOHN ROBERT, lawyer; b. Phila., Aug. 27, 1943; s. Thomas Briggs and Dorothy (O'Hora) L.; m. Karen Kristin Myers, Aug. 28, 1965; children: John Thomas, Michael Dennis. BA, Boston Coll., 1965; LLB, Columbia U., 1968. Bar: N.Y. 1968, Mich. 1976. Assoc. Curtis, Mallet-Prevost, Colt & Mosle, N.Y.C., 1968-69, Davis Polk & Wardwell, N.Y.C., 1969-76; asst. corp. counsel Masco Corp., Taylor, Mich., 1976-77, corp. counsel, 1977-79, v.p., corp. counsel, 1979-88, v.p., gen. counsel, 1988—. Mem. Freedom Twp. Bd. Tax Appeals, 1984-85. Mem. ABA (com. long range issues affecting bus. practice 1976—), Mich. State Bar Assn. Democrat. Roman Catholic. Office: Masco Corp 21001 Van Born Rd Taylor MI 48180

LEEKS, RAYMOND CHARLES FRANK, oil company executive; b. Sudbury, Suffolk, Eng., Mar. 17, 1941; s. Roger and Edith Grace (Richardson) L.; m. Linda Edith Cross, July 14, 1962; children: Paul Raymond, Karen Anne, Mark Leslie. Student, Ipswich Civic Coll., U.K., 1956-59. Chief acct. Total Oil Great Britain, London, 1970-74, dir. corp. planning, 1976-80, dir. fin., 1980-85; v.p. fin. Total Petroleum N.Am. Ltd., Denver, 1985—, also bd. dirs.; secondee Morgan Grenfell & Co. Ltd., London, 1974-76; bd. dirs. Total Petroleum, Inc., Denver, Total Petroleum Can., Ltd., Calgary, Alberta. Fellow Chartered Assn. Cert. Accts., Inst. Chartered Secs. and Adminstrs. Club: Denver. Office: Total Petroleum NAm Ltd Denver Pl 999 18th St Denver CO 80202

LEEMAN, JAMES EDWIN, management consultant; b. Washington, Oct. 3, 1928; s. James Edwin Sr. and Goldie (Ewell) L.; m. Betty L. Sells, June 30, 1950; children: James III, Patti, William, Richard, Charles, Merri. BBA, U. Md., 1950; BD in Theology, Emmaus Bible Coll., Oak Park, Ill., 1952; Cert. in Acctg., LaSalle U., Chgo., 1953; postgrad. in mgmt., Northwestern U., 1977. Controller Indsl. Paper Corp., Chgo., 1952-57; div. controller Mead Corp., Dayton, Ohio, 1957-60, dir. systems, 1960-64; exec. dir. mgmt. info. svcs. Kimberly-Clark Corp., Neenah, Wis., 1964-74; v.p. corp. svcs. Medtronic, Inc., Mpls., 1974-79; exec. dir. mgmt. info. svcs. AMP, Inc., Harrisburg, Pa., 1979-83; pres. James E. Leeman & Assoc., Harrisburg, 1983-85; corp. dir. mgmt. info. svcs. Coulter Electronics, Inc., Hialeah, Fla., 1985—; cons. IBM Corp., Gaithersburg, Md., 1980-83, John Diebold, N.Y.C., 1982; pres. James E. Leeman & Assoc., Coral Springs, Fla., 1985—. Troop chmn. Boy Scouts Am., Appleton, Wis., 1970-74; trustee, bd. dirs. Emmaus Bible Coll., Dubuque, Iowa, 1972—; chmn. YMCA East Br., Mpls., 1977-78, YMCA East Shore, Harrisburg, 1982-83; v.p. Rep. Senate Dist. Minn., Mpls., 1978-79; pres. Lake Geneva (Wis.) Found., 1976—. With U.S. Navy, 1946-48. Mem. Data Processing Mgmt. Assn., Systems Mgmt. Assn., Soc. for Info. Mgmt., Plymouth Brethren, McDowell Male Chorus (Appleton, Wis.), Apollo Male Chorus (Mpls.). Home: 10540 NW 3 Manor Coral Springs FL 33071 Office: Coulter Electronics Inc 600 W Coulter Way Hialeah FL 33010

LEEPER, RAMON JOE, physicist; b. Princeton, Mo., Apr. 1, 1948; s. Joe Edd and Jeanne (Gaul) L.; m. Sumiko Yasuda, Dec. 21, 1976; 1 son, Joe Eric. BS, MIT, 1970; PhD, Iowa State U., 1975. Research assoc. Ames Lab., U.S. Dept. Energy, Iowa, 1975-76; mem. tech. staff Sandia Nat. Labs., Albuquerque, 1976-86, supr. diagnostics div., 1986—; guest scientist Argonne Nat. Lab., Ill., 1971-76; invited lectr. NATO Advanced Study Inst., Italy, summer 1983. Contbr. articles to profl. jours., patentee in field. Recipient Outstanding Teaching award Iowa State U., 1973; NDEA fellow, 1971-73. Mem. Am. Phys. Soc., IEEE (session chmn. 1984), Sigma Xi. Republican. Home: 6905 Rosewood Rd NE Albuquerque NM 87111 Office: Sandia Nat Labs Diagnostics Div 1234 Albuquerque NM 87185

LEET, RICHARD HALE, oil company executive; b. Maryville, Mo., Oct. 11, 1926; s. Theron Hale and Helen Eloise (Rutledge) L.; m. Phyllis Jean Combs, June 14, 1949; children: Richard Hale II, Alan Combs, Dana Ellen. B.S. in Chemistry, N.W. Mo. State Coll., 1948; Ph.D. in Phys. Chemistry, Ohio State U., 1952. Research chemist Standard Oil Co. (Ind.), Whiting, 1953-64; dir. long-range and capital planning, mktg. dept. Am. Oil Co., Chgo., 1964-68; mgr. ops. planning, mfg. dept. Am. Oil Co., 1968-70; regional v.p. Am. Oil Co., Atlanta, 1970-71; v.p. supply Am. Oil Co., Chgo., 1971-74; v.p. planning and adminstrn. Amoco Chems. Corp., Chgo., 1974-75; v.p. mktg. Amoco Chems. Corp., 1975-77, exec. v.p., 1977-78, pres., 1978-83; exec. v.p., dir. Amoco Corp., Chgo., 1983—; bd. dirs. Vulcan Materials Corp., ITW. Chmn. bd. mgrs. Met. YMCA, Chgo.; exec. v.p. Boy Scouts Am.; former chmn. bd. Am. Indsl. Health Council; former bd. visitors Emory U., 1970-71; mem. found. bd. Ohio State U. Served with USNR, 1944-46. Mem. Am. Chem. Soc., Soc. Chem. Industry (exec. com.), Am. Petroleum Inst., Société Industrielle de Chemie, Chem. Mfrs. Assn. (dir.), Phi Sigma Epsilon, Gamma Alpha. Methodist. Office: Amoco Corp 200 E Randolph Dr Chicago IL 60601

LEETS, PETER JOHN, merger and acquisition company executive; b. London, Mar. 12, 1946; came to U.S., 1948; s. Earl Edward and Doris Eileen L.; m. Anne E. Shahinian, May 15, 1982. BS in Mktg., Ind. U., 1969. Salesman Ortho Pharm. Corp., Raritan, N.J., 1969-74; account mgr. Revlon Inc., Indpls., 1974-76; regional dir. Revlon Inc., Cleve., 1976-79; field sales mgr. Revlon Inc., Bay Village, Ohio, 1979-83; nat. field sales mgr. Binney & Smith, Bethlehem, Pa., 1983-85; v.p., dir. sales Dell Publishing Co., Inc., N.Y.C., 1985-87; exec. v.p. Geneva Corp., Irvine, Calif., 1987-88; pres. Geneva Bus. Analysis Co., Costa Mesa, Calif., 1988-89. mem. Orange County Econ. Outlook Conf.; participant high sch. career day. Vol., Big Bros., Detroit; mgr. Little League, Grand Rapids, Mich. Served with USAR. Mem. Sales Execs. N.Y., Am. Mgmt. Assn., Ind. U. Alumni (life), Delta Chi. Home: 26152 Flintlock Ln Laguna Hills CA 92653 Office: Geneva Corp 5 Park Pla Irvine CA 92714

LEFEBVRE, THOMAS WARREN, auditor; b. Portland, Maine, Nov. 8, 1948; s. Edward Philip and Jean (Sawyer) L.; m. Joan Louise Morgan, Sept. 15, 1979. BS in Acctg., Bentley Coll., 1971; BS in Pub. Adminstrn., U. Maine, 1983; MBA, N.H. Coll., 1985. Auditor Maine State Dept. of Audit, Augusta, 1985-88; bank examiner Maine State Bur. of Banking, Augusta, 1988—. Mem. fin. com. Old South Ch., 1985-88, chmn. bd. deacons 1985—. Lt. (j.g.) USCGR, 1983-88. Mem. Maine Soc. CPAs, Soc. Fin. Examiners, Res. Officers Assn. Republican. Office: Maine State Bur of Banking State House Sta 36 Augusta ME 04333

LEFEVRE, ROGER STANLEY, finance company executive; b. Murray, Utah, June 6, 1960; s. Roger A. and Judith Rae (Edens) LeF.; m. Rebecca Hill, Dec. 1, 1980 (div. Mar. 1983); children: Aliza Jennifer, Lauren. Cert. in mortgage, NYU, 1979; cert. in law, Harvard U., 1981. Pres. R.S. LeFevre & Assocs., Salt Lake City, 1975-78; v.p. First Capital Corp., Salt Lake City, 1978-81; v.p. The Consol. Co., Salt Lake City, 1981—, also bd. dirs.; v.p., bd. dirs. Consol Leasing, Salt Lake City; bd. dirs. Consol. Resorts, San Francisco. Intern U.S. Sen. Orrin G. Hatch, Salt Lake City, 1978. Mem. Am. Film Inst., U. Utah Pres. Club. Republican. Mormon. Home: 31 M St Suite 101 Salt Lake City UT 84103 Office: The Consol Cos 175 S Main St Suite 500 Salt Lake City UT 84111

LEFEVRE, THOMAS VERNON, utility company executive, lawyer; b. Dallas, Dec. 5, 1918; s. Eugene H. and Callie E. (Powell) L.; m. Lillian Herndon Bourne, Oct. 12, 1946; children: Eugene B., Nicholas R., Sharon A., Margot P. BA, U. Fla., 1939, LLB, 1942; LLM, Harvard U., 1946. Bar: Fla. 1945, N.Y. 1947, D.C. 1951, Pa. 1955, U.S. Supreme Ct. 1953. Atty. IRS and various firms, N.Y.C., Washington, and Phila., 1946-55; ptnr. Morgan, Lewis & Bockius, Phila., 1956-79; chmn., dir. UGI Corp., Valley Forge, Pa., 1979—; bd. dirs. Mellon Bank (East), Phila. Suburban Corp., Addison Capital Mgmt., Inc.; mem. Commr.'s Adv. Group IRS, 1976-77. Bd. dirs. Zool. Soc. Phila., 1982—, WHYY Inc., 1982—; chmn. bd. trustees Agnes Irwin Sch., 1968-74; chmn. U. Arts; trustee Franklin Inst., 1980—; trustee Fox Chase Cancer Ctr., 1979-88. With USMC, 1942-46. Fellow Am. Bar Found., ABA (vice chmn. govt. rels. sect. of taxation 1976-79); mem. Pa. Bar Assn. Episcopalian. Clubs: Phila., Sunday Breakfast (Phila.); Merion Cricket (Haverford, Pa.); Merion Golf (Ardmore, Pa.); Sankaty Head Golf (Nantucket, Mass.); Feather Sound Country (Clearwater, Fla.). Office: UGI Corp PO Box 858 Valley Forge PA 19482

LEFF, JOEL BASIL, investment advisor; b. N.Y.C., Apr. 4, 1935; s. Morris and Zena (Kahn) L.; 1 child, Adam Bodfish. B.S., U. Pa., 1957; M.B.A., Harvard U., 1961. Mem. faculty Harvard U., Cambridge, Mass., 1961-62; ptnr. Hawkes & Co., N.Y.C., 1963-64, Forstmann-Leff Assocs., N.Y.C., 1968—; exec. v.p. FLA Asset Mgmt., Inc., N.Y.C.; dir. Topps Chewing Gum, Inc., Research Frontiers, Inc. N.Y.C. 1963-70, Guiness Peat Group plc; guest lectr. Columbia U., N.Y.C.; pres. Master Art Sales; speaker, mem. Internat. Fedn. Employee Benefit Plans; speaker instl. investor confs.; mem. investment adv. bd. Honeywell Inc.; mem. pension reporter adv. bd. Bur. Nat. Affairs; mem. adv. com. The Recovery Group. William Cullen Bryant fellow Met. Mus. Art; Joel B. Leff fellow John F. Kennedy Sch. Govt., Harvard U. Mem. Securities Inst. Assn., Internat. Found. Employee Benefits, Soc. Investigation of Recurring Events, N.Y.C. Soc. Security Analysts, Confrerie de la Chaine des Rotisseurs, Nat. Economists Club, Internat. Sporting Club. Clubs: Nat. Economists, Harvard, Atrium, Buckingham Hunt, Nat. Econs., Internat. Sporting.

LEFFERDINK, JOHN RANDALL, real estate services company executive; b. Boulder, Colo., May 10, 1937; s. Allen Jones and Jane Louise (Pratt) L. AA, City Coll. San Francisco, 1968; BS, Nat. U., 1984. V.p. Morey Machine, Inc., Tustin, Calif., 1968-80; sales assoc. Unique Real Estate Co., Encinitas, Calif., 1980-85; pres. The Prudential Lefferdink Real Estate Co., Encinitas, 1985—. Chmn. fund raising North Shores chpt. Am. Cancer Soc., 1988; mem. liason com. Encinitas Econ. Devel. Coun.; mem. Oceanside Econ. Coun., Carlsbad Econ. Enhancement Coun., Encinitas Econ. Coun., 1987-88. With USMC, 1966-67. Recipient Disting. Svc. award Kiwanis Club, N.Y.C., 1967. Mem. LETIP of Carlsbad (1988), Encinitas-Leucadia C. of C. (bd. dirs. 1987-88), San Diego C. of C., Del Mar C. of C., Solana Beach C. of C., Rotary. Republican. Presbyterian. Office: 543 Encinitas Blvd Ste 111 Encinitas CA 92024

LEFKO, JEFFREY JAY, hospital consultant; b. St. Paul, July 15, 1945; s. Morris and Dorothy (Mindell) L.; m. Philomena M. Corno, Mar. 6, 1970 (div. Dec. 1984); children: Melissa Ann, Benjamin Scott, Ellen Rachael; m. Mary Wilson, Jan. 10, 1986. BSBA with distinction, U. Nebr., 1967; M in Hosp. Adminstrn., Washington U., St. Louis, 1969. Adminstrv. resident St. John's Mercy Hosp., St. Louis, 1968-69; nat. fellow Health Services Adminstrn. Am. Hosp. Assn.-Blue Cross Assn., Chgo., 1969-70; v.p. planning/ops. Meth. Hosp. of Ind., Indpls., 1970-75; v.p. Jewish Hosp., St. Louis, 1975-78; v.p. planning Greenville (S.C.) Hosp. System, 1979-88; exec. cons. The Lash Group, Greenville, 1988—; adj. instr. Washington U., 1976-78; guest lectr. Duke U., U. S.C., Clemson U., Ind. U.; instr. Furman U., Greenville, 1982-84. Contbr. articles to profl. jours.; contbr. to (book) Guide to Strategic Plannin g for Hosps., 1981; mem. edit. bd. Health Care Strategic Mgmt., 1984—. Mem. health systems planning com. Appalachian Health Council, Greenville, 1984—, Eastside adv. com., Greenville, 1985—; chmn. pub. affairs com. Community Planning Council, Greenville, 1987; bd. dirs. community planning council United Way, Greenville, 1986—, Duke Endowment-Carl Rowland Library, Charlotte, N.C., 1982-87. Mem. Am. Hosp. Ass. (pres. Soc. for Hosp. Planning and Mktg. 1984-85), Am. Coll. of Health Care Execs., Carolinas Soc. of Hosp. Planning (founding mem.), Innocents Soc., Beta Gamma Sigma. Lodge: Rotary. Office: The Lash Group PO Box 29615 Greenville SC 29604

LEFKOWITH, EDWIN FRANK, communications executive; b. Phila., Jan. 8, 1931; s. Simon Walters and Helen (Friedman) L.; m. Harriet Stern, Sept. 2, 1951 (div. July 1982); children: James Bruce, David Jay, Ann Lefkowith Hicks; m. Christie Antoinette Mayer, Dec. 23, 1983. BA, Pa. State U., 1951, MA, 1952, PhD, 1955. Instr. Pa. State U., University Park, 1951-55; advt. exec. McCann-Erickson, N.Y.C., 1958-60, Batten, Barton, Durstine & Osborn, N.Y.C., 1960-61; sr. v.p. mktg. Lippincott & Margulies, N.Y.C., 1961-68; pres., chief exec. officer Lefkowith, Inc., N.Y.C., 1968—. Served to lt. USN, 1955-58. Office: Lefkowith Inc 845 Third Ave New York NY 10022

LEFKOWITZ, HUGH WALTER, personnel consultant; b. N.Y.C., Sept. 3, 1930; s. Harry and Lillian (Weiss) L.; m. Janet Singer Mayer, June 25, 1955 (div. Sept. 1964); 1 child, Matthew Owen. AB, Dartmouth Coll., 1953. Asst. to pres. , dir. indsl. relations Rowe Mfg. Co., Inc., Whippany, N.J., 1955-62; v.p., dir. personnel L&B Knitting Mills, Bklyn., 1962-66; supr. mgmt. cons. services Ernst & Whinney, N.Y.C. and Boston, 1966-71; dir. personnel Topps Chewing Gum Co., Bklyn., 1971-80; asst. v.p., dir. corp. staffing Premier Indsl. Corp., Cleve., 1980-85; pres. Ivy Cons., Allamuchy, N.J., 1985—. Cons. Office of Mayor, Cleve., 1980-85. Served to cpl. Signal Corps U.S. Army, 1953-55. Recipient Cert. Recognition, Mayor George Voinovich, City of Cleve., 1984. Mem. Morris County C. of C., N.J. (bus. mgmt. com. 1985—), Warren County C. of C., N.J. (bus. mgmt. com. 1985—), Hunterdon C. of C., N.J. (edn. com. 1985—). Jewish. Clubs: Dartmouth (N.Y.C., suburban N.J.), Exchange (Morristown, N.J.). Home: 58 Barn Owl Dr Hackettstown NJ 07840 Office: Ivy Cons PO Box 279 Allamuchy NJ 07820

LEFKOWITZ, JERRY, lawyer, accountant; b. N.Y.C., Jan. 3, 1945; s. Seymour Arthur and Edna (Mann) L.; children: David Scott, Deborah Lynn. BS in Econs., U. Pa., 1966; JD, Boston U., 1969. Bar: N.Y. 1970; CPA, N.Y. Tax mgr. Arthur Andersen & Co., N.Y.C., 1969-77, Main Hurdman, N.Y.C., 1977-82; sr. tax ptnr. Rosenblatt, Slavet & Radezky, CPA's, N.Y.C., 1982—. Home: 80 Arthur Ct Port Chester NY 10573 Office: Rosenblatt Slavet & Radezky l4 W 40th St New York NY 10018

LEFTON, AL PAUL, JR., advertising executive; b. Wilmington, Del., July 11, 1928; s. Al Paul and Clara Belle (Ginns) L.; m. Amarilice Miller, Dec. 28, 1951; children: Alice, Marie, Al Paul III. BA, Yale U., 1950. With Al Paul Lefton Co., Inc., Phila. and N.Y.C., 1950—, v.p., sec., 1961-64, pres., chief exec. officer, 1964—. Bd. dirs. Eaglesville Sanitarium, 1965-79, Mann Music Ctr., Phila. 1975—, Univ. Arts, 1980—, Med. Coll. Pa., 1978-89, No. Home for Children, 1965-86. With AUS, 1951-53. Clubs: Yale (N.Y.C., Phila.); Union League (Phila.). Office: Rohm & Haas Bldg Independence Mall W Philadelphia PA 19106 also: Al Paul Lefton Co Inc 71 Vanderbilt Ave New York NY 10169

LEGATES, JOHN CREWS, information scientist; b. Boston, Nov. 19, 1940; s. Eber Thomson and Sybil Rowe (Crews) LeG. BA in Math., Harvard U., 1962. Edn. svcs. mgr. Telcomp Dept. Bolt Beranek & Newman, Cambridge, Mass., 1966-67; v.p. Washington Engring. Svcs. (later Cambridge Info. Systems), Cambridge, 1967-69; v.p., co-founder Cambridge Info. Systems, 1968-69, Computer Adv. Svc. to Edn., Wayland, Mass., 1966-72; exec. dir. Educom Interuniversity Communications Coun., Boston, 1969-72; founder, mng. dir. Program on Info. Resources Policy Harvard U., 1973—, pres., founder Ctr. Info. Policy Rsch., 1978—; Pvt. cons. Contbr. articles to profl. jours. Bd. dirs. Nat. Telecommunications Conf., Washington, 1979. Kent fellow, 1964. Mem. Nat. Acad. Scis./Nat. Rsch. Coun. (Telecommunications Privacy, Reliability and Integrity Panel), Nat. Sci. Found., IEEE, Soc. for Values in Higher Edn. Episcopalian. Club: Nashuba Valley Hunt (Pepperell, Mass.) (pres. 1974-80). Home: PO Box 331 Lincoln Center MA 01773

LEGO, PAUL EDWARD, corporation executive; b. Centre County, Pa., May 16, 1930; s. Paul Irwin and Sarah Elizabeth (Montgomery) L.; m. Ann Sepety, July 7, 1956; children: Paul Gregory, Debra Ann, Douglas Edward, Michael John. B.S. in Elec. Engring, U. Pitts., 1956, M.S., 1958. With Westinghouse Electric Corp., 1956—; bus. unit mgr. electronic components divs. Pitts., 1974-77; gen. mgr., v.p. lamp divs. Bloomfield, N.J., 1977-80; exec. v.p. electronics and control group Pitts., 1980-83, exec. v.p. control equipment, 1983-85, sr. exec. v.p. corp. resources, 1985-87, pres., chief operating officer, 1988—, also bd. dirs.; bd. overseers N.J. Inst. Tech., 1978—; mem. bd. strategic advs. Pyramid Tech. Corp., 1986—; bd. dirs. Pitts. Nat. Bank, PNC Fin. Corp., USX Corp., USX Found., Inc. Author papers in field. Trustee Carnegie-Mellon U., Pitts., 1987— trustee, exec. com. U. Pitts.; chmn. bd. visitors U. Pitts. Sch. Engring.; bd. dirs. Presbyn.-Univ. Hosp., Pitts., 1988—; mem. citizens' sponsoring com. Allegheny Conf. on Community Devel., Pitts; trustee Com. for Econ. Devel., N.Y.C.; vice chmn. U.S.-Korea Bus. Coun., Washington; exec. adv. bd. Energy Source Edn. Coun., Lakewood, Calif.; bd. overseers N.J. Inst. of Tech., Newark. With AUS, 1948-52. Recipient Westinghouse Order of Merit 1975. Mem. Nat. Elec. Mfrs. Assn. (bd. govs. 1984—), Machinery and Allied Products Assn. (exec. com.), Greater Pitts. C. of C. (vice chmn. 1985—), Elec. Mfrs. Club Chgo., Cherrington Golf Club, Valley Brook Country Club, Duquesne Club (bd. dirs. Pitts. 1988—), Laurel Valley Golf Club, Rolling Rock Club (Ligonier, Pa.), Sigma Xi. Democrat. Roman Catholic.

LE GOFF, RÉNE JEAN, business machine company executive; b. Paris, Apr. 21, 1944; s. Rene Marie and Pierina Modesta (Bertazzon) LeG.; m. Chantal Marie-France Houillon, July 10, 1965; children—Clotilde, Benedicte. Engr., Institut Industriel du Nord, Lille, France, 1967. Adminstrv. asst. Clement Mfg. Co., Paris, 1969; sales rep., mktg. mgr. IBM France, Paris, 1970-81, br. office mgr., Paris, and Orleans, 1982-84, dir. mktg., Paris, 1985; group dir. IBM-France Diffusion, 1985-89; dir. mktg. IBM-Europe Cen. Unit, 1989—, chmn. R.P.B.; dir. MNS, Paris, SIRE, Paris. Gen. sec. Nat. Union Corp. Clubs, 1977-80; mem. Mcpl. Office of Sports, 1976-82. Served to lt. French Navy, 1967-69. Recipient French Sport medal Minister Youth and Sports, 1983, Disting. Citizen award Mayor of Paris, 1985; chevalier Nat. Order Merit, 1986. Clubs: Racing of France (treas. 1984—), IBM Sporting (pres. 1974—). Roman Catholic. Avocation: basketball. Home: 11 Ave de Diane, Saint Maur, 94100 Val de Marne France Office: IBM Europe, Cité Jean Monnet, 92061 Paris La Defense 5, France

LEGUM, JEFFREY ALFRED, automobile company executive; b. Balt., Dec. 16, 1941; s. Leslie and Naomi (Hendler) L.; B.S. in Econs., U. Pa., 1963; grad. Chevrolet Sch. Merchandising and Mgmt., 1966; m. Harriet Cohn, Nov. 10, 1968; children—Laurie Hope, Michael Neil. With Park Circle Motor Co. doing bus. as Legum Chevrolet-Nissan, Balt., 1963—, exec. v.p., 1966-77, pres., 1977—, also dir.; partner Pkwy. Indsl. Center, Dorsey, Md., 1965—; v.p., dir. P.C. Parts Co., 1967—; v.p. Westminster Motor Co. (Md.), 1967-72, pres., dir., 1972—; pres. One Forty Corp., Westminster, 1972—; dir., exec. com. United Consol. Industries, 1970-73; dir. Preakness Celebration, Inc., 1988—; dist. chmn. Chevrolet Dealers Council, 1975-77, chmn. Washington zone, 1982-83. Chmn. auto div. Asso. Jewish Charities,

Balt., 1966-69; mem. Md. Service Acad. Review Bd., 1975-77, Bus. Adv. Bd. to Atty. Gen., 1985-87; trustee The Legum Found., Balt., 1967—; trustee, treas., mem. exec. com., chmn. fin. com., The Park Sch., Balt., 1979—; mem. pres.'s com. U. Toronto, 1983—; bd. dirs. Assoc. Placement Bur., Balt., v.p., 1972-76; adv. bd. The Competitive Edge, Albuquerque, 1977-81; mem. investment com. Balt. Hebrew Congregation, 1980—. Recipient award of honor Assoc. Jewish Charities of Balt., 1967, 68; Cadillac Master Dealer award, 1980-88; Cadillac Pinnacle Excellence award, 1986; Young Pres.'s Orgn. Cert. Appreciation; Nissan Nat. Merit Master award, 1982-88; Chevrolet Nat. Service Supremacy award, annually 1979-89, Wales Giant award Automotive News, 1987. Mem. Md. Auto Trade Assn., Young Pres. Orgn. (pres.'s forum 1977—), Greater Balt. Com., Benjamin Franklin Assocs., Carroll County C. of C., Baltimore County C. of C., Md. Hist. Soc. (exec. com. Library of Md. History 1981—). Clubs: Suburban (Baltimore County); Johns Hopkins Faculty, University of Pa., Center (Balt.); U. Toronto Faculty (hon.). Home: 10 Stone Hollow Ct Baltimore MD 21208 Office: 7900 Eastern Ave Baltimore MD 21224

LEHMAN, JEFFREY H., investment banker; b. N.Y.C., Apr. 23, 1960; s. Joseph L. and Joan B. (Sontag) L.; m. Mallory L. Greenberg, May 16, 1987. BS in Econs. summa cum laude, U. Pa., 1982, MBA with distinction, 1983. Mgr. Candid Litho Co., Inc., N.Y.C., 1977-80; asst. account exec. Grey Advt., Inc., N.Y.C., 1981; assoc. D.H. Blair & Co., Inc., N.Y.C., 1982-83; sr. assoc. Kramer Capital Corp., N.Y.C., 1983-84; asst. mng. dir. Ladenburg, Thalmann & Co. Inc., N.Y.C., 1984-85, mng. dir., 1985—. Mem. charity com. J.D.F., N.Y.C., 1977—. Mem. City Athletic Club, Aspatuck Club (Westhampton Beach, N.Y.). Office: Ladenburg Thalmann & Co Inc 540 Madison Ave New York NY 10022

LEHMAN, KARIN RÓSA, medical clinic administrator; b. Hofsós, Iceland, Apr. 1, 1945; came to U.S., 1968; d. Kristján Jóhannsson Hallsson and Eygerdur A. Bjarnadóttir; m. David A. Lehman, Mar. 31, 1968 (div. 1971); 1 child, Michelle. BS in Mgmt., U. Louisville, 1980, MBA, 1982. Sec. in contractor's office Keflavik, Iceland, 1964-65; bank corr. Handelbanken, Copenhagen, 1966-67; payroll clk. U. Louisville, 1970-71; purchasing agt., administrv. asst. U. Louisville Med. Sch., 1971-74; fin. dir. U. Louisville Coll. Arts and Scis., 1974-80; fin. planner Waddell & Reed Fin. Services, Louisville, 1982-83; dir. Group Health Coop., Seattle, 1983-86; adminstr. Overlake Internal Medicine Assocs., Bellevue, Wash., 1986—; ind. investment and bus. cons., Seattle, 1983—. Dean's scholar U. Louisville, 1979. Mem. Phi Kappa Phi. Home: 614 E Union #104 Seattle WA 98122 Office: Overlake Internal Medicine Assocs 1011 116th Ave NE Bellevue WA 98004

LEHMAN, TIMOTHY JOHN, health care executive, accountant; b. Coshocton, Ohio, Oct. 23, 1947; s. Carl E. and Eloise C. (Walters) L.; m. Suzanne M. Hill, Oct. 16, 1976; children: Andrew J., Matthew A., Kathryn E. BA, Bliss Coll., 1969. Examiner Bur. Fiscal Rev. Ohio Dept. Pub. Welfare, Columbus, 1976-78; reimbursement acct. John P. Nipps and Co., Columbus, 1978-79; v.p. reimbursement Americare Corp., Columbus, 1979-87; pren. Lehman and Assocs., Westerville, Ohio, 1986—. Served with U.S. Army, 1969-72. Mem. Ohio Health Care Assn. (treas. 1987-88—, Pres.'s award 1986, 88), Health Care Fin. Mgmt. Assn. Home: 5809 Lou St Columbus OH 43231 Office: Lehman and Assocs 56 Dorchester Sq Ste B Westerville OH 43081

LEHMANN, ALEXANDER RICHARD, investor relations executive; b. Sorau, Germany, June 8, 1935; s. Herbert and Hedwig (Cora) L.; m. Irene W. Klingner, Aug. 15, 1961; children: Christine, Alexandra. AB, CUNY, 1967; SM, MIT, 1968. Asst. to pres. Carl Zeiss Inc., N.Y.C., 1963-67; v.p. Hayes/Hill Inc., N.Y.C., 1969-79; mng. dir. Sopran, N.Y.C., 1979-81; pres. A.R. Lehmann & Co. Inc., N.Y.C., 1981-83; v.p. investor relations Whitman Corp. (formerly W/C Industries), N.Y.C., 1983—; cons. to investors worldwide. Contbr. articles to profl. jours. Served with U.S. Army, 1960-63, ETO. Mem. Nat. Investor Relations Inst. and Planning Forum. Lutheran. Club: Sky (N.Y.C.). Home: 812 Sleepy Hollow Rd Briarcliff NY 10510

LEHR, JAMES JEROME, bank executive, university public board member; b. Witcha, Kans., Apr. 1, 1931; s. Anton and Vertress (Tucker) L.; m. Rose Marie Shenuk, Aug. 22, 1954; children: Kim Marie, Kathleen Ann, Kevin Anthony, Karen Sue. AA, U. Calif. at Los Angeles, 1955, AB, 1956, MS, 1957. Prodn. news rep. NBC, Burbank, Calif., 1958-61; asst. cashier Union Bank, Los Angeles, Pasadena, Calif., 1962-68; v.p. Bank Calif., Beverly Hills, Calif., 1968-76; pres. Pacific Funding Group, Beverly Hills, 1976-84; v.p. Guardian Bank, Los Angeles, 1984—. Contbr. various articles to Los Angeles Times, 1956, Los Angeles Herald-Examiner, 1957; writer, editor: NBC polit. news., 1960. Mem. San Gabriel Rep. Club, Calif., 1986—. Served to 1st Lt. U.S. Army, 1951-54, Korea. Decorate Bronze Star; recipient cert. commendation Occidential Coll., Los Angeles, 1987; named Calif. State U. Grad. Research Competition juror San Jose State U., 1988. Mem. Am. Bankers Assn., Independent Bankers Assn., Calif. State U. (Univ. Devel. Bd., 1987—), Calif. State U. (The Inter-Colligiate Athletic Bd., 1987—). Republican. Roman Catholic. Club: Los Angeles Stock Exchange. Lodge: Lions. Office: Guardian Bank 800 S Figueroe Los Angeles CA 90017

LEHR, SETH JONATHAN, investment banker; b. Teaneck, N.J., July 21, 1956; s. Robert Lawrence and Shirley (Lichter) L.; m. Ellyn Goodman, May 24, 1981; children: Martin, Audrey, Stephen. BS in Econs., U. Pa., 1978, MBA, 1983. Mktg. rep. IBM Corp., Phila., 1978-80; analyst First Boston Corp., N.Y.C., 1980-81; v.p. Financo Inc., Phila., 1983-85, Shearson Lehman Hutton Inc., Phila., 1985—. Bd. dirs., mem. fin. com. Phila. Geriatric Ctr., 1986—; bd. dirs. nat. young leadership council United Jewish Appeal, Phila., 1986—. Clubs: Locust, Philmont Country (Phila.). Office: Shearson Lehman Hutton 1700 Market St Philadelphia PA 19103

LEHRER, KENNETH EUGENE, real estate advisor, consultant, developer; b. N.Y.C., Apr. 17, 1946; s. Charles Carlton and Evelyn Estelle (Rosenfeld) L.; m. Myrna Sue Newman, Apr. 4, 1981 (div. 1988). BS, NYU, 1967, MBA, 1969, MA, 1972, D in Pub. Adminstrn., 1980. Registered investment advisor; cert. real estate appraiser; lic. real estate broker. Asst. treas. Bankers Trust Co., N.Y.C., 1970-73; dir. devel. Coventry Devel. Corp., N.Y.C., 1974-77; asst. v.p. Affiliated Capital Corp., Houston, 1977-80; dir. fin. Allison/Walker Interests, Houston, 1980-82; mng. dir. Lehrer Devel. and Investments, 1982—; prof. real estate fin. U. Houston, 1985—; chmn. bd. dirs. Acadia Savs. and Loan Assn., Crowley, La., French Market Homestead Savs. Assn., Metairie, La., Twin City Savs. Bank, West Monroe, La., 1st Savs. La., LaPlace. Pres. Cornerstone Mcpl. Utilities Dist., 1978-85; bd. dirs. Ft. Bend County Mcpl. Utility Dist. #106, M.M.H. Equity Fund, Inc. (London); adv. dir. Kaplan Mgmt. Co., Inc., Houston, Lease USA, Inc., Houston, The Clarion Corp., Houston. Mem. Am. Horse Show Assn., Nat. Steeplechase and Hunt Assn. (life), U.S. Tennis Assn. (life), Am. Real Estate and Urban Econs. Assn., Am. Real Estate Soc., Nat. Assn. Bus. Economists, NYU Money Marketeers, Nat. Forensic Ctr., Nat. Assn. Corp. Dirs., Internat. Coll. Real Estate Cons. Profls., Internat. Assn. Corp. Real Estate Execs., Nat. Assn. Forensic Economists, Am. Arbitration Assn., Houston Bus. Economists, Western Econ. Assn., Internat. Real Estate Inst. Fin. Club. NYC., Real Estate Educators Assn., Am. Econ. Assn., N.Am. Econs. and Fin. Assn., So. Econ. Assn., NYU Alumni Fedn. (bd. dirs. 1974-77), Tex. Rep. Assn., Houston C. of C. (mem. govtl. relations com.). Clubs: Atrium, NYU (N.Y.C.); Jockey (Miami, Fla.); World of Tennis (Austin, Tex.). Home: 5555 Del Monte Dr #802 Houston TX 77056-4105 Office: Lehrer Devel & Investments 3 Riverway Ste 1800 Houston TX 77056

LEIBLER, KENNETH ROBERT, stock exchange executive; b. N.Y.C., Feb. 21, 1949; s. Max and Martha (Dales) L.; m. Marcia Kate Reiss, July 15, 1973; children: Jessica Hope, Andrew Ethan. B.A. magna cum laude, Syracuse U., 1971; postgrad., U. Pa., 1972. Mgr. options Lehman Bros., 1972-75; v.p. options Am. Stock Exchange, N.Y.C., 1975-79; sr. v.p. adminstrn. and fin. Am. Stock Exchange, 1979-81, exec. v.p. adminstrn. and fin., 1981-85, sr. exec. v.p., 1985-86, pres., 1986—; instr. N.Y. Inst. Fin.; dir. Securities Industry Automation Corp.; chmn. Amex Commodities Corp. Contbg. author: Handbook of Financial Markets: Securities, Options Futures, 1981. Mem. Fin. Execs. Inst., Securities Industry Assn., Am. Stock Exchange Clearing Corp. (pres.), Phi Beta Kappa, Phi Kappa Phi. Office: Am Stock Exchange Inc 86 Trinity Pl New York NY 10006

LEIBOWITZ, NORMAN, contractor, real estate developer; b. Albany, N.Y., Sept. 21, 1947; s. Morris and Fay (Spiegel) L.; m. Deborah Kirsch, Jan. 10, 1980; children: Jesse Morris, Alex Kirsch. Student, Plattsburgh State U., 1985-89. Chief exec. officer DeGraff-Moffly Gen. Contractors, Albanly, 1983—; real estate cons. First Albany Corp., 1986-87. Chmn. Israel Anniversary Com., Albany; mem. Tri-County Vietnam Vets. Mem. Com. Office: 10 Dewitt St Albany NY 12207

LEIGH, BEVERLY EUGENE, oil company executive; b. Savannah, Ga., Jan. 15, 1924; s. Herbert David and Pauline Catherine (Rehm) L.; m. Mary Pindar, Dec. 22, 1944 (dec. 1968); children—John David, Julia Leigh West; m. Elizabeth LeHardy, Jan. 30, 1971. U. Ga., 1948, Ga. Inst. Tech., 1950. Analyst U.S. Dept. Commerce, Savannah, Ga., 1953; vice chmn., treas. Colonial Oil Industries Inc., Savannah, Ga., 1953—. Served to lt. (j.g.) USNR, 1942-45. Republican. Episcopalian. Home: Rt 6 Box 269A Savannah GA 31410 Office: Colonial Oil Industries Inc PO Box 576 Savannah GA 31402

LEIGH, ROBERT ALFRED, electrical engineer; b. Vienna, Va., Feb. 28, 1945; s. Alfred Day and Mildred Ann (Maitland) L.; m. Cynthia Thrift, Feb. 12, 1983 (div. May 1985); children: Robert Andrew, Heather Maitland. BEE, U. Va., 1967; postgrad., U. Tenn., 1969-71. Registered profl. engr. Va., N.C., S.C., Md., Mich., Ala., Fla. Elec. engr. Olin Corp., Pisgah Forest, N.C., 1967-71, R.S. Noonan of S.C. Inc., Greenville, 1971-78, Blount Internat. Ltd., Greenville, 1978-83; pres. Republic Indsl. Designs Inc., Marietta, Ga., 1983-84, Leigh Engring. Inc., Mauldin, S.C., 1984—. Mem. IEEE (IGA group), Instrument Soc. Am., Nat. Fire Protection Assn., Palmetto Ski. Democrat. Presbyterian. Office: Leigh Engring Inc PO Box 599 Mauldin SC 29662

LEIGHTON, CHARLES MILTON, specialty consumer products executive; b. Portland, Maine, June 4, 1935; s. Wilbur F. and Elizabeth (Loveland) L.; A.B., Bowdoin Coll., 1957; M.B.A., Harvard, 1960; m. Deborah Throop Smith, Aug. 30, 1958; children—Julia Loveland, Anne Throop. Produce line mgr. Mine Safety Appliances Co., Pitts., 1960-64; instr. Harvard Bus. Sch., 1964-65; group v.p. Bangor Punta Corp., Boston, 1965-69; chmn., chief exec. officer CML Group, Inc., Boston, 1969—; bd. dirs. Smart Names, Waltham, Mass., New Eng. Mut. Life Ins. Co. Past pres. Alumni Harvard Bus. Sch., Cambridge, Mass. Republican. Episcopalian. Clubs: New York Yacht (rear commodore); Chatham (Mass.) Yacht (vice commodore 1957); Harvard of N.Y.C. and Boston, Harvard Bus. Sch. (Boston); Somerset. Home: 33 Liberty St Concord MA 01742 Office: CML Group Inc 524 Main St Acton MA 01720

LEIGHTON, DAVID STRUAN ROBERTSON, food products executive, author; b. Regina, Sask., Can., Feb. 20, 1928; s. Gordon Ernest and Mary Haskins (Robertson) L.; m. Margaret Helen House, Aug. 25, 1951; children: Douglas, Bruce, Katharine, Jennifer, Andrew. B.A., Queen's U., Kingston, Ont., 1950; M.B.A., Harvard U., 1953, D.B.A., 1956; LL.D., U. Windsor, 1972. Editor Canadian Press, 1950-51; research assoc. Harvard U., 1953-55, vis. prof., 1974; from asst. prof. to prof. U. Western Ont., 1955-70; pres. Banff (Alta.) Centre, 1970-82; chmn. Nabisco Brands Ltd., Toronto, Ont., Can., 1983-85; dir. Scott's Hospitality, Inc., Gulf Can. Ltd., GSW Ltd., CAMCO, Inc., Acres Internat. Ltd., Rio Algom Ltd., Lornex Mines, John Wiley & Sons Ltd., Montreal Trustco, Telemedia, Inc., Cambridge Shopping Ctrs., Nat. Centre for Mgmt. Research and Devel.;London Free Press Pub. Co. Author: (with McNair, Brown and England) Problems in Marketing, 1957, (with E.J. Fox) Marketing in Canada, 1958, (with Donald H. Thain) Canadian Problems in Marketing, 1959, 66, 72, (with Donald H. Thain and C.B. Johnston) How Industry Buys, 1959 (Media-Scope award as best indsl. market research of 1960), (with Wilding and Wilson) The Distribution of Packaged Consumer Goods: An Annotated Bibliography, 1963, International Marketing: Text and Cases, 1965, (with Donald Thompson) Canadian Marketing: Problems and Prospects, 1973, (with Kenneth Simmonds) Case Problems in Marketing, 1973, (with Peggy Leighton) Artists, Builders and Dreamers, 1982; editor-in-chief: Business Quarterly, 1958-61. Chmn. Canadian Consumer Council, 1968-70; bd. govs. Queen's U/. George F. Baker scholar Harvard U.; recipient Alta. Achievement award, 1978, Alta. Order of Excellence, 1985. Mem. Am. Mktg. Assn. (past pres.). Home: Did River Rd RR3, Komoka, ON Canada N0L 1R6 Office: U Western Ont, Nat Ctr Mgmt R & D, London, ON Canada N6A 3K7

LEIN, DON CURTIS, corporate executive; b. Maquoketa, Iowa, 1934; married. B.S., U. Iowa, 1956; M.B.A., Harvard U., 1962. Pub. acct. Arthur Andersen & Co., 1956-57, 59-60; asst. treas. Crosby Plans, 1962-63; asst. controller Jostens Inc., Mpls., 1963-66, controller, 1966-70, v.p., controller, 1970-72, v.p. fin., 1972-75, exec. v.p. fin. and adminstrn., from 1975, sec., 1975—, now also pres.; dir. Jostens Inc. Served with U.S. Army, 1957-59. Mem. Am. Inst. (C.P.A.'s), Fin. Exec. Inst. Office: Jostens Inc 5501 Norman Center Dr Minneapolis MN 55437 *

LEINEWEBER, J. HUNTZ, marketing executive; b. N.Y.C., Feb. 3, 1947; s. August Charles and Maureen (O'Connell) L.; m. Katherine Marie Keeney, Oct. 2, 1982; children: Heather Marie, Alexa Keeney. BA with honors, Harvard U., 1987. Customer service rep. Memorex, Mountain View, Calif., 1973-75; customer service mgr. No. Telecom, San Mateo, Calif., 1975; account rep., systems analyst Data Point Corp., San Francisco, 1976-79; div. mgr. Remote Computing Corp., Palo Alto, Calif., 1979; mgr. sales NCR, San Francisco, 1980-82; cons. Yankee Bank for Savs., Boston, 1985; sr. v.p. FCAACA Asset Mgmt., Boston, 1982-85; v.p., mgr. pvt. banking Boston Safe Deposit & Trust, 1985-87; mktg. cons., founder Performance Cons., San Francisco, 1987—; sr. cons. State Farm Ins., Orinda, Calif., 1988; cofounder, cons. Movin Movies, Cupertino, Calif., 1988; div. mgr., direct sales Wells Fargo Bank, N.A., San Francisco. Inventor presentation folder binding, 1988. Served with USAF, 1965-70. Mem. Am. Soc. Tng. and Devel. Unitarian. Club: Harvard of Boston. Home and Office: 496 Woodminster Dr Moraga CA 94556

LEIPOLD, WILLIAM CHARLES, JR., plastics company executive, consultant; b. East Reading, Pa., Mar. 30, 1949; s. William Charles Sr. and Patricia (Feehan) L. BS in Chem. Engring., Ohio State U., 1972; MBA, U. Chgo., 1973. Asst. to mfg. mgr. W.R. Grace & Co., Burlington, Mass., 1973; process engr. polyfibron div. W.R. Grace & Co., Owensboro, Ky., 1974, gen. supr. polyfibron div., 1975; mgr. dept. electronics div. Raychem Corp., Menlo Park, Calif., 1976, engring. mgr., 1977-78; U.S. product mgr. pipe protection div. Raychem Corp., Redwood City, Calif., 1978-79; plant mgr., mgr. rsch. and devel. solar div. Sealed Air Corp., Hayward, Calif., 1981; mgr. ops. Custom Coating & Laminating, Worchester, Mass., 1980; pres., chmn. Columbine Plastics Corp., Boulder, Colo., 1982—; cons. Medac, Inc., Bethesda, Md., 1987—. Mem. Soc. Plastic Engrs. (sr. pres. 1970-72, Disting. Service award 1972). Republican. Club: Boulder Country. Office: Columbine Plastics Corp 3195 Bluff St Boulder CO 80301

LEIS, SUSAN SCHOENFELD, accountant; b. Yonkers, N.Y., Aug. 23, 1948; d. David and Madalynne H. (Geller) Schoenfeld; m. Jonathan P. Leis, Dec. 20, 1970; children: Benjamin, Betsy. BS, Cornell U., 1970; MS, Columbia U., 1971; MBA, Case Western Res. U., 1983. CPA, Ohio. Fin. mgr. Urology Services, Cleve., 1983-86; controller Reich, Seidelmann & Janicki, Cleve., 1987—. Troop services dir. Shaker Heights Area Girl Scouts U.S., 1987-88. Mem. Am. Inst. CPA's, Ohio Soc. CPA's, LWV. Home: 3628 Palmerston Rd Shaker Heights OH 44122 Office: Reich Seidelmann & Janicki 30680 Bainbridge Rd Solon OH 44139

LEISNER, ANTHONY BAKER, publishing company executive; b. Evanston, Ill., Sept. 13, 1941; s. A. Paul and Ruth (Solms) L.; B.S., Northwestern U., 1964, M.B.A., 1983; children—Justina, William, Sarah. Salesman, Pitney Bowes Co., 1976-77; with Quality Books Inc., Lake Bluff, Ill., 1968—, v.p., 1972—, gen. mgr., 1979—; adj. faculty Lake Forest (Ill.) Sch. Mgmt., 1983—, Kellogg Grad. Sch. Mgmt. Northwestern U., Evanston, Ill. Pres. bd. dirs. Lake Villa (Ill.) Public Library, 1972-78; bd. dirs. No. Ill. Library Systems, 1973-78; chmn. Libertarian Party Lake County (Ill.), 1980-81; probation officer Lake County CAP, 1981. Mem. ALA, Ill. Library Assn. (Gerald L. Campbell award 1980), Am. Booksellers Assn., Acad. Mgmt., Am. Mktg. Assn., Internat. Platform Assn., World Future Soc., World Isshin Ryu Karate Assn. Author: Official Guide to Country Dance Steps, 1980; also articles. Home: 1174 Cherry St Winnetka IL 60093 Office: Quality Books Inc 918 Sherwood Dr Lake Bluff IL 60044

LEISTEN, ARTHUR GAYNOR, building materials company executive, lawyer; b. Chgo., Oct. 17, 1941; s. Arthur Edward Leisten and Mary (Francis) Gaynor; m. Florence T. Kelly, May 11, 1968; children: Thomas, Hilary. AB magna cum laude, Loyola U., Chgo., 1963; JD, Harvard U., 1966; grad. exec. mgmt. program, Northwestern U., Chgo., 1983 and 1986, Pa. State U., 1985. Bar: Ill. 1966, U.S. Dist. Ct. (no. dist.) Ill. 1967, U.S. Ct. Appeals 1967. Assoc. prof. Sch. Law Loyola U., 1966-69; assoc. Chadwell & Kayser, Ltd., Chgo., 1969-74; staff atty. Texaco, Inc., Chgo., 1974-75; atty. USG Corp., Chgo., 1975-78, sr. atty., 1978-82, sr. gen. atty., 1982-85, assoc. gen. counsel, 1985, v.p., assoc. gen. counsel, 1985-86, v.p., gen. counsel, 1986—. Mem. ABA (corp. counsel com.), Chgo. Bar Assn., Am. Corp. Counsel Assn. Clubs: Univ., Law (Chgo.); Mich. Shores (Wilmette, Ill.). Office: USG Corp 101 S Wacker Dr Chicago IL 60606

LEISY, JAMES FRANKLIN, publisher; b. Normal, Ill., Mar. 21, 1927; s. Ernest Erwin and Elva (Krehbiel) L.; m. Emily Ruth McQueen, June 8, 1949; children: James Franklin, Scot, Rebecca. BBA, So. Meth. U., 1949. Field rep., then editor Prentice-Hall, Inc., N.Y.C., 1949-54; editor Allyn & Bacon, Inc., Boston, 1954-56; founder, exec. editor Wadsworth Pub. Co., Inc., San Francisco, 1956-59, v.p., 1959-60, pres., 1960-77, chmn., chief exec. officer, 1977-85; dep. chmn. Internat. Thomson Orgn., Inc., 1978-85; founder, chmn. Sci. Books Internat., Inc., 1981-83; founder, chmn. Linguistics Internat., Inc., 1983-85; bd. dirs. Mayfield Pub. Co., Inc., Franklin, Beedle and Assocs., Carroll Pub. Co., Scott/Jones, Inc. Author: Abingdon Song Kit, 1957, Let's All Sing, 1958, Songs for Swinging Housemothers, 1960, Songs for Singin', 1961, Songs for Pickin' and Singin', 1962, Beer Bust Song Book, 1963, Hootenanny Tonight, 1964, Folk Song Fest, 1964, Folk Song Abecedary, 1966, Alpha Kappa Psi Sings, 1967, The Good Times Songbook, 1974, Scrooge, The Christmas Musical, 1978, Alice, A Musical Comedy, 1980, Pinocchio, A Musical Play, 1981, Tiny Tim's Christmas Carol, A Musical Play, 1981, The Pied Piper, 1982, The Nutcracker and Princess Pirlipat, 1982, A Visit from St. Nicholas, 1983, Pandora, 1984, Talkin' 'bout America, 1986, Mouse Country, 1987, The Dingaling Circus Holiday, 1987; composer: songs including Keep a Little Christmas In Your Heart, A Little Old Lady in Tennis Shoes, A Personal Friend of Mine, Please Tell Me Why, An Old Beer Bottle. Bd. dirs. Bethel Coll., Ctr. Entrepreneurial Devel., U. Calif.-Santa Cruz; bd. dirs., mem. exec. com. Calif. Council for Econ. Edn., 1968-71; mem. deans council Sch. Bus. Calif. State U., San Jose; mem. Nat. UN Day Com., 1978. Served with USNR, 1945-46. Named to Career Hall of Fame So. Meth. U., 1968; recipient 1st ann. Higher Edn. Achievement award Assn. of Am. Pubs., 1988. Mem. Young Pres.'s Orgn. (bd. dirs. 1970-73), Assn. Am. Pubs. (bd. dirs. 1982-85), ASCAP, So. Meth. U. Alumni Assn. (bd. dirs. 1965-70), Chief Execs. Orgn., World Bus. Council, Bohemian Club, Phi Eta Sigma, Alpha Phi Omega, Alpha Kappa Psi (nat. chmn. song com. 1963-71), Kappa Alpha.

LEITCH, JOHN DANIEL, shipping company executive; b. Winnipeg, Man., Can., Jan. 11, 1921; s. Gordon Clifford and Hilda (Bawden) L.; m. Margaret Beatrice Cartwright, June 14, 1941 (dec. Nov. 1979); children: Mary Francis Leitch Bain, Hilda Jean Leitch Vander Ploeg; m. Catherine Louise Bradshaw, May 16, 1985. Student, Appleby Coll., Trinity Coll., U. Toronto; LLD (hon.), Atkinson Coll. York U., 1980. Pres. Toronto (Ont.) Elevators, 1947-61; chmn. Maple Leaf Mills Ltd. (formerly Toronto Elevators), Toronto, 1961-69; pres., chmn. ULS Internat. Inc. (formerly Upper Lakes Shipping, Ltd.), Toronto, 1952—; v.p., bd. dirs. Can. Imperial Bank of Commerce, Toronto, 1954—; bd. dirs. Am. Airlines, Dallas, Dofasco, Hamilton, Ont. Lt. Royal Can. Navy, 1939-45. Named Gt. Lakes Man of Yr. Sault Ste. Marie Hist. Soc., 1964; recipient Medal of Merit Can. Port and Harbours Assn., Halifax, N.S., 1980. Mem. Toronto Club, York Club. Anglican. Home: 61 Saint Clair Ave W Ste 509, Toronto, ON Canada M4V 2Y8 Office: Thornmark Corp Mgmt Inc, 49 Jackes Ave, Toronto, ON Canada M4T 1E2

LEITER, WILLIAM C., banking corporation executive, controller; b. Akron, Ohio, May 16, 1939; s. Clarence Dailey and Lucille E. (Knecht) L.; m. Sue J. Sullivan, Nov. 5, 1966; children: Jennifer Lynn, Brian Robert, Sonja Lou. BS in Bus. Adminstrn., Kent State U., 1961. CPA, Pa. Various positions Coopers & Lybrand, Pitts., 1961-75; fin. v.p. Wendy's Internat. Inc., Dublin, Ohio, 1975-81; controller Banc One Corp., Columbus, Ohio, 1981—. Mem. Am. Inst. CPAs, Fin. Execs. Inst. (past pres., bd. dirs. 1981—), Assn. Bank Holding Cos. (chmn. acctg. com. 1982—). Republican. Presbyterian. Club: Capital (Columbus). Office: Banc One Corp 100 E Broad St Columbus OH 43271-0251

LEITZKE, JACQUE HERBERT, corporation president, psychologist; b. Watertown, Wis., Dec. 25, 1929; s. Herbert Wilbert and Ruth Valberg (Stavenow) L.; m. Mary Annis Lacey, June 20, 1950 (div. Nov. 1963); children: Keith Alan, Sari Dawn, Thora Jacquelynne. BS, U. Wis., Madison, 1955; MA, Kent State U., 1958. Lic. psychologist, Wis., Ill., N.Y. Sch. psychologist BCG, N.Y.C., 1959-61; clin. psychologist Winnebago County Guidance Ctr., Neenah, Wis., 1961-64; sch. psychologist Waukegan City (Ill.) Sch. Dist. 61, 1965-66; clin. psychologist Wis., Ill., 1967-78; corp. pres., chief exec. officer Psychometrics Internat. Corp., Watertown, 1979—. Author: Definitively Incorporeal Human Intelligence Itself;originator intelligence test Abecedarian Measure of Human Intelligence, 1979. Trustee Human Intelligence Research Found. Served with USAF, 1948-51. Mem. Am. Psychol. Assn., Mensa. Home: 1153 Boughton St #808 Watertown WI 53094 Office: Psychometrics Internat Corp PO Box 247 Watertown WI 53094

LEJEUNE, JOSEPH GUILLAUME, international industrial development projects consultant; b. Maastricht, Netherlands, Feb. 25, 1914; s. Jan Joseph and Elise Agnes (Koumans) Le J.; m. Anna-Maria-Margaretha Huffener, Mar. 9, 1943. Bach. Philosophy, U. Louvain (Belgium), 1942, D.Criminology and Social Scis.; postgrad. U. Utrecht, 1946-50. Head field research Mgmt. Inst., Netherlands, 1950-56; cons. OEEC, European Prodn. Agy., Paris, 1956-58; cons. govt. Peru Internat. Lab. Office, Geneva, 1960-62; sec. gen. of Com. of Leading European Enterprises and Banks, for coop. with Latin Am., Paris, 1963-65; dir. Report on Spain for OECD, Paris, 1966-68; cons. UN Mission, UN Indsl. Devel. Orgn., UNIDO, Vienna, Austria, 1970-76; cons. assignments with European enterprises and banks for indsl. projects in developing countries, 1958-60, 68-70, 1976—. Contbr. articles on indsl. devel. projects to profl. jours. Served to capt. Dutch Army, 1944-47. Decorated Kruis van Verdienste (Order of Merit) Queen of Netherlands, 1947; Verzetscherdenkingskruis (Order of the Resistance Movement) Netherlands Govt. Mem. Soc. for Internat. Devel., Royal Air Forces Assn. Roman Catholic. Club: Stade Francais (Paris). Home: 6 Sq Castiglione, Resid Tuileries, Le Chesnay, 78150 Yvelines France

LEMAHIEU, JAMES JOSEPH, business consultant; b. Milw., Feb. 23, 1936; s. Harold William and Genieveve Azalea (Christman) LeM.; m. Barbara M. Pratt, July 3, 1989; children: Paul George, Ann Genieveve, Charles William. BS, Yale U., 1958; MBA cum laude, Boston U., 1969. System analyst USM Co., Beverly, Mass., 1961-68; system cons. IMF, Inc., Waltham, Mass., 1968-70; mgr. inventory, prodn. control Gorton Group div. Gen. Mills, Gloucester, Mass., 1970-77, dir. forecasting, 1977—; cons. in field, Derry, N.H., 1965—. Chmn. Derry (N.H.) Sch. Survey Com., 1963-66; active Derry Sch. Bd., 1964-79; coach, organizer Derry Recreation Program, 1974-80; trustee, pres. Pinkerton Acad., Derry, 1980—. Mem. Internat. Inst. Forecasters, Beta Gamma Sigma. Lodge: Kiwanis. Home: 1 Edgewood St Derry NH 03038

LE MAISTRE, CHRISTOPHER WILLIAM, educational director; b. Moradabad, India, Aug. 20, 1938; came to U.S., 1978; s. Archibald William and Kathleen Mary (Minas) L.; m. Patricia Margaret Briggs, May 18, 1963; children: Anne Louise, Nicole Marie. B of Applied Sci. in Metallurgy, U. Adelaide, Australia, 1962; PhD, Rensselaer Poly. Inst., 1971. Cert. materials engr. Trainee mettalurgy A. Simpson & Son., Ltd., Adelaide, 1957-60; cadet def. sci. Australian Dept. Supply, Adelaide, 1961-64; exptl. officer Weapons Rsch. Establishment, Adelaide, 1964-68, sr. rsch. scientist, 1971-74; R&D attache Australian High Commn., London, Eng., 1974-77; acting head lab. program Australian Def. Dept., Canberra, 1977-78; assoc. dir. mfg. ctr. Rensselaer Poly. Inst., Troy, N.Y., 1978-84, dir. ctr. for indsl. innovation,

1984—; cons. Xerox Corp., Nortons, Exxon, Bendix Corp., U. Ariz., N.J. State U., 1975—; chmn. peer rev. panel N.J Commn. on Sci. and Tech., Newark, 1987; bd. dirs. tech. adv. com. Hudson Valley Community Coll., Troy, 1988. Author: Computer Integrated Manufacturing, 1987, Technical Innovations and Economic Growth, 1987; editor: Industrial Innovation Productivity and Employment, 1986. Mem. Am. Soc. Metals (chmn. 1983), Am. Ceramic Soc. (chmn. 1984). Home: Joseph St Troy NY 12180 Office: Rensselaer Poly Inst Ctr for Indsl Innovation Troy NY 12180

LEMAN, EUGENE D., meat industry executive; b. Peoria, Ill., Dec. 1, 1942; s. Vernon L. and Viola L. (Beer) L.; m. Carolyn Leman, June 14, 1964; children—Jill C., Jennifer A. B.S., U. Ill., 1964. Dir. various depts. Wilson Foods, Oklahoma City, 1964-78, v.p. fresh and processed pork, 1978-80, v.p. fresh meat group, 1980-81; group v.p. IBP, Inc., Dakota City, Nebr., 1981-86, exec. v.p., 1986—, also bd. dirs. Mem. Am. Meat Inst. (chmn. pork com. 1980-81), Nat. Pork Producers Council (packer rep. Pork Value Task Force 1981-82, 88, pork export com. 1985). Republican. Club: Sioux City Country (Iowa). Office: IBP Inc Hwy 35 Box 515 Dakota City NE 68731

LEMAR, BRUCE RICHARD, human resources executive, lawyer; b. Lincoln, Nebr., Mar. 15, 1946; s. Richard Beverly and Marilyn Helen (Maxey) LeM.; m. Anita Louise D'Alleva, May 15, 1971; children: Andrew Douglas, Reed Anthony. BS in Bus., Ind. U., 1968; JD, U. Mich., 1970. Bar: Colo. 1971. Labor relations atty. Northwest Airlines, St. Paul, 1976-78; sr. dir. employee relations Continental Airlines, Inc., Houston, 1978-85; v.p. personnel Midway Airlines, Inc., Chgo., 1985—; pres. Airline Indsl. Relations Conf., Washington, 1988—, v.p. 1987-88. Served to capt. USAF, 1968-76, Turkey. Mem. ABA, Colo. Bar Assn. Office: Midway Airlines Inc 5959 S Cicero Ave Chicago IL 60638

LEMBERGER, NORMA, financial executive; b. Monticello, N.Y., July 21, 1944; d. Joe J. and Ellen Anna (Rosman) L. BS summa cum laude, Bklyn. Coll., 1965. With IBM, Armonk, N.Y., 1965—; dir. spl. fin. IBM Credit Corp., Stamford, Conn., 1985—; gen. mgr. Rolm Credit Corp. IBM, Santa Clara, Calif., 1985—; pres. Rolm. Credit Corp. and dir. financing programs IBM Credit Corp., Stamford, 1987; treas. IBM Ams. Group, Armonk, 1988-89, program dir. investor rels., 1989—. Mem. Women's Econ. Round Table.

LEMBERSKY, MARK RAPHAEL, computer company executive; b. Pitts., Sept. 30, 1945; s. Herman K. and Alice Lillian (Berger) L.; m. Barbara Jean Diemond, June 6, 1965; 1 child, Carol Sharon. BS, MIT, 1967; MS, Stanford U., 1968, PhD, 1971, grad. exec. program, 1983. Prof. ops. research Oreg. State U., Corvallis, 1971-76; mgr. merchandising and allocation Weyerhaeuser Co., Tacoma, 1976-79, dir. raw materials research and devel. div., 1979-81, dir. forestry and timber products research and devel. div., 1981-83, dir. group fin. and systems, 1983-85, div. gen. mgr. Engineered Products div., 1985-87; pres. Innovis Interactive Techs., Tacoma, 1987—; cons. western U.S., 1972-76. Patentee in field; contbr. articles to profl. jours. Mem. MIT Edn. Council, 1983—, Wash. Council for Tech. Advancement, chmn. subcom. edn., 1984-88; bd. dirs. Sci. Affiliates U. Wash., 1983-86; trustee Somerset Community Assn., Bellevue, Wash., 1977-79. Recipient Carter award Oreg. State U., 1975. Mem. Inst. Mgmt. Sci. (Franz Edelman Internat. prize 1985), Computer and Automated Systems Assn. (sr.), Ops. Research Soc. Am. (edn. com. 1976-77, assoc. editor jour. 1984—), Mgmt. Sci. Roundtable (exec. bd. dirs. 1985-87). Office: Innovis Interactive Techs Park Ctr 11-21 Tacoma WA 98477

LEMCKE, DIXIE LYNN, financial analyst; b. Oklahoma City, Aug. 20, 1964; d. George Martin and Dolly June (Crawford) L. BBA, Cen. State U., Edmond, Okla., 1986. Sec. George Lehmke & Co., Oklahoma City, 1982-84; asst. to v.p. George Lemcke & Co., Edmond, Okla., 1984-86, asst. to pres., 1986-88, cons., 1988—; contract analyst Twister Gas Transmission Co., Oklahoma City, 1988; adminstr. gas contracts, cash mgmt. and investments revenue acct. Ricks Exploration Co., Oklahoma City, Okla., 1988—. Deaconess Univ. Pl. Christian Ch., Oklahoma City, 1988; bd. dirs. Uniform Product Code Coun., Oklahoma City, 1988. Mem. NAFE, Meadows Lady's Aux., Alpha Chi Omega. Republican. Home: 12208 Maple Ridge Rd Oklahoma City OK 73120 Office: Ricks Exploration Co 5600 N May Ste 350 Oklahoma City OK 73112

LEMENS, WILLIAM VERNON, JR., banker, finance company executive, lawyer; b. Austin, Tex., Oct. 26, 1935; s. William Vernon and Lylia (Engberg) L.; m. Jean Lemens, May 29, 1959; children: William Vernon III, Shandra Christine. BA, U. Tex., 1958, LLB, 1962, JD, 1962. Bar: Tex. 1962; lic. real estate broker, Tex. Pvt. practice Austin, 1962—; pres. Standard Fin. Co., Austin, 1963-67, First State Loan, Austin, 1967—; chief exec. officer Southwest Computer Svcs., Inc., Austin, 1965—; pres., chief instr., mgmt. cons. Decision Dynamics, Inc., Austin, 1965-75; exec. v.p., atty. Northwest Savs. Assn., Austin, 1975-78; chmn. bd. First State Bank, Jarrell, Tex., 1975-87; pres., chief exec. officer First Am. Fin. Co., Ft. Worth, 1982—, Eagle Bank, Jarrell, 1987—. Author: Elements of Objective Orientation, 1971, SSAM-The Power of Perfect Decisions, 1972, Successful Financial Institution Operation, 1978, National Standard Financial Company Operations, 1981. Pres. Ballet Austin, 1967, Southwest Regional Ballet Assn., 1968; deacon Univ. Bapt. Ch., Austin, 1979—. Mem. State Bar TEx., Austin Bd. Realtors. Office: 1509 Guadalupe St Ste 200 Austin TX 78701

LEMIEUX, JOSEPH HENRY, manufacturing company executive; b. Providence, Mar. 2, 1931; s. Mildred L. Lemieux; m. Frances Joanne Schmidt, Aug. 11, 1956; children: Gerald Joseph, Craig Joseph, Kimberly Mae Lemieux Wolff, Allison Jo. Student, Stonehill Coll., 1949-50, U. R.I., 1950-51; BBA summa cum laude, Bryant Coll., 1957. With Owens-Ill., Toledo, 1957—, various positions with glass container div. and closure and metal container group; exec. v.p. Owens-Ill. Owens-Ill., Inc., Toledo, 1984, pres. pkg. ops., 1984, pres., chief operating officer, 1986—, also bd. dirs.; chmn. bd. dirs. Health Care & Retirement Corp. Am.; bd. dirs. Ohio Citizens Bank, Toledo, Nat. City Corp. Vice chmn. bd. govs. Edison Indsl. Systems Ctr. U. Toledo, 1986. Served to staff sgt. USAF, 1951-55. Named one of Outstanding Young Men Am., Jaycees, 1965. Mem. Glass Packaging Inst. (chmn. 1984-86), Packaging Edn. Found. (bd. dirs.). Roman Catholic. Clubs: Toledo, Shadow Valley Tennis, Inverness (Toledo). Office: Owens-Ill Inc 1 Seagate Toledo OH 43666

LEMIRE, ANDRE, investment company executive; b. Quebec City, Can., Mar. 15, 1943; s. Adrien and Gabrielle (Martel) L.; m. Ann C. Chisholm, Sept. 6, 1969. BS, U. Ottawa, 1967. Tax analyst Bell Can., Montreal, 1968-69; investment analyst Jones Heward Co., Ltd., Montreal, 1969-72; asst. dir. research Levesque, Beaubien Inc., Montreal, 1972-74, dir. investment research, 1974-78, v.p. investment research, 1978, v.p. internat. and chmn. investment com., 1978—, sr. v.p., 1979-85, exec. v.p., 1985-88; exec. v.p. Levesque, Beaubien & Co., Inc., 1986—; pres., chief exec. officer Levesque Beaubien & Assocs., Inc. Contbr. articles to profl. jours. Mem. Montreal Soc. Fin. Analysts, Montreal Mus. Arts, Montreal Amateur Athletic Assn. Roman Catholic. Clubs: St. James, Montreal Badminton and Squash. Home: 174 Edge Hill Rd, Westmount, PQ Canada H3Y 1E9 Office: Levesque Beaubien & Co Inc, 1155 Metcalfe St, Montreal, PQ Canada H3B 4S9

LEMIRE, JEROME ALBERT, lawyer, geologist, consultant; b. Cleve., June 4, 1947; s. George A. and Matilda (Simon) L.; m. Sandra Marsick, Oct. 1, 1976; children—Laura, Lesley, Thomas. B.S. in Geology, Ohio State U., 1969, M.S. in Geology, 1973, J.D., 1976. Bar: Ohio 1976; cert. fin. planner. Geologist United Petroleum Co., Columbus, Ohio, 1976-77; assoc. Brownfield, Bowen & Bally, Columbus, 1977-79; land mgr. POI Energy Inc., Cleve., 1979-81; cons., Jefferson, Ohio, 1981-83; v.p. Carey Resources Inc., Jefferson, 1984-86; pres. Lemire & Assocs. Inc., Jefferson, 1986—. cons., 1986—. Vice chmn. Tech. Adv. Council, Columbus, 1984—. Served to 1st lt. U.S. Army, 1970-72. Mem. Ohio Bar Assn., Am. Assn. Petroleum Geologists, Am. Assn. Petroleum Landmen, Inst. Cert. Fin. Planners. Democrat. Roman Catholic. Home: 838 State Rte 46 N Jefferson OH 44047

LEMKE, CARL RICHARD, paper company executive; b. Neenah, Wis., Aug. 4, 1943; s. Carl John and Alma Caroline (Berge) L.; m. Jennifer Jane Johnson, Oct. 2, 1976; children—Nicole, Paul, David, Sarah, Joel. B.B.A., U. Wis., 1965. Group leader Bendix Corp., Teterboro, N.J., 1965-67; asst. sec. Consol. Papers, Inc., Wisconsin Rapids, Wis., 1967—; dir. South Wood County Econ. Devel. Corp., Wisconsin Rapids, 1977—; dir. Mead Realty Corp. Avocations: travel; sports; boating. Home: 420 Witter St Wisconsin Rapids WI 54494

LEMKE, CLARK ELLIOTT, scientific research and software development executive; b. Milw., July 29, 1946; s. Nathanael August and Alice Elizabeth (Coffin) L.; m. Colleen Elaine Carson, Dec. 20, 1975; children: Brice Tristan, Adrienne Marie. AB in Econs., Harvard U., 1968, MBA in Fin., 1972. Various positions First Wis. Nat. Bank, Milw., 1968-70; asst. treas. Gould Inc., Rolling Meadows, Ill., 1972-83; treas. Sundstrand Corp., Rockford, Ill., 1983-87; sr. v.p., chief fin. officer Sci. Applications Internat., San Diego, 1987—. Served with USAR, 1968-72. Mem. Fin. Execs. Inst., Nat. Assn. of Corp. Treas., Ill. CPA Soc. Home: 2225 Lagoon View Dr Cardiff CA 92007 Office: Sci Applications Internat Corp 10260 Campus Point Dr San Diego CA 92121

LEMKE, PAUL GUSTAV, distributing company executive; b. North Tonawanda, N.Y., Apr. 8, 1920; s. Fred A. and Mathilda L. (Schulmeister) L.; B.A., U. Buffalo, 1941; m. Lorraine M. McIntyre, July 7, 1945; children—Paul, Michele L. With Buffalo Bolt Co., North Tonawanda, 1939-59, asst. sales mgr., 1953-59; pres., chmn. bd. Thruway Fasteners, Inc., N. Tonawanda, 1959—; pres., chmn. bd. New Schimschack's Inc., 1973—. Mem. bd. Messiah Lutheran Ch., 1968-74; bd. govs. Niagara U.; bd. dirs. Artpark, Inc. Served in U.S. Army, 1941-45. Mem. Nat. Fastener Distbr. Assn. (past pres., chmn. bd., elcted to Hall of Fame), Nat. Assn. Wholesalers (past bd. dirs.). Clubs: Niagara Falls Country (past pres.). Home: 676 Mt View Dr Lewiston NY 14092 Office: 2910 Niagara Falls Blvd N Tonawanda NY 14120

LEMLE, ROBERT SPENCER, lawyer; b. N.Y.C., Mar. 6, 1953; s. Leo Karl and Gertrude (Bander) L.; m. Roni Sue Kohen, Sept. 5, 1976; children: Zachary, Joanna. AB, Oberlin Coll., 1975; JD, NYU, 1978. Bar: N.Y. 1979. Assoc. Cravath, Swaine & Moore, N.Y.C., 1978-82; assoc. gen. counsel Cablevision Systems Corp., Woodbury, N.Y., 1982-84, v.p., gen. counsel, 1984-86, sr. v.p., gen. counsel, sec., 1986—; bd. editors Cable TV and New Media Law and Fin., N.Y.C., 1983—, bd. dirs. Cablevision Systems Corp., 1988—. Mem. ABA, N.Y. State Bar Assn. Home: 7 Grace Dr Old Westbury NY 11568 Office: Cablevision Systems Corp 1 Media Crossways Woodbury NY 11797

LEMOINE, LAWRENCE LOUIS, mortgage company executive; b. Pasadena, Calif., May 23, 1951; s. Louis Lawrence and Ann Elizabeth (Moran) L.; m. Kim Marie Dawson, Feb. 6, 1988. BS in Fin., San Diego State, 1974. Fin. analyst U.S. Borax & Chem. Corp., L.A., 1974-78; acctg. mgr. TRW, L.A., 1978-79; treas. Superscope, Inc., Chatsworth, Calif., 1979-82; controller L.A. Olympic Organizing Com., 1983-84; v.p. servicing mgr. Weyerhauser Mortgage Co., Walnut Creek, Calif., 1984—. Fund raiser U.S. Olympic Com., L.A., 1987-88, cons., 1987-88. Office: Weyerhauser Mortgage Co 1550 Parkside Dr Walnut Creek CA 94596

LEMP, JOHN, JR., telecommunications engineer; b. Trenton, N.J., Dec. 10, 1936; s. John and Helena M. (Braddock) L.; BS in Elec. Engring., Princeton U., 1959; MS in Elec. Engring., Poly. Inst. Bklyn., 1968; MBA, Colo. State U., 1973; grad. Air Command and Staff Coll., 1974; grad. Indsl. Coll. Armed Forces, 1981; m. Susan N. Rose, 1955; children—John, Thomas K., Carl A., Adam F.H. Project engr. Gen. Devices, Inc., Princeton, N.J., 1959-60; with Bell Telephone Labs., N.J. and Colo., 1962-74; mgr. bus. planning Aeronutronic Ford Corp., Willow Grove, Pa., 1974-76; mgr. research and devel. ITT, Corinth, Miss., 1976-78; lectr. Sch. Bus., Temple U., Phila., 1976, Sch. Bus., U. Colo., 1982—; project leader Nat. Telecommunication and Info. Adminstrn., U.S. Dept. Commerce, Boulder, Colo., 1978-82; dir. Info. Access Systems, Inc., 1981-84. Lemp Devel. Co., Inc., 1975—. Mem. CAP, 1970—; pres. Carolyn Heights Civic Assn., 1972-73; treas. Frazier Woods Civic Assn., 1975-76. Served with USAF, 1960-63; served to col. USAFR, 1973-74, 80-81. Decorated Air Force Commendation medal, Meritorious Service medal; named Outstanding Elec. Engr., Armed Forces Communications & Electronics Assn., 1959; cert. instrument flight instr., FAA. Mem. IEEE (sr.), Armed Forces Communications and Electronics Assn., Assn. Computing Machinery, Inst. Mgmt. Sci., Air Force Assn. Patentee in field; contbr. articles to profl. jours. Home: 3745 23d St Boulder CO 80304 Office: U Colo PO Box 419 Boulder CO 80309

LENA, ADOLPH JOHN, specialty steel company executive; b. Latrobe, Pa., Oct. 10, 1925; s. Attilio and Leona (Robb) L.; m. Dolores Ruth Cunningham, June 9, 1948 (div. 1978); m. Beverly Ann Prue, Sept. 15, 1979; children: Mario, Carol, Kathleen, Lisa, Lauren, Lydia. BS in Metallurgy, Pa. State U., 1948; M MetE, Carnegie Mellon U., 1950, D MetE, 1952. Assoc. dir. research Allegheny Ludlum Steel Corp., Pitts., 1953-56, mgr. basic research dept., 1956-63, dir. product devel., 1963-68, dir. research, 1968-69, v.p., tech. dir., 1969-71, v.p., gen. mgr. bar prodn., 1971-76; chmn., chief exec. officer A1 Tech Splty. Steel Corp., Dunkirk, N.Y., 1976-84; exec. v.p., chief operating officer Carpenter Tech. Corp., Reading, Pa., 1986-87, pres., chief operating officer, 1987—, also bd. dirs.; cons. Carpenter Tech. Corp., Reading, 1985-86. Contbr. articles to 20 tech. jours; patentee in field. Trustee Reading (Pa.) Hosp., 1987—. Served to lt. (j.g.) USN, 1944-46, World War II. Recipient McFarland award Pa. State U.; named Disting. Citizen N.Y. State, SUNY Bd. Regents; Pa. State U. alumni fellow. Fellow Am. Soc. Metals (past chmn. Pitts. chpt., past nat. trustee, past nat. sec., Disting. Life Mem. award). Republican. Roman Catholic. Club: Berkshire Country (Reading). Home: 1743 Reading Blvd Wyomissing PA 19610 Office: Carpenter Tech Corp 101 W Bern st PO Box 14662 Reading PA 19612-4662

LENAGH, THOMAS HUGH, lawyer, financial advisor; b. Lawrence, Mass., Nov. 1, 1920; s. Frank Albert and Bethia (Coultar) L.; m. Leila Semple Fellner; children: Katherine, Thomas C., Jessie W. BA, Williams Coll., 1941; LLB, Columbia U., 1948. Analyst Cyrus J. Lawrence, N.Y.C., 1953-59; mgr. research service Goodbody & Co., N.Y.C., 1959-61; asst. treas. Ford Found., N.Y.C., 1961-64, treas., 1964-78; fin. v.p. Aspen Inst., N.Y.C., 1978-80; chmn., chief exec. officer Greiner Engring., Los Angeles, 1982-85; corp. dir. Gintel Inc., Greenwich, Conn., 1985—; bd. dirs. CML Inc., Gintel Funds, Adams Express, U.S. Life, Merrill Lynch Funds, SCI Inc., ICN Biomed., Clemente Capital, Basix, Irvine Sensors. Chmn. N.Y. YWCA, N.Y.C., 1975—. Served with USN, 1941-46, capt. USNR, 1950-53. Mem. Chartered Fin. Analyst, N.Y. Soc. Security Analyst, Conn. Bar Assn. Republican. Club: Williams. Home: 1 Brookside Dr Westport CT 06880 Office: Gintel Inc Greenwich Office Park 6 Greenwich CT 06830

LENGLE, CHARLES DAVID, financial executive; b. Lebanon, Pa., Sept. 20, 1944; s. Charles I. and Elizabeth (Spahn) L.; B.S., Wilkes Coll. cum laude, 1970, M.B.A., 1981; m. Elizabeth Brewer, May 20, 1972. Regional claim supr. Aetna Casualty & Surety Co., Harrisburg and Williamsport, Pa., 1970-76; with Marsh & McLennan, Inc., Sunbury, Pa., 1976-84, asst. v.p., head of office, dir. ins. & safety Weis Markets, Inc., Sunbury, Pa., 1985-88; dir. Spine Fitness Ctr. Evang. Community Hosp., Lewisburg., Pa., 1988—; adj. prof. Wilkes Coll., Bloomsburg U., Susquehanna U. Pres. ch. council Shiloh United Ch. of Christ, 1981. Served with CIC, U.S. Army, 1963-66. Mem. Am. Legion, VFW, Pa. C. of C. (workers compensation com.), Pa. Self Insurer Assn., Am. Risk and Ins. Assn., Risk and Ins. Mgmt. Soc. Republican. Club: Elks. Home: 14th St Riverside PA 17868 Office: Evang Community Hosp 1000 S 2d St Sunbury PA 17801

LENHART, RALPH LEROY, publisher; b. York, Pa., June 27, 1910; s. Thomas F. and Mabel (Strine) L.; divorced; children: Stephanie, Shelly. Student, NYU, Princeton U. Tchr. Post Sch. Advt., Phila.; with Marschalk & Pratt, N.Y.C., Erwin, Wasey & Co., N.Y.C., O.S. Tyson, N.Y.C.; account exec. Internat. Telephone & Telegraph, Fed. Telephone Radio, N. Am. Philips Co., Philips Export Co.; publisher Boca Ratonian mag. Lenhart & Co., Boca Raton, Fla. Active United Way, Princeton (N.J.) First Aid Rescue Squad; life mem. Princeton Hosp. Corp.; pres. Princeton C. of C. With Armed Forces, WWII. Mem. Boca Raton C. of C., Nassau Club (Princeton), Rotary. Home: 1251 S Federal Hwy Boca Raton FL 33432 Office: Lenhart & Co 131 S Federal Hwy Boca Raton FL 33432

LENKER, ROBERT EDWARD, bank executive; b. Millersburg, Pa., Dec. 30, 1928; s. Marion E. and Ferle M. (Klinger) L.; m. Hermine A. Richter, Aug. 28, 1954 (dec. 1974); m. Victoria E. Lehr, Sept. 4, 1980; 1 child, Jarrett Lee. AB in Economics, Brown U., 1951. Mgmt. trainee Prudential Ins. Co., Newark, 1954-55; asst. cashier First Nat. Bank, Millersburg, Pa., 1955-61; owner Keystone Broom Works, Millersburg, 1961-83; deputy exec. dir. Pa. Gen. State Authority, Harrisburg, 1967-71, Pa. Highway and Bridge Authority, Pa. Transp. Assistance, Harrisburg, 1967-71; assoc. v.p. Temple U., Phila., 1971-84; exec. v.p. Community Banks, Inc., Millersburg, 1984—. Bd. dirs. Millersburg Area Sch. Dist, 1984—, Dauphin County Hosp. Authority, Harrisburg, 1985—. Served with U.S. Army, 1951-54. Mem. Am. Assn. Retired Persons. Republican. Methodist. Lodge: Rotary. Home: 318 Johnson St Box 368 Millersburg PA 17061 Office: Community Banks Inc 150 Market St Box 350 Millersburg PA 17061

LENNARTSON, JAMES ROGER, marketing executive; b. Jamestown, N.Y., June 6, 1933; s. Anders Leo and Elna Signey (Bloomberg) L.; B.S., U. Buffalo, 1956; m. Barbara Ann Wilson, Jan. 25, 1958; children—Jennifer Lynn, James Roger. Asst. account exec. power systems Westinghouse Nuclear Center, Pitts., 1962-63, sr. account exec. nuclear communications, 1963-66, asst. mgr. power systems mktg. communications, 1966-68, mgr. power systems mktg. communications, 1968-72, staff mgr. mktg. communications, 1972—. Mem. Atomic Indsl. Forum, Pitts. Conv. and Visitors Bur., Assn. Nat. Advertisers. Republican. Presbyterian. Club: Rotary. Office: Westinghouse Energy Ctr Box 355 Pittsburgh PA 15230

LENNHOFF, DAVID CHARLES, real estate appraiser; b. Ft. Clayton, Panama, Nov. 15, 1946; s. Charles David Thomas and Nancy (Landreth) L.; m. Sandra Margo Sebald, May 5, 1974; children: Katherine, Andrew, Elizabeth. BA, U. Ky., 1969. Constrn. loan officer Standard Fed. Savs. & Loan, Gaithersburg, Md., 1973-75; pres. Real Estate Appraisal Svcs., Inc., Gaithersburg, 1975—. Contbr. articles to profl. jours. 1st lt. U.S. Army, 1969-72. Mem. Soc. Real Estate Appraisers (chpt. pres.), Am. Inst. Real Estate Appraisers (chpt. sec.1988—). Home: 13169 Scarlet Oak Dr Darnestown MD 20878

LENNON, FRANK M., retail executive; b. Boston, Jan. 13, 1938; s. Michael J. and Mary A. (MacDonald); m. Christina J. Barron, Jan. 19, 1970; children: Raymond, Lorraine. BA, St. Paul's Coll., 1963; MS, Am. U., 1982. Tchr. City of Boston, 1963-67; personell mgr. Stop and Shop Cos., Boston, 1967-72; v.p. adminstrn. Value House, Lewiston, Maine, 1972-79; sr. v.p. adminstrn. Golub Corp., Schenectady, N.Y., 1979—; adj. prof. Russell Sage Grad. Sch. Bus., Albany, N.Y., 1985—. Trustee LaSalle Acad., Troy, N.Y., 1988—. Mem. Orgn. Devel. Network, Am. Soc. Personnel Adminstrn., Shaker Ridge Country Club, Elks. Home: 3 Starboard Way Latham NY 12110 Office: Golub Corp 501 Duanesburg Rd Schenectady NY 12306

LENNOX, EDWARD NEWMAN, holding company executive; b. New Orleans, July 27, 1925; s. Joseph Andrew and May Alice (Newman) L.; B.B.A., Tulane U., 1949; m. Joan Marie Landry, Sept. 3, 1949; children—Katherine Sarah, Anne Victoria, Mary Elizabeth, Laura Joan. Mktg. service clk. Shell Oil Co., New Orleans, 1949; with W.M. Chambers Truck Line, Inc., 1950-60, exec. v.p., 1954-60; v.p., gen. mgr. Radcliff Materials, Inc., New Orleans, 1961-71; v.p. Office Pub. Affairs, So. Industries Corp., 1971-88; v.p. Dravo Natural Resources Co., 1982—, pres. Tidelands Industries, Inc., 1982-85; dir. Home Savs. & Loan Assn., 1979—, pres., 1982-88, chmn., 1984—. Pres., La. Tank Truck Carriers, 1954-55; mem. La. Bd. Hwys., 1965-67; chmn. New Orleans Aviation Bd., 1965-66; bd. dirs. Travelers Aid Soc., 1966-68, Met. Area Com., 1967-80, Constrn. Industry Legis. Council, 1968—, Miss. Valley Assn., 1969-72; pres. bd. levee commrs. Orleans Levee Dist., 1969-72; pres. Met. New Orleans Safety Council, 1969-71; bus. and fin. adviser Congregation Sisters of Immaculate Conception; vice chmn. transp. task force Goals for La., 1969-72; mem. New Orleans Bd. Trade, 1971—; mem. Ala. Gov.'s Adv. Council on Econs., 1971-72, Gov.'s Adv. Com. River Area Transp. and Planning Study, 1971-72; area v.p. Pub. Affairs Research Council La., 1972-73; mem. exec. com. La. Good Roads Assn., 1972-74; mem. career advisement com. Tulane U. Grad. Sch. Bus. Adminstrn., 1972—; industry del. La. Constl. Conv., 1973; mem. exec. com. Miss. Valley World Trade Council, 1973-74; bd. dirs., exec. com. Pendleton Meml. Meth. Hosp., 1963-81, dir. emeritus, 1981—; bd. dirs. Boys' Clubs Greater New Orleans, 1973-79; bd. dirs., mem. exec. bd. Goodwill Industries Greater New Orleans, Inc., 1975-79, 81—, treas., 1984-85, first v.p., 1987-88, chmn. 1989-90; bd. dirs. Americanism Forum, 1975—, Tragedy Fund, Inc., 1976—; bd. govs. La. Civil Service League, 1974—, pres., 1977-78; dir. chmn. bd. trustees La. Found. Pvt. Colls. Served to capt. AUS, 1943-46. Recipient Industry Service award Asso. Gen. Contractors Am., 1967; cert. of appreciation Constrn. Industry Assn. New Orleans, 1972; New Orleans Jaycees award, 1960; cert. of merit Mayoralty of New Orleans, 1964, 67; Monte M. Lemann award La. Civil Service League, 1976; named hon. citizen and ambassador at large City of Jacksonville, 1966. Mem. NAM (pub. affairs steering com. So. div. 1979—), La. Motor Transport Assn. (pres. 1963-64), Ala. Trucking Assn. (v.p. 1956-60), So. Concrete Masonry Assn. (pres. 1963-68), Greater New Orleans Ready Mixed Concrete Assn. (pres. 1966-68), La. Shell Producers Assn. (pres. 1966-68), C. of C. New Orleans Area (dir. 1968-73, 75-77, pres. elect 1973), Internat. House (dir. 1977-79), Traffic Club New Orleans, Lakeshore Property Owners Assn. (dir. 1974-86 , pres. 1976-77, 79-80), Tulane Alumni Assn., Mobile Area C. of C. Club: Metairie Country (bd. govs. 1976-82, 89—, pres. 1980-81). Home: 862 Topaz St New Orleans LA 70124 Office: 120 Mallard St Ste 300 Saint Rose LA 70087

LENOIR, GLORIA CISNEROS, small business owner, business manager; b. Monterrey, Nuevo Leon, Mex., Aug. 18, 1951; came to U.S., 1956, naturalized, 1974; d. Juan Antonio and Maria Gloria (Flores) Cisneros; m. Walter Frank Lenoir, June 6, 1975; children: Lucy Gloria, Katherine Judith. Student, Inst. Am. Univs., 1971-72; BA in French Art, Austin Coll., 1973, MA in French Art, 1974; MBA in Fin., U. Tex., 1979. French tchr. Sherman (Tex.) High Sch., 1973-74; French/Spanish tchr, dept. chmn. Lyndon Baines Johnson High Sch., Austin, 1974-77; legis. aide Tex. State Capitol, Austin, Tex., 1977-81; stock broker Merrill Lynch, Austin, 1981-83, Schneider, Bernet and Hickman, Austin, 1983-84; bus. mgr. Holleman Photographic Labs., Inc., Austin, 1984-87, 88—; account exec., stock broker Eppler, Guerin & Turner, 1987-88; group counselor, organizer Inst. Fgn. Studies, U. Strasbourg, France, summer 1976; mktg. intern IBM, Austin, summer 1978; mktg. cons. Creative Ednl. Enterprises, Austin, 1980-81; hon. speaker Mex.-Am. U. of Tex., Austin, 1984; speaker various orgns., bus. classes, Austin, 1981-84; speaker, coordinator small bus. workshops, 1985. Photos published in Women in Space, 1979, Review, 1988; photos exhibited throughout Tex., 1979, 88—. Neighborhood capt. Am. Cancer Soc., Austin, 1982-86, 89; hospitality chmn., first grade coordinator PTA, Austin, 1986; vol. liaison leads program Austin Coll., Austin, 1983—; mem. Advantage Austin, 1988, Laguna Gloria Art Mus.; co-chairwoman fin. Cen. Presbyn. Ch., elder, 1988, elder, 1988—, session clk., 1989—. Recipient Night on the Town award IBM, 1978. Mem. Photo Mktg. Assn., Nat. Fedn. Ind. Businessmen, Austin Investment Assn., Austin C. of C. (mem. Austin Advantage 1988), Hispanic C. of C. (Vol. award 1986). Republican. Presbyterian. Home: 1202 W 29th St Austin TX 78703 Office: Holleman Photog Labs Inc 3018 N Lamar Austin TX 78705

LENOIR, MARIA ANNETTE, management consultant; b. St. Louis, June 11, 1950; d. Jack and Beatrice (Brown) Doyle; m. Howard L. Williams, Sept. 29, 1969 (div. Aug. 1981); 1 child, Howard L. Jr.; m. Aguinaldo Alphonse Lenoir Jr., June 28, 1985; 1 stepchild, Aguinaldo Alphonse III. Student, Florissant (Mo.) Valley Community Coll., 1974-76; BA in Mgmt., Webster U., 1980. Stenographer Internat. Shoe Co., St. Louis, 1968-69; office mgr. Chemplastics Inc., St. Louis, 1969-71; advt./media coord. Ralston Purina Co., St. Louis, 1971-73, sec., 1973-76, adminstrv. asst., 1976-79, sales/mktg. adminstr., 1979-84; pres., chief exec. officer, owner Corp. Image, Inc., St. Louis, 1984—; instr. St. Louis Univ., 1987, St. Louis Community Coll.; pub. rels. advisor Mo. White House Conf. Small Bus., St. Louis, 1986; mem. adv. panel Omni Internat. Hotel, St. Louis, 1986. Contbr. articles to profl. jours. Mktg. advisor Jr. Achievement of Miss. Valley, Hazelwood, Mo., 1983—; mem. Women's Assn. St. Louis Symphony, 1984—, ACE (div. of SCORE), St. Louis, 1985—; role model St. Louis Pub. Schs., 1987; bd. dirs. Community Commitment, Greeley Community Ctr. Youth Emergency Svcs. (YES), St. Louis, 1988—. Named Outstanding Young Women Am., 1987. Mem. Meeting Planners Internat., Nat. Assn. Women Bus. Owners, Assn.

Ind. Meeting Planners (adv. com., bd. dirs.), Florissant Valley Community Coll. Alumni Assn. (v.p. 1985-86, sec./treas. 1987, Alumna of Yr. award 1986 Hall of Fame), Women in Leadership Alumni, NAFE, St. Louis Regional Commerce & Growth Assn., Boulder Yacht Club. Democrat. Pentecostal. Office: Corp Image Inc 4825 Lockwig Saint Louis MO 63033

LENTES, DAVID EUGENE, corporate executive; b. Spokane, Wash., Dec. 14, 1951; s. William Eugene and Ellen Elsie L.; m. Debra Kay White, May 19, 1973 (div. 1984); children: Janette Adele, Damon Arthur. AA, Spokane Falls Community Coll., 1972; BBA, Gonzaga U., 1975. V.p. Dellen Wood Products, Inc., Spokane, 1972—, also bd. dirs.; v.p. Custom Computer Services, Inc., Spokane, 1980-87, also bd. dirs.; mng. ptnr. Com-Lease, 1980-87, Len-Lease, 1980—; v.p., bd. dirs. DWP Trucking, Inc., 1982-85, Sentel Corp., 1983-88, BDR Investment Corp., 1983—; pres., bd. dirs. ASA Mgmt. Corp., 1984—, also Link Internat., Inc., 1985. Treas. Dishman Hills Natural Area Assn., 1970—; elder Bethany Presbyn. Ch., 1980-83; active Spokane Econ. Devel. Council. Mem. Assn. Wash. Bus., Nat. Fedn. Ind. Businessmen, Am. Fedn. Bus., Better Bus. Bur. (Spokane chpt.), U.S. C. of C., Spokane C. of C., Timber Products Mfrs., Hoo-Hoo Internat. Republican. Office: N 3014 Flora Rd Spokane WA 99216

LENTZ, DAVID LEE, data processing executive; b. Hutchinson, Kans., May 31, 1946. AB, Washington U., St. Louis, 1968, AM, 1974; MBA, U. Chgo., 1982. Documentation specialist Harza Engring. Co., Chgo., 1978, mgr. budget and cost sect., 1978-79, programmer/analyst, 1979-81, lead programmer, 1981-83, systems analyst, 1983-84, mgr. info. systems devel., 1984-86, head adminstrv. computer services, 1986—; instr. computer sci. Northwestern U., Chgo., 1988. Served with U.S. Army, 1968-72, Vietnam. Fellow Washington U., 1973-76, U. Zurich, 1976-77. Mem. Assn. for Computing Machinery. Office: Harza Engring Co 150 S Wacker Dr Chicago IL 60606

LENTZ, ROBERT HENRY, lawyer; b. Lake Huntington, N.Y., Dec. 9, 1924; s. Henry Bernard and Mary (Mahony) L.; children—Joanne, Kevin, Robert; m. Gloria Gomes. Student, U. Ky., 1943; B.E.E. magna cum laude, Poly. Inst. Bklyn., 1951; J.D., Loyola U. at Los Angeles, 1956. Bar: Calif. bar 1956. Sr. v.p., gen. counsel Litton Industries, Inc., Beverly Hills, Calif., 1954—; bd. dirs. Peregrine Systems Inc.; past chmn. bd. Topaz Industries. Served with AUS, 1943-46. Fellow Poly. Inst. N.Y., 1983; Mem. Los Angeles Patent Law Assn. Mem. State Bar Calif. (panelist for continuing edn. of bar on corp. law 1973-75, mem. corp. law com. of corp. and bus. law sect. 1978—), Am. Arbitration Assn. (Los Angeles adv. council 1968—, dir. 1984—), ABA, Los Angeles Patent Law Assn., Licensing Execs. Soc., Eta Kappa Nu, Tau Beta Pi. Home: 2877 Nicada Dr Los Angeles CA 90077 Office: Litton Industries Inc 360 N Crescent Dr Beverly Hills CA 90210

LENZ, EDWARD ARNOLD, corporate lawyer; b. White Plains, N.Y., Sept. 28, 1942; s. Frederick and Hildegarde (Bunzel) L.; m. Anna Maria Bartusiak; children: Scott, Eric. BA, Bucknell U., 1964; JD, Boston Coll., 1967; LLM, NYU, 1968. Bar: N.Y. 1968, D.C. 1973, Mich. 1982. Trial atty. U.S. Dept. Justice, Washington, 1970-72; assoc. gen. counsel U.S. Cost of Living Council, Washington, 1973; assoc. Miller & Chevalier, Washington, 1973-80; counsel Health Ins. Assn. Am., Washington, 1980-82; v.p., asst. gen. counsel Kelly Services Inc., Troy, Mich., 1982—; chmn. legis. com. Nat. Assn. Temporary Services, Alexandria, Va., 1985—. Capt. U.S. Army, 1968-70, Vietnam. Decorated Bronze Star. Mem. ABA, N.Y. Bar Assn., D.C. Bar Assn., Mich. Bar Assn., Am. Corp. Counsel Assn., Nat. Health Lawyers Assn. Home: 588 Brookside Birmingham MI 48009 Office: Kelly Svcs Inc 999 W Big Beaver Troy MI 48084

LENZ, HENRY PAUL, management consultant; b. N.Y.C., Nov. 24, 1925; s. Ernest and Margaret (Schick) L.; m. Norma M. Kull, Jan. 25, 1958; children: Susan, Scott, Theresa. A.B., U. N.C., 1946; M.B.A., Coll. Ins., 1974. Underwriter U.S. Casualty Co., N.Y.C., 1948-55; underwriting mgr. Mass. Bonding & Ins. Co., N.Y.C., 1955-60; with Home Ins. Co., N.Y.C., 1960-85; sr. v.p. Home Ins. Co., 1972-75, exec. v.p., dir., 1975-85; chmn. bd., pres. Lenz Enterprises Ltd., Chatham, NJ, 1985—; former pres., dir. Home Indemnity Co.; pres., dir. Home Ins. Co. Ind., Home Ins. Co. Ill., City Ins. Co., Home Group Risk Mgmt.; chmn. bd. Home Reins. Co., Scott Wetzel Services Inc.; chmn., pres. Cityvest Reins. Ltd., City Ins. Co. (U.K.) Ltd.; trustee Am. Inst. Property and Liability Underwriters, Ins. Inst. Am. Served with USNR, 1944-47, 52-53. Decorated Army Commendation medal. Mem. Soc. CPCU's, Phi Beta Kappa, Sigma Nu. Office: Lenz Enterprises Ltd 42 Edgehill Ave Chatham NJ 07928

LENZ, JACK, computer services executive; b. Chgo., Nov. 3, 1934; s. Joseph John and Gertrude B. (Mansell) L.; m. Patricia Ann Tyrcha, May 10, 1958; children: John, Janet, James, Katherine. BS, Lewis U., 1957. Mgr. cost dept. Martin Senour Paint Co., Chgo., 1957-58; mgr. data processing Martin Senour Paint Co., Chgo., 1958-62; asst. mgr. data processing Carson-Pirie Scott & Co., Chgo., 1962-64; data processing application mgr. Motorola Corp., Chgo., 1964-69; mgr. data processing Allis Chalmers Corp., Chgo., 1969-74; dir. data processing Crane Co., Chgo., 1974-80; corp. dir. info. svcs. Union Spl. Corp., Chgo., 1980—. Pres. Sch. Bd., Hazel Crest, Ill., 1976-80; mem. Hazel Crest Traffic Commn. Bd., 1975; mem. adv. bd. Computer Learning Ctr., Chgo., 1984—, Thornton Jr. Coll., Harvey, Ill., 1985—. Served with USAFR, 1957-63. Mem. Ill. Mfg. Assn., KC (various offices), Elks. Roman Catholic. Office: Union Spl Corp 2 N La Salle St Chicago IL 60602

LENZ, JOHN WILLIAM, banker; b. Chgo., Nov. 17, 1946; s. George R. and Margaret (Sanders) L.; m. Carol J. Macy, Aug. 30, 1969; 1 child, Erika. BA in Math., Ill. Inst. Tech., 1970; MBA, U. Utah, 1976. Dir. mgmt. info. systems Gould, Inc., Rolling Meadows, Ill., 1976-80; cons. Peat Marwick, Chgo., 1980-84; v.p. mgmt. info. systems Allied Van Lines, Broadview, Ill., 1986-87; v.p. info. systems Lake Shore Bancorp, Chgo., 1987—. Capt. U.S. Army, 1970-76. Home: 4 Longwood Ct Buffalo Grove IL 60089 Office: Lake Shore Bancorp 605 N Michigan Ave Chicago IL 60611

LENZIE, CHARLES ALBERT, utility company executive; b. South Wilmington, Ill., Sept. 5, 1937; s. Charles and Dorothy Rosita (Fritz) L.; children—Ann Marie, Michael Charles, Jody Ann. Student Ill. State Normal U., 1955-58; B.S. in Acctg., U. Ill., 1960. C.P.A., Ill. Audit Mgr. Arthur Andersen & Co., Chgo., 1960-70, Los Angeles, 1970-74; v.p. fin. Nev. Power Co., Las Vegas, 1974-78, sr. v.p., 1978-83, pres., 1983—, also dir. Bd. dirs. Las Vegas YMCA, Las Vegas Cath. Community Services, Nev. Taxpayers' Assn. Served to cpl. U.S. Army, 1961-63. Lodge: Southwest Las Vegas Rotary. Office: Nev Power Co 6226 W Sahara Ave Las Vegas NV 89151

LEOGRANDE, LOUIS, JR., financial consultant; b. Utica, N.Y., Jan. 1, 1939; s. Louis P. and Mary (Nichol) L.; BA, Utica Coll., 1962; grad. Public Adminstrn. Grad. Course, N.Y. U., 1966; m. Linda LaPone, June 28, 1975. Mgr. L Truck Stop & Service, Inc., Yorkville, N.Y., 1963-70; asst. mgr. McDonalds Restaurant, Whitesboro, N.Y., 1970-71; v.p., fin. cons. Shearson Lehman Hutton Inc, Utica, N.Y., 1971—; guest speaker. Sustaining mem. Republican Nat. Com.; former co-chmn. Greater Utica United Fund Retail div.; active Civil Affairs Assn. Lt. col. USAR, 1962—. Registered rep. N.Y. Inst. Fin. Mem. Nat. Assn. Security Dealers, Commodity Futures Trading Commn., Res. Officers Assn. (past v.p. local chpt.), N.Y. Life Ins. Agts., N.Y. State Notary Publics, New Hartford Hist. Soc. Clubs: U.S. Senatorial; Tyrolean Ski. Home: 16 Gary Ave New Hartford NY 13413 Office: 231 Genesee St Utica NY 13501

LEONARD, GEORGE ADAMS, lawyer, retail food and drug company executive; b. Clinton, Iowa, June 16, 1924; s. George Tod and Lola Frances (Follett) L.; m. Viola Converse, Nov. 5, 1948 (div. 1985); children: Carolyn C., George T., Craig C., Julie A.; m. Donna Kay Battle, July 2, 1986. AB, U. Mich., 1948, JD, 1951. Bar: Mich. 1951, Ohio 1956, U.S. Dist. Ct. (ea. dist.) Mich. 1951, U.S. Ct. Appeals (6th cir.) 1957, U.S. Ct. Appeals (D.C. cir.) 1964. Assoc. Slyfield, Hartman, Reitz & Tait, Detroit, 1951-56; atty. Kroger Co., Cin., 1956-61, supervising atty., 1961-64, mng. atty., 1964-66, gen. atty., 1966-68, v.p., gen. counsel, 1968-86, v.p., sec., gen. counsel, 1968, v.p., gen. counsel, 1986—; dir. Gleaner Life Ins. Soc. Chmn. Greater Cin. United Appeal, 1984; chmn. Cin. chpt. ARC, 1986—, chmn. nat. conv., 1988; bd. dirs. Legal Aid Soc., Cin., 1978-81, Coll. Mt. St. Joseph, Cin., 1986—. Served to maj. USAAF, 1942-45, ETO, ret. Res. 1960. Decorated Air medal with five oak leaf clusters, D.F.C. Mem. ABA, Ohio Bar Assn., Cin. Bar Assn. (chmn. corp. law com. 1965-67, Am. Soc. Corp. Secs. (chmn. Cin. chpt. 1985-86), Am. Corp. Counsel Assn. (pres. Cin. chpt. 1986-87). Clubs: Queen City, Kenwood Country (Cin., trustee). Avocations: golf, running, amateur radio. Office: The Kroger Co 1014 Vine St Cincinnati OH 45202

LEONARD, GEORGE EDMUND, savings and loan executive; b. Phoenix, Nov. 20, 1940; s. George Edmund and Marion Elizabeth (Fink) L.; m. Gloria Jean Henry, Mar. 26, 1965 (div. Feb. 1981); children: Tracy Lynn, Amy Theresa, Kristin Jean. Student, Ariz. State U., 1958-60; BS, U.S. Naval Acad., 1964; postgrad., Pa. State U., 1969-70; M.B.A., U. Chgo., 1973. Commd. ensign, U.S. Navy, 1964, advanced through grades to lt. comdr., 1974; v.p. 1st Nat. Bank Chgo., 1970-75; exec. v.p., chief banking officer Mera Bank, Phoenix, 1975—; pres., chief exec. officer Cen. Savs., San Diego, 1985-87; bd. dirs. Beverly Hills (Calif.) Savs., 1985. Active Phoenix Thunderbirds, 1979—. Mem. Phoenix Met. C. of C. (bd. dirs. 1975-82), Inst. Fin. Edn. (bd. dirs. 1980-87, nat. chmn. 1985-86). Republican. Roman Catholic. Clubs: Paradise Valley Country, Phoenix Country. Lodge: Kiwanis. Home: 3064 E Stella Ln Phoenix AZ 85016 Office: Mera Bank 3003 N Central Ste 2400 Phoenix AZ 85012

LEONARD, JANET TONKA, management consultant, financial planner; b. Indpls., July 31, 1952; d. Clarence and Marjorie (Tuley) Tonka; m. Kenneth Carl Leonard, Mar. 7, 1981. BA, Duke U., 1974; MBA, Columbia Grad. Sch. of Bus., 1983. Sales rep. to dist. account mgr. to asst. nat. account mgr. Gen. Foods Corp., Atlanta, Dallas and White Plains, N.Y., 1974-81; mgmt. cons. Touche Ross, N.Y.C., 1983-85; corp. planning mgr. PepsiCo, Purchase, N.Y., 1985-86; sr. mgmt. cons. The Alexander Group, Inc., N.Y.C., 1987-89; pres., founder Canaan Fin. Mgmt., Inc., New Canaan, Conn., 1989—, JPL Enterprises, New Canaan, Conn., 1988—. Site coordinator IRS Vol. Income Tax Assistance Program, New Canaan, 1989; alumni admissions advisor Duke U. Alumni Admissions Adv. Com., Fairfield City, Conn., 1988-89. Mem. Am. Mgmt. Assn., Young Women's League (New Canaan chpt.), Assn. of Am. Univ. Women, Kappa Kappa Gamma (Delta Beta chpt.). Home: 213 Old Stamford Rd New Canaan CT 06840

LEONARD, JOHN DUNBAR, JR., utility executive; b. Neptune, N.J., Mar. 3, 1933; s. John Dunbar and Marion Scott (MacIntosh) L.; A.A. in Sci., Monmouth Coll., 1951; B.S. in Physics, Duke U., 1953; M.S. in Physics, Naval Postgrad. Sch., 1962; m. Dorothy Ann Jones, Dec. 18, 1954; children—Evelyn Jane, Marion Scott, Robin Ann, Mary Margaret. Commd. ensign USN, 1954, advanced through grades to comdr., 1968, ret., 1974; supr. operational quality assurance Va. Electric Power Co., 1974-76; resident mgr. James A. FitzPatrick Nuclear Power Plant, N.Y. Power Authority, 1976-80, v.p. and asst. chief engr. N.Y. Power Authority, 1980-84; v.p. nuclear ops. L.I. Lighting Co., 1984—. Bd. visitors, Hi Tech adv. com. Monmouth Coll. Mem. Am. Nuclear Soc., U.S. Naval Inst., Oswego (N.Y.) C. of C. (dir. 1976-79), Sigma Xi, Sigma Pi Sigma, Lambda Sigma Tau. Clubs: Shattemuc Yacht, Rotary. Home: 10 Cedar Ln Setauket NY 11733 Office: 618 North Country PO Box 618 Wading River NY 11792

LEONARD, LAURENCE BARBERIE, JR., investment company executive; b. Boston, Apr. 29, 1930; s. Laurence Barberie and Barbara (Beardsell) L.; m. Joan Willenbrok, Dec. 3, 1960; children: George, Susan. B.A., Harvard U., 1952; M.B.A., Stanford U., 1957. With Mfrs. Hanover Bank, N.Y.C., 1957-61; v.p. Eaton & Howard, Boston, 1961-71; v.p. Mass. Fin. Services, Boston, 1971-85, sr. v.p., 1985—; pres. Mass. Income Devel. Fund, Boston, 1981-85, Mass. Investors Trust, Boston, 1985—; trustee 1st Colonial Bank for Savs., Mass., 1975—. Trustee Lynn Hosp., 1965-75; mem. exec. bd. Lynn Family and Children's Service; bd. dirs. Marblehead Youth Soccer Assn., Mass. Served with U.S. Army, 1952-55. Mem. Beach (dir. pres., Swampscott, Mass.), Tedesco Country (dir., sec., Marblehead), Eastern Yacht Club (Marblehead). Republican. Home: 12 Flint St Marblehead MA 01945 Office: Mass Investors Trust 500 Boylston St Boston MA 02116

LEONARD, RAYMOND WESLEY, retired civil and sanitary engineer; b. Lexington, N.C., Dec. 12, 1909; s. John Wesley and Clara Ada (Swing) L.; BS in Civil, Sanitary and Hwy. Engring., N.C. State U., 1932; MPH (fellow), Yale U., 1947; m. Gladys Jane DeHart, June 14, 1934; children: Baxter C. J. and James R. W. (twins). Various engring. assignments N.C. State Hwy., TVA, N.C. State Bd. Health, until 1936; engr. U.S. Geol. Survey, Asheville, N.C. and Pitts., 1936-45, 46-63, C.E., Wilmington, N.C., C.E. Mississippi River Commn., Vicksburg, Miss.; ret., 1973. Registered profl. engr., Vt., Miss. Fellow Royal Soc. Health; mem. N.C. Engrs. Soc., Nat. Soc. Profl. Engrs., ASCE, Am. Assn. Sanitary Engrs. Interam. Assn. Sanitary Engrs., Am. Public Health Assn., Tau Beta Pi, Phi Kappa Phi, Companion of St. Patrick, Masons, Shriners, Eastern Star. Lutheran. Home: PO Drawer HH Bryson City NC 28713

LEONARD, ROBERT BEVERLY, banker, surgeon; b. Spartenburg, S.C., Mar. 11, 1922; s. Paul Holland and Eunice Ruth (Harper) L.; m. Joey Nell Ryan, Nov. 10, 1945 (div 1987); children: Beverly, Joanna, Robert; m. Mary Woodford, Mar. 14, 1987. BS, U. S.C., 1942; MD, Med. Coll. S.C., 1945. Diplomate Am. Bd. Surgery. Intern U.S. Naval Hosp., San Diego, 1945; resident in surgery Med. U. S.C., Charleston, 1949-54; practice medicine specializing in surgery Phoenix, 1954—; bd. dirs. Pacific Wholesale Drug Co., Phoenix, 1959-73, Valley Nat. Bank, Phoenix, 1971—; chief of staff Maricopa County Med. Ctr., St. Joseph's Hosp., Phoenix. Contbr. articles to med. jours. Fellow Am. Coll. Surgeons (pres. Ariz. chpt. 1969-70), Southwestern Surg. Congress (vice councillor 1976-83). Episcopalian. Home: 5702 N 25th St Phoenix AZ 85016 Office: 550 W Thomas Rd #222C Phoenix AZ 85013

LEONARD, SPRING BIXBY, financial consultant; b. Brookline, Mass., Mar. 30, 1953; s. Robert Johnson and Barbara (Bixby) L. BSBA in Fin. with honors, Northeastern U., 1983. Registered investment adv.; cert. fin. planner. Fin. analyst Crosby Valve Co., Wrentham, Mass., 1975-79, USAF, Bedford, Mass., 1980-81; fin. planning and systems dataCon, Inc., Burlington, Mass., 1983-84; assoc. Duffield Fin. Group, Norfolk, Mass., 1985-86; owner SBL Fin. Enterprise, Norfolk, Mass., 1986—; lectr. adult edn. King Philip Regular Sch., 1986—; tchr. Franklin (Mass.) Pub. Schs., 1987—; bd. dirs. Fed. Credit Union, mem. investment com., 1988; bd. trustees Sandcastle/Royal Coachman, 1988. Chmn. Personnel Bd., Norfolk, 1984—; bd. trustees, chmn. planned giving and legacy com., mem. exec. com. Am. Cancer Soc., Neponset Valley Unit, 1986—, bd. dirs. Mass. div., 1988—. Mem. Internat. Assn. Fin. Planners. Home and Office: SBL Fin Enterprise 57 Main St Norfolk MA 02056

LEONARDI, RICHARD COSMO, bank executive; b. Rochester, N.Y., June 9, 1941; s. Orazio and Anna Maria (Almerto) L.; m. Ann Marie Schifano; children: Richard, Lisa Jo, Jennifer, Michael. BS, Rochester Inst. Tech., 1967. Sr. acct. Price Waterhouse & Co., Rochester, 1965-68; mgr. ops., controller George D.B. Bonbright & Co., Rochester, 1968-74; sr. v.p. Chase Lincoln 1st Bank, Rochester, 1974—. Chmn. fin. com. Aquinas Inst., Rochester, 1983-84; mem. N.Y. State Rep. Com., 1985—; Monroe County Rep. Com., Chili, N.Y. 1986—; chmn. Francis J. Russo Campaign, Chili, N.Y., 1986. Mem. N.Y. State Bankers Assn. (trust com. 1976-84, edn. com. 1986-87, exec. com. 1984-87). Roman Catholic. Home: 20 Chi-mar Dr Rochester NY 14624 Office: Chase Lincoln Bank 1 Lincoln First Sq Rochester NY 14643

LEONARDS, DAVID, entertainment company executive; b. Lafayette, Ind., Nov. 20, 1946; s. Gerald and Beryl Leonards; m. Rebecca Jacobs, May 2, 1981; children: Gerald, Brett, Grant. BS, Purdue U., 1968, BS in Chemistry, 1970, MS, 1973. Instr. chemistry Kankakee Valley Sch. Corp., Demotte, Ind., 1968-69; instr. and curriculum cons. Ea. Howard Sch. Corp., Greentown, Ind., 1969-72; founder, pres., chmn. bd. dirs. Internat. Leonards Corp., Indpls., 1973—; exec. dir. Internat. Entertainment Bur., Indpls., 1973—; co-founder Plus Assn. Mgmt., Indpls., 1987—, Conv. & Mktgs. Co., Indpls., 1987—. Chmn. Marion Co. Lic. Rev. Bd., Indpls., 1980—; del. Rep. State Conv., Ind., 1968—; bd. dirs. Mapleton Fall Creek Neighborhood Assn., Indpls., 1978-88. Mem. Mktg. Planners Internat., Indpls. Conv. and Visitors Assn., Ind. Assn. Co. and Dist. Fairs, Ohio Valley Mktg. Planners (v.p.), U.S. C of C., Indpls. C. of C., Am. Soc. Assn. Execs., Ind. Soc. Assn. Execs., Am. Fedn. Muscians, Internat. Assn. Fairs and Expositions, Nat. Music Camp Alumni Assn. (pres.), Rotary Club, Columbia Club. Office: 3612 N Washington Blvd Indianapolis IN 46205

LEONE, PAUL MICHAEL, accountant, lawyer; b. Bklyn., Dec. 6, 1955; s. Vito and Margaret Eileen (Gleason) L.; m. Maureen Ellen Callaghan, Dec. 7, 1986; 1 child, Bridget Anne. BS, Manhattan Coll., 1978; JD, St. John's U., Jamaica, N.Y., 1983; LLM in Taxation, NYU, 1986. Bar: N.Y. 1984, Fla. 1987, U.S. Dist. Ct., 1987, U.S. Tax Ct., 1987; CPA, N.Y. With Arthur Andersen & Co., N.Y.C., 1978-80; estate tax atty. IRS, N.Y.C., 1984-86; assoc. Farrell, Fritz, Caemmerer, Cleary, Barnosky & Armentano, P.C., Uniondale, N.Y., 1986-88; dir. estate planning Hoffman Raich & Fine CPA Group, East Meadow, N.Y., 1988—; mem. Tax and Estate Planning Council L.I., 1987—. Mem. ABA, N.Y. State Bar Assn., Fla. Bar Assn., Am. Inst. CPAs, N.Y. State Soc. CPAs. Home: 77 MacGregor Ave Roslyn Heights NY 11577 Office: Hoffman Raich & Fine CPA Group 90 Merrick Ave East Meadow NY 11554

LEONETTI, MICHAEL EDWARD, financial planner; b. Oak Park, Ill., Aug. 23, 1955; s. Michael Louis and Dolores Mary (DiOrio) L.; m. Elizabeth Anne Goff, June 16, 1979. BA, St. Marys Coll., 1977. Cert. fin. planner; registered investment advisor. Sales rep. Metropolitan Life, Des Plaines and Rosemont, Ill., 1977-80; fin. planner Money Masters Inc., Buffalo Grove, Ill., 1980-82, Leonetti & Assocs., Buffalo Grove, 1982—; instr. fin. planning Harper Coll., 1982-84. Author: Retire Worry Free: Financial Strategies for Tomorrow's Independence; mem. adv. bd. Practical Fin. Planning; contbr. articles to profl. jours. Named One of the Best Fin. Planners in U.S., Money Mag., 1987. Mem. Nat. Assn. Personal Fin. Advisors (pres. 1986-87), United Shareholders Assn., Internat. Assn. Fin. Planning (bd. dirs.), Inst. Cert. Fin. Planners (bd. dirs. 1986—), Registry Fin. Planning Practitioners, Investment Research Inst. Republican. Roman Catholic. Club: St. Mary Coll. Weight Lifting (pres., founder 1973-77). Home: 934 Cambridge Dr Buffalo Grove IL 60089 Office: Leonetti & Assocs 1130 Lake Cook Rd Ste 105 Buffalo Grove IL 60089

LEONG, CAROL JEAN, electrologist; b. Sacramento, Jan. 9, 1942; d. Walter Richard and Edith (Bond) Bloss; m. Oliver Arthur Fisk III, Apr. 12, 1964 (div. 1973); 1 child, Victoria Kay. BA in Sociology, San Jose (Calif.) State Coll., 1963; degree, Western Bus. Coll., 1964; cert. in electrolysis, Bay Area Coll. Electrolysis, 1978. Registered and cert. clin. profl. electrologist, Calif. Model various orgns., Calif., 1951-64; employment counselor Businessmen's Clearinghouse, Cin., 1966-67; dir. personnel Kroger Food Corp., Cin., 1967-68; prin. Carol Leong Electrolysis, San Mateo, Calif., 1978—; prin. Designs by Carol, San Mateo, 1987—; mem. Profl. Women's Forum, 1988—. Contbr. articles to profl. publs. Recipient Cert. of Appreciation San Francisco Lighthouse for the Blind, 1981-82, 83. Mem. Internat. Guild Profl. Electrologists (mem. continuing edn. com.), NAFE, Profl. Women's Forum, Peninsula Humane Soc., San Francisco Zool. Soc., Friends of Filoli, Am. Electrologists Assn., Electrologists Assn. Calif., Chi Omega. Republican. Methodist. Home: 3339 Glendora Dr San Mateo CA 94403 Office: Carol Leong Electrolysis 36 S El Camino Real Ste 205 San Mateo CA 94401

LEONHARD, WILLIAM EDWARD, engineering and construction company executive; b. Middletown, Pa., Dec. 9, 1914; s. Charles Frank and Ruth Eva (Wagner) L.; m. Wyllis Mary Rocker, Feb. 8, 1940; children: William Edward, Richard W., D. Jeanne. BEE, Pa. State U., 1936; MSEE, Mass. Inst. Tech., 1940; LLD, Pepperdine U., 1987. Commd. 2d lt. U.S. Army, 1936; Commd. lt. col. USAF, 1950, advanced through grades to brig. gen., 1960; ret. 1964; with Ralph M. Parsons Co., Pasadena, Calif., 1966—; pres. Ralph M. Parsons Co., 1974—, gen. mgr., 1974-75, chief exec. officer, 1975—, also dir, chmn. bd.; pres., chmn., chief exec. officer The Parsons Corp., 1978—. Bd. visitors, bd. overseers UCLA; assoc. Calif. Inst. Tech.; mem. corp. vis. com. dept. civil engring. MIT; trustee Harvey Mudd Coll., 1986—. Decorated Bronze Star, Legion of Merit (3); recipient Corp. Leadership award M.I.T., 1977; named Chief Exec. of Yr. Fin. World, 1982, 83, 84, 85, Outstanding CEO Wall Street Transcript, 1981, 83; recipient Disting. Alumnus award Pa. State U., 1982, Golden Beaver award in mgmt., 1984. Mem. ASME (Newman award 1961), Nat. Acad. Engring., Council on Fgn. Relations, Los Angeles World Affairs Council. Clubs: California (Los Angeles); Marrakesh Country (Palm Desert, Calif.); Annandale Golf (Pasadena), Pasadena Breakfast, Forum (Pasadena), Twilight (Pasadena).

LEONTIEF, WASSILY, economist; b. Leningrad, Russia, Aug. 5, 1906; s. Wassily and Eugenia (Bekker) L.; m. Estelle Helena Marks, Dec. 25, 1932; 1 dau., Svetlana Eugenia Alpers. Student, U. Leningrad, 1921-25; grad. Learned Economist; PhD, U. Berlin, 1928; PhD honoris causa, U. Bruxelles, Belgium, 1962, U. York, Eng., 1967, U. Louvain, 1971, U. Paris, 1972, U. Pa., 1976, U. Lancaster, Eng., 1976; D honoris causa, Adelphi Coll., 1988; LHD (hon.), Rensselaer Poly. Inst., 1988. Rsch. economist Inst. Weltwirtschaft, U. Kiel, Germany, 1927-28, 30; econ. adviser to Chinese govt. Nanking, 1929; with Nat. Bur. Econ. Rsch., N.Y.C., 1931; instr. econs. Harvard U., Cambridge, Mass., 1932-33; asst. prof. Harvard U., Cambridge, 1933-39, assoc. prof., 1939-46, prof., 1946-75, dir. econ. project, 1948-72, Henry Lee prof. econs., 1953-75; prof. econs. NYU, 1975—, univ. prof., 1983—, founder Inst. Econ. Analysis, 1978-85, mem. rsch. staff, since 1986; cons. Dept. Labor, 1941-47, OSS, 1943-45, UN, 1961-62, Dept. Commerce, 1966-82 , EPA, 1975-80 , UN, 1980—. Author: The Structure of the American Economy, 1919-29, 2d edit., 1976, Studies in the Structure of the American Economy, 1953, 2d edit., 1977, Input-Output Economics, 1966, 2d edit., 1986, Collected Essays, 1966, Theories, Facts and Policies, 1977, The Future of the World Economy, 1977, (with Faye Duchin) The Future Impact of Automation on Workers, 1986; Contbr. articles to sci. jours. and periodicals U.S. and abroad. Mem. Commn. to Study Orgn. of Peace, 1978; trustee N.C. Sch. Sci. and Math., 1978; mem. issues com. Progressive Alliance, 1979; mem. Com. for Nat. Security, 1980. Decorated officer Order Cherubim Univ.Pisa, 1953, Legion of Honor (France), 1967; Order of Rising Sun (Japan), 1984; recipient Bernhard-Harms prize econs. West Germany, 1970, Nobel prize in econs., 1973; Guggenheim fellow, 1940, 50. Fellow Soc. Fellows Harvard (sr. fellow, chmn. 1964-75), Econometric Soc., Royal Statis. Assn. (hon.), Inst. de France (corr.); mem. NAS, Am. Philos. Soc., Am. Acad. Arts and Scis., AAAS, Internat. Statis. Inst., Am. Econ. Assn., Am. Statis. Assn., Royal Econ. Soc., Japan Econ. Rsch. Ctr. (hon.), Brit. Acad. (corr.), French Acad. Scis. (corr.), Royal Irish Acad. (hon.), Brit. Assn. Advancement Sci. (pres. Sect. F 1976), USSR Acad. Scis. (fgn.), Century Club. Mem. Greek Orthodox Church. Office: NYU Inst Econ Analysis 269 Mercer St Rm 203 New York NY 10003

LEOPOLD, IRVING HENRY, physician, medical educator; b. Phila., Apr. 19, 1915; s. Abraham and Dora (Schlow) L.; m. Eunice Robinson, June 24, 1937; children—Ellen Robinson, John. BS, Pa. State U., 1934; MD, U. Pa., 1938, DSc, 1943. Diplomate Am. Bd. Ophthalmology (chmn. bd. 1971-72, examiner 1974-81, subcom. impaired vision and blindness 1967-69, task force on ocular pharmacology, 1967-69, cons. 1975-79, assoc. examiner 1974-81). Intern U. Pa. Hosp., 1938-40; fellow, instr. ophthalmology U. Pa. Hosp., U. Pa. Med. Sch., 1940-45; assoc. Hosp. U. Pa., also U. Pa. Med. Sch., 1945-54; research investigator chem. warfare OSRD, 1941-45; mem. faculty U. Pa. Grad. Sch. Medicine, 1946-64, successively assoc., asst. prof., assoc. prof., 1946-55, prof., head dept. ophthalmology, 1955-64; chief dept. ophthalmology Grad. Hosp., 1955-64; dir. research Wills Eye Hosp., 1949-64, attending surgeon, 1952-64, med. dir., 1961-64, cons. surgeon, 1965-73; chmn. sci. adv. com. Allergan, Inc., 1974, Sr. v.p., 1975; prof., chmn. dept. ophthalmology Mt. Sinai Sch. Medicine, 1965-75; dir. dept. ophthalmology Mt. Sinai Hosp., N.Y.C., 1964-75; prof., chmn. dept. ophthalmology U. Calif. at Irvine, 1975-85, prof. pharmacology, 1982—, prof. emeritus ophthalmology, 1985—; clin. prof. ophthalmolgy Coll. Physicians and Surgeons, Columbia, 1964-67; cons. ophthalmologist St. Joseph's Hosp., 1959-64, Albert Einstein Med. Center, 1959-64; Proctor lectr. U. Calif., 1962; Gifford Meml. lectr., Chgo., 1967; Edwin B. Dunphy lectr. Harvard, 1968; Walter Wright lectr. U. Toronto, 1969; Richardson Cross lectr. Royal Soc. Medicine, 1970; Doyne Meml. lectr. Ophthal. Soc. U.K., 1971; DeSchweinitz Meml. lectr., Phila., 1972; Jules Stein lectr. UCLA, 1974; Bedell lectr., Phila., 1975; Edwin B. Dunphy lectr. Harvard, 1975; Francis H. Adler lectr., Phila., 1980, Dwight Towne lectr., Ky., 1979, C.S. O'Brien lectr., New Orleans, 1979; Disting. vis. lectr. Jefferson Med. Coll., 1980, Moorfields Hosp., Eng., 1980, U. Helsinki, Finland, 1980, Third Francis Heed Adler lectr., 1980, 2d ann. Tullos O. Coston lectr., 1981, Sir Stewart Duke-Elder lectr., 1982,

Everett R. Viers lectr., Scott and White Clinic and Tex. A&M U. Coll. Medicine, Temple, Tex., 1982, U. Phillipines 1st lectr, 1st Irving H. Leopold lectr. Wills Eye Hosp, 1987—. Eye Resident Soc., Eye Referral Ctr., 1982, Royal Soc. Medicine lectr., London, 1985; lectr. Internat. Congress Ophthalmology, Japan, 1978, Phillipine Bd. Opthalmology; cons. Chem. Warfare Service, U.S. Army, 1948-52, 81; surgeon gen. USPHS, 1952-58, FDA, HEW, 1963; mem. med. adv. com. Orange County chpt. Multiple Sclerosis Soc., 1979-81; chmn. ophthalmology panel U.S. Pharmacopeia, 1960-70, mem. revision panel, 1970—; chmn. panel drug efficacy in ophthalmology Nat. Acad. Scis.-NRC, 1966-67, 80—; mem. tng. grants com. USPHS, 1952-58, mem. spl. sensory study sect. research neurol. diseases and blindness, 1954-58; mem. field investigating com. Nat. Inst. Neurol. Diseases and Blindness, 1959-61, mem. neurol. project com., 1961-63, chmn. vision research tng. com., 1967-68; mem. adv. bd. Am. Behcet's Found., Inc., 1980, 81; Expert Agree to Ministry of Health, France, 1981-87; curator ophthalmic pharmaceuticals Found. Am. Acad. Ophthalmology, 1983-89; mem. nat. adv. eye council panel on cataract sect. Nat. Eye Inst. and HEW, 1981-85; mem. med. research and devel. command-chemical welfare U.S. Army, 1981-85. Editor-in-chief: Survey of Ophthalmology, 1958-62; cons. editor, 1962—; editorial bd.: Am. Jour. Diabetes, 1956-73, Investigative Ophthalmology, 1961-74; assoc. editor: Am. Jour. Ophthalmology, 1974-88, now mem. editorial bd.; assoc. editor Archives of Ophthalmology, 1974-81; cons. Jour. AMA, 1974-81; editorial cons. Jour. Ocular Pharmacology, 1985—; editor: Ocular Inflammation and Therapeutics, 1981. Trustee Seeing Eye Guide. Recipient Zentmayer award, 1945, 49; honor award Am. Acad. Ophthalmology, 1955, Sr. Hon. award, 1984; Edward Lorenzo Holmes citation and award, 195iedenwald medal Assn. Research Ophthalmology, 1960; Disting. Research award U. Calif., Irvine, Calif., 1980; Disting. Research award U. Calif. Alumni Assn., 1980, Disting. Service to Opthalmology, 1988; Physician's award Pa. Acad. Ophthalmology and Otolaryngology, 1981; Sir Steward Duke-Elder award, Lederle Medal and Prize for Research in Glaucoma Internat. Glaucoma Congress VI and Am. Soc. Contemporary Ophthalmology, Orlando, Fla., 1982. Mem. N.Y. Acad. Medicine, Am. Ophthal. Soc. (Verhoeff Meml. lectr. 1973, Lucien Howe medal 1974), Am. Acad. Ophthalmology and Otolaryngology (chmn. drug com. ophthalmology 1963-74, Edward Jackson Meml. lectr. 1965, honor guest 1971, 75, Philip M. Corboy Perpetual Excellence award 1988, Disting. Service to Ophthalmology award 1988), Am. Soc. Contemporary Ophthalmology (chief cons. editorial bd. 1981), Assn. Research Ophthalmology (trustee, chmn.), Nat. Soc. Prevention Blindness (dir. 1974-81, v.p., exec. com., hon. bd. dirs.), A.C.S., AAAS, Art Alliance Phila., John Morgan Soc., Coll. Physicians Phila., Am. Diabetes Assn., AMA (chmn. residency rev. com. ophthalmology 1970-72, Physician's Recognition award 1980-87), N.Y. Acad. Sci., Pan Am. Assn. Ophthalmology, Pan Pacific Surg. Assn., Royal Soc. Medicine (London), N.Y. State, N.Y. County, Philadelphia County med. socs., Calif., Orange County med. assns., Orange County Soc. Ophthalmology, Am. Med. Student Assn., Nat. Soc. to Prevent Blindness (hon. bd. dirs. 1986—), Med. Biochemist Club, Vesper Club, Newport Beach Tennis Club, Sigma Xi, Alpha Omega Alpha. Clubs: Medical Biochemist, Vesper (Phila.); Big Canyon Country, Balboa Bay (Newport Beach, Calif.); Century Country, Purchase (N.Y.C.). Home: 1484 Galaxy Dr Newport Beach CA 92660 Office: Allergan Inc 2525 DuPont Dr Irvine CA 92715

LEOPOLD, ROBERT MICHAEL, sewer reconstruction company executive; b. N.Y.C., Feb. 16, 1926; s. Max and Sally (Altman) L.; m. Renee Luria, June 27, 1946; children: Ronni J., Susan G., Barbara L. BS, Ga. Inst. Tech., 1945; postgrad., U. Pa., 1946, NYU, 1966. V.p. L. Luria & Son Inc., N.Y.C., 1946-62; exec. v.p. Savin Corp., Valhalla, N.Y., 1979-82; sr. v.p. N.Y. Hanseatic Corp., N.Y.C., 1962-74; ptnr. Stuart Bros., N.Y.C., 1974-77; chmn., chief exec. officer Richford Industries, N.Y.C., 1976-81; vice chmn. Insituform N.Am., Memphis, 1982-86, chief exec. officer, 1986—; pres. Huguenot Assocs. Inc., Larchmont, N.Y., 1977—; chmn. bd. dirs. Internat. Asset Mgmt. Group, Larchmont; bd. dirs. Campbell Capital Corp., Miami, Fla., Equity Growth Corp., Miami Insituform Mid-Am. Inc., Chesterfield, Mo. Mem. Pvt. Sector Adv. Panel on Infrastructure Financing U.S. Senate Budget Com. Mem. Am. Arbitration Assn., Assn. Corp. Growth, N.Y. Soc. Security Analysts, Beach Point Club, Ga. Tech. Club. Office: Insituform NAm Inc 1890 Palmer Ave Ste 403 Larchmont NY 10538

LEPSINGER, RICHARD LEE, behavioral scientist; b. Pitts., Dec. 11, 1948; s. Norman and Florence (Friedman) L. BS in Behavioral Sci., SUNY, New Paltz, 1970, MS in Edn., 1973; MS in Planning, U. So. Calif., 1979. Tchr. Hyde Park, N.Y., 1970-77; cons. Union Carbide Corp., Danbury, N.Y., 1978-84; v.p. mgmt. devel. Manus Assocs., N.Y.C., 1984—. Mem. Am. Soc. of Tng. and Devel., Human Resource Planning Soc., Instl. Systems Assn. Office: Manus Assocs 175 5th Ave Ste 712 New York NY 10010

LERITZ, DANIEL RAYMOND, pharmaceutical company executive, consultant; b. St. Louis, Jan. 24, 1945; s. Joseph D. and Agnes (Lyons) L.; m. Retta J. Schoen, Nov. 9, 1974; children: Daniel, Retta. BS in Chem., St. Louis U., 1966; MBA, Washington U., 1971. Loss control cons. The Hartford Ins. Group, St. Louis, 1970-71; mgr. new products Carboline Co., St. Louis, 1971-78; acct. exec./dir. mktg. BHN Advt., St. Louis, 1978-80; mgr. sales Carnegie div. Rexall Corp., St. Louis, 1980-81; mgr. western sales The Vitarine Co., Inc., Springfield Gardens, N.Y., 1981-82; mgr. sales Pvt. Formulations, Inc., Edison, N.J., 1982-87; pres. The Leritz Co., Inc., St. Louis, 1985—; bd. dirs. Nutri-Pac Corp., Interstate Foods Mktg., Ltd. Co-authored numerous articles. Bd. dirs. Am. Cancer Soc., Mo., 1980; chmn. bd. trustees York Woods, Mo., 1984. Mem. Am. Chem. Soc., Assn. Drug & Chem. Industry of Mo. Roman Catholic. Home: 1 Cricket Ln Brentwood MO 63144 Office: The Leritz Co Inc 2652 Melvin Ave Saint Louis MO 63144

LERMONDE, VIVIAN CLAIRE, communications consultant; b. Niagara Falls, N.Y., Mar. 14, 1949; d. Rufus Joseph and Marion Catherine (Ryan) L. BA in English, Ursuline Coll., Cleve., 1970; MA in English, John Carroll U., 1972. Legis aide Ohio Ho. of Reps., Columbus, 1973-79; sales mgr. Sheraton-Columbus, 1980-81; media person Ohio Senate, Columbus, 1981-83; cons. Lermonde Communications, Columbus, 1983—; tchr. pub. speaking communications skills dept. Columbus State Community Coll., 1977—. Bd. dirs. Columbus Theater Ballet, 1979-81; mem. publicity com. Ohio Dem. Com., 1980; pres., co-founder Columbus Irish Feis, 1981; mem. Windstar Found., 1989, Nat. Arbor Day Found., 1989, North Shore Animal Protection League, 1987—. Mem. Ancient Order Hibernians (pres. Franklin county 1981-84, chmn. Ohio publicity 1987—, Outstanding svc. award Franklin county 1985), Press Club. Roman Catholic. Home and Office: 5681 Dorsey Dr Columbus OH 43235

LERNER, ALAN CHARLES, financial market economist, educator; b. Bklyn., July 24, 1944; s. Isidore and Florence (Leschinski) L.; m. Bonnie Marilyn Taub, Jan. 28, 1967 (div. Apr. 1980); children: Lisa, Jennifer; m. Linda Joy Hunter, Feb. 1, 1981 (dec. Sept. 1982); 1 child, Kali; m. Wendy Watson, Aug. 20, 1985. B.A., Bklyn. Coll., 1966; M.B.A., NYU, 1968. Instr. econs. NYU, 1969-72; economist Salomon Bros., N.Y.C., 1972-74; economist, sr. v.p. Banker Trust Co., N.Y.C., 1974—; adj. prof. econs. and fin. NYU, 1974—. Author: weekly market letter Prospects for the Credit Markets, 1976—. NDEA fellow, 1967-69. Mem. Am. Fin. Assn., Money Marketeers (v.p. 1981—, past pres.). Jewish. Office: Bankers Trust Co 280 Park Ave New York NY 10017

LERNER, CHARLES SOLOMON, marketing communications professional, consultant; b. Balt., Jan. 10, 1931; s. Harry W. and Florence (Rosenstein) L.; m. Carole Fibus, Sept. 6, 1953; children: Erica, Christopher, Jeffrey. BA, St. John's Coll., Annapolis, Md., 1953; postgrad., U. Chgo., 1953-54, U. Va., 1954-55. Pres. RMC Research Corp., Bethesda, Md., 1970-75; v.p. Kappa Systems, Arlington, Va., 1975-80; dep. asst sec. communications planning U.S. Dept. Health and Human Services, Washington, 1980-81; sr. v.p. The Earle Palmer Brown Co., Bethesda, 1981-85; pres. Charles S. Lerner Assocs., Bethesda, 1985—; chmn. communications planning bd. Cancer Inst., Bethesda, 1987—. Bd. dirs. Adas Israel Congregation, Washington, 1975—, 2d v.p., 1988—. With U.S. Army, 1955-57. Democrat. Jewish.

LERNER, FREDERIC HOWARD, trust company executive; b. Bklyn., Feb. 10, 1957; s. Irving and Judith (Zarchin) L.; m. Sheryl Ann Gorman, June 5, 1983; 1 child, Jacklyn Michele. BS in Acctg., SUNY, 1979. Staff acct. Kipnis & Karchmer, N.Y.C., 1979-81; fin. analyst Bank Leumi Trust Co., N.Y.C., 1981-84; asst. sec. N.J. Trust Co., Jersey City, 1984—; prof. N.Y.U., 1983; prin. sole proprietorship, acct., Jericho, N.Y., 1984—; cons. various orgns. and individuals, N.Y., 1984—. Contbr. articles to profl. jours. Mem. Nat. Comml. Fin. Assn. Home: 32 Peter Ct Jericho NY 11753 Office: Trust Co NJ 35 Joural Sq Jersey City NJ 07306

LERNER, HERBERT J., accountant; b. Newark, Aug. 19, 1938; s. Morris David Lerner and Evelyn L. (Shapiro) Kaplan; m. Dianne Joan Prag, Aug. 23, 1959; children—Joy Ellen, Mark Allen. B.S., Rutgers U., 1959; LL.B., Georgetown U., 1963. Bar: D.C. 1964; C.P.A., D.C. With Ernst & Whinney, Washington, 1963—; ptnr. Ernst & Whinney, 1970-83, nat. dir. tax., 1983-84, vice chmn. tax services, 1984—; mem. IRS Commrs. Adv. Bd., Washington, 1982-83, CCH Tax Transactional Adv. Bd., Washington, 1983—; bd. dirs. Tax Council, Washington, 1984—; mem. tax adv. council United Jewish Appeal Fedn., Washington, 1982—. Author: (with others) Federal Income Taxation of Corporations Filing Consolidated Returns, 3 vols., 1975; contbr.-editor pvt. letter rulings column in Jour. Taxation. Mem. Am. Inst. C.P.A.s (exec. com. 1979-82, 85, 89; chmn. exec. com. 1986-88, mem. exec. com. and immediate past chmn.; mem. Council 1988—), ABA, Internat. Fiscal Assn. Clubs: George Town, City (Washington). Office: Ernst & Whinney 1200 19th St NW 3rd Fl Washington DC 20036

LERNER, JOSEPH, optical retailer; b. N.Y.C., Dec. 7, 1962; s. Harry and Barbara (Smulofsky) L.; m. Laura Debra Leibnitz, Oct. 11, 1987. AAS, N.Y.C. Tech. Coll., 1983. Ophthalmic dispenser Cohen's Fashion Optical, S.I., N.Y., 1982-84, Staten Eye Land, S.I., 1984—. Republican. Jewish. Office: Staten Eye Land 20 Nelson Ave Staten Island NY 10308

LERNER, WILLIAM C., lawyer; b. Phila., July 17, 1933; s. Al and Tillie (Goodman) L.; BA, Cornell U., 1955; LLB, NYU, 1960; m. G. Billie Campbell, Aug. 15, 1957; children—Bonnie, Edwina. Bar: N.Y. 1961. Atty. SEC, 1960-64; asst. v.p. Am. Stock Exch., 1965-68; sr. v.p., sec. Carter, Berlind & Weill, Inc. (predecessor to Shearson, Am. Express, Inc.), N.Y.C., 1968-71, Berg & Cornell, Buffalo, 1970-71, Kavinoky & Cook, Buffalo, 1971-72, Saperston & Day, Buffalo, 1973-78; with firm Robshaw & Lerner, P.C., Buffalo, 1978-80; sr. ptnr. Nasca and Lerner, Buffalo, 1981-85; v.p. and gen. counsel The Geneva Cos., Costa Mesa, Calif., 1986—; bd. dir. Helm Resources, Inc., Seismic Enterprises, Inc., Teletrak Computer, Inc. Chmn., Erie County Pub. Utilities Task Force, 1974-75; mem. Art Coll. Coun. Cornell U. , 1977-85, N.Y. Gov.'s Hazardous Waste Facilities Task Force, 1983-85. 1st lt. Q.M.C., U.S. Army, 1955-57. Mem. ABA, N.Y. State Bar Assn. (regulation of securities com. 1968-86)., Phi Alpha Delta. Club: Buffalo. Contbg. editor The Stock Market Handbook, 1969, The Stock Market Handbook, 1969. Office: The Geneva Cos 5 Park Plaza Irvine CA 92714

LEROUX, MARCEL HENRI, industrial company executive; b. Granville, Manche, France, July 2, 1930; s. Rene Henri and Juliette L.; student Gen. Electric Co. Sch.; m. Christiane Marie Pasturel, Oct. 24, 1951; children—Daniel, Monique, Martine. Electronics engr. Material Electric SW, Paris, 1952-57; project engr. Battell Meml. Inst. Geneva, 1957-60; group leader Brown Boveri, Baden, Switzerland, 1961-68; group leader Gen. Electric Co., Waynesboro, Va., Bridgeport, Conn., 1968-80; pres. Atek NC Corp., 1980-84, pres. ITA 1984—. Past bd. dirs., treas. Va. Mus. of Fine Arts, Waynesboro chpt.; ptnr. Image One Print and Graphics, 1986—. Served with French Navy, 1947-52. Mem. Numerical Control Soc. (pres. program chmn. Liberty Rock chpt.), Swiss Fedn. of Automatic Control, Am. Mgmt. Assn. Patentee in field. Home: 294 Minortown Rd Woodbury CT 06798 Office: 89B S Main St Newtown CT 06470

LEROY, DAVID CHARLES, real estate consultant; b. Wilmington, N.C., Sept. 16, 1946; s. Lemuel David and Mary Margaret (Pridgeon) LeR.; divorced; children: Jennifer Leslie, Melissa Robin. BA in Polit. Sci., W.Va. U., 1968; postgrad., Am. U., 1973-74. Tchr., dir. Leary Sch., Annandale, Va., 1968-70; real estate agt. Long & Foster Realtors, Vienna, Va., 1970-72; real estate appraiser Fairfax (Va.) County Office Real Estate Assessments, 1972-76; broker, co-owner LeRoy & Cannon Realtors & Appraisal Co., Leesburg, Va., 1976—; vice-chmn. Loudoun County Equalization Bd. (court appointed real estate assessment), 1985—; speaker to Va. Gen. Assembly joint com. on cities, counties, and towns, Richmond, 1986; Va. Highway Dept. Condemnation Commr., 1978-83. Author: (property evaluation studies) U.S. Marshall's Service, 1985, 88, IRS, 1985; mem. editorial bd. Realtor Mag., Washington, 1987; contbr. articles to newspapers and mags. on real estate issues. Del. Rep. State Convention, Virginia Beach, Va., 1981. Served with USNR, 1968. Mem. Va. Assn. Realtors (bd. dirs. 1983-87), Loudoun County Bd. Realtors (sec. 1983, v.p. 1984, pres. 1985; State Honor Bd. award 1985, Realtor of Yr. 1986), Nat. Assn. Real Estate Appraisers (cert.), Phi Delta Theta (pres. Morgantown, W.Va. chpt. 1966-67). Republican. Presbyterian. Club: Ruritan Internat. (Lucketts, Va.). Home: PO Box 122 Leesburg VA 22075 Office: LeRoy & Cannon Inc 706 S King St Ste 4 Leesburg VA 22075

LERSCH, DELYNDEN RIFE, engineering manager; b. Grundy, Va., Mar. 22, 1949; d. Woodrow and Eunice Louise (Atwell) Rife; B.S. in E.E., Va. Poly. Inst. and State U., 1970; postgrad. Boston U., 1975—; m. John Robert Lersch, May 9, 1976; children—Desmond, Kristofer. With Stone & Webster Engring. Corp., 1970—, elec. engr., supr. computer applications, Boston, 1978-80, mgr. computer graphics, 1980-84, mgr. engring. systems and computer graphics, 1984-87, div. chief info. techs., 1987—. Named Stone and Webster's Woman Engr. of Yr., 1976, 79; Mass. Solar Energy Research grantee, 1978; honored by Engring. News Record mag. for contbns. to constrn. industry, 1983. Mem. Assn. Women in Sci., Soc. Women Engrs. (sr.), IEEE (sr.), Women in Sci. and Engring., Energy Communicators, Nat. Computer Graphics Assn., Profl. Council New Eng., Nuclear Energy Women (dir. Mass. chpt. 1978, New Eng. region 1979), LWV. Congregationalist. Club: Boston Bus. and Profl. Women's. Author: Cable Schedule Information Systems As Used in Power Plant Construction, 1973, 2d edit., 1975; Information Systems Available for Use by Electrical Engineers, 1976; contbr. articles in field of computer aided design and engring. Home: 6 Blue Skye Dr Hingham MA 02043 Office: 245 Summer St Boston MA 02101

LESCRENIER, CHARLES, manufacturing company executive; b. Laredo, Tex., July 22, 1935; m. Margaret Gebhardt, June 24, 1967; children: Peter, Karen, Jon. BS, Tex. A&M U., 1960; postgrad., U. Tex., Houston, 1960-62, Yale U., 1962-65, U. London, 1964-65; MS, Inst. de Filologia Hispanica, Saltillo, Mex., 1970. Diplomate Am. Bd. Radiology. Chief physicist, asst. prof. Med. Coll. Wis., Milw., 1965-73; chief exec. officer, owner Gammex Inc., Milw., 1969—; adj. prof. Rush Presbyn./Chgo. Med. Sch., 1973-83; lectr. med. physics Rush Presbyn. Med. Ctr., Chgo., 1987—; chief exec. officer, owner Radiation Measurements Inc., Madison, Wis., 1987—; prin. Gammex-Radiation Measurements Inc., Nottingham, Eng., 1987—, also chmn. bd. dirs.; pres., founder Wis. Innovarium Ltd., Milw., 1987—; chmn. bd. dirs. Gammex Internat., Milw., 1987—; chief exec. officer, owner Physics Assocs. Ltd, Benicia, Calif., 1988—; mem. 2 adv. coms. U.S. Dept. Commerce, Small and Minority Bus. for Trade Policy Matters, Washington, 1985—, adv. bd. dept. biology Marquette U., 1986—, adv. bd. Ctr. for Entrepreneurship, 1987—, Industry Adv. Com. on Customs Matters, Washington, 1988—. Inventor in field. Chmn. Civil Service Commn., Wauwatosa, Wis.; mem. steering com. Sch. System-Bus. and Edn. Network, Wauwatosa, 1985-87; mem. exec. bd. Milw. County Boy Scouts Am., 1984—; active Greater Milw. Com., 1988—. Served with USAR, 1954-62. Recipient Wis. Gov.'s Export award, 1985, 87, U.S. SBA Small Bus. Exporter of Yr. award, 1986, Wis. State Profl. Engrs.'-Gov.'s New Product award, 1980, Greater Milw. Initiative honors, 1984, 85, 86, other awards. Mem. Am. Soc. Radiologic Tech. (adv. bd. edn. 1986—), Am. Assn. Physicists in Medicine, Am. Hosp. Radiology Adminstrs., Hosp. Physicists Assn. U.K., Health Physics Soc., Council Ind. Mgrs. (pres. Milw. chpt. 1985-86, nat. chmn. bd. dirs. 1986-87, Outstanding Achievement Presdl. award 1985, 86), Wauwatosa C. of C. (award for invention 1986), Ind. Bus. Assn. (dir. Wis. chpt. 1989—), Inc. Coun. of Growing Cos. (strategic planning com., grand master of Wis., 1988). Methodist. Lodges: Masons, Shriners. Home: 660 Crescent Ct Wauwatosa WI 53213 Office: Gammex Inc PO Box 26708 Milwaukee WI 53226

LESHER, DEAN STANLEY, newspaper publisher; b. Williamsport, Md., Aug. 7, 1902; s. David Thomas and Margaret Eliot (Prosser) L.; m. Kathryn C. Lesher, Nov. 2, 1929 (dec. Mar. 1971); children: Carolyn Lee (dec.), Dean Stanley, Melinda Kay, Cynthia; m. Margaret Louise Lisco, Apr. 2, 1973. BA magna cum laude, U. Md., 1924; JD, Harvard U., 1926. Bar: Mo. 1926. Sole practice Kansas City, 1926-41; gen. counsel Postal Life & Casualty Ins. Co., Kansas City, 1936-41; chmn. bd., pub. East Bay Pub. Co., 1947-60, Lesher Communications, Inc., Walnut Creek, Calif., 1960—; pres. 31 newspaper owning corps. Contbr. articles to trade publs. Trustee Calif. State Univs. and Colls., 1973-81, 85—; regent St. Mary's Coll., 1978-82, John F. Kennedy U., 1981—; mem. Calif. Post-Secondary Edn. Commn., 1979-81. Named News Pub. of Calif., 1977, Best Bus. Leader Walnut Creek Area, 1978, Edn. Pub. of Calif., 1980, Citizen of Yr. Contra Costa County, 1985; recipient Medal of Freedom Valley Forge Freedom Found., 1988. Mem. Am. Newspaper Pubs. Assn., Suburban Newspapers Am. (bd. dirs., Outstanding Pub. award 1982, award named in honor 1982—), Nat. Newspaper Assn. (bd. dirs., spl. award by Pres. Reagan & V.P. Bush in White House 1983), Walnut Creek (Calif.) C. of C. (pres.), Round Hill Country Club, Concord Century Club, Harvard Club, Rotary (past dist. gov.), Masons, Phi Kappa Phi, Phi Delta Theta, Theta Sigma Phi, Sigma Delta Chi. Republican. Home: 6 Sally Ann Rd Orinda CA 94563 Office: Lesher Communications Inc 2640 Shadelands Dr Walnut Creek CA 94598

LESHER, JOHN LEE, JR., financial services company executive; b. Harrisburg, Pa., Feb. 7, 1934; s. John Lee and Mary Alice (Watkeys) L.; m. Nancy Smith, July 11, 1970; children by previous marriage: John David, James Elam, Andrew Gwynne. BA cum laude, Williams Coll., 1956; MBA, Harvard U., 1958. Budget dir., asst. sec. The Barden Corp., Danbury, Conn., 1958-61; cons. Booz, Allen & Hamilton Inc., N.Y.C., 1962-64, assoc., 1964-66, v.p., 1966-76, pres., 1976-85; pres. Mars & Co. Cons. Inc., Greenwich, Conn., 1985-87, Home Group Fin. Services, N.Y.C., 1987-88; v.p. Cresap, McCormick & Paget, N.Y.C., 1988—. Clubs: Harvard Bus. Sch., Williams; Watch Hill Yacht, Misquamicut (Watch Hill, R.I.); Round Hill (Greenwich, Conn.); River (N.Y.C.). Office: Cresap McCormick & Paget 245 Park Ave New York NY 10167

LESHER, RICHARD LEE, association executive; b. Doylesburg, Pa., Oct. 28, 1933; s. Richard E. Lesher and Rosalie Orabelle (Meredith) Lesher Ehrhart; m. Agnes Marie Plocki, June 13, 1981; children by previous marriage: Douglas Allen, Laurie Lynn, Betsy Lee, Craig Collin. BBA, U. Pitts., 1958; MS, Pa. State U., 1960; DBA, Ind. U., 1963, LLD (hon.), 1979; D of Pub. Service (hon.), Ferris State Coll., 1981; DBA (hon.), Lawrence Inst. Tech., 1985. Asst. prof. Coll. Commerce and Adminstrn., Ohio State U., Columbus, 1963-64; cons. NASA, Washington, 1964-65; dep. asst. adminstr. NASA, 1965-66, asst. adminstr., 1966-69; bus. and mgmt. cons. Washington, 1969-71; pres. Nat. Ctr. for Resource Recovery, Washington, 1971-75, U.S. C. of C., Washington, 1975—; bd. dirs. 1st Am. Bank. Author: (book) Economic Progress...It's Everybody's Business, 1980, syndicated newspaper column; participant (weekly syndicated debate show) It's Your Business. Bd. dirs. Wolf Trap Found.; mem. Commn. Voter Participation & Ballot Integrity. Served with U.S. Army, 1954-56. Recipient Superior Achievement award NASA, 1968, Exceptional Service award NASA, 1968, Alumni Achievement award Pa. State U., 1976, Acad. of Alumni Fellows award, Ind. U., 1977, Religious Heritage award, 1978, Horatio Alger award, 1980, Bicentennial Medallian of Distinction U. Pitts., 1987, Golden Exec. medal Gen. C. of C. of Taiwan, 1988. Mem. Am. Soc. Assn. Execs., So. Assn. C. of C. Execs., Washington Soc. Assn. Execs., Internat. Platform Assn., Am. C. of C. Execs. (bd. dirs.), Phi Alpha Kappa, Beta Gamma Sigma (Dir.'s Table, Nat. award 1977). Club: Congressional Country, Met. Office: US C of C 1615 H St NW Washington DC 20062

LESINSKI, ROGER JOHN, corporate counsel; b. Detroit, Mar. 6, 1949; s. Edmond and Frances M. (Grajek) L.; m. Kathleen Mary Mijal, May 25, 1974; children: Roger John Jr., Monika Mary. AB, U. Mich., 1971; JD, U. Detroit, 1977. Legal asst. Blue Cross/Blue Shield, Detroit, 1974-77, assoc. counsel, 1977-80; corp. atty. Cross & Trecker Corp., Bloomfield Hills, Mich., 1980-84; asst. sec., corp. atty. Cross & Trecker Corp., Bloomfield Hills, 1984—; bd. dirs. Am. Corp. Counsel Assn. Mich., Detroit, 1985-88. Cpt. USAR, 1971-79. Mem. State Bar Mich., Detroit Bar Assn., Adv. Bar Assn. Roman Catholic. Home: 1917 Mapleridge Rd Rochester Hills MI 48309 Office: Cross & Trecker Corp 505 N Woodward Ave Bloomfield MI 48013

LESJAK, DAVID MATTHEW, financial planner; b. Cleve., Apr. 22, 1957; s. John William and Gertrude F. (Bair) L.; m. Diana Lynn McDougal, Oct. 13, 1979; children: Rebecca, Bridgett, Daniel, Tegan. Grad. high sch., Fairview Park, Ohio. Cert. fin. planner. Technician Leimknehler Inc., Cleve., 1975-78; registered rep. Anchor Nat. Fin. Service, Cleve., 1976-83; v.p. Lesjak Planning Corp., Westlake, Ohio, 1980—. Mem. Inst. Cert. Fin. Planners (treas. 1985—), C. of C. Republican. Roman Catholic. Office: Lesjak Planning Corp 1991 Crocker Rd Gemini Towers Ste 575 Westlake OH 44145

LESKO, ROBERT TED, accountant, controller; b. Girard, Pa., Feb. 7, 1934; s. John Jerome and Anna Marie (Groff) L.; m. Virginia Ann Olszewski, Nov. 21, 1964; 1 child, Ted John. Cert. in acctg. and fin., Erie Comml. Coll., 1958; BS in Acctg., Gannon U., 1972. Asst. controller Fenestra, Inc., Erie, 1958-63; pres. Meynell Mfg. Co., Erie, 1963-68; asst. controller Erie City iron div. Zurn Indsl., Erie, 1968-71; treas. Techno Corp., Erie, 1971-73, Knobloch Oldsmobile/Toyota, Erie, 1973-80; corp. controller Earl E. Knox Co., Erie, 1980—. Cpl. U.S. Army, 1954-56, ETO. Republican. Roman Catholic. Office: Earl E Knox Co 1111 Bacon St PO Box 1248 Erie PA 16512

LESLIE, HENRY ARTHUR, banker; b. Troy, Ala., Oct. 15, 1921; s. James B. and Alice (Minchener) L.; m. Anita Doyle, Apr. 5, 1943; children: Anita Lucinda, Henry Arthur. B.S., U. Ala., 1942, J.D., 1948; J.S.D., Yale U., 1959; grad., Sch. Banking, Rutgers U., 1964. Bar: Ala. 1948. Asst. prof. bus. law U. Ala., 1948-50, 52-54; prof. law, asst. dean U. Ala. (Sch. Law), 1954-59; v.p. trust officer Birmingham Trust Nat. Bank, Ala., 1959-64; sr. v.p., trust officer Union Bank & Trust Co., Montgomery, Ala., 1964-73; sr. v.p., sr. loan officer Union Bank & Trust Co., 1973-76, exec. v.p., 1976-78, pres., chief exec. officer, 1978—, dir., 1973—; mem. Ala. Oil and Gas Bd., 1984-85; dir. 1st Fin. Mgmt. Corp., Fed. Reserve Bank. Pres. Downtown Unltd., 1983-84; mem. Ala. Bd. Bar Examiners, 1973-78; chmn. bd. dirs. Ala. Bankers Found., 1971-77; trustee Ala. Assn. Ind. Colls.; bd. dirs. Shakespeare Theatre. Served to capt. AUS, 1942-46; to lt. col. JAGC Res. Decorated Bronze Star. Mem. ABA, Ala. Bar Assn., Montgomery Bar Assn., Ala. Ind. Bankers (chmn. 1983-84), Ala. Bankers Assn. (trust div. pres. 1963-65), Ind. Bankers Assn. Am. (dir. 1983—), Farrah Order Jurisprudence (pres. 1973), Order of Coif Alumni, Newcomen Soc. N.Am., Montgomery C. of C. (dir. 1983-84, pres. 1987-88), Delta Sigma Pi, Phi Delta Phi, Omicron Delta Kappa, Pi Kappa Phi. Episcopalian (past sr. warden). Clubs: Maxwell Officers, Montgomery Country (dir. 1987—), Capital City (dir.), Kiwanis. Home: 3332 Boxwood Dr Montgomery AL 36111 Office: Union Bank & Trust Co Commerce St Montgomery AL 36104

LESLIE, JAMES HILL, paper company executive; b. Mpls., Feb. 27, 1930; s. Frank Paul and Ruth (Hill) L.; m. Carol Van Camp, Mar. 23, 1972; children: Laura, Kate, James. B.A., Princeton U., 1952; postgrad., Sloan Sch., M.I.T., 1954-55. With Leslie Paper, Mpls., 1955—; v.p. Leslie Paper, 1960-66, pres., 1966-82, chmn., chief exec. officer, 1982—. Served to lt. USN, 1952-54. Clubs: Minneapolis, Rotary. Office: Leslie Paper PO Box 1351 Minneapolis MN 55440

LESLY, PHILIP, public relations counsel; b. Chgo., May 29, 1918; m. Ruth Edwards, Oct. 17, 1940 (div. 1971); 1 son, Craig.; m. Virginia Barnes, May 11, 1984. BS magna cum laude, Northwestern U., 1940. Asst. news editor Chgo. Herald & Examiner, 1935-37; copywriter advt. dept. Sears, Roebuck & Co., Chgo., 1940-41; asst. dir. publicity Northwestern U., 1941-42; account exec. Theodore R. Sills & Co. (pub. relations), Chgo., 1942; v.p. Theodore R. Sills & Co. (pub. relations), 1943, exec. v.p., 1945; dir. pub. relations Ziff-Davis Pub. Co., 1945-46; exec. v.p. Harry Coleman & Co. (pub. relations), 1947-49; pres. Philip Lesly Co. (pub. rels.), Chgo., 1949—; sr. cons. Polcyn/Lesly Pub. Rels., San Ramon, Calif.; lectr. pub. rels., pub. opinion to bus. and sch. groups. Co-author: Public Relations: Principles and Procedures, 1945, Everything and The Kitchen Sink, 1955; Author: The People Factor, 1974, Selections from Managing the Human Climate, 1979, How We Discommunicate, 1979, Overcoming Opposition, 1984, Bonanzas and Fool's Gold, 1987; bimonthly Managing the Human Climate; also articles in U.S.,

Brit. mags. and trade publs.; Editor: Public Relations in Action, 1947, Public Relations Handbook, 3d rev. edit, 1967, Lesly's Public Relations Handbook, 1971, rev. edit., 1978, 83, 88. Recipient Gold Anvil award Pub. Relations Soc. Am., 1979; voted leading active practitioner Pub. Relations Reporter Survey, 1978. Mem. Pub. Relations Soc. Am., Phi Beta Kappa. Club: Mid-America (Chgo.). Home: 155 Harbor Dr Ste 5311 Chicago IL 60601 Office: 155 Harbor Dr Ste 2201 Chicago IL 60601

LESOK, EDDIE MONROE, lawyer; b. Ft. Worth, Sept. 8, 1948; s. C. Joe and Kathryne Elizabeth (Poulter) L.; m. Janet Small, Nov. 29, 1973. B.B.A., Tex. Tech. U., 1969; J.D., U. Tex., 1971. Bar: Tex. 1971. Atty. Tandy Corp., Ft. Worth, 1972-75; corp. counsel Tandycrafts, Inc., Ft. Worth, 1975-79; exec. v.p., gen. counsel Color Tile, Inc., Fort Worth, 1979-86, chmn. bd. dirs., chief exec. officer, 1986—, also bd. dirs.; Bd. dirs. Tex. Commerce Bank Ft. Worth, Rangaire Corp., Cleburne, Tex. Mem. Am. Bar Assn., Tex. Bar Assn. Republican. Clubs: Colonial Country, Ft. Worth. Office: Color Tile Inc 515 Houston St Fort Worth TX 76102

LESSEM, JAN NORBERT, medical director; b. Malmo, Sweden, Apr. 7, 1948; s. Slom and Frida (Marcus) L.; m. Eva K. Löfquist, July 11, 1976; children: Martin A., Sarah E. MD, U. Lund, 1974, PhD, 1982; AC in Cardiology. Med. diplomate. Intern, then resident in cardiolog; assoc. prof. U. Lund, Sweden, 1981-82; med. dir. Merck, Sharp & Dohme, Rahway, N.J., 1982-83, Bristol-Myers, Evansville, N.D., 1983-85; sect. head cardiology div. Syntex Research, Palo Alto, Calif., 1986-87, sr. dept. head cardiology div., 1987—. Contbr. articles to profl. jours. Fellow Am. Coll. Cardiology, Swedish Soc. Cardiology, Royal Swedish Coll. Med. Jewish. Club: Jewish (Malmo) (pres. 1966-73). Home: 1660 Lloyd Way Mountain View CA 94040 Office: Syntex Rsch 3401 Hillview Ave Palo Alto CA 97303

LESSER, JOSEPH M., business executive, retired retail store executive; b. N.Y.C., July 27, 1928; s. Jacob and Sonia (Gustow) L.; m. Sonia Rabinowitz, Nov. 26, 1948; children: Brett Paul, Peter John. BS in Social Sci., CCNY, 1949; JD, Bklyn. Law Sch., 1953. With Allied Stores Corp., 1955—, personnel and labor relations advisor, 1955-58, dir. cen. services, 1960-68, coordinator control and ops. divs., 1963-65, v.p. control and ops., electronic data processing divs., 1967-80, v.p. food services div., 1967-80, pres. Alcomp Electronic Data Systems div., 1968-75; sr. v.p., exec. group mgr. Allied Stores Corp., N.Y.C., 1980—; dir., sr. v.p. Allied Stores-Penn. Ohio-Inc., N.Y.C., 1981—, Allied Cen. Stores, Inc., N.Y.C., 1984-88; sr. v.p. Allied Stores III, Inc., N.Y.C., 1985-88; dir., exec. v.p. Allied Stores-East, Inc., N.Y.C., 1986-88, ret.; exec. v.p. Internat. Collectibles Inc., 1989—. Pres. Briarcliff Schs., Briarcliff Manor, N.Y., 1973; bd. dirs. North-East Council Schs., N.Y.C., 1967; life trustee Indpls. Mus. Art. Mem. Nat. Retail Mchts. Assn. (bd. dirs. 1977-79), Marco Island Art League, U.S. Power Squadrons, Marco Island Tax Payers Assn., Princeton Club (N.Y.C.), Island Club. Office: 174 S Collier Blvd Ste #202 Marco Island FL 33937

LESTER, JOHN CLAYTON, life insurance company executive; b. Cheyenne, Wyo., Sept. 26, 1940; s. Arthur C. and Harleen E. (Gorman) L.; m. Ruth A. Whatley, Nov. 21, 1959; children: John Clayton, Connie Sue. BBA, Wichita State U., 1965. CLU. Office supr. State Farm Fire & Casualty Co., Greeley, Colo., 1965-69; agt. Equitable Life Assurance Soc., Greeley, 1969-70, from dist. mgr. to agy. mgr., Denver, 1970-78, regional agy. v.p., 1978-84, agy. mgr., Woodland Hills, Calif., 1984—. Served with USN, 1958-61. Mem. Am. Soc. CLU's, San Fernando Valley Life Underwriters, Gen. Agts. and Mgrs. Assn. (past pres. San Fernando Valley chpt.). Republican. Home: 29372 Castlehill Dr Agoura Hills CA 91301 Office: Equitable Life Assurance Soc 21041 Burbank Blvd Ste 200 Woodland Hills CA 91365

LESTER, KATHIANN, media manager; b. Savannah, Ga., Nov. 1, 1957; d. Robert Frederick and Kathryn (McDonald) L. Sec. McCann-Erickson, Inc., Atlanta, 1980, asst. buyer, 1980-81, media buyer, 1981-83, sr. buyer, 1983-85, asst. mgr., 1985-89; buyer, planner Della Femina McNamee, Norcross, Ga., 1989—. Active pub. rels. staff Festival of Trees, Atlanta, 1988. Mem. NAFE. Roman Catholic. Home: 1567 C Loring Dr NW Atlanta GA 30309 Office: Della Femina McNamee IJCRS 5555 Triangle Pkwy Norcross GA 30365

LESTER, WILLIAM WALLACE, financial analyst; b. Seward, Nebr., Jan. 5, 1958; s. Donald Edward and Ruth Elain (Cotton) L.; m. Cynthia Ann Bax, May 24, 1980; children: Nicolle, Brandon, Katherine. BS, U. Nebr., 1980. Rsch. analyst First Mid-Am., Inc., Lincoln, Nebr., 1980-83; securities analyst Bankers Life Nebr., Lincoln, 1983-86; asst. v.p. equity securities Ameritas Investment Advisors, Inc., Lincoln, 1986—. Fellow Life Office Mgmt. Assn., Inc.; mem. Inst. of Fin. Analysts, Omaha-Lincoln Soc. of Fin. Analysts. Office: Ameritas InvestmentAdvisors Inc 210 Gateway Ste 200 Lincoln NE 68505

LESWING, MARK DAVID, investment banker; b. Phila., June 4, 1951; s. Frederick Philip and Shirley (Davis) L.; m. Barbara Casey Donahue, June 18, 1978. BA, Colgate U., 1973; MBA, U. Chgo., 1976. Asst. v.p. Harris Trust and Savs. Bank, Chgo., 1973-78; assoc. The First Boston Corp., N.Y.C., 1978-81; v.p., rep. The First Boston Corp., Tokyo, 1981-83; v.p. The First Boston Corp., N.Y.C., 1984-85; mng. dir. The First Boston Corp., Tokyo, 1986—. Home: 3 5 31 Nishi Azabu Minato Ku, Tokyo 106, Japan Office: First Boston-Japan Ltd, 5 1 Yarakucho 1 chome, Tokyo 100, Japan

LESZAK, JAMES PAUL, maintenance company executive; b. Lackawanna, N.Y., July 26, 1960; s. John J. and Sonia Judith (Wieczorek) L.; m. Charlene Emilie Voelker, Oct. 18, 1986; children: Kara Kristin, James West. BA, Canisius Coll., 1981. Salesman Town Insulation, Amherst, N.Y., 1982-83, Sears, Amherst, 1983-84; pres., owner Direct Home Maintenance of Western N.Y., Inc., Buffalo, 1984—. Mem. Home Improvement Industry Council, Buffalo, Nat. Rep. Com., Washington. Recipient Certs. of Recognition Home Improvement Industry Council, 1984. Mem. Better Bus. Bur., Nat. Remodelers Assn., South Buffalo Businessmen, Greater Buffalo C. of C. Roman Catholic. Office: Direct Home Maintenance Western NY Inc 372 Downing St Buffalo NY 14220

LETSON, JOHNNY LEE, accountant, real estate broker; b. Moulton, Ala., Jan. 7, 1949; s. Omer Henderson Letson and Ida Melinda Sally Jane (Terry) Heflin; m. Brenda Gail Faucett, Oct. 13, 1967 (div. Aug. 1971); children: Donny Lee and Jonny Leon (twins); m. Dany Lidy Libeau, Dec. 1971 (div. 1972); m. Laura May Savery, Dec. 1973 (div. Jan. 1983); m. Barbara Gail Moody, Mar. 28, 1983; children: Chastity Nicole, Sir Waylon Gentry, Heather Elizabeth, Randel Early. AA in Pre-Law, John C. Calhoun Coll., 1977; BS in Pre-Law, Athens (Ala.) State Coll., 1980; postgrad. in taxation, Washington Coll. of Law, Salt Lake City. Franchise owner H&R Block, Moulton, 1975-80; pres., owner John Letson-Acct. (subs. Letson & Letson Entrepreneurs Co., Inc.), Moulton, Ala., 1978—, Twin Real Estate (subs. Letson & Letson Entrepreneurs Co., Inc.), Moulton, 1980—. Mem. Moulton Jaycees (treas. 1977), Am. Legion, VFW, Civitan. Served as sgt., U.S. Army, 1968-71, Vietnam. Democrat. Methodist. Home: 20302 Hwy 33 Moulton AL 35650 Office: 20304 AL Hwy 33 Moulton AL 35650

LETT, THOMAS PATRICK, lamp manufacturing company executive; b. Cin., Aug. 20, 1948; s. Thomas James and Marianne (Howard) L. BS, Boston State Coll., 1976. Sr. technician Sherwin-Williams REsearch, Chgo., 1970-71; assembly technician Thermo-Electron Corp., Waltham, Mass., 1971-72; material foreman Vaco Products Co., Jonesville, Mich., 1976-78; planning supr. G&W Electric Specialty Co., Blue Island, Ill., 1978-80; ind. mgmt. cons. Chgo. and Milw., 1980-82; sr. planner Quality Control Corp., Chgo., 1982-84; sr. scheduler Hermetic Seal Corp., Rosemead, Calif., 1984-85; gen. mgr. Jenkins Ceramic Lamps Inc., Pacoima, Calif., 1985-88; ops. mgr. Toyo Trading Co., Los Angeles, 1988—. Inventor universal lampshade master-pattern fixture. Mem. Am. Mgmt. Assn. Roman Catholic. Office: Toyo Trading Co 13000 S Spring St Los Angeles CA 90061

LETTMANN, JOHN WILLIAM, cereal manufacturing company executive; b. St. Louis, July 5, 1942; s. Henry William and Josephine (Randazzo) L.; m. Vicky Hodges; children: Susan, Jason, Michael. BSBA, U. Kans., 1964; MBA, Ind. U., 1968. Sr. auditor Gen. Mills, Inc., Mpls., 1964-66, with product mgmt. dept., 1968-71; v.p. mktg. and sales Malt-O-Meal Co., Mpls., 1971-85, pres., chief exec. officer, 1985—; bd. dirs. Tech. 80, Inc., Mpls. Recipient Leadership award Bush Found., 1969. Mem. Am. Mgmt. Assn. (council 1987—), Grocery Mfrs. Assn., Mpls. Athletic Club, Interlachen Country Club. Office: Malt-O-Meal Co 2601 IDS Tower Minneapolis MN 55402

LETTOW, CHARLES FREDERICK, lawyer; b. Iowa Falls, Iowa, Feb. 10, 1941; s. Carl Frederick and Catherine (Reisinger) L.; m. Sue Lettow, Apr. 20, 1963; children: Renee, Carl II, John, Paul. BS in Chem. Engring., Iowa State U., 1962; LLB, Stanford U., 1968. Bar: Calif. 1969, Iowa 1969, D.C. 1972. Law clk. to Judge Ben C. Duniway U.S. Ct. Appeals (9th cir.), San Francisco, 1968-69; law clk. to Chief Justice Warren E. Burger U.S. Supreme Ct., Washington, 1969-70; counsel Council on Environ. Quality, Washington, 1970-73; assoc. Cleary, Gottlieb, Steen & Hamilton, Washington, 1973-76, ptnr., 1976—. Contbr. articles to profl. jours. Trustee Potomac Sch., McLean, Va., 1983—, chmn. bd. trustees., 1985-88. 1st lt. U.S. Army, 1963-65. Mem. ABA, D.C. Bar Assn., Iowa Bar Assn., Order of Coif. Republican. Lutheran. Club: International (Washington). Office: Cleary Gottlieb Steen & Hamilton 1752 N St NW Washington DC 20036

LEUBERT, ALFRED OTTO PAUL, international business executive; b. N.Y.C., Dec. 7, 1922; s. Paul T. and Josephine (Haaga) L.; m. Celestine Capka, July 22, 1944 (div. 1977); children: Eloise Ann (Mrs. Kevin B. Cronin), Susan Beth (Mrs. Stephen E. Melvin); m. Hope Sherman Drapkin, June 4, 1978 (div. 1982). Student, Dartmouth Coll., 1943; B.S., Fordham U., 1946; M.B.A., N.Y. U., 1950. Account mgr. J.K. Lasser & Co., N.Y.C., 1948-52; controller Vision, Inc., N.Y.C., 1952-53; with Old Town Corp., 1953-58, controller, 1953-54, sec., controller, 1954-56, sec.-treas., 1956-57, v.p., treas., 1957-58; dir. subsidiaries Old Town Corp. (Old Town Internat. Corp., Old Town Ribbon & Carbon Co., Inc.), Mass. and Calif., 1955-58; v.p., controller Willcox & Gibbs, Inc., N.Y.C., 1958-59; v.p., treas. Willcox & Gibbs, Inc., 1959-65, pres., dir., chief exec. officer, 1966-76; founder, pub., pres. Leubert's Compendium of Bus. (Fin. and Econ. Barometers), 1978—; pres. Alfred O.P. Leubert Ltd., 1981-82; chmn., chief exec. officer Solidyne, Inc., 1982; chmn. bd., pres., chief exec. officer, dir. Chyron Corp., 1983—; chmn. bd., chief exec. officer, bd. dirs. Chyron Group (U.K.) Ltd., 1985—, CMX Corp.; chmn. bd., chief exec officer, dir. CGS Units Inc.,1988—; bd. dirs., Digital Svcs. Corp.; vice chmn. bd. dirs. CMX Laser Systems, Inc.; instr. accountancy Pace Coll., 1955-57. Bd. dirs. United Fund of Manhasset, 1963-69, pres., 1964-65; bd. dirs. Actor's Studio, 1972-76; adv. bd. St. Anthony's Guidance Clinic, 1967-69. Served to 1st lt., inf. USMCR, 1943-46. Decorated Bronze Star; recipient Humanitarian award Hebrew Acad., N.Y.C., 1971. Mem. AICPA, N.Y. State Soc. CPAs, Fordham U. Alumni Assn., Newcomen Soc. N.Am. Roman Catholic. Club: N.Y. Athletic (N.Y.C.). Home: 1 Lincoln Pla New York NY 10023 Office: 265 Spagnoli St Melville NY 11747

LEUM, LEONARD, wholesale grocery company executive. Chmn. bd. dirs. Cert. Grocers of Calif., Ltd., Los Angeles. Office: Cert Grocers Calif Ltd 2601 S Eastern Ave Los Angeles CA 90040 *

LEUNG, IDA MARIE, financial planning company executive; b. Oakland, Calif., Dec. 29, 1951; d. Fook and Yook Moon (Moy) L.; m. Francis Le B. Montgomery, Jan. 1982; 1 child, Sarah. BA, Barnard Coll., 1974; postgrad. Sch. Advanced Internat. Studies, Johns Hopkins U., 1974-75; postgrad., NYU, 1975-78. Cert. fin. planner. Asst. v.p. internat. lending Mfrs. Hanover Trust Co., N.Y.C., 1977-86, mgr. market rsch., 1986-88; fin. planner IDS Fin. Svcs., Poughkeepsie, N.Y., 1988—. Affirmative action chmn. Nat. Women's Polit. Caucus, Washington, 1985-87; pres. Asian Women's Polit. Caucus, N.Y.C., 1987-88. Mem. Internat. Assn. Fin. Planners, Inst. Cert. Fin. Planners, Asian Am. Profl. Women (pres. N.Y.C., 1986-87), Bus. and Profl. Women's Club, Lions. Democrat. Office: IDS Fin Svcs 63 Washington St Poughkeepsie NY 12601

LEUTE, WILLIAM RUSSELL, III, bank executive; b. Phila., Oct. 27, 1945; s. William Russell Jr. and Maverne (Muffitt) L.; m. Landa Braggiotti, June 26, 1976; children: William, Alexander Chadwick. BA in Fin., Lehigh U., 1967; MBA in Internat. Fin., Columbia U., 1971. With internat. div. Irving Trust Co., N.Y.C., 1971-77; regional rep. Irving Trust Co., Paris, 1978-82; exec. v.p., chief operating officer Midland Internat. Trade Services, N.Y.C., 1983—. With U.S. Army, 1969-70, Vietnam. Republican. Episcopalian. Home: 92 Mallard Dr Greenwich CT 06803 Office: Midland Internat Trade Svcs Corp 560 Lexington Ave 11th Fl New York NY 10022

LEVA, JAMES ROBERT, electric utility company executive; b. Boonton, N.J., May 10, 1932; s. James and Rose (Cocci) L.; m. Marie Marinaro, Dec. 19, 1950; children: James, Daniel, Linda, Michael, Christopher. BSEE, magna cum laude, Fairleigh Dickinson U., 1960; JD, Seton Hall Law Sch., 1980. Lineman Jersey Central Power and Light Co., Morristown, N.J., 1952-60, elec. engring. and operating depts., 1960-62, personnel rep., 1962-68, mgr. employee relations, 1968-69, v.p. personnel and services, 1969-79, v.p. consumer affairs, 1979-82, dir., 1976-82; pres., chief operating officer, dir. Pa. Electric Co., Johnstown, 1982-86; pres., chief operating officer Jersey Cen. Power & Light Co., Morristown, N.J., 1986—, also bd. dirs.; bd. dirs. GPU Service Corp., Parsippany, N.J., GPU Nuclear Corp., Parsippany, Utilities Mut. Ins. Co., N.J. Utilities Assn., United Way Morris County, Morris County C. of C., St. Clares Health Care Found.; trustee Tri-County Scholarship Fund and St. Barnabas Burn Found. Served with USMC, 1949-51, Korea. Mem. ABA, N.J. Bar, N.J. Bar Assn. Roman Catholic. Club: Mendham (N.J.) Golf & Tennis. Office: Jersey Cen Power & Light Co Madison Ave at Punch Bowl Rd Morristown NJ 07960

LE VAN, DANIEL HAYDEN, business executive; b. Savannah, Ga., Mar. 29, 1924; s. Daniel Hayden and Ruth (Harner) LeV.; grad. Middlesex Sch., 1943; B.A., Harvard U., 1950; student Babson Inst., 1950-51. Underwriter Zurich Ins. Co., N.Y.C., 1951-52; co-owner, dir. Overseas Properties, Ltd., N.Y.C.; dir. Colonial Gas Co. Served with AUS, 1943-46. Clubs: Harvard (N.Y.C.); Harvard (Boston).

LEVBARG, DIANE, fashion industry executive; b. Mar, 18, 1950; d. Morrison Levbarg and Ann-Louise Lewis; m. Martin I. Klein, May 23, 1974. Cert. in retail studies Coll. for Distributive Trades, London; student Vassar Coll., 1972. Exec. Trainee Harrods, London, 1970-71; exec. trainee, asst. dept. mgr., asst. buyer Saks Fifth Ave, N.Y.C., 1971-73; asst. buyer, buyer Bonwit Teller, N.Y.C., 1973-75; merchandise mgr. Bloomingdale's, N.Y.C., 1975-82; pres., fashion cons. Diane Levbarg & Assocs. Inc., N.Y.C., 1982—; exec. v.p. Missoni U.S.A.; v.p. Nina Ricci; cons. Daniel Hechter, Christian Dior U.S.A., Bogner U.S.A.; adv. bd. Lab Inst. of Mdsing. V.P., James Beard Affiliate, City Meals-on-Wheels. Named One of 100 Women of Promise, Good Housekeeping. Address: 200 E 72d St New York NY 10021

LEVEL, LEON JULES, information services executive; b. Detroit, Dec. 30, 1940; s. Leon and Madeline G. (Mayea) L.; m. Constance Kramer, June 25, 1966; children—Andrea, Aileen. B.B.A., U. Mich., 1962, M.B.A., 1963. CPA, Mich. Asst. accountant Deloitte Haskins & Sells, Detroit, 1963-66, sr. accountant, 1966-69, prin., 1969-71; asst. corp. controller Bendix Corp., Southfield, Mich., 1971-81; v.p. fin. planning Burroughs Corp., Detroit, 1981-82, v.p., treas., 1982-86; v.p., treas. Unisys Corp., Blue Bell, Pa., 1986—; mem. U. Mich. adv. bd., Ann Arbor, 1984—, Providence Hosp. Adv. Bd., Southfield, Mich., 1984-86, Allendale Ins. Adv. Bd., Cleve., 1985—. mem. adv. bd. U. Mich., 1984—, Providence Hosp., Southfield, Mich., 1984-86; trustee Walnut St. Theatre, Phila., 1988—. Mem. Fin. Execs. Inst. (sec. Detroit chpt. 1983-85, v.p. 1985-86, pres. 1986-87), Am. Inst. C.P.A.s, Mich. Assn. C.P.A.s, Nat. Assn. Accts. Office: Unisys Corp PO Box 500 Blue Bell PA 19424

LEVENDECKER, ROBERT GREG, banker; b. Clayton, N.Mex., Jan. 3, 1951; s. Claude E. and Jo (Shubert) L.; m. Georgetta Marston, Feb. 21, 1976; children: Kyle J., Tyson J. BSBA, U. Ark., 1973. Sr. v.p. United N.Mex. Bank at Albuquerque, 1980—. Bd. dirs. Spl. Olympics, N.Mex., 1988, Downtown Neighborhood Housing Assn., Albuquerque, 1987. Mem. N.Mex. Homebuilders Assn. Office: United NMex Bank PO Box 1081 200 Lomas Albuquerque NM 87103

LEVENSON, ALAN BRADLEY, lawyer; b. Long Beach, N.Y., Dec. 13, 1935; s. Cyrus O. and Jean (Kotler) L.; m. Joan Marlene Levenson, Aug. 19, 1956; children—Scott Keith, Julie Jo. A.B., Dartmouth Coll., 1956; B.A., Oxford U., Eng., 1958, M.A., 1962; LL.B., Yale U., 1961. Bar: N.Y. 1962, U.S. Dist. Ct. D.C. 1964, U.S. Ct. Appeals (D.C. cir.) 1965, U.S. Supreme Ct. 1965. Law clk., trainee div. corp. fin. SEC, Washington, 1961-62, gen. atty., 1962, trial atty., 1963, br. chief, 1963-65, asst. dir., 1965-68, exec. asst. dir., 1968, dir., 1970-76; v.p. Shareholders Mgmt. Co., Los Angeles, 1969, sr. v.p., 1969-70, exec. v.p., 1970; ptnr. Fulbright & Jaworski, Washington, 1976—; lectr. Cath. U. Am., 1964-68, Columbia U., 1973; adj. prof. Georgetown U., 1964, 77, 79-81, U.S. rep. working party OECD, Paris, 1974-75; adv. com. SEC, 1976-77; mem. adv. bd. Securities Regulation Inst., U. Calif.-San Diego, 1975—, vice chmn. exec. com., 1979-83, chmn., 1984-88, emeritus chmn., 1988—; mem. adv. council SEC Inst., U. So. Calif., Los Angeles, Sch. Acctg., 1981-85; mem. adv. com. Nat. Ctr. Fin. Services, U. Calif.-Berkeley, 1985—; mem. planning com. Ray Garrett Annual Securities Regulation Inst. Northwestern U. Law Sch.; mem. adv. panel to U.S. Comptroller-Gen. on stock market decline, 1987, panel of cons., 1989—. Mem. bd. editorial advisors U. Iowa Jour. Corp. Law, 1978—; Bur. Nat. Affairs adv. bd. Securities Regulation and Law Report, 1976—; bd. editors N.Y. Law Jour., 1976—; bd. advisors, corp. and securities law advisor Prentice Hall Law & Bus.; contbr. articles to profl. jours.; mem. adv. bd. Banking Expansion Reporter. Recipient Disting. Service award SEC, 1972; James B. Richardson fellow Oxford U., 1956. Mem. ABA (exec. com., fed. regulatory securities com., former chair subcom. on securities activities banks), Fed. Bar Assn. (emeritus mem. exec. com. securities law com.), Am. Law Inst., Practicing Law Inst. (nat. adv. com. 1974), Am. Inst. CPA's (pub. dir., bd. dirs. 1983—, fin. com. 1984—, chmn. adv. council auditing standards bd. 1979-80, future issues com. 1982-85), Nat. Assn. Securities Dealers (corp. fin. com. 1981-87, nat. arbitration com. 1983-87, gov.-at-large, bd. govs. 1984-87, exec. com. 1986-87, long range planning com. 1987—, chmn. legal adv. com. 1988—), numerous adv. coms. Home: 12512 Exchange Ct S Potomac MD 20854 Office: Fulbright & Jaworski 1150 Connecticut Ave NW Washington DC 20036

LEVENSON, RICHARD NEIL, advertising executive; b. Bklyn., Apr. 14, 1942; s. Harry Jack and Mollye (Simon) L.; m. Toby Ann Nadler, June 18, 1966; children: Alexander, Simon. BFA, Pratt Inst., 1963. Art dir. Warren, Muller, Dolobowsky, N.Y.C., 1966-67; art dir., supr. Grey, N.Y.C., 1967-70; assoc. creative dir. Daniel & Charles, N.Y.C., 1970-71; assoc. creative Kenyon & Eckhart, N.Y.C., 1971-77; group creative dir. Benton & Bowles, N.Y.C., 1977-84; exec. creative dir. D'Arcy, Masius, Benton & Bowles, Inc., N.Y.C., 1984—, dep. mng. dir. N.Y. office, 1987—, also bd. dirs.; mem. creative com. 4As, also mem. creative rev. com. 4As. Bd. dirs. Samaritan Found., Queens, N.Y., 1977—, Ellis Island Restoration Com., 1988. Recipient Clio awards, Cannes Film Festival Lion award, Andy awards. Democrat. Office: D'Arcy Masius Benton & Bowles Inc 909 3rd Ave New York NY 10022

LEVENSON, ROBERT HAROLD, advertising agency executive; b. Bronx, N.Y., Nov. 23, 1929; s. William and Frieda L.; m. Kathe Tanous, Dec. 31, 1975; children—Keith, Seth. B.A., N.Y. U., 1950, M.A., 1951. Copywriter Doyle Dane Bernbach Internat. Inc., N.Y.C., 1959-68, copy chief, sr. v.p., 1968-72, exec. v.p. creative, 1972-74, vice chmn. creative, 1974-85, also dir., 1970-85; vice chmn., chief creative officer Saatchi & Saatchi Compton Inc., N.Y.C., 1985-87; vice chmn., creative dir. Scali, McCabe, Sloves, Inc., N.Y.C., 1987—. Served as 1st lt. USAF, 1954-56. Elected to Copywriters Hall of Fame, 1972. Office: Scali McCabe Sloves Inc 800 Third Ave New York NY 10022

LEVENSON, ROBERT J., data processing executive; b. Detroit, June 17, 1941; s. Edward S. Levenson and Lois (Burnstine) Hoffman; m. Mira Mann, Nov. 1988; children from previous marriage: Elizabeth, Sarah. BS, Kent State U., 1963—. Staff acct. Deloitte, Haskins & Sells, 1963-64; mktg. rep. IBM Corp., 1964-66; exec. v.p. Cen. Data Systems Inc., 1966-75, also bd. dirs.; group v.p. data services group, pres. data processing div. Itel Corp., 1975-80; sr. v.p. Exxon Enterprises/Delphi Communications, 1980-81; v.p. bus. planning employer svcs. Automatic Data Processing Inc., Roseland, N.J., 1981-82, pres. midatlantic div., 1982, pres. ea. div., 1982-84, v.p. employer svcs., 1984, group pres. employer svcs. group, corp. v.p., 1984-88, group pres. specialized svcs., 1988—, also bd. dirs. Office: ADP Inc One ADP Blvd Roseland NJ 07068

LEVENTHAL, RICHARD CHARLES, marketing educator; b. Bklyn., June 20, 1943; s. Harry and Rose (Smith) L.; m. Lynn Marie Crandell, Aug. 11, 1975. BS, Cornell U., 1966; MBA, San Francisco State U., 1972; PhD, U. Denver, 1978. Sales, mktg. mgr. Scott Paper Co., Phila., 1966-67, 71-72, Syntex Dental Mfg. Co., Valley Forge, Pa., 1972-76; prof. mktg. Met. State Coll., Denver, 1977—; pres. Leventhal Rsch., Inc., Evergreen, Colo., 1977—. Author: Principle of Marketing , 1985, Marketing by Mandel, 1985, Marketing by Kotler, 1986; author-editor: Readings in Sales Management, 1983, Reading in Retail Management, 1983; mem. editorial bd. Jour. Consumer Mktg. Jour. Bus. & Indsl. Mktg., Journ. Svcs. Mktg., Jour. Managerial Issues, Sales & Mktg. Mgmt.; contbr. articles to profl. jours. Pres. bd. trustees Double D Manor, Evergreen, Colo.; bd. dirs. Cen. Agy. Jewish Edn., Denver, 1984—, Auraria Faculty Club, Denver. Served with USN, 1967-71. Mem. Am. Mktg. Assn., Assn. Instl. Rsch., So. Mktg. Assn., Southwestern Mktg. Assn., Am. Assn. Higher Edn., Am. Soc. Aging, Am. Gerontol. Soc., Mt. Vernon Country Club. Jewish. Home: 7744 Native Dancer Trail Evergreen CO 89439 Office: Met State Coll PO Box 13 1006 11th ST Denver CO 80204

LEVERETT, RONALD HENRY, accountant; b. Seattle, Jan. 6, 1937; s. Ulysses Harrison and Beatrice (Smith) L.; m. Deborah F. Saunders, June 1969 (div. 1976); m. Doris M. Watkins, Dec. 1, 1977; children: Stephen, Robert, Bernadette, John, Robyn, Mark. BS, Portland State Coll., 1964; MBA, U. Oreg., 1972. Tchr. Portland (Oreg.) Pub. Schs., 1965-68; mgr. Albania Corp., Portland, 1968-69; prof. Seattle Community Coll., 1972-73, 77-80; exec. dir. Econ. Resources Devel. Co., Seattle, 1973-76, 82—; auditor Touche Ross & Co., Seattle, 1980-81; acct. Reed Peoples & Co., Seattle, 1985—; lectr. in field. Contbr. articles to profl. jours. Mem. Afro-Am. com. Am. Bicentennial Presdl. Inaugural; mem. Lake Washington Affirmative Action Com., Redmond, 1976-80; bd. dirs. Seattle YMCA, 1980-85, Project Vote, Washington, 1988—. With U.S. Army, 1959-61. Named honoree, Nat. Coun. Negro Women, Inc. and Seattle Times; U. Oreg. MBA fellow, 1969-72. Mem. Nat. Assn. Black Accts. (regional v.p. 1981-84, nat. pres. 1987-88, Disting. Svc. award 1984), Washington Soc. CPAs (mem. com. 1979—), Nat. Assn. Accts., Am. Acctg. Assn., Minority Enterprise Small Bus. Investment Corp. (bd. dirs. 1976-80), Seattle C. of C. (bd. dirs. Leadership of Tomorrow 1988—), Variety Club (mayor's VIP panelist Pacific N.W. chpt.), Kappa Alpha Psi (chpt. pres.), Beta Alpha Psi (bd. dirs. 1988—). Democrat. Baptist. Home: 2222 Sahalee Dr E Redmond WA 98053 Office: Reed Peoples & Co 2301 S Jackson Ste 104 Seattle WA 98144

LEVETOWN, ROBERT ALEXANDER, lawyer; b. Bklyn., July 20, 1935; s. Alfred A. and Corinne L. (Cohen) L.; m. Roberta S. Slobodkin, Oct. 18, 1959. Student, U. Munich, Fed. Republic Germany, 1954-55; AB, Princeton U., 1956; LLB, Harvard U., 1959. Bar: D.C. 1960, N.Y. 1982, Va. 1984, Pa. 1985. Assoc. Pierson, Ball & Dowd, Washington, 1960-62; asst. U.S. atty. Washington, 1962-63; atty. Chesapeake & Potomac Telephone Cos., Washington, 1963-66, gen. atty., 1966-68, gen. solicitor, 1968-73, v.p., gen. counsel, 1975-83; exec. v.p., gen. counsel Bell Atlantic, 1983—, also bd. dirs. Mem. Washington Met. Corp. Counsels' Assn. (bd. dirs. 1981-83), Nat. Legal Ctr. (legal adv. coun. 1986—), ABA (vice chmn. communications com., pub. utility law sect. 1986—). Republican. Jewish. Office: Bell Atlantic Corp 1310 N Court House Rd Arlington VA 22201

LEVEY, PAUL ALBERT, public relations executive; b. Boston, Oct. 22, 1939; s. Albert Jerome and Lillian Blanche (Leate) L.; m. Judith Ann Caron, Oct. 19, 1963; children: Cynthia Ann, Wayne Albert. BS, Northeastern U., 1972, MBA, 1976. Asst. dir. sales promotion Loyal Protective Life Ins. Co., Boston, 1958-66; editor sales publs. Comml. Union Ins. Cos., Boston, 1966-68; mng. editor Northeast Elec. News, Inc., Newton, Mass., 1968-71; v.p. mktg. Prospector Rsch. Svcs., Inc., Waltham, Mass., 1971-76; mktg. mgr. Stonemarketing Corp., Cambridge, Mass., 1976-79; product mgr. Nat. Liberty Corp., Valley Forge, Pa., 1979-82; prin., cons. PAL Assocs., King of

Prussia, Pa., 1982-85; mgr. publs. Subaru Am., Cherry Hill, N.J., 1985—; cons. Lafayette Ambulance Squad, King of Prussia, 1988; mem. curriculum adv. com. Northeastern U., Boston, 1971-73. Author numerous articles to profl. jours. and mags. Staff sgt. USAFR, 1961-67. Mem. Internat. Assn. Bus. Communicators (membership chmn. Phila. chpt. 1986-88, mem. exec. bd., treas. Phila. chpt. 1988—, chmn. U.S. Dist. 1 1988—, EPIC award 1987). Democrat. Congregationalist. Office: Subaru Am Subaru Plaza RR 70 E Cherry Hill NJ 08034

LEVI, KURT, retired banker; b. Wiesbaden, Germany, May 20, 1910; came to U.S., 1937, naturalized, 1942; s. Josef and Martha (Kahn) L.; m. Ruth Neumann, Feb. 17, 1938; 1 son, Peter. LL.B., U. Frankfurt, Germany, 1931. Mdse. mgr. Consol. Retail Stores, Kansas City, Mo., 1937-55; with United Mo. Bank, Kansas City, 1956-80; sr. v.p. United Mo. Bank, 1971-80, Traders Bank, Kansas City, 1980-85; adj. prof. Park Coll., Parkville, Mo., 1985—. Gen. and area chmn. Kansas City (Mo.) United campaign, 1962; chmn. finance com. Camp Fire Girls Am., 1964; chmn. Kansas City Mayor's Prayer Breakfast Club, 1968; gen. chmn. Greater Kansas City Bonds for Israel, 1959; chmn. Greater Kansas City Conf. Soviet Jewry, 1966; vice chmn., mem. exec. bd. Community Relations Bur., 1972; pres. Heart Am. chpt., Religious Zionists Am., 1971; bd. govs. Jewish Fedn. and Council Kansas City, 1972-88, div. chmn. Fedn. campaign, 1986; bd. govs. Kansas City chpt. Am. Jewish Com., nat. bd. dirs.; pres., chmn. bd. Kehilath Israel Synagogue, lifetime hon. Gabbi; bd. govs., ombudsman Temple Sholom, Pompano Beach, Fla., 1988—. Mem. Kansas City C. of C., B'nai B'rith (dist. pres. 1975-76, exec. v.p., bd. govs. Kol Haverim lodge Ft. Lauderdale, Fla. 1988), Kiwanis (v.p. Kansas City Downtown club 1955), Playa Del Sol Social Club (pres. 1989—), Legion of Honor. Home: 3500 Galt Ocean Dr Apt 2405 Fort Lauderdale FL 33308 also: The Sulgrave Apt 1205 121 W 48th St Kansas City MO 64112

LEVIANT, JACQUES, chemical company executive; b. Russia, Oct. 22, 1921; s. Kalman and Riva Leviant; student Lycee Claude Bernard, Paris, Toulouse (France) U.; B.S.B.A., Columbia U., 1944; m. Dolores Smithies, June 8, 1976; 1 son, Alexandre Jacques. Pres., Alloychem, Inc., N.Y.C., ICD Group, Inc., N.Y.C. Mem. Drug, Chem. and Allied Trades Assn., N.E. Petrochem. Assn., others. Trustee St. David's Sch. Club: Meadow (Southampton). Home: 895 Park Ave New York NY 10021 Office: 641 Lexington Ave New York NY 10022

LEVIN, BARTON JOHN, aviation products and services company executive; b. Sioux Falls, S.D., Mar. 3, 1944; s. Arthur Harold Levin and Shirley Thelma (Yonover) Osborn; m. Nancy Ellen MacDonald, Mar. 3, 1972; children—Meredith Ellen, Andrew David. A.B. in Econ., U. Calif., Berkeley, 1965; M.B.A., U. Chgo., 1969. C.P.A., Ill. Exec. Santa Fe Ry. Co., Chgo., 1968-71, 72-78; presdl. interchange exec. U.S. Dept. Transp., Washington, 1971-72; exec. AAR Corp., Elk Grove Village, Ill., 1978-79, v.p., 1979-85, pres., chief operating officer, 1985-89; pres., chief exec. officer Grabill Corp., Oak Forest, Ill., 1989—; dir. AAR Corp., Elk Grove Village. Mem. Ill. Mfrs. Assn. (bd. dirs. 1985-88). Club: Economic (Chgo.). Office: Grabill Corp 15000 Cicero Ave Oak Forest IL 60452

LEVIN, BRUCE ALAN, lawyer, real estate developer; b. Jersey City, Sept. 5, 1939; s. Julius and Toby (Sand) L.; m. Ann Singley, June 1963 (div. Sept. 1967); 1 child, Peter; m. Pamela Jo Dillow, Dec. 23, 1975; children: Sean, Brett, Annalee. Student, Rutgers U., 1957-58; BS in Econs., U. Pa., 1961; JD, Harvard U., 1964. Bar: Calif. 1965, Oreg. 1978, Nev. 1980. Ptnr. Glaser & Levin, L.A., 1968-70, Levin, Saphier & Rein, L.A., 1970-76, Kralow Levin Co., Irvine, Calif., 1976—; v.p., gen. counsel, asst. sec. Golden Nugget, Inc., Las Vegas, 1979—; ptnr. D&L Devel. Co., Las Vegas, 1984. Co-founder, trustee Meadows Sch., Las Vegas, 1984. Mem. Nev. Bar Assn., Oreg. Bar Assn., Calif. Bar Assn. Office: Golden Nugget Inc 129 E Fremont St Las Vegas NV 89101

LEVIN, DAVID MARSHALL, oil industry executive; b. Midland, Tex., Feb. 3, 1954; s. Max and Frances Pearl (Kornblatt) L.; m. Betsy Sue Landsman, Oct. 24, 1981; 1 child, Mark Blair. BS in Geology, U. Tex., 1978; MS in Geology, Albert-Ludwigs U., Freiburg, German Democratic Republic, 1979. Cert. petroleum geologist. Exploration geologist Gulf Oil Corp., Houston, 1978-81, Retamco, Inc., San Antonio, 1981-82; pres. Levin Cons., San Antonio, 1982—, DML Exploration, Inc., San Antonio, 1985—; lectr. Gulf Coast Assn. Geol. Socs., 1983. Contbr. articles to industry publs. Bd. dirs. Jewish Day Sch., San Antonio, 1984-86, Friends of Mc-Nay Mus., San Antonio, 1987. Recipient Cities Service scholarship U. Tex., 1977; Fulbright fellow, 1978-79. Mem. Am. Assn. Petroleum Geologists, So. Tex. Geol. Soc. (asst. editor bull. 1988), San Antonio Assn. Petroleum Landmen, San Antonio Geophys. Soc., Rotary. Democrat. Office: DML Exploration Inc D-408 Petroleum Ctr San Antonio TX 78209

LEVIN, DONALD ROBERT, business and finance executive, motion picture producer; b. Chgo., Oct. 17, 1947; s. Jack Levin and Henrietta (Wolf) Berman. Student pub. schs., Chgo.; m. Kathleen Ann. Pres., Adams Apple Distbg. Co., Chgo., 1969-82, Republic Tobacco, Inc., Chgo., 1982—, D.R.L. Mgmt. Services, Chgo., 1982—; chief exec. officer Adams Apple Film Co., Chgo., 1982—; pres. Top Tobacco Co.; bd. dirs. Scentex Inc., Chgo., Alma Leo USA Co., Republic Entertainment Internat., Chgo., Dr. Levin Family Found. With USMCR, 1965-71. Mem. Nat. Assn. Tobacco Distbrs., Nat. Candy Wholesalers Assn., So. Candy and Tobacco Assn. Jewish. Home: 1196 Oxford Ct Highland Park IL 60635 Office: DRL Mgmt Svcs Inc 5100 N Ravenswood Chicago IL 60640

LEVIN, EDGAR WILLIAM, diversified company executive, marketing educator; b. N.Y.C., Mar. 19, 1932; s. Herman and Frances (Kurland) L.; m. Carole Cynthia Citron, Apr. 3, 1955; children: Randi Sue, Gregg Steven. BA, NYU, 1953; MBA, L.I. U., 1968. Salesman Leigh Assocs., N.Y.C., 1953-54; mgr. statis. unit Am. Assn. Advt. Agys., N.Y.C., 1955-57; market research mgr. Nat. Assn. Elec. Mfrs., N.Y.C., 1958-60; mktg. mgr. Perkin Elmer-Metco div., N.Y.C., 1961-66, Inter-Royal Corp., N.Y.C., 1966-69; sr. v.p. Gulf Western Inc., N.Y.C., 1969—; lectr. Conf. Bd., Am. Mktg. Assn., Nat. Investor Relations Inst., various univs. V.p. Merrick (N.Y.) Rep. Club, 1984—. Served as cpl. U.S. Army, 1953-55. Recipient Humanitarian award Nat. Kidney Found., 1985. Mem. Am. Mktg. Assn., Internat. Execs. Assn., World Trade Club, Bus. Week Corp. Planning 100. Club: Republican (Merrick, N.Y.) (v.p. 1984—). Home: 2123 Beverly Way Merrick NY 11566 Office: Gulf and Western Inc 1 Gulf and Western Pla New York NY 10023-7780

LEVIN, HARVEY JAY, financial institutions facilities consultant, developer; b. Fitchburg, Mass., Apr. 27, 1936; s. Abe and Ila (Friedman) L.; m. Eleanor Soble, June 7, 1959 (div. 1964); 1 dau., Kimberly; m. Patricia Mary Carbino, Feb. 20, 1966; children—Tara, Robin, Vanessa. Student Brandeis U., Boston U., U. Md.; B.B.A. in Fin., U. Mass., 1960; M.A. in Econs., U. N.H., 1970. Lic. real estate broker, Mass., N.H.; lic. comml. pilot. Pres. Central Tool Warehouse, Leominster, Mass., 1959-66; dir. mktg. and sales Spacemakers, Canton, Mass., 1970-72, New Eng. Homes, Biddeford, Maine, 1973-74; gen. mgr. Great No. Homes, Boston, 1966-70; cons. service mgr. Bank Bldg. Corp., St. Louis, 1974-80; v.p. Shelter Resources, Birmingham, Ala., 1972-73; v.p. Fin. Concepts, Natick, Mass., 1980-85; pres. Am. Bank Design, Inc., and Credit Union Bldg. Corp., Exeter, N.H.; cons. Republic Homes, Truro, Can., 1974, Wasco Mfg. Co., Sanford, Maine, 1975. Chmn. sch. bldg. com. Kensington, N.H., 1985; mem. Lake Sunapee Protective Assn., N.H., 1968—. Served with U.S. Army, 1955-57. Recipient Award of Honor, Bank Bldg. Corp. of Am., 1976, 1st Place Design award Bank Bldg. Corp. of Am., 1977, Best Mktg. and Sales Plan award Automation in Housing Assn., 1972, FMHA award for Best Elderly Housing Project; named Hon. Lt. Col. Aide-de-Camp by Gov. of Ala., 1978. Mem. Aircraft Owners and Pilots Assn., Phi Sigma Kappa. Clubs: The River (Kennebunkport, Maine); Hampton River Boat, Portsmouth Power Squadron. Lodge: Masons. Avocations: skiing, tennis, flying, boating.

LEVIN, HOWARD S., company executive; b. Chgo., Feb. 16, 1924; s. Harry and Sara (Pease) L.; children—Janet Levin Rudolph, Wendy. B.S., U. Chgo., 1946. Instr. math. U. Ill., 1946-48; asst. in math. Ill. Inst. Tech., 1949-50; mathematician U.S. Air Force, 1950-53; methods research officer Chesapeake and Ohio Ry. Co., 1953-54; sr. cons. Ebasco Services, 1954-58; nat. mgr. computer applications and ops. research Arthur Young & Co., 1958-61; chmn. exec. com. Computer Resources, Inc., 1970-73, also dir.; pres., chmn. fin. com. Levin-Townsend Computer Corp. and predecessors, N.Y.C., 1961-71, also dir.; Levin Internat. Corp. (name formerly Levin Computer Corp.), N.Y.C., 1971—, also dir. Trans Atlantic Games, Inc., N.Y.C., pres. also dir., 1982—; pilot Lottery Systems, pres., also dir., 1987—. Author: Analytic Geometry, 1949; Office Work and Automation, 1956. Served with U.S. Army, 1943-46. Named founder of computer leasing industry Computer Lessors Assn., 1980. Mem. Ops. Research Soc. Am., Assn. Computing Machinery, IEEE, Am. Statis. Assn., Inst. Mgmt. Scis. Office: Pilot Lottery Systems Inc 224 E 49th St New York NY 10017

LEVIN, JERRY WAYNE, food company executive; b. San Antonio, Apr. 18, 1944; s. Bernard H. and Marion (Bromberg) L.; m. Carol Lee Motel, Dec. 18, 1966; children—Joshua, Abby. B.S.E.E., U. Mich., 1966, B.S.E. in Math., 1966; M.B.A., U. Chgo., 1968. With Tex. Instruments, Dallas, 1968-72; with Marsh & McLennan, Chgo., 1972-74; with The Pillsbury Co., Mpls., 1974—, exec. v.p. corporate devel., treas., 1985—, exec. v.p. corp. devel., chmn. Haagen-Dazs div., 1987-88; exec. v.p. corp. devel. and chmn. S&A Restaurant Corp., 1988—; chmn. Burger King Corp., 1988—; bd. dirs. Apogee Enterprises, Inc. Bd. dirs. Met. Econ. Devel. Assn., Mpls., 1983, Mpls. Fedn., 1982. Mem. Internat. Assn. Corp. Growth (bd. dirs. 1981-83), Corp. Profl. Assn. (bd. dirs. 1982-83). Club: Mpls.; Oak Ridge Country (Hopkins, Minn.); Lafayette (Wayzata, Minn.). Home: 4260 Chimo E Deephaven MN 55391

LEVIN, MICHAEL ELLIOT, lawyer; b. N.Y.C., May 3, 1942; s. Isadore and Selma (Roitman) L.; m. Joy M. Levin, May 8, 1971; children: Joshua David, Jeremy Adam. BA, Washington and Lee U., 1964; LLB, NYU, 1967. Bar: N.J. 1967. Ptnr. Matthews, Levin, Shea and Pfeffer, Jackson, N.J., 1973-85; pres. Levin, Shea and Pfeffer Esquires, Jackson, 1985—; bd. dirs., founder Garden State Bank, Jackson. Elected twp. committeeman Lekewood, N.J., 1971-73, mayor Twp. Lakewood, 1973; mem. planning bd., bd. health Lakewood Twp., 1971-73; past pres. Ocean County (N.J.) Jewish Fedn., 1982-85, campaign chmn., 1988; mem. exec. com. Garden State Polit. Action Com., Roseland, N.J., 1983—. Served with USMC Res., 1960-66. Mem. N.J. Bar Assn., Ocean County Bar Assn. Lodge: Kiwanis (pres. Lakewood chpt. 1980). Home: 1591 N Lake Dr Lakewood NJ 08701 Office: Levin Shea and Pfeffer 255 W County Line Rd Jackson NJ 08527

LEVIN, WILLIAM COHN, physician, former university president; b. Waco, Tex., Mar. 2, 1917; s. Samuel P. and Jeanette (Cohn) L.; m. Edna Seinsheimer, June 23, 1941; children: Gerry Lee Levin Hornstein, Carol Lynn Levin Cantini. B.A., U. Tex., 1938, M.D., 1941; M.D. (hon.), U. Montpellier, 1980. Diplomate: Am. Bd. Internal Medicine. Intern Michael Reese Hosp., Chgo., 1941-42; resident John Sealy Hosp., Galveston, Tex., 1942-44; mem. staff U. Tex. Med. Br. Hosps., Galveston, 1944—, asso. prof. internal medicine, 1948-65, prof., 1965—; Warmoth prof. hematology U. Tex. Med. Br., 1968-86, Ashbel Smith prof., 1986—, pres., 1974-87; past chmn., past mem. cancer clin. investigation rev. com. Nat. Cancer Inst. Exec. com., mem. nat. bd. Union Am. Hebrew Congregations; trustee Houston-Galveston Psychoanalytic Found., 1975-78, Menil Found., 1976-83. Recipient Nicholas and Katherine Leone award for adminstrv. excellence, 1977; decorated Palmes Académiques France. Fellow A.C.P., Internat. Soc. Hematology; mem. Am. Fedn. Clin. Research, Central Soc. Clin. Research, Am. Soc. Hematology, Phi Beta Kappa, Sigma Xi, Alpha Omega Alpha. Office: U Tex Med Br Ashbel Smith Bldg Ste 2.212 301 University Blvd Galveston TX 77550

LEVINE, ARTHUR ALVIN, stockbroker; b. Brookline, Mass., May 20, 1948; s. Manuel and Minnie (Butter) L.; m. Karen Joni Gordon, Sept. 20, 1987. BA in Polit. Sci. and Acctg., U. Denver, 1970; MBA in Fin., Boston Coll., 1972. Investment counselor Profl. Econs., Boston, 1972-73; stockbroker Blyth Eastman Dillon, N.Y.C., 1973-74; v.p. Oppenheimer & Co., Inc., N.Y.C., 1974-78; v.p. L. F. Rothschild, Unterberg, Towbin, N.Y.C., 1978-83, 1st v.p., sr. portfolio mgr., 1981-83, sales and mktg. dir., 1982-83, dir. model cities program and prospecting techniques, 1983; ltd. ptnr., dir. sales and mktg. Prudential-Bache, N.Y.C., 1983-84, sr. v.p. investments-corp. services, 1984—; chmn. bd. Tall Oaks Ins. Agy. Inc.; dir. Gen. Custers Ice Cream Inc.; cons. Saddle River Group Inc.; cons. Group, Inc. Recipient various performance awards. Home: 2 Half Moon Isle Jersey City NJ 07305 Office: 610 Fifth Ave New York NY 10020

LEVINE, BENJAMIN, lawyer; b. New Haven, Conn., May 22, 1931; s. George and Frances (Levovsky) L.; m. Arleen Ella Rosenblatt, Jan. 14, 1962; children: Joshua, Sarah. BA, U. Conn.-Storrs, 1953; JD, Rutgers U., 1963. Bar: N.Mex. 1964, N.Y. 1965, N.J. 1967, U.S. Sup. Ct. 1980; cert. civil trial atty., 1986. Law clk. N.Mex. Sup. Ct., 1963-64; spl. asst. N.J. Commr. Conservation and Econ. Devel., 1965-67; dep. atty. gen. State of N.J., 1967-70; pvt. practice, Summit, N.J. and N.Y.C., 1970—; adj. prof. law Ramapo Coll., Mahwah, N.J., 1978-80. Pres., Environ. Action Inst. N.J., 1977-80; chmn. North Plainfield (N.J.) Environ. Commn., 1974-76; trustee South Branch Watershed Assn., 1976-80. Served to lt. (j.g.) U.S. Navy, 1956-60. Mem. Trial Attys. N.J., Assn. Trial Lawyers Am., N.J. Bar Assn., Summit Bar Assn., N.Y. State Trial Lawyers Assn., N.Y. County Lawyers Assn. (com. on civil cts. 1982—), Am. Arbitration Assn. (arbitrator 1973—, mem. policy com. ins.). Jewish. Club: B'nai B'rith, Anti-Defamation League. Author: Medical Malpractice; (with D. Moore) Zoning Guide For Local Officials; contbr. articles to profl. jours.

LEVINE, CARL MORTON, motion picture exhibition executive; b. Bklyn., Sept. 24, 1931; s. Joseph M. and Frances Pearl (Smith) L.; m. Judith Ann Pollack, June 12, 1955 (div.); m. Miriam Scott Zeldman, June 24, 1973; children—Jonathan Mark, Suzanne Beth; stepchildren—Debra Ellen Wiley, Douglas Reed Duberstein. B.A., Bklyn. Coll., 1953; M.Dramatic Arts, Columbia U., 1955. Unit mgr., floor and stage mgr., asst. dir., assoc. producer Sta. WRCA-TV NBC, N.Y.C., 1952-57; theatre mgr., asst. mgr. Forty Second St. Co., Lawbin Theatre Corp., Inc., N.Y.C., winter 1958-62, supr., 1963-65, gen. mgr., 1965-74; owner, mgr. Double L Ranch, Adirondack Mountains, summers 1958-62; v.p., gen. mgr. Midtown Theatre Corp. Brandt Theatres, N.Y.C., 1974-86; gen. mgr., dir. theatre ops. Sameric Mgmt. Corp., Phila., 1986; comml. ops. mgr. Newmark & Co. Real Estate, Inc., N.Y.C., 1987-88; mng. dir. Loews 84th St. Sixplex Theater, N.Y.C., 1988—; founder, producer, v.p., treas. Mirca Prodns. Ltd., N.Y.C., 1981—; dir. Variety Club, N.Y.C., 1981—, entertainment div. UJA-Fedn., N.Y.C., 1985, mem. Nat. Commn. Anti-Defamation League, 1965—; v.p. Queens Council on Arts, 1977-80, pres., 1980-81. Chmn., producer Vets. Com. Variety Shows, VA Hosp., 1968-71; mem. adv. bd. Nassau County Fine Arts Mus., 1981—. Mem. Acad. TV Arts and Scis., Variety Internat., Motion Picture Pioneer (life), Ind. Theatre Owner's Assn. (v.p. 1967—), League N.Y. Theatres and Producers (labor negotiation com. 1980—). Republican. Jewish. Lodges: Cinema B'nai B'rith (pres. 1970-72).

LEVINE, CHARLES ELLIS, utility company executive; b. Columbus, Ohio, Apr. 1, 1953; s. George Milton and Renee (Katz) L.; 1 child, Lisa Ruth. BA, Trinity Coll., 1974; MBA, Northwestern U., 1977. Brand asst. Procter & Gamble Co., Cin., 1977-78, asst. brand mgr., 1978-80, brand mgr., 1980-83; mgr. new products GE, Portsmouth, Va., 1983-84, mgr. mktg., 1984-85, mgr. ops., 1985-86; dir. product mgmt. AT&T, Parsippany, N.J., 1986-87, v.p. product mgmt., 1987-88, v.p. mktg., product mgmt., 1988—; instr. Rutgers U., New Brunswick, N.J., 1987—. Republican. Jewish. Office: AT&T Gen Bus Systems div 99 Jefferson Rd Parsippany NJ 07054

LEVINE, HAROLD, lawyer; b. Newark, Apr. 30, 1931; s. Rubin and Gussie (Lifshitz) L.; m. Harriet B. Levine; children—Brenda Sue, Linda Ellen Levine Gersen, Louise Abby, Jill Anne Levine Zuvanich, Charles A., Cristina Gussie, Harold Rubin II; m. Cristina Cervera, Aug. 29, 1980. B.S. in Engring., Purdue U., 1954; J.D. with distinction, George Washington U., 1958. Bar: D.C. 1958, Va., 1958, Mass. 1960, Tex. 1972, U.S. Patent Office, 1958. Naval architect, marine engr. U.S. Navy Dept., 1954-55; patent examiner U.S. Patent Office, 1955-58; with Tex. Instruments Inc., Attleboro, Mass., 1959-77, asst. sec., Dallas, 1969-72, asst. v.p. and gen. patent counsel, 1972-77; ptnr. Sigalos & Levine, Dallas, 1977—; chmn. bd. Vanguard Security, Inc., Houston, 1977—; chmn. Tex. Am. Realty, Dallas, 1977—; lectr. assns., socs.; del. Geneva and Lausanne (Switzerland) Intergovtl. Conf. on Revision, Paris Pat. Conv., 1975-76. Mem. U.S. State Dept. Adv. Panel on Internat. Tech. Transfer, 1977. Mem. ABA (chmn. com. 407 taxation pats. and trdmks. 1971-72), Am. Patent Law Assn., Dallas Bar Assn., Assn. Corp. Pat. Csl. (sec.-treas. 1971-73), Dallas-Fort Worth Patent Law Assn., Pacific Indsl. Property Assn. (pres. 1975-77), Electronic Industries Assn. (pres. pat. com. 1972), NAM, Southwestern Legal Inst. on Patent Law (planning com. 1971-74), U.S. C. of C., Dallas C. of C., Alpha Epsilon Pi, Phi Alpha Delta. Republican. Jewish. Club: Kiwanis. Contbr. chpt. to book, articles to profl. jours. Editor: George Washington U. Law Rev., 1956-57; mem. adv. bd. editors Bur. Nat. Affairs, Pat., Trdmk. and Copyright Jour., 1979-87. Office: Sigalos Levine & Montgomery 2700 NCNB Ctr Tower II Dallas TX 75201

LEVINE, JOANN, civic organization executive; b. Cin., Apr. 5, 1945; d. Jerome and Molly (Lucas) Apseloff; m. Marc Samuel Levine, Jan. 29, 1965; children: Ami Jennifer, Shelley, Benjamin. Student Ohio State U., 1963-66, U. Houston, 1984. Sec. Ohio State U., Columbus, 1966-67; sec., treas. United DC Inc., Houston, 1981—. Pres. Sisterhood Agudat Achim, 1972-73, advisor, 1974-81; bd. dirs. Synagogue Agudat Achim, 1972-73; organizer Lead Blood Testing Program Women's Ctr. of Leominster, Mass., 1979-81. Mem. Nat. Assn. Female Execs., Orgn. Rehab. and Tng. Jewish. Club: Hadassah (Houston). Avocations: reading, tennis, swimming. Home: 6235 Queensloch Houston TX 77096 Office: United DC Inc 8947 Market St Houston TX 77029

LEVINE, LAURA AMY, bank executive; b. N.Y.C., May 3, 1959; d. Aaron and Florence (Chaiter) L. AS, Temple U., 1980, BA magna cum laude, 1981; MBA, Georgetown U., 1983. Project mgr. Small Bus. Adminstrn., Washington, 1982-83; fin. analyst R.H. Macys Inc., Newark, 1983-85; cons. Computer Horizens Corp., Parsippany, N.J., 1985-87; corporate fin. asst. v.p. Citicorp Investment Bank, N.Y.C., 1987—. Jewish.

LEVINE, LAWRENCE DAVID, manufacturing executive, consultant; b. Washington, D.C., June 28, 1932; s. Mack and Edith (Kaplan) L.; m. Orabeth Ruderman, June 17, 1956; children: Jill Debra Shirley, Jonathan Daniel, Theodore Samuel. BS, U.S. Coast Guard Acad., 1954; MBA, Northeastern U., 1968. Commd. ensign USCG, 1954, advanced through grades to lt., 1958, resigned, 1959; capt. USCGR, 1975—; cons. Arthur D. Little Inc., Cambridge, Mass., 1966-70; mgr. mfg. engring, shop ops. Gen. Electric, Chgo., 1970-78; dir. Ingersoll. Engrs., Rockford, Ill., 1978-81; v.p. Ogden Corp., Cleve., 1982-84; pres. The Lawrence Group, Northbrook, Ill., 1985-86, Onsrud Machine Corp., Wheeling, Ill., 1986—. Contbr. articles to profl. jours. Mem. Mfg. Mgmt. Assocs. (bd. dirs. 1985—), Wood Machinery Mfrs. Assn. (bd. dirs. 1989—), Numerical Control Soc. (nat. bd. dir. 1970-74, chmn. Yankee chpt. 1969-70). Jewish. Office: Onsrud Machine Corp 110 W Carpenter Ave Wheeling IL 60090

LEVINE, LEON, retail executive; b. 1937; married. Student, Wingate Coll., U. Miami. V.p. Hub Dept. Store Inc., Rockingham, N.C., 1954-57; pres. Union Craft Co. Inc., Wingate, N.C., 1957-59; with Family Dollar Stores, Matthews, N.C., 1959—, pres., chief exec. officer, now chmn., treas., also bd. dirs. Office: Family Dollar Stores Inc PO Box 25800 Charlotte NC 28212 *

LEVINE, MARK JEFFREY, technology business executive; b. Hartford, Conn., Aug. 9, 1954; s. Leon and Anita S. (Schwartz) L.; m. Sara L. Imershein, Feb. 17, 1985; children: Miriam Rose, Samuel Louis. BS, Northeastern U., Boston, 1976; MBA, George Washington U., 1978. Analyst Office Econ. Policy, NOAA, Washington, 1976-78; fin. analyst Office Sec. of U.S. Treasury, Washington, 1978-80; staff dir. energy and environment subcom. Com. on Small Bus., U.S. Ho. of Reps., Washington, 1980-82, staff dir. oversight subcom., 1982-85; dir. corp. devel. Geo-Ctrs., Inc., Boston, 1985—; congrl. del. UN Conf. on New and Renewable Sources Energy, Rome, 1982. Contbr. articles to profl. jours. Mem. com. on govt. affairs Profl. Services Council, Washington, 1985—, chmn. small bus. task force, 1986—. Recipient Innovation Achievement award Nat. Council on Indsl. Innovation, 1983, Participation award Nat. Contract Mgmt. Assn., 1986. Mem. Instrument Soc. Am. Democrat. Jewish. Office: Geo-Ctrs Inc 10903 Indian Head Hwy Ste 502 Fort Washington MD 20744

LEVINE, MARTIN ROBERT, executive search and recruiting company executive; b. Bklyn., Sept. 10, 1943; s. Jack and Minna (Fisher) L.; m. Hilda Lichtenstein, Jan. 28, 1967; 1 child, Jill. BA, Mich. State U., 1965; MA, NYU, 1969. Assoc. dir. placement office NYU, N.Y.C., 1966-69; dir. human resources J.K. Lasser and Co., N.Y.C., 1970-77; mgr. human resources Touche Ross and Co., N.Y.C., 1977-79; exec. v.p., pres. Earley Kielty and Assocs., N.Y.C., 1980—. Bd. dirs. L.I. Regional Am. Jewish Commn., Woodbury, N.Y., 1987—, Student Aid Fund, Great Neck, N.Y., 1984-86; v.p. Temple Beth-El, Great Neck, 1987—. With USNG, 1966-71. Office: Earley Kielty & Assocs Inc 2 Pennsylvania Pla Ste 1990 New York NY 10121

LEVINE, MELVIN CHARLES, lawyer; b. Bklyn., Nov. 12, 1930; s. Barnet and Jennie (Iser) L. BCS, N.Y. U., 1952; LLB, Harvard U., 1955. Bar: N.Y. 1956, U.S. Supreme Ct. 1964. Assoc., Kriger & Haber, Bklyn., 1956-58, Black, Varian & Simons, N.Y.C., 1959; sole practice, N.Y.C., 1959—; devel. multiple dwelling housing. Mem. N.Y. County Lawyers Assn. (civil ct. com., housing ct. com., uniform housing ct. rules com., liaison to Assn. Bar City of N.Y. on selection of housing and civil ct. judge, task force on tort reform). Democrat. Jewish. Home: 146 Waverly Pl New York NY 10014 Office: 271 Madison Ave Ste 1404 New York NY 10016

LEVINE, MICHAEL LAWRENCE, financial planner; b. N.Y.C., Nov. 18, 1947. BA, NYU, 1969. Cert. Fin. Planner; registered investment advisor. Dist. mgr. IDS/Am. Express, Springfield, Mass., 1982-85; pvt. practice Amherst, Mass., 1985—; adj. faculty mem. Coll. for Fin. Planning, 1986—; instr. U. Mass., 1985—. Contbr. articles to profl. jours. Bd. dirs. Holyoke Community Coll. Found., 1986—; treas., bd. dirs. Valley Land Fund, Hadley, Mass., 1977-87, Kestrel Trust, Amherst, Mass., 1988. Named Best Fin. Planning Cons. of Yr., Advocate Newspapers, 1987. Mem. Inst. Cert. Fin. Planners, Internat. Assn. Fin. Planning, Registry Fin. Planning Practitioners, Internat. Bd. Standards and Practices for Cert. Fin. Planners, Estate Planning Council Pioneer Valley., Amherst Club (bd. dirs. 1987—). Office: 664 Main St Amherst MA 01002

LEVINE, RIESA ELLEN, corporate librarian; b. Bklyn., July 1, 1946; d. Morris and Sarah (Lehrer) Alex. BA, Bklyn. Coll., 1967; MLS, Pratt Inst., 1968; postgrad., Drexel U., 1981. Media specialist John Dewey High Sch., Bklyn., 1968-72; reference librarian Cumberland County Library, Bridgeton, N.J., 1972-74; media specialist Greater Egg Harbor Regional High Sch. Dist., Mays Landing, N.J., 1974-86; corp. librarian Atlantic Electric Co., Pleasantville, N.J., 1986—. Mem. Am. Soc. Info. Specialists, Spl. Library Assn., Edison Electric Inst. (library svcs. com.), N.J. Bus. and Profl. Women's Assn. Home: 20 Cresson Woods St Pleasantville NJ 08232 Office: Atlantic Electric Co 1199 Black Horse Pike Pleasantville NJ 08232

LEVINE, SOL, cosmetics company executive; b. 1928. Asst. to chmn. bd. Revlon, Inc., N.Y.C., 1954-69, exec. v.p. cosmetics and fragrances div., 1969-70, exec. v.p., 1970-82, cons., 1982-85, pres., 1985—. With U.S. Army, 1950. Office: Revlon Inc 767 Fifth Ave New York NY 10022 *

LEVINE, STANLEY WALTER, chemical company executive; b. Boston, Dec. 13, 1929; s. Bernard T. and Sonia (Spector) L.; B.S. in Journalism, Butler U., 1952; postgrad. Boston Coll., 1967; children—Robert, Douglas, Elizabeth. Nat. mktg. dir. Bates Mfg. Co., N.Y.C., 1965-68; mgmt. cons. Frederick Chusid Co., N.Y.C., 1971-76, Fashioncade, N.Y.C., 1968-71; pres., chief exec. officer Internat. Coating & Chem. Co. Inc., Fairfield, Conn., 1976—. Mem. Nat. Republican Congl. Com., Rep. Com. Fairfield County (Conn.); mem. Am. Jewish Com., So. Poverty Law Ctr. Served to capt. USAF, 1952-55. Decorated Korean Honor medal. Mem. Am. Mgmt. Assn. Chem. Week Contbrs., Pres.'s Club N.Y., Nat. Chem. Club, N.Y. Acad. Scis., Internat. Platform Assn., Sigma Delta Chi, Sigma Alpha Mu, Alpha Phi Omega. Club: Harmonie N.Y. Contbr. articles to Nat. Chem. Weekly, Harpers. Office: care Intern Coating & Chem Co 1226 Post Rd Fairfield CT 06430 Other: 7742 N 18th St Phoenix AZ 85020

LEVINE, STEVEN ALAN, appraiser, consultant; b. Cin., Aug. 28, 1951; s. E. Pike and Beverly Rae (Friedman) L. BA with honors, U. Cin., 1975;

postgrad., George Washington U., 1975-77. Appraiser Real Estate Evaluators and Cons., Cin., 1969-75; program asst. U.S. Renegotiation Bd., Washington, 1975; appraiser D.C. Govt., Washington, 1976-77; emergency mgmt. specialist Fed. Emergency Mgmt. Agy., Washington, 1977-80; v.p. Am. Res. and Appraisal Ctr., Cin., 1980-82; prin. Steven A. Levine & Assocs., Cin., 1982—; cons. U.S. Army, 1982—. Author: The Renegotiation of Defense Contracts, Military Installation Real Property Management, Property Tax Relief Measures for the Elderly. Coordinator Henry Jackson for Pres., Washington, 1976; mem. Forum for Urban Studies, Washington, 1977; mem. Common Cause, Washington, 1975-78. Served to sgt. USAF, 1969-75. Named to Hon. Order Ky. Cols., Louisville, 1979; named lt. col. aide-de-camp Staff of Gov. of Ga., Atlanta, 1979, lt. col. aide-de-camp Staff of Gov. of Ala., Montgomery, 1983. Mem. Am. Assn. Cert. Appraisers (sr.), Nat. Assn. Realtors, Am. Soc. Pub. Adminstrn. Jewish. Home: 4680 Mission Ln Cincinnati OH 45223 Office: Steven A Levine & Assocs 1617 W North Bend Rd Cincinnati OH 45224

LEVINGSTON, ERNEST LEE, engineering company executive; b. Pineville, La., Nov. 7, 1921; s. Vernon Lee and Adele (Miller) L.; B.M.E., La. State U., 1960; m. Kathleen Bernice Bordelon, June 23, 1944; children—David Lewis, Jeanne Evelyn, James Lee. Gen. foreman T. Miller & Sons, Lake Charles, La., 1939-42; sr. engr., sect. head Cities Service Refining Corp., Lake Charles, 1946-57; group leader Bovay Engrs., Baton Rouge, 1957-59; chief engr. Augenstein Constrn. Co., Lake Charles, 1959-60; pres. Levingston Engrs., Inc., Lake Charles, 1961-85, gen. mgr. SW La., Austin Indsl., 1985-88; pres. Levingston Engrs., 1989—. Mem. Lake Charles Planning and Zoning Commn., 1965-70; mem. adv. bd. Sowela Tech. Inst., 1969—; mem. Regional Export Expansion Council, 1969-70, chmn. code com., 1966—; mem. La. Bd. Commerce and Industry, 1978—; bd. dirs. Lake Charles Meml. Hosp. Served with USNR, 1942-46. Named Jaycee Boss of Year, 1972. Registered profl. engr., La., Tex., Miss., Ark., Tenn., Pa., Md., Del., N.J., D.C., Okla., Colo. Mem. La. Engring. Soc. (pres. 1967-68, state dir. 1967-68), Nat. Inst. Cert. Engring. Technologists (past trustee, mem. exam. com.), Lake Charles C. of C. (dir. 1969-73). Baptist (deacon 1955—). Office: PO Box 1865 Lake Charles LA 70602

LEVINGSTON, JON STUART, furniture company executive; b. Greenwood, Miss., Jan. 19, 1958; s. Douglas Arnold and Barbara Ann (Topol) L. BFA cum laude, U. Ga., 1978. Mgr. Olden Camera and Lens Co., N.Y.C., 1981-82; sales mgr. Storehouse, Inc., Atlanta, 1982-83; exec. v.p. Levingston Furniture Co., Clarksdale and Cleveland, Miss., 1983—; mng. ptnr. Levingston Bros., Clarksdale, 1985—, Levingston Investments, Clarksdale, 1986—. Founder Jon and Bruce Levingston Continuing Fund Humanities, 1985; developer Larry Thompson Ctr. Fine Arts, Clarksdale, 1985; exec. bd. Miss. Arts Commn., Jackson, 1985—, vice chmn., chmn. 1988—; exec. bd. Delta Area council Boy Scouts Am., 1984; bd. dirs. Leadership Miss. Alumni Assn., Jackson, 1986—, So. Arts Fedn., Atlanta, 1988—; pres. and founder Miss. Delta Arts Council, 1984—; co-chmn. Coahoma County Comm. to Elect Ray Mabus Governor, 1987, Gov's Awards in the arts, 1988; rep. Miss. Devel. Bank Bd., 1988—. Recipient Outstanding Achievement award Film Office Miss. Dept. Econ. Devel., Jackson, 1986, Outstanding Achievement award Leadership Miss., Jackson, 1985; named Outstanding Young Men of Am., 1985, 86. Mem. Nat. Home Furnishings Assn., Coahoma County C. of C. (bd. dirs. 1985—), Phi Eta Sigma. Democrat. Jewish. Club: Clarksdale Country. Lodge: Rotary (bd. dirs. Clarksdale chpt. 1985-86). Home: 1214 W 2nd St Clarksdale MS 38614 Office: Levingston Furniture Co PO Box 6 Clarksdale MS 38614

LEVINGSTON, KEITH DAVID, accountant; b. Cleve., Feb. 12, 1957; s. Alfred Aaron and Vivian (Kaplan) L.; m. Bari Rosenfield. BS in Acctg., U. Ala., 1979, M in Tax Acctg., 1980. Tax specialist Coopers & Lybrand, Birmingham, Ala., 1980-82, tax supr., 1982-84, tax mgr., 1984-85; tax mgr. Coopers & Lybrand, Atlanta, 1985-86; tax mgr. Coopers & Lybrand, Memphis, 1986, ptnr., 1986—. Office: Coopers & Lybrand 1000 Morgan-Keegan Tower 50 N Front St Memphis TN 38103

LEVINSON, KENNETH LEE, lawyer; b. Denver, Jan. 18, 1953; s. Julian Charles and Dorothy (Milzer) L.; m. Shauna Titus, Dec. 21, 1986. BA with distinction, U. Colo.-Boulder, 1974; JD, U. Denver, 1978. Bar: Colo. 1978, U.S. Ct. Appeals (10th cir.) 1978. Assoc. atty. Balaban & Lutz, Denver, 1979-83; shareholder Balaban & Levinson, P.C., 1984—. Contbr. articles to profl. jours. Pres., Dahlia House Condominium Assn., 1983-85; intern Reporters Com. For Freedom of the Press, Washington, 1977. Recipient Am. Jurisprudence award Lawyers Co-op., 1977. Mem. ABA, Denver Bar Assn., Colo. Bar Assn., Am. Arbitration Assn. (arbitrator), Internat. Platform Assn. Clubs: Denver Law, Denver Athletic.

LEVINTHAL, MICHAEL JAMES, venture capitalist; b. Palo Alto, Calif., Oct. 11, 1954; s. Elliott Charles and Rhoda Lee (Arons) L. BS, Stanford U., 1976, MS, 1977, MBA, 1981. Mktg. mgr. indsl. products Orion Rsch., Inc., Cambridge, Mass., 1977-79; assoc. spl. ltd. ptnr. New Enterprise Assocs., San Francisco, 1981-83; gen. ptnr. Mayfield Fund, Menlo Park, Calif., 1984—. Bd. dirs. Peninsula Children's Ctr., Palo Alto. Mem. IEEE, Nat. Venture Capital Assn., Western Assn. Venture Capitalists, Alpine Hills Club. Democrat. Jewish. Office: Mayfield Fund 2200 Sand Hill Rd Menlo Park CA 94025

LEVITCH, HARRY HERMAN, retail executive; b. Memphis, Dec. 24, 1918; s. Samuel Arthur and Lena (Feingold) L.; LL.B. cum laude, So. Law U. (now Memphis State U.), 1941; m. Frances Wagner, May 31, 1940; 1 son, Ronald Wagner. Mdse. mgr. Perel & Lowenstein, Inc., 18 yrs.; pres. Harry Levitch Jewelers, Inc., Memphis, 1955—, also treas.; past lectr. on diamonds Memphis State U., Shelby State U. Pres. Leo N. Levi Nat. Arthritis Hosp., Hot Springs Nat. Park, Ark.; del. Conf. on Am.'s Cities, Washington, Regional Conf. U.S. Fgn. Policy, Louisville, Conf. of U.S. Dept. State and So. Center for Internat. Studies; bd. dirs. B'nai B'rith Home and Hosp. for Aged, Memphis, West Tenn. chpt. Arthritis Found.; chmn. Internat. Commn. on Community Vol. Services; adv. bd. dirs. Libertyland and Mid-South Fair Assn.; bd. dirs. W. Tenn. chpt. March of Dimes, NCCJ; lt., spl. dept. sheriff Shelby County (Tenn.). Appointee U.S. Holocaust Meml. Council by Pres. Reagan, 1988—. Served with JAGC, USAAF, 1943-46. Recipient Outstanding Civic Service award City of Memphis; Outstanding Leadership award Christian Bros. Coll.; col. a.d.c. Gov. Tenn.; named Hon. citizen Tex., Ala., Ark., New Orleans. Mem. Memphis Area C. of C., Retail Jewelers of Am., Jewelers Vigilance Com., Nat. Assn. Jewelry Appraisers (sr. appraiser), Internat. Soc. Appraisers, Am. Soc. Appraisers, Diamond Council Am. (cert. gemologist), Jewelry Industry Council. Jewish. Clubs: B'nai B'rith (internat. v.p.), Rotary, Summit, Masons, Shriners. Home: 4972 Peg Ln Memphis TN 38117 Office: Harry Levitch Jewelers Inc Clark Tower Ste 111 5100 Poplar Ave Memphis TN 38137 Also: Levi Arthritis Hosp 300 Prospect Ave Hot Springs AR 71901

LEVITT, ARTHUR, JR., securities executive; b. Bklyn., Feb. 3, 1931; s. Arthur and Dorothy (Wolff) L.; m. Marylin Blauner, June 12, 1955; children: Arthur III, Lauri. BA, Williams Coll., 1952, LLD (hon.), 1980; LLD (hon.), Pace U., 1980, Hamilton Coll., 1981, L.I. U., 1984, Hofstra U., 1985. Asst. promotion dir. Time, Inc., N.Y.C., 1954-59; exec. v.p., dir. Oppenheimer Industries, Inc., Kansas City, Mo., 1959-62; with Shearson Hayden Stone Inc. (now Shearson Lehman Bros., Inc.), N.Y.C., 1962-78, pres., 1969-78; chmn., chief exec. officer, dir. Am. Stock Exchange, N.Y.C., 1978—; trustee East N.Y. Savs. Bank. Chmn. Pres.' Pvt. Sector Survey on Cost Control, 1982-84, Pres.' Task Force on Pvt. Sector Initiatives, 1981-82, White House Small Bus. Conf. Commn., 1978-80; mem. N.Y. State Council Arts, 1969—; chmn. bd. dirs. spl. adv. Task Force on Future Devel. West Side Manhattan; trustee Williams Coll.; bd. dirs. Dole Found., Rockefeller Found., Norman and Rosita Winston Found. Served with USAF, 1952-54; maj. Res. Recipient Medal of Excellence Bd. Regents State of N.Y. Mem. Am. Bus. Cof. (chmn. 1980—), Phi Beta Kappa. Office: Am Stock Exchange 86 Trinity Pl New York NY 10006

LEVITT, BARRY ADNOFF, systems analyst; b. Dover, N.H., Dec. 10, 1950; s. Lionel Levitt and Ruth Marion (Adnoff) Brenner; m. Rita Kay Tess, May 22, 1977 (div. July 1981); 1 child, Esther Leah; m. Pamela Dee Norris, June 1, 1985; stepchildren: Matthew Dennis Krol, Zackary James Krol. BA, Cornell U., 1973; MBA, Ind. U., 1976. CPA, Ind. Asst. systems designer Lincoln Nat. Life Ins. Co., Ft. Wayne, Ind., 1973-75; supr. computer support GTE Sylvania, Winchester, Ky., 1977; cons. Ernst & Whinney, Indpls., 1978-79; system analyst Meridian Mut. Ins., Indpls., 1979-80; system mgr. Geupel DeMars, Indpls., 1980-85; project leader Queens Group Ind., Indpls., 1985-88; programmer analyst Golden Rules Ins., Indpls., 1988—; instr. U. Indpls., 1986. Chmn. Common Cause Ind., Indpls., 1980-82, 87-89. Mem. Ind. CPA's Soc. (chmn. com. 1985-86), Assn. for Computing Machinery (treas. 1983), AICPA, Indpls. Old Tyme Music and Dance Group (treas. 1984—). Democrat. Jewish. Home: PO Box 17353 Indianapolis IN 46227

LEVITT, GERALD STEVEN, natural gas company executive; b. Bronx, N.Y., Mar. 21, 1944; s. Charles and Beatrice (Janet) L.; m. Natalie Lillian Hoppen; children: Mark, Roy. B in Mgmt. Engring., Rensselaer Poly. Inst., 1965; MBA, DePaul U., 1972. Registered profl. engr., Ill. Tech. rep. Worthington Air Conditioning Co., Ampere, N.J., 1965-67; indsl. sales engr. Peoples Gas Light & Coke Co., Chgo., 1967-71; planning specialist Peoples Gas Co., Chgo., 1971-72; v.p. Stone & Webster Mgmt. Cons., Inc., N.Y.C., 1972-82; exec. v.p. South Jersey Gas Co., Folsom, N.J., 1982—. Bd. dirs. Camden County council Boy Scouts Am., West Collingswood, N.J. Mem. Am. Gas Assn., Greater Atlantic City C. of C. (bd. dirs.). Office: S Jersey Gas Co 1 S Jersey Pla Rte 54 Folsom NJ 08037

LEVITT, JAREN, real estate corporation officer; b. N.Y.C., Mar. 19, 1946; s. Seymour and Harriet (Finorsky) L.; m. Estra Matlack, June 15, 1970 (div. 1974); m. Diane Gold, July 16, 1977; children: Jaden, Janna. BS in Psychology and Biology, Syracuse U., 1965; MS in Clin. Psychology, U. Tex., 1967; PhD in Clin. Psychology, UCLA, 1974. Spl. asst Mayor's Office, N.Y.C., 1968-71, Pres. U.S., Washington, 1971; pres. Med. Cons. Internat., Woodland Hills, Calif., 1973-78; mktg. dir. vacation planning Playboy Internat., McAffe, N.J., 1978-80; regional mktg. dir. Gen. Devel. Co., Miami, Fla., 1981-88; asst. v.p. Gen. Devel. Co., Miami, 1988; v.p. Cen. Region and Far East Gen. Devel. Co., Norridge, Ill., 1988—; pres. Am. Real Estate Devel. Corp. Gen. Devel. Co., Fla.; cons. substance abuse projects to bus. and fgn. govts., 1968-78. Contbr. articles to profl. jours. Mem. Heritage Found. Republican. Jewish. Office: Gen Devel Corp 4701 N Cumberland Ave Norridge IL 60656

LEVITT, JEFFREY MILES, controller; b. Tuscaloosa, Ala., July 2, 1962; s. Phillip Russel and Helene (Rosenthal) L. BS in Acctg., U. Md., 1985. CPA, Md. Sr. acct. Coopers and Lybrand, Balt. and Washington, 1985-87; controller Indsl. Coatings Internat., Inc., Balt., 1988—. Mem. Am. Inst. CPAs. Home: 3309 Parkford Manor Dr Apt C Silver Spring MD 20904 Office: 7030 Quad Ave Baltimore MD 21237

LEVITT, LAWRENCE DAVID, insurance agent; b. Los Angeles, Apr. 18, 1944; s. Albert Herbert and Reva (Narvey) L.; m. Cinda Sue Coffee, Apr. 8, 1967; 1 child, Rachel Diane. AA, Solano Community Coll., 1970; B, U. San Francisco, 1976. Officer, detective Fairfield (Calif.) Police Dept., 1968-78; officer, supr. Douglas (Wyo.) Police Dept., 1978-79; comdr. Rock Springs (Wyo.) Police Dept., 1979-83, chief of police, 1983-86; owner CoServe, Rock Springs, 1986—; instr. Solano Community Coll., Fairfield, 1972-78, Western Wyo. Coll., Rock Springs, 1979—; mem. curriculum com. Wyo. Law Enforcement Acad., Douglas, 1985—. Mem. adv. bd. Youth Home, Inc., Rock Springs, 1980, S.W. Wyo. Alcohol Rehab. Assn., Rock Springs, 1984-86; mem. Upper Solano County Assn. For Retarded Children, Fairfield, 1974-78. Recipient Red Cross Life Saving award ARC, 1970; named Police Officer of Yr., Fairfield-Suisun Exchange Club, 1973. Mem. Internat. Assn. Chiefs of Police, Wyo. Assn. Chief's Police (v.p. 1985-86, chmn. edn. com. 1985—), Wyo. Peace Officers Assn., Rock Springs C. of C., Wyo. Assn. Life Underwriters. Democrat. Jewish. Club: Wyo. Paint Horse (Douglas). Lodges: Lions, Shriners, Masons, Elks. Home: 248 Cherokee Dr Rock Springs WY 82901 Office: Allstate Ins 175 Riverview Ste F Green River WY 82935

LEVY, ALAN STEPHEN, oil and mining executive, economist; b. Jamaica, N.Y., Dec. 29, 1948. BA in Geology, CUNY, 1970, MA in Geology, 1977. Regional exploration geologist Brit. Petroleum, Anchorage, 1976-79, Molycorp., Anchorage and Denver, 1980-84; sr. minerals analyst Molycorp., Los Angeles, 1984-86, bus. analyst Unocal Chems. div., 1986-88, mgr. bus. devel., 1988—. Author: Relations of Fordham and Manhattan Formations Near Katonah, N.Y., 1977. Mem. AIME (chmn. So. Calif. sect. 1988—). Office: Molycorp 1201 W Fifth St Los Angeles CA 90017

LEVY, ARNOLD S(TUART), real estate company executive; b. Chgo., Mar. 15, 1941; s. Roy and Esther (Scheff) L.; m. Eva Cichosz, Aug. 8, 1976; children: Adam, Rachel, Deborah. BS, U. Wis., 1963; MPA, Roosevelt U., 1970. Dir. Neighborhood Youth Corps, Chgo., 1966-68; v.p. Social Planning Assn., Chgo., 1968-70; planning dir. Office of Mayor Chgo., 1970-74; dep. dir. Mayor's Office Manpower, Chgo., 1974-75; sr. v.p. Urban Investment & Devel. Co., Chgo., 1975—; pres. JMB/Urban Hotels, Hotel and Resort Devel. Group, JMB/Urban Devel. Co. Pres. Ark, Chgo., 1970-72, Parental Stress Services, Chgo., 1978-79; past lectr. DePaul U., Roosevelt U., Loyola U.; del. Mid-Term Democratic Nat. Conf., Memphis, 1978; v.p. Inst. Urban Life, Chgo., 1983—. Bd. dirs. Chgo. Coun. of Urban Affairs; trustee Spertus Coll. of Judaica. Club: Carlton (Chgo.), Twin Orchard. Home: 535 Park Ave Glencoe IL 60022 Office: JMB/Urban Hotels 900 N Michigan Ave Chicago IL 60611

LEVY, BENJAMIN, medical research executive; b. N.Y.C., June 12, 1937; s. Martin Luther and Alice (Marks) L.; m. Ellen Lois Goldberg, Sept. 1, 1963; children: Michael, Daniel, Mark. BS, Union Coll., Schenectady, N.Y., 1956; MD, N.J. Coll. Medicine, 1960. Diplomate Am. Bd. Internal Medicine. Intern Jersey City Med. Ctr., 1960-61; resident Boston City Hosp., 1961-63; fellow NIH, N.Y.C., 1963-65; gen. practice medicine Hartford (Conn.) Hosp., 1965-83; research dir., pres. Nat. Med. Research Corp., Hartford, 1983—, also bd. dirs.; dir. courses, lectr. Ctr. for Profl. Advancement, New Brunswick, N.J., 1985—. Contbr. articles to profl. jours. Bd. dirs. Conn. Opera Co., Hartford, 1978-82; trustee Westwood Hill Assn., West Hartford, Conn., 1980—. Recipient numerous grants for med. research. Mem. AMA, Am. Soc. Clin. Pharmacology, Conn. Med. Soc., Drug Info. Assn., Soc. for Clin. Trials, Hartford C. of C. (com. mem. 1984—). Clubs: Harford; Tumblebrook Country (Bloomfield, Conn.). Home: 47 Westwood Rd West Hartford CT 06117 Office: Nat Med Rsch Corp 25 Main St Hartford CT 06106

LEVY, DAVID, lawyer; b. Atlanta, July 7, 1937; s. Meyer and Elsie (Reisman) L.; m. Diane L. Lerner; children: Jeffrey Marc, Robert William, Danielle Beth, Margo Shaw; stepchildren: Mitchell S. Haber, Cort A. Haber. B.A., Emory U., 1959, LL.B., 1961; LL.M., Georgetown U., 1964. Bar: Ga. 1961. Atty. SEC, Washington, 1961-65; assoc., partner Arnstein, Gluck, Weitzenfeld & Minow, Chgo., 1965-71; partner Kaler, Karesh & Frankel, Atlanta, 1971-73; sr. v.p., sec., counsel, dir. Nat. Service Industries, Inc., Atlanta, 1973—, also bd. dirs. Mem. Am., Ga. bar assns. Home: 680 River Chase Point Atlanta GA 30328 Office: Nat Svc Industries Inc 1180 Peachtree St NE Atlanta GA 30309

LEVY, JANET CAPLAN, marketing company executive; b. Scranton, Pa., Dec. 30, 1936; d. Sidney Max Caplan and Henrietta Toby (Morrison) Frankel; m. Saul Y. Levy, June 16, 1957; children: Linda Levy Raydo, Jonah. BA, Hunter Coll., 1958; MA, Rutgers U., 1968. Asst. to dir. South Brunswick Twp. Migrant Program, Kendall Park, N.J., 1969-70; freelance writer, editor Paris, 1970-71; writer, editor Transaction, Inc., New Brunswick, N.J., 1971-73; freelance writer N.Y., N.J., 1973-74; staff writer Rutgers U., New Brunswick, 1974-75; mgr. mktg. communications Mathematica Inc., Princeton, N.J., 1975-82; mktg. dir. Data Decisions, Cherry Hill, N.J., 1982-85; pres. TechniConnection Inc., Phila., 1985—. Contbr. articles to profl. jours. Mem. Nat. Assn. Women Bus. Owners. Home: 228 Monroe St Philadelphia PA 19147 Office: TechniConnection Inc 525 S Fourth St Philadelphia PA 19147

LEVY, JOEL HOWARD, research analyst; b. N.Y.C., Jan. 7, 1938; s. David M. and Mildred (Davidoff) L.; m. Renee Fenchel, Aug. 18, 1963; children: Seth Evan, Alissa Cheryl. B of Chem. Engring., City Coll. N.Y., 1960; MS in Chem. Engring., Poly. Inst. Bklyn., 1968; postgrad., Rider Coll. Mgr. devel. Princeton (N.J.) Chem. Research Inc., 1964-71; pilot plant mgr. Hydron Labs., New Brunswick, N.J., 1971-74; mgr. pilot plant Sun Chem. Corp., East Rutherford, N.J., 1974-75; process devel. supr. chem. div. Quaker Oats, Barrington, Ill., 1975-78; mgr. process engring. div. Searle Chem., Skokie, Ill., 1978-80; sr. mktg. research assoc. Allied Corp., Morristown, N.J., 1980—. Served as sgt. USAR, 1961-67. Mem. Am. Inst. Chem. Engrs., Am. Chem. Soc. (chmn. chem., mktg., econs. N.J. sec. 1985-86), Soc. of Plastics Industry (com. on resin stats., exec. com., chmn. nylon resins), European Chem. Mktg. Research Assn., Société de Chimie. Office: Allied Corp Columbia Rd Park Ave PO Box 2332R Morristown NJ 07960

LEVY, JOSEPH LOUIS, publishing company executive; b. Bklyn., June 21, 1947; s. Myron M. and Miriam M. (Glick) L.; m. Carol A. Arschin, July 3, 1973; children: Darren Ross, Marissa Darcel. BBA, Pace U., 1970. Dir. mktg. Frost & Sullivan Inc., N.Y.C., 1966-71; v.p. Internat. Data Corp., Waltham, Mass., 1972-80, v.p. mktg., Framingham, Mass, 1980-86; pres. Pub. and Communications Group, 1986-87, group pres. Internat. Data Corp., 1987; pres., pub. CIO mag., 1988—. Contbr. spl. reports on computer industry and tech. to Fortune mag., 1975-86, Industry Week mag., 1984-85, US News and World Report, 1986, Forbes mag, 1987—. Named Young Exec. of Yr., Internat. Data Corp., 1972-76. Mem. Am. Mktg. Assn. (Mktg. Man of Yr. 1970), Am. Mgmt. Assn., Soc. Mgmt. Info. Systems, Sales Execs. Club. Republican. Home: 137 Rockport Rd Weston MA 02193 Office: 5 Speen St Framingham MA 01701

LEVY, MARIAN MULLER, transportation executive; b. N.Y.C., Mar. 10, 1942; d. Arthur Russ and Diana Elise (Ornstein) Muller; m. Richard Dennis Levy, Nov. 16, 1962; children: Dawn, Nicole, Jason, Adam. Student, Bklyn. Coll., 1959-61, 68-70. Sec. ASCAP, N.Y.C., 1959-61; tchr. spl. edn Garden Park Sch., Phoenix, 1974-76; v.p. Pac Expediters, Ltd., Scottsdale, Ariz., 1976—; cons. ACMRA, 1984-86. Bd. dirs. Outreach, Phoenix, 1982—; co-chmn. Council Jews Spl. Needs, Phoenix, 1987-88. Mem. Scottsdale Ctr. for Arts, Fine Art for Fine Causes, Phoenix Art Mus., The Heard Mus. Home: 7850 E Camelback Rd #602 Scottsdale AZ 85251 Office: Pac Expediters Ltd 3020B N Scottsdale Rd Scottsdale AZ 85251

LEVY, MICHAEL, electronic manufacturing company executive; b. Gainesville, Fla., Dec. 19, 1946; s. Leon and Geneva (Shore) L.; children—Susan Elizabeth, Amanda Christine; m. Jo-Lynn Nelson, July 3, 1986. B.E.E., Ga. Inst. Tech., 1969. Design engr. Harris Corp., Melbourne, Fla., 1969-73; mgr. engring. Racal-Milgo, Inc., Miami, Fla., 1973-78; chmn., chief exec. officer, dir. Lexicon Corp., Ft. Lauderdale, Fla., 1978—, Scope Inc. (subs. Lexicon), Reston, Va., 1985—, also dir.; dir. Cosmo Communications Corp., Miami, Fla., 1986—, Sports-Tech Internat., Ft. Lauderdale, Fla. Patentee electronic dictionary. Named hon. Ky. Col. Mem. Am. Electronics Assn. Republican. Office: Lexicon Corp 2400 E Commercial Blvd Fort Lauderdale FL 33308

LEVY, MILTON ROBERT, plastics, chemical and graphics executive; b. Bklyn., June 28, 1936; s. Nathan and Ruth (Goldstein) L.; B.S., Sch. Commerce, NYU, 1958; m. Corinne Sackman, Aug. 28, 1958; children—Pamela, Norman, Michael. Gen. mgr. Direct Reprodn. Corp., Bklyn., 1959-62; pres. Nation-Wide Plastics Co., Inc., Long Island City, N.Y., 1962—, Non Tox Chem. Corp., Mamaroneck, N.Y., 1969—, Graphics One, Inc., Atlanta, 1971—; treas. Nation-Wide Plastics of Calif., Inc., 1973—; founder Deer Haven Home Products Co., N.Y.C., 1982; ptnr. Levian Investment Co., Golden Realty Co.; dir. Cortes Ward Co. Mem. N.Y.C. Mayor's Com. on Welfare Reform, 1977, Mayor's Voluntary Action Com., 1982; bd. dirs. Hebrew Acad. High Sch., Yonkers, N.Y., 1975-76, Center for Spl. Edn., Bklyn., 1978—, Bklyn. Dodger Baseball Hall of Fame, 1984; pres. Young Israel Scarsdale (N.Y.); 1974-75, 76-77; del. White House Conf. on Small Bus., 1986. Served with U.S. Army, 1958-59. Mem. Nat. Assn. Photo Lithographers, Jewish Alliance Businessmen (officer 1975-76, pres. 1977-78). Home: 42 Stratton Rd New Rochelle NY 10804 Office: 54-18 37th Ave Woodside NY 11377

LEVY, ROBERT I., packaging company executive; b. Chgo., July 21, 1912; s. Charles I. and Celia (Weinshenker) L.; m. Florence Greenblatt, Dec. 17, 1939; children: Maurice Lewis, Burt Samuel. BS in Optometry, OD, No. Ill. Coll., 1933. Pres. optical co. 1933-46; with Milprint, 1947-53, Traver Corp., 1953, Container Corp. Am., 1953-56; pres. Allpak Co., Chgo., 1958—; cons. SacPac, Rolling Meadows, Ill., 1987—, Aargus Div. Belcor Co., Des Plaines, Ill., 1988—; ret. Carolina Fabric Label, Greensboro, N.C., 1978; spl. cons. Allied Paper Co., 1960—; cons. Hipak Industries, Inc., Rolling Meadows, Ill.; bd. dirs. Ampak Co.; v.p. A and S Trading Co. Mem. City of Chgo. Welfare Council, 1963—; adv. council SBA; past trustee Packaging Found., Mich. State U., Lawrence Hall, Chgo.; bd. dirs., past v.p. Chgo. Met. Council Alcoholism; bd. givs. Psychiat. Inst., Northwestern U.; bd. dirs. Cathedral Shelter; past trustee North Shore Congregation Israel; bd. dirs. Congregation Kol Ami; adv. bd. Martha Washington Hosp., C.A.T.C., Salvation Army. Recipient Man of Yr. award Bonds for Israel, 1973. Mem. AIM (pre.'s council 1967-70). Lodge: B'nai B'rith (local pres.). Home: 2800 Lake Shore Dr Chicago IL 60657 Office: 1010 Lake St Oak Park IL 60301

LEVY, (ALEXANDRA) SUSAN, construction company executive; b. Rockville Centre, N.Y., Apr. 26, 1949; d. Alexander Stanley and Anna Charlotte (Galasieski) Jankoski; m. William Mack Levy, Aug. 12, 1977. Student, Suffolk Community Coll., Brentwood, N.Y., 1976. Cert. constrn. assoc. Supr. N.Y. Telephone Co., Babylon, 1970-74; v.p. Aabbacco Equipment Leasing Corp., Lindenhurst, N.Y., 1974-81; pres., owner Femi-9 Contracting Corp., Lindenhurst, 1981—. Mem. affirmative action adv. council N.Y. State Dept. Transp., Albany, 1984—, human resources adv. panel Long Island Project 2000; mem. Presdl. Task Force, Washington, 1982—. Served with U.S. Army, 1967-69. Recipient Henri Dunant Corp. award ARC Suffolk County, 1986. Mem. Nat. Assn. Women in Constrn. (founder L.I. chpt., pres. 1983—, regional chmn. woman-owned bus. enterprise com., nat. chmn. pub. relations and mktg. com., nat. dir. Region 1 1988—, Mem. of Yr. L.I. chpt. 1987, nat. dir., 1988—), Nassau Suffolk Contractors Assn. (sec. 1984-87, sec.-treas. 1987—, bd. dirs.), Women Constrn. Owners and Execs., Nat. Assn. Women Bus. Owners (charter), Am. Plat form Assn. Republican. Roman Catholic. Avocations: reading, writing, golf. Home: 131 Hollins Ln East Islip NY 11730 Office: Femi-9 Contracting Corp 305 E Sunrise Hwy Lindenhurst NY 11757

LEWIN, JACK (JACOB), aerospace company executive; b. Kaunas, Lithuania, Feb. 19, 1932; came to U.S., 1949; s. Morris and Genia (Stark-Masarsky) L.; m. Bernice Eichenbronner, Aug. 26, 1967; children: Elizabeth Anne, Judith Belinda. BSEE, Northeastern U., 1957; MS in Mgmt. Sci., Stevens Inst. Tech., 1967. Sr. mem. tech. staff advanced communications techniques lab., communications systems div. RCA, N.Y.C., 1959-67; sr. systems engr. astro-electronics div. RCA, Princeton, N.J., 1967-73; prin. mem. engring. staff RCA Global/Am. Communications, Inc., Piscataway, N.J., 1973-79; mgr. mission ops./space systems GE/RCA Am. Communications, Inc., Princeton, 1979-88; prin. architect state-of-the-art satellite ground control system The MITRE Corp., Eatontown, N.J., 1988—. Contbr. articles to tech. jours. 1st lt. signal corps U.S. Army, 1957-59. Recipient Cert. Achievement U.S. Army, 1960, awards for inventions and contributions, NASA, 1972. Mem. IEEE (sr.), AIAA,. Jewish. Home: 26 Whitehall Rd East Brunswick NJ 08816-1313 Office: The MITRE Corp 145 Wyckoff Rd Eatontown NJ 07724

LEWIN, JOHN ARTHUR, landscape company executive; b. Quincy, Mass., Sept. 1, 1950; s. Leon Frederic and Marion (Chambers) L.; m. Joanna Lynn, Apr. 13, 1970 (div. July 1977); 1 child, Jennifer; m. Deborah Marie Irvine, June 21, 1981; 1 child, Matthew. BS in Acctg., Bentley Coll., 1972. Acct. Johnson & Johnson Co., Raritan, N.J., 1972-76; controller Biol. Corp. Am., Port Reading, N.J., 1976-80; v.p., controller Cooper Biomed., 1980-85; v.p., treas., controller Technimed Corp., Ft. Lauderdale, Fla., 1985-88; owner A Cut Above, Coral Springs, Fla., 1988—; bd. dirs. Ramblewood Assocs., Inc., Coral Springs, Fla.; cons. Sea Garden Beach and Tennis Resort, Pompano Beach, Fla., 1986—. Treas. Boro of High Bridge (N.J.) 1974-76. Republican. Home: 8741 Shadow Wood Blvd Coral Springs FL 33071 Office: A Cut Above 1877 NW 108 Terr Coral Springs FL 33071

LEWIN, JOHN RICHARD, federal agency administrator; b. St. Louis, Dec. 8, 1946; s. Richard Hyman and Ruth (Hinchliffe) L.; m. Mary Katherine Shannon, Oct. 11, 1975; children: Nora Shannon Lewin, Elizabeth Tannie Lewin. BS, Georgetown U., 1972; MS, Am. U., 1975. Researcher

St. Elizabeth's Hosp., Washington, 1975-78; planner D.C. Govt., Washington, 1978-79; staff asst. U.S. Dept. Justice, Washington, 1979-84; sr. planner U.S. Dept. of Treas., Washington, 1984—. Author numerous articles on criminal justice. Mem. Planning Forum, Am. Mktg. Assn., Am. Soc. Criminology. Home: 4225 Peachtree Pl Alexandria VA 22304 Office: Fin Mgmt Svc 401 14th St SW Washington DC 20227

LEWIS, ANDREW LINDSAY, JR. (DREW LEWIS), transportation executive, natural resource executive; b. Phila., Nov. 3, 1931; s. Andrew Lindsay Sr. and Lucille (Bricker) L.; m. Marilyn S. Stoughton, June 1, 1950; children: Karen Lewis Sacks, Russell Shepherd, Andrew Lindsay IV. BS, Haverford (Pa.) Coll., 1953; MBA, Harvard U., 1955; postgrad., MIT, 1968; hon. degree, Cabrini Coll., Drexel U., Gettysburg Coll., Lehigh U., Widener U. Foreman, job supt., prodn. mgr., dir. Henkels & McCoy, Inc., Blue Bell, Pa., 1955-60; dir. marketing, v.p. sales, dir. Am. Olean Tile Co., Inc., Lansdale, Pa., 1960-68; v.p., asst. to chmn. Nat. Gypsum Co., Buffalo, 1960-70; chmn. Simplex Wire & Cable Co., Boston, 1970-74, chief exec. officer, 1972-74; pres., chief exec. officer Snelling & Snelling, Inc., Boston, 1972-74; fin. and mgmt. cons. Lewis & Assocs., Plymouth Meeting, Pa., 1974-81; sec. U.S. Dept. Transp., Washington, 1981-83; chmn. Warner Amex Cable Communications Inc., N.Y.C., 1983-86; chmn., chief exec. officer Union Pacific R.R., Omaha, 1986; pres. Union Pacific Corp., N.Y.C., 1986-87; chmn., pres., chief exec. officer Union Pacific Corp., Bethlehem, Pa., 1987—; bd. dirs. Am. Express, Ford Motor Co., SmithKline Beckman Corp., AT&T; trustee Com. for Econ. Devel. Rep. candidate for gov., Pa., 1974; mem. Rep. Nat. Com., 1976—, dep. chmn., 1980; dep. polit. dir. Reagan-Bush Campaign, 1980; co-chmn. Nat. Econs. Commn., 1988-89. Mem. Union League Phila., Phila. Aviation Country Club, Saucon Valley Country Club (Bethlehem, Pa.), Bohemian Club (San Francisco), River Club, Links Club (N.Y.C.). Office: Union Pacific Corp Martin Tower Eighth and Eaton Aves Bethlehem PA 18018

LEWIS, ANTHONY HUGH CASSIDY, corporation financial executive; b. Twickenham, Middlesex, U.K., Apr. 6, 1930; came to Can., 1953; s. Sidney Ernest and Muriel Doris (Cassidy) L.; m. Margaret Jean Lewis; children: Simon Deyne, Nicholas Hugh, Rebeca. MA, Cambridge U., U.K., 1952; MBA, McGill U., Montreal, Que., Can., 1958. Trainee Bell Telephone Co., Montreal, 1953-55; credit officer Indsl. Devel. Bank, Montreal, 1955-60; credit asst. Internat. Fin. Corp., Washington, 1960-62; sec./treas. Silhouette Inc., Montreal, 1962-63; treas. RCA Ltd., Montreal, 1963-71; v.p. fin. Rogers Cable Ltd., Toronto, Ont., Can., 1971-75, Datacrown, Inc., Toronto, 1975-81; v.p. treas. Crownx Inc., Toronto, 1981—; owner Proctor Masts Can., Toronto, 1981-87; part-time lectr. McGill U., 1959-60. Served with RAF, 1948-49. Fellow Can. Bankers Assn.; mem. Fin. Execs. Inst. Home: 101 Balmoral Ave, Toronto, ON Canada M4V 1J5 Office: Crownx Inc, 120 Bloor St E, Toronto, ON Canada M4W 1B8

LEWIS, CHARLES SPENCER, professional business manager; b. Syracuse, N.Y., May 15, 1928; s. Spencer H. and Ursula C. Lewis; m. Shirley Bausch, Sept. 3, 1955; children: Pamela, Douglas and Crawford (twins), Mark and Kim (twins). Student, U. Minn., 1945, Rutgers U., 1945; BS, Syracuse U., 1951. Asst. sales mgr. indsl. div. Ruberoid Co., N.Y.C., 1951; account exec. Geyer, Newell & Granger Advt., N.Y.C., 1952-53; dir. mktg. consumer plastics div. Mobil Chem. Corp., Macedon, N.Y., 1954-66; chmn. bd. profl. bus. mgrs. Market Sense, Inc., Rochester, N.Y., 1966—; bd. dirs. Allen Bailey Tag and Label, Inc., Erdle Perforating, Inc., Flower City Printing, Inc.; chmn. bd. Stone Constrn. Equipments, Inc. Bd. dir. Rochester Am. Hockey; past pres. Currewood Assn.; past bd. dirs. Little League Baseball, Rochester, Rochester Gen. Hosp. Found., past v.p., past bd. dirs. Rochester Community Baseball, Inc.; commr. Brighton Aux. Police Dept. Served with U.S. Army, 1945-47. Mem. Am. Mgmt. Assn., Brighton C. of C., Rochester C. of C., Oak Hill Country Club, Boca Grande Club, Mid-Town Tennis Club, Brighton Henrietta Town Line Tennis Club, Country Club of Rochester, Phi Delta Theta. Home: 130 Hollyvale Dr Rochester NY 14618 Office: Market Sense Inc 366 White Spruce Blvd Rochester NY 14623

LEWIS, CRAIG GRAHAM DAVID, public relations executive; b. Dearborn, Mich., Jan. 25, 1930; s. Floyd B. and Elizabeth (Hickey) L. AB, UCLA, 1951; m. Karen Kerns, Oct. 23, 1954; children—Mark, Kern, Arden, Robin. Corr., McGraw-Hill, Inc., Washington, 1952-56; bur. mgr. Aviation Week mag., Dallas, 1957-59, Washington news editor, 1959-61; dep. dir. pub. affairs FAA, Washington, 1961-63; v.p. pub. rels. Air Transport Assn., Washington, 1963-64; dir. pub. rels. Martin Marietta Corp., N.Y.C., 1964-67; assoc. Earl Newsom & Co., N.Y.C., 1967—, dir., 1968—, pres., 1975—, chmn., 1982—; exec. v.p. Adams & Rinehart, Inc., N.Y.C., 1983—, vice chmn., 1986—; vice-chmn. Ogilvy Pub. Rels. Group, 1988—. Mem. Aviation/Space Writers Assn., Am. Inst. Aero-Astro, AIAA, Nat. Press Club, Univ. (N.Y.C.) Club. Home: 6 Avon Rd New Rochelle NY 10804 Office: Adams & Rinehart Inc 708 Third Ave New York NY 10017

LEWIS, CYNTHIA MARIE, infosystems specialist; b. Erie, Pa., July 4, 1957; d. Thomas and Catherine Jean (Drouhard) L.; m. Andrew Lee Spacht, May 24, 1980 (div. 1984). BA in History, Allegheny Coll., 1979; MA in Social Studies, Gannon U., 1987. Adminstrv. asst. Security Bank, Erie, 1979-82; coord. IRA Colony Savs. Bank, Erie, 1982-86, data processing officer, 1986-89; mgr. info. systems Allegheny Coll., Meadville, Pa., 1989—; instr. Inst. Fin. Edn., Erie, 1985. Author biog. sketches for Pa. Hist and Mus. Commn., 1985. Alden scholar, 1978. Mem. NAFE. Democrat. Roman Catholic. Office: Allegheny Coll Devel Office Meadville PA 16335

LEWIS, DALE ARTHUR, financial planning executive, regional franchise company executive; b. Detroit, Jan. 29, 1947; s. Robert Dale and Vernetta (Dibler) Steinmetz L.; m. Cynthia Anne Kopczyk, Apr. 21, 1971; children: Andrew D., Lisa A., Brian A. CLU, Chartered Fin. Cons. Agt., Aid Assn. for Lutherans, Appleton, Wis., 1971-73, bus. ins. adminstr., 1977-80; supr. Conn. Mut. Life, Detroit, 1973-75; 2d v.p. Fed. Home Life Ins. Co., Battle Creek, Mich., 1980-87; pres. Decorating Systems-Great Lakes; sec.-treas. Decorating Den of Farmington Hills, Mich.; mem. Calhoun County Estate Planning Council, 1980-84. Sustaining mem. Republican Nat. Com. With U.S. Army, 1966-68. Mem. Am. Soc. CLUs (Gold Key Soc., pres. S. Mich. chpt.), Nat. Assn. Life Underwriters, Mich. Assn. Life Underwriters, Detroit Assn. Life Underwriters, Battle Creek C. of C., Nat. Assn. Life Underwriters, DAV (life), Midwest Tng. Dirs. Assn. (pres. 1984-85). Lutheran. Home: 30140 Mullane Dr Farmington Hills MI 48018 Office: Decorating Den 31700 W Three Mile Rd Ste 108 Farmington Hills MI 48018

LEWIS, DIANE, entrepreneur; b. Chgo., Jan. 24, 1936; d. George W. and Kathryn (McKinnen) W.; divorced; children: William Brosius, Dwight Scott. Student, U. Ill., Chgo., 1953-57. Exec. officer, founding dir. Interviewing Technicians, Inc., Chgo., 1959-69; exec. officer, founding dir. Interviewing Dynamics, Inc., Chgo., Atlanta and Houston, 1969—, London, 1980—; cons. IDI Profl. Recruitment, Inc., Chgo., 1988—, Indyna Pub. & Pub. Rels., Inc., Chgo., 1988—, Internat. Cons., Inc., Chgo., 1978—; owner I.D. Mgmt., Chgo., 1981—; lectr., pub. speaker TV. Authors: Insider's Guide to Finding the Right Job, 1987, Equal to the Challenge, 1988. Speaker Inner Cir. Rep. Com. Job Seminars, U.S. & Can., 1984—. Trustee Adv. Bd. City Univ. Mem. Am. Mgmt. Assn., Ill. Employment Assn., Aircraft Owners & Pilots Assn., Equal to the Challenge Assn. (pres., founder 1988—).

LEWIS, DIANE PATRICIA, finance executive; b. Elizabeth, N.J., Oct. 9, 1956; d. Walter Charles and Ethel Alida (Worth) L. Assocs. of Bus., Union Coll., 1976; B of Psychology, Rutgers Coll., 1979. Br. mgr. Household Fin. Corp., Wayne, N.J., 1979-85; asst. treas., budget coordinator comml. sector Chase Manhatten Bank, N.Y.C., 1985—; dir. seminars, workshops, classes Eckankar, Rahway, N.J., 1979—; freelance computer cons., N.Y.C., 1986—. Mem. Phi Theta Kappa. Office: 2350 Broadway Ste 1225 New York NY 10024

LEWIS, DOUGLAS GRINSLADE, Canadian minister, parliament member; b. Toronto, Ont., Can., Apr. 17, 1938. Grad. Chartered Acct., 1962; JD, Osgoode Hall Law Sch., 1967. Bar: Ont. 1969. Assoc. Crawford, Lewis, Worling, Ewart & MacKenzie, Orillia, Ont., 1969-79; mem. Ho. Commons, 1979—, parliamentary sec. to minister supply and services, 1979-80, spokesman for housing, 1980, dep. opposition house leader, interim opposition house leader, 1983, chmn. standing com. on pub. accounts, chmn. fed. Ont. Prog. Conservative Caucus, 1983-84, parliamentary sec. to pres. treasury bd., 1984-85, parliamentary sec. to pres. Queen's privy council for Can., 1985-86, parliamentary sec. to dep. prime minister and govt. house leader, 1986-87, minister of state dep. house leader, minister of state treasury bd., 1987-88, minister of justice and atty. gen. Can., govt. house leader, 1989—. Past pres. Toronto Jr. Bd. Trade, Ont. Jaycees, Can. Jaycees; active various polit. campaigns, 1971-79. Named Queen's counsel, 1984; sworn to Privy Coun., 1987. Fellow Inst. Chartered Accts. Conservative. Office: House of Commons, Centre Block Rm 215-S, Ottawa, ON Canada K1A 0A6 also: 41 Peter St N, Orillia, ON Canada L3V 4Y9 also: 517 Dominion Ave, Midland, ON Canada L4R 1P7

LEWIS, DOUGLAS JOEL, financial planner; b. Norfolk, Va., May 10, 1940; s. Albert Samuel and Blanche May (Ablelove) L.; m. Linda Christine Perez, Oct. 23, 1976; children: Deborah, Daniel, Naomi. Pre-law student, Washington and Lee U., 1957-61; BS with honors, Columbia U., 1963, MA with honors, 1965; PhD, U. Tex., 1967. Cert. fin. planner; lic. real estate broker, N.C.; lic. ins. broker, N.C. Tax shelter specialist Bache Halsey Stuart Shields, Raleigh, N.C., 1980-82, Dean Witter Reynolds, Raleigh, 1982; registered rep. FSC Securities, Raleigh, 1982-83, Source Securities, Raleigh, 1983-86; cert. fin. planner Lewis Fin. Mgmt., Raleigh, 1984—; leader numerous seminars and workshops. Author: Dickens on Education, 1965. Served with USCGR, 1960-65. Mem. Internat. Assn. for Fin. Planning, Inst. Cert. Fin. Planners, Investment Cos. Inst. (registered investment advisor), SEC, Better Bus. Bur., Greater Raleigh C. of C., Zeta Beta Tau. Home: 5301 Edington Ln Raleigh NC 27604 Office: Lewis Fin Mgmt PO Box 31648 4600 Marriott Dr Ste 310 Raleigh NC 27622

LEWIS, DUSTIN, management information systems analyst, entrepreneur; b. Appleton, Wis., July 11, 1948; d. Robert George and Martha (Wells) L.; m. Irwin S. Bitter, Nov. 4, 1974 (div. Feb. 1980); m. Donald Erik Kahlson, July 15, 1988. BA in Psychology, U. Wis., 1972, MS in MIS, 1985. Police officer Dept. Police, Middleton, Wis., 1975-78; owner, operator W. Br. Farm, Blue Mounds, Wis., 1975-82; supr. Koppers Co., Pitts., 1985-87; gen. mgr., prin. Architectronics Corp., Morristown, N.J., 1987—. Home and Office: 2 Farragut Pl Morristown NJ 07960

LEWIS, EDWIN A., communications company executive; b. Bronx, N.Y., Oct. 28, 1942. BBA, Baruch Coll., 1964. CPA, N.Y. Acctg. surp. Pall Corp., Sea Cliff, N.Y., 1964-65; various staff positions Deloitte Haskins & Sells, N.Y.C., 1965-75; ptnr. Deloitte Haskins & Sells, 1975-82; with Hearst Corp., N.Y.C., 1983—; v.p., treas. Hearst Corp., 1984—. Mem. Am. Inst. CPA's, N.Y. State Soc. CPA's, Fin. Execs. Inst. Office: Hearst Corp 959 Eighth Ave New York NY 10019

LEWIS, EVELYN, marketing communications executive; b. Goslar, Germany, Sept. 19, 1946; came to U.S. 1952, naturalized 1957; d. Gerson Emanuel and Sala (Mendlowicz) L. BA, U. Ill.-Chgo., 1968; MA, Ball State U., 1973, PhD, 1976. Rsch. analyst Comptr. State Ill., Chgo., 1977-78; lectr. polit. sci. dept. Loyola U., Chgo., 1977; asst. to commr. Dept. Human Svcs., Chgo., 1978-81; group mgr. communications Arthur Andersen & Co., Chgo., 1981-84; dir. communications and pub. rels. Heidrick and Struggles, Inc., Chgo., 1984-88; mgr. change mgmt. svcs. practice Andersen Cons., 1989—; adj. faculty sch. bus. adminstrn. Roosevelt U. , 1988. Mem. priority grants com. United Way of Chgo. Mem. Children of the Holocaust, Chgo., 1982; bd. dirs. Child Abuse Prevention Svcs. Mem. Internat. Assn. Bus. Communicators, Publicity Club Chgo., Coun. of Communication Mgmt, NAFE, B'nai Brith. Jewish. Avocations: writing, poetry, bicycling, hiking. Office: Arthur Anderson & Co 69 W Washington Chicago IL 60606

LEWIS, FRANCIS JAMES, electronics and communications company executive; b. Lorain, Ohio, Nov. 18, 1930; s. Harmon Harrison and Gertrude Ethel (Lunn) L.; m. Nina Louise Dunn, Oct. 20, 1956; children: Michael P., Laura K., Janet L., David J., Kenneth J. B.E.E. with high honors, U. Fla., 1960; postgrad., Fla. Inst. Tech. With Harris Corp., Melbourne, Fla., 1960—, v.p., gen. mgr. govt. communications systems div., 1978-79, v.p., group v.p. govt. systems group, 1979-81, sr. v.p., sector exec., govt. systems sector, 1981-88, sr. v.p., spl. asst. to chmn. and chief exec. officer, 1988—. Served with AUS, 1951-53. Mem. IEEE, Electronic Industries Assn. (bd. dirs.), Armed Forces Communications and Electronics Assn. (bd. dirs.), Security Affairs Support Assn. (bd. dirs.), Aerospace Industries Assn. Roman Catholic. Office: Harris Corp 1025 W NASA Blvd Melbourne FL 32919

LEWIS, GAIL R., investment consultant; b. Pensacola, Fla., July 23, 1943; d. Robert Conley and Mary Opal (Carnes) Robinson; m. J. Frank Harrison (div.); m. Donald E. Lewis, Dec. 17, 1988. Student, U. Tenn.-Chattanooga, 1961-64, N.Y. Sch. Interior Design, 1975. Lic. comml. pilot, fin. cons. Aviation crop duster southeastern states, 1964-65; adminstr. dr.'s office, Chattanooga, 1966-72; interior designer, prin. Chattanooga, 1973-75; pub. relations adminstr. Adios Golf Club, Deerfield Beach, Fla., 1982-84; mktg. exec., adminstr. lawyer's office, Ft. Lauderdale, Fla., 1985-86; ptnr., fin. cons. G & D Investments, Pompano Beach, Fla., 1987—. Membership chmn. United Cerebral Palsy Orgn., Chattanooga, 1973, pres. 1974, treas. 1975; ednl. guide Hunter Mus. Art, Chattanooga, 1975, chmn. aux. guides 1976—arrangements chmn. 1978; mem. Chattanooga Juvenile. Ct. Commn., 1977-79; formerly active Heart Assn. and athletic fund U. Tenn.; bd. dirs. Emerald Tower Assn., 1983-86; mem. Ft. Lauderdale Planned Giving Council, 1985. Named Miss Chattanooga, 1961. Republican. Home: 1508 Riverview Oaks Rd Chattanooga TN 37405 Office: G&D Investments 150 SW 12th Ave Ste 201 Pompano Beach FL 33069 also: 1401 S Ocean Blvd Apt 1001 Pompano Beach FL 33062

LEWIS, GEORGE RALPH, consumer goods company executive; b. Burgess, Va., Mar. 7, 1941; s. Spencer Harcum and Edith Pauline (Toulson) L.; m. Lillian Charlotte Glenn, Oct. 11, 1963; children: Tonya, Tracey. BS, Hampton U., 1963; MBA, Iona Coll., 1968. Product analyst Gen. Foods Corp., White Plains, N.Y., 1963-66; fin. analyst W.R. Grace, N.Y.C., 1966-67; corp. analyst Philip Morris Inc., N.Y.C., 1967-69, sr. planning analyst, 1969-70, mgr. fin. rels., 1970-72, mgr. fin. svcs., 1972-73, asst. treas., 1973-75; v.p. fin. and planning, treas. Philip Morris Indsl., Milw., 1975-82; v.p., treas. Philip Morris Cos., Inc., N.Y.C., 1984—; v.p. fin. The Seven Up Co., St. Louis, 1982-84; bd. dirs. Cen. Fidelity Bank, Richmond, Va. Trustee Meharry Med. Coll., Nashville, Hampton (Va.) U.; bd. dirs. Nat. Urban League, N.Y.C. Recipient Arthur A. Loftus Achievement award in Fin., Iona Coll., 1981, Outstanding Twenty Yr. Alumnus award Hampton U., 1983. Mem. Nat. Corp. Treas. Assn., Nat. Bankers Assn. (corp. adv. bd.), Omega Psi Phi, Sigma Pi Phi. Office: Philip Morris Cos Inc 120 Park Ave New York NY 10017

LEWIS, SIR GEORGE STEPHEN, architect; b. Boston, Dec. 7, 1908; s. William Joseph and Florence Ann (Whitehead) L. Cert., MIT, 1926; grad. (Harvard scholar), Boston Archtl. Sch., 1931; cert., Boston U., 1939; BArch, Boston Archtl. Sch., 1984; grad., Archtl. Sch., Harvard U., 1932, Command and Gen. Staff Coll., 1956, U.S. Army C.E. Sch., 1957, Indsl. Coll. of Armed Forces, 1963. Registered architect, Mass., Maine, Vt., N.H., R.I., Conn., N.Y., Minn. Architect with Maginnis & Walsh, Boston, 1925-31; profl. practice Boston, 1928-41; head architect firm Lewis, Spering & Rogers, Boston, 1941-47; prin. architect George Stephen Lewis & Assos., Boston, 1947—; chief architect Pub. Works Dept., U.S. Navy, Boston, 1953-65; pres. Roslindale Bd. of Trade, 1958-59; mem. Nat. Fed. Agencies Com., 1969, Civic Design Com., 1965-67; participant AIA-HUD Assisted Housing Seminar, 1972, AIA-Cons. Engrs. Council-Profl. Engrs. in Pvt. Practice Conf. Profl. Liability Service, 1972, 75; Cons. Engrs. Council Conf. Occupational, Safety and Health Adminstrn., 1972, 74, Nat. Seminar Architects-Engrs.; Firms on Contracts and Programs, New Orleans, 1971; rep. Nat. Architects-Engrs. Pub. Affairs Conf., Washington, 1972-76. Prin. works include Renovation State Capitol, Mass., 1948-51, Admiral's Residence, Boston Naval Shipyard, 1959-60, San. Bldg, Nahant, Mass., 1948-49, Lodgen's Supermarket, Roslindale, Mass., 1948, modern residences, Boston Housing Authority, 1947-48,; design: Ch. of Annunciation, Danvers, Mass., 1936-37; author: Complet 30 Year History of Boston Chapter of CSI, 1986; also contbr. 416 articles to profl. jours., newspapers. Mem. N.E. regional council; mem. AIA Conf. Nat. and Regional Planning, Ethics and Bus., 1942-86; mem. archtl.-engring. firms contract bd. Boston Naval Shipyard, 1971-73. Served with AUS, 1943-46. Created knight France, 1961, Grand knight, 1962; recipient Great Silver medal of Paris, 1962, Harvard scholar Boston Archtl. Ctr., 1931, Rotch Travelling fellow in architecture, 1933-35, award of honor, citation Nat. Found. Arts and Humanities., 1965, Medaille de la France Libérée, 1982, Churchill medal of Wisdom, Churchill fellow, Wisdom laureate, 1988; inducted to Hall of Fame, 1970. Mem. AIA (nat. legis. minuteman 1968—, del. nat. convs. 1946—, ofcl. recorder 1979), Constrn. Specifications Inst. (chmn. publicity com. Boston chpt. 1974-75, chpt. dir. 1978-80, chpt. historian 1980—, del. N.E. region 1 conf. 1961, 76—, pres.'s cert. Boston chpt. 1977, cert. of appreciation for exceptional disting. service 1980, 86, 40-yr. Chevron award as charter mem. 1988), Boston Soc. Architects (profl. practices com. 1974—, urban design com. 1980—), Order of Lafayette (nat. v.p., dir., historian 1958—), Fed. Profl. Assn., Archtl. Assn. London, Greater Boston C. of C., Inst. Contemporary Art, UN Assn. (charter 1942), Mil. Order World Wars (exec. com. 1973—), Res. Officers Assn. (nominating com., army council chpt. 1974-77, pres. 1960-61). Republican. Episcopalian. Clubs: Harvard (Boston), Republican. Home: 1376 Commonwealth Ave Ste 21 Boston MA 02134 Office: 101 Tremont St Rm 705 Boston MA 02108

LEWIS, HAROLD ALLEN, travel company executive; b. Bronx, Oct. 1, 1945; s. Barney and Bess S. (Feifer) L.; B.B.A., Hofstra U., 1970; M.B.A., N.Y.U., 1971; m. Helene A. Lipitz, May 25, 1968; children—Lyn C., Franci K. Asso. mgr. fin. planning and analysis Dun & Bradstreet Corp., N.Y.C., 1975-77, mgr. budgets/forecasts, 1977-78; mgr. strategic planning Reuben H. Donnelley Corp., N.Y.C., 1978-79; mgr. treasury ops. Dun & Bradstreet, N.Y.C., 1979-80; v.p. fin./planning Corinthian Broadcasting Corp., N.Y.C., 1980-85; v.p. fin. and adminstrn. Thomas Cook Travel, USA, 1985-86, sr. v.p., 1986, pres., 1986—. Served with Army N.G., 1966-71. Mem. N.Am. Soc. Corp. Planning, Hofstra U. Alumni Assn., NYU Alumni Assn. Home: 42 Voorhis Ave Rockville Centre NY 11570

LEWIS, HENRY RAFALSKY, manufacturing company executive; b. Yonkers, N.Y., Nov. 19, 1925; s. Jasper R. and Freda (Rafalsky) L.; m. Barbara Connolly, June 15, 1957; children—Peter, Susan, Abigail. A.B., Harvard U., 1949, M.A., 1951, Ph.D., 1957. Group head Ops. Evaluation Group, Washington, 1955-57; mem. staff Electronic Rsch. Lab. RCA, Princeton, N.J., 1957-66, dir., 1966-70; v.p. rsch./devel. Itek Corp., Lexington, Mass., 1970-74; pres. Optel Corp., Princeton, N.J., 1974; sr. v.p. Dennison Mfg. Co., Waltham, Mass., 1974-85, vice chmn., 1986—, also bd. dirs.; bd. dirs. Dennison Mfg. Co., Delphax Systems, Randolph, Mass., AOI Systems, Lowell, Mass., Genzyme Corp., Boston, Adams-Russell Electronics Co., Inc., Waltham, Mass., Vasocor Corp., Menlo Park, Calif. Contbr. articles to profl. jours. Chmn. investment com. Belmont (Mass.) Music Sch., 1978—. Served with U.S. Army, 1944-46. Mem. IEEE, Am. Phys. Soc., Indsl. Rsch. Inst., Phi Beta Kappa, Sigma Xi. Club: Harvard. Home: 35 Clover St Belmont MA 02178 Office: Dennison Mfg Co 275 Wyman St Waltham MA 02254-9139

LEWIS, JAMES DAVID, finance company executive, management consultant; b. Tazewell, Tenn., Dec. 8, 1947; s. Mark Isaac and Stella (Parkey) L.; m. Ruth Ann Williams, Dec. 20, 1969 (div. Apr. 1981); m. Alice Faye Wilson, Jan. 9, 1983; children: Allison Leah, Mark Isaac. BS in Fin., U. Tenn., 1970, MBA in Mgmt., 1982. Various mgmt. positions Citizens Bank, New Tazewell, 1965-79; sr. v.p. City and Country Bank of Bell County, Middlesboro, Ky., 1981-83; with loan recovery dept. FDIC, Knoxville, Tenn., 1983-84; fin. planner Sequoyah Assocs., Knoxville, 1984-85; owner, pres. Resource Adv. Svcs., Inc., Knoxville, 1985—; investment advisor Holston Conf. United Meth. Ch., 1987—. Mem. Nat. Assn. Personal Fin. Advisors, Internat. Assn. Fin. Planners, Inst. Cert. Fin. Planners. Methodist. Home: 8001 Ember Crest Trail Knoxville TN 37938

LEWIS, JAMES HENRY, communications executive; b. Oneonta, N.Y., July 4, 1949; s. Fred Joseph and Dorothy May (Moore) L.; m. Diane Lynn Hillegas, July 6, 1974; children: Patrick James, Lindsey Diane, Jillian Suzanne. BS in Edn., SUNY, Cortland, 1971. Dist. mgr. Rich Pak, Inc., Vestal, N.Y., 1977-78, TAD, Inc., Johnson City, N.Y., 1978-81; exec. recruiter Dunhill Personnel, Johnson City, 1981-82; dir ops. Software Labs. Corp., Johnson City, 1982-84; v.p. Fabrecon Devel., Johnson City, 1984-87, also bd. dirs.; pres., CEO U.S. Construct, Inc., Johnson City, N.Y., 1987—. Author: Consultant's Guide to Incorporation, 1980, (software) Write Your Own Paycheck, 1984. Membership chmn. Lincoln Sch. PTA, Johnson City, 1986—. Mem. Am. Mgmt. Assn. Republican. Office: Fabrecon Devel Corp 50 Willow St PO Box 706 Johnson City NY 13790

LEWIS, JAMES LUTHER, savings and loan executive; b. Bridgeport, Ohio, Sept. 29, 1912; s. William Luther and Gwen (Evans) L.; grad. Mercersburg Acad., 1931; B.A., Yale U., 1935; m. Mary Anne Glen, Oct. 26, 1943; children—William Luther II, Gwendolyn. Salesman, asst. sales dist. mgr. Chgo. Pneumatic Tool Co., 1935-43, asst. to pres., 1946-55; v.p., adminstrn. and sales, dir. Van Norman Industries, Inc., 1956; pres. Insuline Corp., 1956-58; v.p. corp. devel. Norris Thermador Corp., Los Angeles, 1959-65; chmn. bd., dir. Am. Savs. & Loan Assn., Reno, 1965—, Sierra Fin. Corp., 1968—; dir. Firth Sterling Steel Corp., 1956-58. Served to lt. USNR, 1943-46. Decorated Purple Heart, Presdl. Unit citation. Presbyterian. Home: 7755 Lakeside Dr Reno NV 89511 Office: 67 W Liberty St Reno NV 89501

LEWIS, JEROME A., petroleum company executive, investment banker; b. Wichita, Kans., 1927; B.A. in Geology, U. Okla.; married. With Shell Oil Co., 1950-51; pres. Lewmont Drilling, Inc., 1951-65, Border Exploration Co., 1965-68; pres., chmn. bd., chief exec. officer Petro-Lewis Corp., 1968-87; pres. Princeps Ptnrs., Inc., 1987-88, also bd. dirs.; dir. Leo Energy, 1987-88. Bd. dirs. Young Life Found., Hope Ventures Inc., Denver Leadership Found. Mem. Ind. Petroleum Assn. Am., Oil Investment Inst. (founding gov.), World Bus. Council, Am. Assn. Petroleum Geologists, Am. Petroleum Inst., Chief Execs. Orgn. Office: Princeps Ptnrs Inc 717 17th St Ste 1450 Denver CO 80202

LEWIS, JOHN CLARK, JR., manufacturing company executive; b. Livingston, Mont., Oct. 15, 1935; s. John Clark and Louise A. (Anderson) L.; m. Carolyn Jean Keesling, Sept. 4, 1960; children: Robert, Anne, James. BS, Fresno (Calif.) State U., 1957. With Service Bur. Corp., El Segundo, Calif., 1960-70, Computer Scis. Corp., 1970; with Xerox Corp., El Segundo, 1970-77, pres. bus. systems div., 1977; pres. Amdahl Corp., Sunnyvale, Calif., 1983-87, chief exec. officer, 1983—, chmn., 1987—. Served with USNR, 1957-60. Roman Catholic. Office: Amdahl Corp 1250 E Arques Ave Sunnyvale CA 94088 *

LEWIS, JOHN FURMAN, lawyer, oil company executive; b. Fort Worth, Apr. 24, 1934; s. Ben B. and Minnie W. (Field) L.; m. Beverly Ann George, Feb. 16, 1963; children—Joyce Ann, George Field, William Patrick. Student, Tex. Christian U., summer 1955; B.A. in Econs., Rice U., 1956; J.D. with honors, U. Tex., 1962; postgrad., Princeton U., 1965-66; M.B.A., Bowling Green State U., 1971. Bar: Tex. 1962, U.S. Dist. Ct. 1965, U.S. Supreme Ct. 1967, Ohio 1968, U.S. Ct. Mil. Appeals 1971, Okla. 1987. Atty. Atlantic Richfield Co., 1962-67; with Marathon Oil Co., Findlay, Ohio, 1967-86, gen. atty., 1978, sr. atty., 1978-81, assoc. gen. counsel, 1983-84, v.p., gen. counsel, 1981-83, v.p., gen. counsel., sec., 1985-86; sr. v.p., gen. counsel The Williams Cos., Tulsa, 1986—; mem. adv. bd. Internat. and Comparative Law Ctr. of Southwestern Legal Found.; mem. adv. bd. Internat. Oil and Gas Ednl. Ctr. of Southwestern Legal Found. Contbr. articles to profl. jours. Mem. exec. com., trustee United Way of Hancock County, Findlay, Ohio, 1984-86; bd. dirs. NO-WE-OH council Camp Fire, Inc., Findlay, Ohio, 1974-86, Okla. Green Country council, Tulsa, 1987—. Served to lt. (j.g.) USN, 1956-59. Mem. ABA (subcom. chmn. 1984-85), Tex. Bar Assn., Am. Petroleum Inst. (lawyer-adviser mktg. com. 1982-84, gen. law com. 1983—), Ohio Bar Assn., Okla. Bar Assn., Tulsa County Bar Assn. Republican. Office: Williams Cos 1 Williams Ctr PO Box 2400 Tulsa OK 74172

LEWIS, JOHN OWEN, real estate developer; b. Quanah, Tex., Nov. 20, 1935; s. John O. and Charles Etta (Fisher) L.; m. Mary Jo McPherson, Oct. 22, 1959 (div.); children: John J., Jeanne M.; m. Ashley Wells, Sept. 20, 1985. BA in Econs., U. Calif., Santa Barbara, 1958. Salesman The Seeley Co., Los Angeles, 1959-70, v.p., ptnr., 1970-76; v.p. Cushman and Wakefield, Los Angeles, 1976-77, sr. v.p., 1977-78, exec. v.p., 1978-79; pres. The Lewis Co., Los Angeles, 1979-89, Woodland Hills, Calif., 1989—.

Served to lt. USN, 1959-64. Mem. Am. Soc. Real Estate Counselors, Los Angeles Realty Bd., Malibu Market Club, Jonathan Club. Office: 20969 Ventura Blvd Ste 216 Woodland Hills CA 91304

LEWIS, KENNETH, shipping executive; b. N.Y.C., Aug. 23, 1934; b. Nathaniel and Hana Evelyn (Kotler) L.; A.B., Princeton U., 1955; J.D., Harvard U., 1958; m. Carol Ann Schnitzer, Aug. 3, 1958 (div. 1982); children—Scott, Laurence, Kathleen; m. 2d, Colleen Anne Wesche, Nov. 27, 1983. Admitted to N.Y., Oreg. bars, 1959; law clk. to judge U.S. Dist. Ct., N.Y.C., 1958-59; asso. King, Miller, Anderson, Nash & Yerke, Portland, Oreg., 1959-61; gen. counsel Indsl. Air Products Co., Portland, 1961-63; v.p. to exec. v.p. Lasco Shipping Co., Portland, 1963-79, pres., 1979—; bd. dirs. Britannia Steam Ship Ins. Assn., Ltd., London, 1986—, The Swedish Club, Gothenburg, 1987—, dep. chmn., 1988—. Mem. Port of Portland Commn., 1974-81, treas., 1977, v.p., 1978, pres., 1979; trustee Lewis and Clark Coll., 1974-83; bd. dirs. Columbia River Maritime Mus., 1987—, Oreg. Community Found., 1982—, treas., 1986—; mem. Portland Met. Area Boundary Commn., 1974-74, Portland Met. Mass Transit Dist. Bd., 1973-74; pres. Portland Zool. Soc., 1970, World Affairs Council of Oreg., 1969. Mem. Am., Oreg. Bar Assns., Soc. Maritime Arbitrators, Inc. Democrat. Jewish. Clubs: Multnomah Athletic, Arlington, University, Masons, City (Portland). Office: 3200 NW Yeon Ave Portland OR 97210

LEWIS, MARYANN, auditor; b. Kew Gardens, N.Y., Dec. 28, 1964. BS in Mgmt., St. John's U., 1986. Auditor Irving Trust Co., N.Y.C., 1986-88, J.P. Morgan, N.Y.C., 1988—. Vol. tchr. St. Teresa's Sch., Woodside, N.Y., 1985—. Mem. Nat. Assn. Female Execs., Beta Gamma Sigma, Omicron Delta Epsilon. Republican. Roman Catholic. Home: 48 15 54th Ave Maspeth NY 11378 Office: J P Morgan 23 Wall St New York NY 10015

LEWIS, MICHAEL EDWIN, financial institution executive; b. Toledo, Ohio, Apr. 28, 1956; s. Edwin Neldon Lewis and Lois Blanche (Smith) Lewis Phalen; m. Lori Ann Brueshaber, Sept. 11, 1976; children: Michael Fredrick, Jennifer Christine. Student, U. Toledo, 1974-81. Asst. bus. mgr. Cosmos Broadcasting Corp., Toledo, 1976-81; bus. mgr., controller Heftel Broadcasting Corp., Indpls., 1981-83; comml. loan officer Firstmark Fin. Corp., Indpls., 1983-85; v.p. broadcast fin. Firstmark Fin. Corp., 1985-86, sr. v.p., 1986—. Bd. dirs. Fishers (Ind.) Recreational League, 1987—. Mem. Nat. Assn. Broadcasters, Indpls. Mus. Art. Republican. Baptist. Home: 7726 Sunblest Blvd N Noblesville IN 46060 Office: Firstmark Fin Corp 110 E Washington St Indianapolis IN 46204

LEWIS, MORRIS, JR., wholesale and retail grocery executive; b. Lexington, Miss., Apr. 19, 1911; s. Morris and Julia (Herrman) L.; m. Frederica Lantor, Nov. 21, 1933; children: Morris III, Julia (Mrs. Gerald W. Miller). B.S. in Econs, Wharton Sch., U. Pa., 1932. With Lewis Grocer Co., Indianola, Miss., 1932-86; pres Lewis Grocer Co., 1937-69, chmn. bd., 1969-86; pres. Sunflower Stores, Indianola, 1948-69; chmn. bd. Sunflower Stores, 1969-86; v.p., dir. Super Valu Stores, Inc, Hopkins, Minn., 1965-70; chmn. bd. Super Valu Stores, Inc, 1970-76, dir., chmn. exec. com., 1976-83; pres. Delta Mktg. Co., Indianola, 1981-87; dir. Peoples Bank of Indianola. Mem. Nat. council Boy Scouts Am., also bd. dirs., past pres. Delta council; trustee emeritus Millsaps Coll., Jackson, Food Industry Crusade Against Hunger, 1985—. Served to maj. AUS, World War II. Named Indianola Citizen of Year Indianola C. of C., 1954. Mem. Nat.-Am. Wholesale Grocers Assn. (past nat. pres., past chmn. bd.), Miss. Econ. Council (past chmn.). Club: Rotarian (past pres.). Home: One Arbor Ln Indianola MS 38751 Office: Lewis Grocer Co Hwy 49 Indianola MS 38751

LEWIS, NEIL DENNIS, finance executive; b. Milbank, S.D., July 21, 1934; s. Melbourne and Florence (Lindahl) L.; m. Clarice Kloster, June 1953 (div. 1976); m. Sharon M. Derby, Dec. 31, 1977; children: Steven, Lori, Bradley, Karen, Troy, Terry. Prin. Bowling Lanes Establishment, Milbank, 1957-59, Whetstone Realty, Milbank, 1960-65, Granite Lanes Inc., Milbank, 1965-69; overseas mgr. Ethio Gum Program, Mpls., 1970-72; pres. Internat. Mergers and Acquisitions Inc., Scottsdale, Ariz., 1972—. Patentee granite bowling lanes, granite topped billiard tables. Chmn. Grant County (S.D.) Reps., 1966-67. Served with USNG, 1953-60. Recipient Bus. and Humanitarian award Ethiopian Govt., 1970. Mem. Internat. Real Estate Inst. Lutheran. Office: Internat Mergers & Acquisitions Inc 8100 E Indian School Rd Scottsdale AZ 85251

LEWIS, N(ORMAN) RICHARD, public relations/advertising executive; b. N.Y.C., Aug. 13, 1925; s. David and Jeanne (Miller) L.; m. Margaret Alderson Bowman, Dec. 3, 1962 (div. 1966); 1 child, Ian Richard; m. Sandra Kay Weatherly, Dec. 17, 1970. BS, Ohio U., 1950. Reporter Ala. Post Advocate, 1953-54; news bur. chief Auto Club So. Calif., 1954-57; account exec. Fallon & Co., Los Angeles, 1957-60; pres. Lewis & Assocs., Los Angeles, 1960—; chmn. dean's forum UCLA Grad. Sch. Architecture and Urban Planning. 1st lt. arty. U.S. Army, 1950-53, Korea. Decorated Bronze Star. Mem. Public Relations Soc. Am. (accredited), Soc. for Mktg. Profl. Svcs. (dir. So. Calif. chpt., Profl. of Yr. 1985), Nat. Assn Real Estate Editors, Sigma Delta Chi. Clubs: Jonathan, Mountain Gate Country, Los Angeles Press. Republican. Office: Lewis & Assocs 3600 Wilshire Blvd #200 Los Angeles CA 90010

LEWIS, RALPH JAY, III, management and human resources educator; b. Balt., Sept. 25, 1942; s. Ralph Jay and Ruth Elizabeth (Schmeltz) L. BS in Engring., Northwestern U., 1966; MS in Adminstrn., U. Calif., Irvine, 1968; PhD in Mgmt., UCLA, 1974. Research analyst Chgo. Area Expressway Surveillance Project, 1963-64, Gen. Am. Transp. Co., Chgo., 1965-66; assco. prof. mgmt. and human resources mgmt. Calif. State U., Long Beach, 1972—; cons. Rand Corp., Santa Monica, Calif., 1966-74, Air Can., Montreal, Que., 1972-73, Los Angeles Times, 1973;. Co-author: Studies in the Quality of LIfe, 1972; author instructional programs, monographs; codesigner freeway traffic control system. Bd. dirs. Project Quest, Los Angeles, 1969-71. Mem. AAAS, Am. Psychol. Assn., Assn. for Humanistic Psychology, The World Future Soc., Soc. of Mayflower Desc., SAR (Ill. soc.), Internat. Arabian Horse Assn., Sierra Club, Beta Gamma Sigma. Democrat. Office: Calif State U Dept Human Resources Mgmt Long Beach CA 90840

LEWIS, REGINALD F., venture capitalist; b. Balt., Dec. 7, 1942; married; 2 daughters. AB, Va. State U., 1965; JD, Harvard U., 1968. Bar: N.Y. 1970. Assoc. Paul, Weiss, Rifkind, Wharton & Garrison, N.Y.C., 1968-70; ptnr. Lewis & Clarkson, N.Y.C., 1973—; chmn., chief exec. officer TLC Group, LP, N.Y.C., 1983—. Mem. Assn. of Bar of City of N.Y. (com. on corps.), ABA. Office: Lewis & Clarkson/TLC Group 99 Wall St New York NY 10005

LEWIS, RICHARD JAY, marketing educator, university dean; b. Marion, Ohio, July 14, 1933; s. Harley Franklin and Christina Mary (Anderson) L.; m. Patricia Ruth Montgomery, Sept. 17, 1955; children: Pamela Kay, Gregory Carl, Scott Alan. BS, Miami U., Oxford, Ohio, 1957, MBA, 1959; DBA, Mich. State U., 1964. Mem. faculty Mich. State U., East Lansing, 1964—, prof. mktg., 1970—, dean Coll. Bus., 1975—; dean Faculty of Bus. U. Nigeria, Enugu, 1966-67; bd. dirs. First of Mich. Corp., Detroit, First of Mich. Capital Corp., Dale Computer Corp., Am. Assembly Collegiate Schs. Bus. Author: Logistical Information System for Marketing Analysis, 1970, (with B. von H. Gilmer) Industrial and Organizational Psychology, 1971. Bd. dirs. Edward W. Sparrow Hosp., 1985—. Served with U.S. Army, 1953-55. Decorated Commendation medal. Mem. Am. Mktg. Assn., Lansing Regional C. of C. (bd. dirs. 1980-83), Golden Key, Sigma Xi, Beta Gamma Sigma (bd. govs. 1976-82, nat. pres. 1980-82). Home: 1216 Woodwind Trail Haslett MI 48840 Office: Mich State U Coll Bus East Lansing MI 48824

LEWIS, RITA HOFFMAN, plastic products manufacturing company executive; b. Phila., Aug. 6, 1947; d. Robert John and Helen Anna (Dugan) Hoffman; 1 child, Stephanie Blake. Student Jefferson Med. Coll. Sch. Nursing, 1965-67; Gen. mgr. Sheets & Co. Inc. (now Flower World, Inc.), Woodbury, N.J., 1968-72; dir., exec. v.p., treas. Hoffman Precision Plastics, Inc., Blackwood, N.J., 1973—; ptnr. Timber Assocs.; guest speaker various civic groups, 1974—. Author: That Part of Me I Never Really Meant to Share, 1979; In Retrospect: Caught Between Running and Loving. Mem. Com. for Citizens of Glen Oaks (N.J.), 1979—, Gloucester Twp. Econ. Devel. Com., 1981—, Gloucester Twp. Day Scholarship Com., 1984—; chairperson Gloucester Twp. Day Scholarship Found., 1985—; bd. dirs. Diane Hull Dance Co. Recipient Winning Edge award, 1982, Mayor's award for Womens' Achievement, 1987, Outstanding Community Service award Mayor, Council and Com., 1987. Mem. Sales Assn. Chem. Industry, Blackwood Businessmen's Assn., Soc. Plastic Engrs. Roman Catholic.

LEWIS, ROBERT ALAN, oil field service company executive; b. Brownwood, Tex., Jan. 8, 1949; s. Robert Lee and Joy June (Littlefield) L.; m. Rhonda Sue Nunn, Aug. 25, 1973; children: Robin Michele, Ryan Lee. BS, Tex. A&M U., 1972. Mgr. Bar B Ranch, Brownwood, 1973-78; fluids engr. NL Baroid, Houston, 1978-81; sales rep. NL Baroid-Completion/Workover Fluids, Oklahoma City, 1981-84; tech. sales rep. NL Baroid-C/WOF, Lafayette, La., 1984-87; region mgr. NL Baroid-C/WOF, New Orleans, 1987—. Mem. Soc. Petroleum Engrs. (assoc., membership com. 1985-86), Petroleum Club Lafayette, Aggie Club, Lafayette A&M Club (bd. dirs. 1985-86). Home: 405 Flamingo Rd Slidell LA 70461 Office: NL Baroid 1500 Pere Marquette Bldg New Orleans LA 70112

LEWIS, RONALD ALAN, accountant; b. Chgo., Aug. 15, 1953; s. Milton H. and Rachel (Mevorah) L.; m. Mary Ann Misiewicz, Oct. 5, 1980; 1 child, Alison. BS, U. Ill., Chgo., 1975; M in Taxation, DePaul U., 1983. CPA, Ill. Tax acct. Seidman & Seidman, Chgo., 1976-80; tax mgr., ptnr. Berg, DeMarco, Lewis, Sawatski & Co., Northbrook, Ill., 1980—. Mem. Ill. Soc. CPA's, (chmn. taxation com. proposed regulation 1985—, chmn. tax conf. 1987). Jewish. Office: Berg DeMarco Lewis Sawatski & Co 630 Dundee Rd Ste 425 Northbrook IL 60062

LEWIS, RONALD LOREN, health care executive; b. Clinton, Mo., Mar. 28, 1946; s. Lester Clark Jr. and Lois Arlene (Sell) L.; m. Nancy Louise Price, Nov. 12, 1966; children: Kimberly Dawn, Matthew Ryan. BBA, Roosevelt U., 1976; MBA, Rosary Coll., River Forest, Ill., 1979. Bus. ofc. mgr. Condell Meml. Hosp., Libertyville, Ill., 1970-72; asst. to adminstr. Rehab. Inst. Chgo., 1972-75; corp. dir. materials mgmt. Evang. Hosps. Corp., Oak Brook, Ill., 1975-81, v.p. materials mgmt., 1981-82, v.p. shared services, 1982-84, v.p. corp. services, 1984—; resource maximization com. Health First Network, Oak Brook, 1985-86. V.p. bd. dirs. St. Matthew United Ch. Christ, Wheaton, Ill., 1986—, chmn. planning com., 1985-86, chmn. personnel com., 1985-86, pres., 1987—, chmn. bldg. com., 1988—; bd. dirs. Peace United Ch. Residences, 1987—, Immanuel Ch. Residences, 1987—. Served with USN, 1965-70, Vietnam. Mem. Am. Hosp. Assn., Am. Soc. for Materials Mgrs., Am. Mgmt. Assn. Home: 655 Dorset Dr Wheaton IL 60187 Office: Evang Hosps Corp 2025 Windsor Dr Oak Brook IL 60521

LEWIS, SHELDON NOAH, chemical company executive; b. Chgo., July 1, 1934; s. Jacob Joseph and Evelyn (Mendelsohn) Iglowitz; m. Suzanne Joyce Goldberg, June 17, 1957; children: Sara Lynn, Matthew David, Rachel Ann. B.A. with honors, Northwestern U., 1956; M.S. (Univ. fellow), 1956; Ph.D. (Eastman Kodak fellow), UCLA, 1959; postgrad. (NSF fellow), U. Basel, Switzerland, 1959-60; postgrad. cert. in research mgmt, Indsl. Research Inst., Harvard U., 1973. With Rohm & Haas Co., 1960-78, head lab., 1963-68, research supr., 1968-73, dir. splty. chem. research, 1973-74; gen. mgr. DCL Lab. AG subs., Zurich, Switzerland, 1974-75; dir. European Labs. Valbonne, France, 1975-76; corp. dir. research and devel. worldwide for polymers, resins and monomers Spring House, Pa., 1976-78; with The Clorox Co., Oakland, Calif., 1978—, v.p. research and devel., 1978, group v.p., 1978-84, exec. v.p., 1984—, also bd. dirs., profl. recruiter, univ liaison.; mem. indsl. panel on sci. and tech. NSF. Referee: Jour. Organic Chemistry; patentee in field; contbr. articles to profl. pubs. Mem. World Affairs Council, UCLA Chemistry Adv. Council, Bay Area Sci. Fair Adv. Bd., Mills Coll. Adv. Council for Sci. and Math. Recipient cert. in patent law Phila. Patent Law Assn., 1962, Roon award for coatings research Fedn. Socs. Coatings Tech., 1966, cert. of service Wayne State U. Polymer Conf. Series, 1967, cert. in mgmt. by objectives Am. Mgmt. Research, Inc., 1972. Mem. Soap and Detergent Assn. (bd. dirs.), Indsl. Research Inst., Am. Chem. Soc. (chmn. Phila. polymer sect. 1970-71), Soc. Chem. Industry London, Sigma Xi. Jewish. Home: 3711 Rose Ct Lafayette CA 94549 Office: The Clorox Co 1221 Broadway Oakland CA 94612

LEWIS, SHERMAN RICHARD, JR., investment banker; b. Ottawa, Ill., Dec. 11, 1936; s. Sherman Richard and Julia Audrey (Rusteen) L.; m. Dorothy Marie Downie, Sept. 9, 1967; children: Thomas, Catherine, Elizabeth, Michael. AB, Northwestern U., 1958; MBA, U. Chgo., 1964. With investment dept. Am. Nat. Bank & Trust Co., Chgo., 1961-64; v.p. Halsey, Stuart & Co., N.Y.C., 1964-70, v.p. in charge corp. fin. dept., 1970-73; v.p. C.J. Lawrence & Sons, N.Y.C., 1970; ptnr. Loeb, Rhoades & Co., N.Y.C., 1974-76, ptnr. in charge corp. fin. dept., 1975-76, exec. v.p., bd. dirs., 1976-77, pres., co-chief exec. officer, 1977-78; vice chmn., co-chief exec. officer Loeb Rhoades, Hornblower & Co., N.Y.C., 1978-79; pres. Shearson/Am. Express Inc., N.Y.C., 1979-82, vice chmn., 1983-84; vice chmn. Shearson Lehman/Am. Express Inc., 1984-85, Shearson Lehman Bros. Inc., 1985-87, Shearson Lehman Hutton Inc., 1988—. Mem. President's Commn. on Housing, 1981-82, President's Council on Internat. Youth Exchange, 1982—. Served as commd. officer USMC, 1958-61. Mem. N.Y. Soc. Security Analysts. Clubs: Bond, India House, Ridgewood Country, University, Quogue Field. Office: Shearson Lehman Bros Inc Am Express Tower World Fin Ctr New York NY 10285

LEWIS, SIDNEY ALLISON, financial executive; b. Jacksonville, Fla., Oct. 2, 1945; s. Sidney Lewis and Rachel Elizabeth (Overby) Munson; m. Juliet Ann Thompson, Oct. 3, 1970; children: Matthew, Michael, Ashley. BA, St. Petersburg Jr. Coll., 1965. Loan officer J.K. Kislak Mortgage Co., Atlanta, 1968-70; v.p. Kissell Co., Atlanta, 1970-73; pres. Affiliated Mortgage Investments, Decatur, Ga., 1973-76; exec. v.p. Home Mortgage Investment Corp., St. Petersburg, 1976-80; v.p. Trust Am. Mortgage, Inc., St. Petersburg, 1980—; pres. The Fla. Group, St. Petersburg, 1980-87, exec. v.p., 1987—; chmn., pres. Trust Am. Service Corp., St. Petersburg, 1984—; pres. Equitable Mortgage Resources, Inc., 1988. Chmn. Belleair (Fla.) Regional Soccer League, 1983. Mem. Mortgage Bankers Assn., Mortgage Bankers Assn. Fla., U.S. League Savs., Carlouel Yacht Club, Atlanta Athletic. Office: Trust Am Svcs Corp 1700 66th St N Saint Petersburg FL 33710

LEWIS, STUART CHARLES, investment company executive; b. Houston, June 19, 1940; s. Mitchell Meyer and Grace Celeste (Pollak) L.; m. Donna Gail Glick, Aug. 20, 1961; children: Darryl S., Gregory Kenneth. BS in Econs., U. Pa., Phila., 1962. Registered rep. Bache & Co., Houston, 1962-70; v.p. fin. Primary Med. Communication, Inc., N.Y.C., 1971-74; pres. Cowl Energy Corp., Oakland, Md., 1974-76; pres., chief exec. officer WLG Resources, Inc., Houston, 1976-82; ptnr. Gertner, Aron, Ledet and Lewis Investments Ltd., Houston, 1982—; bd. dirs. Cen. Corp., Ft. Lauderdale, Fla., Rexcom Systems Corp., Houston, IBS Technologies, Ltd., B.C., Can., GAL Laurelwood, Inc. Chmn., bd. dirs. Lawndale Art and Performance Ctr., U. Houston, 1987—. Republican. Jewish. Office: Gertner Aron Ledet & Lewis 1400 Post Oak Blvd Ste 500 Houston TX 77056

LEWIS, SYDNEY, retail company executive; b. Richmond, Va., Oct. 24, 1919; s. Julius Beryl and Dora (Lewis) L.; m. Frances Aaronson, Sept. 3, 1942; children: Sydney Jr., Andrew Marc, Susan (Mrs. Dixon Butler). B.A., Washington and Lee U., 1940, postgrad. in law, 1940-42; postgrad. bus. adminstrn., Harvard, 1942-43; in law, George Washington U., 1946; H.H.D., Va. Commonwealth U., 1983. Bar: Va. 1942, D.C. 1947. V.p. New Standard Pub. Co. Inc., Richmond, 1947-58; pres. New Standard Pub. Co. Inc., 1958—; also dir.; founding pres., chmn. Best Products Co. Inc., Richmond, 1951—; also dir. Best Products Co. Inc. Pres. Richmond Jewish Community Council, 1953—, Va. Mus., 1986—; trustee Washington and Lee U., Lexington, Va., Va. Union Univ., Richmond; trustee Hirshorn Mus., Washington, 1976—, chmn., 1985, pres., 1985—; trustee Inst. Contemporary Art, Phila., 1975—, Sch. Visual Arts, Boston U., 1976—, Va. Environ. Endowment Fund, Va. Found. for Humanities and Public Policy, Hebrew Union Coll., Cin., Hirshorn Mus., 1985—, Bklyn. Acad. Music, N.Y., 1985—; mem. bd. assos. U. Richmond.; Trustee Va. Mus. Fine Arts, 1980—, pres., 1986—; trustee Council of Nat. Gallery Art, Washington, 1983 ; bd. dirs. Jobs for Va. Grads., Commonwealth of Va., 1985. Recipient Disting. Virginian award, 1972; nat. honoree award Beta Gamma Sigma, 1976; ann. award Federated Arts Council of Richmond, 1976; Jackson Davis award for disting. service to higher edn. in Va., 1978; Thomas Jefferson award for public service, 1978; Retailer of Yr. award Va. Retail Mchts. Assn., 1982; Medal of Honor Nat. DAR, 1983; Hon. Degree Dr. of Humanities, Commonwealth of Va., 1983; Gov.'s awards Arts of Va., 1985; Disting. Retailers award Retail Mchts. Assn. Greater Richmond, 1985; Archtl. Medal for Va. Service award Va. Soc. AIA, 1986; Pres.'s Nat. Medal of Arts award, 1987. Club: Lakeside Country. Home: 2601 Monument Ave Richmond VA 23220 Office: Best Products Co Inc PO Box 26303 Richmond VA 23260

LEWIS, WILLIAM ARTHUR, economist, educator; b. St. Lucia, W.I., Jan. 23, 1915; s. George and Ida (Barton) L.; m. Gladys Isabel Jacobs, May 5, 1947; children: Elizabeth Anne, Barbara Jean. Student, St. Mary's Coll., St. Lucia, 1924-29; B.Com., London Sch. Econs., 1937, Ph.D., 1940; M.A. (hon.), Manchester U., 1951, D.Sc., 1973; L.H.D., Columbia U., 1954, Boston Coll., 1972, Coll. of Wooster, 1980, DePaul U., 1981; LL.D., U. Toronto, 1959, Williams Coll., 1959, U. Wales, 1960, U. Bristol, 1961, U. Dakar, 1962, U. Leicester, 1964, Rutgers U., 1965, U. Brussels, 1968, The Open U., 1974, Atlanta U., 1980, U. Hartford, 1981, York U., 1981, Howard U., 1984, Harvard U., 1984; Litt.D., U. West Indies, 1966, U. Lagos, 1974, Northwestern U., 1979; D.Sc., U. London, 1982; D.Social Sci, Yale U., 1983; hon. fellow, London Sch. Econs., 1959, Weizmann Inst., 1962. Asst. lectr., then lectr., reader London Sch. Econs., 1938-48; Stanley Jevons prof. polit. economy U. Manchester, 1948-59; prin., vice chancelor U. West Indies, 1959-63; prof. econs., internat. affairs Princeton U., 1963-83; prin. Bd. Trade, then Colonial Office U.K., 1943-44; mem. Colonial Econ. Adv. Council U.K., 1945-49; dir. Colonial Devel. Corp. U.K., 1950-52; mem. Deptl. Com. on Fuel and Power U.K., 1951-52; econ. adviser Prime Minister of Ghana, 1957-58; dep. mng. dir. UN Spl. Fund, 1959-60; spl. adviser Prime Minister West Indies, 1961-62; dir. Indsl. Devel. Corp., Jamaica, 1962-63, Central Bank of Jamaica, 1961-62; pres. Caribbean Devel. Bank, 1970-73; chancellor U. Guyana, 1967-73; Mem. econ. adv. council NAACP, 1978-80. Author: Economic Problems of Today, 1940, The Principles of Economic Planning, 1949, The Economics of Overhead Costs, 1949, Economic Survey, 1919-39, 1950, The Theory of Economic Growth, 1955, Politics in West Africa, 1965, Development Planning, 1966, Reflections on the Economic Growth of Nigeria, 1967, Some Aspects of Economic Development, 1969, The Evolution of the International Economic Order, 1978, Growth and Fluctuations 1870-1913, 1978, Racial Conflict and Economic Development; editor: Tropical Development, 1970. Decorated Knight Bachelor, 1963; co-recipient Nobel prize in econs., 1979; Corr. fellow Brit. Acad. Mem. Am. Philos. Soc., Royal Econ. Soc. (council 1949-58), Manchester Statis. Soc. (pres. 1956), Econ. Soc. Ghana (pres. 1958), Am. Econ. Assn. (v.p. 1965, Distinguished fellow 1969, pres. 1983); hon. fgn. mem. Am. Acad. Arts and Scis. Office: Princeton U Woodrow Wilson Sch #206 Princeton NJ 08540 *

LEWIS, WILLIAM E., diversified company executive; b. Kansas City, Mo., Sept. 3, 1944; s. Emmor J. and Mary (Brown) L.; m. Laura Sue Dent, June 8, 1968; children: William E., Thomas E., Laura K. BA in Math., U. Kans., 1966, BS in Bus., 1968, MS in Fin., 1969. Asst. contr. Esso Standard Libya, Tripoli, 1971-76; with Exxon Corp., 1969-71; contr. Esso Prospeccao, Rio de Janeiro, 1977-81, Esso Exploradora, Buenos Aires, 1981-83; mgr. fin. systems Esso Colombia, Bogota, 1983-85; chief fin. officer CGF Industries, Topeka, 1986—; v.p., treas. Allen Corp., Indianola, Miss., Dunbarton Corp., Dothan, Ala., Energy Mfg., Monticello, Iowa, Williams Machine & Tool, Omaha, Gordon Sign Co., Denver, Imperial Products, Richmond, Ind., Kistler Graphics, Denver, Norling Studios, High Point, N.C., Williams Printing, Colorado Springs, Colo., Color Control, Seattle. Mem. Fin. Execs. Inst. Home: 3743 SW Canterbury Town Rd Topeka KS 66610

LEWIS, WILLIAM HEADLEY, JR., manufacturing company executive; b. Washington, Sept. 29, 1934; s. William Headley and Lois Maude (Bradshaw) L.; B.S. in Metall. Engring., Va. Poly. Inst., 1956; postgrad. Grad. Sch. Bus. Adminstrn., Emory U., 1978; m. Carol Elizabeth Cheek, Apr. 22, 1967; children—Teresa Lynne, Bret Cameron, Charles William, Kevin Marcus. Research engr. Lockheed-Ga. Co., Marietta, 1956-57, sr. research engr., 1960-63, research group engr., 1963-72, research and devel. program mgr., 1972-79, mgr. engring. tech. services, 1979-83, dir. engring. Getex div., 1983-86; gen. mgr. Inspection Systems div. Lockheed Air Terminal, Inc., 1986-87; pres., chief exec. officer Measurement Systems Inc., Atlanta, 1987—; chmn. Lockheed Corp. Task Force on NDE, 1980-86; pres., Measurement Systems, Inc., 1987—.; mem. Com. to Study Role of Advanced Tech. in Improving Reliability and Maintainability of Future Weapon Systems, Office of Sec. of Def., 1984-85; co-founder, dir., exec. v.p. Applied Tech. Svcs., Inc., 1967—; co-founder, dir. Safetran Corp.; lectr. grad. studies and continuing edn. Union Coll., Schenectady, 1977-82. Served to 1st lt. USAF, 1957-60. Registered profl. engr., Calif. Fellow Am. Soc. for Nondestructive Testing (cert.; nat. dir. 1976-78, chmn. nat. tech. council 1977-78, chmn. aerospace com. 1972-74, nat. nominating com. 1982-83, 1984-85); mem. Am. Inst. Aeronautics and Astronics, Am. Soc. for Metals, Nat. Mgmt. Assn., Nat. Acad. Scis. (mem. com. on compressive fracture 1981-83). Editor: Prevention of Structural Failures: The Role of Fracture Mechanics, Failure Analysis, and NDT, 1978; patentee detection apparatus for structural failure in aircraft. Home: 3127 St Ives Country Club Pkwy Atlanta GA 30136 Office: 2262 Northwest Pkwy Ste A-B Marietta GA 30067

LEWIS, WILLIAM SCHEER, electrical engineer; b. Mt. Vernon, N.Y., Feb. 7, 1927; s. Perley Linwood and Nellie Cora (Scheer) L.; m. Jane Alexander, Feb. 4, 1950 (div. 1972); children: Christopher A., Pamela Scheer Shaw, David Robert; m. Barbara Johnson, June 24, 1972. SB, MIT, 1950, SM, 1950. Registered profl. engr. Mass, N.Y. Sales engr. Gen. Electric Co., Erie, Pa., 1950-53, Morrissey Tractor Co., Burlington, Mass., 1953-56, Hubbs Engine Co., Cambridge, Mass., 1956-57; mgr. contract div. Payne Elevator Co., Cambridge, 1957-69; sales mgr. diversified systems Otis Elevator Co., N.Y.C., 1969-72, mktg. analyst/gen. sales, 1972-78; mgr. vertical transp. Jaros, Baum & Bolles, N.Y.C., 1978—. Editor, ptnr.: (monograph) Tall Buildings-Vertical and Horizontal Transportation, 1978; author: (handbooks) Materials Handling, Freight Elevators, 1985, Building Structural Design-Vertical Tranportation, 1987. Town of Wayland bd. of Assessors, Wayland, Mass., 1954-69, chmn., 1963-69. Recipient 1st prize award N.Y. Assn. Consulting Engrs., 1987, Honor award Am. Consulting Engrs. Council, 1987. Mem. ASME. Republican. Unitarian. Home: 21 Sunset Rd Darien CT 06820-3527 Office: Jaros Baum & Bolles Cons Engrs 345 Park Ave New York NY 10154

LEWIS-KOLBUS, MELINDA ANNE, risk manager, corporate safety administrator; b. Arlington, Va., Oct. 25, 1958; d. Jack Collins and Jacqueline Lucille (Allen) L.; married. Grad., Largo Sr. High, 1973-76. Policy typist Marsh & McLennan Ins. Agy., Washington, 1977-79; account rep. Frank B. Hall & Co., San Antonio, 1979-80, regional mgr., 1980-81; account exec. Charles R. Myers Ins. Agy., San Antonio, 1981-84; risk mgr. James E. Strates Shows, Inc., Orlando, Fla., 1984-85, Reithoffer Shows, Inc., Coral Springs, Fla., 1985—; ins. cons. various outdoor amusement bus., 1984—; pub. relations Boys and Girls Clubs of Am. Mem. Tampa Showmen's Ladies Aux., Miami Showmen's Ladies Aux., Nat. Assn. Female Execs., Outdoor Amusement Bus. Assn. Office: Reithoffer Shows Inc 5332 NW 77th Terr Coral Springs FL 33067

LEWITT, MILES MARTIN, computer engineering company executive; b. N.Y.C., July 14, 1952; s. George Herman and Barbara (Lin) L.; m. Susan Beth Orenstein, June 24, 1973; children: Melissa, Hannah. BS summa cum laude, CCNY Engring., 1973; MS, Ariz. State U., 1976. Software engr. Honeywell, Phoenix, 1973-78; software engr., architect iRMX line ops. systems Intel Corp., Santa Clara, Calif., 1978; engring. mgr. Intel, Hillsboro, Oreg., 1978-80, 1981-89, corp. strategic staff, 1981-82; engring. mgr. Intel, Israel, 1980-81; v.p. engring. Cadre Techs., Inc., Beaverton, Oreg., 1989—; instr. Maricopa Tech. Coll., Phoenix, 1974-75. Contbr. articles to profl. jours. Recipient Engring. Alumni award CCNY, 1973, Eliza Ford Prize CCNY, 1973, Advanced Engring. Program award, Honeywell, 1976, Product of Yr. award Electronic Products Mag., 1980. Mem. IEEE Computer Soc. (voting mem.), IEEE (voting mem.), Assn. Computing Machinery (voting mem.). Democrat. Home: 720 SW Brookwood Ave Hillsboro OR 97123 Office: Cadre Techs Inc 195 45 NW Von Newmann Dr Beaverton OR 97006

LEWKOWICZ, RICHARD, newspaper publisher; b. N.Y.C., Mar. 3, 1937; s. Thomas Anthony and Dorothea (Pflomm) L.; divorced; children: Nancy, Joyce, Mark. V.p., gen. mgr. Gulfstream Newspapers Inc., Pompano Beach,

Fla. Home: 1691 NW 65 Terr Margate FL 33063 Office: Gulfstream Newspapers Inc 3009 NW 25th Ave Pompano Beach FL 33069

LEWNES, PETER A., sales account executive; b. Queens, N.Y., Mar. 15, 1929; s. Andrew P. and Stamateke (Anagnostakos) L.; m. Barbara D. Pappas, Sept. 13, 1953; children: Andrew P., Christina G. Michaels. MS in Fin. Svcs., Am. Coll., 1983. CLU, chartered fin. cons. Structural draftsman Voorhies, Walker, Foley & Smith, N.Y.C., 1950-55, Parco, Inc., N.Y.C., 1956-57; sr. structural draftsman Ford, Bacon & Davis, Inc., N.Y.C., 1958-65; sales rep. Met. Life, Bklyn., 1965—; fin. planner Metlife Securities, Inc., Bklyn., 1986—; moderator Life Underwriter Tng. Council, Bklyn., 1976-79; lectr. SBA Wksp., N.Y.C., 1975-76. Trustee Three Hierarchs Greek Orthodox Ch., Bklyn., 1955-59; youth advisor Three Hierarchs Youth, Bklyn., 1955-65; treas. Holy Order of Three Hierarchs Ch., Bklyn., 1979—. Mem. Nat. Assn. Life Underwriters, Am. Soc. CLU and ChFC, Internat. Assn. Fin. Planners. Republican. Home: 2019 E 15 St Brooklyn NY 11229 Office: Met Life 9920 4th Ave Ste 201 Brooklyn NY 11209

LEYDEN, JOSEPH MICHAEL, lawyer, diversified company executive; b. Akron, Ohio, Dec. 15, 1927; m. Kathleen Fouché, Sept. 3, 1951; children: Michael, John, Laura. LLB, Akron U., 1953. Bar: Ohio 1954. Acct. W.H. Simmons Co., Akron, 1949-53, Chilton, Stump & Daverio, Akron, 1954-57; asst. counsel-tax GenCorp, Akron, 1957-64, asst. to pres., 1964—. Pres. GenCorp Found., 1986—; sec. Akron City Hosp., 1988—. With USN, 1946-47. Mem. Akron Automobile Assn. (pres. 1988—). Republican. Roman Catholic. Office: GenCorp 175 Ghent Rd Fairlawn OH 44313

LEYSON, DATIVO BORCES, economic attaché; b. Cebu, Philippines, Dec. 6, 1930; s. Lucio Velayo and Segunda Borces L.; m. Maria Rosario Karasawa Punsalan, Feb. 17, 1962; children—Leo P., Edmond P., Maria Lisa. Student Far Eastern U., Manila, 1952-55. With Armed Forces of Philippines, 1950-70 (ret.); rep. Central Bank of Philippines, Tokyo, 1971—; econ. attaché Philippine Embassy, Tokyo, 1971—. Roman Catholic. Lodge: Knights of Rizal (Tokyo chpt.). Home: #6 Orchid, Talamban Cebu City, Cebu Philippines Office: 11-24 Nampeidaimachi, Tokyo 150, Japan

LI, BING, XI, mathematics educator, researcher, academic administrator; b. Macao, People's Republic of China, Dec. 15, 1934; parents: Hung Fan and Wai Lan (Lai) Li; m. Dianmei Li, June 7, 1965; 1 child, Jin. BA, Zhongshan U. (Dr. Sun Yat-sen U.), Guangzhou, 1958. Asst. Peking U., Beijing, 1958-63, Zhongshan U., 1963-65; asst. , assoc. prof., prof. Jinan U., Guangzhou, 1965—, chmn. math. dept., 1982-84, v.p., 1984—; vis. scholar U. Calif., Los Angeles, 1979-81. Author: Periodic Orbits of Higher Dimensional Dynamical Systems: Theory & Applications (in Chinese); editor: Annals of Differential Equations, 1985—, Mathematics in Practice and Theory, 1983—; reviewer Zentralblatt für Mathematik, 1983—; also research papers. Hon. Gov. Guangdong Welfare Fund for Handicapped, Guangzhou, 1984—; dep. 6th People's Congress Guangdong Province, 1983-88; mem. standing com. 7th People's Congress, Guangdong Province, 1988—. Recipient Award of Distinction Commn. Sci. Tech. Guangdong. Mem. Math. Soc. People's Republic of China, Am. Math. Soc., Math. Assn. Am., N.Y. Acad. Scis., Am. Biog. Inst. (hon. advisor rsch.). Office: Jinan U, Guangzhou Guangdong People's Republic of China

LI, CHOH-MING, educator; b. Canton, Peoples Republic of China, Feb. 17, 1912; came to U.S., 1930; s. Kanchi and Mewchig (Tsui) L.; m. Sylvia Lu, Sept. 17, 1938; children: Winston, Joan, Tony. BS, U. Calif., Berkeley, 1932, MS, 1933, PhD, 1936; LLD, U. Hong Kong, 1967; postgrad., U. Mich., 1967, Marquette U., 1969, U. Western Ont., 1970, Chinese U. of Hong Kong, 1978; PhD, U. Pa., 1969. Founding vice chancellor Chinese U., Hong Kong, 1963-78; from lectr. to prof. U. Calif., Berkeley, 1950-74, prof. emeritus, 1974—. Author: Economic Development of Communist China, 1959, Political System of Communist China, 1962, The First Six Years 1963-69, 1971, The Emerging University, 1975, A New Era Begins 1975-78, 1979, Li's Chinese Dictionary, 1980. Home: 81 Northampton Ave Berkeley CA 94707

LI, HING KEE, accountant; b. Kowloon, Hong Kong, Dec. 24, 1960; came to U.S., 1976; s. Yip and Shin Wan (Lau) L. BA in Bus. Adminstrn., U. Hawaii, 1983. Night auditor Waikiki Beachcomber Hotel, Honolulu, 1981-83; account clk. II Dept. Hawaii Homeland, State of Hawaii, Honolulu, 1983-84, acct. II, 1984-86, 1987; fin. analyst Bishop Estate, Honolulu, 1987—; tax cons. Li's Co., Honolulu. Mem. Nat. Assn. Accts. Office: Li's Co PO box 37845 Honolulu HI 96837

LIA, GARY PETER, insurance company executive; b. Jersey City, Nov. 8, 1941; s. Peter Alfred and Lucille Marie (Anton) L.; m. Victoria Elizabeth Ranieri, Sept. 19, 1964; children: Kristen, Robert, Dayna, Ryan. BS, Bates Coll., 1964; MBA, Fairleigh Dickinson U., 1970. With Liberty Mut. Ins. Co., East Orange, N.J., 1964-71; dir. product liability service Liberty Mut. Ins. Co., Boston, 1971-76; asst. div. mgr. Liberty Mut. Ins. Co., Weston, Mass., 1976-78; div. loss prevention mgr. Liberty Mut. Ins. Co., Bala Cynwyd, Pa., 1978-81, asst. v.p., asst. div. mgr., 1981-83; v.p., div. mgr. Liberty Mut. Ins. Co., Don Mills, Can., 1983-86; v.p., gen. mgr. Liberty Mut. Ins. Co., Boston, 1986—; bd. dirs. ISO Comml. Risk Services, Inc., Parsippany, N.J. Republican. Roman Catholic. Office: Liberty Mut Ins Co 175 Berkeley St Boston MA 02117

LIAKAS, NICOLAS, publishing company executive, lawyer; b. Salonika, Greece, Sept. 5, 1946; came to U.S., 1955; s. Spyros and Anastasia (Angelidis) L.; m. Olga Tsamisis, June 1, 1969; children: Anastasia, Paula. B.A., CCNY, 1968; J.D., Fordham U., 1972. Bar: N.Y. 1973, U.S. Dist. Ct. (so. and ea. dists.) N.Y. 1973, U.S. Ct. Appeals (2d cir.) 1973, U.S. Supreme Ct. 1976. Sole practice N.Y.C., 1972-76; exec. dir. NYU Inst. Fed. Taxation, 1976-82; pres. Info. Service div. Prentice-Hall, Inc., Paramus, N.J., 1982-85; pres., chief exec. officer Creative Database Pub., Inc., 1985-87, Josephson-Kluwer Legal Edn. Ctrs., Inc., Culver City, Calif., 1985-87; chief oper. officer Valleyfilm Svc., Inc., Van Nuys, Calif., 1988—; dir. Sch. Law, Estate Planning Inst. U. Miami, Fla., 1977—. Editor tax articles. Counsel and trustee Kastorian Soc., N.Y.C., 1972-82; elder Greek Orthodox Ch., Flushing, N.Y., 1979-81. Recipient cert. U. Hartford, 1980. Mem. ABA, N.Y. State Bar Assn., Queens County Bar Assn. Home: 5910 Grey Rock Rd Agoura Hills CA 91301 Office: Valleyfilm Svc Inc 6741 Odessa Ave Van Nuys CA 91406

LIBASSI, FRANK PETER, lawyer, business executive; b. N.Y.C., Apr. 20, 1930; s. Frank G. and Mary (Marino) L.; m. Mary Frances Steen, July 10, 1954; children: Thomas, Timothy, Jennifer. B.A. cum laude with honors in Polit. Sci, Colgate U., 1951; LL.B., Yale U., 1954. Bar: N.Y. 1955, Conn. 1980. Enforcement atty. N.Y. State Housing and Rent Commn., 1954-56; regional dir. N.Y. State Commn. on Human Rights, Albany, 1956-62; dep. staff dir. U.S. Commn. on Civil Rights, 1962-66; spl. asst. to sec., dir. office for civil rights HEW, Washington, 1966-68; exec. v.p. The Urban Coalition, Washington, 1968-71; v.p. Am. City Corp., Columbia, Md., 1971-72; pres., chief exec. officer Greater Hartford Process Inc. (Greater Hartford Community Devel. Corp.), 1971-77; gen. counsel HEW, Washington, 1977-79; partner firm Verner, Liipfert, Bernhard and McPherson, Washington, 1979-82; sr. v.p. Travelers Corp., Hartford, Conn., 1982—; vis. lectr. Anderson Coll., Chatham Coll., Goddard Coll., Ohio Wesleyan U., 1974-76; adj. faculty Grad. Sch. Bus. and Pub. Adminstrn., U. Hartford, 1976-77; mem. Urban Land Inst., 1971-77; adv. bd. Bur. Nat. Affairs Housing and Community Devel. Reporter, 1972-77. Author: The Negro in the Armed Forces, 1963, Family Housing and the Negro Serviceman, 1963, Equal Opportunity in Farm Programs, 1965, Revitalizing Central City Investment, 1977. Bd. dirs. legis. com. Am. Coun. Life Ins., 1987—; bd. dirs., exec. com. Ins. Inst. of Hwy. Safety, 1984-88; mem. pub. relations policy com. Health Ins. Assn. Am., 1988—; incorporator Inst. Living, 1973—, Hartford Hosp., 1973—; mem. adv. com. Democratic Nat. Com., 1974-77; bd. dirs. Ct. Community Care, Inc., 1980-86, Mt. Sinai Hosp., 1982—, Capitol Ptnrships., 1986—; mem. com. on an aging soc. Nat. Acad. Scis., 1982-86; mem. exec. com. Downtown Council Hartford, 1983-86, Greater Hartford Arts Council, 1985-86; chmn. Gov.'s Commn. on Financing Long Term Care, 1986-87; mem. nat. consumer adv. com. Am. Health Care Assn., 1985-86; mem. com. on elderly people living alone The Commonwealth Fund, 1985—; mem. Sec. Bowen's Task Force on Long-term Health Care Policies of Health Care Financing Adminstrn., 1986-87; bd. dirs. Alliance for Aging Research, 1986—; mem. Nat. Retirees Vol. Ctr., 1988—. Recipient Superior Performance award U.S. Commn. on Civil Rights, 1963, Meritorious Service award, 1965; Sec.'s spl. citation, 1967; Disting. Service award HEW, 1968; Woodrow Wilson sr. fellow, 1973-77. Mem. ABA, Fed. Bar Assn., N.Y. State Bar Assn., Conn. Bar Assn., Am. Assn. Retired Persons (nat. steering com. for new roles in soc. 1987—), Greater Hartford C. of C. (bd. dirs. 1985—, exec. com.). Club: Hartford. Home: 580 J Mountain Rd West Hartford CT 06117 Office: The Travelers Corp 1 Tower Sq Hartford CT 06183

LIBBY, JOHN KELWAY, financial service company executive; b. Washington, June 13, 1926; s. John Hermiston and Violet Kelway (Bamber) L.; m. Mary Seymour Kindel, Dec. 30, 1960; children—Carolyn K., Anne K., Virginia K. BA, Haverford Coll., 1945; postgrad., Harvard U., 1946. Vice pres. Kuhn Loeb & Co., N.Y.C., 1960-67, gen. ptnr., 1967-77; mng. dir. Lehman Bros. Kuhn Loeb, Inc., N.Y.C., 1977-80; chmn., chief exec. officer Parkstar, Inc., N.Y.C., 1980—, pres. Parkstar Ltd. Bahamas, 1987—; gen. ptnr. K.L. Assocs., N.Y.C., 1985—; bd. dirs. various U.S. and fgn. corps. Trustee Brearley Sch., N.Y.C., 1977-85, Forest Neighborhood House, Bronx, N.Y., 1965-76, Youth House N.Y.C., 1965-72; committeeman N.Y. County Republican Com. Served to lt. USN, 1944-46, PTO, 1951-53. Episcopalian. Clubs: Sky, Bond, University, N.Y. Yacht; Edgartown Yacht. Avocations: sailing, hunting, jogging. Home: 925 Park Ave New York NY 10028 Office: K L Assocs 450 Park Ave New York NY 10022

LIBERMAN, LEE MARVIN, utility executive; b. Salt Lake City, July 12, 1921; s. Benjamin L. and Sylvia (Goldflam) L.; m. Jeanne Hirsch, Oct. 19, 1946; children: Alise, James, Celia; m. Ann Medler, Aug. 21, 1982. B.S. in Chem. Engring., Yale U., 1942. Registered profl. engr., Mo. With Laclede Gas Co., St. Louis, 1945—; exec. v.p. Laclede Gas Co., 1968-70, pres., 1970—, chief exec. officer, 1974—, chmn., 1976—, also dir.; bd. dirs. Boatmen's Bancshares, Boatmen's Nat. Bank, Angelica Corp., Falcon Products Co., INTERCO Inc., Instituform Mid-Am. Inc., CPI Corp. Mem. Civic Progress, Inc.; chmn. Regional Commerce and Growth Assn.; past pres. Family and Children's Service St. Louis; chmn. St. Louis Symphony Soc.; chmn. bd. trustees Washington U.; chmn. campaign United Way, 1987; past chmn. bd. Jewish Hosp. Served with USAAF, 1944-45. Named St. Louis Man of Yr., 1986. Mem. Nat. Soc. Profl. Engrs., Mo. C. of C., Regional Commerce and Growth Assn. (chmn.). Office: Laclede Gas Co 720 Olive St Saint Louis MO 63101

LIBERT, DONALD JOSEPH, lawyer; b. Sioux Falls, S.D., Mar. 23, 1928; s. Bernard Joseph and Eleanor Monica (Sutton) L.; m. Jo Anne Murray, May 16, 1953; children: Cathleen, Thomas, Kevin, Richard, Stephanie. B.S. magna cum laude in Social Scis., Georgetown U., 1950, LL.B., 1956. Bar: Ohio, D.C. From assoc. to ptnr. Manchester, Bennett, Powers & Ullman, Youngstown, Ohio, 1956-65; various positions to v.p., gen. counsel and sec. Youngstown Sheet & Tube Co., 1965-78; assoc. group counsel LTV Corp., Youngstown and Pitts., 1979; v.p. and gen. counsel Anchor Hocking Corp., Lancaster, Ohio, 1979-87. Served to lt. (j.g.) USN, 1951-54. Mem. ABA, Ohio Bar Assn., Fairfield County Bar Assn., Am. Corp. Counsel Assn., Lancaster C. of C. Republican. Roman Catholic. Club: Lancaster Country. Lodge: Rotary. Office: 127 W Wheeling St Lancaster OH 43130

LICCIARDELLO, DONALD CARMEN, telecommunications company executive; b. Trenton, N.J., May 6, 1946; s. Domenic and Antonette (Fattore) L.; m. Marilyn Lawley, Mar. 24, 1984; children: Kirstin, Aaren, Antonette. BS, U. Scranton, 1968; MS, U. Ill., 1970; PhD, U. Va., 1973. Postdoctoral fellow Ind. U., Bloomington, 1973-74, Birmingham U., Eng., 1974-76; asst. prof. Princeton U., N.J., 1976-84; pres. Princeton TeleCom Corp., N.J., 1984—; cons. Bell Labs, Murray Hill, RCA Labs., various sci. instns., 1974—; speaker in field, 1983—. Contbr. articles to sci. jours. Mem. Dept. Energy Panel on Amorphous Materials. Research grantee Office Naval Research, NSF; recipient Allan Tabott Gwathmey award, 1973. Mem. Am. Phys. Soc., Sigma Xi, Alpha Sigma Nu. Lodge: Rotary. Home: 958 Cherry Valley Rd Princeton NJ 08540 Office: Princeton TeleCom Corp 4 Independence Way Princeton NJ 08540

LICHTENFELS, WILLIAM CHARLES, manufacturing company executive; b. Oswego, N.Y., July 6, 1927; s. Frederick G. and Rose M. Lichtenfels; m. Eileen Anne McGarry, Jan. 2, 1954; children—Beth A., Steven W., W. Andrew, Tara M. Student, Central Conn. State Coll., 1944-46, U. Hartford, 1950; student Advanced Mgmt. Program, Harvard U., 1969. With Emhart Corp., 1951—; pres. Emhart Industries, Farmington, Conn., 1976-79, corp. exec. v.p., 1979-83, pres., 1984—, also chief operating officer. Trustee Hartford Grad. Ctr., 1978—, St. Joseph Coll., Hartford, 1979—; chmn. Cen. Conn. State U. Found., New Britain Meml. Hosp.; chmn. bd. visitors U. Hartford Barney Sch., U. Hartford New Britain Mem. Hosp., St. Francis Hosp. Served with USN, 1945-46. Mem. Builders Hardware Mfrs. Assn. (past pres.), Am. Hardware Mfrs. Assn. (bd. dirs.), Conn. Bus. and Industry Assn. (chmn. bd.). Club: Hartford Golf. Office: Emhart Corp 426 Colt Hwy Farmington CT 06032

LICHTENSTEIN, HOWARD, insurance company executive; b. N.Y.C., Jan. 10, 1947; s. Jules and Ida (Gelman) L.; m. Delores Levitz, Aug. 22, 1970; children: Jason, Jordan. BA, Bklyn. Coll., 1966; postgrad., New Sch. Social Rsch., 1967-69. With Mut. of Am. Life Ins. Co., N.Y.C., 1966—, now exec. v.p. group cons. svcs. Bd. dirs., treas. Jewish Community Svcs. L.I., Rego Park, N.Y., 1985—; bd. dirs. communal planning com. United Jewish Appeal, N.Y.C., 1988—. Office: Mut of Am Life Ins Co 666 Fifth Ave New York NY 10103

LICHTMAN, NEIL, business executive, consultant; b. N.Y.C., Sept. 10, 1945; s. Maxwell Harold and Blanche (Evans) L.; m. Madeline Marie Quaglia, Mar. 23, 1969; 1 child, Melissa Nicole. AS, Bronx Community Coll., 1973; BA in Econs., Bernard Baruch Coll., 1973. Eastern regional mgr. Bell & Howell, Chgo., 1970-77; ea. regional mgr. Douglas Dunhill, Chgo., 1977-78; founder, pres. Lichtman Corp., Spring Valley, N.Y., 1978-85, Am. Marketplace, Spring Valley, N.Y., 1982-85, Gt. Am. Shop, Nyack, N.Y., 1985-87; pres. Interface, Inc., Chestnut Ridge, N.Y., 1988—; speaker Premium Sales Execs., N.Y.C., 1984, Nat. Retail Mchts., N.Y.C., 1982; nat. lectr. Master Card, 1977-80, cons., N.Y.C., 1987—. Author: How to Cash in on the Mail Order Boom, 1979. Mem. St. Anthony Choir; fund raiser St. Anthony Ch., Nanuet, N.Y., 1985-86; pres. County Village Heights Condominium, Spring Valley, 1974; mem. adv. bd. Martin Luther King Ctr., Spring Valley, N.Y., 1987-88; bd. dirs., founder People to People, Rockland, N.Y., 1987-88. With U.S. Army, 1966-69, Vietnam. Mem. Direct Mktg. Assn., N.Y. Direct Mktg.. S.A. Cupboard Club (founder). Democrat. Roman Catholic. Office: 127 S Broadway Nyack NY 10960

LICHTMAN, NEIL PHILIP, manufacturing company executive; b. Akron, Ohio, Dec. 7, 1954; m. Linda Ann Jeffers, Sept. 5, 1982; 2 children. BA in History, Tulane U., 1977. Salesman Alside Inc., Columbus, Ohio, 1977-82, F.A. Kohler Co., Columbus, 1982-84; v.p. Columbus Window Co. Inc., 1984—. Mem. Nat. Assn. Remodeling Industry. Home: 2580 Maryland Ave Columbus OH 43209-1072 Office: Columbus Window Co Inc 2935 E 14th Ave Columbus OH 43219

LICHTY, WARREN DEWEY, JR., lawyer; b. Colorado Springs, Colo., Dec. 17, 1930; s. Warren D. and Margaret (White) L.; m. Margaret Louise Grupy, Dec. 8, 1962. Student Chadron State Coll., 1948-50; BS in Law, U. Nebr., 1952, JD, 1954. Bar: Nebr. 1954, U.S. Dist. Ct. Nebr., 1954, U.S. Ct. Appeals (8th cir.) 1973, U.S. Supreme Ct. 1979. Spl. agt. CIC, 1955-58; county judge Dawes County, Nebr., 1958-61; spl. asst. atty. gen. Nebr. Dept. Justice, Lincoln, Nebr., 1961-69; asst. atty. gen., chief counsel Nebr. Dept. Roads, Lincoln, 1969—; lectr. law Chadron State Coll., 1959-60; mem. com. on eminent domain and land use, transp. research bd. Nat. Acad. Sci.-NRC. Bd. dirs. Scottish Rite Found. Nebr., 1981—, DeMolay Found. Nebr., 1980—, Nebr. Masonic Home Corp., 1979—, Washington Masonic Nat. Meml. Assn. Served with U.S. Army, 1954-58. Mem. editorial bd. New Age mag. Mem. Nebr. Bar Assn., Lincoln Bar Assn., Am. Assn. State Hwy. and Transp. Ofcls. (subcom. on legal affairs), Am. Legion. Republican. Episcopalian. Clubs: Hiram (past pres.), Nebr. (Lincoln). Lodges: Masons (33 deg.; grand master Nebr. 1979, vice chmn. conf. Grand Masters of N.Am., 1980), Shriners, Royal Order of Scotland, Philalithes Soc., Elks. Home: PO Box 2559 Lincoln NE 68502 Office: PO Box 94759 Lincoln NE 68509

LICKISS, EDWIN EMMETT, financial planner; b. Oakland, Calif., Sept. 19, 1947; s. Edwin E. and Norma A. (Hayden) L.; m. Marilyn L. Whelton, Sept. 13, 1969; children—Jennifer, Michael, Thomas, Suzanne. B.A., Calif. State U., 1970, M.A., 1972; Cert. Fin. Planner, Coll. for Fin. Planning, 1979. Tchr. for deaf Concord, Calif., 1971-74; prin., gen. agt. life and disability ins. Orinda (Calif.) Fin. Group, 1974-81; founder Danville (Calif.) Fin. Group, 1981—; registered securities rep., 1976—, gen. securities prin., 1985—. Bd. dirs. San Ramon (Calif.) Home Owners Assn., 1976-77; mem. Parish Council, St. Joan of Arc Ch., San Ramon, 1982-85; v.p., St. Isaidores Found., 1986—; mem. liturgy com., 1980-85. vol. interpretor for deaf, 1971—. Mem. Nat. Assn. Securities Dealers, Internat. Assn. Fin. Planners, Fin. Profl. Advisers Panel, Inst. Cert. Fin. Planners Roman Catholic. Office: 390 Diablo Rd Danville CA 94526

LICKLE, WILLIAM CAUFFIEL, banker; b. Wilmington, Del., Aug. 2, 1929; s. Charles Harold and Hazel (Cauffiel) L.; m. Renee Carpenter Kitchell, Nov. 24, 1950; children: Sydney Cauffiel Lindley, Garrison duPont, Ashley Morgan O'Neil, Kemble Carpenter Lickle O'Donnell. BA, U. Va., 1951, LLB, 1953. Bar: Va. 1953. Registered rep. Laird & Co., Inc., Wilmington, Del., 1953-55; v.p., dir. Nitront & Co. (real estate developers), Wilmington, 1955-56; ptnr. Wheelock & Lickle (realtors), Greenville, Del., 1956-57; registered rep. Laird, Bissell & Meeds, Inc., Wilmington, 1957-73; ptnr. Laird, Bissell & Meeds, Inc., 1962, dir., 1965, exec. v.p., 1967-68, pres., 1968-69, chmn. exec. com., 1969, chmn. bd., chief exec. officer, 1970-73; sr. v.p., dir. Dean Witter & Co. Inc., 1973-77; chief exec. officer, chmn. bd. Del. Trust Co., Wilmington, 1985—, dir. exec. com., 1973—, chmn. trust com., 1979—, vice chmn., 1977-84; bd. dirs. Bessemer Trust Co. N.J., Bessemer Trust Co. N.Y., Bessemer Trust Co. Fla. Dir. United Community Fund Del., 1960-62; dir. treas. Blue Cross-Blue Shield Del., 1963-68; commr. New Castle County (Del.) Airport, 1964-67, New Castle County Trans. Commn., 1967-69; dir. Easter Seal Soc. Del., 1965-75; dir., vice chmn., founder Better Bus. Bur. Del., 1966-72; spl. gifts chmn. Am. Cancer Soc., Del., 1968; trustee Thomas Jefferson U., Phila., 1971-78, Ethel Walker Sch., Simsbury, Ct., 1977-79, Grand Opera House, Wilmington, 1986—; nat. adv. com. Rollins Coll., Winter Pk, Fla., 1973-76; dir. Del. Mus. Natural History, 1974-81; chmn. fin. com. Del. Cancer Network, 1975-77; bus. econ. devel. com. Del. State C. of C., 1979-80; dir. devel. com. Planned Parenthood Palm Beach (Fla.), 1981-85; hon. dir., past dir., treas. Boys' Club Wilmington, 1963—; trustee, dir. emeritus, exec. com., treas., chmn. fin. com. Med. Ctr. Del., 1965—; trustee, chmn. devel. com. Brandywine River Mus., Chadds Ford, Pa., 1982—; dir. Soc. Four Arts, Palm Beach, 1982—; steering com. U. Va. Jefferson Scholars, Charlottesville, 1985—; gov. corp. council Winterthur Mus., Wilmington, 1986—; dir., exec. com., chmn. fin. com. Celebrate '88 Com., Wilmington, 1986—; bd. mgrs. U. Va. Alumni Assn., Charlottesville, 1987—; founder Del. Community Found., 1987—; spl. asst. Gov.'s Econ. Devel., 1987; Del. fin. com. Citizens for Eisenhower, 1956; fin. chmn. Vols. for Nixon, 1960; state coordinator Del. for Goldwater, 1964; treas., exec. com., fin. com. Del. Rep. State Com., 1964-68; chmn. bd. mgrs., race com. Fairhill (Md.) Races, 1975-86; dir., exec. com., treas., chmn. fin. audit com. Breeder's Cup Ltd., Lexington, Ky., 1984—; dir., exec. com. Thoroughbred Racing Communications, 1987—. Mem. SAR, ABA, Va. Bar Assn., Nat. Steeplechase and Hunt Assn. (sr. mem., past steward), Del. Roundtable, Soc. Colonial Wars Wilmington, Kappa Alpha, Phi Alpha Delta. Clubs: Vicmead Hunt (Greenville, Del.) (bd. dirs.); Wilmington Country (Greenville, Del.); Wilmington; Turf (Del. Park, Wilmington) (bd. dirs. 1976-82); Everglades, Seminole Golf, Bath and Tennis (Palm Beach, Fla.); Saratoga Golf and Polo, Reading Room (Saratoga, N.Y.); Rolling Rock (Ligonier, Pa.); Lyford Cay (Nassau, Bahamas). Home: 300 Rockland Rd Montchanin DE 19710 Office: J P Morgan Internat Holding Corp 902 Market St Wilmington DE 19801

LIDDLE, GORDON MCALLISTER, food manufacturing company executive; b. Provo, Utah, Dec. 12, 1940; s. Parley H. and Clare Irene (McAllister) L.; student So. Utah State U., 1959-60; B.S., Utah State U., 1966; M.B.A., U. Utah, 1967; m. Linda Gayle Kirk, Dec. 18, 1964; children—Deborah Ann, Jennifer Irene, David Gordon. Asst. mgr. Christensen Diamond Services, 1967-68, gen. mgr., 1968-69; dir. finance, treas. Christensen Diamond Products Co., Salt Lake City, 1969-81 ; v.p. fin., dir. Christensen Inc., 1974-79, sr. v.p., 1979-83; pres., chief exec. officer Christensen Diamond Tools and Boyles Bros. Drilling Co., 1979-83; pres., chief exec. officer Winder Dairy Inc., 1982—; ptnr. Liddle Farms, U.S. Constrn., Inc.; v.p., dir. Trustco, Inc.; dir. Modern Alloys Inc. Bd. dirs. Utah Safety Council. Republican. Mem. Ch. of Jesus Christ of Latter-day Saints. Office: 4400 W 4100 S Salt Lake City UT 84120

LIDDLE, WILLIAM THOMAS, steel company executive; b. Middlesbrough, Eng., Mar. 19, 1940; came to U.S., 1977; s. Thomas Liddle and Ivy Lilian Nelson; m. Suzanne Crete, Mar. 29, 1969; children: Monique, Grant. BS in Chemistry, Constantine U., Middlesbrough, 1963, postgrad., 1963-64. Supt. steelmaking Georgetown (S.C.) Steel Corp., 1982-83; plant mgr. Reading (Pa.) Industries, 1983-85; supt. steelmaking Sharon Steel Corp., Farrell, Pa., 1985-86, v.p. primary ops., 1986-88; v.p. mfg. Cytemp Splty. Steel div. Cyclops Corp., Titusville, Pa., 1988—. Mem. Iron and Steel Soc., Iron and Steel Engrs., Shenango Valley C. of C. Roman Catholic. Home: PO Box 305 Waterford PA 16441 Office: Cyclops Corp Cytemp Specialty Steel Div PO Box 247 Titusville PA 16354

LIEBAERT, MICHAEL SCOTT, foundation administrator; b. Upland, Calif., Sept. 19, 1953. AA, Chaffey Coll., 1974. Engr. deep-sea diving J. Ray McDermott Contractors, Harvey, La., 1974-75; deep sea diver Global Divers, Harvey, 1975-78; police detective New Orleans Police Dept./Dist. Atty., 1981—; co-executor Estate of Herbert J. Harvey, Jr., New Orleans, 1981—; mng. dir. Azby Fund, New Orleans, 1978—. V.p. Orleans Levee Bd. Tenants Assn., New Orleans, 1986—; donation coordinator of archives Archdiocese of New Orleans, 1979—, Tulane Med. Ctr., 1979—. Sch. of Architecture, 1987-88, New Orleans. Mem. Profl. Assn. Diving Instrs. Republican. Presbyterian. Club: Internat. House. Office: The Azby Fund/ Harvey Estates 1311 Whitney Bank Bldg New Orleans LA 70130

LIEBELER, SUSAN WITTENBERG, lawyer; b. New Castle, Pa., July 3, 1942; d. Sherman K. and Eleanor (Klivans) Levine; BA, U. Mich., 1963, postgrad. U. Mich., 1963-64; LLB (Stein scholar), UCLA, 1966; m. Wesley J. Liebeler, Oct. 21, 1971; 1 child, Jennifer. Bar: Calif. 1967, Vt. 1972, D.C. 1988. Law clk. Calif. Ct. of Appeals, 1966-67; assoc. Gang, Tyre & Brown, 1967-68, Greenberg, Bernhard, Weiss & Karma, L.A., 1968-70; assoc. gen. counsel Rep. Corp., L.A., 1970-72; gen. counsel Verit Industries, L.A., 1972-73; prof. of law law sch. Loyola U., L.A., 1973-84; spl. counsel, chmn. John S. R. Shad, SEC, Washington, 1981-82; commr. U.S. Internat. Trade Commn. Washington, 1984-88, vice chmn., 1984-86, chmn., 1986-88; ptnr. Irell & Manella, Washington, 1988—; vis. prof. U. Tex., summer 1982; cons. Office of Policy Coordination, office of Pres.-elect, 1981-82; cons. U.S. Ry. Assn., 1975, U.S. EPA, 1974, U.S. Price Commn., 1972. Mem. State Bar Calif., L.A. County Bar Assn., D.C. Bar Assn., ABA, ITC Trial Lawyers Assn., Washington Legal Found. (acad. adv. bd.), Asia Pacific R.R. Assn., Internat. Bar Assn., Computer Law Assn., Order of Coif. Jewish. Sr. editor UCLA Law Review, 1965-66; contbr. articles to legal publ.

LIEBER, STEPHEN ANDREW, investment manager; b. N.Y.C., Aug. 30, 1925; s. Samuel and Florence E. (Schwartz) L.; m. Constance E. Emmer, June 4, 1950; children: Janice E., Samuel A. A.B., Williams Coll., 1946; postgrad., Harvard U., 1947-48. Ptnr. Vanden Broeck, Lieber & Co., N.Y.C., 1956-69, Lieber & Co., Harrison, N.Y., 1969—; chmn. Evergreen Total Return Fund, Harrison, 1971—, pres. Evergreen Limited Market Fund, Harrison, 1978—, Evergreen Value Timing Fund, Harrison, 1986—, Evergreen Money Market Trust, Harrison, 1987—, Evergreen Am. Ret. Trust, Harrison, 1988—, Evergreen Tax-Exempt Money Market Trust, Harrison, 1988—. Mem. Fin. Analysts Fedn. Home: 1210 Greacen Point Rd Mamaroneck NY 10543 Office: The Evergreen Total 550 Mamaroneck Ave Harrison NY 10528

LIEBERMAN, ANNE MARIE, financial executive; b. Jersey City, Aug. 28, 1946; d. Ralph Norman and Kathleen Celestine (Dooris) L.; m. Stephen Bruce Oshry, Sept. 21, 1986. BA, Sonoma State U., 1968; MLS, U. Calif., 1970, MBA, 1977. Cert. fin. planner. V.p. Bank of Am., San Francisco, 1977-81, Lawrence A. Krause & Assocs., San Francisco, 1982-86; dir. Lieberman Assocs. Fin. Planning, Larkspur, Calif., 1986—. Author: Marketing Your Financial Planning Practice, 1986, Mastering Money, 1987;

contbg. author: Financial Planning Can Make You Rich, 1987, The Expert's Guide to Managing a Successful Financial Planning Practice, 1988, About Your Future, 1988. Mem. Inst. Cert. Fin. Planners (Fin. Writer's award 1986), Internat. Assn. Fin. Planning, Rotary. Office: Lieberman Assocs Fin Planning 700 Larkspur Landing Circle Ste 100 Larkspur CA 94939

LIEBERMAN, GAIL FORMAN, financial executive; b. Phila., May 26, 1943; d. Joseph and Rita (Groder) Forman. BA in Physics and Math., Temple U., 1964, MBA in Fin., 1977. Dir. internat. fin. Standard Brands Inc., N.Y.C., 1977-79; staff v.p. fin. and capital planning RCA Corp., 1979-82; chief fin. officer, exec. v.p. Scali McCabe Sloves, Inc., 1982—; bd. dirs. Elmer Little Glove Co., Johnstown, Pa., 1983-86. Mem. Fin. Execs. Inst. Office: Scali McCabe Sloves Inc 800 3d Ave New York NY 10022

LIEBERMAN, ROCHELLE PHYLLIS, relocation company executive; b. Bklyn., June 27, 1940; d. Solomon and Freda (Shapiro) Beller; m. Melvyn Lieberman, June 10, 1961; children—Eric Neil, Marc Evan. B.A., Bklyn. Coll., 1961; M.Ed., Duke U., 1977. Tchr., Bklyn. pub. schs., 1961-64; instr. Carolina Friends, Durham, N.C., 1967-70; grad. intern Duke U., Durham, 1974-75, faculty adviser, 1975-76; sales assoc. Kelly Matherly, Durham, 1978-81; pres. Shelli, Inc., Durham, 1981—. Treas. Duke Forest Assn., Durham, 1980-85. Mem. LWV, Durham and Chapel Hill Bd. Realtors, Women's Council of Realtors (sec. 1980-81), Duke U. Eye Ctr. adv. bd., Kappa Delta Pi. Republican. Jewish. Clubs: Duke Faculty, Duke Campus (Durham). Avocations: piano; walking; knitting; writing; reading. Office: Shelli Inc 1110 Woodburn Rd Durham NC 27705

LIEBES, RAQUEL, import/export company owner, partner; b. San Salvador, El Salvador, Aug. 28, 1938; came to the U.S., 1952; d. Ernesto Martin and Alice Bella Juliane (Philip) L.; m. Richard Paisley Kinkade, June 2, 1962 (div. 1977); children: Kathleen Paisley, Richard Paisley Jr., Scott Philip. BA, Sarah Lawrence Coll., 1960; MEd, Harvard U., 1961; MA, Yale U., 1962; postgrad., Yale, 1961-65. Instr. Spanish Sarah Lawrence Coll., Bronxville, N.Y., 1958-60, admissions rep., 1963-68; instr. spanish Yale U., New Haven, 1964-66; exec. stockholder, ptnr., owner Import Export Co., San Salvador, 1968—. Contbr. glossary of Spanish med. terms. Hon. consul Govt. of El Salvador, 1977-80; docent High Mus. of Art, Atlanta, 1972-77; vol. Grady Hosp., Atlanta, 1966-71; instr. Spanish for med. drs. Tucson Med. Ctr., 1966-71; chmn. Atlanta Council for Internat. Visitors, 1966-71; mem. Outreach Group on Latin Am., Washington, 1982-86; founding mem. John Kennedy Ctr. for Performing Arts; lay leader Jewish Community of El Salvador, 1980-88; mem. Folger Library, Smithsonian Inst. Fellow Corcoran Mus. of Art, 1984-85. Mem. Agape of El Salvador, Jr. League of Washington, Anti-Defamation League, Bnai Brith. Republican. Clubs: Harvard (Washington, Boston and N.Y.C.), Yale. Home: 700 New Hampshire Ave Washington DC 20037

LIEBETRAU, RICHARD MARK, business development executive; b. St. Louis, June 29, 1953; s. Richard Ernest and Delores Mae (King) L.; m. Nancy Lee Leighton, Dec. 29, 1974; children: Eric Andrew, Benjamin Richard. BS in Phys. Sci. with honors, Colo. State U., 1975; MS in Speech Pathology with high honors, U. Mich., 1978. Speech pathologist McLaren Gen. Hosp., Flint, Mich., 1978-82; cons. med. sales Support Systems Internat., Detroit, 1982-83, regional mgr., 1983-84, area sales dir., 1985-87; dir. bus. devel. Support Systems Internat., Charleston, S.C., 1987-88, dir. mktg., 1988—. Contbr. articles to profl. lit.; patentee computer program for adult aphasics. Vol. fireman Hartland (Mich.) Fire Dept., 1983; regional coord. Spl. Olympics, Ft. Collins, Colo., 1974; dir. Drug Analysis Lab., 1973-74. Scholarship grantee U. Mich., 1976; named to Pres.'s Club Support Systems Internat., 1983. Mem. Am. Mgmt. Assn., Snee Farm Country Club (Mt. Pleasant, S.C.), Phi Beta Kappa, Sigma Nu. Republican. Home: 1263 S Barksdale Rd Mount Pleasant SC 29464 Office: Support Systems Internat 4349 Corporate Rd Charleston SC 29405

LIEBLING, NORMAN ROBERT, lawyer; b. Chgo., Feb. 17, 1917; s. Louis and Frances (Geller) L.; m. Florence Levinson, Feb. 25, 1950; children: James, Fred. BA, U. Ill., 1937; JD, Harvard U., 1940. Bar: Ill. 1940. Ptnr. Freeman & Liebling, Chgo., 1948-54, Freeman, Liebling, Adelman & Watson, Chgo., 1955-67; sr. ptnr. Liebling, Adelman & Bernstein, Chgo., 1968-81, Liebling, Uriell & Hamman, Chgo., 1976-82, Liebling & Uriell, Chgo., 1982-83; sr. ptnr., gen. counsel Schuyler, Roche & Zwirner, Chgo., 1984—; bd. dirs. The United Equitable Corp., Lincolnwood, Ill. Spl. asst. to atty. gen. State of Ill., Chgo., 1958-61; gen. counsel, bd. dirs. Rosenbaum Found., Chgo., 1982—; bd. dirs. Concission Svcs., Inc. Served to capt. U.S. Army, 1942-46, CBI. Mem. ABA, Chgo. Bar Assn., Harvard Law Soc. Ill. (bd. dirs. 1986—). Clubs: Chgo. Athletic, The Plaza, International (Chgo.). Home: 970 Sunset Ave Winnetka IL 60093 Office: Schuyler Roche & Zwirner One Prudential Pla 130 E Randolph St Chicago IL 60601

LIEBMAN, EMMANUEL, lawyer; b. Phila., Mar. 26, 1925; s. Morris and Pearl (Zucker) L.; m. Anita Forman, Dec. 24, 1953; children—Judith H. Winslow, Lawrence H. B.S. in Econs., U. Pa., 1950; J.D., Rutgers U., 1954. Bar: N.J. 1954, U.S. Tax Ct. 1955, U.S. Supreme Ct. 1960, D.C. 1972, U.S. Ct. Appeals (3d cir.) 1977. Sole practice, Camden, N.J., 1954-70; pres. Emmanuel Liebman, P.A., Cherry Hill, N.J., 1970-72; pres., chmn. Liebman & Flaster, P.A., Cherry Hill, 1972-86; pres. Emmanuel Liebman, Chartered, Cherry Hill, 1986—; lectr., moderator Inst. Continuing Legal Edn., 1962-87. Served with USNR, 1943-46, PTO. Mem. Camden County Bar Assn. (chmn. com. on fed. tax 1964, 68-70, chmn. retirement plan com. 1986—), N.J. State Bar Assn. (chmn. com. on bus. taxes 1967-69, 71-73, chmn. state capitol com. 1973-77, chmn. ad hoc com. on financing legal fees 1976-79, exec. council 1974—), ABA (taxation sect., com. personal svc. corps., real property, probate and trust law sect.), D.C. Bar Assn., N.J. State Bar Found. (trustee 1972-87, pres. 1979-83), Am. Judicature Soc., Am. Arbitration Assn. (panelist 1964-88), Camden County Bar Found. (trustee 1986—). Clubs: Haddon Field (Haddonfield, N.J.); Woodcrest Country (Cherry Hill). Lodge: B'nai B'rith. Home: 46 Dublin Ln Cherry Hill NJ 08003 Office: 409 E Marlton Pike Cherry Hill NJ 08034

LIEBMAN, JUDITH RAE STENZEL, dean, vice chancellor for research; b. Denver, July 2, 1936; d. Raymond Oscar and Mary Madelyn (Galloup) Stenzel; m. Jon Charles Liebman, Dec. 27, 1958; children: Christopher Brian, Rebecca Anne, Michael Jon. BA, U. Colo., Boulder, 1958; PhD, Johns Hopkins U., 1971. Successively asst. prof., head indsl. systems, assoc. prof. U. Ill., Urbana, 1972-84, prof., 1984—; chmn. bd. Ill. Resource Network, U. Ill., 1987—; vis. prof. Tianjin (People's Republic China) U., 1985; acting vice chancellor for research, U. Ill., 1986-87, acting dean, The Grad. Coll., 1986-87, vice chancellor for research, 1987—, dean The Grad. Coll., 1987—. Author: Modeling and Optimization with GINO, 1986; author numerous articles in field. Bd. dirs. United Way, Champaign, Ill., 1986—, East Cen. Ill. Health Systems Agy., Champaign, 1977-82, pres. 1980-82. Mem. Ops. Research Soc. of Am. (pres. 1987-88), Rotary, Sigma Pi Sigma, Sigma Xi, Alpha Pi Mu, Phi Kappa Phi. Home: 113 Whitehall Ct Urbana IL 61801 Office: U Ill 601 E John St 420 Swanlund Champaign IL 61820

LIEBMAN, RONALD STANLEY, lawyer; b. Balt., Oct. 11, 1943; s. Harry Martin and Martha (Altgenug) L.; m. Simma Liebman, Jan. 8, 1972; children: Shana, Margot. BA, Western Md. Coll., Westminster, 1966; JD, U. Md., 1969. Bar: Md. 1969, D.C. 1977, U.S. Dist. Ct. (ea. dist.) Va. 1970, U.S. Dist. Ct. Md. 1970, U.S. Dist. Ct. D.C. 1982, U.S. Ct. Appeals (4th cir.) 1972, U.S. Ct. Appeals (D.C. cir.) 1982, U.S. Ct. Appeals (5th cir.) 1985. Law clk. to chief judge U.S. Dist. Ct. Md., 1969-70; assoc. Melnicove, Kaufman & Weiner, Balt., 1970-72; asst. U.S. atty. Office of U.S. Atty., Dept. Justice, Balt., 1972-78; ptnr. Sachs, Greenebaum & Tayler, Washington, 1978-82, Patton, Boggs & Blow, Washington, 1982—. Author: Grand Jury, 1983; co-editor: Testimonial Privileges, 1983. Recipient spl. commendation award U.S. Dept. Justice, 1978. Mem. ABA, D.C. Bar Assn., Md. Bar Assn. Club: Sergeants Inn (Balt.). Office: 2550 M St NW Washington DC 20037

LIEBMANN, SEYMOUR W., construction consultant; b. N.Y.C., Nov. 1, 1928; s. Isidor W. and Etta (Waltzer) L.; m. Hinda Adam, Sept. 20, 1959; children: Peter Adam, David W. BS in Mech. Engring., Clarkson U. (formerly Clarkson Tech. Coll.), 1948; grad. Indsl. Coll. Armed Forces, 1963, Command and Gen. Staff Coll., 1966, Army War Coll., 1971. Registered profl. engr., N.Y., Mass., Ga. Area engr. constrn. div. E.I. DuPont de Nemours & Co., Inc., 1952-54; constrn. planner Lummus Co., 1954-56; prin. mech. engr. Perini Corp., 1956-62; v.p. Boston Based Contractors, 1962-66; v.p. A.R. Abrams, Inc., Atlanta, 1967-74, pres., 1974-78, also bd. dirs.; founder Liebmann Assocs., Inc., Atlanta, 1979—; bd. dirs. Abrams Industries; mem. nat. adv. bd. Am. Security Council. Author: Military Engineer Field Notes, 1953, Prestressing Miter Gate Diagonals, 1960; contbr. articles to publs. Mem. USO Council, Atlanta, 1968—, v.p., 1978, mem. exec. com., 1975-79; mem. Nat. UN Day Com., 1975; sr. army coordinator, judge Sci. Fair, Atlanta Pub. Schs., annually 1979-88; asst. scoutmaster troop 298 Atlanta area council Boy Scouts Am., 1980-87, Explorer advisor, 1982-86, unit commr., 1985, dist. commr. North Atlanta Dist., Atlanta Area Council, 1988, mem. faculty Commrs. Coll., 1985-87; mem. alumni adv. com. Clarkson Coll. Tech., 1981—, alumni bd. govs., 1983—, Golden Knight award, 1983; mem. exec. com., zoning chmn. neighbor planning unit City of Atlanta, 1982—, chmn., 1988. Col. AUS Corps Engrs., 1948-52, Korea. Decorated Legion of Merit, Meritorious Service medal, U.S. Army Res. medal, 1975; elected to Old Guard of Gate City Guard, 1979; recipient cert. of Achievement Dept. Army, 1978, USO Recognition award, 1979, Order of Arrow award Boy Scouts Am., 1983, 87, Scouters Key Boy Scouts Am., 1988, award Am. Inst. Plant Engrs., 1987. Fellow Soc. Am. Mil. Engrs. (bd. dirs. 1986—, chmn. readiness com. 1986-88, program chmn. Atlanta post 1980-81, v.p. 1982, pres. 1983, program chmn. 1988 nat. meeting, Nat. award of Merit 1982-83, Atlanta post Leadership award 1988); mem. Soc. 1st U.S. Inf., Res. Officers Assn., U.S. Army War Coll. Found. (life mem.), U.S. Army War Coll. Alumni Assn., Nat. Soc. Profl. Engrs., Ga. Soc. Profl. Engrs., Engrs. Club Boston, Assn. U.S. Army, Def. Preparedness Assn., Am. Arbitration Assn. (panel arbitrators 1979—, constrn. adv. com. 1984—), Atlanta C. of C., Mil. Order World Wars. Republican. Jewish. Clubs: Ft. McPherson Officers; Ga. Appalachian Trail. Lodges: Masons (32 deg.), Shriners, Elks, Civitan. Home: 3260 Rilman Dr NW Atlanta GA 30327 Office: 6520 Powers Ferry Rd Ste 200 Atlanta GA 30339

LIEBOVICH, SHELDON BERNARD, steel company executive; b. Madison, Wis., Oct. 5, 1937; s. Joe and Belle (Paley) L.; B.S., Rockford Coll., 1965; m. Rosalie Friedberg, June 28, 1959; children—Michael Louis, Barbara Ann, Jane Susan. Plant mgr. Liebovich Bros., Inc., Rockford, Ill., 1960, corp. sec., 1964, sales mgr., 1968, treas., 1972, exec. v.p., 1979, pres., chief exec. officer, 1982-86; chmn., chief exec. officer, 1986—. pres. Loubess, Inc., Rockford, 1974—, Archtl. Metals, Inc., Rockford, 1988—; v.p. Shanahowe Transp., Inc., Rockford, 1986—. Active Council for Community Services, Rockford, United Way, Rockford Jewish Community Council, Children's Devel. Center. Mem. Assn. Steel Distbrs. Jewish. Club: B'nai B'rith. Office: 2116 Preston St Rockford IL 61102

LIEBOWITZ, SETH JAY, human resource educator; b. N.Y.C., Jan. 13, 1953; s. Jerome and Henrietta (Gersten) L.; m. Jayne A. Berlinger, Sept. 7, 1981; 1 child, Jason Heath. BA in Psychology magna cum laude, SUNY, Cortland, 1975; PhD in Indsl. Organizational Psychology, U. Tenn., 1983. Asst. program evaluator U. Tenn. Environ. Ctr., Knoxville, 1977-79; social sci. analyst TVA, Knoxville, 1979-80; mgr. dept. Sears Roebuck Portrait Studio, Knoxville, 1981-82; cons. Oak Ridge (Tenn.) Nat. Lab, 1982-83; trainer cons. Wilson Learning Corp. (Sequoyah Performance Agy.), Knoxville, 1983-84; asst. prof. sch. bus. and adminstrn. Duquesne U., Pitts., 1984—; cons. human resources T. Boyle Assocs., Pitts., 1984—; faculty advisor Duquesne U. student chpt. Am. Soc. Pers. Adminstrn., Pitts., 1984—. Contbr. articles to profl. jours. Fellow U. Tenn., 1976-77. Mem. Acad. Mgmt., Beta Gamma Sigma, Phi Kappa Phi. Democrat. Jewish. Home: 315 Celestial Dr Freedom PA 15042 Office: Duquesne U Sch Bus & Adminstrn Pittsburgh PA 15282

LIEDEKER, RONALD MORRIS, oil company executive; b. Del Rio, Tex., Dec. 12, 1943; s. Morris Jr. and Shirley (Phillips) L.; m. Phyllis Doughty, Aug. 28, 1965 (div. 1977); children: Drew, Shelby; m. Karen Lindquist, Oct. 5, 1985. BS, Tulane U., 1965. Stock transfer agt. then installment loan collector Nat. Bank Commerce, New Orleans, 1965-66; trainee, systems analyst Tex. Commerce Bank, Houston, 1967-68; loan officer, v.p. Tex. Commerce Bank, Corpus Christi, Tex., 1975-76; loan officer, asst. v.p. Bank of Commerce, Corpus Christi, 1969-73; loan officer, v.p. Guaranty Nat. Bank, Corpus Christi, 1973-75; ind. oil operator Doughty-Liedeker, Corpus Christi, 1976-79; chief fin. officer Sexton Oil & Minerals Corp., Corpus Christi, 1979—; fin. advisor Winston G. Sexton, Corpus Christi, 1979—. Bd. dirs. Corpus Christi chpt. Am. Cancer Soc., 1972-78. Mem. Ind. Petroleum Assn. Am., Corpus Christi Geol. Soc., Beach Combers Club, Corpus Christi Yacht Club. Republican. Jewish. Home: 542 Evergreen St Corpus Christi TX 78412 Office: Sexton Oil & Minerals Corp 600 Bldg Ste 1900 Corpus Christi TX 78473

LIEDTKE, JOHN HUGH, petroleum company executive; b. Tulsa, Feb. 10, 1922; m. Betty Lyn; children: Karen, Kristin, John Hugh, Blake, Kathryn. B.A., Amherst Coll., 1942; postgrad., Harvard Grad. Sch., Bus. Adminstrn., 1943; LL.B., U. Tex., 1947. Pres. Zapata Petroleum Corp., 1953-62; pres., chief exec. officer Pennzoil Co., Houston, 1962-68, chmn., 1968—, also bd. dirs. Trustee Kinkaid Sch., Houston, Baylor Coll. Medicine, U.S. Naval Acad. Found.; council overseers Jesse H. Jones Grad. Sch. Adminstrn. Rice U. Served to lt. USN, 1942-45. Mem. Tex. Mid-Continent Oil and Gas Assn. (dir.), Am. Petroleum Inst. (dir.), Nat. Petroleum Council (dir.), Nat. Petroleum Refiners Assn. (bd. dirs.), Ind. Petroleum Assn. Am. (bd. dirs.), Penn Grade Assn. (bd. dirs.), Houston C. of C. (dir.), Beta Theta Pi, Phi Alpha Delta. Clubs: Houston Country, Ramada, Petroleum; Rolling Rock (Ligonier, Pa.); Racquet (Midland, Tex.); Calgary (Alta., Can.). Office: Pennzoil Co PO Box 2967 Houston TX 77252 *

LIEFF, ANN SPECTOR, music company executive; b. Miami, Fla., Jan. 16, 1952; d. Martin Wilson and Dorothy (Miller) Spector; m. William Allen Lieff, Aug. 24, 1975; 1 child, Laura Rebecca. BA in Sociology, U. Denver, 1974. V.p. Spec's Music, Miami, Fla., 1974-80, pres., chief exec. officer, 1980—. Mem. Jewish Community Ctrs., Miami, 1983—. Mem. Nat. Assn. Retail Merchandisers, Am. Technician Soc., Young Pres.'s Orgn., Hadassah. Democrat. Jewish. Home: 9965 SW 131st ST Miami FL 33176 Office: Spec's Music PO Box 652009 Miami FL 33265

LIEPOLD, ROBERT BRUCE, electrical engineer, consultant; b. Chgo., Oct. 4, 1925; s. Albin Joseph and Jeanette Marion (Hussander) L.; m. Mary Jane Gerrity, Dec. 29, 1964; 1 child, John Robert. BSEE, U. Wis., 1946. V.p. Automatic Electric (GTE), North Lake, Ill., 1947-69; pres. United Bus. Communications, Kansas City, Mo., 1979-74; pres. Robert B. Liepold Inc., St. Louis, 1974-78, Kansas City, 1984—; exec. v.p. United Telecom, Kansas City, 1978-84. pres. Kansas City Ballet, 1983-85; chmn. Jr. Achievement, Kansas City, 1983-84. Served to lt. USN, 1943-46, Atlantic, 1952-54, Korea. Mem. IEEE. Republican. Roman Catholic. Office: 4330 Shawnee Mission Pkwy #211 Shawnee Mission KS 66205

LIES, RICHARD LORENZ, JR., personal care company executive; b. Newark, Sept. 1, 1945; s. Richard L. and Madelon (Thompson) L.; m. Susan Dorothy Lies, July 1, 1967; 1 child, Richard L. III. BA in Econs., Northwestern U., 1967; MBA, U. Chgo., 1978. Maintenance supt. Johnson & Johnson, Chgo., 1972-76; maintenance-mfg. mgr. Armour-Dial Inc., Montgomery, Ill., 1976-78, plant mgr., 1978-86; sr. v.p., gen. mgr. personal care div. The Dial Corp., Phoenix, 1986—. Pres. Aurora (Ill.) YMCA, 1982-83; bd. dirs. United Way Aurora, 1983-84, Ill. Safety Council, Chgo., 1981-86. Capt. USAF, 1967-72, Vietnam. Office: Dial Corp Greyhound Tower #702 Phoenix AZ 85077

LIFFERS, WILLIAM ALBERT, chemical company executive; b. Union City, N.J., Jan. 12, 1929; s. William F. and Gertrude (Wildemann) L.; m. Mary Rafferty, Sept. 5, 1953; children—Steven, Linda, Wendy. B.S. in Bus. Adminstrn., Seton Hall U., 1953. With Am. Cyanamid Co., Wayne, N.J., 1953—; v.p. Cyanamid Internat., 1972-74; pres. Cyanamid Internat. (Cyanamid Americas/Far East), 1974-76, corp. v.p., 1976-77, sr. v.p., dir., 1977-78, vice chmn., 1978—; bd. dirs. CityFed Fin. Corp. and subs. City Fed. Savs. Bank. Bd. dirs. Nat. Fgn. Trade Council, Tax Found., U.S. Council Internat. Bus., N.J. Inst. Tech., Bus.-Industry Polit. Action Com., Ireland-U.S. Council Commerce and Industry, Council U.S. and Italy, Pub. Affairs Research Inst. N.J. Served with Finance Corps U.S. Army, 1951-53. Mem. Nat. Planning Assn. (trustee), Brit.-N. Am. Com., Council on Fgn. Relations. Office: Am Cyanamid Co 1 Cyanamid Pla Wayne NJ 07470

LIFSCHITZ, RALPH See LAUREN, RALPH

LIFSCHULTZ, PHILLIP, financial and tax consultant; b. Oak Park, Ill., Mar. 5, 1927; s. Abraham Albert and Frances Rhoda (Seigel) L.; m. Edith Louise Leavitt, June 27, 1948; children: Gregory, Bonnie, Jodie. BS in Acctg., U. Ill., 1949; JD, John Marshall Law Sch., 1956. Bar: Ill. 1956. Tax mgr. Arthur Andersen & Co., Chgo., 1957-63; v.p. taxes Montgomery Ward & Co., Chgo., 1963-78; fin. v.p., controller Henry Crown & Co., Chgo., 1978-81; prin. Phillip Lifschultz & Assocs., Chgo., 1981—; exec. dir. Dodi Orgn., 1987. Mem. adv. council Coll. Commerce and Bus. Adminstrn. U. Ill., Urbana-Champaign, 1977-78; chmn., Civic Fedn. Chgo., 1980-82; chmn. adv. bd. to Auditor Gen. of Ill., 1965-73; project dir. Exec. Service Corps of Chgo., Chgo. Bd. Edn. and State of Ill. projects, 1980-87. Served with U.S. Army, 1945-46. Mem. Ill. Bar Assn., Chgo. Bar Assn., Am. Inst. CPA's, Ill. CPA Soc., Am. Arbitration Assn. (comml. panel 1983—), Nat. Retail Merchants Assn. (chmn. tax com. 1975-78), Am. Retail Fedn. (chmn. taxation com. 1971). Clubs: Standard, City (bd. govs.). Home: 976 Oak Dr Glencoe IL 60022 Office: 450 E Devon Itasca IL 60143

LIFSCHULTZ, SIDNEY BEN, transportation company executive; b. Chgo., Feb. 10, 1912; s. David and Ida (Arine) L.; m. Charlotte Kessler, Dec. 29, 1940; children: Marsha, David, Lawrence. BS, U. Ill., 1933; MBA, Harvard U., 1935. Pres. Lifschultz Fast Freight Inc., N.Y.C., 1950-65, chmn. bd., 1965—; chmn. bd. Trans Air Freight System, N.Y.C., 1970-80, Wolf and Gerber, N.Y.C., 1973-80. Bd. dirs. United Jewish Appeal, N.Y. area; fellow "The Soc. of 1824," S.C. Med. Sch.; scholar founder NYU. Mem. Solamon Schechter Sch. Bd.; past pres. Westchester Jewish Ctr. Office: Lifschultz Fast Freight 641 W 59th St New York NY 10019

LIGÉ, PETER, retail executive; b. Tallin, Estonia, July 1, 1941; m. June F. Ligé, Dec. 27, 1968; children: Mark, Tara. B Engring. Sci., U. Western Ont., London, 1963-67. Registered profl. engr. Systems engr. IBM Canada Ltd., Toronto, Ont., 1967-69; mktg. rep. IBM Canada Ltd., Toronto, 1969-70, mgr. nat. accounts, 1970-72, mktg. mgr., 1972-75; pres. Marktara Corp., North Battleford, Sask., 1975-85; v.p. Canadian Time Corp. Ltd., Toronto, 1985-86, exec. v.p., 1986—. Office: Can Tire Corp Ltd, 2180 Yonge St, Toronto, ON Canada M4P 2V8

LIGGON, CHARLES ELVIN, III, acoustical products company executive; b. Wilson, N.C., May 29, 1953; s. Charles Elvin Jr. and Marion (Driver) L.; m. Paula Stephens Batchelor, June 23, 1979 (div. Feb. 1986); 1 child, Charles Elvin IV. Student, Atlantic Christian Coll., 1972-73; BS, U. N.C., 1975. Cost acct. J.P. Stevens Corp., Roanoke Rapids, N.C., 1976-77; pres. Five Points Nursery & Floral Co., Wilson, N.C., 1978-84; gen. mgr., sec. S.E. Acoustical Panels, Wilson, 1984—. Mem. Nat. Office Products Assn., Carolina Office Products Assn., Fla. Office Products Assn., Va. Office Products Assn. Democrat. Presbyterian. Lodge: Elks. Home: 419 Westover Ave Wilson NC 27893 Office: Southeastern Acoustical Panels 812 Mercer St PO Box 1385 Wilson NC 27894

LIGHT, KATHY J., electrical components manufacturing company; b. Bucyrus, Ohio, Jan. 12, 1958; d. Edward Rae and Emma Ilene (Winklefoos) L. Gen. mgr. Baystead Precision Screw, Inc., Natick, Mass., 1982-86; mgr. mktg./sales adminstrn. Sprague Electric Co., Mansfield, Mass., 1986—. Mem. Phi Sigma. Avocations: antiques, refinishing furniture, sewing.

LIGHT, KENNETH B., manufacturing company executive; b. N.Y.C., June 2, 1932; s. Max and Mollie (Schein) Lichtenholtz; m. Judith Klein, May 28, 1961; children: Corey, Randi Beth, Allison. B.S., NYU, 1954, LL.B. cum laude, 1957; M.B.A., U. Chgo., 1976. Bar: N.Y. 1957. Partner firm Light & Light, Bklyn., 1958-61; asst. sec. Gen. Bronze Corp., Garden City, N.Y., 1961-69; sec., gen. counsel Allied Products Corp., Chgo., 1969-76; v.p., gen. counsel Allied Products Corp., 1976-79, sr. v.p., 1979-83, exec. v.p., 1983—; pres. Midwest Steel Processing, Inc., 1982-84; dir. Aurora Corp. Ill., Chgo. Mem. Chgo. Bar Assn., N.Y.C. Subcontractors Assn. (v.p. 1967-69), Am. Subcontractors Assn. (dir. 1967-68), Chgo. Assn. Commerce and Industry. Home: 1825 Cavell Ave Highland Park IL 60035 Office: Allied Products Corp 10 S Riverside Pla Chicago IL 60606

LIGHTER, ERIC AARON, real estate developer, consultant; b. Chico, Calif., Aug. 6, 1950; s. Bruce Clyde and Katherine Bernice (Stutsman) L.; m. Gitte Gadix, Dec. 18, 1976 (div. Feb. 1978); m. 2d, Janet Shellen Wong, Apr. 20, 1982 (div. July 1985). Grad. Grad. Realtors Inst., 1973; student U. Hawaii. Salesman Fin. Security Life, Honolulu, 1970; founder, treas. 3d Eye Prodns., Honolulu, 1974-76; pres. Home Rent Hawaii, Honolulu, 1976; pres. A. Lighter Cons., Graphic and Media, 1977—; pres. Lighter Properties Corp., Developers, Honolulu, 1978—; founder Quality Income Systems, Honolulu, 1983; mem. Honolulu Realtor Pub. Relation Com., 1983-84. Editor: Ke Alaka'i, 1984. Bd. dirs. Hawaii Alliance for Arts in Edn., 1984, Inst. Human Services, Honolulu, 1984; Hawaii Statue of Liberty Program Mgr., 1986; founder Diamond Cross Ministries, 1985, performing Gospel guitarist, 1985. Mem. Hawaii Assn. Realtors, Bldg. Industry Assn. Hawaii (Parade of Homes Award of Excellence 1983), Hawaii Jaycees (project initiator Silver Jubilee Project 1983, mgr. Outstanding Hawaii Jaycees program mgr., founding pres. Capital Dist. 1982, chaplin Honolulu Chinese 1982-84, King of King award 1982, 83), Nat. Assn. Bed and Breakfast. Republican. Episcopalian. Club: Scandinavian of Hawaii. Lodge: Lions (Honolulu) (var. offices, including treas.). Avocation: playing Gospel guitar. Home: Honolulu Inn 1045 Spencer St Honolulu HI 96813

LIGHTNER, A. LEROY, JR., advertising agency executive; b. Wyomissing, Pa., Apr. 26, 1921; s. Angus LeRoy and Grace Darling (Thompson) L.; A.B., Franklin and Marshall Coll., 1942; m. Betty Pauline Jenkins, July 22, 1950; children—Karen, Kevin, Laura Lightner Phillips. Prodn. supr. N.W. Ayer & Son, Inc., Phila., 1942-47, account exec., Boston, 1947-52, Phila., 1956-60, account supr., 1961-69, v.p., account supr., N.Y.C., 1970-80; nat. dir. United Meth. Ch. TV Presence and Ministry Campaign, Nashville, 1980-81; v.p. mktg. services Carden & Cherry Advt. Agy., Nashville, 1982—. Mem. Nat. Assn. Conf. Lay Leaders United Meth. Ch., 1973—; trustee Morristown Coll., 1977-87; pres. alumni council Franklin and Marshall Coll., 1960-62, chmn. alumni fund, 1962-70. Mem. Geneal. Soc. Pa., Pub. Utilities Communicators Assn., Am. Gas Assn., New Brunswick Genealogical Soc., Maine Genealogical Soc., Berks County Genealogical Soc., Soc. of Genealogists, New Eng. Hist. Geneal. Soc., SAR, Blue Key, Druids, Lambda Chi Alpha, Pi Gamma Mu. Methodist (lay leader Eastern Pa. Conf. 1971-74, pres. Conf. Bd. Missions and Ch. Extension, 1965-69; pres. Northeastern Jurisdiction Bd. of Laity 1979-80, lay leader No. N.J. Conf. 1976-80). Author: Jenkins-Berry Ancestry, 1970, Lightner-Thompson Family, 1969. Home: 596 Cumberland Hills Dr Hendersonville TN 37075-4361 Office: Carden & Cherry Advt Agy 1220 McGavock St Nashville TN 37203

LIGHTNER, RUTH H., transportation executive; b. N.Y.C., Mar. 9, 1940; d. William Weir and Ruth May (Hayes) McLoughlin; m. John N. Lightner; children: Ruth Marie, Kelly Rachael. Grad. high sch. With NYPA Sand & Gravel, Buffalo, 1964-69, Idamont Ind., Lolo, Mont., 1969-71, Amoco Oil, Missoula, Mont., 1971-74; owner Lightner Brokerage, Missoula, 1974-84; ops. mgr. Bronco Trucking, Downey, Calif., 1984-85; term mgr. Federal Transport, Chino, Calif., 1986—. Mem. Women's Traffic Club of L.A., L.A. Transp. Club, Am. Businesswomen (pres. 1980-82), Delta Nu Alpha. Office: Fed Transport Box 1658 Chino CA 91708

LIGHTSTONE, RONALD, lawyer; b. N.Y.C., Oct. 4, 1938; s. Charles and Pearl (Weisberg) L.; m. Nancy Lehrer, May 17, 1973; 1 child, Dana. AB, Columbia U., 1959; JD, NYU, 1962. Atty. CBS, N.Y.C., 1967-69; assoc. dir. bus. affairs CBS News, N.Y.C., 1969-70; atty. NBC, N.Y.C., 1970; assoc. gen. counsel Viacom Internat. Inc., N.Y.C., 1970-75; v.p., gen. counsel, sec. Viacom Internat. Inc., 1976-80; v.p. bus. affairs Viacom Entertainment Group Viacom Internat., Inc., 1980-82, v.p. corp. affairs, 1982-84, sr. v.p. corp. and legal affairs, 1984-87; exec. v.p. Aaron Spelling Prodns., Inc., West Hollywood, Calif., 1988—, Spelling Intertainment Inc., West Hollywood, 1989—. Served to lt. USN, 1962-66. Mem. ABA (chmn. TV, cable and radio com.), Assn. Bar City N.Y., Fed. Communications Bar Assn. Office: Spelling Entertainment Inc 1041 N Formosa Ave West Hollywood CA 90046

LIGHTWOOD, CAROL WILSON, writer; b. Tacoma, Wash., Oct. 2, 1941; d. Harry Edward and Cora H. Wilson; m. Keith G. Lightwood (div. Dec. 1968; children: Miles Francis, Clive Harry. BA, Smith Coll., 1963. Writer various advt. agencies, 1968-82; v.p. Wakeman & DeForrest, Newport Beach, Calif., 1985-86; owner Lightwood & Ptnrs., Long Beach, Calif., 1986—. Author: Malibu, 1984; contbr. articles to profl. jours. Chair mus. coun. Long Beach Mus. Art. Mem. Sierra Club. Episcopalian.

LIGUORI, FRANK NICKOLAS, temporary personnel company executive; b. Bklyn., July 2, 1946; s. August and Mary (Perotto) L.; m. JoAnn Scioscia, July 7, 1968; children: Frank Jr., Mark. BS in Acctg., St. Francis Coll., Bklyn., 1964. CPA, N.Y. Sr. auditor Coopers & Lybrand, N.Y.C., 1964-71; successively controller, treas., sr. v.p., exec. v.p., pres. Olsten Corp., Westbury, N.Y., 1971—, also bd. dirs.; bd. dirs. WLIW 21, Plainview, N.Y. Mem. Am. Inst. CPAs, N.Y. State Soc. CPAs, Nat. Assn. Temporary Services (bd. dirs.). Home: 2 Talisman Ct Dix Hills NY 11746

LIKER, JACK, ceramic company executive; b. N.Y.C., June 10, 1926; s. Boris and Lucy (Zerulnikova) L.; m. Henriette Handel, Jan. 11, 1948; children: Karin, Jeffrey, Stephen. Floorman Sloves Book Bindery, 1946-51; design engr. Burndy Corp., 1951-59; sales mgr. Molecular Delectrics, 1959-65, Basic Ceramics, Hawthorne, N.J., 1965-71; v.p. sales Mykroy Ceramics, Ledgewood, N.J., 1971-72, v.p., gen. mgr., 1972-80; v.p., gen. mgr. Mykroy/Mycalex div. Spaulding Fibre Co., Clifton, N.J., 1980—; officer Spaulding Composites Corp., Inc., Clifton, N.J., 1987; dir. Ceramic Fabricators, Inc.; ptnr. Liker Travel Agy. Cons. ceramic material dept. chem. engring. Columbia; cons. Karl Roesch Inc.; yearly guest speaker Rutgers U., New Brunswick, N.J. Contbr. articles to profl. jours.; patentee in field. Served with AUS, 1944-46. Mem. Am., Can., N.J. ceramics socs., Ceramic Assn. of N.J. (pres. 1987-88), Internat. Hybrid Microelctronics Soc., Soc. Aerospace Materials and Process Engrs., ASTM, Elec. Insulation Conf., Soc. Plastic Engrs. Lodge: Rotary. Office: 125 Clifton Blvd Clifton NJ 07011

LILES, MALCOLM HENRY, stockbroker; b. Tampa, Fla., Sept. 21, 1950; s. Henry J. and Frances (Bingham) L.; m. Marion Townsend McDougal, May 24, 1975; children; M. Leighton, William N. Student, Valdosta State Coll., 1969-70; BBA, U. Ga., 1972. Mortgage officer Citizens & So. Nat. Bank, Atlanta, 1973-76; v.p., regional mgr. Investors Mortgage Group, Nashville, 1976-81; v.p. investments The Robinson-Humphrey Co., Nashville, 1981—; trustee Arthur & Sylvia Lee Scholarship Found., Brentwood, Tenn., 1986—. Sustaining membership chmn. Mid. Tenn. Explorer Scouts, Nashville, 1986; bd. dirs. Alive Hospice Inc., Nashville, 1986—. Mem. Internat. Assn. Fin. Planning (past pres., bd. dirs. Nashville chpt.), Inst. CFPs, Am. Funds Group (mem. chmn.'s adv. council), Exchange Club (bd. dirs. 1986-87). Home: 3507 Grayswood Ave Nashville TN 37215 Office: The Robinson-Humphrey Co Third Nat Bank Bldg 9th Fl Nashville TN 37219

LILJEBECK, ROY C., transportation company executive; b. 1937; married. BA, U. Puget Sound, 1961. Acct. Touche Ross Bailey and Smart, 1961-67; with Pacific Air Freight Inc., 1967-68; treas., then also v.p. Airborne Freight Corp., Seattle, 1968—, sr. v.p., 1973-84, exec. v.p., 1984—, now also chief fin. officer. Office: Airborne Freight Corp PO Box 662 Seattle WA 98111 *

LILLEY, JOHN MARK, university college provost and dean; b. Converse, La., Mar. 24, 1939; s. Ernest Franklin and Sibyl Arena (Geoghagan) L.; children: Sibyl Elizabeth, Myles Durham; m. Geraldine Murphy Lilley, June 26, 1988; stepchildren: Jason Murphy, Benjamin Murphy. Bachelor in Music Edn., Baylor U., 1961, Bachelor of Music, 1962, Master of Music, 1964; Doctor of Musical Art, U. So. Calif., 1971. Mem. faculty Claremont McKenna, Harvey Mudd, Pitzer and Scripps Colls., Claremont, Calif., 1966-76; asst. dean arts and scis. Kans. State U., Manhattan, 1976-80; provost, dean Pa. State U., Erie, 1980—; bd. dirs. Erie Conf., 1980—. Condr. 1st performances Kubik, 1972, 76, Ives, 1974, (recording) Kubik, 1974. Bd. dirs., v.p. So. Calif. Choral Music Assn., L.A., 1971-76; mem. Archtl. Commn., Claremont, 1974-76; bd. dirs. Erie Philharm., 1980-86, United Way, Erie County, 1981—; mem. Regents Commn. on Nursing Edn., Kansas City, Kans., 1978-79; pres. Pacific S.W. Intercollegiate Choral Assn., L.A., 1969-70. NEH grantee, 1978. Mem. Am. Assn. Higher Edn., Coll. Music Soc., Am. Choral Dirs. Assn., Phi Mu Alpha Sinfonia, Omicron Delta Kappa. Republican. Presbyterian. Clubs: Erie, Kahkwa (Erie), Lake Shore. Lodge: Rotary (bd. dirs. Erie 1979-80, 81—, v.p. 1985-86, pres. 1986-87). Home: 601 Pasadena Dr Erie PA 16505 Office: Pa State U Eric Behrend Coll Station Rd Erie PA 16563

LILLEY, MILI DELLA, entertainment management consultant, insurance company executive; b. Valley Forge, Pa., Aug. 29; d. Leon Hanover and Della Beaver (Jones) L. MBA, Tex. Christian U., 1957, PhD, 1959. Various positions G & G Cons. Inc., Ft. Lauderdale, Fla., 1971-75; v.p. AMEX, Inc., Beverly Hills, Calif. and Acapulco, Mex., 1976-80; pres. The Hanover Group, Ft. Lauderdale, 1981—, mgr. entertainers Ink Spots, Del-Vikings, Moonglows, and Mario Kinsey; dist. agt. Farmers & Traders Life Ins. Co. and other leading cos.; officer, bd. dirs. Arline's World of Travel, Tamarac, Fla.; dist. agt. Farmers & Traders Life Ins. Co. and other leading companies. Named to All Stars Honor Roll Nat. Ins. Sales Mag., 1989. Mem. Fla. Assn. Theatrical Agents, Fla. Guild of Talent Agts., Mgrs., Producers and Orchestras. Executive office: The Hanover Group 1001 W Cypress Creek Rd Ste 314 Fort Lauderdale FL 33309 Office: 3 Sloane Gardens Club, Sloane Sq, London SWI England

LILLIE, JOHN MITCHELL, retail executive; b. Chgo., Feb. 2, 1937; s. Walter Theodore and Mary Ann (Hatch) L.; m. Daryl Lee Harvey, Aug. 23, 1987; children: Alissa Ann, Theodore Perry. B.S., Stanford U., 1959, M.S., M.B.A., 1962-64. Various positions including dir. systems devel., also asst. to pres. Boise Cascade Corp., 1964-68; v.p., chief financial officer Arcata Nat. Corp., Menlo Park, Calif., 1968-70; exec. v.p., chief operating officer Arcata Nat. Corp., 1970-72; pres., chief exec. officer Leslie Salt Co., Newark, Calif., 1972-79; exec. v.p. Lucky Stores Inc., Dublin, Calif., 1979-81, pres., 1981-86, chmn., chief exec. officer, 1986—, also dir. Trustee Stanford (Calif.) U., 1988. Mem. Beta Theta Pi, Tau Beta Pi. Office: Lucky Stores Inc 6300 Clark Ave Dublin CA 94568

LILLIE, RICHARD HORACE, investor, real estate developer, retired surgeon; b. Milw., Feb. 3, 1918; s. Osville Richard and Sylvia Grace (Faber) L.; B.S., Haverford Coll., 1939; M.D., Harvard U., 1943; M.S. in Surgery, U. Mich., 1950; m. Jane Louise Zwicky, Sept. 24, 1949; children—Richard Horace, Diane Louise. Intern, U. Mich. Hosp., Ann Arbor, 1943-44, resident, 1946-50; chief of surgery, Milw. Hosp., 1968-80; practice medicine specializing in surgery, Milw., 1951-81; clin. prof. emeritus Med. Coll. Wis.; pres. Lillie 18-94 Corp.; emeritus trustee Northwestern Mut. Life Ins. Co.; dir. The Lynde and Harry Bradley Found.; trustee State of Wis. Investment bd; investor, real estate developer, 1981—. Bd. dirs. emeritus Goodwill Industries. Served with M.C. AUS, 1944-46. Mem. Am. Bd. Surgery, A.C.S., Central Surg. Assn., AMA, Wis. Surg. Soc. Episcopalian. Clubs: Univ. of Milw., Milw. Yacht, Town. Contbr. articles to surg. jours. Home: 6500 N Lake Dr Milwaukee WI 53217

LILLIS, WILLIAM G., banking executive; b. Ann Arbor, Mich., Oct. 13, 1930; s. William J. and Selina M. (Moss) L.; m. Nancy Wilcox, June 26, 1954; children—Susan, Deborah, Jennifer. B. Civil Engring., Rensselaer Poly. Inst., 1952. Civil engr. Pa. R.R., N.Y.C., 1954-56; asst. operating supt. Bush Terminal Bldg. Co., Bklyn., 1956-66; appraiser, loan officer Met. Life Ins. Co., N.Y.C., 1966-70; exec. v.p. Helmsley Enterprises, N.Y.C., 1970-77; exec. v.p. Empire Savs. Bank, N.Y.C., 1977-79, pres., chief exec. officer, 1979-81; pres. Am. Savs. Bank, N.Y.C., 1981—, also bd. dirs.; trustee, dir. Retirement System for Savs. Instns.; bd. dirs. Joint Computer Ctr., Realty Found. N.Y., Am. Savs. Bank, Retirement System for Savs. Instn., Joint Computer Ctr. Bd. dirs. Community Preservation Corp., 1981—, ; mem. exec. com. March of Dimes Teamwalk, N.Y.C., 1983—. Served with USNR, 1952-54. Fellow Nat. Soc. Real Estate Fin. (cert. real estate financer); mem. Nat. Inst. Real Estate Financing (hon.), Nat. Assn. Real Estate Appraisers (cert.), Nat. Assn. Rev. Appraiser & Mortgage Underwriters (sr.), Real Estate Bd. N.Y., Realty Found. N.Y., Nat. Council Savs. Instns. Republican. Clubs: N.Y. Athletic (N.Y.C.); Leetes Island Assoc. (Guilford, Conn.). Home: Stamford CT Office: Am Savs Bank 99 Church St White Plains NY 10601

LILLY, THOMAS MORE, insurance executive, lawyer; b. Pitts., May 14, 1942; s. Joseph H. and Mary Jo (Lippert) L.; m. Roberta M. Maloney, Dec. 31, 1966. BA, U. Pitts., 1966, JD, 1973. Bar: Pa. 1973, U.S. Dist. Ct. (we. dist.) Pa., 1973; CLU, 1983. Asst. to dir. Assoc. Indsl. Advertisers, N.Y.C., 1966-67; media planner Ketchum, MacLeod & Grove Advt., Pitts., 1967-70; mktg. mgr. Cahners Pub. Co., Chgo., 1970-71; media cons. Thomas M. Lilly, Pitts., 1971-73; asst. dist. atty. Allegheny County, Pitts., 1073-75; law clk. Common Pleas Ct., Pitts., 1975-76; atty. Hickton, Dean, Tighe & Lilly, Pitts., 1976-77; agt. State Mut. Life, Pitts., 1977-86; pvt. practice law and insurance Thomas M. Lilly, Pitts., 1986—. Contbr. articles to profl. jours. Mem. Am. Soc. CLU's and Chartered Fin. Cons., Internat. Assn. Fin. Planners, Allegheny County Bar Assn. Democrat. Roman Catholic. Home: 5 Colonial Pl Pittsburgh PA 15232 Office: 1690 Gateway Two Pittsburgh PA 15222

LIME, JAMES CRAIG, energy industry executive; b. Paterson, N.J., Jan. 29, 1951; s. Daniel Abraham and Barbara Ruth (McDougall) L.; m. Kathy Amanda Buckley; children: Brian James, Kathryn Kimberly. BA in Bus., Rutgers Coll., 1973; MS in Forest Mgmt., Syracuse U., 1975. Sales trainee Westvaco Corp., N.Y.C., 1976, fin. analyst, 1976-77, asst. purchasing agt., 1977-79, mgr. raw materials and fuels, 1979-81, mgr. group purchasing, 1981-84; mgr. raw material purchases Colgate-Palmolive Co., N.Y.C., 1984-87; v.p. corp. purchasing J.M. Huber Corp., Edison, N.J., 1987-88, v.p. purchasing and transp., 1988—. Asst. scout master, Boy Scouts Am., Pluckemin, N.J. Named Eagle Scout, Boy Scouts Am., 1965. Home: 3 Red Hawk Rd S Colts Neck NJ 07722 Office: JM Huber Corp 333 Thornall St Edison NJ 08818

LIMHAISEN, MOHAMMED ABDULRAHAM, banker; b. Al Sulfi, Saudi Arabia, Dec. 29, 1949; s. Abdulrahman Abdul Mohsin; m. Modhi Nasir Abdulaziz Al Nowaiser, June 14, 1978; children: Sarah Mohammed, Abdulrahman Mohammed, Majed Abdulrahman. BS, Washington State U., 1973, BS in Chemistry, 1974; MBA, NW Mo. State U. Credit officer Chase Manhattan Bank, 1976-77; loan officer, project mgr. Saudi Indsl. Devel. Fund, Saudi Arabia, 1977-788, controller gen., 1980; asst. gen mgr. United Saudi Comml. Bank, Riyadh, Saudi Arabia, 1983-86, corp. sec., 1983—, dep. gen. mgr., 1986—; gen. mgr. Saudi Investment Bank, Riyadh, Saudi Arabia, 1988—; chmn. bd. dirs. Riyadh Internat. Med. Co.; bd. dirs. Saudi So. Dairy Co., Riyadh, Saudi Shares Registration Co., Riyadh., Nat. Co. Mfg. Food Stuff, Riyadh. Mem. Am. Mgmt. Assn., Arab Bankers Assn., Minninger Found. Club: Equestrian (Riyadh). Home: PO Box 56013, Riyadh 11554, Saudi Arabia Office: PO Box 3533, Riyadh 11481, Saudi Arabia

LIMPITLAW, JOHN DONALD, publishing company executive; b. N.Y.C., Jan. 4, 1935; s. Robert and Olga (Lang) L.; m. Susan Elizabeth Glover, May 21, 1960; children: Alison, Amy Elizabeth. BA, Trinity Coll., Hartford, Conn., 1956. With Marine Midland Bank Trust Co. N.Y., N.Y.C., 1956-61; asst. mgr. compensation Celanese Corp., N.Y.C., 1961-63; mgr. personnel Westvaco Corp., N.Y.C., 1963-69; v.p. Warnaco Inc., Bridgeport, Conn., 1969-77, Macmillan Inc., N.Y.C., 1977—. Mem. N.Y. Personnel Mgmt. Assn. Democrat. Episcopalian. Club: Fairfield County Hunt (Westport, Conn.). Home: 120 Chelsea St Fairfield CT 06430 Office: Macmillan Inc 866 Third Ave New York NY 10022

LIN, ALICE LEE LAN, physicist, researcher, educator; b. Shanghai, China, Oct. 28, 1937; came to U.S., 1960, naturalized, 1974; d. Yee and Tsing Tsing (Wang) L.; m. A. Marcus, Dec. 19, 1962 (div. Feb. 1972); 1 child, Peter A. Lin-Marcus. AB in Physics, U. Calif.-Berkeley, 1963; MA in Physics, George Washington U., 1974. Research asst. in radiation damage Cavendish Lab., Cambridge U., Eng., 1965-66; statis. asst. dept. math. U. Calif.-Berkeley, 1962-63; info. analysis specialist Nat. Acad. Scis., Washington, 1970-71; teaching fellow, research asst. George Washington U., Catholic U. Am., Washington, 1971-75; physicist NASA/Goddard Space Flight Ctr., Greenbelt, Md., 1975-80, Army Materials Tech. Lab., Watertown, Mass., 1980—. Contbr. articles to profl. jours. Mencius Ednl. Found. grantee, 1959-60. Mem. N.Y. Acad. Scis., AAAS, Am. Phys. Soc., Am. Ceramics Soc., Am. Acoustical Soc., Am. Men and Women of Sci., Optical Soc. Am. Democrat. Avocations: rare stamp and coin collecting, art collectibles, home computers, opera, ballet. Home: 28 Hallett Hill Rd Weston MA 02193 Office: Army Materials Tech Lab Mail Stop MRS Bldg 39 Watertown MA 02172

LIN, PO-AN, energy company executive, controller; b. Fukien, Peoples Republic of China, Nov. 12, 1927; came to U.S., 1961; s. Jung Chi and Kwei-Cheng (Huang) L.; m. Helen Chang-Wan Lee, Apr. 13, 1958. BCS, Soo Chow U., Taipei, Republic of China, 1957; MBA, NYU, 1963, advanced profl. cert. in mgmt. acctg., 1976. Cert. mgmt. accountant. Asst. to fin. sec. Chinese Customs, Taipei, 1948-61; asst. v.p. and controller Interore Corp. div. Occidental Petroleum Corp., N.Y.C., 1965—. Mem. Inst. of Cert. Mgmt. Acctg., Nat. Assn. Accts., Am. Acctg. Assn., Am. Mgmt. Assn. Office: Interore Corp 1230 Ave of the Americas New York NY 10020

LIN, RUTH MEE FUNG, real estate corporation executive; b. Honolulu, July 4; d. William and Betty Ing; widowed, 1971; children : Andrew, Deborah B. Bus. degree, U. So. Calif., 1963. Exec. sec. Dean Witter & Co., Honolulu, 1963-65; fashion coord. Liberty House, 1965-66, SQR, Calif., 1966-68; exec. adminstr. Teledyne Ryan, 1968-71, McGraw Edison PSD, Hawaii, 1971-74; realtor Century 21, 1974-79; pres., chmn. Internat. Planning Cons., 1978—; realtor, pres., chmn. Empress Realty Corp., Honolulu, 1979—. Exec. producer Hawaiian TV series; actress: (TV shows) Hawaii 5-0, Magnum P.I., Jake & the Fat Man, The Vineyard, 1988; contbr. articles to profl. jours. Bd. dirs. Youth Theatre. Named Outstanding Am. Asian Woman, 1988. Mem. Profl. Asian Bus. Women (bd. dirs.), Chinese U. Grads. Soc. (1st v.p.), Elks. Office: Empress Realty Corp 733 Bishop St 2145 Honolulu HI 96813

LINCH, ESTRELLA VINZON, insurance underwriter, small business owner; b. Cavite, Philippines, June 18, 1944; came to U.S., 1961; d. Isidro and Filomena (Dragon) Vinzon. BSEE, Philippine Normal Coll., Manila, 1961; MA, U. Nebr., 1964; student, U. Mex., Mexico City, 1964-65; BA, Calif. State U., Long Beach, 1969; MBA, Loyola Marymount U., 1976. Tchr. Spanish Neligh (Nebr.) Pub. Sch., 1962-63, Linda Vista High Sch., San Diego, 1965-66; budget analyst TRW, Redondo Beach, Calif., 1970-72; fin. analyst Rockwell Internat., El Segundo, Calif., 1972-73; asst. controller Crydom Control, El Segundo, 1973-74; asst. to trustee Beverly Hills (Calif.) Bancorp, 1974-76; owner Sage Fin. and Managerial Co., Los Angeles, 1976—; ins. agt., securities rep. Prudential Ins., Santa Monica, Calif., 1976—. Author: Guidelines for Prospective Entrepreneurs in Small Service Oriented Business, 1976. Mem. Million Dollar Round Table, Top Table, Pilipino for Progress (pres. 1982-86), Gen Trias and Philippine Assn. (pres. 1982). Office: Prudential Ins Co Am 624 S Wilton Pl Los Angeles CA 90005

LINCOLN, EDMOND LYNCH, investment banker; b. Wilmington, Del., Aug. 3, 1949; s. Edmond Earl and Mary Margaret (Lynch) L.; B.A. magna cum laude, Harvard U., 1971, M.B.A., with distinction, 1974; m. Pamela Wick, Sept. 3, 1977; children: Lucy Arms, Emily Lord. Acting rare book librarian Henry Francis duPont Winterthur Mus. (Del.), 1971-72; with Kidder Peabody & Co., Inc., N.Y.C., 1974—, asst. v.p., 1977-79, v.p. 1979—, mgr. govt. agy. fin., 1984-86, transp. group, 1986—; pub. interest dir. Fed. Home Loan Bank of N.Y. Recipient Washburn History prize, Harvard U., 1971. Treas., Fed. Hall Meml. Assocs., 1981-87; mem. vis. com. Harvard Coll. Library, 1981-86, 1988—; exec. com. Friends of Harvard U. Track, 1972—, sec., 1976-87. Mem. Investment Assn. N.Y., Friends of Winterthur (trustee 1976-81, 87—, sec. 1978-81), Assn. Internationale de Bibliophilie, Phi Beta Kappa. Republican. Roman Catholic. Clubs: Odd Volumes, Grolier, Harvard (N.Y.C.); India House, Wilmington, Wilmington Country. Home: 161 E 79th St New York NY 10021 Office: Kidder Peabody & Co Inc 10 Hanover Sq 7th Fl New York NY 10005

LIND, EARL FREDERIC, manufacturing executive; b. Elgin, Ill., Feb. 8, 1934; s. Carl Elmer and Elsie Hilda (Kath) L.; m. Peggy Annette Lorene Hollingsworth, Aug. 1, 1959; children: John Frederic, Eric Christopher. BS, U. State of N.Y. Regents' External Degree Program, Albany, 1981. Mgr. rsch. and devel., tech. adminstrn. Elgin Nat. Watch, Elgin and Rolling Meadows, Ill., 1953-64; liaison engring. and sales adminstrn. Acronetics, Gen. Time, Skokie, Ill., 1964-65; sr. project engr. and supr. engring. Bruning, Mt. Prospect, Ill., 1965-70; gen. supr. prodn. control, materials mgr. Multigraphics Div. of Adress.-Multi., Mt. Prospect, 1970-74; materials mgr. Hach Chem. Co., Ames, Iowa, 1974-75; with Echlin Inc., Branford, Conn., 1975—; materials mgr. ACC div. Kans. Echlin Inc., 1981-86, dir. corp. materials mgmt., 1986-88, staff v.p. corp. materials mgmt., 1986; line v.p. of materials mgmt. Brake Parts, Inc. subs. Echlin, Inc., Branford, 1988—; lectr. in field. Author: Just in Time in a Manufacturing Organization, 1987, Just in Time in a Distribution Center and Finished Goods Warehouse, 1988. Mem. Hoffman-Schaumburg Com. Human Relations, 1969-72; chair pub. relations Independence Arts Council, Kans., 1979—; asst. scoutmaster Branford council Boy Scouts Am., 1985-87; bd. dirs., chair by-laws Weathersfield Homeowners Assns., 1961. Served with U.S. Army, 1957-58. Mem. Am. Mgmt. Assn. Office: Echlin Inc 100 Double Beach Rd Branford CT 06405

LIND, THOMAS OTTO, utility company executive; b. New Orleans, Apr. 24, 1937; s. Henry Carl Lind and Elinor (Rooney) Messersmith; m. Eugenia Niehaus, June 8, 1963; children: Elinor Ashley, Elizabeth Kelly. BS in MechE, Tulane U., 1959, LLB, 1965. Cert. mech. engr., 1959. Assoc. Jones, Walker, Waechter, Poitevent, Carrere and Denegre, New Orleans, 1965-66; v.p., sec., counsel Ingram Corp., New Orleans, 1966-84; v.p. Gulf Fleet Marine Corp., New Orleans, 1984-85; v.p., regulatory counsel, sec. New Orleans Pub. Service, Inc. and La. Power and Light Co., 1985—. Mem. bd. govs. Trinity Sch., New Orleans, 1982-85; vestryman Trinity Ch., New Orleans, 1987—; active Family of Community and Utility Supporters, New Orleans, 1987—. Served to lt. (j.g.) USN, 1959-62. Mem. ABA, Fed. Energy Bar Assn. (bd. dirs. 1987—, treas. 1988-89, sec. 1989—), La. State Bar Assn. (bd. dirs. corp. law sect. 1973-75), New Orleans Lawn Tennis Club (pres. 1986-88). Republican. Episcopalian. Home: 1126 Octavia St New Orleans LA 70115 Office: New Orleans Pub Service Inc 317 Baronne St Mail Unit N-82 New Orleans LA 70112

LINDAHL, HERBERT WINFRED, appliance manufacturing executive; b. Malvern, Ark., Nov. 25, 1927; s. Herbert Winfred and Helen Ester (VanDusen) L.; m. Mary Evalyn Nenon, Feb. 27, 1954; children: Evalyn Nenon, Eric VanDusen. BA, Vanderbilt U., 1950. With State Industries, Inc., Nashville, 1946—, v.p., 1955-68, pres., Ashland City, 1968—. Republican. Clubs: City, Hillwood (Nashville). Office: State Industries Inc By Pass Rd Ashland City TN 37015

LINDARS, LAURENCE EDWARD, retired health care products executive; b. N.Y.C., Oct. 14, 1922; s. Arthur John and Florence Vera (Cunard) L.; m. Mary Gibson Grandy, Jan. 22, 1972; children—John L., William A., Nancy E. Student, Dartmouth Coll., 1943-44; B.S., Columbia U., 1947. Sr. auditor Arthur Young & Co., N.Y.C., 1947-51; chief acct. Deering, Milliken & Co., 1951-53; treas., dir. Poloron Products, Inc., New Rochelle, N.Y., 1953-58; controller Atlas Gen., Inc., N.Y.C., 1958-59; controller, treas., dir. fin. planning Pepperidge Farm, Inc., Norwalk, Conn., 1959-67; with C.R. Bard, Inc., Murray Hill, N.J., 1967-88; dir. C.R. Bard, Inc., 1972—, vice chmn., 1983-88; mem. adv. bd. of Summit Trust Co., 1970-84. Trustee Overlook Hosp., 1973-79, Found., 1988—; trustee Epilepsy Found. N.J., 1985—, pres., 1986-87, chmn., 1988—. Served as lt. (j.g.) USNR, 1943-46. Mem. Fin. Execs. Inst., Delta Upsilon. Presbyterian. Club: Canoe Brook Country, PGA Am.

LINDAUER, THEODORE, psychiatrist; b. N.Y.C., July 17, 1935; s. Harry and Anne (Kurtz) L. AB, Columbia Coll., 1956; MD, U. Pitts., 1960; cert. in adult psychiatry, U. Ill., 1963; cert. in child psychiatry, Harvard U., 1965. Intern Michael Reese Hosp., Chgo.; resident adult psychiatry U. Ill., Chgo.; resident child psychiatry Harvard U., Boston; dir. mental health svcs. L.A. Unified Sch. Dist., 1971-73; asst. clin. profl. UCLA, 1973-75, 79-81; dir. adolescent svcs. Kellogg Psychiat. Hosp., Corona, Calif., 1977-79; med. dir. Hathaway Home for Children, L.A., 1980-82; cons. psychiatrist Chaparral Treatment Ctr., San Bernadino, Calif., 1987-89; cons. mental health AIDS L.A. Project, Long Beach, Calif., 1987-89; cons. psychiatrist Med. Sq. Counseling Ctr., Garden Grove, Cailf., 1987—. Mem., speaker Common Cause, L.A., 1971—; mem., writer Amnesty Internat., L.A., 1971—. Recipient N.Y. State Regents scholar, 1952-56. Mem. Am. Psychiat. Assn., Am. Assn. Child and Adolescent Psychiatry, So. Calif. Psychiat. Soc. Home: 2811 Tucker Ln Los Angeles CA 90720

LINDBERG, FRANCIS LAURENCE, JR., management consultant; b. Jacksonville, Fla., Mar. 13, 1948; s. Francis Laurence and Mildred Hortense (Parrish) L.; m. Anne Louise Stearns, Dec. 29, 1972 (div.); 1 child, Kristen Anne; m. Alexis Jean Parker, Nov. 12, 1983. Student Eckerd Coll., 1965-66; BA, Jacksonville U., 1969; MBA, U. North Fla., 1976. CPA, Ga. Actuarial asst. Gulf Life Ins. Co., Jacksonville, 1967-73; asst. actuary Am. Heritage Life, Jacksonville, 1973-77; asst. sec.-treas., prin. acctg. officer Atlantic Am. Corp., Atlanta, 1977-84; assoc. v.p. fin. Security Benefit Group, Topeka, 1985-86; exec. v.p., chief fin. officer Am. Way Group of Cos., Southfield, Mich., 1986-87; prin. The Lindberg Group, Atlantaand Southfield, 1987—; treas., bd. dirs., bd. advisors Good News Communications, Inc. Mem. Nat. Assn. Accts. (Membership Achievement award 1983), Am. Inst. CPA's, Ga. Soc. CPA's, Acctng. Research Assn. Republican. Episcopalian. Office: The Lindberg Co 1264 Weatherstone Dr Bldg 13 Atlanta GA 30324 also: 2 Pendleton Pl Atlanta GA 30342-3747

LINDBERG, HELGE, airline company executive; b. London, Sept. 17, 1926; arrived in Norway, 1936; s. Carl Andreas and Sigrid Kristine (Bay) L.; m. Kerstin Hildegard Sjunnesson, Oct. 23, 1970; children by previous marriage: Sigrid Kristine, Carl Andreas. Grad., Treiders Handelsskole, Oslo, 1944. With Scandinavian Airlines System, 1946—; dist. mgr. Scandinavian Airlines System, Arabian Gulf, 1958; asst. regional mgr. Scandinavian Airlines System, Middle East, 1959-60; traffic sales mgr., dep. mng. dir. Scanair Charter Co. subs. Scandinavian Airlines System, Copenhagen, 1961-68; div. mgr. Scandinavian Airlines System, Finland and Eastern Europe, 1969-72; v.p. industry assn. affairs Scandinavian Airlines System, Stockholm, 1973-75; v.p. passenger mktg. Scanair Charter Co. subs. Scandinavian Airlines System, Stockholm, 1976-78, exec. v.p. comml., 1979-83, chief operating officer, 1983-86; dep. pres. Scandinavian Airlines System Group, Oslo, Stockholm, 1986—; chmn. Scandinavian Air Tour Prodn., Stockholm, 1976-79, AMADEUS Global Travel distbn., Madrid, 1988—; bd. dirs. Nymann & Schultz Travel Agy., Stockholm, 1976-81, Widerøe's Airline, 1986, Oslo, Diners Nordic A/S, 1986, Bennett Scandinavia Travel Bur., Oslo, 1988—; mem. traffic com. Internat. Air Traffic Assn., Geneva, 1973-74, chmn. 1975-76. Bd. dirs. World Wildlife Fund, 1986—. Mem. Assn. European Airlines (chmn. comml. and air polit. com. 1981-83), Scandinavian Multi Access System for Travel Agts. (chmn. 1983-85). Home: Lappstigen 3, 162 40 Vallingby Sweden Office: Scandinavian Airlines System, 161 87 Stockholm Sweden

LINDBLAD, WILLIAM JOHN, utility executive; b. Oakland, Calif., May 22, 1929; s. William N. and Johnina B. (Moore) L.; B.S. in Elec. Engring., U. Calif., Berkeley, 1951; m. Rosella J. Allender, July 4, 1953; children—Catherine, Nancy, Thomas, Christopher, Margaret, Michael, Therese, Paul. Various engring. and mgmt. positions Pacific Gas & Electric Co., San Francisco, 1954-77; v.p. engring. and constrn. Portland (Oreg.) Gen. Electric Co., 1977-80, pres., dir., 1980—; bd. dirs. Portland Gen. Corp., 1986—. . Mem. adv. bd. Providence Med. Center, 1981—; bd. dirs. Portland State U. Found., 1981—; trustee St. Mary's Acad., Served 1982-83. with USN, 1951-54. Registered profl. engr., Calif. Mem. ASME, Am. Soc. Naval Engrs., IEEE. Republican. Roman Catholic. Club: Univ. Office: Portland GE Co 121 SW Salmon St Portland OR 97204 *

LINDE, RONALD KEITH, corporate executive; b. Los Angeles, Jan. 31, 1940; s. Morris and Sonia Doreen (Hayman) L.; m. Maxine Helen Stern, June 12, 1960. B.S., UCLA, 1961; M.S. (Inst. scholar), Calif. Inst. Tech., 1962, Ph.D. (ACRS scholar, Rutherford scholar), 1964. Cons. Litton Industries, Los Angeles, 1961-63; engr. Litton Industries, 1961; materials scientist Poulter Labs., Stanford Research Inst., Menlo Park, Calif., 1964; head solid state research Poulter Labs., 1965-67, chmn. shock wave physics dept., mgr. tech. services, 1967, dir. shock and high pressure physics div., 1967-68, chief exec. labs., 1968-69; dir. phys. scis. Stanford Research Inst., 1968-69; chmn. bd., chief exec. officer Envirodyne Industries, Inc., Chgo., 1969—. Contbr. articles to various publs.; patentee in field. Mem. Founding Friends Harvey Mudd Coll., 1974—, Northwestern U. Assos., 1978—; mem. Midwestern regional adv. council Calif. Inst. Tech., 1979—. Mem. Sigma Xi, Tau Beta Pi, Phi Eta Sigma. Office: Envirodyne Industries Inc 142 E Ontario St Chicago IL 60611

LINDEMANN, GORDON GILBERT, trust company executive; b. Milw., Sept. 3, 1948; s. Gordon I. and Anne (Prutzlaff) L.; m. Christine Maclay, Sept. 18, 1976; children: Michael, Catherine, Abigail. BBA, U. Wis., 1970; JD, Stanford U., 1973. Bar: Wis., 1973. V.p. First Wis. Trust Co., Milw., 1973—. Office: First Wis Trust Co 777 E Wisconsin Ave Milwaukee WI 53202

LINDEN, HENRY ROBERT, chemical engineering research executive; b. Vienna, Austria, Feb. 21, 1922; came to U.S., 1939, naturalized, 1945; s. Fred and Edith (Lermer) L.; m. Natalie Govedarica, 1967; children by previous marriage: Robert, Debra. B.S., Ga. Inst. Tech., 1944; M.Chem. Engring., Poly. U., 1947; Ph.D., Ill. Inst. Tech., 1952. Chem. engr. Socony Vacuum Labs., 1944-47; with Inst. of Gas Tech., 1947-78, various rsch. mgmt. positions, 1947-61, dir., 1961-69, exec. v.p., dir., 1969-74, pres., trustee, 1974-78; various acad. appointments Ill. Inst. Tech., 1954-86, Frank W. Gunsaulus Disting. Prof. of Chem. Engring., 1987—; chief oper. officer Gas Devel. Corp. (name now GDC, Inc.) subs. Inst. of Gas Tech., Chgo., 1965-73, chief exec. officer, 1973-78, also bd. dirs.; pres., dir. Gas Rsch. Inst., Chgo., 1976-87, exec. advisor, 1987—; dir. Sonat Inc., So. Natural Gas Co., Reynolds Metals Co., UGI Corp., Larimer & Co., Applied Energy Services Inc., Resources for the Future Inc. Author tech. articles; holder U.S. and fgn. patents in fuel tech. Recipient award of merit, oper. sect. Am. Gas Assn., Disting. Svc. award Am. Gas Assn., Gas Industry Rsch. award Am. Gas Assn., 1982, Nat. Energy Resources Orgn. Rsch. and Devel. award, 1986; Walton Clark medal Franklin Inst.; Bunsen-Pettenkofer-Ehrentafel medal Deutscher Verein des Gas- und Wasserfaches.; named to IIT Hall of Fame, 1982. Fellow Am. Inst. Chem. Engrs., Inst. of Fuel; mem. Am. Chem. Soc. (recipient H.H. Storch award, chmn. div. fuel chemistry 1967, councilor 1969-77), Nat. Acad. Engring., So. Gas Assn. (hon. life), Nat. Rsch. Coun. (mem. energy engring. bd.). Office: Gas Rsch Inst 8600 W Bryn Mawr Ave Chicago IL 60631 also: Ill Inst Tech 10 W 33d St Rm 135PH Chicago IL 60616

LINDENBERG, EARL GENE, business consulting executive; b. Percy, Ill., June 23, 1934; s. Louis Henry and Mona (Hornbostel) L.; m. Sandra Sue Emmer, Aug. 30, 1967; 1 child, Amy Michelle. BSBA, Washington U., St. Louis, 1969. V.p. mgmt. info. systems Gardner Advt. Co., St. Louis, 1962-72; dir. mgmt. info. systems Iowa Beef Processors, Sioux City, Iowa, 1972-74; dir. electronic funds transfer St. Louis Savs. & Loan League, 1974-75; v.p., dir. mgmt. info. systems Petrolite Corp., 1975-82; exec. v.p., co-owner Forrest Ford Cons., Inc., 1983-88; pres. Lindenberg & Assocs., Inc., 1988—. Exec. coun. Luth. Family & Children Svcs., 1987-88, chmn. 1989—. With U.S. Army, 1954-56. Mem. Data Processing Mgmt. (pres. 1984), Mo. Athletic Club, Lake Forest Country Club (St. Louis). Republican. Home: 14546 Debbenham Ln Chesterfield MO 63017 Office: 701 Emerson Rd Ste 260 Saint Louis MO 63141

LINDHOLM, CARL EDWARD, electronics company executive; b. N.Y.C., Mar. 8, 1929; s. Carl Edward and Elsie (Krone) L.; m. Louise MacDonald; children—Jeffrey, Julia, Claire. B.S., Webb Inst., N.Y.C., 1950; M.S. in Indsl. Engring, N.Y. U., 1952, M.B.A., 1954. With Motorola Inc., 1967—; v.p., dir. corp. staff, then sr. v.p., dir. corp. staff Motorola Inc., Schaumburg, Ill., 1974-75; sr. v.p., gen. mgr. automotive products div. Motorola Inc., 1975-78, sr. v.p., gen. mgr. automotive and indsl. electronics group, 1978-85, exec. v.p. internat. ops., 1985—. Served with USNR, 1955-58. Office: Motorola Inc 1303 E Algonquin Rd Schaumburg IL 60196

LINDIG, BILL M., food distribution company executive; b. 1936; married. Attended, U. Tex. With Sysco Corp., Houston, 1969—, exec. v.p., from 1984, chief operating officer, 1984—, now also pres., dir. Office: Sysco Corp 1390 Enclave Pkwy Houston TX 77077 also: Sysco Corp 1390 Enclave Pkwy Houston TX 77077

LINDLEY, JAMES GUNN, bank executive; b. Greensboro, N.C., June 13, 1931; s. Paul Cameron and Helen Marie (Gunn) L.; m. Jane Kennedy, Dec. 3, 1954; children: James Gunn, Patricia Van, Julia Anne. BS in Bus. Adminstrn., U. N.C., 1953; MBA in Fin., NYU, 1960. Sr. v.p. Mfrs. Hanover Trust Co., N.Y.C., 1953-75; pres., chief exec. officer Bankshares of N.C. and Bank of N.C., N.A., Raleigh, 1975-79; pres., chief exec. officer S.C. Nat. Bank, Columbia, 1979—, chmn., 1981—; pres. S.C. Nat. Corp., 1979—, chmn., chief exec. officer, 1981—. Served to capt. USNR, 1953-57. Office: SC Nat Corp 1426 Main St Columbia SC 29226

LINDNER, CARL HENRY, financial holding company executive; b. Dayton, Ohio, Apr. 22, 1919; s. Carl Henry and Clara (Serrer) L.; m. Edith Bailey, Dec. 31, 1953; children: Carl Henry III, Stephen Craig, Keith Edward. Co-founder United Dairy Farmers, 1940; pres. Am. Fin. Corp., Cin., 1959-84, chmn., 1959—, chief exec. officer, 1984—; chmn., chief exec. officer, chmn. exec. com. United Brands Co., N.Y.C., 1984—; chmn., chief exec. officer Penn Cen. Corp., Cin., 1983—, also bd. dirs.; chmn., chief exec. officer Gt. Am. Communications Co., 1987—; bd. dirs. Mission Ins. bd. advs. Bus. Adminstrn. Coll., U. Cin. Republican. Baptist. *

LINDNER, ROBERT DAVID, financial company executive; b. Dayton, Ohio, Aug. 5, 1920; s. Carl Henry and Clara (Serrer) L.; m. Betty Ruth Johnston, Mar. 29, 1947; children—Robert David, Jeffrey Scott, Alan Bradford, David Clark. Grad. high sch. Chmn. bd. United Dairy Farmers, Cin., 1940—; With Am. Financial Corp., Cin., 1959—, former v.p., vice chmn. bd., now sr. v.p., vice chmn. bd. dirs. Trustee No. Bapt. Theol. Sem. Served with U.S. Army, 1942-45. Lodges: Masons. Home: 6950 Given Rd Cincinnati OH 45243 Office: United Dairy Farmers 3955 Montgomery Rd Cincinnati OH 45212 also: American Financial Corp 1 E Fourth St Cincinnati OH 45202

LINDOW, LESTER WILLIAM, former telecasters organization executive; b. Milw., Apr. 11, 1913; B.A. in Journalism, U. Wis., 1934; m. Baroness Andree de Verdor, Dec. 7, 1946; 1 dau., Suzanne Helene Lindow Gordon. Assoc. editor Advt. Almanac, Hearst Newspapers, N.Y.C., 1934-35; comml. dept. sta. WCAE, Pitts., 1935-36, nat. sales mgr., 1936-38, comml. mgr., asst. to the gen. mgr., 1938-40; sec., gen. mgr. WFBM, Inc., Indpls., 1940-42; gen. mgr. stas. WRNY and WRNY-FM, Rochester, N.Y., 1946-47; sec., gen. mgr. Trebit Corp. operators sta. WFDF, Flint, 1947-60, sec., dir., 1948-60, v.p., 1954-60; sec.-treas. Landsmore Corp., 1952-57, v.p., 1954-57; mem. exec. com. NBC Radio Affiliates, 1955-57, chmn. exec. com., 1956-57; exec. dir. Assn. Maximum Service Telecasters, Inc., 1957-77, pres., 1977-78; v.p., dir. Grelin Broadcasting, Inc., sta. WWRI, West Warwick, R.I., 1957-69, Radio Buffalo, Inc., sta. WWOL and WWOL-FM, Buffalo, 1959-62. Treas., dir. ARC, 1953-56, Palm Beach County chpt., 1981—; nat. fund vice chmn. for Mich., 1956-57, bd. dirs. Palm Beach County chpt.; dir. Flint YMCA, 1956-57; bd. dirs., mem. exec. com. Radio Free Europe/Radio Liberty, Inc., Washington. Mem. Palm Beach Civic Assn.; Served from 1st lt. to lt. col. AUS, 1942-46; apptd. to Gen. Staff Corps, War Dept., 1946-47; col. U.S. Army Res. (ret.) 1964. Mem. Mich. Assn. Broadcasters, Mich. A.P. Broadcasters' Assn. (dir.), Res. Officers' Assn., Nat. Assn. Radio and TV Broadcasters (dir. AM radio com.), Radio Advt. Bur. (Mich. chmn.), Asso. Press Radio Programming Com. N.Y.C., Assn. Profl. Broadcasting Edn. (dir.), Asso. Press Radio and TV Assn. (v.p., dir.), TV Allocations Study Orgn. (alt. dir.), Ret. Officers Assn., English Speaking Union, Union U. Wis. Alumni Assn., Nat. Broadcasters Club Washington (bd. govs. 1959-61, pres. 1964-65, chmn. 1965-66), Internat. Radio and TV Soc., Radio-TV Pioneers, Soc. of Four Arts, Alpha Chi Rho, Scabbard and Blade, Iron Cross, White Spades, Sigma Delta Chi. Clubs: Flint Golf, Rotary (pres.) (Flint); Broadcast Pioneers, Radio Execs. (N.Y.C.); Internat., Congressional Country (Washington), Elks; Beach, Pundits (Palm Beach, Fla.), Circumnavigators. Home: 3475 S Ocean Blvd Apt 406/7 Palm Beach FL 33480

LINDQVIST, GUNNAR JAN, management consultant, international trade consultant; b. Stockholm, July 12, 1950; s. Bengt Olof Sigfrid and Greta (Nyberg) L.; m. Mary Grady, June 23, 1984; children: Greta Louise, Mary Kerstin. Grad. with honors, Stockholm Sch. Econs., 1974. Asst. acctg. mgr. Granges Shipping, Stockholm, 1975-77; asst. budget mgr. Dynapac AB, Stockholm, 1978-79; asst. treas., controller Peeples Industries, Savannah, Ga., 1980-83; owner, pres. Cash Mgmt., Inc., Savannah, 1983—. Mem. Telfair Acad. of Arts and Scis., Inc., Savannah, 1980—, The Carpenter's Order, Stockholm, 1978—. Served with Swedish Army. Mem. Scandanavian-Am. Found. of Ga. (bd. govs. 1988—), Exchange Club, Internat. Platform Assn., Savannah Area C. of C. (sub-com. chmn. Small Bus. Council). Home and Office: 6800 Sandnettles Dr Savannah GA 31410

LINDSEY, JOHN MORTON, international airline executive; b. Peekskill, N.Y., Jan. 8, 1930; s. Morton Cole and Blodwyn (Price) L.; m. Doris Marie Restein, Sept. 9, 1951; children—Linda Lindsey Meyers, Gail Ann (Cox), Jill Lindsey Auman, Lisa Lindsey Madden. B.A., Duke U., 1951; LL.B., U. Denver, 1957. Bar: Colo. 1958. Atty. CAB, Washington, 1958-63; gen. counsel, sec. Nat. Airlines, Miami, Fla., 1963-80; sr. v.p. adminstrn. Southeast Banking Corp., Miami, 1980-84; sr. v.p. legal corp. Pan Am. World Airways, N.Y.C., 1984—. Served to lt. j.g. USN, 1951-55, Japan; to capt. USNR (ret.). Mem. ABA. Republican. Methodist. Home: 309 E 49th St Apt 9E New York NY 10017 Office: Pan Am World Airways Inc 200 Park Ave New York NY 10166

LINDSEY, MARK KELLY, industrial executive, director; b. Valdosta, Ga., Mar. 15, 1955; s. Paul Neal and Janice Mary (Rhodes) L.; m. Kelly Anne Gilmore, Sept. 19, 1987. BS, Calif. State U., Long Beach, 1979. Supr. Am. Hosp. Supply Corp., Covina, Calif., 1979-82, Johnson & Johnson Corp., Claremont, Calif., 1982-85; mgr. Occidental Petroleum Corp., L.A., 1985-86; dir. Capitol EMI Music, Inc., Hollywood, Calif., 1986—. Mem. Nat. Assn. Mfrs., Internat. Facility Mgrs. Assn., Hollywood C. of C. Republican. Presbyterian. Home: 333 W California Blvd Pasadena CA 91105 Office: Capitol EMI Music Inc 1750 Vine St Hollywood CA 90028

LINDSLEY, HERBERT PIPER, life insurance agent; b. Wichita, Kans., Dec. 16, 1913; s. Herbert Kitchel and Jessie McMahon (Piper) L.; A.B., U. Wichita, 1935; M.B.A., U. Pa., 1937; m. Barbara Irene Benzinger, Dec. 31, 1938; childen—Herbert Benzinger, Barbara Kitchel, Thomas Roland. Agt., Northwestern Mut. Ins. Co., N.Y.C., 1937-38; v.p., edn1. dir. Farmers & Bankers Life, Wichita, 1939-48; gen. agt. Occidental Life Calif., Wichita, 1948—; dir. Electric Furnace Co., Salem, Ohio; chmn. bd. Motel Devel. Corp., Wichita. Mem. Wichita Bd. Edn., 1951-59, pres., 1955; mem. Wichita City Commn., 1959-63, mayor, 1961-62. Republican. Congregationalist. Home and Office: 230 N Terrace Dr Wichita KS 67208

LINDSTROM, NINA LUCILLE, school administrator, director; b. Cleveland, Tenn., Dec. 9, 1940; d. Noah Haskins Jones and Grace (Mae) Burke; m. Larry Lance Lindstrom, June 26, 1966; children: Anton Lee, Kristina Mae. BS in Edn., Biology, U. Tenn., 1963; MS in Edn., Portland (Oreg.) State U., 1970. Cert. tchr., Oreg., Calif. Tchr. sci. Hudson Sch. Dist., LaPuente, Calif., 1963-64, Baldwin (Calif.) Park Dist., 1964-67; tchr. biology Beaverton Sch. Dist. 48, Portland, 1968-70; student tchr. supr. Portland State U., 1971; tchr. Portland Community Coll., 1971-72; prin., dir., founder Belmont Sch., Portland, 1973—; co-owner Riverview Properties, Portland, 1973—; v.p. Mt. Park Vet. Clinic, Lake Oswego, 1978—. Chmn. Sunnyside Neighborhood, Portland, 1987; childcare advisor Portland Pub. Schs., 1976-87. Mem. Portland C. of C. (distinguished service award 1985), Belmont Bus. (treas. 1985-86, sec. 1986-87), Oreg. Fedn. Pvt. Schs. (pre-sch. com. 1986-87, treas. 1988-89). Republican. Baptist. Office: Belmont Sch 3841 SE Belmont Portland OR 97219

LINEBERGER, WALTER FRANKLIN, III, financial company executive; b. Akron, Ohio, Aug. 16, 1943; s. Walter Franklin and Mary (Saalfield) L.; m. Mary Lou Winecki, Oct. 9, 1983. BA, Yale U., 1965; postgrad. in bus., Dartmouth Coll., 1965-66. CLU; chartered fin. cons. Agt. Northwestern Mus. Life, Portland, Oreg., 1971-77; dir. tng. Crown, Boston & Zeigler, Ventura, Calif., 1977-79; asst. dir. brokerage sales Transam. Occidental Life Ins. Co., L.A., 1979-80; regional brokerage dir. Transam. Occidental Life Ins. Co., Milw., 1980-82; v.p. Provident Life & Accident Co., Chattanooga, 1982-85; sr. v.p. mktg. Am. Investors Life Ins. Co., Inc., Topeka, 1985-86; owner, mgr. Personalized Brokerage Svcs., Topeka, 1986—. Author: How To Develop a Life Insurance Brokerage Business, 1980; contbr. articles to profl. jours. Mem. nominating com. Liberatarian Party, Seattle, 1987. Lt USNR, 1966-70. Decorated Bronze Star with combat V, Purple Heart. Home: Rte 2 Box 286 Valley Falls KS 66088 Office: Personalized Brokerage Svcs 506 SW 8th Ave Topeka KS 66603

LINES, BRADLEY MILTON, accountant; b. Mesa, Ariz., Jan. 22, 1957; s. Larry M. and Bette Marie (Davis) L.; m. Julie Nichols, Aug. 31, 1978; children: Treslee, Clifford, Amy, Taylor. BSBA, Ariz. State U., 1980. Staff auditor Coopers & Lybrand, Phoenix, 1980-84; asst. controller Inertia Dynamics Corp., Chandler, Ariz., 1984-86, controller, 1986-88, v.p., controller, 1988—. Mem. Am. Inst. of CPA's, Ariz. Soc. CPA's, Nat. Assn. Accts. Republican. Mormon. Office: Inertia Dynamics Corp 550 N 54th St Chandler AZ 85226

LINEWEAVER, HUGH MARLOW, management consultant; b. Chgo., Nov. 10, 1924; s. Thomas Marlow and Elsie (Evans) L.; m. Margaret Harland, June 6, 1947; children: Margaret, Thomas, James. BA in English, U. Ill., 1947. Copywriter Gerber Advt., Portland, Oreg., 1948-49; account exec. Alport Assocs., Portland, 1949-51; mgr. merchandise Stimpson, Forest Grove, Oreg., 1951-57; from mgr. merchandise to product mgr. Abitibi Corp., Troy, Mich., 1957-72; mgr. mktg. Evans Products, Portland, 1972-74; pres. Mgmt. Search, Portland, 1974—; pres. Keys, Portland, 1976. Exec. Presbyn. Marriage Encounter, 1977-78; mem. com. on ministry Prebytery of the Cascades, Portland, 1985—. Served to lt. (j.g.) USN, 1943-46, PTO. Mem. Nat. Assn. Personnel Cons., Oreg. Assn. Personnel Cons. (bd. dirs. 1986-87), Portland C. of C. (presidents' club 1975—). Republican. Lodge: Rotary. Home: 2161 Hillside Ct Lake Oswego OR 97034 Office: Mgmt Search 621 SW Morrison Portland OR 97205

LINFANTE, CHARLES VINCENT, dental, medical, optical products company executive; b. Bklyn., Oct. 21, 1939; s. Vincent J. and Lea (Rossi) L.; m. Joan Mary Kulha, Jan. 20, 1962; children: Michele, Gene, Kristen, Robert. BS in Acctg., Fairleigh Dickinson U., 1962. CPA, N.Y. Staff acct. Price Waterhouse & Co., N.Y.C., 1962-66, sr. acct., 1966-70, mgr., 1970-72; internal audit dir. IPCO Corp., White Plains, N.Y., 1972, div. controller, 1972-73, corp. controller, 1973-76, v.p., controller, 1976-80, v.p., chief fin. officer, 1980-82, exec. v.p., chief fin. officer, 1982-84, pres., chief fin. officer, 1984—, also bd. dirs. Chmn. Westchester C. of C., White Plains, 1979-80, Westchester Multiple Sclerosis Soc., White Plains, 1984-87; pres. Vis. Nurse Services of Westchester, 1986-87. Mem. Am. Inst. CPA's, N.Y. State Soc. CPA's.

LING, SUILIN, management consultant; b. Shanghai, China, Oct. 13, 1930; s. Chunchen and Maisan (Dunn) L.; came to U.S., 1949, naturalized, 1963; B.S., U. Mich., 1952; Ph.D., Columbia U., 1961; m. Avril Marjorie Kathleen Button, Apr. 4, 1964; children—Christopher Charles, Charmian Avril. Mech. engr. Ebasco Services, Inc., 1953-54; with research div. Foster Wheeler Corp., 1954-64; mgmt. cons. The Emerson Cons., Inc., 1964-65; sr. economist Communications Satellite Corp., 1965-67; chief economist Northrop-Page Communication Engrs., Inc., 1967-70; founder-dir., chief economist Teleconsult, Inc., Washington, 1970-82; founder, pres. Communications Devel. Corp., 1982-87, chmn. bd. dirs., 1987—; lectr. econs. Bernard M. Baruch Sch. Bus. and Pub. Adminstrn., CCNY. Mem. Am. Mgmt. Assn., Am. Econ. Assn., Am. Soc. M.E., Am. Acad. Polit. and Social Sci. Author: Economies of Scale in the Steam-Electric Power Generating Industry, 1964. Home: 2735 Unicorn Ln NW Washington DC 20015 Office: 2828 Pennsylvania Ave NW Washington DC 20007

LING, WILLIAM NORMAN, quality product safety management consultant; b. Elmore, Ohio, Dec. 28, 1937; s. Norman Elmer and Betty Juanita (Frosch) L.; m. Elizabeth Jean Kaiser, Nov. 21, 1956; children: Pamela, Christine, Michelle, Stephanie, Patrick, Lisa. Student, U. Toledo, 1956-61. Registered profl. engr., Calif. Mgr. quality div. Brush Wellman, Inc., Elmore, 1956-79; corp. mgr. quality Owens Corning Fiberglas, Toledo, 1979-87; pres., prin. cons. Ling Mgmt. Devel., Inc., Elmore, 1987—. Contbg. author: Metals Handbook on Quality, 1977; also contbr. papers in field. Mem. NSPE, Ohio Soc. Profl. Engrs., Am. Soc. Quality Control (sr. mem., cert. quality engr., past chmn. Toledo sect., pres. Midwest conf. bd., recipient Toulouse award 1983), Nat. Product Safety Mgmt. Acad., Aircraft Owners and Pilots Assn. Office: Ling Mgmt Devel Inc 510 S Rt 590 Elmore OH 43416

LINGEL, KURT EUGENE, computer engineer; b. Rockford, Ill., May 28, 1962; s. George Merle and Marion Lois (Pihl) L.; m. Darlene Susan Bauer, Jan. 11, 1986. BS in Computer Sci., No. Ill. U., 1984; MS in Computer Sci., Stanford U., 1987. Quality assurance coordinator Woodward-Governor Co., Rockford, 1984—; programmer Amdahl Corp., Sunnyvale, Calif., 1984-87, sr. software engr., 1988—. Home: 3051 Knights Bridge San Jose CA 95132

LINGENFELTER, SHARON MARIE, data processing company executive; b. Nyssa, Oreg., June 17, 1947; d. Floyd LeRoy and Ruth Irene (Bale) Martin; (div.); children: Brian James Lingenfelter, Kevin James Lingenfelter. Student George Fox Coll., 1966, Portland State U., 1968. Vice pres. adminstrn. Century Data, Inc., Portland, 1982—; dir. mktg. and adminstrn. Bus. Prospector, San Francisco Bay Area, 1986—; chief ops. officer Bus. Prospector, Inc., 1989. Editing cons. Century Direct Mktg., Inc., 1983—; office systems analyst C.I. NorCal, San Francisco, 1985—. Mem. Nat. Assn. Female Execs., Am. Mgmt. Assn. Republican. Avocations: skiing, writing, travel, painting, reading. Office: Century Data Inc 2355 NW Quimby St Portland OR 97210

LINGLE, KATHLEEN MCCALL, marketing executive; b. Berea, Ohio, Aug. 24, 1944; d. Arthur Vivian McCall and Mary M. (Maxwell) Miller; m. John Hunter Lingle, Sept. 3, 1968; 1 child, Michael Cameron. BA, Occidental Coll., 1966; MS, Ohio State U., 1977. Research assoc. Ednl. Testing Service, Princeton, N.J., 1978-82; mgr. mktg. services Gulton Industries, Princeton, 1982-84; dir. mktg. research services Applied Data Research, Princeton, 1985-88; regional sales, mktg. mgr. for Europe and Midwestern U.S. Heuristics Software, Inc., Sacramento, 1988—. V.p. ops. Unitarian Ch. of New Brunswick, N.J., 1983-84. Mem. Am. Mktg. Assn., Am. Mgmt. Assn., Princeton Network Profl. Women, NAFE, Am. Field Svc. (Princeton chpt.). Democrat. Home: 988 Princeton Kingston Rd Princeton NJ 08540 Office: Heuristics Inc PO Box 539 New Hope PA 18938

LINK, E. G. (JAY), certified financial planner; b. Portsmouth, Va., Apr. 30, 1952; s. Edward and Hazel (Blalock) L.; m. Pamela Kay Kidwell, Jan. 19, 1955; children: Bethany, Anna, Kara. BA, Cin. Bible Coll., 1974; MDiv, Cin. Christian Sem., 1979; BS, Am. Coll. Nutripathy, 1988, MS, 1989. Minister northern Ky., 1974-79; sales rep. Met. Life Ins., Joplin, Mo., 1979-81, sales mgr., 1981-82; founder, pres. Total Fin. Planners, Inc., Joplin, 1982-85, E.G. Link Leasing Co., Inc., Franklin, Ind., 1982-87; owner, pres. Link & Assocs, Franklin, 1982—; founder, dir. Ind. Food Coop., Franklin, 1986—. Contbr. articles to IN-Joplin mag., 1983-84, Christian Standard Mag., 1972-79. Founder, dir. Stewardship Ministries, Inc., Franklin, 1984—. Mem. Internat. Assn. Fin. Planning, Inst. Cert. Fin. Planners, Fellowship Christian Fin. Advisors, Ind. Organic Growers Assn. Republican. Home and Office: Link & Assocs Rte 5 Box 135B Franklin IN 46131

LINK, JACK JAMISON, property management company executive; b. Maitland, Mo., Oct. 25, 1925; s. Charles M. and Adeline (Jamison) L.; m. Ella Mays, June 16, 1950; children: Timothy, Ted. Student, Boise Jr. Coll., 1943, The Coll. of Idaho, 1946; BA, Washington State U., 1948; postgrad., Northwestern U., 1950. Announcer/salesman Sta. KCID, Caldwell, Idaho, 1948-51; program dir. Sta. KIDO, Boise, 1951-53, Sta. KIDO-TV, Boise, 1953-57, Sta. KING-AM-FM, Seattle, 1957-59; gen. mgr. Sta. KIDO, Boise, 1959-62, William E. Boeing, Jr. Radio Sta., Seattle, 1962-70; property mgr. William E. Boeing Jr. Enterprises, Seattle, 1970—; pres. Tri-Land Corp., Seattle, 1970—; mem. exec. com. NBC Radio Affiliates, 1961-64. Mem. Tukwila (Wash.) City Planning Commn., 1970-77, exec. adv. com. Seattle Pacific U. Sch. Bus., 1980—; pres. Seattle Seafair, 1984; vice chmn. Jr. Achievement, Seattle, 1985; trustee emeritus Coll. Idaho, Caldwell, 1981. Served with USAAF, 1944-46. Recipient Young Man of Yr. Disting. Service award Jaycees, 1960, Bus. Leadership award City of Tukwila, 1986, Disting. Service award Coll. Idaho, 1986, Nat. Bronze Leadership award Jr. Achievement, 1986. Mem. Wash Fedn. Clubs (bd. dirs. 1985—). Republican. Presbyterian. Clubs: Wash. Athletic (pres. 1983-84), 101 (pres. 1985-86). Office: Tri-Land Corp 1325 Fourth Ave Ste 1940 Seattle WA 98101

LINK, ROBERT ALLEN, financial company executive, lawyer; b. Detroit, July 2, 1932; s. Raymond Henry and Helen Emily (Grassley) L.; m. Cynthia Louise Krans, June 15, 1957; children: Charles Nicholas, Frederick Allen. B.S., Wayne State U., 1954; J.D., U. Mich., 1957. Bar: Mich. 1958, U.S. Dist. Ct. (ea. dist.) Mich. 1958, U.S. Ct. Appeals (6th cir.) 1960. Assoc. firm Darden & Bonk, Detroit, 1958-61; sole practice Detroit, 1961-63; assoc. firm Manikoff & Munde, Pontiac, Mich., 1963-64; atty. Chrysler Fin. Corp., Detroit, 1964-67; sr. atty. Chrysler Fin. Corp., Southfield, Mich., 1967-70; sec. Chrysler Fin. Corp., Troy, Mich., 1970—. Mem. ABA, State Bar Mich., Detroit Bar Assn. Home: 945 Harmon Birmingham MI 48009 Office: Chrysler Fin Corp 901 Wilshire Dr 3rd Fl Troy MI 48084

LINKS, SHIRLEY ANN ANDREWS, retail executive; b. Dora, Mo., Dec. 28, 1945; d. Olen Franklin Fish and Edna (Collins) Conley; m. Bill Andrews, Apr. 11, 1970 (div. 1982); children: Kevin, Billy, Kristen; m. C. Glenn Links, Nov. 1, 1986. Grad. high sch., St. Joseph, Mo. Office mgr. R.F. Dickson Co., Inc., Downey, Calif., 1966-73; owner, pres. Turner's Outdoorsman (formerly Andrews Sporting Goods), Orange, Calif., 1971-88, Chino, Calif., 1988—. Office: Turner's Outdoorsman 12615 Colony St Chino CA 91710

LINN, BARBARA JEANNE, real estate executive; b. Newark, Sept. 1, 1952; d. Robert F. and Suzanne (Dougherty) L. BS, U. Ariz., 1977. CPA, Calif.; cert. fin. planner. Sr. auditor Coopers & Lybrand, L.A., 1977-79; audit mgr. Levi Strauss & Co., San Francisco, 1979-81; v.p., dir. fin. RREEF Funds, San Francisco, 1981—. Mem. AICPA, Inst. Cert. Fin. Planners, Internat. Assn. Fin. Planning, Calif. Soc. CPA's, Berkeley Real Estate Assn. Office: 650 California St Ste 1800 San Francisco CA 94108

LINN, JAMES HERBERT, banker; b. Jacksonville, Fla., Nov. 22, 1925; s. Herbert P. and Evelyn Lucile (Gore) L.; m. Betty J. Thatcher, Oct. 22, 1949; children: David, Donald, Charles, Craig, Jill. BA in Liberal Arts, U. Mo., Kansas City, 1948. With various commerce cos. 1948; vice-chmn. Commerce Bancshares, Inc., Kansas City, 1970—; trustee Sci. Pioneers, Inc., Kansas City; v.p., asst. sec., bd. dirs. CBI Ins. Co.; adv. dir. Alaskan Fur Co.; bd. dirs. Commerce Mortgage Corp., Capital for Bus., Inc.; pres., chmn., bd. dirs. Commerce Property and Casualty Ins. With U.S. Army, 1944-46. Mem. Robert Morris Assos., Kansas City C. of C. Club: Univ. Home: 10261 Rosewood Overland Park KS 66207 Office: Commerce Bancshares Inc 1000 Walnut 18th Fl PO Box 13686 Kansas City MO 64199

LINN, ROBERT ALLEN, chemical company executive, lawyer; b. Akron, Ohio, June 9, 1932; s. Robert Albertus and Rita Marie (Hogl) L.; m. Eileen Marie Ryan, Nov. 22, 1956 (div. 1986); children—Nancy Ann, Thomas Patrick, Michael Joseph, Mary Lisa; m. Patricia Moreland Gwinner, Aug. 16, 1986; stepchildren: Kelli Ann Gwinner, Susan Lynne Gwinner. B.S. in Chemistry, Xavier U., Cin., 1954, M.S., 1956; postgrad. Wayne State U., 1956-58; LL.B., U. Detroit, 1961; M.B.A., Mich. State U., 1980. Bar: Mich. 1961, U.S. Dist. Ct. (ea. dist.) Mich. 1962, U.S. Patent & Trademark Office, 1963. Toxicologist, Wayne County, Detroit, 1957-61; patent atty. Ethyl Corp., Ferndale, Mich., 1961-64, mgr. patent sect., 1964-80, economist, Baton Rouge, 1980-81, dir. corp. bus. devel., Richmond, Va., 1981-86, patent atty., Baton Rouge, La., 1986—. Contbr. articles to profl. jours. Mem. Product Devel. and Mgmt. Assn. (pres. 1984-85, Cresheim award for best conf. paper 1982), Assn. Corp. Growth, Am. Intellectual Property Assn. Episcopalian. Office: Eastman Kodak Co 343 State St Rochester NY 14650

LINN, ROBERT BRUCE, insurance company executive; b. Decatur, Ill., Nov. 18, 1943; s. Robert Edson and Mary Katherine (Amman) L.; m. Fleury-Ann Viger, Aug. 26, 1967; children: Brandon James, Paula Katharine,

Nora Elizabeth. BS, U. Ill., 1965; MBA, DePaul U., 1971. CPA, Ill. Sr. audit mgr. Price-Waterhouse, Chgo., 1965-78; asst. controller IC Industries, Inc., Chgo., 1978-81; sr. v.p., treas. Shand, Morahan & Co., Inc., Evanston, Ill., 1981—; bd. dirs. Evanston Ins. Co., Ins. Co. Evanston. Commr. Winnetka Park Dist., Ill., 1987—; chmn. New Trier Rep. Orgn., 1978—. With USAR, 1965-71. Mem. Fin. Execs. Inst., Am. Inst. CPA's, Ill. CPA's Soc., Inst. Acctg. and Systems Assn. Club: Univ. Office: Shand Morahan & Co Inc Shand Morahan Pla Evanston IL 60201

LINNELL, DENISE RAE, accountant; b. Lynnwood, Calif., May 2, 1961; d. Peter Eugene and JoAnn Lauretta (Brenner) Biegel; m. Dennis Richard Linnell, Aug. 18, 1984. BS in Acctg. and Computer Sci., Oreg. State U., 1983. CPA, Alaska. Asst. internal auditor Alaska Mut. Bank, Anchorage, 1982; staff acct. Price Waterhouse, Anchorage, 1983-87; cost acct. Providence Hosp., Anchorage, 1987-88; tax adviser DRL Assocs., Anchorage, 1987—. Vol. fundraiser Sta. KAKM-TV, Anchorage, 1985-87; vol. U.S. Army Corps Quadrathalon Run Providence Hosp. Cardiac Heart-for-Heart Run, Anchorage, 1987-88. Mem. Nat. Assn. Accts. (pres. 1988-89), Alaska Soc. CPAs. Republican. Mem. Church of Nazarene. Home: 7841 Stanley Dr Anchorage AK 99518

LINOFF, ALAN LEE, real estate development company executive; b. Mpls., Minn., June 20, 1934; s. Joseph Louis Linoff and Edith (Modelevsky) Edelman; m. Marian Gottlieb, June 17, 1956 (div. 1969); children: Joseph D., Deborah, Gordon S.; m. Vivian Woods, Jan. 16, 1971; 1 child, Angela D. BA in Bus. and Econs., U. Minn, 1956, student in Physics and Math., 1958-60. Sec., treas. H&L Import, Inc., Miami, Fla., 1969-72; pres. Dimensional Systems, Inc., Miami, 1972-76; prin. Alan Lee Linoff Cons., Miami and Mpls., 1976-84; dir. property devel. Fairview Hosp. and Healthcare Services, Mpls., 1984-86; pres., chief exec. officer Ridges Devel. Co. (A Fairview Co.), Mpls., 1985—; also bd. dirs., pres., chief exec. officer Fairview Devel. Co., Mpls., 1986—; cons. A/E Support Systems, Mpls., 1983—, Fairview Community Hosp., Mpls., 1982-84, Mattson/Macdonald, Inc., Mpls., 1984—. Office: Ridges Devel Co 2312 S Sixth St Minneapolis MN 55424

LINOWES, HARRY MICHAEL, accountant; b. Trenton, N.J., Feb. 4, 1928; s. Joseph and Rose (Oglensky) Linowitz; m. Judith Barbara Bierman, July 6, 1952; children—Jeffrey A., Ronni J., Gary J., Steven D. B.S. in Bus. Adminstrn., Rutgers U., 1948. Mng. ptnr. Leopold & Linowes, CPA's (merged with BDO Seidman, 1986), Washington, 1963—. Treas. Greater Washington Bd. of Trade, 1985, also bd. dirs., pres. Washington Performing Arts Soc., 1985; pres. Jewish Community Ctrs. Greater Washington, 1978-80, also bd. dirs.; exec. com. Boys and Girls Clubs Greater Washington, 1983—; pres. Young Jewish Leadership Coun. of Greater Washington, Nat. Children's Ctr. for Retardation; cons., bd. dirs. Cultural Alliance of Greater Washington, 1985, v.p., 1987, pres., 1988; exec. com. D.C. Pvt. Industry Coun.; bd. dirs. B'nai B'rith Nat. Jewish Mus.; chmn. community adv. bd. Pub. Radio Sta. 88.5-FM, 1985; sec. D.C. Estate Planning Council, 1987-88, treas., 1988-89. editorial adv. bd. mem. The Practical Accountant mag.. Served with U.S. Army, 1950-52. Recipient Ottenstein award for leadership in social welfare Greater Washington Jewish Social Service Agy.; Gulick award Camp Fire Girls; Bronze Stone award Boys Clubs of Am. for outstanding svc. to Boys Clubs movement. Mem. D.C. Inst. C.P.A.s (pres. 1967-68), Am. Inst. C.P.A.s (council mem. 1967-68, 84-86; pub. service award 1982, pub. svc. com. 1987—), C.P.A. Assocs. (chmn. exec. com. 1975-76), Jr. C. of C. (recipient several ann. awards for leadership to orgn. and community). Home: 6220 Clearwood Rd Bethesda MD 20817 Office: Seidman & Seidman 1707 L St NW 8th Fl Washington DC 20036

LINOWES, RICHARD GARY, management educator; b. Washington, Jan. 29, 1951; s. David Francis and Dorothy Lee (Wolf) L. AB in Cybernetics, Princeton U., 1973; MS in Computer, Communication Scis., U. Mich., 1975; D in Bus. Adminstrn., Harvard U., 1984. With Matsushita Electric Indsl. Co., Osaka, Japan, 1974; sr. systems analyst Arthur Andersen & Co., Washington, 1975-77; research asst. Harvard Bus. Sch., Boston, 1978-82; cons. services Goldman Sachs & Co., N.Y.C., 1983-86; asst. prof. mgmt. The Am. Univ., Washington, 1986—; adj. prof. NYU, 1985-86; cons. Digital Equipment Corp., Bedford, Mass., N.Y.C., 1979-82, Dayton Hudson Corp., Detroit, 1981-82, Smithsonian Instn., Washington, 1987—, Am. Council on Edn., Washington, 1987—. Contbr. articles to Harvard Bus. Rev.; contbg. author: Catching Up with the Computer Revolution, 1983, (with R.F. Vancil) Decentralization, 1979; creator experiential exercises for various confs. Mem. Greater Washington Area Bd. Trade, 1987—. Mem. Acad. Mgmt., Organizational Behavior Teaching Soc., Assn. Japanese Bus. Studies (membership com. 1988), Planning Forum, World Affairs Council. Jewish. Clubs: Princeton (N.Y. and Washington). Home: 7425 Democracy Blvd #108 Bethesda MD 20817 Office: The Am Univ KCBA 4400 Massachusetts Ave NW Washington DC 20016

LINOWITZ, SOL MYRON, lawyer, diplomat; b. Trenton, N.J., Dec. 7, 1913; s. Joseph and Rose (Oglenskye) L.; m. Evelyn Zimmerman, Sept. 3, 1939; children: Anne, June, Jan, Ronni. AB, Hamilton Coll., 1935; JD, Cornell U., 1938; LLD (hon.), Allegheny Coll., Amherst Coll., Bucknell U., Babson Inst., Colgate U., Curry Coll., Dartmouth Coll., Elmira Coll., Georgetown U., Hamilton Coll., Ithaca Coll., Oberlin Coll., St. John Fisher Coll., St. Lawrence U., Jewish Theol. Sem., Washington U., St. Louis, U. Miami, Marietta Coll., Muskingum Coll., Notre Dame U., U. Pacific, U. Pa., Rutgers U., Pratt Inst., Rider Coll., Roosevelt U., Chapman Coll., U. Mich., Govs. State U., U. Mo., Syracuse U., Brandeis U.; LHD, Am. U., Yeshiva U., Marietta Coll., U. Judaism, Wooster Coll.; PhD (hon.), U. Haifa. Bar: N.Y. 1938. Asst. gen. counsel OPA, Washington, 1942-44; ptnr. Sutherland, Linowitz & Williams, 1946-58, Harris, Beach, Keating, Wilcox & Linowitz, Rochester, N.Y., 1958-66; chmn. Nat. Urban Coalition, 1970—; chmn. bd. dirs., chmn. exec. com., gen. counsel Xerox Corp., 1958-66; chmn. bd. dirs. Xerox Internat., 1966; sr. ptnr. Coudert Bros., 1969-85, sr. counsel, 1985—; ambassador to OAS, 1966-69; co-negotiator Panama Canal treaties, 1977-78; spl. Middle East negotiator for Pres. Carter, 1979-81; chmn. Am. Acad. of Diplomacy, 1984—; co-chmn. Inter-Am. Dialogue, 1981—; pres. Fed. City Council, 1974-78; chmn. Pres.'s Commn. World Hunger, 1978-79; bd. dirs., co-founder Internat. Exec. Service Corps; chmn. State Dept. Adv. Com. on Internat. Orgns., 1963-66. Author: (memoir) The Making of a Public Man, 1985, This Troubled Urban World, contbr. articles to profl. jours. Trustee Hamilton Coll., Cornell U., Johns Hopkins U., Am. Assembly. Served to lt. USNR, 1944-46. Fellow Am. Acad. Arts and Scis.; mem. Am. Assn. for UN (pres. N.Y. State), Rochester Assn. for UN (pres. 1952), Rochester C. of C. (pres. 1958), ABA, N.Y. Bar Assn., Rochester Bar Assn. (v.p. 1949-50), Am. Assn. UN (bd. dirs.), Council on Fgn. Relations, Order of Coif, Phi Beta Kappa, Phi Kappa Phi. Office: Coudert Bros 1627 I St NW Washington DC 20006

LINSDAY, RICHARD H., insurance agent; b. Oak Park, Ill., Oct. 30, 1947; s. Herbert Robert and Margaret (Boyer) L.; m. Laura Jane Brink, June 16, 1979. BS in Bus., No. Ill. U., DeKalb, 1969. CLU, 1977; Chartered Fin. Cons., Am. Coll., Bryn Mawr, Pa., 1983. Brokerage rep., then mgr. Aetna Life Ins. Co., Los Angeles, 1972-78; brokerage mgr. Mfrs. Life Ins. Co., Los Angeles, 1978-86; exec. v.p. Integrated Fin., 1987—; pres. Linsday Fin. Ins. Services, Inc. (formerly Richard H. Linsday & Assocs., Ltd.), Los Angeles, 1975—; tchr. adult edn. estate planning; affiliate bd. dirs. Devil Pups, Inc. Contbr. articles to profl. jours. Coordinator, W. Los Angeles Spl. Olympics, 1978-79; chmn. planned giving subcommittee Am. Heart Assn., Los Angeles. Served with USMC, 1969-72, Vietnam, maj. Res. Recipient cert. public service Joseph Kennedy Found., 1979. Mem. Nat. Assn. Life Underwriters (v.p. W. Los Angeles chpt. 1980, pres. 1982-83, Philip Grosser Meml. award 1982), Am. Soc. CLU's (dir. Los Angeles chpt. 1982-84, v.p. 1986, pres. 1987-88), Wilshire Estate Planning Council (v.p. 1981, pres. 1982-83), Calif. Assn. Life Underwriters (trustee region 6 1983-85), Cert. Fin. Planners Assn. Methodist. Home: 11417 Sumac Ln Rancho Santa Rosa CA 93010 Office: Integrated Fin 16530 Ventura Blvd Encino CA 91436

LINTON, HEATHER SMITH, accountant; b. Lancaster, Pa., Jan. 17, 1956; d. Hector William and Ann Schroeder (Locher) Smith; m. Richard William Linton, June 12, 1976. BA with highest honors, U. Del., 1976; MBA, U. N.C., 1983. CPA, N.C.; cert. fin. planner. Dept. mgr. Carson, Pirie, Scott & Co., Urbana, Ill., 1976-77; office mgr. sales village Craftsmen, Ltd., Carrboro, N.C., 1977-78; head teller Cen. Carolina Bank, Chapel Hill, N.C., 1978-79, comml. loan processor, 1979-81; staff acct. Nelson & Co., CPAs, Durham, N.C., 1983-86, tax sr., 1986-88, tax mgr., 1988-89; prin. Heather S. Linton, CPA, Chapel Hill, N.C., 1989—; lectr. in field. Contbr. articles to profl. jours. Leader Durham Coun. Girl Scouts U.S.A., 1983-85; fin. officer Ctr. Gallery, Chapel Hill, 1978-81; mem. nominating com. YWCA, Durham, 1986-87; com. mem. Durham Arts Coun., 1987—. Mem. AICPA, N.C. Assn. CPAs (treas. Triangle chpt. 1988—), Durham Orange Estate Planning Coun. (sec. 1987-88), Chapel Hill Country Club, U. N.C. Women's Club, Phi Beta Kappa, Phi Kappa Phi. Home: Fearrington Post Box 70 Pittsboro NC 27312

LINTON, ROBERT DAVID, insurance company executive; b. N.Y.C., Jan. 24, 1954; s. Herbert and Gertrude (Steiner) L. Diploma, Horace Mann Sch., 1972; AB, Princeton U., 1976; MBA, Harvard U., 1979. Fin. analyst Morgan Stanley & Co., N.Y.C., 1976-77; asst. to chmn. Am. Eagle Group, N.Y.C., 1979-81; chmn. Internat. Fin. Group, N.Y.C., 1981—, also bd. dirs.; pres. The Preserver Assurance Co., N.Y.C., 1983-86; also bd. dirs. The Preserver Assurance Co.; bd. dirs., chmn. The Burlington (N.C.) Ins. Co., 1986—; Bd. dirs., chmn. Durton Corp., Burlington, 1984—, MB Realty Corp., 1985—, BGL Holdings Inc., 1986—, Burlington Ins. Group, 1985—, West Pt. Ins. Holding, N.Y.C., 1986—; corp. sec. Bain Dawes Inc., N.Y.C., 1983-86. Club: Harvard (N.Y.C.). Home: 800 Fifth Ave New York NY 10021 Office: The Burlington Ins Co 767 Fifth Ave New York NY 10153

LINTON, ROBERT EDWARD, investment banker; b. N.Y.C., May 19, 1925; s. Adolph B. and Helen (Hirshon) L.; m. Margot R. Tishman, June 19, 1952; children: Roberta Helen, Thomas Norman, Jeffrey Robert, Elizabeth Marie. With Drexel Burnham Lambert Inc., N.Y.C., 1946—; sr. exec. v.p., dir. Drexel Burnham Lambert Inc., 1972-77, pres., dir., chief exec. officer, 1977-82, chmn. bd., chief exec. officer, 1982-85, chmn. bd., chmn. exec. com., 1985—. Served to 2d lt. USAAF, 1943-45. Mem. Securities Industry Assn. (exec. com., treas., dir., chmn. 1983), N.Y. Soc. Security Analysts. Club: Century Country (Purchase, N.Y.). Home: Purchase Ln Rye NY 10580 Office: Drexel Burnham Lambert Inc 60 Broad St New York NY 10004

LINVILLE, THOMAS MERRIAM, engineer; b. Washington, Mar. 3, 1904; s. Thomas and Clara (Merriam) L.; m. Eleanor Priest, Nov. 25, 1939; children—Eleanor, Thomas Priest, Edward Dwight. E.E., U. Va., 1926; grad. advanced mgmt. program, Harvard U., 1950; mod. engrng. program, U. Calif. at Los Angeles, 1960. Various govt. positions 1918-26; with Gen. Electric Co., 1926-66; beginning with Gen. Electric Co. (Advanced Engrng. Program), to 1931, successively at corp. level chmn. rotating machines product com., chmn. rotating machines devel. com., staff asst. to mgr. engrng., 1926-51, mgr. engrng. edn., mgmt. consultation div., 1926-51, mgr. exec. devel., mgr. research operation, mgr. research application and info., 1951-66; chief exec. Linville Co. (Engrs., Research & Devel.), 1966—; mem. USN tech. missions, Pearl Harbor, 1942, Europe, 1945; mem. NRC, 1960-68. Author books (Linville Books) and papers on elec. machine design and application. Chmn. Schenectady City Planning Commn., 1951; pres. N.Y. State Citizens Com. for Pub. Schs., 1952-53; mem. Gov.'s Council Advancement Research and Devel. N.Y. State, 1960—; pres. Schenectady Mus., 1964-69; chmn. Community Chest, 1964, Devel. Council for Sci., Rensselaer Poly. Inst., 1960-67; vis. com. Norwich U., 1970—, Clarkson U., 1959-65; pres. Mohawk-Hudson council ETV-WMHT Channel 17, 1966-70; bd. dirs. Sunnyview Hosp.; pres. Schenectady Indsl. Devel. Corp., 1967-69. Served to lt. USNR, 1940-42. Recipient Charles A. Coffin award, IEEE Centennial medal, USN Certificate of Commendation; Schenectady Profl. Engrs. Soc. Engr.-of-Year award, 1960. Fellow ASME, AAAS, IEEE (dir. 1953-57, Centennial medal 1984); mem. Nat. Soc. Profl. Engrs. (pres. 1966-67), N.Y. State Soc. Profl. Engrs. (pres. 1954-55), Am. Soc. Engring. Edn., Engrs. Joint Council (dir. 1954-59), N.Y. Acad. Scis., Schenectady C. of C. (past dir., v.p.), Raven Soc., Tau Beta Pi (eminent mem., nat. pres. 1974-76), Theta Tau, Delta Upsilon. Unitarian (pres. 1940-45). Clubs: Rotary, Mohawk, Mohawk Golf. Address: 1147 Wendell Ave Schenectady NY 12308

LIPE, LINDA BON, lawyer; b. Clarksdale, Miss., Jan. 10, 1948; s. William Ray and Gwendolyn (Strickland) Lipe; m. Larry L. Gleghorn, Feb. 15, 1983 (div. Feb. 1988). BBA in Accountancy, U. Miss., 1970, JD, 1971. Bar: Miss. 1971, Ark. 1976, U.S. Dist. Ct. (no. dist.) Miss. 1971, U.S. Dist. Ct. (ea. dist.) Ark. 1976, U.S. Ct. Appeals (8th cir.) 1985. Sr. tax acct. Arthur Young & Co., San Jose, Calif., 1971-74, A.M. Pullen & Co., Knoxville, Tenn., 1975; legal counsel to gov. State of Ark., Little Rock, 1975-79; dep. pros. atty. 6th Jud. Dist. Ark., Little Rock, 1979-80; chief counsel Ark. Public Service Commn., Little Rock, 1980-83; asst. U.S. atty. Eastern Dist. Ark., Dept. Justice, Little Rock, 1983—. Mem. ABA, Miss. State Bar, Ark. State Bar Assn., Ark. Bar Assn. Episcopalian. Office: US Atty's Office 600 W Capitol PO Box 1229 Little Rock AR 72203

LIPINSKY DE ORLOV, LUCIAN CHRISTOPHER, marketing representative; b. N.Y.C., Feb. 21, 1962; s. Lino Sigismondo and Leah Safier (Penner) L.; m. Ann Marie Coffey, Aug. 23, 1986. BS in Computer Sci., SUNY, Binghamton, 1984, MS in Advanced Tech., 1985. Part-owner, cons. Computer Solutions Unltd., Johnson City, N.Y., 1983-85; programmer IBM Corp., Tarrytown, N.Y., 1985; assoc. info. ctr. analyst IBM Corp., Tarrytown, 1986-87; mktg. rep. IBM Media Br., N.Y.C., 1987—. Editor: IBM Corp. Hdqtrs. Info. Systems Jour., 1985—, IBM Corp. Hdqtrs. Info. Products and Software Services Product Catalogue, 1985—. Mem. bus. adv. coun. Norman Thomas High Sch., N.Y.C., 1988—; mem. Katonah-Bedford Hills (N.Y.) Vol. Ambulance Corps, 1979-85, North Salem (N.Y.) Vol. Ambulance Corps, 1985—, 2d lt. 1988-89; vol. Caramoor Ctr. for Music and the Arts, Katonah, 1976—, head usher, 1978. Recipient Eagle Scout award Boy Scouts Am., 1977. Mem. IEEE, Assn. Computing Machinery, Soc. Am. Magicians, Internat. Brotherhood Magicians, Nat. Eagle Scout Assn. (life), Mensa, N.Y. State Emergency Med. Technicians. Home: PO Box 524 Rt 22 Goldens Bridge NY 10526 Office: IBM Corp 590 Madison Ave New York NY 10022

LIPPA, DAVID ANTHONY, insurance executive; b. Rochester, N.Y., Sept. 2, 1948; s. Leonard Anthony and Carol Ann (Dobbertin) L.; m. Dianna Rose Shaver, July 19, 1972. Diploma, Coll. Fin. Planning, 1987, Am. Coll., 1988; MS in Fin. Svcs., Am. Coll., 1989. CPCU, CLU; cert. fin. planner, chartered fin. cons. Ins. agt. Prudential, Tustin, Calif., 1972-75, Allstate Ins. Co., Rochester, 1975-79; exec. v.p. Ralph O. Wilcox Co., L.A., 1979—; mem. adv. com. TransAm. Agts., L.A., 1982—; mem. govt. affairs com. PIA Calif. and Nev., L.A., 1987—. Mem. 552 Club Hoag Meml. Hosp., Newport Beach, Calif., 1984—, Performing Arts Fraternity, Costa Mesa, Calif., 1986—. With USN, USMC, 1967-69, Vietnam. Fellow Acad. for Producer Ins. Studies; mem. Soc. Cert. Profl. Ins. Agts. (life), Western Assn. Ins. Brokers, Soc. CPCU, Soc. CLUs and CHFC. Republican. Roman Catholic. Home: 3665 D Bear St Santa Ana CA 92704 Office: 626 Fair Oaks Ave Ste 348 South Pasadena CA 91030

LIPPERT, ALBERT, health service executive; b. Bklyn., Apr. 23, 1925; s. Hyman and Becky (Shapiro) L.; m. Felice Sally Mark, June 21, 1953; children: Keith Lawrence, Randy Seth. B.B.A., Coll. City N.Y., 1949. Asst. buyer Goldrings, 1949-51; buyer, mdse. mgr. Mangel Stores Corp., 1951-67; v.p. Weight Watchers Internat., Inc., Manhasset, N.Y., 1967-68; chmn. bd.. pres. Weight Watchers Internat., Inc., 1968-79, chmn. bd., 1979—, chief exec. officer, 1979-81; treas., past dir. W.W. Twenty First Corp. Active City of Hope; active Mr. and Mrs. League, Grand St. Boys Club. Served with AUS, 1943-46, ETO. Named Man of Yr., N.Y. Council Civic Affairs, 1968. Club: Sands Point Golf. Office: Weight Watchers Internat Jericho Atrium 500 N Broadway Jericho PA 11753-2196

LIPPIATT, BARBARA CASSARD, economist; b. Balt., May 29, 1957; d. Henry DeVries Jr. and Emilie (Leonards) Cassard; m. John William Lippiatt, Sept. 27, 1980; children: John Henry, Sherry Marie. BA in Econs., Hood Coll., 1979; MA in Econs., Am. U., 1982. Economist Nat. Bur. Standards, Gaithersburg, Md., 1977—; staff acct. Maxima Quality Svcs., Hyattsville, Md., 1985-87; owner, mgr. Potomac Enterprises, Rockville, Md., 1986—. Contbr. articles to profl. publs. Mem. Am. Econ. Assn., Md. Tennis Assn. (tournament winner 1987). Episcopalian. Office: Potomac Enterprises PO Box 1088 Germantown MD 20874

LIPPINCOTT, PHILIP EDWARD, paper products company executive; b. Camden, N.J., Nov. 28, 1935; s. J. Edward and Marjorie Nix (Spooner) L.; m. Naomi Catherine Prindle, Aug. 22, 1959; children: Grant, Kevin, Kerry. BA, Dartmouth Coll., 1957; MBA with distinction, Mich. State U., 1964. With Scott Paper Co., Phila., 1959—, staff v.p. corp. planning, 1971, div. v.p., consumer products mktg., 1971-72, corp. v.p., mktg., 1972-75, sr. v.p., mktg., 1975-77, v.p., group exec. packaged products div., 1977, dir., 1978, chief operating officer, 1980-82, pres., 1980—, chief exec. officer, 1982—, chmn., 1983; bd. dirs. Campbell Soup Co., Exxon Corp., The Bus. Coun.; trustee Penn Mut. Life Ins. Co. Bd. overseers Wharton Sch. U. Pa., Dartmouth Inst.; bd. dirs. Fox Chase Cancer Ctr., Phila. Capt. U.S. Army, 1957-59. Mem. Am. Paper Inst. (dir., exec. com.), Paper Distbn. Coun., Grocery Mfrs. Assn. (bd. dirs.), Social Club, Riverton Country Club, Kappa Kappa Kappa, Pi Sigma Epsilon, Beta Gamma Sigma. Mem. Society of Friends. Office: Scott Paper Co Scott Pla Philadelphia PA 19113

LIPPMAN, ALFRED JULIAN, retired real estate executive; b. Newark, May 7, 1900; s. Lewis Isaac and Henrietta (Meyer) L.; m. Rosa Maria Muniz, 1982. With L. Bamberger & Co. Dept. Store, Newark, 1912-22; buyer Symons Dry Goods Co., Butte, Mont., 1922-26; asst. mdse. mgr. Stix, Baer & Fuller Co., St. Louis, 1926-28; mdse. mgr. Union Co., Columbus, Ohio, 1928; supr. N.J. br. offices Eisele & King, mems. N.Y. Stock Exchange, 1928-38; owner real estate bus. 1928-38; salesman, broker Feist & Feist, Newark, 1938-41; ptnr. real estate firm John E. Sloane & Co., Newark, 1941-45; owner, pres. successor firm Alfred J. Lippmann Inc., 1945-80; pres. Fereday & Meyer Co. Inc. Contractors, Newark, 1938-80; exec. dir. Latin Am. Devel. and Ops. Co. V.p. Aerovias Latino Americanos, S.A. of Mexico, 1951-52; N.J. rep. to 3 presdl. inaugurations in Mexico; mem. N.J. Planning Bd., 1936-43; chmn. Sea Bright (N.J.) State Park Commn., 1938; mem. Mcpl. Sanitation Commn., 1952; vice chmn. solid wastes tech. com. N.J. Dept. Health; dir. Children to Children Orgn.; dir. extension course on solid wastes disposal Rutgers U., 1962-71. Served with USN, World War I, USCGR, World War II. Decorated Order of Aztec Eagle (Mexico), 1952, L'Ordre Internacional du Bien Public Comandeur, comdr. Order Holy Cross Jerusalem; named outstanding citizen of N.J. by K.P., 1955, Man of Yr., Acapulco, Mexico, 1971; recipient Disting. Achievement award Advt. Club N.Y., 1964, diploma and Gold medal for extraordinary contbn. Mexican Nat. Tourist Council, 1967, Gold medallion Port Authority N.J. and N.Y., 1975; named Outstanding Citizen of N.J. by K.P., 1955, Man of Yr., Acapulco, Mex., 1971, hon. consul Mex., 1957-77, hon. consul gen. Mex., 1977-78, Consul of Yr., Consular Corps. Coll., 1970, to Hon. Order Ky. Cols. Mem. Am. Legion (life), Soc. Solid Waste Technicians (pres.), Circus Saints and Sinners (nat. v.p.), Nat. Sweepstakes Regatta of Red Bank, N.J. (past rear commodore), Mexican Acad. Internat. Law, Mexican C. of C. of U.S. (pres. 1962-78, chmn. bd. 1978—), N.J. World Trade Com., Consular Corps Coll. Republican. Jewish. Clubs: Old Red Bank Yacht (N.J.) (past commodore); Rio Chumpan Yacht (Mex.) (past commodore). Lodges: Masons, Elks. Home: 2100 S Ocean Ln Fort Lauderdale FL 33316

LIPPMAN, WILLIAM JENNINGS, investment company executive; b. N.Y.C., Feb. 13, 1925; s. Henry J. and Fanny (Schapira) L.; m. Doris Kaplan, July 11, 1948; children—Howard Mark, Deborah Ellen. B.B.A. cum laude, Coll. City N.Y., 1947; M.B.A., N.Y.U., 1957. Marketing mgr. Pavelle Color, Inc., N.Y.C., 1947-50; sales mgr. Terminal Home Sales Corp., N.Y.C., 1950-55; div. mgr. King Merritt & Co., Inc., Englewood, N.J., 1955-60; pres., dir. Pilgrim Distbrs. Inc., Ft. Lee, N.J., 1960-86; pres. L.F. Rothschild Managed Trust L.F. Rothschild Fund Mgmt. Inc., N.Y.C., 1986-88, also dir.; pres. Franklin Managed Trust, New York, 1988—; mem. faculty Fairleigh Dickinson U. Sch. Bus. Adminstrn., 1957-69; bd. govts. Investment Co. Inst. Contbg. author: Investment Dealer Digest. Mem. Nat. Assn. Securities Dealers (investment cos. com.). Home: 18 Daniel Dr Englewood NJ 07631 Office: Franklin Managed Trust 1 Parker Pla Fort Lee NJ 07024

LIPPOLD, JEFFREY HOWARD, oil services company executive; b. Butler, Pa., Apr. 17, 1954; s. Howard T. and Dorothy L. (Protzman) L.; m. Mary Alice Thompson, Sept. 16, 1978; 1 child, Emily. BS, Pa. State U., 1976; MBA, Duquesne U., 1980. CPA, Tex. Acct. Armco Inc., Butler, Pa., 1976-81; supr. fin. Armco Inc., Houston, Tex., 1981-82; subs. controller Armco Inc., Conroe, Tex., 1982-83; mgr. fin. Armco Inc., Houston, 1983-86, controller, 1986-87; chief fin. officer Nat. Oilwell-Armco Inc./USX Corp. J.V., Houston, 1987—. Mem. Fin. Execs. Inst., Am. Inst. CPA's (Houston chpt.), Tex. Inst. CPA's, Fin. Inst. Office: Nat Oilwell PO Box 4638 Houston TX 77210-4638

LIPS, THOMAS DURR, investment advisor, lawyer; b. Wilmington, Del., July 26, 1944; s. Heinz August and Elizabeth Lillian (Engel) L.; m. Margah Ann Brigham, Mar. 14, 1970; children: Emily Margah, Evan Meyjes. BA summa cum laude, Dartmouth Coll., 1966; JD, Harvard U., 1969. Bar: Calif. 1970. Asst. to asst. sec. def. U.S. Dept. Def., Washington, 1970-71; assoc. Bronson, Bronson and McKinnon, San Francisco, 1972-73; legal counsel Trinity Coll., Hartford, Conn., 1973-80; sr. v.p. investments Drexel Burnham Lambert Inc., Hartford, Conn., 1981—; advisor Loan Pricing Corp., N.Y.C., 1986—; bd. dirs. JVS Corp., Simsbury, Conn., Francis S. Jackson Assocs., Hartford, Finec Corp., Hartford. Bd. dirs. Hartford chpt. ARC, 1975-80; trustee Cesari Barbieri Endowment, Hartford, 1978—. With U.S. Army, 1970-71. Mem. State Bar Assn. Calif., University Club, Phi Beta Kappa. Republican. Congregationalist. Home: 105 Foote Rd S Glastonbury CT 06073 Office: Drexel Burnham Lambert Inc 1 Financial Pla Hartford CT 06103

LIPSCHULTZ, HOWARD ELLIOTT, historian, educator, accountant; b. Chgo., Apr. 16, 1947; s. M. Richard and Evelyn (Smolin) L. BS in History, Ill. State U., 1969; cert., Chaim Greenberg Hebrew Coll., Jerusalem, 1972; MA in History, Roosevelt U., 1973, MS in Acctg., 1977. CPA, Ill. Staff acct. Lipschultz Bros. Levin & Gray, Northbrook, 1957-74, Leaf, Dahl & Co., Chgo., 1974-76; pres. LTC Fin. Corp., Northbrook, 1977, Lipschultz & Co. P.C., 1980; cons. U.S. Govt., Chgo., 1977-84; asst. prof. Kendall Coll., Evanston, Ill., 1977-81; adj. prof. Roosevelt U., Chgo., 1980—, Elmhurst (Ill.) Coll., 1982—; lectr. U. Ill., Chgo., 1982-85. Commr. Environ. Quality Commn., Northbrook, 1979-82; bd. dirs. United Way Northbrook, 1980-87, treas., 1985-87, active fin. and allocation, 1984-86. Mem. Orgn. Am. Historians, Acad. Acctg. Historians, Am. Inst. CPAs, Am. Acctg. Assn., Ill. CPA Found. Republican. Jewish. Office: Lipschultz & Co PO Box 203 Northbrook IL 60062

LIPSCOMB, KEITH ANTHWAYNE, vocational evaluator, auditor; b. High Point, N.C., Feb. 15, 1964; s. James William and Dolores LeVarne (Mason) L. BA, John C. Smith U., 1986; postgrad., N.C. A&T State U., 1987—. Rsch. asst. Minority Bio-Med. Rsch. Support, Charlotte, N.C., 1983-85; rehab. coord. Youth Care Inc., Greensboro, N.C., 1986-87; auditor Red Roof Inn, Greensboro, 1987-88; vocat. evaluator Goodwill Industries Inc., Greensboro, 1987—; residential advisor Johnson C. Smith U., Charlotte, 1983-86; program evaluator Mecklenburg County Mental Health, Charlotte, 1986; field suveyor planning dept. Environ. Health, Charlotte, 1986. Mem. Alpha Phi Alpha. Baptist. Office: Goodwill Industries Inc 1235 S Eugene St Greensboro NC 27406

LIPSKY, LINDA ETHEL, business executive; b. Bklyn., June 2, 1939; d. Irving Julius and Florence (Stern) Ellman; m. Warren Lipsky, June 12, 1960 (div. Sept. 1968); 1 child, Phillip Bruce; m. Jerome Friedman, Jan. 17, 1988. BA in Psychology, Hofstra U., 1960; MPS in Health Care Adminstrn., Long Island U., 1979. Child welfare social worker Nassau County Dept. Social Service, N.Y., 1960-64; adminstr. La Guardia Med. Group of Health Ins. Plan of Greater N.Y., Queens, 1969-72; cons. Neighborhood Service Ctr., Bronx, N.Y., 1973-78; dir. ODA Health Ctr., Bklyn., 1978-82; pres. Millin Assocs., Inc., Nassau, N.Y., 1982—. Mem. Health Care Fin. Mgmt. Assn., Nat. Assn. Community Health Ctrs., Nat. Assn. Female Execs., Hofstra U. Alumni Assn. (mem. senate 1984—, chairperson membership com. 1985—), Pi Alpha Alpha. Republican. Jewish. Avocations: cooking, writing, reading. Office: Millin Assocs Inc 521 Chestnut St Cedarhurst NY 11516

LIPTAK, GREGORY JAMES, cable television company executive; b. Streator, Ill., Jan. 4, 1940; s. Clarence John and Genevieve Ann (Comfort) L.; m. Stephanie Anne Smith Liptak, Oct. 29, 1966; children: Christine, Gregory John. BS, U. Ill., 1961, MS, 1964. News dir. WDZ, Decatur, Ill., 1964-65; news, sales WAND-TV, Decatur, 1965-66; asst. gen. mgr. Cox Cable Communications, Lakewood, Ohio, 1966-68; v.p. mktg., ops. United Cable TV Corp., Tulsa, 1968-74; v.p. mktg. Communications Properties,

Inc., Austin, Tex., 1974-79; exec. v.p. Times Mirror Cable TV, Irvine, Calif., 1979-85; group v.p. ops. Jones Intercable , Inc., Englewood, Colo., 1985-88, pres., 1988—. Capt. Signal Corps. U.S. Army, 1961-62. Mem. Cable TV Advt. Bur. (bd. dirs.), Cable TV Adminstrn. and Mktg. Soc. (pres., founder, bd. dirs. 1976-82). Republican. Roman Catholic. Home: 16123 E Crestline Pl Aurora CO 80015 Office: Jones Intercable Inc 9697 E Mineral Ave Englewood CO 80112

LIPTON, CHARLES, public relations executive; b. N.Y.C., May 11, 1928; s. Jack B. and Bertha (Lesser) L.; m. Audrey Williams, Nov. 11, 1951; children—Susan, Jack. A.B., Harvard U., 1948. Market researcher Cecil & Presbury, Inc., N.Y.C., 1948-49; spl. events dir. 20th Century Fox Film Corp., N.Y.C., 1949-52; account exec. Ruder & Finn, Inc., N.Y.C., 1953-58; v.p. Ruder & Finn, Inc., 1958-63, sr. v.p., 1963-69, chmn. bd., 1969—; guest lectr. Boston U., 1967-68. Mem. council Center for Vocat. Arts, Norwalk, Conn., 1966-74; trustee Norwalk Jewish Center, 1966-70, Temple Shalom, Norwalk, 1970—, Nat. Emphysema Soc., 1972—; treas., mem. exec. com. Norwalk Symphony Soc., 1972-85; chmn. parents coun. Washington U., St. Louis, 1976-77, trustee, 1977—, chmn. pub. rels. coun. 1985—; mem. Com. for Corporate Support of Pvt. Univs. Mem. Am. Mgmt. Assn., Nat. Investor Relations Inst., Am. Soc. of Colon and Rectal Surgeon (trustee research found.). Clubs: Harvard (N.Y.C.), Midday (N.Y.C.); Harvard Varsity. Home: 18 Douglas Dr Norwalk CT 06850 Office: Ruder Finn & Rotman Inc 301 E 57th St New York NY 10022

LIPTON, JEFFREY MARC, chemical company executive; b. N.Y.C., July 5, 1942; s. David J. and Ethel (Kuris) L.; m. Adrienne Frank, Dec. 14, 1975; children: Gregory, Dana, Erika. B in Chem. Engring., Rensselaer Poly. Inst., 1963; MBA, Harvard U., 1965. With E. I. DuPont de Nemours & Co., Wilmington, Del., 1965—, v.p. polymer products, 1987. Trustee Med. Ctr. Del. Hosp. Found., Wilmington, 1987; chmn. bd. dirs. Med. Ctr. Del. Holding Co., Wilmington, 1987. Office: E I Du Pont de Nemours & Co 1007 Market St Wilmington DE 19898

LIPTON, MARTIN, lawyer; b. N.J., June 22, 1931; s. Samuel D. and Fannie L.; m. Susan Lytle, Feb. 17, 1982; children: James, Margaret, Katherine, Samantha. BS in Econs., U. Pa., 1952; LLB, NYU, 1955. Bar: N.Y. 1956. Ptnr. Wachtell Lipton Rosen & Katz, N.Y.C., 1965—. Office: Wachtell Lipton Rosen & Katz 299 Park Ave New York NY 10171 *

LIPTON, WILLIAM JAMES, accountant, lawyer; b. N.Y.C., July 11, 1947; s. Irvin Edward and Evelyn Deborah (Morris) L.; m. Carol Anne Miller, Jan. 3, 1982; children: Michael Jon, Bradley Scott, Marissa Kate. BS in Acctg., U. Pa., 1969; JD, St. John's U., N.Y.C., 1973; LLM, N.Y.U., 1977. Bar: N.Y. 1974; CPA, N.Y. Tax assoc. Ernst & Whinney, N.Y.C., 1973-80, ptnr., 1980-87; ptnr.-in-charge Ernst & Whinney, Phila., 1987—; assoc. editor St. John's Law Rev., 1972; contbr. articles to profl. jours. Mem. ABA, N.Y. State Bar Assn., Phila. Bar Assn., Am. Inst. CPAs, N.Y. State Soc. CPAs (chmn. partnership com. 1985-87). Home: 355 Millbank Rd Bryn Mawr PA 19010 Office: Ernst & Whinney 2900 Centre Sq W Philadelphia PA 19102

LIRONES, MICHAEL GEORGE, retail executive; b. St. Joseph, Mich., Apr. 24, 1969; s. George Jr. and Carol (Wolf) L. Student, Lake Mich. Coll., 1987, 88. Prin. Rainbow Painting Svcs., St. Joseph, 1985-87; owner, chief exec. officer Giovani Jewelers, Inc., Benton Harbor, Mich., 1987—; sales rep. Merlite Industries, N.Y.C., 1986-87, nat. salesman Star Cablevision, 1988—. Organizer Salvation Army, Benton Harbor, 1984. Fellow Delta Epsilon Epsilon Chi; mem. St. Joseph Stock Club (pres. 1985-86). Greek Orthodox. Office: Giovani Jewelers PO Box 1261 Benton Harbor MI 49085

LIS, LAWRENCE FRANCIS, facsimile company executive; b. Blue Island, Ill., Jan. 27, 1941; s. Anthony C. and Ann Marion (Galazin) L.; student DeVry Inst. Tech., 1958-59; m. Barbara Jean Lisak, Oct. 19, 1963; children—Christ and Connie (twins), David S. With Telautograph Corp., Chgo., 1959-64; regional mgr. Datalog div. Litton Industries, Chgo., 1964-74; regional mgr. Rapicom Inc., Chgo., 1974-78, nat. dir. field service ops., Hillside, Ill., 1978-79, v.p. customer service div., 1979—, v.p. customer service div. Ricoh Corp. and Ricoh Corp. Ltd. subs. Ricoh Ltd., 1980—. dir. Emergency Services and Disaster Agy., Village of Chicago Ridge, 1977-82; mem. Ill. CD Council. Commander Civil Air Patrol, Ill., 1986—. Mem. Assn. Field Service Mgrs. (pres. Chgo. chpt. 1984-85), Armed Forces Communications and Electronics Assn., Suburban Amateur Radio Assn., Mendel High Sch Alumni Assn. Home: 6704 W 93d Oak Lawn IL 60453 Office: 4415 W Harrison St Hillside IL 60162

LISA, DONALD JULIUS, lawyer; b. Camden, N.J., Apr. 4, 1935; s. Frank Anthony and Frances Theresa (Piccione) L.; m. Isabelle Catherine O'Neill, June 15, 1957; children: Richard Allan, Steven Gregory. BS with distinction, U.S. Naval Acad., 1957; JD, Harvard U., 1965; MBA, U. Chgo., 1987. Bar: N.Y. 1966, N.J. 1974, U.S. Supreme Ct. 1974, Ill. 1976, Ariz. 1980, U.S. Patent and Trademark Office 1967, U.S. Dist. Ct. (no. dist.) Ill. 1983. Commd. ensign USN, 1957, advanced through grades to lt., served as all-weather jet fighter pilot, 1957-62, resigned, 1962; assoc. then ptnr. Kenyon & Kenyon, N.Y.C., 1965-74; div. patent counsel Motorola, Inc., Schaumburg, Ill., 1974-78; exec. dir. technology asset mgmt. Motorola, Inc., Phoenix, 1978-80, v.p., staff gen. patent counsel, 1980-82; v.p., proprietary rights litigation counsel Motorola, Inc., Schaumburg, 1983-84, v.p. dir. acquisitions, 1985-87, pres., 1987; pres. Lisa & Kubida P.C., Phoenix, 1987-89; owner Lisa & Assocs., Phoenix, 1989—. Dir. CD, Millburn (N.J.) Twp. Mem. ABA, N.Y. State Bar Assn., Ariz. Bar Assn., Am. Intellectual Property Law Assn., Maricopa County Bar Assn., Rotary. Republican. Roman Catholic. Home: 10935 E Tierra Dr Scottsdale AZ 85259 Office: Lisa & Assocs 2700 N Central Ave Ste 1225 Phoenix AZ 85004

LISANKIE, BRIAN PATRICK, financial analyst; b. Manhasset, N.Y., Aug. 18, 1960; s. J.R. and Kathryn V. (Casey) L.; m. Jane M. Dall, May 19, 1985; 1 child, Mathew Joseph II. Collection coord. Gen. Electric Credit Corp., Whippany, N.J., 1983-84; internat. fin. analyst Smith & Wesson, Inc., Springfield, Mass., 1984-88; fin. cons. Prime Computer, Inc., Natick, Mass., 1988; internat. fin. analyst Spalding Sports Worldwide, Chicopee, Mass., 1988—. Home: 17 Thorndyke St Springfield MA 01118 Office: Spalding Sports Worldwide Meadow St Chicopee MA 01020

LISCHAK, WALTER HAROLD, sales executive; b. Sryacuse, N.Y., Apr. 4, 1947; s. Walter H. Lischak and Beverly (Beahner) Gill; m. Barbara A. Harbsek, 1969; children: Teresa, Cindy. AS in Phys. Edn., Hudson Valley Community Coll., 1968; BS in Mktg. and Admistn., Siena Coll., 1970. Tchr. phys. edn. Troy (N.Y.) Sch. System, 1971; sales agt. Met. Life Ins., Albany, N.Y., 1971-74, Beech Nut Life Savers, N.Y.C., 1974-76, Orange Ford Motor Co., Albany, 1976-78; new car and gen. sales mgr. Orange Ford Motor Co., Newburgh, N.Y., 1978-81; sales agt. Premier Indsl. Corp., Cleve., 1981-84, dist. mgr., new agt. sch. inst., 1984—. Active Ulster County Hwy. Assn., N.Y., 1982. Mem. Am. Welding Soc., KC. Home: 18 Meadow Ln Modena NY 12548 Office: Pramier Indsl Corp 4500 Euclid Ave Cleveland OH 44103

LISCOM, CLAYTON LEE, investment counselor; b. Goodrich, Mich., Mar. 21, 1947; s. Paul William and Mary Maxine (McKenzie) L.; children by previous marriage: Craig Patrick, Ryan Michael B; m. Diane Elaine Huston, June 17, 1988; Indsl. Engr., Gen. Motors Inst., 1970; M.B.A., U. Mich., 1974. Chartered fin. analyst. Indsl. engr. Buick Motors Gen. Motors Corp., Flint, Mich., 1970-73; sr. fin. analyst Treas. Staff Gen. Motors, Detroit, 1977-78; portfolio mgr. Genesee Bank, Flint, 1973-77, dir. research, 1978-82; dir. equity research First Nat. Bank, Oklahoma City, 1982-84; chief adminstrv. officer First Investment Mgmt., Oklahoma City, 1984-85, chief investment officer, 1985-88; pres. CEO, 1988—; sec. program, chmn. Fin. Analysts Soc. Okla., 1984—. Author: Visual Man-Computer Interface, 1970. Fellow Fin. Analysts Fedn. (pres.). Republican. Methodist. Club: Greens Country. Avocations: golf, tennis, scuba, skiing. Home: 6209 Lansbrook Ct Oklahoma City OK 73132 Office: First Investment Mgmt 120 N Robinson Ste 860W Oklahoma City OK 73102

LISLE, ROBERT WALTON, insurance company executive; b. Butler, Mo., Aug. 18, 1927; s. Henry Harris and Nelle (Walton) L.; m. Donna Moore, Nov. 18, 1950; children: Amy Lisle Albrecht, Thomas W. B.S., U. Mo., 1950, postgrad. Law Sch., 1948-49; grad. Exec. Mgmt. Program, Columbia U., 1972. Vice pres. Prudential Ins. Co., Newark, 1950-82; sr. v.p. real estate investments Travelers Corp., Hartford, Conn., 1982—; pres. PIC Realty Corp., Newark, 1970-82; chmn. bd., chief exec. officer The Prosepct Co., Hartford, 1982-88; chmn. bd. dirs., chief exec. officer Avon The Farnham Corp., Hartford, 1988—. Mem. real estate adv. bd. NYU, 1982—. Served with AUS, 1945-46, ETO. Recipient Citation of Merit U. Mo., 1980. Mem. Urban Land Inst. (trustee), Nat. Assn. Home Builders (mortgage roundtable), Nat. Inst. Bldg. Scis. (dir.), Internat. Council Shopping Centers, Nat. Assn. Corp. Real Estate Execs., Am. Hotel and Motel Assn. Presbyterian. Clubs: Avon (Conn.) Golf, Hartford. Home: 47 Cheltenham Way Avon CT 06001

LISS, HERBERT MYRON, newspaper publisher, communications company executive; b. Mpls., Mar. 23, 1931; s. Joseph Milton and Libby Diane (Kramer) L.; m. Barbara Lipson, Sept. 19, 1954; children: Lori-Ellen, Kenneth Allen, Michael David. BS in Econs., U. Pa., 1952. With mktg. mgmt. Procter & Gamble Co., Cin., 1954-63, Procter & Gamble Internat., various countries, 1963-74; gen. mgr. Procter & Gamble Comml. Co., San Juan, P.R., 1974-78; v.p., mgr. internat. ops. InterAm. Orange Crush Co. subs. Procter & Gamble Co., Cin., 1981-84; pres. River Cities (Ohio) Communications Inc, 1985—; pub. The Downtowner Newspaper, Cin., 1985—. Bd. dirs. Charter Com., Cin., 1958-63, Promotion & Mktg. Assn. U.S., 1978-81, Jr. Achievement, Cin., 1980-87, Downtown Coun., Cin., 1985—. 1st lt. U.S. Army, 1952-54, Korea. Mem. Manila Yacht Club, Manila Polo, Equitacioón De Somos Aguas, Rotary (Cin. club). Home: 8564 Wyoming Club Dr Cincinnati OH 45215 Office: The Downtowner Newspaper 128 E Sixth St Cincinnati OH 45202

LISS, NORMAN RICHARD, insurance executive; b. Bronx, N.Y., May 29, 1947; s. Jacob Melvin and Terry Ruth (Stoppler) L.; student Athens (Ala.) Coll., 1965-67, U. Albuquerque, 1967; m. Orlinda P. Olivas, Apr. 11, 1970; children—Maria, Jacqueline Melissa. With First Nat. Life Ins. Co., Albuquerque, 1969-70; founder, pres. Ins. Planners of N.Mex., Albuquerque, 1970—. Active Heart Fund, United Way, Arthritis Found., Boy Scouts Am.; pres. N.Mex. Track Athletic Congress; bd. dirs. N.Mex. chpt. March of Dimes, N.Mex. Kidney Found. Served with USAF, 1967-69. Recipient various ins. sales awards, Dublin award for public service. Mem. Assn. Life Underwriters (local sec.-treas., bd. dirs., state chmn. pub. service, instr. and moderator Tng. Council), Million Dollar Round Table (life). Republican. Jewish. Lodge: Ct. of Table (chtr. mem.). Home: 11433 Nassau Dr NE Albuquerque NM 87111 Office: JML Profl Bldg 3644 Thaxton SE Albuquerque NM 87108

LISS, SAUL, science administrator; b. Paterson, N.J., July 27, 1925; s. George and Bella (Musicant) L.; m. Lora June Wolfe, 1946 (div. 1974); children: Ronald, Gary; m. Susan B. Seigle, June 19, 1976. BSEE, Purdue U., 1945. Mgr. prodn. Ortho Radio, Paterson, 1949-50; designer electromech. products FADA Radio Co., Belleville, N.J., 1950-51, W.L. Maxson Co., N.Y.C., 1952-56; dir. test equipment and automated systems Kearfott div. Gen. Precision Labs., Little Falls, N.J., 1957-62; pres., chmn. bd. Micro Metrics Inc., Paterson, 1963-74; dir. quality control ABS div. Litton Industries, Clifton, N.J., 1974-75; founder, pres., chmn. bd. Pain Suppression Labs. Inc., Clifton, 1975-85; dir. sci. and tech. Pain Suppression Labs. Inc., Elmwood, N.J., 1986; exec. v.p. Pain Suppression Labs. Inc., Wayne, N.J., 1987—. Patentee in field. Mem. Fair Lawn (N.J.) Planning Adv. Com., 1970-72. Lt. (j.g.) USNR, 1943-45. Mem. Assn. for Advancement Med. Instrumentation (mem. neurosurg. com. 1977—), N.Y. Acad. Scis., Am. Acad. Sci. Jewish. Home: 59 Oxford Pl Glen Rock NJ 07452 Office: Pain Suppression Labs Inc Wayne Pla II 155 Rte 46 W Wayne NJ 07470

LIST, JOHN DEWITT, shipping executive; b. McKeesport, Pa., May 29, 1935; s. John D. and Ida M. List; m. Ruthie Wright, Aug. 2, 1958; children: Deborah, John D., III. BS in Econs., Acctg., Pa. State U., 1957. CPA, N.Y., Ky. Audit mgr. Price Waterhouse & Co., N.Y.C., 1957-66; internal audit mgr. Amerada Hess, Woodbridge, N.J., 1966-70; v.p., chief fin. officer Amerada Hess (V.I.), St. Croix, V.I., 1970-71; adminstrv. asst. to vice chmn. bd. Ashland (Ky.) Oil Co., 1971-74; v.p., chief fin. officer Ecol, Ltd. (Ingram Joint Venture), New Orleans, 1974-76; v.p. corp. devel. Ingram Corp., New Orleans, 1976-78, v.p., treas., 1978-84; sr. v.p., chief fin. officer Lykes Bros. Steamship Co., Inc., New Orleans, 1985-88, sr. v.p. planning and analysis, 1989—; bd. dirs. United Kingdom Mut. Steamship Assurance Assn. (Bermuda) Ltd., 1986. Served to capt. USAF, 1957-60. Mem. Fin. Execs. Inst., Am. Inst. CPA's, N.Y. State Soc. CPA's, Ky. Soc. CPA's. Home: 237 W Livingston Pl Metairie LA 70005 Office: Lykes Bros Steamship Co 300 Poydras St New Orleans LA 70130

LISTER, HARRY JOSEPH, financial company executive, consultant; b. Teaneck, N.J., Jan. 27, 1936; s. Harry and Arline Audrey (Pinera) L.; m. Erika Anna Maria Englisch, Sept. 3, 1960; children: Harry Joseph Jr., Karen P. Lister Lawson, Leslie M. Lister Fidler, Andrea A., Michael P. BS in Fin. and Econs., Lehigh U., 1958. Security analyst Calvin Bullock, Ltd., N.Y.C., 1959-61, assoc. dir. estate planning, 1961-65, dir. estate planning., 1965-72, asst. v.p., 1969-72; v.p. N.Y. Venture Fund, Inc., N.Y.C., 1970-72; registered rep. Johnston, Lemon & Co., Inc., Washington, 1972—, dir., registered prin., 1978—, v.p., 1978-83, corp. sec., 1978-85, sr. v.p., 1984—; v.p. Wash. Mgmt. Corp., 1972-81, corp. sec., 1978-81, exec. v.p., 1981-85, pres., 1985—, also bd. dirs.; pres. JL Fin. Svcs., Inc., Washington, 1975—; v.p. Washington Mut. Investors Fund, Inc., Washington, 1972-81, corp. sec., 1978-81, exec. v.p., 1981-85, pres., 1985—, also bd. dirs.; pres. The Growth Fund of Washington, Inc., 1985—, also bd. dirs.; vice-chmn. Washington Funds Distbrs., Inc., 1985—; pres., trustee The Tax-Exempt Fund of Md., 1986—, The Tax Exempt Fund of Va., 1986—; cons. Capital Group, Inc., L.A., 1972—; regent Coll. for Fin. Planning, Denver, 1979-84, mem. exec. com., 1980-84, chmn. bd. regents, 1981-83; mem. bd. dirs. Internat. Bd. Standards and Practices for Cert. Fin. Planners, 1985-86. Author: Your Guide to IRAs and 14 Other Retirement Plans, 1985. Bd. dirs. cen. Bergen chpt. ARC, Hackensack, N.J., 1968-72, chmn. exec. com., 1970-72; bd. dirs. Westwood, N.J. Planning Bd., 1969-72, vice-chmn., 1970-72; bd. dirs. Westwood N.J. Zoning Bd. Adjustment, 1970-72. Mem. Investment Co. Inst. (pension com., chmn. 1976-81, tax com., rsch. com.), Nat. Assn. Securities Dealers, Inc. (investment cos. com. 1984-87, bd. arbitrators 1987—), University Club. Home: Spinnaker Ct Reston VA 22091 Office: 1101 Vermont Ave NW Washington DC 20005

LISTON, ALAN A., lawyer; b. Hamilton, Ont., Oct. 11, 1946; s. Ambrose James and Kathleen Frances (Burns) L. BA, U. Western Ont., 1968, B. Laws, 1972. Solicitor DomGroup Ltd., Toronto, 1976-81, dir. legal services, 1981-82, gen. counsel, sec., 1982-84, v.p., gen. counsel, sec., 1984-85, sr. v.p., gen. counsel, sec., 1986—, pres., 1988—, also bd. dirs.; bd. dirs. Eplett Dairies Co. Ltd., Toronto. Home: 55 Adelaide St E, Ste 400, Toronto, ON Canada M5C 1K6 Office: Domgroup Ltd, 10 Toronto St, Toronto, ON Canada M5C 2B7

LISTON, ALBERT MORRIS, administrator, educator, investor; b. Carlinville, Ill., Aug. 6, 1940; s. Joseph Bostick and Hazel Marie (Smalley) L.; A.B. in Econs., U. Calif., Davis, 1963; M.A. in Govt., Calif. State U., Sacramento, 1970; m. Phyllis Clayton, Feb. 27, 1967 (div. July 1970). Research analyst Ombudsman Activities Project polit. sci. dept. U. Calif., Santa Barbara, 1970-72; asst. prof. polit. sci. dept. Calif. State U., Fullerton, 1973-79. Served to lt. Supply Corps, USN, 1963-66. Mem. Am. Polit. Sci. Assn., Am. Soc. for Public Adminstrn., Town Hall of Calif., Commonwealth Club Calif., Kappa Sigma, Phi Kappa Phi. Democrat. Contbr. chpt. to Executive Ombudsmen in the United States, 1973. Office: PO Box 96 Tiburon CA 94920

LISY, DEBORAH LEE, marketing professional; b. Joliet, Ill., Apr. 27, 1960; d. Anthony J. and Barbara F. (Palmer) L.; 1 child, Sydney A. BS in Interior Design cum laude, Miami U., Oxford, Ohio, 1982; postgrad., No. Ill. U., 1987—. Program mgr. Kewaunee Sci. Corp., Dallas, 1984-87, 1984-87; dir. mktg. Lyon & Healy Harps, Chgo., 1987—. Editor: The Lyon & Healy Letter. Mem. NAFE, Women Employed, Phi Upsilon Omicron, Sigma Iota Epsilon. Roman Catholic. Home: 655 Glenwood Ave Joliet IL 60435 Office: Lyon & Healy Harps 168 N Ogden Ave Chicago IL 60607

LITOW, JOEL DAVID, controller; b. N.Y.C., Feb. 10, 1947; s. Herbert and Jean (Zaller) L.; m. Lorraine Aziz; children: Jason, Jennifer. BChemE, CCNY, 1968; MBA, Rutgers U., 1973. Chem. engr. Airco, N.Y.C., 1968-69, fin. analyst, 1969-73; mgr. fin. analysis Bali Co., N.J., 1973-75; mgr. cost acctg. M&T Chems. Inc., Rahway, N.J., 1976-77, dir. control devel., 1978-79, controller, 1979-86, v.p. fin., controller, 1986—.

LITSCH, DANIEL GEORGE, sales executive; b. Middletown, Ohio, Sept. 13, 1947; s. Robert Augustus and Mary Elizabeth (Jurgensen) L.; m. Diana Wade Ex, Jan. 30, 1970; children: Joseph Wade, Lucinda Marie. BS, Ohio U., 1969; MBA, So. Ill. U., 1984; cert., Cert. Med. Rep. Inst., Richmond, Va., 1982. Sales rep. Syntex Labs., Evansville, Ind., 1970-74, cert. sales rep., 1974-78; sales mgr. Syntex Labs., St Louis, 1978-85, advanced sales mgr., 1985—. Vol. YMCA, St. Louis, 1978-84, Manchester Athletic Assn., St. Louis, 1982-84, dir., 1984—. Mem. Beta Gamma Sigma, Delta Tau Delta. Home: 1041 Dutch Mill Dr Ballwin MO 63011 Office: Syntex Labs 3401 Hillview Palo Alto CA 94304

LITTELL, JESSICA FULLER, certified financial planner; b. Scranton, Pa., July 24, 1958; d. Gregory Barrett Littell and Kathryn Emaline (Fuller) Hardin; m. Gerald Bruce Birnbaum, July 18, 1987. BS, BA in acctg., Shippensburg U., 1981; cert. fin. planning, Coll. for Fin. Planning, Denver, 1987; student, U. New Haven. Agt. Phoenix Mut. Life Ins. Co., New Haven, 1981-84; fin. planner New Haven Savs. Bank, 1984-89; owner, pres. Fin. Cent$, Madison, Conn., 1989—. Mem. Inst. Cert. Fin. Planners. Republican.

LITTLE, BRIAN F., oil company executive; b. Moncton, N.B., Can., Oct. 28, 1943; s. George E. and Marion M. (McCartney) L.; m. Dianne E. Rogers, Oct. 9, 1969; chldren: Michael William, Sara Elizabeth. BA, Am. Internat. Coll., 1966; LLB, Osgoode Hall Law Sch., 1974; LLM, London Sch. Econs., Eng., 1975. Indsl. devel. asst. Can. Nat., Moncton and Montreal, Can., 1967-71; assoc. McMillan Binch, Toronto, Ont., Can., 1977-82, ptnr., 1982-83; v.p., gen. counsel Dome Petroleum, Calgary, Alta., Can., 1983-88; v.p. law and external affairs Amoco Can. Petroleum Co. Ltd., Calgary, 1988—. Mem. Can. Bar Assn., Law Soc. Upper Can., Can. Tax Found. Office: Amoco Can Petroleum Co Ltd, 240 Fourth Ave SW, Calgary, AB Canada T2P 4H4

LITTLE, CHARLES CURTIS, automotive executive; b. Detroit, Nov. 2, 1954; s. Roy Raymond Little and Alleane Jane (Manion) Kinnison. BBA summa cum laude, Detroit Inst. Tech., 1978. CPA, Mich. Sr. acct. Noteman, Pierce, Cox & Darling, Troy, Mich., 1978-80; audit supr. Coopers & Lybrand, Detroit, 1980-84; asst. treas., acctg. mgr. Trim Trends, Inc., Clawson, Mich., 1984-87; div. controller Trim Trends Div. Harvard Industries, Clawson, 1987—. Mem. Am. Inst. CPA's (Acctg. Research Assn.), Mich. Assn. CPA's, Nat. Assn. Accts. Methodist. Home: 1756 Graefield Birmingham MI 48009 Office: Trim Trends Inc 1271 W Maple Rd Clawson MI 48017

LITTLE, DAVID ALFRED, utility company executive; b. Iowa City, Aug. 4, 1942; s. Henry Alfred and Loretta Rita (Cantoni) L.; children: Leslie, Melissa, Michael. BS, Creighton U., 1964. Personnel asst. Burroughs Corp., Omaha, 1967-68; mgr. compensation benefits Burroughs Corp., Phila., 1968-70; regional personnel mgr. Burroughs Corp., Detroit, 1970-71; dir. personnel Iowa So. Utilities Co., Centerville, 1971-79, dir. personnel and pub. affairs, 1979-82, v.p., 1982—; bd. dirs. Terra Comfort Corp., Centerville, SIDCO, Centerville, SIRCO, Centerville. Mem. Appanoose Indsl. Corp., Centerville, 1981—; state chmn. Job Svc. Employer Com.; bd. dirs. Mary's Cath. Sch. Bd., 1978-84. Capt. USAR, 1964-71. Recipient Outstanding Achievement award Pvt. Industry Council, 1984, Gov.'s Vol. award State of Iowa, 1985, Exemplary Svc. award, 1988. Mem. Mo. Valley Electric Assn., Edison Electric Inst., Centerville C. of C. (bd. dirs. 1975—, Svc. Appreciation award 1983), KC (grand knight, past trustee). Republican. Home: 709 S 16th St Centerville IA 52544 Office: Iowa So Inc 300 Sheridan Ave Centerville IA 52544

LITTLE, DENNIS GAGE, diversified business executive; b. Cambridge, Mass., June 22, 1935; s. Thomas Wolcott and Margaret (deRongé) L.; m. Susan Gay Walker, May 11, 1957 (div.); children: Heather Gage, Jennifer Wolcott; m. Joanne Bowers, Oct. 1, 1983. A.B., Harvard U., 1956, M.B.A. with distinction, 1961. With J.P. Stevens & Co., Inc., 1961-67, asst. to fin. v.p., 1961-67; treas. GK Techs., Inc. (name formerly Gen. Cable Corp.), 1967-82, v.p., 1969-78, v.p. indsl. relations, 1975-78, sr. v.p., chief fin. officer, 1979-82, dir., 1979-82; exec. v.p., chief fin. officer Avco Corp., Greenwich, Conn., 1982-85, also dir.; exec. v.p., chief fin. officer Textron Inc., 1985—; bd. dirs. R.I. Hosp. Trust Nat. Bank, Pine St. Fund, Russell Reynolds Assocs. Trustee Bryant Coll. Served with Supply Corps USNR, 1956-59. Mem. Fin. Execs. Inst. Clubs: Greenwich Country (Conn.); Board Room (N.Y.C.); Agawam Hunt (Providence). Home: 28 Rumstick Dr Barrington RI 02806 Office: Textron Inc 40 Westminster St Providence RI 02903

LITTLE, DOUGLAS KEARNS, industrial hardware company executive; b. Charlotte, N.C., Feb. 26, 1936; s. John Darwin and Ruth Bradley (Short) L.; m. Peggy James, June 28, 1958; children: James Bradley, David Todd, Edward Kearns. BSBA, U. N.C., 1960. With Little Hardware Co. Inc., Charlotte, 1960—, now co-owner, v.p. With U.S. Army, 1954-56. Mem. U.S. Ski Assn., Charlotte Ski Bees (founder). Republican. Home: 16404 MacGregor Ln Charlotte NC 28217 Office: Little Hardware Co Inc 1400 S Mint St Charlotte NC 28203

LITTLE, FREED SEBASTIAN, petroleum equipment manufacturing company executive; b. Ft. Smith, Ark., May 4, 1926; s. Jess Edward and Floy Kimbrough (Witt) L.; B.A., U. Ark., 1950; m. Jana V. Jones, Dec. 9, 1951 (div.); 1 son, Mark McKenna. With Gilbarco Inc., Houston, 1964—, central area mgr., Chgo., 1969-73, Western regional mgr., Houston, 1974-85, Western/Pacific regional mgr., 1986—. Patron, Houston Mus. Fine Arts. Served with USAAF, 1945-46. Mem. Am. Petroleum Inst., Petroleum Equipment Inst., Am. Mgmt. Assn., Sigma Alpha Epsilon. Presbyterian. Clubs: Houston City, Memorial Drive Country. Office: 2909 Hillcroft Ste 210 Houston TX 77057

LITTLE, JOAN DOREEN, savings and loan association executive; b. Winnipeg, Man., Can., May 22, 1943; came to U.S., 1965; d. Charles Lionel and Shirley (Nathanson) Klurfine; m. Steven Robert Little, June 12, 1981. BA in Math., U. Man., 1964. Rsch. dir. Western Fed. Savs., Marina del Rey, Calif., 1969-78, v.p. secondary market, 1978-81; v.p. secondary market 1st Fed. Savs. Bank Calif., Santa Monica, 1981-82, sr. v.p., chief loan officer, 1982-87, exec. v.p., chief loan officer, 1987—. Mem. Calif. Savs. and Loan League (exec. lending com.). Home: 1527 Club View Dr Los Angeles CA 90024 Office: First Fed Savs Bank Calif 401 Wilshire Blvd Santa Monica CA 90401

LITTLE, JOHN WESLEY, retail executive; b. Hinsdale, Ill., Feb. 7, 1935; s. John Earl and Phyllis (Trojan) L.; m. Judith Diane Sehn, June 21, 1938; children: Baird Manion, Suzanne Elyce, Andrea Michelle. BA, Northwestern U., 1957. Mgr. The Squire Shop, Hinsdale, 1957-61; various mgmt. positions Sears Roebuck & Co., Chgo., 1961-76; sr. v.p. Robert Hall Clothes, N.Y.C., 1976-77, Target Stores, Inc., Mpls., 1977-84, Rose's Stores, Inc., Henderson, N.C., 1984-88; pres. Manion Corp., Raleigh, N.C., 1987-88; exec. v.p. merchandising and sales promotion Consol. Stores Internat. Corp., Columbus, Ohio, 1988—. Trustee N.C. Symphony Orchestra, Raleigh, 1985-87; panel member SPARC Awards Com., 1983-87. Mem. Zeta Psi. Republican. Home: 10745 Trego Trail Raleigh NC 27614

LITTLE, LOREN RAY, construction company owner; b. Des Moines, Oct. 27, 1944; s. Howard R. and Rosemary (Reiman) L. Student, Buena Vista Coll., 1963-65, San Jacinto Coll., 1983; cert. tng., Nat. Fire Acad., 1987. Owner A-D Constrn. Co., Austin, Nev., 1970—; project coord. United Contractors, Inc., Dryersburg, Tenn., 1975-76, Houston, 1982-84; adminstrv. asst. United Contractors, Inc., Des Moines, 1978-79; project coord. Argus Resources, Inc., Austin, 1979-82; temp. yard mgr. Carson Masonry Supply Co., Carson City, Nev., 1984-85; maintenance coord. colosseum project Bond Gold, Las Vegas, Nev., 1987-89; purchasing agt., mgr. warehouse bullfrog project Bond Gold, Beatty, Nev., 1989—. Radio coord. Austin Vol.

Fire Dept., 1981—; sustaining mem. Rep. Nat. Com., Washington, 1981—. With USNG, 1966-72. Mem. Internat. Assn. Arson Investigators. Lodge: Moose. Home and Office: Valley and 2nd St PO Box 936 Beatty NV 89003

LITTLE, MARTHA JANE, controller; b. Caruthersville, Mo., May 24, 1953; d. Samuel Jefferson and Helen (Denton) Duckworth; m. Wayne Vaughn, June 1971 (div. 1974); m. Charles M. Little, Oct. 10, 1975; 1 child, Charles Austin. B. of Profl. Accountancy, Miss. State U., 1980. CPA, Ala. Staff acct. Price Waterhouse, Birmingham, Ala., 1980-82; dir. systems and audit North Miss. Health Services, Tupelo, Miss., 1982-86, controller, 1986—. Mem. AICPA, Ala. Soc. CPA's, Nat. Assn. Accts., Healthcare Fin. Mgmt. Assn., Phi Kappa Phi, Beta Alpha Psi. Presbyterian. Office: No Miss Health Svcs 830 S Gloster Tupelo MS 38801

LITTLE, ROBERT CARTER, aerospace executive; b. Kansas City, Mo., Mar. 12, 1925; s. Francis H. and Nelle (Sanborn) L.; B.S. in Mech. Engring., Tex. A. and M. Coll., 1948; m. Betty Jane Kreder, Feb. 10, 1951; children—Susan, Martha, James, Elizabeth. Flight test engr., exptl. test pilot McDonnell Aircraft Corp., St. Louis, 1948-53, chief test pilot, 1953-62, company-wide project mgr. Air Force Phantoms, 1962-64, dir. sales, 1964-68, v.p. mktg., 1968-72, corp. v.p. mktg. McDonnell Douglas Corp., 1972-77, corp. v.p. engring. and mktg., 1977-80, corp. v.p. ops. and mktg., 1980, corp. v.p., group exec., 1982-84, corp. v.p., aerospace group exec., 1984-88, vice chmn., 1988—, also dir. Served with USAAF, 1943-45. Decorated D.F.C., Air medal with 13 oak leaf clusters. Fellow Soc. Exptl. Test Pilots (James H. Doolittle award 1977); assoc. fellow AIAA; mem. Mo. Hist. Soc., Soc. Colonial Wars Mo. Clubs: St. Louis, Old Warson, Burning Tree. Home: 49 Portland Dr Frontenac MO 63131 Office: McDonnell Douglas Corp PO Box 516 Saint Louis MO 63166

LITTLEFIELD, LAWRENCE CROSBY, JR., finance executive; b. Yonkers, N.Y., Mar. 13, 1938; s. Lawrence Crosby and Ursula (Marino) L.; m. Carmella Marion DeMatteo, June 18, 1960; children: Lawrence, Alison, Roger. BBA in Acctg., Manhattan Coll., 1960; MBA in Fin., Pace U., 1971. Sr. acct. Haskins & Sells, N.Y.C., 1960-64; various Avon Products, Inc., Rye, N.Y., 1964-72; regional controller Avon Products, Inc., Rye, 1972-75; div. controller Hertz Corp., N.Y.C., 1975; asst. v.p. fin. and adminstrn. Technical Tape, Inc., New Rochelle, N.Y., 1976; controller Edgcomb Metals Co., Tulsa, 1976-82, v.p. fin., 1982-85; v.p. fin. Edgcomb Steel of New England, Inc., Tulsa, 1985, Edgcomb Metals Co./Edgcomb Corp., Tulsa, 1985-88; exec. v.p. Keller Holdings, Inc., Miami, Fla., 1988—. Vice chmn. United Way, Tulsa, 1986; fin. and exec. advisor Jr. Achievement, Tulsa, 1977-84, bd. dirs. 1983—; bd. dirs. Tulsa Jr. Tennis Devel., 1980-85. Mem. Nat. Assn. Accts. Republican. Roman Catholic. Office: Keller Holdings Inc 18000 State Rd #9 Miami FL 33162

LITTLEFIELD, RONALD LEONARD, insurance executive; b. North Conway, N.H., Apr. 26, 1950; s. Frank E. and Mildred J. (Currier) L.; m. Karen E., Jan. 11, 1979; children: David, Julie. Student, Keene State Coll., 1968-69, Barrington Coll., 1969-70, Fin. Planning Sch., 1973, Am. Coll., 1982—. Cert. Ins. Counselor. Claims adjuster CNA Ins., Chgo., 1970-72; ins. broker Travelers Ins. Co., Hartford, Conn., 1972-75; pres., chief exec. officer The Littlefield Group, Pottstown, Pa., 1976—; cons. in mktg. and adminstrn. The Littlefield Group, Pottstown, 1983—; br. mgr. Harleysville (Pa.) Life Ins. Co., 1983—. Contbr. articles to profl. jours. Mem. Internat. Mgmt. Coun., Profl. Ins. Agts. Am., Am. Assn. Ind. Ins. Agts., Nat. Assn. Life Underwriters, Soc. Cert. Ins. Counselors, Country Music Assn. Home: 4 Tisa Ln East Coventry PA 19464 Office: 1 Littlefield Pl PO Box 617 Collegeville PA 19426

LITTLEFIELD, ROY EVERETT, III, assn. exec., legal educator; b. Nashua, N.H., Dec. 6, 1952; s. Roy Everett and Mary Ann (Prestipino) L.; 1 child, Leah Marie. B.A., Dickinson Coll., 1975; M.A., Catholic U. Am., 1976, Ph.D., 1979. Aide, U.S. Senator Thomas McIntyre, Democrat, N.H., 1975-78, Nordy Hoffman, U.S. Senate Sergeant-at-arms, 1979; dir. govt. relations Nat. Tire Dealers and Retreaders Assn., Washington, 1979-84; exec. dir. Service Sta. and Automotive Repair Assn., 1984—; cons. Am. Retreaders Assn., 1984—; mem. faculty Catholic U. Am., Washington, 1979—. Mem. Nat. Democratic Club, 1978—. Mem. Am. Soc. Legal History, Am. Retail Fedn., Small Bus. Legis. Council, Md. Hwy. Users Fedn. (pres.), Md. Soc. Assn. Execs. (bd. dirs., pres.), Nat. Capitol Area Transp. Fedn. (v.p.), N.H. Hist. Soc., C. of C., Phi Alpha Theta. Roman Catholic. Club: KC (Milford, N.H.). Author: William Randolph Hearst: His Role in American Progressivism, 1980; The Economic Recovery Act, 1982; The Surface Transportation Assistance Act; 1984; contbr. numerous articles to legal jours. Home: 15900 Pinecroft Ln Bowie MD 20716 Office: 9420 Annapolis Rd Ste 307 Lanham MD 20706

LITTMAN, HAROLD, printing company executive; b. N.Y.C., Oct. 3, 1922; s. Henry and Fanny L.; m. Annette Stein, June 8, 1947; children: Joshua, Jonas, Abigail, Jeremy, Jonathan. BA, SUNY, Brookport, 1975; MA, Montclair State Coll., 1979; EdD, NYU, 1987. Gen. mgr. Faultless Press, 1948-54; founder, pres. Seaward Edison Corp., N.Y.C., 1954-69; pres. Serga Corp. div. P&F Industries, L.I. City N.Y., 1969-73, corp. v.p., bd. dirs., 1969-73; v.p. Lasky Co., Millburn, N.J., 1973-84; pres., chief exec. officer Seaward Corp., West Orange, N.J., 1984—; adj. prof. grad. sch. NYU, 1982-88. V.p. Temple Sharey Tefilo-Israel, South Orange, N.J. 1st lt. USAAF, 1942-45. Mem. Am. Arbitration Assn., Craftsmen Club, Assn. Graphic Arts Cons., Printing Industries Am., PRINT, Phi Kappa Phi. Club: Century. Lodge: B'nai Brith. Home: 24 Clonavor Rd West Orange NJ 07052 Office: Seaward Corp 443 Northfield Ave West Orange NJ 07052

LITTMAN, IRVING, forest products company executive; b. Denver, Apr. 21, 1940; s. Maurice Littman and Cecile P. Zohn.; m. Gertrude Pepper, Aug. 16, 1964; children: Margaret R., Michael J., Elizabeth B. BS in Engring. (Applied Math.), U. Colo., 1964; MBA, U. Chgo., 1966. Mgr. corp. systems Boise Cascade Corp., Idaho, 1966-68, mgr. budgeting, 1968-71, asst. to pres., 1971-73; asst. controller realty group Boise Cascade Corp., Palo Alto, Calif., 1973-76; dir. investor relations Boise Cascade Corp., 1976-84, treas., 1984-86, v.p., treas., 1986—. Bd. dirs. Idaho Humanities Council, Boise, 1985-88, vice chair, 1987-88; trustee Bosie High Sch. Band Scholarship Endowment, 1987—; referee US Soccer Fedn., 1982. Served as staff sgt. U.S. Army, 1958-59. Mem. Bogus Basin Ski Area Assn. (bd. dirs. 1988—), Treas. Club of San Francisco, Crane Creek Country Club, Arid Club (Boise). Office: Boise Cascade Corp 1 Jefferson Sq Boise ID 83728

LITZENBOERGER, WOLFGANG, software engineering executive, industrial consultant; b. Hannover, West Germany, June 10, 1935; s. Ernst Joachim and Martha Emma (Althoff) L.; m. Ingeborg Meinhold, May 26, 1940; children: Dominique, Wolf-Rene, Nathalie. Ed., U. Bari (Italy), 1959-60, U. Sorbonne, Paris, 1961, U. Barcelona, Spain, 1962, U. Bologna, Italy, 1963, Pacific Western U., Los Angeles, 1982-83. Gen. mgr. Pisani and Rickertsen, Istanbul, 1956-59; pres., ptnr. INHA Internat. AG, Mauren, Switzerland, 1963-73; mng. dir., owner IDC Indsl. Devel. Cons. GmbH, Duesseldorf, Fed. Republic of Germany, 1972—; owner, mng. dir. PDC Planning and Devel. Cons. GmbH, Duesseldorf, 1981-85; mng. dir., shareholder Indsl. Informatics GmbH, Freiburg, Fed. Republic of Germany, 1985—. Contbr. articles to profl. jours. Fellow Inst. of Dirs. (London); mem. Institut fuer Interdisziplinäre Denkschulung und Publikationen (v.p. 1984—). Home: 34 Am Adels, D 4030 Ratingen Federal Republic of Germany Office: 2i Indsl Informatics GmbH, 20e Haierweg, Freiburg in Breisgall Federal Republic of Germany

LIU, SHING KIN FRANCIS, business executive; b. Hong Kong, Mar. 8, 1953; s. Chung Hin and Fu Har (Lai) L. MBA, Tasman Coll., Australia, 1982; PhD, Calif. U. for Advanced Studies, 1987. Sr. auditor Kwan & Co., CPA, Hong Kong, 1976-79; group internal auditor John D. Hutchison Group Ltd., Hong Kong, 1979-81; EDP audit mgr. Liu Chong Hing Bank Ltd., Hong Kong, 1981-82; chief internal auditor Swiss Bank Corp., Hong Kong, 1982-86; sr. mgr. ops. and control Arab Asian Internat. Ltd., Hong Kong, 1987-87; ops. mgr. Skandinaviska Enskilda, Banken, Hong Kong, 1987—; bd. dirs. Computer Security Cons. Ltd., Hong Kong, 1982—. Mem. St. John Ambulance Assn., Hong Kong, 1968-75. Mem. Inst. Internal Auditors, EDP Auditors Assn. Inc. Hong Kong (pres. 1979-85), EDP Auditors Found. Inc. (CISA exam. chairperson 1979-86), Hong Kong Athletic Assn. Methodist. Club: Hong Kong Overseas Bankers. Mailing Address: GPO Box 9065, Central Hong Kong

LIUZZI, ROBERT C., chemical company executive; b. Boston, 1944; married. AB, Coll. of Holy Cross; LLB, U. Va., 1968. V.p., gen. counsel U.S. Fin., Inc., 1969-74; with CF Industries, Long Grove, Ill., 1975—; exec. v.p., chief fin. officer CF Industries, Lake Zurich, Ill., 1977-80, exec. v.p., operating officer, 1980-84, pres., chief exec. officer, 1985—; chmn. bd. dirs. Agri Trans Corp.; chmn. ad hoc com. Domestic Nitrogen Products, Washington; bd. dirs. Can. Fertilizers Ltd., The Fertilizer Inst., Nat. Council Farmer Coops.; co-chmn. Petrochem. Trade Group, Washington; chmn. Fla. Phosphate Coun., Tampa, Fla. Mem. Northwestern U. Assocs., Evanston. Office: CF Industries Inc Salem Lake Dr Long Grove IL 60047

LIVAS, BASIL LOUIS, management consultant; b. Melrose, Mass., Mar. 8, 1929; s. Frank John and Adah Catherine (Clark) L.; m. Janet Adams Blood, Oct. 15, 1970; children by previous marriage: Mark Basil, Ann Elizabeth. BS in Civil Engr. cum laude, Tufts U., 1951. Sales mgr. Hitchiner Mfg. Corp., Inc., Milford, N.H., 1954-59; prodn., sales mgr. Permattach Diamond Tool Corp., Milford, 1958-59; mgr. mfg. services Bomac, Beverly, Mass., 1959-66; materials mgr. Microwave Assocs., Burlington, Mass., 1966-69; pres. B.L. Livas Assocs., Lawrence, Mass., 1969—; bd. dirs. Cargocaire Eng. Corp., Amesbury, Mass., Info/AVS, Ayer, Mass. Photographer one-man show Shapiro Gallery, Manchester, N.H., 1988. Trustee Wilson Coll. Chamersburg, Pa., 1979-83; mem. N.H. State Occupational Info. Adv. Bd., 1972-73; intern Exec. Service Corp. Served to lt. (j.g.) USN, 1951-54; capt. USNR. Mem. Tau Beta Pi. Republican. Home: 32 Hobbs Rd North Hampton NH 03862 Office: BL Livas Assocs 620 Essex St Lawrence MA 01841

LIVINGSTON, DAVID GLENN, investment banker; b. Van Wert, Ohio, Oct. 28, 1933; s. Glenn Herbert and Helen Ida (Gilliland) L.; m. Joyce Bricker, Aug. 28, 1955; children: Laura Ann, Linda Joy, David B., Douglas G. A.B. in Econs, U. Mich., 1956, M.B.A., 1955. Sr. credit analyst, adminstrv. asst. No. Trust Co., Chgo., 1956-59; br. adminstrn. and credit supr. United Calif. Bank, San Francisco, 1959-62; asst. v.p. Bank of N.Mex., Albuquerque, 1962, v.p., 1962-65, sr. v.p., 1965-68, exec. v.p., 1968-70; chmn. bd. First Nat. Bank, Albuquerque, 1970-75; pres. David Livingston & Assos., Inc., 1975—; chmn. Ventana Internat., Ltd., 1987—; dir. South China Foods Ltd., Cellnet Corp., Walter Peak Resort Ltd. past pres.; trustee Albuquerque Acad.; past pres. Assn. of Commerce and Industry N.Mex., Manzano Sch., Albuquerque YMCA. Kappa Sigma. Presbyterian. Home: 601 Lido Park Dr Newport Beach CA 92663 Office: 2301 Dupont Ste 430 Irvine CA 92715 also: PO Box 25803 Albuquerque NM 87125

LIVINGSTON, LEE FRANKLIN, recreation industry executive, real estate and finance consultant; b. Boston, Feb. 20, 1942; s. William and Frances (Turner) L.; m. Elaine Wiesenfeld, June 9, 1968; children: Eli, Jed. Student Sch. Visual Arts, 1959-62, Georgetown U., 1964. With pub. relations and promotion dept. Cowles Communications Co., N.Y.C., 1961-62, Newsweek, N.Y.C., 1965-70; exec. mng. dir., sec., treas. Carolier Lanes Inc., North Brunswick, N.J., 1970-79; mng. dir., sec., treas. Anasarca Corp., North Brunswick, 1971—; pres. Imperial Cons., Inc.; ptnr. Bess & Co., Phila. Stock Exchange; cons. on charitable fund raising to various charities, 1971—. Active charities for autistic children and retarded citizens, Spl. Olympics. Served with C.E., U.S. Army, 1962-64. Recipient Am. Service award Girl Scouts U.S., Bronze Svc. award Spl. Olympics. Mem. N.J. Soc. for Retarded Citizens, Mu Sigma. Democrat. Clubs: Glenwood Country, Phila. Stock Exchange. Home: 12 Derby Ln RD 4 North Brunswick NJ 08902 Office: Carolier Lanes US Hwy One North Brunswick NJ 08902

LIVINGSTON, W. BRUCE, financial executive; b. Quincy, Mass., May 21, 1945; s. William and Florence Livingston; m. Carole Jane Dickey, June 17, 1941; children: Eric, Beth, Brad. BBA in Mgmt., Northeastern U., 1968, MBA in Fin., 1972. Underwriter USF&G Ins. Co., Boston, 1968-72; regional underwriter Comml. Union Assurance Co., Boston, 1972-75; fin. mgr. IMC Chem. Corp., Boston, 1975-78; mgr. employee benefits financing Raytheon Co., Lexington, Mass., 1978—. Home: 17 Pilgrim Rd Hingham MA 02043 Office: Raytheon Co 141 Spring St Lexington MA 02173

LLEWELLYN, FREDERICK EATON, mortuary executive; b. Mexico, Mo., Mar. 28, 1917; s. Frederick William and Mabel (Eaton) L.; BS, Calif. Inst. Tech., 1938; MBA (Baker scholar), Harvard, 1942; LLD, Pepperdine U., 1976; m. Jane Althouse, Aug. 15, 1940; children: Richard, John, Ann Marie. Asst. gen. mgr., dir. Forest Lawn Life Ins. Co., Glendale, Calif., 1940-41, pres., 1959-61; asst. to gen. mgr. Forest Lawn Meml. Park, Glendale, 1941-42, exec. v.p., 1946-66, gen. mgr., 1966—; pres. Forest Lawn Found., 1961—, Forest Lawn Co., 1967-88; chmn. bd. Am. Security & Fidelity Corp., Forest Lawn Co., 1988—, Founders Fin. Corp., Glendale, 1971—, Upstairs Galleries Inc., 1974—, Met. Computer Center, 1973-81, Calif. Citrus Corp., 1971-80, Forest Lawn Mortgage Corp., 1974-81; dir. Calif. Fed. Savs. & Loan, IT Corp. Recon Optical; chmn. Trust Services Am., Inc., 1983—. Mem. Found. for the 21st Century, 1986—, Orthopaedic Hosp., 1976—, chmn., 1980; chmn. Glendale Meml. Hosp., 1980, trustee, 1982-85; pres. So. Calif. Visitors Council, 1976-77; chmn. Council of Regents, Meml. Ct. of Honor. Mem. Mayor's Ad Hoc Energy Com., Los Angeles, 1973-74, Los Angeles County Reorgn. Commn., 1978; bd. dirs. Los Angeles County Heart Assn., 1957; trustee U. Redlands, 1966-77, chmn. bd., 1969-72; mem. Univ. Bd., Pepperdine Coll., 1966—, chmn. bd. regents, mem. exec. bd., 1977-86 ; bd. dirs. Pasadena Found. Med. Research, 1967-72, So. Calif. Bldg. Funds, 1975—, Met. YMCA Los Angeles, 1975—; trustee San Gabriel Valley council Boy Scouts Am., 1968-74; trustee Calif. Mus. Sci. and Industry, 1977—, pres., 1983-85, chmn., 1985-86; bd. govs. Dept. Mus. Natural History, Los Angeles County, 1968-72; mem. Los Angeles County Energy Commn., 1974-80; chmn. Mayor's Ad Hoc Water Crisis Commn., 1977—. Served with USNR, 1942-45. Decorated knight Order of Merit (Italy). Mem. Nat. Assn. Cemeteries (pres. 1956-57), Los Angeles Area C. of C. (dir. 1969-78, bd. chmn. 1974, pres. 1973), Calif. C. of C. (dir. 1977—), Newcomen Soc., Tau Beta Pi. Clubs: California, San Marino, Lincoln, One Hundred, Twilight, Walnut Elephant. Lodge: Order of St. Hubertus. Contbr. articles to profl. jours. Home: 1521 Virginia Rd San Marino CA 91108 Office: 1712 S Glendale Ave Glendale CA 91205

LLEWELLYN, JOHN SCHOFIELD, JR., food company executive; b. Amsterdam, N.Y., Jan. 10, 1935; s. John S. and Dorothea (Breedon) L.; m. Mary Martha Pallotta, June 9, 1962; children: Mary M., John S. III, Robert J., James P., Timothy J. AB, Holy Cross Coll., 1956; MBA, Harvard U., 1961. With mktg. Gen. Foods Corp., White Plains, N.Y., 1961-69, Sunshine Biscuit div. Am. Brands, N.Y.C., 1973-77; exec. v.p. Morton Frozen Foods div. ITT Continental Baking Co., 1977; pres. ITT Continental Baking Co., Charlottesville, Va., 1977-79; gen. mgr. Continental Kitchens ITT Continental Baking Co., Rye, 1980-81; sr. v.p. Ocean Spray Cranberries Inc., Plymouth, Mass., 1982-86; exec. v.p., chief operating officer Ocean Spray Cranberries Inc., Plymouth, 1986-87, pres., chief exec. officer, 1988—; bd. dirs. Superior Brands Inc., Quincy, Mass. Trustee Derby Acad., Hingham, Mass., 1984-88. Served to capt. USMC, 1957-63. Mem. Nat. Food Processors Assn. (bd. dirs.). Roman Catholic. Home: Steamboat Ln Hingham MA 02043 Office: Ocean Spray Cranberries Inc 1 Ocean Spray Dr Middleboro-Lakeville MA 02349

LLEWELLYN, LEONARD FRANK, real estate broker; b. Harlowton, Mont., Oct. 31, 1933; s. Ralph Emory and Frances Louise (Ewing) L.; m. Patricia Lockrom, Aug. 16, 1951 (div. 1955); m. Corrie J. Spruit, Aug. 16, 1974. BSEE, Eastern Mont. Coll. Edn., 1955. Enlisted USMC, 1956, commisioned capt., 1960, ret., 1967; owner Capitol Fla. Assn., Inc., Alexandra, Va., 1966-74; pres., owner Fla. Properties, Inc., Balt., 1968-74; chmn. Marco Beach Realty, Inc., Marco Island, Fla., 1975-82, Cons., Inc. of S.W. Fla., Marco Island, 1982—; dir. sales Plymouth Realty, Inc., Marco Island, 1987—; served as presdl. pilot for presidents Kennedy and Johnson, 1963-66; bd. dirs. Citizens and Southern Nat. Bank, Naples, Fla. Author: (manual) Aero-Gunnery Tactics, 1958. Bd. dirs. Collier County Conservancy, 1978-83; trustee Naples Community Hosp., 1980-83. Named Top Gun, USN, USMC, 1957, Citizen of Yr. Marco Island N.Y. Times and Marco Island Eagle, 1984. Mem. Marco Island Bd. Realtors (pres. 1982), marco Island C. of C. (pres. 1981-82, pres. emeritus 1984), Naples Forum (pres. 1985-86). Republican. Home: 812 Hideaway Circle E PH-143 Marco Island FL 33937 Office: Cos Inc of SW Fla Marco Island FL 33937

LLOYD, DAVID RICHARD, recreational facilities executive; b. Raleigh, N.C., Apr. 18, 1947; s. Claudie Milton and Letha Mae (Honeycutt) L.; m. Donna Karen Clayton, Aug. 31, 1968; children: David R. Jr., Scott C. BA, East Carolina U., 1969; postgrad., Duke U., 1978-79. Assoc. dir. pub. relations Putt-Putt Golf Courses of Am. Inc., Fayetteville, N.C., 1968-69, nat. franchise dir., 1969-72, pres., 1972-78, vice chmn., chief exec. officer, 1978—; pres. Putt-Putt Golf Courses Internat. Inc., Fayetteville, 1978—; bd. dirs. Peoples Bank & Trust Co., Fayetteville. Dir. tv commls., 1987 (Addy award 1988). Bd. dirs. Human Relations Commn., Fayetteville, 1969-70, Fayetteville Acad., 1982-85. Democrat. Methodist. Home: 1103 Offshore Dr Fayetteville NC 28305 Office: Putt-Putt Golf Courses of Am Inc 3007 Fort Bragg Rd Box 35237 Fayetteville NC 28303

LLOYD, DON KEITH, insurance company executive, lawyer; b. Am. Falls, Idaho, Aug. 7, 1944; s. Keith G. Lloyd and Lois Anderson; m. Judith Lynne Short, Mar. 9, 1967; children: Benjamin, Christopher, Daniel. BA, Portland State U., 1970; JD magna cum laude, Lewis & Clark Coll., 1973. Bar: Oreg. 1973, D.C. 1973. Assoc. Souther, Spalding, Kinsey, Williamson & Schwabe, Portland, Oreg., 1973-79; v.p., gen. counsel First Farwest Corp., 1979-83, exec. v.p., 1983-84, pres., 1984—, chief oper. officer, 1984-88, chief exec. officer, 1988—, also bd. dirs., bd. dirs. subs.; bd. dirs. Bus. Group on Health, Portland, Oreg. Life Guaranty Fund, Portland, UFMC health Systems, Inc., San Francisco. Mem. budget com. City of Troutdale (Oreg.), 1975-76; bd. dirs. Columbia Pacific coun. Boy Scouts Am., Portland, 1988—. Served with USMC, 1966-68, Vietnam. Mem. ABA, University Club, Columbia Edgewater Country Club (Portland). Republican. Mormon. Home: 2150 SE Crown Point Hwy Troutdale OR 97060 Office: First Farwest Corp 400 SW Sixth Ave Portland OR 97204

LLOYD, SCOTT SMITH, accountant; b. Logan, Utah, Sept. 25, 1957; s. Ray Hall and Barbara (Smith) L.; m. Wendy Mae Strachan, Mar. 23, 1985; 1 child, Jameson Scott. BS in Fin., Brigham Young U., 1982; MBA, U. Utah, 1983, BS in Acctg., 1984. CPA, Utah. Mem. staff Legis. Auditor Gen. Utah, Salt Lake City, 1983-85; internal auditor Am. Stores, Salt Lake City, 1985-86, mgr. gen. acctg., 1986, mgr. corp. planning, 1987—. Office: Am Stores Co 19100 Von Karman Ave Ste 500 Irvine CA 92715

LLOYD, SUSAN REBECCA, library technical assistant; b. Akron, Ohio, Apr. 19, 1959; d. Richard Morgan and Lois Irene (Murrin) Fawcett; m. Richard Wilson Lloyd, June 18, 1977; 1 child, Anna Rebecca. AA in Ednl. Tech., U. Akron, 1982. Library tech. asst. Ohio Edison Co. Corp. Library, Akron, 1981—; mem. library tech. adv. com. U. Akron, 1982-84. Home: 500 Marguerite Ave Cuyahoga Falls OH 44221 Office: Ohio Edison Co Corp Library 76 S Main St Akron OH 44308

LOBB, WILLIAM ATKINSON, financial services executive; b. Arlington, Pa., Apr. 21, 1951; s. Anthony William and Annamarie (Hilpert) L.; m. Maureen Veronique O'Hagan, July 7, 1977; children: William Atkinson III, Anthony Hagan. BS, Georgetown U., 1977. Account exec. Johnston Lemon, Washington, 1977-78; sr. account exec. Merrill Lynch, Alexandria, Va., 1979-83; asst. v.p. E.F. Hutton, Washington, 1983-85; sr. v.p., prt.-incharge Oppenheimer and Co., Inc., Atlanta, 1985—. Mem. Ga. Rep. Found., Nat. Assn. Securities Dealers (bd. arbitrators), Nat. Securities Traders Assn., Ga. Securities Assn., Securities Industry Assn. Clubs: University, Army-Navy, Settindown Creek. Office: Oppenheimer & Co Inc 3525 Piedmont Rd Bldg 7 Ste 600 Atlanta GA 30305

LOBBIA, JOHN E., utility company executive; b. 1941; married. BSEE, U. Detroit, 1964. With Detroit Edison Co., 1964—, asst. primary svc. engr. sales dept., 1964-68, acting asst. dist. mgr., dir. svc. planning, 1969-72, project mgr. constrn., 1972-74, dir. generation constrn. dept., 1974-75, mgr. Ann Arbor div., 1975-76, asst. mgr. Detroit div., 1976-78, mgr. Oakland div., 1978-80, asst. vice chmn., 1980-81, asst. v.p., mgr. fuel support, 1981-82, v.p. fin. svcs., 1982-87, exec. v.p., 1987-88, pres., chief operating officer, 1988—, also bd. dirs. Office: Detroit Edison Co 2000 2d Ave Detroit MI 48226 *

LOBEL, IRVING, clothing manufacturing company executive; b. Bklyn., Jan. 18, 1917; s. Benjamin and Jennie (Gross) L.; B.S. in Econs., U. Pa., 1937; m. Selma Agar, Jan. 23, 1943; children—Bonnie, Douglas, Robert. Partner, Lo-Bel Co., N.Y.C., 1937—. Bd. dirs. Cannon Points Coop., 1985—; mem. U. Pa. Ann. Giving Com.; mem. U. Pa. Anniversary com., treas. bd. cooperatives. Served with U.S. Army, 1942-46. Mem. Infants and Childrens Wear Assn. (dir.), Mu Sigma, Sigma Alpha Mu. Democrat. Jewish. Club: Inwood Country. Home: 45 Sutton Pl S New York NY 10022

LOBENFELD, PATRICIA MCCARRON, personal financial planning, debt management consultant; b. Rochester, N.Y., Oct. 1, 1954; d. Robert Joseph and Irene Frances (Wilber) McCarron; m. Eric Jay Lobenfeld, May 3, 1981; 1 child, Claire Anna. AS in Bus. Adminstrn., Monroe Community Coll., 1978; BA in Econs., CUNY, 1983. Sec. Eastman Kodak Co., Rochester, 1974-79; adminstrv. asst. Bradford Nat. Corp., N.Y.C., 1979; adminstrv. asst., office mgr. Bud H. Gibbs, P.C., N.Y.C., 1980-82; investment research asst. Brokaw Capital Mgmt. Co. Inc., N.Y.C., 1982-84; pres. Debt Busters Inc., N.Y.C., 1987—. Mem. NAFE, Internat. Assn. Fin. Planning. Office: Debt Busters Inc 246 W 38th St New York NY 10018

LOBERG, PETER ERIC, photographic company executive; b. Ithaca, N.Y., Apr. 9, 1943; s. Harry John and Aline (Johnson) L.; m. Jeanne Elizabeth Angelone, Nov. 6, 1971; children: Janine, Eric. BME, Cornell U., 1965. With Eastman-Kodak Co., Rochester, N.Y., 1969—, supr. maintenance and engring., 1978-86, dir. materials mgmt., 1987—. Asst. scoutmaster Boy Scouts Am., Honeoye Falls, N.Y., 1985-87. Lt. (j.g.) USN, 1966-69, Vietnam. Mem. Purchasing Mgmt. Assn., Rochester Yacht Club. Republican. Home: 40 Partridge Hill Honeoye Falls NY 14472 Office: Eastman Kodak Co Materials Mgmt Div 1669 Lake Ave Kodak Pk Rochester NY 14652

LOCHIANO, STEPHEN ANTHONY, infosystems specialist; b. Liberal, Kans., Mar. 2, 1949; s. Rocco LoChiano and Margie Louise (Pitts) LoChiano Wooden; m. Ellen Jane Walker, Aug. 28, 1971; children: Anthony Paul, Ryan Michael, Eric Stephen. BS in Bus. Adminstrn., U. Nebr., Lincoln, 1975; postgrad. U. Nebr., Omaha, 1980—. Office mgr. trainee Roberts Dairy, Omaha, 1976-78; controller Security Internat., Omaha, 1978, Jubilee Mfg. Co., Omaha, 1978-80, Omaha Box Co., 1983-85; controller Plastr Glas, Inc., Omaha, 1985-87; plant acct. Weyerhaeuser Co., Omaha, 1980-83, programmer Profl. Adminstrn. Svcs., 1987-88; bus. mgr. Word Data Corp., Omaha, 1988—. Active Coll. Bus. Adminstrn. Action Community, Citizens CBA Action Coun. Sgt. U.S. Army, 1973-75. Mem. Nat. Assn. Accts. (controllers council 1984—), Internat. Soc. Wang Users, Toastmasters (dist. treas. 1980-81), U. Nebr. Alumni Assn. Republican. Lutheran. Club: Park Ave. Health (Omaha). Avocations: camping, computer programming. Home: 10205 R St Omaha NE 68127 Office: Word Data Corp 3172 Dodge St Omaha NE 68131

LOCHTENBERG, BERNARD HENDRIK, chemical company executive; b. Singapore, Mar. 10, 1931; came to U.S., 1979; s. Jan Bernard and Anna Lochtenberg; m. Margaret Lynch, June 16, 1956; children: Jan, Anna, Mark, Michael, Benedict, Margaret, Lucy. B.Engring., U. Western Australia, 1953; D. Phil., Oxford U., 1956. Planning and devel. mgr. ICI Australia, Melbourne, 1971-73; dir. plastics div. ICI PLC Welwyn Garden City, Eng., 1973-79; sr. v.p. ICI Americas, Inc., Wilmington, Del., 1979-88; prin. exec. officer ICI Splty. Chems., Wilmington, 1984-88; pres., chief exec. officer C-I-L, Inc., North York, Ont., Can., 1988—; bd. dirs. Wilmington Savs. Fund Soc., 1987—. Trustee Wilmington Med. Ctr., 1980-88, Sanford Sch., Hockessin, Del., 1982-88, United Negro Coll. Fund, 1987-88; bd. dirs. Del. YMCA, 1982-87, Del. Symphony, 1985-88. Australian Rhodes scholar, 1954-56. Fellow Plastics and Rubber Inst.; mem. Soc. Chem. Industry. Clubs: Leander Rowing (Henley-on-Thames, Eng.); Greenville Country (Del.). Office: C-I-L Inc, PO Box 200 Sta A, North York, ON Canada M2N 6H2

LOCK, RICHARD WILLIAM, packaging company executive; b. N.Y.C., Oct. 5, 1931; s. Albert and Catherine Dorothy (Magnus) L.; m. Elizabeth Louise Kenney, Nov. 2, 1957; children—Albert William, Dorothy Louise

Lock Kuhl, John David. B.S., Rutgers U., 1953; M.B.A., N.Y. U., 1958. Acct. Gen. Electric Co., 1953-54, Union Carbide Co., N.Y.C., 1956-58; div. controller St. Regis Paper Co., Houston, 1959-62; v.p., treas. Owens-Illinois, Inc., Toledo, 1962-64, supr. programmer office methods and data processing, 1964-65, asst. mgr. data processing procedures, 1965-67, mgr. systems analysis and devel., 1967-68, mgr. corp. systems analysis and devel., 1968-70, dir. corp. systems and data processing, 1970-72, gen. mgr. electro/optical display, 1972-75, treas., 1975-80, v.p., dir. corp. planning, 1980-84, v.p., asst. chief fin. officer, treas., 1984—. Mem. adv. bd. Toledo Salvation Army, 1973—, chmn., 1974-77; pres. Toledo Area Govtl. Research Assn., 1978-79; bd. dirs. Riverside Hosp. Found., Toledo, 1982—. Served with USAF, 1954-56. Mem. Fin. Execs. Inst., Am. Soc. Corp. Secs., Phi Beta Kappa. Republican. Lutheran. Club: Toledo. Home: 6110 Jeffrey Ln Sylvania OH 43560 Office: Owens-Ill Inc One Seagate Toledo OH 43666

LOCKE, CHARLES STANLEY, manufacturing company executive, director; b. Laurel, Miss., Mar. 5, 1929; s. Richard C. and Florence (Parker) L.; m. NoraLou Fulkerson, Mar. 15, 1952; children: Cathy, Stanley, Lauren, Pamela. BBA, U. Miss., 1952, MS in Acctg., 1955. With audit staff Price Waterhouse & Co., New Orleans, 1955-58; with Comml. Analysis for Converting div. Westvaco, Inc., 1958-64; controller A.E. Staley Mfg. Co., 1964-69; v.p. fin., dir., mem. exec. com. Brown Co., Pasadena, Calif., 1969-73; sr. v.p., mem. exec. com. Allen Group Inc., Melville, N.Y., 1973-75; v.p. fin., dir. Morton Thiokol, Inc. (formerly Morton-Norwich Products, Inc.), Chgo., 1975-80, pres., chief operating officer, dir., Mar. 1980, pres., chief exec. officer, dir., Apr. 1980, pres., chief exec. officer, chmn. bd., Aug. 1980, chmn. bd., chief exec. officer, dir., 1981-83, chmn. bd., chief exec. officer, pres., dir., 1983-84, chmn. bd., chief exec. officer, dir., 1984—; bd. dirs. Avon Products, Inc., First Chgo. Corp., First Nat. Bank Chgo., NICOR, Inc., No. Ill. Gas Corp. Trustee Mus. Sci. and Industry, Chgo., U. of Chgo.; mem. The Conf. Bd.; bd. dirs. The Lyric Opera, Chgo. With U.S. Army, 1952-54. Mem. Beta Alpha Psi. Clubs: Sky, Chgo., Comml., Econ., Tower, Mid-Am. (com.), Execs. (Chgo.) (mem. adv. bd.), Room One Hundred; Sunset Ridge Country (Northfield, Ill.); Old Elm Country (Lake Forest, Ill.). Home: 1504 N Waukegan Rd Lake Forest IL 60045 Office: Morton Thiokol Inc 110 N Wacker Dr Chicago IL 60606

LOCKETT, CLARENCE EARNEST, corporate executive; b. Kenard, Tex., Oct. 14, 1946; s. Mattie (Vaughn) L.; m. Gloria Hopson, Sept. 5, 1970; children: Kristin, Kara, Karlton. BS in Acctg., Hampton U., 1969; MBA in Mgmt., U. Cent. Ark., 1976; JD, U. Ark., Little Rock, 1980. Bar: Pa. 1984. With Chicopee div. Johnson & Johnson, New Brunswick, N.J., 1969—, asst. corp. controller, 1985-86, v.p. info. and control Chicppee div., 1986—. Pastor 1st Bapt. Ch., Langhorne, Pa.; bd. dirs. Cen. N.J. chpt. ARC, 1985—. Recipient Leadership award Cen. N.J. chpt. ARC, 1987. Mem. Pa. Bar Assn. Home: 919 Pickering Dr Yardley PA 19067

LOCKHART, JAMES BICKNELL, III, insurance brokerage firm executive; b. White Plains, N.Y., May 13, 1946; s. James Bicknell Jr. and Mary Ann (Riegel) L.; m. Carolyn Strahan Zoephel, June 17, 1972; children: James Bicknell IV, Grace Strahan. BA, Yale U., 1968; MBA, Harvard U., 1974. Asst. treas. Gulf Oil(E.H.), London, 1979-80; fin. dir. Gulf Oil Belgium, Brussels, 1980-81; sr. mgr. Gulf Oil Corp., Pitts., 1982-83, asst. treas., 1982-83; v.p., treas. Alexander and Alexander Services, N.Y.C., 1983—. Contbr. articles to profl. jours. Treas. Reps. Abroad, London, 1978-80. Served to lt. USN, 1969-72. Fellow Assn. Corp. Treas. (England); mem. Nat. Assn. Corp. Treas. Office: Alexander and Alexander Svcs 1211 Ave of the Americas New York NY 10030

LOCKLIN, WILLIAM RAY, financial planner; b. Joplin, Mo., Dec. 16, 1942; s. Jack and Audrey R. (Miller) L.; B.S. in Mech. Engring., U. Ariz., 1966, M.B.A., 1968; m. Karen E. Bjorklund, Dec. 29, 1979; children—Kevin Russell, Matthew William. Securities and ins. sales rep. Bell Funding Corp., Los Angeles, 1970-72; gen. agt., mgr., 1972-76; fin. planner Bill Locklin and Co., Santa Monica, Calif.; prin., mgr. Fin. Planners Equity Corp., Santa Monica; now stockholder, registered prin. Associated Planners Securities Corp. Cert. fin. planner; registered investment adv.; C.L.U. Mem. Internat. Assn. Fin. Planning (dir. 1983—, v.p. 1984-87, pres. 1987-88, chmn. bd. 1988—), Inst. Cert. Fin. Planners. Office: 27349 Jefferson Ave Ste 208 Rancho Temecula CA 92390

LOCKTON, DAVID BALLARD, business executive; b. Indpls., Mar. 28, 1937; s. Richard Curtis and Violet (Ballard) L.; m. Mary Shullenberger, Aug. 1961 (div. Dec. 1969); children: Jennifer Anne, Mary Wendell; m. Kathy Austin, Apr. 3, 1971; 1 child, Richard A. BA, Yale U., 1959; JD, U. Va., 1962; cert., Stanford U., 1972. Ptnr. Lockton and Scopelitis, Inc., Indpls., 1965-70; pres., chief exec. officer Ontario (Calif.) Motor Speedway, 1968-71; chief exec. off., publisher, owner Calif. Bus. Mag., L.A., 1972-75; pres., chief exec. officer Lola Grand Prix, Ltd., L.A., 1976-79; founder, chief exec. officer Dataspeed, Inc., San Mateo, Calif., 1980-85; pres., chief exec. officer Network , Inc. (formerly Interactive Game Network, Inc.), Menlo Park, Calif., 1986—; co-founder, bd. dirs. A.Z.L. Resources, Inc., 1964-75; co-founder, chmn. Repair Shop Systems, Inc., 1986; dir. Enseco, Inc., 1986; nationwide lectr. on entrepreneurship, info. tech. Patentee in field. Recipient Meritorious Svc. award Soc. Automotive Engrs., 1970. Mem. Jonathan Club (L.A.), Crooked Stice Golf Club, Penrod Soc. Club (co-founder, Indpls.). Republican. Episcopalian. Home: 97 Hawthorn Dr Atherton CA 94025

LOCKWOOD, FRANK JAMES, manufacturing company executive; b. San Bernadino, Calif., Oct. 30, 1931; s. John Ellis and Sarah Grace (Roberts) L.; children from previous marraige: Fay, Frank, Hedy, Jonnie, George, Katherine, Bill, Dena; m. 2d. Crystal Marie Miller, 1986. Student, Southeast City Coll., Chgo., 1955, Ill. Inst. Tech., 1963-64, Bogan Jr. Coll., Chgo., 1966. Foreman Hupp Aviation, Chgo., 1951-60; dept. head UARCO, Inc., Chgo., 1960-68; pres. XACT Machine & Engring., Chgo., 1968—; chmn. bd., pres., bd. dirs. Lockwood Engring., Inc., Chgo.; Ill. Nat. Corp., Chgo., and cons. engr., Chgo. Patentee printing equipment, beverage cans, gasoline pump dispenser "Super Pin", bus. forms equipment. Participant Forest Land Mgmt. Program; mem. Ill. Ambassadors; commr. Econ. Develop. Commn., Mt. Vernon, Ill., 1985. Served with USN, 1948-50. Named Chgo. Ridge Father of the Yr., 1964. Mem. Ill. Divers' Assn. (pres. 1961-62). Lodge: Masons (32 degree), Shriners (past master 2). Home: RR 1 Texico IL 62889 Office: 7011 W Archer Ave Chicago IL 60638

LOCKWOOD, LEIGH WILLARD, periodical company executive; b. New Rochelle, N.Y., Oct. 16, 1947; s. Robert Arthur and Ellen Estelle (Willard) L.; m. Carol Ann Settle, Sept. 9, 1970; children: Erin, Lisa, Ryan. BA, U. Pacific, 1969; postgrad. Am. Grad. Sch. Internat. Mgmt., 1972, Stanford Exec. Program for Smaller Cos., 1979. Procedures analyst Doubleday & Co., N.Y.C., 1973; asst. mgr. Distribuidora de Impresos S.A., Mexico, 1974-76, gen. mgr., 1977-84; v.p. Feffer & Simons, Inc., 1981-83, exec. v.p., 1983-84, v.p. Periodical Mgmt. Group, San Antonio, 1984-86; chief exec. officer, periodicals div. Clark Group, Trenton, N.J., 1987—. Served with U.S. Army, 1969-71. Decorated Joint Service Commendation medal. Office: The Clark Group PO Box 438 Trenton NJ 08603

LOCKWOOD, MOLLY ANN, communications company executive; b. London, Sept. 19, 1936; d. Warren Sewell and Ann Frances (Gleason) L.; BS, Pa. State U., 1958. With exec. tng. program Lord & Taylor, N.Y.C., 1958-60; assoc. merchandising editor House & Garden Mag., N.Y.C., 1960-65; advt. dir. Status Mag., N.Y.C., 1965-70; merchandising dir. Holiday Mag., N.Y.C., 1970; account mgr. Ladies' Home Journal Mag., N.Y.C., 1970-72; adv. dir. Girl Talk Mag., N.Y.C., 1972-74; mktg. dir./assos. pub. East/West Network Mag., N.Y.C., 1974-77; pres., chief exec. officer, ptnr. Catalyst Communications, Inc., N.Y.C., 1977—; pres. Catalyst Pub. Inc., 1987—; sec. bd. 244 Madison Realty Corp., 1984—; mktg. and sales dir. Mus. Mag., 1979-83. Mem. Advt. Women N.Y., Rear Guard, Kappa Kappa Gamma Alumnae Assn., Liberty Club. Home: 1133 Park Ave New York NY 10128 Office: Catalyst Communications Inc 244 Madison Ave New York NY 10016

LODMELL, DEAN WALTER, investment banker; b. N.Y.C., July 19, 1959; s. Dean Struthers and Marilyn (Maki) L.; m. Diane M. Sweet, Nov. 15, 1985. AB, Dartmouth Coll., 1981; MBA, Harvard U., 1985. Field engr. Ebasco Services, Inc., N.Y.C., 1979-80; assoc. Capital Devel. Co., Olympia, Wash., 1980-83; prin. Kideral Internat., N.Y.C., 1983—. Mem. Harvard Club.

LO DUCA, GERARD CHARLES, manufacturing company executive; b. Malverne, N.Y., Nov. 1, 1954; s. Arnold and Helen (Tiersch) Lo D.; m. Donna Lee Glover, Sept. 8, 1979; 1 child, Aimee. BS in Mktg., St. John's U., 1976. Sales rep. IPCO Hosp. Supply Co., Piscataway, N.J., 1977-79, Med. Electronics Co., Boston, 1979-80; v.p., officer product devel. and mktg. Med. Action Industries, Farmingdale, N.Y., 1980—. Republican. Roman Catholic. Office: Med Action Industries 1934 New Hwy Farmingdale NY 11735

LODWICK, MICHAEL WAYNE, lawyer; b. New Orleans, Sept. 21, 1946; s. Frank Tillman Jr. and Grace Evelyn (Hilty) L.; m. Donna Peirce, June 15, 1968 (div.); children: Sarah Peirce, Jane Durborow, Elizabeth Hilty; m. Dory Scott, Aug. 9, 1986 (div.). BA, La. State U., 1968; MA, Tulane U., 1972, PhD, 1976; JD, Loyola U., New Orleans, 1981. Bar: La., U.S. Dist. Ct. (ea. dist.) La. 1981, U.S. Ct. Appeals (5th cir.) 1981, U.S. Ct. Appeals (D.C. cir.) 1982, U.S. Ct. Appeals (11th cir.) 1986, U.S. Supreme Ct., 1987. Instr. to asst. prof. Tulane U., New Orleans, 1976-78; assoc. Barham & Churchill, New Orleans, 1981-83, O'Neil, Eichin & Miller, New Orleans, 1983-87, ptnr., 1987—. Editor, co-founder and pub. Plantation Soc. in Americas jour., 1979-83, 86—; editor-in-chief Loyola Law Rev., 1980-81; contrbr. articles to profl. jours. Mem. New Orleans Symphony Chorus, 1985—. Tulane U. fellow, 1970-72; recipient Loyola U. Law Rev. Honor award, 1981, Loyola Law Alumni award, 1981. Mem. ABA, La. State Bar Assn., New Orleans Bar Assn., Maritime Law Assn. U.S., Assn. Trial Lawyers Am. Home: 3530 Houma Blvd #908 Metairie LA 70006 Office: O'Neil Eichin & Miller 1 Poydras Plaza Ste 2600 New Orleans LA 70113

LOEB, JAN H., investment banker, securities analyst; b. N.Y.C., Oct. 21, 1958; s. Eric and Sonya (Bechhofer) L.; m. Bluma Irene Steinberg, Apr. 1, 1962; children: Marc David, Leah, Aaron, Ann. BBA in Fin. and Investments, Baruch Coll., 1980. Securities analyst Gruntal & Co., N.Y.C., 1980-83; securities analyst, prin. L.F. Rothschild, N.Y.C., 1983-88; pres. Loeb Fin. Sevcs., 1988—. Mem. Balt. Hebrew Burial Soc., Baruch Coll. Alumni Assn. (bd. dirs. 1983-88). Jewish. Office: Loeb Fin Svc 10451 Mill Run Circle Owings Mills MD 21117

LOEB, JEROME THOMAS, retail executive; b. St. Louis, Sept. 13, 1940; s. Harry W. and Marjorie T. Loeb; m. Carol Bodenheimer, June 15, 1963; children: Daniel W, Kelly E. BS, Tufts U., 1962; MA, Washington U., St. Louis, 1964. Asst. dir. rsch., dir. EDP, div. v.p., dir. mgmt. info. scvs. Famous-Barr div. May Dept. Stores Co., St. Louis, 1964-74, v.p. mgmt. info. svcs./EDP parent co., 1974-77, sr. v.p., chief fin. officer Hecht's div., Washington, 1977-79; exec. v.p. devel. May Dept. Stores Co., St. Louis, 1979-81, exec. v.p., chief fin. officer, 1981—, vice chmn., chief fin. officer, 1986—; also bd. dirs.; bd. dirs. Boatmen's Trust Co. Vice chmn. bd. dirs. Jr. Achievement of Mississippi Valley, 1982—; bd. dirs. Jr. Achievement Nat. Bd., 1988—; vice-chmn., bd. dirs. Jewish Hosp. St. Louis, 1984—. Mem. Westwood Country Club. Office: The May Dept Stores Co 611 Olive St Saint Louis MO 63101

LOEB, MARVIN PHILLIP, entrepreneur; b. Chgo., Sept. 20, 1926; s. Jacob M. and Goldie (Schloss) L.; m. Rhoda M. Finck, Aug. 5, 1950; children: Jacqueline A., Marcia H., Wendy J., Alan. E. BS in Chemistry and Math., U. Ill., 1948. Pres. Tello Corp., Chgo., 1948-62, Mayflower Investors Inc., Chgo., 1962-65, Progressive Fin. Corp., Chgo., 1966-68, Medequip Corp., Chgo., 1969-70; chmn. Telemed Corp, Chgo., 1969-70; pres. Mediclinic Corp., Chgo., 1971—, Loeb & Co., Torrance, Calif., 1965—; chmn. Trimedyne Inc., Tustin, Calif., 1978—, Pharmatec Inc., Gainesville, Fla., 1980—, Gynex Inc., Deerfield, Ill., 1986—, Automedix Scis. Inc., Torrance, 1986—; vice chmn. Petrogen Inc., Arlington Heights, Ill., 1981—; chmn. Cardiomedics Inc., Torrance, 1986—, Xtramedics Inc., Deerfield, 1986—, Ultramedics Inc., Dolton, Ill., 1988—, Contracap Inc., Deerfield, 1988—. Inventor in field. Served with U.S. Navy, 1944-46. Mem. AAAS, N.Y. Acad. Scis., Internat. Soc. for Artificial Organs, Am. Heart Assn., Am. Diabetes Assn. Office: Loeb & Co 19401 S Vermont #B100 Torrance CA 90502

LOEB, PETER KENNETH, investment banker; b. N.Y.C., Apr. 8, 1936; s. Carl M. and Lucille H. (Schamberg) L.; m. Jeanette Winter, Nov. 1, 1980; 1 child, Alexander Winter; children by previous marriage: Peter Kenneth, Karen Elizabeth, James Matthew. BA, Yale U., 1958; MBA, Columbia U., 1961. 1st v.p. Paine Webber Inc., N.Y.C., 1983—; mem. com. on securities Am. Stock Exchange, 1978-80; mem. del. to Beijing Symposium New York Stock Exchange, 1986. Mem. Mus. Modern Art (contbg.), Met. Mus. Art (contbg.), Met. Opera Guild, Friends of the Philharm., Friends of Carnegie Hall, Friends of Kennedy Ctr., Statue of Liberty/Ellis Island Found., Wall St. com. N.Y. Urban Coalition, 1969-71; co-head devel. com., 1985— N.Y. State Spl. Olympics, bd. dirs. 1985—, games official, coach, 1980—; mem. fin. devel. com. Internat. Special Olympics, 1986—; tournament com. Westchester Golf Classic, 1979-83, co-chmn. Marihale, 1984—; vice chmn. Pacesetter com. Greater N.Y. council Boy Scouts Am., 1966-67; mem. exec. bd. new leadership div. Fedn. Jewish Philanthropies, 1963-64; trustee Langeloth Found., 1972—; mem. adv. bd. Atoms Track Club-Bedford-Stuyvesant, 1970—; vice chmn. U.S. Olympic Invitational Track Meet, 1986—; bd. dirs., pres. N.Y.C. Baseball Fedn., 1968—; trustee Columbia U., 1979-85, mem. adv. bd., com. univ. investments 1977-85; trustee N.Y. Infirmary, Beekman Downtown Hosp., 1978-85; trustee Allen-Stevenson Sch., 1969—; vice chmn. alumni bd. Columbia U., mem. com. on univ. investments, 1977-85; mem. adv. council Columbia Bus. Sch., alumni counseling bd., 1970—, pres. Columbia Bus. Assocs., 1971-73, fund chmn., 1964-66. Recipient Disting. Service award N.Y.C. Baseball Fedn., 1976; Alumni medal for conspicuous service Columbia U., 1975; Alumni medal for conspicuous service Bus. Sch., 1976. Mem. Securities Traders Assn. N.Y., Investment Assn. N.Y. (exec. bd. 1969), Securities Industry Assn. (governing council 1977-79, minority capital com. 1980-85, trustee Econ. Edn. Found. 1986—), Nat. Assn. Security Dealers (chmn. dist. 12 com. 1981, gov. 1982-85, chmn. corp. fin. com. 1983-86, vice-chmn. fin. 1984, mem. arbitration com. 1986—), Columbia Grad. Sch. Bus. Alumni Assn. (dir., pres. 1971-74), Columbia U. Alumni Fedn. (bd. dirs. 1971-72), SAR, Beta Gamma Sigma, Alpha Kappa Psi, Phi Gamma Delta. Clubs: City Midday, Bond, Century Country (dir. 1973-77), Madison Square Garden, Doubles. Home: 17 E 89th St New York NY 10128 Office: Paine Webber Inc 1285 Ave of the Americas New York NY 10019

LOEB, WALTER FERDINAND, retail analyst; b. Darmstadt, Fed. Republic of Germany, Jan. 28, 1925; came to U.S., 1940,; s. Charles and Henny (Cohn) L.; m. Phyllis Bell, June 15, 1958; children: Lisa Reneé, Karen Ruth, Martha Ellen. BA, NYU, 1949. Asst. gen. merchandise mgr. May Co., Cleve., 1961-69; sr. retail cons. P.K. Halstead & Assocs., Brussels and N.Y.C., 1969-73; sr. retail analyst Johnson Redbook Svcs., N.Y.C., 1973-74; prin. Morgan Stanley & Co., Inc., N.Y.C., 1974—; speaker at profl. meetings, U.S., France, Japan, Austria and Federal Republic of Germany. Mem. exec. com. Community Synagogue, Rye, N.Y., 1980-86, bd. dirs., 1988—. Cpl. U.S. Army, 1943-46, ETO. Mem. NYU Fin. Club (pres. 1986), Washington Sq. Coll. Alumni Assn. (pres. 1987), Merchandise Analyst Soc. (pres. 1977), N.Y. Soc. Security Analysts, Forecasters Club, All Am. Rsch. Team of Inst. Investors. Home: 7 Stonycrest Rd Rye NY 10580 Office: Morgan Stanley & Co Inc 1251 Ave of Americas New York NY 10020

LOEFFEL, BRUCE, software company executive, consultant; b. Bklyn., Aug. 13, 1943; s. Samuel and Loretta (Bleiweiss) L.; m. Gail Wildman, Dec. 3, 1966; children—Alisa, Joshua. B.B.A., Pace U., 1966; M.B.A., St. John's U., 1971. Certified data processor. Mgr. fin. systems Gibbs & Hill Inc., N.Y.C., 1973-76; mgr. sales/tech. support Mgmt. Sci. Am. Inc., Fort Lee, N.J., 1976-81; dir. mktg. Info. Scis., Inc., Montvale, N.J., 1981-82; dir. bus. devel. Cullinet Software, Inc., Westwood, Mass., 1982-85; v.p. mktg. Online/Data Base Software Inc., Pearl River, N.Y., 1985—; cons. Online/Data Base Specialists, New City, N.Y., 1982-85. Served with U.S. Army, 1966-71. Mem. Inst. Cert. of Computer Profls. Democrat. Jewish. Avocations: sports; electronics. Home: 350 Phillips Hill Rd New City NY 10956 Office: Online Database Software Inc 1 Blue Hill Pla Pearl River NY 10965

LOEFFLER, DAVID E., transportation executive; b. Oswego, Kans., Aug. 25, 1946; s. Edwin H. and Agnes M. (Pinter) L.; m. Cynthia K. Rothove, Feb. 2, 1975; children: Kimberly M., Wesley Todd. BBA, Pittsburg (Kans.) State U., 1969. Audit mgr.in./ Arthur Andersen & Co., Kansas City, Mo., 1969-76; asst. controller Kansas City Power and Light, 1976-78; sr. v.p. fin./adminstrn. Yellow Freight System, Inc., Overland Park, Kans., 1978—. Dean's adv. council Iowa State U., Ames, 1987; mem. mgmt. adv. bd. U. Mo., Columbia, 1987; bd. advisors Pittsburg State U. Sch. Bus. and Econs., 1987. Served with USAR, 1968-74. Named Outstanding Young Alumni Pittsburg State U., 1979. Mem. Nat. Acctg. and Fin. Coun. (pres.-elect 1988), Am. Trucking Assns. Republican. Presbyterian. Club: Blue Hill Country. Office: Yellow Freight SystemInc Del 10990 Roe Ave Box 7563 Overland Park KS 66207

LOEFFLER, WILLIAM ROBERT, quality productivity specialist, engineering educator; b. Cleve., Aug. 31, 1949; s. Harry T. and Frances R. (Pearson) L.; m. Beth Ann Manderfield, Dec. 1978; children—Lindsay Brooke, Kelly Lynn, Robert Jason. B.A., Wittenberg U., 1971; M.A., SUNY-Stony Brook, 1972; Ed. Specialist, U. Toledo, 1979; Ph.D., U. Mich., 1984. Dir. alternate learning ctr. Lucas County Schs., Toledo, 1977-79; dir. chem. and metall. services Toledo Testing Lab., 1979-82; pres. Chem. Resources, Lambertville, Mich., 1982-83; v.p. Benchmark Techs., Toledo, 1983-86; pres. Loeffler Group, Inc., 1986—; pres. Tech. Soc. Toledo, 1985-86; conf. chmn. Am. Soc. Quality Control. Deming Conf., Toledo, 1984; mem. Nat. Task Force ALARA Atomic Indsl. Forum, Washington; congl. sci. counselor PACCOS, Ohio; Ford Motor Co. prof. Statis. quality studies Eastern Mich. U., 1986. . Editor Jour. Toledo Tech. Topics 1982—; asst. editor Jour. English Quarterly, 1976-77. Contbr. articles to profl. jours. Vice chmn. Pvt. Industry Council, Monroe County, Mich., 1983, 84; chmn. Bus.-Industry-Edn. Day Toledo C. of C., 1984; trustee Bedford Pub. Schs., Mich., 1982-85; chmn. Robotics Internat., 1985. Recipient Malcolm Baldrige Nat. Quality award, 1988, 89. Fellow SUNY-Stony Brook 1975-76, Cambridge U. 1976-77. Recipient Harvard Book award 1967. Mem. Am. Chem. Soc. (chmn. Toledo chapt. 1984), Am. Soc. Non-Destructive Testing, Phi Delta Kappa, Phi Kappa Phi. Methodist. Club: U. Mich. (Toledo). Lodge: Rotary. Office: Loeffler Group Inc 3018S Republic Blvd Ste 302 Toledo OH 43615

LOEN, RAYMOND ORDELL, management consultant; b. Howard, S.D., July 15, 1924; s. Lauris and Selina Edith (Langorgen) L.; m. Omeline Janelle, June 17, 1950; children: Kurtis, Jon, Philip, Pamela, Brock. BS, Columbia U., 1948, MS, 1949. Salesman, sales trainer, city sales mgr. Uarco, Inc., N.Y.C. and Phila., 1949-53; staff cons., sr. cons. H.B. Maynard & Co., Inc., Pitts., 1953-59; sales tng. mgr., dir. mgmt. services Fibreboard Corp., San Francisco, 1959-63; prin. R.O. Loen Co., San Anselmo, Calif. and Lake Oswego, Oreg., 1963—; founder, dir. Loen, Brandt Inc., Palo Alto, Calif. 1965-70; bd. dirs., founder Swift Energy Co., Houston. Author: Manage More by Doing Less, 1971; contbr. articles to profl. jours. Served to lt. (j.g.) USNR, 1943-46, PTO. Mem. Salmon and Steelhead Anglers of Oreg., Sons of Norway, Mountain Park Racquet Club, Columbia Univ. Sch. Bus. Alumni Assn., Oreg. Trout, Alpha Kappa Psi. Republican.

LOEVI, FRANCIS JOSEPH, JR., consulting company executive; b. N.Y.C., Mar. 29, 1945; s. Francis J. and Ruth E. (DeJongh) L. B.A. in Labor Mgmt. Relations, Pa. State U., 1967; M.S. Indsl. Relations, Cornell U., 1971. Instr. labor relations U. Mo., Columbia, 1969-70; labor relations advisor HEW, Washington, 1970-74; labor relations officer Dept. Edn., Washington, 1974-77; pres. Axon Assocs., Inc., Washington, 1977—; co-pub. LRP Publs., Washington, 1979—; pres. Potomac Systems, Inc., Washington 1982—; pres. Pub. Adminstrn. Forum, 1985—; mem. AAA Nat. Labor Panel, N.Y.C., 1973—. Author: Arbitration and the Federal Sector Advocate, 1978; Federal Sector Collective Bargaining: A Management Guide, 1980. Contbr. articles to profl. jours. Mem. Soc. Fed. Labor Relations Profls. (pres. 1973-74, dir. 1974-78). Home: 902 Oronoco St Alexandria VA 22314 Office: Axon Group 225 Reinekers Ln Alexandria VA 22314

LOEVINGER, LEE, lawyer; b. St. Paul, Apr. 24, 1913; s. Gustavus and Millie (Strouse) L.; m. Ruth Howe, Mar. 4, 1950; children: Barbara L., Eric H., Peter H. BA summa cum laude, U. Minn., 1933, JD, 1936. Bar: Minn. 1936, Mo. 1937, D.C. 1966, U.S. Supreme Ct., 1941. Assoc. Watson, Ess, Groner, Barnett & Whittaker, Kansas City, Mo., 1936-37; atty., regional atty. NLRB, 1937-41; with antitrust div. Dept. Justice, 1941-46; ptnr. Larson, Loevinger, Lindquist & Fraser, Mpls., 1946-60; assoc. justice Minn. Supreme Ct., 1960-61; asst. U.S. atty. gen. charge antitrust div. Dept. Justice, 1961-63; commr. FCC, 1963-68; ptnr. Hogan & Hartson, Washington, 1968-85; of counsel Hogan & Hartson, 1986—; v.p., dir. Craig-Hallum Corp., Mpls., 1968-73; dir. Petrolite Corp., St. Louis., 1978-83; U.S. rep. com. on restrictive bus. practices Orgn. for Econ. Cooperation and Devel., 1961-64; spl. asst. to U.S. atty. gen., 1963-64; spl. counsel com. small bus. U.S. Senate, 1951-52; lectr. U. Minn., 1953-60; vis. prof. jurisprudence U. Minn. (Law Sch.), 1961; professorial lectr. Am. U., 1968-70; chmn. Minn. Atomic Devel. Problems Com., 1957-59; mem. Adminstrv. Conf. U.S., 1972-74; del. White House Conf. on Inflation, 1974; U.S. del. UNESCO Conf. on Mass Media, 1975, Internat. Telecommunications Conf. on Radio Frequencies, 1964, 66. Author: The Law of Free Enterprise, 1949, An Introduction to Legal Logic, 1952, Defending Antitrust Lawsuits, 1977; author first article to use term-Jurimetrics, 1949; contbr. articles to profl. jours.; editor, contbr.: Basic Data on Atomic Devel. Problems in Minnesota, 1958; adv. bd. Antitrust Bulletin, Jurimetrics Jour. Served to lt. comdr. USNR, 1942-45. Recipient Outstanding Achievement award U. Minn., 1968; Freedoms Found. award, 1977, 84. Mem. ABA (del. of sci. and tech. sect. to Ho. of Dels. 1974-80, del. to joint conf. with AAAS 1974-76, liaison 1984—, chmn. sci. and tech. sect. 1982-83, council 1986—, standing com. on nat. conf. groups), Minn. Bar Assn., Hennepin County Bar Assn., D.C. Bar Assn., FCC Bar Assn., AAAS, Broadcast Pioneers, U.S. C. of C. (antitrust council), Am. Arbitration Assn. (comml. panel), Phi Beta Kappa, Sigma Xi, Delta Sigma Rho, Sigma Delta Chi, Phi Delta Gamma, Tau Kappa Alpha, Alpha Epsilon Rho. Clubs: Cosmos, City Club (Washington). Home: 5600 Wisconsin Ave Apt 17D Chevy Chase MD 20815 Office: Hogan & Hartson 555 13th St NW Washington DC 20004

LOEW, PATRICIA ANN, small business owner; b. Farmville, Va., Aug. 28, 1943; d. Joseph Leo and Delores (McGurk) Dooley; m. Hubert Victor Loew; children: Moritz, Franz. BA, Clarke Coll., Dubuque, Iowa, 1965; MA, Pius XII Inst. Fine Arts, Florence, Italy, 1966. Chmn. fine arts dept. Little Flower High Sch., Chgo., 1966-68; staff painter Otto Galleries, Vienna, Austria, 1968-71; retail store owner Austrian Ski & Sports Haus, Country Club Hills, Ill., 1971—; fashion coord. Marshall Field & Co., Chgo., 1966-67; recreational therapist State of Ill. Mental Health Ctr., Tinley Park, 1966-68; asst. translator Richard Neutra Architect, Vienna, 1971; wholesale importer Franz Klammer USA, Ltd., 1986—. Active Frankfort, Ill. chpt. PTA; mem. Friends of the Libr. Frankfort. Asst. Art Award scholar Pius XII Inst. Grad. Studies, 1966. Mem. Nat. Sporting Goods Owners Am., Ski Industries Am. Democrat. Roman Catholic. Clubs: Prestwick Country, Frankfort Women's. Home: 5556 Fox Hollow Dr Boca Raton FL 33486 Office: The Austrian Ski & Sport Haus 19001 S Cicero Ave Country Club Hills IL 60477

LOEWE, BARBARA, educator; b. Newark, Nov. 11, 1938; d. Oscar U. and Lillian (Freund) L. BS, Fla. So. Coll., 1960; MA, Western Res. U., 1961; postgrad., U. Denver, Fla. State U. Tchr. Manatee County Schs., Bradenton, Fla., 1960-63; instr. SUNY, Brockport, 1965; asst. prof. Bloomsburg (Pa.) State Coll., 1965-68; prof. Hillsborough Community Coll., Tampa, 1969—; guest lectr., counselor, minister Universal Ch. of the Master, Santa Clara, Calif., 1979—; real estate investor, Tampa, 1970—. Bd. dirs. Meadowood Condominium Assn., Tampa, 1979-85, pres., 1979-85; bd. dirs. Hillsborough Community Coll. chpt. Fla. United Services, 1988, Stageworks Theatre, 1989—. Mem. Fla. Communications Assn. (exec. sec., treas. 1986—), Mensa (mem. exec. com. Tampa Bay chpt. 1987—). Home: PO Box 151173 Tampa FL 33684

LOEWY, ARTHUR F., financial executive; b. N.Y.C., Feb. 27, 1929; s. Leopold and Bertha (Mashin) L.; m. Roberta Fifer, May 25, 1952; children: Karen, Richard, Charles. B.S., UCLA, 1952. Fin. mgr. West Coast electronics RCA, 1956; dir. accounting, then asst. controller Mattel Inc., 1964; controller B.V.D. Co., Inc., 1966, v.p. fin., 1968; v.p. fin. and adminstrn. Roblin Industries, Buffalo, 1969; treas. Roblin Industries, 1974; sr. v.p. fin.

Zayre Corp., Framingham, Mass., 1974-82, exec. v.p. fin., 1982—; chief fin. officer TJX Cos., Inc., Natick, Mass., 1987—. Served with U.S. Army, 1952-56, Korea. Mem. Fin. Execs. Inst. Office: The TJX Cos Inc TJX Tower 770 Cochituate Rd Framingham MA 01701

LOFGREEN, PAUL EUGENE, JR., computer company executive; b. Stockton, Calif., June 18, 1946; s. Paul E. and Helen W. (Fotes) L.; student U. Utah, 1965-73; A.A., Thomas Edison Coll., 1975; cert. Center for Real Estate Studies, 1976; m. Clementina Maria Accinno, Aug. 10, 1979; children—Angelina Accinno, Nena Button. Asst. unit mgr. operating room, dept. surgery U. Utah, Salt Lake City, 1966-67, asst. heart-lung pump technician, 1967-69, operating room technician, 1969-70; supr. inbred rodent colony dept. pathology U. Utah, Salt Lake City, 1970-71, contract adminstr., 1971-75; ops. adminstr. Basic Research Program, Frederick (Md.) Cancer Research Center, 1975-76, sr. tech. ops. mgr. animal prodn. area, 1977-83; mgr. Harlan Sprague Dawley, Inc., Walkersville, Md., 1983-86, pres., Computer Systems Plus, Frederick, Md.,1986—.; real estate cons. Imperial Realty Co., Salt Lake City, 1976-77; fiscal mgr. Utah Native Am. Consortium, 1977. Served with USN, 1965-66. Mem. Soc. Research Adminstrs., Internat. Mgmt. Council (chmn. edn. com. 1980-82, v.p. 1982), Am. Assn. Lab. Animal Sci. (parlimentarian 1978-79, co-chmn. nat. capital area br. exhibitors com. 1979, chmn. com. 1980—, chmn. regional examining bd. 1982-84, pres. nat. capital area br. 1984-85 ; editorial adv. bd. Lab Animal mag. 1979—), Assn. Gnotobiotics. Baptist. Home and Office: 1345 Butterfly Ln Frederick MD 21701

LOFTIN, RAYMOND VICTOR, JR., oil and gas company executive; b. Houston, Dec. 24, 1927; s. Raymond Victor and Helen Viola (Jones) L.; m. Martha McBride, Apr. 4, 1959 (div. May 1986); children: Helen Louise, Stephen McBride. BA, Rice U., 1948; LLB, U. Tex., 1951. Bar: Tex., U.S. Ct. Appeals (5th cir.), U.S. Supreme Ct. Briefing atty. Tex. Supreme Ct., Austin, 1957-58; from atty. to sr. v.p., assoc. gen. counsel Transco Energy Co., Houston, 1961—. With U.S. Army, 1952-54, Korea. Fellow Tex. Bar Found. (life); mem. State Bar Assn. Tex. (chmn. corp. counsel sect. 1977-78), Federal Energy Bar, Houston Bar Assn. Republican. Episcopalian. Office: Transco Energy Co PO Box 1396 Houston TX 77251

LOFTUS, THOMAS DANIEL, lawyer; b. Seattle, Nov. 8, 1930; s. Glendon Francis and Martha Helen (Wall) L. BA, U. Wash., 1952, JD, 1957. Bar: Wash. 1958, U.S. Ct. Appeals (9th cir.) 1958, U.S. Dist. Ct. Wash. 1958, U.S. Ct. Mil. Appeals, U.S. Supreme Ct. Trial atty. Northwestern Mut. Ins. Co., Seattle, 1958-62; sr. trial atty. Unigard Security Ins. Co., Seattle, 1962-68, asst. gen. counsel, 1969-83, govt. rels. counsel, 1983—; mem. Wash. Commn. on Jud. Conduct (formerly Jud. Qualifications Commn.), 1982-88, vice-chmn., 1987-88; judge pro tem Seattle Mcpl. Ct., 1973-81. Sec., treas. Seattle Opera Assn., 1980—; pres., bd. dirs. Vis. Nurse Svcs., 1979-88; pres., v.p. Salvation Army Adult Rehab. Ctr., 1979-86; vice chmn. Young Rep. Nat. Fedn., 1963-65; pres. Young Reps. King County, 1962-63; bd. dirs. Seattle Seafair, Inc., 1975; bd. dirs., gen. counsel Wash. Ins. Coun., 1984-86, sec., 1986-88, v.p., 1988—; bd. dirs. Arson Alarm Found. 1st lt. U.S. Army, 1952-54, col. Res., 1954-85. Fellow Am. Bar Found.; mem. Am. Arbitration Assn. (nat. panel arbitrators 1965—), Wash. Bar Assn. (gov. 1981-84), Seattle King County Bar Assn. (sec., trustee 1977-82), ABA (ho. of dels. 1984—), Internat. Assn. Ins. Counsel, Def. Rsch. Inst., Washington Def. Trial Lawyers Assn., Am. Judicature Soc., Res. Officers Assn., Judge Advocate General's Assn., U. Wash. Alumni Assn., Pi Sigma Alpha, Delta Sigma Rho, Phi Delta Phi, Theta Delta Chi. Republican. Presbyterian. Clubs: Coll. of Seattle, Wash. Athletic. Lodges: Masons, Shriners. Home: 3515 Magnolia Blvd West Seattle WA 98199 Office: 1215 Fourth Ave 18th Fl Seattle WA 98161

LOFTUS, WILLIAM FREDERICK, corporate financial executive, lawyer; b. Niagara Falls, Sept. 26, 1938; s. William H. and Mary O. (Kirchner) L.; m. Bonnie Braxton Geiger, Aug. 26, 1961; children: Stephen Geiger, William Kirchner. A.B., Yale U., 1960; J.D., U. Mich., 1963; LL.M. in Taxation, NYU, 1968. Bar: N.Y. 1963. Practice law N.Y.C., 1963-68; various mgmt. positions E.I. duPont de Nemours & Co., Wilmington, Del., 1963-79; dir. tax Allied Signal Corp., Morristown, N.J., 1979-82, v.p., treas., 1982-88; sr. v.p., chief fin. officer US Air Group Inc., Arlington, Va., 1989—. Active Legal Advocacy for Handicapped Children; founder, trustee N.J. Assn. for Hearing Impaired, Inc.; bd. dirs. Deafness Research Found. Mem. Nat. Assn. Corp. Treas., N.Y. State Bar Assn. Clubs: Yale of Central N.J. (Summit) (trustee and officer 1979, sec. 1981-83); Beacon Hill Country; Am. Yacht (Rye, N.Y.). Home: 127 Bellevue Ave Summit NJ 07901 Office: US Air Group Inc 2345 Crystal Dr Arlington VA 22227

LOGAN, CAROLYN ELIZABETH, furniture company executive; b. Pontotoc, Miss., May 9, 1943; d. Hershell Eddmon and Cordie (Brown) F.; m. John W. Logan, Mar. 23, 1939; children: Michael. John, Kristy. BBA, U. Miss., 1981. Prodn. worker Rivera, Inc., Pontotoc, 1965-72; asst. mgr. Buckhorn Gen. Store, Randolph, Miss., 1976-81; cons. L & M Frame Shop, Randolph, 1976-81, fin. mgr., 1981-82; gen. mgr., sec-treas. L & M Frames, Inc., Randolph, 1982—; cons. loans Ind. Farmers , Randolph, 1984—. Vol., fund raiser 4-H Club Am., Pontotoc County, 1983—; fund raiser Heart Assn., 1984—, Lung Assn., 1986—, Miss. Sheriffs Boys Ranches, Pontotoc, 1982—; mem. Pontotoc County Adv. Com., County Dem. Com. Democrat. Baptist. Home and Office: Rt 1 Box 185 Randolph MS 38864

LOGAN, DAVID SAMUEL, investment banker; b. Chgo., Jan. 10, 1918; s. Morris and Gertrude (Irving) L.; m. Reva Frumkin, Jan. 24, 1943; children: Daniel Joel, Richard Elliot, Jonathan Charles. BA, U. Chgo., 1939, JD, 1941. Bar: Ill., 1941, U.S. Supreme Ct., 1950. Lawyer Bd. of Econ. Warfare, Washington, 1942-46; mng. ptnr. Associated Hotels, Chgo., 1947-55, Mercury Investments, Chgo., 1955—. Chmn. Artists-in-Residence, Lit., Budget, Ill. Arts Council, Chgo., 1982—; exec. com. Nat. Archives Council, Chgo., 1975-80, Ill. State Arts Council, Chgo., 1977—; donor of the Reva and David Logan grants in support of New Writing on Photography, The Logan Scholarship at U. Mich. Sch. Law, and the Reva and David Logan Ctr. for Clin. Rsch. U. Chgo. Recipient Civil Govt. award U. Chgo. Mem. Ill. State Bar Assn., Chgo. Bar Assn. Jewish. Clubs: Arts, Grolier (N.Y.C.), Caxton. Home: 209 E Lake Shore Dr Chicago IL 60611 Office: Mercury Investments 919 N Michigan Ave Ste 3301 Chicago IL 60611

LOGAN, HENRY VINCENT, transportation executive; b. Phila., Nov. 7, 1942; s. Edward Roger and Alberta (Gross) L.; m. Mary Genzano, Sept. 28, 1963; children: Michele Leah, Maureen Laura, Monica Lynn. BS in Commerce, DePaul U., 1975; M in Mgmt., Northwestern U., 1984. Successively supr. corp. acctg., asst. mgr. gen. acctg., mgr. gen. acctg., dir. corp. acctg. and taxes Trailer Train Co., Chgo., 1962-70, controller, 1970-78, dir. fin. planning, 1978-83, mng. dir., fin. adminstr., 1983-85, v.p., chief fin. officer, 1985-88, sr. v.p. fleet mgmt., 1988—; bd. dirs. Calpro Co., 1983—, Mira Loma, Calif., RailGon Co., Chgo., 1983—. Treas. Trailer Train Co. Polit. Action Com., Chgo., 1980; vol. Sch. Dist. 87 Task Force, Glen Ellyn, Ill., 1986. Mem. Nat. Freight Transp. Assn., Assn. Am. Railroads (treas. div.), Union League Club (reception com. 1987—), Medinah (Ill.) Country Club. Republican. Roman Catholic. Home: 812 Abbey Dr Glen Ellyn IL 60137

LOGAN, JOHN FRANCIS, electronics company executive; b. Norristown, Pa., Apr. 10, 1938; s. Francis Michael and Elizabeth V. Logan; m. Margaret Louise Mott, Nov. 13, 1982. BS in Bus. Adminstrn., Drexel U., 1961. CPA, N.Y. Auditor Hurdman and Cranston CPA's (merger Peat Warwick Main & Co.), N.Y.C., 1961-69; v.p. fin., chief fin. officer, treas. Aero Flow Dynamics, Inc., N.Y.C., 1969-84; v.p. fin. and adminstrn., chief fin. officer, treas. Codenoll Tech. Corp., Yonkers, N.Y., 1985—. Served with U.S. Army, 1962-64. Mem. Am. Inst. CPA's, N.Y. State Soc. CPA's, Pa. Soc. Home: 212 W 22d St New York NY 10011 Office: Codenoll Tech Corp 1086 N Broadway Yonkers NY 10701

LOGAN, RENEE MARIE, healthcare finance director; b. Aberdeen, S.D., Sept. 10, 1953; d. Robert Dewey and Caroline (Engelhart) Orr; m. Steven Walter Logan, Apr. 8, 1972; children: Tamara, Barney. BA, U. S.D., 1974. CPA, N.D. Dir. fiscal services McIntosh County Meml. Hosp., Ashley, N.D., 1980-83; dir. fin. Mercy Hosp., Valley City, N.D., 1983-85; staff acct. William G. Neale, CPA, Watertown, S.D., 1985; dir. fin. Prairie Lakes Health Care Ctr., Watertown, 1986—. Mem. N.D. Soc. CPA's, Health Care Fin. Mgmt. Assn. (treas. Sioux Falls, S.D. chpt.). Democrat. Lutheran. Home: RR 3 Box 209 Watertown SD 57201

LOGAN, VERYLE JEAN, retail executive, realtor; b. St. Louis, Oct. 24; d. Benjamin Bishop and Eddie Mae (Williams) Logan. BS, Mo. U., 1968; postgrad. Wayne State U., 1974, 76, U. Mich.-Detroit, 1978, 80. With Hudson Dept. Store, Detroit, 1968-84, Dayton Hudson, Mpls., 1984-86, div. mdse. mgr., 1983-84, retail exec. div. mdse. mgr. Coats and Dresses, 1984-86; pres. Ultimate Connection, Inc., Mpls., 1987—. Mem. Pilgrim Bapt. Ch., Golden Valley Black History Month Com., 1987—, also bd. dirs.; trustee Harry Davis Found., 1988. Named Woman of Yr., Am. Bus. Women, 1984. Mem. Grad. Realtors Inst., Am. Bus. Womens Assn. (v.p. 1983-84, named Woman of Yr. 1984), Minn. Black Networking (exec. bd. 1985—), Delta Sigma Theta Mpls.-St. Paul Alumnae Assn. (life mem., recording sec. 1985-87, chmn. arts and letters, corresponding sec. 1987-88, chmn. heritage and archives 1988-89, named Delta of the Yr., 1988). Club: M.L. King Tennis Buffs. Office: PO Box 16438 Minneapolis MN 55416

LOGLER, FRANK JOSEPH, JR., club manager; b. Newport, R.I., July 6, 1948; s. Frank J. and Martha (Conway) L.; m. Donna Gemmellaro, May 17, 1969 (div. Oct. 1975); m. Susan A. Badwey, Jan. 13, 1979; children: Samantha A., Nicholas T., Tracey C., Frank J. Student, R.I. Jr. Coll., 1966-67, Roger Williams Coll., 1971-73, Mich. State U., 1979. Owner, mgr. Bojangles Pub. Co., Middletown, R.I., 1975-76; asst. mgr. Spouting Rock Beach Assocs., Newport, 1971-81; mgr. Greenwich Club Inc., E. Greenwich, R.I., 1981—; cons. to pvt. clubs; pres. Logler Assocs. dba Troll Ltd. Mem. R.I. Rep. com., 1978-84. Served with USCG, 1967-72. Mem. Am. Culinary Fedn., Am. Beverage Assn., Nat. Orgn. Career Profls. (life mem. Concord group), Newport Preservation Soc., Norman Bird Sanctuary, U.S. Coast Guard Aux. (vice comdr. Newport 1973—). Roman Catholic. Home: 110 Indian Hill Rd Middletown RI 02840 Office: Greenwich Club Inc 5426 Post Rd East Greenwich RI 02818

LOGSDON, ROBERT LESTER, library administrator; b. Covington, Ky., Apr. 13, 1947; s. Arlan V. and Margaret Louise (Fornash) L.; m. Marilyn B. Flowers, Aug . 29, 1970; children: Robyn Michelle, Jonathan Richard. BA, Ea. Ky. U., 1970; MLS, Ind. U., 1976, Cert. in Pub. Mgmt., 1980. Reference librarian Indpls. Pub. Library, 1970-74; br. head Evansville (Ind.) Pub. Library, 1974-77; asst. dept. head Ind. State Library, Indpls., 1977-82, dept. head, 1982-86, assoc. dir., 1986—; instr. part-time Ind. U., Indpls., 1987—. Contbr. articles to profl. jours., chpts. to books. Mem. ALA, Ind. Library Assn. (sec. 1976-78), Ind. Assn. Adult and Continuing Edn., Ind. Hist. Soc. Home: 11253 Maze Rd Indianapolis IN 46259 Office: Ind State Libr 140 N Senate Ave Indianapolis IN 46204

LOGSDON, THOMAS JOHN, marketing executive; b. Chgo., Dec. 28, 1960; s. John Clarence and Genevieve (Morrison) L. BA in Mktg., Western Ill. U., 1983. Acct. coordinator Frankel & Co., Chgo., 1984-86; sales rep. Dictaphone Corp., Chgo., 1986-87; rep. midwest accts. Mfg. Hanover Trust, Chgo., 1987—. Mem. Phi Sigma Epsilon Alumni Assn., Mfgs. Hanover's Midwest Mktg. Com., Nat. Assn. of Bankruptcy (trustees), Am. bankruptcy Inst. Republican. Home: 9275 W Noel Des Plaines IL 60016 Office: 10 S LaSalle Ste 2300 Chicago IL 60603

LOHAFER, DOUGLAS ALLEN, chemical engineer; b. Holstein, Iowa, June 7, 1949; s. Walter Jessen and Dorothy Ann (Thies) L. AA in Liberal Arts magna cum laude, Waldorf Coll., 1975; student, Mayo Sch. Health-Related Scis., Iowa State U., 1976; BA in Biology, Chemistry, Luther Coll., 1977, St. Olaf Coll., 1977; postgrad., San Jose State U. Sr. satellite ops. engr. Lockheed Missiles & Space Co., Inc., Sunnyvale, Calif., 1978-87, Lockheed Tech. Ops. Co., Inc., Sunnyvale, Calif., 1987—. Active Gideons Internat. Mem. Calif. Acad. Scis., Nat. Eagle Scout Assn., Am. Chem. Soc. (assoc. Santa Clara Valley sect. 1979, div. biol. chemistry 1979, div. nuclear chemistry and tech. 1986), Health Physics Soc. (assoc. No. Calif. chpt.), Ctr. for Theology and Natural Scis., Internat. Platform Assn., N.Y. C.S. Lewis Soc., U.S.A. Søren Kierkegaard Soc., Phi Theta Kappa. Democrat. Lutheran. Home: 403 Los Encinos Ave San Jose CA 95134

LOHMAN, WILLIAM FRANCIS, metals and specialty products company executive; b. N.Y.C., Feb. 26, 1948; s. William Frederick and Cathleen Theresa (Cunningham) L.; m. Patricia Ann Devlin, Aug. 8, 1970; children: Jason Devlin, Ashley Caralyn. BS in Math., Iona Coll., 1970; MBA in Fin., NYU, 1972. Fin. analyst Amax Inc., N.Y.C., 1972-74, mgr. precious metals raw material, 1976-79; asst. to v.p. fin. base metal group Amax Inc., Greenwich, Conn., 1974-75, asst. to pres. copper div., 1975-76, sr. v.p. base and precious metals div., 1984-85; mgr. copper scrap Amax Copper Inc., N.Y.C., 1979-80, asst. v.p. precious metals, 1980-82, v.p. precious metals, 1982-84; exec. v.p., gen. mgr. Engelhard Metals Corp., Iselin, N.J., 1985—. Mem. Internat. Precious Metals Inst. (treas. 1984-85, sec. 1985-86, 2d v.p. 1986-87, 1st v.p. 1987-88, pres. 1988—). Republican. Roman Catholic. Home: PO Box 138 Liberty Corner NJ 07938 Office: Engelhard Metals Corp 70 Wood Ave S #CN770 Iselin NJ 08830

LOHMANN, DONALD GENE, financial company executive; b. Perryville, Mo., Feb. 9, 1940; s. Walter R. and Ruth H. L.; m. Jill, Jan. 30, 1960; 1 dau., Lorri. B.A., Northwestern U., M.B.A. With Household Fin. Corp., Prospect Heights, Ill., 1962—; now exec. v.p. Household Fin. Corp.; pres. Household Comml. Fin. Svcs. Mem. Fin. Mgrs. Assn. Chgo. Club: Exmoor Country (Highland Park, Ill.). Office: Household Fin Svcs 2700 Sanders Rd Prospect Heights IL 60070

LOHN, ALOIS JOSEF, apparel company executive; b. Leverkusen, Fed. Republic Germany, Oct. 3, 1934; came to U.S., 1956; s. Alois Johann and Wilhelmine (Schneider) L.; m. Heide Marie Riechen, June 6, 1959; children: Henry Alois, Christina Heide, Michael John. Mgr. mfg. dept. Brooks Van Horn, Phila., 1957-66; plant mgr. Weintraub Bros., Phila., 1966-69; designer Campus Sweater & Sportswear, N.Y.C., 1969-75; product dir. Robert Lewis, Inc., West Long Branch, N.J., 1975-81; prodn. mgr. Tahari, N.Y.C., 1981-82; sr. v.p. mfg. Liz Claiborne, Inc., N.Y.C., 1982—. Office: Liz Claiborne Inc 1 Claiborne Ave North Bergen NJ 07047

LOHR, JAMES A(BRAHAM), electronics manufacturing company executive; b. Norristown, Pa., Feb. 4, 1944, s. James Gasgoin and Helen Frances (Coffman) L.; m. Billie Marie Supplee, Nov. 21, 1966; children: James E., Bruce A., Melissa E., Daniel E., Christine E. Vice pres. engring. Aydin Controls, Fort Washington, Pa., 1979-81; exec. v.p. engring. Aydin Computer Systems, Horsham, Pa., 1981-83, exec. v.p. sales mktg., 1983-84, pres., 1984-87; v.p. Aydin Corp., Horsham, 1985-88; exec. v.p. Aydin Computor and Monitor div., 1988—. Contbr. articles to profl. jours. Recipient award of merit Signal, 1980. Mem. IEEE, Assn. Computing Machinery, Armed Forces Communications and Electronic Assn. (appreciation award 1985), Air Traffic Controllers Assn., Nat. Computer Graphics Assn. Mil Graphics, NSIA. Republican. Lutheran. Club: Mensa (Norristown, Pa.). Home: 1905 Valley Forge Rd Lansdale PA 19446 Office: Aydin Computer and Monitor div 700 Dresher Rd Horsham PA 19044

LOHRE, JOHN OWEN, leasing company executive; b. Vermillion, S.D., Apr. 21, 1932; s. George Herman and Sanna (Nelson) L.; m. Mary Belle Biggert, Aug. 6, 1960; children: Kathryn, Philip. BS, U. S.D., 1954; MBA, Harvard U., 1959. With Chgo. Bridge and Iron Co., 1959-65; v.p. First Nat. Bank of Chgo., 1965-74; with First Mcpl. div. BancOne Leasing Corp., Denver, 1974—, pres., 1980—; bd. dirs. Resort Breweries Inc. Treas. Community Renewal Soc., Chgo., 1973-74; bd. dirs. Crow Canyon Ctr. for Southwestern Archaeology, 1985—, Cascade Village Met. Dist., 1985—. 1st lt. U.S. Army, 1955-57. Presbyterian. Clubs: University (Chgo.); Harvard (N.Y.C.); Harvard Bus. Sch. of Colo. (v.p. 1979-80, dir. 1980—, pres. 1986-87), Cherry Hills Country; Denver Athletic. Home: 3333 E Florida Ave #122 Denver CO 80210 Office: 857 Grant St Denver CO 80203

LOKHORST, JONATHAN ROBERT, accountant; b. Mpls., June 6, 1962; s. Robert John and Janet Kerith (Anderson) L.; m. Barbara Kay Felton, July 22, 1983; 1 child, Robert Scott. BA cum laude, Bethel Coll., 1983. CPA, Minn. Supr. W. Scott Wallace, CPA, St. Paul, 1983—. Mem. Bethel Coll. Communications Bd., St. Paul, 1981-83; chmn. stewardship com. Redeemer Covenant Ch., Brooklyn Park, Minn., 1985-86, allocations com. local chpt. United Way, 1988—. Lee Journalism scholar Bethel Coll., 1982-83. Mem. Am. Inst. CPA's, Minn. Soc. CPA's (nonprofit orgn. com., 1987). Republican. Home: 849 Sherwood Rd Shoreview MN 55126 Office: W Scott Wallace CPA 1700 W Hwy 36 Roseville MN 55113

LOLLAR, ROBERT MILLER, management consultant; b. Lebanon, Ohio, May 17, 1915; s. Harry David and Ruby (Miller) L.; Chem E., U. Cin., 1937, MS, 1938, PhD, 1940; m. Dorothy Marie Williams, Jan. 1, 1941; children—Janet Ruth (Mrs. David Schwarz), Katherine Louise (Mrs. James Punteney, Jr.). Cereal analyst Kroger Food Found., Cin., 1935-37; devel. chemist Rit Product div. Corn Products, Indpls., 1937-39, 40-41; assoc. prof. U. Cin., 1941-59; tech. dir. Armour & Co., Chgo., 1959-73; mgmt. and tech. cons., pres. Lollar and Assocs., 1973—; tech. dir. Leather Industries Am., Cin., 1975-86, cons., 1986—. Dir. OSRD, 1942-45. Recipient Alsop award Am. Leather Chemists Assn., 1954, Disting. Svcs. award, 1985, 86, Fraser Muir Moffat medal Leather Industries Am. Mem. Am. Leather Chemists Assn. (pres., editor-in-chief), Inst. Food Technologists, Am. Chem. Soc. (nat. councillor), Am. Soc. Quality Control, World Mariculture Soc., Sigma Xi, Tau Beta Pi, Alpha Chi Sigma. Address: 5960 Donjoy Dr Cincinnati OH 45242

LOLLI, ANDREW RALPH, industrial engineer, former army officer; b. Seatonville, Ill., Oct. 15, 1917; s. Joseph Fredrick and Adolfa (Fiocchi) L.; student Armed Forces Staff Coll., 1950, Nat. War Coll., 1957, N.Y. Inst. Fin., 1971; B.S., Dickinson Coll., 1952; postgrad. Fordham U., 1952; m. Mary H. Tatsapaugh, Jan. 14, 1983. Enlisted in U.S. Army, 1940, advanced through grades to maj. gen., 1960; chief plans and priorities Allied Forces So. Europe, 1952-56; comdr. Air Def. units, N.Y. and San Francisco, 1957-60; comdr. XX U.S.A. Corps, 1961-62, XV, 1962-63, comdr. Western NORD Region, Hamilton AFB, Calif., 1963-66; ret., 1966; exec. asst. Hughes Aircraft Co., Fullerton, Calif., 1967; dir. gen. services State of Calif., Sacramento, 1967-70; v.p. Sigmatics, Newport Beach, Calif., 1970-73, Intercoast Investments Co., Sacramento, 1975-76; pres. Andrew R. Lolli Assos. Inc., San Francisco, 1973—, Lolman Inc., San Francisco, 1976—; commr. Small Bus. Adv. Commn., San Francisco, 1989—; pres. bd. trustees Commonwealth Equity Trust, 1974-80; vice chmn. Calif. Pub. Works bd., 1967-69; mem. adv. panel Nat. Acad. Scis. and Engring. in Research, Washington, 1968-70; mem. fed., state and local govt. adv. panel Fed. Gen. Services, Washington, 1968-69. Bd. dirs. Columbia Boys Park Club, San Francisco, Lab. for Survival, San Francisco. Decorated D.S.M., Legion of Merit with oak leaf cluster, Bronze Star with oak leaf cluster; named Man of Year, Italian Sons of Am., 1964. Mem. Nat. Assn. Uniformed Services, Assn. U.S. Army, Ret. Officers Assn. Roman Catholic. Clubs: Presidio San Francisco, Golf. Developed short notice inspection system for army air def. missiles, 1960. Home: 1050 North Point San Francisco CA 94109 Office: 286 Jefferson St San Francisco CA 94133

LOMASON, HARRY AUSTIN, II, automotive company executive; b. Detroit, Oct. 6, 1934; s. William Keithledge and Neva L.; children by previous marriage: Kimri Elizabeth Lomason Massey, Krista Anne Lomason Massell, William Keithledge, Peter Kevin; m. Mary Alice Pushkarsky, June 26, 1971; children: Harry Austin, Heather Alice. Student, Ga. Inst. Tech., 1953-56; B.B.A., Ga. State U., 1959. With Douglas & Lomason, Farmington Hills, Mich., 1960—, asst. sec., 1966-72, v.p., sec., 1972-76, pres., chief operating officer, 1976-82, pres., chief exec. officer, 1982—, also bd. dirs.; v.p. bd. dirs. Douglas y Lomason de Mex. S.A. de C.V.; chmn., bd. dirs. Mich. Mut. Ins., Detroit, Bloomington-Normal (Ill.) Seating Co., The Am. Supplier Inst.; bd. dirs., mem. exec. com. The Amerisure Cos., Detroit; bd. examiners Malcolm Baldridge Nat. Quality Award com. Bd. dirs. Detroit Symphony Orch. Hall, 1979—; bd. dirs. Mich. Thanksgiving Parade Found., Harper-Grace Hosp. Mem. Engring. Soc. Detroit, Soc. Automotive Engrs., Mich. Mfg. Assn. (chmn.). Episcopalian. Clubs: Detroit, Detroit Athletic, Detroit Golf; Cherokee Town and Country (Atlanta); Marianna (Ark.) Country; Pine Lake Country (Orchard Lake, Mich.). Home: 2900 Pine Lake Rd Orchard Lake MI 48033 Office: Douglas & Lomason Co 24600 Hallwood Ct Farmington Hills MI 48331-4508

LOMASON, WILLIAM KEITHLEDGE, automotive company executive; b. Detroit, July 12, 1910; s. Harry A. and Elizabeth (Bennett) L.; m. Neva C. Wigle, 1930 (dec. 1965); m. Ruth M. Martin, 1970. AB, U. Mich., 1932, AM, 1933. With Douglas & Lomason Co., Detroit, 1934—; treas. Douglas & Lomason Co., 1943-52, v.p., 1945-50, pres., gen. mgr., 1950-75, chmn. bd., chief exec. officer, 1976-82, chmn. bd., 1982—, also bd. dirs.; pres. Shamrock Air Lines, 1968-76. Co-author: When Management Negotiates, 1967. Bd. dirs., mem. exec. com. Nat. Right to Work Com.; bd. dirs. past chmn. and pres. Bus. Council of Ga.; dir. emeritus Mich. Mfrs. Assn. Recipient Man of Yr. award, Carrollton, Ga., 1967; named lt. col. aide de camp Gov.'s Staff, Ga., 1956. Mem. Engring. Soc. Detroit, Am. Electroplaters Soc., Alpha Chi Rho. Episcopalian. Office: Douglas & Lomason Co 24600 Hallwood Ct Farmington Hills MI 48018

LOMBARD, JOHN JAMES, JR., lawyer; b. Phila., Dec. 27, 1934; s. John James and Mary R. (O'Donnell) L.; m. Barbara Mallon, May 9, 1964; children—John James, William M., James G., Barbara E., Laura K. B.A. cum laude, LaSalle Coll., Phila., 1956; J.D., U. Pa., 1959. Bar: Pa. 1960. Assoc., Obermayer, Rebmann, Maxwell & Hippel, Phila., 1960-65, ptnr., 1966-84, fin. ptnr., 1980-84; ptnr. Morgan, Lewis & Bockius, Phila., 1985—, mgr. personal law sect., 1986—; sec., dir. Airline Hydraulics Corp., Phila., 1969—. Bd. dirs. Redevel. Authority Montgomery County, Pa., 1980-87, Gwynedd-Mercy Coll., Gwynedd Valley, Pa., 1980. Served with N.G., 1959-60. Mem. ABA (chmn. com. simplification security transfers 1972-76, chmn. membership com. 1978-84, mem. council real property, probate and trust law sect. 1979-85, sec. 1985-87, div. dir. probate div. 1987—), Pa. Bar Assn. (ho. of dels. 1979-81), Phila. Bar Assn. (chmn. probate sect. 1972), Am. Coll. Probate Counsel (editor Probate Notes 1983, bd. regents 1985—), Internat. Acad. Estate and Trust Law (exec. com. 1985—), Am. Bar Found., Internat. Fish and Game Assn. Clubs: Aviation Country (Blue Bell, Pa.); Union League (Phila.); Ocean City (N.J.) Marlin and Tuna. Co-author: How to Live and Die with Pennsylvania Probate, Durable Power of Attorney—A Systems Approach, 1984, 2d edit. 1988; contbr. articles to profl. jours. Office: Morgan Lewis & Bockius 2000 One Logan Sq Philadelphia PA 19103

LOMBARDO, (GUY) GAETANO, venture capitalist; b. Salemi, Italy, Feb. 4, 1940; came to U.S., 1947; s. Salvatore and Anna Maria L.; Sc.B. with honors, Brown U., 1962; Ph.D. in Physics, Cornell U., 1971; m. Nancy B. Emerson, Sept. 2, 1967; children—Nicholas Emerson, Maryanne Chilton. Sr. staff Arthur D. Little Inc., Cambridge, Mass., 1967-77; v.p. logistics Morton Salt Co., Chgo., 1977-78; dir. logistics and distbn. Gould Inc., Chgo., 1978-80; corp. dir. Bendix Corp., Southfield, Mich., 1980-82; group v.p. worldwide bus. devel. Bendix Indsl. Group, 1982-84; pres., chief exec. officer Comau Productivity Systems, 1984-86; pres. Nelmar Corp., 1986-88; chmn., chief exec. officer Courtesy Mfg. Co., Elk Grove, Ill., 1988—; vis. prof. ops. mgmt. Boston U., 1973. Contbr. articles on physics and bus. mgmt. to profl. jours. Home: 900 Timberlake Dr Bloomfield Hills MI 48013 Office: Nelmar Corp 2000 Town Ctr Ste 1900 Southfield MI 48075

LONDON, SHERI FAITH, financial planner; b. Hackensack, N.J., Dec. 6, 1955; d. Julius and Millie (Dier) L. BA, Rutgers U., 1977; postgrad., Emory U., 1978-80. Cert. fin. planner. Research asst. grad. sch. Emory U., Atlanta, 1978-79; registered rep. Donald & Co. Securities Inc., Jersey City, 1980—, v.p., registered options prin., 1984—, gen. prin., 1986—; researcher, office mgr. Pub. Citizen's Congress Watch, Washington, 1982-83; pres. S.F.L. Fin. Planning, Inc., Hackensack, 1985—; life, health ins. rep. Berger Agy., Neptune, N.J., 1987—; sr. v.p. Donald & Co. Securities, inc., 1989—; fin. planner seminars for orgns. and high schs.; cons. in field, 1986—. Contbr. articles to profl. jours. Bd. dirs. Bergen County chpt. ACLU, N.J., 1983—. Emory U. Grad. Sch. grantee, 1978. Mem. No. N.J. Inst. Cert. Fin. Planners (cert., bd. dirs.). Office: SFL Fin Planning Inc 15F Coles Ave Hackensack NJ 07601

LONEGAN, THOMAS LEE, restaurant corporation executive; b. Kansas City, Mo., July 4, 1932; s. Thomas F. and Edna L. (Payton) L.; m. Donna F. Ednie, Apr. 11, 1958; children: Timothy L., John M. BSME, Gen. Motors Inst., 1955; MS in Mgmt., USN Post Grad Sch., 1963; grad., Indsl. Coll. Armed Forces, Washington, 1970; postgrad., Calif. State U., Long Beach, 1979-83; grad., Coll. for Fin. Planning, Denver, 1984. Registered profl.

engr.; cert. fin. planner. Commd. ensign USN, 1956, advanced through grades to comdr., 1978; dir. pub. works Naval Weapons Sta., Seal Beach, Calif., 1974-78; dir. cen. staff McAthco Enterprises, Inc., Camarillo, Calif., 1985, exec. v.p., chief fin. officer, 1986—; gen. ptnr. 6 Sizzler Restaurants, 1985—. Author: Analysis and Attenuation of Air Borne Noise in Industrial Plants, 1955, Formalized Training of Maintenance Personnel, 1963. Vol. various couns. Boy Scouts Am., 1968-74. Decorated Bronze Star; recipient Order of Chamoro Govt. of Guam; named Engr./Arch Yr. Naval Facilities Engr. Command, 1972. Fellow Soc. Am. Mil. Engrs., Inst. Cert. Fin. Planners, Internat. Assn. Fin. Planning, Retired Officers Assn., Beta Gamma Sigma. Home: 8578 Amazon River Circle Fountain Valley CA 92708 Office: McAthco Enterprises Inc 3687 Las Posas Rd Ste 188 Camarillo CA 93010

LONG, ALFRED B., former oil co. exec., cons.; b. Galveston, Tex., Aug. 4, 1909; s. Jessie A. and Ada (Beckwith) L.; student S. Park Jr. Coll., 1928-29, Lamar State Coll. Tech., 1947-56, U. Tex., 1941; m. Sylvia V. Thomas, Oct. 29, 1932; 1 dau., Kathleen Sylvia (Mrs. E.A. Pearson, II). With Sun Oil Co., Beaumont, Tex., 1931-69, driller geophys. dept., surveyor engring. dept., engr. operating dept., engr. prodn. lab., 1931-59, regional supr., 1960-69, cons., 1969—. Mem. Jefferson County Program Planning Com., 1964; mem. tech. adv. group Oil Well Drilling Inst., Lamar U., Beaumont. Mem. Soc. Petroleum Engrs., Am. Petroleum Inst., Am. Assn. Petroleum Geologists, IEEE, Houston Geol. Soc., Gulf Coast Engring. and Sci. Soc. (treas. 1962-65), U.S. Power Squadron, Soc. Wireless Pioneers. Inventor various oil well devices. Office: PO Box 7266 Beaumont TX 77726

LONG, ANNA MARIBETH, electrical engineer; b. Nashville, Aug. 18, 1960; d. George William and Martha Elizabeth (Love) Long; m. Arvind M. Parikh, June 11, 1988. BS in Applied Sci., U. Louisville, 1982, M in Elec. Engring., 1983. Policy analyst intern U.S. Govt., Washington, 1980-81; master control programmer Sta. WKPC-TV, Louisville, 1982-83; system devel. engr., network analyst IBM, Gaithersburg, Md., 1983—; del. Internat. Student Pugwash Conf., Ann Arbor, Mich., 1983; instr. Montgomery Coll., Germantown, Md., 1984-86, U. Md., College Park, 1986—. Counselor Montgomery County Fin. Counseling Service, 1986-87. Mem. IEEE, NSPE, Omicron Delta Kappa, Tau Beta Pi, Eta Kappa Nu. Office: IBM Systems Div 18100 Frederick Pike Gaithersburg MD 20879

LONG, DONALD GREGORY, industry consultant; b. Lima, Ohio, Mar. 19, 1937; s. Chester Vernon and Margaret Francis (Packard) L.; m. Linda Ann Bosking, Aug. 1, 1964: Karen Elizabeth, Joanne Deborah. BS, U. Ill., Urbana, 1959; MBA, Stanford U., 1964. Systems engr. IBM Corp., N.Y.C., 1964-68; product mgr. IBM Corp., Princeton, N.J., 1969-75; elec. funds transfer project mgr. IBM Corp., Princeton, 1975-78, industry cons., 1979—; IBM liaison pres.'s nat. commn. elec. funds transfers, Washington, 1975-77; faculty mem. Stonier Grad. Sch. of Banking, Rutgers U., N.J., 1979-83, Grad. Sch. Banking, U. Wis., 1978-86, Grad. Sch. Retail Bank Mgmt., U. Va., 1980-85, Sch. Elec. Funds Transfer, Northwestern U., 1985—, Payment Systems Inst., U. Colo., 1986—; bd. dirs. Montgomery Nat. Bank, Rocky Hill, N.J., 1981—; trustee New Money Inst., Washington, 1987. Contbr. articles to fin. mags. Pres. Rep. orgn., Belle Mead, N.J., 1976-77; chmn. Montgomery Township N.J. planning bd., Belle Mead, 1981-88; trustee Foundation for Hosp. Art, Atlanta, 1986—. Served to capt. with USAF, 1960-62. Mem. Elec. Funds Transfer Hall of Fame, Princeton area C. of C., Electronics Funds Transfer Assn. (bd. dirs. 1982—), Nat. Assn. Watch and Clock Collectors. Republican. Methodist. Club: Antique Auto. Lodge: Masons, Shriners. Home: 61 Jamestown Rd Belle Mead NJ 08502 Office: IBM Corp 301 College Rd Princeton NJ 08540

LONG, E(VELYN) CLAUDINE, finance planning executive, educator; b. Laurel, Miss.; d. William Andy and Ada Eunice (Clearman) Parrish; m. Jack M. Long, Sept. 26, 1948; children: John R., Jaime E., Susan E., Mary E. AA in Bus., Mundelein Coll., 1981; grad., Coll. Fin. Planning, 1987. Cert. fin. planner. Mgr. women's div. Manpower, Inc., Oklahoma City, 1964-65; with. Liberty Nat. Bank and Trust Co., 1965-87, sr. v.p., 1981; v.p. Banks of Mid-Am., Inc., 1987; v.p., mgr. Liberty Found., Inc., 1987; dir. fin. planning Seidman Fin. Services, Oklahoma City, 1987—; adj. prof. Coll. Fin. Planning, Oklahoma City U., 1987, selection com. Parry scholarship Coll. Nursing; mem. Better Bus. Bur. Mem. exec. com. Last Frontier council Boy Scouts Am., 1988; mem. exec. com. Oklahoma City Beautiful, chmn. Penny Campaign, 1988; pres. Oklahoma City Pub. Sch. Found., Inc., 1988; mem. Heritage Hills Assn., YMCA Fund Drive, 1987, YWCA Fund Drive Rape Crisis Ctr., Okla. Heritage Assn. Hall of Fame Program com., Jour. Record Corp. Woman of Yr. com.; bd. dirs. Downtown Now, Okla. Arts Inst., Okla. Mus. Art, Allied Arts Found., YWCA Assoc., Deskset. Named one of Outstanding Ladies in the News, Okla. Hospitality Club, 1975, 86; recipient Byliners award/Fin. Women in Communication, 1987, Outstanding Vol. award Fund Raiser Execs., 1988. Mem. Inst. Chartered Fin. Planners, Exec. Women Internat. (past pres. Oklahoma City chpt.), Charter 35, Econ. Club for Women, Contbrs. Adv. Group, Oklahoma City C. of C. Republican. Baptist. Club: Toastmasters. Home: 423 NW 21st St Oklahoma City OK 73103 Office: BDO Seidman 2 Leadership Sq Ste 300 Oklahoma City OK 73102

LONG, GERALD BERNARD, accountant; b. Bessemer, Ala., Oct. 19, 1956; s. Edward Beckon Sr. and Ruby Stein (Hubbert) L.; m. Darlene Gillon, Oct. 20, 1980; children: Claudia Miranda. Assoc. in Applied Sci., Bessemer State Tech. Coll., 1977; BS, U. Ala., Birmingham, 1983. CPA. Sr. auditor Peat, Marwick, Mitchell & Co., Birmingham, Ala., 1983-86, supervising sr. auditor, 1986-88; v.p., dir. internat. audit Booker T. Washington Ins., Co., Birmingham, 1988—; pres., owner Long & Assocs., Birmingham, 1988—; adv. staff CPA Ala. Pub. Svc. Commn., 1988—. Adv. bd. A.G. Gaston Boys Club Bessemer, 1988—. Fellow Ala. Soc. CPA's (researcher 1986-87); mem. Bessemer Area C. of C. (leadership participant 1986), Nat. Assn. Accts. (mem. Vulcan chpt.), Inst. Internal Auditors, AICPA. Democrat. Methodist. Lodge: Kiwanis (mem. Vulcan chpt.). Home: 3024F Southmall Cir Montgomery AL 36116 Office: 1 Court Sq Ste 321 Montgomery AL 36103

LONG, HENRY ARLINGTON, real estate executive; b. Arlington, Va., May 18, 1937; s. William Armstead and Emily Pearl (Garland) L.; m. Betty Mae Horner, Dec. 28, 1963; children: Andrea Long Selfe, Elissa Michelle, Elizabeth Kristen, Henry Arlington II. BS, Va. Poly. Inst., 1959. Cert. comml. investment mem., 1977. Ind. comml. real estate sales Va. and Washington, 1965-68; co-owner Long & Foster Real Estate, Inc., Fairfax, Va., 1968-79; owner Henry A. Long Co., Westfields, Va., 1979—; co-owner Scott, Long Constrn., 1978—; mng. gen. ptnr. Snowden Village Assocs., 1972-85, Manassas Forum Assocs., 1973-86, Eskridge Indsl. Assocs., 1974-86, Reston Racquet Club Assocs., 1976-86, Westwood Corp. Ctr. Assocs., 1979—, Westfields Corp. Ctr. Assocs., 1984—, Internat. Conf. Resorts Am., 1987—; bd. dirs. No. Va. Bd. Realtors, 1973, 74. Trustee The Potomac Sch., McLean, Va., 1979-85; chmn. fund raising com. Potomac Secondary Sch., 1986—, Fairfax County Chair of Local Govt. at George Mason U., 1987—; bd. dirs. Wolf Trap Assocs., 1985—; vestry Truro Episcopal Ch., Fairfax, Va., 1981-84, vestry Ch. of the Epiphany, 1986—. Served with USAF, 1959-65, with Res. 1966-70. Recipient award for Mil. Merit, Chgo. Tribune, 1959, Disting. Service award No. Va. Bd. Realtors, 1972, 73. Mem. Nat. Assn. Realtors, Real Estate Securities and Syndication Inst., MIT Ctr. Real Estate Devel., Realtors Nat. Mktg. Inst., Jaycees, The Econ. Club (Washington), Georgetown Club, Tower Club, Pi Delta Epsilon. Lodge: Kiwanis (dir. Fairfax chpt. 1970-71). Home: 1234 Meyer Ct McLean VA 22101 Office: Henry A Long Co 14800 Conference Center Dr Ste 400 Westfields VA 22021-3806

LONG, I. A., banker; b. Herndon, Va.; m. Lydia Ann Kimbrough Allen; children—Claxton Allen, Lydia Long Baer, Ada White. Ed., U. Va., Am. Inst. Banking. Mem. staff N.Y. br. Royal Bank of Can., 1919-20; asst. cashier Peoples Nat. Bank, Leesburg, Va., 1920-27; v.p. Mercantile Trust Co., St. Louis, 1928-53; pres. S.W. Bank of St. Louis, 1953-77, chmn bd., chief exec. officer, 1977-84, chmn. emeritus, 1984—. mem. faculty Sch. of Banking, U. Wis. Pres. bd. trustees Mary Inst.; pres. Central Inst. for the Deaf, St. Louis Mcpl. Bond Club, St. Louis Corp. Fiduciaries Assn.; chmn. St. Louis Housing Authority, St. Louis Land Clearance Authority, Citizens Sch. Improvement Com., Fifth War Loan Drive, Met. St. Louis; chmn. emeritus bd. trustees Jefferson Nat. Expansion Meml. Assn.; chmn. emeritus Mo. Hist. Soc.; mem. Mo. Acad. Squires. Named Ky. Col., Ark. Traveler. Mem. Investment Bankers Assn. Am. (chmn. Miss. Valley group) (bd. dirs.). Clubs: St. Louis Country, Noonday (past pres.), Racquet (past pres.), Profl. and Bus. Men's of the Hill. Home: 5155 Westminster Pl Saint Louis MO 63108 Office: SW Bank 2301 S Kings Hwy Saint Louis MO 63139

LONG, JAMES ALFRED, financial services company executive; b. Oceanside, N.Y., July 4, 1942; s. Clymer Alfred and Gladys (Serbe) L.; m. Susan Miller, Sept. 30, 1972; children: Jennifer, Allison, Andrew. AB, Dartmouth Coll., 1964; MBA, Columbia U., 1966. Dir. mergers and acquisitions Sperry & Hutchinson Co., N.Y.C., 1970-73, asst. to pres. furnishings div., 1974-75; dir. asset mgmt. Am. Can Co., Greenwich, Conn., 1976-78, v.p. mergers and acquisitions, 1979-81, sr. v.p mergers and acquisitions, 1982-86, exec. v.p. mergers and acquisitions, 1987—. Contbg. author: Leveraged Buyout, 1985. Served to lt. USN, 1966-69. Mem. Assn. Corp. Growth. Methodist. Office: Primerica Corp American Ln Greenwich CT 06830

LONG, JOHN HOLMES, manufacturing company executive; b. Chgo., June 4, 1947; s. Richard Alan Grest and Audrey (Holmes) Rhodes; m. Lynn M. Cancellieri, Sept. 18, 1976. BA in Chemistry, Ill. Wesleyan U., 1970; MBA in Mgmt., Pepperdine U., 1982. Factory mgr. Chemold Corp., Maspeth, N.Y., 1972-76; chief process engr. AMF Voit, Santa Ana, Calif., 1976-81, factory mgr., 1982-85; mng. coordinator South Coast Carriers, Vernon, Calif., 1985, pres., 1987—. Bd. dirs., pres. Harbor View Knoll Community Assn., Newport Beach, Calif., 1977-88. Mem. Am. Chem. Soc., Los Angeles Rubber Group Inst. Republican. Home: 2745 Hillview Dr Newport Beach CA 92660 Office: S Coast Carriers 4376 Soto St Vernon CA 90058

LONG, JOSEPH M., retail drug company executive; b. Covelo, Calif., 1912; m. Vera Mai Skaggs. Ed., U. Calif., 1933. Asst. to city mgr. City of Berkeley, Calif., 1933-36; with Safeway Stores Inc., 1936-37; with Longs Drug Stores Inc., Walnut Creek, Calif., 1938—, pres., chief exec. officer, 1946-75, chmn. bd., chief exec. officer, 1975-77, chmn. bd., dir., 1977—. Office: Longs Drug Stores Inc 141 N Civic Dr Box 5222 Walnut Creek CA 94596

LONG, MICHAEL RAYMOND, investment company executive; b. Columbia, S.C., July 26, 1949; s. Raymond Francis and Elaine Mary (Mogilka) L.; m. Heather Ann Hirson, Oct. 24, 1980; 1 child, Amanda Ellis. BA, Washington and Lee U., 1972. Acct. exec. Reynolds Securities, N.Y.C., 1973-74; v.p. Shearson Am. Express, N.Y.C., 1974-80; exec. v.p., dir. trading The Millburn Corp., N.Y.C., 1980-88; pres. Rockbridge Asset Mgmt., N.Y.C., 1988—. Club: Metropolitan (N.Y.C.). Home: 16 Hudson St Apt 6B New York NY 10013

LONG, PHILIP LEE, information systems executive; b. Cleve., Jan. 24, 1943; s. Philip Joseph and Anne Catherine (Woodward) L.; B.E.E., Ohio State U., 1968, M.Sc., 1970; m. LeAnn Boyack Edvalson, Apr. 22, 1982; children—Sarah J., Caitlin T.; children by previous marriage—Philip Imants, Michael Oskar; Assoc. dir. Ohio Coll. Library Center, 1969-73; asso. for computer systems devel. SUNY, Albany, 1974-75; pres. Philip Long Assos., Inc., Salt Lake City, 1975-81; v.p. Novell Data Systems, 1981-82; v.p. Telerate Systems, Inc., 1983—; instr. computer sci. Ohio State Univ., library sci. SUNY, Catholic U. Am.; cons. to UNESCO, Bibliotheque National de France, Lib. Congress, Nat. Comm. Library and Info. Sci. Grantee, Nat. Research Council, Nat. Acad. Sci., 1971. Mem. Am. Soc. Info. Sci., IEEE, ALA, Assn. Computing Machinery, Am. Nat. Standards Inst. Contbr. articles to profl. jours. Home: 397 Thornden St South Orange NJ 07079 Office: Telerate Systems Inc World Trade Center 104th Floor New York NY 10048

LONG, PHILLIP CLIFFORD, banker; b. Tucson, Oct. 11, 1942; s. Hugh-Blair Grigsby and Phyllis Margaret (Clay) L.; m. Martha Whitney Rowe, Aug. 26, 1972; children—Elisha Whitney, Charlotte Clay, Elliot Sherlock. B.A., Tulane U., 1965. Sec. Fifth Third Bancorp, Cin., 1976—; asst. sec. Fifth Third Bank, Cin., 1975-76, sec., 1976-77, asst. v.p., 1977-79, sr. v.p., sec., 1979-88. Trustee Art Acad. Cin., 1980—, Cin. Symphony Orch., 1981-87, Contemporary Arts Ctr., 1974-84, Cin. Nature Ctr., 1982-88, Taft Mus., 1987—; trustee, treas. Cin. Music Hall, 1981—, Convalescent Hosp., 1989—. Served to capt. U.S. Army, 1966-67. Mem. Cin. Council on World Affairs. Clubs: The Camargo, Queen City. Home: 4795 Burley Hills Dr Cincinnati OH 45243 Office: Fifth Third Bank 38 Fountain Square Pla Cincinnati OH 45263

LONG, ROBERT ALBERT, JR., educational and business administrator; b. Oakland, Calif., Nov. 29, 1934; s. Robert Albert and Lillian Long; m. M. Ann Haynes, June 25, 1983. BA, San Francisco State U., 1961, MA in Edn., 1967; MBA, U. Phoenix, 1984. Asst. mgr. H.E.B. Retail Ctrs., San Antonio, 1955-57; engring. specialist Woodward, Clyde, Assoc., San Francisco, 1957-61; faculty mem. San Francisco State U., 1961-62; bus. adminstr. Oakland Unified Sch. Dist., 1961-82, Sequoia Union High Sch. Dist., Redwood City, Calif., 1982—; adv. fin. State of Calif., Sacramento, 1980—; cons. edn. and bus., Calif., 1982—; lectr., adj. faculty Calif. State U., San Francisco, 1986—. Rep. Recreation Commn., Oakland, 1974-76; vice chmn. Civic Arts Commn., Oakland, 1978-80; chmn. Library Commn., Oakland, 1980-82; advisor State Commn. Fin. and Agy. Governance, Sacramento, 1984-86. Recipient Life Membership Service award Nat. PTA, 1971, Meritorious Commn. Service, City of Oakland, 1980, Service Commendation, Oakland Unified Sch. Dist., 1982. Mem. AAUP, Am. Assn. Sch. Adminstrs., Council Ednl. Planners Internat., Calif. Coalition Edn. Facilities (regional chmn. 1984—), Calif. Assn. Sch. Bus. Officials Commn. (chmn. 1984—), Oakland C. of C. Club: Lake Merit Breakfast. Lodges: Kiwanis (sec., treas. 1977-80, Activity Commendation award 1978), Masons, Shriners. Home: 16635 Springbrook Ln Castro Valley CA 94552 Office: Sequoia Union High Sch Dist 480 James Ave Redwood City CA 94062

LONG, ROBERT MERRILL, retail drug company executive; b. Oakland, Calif., May 19, 1938; s. Joseph Milton and Vera Mai (Skaggs) L.; m. Eliane Quilloux, Dec. 13, 1969. Student, Brown U., 1956-58; B.A., Claremont Men's Coll., 1960. With Longs Drug Stores Inc., Walnut Creek, Calif., 1960—, dir., 1968—, pres., 1975-77, pres., chief exec. officer, 1977—. Mem. Nat. Assn. Chain Drug Stores (dir.). Office: Longs Drug Stores Corp 141 N Civic Dr Walnut Creek CA 94596

LONG, RONALD ALEX, real estate consultant, educator; b. Scranton, Pa., Dec. 9, 1948; s. Anthony James and Dorothy Agnas (Posgay) L.; m. Geraldine Sinneway, July 17, 1976; 1 child, Elizabeth Dorothy. BA, Bethany Coll., Lindsburg, Kans., 1971; MAT, Trenton (N.J.) State Coll., 1973; BS, Spring Garden Coll., 1980; MBA, St. Joseph's U., Phila., 1985. Cert. tchr., N.J., Pa., real estate instr., Pa. Substitute tchr. Hackettstown and Roxbury (N.J.) Sch. Bds., 1971-72; prof. Spring Garden Coll., Phila., 1973—; sales assoc. Red Carpet Real Estate, Doylestown, Pa., 1980—; cons. real estate Doylestown, 1980—; cons. mgmt. Budd Wheel Corp., Phila., 1978-82. Co-author: Explorations in Macroeconomics, 1988, Explorationsin Microeconomics, 1987; contbr. articles to area newspapers. Site dir. ARC Blood Mobile, 1975—; bd. dirs. Buckingham (Pa.) PTA, 1984—. Recipient Legion Honor award Chapel of the 4 Chaplains, Phila., 1984. Mem. Nat. Assn. Realtors, Pa. Assn. Realtors, Bucks County Assn. Realtors, Profl. Assn. Diving Instrs. (cert.), Bus. Club (treas. 1969-71, pres. 1970-71), Alpha Chi, Pi Sigma Chi, Eta Beta Phi. Republican. Home: 2698 Cranberry Rd Doylestown PA 18901 Office: Spring Garden Coll 7500 Germantown Ave Philadelphia PA 19119

LONG, WILLIAM ARTEE, JR., controller; b. Daytona Beach, Fla., Dec. 29, 1950; s. William A. Sr. and Ruth (Carroll) L.; m. Patricia Claire O'Neal, May 19, 1979; children: Amanda Lynn, William A. III. BBA, U. Cen. Fla., 1974; MA, Fla. State U., 1976. CPA. Supervising sr. Peat, Marwich, Marwick & Co., Tampa, 1977-81; mgr. accting. Jack Eckerd Corp., Clearwater, Fla., 1981-82; sr. fin. analyst Jack Eckerd Corp., Clearwater, 1982-83, asst. controller, 1983-86; controller Robbins Mfg. Co., Tampa, 1986—. Treas. Gorrie Elem. PTA, Tampa, 1985-87. Mem. Am. Inst. CPA's, Fla. Inst. CPA's, Fin. Exec. Inst. (bd. dirs. 1988—, chmn. com. 1987-88), Tampa Yacht Club, Krewe of Gasparilla. Republican. Presbyterian. Office: Robbins Mfg Co PO Box 17939 Tampa FL 33682

LONG, WILLIAM JERRY, metal processing executive; b. Knoxville, Tenn., Oct. 1, 1942; s. William J. and Martha Pauline (Holmes) L.; m. Carol Rudder, July 16, 1943; children: Jay, Chad. BS in Bus., U. Tenn., 1965, MBA in Bus., 1976. Salesman ALCOA, Atlanta, Tampa and Nashville, 1970-77; mktg. mgr. ARCO (ANACONDA), Louisville, 1977-80; planning and mktg. mgr. ARCO-Packing, Louisville, 1981-82; mgr. new ventures Arco-Metals, Louisville, 1982-84; mktg. cons. ALCAN-USA, Louisville and Cleve., 1985; mktg mgr. nat. sales Revere Copper & Brass, Newport, Ark., 1985-86; dir. strategic planning Commonwealth Aluminum Corp., Bethesda, Md., 1987—. Author of numerous comml. rsch. studies. Capt. U.S. Army, 1965-69, Vietnam, Korea. Home: 422 Blanken Baker Ln Louisville KY 40207 Office: Commonwealth Aluminum 1200 Meidinger Tower Ste 1200 Louisville KY 40202

LONGAN, WILLIAM JOSEPH, JR., investment company executive; b. Richmond, Va., Apr. 10, 1953; s. William Joseph and Rowena (Seale) L.; m. Mary Cabell Smith, Sept. 5, 1981; children: Mary Cabell, Robert Spencer. BA, U. N.C., 1976. Broker Anderson & Strudwick, Richmond, 1977-79, Dean Witter Reynolds, Richmond, 1979-85; portfolio mgr., mgr. dividend capture program Capitoline Investment Svcs., Richmond, 1985—. Mem. Nat. Options and Future Soc. (bd. dirs. 1988—), Hist. Richmond Found. (bd. trustees 1988), Bull and Bear Club, Westwood Racquet Club, Rotary. Home: 8702 Standish Ln Richmond VA 23229 Office: Capitoline Investment Svcs 919 E Main St Richmond VA 23219

LONGBERG, LESLIE CLINTON, found. fin. officer; b. Manhattan, Kans., June 21, 1946; s. Harry Wilbur and Parthena Louise (Watson) L.; B.S. magna cum laude, Kans. State U., 1968; M.B.A., U. W. Fla., 1973; m. Marcia Lowther, June 2, 1973; children—Michelle, Christina, Benjamin. Staff acct. Arthur Andersen & Co., C.P.A., Kansas City, Mo., 1972-74; internal auditor Garvey Industries, Inc., Wichita, 1974-77; controller Kans. State U. Found., Manhattan, 1977—. Served with USAF, 1968-72. C.P.A., Kans. Mem. Am. Inst. C.P.A.s, Kans. Soc. C.P.A.s, Nat. Assn. Accts., Alpha Kappa Psi, Alpha Kappa Lambda (pres. corp. bd.), Phi Kappa Phi (sec.). Republican. Mem. Ch. Nazarene (treas., dir.). Home: 15020 W Highway 24 Wamego KS 66547 Office: 1408 Denison St Manhattan KS 66502

LONGLEY, ALICE BEEBE, financial analyst; b. Kalamazoo, Mich., June 6, 1948; d. Clifford Deming and Mildred (Dunn) Beebe; m. Frank Alan Longley, Aug. 22, 1981; children: Jonathan Thatcher, Andrew Deming. BA, Wellesley Coll., 1970; MA, Columbia U., PhD, 1981. Prof. Columbia U., N.Y.C., 1978-80; v.p. research Donaldson, Lufkin & Jenrette, N.Y.C., 1982—. Mem. N.Y. Soc. Security Analysts, Phi Beta Kappa. Office: Donaldson Lufkin & Jenrette 140 Broadway New York NY 10005

LONGMAN, GARY LEE, accountant; b. Kewanee, Ill., Apr. 25, 1948; s. Howard L. and Dorothy (Wenk) L.; m. Ruth Ann Biesboer; children: Gregory, Rebecca. AA, Joliet (Ill.) Jr. Coll., 1968; BS in Acctg., No. Ill. U., 1970. CPA, Ill. Staff acct. Peat Marwick Main & Co., Chgo., 1970-72, sr. acct., 1972-74, mgr., 1974-80, ptnr., 1980—. Pres. Mental Health Assn. DuPage County, Lombard, Ill. 1982-84; treas. Mental Health Assn. Greater Chgo., 1986-87, also bd. dirs. 1984—. Mem. Am. Inst. CPA's, Ill. CPA Soc. Office: Peat Marwick Main & Co 303 E Wacker Dr Chicago IL 60601

LONGMOORE, JOHN THOMAS, insurance company executive; b. Fredericton, N.B., Can., Sept. 23, 1934; s. Earle Richard and Annie Elizabeth (Crone) L.; m. Sally Jo Brown, Oct. 26, 1963; children: Thomas, Linda. BS, McGill U., 1956; postgrad., U. Mich., 1956-57. Actuarial asst., then sr. actuarial asst. Prudential Ins. Co., Newark and Toronto, Ont., Can., 1957-62; with John Hancock Mut. Life Ins. Co., Boston, 1962—, assoc. actuary, 1966-69, 2d v.p., 1969-74, v.p., 1974-83, sr. v.p. individual equity and pension products, 1983-87, sr. v.p. group pension products, 1987—; vice chmn. bd. mgrs. John Hancock Variable Accounts, Boston, 1977—; pres. John Hancock Variable Life Ins. Co., Boston, 1979-87; bd. dirs. Maritime Life Assurance Co. Fellow Soc. Actuaries (enrolled actuary); mem. Nat. Assn. Securities Dealers (registered prin.), Am. Council Life Ins. (com. pensions 1989—), Life Ins. Mktg. and Rsch. Assn. (pension officers round table 1988—), Boston Actuaries Club, Assn. Pvt. Pension and Welfare Plans (bd. dirs. 11987—. Home: 47 Blue Hill Dr Westwood MA 02090 Office: John Hancock Mut Life Ins Co PO Box 111 Boston MA 02117

LONGWORTH, RICHARD COLE, journalist; b. Des Moines, Mar. 13, 1935; s. Wallace Harlan and Helen (Cole) L.; m. Barbara Bem, July 19, 1958; children: Peter, Susan. BJ, Northwestern U., 1957; postgrad., Harvard U., 1968-69. Reporter UPI, Chgo., 1958-60; parliamentary corr. UPI, London, 1960-65; corr. UPI, Moscow, 1965-68, Vienna, 1969-72; diplomatic corr. UPI, Brussels, 1972-76; econ. and internat. affairs reporter Chgo. Tribune, 1976-86, bus. editor, econ. columnist, 1987—; internat. affairs commentator Sta. WBEZ-FM, Chgo., 1984—. Served with U.S. Army, 1957-58. Nieman fellow, 1968-69; recipient award for econ. reporting U. Mo., 1978, 80, John Hancock award for econ. reporting, 1978, 79, 82, Gerald Loeb award for econ. reporting, 1979, Media award for econ. understanding Dartmouth Coll., 1979, award Inter-Am. Press Assn., 1979, Peter Lisagor award Sigma Delta Chi, 1979, Sidney Hillman award, 1985, Lowell Thomas award for travel writing, 1985, Beck award for fgn. corr., 1986, Domestic Reporting award, 1987. Mem. Chgo. Com. of Council Fgn. Relations. Office: Chgo Tribune 435 N Michigan Ave Chicago IL 60611

LOOK, KENNETH WILLIAM, pharmaceutical company executive; b. Appleton, Wis., Apr. 17, 1939; s. Arthur Clarence and Lorraine Elizabeth (Radder) L.; m. Virginia Lee Bailey, Feb. 8, 1975; children: Heather Amy, Kevin Andrew. BS in Pharmacy, U. Wis., 1961, MS in Pharmacy Adminstn., 1968, PhD in Pharmacy Adminstrn., 1974; postgrad., U. Nottingham, Eng., 1962-63. Retail and hosp. pharmacist Wis. and Tex., 1963-69; teaching asst. U. Wis., Madison, 1968-69; dir. corporate mktg. research G.D. Searle & Co., Skokie, Ill., 1969-79; dir. bus. rsch. and acqusitions Searle Pharms., Skokie, Ill., 1979-84; mgr. market planning and rsch. Monsanto Co., St. Louis, 1984-85; mgr. bus. devel. G.D. Searle & Co., Skokie, 1986-87, mgr. mktg. rsch.internat., 1988—. Capt. AUS, 1963-65. Mem. Am. Pharm. Assn., Am. Mktg. Assn., Rho Chi, Kappa Psi, Sigma Phi Epsilon. Home: 2818 Knollwood Ln Glenview IL 60025 Office: 5200 Old Orchard Rd Skokie IL 60077

LOOMIS, ARTHUR LAURENCE, II, investment banker; b. Kansas City, Mo., May 17, 1955; s. Howard Krey and Florence (Porter) L.; m. Patricia Ann Allen, June 30, 1979; 1 child, Genevieve E. BA, Cornell U., 1977, MBA, 1981. Bank examiner Fed. Res. Bank of N.Y., N.Y.C., 1977-79; mgmt. cons. Warburg, Paribas, Becker/A.G. Becker, N.Y.C., 1980; asst. to pres. Bank One of Columbus, N.A., Ohio, 1981-86; assoc. v.p. corp. fin. Ryan, Beck & Co., West Orange, N.J., 1986-88, v.p. corp. fin., 1988-89; v.p. corp. fin. Lyons, Zomback & Ostrowski, Inc., N.Y.C., 1989—; bd. dirs. Cen. States Fin. Co., Pratt, Kans. Div. head United Way Campaign for Bank One Corp., Columbus, 1981, chmn., 1985. Presbyterian. Clubs: Cornell (Cen. N.J.); Cornell (Cen. Ohio) (chmn. Secondary Schs. com. 1984-86). Office: Lyons Zomback & Ostrowski Inc 70 Pine St 54th Fl New York NY 10270

LOOMIS, HOWARD KREY, banker; b. Omaha, Apr. 9, 1927; s. Arthur L. and Genevieve (Krey) L.; AB, Cornell U., 1949, MBA, 1950; m. Florence Porter, Apr. 24, 1954; children: Arthur L. II, Frederick S., Howard Krey, John Porter. Mgmt. trainee Hallmark Cards, Inc., Kansas City, Mo., 1953-56; sec., controller, dir. Mine Service Co., Inc., Ft. Smith, Ark., 1956-59; controller, dir. Electra Mfg. Co., Independence, Kans., 1959-63; v.p., dir. The Peoples Bank, Pratt, Kans., 1963-65, pres., 1966—; pres., dir. Gt. Plains Leasing, Inc., Pratt, 1966-80, Central States Inc., Pratt, 1970-76, Krey Co. Ltd., Pratt, 1978—; dir. Garland Coal & Mining Co., Ft. Smith, All Ins., Inc., Pratt, Kans. Devel. Credit Corp., Topeka. Past pres. Pratt County United Fund; bd. dirs., past chmn. Cannonball Trail chpt. ARC; past pres. Kanza council Boy Scouts Am. Served with AUS, 1950-52. Mem. Kans. (past transp. chmn., v.p., dir.) Pratt Area (past pres., dir.) chambers commerce, Kans. Bankers Assn. (past dir.), Fin. Execs. Inst. (Wichita chpt.), Sigma Delta Chi, Chi Psi. Republican. Presbyterian. Club: Park Hills Country (past pres.). Lodges: Elks, Rotary. Home: 502 Welton St Pratt KS 67124 Office: The Peoples Bank 222 S Main St Pratt KS 67124

LOONEY, CLAUDIA ARLENE, fund raising executive; b. Fullerton, Calif., June 13, 1946; d. Donald F. and Mildred B. (Gage) Schneider; m. James K.

Looney, Oct. 8, 1967; 1 child, Christopher K. BA, Calif. State U., 1969. Dir. youth YWCA No. Orange County, Fullerton, Calif., 1967-70; dir. dist. Camp Fire Girls, San Francisco, 1971-73; asst. exec. dir. Camp Fire Girls, Los Angeles, 1973-77; asst. dir. community resources Childrens Hosp., Los Angeles, 1977-80; dir. community devel. Orthopaedic Hosp., Los Angeles, 1980-82; sr. v.p. Saddleback Health Found. and Hosp. & Health Ctr., Laguna Hills, Calif., 1982—. Mem. steering com. United Way, Los Angeles, 1984-86. Fellow Nat. Assn. Hosp. Devel. (chmn. program Nat. Edn. Conf. 1986); mem. Nat. Soc. Fund Raising Execs. Found. (vice- chmn. 1985—), Nat. Assn. Hosp. Devel. (regional dir. 1985—), So. Calif. Assn. Hosp. Devel. (past pres., bd. dirs.), Profl. Ptnrs. (chmn. 1986), Philanthropic Ednl. Orgn. (past pres. 1968, 70, 72). Office: Saddleback Health Found 24451 Health Ctr Dr Laguna Hills CA 92653

LOONEY, WILTON D., automotive supplies company executive; b. 1919; married. With Genuine Parts Co., Atlanta, 1938—, purchasing agt., 1945-46, mgr. New Orleans wholesaling ops., 1946-55, pres., 1955-73, chief exec. officer, 1964-73, chmn., chief exec. officer, 1973—, also bd. dirs. Served with U.S. Army, World War II. Office: Genuine Parts Co 2999 Circle 75 Pkwy Atlanta GA 30339 *

LOPATIN, FLORENCE, comptroller, financial management executive; b. Detroit, May 28, 1928; d. Leo and Edith (Atkins) Grossman; m. Lawrence Harold LoPatin, Dec. 3, 1950; children—Mark Bruce, Norman Stuart. B.A., U. Mich., 1949; postgrad. Wayne U., 1949-50; B.Acctg., Walsh Coll., Troy, Mich., 1978. Mng. ptnr., Trade Markets, catalogue bus., Southfield, Mich., 1976-78; comptroller Bagel Nosh of Mich., Southfield and Detroit, 1978-85; comptroller L.H. LoPatin & Co., Southfield, 1978—; gen. ptnr., chief operating officer Trees of Life Mgmt. Co., Southfield, Mich., 1978—; comptroller, v.p., treas. River Crest Properties, Inc.; comptroller Westpoint Manor Mobile Home Park, Westridge Mobile Home Park; comptroller, mgr. Willow Oak Profl. Bldg. Brichwood Profl. Bldg.; ptnr., cons. Westpoint Manor Devel. Co., Nottingham Estates, W.R. Southfield Assocs., Birchwood Med. Ctr., Willow Oak Med. Ctr. Chmn. United Fund, Southfield, 1970; bd. dirs. Nat. Council Jewish Women, 1974-78; mem. Women's Assn. Detroit Symphony, 1975—. Mem. Southfield C. of C., Walsh Coll. Alumni Assn. Office: 3000 Town Ctr Suite 1000 Southfield MI 48075

LOPEZ-LOPEZ, MANUEL ANTHONY, utilities executive; b. Camuy, P.R., July 13, 1943; came to U.S., 1966; s. Manuel Lopez-Cordero and Elba Lopez-Lopez; m. Rosalie L. Calcagno, Sept. 2, 1972; children: Lisa C., Lori D. BEE, NYU, 1973; MEE, N.J. Inst. Tech., 1977; MBA, N.Mex. Highlands U., 1983. Registered profl. engr. Assoc. engr. Am. Electric Power Co., N.Y.C., 1974-77; sr. planning engr. Pub. Service Co. N.Mex., Albuquerque, 1978-81, mgr. fin. planning, 1982-85, mgr. strategic planning, 1986-88; mgr. interconnected systems EBASCO Services Inc., N.Y.C., 1988—; bd. dirs. Transitional Living Services, Inc., 1987—. Mem. council YMCA, 1986—. Served with USAF, 1966-70. Mem. IEEE, Nat. Soc. Profl. Engrs., Edison Electric Inst., East Central Area Reliability. Democrat. Roman Catholic. Office: EBASCO Services Inc 2 World Trade Ctr New York NY 10048

LOPEZ-MUNOZ, MARIA ROSA P., land development company executive; b. Havana, Cuba, Jan. 28, 1938; came to U.S., 1960; d. Eleuterio Perfecto and Bertha (Carmenati Colon) Perez Rodriguez; m. Gustavo Lopez-Munoz, Sept. 9, 1973. Student, Candler Coll., Havana, 1951-53; Sch. Langs., U. Jose Marti, Havana, 1954-55. Lic. interior designer. Pres. Fantasy World Acres, Inc., Coral Gables, Fla., 1970-84, pres., dir., 1984—; sec. Sandhills Corp., Coral Gables, Fla., 1978-85, dir., 1978—. Treas. Am. Cancer Soc., Miami, Fla., 1981, also sec. Hispanic Bd., 1987, and bd. dirs. aux. treas.; bd. dirs. Am. Heart Assn., Miami, 1985, also chmn. Hispanic div.; bd. dirs. YMCA, Young Patronesses of Opera, Miami, 1985, Lowe Mus. of U. Miami, 1986—. Recipient Merit award Am. Cancer Soc., 1980, 81, 82, 83, 84; Woman with Heart Award, Am. Heart Assn., 1985, Merit awards, 1980-84, Women of Yr., 1986; named to Gt. Order of José Marti, 1988. Mem. Real Estate Commn. Republican. Roman Catholic. Clubs: Ocean Reef (Key Largo, Fla.); Opera Guild (Miami); Key Biscayne Yacht; Regine's International (Paris), Jockey. Avocations: yachting, snow skiing, scuba diving, guitar. Office: Fantasy World Acres Inc 147 Alhambra Circle Suites 220-21 Coral Gables FL 33134

LORD, ESTHER A., corporate executive; b. 1932. Student, Ind. U., Am. Inst. Banking. With Assocs. Corp. N.Am., N.Y.C., 1965—, asst. treas., 1976-80, asst. v.p., 1980-82, v.p., 1982-87, sr. v.p., asst. treas., 1987—. Office: Assocs Corp of NAm 1 Gulf and Western Pla New York NY 10023 *

LORD, JACQUELINE WARD, accountant, photographer, artist; b. Andalusia, Ala., May 16, 1936; d. Marron J. and Minnie V. (Owen) Ward; m. Curtis Gaynor, Nov. 23, 1968. Student U. Ala., 1966, Auburn U., 1977, Huntingdon Coll., 1980, Troy State U., 1980; B.A. in Bus. Adminstrn., Dallas Bapt. U., 1985. News photographer corr. Andalusia (Ala.) Star-News, 1954-59, Sta. WSFA-TV, Montgomery, Ala., 1954-60; acct., bus. mgr. Reihardt Motors, Inc., Montgomery, 1962-69; office mgr., acct. Cen. Ala. Supply, Montgomery, 1969-71; acct. Chambers Constrn. Co., Montgomery, 1972-75; pres. Foxy Lady Apparel, Inc., Montgomery, 1973-76; acct. Rushton, Stakely, Johnston & Garrett, attys., Montgomery, 1975-81; acctg. supr. Arthur Andersen & Co., Dallas, 1981-82; staff acct. Burgess Co., C.P.A.s, Dallas, 1983; owner Lord & Assocs. Acctg. Service, Dallas, 1983—; tax acct. John Hasse, C.P.A., Dallas, 1984-86; Dallas Bapt. Assn., 1986—. Vol. election law commr. Sec. of State of Ala. Don Siegelman, Montgomery, 1979-80; mem. Montgomery Art Guild, 1964-65, Ala. Art League, 1964-65, Montgomery Little Theatre, 1963-65, Montgomery Choral Soc., 1965. Recipient Outstanding Achievement Bus. Mgmt. award Am. Motors, 1968. Mem. Am. Soc. Women Accts. (pres. Montgomery chpt. 1976-77, area day chmn. 1978, del. ann. meeting 1975-78). Home: 5209 Meadowside Dr Garland TX 75043

LORD, MARVIN, apparel company executive; b. N.Y.C., Sept. 22, 1937; s. Harry and Irene (Taub) L.; m. Joan Simon, Aug. 5, 1961; children—Elisa Anne, Michael Harris. B.S., Long Island U., Bklyn., 1959. Mdse. mgr. Oxford Industries, Inc., N.Y.C., 1964-66, gen. mdse. mgr., 1966-70, v.p., gen. mgr., 1970-73; pres. Holbrook Co., Inc. Div Oxford Industries, Inc., N.Y.C., 1970-85; pres., chief exec. officer Crystal Brands, Inc.-Youthwear Group, N.Y.C., 1985—; pres. Cluett Shirtmakers, N.Y.C., 1988—. chmn. Fathers Day Council, N.Y.C., 1984—. Recipient Disting. Alumni award L.I. U., 1987. Mem. Mens Fashion Assn., Young Menswear Assn. Jewish. Home: 53 Parkway Dr Roslyn Heights NY 11577 Office: Crystal Brands Inc Youthwear Group II Pennsylvania Pla New York NY 10001 also: 1372 Broadway New York NY 10118

LORDEMAN, JAMES ENGELBERT, financial company executive; b. Altoona, Pa., Aug. 20, 1923; s. James Engelbert and Aurelia Agnes (Dumm) L.; m. Erma Ilene Heinze, Sept. 4, 1947; children: Ann Marie, Nancy Jo, Jane Louise, James Charles. BS in Acctg., St. Vincent Coll., 1947; MBA, Northwestern U., 1948. Cert. internal auditor. Asst. prof. acctg. Pa. State U., State College, 1948-51; cost acctg. mgr. Ford Motor Co., Dearborn, Mich., 1951-58; dir. adminstrn. and fin. Renault, USA, N.Y.C., 1958-62; treas. Bulova Watch Co., Jackson Heights, N.Y., 1962-64; v.p. fin. Landers, Frary & Clark, New Britain, Conn., 1964-65; asst. corp. comtroller ITT World Headquarters, N.Y.C., 1965-83; chief fin. officer Am. Hotel and Motel Assn., N.Y.C., Washington, 1984—. Office: Am Hotel and Motel Assn 1201 New York Ave NW Washington DC 20005

LORENSON, HAROLD WALFRED, manufacturing company executive; b. Bristol, Conn., July 8, 1928; s. Oscar W. and Edith Marion (Anderson) L.; m. Phoebe Laura Blomstrann, Oct. 27, 1951; children: Linda Lysaght, Karen Tracey, David, Greta Robbins. AS in Elec. Engring., Hartford State Tech. Inst., 1948. Dist. sales mgr. Superior Electric Co., Cleve., 1954-63; internat. sales mgr. Superior Electric Co., Bristol, 1969-75, v.p. sales, 1977-86, pres. specialty products div., 1986—; mgr. European sales Superior Electric Nederland BV, Hague, Netherlands, 1963-69; mng. dir. Superior Electric Nederland BV, 1975-77, bd. dirs., 1977—; pre. Electro-Kinesis, Inc., 1987—. With USMC, 1952-54. Mem. Electronic Motion Control Assn. (sec., treas. 1982-88, bd. dirs.), Chippanee Golf Club (Bristol). Republican. Congregationalist. Home: 15 Tanglewood Rd Bristol CT 06010 Office: Superior Electric Co 383 Middle St Bristol CT 06010

LORENTZEN, CARL WARREN, chemical company executive; b. N.Y.C., Dec. 23, 1929; s. Carl P. and Elvira C. (Kallies) L.; m. Karen M. Hansen, Apr. 22, 1956; children: Eric Carl, Leif Parker, Kyle David, Kristen Anne, Keira Jean. B.A., Adelphi Coll., 1951; grad., Advanced Mgmt. Program, Harvard Bus. Sch., 1977. Dir. mktg. Charles Pfizer, N.Y., 1962-64; dir. mktg. chem. div. S.C. Johnson & Sons, Inc., N.Y., 1964-66, v.p. mktg. organic div., 1967-69; pres. polymers div. W. R. Grace & Co., N.Y., 1969-71; exec. v.p. Dewey & Almy subs. W.R. Grace, N.Y., 1971-75, pres. organic chem. div., 1975-78, v.p., 1978-85, sr. v.p. specialty chem. div., 1986—; dir. Cambridge Trust Co.; adj. faculty mem. U. Lowell, Mass. Served to 1st lt., inf. U.S. Army, 1951-54. Mem. Soc. Chem. Industry, Comml. Devel. Assn., Drug, Chem. and Allied Trades Assn. (pres.), Chem. Mfrs. Assn. (bd. dirs.). Clubs: Southport (Maine); Yacht. Office: W R Grace & Co 1114 Ave of the Americas New York NY 10036

LORENTZEN, KENNETH NEIL, financial services executive; b. Detroit, Dec. 28, 1951; s. Lawrence C. and Helen Jule (Hare) L.; m. Lee Ann Johnson, May 18, 1985; 1 child, Ann Elizabeth. BA, Denison U., 1974; JD, Wayne State U., 1977. Sole practice Jackson, Mich., 1977-79; loan officer County Savs. Bank, Newark, Ohio, 1979-81; dept. mgr., retail banking Equitable Fed. Savs. Bank, Lancaster, Ohio, 1981-83; cons. Ohio Fin. Cons., Inc., Columbus, Ohio, 1983-85; prin. Thrift Cons., Inc., Columbus, Ohio, 1985-87; project dir. Whirlpool Fin. Corp., Benton Harbor, Mich., 1987—. Office: Whirlpool Acceptance Corp 553 Benson Rd Benton Harbor MI 49022

LORENZ, JAMES MICHAEL, stockbroker; b. Boston, Mar. 10, 1965; s. Paul Daniel and Janice Marie (Grafton) L. BS, Roger Williams Coll, 1987; car. Registered rep. First Investors Corp., Cranston, R.I., 1987; stockbroker Equities Internat. Securities, Providence, 1987-88, Josephthal & Co., Inc., Boston, 1988—. Home: PO Box 35 Portsmouth RI 02871

LORENZ, JUDITH MABLE, aviation executive, accountant; b. Manitowoc, Wis., Oct. 17, 1947; d. Minor J. Vanschepen and Olive M. (Gustaveson) Karstaedt; m. John G. Lorenz, jan. 21, 1967; children: Anne M., Donna L., John M., Paul M.G. Pres. Chgo. Skyline Ltd., 1980—. Mem. St. Thomas More Home Sch. Assn., Chgo.; pres., bd. dirs. Midway Airport Tenants Assn., Chgo. Mem. Aircraft Owners and Pilots Assn., Ill. Pilots Assn., Chgo. Assn. Commerce and Industry. Republican. Roman Catholic. Office: Chgo Skyline Ltd 5245 W 55th St Room 106 Chicago IL 60638

LORENZO, FRANCISCO A., airline companies executive; b. N.Y.C., May 19, 1940; s. Olegario and Ana (Mateos) L.; m. Sharon Neill Murray, Oct. 14, 1972. BA, Columbia U., 1961; MBA, Harvard U., 1963. Fin. analyst TWA, 1963-65; mgr. fin. analysis Eastern Airlines, 1965-66; founder, chmn. bd. Lorenzo, Carney & Co. (fin. advisers), N.Y.C., from 1966; chmn. bd. Jet Capital Corp. (fin. advisers), Houston, from 1969; pres. Tex. Internat. Airlines, Inc., Houston, 1972-80, chmn. exec. com., 1980—; pres. Tex. Air Corp., 1980-85, chmn., chief exec. officer, 1986—; chmn. N.Y. Airlines, 1980-87, Continental Airlines Corp., Houston, 1982-88, Eastern Air Lines, Inc. (subs. Tex. Air Corp.), Miami, 1987—; chmn. bd. dirs. Eastern Airlines. Served with AUS, 1963. *

LORING, ARTHUR, lawyer, financial services company executive; b. N.Y.C., Oct. 13, 1947; s. Murray and Mildred (Rogers) L.; m. Vicki Hootstein, June 4, 1978. B.S. in Commerce, Washington and Lee U., 1969; J.D. cum laude, Boston U., 1972. Bar: Mass. 1972. Atty. Fidelity Mgmt. & Research Co., Boston, 1972; sr. legal counsel Fidelity Mgmt. & Research Co., 1980-82, v.p., gen. counsel, 1984—; v.p.-legal FMR Corp., Boston, 1982—; sec. Fidelity Group of Funds, Boston, 1983—; bd. govs. Investment Co. Inst., 1988—. Mem. ABA (securities regulation com.), Boston Bar Assn., Am. Corp. Counsel Assn., Cavendish (dir. 1981-84), Boston Chess (pres. Brookline, Mass. 1981-83), Pinebrook Country Club. Republican. Jewish. Home: 37 Brimmer St Boston MA 02108 Office: Fidelity Mgmt & Rsch Co 82 Devonshire St Boston MA 02109

LORING, CALEB, JR., investment company executive; b. Boston, Feb. 5, 1921; s. Caleb and Suzanne (Bailey) L.; m. Rosemary Merrill, Feb. 12, 1943; children—Caleb, David, Rosemary, Keith. A.B., Harvard U., 1943, LL.B., 1948. Bar: Mass. 1948. Asso., then partner firm Gaston, Snow, Motley & Holt, Boston, 1948-70; dir., trustee Loring, Wolcott and Coolidge Office-Fiduciary Services, Boston, 1948-86; v.p., dir. Puritan Fund, Inc., and all other funds in Fidelity Group of Funds, Boston, 1973-86; treas. Fidelity Mgmt. & Research Co., Boston, 1977-86, ret., 1986; dir. Fidelity Mgmt. & Research Co., 1959-86; mng. dir. FMR Corp. (parent co. Fidelity Mgmt. & Rsch. Co.), Boston, 1986—. Served with USNR, 1943-46. Mem. Am. Bar Assn., Mass. Bar Assn., Boston Bar Assn. Home: Paine Ave Prides Crossing MA 01965 Office: FMR Corp 82 Devonshire St #54A Boston MA 02109

LORINSKY, LARRY, international trade executive, consultant; b. New Britain, Conn., July 31, 1944; s. Jacob and Bernice Edythe (Horn) L.; BA, U. Conn., 1966, MA, 1968; m. Laurie Clark Griffin, June 9, 1968; children: Michael Bliss, Jennifer Bartlett, Jessica Clark. Ops. mgr., then trading mgr. Norwich Iron & Metal Co. (Conn.), 1965-75; ferrous export mgr. Comml. Metals Co., Dallas, 1975-77, br. mgr., San Francisco, 1977-81 , West Coast area mgr., 1980-81; exec. v.p. Technalloy Inc., San Jose, Calif., 1981-83; dir. nonferrous alloys David Joseph Co., 1983-84; pres., chief exec. officer Lornat Metals Trading, Inc., 1984-87; project mgr. Mindseed Corp., 1987—; ltd. dir., rep. METALSASIA Internat. Mem. Nat. Inst. Scrap Iron and Steel (nat. export council), Seaguard Svcs. Inc. (dir.), Locell Assocs. Ltd., Nat. Assn. Recycling Industry (nat. traffic com.), Brisbane (Calif.) C. of C. (dir. 1977-81). Democrat. Jewish. Club: Masons.

LORION, DIANE ALISON, computer company manager, editor, graphic artist; b. Fitchburg, Mass., July 1, 1955; d. Harold Arthur and Alice Mary (LeBlanc) Lacroix; m. Dennis Francis Lorion, Aug. 16, 1975 (div.); 1 child, Alison Judith; m. Andrew Maxwell Levin, May 20, 1989. Student Lake Erie Coll., Painesville, Ohio, 1973-74, Fitchburg State Coll., 1974; A. in Bus. Adminstrn., Mount Wachusett Community Coll., Gardner, Mass., 1979; B.B.A., Fitchburg State Coll., 1980; M.B.A., Suffolk U., Boston, 1983. Cert. stage presence judge. Hostess, cashier, asst. buyer Old Mill Restaurant, Westminster, Mass., 1974-75; inventory control clk., stockroom attendant Digital Equipment Corp., Westminster, 1975-78, bill of material engr., Westminster and Marlboro, Mass., 1978-81, new products mfg. planner, 1981-82, sr. engring. tech. support adminstr., 1982, corp. newsletter editor, 1980-84, product mgr., 1982-86, sr. product mgr., Stow, Mass., 1986-87; sr. product mktg. mgr., 1988— . Editor, graphic artist: The Key-Note, 1984-88, Harmony From Our Hearts, 1985. Chmn. troop com. Montachusett Coun. Girl Scouts U.S.A., 1985-86, 88—. Mem. Harmony, Inc., (chpt. pres. 1983-84, area parliamentarian 1984-88, internat. bd. asst. 1984—, cert. stage presence judge 1986—, chmn. judges candidate 1986—, stage presence coach 1984—), Nat. Assn. Female Execs., Inc., Mt. Wachusett Community Coll. Alumni Assn., Fitchburg State Alumni Assn., Suffolk U. Alumni Assn., Digital Equipment Computer Users Soc. Democrat. Roman Catholic. Home: 15 Overlook Rd Westminster MA 01473 Office: Field Svc Mktg Digital Equipment Corp 40 Old Bolton Rd 0G01-2/G16 Stow MA 01775

LORNE, SIMON MICHAEL, lawyer; b. Hampton, Eng., Feb. 1, 1946; came to U.S., 1952, naturalized, 1961; s. Henry Thomas and Daphne Mary (Brough) L.; A.B. cum laude, Occidental Coll., 1967; J.D. magna cum laude, U. Mich., 1970; m. Patricia Ann Coady, Aug. 12, 1967; children—Christopher, Michele, Allison, Nathan James, Katrina. Admitted to Calif. bar, 1971; assoc. firm Munger, Tolles & Olson, Los Angeles, 1970-72, ptnr., 1972—; vis. assoc. prof. law U. Pa., 1977-78, acting dir. Ctr. Study of Fin. Instns., 1977-78; lectr. in law, corp. fin. U. So. Calif., 1986—. Author: Acquisitions and Mergers: Negotiated and Contested Transactions, 1985. Mem. Los Angeles Mayor's Com. on Internat. Trade Devel., 1979-81; bd. dirs., sec. Los Angeles Internat. Trade Devel. Corp., 1982-85; mem. adv. com. to U.S. Senator S.I. Hayakawa on Internat. Trade, 1979-82; bd. govs. Econ. Literacy Council Calif., 1981-87; mem. Nat. Legal Adv. Commn., Nat. Assn. Security Dealers, 1988—. Served with USMCR, 1967-68. Mem. Los Angeles Area C. of C. (exec. com., internat. commerce com., leadership mission to People's Republic of China, 1980), ABA, Los Angeles County Bar Assn. (exec. com. bus. and corps. law sect., chmn. 1984-85). Republican. Roman Catholic. Clubs: Jonathan; Lake Arrowhead Yacht. Home: 14951 Altata Dr Pacific Palisades CA 90272 Office: Munger Tolles & Olson 355 S Grand Ave 35th Fl Los Angeles CA 90071

LORSCH, JAY WILLIAM, human relations educator; b. St. Joseph, Mo., Oct. 8, 1932; s. Hans R. and Serina B. (Levin) L.; m. Patricia Welbourn, July 1, 1978; children by previous marriage: Robin, Jon, David. AB, Antioch Coll., 1955; MS, Columbia U., 1956; DBA, Harvard U., 1964. Rsch. fellow Harvard U. Grad Sch. Bus. Adminstrn., Boston, 1964-65; from asst. prof. to prof. Harvard U. Grad. Sch. Bus Adminstrn., Boston, 1965—; Louis E. Kirstein prof. human relations Harvard U. Grad. Sch. Bus. Adminstrn., Boston, 1977—, sr. assoc. dean, dir. rsch., 1986—; with controller's dept. Hallmark Cards, Inc., 1959; bd. dirs. Brunswick Corp., Sandy Corp. Author: Product Innovation and Organization, 1965, (with Gene Dalton and Paul R. Lawrence) Organizational Structure and Design, 1967, (with Lawrence) Organization and Environment: Managing Differentiation and Integration, 1967, Organizational Development: Diagnosis and Action, 1969, Studies in Organization Design, 1970, (with Louis B. Barnes) Managers and Their Careers: Cases and Readings, 1972, (with Lawrence) Organization Planning: Cases and Concepts, 1972, Managing Groups and Intergroup Relations, 1972, (with Stephen A. Allen) Managing Diversity and Interdepndence: An Organizational Study of Multidivisional Firms, 1973, (with John J. Morse) Organizations and Their Members: A Contingency Approach, 1975, (with Lawrence and Barnes) Organizational Behavior and Adminstration, 1976, Understanding Management, 1978, Decision Making at the Top, 1983, Handbook of Organizational Behavior, 1987; Pawns or Potentates, 1989; contbr. to bus. and mgmt. jours., 1983. Lt. U.S. Army, 1956-59. Recipient Book of Yr. award Acad. of Mgmt., 1978. Office: Harvard U Grad Sch Bus Adminstrn Boston MA 02163

LORUSSO, JOSEPH ANTHONY, investment officer; b. Bklyn., July 14, 1957; s. Pat and Mary (Lupo) L.; m. Rose Marie Kelley, May 11, 1980; children: Joseph P., James R. BA, Merrimack Coll., 1979; MBA, Drexel U., 1982. Budget analyst City of N.Y. Office of Mgmt. and Budget, 1979-81; investment analyst Penn Mut. Life Ins. Co., Phila., 1983-85; investment officer Conn. Mut. Life Ins. Co., Hartford, 1985—. Mem. Fin. Analysts Soc. Republican. Roman Catholic.

LOSCH, DAVID EDWARD, chemical company executive; b. Upland, Calif., June 2, 1954; s. Edward Dougherty and Shirley Diane (Martin) L.; m. E. Marianne Feenstra, June 12, 1976; children: Matthew, Elizabeth. BSE, Princeton U., 1975; MBA, Harvard U., 1977. With Olin Corp., Pasadena, Tex., 1977-78; process engr. Olin Corp., Stamford, Conn., 1978—, econ. evaluator, market mgr., mgr. treasury analysis, mgr. venture and corp. devel., 1986—. Mem. Am. Inst. Chem. Engrs. Republican. Presbyterian. Home: 33 Fawnfield Rd Stamford CT 06903 Office: Olin Corp 120 Long Ridge Rd Stamford CT 06904

LOSI, MAXIM JOHN, medical communications executive; b. Jersey City, Dec. 27, 1939; s. Maxim Fortune and Carrie (Rivoli) L.; m. Mary Ann De Grandis, May 30, 1968; children: Christopher, Benjamin. AB, Princeton U., 1960; postgrad. Albert Einstein Coll. Medicine, NYU, 1960-62, PhD, 1972. Lectr. English C.W. Post Coll. L.I. U., Greenvale, N.Y., 1965-67; instr. English, Centenary Coll. for Women, Hackettstown, N.J., 1967-71, chmn. dept., 1970-71; med. abstractor/indexer Coun. for Tobacco Rsch., N.Y.C., 1972-73; freelance med. writer, 1973-74; sr. clin. info. scientist Squibb Inst. Med. Rsch., Princeton, N.J., 1974-77, project team leader, 1975-77; chief med. writer ICI Ams., Wilmington, Del., 1977-79; dir. biomed. communications Revlon Health Care Group, Tuckahoe, N.Y., 1979-86; pres. Max Losi Assocs. Biomed. Writers, Trenton, N.J., 1986-87; dir. project mgmt., sci. documentation G.H. Besselaar Assocs., Princeton, N.J., 1987—; FDA cons. Microbiol. Assocs., Bethesda, Md., 1973; mgmt. cons. Robert S. First Assocs., N.Y.C., 1974; vis. lectr. med. writing techniques med. sch. St. George U. , Grenada, W.I., 1977. Mem. Am. Med. Writers Assn. (nat. pres. 1987-88), Drug Info. Assn., Sierra Club, Council of Biology Editors, Soc. Tech. Communication. Roman Catholic. Home: 1194 Parkside Ave Trenton NJ 08618

LOSS, IRA S(AUL), investment advisor; b. N.Y.C., Jan. 3, 1945; s. Benjamin and Sara (Eliasoph) L.; m. Lynn B. Kedan, Nov. 21, 1981; children: Samantha Jory, Zachary Ryan. BA, U. Conn., 1966; JD with honors, George Washington U., 1969. Bar: Conn. 1969. Legis. asst. to Congressman E.Q. Daddario U.S. Ho. of Reps., Washington, 1970; assoc. counsel Am. Ins. Assn., Washington, 1971; sr. policy analyst Govt. Research Corp., Washington, 1972-73; v.p. Washington (D.C.) Analysis Corp., 1973—, also bd. dirs. Mem. Am. Jewish Com. Served with USAR, 1969-75. Mem. Conn. Bar Assn., Archons Soc., Phi Sigma Delta. Home: 8001 Split Oak Dr Bethesda MD 20817 Office: Washington Analysis Corp 1612 K St NW Washington DC 20006

LOTA, GERD-PETER EMIL, association executive, marketing educator; b. Ahlbeck, Germany, May 5, 1944; came to U.S., 1979; s. Franz Michael and Gerda Helene M. (Buss) L.; divorced; 1 child, Thomas Herbert. M.B.A. in Internat. Bus., U. Hamburg, 1964; degree Royal Soc. Arts and Lang., Greater London Council, 1967; postgrad. U. Paris, 1975-77. Circulation dir. Vision, Paris, 1970-76; dir. gen. export Cozelem S.A., Paris, 1977-79; v.p. mktg. Diversified D Industries, N.Y.C., 1979-80; assoc. prof. mktg. CUNY, N.Y.C., 1980—; exec. v.p. FCIB-NACM Corp., N.Y.C., 1980—; lectr., organizer internat. trade workshops and seminars, U.S., Europe. Editor FCIB Internat. Bull. and Newsletters; columnist World Trade Notes, Bus. Credit; contbg. editor internat. sect. Credit Manual of Commercial Laws of the World, Northeast International Business, Global Trade mag. Recipient Pres.'s E Star, U.S. Sec. Commerce, 1982. Mem. N.Y. Inst. Credit, N.Y. Dist. Export Council, Internat. Fiscal Assn., Nat. Assn. Credit Mgmt. (v.p. 1983—), Internat. FCIB Industry Groups (sec. 1980—). Roman Catholic. Office: FCIB-NACM Corp 520 8th Ave Ste 2201 New York NY 10018-6571

LOTEMPIO, JULIA MATILD, accountant; b. Budapest, Hungary, Oct. 14, 1934; came to U.S., 1958, naturalized 1962; d. Istvan and Irma (Sandor) Fejos; m. Anthony Joseph, Mar. 11, 1958. AAS in Lab. Tech. summa cum laude, Niagara County Community Coll., Sanborn, N.Y., 1967; BS in Tech. and Vocat. Edn. summa cum laude, SUNY, Buffalo, 1970; MEd in Guidance and Counseling, Niagara U., 1973, BBA in Acctg. summa cum laude, 1983. Sr. analyst, researcher Great Lakes Carbon Co., Niagara Falls, N.Y., 1967-71; tchr. sci. Niagara Falls Schools, 1973-75; tchr. sci. and English Starpoint Sch. System, Lockport, N.Y., 1975-77; instr. applied chem. Niagara County Community Coll., Sanborn, 1979; club adminstr., acct. Twinlo Racquetball, Inc., Niagara Falls, 1979-81; bus. cons. Twinlo Beverage, Inc., Niagara Falls, 1981-85; staff acct. J.D. Elliott & Co. PC, CPAs, Buffalo, 1986-87; acct. Lewiston, N.Y., 1988—; bd. dirs. Niagara Frontier Meth. Home Inc., Niagara Frontier Nursing Home Inc., The Blocher Homes Inc., Buffalo. Mem. faculty continuing edn., speaker, chairperson fin. and community rels. coms. United Meth. Ch., Dickersonville, N.Y., 1985—; guest speaker, counselor, tchr. Beechwood Service Guild, Buffalo, 1987—; bd. dirs. Niagara Frontier Meth. Home, Inc., Getzville, N.Y., 1988—; bd. dirs., mem. fin., investment, pension, ins., and community rels. coms. Niagara Frontier Nursing Home Co., Inc., Getzville, 1988—, Blocher Homes, Inc., Williamsville, N.Y., 1988—. Mem. Nat. Assn. Accts., Nat. Assn. Female Execs., Nat. Fedn. Bus. and Profl. Women's Club, Internat. Platform Assn., Niagara U. Alumni Assn., SUNY Coll. at Buffalo Alumni Assn., Niagara County Community Coll. Alumni Assn. Home and Office: 1026 Ridge Rd Lewiston NY 14092

LOTMAN, ALLEN MURRAY, financial executive; b. Phila., Mar. 16, 1946; s. David and Bella (Bromberg) L.; m. Marian Orrell Taylor, Sept. 10, 1970; children: Shayna Beth, Jonathan Taylor. BS, Pa. State U., 1969; MBA, Ea. N.Mex. U., 1981. CPA, Pa. Acct. Coopers-Lybrand, Phila., 1969-72; controller Johnson March corp., Phila., 1972-74, Caldwell Dress Co., Phila., 1974, Estacado, Inc., Hobbs, N.Mex., 1977-82; sr. fin. analyst Wells Fargo Alarm Svcs., Horsham, Pa., 1975-77; v.p. fin., sec., chief fin. officer WB Supply Co., Pampa, Tex., 1982—. Mem. Pampa council Boy Scouts Am., 1988. Mem. Am. Inst. CPA's, Pa. Inst. CPA's, Phi Kappa Phi. Home: 2634 Chestnut Dr Pampa TX 79065 Office: WB Supply Co 111 N Naida Rd Pampa TX 79065

LOTZ, JOHN JACOB, building contractor; b. Phila., Aug. 19, 1922; s. William F. and Amelia (Albright) L.; m. Evelyn L. Buckley, Sept. 16, 1944; children: Joan Lotz Subotnick, Mary Lotz Dare. BSCE, Lehigh U., 1947,

DHL, Combs Coll., 1970. Pres., chmn. Lotz Designers, Engrs., Constructors, Horsham, Pa.; dir. Frankford Trust Co. Past mem. Cheltenham Twp. Bd. Edn., Sch. Authority Abington Twp.; vice chmn. bd. trustees Spring Garden Coll.; past pres. Carpenters' Co. Phila. (Carpenters Hall); bd. dirs. YWCA, Pen Jer Del council. Served with Combat Engrs. U.S. Army, World War II. Benjamin Franklin fellow Royal Soc. Arts, London, 1976; named Engr. of Yr., Delaware Valley Engring. Soc., 1977. Fellow ASCE, Soc. Am. Mil. Engrs. (past pres.), ASCE; mem. Gen. Bldg. Contractors Assn. Phila. (dir., past pres.), Montgomery County Indsl. Devel. Corp. (dir.), Nat. Assn. Indsl. and Office Parks (past pres., chmn. Edn. Found.), N.E. Mfrs. Assn. (past pres.), Mfrs. Assn. of Delaware Valley (dir.), Engrs. Club Phila. (George Washington Gold medal for Engring. Excellence 1983), Am. Concrete Inst., Northeastern Ind. Devel. Assn., Am. Indsl. Devel. Council, Indsl. Developers Research Council, Prudential Bus. Campus Assn. (past pres.), Soc. Indsl. Realtors, Council Urban Econ. Dirs., Urban Land Inst., Landmarks Soc. Phila. (dir.), Beta Theta Pi (past chpt. pres.). Clubs: Masons, Shriners (trustee), Kiwanis, Seaview Country, Mfrs. Country. Contbr. articles to profl. jours.; nat. lectr. on balanced econ. growth, environ. concerns and economic need, indsl. and office park devel. Home: 1846 Hemlock Circle Abington PA 19001 Office: 601 Dresher Horsham PA 19044

LOUCKS, RALPH BRUCE, JR., investment company executive; b. St. Louis, Dec. 10, 1924; s. Ralph Bruce and Dola (Blake) L.; m. Lois Holloway, June 4, 1949 (dec. Sept. 1983); children: Elizabeth, Mary Jane; m. 2d, Mary Sutliffe Stahl, June 2, 1984. BA, Lake Forest Coll., 1949; postgrad. U. Chgo., 1950-52. Investment fund mgr. No. Trust Co., Chgo., 1950-53, Brown Bros. Harriman & Co., Chgo., 1953-55; investment counsel, pres. Tilden, Loucks & Grannis, Chgo., 1955-80; sr. v.p. Bacon, Whipple & Co., 1981-88; sr. v.p. Roberts, Loucks & Co., 1988—. Served with 11th Armored Div., AUS, 1943-45. Decorated Bronze Star medal, Purple Heart. Mem. Investment Analysts Soc., Investment Counsel Assn. Am., Huguenot Soc. Ill. (pres. 1960-61), Soc. Colonial Wars. Clubs: Economic, Racquet, Chgo. Yacht (Chgo.). Office: 250 S Wacker Dr Chicago IL 60606

LOUCKS, THOMAS ALEXANDER, mining industry analyst; b. Bronxville, N.Y., Jan. 23, 1949; s. William Dewey Jr. and Carolyn (Bade), L.; m. Dominique MarieúSolange Chesneau, Aug. 11, 1973; children: Christopher Stewart, Averil Melissa, Frances Alexandra. BA in Geology, Dartmouth Coll., 1971, MA in Geology, 1973; MBA, Stanford U., 1985. Research geologist Kennecott Copper, Salt Lake City, 1974-76; exploration geologist Bear Creek Mining Co., Tucson, Ariz., 1976-80; project geologist Climax Molybdenum, Golden, Colo., 1980-83; sr. project geologist AMAX Exploration, Golden, 1983; bus. analyst Newmont Mining Corp., N.Y.C., 1985-88; v.p. corp. devel. Royal Gold States Exploration, 1988—; v.p. Denver Mining Fin. Co., 1988—, States Exploration Ltd., 1988—. Contbr. articles to profl. jours.; photographer photos in maga. Bd. dirs. Flying Dutchman Homeowner's Assn., Keystone, Colo., 1987-89; trip leader Boy Scouts Am., New Canaan, Conn., 1986-88. Sigma Xi grantee, 1972. Mem. Geol. Soc. Am. (Penrose Bequest grant, 1972), Soc. Mining Engrs., Am. Inst. Mining Engrs. (exec. com. sec.), Dartmouth Club, Club of N.Y. Republican. Home: 5270 S Logan Dr Littleton CO 80121 Office: Denver Mining Fin Co 1660 Wynkoop St Ste 1000 Denver CO 80202

LOUCKS, URSULA Z., venture capitalist; b. Springs, South Africa, Nov. 27, 1951; came to U.S., 1960, naturalized, 1976; d. Chester A. and Cecylia Zawistowski; m. Terry Lee Loucks, Apr. 16, 1977. B.A. in Biochemistry, U.Calif.-Berkeley, 1976; M.B.A., Wright State U., 1982; stepchildren—Todd L., Tadd L., Jon D. Mem. tech. staff Rockwell Internat., Thousand Oaks, Calif., 1974-77; pres. Priority Assocs., Red Bank, N.J., 1977—; dir. Infolink Corp., Northbrook, Ill.; v.p. UNC Ventures, Inc., Boston. Home: 183 Commonwealth Ave Boston MA 02116

LOUCKS, VERNON R., JR., hospital supply company executive; b. Evanston, Ill., Oct. 24, 1934; s. Vernon Reece and Sue (Burton) L.; m. Linda Kay Olson, May 12, 1972; children: Charles, Greg, Suzy, David, Kristi, Eric. B.A. in History, Yale U., 1957; M.B.A., Harvard U., 1963. Sr. mgmt. cons. George Fry & Assos., Chgo., 1963-65; with Baxter Travenol Labs., Inc. (now Baxter Internat. Inc.), Deerfield, Ill., 1966—, exec. v.p., 1973-76, pres., chief oper. officer, 1976-80, chief exec. officer, 1980—, chmn., 1987—, also bd. dirs.; dir. Dun & Bradstreet Corp., Emerson Electric Co., Quaker Oats Co., Anheuser-Busch Cos. Chmn. Met. Crusade of Mercy, 1977; bd. dirs. Lake Forest Hosp.; trustee Rush-Presbyn.-St. Lukes Med. Center; assoc. Northwestern U.; successor trustee Yale Corp.; chmn. Yale Devel. Bd. Served to 1st lt. USMC, 1957-60. Recipient Citizen Fellowship award Chgo. Inst. Medicine, 1982, Nat. Health Care award B'nai B'rith Youth Services, 1986; named 1983's Outstanding Exec. Officer in the health-care industry Financial World; elected to Chgo.'s Bus. Hall of Fame, Jr. Achievement, 1987. Mem. Health Industry Mfrs. Assn. (chmn. 1983), Bus. Roundtable (conf. bd.), Chgo. Com. of Chgo. Council on Fgn. Relations. Clubs: Chgo. Commonwealth, Commercial, Mid-America. Office: Baxter Internat Inc One Baxter Pkwy Deerfield IL 60015

LOUDERBACK, PETER DARRAGH, consultant; b. N.Y.C., July 16, 1931; s. Darragh and Constance (Clemens) L.; m. Roberta Widow, Jan. 7, 1978; children by previous marriage: John, Jim, Susan, Tom. BA, U. Vt., 1955. With Bell Telephone of Pa., Phila., 1955-61, supr. revenue accounting, 1959-61; cons. Peat, Marwick, Mitchell & Co., Newark, 1962-71, ptnr., 1971-79, ptnr. in charge comml. bank cons. practice, 1979-81, dir. fin. instns. cons. practice, 1981-85, prin. owner earnings performance group, 1985—. Served to capt. U.S. Army, 1961. Republican. Episcopalian. Home: 12 Woods Ln Chatham NJ 07928 Office: 383 Main St PO Box 239 Chatham NJ 07928

LOUDERBACK, ROBERTA WILDOW, financial executive; b. N.Y.C., Mar. 15, 1945; d. Robert Fritz and Mary (Kirechuck) Wildow; m. Peter Darragh Louderback, Jan. 7, 1978; stepchildren: John, James, Susan, Thomas. BA, NYU, 1965. Clk. Venet Advt. Agy., Union, N.J., 1965-68; supr. Raymonds Richards Advt., Springfield, N.J., 1969-71; mgr. media acctg. Young & Rubicam, N.Y.C., 1972-75; v.p. Benton & Bowles, N.Y.C., 1975-87; chief fin. officer Keyes, Martin, Gaby, Linett, Springfield, 1987-88; pvt. practice Chatham, N.J., 1988—.

LOUGHEED, THOMAS ROBERT, solar energy construction company executive; b. Detroit, July 8, 1941; s. Aloysius V. and Ruth S. (Stait) L.; m. Nancy E. Godt, Mar. 28, 1970; children—Thomas S., Patrick R. Student Wayne State U., 1961, postgrad., 1969-74; student Welch Sch. Acctg., Detroit, 1962; B.S., Central Mich. U., 1964, M.B.A., 1966, M.A., 1967; postgrad., MIT, 1968. Cost auditor Fisher Body div. Gen. Motors Co., Flint, Mich., 1964; staff acct. Jim Robbins Co., Troy, Mich., 1964-66; owner Dyn-A-Systems, Flint, 1966-83; treas., sec., ptnr. Talo Enterprises, Ltd., Fenton, Mich., 1976-77; v.p., treas. Dyn Am. Land, Inc., Swartz Creek, Mich., 1972-76, pres., 1976—; officer Creative Ekistic Systems and Solar Unique Networks, Ltd., Swartz Creek, 1980—; instr. statis/research design Eastern Mich. U., Flint, 1970-71; prof. Mott Community Coll., Flint, 1966-85; instr. Mich. Dept. Treasury, Mich. State U., Flint, 1972-77. Councilman City of Swartz Creek, 1976-80, mem. Planning Commn., 1976-80. Mem. Nat. Home Builders Genesee County, Am. Solar Soc., Mich. Soc. Planning Ofcls., Assn. Govtl. Accts., Pi Sigma Alpha, Alpha Kappa Psi. Democrat. Lutheran. Avocations: music, water sports. Office: 6449 Bristol Rd Swartz Creek MI 48473

LOUGHRIDGE, ROBERT FOSTER, JR., oil company executive; b. Ft. Worth, Nov. 15, 1935; s. Robert Foster and Elizabeth (Hamlet) L.; m. Celeste Page, June 15, 1962 (div. 1986); children—Christopher, Mark; m. Mary Holt, Aug. 8, 1987. B.A. summa cum laude, U. Tex., 1958; M.B.A., Harvard U., 1961. Various positions Exxon Corp., N.Y.C., Venezuela, Brazil, Argentina, Paraguay, Hong Kong, Spain, Houston, 1961-78; dir. econ. and strategic planning, chief economist Goodyear Tire & Rubber Co., Akron, Ohio, 1978-82; sr. v.p., chief fin. officer Pacific Resources, Inc., Honolulu, 1982—. Pres. Hawaii Opera; bd. dirs. Aloha United Way, Japan-Am. Soc. Served to 1st lt. AUS, 1959. Mem. Planning Execs. Inst. (pres. Akron-Canton chpt. 1981), Fin. Execs. Inst., Am. Mktg. Assn. (bd. dirs.), Internat. Bus. Coun., Nat. Assn. Bus. Economists, Mensa (pres. East Ohio group 1980), Oahu Club, Pacific Club. Republican. Home: PO Box 1192 Honolulu HI 96807 Office: Pacific Resources Inc PO Box 3379 Honolulu HI 96842

LOUIS, JOHN RAYMOND, forging equipment dealer, consultant; b. Cleve., Aug. 5, 1932; s. Cornelius W.H. and Hendreka (Bosch) L.; m. Janice Marjorie Meyers, July 15, 1955; children: John, Carol, Jim, Steve. Student, Calvin Coll., 1954-55, Cleve. State U., 1956. Plant engr. Champion Rivet, Cleve., 1955-62; forging engr. Nat. Machinery, Inc., Tiffin, Ohio, 1963-66, Champion Comml. Corp., Cleve., 1967-70; forging engr. Wodin, Inc., Bedford Heights, Ohio, 1970-73, v.p., ops., 1980-83; sr. mfg. engr. SPS Techs., Cleve., 1973-80; owner, pres. Forgedynamics, Inc., Sagamore Hills, Ohio, 1983—. Active bldg. com. Christian Reformed Ch., Warrensville Heights, Ohio, 1960, deacon, treas, bldg. fund, 1969-72, gen. fund, 1975-78; treas. Boy Scouts Am. troop, 1968. Served with USN, 1951-52. Mem. Soc. Mfg. Engrs. (sr.), Am. Soc. for Metals, Forging Industry Assn., Nat. Ry. Hist. Soc., Midwest Ry. Hist. Found. Home: 855 W Highland Rd Sagamore Hills OH 44067 Office: Forgedynamics Inc PO Box 48 Northfield OH 44067

LOUTSENHIZER, MARVIN JERRY, manufacturing executive; b. Bryan, Ohio, May 19, 1938; s. Harold Kenneth and Hazel Sarah (Martin) L.; m. Sara Ruth Loutsenhizer; children—Troy Kevin, Bradley Marvin, Natalie Joy. B.S., Manchester Coll., 1960; M.B.A., Ind. U., 1965. Various positions Gen. Telephone Co., Fort Wayne, Ind., 1966-71; acctg. mgr. Hardware Wholesalers, Fort Wayne, 1971-76, controller, 1976-78, dir. fin., 1978-80, v.p. fin., 1980—; v.p., dir. Travel Place, Fort Wayne, 1978-88. Chmn. Manchester Coll. Alumni Northeastern Ind., Fort Wayne, 1983; bd. dirs. Alumni Leadership Fort Wayne, 1988, 89; v.p., bd. dirs. Manchester Coll. Alumni, 1988-89; treas. United Way of Allen County, Fort Wayne, 1985—; chmn. bd. dirs., exec. com. Lincolnshire Ch. of Brethren, Fort Wayne, 1984—. Recipient Outstanding Alumni Services award Manchester Coll., 1984. Mem. Nat. Assn. Accts. (pres. 1979-80, pres. Lincoln Trails Regional Coun. 1983-84), Fin. Execs. Inst., Manchester Coll. Alumni Assn. (nat. v.p.). Republican. Home: 6027 Landover Pl Fort Wayne IN 46815

LOVATT, ARTHUR KINGSBURY, JR., manufacturing company executive; b. Ventura, Calif., Mar. 12, 1920; s. Arthur Kingsbury and Flora (Mercedes) L.; B.S., U. So. Calif., 1941; M.B.A., Queens U., 1943; m. Juanita Gray, Feb. 1, 1946; children—Sherry Lynn, Tim Arthur. Leaseman, Shell Oil Co., Los Angeles, 1946-51; dir. indsl. relations Willys-Overland Motors, Inc., Los Angeles, 1952-55; asst. to pres. and gen. mgr. Pastushin Aviation Corp., Los Angeles, 1955-57; pres. Lovatt Assos., Los Angeles, 1957-66; chemn. bd., pres., gen. mgr. Lovatt Tech. Corp., Santa Fe Springs, Calif., 1966—, also dir.; chmn. bd. Lovatt Sci. Corp., Santa Fe Springs, Metal Ore Processes, Inc., Santa Fe Springs; dir. Lovatt Industries, Inc., others. Mem. Calif. Republican State Central Com., 1964—; state adviser U.S. Congl. Adv. Bd.; chartered mem. Republican Pres. Task Force. Served with U.S. Army, 1943-45. Mem. Am. Legion (post comdr. 1946), AAAS, Nat. Space Inst., Am. Soc. Metals, Los Angeles C. of C., U. So. Calif. Alumni Assn. (life), Nat. Hist. Soc. (founding assoc.), N.Y. Acad. Scis., Internat. Oceanographic Found., Smithsonian Assos., Am. Ordnance Assn., Disabled Am. Vets., U.S. Senatorial Club, Nat. Rifle Assn. Club: Masons (past master, Shriner). Inventor, developer tech. processes. Office: Lovatt Tech Corp 10106 Romandel Ave Santa Fe Springs CA 90670

LOVE, DAVID, accountant; b. Cambridge, Mass., Jan. 31, 1935. BS in Econs., U. Pa., 1956; JD, Harvard U., 1959. Bar: Mass.; CPA, Mass. Mng. ptnr. Laventhol & Horwath, Boston, 1974—. Office: Laventhol & Horwath Two Center Pla Boston MA 02108

LOVE, HOWARD MCCLINTIC, diversified company executive; b. Pitts., Apr. 5, 1930; s. George Hutchinson and Margaret (McClintic) L.; B.A., Colgate U., 1952; M.B.A., Harvard U., 1956; m. Jane Vaughn, June 9, 1956; children—Marion Perkins, George Hutchinson II, Howard McClintic Jr., Jane Vaughn, Victoria Elizabeth. Mgmt. trainee Gt. Lakes Steel div. Nat. Steel Corp., Ecorse, Mich., 1956-58, operating mgmt. Gt. Lakes Steel div., 1958-63, asst. gen. mgr. sales Midwest Steel div., 1963-64, Gt. Lakes Steel div., 1964-65, asst. to pres., 1965-66, pres. Midwest Steel div., 1966—, pres. Granite City (Ill.) Steel div., 1972—, corp. pres., chief operating officer, 1975—, chief exec. officer, 1980—, also dir., mem. exec. com.; chmn. bd. Nat. Intergroup, Inc., Nat. Steel Corp., 1981—; chmn. bd. Nat. Steel Corp., 1974—; dir. Monsanto Co., St. Louis, Hamilton Oil Corp., TW Services, Inc. Trustee Colgate U., Hamilton, N.Y., U. Pitts., Pitts. Ballet Theatre, Inc.; pres. Allegheny Conf. Community Devel.; bd. dirs., pres. United Way Allegheny County, Pitts. Regional Planning Assn.; mem. exec. bd. Allegheny Trails Area council Boy Scouts Am. Served with USAF, 1952-54. Mem. Am. Iron and Steel Inst. (exec. com., dir.), Bus. Council, Bus. Roundtable, City of Pitts.-Allegheny County Pvt. Industry Council (chmn. 1981-82), Nat. Bd. Smithsonian Assocs., Beta Theta Pi. Republican. Episcopalian. Club: Masons. Office: Nat Intergroup Inc 20 Stanwix St Pittsburgh PA 15222

LOVE, JOSEPH WILLIAM, JR., retired oil company executive, real estate broker; b. Tulsa, Mar. 31, 1928; s. Joseph William and Eva Elizabeth (Henderson) L. Student Okla. State U., 1945-47; BS, U. Tulsa, 1949; postgrad. U. Houston, 1957-60. Lic. real estate broker, Tex. Various mgmt. positions Union Tex. Petroleum Corp., 1956-84; cons. in field. Pub. The Propane Futures Market Letter. Capt., USAF, 1951-55. Decorated Air Medal. Mem. Nat. Assn. Bus. Economists, Aircraft Owners and Pilots Assn., SW Chem. Assn., Realty Investment Club, Sigma Phi Epsilon. Methodist. Club: Waterwood Nat. Country. Home: 4022 Norfolk Houston TX 77027

LOVE, ROBERT JOHN, JR., financial planner. s. Robert and Florence June (Maron) L.; m. Gemma Fulgar, Nov. 27, 1987. AAS in Bus., Ocean County Coll., 1970; BS in Forestry, Colo. State U., 1976, MS in Econs., 1978. Cert. fin. planner. Forestry technician U.S. Forest Svc., Western U.S. area, 1973-76; rsch. asst. U.S. Forest Svc., Ft. Collins, Colo., 1976-78; forester U.S. Forest Svc., Hill City, S.D., 1978-86; fin. planner Waddell & Reed, Inc., Rapid City, S.D., 1986—; cons. in field. Mem. Mil. Affairs Com., Rapid City, 1987. Lt. comdr. USNR, 1970—. Mem. Inst. Assn. Cert. Fin. Planners, Soc. Am. Foresters, Toastmasters, Kiwanis, Gamma Sigma Delta. Roman Catholic. Office: Waddell & Reed Inc 2525 W Main Ste 210 Rapid City SD 57702

LOVE, ROBERT MITCHELL, mamufacturing executive; b. Chgo., Aug. 7, 1928; s. Quill Horace and Jemma (Mitchell) L.; student Monterey Peninsula Jr. Coll., 1960-61, Inst. for Orgn. Mgmt. U. Houston, 1966, 67, Tex. Christian U. Advanced Mgmt. Studies, 1968-70; m. Shari Lee Cook, Dec. 12, 1964; children—Mark, Gregory, Wendi. Customer service agt. Am. Airlines, Memphis, 1951-55, customer service mgr., Washington, 1955-59, mgr. mil. traffic office, San Francisco, 1959-63; mgr. customer service and operations Mohawk Airlines, N.Y.C., 1963-65; mgr. conv. and visitors bur. Little Rock C. of C., 1965-67; exec. v.p., gen. mgr. Jonesboro (Ark.) C. of C., 1967-71; dir. indsl. services Knoxville (Tenn.) C. of C., 1971-72; exec. v.p. Melton Hill Regional Inds. Devel. Assn., 1972-73; exec. v.p., sec. Indsl. Devel. Bd. Scott County (Tenn.), 1974-79; pres. Cumberland Wood Products, Inc., 1976—. Served with AUS, USAF, 1946-51. Decorated Bronze Star, Purple Heart. Mem. Am. Indsl. Devel. Assn., So. Indsl. Devel. Council, East Tenn. Indsl. Council, Tenn. Indsl. Devel. Council. Methodist. Mason. Office: Box 496 Oneida TN 37841

LOVEALL, JERRY DEE, controller; b. Washington, Ind., Sept. 13, 1947; s. Ernest Dee and Carrie Ann (Deffendoll) L.; m. Donna Sue Gramelspacher, Apr. 16, 1966; children: Michelle, Traci. BS in Acctg., Ind. State U., 1978. Staff acct. Leo Buttrum, CPA, Evansville, Ind., 1978-80; controller Holland (Ind.) Excavating, 1977-78, also bd. dirs.; controller Bicknell (Ind.) Minerals, Inc., 1981-87, Tri-States Double Cola Bottling Co., 1987—. Served with USN, 1965-68. Recipient Presdl. citation USN, 1967. Mem. Nat. Assn. Accts., VFW, DAV. Home: 6555 Yorktown Ct Newburgh IN 47630 Office: Tri-States Double Cola Bottling Co Inc PO Box 3209 Evansville IN 47731

LOVEJOY, GEORGE MONTGOMERY, JR., real estate executive; b. Newton, Mass., Apr. 15, 1930; s. George Montgomery and Margaret (King) L.; m. Ellen West Childs, June 30, 1956; children: George Montgomery III, Edward R., Philip W., Henry W. BA, Harvard U., 1951. V.p. Minot, DeBlois & Maddison, Boston, 1955-72; exec. v.p. Meredith & Grew, Inc., Boston, 1972-78, pres., 1978-88, chmn., 1988—; trustee Scudder Cash Investment Trust, Scudder GNMA Fund, Scudder Growth and Income Fund, Scudder Income Fund, Scudder Mcpl. Trust, Scudder Tax Free Money Fund, Scudder Treasurers Trust. Mem. planning bd. Town of Weston, Mass., 1961-68, chmn., 1965-67; selectman, Town of Weston, 1968-71, chmn. selectmen, 1970-71; bd. dirs., past chmn. Boston Mcpl. Research Bur., 1966—; mem. sr. adv. group Econ. Edn. Council Mass.; mem. com. Fund for Preservation of Wildlife and Natural Areas; trustee Mass. Eye and Ear Infirmary; bd. govs. New Eng. Aquarium; trustee Radcliffe Coll.; mem. corp. Northeastern U. Mem. Am. Soc. Real Estate Counselors (past pres., bd. govs.), Greater Boston Bldg. Owners and Mgrs. Assn. (past pres.), Internat. Council Shopping Ctrs., Inst. Real Estate Mgmt. (past pres. New Eng. chpt.), Greater Boston Real Estate Bd. (past pres.), Mass. Assn. Realtors, Nat. Assn. Realtors, Urban Land Inst., Harvard Alumni Assn. (bd. dirs.), Harvard Club of Boston (past pres.). Home: 81 Beacon St Boston MA 02108 Office: Meredith & Grew Inc 160 Federal St Boston MA 02110

LOVEJOY, LEE HAROLD, investment company executive; b. Aurora, Mo., July 19, 1936; s. Harold B. and Lorene E. (Spangler) L.; B.S., Drake U., 1958; m. Carol L. Nellis, Feb. 14, 1976; children by previous marriage—Steven Lee, Kristin Ann. With Paine Webber Jackson & Curtis, St. Paul, 1965-68, mgr. Twin Cities instl. dept., Mpls., 1968-72, v.p./mgr. New Eng., Boston, 1972-74, sr. v.p./mgr. nat. instl. equity dept., 1974-77; sr. v.p., dir., chief adminstrv. officer, dir. mktg. Paine Webber Mitchell Hutchins Inc., N.Y.C., 1977-83, sr. v.p. consumer products group, Phila., 1983-88, Tucker Anthony & R.L. Day, Inc., Phila., 1988—. Mem. St. Paul Mayor's Legal and Fin. Adv. Com. Bd. dirs. Presbyn. Homes Found.; trustee Drake U. Served to capt. USAF, 1958-65. Mem. Internat. Golf Sponsors Assn., Security Industry Assn., Boston Security Traders, Boston Investment Club, Security Traders N.Y., Sigma Alpha Epsilon, Omicron Delta Kappa, Arnold Air Soc. Republican. Home: Hideaway Farm RD 2 Hampton NJ 08827 Office: 1760 Market St Philadelphia PA 19103

LOVEJOY, WILLIAM JOSEPH, marketing executive; b. Bklyn., Sept. 2, 1940; s. William G. and Catherine J. (Barry) L.; m. Geraldine V. Smith, Feb. 12, 1966; children: William Jerome, Catherine Elizabeth. BS, St. Francis Coll., 1975; MBA, Fairleigh Dickinson U., 1981. Teller First Nat. City Bank, Bklyn., 1959-62; mem. credit staff GMAC, Bklyn., 1962-71; mgr. GMAC, Parsippany, N.J., 1974-75; asst. control mgr. GMAC, Washington, 1975-78; regional mgr. GMAC, Denver, 1981-84; group v.p. mktg. GMAC, Detroit, 1984—, v.p. ops., 1985-88, also bd. dirs. With U.S. Army, 1961-62. Office: GMAC 3044 W Grand Blvd Detroit MI 48202

LOVELACE, JON B., investment management company executive; b. Detroit, Feb. 6, 1927; s. Jonathan Bell and Marie (Andersen) L.; m. Lillian Pierson, Dec. 29, 1950; children: Carey, James, Jeffrey, Robert. A.B. cum laude, Princeton U., 1950. Personnel asst. Pacific Finance Co., 1950-51; with Capital Research & Mgmt. Co., L.A., 1951—, treas., 1955-62, v.p., 1957-62, exec. v.p., 1962-64, pres., 1964-75, 82-83, chmn. bd., 1975-82, 83—, also dir.; chmn. bd. Investment Co. Am., 1982—, Capital Income Builder, 1987—, Am. Mut. Fund Inc., 1971—; bd. dirs. Capital Research Co., 1967—, Am. Pub. Radio; pres., dir. New Perspective Fund; vice chmn. Capital Group, Inc. Trustee Claremont McKenna Coll.; mem. bd. fellows Claremont U. Ctr.; mem. adv. bd. Stanford U. N.E. Asia/U.S. Forum on Internat. Policy; mem. adv. council Stanford U. Grad. Sch. Bus.; trustee Calif. Inst. Arts, chmn., 1983-88; trustee Santa Barbara Med. Found. Clinic, J. Paul Getty Mus., chmn. 1988—. Mem. Council on Fgn. Relations, Sierra Club. Clubs: Princeton (N.Y.C.), University (N.Y.C.); Calif. (Los Angeles). Home: 800 W First St Los Angeles CA 90012 also: 780 El Bosque Rd Santa Barbara CA 93108 Office: Capital Rsch & Mgmt Co 333 S Hope St Los Angeles CA 90071

LOVELAND, HOLLY STANDISH, information systems executive; b. Slater, S.C., Aug. 28, 1947; d. Albert C. and Lucille E. (Standish) L. AA, Macomb Coll., 1974; BA Siena Heights Coll.,1985. Applications analyst Burroughs Corp., Detroit, 1977-79; programmer analyst Ford Hosp., Detroit, 1979-80, project leader applications support, 1980, project mgr. applications support, 1980-82, mgr. systems services, 1982-84; dept. exec. VI, info. services Wayne County, Detroit, 1984-86, dir. data services City of Milw., 1986—; computer cons. Cons. mem. MIS adv. bd. Marquette U. Mem. Soc. for Info. Mgmt. (Wis. chpt. sec.). Home: 2538 S Wentworth Ave Milwaukee WI 53207 Office: 809 N Broadway Rm 400 Milwaukee WI 53202

LOVELL, FRANCIS JOSEPH, III, investment company executive; b. Boston, Mar. 21, 1949; s. Frank J. and Patricia Anna (Donnellan) L.; BBA, Nichols Coll., 1971. With Brown Bros. Harriman & Co., Boston, 1971, asst. mgr., 1984—. Mem. New Eng. Hist. Gen. Soc., United Way Loaned Exec. Assn. (v.p.). Republican. Home: 25 Pomfret St West Roxbury MA 02132 Summer Home: 48 Hidden Village Rd West Falmouth MA 02574 Office: 40 Water St Boston MA 02109

LOVELL, JAMES C., business executive; b. Nashville, Sept. 24, 1926; s. James and Pauline (Bernhardt) L.; m. Mary Jordan, Sept. 23, 1950; Mary Paula, Jane Clarice, Beth Ann. B.S., U. Tenn., 1949. Pres., J.B. White Co., Columbia, S.C., 1957-64; gen. mdse. mgr. N.Y.O.-Mercantile, N.Y.C., 1964-68; group pres. Castner Knott Co., Nashville, 1968-75; corp. pres. Mercantile Stores Co., Inc., N.Y.C., 1975—, also dir. Bd. dirs. Better Bus. Bur., Nashville, 1969, YMCA, Nashville, 1969, Jr. Achievement, Nashville, 1970, Travelers Aid, Nashville, 1970. Served with U.S. Army, 1944-47. Clubs: Union League, Nashville City. Home: 177 Rumson Rd Rumson NJ 07660 Office: Merc Stores Co Inc 128 W 31st St New York NY 10001

LOVELL, ROBERT MARLOW, JR., investment manager; b. Orange, N.J., June 24, 1930; s. Robert Marlow and Agnes Whipple (Keen) L.; m. Barbara Jane Cronin, Jan. 16, 1960; children—Kimberley, Kerry, Anthony, Matthew. B.A. with honors in History, Princeton U., N.J., 1952. Trainee Halsey, Stuart & Co., N.Y.C., 1955-57; assoc. Lehman Bros., N.Y.C., 1957-64, assoc. dir., investment adv. service, 1965-67; v.p. New Court Securities Corp., N.Y.C., 1968-70; fin. v.p. Crum & Forster, Morristown, N.J., 1970-73, sr. v.p. fin., 1973-85; pres. First Quadrant Corp., 1985-88, chmn. bd., 1988—; trustee Coll. Retirement Equities Fund, 1976-88; dir. Horizon Bank, N.J.; bd. dirs. Princeton Trust, N.J. Contbr. articles to profl. jours. Trustee, Morristown Meml. Hosp., 1977-84, treas., chmn. fin. com., 1979-84; sec. Princeton's Class of 1952, 1977-82. Served to lt. (j.g.) USNR, 1955-57. Mem. Fin. Analysts Fedn., N.Y. Soc. Securities Analysts. Ins. Investment Officers, Am. Fin. Assn. Republican. Presbyterian. Club: Princeton Quadrangle. Home: Featherbed Ln New Vernon NJ 07976 Office: First Quadrant Corp 305 Madison Ave Morristown NJ 07962

LOVELL, THEODORE, electrical engineer, consultant; b. Paterson, N.J., May 10, 1928; s. George Whiting and Ethel Carol (Berner) L.; m. Wilma Syperda, May 8, 1948 (div. Oct. 1961); m. Joyce Smelik, July 15, 1962; children: Laurie, Dorothy Jane, Valerie, Cynthia, Karen, Barbara. BEE, Newark Coll. Engring., 1948; postgrad., Canadian Inst. Tech., 1950. Exec. dir. Lovell Electric Co., Franklin Lakes, N.J., 1955-82; ptnr., exec. dir. Lovell Design Services, Swedesboro, N.J., 1982-86. Author engring. computer software, 1982. Pres. Bloomingdale Bd. Edn., N.J., 1970-82; mem. Mcpl. Planning Bd., Bloomingdale, 1980-82, Swedesboro/Woolwich Bd. Edn., 1987—; mayoral candidate Borough of Bloomingdale, 1982. Recipient Outstanding Service award Lake Iosco Co., Bloomingdale, 1985. Mem. Am. Soc. Engring. Technicians, Radio Club Am., Dickinson Theater Organ Soc. Republican. Presbyterian. Home: 502 Liberty Ct Woolwich Township NJ 08085 Office: Lovell Design Svcs 530 Commerce St Franklin Lakes NJ 07417

LOVELL, WALTER CARL, engineer, inventor; b. Springfield, Vt., May 7, 1934; s. John Vincent and Sophia Victoria (Klementowicz) L.; m. Patricia Ann Lawrence, May 6, 1951; children: Donna, Linda, Carol, Patricia, Diane, Walter Jr. B of Engring., Hillyer Coll., Hartford, Conn., 1959. Project engr. Hartford Machine Screw Co., Windsor, Conn., 1954-59; design engr. DeBell and Richardson Labs., Enfield, Conn., 1960-62; cons. engr. Longmeadow, Mass., 1962—; freelance inventor Wilbraham, Mass., 1965—. Numerous patents include Egg-Stir mixer, crown closure sealing gasket and circular unleakable bottle cap; composer over 50 country-and-Western songs. Office: 348 Mountain Rd Wilbraham MA 01095

LOVEN, ANDREW WITHERSPOON, environmental engineering company executive; b. Crossnore, N.C., Jan. 31, 1935; s. Andrew Witherspoon Loven and Annie Laura (Crowell) Stewart; m. Elizabeth Joann DeGroot, June 20, 1959; children: Laura Elizabeth, James Edward. BS, Maryville

Coll., 1957; PhD, U. N.C., 1962. Registered profl. engr., Va., Ga., Iowa, Md., N.C., S.C., D.C., Ohio, Fla. Rsch. assoc. U. N.C., Chapel Hill, 1962-63; sr. rsch. chemist Westvaco Corp., Charleston, S.C., 1963-66; mgr. carbon devel. Westvaco Corp., Charleston, 1966-71, mgr. Westvaco Wastewater Cons. Service, 1967-71; mgr. engring. concepts Engring.-Sci. Inc., McLean, Va., 1971-74; v.p., regional mgr. Engring.-Sci. Inc., Atlanta, 1974-80, group v.p., 1980-86; pres. Engring. Sci. Inc., Pasadena, Calif., 1986—. Contbr. articles to profl. jours. NSF grantee, 1958-59. Mem. Am. Acad. Environ. Engrs. (membership com. 1985—), Water Pollution Control Fed., Am. Inst. Chem. Engrs., Am. Water Works Assn., Nat. Soc. Profl. Engrs., Am. Pub. Works Assn., Willow Springs Club, Alpha Gamma Sigma, Sigma Xi. Home: 514 Starlight Crest Dr La Cañada CA 91011 Office: Engring-Sci Inc 75 N Fair Oaks Pasadena CA 91103

LOVETT, RADFORD DOW, real estate and investment company executive; b. Jacksonville, Fla., Sept. 6, 1933; s. William Radford and Agnes (Dow) L.; AB, Harvard U., 1955; m. Katharine Rutledge Howe, June 25, 1955; children: Katharine, William Radford, Philip, Lauren. With Merrill Lynch, Pierce, Fenner & Smith Inc., N.Y.C., 1958-78; mng. dir., Capital Markets Group, 1975-78; pres. Piggly Wiggly Corp., Jacksonville, 1978-82; chmn. bd. Commodores Point Terminal Corp., Jacksonville, 1978—, India Wharf Assocs., Inc., Boston, 1982—; dir. First Union Corp., Fla. Rock Industries Inc., FPR Enterprises, Inc., Am. Heritage Life Investment Corp., Winn-Dixie Stores, Inc. Trustee, Drew U., 1976-79, St. Vincent's Found. Lt., F.A., U.S. Army, 1955-57. Episcopalian. Office: 1010 E Adams St PO Box 4069 Jacksonville FL 32202

LOVIG, LAWRENCE, III, management consultant; b. Norfolk, Va., Nov. 17, 1942; s. Lawrence Jr. and Edith McDowell (Burfoot) L.; m. Gail Helena Halsted, Aug. 27, 1966 (div. Dec. 1984); children: Justine Helene, Jessica, Lydia Charlotte; m. Annika Marie Olsson, Apr. 05, 1985. BS, U.S. Naval Acad., 1964; MBA, Harvard U., 1970. Cmmd. ensign USN, 1964, advanced through grades to lt. comdr., 1971, resigned, 1974; asst. to N.Am. head First Nat. Bank Chgo., 1974-75; sr. engagement mgr. McKinsey & Co., Inc., Chgo., Copenhagen and Stockholm, 1976-82; pres. Larlo, Westport, Conn., 1983-84; v.p. mktg. Kontron, Inc., Everett, Mass., 1984; mgr. Bain & Co., Inc., Boston, 1985-89, Putnam, Hayes & Bartlett, Cambridge, Mass., 1989—. Bd. dirs. Chgo. Lung Assn., 1976-79. Mem. ASTM (dir. com. on rsch. and tech. planning 1986—). Home: 377 Commonwealth Rd Wayland MA 01778 Office: Putnam Hayes & Bartlett 124 Mt Auburn St Cambridge MA 02138

LOVINGOOD, JUDSON ALLISON, aerospace industry executive; b. Birmingham, Ala., July 18, 1936; s. Samuel and Margaret Viola (Allison) L.; m. Patricia Ann Plummer, July 29, 1955 (div. 1983); children: Patricia Allison, Mary Beth, Lee Ann, Judson Samuel; m. Paulette Marie Dauro, May 27, 1983. BEE, U. Ala., 1958, PhD, 1968; MS, U. Minn., 1963. Dep. mgr. control systems NASA, Huntsville, Ala., 1968-73, mgr. dynamics and control, 1973-79, dir. systems dynamics lab., 1979-83, mgr. space shuttle main engine, 1983-86, dep. mgr. space shuttle, 1986-88, assoc. dir. space transp. system, 1988; tech. dir. Morton-Thiokol Inc., Huntsville, Ala., 1988—. Contbr. 200 articles to profl. jours. Home: 117 Hickory Hill Gurley AL 35748 Office: Morton Thiokol Inc Huntsville Div Huntsville AL 35807

LOW, JOHN HENRY, banker; b. N.Y.C., Apr. 5, 1954; s. Henry John and Vaike M.L.; B. Sci. Engring., Princeton U., 1976; M.B.A., Wharton Sch. U. Pa., 1985. Mgmt. trainee Mellon Bank, Pitts., 1976-78, credit analyst, Frankfurt, W. Ger., 1978-80, internat. rep., N.Y.C., 1980, Asst. internat. officer, 1980-81, internat. officer, 1981-82, asst. v.p., 1982-85, v.p., 1986—. Mem. AIAA, IEEE, Aircraft Owners and Pilots Assn. Clubs: Univ., Princeton (N.Y.C.); Rolling Rock; Harvard-Yale-Princeton (Pitts.). Home: 64 E 86th St New York NY 10028 Office: Mellon Bank Mellon Fin Ctr 551 Madison Ave New York NY 10022

LOW, KENNETH GORDON, leasing company owner; b. Urbana, Mo., Apr. 26, 1924; s. J. Claude and Ada Leona (Payne) L.; m. Mary Ellen Leonard, June 21, 1953; children: Karen Denise Camm, David, Linda Kay Blackburn. BS in Agr., U. Mo., 1952; postgrad., Colo. A&M U., 1954, Drury Coll., 1954-57. County ext. agt. agr. U. Mo., Mount Vernon, 1952-56; sales rep. Beechcraft Outlet Ctr., Vandalia, Ohio, 1957-85; pres. Superior Aircraft Leasing Co., Lebanon, Mo., 1978—. Mem. Miami county Rep. Party, Ohio Rep. Party, Nat. Rep. Com., Washington, 1971—. U. Mo. scholar, 1954. Mem. Aircraft Owners and Pilots Assn. Methodist.

LOW, PAUL REVERE, business machine company executive; b. Elizabeth, N.J., Mar. 16, 1933; s. Paul R. and Bertha (Branch) L.; m. Anne Goodrich; children: John, Paul Jr., Lynda, Scott. BSEE, U. Vt., 1955, MS in Physics, 1957; PhD in EE, Stanford U., 1963. Dir. East Fishkill (N.Y.) Lab. IBM Corp., 1969-70; asst. gen. mgr. mfg. IBM Corp., Burlington, Vt., 1970-71; gen. mgr. IBM Corp., Burlington, 1971-74; dir. devel. System Products div. IBM Corp., East Fishkill and Poughkeepsie, N.Y., 1974-75, v.p. devel. and mfg., System Products div., 1975; devel. lab. dir. East Fishkill div. IBM Corp., 1979-80, gen. mgr. East Fishkill div., 1981-83; v.p. Gen. Tech. div. IBM Corp., N.Y., 1983-84; v.p. IBM Corp., White Plains, N.Y., 1984—; bd. dirs. Dutchess Bank & Trust Co, Poughkeepsie; trustee Rensselaer Poly. Inst. Trustee Marist Coll., Poughkeepsie, 1982—; gen. mgr. United Way Dutchess County, 1983. Fellow IEEE; mem. Am. Electronics Assn., Sigma Xi, Nu Beta Pi. Club: Indian Harbor Yacht (Greenwich, Conn.). Office: IBM Corp 44 S Broadway White Plains NY 10601

LOW, ROBERT BRUCE, marketing professional; b. Detroit, Apr. 1, 1943; s. Robert Hamilton and Hele Catherine (Farkas) L.; m. Joanne A. Humpal; children: John, Jennifer. BA, Albion Coll., Mich., 1965; MEd, Wayne State U., 1976; PhD, Columbia Pacific U., San Rafael, Calif., 1983. Test technician, occupational analyst Mich. Employment Security Commn., Detroit, 1968-69; personnel research tng. mgr. Fred Sanders Co., Detroit, 1969-71, personnel mgr., indsl. relations, 1971-76, prodn. and inventory mgr., 1976-77; adminstr., research and statis. analysis Comprehensive Health Services, Detroit, 1977-81, dir. mgmt. services, 1981-85, asst. v.p. mgmt. services, pub. sales, 1985-87, v.p. mgmt. and mktg. services, 1987—; cons. Wayne State U., 1965-68, Gen. Motors Personnel Evaluation System Dept., Detroit, 1965-68; instr. Oakland Community Coll., Detroit, 1978-87. Mem. Am. Pub. Health Assn., Group Health Assn. of Am., Am. Mgmt. Assn., Coll. of Health Care Mktg. Methodist. Office: Comprehensive Health Svcs 6500 John C Lodge Detroit MI 48202

LOWDER, LONI, equipment leasing executive, consultant; b. Burley, Idaho, July 27, 1948; s. Eldon Lewis and Maxine (Preal) L.; m. Nancy Christine Poulson, Mar. 17, 1966; children: Lisa, Gregory Michael, Ryan Paul. BA in Polit. Sci., Brigham Young U., 1970; MBA, U. Utah, 1972. V.p. Interior World, Salt Lake City, 1972-76; account exec. IBM Corp., 1976-79; exec. v.p. PFC, Inc., 1979-84, pres., 1983-88; v.p. mktg. Zions Credit Corp., 1986—; mem. cons. bd. Amembal & Isom, Salt Lake City, 1987—. Mem. Am. Assn. Equipment Lessors, Western Assn. Equipment Lessors (regional chmn. 1987—), MBA Assn. U. Utah (v.p.), Mastermind Club (founding mem. Salt Lake City chpt. 1983). Home: 7 Cherrywoods Sandy UT 84092 Office: Zions Credit Corp 310 S Main Mezzanine Salt Lake City UT 84101

LOWE, GEORGE WATSON, JR., sales executive; b. Evanston, Ill., Dec. 31, 1936; s. George Watson and Elsie (Wehrmann) L. Assoc. in Applied Sci. and Bus. Data Processing, McHenry Coll., 1985. Owner Lowe Oil Co., Cary, Ill., 1962-82; dir. data processing Teledyne Big Beam, Crystal Lake, Ill., 1984-87; dir. sales Advanced Computer Systems, Crystal Lake, 1988—. Mem. McHenry County Bd., Woodstock, Ill., 1974-86, McHenry County Bd. of Health, Woodstock, Ill., 1976-78, Cary Village Bd., 1970-72, Health Systems Agy. for Kane, Lake and McHenry Counties, Inc., 1979—. Served with U.S. Army, 1960-62. Mem. Phi Theta Kappa. Republican.

LOWE, RICHARD GERALD, JR., computer programmer manager; b. Travis AFB, Calif., Nov. 8, 1960; s. Richard Gerald and Valerie Jean (Hoefer) L. Student, San Bernardino Valley Coll., 1978-80. Tech. specialist Software Techniques Inc., Los Alamitos, Calif., 1980-82, sr. tech. specialist, 1982-84, mgr. tech. services, 1984-85; mgr. cons. services Software Techniques Inc., Cypress, Calif., 1985-86; sr. programmer BIF Accutel, Camarillo, Calif., 1986-87; systems analyst BIF Accutel, Camarillo, 1987-88; mgr. project Beck Computer Systems, Long Beach, Calif., 1986—. Contbr. articles to profl. jours. Mem. Assn. Computing Machinery, Digital Equipment Corp. Users Group. Office: Beck Computer Systems 5372 Long Beach Blvd Long Beach CA 90805

LOWE, RONALD LEON, sales executive; b. Crawfordsville, Ind., July 11, 1926; s. Ora E. and Evangeline M. (Layne) L.; m. Barbara Marie Jones, Aug. 26, 1950; children: Nancy M., David D., Steven T. AB, DePauw U., 1950. From salesperson to mgr. sales promotion Diamond Internat., N.Y.C. and Springfield, Mass., 1951-61; mgr. mktg. planning and svcs. Am. Standard, N.Y.C., 1961-72; from eastern regional sales mgr. to nat. sales mgr. Roscoe Tools, Smithtown, N.Y., 1972-74; nat. sales mgr. Bemis Mfg. Co. div. Mayfair Co., Sheboygan Falls, Wis., 1974—. Contbr. articles to profl. jours. Scoutmaster Boy Scouts Am., Springfield and Darien, Conn., 1955-68; mem Young Reps., Darien, 1962-66. Served to sgt. USAF, 1942-45, PTO. Mem. Nat. Hardware Mfrs. Assn., Nat. Wholesale Hardware Assn. (assoc.), Sports Core Club (Kohler, Wis.), Elks, Masons. Republican. Episcopalian. Home: 313 Timberlake Rd Sheboygan WI 53081 Office: Bemis Mfg Co Mayfair div 300 Mill St Sheboygan WI 53085

LOWE, STEVEN WARREN, finance company executive; b. Lafayette, Ind., Jan. 30, 1948; s. Phillip Charles and Edna May (Warren) L. BS in Bus. Econs., Purdue U., 1971; MS in Mgmt., —, 1975. Fin. analyst Amoco Corp., Chgo., 1975-77; sr. fin. analyst Chemetron Corp., Chgo., 1977-78; mgr. ops. and fin. analyst DWG Corp., Miami Beach, 1978-80; sr. v.p. Jartran Inc., Miami, 1980-86; v.p. fin. Lexicon Corp., Ft. Lauderdale, Fla., 1986—; bd. dirs. Scope Inc., Rston, Va., Sigtech Corp., Reston, Lexicon Sports Corp., Ft. Lauderdale, Origin Tech. Inc., Miami. Served with Va. N.G., 1970-76. Mem. Am. Electronics Assn. Office: Lexicon Corp 2400 E Commercial Blvd Fort Lauderdale FL 33308

LOWE, TODD PARKER, investment executive; b. Dayton, Ohio, Oct. 18, 1959; s. Alfred J. and Jane (Jones) L. BS in Fin., Western Ky. U., 1981. Cert. fin. planner, Ky. Fin. cons. Merrill Lynch, Louisville, 1982-86; v.p. Future Fed. Savs. Bank, Louisville, 1986-87; portfolio mgr., analyst J.J.B. Hilliard W.L. Lyons Inc., Louisville, 1987—. Profl. musician with Tommy Dorsey Orch., Rich Little Orch., Duke Ellington Orch., Billy Vaughn Orch., Todd Lowe Dance Band, Owensboro Symphony, Flying Monkees, Four Most, 1975—. First v.p. Downtown Bus. Assn., Bowling Green, 1985-86; founder, pres. Young Assocs. at Capital Arts Ctr., Bowling Green, Ky., 1986; bd. dirs. Horse Cave (Ky.) Theatre, 1986, Louisville Jazz Soc.; chmn. arts div. Bowling Green C. of C., 1986; project exec. Econ. Impact of Arts on Ky.; co-founder Not Ready for Yuletide Players; v.p. ways and means com. Progressive Arts Soc. Mem. Internat. Assn. Fin. Planners (bd. dirs.), Inst. Cert. Fin. Planners (cert.), Ky. Chpt. Inst. Cert. Fin. Planners (bd. dirs. 1986—), Lower Ashmolian Marching Soc., Louisville Jazz Soc. (bd. dirs.), Kappa Alpha. Lodge: Rotary (chmn. Bowling Green chpt. found. 1986). Office: JJB Hilliard WL Lyons Inc Pvt Fin Svcs Group Hilliard Lyons Ctr 501 S 4th St Louisville KY 40202

LOWELL, ARTHUR HAROLD, airplane manufacturing company executive; b. Juneau, Alaska, Jan. 11, 1928; s. John and Anna Marie (Aase) L.; m. Suzanne Marie Ladner, Sept. 13, 1952; children: Barbara Ann, Michael Peter, Mary Kathryn, Patricia Renee, Sally Jane and Susan Marie (twins). BS in Acctg., Seattle U., 1952. Cost acct. Boeing Co., 1952-60, chief fin. controls Minuteman program, 1960-65, dir. fin. supersonic transport div., 1966-67, asst. dir. fin. 747 div., 1968-70, dir. fin. engring. and rsch. div., 1970-71, dir. cost control corp. office, 1971-72; dir. fin. Boeing Vertol Co., Phila., 1972-77; controller Boeing Comml. Airplane Co., 1977-81, corp. controller, 1981-84, corp. v.p. controller, 1984—; Mem. Boeing Mgmt. Assn., 1956—. Mem. acctg. assoc. adv. bd. Seattle U., 1982—, acctg. bd. visitors Pacific Luth. U., Tacoma, Wash., 1982—, Cen. Wash. U., 1988—; trustee Fin. Execs. Rsch. Found, 1985-88. With USN, 1946-47. Mem. Fin. Execs. Inst. (pres. Seattle chpt. 1985-86, chmn. com. on govt. bus. 1987—), Aerospace Industries Assn. (procurement and fin. council 1981—), Nat. Adv. Forum, Machinery and Allied Products Inst. (fin. council III 1981—), Beta Alpha Psi (nat. adv. forum 1985-88). Home: 1011 Vista Way Edmonds WA 98020 Office: The Boeing Co PO Box 3707 M/S 10-18 Seattle WA 98124-2207

LOWENFELS, FRED M., lawyer; b. Richmond, Va., Mar. 22, 1944; s. Fred C. and Joan (Weber) L.; m. Joan Roberta Brafman, June 10, 1974; children: Erica Anne, Helene Beth. AB, Harvard U., 1965, JD, 1968; postgrad., Univ. Libre de Bruxelles, 1968-69. Bar: N.Y. 1969. Assoc. Wolf, Haldenstein, Adler, Freeman & Herz, N.Y.C., 1970-74; v.p., gen. counsel Transammonia Inc., N.Y.C., 1974—. Trustee Jewish Home and Hosp. for the Aged, N.Y.C., 1974—. Mem. Assn. Bar City N.Y. Club: Harvard (N.Y.C.). Office: Transammonia Inc 350 Park Ave New York NY 10022

LOWENSTEIN, IRWIN LANG, retail furniture chain executive; b. Louisville, Aug. 17, 1935; s. Stanley Ben and Fannie Georgie (Lang) L.; m. Joel Annette Dampf, June 15, 1957; children—Jo-Anne, Suzanne, Ruth, Ellen, Stanley. B.A., Vanderbilt U., 1957. Pres. Biederman Furniture, St. Louis, 1971-72, Duchess Furniture, Florence, Ky., 1972—, Crossroads Furniture, Houston, 1972-77; Pres. Rhodes, Inc., Atlanta, 1977—, also bd. dirs.; pres. Future, Inc., Atlanta; bd. dirs. Atlantic Am. Corp., Rhodes, Inc. Trustee, v.p. The Temple; bd. dirs. Jewish Children's Services. Served with U.S. Army, 1957. Honoree Scholarship and Fellowship Fund Brandeis U., 1982; recipient Human Relations award Am. Jewish Com., 1983; bldg. named in his honor bd. trustees Bapt. Hosp., 1987. Mem. Nat. Home Furnishings Assn. (bd. dirs.). Republican. Jewish. Club: Standard (Atlanta). Home: 6275 Old Hickory Point NW Atlanta GA 30328 Office: Rhodes Inc 4370 Peachtree Rd NE Atlanta GA 30319

LOWENTHAL, HENRY, greeting card company executive; b. Frankfurt, Ger., Oct. 26, 1931; came to U.S., 1940, naturalized, 1945; s. Adolf and Kella (Suss) L.; m. Miriam Katzenstein, June 29, 1958; children—Sandra, Jeffry, Joan Chana, Benjamin, Avi. B.B.A. cum laude, City U. N.Y., 1952, M.B.A., 1953; J.D., N.Y. U., 1962. CPA. Lectr. acctg. Baruch Coll., N.Y.C., 1952-53; auditor Price Waterhouse & Co., N.Y.C., 1955-62; v.p., controller Am. Greetings Corp., Cleve., 1962-68, controller, 1966-68, sr. v.p. fin., 1977—; v.p. fin., treas. Tremco Inc., Cleve., 1968-77; mem. adv. bd. Case Western Res. U. Dept. Accountancy, 1986—. Chmn. bd. dirs. Rabbinical Coll. Telshe, 1974-77, v.p., 1977—; v.p. Hebrew Acad. Cleve., 1977—; pres. Cleve. chpt. Agudath Israel Am., 1978—; bd. dirs. Jewish Community Fedn. Cleve., 1979—; chmn. citizens rev. com. Cleveland Heights-University Heights Sch., 1972-73, mem. lay fin. com., 1974-79; mem. Cleveland Heights Citizens Adv. Com. for Community Devel., 1976-79. Served with AUS, 1953-55. Mem. AICPA, Nat. Assn. Over the Counter Cos. (budget & fin. com. 1986—, bd. dirs. 1987—), Fin. Execs. Inst. (sec. N.E. Ohio chpt. 1979-80), N.Y. Soc. CPA's, Ohio Soc. CPA's, Greater Cleve. Growth Assn., Beta Gamma Sigma, Beta Alpha Psi. Home: 3394 Blanche Ave Cleveland Heights OH 44118 Office: Am Greetings Corp 10500 American Rd Cleveland OH 44144

LOWENTHAL, MORT, investment banker; b. N.Y.C., Feb. 22, 1931; s. Martin and Essie (Albert) L.; m. Eleanor LeVine, Sept. 12, 1954; children: Leslie, Terri Ann, Emily, Meg Akabus. BS in Chem. Engring., Cornell U., 1954; MBA, Harvard U., 1956. Planning mgr., chem. mgr. products dept. Mobil Corp., N.Y.C., 1956-68, mng. dir. Donaldson, Lufkin & Jenrette, N.Y.C., 1970-78; gen. ptnr. Wertheim & Co., N.Y.C., 1978—; now mng. dir. Wertheim Schroder & Co.; bd. dirs. MidSouth Corp., MidSouth Rail Corp., Southrail Corp., Jackson, Miss., 1986—, Mont. Rail Link, Missoula, 1987—, Livingston Rebuild Ctr., Missoula, 1986—, Ideal Basic Industries, Denver, 1983-87, Stamford Econ. Assistance Corp., Conn., 1978-87. Vice-chmn. Cornell U. Council, Ithaca, N.Y., 1987—; bd. govs. Am. Jewish Com., 1987—. Mem. Cornell Alumni Assn. (pres. 1988—). Republican. Office: Wertheim Schroder & Co Equitable Ctr 787 7th Ave New York NY 10019

LOWERY, MARY BEASLEY, banker; b. Albertville, Ala., Oct. 29, 1944; d. Charlie Alvin and Mary Nell (Hearn) Beasley; m. Andrew Jackson Lowery III, July 1, 1967; children: Andrew Jackson IV, Sarah Elizabeth. BA, U. Ala., 1967. Cert. secondary tchr., Ala. Tchr. Gadsden (Ala.) City Sch. System, 1967, Huntsville (Ala.) City Sch. System, 1968-71; v.p. pub. rels. and bus. devel. Colonial Bank, Huntsville, 1982—; bd. dirs. Huntsville Hosp. Found.; chmn. advt. com. Huntsville Banks Reps., 1987-88. Mem. state conv. cabinet Pub. Rels. Coun. Ala., 1986; chmn. Summer Youth Vol. Program, Huntsville, 1977, Jail Bail for Heart Am. Heart Assn., 1986; v.p. Better Bus. Bur., Huntsville, 1987—; bd. dirs. United Way, 1988; pres. Jr. League Huntsville, 1981-82. Recipient United Negro Coll. Fund award Oakwood Coll., 1987. Mem. Huntsville C. of C. (bd. dirs. 1988-91), U. Ala. Alumni Assn. (pres. Madison County chpt. 1987-88). Presbyterian. Home: 608 Franklin St Huntsville AL 35801 Office: Colonial Bank 101 Governors Dr Huntsville AL 35801

LOWERY, ROBERT, real estate broker; b. Crockett County, Tenn., June 10, 1924; s. Roy Lowery Fergunson and Wilma Burl (Woodside) Lowery; m. Glorianna Menginou Rivera; children: Jennifer W., Robert B., Michael R., Carolina G., Viviana D., Leonora I., Roy A. BS, Miss. State U., 1949. Engring. asst. Coast & Geodetic Survey, various, 1942-44; farm gen. mgr. Nelson Rockefeller Farms Inc., Venezuela, 1949-80; real estate broker/appraiser ForKeDeer Agy., Trenton, Tenn., 1980—; cons. Entero Inc., Odem, Tex., 1986-88, Agriculture Trade Group Internat., San Diego, 1987—. Co-author: (textbook) Animal Science Ganaderia Venezolana, 1976. Gibson County Commr., Trenton, 1988; Sunday sch. tchr. Meth. Ch., Trenton, 1985—; candidate for state rep., Tenn., 1982. Served with USN, 1944-46, PTO. Mem. Am. Inst. Real Estate Appraisers, Alpha Zeta. Lodges: Masons, Trenton Lodge #86. Home: 76 Lowery Lane Rd Trenton TN 38382 Office: ForKeDeer Agy PO Box 182 Trenton TN 38382

LOWREY, E. JAMES, food service company executive; b. Lubbock, Tex., Feb. 21, 1928; s. E. J. and Sarah Ruth (Cooper) L.; m. Stella Jean Oates, Apr. 28, 1950; children—Jane Lynwood Tierney, Ernest James Jr. BBA, U. Tex., 1949. CPA, Tex. With Howard T. Cox & Co., Austin, Tex., 1949-51; ptnr. Frazer & Torbet, Houston, 1951-55, 59-70, Elgin-Butler Brick Co., Austin, 1955-59; sr. v.p. River Oaks Bank and Trust Co., Houston, 1971-73; v.p. fin., treas. SYSCO Corp., Houston, 1973-76, sr. v.p. adminstrn. and fin., 1976-78, exec. v.p. fin. and adminstrn., 1978—; also dir. SYSCO Corp. Mem. Am. Inst. CPA's, Tex. Soc. CPA's, (pres. Houston chpt. 1970-71). Republican. Presbyterian. Office: SYSCO Corp 1390 Enclave Pkwy Houston TX 77077-1430

LOWREY, RICHARD WILLIAM, architect; b. Phila., June 11, 1938; s. Charles William and Ethel May (Straley) L.; m. Eileen Joanne Wallace, Jan. 28, 1989; children: Jodi, Erika, Melanie, Ian. B.Arch., Pa. State U., 1962. Registered architect Mass., Pa. Project mgr. Nolen, Swinburne & Assocs., Phila., 1962-64, project architect, 1968-69; project architect Harold E. Wagoner, FAIA, Phila., 1964-68; constrn. mgr. Cape Lands Realty & Bldg. Corp., Brewster, Mass., 1969-70; v.p. David M. Crawley Assocs., Inc., Plymouth, Mass., 1970-75; owner Lowrey Assocs., Architects, 1975-84; pres. Architects Lowrey & Blanchard, Inc., 1984-88, owner Richard W. Lowrey, R.A., 1988—. Mem. Plymouth Hist. Dist. Commn., 1979—; trustee Old Colony Natural History Soc., 1979—; corp. mem. Plymouth Pub. Library, 1984—, Old Colony Club, 1986—. Recipient Plymouth County Renaissance award, 1980, 87, 88. Congregationalist. Mem. Masons, Kiwanis (disting. past pres. Plymouth chpt. 1980-81). Avocations: music, photography, reading, racquetball, darts.

LOWRIE, GERALD M., communications executive; b. Elaine, Alaska, July 13, 1935; m. Shirley Ruth Johnston; children: Lynn, Richard. BS, Memphis State U., 1957. With sales and mktg. IBM, 1961-68; exec. dir. Am. Bankers Assn., Washington, 1968-85; sr. v.p. corp. hdqrs. AT&T, Washington, 1985—, also bd. dirs.; mem. adv. bd. Am. Security Bank. Mem. Washington Steering Com.; chmn. com. Bus.-Govt. Rels. Coun.; bd. dirs. Greater Washington Bd. of Trade. Mem. Circle Nat. Gallery Art, Computer and Bus. Equipment Mfrs. Assn. (bd. dirs.), John F. Kennedy Ctr. Performing Arts, U.S. League Women Voters (corp. adv. com.), Nat. Mus. Women in Art (bd. dirs.), Nat. Planning Assn. (com. mem.), Washington Performing Arts Soc. (bd. dirs., exec. com.), Memphis State U. Alumni Assn., Burning Tree Club, Capitol Hill Club, City Washington Club, City Tavern Club, Georgetown Club, One 16 Club. Office: AT&T Corp Hdqrs 1120 20th St NW Ste 1000 Washington DC 20036

LOWRIE, WILLIAM G., oil company executive; b. Painesville, Ohio, Nov. 17, 1943; s. Kenneth W. and Florence H. (Strickler) L.; m. Ernestine R. Rogers, Feb. 1, 1969; children: Kristen, Kimberly. B.Chem. Engring., Ohio State U., 1966. Engr. Amoco Prodn. Co. subs. Standard Oil Co. (Ind.), New Orleans, 1966-74, area supt., Lake Charles, La., 1974-75, div. engr., Denver, 1975-78, div. prodn. mgr., Denver, 1978-79, v.p. prodn., Chgo., 1979-83; v.p. supply and marine transp. Standard Oil Co. (Ind.), Chgo., 1983-85; pres., Amoco Can., 1985-86; sr. v.p. prodn., Amoco Prodn. Co., 1986-87, exec. v.p. USA, 1987-88; exec. v.p. Amoco Oil Co., Chgo., 1989—. Bd. dirs. Colo. Civic Edn. Found., Denver, 1978. Named Outstanding Engring. Alumnus, Ohio State U., 1979, Disting. Alumnis Ohio State U., 1985. Mem. Soc. Petroleum Engrs., Am. Petroleum Inst., Healthcare Affiliates, Mid-Am. (Chgo.). Republican. Presbyterian. Office: Amoco Oil Co PO Box 87707 Chicago IL 60680-0707

LOWRY, JAMES HAMILTON, management consultant; b. Chgo., May 28, 1939; s. William E. and Camille C. L.; BA, Grinnel Coll., 1961; M in Polit. and Instl. Adminstrn., U. Pitts., 1965; PMD, Harvard U., 1973; 1 child, Aisha. Asso. dir. Peace Corps, Lima, Peru, 1965-67; spl. asst. to pres., project mgr. Bedford-Stuyvesant Restoration Corp., Bklyn., 1967-68; sr. asso. McKinsey & Co., Chgo., 1968-75; pres. James H. Lowry & Assos., Chgo., 1975—; mem. Small Bus. Edv. Com.; bd. dirs. Independence Bank, Johnson Products Co. Mem. vis. com. Harvard U., adv. bd. J.L. Kellogg Grad. Sch. Mgmt. Northwestern U.; trustee Grinnell Coll.; bd. dirs. Chgo. United, Northwestern Hosp., Chgo. Pub. Library, Ptnrs. in Internat. Edn. John Hay Whitney fellow, 1963-65; co-chmn. Chgo. United. Mem. Harvard Alumni Assn. (dir., vis. com.), Inst. Mgmt. Cons. Clubs: Econ., Monroe, Univ., Comml. of Chgo. Home: 3100 Sheridan Rd Chicago IL 60657 Office: 303 E Wacker Dr Chicago IL 60601

LOWRY, LARRY LORN, management consulting company executive; b. Lima, Ohio, Apr. 12, 1947; s. Frank William and Viola Marie L.; m. Jean Carroll Greenbaum, June 23, 1973; 1 child, Alexandra Kristin. BSEE, MIT, 1969, MSEE, 1970; MBA, Harvard U., 1972. Mgr. Boston Consulting Group, Menlo Park, Calif., 1972-80; sr. v.p. Booz, Allen & Hamilton Inc, San Francisco, 1980—; pres. Booz,Allen Capital Inc., San Francisco, 1987—. Western Electric fellow, 1969, NASA fellow, 1970. Mem. Sigma Xi, Tau Beta Pi, Eta Kappa Nu. Presbyterian. Home: 137 Stockbridge Ave Atherton CA 94025

LOWRY, WILLIAM KETCHIN, JR., insurance company executive; b. Columbia, S.C., Oct. 4, 1951; s. William Ketchin and Beverly Hubbard (Frazee) L.; m. Elaine Diana Kent, June 22, 1984; children: Jennifer Lyn, Julia Ann. BS in Bus. Adminstrn., U. S.C., 1972, M in Acctg., 1973. CPA, S.C. Supr. Ernst & Whinney, Columbia, 1973-81; sr. mgr. Price Waterhouse, Hartford, Conn., 1981-83, Phila., 1983-84; dir. corp. systems devel. and analysis Am. Can Co., Greenwich, Conn., 1984-86; v.p., treas., chief fin. officer Phoenix Re Corp. and Reinsurance Co., N.Y.C., 1986—; mem. faculty Midlands Tech. Coll., Columbia, S.C., 1980-81. Pres., bd. dirs. Groves Homes Assn., Columbia, 1980-81. Fellow Life Office Mgmt. Soc.; mem. Am. Inst. CPAs, S.C. Assn. CPAs, Fin. Execs. Inst., Am. Soc. CLUs, Beta Gamma Sigma, Omicrom Delta Kappa, Beta Alpha Psi, Omicron Delta Epsilon, Sigma Phi Epsilon. Presbyterian. Club: Forest Lake (Columbia). Home: 314 Elizabeth Ave Ramsey NJ 07446 Office: Phoenix Re Corp 80 Maiden Ln New York NY 10038

LOWTHER, FRANK EUGENE, research physicist; b. Orrville, Ohio, Feb. 3, 1929; s. John Finger and Mary Elizabeth (Mackey) L.; m. Elizabeth E. Koons, Apr. 21, 1951; children—Cynthia E., Victoria J., James A., Frank Eugene. Grad. Ohio State U., Columbus, 1952. Scientist missile systems div. Raytheon Corp., Boston, 1952-57, Gen. Electric Co., Syracuse, N.Y., and Daytona Beach, Fla., 1957-62; mgr. ozone research and devel. W.R. Grace Co., Curtis Bay, Md., 1972-75; sr. engring. assoc. Linde div. Union Carbide Corp., Tonawanda, N.Y., 1975-79; chief scientist, Purification Sci. Inc., 1979-81; chief scientist, Atlantic Richfield-Energy Conversion and Materials Lab, 1981-83; prin. scientist Atlantic Richfield-Corp. Tech., 1983-85, sci. advisor, 1985-88, research advisor, 1988—. Recipient Inventor of Yr. award Patent Law Assn. and Tech. Socs. Council, 1976. Assoc. fellow AIAA; mem. IEEE (sr.). Club: Masons. Patentee in field of ozone tech., plasma generators, solid state power devices, internal combustion engines, electro-desorption, thermoelectrics, virus and bacteria disinfection systems. Home: 2928 Clear Spring Plano TX 75075-7602 Office: 2300 W Plano Pkwy Plano TX 75075

LOYLESS, P. EDWARD, JR., mortgage banker; b. Blakely, Ga., Oct. 13, 1949; s. Perry Edward and Helen (Peek) L.; m. Barbara Sharon Robinson, June 24, 1977 (div. Aug. 1980); m. Paulette Suzanne Nagel, Oct. 23, 1982. B in Bus., Ga. State U., 1972. Loan officer Nat. Homes Acceptance Corp., Atlanta, 1977; sr. loan officer Delson Fin. Corp., Atlanta, 1977-78, Trust Co. Mortgage, Atlanta, 1978-81; v.p. Pine State Securities Corp., Tucker, Ga., 1981-85; pres. Dunwoody (Ga.) Mortgage, Inc., 1985-88, chmn., chief exec. officer, 1988—. Contbr. articles to profl. jours. Mem. Am. Inst. Mortgage Brokers, Mortgage Bankers Assn. Ga., Ga. Assn. Realtors, Nat. Assn. Home Builders, Mortgage Bankers of Am., Home Builders Assn. Met. Atlanta, Atlanta Mortgage Bankers Assn. (bd. dirs. 1987—), Ga. Inst. Mortgage Brokers (founder, bd. dirs. 1985—), Mortgage Bankers Assn. of Ga. (com. chmn.), Gwinnett County C. of C., Atlanta C. of C., Dekalb C. of C., Ducks Unltd., NRA, Citizens Right to Bear and Keep Arms, Ravinia Club (Atlanta), Bama Hunting Club, Sigma Nu. Republican. Methodist. Home: 15450 Alpha Woods Dr Alpharetta GA 30201 Office: Dunwoody Mortgage Inc 10 Perimeter Center East NE Atlanta GA 30346

LOYND, RICHARD BIRKETT, athletic footwear company executive; b. Norristown, Pa., Dec. 1, 1927; s. James B. and Elizabeth (Geigus) L.; m. Jacqueline Ann Seubert, Feb. 3, 1951; children: Constance, John, Cynthia, William, James, Michael. B.S. in Elec. Engring., Cornell U., 1950. Sales engr. Lincoln Electric Co., Cleve., 1950-55; with Emerson Electric Co., St. Louis, 1955-68; pres. Builder Products div. Emerson Electric Co., 1965-68, v.p. Electronics and Space div., 1961-65; v.p. ops. Gould, Inc., Chgo., 1968-71; exec. v.p. Eltra Corp., N.Y.C., 1971-74; pres. Eltra Corp., 1974-81; chmn. Converse, Inc., Springfield, N.J., 1982—. Home: 19 Randall Dr Short Hills NJ 07078 Office: Converse Inc 505 Morris Ave Springfield NJ 07081 also: Converse Inc 1 Fordham Rd North Reading MA 01864

LU, MARY, federal contract auditor; b. Uchitomari, Okinawa, Japan, Aug. 3, 1954; d. Peter Konan and Helen (Sun) L. Student, George Mason U., 1977-78; BA, U. Va., 1977. CPA, Va.; cert. systems profl. Auditor Naval Audit Service, Falls Church, Va., 1979-82; project mgr. Dept. Def. Insp. Gen., Arlington, Va., 1982—. Mem. Nat. Contract Mgmt. Assn. Mem. Assn. of the Inst. for Cert. of Computer Profls., Assn. Govt. Accts.

LUBBOCK, JAMES EDWARD, writer, photographer, publicity consultant; b. St. Louis, Sept. 12, 1924; s. Winans Fowler and Hildegard Beauregard (Whittemore) L.; BA in English, U. Mo., 1949; m. Charlotte Frances Ferguson, Aug. 24, 1947; children: Daniel Lawrason (dec.), Brian Wade, Kathleen Harper. Asst. editor St. Louis County Observer, 1949-51; staff writer St. Louis Globe-Democrat, 1951-53, state editor, 1954-56; mng. editor Food Merchandising mag., 1956-57; free-lance indsl. writer-photographer, cons., St. Louis, 1958—; pres. James E. Lubbock, Inc., 1981—. Served with Signal Corps, U.S. Army, 1943-46. Mem. Soc. Profl. Journalists, St. Louis Press Club, ACLU, Common Cause. Democrat. Home and Office: 10734 Clearwater Dr Saint Louis MO 63123

LUBERT, IRA MARK, venture capital executive; b. Moorestown, N.J., Mar. 31, 1950; s. Sidney and Ethal (Brody) L.; m. Karen Lee Mathany, Dec. 2, 1973; children: Jonathan, Kristine. BS, Pa. State U., 1973. Mktg. mgr., product planner IBM, 1973-81; v.p. N.Am. sales ITT Courier (subs. ITT Corp.), 1981-82; v.p. worldwide sales Decision Data Computer Corp., 1983-84; v.p. mktg. and sales Mnemos, Inc. (subs. Combined Technologies PLC), 1984-86; pres., owner IL Mgmt., Inc., 1986—; v.p. acquisitions Safeguard Scientifics, Inc., King of Prussia, Pa., 1986-88; pres. CompuCom Systems, Inc., Cherry Hill, N.J., 1987-88; chmn. bd. CompuCom Systems, Inc., 1988—, mem., bd. dirs.; mng. dir. Radnor (Pa.) Venture Ptnrs. L.P., 1988—; Mem., bd. dirs. Sanchez Computer Assocs., Triangle Electronics, Inc., DDI Fin. Systems, Inc., Fisher Restaurant Systems, Inc., Telemarketing Concepts; bd. dirs. Data Devel., Inc. Head South N.J. fund raising Pa. State U., 1988. Mem. Union League Club, Moorestown Field Club. Office: Radnor Venture Ptnrs 259 Radnor-Chester Rd Ste 390 Radnor PA 19087

LUCANDER, HENRY, investment banker; b. Helsingfors, Finland, Dec. 21, 1940; came to U.S., 1965, naturalized, 1974; student Gronesche Handelsschule, Hamburg, W.Ger., 1961-62, Pontificia Universidade Católica, Rio de Janeiro, 1963-64; diploma Brazilian Coffee Inst., Rio de Janeiro, 1965; M.B.A., Columbia U., 1968; m. Karen-Jean Olson, Aug. 22, 1981. With Schenkers Internat. Forwarders, Inc., N.Y.C., 1965-66; coffee merchandizer Anderson Clayton & Co., Inc., N.Y.C., 1966-68; with Smith Barney & Co., Inc., N.Y.C., 1968-69, Kidder Peabody & Co., Inc., N.Y.C., 1969-70; with Lucander & Co., Inc., investment bankers, N.Y.C., 1970—, pres., 1972—. Served to lt. Finnish Army, 1960-61. Home: 8 Washington Ave Westport CT 06880 Office: Lucander & Co Inc 40 Wall St #538 New York NY 10005

LUCAS, DANA RICHARD, accountant; b. Weymouth, Mass., Mar. 5, 1960; d. Richard A. and Elizabeth A. (Reiss) L. BS in Acctg., Babson Coll., 1982. Assoc. acct. Prime Computer, Inc., Natick, Mass., 1982-83; staff acct. Prime Computer, Inc., Natick, 1983-84, sr. acct., 1984; sr. acct. Stratus Computer, Inc., Marlboro, Mass., 1984-85; supr. revenue adminstrn. Stratus Computer, Inc., Marlboro, 1985-87; supr. acctg. Crosby Valve & Gage Co., Wrentham, Mass., 1987-88, acctg. mgr., 1988—. Mem. Theta Chi. Roman Catholic. Home: 17 Precinct St Lakeville MA 02347

LUCAS, JAMES RAYMOND, manufacturing executive, management consultant; b. St. Louis, Mar. 9, 1950; s. James Earl and Anna LaVerne (Ryan) L.; m. Pamela Kay Petersen, June 10, 1972; children: Laura Christine, Peter Barrett, David Christopher, Bethany Gayle. BS in Engring. Mgmt., U. Mo., Rolla, 1972. Registered profl. engr., Mo., Kans. Product analyst The Lee Co., Westwood, Kans., 1971-73; mgr. planning Black & Veatch, Kansas City, Mo., 1973-79; dir. constrn. Hallmark Cards, Kansas City, Mo., 1979-81; project mgr. The Pritchard Corp., Kansas City, Mo., 1981-83; freelance author Overland Park, Kans., 1983—; gen. mgr., pres., chief exec. officer EPIC Mfg., Kansas City, Mo., 1984-86; pres. Luman Cons., Prairie Village, Kans., 1983—; bd. dirs. Emergency Systems Services Workshop, Inc.; ops. mgr. PSM, Inc., 1987—. Author: Weeping In Ramah, 1985. Spokesman Mother and Unborn Baby Care, Overland Park, 1985—; elder Ch. of Living Faith in Jesus, 1985—. Mem. Soc. Mfg. Engrs. (sr.), Bible Sci. Assn., Creation Sci. Assn. Mem. Bible Believing Christian Ch. Home: 7303 Rosewood Prairie Village KS 66208 Office: Luman Cons PO Box 2566 Shawnee Mission KS 66201

LUCAS, RAYMOND DAVID, services company executive; b. Webster Groves, Mo., Nov. 21, 1937; s. Raymond Lyle and Dorothy Florence (Warren) L.; m. V. Jo Payton, Nov. 18, 1961; children: James S., Jennifer L., Andrea A. BA, Rice U., 1959, BS in Elec. Engring., 1960; MS in Elec. Engring., Stanford U., 1962. Engr. GTE Govt. Systems, Mountain View, Calif., 1960; supr. GTE Govt. Systems, Mountain View, 1966, dept. mgr., 1967, bus. area mgr., 1974; v.p. bus. analysis GTE Products Corp., Stamford, Conn., 1979, GTE Svc. Corp., Stamford, 1980; v.p. planning, bus. devel. GTE Communications Systems, Stamford, 1981, GTE Products & Systems, Stamford, 1987—; bd. dirs. Fujitsu GTE Bus. Systems, Tempe, Ariz., 1987—, Siemens Transmission Systems, Phoenix, 1989—; fellow mem., adv. com. grad. sch. Sloan program Stanford U., Palo Alto, 1974-77. Inventor in filed. Deacon Long Ridge Congl. Ch., Stamford, 1984-86. Mem. IEEE, Am. Def. Preparedness Assn., Japan Soc., Inc. Republican. Congregationalist. Office: GTE 1 Stamford Forum Stamford CT 06904

LUCAS, WILLIAM DANE, excursion boats company executive; b. Tupelo, Miss., Jan. 26, 1940; s. Luther Herman and Birdie Lavene (Brooks) L. BS in Bus. and Law, U. Western Ky., 1962. Adminstr., cons. C.N.A. Ins. & City of Chgo., 1967-75; owner, pres. Dane's Restaurant, Jacksonville, Fla., 1975-84; owner River Entertainment, Jacksonville, 1985—, A'La Mode Caterers, Inc., Jacksonville, 1985-88, World Importers, Inc., Jacksonville, 1985—, Internat. Glass Etch, Jacksonville, 1987—. Author: You are Your Own Best Psychiatrist, 1985. Mem. Gator Bowl Assn., United Way, Cancer Soc., Symphony Assn. Mem. Fla. Restaurant Assn. (past pres.), Sales and Mktg. Execs. Assn., Hotel and Motel Assn., Jacksonville C. of C. (past com. mem.), Southside Bus. Club. Republican. Office: River Entertainment Inc 1884 Southampton Rd Jacksonville FL 32207

LUCAS, WILLIAM JASPER, transportation executive; b. Red Oak, Okla., June 13, 1926; s. Raymond Haskell and Carrie P. (Butler) L.; student Okla. State U., 1946-48, St. Michaels U., 1954, U. N.Mex., 1974; m. Martha Joye Hines, Aug. 29, 1948; children—Mark William, Bret Raymond, Kurt Jonathan, Lane. Terminal mgr. Santa Fe Storage & Transfer Co. (N.Mex.), 1952-60; mgr. traffic and sales Dalton Transfer & Storage, Albuquerque, 1960-68; exec. v.p. H-K Moving & Storage, Albuquerque, 1968-77, pres., treas., 1977-88, also dir., ret. 1988; rate and traffic cons. N.Mex., 1961-88; practitioner ICC, 1961—; mem. mil. and govt. affairs com. Mayflower Warehousemen's Assn., 1978—; guest lectr. art U. N.Mex., 1977—. Served with Horse Cavalry, U.S. Army, 1944-46, adj. gen. dept., 1950-52. Mem. Am. Soc. Traffic and Transp., Assn. Interstate Commerce Practitioners, Nat. Def. Exec. Res., Soc. for Photog. Edn., Albuquerque C. of C. Republican. Club: Tennis of Albuquerque. Contbr. articles to profl. jours.; numerous exhibits of photography. Office: 1310 Calle del Ranchero NE Albuquerque NM 87106

LUCCHESI, NELLO WILLIAM, finance company executive; b. Houston, Oct. 23, 1955; s. Claude A. and Ruth A. (Wellstein) L.; m. Janice L. Gillette, Sept. 15, 1979. BA, Northwestern U., 1977, MS in Mgmt., 1979. Cert. CPA, CDP, CFA. Sr. cons. Arthur Andersen & Co., Chgo., 1979-80, Deloitte Haskins & Sells, Chgo., 1980-82; asst. mgr. Northwest Industries, Chgo., 1982-85; asst. v.p. First Nat. Bank of Chgo., 1985-86; sr. v.p. Household Comml. Fin. Svcs., Prospect Heights, Ill., 1986—. Mem. Am. Inst. CPA's, Am. Prodn. and Inventory Control Soc., Fin. Analysts Fedn., Ill. CPA Soc., Investment Analysts Soc. Chgo. Home: 900 South River Rd Des Plaines IL 60016 Office: Household Comml Fin Svcs 2700 Sanders Rd Prospect Heights IL 60070

LUCE, GORDON COPPARD, savings and loan association executive; b. 1926; married. BA, Stanford U., 1950, MBA, 1952. Former Sec. of Bus. & Transp. State of Calif.; former sr. v.p. branches mktg. & adminstrn. Home Fed. Savs. & Loan Assn., San Diego; pres. Great Am. First Savs. Bank, San Diego, 1969-79, chief exec. officer, 1969—, chmn., 1979—, also dir. Served with U.S. Army, 1944-46. Office: Gt Am 1st Savs Bank San Diego Fed Bldg 600 B St San Diego CA 92183 *

LUCEY, LAWRENCE HAYDN, investment counselor, lawyer; b. Henderson, Nev., Dec. 17, 1947; s. Lawrence Young and Elizabeth Ruth (Fischer) L.; m. Nancy Gina Scaramella, Nov. 6, 1981; children: Clare Poole, Peter James. BS, Purdue U., 1969; MBA, U. Chgo., 1975; JD, Loyola U., 1982. Bar: Ill. 1982; chartered fin. analyst, 1975. V.p. Continental Ill. Nat. Bank, Chgo., 1969-83; sr. v.p. Chgo. Corp., 1983—. Author, editor Ready Reference of Investment Sect. Ill. Ins. Code, 1984; co-author: Investment Regulations for Illinois Insurance Agents and Brokers, 1982. Fellow Fin. Analysts Fedn.; mem. Ill. State Bar Assn., Investment Analysts Soc., Chgo., Fin. Stock Assn., Inst. Chartered Fin. Analysts, Nat. Assn. Life Cos., Union League Club of Chgo., Mich. Shores Club. Republican. Roman Catholic. Office: Chgo Corp 208 S LaSalle St Chicago IL 60604

LUCHT, JOHN CHARLES, management consultant, executive recruiter; b. Reedsburg, Wis., June 1, 1933; s. Carl H. and Ruth A. (Shultis) L.; m. Catherine Ann Seyler, Dec. 11, 1965 (div. 1982). BS, U. Wis., 1955, LLB, 1960. News dir. Sta. WISC-AM/FM, Madison, Wis., 1952-55; merchandising dir. The Bartell Group (radio and TV stas.), Milw., 1955-56; instr. U. Wis. Law Sch., 1959-60; TV contracts exec., account exec. J. Walter Thompson Co., N.Y.C., 1960-64; product mgr., new products supr., dir. new product mktg. Bristol-Myers Co., N.Y.C., 1964-69; dir. mktg. W.A. Sheaffer Pen Co., Ft. Madison, Iowa, 1969-70; gen. mgr. Tetley Tea div. Squibb Beech-Nut Inc., N.Y.C., 1970-71; v.p. Heidrick & Struggles, N.Y.C., 1971-77; pres. The John Lucht Consultancy, Inc., N.Y.C., 1977—; Lectr. in field. Author: Rites of Passage at $100,000 Plus, The Insider's Guide to Executive Job-Changing. Mem. State Bar Wis., N.Y. Bd. Trade, Assn. Exec. Search Cons., Nat. Assn. Corp. and Profl. Recruiters, N.Y. Acad. Scis., Phi Beta Kappa, Phi Eta Sigma, Phi Kappa Phi, Phi Delta Phi, Sigma Alpha Epsilon. Clubs: Metropolitan, Canadian (N.Y.C.). Office: Olympic Tower 641 Fifth Ave New York NY 10022

LUCHTERHAND, RALPH EDWARD, financial planner; b. Portland, Oreg., Feb. 9, 1952; s. Otto Charles II and Evelyn Alice (Isaac) L.; m. JoAnn Denise Adams, Aug. 13, 1983; children: Anne Michelle, Eric Alexander. B.S., Portland State U., 1974, MBA, 1986. Registered profl. engr., Oreg., Wash.; gen. securities broker NYSE/NASD. Mech. engr. Hyster Co., Portland, 1971-75, service engr., 1975-76; project engr. Lumber Systems Inc., Portland, 1976-79; prin. engr. Moore Internat., Portland, 1979-81, chief product engr., 1981-83; project engr. Irvington-Moore, Portland, 1983, chief engr., 1983-86; ind. cons. engr., 1986; engring. program mgr. Precision Castparts Corp., Portland, 1986-87; reg. rep./personal fin. planner IDS Fin. Services, Clackamas, Oreg., 1987—. Treas. Village Bapt. Ch., Beaverton, Oreg., 1988—. Mem. ASME (pres. student chpt. 1973-74). Republican. Home: 3000 NW 178th Ave Portland OR 97229 Office: IDS Fin Svcs Inc 8800 SE Sunnyside Rd Ste 300 Clackamas OR 97015

LUCIA, PHILIP JOHN, insurance company executive; b. Tarrytown, N.Y., Dec. 9, 1928; s. Pasquale Joseph and Winifred Edna (McGuinn) L.; m. Ruth Marie Zong, May 17, 1952; children: Maria, Patrick, Wendy. BS in Acctg., Lasalle U., Phila., 1951. Underwriting mgr. Allstate Ins. Co., White Plains, N.Y., 1954-63, Fireman's Fund, N.Y.C., 1963; v.p., regional mgr. Nationwide Ins. Co., Harrisburg, Pa., 1963—. Bd. trustees Community Gen. Osteo. Hosp., Harrisburg, 1987—, mem. audit com., human resource com., strategic planning com.; vice chmn. Pa. Ins. Polit. Action com., Phila., 1988—. With U.S. Army, 1951-53. Republican. Lutheran. Office: Nationwide Mut Ins Co 1000 Nationwide Dr Harrisburg PA 17110

LUCIANO, ROBERT PETER, pharmaceutical company executive; b. N.Y.C., Oct. 9, 1933; s. Peter and Jennie (Mastro) L.; m. Barbara Ann Schiavone, June 21, 1953; children: Susan Ann, Richard Peter. BBA, CCNY, 1954; JD, U. Mich., 1958. Sr. tax assoc. Royall, Koegel & Rogers (now Rogers & Wells), N.Y.C., 1958-66; atty. CIBA Corp., Summit, N.J., 1966-68, asst. sec., 1968-70; asst. gen. counsel, dir. pub. affairs CIBA Pharm. Co., Summit, 1970-71, v.p. mktg., 1973-75; v.p. planning and adminstrn. pharm. div. CIBA-GEIGY Corp., Summit, 1971-73, pres. pharm. div., 1975-77; pres. Lederle Labs. div. Am. Cyanamid Co., Pearl River, N.Y., 1977-78; sr. v.p. adminstrn. Schering-Plough Corp., Kenilworth, N.J., 1978-79, exec. v.p. pharm. ops., 1979-80, pres., chief operating officer, 1980-82, pres., chief exec. officer, 1982-84, chmn. bd., pres., chief exec. officer, 1984-86, chmn. bd., chief exec. officer, 1986—; bd. dirs. C.R. Bard, Inc., Murray Hill, N.J., Bank of N.Y. Co., Inc., N.Y.C. Asst. editor: U. Mich. Law Rev., 1957-58. Served with U.S. Army, 1954-56. Mem. ABA, N.Y. Bar Assn., Nat. Assn. Mfrs. (bd. dirs. 1982—), N.J. State C. of C. (bd. dirs. 1986—). Republican. Clubs: Union League, Sky, Econ. (N.Y.C.). Office: Schering-Plough Corp 1 Giraldi Farms Madison NJ 07940-1000

LUCKMAN, STANLEY, food products executive; b. N.Y.C., Dec. 25, 1922; s. Morris and Anna (Brown) L.; student Kans. State U., 1940-42; B.S. in Commerce and Fin., Bucknell U., 1948; m. Rosalyn Shapiro, Aug. 20, 1949; 1 child, Elizabeth. Dir. research and devel. Zion Kosher Provisions Co. N.Y.C., 1966-70; v.p., dir. research and devel. Empire Kosher Poultry, Inc., Mifflintown, Pa., 1970-88; cons. Nat. Foods, 1988, Hebrew Nat. Foods, 1988—; cons. in field. Served as lt. (j.g.) USN, 1942-46; ETO. Recipient merit award Union Carbide Corp.; Canner Packer award New Product Contest, 1977. Mem. Inst. Food Technologists, N.Y. Acad. Scis., Packaging Inst. U.S.A., Nat. Geog. Soc., Kennedy Center for Performing Arts, Audubon Soc., Met. Opera Guild, Smithsonian Inst., Sigma Alpha Mu. Clubs: Hershey Racquet, B'nai B'rith. Home: 2853 Vista Circle Camp Hill PA 17011 Office: RD 3 PO Box 165 Mifflintown PA 17059

LUDEMANN, ROGER REO, finance company executive; b. Burke, S.D., Dec. 4, 1948; s. Reo Wayne and Marguerite H. (Rockholm) L.; m. Barbara Jo Hellwig, June 17, 1978; children: Robert R., Kathryn A. BA, U. Nebr., 1971. Broadcast newsman Stuart Broadcasting, Sioux City, Iowa, 1971-73; with broadcast sales dept. Stuart Broadcasting, Grand Island, Nebr., 1973-75; ptnr. Miller Friendt Ludemann, Inc., Lincoln, Nebr., 1975-85; sr. v.p. Am. Charter Fed. Savs. and Loan, Lincoln, 1985—. V.p. Boy Scouts Am., Lincoln, 1984-88, Lincoln Symphony Orch. Assn., 1985—, pres., 1989—; bd. dirs. United Way Grand Island, 1976-77, Lincoln Community Playhouse, 1986-88. Mem. Fin. Instns. Mktg. Assn., Advt. Fed. Lincoln, Univ. Club, Rotary (pres. 1988—). Republican. Club: Univ. Lodge: Rotary (pres. 1988-89). Home: 1730 Memorial Dr Lincoln NE 68502 Office: Am Charter Fed Savs 206 S 13th St Ste 420 Lincoln NE 68508

LUDINGTON, JOHN SAMUEL, manufacturing company executive; b. Detroit, May 7, 1928; s. Samuel and Fredda (Holden) L.; m. Dorothy Lamson, Feb. 14, 1953; children: Thomas, Laura, Ann. B.S. in Econs, Albion (Mich.) Coll., 1951; LL.D. (hon.), Saginaw Valley State Coll.; D.B.A. (hon.), S.D. Sch. Mines and Tech.; H.H.D. (hon.), Northwood Inst. With Dow Corning Corp., Midland, Mich., chmn.; dir. Comerica Bank-Midland. Chmn. bd. trustees Albion Coll.; trustee Midland Community Ctr., Strosacker Found. Served with AUS. Methodist. Office: Dow Corning Corp 220 W Salzburg Rd Box 994 Midland MI 48686

LUDLOW, THOMAS HIBBARD, publishing executive; b. Buffalo, May 9, 1946; s. Norman Hibbard and Anne (McCarthy) L.; m. Madeleine Weigel, Jan. 16, 1982. BA, Allegheny Coll., 1968; MA, Syracuse U., 1970; MBA, Columbia U., 1980. Copywriter, McCann Erickson, Inc., Atlanta, 1972-74; creative dir. J. Walter Thompson, Atlanta, 1975-77; dir. mktg. Home Box Office, N.Y.C., 1980-83; v.p. mktg. Preview STV, Time Inc., N.Y.C., 1983-84; dir. account services Ventura Assocs., Inc., N.Y.C., 1984-85; pres. Red Lion Pub. div. Thomas H. Ludlow Inc., Chatham, N.J., 1985-88; assoc. pub., dir. mktg. Successful Meetings Mag., Bill Communications, N.Y.C., 1988—; adj. assoc. prof. Columbia U., N.Y.C., 1983-84. Served to 1st lt. USAF, 1970-72. Clubs: Fairmount Country (Chatham, N.J.); University (N.Y.C.). Home: 10 Wickham Way Chatham NJ 07928-1366

LUDMER, IRVING, retail company executive; b. Montreal, Que., Can., May 24, 1935; s. Joseph and Tillie (Lapidus) L.; m. Mona Vivian, Aug. 16, 1959; children: Brian, Cindy, David. Various positions Steinberg Inc., Montreal, 1957-71, pres., chief operating officer, 1984-85, pres., chief exec. officer, 1985—; pres. Irving Ludmer & Assocs., Inc., 1971; ptnr., v.p. Iberville Devel. Ltd., 1971; owner, pres. Ludco Enterprises Ltd., 1975; pres., chief exec. officer Ivanhoe, Inc., 1983-84. Office: Steinberg Inc, 3500 de Maisonneuve W, 2 Place Alexis Nihon, Westmount, PQ Canada H3Z 1Y3

LUDOVICI, ANTHONY, security investment executive; b. Bronxville, N.Y., June 11, 1927; s. Angelo and Mary (Santucci) L.; m. Matilda Margaret Mary McCormick, Apr. 8, 1961; 1 child, Michael Anthony. Student NYU, N.Y. Inst. Fin. Dir. research Gude Winmill & Co., N.Y.C., 1964-70, Peter P. McDermott & Co., N.Y.C., 1970-73; mgr. research dept. Wood Walker & Co., N.Y.C., 1973-74; v.p., sr. investment analyst Tucker Anthony & R.L. Day, Inc., N.Y.C., 1974—; fin. cons. Market Chronicle. Chmn. Eastchester Narcotics Coun., 1970-74, Office Drug Abuse Eastchester, 1974-76, feasibility com. to purchase country club for Eastchester, 1979, recreation commn., Eastchester, 1982-84; rep. on Westchester County Urban Devel. Adv. Group, Eastchester, 1978-79; mem. blue ribbon panel to study feasibility of Westchester County owned electric utility, 1980. Recipient Town Eastchester Appreciation Award, Westchester County Proclomation Award, appreciation award for drug abuse prevention activites. Mem. Nat. Assn. Petroleum Analysts, Diversified Industry Analysts, Electrical Equipment Analyst Group, Lake Isle C. of C. (chmn. bd. 1980-84), Westchester County Med. Ctr. (bd. dirs. 1987—), N.Y. Soc. Security Analysts, Fin. Analysts Fedn., Am. Stock Exchange Club (charter, membership com.), Auto Analysts Group, Elec. Products Analysts Group, Kiwanis. Office: Tucker Anthony & R L Day Inc 120 Broadway New York NY 10271

LUDSIN, STEVEN ALAN, brokerage house executive; b. Passaic, N.J., July 27, 1948; s. Samuel and Sonja (Gottlieb) L. BS, Cornell U., 1970; JD, Fordham U., 1975. Bar: N.Y. 1975. Assoc. Salomon Bros., N.Y.C., 1976-80; dir. instl. sales Ladenburg Thalmann & Co., Inc., N.Y.C., 1980-81; v.p. investments Drexel Burnham Lambert, Inc., N.Y.C., 1981-83; v.p. Ehrlich Bober Advisors, N.Y.C., 1983-84; pres. S.A. Ludsin & Co., N.Y.C., 1984—; chmn. N.Y.C. Small Bus. High. Tech. Inst., 1988. Active Pres.'s Commn. on Holocaust, Washington, 1979, U.S. Holocaust Meml. Coun., Washington, 1980—, Roundtable Polit. Action Com., N.Y.C., 1984—; rep. class and founders fund Cornell U., Ithaca, N.Y., 1986. Mem. N.Y. State Bar Assn., Harmonie Club (forum com. 1986). Democrat. Jewish. Office: SA Ludsin & Co 767 Fifth Ave 9th Fl New York NY 10153

LUDVIGSON, DAVID LEE, utility company executive; b. Grand Meadow, Minn., Sept. 28, 1938; s. Harold and Helen Lucille (Betz) L.; children: Brent Aaron, Eric Nordahl, Adam Scott. BA, U. Iowa, 1960, LLB, 1963. Bar: Calif. 1964, U.S. Dist. Ct. (no. dist.) Calif. 1964, U.S. Ct. Appeals (9th cir.) 1964. Assoc. Pillsbury, Madison & Sutro, San Francisco, 1963-70; v.p., gen. counsel, sec. Natomas Co., San Francisco, 1970-75; pvt. practice law, San Francisco, 1975-79; atty. Pacific Gas & Electric, San Francisco, 1979-84; exec. v.p. Calif. Energy Co., Inc., San Francisco and Santa Rosa, Calif., 1984—. Mem. Order of Coif. Home: 160 Seminary Dr Mill Valley CA 94941 Office: Calif Energy Co Inc 601 California St San Francisco CA 94108

LUDWIG, DAVID WILLARD, corporate professional; b. Wilkinsburg, Pa., June 17, 1926; s. Harold Louis and Frances (Willard) L.; m. Kathryn Leanna Scofield, Sept. 2, 1950; children: David Willard Jr., Thomas Arthur, Scott Edward. BS in Ceramic Engring., Pa. State U., 1951. Cert. fin. planner. Shift supr. Harbinson Walker, Clearfield, Pa., 1951-52; tech. devel. PPG Industries, Pitts., 1952-60, tech. sales engr., 1960-64, sales mgr., 1964-69, gen. mgr., 1969-72; exec. v.p., chief fin. officer MART Inc., Huntsville, Ala., 1972-74; pres. Tenn. Valley Industries, Inc., Huntsville, Ala, 1974—. Editor Gt. Am. Outdoors mag., 1983—. Served with U.S. Army, 1943-46. Mem. Inst. Cert. Fin. Planners, Internat. Assn. Fin. Planners, Estate Planning Council. Republican. Methodist. Lodges: Rotary, Masons. Home: 712 Corlett Dr SE Huntsville AL 35802 Office: Tenn Valley Industries Inc 2707 Artie St Suite 4 300 Exec Pkwy S Huntsville AL 35805

LUDWIG, JACK LEWIS, financial executive; b. Phila., Sept. 4, 1938; s. Reubin Litvak nd Frances (Kurman) L.; m. Barbara G. Switt, July 6, 1963; children: Jon Scott, Gail Susan. BSBA, Temple U., 1964; cert. fin. planner, Coll. Fin. Planning, 1983. Systems engr. IBM, Phila., 1963-67; sr. engring. programmer Burroughs Corp., Paoli, Pa., 1967-69; systems analyst Comserv, Phila., 1969-71, Memorex, Phila., 1971-75; pvt. practice computer cons. Data Gen. Corp., Marlboro, Mass., 1975-76, Data Pro Research, Rivton, N.J., 1976; rep. Clayton Brokerage, Valley Forge, Pa., 1976-80; fin. cons. Shearson Lehman Hutton, Phila., 1980ú; tchr. Main Line Sch., Radnor, Pa., 1985—, Unisys After Hours., Phila., 1988—; cons., presenter in field. Author: Computer Output Microfilm, 1974, Financial Planning Made Simple, 1988; editor: Computer Communication, 1976. Group leader Leadership Inst., King of Prussia, Pa., 1978-84. Served with USAF, USNG, 1955-61. Mem. Internat. Bd. Cert. Fin. Planners (bd. dirs. 1985-86), Internat. Assn. Fin. Planners, Main Line C. of C. (organizer fin. fair 1981-85). Republican. Jewish. Lodge: B'nai B'rith. Office: Shearson Lehman Hutton 1818 Market St Philadelphia PA 19103

LUDWIG, LEROY FRANK, retail store executive; b. Remsen, Iowa, Apr. 28, 1923; s. Joseph Francis and Lela Marie (Pitz) L.; m. Genevieve Frances Boet, Nov. 22, 1945; children—LaRinda Ludwig Saylor, LeRoy Frank, Geri Ludwig Dempsey. Student, Chgo. Tech. Coll., 1941-42, Drury Coll., Springfield, Mo., 1943, U. Calif.-Berkeley Extension; cert. in real estate, Chabot Coll., Hayward, Calif., 1978. Archtl. drafter Safeway Stores, Inc., Oakland, Calif., 1945-57; design mgr. Safeway Stores, Inc., Oakland, 1957-74, project engr., 1974-77; div. property mgr. Safeway Stores, Inc., Fremont, 1979-82, real estate dir., 1982-84; v.p., real estate div. mgr. Safeway Stores, Inc., Oakland, 1984-86, v.p. real estate, div. mgr. facilities engring., 1986—. Pres., Oakland Zool. Soc., 1972-73. Served with USAAF, 1943-45, ETO. Decorated Air medal with four oak leaf clusters. Mem. Internat. Council of Shopping Ctrs., Nat. Assn. Corp. Real Estate Execs., Am. Legion. Roman Catholic. Home: 3221 Round Hill Dr Hayward CA 94542 Office: Safeway Stores Inc 201 Fourth St Oakland CA 94660

LUDWIG, VERNELL PATRICK, gas pipeline company executive, mechanical engineer; b. Algona, Iowa, Nov. 5, 1944; s. Vernell Peter and Alice Marcella (Joynt) L.; m. Susan Lee, Nov. 30, 1968; children—Maryanne, David. B.S.M.E., Iowa State U, Ames, 1966; M.B.A., Harvard U., Cambridge, 1972. Sr. cons. Resource Planning Assocs., Cambridge, Mass., 1974-77; mgr. Tex. Eastern Gas Pipeline Co., Houston, 1977-80, asst. to pres., 1980-81, gen. mgr., 1981-82, v.p., 1982-83, sr. v.p., 1983-86; v.p. Transwestern Pipeline Co., Houston, 1982-83, sr. v.p., 1983-84; exec. v.p. Algonquin Energy, Inc., Boston, 1986—; bd. dirs. New Eng. Gas Assn. Served to lt. USN, 1967-70; Vietnam. Mem. ASME, Interstate Natural Gas Assn., Am. Gas Assn., New Eng. Gas Assn. (bd. dirs.), Pi Tau Sigma. Office: Algonquin Gas Transmission Co 1284 Soldiers Field Rd Boston MA 02135

LUECKE, JOSEPH E., insurance company executive; b. 1927; married. BA, La Salle Coll., 1950. With Lumbermen's Mut. Casualty Co., 1951—, chmn., chief exec. officer, dir., 1981—; with Kemper Corp., 1951—; chmn. bd. dirs., chief exec. officer Kemper Corp., Long Grove, Ill.; chmn., chief exec. officer Am. Motorists Ins. Co., Long Grove, also bd. dirs.; bd. dirs. Kemper Fin. Svcs. Inc., Chgo., Kemper Internat. Corp., Chgo., Kemper Reinsurance Co., Long Grove. Office: Kemper Group Rte 22 Long Grove IL 60049 *

LUEDDE, CHARLES EDWIN HOWELL, lawyer, corporation executive; b. St. Louis, Apr. 4, 1944; s. Henry William and Jane Elisabeth (Howell) L.; m. Jane Richmond Smallridge, Sept. 21, 1974; children: William Heath, Robert Chalmers. Bar: Mo. 1969. Jr. ptnr. Bryan, Cave, McPheeters & McRoberts, St. Louis, 1969-74, 76-77, sr. ptnr., 1978-83; exec. v.p., gen. counsel, sec. AMEDCO, Inc., St. Louis, 1983-87; ptnr., officer Greensfelder, Hemker, Wieses, Gale & Chappelow PC, St. Louis, 1987—; spl. counsel, atty. fellow Office of Gen. Counsel SEC, Washington, 1974-75; bd. dirs., cons. Huntco Inc., St. Louis, 1986—; bd. dirs. Community LifeCare Enterprises, Springfield, Ill. Bd. dirs. St. Louis Charitable Found., 1986—. Mem. ABA, Bar Assn. Metro St. Louis (chmn. bus. law sect. 1980-81), Am. Soc. Corp. Secs., Order of Coif. Home: 750 Cella Rd Saint Louis MO 63124 Office: 1800 Equitable Bldg 10 S Broadway Saint Louis MO 63102

LUELLEN, CHARLES J., oil company executive; b. Greenville, S.C., Oct. 18, 1929; s. John B. and Dorothy C. (Bell) L.; m. Jo S. Riddle, July 11, 1953; children: Margaret A., Nancy J. B.S., Ind. U., 1952. Sales rep. Ashland Oil, Inc., Ky., 1952-70, v.p. sales, 1970-72, group v.p. sales, 1972-80, pres., chief operating officer, 1986—, also dir.; pres. Ashland Petroleum Co., 1980-86; bd. dirs., budget adv. com. Am. Petroleum Inst., Washington, 1982—, Asphalt Inst., Washington, 1974-76; bd. dirs. Ashland Coal Inc. Bd. dirs. Kings Daus., Hosp., Ashland, 1981—, Ashland area YMCA, 1980—, Nat. Chamber Found., Washington, 1987; trustee Centre Coll., Danville, Ky., 1988, Joint Council on Econ. Edn., N.Y.C. Mem. Ind. Univ. Fellows, U.S. C. of C. (mem. energy & natural resources com.), Beta Gamma Sigma. Club: Bellefonte Country (Ashland); Pendennis (Louisville), 25 Yr. (Washington). Home: 4400 Oak Hollow Dr Ashland KY 41101 Office: Ashland Oil Inc PO Box 391 Ashland KY 41114 also: Ashland Oil Inc 1000 Ashland Dr Russell KY 41169

LUERSSEN, FRANK WONSON, steel company executive; b. Reading, Pa., Aug. 14, 1927; s. George V. and Mary Ann (Swoyer) L.; m. Joan M. Schlosser, June 17, 1950; children: Thomas, Mary Ellen, Catherine, Susan, Ann. B.S. in Physics, Pa., State U., 1950; M.S. in Metall. Engring, Lehigh U., 1951; LL.D. hon., Calumet Coll. Metallurgist research and devel. div. Inland Steel Co., East Chicago, Ind., 1952-54; mgr. various positions Inland Steel Co., 1954-64, mgr. research, 1964-68, v.p. research, 1968-77, v.p. steel mfg., 1977-78, pres., 1978-85, chmn., 1983—; dir. Continental Ill. Corp., Morton Thiokol, Inc. Author various articles on steelmaking tech. Trustee Calumet Coll., Whiting, Ind., 1972-80, Northwestern U., 1980—; v.p., bd. dirs. Munster (Ind.) Med. Research Found., 1972-84; trustee, sec., treas. Munster Sch. Bd., 1957-66. Served with USNR, 1945-47. Named disting. alumnus Pa. State U. Fellow Am. Soc. Metals, Nat. Acad. Engring.; mem. AIME (Disting. life mem., B.F. Fairless award), Am. Iron and Steel Inst. Home: 8226 Parkview Ave Munster IN 46321 Office: Inland Steel Industries Inc 30 W Monroe St Chicago IL 60603

LUFT, WALTER, steel trading executive; b. Braunschweig, Federal Republic of Germany, Aug. 8, 1928; came to U.S., 1967; s. Gerhard Ludwig Ernst and Gertrud Adele (Camphausen) L.; m. Charlotte Marie Schmidt, Aug. 27, 1955; children: Dagmar, Norbert. Abitur, Raabeschule, Braunschweig, Germany, 1948; MBA, Adelphi U., 1975. With Braunschweigische Staatsbank, Fed. Republic Germany, 1948-54, Rhein-Ruhr Bank, Duisburg, Fed. Republic Germany, 1954-55, Kloeckner & Co., Duisburg, 1955-56; treas. Klockner Inc., Garden City, N.Y., 1966—. Lutheran. Home: 8 Willowood Ln Coram NY 11727 Office: Klockner Inc 666 Old Country Rd Garden City NY 11530

LUFTGLASS, MURRAY ARNOLD, manufacturing company executive; b. Bklyn., Jan. 2, 1931; s. Harry and Pauline (Yaged) L.; children by previous marriage: Paula Jean, Bryan Keith, Robert Andrew, Richard Eric; m. Christine L. Novick, May 29, 1988. BS, Ill. Inst. Tech., 1952; MS, U. So. Calif., 1959; MBA, U. Conn., 1972.With Shell Chem. Co., Torrance, Calif., 1955-60, N.Y.C., 1960-61, Wallingford, Conn., 1961-64, Torrance, 1964-66, N.Y.C., 1966-69; asst. gen. mgr. Westchester Plastics div. Ametek, Inc., Mamaroneck, N.Y., 1969-75; dir. corp. devel. Ametek, Inc., N.Y.C., 1975-76, v.p., 1976-83, sr. v.p. corp. devel., 1984—; instr. survey modern plastics Soc. Plastics Industry, Los Angeles. Bd. dirs. Sunny Hill Children's Center. Served to lt. (j.g.) USN, 1952-55. Mem. NAM, Soc. Plastics Industry, Assn. Corp. Growth, Soc. Plastics Engrs., Tau Beta Pi, Beta Gamma Sigma, Phi Lambda Upsilon. Club: University (N.Y.C.). Contbr. articles to profl. jours., publs. Patentee in field. Home: PO Box 552 Hoboken NJ 07030 Office: Ametek Inc 410 Park Ave New York NY 10022

LUGER, DONALD R., engineer; b. Elizabeth, N.J., May 12, 1938; s. George A. and Elizabeth M. L.; m. Pat Sanders, Feb. 17, 1968 (dec. 1982); m. Sharon L. Luger, May 14, 1983; children: Christopher, Morgan Kathleen. BCE, Auburn U., 1962, MSCE, Auburn U., 1964, course in exec. program Stanford U., 1979. Registered profl. engr., N.C., Ga., Mich., Va, N.Y. structural engr. NASA, Huntsville, Ala., 1962; constrn. engr. E.I. DuPont Co., Old Hickory, Tenn., 1964; structural engr. Hayes Internat. Corp., Huntsville, 1964-65; resident engr. Fibers Industries, Inc., Shelby, N.C., 1965-66, Greenville, S.C., 1966-67; project mgr. Lockwood Greene Engrs., Inc., Atlanta, 1967-71, sr. project mgr., 1971-74, v.p., mgr. ops., corp. dir., 1974-78, sr. v.p., mgr. Atlanta office, corp. dir., 1978-82, pres., 1982—, chief exec. officer, 1983—. Mem. ASCE, Nat. Soc. Profl. Engrs., Ga. Soc. Profl. Engrs., So. Ctr. for Internat. Studies, Auburn U. Alumni Assn., Commerce Club, Athletic Club

LUHRS, H. RIC, toy manufacturing company executive; b. Chambersburg, Pa., Mar. 22, 1931; s. Henry E. and Pearl (Beistle) L.; m. Grace Barnhart, June 12, 1973; children by previous marriage—Stephen Frederick, Christine Michelle, TerriAnn, Patricia Denise. B.A., Gettysburg Coll., 1953. With The Beistle Co., Shippensburg, Pa., 1948-53, 1959—; pres., gen. mgr. Beistle Co., 1962—, chmn. bd., 1978—; dir. First Nat. Bank of Shippensburg, 1964-80, Commonwealth Nat. Bank, 1980—, Commonwealth Nat. Fin. Corp., 1981—, Capital Tech. Corp., 1984—, Fla. Atlantic U. Found., 1988—; dir., vice chmn. CompuPix Tech. Inc., 1984—, pres., 1986—; gemologist, 1977—; pres. South Lac Devel. Co., 1986—; owner Luhrs Gem Testing Lab., 1977—, Luhrs Jewelry, 1976—, Allied Leasing Co., Shippensburg, 1968; pres. South Lac Devel. Co., 1986—. Pres. Shippensburg Public Library, 1964-66, 1970-72, 76-78, bd. dirs., 1963-82; pres. Community Chest, 1965, dir., 1963-72; pres. Shippensburg Area Devel. Corp., 1966-72; bd. dirs., trustee Carlisle (Pa.) Hosp., 1967-71, Chambersburg Hosp., 1969-75; mem. consumer advisor council Capital Blue Cross, 1976-78; bd. dirs. Fla. Atlantic U. Found., 1988—. Served to capt. USAF, 1953-59. Mem. Shippensburg Hist. Soc. (dir. 1968), Nat. Sojourners, SAR (life), Shippensburg C. of C. (pres. 1965, dir. 1964-65), Toy Mfrs. Assn. (dir. 1969-71), Nat. Small Businessmen's Assn., Nat. Rifle Assn. (life), Shippensburg Fish and Game Assn. (pres. 1963), Am. Legion. Lutheran. Clubs: Cumberland Valley Indsl. Mgmt, York of Printing House Craftsmen. Lodges: Masons (32 deg.), Shriners, Elks, Tall Cedars of Lebanon. Office: 14-18 E Orange St Shippensburg PA 17257

LUISO, ANTHONY, international food company executive; b. Bari, Italy, Jan. 6, 1944; s. John and Antonia (Giustino) L.; m. Nancy Louise Bassett, June 26, 1976. B.B.A., Iona Coll., 1967; M.B.A., U. Chgo., 1982. Audit sr. Arthur Andersen & Co., Chgo., 1966-71; supr. auditing Beatrice Foods Co., Chgo., 1971-74, adminstr. asst. to exec. v.p., 1974-75, v.p. ops. internat. div., dairy div., 1975-77, exec. v.p. internat. div., 1977-82, prof. internat. div., 1982-83, chief operating officer internat. food group, 1984-86, pres. U.S. Food segment, 1986—; group v.p. Internat. Multifoods Corp., Mpls., until 1988, pres., 1988—, chief operating officer, 1988-89. Mem. adv. council U. Chgo. Grad. Sch. of Bus. Served with USAR, 1968-74. Mem. Am. Inst. C.P.A.s. Republican. Roman Catholic. Clubs: Univ. (Chgo.), Internat. (Chgo.). Office: Internat Multifoods Corp Multifood Tower Box 2942 Minneapolis MN 55402 *

LUKACH, ARTHUR S., JR., manufacturing executive; b. N.Y.C., Feb. 14, 1935; s. Arthur S. and Marion (Long) L.; m. Joan Sherring Mickelson, Mar. 27, 1961; 1 child, Justin A. C. BSME, Rensselaer Poly. Inst., 1956; MBA, Harvard U., 1964. V.p. Systemation Inc., Boston, 1967-70; prin. Lukach & Assocs., Cambridge, Mass., 1970-74; mgr. McKinsey & Co. Inc., N.Y.C., 1975-81; chmn., chief exec. officer Micromold Products Inc., Yonkers, N.Y., 1982—; guest lectr. Harvard U., Stanford U. Grad. Schs. Bus. Adminstrn. Bd. dirs. Vis. Nurse Svc., N.Y.C. Mem. ASME, Soc. Plastics Engrs. Clubs: Harvard Bus. Sch. (N.Y.C.), Harvard (N.Y.C.), Rensselaer Poly. Inst. of N.Y. (N.Y.C.). Home: Halls Ln Kent CT 06757 Office: Micromold Products Inc 660 Saw Mill River Rd Yonkers NY 10710 also: 61 E 90th St New York NY 10128

LUKACS, MICHAEL EDWARD, communications researcher; b. N.Y.C., Mar. 25, 1946; s. William and Hannah (LeWitter-Wolf) L.; m. Diane Harriet Katz, Oct. 29, 1967. Student, CUNY, Queens, 1965-68; T-3, R.C.A. Inst. now Tech Careers Inst., N.Y.C., 1968-69. Tech. aide Bell Telephone Labs., Holmdel, N.J., 1969-72, sr. tech. aide, 1972-77, assoc. mem. tech. staff, 1977-81, mem. tech. staff, 1981-83; mem. tech. staff Bell Communications Research, Red Bank, N.J., 1983-89. Patentee cathode ray tube dynamic focus apparatus, cathode ray tube electro-optic linearization device; (co-inventor) pel recursive motion compensated video coder; (inventor) "Lukacs" coding, disparity corrected predictive coding for 3-D video. Recipient Notable Achievement award Bell Labs Research Lab. 113, 1983. Mem. Assn. for Computing Machinery, Inst. Elec. and Electronic Engrs., Soc. Motion Picture TV Engrs. Office: Bell Communications Research 331 Newman Springs Rd Red Bank NJ 07701-7040

LUKAS, GAZE ELMER, accountant; b. Austria, Hungary, Nov. 9, 1907; s. Victor and Theresa (Dinzenberger) L.; came to U.S., 1909, naturalized, 1920; B.S. in Accountancy with honors, U. Ill., 1930, M.S., 1933, J.D. first in class, 1956; m. Frances Adelaide Lyman, Nov. 25, 1932 (dec.); 1 son, Victor Thomas; m. Adelaide W. Bosselman, Jan. 7, 1987; Instr. U. Ill., Urbana, 1930-35, asst. prof., 1954-55, asso. prof., 1955-56, prof., 1956-69, prof. emeritus, 1969—; dir. fin. U.S. Farm Security Adminstrn., Washington, 1935-42; chief accountant UNRRA, Washington, 1945-46; chief of renegotiation Quartermaster Gen.'s Office, Fgn. Service, State Dept., Rome, New Delhi, 1947-54; partner Paul M. Green & Assos., Bus. Edn. Cons., Champaign, Ill., 1955-68; Elmer Fox vis. prof. accounting Wichita (Kans.) State U., 1970-71; vis. prof. accounting Fla. Tech. U., Orlando, 1968-70, Fla. Atlantic U., Boca Raton, 1971-72; comptroller Palm Beach Atlantic Coll., West Palm Beach, Fla., 1979-81, cons., 1981-85. Mem. County Audit Adv. Bd. of Ill., 1962-68, chmn., 1964-66, recipient pub. service award, 1968. Served to maj. AUS, 1942-45; ETO. Decorated Bronze Star; recipient Meritorious Civilian Service award Q.M. Gen., 1947, Americanism medal Nat. Soc. DAR, 1986. C.P.A., Ill. Mem. Am. Inst. C.P.A.'s, Ill. C.P.A. Soc. (life), Appraisers Assn. Am., Order of Coif, Beta Gamma Sigma, Beta Alpha Psi, Pi Kappa Phi, Phi Eta Sigma, Sigma Alpha Epsilon, Phi Delta Phi, Alpha Kappa Psi. Contbr. articles to profl. jours. Address: 719 Lori Dr #19-210 Palm Springs FL 33461

LUKE, DAVID LINCOLN, III, paper company executive; b. Tyrone, Pa., July 25, 1923; s. David Lincoln and Priscilla Warren (Silver) L.; m. Fanny R. Curtis, June 11, 1955. AB, Yale U., 1945; LLD (hon.), Juniata Coll., 1967, Lawrence U., 1976, Salem Coll., 1983, W. Va. U., 1984. Vice pres., dir. Westvaco Corp., N.Y.C., 1953-57, exec. v.p., dir., 1957-62, pres., dir., after 1962, chief exec. officer, 1963-88, chmn. bd., 1980—; bd. dirs. B.F. Goodrich Co., Clupak, Inc., McGraw Hill Inc., Grumman Corp. Trustee Cold Spring Harbor Lab.; bd. dirs. Josiah Macy Jr. Found.; past chmn., trustee emeritus Hotchkiss Sch. Served from aviation cadet to capt. USMCR., 1942-45. Mem. Am. Paper Inst. (dir., past chmn.), Inst. Paper Chemistry (trustee, past chmn.). Clubs: Links, The River (N.Y.C.); Piping Rock, Megantic Fish and Game Corp. Home: 775 Park Ave New York NY 10021 also: Shelter Ln Locust Valley NY 11560 Office: Westvaco Corp 299 Park Ave New York NY 10171

LUKE, HENRY, management consultant; b. Newton, Miss., Jan. 4, 1937; s. Henry and Mary Francis L.; m. Barbara Ann Hunter, Dec. 21, 1962; children: Linda, David. BS, Miss. State U., 1959; MS, U. Tenn., 1965. Registered profl. engr., Fla., Miss.; lic. real estate broker, Fla. Engr. Miss. Hwy. Dept., Newton, 1959-61, TVA, Knoxville, 1961-65; with Reynolds, Smith and Hills Architects, Engrs. and Planners, Inc., Jacksonville, Fla., 1965—, sr. v.p., 1988—; pres., Plantec subs. Reynolds, Smith and Hills, 1974—; chmn. bd. The Fla. Cos., 1982-83; bd. dirs. Reynolds, Smith & Hills Architects-Engrs.-Planners, Inc.; speaker in field. Mem. Gov. of Fla. Econ. Adv. Com., 1980-84, chmn., 1983-84; apptd. mem. 1st Coast Transp. Study, 1986—; chmn. fin. com. 1st Bapt. Ch., Jacksonville, 1983, chmn. bd. deacons, 1984, 87, 88; mem. Mayor's High Tech. Task Force, 1984; mem. Duval County Research and Devel. Authority, 1984—, chmn. 1986—; chmn. Jacksonville Commn. on Crime, 1988; gen. chmn. First Coast Planning Conf., 1987. Mem. ASCE, Am. Planning Assn., Fla. Engring. Soc., NSPE, Planning Execs. Inst., Northeast Fla. Builders Assn. (bd. dirs. 1982), Jacksonville C. of C. (chmn. legis. policy task force 1982-83, chmn. strategic planning task force 1983, mem. exec. com. 1984-85, bd. govs. 1984-85, 86—, v.p. community devel. 1984, v.p. internat. devel. 1985, chmn. jail relocation task force 1986, co-chmn. tech. task force 1988), Fla. C. of C. (bd. govs. 1988—), Phi Kappa Phi. Republican. Home: 345 Greencastle Dr Jacksonville FL 32225 Office: PO Box 52507 Jacksonville FL 32225

LUKE, JOHN ANDERSON, paper company executive; b. Tyrone, Pa., Nov. 30, 1925; s. David Lincoln and Priscilla Warren (Silver) L.; m. Joy Carter, Dec. 21, 1946; children: John Anderson, Hope S., Jane T., William H. B.A., Yale U., 1949. Personnel asst. Westvaco Corp., Charleston, S.C., 1949-51; personnel mgr. Westvaco Corp., 1951-53, asst. mgr. adminstrn., 1953-55; mill mgr. Westvaco Corp., Luke, Md., 1955-60; mgr. fine papers div. Westvaco Corp., 1960-74; v.p. Westvaco Corp., N.Y.C., 1966-74, sr. v.p., 1974-76, exec. v.p., 1976-80, pres., 1980-88, pres., chief exec. officer, 1988—; also dir. Westvaco Corp., pres., chief exec. officer, 1988—; dir. Arkwright Ins. Co., Discount Corp. of N.Y., Landauer Assocs., Inc., Clupak. Served with USAAF, 1943-45. Clubs: Bedford Golf and Tennis, River. Office: Westvaco Corp 299 Park Ave New York NY 10171

LUKE, WARREN K. K., investment company executive; b. Honolulu, May 22, 1944; s. Kan Jung and Beatrice (Lum) L.; B.S. in Bus. Adminstrn., Babson Inst. Bus. Adminstrn., 1966; M.B.A., Harvard U., 1970; m. Carolyn Ching, 1970; children—Kevin James, Catherine, Bryan, Joanne. Pres., dir. Indsl. Investors, Inc., Honolulu, 1970—; vice chmn., dir. Hawaii Nat. Bank, Honolulu, 1972—; v.p., dir. Bancard Assn. Hawaii Inc., 1976—; treas., dir. Computer Systems Internat. Inc.; v.p., sec., dir. KJL, Inc., Honolulu, 1974—; pres., dir. Loyalty Devel. Co., Ltd., Honolulu, 1970—, Hawaii Nat. Bancshares, Inc., 1987—; pres., dir. Mgmt. Resources Cons., Inc., Honolulu, 1973—; dir. Loyalty Enterprises, Ltd., Honolulu, Loyalty Ins. Co., Ltd., Honolulu, Barclay Corp., Honolulu. First vice chmn. Hawaii State chpt. ARC, 1973-77, bd. dirs. 1972—, mem. exec. com., 1974-78, 85—, chpt. chmn., 1977-78, mem. Pacific div. adv. council, 1976-80, mem. Western field office adv. council, 1979—, chmn., 1979-80, nat. bd. govs., 1983—; treas., exec. com. mem. Community Scholarship Program, Honolulu, 1974-85; mem. Gov.'s Task Force Jobs for Vets., 1975-76; dir. Hawaii Theater Ctr., 1988—; trustee Honolulu Jr. Acad., 1979-85, Hawaiian Meml. Park Cemetery Assn., Honolulu, 1975-85, Punahou Sch., 1989—; mem., trustee U. of Hawaii Found., 1986—; mem. deans adv. council U. Hawaii Coll. Bus. Adminstrn., 1975—. Mem. Navy League U.S. (treas. Honolulu council 1974-76, dir. 1973-76, adv. com. 1977—), Chinese C. of C. (dir. 1980—, pres. 1985-86), Robert Morris Assocs., The Deputies, Western Ind. Bankers Assn. (pres. 1986-88). Office: 84 N King St Honolulu HI 96817

LUKENS, BARBARA, cable television company executive; b. Phila., Aug. 15, 1930; d. Adrian W. and Verna E. (Rhine) Woegelin; m. Matthias Peter, Ardis Amanda, Jon Mahlon. BA magna cum laude, U. Pa., 1973, MA, 1975. Cons. Pa. House Minority Caucus, Harrisburg, 1975-77, 78; field dir. Butera for Gov. Com., Harrisburg, 1977; exec. dir. Comcast Cable Communications Inc., Bala-Cynwyd, Pa., 1979-82, v.p. planning, 1982-83, v.p. pub. affairs, 1983—; also bd. dirs. Comcast Cablevision of Phila., Inc., Bala-Cynwyd. Active Montgomery County Rep. Com., Pa., 1967-73; vice chmn. Montgomery County (Pa.) Gov. Study Commn., 1974; mem. adv. bd. Bus. Women's Network, Phila., 1983-85; trustee United Way Southeastern Pa., Phila., 1983—; dir. Movement Disorder Bd. Grad. Hosp., Phila., 1986—; bd. dirs. Montgomery County Citizens Council, Norristown, Pa., 1976-79. Recipient Woman of Achievement award YMCA of Germantown, Phila., 1985. Mem. Nat. Acad. TV Arts and Scis. (sec. Phila. chpt. 1985-86, gov. 1986—), Nat. Acad. Cable Programming, Women in Cable (nat. dir. 1982-83, founding dir. Valley chpt. 1980-82). Office: Comcast Cable Communications Inc One Belmont Ave Bala-Cynwyd PA 19004

LUKENS, KENNETH B., banking executive; b. Pottstown, Pa., Apr. 28, 1951; s. Clarence G. and Anna (Howresko) L.; m. Carolyn Walker, June 11, 1977. BS in Fin., Pa. State U., 1973. Credit analyst Am. Bank & Trust Co. Pa., Reading, 1974, loan rev. analyst, 1974-75; sr. credit analyst First Nat. Bank Md. (subs. First Md. Bancorp), Balt., 1975-77, loan officer, then loan exec., 1977-79, sr. loan exec., 1979-81, v.p., 1981-84; pres. First Md. Leasecorp. (subs. First Md. Bancorp.), Balt., 1984—; acting chmn. First Md. Leasecorp. (subs. First Md. Bancorp.), 1984—. Mem. Delta Sigma Phi (fin. chmn., bd. dirs. 1978-87). Office: First Md Leasecorp Mail Code 109-910 PO Box 1596 Baltimore MD 21203

LUKENS, PAUL BOURNE, financial executive; b. Meriden, Conn., Oct. 29, 1934; s. George Price and Elsie (Bourne) L.; m. Gail Perry Todd, July 7, 1956; children: Jennifer C. Lukens Holmes, Julie B. B.S. in Accounting, U. Conn., 1956. C.P.A. Sr. accountant Webster Blanchard & Willard (merged with Price Waterhouse & Co. 1962), 1956-62; audit mgr. Price Waterhouse & Co., Hartford, Conn., 1962-69; with Aetna Life & Casualty Co., Hartford, Conn., 1969-77; v.p. treas. Aetna Variable Annuity Life Ins. Co. (subs), 1972-75, v.p. corp. planning dept. parent co., 1975-77; v.p., controller INA Corp., 1977-82, Cigna Corp., 1982—. Contbg. author: Property-Liability Insurance Accounting, 1974. Trustee Episcopal Hosp., Phila., 1981-85. Mem. Am. Inst. C.P.A.s (acctg. standards exec. com. 1983-85), Conn. Soc. C.P.A.s (bd. govs. 1973-75), Fin. Execs. Inst. (com. on corp. reporting 1979—, bd. dirs. Phila. chpt. 1982-85), Fin. Acctg. Standards Bd. (emerging issues task force). Home: 546 Woodlea Ln Berwyn PA 19312 Office: Cigna Corp One Logan Sq Philadelphia PA 19103

LUKINS, BETTY SUE, real estate developer; b. Louisville, Jan. 4, 1940; d. Harry Nute and Cornelia (Elliott) Lukins; 1 child, Michael Harry. BA, Rollins Coll., 1960; MA, Columbia U., 1962. Researcher The Tax Found., Inc., N.Y.C., 1961-64; rsch. analyst Downtown Devel. Com., Salt Lake City, 1966-67; mgr. J.C. Penny, 1967-69; health program coordinator Office of the Gov., 1970-71; mgmt. cons. Ultra Systems, Inc., Newport Beach, Calif., 1971; with pub. relations Architects and Engrs. Svc., L.A., 1972-74; pres. Lukins Devel. Co., Inc., Ojai, Calif., 1974-88, Topa Vista Ranch, Inc., Ojai, 1985—. Bd. mem. Orange County Ctr. Performing Arts, 1979-85. Mem. Big Canyon Philharmonic Soc., Lobrero Theatre, Nat. Assn. Home Builders, Bldg. Industry Assn., Am. Assn. Individual Investors, Balboa Bay Club, Coral Casino Swim Club, The Tower Club. Presbyterian. Office: Lukins Devel Co PO Box 1838 Ojai CA 93023

LUMADUE, DONALD DEAN, hobby and crafts executive; b. El Reno, Okla., Sept. 30, 1938; s. Harry Basil and Muriel Ellen (Craven) L.; m. Joyce Anne Hayes, June 28, 1958; children: Dawnia, Donald, Robert, Ronald. Student USCG Acad., 1956-57. Lab. technician Charles Pfizer & Co., Groton, Conn., 1957-60; indsl. engr. Sonoco Products, Mystic, Conn., 1960-67; partner Joydon's, New London, Conn., 1958—, House of Leisure, New London, 1965—; Hobby Crafts, New London, 1968—; pres. NEI, Inc., New London, 1968-83. Mem. New Eng. Hobby Industry Assn. (pres. 1973-74, 86-88, bd. dirs. 1983—), Hobby Industry Assn. Am. (chmn. Wholesaler bd. 1976-78, 82—, exec. show bd. 1985—, Pres.'s award 1986), Nat. Assn. Wholesalers (trustee 1976—), Mgmt. Club S.E. Conn. (pres. 1961-62, 77-78). Office: 78-88 Captain's Walk New London CT 06320

LUMINGKEWAS, STEFANUS BUANG, mechanical engineer; b. Semarang, Indonesia, Dec. 19, 1937; s. Henry Budiono and Molly (Kamini) Budiono Suliando; m. Wulan Maramis Lumingkewas, Oct. 1, 1965; children—Ingrid, Maudy Pingkan. M.S. in Mech. Engring., Inst. Tech. Bandung (Indonesia), 1962. Mgr. P.T. Gruno Nasional, Surabaya, Indonesia, 1963-78, mng. dir., 1978-82; pres. P.T. Encoxim, Surabaya, 1982—. Lodge: Rotary Surabaya Selatan (pres. 1988-89). Avocations: swimming; reading; body building. Home: Trunojoyo 62, Surabaya 60264, Indonesia Office: PT Encoxim, KBPM Duryat 20, Surabaya 60262, Indonesia

LUMRY, ROGER WAYNE, retail executive; b. Sacramento, Mar. 12, 1947; s. Carlton E. and Gertrude V. (Raabe) L.; m. Carol A. Lumry, June 22, 1968; children: Lisa M., Sheri N. BA in History, U. Calif., Davis, 1968. Mgr. J.C. Penny Co., San Jose, Calif., 1968-71; div. mgr. Liberty House, San Jose, 1971-72; asst. to v.p. ops. Liberty House, San Francisco, 1972-73, ops. mgr., 1973-75; dist. ctr. div. mgr. Mervyn's, Hayward, Calif., 1975-80, dir. shortage control, 1980-86; v.p. ops. The Good Guys, Burlingame, Calif., 1986—. Sgt. with USMC, 1968-75. Republican. Roman Catholic. Office: The Good Guys 1649 Adrian Rd Burlingame CA 94010-2181

LUNA, PATRICIA ADELE, food manufacturing company executive; b. Charleston, S.C., July 22, 1956; d. Benjamin Curtis and Clara Elizabeth (McCrory) L. BS in History, Auburn U., 1978, MEd in History, 1980; MA in Adminstrn., U. Ala., 1981, EdS in Adminstrn., 1984, PhD, ABD in Adminstrn., 1986. Cert. tchr., Ga., Ala. History tchr. Harris County Middle Sch., Ga., 1978-79, head dept., 1979-81; residence hall dir. univ. housing U. Ala., 1981-83, asst. dir. residence life, 1983-85; intern Cornell U., Ithaca, N.Y., 1983; dir. of mktg. Golden Flake Snack Foods, Inc., Birmingham, Ala., 1985—; cons., lectr. in field. Author: Specialization: A Learning Module, 1979, Grantsmanship, 1981, Alcohol Awareness Programs, 1984; University Programming, 1984; Marketing Residential Life, 1985; The History of Golden Flake Snack Foods, 1986; Golden Flake Snack Foods, Inc., A Case Study, 1987. Fundraiser, U. Ala. Alumni Scholarship Fund, Tuscaloosa, 1983, Am. Diabetes Assn., Tuscaloosa, 1984, Urban Ministries, Birmingham, 1985-88; fundraiser, com. chmn. Spl. Olympics, Tuscaloosa, 1985; fundraiser Am. Cinema Soc., 1988; chmn. Greene County Relief Project, 1982-89; bd. dirs. Cerebral Palsy Found., Tuscaloosa, 1985-86; lay rector and com. chmn. Kairos Prison Ministry, Tutwiler State Prison, Ala., 1986—; lobbyist, com. chmn. task force Justice Fellowship, 1988-89; bd dirs. Internat. Found. Ewha U., Seoul, Korea. Recipient Dir. of Yr. award U. Ala., 1982, 83; Skeets Simonis award, U. Ala., 1984, nat. award Joint Council on Econ. Edn., 1979, rsch. award NSF, 1979; named to Hon. Order Ky. Cols. Commonwealth of Ky., 1985—, Rep. Senatorial Inner Circle, 1986; Mem. Sales and Mktg. Execs. (chmn. com. 1985-86), Leadership Ala. (pres. 1982-83), Am. Mktg. Assn. (Disting. Leadership award 1987, Commemorative Medal of Honor 1988), Assn. Coll. and Univ. Housing Officers (com. chmn. 1983-85), Nat. Assn. Student Personnel Officers, Snack Food Assn. (mem. mktg. com. and conf. presenter), Commerce Exec. Soc., Emmaus Club (chmn. com. 1985-89), Snow Skiing Club, Sailing Club, Omega Rho Sigma (pres. 1983-84), Omicron Delta Kappa, Phi Delta Kappa, Kappa Delta Pi, Phi Alpha Theta. Republican. Methodist. Avocations: skiing, racquetball, community work, public speaking. Home: 11 Vestavia Hills Northport AL 35476 Office: Golden Flake Snack Foods Inc 110 Sixth St S Birmingham AL 35201

LUND, ARTHUR KERMIT, lawyer; b. Chinook, Wash., May 2, 1933; s. Arthur K. and Lillian (Lee) L.; children: Michael Lee, Karen Elizabeth Near, Nancy Marie; m. Agnieszka Winkler. AB in Bus. Adminstrn., San Jose State U., 1955; JD, U. Calif., Berkeley, 1961. Bar: Calif. 1962 U.S. Dist. Ct. (no. dist.), Calif., U.S. Ct. Appeals (9th cir.), U.S. Dist. Ct. (no. dist.) Calif.,

U.S. Supreme Ct.1971. Ptnr. Rankin, Oneal, Center, Luckhardt & Lund, San Jose, Calif.; chmn. bd. San Jose Nat. Bank; bd. dirs. Coast Counties Truck & Equipment Co., Semi Con Systems, Inc., Winkler McManus; pres. O'Connor Profl. Bldg., Inc.; adv. bd. San Jose State U.; past lectr. law sch. Lincoln U., San Jose. Chmn. bd. O'Connor Found.; bd. trustees Presentation High Sch.; bd. dirs. San Jose Conv. and Visitors Bur.; past pres., bd. dirs. Spartan Found. San Jose State U.; past pres. Health Facilities Planning Council Santa Clara County. 2d lt. USMC, 1955, capt. USMCR. Mem. ABA, Am. Acad. Hosp. Attys., State Bar Calif., Santa Clara County Bar Assn., San Jose C. of C. (chmn. aviation com.), Aircraft Owners and Pilots Assn., Navy League, San Jose State U. Alumni Assn. (life, past pres.). Clubs: St. Claire. Lodge: Rotary (past pres.). Home: 52 Isabella Ave Atherton CA 94025 Office: 152 N Third St Ste 400 San Jose CA 95115

LUND, HARRY AUSTIN, investment banking executive; b. Metuchen, N.J., Apr. 20, 1936; s. Harry Anthony and Theresa Marie (Hanley) L.; m. Elaine Barbara Foss, Oct. 7, 1961; children: Mark, Sharon. BA, Catholic U. Am., 1958; MBA, U. Va., 1960; JD, NYU, 1966. Fin. analyst E.I. DuPont de Nemours & Co., Wilmington, Del., 1960-62; strategic planner Esso Research & Engring. Co., Florham Park, N.J., 1962-66; capital mgmt. officer Am. Brand, Inc., N.Y.C., 1966-67; investment banker Irving Trust Co., N.Y.C., 1967—. Home: 37 Overlook Dr Berkeley Heights NJ 07922 Office: Irving Trust Co 1 Wall St New York NY 10015

LUND, VICTOR L., retail food company executive; b. Salt Lake City, 1947; married. BA, U. Utah, 1969, MBA, 1972. Audit mgr. Ernst and Whinney, Salt Lake City, 1972-77; sr. v.p. Skaggs Cos. Inc., from 1977; v.p., contr. Am. Stores Co., 1980-83, sr. v.p., contr., from 1983, exec. v.p., now vice-chmn., chief fin. and adminstrv. officer. Office: Am Stores Co PO Box 27447 Salt Lake City UT 84127-0447 also: Am Stores Co 19100 Von Karman Ave Irvine CA 92715 *

LUNDAHL, MARGARET ANN, law librarian; b. Chgo., Nov. 26, 1948; d. John E. and Lois N. (Olausson) L.; m. Gary L. Tucker, June, 1971 (div. 1974). Student, U. Chgo., 1966-68, MBA, 1969, MA, 1976; JD, Ill. Institute Tech., 1980. Bar: Ill. 1980. Asst. bus. librarian U. Chgo. Grad. Sch. Bus., 1969-71; cataloger U. Chgo. Law Library, 1971-76; librarian Isham, Lincoln, & Beale, Chgo., 1976-83; prin. Lundahl Enterprises, Chgo., 1981—. Mem. Am. Assn. Law Libraries, ABA, Spl. Libraries Assn., Chgo. Bar Assn. Home and Office: Lundahl Enterprises 10128 Ave J Chicago IL 60617

LUNDBERG, CHARLES LOUIS, automotive industry executive; b. Ludington, Mich., Sept. 13, 1949; s. Louis Lowell and Betty Ann (Knudsen) L.; m. Janice Lynn Steen, Oct. 21, 1972; children: Robert Louis, William Charles. BE and BS in Engring. Mechanics/Aerospace, U. Mich., 1971, MBA, 1985. Engr. design and devel. Ford Motor Co., Dearborn, Mich., 1978-80; mgr. mktg. and engring. Echlin Inc., Owosso, Mich., 1980-86; dir. engring. and mktg. Holset Engring. Co. div. Cummins Engine Co., Farmington Hills, Mich. and Madison, Ind., 1986—; instr. U. Wis. Mgmt. Inst., Madison, 1985—. pilot, ops. plans officer USAF Air Nat. Guard, Battle Creek, Mich., 1985—. Served to maj. USAF, 1971-78. Mem. Soc. Automotive Engrs., Maintenance Council, Automotive Parts Rebuilders Assn., Res. Officers Assn., Nat. Guard Assn., Mich. Republican. Methodist. Home: 1914 Village Green Blvd Apt #192 Jeffersonville IN 47130 Office: Holset Engring Co Inc 38855 Hills Tech Dr Farmington Hills MI 48331

LUNDEEN, ROBERT WEST, electronics company executive; b. Astoria, Oreg., June 25, 1921; s. Arthur Robert and Margaret Florence (West) L.; m. Betty Charles Anderson, Dec. 26, 1942; children: John Walter, Peter Bruce, Nancy Patricia. B.S., Oreg. State U., 1942; postgrad., Inst. Meteorology, U. Chgo., 1942-43. With Dow Chem. Co., 1946-87; dir. bus. devel. Dow Chem. Internat., Midland, Mich., 1963-66; pres. Dow Chem. Pacific, Hong Kong, 1966-77, Dow Chem. Latin Am., from 1978; exec. v.p. Dow Chem. Co., 1978-82, chmn. bd., 1982-87, dir., 1973-87; chmn. Tektronix Inc., Beaverton, Oreg., 1987—. Chmn. City Planning Commn., Concord, Calif., 1960-61; trustee Kettering Found., Dayton, Ohio, Monterey Inst. Internat. Studies, Calif., Oreg. State U. Found., Corvallis, Orcas Island Library Dist., 1987—. Served with U.S. Army, 1942-46. Decorated Bronze Star. Mem. AICE, Am. Chem. Soc. Republican. Clubs: Hong Kong, Royal Hong Kong Yacht; Orcas Tennis, Orcas Island Yacht, Beach and Tennis Club (Pebble Beach, Calif.). Office: Tektronix Inc PO Box 500 Beaverton OR 97077 *

LUNDGREN, CLARA ELOISE, public affairs officer, journalist; b. Temple, Tex., Mar. 7, 1951; d. Claude Elton and Klara (Csirmaz) L. AA, Temple Jr. Coll., 1971; BJ, U. Tex., 1973; MA, Columbia Pacific U., 1986. Reporter Temple Daily Telegram, 1970-72; news editor Austin (Tex.) Am.-Statesman, 1972-75; mng. editor Stillhouse Hollow Pubs., Inc., Belton, 1975-77; pub. affairs officer Darnall Army Community Hosp., Ft. Hood, Tex., 1978-80; editor Ft. Hood Sentinel III Corps, 1980-85; command info. officer Pub. Affairs Office III Corps, Ft. Hood, 1985-87, community relations officer, 1987-88, dep. pub. affairs officer, 1988—. Recipient Nat. Observer Journalistic Achievement award Dow Jones and Co., 1971. Mem. NOW, Tex. Press Women, Fed. Women's Program, Assn. of U.S. Army, Jaycees. Home: 1305 S 13th Temple TX 76504 Office: III Corps Pub Affairs Office Fort Hood TX 76544-5056

LUNDHOLM, WILLIAM ROBERT, sales executive; b. Rockford, Ill., June 23, 1937; s. Joseph T. and Jessie J. (Coddington) L.; m. Patricia M. Cullen, Aug. 6, 1960; children: Michael R. and Lori A. BBA, U. Nebr., 1960. Sales rep. Nat. Lock Co., Rockford, 1962-65; sales rep. Palnut div. TRW, Chgo. and Cleve., 1965-69; dist. mgr. Palnut div. TRW, Chgo., 1969-71; with Carr Fastner div. TRW, Cambridge, Mass., 1971-80, gen. sales mgr., 1977-80; dir. dist. sales/mktg. tools div. TRW, Cleve., 1980-84; dir. sales, mktg. MRC div. TRW, Jamestown, N.Y., 1984-86; v.p. sales SKF Bearing Industries, King of Prussia, Pa., 1986-87, v.p. machinery bus. unit, 1987—. V.p. Jamestown C. of C., 1984-86. Served with U.S. Army, 1960-62. Mem. Am. Mgmt. Assn., Anti-Friction Mfgs. Assn. (govt. realtions, internat. trade coms. 1984—). Republican. Lutheran. Office: SKF Bearing Industries 1100 First Ave King of Prussia PA 19406-1352

LUNDY, AUDIE LEE, JR., lawyer; b. Columbus, Ga., Mar. 10, 1943; s. Audie Lee and Mary Blanche (Snipes) L.; m. Ann Porter, June 11, 1966; children: Travis Stuart, Katherine Porter. B.A., Yale U., 1965; LL.B. magna cum laude, Columbia U., 1968. Bar: N.Y. 1968, D.C. 1976, Pa., 1988. Assoc. firm White & Case, N.Y.C., 1968-71, 74-75, London, 1971-74, Washington, 1975-78; asst. gen. counsel Campbell Soup Co., Camden, N.J., 1978, gen. counsel, 1979-88, v.p., gen. counsel, 1988—. Bd. mgrs. St. Christopher's Hosp. for Children, Phila., 1980—, vice chmn. 1986—; trustee Food and Drug Law Inst., Washington, 1982—. Mem. ABA, Am. Soc. Internat. Law, Assn. Gen. Counsel. Republican. Presbyterian. Clus: Merion Cricket. Home: 810 Waverly Rd Bryn Mawr PA 19010 Office: Campbell Soup Co Campbell Pl Camden NJ 08101

LUNDY, SADIE ALLEN, small business owner; b. Milton, Fla., Mar. 29, 1918; d. Stephen Grover and Martha Ellen (Harter) Allen; m. Wilson Tate Lundy, May 17, 1939 (dec. 1962); children: Wilson Tate Jr., Houston Allen, Michael David, Robert Douglas, Martha Jo-Ellen. Degree in acctg., Graceland Coll., 1938. Acct. Powers Furniture Co., Milton, Fla., 1939-40, Lundy Oil Co., Milton, 1941-52; controller First Fed. Savs. & Loan, Kansas City, Mo., 1953-55, Herald Pub. Co., Indepenence, Mo., 1956-58; mgr. Baird & Son Toy Co., Kansas City, Mo., 1959-62; regional mgr. Emmons Jewelers of N.Y., Kansas City, 1963-65; owner, pres. Lundy Tax Service, Independence, 1965-85; acct. Optimation, Inc., Independence, 1974-85, mgr., 1985—; v.p. Lundy Oil Co., Milton, 1941-52. Contbr. articles to profl. jours. Mem. com. Neighborhood Council, Independence, 1985. Mem. Am. Bus. Women's Assn., Independence C. of C. (mem. com. 1965-85). Republican. Mem. Reorganized Ch. of Jesus Christ of Latter Day Saints. Club: Independence Women's. Home: PO Box 520238 Independence MO 64052 Office: Optimation Inc 645 N Powell Rd Independence MO 64050

LUNG, DAVID D(ARLING), restaurant owner, exporter, investment specialist, commodity broker; b. Kwei Chow, China, Feb. 28, 1947; came to U.S., 1973; s. Chi-Kwei and Ai-Yuan (Su) L.; m. Ingrid W. Fang, Sept. 20, 1975; children: Jannie J., Bryan T. BA in Social Work, Nat. Taiwan U., Republic of China, 1970; MA in Sociology, No. Ill. U., 1980. Cert. restaurant mgr.; lic. commodity broker. Mgr. Charlie Lui Restaurant, Chgo., 1976-78, Yen Ching Restaurant, Urbana, Ill., 1978-79, 79-80, Chung King Inn, St. Charles, Ill., 1979; owner China Inn Restaurant, Champaign, Ill., 1980—; pres. China Inn Enterprises, Inc., Champaign, 1982—, China Inn II, Urbana, 1985—, Creative Investment Mgmt. Corp., Champaign, 1986—; v.p. Amerasia Internat., Champaign, 1984—; exclusive sales agt. Far East sect. New Generation Products Health System Internat., Reno, Nev. Mem. Rep. Presdl. Task Force, Washington, 1980, U.S. Senatorial Club, Nat. Rep. Senatorial Com., Washington, 1982—. Recipient Award Cert. Consulate-Gen. Republic of China, 1979, Award Cert. Coordination Council N.Am. Affairs, 1980, Award Cert. The Nat. Rep., 1982, Award Cert. Congl. Com., 1983-84. Mem. Am. Assn. Ind. Investors, Ill. Restaurant Assn., Cen. Ill. Better Bus. Bur., U.S. C. of C., Free Chinese Assn. (consul midwest chpt. 1975-76). Lodge: Lions. Home: 1907 S Prospect Champaign IL 61821 Office: China Inn Enterprises Inc 2312 W Springfield Champaign IL 61821

LUNGER, CHARLES WILLIAM, diversified company executive; b. Williamsport, Pa., Nov. 28, 1927; s. Charles L. and Mabel C. (Taylor) L. B.S., Western Mich. U., 1951. Plant mgr. Studebaker Corp., South Bend, Ind., 1962-64; plant mgr. Allied Products Corp., South Bend, 1964-71, div. pres., 1971-75, sr. v.p., 1975-82; exec. v.p. Allied Products Corp., Chgo., 1983—. Served with USN, 1945-47. Home: 3887 N Mission Hills Rd Northbrook IL 60062 Office: Allied Products Corp 10 S Riverside Pla Chicago IL 60606

LUNKA, VICTOR WILLIAM, JR., investment broker, financial planner; b. Painesville, Ohio, Sept. 21, 1955; s. Victor William Sr. and Marcia Louise (Payne) L.; m. Karen Elizabeth Korhely, Oct. 13, 1984; 1 child, Derek. BS in Bus., Miami U., Oxford, Ohio, 1977; cert., Coll for Fin. Planning, Denver, 1987. Cert. fin. planner, lic. commodities broker. Credit adjustor Huntington Bancorp, Columbus, Ohio, 1977-78; bank examiner div. banks State of Ohio, Columbus, 1978-83; sr. investment broker A.G. Edwards & Sons, Mentor, Ohio, 1983—. Mem. Inst. Cert. Fin. Planners, Rotary, Elks. Republican. Roman Catholic. Home: Chestnut Run Gates Mills OH 44040 Office: AG Edwards & Sons 8500 Station St Ste 300 Mentor OH 44060

LUNTZ, THEODORE MICHAEL, recycling company executive; b. Canton, Ohio, June 4, 1926; s. Abe M. and Fanny (Telpansky) L.; m. Idarose Schock, Aug. 23, 1953; children: W. Jean, Pamela, Brian, Jill. BA, Yale U., 1948. Pres. Marquette Steel Co., Cleve., 1952; v.p., treas. Luntz Corp., Canton, 1952-72, exec. v.p., 1972-84, pres., 1984—; v.p. 62 Land Inc., Canton, 1972—. Bd. dirs. Baldwin Wallace Coll., Montefiore Home, Hawken Sch., Boy Scouts Am., NCCJ, Cleve. Coll. Jewish Studies; chmn. Schnurmann House, Cathedral Latin Sch., Beachwood Am. Field Svcs. With U.S. Army, 1950-52. Mem. Nat. Inst. Scrap Iron and Steel (pres. No. Ohio chpt. 1970-74, nat. bd. dirs. 1975, co-chmn. fin. com. 1985-87), Oakwood Club, Rotary (bd. dirs.Cleve. club). Republican. Home: 29776 Gates Mills Blvd Pepper Pike OH 44124 Office: Luntz Corp 4250 E 68th St Cleveland OH 44105

LUPE, JOHN EDWARD, JR., finance executive; b. Columbus, Ohio, Jan. 4, 1939; m. Betty Jo Davis; children: Teresa, John. BS, Ohio U., 1960. CPA, Ohio. Staff acct. Haskins & Sells, Columbus, 1960-65; sr. tax acct. Rockwell Internat., Pitts., 1965-67; tax mgr. Roadway Services, Akron, Ohio, 1967-70, Nat. Standard, Niles, Mich., 1970-76; controller Nat. Standard, Niles, 1976; controller Lennox Internat., Dallas, 1976-79, v.p., controller, 1979-83, exec. v.p. fin. and treas., 1983—. Mem. Fin. Execs. Inst., Tax Execs. Inst., Nat. Assn. Mfrs. Lodge: Masons. Home: 7611 Chattington Dr Dallas TX 75248 Office: Lennox Internat Inc 7920 Belt Line Rd Dallas TX 75240-8145

LUPIEN, ADRIAN JOHN, JR., consumer products company executive; b. Malden, Mass., Jan. 19, 1941; s. Adrian John Sr. and Dorothy Mae (O'Brien) L.; m. Barbara Goldberg, Sept. 4, 1971; children: Daniel, Beth. BS, Northeastern U., 1964. Mgr. field sales profl. products div. Bausch & Lomb Co., Rochester, N.Y., 1971-78, v.p. sales profl. products, 1979-84; v.p. gen. mgr. PCI div. Bausch & Lomb Co., Woburn, Mass., 1984-86; gen. mgr., chief oper. officer Bernat Yarn & Craft Co., Uxbridge, Mass., 1986—. Home: 208 Carlton Ln North Andover MA 01845 Office: Bernat Yarn and Craft Co Depot St Uxbridge MA 01569

LUPINSKI, THOMAS MARION, wholesale trade company executive, accountant; b. Goshen, N.Y., Nov. 19, 1952; s. John Walter and Theresa (Lewandowski) L. AB cum laude, Colgate U., 1974; MBA, Northwestern U., 1976. CPA, N.Y. Sr. auditor Arthur Andersen & Co., Stamford, Conn., 1976-82; fin. mgr. internat. ops. and over the counter divs. Revlon Health Care Group, Tarrytown, N.Y., 1982-86; v.p., controller Forschner Group, Inc., Shelton, Conn., 1986—. Chmn. admmissions Colgate U. Alumni Orgn., Fairfield County, Conn., 1984-87. Alumni Meml. scholar Colgate U., 1970-74. Mem. Am. Inst. CPAs, N.Y. Soc. CPAs. Republican. Office: Forschner Group Inc 151 Long Hill Crossroads Shelton CT 06484-0874

LUPO, ROBERT EDWARD SMITH, real estate developer, investments; b. New Orleans, May 27, 1953; s. Thomas Joseph and Alvena Florence (Smith) L.; m. Mary Lynn Puissegur, June 16, 1980; 1 child, Robert Thomas Smith. BArch, Tulane U., 1977. Owner Robert Edward Smith Lupo Properties, New Orleans, 1976—; cons. various firms, New Orleans, 1977-81; chief operating officer Commodore Thomas J. Lupo Enterprises, Williams-Lupo, Smith-Lupo, New Orleans, 1981—; pres. Hedwig, Inc., Zephyr, Inc., Noroaltom Devel. Co., Inc., New Orleans, 1981—; cons. Mrs. Thomas J. Lupo properties, 1981—; bd. dirs. Pelican Savs. & Loan Assn., Metairie, La. Grad. Met. Area Leadership Forum, New Orleans, 1980; bd. dirs., v.p. New Orleans Mun. Yacht Harbor, 1981—; life mem. Friends of Audubon Zoo, 1983; bd. dirs. Met. Area Com., New Orleans, 1985—. Recipient Gov.'s award State of La., 1980, Tulane Assoc. award Tulane U., 1986; named one of 10 Best Dressed Men, Men of Fashion, 1983. Mem. Sigma Alpha Epsilon (founding). Republican. Roman Catholic. Club: Semreh; Tulane Green Wave. Office: Smith Lupo Ctr 145 Robert E Lee Blvd Penthouse Ste New Orleans LA 70124

LUPPENS, CARL HENRY, real estate broker and developer; b. Long Beach, Calif., Aug. 25, 1952; s. Charles Louis and Marguerite Mae (Schmidt) L.; m. Diane Hagnaur Muckerman, Sept. 15, 1979; children: Laura Marguerite, Carolyn Leigh. BA, Claremont McKenna Coll., 1974; JD, U. Colo., 1978. Bar: Mo. 1978, Co. 1981. Field engr. Alaskan Resource Sci. Corp., Fairbanks, 1974-75; jr. ptnr. Bryan, Cave, McPheeters & Roberts, St. Louis, 1978-80; atty. Manville Corp., Denver, 1980-81; sr. v.p. Vantage Properties, Inc., Aurora, Coll., 1981-84; v.p. Riva Cos., Denver, 1984-86; ptnr. Argus Real Estate Ptnrs., Inc., Denver, 1986-88; v.p. Cushman Realty, Denver, 1989—; lectr. real estate Grad. Sch. Bus. Adminstrn. U. Denver. Developer Country Club Towers, 1987, Washington Ctr., 1988. Mem. 50 for Colo., Denver, 1988—, task force Downtown Denver Plan, 1986-87. Recipient Merit award Am. Soc. Landscape Architects, 1987. Mem. Urban Land Inst., Denver Bar Assn., Denver Athletic Club. Republican. Presbyterian. Office: Cushman Realty Corp 370 17th St Denver CO 80202

LURIX, PAUL LESLIE, JR., chemist; b. Bridgeport, Conn., Apr. 6, 1949; s. Paul Leslie and Shirley Laurel (Ludwig) L.; m. Cynthia Ann Owens, May 30, 1970; children—Paul Christopher, Alexander Tristan, Einar Gabrielson. B.A., Drew U., 1971; M.S., Purdue U., 1973; postgrad., 1973—. Tech. dir. Analysts, Inc., Linden, N.J., 1976-77; chief chemist Caleb Brett USA, Inc., Linden, 1977-80; v.p. Tex. Labs., Inc., Houston, 1980-82; pres. Lurix Corp., Fulshear, Tex., 1982—; cons. LanData, Inc., Houston, 1980—, Nat. Cellulose Corp., Houston, 1981—, Met. Transit Authority, Houston, 1981—, Phillips 66, Houston, 1986—; dir. research and devel. Stockbridge Software, Inc., Houston, 1986—; v.p. Diesel King Corp., Houston, 1980-82. Contbr. article to profl. jour. Patentee distillate fuel additives. Fellow Am. Inst. Chemits; mem. Am. Chem. Soc., ASTM, AAAS, Soc. Applied Spectroscopy, N.Y. Acad. Sci., Phi Kappa Phi, Phi Lambda Upsilon, Sigma Pi Sigma. Republican. Methodist. Lodge: Kiwanis (pres. 1970-71). Current work: Infrared spectroscopy; data base programming for science and industrial applications. Subspecialties: Infrared spectroscopy; Information systems, storage, and retrieval (computer science). Avocations: tennis, golf, piano. Home: 32602 Hepple White Dr Fulshear TX 77441

LURTON, H. WILLIAM, retail executive; b. Greenwich, Conn., Sept. 18, 1929; s. William Pearl and Elizabeth (McDow) L.; m. Susan Harvey, Oct. 26, 1980; children: Scott, Carrie, Nancy, Jennifer. B.A., Principia Coll., 1951. Sales rep. Jostens Inc., Mpls., 1955-61; yearbook sales and plant mgr. Jostens Inc., Visalia, Calif., 1961-66; gen. sales mgr. yearbook div. Jostens Inc., v.p., gen. mgr. yearbook div., 1969-70, corp. exec. v.p., 1970-71, mem. exec. com., 1970-72, pres., 1971-75, chief operating officer, 1971-72, chief exec. officer, 1972—, chmn. bd., 1975—, also dir.; dir. Deluxe Check Printers, Pentair, Inc. Bd. dirs. U.S. C. of C., Mpls. YMCA. Served with USMC, 1951-53. Mem. Mpls. C. of C. (bd. dirs.). Clubs: Wayzata (Minn.) Country, Minneapolis. Home: 3135 Jamestown Rd Long Lake MN 55356 Office: Jostens Inc 5501 Norman Center Dr Minneapolis MN 55437

LUSSIER, BARBARA M., architectural services company executive; b. Phila., June 21, 1956; d. Ronald E. and Barbara (Brennan) Miller; m. Grant P. Lussier, Aug. 8, 1981. B.S., Sch. Mgmt., Boston Coll., 1978. Asst. buyer designer sportswear Lord & Taylor, N.Y.C., 1978-81; v.p. mktg., co-owner 3XM Inc., Houston, 1981—; co-owner 3XM Inc., Phila., 1987—. Mem. Urban Land Inst (assoc.), Houston C. of C., Boston Coll. Alumni Club. Home: 136 N Bread St Ste 322 Philadelphia PA 19106 Office: 3XM Inc 18 S Strawberry St Philadelphia PA 19106

LUSTE, JOSEPH FRANCIS, JR., land use, planning and housing specialist; b. Troy, N.Y., Dec. 7, 1940; s. Joseph Francis and Catherine (Coler) L.; m. Migdalia Malissa Gallardo, Jan. 31, 1970; children: Kimberly, Jonathan. AAS in Engring., Hudson Valley Community Coll., 1960; BA in Planning, Rutgers U., 1979; M in Aviation Mgmt., Embry-Riddle Aero. U., 1985; PhD in Property Mgmt., Western States U., 1987. Jr. engr. Tallamy Assocs., Inc., Washington, 1965-71; staff engr., planner Barrett & Hale, Inc., Hato Rey, P.R., 1971-73; sr. engr., planner T&M Assocs., Inc., Middletown, N.J., 1973-80; dir. planning and devel. Twp. of Middletown, 1980-82; head planning, engring. and devel. County of Atlantic, Atlantic City, 1982-84; prin. planner, office mgr. Edwards and Kelcey, Inc., Atlantic City, 1984-86; dir. planning, assoc. Pennoni Assocs., Inc., Haddon Heights, N.J., 1986—. Author planning/housing reports. Dir. aerospace edn., USAF, CAP, McGuire AFB, N.J., 1984. Served with USN, 1961-65. Recipient Assistance award Sr. Citizens Council, 1981., Cert. Appreciation Atlantic County Pvt. Industry Council, 1983. Mem. Am. Planning Assn. (charter, exec. com. N.J. chpt. 1982), Coll. Real Estate Appraisers, Urban Land Inst., Met. Assn. Urban Designers and Environ. Planners, Internat. Real Estate Inst., Greater Atlantic City C. of C. (chmn. transp. com. 1986—), South Jersey C. of C. (transp. com. 1986—), Greater Mainland C. of C. (bd. dirs.). Republican. Seventh Day Adventist. Home: 28 Harding Ave Cherry Hill NJ 08002 Office: Pennoni Assocs Inc 515 Grove St Ste 2A Haddon Heights NJ 08035

LUSTGARTEN, ELI SIMON, security analyst; b. N.Y.C., June 10, 1945; s. Samuel and Elsie (Cohen) L.; m. Jacqueline Siegel, Apr. 12, 1970; children: Ephram, Jonathan. BSEE, Poly. Inst. N.Y., 1966; MSEE, U. Pa., 1968; MBA, Harvard U., 1972. Sr. engr. Raytheon, Bedford, Mass., 1968-71; first v.p. Paine Webber, N.Y.C., 1972—. Ford Found. fellow, 1966-67; Baker scholar Harvard U., 1972. Fellow N.Y. Soc. Secutiry Analysts; mem. (charter) Robotics Internat. Soc. Mech. Engrs., Harvard Bus. Sch. Assn. Home: 12 Country Club Way Demarest NJ 07627 Office: Paine Webber Inc 1285 Ave of the Americas New York NY 10019

LUSTGARTEN, STEWART J., dental marketing executive; b. N.Y.C., Jan. 4, 1943; s. Samuel H. and Kate (Motelson) L.; m. Susan Figa, Aug. 14, 1969; children: Jennifer, Shelby, Jillian. Student U. Miami, Fla., 1960-63. Asst. v.p. Columbia Dentoform Corp., N.Y.C., 1964-77; dir. bio-materials div. Parkell Inc., Farmingdale, N.Y., 1977; v.p. Healthco Internat., Inc., Boston, 1977-86; chief exec. officer Lustgarten Multi-Tech Internat. Inc., Framingham, Mass., 1986—; v.p., bd. dirs. Roeko U.S.A., Inc., Framingham, 1987—; cons. Roeko GmbH, Langenau, Fed. Republic Germany, 1987—, Accutek, Inc., Cranston, R.I., 1988; Adiesse Founitures Dental, Florence, Italy, 1986—, P.S.P. Dental Ltd, Belv. Kent, England, 1986, Macrochem Corp., Woburn, Mass., 1987—, Biodmed. Devel. Corp., San Antonio, 1989—, Avitar Corp, Canton, Mass., 1989—, Warner Lambert Corp., Morristown, N.J., 1972-74, Primary Med. Communications, Inc., N.Y.C., 1971-74, Denar Corp., Anaheim, Calif., 1977-78, dept. dental materials Coll. Dentistry, NYU, 1974-77, dept. dental materials N.J. Coll. Dentistry, Newark, 1974-77 and numerous other cos.; bd. dirs. Dental Mfrs. Am., Phila., 1974-77. Patentee dental materials and methods. Served with USNR, 1964-70. Recipient cert. of appreciation Mass. Dental Assts. Assn., 1983, 84. Mem. Am. Assn. Dental Schs., Am. Assn. for Dental Research, Acad. Operative Dentistry. Avocations: boating; dancing; music, writing. Home: 73 Dalton Rd Holliston MA 01746 Office: 1661 Worcester Rd Framingham MA 01701

LUSZTIG, PETER ALFRED, university dean, educator; b. Budapest, Hungary, May 12, 1930; s. Alfred Peter and Susan (Szabo) L.; m. Penny Bicknell, Aug. 26, 1961; children: Michael, Cameron, Carrie. B in Com., U. B.C., Vancouver, Can., 1954; MBA, U. Western Ont., London, Can., 1955; PhD, Stanford U., 1964. Asst. to comptroller B.C. Electric, Vancouver, 1955-57; instr. fin. U. B.C., 1957-60, asst. prof. fin., 1962-64, assoc. prof., 1964-68, Killam sr. research fellow, 1968-69, prof., 1968—; dean Faculty Commerce, 1977—; pub. gov. Vancouver Stock Exchange; bd. dirs. Canfor Corp., Canfor Capital, Tree Island Industries; mem. univ. senate, 1976—; vis. prof. IMEDE, Switzerland, 1973-74, London Grad. Sch. Bus. Studies, 1968-69, Pacific Coast Banking Sch., 1977—; bd. govs. Banff Sch. Advanced Mgmt. Author: Report of the Royal Commission on Automobile Insurance, 2 vols, 1968, Financial Management in a Canadian Setting, 4th. rev. edit, 1988. Bd. dirs. Vancouver Gen. Hosp. Found. Ford Found. faculty dissertation fellow, Stanford U., 1964. Mem. Am. Fin. Assn., Council Deans, Fin. Mgmt. Assn., Vancouver Club. Lutheran. Office: Dept Commerce & Bus, Adminstrn BC, Vancouver, BC Canada V6T 1W5

LUTER, JOSEPH WILLIAMSON, III, meat packing and processing company executive; b. Smithfield, Va., 1939; married. BBA, Wake Forest Coll., 1962. Pres. Smithfield Packing Co., Arlington, Va., 1964-69, Bryce Mountain Resort Inc., 1969-75; with Smithfield Foods Inc., Arlington, 1975—, pres., 1975-86, chief exec. officer, 1975—, chmn., 1977—, also bd. dirs. Office: Smithfield Foods Inc 501 N Church St Smithfield VA 23430 *

LUTGEN, LARRY GENE, controller; b. Zanesville, Ohio, Sept. 9, 1948; s. Virgil H. Lutgen and Dorothy J. (Heslup) Urban; m. Gloria J. Dillon, Oct. 20, 1974 (div.); children: Larry Lee, Beth Ann; m. G. Gayle Howell, Dec. 13, 1984; 1 child, Kimberly H. Young. BBA, Ohio U., 1976, MBA, 1978. CPA, Ga. Controller ITT Rayonier, Atlanta, 1977-82, Container Corp. Am., Atlanta, 1982-83, Talley Metals, Hartsville, S.C., 1983-86, La-Z-Boy Co. East, Florence, S.C., 1986—. Mem. Church of the Pentecostal Holiness. Home: 956 Swan Circle Florence SC 29501 Office: La-Z-Boy East 901 N Douglas St Florence SC 29501

LUTH, JAMES CURTIS, programmer analyst; b. Fairmont, Minn., May 19, 1961; s. Richard H. and Doris M. (Shockley) L. BA, Wartburg Coll., Waverly, Iowa, 1983. Programmer, analyst Grinnell (Iowa) Mut. Reins Co., 1984-86, Analyst Internat. Corp., Rochester, Minn., 1986—. George A. Hormel Co. merit scholar, 1979; Wartburg Coll. scholar, 1979. Methodist. Home: 1160 Cushing Circle Apt 206 Saint Paul MN 55108

LUTH, ROBERT J., communications company executive; b. N.Y.C., July 20, 1943; s. Kathleen Hunter; children: Christine, Robert J. Jr., Cindy. Student, NYU, 1963; BA, Susquehanna U., 1966. CPA, N.Y. With Deloitte, Haskins & Sells, N.Y.C., 1966-73, Norton Simon, Inc., N.Y.C., 1973-76, Max Factor & Co., L.A., 1976-79; controller Norton Simon, Inc., L.A., 1982-84; v.p. Halston Fragrances & Orlane, N.Y.C., 1979-82; exec. v.p. Mura Corp., Hicksville, N.Y., 1984, pres., 1984-85; pres. HCL Leasing Corp., Parsippany, N.J., 1984-86; treas. TIE/Communications, Inc., Shelton, Conn., 1986-88; v.p. fin., chief exec. officer Telesphere Internat., Inc., Oakbrook Terrace, Ill., 1988—. Mem. Am. Inst. CPA's, N.Y. State Soc. CPA's (real estate acctg. com. 1974-76). Office: Telesphere Internat Inc 2 Mid-America Pla Oakbrook Terrace IL 60181

LUTHE, FRANK, sales executive; b. Camden, N.J., Jan. 25, 1948; s. William C. and Rose Anne (Donato) L.; m. Kathleen Abel, Sept. 30, 1972; children: Kristin Ann, Lindsay Erin. Student, Rider Coll., Lawrenceville,

N.J., 1965-67; grad., Antonelli's Sch. of Photography, Phila. Photographer, lab. technician Crown Photo, Gloucester, N.J., 1972-77; sales rep. Rieke Corp., Linden, N.J., 1977-82, Russell-Stanley Corp., Woodbridge, N.J./Houston, 1982; dist. sales mgr. Russell-Stanley Corp., various locations, 1983—, Woodbridge, 1987—. Bd. dirs. Northwoods Unitarian Ch., The Woodlands, Tex., 1985; publicity com. chmn. Lexington Woods Recreation Assn., Spring, Tex., 1983-85. Served with USAF, 1967-71. Unitarian. Office: Russell-Stanley East Convery Blvd and Bey St Woodbridge NJ 07095

LUTHER, JAMES HOWARD, lawyer, retired pharmaceutical company executive; b. West New York, N.J., Jan. 27, 1928; s. James Howard and Margaret Mary (Leyden) L.; m. Frances Audrey Lynch, July 14, 1951; children—David Gerard, Stephanie Lynch. A.B. magna cum laude, Fordham U., 1948, J.D. cum laude, 1951. Bar: N.Y. bar 1951. Assoc. Donovan, Leisure, Newton & Irvine, N.Y.C., 1951-55; with Sterling Drug Inc., N.Y.C., 1955-88, v.p., 1968-78, dir., 1973-88, gen. counsel, 1976-88, sr. v.p., gen. counsel, 1978-88, ret.; pvt. practice N.Y.C., 1988—. Mem. ABA, Proprietary Assn. (v.p. 1972-85, dir. 1972-88, chmn. bd. 1985-87). Roman Catholic. Home and Office: 1175 York Ave New York NY 10021

LUTHER, WILLIAM MARTIN, management executive; b. Chgo., July 10, 1931; s. Arleigh James and Clarice Alfredia L.; m. Elizabeth Terese Stemper, Jan. 19, 1958; children: Jeannie, Michael, Susan, Ann. BBA, U. Minn., 1953. Account exec. Campbell-Mithun, Mpls., 1956-58, Phillips-Ramsey, San Diego, 1959-61, McCann-Erickson, Honolulu, 1961-63; account supr. Marshalk, San Francisco, Dallas and Atlanta, 1964-66; v.p. Grey Advt., N.Y.C., 1967-70; pres. Luther Mgmt. Inc., Stamford, Conn., 1971—. Author: The Marketing Plan, 1982, How to Develop a Business Plan in 15 Days, 1987; author computer software on mktg. planning and strategic planning. Served with U.S. Army, 1953-55, Korea. Office: Luther Mgmt Inc 211 Riverbank Dr Stamford CT 06903

LUTKEN, DONALD C., utility company executive; b. Jackson, Miss., Mar. 26, 1924; s. Peter Koch and Erma (Curry) L.; m. Melissa Turner, June 11, 1946; children: Melissa (Mrs. Hugo Newcomb, Jr.), Isabel Poteat (Mrs. W.L. Eggart), Donald C., Edwin Poteat. BS, U.S. Naval Acad., 1946. With Miss. Power & Light Co., Jackson, 1949—, exec. v.p. ops., 1969-70, pres., 1970—, chief exec. officer, 1971—, chmn., 1984-89, chmn. emeritus, 1989, also bd. dirs.; v.p. Mid. South Energy, Inc.; bd. dirs. Unifirst Fed. Savs. and Loan Assn., Lamar Life Corp.; Miss. chmn. payroll U.S. Savs. Bond div. Treasury Dept. Mem. exec. bd. Andrew Jackson council Boy Scouts Am., adv. bd. S.E. region Area IV; trustee Belhaven Coll., Mary Baldwin Coll., So. Research Inst., Miss. Found. Ind. Colls.; past deacon Jackson Presbyn. Ch.; bd. dirs. Cen. Miss. Growth Found., Jackson State U. Devel. Found. Served with USNR, 1946-49. Mem. Jackson C. of C., Jackson Symphony League, Newcomen Soc., Miss. State U. Alumni Found., Nat. Assn. Electric Cos., Miss. Soc. Profl. Engrs., ASME, IEEE, Edison Electric Inst., Miss. Mfrs. Assn., Miss. Econ. Assn., Miss. Hist. Soc. Clubs: Jackson Country, Univ., Capital City Petroleum (Jackson). Lodge: Rotary. Home: Rte 2 Box 250 Sub Rosa Jackson MS 39209 Office: Miss Power & Light Co PO Box 1640 Jackson MS 39215-1640

LUTKOWITZ, MARK, market research executive; b. N.Y.C., Oct. 1, 1960; s. Morris Murray and Jeanette (Cooperman) L. BA, NYU, 1983. Sr. analyst No. Bus. Info., N.Y.C., 1983-86; pres. Trans-Formation Inc., Tulsa, 1986—. Republican. Jewish. Office: Trans-Formation Inc One Memorial Pl Ste 324 7633 E 63rd Pl Tulsa OK 74133

LUTSKY, SHELDON JAY, financial and marketing consultant, writer; b. New Kensington, Pa., Jan. 13, 1943; s. Hyman I. and Rose S. (Schwartz) L.; B.S., Kent State U., 1967; postgrad. U. Colo., 1969-70. Chemist B.F. Goodrich, Akron, Ohio, 1966; with United Bank of Denver, 1968-75; founder Mountain States Ski Assn., pub. Mountain States Recreation, Denver, 1976-81; pres. Dolphin Assocs., Denver, 1981—; instr. penny stocks Denver U. Bd. mem. Colo. 4-H Adv. Council. Recipient Burr Photog. Achievement award Kent State U., 1965. Mem. Denver C. of C., Denver Conv. Bur., Nat. Ski Writers Assn., Rocky Mountain Ski Writers Assn., Rocky Mountain Fin. Writers Assn. (pres. 1982-84). Developer Slope Scope, ski slope evaluation system. Home: 4807 S Zang Way Morrison CO 80465 Office: Lutsky & Assocs 2124 S Dayton St Denver CO 80231

LUTTRELL, MICHAEL JOSEPH, medical products company executive; b. Chester, Pa., Sept. 12, 1948; s. Joseph Irving and Anna Jean (White) L.; m. Nell Louise Dewald, Nov. 17, 1973; 1 child, Margaret Louise. BS in History, Mt. St. Mary's Coll., Emmitsburg, Md., 1970; MBA in Mgmt. with highest honors, Lake Forest Coll., 1985. Lic. funeral dir. Pa. Funeral dir. G.J. White Funeral Home, Ridley Park, Pa., 1971-79; sales rep. Flint div. Baxter Healthcare Corp. (formerly Travenol Labs.), Washington, 1979-80; asst. to nat. sales mgr. Baxter Healthcare Corp. (formerly Travenol Labs.), Deerfield, Ill., 1980-82, asst. to pres., 1982, product mgr., 1982-83, mktg. specialist respiratory homecare div., 1983-84, mgr. sales devel. respiratory homecare div., 1984-85; mgr. tng. and devel. home respiratory therapy Travenol Labs., Deerfield, Ill., 1985-87; v.p. mktg. The John Bunn Co., Tonawanda, N.Y., 1988—; bd. dirs. Baxter Travenol Employees Credit Union; editorial adv. bd. Tng. Dirs. Forum. Mem. curriculum rev. com. Lake Forest (Ill.) Grad. Sch., 1986—, Ridley Park Bicentennial Commn., 1976, Ridley Park Bus. Assn., 1971-79; chmn. Ridley Park Zoning Bd., 1977-79; mem. relief assn. Ridley Park Fire Dept., 1975-79, adv. bd. Sch. Dist. 15, Palatine, Ill. Mem. Am. Soc. Tng. and Devel., Nat. Soc. Sales Tng. Execs., Healthcare Mfrs. Mktg. Council. Republican. Roman Catholic. Office: 290 Creekside Dr Tonawanda NY 14150

LUTVAK, MARK ALLEN, computer company marketing executive; b. Chgo., Feb. 9, 1939; s. Joseph Issac and Jeanette Nettie (Pollock) L.; B.S. in Elec. Engring., U. Mich., 1962; M.B.A., Wayne State U., Detroit, 1969; m. Gayle Helene Rotofsky, May 24, 1964; children—Jeffrey, Eric. Sales rep. IBM Corp., 1962-64; successively sales rep., product mktg. mgr., corp. product mgr. Burroughs Corp., Detroit, 1964-76; mgr. product mktg. Memorex Corp., Santa Clara, Calif., 1976-80, product program gen. mgr., 1980-81; dir. product mktg. Personal Computer div. Atari, Inc., Sunnyvale, Calif., 1981-83; dir. mktg., v.p. Durango Systems, San Jose, Calif., 1983-85; dir. mktg. ITTQUME Corp., San Jose, 1985-87; v.p. mktg. Optimem, Mountain View, Calif., 1987-88; dir. mktg. Priam Corp., San Jose, 1988—; prof. Applied Mgmt. Center, Wayne State U., 1967-72, Walsh U., Troy, Mich., 1974-76, West Valley Coll., Saratoga, Calif., 1977-78. Trustee, pres. brotherhood Temple Emanuel, San Jose, Calif., 1979-80. Mem. IEEE, Soc. Applied Math., Alpha Epsilon Pi. Home: 1364 Box Canyon Rd San Jose CA 95120

LUTZ, JOHN SHAFROTH, lawyer; b. San Francisco, Sept. 10, 1943; s. Frederick Henry and Helena Morrison (Shafroth) L.; m. Elizabeth Boschen, Dec. 14, 1968; children: John Shafroth, Victoria. BA, Brown U., 1965; JD, U. Denver, 1971. Bar: Colo. 1971, U.S. Dist. Ct. Colo. 1971, U.S. Ct. Appeals (2d cir.) 1975, D.C. 1976, U.S. Supreme Ct. 1976, U.S. Dist. Ct. (so. dist.) N.Y. 1977, U.S. Tax Ct. 1977, U.S. Ct. Appeals (10th cir.) 1979, N.Y. 1984. Trial atty. Denver regional office U.S. SEC, 1971-74; spl. atty. organized crime, racketeering sect. U.S. Dept. Justice, So. Dist. N.Y., 1974-77; atty. Kelly, Stansfield and O'Donnell, Denver, 1977-78; gen. counsel and gen. ptnr. Boettcher & Co., Denver, 1978-87, Kelly, Stansfield and O'Donnel, Denver, 1987; spl. counsel, 1987-88, ptnr., 1988—. allied mem. N.Y. Stock Exch., 1978-87; speaker on broker, dealer, securities law and arbitration issues to various profl. orgns. Contbr. articles to profl. jours. Bd. dirs. Cherry Creek Improvement Assn., 1980-84, Spalding Rehab. Hosp., 1986—. Lt. (j.g.), USNR, 1965-67. Mem. ABA, Colo. Bar Assn., Denver Bar Assn., Am. Law Inst., Securities Industry Assn. (state regulations com. 1982-86), Nat. Assn. Securities Dealers, Inc. (nat. arbitration com. 1987—), St. Nicholas Soc. N.Y.C., Denver Law Club, Denver Country Club, Denver Tennis Club, Denver Athletic Club, Rocky Mountain Brown Club (founder, past pres.), Racquet and Tennis Club. Republican. Episcopalian. Home: 144 Race St Denver CO 80206 Office: Kelly Stansfield & O'Donnell 550 15th St Denver CO 80202

LUTZ, NANCY ANNE, economist educator; b. Chgo., Sept. 17, 1960; d. Walter Frederick and Marianne (Lindener) L. BA, MA, Northwestern U., 1982; PhD, Stanford U., 1987. Asst. prof. econs. Yale U., New Haven, Conn., 1986—. Mem. Am. Econ. Assn., Econometric Soc., Phi Beta Kappa, Gamma Phi Beta. Roman Catholic. Office: Cowles Found for Econ Rsch PO Box 2125 Yale Sta New Haven CT 06511

LUTZ, WILLIAM ANDREW, sales and marketing executive; b. Maspeth, N.Y., Nov. 11, 1944; s. William Charles and Constance (Dwyer) L.; m. Susan Anthony, Sept. 20, 1970; 1 child, Erin Kimberly. Student, Princeton U., 1962-65, La Sorbonne, Paris, 1966; AB, Princeton U., 1971; MA, Ind. U., 1977. Indsl. engr. Grumman Aerospace Corp., Bethpage, N.Y., 1966-69; account exec. Dean Witter Reynolds, Chgo., 1975-78; mktg. rep. Control Data Corp., Chgo., 1978-80; mgr. industry mktg. Control Data Corp., N.Y.C., 1980-81, mktg. mgr., 1981-83; v.p. sales, mktg. Ziff-Davis Corp., N.Y.C., 1983-84; cons. sales, mktg. Touche Ross & Co., N.Y.C., 1984-86, dep. nat. dir. mktg. and communications, 1986-88, nat. dir. mktg. and communications, 1988—. Mem. Am. Mgmt. Assn., Am. Mktg. Ass., Internat. Assn. Fin. Planners, Internat. Assn. for Tng. and Devel., The Planning Group. Lutheran. Club: Princeton (N.Y.C.). Office: Touche Ross & Co 1633 Broadway New York NY 10019

LUX, JOHN H., corporate executive; b. Logansport, Ind., Feb. 3, 1918; s. Carl Harrison and Mary Emma (Dunn) L.; m. Betty F. Passow, Aug. 27, 1940; children—John Ernst, Courtney Rae; m. Bernice Weitzel Brown, 1965; m. Linda Merrill Brown, Mar. 2, 1978; children—Julia Elizabeth, Jenifyr Claire. B.S., Purdue U., 1939; Ph.D., 1942. Asst. dir. research and devel. The Neville Co., 1943-46; v.p., cons. Atomic Basic Chems. 1946-47; dir. research Witco Chem. Co., 1947-50; mgr. new product devel. Gen. Electric Co., 1950-52; v.p. Shea Chem. Co., 1952-55; pres., dir. Haveg Industries, Inc., Wilmington, Del., 1955-66, Haveg Corp., Tourlux Mgmt. Corp. (P.R.); chmn. bd. Hemisphere Products Corp. (P.R.), Reinhold Engring. & Plastics Co., Norwalk, Calif., Am. Super-Temperatures Wires Co.; pres. Ametek, Inc., 1966-69, chmn. bd., chief exec. officer, 1969—. Mem. Am. Inst. Chem. Engrs., Am. Chem. Soc., Phi Lambda Upsilon. Club: Met. Office: Ametek Inc PO Box 8266 Rancho Santa Fe CA 92067 also: 410 Park Ave 21st Fl New York NY 10022

LYALL, MICHAEL RODNEY, investment banker; b. Oxford, Eng., Aug. 28, 1945; came to U.S., 1970; s. Rodney and Joan (Morgan) L.; m. Alice Jackson Myers, June 28, 1973 (div. 1976). BA, Oxford U., Eng., 1967; MBA, Harvard U., 1973. Assoc. Bankers Trust Internat. Ltd., N.Y.C., London, 1973-75; v.p. Chase Manhattan Bank, N.Y.C., 1975-80; mng. dir. Carr Sebag Ltd., N.Y.C., 1981-82; exec. v.p. Hoare Govett, Inc., N.Y.C., 1982-86; mng. dir. Woolcott & Co., N.Y.C., 1987-88, The Am. Acquisition Co., N.Y.C., 1988—; bd. dirs. Matrix Membranes, Inc., Societe Textile de Kaolack, Dakar, Senegal. Named Chevalier de l'Ordre du Grand Lion (Senegal). Episcopalian. Clubs: White's (London); Racquet and Tennis (N.Y.C.). Home: 145 E 74th St New York NY 10021 also: Doodle House Ancram NY 12502

LYKES, JOSEPH T., III, shipping company executive; b. Galveston, Tex., Mar. 6, 1948; m. Dianne Bland Cuevas, Oct. 10, 1987. BA, Washington and Lee U., 1970. Asst. mgr. Lykes Lines Agy., Antwerp, Belgium, 1971-73; owners rep. Lykes Lines Agy., Tokyo, 1973-75; townage controller Lykes Bros. Steamship Co., New Orleans, 1975-78; dir. traffic Lykes Bros. Steamship Co., San Francisco, 1979-81; asst. v.p. Lykes Bros. Steamship Co., New Orleans, 1982-84, v.p. pricing, 1984-86, v.p., treas., 1986-88, sr. v.p., chief fin. officer, 1988—; bd. dirs. Lykes Bros., Inc., Tampa, Fla., Shore Mmgt., Inc., Tampa, Lykes Energy, Inc., Tampa. Office: Lykes Bros Steamship Co Inc Lykes Ctr 300 Poydras St New Orleans LA 70130

LYKINS, JAY ARNOLD, economic development director; b. Shattuck, Okla., Feb. 13, 1947; s. George Eldridge and Lucy Lee (Croom) L.; m. (Mary) Lynn Turner, Jan. 3, 1970; children: Mary Lee and Amy Lynn (twins), Jason. BA, Covenant Coll., 1973; MBA in 3rd World Econ. Devel., Kennedy-Western U., 1987, PhD in Internat. Bus., 1988. Credit specialist Gen. Electric Supply Co., Nashville, 1974-75; owner, mgr. Environment Control Co., Nashville, 1975-78; bus. adminstr. Youth for Christ, Atlanta, 1978-81; controller Young Life, Colorado Springs, Colo., 1981-82, internat. adminstr., 1982-86; exec. dir. Global Reach, Milpitas, Calif., 1982—; cons. Royal Donuts, Lima, Peru, Barnabas Group, Vancouver. B.C, Manna Corp., Bulawayo, Zimbabwe, Denver Bridge Corp. Author: Values in the Marketplace, 1985, Development and Technology: Economics for the Third World, 1987, Islamic Business: Philosophy and Methods, 1988. Served with USN, 1966-68. Mem. Internat. Council for Small Bus., Am. Cons. League, Assn. MBA Execs., Ctr. Enterpreneurial Mgmt. Club: Nob Hill Country (Snellville, Ga.) (pres. 1980). Office: Global Reach 25 Corning Ave Milpitas CA 95035

LYMAN, JERRY ROSS, radio executive; b. Richmond, Va., Jan. 12, 1941; s. Carson F. and Elizabeth P. Lyman; m. Judith Dennard, Mar. 6, 1965; children: Erin Samantha, Derek Ross. BS in Radio and TV Prodn., U. Wis., 1963. Sales mgr. RKO Radio Reps., Los Angeles, 1969; gen. sales mgr. Sta. WGMS-AM-FM, Washington, 1971, gen. mgr., 1972, v.p., gen. mgr., 1972-84; sr. v.p. RKO Radio, Washington, 1974, pres. FM div., 1977-82; v.p. govt. relations RKO Gen., Washington, 1982-84; pres. RKO Radio, N.Y.C., 1984-89; pres., chief exec. officer Radio Ventures I, L.P., Washington, 1989—; mem. adv. bd. Am. Security Bank Washington, 1983-85; bd. dirs. Radio Advt. Bur., N.Y.C., 1987. Bd. dirs. Nat. Symphony Orch., Washington, 1975-80, Children's Hosp. Nat. Med. Ctr., Washington, 1981-85, corp. bd., 1976-87; mem. state productivity bd. U.S. Senate, Md., 1983-84. Mem. Nat. Assn. Broadcasters (radio bd. vice chmn. 1986-87, chmn. 1987-88), Washington Area Broadcasters Assn. (bd. dirs. 1974-84, vice chmn. 1979-80, chmn. 1980-82). Home: 18 Mercy Ct Poromac MD 20854 Office: Radio Ventures I LP 1001 Penn Ave NW Ste 220S Washington DC 20004 also: Sta WRKO 3 Fenway Pla Boston MA 02215

LYMAN, JOHN ROOT, oil company executive; b. Washington, Aug. 2, 1939; s. John Root and Mary Mutter (Moore) L.; m. Constance Rose Nagel, May 18, 1968; children: John Miller, Suzanne Marie. BA in Econs., Yale U., 1961; MS in Indsl. Mgmt., MIT, 1963. Spl. asst. East African Rys., 1963-65; research assoc. MIT, Cambridge, 1965-66; economist Amoco Internat. Oil Co., Chgo., 1966-69, environ. analyst, 1969-72, contr., 1975-80; asst. treas. Amoco Corp., Chgo., 1980-81, gen. mgr. auditing, 1981-84, gen. mgr., v.p. info. services, 1984-87, v.p. planning and econs., 1987—; mgr. budgets Standard Oil Co., Chgo., 1972-75. Pres. Nat. Lekotek, Evanston, Ill., 1985-87; mem. Citizens for Evanston's Future, 1986—; mem. Chgo. com. Coun. on Fgn. Rels. Mem. Soc. for Info. Mgmt., Fin. Execs. Inst., Am. Petroleum Inst. (various coms.), Conf. Bd. (various coms.). Clubs: Mid-Am., Economic (Chgo.). Office: Amoco Corp 200 E Randolph Dr Mail Code 2904A Chicago IL 60601

LYNCH, CHARLES ALLEN, home furnishings executive; b. Denver, Sept. 7, 1927; s. Laurence J. and Louanna (Robertson) L.; m. Linda Bennet, June 14, 1952; children: Charles A., Tara O'Hara, Casey Alexander. B.S., Yale U., 1950. With E.I. duPont de Nemours & Co., Inc., Wilmington, Del., 1950-69, dir. mktg., 1965-69; corp. v.p. SCOA Industries, Columbus, Ohio, 1969-72; corp. exec. v.p., also mem. rotating bd. W.R. Grace & Co., N.Y.C., 1972-78; chmn. bd., chief exec. officer Saga Corp., Menlo Park, Calif., 1978-86, also dir.; chmn., chief exec. officer DHL Airways, Inc., Redwood City, Calif., 1986-88; pres., chief exec. officer Levolor Corp., 1988—; bd. dirs. Pacific Mut. Life Ins. Co., Nordstrom, Inc., SRI Internat., Palo Alto Med. Found., Syntex Corp.; trustee Conf. Bd. Bd. dirs. San Francisco YMCA; vice chmn. Bay Area Council; former chmn. Calif. Bus. Roundtable; trustee Occidental Coll., 1987; adv. bd. U. Calif., Berkeley Bus. Sch., Governance Bd., Coll. of Notre Dame, Belmont, Calif.; chmn. Bay area campaign United Way. Served with USNR, 1945. Republican. Clubs: Yale (N.Y.C.); Internat. Lawn Tennis; Menlo Country (Calif.), Menlo Circus (Calif.); Pacific Union (San Francisco); Ponte Vedra (Fla.); Beach and Tennis; Coral Beach and Tennis (Bermuda); Vintage (Indian Wells, Calif.). Office: Levolor Corp One Upper Pond Rd Parsippany NJ 07054

LYNCH, DAVID DILLON, transportation executive, educator; b. Richmond Heights, Mo., July 24, 1940; s. David Dillon and Alice Ann (Eubank) L.; m. Judy Anton, Aug. 13, 1960; children: Gwynn, Christine, Jennifer. BSEE, Washington U., Clayton, Mo., 1962, MSEE, 1965; postgrad., Bklyn. Poly. Inst., 1966, UCLA, 1974, 84. Project engring. asst. Union Electric Co., St. Louis, 1961; project engr. Mo. Research Lab., St. Louis, 1962-64; mem. tech. staff Bell Labs., Murray Hill, N.J., 1964-65; group supr. Emerson Electric Co., St. Louis, 1966-70; program mgr., group v.p. and mgr. engring. div. Hughes Aircraft Co., Los Angeles, 1970—; bd. dirs. Hughes S.C. Inc.; instr. UCLA, 1971-76, U. So. Calif., Los Angeles, 1973-76; asst. prof. U. Mo., Rolla, 1964-67; cons. Evolving Technology, San Diego, 1973—. Co-author books on radar and signal processing; contbr. articles to profl. jours.; patentee in field. Recipient Hyland Patent award Hughes Aircraft Co., 1978. Sr. mem. IEEE, AIAA; mem. Computer Soc. of IEEE (pres. and v.p. chpt.), Am. Soc. Metals, Hughes Mgmt. Club, Sigma Xi, Phi Delta Theta. Episcopalian. Home: 18651 Gledhill St Northridge CA 91324 Office: Hughes Aircraft Co Radar Systems Group PO Box 92426 Los Angeles CA 90009

LYNCH, DERRELL SEVIER, manufacturing executive; b. Lowell, Mass., Oct. 10, 1935; s. David O. and Marion A. (Asquith) L.; m. Jane C. Smith, Sept. 20, 1958; children: Jeffrey A., Philip C. Attended, Tufts U., 1953-54, U.S. Mil. Acad., 1957-58; BBA cum laude, U. Mass., 1962; postgrad., NYU, 1962-65. V.p. fin., treas. Gleason Corp., Rochester, N.Y., 1982-84, sr. v.p. fin., adminstrn., 1984—, also bd. dirs. Dir. Rochester Friendly Home, 1986—. Mem. Fin. Execs. Inst. (bd. dirs. Rochester chpt. 1984-86), Machinery and Allied Products Inst. (fin. council 1983-89), Beta Gamma Sigma. Club: Genesee Valley (Rochester). Office: Gleason Corp 30 Corporate Woods Box 22856 Rochester NY 14692

LYNCH, FRAN J., real estate development executive; b. Bklyn., Dec. 15, 1948; d. William R. and Ruth (Slaiman) Diamondstein; m. James P. Lynch, Jan. 8, 1969; children: Cheryl Ann, Christopher, Kevin. BA, Bklyn. Coll., 1969; student, Suffolk Community Coll., Brentwood, N.Y., 1980-82; postgrad, L.I. U., 1983. V.p. Castle Capital Corp., N.Y.C., 1971-74; agt. Jerome Castle Found., N.Y.C., 1970-74; dir. office services Penn-Dixie Industries, N.Y.C., 1970-74; exec. asst. Med. Fin. Advisor, N.Y.C., 1974; v.p. Sept. Capital Corp., Glen Cove, N.Y., 1977-80; controller Bobgar Inc., Wallweaves Inc. and N.Y. Twine, Syosset, N.Y., 1980-86, The Kapson Group, Commack, N.Y., 1987—; cons. Women's Times, Queens, N.Y., 1987. Sec. Elwood Booster Club, East Northport, N.Y., 1987; mem. Harley Ave. PTA, 1980-87; coach Northport Youth Soccer, 1982; tchr. Confraternity Christian Doctrine Project St. Elizabeth's Ch., 1972-80, bd. dirs. Parish council, S. Huntington, N.Y., 1978-80. Home: 25 Hooper Ct East Northport NY 11731

LYNCH, FRANK JOSEPH, insurance company executive; b. S.I., N.Y., Mar. 19, 1930; s. Frank J. and May (McBreen) L.; m. Patricia Crane, Apr. 27, 1957; children—Frank, Michael, Megan, Carmel. B.A., Wagner Coll., 1951; LL.B., N.Y. Law Sch., 1962. Bar: N.Y. 1962. Underwriter Fireman's Fund Ins. Co., N.Y.C., 1950-53; analyst Ebasco Services, Inc., N.Y.C., 1954-55; with U.S. Aviation Underwriters, Inc., N.Y.C., 1956—, sr. v.p., chief underwriter, 1971-72, pres., 1972-77, chmn. bd., chief exec. officer, 1977—. Trustee Delbarton Prep Sch., Morristown, N.J., 1982—, Chestnut Hill Coll., Pa., 1984—, Morris Mus., Morristown, 1984—, Tri-County Scholarship Fund, Paterson, N.J., 1984—. Served with USNR, 1947-51, USAF, 1951. Republican. Roman Catholic. Clubs: Wall St. Club; Springbrook Golf (N.J.), Baltusrol Golf (N.J.). Home: Crestley Van Beuren Rd Morristown NJ 07960 Office: US Aviation Underwriters Inc One Seaport Pla 199 Water St New York NY 10038

LYNCH, FRANK WILLIAM, aerospace company executive; b. San Francisco, Nov. 26, 1921; s. James Garfield and Med (Kelly) L.; m. Marilyn Leona Hopwood, June 24, 1950; children: Kathyn Leona, Molly Louise. A.B., Stanford U., 1943, postgrad., 1946-48. Research engr. Boeing Airplane Co., Seattle, 1948-50; with Northrop Corp., Hawthorn, Calif., 1950-57, Los Angeles, 1959—; sr. v.p. ops. corp. hdqrs. Northrop Corp., 1974-78, sr. v.p. and group exec. Tactical and Electronic Systems Group, 1978-82, pres., chief operating officer, 1982-87, vice chmn. of bd., 1987—; div. v.p. engring. Lear-Siegler Corp., Anaheim, Calif., 1957-59. Vice-chmn. Found. for Sitery Ballet; trustee Calif. State U. Found., L.A.; bd. govs. L.A. Music Ctr. Served with AC U.S. Army, 1942-46. Mem. IEEE (sr. mem.), AIAA (sr. mem.), Assn. U.S. Army, Am. Def. Preparedness Assn., Air Force Assn., Navy League, Balboa Yacht Club, City Club, Ctr. Club. Home: 1933 Altura Dr Corona Del Mar CA 92625 Office: Northrop Corp 1840 Century Park E Los Angeles CA 90067

LYNCH, JAMES PATRICK, computer scientist, educator, consultant; b. Oklahoma City, Okla., Mar. 19, 1952; s. Raymond Warren and Elizabeth Johnson (Vann) L.; m Elizabeth Jean Luckhart, Aug. 6, 1971; children: Laura Ann, Max William, Megan Elizabeth. Student, Cen. State U., 1970-72, BS, 1982; BS, Oklahoma City U., 1974, MA in Edn., 1983; postgrad., U. Okla., 1974-75. Cert. secondary edn. tchr., Okla. Sci. tchr. Bishop McGuinness High Sch., Oklahoma City, 1975-76; electron microscopist Okla. Children's Meml. Hosp., Oklahoma City, 1976-78, chief electron microscopist, 1979-82; instr. tech. br. Okla. State U., Oklahoma City, 1983-89; pres., lab. dir. T.E.M. Testing Corp., Oklahoma City, 1989—; owner Lynch Computer Enterprises, Edmond, 1987—; computer programmer Okla. Children's Meml. Hosp., 1983-86; lectr. Cen. State U., Edmond, Okla., 1984—; cons. Kirkpatrick Ctr./Complex, Oklahoma City, 1984-85; ptnr. Fin. Systems Services, Edmond, 1986-87. Author software programs, 1985. Mem. bd. edn. John Carroll Sch., Oklahoma City, 1983-84. Mem. Electron Microscopy Soc. Am. (cert.), Beta Beta Beta. Republican. Roman Catholic. Home: 526 SE 28th St Edmond OK 73013 Office: TEM Testing Corp 5013 NW 24th Pl Oklahoma City OK 73107

LYNCH, JOHN JOSEPH, electronics company executive; b. Boston, Dec. 23, 1931; s. John James and Margaret Joan (Crowley) L.; m. Christine Mary Sullivan, Feb. 13, 1954; children: John J. II, Christine M. O'Hurley, Michael J., Kevin C., James M. BSBA, Boston Coll., 1953; MBA, Harvard, 1958. Asst. mgr. internat. audit Raytheon, Lexington, Mass., 1958-61; contr. U.S. Sonics Corp., Cambridge, Mass., 1961-62; treas., bus. mgr. Adams-Russell Electronics Co., Inc., Waltham, Mass., 1962-70; dir. Adams-Russell Electronics Co., Inc., 1964—, v.p. fin., 1970-80, pres., chief ops. officer, 1980-82, pres., chief exec. officer, 1982-88; chmn., chief exec. officer Adams-Russell Electronics Co., Inc. (name changed to Adams-Russell, Inc.), 1988—; bd. dirs. SofTech, Inc., Waltham, Mass. High Tech. Coun., Boston. Trustee Associated Cath. Hosps., Brighton, Mass., 1984—, Mass. Eye and Ear Infirmary, Boston, 1986—; bd. dirs. Am. Heart Assn. Mass. Affilitate, Needham, 1984-88. Lt. USNR, 1953-56, Western Pacific and Newport, R.I. Office: Adams-Russell Inc 1380 Main St Waltham MA 02154

LYNCH, KATHLEEN MARIE, real estate executive, lawyer; b. N.Y.C., Dec. 30, 1949; d. Daniel Francis and Mary Margaret (Flynn) L. BA in Math. cum laude, Coll. of Mt. St. Vincent, 1970; postgrad., U. Pa., 1976-77; JD cum laude, U. Md., 1977. Bar: Pa. Supreme Ct. 1977, N.J. Supreme Ct. 1978, U.S. Ct. Appeals (3d cir.) 1980, U.S. Supreme Ct. 1981, N.Y. Supreme Ct. 1984, D.C. 1984. Research analyst, claims rep. Social Security Adminstrn., Balt., 1973-76; assoc. Drinker, Biddle & Reath, Phila., 1977-84, ptnr., 1984-86; v.p., gen. counsel M. Alfieri Co., Inc., Edison, N.J., 1986—; instr. Inst. for Paralegal Tng., Phila., 1984-85; bd. dirs. ViraSearch, Inc., Phila., 1985—. Vol. atty. Support Ctr. for Child Advocates, Phila., 1979-86, Queen Village Neighbors Assn., Phila., 1984-86; pres. Soc. Hill Towers Buyers Assn., Phila., 1979-80; bd. dirs. Soc. Hill Civic Assn., 1980. Mem. ABA, Pa. Bar Assn., Phila. Bar Assn. (chair zoning and land use com. 1985-86), N.J. Bar Assn. Office: M Alfieri Co Inc 399 Thornall St Edison NJ 08837

LYNCH, M(ARGARET) TERI, holding company executive; b. Akron, Ohio, Apr. 14, 1952; d. Daniel M. Lynch. BS, U. Akron, 1974, MS, 1978, JD, 1986. CPA, Ohio. Various acctg. positions leading to corp. controller Mohawk Rubber Co., Akron, 1975-85; corp. controller Danaher Corp., Washington, 1985-87, treas., 1987—; bd. dirs. Mohawk Rubber Co. and various subs. of Danaher Corp. Mem. Am. Inst. CPA's. Democrat. Roman Catholic.

LYNCH, MARY PATRICIA, insurance sales executive; b. Chgo., Oct. 31, 1932; d. Thomas and Nora Marie (Cooney) Lavelle; m. Terrence Brons Lynch, Oct. 9, 1954 (div. 1985); children: Patrice M., Michael J., Thomas F., Teresa J. Student, Loyola U., Chgo., 1951-53, U. Calif., Sacramento, 1956, Rollins Coll., 1981, Valencia Community Coll., 1982; cert., Am. Coll., Bryn Mawr, Pa., 1980-86. CLU, chartered fin. cons. Office mgr. Guardian Life Ins. Co. Am., Orlando, Fla., 1971-80; ptnr. Macsay, Lynch & Assocs.,

Casselberry, Fla., 1980-85; owner, operator Mary "Pat" Lynch, CLU, Chartered Fin. Cons. & Assocs., Longwood, Fla., 1985—; moderator Life Underwriter Tng. Course, Orlando, 1989—. Mem. Internat. Assn. Fin. Planning, Women's Life Underwriters Confdn. (bd. dirs. 1985—), Soc. CLU (chmn. Huebner Sch. 1983-84), Cen. Fla. Life Underwriters, Cen. Fla. Soc. CLU (bd. mem. 1983-84), Seminole County C. of C. Democrat. Roman Catholic. Home: 436 Evesham Pl Longwood FL 32779 Office: 2917 W SR 434 Ste 141 Longwood FL 32779

LYNCH, MAUREEN, financial planner; b. Orange, N.J., June 18, 1953; d. Isabel Ellen (Meekins) Chamberlain. BS, Cen. State U., 1979; M in Human Relations, Okla. U., 1988. Fin. planner IDS Fin. Services, Oklahoma City, 1979—. Mem. Master Millionaire Club, Inst. Cert. Fin. Planners, Internat. Assn. Fin. Planners, Okla. Soc. Cert. Fin. Planners (bd. dirs.). Home: 2529 NW 44th St Oklahoma City OK 73112 Office: IDS Fin Svcs Union Plaza Ste 900 3030 NW Expressway Oklahoma City OK 73112

LYNCH, MICHAEL JOSEPH, sportscaster; b. Lynn, Mass., Sept. 25, 1953; s. Richard Joseph and Joann (Joyce) L.; m. Mary Ellen Mullaney, June 20, 1980; children: Kelly Ann, Molly, Katey. BA, Harvard U., 1976. Sports announcer Sta. WITS Radio, Boston, 1977-82, Sta. WCVB-TV, Boston, 1982—. Named Sportscaster of Yr. Nat. Assn. Sportscasters, 1985, 86, 87, 88; recipient New Eng. Emmy award, 1987. Roman Catholic. Home: 48 Amberwood Dr Winchester MA 01890 Office: Sta WCVB-TV 5 Televison Pl Needham MA 02192

LYNCH, RAY JOSEPH, gas pipeline company executive; b. Chgo., Oct. 10, 1922; s. Rollin John and Eva (Schoeller) L.; m. Leila Mariotti, June 11, 1949; children: Dawn, Mary Joy, Tim, Cheryl, Jane, Martha, Christopher, John, Robert. B.S. in Commerce, U. Ill., 1948. C.P.A. With Arthur Andersen & Co. (C.P.A.s), Chgo., 1948-53, Mich. Wis. Pipe Line Co., Detroit, 1953—; treas. Mich. Wis. Pipe Line Co., 1960-62, v.p., 1962-69, exec. v.p., 1969-73, pres., 1973-83, chmn., chief exec. officer, 1982—; dir. Mich. Wis. Pipe Line Co., Mich., Wis.; vice chmn., dir. parent co. Am. Natural Resources Co. and affiliates, 1982-86, cons., 1986—; dir. Mich. Nat. Bank, Detroit; bd. dirs. Bon Secours Hosp. Bd. dirs. Boysville of Mich. Served as pilot USAAF, World War II. Home: 529 Ballantyne Rd Grosse Pointe Shores MI 48236 Office: ANR Pipeline Co 1 Woodward Ave Detroit MI 48226

LYNCH, ROBERT MARTIN, lawyer, educator; b. St. Louis, Mar. 28, 1950; s. Raymond Burns and Nancy Winn (Roeder) L.; m. Cynthia Kay Allmeyer, June 7, 1974; children: Christopher, Kelly, Stephanie. AB, St. Louis U., 1972, JD, 1975. Bar: Mo. 1975, D.C. 1985. Law clk. to presiding justice Mo. Ct. Appeals, St. Louis, 1975-76; atty. Southwestern Bell Telephone Corp., St. Louis, 1976-79, atty. network, 1979-83, gen. atty., 1983-88, v.p., asst. gen. counsel, 1988—; instr. paralegal studies St. Louis Community Coll., 1977—. Mem. ABA, Mo. Bar Assn. (adminstrv. law com. council), St. Louis Bar Assn. (chmn. adminstrv. law com. 1981-82). St. Louis Chpt. Am. Corp. Counsel Assn. (chmn. communications com.). Republican. Office: Southwestern Bell Corp One Bell Ctr 40-Z-01 Saint Louis MO 63101-3099

LYNCH, SONIA, data processing consultant; b. N.Y.C., Sept. 17, 1938; d. Espriela and Sadie Beatrice (Scales) Sarreals; m. Waldro Lynch, Sept. 18, 1981 (div. Oct. 1983). BA in Langs. summa cum laude, CCNY, 1960; cert. in French, Sorbonne, 1961. Systems engr. IBM, N.Y.C., 1963-69; cons. Babbage Systems, N.Y.C., 1969-70; project leader Touche Ross, N.Y.C., 1970-73; sr. programmer McGraw-Hill, Inc., Hightstown, N.J., 1973-78; staff data processing cons. Auxton Computer Enterprises, Piscataway, N.J., 1978—. Mem. bd. fellowship St. Andrew Luth. Ch., Silver Spring, 1987—. Downer scholar CUNY, 1960, Dickman Inst. fellow Columbia U., 1960-61. Mem. Assn. for Computing Machinery, Phi Beta Kappa. Democrat. Home: 13705 Beret Pl Silver Spring MD 20906 Office: Auxton Computer Enterprises 1100 Wayne Ave Silver Spring MD 20910

LYNCH, THOMAS WIMP, lawyer; b. Monmouth, Ill., Mar. 5, 1930; s. William Brennan and Mildred Maurine (Wimp) L.; m. Elizabeth J. McDonald, July 30, 1952; children: Deborah, Michael, Maureen, Karen, Kathleen. BS in Geology, U. Ill., 1955, MS in Geology, 1958, JD, 1959. Bar: Ill. 1960, Okla. 1960, U.S. Supreme Ct. 1971, Tex. 1978. Staff atty. Amerada Hess Corp., Tulsa, 1959-72, asst. gen. counsel, 1972-75; ptnr. Hall, Estill, Hardwick, Gable, Collingsworth & Nelson, Tulsa, 1975; v.p. gen., counsel Tex. Pacific Oil Co., Inc., Dallas, 1975-80; v.p., gen. counsel Sun Exploration & Prodn. Co., Dallas, 1980—; adj. prof. law U. Tulsa, 1974. Served with USN, 1948-49, U.S. Army, 1951-53. Mem. ABA, Southwestern Legal Found. (chmn., lectr. ann. oil and gas shortcourse 1976—, chmn. Oil and Gas Edn. Ctr.), Am. Petroleum Inst. (past chmn. task group on unit ops.), Interstate Oil Compact Commn. (mem. legal com.), Tex. State Bar Assn., Dallas County Bar Assn. Roman Catholic. Club: Dallas Petroleum. Office: Sun Exploration & Prodn Co 5656 Blackwell Dallas TX 75231

LYNCH, TIMOTHY MICHAEL, broadcasting executive; b. Ithaca, N.Y., Jan. 1, 1949; s. William Henry Lynch and Jean Francis (Babbit) Branigan; m. Mary Ann Walsh, May 24, 1974; children: Jessica Ann, Ryan Wendall. Student, Ithaca Coll. With local sales WTKO Radio, Ithaca, 1973-74, WSYR-TV, Syracuse, N.Y., 1974-77, WXEX-TV, Richmond, Va., 1977-79; mgr. nat. sales WILX-TV, Lansing, Mich., 1979-80; with regional sales WVEC-TV, Norfolk, Va., 1980-83; mgr. gen. sales WTVZ-TV, Norfolk, 1983-84; v.p., gen. mgr. WMKW-TV, Memphis, 1984-87, WDCA-TV, Washington, 1987—; advisor MAC com. INTV, N.Y.C., 1983-84. Served with spl. forces U.S. Army, 1969-70, Vietnam. Decorated Bronze Star with V, Air medal, Vietnamese Cross of Gallantry. Mem. Jaycees, Spl. Forces Assn., Ad Club Washington, Washington Area Broadcasters. Republican. Roman Catholic. Home: 1709 Montafia Ln Vienna VA 22180 Office: TVX Broadcast Group Inc 5501 Greenwich Rd Virginia Beach VA 23462

LYND, LLOYD ALBERT, JR., insurance executive; b. Tulsa, Mar. 1, 1929; s. Lloyd Albert and Lois Margaret (Hanna) L.; m. Virginia Atkins, Nov. 24, 1956; children—Lloyd A. III, Elizabeth, Kathryn. B.S., Okla. U., 1950; B.B.A., 1951. Engr. trainee Ins. Co. N.Am., Dallas, 1950-51; acct. Central Securities, Inc., Newton, Kans., 1951-52; sr. v.p. R.B. Jones, Inc., Kansas City, Mo., 1953—, Alexander & Alexander, Inc., Kansas City, Mo., 1979—. Elder, Presbyterian Ch. Served with USAF, 1952-53. Mem. Tau Beta Pi, Sigma Tau, Beta Theta Pi. Republican. Clubs: University, Mission Hills Country. Lodge: Masons. Home: 38 Coventry Ct Prairie Village KS 66208-5206 Office: Alexander & Alexander Inc PO Box 13647 Kansas City MO 64199

LYND, WILLIAM, computer company executive; b. Boston, Nov. 24, 1942; s. Joseph Mearle and Alice (Campbell) L.; m. Nancy Hellman Herman,July 3, 1973; children: Allyn David, Barry Henry, Bradford Joseph. AA, Menlo Coll., 1963; BS in Indsl. Mgmt., U. Calif., San Jose, 1965; BSEE, Lawrence U., 1965; MBA, Pacific Northwestern U., 1968; MS, Bruckner U., 1969, PhD, 1969. Project analyst U. Calif., 1962-64; salesman Control Data Corp., Palo Alto, Calif., 1964-67; regional mgr. DPF & G Co., Westwood, Calif., 1967-71; v.p. sales, founder Logicon Intercomp., Torrance, Calif., 1971-75; dir. mktg./sales MacArco div. MacDonald Douglas Co., Carson, Calif., 1975-77; founder, then exec. v.p. MRP, Inc., Santa Ana, Calif., 1977-80; pres. M-Systems, Santa Ana, 1980—, also bd. dirs.; dir. CIT, Inc., Santa Ana, B.G. Enterprises, Inc.; lectr. U. Calif., Irvine, 1979-80, Saddleback Coll., 1977-79. Mem. Am. Prodn. and Inventory Control Soc. (cert.). Home: 25051 Linda Vista Dr Laguna Hills CA 92653 Office: M-Systems 4501 Birch St Newport Beach CA 92660

LYNFORD, JEFFREY HAYDEN, investment banker; b. N.Y.C., Oct. 7, 1947; s. Franklyn Jerome and Ruth (Kahn) L.; m. Carol Lynford, Sept. 2, 1974; children: Victoria, Andrew. BA, SUNY, Buffalo, 1969; M in Pub. Affairs, Princeton U., 1971; JD, Fordham U., 1975. Bar: N.Y. V.p. Internat. Paper Realty, N.Y.C., 1974-77; assoc. White, Weld & Co., Inc., N.Y.C., 1977-78; mng. dir. A.G. Becker Paribas, N.Y.C., 1978-84; ptnr. Bear Stearns, N.Y.C., 1984-86; chmn. bd. Wellsford Group, Inc., 1986—; mem. investment com. Calif. Fed. Syndications, Inc., L.A., 1984—; bd. dirs. Keaau Macadamia Corp., Honolulu, 1983—, Real Estate Securities Income Fund, Inc, N.Y.C., 1988—; chmn. Quality Hill Redevel. Corp., Kansas City, 1985—; trustee Lynford Family Charitable Trust, N.Y.C., 1985. Trustee Nat. Trust for Hist. Preservation, 1987; bd. dirs. Alan Guttmacher Inst., N.Y.C., 1987—. Mem. ABA, N.Y. Bar Assn. Democrat. Club: Princeton (N.Y.C.).

LYNG, DIANA LOUISE, retail executive; b. Malone, N.Y., Sept. 1, 1959; d. Edward Phillip and Gertrude Thelma (Perry) L. AAS, State U., Canton, N.Y., 1978; postgrad., U. Plattsburgh. Clk., bookkeeper Hallmart Food Shoppe, Malone, 1976-89; bookkeeper JES Trucking, Inc., Malone, 1980-81; bank courier Gelco Courier Svc., Utica, N.Y. and Malone, 1981-82; mgr. Paul Smith's (N.Y.) Coll. Bookstores, 1984—. Co-leader Girl Scouts U.S., Malone, 1987-89. Mem. Nat. Assn. Female Execs., Nat. Assn. Coll. Bookstores. Democrat. Roman Catholic. Office: Paul Smith's Coll Rts 192 & 30 Paul Smiths NY 12970

LYNG, RICHARD EDMUND, former secretary of agriculture; b. San Francisco, June 29, 1918; s. Edmund John and Sarah Cecilia (McGrath) L.; m. Bethyl Ball, June 25, 1944; children: Jeanette (Mrs. Gary Robinson), Marilyn (Mrs. Daniel O'Connell). Ph.B. cum laude, U. Notre Dame, 1940; PhD (hon.), Carroll Coll., 1988. With Ed J. Lyng Co., Modesto, Calif., 1945-66, pres., 1949-66; dir. Calif. Dept. Agr., 1967-69; asst. sec. Dept. Agr., Washington, 1969-73, dep. sec., 1981-85; vice chmn. Commodity Credit Corp., 1981-85; pres. Lyng & Lesher, Inc., Washington, 1985-86; Sec. of Agr. Dept. Agr., Washington, 1986-89; pres. Am. Meat Inst., Washington, 1973-79; pvt. cons., 1980; dir. Commodity Credit Corp., 1969-73, Nat. Livestock and Meat Bd., 1973-76, Tri-Valley Growers, 1975-81; bd. govs. Refrigeration Research Found., 1974-77, Chgo. Merc. Exchange; chmn. food industry trade adv. com. Commerce Dept.; chmn. U.S. Child Nutrition Adv. Com., 1971-73; mem. animal health com. NAS; sr. rsch. fellow Harvard U. Sch. Bus. Adminstrn., 1989—. Chmn. Stanislaus County (Calif.) Republican Central Com., 1961-62; dir. agr. div. Pres. Ford Com., 1976; co-dir. farm and food div. Reagan-Bush Campaign, 1980. Served with AUS, 1941-45. Roman Catholic. Clubs: Washington Golf and Country, Capitol Hill. Lodge: Rotary. *

LYNHAM, C(HARLES) RICHARD, ceramics company executive; b. Easton, Md., Feb. 24, 1942; s. John Cameron and Anna Louise (Lynch) L.; m. Elizabeth Joy Card, Sept. 19, 1964; children: Jennifer Beth, Thomas Richard. BME, Cornell U., 1965; MBA with distinction, Harvard U., 1969. Sales mgr. Nat. Carbide Die Co., McKeesport, Pa., 1969-71; v.p. sales Sinter-Met Corp., North Brunswick, N.J., 1971-72; sr. mgmt. analyst Am. Cyanamid Co., Wayne, N.J., 1972-74; gen. mgr. ceramics and additives div. Foseco Inc., Cleve., 1974-77, dir. mktg. steel mill products group, 1977-79; pres., chief exec. officer Exomet, Inc. subs. Foseco, Inc., Conneaut, Ohio, 1979-81, Fosbel Inc. subs. Foseco, Inc., Cleve., 1981-82; gen. mgr. splty. ceramics group Ferro Corp., Cleve., 1982-84, group v.p. splty. ceramics, 1984—; bd. dirs. Hi-Temp Inc., Cleve., Chick Master Incubator Inc.; sci. adv. bd. Cleve. Sci. Collaborative, Cleve. City Schs. Patentee teapot ladle, desulphurization of metals. Chmn. Medina (Ohio) Cable TV Commn.; dir. sci. collaborative Cleve. Pub. Schs.; mem. sci adv. bd. Cleve. Bd. Edn., East Asta program Cornell U. Served to lt. C.E., U.S. Army, 1965-67. Decorated Bronze Star with one oak leaf cluster. Mem. Am. Soc. Metals, Am. Ceramic Soc. (mem. adv. bd.), Iron and Steel Soc., AIME, Am. Soc. Iron and Steel Engrs., U.S. Advanced Ceramics Assn. (bd. dirs.), Cleve. Bd. Edn. (mem. Sci. Adv. Bd.), Cornell U. Alumni Council, Cornell Alumni Class 1963 (past v.p., past pres.), Cornell Assn. Class Officers (past pres.), Cornell Alumni Assn. (v.p., past bd. dirs.), Cornell U. East Asia Program (mem. adv. bd.), Chippewa Yacht Club (commodore 1982), Cornell Club of N.E. Ohio (pres.). Republican. Congregationalist. Home: 970 Hickory Grove Medina OH 44256 Office: Ferro Corp 1000 Lakeside Ave Cleveland OH 44114

LYNN, C(HARLES) STEPHEN, franchising company executive; b. LaGrange, Ga., July 27, 1947; s. Charles Hubert and Norma Lee (Batey) L.; m. Milah Faith Pass, Sept. 4, 1976. B.S. in Indsl. Engring., Tenn. Tech. U., 1970; M.B.A., U. Louisville, 1973. Indsl. engr. Brown & Williamson Corp., Louisville, 1970-73; dir. distbn. div. Ky. Fried Chicken Corp., Louisville, 1973-77; pres., chief exec. officer MarQuest, Inc. subs. Century 21 Real Estate Corp., Irvine, Calif., 1978-80; v.p. Century 21 Real Estate Corp., Irvine, 1978-80; exec. v.p., dir., chief operating officer Burtson Corp., Marina Del Rey, Calif., 1980-83; chmn., pres., chief exec. officer Sonic Industries, Inc., Oklahoma City, 1983—, also dir.; bd. dirs. Century Bank, Oklahoma City, Eateries Inc., Okla. Healthcare Corp., Am. First Corp. Bd. dirs. editorial bd. Restaurant Insights. Bd. dirs. Salvation Army, Oklahoma City, U. Okla. Sch. of Bus.; past bd. dirs. Jr. Achievement, fund drive chmn. Mem. Inst. Indsl. Engrs. (pres. 1973), Assn. M.B.A.s, Pres.'s Assn. of Am. Mgmt. Orgn., Young Pres.'s Assn., Downtown C. of C. (vice chmn.), Nat. Restaurant Assn., Internat. Franchise Assn. Republican. Presbyterian. Lodge: Rotary (bd. dirs.). Home: 12801 Deerfield Circle Oklahoma City OK 73142 Office: Sonic Industries Inc Sonic Ctr 120 Robert S Kerr Oklahoma City OK 73102

LYNN, DAVID S., finance executive, communications executive. BS in Bus., Ea. Ill. U., 1979; MBA, U. Colo., 1987. Acct. Hyster Co., Danville, Ill., 1979-82; fin. analyst Am. TV and Communications Co., Englewood, Colo., 1982-84, mgr. fin., 1984—. Office: Am TV and Communications Co 160 Inverness Dr W Englewood CO 80112

LYNN, EVADNA SAYWELL, investment analyst; b. Oakland, Calif., June 1935; d. Lawrence G. Saywell; m. Richard Keppie Lynn, Dec. 28, 1962; children: Douglas, Lisa. BA, U. Calif., Berkeley, MA in Econs. Chartered fin. analyst. V.p. Paine Webber, N.Y.C., 1974-77, Wainwright Securities, N.Y.C., 1977-78; 1st v.p. Merrill Lynch Capital Markets, N.Y.C., 1978—. Mem. N.Y. Soc. Security Analysts, San Francisco Security Analysts (treas. 1973-74). Mem. Fin. Women's Club of San Francisco (pres. 1967). Office: Merrill Lynch Capital Markets N Tower World Finance Ctr New York NY 10281

LYNN, FREDERICK ANSON, investment counselor; b. Memphis, Aug. 7, 1946; s. Harvey Don and Marcia Helen (Diamond) L.; m. Ann M. Coleman, Nov. 24, 1973; 1 child, Jeffrey Anson. AB, Tulane U., 1968. Securities analyst Mfrs. Nat. Bank Detroit, 1969-71, Goldman, Sachs & Co., N.Y.C., 1971-72, Pershing & Co., N.Y.C., 1972-74; prin. Lynn Capital Mgmt., N.Y.C., 1974-75; pres. F.A.L. Capital Mgmt., Mt. Kisco, N.Y., 1976—. Bd. dirs. 92d St. YM & YWHA, N.Y.C., 1975-84. Mem. Amex Club N.Y., N.Y. Soc. Securities Analysts. Republican. Club: City Athletic (N.Y.C.). Home: 183 Lantern Ridge Rd New Canan CT 06840 Office: FAL Capital Mgmt 103 S Bedford Rd Mount Kisco NY 10549

LYNN, JAMES F., banker. V.p. Liberty Mut. Ins. Co., Boston. Office: Liberty Mut Ins Co 175 Berkeley St Boston MA 02117 *

LYNN, JAMES T., insurance company executive, lawyer; b. Cleve., Feb. 27, 1927. B.A., Western Res. U., 1948; LL.B., Harvard U., 1951. Bar: Ohio 1951, D.C. 1977. Gen. counsel U.S. Dept. Commerce, 1969-71; under sec. U.S. Dept. State, 1971-73; sec. HUD, 1973-75; dir. Office Mgmt. and Budget, 1975-77; asst. Pres. U.S., 1975-77; with Jones, Day, Reavis & Pogue, 1951-69, 77-84, ptnr., 1960-79, mng. ptnr., 1979-84; with Aetna Life & Casualty Co., Hartford, Conn., 1984—, vice chmn., 1984-85, chmn., 1985—, chief exec. officer, from 1985, now also pres., also bd. dirs. Case editor Harvard Law Rev., 1950-51. Served with USNR, 1945-46. Mem. Phi Beta Kappa. Office: Aetna Life & Casualty 151 Farmington Ave Hartford CT 06156 *

LYNN, KARYL V., retired manufacturing company executive, consultant; b. Bklyn., Mar. 20, 1922; s. Karyl V. and Hazel M. (Wendell) L.; m. Lorraine W. Mullen, July 21, 1946; children: Kevin V., Keith J., Kathleen A. BBA with distinction, U. Mich., 1948, MBA with distinction, 1949. Personnel dir. Dairypak, Inc., Cleve., 1949-54; personnel mgr. Gen. Mills Corp., Mpls., 1954-56; plant mgr. Dairypak, Inc., Toledo, 1958-63, Mercury Packaging Co., Toledo, 1963-66; group dir. indsl. relations Hoover Ball BearingCo., Ann Arbor, Mich., 1966-67, Crucible Steel Corp., Pitts., 1967-68; dir. personnel adminstrn. Colt Industries, Inc., N.Y.C., 1968-87, cons., 1987—; lectr. indsl. relations John Carroll U., Cleve., 1949-54; mem. steering com. Mgmt. Compensation Services, Scottsdale, Ariz., 1975-82; mem. adv. com. T.P.F. & C. Compensation Data Bank, N.Y.C., 1977-87; seminar speaker. Contbr. articles to profl. jours. Served with USAF, 1943-46. U. Mich. Club scholar, 1947-48, 49. Mem. Northwestern Ohio Tennis Assn. (chmn. jr. devel. 1965-66), Am. Soc. Personnel Adminstrn., Am. Compensation Assn. (bd. dirs. 1986-88, life mem., symposium leader, tchr. exec. compensation courses), Assn. Practical Tng. (mem. bd. 1966—, chmn. bd. 1971-85), Am. Mgmt. Assn., Internat. Exec. Svc. Corps (vol. in Sri Lanka 1989), Beta Gamma Sigma, Phi Kappa Phi. Republican. Unitarian. Lodge: Kiwanis (dir. 1963-64). Home and Office: 203 Forest Dr Hillsdale NJ 07642

LYNN, LAWRENCE RICHARD, public broadcasting company executive; b. Bklyn., Apr. 9, 1948; s. David and Shirley (Dubin) L.; m. Vanessa Stanger, Jan. 24, 1970. BA, SUNY, Binghamton, 1969; MA, U. R.I., 1971. Dir. devel. Human Resources Ctr., Albertson, N.Y., 1974-79, Am. Ballet Theatre, N.Y.C., 1979-87; sr. v.p. WNET-TV, N.Y.C., 1987—. Trustee Aerodance Group, N.Y.C., 1982—. Mem. Nat. Soc. Fund Raising Execs. Home: 120 Carstairs Rd Valley Stream NY 11581 Office: Sta WNET-TV 356 W 58th St New York NY 10019

LYNNE, JANICE C., sales executive; b. Eugene, Oreg., Feb. 4, 1954; d. Ralph L. and Mary Ann (McFarlane) Nafziger; m. Glenn R. Caddy, July 30, 1977 (div. Feb. 1989); stepchild: Gavin David. BA, Wash. State U., Bellingham, 1976. Probation counselor Snohomish County, Everett, Wash., 1974-76; substitute tchr. Norfolk (Va.) Pub. Schs., 1976; probation and parole officer State of Va., Norfolk, 1977-78; account exec. Cruise Internat., Norfolk, 1978-80; mgr. sales Carnival Cruise Line, Miami, Fla., 1981-87, dir. sales, 1987—; adv. bd. Fla. Atlantic U., 1984—, South Fla. Travel Acad., 1989—; speaker in field, Fla., 1981—. Mem. Bons Vivants (1st v.p. 1988, bd. dirs. 1986-87, pres. 1989), Thespians. Lutheran. Office: Carnival Cruise Lines 5225 NW 87th Ave Miami FL 33178

LYON, JAMES BURROUGHS, lawyer; b. N.Y.C., May 11, 1930; s. Francis Murray and Edith May (Strong) L. BA, Amherst Coll., 1952; LLB, Yale U., 1955. Bar: Conn. 1955, U.S. Tax Ct. 1970. Asst. football coach Yale U., 1953-55; assoc. Murtha, Cullina, Richter and Pinney (and predecessor), Hartford, Conn., 1956-61, ptnr., 1961—; mem. adv. com., lectr. and session leader NYU Inst. on Fed. Taxation, 1973-86. Chmn. 13th Conf. Charitable Orgns. NYU on Fed. Taxation, 1982, chmn. adv. com. Hartford Downtown Council, 1986—; trustee Kingswood-Oxford Sch., West Hartford, Conn., 1961—, chmn. bd. trustees, 1975-78; trustee Old Sturbridge Village, Mass., 1974—, vice chmn. bd. trustees, 1988—, Ella Burr McManus Trust, Hartford, 1980—, Howard and Bush Found., Hartford, 1987—, Hartford YMCA, 1985—, Conn. River Mus. at Steamboat Dock, Essex, 1985—; trustee Wadsworth Atheneum, Hartford, 1968—, pres., 1981-84; corporator Inst. of Living, 1981—, Mt. Sinai Hosp., Hartford, 1972—, Hartford Hosp., 1975—, St. Francis Hosp., Hartford, 1976, Hartford Art Sch., 1979—, Hartford Pub. Library, 1979—. Recipient Eminent Service medal Amherst Coll., 1967, Nathan Hale award Yale Club Hartford, 1983, Disting. Am. award No. Conn. chpt. Nat. Football Hall of Fame, 1983. Fellow Am. Coll. Tax Counsel, Am. Bar Found.; mem. ABA (tax sect. exempt orgn. com., chmn. com. mus.'s and other cultural instns. 1987—), Conn. Bar Assn. (lectr. continuing legal edn. programs 1963—), Hartford County Bar Assn. (mem. editorial adv. com. Conn. Law Tribune 1988—), Assn. Bar City N.Y., Conn. Bar Found. (bd. dirs. 1975-86), Am. Law Inst., Phi Beta Kappa (assocs.). Republican. Roman Catholic. Clubs: Hartford, Hartford Golf, Univ. (pres. 1976-78), Tennis (Hartford); Yale, Union (N.Y.C.); Limestone Trout (East Canaan, Conn.); Univ. (Washington); Dauntless (pres. 1989—)(Essex, Conn.); Mariner Sands (Stuart, Fla.). Office: City Place 185 Asylum St City Pl Hartford CT 06103

LYON, L(YMAN) MAX, biotechnology executive; b. Cin., Apr. 23, 1944; s. Lyman M. and Alfreda (Harris) L.; m. Amanda Jane Poe, July 10, 1976; children: Serena, Johanna. BA, Cornell U., 1966; MBA, City U., Seattle, 1979. Dir. planning Weyerhaeuser Co./Westwood Lines, Tacoma, 1980-82; v.p. Genetic Systems Corp., Seattle, 1982-85; founder , dir., pres., chief operating exec. Biocontrol Systems, Inc., Seattle, 1985-88; chief exec. officer Bainbridge Labs., Seattle, 1988—; bd. dirs. Oncogen Co., Seattle, 1982-85. Served as lt. USNR, 1966-69. Office: Bainbridge Labs 7861 Day Rd W Bainbridge Island WA 98110

LYON, PHILIP K(IRKLAND), lawyer; b. Warren, Ark., Jan. 19, 1944; s. Leroy and Maxine (Campbell) L.; m. Jayne Carol Jack, Aug. 12, 1982; children by previous marriage: Bradford F., Lucinda H., Bruce P., Suzette P., John P., Martin K., Meredith P.; JD with honors, U. Ark., 1967. Bar: Ark. 1967, U.S. Supreme Ct. 1970. Sr. ptnr., dir. ops. House, Wallace, Nelson & Jewell, P.A., Little Rock, 1967-86; pres. Jack, Lyon & Jones, P.A, Little Rock, 1986—. Instr. bus. law, labor law, govt. bus. and collective bargaining U. Ark., Little Rock, 1969-72, lectr. practice skills and labor law, U. Ark. Law Sch., 1979-80. Co-author: Schlei and Grossman Employment Discrimination Law, 2d edit., 1982. Bd. dirs. Ark. Law Rev., 1978—, Southwestern Legal Found., 1978—. Mem. Ark. State C. of C. (bd. dirs. 1984-88), Greater Little Rock C. of C. (chmn. community affairs com. 1982-84, minority bus. affairs 1985), ABA (select com. for liason with office of fed. contract compliance programs 1982—, select com. liason with EEOC 1984—, select com. immigration law), Ark. Bar Assn. (chmn. labor law com. 1977-78, chmn. labor law sect. 1978-79), Pulaski County Bar Assn., Assn. Trial Lawyers Am., Ark. Trial Lawyers Assn., Am. Soc. Personnel Adminstrn., Little Rock Racquet, Capitol. Home: 17 Heritage Park Circle North Little Rock AR 72116 Office: Jack Lyon & Jones PA 3400 TCBY Tower Capitol at Broadway Little Rock AR 72201

LYON, SHERMAN ORWIG, rubber and chemical company executive; b. Greenwich, Conn., Sept. 4, 1939; s. James R. and June K. (Orwig) L.; m. Nell Collar, June 15, 1968; children—Jeffrey, Michelle. B.S. in Chem. Engring., Purdue U., 1961; grad. exec. program, Stanford U., Palo Alto, Calif., 1978. Process engr., prodn. supt. Monsanto Co., St. Louis, 1961-69, mktg. mgr., 1969-72; gen. mgr. chem. div. Mallinckrodt, Inc., St. Louis, 1972-78, v.p. specialty chems., 1978-80; group v.p. Celanese Corp., Chatham, N.J., 1980-82; pres. Copolymer Rubber & Chem. Corp., Baton Rouge, 1982—; sr. v.p. Armstrong Rubber Co., New Haven, 1983—; exec. v.p. Armtek Corp., 1987; pres., chief exec. officer Lyon Investment Corp., 1986—; dir. City Nat. Bank. Mem. exec. bd. Istrouma area council Boy Scouts Am., Baton Rouge, 1984; bd. dirs. Gulf South Research Inst., Baton Rouge, 1984, Woman's Hosp. (dir. 1985-86), United Way Baton Rouge Area (dir. 1985-87), Baton Rouge C. of C. (dir. 1985-87). Recipient Iron Key, Purdue U., 1961. Mem. Internat. Inst. Synthetic Rubber Producers (dir. 1983—, pres. N.Am. sect. 1985-86), Synthetic Organic Chem. Mfg. Assn. (bd. govs. 1981-82), Am. Inst. Chem. Engrs., Baton Rouge C. of C. (bd. dirs.), Tau Beta Pi, Omicron Delta Kappa (founding mem. Purdue chpt. 1961), Sigma Phi Epsilon. Republican. Clubs: City, Baton Rouge Country, Camelot (Baton Rouge). Office: Copolymer Rubber & Chem Corp PO Box 2591 Baton Rouge LA 70821

LYON, WAYNE BARTON, corporate executive; b. Dayton, Oct. 26, 1932; m. Maryann L., 1961; children: Karen, Craig, Blair. BChemE, U. Cin., 1955; MBA in Mktg., U. Chgo., 1969. Registered profl. engr., Mich. Tech. rep. Union Carbide, Chgo., 1955-62; product devel. mgr., v.p. bus. devel. Ill. Tool Works, Chgo., 1962-72; group v.p., exec. v.p., pres. Masco Corp., Taylor, Mich., 1972—; bd. dirs. Emco Ltd., London, Ont., Can., Mech. Tech. Inc., Latham, N.Y., 1973, Masco Corp., Taylor, Mich., Mfrs. Nat. Corp., Payless Cashways Inc.; lectr. AMA. Patentee in field. Bd. govs., trustees Cranbrook Kingswood Schs., Bloomfield Hills, Mich., 1984—, Orchard Lake Country Club, Mich., 1985—. Served to capt. U.S. Army, 1955-63. Clubs: Fairlane (Dearborn, Mich.); Renaissance (Detroit), Detroit Athletic, Orchard Lake Country; Bloomfield Hills Country. Office: Masco Corp 21001 Van Born Rd Taylor MI 48180

LYON, WILLIAM SCHUYLER, JR., accountant; b. Seattle, Jan. 27, 1956; s. William Schuyler Lyon Sr. and Jodene (Law) Daly; m. Mary Kathryn Kuehne, Oct. 13, 1984. BS in Acctg., U. Minn., 1980. CPA, Minn. Acct. Blue Ink Graphics, Mpls., 1980-84; staff CPA Julius & Nordstrom, Plymouth, Minn., 1984-87; sr. CPA O'Connor & Assocs., Golden Valley, Minn., 1987-88; sr. acct. Johnson Giere Co., 1988—. Mem. AICPA, Minn. Soc. CPA's. Home: 9145 Larch Ln N Maple Grove MN 55369

LYONS, DENNIS G., pharmacist; b. Boston, Mar. 22, 1952; s. Augustus J. and Helen (McGaffigan) L.; m. Frances M. Lyons, Sept. 22, 1979; lhild,

Mary Ellen. BS, Mass. Coll. Pharmacy, Boston, 1975. Pharmacy auditor Pilgrim Health Applications, Bedford, Mass., 1976-77; asst. dir. pharmacy Medicaid program Mass. Dept. Pub. Welfare, Boston, 1977-78; dir. ops. Profl. Health Systems, Burlington, Mass., 1978-79, Programs & Analysis, Burlington, 1979-83; dir. mgmt. info. systems Thayer Pharmacies, Inc., Stoughton, Mass., 1983—; pres. Masscript Inc., Burlington, 1987—; treas. Pharmacist Polit. Action Com., Mass., 1987. Mem. Mass. Pharm. Assn. (pres. 1987-88). Democrat. Roman Catholic. Office: Thayer Pharmacies Inc 175 Campanelli Pkwy Stoughton MA 02072

LYONS, DONALD EDWIN, manufacturing executive, educator, consultant; b. Metcalf, Ill., Sept. 15, 1932; m. Ruth J. Graham, Dec. 31, 1953; children: Stephen, Stephanie, Jacqueline Lyons Sale. BS in Econs., Purdue U., 1959, MS in Indsl. Relations, 1961. Staff asst. Order of R.R. Telegraphers, St. Louis, 1961-63; asst. dir. personnel Chgo. and Ea. Ill. R.R. Co., Chicago Heights, Ill., 1963-68; asst. dir. labor relations Chesapeake & Ohio R.R., Huntington, W.Va., 1968-70; dir. indsl. relations Chgo. Rawhide Mfg. Co., 1970-72; group mgr. employee relations Clow Corp., Chgo., 1972-78; mgr. labor relations Snap-on-Tools Corp., Kenosha, Wis., 1978-79, dir. labor relations, 1979-82, v.p. human resources, 1982—; adj. asst. prof. U. Wis., Kenosha, 1982-83; lectr. Lake Forest Grad. Sch. Mgmt., Ill., 1985-86; bd. dirs. Am. Assembly Tool, Inc., Cleve. Mem. Nat. R.R. Commn. on Scouting; mem. exec. bd. Calumet Council Boy Scouts Am., Chicago Heights; mem. adv. council U. Wis., Milw., 1986—; bd. dirs. Kenosha Area Labor Mgmt. Council, 1980—, Kenosha Achievement Ctr. Recipient Outstanding Service award Nat. R.R. Commn., 1965, Boy Scouts Am., 1968. Mem. ASTD, Human Resource Planning Soc., Indsl. Relations Research Assn., Am. Soc. Personnel Adminstrn., Am. Radio Relay League, Nat. Assn. Mfrs. (mem. human resources coun.), Sierra Club. Methodist. Home: 1471 Lawrence Ave Lake Forest IL 60045 Office: Snap On Tools Corp 2801 80th St Kenosha WI 53141

LYONS, FREDERICK WILLIAM, JR., pharmaceutical company executive; b. Youngstown, Ohio, Nov. 7, 1935; s. Frederick William and Edith (Barnes) L.; m. Carol Lee deBruin, Aug. 30, 1957; children: Linda Kay, Stephen Frederick. B.S., U. Mich., 1957; M.B.A., Harvard U., 1959. Div. mgr. cost acctg. and purchasing Alcon Labs., Inc., Fort Worth, 1959-61; salesman Alcon Labs., Inc., 1961-62; dir. mktg. Conal Pharms., Inc., Chgo., 1962-64, gen. mgr., 1964-65, v.p., gen. mgr., 1965-70; v.p., gen. mgr. Marion Labs., Inc., Kansas City, Mo., 1970-72, sr. v.p., dir., pres. Pharm div., 1972-74, exec. v.p., dir., 1974-77, pres., dir., 1977—, chief operating officer, from 1977, now also chief exec. officer; dir. Commerce Bank of Kansas City (N.A.). Mem. nat. adv. council Ariz. Heart Inst. Mem. Pharm. Mfrs. Assn. (dir.), ACT Found., Rho Chi, Phi Kappa Phi, Phi Gamma Delta. Office: Marion Labs Inc PO Box 8480 10236 Marion Park Dr Kansas City MO 64137 *

LYONS, HENRY EARNEST, real estate developer; b. Kansas City, Mo., Jan. 10, 1952; s. Dewey Alford Foote and Normajene Smallwood. BS, U. Mo., Kansas City, 1968, MPA, 1974. Insp. FDA, Kansas City, 1968; budget analyst City of Kansas City, 1974-75; cost analyst Ford Motor Co., Kansas City, 1975-77; credit specialist Upjohn Co., Kansas City, 1977-79; pres. Henry E. Lyons & Co., Kansas City, 1979—, Urban Pioneers, Kansas City, 1983—; mgr. Westport Devel. Co., Kansas City, 1987—. Treas. Kansas City Citizens Assn., 1987-88. With USAF, 1968-72. Mem. Landlords Inc. (Outstanding Svc. award 1984, 85, bd. dirs., v.p. 1985-87, pres. 1987-88), Alpha Phi Alpha. Methodist. Office: PO Box 6171 Kansas City MO 64110

LYONS, JACK, sales executive; b. Paterson, N.J., Apr. 18, 1964; s. John Edward and Ellen Catherine (Seymour) L. BS in Biology, Montclair State Coll., 1986. Telemktg. supr. Sandoz Pharms., East Hanover, N.J., 1986; sales rep. Marion Labs., Inc., Kansas City, Mo., 1987—. Active Child's Wish Come True, West Paterson, N.J., 1988—; acting vol. Big Bro. & Big Sisters Am. Mem. No. N.J. Pharm. Rep. Assn., Montclair State Alumni Assn. Home: 44 Emerson Ave Paterson NJ 07502

LYONS, JOHN EDWARD, health care company executive. married. BS, Fordham U. With Merck & Co. Inc., Rahway, N.J., 1950—, various sales and mgmt. positions, 1950-71, v.p. sales and mktg., 1971-75, pres. pharm. div., 1975-85, exec. v.p., 1985-88, vice chmn., 1988—, also bd. dirs. Mem. Pharm. Mfrs. Assn. (chmn. bd. dirs., 1989). Office: Merck & Co Inc PO Box 2000 Rahway NJ 07065

LYONS, JOSEPH, software company executive; b. N.Y.C., June 20, 1945; s. Joseph Charles and Jane (Rock) L. MusB, Juilliard Sch., 1968, MS, 1973; MA, CUNY, 1970. Faculty Julliard Sch., N.Y.C., 1966-69, 70-73; pres. Enhanced Tech. Assocs., Inc., N.Y.C., 1984—; pres. Virtusonics Corp., N.Y.C., 1986-88. Patentee in field. Julliard scholar, 1962-72. Home: Philipsebrook Rd Garrison NY 10524 Office: Enhanced Tech Assocs Inc 1123 Rt 52 Ste 46 Fishkill NY 12524

LYONS, LAURENCE, securities executive; b. Jersey City, Aug. 11, 1911; s. Louis and Teresa (Serge) L.; m. Gertrude Starr, Sept. 1, 1945; 1 son, Jonathan. BS, NYU, 1934, postgrad., 1935. Securities analyst Allen & Co., N.Y.C., 1935-52; exec. corp. pres. Allen Co., Inc., N.Y.C., 1952—. Mem. Soc. Security Analysts, Security Industries Assn. Club: NYU (N.Y.C.). Home: 13 Grace Ct N Great Neck NY 10021 Office: Allen & Co Inc 711 Fifth Ave New York NY 10022

LYONS, PHILLIP MICHAEL, SR., insurance, accounting and real estate executive; b. Gueydan, La., Nov. 22, 1941; s. Joseph Bosman and Elder (Richard) L.; student McNeese State Coll., 1959-62, Alvin Jr. Coll., 1964, Coll. of Mainland, 1974; BBA, U. Houston, 1977, postgrad., 1984; children from previous marriage: Phillip M., Wilton J. Adminstrv. trainee Am. Nat. Ins. Co., Galveston, Tex., 1965, asst. mgr., acting mgr. policy issue dept., 1966-67, mgr., 1967-68, mgr. pre-issue dept., 1968-71, systems analyst, 1971-72, div. mgr., policyholders service div., 1972-76, dir. ordinary policyholder's service, 1976-77, dir. combination policy records, 1977-79; supervising acct. materials acctg. comptroller's dept. Aramco Services Co., Houston, 1977-79, ins. adviser treas.'s dept., 1979-80, adminstr. risk mgmt. and ins. div., treas.'s dept., 1980—; ptnr. Lyons Real Estate, Sulphur, La., 1966—, L&L Enterprises, Sulphur; owner Phil and Nonie's Agy., Sulphur; bd. dirs. Studio B, Inc., Houston. Solicitor, United Fund, 1966-69. Fellow Life Office Mgmt. Assn.; mem. Risk and Ins. Mgmt. Soc. (assoc. in risk mgmt.), Internat. Found. Employee Benefit Plans, Jr. C. of C. (dir. 1972, state dir. 1972—, Sparkplug of Yr., 1972-73, Roadrunner of Year 1972-73). Lodges: Masons, Shriners, K.C. Home: 223 W Sherwood Dr Alvin TX 77511 Also: 1012 S Stanford St Sulphur LA 70663 Office: PO Box 4536 Houston TX 77210

LYONS, ROBERT JOHN, manufacturing executive; b. Pitts., Dec. 14, 1954; s. Robert Herbert and Joan (Forsythe) L.; m. Debra Ann Fusca, June 26, 1976; children: melissa Ann., Bethany Lynn. BBA, Grove City Coll., 1976; cert. in paper mgmt., Miami U., Oxford, Ohio, 1987. Mem. outside sales staff Alling & Cory Co., Cleve., 1976-82, mgr. sales div. printing paper, 1982-85, v.p., gen. mgr., 1985—. Mem. Avon Oaks Country Club. Office: Alling & Cory Co 12555 Berea Rd Cleveland OH 44111

LYSTAD, HOLLY ANN, research scientist; b. Oakland, Calif., June 27, 1959; d. Stanley Fritjof and Carol Virginia (Jensen) L. BS, Mich. State U., 1981. Lab. asst. dept. phys. chemistry Mich. State U., East Lansing, 1978-80; physicist Physics Internat., San Leandro, Calif., 1981-84; research scientist, project leader Calif. Research & Tech., Inc., Pleasanton, 1984—. Contbr. articles to profl. jours. Pres. Homeowners Assn., Tracy, Calif.; chmn. nominating com. Alameda Contra Costa council Camp Fire Inc., 1984-86, chmn. Leader's Assn. Cen. Valley Council, Stockton, Calif., 1986-87. Nat. Merit scholar. Mem. Nat. Assn. Female Execs., Calif. Scholarship Fedn. (life), Phi Kappa Phi (life). Home: 2161 Costa Ct Tracy CA 95376 Office: Calif Rsch and Tech Inc 5117 Johnson Dr Pleasanton CA 94566

MAAS, GERALD LEE, railroad company executive; b. Indpls., Jan. 13, 1937; s. Gerald E. and Helen Louise (Hanson) M.; m. Raenota Lee Storm, Oct. 1, 1961; children: Brian, Leanne, Michelle. BA, Ea. Ill. U., 1960; cert. advanced mgmt. program, Harvard U., 1980-81. From agt. to supt. N.Y. Cen. R.R., 1955-70, div. supt., 1971-76; gen. mgr. Cen. Vt. Ry., St. Albans, 1976-77, pres., 1986—, also bd. dirs.; from gen. mgr. to v.p. Grand Trunk Western R.R., Detroit, 1977-84, exec. v.p., 1984-86, pres., 1986—, also bd. dirs.; pres. Grand Trunk Corp., Detroit, 1986—, also bd. dirs., 1986—; pres., bd. dirs. Duluth, Winnipeg & Pacific Ry., Superior, Wis., 1986—, Cen. Vt. Ry., St. Albans, 1986—; bd. dirs. Belt Ry. Co. Chgo., Chgo. and Western Ind. R.R. Co. Mem. Am. Assn. R.R. Supts. (bd. dirs. 1986—), Mich. C. of C. (bd. dirs. 1986—), Detroit C. of C. Office: Grand Trunk Western RR Co 1333 Brewery Park Blvd Detroit MI 48207

MAATMAN, GERALD LEONARD, insurance company executive; b. Chgo., Mar. 11, 1930; s. Leonard Raymond and Cora Mae (Van Der Laag) M.; children: Gerald L. Jr., Mary Ellen; m. Bernice Catherine Brummer, June 3, 1971. BS, Ill. Inst. Tech., 1951. Asst. chief engineer Ill. Inspection & Rating Bureau, Chgo., 1951-58; prof., dept. chmn. Ill. Inst. Tech., Chgo., 1959-65; v.p. engring. Kemper Group, Chgo., 1966-68, pres. Nat. Loss Control Service Corp., 1969-74; v.p. corp. planning Kemper Group, Long Grove, Ill., 1974-79; sr. v.p. info. services group Kemper Group, Long Grove, 1979-85, exec. v.p. ins. opers., 1985-87; pres. Kemper Nat. P & C Ins. Cos., Long Grove, 1987—; bd. dirs. Ins. Info. Inst., N.Y.C., 1985—; chmn. Ins. Services Orgn., N.Y.C.,1989—; bd. trustees Underwriters Labs., Inc., 1989. Lt. (j.g.) USCGR, 1952-54. Mem. Soc. Fire Protection Engrs. (J.B. Finnegan award 1965), Wynstone Golf Club, Tau Beta Pi. Republican. Roman Catholic. Office: Am Motorists Ins Co Kemper Ctr Long Grove IL 60049

MABE, DONALD W., food products company executive. Pres. Perdue Farms Inc., Salisbury, Md.; vice chmn. Perdue, Inc, Salisbury, Md. Office: Perdue Farms Inc PO Box 1537 Salisbury MD 21801 *

MABRY, GUY O., manufacturing company executive; b. 1926. BS, U. Kans., 1950. V.p. Owens Corning Fiberglass Corp., 1964-80, sr. v.p., 1980-86, exec. v.p., 1986—. Office: Owens-Corning Fiberglas Corp Fiberglas Tower Toledo OH 43659 *

MACALLISTER, JACK ALFRED, telephone company executive; b. Humeston, Iowa, July 12, 1927; s. Maxwell A. and Opal E. (Caldwell) MacA.; m. Marilyn Anderson, June 12, 1950; children: Steven, James, Sue. B.Commerce, Iowa State U., 1950; student, Iowa State Tchrs. Coll., Cedar Rapids, 1947-48. With Northwestern Bell Telephone Co., 1950-65, 67-83; v.p. ops. Northwestern Bell Telephone Co., Omaha, 1974-75, pres., 1965-82, chmn., 1982-83; pres., chief exec. officer U.S. West, Inc., Englewood, Colo., 1984-86, chmn. bd. dirs., chief exec. officer, 1986—; mem. staff AT&T, N.Y.C., 1965-67; bd. dirs. 1st Interstate Bank of Los Angeles, The St. Paul Cos., Western Strategy Ctr. for Regional Devel.; mem. adv. bd. U. Pa. Wharton Sch. Fishman-Davidson Ctr. for study of service sector; mem. nat. adv. bd. U. Ariz.; mem. internat. adv. bd. Stanford Research; mem. Bus. Higher Edn. Forum. Mem. Found. Bd. Denver Art Mus.; mem. exec. bd. Denver Area council Boy Scouts Am.; bd. dirs. U. Iowa Found.; co-chair Ednl. Commn. of the States. Office: US West Inc 7800 E Orchard Rd Englewood CO 80111

MACARTHUR, BRIAN HENRY, hotel executive; b. Bronxville, N.Y., July 25, 1949; s. Chester Wallace and Arline (Simmen) MacA. BS in Hotel and Restaurant Adminstrn., Okla. State U., 1971. Cert. hotel adminstr. Mgr. food and beverage Quality Inn Cen., Arlington, Va., 1971; budget and cost analyst Quality Hotels & Resorts Inc., Silver Spring, Md., 1972-82, contr. hotel ops., 1982-86; contr. Quality Inns, Inc., 1986-89, Manor Care, Inc., Hotel div., 1989—. Mem. Internat. Assn. Hospitality Accts. Republican. Presbyterian. Avocations: coin collecting, bowling, computer programming. Home: 11411 Oak Leaf Dr Silver Spring MD 20901 Office: Manor Care Inc Hotel div 10750 Columbia Pike Silver Spring MD 20901

MACARTHUR, DIANA TAYLOR, business executive; b. Santa Fe, July 7, 1933; d. Antonio J. and Elizabeth (Steele) Taylor; student U. Geneva, 1953-54, B.A., Vassar Coll., 1955; children—Elizabeth, Alexander Tschursin; m. Donald Malcolm MacArthur, Mar. 31, 1962. Cons. economist Checchi & Co., Washington, 1957-61; v.p. Thomas J. Deegan Co., dir. Washington office, 1961-62; dep. chief W. Africa, Peace Corps, 1963, regional program officer N. Africa, Near East, South Asia, 1964, dir. div. pvt. and internat. orgns., 1965-66; coordinator Nat. Youth Conf. on Natural Beauty and Conservation, 1966-68; self-employed cons. public affairs to corps., assns., govt., Washington, 1968-76; pres. Consumer Dynamics, Inc., 1976-81; dir. Dynamac Internat., Inc., 1978-88, v.p., dir., 1980-88; chmn. bd., chief exec. officer Dynamac Corp., 1988—; chmn., chief exec. officer Rsch., Analysis and Mgmt. Corp., 1988—; pres. Fgn. Traders, Inc., 1980-86 . Mem. citizens adv. bd. Pres.'s Council on Youth Opportunity, 1968-69; trustee Menninger Found., Topeka, 1972—; bd. dirs. Washington Area Council Alcoholism and Drug Abuse, chmn. bd., 1974. Mem. Phi Beta Kappa. Home: 5103 Cape Cod Ct Bethesda MD 20816 Office: Dynamac Bldg 11140 Rockville Pike Rockville MD 20852

MACAULAY, JOHN CLINTON, financial executive; b. Long Beach, Calif., Oct. 11, 1943; s. Warren Lowell and Dorothy Mae (McVeety) M.; m. Susan Tucker Woodruff, June 14, 1969; children: Craig, Todd. BA in Biology and Chemistry, St. Olaf Coll., 1965; MBA in Fin. and Acctg. and Info. Systems with distinction, Northwestern U., 1972, cert. in mgmt. acctg., 1974. Personnel adminstrn. mgr. Harvard Trust Co., Cambridge, Mass., 1969-70; fin. analyst Gen. Mills, Mpls., 1972-73; mgr. budget and analysis Gen. Mills, Salem, Mass., 1973-75; fin. analyst Dresser Industries, Inc., Dallas, 1975-77; controller Harbison Walker Internat. div. Dresser Industries, Inc., Pitts., 1977-82; controller tool group Dresser Industries, Inc., Chgo., 1982-84, dir. ops. analysis and planning, 1984—; instr. acctg. and info. systems U. Tex., Dallas, 1977. Author: (with Bulloch, Keller, Vlasho) Long Range Planning, Accountant's Cost Handbook, 1983. Vestryman, St. Paul's Episcopal Ch., Mt. Lebanon, Pa., 1982-83; vestryman jr. warden Episcopal Ch. of Epiphany, Richardson, Tex., 1986-89. Served with USN, 1965-69. Named Disting. scholar Kellogg Sch. Bus., Northwestern U., 1972. Mem. Nat. Assn. Accts. (nat. bd. dirs. 1987-89, Dallas chpt. pres., chmn. 1985-88, officer Tex. council 1987—), Fin. Execs. Inst., Stuart McLeod Soc., Beta Gamma Sigma. Republican. Office: Dresser Industries Inc 1600 Pacific Ave Dallas TX 75201

MACAVOY, PAUL WEBSTER, economist, educator; b. Haverhill, Mass., Apr. 21, 1934; s. Paul Everett and Louise Madeline (Webster) MacA.; m. Katherine Ann Manning, June 13, 1955; children: Libby, Matthew. A.B., Bates Coll., 1955, LL.D., 1976; M.A., Yale, 1956, Ph.D., 1960. Asst. to full prof. MIT, Cambridge, Mass., 1963-74, Henry R. Luce prof.pub. policy, 1974-75; mem. Pres.'s Council Econ. Advisers, 1975-76; prof. econs. and mgmt. Yale U., 1976-81, Beinecke prof. econs., 1981-83; dean W.E. Simon Grad. Sch. Bus. Admin. U. Rochester, 1983—, John M. Olin prof.; bd. dirs. Amax Corp., Atlantic Legal Found., Inc., Combustion Engring., Am. Cyanamid Corp., Gleason Corp. Author: Price Formation in Natural Gas Fields, 1962, Economic Strategy for Developing Nuclear Breeder Reactors, 1969, (with Stephen Breyer) Energy Regulation by the Federal Power Commission, 1974, (with R. Pindyck) The Economics of the Natural Gas Shortage, 1975, The Economics and Politics of International Commodity Agreements, 1977, The Regulated Industries and the Economy, 1979, World Crude Oil Prices, 1981, Energy Policy, 1983, Explaining Metals Prices, 1988; editor: Ford Administration Papers on Regulatory Reform, 8 vols, 1977-78, Privatization and State-Owned Enterprise: Assessment for the United Kingdom, Canada and the United States, 1988. Home: 3333 Elmwood Ave Rochester NY 14610 Office: U Rochester Simon Grad Sch Bus Adminstrn Rochester NY 14627

MAC AVOY, THOMAS COLEMAN, glass manufacturing executive, educator; b. Jamaica, N.Y., Apr. 24, 1928; s. Joseph V. and Edna M. MacA.; m. Margaret M. Walsh, Dec. 27, 1952; children: Moira MacAvoy Brown, Ellen, Christopher, Neil. B.S. in Chemistry, Queens Coll., 1950; M.S. in Chemistry, St. John's U., 1952, D.Sc. (hon.), 1973; Ph.D. in Chemistry, U. Cin., 1952. Chemist, Charles Pfizer & Co., Bklyn., 1957-60; mgr. electronics research Corning Glass Works, N.Y., 1960-64; dir. phys. research Corning Glass Works, 1964-66, v.p. electronic products div., 1966-69, v.p. tech. products div., 1969-71, pres., 1971-83, vice-chmn., 1983-87; prof. mgmt. grad. sch. U. Va., 1988—; bd. dirs. Quaker Oats Co., Chubb Corp., Lubrizol Corp. Patentee in field; contbr. articles to tech. jours. Trustee Corning Mus. Glass; past pres. Boy Scouts Am. With USN, 1946; with USAF, 1952-53. Recipient Silver Antelope award Boy Scouts Am., 1976, Silver Beaver award, 1975, Silver Buffalo award, 1982, Bronze Wolf award, 1988. Roman Catholic. Club: Univ. (N.Y.C.). Office: U Va Darden Grad Sch Bus Adminstrn Charlottesville VA 22096

MACBETH, HUGH JAMES, data processing and telecommunications executive; b. N.Y.C., Jan. 19, 1947; s. John Brown and Josephine Earl (Olsen) Macb. BA, Hiram Coll., 1968. Gen. mgr. 9-20 Inc., Great Barrington, Mass., 1971-73; acct. Chem. Constrn. Corp., N.Y.C., 1973-75; owner, gen. mgr. The Fairfield Inn, Great Barrington, 1975-78; v.p. Am. Agy. Data Systems, Merritt Island, Fla., 1978-80; pres. Advanced Info. Mgmt., Cocoa Beach, Fla., 1980-81; mgr. info. systems and telecommunications Greater Orlando (Fla.) Aviation Authority, 1981—; pres. Exec. Info. Services, Cocoa Beach, 1985—. Columnist: Orlando Bus. Jour., 1984—. Mem. U.S. working party to UN Jt. Commn. on Electronic Document Interchange. Mem. Airport Ops. Internat. (chmn. info. systems sub-commn. 1985-86, chmn. internat. airport ops. computer fair, 1988, chmn. 1990 fair), Am. Assn. Airport Execs. (chmn. computer com.,). Republican. Episcopalian. Home: 2815 S Atlantic Ave 102 Cocoa Beach FL 32931 Office: Greater Orlando Aviation Auth Orlando Internat Airport Orlando FL 32812

MACCAULEY, HUGH BOURNONVILLE, banker; b. Mt. Vernon, N.Y., Mar. 12, 1922; s. Morris Baker and Alma (Gardiner) MacC.; m. Rachael Gleaton, Aug. 30, 1943 (div. May 1980); m. Felice Cooper, Dec. 2, 1980. Student, Rutgers U., 1939-41, Tex. Christian U., 1948-50, U. Omaha, 1957-59. Commd. 2d lt. U.S. Army, 1943; advanced through grades to col. U.S. Army, USAF, Washington, 1943-73; v.p. Great Am. Securities, San Bernardino, Calif., 1979—; chmn. bd. Desert Community Bank, Victorville, Calif., 1980—. bd. dirs. Air Force Village West, 1986-88; chmn. bd. Gen. and Mrs. Curtis E. Lemay Found., 1987—. Decorated Air medal, Legion of Merit. Mem. Daedalian Soc. Republican. Presbyterian. Lodge: Rotary. Home: 1630 Monroe St Riverside CA 92504 Office: Great Am Securities Inc 334 W Third Ste 201 San Bernardino CA 92401

MACCAUSLAND, PAUL JOSEPH, corporation executive; b. Winchester, Mass., Mar. 14, 1965; s. Frank G. and Geraldine Francis (Lynch) MacC. BS, Merrimack Coll., 1986. Auctioneer Carl W. Stinson, Inc., Reading, Mass., 1980-82; pres., chief exec. officer The Young Auctioneers, Inc., Reading, 1982-83; pres., chief exec. officer MacCausland Acquisition Corp., Woburn, Mass., 1983-85, chmn., 1985—; pres., chief exec. officer Macquisition, Inc., Reading, 1975—; lectr. in field, 1984—; founder The First Internat. Bank Am., Ltd., 1987, spl. advisor to bd. dirs., 1987—; founder First Internat. Capital, Ltd., Hong Kong, 1988. Dir. budgeting com. Merrimack Coll., North Andover, Mass. 1985-88; treas. Commuter Council, North Andover, 1984-87. Mem. Soc. for the Advancement Mgmt. (bd. dirs. 1985-87), New Eng. Auctioneers Assn. Roman Catholic. Home: 252 Haverhill St Reading MA 01867-1808

MACCHI, EUGENE EDWARD, package company executive; b. Kearney, N.J., July 20, 1926; s. Louis Robert and Teresa D. (Maher) M.; student Army spl. tng. program, Carnegie Inst. Tech., 1943-44; student Swarthmore Coll., 1945-47; BA, Kalamazoo Coll., 1948; m. Josephine M. Towle, May 5, 1951; children—Eugene E., Michael S., Mary Jo, Karen M., Robert C., Thomas J., Charles J.; m. 2d, Constance A. Dill, June 28, 1981; children—Robin, Rhys, Rhett, Ryan, Rourke, Rowan. Sales supr. Wyandotte Chems. Corp., 1948-54; mgr. Eastern div., Hankins Container div. MacMillan Bloedell, Union, N.J., 1954-62; pres., chmn. bd. Continental Packaging Corp., Kenilworth, N.J., New Castle, Pa., Macon, Ga., 1962-75, also dir.; pres., chmn. bd. Ind. Corrugated Container Corp. Am., Paterson, N.J., 1975—. Commr. NW Bergen County Sewer Authority, 1966-69, 75-80, chmn., 1967-69, 76-80. Served with USAAF, World War II. Mem. Assn. Eastern Corrugated Box Mfrs. (pres. 1973-75), Fibre Box Assn., Assn. Ind. Corrugated Converters (pres. 1975-77), C. of C., Young Pres. Orgn., Phi Sigma Kappa. Contbr. articles to trade mags. Home: 63 Arbor Dr Ho-Ho-Kus NJ 07423 Office: Ind Corrugated Container Corp 2 Waite St Paterson NJ 07524

MACCHIA, ANTHONY FRANCIS, economist, management consultant; b. N.Y.C., Dec. 21, 1952; s. Frank and Stella M.; m. Irene Leung, Sept. 11, 1982. BA in Econs., SUNY-Stony Brook, 1973, B Engring., 1973; PhD, U. Pa., 1979. Economist, Office of Sec., Dept. Interior, Washington, 1976; instr. Wharton Sch.-Fels Ctr., U. Pa., Phila., 1977-78; sr. economist, antitrust div. Dept. Justice, Washington, 1979-81; mem. Atty. Gen.'s AT&T Relief Task Force, Washington, 1980-81; sr. assoc. Mgmt. Analysis Ctr., Washington, 1981-83; pres. Macchia & Co., Phila., 1983—; chief cons. mergers, acquisitions and bus. disputes Japanese and U.S. cos. Author: The Hospital and the Industrial Organization of the Hospital Market, 1979, The Challenges of a New Era: Competitive Strategy, Value Creation and Securitization, 1987, The Securitization of Real Estate: Strategies for Investment Banking, 1987; mem. bd. contbg. editors The Real Estate Fin. Jour., 1987—. Wharton-Fels fellow U. Pa., 1973-77; recipient U.S. Atty. Gen.'s Spl. Achievement award Dept. Justice, 1980. Fellow Tau Beta Pi; mem. Am. Econ. Assn., Am. Fin. Assn., Omicron Delta Epsilon. Roman Catholic. Home: 1945 Panama St Philadelphia PA 19103 Office: Macchia & Co 1411 Walnut St Suite 200 Philadelphia PA 19102

MACCHIA, JOSEPH DOMINICK, insurance company executive; b. N.Y.C., Mar. 10, 1935; s. Michael Joseph and Grace Marie (Amico) M.; m. Harriet Katherine Ruggles, June 27, 1959; children: Leah Marie, David Joseph, Alysia Katherine. BS, Fairfield U., 1957; postgrad., Western Mich. U., 1971-75. Dist. mgr. Liberty Mut. Ins. Co., East Orange, N.J., 1961-66; product mgr. Great Am. Ins. Co., N.Y.C., 1966-69; v.p. Foremost Ins. Co., Grand Rapids, Mich., 1969-75; pres. Early Am. Ins. Co., Ft. Worth, 1975-78; pres., chmn. bd. Gen. Agts. Ins. Co. Am., Inc., Ft. Worth, 1978—; pres., chmn., chief exec. officer, bd. dirs. GAINSCO, Inc., MGA Ins. Co., Inc., Gen. Agts. Premium Fin., Risk Retention Adminstrs., Agts. Processing Systems, Inc. Del. Tex. State Rep. Conv., 1986. 1st lt. USMC, 1957-61. Mem. Nat. Assn. Ind. Insurers, Nat. Assn. Profl. Surplus Lines Offices Ltd., Internat. Ins. Co. (gov.), Petroleum Club, Ridglea Country Club. Republican. Roman Catholic.

MACCURDY, JOHN A., real estate appraiser, consultant; b. Ft. Worth, Mar. 6, 1947; s. Robert Earl and Constance (Pontius) MacC.; m. Kathryn Blitch, Feb. 11, 1967; 1 child, Kristen. BBA, U. Miami, 1974; MSM, Fla. Internat. U., 1977. Supr. Fed. Res. Bank, Miami, Fla., 1971-73; realtor, assoc. Chas. SandeFur Realty, Miami, 1963-75; grad. asst. Fla. Internat. U., Miami, 1975-77; appraiser Jos. J. Blake & Assoc., Inc., Miami, 1977-80; exec. v.p. Chas. V. Failla & Assoc., Inc., Coral Gables, Fla., 1980-87; pres. J.A. MacCurdy & Assoc., Inc., Boca Raton, Fla., 1987—; spl. master Palm Beach (Fla.) County Property Appraisal Adjustment Bd., 1987, 88. Mem. Boca Forum. Served to sgt. USAF, 1966-70, Korea. Mem. Urban Land Inst., Boca Raton Bd. Realtors, Am. Inst. Real Estate Appraisers, Boca Raton C. of C. Republican. Presbyterian. Office: 215 N Federal Hwy Boca Raton FL 33432

MAC DONALD, ALAN DOUGLAS, lawyer; b. Springfield, Mass., Oct. 23, 1939; s. Alexander Stuart and Josephine Ann (Czaja) MacD.; m. Jill Nickerson, May 20, 1978. B.S.S., Fairfield U., 1961; M.B.A., U. Mass., 1963; B.C.L., Coll. William and Mary, 1966. Bar: Va. 1966, N.Y. 1967, Ill. 1974. Assoc. firm Carter, Ledyard & Milburn, N.Y.C., 1966-71; v.p. law dept., sr. staff counsel Motorola, Inc., Schaumburg, Ill., 1972-80; v.p., gen. counsel, sec. Ex-Cell-O Corp., Troy, Mich., 1980-86; of counsel Fitzgerald, Hodgman, Cox, Cawthorne & McMahon, Detroit, 1988-89; sr. v.p., gen. counsel, sec. Mortgage Guaranty Ins. Corp., Milw., 1989—. Mem. ABA. Office: Mortgage Guaranty Ins Corporate Pla Milwaukee WI 53201

MACDONALD, DONALD ARTHUR, publishing executive; b. Union City, N.J., Nov. 30, 1919; s. Richard A. and Marie (McDonald) M.; m. Ruth Moran, Dec. 21, 1942; children: Ronald A., Martha J., Marie C., Donald A., Charles A. BS cum laude, NYU, 1948, MBA, 1950. Advt. sales rep. Wall St. Jour., Dow Jones & Co., Inc., N.Y.C., 1953-55, mgr. New Eng. and Can. ter., 1955-58, ea. advt. mgr., 1958-61, exec. advt. mgr., 1961-63, advt. dir. sales promotion and prodn. depts., 1963-67, v.p. advt. sales, 1970-74, sr. v.p., 1974—, also dir.; vice chmn. Dow Jones & Co. Inc., N.Y.C., 1979—; also dir. Dow Jones & Co. Inc.; dir. Far Ea. Econ. Rev., Hong Kong; chmn. coun. judges Advt. Hall of Fame, 1972-78. Served to capt. AUS, 1942-46. Named to Advt. Hall of Fame, 1986. Mem. Am. Advt. Fedn. (dir. 1962—, past chmn.), Advt. Fedn. Am. (past gov. 2d dist., past chmn. joint commn., past chmn.), Advt. Council (dir.), N.Y. Advt. Club (past dir., Silver medal award 1965), Beta Gamma Sigma. Clubs: Downtown Athletic (N.Y.C.), Yale (N.Y.C.); Rumson Country (N.J.). Home: 15 Buttonwood Ln Rumson NJ 07760

MAC DONALD, JAMES GORDON, retired insurance executive; b. N.Y.C., June 16, 1925; s. Daniel M. and Anne C. (Macdonald) MacD.; m. Imogene Williamson, Feb. 4, 1950; children—James Gordon, Patricia J., Nancy C. B.A., Hobart Coll., 1948. With Liberty Mut. Ins. Co., Newark, 1948-52; Mich. and N.Y. group supr. New York Life Ins. Co., 1952-56; group underwriter Tchrs. Ins. & Annuity Assn., Coll. Retirement Equities Fund, N.Y.C., 1956-58; group officer Tchrs. Ins. & Annuity Assn., Coll. Retirement Equities Fund, 1958-60, asst. v.p., 1960-63, v.p., 1963-72, exec. v.p. adminstrn., 1972-79, pres., 1979-84, chmn., chief exec. officer, 1984-87. Trustee Saugatuck Congl. Ch., 1974—, Coll. Retirement Equities Fund, 1978-87; Tchrs., Ins. and Annuity Assn., 1979—. Served to lt. (j.g.) USN, 1943-47. Mem. Am. Pension Conf., Health Ins. Assn. Am. (dir. 1982-85), Regional Plan Assn. (dir. 1981), Life Office Mgmt. Assn. (dir. 1982-85), Life Ins. Council N.Y. (dir. 1982-85), St. Andrews Soc. New York. Republican. Clubs: Patterson Country (dir. Fairfield, Conn.); Hobart (N.Y.C.). Office: Tchrs Ins & Annuity Assn Am 730 3rd Ave New York NY 10017

MACDONALD, JOSEPH ALBERT FRIEL, lawyer; b. Halifax, N.S., Canada, Dec. 10, 1942; s. Charles F.H. and Mary E. (Friel) M.; m. Linda Lee Bergstrom, Sept. 15, 1967; children: Charles Lloyd, Mary Georgette. B.A., Dalhousie U., Halifax, 1963, LL.B., 1966; LL.M., NYU, 1967. Bar: N.S. 1967, Queen's Counsel 1983. Assoc. McInnes, Cooper & Robertson, Halifax, 1967-74, ptnr., 1975—; chmn. bd. N.S. Power Corp., 1980—; gov. Mt. St. Vincent U., 1987—. Mem. N.S. Barristers Soc., Can. Bar Assn., Can. Tax Found. Conservative. Roman Catholic. Club: Halifax. Home: 2915 Somerset Ave, Halifax, NS Canada B3L 3Z4 Office: NS Power Corp PO Box 910, 1894 Barrington St, Halifax, NS Canada B3J 2W5

MACDONALD, R. FULTON, venture developer, business educator; b. Monmouth County, N.J., Dec. 24, 1940; s. James Fleming Smith Macdonald and Jane Macfarlane Barnes Abbott; m. Carol Jean Archer, Mar. 29, 1963 (div. Jan. 1982); 1 child, Paige Brubaker Smith; m. Laura Boswell, Jan. 13, 1989. A.B., U. Pa., 1963; M.B.A., 1969; Sr. mktg. mgmt. cert. Stanford U., 1979. Systems mgr., mcht. John Wanamaker, Inc., Phila., 1969-74; prin. Booz, Allen & Hamilton, N.Y.C., 1974-79; pres. Irwill Industries, N.Y.C., 1979-82; pres. Internat. Bus. Devel. Corp., N.Y.C., 1982—; chmn. IBEX Mktg. Corp., N.Y.C., 1988—; pres. Simfer Operational Internat., Inc., N.Y.C., 1984; vice chmn. Neusteter Co., Denver, 1984-85; dir. Fragrances Selective, Inc., 1985-87; mng. dir. Stuyvesant Group Internat., Dutch Am. Bus. Advisors, N.Y.C. and Amsterdam, 1987-88; adj. prof. Grad. Bus. Sch., Columbia U., N.Y.C., 1984-85. Designer Manpower Mgmt. Concepts computer system, 1972—; contbr. articles to bus. publs. Served to capt. inf. U.S. Army, 1963-67, Fed. Republic Germany, Vietnam. Decorated Bronze Star. Mem. Ripon Soc., Inst. Mgmt. Consultants, Global Econ. Action Inst., Soc. Mayflower Descendants, Soc. Coll. Alumni U. Pa. (pres. 1973-74). Republican. Christian Scientist. Avocation: squash. Home: Trump Tower 721 Fifth Ave New York NY 10022

MACDONALD, RALPH LEWIS, JR., banker; b. White Plains, N.Y., Jan. 9, 1942; s. Ralph Lewis and Marjorie (Beaird) MacD.; m. Virginia Elizabeth Whittet, June 29, 1968; children: Thomas, Cynthia, Ralph Lewis III. A.B., Williams Coll., 1963; postgrad., NYU, 1964-65, Northwestern U., 1978. With Bankers Trust Co., N.Y.C., 1964—, sr. v.p. energy group, 1978-79, sr. v.p. employee benefit div., 1980-82, exec. v.p. world corporate dept., 1983-86, mng. dir. corp. fin., 1986—; bd. dirs. United Meridian Corp., Dallas. Mem. Assn. Res. City Bankers, Bank Capital Markets Assn. (bd. dirs.). Office: Bankers Trust NY Corp 280 Park Ave New York NY 10017

MACDONALD, RICHARD BRUCE, pharmaceutical sales executive; b. Boston, Jan. 23, 1942; s. Angus and Edna Margaret (Clark) MacD.; m. Theresa Angeline Podkowka, Sept. 1964; children James Richard, Karen Elizabeth. AA, Schoolcraft Coll., Livonia, Mich., 1975; BS, Madonna Coll., 1976, MSA, 1986. Sales rep. Hoechst-Roussel Pharm. Co., Somerville, N.J., 1968-72; hosp. sales rep. Hoechst-Roussel Pharm. Co., Somerville, 1972-74, div. mgr., 1974-85, sr. div. mgr., 1985—. With USAF, 1959-66. Mem. Southeast Mich. Hosp. Pharm. Assn., Mich. Pharmacists Assn., Toastmasters, Delta Mu Delta. Republican. Roman Catholic. Home: 16241 Ronnie Ln Livonia MI 48154 Office: Hoechst-Roussel Pharm Co Rte 202-206 North Somerville NJ 08876

MACDONALD, ROBERT ROGER, venture capital company executive; b. Wilmington, Del., Oct. 31, 1944; s. Milford Webster and Elizabeth (Melchior) MacD.; m. Barbara Jane Schroeder, Oct. 19, 1968; children: Bill, Nathaniel, Bob. BS in Engring. Physics, Cornell U., 1966, MEE, 1967; MBA, Harvard U., 1973. Asst. to v.p. Emerson Electric Co., St. Louis, 1967-68; gen. ptnr. Idanta Ptnrs., San Diego, 1973-78; pres., chief operating officer Lifeline Systems, Inc., Watertown, Mass., 1978-84, Profit Key Internat., Inc., Salem, N.H., 1984-86; gen. ptnr. Plant Resources Venture Funds, Cambridge, Mass., 1986—; bd. dirs. Zynaxis Cell Scis., Phila., Aqua Group, Inc., Tampa, Fla., BioTrol, Inc., Chaska, Minn., Meridian Instruments, Inc., Okemos, Mich. Served to 1st lt. U.S. Army, 1968-71. Baker scholar Harvard U. Grad. Sch., 1973. Mem. Nat. Venture Capital Assn., New Eng. Venture Capital Assn. Office: Plant Resources Venture Funds 124 Mt Auburn St Ste 310 Cambridge MA 02138

MACDONALD, THOMAS J., JR., trust company executive; b. Providence, Sept. 17, 1940; s. Thomas J. and Elizabeth (Dion) MacD.; m. Kathleen J. Purnell, Aug. 26, 1961. BA, U. R.I., 1962; MA, Stanford U., 1965. Trust officer Lincoln Rochester (N.Y.) Trust Co., 1968-70; trust officer Hawaiian Trust Co. Ltd., Honolulu, 1970-72, mgr. probate dept., 1973-78, mgr. trust dept., 1979-83, mgr. personal trust group, 1983-87, exec. v.p., 1987—. Bd. dirs. YMCA of Honolulu, 1986—; bd. dirs., treas. Aloha United Way, 1987—; bd. dirs., pres. Hawaii Planned Parenthood, 1973-75. Capt. U.S. Army, 1966-68. NDEA fellow, 1962-65. Mem. Fin. Execs. Inst., Rotary. Home: 344 Wailupe Circle Honolulu HI 96821 Office: Hawaiian Trust Co Ltd PO Box 3170 Honolulu HI 96802

MACDOUGAL, GARY EDWARD, electronic controls manufacturing executive; b. Chgo., July 3, 1936; s. Thomas William and Lorna Lee (McDougall) MacD.; m. Julianne Laurel Maxwell, June 13, 1958; children: Gary Edward, Michael Scott. BS in Engring., UCLA, 1958; MBA with distinction, Harvard U., 1962. Cons. McKinsey & Co., L.A., 1963-68, ptnr., 1968-69; chmn. bd., chief exec. officer Mark Controls Corp. (formerly Clayton Mark & Co.), Evanston, Ill., 1969-87, hon. chmn. bd., 1988—, also pres., 1971-76, 81-87; sr. advisor and asst. campaign mgr. George Bush for Pres., Washington, 1988; bd. dirs. United Parcel Svc. Am., Inc., Greenwich, Conn., Union Camp Corp., Wayne, N.J., CBI Industries, Oak Brook, Ill., France Fund, N.Y.C.; instr. UCLA, 1969. Contbr. articles to profl. jours., chpts. to books. Trustee UCLA Found., 1973-79, Annie E. Casey Found., Greenwich, Com. for Econ. Devel., N.Y.C.; chair Russell Sage Found., N.Y.C.; hon. dir. Am. Refugee com.; commr. Sec. Labor's Commn. on Workforce Quality and Productivity, Washington, 1988-89; sr. advisor, asst. campaign mgr. George Bush for Pres. Campaign, 1988. Lt. USNR, 1958-61. Mem. Harvard Club, Econ. Club, Harvard Bus. Sch. Club, Kappa Sigma. Episcopalian. Home: 505 N Lake Shore Dr Apt 2711 Chicago IL 60611

MACE, DAVID M., banker; b. 1938. B.A., Amherst Coll., 1960; LL.B., U. Va., 1964. Assoc. Cadivalader, Wickersham & Taft, 1964-65; sec. Irving Bank Corp., 1967; with Irving Trust Co., N.Y.C., 1966—, resident counsel, 1966-70, v.p. loan adminstrn., 1970-71, v.p. internat. ops., 1971-74, v.p., mgr., Tokyo branch, 1974-79, sr. v.p. internat. corp. banking, 1979-80, exec. v.p. internat. banking group, 1980-82, sr. exec. v.p. internat. banking activities, 1982-84, pres., 1984—, dir. Office: Irving Trust Co 1 Wall St New York NY 10005 *

MACE, STEPHEN ALAN, lawyer, banker; b. Springfield, Mo., Dec. 30, 1957; s. Leslie Jasper and Virginia Sue (Dunaway) M.; m. Deborah Marie Smith, Dec. 3, 1983; 1 child, Andrew Stephen. BA, William Jewell Coll., 1979; JD, U. Mo., 1982. CPA, Mo. Tax specialist Coopers & Lybrand, St. Louis, 1982-85; atty. Blumenfeld, Sandweiss, et al, St. Louis, 1985-86; sr. trust officer Boatmen's Nat. Bank, St. Louis, 1986—. Mem. ABA, Mo. Bar, Bar Assn. Met. St. Louis (speaker's bur. 1982—), Am. Inst. CPA's, Mo. Soc. CPA's, Internat. Assn. Fin. Planning. Republican. Baptist. Lodge: Kiwanis Internat. (charter pres. St. Ann, Mo. chpt. 1982-83, Disting. Club Pres. 1983).

MACEWEN, EDWARD CARTER, communications executive; b. Cleve., Feb. 12, 1938; s. Kenneth Donald and Helen (von Den Steinen) MacE.; m. Janet Ellen Sandrock; children: Michael, Bonnie. BFA, Carnegie Mellon U., 1960; MA, Fairfield U., 1984. Art dir. Andrews, Bartlett & Assocs., Cleve., 1960-63; producer Wilding, Inc., Cleve., 1963-66; dir. corp. advt. PPG Industries, Inc., Pitts., 1966-79; v.p. corp. communications GTE Corp., Stamford, Conn., 1979—. Bd. trustees Williamstown Regional Art Conservation Lab., Mass.; bd. dirs. Pro Arte Chamber Singers. Mem. Assn. of Nat. Advertisers, Pub. Relations Soc. Am., Nat. Advt. Rev. Bd., Ad Council. Home: 208 Chestnut Hill Rd Wilton CT 06897 Office: GTE Corp One Stamford Forum Stamford CT 06904

MACFADYEN, ALEXANDER HUGH, corporate financial executive; b. Tarrytown, N.Y., Oct. 6, 1931; s. Andrew Aird and Joan (Fraser) MacF.; m. Constance De Michelle, Apr. 29, 1961; children: Hugh, Alison. BBA, Iona Coll., 1959. Auditor Touche Ross and Co., N.Y.C., 1959-63; asst. contr. Westrex div. Litton Inds., New Rochelle, N.Y., 1964-68; treas. Litton Ednl. Publs., Inc., N.Y.C., 1969-71, v.p. fin., 1972-75; v.p., controller Litton Inds. Pub. Group, Oradell, N.J., 1975-81; v.p. fin., adminstrn. sec., treas. NFL Properties, Inc., N.Y.C., 1982—. Staff sgt. USAF, 1951-55. Mem. Nat. Assn. Accts., Mag. Pubs. Assn., Contrs. Coun., The Bus. Planning Bd. Republican. Clubs: Pascack Valley Radio Control Flying (pres. 1984-87), Rockland Radio Control Flying. Home: 12 Edgebrook Ln Monsey NY 10952 Office: NFL Properties Inc 410 Park Ave New York NY 10022

MAC FADYEN, SCOTT DOUGLAS, retail executive; b. Neptune, N.J., Mar. 31, 1961; s. Alexander Smith and Jean Helen (Van Brakle) Mac F.; m. Dorene Kaley Smith, Sept. 19, 1987. BS in Mktg., Richard Stockton State Coll., 1984. Cons. Control Assocs., N.Y.C., 1984; mgr. Cargo Furniture, Atlanta, 1984-86; dist. mgr. Cargo Furniture, Ft. Worth, 1986-87; gen. mgr. outlet Pa. House Furniture, Lewisburg, 1987-88; promoted mgr. of retail ops. Pa. House Furniture, 1988—. Republican. Methodist.

MACFARLAND, ROBERT F., bank executive; b. Newburgh, N.Y., Dec. 10, 1931; s. Frederick R. and Martha (Neubert) M.; m. Nancy L. Henderson, Dec. 4, 1950; 1 child, Sharon MacFarland Dillon. BA, Trinity Coll., Hartford, Conn., 1950; cert. banking, Stonier Grad. Sch. Rutgers U., 1968. From br. mgr. to pres. Highland Nat. Bank, Newburgh, N.Y., 1951-81; chmn., chief exec. officer Norstar Mid-Hudson Bank Group, 1981-82, Norstar Long Island Bank Group, 1982-84; exec. v.p. Norstar Bancorp Inc., Albany, N.Y., 1984-86; pres. Norstar Bank of Upstate N.Y., Albany, 1986-87, chmn., chief exec. officer, 1987—. Dir. Capital Region Tech. Devel. Council, 1987—, Albany Area Econ. Devel. Commn., 1987—, N.Y. State Council on Econ. Edn., 1988—; trustee Albany Meml. Hosp.; bd. dirs. Albany Symphony Orch. Mem. Fort Orange Club, Schuyler Meadows Country Club (Loudonville, N.Y.). Office: Norstar Bank Upstate NY 69 State St Albany NY 12201

MACFARLANE, GORDON FREDERICK, telephone company executive; b. Victoria, B.C., Can., Sept. 21, 1925; s. Frederick Randolph and Nora Margaret (La Fortune) MacF.; m. Hazel Louise Major, June 1946; children: Michael Gordon, Ann L. MacFarlane Patterson, Katherine M. MacFarlane Bernard. B.S.E.E., U. B.C. Chief engr., dir. plant services B.C. Telephone Co., Vancouver, 1966-67, v.p. ops., 1967-70, v.p. corp. devel., 1970-76, v.p. adminstr., 1976; chmn., chief exec. officer B.C. Telephone Co., Burnaby, 1977—; pres., chief exec. officer GTE Automatic Elec., Brockville, Ont., Can., 1976-77; chmn. Microtel Pacific Research Ltd.; chmn. Microtel Ltd.; chmn., pres., chief exec. officer North-West Telephone Co., dir. Air Can., Fletcher Challenge Canada Ltd., Telecom Leasing Can. Ltd., Can. Telephones and Supplies Ltd., BC Gas Inc.; bd. trustees Advanced Systems Found., Advanced Systems Inst. Mem. bd. govs. Vancouver Pub. Aquarium Assn. Recipient First Communications Can. award, 1988. Mem. IEEE, Assn. Profl. Engrs. B.C., Telephone Pioneers Am., Premier Econ. Adv. Council. Office: BC Telephone Co, 21-3777 Kingsway, Burnaby, BC Canada V5H 3Z7

MACGREGOR, CLARK, retired manufacturing company executive; b. Mpls., July 12, 1922; s. William Edwin and Edith (Clark) MacG.; m. Barbara Porter Spicer, June 16, 1948; children: Susan Clark, Laurie Miller, Eleanor Martin. Grad. cum laude, Dartmouth, 1946; J.D., U. Minn., 1948. Bar: Minn. 1948. Practiced in Mpls., until 1961; partner firm King & MacGregor, 1952-61; mem. 87th-91st Congress, 3d Dist. Minn., mem. jud. com., com. on banking and currency; counsel to Pres. for congl. affairs, 1971-72; Nixon campaign dir. 1972; sr. v.p. United Technologies Corp., 1972-87. Bd. dirs. Nat. Symphony Orch. Assn., Wolf Trap Found. Served to 2d lt. AUS, 1942-45, CBI. Decorated Bronze Star, Legion of Merit. Mem. Nat. Security Indsl. Assn. Republican. Presbyn. Clubs: Burning Tree, Metropolitan, Chevy Chase. Home: 2834 Foxhall Rd NW Washington DC 20007

MACHAFFIE, FRASER GLEN, accountant, educator; b. Sutton, Surrey, Eng., Mar. 2, 1941; came to U.S., 1976; s. Cecil Reid and Margaret Watt (Glen) MacH.; m. Barbara Jane Zink, Sept. 8, 1972. BS, U. Glasgow, Scotland, 1963; BD, U. Edinburgh, Scotland, 1972; MA, Princeton Theol. Sem., 1977; MBA, Cleve. State U., 1981. CPA, chartered acct., Scotland. Acct. Richardson & Lawson, Glasgow, 1962-66; acct. Penisular and Oriental Steam Navigation Co., London, 1966-67, asst. to sec., 1967-69; asst. minister Ch. of Scotland, Edinburgh, 1972-74; pvt. practice as chartered acct. Edinburgh, 1974-76; acct. McCarthy & Hicks, Princeton, N.J., 1976-80; asst. prof. acctg. Marietta (Ohio) Coll., 1982-88, assoc. prof. acctg., 1988—. Author: The Short Sea Route, 1975; (with others): The Civil War: A Selective Annotated Bibliography, 1987. Mem. Inst. Chartered Accts. Scotland, Am. Inst. CPAs, Am. Acctg. Assn., Tau Pi Phi (trustee 1987—). Office: Marietta Coll Dept Econs Marietta OH 45750

MACHIZ, LEON, electronic equipment manufacturing executive; b. Bklyn., June 23, 1924; s. Isadore and Fanny (Klonsky) M.; m. Lorraine Block, Mar. 31, 1951; children: Marc, Linda, Gary. Grad., Cooper Union. Salesman Sun Radio Co., 1942-52; founder Time Electro Sales Co. (merged with Avnet, Inc. 1952-68), Electro Air of Ga. (merged with Avnet, Inc. 1968), 1957-68, Electro Air of Fla., 1960-68; sr. v.p., dir. Avnet, Inc., N.Y.C., 1968-80, pres., dir., 1980—, vice chmn., 1986—, chief exec. officer, from 1986, now also chief operating officer, dir., chmn., chief exec. officer, 1988—. Trustee North Shore Univ. Hosp., Boys' Brotherhood Republic. Office: Avnet Inc 767 Fifth Ave New York NY 10153 also: Avnet Inc 80 Cutter Mill Rd Great Neck NY 11021 *

MACHLER, ERWIN, cement company executive; b. Rueti, Switzerland, Feb. 2, 1925; s. Paul and Lydia (Honegger) M.; m. Erna Honegger, July 7, 1951; children: Felix, Susanne, Monica. Dr. publ., U. Zurich, Switzerland, 1952. Asst. sec. Schmidheiny Group Cos., Heerbrugg, Switzerland, 1968-72; mng. dir. Holderbank Financiere Glarus S.Am., Heerbrugg, 1972—, chmn. exec. com., 1976-78; chmn. bd., pres., chief exec. officer Hofi N.A. (Holnam); chmn. bd. St. Lawrence Cement Inc., Montreal, Que., Can., Dundee Cement Co.; bd. dirs. Ideal Basic Industries Inc., Alsen-Breitenburg, Hamburg, Fed. Republic Germany, Nordcement AG, Hannover, Fed. Republic Germany, Kredietbank Suisse S.A. Col. Swiss Air Force, 1945-80. Mem. Can.-Swiss Bus. Men's Assn., Rotary. Home: Wolkenberg, 9445 Rebstein Saint-Gall Switzerland Office: St Lawrence Cement Inc, 1945 Graham Blvd, Mount Royal, PQ Canada H3R 1H1

MACILVAINE, WILLIAM RODMAN, banker; b. N.Y.C., Jan. 5, 1929; s. Francis Shippen and Irene MacI.; m. Lucy Swann Barham, June 28,1952; children: W. Rodman III, Susan S., Katherine B., Elizabeth F. BA, Princeton U., 1952. Salesman, mgr. Standard Packaging Corp., Clifton, N.J., 1954-72; div. sales mgr. Milprint div. Philip Morris, Inc., Milw., 1972-78; pres. Sunrise Packaging, Inc., Oak Creek, Wis., 1978-81; registered rep. Equitable Life Ins. Co., Milw., 1981-83; v.p., mgr. M&I Marshall and Ilsley Bank, Milw., 1983—; registered prin. M&I Capital Corp., Milw., 1987—. Pres. Brookhaven Civic Assn., Short Hills, N.J., 1965; chmn. Children's Hosp. of Wis. Telethon, Milw., 1986; treas. Eastbrook Ch., Milw., 1979-85; mem. adv. bd. 411 YMCA, Milw., 1986—, Oakton Manor, 1986—. Mem. Kiwanis (bd. dirs. 1988—, trustee Milw. Kiwanis Found. 1988—), Princeton Alumni Assn. (treas. Wis. area 1988—). Republican. Club: Lake Shore (Mequon, Wis.). Home: 6301 N Berkeley Blvd Whitefish Bay WI 53217 Office: M&I Marshall & Ilsley Bank 770 N Water St Milwaukee WI 53202

MACINTOSH, ALEXANDER JOHN, lawyer, business executive; b. Stellarton, N.S., Can., July 10, 1921; s. Hugh Ross and Katherine Elizabeth (Stewart) M.; m. Elizabeth Agnes Allen, Apr. 5, 1944; 1 child, Donald Alexander. BA, Dalhousie U., 1942, LLB, 1948; LLD, Brock U., 1987. Bar: N.S. 1948, Ont. 1948; created Queen's counsel 1961. Read law T.D. MacDonald, Q.C., Dep. Atty. Gen., N.S.; ptnr. Blake, Cassels & Graydon, Toronto, 1948—; chmn. Varta Batteries Ltd.; mem. Ont. Task Force on Fin. Instns.; bd. dirs. Can. Imperial Bank of Commerce, Torstar Corp., John Labatt Ltd., Stelco, Inc., Fluor Daniel Canada, Inc., Markborough Properties, Ltd, Ont. Hydro., Honeywell Inc. Bd. govs. Dalhousie U. Lt. Royal Can. Naval Vol. Res., 1942-45. Clubs: Toronto; York. Office: Blake Cassels & Graydon, PO Box 25, Commerce Ct W, Toronto, ON Canada M5L 1A9

MACINTYRE, R. DOUGLAS, computer software executive; b. Bennettsville, S.C., Aug. 6, 1951; s. Wade Hampton and Lucy Allen (Tison) M.; m. Elizabeth Wallace, June 30, 1973; children—Robert, Carter, Stewart. BA, U.S. Mil. Acad., West Point, 1973; MSBA with honors, Boston U., 1976; postgrad., Harvard U., Boston, 1985, U. Pa., 1987. Mktg. rep. McDonnell Douglas, Atlanta, 1978-79; mktg. rep. Mgmt. Sci. Am. Inc., Atlanta, 1980-81, dist. mgr., 1982, regional mgr., 1983, v.p., 1984, sr. v.p. mktg., 1985-87, div. pres., 1987-88, exec. vp. U.S. ops., 1988—. Bd. dirs. U.S. Mil. Acad. Assn. of Grads., 1988-89; bd. dirs. Sci. and Tech. Mus. Atlanta, 1986—. Capt. U.S. Army, 1973-78. Named Outstanding Young Man of Am., 1984. Mem. Willow Springs Country Club. Methodist. Home: 145 May Glen Way Roswell GA 30076 Office: Mgmt Sci Am 3445 Peachtree Rd NE Atlanta GA 30326

MACIVER, LINDA B., information services administrator; b. Manchester, N.H., Apr. 7, 1946; d. George Donald and Vera B. (Arlin) MacI. BA in History, U. N.H., 1968; MEd, Boston U., 1981; MS, Simmons Coll., Boston, 1982. Tchr. social sci. Meml. High Sch., Manchester, 1968-72, library-media specialist, 1972-80; media services librarian Simmons Coll., Boston, 1981-82; info. specialist Schneider Parker Jakuc, Inc., Boston, 1982-85; mgr. info. services Ingalls, Quinn & Johnson (formerly Ingalls Assocs.) Boston, 1985—. Mem. Am. Soc. Info. Sci. (treas. New Eng. chpt. 1984-86), Spl. Libraries Assn., ALA., NELA. Unitarian-Universalist. Home: 123 Commonwealth Ave Apt 3 Boston MA 02116 Office: Ingalls Quinn & Johnson 855 Boylston St Boston MA 02116

MACK, EARLE IRVING, real estate company executive; b. N.Y.C., July 11, 1939; s. H. Bertram and Ruth (Kaufman) M. BBA, Drexel U., 1960; postgrad., Fordham Law Sch., 1961-62. Owner, breeder thoroughbred horses, Fla., Ky., N.J., Md., 1964—; sr. ptnr., chief fin. officer Mack/Taylor Prodns. Inc., Rochelle Park, N.J., 1964—; chief exec. officer Mack/Taylor Prodns., Inc., N.Y.C., 1985—. Producer (film) The Children of Theater Street, 1977 (Acad. Award nomination). Dir. Briansky Ballet Sch., Saratoga, N.Y., 1977—; bd. dirs. Benjamin N. Cardozo Sch. of Law Yeshiva U., N.Y.C., 1980—, N.Y.C. Ballet, 1988—; chmn. N.Y. State Racing Commn., 1983—; mem. bldg. devel. com. N.Y.C. Holocaust Commn., 1985—, N.Y. State Thoroughbred Racing Capital Investment Fund, 1987—; bd. dirs. Dance Theater of Harlem, N.Y.C., 1987; elected co-chmn. Dance Theatre of Harlem. Served as 1st lt. U.S. Army Reserve, 1960-68. Nominated for Acad. award (film) The Children of Theatre Street, 1977. Mem. Nat. Realty Com. (bd. dirs., exec. com. 1986—), Urban Land Inst. Clubs: Union League; Univ.; Reading Room; Turf & Field. Office: The Mack Co 370 W Passaic St Rochelle Park NJ 07662

MACK, JEROME D., banker; b. Albion, Mich., Nov. 6, 1920; s. Nate and Jennie (Solomon) M.; m. Joyce Jean Rosenberg, Mar. 30, 1947; children; children: Barbara Joan, Karen Diane, Marilynn Susan. BA, AA, UCLA, 1943; D.Law (hon.), U. Nev., Las Vegas, 1983. Vice chmn. Valley Capital Corp. (formerly Valley Bank of Nev.), Las Vegas, 1965—; chmn., commnr. Nev. State Tax Commn., 1970—. Mem. Dem. Nat. Fin. Com., Washington; nat. coordinator Humphrey for Pres., Las Vegas, 1968; fin. chmn. Nev. State Dem. Party, 1968; state coordinator, treas., Cannon for Senate Com., 1958; trustee Boy Scouts Am., 1965-87, U. Nev. Las Vegas Land Found., 1965-87; trustee, bd. overseers UCLA. Recipient Israel's Peace award, 1981; named Outstanding Nev. Citizen U. Nev. Las Vegas Alumni, 1981. Democrat. Jewish. Club: Boys (founder, dir.). Office: Valley Capital Corp PO Box 98600 Las Vegas NV 89193

MACK, JOHN EDWARD, finance company executive; b. Cleve., July 16, 1947; s. Edward John and Lorraine (Loriaux) M.; m. Janne Himes, May 24, 1975. BA in Econs., Davidson (N.C.) Coll., 1972; MBA, Darden Bus. Sch., Charlottesville, Va., 1974. Credit analyst N.C. Nat. Bank, Charlotte, N.C., 1974, mgr. profit planning, 1974-76, analyst asset liability, 1976-78; account officer London, 1978-80; mgr. corp. fin. Charlotte, 1980-83; dir. corp. planning N.C. Nat. Bank Corp., Charlotte, 1983-87, sr. v.p., treas., 1987—. Democrat. Presbyterian. Office: NCNB Corp 1 NCNB Pla Charlotte NC 28255

MACK, ROBERT FRANK, banker; b. Pittston, Pa., Nov. 2, 1948; s. Dominick Thomas and Catherine Marie (Miceli) M.; m. Patricia Linda Wells, Nov. 7, 1970. Asst. comptroller 1st Peoples Bank N.J., Haddon Twp., 1970-75; fin. officer Provident Nat. Bank, Phila., 1975-78; controller Bank of Mid-Jersey, Bordentown, N.J., 1978-81; asst. v.p. 1st Jersey Nat. Corp., Jersey City, 1981-83; v.p., controller 1st Jersey Nat. Bank Cen., Perth Amboy, N.J., 1985-86; sr. v.p., chief fin. officer Hansen Savs. Bank, SLA, East Brunswick, N.J., 1986—. Chmn. Haddon Twp. Rent Control Bd., 1983-86; mem. Haddon Twp. Zoning Bd., 1986—; pres. N.J. Jaycees, 1979-80 (Dennis Hamilton Meml. award 1979), N.J. Jaycees Senate, 1984-85, Regular Rep. Club Haddon Twp., 1985-86; bd. dirs. U.S. Jaycees, 1979-81; chmn. N.J. Jaycee Found., 1980-81; commr. Haddon Twp. Fire Dist. #3, 1984—; mem. Gov.'s Commn. on Voter Registration, 1979-80. Republican. Roman Catholic. Home: 1 E Cedar Ave Haddon Township NJ 08107 Office: Hansen Savs Bank SLA Rt 18 East Brunswick NJ 08816

MACK, STEPHEN W., financial planner; b. Chgo., Mar. 4, 1954; s. Walter M. and Suzanne (Charbonneau) M.; m. Dayle A. Rothermel, Nov. 19, 1983; children: Michael, Veronica, Kevin. BBA in Fin., U. Mich., 1976; cert., Coll. Fin. Planning, Denver, 1987. Gen. sales mgr. Mack Cadillac Corp., Mt. Prospect, Ill., 1976-81; sales rep. Merrill Lynch Co., Chgo., 1981-84; resident mgr. Merrill Lynch Co., Rockford, Ill., 1984-85; asst. v.p. Merrill Lynch Co., Skokie, Ill., 1985-86; pres., chief exec. officer Mack Investment Securities, Inc., Northfield, Ill., 1986—. Mem. Nat. Assn. Securities Dealers, Internat. Assn. Fin. Planners, Am. Assn. Cert. Fin. Planners, Am. Assn. Registered Fin. planners, Am. Assn. Registered Investment Advisers, Mensa. Office: Mack Investment Securities Inc 1939 Waukegan Rd Glenview IL 60025

MACKAY, ANDREW DOUGAL, electronics equipment company executive; b. Long Beach, Calif., Feb. 22, 1946; s. Dougal Donald and Virginia Francis (Morris) M.; m. Helen Grace Hall, May 27, 1971. B.S. in Physics, Calif. Inst. Tech., 1967; M.A. in Physics, U. Calif.-Berkeley, 1969, M.B.A., 1975. Physicist, Lawrence Livermore Lab., Calif., 1967-71; v.p. Controlled Fusion Inc., San Ramon, Calif., 1971-73; v.p., controller Magna-Tek Systems, Inc., Hayward, Calif., 1973-76; dir. tech. ventures Combustion Engring. Inc., Stamford, Conn., 1976-84; chief operating officer, chief fin. officer Spire Corp., Bedford, Mass., 1984-87; pres. Maccor, Inc., Tulsa, 1987—, also dir.; dir. Internat. Biotech. Labs, Inc., Cambridge, Mass., Shawmco, Inc., Tulsa. Nat. Merit scholar, 1963; NASA fellow, 1967. Mem. IEEE, Instrument Soc. Am. Republican. Office: Maccor Inc 2805 W 40th St Tulsa OK 74107

MACKAY, MALCOLM, management consultant; b. Bklyn., Nov. 6, 1940; s. John F. and Helen (Pflug) MacK.; m. Cynthia Johnson, Aug. 29, 1964;

children: Robert Livingston, Hope Winthrop. A.B. Cum laude, Princeton U., 1963; J.D., Harvard U., 1966. Bar: N.Y. 1967. Assoc. Milbank, Tweed, Hadley and McCloy, N.Y.C., 1966-69; dep. supt. N.Y. State Ins. Dept., N.Y.C., 1969-71; 1st dep. supt. N.Y. State Ins. Dept., 1971-73; vice chancellor L.I. U., Greenvale, N.Y., 1973-75; sr. v.p. Blue Cross & Blue Shield of Greater New York, 1975-77, N.Y. Life Ins. Co., N.Y.C., 1977-88; mng. dir. Russell Reynolds Assocs., N.Y.C., 1988—; bd. dirs. Independence Savs. Bank, Bklyn. Author several local histories; contbr. articles on ins. to profl. publs. Bd. dirs. N.Y. Assn. of the Blind, N.Y. Urban Coalition, Citizens Union of N.Y., Sch. Am. Ballet, Met. Mus. Art; trustee Bklyn. Botanic Garden, The Green-Wood Cemetery, Pratt Inst. Mem. Assn. of Bar of City of N.Y., Century Assn., Piping Rock Club. Home: 166 Columbia Heights Brooklyn Heights NY 11201 Office: NY Life Ins Co 51 Madison Ave New York NY 10010

MACKAY, MARIA PILLON, international trade administrator; b. Vicenza, Italy, Jan. 24, 1941; came to U.S., 1969.; Doctorate in Russian Lang. and Lit., Ca'Foscari, Venice, Italy, 1965; MA in Internat. Econs., Georgetown U., 1982. Pres. MacKay & Liddle Enterprises, Bethesda, Md., 1982-84; pvt. practice Washington, 1984-85; internat. trade analyst U.S. Internat. Trade Commn., Washington, 1985-88; program mgr. Voluntary Restraint Arrangements for steel products with Latin Am. countries U.S. Dept. Commerce, Washington, 1988—. Mem. Am. Econ. Assn., Am. Translators Assn., Washington Internat. Trade Assn., Washington Women in Internat. Trade. Home: 5311 Massachusetts Ave Bethesda MD 20816 Office: US Dept of Commerce 14th & Constitution Ave NW Washington DC 20230

MACKE, KENNETH A., retail executive; b. Templeton, Iowa, Dec. 16, 1938; B.S., Drake U., 1961; m. Kathleen O'Farrell; children: Michael, Jeffrey. With Dayton Hudson Corp., and affiliates, 1961—, former chmn., chief exec. officer Target Stores, sr. v.p. corp., 1977-79, pres. corp. 1981-84, cor. chmn., chief exec. officer, chmn. exec. com., 1984—; also dir.; mem. bd. bus. and indsl. advisers U. Wis., Stout, 1978-80. Bd. dirs. Walker Art Center, Urban Coalition Mpls.; trustee Drake U.; bd. regents Augsburg Coll., Mpls., 1979-80; div. chmn. United Way Mpls., 1977, 79-80. Mem. Nat. Mass. Retailing Inst. (dir. 1977-81), Nat. Retail Mchts. Assn. (dir. 1982-83), Greater Mpls. C. of C. (dir. 1980-82). Office: Dayton-Hudson Corp 777 Nicollet Mall Minneapolis MN 55402 *

MACKE, PATRICIA JEAN, marketing company official; b. Indpls., July 14, 1952; d. Hershel Beecher and Ellen Maxine (Wallace) Owen; m. Darrell Wayne Macke, Feb. 6, 1972; children: Darrell Clifford, Kimberly Sue, Steven Christopher. AS, Ivy Tech. Sch., Terre Haute, Ind., 1985. Group leader Cen. Electronics, Paris, Ill., 1975-83; with Terre Haute Maintenance Co., 1985; ins. producer Pan Am. Mktg Co., Taylorville, Ill., 1985—; owner Macke's Trophies and Engraving, Marshall, Ill., 1987; with ML Express Printing, Terre Haute, 1988—; loan processor Mut. Fed. Savs. & Loan Assn., 1989—. Coach minor league soccer team boys and girls, Paris, 1988; leader Girl Scouts U.S.A., Paris, 1985—; sunday sch. tchr. Trinity Meth. Ch., Marshall, 1986—; vol. Paris Dem. Com., 1985. Mem. Am. Mktg. Assn., Delta Epsilon Chi (state v.p. 1984-85). Home: RR 3 Box 253A Marshall IL 62441

MACKENZIE, JOHN, retired corporation executive; b. 1919. B.S., N.Y. U., 1948. Accountant S.Am. Devel. Co., N.Y.C., 1938-41; financial comptroller French Oil Ind. Agy.-Groupment D'Achat des Carburants, N.Y., 1946-53; v.p., treas. George Hall Corp., 1954-56; asst. treas. Am. Petrofina, Inc., 1956-61, sec., 1961-64, v.p., sec., 1964-68, sr. v.p., sec., 1968-84; ret. 1984. Decorated comdr. Order of Crown (Belgium). Address: 9225 Middle Glen Dr Dallas TX 75243

MACKENZIE, KENNETH ALLEN, treasurer, controller; b. Chgo., July 31, 1934; s. John Doyle and Helen Charlotte (Carbonel) MacK.; m. Joan Margaret Mary Nolting, July 23, 1960; children: Kenneth, Mary, Noreen, Eileen, John. BS, DePaul U., 1956; MS, Lake Forest Coll., 1974. CPA Ill. Controller Jewel Food Stores, Chgo., 1971-74, v.p. service ops., 1974-77; v.p. fin. Stein Drugs Inc., Milw., 1977-79; controller Marc's Big Boy, Milw., 1979-81; treas. controller Marcus Corp., Milw., 1981—. Served with U.S. Army, 1956-58. Mem. Wis. Retail Fin. Execs. (pres. 1987—), Ill. Soc. of CPA's. Office: Marcus Corp 212W Wisconsin Ave Milwaukee WI 53203

MACKEY, ALLAN NORMAN, management consultant; b. Phila., Aug. 16, 1937; s. W. Norman Mackey and Celeste (Parvin) Mackey Barley; m. Helen Christine Riegels, Apr. 25, 1962; children: Scott Riegels, Blake Parvin. Student, Swarthmore Coll., 1955-58; BA in History, Temple U., 1967; MBA, Harvard U., 1970. Service mgr. John Wanamaker Stores, Phila., 1962-63, sales audit mgr., 1964-67, sr. systems cons., 1967-68; dir. manpower devel. State of Vt., Montpelier, 1972-73; assoc. Am. Mgmt. Assn., N.Y.C., 1974-75, dir. govt. svcs., 1976; pres. Allan Mackey Assocs., Montpelier, 1977—; founding prin. Vt. Cons. Group, 1982-87; cons., tchr. Nat. Tng. Devel. Service, Washington, 1974-78; tchr. Goddard Coll., Plainfield, Vt., 1976-78; tchr., advisor Johnson (Vt.) State Coll., 1982-85. Fund raising dir. Amestoy for Atty. Gen., Montpelier, 1984; bd. dirs. Men for ERA, Burlington, Vt., 1986; moderator East Calais Water Bd., East Calais, Vt., 1985-86; mem. Jim Jeffords Congl. Club, Washington, 1986—. Served with USNG, 1960-66. Baker scholar Swarthmore Coll., 1955-57; Macy fellow Harvard U., 1969, Goldston fellow, 1968. Quaker. Office: Allan N Mackey Assocs 137 Elm St Box 1020 Montpelier VT 05602

MACKEY, EMILY JAN, pharmacy administrator; b. Brunswick, Ga., Feb. 20, 1955; d. George and Alva (Doss) M.; m. Brian D. Parker, June 10, 1983. BS in Pharmacy, U. Ga., 1978. Intern Med. Ctr. Cen. Ga., Macon, 1973-75; supr. Med. Coll. Ga., Augusta, 1978-81; dir. HPI Hosp. Pharmacies, Atlanta, 1981, Cobb Gen. Hosp., Austell, Ga., 1981—; mem. pharm. adv. council Vol. Hosps. Am., Dallas, 1987—, hosp. adv. bd. McKesson Drug Co., San Francisco, 1987—. Mem. Am. Soc. Hosp. Pharmacists, Am. Pharm. Assn., Ga. Pharm. Assn., Ga. Soc. Hosp. Pharmacists, Southeastern Soc. Hosp. Pharmacists. Democrat. Baptist. Club: Toastmasters. Office: Cobb Gen Hosp 3950 Austell Rd Austell GA 30001

MACKIE, FRANK IRVING, metal processing company executive; b. Troy, N.Y., Nov. 10, 1936; s. Frank Irving and Laura Margaret (Condon) M.; m. Madeline Claire Addis, Oct. 4, 1958; children: Elizabeth Anne, Thomas Francis, Christopher Paul. AA in Metall. Engring., Erie Tech. U., 1956; BS Metall. Engring., Rensselaer Poly. Inst., 1958; postgrad., U. Pa., 1962. Metall. engr. Allegheny Ludlum Co., Watervliet, N.Y., 1956-58, Midvale Heppenstall, Phila., 1958-65; chief metallurgist Heppenstall, Bridgeport, Conn., 1965-68; tech. dir. Whittaker, L.A., 1968-72; v.p. Southwestern Alloys, Paramount, Calif., 1972-78, Aerospace Metals, Irvine, Calif., 1978-83; gen. mgr. United Alloys, L.A., 1983—. Served with U.S. Navy, 1961-62. Democrat. Roman Catholic. Home: 2231 Yucca Ave Fullerton CA 92635 Office: United Alloys 2627 S Soto Los Angeles CA 90023

MACKILLOP, SCOTT ANDREW, lawyer; b. Stockton, Calif., May 2, 1951; s. Malcolm Andrew and Shirley (Cobb) MacKillop Fitch; m. Debra Jean Poor, May 24, 1984; children: Jamie Andrew, Malcolm Ian. BA, Stanford U., 1972; JD, George Washington U., 1976. Bar: Va. 1976, D.C. 1977. Assoc. Freedman, Levy, Kroll & Simonds, Washington, 1976-80, Steptoe & Johnson, 1980-84; v.p., gen. counsel Capital Assoc., 1984-85; ptnr. MacKillop & Hackford, Herndon, Va., 1985-88, Michaels & Wishner, Washington, 1988—. bd. dirs. Health Innovations, Inc., Herndon. Mem. D.C. Bar Assn., Va. Bar Assn., Balt.-Washington Venture Group, Entrepreneurship Group, The Entrepreneurship Inst. Republican. Episcopalian. Office: Michaels & Wishner 1726 M St NW Ste 500 Washington DC 20036

MACKINNON, MALCOLM D(AVID), insurance company executive, information systems executive; b. Guelph, Ont., Can., Mar. 9, 1931; came to U.S., 1955; s. A.L. and Jean (Butchart) MacK.; m. Betty Campbell, June 18, 1955; children: Sandra, Katherine, Donald. BA, U. Toronto, 1953. CLU; chartered fin. analyst. With Prudential Ins. Co., 1954—, v.p., Newark, 1979-81, sr. v.p., 1981-82, sr. v.p., Roseland, N.J., 1982—. Fellow Soc. Actuaries; mem. N.Y. Soc. Security Analysts. Club: Canoe Brook Country (Summit, N.J.). Office: The Prudential Ins Co Am 55 N Livingston Ave Roseland NJ 07068

MACKINNON, WILLIAM HOWARD, airline executive; b. Sumatra, Indonesia, May 21, 1938; came to U.S., 1941; s. William and Marion Howard (Baker) MacK.; m. Ramona Reames, Dec. 17, 1960; children: Heather, Kevin, Kyle, Adam. BBA, Emory U., 1960; MBA, Ga. State U., 1967. cert. mgmt. acctg. Bus. rep. internat. dept. Trust Co. Bank, Atlanta, 1964-68; v.p. Conway Research, Atlanta, 1968-71; asst. treas. Southern Airways, Atlanta, 1971-79; v.p., treas. Republic Airlines, Mpls., 1979-83, Piedmont Aviation, Inc., Winston-Salem, N.C., 1983-84; sr. v.p., treas. Piedmont Aviation, Inc., Winston-Salem, 1984-86, sr. v.p. fin., 1986-88; exec. v.p. fin. and adminstrn. Braniff Airlines, Dallas, 1988—. Contbr. articles to Travel Investment Mag., 1968-71. Bd. dirs., chmn. loaned execs. Forsyth County (N.C.) United Way, 1986-87. Served as lt. (j.g.) USN, 1961-64. Recipient Excellence Studies in Internat. Fin. award, World Trade Council, Atlanta, 1968. Mem. Nat. Assn. Corp. Treas., Nat. Assn. Accts., Fin. Execs. Inst., Air Transport Assn. (exec. and fin. council 1984-87), U.S. C. of C. (econ. policy com. 1985-87). Republican. Epscopalian. Club: Piedmont (Winston-Salem). Home: 2675 Reynolds Dr Winston-Salem NC 27104 Office: Piedmont Aviation Inc One Piedmont Pla Winston-Salem NC 27156

MACLACHLAN, ALEXANDER, chemical company executive; b. Boston, Jan. 22, 1933; s. Hugh and Catherine (Sullivan) MacL.; m. Elizabeth Pegues, Jan. 25, 1958; children: Katherine Ellen, Amy Elizabeth, Mary Emily, Alexander, Hugh. BS in Chemistry, Tufts U., 1954; PhD in Organic Chemistry, Mass. Inst. tech., 1957. Mktg. dir., printing product dir. E. I. du Pont Nemours & Co., Wilmington, Del., 1976-78, dir. plastics dept., 1978-80, dir. research and devel. div. chemical and pigments div., 1980-82, asst. dir. cen. research and devel. dept., 1982-83, dir. cen. research and devel. dept., 1983-86, sr. v.p. tech., 1986—. Nat. sci. adv. bd. Howard U., Washington, 1985—; chmn. tech. com. Gov.'s High Tech. Task Force, Wilmington, 1986-88; trustee Mt. Cuba Atron. Observatory, Wilmington, 1986—. Mem. Am. Chemical Soc., Nat. Sci. Assn. of U. Pa. Office: E I Du Pont de Nemours & Co 1007 Market St Wilmington DE 19898

MAC LAREN, DAVID SERGEANT, manufacturing corporation executive; b. Cleve., Jan. 4, 1931; s. Albert Sergeant and Theadora Beidler (Potter) MacL.; children: Alison, Catherine, Carolyn. AB in Econs., Miami U., Oxford, Ohio, 1955. Chmn. bd., pres., Jet, Inc., Cleve., 1961—; founder, chmn. bd., pres. Air Injector Corp., Cleve., 1958-78; founder, pres., chmn. bd. Fluid Equipment, Inc., Cleve., 1962-72; founder, chmn. bd., pres., T&M Co., Cleve., 1963-71, Alison Realty Co., Cleve., 1965—, Sergeant Realty, Inc., 1979-86; bd. dirs. Gilmore Industries, Cleve., 1975-77, MWL Systems, Los Angeles, 1979-85; mem. tech. com. Nat. Sanitation Found., Ann Arbor, Mich., 1967—. Patentee in field. Mem. Rep. State Cen. Com., 1968-72; bd. dirs. Cleve. State U. Found., 1986—. Served with arty. AUS, 1955-58. Fellow Royal Soc. Health (London); mem. Nat. Environ. Health Assn., Am. Pub. Health Assn., Nat. Water Pollution Control Fedn., Cen. Taekwondo Assn. (2d Dan), Jiu-Jitsu/Karati Black Belt Fedn. (black belt instr.), Mercedes Benz Club N.Am. (pres. 1968), H.B. Leadership Soc. (sch. headmaster soc., devel. com. 1976-78), SAR, Soc. Mayflower Descendants, Mentor Harbor Yachting Club, The Country Club, Cotillion Soc., Union League, Yale Club, Deke Club, Delta Kappa Epsilon (nat. bd. dirs. N.Y.C. chpt. 1974-86, bd. dirs. Kappa chpt. 1969—). Home: West Hill Dr Gates Mills OH 44040 Office: Jet Inc 750 Alpha Dr Cleveland OH 44143

MACLAUCHLAN, DONALD JOHN, JR., real estate company executive; b. S.I., N.Y., Mar. 2, 1935; s. Donald John and Alice Lucy (Macklin) MacL.; B.A. magna cum laude, Harvard U., 1957; m. Mary Eleanor Manor, Oct. 14, 1967; children—Douglas Laird, Phyllis Ann, Donald John III. Mortgage analyst Conn. Gen. Life Ins. Co., Hartford, 1957-60; mortgage broker James W. Rouse & Co., Balt., 1960-62; devel. mgr. Devel. & Constrn. Co., Inc., Balt., 1962-66; v.p. Nat. Homes Corp., Lafayette, Ind., 1966-75; pres., dir. The Criterion Group, Lafayette, 1975—, Park 65 Inc., 1986—; chmn. bd. Insight Unltd., Inc.; dir. Lafayette Parking, Inc., Sagamore Food Services, Inc. Elder, Central Presbyn. Ch., Lafayette, 1971—; mem. gen. council Presbytery of Wabash Valley, 1976-78; bd. dirs. Greater Lafayette Progress, Inc., 1987—, United Way of Greater Lafayette, 1989—; bd. dirs. Tippecanoe County Apt. Assn, 1977—, pres., 1980, 87. Mem. Lafayette Bd. Realtors (dir. 1986—), Greater Lafayette C. of C., Ind. Apt. Assn. (bd. dir. 1980—), Lafayette Country Club, Romwell Foxhounds (joint master). Republican. Office: PO Box 275 Lafayette IN 47902

MACLEAN, DANIEL CRAWFORD, III, lawyer; b. N.Y.C., Sept. 15, 1942; s. Daniel Crawford and Elsie O. (Reeh) M.; m. Hildi Starstrom; 1 son, James; 1 dau. by previous marriage—Lisa. A.B., Columbia U., 1964; Certificat, U. Paris, 1964; J.D., Georgetown U., 1967. Bar: Conn. 1967. Atty. SEC, Washington, 1967-72; mem. firm Reavis & McGrath, N.Y.C., 1972-73; asso. gen. counsel Dreyfus Corp., N.Y.C., 1973-78; gen. counsel, sec. Dreyfus Corp., 1978-83, v.p., gen. counsel, 1983—. Mem. ABA. Home: Contentment Island Rd Darien CT 06820 Office: Dreyfus Corp 767 Fifth Ave New York NY 10153

MACLEAN, WILLIAM BRADLEY, investment analyst; b. Mpls., Feb. 18, 1953; s. Alan Lockwood and Charlotte (Lacey) MacL.; m. Laurie Jo Anderson, Sept. 12, 1981; children: Edward, Anna. BA, Rollins Coll., 1976. CPA, Minn. Asst. nat. bank examiner Comptroller of Currency, Atlanta, 1977-79; staff acct. Lurie, Eiger, Besikof & Co., CPA's, Mpls., 1979-82; investment analyst TCF Banking & Savs., F.A., Mpls., 1982—. Mem. Am. Inst. CPA's, Minn. Soc. CPA's. Home: 4604 Edina Blvd Edina MN 55424 Office: TCF Banking and Savs FA 801 Marquette Ave Minneapolis MN 55424

MACLEOD, IAN ROBERTS, lawyer; b. Erie, Pa., Aug. 6, 1931; s. Donald Ridgway and Dorothy (Roberts) M.; m. Jane Zeta Davidson, June 10, 1953; children: Douglas, Andrew, Stewart, Laurie. AB with honors, U. Rochester, 1953; JD, Harvard U., 1959. Bar: N.Y. 1960, Ohio 1967. Assoc. Cadwalader, Wickersham & Taft, N.Y.C., 1959-65; asst. counsel Firestone Tire & Rubber, Akron, Ohio, 1965-69, asst. sec, asst. counsel, 1969-79; sec. Interlake, Inc., Oak Brook, Ill., 1979-86, Interlake Corp., Oak Brook, 1986—. Chmn. Little Hoover commn. Pub. Safety Task Force, Akron, 1973. Served to lt. (j.g.) USN, 1953-56. Mem. ABA, Am. Soc. Corp. Secs., Sigma Chi. Republican. Episcopalian. Home: 1493 Garywood Dr Burr Ridge IL 60521 Office: Interlake Corp 701 Harger Rd Oak Brook IL 60521-1488

MACLEOD, JOHN AMEND, lawyer; b. Manila, June 5, 1942; s. Anthony Macaulay and Dorothy Lillian (Amend) M.; children—Kerry, Jack. B.B.A., U. Notre Dame, 1963, J.D., 1969. Bar: D.C. 1969, U.S. Supreme Ct. 1980. Assoc., Jones, Day, Reavis & Pogue, D.C., 1969-73; ptnr., 1974-79; ptnr. Crowell & Moring, Washington, 1979—, mem. mgmt. com., 1979-82, 83-86, chmn., 1984-85. Trustee, mem. exec. com. Eastern Mineral Law Found.; bd. dirs. St. Francis Ctr. Served to lt. U.S. Army, 1963-65. Mem. ABA, D.C. Bar Assn., Notre Dame Law Assn. (dir., exec. bd.). Club: Metropolitan (Washington). Editor-in-chief Notre Dame Law Rev., 1968-69. Contbr. articles to profl. jours. Home: 1733 Que St NW Washington DC 20009

MACLIN, RUSSELL CHEVES, software company executive, consultant; b. Baldwin, N.Y., Oct. 24, 1942; s. Russell Cheves and Evelyn Fermine (Suits) M.; m. Jane Kronmann (div. 1978). BA, Rutgers U., 1964. Supr. Am. Airlines, N.Y.C., 1968-69; communicaitons cons. N.Y. Tel. Co., N.Y.C., 1969-73; data systems specialist So. Bell, Miami, Fla., 1973-78; chmn., v.p. Dynamic Resources, Inc., Atlanta, 1978—; ptnr. DRI Leasing Co., Atlanta, 1980—; chmn., pres. Dynamic Exec. Svcs., Atlanta, 1983—. Bd. dirs. D'Youville Condominium Assn., Atlanta, 1986-87, Dunwoody (Ga.) Place North Condominium Assn., 1986—. Lt. USN, 1964-68. Republican. Home: 4198 D'Youville Trace Atlanta GA 30341 Office: Dynamic Resources Inc 1866 Independence Sq Atlanta GA 30338

MACMANUS, SUSAN ANN, political science educator, researcher; b. Tampa, Fla., Aug. 22, 1947; d. Harold Cameron and Elizabeth (Riegler) MacM. BA cum laude, Fla. State U., 1968, PhD, 1975; MA, U. Mich., 1969. Instr. Valencia Community Coll., Orlando, Fla., 1969-73; research asst. Fla. State U., 1973-75; asst. prof. U. Houston, 1975-79, assoc. prof., 1979-85, dir. M of Pub. Adminstrn. program, 1983-85, research assoc. Ctr Pub. Policy 1982-85; prof., dir. PhD program Cleve. State U., 1985-87; prof. pub. adminstrn. and polit. sci. U. South Fla., Tampa, 1987—; vis. prof. U. Okla., Norman, 1981—; field research assoc. Brookings Instn., Washington, 1977-82, Columbia U., summer 1979, Princeton (N.J.) U., 1979—, Nat. Acad. Pub. Adminstrn., Washington, summer 1980, Cleve. State U., 1982-83, Westat, Inc., Washington, 1983—. Author: Revenue Patterns in U.S. Cities and Suburbs: A Comparative Analysis, 1978, (with others) Governing A Changing America, 1984; writer manuals in field; mem. editorial bds. various jours.; contbr. articles to jours. and chpts. to books. Bd. dirs. Houston Area Women's Ctr., 1977, past pres., v.p. fin., treas.; mem. LWV, Gov.'s Council Econ. Advisers, 1988—, Harris County (Tex.) Women's Polit. Caucus, Houston. Recipient U. Houston Coll. Social Scis. Teaching Excellence award, 1977, Herbert J. Simon Award for best article in 3d vol. Internat. Jour. Pub. Adminstrn., 1981; Ford Found. fellow, 1967-68; grantee Valencia Community Coll. Faculty, 1972, U. Houston, 1976-77, 79, 83. Mem. Am. Polit. Sci. Assn. (program com. 1983-84, chair sect. intergovtl. relations), So. Polit. Sci. Assn. (V.O. key award com. 1983-84), Midwest Polit. Sci. Assn., Western Polit. Sci. Assn., Southwestern Polit. Sci. Assn. (local arrangements com. 1982-83, profession com. 1977-80), Am. Soc. Pub. Adminstrn. (nominating com. Houston chpt. 1983), Policy Studies Orgn. (mem. editorial bd. jour. 1981—, exec. council 1983-85), Women's Caucus Polit. Sci. (portfolio pre-decision rev. com. 1982-83, projects and programs com. 1981, fin.-budget com. 1980-81), Acad. Polit. Sci., Mcpl. Fin. Officers Assn., Phi Beta Kappa, Phi Kappa Phi, Pi Sigma Alpha. Republican. Methodist. Home: 746 Collier Pkwy Land O'Lakes FL 34639 Office: U South Fla Dept Pub Adminstrn Soc 107 Tampa FL 33620

MACMILLAN, DAVID PAUL, oil company executive; b. East Orange, N.J., Nov. 16, 1943; s. Hugh Dame and Marie Ann (Hahn) MacM.; B.S. in M.E. Summa Cum Laude, N.J. Inst. Tech., 1969; m. Rosemary Longo, Nov. 16, 1969; children—Melanie, Hugh. With Exxon Research & Engring. Co., various locations, 1969-85, sect. head, Florham Park, N.J., 1978-80, project mgr., Denver, 1980-82, spl. assignment to sr. gen. mgr., Florham Park, 1982-83, project mgr.-Belgium, 1983-85, staff advisor controllers dept., Exxon Co. Internat., Florham Pk, N.J., 1986-88; materials mgr. Exxon Cen. Svcs., Florham Park, 1989—. Served with USMC, 1961-65. Mem. Tau Beta Pi, Pi Tau Sigma. Republican. Presbyterian. Home: 55 Village Rd Florham Park NJ 07932 Office: Exxon Internat PO Box 300 Florham Park NJ 07932

MACMILLAN, ROBERT SMITH, electronics engineer; b. L.A., Aug. 28, 1924; s. Andrew James and Moneta (Smith) M.; BS in Physics, Calif. Inst. Tech., 1948, MS in Elec. Engring., 1949, PhD in Elec. Engring. and Physics cum laude, 1954; m. Barbara Macmillan, Aug. 18, 1962; 1 son, Robert G. Rsch. engr. Jet Propulsion lab. Calif. Inst. Tech., Pasadena, 1951-55, asst. prof. elec. engring., 1955-58; assoc. prof. elec. engring. U. So. Calif., L.A., 1958-70; mem. sr. tech. staff Litton Systems, Inc., Van Nuys, Calif., 1969-79; dir. systems engring. Litton Data Command Systems, Agoura Hills, Calif., 1979—; treas., v.p. Video Color Corp., Inglewood, 1965-66. Cons. fgn. tech. div. USAF, Wright-Patterson AFB, Ohio, 1957-74, Space Tech. Labs., Inglewood, Calif., 1956-60, Space Gen. Corp., El Monte, Calif., 1960-63. With USAAF, 1943-46. Mem. IEEE, Am. Inst. Physics, Am. Phys. Soc., Sigma Xi, Tau Beta Pi, Eta Kappa Nu. Research in ionospheric, radio-wave, propagation; very low frequency radio-transmitting antennas; optical coherence and statist. optics. Home: 350 Starlight Crest Dr La Canada CA 91011 Office: Litton Data Command Systems 29851 Agoura Rd Agoura Hills CA 91301

MACMILLEN, WILLIAM CHARLES, JR., investment banker; b. Troy, N.Y., May 24, 1913; s. William C. and Anna C. (Dugan) MacM.; m. Barbara Christy Downing, Mar. 6, 1942; children: Paul Downing, Sally, Anita, William, Nancy. Student, William Coll., 1931-34; LLB, Albany Law Sch., 1937. Ptnr. MacMillen & Filley, 1939-41; asst. to chmn. Allegheny Corp., 1946; pres. Fedn. Ry. Progress, 1947-48, Eagle Lion Films, Inc., 1949-50, Chesapeake Industries, Inc., 1950-57, Colonial Trust Co., 1957-59; cons. Kuhn, Loeb & Co., 1960-61; chmn., dir. Lexington Internat., Inc., 1962; pres. Cosmos Am. Corp., 1963-64, Internat. Bus. Relations Corp., 1965-66, Tower Internat., Inc., 1967-68; pres., dir. William C. MacMillen & Co., Inc., 1969—; racehorse owner and breeder; dir. Corroon & Black Corp., Republic Nat. Bank N.Y. (and subs.), Eutectic Welding Alloys Corp., Republic N.Y. Corp., Williamsburg Savs. Bank. Served as maj. USAAF, 1942-45. Decorated Legion of Merit. Mem. Mgmt. Execs. Soc., Jockey Club. Clubs: Jockey, Saratoga Golf, Rockaway Hunting, Turf and Field, Racquet and Tennis. Home: 254 Victoria Pl Lawrence NY 11559

MACNAUGHTON, ANGUS ATHOLE, finance company executive; b. Montreal, Que., Can., July 15, 1931; s. Athole Austin and Emily Kidder (MacLean) MacN.; children—Gillian Heather, Angus Andrew. Student, Lakefield Coll. Sch., 1941-47, McGill U., 1949-54. Auditor Coopers & Lybrand, Montreal, 1949-55; acct. Genstar Ltd., Montreal, 1955; asst. treas. Genstar Ltd., 1956-61, treas., 1961-64, v.p., 1964-70, exec. v.p., 1970-73, pres., 1973-76, vice chmn., chief exec. officer, 1976-81, chmn. or pres., chief exec. officer, 1981-86; pres. Genstar Investment Corp., 1987—; bd. dirs. Can. Pacific Ltd., Sun Life Assurance Co. Can. Ltd., Am. Barrick Resources Corp., Stelco Inc., Varian Assocs. Inc., Stelco Inc.; past pres. Montreal chpt. Tax Exec. Inst. Bd. govs. Lakefield Coll. Sch.; sr. mem. Conf. Bd. N.Y.; bd. dirs. San Francisco Bay Area Council, Boy Scouts Am. Mem. Pacific Union, World Trade Club (San Francisco), Mount Royal (Montreal), Toronto Club. Office: Genstar Investment Corp 801 Montgomery St Ste 500 San Francisco CA 94133 also: Am Barrick Resources Corp, 24 Hazelton Ave, Toronto, ON Canada M5R 2E2

MACON, IRENE ELIZABETH, designer, consultant; b. East St. Louis, Ill., May 11, 1935; d. David and Thelma (Eastlen) Dunn; m. Robert Teco Macon, Feb. 12, 1954; children: Leland Sean, Walter Edwin, Gary Keith, Jill Renee Macon Martin, Robin Jeffrey, Lamont. Student Forest Park Coll., Washington U., St. Louis, 1970, Bailey Tech. Coll., 1975, Lindenwood Coll., 1981. Office mgr. Cardinal Glennon Hosp., St. Louis, 1965-72; interior designer J.C. Penney Co., Jennings, Mo., 1972-73; entrepreneur Irene Designs Unltd., St. Louis, 1974—; vol. liaison Pub. Sch. System, St. Louis, 1980-82; cons. in field. Inventor venetian blinds for autos, 1981, T-blouse and diaper wrap, 1986; author 26th Word newsletter, 1986. Committeewoman Republican party, St. Louis, 1984; vice chair 4th Senatorial Dist. of Mo., 1984, vol. St. Louis Assn. Community Orgns., 1983; instr. first aid Bi-State chpt. ARC, St. Louis, 1984; cubmaster pack #80 Keystone dist. Boy Scouts Am.; block capt. Operation Brightside, St. Louis, 1984; co-chair Status and Role of Women, Union Meml. United Meth. Ch., 1986—; trustee Wofit Found., 1989. Named One of Top Ladies of Distinction St. Louis, 1983. Mem. Am. Soc. Interior Designers (assoc.), NAACP, Nat. Mus. Women in the Arts (charter), Internat. Platform Assn., Nat. Council Negro Women (1st v.p. 1984), Invention Assn. of St. Louis (subcom. head 1985), Coalition of 100 Black Women, St. Louis Assn. Fashion Designers, Pres. Club. Methodist. Avocations: reading; designing personal wardrobe; modeling; horseback riding; boating. Home and Office: PO Box 20370 Saint Louis MO 63112-0370

MACQUEEN, JAMES HENRY, banker, real estate executive; b. Chgo., Jan. 13, 1962; s. Kenneth Henry and Janet Kay (Dietrich) M. BA in Econs., Duke U., 1984; MBA, Rice U., 1986. Sr. fin. analyst Century Investments, Inc., Houston, 1986-87; project mgr. Century Real Estate Advisors, Houston, 1987-88; asst. to the chmn. The Kislak Orgn., Miami Lakes, Fla., 1988-89, planning mgr., 1989—; asset mgr. Kislak Real Estate Ventures, Miami Lakes, Fla., 1988—; bd. dirs., cons. Marteg Realty Inc.; cons. Blackwell Real Estate Investments, Nashville, 1987—. Mem. Japan-Am. Soc., Mortgage Banking Soc., Psi Upsilon. Republican. Presbyterian. Home: 6700 Bull Run Rd A-469 Miami Lakes FL 33014

MACRAE, JOHN SUMTER, III, architect; b. Charlotte, N.C., Aug. 3, 1937; s. John Sumter and Agnes (Thorne) M.; m. Eugenia Hickerson; children: John Douglas, Robert Thorne. BArch., N.C. State U., 1961. Registered architect, N.C., S.C., Va., Fla. Designer J. Hyatt Hammond Assocs., Ashboro, N.C., 1961-62; designer, architect William F. Freeman Assocs., High Point, N.C., 1964-67; architect, v.p. Woodroof and MacRae Architects, Greensboro, N.C., 1967-68; pres. John MacRae Assocs., Greensboro, N.C., 1968-72, MacRae, Funderburk, Marshall, Greensboro, N.C., 1972-74, MacRae-Bell Assocs., Greensboro, N.C., 1974—. Prin. works include numerous comml., recreational, institutional, multi-family and religious bldgs. in N.C., S.C., Va. Served as capt. U.S. Army, 1962-64. Mem. AIA (pres. Piedmont sect., bd. dirs. N.C. chpt.), Kiwanis, Greensboro City Club. Presbyterian. Home: 2107 Medford Ln Greensboro NC 27408 Office: MacRae Bell Assocs 125 Summit Ave Greensboro NC 27401

MACRE, ROBERT ALFRED, controller; b. Bayonne, N.J., July 18, 1943; s. Joseph and Mary (Cortese) M.; m. Rosetta Hurst, Feb. 14, 1970 (div. Jan. 1978); children: Maria, Gina; m. Joan Demko, May 30, 1988. BS, Rutgers U., 1972. Various clerical positions U.S. Trust Co., N.Y.C., 1961-63, 65-67; acctg. clk., sr. clk., jr. acct., sr. cost acct. Otto B. May, Inc., Newark, 1967-75; staff cost acct. Amerace Esna, Union, N.J., 1975-78, plant contr., 1978-87; plant and div. contr. Harvard Esna, Union, 1987—. With U.S. Army, 1963-65. Roman Catholic. Office: Harvard Esna 2330 Vauxhall Rd Union NH 07083

MACRURY, KING, management counselor; b. Manchester, N.H., Oct. 14, 1915; s. Colin H. and Lauretta C. (Shea) MacR.; 1 son, Colin C. A.B., Rollins Coll., 1938; postgrad., St. Anselms Coll., L.I. Coll. Medicine, Princeton. Asst. personnel dir. Lily-Tulip Cup Corp., 1939; asst. dir. market research Ward Baking Co., 1940-41; staff mem. Nat. Indsl. Conf. Bd., 1941-43; cons. indsl. relations and orgn. planning McKinsey & Co., 1946-48; internal cons. Oxford Paper Co., 1949-50; installer, dir. indsl. relations Champion Internation Co., 1950-51; pvt. practice mgmt. counselor 1951—; lectr. Indsl. Edn. Inst., 1962-68, Mgmt. Center, Cambridge, 1968-71, Dun & Bradstreet, 1979—; extension div. U. N.H., 1968—; extension program U. Maine, 1978—; also U. Bridgeport, extension program U. Conn.; coordinator mgmt. edn. extension div. U. Conn., 1964-68, Philippine Council Mgmt., 1969—, Econ. Devel. Found. Philippines, 1969—, Am. Metal Stamping Assn., 1969—; condr. mgmt. seminars for Asian Assn. Mgmt. Orgns. C.I.O.S., 1972; Mem. Indsl. Devel. Commn. Andover, 1957-58; manpower com. U.S. Dept. Labor Bus. Adv. Council, 1958-61. Author: Developing Your People Potential; Contbr. numerous articles in field to profl. jours. Served to lt. USNR, 1943-46. Mem. N.H. Dental Soc. (hon.). Office: Box 215 Rye NH 03870

MACUR, PATRICIA A., computer programmer, analyst; b. Chgo.; d. Alexander J. and Alice Mary (Styburski) Mackiewicz; m. George J. Macur, 1960; children: Alexander, Cindy Macur Conti. BS, SUNY, 1978; MS, Thomas J. Watson Sch. of Engring., 1984. System control analyst IBM Corp., Endicott, N.Y., 1977; programmer trainee intelligent systems NCR, Ithaca, N.Y., 1978-79, assoc. programmer software integration, 1980, assoc. programmer I gen. purpose systems, 1980-81, programmer, analyst terminal software div., 1981-84; applications analyst material mgmt. systems Eastman Kodak Co., Rochester, N.Y., 1984-86, applications analyst planning and control systems, 1986—; sr. programmer, analyst mfg. systems Ingersoll-Rand Systems, Athens, Pa., 1986-88; sr. assoc. programmer copics packaging, applications system div. IBM, Atlanta, 1988—. Mem. IMC, AMA (assoc.). Home: 202 Vinings Pkwy Smyrna GA 30080 Office: IBM 1500 River Edge Pkwy Atlanta GA 30328

MACZULSKI, MARGARET LOUISE, association executive; b. Detroit, Apr. 1, 1949; d. Bohdan Alexander and Olga Louise (Martinuick) M. BS, Mich. State U., 1972. Mgr. meetings Nat. Assn. Realtors, Mktg. Inst., Chgo., 1977-82, mgr. mktg., 1982-83; regional sales mgr. Fairmont Hotels, Chgo., 1982; dir., mgr. trade shows and confs. Am. Broadcasting Co./Pub. Div., Wheaton, Ill., 1983-85; mgr. meeting and conf. planning Am. Soc. Personnel Adminstrn., Alexandria, Va., 1985—. Mem. Meeting Planners Internat., Greater Washington Soc. Assn. Execs. (chmn. site inspection com.), Am. Soc. Assn. Execs., Nat. Assn. Exposition Execs., Mich. State U. Alumni Assn. (treas. D.C. chpt. 1987—). Republican. Roman Catholic. Avocations: piano, swimming. Home: 5340 Holmes Run Pkwy #219 Alexandria VA 22304 Office: Am Soc Personnel Adminstrn 606 N Washington Alexandria VA 22314

MADARA, MAUREEN DIANE, bank officer; b. Erie, Pa., June 15, 1961; d. William George and Antoinette May (Potthoff) M. Student, Thiel Coll., 1981-83; BS, Villa Maria Coll., 1986. Mktg. asst. IBM, Erie, 1985-86; asst. mgr. 1st Nat. Bank Pa., Erie, 1986-87. Sec. exec. com. Erie Arts Council, 1987—; active mem. Jr. League Erie, 1987—. Mem. Nat. Assn. Banking Women, Am. Inst. Banking, Nat. Assn. Female Execs., Soc. for Advancement of Mgmt. (pres. 1985-86). Republican. Roman Catholic. Home: 1200 Wilkins Rd Erie PA 16505 Office: 4645 Westlake Rd Erie PA 16505

MADDEN, PETER E., banker; b. Wellesley, Mass., Mar. 16, 1942; s. Edward Aloysius and Mary (O'Neal) M.; m. Cynthia Shreve, May 5, 1981; children—Amy, Mark, William, Michael, Daniel. B.S. in Bus. Adminstrn., Babson Coll., 1964; A.M.P., Harvard Grad. Sch. Bus. Adminstrn., 1977. With sales and mgmt. depts. IBM, Mass., 1966-73; with State St. Boston Corp., 1973—, vice chmn. bd., 1981-85, pres., chief operating officer, 1985—, also dir.; bd. dirs. VISA U.S.A., Inc., San Francisco. Chairperson United Way, Boston, 1981, United Way Mass. Bay, 1989; bd. dirs. Family Counseling and Guidance Ctrs., Inc., Boston; mem. corp. of Northeastern U.; trustee Babson Coll. Corp.; trustee Lahey Clinic Found. Assn. Res. City Bankers, Greater Boston C. of C. (bd. dirs.). Roman Catholic. Clubs: Wellesley Country (Mass.); The Country (Brookline, Mass.). Office: State St Boston Corp 225 Franklin St Boston MA 02101

MADDEN, RICHARD BLAINE, forest products executive, educator; b. Short Hills, N.J., Apr. 27, 1929; s. James L. and Irma (Twining) M.; m. Joan Fairbairn, May 24, 1958; children: John Richard, Lynn Marie, Kathryn Ann, Andrew Twining. B.S., Princeton U., 1951; J.D., U. Mich., 1956; M.B.A., NYU, 1959. Bar: Mich. 1956, N.Y. 1958. Gen. asst. treas.'s dept. Socony Mobil Oil Corp., N.Y.C., 1956-57; spl. asst. Socony Mobil Oil Corp., 1958-59, fin. rep., 1960; asst. to pres. Mobil Chem. Co.; also dir. Mobil Chems. Ltd. of Eng., 1960-63; exec. v.p., gen. mgr. Kordite Corp.; also v.p. Mobil Plastics, 1963-66; v.p. Mobil Chem. Co., N.Y.C., 1966-68; group v.p. Mobil Chem. Co., 1968-70; asst. treas. Mobil Oil Corp., 1970-71; chmn. Mobil Oil Estates Ltd., 1970-71; pres., chief exec. to chmn., chief exec. officer Potlatch Corp., San Francisco, 1971—; bd. dirs. Pacific Gas and Electric Co.; from lectr. to adj. assoc. prof. fin. NYU, 1960-63. Bd. dirs. Am. Paper Inst., Nat. Park Found.; trustee, exec. com. Am. Enterprise Inst.; bd. govs. San Francisco Symphony; bd. dirs. San Francisco Opera Assn. Lt. (j.g.) USNR, 1951-54. Mem. N.Y., Mich. bar assns. Roman Catholic. Clubs: University (N.Y.C.); Pacific Union (San Francisco), Bohemian (San Francisco); Lagunitas (Ross, Calif.); Metropolitan (Washington).

MADDEN, WALES HENDRIX, JR., lawyer; b. Amarillo, Tex., Sept. 1, 1927; s. Wales Hendrix and Kathryn (Nash) M.; m. Alma Faye Cowden, Nov. 8, 1952; children: Wales Hendrix III, Straughn. B.A., U. Tex., 1950, LL.B., 1952. Bar: Tex. 1952. Practiced in Amarillo; bd. dirs. First Nat. Bank of Amarillo, Mesa Ltd. Partnership, Nowlin Mtg. Co.; mem. Tex. Constnl. Revision Commn., 1973. Bd. regents Amarillo Coll., 1958-59, U. Tex., 1959-65; mem. Tex. Coll. and Univ. System Coordinating Bd., 1964-69, Amarillo Area Found., Cal Farley's Boys Ranch, Pres.'s Export Council, 1981; trustee Trinity U., San Antonio; mem. Select Com. Higher Edn., 1985, 87. Served with USNR. Named Outstanding Man of Amarillo, 1972; Disting. Alumnus U. Tex., 1979, U. Tex. Law Sch., 1986. Mem. ABA, Amarillo Bar Assn. (pres. 1956), Tex. Philos. Soc., Amarillo C. of C. (pres. 1968), State Bar Tex., State Jr. Bar Tex. (pres. 1956), Friar Soc., Phi Alpha Delta, Phi Delta Theta, Phi Eta Sigma, Pi Sigma Alpha. Presbyterian (elder). Home: 2701 Teckla St Amarillo TX 79106 Office: 712 W 9th St Amarillo TX 79101

MADDOX, RUSSELL HOWARD, pharmaceutical company executive; b. Atlanta, Dec. 31, 1940; s. Edward Quincy and Louise (Nort) M.; m. Martha Spink, June 24, 1960 (div. Jan. 1974); children: Russell Howard II, Robin Lynette; m. Susan Flynn, July 7, 1979; children: Kelley Lynn Laughlin, Leigh Ann Laughlin. With Russ Pharm, Inc., Birmingham, Ala. Mem. Vestavia Hills Zoning Bd., 1980-85; bd. dirs. Entrepreneurship Forum, Birmingham, 1986—, Birmingham Bus. Assistance Network, 1986—, Ala. Ind. Colls., 1987—; adv. bd. Sch. Pharmacy, Sanford U. Named Small Bus. Person of Yr., State of Ala., 1987, Birmingham C. of C., 1987. Mem. Riverchase Country Club, Shoal Creek Country Club, Masons. Republican. Presbyterian. Home: 147 Mountain Brook Park Dr Birmingham AL 35213 Office: Russ Pharm Inc 22 Inverness Ctr Pkwy Ste 400 Birmingham AL 35242

MADDOX, YVONNE TARLTON, medical communications company executive; b. Lubbock, Tex.; m. George Allman, Nov. 2, 1974. B.A., Okla. State U. Pres., World Health Info. Services, Inc., N.Y.C., 1970-83; v.p. Health Edn. Technologies, Inc. div. Batton, Barton, Durstine & Osborn, Inc., N.Y.C., 1984-86; pres. Internat. Communications in Medicine, Inc., N.Y.C., 1986—; v.p. S.E.R.A.D., Inc., San Francisco, 1988—. Mem. Pharm. Advt. Council, Am. Women in Radio and TV (past dir.). Home: 340 E 64th St New York NY 10021

MADERA, CORNELIUS J. J., JR., supermarket chain executive, lawyer; b. July 24, 1949; s. Cornelius J. Sr. and Adele (Dobrowolski) M.; m. Marjorie Jones, Aug. 24, 1974; children: Meghan, Caitlin, Morgan. AB, MIT, 1970, Brown U., 1971; JD, Boston U., 1974. Bar: N.J. 1974, Mass. 1974, N.Y. 1981. Assoc. Riker, Danzig, Scherer & Debevoise, Morristown, N.J., 1974-78; real estate atty. Gt. Atlantic and Pacific Tea Co., Montvale, N.J., 1978-79; gen. counsel Village Supermarket, Inc., Springfield, N.J., 1979-82; sr. v.p., gen. counsel Big V Supermarkets, Inc., Florida, N.Y., 1982—; instr. U. Shopping Ctrs., Atlanta, 1987; sec. N.J. Atty.'s Ethics Com., Morristown, 1976-78. Trustee Village Tuxedo park, N.Y., 1984—; dep. mayor Tuxedo Park; v.p. Tuxedo Park Sch. Mem. ABA, Fed. Bar Assn., N.Y. Bar Assn., N.J. Bar Assn., Mass. Bar Assn. Club: Tuxedo (Tuxedo Park). Home: Lorillard Rd Tuxedo Park NY 10987 Office: Big V Supermarkets Inc 176 N Main St Florida NY 10921

MADIGAN, JOHN WILLIAM, publishing executive; b. Chgo., June 7, 1937; s. Edward P. and Olive D. M.; m. Holly Williams, Nov. 24, 1962; children: Mark W., Griffith E., Melanie L. B.B.A., U. Mich., 1958, M.B.A., 1959. Fin. analyst Duff & Phelps, Chgo., 1960-62; audit mgr. Arthur Andersen & Co., Chgo., 1962-67; v.p. investment banking Paine, Webber, Jackson & Curtis, Chgo., 1967-69; v.p. corp. fin. Salomon Bros., Chgo., 1969-74; v.p., chief fin. officer, dir. Tribune Co., Chgo., 1975-81, exec. v.p., 1981-88; pres., chief exec. officer Chicago Tribune Co., 1988—. Trustee Rush-Presbyn.-St. Luke's Med. Center, Robert R. McCormick Charitable Trust, Ill. Inst. Tech.; mem. vis. com. Sch. Bus. Adminstrn. U. Mich., Med. Sch. Northwestern U. Served with USMC, 1959. Clubs: Tavern, Commonwealth, Chicago, Commercial, University, Indian Hill, U. Mich., Economic (Chgo.). Home: 435 N Michigan Chicago IL 60611 Office: Tribune Co 435 N Michigan Ave Chicago IL 60611

MADIGAN, JOSEPH EDWARD, restaurant executive; b. Bklyn., June 26, 1932; s. James Peter and Mary (Goldman) M.; m. Catherine Cashman, July 26, 1980; children: Kerri Ann, Kimberly Ann, Jeffrey Charles, Elizabeth Ann. BBA cum laude, Baruch Sch., CUNY, 1958; MBA, NYU, 1963. Adminstrv. asst. Asso. Metals & Minerals Corp., 1961-63; fin. analyst, fgn. exch. trader, corp. portfolio trader AMAX, Inc., 1963-65; mgr. corp. portfolio, dir. cash mgmt., asst. treas. TWA, Inc., 1965-68; treas. Borden, Inc., 1968-76, v.p., treas., 1976-80; exec. v.p., chief fin. officer Wendy's Internat., Inc., Dublin, Ohio, 1980-87; dir. Wendy's Internat., Inc., 1981-88; pvt. corp. fin. cons. 1977; trustee NCC Funds; corp. fin. cons. Served with USN, 1951-55. Mem. Fin. Execs. Inst. (bd. dir. Cen. Ohio chpt.), Assn. Corp. Growth, Baruch Sch.-CUNY Alumni Assn., NYU Alumni Assn., Nat. Investor Rels. Inst., NYU Finance Club, Treas. Club, Beta Gamma Sigma, NYU Club, Country At Muirfield Coub, Capital Club (Columbus, Ohio). Republican. Roman Catholic. Home: 4341 Shelbourne Ln Columbus OH 43220

MADISON, CATHERINE BOYSEN, magazine editor, communications executive; b. Tacoma, Oct. 7, 1949; d. Alexander M. and Margaret E. (Levan) Boysen; m. James D. Madison, Mar. 28, 1970 (div. Mar. 1988); children: Kristin, Erika. BA in Journalism summa cum laude, U. Minn., 1973. Asst. editor St Anthony Park Bugle newspaper, St. Paul, 1977-81; editor, pub. Format mag., Mpls., 1981-84; exec. dir. Advt. Fedn. Minn., 1981-84; editor Am. Advt. mag., Washington, 1984-88; communications dir. Carmichael Lynch, Mpls., 1984-88; sr. editor Adweek mag., 1988—. Mem. mktg. com. Women's Intercoll. Athletics, Mpls., 1987—. Recipient 1st Place prize for publs. Am. Advt. Fedn., 1983, 84; named one of Outstanding Young Women Am., 1982. Mem. Advt. Fed. Minn. (com. chmn. 1987-88, Paul Foss award 1985), Am. Assn. Advt. Agencies (mem. pub. rels. com.), Phi Beta Kappa, Kappa Tau Alpha. Office: Adweek 10 S 5th St #700 Minneapolis MN 55402

MADISON, T. JEROME, business executive; b. N.Y.C., June 2, 1940; s. Theodore H. and Eleanor E. (Eveland) M.; m. Marsha A. Heeb, Sept. 26, 1964; children: Jill, Kim, Ryan. BS, U. Pa., 1962; MBA, Monmouth Coll., 1975. CPA, N.J. Mgr., Peat, Marwick, Mitchell & Co., Newark and Princeton, N.J., 1970-75; mgr. Abbott Labs., North Chicago, Ill., 1976; chief internal auditor Rorer Group, Inc., Fort Washington, Pa., 1977-78, corp. controller, 1979-82; v.p. fin. Cytogen Corp., Princeton, N.J., 1982-86; pres., dir. Outwater & Wells Ventures, Inc., 1981-85, Atlantic Capital Resources Group, Inc., 1985-87, Founders Court Investors Inc., Princeton, N.J., 1986—; chmn., chief exec. officer Pilling Co., 1986—; chmn. Capital Controls Corp, 1987—; chmn. MEECO Industries, Inc., 1988—, Prince Gardner, Inc., 1989—; dir., chmn. fin. com. Carrier Found.; dir. Dycast, Inc., Pendot Holdings, Inc. Served with USN, 1962-66. Mem. Delaware Valley Venture Group, Fin. Execs. Inst., Am. Inst. CPA's. Lodge: Rotary. Office: Founders Ct Investors Inc 92 Nassau St Princeton NJ 08542

MADOLE, DONALD WILSON, lawyer; b. Elkhart, Kans., July 14, 1932. Student Kans. State Tchrs. Coll., 1950-51; B.S., U. Denver, 1959, J.D., 1959. Bar: Colo. 1960, U.S. Dist. Ct. Colo. 1960, U.S. Ct. Appeals (10th cir.) 1960, D.C. 1971, U.S. Supreme Ct. 1972, U.S. Ct. Appeals (1st cir.) 1976, U.S. Ct. Appeals (5th cir.) 1977, U.S. Ct. Appeals (6th cir.) 1982, U.S. Ct. Appeals (7th and 9th cirs.) 1975, U.S. Ct. Appeals (11th cir.) 1981. V.p. Mountain Aviation Corp., Denver, 1958-59; trial atty. FAA, Washington, 1960-62; sr. warranty adminstr. Am. Airlines, Tulsa, 1962-63; chief hearing and reports div., atty. adviser CAB, Washington, 1963-66; ptnr. Speiser, Krause & Madole, Washington, 1966—; pres. Aerial Application Corp., Burlingame, Calif., 1968-69; v.p., dir. Environ. Power Ltd., Pitts., 1972—; bd. dirs. Equipment Leasing Co., San Antonio, Unitrade Ltd., Washington, Bus. Ins. Mgmt. Inc., Bethesda, Md., Entertainment Capitol Corp., N.Y.C.; gen. counsel Nat. Aviation Club, 1978-80, Internat. Soc. Air Safety Investigators, 1977—; mem. blue ribbon panel on airworthiness Nat. Acad. Sci., 1980; adviser U.S. Govt. del. Internat. Civil Aviation Orgn., 1965; U.S. Govt. rep. Aircraft Inquiry, Montreal, P.Q., Can., 1964. Author: Textbook of Aviation Statutes and Regulations, 1963; International Aspects of Aircraft Accidents, 1963; CAB, Aircraft Accident Investigation, 1964. Mem. chancellor's soc. U. Denver, 1982—. Served to comdr. USNR, 1953-57. Recipient Outstanding Performance award FAA, 1961; Meritorious Achievement award Am. Airlines, 1962; Outstanding Performance awards CAB, 1963-65; Fed. Govt. Outstanding Pub. Service award Jump-Meml. Found., 1966. Fellow Internat. Acad. Trial Lawyers; mem. ABA, Colo. Bar Assn., Fed. Bar Assn., D.C. Bar Assn., Assn. Trial Lawyers Am., Lawyer-Pilots Assn., Am. Law Inst., Phi Delta Phi, Phi Mu Alpha. Clubs: Congl. Country, Nat. Aviation, Nat. Press. Home: 2800 Jenifer St NW Washington DC 20015 Office: 1216 16th St NW Washington DC 20036

MADRID, DONNA KAY, personnel executive; b. Mt. Ayr, Iowa, May 29, 1937; d. Clete Hewitt and Murice Marjorie (Cornwall) Madison; married; children: Murice Elaina Scanlon, Cathy Lynne Carlson. AA, Interior Designers Guild, Sherman Oaks, Calif., 1987. Owner Home Cleaning Service, Canoga Park, Calif., 1970-79; designer Beam Interiors, Northridge, Calif., 1979-80; owner, mgr. Innovative Interiors, Chatsworth, Calif., 1980-81; office mgr. Jardine Emett & Chandler, Los Angeles, 1981—, asst. v.p., 1988—. Mem. Personnel and Indsl. Rels. Assn., NAFE, Women Referral Svc. Office: Jardine Emett & Chandler Los Angeles Inc Ins Brokers 11835 W Olympic Blvd Los Angeles CA 90021

MADSEN, RODNEY KENT, manufacturing executive, mechanical engineer; b. Aberdeen, S.D., Mar. 29, 1935; s. Emil and Phyllis Marie (Muller) M.; m. Polly Ann Downs, Feb. 2, 1958; children: Kent, Matthew. BS in Mech. Engring., U. Nebr., 1958; MS in Mech. Engring., U. Pa., 1966. Registered profl. engr., Pa., Ca. Engring. supr. Honeywell, Ft. Washington, Pa., 1961-66; v.p. engring. Emerson Elect. div. Brooks Instrument, Hatfield, Pa., 1966-75; v.p., gen. mgr. Varec div. Brooks Instrument, Garden Grove, Calif., 1975-80; pres., chief exec. officer Gary Safe Co., Industry, Calif., 1980-82; v.p. CETEC Corp., El Monte, Calif., 1982—. Lt. USN, 1958-61. Mem. Pi Tau Sigma, Sigma Tau. Republican. Presbyterian. Office: CETEC Corp 9900 Baldwin Pl El Monte CA 91731

MAEDA, J. A., data processing executive; b. Mansfield, Ohio, Aug. 24, 1940; d. James Shunso and Doris Lucille (Moore) M.; m. Robert Lee Hayes (div. May 1970); 1 child, Brian Sentaro Hayes. BS in Math., Purdue U., 1962, postgrad., 1962-63; postgrad., Calif. State U., Northridge, 1968-75; cert. profl. designation in tech. of computer operating systems and tech. of info. processing, UCLA, 1971. Cons., rsch. asst. computer ctr. Purdue U., West Lafayette, Ind., 1962-63; computer operator, sr. tab operator, mem. faculty Calif. State U., Northridge, 1969, programmer cons., tech. asst. II, 1969-70, supr. acad. applicatons, EDP supr. II, 1970-72, project tech. support coord. programmer II, office of the chancellor, 1972-73, tech. support coord. statewide timesharing tech. support, programmer II, 1973-74, acad. coord., tech. support coord. instrn., computer cons. III, 1974-83; coord. user svcs. info. ctr., mem. tech. staff IV CADAM INC subs. Lockheed Corp., Burbank, Calif., 1983-86, coord. end user svcs., tech. specialist computing dept., 1986-87; v.p., bd. dirs. Rainbow Computing, Inc., Northridge, 1976-85; pres. Akiko Maeda Tech./Design Cons., Northridge, 1980—; mktg. mgr. thaumaturge Taro Quipu Tech./Design Cons., Northridge, 1987—; tech. cons. Digital Computer Cons., Chatsworth Calif., 1988; cons. computer tech., fin. and bus. mgmt., systems integration, 1988—. Author 100 user publs., 1969-83, 98 computer user publs., 1983-87, basic computer programming language; contbr. articles and papers and photos to profl. jours. Mem. IEEE, SHARE, Digital Equipment Computer Users Soc. (author papers and presentations 1977-81, ednl. spl. interest group 1977-83, steering com. Resource Sharing Timesharing System/Extended (RSTS/E), 1979-82). Home: 18257 Shepley Pl Northridge CA 91326

MAFFIA, PAUL MARIE, internal controls and finance consultant; b. Chgo., July 14, 1936; s. Anthony and Clara (Leo) M.; m. Mary Ellen McLane, June 25, 1960; children: Timothy, Felicia. BS in Commerce, Loyola U., Chgo., 1958; MBA, U. Wash., 1974. Cert. internal auditor, cert. fin. planner. Sales clk. Montgomery Ward and Co., Chgo., 1955-58; internal auditor The Boeing Co., Seattle, 1962-70; state examiner Office of State Auditor, Olympia, Wash., 1975-81; pres. PM-LA Services, Bainbridge Island, Wash., 1981—; instr. Cogswell Coll. N., Seattle, 1980-81, City U., 1988—. Served to 1st lt. U.S. Army, 1958-62. Recipient Silver medal Chgo. Tribune, 1956, 58. Mem. Assn. MBA Execs., Inst. Cert. Fin. Planners (cert.), Inst. Internal Auditors (cert., gov., CIA chmn., audit chmn., bd. dirs. Puget Sound chpt. 1982—), Internat. Assn. Fin. Planners., Internat. Assn. Cert. Fin. Planners. Roman Catholic. Office: PM-1A Svcs 4574 Drystal Springs Dr NE Bainbridge Island WA 98110

MAFFIE, MICHAEL OTIS, utility executive; b. Los Angeles, Jan. 26, 1948; s. Cornelius Michael and Elaine Minie (Wack) M.; m. Nickie Neville, Apr. 10, 1971; children—Wendy, Zachary. B.S. in Acctg, U. So. Calif., 1969, M.B.A. in Fin, 1970. Audit mgr. Arthur Andersen & Co., C.P.A.s, Los Angeles, 1970-78; exec. v.p. S.W. Gas Corp., Las Vegas, 1978—.

MAGARY, ALAN BRUCE (SKY), airline company executive; b. Chgo., Sept. 20, 1942; m. Susan Bane; children—Alexander, Amanda, Andrew. B.A. with honors in Econs., Yale U., 1963; M.B.A., Harvard U., 1967. Various positions Chessie System, Balt., 1963-65; with Pan Am., N.Y.C., 1967-72, staff v.p., 1972-75; mng. dir. Pan Am South Pacific, Sydney, Australia, 1975-77; v.p. Pan Am., N.Y.C., 1977-82; pres. Hyatt Chain Services Ltd., Hong Kong, 1983-84; v.p. Hyatt Internat. Corp., Chgo., 1982-84; sr. v.p. mktg. Republic Airlines, Mpls., 1984-86; exec. v.p. mktg. Northwest Airlines, St. Paul, 1986—; bd. dirs. MLT Vacations, Inc., Minnetonka, Minn., PARS, Kansas City, Mo. Office: NW Airlines Inc Mpls-St Paul Internat Airport Saint Paul MN 55111

MAGDALENSKI, VIRGINIA REGINA, association administrator; b. Boston, Dec. 22, 1922; d. Lawrence and Mary Katherine (Zaik) Malcik; m. Stanley Martin Magdalenski, Nov. 8, 1941; children: Sandra Magdalenski Pozzetta, Lawrence M., Margaret Magdalenski Tringali. Grad., Pittsfield (Mass.) High Sch., 1940. Clk. GE Co., Pittsfield, 1939-41; Clk. Assn. Marian Helpers, Stockbridge, Mass., 1957-58, supr. data entry, data processing, 1958-76, unit mgr., 1976-84, asst. dir., 1984—. Pres. Pittsfield area Campfire Orgn., 1937, Housatonic (Mass.) PTA, 1950. Republican. Roman Catholic. Office: Assn Marian Helpers Eden Hill Stockbridge MA 01263

MAGEE, CATHERINE LOUISE, marketing executive; b. Richmond, Va., July 13, 1954; d. Stanley Earl and Louise (Allman) Magee. B.A. in History, Westhampton Coll., 1976. Govt. bond trader Wheat First Securities Inc., Richmond, Va., 1977-78; mcpl. bond retail trader Wheat First Securities, 1978-80; mcpl. bond retail sales Dean Witter Reynolds, Inc., N.Y.C., 1980-81; dir. retail mcpl. bond mktg. Moseley, Hallgarten, Estabrook & Weeden Inc., N.Y.C., 1981-82; account exec. Dean Witter Reynolds, Inc., Richmond, Va., 1984; mktg. rep. HCW, Inc., Boston, 1985; mktg. rep. Liberty Securities Corp., Boston, 1986, mktg. mgr. Liberty Real Estate Corp., 1986-88; investment cons. Inland Securities Corp, Clearwater, Fla., 1988—; key career cons. U. Richmond, Va., 1978-80. Recipient Key award, U. Richmond, 1980. Mem. Nat. Assn. Securities Dealers, Nat. Honor Soc., Phi Alpha Theta. Republican. Baptist. Clubs: Richmond Municipal Bond, Municipal Bond of N.Y. Avocations: photography; painting; jazz dance; racquetball; tennis. Home: 3760 Preakness Pl Apt 1807 Palm Harbor FL 34684 Office: Inland Securities Corp 2535 Landmark Dr Ste 103 Clearwater FL 34621

MAGEE, JOHN FRANCIS, research company executive; b. Bangor, Maine, Dec. 3, 1926; s. John Henry and Marie (Frawley) M.; m. Dorothy Elma Hundley, Nov. 19, 1949; children: Catherine Anne, John Hundley, Andrew Stephen. AB, Bowdoin Coll., 1947; MS, U. Maine, 1952; MBA, Harvard U., 1948. With Arthur D. Little, Inc., Cambridge, Mass., 1950—, v.p., 1961-72, pres., 1972-86, chief exec. officer, 1974-88, chmn., 1986—, also dir.; dir. John Hancock Mut. Life Ins. Co., Boston, Houghton-Mifflin Co., Boston, Bank of New Eng. Corp., Boston. Author: Physical Distribution Systems, 1967, Industrial Logistics: Analysis and Management of Physical Supply and Distribution Systems, 1968, (with D. M. Boodman) Production Planning and Inventory Control, 1968; (with W. Capacino and W. Rosenfield) Modern Logistics Management, 1985. Trustee New Eng. Aquarium, Boston, Univ. Med. Center, U.S.S. Constitution Mus., Bowdoin Coll., Woods Hole Oceanographic Instn. Served with USNR, 1944-46. Mem. Ops. Research Soc. Am. (pres. 1966-67), Inst. Mgmt. Scis. (pres. 1971-72), Phi Beta Kappa, Phi Kappa Psi. Clubs: Concord (Mass.) Country (gov. 1971-74); The Country (Brookline, Mass.); Somerset (Boston). Office: Arthur D Little Inc 25 Acorn Pk Cambridge MA 02140

MAGEE, WILLIAM H., chemical company executive; b. Bayonne, N.J., Feb. 5, 1938; s. William Henry and Vera (Cavanaugh) M.; m. Helmtrud Maria Fellermayer, Jan. 21, 1961 (div. Dec. 1980); children: Christina, Thomas, Robert; m. Linda Louise Warren, Feb. 14, 1981. BS, St. Peter's Coll., Jersey City, 1967. Adminstrv. mgr. ARCO Chem. Co., Chgo., 1968-70; mgr. performance reporting and capital ARCO Petroleum Products, N.Y.C., 1970-72; mgr. ops. analysis ARCO Petroleum Products, Los Angeles, 1973, controller, 1973-76, mgr. planning and analysis, 1976-77, v.p. planning and control, 1977-81; v.p., controller Atlantic Richfield Co., Los Angeles, 1981-87; sr. v.p., chief fin. officer Arco Chem. Co., Newtown Sq., Pa., 1987—; also bd. dirs. Arco Chem. Co. Mem. Pres.'s adv. bd. Calif. State U., Los Angeles, 1982-87; pres., chmn. bd. dirs. Los Angeles Internat. Film Exposition, 1983—; chmn. Child Care Study program United Way, Los Angeles, 1982-83. Served with U.S. Army, 1958-60. Mem. Am. Petroleum Inst., Fin. Execs. Inst. Club: University (Los Angeles). Office: ARCO Chem Co 3801 W Chester Pike Newtown Square PA 19073

MAGENHEIMER, FRED EDWARD, JR., industrial fabric company executive; b. Bklyn., Nov. 29, 1939; s. Fred. E. Sr. and Mary M. (Hottenroth) M.; m. Paula Slawter, Jan. 15, 1964; children: Richard, Jeffrey. BA, Spring Hill Coll., 1961. Sales trainee Internat. Paper Co., N.Y.C., 1964-65; salesman USI Film Products, Phila. and San Francisco, 1965-67; mgr. regional sales USI Film Products, N.Y.C., 1967-70; salesman Rexham Corp., N.Y.C., 1970-74; mgr. nat. sales Herculite Products Inc., N.Y.C., 1974-78, v.p. sales, 1978-82, exec. v.p., 1982-85, pres., 1985—; v.p., bd. dirs. Health-Chem Corp., N.Y.C. Advisor Friends of Arts, 1984—. 1st lt. U.S. Army, 1962-64, Korea. Mem. Port Washington Homeowners Assn. (pres. 1974), Indsl. Fabrics Assn. (bd. dirs. 1988—), Internat. Sleep Products Assn. (suppliers council 1985—, bd. dirs. 1988—), U.S. Indsl. Fabric Inst. (bd. dirs.). Roman Catholic. Home: 15A Hillside Ave Port Washington NY 11050 Office: Herculite Products Inc 1107 Broadway New York NY 10010

MAGGARD, WOODROW WILSON, JR., management consultant; b. Quincy, Ill., Feb. 5, 1947; s. Woodrow Wilson and Claire Lorene (Lyons) M.; BA, Brigham Young U., 1971; MPA, Consortium of Calif. State U., 1978; m. Linda Margaret Davis, Dec. 30, 1967; children: Jared Isaac, Erin Leigh-Taylor, Solveig Kirsten, Christian Heinrich, Anica May, Kayla Margaret. Div. mgr. Sears, Roebuck & Co., Provo, Utah and Ventura, Calif., 1967-74; adminstrv. officer County of Ventura (Calif.), 1974-78; founding ptnr. Maggard, Maughan, Gress and Assocs., Ventura, 1976-83; founder Intermountain Property Services, Ventura, 1974—; v.p. econ./bus. devel. Dineh Coops., Inc., Chinle, Navaho Nation, Ariz., 1978-80; dir. econ. devel. City of Scottsdale (Ariz.), 1980-81; exec. dir., chief exec. officer Fairbanks Devel. Auth. (Alaska), 1981-87; co-founder Pacific Rim Inst., 1984—; founder Maggard & Maggard, Fairbanks, 1983—; exec. dir., chief exec. officer Orange County R & D Authority, Cen. Fla. Rsch. Park, Orlando, 1988—; instr. real estate econs./appraisal Oxnard (Calif.) Coll., 1975-78; instr. bus. Utah Tech. Coll., Provo, 1978; Active Boy Scouts Am.; high priest Ch. of LDS; econ. dir. City of Dover, N.H., 1988; bd. dirs. Dover Indsl. Devel. Authority. Recipient Nat. Merit award for Excellence in comml. devel., 1987, Dixwell Pierce award, 1975, Alaska Environ. Enhancement award, 1983; cert. rev. appraiser; registered mortgage underwriter. Mem. Am. Soc. Public Adminstrn., Internat. Right-of-Way Assn. (internat. property mgmt. com.), Nat. Assn. Rev. Appraisers and Mortgage Underwriters (sr.), Nat. Council on Urban Econ. Devel., Urban Land Inst., Acad. Polit. Sci., United Indian Planners., Phi Alpha Theta, Rotary. Democrat. Contbr. articles to profl. jours. Home: 804 Mimosa Dr Altamonte Springs FL 32714 Office: Orange County R & D Authority 12424 Research Pkwy Ste 100 Orlando FL 32826

MAGID, MARGO, financial executive; b. Rye, N.Y., May 21, 1947; d. Meyer and Helaine (Goldberg) M.; m. Gerard M. McCaffery, Oct. 13, 1985. BA, Goucher Coll., 1969; MA, Johns Hopkins U., 1970; MSW, SUNY-Stonybrook, 1974. Dir. office of program devel. Health, Edn., and Welfare Region II, 1974-76; dir. office program, policy devel. Human Resources Adminstrn., N.Y.C., 1976-81; v.p., dir. strategic planning, info. group Citicorp, 1981-88; exec. v.p. Benton Internat. Fin. Svcs. Consulting, N.Y.C., 1988—; cons. grants Ford Found., Rand Corp., pvt. agys., 1974-76. Office: Benton Internat 747 3d Ave New York NY 10017

MAGINNIS, NINAMARY BUBA, journalist, promotional writer; b. Peabody, Mass., Nov. 3, 1956; d. Karol John and Nina Therese (Rechetnuck) Buba; m. Thomas Maginnis, May 10, 1986; 1 child, Karol John. BA in Journalism and English, U. Mass., 1979; MS in Journalism, Boston U., 1982. Journalist Salem (Mass.) Evening News, 1978-79, Lawrence Eagle-Tribune, North Andover, Mass., 1979-81; prin. writer Wang Labs., Inc., Lowell, Mass., 1981-83; mktg. specialist Wang Labs., Inc., Lowell, 1983; promotional writer Digital Equipment Corp., Maynard, Mass., 1984-86; sr. writer Computerworld, Framingham, Mass., 1986-87; freelance journalist, promotional writer Webster, Mass., 1987—; media cons. Digital Equipment Corp., Maynard, 1987—; police reporter Worcester (Mass.) Telegram. Hotline vol. Samaritans, Lawrence, Mass., 1984; pub. relations cons. Little Bros. of the Elderly, Boston, 1986. Mem. Kappa Kappa Gamma. Roman Catholic.

MAGNER, FREDRIC MICHAEL, financial services executive; b. June 27, 1950; m. Rachel Harris, May 14, 1972. B.A. in Internat. Studies, U. S.C., 1971, M.B.A., 1972; M.Accountancy, U. So. Calif., 1976. Cert. in mgmt. acctg. Mktg. rep. IBM, L.A., 1976-79; v.p. First Interstate Services Co., El Segundo, Calif., 1979-82, First Interstate Bancorp, Los Angeles, 1982-83; sr. v.p. First Interstate System, L.A., 1983-86, First Interstate Bancorp, L.A., 1986— . Served to capt. USAF, 1973-76. Home: 2200 Pine Ave Manhattan Beach CA 90266 Office: First Interstate Bancorp PO Box 54068 Los Angeles CA 90054

MAGNER, RACHEL HARRIS, banker; b. Lamar, S.C., Aug. 5, 1951; d. Garner Greer and Catherine Alice (Cloaninger) Harris; B.S. in Fin., U. S.C., 1972; postgrad. UCLA, 1974, Calif. State U., 1975; m. Fredric Michael Magner, May 14, 1972. Mgmt. trainee Union Bank, Los Angeles, 1972-75, comml. loan officer, 1975-77; asst. v.p. comml. fin. Crocker Bank, Los Angeles, 1978, asst. v.p., factoring account exec. subs. Crocker United Factors, Inc., 1978-81; v.p. comml. services div. Crocker Bank, 1981-82, v.p., sr. account mgr. bus. banking div., 1982-83; v.p. corporate banking Office of Pres., Sumitomo Bank Calif., 1983—. Home: 2200 Pine Ave Manhattan Beach CA 90266 Office: Sumitomo Bank of Calif 101 S San Pedro Ste 500 Los Angeles CA 90012

MAGNESS, BOB JOHN, telecommunications executive; b. Clinton, Okla., 1924. Attended, South Western State Coll. Chmn. Tele-Communications, Inc., Denver. Office: Tele-Communications Inc 4643 S Ulster St #360 Denver CO 80237-2863

MAGOUIRK, ROBERT D., electrical engineering company executive; b. Shawmut, Ala., Feb. 12, 1930; s. Rance O. and Annie M. (Crowdee) M.; m. Patricia Williams, Feb. 21, 1981; 1 child, Sara Louise. BSEE, U. Alaska, 1967. Jr. engr. Ga. Power Co., Atlanta, 1971-74; sr. engr. Ebasco, N.Y.C., 1974-75; elec. engr. United Engrs. and Constructors, Phila., 1975-78, system project engr., 1980-82; project engr. in Indonesia. Gibbs/Hill, N.Y.C., 1978-80; system project engr. Impell Corp., Walnut Creek, Iowa, 1983-84; sr. engr. Iowa Electric Co., Cedar Rapids, 1983-84; pres. Midwest Engring. Cons., Jacksonville, N.C., 1988—. With USAF, 1947-69, Korea. Mem. IEEE, Am. Nuclear Soc. Home: 2527 Country Club Rd Jacksonville NC 28540 Office: Midwest Engring Cons 103 El Dorado Ct Jacksonville NC 28540

MAGOWAN, PETER ALDEN, grocery chain executive; b. N.Y.C., Apr. 5, 1942; s. Robert Anderson and Doris (Merrill) M.; m. Jill Tarlau (div. July 1982; children—Kimberley, Margot, Hilary; m. Deborah Johnston, Aug. 14, 1982. B.A., Stanford U.; M.A., Oxford U., Eng.; postgrad., Johns Hopkins U. Store mgr. Safeway Stores Inc., Washington, 1968-70; dist. mgr. Safeway Stores Inc., Houston, 1970-71; retail ops. mgr. Safeway Stores Inc., Phoenix, 1971-72; div. mgr. Safeway Stores Inc., Tulsa, 1973-76; mgr. internat. div. Safeway Stores Inc., Toronto, Ont., Can., 1976-78; mgr. western region Safeway Stores Inc., San Francisco, 1978-79; chmn. bd., chief exec. officer Safeway Stores Inc., Oakland, Calif., 1980—; also pres. Safeway Stores Inc., Oakland, 1988—; bd. dirs. Pacific Gas and Electric, Chrysler Corp., Vons Cos. Inc. Mem. U.S. C. of C., Food Mktg. Inst. (bd. dirs.), Bus. Roundtable. Office: Safeway Stores Inc 201 4th St Oakland CA 94660 *

MAGUINA, JAIME JOHN, marketing communications consultant; b. Lima, Peru, Aug. 30, 1944; came to U.S., 1969; s. Juan Maguina and Nicolasa (Yolanda) Salinas; m. Joan Flanagan, Feb. 8, 1974; 1 child, Jennifer. BBA, Villareal Nat. U., 1965; MBA, U. Lima, 1968. Dir. tour devel. EST Travel, N.Y.C., 1970-76; regional dir. Thompson Travel Mktg./Am. Express Destination Svcs., N.Y.C., 1976-81; sr. v.p. mktg. and sales Melia Internat. Travel Mgmt. Co., N.Y.C., 1982-86; pres., chief exec. officer J.J. Maguina and Assocs., Pearl River, N.Y., 1987—; exec. dir. PBI meetings and Incentives, River Vale, N.J., 1986-87. Mem. Soc. Assn. Execs., Travel and Tourism Rsch. Assn., Am. Mktg. Assn., Soc. of Incentive Travel Execs. Republican. Roman Catholic. Office: JJ Maguina & Assocs 367 Laurel Rd Pearl River NY 10965

MAGUIRE, JOHN PATRICK, financial executive; b. Waltham, Mass., Feb. 19, 1940; s. John Joseph and Ellen (Gavin) M.; m. Jean A. Lifrieri, Sept. 11, 1965; children: Diane, Linda. BBA, Boston Coll., 1961; MBA, Northeastern U., 1968. Cost acct. Carter Ink Co., Cambridge, Mass., 1962-72; controller Nashua (N.H.) Corp., 1972-82, regional controller, 1982-84; dir. fin., officer Costello, Lomasney & de Napoli, Inc., Manchester, N.H., 1986—. Mem. council parish St. John Neumann, Merrimack, N.H. Served with USCGR, 1961-69. Mem. Fin. Execs. Inst., Boston Coll. Club N.H. Home: 21 Fletcher Ln Hollis NH 03049 Office: Costello Lomasney & de Napoli Inc 540 N Commercial St Manchester NH 03101

MAGUIRE, ROBERT EDWARD, public utility executive; b. Somerville, Mass., Jan. 25, 1928; s. Hugh Edward and Alice Theresa (Garrity) M.; m. Leona Rosemarie Beaulieu, June 21, 1952; children—Lynne Marie, Steven Francis, Judith Anne, David Robert. B.S. in Chem. Engring., Northeastern U., 1950, B.B.A. in Engring. and Mgmt., 1953. Vice pres., mgr. Lawrence Gas Co., Mass., 1960-68; vice pres., mgr. Mystic Valley Gas Co., Malden, Mass., 1968-70; v.p., regional exec. Mass. Electric Co., North Andover, 1970-71; v.p. New Eng. Power Service Co., Westboro, Mass., 1971-72, New Eng. Electric System, Westboro, Mass., 1972-75; exec. v.p., trustee Eastern Utilities Assocs., Boston, 1975—; exec. v.p., dir. EUA Service Corp., Boston, 1975—, Montaup Electric Co., Somerset, Mass., 1975—, EUA Power Corp., 1987—, EUA Cogenex Corp., 1987—; vice chmn., dir. Eastern Edison Co., Brockton, Mass., 1975—, Blackstone Valley Electric Co., Lincoln, R.I., 1975—. Contbr. to Gas mag., 1959. Vice chmn. Greater Lawrence United Fund Budget Com., 1967; treas., dir. ARC, Lawrence, 1966; trustee Essex-Broadway Savs. Bank, Lawrence, 1966-78; pres., dir. Greater Lawrence C. of C., 1962-64. Recipient Paul Revere Leadership medal Boston C. of C., 1963. Roman Catholic. Club: Lanam (Andover, Mass.). Home: 22 Ivy Ln Andover MA 01810 Office: Ea Utilities Assocs 1 Liberty Sq PO Box 2333 Boston MA 02107

MAGUIRE-KRUPP, MARJORIE ANNE, corporate executive, developer; b. Stamford, Conn., Apr. 29, 1955; d. Walter Reeves and Jean Elisabeth (Cook) M.; m. Joseph Michael Krupp, Jr., Nov. 26, 1983; children: Parnell Joseph Maguire Krupp; stepchildren: Theresa Margaret, Donna Marie, Maura Elizabeth. BA in Acctg. cum laude, Franklin and Marshall Coll., 1977; MBA in Fin. with honors, NYU, 1983, cert. in real estate, 1986; cert. in French, U. Strasbourg, France, 1971. CPA, Conn.; lic. real estate sales agt., N.J. Supervisory auditor Arthur Young & Co., Stamford, 1976-80; mgr. fin. planning Combustion Engring., Stamford, 1980-84; asst. v.p., mgr. fin. planning and analysis Kidder Peabody & Co., N.Y.C., 1984-87; pres. Parnell Devel. Corp., 1987—; v.p. fin. Jeremiah Devel. Co., 1987-89; fin. cons. to brokerage industry, 1988—; prin., v.p. Port Liberte Marina Corp., 1989—. Advisor Jr. Achievement, Stamford, 1979-80; mem. Met. Opera Guild, N.Y.C., 1985-89, Met. Mus. Art, N.Y.C., 1983—, Mus. Modern Art, N.Y.C., 1983—; treas., bd. dir. Cliffhouse Condo Assn., Cliffside Park, N.J., 1983-85. Mem. Am. Inst. CPA's, NAFE, Stamford Jaycee Women Club (pres. 1980-81, chmn. bd. 1981-82, Stamford Disting. Svc. award, Outstanding Young Woman of Yr. award, 1980), Phi Beta Kappa (honor soc.), Beta Gamma Sigma (bus. honor soc.). Republican. Presbyterian. Avocations: travel, skiing, sailing, gourmet cooking, piano. Home: 107 Shearwater Ct Port Liberte NJ 07305

MAHADEVA, MANORANJAN, controller; b. Colombo, Sri Lanka, Feb. 12, 1955; came to U.S., 1977; s. Kandiah and Rupavathy (Ponniah) M.; m. Donna Sue Martin, May 12, 1986; 1 child, Danielle. BBA, U. Tex., 1981; MBA, N. Tex. State U., 1985. Asst. contr. Presbyn. Village North, Dallas, 1981-84; chief fin. officer Dallas Meml. Hosp., 1984-86; contr. Associated Orthopedics & Sports Medicine, Plano, Tex., 1986—; gen. mgr. Yogurt North Metroplex, Inc., Plano, 1987—; chief fin. officer Access Med. Supply, Inc., 1988—; bd. dirs. Gibraltar Mgmt. Enterprises, Dallas, 1982—. Presdl. scholar Wayne (Nebr.) State U., 1977-78. Mem. Nat. Assn. Accts. (bd. dirs. N. Dallas chpt. 1985, 86), Am. Hosp. Assn., Nat. Restaurant Assn., Internat. Students Assn., Plano C. of C., McKinney C. of C., Dallas C. of C., Lions, Delta Sigma Pi. Home: 3313 Claymore Dr Plano TX 75075 Office: Associated Orthopedics & Sports Medicine 3801 W 15th St Bldg 2 Ste 350 Plano TX 75075

MAHALIK, PAUL YASUNAS, landscape architect; b. Bridgeport, Conn., Jan. 20, 1956; s. John and Ann (Yasunas) M. BS in Landscape Architecture, U. Conn., 1977, Sorbonne, Paris, 1979. Project supr. Environ. Industries, El Cajon, Calif., 1979-81; project architect Ralph Stone & Assocs., Solana Beach, Calif., 1981-83; landscape architect PYM Assocs., Del Mar, Calif., 1983—; asst. Robert Irwin Art, San Diego, 1985—. Mem. San Diego County Pub. Arts Bd., 1981—, Balboa Park Task Force, San Diego, 1982—. Mem. Am. Soc. Landscape Architects, Am. Assn. Botanical Gardens and Arboretums, Internat. Palm Soc. (bd. dirs. 1989). Home and Office: PYM Assocs 740 Crest Rd Del Mar CA 92014

MAHAN, (DANIEL) DULANY, JR., lawyer, real estate developer; b. Hannibal, Mo., Dec. 22, 1914; s. D. Dulany and Sarah (Marshall) M.; m. Eleanor F. Bethea, Sept. 14, 1948 (div. 1953). AB, U. Mo., Columbia; J.D., Harvard U., 1940. Assoc., Office of George M. Clark, N.Y.C., 1940-42; asst. atty. FTC, Washington, 1948-51; assoc. Adams & James, N.Y.C., 1951-68; assoc. Kurnick & Hackman, N.Y.C., 1968—; ptnr. Tall Pines Estates Devel., Jacksonville, Fla., 1971—; atty., prin. Magnolia Grove Real Estate Devel., Dunedin, Fla., 1976—. Served with U.S. Army, 1942-46. Mem. ABA, Internat. Bar Assn., World Assn. Lawyers, N.Y. Bar Assn., Fed. Bar Assn. Republican. Clubs: Harvard (N.Y.C.); Nat. Lawyers (Washington). Home: 98 Ralph Ave White Plains NY 10606 Office: 660 Madison Ave New York NY 10021

MAHANES, DAVID JAMES, JR., distillery executive; b. Lexington, Ky., June 19, 1923; s. David James and Ethel (Brock) M.; m. Dorothy Jean Richardson, Oct. 28, 1950; 1 son, David James III. B.S., U. Ky., 1947; M.B.A., Harvard U., 1950. Regional mgr. Jack Daniel Distillery, Nashville, 1960-65, v.p., 1965-70, sr. v.p., 1970-71, exec. v.p., 1971-85, pres., 1985-88, also chmn. bd. dirs. Served to lt. col. inf. AUS, 1943-45, ETO. Runnerup as outstanding sales exec. Gallagher Report, 1982. Mem. SAR, English Speaking Union, So. Srs. Golf Assn., Tenn. Profl. Golfers Assn. (hon.), Kappa Alpha, Beta Gamma Sigma. Republican. Presbyterian. Clubs: Belle Meade Country, Nashville City; Exchange (Nashville). Home: 104 Adams Park Nashville TN 37205

MAHER, FRAN, advertising agency executive; b. Chgo., June 22, 1938; d. Edward Stephan and Virginia Rose (Harrington) M.; m. Anthony Peter Petrella, Sept. 17, 1957; children: Roland, Louis, Marcus. Student (univ. scholar) U. Minn., 1956-57; student Spectrum Inst., 1968-71; BA summa cum laude, Kean Coll. N.J., 1979. Office mgr. Lead Supplies, Inc., Mpls., 1957-59; freelance artist and writer, Warren, N.J., 1968-72; prin. Visuals, Warren, N.J., 1974-79; pres. Fran Maher, Inc., Stirling, N.J., 1980—; dir. Parent Edn. Advocacy Tng. Center, Alexandria, Va., 1979-85. Officer Friends of Weigand Farm, Milton, N.J., 1977-80, Somerset County Assn. for Retarded Citizens, 1982—, pres., bd. dirs. 1987—; founding mem. Flintlock Boys' Club. Recipient N.J. Art Dirs. Show award, 1978, 1st place award in graphics Watchung Art Center, 1980. Mem. Art Dirs. Club N.J., Am. Women's Econ. Devel. Corp., Advt. Agy. Network Internat., Internat. Platform Assn. Office: 1390 Valley Rd Stirling NJ 07980

MAHER, JOHN FRANCIS, financial executive; b. Berkeley, Calif., Apr. 25, 1943; s. Edward John and Emilia A. (Radovan) M.; m. Ann Elizabeth Breeden (div. 1975); children: Edward John II, Elizabeth Ann; m. Helen Lee Stillman, Mar. 20, 1976; children: Michael Stillman, Helen Cathline. BS, Menlo Coll., 1965; MBA, U. Pa., 1967. Gen. ptnr. Eastman Dillon, N.Y., 1971; 1st v.p. Blyth Eastman Dillon, N.Y., 1972; exec. v.p. Blyth Eastman Dillon, Los Angeles, 1976-79; exec. v.p., chief fin. officer Gt. Western Fin., Beverly Hills, Calif., 1973-76, also bd. dirs.; mng. dir. Shearson Lehman Bros., Los Angeles, 1979-86; pres., chief operating officer Great Western Fin. Corp., Beverly Hills, 1986—; bd. dirs. Gt. Western Fin. Corp., Beverly Hills, Baker Hughes Internat. Bd. dirs. Los Angeles Big Bros., Inc., Baker Hughes, Inc. Joseph Wharton fellow U. Pa., 1965-67. Office: Gt Western Fin Corp 8484 Wilshire Blvd 10th Fl Beverly Hills CA 90211-3212

MAHER, PATRICK JOSEPH, utility company executive; b. Dublin, Ireland, Apr. 20, 1936; came to U.S., 1946, naturalized, 1955; s. Pierce Albeus and Mary (Brady) M.; m. Catherine M. Sullivan, Oct. 13, 1962; children: Kathy, Kevin, Erin, Megan. BBA, Iona Coll., 1959; MBA, N.Y. U., 1965. With spl. devel. program Chase Manhattan Bank, N.Y.C., 1961-64, 2d v.p. fiduciary dept., 1964-68; asst. v.p. Nat. Comml. Bank, Albany, N.Y., 1968-70; chief sect. utility fin. N.Y. State Pub. Svc. Commn., Albany, 1970-74; v.p., chief fin. officer Washington Gas Light Co., 1974-80, exec. v.p. fin. and adminstrn., 1980-87, pres., 1987—; bd. dirs. Harvest Bancorp, Inc., Washington Gas Light Co. Served with USAR, 1960-61. Mem. Am. Gas Assn., Nat. Soc. Rate of Return Analysts, Natural Gas Men's Roundtable, Greater Washington Bd. Trade, U.S. C. of C., Rotary, N.Y. Athletic Club, Washington City Club. Roman Catholic. Home: Route 2 Box 166-H Leesburg VA 22075 Office: Washington Gas Light Co 1100 H St NW Washington DC 20080

MAHER, WILLIAM JAMES, entertainment industry executive; b. Chgo., Feb. 23, 1937; s. Alexander E. and Merle G. M.; B.B.A., Marquette U., 1961. Merchandising exec. Montgomery Ward & Co., Inc., Chgo., 1962-68; mgmt. cons. Cresap, McCormack & Paget, N.Y.C., 1968-69; v.p., treas. Solar Prodns., Inc., Hollywood, Calif., 1969-72; v.p., sec., treas. Creative Mgmt. Assocs., Los Angeles, 1972-74; v.p., dir. Josephson Internat., Inc., Los Angeles, 1974-83; pres. Tipperary Prodns., Inc., Beverly Hills, Calif., 1983—. Office: Tipperary Prodns Inc 1930 N Beverly Dr Beverly Hills CA 90210

MAHESHWARI, ARUN KUMAR, data processing executive; b. Jaipur, Rajasthan, India, Nov. 9, 1944; came to U.S., 1967; s. Chandmal and Kamala (Sharda) M.; m. Vijaylakshmi Jhaver, Jan. 16, 1974; children: Aditi, Amit. BS, U. Rajasthan, Jaipur, 1964; MBA, Columbia U., 1970; PhD, U. Pa., 1973; MS, Stanford U., 1977. Cons. Tata Consultancy Svcs., Bombay, 1974-76, McKinsey and Co., N.Y.C., 1977-81; asst. v.p. Reliance Inc., Phila., 1981-85; v.p. Continental Ins., Neptune, N.J., 1985—. Republican. Hindu. Home: 49 Acadia Dr Voorhees NJ 08043 Office: Continental Ins 3501 Hwy 66 Neptune NJ 07753

MAHFOOD, STEPHEN MICHAEL, state agency director; b. Evansville, Ind., Feb. 12, 1949; s. George Mahfood and Bonnie (Short) Morse; m. Bernadette Scarani, Oct. 16, 1976; children: Nadia Joan, Leila Emma. BS, Rutgers U., 1971. Planning cons. Area V Health Services Adminstrn., Poplar Bluff, Mo., 1976-77; planner Mo. State Health Planning & Devel. Agy., Jefferson City, Mo., 1977-78, chief of planning, 1978-80, dir., 1980-82; gen. mgr. Chimney Rock (N.C.) Co., 1982-84; dir. Mo. Environ. Improvement & Energy Resources Authority, Jefferson City, 1984—; tchr. courses related to environ. and mgmt. agy. topics. Vol. YMCA, Beirut, Lebanon, 1974; bd. dirs. Jefferson City Montessori Sch. (pres.), 1980, Council of Pollution Control Fin. Agys., Midwest Recycling Coalition appointed Nat. Govs. Assn. Hazardous Minimization Assurance Adv. Group; appointed Congressman Anthony's House Ways and Means Task Force on Pub. Fin. Recipient Disting. Service award Mo. Div. of Health and Mo. Dept. Social Services, Achievement award Mo. Waste Control Coalition, 1986. Mem. Am. Soc. for Pub. Adminstrn., Am. Mgmt. Assn., Am. Planning Assn., Nat. Assn. Environ. Profl., Am. Pub. Health Assn. Home: 1416 Herron Dr Jefferson City MO 65191 Office: Mo Environ Improvement & Energy Resources Authority PO Box 744 Jefferson City MO 65101

MAHIN, CHARLES DOUGLAS, automobile company executive; b. Evanston, Ill., Feb. 17, 1940; s. Charles Boyd and Wanda (Spray) M.; m. Angela Carillo; children: Gina L., Laura W., Elizabeth C. BA, U. Wichita, 1963; MBA, U. Tex., 1967. Mem. sales staff Ford Motor Co., Denver, 1967-72; mem. nat. advt., merchandising staff Ford Motor Co., Detroit, 1972-73; gen. field mgr. Ford Motor Co., Boston, 1973-75; nat. sales promotion mgr. Ford Motor Co., Detroit, 1975-79; sales mgr. Ford Motor Co., Atlanta, 1979-82; dir. mktg. devel. Subaru Am., Cherry Hill, N.J., 1982-83, v.p. distbr. div., 1983-84, v.p. mktg., 1984-86, group v.p. sales and mktg., 1986—; bd. dirs. Subaru Am. subs. cos. Served with U.S. Army, 1963-65. Recipient Clio award, 1985, 86, 87, 88, Andy award 1986, Best of 85 award Automotive, Advt. Age, 1985, Mobius award U.S. TV and Radio Festival, 1986, Silver Lion award Cannes Festival, 1985. Mem. Phi Kappa Phi, Beta Gamma Sigma. Office: Subaru Am PO Box 6000 Cherry Hill NJ 08034

MAHLER, STEPHANIE IRENE, marketing executive; b. Bennington, Vt., Jan. 29, 1952; d. Guenther Alexander and Barbara Irene (Overlock) M. BA, Allegheny Coll., 1973. Customer service rep. Albany (N.Y.) Felt Co., 1974-77; order systems analyst Miller Brewing Co., Milw., 1977-78, area mgr., 1978-80, regional adminstr., 1980-83, price promotions mgr., 1983-85, asst. brand mgr., 1985-88, mgr. mktg. projects, 1988—. Mem. pres.'s club Albany Area C. of C., Albany, 1975-76; mgmt. advisor Jr. Achievment, 1973-74. Named One of Outstanding Young Women of Am., Montgomery, Ala., 1983; Presdl. scholar, 1969, Alden scholar Allegheny Coll., Meadville, Pa., 1970-73. Mem. NOW (at-large), Phi Beta Kappa. Home: 8325 N Links Way Fox Point WI 53217 Office: Miller Brewing Co 3939 W Highland Blvd Milwaukee WI 53201

MAHLMANN, KARSTEN, trading executive. came to U.S., 1957; Grad. high sch., Fed. Republic Germany. Runner Daniel F. Rice & Co., 1957, with wire room, margin dept., settlement dept., cash grain dept.; exec. com. ptnr., chief exec. officer, mng. ptnr. Stotler and Co.; mem. Chgo. Bd. Trade, 1963—, dir., 1983-85, vice chmn. bd. dirs., 1986-87, chmn. bd. dirs., 1987—, chmn. exec. com. on competitive stance, chmn. exec. com.; chmn. MidAm. Commodity Exchange, chmn. exec. com.; chmn. Chgo. Rice and Cotton Exchange; past mem. spl. com. on long range planning and internat. expansion, ad hoc com. on competitive stance, spl. com. on bankruptcy regulations, rev. com. on income stream of Exchange, spl. com. to rev. future uses of North Room; past co-chmn. mem. services com.; past vice chmn. ad hoc com. for regulatory policy; past chmn. fin. com., ad hoc com. to rev. fin. standards, metals com., margin com. Office: Chgo Bd of Trade 141 W Jackson Blvd Chicago IL 60604 *

MAHON, MARGARET MARY, manufacturing company executive; b. Crossmolina, Ireland, Nov. 19, 1928; came to U.S., 1951, naturalized, 1970; d. Patrick John and Mary Christina (McNamara) M.; B.S., Fordham U., 1974, M.B.A., 1977. Sec., NCR Corp., N.Y.C., 1951-54, 63-74, adminstrv. specialist, 1974-77, dist. sect. mgr., 1977-78, N.Y. dist. adminstrv. mgr., 1978—; mgr. family bus., 1954-63. Mem. Assn. M.B.A. Execs., Grad. Bus. Alumni Assn. Fordham U., N.Y. C. of C. and Industry. Roman Catholic. Club: Lake Isle Country. Home: 12 Yonkers Ave Tuckahoe NY 10707 Office: NCR Corp 50 Rockefeller Pla New York NY 10020

MAHONE, JOAN JENKINS, tire company executive; b. Morgantown, W.Va., Jan. 16, 1926; d. Frank Roy and Edna E. (Jenkins) Yoke; widowed; children: Kenneth Barry, Jeffrey Kent, Joan K. Mahone Davis, Philip Kirk, Marla K. AB, W.Va. U., 1949. Announcer, programmer Sta. WCOM, Parkersburg, W.Va., 1949-51; pres. Mahone Tire Svc., Inc., Parkersburg, 1975—. Mem. Bus. Women Assn. Democrat. Lutheran. Home: 1700 15th St Parkersburg WV 26101

MAHONEY, MICHAEL JAMES, management consultant; b. Spokane, Wash., July 18, 1960; s. James Lyle and Frances Edith (Castle) M. BA in History cum laude, Whitman Coll., Walla Walla, Wash., 1982. Fin. analyst E.F. Hutton & Co., Inc., N.Y.C., 1982-85; assoc. cons. Bain & Co., Inc., Boston, 1985-87, cons., 1987—. Pres. Spokane County Young Reps., 1976-78; campaign mgr. Malone for U.S. Senate, Boston, 1988. Mem. Sigma Chi (com. chmn. 1979-80), Phi Beta Kappa. Home: 151 Park Dr Boston MA 02215

MAHONEY, RICHARD JOHN, manufacturing company executive; b. Springfield, Mass., Jan. 30, 1934; m. Barbara Marsden Barnett, Jan. 26, 1956; 3 children. BS in Chemistry, U. Mass., 1955, LLD, 1983. Product devel. specialist Monsanto Co., 1962; market mgr. new products Monsanto Co., St. Louis, 1965-67; plastic products and resins div. Monsanto Co.; market mgr. bonding products, div. sales dir. Monsanto Co., Kenilworth, N.J., 1967-71; sales dir. Agrl. div. Monsanto Co., St. Louis, 1971-74, dir. internat. ops., 1974-75, gen. mgr. overseas div., 1975; corp. v.p., mng. dir. Monsanto Agrl. Products Co., 1975-76; group v.p., mng. dir. Monsanto Plastics & Resins Co., 1976-77, exec. v.p., 1977-80, pres., 1980, chief operating officer, 1981, bd. dirs., 1979—; pres., chief exec. officer Monsanto Co., St. Louis, 1983-86; chmn., chief exec. officer Monsanto Co., 1986—; bd. dir. Met. Life Ins. Co., G.D. Searle & Co., Fisher Controls Internat. Bd. dirs. U.S.-USSR Trade and Econ. Coun., Coun. Aid to Edn., trustee Washington U., St. Louis; adv. bd. St. John's Mercy Med. Ctr.; bd. mgrs. Cen. Inst. Deaf. Recipient Frederick S. Troy Alumni Achievement award U. Mass., Amherst, 1981; hon. fellowship Exeter Coll., Oxford, 1986. Mem. Chem. Mfrs. Assn., Soc. Chem. Industry, Bus. Coun., Bus. Round Table. Clubs: Log Cabin, St. Louis, Bellerive Country. Office: Monsanto Co 800 N Lindbergh Blvd Saint Louis MO 63167

MAHONEY, ROBERT WILLIAM, electronic and security systems manufacturing executive; b. N.Y.C., Sept. 10, 1936; s. Francis Joseph and Margaret (Colleton) M.; m. Joan Marie Sheraton, Oct. 3, 1959; children: Linda Marie, Stephen Francis, Brian Michael. BS, Villanova U., 1958, MBA, Roosevelt U., Chgo., 1961. With sales dept. NCR, Inc., Phila., 1961-70, sales mgr., Allentown, Pa. and Atlanta, 1971-76, v.p., Dayton, Ohio, 1977-

80; pres. NCR Can. Ltd., Toronto, 1981-82; sr. v.p. Diebold, Inc., Canton, Ohio, 1983-84, pres., chief op. officer, 1984-85, pres., chief exec. officer, 1985-88, chmn. bd., chief exec. officer, 1988—, also bd. dirs. Bd. dirs. Timken Mercy Med. Ctr., Canton, 1983—, Northeast Ohio Council, Cleve., 1986—, Profl. Football Hall of Fame, Canton, 1987—, Stark County Devel. Bd., Canton, 1986—, Canton Symphony Orch., 1985, Jr. Achievement, Canton, 1984, Akron (Ohio) U. Econ. Devel. Bd., 1982; trustee Canton City Schs., 1986, Mount Union Coll., 1988—, Ohio Found. Ind. Colls., 1988—; mem. adv. bd. C. of C. Leadership Canton, 1987. Served with USN, 1958-61. Republican. Roman Catholic. Clubs: Firestone Country (Akron); Brookside Country (Canton). Office: Diebold Inc 5995 Mayfair Rd North Canton OH 44711

MAHONEY, THOMAS HENRY, investment banker; b. Cambridge, Mass., May 27, 1952; s. Thomas Henry Donald and Katherine Phyllis (Norton) M. A.B., Harvard Coll., 1973; M.B.A., U. Pa., 1976. Assoc. corp. fin. Dillon, Read & Co. Inc., N.Y.C., 1976-80; v.p. corp. fin., 1981-84; v.p. corp. fin. Oppenheimer & Co., Inc., N.Y.C., 1984-86; v.p. debt fin. Merrill Lynch Capital Markets, N.Y.C., 1986-87, dir. product devel., 1988-89, mng. dir., 1989— . Mem. New Eng. Soc. in City N.Y., English-Speaking Union of U.S. Republican. Roman Catholic. Clubs: Doubles, Harvard (N.Y.C.). Home: 1045 Park Ave Apt 7-B New York NY 10128 Office: Merrill Lynch Capital Markets World Fin Ctr North Tower New York NY 10281-1323

MAHONY, JAMES PATRICK, holding company executive; b. Kew Gardens, N.Y., Mar. 4, 1938; s. James P. and Agnes C. Mahony. BBA, St. Bonaventure U., 1963. Trader, B.J. Conlon & Co., N.Y.C., 1960-70; trader, mgr. trading dept. Edwards & Hanly, N.Y.C., 1970-76; pvt. investor, mgr. family assets, 1976-79; salesman, trader, money mgr. Laidlaw, Adams & Peck, N.Y.C., 1979-80, Bruns, Nordeman & Rea, 1980-81; mgr. Bache Halsey Stuart Shields, Water Mill, N.Y., 1981-83, Merrill Lynch, Riverhead, L.I., N.Y., 1983—. Served with USMC, 1957-59. Mem. Security Traders Assn. N.Y. Republican. Roman Catholic. Clubs: N.Y. Athletic, Kiwanis. Home: 48 Sherwood Ln East Hampton NY 11937 Office: Merrill Lynch 806 E Main St Riverhead NY 11901

MAHOOD, JAMES ANDREW, security systems corporation executive; b. Washington, Pa., Jan. 13, 1939; s. John Christopher and Charlotte Lucille (Bullaman) M.; m. Cynthia Jeanette Richter, Aug. 13, 1960; children: Shelley Lee, Lisa Marie, James Daniel. Student, Slippery Rock Coll., 1961, Fisher Jr. Coll., 1974-75. Repairman Simplex Time Co., Pitts., 1961-65; service mgr. Simplex Time Co., Flint, Mich., 1965-67; tech. rep. mgr. Simplex Time Co., Toronto, Ont., Can., 1967-70, Toledo, 1970-74, Boston, 1974-78; sales rep. Simplex Time Co., Portland, Maine, 1978-81; owner, ptnr. Timelo Systems, Inc., Westbrook, Maine, 1981-83; pres. Timelo Systems, Inc., Gorham, Maine, 1983—; fire alarm system technician instr., Mass. Bd. Higher Edn., Boston, 1974-78. Served with USAF, 1956-60; also with USAR, 1972—. Mem. Internat. Mcpl. Signalmans Assn., Maine Fire and Burglar Alarm Assn., N.H. Signalmans Assn., NRA. Home: 457 McLellan Rd Gorham ME 04038 Office: Timeco Systems Inc PO Box 316 Gorham ME 04038-0316

MAHRER, A. JAMES, real estate developer; b. Long Beach, Calif., Sept. 10, 1956; s. Albert Henry and Bruna Giordana (Di'Piatti) M.; m. Monte Ann Alexander, Aug. 21, 1982; 1 child, Andrew. BS in Constrn. Tech., East Tex. State U., 1979. Project engr. Luther Hill & Assocs., Dallas, 1979-83; project mgr. Sumner & Greener, Dallas, 1983, v.p., 1984; project coord. Bramalea Tex., Inc., Dallas, 1984-86; constrn. mgr. Bramalea Ctrs. Inc., Dallas, 1987-88, dir. constrn., 1988—. Mem. Internat. Coun. Shopping Ctrs., Assoc. Gen. Contractors (edn. and careers com., curriculum rev. com. for East Tex. State U. 1979-80, scholar 1977-79), Am. Inst. Constructors, Sigma Chi. Republican. Office: Bramalea Ctrs Inc 901 Main St Ste 4912 Dallas TX 75202

MAI, FRIEDA JEAN, steel service center executive, accountant; b. Council Grove, Kans., Mar. 6, 1960; d. Paul Karl and Betty Jo (Files) M. BSBA, Creighton U., 1982. V.p. Salina (Kans.) Steel Supply, Inc., 1977—. Exec. sec. endowment bd. Sacred Heart Jr.-Sr. High Sch., Salina, 1988—. Mem. Am. Mgmt. Assn., Salina Area C. of C. (bd. dirs. 1989—), Salina German-Am. Club (sec. 1983-85, pres. 1986, exec. coun. 1986—). Office: Salina Steel Supply Inc 234 E Ave A Salina KS 67401

MAI, KLAUS L., oil research company executive; b. Changsha, China, Mar. 7, 1930; s. Ludwig H. and Ilse (Behrend) M.; m. Helen M. Martinchek, July 14, 1957; children: Martin, Michael, Mark, Matthew. BS in Chem. Engring., Gonzaga U., Spokane, Wash., 1951; MS, U. Wash., Seattle, 1952, PhD, 1954. Registered profl. engr., Wash. With Shell Chem. Co., 1957-74, 77-81, various overseas assignments, 1974-75; v.p. Shell Chem. Co., Houston, 1977-81; v.p. transp. and supplies Shell Oil Co., 1976-77; pres. Shell Devel. Co., Houston, 1981—; chmn., pres. various subs. Shell Oil Co. Contbr. articles to profl. publs.; patentee. Trustee, bd. dirs. S.W. Rsch. Inst., San Antonio; mem. Gov.'s Sci. and Tech. Coun.; bd. govs. St. Joseph's Hosp., Houston; pres., chmn. bd. dirs. World Petroleum Congresses; bd. dirs. Keystone Ctr. Recipient Disting. Alumnus award Gonzaga U., 1982, U. Wash., 1988. Fellow Am. Inst. Chem. Engrs. (bd. dir.); mem. Soc. Chem. Industry, Am. Chem. Soc. (adv. bd.), Am. Petroleum Inst., Coun. Chem. Rsch. (chmn., bd. dir.), World Petroleum Congresses (pres., chmn. exec. com.), Am. Ind. Health Coun. (bd. dirs.), Chem. Indsl. Inst. Toxicology (bd. dirs.), Sigma Xi, Tau Beta Pi. Clubs: Lakeside Country (Houston), Petroleum (Houston). Office: Shell Oil Co PO Box 2463 Houston TX 77001

MAIA, FREDERICK OLIVER, marketing executive; b. Brockton, Mass., Aug. 28, 1935; s. Antonio O. Maia; children: Diane M., Karen A.; m. Doris M. Neely, 1984. Student, Richland Coll. Mgmt. trainee W.T. Grant Co., N.Y.C., 1958-64, asst. buyer, 1965-69, gen. mgr., 1970-73; regional sales mgr. Joseph Markovits, Inc., Dallas, 1973-84; mktg. v.p. Designer Accents, Inc., Dallas, 1984—; pres. promotional Concepts, Inc., Arlington, Tex., 1982—. Author newsletter The W5YI Report, 1978—. Served with USAF, 1953-57, Korea. Mem. Am. Mktg. Assn., Amateur Radio Service (nat. vol. examiner coordinator), Mensa. Home: 1020 Byron Ln Arlington TX 76012 Office: Designer Accents Inc 10676 King William Dr Dallas TX 75220

MAIBACH, BEN C., JR., business executive; b. Bay City, Mich., 1920. With Barton-Malow Co., Detroit, 1938—; v.p., dir.-in-charge field ops. Barton-Malow Co., 1949-53, exec. v.p., 1953-60, pres., 1960-76, chmn. bd., 1976—; chmn. bd. Barton-Malow II and Barton-Malow Thatcher, Sarasota, Fla., Cloverdale Equipment Co.; chmn., dir. S-C-P Leasing Corp.; dir., mem. exec. com. Amerisure Ins. Co., Amerisure Life Ins. Co., Mich. Mut. Ins. Co.; dir. Amerisure, Inc.; chmn., dir. Hasper Equipment Co., Sunbelt Crane & Equipment; chmn. bd. Armstrong/Cloverdale Equip. Trustee Barton-Malow Found.; asst. sec., trustee Greater Del Safety Coun.; chmn. Apostolic Christian Woodhaven, Detroit; bishop Apostolic Christian Ch., Mich., Ohio, Fla.; bd. dirs. S.E. Mich. chpt. ARC, United Found., Rural Gospel and Med. Missions of India; trustee Lawrence Inst. Tech. Home: 34050 Ramble Hills Dr Farmington Hills MI 48331 Office: Barton-Malow Co PO Box 5200 Detroit MI 48235 also: Barton-Malow Enterprises 27777 Franklin Rd Southfield MI 48034

MAICHEL, JOSEPH RAYMOND, lawyer, business executive; b. Stanton, N.D., Nov. 24, 1934; s. John and Sarfina (Hoffman) M.; m. Hilda Deichert, Jan. 7, 1961; children: Mary, Mark, Scott. B.S. in Acctg., U. N.D., 1957, J.D. with distinction, 1959. Bar: N.D. 1959. Spl. asst. atty. gen. State of N.D., 1959-71; atty. Mont.-Dakota Utilities Co., Bismarck, N.D., 1971-76, gen. counsel, sec., 1976-82, v.p., gen. counsel, sec., 1979-82, pres., 1985—, also bd. dirs.; gen. counsel Knife River Coal Mining Co., Bismarck, 1979-82; also dir.; pres. Grassland, Inc., Bismarck, 1978-84; sec., dir. Fidelity Oil Co., 1980-83, Welch Coal Co., 1980-83, Wibaux Gas Co., 1980-83; bd. dirs. First Fed. Savs. & Loan, Bismarck; tchr. bus. law, 1968—. Contbr. articles to legal jours. Mem. ABA, Am. Soc. Corp. Secs., North Central Electric Assn., Midwest Gas Assn., Edison Electric Inst., N.D. Bar Assn., Burleigh County Bar Assn. (atty. standards com., law sch. com.), Delta Sigma Pi, Phi Alpha Delta. Roman Catholic. Office: Montana-Dakota Utilities Co 400 N 4th St Bismarck ND 58501

MAIDMAN, RICHARD HARVEY MORTIMER, lawyer; b. N.Y.C., Nov. 17, 1933; s. William and Ada (Seegle) M.; m. Lynne Rochelle Lateiner, Apr. 3, 1960 (div. Sept. 1987); children: Patrick, Mitchel, Dagny. BA, Williams Coll., 1955; JD, Yale U., 1959; postgrad. N.Y. U. Grad. Sch. Bus., 1957, Grad. Sch. Law, 1960, 77. Bar: N.Y. 1961, Fla. bar, 1961, U.S. Dist. Ct. 1962, 79, U.S. Ct. Appeals 1966, U.S. Supreme Ct., 1978. Assoc. Saxe, Bacon & O'Shea, N.Y.C., 1962-64; ptnr. Weiner, Maidman & Goldman, N.Y.C., 1964-67; pvt. practice, N.Y.C., and Fla., 1968—; dir. Microbiol. Scis., Inc.; Nat. Over-the-Counter List, Providence, 1971—, sec., 1971—; pres. MBS Equities, Inc., Fashion Wear Realty Co., Inc., N.Y.C., 1975—; mng. gen. ptnr. Richard and David Maidman, N.Y.C., 1972—, New Haven Projects Co., 1987; legis. counsel Theodore R. Kupferman, 17th Congl. Dist. N.Y., 1966-68; of counsel Shwal, Thompson & Bloch, N.Y.C. and Geneva, 1976-87; receiver Halloren House Hotel, N.Y.C., 1981. Contbr. articles to profl. jours. Mem. ABA, N.Y. State Bar Assn., Fla. Bar Assn., Assn. Bar City N.Y., Bankruptcy Lawyers Assn. N.Y.C., Real Estate Bd. of N.Y. Home: Steamboat Landing Sands Point NY 11050 also: 1155 21st St NW Washington DC 20036

MAIER, ROBERT ANDREW, healthcare financial consulting executive, hospital administrator; b. Washington, Sept. 6, 1949; s. John Anthony and Gloria (Nevers) M.; children: Natalie, Brendan. BS in Acctg. summa cum laude, U. Albuquerque, 1975; postgrad. in mgmt., U. N.Mex., 1977. CPA, N.Mex. Sr. auditor Ernst & Whinney, Albuquerque, 1975-77; v.p. fin. Univ. Heights Hosp., Albuquerque, 1977-81; pres. Heights Gen. Hosp., Albuquerque, 1981-84, LINC Mgmt. Services Co., Chgo., 1984—; chmn. N.Mex. Health Systems Agy., 1981-84; pres. Albuquerque Hosp. Council; lectr. in field; bd. dirs. LINC Venture Lease Ptnrs., Chgo. Contbr. articles to profl. jours. Named Outstanding Jaycee, 1972. Mem. Am. Inst. CPA's, N.Mex. Inst. CPA's. Office: LINC Group Inc 303 E Wacker Dr Chicago IL 60601

MAIMAN, GEORGE, accountant, finance consultant; b. Hungary, Aug. 30, 1939; s. Al and Anna (Stern) M.; B.A., Concordia U., 1965, Bernard Baruch Coll., City U. N.Y., 1975; m. Edith Schwartz, Nov. 13, 1966; children—Ronald E., Andrew D. Controller, Unimet Corp., N.Y.C., 1973-75, Pickwick Internat. Inc., Woodbury, N.Y., 1975-77; prin. Maiman & Co., C.P.A.'s, N.Y.C., 1977—; cons. C.P.A., N.Y. State. Mem. Am. Inst. C.P.A.'s. Office: 250 W 57th St New York NY 10107

MAIN, ROBERT GAIL, communications and training consultant, television and film producer, educator, former army officer; b. Bucklin, Mo., Sept. 30, 1932; s. Raymond M. and Inez L. (Olinger) M.; m. Anita Sue Thoroughman, Jan. 31, 1955; children: Robert Bruce, David Keith, Leslie Lorraine. BS magna cum laude, U. Mo., 1954; grad. with honors, Army Command and Gen. Staff Coll., 1967; MA magna cum laude in Communications, Stanford U., 1968; PhD, U. Md., 1978. Commd. 2d lt. U.S. Army, 1954, advanced through grades to lt. col., 1968; various command and staff assignments field arty., 1954-64; sr. instr. and div. chief Pershing missile div. U.S. Army Arty. and Missile Sch., Ft. Sill, Okla., 1964-66; mem. faculty U.S. Army Command and Gen. Staff Coll., 1968-70; chief speechwriting and info. materials div. U.S. Army Info. Office, 1971, chief broadcast and film div., 1972-73; dir. def. audiovisual activities Office of Info. for Armed Forces, 1973-76, ret., 1976; prof., grad. adv. Coll. Communications, Calif. State U., Chico, 1976-87; pres. Grant & Main, Inc., corp. communications and tng. cons. Author: Rogues, Saints and Ordinary People, 1988; contbr. articles on audiovisual communications to profl. publs.; producer: Walking Wounded, TV documentary, 1983; producer army info. films, army radio series, 1972-73; creating family heritage videos. Decorated Legion of Merit, Meritorious Service medal, Commendation medal with oak leaf cluster, combat Inf. Badge; Vietnamese Cross of Gallantry; recipient Freedom Found. awards, 1972, 73, 74; Bronze medal Atlanta Film Festival, 1972; Best of Show award Balt. Film Festival, 1973; Creativity award Chgo. Indsl. Film Festival, 1973; Cine gold award Internat. Film Producers Assn., 1974; named an Outstanding Prof. Calif State U., 1987-88. Mem. Assn. for Ednl. Communications Tech., Am. Soc. of Curriculum Developers, Nat. Assn. Ednl. Broadcasters, Phi Eta Sigma, Alpha Zeta, Phi Delta Gamma, Omicron Delta Kappa, Alpha Gamma Rho. Mem. Christian Ch.

MAINE, RUSSELL CLAY, manufacturing executive; b. Denison, Tex., May 13, 1964; s. Ralph Cecil and Rita Mae (Larson) M.; m. Jane Ann Cannaday, June 4, 1983; 1 child, Loren Michelle. BS, Southeastern Okla. State U., 1987. Draftsman Swartout Industries, Inc., Sherman, Tex., 1982-83; acct. Donna Self, CPA, Altus, Okla., 1985-86; mfg. supr. Tex. Instruments, Sherman, 1987—. Staff sgt. USAF, 1983-86. Mem. Durant Acctg. Club. Republican. Home: 702 Valentine Sherman TX 75090 Office: Tex Instruments Hwy 75 S Sherman TX 75090

MAINES, CLIFFORD BRUCE, insurance company executive; b. Tacoma, Wash., Aug. 14, 1926; s. Clifford McLean and Ida Vera (Wardall) M.; m. Mary Jean Marshall, Sept. 4, 1948; children—Molly, Janet Lynn. Student, Central Coll., Fayette, Mo., 1944-45, U. Mich., 1945-46; B.S., U. Wash., 1948, LL.B., 1949, J.D., 1949. Bar: Wash. bar 1950. Mem. legal staff Safeco Corp., Seattle, 1950-62, asso. gen. counsel, 1962-66, gen. counsel, 1966-68, v.p., gen. counsel, 1968-74, sr. v.p., 1974-81, pres., 1981—, pres., chief exec. officer, 1986—, dir., 1977—; exec. v.p., chief operating officer, dir. Gen. Ins. Co. Am., 1974-77, pres., 1977-81; now dir.; exec. v.p. 1st Nat. Ins. Co. Am., 1974-77, pres., 1977-81; now dir.; exec. v.p. Safeco Ins. Co., 1974-77, pres., 1977-81, now dir.; dir. Safeco Life Ins. Co.; exec. v.p. GSL. Served with USNR, 1944-46. Mem. ABA, Wash. Bar Assn., Seattle-King County Bar Assn. (past trustee), Wash. Ins. Council (past pres.), Pacific Ins. and Surety Conf., Washington Athletic Club, Broadmoor Golf Club, Seattle Golf Club, Columbia Tower Club, Beta Theta Pi. Methodist. Office: Safeco Corp Safeco Pla Seattle WA 98185

MAIRA, AJIT NATH, marketing automation entrepreneur, sales and marketing consultant; b. Lahore, Punjab, India, June 30, 1945; s. Amar Nath and Usha (Puri) M.; m. Lynn Harwood Reindollar, June 19, 1970; children: Ravi, Karam. B in Tech., Indian Inst. Tech., 1967. Registered profl. engineer, Mass. Mktg. rep. IBM, Boston and India, 1968-76; mgr., gen. internat. area Digital Equipment, Merrimack, N.H., 1976-81; v.p. mktg. Raytheon, Norwood, Mass., 1983; v.p. sales, mktg. Concord Data Systems, Waltham, Mass., 1984-86; pres. Market Builders Int., Sudbury, Mass., 1986—. V.p. Sudbury Youth Soccer Assn., 1987-88, dir., 1985—. Mem. Soc. Mfg. Engrs. Republican. Home: 42 Hawes Rd Sudbury MA 01776 Office: Market Builders Internat 121 Boston Post Rd Sudbury MA 01776

MAISEL, DARRELL KEITH, manufacturing executive; b. East St. Louis, Ill., Mar. 5, 1947; s. Charles Earl and Lonah Belle (Harrison) M.; m. Darlyn Marie Range, Nov. 27, 1974; children: Tracy, Richard, Donald, James. Student, Wash. U., St. Louis, 1975-81, Belleville Area Coll., 1975-79, U. Mo., 1981-82; cert., Ranken Tech. Trade Sch., St. Louis, 1969-71. Assembly line workerChevrolet div. GM, St. Louis, 1965-66; mgr. svc. sta. Standard Oil Co., Cahokia, Ill., 1966-67; millwright Cerro Copper Products Co., Sauget, Ill., 1967-70, electrician, 1970-72, maintenance supr., 1972-76, elec. engr., 1976-78; maintenance supt. Cerro Copper Products Co., Sauget, 1978-81; tech. mgr. Cerro Copper Products Co., Shelbina, Mo., 1981-82; plant gen. mgr. Cerro Copper Tube Co., Shelbina, Mo., 1982—. Treas. Zion Luth. Ch., Macon, Mo., 1985-86. Mem. Am. Soc. Metals, Internat. Tube Assn., Am. Tube Assn. Office: Cerro Copper Tube Co 516 W Chestnut St Shelbina MO 63468

MAISEL, MICHAEL, shoe designer and manufacturer; b. Newark, Oct. 19, 1947; s. Irving and Betty (Markin) M.; m. Arlette Bernstein, Oct. 18, 1980; children: Ian Albert, Alicia Beth, Noah Shawn, Bette Gabrielle. B.S. in Mktg., B.A. in Gen. Bus. Adminstrn., Ariz. State U., 1969. Asst. sales mgr. Mid-Atlantic Shoe Co. div. Beck Industries, N.Y.C., 1969-71; dir. imports Felsway Corp., Totowa, N.J., 1972-73; exec. v.p. Carber Enterprises, N.Y.C., 1973-80; v.p. S.R.O. div. Caressa, N.Y.C., 1980-84; pres. Sandler of Boston, N.Y.C., 1984-85, chmn. bd., 1986—; cons. in field. Mem. 210 Shoe Industry (life), Nat. Shoe Retailers Assn. (bd. dirs.), Nat. Shoe Mfrs. Assn. Republican. Jewish. Designer Carber's shoe, displayed in Met. Mus. Art; nominated for Coty design award, 1974-78. Office: China Clipper 350 Fifth Ave Ste 7100 New York NY 10118

MAJKA, JOHN ROBERT, engineer, retail executive; b. Chgo., Sept. 3, 1942; s. John J. Majka and Violet M. (Krolikowski) Binczyk; m. Barbara A. Batts, Aug. 21, 1976. BS in Engring., U. Ill., Chgo., 1974. Engr. Marsh Instrument Co., Skokie, Ill., 1971-72, Lake Ctr. Industries, Winona, Minn., 1972-73, Internat. Harvester, Libertyville, Ill., 1974-75; sr. engr. ICI Ams., Inc., Charlestown, INd., 1975—; v.p. The Craft Sampler Corp., Louisville, 1986—. With U.S. Army, 1963-66, Vietnam. Republican. Office: ICI Ams Inc Hwy 62 Charlestown IN 47111

MAJOR, RICHARD DEMAREST, manufacturing company executive; b. Pitts., Apr. 10, 1935; s. Alfred Job and Marjorie Eleanor (Demarest) M.; m. JoAnn Detwiler, June 25, 1977; children: Keith Richard, Barbara Lynn, Jeffrey Briggs. BS in Math., Carnegie-Mellon U., 1956; MBA, U. Pitts., 1961, PhD in Bus. Adminstrn., 1973. Prodn. engr. E.I. duPont de Nemours & co., Niagara Falls, N.Y., 1956-60; mgr. Touche ross & Co., N.Y.C., 1963-69; dept. mgr., fin. staff Ford Motor Co., Dearborn, Mich., 1969-70; pres. Energy Conversion Devices, Inc., Troy, Mich., 1970-73, Hauserman, Inc., Cleve., 1973-84, Hiebert, Inc., Carson, Calif., 1984-87, GF Corp., Youngtown, OH, 1987—. Trustee Leukemia Soc. Am., Cleve., 1979-81, St. Vincents Charity Hosp., 1979-81, Cleve. Ballet, 1981-84, Joffrey Ballet, Los Angeles, 1986; bd. dirs. Youngstown Symphony Soc., 1988—; mem. Leadership Cleve., 1977-78, Leadership Youngstown, 1987-88, bd. dirs. Recipient Leadership Youngstown award, 1987-88; predoctoral fellow Ford Found., Pitts., 1962-63. Mem. Youngstown C. of C. (bd. dirs. 1988), Youngstown Country Club, Pi Mu Epsilon, Beta Gamma Sigma, Beta Alpha Psi. Home: 151 Newport Dr Boardman OH 44512 Office: GF Corp 4944 Belmont Ave Youngstown OH 44512

MAJOR, WILLIAM ALEXANDER, JR., gas pipeline company executive, lawyer; b. Birmingham, Ala., Dec. 2, 1942; s. William Alexander and Lucia Noel (Beddow) M.; m. Emily Frances Chenoweth, Aug. 22, 1965 (div. Apr. 1985); children—Frances, Barbara, Emily; m. Jacqueline J. Zoch. A.B., U. Ala., 1964; LL.B., U. Va., 1967. Bar: Ala. 1967. Clk. fed. cts. Birmingham, Ala., 1967-68; assoc. Cabaniss, Johnston, Birmingham, Ala., 1968-71; with So. Natural Gas Co., Birmingham, Ala., 1971—, sr. v.p., gen. counsel, 1983—; pres. SNG Intrastate Pipeline Inc., Bear Creek Storage Co., So. Deepwater Pipeline, Birmingham; pres., mem. bd. dirs. Bear Creek Capital Co.; bd. dirs. So. Ga. Nat. Gas, So. Energy, So. Gas Storage; chmn. mgmt. com. Sea Robin Pipeline Co.; v.p., dir. So. Frontier Pipeline. Bd. dirs. Lakeshore Hosp., Birmingham, Ala., 1980. Served to 1st lt. Air N.G., 1967-73. Mem. Interstate Natural Gas Assn. Am. (chmn. legal com. 1982-83), Am. Gas Assn. Episcopalian. Clubs: Redstone, Mt. Brook (Birmingham, Ala.). Office: So Natural Gas 1900 5th Ave N Birmingham AL 35202

MAKADOK, STANLEY, management consultant; b. N.Y.C., Mar. 30, 1941; s. Jack and Pauline (Speciner) M.; BME, CCNY, 1962; MS in Mgmt. Sci., Rutgers U., 1964; m. Lorraine Edith Dubin, Aug. 24, 1963 (div. 1988); 1 son, Richard. Bus. systems analyst Westinghouse Electric Corp., Balt., 1964-65; project engr., corp. cons. Am. Cyanamid Corp., Pearl River, N.Y., Wayne, N.J., 1965-68; v.p., bus. devel. and planning Pepsico Inc. and affiliates, Purchase, N.Y., Miami, Fla., 1968-75; mgr. fin. and planning cons. Coopers & Lybrand, N.Y.C., 1975-77; pres. Century Mgmt. Cons., Inc., Ridgewood, N.J., N.Y.C., 1977—. Contbr. articles to profl. jours. Office: Century Mgmt Cons Inc 4 Wilsey Sq Ste 9 Ridgewood NJ 07450

MAKALOU, OUMAR, economic advisor; b. Kita, Mali, Jan. 1, 1934; s. Sambou and Coumba (Tounkara) M.; m. Morimoussou Koite, July 30, 1944; children: Modibo Mao, Kalle, Mamaye, Sambou, Coumba. BA in Law, Paris U., 1960, MA in Econs., 1968; PhD in Econs., U. Paris-Sorbonne, 1970. Insp. Fin. Services, Paris, 1956-60; pres. Devel. Bank, Bamako, Mali, 1961-63; state controller Office of Pres., Koulouba, Mali, 1963-68; dir. gen. Treasury Banks and Ins., Koulouba, 1968-71, Internat. Corp., Koulouba, 1971-73; chmn. bd. dirs. Cen. Bank, Bamako, Mali, 1973-77; chief of staff Office of Pres., Bamako; dep. dir. African dept. IMF, Washington, 1977-84; sr. advisor IMF Inst., Washington, 1984—; vis. prof. U. Montreal, Que., Can., 1983. Author: Budget Equilibrium in Developing Countries, 1970. Named Grand Officer of the Cross of Merit, Fed. Republic of Germany, Officer of Merit Order of France, Knight of the Nat. Order of Mali. Mem. Soc. for Internat. Devel. (bd. dirs. 1986-87). Home: 5915 Bradley Blvd Bethesda MD 20814 Office: IMF 700 19th St NW Washington DC 20431

MAKAREM, ESSAM FAIZ, manufacturing company executive; b. Lagos, Nigeria, Aug. 20, 1936; s. Faiz Mahmoud and Jamal Mohammed Makarem; Diploma in English and Arabic, Nat. Coll., Aley Lebanon, 1953; BS in Bus. Adminstrn. U. Beverly HIlls, 1987; m. Ghada Mahmoud Aawar, Oct. 5, 1969; children—Hitaf, Wael, Nader, Joumana, May, Ussama. Dir., gen. mgr. Faiz Moukarim & Sons Ltd., Kano, Nigeria, 1954—, also dir.; mng. dir. Moukarim Metalwood Factory Ltd., Kano, Ikeja, Katsina and Jos Nigeria, 1959—; dir. Borno Engring. and Steel Mfrs. Ltd., Nigeria Gas Industries Ltd., Moukarim Bros. Ltd.; Mgmt. and Fin. Internat. Ltd., Beirut, United Devel. Corp. (Holding), Beirut. Pres. Nat. Council Nigeria, World Lebanese Cultural Union, 1972-73, v.p. world council, 1976-83; sec. gen. Druse Found. for Soc. Welfare, Beirut, 1983—, Kamal Jumblatt Soc. Found., Beirut, 1981—. Mem. C. of C. and Industry of Kano, Assn. Steel Tube Mfrs. (chmn. 1979-80), Assn. Foam Mfrs. Druse Moslem. Lodges: Rotary (pres. local club 1971-72), Kano Lebanon (pres. 1973-76) (Kano); Masons, Odd Fellows. Office: Plot M Awosika Ave, PO Box 160, Ikeja Lagos Nigeria

MAKEPEACE, DARRYL LEE, manufacturing company executive; b. Pitts., Oct. 24, 1941; s. Thomas Henry Makepeace and Nevada Ruth (Wagner) Desin; m. Maryanne Stright, Aug. 16, 1977; children: Krisanne, Erin. BS in Indsl. Engring., Pa. State U., 1969; MBA, Pepperdine U., 1982. Dept. mgr. Procter & Gamble, Cin., 1969-72; plant mgr. CBS Mus. Instruments, Fullerton, Calif., 1972-76; dir. mfg. Frigid Coil/Wolf Range, Whittier, Calif., 1977-79; mgr. materials mgmt. Nat. Supply, Los Nietos, Calif., 1979-85, mgr. mfg., 1985-86; program mgr. Armco Cumberland Group, Middletown, Ohio, 1986; ptnr., cons. Armco Cumberland Group, Mason, Ohio, 1986-87, ptnr., prin., 1988—; assoc. prof. mgmt. Wright State U., Dayton, Ohio, 1987-88, Miami U., Oxford, Ohio., 1988—. Contbr. articles to profl. jours. Served with U.S. Army, 1960-61. Named to Honorable Order of Ky. Cols. Mem. Am. Prodn. and Inventory Control Soc., Inst. Indsl. Engrs., Alpha Pi Mu, Tau Beta Pi, Sigma Tau. Home: 726 Eagle View Ct Mason OH 45040

MAKOSKI, MILTON JOHN, human resources executive; b. Poughkeepsie, N.Y., Jan. 19, 1946; s. Milton Cornelius and Marie Elizabeth (Kimlin) M; m. Mary Helen Staskiewicz, aug. 8, 1972; children: Milton Kimlin, Marek Laban, Manya Janine. BS in Mgmt. Sci., Rensselaer Poly. Inst., 1968; MBA, U. New Haven, 1972; JD, U. Conn., 1977. Mgr. employee rels. TRW, New Haven, 1973-77; mgr. labor rels. Monsanto, St. Louis, 1977-79; dir. employment, EEO and tng. GTE, Stamford, Conn., 1979-81; mgr. employee rels. Gen. Electric, Fairfield, Conn., 1981-84; v.p. adminstrn., chief adminstrv. officer Sealectro Corp., Trumbull, Conn., 1984-86; v.p. human resources Echlin Inc., Branford, Conn., 1986—. Mem. Nat. Assn. Corp. and Profl. Recruiters, Employment Mgmt. Assn., Am. Soc. for Personnel Adminstrn. Republican. Home: 19 Sallyann Dr Trumbull CT 06611 Office: Echlin Inc 100 Double Beach Rd Branford CT 06405

MAKOSKY, JOHN PAUL, insurance comany executive; b. Boonton, N.J., Dec. 4, 1942; s. John J. and Ann H. (Mayerhcak) M. AA, Morris County Coll., 1972; A. in Sci. Mgmt., Edison State Coll., 1984; A. in Specialized Bus., Ctr. for Degree Studies, 1984. Asst. claims examiner Prudential Ins. Co. Am., Wayne, N.J., 1972-78; sales approver Prudential Ins. Co. Am., Wayne, 1978-88; sales rep. Sears Roebuck Co., Rockaway, N.J., 1988—. Mem. Am. Mktg. Assn., Nat. Assn. Investment Clubs. Office: Sears Roebuck Co Rockaway NJ 07866

MAKOSKY, THOMAS, computer company executive; b. Morristown, N.J., July 29, 1948; s. John Joseph and Ann Helen (Mayerchak) M.; m. Catherine Virginia Alonge, June 14, 1969; children: Dianne, Christine. BS in Math., Drew U., 1970; postgrad., NYU, 1971-73; MS in Computer Sci., Rutgers U., 1981. Mgr. computer ctr. Drew U., Madison, N.J., 1970-74, dir. computer services, 1974-81; dir. application systems AXXESS Info. Systems, Mountainside, N.J., 1981-83; pres. APT Computer Solutions, Inc., East Hanover, N.J., 1983—. Mem. Assn. PICK Profls. and Users, MICRU Internat., Assn. Small Computer Users in Edn. Roman Catholic. Office: APT Computer Solutions Inc 25 Hanover Rd PO Box 569 Florham Park NJ 07932

MAKOVSKY, KENNETH D., public relations executive; b. St. Louis, Oct. 3, 1940; s. Jack and Minnie (Freedman) M.; m. Phyllis Ann Peck, Oct. 15, 1972; children: Evan, Matthew. BA, Washington U., St. Louis, 1962, JD, 1965. Asst. account exec. Curtis Hoxter Inc., N.Y.C., 1965-66; account exec. Ruder & Finn Inc., N.Y.C., 1966-69; account exec. Harshe-Rotman & Druck, N.Y.C., 1970-72, v.p., 1973-75, sr. v.p., 1975-79, sr. v.p., dep. gen. mgr. N.Y. office, 1978-79; founder, pres. Makovsky & Co., Inc., N.Y.C., 1979—; Pres., founder Pub. Relations Exch., 1986-88. Contbr. articles to profl. pubs. Speechwriter 17th Distr. Congl. Campaign, N.Y.C., 1972; v.p. Am. Jewish Com. N.Y., N.Y.C., 1985—, bd. dirs. 1978—, chmn. Diplomatic Outreach, 1987—; bd. dirs. Postgrad. Ctr. for Mental Health, N.Y.C., 1981—. Co. named one of ten fastest growing pub. rels. firms in U.S. O'Dwyer rankings, 1985, 86, 87; named one of four top smaller pub. rels. firms in N.Y.C. trade mag. survey, 1988. Mem. Pub. Rels. Soc. Am. (Silver Anvil award 1978), Nat. Investor Rels. Inst., Pub. Rels. Exchange (founder, 1984, pres. 1986-88), Washington U. Alumni Club N.Y.C. (pres. 1970), Broad St. Club, 200 East Club (N.Y.C.). Office: Makovsky & Co Inc 245 Fifth Ave New York NY 10016

MAKRIANES, JAMES KONSTANTIN, JR., management consultant; b. Springfield, Mass., Jan. 15, 1925; s. James K. and Clara (Allen) M.; m. Judith Alden Erdmann, Sept. 30, 1960; children—Mary, James, Susan, Jane, Mahady. B.A., Amherst Coll., 1949. V.p., gen. mgr. Nat. Paper Box Co. and Nat. Games, Inc., Springfield, 1949-59; merchandising and acct. exec. Young & Rubicam, Inc., N.Y.C., 1959-63; v.p., acct. supr. Young & Rubicam, Inc., 1963-67, sr. v.p., mgmt. supr., 1963-73, exec. v.p., dir., 1973-78; sr. v.p., dir. Haley Assocs., Inc., N.Y.C., 1978-80, pres., 1980—, chief exec. officer, 1985-89; ptnr., dir. Ward & Howell Internat., Inc., N.Y.C., 1989—. Trustee Boys' Club N.Y., 1976—. Served with USNR, 1943-46. Clubs: Union, Links, Maidstone., Racquet and Tennis. Home: 60 East End Ave New York NY 10028

MALABRE, ALFRED LEOPOLD, JR., journalist, author; b. N.Y.C., Apr. 23, 1931; s. Alfred Leopold and Marie (Leonard) M.; m. Mary Patricia Wardropper, July 28, 1956; children: Richard C., E. Ann, John A. B.A., Yale U., 1952. Copy editor Hartford (Conn.) Courant, 1957-58; successively reporter, Bonn bur. chief, econs. editor, news editor and Outlook columnist Wall St. Jour., 1958—, news editor, 1969—. Author: Understanding the Economy: For People Who Can't Stand Economics, 1976, America's Dilemma: Jobs vs. Prices, 1978, Investing for Profit in the Eighties, 1982, Beyond Our Means, 1987, Understanding the New Economy, 1988. Served with USNR, 1953-56, Korea. Poynter fellow, 1976; recipient Eccles prize Columbia U., 1988. Mem. Authors Guild, Pilgrims Soc. U.S., Union Club. Address: 150 E 73rd St New York NY 10021

MALACH, HERBERT JOHN, lawyer; b. N.Y.C., Aug. 3, 1922; s. James J. and Therese (Lederer) M.; A.B., Iona Coll., 1951; J.D., Columbia U., 1955; m. Patricia Sweeny, Sept. 12, 1953 (dec. 1972); children: Therese, Herbert John, Helen. Bar: N.Y. 1957, D.C. 1958, U.S. Dist. Ct. (ea. and so. dists.) N.Y. 1958, U.S. Ct. Appeals (2d cir.) 1960, U.S. Supreme Ct. 1961, U.S. Dist. Ct. (no. and we. dists.) N.Y. 1988, U.S. Ct. Appeals (Fed. cir.) 1988, U.S. Tax Ct. 1988. Practiced in N.Y.C., 1957-72, New Rochelle, N.Y., 1960—; lectr. bus. law Iona Coll., New Rochelle, 1957-59, asst. to pres. for community services, 1959-62. Vice chmn., exec. dir. Iona Coll. Westchester County Law Enforcement Inst.; spl. counsel N.Y. State Temporary Commn. on Child Welfare; mem. Westchester County Youth Adv. Council, 1969-73; mem. Law Enforcement Planning. Agy., New Rochelle, 1968-69; adv. counsel Westchester Police Youth Officers Assn.; mem. Westchester County Child Abuse Task Force; mem. New Rochelle Narcotics Guidance Council, 1972-75; adv. council New Rochelle Salvation Army, 1976-79; legal adviser East-End Civic Assn.; law guardian Westchester County Family Ct.; referee New Rochelle City Ct.; arbitrator Civil Ct., Bronx; arbitrator Supreme and County Ct., Westchester. Bd. dirs. Art Inst., Iona Coll., mem. adv. bd. radio activities, adv. bd. criminal justice Iona Coll., bd. dirs. Westchester County Youth Shelter. Served with AUS, 1942-46. Recipient Patrick B. Doyle award for outstanding service, 1969, William B. Cornelia Founders award, 1976 (both Iona Coll.). Hon. dep. sheriff Westchester County. Mem. Am. (family law sect.), N.Y. State (com. child welfare, com. family ct.), Bronx County (com. family ct.), Westchester County, New Rochelle Bar assns., Am. Judicature Soc., N.Y. County Lawyers Assn. (family ct. com.), Criminal Cts. Bar Assn. Westchester County, Am. Fedn. Police, Internat. Narcotic Enforcement Officers Assn., Internat. Acad. Criminology, Am. Acad. Polit. and Social Sci., Am. Profl. Soc. on Abuse of Children, Law Guardians Assn. Westchester County (pres.), Am. Psychology-Law Soc., Internat., N.Y. State, Bergen County chiefs of police, Nat. Assn. Council for Children, Nat. Sheriffs Assn., Am. Soc. Internat. Law, Iona Coll. Alumni Assn., Inc. (pres., chmn. bd. dirs. 1958-60, 62-64, 72-74, 74-76, dir. 1954-58, 68-72, 76-86, v.p. 1966-68). Address: 105 Harding Dr New Rochelle NY 10801

MALAHOSKI, JOHN JOSEPH, accountant; b. Carbondale, Pa., Aug. 27, 1947; s. John Joseph and Veronica Julia (Lubash) M.; m. Patricia Ann Lachovich, Nov. 8, 1980. BS cum laude, U. Scranton, 1969; MBA, U. Pitts., 1970. CPA, Pa., N.Y. Sr. auditor Arthur Andersen & Co., N.Y.C., 1969-74; mgr. internal audit dept. The Soc. of N.Y. Hosp., N.Y.C., 1974-77; ptnr. Parente, Randolph, Orlando, Carey & Assocs., Wilkes-Barre, Pa., 1977—; instr. courses for accts., Pa., 1980—. Active Leadership Wilkes-Barre, 1988; bd. dirs. Assn. Retarded Citizens, 1988. Mem. Am. Inst. CPAs, Pa. Inst. CPAs, N.Y. State Soc. CPAs, Consol. Hunting Club (Peckville, Pa.) (treas. 1983—). Office: Parente Randolph Orlando Carey & Assocs 46 Public Sq Wilkes-Barre PA 18701-2681

MALAND, TIM, hospitality company executive; b. Mineola, N.Y., May 25, 1953; s. Einar Reidar and Grace Sarah (McDonough) M.; m. Carol Ann Jones, June 21, 1977 (div. May 1979); m. Donna Eliakis, June 27, 1987. BS in Quantitative Systems, Ariz. State U., 1975; internat. exec. program, Insead, 1985; cert., Goethe Inst., 1983. CPA, Nev. Acct. Deloitte, Haskins & Sells, Las Vegas, 1977-79; systems analyst Del E. Webb Corp., Las Vegas, 1979-80; controller Tropicana Hotel, Las Vegas, 1980-81; internat. auditor Ramada Inc., Phoenix, 1981-82, internat. controller, 1982-85; v.p. devel. Asia, Pacific Ramada Inc., Hong Kong, 1985-86; sr. v.p., hotel group controller Ramada Inc., Phoenix, 1987—. Bd. dirs., Big Brother Valley Big Brother Assn., Phoenix, 1983-85. Mem. Internat. Assn. Hospitality Accts., AICPA, Am. Hotel and Motel Assn., Western Res. Club, Beta Gamma Sigma, Alpha Iota Delta, Beta Alpha Psi. Republican. Roman Catholic. Office: Ramada Inc 3838 E Van Buren St Phoenix AZ 85008

MALASKY, ILENE POST, stockbroker; b. Columbus, Ohio, July 4, 1938; d. Harry S. and Jeanne (Stone) Post; student Harcum Jr. Coll., 1958; B.S., Youngstown State U., 1961; children—Bruce A., Stephen P. With Murch & Co., Youngstown, Ohio, 1969-70; with Prescott Ball & Turben, Youngstown, 1970—, v.p., 1981—; pres. The 759 Corp. Trustee Rodef Sholom Temple, 1982-86; mem. Jr. Guild of St. Elizabeth Hosp., 1970-86; mem. faculty awards com. Youngstown State U., 1984-87. Jewish. Clubs: Youngstown, Squaw Creek Country. Home: 3038 Greenacres Dr Youngstown OH 44505 Office: 201 E Commerce St Ste 100 Youngstown OH 44503

MALASPINA, ALEX, soft drink company executive; b. Athens, Greece, Jan. 4, 1931; came to U.S., 1948; s. Spiros and Mary (Souyiouljoglou) M.; m. Doris Woodruff Gould, Sept. 25, 1954; children: Spiros, Ann, Paul, Mark. B.S., MIT, 1952, Ph.D., 1955. Coord. new products Pfizer, Inc., N.Y.C., 1955-61; mgr. quality control Coca-Cola Export Corp., N.Y.C., 1961-69, v.p., 1969-78; v.p. Coca-Cola Co., Atlanta, 1978-86, sr. v.p., 1986—; pres. Internat. Life Scis. Inst., Washington, 1978—, Internat. Tech. Caramel Assn., Washington, 1977—; v.p. Toxicology Forum, Washington, 1979—. Mem. N.Y. Acad. Scis., Am. Inst. Chemists, Inst. Food Technologists, AAAS, Am. Chem. Soc. Greek Orthodox. Home: 425 Kenbrook Dr NW Atlanta GA 30327 Office: Coca-Cola Co 1 Coca-Cola Pla NW Atlanta GA 30313

MALCOLM, JOHN GRANT, government official; b. Missoula, Mont., Apr. 15, 1941; s. Grant and June (Smith) M.; m. Sharon Lee McDonald, 1960; children: Lynn Conrad Linda Kim. BA with honors, U. Md., 1970, MBA, 1971. Sales rep. Olivetti Corp., Washington, 1971-72; mgmt. analyst USPHS, Washington, 1972-78; chief, Mgmt. Systems Div. Nat. Hwy. Traffic Safety Adminstrn., U.S. Dept. Transp., 1978-79; printing officer Dept. HHS, Washington, 1979-88; sr. analyst Dept, HHS, Washington, 1988— ; v.p. Mgmt. Factors Orgn., McLean, Va.; pres. Puffin Projects, Silver Spring, Md.; lectr. U. Md., 1975—. Bd. dirs. World Nature Assn., King Realty. Served with U.S. Army, 1960-68. Def. Dept. fellow, 1970-71. Mem. Am. Mktg. Assn., Am. Mgmt. Assn., World Future Soc., Am. Ornithology Union, Md. Ornithol. Assn. (bd. dirs.) Episcopalian. Office: US HHS 200 Independence Ave SW Room 514G Washington DC 20201

MALDONADO-BEAR, RITA MARINITA, economist, educator; b. Vega Alta, P.R., June 14, 1938; d. Victor and Marina (Davila) Maldonado; B.A., Auburn U., 1960; Ph.D., N.Y.U., 1969; m. Larry Alan Bear, Mar. 29, 1975. With Min. Wage Bd. & Econ. Devel. Adminstrn., Govt. of P.R., 1960-64; asso. prof. fin. U. P.R., 1969-70; asst. prof. econs. Manhattan Coll., 1970-72; assoc. prof. econs. Bklyn. Coll., 1972-75; vis. assoc. prof. fin. Stanford (Calif.) Grad. Bus. Sch., 1973-74; assoc. prof. fin. and econs. Grad. Sch. Bus. Adminstrn., N.Y.U., N.Y.C., 1975-81, prof., 1981—; cons. Morgan Guaranty Trust Co., N.Y.C., 1972-77, Bank of Am., N.Y.C., 1982-84, Res. City Bankers, N.Y.C., 1978-87, Swedish Inst. Mgmt., Stockholm, 1982—, Empresas Master of Puerto Rico, 1985— ; dir. Medallion Funding Corp., 1985-87. P.R. Econ. Devel. Adminstrn. fellow, 1960-65; Marcus Nadler fellow, N.Y.U., 1966-67, Phillip Lods Dissertation fellow, 1967-68. Mem. Am. Econs. Assn., Am. Fin. Assn., Metro. Econ. Assn. N.Y., Assn. for Social Econs. Author: Role of the Financial Sector in the Economic Development of Puerto Rico, 1970; contbr. articles to profl. jours. Home: 95 Tam O'Shanter Dr Mahwah NJ 07430 Office: 40 W Fourth St New York NY 10003

MALECKI, CHERYL ANN, accountant, financial analyst; b. Jackson Hts., N.Y., Dec. 9, 1958; d. Joseph Peter and Lorraine Marie (Zaino) M. BBA magna cum laude, Dowling Coll., 1980; MBA in Mgmt. Info. Services with distinction, N.Y. Inst. Tech., 1986. CPA, N.Y. Bookkeeper Various firms, L.I., N.Y., 1975-78; asst. fin. controller So. Container Corp., Hauppage, N.Y., 1978-80; staff acct. Estee Lauder, Inc., Melville, N.Y., 1980-82; sr. acct. Ralph Conti, CPA, Garden City, N.Y., 1982-85; bus. analyst Citicorp, N.Y.C., 1985-88; pvt. practice acctg. N.Y.C., 1985—; confidential fin. analyst Newspaper div. N.Y. Times Co., N.Y.C., 1988-89; head finance dept. Citicorp Internat. Corp., N.Y.C., 1989—; treas. Frost House Coop. Corp., 1988—; acct. Clinton Ave Coop. Corp., 1985—, 501 E. 12th St. Coop. Corp., 1987—, 546 E. 11th St. Coop. Corp., 1987—; implemented fin. system for Citicorp. Satellite Corp., 1986; project/system mgmt. N.Y. Times Corp., 1988. Author Policy Manual for Citicorp. Satellite Corp., 1986. Mem. Am. Inst. CPAs, N.Y. Soc. CPAs (mem. com. for cooperation with investment bankers and stock brokers, 1987—, com. fin. analysis, 1986-87), Delta Mu Delta. Home: 1160 3rd Ave 8F New York NY 10021 Office: Citicorp Internat Corp Finance Dept 399 Park Ave 10th Fl Zone 10 New York NY 10043

MALEK, FREDERIC VINCENT, banker; b. Oak Park, Ill., Dec. 22, 1936; s. Fred W. and Martha (Smickilas) M.; m. Marlene A. McArthur, Aug. 5, 1961; children: Fred W., Michelle A. BS, U.S. Mil. Acad., 1959; MBA, Harvard U., 1964; D of Humanities (hon.), St. Leo Coll., St. Petersburg, Fla., 1970. Assoc. McKinsey & Co., Inc., Los Angeles, 1964-67; chmn. Triangle Corp., Columbia, S.C., 1967-69; dep. under sec. HEW, Washington, 1969-70; spl. asst. to Pres. U.S., Washington, 1970-73; dep. dir. U.S. Office of Mgmt. and Budget, Washington, 1973-75; with Marriott Corp., Washington, 1975-88, sr. v.p., 1975-77, exec. v.p., 1978-88; pres. Marriott Hotels and Resorts, Washington, 1981-88; sr. adviser Carlyle Group, Washington, 1989—; co-chmn. comml. group Coldwell Banker, 1989—; bd. dirs. Automatic Data Processing Corp., Avis Inc., Nat. Edn. Corp., FPL Group, Inc., Paine Webber Funds, Gibson Greetings, Inc.; adj. prof. U. S.C., 1968-69; lectr. Kennedy Sch. Govt. Harvard U., 1976. Author: Washington's Hidden Tragedy: The Failure to Make Government Work, 1978; contbr. articles to mgmt. jours. Mem. President's Commn. on White House Fellows, 1971-75, President's Commn. on Pvt. Sector Initiatives, White House Domestic Council, 1974-75, President's Commn. on Personnel Interchange, 1974-76; dep. dir. com. for Re-election of Pres., 1972; dir. conv. Bush for Pres., 1988; nat. adv. bd. Nat. Center Econ. Edn. of Children, 1980—; mem. Pres.' Council on Phys. Fitness and Sports, 1986—. Served to 1st lt. AUS, 1959-62. Mem. Harvard Club of So. Calif. (bd. dirs., 1st v.p. 1965-67), University Club (com. chmn. 1966-68). Episcopalian. Office: Carlyle Group 1000 Pennsylvania Ave NW Washington DC 20004

MALEK, ILHAM MOUSSA, real estate executive; b. Beirut, July 1, 1956; came to U.S., 1976; d. Moussa Aziz and Mounira (Korio) M. BA, Barnard Coll., 1979; SM, MIT, 1986. Project analyst MAM Trading & Contracting Co., Sharjah, UAE, 1979-81; ops. officer Bank Audi USA, N.Y.C., 1987-88, mktg. officer, 1988; v.p. The Malek Group, Inc., Natick, Mass., 1988—; also bd. dirs. The Malek Group, Inc., Natick. Active Am. Task Force for Lebanon, Washington, 1988; exec. com. MIT Alumni Ctr., N.Y.C., 1988-89. Mem. Arab Bankers Assn. N.Am., Carnegie Council on Ethics and Internat. Affairs, World Affairs Council Boston, MIT Alumni Club Boston. Republican. Syrian Orthodox. Home: 47 Radcliffe Rd Weston MA 02193 Office: The Malek Group Inc 313 Speen St Natick MA 01760

MALESKA, MARTIN EDMUND, publishing company executive; b. Yonkers, N.Y., Apr. 3, 1944; s. Edmund Joseph and Marian (Kolton) M.; m. Elissa Mary Delfini, Apr. 27, 1968; children: Christine, Matthew, Danielle. BS in Chemistry, Fordham U., 1966; MBA in Fin., NYU, 1968. Dir. fin. Celanese do Brasil, São Paulo, Brazil, 1972-77; mng. dir. internat. ops. Pfizer Med. Systems, N.Y.C., 1977-80; dir. planning Macmillan Inc., N.Y.C., 1980-82, v.p., group exec., 1984—; pres. Nat. Register Pub. Co., N.Y.C., 1982-83, Media Plan Mgmt. Co., N.Y.C., 1983-84; bd. dirs. Intertec Pub. Co., Macmillan Inc., Maxwell Communications PLC. Served to capt. USAF, 1968-72. Mem. Info. Industry Assn., Chappaqua Swim and Tennis Assn. (dir.). Republican. Roman Catholic. Home: 3 Deborah Ln Chappaqua NY 10514 Office: Macmillan Inc 866 3rd Ave New York NY 10022

MALIK, HELEN THERESA, corporate officer; b. Owosso, Mich., Jan. 23, 1943; d. Anthony Joseph and Helen Ann (Kleinedler) Sovis; m. Frederick Malik, May 22, 1965; 1 child, Frederick Fabian. Student, Charles Stewart Mott Community Coll., Flint, Mich., 1975, Gen. Motors Inst., Flint, Mich., 1985, Lansing (Mich.) Community Coll., 1988. Clk. accts receivable Mitchell Corp. of Owosso, Mich., 1964-67, sec. purchasing dept., 1967-70, clk. payroll dept., 1970-72, sr. clk. payroll and ins. benefits, 1972-82, asst. corp. sec., adminstr. pension, benefits, payroll, 1982-89; corp. sec. Mitchell Corp. of Owosso, 1989—. Treas. Corunna Band Boosters, Corunna, Mich., 1981-83; mem. Owosso Personnel Group, 1986. Mem. Am. Compensation Assn., Am. Payroll Assn., Bar Code User's Group. Roman Catholic. Home: 1425 New Lothrop Rd Lennon MI 48449 Office: Mitchell Corp of Owosso 123 N Chipman St Owosso MI 48867

MALIK, ROBERT KEVIN, financial services company official; b. New York City, Dec. 8, 1942; s. Robert and Sylvia Malik; m. Georgette Cullen, Sept. 10, 1966; children: Robert, Lisa. BBA, Hofstra U., 1971; MS in Computer Sci., Pratt Inst., 1982; postgrad. in exec. mgmt., Pa. State U., 1987; postgrad. in strategic planning, Babson Coll., 1988. Analyst Allied Chemical Corp., N.Y.C., 1966-69; cons. Mobil Oil Corp., N.Y.C., 1969-73; dir. W.R. Grace & Co., N.Y.C., 1973-76; v.p. data processing Md. Nat. Bank, Balt., 1976-78; mgr. Touche Ross & Co., Washington, 1978-83; dir. group ins. systems Cigna Corp., Hartford, Conn., 1980-83, asst. v.p. systems, 1983-85; v.p. corp. fin. and investment groups systems div. Travelers Corp., Hartford, 1985-87; v.p. corp. tech. The Travelers Cos., Hartford, 1987-88, v.p. corp. tech. and agy. mktg. group property and casualty group, 1988—; tchr. computer sci U. Hartford, 1982, exec. mgmt. program Pa. State U.; mem. MIT Enterprise Forum. Chmn. United Way Campaign, 1983-84. Republican. Roman Catholic. Home: 38 Copplestone Avon CT 06001 Office: Travelers Corp Corp Fin and Investment Groups Systems Div Hartford CT 06152

MALIK, RONALD ANTHONY, food products executive; b. Chgo., Apr. 24, 1938; s. Anthony Aloious and Julia Elizabeth (Vargo) M.; m. Patricia Lynn Perry, Nov. 12, 1960; children: Jayme Lynn, Scott Anthony, Jeffrey James. BSBA, Marquette U., 1960. Salesman Marhoefer Packing Co., Muncie, Ind., 1960-61; broker United Brokers, Inc., Chgo., 1961-69; broker, wholesaler Malik Melin Brokers and Mac's Foods Inc., Park Ridge and Des Plaines, Ill., 1969-79; wholesaler Jason's Foods, Inc., Northbrook, Ill., 1979-82; wholesaler, owner Mac's Foods, Inc., Des Plaines, 1982—. Bd. dirs. Glenview (Ill.) Youth Baseball, 1971-89, pres., 1982-88, 89. Mem. Am. Meat Inst. Republican. Roman Catholic. Home: 932 Kenilworth Glenview IL 60025 Office: Macs Foods Inc 1785 Oakton Des Plaines IL 60018

MALIN, RANDALL, airline executive; b. Phila., May 3, 1937; s. Patrick Murphy and Caroline Cooper (Biddle) M.; m. Lucinda Taylor Lusby, Oct. 26, 1962 (div. July 1982); children—Katherine Murphy, Sarah Biddle; m. Constance Louise Meakin, Mar. 26, 1983. B.A., Dartmouth Coll., 1959; M.B.A., Amos Tuck Sch. Bus. Adminstrn., Hanover, N.H., 1960. With fin. and planning dept. Am. Airlines, Inc., N.Y.C., 1961-67, asst. to pres., 1967-68, dir., asst. v.p. mktg. plans, 1968-70, v.p. resource planning, 1970-74, v.p. mktg. planning, 1974-75, v.p. passenger sales and advt., 1976-79; v.p. passenger sales and advt. Am. Airlines, Inc., Dallas, 1979-80; sr. v.p. mktg. USAir, Inc., Washington, 1980-83, exec. v.p. mktg., 1983—; dir. Airline Tariff Publishing Co., Washington. Served with U.S. Army, 1960-61. Mem. Inst. Cert. Travel Agts. (trustee 1979—). Home: 1104 N Pitt St Alexandria VA 22314 Office: USAir Inc Washington Nat Airport Washington DC 20001

MALIN, ROBERT ABERNETHY, investment banker; b. Mt. Vernon, N.Y., Dec. 13, 1931; s. Patrick Murphy and Caroline Cooper (Biddle) M.; m. Gail Lassiter, Nov. 5, 1960; children: Alison Campbell, Robert Lassiter. A.B., Dartmouth Coll., 1953, M.B.A., 1954. Asst. to comptroller Biddle Purchasing Co., N.Y.C., 1958-59; with Blyth & Co., Inc., N.Y.C., 1960-71; v.p. Blyth & Co., Inc., 1965-71, dir., 1968-71, sr. v.p., mem. exec. com., 1971-72; sr. v.p. corp. fin. Reynolds Securities Inc., N.Y.C., 1972-74; dir. Reynolds Securities Inc., 1973-74; mng. dir. First Boston Corp., N.Y.C., 1974—. Mem. adv. council Fin. Acctg. Standards Bd., 1973-78. Served as lt. (j.g.) USNR, 1954-57. Mem. Investment Bankers Assn. Am. (v.p., exec. com. 1970-71), Securities Industry Assn. (accounting com.), N.Y. Soc. Security Analysts. Republican. Clubs: Links, Bond, Midday Club (N.Y.C.) (gov. 1971—); Calif. (Los Angeles); Beacon Hill (Summit, N.J.); Morris Country (N.J.), Harbour Ridge (Stuart, Fla.). Home: 105 Whittredge Rd Summit NJ 07901 Office: First Boston Corp Park Avenue Pla New York NY 10055

MALINO, JOHN GRAY, real estate executive; b. N.Y.C., Oct. 15, 1939; s. Joseph and Dorothy (Gray) M.; m. Geraldine Seibel, 1964 (div.); m. Phyllis Susan Alter, Mar. 29, 1987; children: Joanne, Linda. BA, NYU, 1961. Lic. real estate broker, N.Y. Real estate broker Robert Joseph, N.Y.C., 1961-64; asst. v.p. Loews Corp., N.Y.C., 1964-83, v.p., 1983—. Chmn. Young Men's and Women's Real Estate Assn., N.Y., 1974, N.Y.C. Real Estate Bd., 1982. Lodge: B'nai B'rith (pres. real estate div.). Home: 553 Barnard Ave Woodmere NY 11598 Office: Loews Corp 667 Madison Ave New York NY 10021

MALLAN, FRANCIS SCOTT, retail executive; b. Ft. Gordan, Ga., Oct. 24, 1964; s. Edward Michael and Connie Elizabeth (Taylor) M. Student, U. S.C., 1982-83, 85-88. Night mgr. Chick-Fil-A, Columbia, S.C., 1980-82; asst. mgr. Showbiz Pizza, Columbia, 1983-85; credit mgr. Cir. City Stores, Inc., Columbia, 1985-89, ops. mgr., 1989—. Pres. S.C. chpt. Students Against Multiple Sclerosis, 1989—. Mem. Assn. for Soc. Personnel Adminstrs., Am. Mgmt. Assn., Kappa Sigma (pres. 1988-89, v.p. 1987-88, asst. alumnus advisor, Treas. Efficiency award 1987). Home: PO Box 11411 Columbia SC 29211

MALLARD, STEPHEN ANTHONY, utility company executive; b. Jersey City, Sept. 15, 1924; s. Stephen F. and Gertrude V. (Donahue) M.; m. Winifred Anne Carey, June 7, 1947; children: Stephen Kevin, Catherine Anne, Eileen Rosemary Mallard McClenehan. M.E., Stevens Inst. Tech, Hoboken, N.J., 1948, M.S.E.E., 1951. With elec. distbn., system planning and devel. Pub. Service Electric and Gas Co., Newark, 1951-77, v.p. system planning, 1977-80, sr. v.p. planning and research, 1980-88, sr. v.p. transmission systems, 1989—. Bd. dirs. Essex chpt. ARC, East Orange, N.J., 1985—, ARC No. N.J., 1988—; Essex County Grand Jury Assn., 1978-87. Served with USN, 1944-46, PTO. Fellow IEEE; mem. Nat. Soc. Profl. Engrs., , Conf. Internationale des Grands Reseaux Electriques a Haute Tension, Eta Kappa Nu, Tau Beta Pi. Roman Catholic. Club: Essex (Newark). Office: Pub Svc Electric & Gas Co 80 Park Pla PO Box 570 Newark NJ 07101

MALLERY, GARY DEAN, accountant; b. McMinnville, Oreg., Sept. 14, 1939; s. Albert James and Anne Verta (Williams) M.; m. Sharon Margaret Peyree, Sept. 10, 1960; children: Lynnette, Susan, Michelle. BS, U. Oreg., 1961, MS, 1968. CPA, Md. Acct. Deloitte Haskins & Sells, Portland, Oreg., 1962-68; acct. Deloitte Haskins & Sells, N.Y.C., 1968-74, ptnr., 1974-76; ptnr. Deloitte Haskins & Sells, Washington, 1976-86; ptnr.-in-charge Deloitte Haskins & Sells, Balt., 1986—. Mem., bd. dirs. Washington-Balt. Region Assn., 1986; com. chmn. Greater Balt. Com., 1987; v.p. Bus. Adv. Coun. U. Balt., 1987; bd. dirs. Batt County Econ. Devel. Rehab. Alliance, 1988; bd. dirs., treas. Shared Housing of Va., 1988. Mem. Am. Inst. CPA's, D.C. Soc. CPA's, Md. Assn. CPA's, Md. C. of C. (treas., bd. dirs.), Ctr. Club (Balt.), River Bend Club (Great Falls, Va.). Republican. Presbyterian. Home: 327 Warren Ave J Baltimore MD 21230 Office: Deloitte Haskins & Sells 2 Hopkins Pla Ste 1100 Baltimore MD 21201-2983

MALLETT, WILLIAM BRYAN, metal processing company executive; b. Galveston, Tex., Mar. 24, 1943; s. William Bryan and Lillian (Lusty) M.; m. Joan Glennis Lay, Aug. 1, 1964; children: Bethany Michelle, Joanna Ashley. BME, Ga. Inst. Tech., 1970; MS in Engring. Mgmt., Vanderbilt U., 1980. Registered profl. engr., Tex., Wash. Staff engr. Aluminum Co. Am. (Alcoa), Point Comfort, Tex., 1970-75; engring. sect. mgr. Aluminum Co. Am. (Alcoa), Pitts., 1979-83; chief mech. engr. Suriname Aluminum Co., Paramaribo, 1975-79; engring. mgr. Alcoa Minerals Of Jamaica, Kingston, 1983-88; engr. mgr. Wenatchee (Wash.) Works (Alcoa), 1988—. Sgt. U.S. Army, 1964-68, Vietnam, Fed. Republic Germany. Mem. Nat. Soc. Profl. Engrs., Am. Soc. Engring. Mgmt., Am. Soc. Mech. Engrs. Republican. Baptist. Office: Aluminum Co Am PO Box 221 Wenatchee WA 98801

MALLON, EDWARD JOHN, financial executive; b. N.Y.C., July 2, 1944; s. Edward John and Helen (Will) M.; B.B.A., Pace Coll., 1968; postgrad. Baruch Coll., 1968-69; m. Frances Raye Simpson, Aug. 27, 1966; children—Kathryn Elaine, Melinda Mary, Edward John. Asst. contr. Dishey Easton & Co., N.Y.C., 1966-68; control mgr. Glore Forgan/Wm. R. Staats, Inc., N.Y.C., 1968-69; v.p., treas., chief operating officer Chubb Securities Corp. (ULAICO Equity Services) and Hampshire Funding Inc., Concord, N.H., 1969-77, pres., chief exec. officer, 1977-86; pres. Chubb Investment Adv. Corp., 1985-86; v.p. United Life and Accident Ins. Co., Concord, 1978-82, sr. v.p.; v.p. Chubb Life Ins. Co. Am., Concord, 1980-82; v.p. Chubb Am. Service Corp., 1980-82; sr. v.p. Chubb Life Ins. Co. Am., Chubb Am. Service Corp., Concord, 1982-86, Chubb/Colonial Life Ins. Co. Am., 1982-86; sr. v.p. Vol. State Life Ins. Co., 1984-86; treas. Chubb Life Ins. Co. Am., Chubb Am. Service Corp., United Life and Accident Ins. Co., Colonial Life Ins. Co. Am., Chubb/Colonial Life Ins. Co. Am., 1983-86, pres., chief exec. officer Monarch Securities, Inc., Springfield, Mass., 1986—, also bd. dirs.; pres., chief exec. officer Monarch Fin. Svcs., Inc., 1988—, First Variable Life Ins. Co, 1987—, also bd. dirs.; pres. Retirement Svc. Corp., 1987—; chmn. bd. Variable Investors Series Trust. Mem. investment co. Am. Coll., 1977; bd. regents Coll. Fin. Planning, 1977-78; mem. council fin. and adminstrn. N.H. conf. United Meth. Ch., 1972-76; chmn. Concord chpt. N.H. Heart Assn., 1974; mem. Eagle Honor Ct. Merrimack county coun. Boy Scouts Am., 1981-86; council League N.H. Craftsmen, 1981-86, treas., 1983-86; bd. dirs. Concord chpt. ARC, 1982-86; bd. dirs., treas., former pres. Central N.H. Community Mental Health Center, 1978-82. C.L.U., cert. fin. planner; registered prin. NASD. Mem. Internat. Assn. Fin. Planners, Am. Coll. Life Underwriters, Nat. Assn. Security Dealers, Fin. Execs. Inst., Concord C. of C. (past pres.). Home: 4 Hemlock Circle Wilbraham MA 01095 Office: Monarch Securities Inc 1 Financial Pla Springfield MA 01102

MALLON, ROBERT JAMES, lawyer; b. Jersey City, May 7, 1948; s. William J. and Gloria M. (Calamano) M.; m. Janice L. Duphorn, Nov 11, 1978; 1 child, Christopher. BA in Econs., Rutgers U., 1970; postgrad., Fairleigh-Dickinson U., 1971; JD, St. John's U., N.Y., 1974. Trial counsel N.J Dept. Transpn., Maplewood, 1975-80; spl. counsel Gov. N.J., Maplewood/Trenton, 1980-81; trial atty. Sellar, Richardson & Stuart, Newark, 1981-83; ptnr. Masslar & Mallon, Mountainside, N.J., 1983-84; prin. Robert J. Mallon Esq., Union, N.J., 1984-86; ptnr. Vit & Mallon,

Hillside, N.J., 1986—; dir. bd. Regional Funding Corp., Mountainside, 1983-85; cons. Cellular Am. Inc., DALT Internat., Bestway Group, Better Bus. Bur.; lectr. Rutgers U., Farleigh dickinson U., Marymount Coll. Editor: (jour.) Public Employment, 1975. Dir. Boys Club-Girls Club, Union, 1984—; bd. dirs. atty. Hillside Bd. Health, 1986-87; mem. state rep. com. Served to sgt. 1st class U.S. Army, 1970-71. Mem. NRA, U.S. Power Squadron. Roman Catholic. Lodges: Rotary, Masons. Home: 23 Garden Oval Springfield NJ 07081 Office: Axco Inc 1089 Cedar Ave Ste 9 Union NJ 07083

MALLORY, TROY L., accountant; b. Sesser, Ill., July 30, 1923; s. Theodore E. and Alice (Mitchell) M.; m. Magdalene Richter, Jan. 26, 1963. Student So. Ill. U., 1941-43, Washington and Jefferson Coll., 1943-44; BS, U. Ill., 1947, MS, 1948. Staff sr., supr. Scovell, Wellington & Co., CPA's, Chgo., 1948-58; mgr. Gray Hunter Stenn, CPA's, Quincy, 1959-62, ptnr., 1962—. Mem. fin. com. United Fund, Adams County, 1961-64. Bd. dirs. Woodland Home for Orphans and Friendless, 1970—, pres., 1981-84, 87—. Served with 84th Inf. Div. AUS, 1942-45. Decorated Purple Heart, Bronze Star. Mem. Quincy C. of C. (bd. dirs. 1970-76), Am. Inst. CPA's, Ill. CPA Soc. Lodges: Rotary (bd. dirs. Quincy 1967-70, pres. 1978-79), Shriners (bd. dirs. Quincy 1982-85, pres. 1988). Home: 51 Wilmar Dr Quincy IL 62301 Office: 200 Am Savs Bldg Quincy IL 62301

MALLOY, JAMES B., paper goods company executive; b. 1927. BS, Babson Coll., 1951. With U.S. Gypsum Co., Chgo., 1951-52, Internat. Paper Co., N.Y.C., 1952-78; with Jefferson-Smurfit Corp., Alton, Ill., 1978—, sr. v.p., 1980-82, pres., chief operating officer, 1982—, also bd. dirs. Office: Jefferson Smurfit Corp PO Box 66820 Saint Louis MO 63166

MALLOY, JOHN RICHARD, lawyer, chemical company executive; b. Boston, Nov. 26, 1932; s. Thomas Francis and Mary (Field) M.; m. Maraleta Ellerson, May 24, 1960; children: Maureen, John, Megan, Elizabeth. BA, St. John's Sem., Brighton, Mass., 1954; LLB, Boston Coll., 1957. Bar: Mass. 1957. V.p., dir. fin. Remington Arms Co., Inc., Bridgeport, Conn., 1975-78; chief counsel, energy and raw materials E. I. du Pont de Nemours and Co., Wilmington, Del., 1978-79, asst. gen. counsel legal, 1979-83, dir. pub. affairs, 1983-85, v.p. pub. affairs, 1983-85, sr. v.p. external affairs, 1985—. Chmn. Jobs for Del. Grads., Wilmington, 1985—; trustee Del. Multiple Sclerosis Soc., 1980—, Med. Ctr. of Del., Christiana, 1985—; bd. dirs. Del-Mar-Va council Boy Scouts Am., Wilmington, 1984—, WHYY, Wilmington, 1987—. Served to lt. JAGC, U.S. Army, 1958-60. Mem. ABA, Fed. Bar Assn., Bus. Roundtable (pub. affairs com.), Del. Bar Assn., Pub. Relations Seminar. Democrat. Roman Catholic. Office: E I du Pont de Nemours & Co 1007 Market St Wilmington DE 19898

MALLOY, KATHLEEN SHARON, lawyer; b. Evergreen Park, Ill., Apr. 7, 1948, d. Clarence Edmund and Ruth Elizabeth (Petrini) M.; m. Randall Kleinman, Aug. 5, 1978; children: Brighid, Ellena, Grant. BA in Psychology, St. Louis U., 1970; JD, Loyola U., Chgo., 1976. Bar: Ill. 1976, Calif. 1977. CPCU. Account exec. Complete Equity Mkts., Wheeling, Ill., 1970-76, corp. counsel, 1976-80, v.p., gen. counsel, 1980-83, exec. v.p., gen. counsel, 1983, chief operating officer, gen. counsel, 1984-85, vice chmn. bd., gen. counsel, 1986—; founding ptnr. firm Malloy & Kleinman, P.C., Des Plaines, Ill., 1985—. Vol. atty. legal aid orgns., Calif., 1976-79. Mem. ABA, Calif. State Bar Assn., Mensa, Women's Bar Assn., Northwest Suburban Bar Assn., Nat. Legal Aid and Defender Assn. (ex-officio mem. ins. com. 1986—), Am. Soc. Chartered Property Casualty Underwriters. Office: Malloy & Kleinman PC 640 Pearson St Ste 206 Des Plaines IL 60016

MALM, RITA P., securities executive; b. May 8, 1932; d. George Peter and Helen Marie (Woodward) Pellegrini; student Packard Jr. Coll., 1950-52, N.Y. Inst. Fin., 1954, Wagner Coll., 1955; m. Robert J. Malm, Apr. 19, 1969. Sales asst. Dean Witter & Co., N.Y.C., 1959-63, asst. v.p., compliance dir., 1969-74; v.p., dir. Securities Ind. Assocs., N.Y.C., 1969-72; chief exec. officer Muriel Siebert & Co., Inc., N.Y.C., 1981-83; pres. Madison-Chapin Assocs., N.Y.C., 1984—; art mktg. cons. Mem. Women's Bond Club N.Y. (dir., v.p., program chmn., pres. 1980-82). Office: 3 Hanover Sq New York NY 10004

MALONE, RICHARD WAYNE, insurance company official; b. Bruce, Miss., Aug. 4, 1951; s. William Rupert and Jewel (Caperton) M.; m. Holley Susan Miller, Nov. 21, 1975; children: Bradley Wayne, Jenna Elise. BS, U. So. Miss., 1973; MDiv, New Orleans Bapt. Theol. Sem., 1975. Ordained to ministry Bapt. Ch., 1972. Minister youth and evangelism Main St. Bapt. Ch., Hattiesburg, Miss., 1976-79; minister music and youth Calvary Bapt. Ch., De Soto, Tex., 1979-82, Collins (Miss.) Bapt. Ch., 1982-83; career agt. Southwestern Life Ins. Co., Dallas, 1983-85, v.p., 1985-87; product and competition analyst Fidelity Union Life Ins. Co., Dallas, 1987—. Mem. Nat. Assn. Life Underwriters, Dallas Assn. Life Underwriters, Ins. Industry Citizen Action Network, Grand Prairie Soccer Assn. (coach). Republican. Home: 2550 Slaton Dr Grand Prairie TX 75052 Office: Fidelity Union Life Ins Co 2323 Bryan St Dallas TX 75201

MALONE, STEPHEN MICHAEL, data processing executive; b. Malden, Mass., June 20, 1955; s. James Patrick and Jane Theresa (Gately) M. m. Debra Jayne Collins, Nov. 1, 1980; children: Sean Patrick, Michael Stephen. BS in Bus. Edn., Salem State Coll., 1978. Supr. inside sales W.W. Grainger, Inc., Woburn, Mass., 1979-84; instr. bus. Adult Edn. Program, Woburn, 1984-87, pres. Midland dist., 1984—; instr. bus. Adult Edn. Program, Medford, Mass., 1987—; sr. contract adminstr. Computervision div. Prime, Bedford, Mass., 1984—, govt. contract mgr., 1988—. Coach Am. Softball Assn., Woburn, 1985-87. Mem. Am. Legion, K.C., Elks, Phi Beta Lambda. Democrat. Roman Catholic. Home: 22 Lexington St Woburn MA 01801 Office: Computervision 100 Crosby Dr Bedford MA 01730

MALONE, WILLIAM GRADY, lawyer; b. Minden, La., Feb. 19, 1915; s. William Gordon and Minnie Lucie (Hortman) M.; m. Marion Rowe Whitfield, Sept. 26, 1943; children—William Grady, Gordon Whitfield, Marion Elizabeth, Helen Ann, Margaret Catherine. BS, La. State U., 1941; JD, George Washington U., 1952. Bar: Va. 1952, U.S. Supreme Ct 1971. Statis. analyst Dept. Agr., Baton Rouge, 1941; investigator VA, Washington, 1946-59; legal officer, dep. gen. counsel, asst. gen. counsel 1959-79; individual practice law Arlington, Va., 1979—. Editor: Fed. Bar News, 1972-73. Pres. Aurora Hills Civic Assn., 1948-49; spl. asst. to treas. Com. of 100, 1979-81, chmn., 1982-83; pres. Children's Theater, 1968-69; trustee St. George's Episc. Ch., 1979—; chmn. Arlington County Fair Assn., 1979-83. Lt. col. AUS, 1941-46, ETO. Decorated Legion of Merit; recipient Disting. Svc. award, 1979, 3 Superior Performance awards, 1952-72, Outstanding Alumni award George Washington Law Sch., 1978. Mem. Fed. Bar Assn. (pres. D.C. chpt. 1970-71, nat. pres. 1978-79), Va. Bar Assn., Arlington County Bar Assn., Nat. Lawyers Club (dir.), Arlington Host Lions, Ft. Myer Officers Club. Home: 224 N Jackson St Arlington VA 22201 Office: 2060 N 14th St Ste 310 Arlington VA 22201

MALONEY, CLEMENT GARLAND, international marketing consultant; b. Hot Springs, Ark., July 4, 1917; B.A. in Bus. Adminstrn., Northwestern U., 1940; m. Monique Pearl Nguyen; 1 son, Thomas C. Dep. dir. Chgo. unit War Assets Adminstrn., 1946-48; chief major procurement USAF, Washington, 1948-51; chief aircraft div. office Asst. Sec. Def., Washington, 1951-53, program adminstr., Paris, France, 1953-55; spl. asst. for financial control air force resources to asst. sec. Air Force, 1955-58; spl. asst. to pres. Hoffman Electronics, Los Angeles, 1958-59; spl. asst. to pres. for domestic and internat. mktg. Gen. Dynamics-Electronics div. Gen. Dynamics Corp., N.Y., 1959-61; v.p. charge domestic and internat. mktg. Kollsman Instrument Corp., Elmhurst, N.Y., 1961-64; cons. to U.S. sec. def., 1964-66, 67-69; internat. mktg. cons. Philco Corp. div. Ford Motor Co., 1966-67; internat. mktg. cons. to sec. Def., 1967-69; spl. asst. to pres. Control Data Corp., 1969-72; fin. mgmt. and mktg. cons., 1972—; commr. Armed Services Commn., Long Beach, Calif. Mem. adv. bd. Salvation Army. Served to col. USAAF, World War II, Korea, Vietnam; col. Calif. State Mil. Res. Recipient Exceptional Civilian Service award USAF. Mem. Air Force Assn., Am. Def. Preparedness Assn., Mil. Order World Wars, Am. Mgmt. Assn., Mil. Order of Carabao, Res. Officers Assn. Home: Galaxy Towers 2999 E Ocean Blvd Apt 2040 Long Beach CA 90803

MALONEY, GEORGE THOMAS, health industry executive; b. Phila., Aug. 28, 1932; s. John J. and Clara (Becker) M.; m. Sara Marie Carroll, Apr. 26, 1969. B.S., Siena Coll., 1954. Labor relations rep. Gen. Motors, Linden, N.J., 1957-58; salesman C.R. Bard, Inc., Murray Hill, N.J., 1959-63; div. mgr. C.R. Bard, Inc., 1963-64, mdse. mgr., 1965-66, v.p. mdse., 1967-68, corp. v.p. planning, 1969-70, group v.p., 1976-77, exec. v.p., 1977-78, pres., chief operating officer, 1978-88, pres., chief exec. officer, 1989—, also dir.; v.p. mktg. services (Bard Mktg. div.), 1974, (U.S. Catheter & Instrument Co.), 1970-73; v.p., gen. mgr. Inspiron div. C.R. Bard, Inc., 1974-75, pres., 1975-76; dir. Electro-Nuleonics, Inc., Fairfield, N.J., 1977-88, Electro-Biology, Inc., Fairfield, 1985-88; Trustee Atlantic Health Systems. Patentee in field med. edn. Trustee Overlook Hosp., 1985, N.J. Hemophilia Assn., 1978—; bd. assoc. trustees Siena Coll. Served to 1st lt. U.S. Army, 1955-56. Office: C R Bard Inc 731 Central Ave Murray Hill NJ 07974

MALONEY, GERALD P., utility executive; b. Lawrence, Mass., Mar. 9, 1933; s. Thomas P. and Concetta M.; m. Dorothea Ames. BSEE, MIT, 1955, BSBA, 1955; MBA, Rutgers U., 1962. With Am. Electric Power Co., Inc., Columbus, Ohio, 1955—; controller Am. Electric Power Co., Inc., 1965-70, v.p. fin., 1970-75, sr. v.p. fin., 1975—; dir., v.p. fin. Appalachian Power Co., Ind. and Mich. Electric Co., Ohio Power Co., Ky. Power Co., Mich. Power Co., Wheeling Electric Co., Kingsport Power Co., Columbus & So. Ohio Electric Co. Mem. Edison Electric Inst. (fin. com.), Beta Gamma Sigma. Office: Am Electric Power Co 1 Riverside Pla Columbus OH 43216

MALONEY, KATHLEEN RAE, lawyer, corporate executive; b. Santa Monica, Calif., Aug. 20, 1951; d. Raymond LeRoy Long and Joanne Marguerite (Arseneault) Madison; m. Kevin Michael Maloney, Dec. 12, 1974; 1 child, David Sean. BA, Northwestern U., 1973; JD, Boston U., 1977. Bar: Mass. 1977. Assoc. Field & Schultz, Boston, 1977-82; asst. gen. counsel Chancellor Corp., Boston, 1982-86, v.p., 1985—, gen. counsel, 1986—. Mem. ABA, Mass Bar Assn. Office: Chancellor Corp Fed Reserve Plaza Boston MA 02210

MALONEY, SIMONE, accountant; b. Manchester, N.H., Sept. 11, 1936; d. Henri and Emilia Carignan; m. Anthony Maloney, Aug. 30, 1958; children: Paul, Charles, James. BS in Acctg., N.H. Coll., 1981. Cert. tax profl. Receptionist, telephone operator, acctg. supr. Travelers Ins. Co., Manchester, 1966-76, auditor, 1976-79; pvt. practice as acct., bookkeeper, tax caseworker Manchester, 1981—. Vol. Boy Scouts Am., campaign to reelect Robert Shaw for Mayor, City of Manchester, 1985, presdl. campaign Congressman Phil Crane, 1980; candidate for Alderman, City Manchester, 1983; office mgr. campaign Congressman Bob Smith, 1983-84 (treas. 1985-86); sec., chmn. Ward 2 Rep. Com., 1987-88, treas. 1988—; mem. N.H. State Rep. Com.; bd. dirs. Manchester Rep. Com., treas. 1989—; sec. Greater Manchester Federated Rep. Women's Club, 1987. Mem. Nat. Soc. Tax Profls., Smithsonian Inst. Republican. Roman Catholic. Home: 171 Russell St Manchester NH 03104

MALONEY, THERESE ADELE, insurance company executive; b. Quincy, Mass., Sept. 15, 1929; d. James Henry and F. Adele (Powers) M.; B.A. in Econs., Coll. St. Elizabeth, Convent Station, N.J., 1951; A.M.P., Harvard U. Bus. Sch., 1981. With Liberty Mut. Ins. Co., Boston, 1951—, asst. v.p., asst. mgr. nat. risks, 1974-77, v.p., mgr. nat. risks, 1977-79, v.p., mgr. nat. risks, 1979-86, sr. v.p. underwriting mktg. and adminstrn. 1986-87, exec. v.p. underwriting, policy decision, 1987—; also bd. dirs.; pres. and bd. dirs. subs. Liberty Mut. (Bermuda) Ltd., 1981—, LEXCO Ltd.; bd. dirs., dep. chmn. Liberty Mut. (Mass.) Ltd., London; bd. dirs. Liberty Mut. Fire Ins. Co.; mem. faculty Inst. Inst., Northeastern U., Boston, 1969-74; mem. adv. bd., risk mgmt. studies Ins. Inst. Am., 1977-83; mem. adv. council Suffolk U. Sch. Mgmt., 1984—; mem. adv. council to program in internat. bus. relations Fletcher Sch. Law and Diplomacy, 1985—. C.P.C.U. Mem. Soc. C.P.C.U.s (past pres. Boston chpt.). Club: University, Algonquin (Boston). Office: Liberty Mut Ins Co 175 Berkeley St Boston MA 02117

MALOOLEY, DAVID JOSEPH, electronics and computer technology educator; b. Terre Haute, Ind., Aug. 20, 1951; s. Edward Joseph and Vula (Starn) M. B.S., Ind. State U., 1975; M.S., Ind. U., 1981, doctoral candidate. Supr., Zenith Radio Corp., Paris, Ill., 1978-79; assoc. prof. electronics and computer tech. Ind. State U., Terre Haute, 1979—; cons. in field. Served to 1st lt. U.S. Army, 1975-78. Mem. Soc. Mfg. Engrs., Nat. Assn. Indsl. Tech., Am. Vocat. Assn., Instrument Soc. Am. (sr.), Phi Delta Kappa, Pi Lambda Theta, Epsilon Pi Tau. Democrat. Christian. Home: RR 52 Box 594D Terre Haute IN 47805 Office: Ind State U Terre Haute IN 47809

MALOTT, ROBERT HARVEY, manufacturing company executive; b. Boston, Oct. 6, 1926; s. Deane W. and Eleanor (Thrum) M.; m. Elizabeth Harwood Hubert, June 4, 1960; children: Elizabeth Hubert, Barbara Holden, Robert Deane. A.B., U. Kans., 1948; M.B.A., Harvard U., 1950; postgrad., N.Y. U. Law Sch., 1953-55. Asst. to dean Harvard Grad. Sch. Bus. Adminstrn., 1950-52; with FMC Corp., 1952—; asst. to exec. v.p. chems. div. FMC Corp., N.Y.C., 1952-55; controller Niagara Chem. div. FMC Corp., Middleport, N.Y., 1955-59; controller organic chems. div. FMC Corp., N.Y.C., 1959-62; asst. div. mgr. FMC Corp., 1962-63, div. mgr., 1963-65, v.p., mgr. film ops. Am. Viscose div., 1966-67, exec. v.p., mem. president's office, 1967-70; mgr. machinery divs. FMC Corp., Chgo., 1970-72; pres., chief exec. officer FMC Corp., 1972—, chmn., 1973—; dir. FMC Corp., FMC Gold Co., Amoco Corp., United Techs. Corp. Trustee U. Chgo.; bd. govs. Argonne Labs.; bd. overseers Hoover Instn. Served with USNR, 1944-46. Mem. Chem. Mfrs. Assn., Bus. Council, Bus. Roundtable, U.S. C. of C., Phi Beta Kappa, Beta Theta Pi, Alpha Chi Sigma. Clubs: Econ. (Chgo.), Chgo. (Chgo.), Mid-Am. (Chgo.); Links (N.Y.C.), Explorers (N.Y.C.); Indian Hill (Kenilworth, Ill.); Bohemian (San Francisco). Office: FMC Corp 200 E Randolph Dr Chicago IL 60601

MALPAS, ROBERT, petroleum company executive; b. Birkenhead, Eng., Aug. 9, 1927; came to U.S., 1978; s. Cheshyre and Louise M.; m. Effie Josephine Dickenson, June 30, 1956. BSc with honors, Durham (Eng.) U., 1948. With ICI, Ltd., Millbank, London, 1948-78; pres. Halcon Internat., Inc., N.Y.C., 1978-82; mng. dir., mem. bd. Brit. Petroleum PLC, London, 1983—; bd. dirs. BOC Group PLC, Eurotunnel PLC, Barings PLC. Decorated comdr. Order Brit. Empire; recipient Order of Civil Merit, Spain, 1967. Fellow Inst. Chem Engrs., Inst. Mech. Engrs., Royal Soc. Chemistry (hon.); mem. Inst. Dirs., Am. Acad. Engring. (fgn. assoc.), River Club (N.Y.C.), RAC Club (London), Royal Automobile de España Golf Club (Madrid), Mill Reef Club (Antigua).

MALPHURS, ROGER EDWARD, insurance company executive; b. Lake Worth, Fla., Dec. 15, 1933; s. Cecil Edward and Muriel Thelma (Ward) M.; m. Carolyn Sue Calapp, Feb. 2, 1963; children: Steven, Brian, Darren, Regina, Victoria. BS, U. Utah, 1961. Cert. med. technologist. Supr. spl. chemistry Cen. Pathology Lab., Santa Rosa, Calif., 1968-73; mgr. lab. Community Hosp., Santa Rosa, 1973-76; supr. chem., staff asst. Meml. Hosp., Santa Rosa, 1976-85; pres., chief exec. officer R.E. Malphurs Co., Sunnyvale, Calif., 1972—; owner, developer REMCO Mktg. Assocs., Santa Rosa, 1970-72, Better Bus. Forms and Typeset, Santa Rosa, 1977-81. Author: A New, Simple Way to Win at Blackjack, 1972. Served as squadron commdr. CAP USAF Aux., 1982-84. Mem. Am. Chiropractic Assn., Calif. Chiropractic Assn., Optimists Internat. (Santa Rosa) (youth awards chmn. 1969-74), Mem. Am. Pub. Health Assn. Republican.

MALSKY, STANLEY JOSEPH, physicist; b. N.Y.C., July 15, 1925; s. Joseph and Nellie (Karpinski) M.; m. Gloria E. Gagliardi, Oct. 15, 1965; 1 son, Mark A. B.S., NYU, 1949, M.A., 1950, M.S., 1953, Ph.D., 1963. Nuclear physicist Dept. Def., 1950-54; chief physicist VA, 1954-73; from instr. to asst. prof. physics NYU, 1960-64; adj. asso. prof., then prof. radiol. sci. Manhattan Coll., Bronx, N.Y., 1960-74; non-resident research collaborator med. div. Brookhaven Nat. Labs., Upton, N.Y., 1964-69; research prof. radiology NYU Sch. Medicine, N.Y.C., 1975-77; pres. Radiol. Physics Assn., White Plains, N.Y., 1965—, Therapy Physics Services, 1980—, Sigmasel Dosimetry, 1986—; bd. trustees Doggs Ferry Hosp., N.Y. Contbr. chpts. to books. Served with U.S. Army, 1945-46. Recipient James Picker Found. award, 1963-67; Founder's Day award NYU, 1964; Leadership award Manhattan Coll., 1969; AEC grantee, Bureau of Radiological Health grantee, Nat. Cancer Inst. grantee. Fellow Am. Public Health Assn., AAAS, Royal Soc. Health; charter mem. Am. Assn. Physicists in Medicine, Health Physics Soc., Sigma Xi, Sigma Pi Sigma, Phi Delta Kappa. Roman Catholic. Address: 119 Lansdowne Westport CT 06880

MALSON, REX RICHARD, drug and health care corporation executive; b. Stanberry, Mo., Nov. 26, 1931; s. Albert J. Curtis and Nellie E. Coburn (Bussey) M.; m. Jimmie S., May 25, 1956 (dec. 1980); children: Richard Gary, Gregory Neil; m. Vicki L., Feb. 10, 1983 (div. Aug. 1984). B.B.A., Ga. State U., 1961; postgrad. exec. program hon., Stanford U., 1983. Gen. transp. mgr. John Sexton & Co., Chgo., 1964-68; dir. distbn. system Keebler Co., Chgo., 1968-73; with drug and health care group McKesson Corp., San Francisco, 1973—, vice pres., 1984-86, exec. v.p. ops., 1986—, also bd. dirs.; bd. dirs. Sunbelt Beverage Co., Balt., Stationers Distbg. Co., Ft. Worth. Served with U.S. Navy, 1951-55, Korea. Mem. Am. Soc. Traffic and Transp. Republican. Office: McKesson Corp One Post St San Francisco CA 94104

MALT, RONALD BRADFORD, lawyer; b. Boston, Aug. 1, 1954; s. Ronald A. and Geraldine (Sutton) M.; m. Sharon Lynn Harford, Feb. 14, 1981; 2 children. AB, Harvard U., 1976, JD, 1979. Bar: Mass. 1979. Assoc. Ropes & Gray, Boston, 1979-86, ptnr., 1987—; bd. dirs. Pannill Knitting Co., Inc., Martinsville, Va., Data Translation, Inc., Marlboro, Mass. Mem. corp. Mass. Gen. Hosp., Boston. Mem. Republican. Episcopalian. Office: Ropes & Gray One International Pl Boston MA 02110

MALVEY, KENNETH PETER, banker; b. St. Paul, May 3, 1965; s. Peter Erick Malvey and Sharon Lee (Duden) Kessler. BS cum laude, Winona State U., 1987. With Advance Tool, Inc., St. Paul, 1983-85; v.p., exec. mgr. Video Action, St. Paul, 1986-87; library asst. Winona (Minn.) State U., 1986-87, fin. tutor, 1986-87; bank examiner Fed. Deposit Ins. Corp., Rochester, Minn., 1987—. Del. Rep. Party, Winona, 1984-85. Mem. Fin. Mgmt. Assn., Nat. Honor Soc., Winona U. Fin. Assn. (pres. 1986-87), U.S. C. of C. Lutheran. Home: 421 1/2 13th Ave NW Rochester MN 55901 Office: Fed Deposit Ins Corp PO Box 6608 Rochester MN 55903

MAMAT, FRANK TRUSTICK, lawyer; b. Syracuse, N.Y., Sept. 4, 1949; s. Harvey Sanford and Annette (Trustick) M.; m. Kathy Lou Winters, June 23, 1975; children: Jonathan Adam, Steven Kenneth. BA, U. Rochester, 1971; JD, Syracuse U., 1974. Bar: D.C. 1976, Fla. 1977, Mich. 1977, U.S. Dist. Ct. (no. dist.) Ind. 1984, U.S. Dist. Ct. (ea. dist.) Mich. 1983, U.S. Ct. Appeals (D.C. cir.) 1976, U.S. Dist. Ct. (D.C. cir.) 1976, U.S. Ct. Appeals (6th cir.) 1983, U.S. Supreme Ct. 1979. Atty., NLRB, Washington, 1975-79; assoc. Proskauer, Rose, Goetz & Mendelsohn, Washington, N.Y.C., and Los Angeles, 1979-83; assoc. Fishman Group, Bloomfield Hills, Mich., 1983-85, ptnr., 1985-87, ptnr. Honigman, Miller, Schwartz and Cohn, 1987—; bd. dirs. Covenant Credit Union, Associated Builders and Contractors. Gen. counsel Rep. Com. of Oakland County, 1987—, bd. dirs. 300 Club, Mich., 1984—; mem. Rep. Nat. Com., Nat. Rep. Senatorial Com., Presdl. Task Force; City dir. West Bloomfield, 1985-87; pres. West Bloomfield Rep. Club, 1985-87; fin. com. Rep. Com. of Oakland County, 1984—; pres. Oakland County Lincoln Rep. Club, 1989—; vice. chmn. lawyers for Reagan-Bush, 1984; v.p. Fruehauf Farms, West Bloomfield, Mich., 1985—; mem. staff Exec. Office of Pres. Of U.S. Inquiries/Comments, Washington, 1981-83. Mem. ABA, Oakland County Bar Assn., D.C. Bar Assn., Fed. Bar Assn., Mich. Bar Assn., Detroit Bar Assn., Fla. Bar Assn. (labor com. 1977—), Founders Soc. (Detroit Inst. of Art), Econ. Club of Detroit, B'nai Brith (v.p. 1982-83, pres. 1985—, trustee Detroit council, 1987-88, bd. dirs. Detroit Barristers Unit 1983—, pres. 1985-87), Detroit Athletic Club, Renaissance Club, Skyline Club, Fairlane Club, Savoyard Club. Office: Honigman Miller et al 2290 First National Bldg Detroit MI 48226

MAMMEL, RUSSELL NORMAN, food distribution company executive; b. Hutchinson, Kans., Apr. 28, 1926; s. Vyvian E. and Mabel Edwina (Hursh) M.; m. Betty Crawford, Oct. 29, 1949; children: Mark, Christopher, Elizabeth, Nancy. BS, U. Kans., 1949. Sec.-treas. Mammel's Inc., Hutchinson, 1949-57, pres., 1957-59; retail gen. mgr. Kans. div. Nash Finch Co., Hutchinson, 1959-61, retail gen. mgr. Iowa div., Cedar Rapids, 1961-66, dir. store devel., Mpls., 1966-75, v.p., 1975-83, exec. v.p., 1983-85, pres., chief operating officer, 1985—, also bd. dirs. Served with AUS, 1944-46. Home: 6808 Cornelia Dr Edina MN 55435 Office: Nash Finch Co 3381 Gorham Ave Saint Louis Park MN 55426

MAMON, DEBORAH ELAINE, hotel executive; b. Chgo., Sept. 3, 1966; d. Joseph Anthony and Doris Elaine (Bonk) M. Student, William Rainey Harper Coll., 1984-85, Milw. Area Tech. Coll., 1985—. Reservationist Astor Hotel, Milw., 1986, reservations mgr., 1986-87; front office clk. Hyatt Regency Milw., 1987-88, night audit mgr., 1988-89; adminstrv. asst. Good Samaritan Hosp., Milw., 1989—. Office: Hyatt Regency 7168 W Appleton Ave 3 Milwaukee WI 53216

MANARY, RICHARD DEANE, manufacturing executive; b. Des Moines, Nov. 11, 1944; s. Robert Claude and Veronica (Cornwell) M.; m. Eileen Cecile, Aug. 16, 1986; children: (Erica (dec.), Matthew, Stephen, Lauren. AA in Indsl. Engring., Southwestern Coll., 1976; BA in History, Calif. State U., San Diego, 1967, BS in Edn., 1973. Registered profl. engr., Calif. Mfg. engr. Rohr Industries, San Diego, 1967-78; chief research and devel. space products div. Rohr Industries, Riverside, Calif., 1978-80, project mfg. mgr., 1980-84; dep. program mgr. Rohr Industries, Wichita, Kans., 1984-87; mgr. Titan 3d, Titan IVmissle programs Rohr Industries, Riverside, 1987—. Contbr. articles to profl. jours. Chmn. Rohr Industries Co. Employee and Community Assistance Program, Riverside, 1981-85; adv. Jr. Achievement, Riverside chpt., 1978-79. Mem. Soc. Mfg. Engrs. (sr., assoc., chmn. 1978-79), Soc. Automotive Engrs., Soc. Material and Process Engrs., Am. Soc. Metals, Nat. Mgmt. Assn. (chmn. 1980-81), Air Force Assn. Democrat. Roman Catholic. Home: 23816 West View Dr Riverside CA 92506 Office: Rohr Industries 8200 Arlington Blvd Riverside CA 92503

MANASSAH, JAMAL TEWFEK, electrical engineering and physics educator, consultant; b. Haifa, Palestine, Feb. 23, 1945; s. Tewfek George and Alia Nasrallah (Kardoush) M.; m. Azza Tarek H.I. Mikdadi, Mar. 16, 1979; children—Tala, Nigh. B.Sc., Am. U. Beirut, Lebanon, 1966; M.A., Columbia U., 1968, Ph.D., 1970. Mem. Inst. Advanced Study, Princeton, N.J., 1970-72, 74-79; asst. prof. Am. U. Beirut, 1972-75; chief sci. adviser Kuwait Inst. Sci. Rsch., 1976-81; chief operating officer Kuwait Found., 1979-81; prof. dept. elec. engring. CUNY, N.Y.C., 1981—; cons. Columbia Radiation Labs., N.Y.C., 1970-73, Ford Found., N.Y.C., 1973-79, NSF, Washington, 1978-83; chmn. Internat. Symposium Series, Kuwait, 1979-81; bd. dir. Technopro, N.Y.C., 1982-86; mng. dir. Khayatt and Co., Inc., N.Y.C., 1982—; mem. organizing com. Chem. Rsch. Applied to World Needs II, Internat. Union Pure and Applied Chemistry, 1980-83; mem. Welfare Assn., Geneva, 1984—. Editor: Alternate Energy Sources (2 vols.), 1981; (with others) Advances in Food Producing Systems for Arid and Semiarid Lands (2 vols.), 1981, Innovations in Telecommunication (2 vols.), 1982. Commr. Lebanese Boy Scouts Assn., Beirut, 1972-75; adviser internat. program NSF, 1979-83. Columbia U. faculty fellow, 1966-68, Pfister fellow, 1968-70; grantee NSF, 1982-87; recipient ABI Key award, 1987. Mem. Optical Soc. Am., AAAS, N.Y. Acad. Sci., Assn. Mems. of Inst. for Advanced Study., Internat. Platform Assn. Christian Orthodox. Club: Princeton (N.Y.C.). Home: 55 E 87th St Apt 15G New York NY 10128 Office: CUNY Dept Elec Engring Convent Ave at 140th St New York NY 10031

MANATT, KATHLEEN GORDON, publishing company executive; b. Boone, Iowa, June 3, 1948; d. Richard Condon and Lewise Ryan (Gordon) M.; BA, Coll. Wooster, 1970. Prodn. coordinator Scott, Foresman & Co., Glenview, Ill., 1970-73, editor, 1973-81, product mgr., 1981-87; exec. editor McDougal, Littell & Co., Evanston, Ill., 1987—. Mem. Assn. for Supervision and Curriculum Devel., Nat. Council Social Studies, Ill. Council Social Studies, Nat. Assn. for Bilingual Education, N.E. Conf. for the Teaching of Fgn. Langs., Common Cause, People for the Am. Way, So. Poverty Law Ctr., Chgo. Council Fgn. Relations, Amnesty Internat. Presbyterian. Home: 3270 N Lake Shore Dr Chicago IL 60657 Office: McDougal Littell & Co PO Box 1667 Evanston IL 60204

MANCERA, AGUAYO MIGUEL, banker; b. Mexico City, Dec. 18, 1932; s. Rafael and Luisa (Aguayo) Mancera; m. Sonia Corcuera, July 18, 1959; children: Miguel, Carlos, Alvaro, Jaime, Gonzalo. Officer Banco de Comercio, Mexico City, 1953-56; economist Govt. of Mex., Mexico City,

1957-58; economist Banco de Mex., Mexico City, 1958-62, adminstr. Fomex div., 1962-67, mgr. internat. affairs, 1967-71, dep. dir., 1971-73, gen. dep. dir., 1973-82, dir. gen., 1982—. Home: Salvador Novo No 94, 04000 Mexico City Mexico Office: Bank of Mexico, Apdo 98 bis, Avda 5 de Mayo 2, 06059 Mexico City Mexico

MANCHESKI, FREDERICK JOHN, automotive company executive; b. Stevens Point, Wis., July 21, 1926; s. John Stanley and Luella (Zwaska) M.; m. Judith Knox; children: Mary Lou, Laura, Marcia, Bruce, Amy Frederick-a. B.S. in Mech. Engring., U. Wis., 1948. With Timken Roller Bearing Co., Canton, Ohio, 1948-57, McKinsey & Co. (mgmt. cons.), N.Y.C., 1957-63, Echlin Inc., Branford, Conn., 1963—; chmn. bd., chief exec. officer Echlin Inc., 1969—; dir. Russell, Burdsall & Ward Inc., The Conn. Nat. Bank. Contbg. author: Turnaround Management, 1974. Former Mem. New Haven Devel. Commn.; former Mem. U.S. Indsl. Council Commn.; former bd. dirs. Quinnipiac council Boy Scouts Am.; trustee Hosp. of St. Raphael, Conn. Hospice, Albertus Magnus Hopkins, Quinnipiac Coll.; bd. dirs. Jr. Achievement; former trustee Conn. Pub. Expenditure Council. Recipient Gold award Wall Street Transcript, 1985; named Automotive Man of Yr., Automotive Warehouse Distbrs. Assn., 1973, Chief Exec. of Decade (Bronze award), Fin. World, 1989; named to Automotive Hall of Fame, 1985. Mem. World Bus. Council, Young Pres.'s Orgn., Nat. Soc. Profl. Engrs., NAM (former dir.), Conn. Bus. Industry Assn. (former dir.), Greater New Haven Co. of C. (former dir.), Sigma Alpha Epsilon. Clubs: Pine Orchard Country (New Haven), Quinnipiack (New Haven), New Haven Country (New Haven). Home: 10 Old Farm Rd North Haven CT 06473 Office: Echlin Inc 100 Double Beach Rd PO Box 451 Branford CT 06405

MANCHISI, JAMES, engineer; b. Astoria, N.Y., Oct. 21, 1957; s. Peter and Alice (McCue) M.; m. Margaret M. Canovan, Aug. 7, 1981; children: John Peter, Matthew James, Michael Thomas. BEE, Cooper Union, 1979; MS, SUNY, Binghamton, 1982. Program engr. Gen. Electric Aerospace, Johnson City, N.Y., 1979-81, devel. engr., 1981-84, staff engr., 1984-86, mgr. mktg., 1986-88; mgr. engr. Gen. Electric Aerospace, 1988—. Coach Cath. Youth Orgn., 1974-85. Recipient Bishop McGovern Outstanding Service to Youth award, 1977, Coach of Yr. award, 1981. Republican. Roman Catholic. Home: 516 Riverside Dr Johnson City NY 13790 Office: Gen Electric Aerospace 600 Main St Johnson City NY 13790

MANCINELLI, JACOB EMIL, corporate executive, consultant; b. Smock, Pa., Oct. 1, 1919; s. Joseph and Claudia (Di Russo) M.; BA, Harvard U., 1948; m. Sumiko Ogura; children: Teresa Ann, Kathryn Jean, Robin. With fin. dept. Gen. Electric Co. and G.E. C.C., Louisville, 1948-62; sr. v.p. U.S. Leasing Corp., San Francisco, 1962-69; sec., dir. Silver State Leasing Corp.; v.p., dir. Air Lease Corp., Barrel Leasing Corp., Cargo Vans Ltd., Comml. Pacific Corp., Fleet Leasing Corp., San Francisco, 1962-69; pres., dir. Compass Fin. Corp. (formerly Whittaker Leasing Corp.), Burlingame, Calif., 1969-73; pres., dir. TRE Fin. Corp., San Mateo, Calif., 1973-74; chmn. bd., pres. Dome Fin. Corp., Burlingame, 1974—; chmn. bd. Highridge, Inc., Redwood City, Calif., 1974-81; owner The Dome Co., Dome Realty, San Mateo, Calif., 1980—; instr. U. Calif. Extension. Pres., Foster City (Calif.) Home Improvement Assn., 1964-66, Pioneer Community Assn., 1985—; mem. Foster City Park and Recreation Commn., 1968—; chmn. Foster City Com. for Better Govt., 1973—; exec. bd. San Mateo council Boy Scouts Am.; bd. dirs. Foster City Community Assn., 1972—, pres., 1973—. Served as officer USAF, 1939-54. Decorated Air medal with 2 clusters, Presdl. citation. Mem. Nat. Comml. Fin. Conf. (dir. 1967—), Greater San Francisco (mcpl. legis. com. 1967-69), Foster City (dir. 1972) C. of C., Internat. Platform Assn., Res. Officers Assn., World War II 315th Troop Carrier Group Assn. (dir. 1988), Pioneer Dist. Community Assn., 1985—. Roman Catholic (council 1972—). Clubs: Commonwealth of Calif., Marina Point Tennis (pres.), Arnhem 1944 Vets. Author: Love Thoughts and Other Things, 1980. Home: 4927 Antioch Loop Union City CA 94587 Office: PO Box 381 Union City CA 94587

MANCUSI UNGARO, ALVIN PETER, international investment banking executive, plastic/reconstructive surgeon, chemist; b. Newark, July 24, 1921; s. Arnold and Anna (Marquardt) M.; m. Jeanne Reimer, June 6, 1944 (dec. May 1978); children: Judith Buff, Alan P., Philip. BS in Chemistry, Rutgers U., 1942; MD, Hahnemann Med. Coll., 1946. Diplomate Am. Bd. Plastic Surgery. Chemist Hoffman La Roche, Nutley, N.J., 1942, Wallace Tiernan, Belleville, N.J., 1943; intern Newark City Hosp., 1946-47; chief resident in surgery Presbyn. Hosp., Belleville, 1952-53; resident in plastic surgery St. Barnabas Hosp., Livingston, N.J., 1953-55; resident in hand surgery Roosevelt Hosp., N.Y.C., 1955-56; pvt. practice specializing in plastic, reconstructive and hand surgery Saint Barnabas, N.J., 1956-82; chief plastic surgery residency St. Barnabas Hosp., Livingston, 1968-80; cons. A&P Surg. Instruments, Newark, 1962-70; ltd. ptnr. Layton Oil, Tulsa, 1969-78; pres. Mancusi-Wingaro R.S.P.D. P.A. and P.S.F.D. P.A., Key Largo, Fla., 1983—; parliamentarian Internat. Soc. Plastic and Reconstructive Surgery, Rio de Janeiro, 1978; pres. Plastic and Reconstructive Surgery N.Y. Regional Socs., N.Y.C., 1978-79; instr. in field; cons. for pvt. placement of govt. borrowings internat. Contbr. numerous articles to profl. jours. Capt. USMC, 1947-49. Fellow Internat. Coll. Surgeons, ACS; mem. N.J. Surg. Soc., AMA, Practitioner Club. Republican. Presbyterian.

MANCUSO, GEORGE PHILIP, management consultant, educator; b. Chgo., Nov. 11, 1931; s. George Anthony and Josephine Rose (Pizzuto) M.; m. Concetta Faith Tamburo, May 15, 1987; children: George, Gary, Mark, Paul, Anne, Tricia, John. BBA, Loyola U., L.A., 1955; MS in Hosp. Adminstrn., Northwestern U., 1959. Assoc. adminstr. St. Mary's Hosp., Marquette, Mich., 1959-64; instr., dir. assn. svcs. St. Louis U. & Cath. Health Care Assn., 1964-71; assoc. dir. Alliance for Regional Community Health, St. Louis, 1971-72; asst. prof. Sch. Dental Medicine So. Ill. U., Edwardsville, 1972-76; exec. dir. St. Joseph Riverside Hosp., Warren, Ohio, 1976-83; dir. regional mktg. Fischer-Mangold Group, Pleasonton, Calif., 1983-84; pres. Mancuso Assoc., Columbus, Ohio, 1984—; lectr. mgmt. devel. seminars. Author: The Successful Manager 1986; contbr. articles to profl. jours. 1st. lt. USAF, 1955-57. Mem. Ohio Health Care Assn. (profl. devel. com. 1986—), Assn. of Ohio Philanthropic Homes for the Aging. Roman Catholic. Office: Mancuso & Assoc PO Box 29272 Columbus OH 43229

MANCUSO, JAMES VINCENT, automobile dealer; b. Batavia, N.Y., June 18, 1916; s. Benjamin J. and Laura (LaRussa) M.; student Gen. Motors Inst., Flint, Mich., 1949; m. Clarissa R. Pope, Sept. 8, 1945; children—Richard J., Robert P., Linda M., Laura Lee. Auto salesman C. Mancuso & Son, Inc., 1934-39, gen. mgr., 1939-42; gen. mgr. Batavia Motors (N.Y.), 1945-49; sales rep. Cadillac Motor Car div. Gen. Motors Corp., 1950-53; pres., gen. mgr. Mancuso Chevrolet, Inc., Skokie, Ill., 1953-74, chmn. bd., 1974-84; pres. Mancuso Cadillac/Honda, Inc., Barrington, Ill., 1974-76, chmn. bd., 1976—; pres. Mancuso Co., 1984—; pres., Service Survey Systems, 1985—; adv. council Consol. Am. Life Ins. Co.; dir. Lake States Life Ins. Co.; mem. faculty Chevrolet Acad., Wayne State U., 1964; dir. Auto Industries Hwy. Safety Com. Chmn. Niles Twp. Jud. Reform Com.; gen. mgr. Niles Twp. Community Fund, 1955; chmn. Skokie's All Am. City Com., 1961. Served from pvt. to maj. USAAF, 1942-46. Mem. Am. Legion, Nat. Auto Dealers Assn. (dir. chmn. pub. relations com.), Chgo. Better Bus. Bur. (dir.), Asso. Employers Ill. (dir.), Skokie C. of C. (pres. 1956), Chgo. Auto Dealers Assn. (dir. 1959-68), Chgo. Auto Trade Assn. (v.p. 1959-60), Chgo. Met. Chevrolet Dealers Assn. (pres. 1957-59), Chgo. Chevrolet Dealers Advt. Assn. (pres. 1969-70). Roman Catholic. Clubs: Rotary (pres. 1960-61), Evanston Golf (pres. 1969-70); Boca (Boca Raton, Fla.). Home: 17 Longmeadow Rd Winnetka IL 60093 Office: Box 278 Winnetka IL 60093

MANCUSO, ROBERT JAMES, insurance company executive; b. Jersey City, May 29, 1949; s. Robert Alar and Dorothy Roche; m. Linda Bielik (div. 1984); children: Eve Vera, Robin Marie. Student, Marlboro U., 1966-68; Assoc. in Paramedicine, Yavapai U., 1984. Exec. dir. Jean Paul Modeling Inc., San Diego, 1974-77, Thin Systems Inc., Prescott, Ariz., 1979-82; gen. mgr. Nevada Medi-Car Inc., Las Vegas, 1982-84; pres. R.J. Mancuso & Assocs., Inc., Belleville, N.J., 1984—. Creator fashion modeling piece, 1974. Eucharistic minister, lector St. Paul of the Cross Ch., Jersey City, 1984—. Served as cpl. USMC, 1969-71, Vietnam. Recipient MAn of Yr. award Criminal Justice Police News, 1988. Mem. Life Underwriting Tng. Council, U.S. Chess Fedn., ACLU. Roman Catholic. Lodge: KC. Office: 41 Watchung Ave Belleville NJ 07109

MAND, MARTIN G., financial executive; b. Norfolk, Va., Sept. 26, 1936; s. Meyer J. and Lena (Sutton) M.; m. Shelly Cohen, Aug. 29, 1965; children: Gregory S., Michael E., Brian C. BS in Commerce, U. Va., 1958; MBA, U. Del., 1964. Various fin. staff and mgmt. positions E.I. du Pont de Nemours & Co., Wilmington, Del., 1961-83, v.p. taxes and fin. services, 1983-84; v.p., comptroller, 1984-88, v.p., treas. 1989— ; dir. First Fed. Savs. and Loan, Wilmington, 1977-83; pres. Fin. Execs. Research Found., 1988—. Lt. USN, 1958-61. Mem. Fin. Execs. Inst. Office: E I du Pont de Nemours & Co 1007 Market St D-8000 Wilmington DE 19898

MANDAR, WILLIAM L., lawyer; b. N.Y.C., Nov. 21, 1947; s. Alexander J. and Babette E. (Katz) M.; m. Gwenn E. Drucker, Aug. 28, 1975 (div. 1980); m. Silvana Toueg, Dec. 30, 1986. BA, Queens Coll., 1968; JD, NYU, 1971, LLM in Taxation, 1979. Bar: N.Y. 1972, Fla. 1974, U.S. Dist. Ct. (ea. and so. dists.) N.Y., U.S. Tax Ct., U.S. Cir. Ct. (2d cir.). Estate tax atty. IRS, Bklyn., 1972-79; mem. counsel Sperduto Spector & Co., N.Y.C., 1979-80, Padell, Nadel, Fine, Weinberger & Co., N.Y.C., 1981—. Mem. Fla. Bar Assn. Home: 68-10 108th St Forest Hill NY 11375 Office: Padell Nadell Fine Weinberger & Co 1775 Broadway 7th Fl New York NY 10019

MANDARICH, DAVID D., real estate corporation executive; b. 1948. With Majestic Savs. and Loan, 1966-67; formerly chief operating officer, exec. v.p. MDC Holdings Inc.; pres., co-chief operating officer MDC Holdings Inc., Denver, from 1986, now pres., chief operating officer. Office: MDC Holdings Inc 3600 S Yosemite St Denver CO 80237 *

MANDEL, HERBERT MAURICE, civil engineer; b. Port Chester, N.Y., May 11, 1924; s. Arthur William and Rose (Schmeiser) M.; m. Charlotte Feldman, Aug. 22, 1954; children—Rosanne Mandel Levine, Elliott D., Arthur M. B.S.C.E., Va. Poly. Inst., 1948, M.Engring., Yale U., 1949. Registered profl. engr., N.Y., Conn., Md., Mich., Minn., Ohio, Pa., R.I., Va., W.Va. Structural engr. Madigan Hyland Co., Long Island City, N.Y., 1949-50; with firm Parsons, Brinckerhoff, Quade & Douglas, Inc., 1950-86; v.p. GAI Cons. Inc., 1986—, project mgr., Atlanta, 1962, N.Y.C., 1963-70, Honolulu, 1970-74, v.p., 1975, sr. v.p., Pitts., 1977-86; faculty Yale U., 1948-49; adj. faculty Bklyn. Poly. Inst., 1956-64, U. Pitts., 1986; gen. chmn. 6th Internat. Bridge Conf., Pitts., 1989. Author tech. papers. Served to 1st lt. U.S. Army, 1943-46, 50-52; ETO. Fellow ASCE; mem. Am. Ry. Engring. Assn. (steel structures specifications com., 1974—), Soc. Am. Mil. Engrs. (pres. Pitts. post 1987-88), Nat. Soc. Profl. Engrs., Profl. Engrs. in Pvt. Practice, Internat. Assn. Bridge and Structural Engring, Cons. Engrs. Council of Pa. (govt. affairs com.), Tau Beta Pi, Chi Epsilon, Omicron Delta Kappa, Phi Kappa Phi, Pi Delta Epsilon, Scabbard and Blade. Jewish. Club: Engineers (Pitts.). Home: 920 Parkview Dr Mount Lebanon PA 15243 Office: GAI Cons Inc 570 Beatty Rd Monroeville PA 15146

MANDEL, JACK N., manufacturing company executive; b. Austria, July 16, 1911; s. Sam and Rose M.; m. Lilyan, Aug. 14, 1938. Student, Fenn Coll., 1930-33. Founder, now chmn. fin. com. Premier Indsl. Corp., Cleve. Mem. exec. com. NCCJ; trustee Wood Hosp., 1969—, Fla. Soc. for Blind, South Broward Jewish Fedn.; life trustee Cleve. Jewish Welfare Fedn.; pres. Montefiore Home for Aged; pres. adv. bd. Barry U.; hon. trustee Hebrew U.; trustee Tel Aviv U. Mus. of the Diaspora; life trustee The Temple. Clubs: Emerald Hills Country, Beachmont Country, Commede. Office: Premier Indsl Corp 4500 Euclid Ave Cleveland OH 44103

MANDEL, KARYL LYNN, accountant; b. Chgo., Dec. 14, 1935; d. Isador J. and Eve (Gellar) Karzen; m. Fredric H. Mandel, Sept. 29, 1956; children: David Scott, Douglas Jay, Jennifer Ann. Student, U. Mich., 1954-56, Roosevelt U., 1956-57; AA summa cum laude, Oakton Community Coll., 1979. CPA, Ill. Pres., nat. bd. mem. Women's Am. Orgn. for Rehab. through Tng., 1961-77; pres. Excel Transp. Service Co., Elk Grove, Ill., 1958-78; tax mgr. Chunowitz, Teitelbaum & Baerson, CPA's, Elk Grove, Ill., 1958-78; tax mgr. Chunowitz, Teitelbaum & Baerson, CPA's, Northbrook, Ill., 1981-83, tax ptnr., 1984—; sec-treas. Lednam, Inc., Coffee Break, Inc.; mem. acctg. curriculum adv. bd. Oakton Community Coll., Des Plaines, Ill., 1987—. Contbg. author: Ill. CPA's News Jour. Recipient State of Israel Solidarity award, 1976. Mem. AICPA, Am. Soc. Women CPA's, Women's Am. ORT, Ill. CPA Soc. (vice chmn. estate and gift tax com. 1985-87, chmn. estate and gift tax com., 1987-89, mem. legis. contact com. 1981-82, pres. North Shore chpt., award for Excellence in Acctg. Edn., bd. dirs. 1989—), Chgo. Soc. Women CPA's, Chgo. Estate Planning Council, Nat. Assn. Women Bus. Owners. Office: 401 Huehl Rd Northbrook IL 60062

MANDEL, LESLIE ANN, financial advisor, fundraiser, entertainment company executive; b. Washington, July 29, 1945; d. Seymour and Majorie Syble (Perlman) M. BA in Art History, U. Minn., 1967; cert., N.Y. Sch. Interior Design, 1969. Pres. Leslie Mandel Enterprises, Inc., N.Y.C., 1972—; sr. v.p. Maximum Entertainment Network, L.A. and N.Y.C., 1988—; fin. advisor Osmed Inc., Mpls., 1986—, Devine Communication/Allen & Co., N.Y., Del., Utah, N.Mex., 1984—, Am. Kefir Corp., N.Y., 1983—, Sta. KVBC-TV, Los Vegas, 1983—, Shore Group (Internat., Guyana); owner 11 nationwide catalogues, fundraising lists. Photographer: Vogue, 1978, Fortune mag.; braille transcriber: The Prophet (Kalil Gibran), 1967, Getting Ready for Battle (R. Prawe Jhabuala), 1967; exec. producer film: Hospital Audiences, 1975 (award at Cannes 1976). Fin. advisor Correctional Assn., Osborn Soc., 1977—; founder, treas. Prisoners Family Transportation and Assistance Fund, N.Y., 1972-77; judge Emmy awards of Acad. TV Arts and Scis., N.Y.C., 1970. Recipient Inst. for the Creative and Performing Arts fellowship, N.Y.C., 1966, Appreciation cert. Presdl. Inaugural Com., Washington, 1981. Fellow N.Y. Women in Real Estate; mem. Com. on Am. and Internat. Fgn. Affairs, Lawyers Com. on Internat. Human Rels., Sigma Delta Tau, Sigma Epsilon Sigma. Democrat. Jewish. Club: Venture Capital Breakfast (fellow). Home: 4 E 81st St Penthouse New York NY 10028 Office: Maximum Entertainment Network 1901 Ave of the Stars Ste 1774 Los Angeles CA 90067

MANDEL, MORTON LEON, industrial corporation executive; b. Cleve., Sept. 19, 1921; s. Simon and Rose (Nusbaum) M.; m. Barbara Abrams, Feb. 27, 1949; children: Amy, Thomas, Stacy. Student, Case Western Res. U., 1940-42, Pomona Coll., 1943; LHD (hon.), Gratz Coll., 1984, Hebrew Union Coll., 1986. With Premier Indus Corp., Cleve., 1946—, sec.-treas., 1946-58, pres., 1958-70, chmn., 1970—; also bd. dirs. Premier Indsl. Corp., Cleve. Pres. Jewish Community Ctrs. of Cleve., 1952-58, now life trustee; v.p. Jewish Community Fedn., 1971-74, pres., 1974-76, now life trustee; trustee Nat. Jewish Welfare Bd., v.p., 1964-70, pres., 1970-74, now hon. pres.; chmn. Found. Adv. Council, 1967-75; v.p. United Way Cleve., 1971-77, pres., 1977-79, chmn., 1979-81, now life trustee; v.p. Council Jewish Fedns., 1971-74, pres., 1978-81, now life trustee; pres. Bur. Careers in Jewish Service, 1967-70; mem. Commn. on Health and Social Services, City of Cleve., 1970-71; mem. ways and means com. Ops. Task Force, 1980; mem. vis. com. Sch. Applied Social Sci., Case Western Res. U., 1958-74, trustee, 1977—; trustee Mt. Sinai Hosp., Cleve., 1970-79, now trustee emeritus; trustee Cleve. Zool. Soc., 1970-73, Greater Cleve. Roundtable, 1981-83; founding pres. World Confedn. Jewish Community Centers, 1977-81, now hon. pres.; bd. govs. Jewish Agy., 1979-88; trustee United Israel Appeal, 1977-88, United Jewish Appeal, 1978-82; trustee Am. Jewish Joint Distbn. Com., 1975-88, mem. exec. com., 1978-82; founder Cleve. Project MOVE, 1981; founder Clean-Land Ohio, 1981, trustee, 1981—; vice chmn. Cleve. Tomorrow, 1982-88, trustee, 1982—; founder, chmn. Mid-Town Corridor, 1982-85; trustee United Way of Am., 1985—, exec. com., 1986—; mem. Ctr. Social Policy Studies, 1983—; co-chmn. Operation Independence, 1985-88. Recipient Outstanding Young Man of Yr. award Cleve. Jr. C. of C., 1956, Businessman of Yr. award Urban League of Cleve., 1973, Frank L. Weil award Nat. Jewish Welfare Bd., 1974, Charles Eisenman award Cleve. Jewish Community Fedn., 1977, Citizen of Yr. award Cleve. Area Bd. Realtors, 1973, Mgmt. Performance award Case Western Res. U., 1982, Business Statesman of Yr. award Harvard Bus. Sch. Club of Cleve., 1985, Dively award Corp. Leadership in Urban Devel., 1986, Ben-Gurion Centennial medal State of Israel Bonds, 1986; named Man of Yr. B'nai B'rith, 1980, Leader of Yr., Clean-Land Ohio, 1983. Home: 17250 Parkland Dr Shaker Heights OH 44120 Office: Premier Indsl Corp 4500 Euclid Ave Cleveland OH 44103

MANDELBAUM, FRANK, pharmaceutical company executive; b. Bklyn., Jan. 12, 1934; s. Sidney and Judith (Rosenbaum) M.; m. Elaine Sue Projan, Feb. 1, 1964 (div. Jan. 1976); children: Robert Michael, David Lawrence; m. Frances Ann DeToro, Apr. 16, 1981. BA, NYU, 1955. Pres. Aero-Shield Plastics Inc., N.Y.C., 1970-72, Integrated Plastics Inc., Long Island City, N.Y., 1972-74, J.R.D. Sales Inc., Long Island City, 1974—; exec. v.p., treas. Choice Drug Systems Inc., Inwood, N.Y., 1986—; chmn. bd. True Type Printing Co. Inc., N.Y.C., 1978—. Served with U.S. Army, 1957-59. Republican. Jewish. Lodge: Masons (master 1970, meritorious service award 1972). Office: Choice Drug Systems Inc 457 Doughty Blvd Inwood NY 11696

MANDELL, GARY LEE, financial planning firm executive; b. Cleve., June 27, 1957; s. Harvey M. and Mildred S. (Ginsburg) M. BS in Econs. cum laude, U. Pa., 1979; MBA, U. Chgo., 1982. Cert. fin. planner, registered fin. planning practitioner, registered prin., life and health broker; CPA, Ill. Staff acct. Cohen & Co., CPAs, Cleve., 1979-80; investment intern Gofen & Glossburg, Chgo., 1981-82; fin. planner Fin. Strategies, Chgo., 1982-84; pres. The Mandell Group, Chgo., 1984—. Mem. Am. Arbitration Assn. (panel of arbitrators 1988—), Internat. Assn. Fin. Planning (bd. dirs. 1986—), Inst. Cert. Fin. Planners, Ill. CPA Soc. (bd. dirs.), Million Dollar Round Table. Office: The Mandell Group 222 S Riverside Pla Ste 1800 Chicago IL 60606

MANDELL, STEPHEN ELLIOT, business consultant; b. Bklyn., Apr. 28, 1944; s. Herman and Estelle (Minchenberg) M.; BS in Mech. Engring., N.Y. U., 1965, MBA, 1978, PhD/ABD, 1978; MS in Mgmt. Sci., Stevens Inst. Tech., 1971; m. Barbara Cooper, Dec. 31, 1971; children—David Herman, Iris Morrisa. Engr. in tng. Combustion Engring. Inc., Windsor, Conn., 1965-66; project engt. Bendix Corp., Teterboro, N.J., 1966-67; successively project engr., mgmt. cons., chief mgmt. scientist U.S. Army Material Command, Dover, N.J., 1967-76; mgr. ops. Operating Group Citibank, N.A., N.Y.C., 1976-77, mgr. fin. ops. Investment Mgmt. Group, 1977-78; bd. dir. NE Health Survival, Inc., Maplewood, N.J., 1977-82; pres. Morgan/Tech. Corp., 1980—; cons. various stages of computerization businesses, specialist in computerization of med. office and ins. reimbursement, Cedarhurst, N.Y.; owner, founder Enchanted Valley Toy and Bear Refuge, 1980-86; founder, pres. Temple Ohr Tikvah Reform Jewish Synagogue, 1985-86. U.S. Army fellow, 1971-73. Mem. Inst. Mgmt. Scis., Assn. Computing Machinery, Modesto Jaycees (past v.p.), Boston Computer Soc., Healthcare Users Group Newsletter (editor), N.Y. Mcintosh Users Group (pres.), Healthcare Mgmt. Group, United Martial Arts (red belt), Omega Rho (nat. sec. ops. rsch. honor soc.), Beta Gamma Sigma (past pres.). Clubs: Teddy Bear Lovers. Home and Office: 8 Lotus St Cedarhurst NY 11516

MANDICH, DONALD RALPH, banker; b. Milw., Sept. 1, 1925; married. B.B.A., U. Mich., 1946, M.B.A., 1950. With Comerica Bank-Detroit (formerly Detroit Bank & Trust Co.), Detroit, 1950—, asst. cashier, 1957-61, asst. v.p., 1961-63, v.p., 1963-69, sr. v.p., 1969-74, exec. v.p., 1974-77, pres., 1977-81, chmn., 1981—; chmn. bd. Comerica Inc. (formerly Detroitbank Corp.). Office: Comerica Inc 211 W Fort St Detroit MI 48275-1045

MANDINE, SALVADOR G., insurance executive; b. N.Y.C., Dec. 31, 1921; s. Salvador Garcia and Asuncion Mandine; m. Carmen Alonso, Nov. 1, 1958; 1 child, Rosalind. BA, CUNY, 1950; LLB, Bklyn. Law Sch., 1953; postgrad., Adelphi U., 1973-74, U. Conn., 1974. Acct. various cos. in internat. trade, N.Y.C., 1945-57; reinsurance acct. Godoy-Sayan Ins. & Banking Orgn., N.Y.C., Havana, 1957-60; controller Barnett Internat. Forwarders, Inc., N.Y.C., 1960-63; asst. treas. Gen. Reinsurance Corp., N.Y.C., 1963-74, Greenwich, Conn., 1974-84, Stamford, Conn., 1984—. Active Rep. Town Meeting, Darien, Conn., 1979-84. With USN, 1942-45. Mem. Horatio Alger Soc., Am. Assn. Retired Persons, Am. Legion, KC. Republican. Roman Catholic. Home: 59 Du Bois St Darien CT 06820 Office: Gen Reinsurance Corp 695 E Main St PO Box 10350 Stamford CT 06904

MANDL, ALEX J(OHANN), transportation, energy, properties, and technology company executive; b. Vienna, Austria, Dec. 14, 1943; came to U.S., 1958, naturalized, 1968; s. Otto William and Charlotte J. (Peshek) M.; m. Nancy J. Scott, June 10, 1967; 1 dau., Melanie. B.A., Willamette U., Salem, Oreg., 1967; M.B.A., U. Calif., Berkeley, 1969. With Boise Cascade Corp., 1969-80; dir. internat. fin., asst. treas., then fin. chmn. Boise Cascade Corp., Boise, Idaho, 1973-80; sr. v.p. fin. and corp. planning Seaboard System R.R. Co., Jacksonville, Fla., 1980-85; sr. v.p. corp. devel. and adminstrn. CSX Corp., Richmond, Va., 1985-86; chmn., chief exec. officer CSX Tech., 1986-88, Sea-Land Corp. subs. CSX Corp., Iselin, N.J., 1988—; also bd. dirs. CSX Communications Inc., CSX Transp. Inc., Richmond Renaissance; bd. dirs. Cybernetics and Systems Inc. Trustee Jacksonville Art Mus. Mem. Fin. Execs. Inst., Soc. Internat. Treasurers, Young Pres. Orgn., Bus. Week Corp. Planning 100, Mgmt. Policy Council, Council Planning Execs. (conf. bd.), Fin. Execs. Inst. (com. on corp. fin.). Clubs: River, University, The Bull and Bear. Office: Sea-Land Corp PO Box 800 Iselin NJ 08830

MANDULA, MARK STEPHEN, financial institution consultant; b. Wichita, Kans., Jan. 15, 1957; s. John Jr. and Margaret (Ramusack) M.; m. Kathy Brumenshenkel, Apr. 26, 1986. BBA, U. Toledo, 1979, MBA, 1981. Rsch. analyst Austin Assocs. Inc., Toledo, 1979-80, dir. rsch., 1980-81; v.p. Austin Assocs., Inc., Toledo, 1981-85, sr. v.p., prin., 1985-87, exec. v.p., prin., 1987—; instr. Dept. Fin., Coll. Bus. Adminstr. U. Toledo, 1987—; chmn. bd. dirs. Internat. Credit Svc. Group, 1988—. Author: Banker's Handbook for Strategic Planning, 1985; contbr. articles to

MANEATIS, GEORGE A., utility company executive; b. 1926. BS in Elec. Engring., Stanford U., 1949, MS in Elec. Engring., 1950. With Gen. Elec. Co., 1950-53; with Pacific Gas & Elec. Co., San Francisco, 1953—, v.p., 1979-81, sr. v.p., 1981-82, exec. v.p., 1982-86, pres., 1986—, also dir. Office: Pacific Gas & Electric Co 77 Beale St San Francisco CA 94106 *

MANFREDI, JOSEPH JOHN, process distribution and design company executive; b. Weehawken, N.J., Jan. 1, 1952; s. John Carmen and Gladys Winifred (Rankin) M.; m. Lynne Yvonne Neukirchner, Sept. 21, 1985. BS in Indsl. Engring., Newark Coll. Engring., 1974; postgrad. in E.M., N.J. Inst. Tech. Sales engr. Trane Co., LaCrosse, Wis. and Livingston, N.J., 1974-76; applications engr. Process Pumps Inc., Kenilworth, N.J., 1976-77; dist. sales engr. Mooney Bros. Corp., Little Falls, N.J., 1977-79; N.J. sales engr. Eastern Dairy Equipment, N.Y.C., 1979-80; pres. GMP Systems Inc., Pine Brook, N.J., 1980—; pres. Sea & Ski Realty Co., West Milford, N.J., 1981—. Pres. Scribner Hollow Homeowners Assn., Hunter, N.Y., 1981—. Edwin Aldrin grantee, 1973. Mem. Parenteral Drug Assn., Internat. Soc. Pharm. Engrs. (lectr., mem. editorial bd. 1981-88), Am. Welding Soc., N.J. Inst. Tech. Alumni Assn. (past pres., mem. Pres.'s Gift Club), Pi Kappa Phi, Indsl. Sports Assn. Roman Catholic. Home: 1662 Macopin Rd West Milford NJ 07480 Office: 101 Rt 46 Suite 137 Pine Brook NJ 07058

MANFRO, PATRICK JAMES (PATRICK JAMES HOLIDAY), radio artist; b. Kingston, N.Y., Dec. 30, 1947; s. Charles Vincent and Anna Agnes (Albany) Manfro; Asso. Sci. in Acctg., Ulster Coll., 1968; diploma Radio Electronics Inst., 1969; student St. Clair Coll., 1974—; m. Janice Lynn Truscott, July 5, 1975; children: Wesley Patrick, Whitney Dawn. Program dir., radio artist WKNY, Kingston, 1966-70; radio artist WPTR, Albany, N.Y., 1970, WPOP, Hartford, Conn., 1970, CKLW, Detroit, 1970-71, WOR-FM, N.Y.C., 1971-72; radio artist CKLW Radio, Detroit, 1972—, asst. program dir., 1978-80, program dir., 1980-83; v.p. programming CKLW/CFXX, Detroit, 1983-84 ; pres. Musicom Inc., radio cons. co., Detroit; pres., chief exec. officer Internat. Data Corp., Wilmington, Del.; adviser New Contemporary Sch. Announcing, Albany, 1973—; comml. announcer radio, television, 1970—. Judge, Miss Mich. Universe Pageant, 1970. Mem. N.Y. State N.G., 1968-74. Recipient 5 Year Service ribbon N.Y. State, 1973; named Runner-up Billboard Air Personality awards, 1971. Mem. AFTRA, Screen Actors Guild, Internat. Platform Assn., Smithsonian Assos., BMI Songwriters Guild. Club: Dominion Golf and Country. Home: 3466 Wildwood St, Windsor, ON Canada N8R 1X2 Office: PO Box 186 Dearborn MI 48121

MANGAM, JAMES FREDERICK, financial planner; b. Bklyn., Aug. 16, 1946; s. James Frederick and Jean Margaret (Hoskin) M.; divorced; 1 child, Kevin Conrad. Student, Rockland Community Coll., 1965-67; BS, Western

Carolina U., 1970. Cert. fin. planner, CLU. Sales rep. Met. Life, Glen Rock, N.J., 1972-74, sales mgr., 1974-75, sales rep., 1975-77; owner The Mangam Agy., Paramus, N.J., 1977—. Served with U.S. Army, 1970-72, Vietnam. Recipient Sales Achievement award Chubb Life Ins., 1984-86, Leading Sales Rep. award BNL Securities, Inc., 1987, award Pres.'s Conf. Bankers Nat. Life, 1982-88. Mem. Nat. Assn. Life Underwriters, CLUs Soc., Internat. Bd. Cert. Fin. Planners, Internat. Assn. Fin. Planners, Inst. Cert. Fin. Planners, Employers Coun. Flexible Compensation. Republican. Office: The Mangam Agy 350 W Passaic St Rochelle Park NJ 07662

MANGAN, CHARLES VINCENT, utility company executive; b. N.Y.C., July 12, 1939; s. James Francis and Anne Frances (Farrell) M.; m. Edna Joyce Planz, July 23, 1966; children: Christopher, Michele, Suzanne, Theresa, Linda. BSME, Manhattan Coll., 1961; cert. in nuclear tech., Oak Ridge (Tenn.) Sch. Reactor Tech., 1964. Steam turbine engr. Allis-Chalmers Mfg. Co., Milw., 1961-63; nuclear engr. Niagara Mohawk Power Corp., Buffalo, 1963-69; supr. thermal generation planning Niagara Mohawk Power Corp., Syracuse, N.Y., 1969-73, mgr. system engring., 1973-75, mgr. prodn. plant engring., 1975-78, mgr. staff engring., 1978-81, mgr. design engring., 1981-82, v.p. nuclear engring. and licensing, 1982-85, sr. v.p., 1985—. Scoutmaster Boy Scouts Am., Liverpool, N.Y., 1978-83; cubmaster Cub Scouts Am., Liverpool, 1976-78; mem. Sch. Dist. Adv. Com., Liverpool, 1973. Mem. Am. Nuclear Soc., ASME (vice chmn. local chpt.), Atomic Indsl. Forum. Republican. Roman Catholic. Office: Niagara Mohawk Power Corp 301 Plainfield Rd Syracuse NY 13212

MANGAN, EDMUND LAWRENCE, technical and business consultant, business executive; b. Los Angeles, Dec. 20, 1938; s. Francis A. and Edith D. (Perry) M.; m. Suzanne Marie Yelle, Feb. 2, 1960; children: Alan, Michele, Meredith, Maureen. BS in Engring., U.S. Naval Acad, 1960; MBA, Lehigh U., 1975. With Bethlehem Steel Corp. (Pa.), 1964-82, tech. and managerial positions research and devel., 1964-77, in steel ops. 1978-82; ind. tech. and bus. cons., 1983—; v.p. engring. and mktg. SI Handling Systems, Easton, Pa., 1983-86; sr. industry exec. World Bank, Washington, 1986—. Served as ensign U.S. Navy, 1960. Mem. IEEE, Assn. Iron and Steel Engrs. (Kelly award 1973). Contbr. articles on indsl. measurement and control to profl. jours.; patentee indsl. measurement and control equipment.

MANGELS, JOHN DONALD, banker; b. Victoria, B.C., Can., Apr. 14, 1926; s. August and Marguerite E. M.; m. Mary Ann Hahn, Nov. 25, 1954; children: Susan, Meg, John Donald. BA in Bus. and Econs., U. Wash., 1950. With Security Pacific Bank Wash., Seattle, 1950—, pres., 1984-87, chmn., chief exec. officer, 1987—, pres., 1976-86, chmn. bd. dirs., 1986-87, chmn., chief exec. officer, 1987—; vice-chmn. Security Pacific Bancorp. N.W., Seattle, 1975-84; bd. dirs. PEFCO, ISC Systems, Inc. Trustee Downtown Seattle Assn., Corp. Council for Arts, 5th Ave. Theatre Assn., Seattle-King County Econ. Devel. Council, U. Wash. Devel. Bd., Wash. Roundtable, Children's Hosp. Found. Served with USAAF, 1944-46. Mem. Wash. Inst. C.P.A.s, Assn. Res. City Bankers, Robert Morris Assocs. Presbyterian. Clubs: Rainier, Broadmoor Golf, Seattle Tennis.

MANGES, JAMES H., investment banker; b. N.Y.C., Oct. 8, 1927; s. Horace S. and Natalie (Bloch) M.; m. Joan Brownell, Oct., 1969 (div.); m. Mary Seymour, Mar. 28, 1974; children: Alison, James H. Jr. Grad., Phillips Exeter Acad., 1945; BA, Yale U., 1950; MBA, Harvard U., 1953. With Kuhn, Loeb & Co., N.Y.C., 1954-77, ptnr., 1967-77; mng. dir. Lehman Bros., Kuhn Loeb Inc., N.Y.C., 1977-84, Shearson Lehman Hutton, Inc., N.Y.C., 1984—; dir. Baker Industries, Inc., 1967-77; dir., exec. com. Metromedia, Inc. 1970-86. Trustee The Episcopal Sch., 1978—, St. Bernard's Sch., 1985—, Phillips Exeter Acad., 1984—. Served with CIC, AUS, 1946-48. Clubs: Bond, Yale (N.Y.C.); City Midday, Century Country (Purchase, N.Y.). Home: 875 Park Ave New York NY 10021 Office: Shearson Lehman Hutton Inc World Fin Ctr Am Express Tower New York NY 10285

MANGHIRMALANI, RAMESH, international trade corporation executive; b. Bombay, Dec. 31, 1953; came to U.S., 1968; s. Chatur Thakurdas and Maya Mansukhani; m. Mona Gour, 1988. BA in History, Oxford U., 1975; MBA, London Sch. Econs., 1977; cert. internat. law and trade, U. Paris, 1979; diploma Exec. Devel. Program, Harvard U., 1984. Chief planner UN, Geneva, 1977-81; cons. Fin. Corp. Am., L.A., 1981-85; mgr. mktg. Calif. Fed. Savs. and Loan, L.A., 1985-86; pres. Marco Polo Assocs., San Francisco, 1986—; dir. Wall St. Cons. Assn., 1986—; pres. Indian Tourism Devel. Corp., 1988—. Author: Third World Debt Solution, 1987, Marketing of Financial Instruments, 1988, India's Role in International Economy, 1988. Dir. Indian Children's Assn., New Delhi; pres. Children's World. Mem. Am. Mgmt. Assn., World Affairs Coun., Commonwealth Club. Home: PO Box 26427 San Francisco CA 94126 Work: Marco Polo Assocs Inc 1540 Market St #425 San Francisco CA 94102

MANGIAPANE, JOSEPH ARTHUR, consulting company executive, applied mechanics consultant; b. N.Y.C., Aug. 1, 1926; s. Michael and Rose D'Amico M.; m. Marcia Balut, Oct. 30, 1954 (div. Apr. 1974); children: Rosemarie, Michael, Diana, Joseph J., Susan. BS, Fordham U., 1950. Stress analyst Republic Aviation, Farmingdale, N.Y., 1951-55; pvt. practice tech. cons. 1955-58; sect. mgr. Aerojet-Gen., Sacramento, 1958-61; project engr. Pratt & Whitney Aircraft, East Hartford, Conn., 1961-71; pvt. practice tech. cons. 1971-79; pres. Joseph A. Mangiapane & Assocs., Inc., Tampa, Fla., 1979—. Author numerous tech. reports. Served as cpl. USAAF, 1945-47, ETO. Assoc. fellow Am. Inst. Aeronautics and Astronautics; mem. ASME. Republican. Roman Catholic. Club: Pine Acres (Wethersfield, Conn.) (pres. 1968-69). Home: 4713 San Rafael St Tampa FL 33629 Office: PO Box 18876 Tampa FL 33679

MANGIN, CHARLES-HENRI, electronics company executive; b. Riom, France, Apr. 16, 1942; s. Louis Eugene and Monique (Mathivon) M.; m. Marguerite Stern, Nov. 27, 1974; children: Charlotte, Louis-David, Maxence. MBA, Ecole Superieure de Commerce, Reims, France, 1965. Computer salesman IBM, Paris, 1967-68; asst. to pres. EDC, Rome, 1969-71; gen. mgr. CEGI, Paris, 1971-77; pres. CEERIS, Paris, 1977-81, CEERIS Internat., Inc., Old Lyme, Conn., 1982—; cons. The Mitre Corp., Washington, 1973-78, Coyne & Bellier, Paris, 1973-76, IITRI, Chgo., 1979-81, PRC, London, 1980-81. Author: Lebanon, 1965, Surface Mount Technology, 1986; editor: SMT Today in Assembly Engineering; contbg. editor: Electronic Packaging and Production; contbr. articles to profl. jours. Mem. Soc. Mfg. Engrs., Internat. Electronics Packaging Soc., Am. Soc. Test Engrs., Internat. Soc. for Hybrid Microelectronics. Roman Catholic. Club: Ski (Les Arcs, France). Office: Ceeris Internat Inc PO Box 939 Old Lyme CT 06371

MANGO, LOUIS ALBERT, JR., sales executive; b. Jacksonville, Fla., Aug. 23, 1959; s. William Oberion and Harriet Susan (Lubell) Meeks; m. Dawn Lucinda Tesmer, July 13, 1985; 1 child, Christopher. BS in Edn., U. Ala., Tuscaloosa, 1982. Salesman Cutco, Birmingham, Ala., 1979-80; adminstrv. asst. Custom Food Co., Birmingham, 1982-83, field rep. Birmingham and Houston, 1983-84, regional mgr. Denver and Fremont, Calif., 1984-86, nat. sales mgr., 1986, v.p. sales deli-products group, 1986-87, v.p. Convenience Store Food Service div., 1987—. Vol. Red Cross, Birmingham, 1977-79. Mem. Ala. Ins. Soc., U. Ala. Nat. Alumni Assn., Nat. Deli Assn., Kappa Sigma (sports chmn., Athlete of the Year 1985). Republican. Baptist. Club: Interact (sec. 1975-77). Home: 801 Mill Run Ln Birmingham AL 35226 Office: Custom Food Co 19 W Oxmoor Rd Birmingham AL 35209

MANGO, WILFRED GILBERT, JR., consruction company executive; b. Weehawkin, N.J., July 11, 1940; s. Wilfred Gilbert and Mildred B. M.; children from previous marriage: Christian P., Peter H.; m. Charlene Holt, Feb. 14, 1985. B.S., Lehigh U., 1963; M.B.A., NYU, 1969. Auditor Hurdman & Cranstown, N.Y.C., 1963-69; dir. fin. Thomas Crimmins Contracting Co., N.Y.C., 1969-77; v.p. fin., mgr. fin. controls ITT Teleplant, Inc., N.Y.C., 1977-78; v.p. fin. George A. Fuller Co. div. Northrop Corp., N.Y.C., 1978-81, now pres., chief exec. officer, dir., 1981—. past chmn. bd. trustees, Marymount Manhattan Coll. Mem. Am. Soc. C.P.A.s, N.Y. State Soc. C.P.A.s. Clubs: Lehigh U. of N.Y.; University (N.Y.C.); Tokeneke. Home: 1 Tiffany Ln Westport CT 06880 Office: George A Fuller Co 919 3rd Ave New York NY 10022

MANILLA, JOHN ALLAN (JACK MANILLA), furniture company executive; b. Sharon, Pa., July 17, 1941; s. Vito John and Helen Elizabeth (Papai) M.; B.S., Youngstown State U., 1966; postgrad. Duquesne U., 1967-68; M.S. in Mgmt., Aquinas Coll., 1984; m. Paula Gale Jurko, 1960; children—Jacqueline Lee, John Paul, Paul Allan, Bradley James. V.p. Yankee Lake Amusement Co., Yankee Lake Village, Ohio, 1961-66, 70-71; sr. staff asst. Elevator Co., Westinghouse Electric Corp., Pitts., 1966-68, salesman I, 1968-70, salesman II, Union, N.J., 1971, Miami, Fla., 1971-72, dist. mgr., Indpls., 1973-77, regional mgr. archtl. and furniture systems div., Grand Rapids, Mich., 1977-79, nat. field sales mgr., 1979-81; mgr. strategic programs Herman Miller, Inc., Zeeland, Mich., 1981, group mktg. mgr., 1981, dir. mktg., 1981-84, dir. corp. distbn. resources, 1984; dir. sales and mktg. Gen. Office Equipment Co., Inc., Saddle Brook, N.J., 1984-86, v.p. sales and mktg., 1987—; elevator and office environment cons. architects, engrs., bldg. owners and facilities mgrs., contractors. Chief, YMCA Indian Guides, Allison Park, Pa., 1970; asst. scoutmaster Boy Scouts Am., Dania, Fla., 1971-72; asst. to Boy Scouts Am., Ind. Sch. for Blind, Indpls., 1973; jr. high sch. prin., instr. Christian Doctrine, St. Ursula Ch., Allison Park, 1968-70, St. Sabastion Ch., Masury, Ohio, 1970-71; pres. bd. edn. Our Lady of Mt. Carmel Sch., Carmel, Ind., 1973-76; mem. Carmel Dad's Club, 1973-74; pres. Princeton Estates Homeowners Assn., 1982; co-chmn. capital endowment campaign-continuing edn. div. Aquinas Coll., 1982, mem. master's program scholarship fund com., 1983-84; active Grand Rapids Bishop's Service Appeal, 1982, Grand Rapids Arts Council, 1980; mem. fin. and bldg. fund cons. St. Mary Magdalen Ch., 1984—; exec. com. Kentwood High Sch. Acad. Boosters, Mich., 1984. Recipient First in Performance award Westinghouse Electric Corp., 1972, 120 Club Honor Roll, 1968, 69, 70, 71, 72. Mem. Bldg. Owners and Mgrs. Assn., Constrn. Specification Inst., Assn. Gen. Contractors Ind., Am. Water Ski Assn. (torunament official), Mich. Water Ski Assn., West Mich. Water Ski Assn., Lake Mohawk Ski Hawks (trustee, v.p., chief tow boat driver), N.J. Garden State Games (asst. chmn. waterskiing), N.J. State Water Ski Fedn. (v.p., asst. chair), Cornerstone Playhouse (lighting director), Clubs: Rotary, Indpls. Athletic; Yankee Lake (Ohio) Water Ski (pres.); Renaissance (Detroit). Office: Gen Office Equipment Co Inc 94 Wagon Wheel Rd Sparta NJ 07871

MANLEY, CATHEY NERACKER, interior design executive; b. Rochester, N.Y., Feb. 10, 1951; d. Albert John and Eleanor (Roberts) Neracker; m. Keith Howard Manley, Dec. 2, 1972 (div. Sept. 1977). AS, Endicott Jr. Coll., Beverly, Mass., 1971. Interior designer Bayles Furniture Co., Rochester, 1971-78, dir. mktg. and design, 1978-81; pres. Fabric PROTECTION Rochester, 1982—; bus. cons. Susanne Wiener & Assocs., Stamford, Conn., 1981—; owner Cathey Manley Assocs., Rochester, 1981—; cons. Womens' Career Ctr., Rochester, 1976—. Contbr. to book: What Do You Say To A Naked Room, 1981; designer TV show Great American Home; writer, hostess video How to Sell Accessories. Mem. bldg. com. Rochester Health Assn., 1978-83; dir. Family Service of Rochester at Greece (N.Y.), 1973-76, Town of Greece Youth Bd., 1973-77; founder "The Point", Greece, 1971. Fellow Interior Design Soc. (pres. Rochester chpt. 1977-78, nat. bd. dirs. 1977—, nat. pres. at Chgo. 1983-85). Home: 2777 Enterprise Rd E #54 Clearwater FL 34619

MANLEY, HENRY SPARKS, human resources and labor relations director; b. N.Y.C., Feb. 8, 1944; s. Henry Miles and Charity (Sparks) M.; m. Muriel V. Wiggins, May 8, 1965 (div. Sept. 1971); children: Henry Kevin, Kyle Royce; m. Rosa Mary Merritt, Aug. 31, 1980; 1 stepchild, Kevin Alan. BA, Fordham U., 1977; M Pub. Adminstrn., NYU, 1980; Cert. in Labor Studies, Cornell U., 1987. Police officer N.Y.C. Transit Police, Bklyn., 1965-78; clinic adminstr. Albert Einstein Coll., Bronx, 1979-80; personnel mgr. Montefiore Hosp., Bronx, 1980-83, Columbia U., N.Y.C., 1983-84; dir. personnel Harlem Hosp. Ctr., N.Y.C., 1984-86; med. adminstr. N.Y.C. Transit Authority, Bklyn., 1986-87; dir. human resources Riverbay Corp., Bronx, 1987—; adj. prof. Coll. of New Rochelle, 1981—; bd. dirs. Queensboro Soc. For Prevention of Cruelty to Children, Queens, N.Y., cons., 1986—. Author: The Zulu-Health Services in South Africa, 1976. Bd. dirs. Hutchinson River Boys and Girls Club Inc., Bronx, 1987—; active 100 Black Men, Inc., N.Y.C., 1984—. Mem. Internat. Union Operating Engrs. Local 94-94A AFL-CIO (bd. trustees pensio and annuity fund). Republican. Baptist.

MANLEY, MARSHALL, lawyer; b. Newark, May 3, 1940; s. Nathan and Faye (Rosen) M.; m. Johanna Kallenberg, June 26, 1986; 1 child, Chase. BA, Bklyn. Coll., 1962; JD cum laude, NYU, 1965; LittD (hon.), Bklyn. Coll., 1987. Bar: Calif. 1966, D.C. 1985, N.Y. Pres., chief exec. officer, dir. The Home Group, Inc., Newark, Del., 1985—; chmn. bd. dirs. The Home Ins. Co.; dir. Gen. Devel. Corp.; mem. adv. bd. Fed. Home Loan Mortgage Corp.; mem. Calif. State Senate Adv. Council on Ins. Problems of Fin. Insts., 1984—. Mem. Motion Picture Devel. Coun., 1977-79, Commn. of Califs., from 1980, trustee Bklyn. Coll., Am. Mus. Nat. History, N.Y.C.; co-chmn. bus. com. N.Y. Zool. Soc.; mem. bus. com. Met. Mus. Art; mem. leadership com. Lincoln Ctr. Recipient Horatio Alger award, 1987, Alumnus of Yr., 1987. Mem. ABA, Calif. Bar Assn., Bd. Room Club., Met. Club, Rockefeller Ctr., Regency Club, Downtown Athletic City Club. Office: Home Group Inc 59 Maiden Ln New York NY 10038

MANLEY, NANCY JANE, civil engineer; b. Ft. Smith, Ark., Sept. 13, 1951; d. Eugene Hailey and Mary Adele (Chave) M. BSE, Purdue U., 1974; MSE, U. Wash., 1976; postgrad., U. Minn., 1976-77; grad., Air Command and Staff Coll., 1984, Exec. Leadership Devel. Program Dept. Def., 1988. Lic. profl. engr., Ga. Sanitary engr. Minn. Dept. Health, Mpls., 1976-77; sanitary engr. water supply EPA, Chgo., 1977; leader primacy unit water supply EPA, Atlanta, 1977-79, leader tech. assistance team, 1979-82; chief environ. and contract planning, project mgr. Grand Bay Range design USAF, Moody AFB, Ga., 1982-84; dep. base civil engr. USAF, Carswell AFB, Tex., 1984-86; dep. base civil engrs. USAF, Scott AFB, Ill., 1986—; mem. tech. adv. com. Scott AFB master plan study Belleville, Ill., 1986—; mem. Fla. Tech. Adv. Com. for Injection Wells, Tallahassee, 1980-82, Nat. Implementation Team for Underground Injection Control Program, Washington, 1979-82, tech. panel Nat. Groundwater Protection Strategy Hearings, 1981; judge Internat. Sci. and Engring. Fair, 1986. Active various church support activities, 1969-74; vol. Meals-on Wheels, Girls Scouts, others, various towns, 1982—; founder, crisis intervention counselor Midwest Alliance, West Lafayette, Ind., 1970-74; active St. Louis Math. and Sci. Network Day, 1989, Adopt-a-School Program, Lebanon, Ill., 1987—. Recipient Disting. Govt. Service award Dallas/Ft. Worth Fed. Exec. Bd., 1986. Mem. NSPE, Soc. Women Engrs. (sr. mem.; local offices 1979-82, 84-86), ASCE, Am. Women in Sci., Soc. Am. Mil. Engrs. (local membership and contingency engring. coms.). Office: USAF Civil Engring 375 ABG/DED Scott AFB IL 62225-5045

MANLEY, RICHARD W., insurance executive; b. Malone, N.Y., Dec. 26, 1934; s. Walter E. and Ruth (St. Mary) M.; m. Linda Kimberlin, Dec. 18, 1965; children: Stephanie, Christopher. BS in Bus., U. So. Miss., 1960. Cert. real estate broker. Account exec. Colonial Life and Accident, Hattiesburg, Miss., 1960-63; dist. mgr. Colonial Life and Accident, Oklahoma City, 1963-66; regional dir. Colonial Life and Accident, Denver, 1966-76, zone dir., 1976-82; pres. Commonwealth Gen. Group, Denver, 1982-88, Commonwealth Flex Comp. Co. Inc., Denver, 1986-88, Manley Properties Inc., Denver, 1982-88; cons. Capitol Am. Life Ins. Co., Cleve., 1987-88, bd. dirs. (Merco) Mercy Hosp., Denver, 1982-87. With USAF, 1956-59. Mem. Nat. Life Underwriters, Colo. Bd. Realtors, Sertoma, Cherry Hills C. of C., Rotary, Elks, Alpha Tau Omega. Roman Catholic. Home: 1518 Cottonwood Lane Littleton CO 80121 Office: Commonwealth Gen Group Inc 5000 S Quebec Suite 430 Denver CO 80237

MANLY, WILLIAM DONALD, metallurgist; b. Malta, Ohio, Jan. 13, 1923; s. Edward James and Thelma (Campbell) M.; m. Jane Wilden, Feb. 9, 1949; children—Hugh, Ann, Marc, David. Student, Antioch Coll., 1941-42; B.S., U. Notre Dame, 1947, M.S., 1949; postgrad., U. Tenn., 1950-55. Metallurgist Oak Ridge Nat. Lab., 1949-60, mgr. gas cooled reactor program, 1960-64; mgr. materials research Union Carbide Corp., N.Y.C., 1964-65; gen. mgr. Union Carbide Corp. (Stellite div.), N.Y.C., 1967-69; v.p. Union Carbide Corp. (Stellite div.), Kokomo, Ind., 1969-70; sr. v.p. Cabot Corp., Boston, 1970-83; exec. v.p. Cabot Corp., 1983-86; ret. 1986; also dir. chmn. adv. com. for reactor safety AEC, 1964-65. Served with USMC, 1943-46. Recipient Honor award U. Notre Dame, 1974. Fellow Am. Soc. Metals (pres. 1972-73), AIME, Am. Nuclear Soc. (Merit award 1966); mem. Nat. Acad. Engring., Nat. Assn. Corrosion Engrs., Metall. Soc. Presbyterian. Clubs: Cosmos, Masons. Home: Box 197A Rte 1 Kingston TN 37763

MANN, DONA JANE, real estate agent; b. Satanta, Kans., Apr. 10, 1933; d. Dwight Custer and Mable Pearl (Jones) Stevens; m. Earl Russell, June 23, 1951; children: Nedra Ann Mann Jennings, Douglas Claude, Darla Jean Olenick Mann Deck, Donald Dean. Grad. high sch., Florence, Kans. Br. mgr. Emmons Jewelers, Newark, N.Y., 1961-68; regional sales mgr. Deborah Dow Creations, Chgo., 1968-73; v.p. Jewels by Park Lane, Chgo., 1973-84; realtor, residential specialist Century 21 Challenge Realty, Wichita, Kans., 1983—; co-owner Mann's Siding Co., Wichita, 1977—, Midwest Mgmt. & Devel. Co., Wichita, 1984-86. Recipient numerous sales awards; Million Dollar Club, 1985-86, 87. Mem. Century 21 Investment Soc. Republican. Home: 1606 N Wheatridge Wichita KS 67235 Office: Challenge Realty 3540 W Douglas Wichita KS 67203

MANN, GEORGE STANLEY, real estate and financial services corporation executive; b. Toronto, Ont., Can., Dec. 23, 1932; s. David Philip and Elizabeth (Green) M.; m. Saundra Sair, Jan. 2, 1955; children: Michael, Tracy. Attended, North Toronto Collegiate Sch. Ptnr. Mann & Martel Co. Ltd., 1959-68, chief exec. officer, 1968-70; chief exec. officer United Trust Co., 1970-76; pres. Unicorp Canada Corp., Toronto, 1972-76, chmn. bd., controlling shareholder, 1976—; chmn. bd., dir. Unicorp American Corp., N.Y.C., Union Enterprises Ltd., Toronto, Union Gas Ltd., Chatham, Ont.; bd. dirs. Lincoln Savs. Bank, Nat. Bank Can. Bd. govs. Mt. Sinai Hosp., Toronto. Clubs: Oakdale Golf & Country (Toronto); High Ridge Country (Palm Beach, Fla.). Home: 18 Old Forest Hill Rd, Toronto, ON Canada M5P 2P7 also: Palm Beach FL 33480 Office: Unicorp Can Corp, 21 St Clair Ave E P/H, Toronto, ON Canada M4T 2T7

MANN, GORDON LEE, JR., insurance broker; b. Taylor, Tex., May 5, 1921; s. Gordon L. and Ruth (Kirkpatrick) M.; student, UCLA, 1939, Loyola U., L.A., 1961. Claims mgr. Traders and Gen. Ins. Co., L.A., 1948-52, Fireman's Fund Am. Ins. Cos., 1952-70; account exec., claims cons. Behrendt-Levy Ins. Agy., 1970-72; asst. div. mgr. Argonaut Ins. Co., L.A., 1972-78; v.p. Frank B. Hall & Co., L.A., 1978—. Lt. USNR, 1946. Recipient Meritorious Pub. Svc. citation Dept. Navy, 1965; Nat. Scroll of Honor, Navy League, 1968. CPCU. Mem. Am. Soc. CPCUs (pres. L.A. chpt. 1972, gen. chmn. nat. conv. 1970), Navy League U.S. (nat. dir. 1963-75, v.p. for adminstrn. 11th region 1974-75, pres. L.A. council 1962, state pres. 1965), Am. Legion (past comdr.) Nat. Soc. Colonial Wars (gov. Calif. soc. 1967, nat. dep. gov. gen. 1969), Children Am. Revolution (past nat. com. chmn.), S.R., Mil. Order World Wars, Men of All Saints' Soc. (past pres.), Naval Order U.S. Rep., Masons, L.A. Club, American Club. Episcopalian. Speaker and writer on ins. and patriotic subjects. Home: 435 S Curson Ave Los Angeles CA 90036 Office: 3200 Wilshire Blvd Los Angeles CA 90010

MANN, HENRY DEAN, accountant; b. El Dorado, Ark., Feb. 8, 1943; s. Paul L. and Mary Louise (Capps) M.; m. Rebecca Balch, Aug. 14, 1965; children: Julie Elizabeth, Betsey Sawyer Mann. BBA, U. Ark., 1965. CPA, Mo., Tex. Staff acct., mgr. Ernst & Whinney, Houston, 1967-76, ptnr., 1976-77; regional personnel ptnr. Ernst & Whinney, St. Louis, 1977-78, mng. ptnr., 1978-88; pres. Mann Industries, Inc., St. Louis, 1988—; mem. adv. bd. Sch. Accountancy, U. Mo., Columbia, 1979-82. Treas., bd. dirs., Jr. Achievement, St. Louis, 1986—, United Way, St. Louis, 1986, Art and Edn. Council, St. Louis, 1986—; bd. dirs., St. Louis Symphony, 1986—, Kammergild Chamber Orch., St. Louis, 1986, pres., 1983-85. Served to 1st lt. U.S. Army, 1965-67. Mem. Am. Inst. CPA's, Mo. Soc. CPA's, Beta Gamma Sigma, Beta Alpha Psi. Presbyterian. Club: Bellerive Country (treas. 1986, v.p. 1988—), Saint Louis.

MANN, JAMES MICHAEL, construction and real estate executive; b. Chgo., Apr. 21, 1946; s. Charles Hubert and Margaret (Hayden) M. BS in Civil Engring., Marquette U., 1969; MBA, Loyola U., Chgo., 1975. Pres. Joseph J. Duffy Co., Chgo., 1974—. Mem. ASCE, Constrn. Specifications Inst., Evanston Golf Club. Roman Catholic. Office: Joseph J Duffy Co 4994 N Elston Ave Chicago IL 60630

MANN, MARVIN L., electronics executive; b. Birmingham, Ala., Apr. 22, 1933; s. Jesse Marvin and Nannie Leola (Thomason) M.; m. Frances Nell Marlin, Dec. 24, 1953; children: Tara Jane, Jeffery Loy. BS, Samford U., 1954; MBA, U. Ala., 1958. V.p., gen. mgr. svcs. industries IBM Corp., White Plains, N.Y. Office: IBM Corp 44 S Broadway White Plains NY 10601

MANN, MICHAEL MARTIN, electronics company executive; b. N.Y.C., Nov. 28, 1939; s. Herbert and Rosalind (Kaplan) M.; m. Mariel Joy Steinberg, Apr. 25, 1965. BSEE, Calif. Inst. Tech., 1960, MSEE, 1961; PhD in Elec. Engring. and Physics, U. So. Calif., 1969; MBA, UCLA, 1984. Mgr. high power laser programs office Northrop Corp., Hawthorne, Calif., 1969-76; mgr. high energy laser systems lab. Hughes Aircraft Co., El Segundo, Calif., 1976-78; mgr. E-0 control systems labs. Hughes Aircraft Co., El Segundo, 1978-83, asst. to v.p., space & strategic, 1983-84; exec. v.p. Helionetics Inc., Irvine, Calif., 1984-85, pres., chief exec. officer, 1985-86, also bd. dirs.; ptnr. Mann Kavanaugh Chernove, 1986—; sr. cons. Arthur D. Little, Inc., 1987—; chmn. bd., pres., chief exec. officer Blue Marble Devel. Group, Inc., 1988—; mem. Army Sci. Bd., Dept. Army, Washington, 1986—; cons. Office of Sec. of Army, Washington, 1986—, Inst. of Def. Analysis, Washington, 1978—, Dept. Energy, 1988—; bd. dirs. Datum, Inc., Safeguard Health Enterprises, Inc., Am. Video Communications, Inc., Meck Industries, Inc.; bd. dirs., mem. adv. bd. Micro-Frame, Inc., 1988—; chmn. bd. HLX Laser, Inc., 1984-86; research assoc., mem. extension teaching staff U. So. Calif., Los Angeles, 1964-70. Contbg. editor, mem. adv. bd. Calif. High-Tech Funding Jour., 1988—; contbr. over 50 tech. articles; 12 patents. Adv. com. to Engring Sch., Calif. State U., Long Beach, 1985—; chmn. polit. affairs Am. Electronics Assn., Orange County Council, 1986—, mem. exec. com. , 1986—; adv. com. several Calif. congressmen, 1985—; mem. dean's council UCLA Grad. Sch. Mgmt., 1984-85; bd. dirs. Archimodes Circle U. So. Calif., 1983-85, Ctr. for Innovation and Entrepreneurship, 1986—, Caltech/MIT Venture Forum, 1987—. Hicks fellow in Indsl. Relations, Calif. Inst. Tech., 1961, Hewlett Packard fellow. Mem. So. Calif. Tech. Execs. Network, IEEE (sr.), Orange County CEO's Roundtable, Aerospace/Def. CEO's Roundtable, Am. Defense Preparedness Assn., Security Affairs Support Assn., Internat. Platform Assn., King Harbor Yacht Club. Republican. Home and Office: 4248 Via Alondra Palos Verdes Estates CA 90274

MANNERS, TIMOTHY GEORGE, public relations executive; b. Norwalk, Conn., Oct. 6, 1957; s. David X. and Ruth Ann (Bauer) M.; m. Beth Sydnie Dalis, Sept. 30, 1984. BA in History magna cum laude, Tufts U., 1979. Newscaster Westport Broadcasting Inc., Stamford, Conn., 1979-81; v.p. David X. Manners Co. Inc., Norwalk, 1981-84, pres., 1984—. Editor: The Gundersen Report, N.Y.C.; contbr. articles in field. Cons. Collins for Mayor, Norwalk, 1985, Bruce Babbitt for Pres., 1987-88, John Loeser for U.S. Congress, 1988; St. Sergius High Sch., N.Y.C., 1987-88. Mem. Fairfield County Pub. Rels. Assn. Democrat. Home: 58 Glen View Wilton CT 06897 Office: David X Manners Co Inc 84 W Park Pl Stamford CT 06901

MANNEY, RICHARD, advertising company executive; b. N.Y.C., June 19, 1936; s. Irving and Paula Manney; m. Gloria Peltz, Apr. 7, 1963; 1 child, Patricia. Student Baruch Sch. Bus. and Pub. Adminstrn., 1953-58. Sec., treas. Fine Art Productions, Inc., 1958-60; pres. Richard Manney Corp., 1960-66; pres., chmn. bd. The Mediators Inc., N.Y.C., 1966—. Chmn. Com. U.S. Senatorial Bus. Adv. Bd., Washington; chmn. com. Met. Mus. Art; mem. mus. bd. Nat. Acad. Design; mem. adv. council dept. art Columbia U.; mem. com. Am. arts Art Inst. Chgo.; mem. com. rsch. libs. N.Y. Pub. Library.founding trustee, bd. dirs. Irvington Hist. Soc.; trustee Winterthur Mus. Contbr. articles to profl. jours., newspapers. Named Man of Yr., Boys Town Italy, 1983; recipient Order of Merit, Rep. Italy, 1984. Mem. Am. Antiquarian Soc. Republican. Clubs: Explorers, Metropolitan, Grolier. Avocations: collecting 19th Century American art and furniture; arctic explorations; hot air ballooning. Office: The Mediators Inc 667 Madison Ave 11th Fl New York NY 10021

MANNING, BURT J., advertising executive; b. May 31, 1931. Assoc. creative dir. Leo Burnett Co., Chgo., 1964-66; vice chmn. creative resources J. Walter Thompson Co. Worldwide, N.Y.C., 1977-80; chmn., chief exec. officer J. Walter Thompson U.S.A., Inc., 1980-86; prin., chmn. exec. com. Jordan, Manning, Case, Taylor & McGrath Inc., N.Y.C., 1986-87; chmn., chief exec. officer J. Walter Thompson Co., N.Y.C., 1987—. Dir. Nat. Coun. for Depressive Illness. Mem. Am. Assn. Advt. Agencies (bd. dirs.), Advt. Edn. Found. (bd. dirs.), N.Y.C. Partnership (bd. dirs.), Neurosciences Inst. (trustee). Office: J Walter Thompson Co 466 Lexington Ave New York NY 10017

MANNING, CHRISTOPHER ASHLEY, venture capital executive; b. Los Angeles, June 26, 1945; s. Ashley and Vivian LaVerne (Wagner) M.; m. Cathy Ann Nichols, July 30, 1977. BS, San Diego State U., 1967; MBA, Northwestern U., 1971; PhD, UCLA, 1983. Corp. loan officer Security Pacific Nat. Bank, Los Angeles, 1971-75; v.p. fin. Solitude Ski Resort, Bravo Ski Corp., Salt Lake City, 1975-78; pres. Sequoia Spa Co., Los Angeles, 1976-79; pres. Manning and Co., Los Angeles, 1971-86, Manning's Little Red Piano Shop, Los Angeles, 1971-86; instr. corp. fin. Pepperdine U., Los Angeles, 1979-83; instr. corp. fin. and real estate Long Beach State U. (Calif.), 1983-86; assoc. prof. fin. Loyola Marymount U., Los Angeles, 1986—. Served to 1st lt. U.S. Army, 1967-70. Decorated Bronze Star medal. Mem. Beta Gamma Sigma. Republican. Episcopalian. Club: Caballeros and Rolling Hills Tennis. Home: 14 Crest Rd W Rolling Hills CA 90274 Office: 29438 Quailwood Dr Rancho Palos Verdes CA 90274

MANNING, JOSEPH A., banker; b. Worcester, Mass., Feb. 1, 1946; s. Joseph A. and Martha M. (Edgecomb) M.; m. Stephanie M. Pielaszczyk, Apr. 6, 1968; children: Ted, Tiffany, Jared. BBA in Fin., Nichols Coll., 1968. Substitute tchr. Worcester-Holden Sch. Systems, 1969; asst. v.p., mgr. Mechanics Nat. Bank, Worcester, 1969-78; mgr. Vt. Nat. Bank, Rutland, 1978-79, asst. v.p., 1979-82, v.p., 1982; sr. v.p. Vt. Nat. Bank; sr. v.p., sr. loan officer Marble Bank, Rutland, 1982-87, exec. v.p., sr. loan officer, 1987-88, pres., chief exec. officer, 1988—; v.p., sec. Marble Fin. Corp., 1986-88, pres., chief exec. officer, 1988—; sr. assoc., pres. Robert Morris Assocs., Rutland, 1987—. Bd. dirs. Entrepreneurship Inst. Vt. Inc., 1987; capt. Rutland County United Way, 1982; pres-elect, dir. Vt. Achievement Ctr., 1989—. With U.S. Army, 1968-69. Home: 69 HIgh St Proctor VT 05765 Office: Marble Bank 47 Merchants Row Rutland VT 05701

MANNING, L(YNNE) COLLEEN, computer specialist; b. Pasco, Wash., July 28, 1941; d. Verne Leroy and Dorothy Lorraine (Boehmer) Foraker; divorced; children: Angela Michelle, Mark Wayland. Student, Seattle Pacific U., 1959-61; BS in Acctg., City U., Seattle, 1985. CPA, Wash. Engring. design progress estimator Boeing Comml. Airplane Co., Seattle, 1965-71; office supr. fin. svcs. Brigham Young U., Provo, Utah, 1971-78; engring. resources contr. Boeing Comml. Airplane Co., Seattle, 1978-84, cost acct., 1984-86, fin. planner, 1986-87, artificial intelligence specialist, 1987—. Mem. Am. Assn. Artificial Intelligence, Assn. for Computing Machinery, Everett Sister Cities Assn. Office: Boeing Comml Airplane Customer Svcs PO Box 3707 Seattle WA 98124-2207

MANNING, WALTER SCOTT, accountant, former educator, consultant; b. nr. Yoakum, Tex.; B.B.A., Tex. Coll. Arts and Industries, 1932; M.B.A., U. Tex., 1940; m. Eleanor Mary Jones, Aug. 27, 1937; children—Sharon Frances, Walter Scott, Robert Kenneth. Asst. to bus. mgr. Tex. Coll. Arts and Industries, Kingsville, 1932; tchr. Sinton (Tex.) High Sch., 1933-37, Robstown (Tex.) High Sch., 1937-41; prof. Tex. A&M U., College Station, 1941-77; cons. C.P.A. C.P.A., Tex. Walter Manning Outstanding Jr. and Outstanding Sr. awards at Coll. Bus. Adminstrn., Tex. A&M U. named in his honor. Mem. AAUP, Am. Acctg. Assn., Am. Inst. C.P.A.s, Tex. Soc. C.P.A.s, College Station C. of C. (past pres.), Tex. Assn. Univ. Instrs. Acctg. (pres. 1963-64), Knights York Cross of Honor, Alpha Chi, Beta Gamma Sigma, Beta Alpha Psi. Democrat. Presbyterian (elder). Clubs: Masons, (32 deg.), Shriners, K.T., Kiwanis (past pres., past lt. gov. div. IX Tex. Okla. dist.). Home: 405 Walton Dr E College Station TX 77840

MANNING, WHIPPLE HALL, savings and loan executive, real estate finance consultant; b. Oakland, Calif., Oct. 23, 1936; s. John Hudson and Anne Crellin (Hall) M.; m. Jacqueline Long, Sept. 5, 1963; children: Thomas Crellin, Elizabeth Anne. BS in Bus., U. Ariz., 1961. Trainee to regional mgr. Pacific Mut. Life Ins. Co., various cities, 1961-78; sr. v.p. Calif. Fed. Savs. & Loan, Los Angeles, 1978-83; exec. v.p. Coast Savs. and Loan, Los Angeles, 1983—; bd. dirs. Coast Fed. Properties, Beverly Hills, Calif., Nat. Ptrnship. Investment Co., Los Angeles, Coast Mortgage & Realty Investors, Los Angeles; mem. Los Angeles adv. bd. Chgo. Title Co. Past trustee Orme Sch., Mayer, Ariz., 1984-86; past bd. dirs. Calif. Bus. Properties Assn., Sacramento, 1984-87, mem. adv. bd., 1987—; past officer, dir. Flintridge Aquatics, La Canada, Calif., 1976-82. Mem. Urban Land Inst., Internat. Coun. of Shopping Ctrs., So. Calif. Mortgage Bankers, Nat. Assn. Indsl. and Office Parks. Republican. Episcopalian. Clubs: Los Angeles Athletic, Annandale Golf (Pasadena). Office: Coast Savs & Loan Assn 1000 Wilshire Blvd 22d Fl Los Angeles CA 90017

MANNING, WILLIAM DUDLEY, JR., specialty chemical company executive; b. Tampa, Fla., Mar. 7, 1934; s. William Dudley and Rebecca (Reid) M.; m. Carol Randolph Gillis, June 30, 1962; children: Carol Randolph, Rebecca Barrett, Anne Gillis. BA in Chemistry, Fla. State U., 1957. Sales rep. Amoco Chem. Co., St. Louis and Cleve., 1959-63; sales engr. The Lubrizol Corp., Tulsa, 1963-64, southwestern regional sales mgr., 1964-66; mgr. chem. product sales The Lubrizol Corp., Wickliffe, Ohio, 1966-72, sales mgr., western U.S., 1972, gen. sales mgr., asst. div. head-sales, 1972-79, mktg. mgr., asst. div. head-sales, 1979-80, v.p. mktg., 1980-81, v.p., bus. devel. div., 1981-85, sr. v.p. sales and mktg., 1985-87; pres. Lubrizol Petroleum Chems. Co., Wickliffe, 1987—. Trustee Soc. for Crippled Children, Cleve., 1985—. Served with USAR, 1957-63. Mem. Soc. Automotive Engrs. (assoc.), Am. Petroleum Inst., Nat. Petroleum Refiners Assn., Soc. of Chem. Industry. Republican. Roman Catholic. Clubs: Kirtland Country (Ohio) (v.p. 1986-88, pres. 1988-89); Tavern (Cleve.) (trustee 1986—); Chagrin Valley Hunt (Gates Mills, Ohio), Firestone Country (Akron). Office: Lubrizol Petroleum Chems Co 29400 Lakeland Blvd Wickliffe OH 44092

MANNINO, ANTHONY JAMES, JR., real estate executive; b. Trenton, N.J., Dec. 17, 1951; s. Anthony James and Barbara Rita (Salkauski) M.; m. Vivian Patricia Cassetta, Aug. 25, 1973; children: Mark Vincent, Alexander Paul. BA in Polit. Sci. and Acctg., Rutgers U., 1973. Staff acct. audit Price Waterhouse, Phila., 1973-74, staff acct. tax, 1974-76, sr. acct. tax, 1976-79, tax mgr., 1979-80; controller The Core Group, Phila., 1980-81, v.p., treas., dir., 1981-86, chief fin. officer, 1986-88; pres. Lewis and Co., N.Y.C. and Phila., 1988—; bd. dirs. Phila. Ball and Roller Bearing Co., Health Enterprises Mgmt., Inc., Albany, N.Y. Mem. AICPA, Pa. Inst. CPAs, Racquet Club of Phila. Republican. Roman Catholic. Office: Lewis and Co 2005 Pine St Philadelphia PA 19103

MANO, RONALD MAKOTO, accounting educator; b. Ogden, Utah, Aug. 28, 1942; s. Eisaku and Michi (Morio) M.; m. Cheryl Sei Shimizu, Mar. 22, 1969; children: Tiffany Taka, Patrice Michiko, Tisha Misa, Karisa Kazuko, Rhett Makoto, Darin Masao. BS, U. Utah, 1968, MBA, 1970; PhD, U. Nebr., 1978. Staff acct. Hansen, Barnett & Maxwell CPAs, Salt Lake City, 1968-70; audit sr. Ernst & Whinney, Salt Lake City, 1970-73; instr. acctg. U. Utah, Salt Lake City, 1973-78, asst. prof., assoc. prof., 1978-85; assoc. prof. Weber State Coll., Ogden, 1985-86, prof. acctg., 1986—; vis. prof. Brigham Young U., Provo, summer 1985; Williard L. Eccles vis. prof. Weber State Coll., 1982-83; vis. asst. prof. U. Nebr., Lincoln, 1976-77; cons. in field; conductor seminars in field; lectr. in field. Contbr. articles to profl. jours. Bd. dirs. Sandy Edn. Found., Utah, 1987—; del. State Rep. Conv., Salt Lake City,1987-88. U. Utah research grantee 1979-84; Weber State Coll. grantee, 1982, 85, 86, 87, 88. Mem. Utah Assn. CPAs, Am. Acctg. Assn., Am. Inst. CPAs, Inst. Internal Auditors, Nat. Assn. Accts. (dir. publicity 1987-88, v.p. communications 1986-87, dir. manuscripts 1988—), Western Risk and Ins. Assn. Republican. Mormon. Home: 8640 Snowville Dr Sandy UT 84093 Office: Weber State Coll Sch Bus & Econs Acctg Dept Ogden UT 84408

MANOOGIAN, RICHARD ALEXANDER, manufacturing company executive; b. Long Branch, N.J., July 30, 1936; s. Alex and Marie (Tatian) M.; children: James, Richard, Bridget. B.A. in Econs, Yale U., 1958. Asst. to pres. Masco Corp., Taylor, Mich., 1958-62, exec. v.p., 1962-68, pres., 1968-85, chmn., 1985—, chief exec. officer, from 1985, also dir.; chmn., dir. Masco Industries, Inc.; dir. Emco Ltd., London, Ont., Can., Nat. Bank of Detroit, Flint & Walling, Kendallville, Ind., R.P. Scherer Corp., Do It Yourself Inst. Trustee U. Liggett Sch., Assocs. of Am. Wing, Detroit Inst. Arts, Founder's Soc., Detroit Inst. Arts, Center for Creative Studies. Mem. Young Presidents Orgn., Am. Bus. Conf. Clubs: Grosse Pointe Yacht, Grosse Pointe Hunt, Country of Detroit, Detroit Athletic. Office: Masco Corp 21001 Van Born Rd Taylor MI 48180 *

MANOS, PETE LAZAROS, supermarket executive; b. Washington, Dec. 29, 1936; s. George and Ardemecia (Saranides) M.; m. Barbara Lorraine Isper, July 16, 1960; children—Helene Deborah, Cynthia Denise. B. Comml. Sci., Benjamin Franklin U., Washington, 1956, M. Comml. Sci., 1962. C.P.A., Md. Buyer Giant Food Inc., Washington, 1961-63, sr. buyer, 1963-70, mgr., 1970-74, dir., 1974-77, v.p., 1977-81, sr. v.p., 1981—; pres. Giant Food Fed. Credit Union, Greenbelt, Md., 1980-86. Mem. Prince Georges' Environ. Trust, Prince Georges' County, Md., 1969-70; mem. U.S. Selective Service Bd., Prince George County, 1974-76; mem. Prince George Solid Waste Disposal Task Force, 1972-73. Served with USN, 1956-59. Mem. United Fresh Fruit and Vegetable Assn. (bd. dirs. 1983-86), Product Mktg. Assn. Democrat. Greek Orthodox. Lodge: Masons. Home: 947 Coachway St Annapolis MD 21401 Office: Giant Food Inc 6300 Sheriff Rd Landover MD 20785

MANSELL, JAMES R., engineering and construction company executive; b. Tupelo, Miss., Aug. 18, 1929; s. Robert Quinton and Corinne (Threldkeld) M.; m. Alice Ann Appleton, Apr. 26, 1952; children: Robert Dudley, James Quinton. B.S.C.E., Miss. State U., 1951. Registered profl. engr., Tex. Engr. Chgo. Bridge & Iron Co., 1955-68; dist. sales mgr. Chgo. Bridge & Iron Co., N.Y.C., 1968-74, Chgo. Bridges & Iron Co., Houston, 1974-76; v.p. engring. Chgo. Bridge & Iron Co., Oak Brook, Ill., 1976-79; sr. v.p. engring. and research Chgo. Bridge & Iron Co., Oak Brook, 1979-83; sr. v.p., chief tech. officer CBI Industries, Oak Brook, 1983—; dir. Harris Bank, Hinsdale, Ill., FluiDyne Engring. Corp., Mpls., Hydra Fab, Houston, Petroterminal de Panama, S.A., Panama City. Active Hinsdale Washington Sq., 1983—. Served to 1st lt. USAF, 1951-53. Fellow ASCE; mem. Western Soc. Engrs. (dir.), Am. Petroleum Inst. Mem., United Ch. of Christ. Club: Hinsdale Golf. Home: 836 S Oak St Hinsdale IL 60521 Office: CBI Industries 800 Jorie Blvd Oak Brook IL 60521

MANSEN, STEVEN ROBERT, manufacturing company executive; b. Chgo., Nov. 26, 1955; s. Robert Lee and Dorothy Nora (Nichols) M.; m. Leesa, May 7, 1988; 1 child, Ambur. B.in Indsl. Adminstrn., Gen. Motors Inst., 1978. Data processing system analyst in traffic Gen. Motors Corp., Oklahoma City, 1979-81, premium freight system coordinator, outbound distbn. rate analyst in traffic, 1981-83; sr. mfg. system analyst Tech. Oil Tool Co. div. Baker Internat., Norman, Okla., 1983-86; v.p. mgmt. info. systems W. Pat Crow Forgings, Inc., 1986-88; material mgr., Aerospace Technologies, Inc. div. Alco Standard Group, Ft. Worth, 1988—. Mem. S.W. States ASK Users Group (v.p. 1984-86, pres. 1986). Home: 2600 Stoneridge Ct Arlington TX 76014 Office: Aerospace Technologies Inc 7445 E Lancaster Fort Worth TX 76112

MANSFIELD, HARRY EDGAR, data processing executive; b. Wamego, Kans., Feb. 10, 1942; s. James and A. Irene (Hatcher) M.; m. Shirley Nadine Lamkin, July 13, 1963; children: Marsha, Denise, James, William. Student, Kans. State U., 1960-62, Abilene (Tex.) Christian U., 1964-65. Cost control mgr. O'Brien Homes, Inc., Rochester, N.Y., 1967-73; data processing mgr. Boling Bldrs., Kansas City, Mo., 1974-76; systems mgr. Lear-Seigler Safelite, Wichita, Kans., 1976-78; data processing mgr. Pester Corp., Des Moines, 1978-80; pres. H.E. Mansfield & Assocs., Wamego, 1980-83; dir. info. services Kans. State Network, Inc., Wichita, 1983-88; exec. v.p. Allegro Info Systems, Overland Park, Kans., 1988—; cons. Midwest Fire & Casualty, Wellington, Kans., 1980-82, Derby (Kans.) Police Dept., 1981-82. Mem. Wichita Area Assn. of System 34-36-38 Users (v.p. 1985), Broadcast Fin. Mgmt. (chmn. data processing standards 1985-86, bd. dirs. 1987—, chmn. MIS com. 1987-89), Data Processing Mgrs. Assn., COMMON (communication hotline 1986). Office: Allegro Info Systems 11879 W 112th Overland Park KS 66210

MANSFIELD, KENNETH EUGENE, retail executive; b. Nashville, Feb. 25, 1946; s. Jack and Roberta (Corlew) M. BA in Polit. Sci., Vanderbilt U., 1971, MBA, 1985. Export sales mgr. Genesco Inc., Nashville, 1971-74, dir. world licensing, 1976-81, dir. mktg., 1981-84, dir. ops. (retail group), 1984-86; Pacific regional sales mgr. J.K. Kealy Co., Honolulu, 1974-76; pres. retail group Endicott Johnson, Endicott, N.Y., 1986-88; pres. retail div. G.H. Bass and Co., Falmouth, Maine, 1988—. Active United Way, Binghampton, N.Y., 1986—; mem. adv. council Owen Grad. Sch. Mgmt. Vanderbilt U., Nashville, 1985—, alumni bd. dirs., 1988—. Mem. Footwear Retailers Am. (bd. dirs.). Office: G H Bass & Co 360 US Rte 1 Falmouth ME 04105

MANSFIELD, MARY KATHERINE, marketing professional; b. Framingham, Mass., July 20, 1965; d. James Martin Glynn and Patricia Ann (Nichols) Heath; m. Edward Paul Mansfield, Sept. 6, 1986. AS in Fashion Merchandising/Mktg., Fisher Jr. Coll., 1985. Lic. realtor, Mass. Asst. buyer Grover Cronin, Inc., Waltham, Mass., 1981-85; mgr. ops. Bay Colony Devel., Waltham, 1985—; coord. mktg. Better Homes & Gardens, Millbury, Mass., 1987-89; pres. Mansfield Properties, Northbridge, Mass., 1989—; freelance interion design cons., Millbury, 1987—; corp. clk. Bay Colony Devel. Corp., 1985—. Trustee Paul Revere Village Assn., Millbury, 1987-88. Parents Without Ptnrs. scholar, 1983, Fisher Jr. Coll. Acad. Excellence scholar, 1983, 84. Mem. Distributive Edn. Club of Am. (pres. 1982-83), Phi Theta Kappa. Home: 44 Violette Circle Northbridge MA 01534 Office: Mansfield Properties 44 Violette Circle Northbridge MA 05134

MANSON, RICHARD HENRY, marketing professional; b. Boston, Mar. 10, 1943; s. Henry I. and Katherine C. (O'Donnell) M.; m. Rochelle Summers, May 27, 1987; children: Jill, Jeffrey; stepchildren: Shaun, Amy. BS in Biology, Norwich U., 1964. Sales rep. Squibb Pharm. Co., New Brunswick, N.J., 1968-70, Brockway Plastics div. Brockway Glass Co., East Orange, N.J., 1970-74, Gibson Assocs., Cranford, N.J., 1974-80; mktg. mgr. Thatcher Plastics, Paramus, N.J., 1980-84; v.p. sales and mktg. Arpak Plastics div. Plant Industries, Hackensack, N.J., 1984-86, Guest Packaging div. Guest Supply Co., North Burnswick, N.J., 1986-87; dir. mktg. and sales Cairns & Bros., Inc., Clifton, N.J., 1987—. 1st lt. U.S. Army, 1964-67. Mem. Packaging Inst. U.S.A. Home: 874 Ridgewood Blvd E Westwood NJ 07675

MANSUETO, JOSEPH DANIEL, publisher; b. East Chicago, Ind., Sept. 3, 1956; s. Mario Daniel and Sara Wilda (Smart) M. BA, U. Chgo., 1978, MBA, 1980. Securities analyst Harris Assocs., Chgo., 1983-84; prin. Morningstar, Chgo., 1984—. Office: Morningstar Inc 53 W Jackson Blvd Chicago IL 60604

MANTILLA, NECTARIO RUBÉN, banker; b. Guayaquil, Guayas, Ecuador, July 26, 1940; s. Nectario and Juanita (Zambrano) M.; m. Helen Mantilla, Sept. 8, 1965; 1 child, Xavier. BS, NYU, 1971, MBA, 1972; postgrad., Stanford U., 1981. Mktg. asst. Hallmark Cards, Inc., N.Y.C., 1966-72; account mgr. Citibank N.A., Guayaquil, Ecuador, 1973-75, br. mgr., 1976-78, corp. bank head, v.p., 1979-82; exec. v.p. Banco Continental, Guayaquil, 1983-86; pres., founder Interleasing S.A., Guayaquil, 1987—, Interconsult SA, Guayaquil, 1988—; prof. Guayaquil U., 1974-75; participant, guest speaker numerous bank and mgmt. seminars, 1984—; cons. Jouvin Group, 1983-84, Massuh Group, 1983-86, Banco del Litoral, 1989—. Author: Financial Structure and the Cost of Capital, 1972, Account Management: A Dynamic Marketing Approach, 1981, Micro/Macroeconomic Analysis of the Sugar Industry, 1975, Risk Analysis in the Extension of Credit, 1985, Ecuador's Economic Survey, 1986, How to Invest In Ecuador, 1988, Analysis of Ecuador's Stabilzation Program, 1988. Served with U.S. Army, 1960-62. Recipient Western Hemisphere award Citibank, 1978, Exec. award Stanford U., 1981. Mem. Ecuadorian-Am. C. of C., V. Rocafuerte High Sch. Alumni Assn. (pres. 1981-82). Roman Catholic. Clubs: Union, Country. Home: PO Box 10383, Guayaquil Ecuador

MANTON, EDWIN ALFRED GRENVILLE, insurance company executive; b. Earls Colne, Essex, Eng., Jan. 22, 1909; came to U.S., 1933; s. John Horace and Emily Clara (Denton) M.; m. Florence V. Brewer, Feb. 1, 1936; 1 child, Diana H. Manton Morton. Student, London (Eng.) U., 1925-27, N.Y. Ins. Soc., 1933-35. Trainee B.W. Noble Ltd., Paris, 1927-33; casualty underwriter Am. Internat. Underwriters Corp., N.Y.C., 1933-37, sec., 1937-38; v.p. Am. Internat. Underwriters Corp., 1938-42, pres., 1942-69, chmn., 1969-75, also dir.; dir. & sr. advisor Am. Internat. Group, Inc., also subs.; dir. C.V. Starr & Co. Inc., also subs.,. Trustee St. Luke's-Roosevelt Hosp., N.Y.C. Mem. Salmagundi Club, City Midday Drug and Chem. Club, Mendelssohn Glee Club, Williams Club, St. George's Soc. (v.p.). Episcopalian. Home: 40 Fifth Ave New York NY 10011 Office: Am Internat Group Inc 70 Pine St New York NY 10270

MANTOR, PHILIP DAVID, oil company executive; b. Tyler, Tex., Sept. 12, 1936; s. Philip and Elizabeth (Blackshear) M.; m. Kay, Aug. 26, 1958 (div. 1981); children: Philip Cameron, Meredith P. Cook, David B.; m. Sharon K. Pratt, Feb. 26, 1983. BA ChemE, Rice U., 1958, MS ChemE, 1960. Engr., then div. planning mgr., then reservoir engr. and dist. mgr. Exxon Corp., 1960-75; successively ops. v.p., exec. v.p., pres. Tex. Internat. Petroleum Corp., Oklahoma City, 1975-80; exec. v.p., then pres. Hamilton Internat. Oil Co., Denver, 1980—; sr. exec. v.p. Hamilton Oil Corp., Denver, 1980—, also bd. dirs. Served to 2d lt. U.S. Army, 1960-61. Mem. Soc. Petroleum Engrs. of AIME, Tex. State Profl. Engrs., Am. Petroleum Inst., Independent Petroleum Assn. Am. Republican. Episcopalian. Clubs: Denver, Glenmoor Country. Office: Hamilton Oil Corp 1560 Broadway Ste 2000 Denver CO 80202

MANTZ, RICHARD FREDERICK, accountant, researcher; b. Allentown, Pa., Dec. 10, 1956; s. Richard Frederick Sr. and Jacqueline (Marline) M. BS, Pa. State U., 1978; MBA, Lehigh U., 1986. Mgr. acctg. Perdue Farms, Inc., Salisbury, Md., 1986-87, sr. sales analyst, 1987-88; ops. acct. Sonoco Products Co., Hartsville, S.C., 1988—; cons. in field. Dist. dir. Pa. Jaycees, 1985-86, regional dir., 1986; dist. dir. Mo. Jaycees, 1985; pres. Allentown chpt. Jaycees, 1984. Home and Office: PO Box 941 Hartsville SC 29550

MANTZAVINOS, ANTHONY G., banker; b. Athens, Greece, May 9, 1928; s. George and Irene (Papaleonardos) M.; m. Anita Boukydis; children—George, Irene. B.A., McGill U., 1951, M.A., 1952. Fin. mgr. Powder & Cartridge Co. Ltd., Athens, 1955-60; dir. for capital investments Hellenic Indsl. Devel. Bank, Athens, 1960-64; various assignments Citibank, Greece, 1964—, Spain, Portugal, Canada, N.Y.; now group exec. Citibank, N.Y.C., also dir. Dep. minister of econ. coordination Greek Govt., Athens, 1966-67. Served to 2d lt. Greek Coast Guard. Mem. Pres.'s Coun. Asia Soc. (trustee 1982-88), Alexander S. Onassis Found. (dir. 1982—), Alexander S. Onassis Public Benefit Found. (dir. 1982—). Mem. Greek Orthodox Ch. Office: Citicorp 399 Park Ave New York NY 10043

MANUSO, JAMES S. J., management consultant, real estate developer; b. N.Y.C., Nov. 9, 1948; s. John D. and Eleanor S. Manuso; m. Susan Alexander, 1982. AB in Econs. with honors, NYU, 1970, cert. in real estate, 1984, 87; AM, New Sch. for Social Research, 1972, PhD in Psychology, 1978; cert., Harvard Bus. Sch., 1981; MS in Bus., Columbia U., 1983. Lic. real estate broker. Mgr. equipment control dept. Am. Export Isbrandtsen Lines, N.Y.C., 1966-67; rehab. counselor N.Y. State Office Drug Abuse Services, N.Y.C., 1970-72, dir. psychology dept., 1973-74; cons. in psychology 1972-73; clin. supr. occupational clin. psychology New Sch. for Social Research, N.Y.C., 1976-81, dir. psychology intern program, 1976-81; dir. program planning and devel. Equitable Life Assurance Soc. U.S., N.Y.C., 1978-83, chief psychologist, 1974-78, dir. psychol. services, 1978-80, asst. v.p., 1980-83; cons. James S.J. Manuso and Assocs., N.Y.C., 1982-83; pres. Dellman Constrn. Corp., N.Y.C., 1983-84; mng. gen. ptnr. Bromanna Realty, N.Y.C., 1983-85; real estate salesman Brown and Gilbert, N.Y.C., 1983-88; owner, sole propr. Woodstock Enterprises, N.Y.C., 1983—; v.p. The Neil Michael Group Inc., N.Y.C., 1988—; founder Biofeedback Lab., N.Y., 1976; adv. to Pres.'s Commn. on Mental Health, 1977-78, Senate subcom. on Health and Sci. Research, 1979; cons. occupational health to various health orgns. in U.S. and abroad, 1977—. Author: Occupational Clinical Psychology, 1983; contbr. articles on occupational health and psychology to profl. jours.; appearances various radio and TV programs, 1976—. Mem. N.Y. Biofeedback Soc. (pres. 1981-82), Am. Inst. Stress (sec., treas. 1980-85), Am. Psychol. Assn., N.Y. State Psychol. Assn., Soc. Behavioral Medicine, N.Y. Soc. Clin. Psychologists. Episcopalian. Club: Columbia (N.Y.C.). Home: 529 W 42d St #6Q New York NY 10036 Office: Neil Michael Group Inc 305 Madison Ave Ste 819 New York NY 10165

MANZELLA, FRANK, holding company executive; b. Bklyn., Dec. 10, 1939; s. Peter Fred and Mary Rose (Angelone) M.; m. Joan Mary Delapina, May 3, 1964; children: Frank Joseph, Michael Peter. BA, Manhattan Sch. Music, N.Y.C., 1963, MA, 1964. Treas. Iquinta Industries, N.Y.C., 1963-68; pres. Topper Enterprises, Inc., Queens, N.Y., 1969-79; chmn., pres. Rockville Group Ltd., Rockville Centre, N.Y., 1979—; bd. dirs. United Steel Products, Inc., Trenton, N.J., West Window Corp., Martinsville, Va., SouthWest Rebar Fabricators, Inc., Phoenix, CPM Computer Software Devel., Inc., Rockville Centre, Southtech Industries, Inc., N.Y.C. Cubmaster Boy Scouts Am., N.Y.C., 1978-81. Office: Rockville Group Ltd 100 Merrick Rd Ste 312-E Rockville Centre NY 11570

MANZI, JIM PAUL, computer software company executive; b. N.Y.C., Dec. 22, 1951; s. Walter Edward and Ann (Smirka) M.; m. Glenda Baugh, May 20, 1978. B.A., Colgate U., 1973; M.A.L.D., Fletcher Sch., Tufts U., 1979. Editorial asst. Nat. Rev. Mag., N.Y.C., 1973-74; news reporter Gannet Newspapers, Port Chester, N.Y., 1974-77; cons. McKinsey & Co., Los Angeles, Boston and N.Y.C., 1979-83; v.p. mktg. and sales Lotus Devel. Corp., Cambridge, Mass., 1983-84, pres., 1984-86, 89—, chmn., chief exec. officer, 1986—. Recipient In-Depth Reporting award AP, N.Y., 1976, 77, Investigative Reporting award N.Y. State Pubs. Assn., 1976, 77. Office: Lotus Devel Corp 55 Cambridge Pkwy Cambridge MA 02142 *

MAPELLI, ROLAND LAWRENCE, food company executive; b. Denver, June 10, 1922; s. Herman M. and Della (Borelli); m. Neoma Robinson, Apr. 1942; children—Terralyn Mapelli DeMoney, Geraldine Mapelli Gustafson. Student, Regis Coll., 1959-61. Pres. Mapelli Bros. Distbg. Co. div. Monfort of Colo., Greeley, 1969—; chmn. bd., sr. v.p. Monfort of Colo., Inc., Greeley, 1971—; owner, operator Mapelli Farms, Eaton, Colo., 1974—; chmn. bd. Denver Union Stock Yards Co., 1969-70; dir. United Banks Colo., United Bank of Greeley; mem. Colo. Bd. Agr.'s Frozen Food Provisioners Bd., 1967-71; mem. Colo. Agrl. Adv. Com., 1966-73. Chmn. Denver Off-Street Parking Commn., 1960-72; mem. Denver City Coun., 1955-59, Colo. Ho. of Reps., 1961-62, Colo. State Senate, 1962-66; mem. adv. bd. Ft. Logan Mental Health Ctr., 1961-64, St. Anthony's Hosp., 1960-65; bd. dirs. N. Denver Civic Assn., 1955-65, Better Bus. Bur., 1966-69; mem. bd. Ambassadors Loretto Heights Coll., 1960-65; bd. dirs., exec. com. Nat. Western Stock Show, 1966—; dir. Colo. State U. Land Coun., 1984—. 2d lt. USAF, 1942-46, ETO. Recipient Knute Rockne award, 1961; Water for Colo. Conservation award, 1985. Mem. Mountain/Plains Meat Assn. (pres. 1968-69), Colo. Cattlemen's Assn., Colo. Cattlefeeders Assn., Colo.-Wyo. Restaurant Assn., Nat. Assn. Meat Purveyors. Roman Catholic. Home: 18979 Weld County Rd 78 Eaton CO 80615 Office: PO Box G Greeley CO 80632

MAPES, PIERSON, TV broadcasting company executive; m. Patricia Carlson. Grad. Norwich Univ. With NBC, 1963-72; account exec., sales mgr., v.p. Blair TV, 1972-79; v.p. NBC TV Network, 1979-82, now pres., NBC TV Network, NBC-TV, N.Y.C., 1982—; chmn. bd. dirs. Ramapo Land Co., Sloatsbury, N.Y.; bd. dirs. Broadcast Pioneers, Broadcast Pioneers Library. Trustee Norwich Univ. Capt. U.S. Army, 1959-63. Mem. Internat. Radio and TV Soc. Office: NBC-TV Network 30 Rockefeller Pla New York NY 10112 *

MAPLES, ROBERT CARL, stock brokerage executive; b. Plainfield, N.J., Apr. 19, 1957; s. Francis K. and Lois Randolph (Cooley) M. AB, Dartmouth Coll., 1979; MBA, Harvard U., 1986. Legis. asst. office of Rep. Millicent Fenwick U.S. Ho. of Reps., Washington, 1979-82; vol. Peace

Corps, Atenas, Costa Rica, 1982-84; asst. v.p. Piper, Jaffray & Hopwood, Inc., Mpls., 1986—. Office: Piper Jaffray & Hopwood Inc Box 28 Minneapolis MN 55440

MARAFINO, VINCENT NORMAN, aerospace company executive; b. Boston, June 8, 1930; m. Doris Marilyn Vernall, June 15, 1958; children: Marli Ann, Sheri Louise, Wendi Joan. A.B. in Acctg. and Econs., San Jose State Coll., 1951; M.B.A., Santa Clara U., 1964. Chief acct. Am. Standard Advance Tech. Lab., Mountain View, Calif., 1956-59; with Lockheed Missiles & Space Co., Sunnyvale, Calif., 1959-70; chief acct. Lockheed Missiles & Space Co., 1967-68, dir. fin. mgmt. and controls, R & D div., also asst. dir. fin. ops., 1968-70; asst. controller Lockheed Corp., Burbank, Calif., 1970-71, v.p., controller, 1971-77, sr. v.p. fin., 1977-83, exec. v.p., chief fin. and adminstrv. officer, 1983-88, vice chmn. bd., chief fin. and adminstrv. officer, 1988—, also dir.; bd. dirs. Lockheed Missiles & Space Co., Inc., Dataproducts Corp., Woodland Hills, Calif., Newport Corp., Fountain Valley, Calif.; chmn. bd. dirs. Lockheed Fin. Corp. Chmn. bd. trustees Holy Cross Med. Ctr., Mission Hills, Calif. Served with USAF, 1953-56. Mem. Fin. Execs. Inst., Am. Inst. CPAs, Jonathan Club, North Ranch Country Club. Office: Lockheed Corp 4500 Park Granada Blvd Calabasas CA 91399

MARAKAS, JOHN LAMBROS, insurance company executive; b. Connellsville, Pa., July 16, 1926; s. Gust John and Elizabeth Hamilton (Cutler) M.; m. Alice Dixon, Dec. 26, 1948; children: Andy, Nancy, Donna. A.B., U. Mich., 1949. Actuarial asst. Acacia Mut., Washington, 1949-50; actuary Continental Assurance, Chgo., 1950-53; v.p., actuary, exec. v.p., pres. Res. Life Ins. Co., Dallas, 1953-70; v.p. Nationwide Corp., Columbus, Ohio, 1971-72, pres., 1972—, also bd. dirs.; pres., dir. Nationwide Life Ins. Co., Columbus, 1981—, gen. mgr.; pres., dir. Nationwide Property Mgmt., Inc., Fin. Horizons Life Ins. Co.; vice-chmn. Nationwide (PEBSCO Inc.); dir. Farmland Life Ins. Co., Nationwide Agribus. Ins. Co., Farmland Mut. Ins. Co., Gulf Atlantic Life Ins. Co., Nat. Casualty Co., Nationwide Investors Services, Inc., Nationwide Community Urban Redevelopment Corp., Hickey-Mitchell Ins. Agy., Inc., Nationwide Fin. Services Inc., Nationwest Ins. Services, West Coast Life Ins. Co., Nationwide Cash Mgmt. Co., Calif. Cash Mgmt. Co., Nat. Casualty Co. of Am., Ltd., Nat. Premium and Benefit Adminstrn. Co., Wausau Service Corp.; trustee Nationwide Found., Nationwide Investing Found., Nationwide Separate Account; chmn., trustee N.W. Tax Free Fund, N.W. Separate Account; bd. dirs., sr. v.p. Employers Ins. of Wausau A Mut. Co.; dir., chmn. bd. Nationwide Health Care Corp. Bd. dirs. Ohio affiliate Nat. Soc. to Prevent Blindness. Served with U.S. Army, 1946-47. Mem. Am. Acad. Actuaries, Health Ins. Assn. Am. (chmn. 1988-89), Assn. Ohio Life Ins. Cos. Office: Nationwide Life Ins Co One Nationwide Pla Columbus OH 43216

MARANDE, E. DAVID, JR., financial analyst; b. Detroit, Mar. 1, 1961; s. Edward David Sr. and Betty Lowe M. BA, St. Mary's Coll., 1984. Cert. fin. planner. Assoc. The Am. Group, Farmington Hills, Mich., 1984-87; exec. v.p. Fin. Fitness, Grosse Pointe, Mich., 1986—; chmn. Mich. Fin. Adv. Service, Inc., Farmington Hills, 1987—; dir. fin. planning The Am. Group, Farmington Hills, 1987—; fin. educator St. Mary's Coll., Orchard Lake, Mich., 1988—. Author: Financial Fitness, 1986, revised, 1987. Mem. Internat. Assn. Fin. Planning, Inst. Fin. Planning, Inst. Cert. Fin. Planners, Nat. Assn. Security Dealers, Nat. Assn. Life Underwriters, Midwestern Assn. Fin. Planning. Club: Gen. Motors Ski (Detroit). Home: 351 Neff Rd Grosse Pointe MI 48230 Office: The Am Group 30600 Northwestern Hwy Suite 300 Farmington Hills MI 48018

MARANO, SUSAN ELIZABETH, construction company executive, horse breeder and trainer; b. Rochester, N.Y., Dec. 4, 1955; d. Robert Irving and Marion Helen (Bendix) Morris; m. Daniel Joseph Marano, Aug. 21, 1982; children: David Benjamin, Rachel Catherine, Allison Sarah. AS in Animal Sci., So. Sem., Buena Vista, Va., 1975; BS in Psychology, Va. Commonwealth U., 1977. Riding instr., trainer Hanover Equestrian Ctr., 1975-79, Woodinville Riding Club, 1979-80; with real estate sales dept. Century 21/Donald H. Hibberd, Media, Pa., 1980-84; collection rep. Clement Communicatoins, Inc., Concordville, Pa., 1981-84, collection mgr., 1984-85; co-owner Marano Plumbing & Heating, Chadds Ford, Pa., 1984-86, v.p., sec., 1987—; owner Willow Tree Farm, West Chester, Pa., 1984—; co-owner Marano-Stevenson Partnership, West Chester, 1986—. Mem. Am. Horse Show Assn. Jewish. Home: 1072 W Street Rd West Chester PA 19382 Office: 402 N Mill Rd Kennett Square PA 19348

MARASCO, FRANCIS ANTHONY, human resources executive; b. Punxsutawney, Pa., Jan. 23, 1943; s. Reese and Josephine (Serriani) M.; m. Marilyn Kay Mastro, Aug. 17, 1968; children: Matthew, Lauren. BS, St. Vincent Coll., 1964; postgrad., W.Va. U., 1964-67. Personnel asst. PPG Industries, Inc., Harmar Twp., Pa., 1968-69; successively staff asst., mgr. personnel relations, dir. personnel, v.p. personnel Thrift Drug Co., Pitts., 1969-87, sr. v.p., 1987—. Div. chmn. Literacy Task Force United Way, 1986—, sect. campaign chair 1984, 88; sec. RIDC Park Assn., 1986—; bd. dirs. Arthritis Found. Western Pa., 1987. Sgt. USMC Res. 1967-73. Mem. Pitts. Personnel Assn., Nat. Assn. Chain Drug Stores (chair human resource com. 1982-84). Roman Catholic. Home: Box 153 RD #8 Greensburg PA 15601 Office: Thrift Drug Co 615 Alpha Dr Pittsburgh PA 15238

MARASH, STANLEY ALBERT, consulting firm executive; b. Bklyn., Dec. 18, 1938; s. Albert Samuel and Esther (Cunio) M.; m. Muriel Sylvia Sutchin, June 24, 1961; children: Judith Ilene, Alan Scott. Student, Bklyn. Coll., 1956-58; BBA, CCNY, 1961; student, U. Idaho, 1962-63, Boston U., 1964-66; MBA, Baruch Coll., 1970. Registered profl. engr., Calif.; cert. quality engr., reliability engr. Statistician Electric Boat Gen. Dynamics, Groton, Conn., 1961-62; statistician Idaho Nuclear Energy Lab. Electric Boat Gen. Dynamics, Idaho Falls, 1962-63; mgr. quality assurance memory product ops. RCA, Needham, Mass., 1963-65; cons. engr. astroelectronics div. RCA, Princeton, N.J., 1965-66; corp. mgr. quality assurance Ideal Corp., Bklyn., 1966-68; mgr. quality assurance Gen. Instrument, Signalite, Neptune, N.J., 1968; pres. STAT-A-MATRIX, Inc., Edison, N.J., 1968—, chmn. bd., 1975—; trustee Ellis R. Ott Found., Edison, 1982—; advisor, quality tech. Middlesex County Coll., Edison, 1970—; vis. prof. U. Sao Paulo, Brazil, 1974, 75, 77, Madrid Poly. U., 1976; expert cons. Internat. Atomic Energy Agy., Vienna, 1974-77; cons. various govt. agys. and pub. and pvt. cos., 1972—; mem. indsl. adv. com. statistics dept. Rutgers U., New Brunswick, 1977-78, exec. standards council Am. Nat. Standards Inst., N.Y.C., 1979-80. Author: (tng. manual) Statistically Aided Management: What Every Executive Needs to Know, 1987; contbr. numerous articles, manuals and tng. texts. Fellow Am. Soc. Quality Control (chmn. 1966-68, Ellis R. Ott award 1981, chmn. internat. com. 1989)); mem. IEEE (sr.), ASTM, ASME, Am. Statis. Assn., Am. Soc. Tng. Devel., Am. Nuclear Soc. Office: STAT-A-MATRIX Group 2124 Oak Tree Rd Edison NJ 08820-1059

MARCARI, DANIEL, accountant, controller, consultant; b. Flushing, N.Y., Oct. 30, 1958; s. Gerard Albert and Patricia (Cosgrave) M.; m. Nancy Mary Maier, Aug. 30, 1986. AA, Suffolk Community Coll, 1979; BBA in Acctg., Hofstra U., 1988. Staff acct. Huntington (N.Y.) TV Cable, 1981-83; asst. mgr. acctg. Photocircuits div. Kollmorgen, Glen Cove, N.Y., 1983-85; asst. contr. IMC Magnetics Corp., Jericho, N.Y., 1985—; lectr. NYU, N.Y.C., 1985; pres. PCK Employee Fed. Credit Union, Glen Cove, 1983-87; with profl. recruitment, 1983-85; cons. Small Bus. Bur. Foster parents Christian Children's Fund, Richmond, Va.; counselor St. Joseph Youth Group, Kings Park, N.Y., 1986. Recipient Hofstra U. scholar, 1980. Republican. Roman Catholic. Home: 365 Rte 111 Smithtown NY 11787 Office: IMC Magnetics Corp 100 Jericho Quadrangel Jericho NY 11753

MARCELLAS, THOMAS WILSON, electronics company executive; b. Owings, Md., June 22, 1937; s. Carroll Wilson and Mabel Ellice (Hardesty) M.; B. Engring. Sci., Johns Hopkins U., 1960; M.Engring. Adminstrn., George Washington U., 1980; m. Janet Fay Hardesty, June 20, 1964; children: David Carroll, Diane Elizabeth. Project engr. Bendix Radio Corp., Towson, Md., 1960-61, 63-66; electronic systems engr. Electronic Modules Corp., Hunt Valley, Md., 1966-78, product devel. mgr., 1978-81; dir. research and devel. EMC Controls Inc., Hunt Valley, 1981-82, v.p. research and devel., 1982-84; v.p. research and devel. EMC Ops. Div., Hunt Valley, 1984-85; v.p. research and devel. Rexnord Automation Inc., Hunt Valley Md., 1986-87, v.p. mfg. and engring. Electronic Ops. Group, 1987-89; prodn. program mgr. Bendix Communications div. Allied Signal Aerospace Co, Towson, 1989—. Mem. adv. bd. Dundalk Community Coll. Served to 1st lt. U.S. Army, 1961-63. Mem. IEEE, Am. Mgmt. Assn., Surface Mount Tech. Assn., Assn. Mfg. Excellence. Democrat. Methodist. Home: 13804 Princess Anne Way Phoenix MD 21131 Office: Allied Signal Aerospace Co Bendix Communications Div 1300 E Joppa Rd Towson MD 21204

MARCHAND, CLAUDE R., corporate executive; b. Victoriaville, Que, Can., Apr. 20, 1931; s. Louis-Philippe and Thérèse (Favreau) M.; m. Lucille Jarry, Dec. 11, 1954 (div. Nov. 1974); children: Hélène, Philippe; m. Danielle Blanchet, Nov. 30, 1974; 1 child, Julie. BA, U. Montreal, 1950, licence in law, 1953; postgrad., Inst. European Studies, Torino, Italy, 1955. Sole practice Montreal, 1954-62; legal counsel Steinberg's Ltd., Montreal, 1962-63; legal advisor Corp. Engrs. Quebec, Montreal, 1964-68; exec. sec. Montreal Bar Assn., 1968-69; sec., corp. solicitor Microsystems Internat. Ltd., Montreal, 1969-72; sec., gen. counsel Can. Devel. Corp. (now Polysar Energy and Chem. Corp.), Toronto, Can., 1972-76, v.p., sec., gen. counsel, 1976-79, sr. v.p., sec., 1979—; bd. dirs. Canterra Energy Ltd., Calgary, Polysar Ltd., Sarnia, Zycor, Inc., Toronto. V.p. Toronto French Theatre, 1985-88. Mem. Barreau du Quebec, Jr. Bar Montreal (treas. 1959-60), French C. of C. (dir. 1979-83), U. Montreal Alumni Assn. (pres. 1968-69, Prix Arthur Valle award 1954), France-Can. (pres. 1978, 79), Cercle Canadien (v.p. 1987), U. Montreal Athletic Union (pres. 1952-54). Clubs: Ontario, Granite. Office: Polysar Energy & Chem Corp, 444 Yonge St, Toronto, ON Canada M5B 2H4

MARCHMAN, DENNIS LEROY, accountant; b. White Plains, Ga., Feb. 20, 1915; s. Clarence Moore and Lillie Mae (Darnell) M. Student Oglethrope U., 1934, Southern Brothers Law Sch., 1936-37. With Miami (Fla.) Herald, 1936-38; bookkeeper Vultee Aircraft Co., Miami, 1941-42; acct. C.F. Wheeler Builder, Miami, 1946-49; controller Hardy Houses, Laurel, Md., 1949-50; v.p. Tec-Bilt Homes, Miami, 1950-55, Carl G. Fisher Corp., Nassau, Bahamas, 1955-57; controller Brook Gas Co., Miami, Fla., 1957-67; controller Auto-Marine Engrs., Inc., Miami, 1967—; v.p., dir. Aviation Marine and Auto Supply, Inc., 1975—. Served with USNR, 1942-45. Democrat. Baptist. Home: 5330 SW 62d Ave Miami FL 33155

MARCUM, JOSEPH LARUE, insurance company executive; b. Hamilton, Ohio, July 2, 1923; s. Glen F. and Helen A. (Stout) M.; m. Sarah Jane Sloneker, Mar. 7, 1944; children: Catharine Ann Marcum Lowe, Joseph Timothy (dec.), Mary Christina Marcum Manchester, Sarah Jennifer Marcum Shuffield, Stephen Sloneker. B.A., Antioch Coll., 1947; M.B.A. in Fin, Miami U., 1965. With Ohio Casualty Ins. Co. and affiliates, 1947—, now chmn. bd., chief exec. officer, also bd. dirs.; bd. dirs. First Nat. Bank S.W. Ohio; bd. dirs., chmn. exec. com. First Fin. Bancorp., Monroe, Ohio. Trustee Miami U., Oxford, Ohio. Capt., inf. U.S. Army. Mem. Soc. C.P.C.U. (nat. dir.), Am. Inst. Property and Liability Underwriters (trustee), Queen City Club, Bankers Club, Can. Club, Met. Club, Princeton Club of N.Y., Eldorado Country Cblu, Little Harbor Club, Walloon Lake Country Club, Mill Reef Club. Presbyterian. Home: 475 Oakwood Dr Hamilton OH 45013 Office: Ohio Casualty Corp 136 N 3rd St Hamilton OH 45025

MARCUM, WALTER PHILLIP, oil company executive; b. Bemidji, Minn., Mar. 1, 1944; s. John Phillip and Johnnye Evelyn (Edmiston) M.; m. Barbara Lynn Maloof, Apr. 17, 1976. BBA, Tex. Tech U., 1967. Researcher Collins Securities, Denver, 1968-70, Hanifin Imfoff, Denver, 1970-71; cons. Marcum-Spillane, Denver, 1971-76; with MGF Oil Corp., Midland, Tex., 1976-87, sr. v.p., 1978, exec. v.p., 1979-83, pres., chief exec. officer, 1983-87; sr. v.p. corp. fin. Boettcher & Co., Denver, 1987—; dir. Aristek Corp., Homefree Village Resorts & Enerco, Inc., Mallon Resources Corp. Republican. Presbyterian. Home: 676 Monroe Denver CO 80206 Office: Boettcher & Co PO Box 54 Denver CO 80201-0054

MARCUM, WILLIAM IRA, land manager; b. Stepptown, W.Va., Dec. 29, 1950; s. Ira and Charlene (Asbury) M. AB, Marshall U., 1972, MA, 1974. Teaching asst. Marshall U., Huntington, W.Va., 1972-74; tchr. Wayne County (W.Va.) Schs., 1974-79; sr. advisor Dept. Housing and Urban Devel., Holden, W.Va., 1979-80; edn. coordinator McDowell County Health Program, Welch, W.Va., 1980-82; land mgr. Wolf Creek Resource Group, Inez, Ky., 1982—. Commr. 37th Precinct, Wayne County, W.Va., 1974—; advisor Village Council, Stepptown, 1987—. Mem. Am. Mgmt. Assn., Am. Assn. Univ. Profs., W. Va. State Health Council (pres. 1981-82), K.C. (sec. Welch chpt. 1980-82). Home: Box 333 Stepptown WV 25674 Office: Wolf Creek Resource Group Box 413 Inez KY 41224

MARCUS, ALAN C., public relations consultant; b. N.Y.C., Feb. 26, 1947; s. Percy and Rose (Fox) M.; m. Judith Lamel, June 21, 1979. Student Hun Sch., Princeton, 1966. Dir. pub. relations Bergen County Rep. Com., Hackensack, N.J., 1968; clk. N.J. Gen. Assembly, Trenton, 1969, sec. to majority party of assembly, 1970; pres. Alan C. Marcus Assocs., Secaucus, 1971—, The Marcus Group, Inc., Secaucus, 1976—; adj. prof. Rutgers U. Grad. Sch., 1986-88. Trustee Nat. Leukemia Assn., 1976-82, Hun Sch. of Princeton, 1977-88, Passaic River Coalition, 1980-82. Recipient Youth Enterprise award Jim Walter Corp., 1972. Mem. Pub. Relations Soc. Am. (N.J. chpt. pres.'s award 1975, past pres. and bd. dirs. N.J. chpt. 1976-77), N.J. C. of C., Meadowlands C. of C., N.J. Bus. and Industry Assn., N.J. Broadcasters Assn., N.J. Press Assn., Capitol Hill, Fed. City (Washington); Essex, Mayfair. Office: 500 Plaza Dr PO Box 3309 Secaucus NJ 07096-3309 also: 240 W State St Trenton NJ 08608 also: 1030 15th St NW Washington DC 20005

MARCUS, MARSHALL MATTHEW, sales executive; b. Boston, June 9, 1933; s. Jacob and Elizabeth (Rotman) M.; m. Joyce Elaine Hellerman, Apr. 17, 1961; children: Lloyd S., Debra M. Haluska. AA, Suffolk U., 1950, JD, 1955. Salesman Cen. States Diversified Corp., Boston, 1971-74; product mgr. Cen. States Diversified Corp., St. Louis, 1974-76, dept. mgr., 1976-78; mgr. sales div. Cen. States Diversified Corp., N.Y.C., 1978-84; v.p. Cen. States Diversified Corp., Stamford, Conn., 1984—; bd. dirs. Cen. States Diversified Corp., St. Louis, 1978-84. Served with U.S. Army, 1958-61. Decorated Purple Heart. Hebrew. Lodge: B'nai Brith (v.p. Rye, N.Y. chpt. 1978-79, pres. 1979-80, chmn. 1980-81, chaplain 1981-82). Home: 180-24 Glenbrook Rd PO Box 2549 Stamford CT 06906-0549 Office: Cen States Diversified Inc 447 Glenbrook Rd Stamford CT 06906

MARCUS, STEPHEN CECIL, printing company executive; b. Phila., Mar. 8, 1932; s. Jerome Milton and Helen Gertrude (Jacobs) M.; m. Seena Hymowitz, Nov. 2, 1958; children: Nancy Joy, Julie Bea; m. Lois Simon, Oct. 7, 1984. BS, Drexel U., 1957. Jr. partner Liess-Marcus Co., Inc., Phila., 1957-59; v.p. sales Mid-City Press, Inc., Phila., 1959-70; pres., chief exec. officer, founder Mars Graphic Services, Inc., Westville, N.J., 1970-86, chmn. 1986—; mem. Phila. Mgmt. Negotiating Com., Jr. Execs./Graphic Arts, Phila. br. Trustee, Friends' Central Sch., 1977-80; trustee/co-founder Beth Tovin Synagogue, Phila., 1972—; active Am. Cancer Soc., Phila. Big Bros. Served with U.S. Army, 1953-55. Recipient Annual award Exchange Club N.J., 1981; awards Big Bros. Am., Am. Cancer Soc. Mem. Am. Arbitration Assn. (various awards), Nat. Direct Mail Mktg. Assn., Graphic Arts Tech. Found., South Jersey Graphic Arts Assn., Graphic Arts Assn. of Del. Valley (bd. dirs. 1988), Radnor Valley Country Club (Villanova, Pa.), Poor Richard Club (Phila.), Tau Kappa Epsilon. Republican. Jewish. Home: 644 Robinson Ln Haverford PA 19041 Office: 1012 Edgewater Ave Westville NJ 08093

MARCUS, STEPHEN GARRETT, physician, biotechnology executive, researcher; b. Bklyn., Sept. 5, 1953; s. Seymour and Miriam Marcus. BS, Bklyn. Coll., 1973; MD, N.Y. Med. Coll., 1976. Diplomate Am. Bd. Internal Medicine. Intern, then resident Lenox Hill Hosp., N.Y.C., 1976-79; fellow cancer rsch. inst. U. Calif., San Francisco, 1979-81; emergency physician Children's Hosp., San Francisco, 1981-84; assoc. dir. clin. rsch. Triton Bioscis., Alameda, Calif., 1985-86, dir. clin. rsch., 1986-88; sr. dir. med. affairs Triton Bioscis. sub. Shell Oil Co., Alameda, Calif., 1988—. Aem. AMA (Recognition award 1981), Internat. Soc. Inteferon Rsch., Am. Acad. Med. Dirs., Soc. for Biolog. Therapy, Internat. AIDS Soc., Calif. Med. Assn. Home: 9 Captain's Dr Alameda CA 94501 Office: Triton Bioscis 1501 Harbor Bay Pkwy Alameda CA 94501

MARCUS, STUART ALLEN, sales executive; b. Hagerstown, Md., Dec. 29, 1956; s. E. Mason and Roxanna (Tauer) M. BS, Northeastern U., 1979. Western sales mgr. Towle Housewares Group, Boston, 1979-80, Leonard Silver Mfg., Boston, 1980-81; v.p. sales Gold Lance div. Town & Country, Houston, 1981—. Patentee in field. Mem. So. Jewelers Travelers Assn. Home: Town & Country Gold Lance Div 1920 N Memorial Way Houston TX 77007

MARDELL, FRED ROBERT, alcoholic beverages company executive; b. Chgo., Oct. 2, 1934; s. Sam and Clara (Feldman) M.; m. Susan Mardell; children: Elizabeth, Caleb, Sarah. B.S., DePaul U., 1955; J.D., U. Chgo., 1958. Bar: Ill. 1958. Practice in Chgo., 1961-65; law clk. Justice U.S. Schwartz, Ill. Appellate Ct., 1958-59; research asso. U. Chgo. Law Sch., 1959; assoc. Miller, Shakman, Nathan & Hamilton, 1961-65; v.p., dir., exec. v.p., sec. Barton Brands, Ltd., Chgo., 1965—. Assoc. editor: U. Chgo. Law Rev, 1957-58. Served with AUS, 1959-61. Mem. Pi Gamma Mu. Home: 838 Michigan Evanston IL 60202 Office: Barton Brands Ltd 55 E Monroe St Chicago IL 60603

MARDIGIAN, EDWARD STEPHAN, machine tool company executive; b. Stambul, Turkey, Oct. 25, 1909; s. Stephan and Agavine (Hagopian) M.; came to U.S., 1914, naturalized, 1929; student Wayne U., 1932-34; m. Helen Alexander, June 5, 1938; children—Marilyn, Edward, Robert. Asst. tool engr. Briggs Mfg. Co., Detroit, 1935-37, chief tool engr., Eng., 1937-45, chief project engr., 1945; owner, operator Mardigian Corp., Warren, Mich., 1948-69, Marco Corp., Warren, 1954, bought Buckeye Aluminum Co., Wooster, Ohio, 1956, Mardigian Car Corp., Warren, 1966—; pres. Hercules Machine Tool & Die Co., Warren, 1973—; chmn. bd. Central States Mfg. Co., Warren, 1973—. Pres. Armenian Gen. Benevolent Union Am., 1972—; chmn. Chief Exec. Orgn., Warren, 1974, Chief Exec. Orgn. Internat. Decorated medal St. Gregory by Vasken 1st Supreme Patriarch of All Armenians, 1966; named Man of Year Diocese Armenian Ch. N.Am., 1977. Home: 1525 Tottenham Rd Birmingham MI 48009 Office: Hercules Machine Tool & Die Co E Ten Mile Rd Warren MI 48089

MAREE, ANDREW MORGAN, III, business management and investment advisor; b. Detroit, Mar. 9, 1927; s. Andrew Morgan, Jr., and Elizabeth Lathrop (Cady) M.; B.A., Claremont Men's Coll., 1950; M.B.A., U. Chgo., 1951; J.D., Whittier Coll., 1982; m. Wendy Patricia Haymes, Dec. 20, 1980; children: Samantha, Andrew Morgan, IV. Trust analyst Hanover Bank & Trust Co., N.Y.C., 1951-52; pres. A. Morgan Maree, Jr., & Assocs. Inc., Los Angeles, 1952-86, chmn. bd., 1987—; dir. Carson Estate Co. Served with USNR, 1944-46. Mem. Acad. Motion Picture Arts and Scis., The Players, Am. Film Inst. Office: PO Box 960 Lake Arrowhead CA 92352

MARESCO, STEPHEN PETER, financial services executive; b. Bridgeport, Conn., Feb. 18, 1928; s. Stephen Sr. and Mary (Orsaio) M.; married, June 25, 1955; children: Catherine Mary Racioppo, Peter Frank. BBA, Manhattan Coll., 1959; MBA, St. John's U., 1976; MS, Manhattan Coll., 1978. Computer programmer, ops. research analyst Chase-Manhattan Bank, N.Y.C., 1947-71; methods specialist hosp. efficiency Blue Cross Blue Shield, N.Y.C., 1971-78; sect. mgr. systems and procedures E.F. Hutton & Co., Inc., N.Y.C., 1979-87, mgr. internal control evaluation dept., 1987-88; internal revenue agt. IRS, N.Y.C., 1988; adminstrv. analyst N.Y.C. Housing Authority, 1989—. Contbr. articles to profl. jours. With Chase-Manhattan Bank, 1966; chmn. Cub Scouts Boy Scouts Am., N.Y.C.; baseball, basketball coach, Wood-Lean Boys Club, Yonkers, 1969-71. Served as cpl. U.S. Army, 1951-52, Korea. Mem. Inst. for Econometric Research, Am. Legion (chaplain). Republican. Roman Catholic. Office: New York CIty Housing Authority 250 Broadway New York NY 10007

MARGARITOFF, DIMITRI ANDREJ, business executive; b. Berlin, Germany, Sept. 12, 1947; s. Peter and Tamara (Holl) M.; m. Karen Andrea Hollihan, Aug. 2, 1985; 2 children: Peter Andrej, Marco Alexander. MEE, Swiss Fed. Inst. Tech., Zürich, 1973; MBA, U. Rochester, 1975. Mktg. engr. Edmac Assocs., Rochester, N.Y., 1975-76; mktg. mgr. Hawesko GmbH, Hamburg, Fed. Republic Germany, 1977-80, pres., 1981—, co-owner, 1987—; bd. dirs., co-owner CWD GmbH, Hamburg, 1986—; bd. dirs. Chateaux & Domaines GmbH, Hamburg. Home: Weetenkamp 1, 2000 Hamburg 52, Federal Republic of Germany Office: Hawesko GmbH, Hamburger Str 14, 2082 Tornesch-Hamburg Federal Republic of Germany

MARGESON, WILLIAM, investment counselor; b. New Bedford, Mass., May 6, 1914; s. Thomas Harry and Jane (Haworth) M.; A.B., Brown U., 1937; m. Mary Bowers, 1940 (dec. 1982); children: Mary Jane, William Frederic; m. Lillian Dorsey Colby, Nov. 26, 1983. Dir. sales research, head new bus. Kircher Helton & Collett, Dayton, 1946-48; pres. Bramble Margeson & Odiorne, Dayton, 1948-50; pres. William Margeson Co., Syracuse, 1950-53; v.p. Waddell & Reed Inc., Kansas City, Mo., 1953-59; pres. Family, Industry & College Planning Co., Inc., Syracuse, 1959—; cons. mut. funds St. Paul's Cathedral, N.Y. Served to lt. USNR, 1942-46. Mem. Nat. Assn. Securities Dealers. Episcopalian. Clubs: Brown Univ. (pres. Central N.Y. 1963-64), Ivy League (pres. Cen. N.Y. 1967-68). Originated "Pay-Back Check-A-Month" plan, "Margeson Plan", a Tax-Sheltered Investment Program of Estate Planning for Donor and Eleemosynary Instns.; cons. Mut. Funds to St. Paul's Cathedral Diocese of Cen. N.Y. Home: 113 Archer Rd Syracuse NY 13207 Office: 528 Oak St Syracuse NY 13203

MARGOLIN, ARTHUR STANLEY, distillery company executive; b. N.Y.C., Aug. 7, 1936; s. Samuel and Belle (Gelb) M.; m. Barbara Jane Lester, June 27, 1965; children: Sarah Jennifer, Julie Ellen, Carolyn Leigh. BA in Econs., NYU, 1957, postgrad. in bus., 1961. Analyst, sr. analyst Asch Market Research (div. JES), N.Y.C., 1961-63; field asst. to eastern div. mgr. Calvert Distillers, N.Y.C., 1963-64, asst. to asst. and met. N.Y. mgr., 1964-72, asst. to exec. v.p. sales, asst. to pres., 1972-78; exec. asst. to pres. House of Seagram, N.Y.C., 1978-80; dir. U.S. ops. Seagram Europe, London, 1980-82; asst. to pres. Seagram Internat. Joseph E. Seagram & Sons Inc., N.Y.C., 1982, asst. to office of chmn. and pres., 1982-85, v.p. spl. asst. to office of chmn. and pres., 1985—; bd. dirs. Forhan Forwarding and Handling Co., N.V., Antwerp, Belgium. Mng. editor Heights Daily News, 1956-57. Bd. dirs. Fifth Ave. Assn., N.Y.C., 1987. Capt. USAF, 1957-60. Republican. Jewish. Office: Joseph E Seagram & Sons Inc 375 Park Ave New York NY 10152-0192

MARGOLIS, DAVID I(SRAEL), corporate executive; b. N.Y.C., Jan. 24, 1930; s. Benjamin and Celia (Kosofsky) M.; m. Barbara Schneider, Sept. 7, 1958; children: Brian, Robert, Peter, Nancy. B.A., Coll. City N.Y., 1950, M.B.A., 1952; post-grad., N.Y.U., 1952-55. Security analyst Josephthal Co., 1952-56; asst. treas. Raytheon Co., 1956-59; treas. IT&T, N.Y.C., 1959-62; with Colt Industries Inc. (formerly Fairbanks Whitney Corp.), N.Y.C., 1962—, now chmn., pres., chief exec. officer. Mem. N.Y. State Emergency Fin. Control Bd. for City N.Y., 1975-77. Mem. Fin. Execs. Inst., N.Y. Chamber Commerce and Industry (dir.), Conf. Bd. ((mem. corp.)). Office: Colt Industries Inc 430 Park Ave New York NY 10022

MARGOLIS, SIDNEY O., textile and apparel company executive; b. Boston, Dec. 13, 1925; s. Joseph and Lillian (Frank) M.; m. Phyllis Teichberg, June 24, 1950; children—Jonathan S., Dean F., Brian B. B. Indsl. Engring., Ohio State U., 1949. Indsl. engr. ACME Backing Corp., Bklyn., 1949-53; purchasing agt. Flexible Barriers Inc., Stamford, Conn., 1953-57; office mgr. United Mchts. and Mfrs. Inc., N.Y.C., 1957-69, comptroller merchandising, 1970-77, v.p. adminstrn., 1977-80, sr. v.p. adminstrn., 1980—, exec. v.p. adminstrn., 1984—, also bd. dirs.; bd. dirs. 10 West 86 St. Corp., N.Y.C. Served with USAAF, 1943-44. Mem. IIE (recipient 25-yr. disting. svc. award N.Y.C. chpt. 1985), Am. Inst. Indsl. Engrs. (Service award 1984), Administrative Mgmt. Soc., Textile Distributors Assn., Am. Textile Mfrs. Inst. Office: United Mchts & Mfrs Inc 1407 Broadway New York NY 10018

MARIANAK, CHARLES GABOR, electronics company executive; b. Budapest, Hungary, July 29, 1946; came to U.S., 1984; s. Karoly and Angela Elizabeth (Agota) M.; m. Rosemary Halsal, Sept. 25, 1965 (div. Sept. 1980); 1 child, Charles; m. Patricia Brier, Sept. 6, 1986; children: Barbara, Richard. BS in Chemistry, U. Western Ont., London, Can., 1971, MBA, 1976. Pres., chief exec. officer Photochem. Research Assocs. Inc., London,

1976-83; pres., chief exec. officer Photon Tech. Internat. Inc., Princeton, N.J., 1983—, also chmn. bd. dirs.; bd. dirs. Flow Vision Inc., Clifton, N.J. Mem. govs. adv. com. on photonics State N.J., Princeton, 1988—. Mem. Fellow Am. Chem. Soc.; mem. Am. Optical Soc., Soc. Photo-Optical Instrumentation Engrs. Office: Photon Tech Internat Inc 601 Ewing St C-2 Princeton NJ 08540

MARIENCHILD, EVA, management consultant; b. N.Y.C., Mar. 24, 1957; d. Benjamin Beauchamp de Jesus Rodriguez-Martinez and Marien (Engracia) Martinez-Ceberio. Student, Dominican Comml. Sch., 1976. Account mgmt. exec. sec. Warwick, Welsh & Miller, N.Y.C., 1978-80; chem. patent trademark paralegal Davis, Hoxie, Faithfull & Hapgood, N.Y.C., 1980-82; dir. publicity, exec. sec. Waring & LaRosa Advt., N.Y.C., 1981-82; assoc. account exec. Stiefel/Raymond Advt., N.Y.C., 1982-83; copy editor personal fin. E.F. Hutton, N.Y.C., 1983-84; account exec. Anderson Stone & Jason, N.Y.C., 1984-85; v.p. sales Computer Research Tabs, N.Y.C., 1985-86; pres., chief exec. officer Collection Resource Team, N.Y.C., 1986—, Eva Marienchild Cons., N.Y.C., 1988—; dir. promotion Motion Picture & TV Media Registry, N.Y.C., 1983. Editor, pub. Sidelines mag., 1984, various newsletters; contbr. to Seventeen mag., others. Graphic artist fin. div. UNICEF, N.Y.C., 1983; collaborator sci. and tech. entry program Manhattan Coll. Mem. NAFE. Home: 34 W 12th St Ste 3F New York NY 10011 Office: 80 E 11th St New York NY 10003

MARIN, GEORGE EDWARD, computer systems company executive; b. Phila., Aug. 29, 1950; s. George Anthony and Evelyn Lorraine (Harbert) M.; A.A.S., Montgomery County Coll., 1971; B.S. cum laude, Point Park Coll., Pitts., 1973; postgrad. Lehigh U., Bethlehem, Pa., Villanova (Pa.) U.; m. Susan Clare Nolan, June 27, 1970; children—Steven William, Michael Frederick, Jennifer Clare. Dir. Rotelle Mgmt., Inc., West Point, Pa., 1973—; pres. Data Tech. Svcs., Inc., 1982—. Mem. Eastern Montgomery County Area Vocat. Tech. Sch. Data Processing Craft Com., 1974—. Mem. Data Processing Mgmt. Assn. (past chpt. sec.). Designer computer systems IBM 4300 CMO. Home: 1332 Highland Ave Fort Washington PA 19034 Office: Data Tech Svcs Rotelle Complex 301 Morris Rd West Point PA 19486

MARINE, CLYDE LOCKWOOD, agribusiness company executive; b. Knoxville, Tenn., Dec. 25, 1936; s. Harry H. and Idelle (Larue) M.; m. Eleanor Harb, Aug. 9, 1958; children: Cathleen, Sharon. B.S. in Agr., U. Tenn., 1958; M.S. in Agrl. Econs., U. Ill., 1959; Ph.D. in Agrl. Econs., Mich. State U., 1963. Sr. market analyst Pet Milk Co., St. Louis, 1963-64; mgr. market planning agr. chems. div. Mobile Chem. Co., Richmond, Va., 1964-67; mgr. ingredient purchasing Central Soya Co., Ft. Wayne, Ind., 1970-73, corp. economist, 1967-70, v.p. ingredient purchasing, 1973-75, sr. v.p., 1975—. Bd. dirs. Ft. Wayne Fine Arts Found., 1976-79; bd. dirs. Ft. Wayne Pub. Transp. Corp., 1975-83; v.p. Ft. Wayne Philharm., 1974-76. Served with U.S. Army, 1959-60. Mem. Nat. Soybean Processors Assn. (chmn.), U.S. C. of C., Am. Agrl. Econs. Assn., Am. Feed Mfrs. Assn. (chmn. purchasing council), Chgo. Bd. Trade, Chgo. Merc. Exchange. Episcopalian. Club: Ft. Wayne Country. Office: Cen Soya Co Inc PO Box 1400 Fort Wayne IN 46801-1400

MARINEAU, PHILIP ALBERT, food company executive; b. Chgo., Oct. 4, 1946; s. Philip Albert and Bernice (Collins) M.; m. Susan Anne Graf, June 28, 1969; children: Philip Albert III, Anne Elizabeth. AB in History, Georgetown U., 1968; MBA, Northwestern U., 1970. Coordinator sales research The Quaker Oats Co., Chgo., 1972-73, mktg. asst., 1973-74, asst. brand mgr., then brand mgr., 1974-78, product group mgr., 1978-80, dir., then v.p. product mgmt., 1980-85, pres. grocery specialties div., 1985-87, exec. v.p. grocery specialties and market devel., 1987-88, exec. v.p. internat. grocery products, 1988—. Bd. dirs. Travelers and Immigrant Aid, Chgo., 1987—; trustee Northlight Theatre, Evanston, Ill., 1985—. Mem. Am. Mktg. Assn. (Steuart Hendersen Britt award 1987), Westmoreland Country Club (Wilmette, Ill.). Office: The Quaker Oats Co Quaker Tower 321 N Clark St Chicago IL 60610

MARINI, MATTHEW ANTHONY, finance company executive; b. Jacksonville, Fla., July 11, 1955; s. Anthony J. and Donna (Armstrong) M.; m. Donna L. Marini, Apr. 8, 1983; children: Dana, Megan. BS, Pa. State U., 1977; MBA, Drexel U., 1978. Various positions GE Credit Corp., Menlo Park, Calif., 1979-85, regional mgr., 1985-87; sr. v.p. corp. fin. group GE Capital Co., N.Y.C., 1987—. Office: GE Capital Co Corp Fin Group 535 Madison Ave Suite 2200 New York NY 10022

MARINO, JOHN HARRISON, railway executive; b. Middletown, N.Y., July 18, 1939; s. Orlando Nicholas and Mary Lorraine (Dunn) M.; B.S. in Engring. (Allegheny-Ludlum achievement award scholar), Princeton U., 1961; M.S. in Transp. Engring. (Automotive Safety Found. fellow), Purdue U., 1963; m. Ann Southerlyn Dozier, Oct. 15, 1966; children—John Harrison Jr., Ann Southerlyn. Indsl. engr. Reading R.R., Phila., 1966-68; assoc. Kearney Mgmt. Cons., Chgo., 1968-73; mgr. indsl. engring. Seatrain Lines, 1973-74; chief ops. planning U.S. Ry. Assn., Washington, 1974-76; pres. Hillsdale County Ry. Co. (Mich), 1976-83, Lenawee County R.R. Co., Adrian, Mich., 1977-83, Canton R.R., Balt., 1982-84, pres., treas., 1984-87; exec. v.p. No. Mo. R.R., 1984-85; pres. Transp. Mgmt. Services, Inc., 1976—; v.p. Corp. Strategies, Inc., Springfield, Va., 1980-87; pres. Huron and Eastern Ry. Co., Bad Axe, Mich., 1986—. Lt. U.S. Army Corps Engrs., 1963-65. Registered profl. engr., N.Y., Pa., Conn. Mem. ASCE, NRC, Inst. Transp. Engrs., Am. Ry. Engring. Assn. Republican. Roman Catholic. Clubs: Princeton (N.Y.C.), Tantallon Yacht. Home: 6189 Deer Path Ct Manassas VA 22111 Office: 12864B Harbor Dr Lake Ridge VA 22192

MARINO, ROBERT JAMES, telecommunications company executive; b. N.Y.C., Apr. 3, 1947; s. Vincent James and Martha C. (D'Agnillo) M.; m. Nancy Louise Beatty, July 19, 1969; children: Kristin, Kara, Kathleen. BS in Econs., SUNY, Brockport, 1969. Various mgmt. and tech. positions Rochester (N.Y.) Telephone Corp., 1969-77; div. sales mgr., gen. mktg. mgr. United Telephone Co. Ohio, Mansfield, 1977-82; v.p., gen. mgr. United Tele System, Inc., Westwood, Kans., 1982-85; pres. United TeleSpectrum, Inc., Kansas City, Mo., 1985--; speaker in field, 1985--. Contbr. articles to profl. publs. Mem. Cellular Telephone Industry Assn. (bd. dirs. 1985-87), Kansas City C. of C. (steering com. 1986-87), Kansas City Club, Milburn Country Club (Kans.). Republican. Roman Catholic. Office: United TeleSpectrum Inc 2546 Broadway PO Box 418070 Kansas City MO 64141 also: PO Box 7942 Shawnee Mission KS 66207

MARIO, ERNEST, pharmaceutical company executive; b. Clifton, N.J., June 12, 1938; s. Jerry and Edith (Meyer) M.; m. Mildred Martha Daume, Dec. 10, 1961; children—Christopher Bradley, Gregory Gerald, Jeremy Konrad. B.S. in Pharmacy, Rutgers U., 1961; M.S. in Phys. Scis., U. RI., 1963, Ph.D. in Phys. Scis., 1965. Registered pharmacist, R.I., N.Y. Vice pres. mfg. Smith Kline Corp., Phila., 1975-77; v.p. mfg. ops. U.S. Pharm. Co. div. E. R. Squibb, New Brunswick, N.J., 1977-79; v.p., gen. mgr. chem. div. E. R. Squibb, Princeton, N.J., 1979-81; pres. chem. and engring. div., sr. v.p. Squibb Corp., Princeton, 1981-84; v.p. Squibb Corp., 1984-86; pres., chief operating officer Glaxo Inc., 1986-88, chmn., chief exec. officer, 1988—; grad. asst., instr. U. R.I., Kingston, 1961-66; research fellow Inst. Neurol. Diseases, Bethesda, Md., 1963-65. Contbr. articles to profl. jours. Pres.'s Council, Am. Lung Assn.; chmn. Nat. Found. for Infectious Diseases; trustee Rutgers U. Mem. Pharm. Mfrs. Assn. (bd. dirs.). Office: Glaxo Inc 5 Moore Dr PO Box 13408 Research Triangle Park NC 27709

MARION, JOHN LOUIS, fine arts auctioneering and appraiser; b. N.Y.C., Nov. 27, 1933; s. Louis John and Florence Adelaide (Winters) M.; children: John L., Deborah Mary, Therese Marie, Michelle Marie; m. Anne Burnett Windfohr, May 26, 1988. BS, Fordham U., 1956; postgrad., Columbia U., 1960-61. With Sotheby Parke Bernet Inc., N.Y.C., 1960—, dir., 1965—, v.p., 1966-70, exec. v.p., 1970-72, pres., 1972-87, chmn. bd., 1975—; bd. dirs. Sotheby Holdings Inc., London. Chmn. fine arts N.Y.C. div. Am. Cancer Soc., 1983—; vice chmn. bldg. steering com. Dobbs Ferry (N.Y.) Hosp., 1975; bd. dirs. Internat. Found. Art Research, Ctr. for Hope. Served as lt. (j.g.) USN, 1956-60. Mem. Appraisers Assn. Am., Inc. Clubs: Castle Pines, Siwanoy Country, Lotos. Lodge: Knights of Malta. Home: 1400 Shady Oaks Ln Fort Worth TX 76107 Office: Sotheby's 1334 York Ave New York NY 10021

MARIONE, DONALD PETER, telephone company executive; b. North Bergen, N.J., Oct. 31, 1926; s. Raphael A. and Concetta (Petrecca) M.; m. Claire E. Archbold; children: Cynthia, David. B in Econs., Rutgers U., 1949. Sales rep. N.J. Bell Telephone Co., Paterson, 1952-74; gen. mgr. Hudson, Hackensack, N.J., 1974-83; v.p. external affairs Newark, 1983-87, v.p. ops., chief operating officer, 1987—, also bd. dirs. Mayor, Wyckoff, N.J., 1967; chmn. bd. Bergen County C. of C., Hackensack, 1976; trustee Bergen County Econs. Edn. Found., Hackensack, 1974. Served with USN, 1944-46. Mem. N.J. Utilities Assn. (bd. dirs.), Commerce & Industry Assn. N.J. (bd. dirs.), Boys' and Girls' Club of Newark. Republican. Roman Catholic. Clubs: Essex (Newark); Hackensack Golf; Indian Trail (Franklin Lakes, N.J.). Office: NJ Bell Telephone Co 540 Broad St Newark NJ 07101

MARISCALCO, MICHAEL GUY, engineering company executive; b. Dayton, Ohio, Oct. 10, 1952. BSME, U. Dayton, 1975, MSME, 1976. Registered profl. engr. Ohio, Ky., Pa., Ark., N.J., Ind., Miss. Sr. project engr. Bruce Menkel and Assoc. Inc., Franklin, Ohio, 1979-84; pres. Qsource Engring., Inc., Dayton, 1984-88; dir. Mayo Control and Technology, Inc., Dayton, 1988—; bd. trustees Dayton Art Inst., 1989—. Bd. dirs. Unified Bd. of Bldg. Appeals, Montgomery County, Ohio, 1986—; mem. adv. bd. Sinclair Community Col., 1988—. Recipient Dayton Area Up and Comers award, 1988. Mem. ASME, ASHRAE, Nat. Soc. Profl. Engrs., Am. Mgmt. Assn., Am. Assn. Energy Engrs., Racquet Club, Engrs. Club. Home: 1009 Fleming Ct Spring Valley OH 45370 Office: Qsource Engring Inc 288 Byers Rd Miamisburg OH 45342

MARK, HENRY ALLEN, lawyer; b. Bklyn., May 16, 1909; s. Henry Adam and Mary Clyde (McCarroll) M.; m. Isobel Ross Arnold, June 26, 1940; BA, Williams Coll., 1932; JD, Cornell U., 1935. Bars: N.Y. 1936, Conn. 1981, U.S. Dist. Ct. (so. dist.) N.Y. 1943. Assoc. firm Allin & Tucker, N.Y.C., 1935-40; mng. atty. Indemnity Ins. Co. of N.Am., N.Y.C., 1940-43; assoc. firm Mudge, Stern, Williams & Tucker, N.Y.C., 1943-50, Cadwalder, Wickersham & Taft, N.Y.C., 1950-53; ptnr. Cadwalader, Wickersham & Taft, 1953-74, of counsel, 1974—; lectr. Practicing Law Inst., N.Y.C., 1955-68. Mem. adv. com. zoning Village of Garden City (N.Y.), 1952-54, planning comm., 1957-59, zoning bd. appeals, 1959-61, trustee, 1961-65, mayor, 1965-67; chmn. planning commn. Town of Washington (Conn.), 1980-84. Mem. ABA, N.Y. Bar Assn., Assn. Bar City of N.Y., Conn. Bar Assn., Litchfield County Bar Assn., Cornell Law Assn. (pres. 1971-73), St. Andrew's Soc., Phi Beta Kappa. Republican. Congregationalist. Lodge: Masons. Address: 10 Millay Ct Litchfield CT 06759

MARK, REUBEN, consumer products company executive; b. Jersey City, N.J., Jan. 21, 1939; s. Edward and Libbie (Berman) M.; m. Arlene Slobzian, Jan. 10, 1964; children: Lisa, Peter, Stephen. AB, Middlebury Coll., 1960; MBA, Harvard U., 1963. With Colgate-Palmolive Co., N.Y.C., 1963—; pres., gen. mgr. Venezuela, 1972-73, Can., 1973-74; v.p., gen. mgr. Far East div. 1974-75, v.p., gen. mgr. household products div., 1975-79, group v.p. domestic ops., 1979-81, exec. v.p., 1981-83, chief operating officer, 1983-84, pres., 1983—, chief exec. officer, 1984—, chmn. bd., 1986—; lectr. Sch. Bus. Adminstrn., U. Conn., 1977. Served with U.S. Army, 1961. Mem. Soap and Detergent Assn. (bd. dirs.), Grocery Mfrs. Am. (dir.), Nat. Exec. Service Corp. Office: Colgate-Palmolive Co 300 Park Ave New York NY 10022 *

MARKER, MARC LINTHACUM, lawyer, leasing company executive; b. Los Angeles, July 19, 1941; s. Clifford Harry and Voris (Linthacum) M.; m. Sandra Yocom, Aug. 29, 1965; children—Victor, Gwendolyn. B.A. in Econs. and Geography, U. Calif.-Riverside, 1964; J.D., U. So. Calif., 1967. Asst. v.p., asst. sec. Security Pacific Nat. Bank, Los Angeles, 1970-73; sr. v.p., chief counsel, sec. Security Pacific Leasing Corp., San Francisco, 1973—; pres. Security Pacific Leasing Services Corp., San Francisco, 1977-85, dir., 1977—; bd. dirs., sec. Voris, Inc., 1973-86; bd. dirs. Refiners Petroleum Corp., 1977-81, Security Pacific Leasing Singapore Ptc Ltd., 1983-85; lectr. in field. Served to comdr. USCGR. Mem. ABA, Calif. Bar Assn., D.C. Bar Assn., San Francisco Bar Assn., Am. Assn. Equipment Lessors. Republican. Lutheran. Club: University (Los Angeles). Office: Security Pacific Leasing Corp 4 Embarcadero Ctr #1200 San Francisco CA 94111

MARKERT, JAMES MACDOWELL, construction and real estate company executive; b. Cleve., Mar. 13, 1934; s. Frederick Schaefer and Francine (MacDowell) M.; m. Barbara Yazdi, Nov. 8, 1958; children: Dorothy, James MacDowell, Marion. B.S.Ch.E., Princeton U., 1956; M.B.A., Harvard U., 1958. Devel. rep. Chevron Chem., San Francisco, 1958-66; planning mgr. Xerox Corp., Rochester, N.Y., 1966-70; treas. Fluor Corp., Irvine, Calif., 1970-84; sr. v.p. fin., dir. Perini Corp., Framingham, 1984—; mem. adv. coun. Framingham Union Hosp. Club: Princeton (N.Y.C.). Home: 91 Royalston Rd Wellesley MA 02181 Office: Perini Corp 73 Mt Wayte Ave Framingham MA 01701

MARKEY, TERENCE FARLEY, investment executive; b. Stamford, Conn., Feb. 15, 1957; s. Richard Anthony and Joan (Farley) M.; m. Constance Anne Crabtree, Mar. 30, 1985. BS magna cum laude, Boston Coll., 1979. Key account mgr. Cheseborough Pond, Greenwich, Conn., 1979-80; account exec. Dean Witter Reynolds, N.Y.C., 1980-82, assoc. v.p., 1982-84, v.p., br. mgr., 1984-86, br. mgr. northeast region, 1986—; cons. Western Electric Co., N.Y.C., 1983-85; conducted numerous seminars for assns., orgns., N.Y.C. area, 1983—. Republican. Roman Catholic. Clubs: Greenwich (Conn.) Country; N.Y. Athletic. Office: Dean Witter Reynolds 1 N Broadway White Plains NY 10601

MARKHAM, LINCOLN ROCK, mechanical engineer; b. Albany, N.Y., Aug. 8, 1963; s. Lowell E. and Margaret D. (Mazzaferro) M.; m. Lynn M. Yaroschck, June 6, 1987. AS in Engring. Tech., Hudson Valley Community Coll., 1984; BS in Engring. Tech., Rochester Inst. Tech., 1987; postgrad., U. Rochester, 1987—. Mech. engring. trainee Rochester (N.Y.) Gas and Elec. Corp., 1985-87, corp. mech. engr., 1987—. Mem. ASHRAE (assoc. mem., acad. excellence award 1984, 86), Tau Alpha Pi (pres. student chpt. 1986-87). Roman Catholic. Home: 35 Andony Ln Rochester NY 14624 Office: Rochester Gas and Elec Corp 89 East Ave Rochester NY 14649

MARKHAM, LINDA GAIL, accountant; b. St. Petersburg, Fla., Apr. 22, 1951; d. Peggy Ann (Daughtry) MacDonald; m. Wayne S. Markham, June 12, 1971. BS cum laude, U. Md., 1974. CPA, Fla.; cert. fin. planner. Prin. Markham, Norton & Co., PA, CPA, Cape Coral and Ft. Myers, Fla., 1979—; bd. dirs., sec. Community Nat. Bank, Cape Coral; treas. South Fla. Fin. Corp.; active Southwest Fla. Tax Council, 1981—; trustee Lee County Electric Coop. Chmn. Cape Coral United Way Campaign, 1981-84 (agy. rev. com. 1980, budget rev. com. 1981-83); bd. dirs. United Way of Lee County, 1980-86; steering com., treas. Celebration of Women, 1982; mem. Pres.'s Adv. Com., Inst. for Mgmt. Devel. Edison Community Coll., 1982-84; gov.'s commns. on crime, leadership, small bus., 1982-84; State Sen. Fred Dudley's liaison between State Legislature and CPA's; mem. adv. bd. Lee County Indsl. Develop. Authority, 1988—; mem. steering com. Lee County Task Force on Infrastructure, 1988—; mem. charter class, steering com. Leadership Lee County, 1986—; adv. bd. Better Bus. Bur., 1986; mem. adv. council U.S. Small Bus. Adminstrn. region IV, 1987-89. Recipient Outstanding Businessperson of Yr. award Service Corps of Ret. Execs., 1984; named Acct. Advocate of Yr. for Fla., SBA, 1985, Career Woman of Yr. for Lee County, 1985. Mem. Am. Inst. CPA's, Fla. Inst. CPA's (chmn. speakers bur. 1979-80, pub. relations com. 1981, bd. dirs. Southwest Fla. chpt. 1978, v.p. 1979), Am. Womens' Soc. CPA's, Southwest Fla. Local Practitioners, Inst. Cert. Fin. Planners, Southwest Fla. Soc. Inst. Cert. Fin. Planners, Chamber of Southwest Fla. (bd. dirs. 1988—, exec. com. 1988, vice chmn. bd. bus. and econ. affairs 1988), Fort Myers Womens' Forum, Fort Myers C. of C., Cape Coral Contractors Industry Assn., Cape Coral C. of C. (chmn. task force on women in bus. 1980, chmn. membership com. 1980-81, exec. com. bd. dirs. 1982-85, chmn. leadership com. 1986, pres. 1984). Republican. Office: 1003 Del Prado Blvd Ste 300 Cape Coral FL 33990 also: 6361 Presidential Ct Fort Myers FL 33919

MARKIEWICZ, MICHAEL, accountant, financial planner; b. Boston, Feb. 17, 1953; s. Joseph and Ruth (Ackerman) M. BA in Sociology and Econs., Tufts U., 1974; MS in Acctg., Northeastern U., 1975. CPA, Mass., N.H.; cert. secondary edn. tchr., Mass. Acct. Deloitte Haskins & Sells, Boston, 1975-78; controller L.M. Ericsson Telecommunications, Inc., Framingham, Mass., 1978-79; mgr. planning and devel. Boston Co., 1979-83; rep. Alt. Investment Corp., Boston, 1983-84; acct., fin. planner Smith, Batchelder & Rugg, Hanover, N.H., 1984-87; owner, mgr., fin. planner, acct. Markiewicz & Co., Lebanon, N.H., 1987—; speaker numerous seminars on tax and fin. planning. Contbr. articles to profl. jours. Trustee, treas. Upper Valley Community Land Trust. Mem. AICPA, Mass. Soc. CPA's, N.H. Soc. CPA's (chmn. personal fin. planning com.), Mass. Soc. CPA's, Inst. Cert. Fin. Planners, Internat. Assn. Fin. Planning. Office: PO Box 660 Lebanon NH 03766

MARKLE, ROGER A(LLAN), oil company executive; b. Sidney, Mont., Dec. 12, 1933; s. Forrest William and Mary Elizabeth (Hartley) M.; m. Mary Elizabeth Thompson, Jan. 13, 1967. B.S. in Mining Engring, U. Alaska, 1959; M.S., Stanford U., 1965; M.B.A., U. Chgo., 1972. Mgr. mine devel. Amoco Minerals, Inc., Chgo., 1973-74; pres. western div. Valley Camp Coal Co., Salt Lake City, 1974-78; pres., chief exec. officer Valley Camp Coal Co., Cleve., 1979-82; pres. Quaker State Corp., Oil City, Pa., 1982-86, chief operating officer, 1986-88, also bd. dirs.; vice chmn. Quaker State Corp., Oil City, 1988—; dir. U.S. Bur. Mines, Washington, 1978-79. Served with USN, 1951-54. Mem. AIME, Nat. Coal Assn. (dir.). Clubs: Alta (Salt Lake City); Duquesne (Pittsburgh); Oil City (Oil City, Pa.); Wanango Country (Reno, Pa.). Office: Quaker State Corp 255 Elm St Oil City PA 16301

MARKLUND, RICHARD GUSTAV, trade company executive; b. Rockford, Ill., Jan. 18, 1945; s. Gustau Herbert and Berta (Lilgigren) M.; m. Lynn Porter, Apr. 12, 1966 (div. 1978); children: Brant, Erick; m. Julie Lynn Slater, May 8, 1982. BA in Polit. Sci., Rockford Coll., 1967. Dir. European sales and mktg. Riegel paper Corp., Rockford, 1967-73; dir. advt. Tonka Corp., Mpls., 1973-79; v.p. mktg., dir. ITT Consumer Fin. Corp., Mpls., 1979-82; pres., chief exec. officer Magnetic Technologies, Inc., Mpls., 1982-87; chmn., chief exec. officer Teclink Internat., Ltd., Mpls., 1987—; dir. Infinite Graphics, Inc., Mpls., 1985—, Consul Restaurant Corp., Mpls., 1986—, World Containers Corp., Mpls., 1987—, Playtronics Corp., Mpls., 1987—. Author: Modern Packaging, 1972. Platform chmn. Young Reps., Ill., 1966; dir. Medina Home Farm Assn., Minn., 1976. Mem. Licensing Execs. Soc. Internat. Lutheran. Office: Teclink Internat Ltd 1000 Shelard Pkwy Ste 360 Minneapolis MN 55426

MARKMAN, SHERMAN, mortgage banker, venture capital investor, corporate financier; b. Denver, Aug. 21, 1920; s. Abe and Julia (Rosen) M.; m. Paula Elaine Henderson. Student So. Meth. U., 1962-64; children—Michael, Joan, Lori Ann. V.p. Lester's, Inc., Oklahoma City, 1940-59; exec. v.p. Besco Enterprises, San Francisco, 1960-61; sr. v.p. Zale Corp., Dallas, 1962-69; pres., chief exec. officer Leased Jewelry div., 1965-69, pres. Designcraft Industries, N.Y.C., 1969-75, chief exec. officer, 1969-75; pres. Tex. Internat. Export Co., Dallas, 1975—, CAC Fin. Group (Tex.), Dallas, 1982—; former bd. dir. Pipelife Svc. Corp., Chem. Applicators, Lafayette, La., Coverage Cons., N.Y.C.; bd. dir. Transworld Ins. Intermediaries, Ltd.; cons. Homecare Mgmt., Patchouge, N.Y.; charter mem. N.Y. Ins. Exch.; guest lectr. fin. risk confs., 1982—; pres., chief exec. officer The Myers Fin. Orgn., N.Y., 1975-86, The Markman Fin. Orgn., Dallas, 1985— ; cons. Cinema 'N' Drafthouse, Chgo., The Windy City Group, Chgo. Contbr. articles to profl. jours. Vol. social worker Presbyn. Hosp., Dallas; mem. Dallas Coun. World Affairs, 1962—; active NCCJ. With USMCR, 1942-45; PTO. Mem. Young Men's Philanthropic League N.Y. Clubs: Press, Columbian, City (Dallas); India Temple (Oklahoma City); L.A. Athletic. Avocations: gardening, golf, nature studies. Office: Premier Pl 5910 North Central Expwy Ste 1000 Dallas TX 75206

MARKO, HAROLD MEYRON, diversified industry executive; b. Detroit, Oct. 29, 1925; s. Louis Meyron and Mae (Goldberg) M.; m. Barbara Soss, July 2, 1951; children—Clifford S., Neil L., Matthew P. B.A., U. Mich., 1948. Salesman Core Industries Inc (formerly SOS Consol. Inc.), Bloomfield Hills, Mich., 1951-57; v.p. sales Core Industries Inc (formerly SOS Consol. Inc.), 1957-60, pres., 1960—, also dir., chmn. bd. dirs., chief exec. officer, 1986. Contbr. chpt. to book. Mem. Founders' Soc., Detroit Inst. Arts; trustee Nat. Jewish Hosp., Denver; bd. dirs. Detroit Symphony Orch.; mem. adv. bd. Greater Detroit Round Table; bd. govs. Cranbrook Acad. Art. Served with AUS, 1943-45. Club: Bloomfield Open Hunt. Home: 530 E Long Lake Rd Bloomfield Hills MI 48013 Office: Core Industries Inc 500 N Woodward Ave Bloomfield Hills MI 48013

MARKOFF, GARY DAVID, investment executive; b. Brookline, Mass., July 29, 1956; s. Leon Fred and Marylyn Sue (Goldstein) M. BA in Econs., Trinity Coll., Hartford, Conn., 1978. Account exec. E.F. Hutton & Co. Inc., Chestnut Hill, Mass., 1978-83, asst. v.p., 1984-85, v.p., 1986-88; v.p. sales div. Smith Barney & Co. Inc., Boston, 1988—. Fundraiser Hunger Project, 1985—; active Spl. Olympics, 1988; founding mem. fin. profls. unit B'nai B'rith, 1988. Named one of Best Stockbrokers in Am., Money mag., 1987. Mem. Boston Jaycees. Club: World Runners (San Francisco). Home: 100 Pond St Apt 7 Boston MA 02130 Office: Smith Barney & Co Inc Exchange Pl 38th Fl 53 State St Boston MA 02109

MARKOVICH-TREECE, PATRICIA HELEN, economist; b. Oakland, Calif.; s. Patrick Joseph and Helen Emily (Prydz) Markovich; BA in Econs.; MS in Econs., U. Calif.-Berkeley, postgrad. (Lilly Found. grantee) Stanford U., (NSF grantee) Oreg. Grad. Rsch. Ctr., DD World Christian Ministries; children—Michael Sean, Bryan Jeffry, Tiffany Helene. With pub. rels. dept. Pettler Advt., Inc.; pvt. practice polit. and econs. cons.; aide to majority whip Oreg. Ho. of Reps.; lectr., instr., various Calif. instns., Chemeketa (Oreg.) Coll., Portland (Oreg.) State U. Commr., City of Oakland (Calif.), 1970-74; coord. City of Piedmont, Calif. Gen. Planning Commn. Mem. Mensa, Bay Area Artists Assn. (coord., founding mem.), Piedmont Civic Assn., CFRTP (bd. dirs.), BACA, San Francisco Arts Commn. File, Index for Contemporary Arts, Pro Arts.

MARKOWITZ, STEPHAN ALAN, business consultant; b. White Plains, N.Y., June 27, 1960; s. Gerald Harvey and Sandra Lee (Schulner) M.; m. Fiona Elizabeth Victoria Polun, Mar. 20, 1988. BA in Psychology, SUNY, Purchase, 1983; MS in Organizational Psychology, San Diego State U., 1987; postgrad. in behavioral sci., La Jolla U., 1987—. Pres., cons. EXP Networking Cons., San Diego, 1984—; cons. Performax Cons., La Jolla, Calif., 1986—; cons. Robert Allen, Del Mar, Calif., 1988; assoc. Dyad Systems, La Jolla, 1987—. Editor Statement to Congress Subcom. on Human Resources, 1988; numerous TV performances. Nat. program dir. Internat. Missing Children's Found., San Diego, 1985-87, fundraiser, coordinator, 1986—; fundraiser deaf communications services YMCA, San Diego, 1986-88; ednl. rep. La Jolla U., 1988—, mktg. rep., 1988—; coordinator Holiday Project, San Diego, 1985-88. Named one of Outstanding Young Men of Am., 1987, Man of Yr., Internat. Missing Children Found., 1987. Mem. Organizational Devel. Network, Personal Progress Library, Psi Chi. Jewish. Office: 2445 Morena Blvd #200 San Diego CA 92101

MARKS, ALBERT AUBREY, JR., brokerage house executive; b. Phila., Dec. 19, 1912; s. Albert A. and Edythe (Lilian) M.; grad. Harrisburg (Pa.) Acad., 1928; student Williams Coll., 1928-30; B.S., U. Pa., 1932; m. Mary Kay Bryan; children—Albert Aubrey, Christina M., Robert B. Br. office mgr. Newburger & Co., Phila., 1934-42, gen. ptnr. Newburger & Co., Atlantic City, N.J., 1946—, Advest Co.; pres. Atlantic Co. N.J.; dir. Guarantee Bank & Trust Co., Atlantic City, Anchor Savs. and Loan Assn.; allied mem. Am., N.Y., Phila., Balt. stock exchanges. Vice pres. N.J. Mid-Atlantic Farm Show, 1952-54; dir. Atlantic City Conv. Bur., 1951-54, treas., 1962; pres. Miss Am. Pageant, 1962-64, chmn. bd., 1966; chmn. Boardwalk Adv. Commn.; mem. Bd. Edn., Margate, N.Y.; vice chmn. Com. Adult Edn. So. N.J.; pres. Atlantic County Community Chest and Welfare Council, 1953; gen. campaign chmn. Community Chest, 1956; former pres. 4-Club Council; mem. exec. council Boy Scouts Am., Atlantic County; trustee So. N.J. Devel. Council, 1951-54; mem. N.J. Legis. Study Commn., Securities Adv. Com. N.J. State, Conflict Interest Com. Gov. Betty Bacharach Home Afflicted Children; chmn. Com. of 50, Atlantic City, 1972—, Atlantic County Improvement Authority, 1975; pres. Atlantic City Med. Ctr. Found., 1986—. Served from 2d lt. to lt. col. USAAF, 1942-46. Named Citizen of Year, Atlantic City, 1953; Citizen of Decade, Elks, 1972. Mem. Investment Bankers Assn., Security Traders Assn., Nat. Assn. Security Dealers, Assn. Stock Exchange Firms, Atlantic City (pres. 1952-53), So. N.J. (chmn. devel. council 1951-54) C.'s of C., Atlantic City Centennial Assn. (v.p. 1953-54), Mil. Order World Wars (companion), Res. officers Assn., Air Force Assn.,

Newcomen Soc., Pa. Soc., Newcomen Soc. Roman Catholic. Clubs: Masons, Kiwanis (pres. 1954), Press, Haddon Hall Racquet, Osborne Beach; Williams, Marco Polo (N.Y.C.). Home: 1 N Osborne Ave Margate NJ 08402 Office: Box 222 Northfield NJ 08255

MARKS, ALVIN MELVILLE, scientist, consultant; b. N.Y.C., Oct. 28, 1910; s. John Adams and Carlotta (Marks) Inslee; m. Beatrice Lawrence (div.); children—Sara Marks Tabby, Douglas Merydith; m. Molly Bennett, Aug. 25, 1965 (div. 1977); children—Bridget Grace, Sean Christopher, Frederick Peter, Jacqueline Lee. B.S., Cooper Union Inst. Tech., 1932; postgrad. Bklyn. Poly. Inst., 1935-36, Harvard U., 1944-45, MIT, 1944-45, N.Y.U., 1946-47. Founder, pres., dir. Polalite Corp., Whitestone, N.Y., 1935-53, Marks Polarized Corp., Whitestone, 1953-81; founder, dir. Phototherm Inc., Nashua, N.H.; founder, pres. Advanced R & D, Inc., Athol, Mass. Mem. Pres. Kennedy's Power Panel, 1960; founder, sci. adviser World Energy Found., N.Y.C., 1981—. Patentee in polarizing and photovoltaic materials, over 125 patents. Served to lt. USN, 1944-46. Recipient Gano Dunn Medal Cooper Union, 1973, Man of Yr. award, 1973, Disting. Alumnus award, 1986; grantee NSF, 1975, Dept. Energy, 1979, Mem. AAAS, Am. Inst. Physics, N.Y. Soc. Profl. Inventors, N.Y. Acad. Scis., AAAS, Second Century Soc. (founding). Office: Advanced R & D Inc 359 R Main St Athol MA 01331

MARKS, IRA ALAN, executive search company executive; b. Bklyn., Apr. 11, 1942; s. Samuel Alex and Sylvia Ruth (Schiller) M.; m. Jo-Ann Marks, July 11, 1968; children: Meredith, Marissa. BA, Pace Coll., 1965. Tchr. N.Y.C. Sch. System, Bklyn., 1965-71; N.Y. sales mgr. Harper & Row Pub., N.Y.C., 1971-77; pres. J.M. Meredith & Assoc. Inc., Phoenix and Santa Cruz, Calif., 1977—; v.p. Nova Strategies, Santa Cruz, 1987—; founder Ariz. Search Assn., 1981. Bd. dirs. Paradise Valley Soccer Club, Phoenix, 1979-84. Mem. Ariz. Assn. Personnel Cons. (v.p. 1979-80). Republican. Jewish. Home: 2240 N Rodeo Gulch Rd Soquel CA 95073

MARKS, LAWRENCE IRWIN, consumer products company executive; b. Bklyn., May 7, 1925; s. Nathan and Sadie (Myers) M.; m. Barbara Etta Katzman, Sept. 1, 1946; children—Sheila Jay, Nancy Sharman. A.B., Harvard U., 1946, M.B.A., 1948. Office methods specialist Johns Manville Corp., N.Y.C., 1948-51; sr. acct. Touche Niven, N.Y.C., 1951-53; v.p., treas. Adler Electronics, New Rochelle, N.Y., 1956-63; group v.p. Litton Industries, New Rochelle, 1963-65; exec. v.p. Culbro Corp., N.Y.C., 1965—, also dir. Interviewer Harvard Schs. Com., N.Y.C., 1971—. Served as lt. USNR, 1944-46, 51-53. Mem. Am. Inst. C.P.A.s. Democrat. Jewish. Home: 86 Greenway Terr Forest Hills NY 11375 Office: Culbro Corp 387 Park Ave S New York NY 10016

MARKS, MICHAEL J., corporate executive, lawyer; b. 1938. AB, Cornell U., 1960; JD, U. Chgo., 1963. Assoc. Stroock & Stroock & Lavan, 1964-70, Chun, Kerr & Dodd, 1970-72; counsel Kelso, Spencer, Snyder & Stirling, 1972-75; asst. gen. counsel Alexander & Baldwin Inc., Honolulu, 1975-80, v.p., gen. counsel, 1980-84, v.p., gen. counsel, sec., 1984-85, sr. v.p., gen. counsel, sec., 1985—. Office: Alexander & Baldwin Inc 822 Bishop St Honolulu HI 96813

MARKS, RAYMOND H., chemical company executive; b. N.Y.C., July 4, 1922; s. Harry S. and Rebecca (Pollak) M.; m. Anne Cohen, Nov. 30, 1952; children: Victoria, Michael, Andrea. B.S., N.C. State Coll., 1943. Sales exec. Monsanto Chem. Co., Springfield, Mass., 1946-51, Chgo., 1951-52; Sales exec. Monsanto Chem. Co., N.Y.C., 1952-55; sales exec. Knickerbocker Toy & Plastic, N.Y.C., 1955-57; with Cary Chems., Inc., East Brunswick, N.J., 1957-65; exec. v.p. Cary Chems., Inc., 1960-65, pres., 1965-68; v.p. Tenneco Chems., Inc. (absorbed Cary Chems.), N.Y.C., 1968-70; pres. Tenneco Chems., Inc. (absorbed Cary Chems.), 1970-82; sr. v.p. Tenneco, Inc., 1983-85; chmn. Tenneco Europe Ltd., 1985-87; cons. Houston, 1987; ret. 1987; dir. Kalama Chem. Inc., Myron Mfg. Corp., Tenneco Chems. Europe Ltd., Bristol, Eng., Tenneco Resins, Inc., Albright & Wilson Ltd., London, Tenneco Polymers, Inc., AMA Internat., Tenneco Eastern Realty, Inc. Served to 1st lt. Signal Corps, AUS, 1943-46. Mem. Soc. Plastics Engrs., Soc. Plastics Industry, Chem. Mfrs. Assn. Office: Tenneco Inc Tenneco Bldg Houston TX 77002 Summer: Box 1305 Amagansett NY 11930 Winter: 1311 Bridgewood Dr Boca Raton FL 33434

MARKUM, ARLENE, banker; b. N.Y.C., June 15, 1942; d. John Thomas and Mary Louise McAllister; student Pace U., 1975—; m. Onzelo Markum Jr., July 28, 1960; children—Onzelo III, Andrea Gail. Credit adminstrn. clk. Franklin Simon, N.Y.C., 1963; supr. Lord & Taylors, N.Y.C., 1963-68; with Citibank N.Y., N.Y.C., 1969—, asst. mgr., 1974-81, mgr., 1981-85, asst. v.p., 1986—. Mem. Nat. Assn. Female Execs., Nat. Spkty. Mdse. Assn., Am. Soc. Profl. & Exec. Women, Urban Banking Coalition (N.Y. chpt.). Republican. Home: 8400 Shore Front Pkwy Rockaway Beach NY 11693

MARKUN, FRANK O., food services executive; b. Des Moines, Oct. 22, 1947; s. Frank Oliver and Grace Ellen (Marshall) M.; m. Milagros Macuja, Dec. 29, 1971; children: Michael Allen, Jeffrey Patrick. BS, Iowa State U., 1969; MBA, Eastern Mich. U., 1974. Registered dietitian; disting. health care foodservice adminstr. Dietitian II, South Quadrangle, U. Mich., Ann Arbor, 1969-71, food service supr. II Bursley Hall, 1971-77, food service mgr. II, Residential Coll., 1977-80, West Quadrangle Complex, 1980-81; dir. food services Cabell Huntington Hosp. (W.Va.), 1981—. Contbr. articles to profl. jours. Participant various nat. recipie contests; Statler Found. scholar, 1965; Mem. Am. Dietetic Assn., W.Va. Dietetic Assn. (pres. 1984-85; Outstanding W.Va. dietitian 1983-84, various coms. 1981-89, adv. bd. 1985-88), W.Va.-Ohio-Ky. Dist. Dietetic Assn. (chmn. council on practice 1981, pres. 1982-83, chmn. nominating com. 1984-85, various coms. 1985-88), Am. Soc. Hosp. Food Service Adminstrs. (pres. W.Va. chpt. 1985-86, nat. nominating com. 1988-89, legis. com. 1987-88, publs. com. 1988-89, various coms. 1986—). Republican. Roman Catholic. Home: 54 Twin View Ln RR 4 Huntington WV 25704 Office: Cabell Huntington Hosp 1340 Hal Greer Blvd Huntington WV 25701

MARKUS, JOSEPH FRANCIS, financial executive; b. St. Louis, Oct. 24, 1952; s. Francis Henry and Dolores L. (Murray) M.; m. Faith Ann Ploesser, Jan. 27, 1979; children: Richard, Lisa, Cecily, Joseph, Blake. Student, St. Mary's Sem.; BA, Webster U. V.p. Murray Tile Co., St. Louis, 1976-80; pres. Markus & Assocs., Ltd., St. Louis, 1980-82; v.p. Galway Distbg. Co., St. Louis, 1982-83; controller Aspen Holding Co., St. Louis, 1983-86; v.p., chief fin. officer CG&T Industries Inc., Paducah, Ky., 1986-89; cons. Markus & Assocs., St. Louis, 1980—; bd. dirs. Transp. and R.R. Assurance Co. Ltd., Hamilton, Bermuda. Dem. candidate for state rep., St. Louis, 1984. Served as sgt. USAF, 1974-75. Named Ky. Col., 1987. Mem. Assn. Am. R.R.s., R.R. Ins. Mgmt. Assn. Roman Catholic. Home: 528 Drawbridge Trace Paducah KY 42003

MARLAND, ALKIS JOSEPH, leasing company executive, computer science educator, financial planner; b. Athens, Greece, Mar. 8, 1943; came to U.S., 1961, naturalized, 1974; s. Basil and Maria (Pervanides) Mouradoglou; m. Anita Louise Malone, Dec. 19, 1970; children: Andrea, Alyssa. BS, Southwestern U., Tex., 1963; MA, U. Tex., Austin, 1967; MS in Engring. Adminstrn., So. Meth. U., 1971. Cert. data processing; chartered fin. cons.; cert. fin. planner. With Sun Co., Richardson, Tex., 1968-71, Phila., 1971-76, mgr. planning and acquisitions Sun Info. Services subs. Sun Co., Dallas, 1976-78, v.p. Helios Capital Corp. subs. Sun Co., Radnor, Pa., 1978-83; pres. ALKAN Leasing Corp., Wayne, Pa., 1983—; prof. dept. computer scis. and bus. adminstrn. Eastern Coll., St. Davids, Pa., 1985-87; prof. math. Villanova (Pa.) U., 1987—. Bd. dirs. Radnor Twp. Sch. Dist., 1987—. Recipient Phila. Fin. Assn. award, 1988. Mem. Assn. Computing Machinery, IEEE, Internat. Assn. Fin. Planners, Am. Soc. CLU & ChFC, Am. Assn. Equipment Lessors, Inst. Cert. Fin. Planners, Fin. Analysts Phila., Phila. Fin. Assn., World Affairs Council Phila., Rotary (pres.-elect Wayne Club 1989—), Masons. Republican. Home: 736 Brooke Rd Wayne PA 19087 Office: PO Box 153 Radnor PA 19087

MARLAND, SIDNEY PERCY, JR., educational company executive; b. Danielson, Conn., Sept. 19, 1914; s. Sidney Percy and Ruth (Johnson) M.; m. Virginia Partridge, June 29, 1940; children: Sidney Percy III, Pamela, Judith. AB, U. Conn., 1936, MA, 1950; PhD, N.Y.U., 1955; LLD (hon.), U. Pitts., 1967, N.Y.U., 1971, Northwestern U., 1971; DHL, Ripon Coll., 1972, Denison U., 1972, Bishop Coll., 1973, R.I. Coll., 1973, Fairfield U., 1973, U. Akron, 1973. Tchr. English W. Hartford (Conn.) High Sch., 1938-41; supt. schs. Darien (Conn.) Sch. Dist., 1948-56, Winnetka (Ill.) Pub. Schs., 1956-63, Pitts. Pub. Schs., 1963-68; pres. Inst. Ednl. Devel., Pitts., 1968-70; U.S. commr. edn. Washington, 1970-72; asst. sec. for edn. HEW, Washington, 1972-73; pres. Coll. Entrance Exam Bd., N.Y.C., 1973-79; chmn. Editorial Bd. Scholastic, Inc., Hampton, Conn., 1979—; bd. dirs. Altantic Mutual Cos., 1974—, Mutual of N.Y., 1974—, Scholastic, Inc., 1975—; adj. prof. Columbia U.; vice chmn. White House Conf. on Edn., 1965; chmn. bd. dirs. Merit Scholarship, 1968; lectr. in Harvard, U., Northwestern U., Nat. Coll. Edn., U. Mont. Author (book): Career Education: A Proposal on Reform, 1975, (co-author) The Unfinished Journey, 1968, Religion in the Public Schools, 1963, Winnetka: The History and Significance of an Educational Experiment, 1963; editor: Essays on Career Education, 1972. Asst. dir. YMCA Camp, Hartford, Conn., 1937-40; pres. bd. Darien Library Assn., 1949-56, Isaac Walton League, Winnetka, 1957-61; mem. commn. Ch.-State Relations, nat. adv. council office Econ. Opportunity, 1960-68, Edn. Disadvantaged Children, 1964-68; trustee John F. Kennedy Ctr. for Performing Arts, 1970-74; pres. Great Cities Sch. Improvement Council, 1967-68, Nat. Ednl. TV, 1962-70; bd. trustees U. Pitts., 1965-68, Am. Coll., 1975—; bd. dirs. Joint Council on Econ. Edn., Urban League Pitts., 1963-68; bd. govs. Conn. Higher Edn., 1984—; warden, vestryman Episcopalian Ch., 1948-56, 57-63. Served to Col. AUS, 1941-47. Decorated Distinguished Service Cross, Legion of Merit, Bronze Star medal. Mem. VFW, NEA, Am. Assn. Sch. Adminstrs., Am. Legion, Rotary. Home: Bigelow Rd Hampton CT 06247 Office: Scholastic Inc 730 Broadway New York NY 10003

MARLAS, JAMES CONSTANTINE, holding company executive; b. Chgo., Aug. 22, 1937; s. Constantine J. and Helen (Cotsirilos) M.; m. Kendra S. Graham, 1968 (div. 1971); m. Glenn Close, 1984 (div. 1987). A.B. cum laude, Harvard U., 1959; M.A. in Jurisprudence, Oxford (Eng.) U., 1961; J.D., U. Chgo., 1963. Bar: Ill. 1963, N.Y. 1966. Assoc. firm Baker & McKenzie, London and N.Y.C., 1963-66; exec. v.p. South East Commodity Corp., N.Y.C., 1967-68; chmn. bd. Union Capital Corp., N.Y.C., 1968—; vice chmn. bd. Mickelberry's Food Products Co., N.Y.C., 1970-71; pres., dir. Mickelberry Corp., N.Y.C., 1972—; chief exec. officer Mickelberry Corp., 1973—, chmn. bd., 1984—; chmn. bd., chief exec. officer Newcourt Industries, Inc., 1976—; chmn. bd. Bowmar Instrument Corp., 1976-83, chmn. exec. com., 1983—; bd. dirs. Brasenose Coll. Charitable Found. Co-editor: Univ. Chgo. Law Rev, 1962-63; Contbr. articles to profl. jours. Bd. dirs. N.Y.C. Opera, Commanderie de Bordeaux, Brasenose Coll. Charitable Found. Mem. Am. Fgn. Law Assn., Young Pres.'s Orgn. Clubs: Boodle's (London); Racquet and Tennis (N.Y.C.). Office: Mickelberry Corp 405 Park Ave New York NY 10022

MARLEY, JAMES EARL, manufacturing company executive; b. Marietta, Pa., July 18, 1935; s. Earl W. and Elsie H. (Fahringer) M.; m. Kathleen Y. Robinson, Nov. 22, 1974; children—Kathy L., Robert B., Kimberly J., Lora B. B.S. in Aero. Engring., Pa. State, 1957; M.S. in Mech. Engring., Drexel Inst., 1963. Group dir. automachine AMP Inc., Harrisburg, Pa., 1969-70, v.p. automachine group, 1970-79, v.p. mfg. resources, 1979-80, v.p. mfg., 1980-81, corp. v.p. mfg., 1981-83, corp. v.p. ops., 1983-86, pres., 1986—, also bd. dirs. Inventor and patentee in field. Mem. IEEE, Am. Soc. Mech. Engrs., Am. Mgmt. Assn., Mfg. Council of the Machinery and Allied Products Inst., Harrisburg C. of C. Republican. Club: Harrisburg Country (Pa.) (bd. govs. 1983—). Home: 1230 Mountain View Blvd Dauphin PA 17018 Office: AMP Inc 470 Friendship Rd PO Box 3608 Harrisburg PA 17105 *

MARLIER, JOHN THOMAS, communication educator; b. Pitts., Nov. 25, 1948; s. Raymond Murray Jr. and Gladys Marie (Johnson) M.; m. Ada Jane Focer, July 31, 1971; children: Ian, Grace. BA, Bucknell U., 1970; MA, W.Va. U., 1973; PhD, Mich. State U., 1976. News writer Sta. WKOK, Sunbury, Pa., 1970; salesman Sta. WUDO, Lewisburg, Pa., 1970-71, sales mgr., 1971; grad. asst. W.Va. U., Morgantown, 1971-73, Mich. State U., East Lansing, 1973-76; asst. prof. Northeastern U., Boston, 1976-83; assoc. prof. Curry Coll., Milton, Mass., 1983-84; prin. cons. Marlier & Assocs., Boston, 1983—; assoc. prof. communication Emerson Coll., Boston, 1984—. Author: (with others) Multidimensional Scaling Software Galileo, 1977; contbr. articles to profl. jours. Disposition panelist and trainer Urban Ct. Program Dorchester Dist. Ct., 1979-81; founder, charter mem. bd. dirs. Codman Sq. Community Devel. Corp., Boston, 1979; vol. cons. The Boston Com., 1980-83, City of Boston Neighborhood Devel. Agy., 1980-81; bd. dirs. New England Hemophilia Assn., Dedham, Mass., 1982-84, Dorchester YMCA, Boston, 1981-84. Mem. Am. Arbitration Assn., Internat. Communication Assn. (top paper award 1983), Speech Communication Assn. (top paper award 1974), Indsl. Relations Research Assn., Am. Bus. Communication Assn., Boston Athletic Club. Mem. Soc. of Friends Ch. Home: 107 Ocean St Boston MA 02124 Office: Emerson Coll 100 Beacon St Boston MA 02116

MARMON, DENNIS CARL, accountant, auditor; b. Kew Gardens, N.Y., Dec. 20, 1949; s. Carmine Alphose and Marie (Tersigni) M.; m. Phyllis Theresa Marmon, May 24, 1981; 1 child, Karla Denise Marmon; student SUNY, Farmingdale, 1968-70; A.A.S. cum laude, Nassau Community Coll., 1971; B.B.A., Adelphi U., 1973. Acct., Electronic Systems div. Gen. Instruments Corp., Hicksville, N.Y., 1973-75, Exxon Internat., Exxon Corp., N.Y.C., 1975-76; acct./auditor N.Y. State Dept. Taxation and Fin., Mineola, 1976-85. Mem. Inst. Mgmt. Acctg. (profl.), Assn. Spl. Tax Auditors N.Y. State. Republican. Roman Catholic. Club: Rockville Centre Advanced Intermediates Tennis League (N.Y.); Beverly Hills., Lions. Home and Office: 3288 N Maidencane Dr Beverly Hills FL 32665

MAROONEY, KIMBERLY JO, financial planenr; b. Burney, Calif., Nov. 10, 1956; d. Joseph Heber and Donna Mae (Hilliard) Robertson; m. James Whitney, Jan. 1, 1988. Student, Occidental Coll., 1974-76, San Francisco State U., 1976-78; MusB, San Diego State U., 1980; postgrad., Am. Coll., 1983—. Ins. agt. State Mut. Life Assurance, San Diego, 1980-82, New Eng. Life, 1982—; co-owner Corp. Employee Communications Systems, 1983-86; fin. planner New. Eng. Fin. Advisors, 1986—. Author: (with others) The Miracle Book, 1988; guest on TV program, 1986; guest talk show Spirit Flight, 1988. Instr. Gateway Community, San Diego, 1987—. Mem. NASD, Nat. Assn. Life Underwriters (committeeman 1982-84, Nat. Quality award 1985), Internat. Assn. Fin. Planning, Life Ins. Leaders Club San Diego (pres. 1984-85). Republican. Office: New Eng Fin Advisors 1455 Frazee Rd Ste 700 San Diego CA 92108

MAROTTA, NICHOLAS G(ENE), specialty chemicals company executive; b. Conflenti, Italy, 1929; married. BS, Long Island U., 1952. With Nat. Starch & Chem. Corp., Bridgewater, N.J., 1959—, v.p. mktg. Starch div., 1972-73, corp. asst. v.p., 1973-76, corp. v.p., 1976-77, group v.p. Starch div., 1977-84, pres., chief operating officer, 1984-85, pres., chief exec. officer, 1985—, dir. Office: Nat Starch & Chem Corp 10 Finderne Ave Bridgewater NJ 08807 *

MAROUS, JOHN CHARLES, JR., manufacturing company executive; b. Pitts., June 25, 1925; s. John Charles and Mary Ellen (Ley) M.; m. Lucine O'Brien, May 25, 1957; children: Julia, John, Leslie. B.S. in Elec. Engring, U. Pitts., 1949, M.S., 1953. With Westinghouse Electric Corp., 1949—; gen. mgr. div. Westinghouse Electric Corp., Youngwood, Ohio, 1968-70; gen. mgr. 5 divs. Westinghouse Electric Corp., 1970-72; exec. v.p. constrn. group Westinghouse Electric Corp., Pitts., 1973-79; pres. Internat. Westinghouse Electric Corp., 1979-83, pres. industries and internat. group, 1983-87, chmn., chief exec. officer, 1987—; bd. dirs. Bell Atlantic, Conn. Mut., Mellon Bank. Bd. dirs. World Affairs Council Pitts.; chmn. trustees U. Pitts.; chmn. bd. visitors Engring. Sch. U. Pitts.; overseer exec. council on Fgn. Diplomats; chmn. bd. dirs. River City Brass Band, Pitts. Served with U.S. Army, 1943-46. Mem. Council Fgn. Relations, Fgn. Policy Assn., Conf. Bd. (internat. council), Am. Soc. Corp. Execs., Bus. Council Internat. Understanding (vice chmn., dir.), Internat. C. of C. (trustee U.S. council). Republican. Roman Catholic. Clubs: Duquesne, Pitts. Field; Laurel Valley Golf and Rolling Rock (Ligonier, Pa.); Congressional Country (Washington); Pelican Bay (Naples, Fla.). Office: Westinghouse Electric Corp Westinghouse Bldg 6 Gateway Ctr Rm 2300 Pittsburgh PA 15222 *

MARQUARD, WILLIAM ALBERT, diversified manufacturing company executive; b. Pitts., Mar. 6, 1920; s. William Albert and Anne (Wild) M.; m. Margaret Thoben, Aug. 13, 1942; children: Pamela, Suzanne, Stephen. BS, U. Pa., 1940; HHD (hon.), U. Puebla (Mex.). With Westinghouse Electric Corp., Pitts. and Mexico City, 1940-52; with Mosler Safe Co., Hamilton, Ohio, 1952-67, sr. v.p., 1961-67, pres., 1967-70; with Am. Standard, Inc., N.Y.C., 1967—, sr. exec. v.p., 1970, pres., chief exec. officer, 1971-85, also chmn., 1971-86, chmn. exec. com., from 1985, now chmn.; bd. dirs. Chem. N.Y. Corp., Chem. Bank, N.Y. Life Ins. Co., Shell Oil Co., N.L. Industries, Inc., Allied Stores; chmn., bd. dirs. Arkansas Best Corp. Trustee U. Pa., N.Y.C. Citizens Budget Commn., N.Y. Infirmary-Beekman Downtown Hosp., Washington Opera, Found. of U. Ams., Com. Econ. Devel.; bd. overseers Wharton Sch. Bus., Bus. Com. for Arts, Brit.-N. Am. Com.; mem. Com. Corp. Support Pvt. Univs.; bd. dirs. Nat. Minority Purchasing Council. Mem. Conf. Bd. (sr.). Office: Am Standard Inc 40 W 40th St New York NY 10018 *

MARQUARDT, KATHLEEN P., business executive; b. Kalispell, Mont., June 6, 1944; d. Dean King and Lorraine Camille (Buckmaster) Marquardt; m. William Wewer, Dec. 6, 1987; children—Shane Elizabeth, Montana Quinn. Purser, Pan Am. World Airways, Washington, 1968-75; info. specialist Capital Systems Group, Kensington, Md., 1979-81; dir. pub. affairs Subscription TV Assn., Washington, 1981-83, exec. dir., 1983-86 ; pres. Internat. Policy Studies Orgn., 1983—, pres., designer Elizabeth Quinn Couture, 1986—. Bd. dirs. Am. Tax Reduction Movement, 1983—; chmn. bd. Friends of Freedom, 1982—. Mem. Nat. Women's Polit. Caucus, NOW, Women in Communications, Nat. Assn. Women Bus. Owners. Home: 11 E Irving St Chevy Chase MD 20815 Office: 7201 Wisconsin Ave Ste 705 Bethesda MD 20814

MARQUES, CHARLES ANTHONY, banker; b. Bridgeport, Conn., Oct. 29, 1939; s. Antonio and Tercina (Candito) M.; m. June Helen Duback, May 31, 1959; children: Carolynn, Karen, Tresa, Charles, Gale, Douglas, David. BBA, SUNY, Albany, 1986. Data processing mgr. Finch, Pruyn and Co., Glen Falls, N.Y., 1970-75; adj. prof. Adirondack Community Coll., Glen Falls, 1975-77; ops. mgr. Blue Cross, Blue Shield, Albany, 1977-80; project mgr. Comml. Union, Boston, 1980-83; asst. v.p. Goldome, Buffalo, N.Y., 1983—; dir. Advance Computer Svc., Buffalo. Mem. Willowridge Community Assn., Amherst, N.Y., 1987; com. mem. Buffalo Assn. Retarded Children, 1987—. Mem. Assn. Systems Mgmt. (pres. 1975). Office: Goldome 325 Delaware Ave Buffalo NY 14202

MARRIE, THOMAS PHILLIP, bank executive; b. N.Y.C., Feb. 13, 1938; s. Thomas P. Marrie; m. Elizabeth Marrie Schneeman; 1 child, Crystal. BEE, Manhattan Coll., 1960; MS in Engring., Yale U., 1962; MS in Indsl. Mgmt., MIT, 1964. Various positions Am. Express Co., Fireman's Fund Ins. Co., Rockwell Internat. Corp, W.R. Grace Co., N.Y.C., 1964-78; sr. v.p., chief fin. officer Am. Express Bank, N.Y.C., 1979-81; treas., chief fin. officer No. Trust Co., Chgo., 1981-84; exec. v.p., chief fin. officer First Interstate Bank of Calif., L.A., 1984-88, First Interstate Bancorp, L.A., 1988—. Office: 1st Interstate Bancorp 707 Wilshire Blvd W25-12 Los Angeles CA 90017

MARRINAN, SUSAN FAYE, lawyer; b. Vermillion, S.D., May 29, 1948; d. H. Lyal and Ada Myrtle (Hollingsworth) Abild; children: Molly, Cara. BA, U. Minn., 1969, JD, 1973. Bar: Minn. 1973. Atty. Carlson Cos., Plymouth, Minn., 1973-74, Prudential Ins. Co., Mpls., 1974-75; v.p., gen. counsel, corp. sec. H.B. Fuller Co., St. Paul, 1977—. Fundraiser Am. Cancer Soc., St. Paul, 1984—; bd. dirs. Family Services of St. Paul, 1985, Childrens Theatre Co. Mem. Corporate Counsel Assn. (pres. 1986—), Am. Assn. Corporate Counsel (bd. dirs. Minn. chpt. 1986—). Republican. Office: H B Fuller Co 8 Pine Tree Dr Saint Paul MN 55112

MARRIOTT, JOHN WILLARD, JR., hotel, restaurant and food service chain executive; b. Washington, Mar. 25, 1932; s. John Willard and Alice (Sheets) M.; m. Donna Garff, June 29, 1955; children: Deborah, Stephen Garff, John Willard, David Sheets. B.S. in Banking and Fin, U. Utah, 1954. Vice pres. Marriott Hot Shoppes Inc., 1959-64, exec. v.p., 1964; pres., dir. Marriott Corp., 1964—, chief exec. officer, 1972—, chmn. bd., 1985—; bd. dirs. Outboard Marine Corp., Waukegan, Ill. Trustee Mayo Found., Nat. Geographic Soc., Woodrow Wilson Internat. Ctr. for Scholars; adv. council Stanford U. Grad. Sc. Bus.; mem. nat. exec. bd. Boy Scouts Am. Served to lt. USNR, 1954-56. Recipient Bus. Leader of Yr. award, Georgetown U. Sch. Bus. Adminstrn., 1984, Svc. Above Self award, Rotary Club at JFK Internat. Airport, 1985, Am. Mgr. of Yr. award, Nat. Mgmt. Assn., 1985, Golden Chain award, Nations's Restaurant News, 1985, Hall of Fame award, Consumer Digest Mag., 1985, Citizen of Yr. award, Boy Scouts of Am., 1986, Restaurant Bus. Leadership award, Restaurant Bus. Mag., 1986, Gold Plate award, Am. Acad. Achievement, 1986, Hall of Fame, Am. Hotel and Motel Assn., 1986, Hall of Fame award, Culinary Inst. of Am., 1987, Hospitality Exec. of Yr. award, Pa. State U., 1987, Bronze winner in Fin. World's Chief Exec. Officers award, 1988. Mem. Conf. Bd., U.S. C. of C. (dir.), Sigma Chi. Mormon. Clubs: Burning Tree (Washington), Met. (Washington). Office: Marriott Corp Marriott Dr Washington DC 20058

MARRON, DARLENE LORRAINE, real estate development executive, financial and marketing consultant; b. Auburn, N.Y., July 20, 1946; d. William Chester and Elizabeth Barbara (Gervaise) Kulakowski; m. Edward W. Marron, Jr., Apr. 28, 1973. BS cum laude, Rider Coll., 1968; MBA, NYU, 1970. Lic. securities broker. Dir. mktg. Am. Airlines, N.Y.C., 1970-79; asst. v.p. Merrill Lynch, N.Y.C., 1979-83; v.p. Kidder, Peabody & Co., N.Y.C., 1983-86; owner, principal, Marron Cos., Upper Saddle River, N.J., 1986—; fin. and mktg. cons. to real estate devel. industry. Avocations: pianist, flutist, skiing, fly fishing. Home: 743 W Saddle River Rd Ho-Ho-Kus NJ 07423 Office: Marron Cos 118 Hwy 17 Upper Saddle River NJ 07458

MARRS, DOYLE G., oil company executive. Formerly pres. Mobil Oil Can. Ltd., Calgary, Alta., to 1988; now v.p. internat. producing ops. Mobil Oil Corp., N.Y., 1988—. Office: Mobil Corp 150 E 42nd St New York NY 10017 *

MARRS, PATRICK MICHAEL, communications executive; b. Seldovia, Alaska, Mar. 25, 1947; s. Rollen Charles and Elsie Katherine (Carlough) M.; m. Sheila Joyce Morrow, mar. 18, 1967; children: Jessie Michelle, P.J. Keegan. AA, Shoreline Community Coll., Seattle, 1972; BSEE, U. Washington, Seattle, 1975. Technician Raytheon Marine Co., Seattle, 1969-74, No. Radio Co., Seattle, 1974-75; br. mgr. Radar Electric Co., Seward, Alaska, 1975-77; owner, pres. Communications North, Seward, 1977—; treas. Cook Inlet Region, Inc., Anchorage, 1977—, also bd. dirs.; chmn. bd. Cook Inlet Tribal Council, 1985—; sec., treas. Cook Inlet Communications, Inc., 1986—. Chmn. Seward C. of C., 1984. With USN, 1966-69. Mem. Nat. Marine Electronics Assn., Radio Tech. Council Marine (assoc.), Inst. Naviation. Home: Mile Seven Old Mill Seward AK 99664 Office: Communications North 1607 Leirer Rd Seward AK 99664

MARRS, RICHARD E., insurance company executive. married. BS, W.Va. Wesleyan Coll., 1955; JD, U. Md., 1959. Sr. v.p. Travelers Corp., 1984—, Travelers Indemnity Co., Hartford, Conn., 1984—; also sr. v.p. Phoenix Ins. Co.; sr. v.p. Travelers Life and Annuity Co.; bd. dirs. Underwriters Salvage Co. Office: The Travelers Corp 1 Tower Sq Hartford CT 06183 *

MARRUS, STEPHANIE KRISTINA, business executive; b. N.Y.C., Apr. 25, 1947; m. Richard Lee Rotnem, Dec. 21, 1980; children: Brant Edwards, Wells Cransbrook. AB, Cornell U., 1968; MA, Columbia U., 1969; MBA, U. Pa., 1982. Dir. market planning Atex, Inc., Bedford, Mass., 1981-84; product mgr. Computervision Corp., Bedford, 1984-85; pres. Brant Co., Weston, Mass., 1985—; dir. corp. devel. Symbolics, Inc., Cambridge, Mass., 1986-87, dir. cons. group, 1988; dir. bus. devel. Apollo Computer, 1988—; lectr. Northeastern U., Boston, 1986. Author: Building the Strategic Plan, 1984. Mem. Am. Electronics Assn. (dir. mktg. programs New Eng. chpt. 1988), Wharton Club Boston Club (pres. 1984-85, bd. dirs. 1982—). Home: 19 Nash Ln Weston MA 02193 Office: Apollo Computer 330 Billerica Rd Chelmsford MA 01824

MARS, FORREST, JR., candy company executive. s. Forrest Mars Sr.; married. Grad., Yale U., 1953. Co-pres. Mars Inc., 1973—. Office: Mars Inc 6885 Elm St McLean VA 22101 *

MARS, FORREST E., SR., candy company executive. s. Frank and Ethel Mars; children: Forrest Jr., John, Jacqueline. Chmn. Mars Inc. Office: Mars Inc 6885 Elm St McLean VA 22101 *

MARS, JOHN, candy company executive; b. 1935; married. Student, Yale U., 1957. Chmn. Kal Kan Foods Inc.; co-pres. Mars Inc., 1973—. Office: Mars Inc 6885 Elm St McLean VA 22101 *

MARSALA, CHARLES EUGENE, sales manager; b. June 13, 1960; s. Joseph Peter and Beatrice (Bruscato) M., m. Shelly Maria Ferro, May 3, 1986. BSME, Tulane U., 1983. Registered profl. engr., Calif. Field engr. Gearhart Industries, Ft. Worth, 1982-83; sales engr. Lista Internat. Corp., San Jose, Calif., 1983-84; regional mgr. sales Lista Internat. Corp., San Jose, 1984—; student tchr. Dale Carnegie Sales Course, Santa Ana, Calif., 1983. Mem. Am. Mgmt. Assn., ASME, Soc. Petroleum Engrs. Republican. Roman Catholic. Club: Bacchus. Office: Lista Internat Corp 2520 Mira Mar Ave Long Beach CA 90815

MARSCHING, RONALD LIONEL, lawyer; b. N.Y.C., Mar. 30, 1927; m. Marjory Fleming Duncan, Dec. 31, 1964; children: Christine, Jane. BA, Princeton U., 1950; JD, Harvard U., 1953. Bar: N.Y. 1954. With Timex Corp. Waterbury, Conn., 1967; vice chmn., gen. counsel Timex Corp., Waterbury, Conn., 1980-86, also bd. dirs. Served with U.S. Army, 1953-54. Mem. ABA, Nat. Assn. Dirs., Assn. of Bar of City of N.Y., Westchester-Fairfield Corp. Counsel Bar Assn. Club: University (N.Y.C.); Waterbury. Home: 41 E Hill Rd Woodbury CT 06798

MARSEE, DONALD JAMES, financial executive; b. Cin., Dec. 1, 1943; s. Athel C. Marsee and Elizabeth (Endejann) Cardon; m. Claudia Ann Welles, June 15, 1964 (div. Feb. 1975); children: Dane, Carol, Derek, Robert, Mary; m. Nelly C. Cadena, Dec. 3, 1977; 1 child, Brian. BA in Acctg., U. Dayton, 1966; postgrad., Duquesne U., 1969. Controller Wayne Corp., Richmond, Ind., 1969-72; gen. mgr. Wayne Sales Fin., Detroit, 1972-75; v.p. ops. Data Mgmt. Co. div. Indian Head Inc., Hawthorne, Calif., 1975-78; v.p., controller Info. Techs. Indianhead, Inc., Denver, 1978-81; v.p., chief fin. officer, dir. Bio Rad Labs., Richmond, Calif., 1981-82; sr. v.p., chief fin. officer Vendo Co., Fresno, Calif., 1982-86; v.p. corp. devel. Telautograph Corp., Los Angeles, 1986—; pres. G.P.S. Industries, 1987—; keynote speaker Nat. Assn. Accts. Conv., Fresno, 1985. Treas. Blytheville (Ark.) Jaycees, 1972-74, pres., 1975. Named Profl. of Yr., Indian Head, Inc., N.Y.C., 1977. Mem. Fin. Execs. Inst. Home: 1545 Monte Viento Dr Malibu CA 90265 Office: Telautograph Corp 8700 Bellanca Ave Los Angeles CA 90045 Other: GPS Industries 13280 Amar Rd City of Industry CA 91746

MARSH, DON E., supermarket executive; b. Muncie, Ind., Feb. 2, 1938; s. Ermal W. and Garnet (Gibson) M.; m. Marilyn Faust, Mar. 28, 1959; children: Don Ermal, Jr., Arthur Andrew, David Alan, Anne Elizabeth, Alexander Elliott. BA, Mich. State U., 1961. With Marsh Supermarkets, Inc., Yorktown, Ind., 1961—; pres. Marsh Supermarkets, Inc., Yorktown, 1968—; also dir. Marsh Supermarkets, Inc.; bd. dirs. Mchts. Nat. Bank, Indpls., Ind. Energy, Inc., Indpls. Bd. dirs. Ball State U. Found., Hanover Coll., St. Vincent Hosp. Found. Mem. Am. Mgmt. Assn. (Gen. Mgmt. Assn.), Internat. Food Congress, Nat. Assn. Over-the-Counter Cos. (bd. dirs., chmn. Washington), Food Mktg. Inst. (bd. dirs.), Indpls. C. of C., Ind. State C. of C. (bd. dirs.), Ind. Retail Coun. (bd. dirs.), Ind. Soc. Chgo., Chief Execs. Orgn., Young Pres.'s Orgn. (alumnus), World Bus. Coun., Newcomen Soc. N.Am., Internat. Assn. Food Chains (chmn. Paris), Crooked Stick Golf Club, Columbia Club, Delaware Country Club, Hundred Club, Indpls. Athletic Club, Marco Polo Club, Meridian Hills country Club, Skyline Club, Masons, Elks, Pi Sigma Epsilon, Lambda Chi Alpha. Republican. Presbyterian. Office: Marsh Supermarkets Inc 501 Depot St Yorktown IN 47396

MARSH, JOHN EDWARD, residential services system manager; b. Ft. Belvoir, Va., Jan. 9, 1949; s. Edward Thomas and Harriet (Bryant) M.; m. Marjory Jayne Rauhauser, Dec. 30, 1972; children: Amanda, Laura, Jonathan. BS in Geology, U. Wis., 1972; MA in Exec. Devel., Ball State U., 1976. Commd. U.S. Army, 1972, advanced through grades to; lt. armor br. U.S. Army, Fed. Republic of Germany, 1972-73; capt. mil. intelligence U.S. Army, 1974-77; capt. Def. Intelligence Agy. U.S. Army, Washington, 1977-79; resigned U.S. Army, 1979; staff mem. BDM Corp., Albuquerque, 1979-82, asst. mgr. engring. applications, 1982-84, mgr. engring. systems, 1984-86, dir. engring. tech., 1986-87; program mgr. Sparton Tech. Inc., Albuquerque, 1987—; cons. remote sensing BDM Corp., Albuquerque, 1987—. Maj. USAR, 1980—. Office: Sparton Tech Inc 4901 Rockaway Blvd SE Rio Rancho NM 87124

MARSH, JOSEPH VIRGIL, commercial real estate and investment broker; b. Winston-Salem, N.C., Apr. 28, 1952; s. Gilliam Hughes and Dovie Elizabeth (Watson) M.; student Surrey Community Coll., 1970-72; Coop. Engring. Program, U.S. Govt. Schs., Md., S.C., Washington, 1972-74; grad. N.Y. Inst. Fin., 1978. With Joint Armed Services Tech. Liaison, Washington, 1974-75; cons. U.S. Govt., 1975-76; corr., cons. individuals, bus. on tech. matters, Ararat, N.C., 1977—; registered adviser SEC, 1981—. Mem. U.S. Presdl. Task Force, 1981—. Comml. real estate broker, N.C. Mem. Internat. Entrepreneurs Assn., VFW (hon.), Armed Forces Assn., Ind. Consultants Assn., Internat. Assn. Sci. Devel., Council Civilian Tech. Advisers. Republican. Office: PO Box 12 R 1 NC 2019/2026 Ararat NC 27007-0012

MARSHAK, RON WINSTON, marketing executive; b. N.Y.C., Mar. 22, 1941; s. Albert Abraham and Linda May (Getz) M.; m. Pirkko Helena Siirala, Aug. 21, 1965; children: Gregory Harris, David Michael, Vanessa Johanna. BA with honors, Sir Wilfred Laurier U., 1968; MA, U. Toronto, Can., 1969. Dir. rsch. Ont. Fedn. Constrn. Assns., Toronto, 1969-71; mem. faculty Canadore Coll., North Bay, Ont., Can., 1971-74; dir. mktg. Bus. Supplies, Inc., Toronto, 1974-78; pvt. practice mktg. cons. Toronto, 1978-86; dir. mktg. Performance Seminar Group, Bridgeport, Conn., 1986-88; pvt. practice as direct mail cons. 1988—; seminar speaker Bus. and Profl. Rsch. Inst., Princeton, N.J., 1981-87, Ctr. for Direct Mktg., Westport, Conn., 1984-88. Province Ont. grad. fellow, 1969. Home and Office: 22 Peace St, Cannington, ON Canada LOE 1EO

MARSHALL, ALLAN STANLEY, investment executive, research analyst; b. Tarrytown, N.Y., June 7, 1926; s. Maxwell Robert and Jennie M. Marshall; m. Joan Slater, Apr. 8, 1951; children: Robert, Sally Anne. BA, Syracuse U., 1949, MA, 1950. Registered rep. Paine, Weber Co., N.Y.C., 1968-70; dir. mktg. Reich & Co., N.Y.C., 1970-75; v.p. mktg. Dreskin & Co., Inc., N.Y.C., 1975-81; exec. v.p. R.M. Furman Co., N.Y.C., 1981-82; pres. Marshall Investment Group, N.Y.C., 1982—; exec. coordinator Wall St. Securities Forum, 1987—; bd. dirs. Rent-A-Vault, Inc., Ft. Worth. Contbr. articles to profl. jours. Trustee Barnert Meml. Temple, Franklin Lakes, N.J., 1971—. Served with USN, 1944-46, PTO. Mem. Fin. Research Analysts Assn. (charter; pres. 1985—). Hebrew. Club: Westmount Country. Lodge: Masons. Home: 94 Chadwick Pl Glen Rock NJ 07452 Office: Marshall Investment Group Wall Street Sta PO Box 901 New York NY 10268

MARSHALL, C. TRAVIS, manufacturing executive, government relations specialist; b. Apalachicola, Fla., Jan. 31, 1926; s. John and Estelle (Marks) M.; m. Katherine Rose Lepine; children: Melanie, Monica, Katharine. BS, U. Notre Dame, 1948. Chief clk. Firestone Tire & Rubber Co., Detroit, 1948-51; gen. sales mgr. The Hallicrafters, Chgo., 1952-65; v.p. mktg. E. F. Johnson, Waseca, Minn., 1965-70; v.p. mktg. ops. Motorola, Inc., Schaumburg, Ill., 1970-72, dir., govt. relations, communications div., 1972-74; v.p., dir. govt. relations Motorola, Inc., Washington, 1974-85, sr. v.p., dir., gov. relations, 1985—. Appointed ambassadorby Pres. Bush to Internat. Telecommunications Union Conf. Recipient Disting. Service award Electronics Industries Assn., Washington, 1987. Mem. Electronics Industries Assn. (treas. 1982—, v.p. 1975-88). Republican. Roman Catholic. Clubs: Burning Tree Country (Bethesda), Columbia Country (Chevy Chase), Georgetown Club (Washington), Crystal Downs Country (Frankfort, Mich.), International (bd. dirs. 1987), Metropolitan. Office: Motorola Inc 1776 K St NW Washington DC 20006

MARSHALL, CHARLES, communications company executive; b. Vandalia, Ill., Apr. 21, 1929; s. William Forman and Ruth (Corson) M.; m. Millicent Bruner, Jan. 2, 1953; children: Ruth Ann, Marcia Kay Marshall Rinek, William Forman, Charles Tedrick. B.S. in Agr, U. Ill., 1951. With Ill. Bell Telephone Co., 1953-59, 61-64, 65-70, 71-72, 77—; pres., chief exec. officer Ill. Bell Telephone Co., Chgo., 1977-81; with AT&T, 1959-61, 64-65, 70-71, 1976-77; chmn., chief exec. officer Am. Bell, Morristown, N.J., 1983-84, AT&T Info. Systems, 1984-85; vice chmn. AT&T, N.Y.C., 1985—; also bd. dirs. AT&T; bd. dirs. Sonat, Hartmarx. Served to 1st lt. USAF, 1951-53. Mem. Econ. Club Chgo. Clubs: Somerset Hills Country; Metropolitan (Washington). Office: AT&T Co 550 Madison Ave New York NY 10022

MARSHALL, CHARLES NOBLE, railroad executive; b. Phila., Feb. 18, 1942; s. Donnell and Cornelia Lansdale (Brooke) M.; m. Ann Shaw Donovan, Jan. 12, 1971; children—Elizabeth, Caroline, Cornelia, Edward. B.S. in Engring., Princeton U., 1963; J.D., U. Mich., 1967. Bar: Pa., Md., D.C. Atty. Balt. & Ohio R.R., Balt. and Cleve., 1967-73; gen. atty. So. Ry., Washington, 1973-78; gen. counsel commerce Conrail, Phila., 1978-83, v.p. mktg., 1983-85, sr. v.p. mktg. and sales, 1985—; bd. dirs. Provident Nat. Bank, Phila. Mem. Pa. Bar Assn., D.C. Bar, Md. Bar. Republican. Episcopalian.

MARSHALL, FREDERICK STOWE, oil company executive; b. Boston, Apr. 26, 1953; s. Walton H. and Ruth (Humiston) M.; m. Kathryn E. Johnson, Sept. 12, 1973. BA in Econs., U. Tex., 1975, MBA, 1980. Acct. Mobil Corp., Houston, 1978; cash mgr. Pennzoil Co., Houston, 1981, fin. analyst, 1981-84, fin. analyst treasury dept., 1984-86, corp. cash mgr., 1986-88, corp. cash mgr., mgr. pension funds, 1988—. Home: 536 W 32d St Houston TX 77018 Office: Pennzoil Co 700 Milam Houston TX 77001

MARSHALL, JOHN LESLIE, dealership executive; b. Dayton, Ohio, May 21, 1947; s. Charles Lee and Gertrude Aurelia (Bucher) M.; m. Sandra Jean Miller, Nov. 23, 1979. Student, Miami U., Oxford, Ohio, 1965-66; BS, Ohio State U., 1969. V.p. prodn. Grismer Tire Co., Dayton, Ohio, 1969-71, v.p. retail ops., sec., treas., bd. dirs., 1971—; pres., chief exec. officer Dayton Tire Sales, 1972—; bd. dirs. Assocs. Tire & Svc., Inc., Dayton, Morris & Marshall, Inc. Fin. chmn. election com. Farquhar for Judge, Dayton, 1987. Mem. Dayton Bicycle Club, Optimists (bd. dirs. Dayton chpt.), Beta Gamma Sigma, Sigma Pi. Office: Grismer Tire Co PO Box 337 Dayton OH 45401

MARSHALL, JOHN PAUL, broadcast engineer; b. Hadjeb El-Aioun Gare, Tunisia, Dec. 21, 1941; came to U.S., 1967; Degree, de l'Academie de Grenoble (France), 1963, Univ. Munich, Germany, 1965; student, San Francisco State, 1969-71. Filmmaker Cinemalab, San Francisco, 1970; engr. film and TV Able Studios, San Francisco, 1971-73; radio and TV engr. Sta. KALW-FM-TV (Nat. Pub. Radio), San Francisco, 1973-74; broadcast engr. Sta. KRON-TV (NBC), San Francisco, 1974—; freelance audio visual tech. advisor, San Francisco area, 1975—, lectr. radio, TV, motion pictures, 1975—, cons. customized electronic effects. Translator tech. pubs. and manuals, 1975—. Mus. dir., participant in theater prodns., 1950-59; worked with Boy Scouts. Club: Rolls Royce Owners. Home: Cathedral Hill Pla 1333 Gough St No 4G San Francisco CA 94109

MARSHALL, LARRY, executive search consultant; b. Newark, N.J., Nov. 17, 1941; s. Solomon and Adeline (Levy) Minsky; m. Isabel Cabrera, May 22, 1971; 1 child, Donald. Student, Queens Coll. Actor, performer Broadway shows N.Y.C., 1955-61; v.p. Reston & Carroll Advt., N.Y.C., 1961-62; mgr. communications placement Howard Sloan Personnnel, N.Y.C., 1962-67; pres., chief exec. officer Marshall Cons., Inc., N.Y.C., 1967—. Contbr. articles to profl. jours.; speaker in field. Mem. Nat. Assn. Corp. Profl. Recruiters, Nat. Investor Rels. Assn., Internat. Assn. Bus. Communicators, Internat. Pub. Relations Assn., Aircraft Owners and Pilots Assn. Home: N Mountain Rd Copake Falls NY 12517 Office: Marshall Cons Inc 360 E 65th St PH-B New York NY 10021

MARSHALL, MICHAEL MURPHY, chemical company executive; b. Washington, June 18, 1931; s. Charles Van Lennop and Margaret Agnes (Murphy) M.; m. Paddy Joan Lether; children: Kathleen, Michael. BS in Chem. Engring., U. Miss., 1952. Engring. mgr. Dow Chem. Co., Rotterdam, The Netherlands, 1976-80; v.p. mfg. Enoxy Chem. A.G., Zurich, Switzerland, 1981-84; v.p. mfg., engring. Lonza Inc., Fair Lawn, N.J., 1984-87. Pres. Ironton C. of C., Ohio, 1975; pres. Jr. Achievement of Ohio Valley, Ashland, Ky., 1975. Served to lt. USN, 1952-55, Korea. Mem. Chem. Mfrs. Assn. (health and safety com.). Home: 416 Glendale Rd Wyckoff NJ 07481 Office: Lonza Inc 2100 Rt 208 Fair Lawn NJ 07410

MARSHALL, ROBERT CHARLES, research scientist; b. Brisbane, Queensland, Australia, Oct. 5, 1945; s. Raymond Alexander and Dorothy Mabel (Enever) M.; m. Wendy Olive Moore, Jan. 10, 1970; children: Scott Robert, Brenton Charles, Michelle Wendy. BSc, U. Queensland, 1966, BSc with honors, 1967, PhD, 1971. Research assoc., chemistry dept. Ind. U., Bloomington, 1971-73; research scientist, sr. prin. research scientist CSIRO, Div. Wool Technology, Melbourne, Victoria, Australia, 1973—, leader wool and fibrous proteins program, 1981—. Contbr. over 65 articles to profl. jours. Recipient University medal, 1967, CSR Chems. prize, 1968, Philip Allen award, 1982; Fulbright-Hays exch. scholar Australian-Am. Edn. Found., 1971-73; Alexander von Humboldt rsch. fellow, Fed. Republic Germany, 1982-83, fellow Royal Australian Chem. Inst. Mem. Australian Biochem. Soc., Australian Soc. Cosmetic Chemists (Lester Conrad Meml. award 1987), Textile Inst., Australian Inst. Mgmt. Mem. Anglican Ch. Home: 84 Astons Rd, 3091 Yarrambat Australia Office: CSIRO Div Wool Tech, 343 Royal Parade, 3052 Parkville Australia

MARSHALL, ROBERT CHARLES, computer company executive; b. Berwyn, Ill., June 19, 1931; s. Joseph H. and Rose M.; m. Sarane Virruso, Aug. 1, 1954; children—Joseph, Lisa, Jim. B.S.E.E., Heald Engring. Coll., 1956; M.B.A., Pepperdine U., 1976. Engr. Lawrence Radiation Lab., Livermore, Calif., 1956-64; systems engr. Electronics Assos., Palo Alto, Calif., 1964-69; v.p. mfg. Diablo Systems, Hayward, Calif., 1969-75; with Tandem Computers, Inc., Cupertino, Calif., 1975—; sr. v.p., chief operating officer, dir. Tandem Computers, Inc., 1979—. Served with U.S. Army, 1952-54. Office: Tandem Computers Inc 19333 Vallco Pkwy Cupertino CA 95014

MARSHALL, THOMAS MATTHEW, relocation consultant; b. Wilmington, Del., Mar. 13, 1950; s. Thomas and Beatrice (Gray) M.; m. Marie Anita Marusco, Jan. 3, 1981; children: Diana M., Amanda C. BA in Sociology, U. Del., 1972. Supr. contracts Du Pont & Co., Deepwater, N.J., 1974-79; personnel rep. Du Pont & Co., Newark, Del., 1979-80, relocation coordinator, 1980—. Chmn. staging benefit Del. Found. Retarded Children, Longwood, Pa., 1983—; mem. vestry Grace Episc. Ch., Wilmington, 1986—, warden, 1986-89; pres. Delaware Valley Relocation Coun., mem. program com., 1988—; mem. Employee Relocation Coun., internat. planning com., 1988—. Mem. Artists Theatre Assn., Inc. (pres. 1989, treas. 1987), Brandywiners, Ltd. (mgr. bus. 1977, asst. dir.). Office: E I duPont de Nemours & Co Barley Mill Pla-12/2150 PO Box 80012 Wilmington DE 19880-0012

MARSHALL, WILLIAM DAVID, insurance company official; b. Columbus, Ohio, Mar. 27, 1959; s. John David and Hilda (Hagwood) M.; m. Veronica Francine Lane, Dec. 18, 1981; children: LaShawna Monique, Lauren Michelle, Cameron David. With Buckeye Union Ins. Co., Columbus, 1978-81, Hart Stores, Inc., Columbus, 1981; social svc. counsel Ohio Dept. Mental Health, Columbus, 1981-85; supr. group adminstrn. John Alden Life Ins. Co., Dublin, Ohio, 1985-87; bus. systems analyst Nationwide Ins. Co., Columbus, 1987—; sales rep. Da'Nor Realtors, Columbus, 1985—. Mem. Woodland Terrace Civic Assn., Columbus, 1986—, Nationwide Civic Action Program, Columbus, 1988—; active PTA, 1987—. Mem. Columbus Bd. Realtors, Columbus Jaycees (dir. community rels. 1986-87, pub. rels. 1987-88), Nationwide Ins. Activities Assn. (svc. coun. bd. 1987—), Action Alliance Black Mgrs., Kings Men Club (charter), Toastmasters (ednl. v.p. 1979-80). Democrat. Home: 1709 Marina Dr Columbus OH 43219-1255

MARSTELLER, THOMAS FRANKLIN, JR., lawyer; b. Phila., Oct. 18, 1951; s. Thomas Franklin and Hannah Henrietta (Bender) M. BS in Physics, Rensselaer Poly. Inst., 1973; JD, U. Houston, 1979. Bar: Tex. 1980, U.S. Ct. Claims 1980, U.S. Ct. Internat. Trade 1980, U.S. Patent Office 1980, U.S. Dist. Ct. (ea. and no. dists.) Tex. 1981, U.S. Ct. Appeals (5th and 11th cirs.) 1981, U.S. Supreme Ct. 1983, U.S. Dist. Ct. (we. dist.) Tex. 1984, U.S. Dist. Ct. (so. dist.) Tex. 1985, D.C. 1986, Fla. 1987. Assoc. Pravel, Gambrell, Hewitt, Kirk & Kimball, Houston, 1979-84; shareholder Marsteller & Assocs., P.C., 1984—; panelist Am. Arbitration Assn. Editor: Houston Jour. Internat. Law, 1978-79; contbr. articles to profl. jours. Host Houston Grand Opera. Served with USAF, 1973-77. Recipient Am. Jurisprudence award U. Houston, 1978. Mem. ABA, Internat. Bar Assn., Fed. Bar Assn. (treas. local chpt. 1984-87, pres.-elect 1987-88, pres. 1988-89), Tex. Young Lawyers Assn., (pres. 1987-88, 89), Houston Bar Assn. (sec. Internat. law sect. 1983-84), Houston Engring. and Sci. Soc., Houston Young Lawyers Assn. (chmn. Bill of Rights com. 1980-81). Lodges: Masons, Shriners. Home: PO Box 27580 Houston TX 77227 Office: Marsteller & Assocs PC PO Box 56265 Houston TX 77256-6265

MARSTON, ALFRED J., economist, business executive; b. Silesia, Poland, July 22, 1924; s. Alovsius and Martha (Von Stackberg) M.; Ph.D., U. Paris, 1950; postgrad. Ecole des Sci. Politiques, 1945-47; m. Vilma Mercaldi, Nov. 30, 1956. Analyst, Internat. Public Opinion Research, N.Y.C., supr. European research operation, 1951-52; analyst, research supr. UNGRAN, N.Y.C., 1953-55; econ. analyst terminals Port of N.Y. Authority, 1956-60, asst. transp. economist, 1961-62, economist, 1962-79; v.p., econ. and bus. cons. Inversion, Inc., N.Y.C., 1980—; dir., pres. Chatham Towers Inc., N.Y.C. Pres., Manhattan Downtown Community Council; mem. steering com. Health Systems Agy. N.Y.C.; dir. Elisabeth Blackwell Found.; trustee, chmn. adv. bd. N.Y. Infirmary-Beekman Downtown Hosp.; mem. N.Y.C. Local Planning Bd.; pres., dir. POMOC, Inc., N.Y.C. Served with French Army, 1943-45. Mem. Am. Econ. Assn., Am. Statis. Assn., Nat. Acad. Scis. (transp. research bd.), Polish Inst. Arts and Scis., URISA (chmn. internat. sig. com.). Author: The French Legion of Haiti, 1952; contbr. to publs. in transp. field, articles to profl. jours. Home: Indian Neck Ln Peconic NY 11958 Office: 170 Park Row New York NY 10038

MARSTON, EDGAR JEAN, III, cement, oil and gas executive; b. Houston, July 5, 1939; s. Edgar Jr. and Jean (White) M.; m. Graeme Meyers, June 21, 1961; children: Christopher Graham, Jonathan Andrew. BA, Brown U., 1961; JD, U. Tex., 1964. Bar: Tex. 1964. Law clk. to presiding justice Supreme Ct. Tex., Austin, 1964-65; assoc. Baker & Botts, Houston, 1965-71; ptnr. Bracewell & Patterson, Houston, 1971-87; exec. v.p., gen. counsel Southdown, Inc., Houston, 1987—; also bd. dirs. Southdown, Inc.; bd. dirs. Gemcraft Inc., Houston. Mem. ABA, Tex. Bar Assn., Tex. Bar Found., Houston Bar Assn., Houston Country Club, Coronado Club, Tejas Club. Episcopalian. Office: Southdown Inc 1200 Smith St Ste 2200 Houston TX 77002

MARSTON, MARIA BARROS, accountant; b. Pontevedra, Spain, Aug. 1, 1952; came to U.S., 1963; d. Jose Vietez and Concha (Seara) Barros; m. Robert D. Marston, Aug. 19, 1978; children: Lisa Marie, Lauren Michelle. BA, U. Va., 1975; MS, Georgetown U., 1977; BS summa cum laude with distinction, U. N.C., Greensboro, 1986. CPA, Va. Clk. OAS, Washington, 1977-79; tchr. Madison (Va.) County High Sch., 1979-82; staff acct. Omni Svcs., Inc., Culpeper, Va., 1986-88, Hantzmon, Wiebel & Co., Charlottesville, Va., 1988—. Mem. AICPA, Va. Soc. CPAs, Beta Apha Psi. Episcopalian. Home: 216 Boxley Ln Orange VA 22960

MARSTON, MICHAEL, urban economics, real estate asset manager; b. Oakland, Calif., Dec. 4, 1936; s. Lester Woodbury and Josephine (Janovic) M.; m. Alexandra Lynn Geyer, Apr. 30, 1966; children: John, Elizabeth. BA, U. Calif., Berkeley, 1959; postgrad. London Sch. Econs., 1961-63. V.p. Larry Smith & Co., San Francisco, 1969-72, exec. v.p. urban econ. div., 1969-72; chmn. bd. Keyser Marston Assocs., Inc., San Francisco, 1973-87; gen. partner The Sequoia Partnership, 1979—; pres. Marston Vineyards and Winery, 1982—, Marston Assocs., Inc., 1982—. Cert. rev. appraiser Nat. Assn. Rev. Appraisers and Mortgage Underwriters, 1984—. Chmn., San Francisco Waterfront Com., 1969-86; chmn. fin. com., bd. dirs., mem. exec. com., treas. San Francisco Planning and Urban Research Assn., 1976-87, Napa Valley Vintners, 1986—; trustee Cathedral Sch. for Boys, 1981-82, Marin Country Day Sch., 1984—; v.p. St. Luke's Sch., 1986—; pres. Presidio Heights Assn. of Neighbors, 1983-84; v.p., bd. dirs., mem. exec. com. People for Open Space, 1972-87, chmn. adv. com., 1988—; mem. Gov.'s Issue Analysis Com. and Speakers Bur., 1966; mem. speakers bur. Am. embassy, London, 1961-63; v.p., bd. dirs. Democratic Forum, 1968-72; v.p., trustee Youth for Service. Served to lt. USNR. Contbr. articles to profl. jours. Mem. Nat. Assn. Rev. Appraisers and Mortgage Underwriters (cert. 1984—), Napa Valley Vintners, Urban Land Inst., World Congress Land Policy (paper in field), Order of Golden Bear, Commanderie de Bordeaux, Bohemian Club, Pacific Union Club, Lambda Alpha. Contbr. articles to profl. articles. Home: 3375 Jackson St San Francisco CA 94118

MARSTON, ROBERT ANDREW, public relations executive; b. Astoria, N.Y., Aug. 6, 1937; s. Frank and Lena (DiDomenico) M.; m. Carolyn Barris, June 30, 1973 (div. June 1982). B.A., Hofstra U., 1959. Sr. v.p. Rowland Co., N.Y.C., 1959-68, Rogers & Cowen, Inc., N.Y.C., 1968-70; founder, pres. Robert Marston and Assocs., N.Y.C., 1970—. Contbr. articles and photographs to profl. jours. and popular mags. Mem. Public Relations Soc. Am. (counselors sect.). Roman Catholic. Clubs: Madison Sq. Garden, N.Y. Athletic, Marco Polo, Doubles, Board Room; Tryall Beach and Golf (Jamaica). Home: 570 Park Ave New York NY 10021 Office: Robert Marston & Assocs Inc 485 Madison Ave New York NY 10022 *

MARTAN, JOSEPH RUDOLF, lawyer; b. Oak Park, Ill., Mar. 28, 1949; s. Joseph John and Margarete Paulina (Rothenbock) M. BA with honors, U. Ill., 1971; JD with honors, Ill. Inst. Tech., Chgo.-Kent Coll. Law, 1977. Bar: Ill. 1977, U.S. Dist. Ct. (no. dist.) Ill. 1977. Assoc. V.C. Lopez, Chgo., 1978-80; litigation counsel Goldblatt Bros., Inc., Chgo., 1980-81; br. counsel Ill. br. Am. Family Ins. Group, Schaumburg, 1981-87; atty. Judge & Knight Ltd., Park Ridge, Ill., 1987—. Mem. West Suburban Community Band, Inc., Western Springs, Ill., 1975—, pres., 1979-81. Served with U.S. Army, 1972-74, to capt. USAR, 1974-85. Decorated Army Commendation medal. Mem. Ill. State Bar Assn., Chgo. Bar Assn., Du Page County Bar Assn. (mem. civil practice com.), Bohemian Lawyer's Assn. Chgo. (sec. 1987, 2d v.p. 1988), Def. Research Inst., Assn. Trial Lawyers Am., Res. Officer's Assn., Assn. U.S. Army, Met. Opera Guild, Pi Sigma Alpha, Pi Sigma Alpha. Home: 4056 Gilbert Ave Western Springs IL 60558 Office: Judge & Knight 422 N Northwest Hwy Park Ridge IL 60068

MARTEL, EUGENE HARVEY, engineering company executive; b. Webster, Mass., Sept. 15, 1934; s. Eugene P. and Rose A. (Lemay) M.; m. Audrey Renee Ballou, Sept. 1, 1958; children: Neil A., Denise M., Kevin E., Lisa A. B.S. in Chem Engring., U. R.I., 1956. Registered profl. engr., Mass. Process engr. Badger, Cambridge, 1956-71; v.p. Badger Tomoe, Tokyo, 1971-73; pres. China Badger, Taipei, Taiwan, 1973-75; v.p. Asia/Pacific The Badger Co., Inc., Cambridge, Mass., 1975-81, sr. v.p. bus. devel., 1981-83; sr. v.p. Western hemisphere and Far East Lummus Crest, 1984-87, exec. v.p., 1987—. Served to 2d lt. U.S. Army, 1957-63. Mem. Am. Inst. Chem. Engrs. Office: Lummus Crest Inc 1515 Broad St Bloomfield NJ 07003

MARTEL, ROBERT JOHN, financial planner; b. Somerville, Mass., Aug. 9, 1936. AS, Tufts U., 1958; BS, Boston U., 1962; MS, MIT, 1966. Mgr. Price Waterhouse & Co., Boston, 1966-69; div. mgr. Tasc, Reading, 1969-72; pres. R.J. Martel Assocs., Inc., Lexington, Mass., 1973-85, Fin. Planning & Mgmt., Lexington, 1985—. Mem. Inst. Cert. fin. Planners (bd. dirs. 1986-87, sec. 1987-88), Internat. Assn. Fin. Planning (bd. dirs. 1984-85). Office: Fin Planning & Mgmt In 3 Militia Dr Lexington MA 02173

MARTENS, JOHN DALE, telecommunications company executive; b. Wayne, Nebr., Nov. 12, 1943; s. Leonard William and Irma Bertha (Von Seggern) M.; m. Laura Elizabeth Price, Dec. 28, 1966. BSBA, U. Colo., 1966; MS, Thurderbird Grad. Sch. Internat. Mgmt., 1972; postgrad. Queen Mary Coll., U. London, 1976. Analyst overseas ops. Ford Motor Co., Dearborn, Mich., 1972-73; internat. mktg. ofcl. Agrico Chem. Co., Tulsa,

1973-76; tech. and comml. devel. ofcl. Resource Scis. Co., Tulsa, 1976-78, planning and corp. devel. ofcl., 1978-80; chief exec. officer, pres., treas., dir. Sterling Oil of Okla., Inc., Tulsa, 1980-82; dir. strategic devel. MCI Communications Corp., Washington, 1983-84, v.p. corp. devel., 1984-86; v.p. mktg. So. New Eng. Telecommunications Co. Inc., New Haven, 1986. Capt. USAF, 1967-70. Episcopalian. Mem. Quinnipiack Club (New Haven), New Haven Country Club. Office: So New Eng Telecommunications Co Inc 195 Church St 10th Floor New Haven CT 06510

MARTENS, ROY MICHAEL, lease finance representative; b. Des Moines, Feb. 7, 1950; s. Roy Edwin and Maxine Hayworth M. BA, Luther Coll., 1972; MBA, U. Minn., 1978. Auditor Honeywell, Mpls., 1972-75; supr. Northwest SW, Mpls., 1975-78; fin. analyst Amhoist, St. Paul, 1979-81; sr. fin. analyst Farm Credit Services, St. Paul, 1981-88; lease finance rep. Dataserv, Eden Prairie, Minn., 1988-89. Mem. Twin City Cash Mgmt. Assn. (program com. 1987-89), Epsilon Delta Omicron. Republican. Lutheran. Club: Wayzata Yacht (measurer 1985, sec. 1988), Minnetnka Yacht. Home: 2511 Chestnut Ave W Minneapolis MN 55405

MARTENSON, JOHN RAYMOND, computer company executive; b. Eau Claire, Wis., Mar. 21, 1955; s. Albert Emil and Charlotte Mary (Poe) M.; m. Sally Jo Schiedegger, Dec. 26, 1978. BBA, U. Wis., 1977, MBA, 1979. Budget analyst ITT Life Ins. Co., Mpls., 1977-78; sr. adminstr. Cray Rsch., Inc., Mpls., 1980—; entrepreneurship instr. Chippewa Valley Tech. Coll., Eau Claire; owner, pres.. G.D. Odds, Ltd., Eau Claire, 1984—. Mem. Am. Mgmt. Assn. Republican. Roman Catholic.

MARTIN, ARTHUR RAYMOND, media company executive; b. Evanston, Ill., Apr. 7, 1949; d. Arthur R. and Catherine L. (Burke) M.; m. Janice S. Filardo, May 6, 1978. BA, U. Notre Dame, 1971; MBA, U. Chgo., 1978. CPA, Ill. Asst. treas. Bradner Cen. Co., Chgo., 1978-81, treas., 1981-84; real estate mgr. Tribune Co., Chgo., 1984-85, dir. real estate, 1984-85, 88—; v.p. Tribune Properties, Chgo., 1988—. Mem. adv. com. Chgo. Local Iniatives Support Corp., 1986—. Capt U.S. Army, 1971-78. Mem. Ill. CPA Soc., Comml. Investment Coun., Nat. Assn. Realtors. Office: Tribune Co 435 N Michigan Ave Chicago IL 60611-4041

MARTIN, BARBARA JESSICA, clothing company executive; b. Hackensack, N.J., Nov. 27, 1950; d. John M. and Jessica B. (Keller) M. BA, U. Vt., 1972. Asst. buyer Lord & Taylor, N.Y.C., 1972-75; buyer, mgr. Lonergans, N.Y.C., 1975-78; saleswomen Tanner of N.C., N.Y.C., 1978-80; sales dir. Marisa Christina, N.Y.C., 1980-84; nat. sales mgr. Accessory Club, N.Y.C., 1985-86; nat. sales mgr. Pierre Cardin div. Beldoch Industries, 1986-88; nat. mktg. rep. Shapely div. Leslie Fay, N.Y.C., 1988—; cons. regional alumnae U. Vt., 1980—; cons. regional networking for alumnae Sweet Briar Coll., 1986—. Mem. U. Vt. Alumnae Assn., Sweet Briar Coll. Alumnae Assn. Republican. Methodist.

MARTIN, DARRYL WAYNE, accountant, engineer; b. Lyons, Nebr., Feb. 1, 1948; s. Lyle W. and Joan (Neil) M.; m. Elizabeth Eileen Stewart, Feb. 1, 1979; children: Layke Anne, Dorain Elizabeth. BSEE, U. Nebr., 1972. Registered profl. engr., Nev.; CPA, Nev. Founder, dir. ops. CSW subs. San Francisco Chronicle Pub. Co.; chief exec. officer S.W. Resource Group, Las Vegas, Nev., 1980—; bd. dirs. Syncomp Sci., Las Vegas. Contbr. articles to profl. jours. Mem. IEEE. Office: SW Resource Group 5530 Evaline Las Vegas NV 89120

MARTIN, DAVID, manufacturing company executive; b. Hackensack, N.J., 1945. Grad., Princeton U., 1967. With Nat. Semiconductor Corp., 1973—, now exec. v.p.; pres. Nat. Advanced Systems, Santa Clara, Calif. Office: Nat Advanced Systems 750 Central Expwy Santa Clara CA 95054-0996

MARTIN, DAVID LOUIS, financial systems analyst; b. Oak Park, Ill., Dec. 20, 1950; s. Donald Maxwell and Marian Sylvia (Goers) M.; m. Norma Kay Allen, June 7, 1975. BA, Calif. State U., Fullerton, 1972. Mgr. programming Mortgage Systems, Anaheim, Calif., 1974-79; sr. programmer McDonnell Douglas, Huntington Beach, Calif., 1979-80; systems analyst Downey Savs., Costa Mesa, Calif., 1980-83; sr. project mgr. Columbia Savs., Irvine, Calif., 1983-89; free lance data processing cons. 1989—; cons., Santa Ana, Calif., 1973—. Lutheran. Home: 2041 N Ross Santa Ana CA 92706 Office: Columbia Savs and Loan 17911 Von Karman Ave Irvine CA 92714

MARTIN, DONALD TIMOTHY, financial executive, accountant; b. Columbia, S.C., Apr. 8, 1957; s. David Sr. and Gladys (Locklair) M.; m. Donna Williams, June 6, 1981; children: Alison M., Donald Timothy Jr. BS, U. S.C., 1979. CPA, S.C. Acct. Brittingham, Dial & Jeffcoat, CPAs, West Columbia, S.C., 1978-84; dir. fin. Columbia Met. Airport, 1984—. Mem. AICPA, S.C. Assn. CPAs (Cen. chpt.), Am. Assn. Airport Execs. (S.E. chpt.). Republican. Baptist. Office: Columbia Met Airport 3000 Aviation Way West Columbia SC 29169

MARTIN, DOTTY, newspaper publisher; b. Kingston, Pa., Mar. 10, 1955; d. David Thomas and Kathryn Joanne (Schooley) M. BA in English and Journalism, Wilkes Coll., 1977. Reporter Sunday Dispatch, Pittston, Pa., 1973-78; dir. pub. rels. Am. Cancer Soc., Wilkes-Barre, Pa., 1977-78; sportswriter, copy editor The Times Leader, Wilkes-Barre, 1978-81; editor The Dallas (Pa.) Post, 1983-87; editor, pub., pres. West Side Weekly/Grapevine Pub., Inc., Kingston, 1987—. Vol. Spl. Olympics, Luzerne County, Pa., 1987—. Mem. Sigma Delta Chi. Democrat. Home: 1137 Murray St Forty Fort PA 18704 Office: Rear 649 Wyoming Ave Kingston PA 18704

MARTIN, DRUSILLA LYNN, accountant; b. Nashville, Mar. 22, 1958; d. George Herbert and Ruby Jean (Dartis) Darden; m. Michael Martin, Feb. 16, 1988; 1 child, Christopher Ryan. BBA, Tenn. State U., 1982. CPA. Revenue agt. IRS, Nashville, 1981—. Democrat. Baptist. Home: 1313 Calvin Ave Nashville TN 37206 Office: IRS 1101 Kermit Dr Nashville TN 37217

MARTIN, EARLE WILSON, computer services and pharmaceutical research executive; b. New Orleans, Oct. 17, 1952; s. James Henry Jr. and Charlotte Elmyra (Danner) M.; m. Elizabeth Stone Thiele, June 6, 1977; children: Jonathan, Christopher, Annie. BA, U. Va., 1975. Resch. asst. Sch. Medicine U. Va., Charlottesville, 1975-77; resch. computing mgr. Hartford (Conn.) Ins. Group, 1977-79; tech. specialist Automatic Data Processing, Waltham, Mass., 1979—, account rep., 1980-81, sales mgr., 1981-82; regional sales mgr. Artificial Intelligence Corp., Waltham, 1982-85, dir. mktg., 1985-86; dir. mktg. Bachman Info. Systems, Cambridge, Mass., 1987; gen. mgr. Pharm. Rsch. Assn., Charlottesville, Va., 1987—, also bd. dirs. Home: 10208 Conover Dr Silver Spring MD 20902 Office: Pharm Rsch Assn Inc Rte 1 Box 380 Charlottesville VA 22901

MARTIN, EDWARD LEE, manufacturing executive; b. Boston, Apr. 27, 1954; s. Alan and Charlotte (Kaufman) M.; m. Janet Lynn Johnson, Sept. 15, 1984; 1 child, Amanda Leone. BA in Psychology, U. Mass., 1976, MS in Indsl. Engring. and Ops. Rsch., 1978. With materials mgmt. dept. Digital Equipment Corp., Westfield, Mass., 1978; with operating and strategic planning dept. IBM, Raleigh, N.C., 1979-81; cons. productivity div. IBM, Raleigh, 1980-84, mgr. productivity improvement planning, indsl. engring. systems, 1982-84; v.p. mfg., fin. Creative Engring., Taunton, Mass., 1984—; productivity cons. to IBM World Trade, 1982. Organizer United Way, Raleigh, 1979-84; active Big Bros., Durham, N.C., 1980-81. Mem. Am. Inst. Indsl. Engring. (sr.). Jewish. Office: Creative Engring Inc 475 Myles Standish Blvd Taunton MA 02780

MARTIN, EMILY FRANCES, accountant; b. Bklyn., Oct. 14, 1958; d. Henry F. and Emiko E. (Endo) Stanfield. AA, St. Petersburg Jr. Coll., 1977; BA in Acctg., U. South Fla., 1982; M in Acctg. with honors, Nova U., 1985. CPA, Fla. File and systems clk. GTE Directories, St. Petersburg, Fla., 1975-81; bookkeeper Dara-Hennessy, St. Petersburg, 1981-83; staff acct. Spence Marston & Bunch, Clearwater, Fla., 1983; staff acct. Aero Systems, Miami, Fla., 1983-85, acctg. supr., 1985; chief acct., dep. dir. bus. Pan Am World Services, Medley, Fla., 1985-88; dir. fin. 1988—, Carnival Cruise Lines, 1988—; adjunct faculty mem. Broward Community Coll., 1986—. Coordinator Neighborhood Crime Watch, St. Petersburg, 1982. Mem. Nat. Assn. Accts., Nat. Assn. Female Execs., Nat. Notary Assn., Fla. Inst. CPAs, Am. Inst. CPAs. Avocations: reading,; ballet, sewing, shooting. Home: PO Box 8125 Fort Lauderdale FL 33310

MARTIN, FRANK JAMES, JR., marketing company executive; b. Chgo., Jan. 28, 1931; s. Frank James and Claire Victoria (Praiter) M.; m. Ruth Ann Hennigar, Oct. 3, 1952; children: Vickilee J., Frank J. III, Jon J., Kerry J. BS in Bus., Ind. U., 1953. Supr. Jefferson Standard, Goldsboro, N.C., 1961-63; exec. sales Alside Homes Corp., Akron, Ohio, 1963-64; ter. sales mgr. Armco Steel Corp., Middletown, Ohio, 1964-66; sales mgr. Ryan Homes, Inc., Cin., 1966-68; v.p. mktg. services, dir. mktg., div. mgr. The Ryland Group, Columbia, Md., 1968-80; pres. Martin Corp., Annapolis, Md., 1979—. Contbr. articles to profl. jours. Mem. mktg. com. Mayor's Pvt. Industry Council, Balt., 1983-86. Capt. USAF, 1953-61. Recipient awards of honor Automation in Housing, Miami, Fla., 1972. Mem. Nat. Home Builders Assn. (com. chmn., life mem. Million Dollar Circle and Life Spike), Inst. Residential Mktg. (nat. pres. 1986), Nat. Sales and Mktg. Council, Md. Home Builders Assn. (bd. dirs.), Order of Ky. Cols., Alpha Tau Omega. Republican. Lutheran. Office: Martin Corp 1202 Chrisland Ct Annapolis MD 21403

MARTIN, FRED L., banker; b. Alamogordo, N.Mex., Nov. 3, 1947; s. Edward Lowell and Miriam Irene (Patterson) M. BA, N.Mex. State U., 1969. With acctg., bookkeeping dept. Alamogordo Fed. Savs. and Loan, 1970, v.p., treas., 1970-84, chief fin. officer, 1984-86, sr. v.p., 1986—. Mem. Fin. Mgrs. Soc., Fin. Mktg. Assn., Rotary (chmn. 1982-88), Masons. Office: Alamogordo Fed S&L 400 10th St Alamogordo NM 88310

MARTIN, FREDERICK, securities dealer, broker; b. Indpls., Mar. 24, 1908; s. William Nelson and Ida Martin; A.B., Butler U., 1928; postgrad. Harvard Law Sch., 1929; M.B.A., Harvard U., 1931; m. Eleanor Lauderdale Rankin, Feb. 14, 1942; children—Frederick, Melissa, Laurel. Round-the-world seaman S.S. Isthmian, 1932; acct. Cooney Mining Co., Silver City, N.Mex., 1933; security analyst Thomson & McKinnon, N.Y.C., 1934-39, Nat. Investors, 1940-41, Sterling Grace & Co., 1945-48, Joseph Faroll & Co., 1948-50; treas. Standard Cable Corp., Okla., 1951-52; exec. v.p. Dorsett Labs., 1952-58; owner Fred Martin & Co., Norman, Okla., 1959-68, La Jolla, Calif., 1969—; chmn. Naturizer Inc., Norman, 1958-59; pres. Investment Securities Assn., Oklahoma City, 1966; mem. N.Y. Soc. Security Analysts, 1946-61; spl. instr. bus. fin. Okla. U., 1958, 68; mem. U.S. Senatorial Bus. Adv. Bd., 1982. Sec., Park Bd. Norman, 1955-57, Bd. Adjustment Norman, 1958-60; mem. La Jolla Town Council, 1973. Served to lt. comdr. USNR, 1942-45. Recipient award San Diego Union Review, 1980. Mem. Stock & Bond Club, Nat. Assn. Securities Dealers, Securities Investor Protection Corp. Club: La Jolla Beach and Tennis. Contbr. articles, book reviews to profl. jours. Home and Office: 5551 Warbler Way La Jolla CA 92037

MARTIN, HARVEY CARR, building supply dealer, investor; b. Muskegon, Mich., Nov. 2, 1911. Grad. high school, Muskegon Heights. With M. K. Investment Co., Muskegon. Mem. Sr. Services of Muskegon County, pres., 1987-88. Mem. Mich. Builders Supply Assn. (pres. state chpt., 1976), Nat. Assn. Credit Execs. (Muskegon chpt. pres., 1965, 1979). Republican. Congregationalist. Club: Optimist (Muskegon pres. 1964-65). Lodge: Masons. Home: 18911 N Fruitport Rd Spring Lake MI 49456 Office: M K Investment Co 1960 S Roberts St Muskegon MI 49442

MARTIN, JAMES ALAN, banker; b. Wilson, N.C., Oct. 21, 1954; s. Claude Durwood and Joyce Ann (Hellman) M.; m. Frances Kay Cameron, Jan. 8, 1983; 1 child, Ryan Cameron. BS, U. Tex., 1977, MBA, 1980. Fin. analyst Ft. Worth div. Gen. Dynamics Corp., 1979-80; staff acct. Alcon Pharms., Inc., Ft. Worth, 1980-81; asst. v.p. planning MCorp, Dallas, 1981-85; v.p. planning and reporting MBank, Ft. Worth, 1986, controller, v.p., 1986—. Mem. mgmt. com. Bus. Vols. for Arts, Ft. Worth, 1986; fund-raising vol. Am. Heart Assn., Ft. Worth, 1986. Mem. Fin. Execs. Inst., Planning Forum, Ft. Worth C. of C. (fund-raising vol. 1988). Republican. Methodist. Home: 2106 Riverforest Ct Arlington TX 76017 Office: MBank 777 Main St Fort Worth TX 76102

MARTIN, JAMES JAY, management consultant; b. Wilkes Barre, Pa., July 15, 1948; s. Wilbur James and Agnes I. (McGinnis) M.; m. Dorothy Jane, June 28, 1975; children: Patrick James, Steven David, Sara Jane. AS, York Coll., 1968; BS in Mktg., U. Del., 1974. Mgr. in tng. A&P Food Stores, Rehoboth Beach, Del., 1975-76; salesman Bruce Indsl. Co., Wilmington, Del., 1976-77; with ops. dept. Alexander Proudfoot Co., Chgo., 1977-79, mgr. installation, 1979-81, bus. analyst, 1981-82; chief productivity improvement installations Alexander Proudfoot Co., West Palm Beach, Fla., 1982-86; chief installations APC Skills Co, West Palm Beach, 1986; v.p. ops. The Systems Cons. Group, Bryn Mawr, Pa., 1986—; bd. dirs. That Patchwork Place, Woodinville, Wash. Bd. dirs. Main St. Assn., Kennett Square, Pa., 1987—, now v.p.; coach Youth Soccer. With U.S. Army, 1969-71. Home: 240 N Broad St Kennett Square PA 19348 Office: The Systems Cons Group 25 Elliott Ave Bryn Mawr PA 19010

MARTIN, JAMES JOHN, JR., consulting research firm executive, systems analyst; b. Paterson, N.J., Feb. 3, 1936; s. James John and Lillian (Lea) M.; m. Lydia Elizabeth Bent, June 11, 1954; children—David, Peter, Laura, Daniel, Lucas. B.A., U. Wis.-Madison, 1955; postgrad., Div. Sch., Harvard U., 1955-57; M.S., Navy Postgrad. Sch., 1963; Ph.D., MIT, 1965. Commd. ensign U.S. Navy, 1957; advanced through grades to comdr. 1971, ret., 1977; group sr. v.p. Sci. Applications Internat. Corp., La Jolla, Calif., 1977—. Author: Bayesian Decision Problems and Markov Chains, 1967; also articles on nat. security. Bd. dirs. Mil. Conflict Inst., 1986—. Decorated Legion of Merit. Mem. Internat. Inst. Strategic Studies, Ops. Research Soc. Am., Mil. Ops. Research Soc. (bd. dirs. 1974-77). Republican. Home: 6603 Aranda Ave La Jolla CA 92037 Office: Sci Applications Internat Corp 10260 Campus Point Dr San Diego CA 92121

MARTIN, J(AMES) PHILLIP, church official; b. Huntsville, Ala., Mar. 4, 1952; s. John Paul and Marguerite (James) M.; m. Gloria L. Little, June 23, 1973; children: Lauren, Andrea. MusB, Samford U., 1974; MA in Religious Edn., Southwestern Bapt. Theol. Sem., 1976, MA, 1983. Minister edn. and music 1st Bapt. Ch., Richmond, Tex., 1976-78; minister edn. South Avondale Bapt. Ch., Birmingham, Ala., 1978-82; ministry edn. adminstrn. 1st Bapt. Ch. Chamblee, Atlanta, 1982-86; sr. educator, staff adminstr. South Main Bapt. Ch., Houston, 1986—. Named Outstanding Young Man of Am., Jaycees, 1975. Mem. Nat. Assn. Ch. Bus. Adminstrn., ea. Bapt. Religion Edn. Assn., Ea. Bapt. Religion Edn. Assn., Birmingham Bapt. Religious Educators. Office: South Main Bapt Ch 4100 Main St Houston TX 77002

MARTIN, JAMES SMITH, insurance executive; b. Hartford, Conn., Mar. 10, 1936; s. John G. and Elis (Parsons) M.; student Loomis Inst., 1954; BS, Yale U., 1958; MBA, Columbia U., 1961; m. Ann Louise Willem, Feb. 11, 1961; children: James Smith, Lawrence Hedrick. With Chase Manhattan Bank, N.Y.C., 1961-74, v.p., 1969-74; with Tchrs. Ins. & Annuity Assn. Am., N.Y.C., 1974—, exec. v.p., 1979-83, chmn. fin. com., 1984—; trustee Coll. Retirement Equities Fund; dir. United Kingdom Fund. Office: Tchrs Ins & Annuity Assn Am 730 3rd Ave New York NY 10017

MARTIN, JERRY C., oil company executive; b. Indpls., May 10, 1932; s. Joel C. and Blanche J. (Traubel) M.; m. Marilyn L. Brock, Sept. 7, 1952 (div. May 1976); children: Cathy J. Keiffer, Douglas E.; m. Connie B. Young, May 8, 1979 (div. July 1988); 1 son, Michael. BS in Acctg., Butler U., 1953. Acct. Allison div. Gen. Motors, Indpls., 1953-57; acctng. and budget mgr. Standard Oil, Indpls., 1957-60; budget dir. Inland Container Corp., Indpls., 1960-71; corp. controller Storm Drilling and Marine Co., Chgo., 1971-75; v.p. Scottsman Norwood, Houston, 1975-76; corp. controller Internat Systems and Controls, Houston, 1976-79; v.p., controller Global Marine Drilling Co., Houston, 1979-85; sr. v.p., chief fin. officer Global Marine, Inc., Houston, 1985—. Mem. Fin. Execs. Inst., Mensa, Westlake Club, Westside Tennis Club. Republican. Office: Global Marine Inc 777 N Eldridge Houston TX 77079

MARTIN, JOHN JOSEPH, manufacturing company executive, lawyer; b. N.Y.C., July 11, 1931; s. John J. and Vera (Moran) M.; m. Marilyn E. Hughes, Jan. 5, 1955; children: John Joseph, Kieran, Robert, Paul. BA, NYU, 1958, JD, 1962. Bar: N.Y. 1962, Conn. 1975. Assoc. Huber, Magill, Lawrence & Farrell (and predecessor firm), N.Y.C., 1962-68; v.p., sec., assoc. gen. counsel Bangor Punta Corp., Greenwich, Conn., 1968-79; sr. v.p., gen. counsel, sec. Lone Star Industries, Inc., 1979—; v.p., sec., dir. Piper Aircraft Corp., 1970-79. Served to cpl. U.S. Army, 1951-53. Mem. Am. Soc. Corp. Secs., N.Y. State Bar Assn., Conn. Bar Assn., Westchester-Fairfield Corp. Counsel Assn., Inc. (bd. dirs. 1986—). Roman Catholic. Club: Burning Tree (Greenwich) (gov. 1987). Office: Lone Star Industries Inc 1 Greenwich Pla Box 5050 Greenwich CT 06830

MARTIN, JOHNNY BENJAMIN, accountant; b. Gainesville, Ga., June 9, 1947; d. John Daniel and Helen Amanda (Meeks) M.; m. Mary Sue West, June 8, 1969; 1 child, Tammy Michelle. BBA, U. Ga., Athens, 1969, MA, 1971. CPA, Ga. Tchr. high sch. Hall County Sch. Systems, Gainesville, 1969-70; instr. in acctg. Austin Peay State U., Clarksville, Tenn., 1972-76; instr. in bus. Gainesville Jr. Coll., 1976-77; controller Home Fed. Savs. and Loan, Gainesville, 1977-83; ptnr. Kendrick & Jessup, CPA's, Gainesville, 1983—. Mem. Am. Inst. CPA's, Ga. Soc. CPA's, Tenn. Soc. CPA's, Phi Kappa Phi, Beta Gamma Sigma. Democrat. Baptist. Lodge: Civitan (bd. dirs., treas. 1981-82, treas. 1986-87). Home: 3751 Robinson Dr Oakwood GA 30566

MARTIN, JOSEPH, JR., lawyer, diplomat; b. San Francisco, May 21, 1915; m. Ellen Chamberlain Martin, July 5, 1946; children: Luther Greene, Ellen Myers. AB, Yale U., 1936, LLB, 1939. Assoc. Cadwalader, Wickersham & Taft, N.Y.C., 1939-41; ptnr. Wallace, Garrison, Norton & Ray, San Francisco, 1946-55, Pettit & Martin, San Francisco, 1955-70, 73—; gen. counsel FTC, Washington, 1970-71; ambassador, U.S. rep. Disarmament Conf., Geneva, 1971-76; mem. Pres.'s Adv. Com. for Arms Control and Disarmament, 1974-78; bd. dirs. Arcata Corp., Allstar Inns, Astec Industries, Inc., Opco Holding, Inc. Pres. Pub. Utilities Commn., San Francisco, 1956-60; Rep. nat. committeeman for Calif., 1960-64; treas. Rep. Party Calif., 1956-58; bd. dirs. Patrons of Art and Music, Calif. Palace of Legion of Honor, 1958-70, pres., 1963-68; bd. dirs. Arms Control Assn., 1977-84; pres. Friends of Legal Assistance to Elderly, 1983-87. Lt. comdr. USNR, 1941-46. Recipient Ofcl. commendation for Outstanding Service as Gen. Counsel FTC, 1973, Distinguished Honor award U.S. ACDA, 1973, Lifetime Achievement award Legal Assistance to the Elderly, 1981. Fellow Am. Bar Found. Clubs: Burlingame Country, Pacific Union. Home: 2580 Broadway San Francisco CA 94115 Office: Pettit & Martin 101 California St 35th fl San Francisco CA 94111

MARTIN, JOSEPH ROBERT, financial executive; b. Phila., Dec. 9, 1947; s. Robert and Elva Ruth (Griffen) M.; m. Catherine Marie Kelly, Sept. 5, 1970; children: Joseph Robert, Jennifer H., Patrick F., Kathleen K. BS, Embry Riddle U., 1974; MBA, U. Maine, 1976. Sr. corp. fin. analyst Keyes Fibre Co., Waterville, Maine, 1976-80; mfr. fin. analysis and planning Schlumberger, Fairchild, South Portland, Maine, 1980-83; div. controller Schlumberger, Factron, Clifton Park, N.Y., 1983-84; corp. controller VTC, Inc., Bloomington, Minn., 1984-87; v.p. fin., chief fin. officer VTC, Inc., Bloomington, 1987—. Served to capt. U.S. Army, 1967-72, Vietnam. Decorated D.F.C., Purple Heart, Bronze Star medal, Air medal. Home: 13635 Havelock Trail Apple Valley MN 55124 Office: VTC Inc 2401 E 86th St Minneapolis MN 55420

MARTIN, LAURA ANNE, banker; b. Pasadena, Calif., Dec. 11, 1958; d. Warren Leicester and Laura Paez (Reed) M.; m. Daniel Andrew Medina, July 16, 1983. Student Wellesley Coll., 1976-78; BA, Stanford U., 1980; MBA, Harvard U., 1983. Fin. analyst AG Becker, Los Angeles, 1980-81; assoc. Drexel Burnham Lambert, Los Angeles, 1983-86, v.p., 1986-88, 1st v.p. 1988—. Office: Drexel Burnham Lambert 131 S Rodeo Dr Suite 300 Los Angeles CA 90212

MARTIN, LEE, business executive; b. Elkhart, Ind., Feb. 7, 1920; s. Ross and Esther Lee (Schweitzer) M.; m. Geraldine Faith Fitzgarrald, July 20, 1945; children: Jennifer L., Casper, Rex, Elizabeth L. B.S.M.E. and M.S.M.E., MIT, 1943. With Gen. Electric Co., 1940-42; with NIBCO Inc., Elkhart, 1946—; successively v.p., gen. mgr. NIBCO Inc., 1950-56, pres, pres., 1957-76, chief exec. officer, 1976—; bd. dirs. AmeriTrust Ind. Corp., Indpls. Chmn. Samaritan Inst., Denver, 1980—; dir. Interlochen (Mich.) Ctr. for Arts, 1983—. Republican. Presbyterian. Clubs: Union League (Chgo.), Mid-Am. (Chgo.). Office: NIBCO Inc 500 Simpson Ave PO Box 1167 Elkhart IN 46515

MARTIN, MICHAEL TOWNSEND, racing horse stable executive, sports marketing consultant; b. N.Y.C., Nov. 21, 1941; s. Townsend Bradley and Irene (Redmond) M.; m. Jennifer Johnston, Nov. 7, 1964 (div. Jan. 1977); children: Ryan Bradley, Christopher Townsend; m. Jean Kathleen Meyer, Mar. 1, 1980. Grad. The Choate Sch., 1960; student Rutgers U., 1961-62. Asst. gen. mgr. N.Y. Jets Football Club, N.Y.C., 1968-74; v.p. NAMANCO Prodns., N.Y.C., 1975-76; v.p., gen. mgr. Cosmos Soccer Club, N.Y.C., 1976-77; exec. asst. Warner Communications, N.Y.C., 1978-84; owner, operator Martin Racing Stable, N.Y.C., 1983—; chmn., chief exec. officer Hydro-Train Systems Inc., 1987—; ptnr. Halstead Property Co., 1987—; bd. advisors N.Y. Zool. Soc., N.Y.C., 1984—, N.Y. Aquarium, Coney Island, 1983—. Bd. dirs. Old Westbury Gardens, Westbury, N.Y., 1983—, Phipps Houses, 1986—; trustee The Pennington Sch.; trustee, pres. Alumni and Parents Assn. Choate Rosemary Hall Sch.; bd. dirs. Very Spl. Arts, 1982—. Served to E-4 USN, 1963-67. Mem. Athletics Congress (life, cert. official 1984—), U.S. Tennis Assn. (life), Internat. Oceanographic Found. (Miami life mem.), Eastern N.Y. Thoroughbred Breeders Assn. (bd. dirs. 1987—), Fla. Thoroughbred Breeders Assn. Republican. Episcopalian. Clubs: N.Y. Athletic; Quogue Field (N.Y.). Avocations: major collection Inuit (Eskimo) art; marathon running. Home: 131 E 69 St Apt 11-A New York NY 10021 Office: 575 Madison Ave Suite 1006 New York NY 10022

MARTIN, PATRICIA J., real estate executive; b. Hackensack, N.J., Sept. 30, 1954; d. William E. Martin and Dorothy J. (Salmon) Schindler. BA, Ramapo Coll., 1976; MBA, Pace U., 1985. Cert. broker. Asst. mgr. promotions Keyes Fibre Co., Stamford, Conn., 1977-82; supr. mktg. svcs. Clairol div. Bristol-Myers Co., N.Y.C., 1982-84; product mgr. Berkey Mktg. Co., Woodside, N.Y., 1984; v.p. mktg. NOAH/Hearthstone Realtors, Montvale, N.J., 1984—. Driver Pascack Valley Meals on Wheels, Westwood, N.J., 1987—; bd. dirs. Christian edn. Park Ridge (N.J.) Congl. Ch., 1986—, adviser youth group, 1986—. Mem. Nat. Assn. Realtors (Million Dollar Sales award 1986, 87), Pascack Valley Bd. Realtors (com. chairs realtor protection, profl. standards), Greater Montvale Bus. Assn. Office: NOAH/Hearthstone Realtors 2 Railroad Ave Montvale NJ 07645

MARTIN, PAUL, Canadian provincial official; b. Windsor, Ont., Can., Aug. 28, 1938; s. Paul Joseph and Eleanor (Adams) M.; m. Sheila Ann Cowan, Sept. 11, 1965; children—Paul William James, Robert James Edward, David Patrick Anthony. BA in Philosophy and History, U. Toronto, Can., 1962, LLB, 1965; LLB, U. Toronto, Can., 1965. Bar: Ont. 1966. Exec. asst. to pres. Power Corp. Can. Ltd., 1966-69, v.p., 1969-71; v.p. spl. projects Consol.-Bathurst Ltd., 1971-73; v.p. planning and devel. Power Corp., Can., 1973-74; pres. Can. S.S. Lines Ltd., Montreal, 1974-80, chief exec. officer, 1976-80; pres., chief exec. officer CSL Group Inc., 1980-89; M.P. Ho. of Commons, 1989—; past chmn. bd., chief exec. officer, Can. Steamship Lines Inc. Mem. C.D. Howe Inst. Policy Analysis Com., Brit. N.Am. Com., Ctr. Rsch. Action on Race Rels.; mem. adv. bd. Can. Ctr. Arms Control; bd. dirs. Can. Council Christians and Jews; founding dir. emeritus North-South Inst., Can. Council Native Bus.; bd. govs. Concordia U., council v.p. Mem. Chartered Inst. Transport, Amnesty Internat., Dominion Marine Assn., University Club, Mt. Bruno Country Club, Mt. Royal Club. Office: House of Commons, Confederation Bldg Rm 481, Ottawa, ON Canada K1A 0A6

MARTIN, PAUL EDWARD, lawyer; b. Atchison, Kans., Feb. 5, 1928; s. Harres C. and Thelma F. (Wilson) M.; m. Betty Lou Crawford, Aug. 28, 1954; children: Cherry G., Paul A., Marylou. BBA, Baylor U., 1955, LLB, 1956; LLM, Harvard U., 1957. Bar: Tex. 1956, Pa. 1958. Assoc. Ballard, Spahr, Andrews & Ingersoll, Phila., 1957-58; ptnr. Fulbright & Jaworski, Houston, 1959-77; sr. ptnr. Chamberlain, Hrdlicka, White, Johnson & Williams, 1977—; instr. in estate planning U. Houston. Exec. com. Met. Houston March of Dimes, 1980-82 ; chmn. deacons West Meml. Baptist Ch., 1979-80; trustee Baylor U., 1970—, Meml. Hosp. System, 1980—, Fgn.

Mission Bd., So. Bapt. Conv.; pres. Baylor U. Devel. Council, 1973-74. Lt. comdr. USN, 1947-53. Fellow Am. Coll. Probate Council; mem. ABA (sect. real property, probate and trust law and sect. taxation), State Bar Tex., Houston Bar Assn., Houston Estate and Fin. Forum (pres. 1965-66), Houston Bus. and Estate Planning Council, Houston Club, Phi Delta Phi. Republican. Co-author: How to Live and Die with Texas Probate. Office: Chamberlain Hrdlicka White Johnson & Williams 1400 Citicorp Ctr 1200 Smith St Houston TX 77002

MARTIN, PAUL LAWRENCE, JR., investment consultant; b. Ft. Sill, Okla., Mar. 6, 1933; s. Paul Lawrence and Catherine Ann (Nichols) M.; m. Marlene G. Goodwin, June 12, 1955; children: Linda, Jeffrey. BS, U.S. Mil. Acad., 1955; MSE, Purdue U., 1961; MBA, Auburn U., 1976. Commd. 2d lt. USAF, 1955, advanced through grades to col., ret., 1980; mgr. Analytic Scis. Corp., Arlington, Va., 1980-82; pvt. practice fin. planning Annandale, Va., 1982-85; chmn., chief exec. officer Windsor Advisors, Inc., Longwood, Fla., 1986—, Windsor Fin. Group, Inc., Longwood, Fla., 1986—; bd. dirs. Star Enterprises, Inc., Annandale, Eastern Am. Bank, McLean, Va. Mem. Inst. Cert. Fin. Planners, Longwood C. of C., Rotary. Office: Windsor Advisors Inc 2180 State Rd 434 Sanlando Ctr Ste 2180 Longwood FL 32779

MARTIN, PRESTON, savings and loan executive; b. L.A., Dec. 5, 1923; s. Oscar and Gaynell (Horne) M.; 1 child, Pier Preston. BS in Fin., U. So. Calif., 1947, MBA, 1948; PhD in Monetary Econs., U. Ind., 1952. Rsch. fellow U. Ind., Bloomington, 1948-49; prin. in housebldg. firm 1952-56; with mortgage fin. and consumer fin. instns., 1954-57; prof. econ. rsch. group specializing in savs. and loan matters, 1956-66; developer, adminstr. Pakistan Project for Grad. Bus. Edn., L.A., 1960-63; developer, dir. Programs for Bus. and Govt. Execs. U. So. Calif., L.A., 1959-63; commr. savs. and loan State of Calif., 1967-69; chmn. Fed. Home Loan Bank Bd., Washington, 1969-72; chmn., chief exec. officer PMI Mortgage Ins. Co., 1972-80; chmn., chief exec. officer Seraco Group subs. Sears, Roebuck & Co., 1980-81, also bd. dirs. parent co.; chmn., chief exec. officer H.F. Holdings, Inc., San Francisco, 1988—; chmn. bd. Fed. Home Loan Bank Bd., 1969-72; vice chmn. Fed. Res. Bd., Washington, 1982-86; vice chmn. Fed. Res. Bd. Govs., 1982-86; bd. dirs. Honolulu Fed. Savs. Bank, Fed. Home Loan Mortgage Corp. Adv. Com.; Policy Adv. Bd. Ctr. for Real Estate and Urban Econs. U. Calif.; chmn., chief exec. officer SoCal Holdings, Inc., San Francisco, 1987—, WestFed Holdings, Inc., San Francisco, 1988—, Wespar Fin. Svcs., Inc., San Francisco, 1987—. Author: Principles and Practices of Real Estate, 1959; contbr. articles to profl. jours. Mem. Joint Ctr. Urban Studies MIT; sr. advisor Reagan Adminstrn. Commn. on Housing, 1980-81. With AUS, 1943-46. Recipient House and Home award, 1969, award Engring. News Record, 1971, NAHB Turntable award, 1973. Mem. Am. Econs. Assn., Am. Fin. Assn., Lambda Chi Alpha. Presbyterian.

MARTIN, RAY, banker; b. 1936. With Coast Savs. and Loan Assn., L.A., 1959—, pres., 1980-84, pres., chief exec. officer, from 1984, now chmn., chief exec. officer, also bd. dirs. Office: Coast Savs & Loan Assn 855 S Hill St Los Angeles CA 90014 *

MARTIN, RAYMOND EDWARD, business manager; b. N.Y.C., Sept. 17, 1957; m. Deborah Ann Martin. BBA, Cleve. State U. Cons. Ernst & Whinney, Cleve., 1980-82, Scott Fetzer, Cleve., 1982-83; bus. cons. Am. Consumer Products, Cleve., 1983-87; bus. mgr. APCOA, Inc., Cleve., 1988—. bd. dirs. United Way, Cleve., 1981. Roman Catholic.

MARTIN, RICHARD N., electronics executive; b. Clifton Springs, N.Y., Aug. 22, 1922; s. Douglas and Evelyn (Hilton) M.; m. Hutson Weber, Dec. 26, 1949 (div. Dec. 1958); children: Jeffrey, Peter, Bradford; m. Barbara E. Hener, Oct. 24, 1963; 1 child, Lisa. Student, Alfred U., 1940-41; BA, Hofstra U., 1948; MS, Syracuse U., 1950. Chief lab. tech. Westlake Hosp., Melrose Park, Ill., 1950-51; immunologist B.H. Kean M.D., N.Y.C., 1951-53, St. Francis Hosp., Poughkeepsie, N.Y., 1953-57; dir. tech. services Am. Hosp. Supply, Miami, Fla., 1957-68; v.p. internat. Coulter Electronics Inc., Hialeah, Fla., 1968—; cons., dir. numerous cos. world-wide. Contbr. numerous articles in field. Mem. parish council St. John's Ch., Harpenden, Eng., 1980-83, local council Harpenden Village, 1980-82. With USN, 1942-45, PTO. Recipient Queen's Award to Industry Govt. U.K., 1970, 71. Mem. AAAS, Am. Inst. Biol. Scis., Am. Assn. Blood Banks, Am. Soc. Microbiology, N.Y. Acad. Scis., Am. Horticulture Soc., Royal Brit. Horticulture Soc. Republican. Episcopalian. Home: Harpenden House Rt 2 Box 71 Daleville VA 24083 Office: Coulter Electronics 600 W 20th St Hialeah FL 33031

MARTIN, ROBERT A., electronics company executive. Chmn., pres. NES, Inc., Carpentersville, Ill. Office: NES Inc 3003 Wakefield Dr Carpentersville IL 60110 *

MARTIN, ROBERT BRIDGES, insurance executive; b. Gary, Ind., Mar. 14, 1933; s. James Renick and Isabel (Lucas) M.; m. Nancy Jo Talley, June 11, 1955; children: Jeffrey L., Michael S., Scott D., Judith L. Anderson, Jill R. BA, Ohio Wesleyan U., 1955. Home office rep. Aetna Life Inc. Co., Chgo., 1959-61, Joliet, Ill., 1961-66; mgr. group div. Aetna Life Inc. Co., Oak Brook, Ill., 1966-76; sr. account exec. Aetna Life Inc. Co., Chgo., 1976-78, asst. mgr. group div., 1978-79; dir. group div. Aetna Life Inc. Co., Hartford, Conn., 1979-81, asst. v.p. div. employee benefits, 1981-82, v.p. div. employee benefits, 1982—. Treas. Nat. Fund for Med. Edn., Boston, 1984-87, bd. dirs., mem. exec. com., 1988—. 1st lt. USMC, 1955-59. Mem. Middlesex County (Conn.) C. of C. (bd. dirs. 1984-88).

MARTIN, SHIRLEY MARIE, insurance company executive; b. Tekamah, Nebr., Apr. 15, 1944; d. J. Clinton Martin and N. Marie (McKain) Grant; m. Michael P. Burnett, Apr. 19, 1963 (div. Oct. 1980); children: Todd Burnett, Tara Burnett. Student, Everett (Wash.) Jr. Coll., 1962-64; grad., Bell and Howell Sch. Acctg., Chgo., 1974. Fin. coordinator, collection mgr. The Continental Ins. Co., Seattle, 1963-70; audit reviewer The Home Ins. Co., Seattle, 1970-75, premium field auditor, 1975-80; owner Martin & Assocs., Bellingham, Wash., 1980—; author, pub. S.M. Martin Co., Bellingham, 1986—. Mem. Nat. Assn. Premium Auditors, Nat. Assn. Life Underwriters, Nat. Assn. Female Execs., Whatcom C. of C. Democrat. Roman Catholic. Home and Office: PO Box 5523 Bellingham WA 98227

MARTIN, THOMAS BROOKS, electrical engineer; b. Burlington, Iowa, June 23, 1935; s. Paul J. and Eleanor (Brooks) M.; B.E.E., U. Notre Dame, 1957; M.E.E., U. Pa., 1960, Ph.D., 1970. Group leader RCA Corp., Camden, N.J., 1957-70; chmn. bd. dirs., pres., dir. Threshold Tech. Inc., Delran, N.J., 1970-82, cons., 1982-83; pres. RFL Industries Inc., Boonton, N.J., 1983-86, cons. 1986—; cons. Bell Tel. Labs, 1982-84; mem. adv. council dept. elec. engring. and sci. U. Pa., 1977-85; adj. assoc. prof. dept. physiology Thomas Jefferson U., 1971-74. Douglas scholar, 1956-57. Mem. Tau Beta Pi. Roman Catholic. Address: 51 Stoney Brook Rd Montville NJ 07045

MARTIN, THOMAS DAVID, accountant, auditor; b. Coshocton, Ohio, Jan. 1, 1948; s. Joseph Edward and Eloise Francis (Carton) M.; m. Claressa Kay Jackson, Oct. 4, 1980; children: Michele, Heather. BS in Indsl. Mgmt., Kent State U., 1972. CPA, Tex. Auditor Roadway Express, Akron, Ohio, 1972-77; mgr. Consol. Freightways, Houston, 1977-79; cons. Martin Assocs., Houston, 1979-80; audit mgr. Enterprise Cos. Inc., Houston, 1980-84; audit dir. Intermedics Inc., Angleton, Tex., 1984—. Mem. Am. Inst. CPAs, Tex. Soc. CPAs, Christian Renew Club (Houston). Republican. Roman Catholic. Home: 12400 Brockglade Circle Apt 11 Houston TX 77099 Office: Intermedics Inc 4000 Technology Dr Angleton TX 77515

MARTIN, THOMAS RHODES, communications executive, writer; b. Memphis, July 10, 1953; s. Otis Knox and Joe Anne (Coggin) M.; m. Wanda C. Benderman, Dec. 1, 1984; children: Seth Knox, Cyrus Rhodes. BA, Vanderbilt U., 1975. Sales communication writer Schering-Plough Corp., Memphis, 1976-78; media devel. specialist Fed. Express Corp., Memphis, 1978-81, sr. media devel. specialist, 1981-82, mgr. of mgmt. communication, 1982-84, mng. dir. employee communication, 1984—. Contbg. editor Memphis mag., 1984—; contbr. numerous articles to mags. Bd. dirs. Big Bros./Big Sisters, Memphis, 1983-87, Memphis Oral Sch. for the Deaf, 1985—, Leadership Memphis, 1986-87. Recipient Journalism award Sigma Delta Chi, 1983. Mem. Internat. Assn. Bus. Communicators, Internat. TV Assn. Office: Fed Express Corp 3003 Airways Ste 1102 Memphis TN 38194

MARTIN, VINCENT JOSEPH, JR., stock broker; b. Trenton, N.J., July 24, 1945; s. Vincent J. Sr. and Arline Doris (Clay) M.; m. Mary Ellen Danchak, June 21, 1970; children: Vincent J. III, Thomas P., Daniel J. BBA magna cum laude, Seton Hall U., 1972. Cert. fin. planner. Mgr. N.Y. mcpl. bond dept. Janney Montgomery Scott Inc., N.Y.C., 1977-81; v.p., dir. retail sales Mabon-Nugent & Co., N.Y.C., 1981-83; v.p., resident mgr. Prudential Bache Securities, N.Y.C., 1983-85; v.p. sales Drexel Burnham Lambert, Paramus, N.J., 1985—. Mem. Vets. Adv. Bd. on Agt. Orange Settlement to U.S. Dist. Ct. Bklyn., 1985—. Served as lt. U.S. Army, 1968-69, Vietnam. Roman Catholic. Home: 41 Glendale Rd Summit NJ 07901 Office: Drexel Burnham Lambert E 140 Ridgewood Ave Mack Centre III Paramus NJ 07652

MARTIN, WAYNE MALLOTT, lawyer; b. Chgo., Jan. 9, 1950; s. Mallott Caldwell and Helen (Honkisz) M.; m. Jo Ann Giordano, Mar. 18, 1978; 1 child, Bradley. BA, Drake U., 1972; JD, DePaul U., 1977. Bar: Ill. 1978, U.S. Dist. Ct. (no. dist.) Ill. 1978. Dir. sales Inland Real Estate Corp., Chgo., 1977-78; asst. v.p. Inland Real Estate Corp., Oak Brook, Ill., 1979; v.p. Inland Real Estate Corp., 1980-81; pres. Inland Property Sales Corp., Palatine, Ill., 1981-85; sr. v.p. Inland Investment Corp., Oak Brook, 1985-86, Bramar Mortgage Corp., Long Grove, 1987—. Trustee, Chgo. Realtors Polit. Action Com. Mem. ABA, Ill. Bar Assn., Chgo. Bar Assn., Nat. Assn. Realtors, Ill. Assn. Realtors, Chgo. Bd. Realtors (bd. dirs. 1986-88), West Side Real Estate Bd. (bd. dirs. 1982-84, pres. 1984-88, gen. counsel 1988—), Chicagoland Assn. Real Estate Bds. (chmn. 1987-88). Home and Office: 1618 RFD Picardy Ct Long Grove IL 60047

MARTIN, WILBUR WESLEY, business broker; b. Chgo., Sept. 4, 1928; s. Emil Julius and Clara (Kreuger) M.; m. Patricia Elaine Daggett, Aug. 17, 1957; children: Suzanne, Cassandra. AA, Wilson Jr. Coll., 1947; student, Northwestern U., 1948; BS, Bradley U., 1949. Pres. Martin Cos., Chgo., 1949-60, Maco Corp. Import-Export, Chgo., 1960-68, Bus. Appraisal Co., Oak Brook, Ill., 1968—. Bd. dirs. Moraine Valley Community Coll., Palos Hills, Ill., 1972-78, chmn., 1977-78. Served with U.S. Army, 1950. Recipient cert. of merit, Ill. Community Coll. Trustee Assn., 1978. Mem. Pres.'s Assn. (bd. dirs. 1980-83), Assn. Corp. Growth, Warbirds of Am., Exptl. Aircraft Assn. Club: Chgo. Yacht. Home: 112 Old Creek Rd Palos Park IL 60464 Office: Bus Appraisal Co One Lincoln Ctr Ste 1090 Oakbrook Terrace IL 60181

MARTIN, WILFRED SAMUEL, management consultant; b. Adamsville, Pa., June 11, 1910; s. Albert W. and Elizabeth (Porter) M.; B.S., Iowa State U., 1930; M.S., U. Cin., 1938; m. Elizabeth Myers, July 9, 1938; children—Peter, Judith (Mrs. Peter Kleinman), Nancy (Mrs. Richard Foss), Paula (Mrs. Dale Birdsell). Chem. engr. process devel. dept. Procter & Gamble Co., Cin., 1930-50, mgr. drug products mfg., 1950-51, asso. dir. chem. div., 1952-53, dir. product devel., soap products div., 1953-63, mgr. mfg. and products devel. Food Products div., 1963-71, sr. dir. research and devel., 1971-75; mgmt. cons., 1975—. Mem. Wyoming (Ohio) Bd. Edn., 1961-69, pres., 1965-68. Bd. dirs. Indsl. Research Inst., 1964-68, v.p., 1968-69, pres., 1970-71; chmn. trustee Ohio Presbyn. Homes, Columbus, Ohio, 1959-69, 73-77; vice chmn. bd. trustees Pikeville (Ky.) Coll., 1973-76, 80-86, trustee emeritus, 1986—, chmn. bd. trustees, 1976-78, 83-84, mem., 1980-84. Adv. council Clarkson Coll., Potsdam, N.Y., 1975-81. Fellow AAAS, Am. Inst. of Chemists; mem. Am. Chem. Soc., Am. Inst. Chem. Engrs., Soc. Chem. Industry, Am. Oil Chemist Soc., Engring. Soc. Cin. (dir. 1972-75), N.Y. Acad. Scis., Am. Mgmt. Assn. (research devel. council 1974-81), Soc. Research Adminstrs. Club: Wyoming Golf (Cin.). Home: 504 Hickory Hill Ln Cincinnati OH 45215

MARTIN, WILLIAM FLYNN, federal agency administrator; b. Tulsa, Oct. 4, 1950; s. Wilfred Wright and Ailene (Flynn) M.; m. Jill Wheaton, Sept. 22, 1954; children: Nicholas Carl, Christopher Flynn. BS, U. Pa., 1972; MS, MIT, 1974. Program officer MIT Energy Lab., Cambridge, Mass., 1974-77; spl. asst. to exec. dir. Internat. Energy Agy., Paris, 1977-81; spl. asst. to undersec. of state Dept. State, Washington, 1981-82; dir. internat. econ. affairs Nat. Security Council, Washington, 1982-83, exec. sec., 1985-86; spl. asst. to Pres. The White House, Washington, 1983-85; dep. sec. Dept. Energy, Washington, 1986—. Mem. Council on Fgn. Relations. Republican. Office: Dept Energy 1000 Independence Ave SW Washington DC 20585

MARTIN, WILLIAM HARRY, financial planner; b. Phila., Dec. 8, 1955; s. Abraham William and Elizabeth (Platt) M.; m. Amy Sue Martin, June 12, 1983; children: Scott Abraham, Christian William. BS in Fin., Pa. State U., 1977. CLU, chartered fin. cons., cert. fin. planner. Assoc. mgr. Wienken & Assocs., State College, Pa., 1977—. Named to Pres. Club, nat. assoc. Squad Club Mut. Benefit Life, Newark, 1983, 84, 85, 86, 87. Mem. Inst. Cert. Fin. Planners, Soc. CLUs, Million Dollar Roundtable, Center Counties Assn. Life Underwriters, Center Counties Cert. Fin. Planners, Elks. Republican. Methodist. Office: Wienken & Assocs 3939 S Atherton State College PA 16801

MARTIN, WILLIAM RAYMOND, financial planner; b. Phila., Oct. 16, 1939; s. Clyde Davis and Mary Anna (Coates) M.; m. Michaela Smink, Sept. 8, 1962 (div. 1969); 1 child, James; m. Margaret Scouten, Oct. 16, 1970 (div. 1983); children: Mary Frances, Susanna; m. Joan Friedman Kennedy, Jan. 29, 1988. BSME, Lehigh U., 1960; MBA, U. Pa., 1973. Mem. engring. staff Pa. R.R., 1960-65; asst. gen. mgr. Excelsior Truck Leasing, Phila., 1965-71; sr. analyst Assn. Am. R.R.s, Washington, 1973-76, mgr. engring. econ., 1976-78; mgr. fin. analysis So. Ry., Washington, 1978-83; dir. fin. planning Norfolk So. Corp., Va., 1984—. Contbr. articles to profl. jours. Bd. dirs. The Williams Sch., Norfolk, 1988—. Mem. Soc. Automotive Engrs., ASME. Home: 2605 Ridley Pl Virginia Beach VA 23454 Office: Norfolk So Corp Three Commercial Pl Norfolk VA 23510

MARTIN, WILLIAM WOODROW, tractor company executive; b. Ottawa, Kans., June 19, 1924; s. Charles Henry and Mary Elizabeth (Koontz) M.; BS in Indsl. Mgmt., U. Kans., 1949; m. Betty Louise Chubb, Dec. 20, 1947; children: Gregory Jennings, Janet Louise, Judith Ellen. Propr., W.W. Martin Constrn. Co., Fort Scott, Kans., 1946-49; chmn. bd. Martin Tractor Co., Inc., Topeka, 1957—; chmn. bd. Martin Co. Inc., Topeka, 1967—; dir. Bank IV, Topeka, Southwestern Bell Corp., Stormont-Vail Health Svcs., Oread Cabs, Inc.; Vice chmn. Topeka Urban Renewal Agy., 1960-64; chmn. Gov.'s Task Force on Effective Mgmt., Hwy. Task Force, 1987. Past precinct committeeman Rep. Party, Topeka; past mem. exec. com. Kans. Rep. Com.; chmn. 2d Congressional Rep. Dist. Exec. bd. Kans. U. Sch. Bus.; exec. com. Kans. U. Endowment Assn.; bd. dirs. Bipartisan Indsl. Polit. Action com.; trustee Kans. U. Endowment Assn., also mem. exec. com; bd. govs. Kans U. Alumni Center Bldg.; mem. Kans. Hwy. Commn., 1988—. With Q.C., AUS, 1943-46; PTO. Mem. Kans. Assn. Commerce and Industry (past chmn. bd., pres., dir.), Greater Topeka C. of C. (past pres.), Associated Industries Kans. (pres. 1968-70), Kans. U. Alumni Assn. (past pres., bd. dirs.), Phi Delta Theta, Masons, Shriners, Rotary (past pres. Topeka). Methodist (trustee 1971-76). Home: 2338 Mayfair Pl Topeka KS 66611 Office: 1737 SW 42d St Box 1698 Topeka KS 66601

MARTINDALE, LANNY ROBERT, bank executive; b. Woodville, Tex., Mar. 25, 1960; s. R.L. Martindale. BS, Howard Payne U., 1983; MBA, Tex. A&M U., 1985. Credit analyst First Nat. Bank, Killeen, Tex., 1986-87, asst. v.p. comml. lending, 1987—; affiliate instr. Am. Tech. U., Killeen, 1987—; counselor Small Bus. Devel. Ctr., 1988. Nat. Merit scholar, 1978-82. Mem. Robert Morris Assocs., Killeen C. of C., Assn. Former Students Tex. A&M U., Exch. Club, Masons (32d degree), Pi Gamma Mu. Republican. Baptist. Office: First Nat Bank 507 Gray St Killeen TX 76540

MARTINEZ, BETTY ELNORA, chemical company executive; b. Oklahoma City, Jan. 7, 1947; d. Jim and Jewell Frances Smith; B.S., Oklahoma City U., 1974, M.B.A., 1975; divorced. Pvt. booking agt. and bus. mgr. local rock and roll bands, Okla., Colo., 1960-67; with Kerr McGee Corp., Oklahoma City, 1965-81, acct., 1974-76, solvent sales rep., from 1975, assoc. sales rep. until 1981; petrochems. sales rep. No. Petrochem. Co., Ramsey, N.J., 1981-85; Southern area sales rep. AC Polyethylene Allied/Signal Corp., Morristown, N.J., 1985—. Del. Okla. Democratic Conv., 1972; vol. Grady Hosp., Atlanta, Ga. Rape Crisis Ctr. Mem. M.B.A. Club Oklahoma City U. (pres. 1975), ACLU, Soc. Plastic Engrs. (bd. dirs. 1987-88), Toastmasters (adminstrv. v.p., 1988). Home and Office: PO Box 70426 Marietta GA 30007

MARTINEZ, LUIS A., import-export company executive; b. Colombia, S.Am., Apr. 25, 1955; s. Luis H. and Celina (Llamas) de Martinez; A.A., Queensborough Community Coll., 1978; B.A., Queens Coll., 1981. Pres. Onyx Enterprises, Inc., N.Y.C., 1977—; v.p. Trade N Investments, Ltd., N.Y.C., 1981—; engaged in internat. commodities and financing. Clubs: World Trade, Masons, KP. Office: 35-15 190th St 1st Fl Bayside NY 11358

MARTINEZ, MARIA ELENA, accountant; b. Laredo, Tex., Aug. 11, 1935; d. Blas and Elvira (Gonzalez) M. AA, Laredo Jr. Coll., 1955. Credit mgr. Hachar's, Inc., Laredo, 1955-58; teletype setter Laredo Morning Times, 1959-60; sec. to v.p. DeLlano's Mexican Products Co., Laredo, 1960-83; acct. Wilkinson Bros. Iron and Metal, Laredo, 1983-86; owner, acct. Martinez Tax and Bookkeeping Service, Laredo, 1986—; owner, pres. A Touch of Green garden ctr. Mem. Laredo Women's Bowling Assn. (pres. 1978-79), Tex. Assn. Pub. Advisors (treas. 1987-88). Republican. Roman Catholic. Home and Office: 1606 Garfield St Laredo TX 78040

MARTINI, EMIL P., JR., wholesale pharmaceutical distribution company executive; b. Teaneck, N.J., 1928. Grad., Purdue U., 1950. With Bergen Brunswig Corp., Los Angeles, 1952—, now chmn., chief exec. officer; pres., mgr. Bergen Drug Co. div., Los Angeles, 1956-69, corp. pres., chief exec. officer, from 1969, also dir.; dir. Bro-Dart Industries. Office: Commtron Corp 1501 50th St West Des Moines IA 50265 also: Bergen Brunswig Corp 4000 Metropolitan Dr Orange CA 92668 *

MARTINI, ROBERT E., wholesale pharmaceutical and electronic products company executive; b. Hackensack, N.J., 1932. B.S., Ohio State U., 1954. With Bergen Brunswig Corp., Orange, Calif., 1956—, v.p., 1962-69, exec. v.p., 1969-81, pres., chief operating officer, dir., 1981—, now chmn. exec. com., pres., dir.; also chmn., dir. Bergen Brunswig Drug Co., Orange, Calif. Served to capt. USAF, 1954. Office: Bergen Brunswig Corp 4000 Metropolitan Dr Orange CA 92668 *

MARTINO, DENNIS, finanacial executive; b. Newark, Jan. 7, 1952; s. Orlando and Louise (Sagarese) M.; m. Joann Smith; children: Ryan, Kristin. BBA, Pace U., 1974. Cert. fin. planner. Regional buyer Kinney Shoe Corp., N.Y.C., 1972-78; pres. Foursome Corp., Clearwater, Fla., 1978-80; v.p. investments Prudential-Bache Securities, Clearwater, 1980—. Recipient Portfolio Mgr. Yr. award Prudential Bache Securities, 1987. Mem. Internat. Assn. Fin. Planners. Republican. Roman Catholic. Lodge: Optimists. Office: Prudential Bache Securities 2536 Countryside Blvd Ste 110 Palm Harbor FL 33563

MARTINO, JAMES BOYD, lingerie manufacturing executive; b. Denton, Tex., Mar. 28, 1951; s. Frank Nilson and Betty Jean (Newman) M.; m. Jennie Marie Barron, Aug. 18, 1973; children: Kimberly, Karina, Emily, Lauren, Benjamin. BS in Fin., Brigham Young U., 1974. Purchasing agt. Russell-Newman, Denton, 1974-77, sec., treas., 1977-81, v.p., treas., 1981-86, exec. v.p., 1986—; dir. Martino Realty, Denton, Tex., 1975-87, 5M & R Ranch, Aubrey, Tex., 1975-87. Dir. YMCA, Denton, United Way, Denton, Big Bros./Big Sisters Am., Denton, Denton C. of C.; chmn. John Tower for Senate campaign, Denton, 1978, Occupational Tech. Adv. Comm., Denton, 1984. Mem. Am. Apparel Mfgs. Assn. (dir. intimate apparel council 1985-87), Beta Gamma Sigma, Phi Beta Kappa. Republican. Mormon. Lodge: Rotary (local dir. 1978-87).

MARTINO, MICHAEL, computer network consultant; b. Bklyn., Nov. 19, 1958; s. Michael Amadeo and Stella Mary M. Student, Fla. State U., 1980-82. Mgr. tech. service Data Access Corp., Miami, Fla., 1982-84; sr. database cons. Cache Data Products, Inc., St. Louis, 1984-86; LAN cons. Novell, Inc., St. Louis, 1986—; database cons. Databridge, St. Louis, 1984-87; presenter Auburn/Interact Conf., Atlanta, 1986—. Mem. Oracle Users Group, Am. Mgmt. Assn. Office: Novell 1938 Innerbelt Bus Ctr Saint Louis MO 63130

MARTINO, ROCCO LEONARD, data processing executive; b. Toronto, Ont., Can., June 25, 1929; s. Domenic and Josephine (DiGiulio) M.; BSc, U. Toronto, 1951, MA, 1952; PhD, Inst. Aerospace Studies, 1955; m. Barbara L. D'lorio, Sept. 2, 1961; children: Peter Domenic, Joseph Alfred, Paul Gerard, John Francis. Dir., Univac Computing Svc. Ctr., Toronto, 1956-59; pres. Mauchly Assos. Can. Ltd., Toronto, 1959-62, v.p. Mauchly Assos., Inc., Ft. Washington, Pa., 1959-61; mgr. advanced systems Olin Mathieson Chem. Corp., N.Y.C., 1962-64; dir. advanced computer systems Booz, Allen & Hamilton, N.Y.C., 1965-70; pres., chmn. bd. Info. Industries, Inc. and subs.'s, Wayne, Pa., 1965-70; chmn. bd., chief exec. officer XRT, Inc., Malvern, Pa., 1970—; chmn. bd. MBF Computer Ctr. for Handicapped Children; mem. bd. St. Joseph's U., Phila., Gregorian U. Found., N.Y.; mem. exec. com. Gregorian U., N.Y. and Rome, 1987—, bd. dirs. 1984—, pontifical circle, 1985—, active, 1982—; asso. prof. math. U. Waterloo, 1959-62, prof. engring., dir. Inst. Systems and Mgmt. Engring., 1964-65; adj. asso. prof. N.Y. U., 1963-64, adj. prof. math., 1964-65, 66; lectr. on computers mgmt.; chmn. Gov. Ill. Task Force, 1970-71, Ill. Bd. Higher Edn. Task Force, 1971-72, Computer-Use Task Force FCC, 1972-73, Computer-Use Planning Task Force U.S. Postal Svc., 1973-74. Trustee Gregorian Found., N.Y.C. and Rome, 1984—; bd. govs. St. Joseph's U. Sch. Bus., 1983—. Mem. Assn. Computing Machinery, Ops. Rsch. Soc. Am., Porfl. Engrs. Ont., Computing Soc. Can., ITEST (bd. dirs.), K.C., Lions, Overbrook Golf and Country Club, Yacht of Sea Isle City Club (commodore 1973-74, trustee 1975-86, chmn. 1983-86), Commodores Club, S. Jerry Yacht Racing Club (commodore 1979-81, sec. 1981-83, officer 1983—), Papal Knight, Equestrian Order Holy Sepulchre (knight 1986), Order of Malta, Knights of Malta (knight 1988). Author books, most recent being: Resources Management, 1968; Dynamic Costing, 1968; Project Management, 1968; Information Management: The Dynamics of MIS, 1968; MIS-Management Information Systems, 1969; Decision Patterns, 1969; Methodology of MIS, 1969; Personnel Information Systems, 1969; Integrated Manufacturing Systems, 1972; APG-Virtual Application Systems, 1981; contbr. numerous articles on mgmt., computers and planning in profl. publs.; designer, developer Application Program Generator computer system, 1974-75; developer cash mgmt. and on-line internat. trading systems, 1984. Home: 512 Watch Hill Rd Villanova PA 19085 Office: 989 Old Eagle Sch Rd Ste 806 Wayne PA 19087

MARTINSON, KENNETH NEIL, investment management executive; b. Puyallup, Wash., Mar. 5, 1952; s. R. Del and Ruth Marie (Brackman) M.; m. Marilyn Evon Michalsen, Sept. 7, 1973 (div. 1979); m. Jace Charlesworth, Mar. 28, 1980. BBA, Seattle Pacific U., 1974. CPA, Alaska. Staff acct. Ernst & Ernst, Anchorage, 1974-78; audit supr. Ernst & Whinney Internat., Anchorage, 1978-80; corp. controller Alaska Brick Group of Cos., Anchorage, 1980-82; ind. fin. and acct. cons. Anchorage, 1982; v.p. fin. Restaurants N.W., Inc., Anchorage, 1983-84; account exec. Integrated Resources Equity Corp., N.Y.C., Anchorage, 1984-87, mmng. exec., exec. v.p., 1987—; chief operating officer Fin. Resources Group, also bd. dirs.; bd. dirs. Alaska Party Sales, Inc., Anchorage, Frontier Investment Corp., Anchorage, Al-Cal Investment Co., Anchorage. State treas. Reagan-Bush Re-election Com., 1984. Mem. NASD, Am. Soc. CPAs, Downtown Club, Rotary. Republican. Lutheran. Home: 2231 Sue's Way Anchorage AK 99516 Office: Fin Resources Group 1600 A St Ste 300 Anchorage AK 99501

MARTUCCI, GLORIA MARTHA, educator, former insurance agent; b. Bronx, N.Y., Dec. 19, 1934; d. Thomas Angelo and Martha Marie (De Marco) M.; BA, Fla. State U., 1960; MS, SUNY at New Paltz, 1973; cert. of mgmt. Mercy Coll., Yorktown Heights, N.Y., 1979. Tchr. French and history, Bunnell, Fla., 1960-62, Dept. of Army, Okinawa, 1962-63, U.S. Air Force, Itazuke, Japan, 1963-64; tchr. langs. Yorktown Jr. High Sch., Yorktown Heights, N.Y., 1965; tchr. French and bus. Mahopac (N.Y.) Sr. High Sch., 1966-78, Mahopac Jr. High Sch., 1979-85; ins. agt. Mut. of Omaha, Poughkeepsie, N.Y., 1985-87. Pinellas County (Fla.) teaching scholar, 1958-60. Mem. Am. Assn. Tchrs. French, N.Y. State Assn. Fgn. Lang. Tchrs., Nat. Bus. Edn. Assn., Bus. Tchrs. Assn. N.Y. Republican.

Roman Catholic. Club: Single Profls. Westchester (2d v.p. 1978-79). Home: 4381 E Orchard Dr Tucson AZ 85712

MARUVADA, RAJESWARA RAO, accountant; b. Bhimuni Patnam, Andhra Pradesh, India, Sept. 1, 1945; came to U.S., 1981; s. Rama Krishnamma and Meenakshi (Karra) M.; m. Vindhyavasini Nookala, Dec. 14, 1972; 1 child, Prabhakar. BS in Acctg., G.M. Coll., 1968; MBA in Fin., St. Joseph's U., Phila., 1985. CPA, Pa. Audit mgr. A.F. Ferguson & Co., New Delhi, 1973-79; br. acct. Parry & Co. Ltd., New Delhi, 1979-81; payroll supr. ARA Svcs., Inc., Phila., 1981-84, fin. analyst, 1984-85, adminstr. fin. reporting, 1985—. Mem. AICPA, Pa. Inst. CPA's, Nat. Assn. Accts. Home: 108 E Harvard Ave Somerdale NJ 08083 Office: ARA Svcs Inc 1101 Market St Philadelphia PA 19107

MARVIN, DANIEL EZRA, JR., bank executive; b. East Stroudsburg, Pa., Apr. 25, 1938; s. Daniel E. Marvin Sr. and Hazel (Meitzler) Marvin Doll; m. Maxine James, June 15, 1958; children: Brian, Laurie, Amy. Student, Susquehanna U., 1956-58; BS in Edn., E. Stroudsburg State Coll., 1960; MS in Zoology, Ohio U., 1962; PhD in Physiology, Va. Poly. Inst., 1966; DLitt (hon.), Hanyang U., Seoul, Republic of Korea, 1981. Asst. prof. biology Radford (Va.) Coll., 1962-67, prof., dean div. natural scis., 1967-68, v.p. acad. affairs, 1968-70, acting pres., 1968-69; assoc. dir., then dir. Va. State Council on Higher Edn., Radford, 1970-77; pres. Eastern Ill. U., Charleston, 1977-83, First Nat. Bank, Mattoon, Ill., 1983—, First Mid-Ill. Bancshares, Inc., Mattoon, 1983—; bd. dirs. Ill. Consol. Telephone Co., Appalachia Ednl. Lab., Cen. Va. Ednl. TV Corp., Nat. Ctr. Higher Edn. Mgmt. Systems, Resource Ctr. Planned Change at State Colls. and Univs.; chmn. State Policy Bd. Automated Data Processing in Higher Edn., Nat. Adv. Council on Extension and Continuing Edn.; past pres. Gateway Collegiate Athletic Conf.; mem. U.S. del. univ. pres. to Poland, 1980, 82. Mem. editorial bd. Community/Jr. Coll. Research Quar.; contbr. to profl. jours.; subject of mag. interviews. Mem. Gov.'s Manpower Planning Council, State of Va.; bd. dirs. Sarah Bush Lincoln Health Ctr.; pres. East Cen. Ill. Devel. Corp., 1985-88; bd. dirs. Lakeland Coll. Found. Recipient Strategic Planning of Higher Edn. award, Ministry Edn., Republic of China, 1976, 81; grantee NSF, Ford Found. Mem. Ill. Ednl. Consortium (bd. dirs.), Am. Council Edn., Am. Assn. State Colls. and Univs., Ill. Bankers Assn. (bd. dirs.), Am. Bankers Assn., Community Bankers Council and Adv. Bd., Sigma Xi. Republican. Presbyterian. Home: 12 Saint Andrews Pl Mattoon IL 61938

MARVIN, EARL, lawyer; b. N.Y.C., Mar. 17, 1918; s. Benjamin and Rose Lillian (Salmow) M.; m. Helaine F. Kaplan, Nov. 2, 1941 (div. Jan. 1962); children: Peter F. Benjamin A., Elizabeth C.; m. Eleanor Dreyfus, June 14, 1964. AB, Harvard U., 1938, LLB, 1941, JD, 1967. Bar: Mass. 1941, N.Y. 1942. Assoc. Goldwater & Flynn, N.Y.C., 1946-48; pvt. practice N.Y.C., 1948—; of counsel Goldstein, Schrank, Segelstein & Shays, N.Y.C., 1970—; bd. dirs. Superior Surg. Mfg. Co. Inc., Seminole, Fla., Bleyer Industries Inc., Lynbrook, N.Y. Mem. New York County Lawyers Assn., Harvard Club (N.Y.C.), Inwood Country Club (L.I., N.Y., bd. govs. 1971-73), Countryside Country Club (Clearwater, Fla.). Home: 1660 Gulf Blvd Apt 1001 Clearwater FL 34630 Office: Superior Surg Mfg Co Inc Seminole Blvd PO Box 4002 Seminole FL 34642-0002

MARZULLO, JOHN PHILIP, financing company executive; b. Bklyn., Dec. 18, 1945; s. Gaetano Philip and Florence Nancy (Guastella) M.; m. Phyllis Mary LoCicero, July 4, 1968; children: Dina, Jennifer, David and Jonathan (twins). BS, St. John's U., Jamaica, N.Y., 1967, JD, 1969. Pres., chmn. bd. Dalin Pharms., Inc., Farmingdale, N.Y., 1986-89; pres., chmn. bd. dirs. Sun Sci. Group Inc., Clearwater, Fla., 1989—; chmn. bd. dirs. Whitney Group Inc., Clearwater, Chemi-Tech Labs. Inc., Farmingdale. Dem. committeeman, Nassau County, N.Y., 1976; charter mem. Rep. Presdl. Task Force, Washington. Recipient Cert. of Merit, Rep. Presdl. Task Force, 1986. Mem. Internat. Soc. Pharm. Engrs., Am. Judicature Soc., Am. Chem. Soc. Home: 13882 Whisperwood Dr Clearwater FL 34622 Office: Sun Sci Group Inc 1393 Missouri Ave S Clearwater FL 34616

MASBRUCH, RANDAL JOHN, financial executive; b. Platteville, Wis., Jan. 13, 1954; s. Robert Louis and Aletha Jane (Dearth) M.; m. Laurie Jaye Meltz, April 22, 1978; children: Jeffrey Robert, Jody Lynne, Jennifer Leigh. BS in Acctg., U. Wis., Platteville, 1976; MBA, Lewis U., 1980. CPA, Wis., Ill. Internal auditor Inryco, Inc., Milw., 1976-77, supr. acctg., 1977; supr. acctg. Inryco, Inc., Bedford Park, Ill., 1977-80, Melrose Park, Ill., 1980-81; mgr. acctg. Inryco, Inc., Melrose Park, 1981-82; div. controller Inryco, Inc., Milw., 1982-84; corp. controller Inryco, Inc., Bannockburn, Ill., 1984-88; v.p. fin. Peterson/Puritan, Inc., Danville, Ill., 1988—. Treas. Risen Savior Luth. Ch., Indian Creek, Ill., 1985-88. Mem. Wis. Inst. CPAs. Home: 3008 Golf Terr Danville IL 61832 Office: Peterson/Puritan Inc 1 W Hegler Ln Danville IL 61832

MASCAVAGE, JOSEPH PETER, sales executive; b. Allentown, Pa., July 7, 1956; s. John Joseph and Florence M.; m. Jo Ellen Huhnke, Aug. 8, 1981; children: Lauren Christine, Gregory Joseph. BS in Environ. Resource Mgmt., Pa. State U., 1978. Tech. sales rep. Am. Cyanamid Co., Los Angeles, 1978-82; supr. utilites application Am. Cyanamid Co., Azusa, Calif., 1982-83; asst. to mktg. mgr. Am. Cyanamid Co., Wayne, N.J., 1983; dist. sales mgr. Am. Cyanamid Co., Houston, 1984-86; mgr. sales tng. Am. Cyanamid Co., Wayne and Charlotte, N.C., 1986—. Author, editor Chem. Group Sales Manual, 1986. Mem. Am. Soc. for Tng. and Devel., N.J. Sales Tng. Assn. Office: Am Cyanamid Co 8309 Wilkinson Blvd Charlotte NC 28210

MASI, DALE A., research company executive, social work educator; b. N.Y.C.; d. Alphonse E. and Vera Avella; children: Eric, Renee, Robin. B.S., Coll. Mt. St. Vincent, 1951; M.S.W., U. Ill., 1957; D.S.W., Cath. U., 1965. Project dir. occupational substance abuse program, asso. prof. Boston Coll. Grad. Sch. Social Work, 1972-79; dir. Office Employer Counseling Service, Dept. Health and Human Services, Washington, 1979-84; pres. Masi Research Cons., Inc.,, 1984—; prof. U. Md. Grad. Sch. Social Work, 1980—; adj. prof. U. Md. Coll. Bus. and Mgmt., 1980—; lectr. Sch. Social Services, Ipswich, Eng., 1970-72; cons. NIMH, IBM, White House, WHO, Bechtel Corp., other orgns. in pub. and pvt. sector; bd. advisors Employee Assistance mag. and Nat. Security Inst. Author: Human Services in Industry, Organizing for Women, Designing Employee Assistance Programs, Drug Free Workplace; mem. edit. bd. Testing in the Law; contbr. numerous articles to profl. jours. Fulbright fellow, 1969-70; AAUW postdoctoral fellow; NIMH fellow, 1962-64; recipient award Employee Assistance Program Digest; named to Employee Assistance Program Hall of Fame. Mem. Nat. Assn. Social Workers, Acad. Cert. Social Workers, (ALMACA) Assn. Labor Mgmt. Adminstrs. and Cons. on Alcoholism (nat. individual achievement award 1983), AAUW. Democrat. Roman Catholic. Office: Watergate 180 600 New Hampshire Ave NW Washington DC 20037

MASI, JANE VIRGINIA, marketing and sales consultant; b. N.Y.C., June 6, 1947; d. Vincent Joseph and Virginia Marie (Beddow) Masi; m. Charles Walter Friedman, Feb. 14, 1976. BA in Communications and Psychology, Mercy Coll., N.Y., 1969; MA, New Sch. Social Research, 1979, now PhD candidate. Asst. sales mgr. Chevron Chem., N.Y.C., 1969-71; writer, 1973-75; ptnr. Masi-D'Angelo Constrn. and Devel. Assocs., N.Y.C., 1979-83; pres., founder Beddow Mills Inc., N.Y.C., 1982-85, Beddow Mfg. Ind., 1983-85; co-pres. TRS Mktg. Inc., N.Y.C., 1985—; founder Energy Works, 1985, Did You Know, 1989, Range Burgers, 1989, Terramor, 1989; founder, dir. TRS Inc. Profl. Suite, 1986—. Author 38 novellas. N.Y. Regents scholar, 1965-69. Mem., Trans-Species Unltd., Soc. Ethical Treatment of Animals. Avocations: woodworking, carpentry, advocating animal rights, design psychology. Office: TRS Mktg Inc 7 E 30th St New York NY 10016

MASKALUNAS, RONALD, accounting company executive; b. Chgo., Dec. 28, 1940; s. Stanley and Bernice (Schimalus) M.; m. Georgia D'Angela, Oct. 30, 1966; children: Mark A., Scott, Eric. BS, Purdue U., 1963; MBA, U. Chgo., 1969. CPA. Mgr. prodn. Wester Electric, Chgo., 1963-69; mem. staff then mgr. Coopers & Lybrand, Chgo., 1969-76, ptnr., 1976-85, ptnr.-in-charge gen. practice, 1985—. Mem. Civic Fedn. Adv. Com., Chgo., 1978, adv. bd. Sch. Pub. Mgmt. Northwestern U., Evanston, Ill., 1979; bd. govs. Sch. Art Inst., Chgo., 1985—. Presdl. Interchange Program fellow, Washington, 1973. Mem. AICPA, Mcpl. Fin. Officers Assn., Ill. Soc. Cert. Pub. Accts., Bob O'Link Club (Highland Park, Ill.), River Club (bd. govs. Chgo. chpt.), Rolling Green Country Club (Arlington Heights, Ill.), Lions (past pres. Prospect Heights, Ill. club). Office: Coopers & Lybrand 203 N LaSalle St Chicago IL 60601

MASKER, GERALD SEELY, computer company executive; b. Mt. Kisco, Apr. 20, 1944; s. Seely Ora and Marjorie Francis (Baker) M.; m. Natalie Pollack, June 10, 1968; 1 child, Sally Ann. AAS in Elec. Tech., Westchester Community Coll., 1964; BSEE, SUNY, Buffalo, 1968; MSEE, SUNY, 1971. Systems engr. Comptek Rsch., Inc., Buffalo, 1969-73, asst. mgr. systems engring., 1973-76, prin. systems engr., 1976-80, mgr. rsch. and devel., 1980-82; v.p. rsch. and devel. Barrister Info. Systems Corp., Buffalo, 1982—. Mem. Nat. Benchrest Shooters Assn. (world record 1984), Internat. Benchrest Shooters Assn. (Nat. Champion 1985, 86, 87), Am. Radio Relay League, Am. Contract Bridge League. Presbyterian. Home: 54 Woodshire S Getzville NY 14068 Office: Barrister Info Systems Corp 45 Oak St Buffalo NY 14203

MASLYK, CHERI ANN, marketing professional, consultant; b. Fort Wayne, Ind., Dec. 25, 1949; d. Van Watt Gardner and Margaret Joann (Little) Moore; m. Brian Joseph Maslyk, June 18, 1971. Cert. of Airline Op., Atlantic Sch., Kansas City, Mo., 1968; student, U. Ky., 1969, Ind. Inst. Tech., 1982-88. Owner Concept Advt. and Mktg., Kalamazoo, 1975-80; major accounts mgr., new product devel. mgr. Fort Wayne Newspapers, 1980-85; dist. mgr. Modern Metals, Chgo., 1985-87; dir. product devel. Rho Lyn Engring., Detroit, 1985; exec. dir. Small Bus. Devel. Ctr., Fort Wayne, 1987; mem. adv. bd. Indiana/Purdue U. Mktg. Club, 1987-88, Young Entrepreneurs Success Program. Event organizer Run Jane Run, 1983-84; fund raiser United Way, 1984, Fort Wayne Ballet, 1988; mem. Leadership Ft. Wayne; mem. Citizens Adv. Com., City Ft. Wayne, 1988—. Recipient Cert. of Recognition Crossroads Children's Home, Cert. Nat. Safety Council, 1988, Cert. of Profl. Contbn. Delta Sigma Pi. Mem. Women's Bur., Small Bus. Inst. Dirs. Assn., Friends of the Urban League, Women's Bus. Owner's Assn. (speaker 1988), Am. Cancer Soc. Republican. Roman Catholic. Home: 2330 Springmill Rd Fort Wayne IN 46825 Office: Small Business Devel Ctr 1830 Wayne Trace Fort Wayne IN 46803

MASON, CRAIG WATSON, corporate planning executive; b. Stamford, Conn., June 4, 1954; s. Harry Leeds and Alice Henrietta (Watson) M.; m. Lisa Ellen Boe, Aug. 30, 1980; 1 child, Katherine Anne. BA in English, Yale U., 1976. Brand asst. Procter & Gamble Co., Cin., 1976-77, sales trainee, St. Louis, 1977, asst. brand mgr., Cin., 1978-79, Instant Folger's brand mgr., 1979-82, Biz and Mr. Clean brand mgr., 1982-83; dir. brand mgmt. Beecham Products USA, Pitts., 1983-87, dir. bus. planning, 1987-88, dir. bus. and logistics planning, 1988—. Editor: The Insiders Guide to the Colleges, 1975; contbr. articles to profl. jours. Class agt. Yale Alumni Fund, 1976—; trustee Peters Twp. (Pa.) Pub. Library, 1986—. Republican. Episcopalian. Club: Yale of N.Y.C. Avocations: photography; personal computers. Home: 230 King Richard Dr McMurray PA 15317 Office: Beecham Products USA 100 Beecham Dr Pittsburgh PA 15205

MASON, DAVID ERNEST, management consultant, author, clergyman; b. Natchitoches, La., Jan. 3, 1928; s. Charles Culberson and Marjorie (O'Bannon) M.; m. Betty D. Oxford, Aug. 11, 1950 (div.); m. Alberta Martin, July 2, 1964; children: David Ernest, Paul Alexander; stepchildren: Hobart, Jeffrey, William, Suzanne. BA, La. State U., 1949; BD, So. Bapt. Theol. Sem., 1952, ThM, 1952; DD (hon.), U. Corpus Christi, 1958; MA in Journalism, Syracuse U., 1964, PhD in Communications, 1968. Ordained to ministry Bapt. Ch., 1950. Student dir. Bapt. Student Union La. Poly. Inst., 1950; asst. to pastor 2d Ponce de Leon Ch., Atlanta, 1952-53; pastor 1st Ch., Jefferson, Ga., 1953-55, Jonesboro, La., 1955-60, Alice, Tex., 1960-62; assoc. dir. Laubach Literacy, Inc., Syracuse, 1963-66, exec. dir., 1967-68; dir. Manpower Ednl. Corp., N.Y.C., 1968-69; chmn. bd. Supportive Services, Inc., N.Y.C., 1969-74; also chmn. bd. Westchester Learning Ctr., 1971-74, N.Y. Jobs Consortium, Inc., 1971-74; cons. to Internat. Paper Co., Am. Cyanamid, U.S. Industries, Hertz, Inc., Indian Head Corp., Prudential Life Ins. Co., Nat. Bank N.Am., others. Author: Now Then, 1957, The Charley Matthews Story, 1958, Eight Steps Toward Maturity, 1962, The Vacant Hearted, 1963, Apostle to the Illiterates, 1965, Frank C. Laubach, Teacher of Millions, 1967, Reaching The Silent Billion, 1967, The Compulsive Christian, 1968, Voluntary Nonprofit Enterprise Management, 1984; numerous articles. Mem. L.I. Econ. Devel. Corp., 1969-72; mem. Mayor's Com. on Jobs for Vets., 1972-87, New Orleans Civic Council, 1972-87, New Orleans Human Relations Commn., Orleans Parish Prison Bd., 1972-87, Legal Aid Bur. Chmn. home missions com. La. Bapt. Conv., 1957; chmn. New Orleans White Collar Crime Com., 1979; mem. Sch. Bd. Sch. Fin. Com., 1979; pres. Greater New Orleans Fedn. Chs., 1972-87; La. chmn. James P. Boyce Library Fund, 1957-59; trustee So. Bapt. Theol. Sem., 1959-60; bd. dirs. Am. Council of Vol. Agys. for Fgn. Service, 1967-68, Koinoia Found., Balt., 1967-68; chmn. adv. bd. Afrlo-Lit., Africa.; bd. overseers Dag Hammarjskold Coll., 1970-72; mem. bd. Greater New Orleans Housing Corp., 1972-76, Inst. Human Understanding, 1972-78, New Orleans Tragedy Fund, 1973-78; mem. steering com. Goals Found., 1972-77; chmn. New Orleans Nat. Alliance Businessmen JOBS program, La. Renaissance, Religion and Arts, 1976-77; bd. dirs. Luth. Home New Orleans, 1976-84; mem. Westchester County (N.Y.) Council on Arts.; v.p. Community Access Corp., 1981-85, pres., 1986-87; exec. chmn. Greater New Orleans 1984 World's Fair Com.; chmn. Religious Ecumenical Access Channel. Mem. Assn. Internat. Vol. Orgns. (chmn. 1966-69), Adult Edn. Assn., Bapt. Writers Assn. (past chmn.), Fellowship of Religious Journalists (pres.), Soc. Internat. Assn. Voluntary Action Scholars (bd. dirs. 1985-87), Devel., Religious Pub. Relations Assn., Financing the Future Coalition. Baptist. Clubs: Internat. Trade Mart, Internat. House, Tower. Lodge: Rotary. Home: 3352 Ocean Dr Corpus Christi TX 78411 also: Martin-Mason Ranches PO Box 161 Tilden TX 78072

MASON, EDWARD ARCHIBALD, chemical and nuclear engineer; b. Rochester, N.Y., Aug. 9, 1924; s. Henry Archibald and Monica (Brayer) M.; m. Barbara Jean Earley, Apr. 15, 1950; children—Thomas E., Kathleen M., Paul D., Mark J., Anne M., Mary Beth. B.S., U. Rochester, 1945; M.S., Mass. Inst. Tech., 1948, Sc.D., 1950. Asst. prof. chem. engring. Mass. Inst. Tech., Cambridge, 1950-53; asso. prof. nuclear engring. Mass. Inst. Tech., 1957-63, prof., 1963-77, dept. head, 1971-75; commr. Nuclear Regulatory Commn., Washington, 1975-77; v.p. research Standard Oil Co. (Ind.) (now Amoco Corp.), Chgo., 1977—; dir. research Ionics, Inc., Cambridge, Mass., 1953-57; sr. design engr. Oak Ridge Nat. Lab., 1957; mem. adv. com. reactor safeguards AEC, 1972-75; cons. other govt. agys., industry; dir. Cetus Corp., Commonwealth Edison Co., XMR, Inc. Patentee in field; contbr. articles to profl. jours. Mem. adv. com. M.I.T., U. Chgo., U. Tex., Ga. Inst. Tech., U. Calif., Berkeley; bd. dirs. John Crerar Library. Served with USNR, 1943-46. NSF Sr. Postdoctoral fellow, 1965-66. Fellow Am. Acad. Arts and Scis. (councillor 1987—), Am. Nuclear Soc., Am. Inst. Chemists; mem. Nat. Acad. Engring. (councilor 1978-84), N.Y. Acad. Scis., Am. Inst. Chem. Engrs. (R.E. Wilson award in nuclear chem. engring. 1978), Western Soc. Engrs., Am. Chem. Soc., AAAS, Phi Beta Kappa, Sigma Xi, Tau Beta Pi. Clubs: Execs. (Chgo.); Hinsdale (Ill.) Golf. Home: 145 Hillcrest Ave Hinsdale IL 60521 Office: Amoco Research Ctr Warrenville Rd PO Box 400 Naperville IL 60566

MASON, FRANK HENRY, III, automobile company executive; b. Paris, Tenn., Nov. 16, 1936; s. Frank H. and Dorothy (Carter) M.; m. Judith Payne, June 2, 1958; children—Robert C., William C. B.E.E., Vanderbilt U., 1958; M.S. in Indsl. Mgmt., MIT, 1965. With Ford Motor Co., 1965-71, asst. controller Ford Brazil, Sao Paulo, Brazil, 1971-74, mgr. overseas financing dept., Dearborn, Mich., 1974-76, asst. controller engine div., 1976-78, mgr. facilities and mgmt. services, 1978-81; controller Ford Motor Credit Co., Dearborn, 1981-87; dir. finance Ford Fin. Services Group, Dearborn, 1987— . Served to lt. U.S. Navy, 1958-63. Office: Ford Motor Credit Co American Rd Dearborn MI 48121

MASON, FRANKLIN ROGERS, financial executive; b. Washington, June 16, 1936; s. Franklin Allison and Jeannette Morgan (Rogers) M.; m. Aileen Joan Larson, July 29, 1961; children: William Rogers, Elisa Ellen. BS in Engring, Princeton U., 1958; MBA, Northwestern U., 1959. With Ford Motor Co., 1960-75, finance mgr., Portugal, 1969-72; fin. analysis mgr. Ford subs. Richier S.A., France, 1972-75; sr. v.p. finance Raymond Internat. Inc., Houston, 1975-86; chief fin. officer Quanex Corp., Houston, 1986-87; group v.p., chief fin. officer Gulf States Toyota, Inc., Houston, 1987—; bd. dirs. First City Bank-Westheimer, Houston. Served with arty. U.S. Army, 1960. Mem. Princeton U. Alumni Assn., Univ. Club, Racquet Club, Princeton Club. Republican. Episcopalian. Home: 5765 Indian Circle Houston TX 77057 Office: Gulf States Toyota Inc 7701 Wilshire Place Dr Houston TX 77040

MASON, JOHN FRANKLIN, JR., accountant, accounting educator; b. Balt., Oct. 7, 1950; s. John Franklin Sr. and Ester Marie (Hilton) M.; m. Christine Marie Duni, June 19, 1971; children: Kimberly, John William. BS in Bus. Mgmt., U. Md., Balt., 1976. CPA, Md. Acct. U. Md., Balt., 1977-79; mgr. cost analysis Johns Hopkins U., Balt., 1979-85; acct. Farboil Co., Balt., 1985—; part-time instr. Dundalk Community Coll., Balt., 1987—. Mem. Nat. Assn. Accts. Republican. Presbyterian. Home: 3018 Liberty Pkwy Baltimore MD 21222

MASON, JOHN WHITTIER, pathologist; b. Milw., Wis., July 18, 1938; s. Elwood Whittier and Mary (Wing) M.; m. Parsla Krievs, Jan. 23, 1965; children: Christopher, Julie. BS, Trinity Coll., 1960; MD, Case Western Res. U., 1964. Diplomate Am. Bd. Pathology in Anat. and Clin. Pathology, Blood Banking and Hematology. Intern Cleve. Met. Gen. Hosp., 19764-65; resident in patholgy Mass. Gen. Hosp., Boston, 1965-69; dir. lab. 48th Tac Hosp. USAF, Eng., 1969-71; pathologist, dir. blood bank and hematology Berkshire Med. Ctr., Pittsfield, Mass., 1971-76; chmn. pathology and lab. medicine Christ Hosp. and Med. Ctr., Oaklawn, Ill., 1976—; Bd. dirs., treas. SIPA, Inc., Oak Lawn, 1985-88; bd. dirs. Lifesources, Inc., Glenview, Ill.; chmn. bd. dirs. ISP, Inc. Contbr. articles to profl. jours. Mem. Midwest adv. council ARC, St. Louis, 1987—, resolutions com., 1985; bd. dirs. Mid-Am. Chpt., Chgo., 1977—. Maj. USAF, 1969-71. Mem. AMA, Am. Coll. Physician Execs., Coll. Am. Pathologists, Internat. Acad. Pathology. Office: Christ Hosp and Med Ctr 4440 W 95th St Oak Lawn IL 60453

MASON, LEON VERNE, financial planner; b. Lawrence, Kans., Jan. 13, 1933; s. Thomas Samuel and Mabel Edith (Hyre) M.; m. Martha Harryann Sippel, Aug. 26, 1955; children: Mark Verne, Kirk Matthew, Erik Andrew. BS in Engring. with honors, U. Kans., 1955; MS in Mgmt. with honors, U. Colo., 1970. Engr., Pittsburg Des Moines Steel Co., 1955-56; with IBM, 1958—, sr. engr., San Jose, Calif., 1975-77, Boulder, Colo., 1977—; sr. engr. on loan, dir. capital campaign Vols. of Am., 1980-81. Pres., Boulder Interfaith Housing; dir. Golden West Manor, 1978-84, pres., 1983-84; dir. Ret. Sr. Vol. Program, 1979-86; chmn. elders 1st Christian Ch., Boulder, 1977-79. Served with USAF, 1955-57; col. Res. Cert. fin. planner; registered profl. engr.; trustee 1st Christian Ch., 1989—; supervisory faculty Regis Coll., 1988—. Mem. Internat. Assn. Fin. Planners, Am. Soc. Quality Control, Soc. Mfg. Engrs. Club: Kiwanis. Home: 660 S 42d Boulder CO 80303

MASON, PETER IAN, lawyer; b. Bellfonte, Pa., Mar. 20, 1952; s. Robert Stanley and Abelle (Dinkowitz) M.; m. Margaret Ellen Bremner, July 9, 1983; children: Henry Graham, Ian Peter. AB Bard Coll., 1973; JD cum laude, Boston U., 1976. Bar: Ill. 1976, U.S. Dist. Ct. (no. dist.) Ill. 1976, N.Y. 1981. Assoc. Rooks, Pitts, Fullagar and Poust, Chgo., 1976-80, 81-83, Shearman & Sterling, N.Y.C., 1980; mng. ptnr. Freeborn & Peters, Chgo., 1983—; dir. U.S. Robotics, Inc., Chgo., 1983—; gen. counsel Graphisphere Corp., Bradley Printing Co., Lavelle Industries Inc. Mem. ABA, Ill. State Bar Assn., Chgo. Bar Assn. Republican. Episcopalian. Clubs: The Attic, Union League of Chgo. Office: Freeborn & Peters 11 S LaSalle St Chicago IL 60603

MASON, RAYMOND ADAMS, brokerage company executive; b. Lynchburg, Va., Sept. 28, 1936; s. Raymond Watsi and Marion (Adams) M.; children: Paige Adams, Pamela Ann, Carter Meade. BA in Econs., Coll. William and Mary, 1959. Rep. Mason & Lee Inc., Richmond, Va., 1960-62; founder, pres. Mason & Co. Inc., Newport News, Va., 1962-70; pres. Legg, Mason & Co., Inc., Washington, 1970-73; pres. Legg, Mason Wood Walker, Inc., Balt., 1973—, chmn. bd. dirs.; pres. Legg Mason, Inc., 1981—, also bd. dirs.; mem. adv. bd. Potomac Investment Assocs.; chmn. bd. dirs. Environ. Elements Corp.; chmn. regional firms com. N.Y. Stock Exchange, 1978-81; chmn. Legg Mason Value Trust; bd. dirs. Legg Mason Value Trust, Legg Mason Masten, Howard Weil Fin., Western Asset Mgmt. Trustee emeritus Endowment Assn., Coll. William and Mary; dir. emeritus William and Mary Sch. Bus. Adminstrn. Sponsors, Inc.; trustee Balt. Mus. Art, Johns Hopkins Hosp.; bd. dirs. Nat. Aquarium, Balt., John Hopkins Hosp., John Hopkins U.; chmn. bd. sponsors Sch. Bus. and Mgmt., Loyola Coll., Balt.; bd. dirs., chmn. Greater Balt. Com.; chmn. United Way of Central Md., 1985. Mem. Nat. Assn. Securities Dealers (bd. govs. 1971-75, chmn. bd. govs. 1974-75), Securities Industry Assn. (bd. dirs. 1982—, chmn. 1985-86), Washington/Balt. Regional Assn. (bd. dirs.). Clubs: Center, Merchants, Md., Balt. Country, L'Hirondelle. Home: 5700 Coley Ct Baltimore MD 21210 Office: Legg Mason Wood Walker Inc 111 S Calvert St Baltimore MD 21202

MASON, RICHARD GORDON, lawn and garden tool manufacturing company executive; b. Woonsocket, R.I., Dec. 5, 1930; s. Stephenson and Marion Irons (Cook) M.; m. Joan Elizabeth Morrison, June 29, 1957; children: Lydia Gordon, Jonathan Whitcomb, James Stephenson. BS, Yale U., 1952; MBA, Harvard U., 1957. With Stanley Works Co., New Britain, Conn., 1957-62; prodn. supt. Thomas Smith Co., Worcester, Mass., 1962-65; v.p. mfg. Stanley Tools, New Britain, 1965-75; v.p. Ames Co., Parkersburg, W.Va., 1975-78; pres. Ames Co., Parkersburg, 1978—; Dir., past pres. Am. Hardware Mfrs. Assn., Schaumburg, Ill., 1979—. Chmn. Parkersburg Community Found., 1979—; bd. advisors Parkersburg Community Coll., 1987—; bd. dirs. W.Va. Found. for Ind. Colls., 1980—. Served to lt. USNR, 1952-55, ETO, PTO. Mem. Greater Parkersburg Area C. of C. (bd. dirs. 1978-85), Am. Hardware Mfg. Assn. (officer, bd. dirs. 1978—). Republican. Episcopalian. Lodge: Rotary. Home: 43 Lake Dr Parkersburg WV 26101 Office: Ames Co Box 1774 Camden & Broadway Aves Parkersburg WV 26102

MASON, ROBERT LOUIS, limousine rental company executive; b. Albany, N.Y., July 14, 1949; s. Walter Stocks and Catherine (Pratt) M.; m. Joanne E. Whitney Zink, May 4, 1974 (div. Apr. 1988); 1 child, Alecia Lindsay. Automotive cert., Hudson Valley Community Coll., 1970. Owner, mgr. Mason Automotive Co., Clifton Park, N.Y., 1968-73, Bob Mason's Sunoco Svc. Ctr., East Greenbush, N.Y., 1973-80; pres., chief exec. officer Bob Mason Enterprises Inc., East Greenbush, 1980-82, Turnpike Towing and Automotive Inc., East Greenbush, 1982-85, Hi Tech Automotive Inc., Schenectady, N.Y., 1985—, Hi Tech Limousine Svc Inc., Schenectady, 1987—, Hi Tech Sales and Leasing Co., Schenectady, 1987—; motor vehicle insp. N.Y. State Dept Motor Vehicles, Albany, 1973—; instr. Nat. Safety Council, 1984—, N.Y. State Motor Vehicles Emission Control Dept., 1985—; tech advisor arbitration bd. Chrysler Corp., Syracuse, 1985-87. Recipient Civic Appreciation award East Greenbush Garden Club, 1973-78. Mem. Gasoline Retailers Assn. (sec. 1982-85), Tri Vettes Ltd. Corvette Club (hon., pres. 1980-85), John Birch Soc., Mended Hearts. Republican. Methodist. Home: 507 Cimino Ln Schenectady NY 12306 Office: Hi Tech Automotive Group 1021 Altamont Ave Schenectady NY 12303-1831

MASON, ROBERT MITMAN, JR., finance company executive; b. Little Rock, Jan. 2, 1950; s. Robert M. Mason Sr. and Floris (Lockard) Farrand; m. Kathleen Kawakami (div. 1980); m. Christine Marie Eckman, Sept. 6, 1981. BS, Colo. State U., 1973. Personal banking official Colo. Nat. Bank, Denver, 1978-79; exec. banker United Bank of Skyline, Denver, 1979-81; account rep. VALIC, Fort Collins, Colo., 1981-88; dist. mgr. VALIC, Lakewood, Colo., 1988—. Capt. U.S. Army, 1973-77. Republican. Home: 103 S Indiana Way Golden CO 80401 Office: VALIC 390 Union Blvd Ste 600 Lakewood CO 80228

MASON, STEVEN CHARLES, forest products company executive; b. Sarnia, Ont., Can., Feb. 22, 1936. B.S., MIT, 1957. Pres. div. Mead Corp., Dayton, Ohio, 1978-79, group v.p., 1979-82, sr. v.p. ops., 1982, pres., 1983—. Office: The Mead Corp Courthouse Pla NE Dayton OH 45463

MASON, WILLIAM PHILIP, sales executive; b. Mexico City, Aug. 30, 1952; came to U.S., 1965; s. Alfred Lewis and Elena (Oseguera) M.; m. Lois Marie Harrington, June 15, 1976; children: Paulina Marie, Michael Philip. BS, B of Commerce, U. Santa Clara, 1974; MBA, Harvard U., 1976.

Controller Foster Farms Inc., Modesto, Calif., 1976-79; v.p. Agribus Assocs., Wellesley, Mass., 1979-84; v.p. fin. WearGuard Corp., Norwell, Mass., 1984-85, gen. mgr. retail div., 1985-87, sr. v.p., 1987—. Author: Soybeans: Brazil as a Competitive Force, 1976 (Uhlman Prize). Mem. Profl. Appraisal Assn. (bd. dirs. Phila. chpt. 1988—). Office: WearGuard Corp 141 Longwater Dr Norwell MA 02061

MASON, WILLIAM RANDY, sales executive; b. Quantico, Va., Aug. 10, 1944; s. Wilbur Randall and Anne (Kelly) M.; m. Maureen Middlecamp, Feb. 22, 1969; children: Erin, Shannon. Student, Roanoke Coll., 1963-65. Technician Gen. Electric, Salem, Va., 1965-70; sales rep. Am. Greetings, Roanoke, Va., 1970-72; field mgr. Am. Greetings, Raleigh, N.C., 1972-74; dist. mgr. Am. Greetings, Atlanta, 1974-76; regional dirs. Am. Greetings, Cleve., 1976-78; regional v.p. Am. Greetings, San Francisco, 1978-80; nat. sales mgr. Am. Greetings, Cleve., 1980-81, sone v.p., 1981-83, v.p., mgr. gen. sales, 1983—. Served with USMC. Named Eagle Scout with gold palm Boy Scouts Am. Mem. Internat. Mass Retail Assn., Nat. Assn. Chain Drug Stores, Food Market Inst. Republican. Roman Catholic.

MASOTTI, LEWIS RICHARD, utility company executive; b. Stamford, Conn., Dec. 15, 1933; s. Peter Vincent and Lee (Bohiem) M.; m. Florence L. Masson, Aug. 18, 1956 (div.); children: Patricia Smith, Carol, Peter, Richard; m. Judy Patton, Mar. 19, 1988. BS in Acctg., U. R.I., 1955. Acct. Masotti & Masotti, Stamford, 1955; treas. Bertie, Inc., Stamford, 1955-57; controller Citizens Utility Co., Stamford, 1957-65; dir. acctg. services Gilbert Assocs., N.Y.C., 1965-66; sr. v.p. fin. Gen. Waterworks Corp., Bryn Mawr, Pa., 1966—; prin. fin. officer GWC Corp., Claymont, Del., 1982—; Bd. dirs. 36 subs. co's. Gen. Waterworks Corp.; guest lectr. Drexel U., Phila., 1967. Recipient Ark. Traveler award Gov. of Ark., 1968. Mem. Nat. Assn. Water Cos. (bd. dirs. 1974—), Am. Water Works Assn., Am. Mgmt. Assn. Republican. Roman Catholic. Clubs: Toastmasters (treas. 1970-71), Blue Line-Firebird Hockey (Phila.) (bd. dirs. 1974-79). Home: 3108 Stoneham Dr West Chester PA 19380 Office: Gen Waterworks Corp 950 Haverford Rd Bryn Mawr PA 19010

MASOTTI, LOUIS HENRY, management educator, consultant; b. N.Y.C., May 16, 1934; s. Henry and Angela Catherine (Turi) M.; m. Iris Patricia Leonard, Aug. 28, 1958 (div. 1981); children: Laura Lynn, Andrea Anne; m. Ann Randel Humm, Mar. 5, 1988. A.B., Princeton U., 1956; M.A., Northwestern U., 1961, Ph.D., 1964. Fellow Nat. Ctr. Edn. in Politics, 1962; asst. prof. polit. sci. Case Western Res. U., Cleve., 1963-67, assoc. prof., 1967-69, dir. Civil Violence Research Ctr., 1968-69; sr. Fulbright lectr. Johns Hopkins U. Ctr. Advanced Internat. Studies, Bologna, Italy, 1969-70; assoc. prof. Northwestern U., Evanston, Ill., 1970-72, prof. polit. sci. and urban affairs, 1972-83, prof. mgmt. and urban devel. Kellogg Sch. Mgmt., 1983—, dir. Ctr. Urban Affairs, 1971-80, dir. Program in Pub. and Not-for-Profit Mgmt., Kellogg Sch. Mgmt., 1979-80, dir. Real Estate Research Ctr., 1986-88; cons. to numerous pubs., govt. agys. real estate devels. and corps.; vis. assoc. prof. U. Wash., summer 1969; exec. dir. Mayor Jane Byrne Transition Com., Chgo., 1979; vis. prof. Stamford Sch. Bus., UCLA Sch. Mgmt., 1989. Author: Education and Politics in Suburbia, 1967, Shootout in Cleveland, 1969, A Time to Burn?, 1969, Suburbia in Transition, 1973, The New Urban Politics, 1976, The City in Comparative Perspective, 1976, co-editor: Metropolis in Crisis, 1968, 2d edit., 1971, Riots and Rebellion, 1968, The Urbanization of the Suburbs, 1973, After Daley: Chicago Politics in Transition, 1981 ; editor Edn. and Urban Soc., 1968-71, Urban Affairs Quar., 1973-80; sr. editor Econ. Devel. Quar., 1986—; vice chmn. bd. Illinois Issues jour., 1986—. Research dir. Carl Stokes for Mayor of Cleve., 1967; mem. Cleveland Heights Bd. Edn., 1967-69; devel. coordinator for high tech. State of Ill.-City Chgo.; adviser to various congl. and gubernatorial and mayoral campaigns, Ohio, Ill., N.J., Calif. Served to lt. USNR, 1956-59. Recipient Disting. Service award Cleve. Jaycees, 1967; numerous fed. and found. research grants, 1963—. Mem. Urban Land Inst., Nat. Council Urban Econ. Devel., Nat. Assn. Corp. Real Estate Execs., Nat. Trust for Hist. Preservation, Lambda Alpha. Home: 50 E Bellevue Pl Chicago IL 60611

MASSA, DONALD MICHAEL, brokerage company executive; b. Cin., Jan. 22, 1945; s. Donald Arthur and Ruth Mary (Bonfield) M.; B.S. in Econs., Xavier U., 1967; m. Juanita Jean Dickman, Jan. 28, 1967; children—Michael, Gina. Sales and mgmt. trainee Conn. Mut. Life Ins. Co., 1967-69; stockbroker W.E. Hutton & Co., 1969-74, Thompson McKinnon, 1974-75; with Paine Webber Jackson & Curtis, Cin., 1975—, br. mgr., v.p., 1979—. Mem. Cin. Stock and Bond Club (trustee). Roman Catholic. Club: Hyde Park Golf and Country. Home: 2974 Alpine Terr Cincinnati OH 45208

MASSAH, CHERILYN, auditor; b. Dallas, Jan. 31, 1951; Herman Hiram and Mary Charleene (Thomas) Hill; m. Fathollah Massah, June 30, 1979. AA with highest honors, Tarrant County Jr. Coll., Hurst, Tex., 1982; BBA, U. Tex., Arlington, 1987. Auditor Def. Contract Audit Agy., Dallas, 1987—. Spl. Interest grantee Tarrant County Jr. Coll., 1982; nominated to Nat. Dean's List U. Tex.-Arlington, 1986-87. Mem. Assn. Govt. Accts., Beta Alpha Psi. Home: 4708 Michelle Dr Arlington TX 76016 Office: Def Contract Audit Agy 1100 Commerce St 3B17 Dallas TX 75242

MASSANISO, PETER ANTHONY, investment counselor; b. Phila., Aug. 18, 1936; s. Frank Paul and Emily Elena (Finocchiaro) M.; m. Karen Wibbing; children—Gia Elise, Peter Jr. A.B., Williams Coll., 1958; M.B.A. in Finance, Wharton Sch. of U. Pa., 1961. Sr. investment analyst, comml. and indsl. loan dept. Prudential Life Ins. Co., 1961-65; v.p. securities Ind. Life and Accident Ins. Co., Jacksonville, Fla., 1965-69; pres. Bus. and Fin. Mgmt., Inc., Jacksonville, 1969-71; v.p. corporate planning, dir. Fisco, Inc., ins., Phila., 1971-74; pres. Profl. Capital Mgmt., Inc., Jacksonville, 1974-84, Peter A. Massaniso & Co., Inc., 1984—; dir., mem. exec. com. Hickory Furniture Co. (N.C.), Presco Holding Corp., Chgo. Mem. adv. bd. and trust fund com. North Fla. council Boy Scouts Am.; trustee, chmn. investment com., pres. Mus. Sci. and History Jacksonville Inc, Jacksonville Art Mus. Served with Pa. N.G., 1958-61. Mem. Phila., Jacksonville Fin. Analysts Socs., Delta Kappa Epsilon. Clubs: Tournament Players; Ponte Verda, The River (bd. dirs.), Sawgrass. LeClub (N.Y.C.). Contbr. articles to profl. jours. Home: 839 Ponte Vedra Blvd Ponte Vedra Beach FL 32082 Office: 2250 Gulf Life Tower Jacksonville FL 32207

MASSÉ, LAURENCE RAYMOND, personnel search firm executive; b. Holland, Mich., July 27, 1926; s. Lawrence Joseph and Gladys Lucille (Tidd) M.; m. Barbara Anne Kranendonk, Dec. 23, 1948 (div. 1970); children: Laurel, Babette; m. Pamela Bateman, Feb. 3, 1982; children: Heather, Edward. BA in English, Hope Coll., 1950. Tchr. Pub. Sch. System, Holland, 1950-53; cons. Gen. Motors Corp., Flint, Detroit, Mich., 1953-56; dir. personnel Gen. Foods Corp., White Plains (N.Y.), London, Paris, 1956-66; dir. adminstrn. & personnel Internat. Telephone & Telegraph Co., Brussels, 1966-68; cons. Heidrick & Struggles, N.Y.C., 1968-69; v.p. indsl. relations REA Express Inc., N.Y.C., 1969-72; sr. ptnr. Ward Howell Internat., N.Y.C., Chgo., 1972—. Dir. Ridgefield (Conn.) Community Ctr., 1960-63. With U.S. Navy, 1945-46. Mem. AMA, Chgo. Council Fgn. Relations, Nat. Indsl. Conf. Bd., U.S. C. of C. Republican. Presbyterian. Home: 400 Westwood Dr Barrington IL 60010 Office: Ward Howell Internat Inc 1250 Grove Ave Ste 201 Barrington IL 60010

MASSELLI, SANDY JOHN, JR., financial consultant; b. New Brunswick, N.J., Sept. 11, 1962. BA in Polit. Sci. and Econs., Monmouth Coll., 1984. Corp. intern Merrill Lynch & Co., N.Y.C., 1983-85; exec. corp. fin. cons. Merrill Lynch & Co., Newark, 1985-88; sr. v.p. Drexel Burnham Lambert, Inc., N.Y.C., 1989—; bd. dirs. Broadway Restaurant Equipment Co., Essex Reprographics, Inc. Contbr. articles to profl. jours. Pres. Rep. Assn. of Monmouth County, Freehold, N.J., 1982-83; exec. dir. Delta Sigma Phi Fraternity and Alumni Assn. of Monmouth Coll. 1984-85. Mem. Am. Mgmt. Assn. Roman Catholic. Home: 448 Ocean Ave West End NJ 07740 Office: Drexel Burnham Lambert Inc 555 Madison Ave New York NY 10022

MASSEY, DAVID MONTGOMERY, management consultant; b. Dry Creek, W.Va., June 22, 1956; s. Winifred Nelson and Aline Bonnie (Cook) M. BBA, U. Toledo, 1982, MBA, 1983, JD, 1988. Bar: Ohio 1988. Programmer, analyst U. Toledo, 1982-87; personnel cons. Ohio Compensation Svcs., Toledo, 1987-88; instr. bus. law U. Toledo, 1988—; pres. Soft Sell Midwest Cons., Toledo, 1985-88. Mem. ABA, Ohio Bar Assn., Assn. for Computing Machinery, Assn. Systems Mgmt., Am. Mgmt. Assn., Mensa (membership coord. Toledo chpt.). Republican. Roman Catholic. Home: 5536 Winona Toledo OH 43613-2157 Office: U Toledo Stranahan Hall 2801 W Bancroft Toledo OH 43606

MASSEY, DONALD WAYNE, microfilm consultant, small business owner; b. Durham, N.C., Mar. 7, 1938; s. Gordon Davis and Lucille Alma (Gregory) M.; student U. Hawaii, 1959, U. Ky., 1965, U. Va., 1970, Piedmont Community Coll., 1982; m. Violet Sue McIlvain, Nov. 2, 1958; children—Kimberly Shan (dec.), Leon Dale, Donn Krichele. Head microfilm sect. Ky. Hist. Soc., Frankfort, 1961; dir. microfilm center U. Ky., Lexington, 1962-67; dir. photog. services and graphics U. Va., Charlottesville, 1967-73; pres. Micrographics II, Charlottesville, Va. & Charleston, S.C., 1973—; owner Roseraie Nursery Ctr., 1988—; pub. Micropublishing Series, 18th Century Sources for Study English Lit. and Culture; instr. U. Va. Sch. Continuing Edn., 1971-72, Central Va. Piedmont Community Coll., 1976; cons. Microform Systems and Copying Centers; owner Massland Farm, Shadwell, Va.; basketball coach Rock Hill Acad., 1975-77. Author: Episcopal Churches in the Diocese of Virginia, 1988. Pres., Rock Hill Acad. Aux., 1975-76; pres. bd. Workshop V for handicapped, Charlottesville, Va., 1972-73; mem. Emmanuel Episc. Ch., Greenwood, Va. Served with USMCR, 1957-60. Named Ky. Col.; recipient Key award Workshop V. Mem. Am., Va. library assns., Soc. Reprodn. Engrs., Nat. (library relations com. 1973-—), Va. (Pioneer award 1973, pres. 1971-72, v.p. 1973-74, program chmn. ann. conf. 1974), Ky. (Outstanding award 1967, pres. 1964-67) microfilm assns., Assn. for Info. and Image Mgmt., Thoroughbred Owners and Breeders Assn., Am. Rose Soc., Thomas Jefferson Rose Soc. (charter), Nat. Rifle Assn. Contbg. editor Va. Librarian, 1970-71, Micro-News Va. Microfilm Assn., 1970-71, Plant & Print Jour., 1983-85; contbr. articles to profl. publs. Home: Rte 2 Box 44 Keswick VA 22947 Office: PO Box 191 Keswick VA 22947

MASSEY, JAY RICHARDSON, JR., investment advisory company executive; b. Phila., Dec. 30, 1938; s. Jay Richardson and Marian Virgina (Boles) M. BA with honors, Coll. Holy Cross, Worcester, Mass., 1960; MA, Bryn Mawr Coll., 1962. Tchr. Latin Friends Cen. Sch., Phila., 1961; stockbroker Reynolds & Co., Phila., 1962-65; mktg. analyst Smith Kline Overseas Co., Phila., 1965-68; 1st v.p. Drexel Burnham Lambert, Phila., 1968-81; pres., chief exec. officer Addison Capital Mgmt., Phila., 1981—; bd. dirs., pres., chief exec. officer Addison Capital Shares, investment co. Bala Cynwyd, Pa., 1986—. Pres. Fabric Workshop, Phila., 1977-81; chmn. Friends Phila. Mus. Art, 1980-82; bd. dirs. Fleisher Art Meml., Phila., 1983—. Served with USN, 1960-61. Rotary Club Phila. traveling fellow, Chile, 1968. Fellow Chartered Fin. Analysts Soc. (chartered); mem. Fin. Analysts Phila., Soc. War of 1812, Print Club Phila. (v.p. 1970-80), Shakspere Soc. (treas.). Democrat. Roman Catholic. Clubs: Phiadelphia, Rittenhouse (Phila.). Home: 2017 Waverly St Philadelphia PA 19146 Office: Addison Capital Mgmt 1608 Walnut St Philadelphia PA 19103

MASSEY, LEROY GAVANE, insurance company executive; b. Jal, N.Mex., Aug. 22, 1939; s. LeRoy and Cora (Davidson) M.; m. Catherine Theresa Carucci, June 26, 1965; children: Helen Jo, Mary Anne, Catherine Louise. Student, Fresno (Calif.) Pub. Schs., 1969—. Bd. dirs. YMCA, Fresno, 1969-86, others; chmn. Guard-A-Kid, Fresno, 1985-86. Served with USN, 1961-68. Mem. Fresno Life Underwriters Assn. (pres. 1984-85, mem. of the yr. 1984), Fresno C. of C. (Ambassador's Club). Roman Catholic. Clubs: Fresno Trade, Fresno Leadership. Lodge: Rotary (sec. 1988). Office: Roy Massey Ins Svcs 1550 E Shaw Ste 114 Fresno CA 93710

MASSEY, SAMUEL NICK, banker; b. Sioux City, Iowa, Nov. 3, 1947; s. Samuel Oliver and Helen Mae (Brower) M.; m. Judy Darlene Hayes, Aug. 19, 1973; children: Wendy, Michelle, Katherine Anne. BSBA, U. San Francisco, 1975. Stockbroker Dean Witter Reynolds, Cupertino, Calif., 1977-81; stockbroker, asst. mgr. Merrill Lynch, Pierce, Fenner & Smith, San Jose, Calif., 1981-84; investment rep. and mgr. Alex Brown & Sons, San Francisco, 1984-86; v.p., mgr. asset mgmt. div. Cen. Bank, San Francisco, 1986-87; v.p., mgr. investment products group Cen. Bank, Walnut Creek, Calif., 1987—. Sgt. 1st class U.S. Army, 1967-77, ETO. Mem. Nat. Assn. Securities Dealers, Crow Canyon Country Club (San Ramon, Calif.). Republican. Methodist. Home: 209 Salamanca Ct San Ramon CA 94583 Office: Cen Bank 1450 Treat Blvd Walnut Creek CA 94596

MASSEY, STEVEN ALLAN, financial executive; b. Warwick, R.I., Sept. 3, 1957; s. Alfred H. and Gertrude A (Beniot) M.; m. Irmgard K. Hutter, Aug. 10, 1985; 1 child, Jenna M. BSME, Worcester Poly. Inst., 1980. Cert. fin. planner. Engr. Warner & Swasey/Bendix, Worcester, Mass., 1978-82; ins. agt. New Eng. Life Ins. Co., N.Y.C., 1982-85; pvt. practice fin. planning Jericho, N.Y., 1986—. Mem. Internat. Assn. Fin. Planners, Inst. Cert. Fin. Planners, Internat. Assn. Registered Fin. Planners. Republican. Lodge: Masons. Office: 555 N Broadway Jericho NY 11753

MASSEY, STEVEN JAMES, venture capitalist; b. Milw., May 1, 1959; s. Theodore Robert and Lois Lorraine (Flament) M. BS in Econs., U. Pa., 1981. CPA, Ill. Sr. auditor Arthur Young & Co., Chgo., 1981-83; investment officer Moramerica Capital Corp., Milw., 1983-85; v.p., asst. treas. InvestAmerica Venture Group, Inc., Milw., 1985—; also bd. dirs. InvestAmerica Venture Group, Inc., Cedar Rapids, Iowa; bd. dirs. Plastocon, Inc., Milw.; v.p., asst. treas. Clean Duds, Inc., Des Moines., also bd. dirs. Mem. Ind. Bus. Assn. Wis., Wis. Inst. CPAs. Office: InvestAmerica Venture Group Inc 600 E Mason St Suite 300 Milwaukee WI 53202

MASSIALAS, MARGARET OLIVE, investment service officer, business consultant; b. Hillingdon, Middlesex, Eng., May 22, 1933; came to U.S., 1966; d. James and Annie E. Mary (Fuller) MacKenzie; m. Frixos George Massiales, Dec. 23, 1954 (div. Oct. 1987); children: Gregory David Demetrius, Christina Alexandra. Diploma, St. Godric's Coll., London, 1951; BGS, U. Mich., 1979. Appeals organizer I.S.T.D., London, 1951-52; mgr. Clinic for Psychotherapy, London, 1952-53; ins. asst. Nestle Co., Vevey, Switzerland, 1953-55; prof. office mgr. Merritt-Chapman, Crete, Greece, 1955-56; cultural attache asst. Brit. Council, Athens, Greece, 1957-66; asst. to chmn. U. Microfilms, Ann Arbor, Mich., 1967-70; office mgr. Eugene B. Power, Ann Arbor, 1970—; sr. ptnr. Bus. Cons. Internat., Ann Arbor, 1985—; exec. sec., trustee The Power Found., Ann Arbor, 1982—; v.p., trustee Ann Arbor Summer Festival, Mich.. 1978—; trustee Eskimo Art, Inc., 1976—, Marcel Marceau World Ctr. Mime, Ann Arbor, 1986—. V.p., trustee Planned Parenthood of Mid-Mich., 1977-83; bd. dirs. Soundings, Inc., 1983-88; sec. Mich. chpt. Amateur Fencers League of Am., 1977-78; com. mem. Citizens for Pub. Art. Mem. Acad. Polit. Sci. Club: Zonta Internat. (pres.). Home: 3187 Plymouth Rd Ann Arbor MI 48105 Office: Eugene B Power 2929 Plymouth Rd Ann Arbor MI 48105-3291

MASSIE, EDWARD LINDSEY, JR., publishing company executive; b. Louisville, Sept. 16, 1929; s. Edward Lindsey and Ruth Sarah (Walts) M.; m. Betty Ann Hart, June 13, 1953; children: Steven, Cornelia, Diana. B.S., U. Ky., 1953. Trainee Gen. Electric Co., Louisville, 1953-54; exec. v.p. Commerce Clearing House, Chgo., 1954—. Served to 1st lt. USAF, 1955-56. Presbyterian. Office: Commerce Clearing House Inc 2700 Lake Cook Rd Riverwoods IL 60015

MASSIE, ROBERT JOSEPH, publishing company executive; b. N.Y.C., Mar. 19, 1949; s. Franklin Joseph and Genevieve Helen (Savarese) M.; m. Barbara Ellen Batchelder, Apr. 16, 1982; children—David Chance, Caroline Courtenay, Laura Brett. B.A., Yale U., 1970; M.B.A., Columbia U., 1974, J.D., 1974; Diploma, U. d'Aix en Provence, France, 1969. Bar: D.C. 1974. Assoc. Covington & Burling, Washington, 1975-79; mgmt. cons. McKinsey & Co., N.Y.C., 1979-82; v.p. Harlequin Enterprises, Toronto, Ont., Can., 1982-84, exec. v.p. overseas div., 1984—; chmn. bd. dirs. Harlequin Mondadori, Milan, Italy, 1985—; dir. Harlequin Hachette, Paris, Cora Verlag, Hamburg, Fed. Republic Germany, Mills & Boon, Sydney, Australia, Harlenik Ltd., Athens, Greece. Contbr. articles to law jours. Harlan Fiske Stone scholar, 1974. Mem. Bd. Trade Toronto. Club: Yale (N.Y.C.). Home: 23 Eastbourne Ave, Toronto, ON Canada M5P 2E8 Office: Harlequin Enterprises, 225 Duncan Mill Rd, Don Mills, ON Canada M3B 3K9

MASTBAUM, WILLIAM EDWARD, container manufacturing company executive; b. Dayton, Ohio, Feb. 28, 1923; s. Herman J. and Dorothy (Thurman) M.; student U. Ill., 1946-48; B.S.C., Ohio U., 1949; M.B.A., Harvard U., 1951; m. Carole S. Baloun, Mar. 1, 1986; children—Shelley Mastbaum Weathered, Thomas L. With Container Corp. Am., 1951-82, sr. v.p. employee relations, Chgo., 1977-79, group v.p. for Timber, Pulp Paperbd. Mills and Container div., 1979-80, group v.p. for Domestic Fabricating—Composite Cans, Plastics, Folding Cartons, Corrugated Shipping Containers & Doerfer and staff depts. communication and market research, 1980-82, also dir.; cons., 1982-84; chmn., dir. Belkin Packaging of Am., 1984—; dir. Hawthorne Bank of Wheaton, Belkin, Inc. Bd. dirs., mem. exec. com. Jr. Achievement Greater Chgo., 1975-82. Served to lt. s.g. AC, USN, 1942-46. Mem. Paperbd. Packaging Council (chmn.), Boxboard Research & Devel. Assn (trustee). Roman Catholic. Clubs: Harvard Bus. Sch. of Chgo., Univ. of Chgo. Office: 15 Spinning Wheel Rd Ste 116 Hinsdale IL 60521

MASTERS, GEORGE WILLIAM, biotechnology company executive; b. Toronto, Ont., Can., Sept. 27, 1940; came to U.S., 1973; s. George Vincent and Audrey Alice (Steeley) M.; m. Patricia Agnes Carrigan, Aug. 26, 1961; children: Warren Scott, Kelly Elizabeth. BSc, Hamilton Inst. Med. Tech., Ont., 1962. Mktg. mgr. Warner-Lambert Co., Toronto, 1964-72, dir. internat., 1972-76, div. pres., 1976-81, group pres., 1981-83; chief oper. officer Ventrex Labs., Portland, Maine, 1983-84; pres., chief exec. officer, dir. Xenogen, Inc., Storrs, Conn., 1984-85; pres., chief operating officer Immunomedics, Inc., Warren, N.J., 1985-89; pres., chief exec. officer Hemosol Inc., Toronto, Ont., Can., 1989—, also bd. dirs. Bd. dirs. Morris Ctr. YMCA, Cedar Knolls, N.J., 1986—. Mem. Assn. Biotech Cos. (bd. dirs. 1988—), Health Industry Mfrs. Assn. (mem. small bus. adv. com. 1986—), Woodlands Golf Club (Falmouth, Maine). Republican. Episcopalian. Home: 5 Wildwood Blvd Cumerland Foreside ME 04110 Office: Hemosol Inc, 100 International Blvd, Etobicoke, ON Canada M9W 6J6

MASTERS, STEPHEN CHESLEY, banker; b. Winchester, Mass., Dec. 6, 1942; s. Robert Chenery and Ruth Libby (Chesley) M.; m. Claudette Gabriella Artini, Nov. 13, 1965 (div. Oct. 1980); children: Douglas Andrew, Robert Chenery II, Gregory Artini; m. Mary Sherwood Newton, Jan. 24, 1981. AB, Princeton U., 1964; MBA, Temple U., 1972. Staff officer br. ops. First Pa. Banking & Trust Co., Phila., 1969-71, br. mgr., 1971-72, div. head br. ops., 1973-74; dept. comptroller br. First Pa. Bank, Phila., 1974, area v.p. brs., 1975-78, head deposit svcs., 1980-83, dir. MIS, 1983-86, dir. corp. planning, 1986—; pres. 3-2 Ctrs. (subs. First Pa. Bank), Phila., 1978-80. Served with U.S. Army, 1964-65. Mem. Delaware Valley Assn. RR Passengers (acting treas. 1987-88), Princeton Terr. Club. Democrat. Unitarian. Office: First Pa Bank 1500 Market St Philadelphia PA 19101-7558

MASTERSON, KENNETH RHODES, lawyer; b. Memphis, Feb. 22, 1944; s. H. Byron and Mary (Rhodes) M.; m. Nancy Frederickson, Feb. 28, 1980; children—Michael K., Elizabeth Megel, Grace Megel. BA, Westminster Coll., 1966; JD, Vanderbilt U., 1970. Bar: Mo. 1970, Tenn. 1976. Ptnr. Thomason, Crawford & Hendrix, Memphis, 1976-79; v.p. legal Fed. Express Corp., Memphis, 1980-81, sr. v.p., gen. counsel, 1981—. Mem. ABA, Mo. Bar Assn., Am. Corp. Counsel Assn., Memphis and Shelby County Bar Assn. Home: 2461 Brandemere Dr Germantown TN 38138 Office: Fed Express Corp 2005 Corporate Ave Memphis TN 38132-1842

MASTERSON, WILLIAM LLOYD, sports association executive ; b. Chgo., Aug. 19, 1949; s. Lawrence and Lorraine Mae (Shaw) M. Student pub. schs., Chgo. Organizer United Farm Workers, various locations, 1968-72; innkeeper Holiday Inns, Skokie, Ill., 1972-74; sec. Ill. Racing Bd., Chgo., 1974-79; gen. mgr. Maywood Park (Ill.) Race Track, 1979-83; pres. N.Am. Grain Co., Chgo.; exec. v.p., gen. mgr. Racing Assn. Cen. Iowa, 1988—; sr. project mgr. The JNC Cos., v.p. devel., 1987; v.p. devel. and constrn. JNC Cos.; exec. v.p., gen. mgr. Racing Assn. Cen. Iowa, 1988—; lectr. U. Ariz. Civic leader tour USAF, 1986. Recipient Outstanding Achievement award Chgo. div. Horsemen's Benevolent and Protective Assn., 1976. Mem. Internat. Assn. Auditorium Mgrs., Nat. Assn. State Racing Commrs. (hon. life), Harness Tracks of Am. (bd. dirs. 1979-83), Am. Horse Council, Chgo. Symphony Soc., Irish Am. Cultural Inst., Art Inst. Chgo. Democrat. Lutheran. Club: Irish Fellowship (Chgo.). Home: 300 Walnut St Box 127 Des Moines IA 50309 Office: Racing Assn Cen Iowa One Prarie Meadows Dr Altoona IA 50009

MATA, PEDRO FRANCISCO, food products executive; b. Guayaquil, Ecuador, May 27, 1944; s. Isabel Mata; m. Carol Morehouse, Mar. 25, 1967. BS in Indsl. Engring., Cornell U., 1967, M of Indsl. Engring., 1968. Fin., MIS cons. W.R. Grace & Co., N.Y.C. and Lima, Calif., 1968-73; asst. to chmn. Office of J.P. Grace, Jr., N.Y.C., 1974-75; pres., chief exec. officer Allied Food Industries, Singapore, 1976; v.p. devel. Grace Home Ctrs., N.Y.C., 1977-80; pres., chief exec. officer Ambrosia Chocolate, Milw., 1981-83, Baker & Taylor, N.Y.C., 1983-85; dep. group exec. W.R. Grace Retail Group, N.Y.C., 1985-86; pres., chief exec. officer Grace Cocoa, N.Y.C., 1986—. Bd. dirs. Westport (Conn.)/Weston United Way. Mem. Young Pres's. Orgn., Union League Club of N.Y.C., Aspetuck Valley Club of Westport. Office: W R Grace & Co 1114 Ave of the Americas New York NY 10036

MATALON, NORMA, travel and public relations executive; b. N.Y.C., Jan. 20, 1949; d. Albert and Suzanne Matalon. BA, Skidmore Coll., 1970. Cert. market mgmt., fin. mgmt. Am. Mgmt. Assn., computer automation. Cons., regional sales mgr. Revlon, N.Y.C., 1970-76; dir. sales, mktg. Diane Von Furstenberg Inc., N.Y.C., 1976-78; pres. Norma Matalon Cosmetic Cons., N.Y.C., 1978—, Norma Matalon Internat. Ltd., N.Y.C., 1982—; cons. to overseas cosmetic and fragrance cos., 1986—. Patentee in field. Com. mem., April in Paris Charities, 1976—, Project Hope, 1986—, United World Coll. Schs., 1983—, Northwood Inst., 1978—, Internat. Debutante Found. Charities, Princess Grace Found. for Arts U.S., 1984—, Am. Cancer Soc., 1976. Recipient Outstanding Performance award Revlon, N.Y.C., 1972. Mem. Foreign Policy Assn., N.Y.C. (Nat. Adv. Bd. 1985—), Am. Cancer Soc. (raffle chmn. 1985, 86, 87), The Fragrance Found., Am. Mgmt. Assn., The Foragers of Am. Unitarian. Clubs: The Lansdowne (London); Cosmopolitan (N.Y.C.), The Tuxedo (N.Y.C.), St. Anthony (N.Y.C.); The American (London); New Eng. Soc. Home: 445 E 77th St New York NY 10021

MATASAR, ANN B., business educator, university dean; b. N.Y.C., June 27, 1940; d. Harry and Tillie (Simon) Bergman; m. Robert Matasar, June 9, 1962; children—Seth Gideon, Toby Rachel. A.B., Vassar Coll., 1962; M.A., Columbia U., 1964,, Ph.D., 1968; M.M. in Fin., Northwestern U., 1977. Assoc. prof. Mundelein Coll., Chgo., 1965-78; prof. dir. Ctr. for Bus. and Econ. Elmhurst Coll., Elmhurst, Ill., 1978-84; dean, prof. mgmt. Walter E. Heller Coll. Bus. Adminstrn. Roosevelt U., Chgo., 1984—; dir. Corp. Responsibility Group, Chgo., 1978-84; chmn. long range planning Ill. Bar Assn., 1982-83; mem. edn. com. Ill. Commn. on the Status of Women, 1978-81. Author: Corporate PACS and Federal Campaign Financing Laws: Use or Abuse of Power?, 1986; (with others) Research Guide to Women's Studies, 1974. Contbr. articles to profl. jours. Dem. candidate 1st legis. dist., Ill. State Senate, no. suburbs of Chgo., 1972; mem. Dem. exec. com., New Trier Twp., Ill., 1972-76; research dir., acad. advisor Congressman Abner Mikva, Ill., 1974-76; bd. dirs. Ctr. Ethics and Corp. Policy. Named Chgo. Woman of Achievement Mayor of Chgo., 1978. Fellow AAUW; mem. Am. Polit. Sci. Assn., Midwest Bus. Adminstrn. Assn., Acad. Mgmt., Women's Caucus for Polit. Sci. (pres. 1980-81), John Howard Assn. (bd. dirs.), Beta Gamma Sigma. Democrat. Jewish. Office: Roosevelt U Coll Bus Adminstrn 430 S Michigan Ave Chicago IL 60605-1394

MATCZAK, THOMAS M., corporate finance executive; b. Chgo., Dec. 28, 1953; s. Michael S. and Mary E. (Koziatek) M.; m. Lynne A. Barry, Nov. 19, 1977; children: Jennifer, Scott. BS in Fin., U. Ill., Chgo., 1976; MBA, No. Ill. U., 1983. Staff acct. Stewart Warner Electronics Co., Chgo., 1976-77; sr. analyst Shure Bros. Electronics Co., Evanston, Ill., 1977-78; asst. contr. Infolink Corp., Northbrook, Ill., 1978-84; contr. Quantum Data, Inc., Carol Stream, Ill., 1984-86; v.p. fin. Comfab Techs., Inc., Addison, Ill., 1986—. Mem. Lake Zurich Jaycees (pres., treas. 1985). Republican. Catholic. Home: 212 Alpine Rd Lake Zurich IL 60047 Office: Comfab Techs Inc 409 Vista Ave Addison IL 60101

MATELES, RICHARD ISAAC, biochemist; b. N.Y.C., Sept. 11, 1935; s. Simon and Jean (Phillips) M.; m. Roslyn C. Fish, Sept. 2, 1956; children: Naomi, Susan Rachel, Sarah Frances. BS, MIT, 1956, MS, 1957, DSc, 1959. USPHS fellow Laboratorium voor Microbiologie, Technische Hogeschool, Delft, The Netherlands, 1959-60; mem. faculty MIT, 1960-70, assoc. prof. biochem. engring., 1965-68; dir. Fermentation unit MIT, Jerusalem, 1968-77; prof. applied microbiology Hebrew U., Hadassah Med. Sch., Jerusalem, 1968-80; vis. prof. dept. chem. engring. U. Pa., Phila., 1978-79; asst. dir. rsch. Stauffer Chem. Co., Westport, Conn., 1980, dir. rsch., 1980-81, v.p. rsch., 1981-88; sr. v.p. IIIT Rsch. Inst., Chgo., 1988—; sr. v.p. Applied Scis., Ill. Inst. Tech. Rsch. Inst., Chgo., 1988—. Editor: Biochemistry of Some Foodborne Microbial Toxins, 1967, Single Cell Protein, 1968; mem. editorial bd.: Biotech. and Bioengring., 1971—, Jour. Chem. Tech. and Biotech., 1972—; contbr. articles to profl. jours. Mem. Conn. Acad. Sci. Engring., 1981—; mem. vis. com., dept. applied biol. sci. MIT, 1980-88; mem. exec. com. Coun. on Chem. Rsch., 1981-85. Mem. Am. Chem. Soc., Am. Inst. Chem. Engrs., Am. Soc. Microbioloby, Soc. for Gen. Microbiology U.K., Inst. Food Technologists, AAAS, SAR, Sigma Xi. Home: 5 E Meadow Rd Westport CT 06880 Office: Ill Inst Tech Rsch Inst 10 W 35th St Chicago IL 60616

MATES, LAWRENCE A., II, medical company executive, consultant; b. Toledo, Oct. 10, 1954; s. Lawrence A. and Phyllis A. (Thomas) M.; m. Ulrike D. Heermann, Dec. 23, 1977; children: Lawrence A. III, Jessica M. BEE, BS in Mktg. cum laude, Case Western Res. U., 1976, MBA, 1978. Dist. mgr. Technicare Corp., Cleve., 1977-81; v.p. Med. Imaging div. Siemens Med., Iselin, N.J., 1981-85; pres., cons. Med. Systems Assocs., Toledo, 1985—; bd. dirs. Am. Hosp. Group, Chgo. Mem. United Way, 1985-86. Mem. Med. Researchers Assn., Am. Hosp. Assn., Toledo Bus. Assn. (v.p. 1984-85), Ohio Young Mens Bus. Assn. (pres. 1985), Toledo Investors LTD (pres. 1986). Republican. Roman Catholic. Clubs: Toledo; University (asst. v.p. 1985-86). Home: 2521 Challedon Ct Toledo OH 43615

MATHER, HAL FREDERICK, management consultant; b. London, Oct. 2, 1935; came to U.S., 1966; s. Stanley Arthur and Elizabeth (Gibson) M.; m. Jean Richardson, Oct. 6, 1956; 1 child, Carol Ann. BSc, Southall Tech. Coll., 1956. Test engr. Fairey Aviation, Hays, Eng., 1952-58; project engr. Fairey Aviation, Dartmouth, N.S., Can., 1958-66; mgr. Nat. Rsch. Corp., Boston, 1966-69; materials mgr. Gilbarco div. Exxon Corp., Greensboro, N.C., 1969-73; v.p. Mather & Plossl, Atlanta, 1973-78; pres. Hal Mather Inc., Atlanta, 1978—. Author: Bills of Materials, 1982, How To Really Manage Inventories, 1984, Competitive Manufacturing, 1988; contbr. articles to profl. jours. Fellow Instn. Mech. Engrs., Am. Prodn. and Inventory Control Soc.; mem. Soc. Mfg. Engrs. (sr.), Inst. Indsl. Engrs., Assn. for Mfg. excellence. Home and Office: 4412 Paces Battle NW Atlanta GA 30327

MATHESON, WILLIAM ANGUS, JR., farm machinery company executive; b. Oregon City, Oreg., Dec. 6, 1919; s. William Angus and Maude (Moore) M.; BS in Bus. Adminstrn., Lehigh U., 1941; m. Jeanne Elyse Manley, Feb. 14, 1942; children: Jeanne Sandra, Susan Manley, Bonnie Ann. Procurement engr. Office Chief of Ordnance, 1942-43; mgr. contract sales Eureka-Williams Corp., Bloomington, Ill., 1946-49; dist. sales mgr. Perfex Corp., Milw., 1949-51; v.p. sales Internat. Heater Co., Utica, N.Y., 1951-53; sales mgr. heating div. Heil Co., Milw., 1953-55; v.p. sales, dir. Portable Elevator Mfg. Co., Bloomington, 1955-70; exec. v.p. portable elevator div. Dynamics Corp. Am., 1971-85, dir., pres., 1975-84; owner Matheson Enterprises, 1985—. Bd. dirs. Jr. Achievement Central Ill., 1959-71, pres. Bloomington dist., 1964. Served from pvt. to 1st lt. AUS, 1943-46. Mem. Farm Equipment Mfrs. Assn. (dir. 1961-80, pres. 1969, treas. 1970-80), Ill. C. of C. (dir. 1978-84, vice chmn. 1984), McLean County Assn. Commerce and Industry (pres. 1974), Truck Equipment and Body Distbrs. Assn. (co-founder 1963), Am. Legion, Flying Farmers, Nat. Pilots Assn., Sarasota Yacht Club, Longboat Key Club, Bloomington Country Club, Masons, Shriners, Elks, Chi Phi. Republican. Presbyterian. Home: 1404 E Washington St Bloomington IL 61701 Office: 105 W Market St Bloomington IL 61701

MATHEWS, GEORGE W., JR., manufacturing company executive; b. Ft. Lauderdale, Fla., Sept. 7, 1927; s. George William and Weeta (Watts) M.; m. Jane Kerr, May 13, 1961; children: Kathleen, George III. BS, Ga. Inst. Tech., 1948; MBA, Harvard U., 1950. Various positions Blue Bird Body Co., Ft. Valley, Ga., 1948-58; v.p., gen. mgr. Southeastern Mdse. Mart, Inc., Atlanta, 1959-60; exec. v.p. Columbus (Ga.) Iron Works div. W.C. Bradley Co., 1960-69; v.p. ops. Peachtree Doors, Inc., Atlanta, 1969-71; founder, chief exec. officer Columbus Foundries, Inc., 1971-84; chief exec. officer Intermet Corp., Atlanta, 1984—, also chmn. bd. dirs. Past pres. Chattahooche council Boy Scouts Am.; past deacon First Presbyn. Ch. Atlanta; past dir. So. Indsl. Relations Conf., Big Canoe Property Owners Assn.; active Ga. Bd. Industry and Trade, U.S. Sen. Bus. Adv. Bd., coll. mgmt. Ga. Inst. Tech., Ga. Tech Athletic Hall of Fame; bd. trustees Ga. Tech Found. Recipient Spirit of Ga. award, 1988; named Entrepreneur of Yr. Assn. for Corp. Growth, 1986. Mem. Am. Mgmt. Assn., Ga. Tech Alumni Club (past pres.), The Vinings Club (bd. gov's.), Capital City Golf Club, Peachtree Golf Club, Piedmont Driving Club, Georgian Club, Rotary. Office: Intermet Corp 2859 Paces Ferry Rd Ste 1600 Atlanta GA 30339

MATHEWS, LOUISE ROBISON, real estate broker; b. Tecumseh, Okla., Sept. 22, 1917; d. Clarence and Irene (Buzzard) Robison; student E. Central State Coll., 1935, 38, Okla. Bapt U., 1936-37; m. William F. Mathews (dec.); 1 son, William F. Law sec. firm Robison-McKinnis, Shawnee, Okla., 1932-36; with Greene's Women's Specialty Shop, Shawnee, 1944-47; v.p. Streets Women's and Children's Splty. Shops, Oklahoma City, 1947-79; broker Assoc. Stewart-Van Cleef Realtors, 1979-86; chmn. Oklahoma City Fashion Week, 1973-75. Pres. Oklahoma County Council for Mentally Retarded Children, 1953-55, 1969-71: parent-observer White House Conf. Mental Retardation, 1963; chmn. 1st Ladies Okla. Gown Collection; Gov.'s Task Force Mental Retardation; mem. Okla. Mental Health Planning Com., 1963-65; hon. curator First Ladies Okla. Gown Collection. Mem. Okla. Retail Mchts. Assn. (dir. 1971-85), Oklahoma City Regional Fashion Group (dir., pres. 1969-70), Nat. Assn. Realtors, Okla. Hist. Soc., Okla. Assn. Mentally Retarded (past pres.), Nat. Assn. for Mentally Retarded Citizens (bd. dirs. 1958-60), Better Bus. Bur., DAR, Oklahoma City Retailers Assn. Democrat. Presbyn. Club: Altrusa, Women's Econ., Greens County. Home: 2700 NW Grand Blvd Oklahoma City OK 73116

MATHEWS, MICHAEL STONE, investment banker; b. Ohio, Oct. 23, 1940; s. Robert Green and Dallas Victoria (Stone) M.; m. Cecilia Aall, May 13, 1967; children: Brandon, Mark, Alexander. AB, Princeton U., 1962; JD, U. Mich., 1965. Bar: N.Y. 1966. Assoc. White & Case, N.Y.C., 1965-69; v.p. Smith Barney Harris Upham & Co., N.Y.C., 1969-77; sr. v.p. Scandinavian Securities Corp., N.Y.C., 1977-79; sr. v.p. DNC Am. Banking Corp., N.Y.C., 1979—; pres. DNC Capital Corp., 1986—; bd. dirs. St. Mary's Paper Co., Inc. Mem. Council Fgn. Relations. Clubs: Univ., Downtown, Sky, Bond. Home: 193 Elm Rd Princeton NJ 08540 Office: 600 Fifth Ave New York NY 10020

MATHEWS, ROBERT DANIEL, manufacturing executive; b. Thomson, Ga., Mar. 20, 1928; s. John Dewey and Duffie Irene (Rabun) M.; m. Louise Brown, June 20, 1953; children—Joy, Dawn, Mary, Holly. B.A. cum laude, Mercer U., 1951; postgrad. in indsl. mgmt. and textile engring., Ga. Tech. Inst., 1952-55, N.C. State U., 1958-69, Marquette U., 1955. Mgmt. trainee United Mchts., Clearwater, S.C., 1952-55; gen. mgr. Langley Processing div. United Mchts. and Mfrs., Inc., Statesville, N.C., 1956-69, asst. gen. mgr. Uniglass Industries div., 1969-72, v.p. Uniglass Industries div., 1972-74, exec. v.p., gen. mgr. Uniglass Industries div., 1974-80; asst. v.p. United Mchts. and Mfrs., Inc., Greenville, S.C., 1980, asst. mgr. mfg. div., 1981, v.p. corp. staff functions-domestic and fgn., 1981-82, sr. v.p., 1982-84, exec. v.p., 1984—, dir., 1983—; chmn. Spun Glass Ltd., London; dir. Blue Cross/Blue Shield, Columbia. Bd. dirs. J.E. Sirrine Textile Found., Greenville, 1984—. Mem. N.C. Textile Mfrs. Assn., N.C. Citizens Assn., Am. Textile Mfrs. Assn., S.C. Textile Mfrs. Assn. (bd. dirs. 1984—, transp. com. 1985-86). Clubs: Statesville City (v.p., dir. 1969-79); Commerce, Greenville City, Pebble Creek Country (Greenville). Lodges: Elks, Masons, Shriners.

MATHEY, FRANK ALBERT, state financial official; b. Quincey, Ill., July 14, 1935; s. Frank Albert and Elsie Julia (Vandevelde) M.; m. Agnes Eichier, Aug. 20, 1966; children: Nanette Marie, Frank Albert III. BBA, U. Miami, 1957. Auditor Fla. Dept. Beverage, Tallahassee, 1960-68, dist., auditor, 1968-70, cigarette tax supr., 1970-72, dir. fin. and acctg., 1972—. Youth coordinator Good Shepherd Ch., 1981-84; mem. Youth Commn. Diocese Pensacola/Tallahassee Roman Catholic Ch., 1981-84; mem. U. Miami Symphony Orch. 1954-57. With USAF, 1958-60. Mem. Fla. Govtl. Acctg. and Mgmt. Assn. (pres.), Govt. Fin. Officers Assn., State Automated Mgmt. Accts. System (chmn. accounts receivable and revenue sub system devel. com. 1982, chmn. purchasing subcom. 1985), Phi Mu Alpha. Club: KC. Home: 7043 Dardwood Ln Tallahassee FL 32312 Office: 725 S Bronough St Tallahassee FL 32304

MATHIAS, CORINNE FLORENCE, consultant company executive; b. Buffalo, June 10, 1926; d. Sidney and Florence (Vincent) O'Neill; m. Richard Charles Mathias, Sept. 6, 1947 (dec. Apr. 20, 1972); children—Richard Charles, Micheal William, Corinne Mary, Marc Francis. A.A., Citrus Coll., 1979. Dir. Universal Product Code and Direct Store Set-UP, Vons Grocery Co., El Monte, Calif., 1958-78; pres., owner Direct Delivery Data, Glendora, Calif., 1978—. Author receiving clerk's manual, 1966. Fellow mem. Los Angeles Art Mus., 1984—, Com. Against Govt. Waste, Washington, 1984—, Redlands Community Music Assn., Calif., 1984—. Women in Mgmt. scholar, 1979. Fellow So. Calif. Grocers Assn., Bus. and Profl. Women. Democrat. Roman Catholic. Avocations: bridge; golf; tennis; travel; photography.

MATHIAS, EDWARD JOSEPH, investment management company executive; b. Camden, N.J., Nov. 11, 1941; s. Edward Joseph and Zelma (Pollack) M.; m. Ann Robyn Rafferty, Aug. 3, 1968. B.A., U. Pa., 1964; M.B.A., Harvard U., 1971. V.p. T. Rowe Price Assocs., Inc., Balt., 1971—, also bd. dirs.; chmn. T. Rowe Price Threshold Funds, L.P., Balt., 1984—, New Frontiers L.P., 1985—; chmn., also bd. dirs. T. Rowe Price New Horizons Fund, 1982—, Sci. and Tech. Fund, 1987—, Small Cap/Value Fund, 1987—. Mem. nat. adv. bd. Am. Univ., Washington; bd. overseers Sch. Arts and Scis., U. Pa. Served to lt. USN, 1964-69. Republican. Clubs: Harvard, University (N.Y.C.); Columbia Country (Chevy Chase, Md.); Coral Beach (Bermuda); Merchants, Center (Balt.). Home: 5120 Cammack Dr Bethesda MD 20816 Office: T Rowe Price Assoc 100 E Pratt St Baltimore MD 21202

MATHIAS, MARGARET GROSSMAN, manufacturing company executive, leasing company executive; b. Detroit, June 26, 1928; d. D. Ray and Lila May (Skinner) Grossman; m. Robert D. Mathias, Oct. 1, 1955 (div. Feb. 1983); children: Deborah, Robert, Lesley, Jennifer, Mary. BA, Mt. Holyoke Coll., 1949; cert., Am. Acad. Art, 1951. Artist and co-mgr. Mary Chase Marionettes, N.Y.C., 1951-54; exec. v.p. L & J Press Corp., Elkhart, Ind., 1970—, also bd. dirs., sec., chmn. bd., 1985—; exec. v.p. Star Five Corp., Elkhart, 1978-85, pres., treas., chmn. bd., 1985—; chmn. MAGCo Inc., Elkhart, 1986—. Mem. fin. com. United Fund, Elkhart, 1960-64, parents adv. bd. Furman U., Greenville, S.C., 1978-83, art adv. bd. Mount Holyoke Coll., South Hadley, Mass., 1982—; pres. Tri Kappa Service Orgn., Elkhart, 1965-66; trustee Stanley Clark Sch., South Bend, Ind., 1977-87. Mem. Elkhart C. of C. Republican. Clubs: Elcona Country (Elkhart), Woman's Athletic (Chgo.), Thursday (Elkhart) (pres. 1976).

MATHIESON, ROBERT FRANCIS, director, international relations; b. N.Y.C., Aug. 11, 1932; s. Oliver and Loretta (Coleman) M.; B.A., Hunter Coll., 1960; M.A., N.Y. U., 1962; m. Mary J. McCaffery, Sept. 6, 1952; children—Christine, Michael, Kevin. Div. chief Fed. Res. Bank of N.Y., 1964-66; mgr. corp. planning Gen. Electric Co., N.Y.C., 1966-68; sr. v.p. Scudder Stevens & Clark, N.Y.C., 1968-73; v.p. econs. Merrill Lynch, N.Y.C., 1973-76; div. mgr. demand analysis AT&T, N.Y.C., 1976-83, div. mgr. internat. relations, 1983—; adj. prof. internat. mgmt. Pace U.; advisor Japan affairs U. Md. INFORUM Project; mem. Columbia U. China Bus. Devel. Project; mem. econ. adv. com. U.S. Dept. Commerce; bd. dirs. YMCA Ctr. for Internat. Mgmt. Studies. Named to Hunter Coll. Hall of Fame, 1974. Mem. U.S. C. of C. (Can.-U.S. relations com.; banking, monetary and fiscal affairs com.), Soc. for Internat. Devel. (dir.), Soc. Applied Econs. (dir. 1981), N. Am. Soc. Corp. Planning. Clubs: Met., Canadian (N.Y.C.). Office: Hofstra U Econ Dept Hempstead NY 11550

MATHIEU, PETER LOUIS, physician, banker; b. Woodstock, Vt., June 23, 1924; s. Pierre L. and Ida Veronica (Racine) M.; m. Betty Burkhardt, May 30, 1950; children: Elizabeth, Gretchen, Joan, Amy. BS in Biology-Chemistry, Coll. of Holy Cross, 1946; MD, St. Louis U., 1948. Diplomate Am. Bd. Pediatrics, Am. Bd. Allergy and Immunology. Resident R.I. Hosp., 1948-50; resident in pediatrics Boston Children's Hosp., 1950-52; pvt. practice Providence, 1955—; dir. pediatrics St. Joseph's Hosp., Providence, 1971-82; mem. staff Roger Williams, Pawtucket Meml. hosps.; clin. asst. prof. pediatrics Med. Sch., Brown U., Providence, 1974—; dir. metabolic svcs. R.I. Health Dept., Providence, 1955-74; med. dir. St. Vincent's Ctr., 1955—, St. Aloysius Home for Adolescents, Greenville, R.I., 1960-84, R.I. Sch. for Deaf, Providence, 1960—; dir. Cath. Social Svcs., Providence, 1955—; bd. dirs. 1st Fin. Corp., Providence. Author: Allergy Equilibrium, 1960; former newspaper columnist, host weekly radio program. Mem. AMA, Am. Acad. Pediatrics, Am. Acad. Allergy, New Eng. Med. Soc. (pres. 1982-83), R.I. Med. Soc. (pres. 1981), Providence Med. Assn. (pres. 1974), Nat. Assn. State Med. Socs. (pres. 1983), Staff Phys. Soc. R.I. (pres. 1975), Rotary. Roman Catholic. Home: Parkman Rd Narragansett RI 02882 Office: Comprehensive Health Svcs 255 Waterman St Providence RI 02906

MATHIS, EARNEST, JR., financial services executive; b. Dalton, Ga., Dec. 4, 1959; s. Earnest and Jesse (Aragon) M.; m. Valere Ann Skufca, May 25, 1985. Student, Denver U., 1984. Sales assoc. Franklin Life Ins. Co., Denver, 1979-82; owner Earnest Mathis Floor Coverings, Denver, 1980-87; bus. analyst Dun & Bradstreet Inc., Aurora, Colo., 1983-84; ptnr. Chenault & Assocs. Inc., Englewood, Colo., 1985-88; owner Inverness Investments, Denver, 1987—; pres. Laguna Capital Corp., Norcap Inc., Denver, 1986-88, P.R. Ink Inc., Englewood, 1985-87, Menlo Capital Corp., 1986-87, Monterey Capital Corp., 1986—; chief fin. officer, sec.-treas. Met Capital Corp., 1987—, Galt Fin. Corp., 1988—. Mem. Am. Mgmt. Assn., Denver Soc. Security Analysts (assoc.). Republican. Roman Catholic. Home: 12708 E Wyoming Circle Aurora CO 80012 Office: Inverness Investments 6160 S Syracuse Way Suite 310 Englewood CO 80111

MATHIS, JACK DAVID, advertising executive; b. La Porte, Ind. Nov. 27, 1931; s. George Anthony and Bernice (Bennethum) M.; student U. Mo., 1950-52; B.S., Fla. State U., 1955; m. Phyllis Dene Hoffman, Dec. 24, 1971; children—Kane Cameron, Jana Dene. With Benton & Bowles, Inc., 1955-56; owner Jack Mathis Advt., 1956—; cons. films, including That's Action!, 1977, Great Movie Stunts: Raiders of the Lost Ark, 1981, The Making of Raiders of the Lost Ark, 1981, An American Legend: The Lone Ranger, 1981; Heroes and Sidekicks: Indiana Jones and the Temple of Doom, 1984. Mem. U.S. Olympic Basketball Com. Recipient citation Mktg. Research Council N.Y. Mem. Alpha Delta Sigma. Author: Valley of the Cliffhangers. Office: Box 738 Libertyville IL 60048

MATHIS, JAMES FORREST, retired petroleum company executive; b. Dallas, Sept. 28, 1925; s. Forrest and Martha (Godbold) M.; m. Frances Ellisor, Sept. 4, 1948; children: Alan Forrest, Lisa Lynn. BS in Chem. Engring., Tex. A&M U., 1946; MS, U. Wis., 1951, PhD, 1953. Research engr. Humble Oil & Refining Co., Baytown, Tex., 1946-49, 53-61, mgr. research and devel., 1961-63, mgr. Splty. products planning, 1963-65; v.p. Exxon Research & Engring. Co., Linden, N.J., 1966-68; sr. v.p., dir. Imperial Oil Ltd., Toronto, Ont., Can., 1968-71; v.p. tech. Exxon Chem. Co., Florham Park, N.J., 1971-80; v.p. sci. and tech. Exxon Corp., N.Y.C., 1980-84; ret., 1984; cons. Arthur D. Little, Inc., 1984—; dir. NL Industries, 1985-86; chmn. N.J. Commn. Sci and Tech., 1988—. Bd. dirs. Chem. Industry Inst. Toxicology, 1975-83, treas., 1977-80, chmn., 1980-83; trustee Wis. Alumni Research Found., 1984—; bd. chem. sci. and tech. of Nat. Research Council, 1987—. Served with AC, USNR, 1944-45. Fellow Am. Inst. Chem. Engrs. (interim exec. dir., sec. 1987-88, chmn. N.J. State Commn. on Sci. and Tech. 1988—); mem. Am. Chem. Soc., AAAS, Sigma Xi, Phi Lambda Upsilon, Tau Beta Pi. Presbyterian. Home: 96 Colt Rd Summit NJ 07901 Office: Box 3 Summit NJ 07901

MATHIS, MARSHA DEBRA, management consulting firm executive; b. Detroit, Dec. 22, 1953; d. Marshall Junior and Anita Willene (Biggers) M. BS, Fla. State U., 1978; MBA, Miss. Coll., 1982. With telecommunications dept. Fla. State Dept. Safety, Tallahassee, 1973-76; asst. to chmn. Tallahassee Savs. and Loan Assn., 1976-78; sales engr. Prehler, Inc., Jackson, Miss., 1978-82; mktg. mgr. Norand Corp., Arlington, Tex., 1982-87; v.p. mktg. and sales Profl. Datasolutions, Inc., Irving, Tex., 1987-88; v.p. mktg. and sales, ptnr. Target Systems, Inc., Irving, 1988—, also bd. dirs. Contbr. articles in industry trade jours. Advisor Am. Diabetes Assn., Jackson, 1983—. Mem. Internat. Platform Assn., Nat. Adv. Group, Nat. Assn. Convenience Stores (Industry Task Force 1987-88), Furniture Cons. Ctr., S.W. Home Furnishings Assn. Republican. Roman Catholic. Home: 600 Eagle Nest Irving TX 75063 Office: Target Systems Inc 5605 N MacArthur Blvd Ste 280 Irving TX 75038

MATHIS, WELDON LAMAR, labor union administrator; b. Sylvester, Ga., Apr. 2, 1926; m. Myrtle Mathis; five children. Bus. agt. Local 728 Internat. Brotherhood Teamsters, Atlanta, 1950-53, sec.-treas. Local 728, 1953, pres. Local 728, 1966—; organizer So. Conf. Internat. Brotherhood Teamsters, 1957, gen. organizer, 1967; exec. asst. to gen. pres. Internat. Brotherhood Teamsters, Washington, 1967-78, dir. div. bldg. material and constrn., 1978-85, gen. sec.-treas., 1985—. Active Little City Found., Bapt. Children's Home, Bethesda, Md. With USAAF, World War II. Named Labor Man of Yr., State of Ga., 1983, Man of Yr. Teamsters Lodge 2201 B'nai B'rith, 1985. Mem. Shriners, Masons. Office: Internat Brotherhood of Teamsters 25 Louisiana Ave NW Washington DC 20001

MATHISEN, HAROLD CLIFFORD, investment analyst; b. East Orange, N.J., Apr. 1, 1924; s. Harold and Ottilie Christine (Nordland) M.; A.B., Princeton U., 1943; M.B.A., Harvard U., 1948; m. Dora Elizabeth Bachtel, Sept. 14, 1946; children—Margaret Bennett, Harold, Elizabeth Mathisen Andersen, Barbara. Asst. to controller Kaiser Frazer Corp., Willow Run, Mich., 1948-52; investment analyst Smith Barney & Co., N.Y.C., 1952-61; pres. Alliance Found., N.Y.C., 1961—; treas. AGF Mgmt. Co., N.Y.C., 1969-85; asst. treas., investment mgr. Christian and Missionary Alliance, Nyack, 1978-80; pres. Alliance Growth Fund, N.Y.C., 1968-78; asst. treas. N.Y. Internat. Bible Soc., N.Y.C., 1980-82; portfolio mgr. Legg Mason Wood Walker, Inc., N.Y.C., 1967-78, 82—. Trustee, treas. McAuley Water St. Mission, N.Y.C., 1967—. Served as lt. USNR, 1944-46. Mem. N.Y. Soc. Securities Analysts, Inst. Chartered Fin. Analysts, Phi Beta Kappa, Sigma Xi. Home: 29 Union Hill Rd Madison NJ 07940 Office: 63 Wall St New York NY 10005

MATLINS, STUART M., management consultant; b. N.Y.C., July 25, 1940; s. Louis Karl and Lillian (Keit) M.; student London Sch. Econs., 1958-59; BS, U. Wis., 1960; AM, Princeton U., 1962, postgrad., 1962-63; m. Andrea Cines, June 20, 1960 (div.); children: Seth, Andrew; m. Antoinette Leonard, Oct. 9, 1977. Internat. economist Bur. Internat. Commerce, U.S. Dept. Commerce, Washington, 1963-66; cons. Booz Allen & Hamilton, Inc., N.Y.C., 1966-67, asst. to pres. internat./adminstrv. dir., 1967-70, v.p. internat. ops., 1970-71, v.p./mng. officer, instl. and pub. mgmt. div., 1971-74; pres. Stuart Matlins Assocs., Inc., mgmt. cons., South Woodstock, Vt., 1974—; chmn. bd., dir. LongHill Ptnrs., Inc.; dir. Johnson, Smith & Knisely, Inc., Comprehensive Addiction Programs, Inc., The Fur Vault, Inc., Gemstone Press. Bd. dirs. Health Edn. Found.; mem. assembly of overseers, Mary Hitchcock Meml. Hosp.; mem. Woodstock Town Fin. Com. Woodrow Wilson fellow, 1960-61; Herbert O. Peet fellow, 1961-62; Phillip A. Rollins fellow, 1962-63 Mme. Princeton Club. Home: High Riding South Woodstock VT 05071 Office: PO Box 276 South Woodstock VT 05071

MATLOCK, KENNETH JEROME, building materials company executive; b. Oak Park, Ill., May 30, 1928; s. Harvey and Lillian (Sivertsen) Samuelson; m. Dorothy Belowski, Nov. 3, 1956; children—Geoffrey, Barbara, Gail, Paul. Student, James Millikin U., 1946-48; B.S. in Accountancy, U. Ill., 1950; postgrad., Northwestern U. Inst. Mgmt., summer 1963. C.P.A., Ill., Fla. Sr. audit mgr. Price Waterhouse & Co., Chgo., 1950-64; with Celotex Corp., Chgo., 1964-65; v.p. fin. ops. Celotex Corp., Tampa, Fla., 1965-74; asst. to v.p. Jim Walter Corp., Tampa, 1966-69; controller Jim Walter Corp., 1970-72, v.p., 1972-74, v.p., chief fin. officer, 1974-84, sr. v.p., chief fin. officer, 1984-88; sr. v.p., chief fin. officer, aslo bd. dirs. Walter Industries, Inc., 1987—; sr. v.p., chief fin. officer, also bd. dirs. Hillsborough Holdings Corp., 1987—. Adviser Jr. Achievement, Chgo., 1958-60; active Heart Fund, United Fund, 1956-58. Served with USNR, 1945-46. Mem. Am. Inst. C.P.A.s, Ill., Fla. socs. C.P.A.s, Fin. Execs. Inst. Home: 1401 87th Ave N Saint Petersburg FL 33702 Office: Walter Industries Inc 1500 N Dale Mabry Hwy Tampa FL 33607

MATOS, PHILIP WAITE, oil company executive; b. Washington, May 29, 1936; s. Andrew E. and Agnes Louise (Waite) M.; m. Susan Maczka; children: Lora, Julie Magar, Lisa. BS ChemE, Ga. Inst. Tech., 1958; postgrad., St. Louis U., 1959, NYU, 1966-70. Various positions Mobil Oil, Tex. and N.Y., 1958-76; v.p. Mobil Pipeline Co., Dallas, 1977-80; v.p. planning U.S. Mktg. and Refining div., Fairfax, Va., 1980-82; treas., mktg. and refining Mobil Corp., N.Y.C., 1982-83, v.p., regional exec. Far East, 1983-84, controller, mktg. and refining, 1984-85, dep. controller, 1985-86, corp. controller, 1986-88; pres. Mobil Chem. Company, Stamford, Conn., 1988—. Served to 1st lt. USAF, 1958-63, Vietnam. Mem. Fin. Execs. Inst., Am. Petroleum Inst. (fin. and acctg. exec. com. 1986-88). Republican. Office: Mobil Chem Co 100 First Stamford Pl Stamford CT 06904-2070

MATRAS, JAMES ALLEN, transportation executive; b. Chgo., Jan. 16, 1954; s. Chester Stanley and Emily Therese (Lewicki) M.; m. Elizabeth Ann Nagan, Aug. 31, 1974; children: Michelle Therese, Cassandra Lynn. AAS in Transpn. Mgmt., Prairie State Coll., 1974; diploma in ICC Law, Practice and Procedure, Coll. Advanced Traffic, Chgo., 1975; BA in Transpn. and Law, Gov.'s State U., 1977. Billing clk., dispatcher Spector Freight Systems Inc., Gary, Ind., 1972-73; hearings examiner ICC, Chgo., 1973-77; dir. pricing and tariff adminstrn. Great Lakes & European Lines Inc., Chgo., 1977-78; assoc. dir. commerce Rocor Internat., Palo Alto, Calif., 1979; supr. commerce Schneider Transport Inc., Green Bay, Wis., 1979-80; dir. traffic and commerce Pirkle Freight Lines, Madison, Wis., 1980-83; exec. v.p. adminstrn. Wis. Farm Lines Ltd., Wisconsin Dells, 1986-87; pres. Interstate Transp. Services Inc., Madison, 1983—; v.p. Interstate Ins. Svcs. Inc., Madison, 1986-88, pres., 1988—; instr. Coll. Advanced Traffic, 1977-78, Northeast Wis. Tech. Inst., Green Bay, 1979-80; program leader U. Wis. Mgmt. Inst., 1988—. Mem. Trasnp. Practitioners' Assn., Transp. Club (bd. dirs. 1986-88), Wis. Motor Carrier Assn. (program leader 1988—), Delta Nu Alpha (bd. dirs. 1985-87, pres. 1988—), Exchange Club. Roman Catholic. Home: 621 Yorktown Rd De Forest WI 53532 Office: Interstate Transp Svcs 16 N Carroll St Ste 600 Madison WI 53703

MATSCHULAT, NATEL KYPRIOTOU, marketing professional; b. Greece, Mar. 29, 1944; came to U.S., 1960; d. Philip Kypriotis and Beatrice (Zarifakis) Millar. Student, Calif. State Poly. U., 1962-64; BS in French, Math., German, Mount Mary Coll., Milw., 1967; postgrad., NYU, 1974. Media exec., asst. group head Grey Advt., Inc., N.Y.C., 1967-73; acct. exec. Foote, Cone & Belding, Inc., N.Y.C., 1973-74; group product mgr. Lever Bros. Co., N.Y.C., 1974-79; sr. dep. commr. N.Y. State Dept. Commerce, N.Y.C., Albany, 1979-83; pres., founder Natel, Inc., N.Y.C., 1983—; v.p. mktg., pub. affairs and devel. The Mt. Sinai Med. Ctr., N.Y.C., 1986-89; v.p., dir. strategic mktg. pvt. banking Citicorp/Citibank, N.Y.C., 1989—; mgmt. cons. Exxon, USA, Houston, 1985; mktg. cons. Am. Standard, Inc., N.Y.C., 1985, The Comite Colbert of France, Paris, 1983-86, J. Walter Thompson, USA, N.Y.C., 1984. Dir. advtg. campaigns, I Love N.Y., 1979-83 (numerous awards), Made in New York, 1979-83. Mem. Ptnrship. for the Homeless, 1986—; exec. com. mem. Assn. for a Better N.Y., 1982—; dir. N.Y.C. Coll. Town; com. mem., Madison Sq. Boys and Girls Club, N.Y.C., 1986—. Named one of Top 10 Women in Advtg. Esquire Mag., 1984, Internat. Travel Dir. Yr. Brazilian Press Assn., 1983; recipient Am. Traditions award B'nai B'rith, 1982, Medal for Profl. Excellence Mount Mary Coll., 1984. Fellow Am. Coll. Healthcare Mktg. (Health Marketer of Yr. 1988); mem. Travel Industry Am. (bd. dirs.), Am. Mktg. Assn., Soc. Healthcare Planning and Mktg., Am. Soc. Hosp. Mktg. and Pub. Relations, Pub. Relations Soc. Am., Assn. Am. Med. Colls. (mem. group on pub. affairs), Club of Clubs Internat. (Munich), Kappa Mu Epsilon, Alpha Mu Gamma, KME, AMF. Greek Orthodox. Office: Citicorp 399 Park Ave New York NY 10022

MATSON, JAMES HERBERT, cosmetics manufacturing executive; b. Mankato, Minn., Feb. 24, 1940; m. Jane Hall, May 23, 1964; 1 child, Tracey. BS, Mankato State U., Minn., 1963; MBA, U. Chgo., 1967. Supr. Avon Products, Inc., Chgo., 1970-72; mfg. mgr. Mallinkrod, Inc., St. Louis, 1972-75; dir. ops. Bristol-Meyers Inc., Buffalo, N.Y., 1975-82; sr. v.p. ops. Noxell Corp., Balt., 1982—. Served to capt. USAF, 1964-70, Vietnam. Decorated Bronze Star. Mem. Am. Production and Inventory Control Soc., NAM. Home: 5 Hunt Valley View Terr Phoenix MD 21131 Office: Noxell Corp 11050 York Rd Hunt Valley MD 21030

MATSUKAWA, MICHIYA, securities company executive; b. Aizu-wakamatsu, Fukushima, Japan, Dec. 22, 1924; s. Tomiyasu and Koh Matsukawa; m. Ryoko Sakakibara, June 12, 1931; children: Makiko Watanabe, Kikuko Murofushi. BA in Polit. Sci., Tokyo Imperial U., 1947; MA in Economics, U. Ill., 1951. Various positions held throughout Japan Ministry of Fin., 1947-73, dir. gen. internat. fin. bur., 1973-74, dep. vice minister fin., 1974-75, dir. gen. fin. bur., 1975-76, vice minister fin. internat. affairs, 1976-78, spl. advisor to Minister Fin., 1978-80; advisor Tohmatsu Aoki and Sanwa, Tokyo, 1982—; chmn. inst. Nikko Research Ctr. Ltd., Tokyo, 1982—; chmn. bd. dirs. Nikko Internat. Capital Mgmt. Co. Ltd., Tokyo; bd. dirs. Nippon Investors Service Inc., Tokyo; sr. advisor to pres. Nikko Securities Co. Ltd., Tokyo, 1980—; mem. adv. bd. Morgan Stanley Co. Inc., N.Y.C., 1986; dir. Fedn. Economic Orgns., Tokyo, Japan Inst. Fgn. Affairs; mem. U.N. investment com. U.N. Pension Fund, N.Y.C., U.N. U., N.Y.C. Trustee Soc. Internat. Cultural Exchange; mng. dir. Eisaku Sato Meml. Found. Cooperation with U.N. U., pres. Served with Japanese Navy, 1944-45. Mem. Japan Securities and Economics Club (counsellor). Clubs: Tokyo, Keidanren. Office: Nikko Securities Co Ltd, 3 3 1 Marunouchi, Chiyoda ku, Tokyo 100, Japan

MATSUURA, TAKANORI, business administration educator; b. Hokkaido, Japan, July 5, 1940; s. Sueji and Miyoshi Matsuura; m. Kazuko Hashimoto, Oct. 25, 1943; 1 child, Masa. JD, Chuou U., 1963. Mem. editorial staff Mgmt. Today, Diamond, Inc., Tokyo, 1967-71, asst. to pres., 1971-73; researcher Inst. Social Engring., Tokyo, 1975-82; caster NHK ETV Culture Series, Tokyo, 1978-82; assoc. prof. Chubu Inst. Tech., Kasugai, Aichi-Ken, Japan, 1982-84; assoc. prof. Coll. Bus. Adminstrn. and Info. Sci. Chubu Inst. Tech., Kasugai, Japan, 1984-89; prof. TAMA Inst. Mgmt. and Info. Sci., Tokyo, 1989—; part time lectr. faculty bus. adminstrn. Meiji U., Tokyo, 1981—. Author: Recruiting--Company and Undergraduate on the Job Market in Japan, 1978, The Research of Japanese Corporation and Management Climate, 1983, The New Research of Japanese Corporation and Management Climate, 1987. Mem. Acad. Assn. Orgnl. Sci. Home: 1-7-14 Takaban, Meguro-ku, Tokyo Japan 152 Office: Chubu U Coll Bus Adminstrn and Info Sci, 1-7-14 Takaban, Meguro-ku, Tokyo 152, Japan

MATTESON, E. DAVID, sales and marketing executive; b. Erie, Pa., Sept. 23, 1939; s. Emory Fenn and Johanna Regina (Jeffrey) M.; m. Coreen Mary Shaughnessy, Aug. 30, 1965; children: E. Paul, Guy, Eric. AEE, Westchester Coll., 1961; student, U. Bridgeport, 1961-68. Sales engr. New Britain (Conn.) Machine div. Litton Industries, 1967-69, Detroit and Dayton, Ohio, 1969-80; dist. sales mgr. New Britain (Conn.) Machine div. Litton Industries, Dayton, 1980-83; regional sales mgr. New Britain (Conn.) Machine div. Litton Industries, Dayton and midwestern states, 1983-85; v.p. sales and mktg. New Britain (Conn.) Machine div. Litton Industries, New Britain, 1985—. Served with USAR, 1963-69. Mem. Numerical Control Soc., Internat. Platform Assn. Republican. Roman Catholic. Office: New Britain Machine Div Litton South St PO Box 2200 New Britain CT 06050-2200

MATTEUCCI, DOMINICK VINCENT, real estate developer; b. Trenton, N.J., Oct. 19, 1924; s. Vincent Joseph and Anna Marie (Zoda) M.; BS, Coll. of William and Mary, 1948; BS, Mass. Inst. Tech., 1950; m. Emma Irene DeGuia, Mar. 2, 1968; children: Felisa Anna, Vincent Eriberto. Owner, Matteucci Devel. Co., Newport Beach, Calif.; pres. Nat. Investment Brokerage Co., Newport Beach. With USAAC, 1943-46. Recipient NASA achievement award, 1974; registered profl. engr., Calif.; lic. gen. bldg. contractor, real estate broker. Home: 2104 Felipe Newport Beach CA 92660 Office: PO Box 8328 Newport Beach CA 92660

MATTHEWS, BRUCE ALLEN, insurance company executive; b. Milw., Aug. 22, 1944; s. Frederick A. and Margaret (King) M.; m. Joanne L. Haberer, Aug. 2, 1969; children: Ursula H., Rachel L., Jessica L. BA, Miami U., 1969. Tchr., coach Batavia (Ohio) Pub. Schs., 1969-70; agt., mgr. N.Y. Life Ins. Co., Cin., 1970-73; asst. dir. tng. Union Cen. Life, Ohio, 1973-78; dir. regional sales Provident Mut. Life, Phila., 1978-83; agy. head Mut. of N.Y., Washington, 1983-85; regional v.p. Nat. Life Vt., Scottsdale, Ariz., 1985—; CLU. Bd. dirs. Wilder Acad., Louisville, 1977. Faculty fellow Miami U., 1968-69. Mem. Nat. Assn. Life Underwriters, Gen. Agts. Officers Assn., Am. Soc. CLU's, Gainey Estate Club. Republican. Roman Catholic. Home: 7878 Gainey Ranch Rd 53 Scottsdale AZ 85258 Office: Nat Life Vt 8777 E Via De Ventura Ste 340 Scottsdale AZ 85258

MATTHEWS, CLARK J(IO), II, retail executive, lawyer; b. Arkansas City, Kans., Oct. 1, 1936; s. Clark J. and Betty Elizabeth (Stewart) M.; m. Janice Eleanor Hill, June 28, 1959; children: Patricia Eleanor, Pamela Elaine, Catherine Joy. B.A., So. Meth. U., 1959, J.D., 1961. Bar: Tex. 1961. Trial atty. Ft. Worth Regional Office, SEC, 1961-63; law clk. to chief U.S. dist. judge No. Dist. Tex., Dallas, 1963-65; atty. Southland Corp., Dallas, 1965-73; v.p., gen. counsel Southland Corp., 1973-79, exec. v.p., chief fin. officer, 1979-83, sr. exec. v.p., chief fin. officer, 1983-87, exec. v.p., chief fin. officer, 1987—. Mem. ABA, Tex., Dallas, Bar Assns., Am. Judicature Soc., Alpha Tau Omega, Pi Alpha Delta. Methodist. Club: DeMolay. Home: 7005 Stefani St Dallas TX 75225 Office: Southland Corp 2828 N Haskell Ave Dallas TX 75204

MATTHEWS, CRAIG GERARD, gas company executive; b. Bklyn., Mar. 8, 1943; s. William A. and May M. (Aldag) M.; m. Carol O. Olsen, Sept. 10, 1971; children: Kenneth C., Bradford P., Melinda M. BCE, Rutgers U., 1965; MS in Indsl. Mgmt., Polytech. Inst. Bklyn., 1971. Trainee Bklyn. Union Gas Co., 1965, engr. indsl. sales, 1968-71, chief analyst, 1971-73, asst. mgr., 1973-74, mgr., 1974-76, asst. v.p., 1977-81, v.p., 1981-83, sr. v.p., 1984-86, chief fin. officer, 1986, group sr. v.p., chief fin. officer, 1988—; mem. exec. com. Associated Gas Distbrs., Washington. Bd. dirs. Bklyn. Philharm. Served to capt. U.S. Army, 1966-68. Mem. Am. Gas Assn. (various coms., Mktg. award, Meritorious Service award), Bklyn. C. of C. (bd. dirs.). Republican. Presbyterian. Home: 17 Wynwood Rd Chatham NJ 07928 Office: Bklyn Union Gas Co 195 Montague St Brooklyn NY 11201

MATTHEWS, DREXEL GENE, quality control executive; b. Vanzant, Ky., Feb. 1, 1952; s. Marcus Ivan and Lillia Mae (Lake) M.; m. Roberta June Eby, Oct. 16, 1971; children: Tracie Marie, Marcia Nichole. Student, Brescia Coll., Owensboro, Ky., 1976-79, Morehead State U., 1969-71. With Nat. Aluminum div., Nat. Steel Corp., Hawesville, Ky., 1971-78; customer service mgr. Nat. Aluminum div., Nat. Steel Corp., Hawesville, 1977-78; quality control mgr. Hunter Douglas Bldg. Products div., Roxboro, N.C., 1979-81; process engring. mgr., mgr. quality control and specification engring. MEPCO-ELECTRA Co., Roxboro, N.C., 1981-84; quality assurance sr., mng. engr. Sumitomo Electric Co., Research Triangle Park, N.C., 1984-87; quality assurance supplier Consol. Diesel Co., Whitakers, N.C., 1987—. Mem. Am. Soc. Metals, Am. Soc. Quality Control (guest speaker 1987), Am. Nat. Standards Inst. (fiber optics com. 1986—), Durham (N.C.) Kennel Club, Cen. N.C. Siberian Husky Club. Republican. Baptist. Home: 5057 Netherwood Rd Rocky Mount NC 27803

MATTHEWS, GAIL THUNBERG, marketing executive; b. Hartford, Conn., July 29, 1938; d. Harold Einar and Mildred (Wentland) Thunberg; m. Glenn Holbrook Matthews, Aug. 9, 1959; children: Scott Holbrook, Brett Holbrook. Student Boston U., 1958-59. Hostess show, copywriter Sta. WJDA, Boston, 1956-58; fashion coordinator Jordan Marsh, Boston, 1958-59, Miller & Rhoades, Richmond, Va., 1959-60, Sage Allen, Hartford, 1960-61; columnist Boston Globe, 1962-63, Hartford Times, 1961-63; free-lance writer, contbr. articles to New Englander mag., Christian Sci. Monitor, Yankee, 1961-65; v.p., treas. Coll. Mktg. Group, Inc., Winchester, Mass., 1968-86; corporator Reading Savs. Bank; mem. adv. council Baybank Middlesex. Chmn. Love Lights a Tree, Am. Cancer Soc., New London, 1988. Author: Hor'doeuvre Cooking, 1966, Gourmet Cooking, 1966, Birthday Fortune Book, 1967, (children's series) The Adventures of a Shih Tzu The Gook Luck Puppy, 1980. Choral dir. Barrows Sch., Reading; pres. local PTA; chmn. Heart Fund Reading; founder, chmn. Reading chpt. Am. Cancer Soc., Love Lights A Tree chpt. New London Am. Cancer Soc., named citizen of yr., 1983-84; pres. Kimpton Brook Gardens Restorations. Recipient Service to Youth award Reader's Digest, 1967; CAP award 1965; Spl. award Am. Cancer Soc., 1981-82; Citizenship award Reading Tchrs. Assn., 1980. Mem. Antiquarian Soc., Dartmouth Coll. Women's (bd. dirs.).

MATTHEWS, JEANNE PEARSON, logistic support analyst, company executive; b. Marietta, Ga., July 2, 1941; d. Silas Leon and Edith Mae (Rich) Pearson; m. William Dean Bottoms, Apr. 2, 1960 (div. 1973); 1 child, William Dave; m. William Glenn Matthews, Sept. 4, 1976. Typist, stenographer, sec. Lockheed-Ga. Co., Marietta, 1962-82, gen. acct., price estimator, 1982-84, logistic support analyst, 1984—; pres. J&B Office Service, Inc., Villa Rica, Ga., 1984-87. Mem. Nat. Platform Com. Named Hon. Lt. Col. Aide-de-Camp Ala. State Militia, 1976; named Ms. Lockheed, Lockheed-Ga. Co., 1972, 74. Mem. Nat. Assn. Female Execs., Nat. Film Inst., Nat. Assn. Mature People, Paulding County C. of C., AFL-CIO (recording sec. Lodge 709 1973-79). Democrat. Baptist. Clubs: Kennesaw Mountain Beagle (sec.-treas. Dallas, Ga. 1980—), Atlanta Braves Fan. Lodge: Order Eastern Star. Avocations: Beagles; baseball; swimming. Home: Rte 2 Box 519 Villa Rica GA 30180

MATTHEWS, L. WHITE, III, railroad executive; b. Ashland, Ky., Oct. 5, 1945; s. L. White and Virginia Carolyn (Chandler) M.; m. Mary Jane Hanser, Dec. 30, 1972; children—Courtney Chandler, Brian Whittlesey. B.S. in Econs, Hampden-Sydney Coll., 1967; M.B.A. in Fin. and Gen. Mgmt, U. Va., 1970. Cons. fin. Chem. Bank, N.Y.C., 1970-72, asst. sec., 1972-74, asst. v.p., 1974-75, v.p., 1976-77; treas. Mo. Pacific Corp., St. Louis, 1977-82; v.p. fin. Mo. Pacific R.R. Co. subs. Mo. Pacific Corp., St. Louis, 1979-82; v.p., treas. Union Pacific Corp. and Union Pacific R.R. Co., N.Y.C., 1982-87, sr. v.p. fin., 1987—; bd. dirs. First Am. Bank of N.Y. Trustee Centerland Fund, St. Louis.

MATTHEWS, NORMAN STUART, department store executive; b. Boston, Jan. 13, 1933; s. Martin W. and Charlotte (Cohen) M.; m. Joanne Banks, June 11, 1956; children: Gary S., Jeffrey B., Patricia A. B.A., Princeton U.; M.B.A., Harvard U. Ptnr. Beacon Mktg. and Advt. Assocs., N.Y.C., 1956-71; sr. v.p. Broyhill Furniture Co., Lenoir, N.C., 1971-73, E.J. Korvettes, N.Y.C., 1973-78; chmn., chief exec. officer Gold Circle Stores, Columbus, Ohio, 1978-82; with Federated Dept. Stores, Cin., from 1982, pres., chief operating officer, 1987-88, retail cons., 1988—; dir. Progressive Corp., Cleve., Loehmann's, N.Y.C., Best Products, Richmond, Gitano Corp., N.Y.C. Office: 101 E 52d St New York NY 10022

MATTHEWS, PATRICK JOHN, financial executive; b. Winnipeg, Manitoba, Can., Mar. 17, 1942; m. Clarice Marie Carstens; children: Brian, Richard. B of Commerce, U. Manitoba, 1968. Chartered acct., Manitoba. Various positions Peat, Marwick, Mitchell & Co., Winnipeg, Manitoba, 1968-75, ptnr., 1975-79; v.p. corp. planning Gendis Inc., Winnipeg, Manitoba, 1979-82, v.p. fin., 1982—. Mem. Inst. Chartered Accts. Manitoba. Office: Gendis Inc, 1370 Sony Pl PO Box 9400, Winnipeg, MB Canada R3C 3C3

MATTHEWS, PAUL DEACON, steel company executive; b. Thunder Bay, Ont., Can., Sept. 3, 1929; s. Wilbert Jamieson and Emily Josephine (Stagg) M.; m. Kathleen Joanna Cooper, Sept. 12, 1959; children—Ian, Catharine, Sarah. B.Commerce, McGill U., Montreal, Que., Can., 1952; M.B.A., Wharton Sch. U. Pa., 1953. Cert. gen. acct., Ont. Cons. Woods Gordon Co., Toronto, Ont., 1953-57; control mgr. Union Carbide Corp., Toronto, 1957-69; controller Toronto Star, 1969-72; dir. fin. and adminstrn. Southam Murray Printing Co., Toronto, 1972-75; treas. Stelco Inc., Toronto, 1975-85, v.p., treas., 1985—. Mem. Cert. Gen. Accts., Fin. Execs. Inst., Soc. Internat. Treasurers (chmn. Toronto chpt.). Club: Royal Can. Yacht. Office: Stelco Inc, PO Box 205, Toronto Dominion Ctr, Toronto, ON Canada M5K 1J4

MATTHEWS, ROBERT EMIL, utility company executive; b. Elizabeth, N.J., May 1, 1925; s. Emil Charles and Mae Margaret (McLaughlin) M.; m. Jeanne Frances Corbett, Jan. 20, 1951; children: Robert Edward, Patricia, Thomas, John, Anne. BME, Cath. U. Am., 1950; MBA, Morehead State U., 1978. Mech. engr. Am. Gas & Electric Service Corp. (now Am. Electric Power Service Corp.), N.Y.C., 1950-58, head engring. sect., 1958-64, dir. sales engring., 1964-67, dir., 1978—; comml. mgr. Ky. Power Co., Ashland, 1967-74, div. mgr., 1974-78, exec. v.p., 1978-80, pres., 1980—, also dir.; chmn. bd. First Am. Bank, Ashland, Ky. Energy Research Bd., 1980-83. Former bd. dirs. Hack Estep Home for Boys, Boyd County; trustee Huntington Mus. Art, 1984-87, Ky. Ind. Coll. Fund, 1983—; bd. dirs., vice chmn. Ky. Appalachian Found., 1987—; bd. mgrs. Kings Daus. Med. Ctr., Ashland, 1986—. Mem. Ky State Sch. Bd. for Vocat., Adult and Rehab. Edn., 1989—; bd. dirs. Leadership Ky.; mem. adv. bd. Project 21. With AC U.S. Army, 1943-46. Mem. ASHRAE, Ashland Area C. of C. (dir. 1975-78, pres. 1977), Associated Industries of Ky. (bd. dirs.), Ky. State C. of C. (dir. 1980-84), Rotary (past dir. club), Elks. Roman Catholic. Office: Ky Power Co 1701 Central Ave Ashland KY 41101

MATTHEWS, ROBERT LLOYD, banker; b. Omaha, Sept. 23, 1937; s. Lloyd Dale and Henrietta Anna (Voss) M.; m. Elizabeth Ann Martell, Feb. 17, 1962; children: Charles Robert, John Lloyd. B.A., U. Nebr.-Omaha, 1959; grad., Am. Inst. Banking, 1968, Pacific Coast Banking Sch., 1970. With Ariz. Bank, Phoenix, 1959—, beginning as mgmt. trainee, successively loan officer, br. mgr., loan supr., asst. to pres., exec. v.p. charge loan div., 1959-75, exec. v.p. charge earning assets div., 1975-77, pres., 1978-85, pres., chief operating officer, 1985-87, pres., chief exec. officer, 1987-88, chmn. bd. dirs., chief exec. officer, 1988—; bd. dirs., past chmn. Pacific Coast Banking Sch.; bd. dirs. Babbitt Bros. Trading Co., U.S. West Communications; bd. dirs., pres., mem. exec. com. COMPAS. Life mem. Phoenix Thunderbirds, Fiesta Bowl Adv. Bd.; mem. bd. regents, Brophy Prep. Coll.; adv. bd. Sun Angel Found.; bd. dirs. Phoenix Community Alliance, Heard Mus., Herberger Theater Ctr., Phoenix Civic Ctr., Phoenix Together, Valley Big Bros., adv. dir., former pres.; chmn. bd. dirs. United for Ariz.; trustee emeritus, hon. bd. dirs. St. Luke's Health System; mem. adv. coun. Engring. Sch., Ariz. State U.; mem. bd. advisors U. Ariz. Bus. Sch. With Air N.G., 1959-65. Mem. Robert Morris Assos. (past pres.), Ariz. Bankers Assn. (dir., past pres.), Am. Bankers Assn. (past council), Phoenix Met. C. of C. (dir., past chmn.), Phoenix 40. Republican. Roman Catholic. Office: Ariz Bancwest Corp 101 N 1st Ave Phoenix AZ 85003 also: Security Pacific Nat Bank PO Box 2097 Terminal Annex Los Angeles CA 90051

MATTHEWS, WILLIAM D(OTY), lawyer, consumer products manufacturing company executive; b. Oneida, N.Y., Aug. 25, 1934; s. William L. and Marjorie L. (Doty) M.; m. Ann M. Morse, Aug. 4, 1956; children: Judith Anne, Thomas John. A.B., Union Coll., 1956; LL.B., Cornell U., 1960. Bar: N.Y. 1960, D.C. 1962. Atty. div. corp. fin. SEC, Washington, 1960-62; assoc. Whitlock, Markey & Tait, Washington, 1962-69; gen. counsel Oneida (N.Y.) Ltd., 1973-86, v.p., 1977-78, sr. v.p., 1978-86, exec. v.p., 1986, also dir., chmn., chief exec. officer, 1986—, pres., 1989—; bd. dirs. Oneida Can. Ltd., Chase Lincoln First Bank N.A., Camden Wire Co., Inc., Buffalo China Co., Inc., N.Y. State Bus. Council, Sta. WCNY-TV. Alderman City of Oneida, 1972-79; mem. Madison County Bd. Suprs., 1984-86. Mem. ABA, Madison County Bar Assn. Presbyterian. Home: 621 Patio Circle Dr Oneida NY 13421 Office: Oneida Ltd Adminstrn Bldg Kenwood Ave Oneida NY 13421

MATTHEWS, WILLIAM ELLIOTT, IV, gas company executive; b. Birmingham, Ala., Sept. 11, 1929; s. William Elliott and Julia Lovett (Murfee) M. III; m. Wahwiece Coe, Feb. 17, 1962; children—Martha Wahwiece, William Elliott V, Julia Lovett, Mary Elizabeth. B.E.E., Ga. Inst. Tech., 1950; postgrad. Advanced Mgmt. Program, Harvard U., 1977. With So. Natural Gas Co., Birmingham, 1950—, pres., 1984—, chmn. bd. dirs., 1989—; sr. v.p. Sonat Inc., Birmingham, 1987—. Bd. dirs. YMCA, Birmingham, Jefferson-Shelby div. Am. Heart Assn., 1982-85. Served to lt. USN, 1954-56. Mem. Am. Gas Assn., Interstate Natural Gas Assn. Am., So. Gas Assn. (bd. dirs. 1979-82), Newcomen Soc. N.Am. Presbyterian. Lodge: Kiwanis. Office: So Natural Gas Co First Nat-So Nat Bldg PO Box 2563 Birmingham AL 35203 also: Sonat Inc 1900 5th Ave N Birmingham AL 35203

MATTICK, WILLIAM OSCAR, automotive executive; b. Detroit, July 18, 1945; s. Oscar William and Bernice Ann Mattick; m. Louise Marilyn Miller, Aug. 24, 1968; children: Elizabeth, Michael. BS in Engring., U. Mich., 1967, MS in Engring., 1970. Mgr. quality control Kelsey-Hayes Co., Romulus, Mich., 1968-72; mgr. product engring. Ford Motor Co., Dearborn, Mich., 1972-85; v.p., sec., owner Huron Plastics Group, St. Clair, Mich., 1985—, also bd. dirs.; bd. dirs. Ostec Corp., New Haven, Mich. Asst. leader Rochester Hills (Mich.) coun. Cub Scouts Am., 1987; coach Rochester Area Recreational Assn., 1987-89. Mem. Soc. Plastic Engrs., Soc. Automotive Engrs., Fairline Club, Radrick Farms Country Club, Oakland Univ. Pres.'s Club, Radrick Farms Golf Club. Office: Huron Plastics Group 1362 N River Rd Saint Clair MI 48079

MATTINGLY, ROBERT KERKER, entreprenuer; b. Zanesville, Ohio, Mar. 12, 1921; s. John Clement and Olive (Kerker) M.; m. Bette Louise Allen, Dec. 27, 1941; 1 child, Barbara Kay. Grad., High Sch., Zanesville, 1939. Pres. Mattingly Foods, Inc., Zanesville, 1945—. Bd. dirs. Goodwill Industries, Zanesville, 1970-76, Zanesville Trace, 1981—. Served to 1st lt. U.S. Army, 1942-45. Named So. Ohio Gentleman Farmer, Bob Evans, 1979, Ohio Commodore, Gov. Rhodes, 1979; recipient Pres.'s award, Syracuse China, 1978-85. Mem. Zanesville C. of C. (pres. 1976-77). Home: 3675 Frazeysburg Rd Zanesville OH 43701 Office: Mattingly Foods Inc 302 State St Zanesville OH 43701

MATTIS, LOUIS PRICE, pharmaceutical and consumer products company executive; b. Balt., Dec. 12, 1941; s. Louis Wadsworth and Sara Helene (Myers) M.; m. Patricia Diane Brown, Nov. 29, 1963; children—Louis Wadsworth, Deborah Cook. A.B. in Internat. Affairs, Lafayette Coll., Easton, Pa., 1962; M.B.A., Tulane U., 1964. V.p., gen. mgr. Warner Lambert Co., Manila, 1971-74; regional dir. Warner Lambert Co., Hong Kong, 1974-76; region pres. Warner Lambert Co., Sydney, Australia, 1976-79; exec. v.p. Americas-Far East Richardson-Vicks, Inc., 1979-81, pres. Americas-Far East, 1981-84, exec. v.p., 1985-87; group v.p. Sterling Drug Inc., N.Y.C., 1987-88, pres., chief operating officer, 1988—. Republican. Episcopalian. Clubs: Union League of N.Y., New Canaan (Conn.) Country; Sea Island (Ga.) Golf; Manila Polo; Skek-o. Home: 156 Kemble Dr Sea Island GA 31561 Office: Sterling Drug Inc 90 Park Ave New York NY 10016

MATTONE, JOSEPH MICHAEL, real estate developer; b. Bklyn., Sept. 15, 1931; s. Vincent James and Julia (D'Amato) M.; m. Irene Marie Ficarra, July 14, 1956; children: Julia, Irene, Carl, Joseph Jr., Francesca, Teresa, Michael. BA, St. John's U., N.Y., 1952, LLB, 1955. Bar: N.Y., U.S. Dist. Ct. (ea., so. dists.) 1956. Sole practice Bklyn., 1955-76; real estate developer Mannix and Mattone, Flushing, N.Y., 1963—; sr. ptnr. Mattone, Mattone, Mattone, Megna & Modena, Flushing, 1976—; reps. Citibank N.A., Dime Savs. Bank; counsel Marine Midland. Fund raiser Jackson St. Settlement Assn., St. John's U., C.Y.O., Cerebral Palsy, Muscular Dystrophy, St. Vincent's Home, Am. Cancer Soc., Booth Meml. Hosp.; trustee, Anthropology Mus. People of N.Y.; candidate Supreme Ct. N.Y. 1968; active in gubernatorial campaigns 1974, 78-82; mem. St. Anastasia parish council 1977-78. Named Man of Yr. United Cerebral Palsy, 1981, Italian Charities Am., 1983, Flushing Boys Club, 1983, Cath. Youth Orgn., 1985; recipient Top Hat award Am. Cancer Soc., 1989. Mem. N.Y. State Bar Assn., Queens Bar Assn., Bklyn. Bar Assn., Columbian Lawyers Assn. Queens County (sec. 1985, v.p. 1986), Columbia Soc. Real Estate Appraisers, Queens County Builders Assn., Delta Theta Pi, KC, Knights Equestrian Order, Holy Sepulchre Jerusalem, Knights of Malta, Sons of Italy. Office: Mattone Mattone Mattone Mattone Megna & Todd 159-18 Northern Blvd Flushing NY 11358

MATTSON, WALTER EDWARD, publishing company executive; b. Erie, Pa., June 6, 1932; s. Walter Edward and Florence Evelyn (Anderson) M.; m. Geraldine Anne Horsman, Oct. 10, 1953; children: Stephen, William, Carol. B.S., U. Maine, 1955; A.S., Northeastern U., 1959, hon. doctorate, 1980; postgrad., Harvard U. Advanced Mgmt. Program, 1973. Printer various cos. 1948-53; advt. mgr. Anderson Newspapers Co., Oakmont, Pa., 1954; asst. prodn. mgr. Boston Herald Traveler, 1955-58; cons. Chas. T. Main Co., Boston, 1959; with N.Y. Times Co., N.Y.C., 1960—, sr. v.p., 1972-74, exec. v.p., 1974-79, pres., 1979—, chief operating officer. Bd. dirs. nat. council Northeastern U. Served with USMC, 1951. Named Distinguished Alumni Northeastern U., 1974. Mem. ANPA (vice chmn. prodn. mgmt. com.). Office: NY Times Co 229 W 43rd St New York NY 10036 *

MATZ, JEFFREY R., business executive; b. Battle Creek, Mich., Aug. 12, 1960; s. Edward Gustave and Blanche Ann (Bieck) M.; m. Jacquelyn Kay Harper, Dec. 13, 1987. BS in Acctg. and Econs., Hope Coll., 1982. Spl. project adminstr. Anixter Bros., Skokie, Ill., 1982-83; ops. mgr. Anixter Bros., Portland, Oreg., Austin, Tex., and Boston, 1983-85; ops. analyst Anixter Bros., Skokie, Ill., 1985-87; nat. ops. project mgr. Anixter Bros., Skokie, 1987—. Vol. Spl. Olympics, Luth. Gen. Hosp., Des Plaines, Ill., 1986, 87, 88. Republican. Lutheran. Home: 3459 N Marshfield 2d Fl Chicago IL 60657 Office: Anixter Bros 4711 Golf Rd Skokie IL 60076

MATZDORFF, JAMES ARTHUR, investment banker; b. Kansas City, Mo., Jan. 3, 1956; s. Ralph G. and Sophia (Barash) M. BS, U. So. Calif., 1978; MBA, Loyola U., Los Angeles, 1980. Comml. loan officer Bank of Am., Los Angeles, 1976-78; mng. ptnr. James A. Matzdorff & Co., Beverly Hills, Calif., 1978—. Mem. Rep. Nat. Com., 1980—. Mem. NRA, Am. Fin. Assn., Porsche Car Club, Phi Delta Theta. Office: 9903 Santa Monica Blvd Ste 374 Beverly Hills CA 90212

MATZIORINIS, KENNETH N., economist; b. N.Y.C., May 4, 1954; s. Neocles N. and Penelope (Gregoratos) M.; m. Catherine Marina Astrakianakis, July 27, 1985. B.A., McGill U., 1976, M.A., 1979, Ph.D., 1985. Cert. mgmt. cons. Asst. economist Nat. Bank Greece (Can.), Montreal, 1978-81; lectr. econs. McGill U., Montreal, 1977—; prof. econs. John Abbott Coll., Montreal, 1981—; pres. Canbek Econ. Cons., Inc., Montreal, 1983—. Econs. adviser to bd. dirs. Internat. Orgn. Psychophysiology, 1982—; bd. dirs. Can. Inst. Study Pub. Enterprise, 1980—. Author: Introduction to Macro Economics: An Applied Approach, 1988; editor: Vital Graphs of Canadian Economy, 1984; contbr. articles to profl. jours. Vice pres. Westmount Liberal Riding Assn., Montreal, 1975-77; bd. govs. McGill U., 1978-81; bd. govs. John Abbott Coll., 1988—; chmn. bd. dirs. Community Service Ctr. St. Louis, Montreal, 1978-80. Mem. Am. Econ. Assn., Can. Econ. Assn., Can. Assn. Bus. Economists, Internat. Orgn. Psychophysiology, Assn. Evolutonary Econo., Que. Inst. Cert. Mgmt. Cons. Greek Orthodox. Club: Graduate (Montreal). Home: 619 67th Ave, Laval, PQ Canada H7V 3N9

MAUCK, WILLIAM M., JR., executive recruiter; b. Cleve., Mar. 30, 1938; s. William M. and Elizabeth Louise (Stone) M.; m. Paula Jean Mauck, Aug. 15, 1969 (div. Mar. 1983); children: Brian, David; m. Jeanne Lee Mauck, May 21, 1987. BS in Bus., Ind. U., 1961. Sales engr. Inland Container Corp., Louisville, 1961-69; sales mgr. Dixie Container Corp., Knoxville, Tenn., 1969-70, gen. mgr., 1970-75; v.p., ptnr. Heidrick & Struggles, Inc., Houston, 1975-81; pres. Booker & Mauck, Inc., Houston, 1981-85; ptnr. Ward Howell Internat. Inc., Houston, 1985-89; prin. William M. Mauck, Jr., Houston, 1989—; mem. adv. bd. Women's Sports Found., N.Y.C., 1985—. Mem. Plaza Club (Houston) (chmn. bd. govs. 1987-88), Sertoma Club (Knoxville 1972-75) (pres. 1974-75). Republican. Methodist. Home: 190 Old Bridge Lake Houston TX 77069 Office: 16825 Northchase Dr Ste 705 Houston TX 77060

MAUGANS, EDGAR HURLEY, utility company executive; b. Harrisburg, Pa., Jan. 14, 1935; s. Edgar Hurley and Grace Lenore (English) M.; m. Fern Shaw, Sept. 3, 1955 (div. Dec. 1982); children: Edgar Hurley, Todd D., Elizabeth, Jennifer; m. Barbara Schulte, Dec. 28, 1982. BS, Findlay Coll., 1956; grad. advanced mgmt. program, Harvard U., 1987. With Cleve. Electric Illuminating Co., 1956-86, supt., 1972-73, controller, 1973-79, v.p., 1977-79, v.p. fin., chief fin. officer, 1979-86; sr. v.p. fin., chief fin. officer Centerior Energy Corp., 1986—. Trustee Gt. Lakes Theater Festival, 1979—, Fairview Gen. Hosp., 1986—, Friends of Cleve. Pub. Library, 1982-88, Findlay (Ohio)

Coll., 1988—. Mem. Edison Electric Inst., Fin. Execs. Inst., Am. Statis. Assn. Republican. Lodge: Lakewood-Rocky River Rotary. Home: 12550 Lake Ave #1407 Lakewood OH 44107 Office: Centerior Energy Corp 6200 Oak Tree Blvd Cleveland OH 44131

MAULDIN, JEAN HUMPHRIES, aviation company executive; b. Gordonville, Tex., Aug. 16, 1923; d. James Wiley and Lena Leota (Noel-Crain) Humphries; B.S., Hardin Simmons U., 1943; M.S., U. So. Calif., 1961; postgrad. Westfield Coll., U. London, 1977-78, Warnborough Coll., Oxford, Eng., 1977-78; m. William Henry Mauldin, Feb. 28, 1942; children—Bruce Patrick, William Timothy III. Psychol. counselor social services 1st Baptist Ch., 1953-57; pres. Mauldin and Staff, public relations, Los Angeles, 1957-78; pres. Stardust Aviation, Inc., Santa Ana, Calif., 1962—. Mem. Calif. Democratic Council, 1953-83; mem. exec. bd. Calif. Dem. Central com., 1957—, Orange County Dem. Central Com., 1960—; mem. U.S. Congl. Peace Adv. Bd., 1981—; del. Dem. Nat. Conv., 1974, 78, Dem. Mid-Term Conv., 1976, 78, 82, 86, Dem. Nat. Issues Conf.; mem. nat. advisor U.S. Congl. Adv. Bd. Am. Security Council; pres. Santa Ana Friends of Public Library, 1973-76, McFadden Friends of Library, Santa Ana, 1976-80; chmn. cancer crusade Am. Cancer Soc., Orange County, 1974; mem. exec. bd. Lisa Hist. Preservation Soc., 1970—; lay leader Protestant Episcopal Ch. Am., Trinity Ch., Tustin, Calif. Named Woman of Yr., Key Woman in Politics, Calif. Dem. Party, 1960-80. Am. Mgmt. Assn. (pres.'s club), Bus. and Profl. Women Am., Exptl. Aircraft and Pilots Assn., Nat. Women's Polit. Caucus, Dem. Coalition Central Coms., Calif. Friends of Library (life), Women's Missionary Soc. (chmn.), LWV, Nat. Fedn. Dem. Women, Calif. Fedn. County Central Com. Mems., Internat. Platform Assn., Peace Through Strength, Oceanic Soc., Nat. Audubon Soc., Sierra Club, Nat. Wildlife Fedn., Internat. Amnesty Assn., Am. Security Council, Nat. Women's Pilot. Club: U. So. Calif. Ski, Town Hall of Calif. Author: Cliff Winters, The Pilot, The Man, 1961; The consummate Barnstormer, 1962; The Daredevil Clown, 1965. Home: 1013 W Elliott Pl Santa Ana CA 92704 also: 102 E 45th St Savannah GA 31405 Office: 16542 Mount Kibby St Fountain Valley CA 92708

MAUNEY, MARGARET STEVENS, textile and apparel company executive; b. Washington, N.C., Feb. 3, 1954; d. Charles Edgar and Margaret Mann (Swindell) Stevens; m. Fred Kevin Mauney, Oct. 10,1 987. AA, St. Mary's Coll., Raleigh, N.C., 1974; BSBA, East Carolina U., 1976. CPA, N.C. Tax supr. Ernst & Whinney, Raleigh, 1976-80; tax mgr. Leggs Products, Winston-Salem, N.C., 1980-85; dir. fin. planning and analysis Sara Lee Knit Products, Winston-Salem, 1985—. Vol. in museum shop Southeastern Ctr. for Contemporary Art, Winston-Salem, 1985—. Named one of Outstanding Young Women of Am., 1985. Mem. Am. Inst. CPAs, N.C. Assn. CPAs. Democrat. Baptist. Club: YMCA Women. Home: 3401 Buena Vista Rd Winston-Salem NC 27106 Office: Sara Lee Knit Products 450 Hanes Mill Rd Winston-Salem NC 27105

MAURER, C(HARLES) F(REDERICK) WILLIAM, 3D, food brokerage executive; b. Jersey City, July 12, 1939; s. William and Daisy L. (Knight) M.; BA, Va. Mil. Inst., 1961, MA in Humanities, Manhattanville Coll., 1988; m. Shon Hooker, June 6, 1964; children: Melissa, Adam. Adminstrv. sec. Marshall Research Found., 1961-62; adminstrv. sec. Morse, Maurer & Kopple, Englewood Cliffs, N.J., 1965-72; v.p. instl. sales HMM&K, Englewood Cliffs, 1972-78; v.p. Maurer & Kopple, Englewood Cliffs, 1978-84, pres., 1984-88; exec. v.p. Foodservice, div. M&H Co., Purchase, N.Y., 1978—. Author: Third Continental Dragoons Diary, 1776-1784, 1979. Pres., Park Ridge (N.J.) Bd. Health, 1980-83, councilman, 1984—. Maj., inf., U.S. Army, 1962-64. Mem. Co. Mil. Historians, Pascack Hist. Soc. (pres. 1978-80), Gideon Club. Methodist. Home: 3 Tulip Ct Park Ridge NJ 07656

MAURER, CLAUDE EMILE, oil and gas mining executive; b. Chatillon sur/Seine, Cote d'or, France, Dec. 21, 1924; s. Robert and Yvonne (Chanonat) M.; Gladys May Espinosa, Sept. 7, 1966; children: Victor, Valerie, Yves. Degree engring., E.N.S.A.M., Paris, 1945. Research engr. Soc. Nat. De Constrn. Aeronautique Du Nord, Paris, 1945-46; field engr. Schlumberger Overseas S.A., Indonesia, 1947-50; research engr. Ste. Prospection Electrique, Paris, 1950-56; field ops. supr. Schlumberger Surenco, Venezuela, Peru, Brazil and Argentina, 1956-62; mgr. field ops. Schlumberger Surenco, Caracas, Venezuela, 1962-64; pres., chief exec. officer Minar SAPS, Buenos Aires, Argentina, 1966—; pres., chief exec. officer Precimeca, Buenos Aires, 1974—, Maurer Tools Inc., Houston, 1979—, WYC, Inc., Houston, 1981—. Served to lt. French Navy, 1946-47. Mem. Soc. Petroleum Engrs., Inst. Argentino Petróleo. Roman Catholic. Clubs: River Plate (Capital Federal) Tiro Federal Argentina. Office: Minar SAPS, Maipu 267 piso 20, 1084 Buenos Aires Argentina

MAURER, FREDERIC GEORGE, III, banker; b. Grand Rapids, Mich., May 15, 1952; s. Frederic George and Rhea Marie (Annesser) M. B.A., St. Louis U., 1974, M.B.A., 1977. Dir. residence Marguerite Hall, St. Louis U., 1977-79; internat. banking analyst Merc. Trust Co., St. Louis, 1979-80, banking rep. Latin Am., 1980-81, internat. officer, 1981-83, asst. v.p., 1983; asst. v.p. Union Bank, Los Angeles, 1983-86; asst. v.p. internat. sect. Centerre Bank, N.A., St. Louis, 1986-87, portfolio mgmt. sect.,1987-88, pvt. banking dept. Boatmen's Nat. Bank St. Louis, 1988, v.p., 1989—. Bd. dirs. Assocs. St. Louis U. Libraries, 1975-79. Internat. Bus. fellow, 1975-77. Mem. Assocs. St. Louis U. Libraries, Ctr. Internat. Banking Studies, U. Va., Charlottesville; mem. Robert Morris Assocs., Alumni Council St. Louis U., Opera Guild, Performing Arts Council-In the Wings, Los Angeles. Mem. dir.'s assn. Mo. Botanical Garden, 1986—, mem. World Affairs Coun., St. Louis; mem. DuBourg Soc. St. Louis U. Mem. Japan-Am. Soc., U.S.-Mexico C. of C. (Pacific chpt.), English-speaking Union. Republican. Roman Catholic. Clubs: American (London); Noonday, Mo. Athletic (St. Louis); Los Angeles Athletic. Home: 4225 W Pine Blvd Saint Louis MO 63108 Office: Boatmen's Nat Bank Saint Louis One Boatmen's Pla Saint Louis MO 63101

MAURER, J. PIERRE, insurance company executive; b. Montreal, Que., Can., June 10, 1924; came to U.S., 1978; s. Alexis Antoine and Jeanne (Marcotte) M.; m. Armande Crete, Feb. 15, 1947; 1 son, Michel. B.A., St. Ignatius Coll., Montreal, 1946; hon. degree, Ottawa U., 1978. With Met. Life Ins. Co., N.Y.C., 1950—, pres. Can. ops., 1974-78, exec. v.p., mem. exec. com., 1978-86, vice chmn. bd., 1986—, also dir.; dir. Royal Bank Can.; chmn. Century 21 Real Estate Corp., 1985—. Trustee Am. Coll. and Bus. Council for the U.N. Mem. Life Ins. Mktg. Research Assn. (past chmn.). Clubs: Rideau (Ottawa, Ont. Can.); Mt. Royal (Montreal); Ont. (Toronto); Metropolitan (N.Y.C.). Home: 8 Peter Cooper Rd New York NY 10010 Office: Met Life Ins Co 1 Madison Ave New York NY 10010

MAURER, P(AUL) REED, JR., pharmaceutical company executive; b. Minersville, Pa., Sept. 20, 1937; s. Paul Reed and Ruth Lillian (Daniel) M.; m. Beverly Mae Seaman, June 22, 1963 (div. Feb. 1984); children: Paul Reed, Glenn Charles; m. Yuko Arai, June 30, 1984; children: Michelle Aoi, Tricia Haruna. BS, Kutz U., 1959; MS, U. Pa., 1962. Asst. prof. Bucknell U., Lewisburg, Pa., 1963-64; salesman Eli Lilly & Co., Wilmington and Washington, N.D., 1964-66; corp. trainee Eli Lilly & Co., Indpls., 1967-69; dir. mktg. Eli Lilly Internat. Corp., Kobe, Japan, 1970; v.p. Eli Lilly K.K., Kobe, Japan, 1971-76; chmn. MSO Co. Ltd., Tokyo, 1976-85; v.p. Merck & Co., Rahway, N.J., 1977-86; pres. Metpac Ltd., 1986—; cons. Merck & Co. Inc., 1986—. Contbr. articles to profl. jours. Mem. Pharm. Mfrs. Assn. (Japan rep.), Am. C. of C. (Tokyo). Lodge: Rotary (Found. fellow 1960). Home and Office: care 220 S King St Ste 1600 Honolulu HI 96813

MAURIEL, JOHN JOSEPH, management educator; b. Schenectady, N.Y., May 4, 1932; s. John J. and Rosemary (Araneo) M.; m. Maryanne Kennedy, Aug. 25, 1962; 1 child, Michael. AB in Econs., U. Mich., 1953; MBA, Harvard U., 1961, Dr. Bus. Adminstrn., 1964. Sales rep. IBM, Schenectady, 1956-59; lectr. Harvard U., Cambridge, Mass., 1963-64; lectr. bus. sch. Harvard U., 1964-65; prof. sch. mgmt. U. Minn., Mpls., 1965—; bd. dirs. exec. fellow program Bush Pub. Sch., St. Paul, 1975—, Bush Prins. Leadership Program, St. Paul, 1985—, H.B. Fuller Co., St. Paul; vis. prof. North European Mgmt. Inst., Oslo, Norway, 1975-76. Author: Logic of Strategy, 1988; contbr. articles in field to profl. jours. Bd. dirs. Golden Valley Sch. Bd., 1977-80, Learning Ctr. for Econs., Mpls. Pub. Sch., 1986—; chmn. Rotary Scholarship com., Mpls., 1987-88; chmn. bd. dirs. Mercy Missionaries, Mpls., 1986—. Lt. USNR, 1953-56, PTO. Mem. Acad. Mgmt. Assn., Am. Ednl. Rsch. Assn., Rotary. Home: 4521 Westwood Ln Minneapolis MN 55416 Office: U Minn Sch Mgmt 271 19th Ave S Minneapolis MN 55455

MAURO, GEORGE THEODORE, corporate executive; b. N.Y.C., Mar. 7, 1938; s. Peter Terzo and Bella (Cohn) M.; m. Mary Ann Stoehr, Feb. 15, 1964; children: Mary Patricia, Christine. BA, U. N.H., 1959; MBA, U. Pa., 1972. Sr. cons. Booz, Allen & Hamilton, Inc., Phila., 1972-75, v.p., 1975-77; dir. Asset Value Analysis, U.S. Ry. Assn., Washington, 1977-79; sr. assoc. Temple Barker & Sloane, Inc., Lexington, Mass., 1979-83; dir. transp. FMC Corp., Chgo., 1984-85, dir. logistics, 1985—. Served with USAF, 1960-70. Decorated Meritorious Service medal Dept. Def., Air Force Commendation medal. Mem. Ops. Mgmt. Assn., Council Logistics Mgmt., Nat. Indsl. Transp. League, Nat. Freight Transp. Assn., Assn. for Mfg. Excellence, Beta Gamma Sigma, Tau Kappa Alpha, Psi Chi, Pi Kappa Alpha. Office: 200 E Randolph Dr Chicago IL 60601

MAUS, RALPH DALE, sales executive; b. Parsons, Kans., Mar. 27, 1903; s. L.T. and Anna L. (Smith) M.; m. Florence Luella Adkins, Nov. 14, 1928; 1 child, Constance Lorraine Maus Hammond. BS in Pharm., Kans. U., 1928. Registered pharmacist, Kans., Ind. Territory salesman The Upjohn Co., Okla., 1928-31; salesman, sales mgr. Pitman Moore Co., Dow Chem., 1931-61, asst. v.p. sales, 1961-66; indsl. salesman, sales trainer Bus. Furniture Co., Ind., 1966-71; sales and mktg. exec. Parsons Bishop Nat. Collections, Indpls., 1971-76; security salesman Beta Med. Pharm., Indpls., 1976-80; sales councilor, trainer various cos., Ind., 1980—; sales instr. Butler U., Indpls., 1965—; lectr. human relations to pharmacy schs., med. schs., vet. and dental schs., clubs, others. Active United Fund Indsl. Div., Indpls., 1960-63; chmn. Marion County March of Dimes, Indpls., 1964—. Mem. Sales Exec. Council (program chmn. 1979—), Rotary (exec. council 1980), Masons, Shriners. Baptist. Home: 675 S Ford Rd E007 Zionsville IN 46077

MAUTER, WARREN EUGENE, chemist, business development manager; b. Denver, Aug. 27, 1951; s. Jacob Martin and Harriette June (Kaiser) M.; m. Deborah Lee Long, Jan. 22, 1983 (div. 1987). BS in Chemistry, Met. State Coll., 1976; MBA, U. Colo., 1986. Rech. chemist Manville Corp., Denver, 1973-80, group leader, 1980-83; applications mgr. Cardinal Chem., Columbia, S.C., 1983-84; prin. Alpine Cons., Denver, 1984-88; corp. mgr. COBE Labs., Inc., Lakewood, Colo., 1988—; instr. econs. and fin. U. Colo. Coll. Engring, 1987-89; mem. bd. advs. Shock Found., 1986-88. Bd. reviewers Jour. Vinyl Tech., 1981-83; contbr. articles to profl. jours. Sci. and Tech. Colo. scholar Met. State Coll., 1972-75. Mem. ASTM, Soc. Plastics Engrs. (bd. dirs. vinyl div. 1982-86), Nat. Sanitation Found. (industry adv. bd. 1980-84), Am. Chem. Soc., Am. Mgmt. Assn., Colo. Mountain Club, U. Colo. Execs. Club (Denver, v.p. 1987, pres. 1988). Republican. Home: 1649 S Marion St Denver CO 80210 Office: COBE Labs Inc 1185 Oak St Lakewood CO 80215

MAVROS, GEORGE S., clinical laboratory director; b. Adelaide, Australia, Oct. 14, 1957; came to U.S., 1970; s. Sotirios George and Angeliki (Korogiannis) M.; m. Renee Ann Cuddeback, June 24, 1979. BA in Microbiology, U. South Fla., 1979, MS in Microbiology, 1987; postgrad. MBA, Nova U., 1987—. Diplomate Lab Mgmt.; cert. clin. lab dir. Med. technologist Jackson Meml. Hosp., Dade City, Fla., 1979-81; microbiology supr. HCA Bayonet Point-Hudson Med. Ctr., Hudson, Fla., 1981-82, dir. labs., 1982-88; dir. labs. Citrus Meml. Hosp., Inverness, Fla., 1988—; lab. cons. HCA Oak Hill Hosp., Spring Hill, Fla., 1983-84; cons. lab. info. systems Citation Computer Systems, St. Louis, 1983—, Hosp. Corp. of Am., Nashville, 1986; instr. Microbiology Pasco Hernando Com. Coll., New Port Richey, Fla., 1986-88, Inst. Biolog. Scis. Cen. Fla. Community Coll., Lecanto, 1989—; bd. dirs. Gulf Coast chpt. Clin. Lab. Mgrs. Assn., Tampa, Fla., 1987, pres., 1987-89. Parish pres. Greek Orthodox Ch. of West Cen., Inverness, Fla.; chmn. Bayonet Point Hosp. Good Govt. Group, Hudson, 1986-88. Mem. Am. Mgmt. Assn., Am. Soc. Microbiology, Am. Soc. Clin. Pathologists (cert.), Am. Soc. Med. Technologists, Am. Med. Technologists (cert.), Fla. Soc. Med. Technologists, Clin. Lab. Mgmt. Assn. (pres. Gulf Coast chpt. 1988—), Am. Assn. Clin. Chemists, Am. Pub. Health Assn., Am. Acad. Microbiology (cert.), Nat. Cert. Agy. for Clin. Lab. Personnel (cert. specialist in microbiology). Democrat. Clubs: Greek Orthodox Youth Am. (Clearwater, Fla.). Lodges: Order of DeMolay, Sons of Pericles (sec.). Home: 6 Mastic Ct E Homosassa FL 32646-8719 Office: HCA Bayonet Point-Hudson Med Ctr 14000 Fivay Rd Hudson FL 33567

MAW, JAMES GORDON, forest products company executive; b. Hamilton, Ont., Can., June 2, 1936; s. John Lawrence and Holly Alexandra (Stitt) M.; m. Patricia Ann McCaghey, Dec. 23, 1961; children: Sean, Jay. B.A., Queens U., Kingston, Ont., Can., 1957, B.Commn., 1958; M.B.A., Harvard U., 1960. Corp. fin. analyst Stelco, Hamilton, 1965-66, spl. duties-systems positions, 1966-67; bus. analyst Abitibi-Price Inc., Toronto, Ont., 1967-70, corp. planner, 1970-73, mgr. fin. planning, 1973-80, treas., 1980-82; v.p., treas. Abitibi-Price Inc., 1982-87, v.p. fin., 1987-88, sr. v.p. fin., 1988—. Author: Return on Investment: Concept and Application, 1968. Bd. dirs. Hamilton Jaycees, 1962-64. Mem. Fin. Execs. Inst., Conf. Bd. Fin. Execs., Toronto Bd. Trade, Port Credit Yacht Club. Progressive Conservative. Home: 132 Oakes Dr, Mississauga, ON Canada L5G 3M1 Office: Abitibi-Price Inc, 2 First Canadian Pl Box 39, Toronto, ON Canada M5X 1A9

MAWHINNEY, KING, insurance company executive; b. Richmond, Va., Sept. 13, 1947; s. John A. and Ellen E. (King) M.; m. Jeanne Dale Smothers, June 8, 1976 (div. Oct. 1984); m. Cathryn C. Morley, Nov. 15, 1986. A.B., Davidson Coll., 1971; M.A., Pacific Lutheran U., 1973. C.L.U.; chartered fin. cons. Devel. mgr. Prudential Ins. Co., Newark, 1977-80; sr. sales rep. USAA Life Ins. Co., San Antonio, 1980-81, sales tng. adminstr., 1981-82, dir. procedures and tng., 1983-85, dir. group/bus. sales, 1985-86, sr. dir. USAA Ednl. Services, 1986-88, exec. dir. individual sales, FSD Mktg., 1989—. Active United Way, Am. Heart Assn.; mem. choir Alamo Heights Presbyterian Ch., 1981-83, deacon, 1982-83; mem. bd. gov's. San Antonio Estate Planners Coun. Served to capt. U.S. Army, 1972-77; Korea. Fellow Life Mgmt. Inst. (coun. chmn. 1988—, soc. com. 1988—); mem. Davidson Coll. Alumni Assn. (chpt. pres. 1983—), San Antonio Chpt. C.L.U. (bd. dirs., v.p. programs, v.p. fin., v.p. adminstrn., pres.-elect, pres.), FLMI Soc. So. Cen. Tex. (chpt. pres. 1986—), Am. Soc. Tng. and Devel., Phi Kappa Phi, Sigma Nu. Republican. Avocations: dog training and showing; stamp collecting; swimming; aerobic exercise. Home: 6010 Bloomwood Dr San Antonio TX 78249 Office: USAA FSD Mktg USAA Bldg D3W San Antonio TX 78288

MAXFIELD, MICHAEL GERALD, forest products company executive, accountant; b. Pontiac, Mich., Feb. 27, 1954; s. Gerald E.L. and Mildred (Lewis) M. BS, Mich. State U., 1973, MBA, 1975. CPA, Mich. Mgr. Deloitte, Haskins & Sells, Detroit and Grand Rapids, Mich., 1975-86; v.p. fin. The Universal Cos., Inc., Grand Rapids, 1986—, also bd. dirs., treas. Treas. Kent County Rep. Com., Grand Rapids, 1984—, 5th dist. fin. chmn. Mem. AICPA, Mich. Assn. CPAs, Grand Rapids C. of C. (chmn. 1984-88). Republican. Home: 7737 Kenrob SE Grand Rapids MI 49508 Office: The Universal Cos Inc 2801 E Beltline NE Grand Rapids MI 49505

MAXON, DON CARLTON, construction company executive, mining company executive; b. Downers Grove, Ill., Dec. 23, 1914; s. Norman T. and Agnes M. (Matteson) M.; student public schs., Barrington, Ill.; m. Mary T. Quirk, June 14, 1941; children—Maureen, Don, Paul, Anne, Lee; m. 2d, Ella Luanne Roy, Dec. 10, 1971; 1 stepson, Tom Roy. Founder, pres. Maxon Constrn. Co., Tucson, 1936—, Gen. Mining & Devel. Co., Tucson, 1967—; rancher; internat. fin. cons. Mem. pres.'s club Pres. Johnson and Kennedy; mem. Pockets of Poverty Commn. Served with Seabees, USN, 1942-45. Recipient awards for designing family communities of Streamwood, Ill. and Green Valley, Ariz., Parents' mag., 1953, 59, 60; Tenn. Squire. Mem. Nat. Assn. Home Builders (Nat. Homes Pres.'s Land Planning award 1954), Gov.'s Club Ariz. Democrat. Roman Catholic. Research on methods for testing and extracting gold from complex ores; builder U.S. Gypsum Co. Research Village, Barrington, Ill. Home: 2586 E Avenida de Maria Tucson AZ 85718

MAXWELL, DAVID OGDEN, federal mortgage association executive; b. Phila., May 16, 1930; s. David Farrow and Emily Ogden (Nelson) M.; m. Joan Clark Paddock, Dec. 14, 1968. BA, Yale U., 1952; LLB, Harvard U., 1955. Bar: Pa. 1955, D.C. 1955. Assoc. Obermayer, Rebmann, Maxwell & Hippel, Phila., 1959-67, ptnr., 1963-67; ins. commr. State of Pa., 1967-69, adminstrn. and budget sec., 1969-70; gen. counsel HUD, Washington, 1970-73; pres., chief exec. officer Ticor Mortgage Ins. Co., 1973-81; chmn. bd., chief exec. officer Fed. Nat. Mortgage Assn., Washington, 1981—; bd. dirs. Kaufman and Broad, Inc.; trustee The Urban Inst., The Enterprise Found. Bd. dirs. Alliance to Save Energy. Served with USNR, 1955-59. Mem. ABA, Am. Bar Found. Home: 3525 Springland Ln NW Washington DC 20008 Office: Fed Nat Mortgage Assn 3900 Wisconsin Ave NW Washington DC 20016 *

MAXWELL, DONALD STANLEY, publishing executive; b. Los Angeles, May 30, 1930; s. Harold Stanley and Margaret (Trenam) M.; m. Martha Helen Winn, Dec. 5, 1952; children: Sylvia Louise, Cynthia Lynn, Bruce Stanley, Bradley Erl, Walter James, Wesley Richard, Amy Bernice. Student, Long Beach City Coll., 1948-50; B.B.A., Woodbury Coll., 1956. C.P.A. Ptnr. Robert McDavid & Co. (C.P.A.'s), Los Angeles, 1955-61; controller Petersen Pub. Co., Los Angeles, 1961-68; v.p. fin. Petersen Pub. Co., 1969; controller Los Angeles Times, 1969-79, v.p., 1977-79, v.p. fin., 1979-81; asst. treas. Times Mirror Co., 1971-82, v.p., controller, 1982-87, v.p., chief acctg. officer, 1987—. Trustee Woodbury U., 1981—, chmn. bd. trustees, 1984-87. Served with AUS, 1950-52. Mem. Fin. Execs. Inst. (dir. 1979-82, pres. Los Angeles chpt. 1973-74), Internat. Newspaper Fin. Execs. (dir. 1978-82, pres. 1980-81), Am. Inst. CPAs, Calif. Soc. CPAs, Am. Horse Council, Internat. Arabian Horse Assn., Arabian Horse Assn. So. Calif., Friendly Hills Country Club. Republican. Baptist. Home: 2160 LeFlore Dr La Habra Heights CA 90631 Office: Times Mirror Sq Los Angeles CA 90053

MAXWELL, HAMISH, diversified consumer products company executive; b. 1926. BA, Cambridge U., Eng., 1949. With Thomas Cook Sons & Co., 1949-54, Philip Morris, Inc., 1954-85; salesman Philip Morris, Inc., Richmond, Va., 1954-69; v.p. Philip Morris, Inc., 1969-76, sr. v.p., 1976-78, exec. v.p., 1978-83, pres., chief operating officer, 1983-84, chmn., chief exec. officer, 1984-85, also bd. dirs.; with Philip Morris Internat., 1961-83, advt. dir., 1961-63, v.p. mktg., 1963-65, regional v.p., Asia/Pacific region, 1965-73, exec. v.p. Canadian & Asia/Pacific regions, 1973-75, exec. v.p. Can./Asia & Europe/Middle East/Asia regions, 1975-78, pres., chief exec. officer, 1978-85, chmn., chief exec. officer; also bd. dirs. Philip Morris Cos., Inc. (holding co. of Philip Morris Inc. & Philip Morris Internat.), 1985—. Served with RAF, 1944-47. Office: Philip Morris Cos Inc 120 Park Ave New York NY 10017 *

MAXWELL, IAN, communications corporation executive. Grad., Balliol Coll. Oxford (Eng.) U. Various sr. mgmt. positions Pergamon Press, France, Fed. Republic Germany, U.S., 1978-83; joint mng. dir. worldwide mktg. ops. Maxwell Communication Corp., 1985—; bd. dirs. Hollis plc, Mirror Group Newspapers Ltd., TF1, France; chmn. bd. dirs. Agence Centrale de Presse, France. Active Prince's Charitable Trust, England, 1983-84. *

MAXWELL, J. DOUGLAS, JR., photographic company executive; b. Glen Cove, N.Y., Sept. 26, 1941; s. John Douglas M. and Marie Elise (Powers) Cummings; m. Hanne Agnete Kristensen, June 6, 1970; children: Scott Rogers, Samuel Douglas, Whitney Bodil. BA, Williams Coll., 1963; MBA, L.I.U., 1970. With Photocircuits Corp., Glen Cove, 1963-70; mgr. epuipment mktg. Chemco Techs., Inc., Glen Cove, 1970-76, treas., 1976-79, mng. dir., 1979-84, pres., 1984—, also bd. dirs.; dir. Kellmorgen Corp., Stamford, Conn., Slater Electric Corp., Glen Cove, First Nat. Bank L.I., Glen Head. Bd. dirs., v.p. Glen Cove Boys & Girls Club, 1970; bd. dirs., treas. L.I. Coun. on Alcoholism, Mineola, 1980; trustee Green Wood Cemetery, Bklyn., 1984, Green Vale Sch., Glen Head, 1986. Home: Cherry Ln Glen Head NY 11545 Office: Chemco Tech Inc Charles St Glen Cove NY 11542

MAXWELL, JEROME EUGENE, electronics co. exec.; b. Princeton, Ill., June 2, 1944; s. Emmett Eugene and June (Erickson) M.; BSEE, So. Meth. U., 1967, MSEE, 1971; m. Cynthia Jane O'Connell, July 30, 1977; children: Eric Vaughn, Christina Dawn, Jeremy Emmett, Jason Daniel, Nicholas Mark. Maintainability engr. product support div. Collins Radio Co., Richardson, Tex., 1965-67; jr. engr. computer systems div., 1967-70; sr. engr. TRW Electronic Products, Inc., Colorado Springs, 1970-73, mgr. engring., 1973-79, mgr. program mgmt. office, 1979-81, gen. mgr. space electronics mfg. div., 1981-86; pres., chief exec. officer G&S Systems, Inc., Bedford, Mass., 1986-87; pres., chief exec. officer Atec, Inc., Houston, 1987—. Mem. adv. council U. Colo., Colorado Springs, 1973-86, U. So. Colo., Pueblo, 1974-78; Weblo leader, asst. pack leader Boy Scouts Am., 1976-77; fin. chmn. Ascension Luth. Ch., 1981-86; cons. to community edn. coordinator for computer systems and equipment, 1980-86. Republican. Patentee in field. Home: 3119 Baywood Park Dr Houston TX 77068 Office: 8219 Kempwood Dr Houston TX 77055

MAXWELL, KEVIN F. H., publisher; b. Paris, Feb. 20, 1959; s. Ian Robert and Elisabeth (Meynard) M.; m. Pandora Deborah Warnford-Davis, May 5, 1984; children: Matilda, Edward, Elouise. Student, Oxford U., Eng., 1980. Mng. dir. Maxwell Communication Corp. plc, London; vice chmn. Macmillan, Inc., N.Y.C., 1988—. Office: Macmillan Inc 866 Third Ave New York NY 10020

MAXWELL, (IAN) ROBERT, publisher, film producer; b. Selo Slatina, Czechoslovakia, June 10, 1923; naturalized, 1945; s. Michael and Ann Hoch; m. Elisabeth Meynard, Mar. 15, 1945; children: Anne, Philip, Christine, Isabel, Ian, Kevin, Ghislaine. Self-educated; DSc (hon.), Moscow U., 1983, Poly Inst. N.Y., 1985; LLD (hon.), U. Aberdeen, 1988; Doc honoris causa, Adama Mickiewicza U., Poland, 1989; LLD (hon.), Temple U., 1989. Head press and publs. div. German sect. British Fgn. Office, 1945-47; founder, chmn., pub., dir. Pergamon Press Ltd., Oxford, Eng., N.Y.C. and Paris, 1949—; chmn. bd., pres. Pergamon Press Inc., N.Y.C., 1950—; chmn., chief exec. officer Maxwell Communication Corp. plc (formerly British Printing & Communications Corp. Ltd.), 1981—, Central TV plc., 1983—; chmn. Mirror Group Newspapers Ltd., pub. Daily Mirror, Daily Record, Sunday Mail, Sunday Mirror, The People, Sporting Life, Sporting Life Weekender, 1984—, Brit. Cable Services Ltd. (Rediffusion Cablevision), 1984—; chmn., chief exec. officer The Solicitors' Law Stationery Soc. plc, 1985—; chmn. Mirrorvision, 1985—, Robert Maxwell and Co. Ltd., 1948-86; chmn., chief exec. officer Clyde Cablevision Ltd., 1985—, Premier, 1986—, Maxwell Pergamon Pub. Corp. plc. (formerly Pergamon BPCC Pub. Corp. plc.), 1986-89, BPCC plc (formerly BPCC Printing Corp. plc., 1986—, MTV Europe, 1987—, Maxwell Communication Corp. Inc., N.Y., 1987—, Macmillan Inc., N.Y.C., 1988—; pub. China Daily in Europe, 1986—, The London Daily News, 1987; pub. English edition Moscow News, 1988—; pub., editor-in-chief The European, 1988—; bd. dirs. Pergamon AGB plc (formerly Hollis plc), 1983—, chmn., 1988—; bd. dirs. SelecTV plc, 1982—, Central TV plc, 1983—, Reuters Holdings plc, 1986—, TF1, 1987—, Agence Centrale de Presse, 1987—, Maxwell Media, Paris, 1987—, Solicitors' Law Stationery Soc. plc, 1985—, Philip Hill Investment Trust, 1986—; pres. European Satellite TV Broadcasting Consortium, 1986—; chmn. Gt. Britain-Sasakawa Found., 1985—;. Co-producer films: Mozart's Don Giovanni, Salzburg Festival, Bolshoi Ballet, 1957, Swan Lake, 1968; producer children's TV series DODO the Kid from Outer Space, 1968; author: Public Sector Purchasing, 1968; Editor: Progress in Nuclear Energy: The Economics of Nuclear Power, 1963; Gen. editor: Leaders of the World series, 1980—, The Econs. of Nuclear Power, 1965, Pub. Sector Purchasing, 1968; co-author: Man Alive, 1968. Labour mem. Parliament for Buckingham, 1964-70; chmn. Labour Fund Raising Found., 1960-69; chmn. labour working party on sci., govt. and industry, 1963-64; mem. Council of Europe, vice-chmn. com. on sci. and tech., 1968; treas. Round House Trust Ltd., 1965-83; chmn. Commonwealth Games (Scotland 1986), Ltd., 1966; chmn. Nat. Aids Trust fundraising group, 1987—; trustee Internat. Centre for Child Studies; mem. senate U. Leeds, 1986—; trustee Poly. Univ. N.Y., 1987—; pres. State of Israel Bonds, U.K., 1988—; dir. Bishopsgate Trust Ltd., 1984; chmn. media com. NSPCC Centenary Appeal, 1984; chmn. United Oxford Football Club plc, 1982-87; chmn. Derby County Football Club, 1987—. Decorated Officer 1st class Royal Swedish Order of Polar Star, 1983, Officer 1st class Order Stara Planina, Bulgaria, 1983, Comdr. Order of Merit with Star, Poland, 1986, 1st class Order of the White Rose, Finland, 1988; Kennedy fellow Harvard, 1971. Mem. Newspaper Pubs. Assn. (council 1984—), Human Factors Soc., Fabian Soc. Gt. Brit., Internat. Acad. Astronautics (hon.), Club of Rome (exec. dir. Brit. Group). Address: Holburn Circus, London EC1A 1DQ, England Office: Macmillan Inc 866 3rd Ave New York NY 10022

MAXWELL, ROBERT OLIVER, insurance company executive; b. Sioux City, Iowa, Sept. 23, 1940; s. Lyle Charles and Corinne Zenobia (Knudson) M.; m. Carol Marie Lejchar, June 23, 1973; 1 child, Todd Robert. BS in Mktg., Drake U., 1962. Office mgr. Occidental Life Ins. Co., L.A., 1962-68; sales rep. William Volker & Co., L.A., 1968-70; mgr. sales office State Farm Ins. Co., Palos Verdes, Calif., 1970-71; pres. Congress Life Ins. Co., Mpls., 1971—; also bd. dirs. Congress Life Ins. Co.; exec. v.p. Security Ins. Co., Mpls., 1971—; also bd. dirs. Security Ins. Co. With U.S. Army, 1963-69. Mem. Hazeltine Golf Club. Republican. Lutheran. Home: 7269 Tartan Curve Eden Prairie MN 55346 Office: Security Life Ins Co 6681 Country Club Dr Minneapolis MN 55427

MAXWELL, THOMAS EUGENE, financial sales professional, consultant; b. Alliance, Ohio, May 8, 1945; s. Harry Paul and Arletta Mae (Greathouse) M.; m. Cheryl Ann Eaton, Sept. 24, 1977 (div. 1984); 1 child, Krysta Nicole. Student, Dale Carnegie Inst., 1980-81. Lending officer 1st Nat. City Bank, Alliance, 1967-70; ops. officer United Calif. Bank, Los Angeles, 1970-72; customer service rep. Delimus Corp., Los Angeles, 1972-75, sales rep., 1980-83; trainer Delimus Corp., Piscataway, N.J., 1975-79; v.p. mktg. 1st Alliance Fin. Services, Santa Ana, Calif., 1983; pres. Maxwell Enterprises, Downey, Calif., 1983-85; mem. sales dept. Nixdoif Computer Corp., Culver City, Calif., 1985-87; with fin. sales staff GL Services Corp., Orange, Calif., 1987—. Writer various tng. materials. Named Alliance Jaycee of Month, 1968. Republican. Office: Credit Claims and Collections 1717 S State College #260 Anaheim CA 92806

MAY, ADDISON CUSHMAN, commerical bank executive; b. N.Y.C., Dec. 25, 1933; s. Byron Britton and Martha (Fay) M.; m. Jean Beattie, Sept. 2, 1961; children: Julia Cushman, Emily Beattie. BA, Yale U., 1956; postgrad., NYU, 1957-58. Ofcl. asst. Citibank of N.Y.C., 1956-60; v.p. Intercredit Agy., Inc., N.Y.C., 1960-66; asst. v.p., v.p., sr. v.p. Chase Manhattan Bank, N.Y.C. and Tokyo, 1966-77; sr. v.p., exec. v.p., vice chmn., bd. dirs. Conn. Bank & Trust Co., Stamford, Conn., 1977—; bd. dirs. Maritime Ctr. Inc., Norwalk, Conn. Bd. visitors U. Conn. Sch. Bus. Adminstrn.; adv. bd. U. Bridgeport, Conn., 1980—; bd. dirs. New Canaan Community Found., 1984—; mem. bd. trustees Stamford Ctr. Arts, Stamford, Conn. Served to 1st lt. U.S. Army, 1956-61. Mem. Southwestern Conn. Bus. & Industry Assn. (exec. com., bd. dirs. 1984—), NCCJ (exec. com. 1983—). Presbyterian. Clubs: Yale (N.Y.C.), University (N.Y.C.); Country (New Canaan, Conn.); Landmark of Stamford (Conn.) (bd. dirs. 1988—).

MAY, AMELIA RUTH, telemarketing executive; b. Akron, Ohio, July 19, 1956; d. John Dean and Marilyn Ann (Resley) M.; m Leonard Earl Everette, Dec. 13, 1987. BS in Mktg., Miami U., Oxford, Ohio, 1978; MBA, U. Phoenix, 1985. Mktg. rep. NCR Corp., Akron, 1978-80; nat. account exec. AT&T, Phoenix and Santa Clara (Calif.), 1980-84; account mgr. Multi-Systems Inc., Mountain View, Calif., 1984-85; co-owner, sr. cons. Mktg. Connections Corp., San Ramon, Calif., 1985-87; pres. Amtech Mktg. Inc., Parker, Colo., 1987—. Mem. Easter Seals Devel. Council, San Jose, Calif., 1984-86. Mem. Am. Mktg. Assn., Am. Telemktg. Assn., Rocky Mountain Telemktg. Assn. (exec. v.p. 1988-89, pres. 1989—). Office: Amtech Mktg Inc 13350 Hilary Pl Parker CO 80134

MAY, EDWARD JOSEPH, III, graphic arts executive; b. Portsmouth, Va., Mar. 12, 1946; s. Edward Joseph and Frances Katherine (Quinn) M.; m. Janet Ann Lehmann, Aug. 29, 1970; children: Elizabeth, Mark, Amanda, Kathleen. BS in Acctg. with Honors, N.Y. Inst. Tech., 1972. Staff acct. Laventhol & Horwath, Melville, N.Y., 1972-74; controller Angenieux Corp. of Am., Bohemia, N.Y., 1974-80, AMBICO, Inc., Lynbrook, N.Y., 1980-82; chief fin. officer, treas. TREBOR Conf. Ltd., Melville, 1982-86; v.p. Liberty Bus. Forms and Systems, Inc., Plainview, N.Y., 1986—. Sch. bd. chmn. North Shore Christian Sch., Port Jefferson, N.Y. 1986-88. With USN, 1964-68, Vietnam. Mem. Nat. Assn. of Accts., N.Y. State CPAs. Republican. Home: 56 Peachtree Ln Mount Sinai NY 11766 Office: Liberty Bus Forms 265 Exec Dr Plainview NY 11803

MAY, KENNETH LEE, diversified financial company executive, consultant; b. Reading, Pa., Apr. 21, 1946; s. Alfred C. and Frances V. (Laniecki) M.; 1 adopted child, Harvey W. BS in Biology, U. Notre Dame, 1968. Tchr., Gov. Mifflin Sch., Shillington, Pa., 1968-69, Reading Muhlenberg Sch., Reading, 1969-72; analyst, programmer Deiner Industries, Leesport, Pa., 1972-73; mgr. EDP, Cinderella Knitting, Denver, Pa., 1973-77; v.p. info. systems Horrigan Am., Reading, 1977—; instr. Reading Community Coll., 1979—; mem. EDP adv. coms., Reading, 1974—. Vol. ARC, Reading, 1969—, bd. dirs., 1983—; vol. Berks County Prison Soc., 1972—; foster parent Berks County Children Svc., 1979—. Mem. Data Processing Mgr. Assn., Fedn. NCR User's Groups (chmn. software adv. com. 1984—, bd. dirs. 1986—), Mid Atlantic NCR User's Group (sec. 1983—). Republican. Roman Catholic. Home: RD 4 Box 4280 Mountain PA 19540 Office: Horrigan Am Inc PO Box 13428 Reading PA 19611

MAY, KENNETH NATHANIEL, food products executive; b. Livingston, La., Dec. 24, 1930; s. Robert William and Mary Hulda (Caraway) M.; m. Patsy Jean Farr, Aug. 4, 1953; children: Sherry Alison (dec.), Nathan Elliott. BS in Poultry Sci., La. State U., 1952, MS in Poultry Sci., 1955; PhD in Food Tech., Purdue U., 1959, DAgr, 1988. Asst. prof. U. Ga., Athens, 1958-64, assoc. prof., 1964-67, prof., 1967-68; prof. Miss. State U., State College, 1968-70; dir. research Holly Farms Poultry, Wilkesboro, N.C., 1970-73, v.p., 1973-85, pres., 1985-88, chmn., chief exec. officer, 1988—; bd. dirs. Nat. Broiler Council, Washington, 1982—; adjunct prof. N.C. State U., 1975. Contbr. over 60 articles to profl. jours.; patentee treatment of cooked poultry. Bd. trustees Appalachian State U., 1987—. Recipient Industry Service award Poultry and Egg Inst. Am., 1971, Meritorious Service award, Ga. Egg Commn., 1964, Disting. Service award Agribus. N.C., 1986. Fellow Poultry Sci. Assn.; mem. Nat. Poultry Hist. Soc. (bd. dirs. 1982-88), Inst. Food Technologists. Methodist. Office: Holly Farms Foods Inc 1203 School St Wilkesboro NC 28697

MAY, PETER WILLIAM, business executive; b. N.Y.C., Dec. 11, 1942; s. Samuel D. and Isabel (Meyer) M.; m. Leni Finkelstein, Aug. 16, 1964; children: Jonathan Paul, Leslie Ann. AB, U. Chgo., 1964, MBA, 1965. CPA, N.Y. Mgr. Peat, Marwick, Mitchell & Co., N.Y.C., 1965-72; exec. v.p. Flagstaff Corp., N.Y.C., 1972-78; pres., chief operating officer Trian Group. L.P. (formerly Triangle Industries, Inc.), N.Y.C., 1978—, also bd. dirs.; bd. dirs. Avery, Inc., N.Y.C. Bd. govs. Ethical Culture Schs., N.Y.C., exec. com.; founding mem. Laura Rosenberg Meml. Fund for Pediatric Leukemia Research; trustee Robert Hirsch Charitable Trust; alumni dir. U. Chgo. Grad. Sch. of Bus.; chmn. endowment fund Ethical Culture Schs., N.Y.C.; bd. dirs. 92d St. YMCA. Mem. Am. Inst. CPA's, N.Y. Soc. of CPA's. Office: Trian Group 900 3rd Ave New York NY 10022

MAY, PHYLLIS JEAN, corporate executive; b. Flint, Mich., May 31, 1932; d. Bert A. and Alice C. (Rushton) Irvine; m. John May, Apr. 24, 1971. Grad. Dorsey Sch. Bus., 1957; cert. Internat. Corr. Schs., 1959, Nat. Tax Inst., 1978; MBA, Mich. U., 1970. Registered real estate agt. Office mgr. Comml. Constrn. Co., Flint, 1962-68; bus. mgr. new and used car dealership, Flint, 1968-70; contr. various corps., Flint, 1970-75; fiscal dir. Rubicon Odyssey Inc., Detroit, 1976-78, Wayne County Treas.'s Office, 1987—; acad. cons. acctg. Detroit Inst. Commerce, 1980-81; pres. small bus. specializing in adminstrv. cons. and acctg., 1982—; supr. mobile svc. sta., upholstery and home improvement businesses; owner retail bus. Pieces and Things. Pres. PTA Westwood Heights Schs., 1972; vol. Fedn. of Blind, 1974-76, Probate Ct., 1974-76; mem. citizens adv. bd. Northville Regional Psychiat. Hosp., 1988, sec. 1988-89. Recipient Meritorious Svc. award Genesee County for Youth, 1976, Excellent Performance and High Achievement award Odyssey Inc., 1981. Mem. Am. Bus. Women's Assn. (treas. 1981, rec. sec. 1982, v.p. 1982-83, Woman of Yr. 1982), NAFE (bd. dirs.), Womens Assn. Dearborn Orch. Soc., Internat. Platform Assn., Pi Omicron (officer 1984-85). Baptist. Home: 12050 Barlow St Detroit MI 48205 Office: 400 Monroe St Detroit MI 48226

MAY, RICHARD DEN, restaurant executive; b. Phila., Nov. 26, 1952; s. Den and Florence Jean (Brown) M.; m. Deborah Ann Crouch, May 21, 1977; 1 child, Warren Richard. BA in Polit. Sci., Wake Forest U., 1974; MBA, Vanderbilt U., 1987. Mgr., supr. restaurant Winners Corp., Columbia, S.C., 1978-79; dir. tng. Winners Corp., Atlanta, 1979-80, regional dir. ops., 1980-82; regional dir. franchise ops. Winners Corp., Nashville, 1982-84, v.p. franchise services, 1984-86, group v.p., 1986—; bd. dirs. M&W Mgmt. Co., Topeka. Republican. Home: 134 N Berwick Ln Franklin TN 37064 Office: Winners Corp 101 Winners Circle Brentwood TN 37027

MAY, THOMAS DANIEL, financial executive; b. Sandusky, Ohio, Aug. 9, 1950; s. James Irvin and Della Rose (Hemker) M.; m. Huguette Despault, June 19, 1972; 1 child, Noah Ryan. BS in Econs., John Carroll U., 1972. Program analyst fiscal, logistics and mgmt. br. Dept. Energy, Washington, 1977-79; mgr. fin. and adminstrn. naval reactors Dept. Energy, Idaho Falls, Idaho, 1979-85; dir. fin. Balt. Symphony Orch., 1985—. Lt. USN, 1971-77. Recipient Spl. Resolution of Recognition award Md. Senate, 1988. Democrat. Mem. Unitarian Ch. Home: 3531 Northway Dr Baltimore MD 21201 Office: Balt Symphony Orch 1212 Cathedral St Baltimore MD 21201

MAYALL, ROBERT LYON, international venture capital and finance consultant; b. Southampton, N.Y., Nov. 23, 1936; s. Herschel Johnson and Caroline Hollins (Lyon) M.; m. Jennifer Adler, 1978; children: Phanella, Myles, Student Harvard U., 1955; BA, Johns Hopkins U., 1958; MA, Columbia U. Fgn. Relations 1967. Mgr. corp. fin. Liggett Group Inc., N.Y.C., 1970-73; v.p., fin. group mgr. Bell & Stanton, Inc., (merged with Manning, Selvage & Lee), N.Y.C., 1974-76; sr. v.p., internat. group mgr. Manning, Selvage & Lee, Inc., N.Y.C., 1976-79; pres. The Gray Fin. Cons. Group, Inc. (merged with EPR Fin. Am.), N.Y.C. and Washington; mng. dir. R.L. Mayall & Co., Ltd., N.Y.C., London, 1979-87, pres. 1988—; dir. EPR Financial Am. Inc., 1983—, pres., 1984—; sr. ptnr. Reitenbach, Mayall Venture Capital Ptnrs., 1986—. Bd. dirs. N.Y. Republican Vol. Orgn.; mem. U.S. Def. Com. Served to maj. U.S. Army. Mem. Fgn. Policy Assn., Japan Soc., China Inst., Asia Soc., Assn. for Asian Studies, U.S. Naval Inst., Navy League of U.S., Nat. Investor Relations Inst., Nat. Alliance Vietnam Vets, War of 1812 Assn., Civil War Roundtable, SAR. Episcopalian. Author: New Fires from Old Ashes; Southeast Asia Since World War II, 1964; Yaun Shi-Kai, The Chinese Republic and The International Banking Community, 1967; Japan's Trade Surplus with the U.S.; Causes and Cures, 1978; High Technology Investment and Venture Capital Techniques, 1984, Back Home on the Red Ball Express, 1986, (novel) Samuel Smith of Maryland and the Dawn of American Empire, 1987, The Second War of American Independence 1812-14, 1988. Office: RL Mayall & Co Inc 200 Park Ave Ste 303E New York NY 10166

MAYCEN, DALE F., manufacturing company executive; b. Chgo., Apr. 5, 1938; s. Rudolph F. and Agnes S. Maycen; m. Jacquelyn Woodruff, Sept. 8, 1963; (div. June 1975); children: J. Andrew, Deanna Lynne; m. Kathleen Susan Stapleton, June 26, 1983. BA, U. Tulsa, 1962; MBA, Northwestern U., Evanston, Ill., 1963. Fin. analyst Texaco Inc., N.Y.C., 1963-66, Sinclair Oil Corp., N.Y.C., 1966-69; asst. treas. Am. Standard Inc., N.Y.C., 1969-71, gen. auditor, 1971-78, v.p. auditing and mktg. info. systems, 1978-83, v.p., treas., 1983—. Mem. Fin. Exec. Inst. Episcopalian. Clubs: Union League, Pine Orchard Yacht and Country (Conn.). Home: 671 Westover Rd Stamford CT 06902 Office: Am Standard Inc 40 W 40th St New York NY 10018

MAYER, MARILYN GOODER, steel company executive; b. Chgo.; d. Seth MacDonald and Jean (McMullen) Gooder; m. William Anthony Mayer, Nov. 14, 1959; children—William Anthony Jr., Robert MacDonald. grad. Career Inst. Chgo., 1941; student Lake Forest Coll., Ill., 1942. Adminstrv. asst. Needham, Louis & Brorby, Chgo., 1949-53; v.p. RMB Corp., Chgo., 1963-71, Mayer Motors, Ft. Lauderdale, Fla., 1965-74, Gooder-Henrichsen, Chicago Heights, Ill., 1975—; dir. Barnett Bank, West Palm Beach, Fla. Trustee Gulf Stream (Fla.) Sch., St. Andrew's Sch., Boca Raton, Fla.; bd. dirs. Bethesda Hosp. Assn., Boynton Beach, Fla., pres. 1981-82; bd. dirs. Gulf Stream Civic Assn. Mem. Soc. Four Arts. Republican. Episcopalian. Clubs: Little, Gulf Stream Bath and Tennis. Avocation: travel. Home: 2925 Polo Dr Gulf Stream FL 33483

MAYER, PATRICIA JAYNE, finance executive; b. Chgo., Apr. 27, 1950; d. Arthur and Ruth (Greenberger) Hersh; m. William A. Mayer Jr., Apr. 30, 1971. AA, Diablo Valley Coll., 1970; BSBA in Acctg., Calif. State U., Hayward, 1975. Staff acct., auditor Elmer Fox Westheimer and Co., Oakland, Calif., 1976; supervising auditor Auditor's Office County of Alameda, Oakland, 1976-78; asst. acctg. mgr. CBS Retail Stores doing bus. as Pacific Stereo, Emeryville, Calif., 1978-79; contr. Oakland Unified Sch. Dist., 1979-84; v.p. fin. YMCA of San Francisco, 1984—; instr. acctg. to staff YMCA, San Francisco, 1984—, CBS Retail Stores, 1978-79. Draft counselor Mt. Diablo Peace Ctr., Walnut Creek, Calif., 1970-72; dep. registrar of voters Contra Costa County Registrar's Office, Martinez, Calif., 1972-77. Mem. Nat. Assn. Accts. Democrat. Jewish. Club: Dalmatian of No. Calif. (bd. dirs. 1988-89), Dalmation Club of Am. Home: 2395 Lake Meadow Circle Martinez CA 94553 Office: YMCA 220 Golden Gate Ave 3rd Fl San Francisco CA 94102

MAYER, STEVEN CHARLES, corporate professional; b. Washington, May 21, 1953; s. Charles H. and Antoinette (Colijn) M.; m. Deborah Page Laughlin, Aug. 29, 1979; children: Suzanne, Karen. BA in Econs. cum laude with honors, Williams Coll., 1975; MBA, Stanford U., 1979. Assoc. corp. fin. Smith Barney and Harris Upham, N.Y.C., 1979-80; fin. planning mgr. Martin Marietta Corp., Bethesda, Md., 1980-82; contr. Martin Marietta Corp., Bethesda, 1982-83, acquisitions dir., 1983-85; chief fin. officer Native Plants, Inc., Salt Lake City, 1985—; bd. dir., exec. com. Phytotec, S.A. Home: 828 E 17th Ave Salt Lake City UT 84103 Office: Native Plants Inc 417 Wakara Way Salt Lake City UT 84108

MAYER, WILLIAM EMILIO, investment banker; b. N.Y.C., May 7, 1940; s. Emilio and Marie Mayer; m. Katherine Mayer, May 16, 1964; children: Kristen Elizabeth, William Franz. BS, U. Md., 1966, MBA, 1967. Pres., chief exec. officer First Boston Corp., N.Y.C., 1967—; bd. dirs. Modular Computer Systems, Ft. Lauderdale, Fla. Bd. dirs. U. Md. Found., College Park, 1984—; trustee Cancer Research Inst. Served to 1st lt. USAF, 1961-65. Mem. Bond Club N.Y., Investment Assn. of N.Y. Clubs: Manhasset Bay (N.Y.); Univ. (N.Y.C.); Mashomack Fish & Game. Home: 172 Long Neck Point Darien CT 06820 Office: The First Boston Corp Park Ave Pla New York NY 10055

MAYERS, LESLIE LEE, marketing executive; b. Los Angeles, Jan. 30, 1945; s. Louis Spencer and Helen Septima (Grossman) M.; m. Kathy Ann Kent, July 3, 1977; 1 child, Samantha Lee. BS, U. So. Calif., 1967. Acct. exec. trainee Doyle, Dane, Bernbach, Los Angeles, 1967-68; nat. sales mgr. Monogram Industries, Inc., Los Angeles, 1968-73; Western sales mgr. Meyers Mfg. Co., N.Y.C., 1976-81; pres. Les Mayers & Co., Los Angeles, 1975—; pres., chief exec. officer Gen. Merchandising Corp., Los Angeles, 1985-87; nat. mktg. dir. Broco, Inc., Rialto, Calif., 1988—. Jewish. Home: 14423 Dickens St #8 Sherman Oaks CA 91423

MAYES, LINDA SHERRILL, paralegal specialist; b. Annapolis, Md., Feb. 9, 1951; d. Luther Eugene and Florence (Myers) M. BA in Spanish and Lit., Mt. Holyoke Coll., 1973; MPA, Am. U., 1986. Rsch. specialist Watergate Spl. Prosecution Task Force Dept. Justice, Washington, 1973-74, rsch. analyst criminal div., 1975-76, paralegal specialist antitrust div., 1976-78, paralegal civil rights div., 1978—. Democrat. Episcopalian. Office: Dept Justice Civil Rights Div 10th and Pennsylvania Ave NW Washington DC 20530

MAYFIELD, EDGAR, telephone company executive, lawyer; b. Lebanon, Mo., July 14, 1925; s. Winan I. and Mary J. (Turner) M.; m. Martha Ellen Burton, July 24, 1949; children—JoEllen Mayfield Essman, Cynthia Mayfield Dobbs, Andrew. Diploma Navy V-12 program, Central Meth. Coll., Fayette, Mo., 1944; LLB, U. Mo., Columbia, 1949. Bar: Mo., 1949, Ark. 1960, Tex. 1965, N.Y. 1975. Pros. atty. Laclede County, Mo., 1949-52; atty. Southwestern Bell Telco., St. Louis, 1956-60; gen. atty. Southwestern Bell Telco., Little Rock, 1960-64; solicitor Southwestern Bell Telco., Dallas, 1964-68; solicitor Southwestern Bell Telco., St. Louis, 1968-69, gen. atty., 1970, gen. solicitor, 1970-74; v.p., gen. atty. AT&T, Long Lines, N.Y.C., Bedminster, N.J., 1975-80; v.p. Southwestern Bell Tel. Co., St. Louis, 1980; v.p., gen. counsel Southwestern Bell Corp., St. Louis, 1981-86, sr. v.p., gen. counsel, 1986-88; sr. exec. v.p., gen. counsel Southwestern Bell Corp., 1988—. Lt. (j.g.) USN, 1943-46. Recipient Disting. Alumni award Cen. Meth. Coll., 1981, Citation of Merit U. Mo. Law Sch, 1986. Mem. ABA, St. Louis Bar Assn., Noonday, St. Louis Club, Bellerive Country Club, Masons. Clubs: Noonday, St. Louis, Bellerive Country (St. Louis). Lodge: Masons. Office: Southwestern Bell Corp 1 Bell Ctr Rm 4208 Saint Louis MO 63101

MAYHEW, KENNETH EDWIN, JR., transportation company executive; b. Shelby, N.C., Sept. 27, 1934; s. Kenneth Edwin and Evelyn Lee (Dellinger) M.; m. Frances Elaine Craft, Apr. 7, 1957; 1 dau., Catherine Lynn Prince. A.B., Duke U., 1956. CPA, N.C. Sr. auditor Arthur Andersen & Co., Atlanta, 1956-58, 60-63; controller Trendline, Inc., Hickory, N.C., 1963-66; with Carolina Freight Carriers Corp., Cherryville, 1966—, treas., 1969-74, v.p., 1971-72, exec. v.p., 1972-85, pres., chief ops. officer, 1985-89, also dir., pres., chief exec. officer, 1989—; pres., dir. Robo Auto Wash, Shelby, Inc., 1967-73, Robo Auto Wash Cherryville, Inc., 1968-73; dir. Cherryville Nat. Bank. Mem. adv. bd. N.C. bus., Fuqua Sch. Bus., Duke U. Served with AUS, 1958-60. Mem. Am. Inst. CPA's (vice chmn.), Am. Trucking Assn. (dir. Regular Common Carrier Conf.), N.C. Trucking Assn. (v.p.), Gaston County C. of C. (v.p. public affairs), Phi Beta Kappa, Omicron Delta Kappa, Phi Eta Sigma. Methodist. Club: Lion (pres. Cherryville 1972-73). Home: 507 Spring St Cherryville NC 28021 Office: Carolina Freight Carriers Corp PO Box 697 Cherryville NC 28021 also: Carolina Freight Corp PO Box 545 Cherryville NC 28021

MAYNARD, JOHN RALPH, lawyer; b. Seattle, Mar. 5, 1942; s. John R. and Frances Jane (Mitchell) Maynard Kendryk; m. Mary Ann Mascagno, May 1, 1945; children: Bryce James, Pamela Ann. BA, U. Wash., 1964; JD, Calif. Western U., San Diego, 1972; LLM, Harvard U., 1973. Bar: Calif. 1972, Wis. 1973. Assoc. firm Whyte & Hirschboeck, Milw., 1973-78, firm Minahan & Peterson, Milw., 1979—. Bd. dirs. Am. Heart Assn. of Wis., Milw., 1979-82. Mem. Wis. Adv. Council to U.S. SBA, 1987—. Served to lt. USN, 1964-69. Mem. ABA. Republican. Clubs: University (Milw.); Harvard (Wis.). Home: 6110 N Bay Ridge Ave Milwaukee WI 53217 Office: Minahan & Peterson SC 411 E Wisconsin Ave Milwaukee WI 53202

MAYNARD, PETER MONTMORENCY, investment banker; b. Auckland, New Zealand, Oct. 30, 1929; s. Fortescue de Trafford and Gertrude Sophia (Cohen Taylor) M.; m. Danielle La Rue, June 4, 1948 (dec. 1950); 1 child, Sosthenes; m. Alice Rosen, June 15, 1970; children: Reoch, Abraham, Sally-Ruth. BA, Rampton U., Nottingham, Eng., 1950; MBA, U. Oxford, Eng., 1954; LLB, Borstal Law Sch., Eng., 1955. Registered rep. New York Stock Exchange Seiden & De Cuevas, N.Y.C., 1956-58; ptnr. Bertner Bros., N.Y.C., 1958-63; chief exec. officer Seligman, Erlanger & Co., London, 1969-74, Sebag's, London, 1969-74; chmn. SIMKO Equities Internat., N.Y.C., 1974—; cons. Hong Kong C. of C., 1980—; bd. dirs. Burke, Hampton wick & Jodrell Ltd., Singapore. Author: The Wanking Oyster, 1981. Trustee Amateur Mendicant Soc., London, 1965, Midas Found., Nassau, 1974—; fundraiser Cinders Found., N.Y.C., 1972. Served to capt. Brit. Army, 1954-56. Decorated Victoria Cross, Mil. Cross with bar. Mem. Friends of Africa, Broederbund, Plankton Inst. Republican. Episcopalian. Clubs: Whites (London), Muthaiga (Kenya). Lodge: Elks.

MAYNE, JACK EVERETT, food products executive; b. Petersborough, Ont., Can., Aug. 10, 1924; came to U.S., 1981; m. Verlin Bruner, May 3, 1947; children: Brian, Donald, Jane Mayne Cohen. BA in Chem. Engring., U. Toronto, 1946. Var. mgmt. positions Internat. Multifoods, Mpls., 1948-88, sr. v.p., 1988—, 1988—. Mem. Assn. Operative Millers. Club: Minneapolis. Office: Internat Multifoods Corp Box 2942 Minneapolis MN 55402

MAYO, A. DALE, banker; b. N.Y.C., July 19, 1941; s. Dominick F. and Helen (Sanzo) M.; m. Arlene Shale, Apr. 11, 1964 (div. July 1983); children: Melanie, Stacey; m. Sueanne Hall, Aug. 28, 1983; 1 child, A. Drew. BS, NYU, 1964, postgrad., 1965-68. Mktg. rep. data processing IBM, White Plains, N.Y., 1963-67; exec. v.p. Strategic Systems Inc., N.Y.C., 1967-69; pres. Genesis Indsl. Corp., N.Y.C., 1970; 1st v.p., dir. corp. fin. Filor, Bullard & Smith, N.Y.C., 1971-73; pres., founder A. Dale Mayo & Assocs. Inc., Dumont, N.J., 1969—; pres. Clearview Leasing Corp., Dumont, 1976—; pres. Clearview Group, Dumont, 1986—. Bd. dirs. Millay Colony for the Arts, Austerlitz, N.Y.; pres. John Harms Ctr. for Performing Arts, Englewood. Mem. Am. Assn. Equipment Lessors, Real Estate Syndicate Inst., Knickerbocker Country Club, Englewood Field Club. Republican. Episcopalian. Office: Clearview Group 47 E Madison Ave Dumont NJ 07628

MAYO, JOHN SULLIVAN, telecommunications company executive; b. Greenville, N.C., Feb. 26, 1930; s. William Louis and Mattie (Harris) M.; m. Lucille Dodgson, Apr. 1957; children—Mark Dodgson, David Thomas, Nancy Ann, Lynn Marie. B.S., N.C. State U., 1952, M.S., 1953, Ph.D., 1955. With AT&T Bell Labs., Murray Hill, N.J., 1955—, exec. dir. toll electronic switching div., 1973-75, v.p. electronics tech., 1975-79, exec. v.p. network systems, 1979—; mem. N.Y.C. Partnership's High Tech. Com.; adv. bd. Coll. Engring., U. Calif., Berkeley; mem. com. on engring. utilization Am. Assn. Engring. Socs.; bd. dirs. Johnson & Johnson, Polytechnic U. Corp., Western Digital Corp. Contbr. articles to profl. jours.; patentee in field. Named Outstanding Engring. Alumnus N.C. State U., 1977. Fellow IEEE (Alexander Graham Bell award 1978, Simon Ramo medal 1988, C&C prize 1988); mem. Nat. Acad. Engring., Sigma Xi, Phi Kappa Phi. Baptist. Office: AT&T Bell Labs 600 Mountain Ave Murray Hill NJ 07974

MAZANKOWSKI, DONALD FRANK, Canadian government official; b. Viking, Alta., Can., July 27, 1935; s. Frank and Dora (Lonowski) M.; m. Lorraine Poleschuk, Sept. 6, 1958; children: Gregory, Roger, Donald. Student, pub. schs. Mem. Progressive Conservative House of Commons, 1968—, chmn. com. transp., 1972-74, mem. com. govt. ops., 1976-77, mem. com. trans. and communication, 1977-79; minister of transp. Can. Govt., 1979-80, 84-86; minister responsible for Can. Wheat Bd., 1979-80; pres. Treas. Bd., 1986-88; dep. prime minister, pres. Queen's Privy Council, govt. leader in House of Commons, minister responsible for privatization and regulatory affairs Govt. of Can., 1986—; apptd. minister responsible for Privatization and Regulatory Affairs, 1986-88, min. agriculture, 1988—. Trustee Vegreville Sch. Bd., 1963-68; mem. Vegreville and Dist. Credit Union; regional dir. Alta. Progressive Conservative Assn., 1962, No. v.p., 1963, No. chmn. orgn., 1964; pres. Vegreville Progressive Conservative Assn., 1963-68. Mem. Commonwealth Parliamentary Assn., Interparliamentary Union, Can. NATO Parliamenty Assn., Can. World Federalist Parliamentary Assn., Vegreville C. of C., Royal Can. Legion (hon.), Alta. Fish and Game Assn., Indian Assn. Alta. Roman Catholic. Club: Vegreville Rotary (past dir.). Lodge: KC. Office: House of Commons, Parliament Bldgs, Ottawa, ON Canada K1A 0A6

MAZEL, JOSEPH LUCAS, corporate publications executive; b. Paterson, N.J., Oct. 1, 1939; s. Joseph Anthony and Anne (Kidon) M.; children—Joseph William, Jeanne Eileen. B.M.E., Newark Coll. Engring., 1960. Mech. engr. Austin Co., Roselle, N.J., 1960-61; engr. Western Electric Co., Newark, Atlanta, 1961-62; asst. asso., sr. editor Factory mag. McGraw-Hill Pubs. Co., N.Y.C., 1962-71, editor-in-chief, sr. editor 33 Metal Producing mag., 1971-85, chmn. editorial bd., 1980-82; pub. relations account supr. Hammond Farrell Inc., N.Y.C., 1985-87; mgr. publs. Siemens Corp., Iselin, N.J., 1987—; guest lectr. Writers Conf., N.J. Inst. Tech., 1972-83; mem. editorial adv. com. Tech. and Soc. publ., 1981-85. Mem. N.G., 1963-69. Recipient Apolloneer award Gen. Electric Co., 1966; Jesse H. Neal cert. of merit, 1977, 79, 83; Jesse H. Neal Editorial Achievement award, 1979; named to Alumni Achievement Honor Roll, N.J. Inst. Tech., 1979, Wise Old Owl award U.S. Steel Corp. Mem. Soc. Profl. Journalists, Sigma Delta Chi. Lodge: KC (grand knight 1967-68, trustee); Pitts. Press; Deadline. Home: 40-22 Tierney Place Fair Lawn NJ 07410

MAZO, MARK ELLIOTT, lawyer; b. Phila., Jan. 12, 1950; s. Earl and Rita (Vane) M.; m. Fern Rosalyn Litman, Aug. 19, 1973; children: Samantha Lauren, Dana Suzanne, Ross Elliott, Courtney Litman. AB, Princeton U.,

1971; JD, Harvard Law Sch., 1974. Bar: D.C. 1975, U.S. Dist. Ct. D.C. 1975, U.S. Claims Ct. 1975, U.S. Ct. Appeals (D.C. cir.) 1976, U.S. Supreme Ct. 1979. Assoc. Jones, Day, Revis & Pogue, Washington, 1974-79; Crowell & Moring, Washington, 1979-81; ptnr. 1981—. Contbr. articles to profl. jours. White House intern Exec. Office of Pres., Washington, 1972. Served to capt. USAR, 1971-79. Mem. Harvard Law Sch. Assn., ABA, D.C. Bar Assn., Phi Beta Kappa. Republican. Clubs: University (Washington); Columbia Country., Princeton, (N.Y.C.); Colonial. Home: 3719 Cardiff Rd Chevy Chase MD 20815 Office: Crowell & Moring 1001 Pennsylvania Ave NW Washington DC 20004-2505

MAZUJIAN, DAVID ARAM, banker; b. Belleville, N.J., Nov. 25, 1960; s. Joseph and Ann (Broojian) M. BA in Bus. Adminstrn., Rutgers U., 1982; MBA in Fin. and Internat. Bus., NYU, 1986; grad. internat. mgmt. program, London Bus. Sch., 1986. Asst. sec. Mfrs. Hanover Trust Co., N.Y.C., 1982-84; strategic bus. analyst Am. Cyanamid Co., Wayne, N.J., 1985; sr. cons. Touche Ross and Co., N.Y.C., 1986-88; assoc. account officer real estate sect. Bank of Montreal, N.Y.C., 1988—. Mem. Grad. Fin. Assn., Entrepreneurs Exchange Inc., Beta Gamma Sigma. Home: 1590 Anderson Ave #12-D Fort Lee NJ 07024 Office: Bank of Montreal 430 Park Ave New York NY 10022

MAZUR, CONNIE MOAK, investment executive; b. Ft. Worth, Feb. 5, 1947; d. David Clark and Dorothy Carol (Jackson) Moak; m. Jay Mazur, May 31, 1987. BBA, N. Tex. State U., 1969. V.p. Lionel D. Edie and Co., N.Y.C., 1969-77; mgr. Peat, Marwick, Mitchell and Co., N.Y.C., 1977-80; v.p. Shaw Data, N.Y.C., 1980, Fred Alger Mgmt., N.Y.C., 1980-82; ptnr. Glickenhaus and Co., N.Y.C., 1982—. Contbr. articles to profl. jours. Mem. Fin. Women's Assn., Am. Pension Conf., Internat. Found. Employee Benefit Plans, Nat. Coun. Tchrs. Retirement, Assn. Investment Mgrs. (dir. 1987—). Office: Glickenhaus and Co 6 E 43d St New York NY 10017

MAZZA, CLARKE OLIN, music and multi media company owner, musician; b. Jacksonville, Fla., Apr. 30, 1957; s. Ralph N. and Marilyn (Wilson) M.; m. Martha Taft, Dec. 27, 1981; 1 child, Cristina Anne. AA, Fla. Jr. Coll., 1979. Owner, pres. Mazza Studio of Music, Jacksonville, 1975—, Pot O' Gold Multi-Cinema Prodns., Jacksonville, 1984—; owner, v.p. Touch of Class Band, Jacksonville, 1976-78; organist, choir dir. St. Catherine's Episc. Ch., Jacksonville, 1978-79, 103d St. Episc. Ch., Jacksonville, 1981-82; organist St. Pauls Episc. Ch., Mandarin, Fla., 1978-79. Mem. Jacksonville Exec. Assn. (, pres. 1989, bd. dirs. 1988-89). Republican. Baptist. Home and Office: 1639 Bearskin Ln Jacksonville FL 32225

MAZZAGETTI, DOMINICK ANTHONY, banker; b. Newark, July 26, 1948; s. Dominick and Grace (Grimaldi) M.; m. Marianne Cunniff, Nov. 23, 1974; children: Elizabeth, Leigh. BA in Polit. Sci., Rutgers U., 1969; JD, Cornell U., 1972. Bar: N.J. 1972. Law sec. to Chief Justice Joseph Weintraub N.J. Supreme Ct., Trenton, 1972-73; assoc. Lum, Biunno and Tompkins, Newark, 1973-79; ptnr. Bennett, Hueston, Mueller and Mazzagetti, Florham Park, N.J., 1979-82; dep. commr. N.J. Dept. Banking, Trenton, 1982-85, acting commr., 1984; v.p. gen. counsel Cenlar Fed. Savs. Bank, Princeton, N.J., 1985-87, exec. v.p., 1987—. Mem. Morris County Mental Health Bd., 1979-86, chmn., 1982-83; bd. dirs. Madison Area YMCA, 1979-86, treas., 1982-83; bd. dirs. Madison-Florham Park United Fund, 1980-82, Consumer Credit Counseling Service N.J., 1986—; treas. Florham Park Independence Day Celebration Com., 1978, vice chmn., 1979, chmn., 1980; mem. N.J. New Horizons Task Force, 1985-86; mem. Raritan Twp. Parks and Recreation Com., 1988. Mem. ABA, N.J. Bar Assn., N.J. Savs. League (legal com. 1985—), Florham Park Jaycees (chmn. 1976-77). Office: Cenlar Fed Savs Bank 101 Carnegie Ctr Princeton NJ 08540

MAZZEI, AUGUSTINE ANTHONY, JR., lawyer; b. Stonewood, W. Va., Sept. 22, 1936; s. Augustine Anthony and Anna Jean (Fazio) M.; m. Carol Ann Shumaker, Jan. 28, 1961; children: Mark, Marci, Megan. BA, W. Va. U., 1962, JD, 1965. Bar: W. Va. 1965, Pa. 1972. Atty. W.Va. Pub. Service Commn., Charleston, 1965-67, asst. gen. counsel, 1967-72; atty. Equitable Gas Co., Pitts., 1972-77, asst. gen. counsel, 1977-78, gen. counsel, 1978-80, v.p., gen. counsel, 1980-88, sr. v.p., gen. counsel, 1988—. Committeeman Monroeville council Boy Scouts Am., Pa., 1975-80; co-chmn. Dem. Mayoral Campaign, Monroeville, 1976, chmn., 1980; bd. trustees, exec. com. Ea. Mineral Law Found. With USAF, 1954-58. Mem. Pa. Bar Assn., W. Va. Bar Assn., Fed. Energy Bar, Allegheny County Bar, Pa. Gas Assn. (chmn. regulatory matters com. 1977-78), Am. Gas Assn. (mng. com. legal sect., chmn. legal sect. 1987—), Am. Corp. Counsel Assn. (bd. dirs. Western chpt.), UDC Exec. Com. Roman Catholic. Home: 119 Trotwood Dr Monroeville PA 15146 Office: Equitable Resources Inc 420 Blvd of Allies Pittsburgh PA 15219

MAZZONI, MICHAEL JAMES, beer company executive; b. St. Louis, Apr. 22, 1946; s. John A. and Genevieve A. (Jamboretz) M.; m. Cheryll Delsig, Aug. 10, 1968; children: Laura Kristine, Christopher Michael. BS, U. Mo., 1968, MBA, 1973. Various positions Anheuser-Busch, Inc., St. Louis, 1973-80; regional sales mgr. Pabst Brewing Co., Milw., 1980-81; exec. dir. St. Louis Conv. and Visitors Bur., 1982-83; exec. v.p., gen. mgr. Barton Beers, Ltd., Chgo., 1983—. Served to lt. USN, Vietnam. Mem. Union League. Republican. Roman Catholic. Office: Barton Beers Ltd 55 E Monroe St Chicago IL 60603

MBAH, BRIAN CHIBUIKE, synthetic and yarn manufacturing company administrator; b. Obohia Okike, Imo, Ikwuano, Nigeria, May 5, 1956; s. Abraham and Aforinwa (Ezekwu) M.; m. Catherine Chinyere, July 3, 1984; children: Uloma Ihuoma L., Osinachi Mc Wisdom. Student Inst. Chartered Secs. and Adminstrs. London. Exec. sec. Stokvis Nigeria Ltd., Kano, Nigeria, 1976-78; adminstrv. asst. Universal Spinners Ltd., Kano, 1978—. Author: Gods Never Lie, 1985. Fin. dir. Obohia Devel. Union, Kano State, vice chmn. Assoc. mem. Inst. Export London; mem. Nigerian Inst. Mgmt., Nigerian Inst. Personnel Mgmt. Avocations: reading; motor race. Home: Independence Rd, Kano Nigeria 2471 Office: Universal Spinners Ltd, PO Box 2471, Kano Nigeria

MCAFEE, LAWRANCE WILEY, finance executive; b. Huntsville, Tex., Jan. 31, 1955; s. Raymond Mack McAfee and Moira Jean (Wiley) Attwell; m. Martha Jane O'Neal, Apr. 21, 1984. BBA, U. Tex., 1977; MBA, So. Meth. U., 1978. Analyst First Nat. Bank in Dallas, 1979, banking assoc., 1979-80, loan officer, 1979-81; corp. fin. Transco Energy Co., Houston, 1981-82; dir. fin. U.S. Home Corp., Houston, 1982-85, treas., 1985-87, v.p., treas., 1987, v.p., chief fin. officer, 1987-89; sr. v.p., treas. Stillbrooke Corp., 1989—. Mem. Fin. Execs. Inst. Episcopal. Home: 5430 Judalon Houston TX 77056 Office: Stillbrooke Corp 700 Louisiana Ste 3320 Houston TX 77002

MCAFEE, WILLIAM GAGE, lawyer; b. N.Y.C., Mar. 23, 1943; came to Hong Kong, 1976; s. Horace J. and Kathryn (Gage) McA.; m. Linda June 3, 1978; children—Zachary, Dallas, Matthew. A.B., Harvard U., 1965; J.D., Columbia U., 1968. Bar: N.Y. 1969, D.C. 1979, U.S. Supreme Ct. 1973. Legal adviser AID, Dept. State, Saigon, Vietnam, 1969-71; adj. prof. Saigon U. Faculty Law, 1970-71; assoc. Davis Polk Wardwell, N.Y.C., 1971-73; with Coudert Bros., Singapore, Hong Kong, 1973-76; ptnr. 1976—; advisor consultative com. for the basic law of Hong Kong; pres. AmCham, 1984-86, chmn. govt. relations com., trustee Charitable Found.; mem. Hong Kong C. of C., chamber coun., gen. com., legal com., chmn. corp. contbn. program; campaign com. Community Chest of Hong Kong; sec. Law Assn. for Asia and the Western Pacific Energy Section. Editor Energy Law and Policy in Asia and the Western Pacific, 1985, Introduction to the Energy Laws of Asia, 1984; contbg. editor Oil & Gas Law & Taxation Rev.; hon. cons. Econ. & Law Rev.; adv. com. China Oil mag.; adviser Asian Devel. Bank; assoc. Urban Land Inst.; comml. panel arbitrators Am. Arbitration Assn. Mem. ABA, Internat. Bar Assn., D. C. Bar Assn., N.Y. Bar Assn., Internat. Inst. Strategic Studies, Chartered Inst. Arbitrators (legal panel Hong Kong br.). Episcopalian. Clubs: Porcellian (Cambridge); Harvard (N.Y.C., Hong Kong); Pacific (bd. govs.), Fgn. Correspondents'. Home: Severn Villa, 3 Severn Rd The Peak, Hong Kong Hong Kong Office: 31/F Alexandra House, 20 Chater Rd Central, Hong Kong Hong Kong

MCALISTER, EDGAR RAY, business administration education; b. Texarkana, Ark., Dec. 5, 1935; s. Edgar Otis and Gladys (Agee) McA.; m. Gloria Anita Martin, Sept. 2, 1957; children: Stephen Ray, Deanna, Stuart Russell, Mark Edward. BS, Harding U., 1958; MBA, U. North Tex., 1960; PhD, Ohio State U., 1963. Teaching asst. U. North Tex., Denton, 1958-60, prof. bus. administrn., 1963—; teaching asst. Ohio State U., Columbus, 1960-63. Author: Retail Installment Credit, 1964; contbr. articles to profl. jours. Mem. Ch. of Christ. Home: 405 Ridgecrest Circle Denton TX 76205 Office: U North Tex Ave A and Mulberry Denton TX 76203

MCALLISTER, GENE ROBERT, electronics company executive, electrical engineer; b. La Porte, Ind., Apr. 28, 1930; s. Leonard Leroy and Ethel May (Kellog) McA.; m. Diane Stanton, Jan. 29, 1955; children: Jean Anne, Thomas Michael. BSEE, Purdue U., 1959. Jr. engr. No. Ind. Pub. Service Co., La Porte, 1948-59; engr. Magnavox G&I Electronics Co., Ft. Wayne, Ind., 1959-60, asst. product mgr., 1960-63, product mgr., 1963-68, dir. mktg., 1968-74, v.p., gen. mgr. sensors, 1974-82; also bd. dirs. Magnavox G&I Electronics Co.; v.p., dir. ops. Magnavox Electronic Systems Co., Ft. Wayne, 1982-85, group v.p., 1985-87, exec. v.p., 1987—. Mem. Leadership Ft. Wayne, 1981—. With U.S. Army, 1951-53, Korea. Mem. Nat. Security Indsl. Assn. (bd. dirs., ASW exec. com.), Machinery and Allied Products Inst. (govt. contracts council 1970—), Magnavox Mgmt. Club (bd. dirs. 1984—), Ft. Wayne C. of C. (legis. com. 1982—), Assn. U.S. Army, Navy League. Clubs: Pine Valley Country (bd. dirs. 1978-82), Ft. Wayne Racquet, Olympia (bd. dirs 1970-79). Office: Magnavox Electronic Systems Co 1313 Production Rd Fort Wayne IN 46808

MCALLISTER, ROBERT COWDEN, retail company executive; b. Birmingham, Ala., July 8, 1940; s. Melvin Mobley and Lucile (Cowden) McA.; m. Frances Earle Adair, Aug. 9, 1963; children: William Robert, Pamela Frances. BS in Bus. Adminstrn., Samford U., 1965. Store mgr. southeastern states, K Mart Corp., 1970-78; dist. mgr. K Mart Corp., Tampa, Fla., 1978-82; dir. store merchandising K Mart Corp., Atlanta, 1982-84, regional mgr., 1984-85, v.p., 1985—; Mem. Bus. Sch. Adv. Bd. Nash Community Coll., Rocky Mount, N.C., 1974-75. Recipient Disting. Alumnus award Samford U. Sch. Bus., 1987. Pi Kappa Alpha, Alpha Kappa Psi. Methodist. Lodge: Rotary. Office: K Mart Corp So Regional Office 2901 Clairmont Rd NE Atlanta GA 30029

MCALLISTER, THOMAS JAY, SR., financial planning consultant; b. Terre Haute, Ind., Nov. 15, 1937; s. Thomas Joseph and Vera Beatrice (Brown) McA.; m. Janice Kay Preusz, Sept. 17, 1955 (div. Apr. 1974); children: Deborah, Denise, Donna, Darlene, T. Jay, DeAnn; m. Mary Jane Pickard, Apr., 1978. AS in Engring., Vincennes (Ind.) U., 1957; BA in Psychology, Internat. Coll., Los Angeles, 1977. Cert. fin. planner. Mgr. Preston Chem., Columbus, Ind., 1958-62; acct. exec. Merrill Lynch, Indpls., 1962-69; v.p., mgr. R.W. Baird & Co., Indpls., 1969-75; pres. McAllister Finl. Planning, Indpls., 1975—; Mem. Registry of Fin. Planners, Atlanta, Ga., 1985—, Fin. Products Standards Bd., Denver, 1984-87. Author: Your Book for Financial Planning, 1983; contbr. articles to profl. jours. Rep. ward chmn, Indpls., 1969-72, precintct commn., Columbus, 1962-64, Indpls., 1964-68. Mem. U.S. Jaycees (McCall award 1967), Inst. Cert. Fin. Planners, Internat. Assn. Fin. Planner (state pres. 1980-81), Nat. Assn. Securities Dealers (direct participation com. 1978-81, qualifications com. 1982-88, dist. com. 1984-87), Indpls. Bond Club (pres. 1977-78), KC (Dep. Grand Knight 1962-64), Kiwanis (pres. 1988-89). Roman Catholic. Home: 7656 Bay Shore Dr Indianapolis IN 46240 Office: McAllister Fin Planning 8445 Keystone Crossing #102 Indianapolis IN 46240

MCANDREW, MICHAEL KENNETH, hospital executive; b. Holyoke, Mass., Mar. 21, 1948; s. Michael Kenneth Sr. and Florence (Salha) McA.; m. Sandra Johnson, Oct. 18, 1984; children: Joshua Wayne, Michael Johnson. BS in English, Boston State Coll., 1978; M in Health Adminstrn., Va. Commonwealth U., 1981. V.p. profl. svcs. Galesburg (Ill.) Cottage Hosp., 1981-83; v.p. outreach svcs. Jackson (Tenn.) Madison County Gen. Hosp., 1983-86; pres., chief exec. officer Flaget Meml. Hosp., Bardstown, Ky., 1986-88; chief oper. officer Brazosport Meml. Hosp., Lake Jackson, Tex., 1988—; speaker at seminars. Mem. mayor's adv. com., City of Bardstown, 1988. Named Ky. Col. Mem. Am. Coll. Healthcare Execs., Am. Hosp. Assn., Ky. Hosp. Assn., Nat. Rural Health Assn., Bardstown C. of C. Democrat. Roman Catholic. Home: 303 Raintree Lake Jackson TX 77566 Office: Brazosport Meml Hosp 100 Medical Dr Lake Jackson TX 77506

MCANENY, EVELYN LOUISE, banker; b. Johnstown, Pa., Aug. 29, 1949; d. Donald Richard and Rita Catherine (Bieter) Forgas; m. Joseph Benedict McAneny, June 24, 1972. BS in Psychology, U. Pitts., 1972; MS in Labor Rels., Indiana U. of Pa., 1985. Social worker Family Welfare Soc., Johnstown, 1973-75; asst. mgr. Household Fin. Co., Johnstown, 1975-79; mgr. loan dept. UMWA Fed. Credit Union, Johnstown, Pa., 1979; bus. mgr. Dewar's Car World, Johnstown, Pa., 1979-80; pers. officer Mercy Hosp., Nanty Glo, 1980-84; asst. v.p. Johnstown Savs. Bank, 1984—, lectr., 1986—; instr. Am. Inst. Banking, 1986—. Chmn. pers. com., mem. exec. com. YWCA, Johnstown, 1983-85, bd. dirs. 1982-85. Office: Johnstown Savs Bank Main & Market Sts Johnstown PA 15901

MCARTOR, (TRUSTEN) ALLAN, federal agency administrator; b. St. Louis, July 3, 1942; s. John Trusten and Nina Florence (Starbuck) McA.; m. Grace Whiting Mitchell; children: Andrew Allan, Scott David, Kelley Leigh (dec.). BS in Aero. and Astronautical Engring., USAF Acad., 1964; MS in Engring. Mechanics, Ariz. State U., 1971. Commd. 2d lt. USAF, 1964, advanced through grades to maj., 1970; fighter pilot, acad. instr. USAF, various locations, 1964-74; officer, dir. Tenn. Investment Properties, Memphis, 1974-79, Delta Internat Inc., Memphis, 1974-79; sr. v.p. Fed. Express Corp., Memphis, 1979-87; adminstr. FAA, Washington, 1987—; Mem. USAF Thunderbirds air demonstration team. Mem. Exec. Level Presdl. Appointees Orgn., Washington, 1987—, adv. com. Boy Scouts Am., Memphis, 1987—, speakers bur. Rep. Nat. Com., Washington, 1987—; nat. bd. dirs. Youth Service USA, Washington, 1987—; bd. dirs. Challenger Ctr. for Space Sci. Edn., Alexandria, Va., 1987—. Decorated Silver Star, D.F.C., Air medal with 9 oak leaf clusters. Mem. AIAA (exec. advisor), Air Force Assn., Ariz. State Alumni Assn., Falcon Found. (trustee), Nat. Aviation Club (bd. govs.), Order Daedalians, Optimists, Thunderbird Alumni Assn., Wings Club, Ninety-Nines (judge scholarship program), USAF Acad. Assn. Graduates (com. fund raising), Tau Beta Pi. Episcopalian. Office: FAA 800 Independence Ave SW Washington DC 20591

MCARTOR, MICHAEL MITCHELL, real estate investment executive; b. Harvey, Ill., Dec. 3, 1952; s. Walter P. and Dorothy (Mitchell) McA.; 1 child, Michael C. M. BS in Bus., U. Colo., 1975; MBA, So. Methodist U., 1977; postgrad., Am. Graduate Sch. Internat. Mgmt., 1977. Real estate lending officer Chem. Bank, N.Y.C., 1977-81; treas. Carma Developers, Inc., San Francisco, 1981-83; pres. Independence Investment Co., Tampa, Fla., 1983—; chmn., chief exec. officer Freedom Mortgage Co., Tampa, 1986-87, also bd. dirs.; exec. v.p. Freedom Savs., Tampa, 1987—; bd. dirs. Banner Equities, Inc., Tampa, 1983—, Sunshine State Service Co., Tampa, 1983—. Mem. Nat. Assn. Homebuilders, Mortgage Bankers Assn., Beta Gamma Sigma. Republican. Episcopalian. Clubs: Centre (Tampa), Tower (Tampa), Harbor Island Athletic (Tampa). Office: Freedom Savs & Loan Assn 2002 N Lois Ave Tampa FL 33607

MCATEE, JAMES WAYNE, investment company executive; b. Davenport, Iowa, Mar. 11, 1945; s. J.W. and Euphia Dee (McLaughlin) McA.; m. Mary Joy Honore, May 19, 1979; children: Joseph Honore, Alexandria Heather. Cost. acct. Bell & Howell Corp., Skokie, Ill., 1971-73; acct., div. contr. Masonite Corp., Rock Falls, Ill., 1973-76; hosp. contr. Hosp. Affiliates Internat., Tex., La. N.J., 1976-79; regional contr. Hosp. Affiliates Internat., Los Angeles, 1979-80; div. contr. Hosp. Affiliates Internat., Dallas, 1980-81; v.p., chief fin. officer Horizon Health Corp., Dallas, 1981-83, exec. v.p., chief operating officer, 1983-84; exec. v.p., chief fin. officer Republic Health Corp., Dallas, 1985-87; gen. ptnr., mng. dir. Horizon Ptnrs., Horizon Acquisition, Horizon Cos., Lewisville, Tex., 1987—; bd. dirs. Horizon Plastics, Houston, 1983—; mem. adv. bd. Protection Mut. Ins., Park Ridge, Ill, 1985-87, Harpool Seed Inc., Dallas, Tex., 1987—, Auburn Systems, Dallas, 1987-88, GRG S.W., Inc., Dallas, 1988—, Fast Times Automotive, Inc., 1988—, Harpool Farm and Garden, 1989—; pres. GRG S.W. Inc., 1988—. Mem. fin. coun. Dem. Nat. Com., Washington, 1986-88. With U.S. Army, 1965-67. Mem. Assn. for Corp. Growth, Fedn. Am. Health Systems (bd. govs. 1986-87), Univ. Club (Dallas). Home: 4348 Millcreek Rd Dallas TX 75244

MCAULAY, JEFFREY JOHN, new business analysis manager; b. Yonkers, N.Y., Jan. 5, 1953; s. John and Regina (Pryzgoda) McA.; m. Patricia Bouley, Sept. 15, 1979. BA in Economics, Yale U., 1975; MBA, N.Y.U., 1978. Sr. auditor Authur Andersen & Co., N.Y.C., 1975-79; fin. analyst W.R. Grace, Paris, 1979-82; fin. planning mgr. Grace Splty. Chem. subs. W.R. Grace & Co., N.Y.C., 1982-83; asst. controller Grace Splty. Chem. subs. W.R. Grac & Co., N.Y.C., 1983-87; interim chief fin. officer Japan Chem. div. subs. W.R. Grace & Co., N.Y.C., 1987; new business analysis mgr. Grace Splty. Chem. subs. W.R. Grace & Co., N.Y.C., 1987—; adj. prof. Am. Coll., Paris, 1981-82. Treas. 315 W. 23rd Owners Corp., N.Y.C. Mem. Am. Inst. CPAs, Comml. Devel. Assn. Roman Catholic. Club: Yale (N.Y.C.). Home: 315 W 23rd St New York NY 10011 Office: W R Grace & Co 1114 Ave of the Americas New York NY 10036

MCAULIFFE, PATRICIA MARIE, accountant; b. Cleve., Nov. 13, 1961; d. John Peter and Clare Marie (McCauley) McA. BS, Madonna Coll., Livonia, Mich., 1985. CPA, Mich. Auditor Coopers & Lybrand, Detroit, 1985—. Mem. area council Big Bros./Big Sisters, Detroit, 1986—. Mem. Inst. Internal Auditors (counselor 1983—). Office: Coopers & Lybrand 400 Renaissance Ctr Detroit MI 48243

MCAVOY, KENNETH, manufacturing executive; b. Balt., Oct. 18, 1951; s. Kenneth and Irene (Smith) McA.; m. Joyce Alice Chadbourne, Oct. 23, 1971; children: Angela, Amy, Nicholas. AA, Essec Community Coll., 1971; BS in Bus., Jackson State Coll., 1974. Sales rep. Eastern Stainless, Balt., 1971-75; dist. mgr. Mark Controls, Lake Zurich, Ill., 1975-77; exec. v.p. Main Steel, Balt., 1977—. Leader Kingsville council Cub Scouts Am., 1987. Republican. Roman Catholic. Office: Main Steel 1301 Boyle St Baltimore MD 21230

MCBEE, FRANK WILKINS, JR., industrial executive; b. Ridley Park, Pa., Jan. 22, 1920; s. Frank Wilkins and Ruth (Moulton) McB.; m. Sue U. Brandt, Apr. 10, 1943; children: Marilyn Moore, Robert Frank. BS in Mech. Engring., U. Tex, 1947, MS in Mech. Engring., 1950; PhD (hon.), St. Edward's U., Austin, 1986. Instr. to asst. prof. mech. engring. U. Tex., Austin, 1946-53, supr. mech. dept. Def. Research Lab., 1950-59; co-founder Tracor, Inc., Austin, 1955, treas., sr. v.p., 1955-67, exec. v.p., 1967-70, pres., 1970-86, chief exec. officer, 1970-88, chmn. bd., 1972-88, exec. cons., 1988—; bd. dirs. MCorp, Dallas, KMW Systems Corp., Austin, Med. Systems Support, Inc., Dallas, Radian Corp., Austin, Pritronix, Dallas; chmn. bd. Electrosource Inc., Austin, Research Applications Inc., Austin. Sr. active mem. adv. council U. Tex. Engring. Found.; mem. chancellor's council, U. Tex.; mem. Gov.'s task force on bus. devel. and jobs creation, Gov.'s Super Collider Adv. Council, Lt. Gov's. Select Com. on Tax Equity; chmn. adv. bd. Discovery Hall; corp. cabinet Am. Heart Assn. Tex. Affiliate, Inc.; chmn. bd. trustees Laguna Gloria Art Mus; fin. council Seton Med. Ctr.; past chmn. Austin Area Research Orgn.; trustee emeritus Southwest Tex. Pub. Broadcasting Council; contbg. mem. N.Y. Met. Mus. Art; vice chmn. Headliners Found.; chmn. Headliners Club; co-chmn. Advantage Austin. Served to capt. USAAF, 1944-46. Recipient Free Enterprise award Austin Sales and Mktg. Execs. Club, 1976, Benefactor award Austin Community Found., 1980, Spl. award Austin C. of C. Econ. Devel. Council, 1982, Clara Driscoll award Laguna Gloria Art Mus., 1987, Disting. Alumnus award U. Tex. Coll. Engring., 1978, Austinite of Yr. award Austin C. of C., 1986, Disting. Alumnus award U. Tex., 1988; named to Stephen F. Austin High Sch. Hall of Honor, 1981. Mem. NSPE, Tex. Soc. Profl. Engrs. (Outstanding Engr. of Yr. 1983), Tex. Assn. Bus., Tex. Taxpayers Assn. (bd. dirs.), Am. Electronics Assn. (bd. dirs.), Austin Heritage Soc. (life), Austin History Ctr. Assn. (founding), Nat. Trust for Hist. Preservation (sustaining mem.), U. Tex. Pres.'s Assocs., Austin C. of C., Tau Beta Pi, Sigma Xi, Pi Tau Sigma. Clubs: Austin Yacht (former commodore, vice chmn.); Headliners (chmn. exec. com., Found. trustee, chmn. club); Austin; Metropolitan. Office: 705 San Antonio Austin TX 78701

MCBRIDE, JACK J., life and financial services executive; b. Orient, Iowa, June 24, 1936; s. Marvin Clair and Ruth (Jones) McB.; m. Mary Ann Garden, June 16, 1957; children: Jeffry J., Beth Ann, Kelley Lynn, Grant G. BA, Simpson Coll., Indianola, Iowa, 1958; postgrad. U. Conn., 1963. Spl. agt. Bankers Life Co., Des Moines, 1958-60; agy. supr. Aetna Life Annuity, Fin. Services, Inc., Hartford, Conn., 1960-65, gen. agt., Springfield, Ill., also Milw., 1972-82; agy. mgr. Equitable Life Iowa, E.I. Sales, Inc., Omaha, also Davenport, Iowa, 1965-72; supt. personal fin. security div., Aetna Life & Casualty Co., Chgo., 1982-84; instr. Life Underwriters Tng. Council, Quad Cities, 1968-69; lectr. to various univs. and colls. Contbr. articles to profl. jours. Chmn. friends bd. So. Ill. U. Med. Sch., 1975-77, bd. dirs., 1973-77; co-chmn. 1st Day Care Ctr., Springfield, Ill., 1973-77; charter chmn. stewardship St. Luke's Ch., Omaha, 1966; mem. steering com. devel. council Simpson Coll. Named Outstanding Young Man Am., 1966. Mem. Nat. Assn. Life Underwriters (past co-chmn. edn. com., chmn., dir. Iowa State com.), Springfield Gen. Agts. and Mgrs. Assn. (past pres., dir.), Sangamon Estate Planners Council (charter mem.), Adminstrv. Mgmt. Soc., Quad Cities C. of C. (speakers bar). Republican. Mem. Union Ch. Club: Merrill Hills (Waukesha, Wis.). Lodge: Masons (32 deg.), St. Andrew Soc., Rotary.

MCBRIDE, JONATHAN EVANS, exec. search cons.; b. Washington, June 16, 1942; s. Gordon Williams and Martha Alice (Evans) McB.; BA, Yale U., 1964; m. Emilie Evans Dean, Sept. 5, 1970; children: Webster Dean, Morley Evans. Account exec. Merrill Lynch & Co., Washington, 1968-72; v.p. dept. mgr. Lionel D. Edie & Co., N.Y.C., 1972-76; v.p., exec. search cons. Simmons Assocs., Inc., Washington, 1976-79; pres. McBride Assocs., Inc., Washington, 1979—. Bd. dirs. Yale U. Alumni Fund, 1974-79. Served to lt. USNR, 1964-68. Clubs: Yale (N.Y.C.); Met. (Washington); Chevy Chase (Md.). Office: 1511 K St NW Washington DC 20005

MCBRIDE, KEITH L., investment banker; b. Steubenville, Ohio, Dec. 22, 1947; s. Charles E. and Catherine T. (Woodstuff) McB.; m. Therese Samodell, June 11, 1971; children: Cameron K., Evan C., Brandon C., Amber T. BA, Case Western Res. U., 1974, MS in Mgmt., 1975; postgrad., U. Pa., 1981. Mgr. mktg. Indsl. Distbns., Atlanta, 1975-76; co-owner McDonald & Co., Cleve., 1976-85; v.p. Underwood Neuhaus & Co., Houston, 1985-87, sec., 1987—, also bd. dirs.; bd. dirs. Underwood Neuhaus Fin. Corp., Houston, Underwood Neuhaus Corp., Gateway Fin. Corp., Commodities Future Corp. Sgt. N.G., 1972-78. Mem. Mcpl. Bond Club Houston (gov. 1982-85, pres. 1984-85), Cleve. Bond Club (pres. 1984-85), Securities Industry Assn., Pub. Securities Assn., N.Y. Stock Exch. (allied mem.). Republican. Office: Underwood Neuhaus & Co 909 Fannin Houston TX 77010

MCBRIDE, ROBERT JOHN, gas and water company executive; b. Wilkes Barre, Pa., Nov. 8, 1931; s. Joseph A. and Alma (Dann) McB.; m. Theresa A. Walsh, July, 1952; children: Joseph, Michael, Molly, Colleen. BS in Acctg., King's Coll., 1953. With Pa. Gas and Water Co., Wilkes-Barre, 1953-68, asst. treas., 1968-78, treas., 1978—. Mem. Pa. Gas Assn., Wilkes Barre C. of C. Democrat. Roman Catholic. Office: Pa Gas and Water Co Wilkes Barre Ctr 39 Pub Square Wilkes-Barre PA 18701

MCBRIDE, WILLIAM BERNARD, financial executive; b. N.Y.C., May 22, 1931; s. William and Nora (Hughes) McB.; m. Lorraine Barry, May 27, 1956; children: Mary, William, Stephen, Anne. B.S., Fordham U., 1952; M.B.A., Baruch Sch., 1963. C.P.A., N.Y. Staff auditor Touche, Ross, Bailey & Smart (C.P.A.s), N.Y.C., 1952-58; asst. v.p. Bankers Trust Co., N.Y.C., 1959-67; treas. Kidde, Inc., Saddle Brook, N.J., 1967—; v.p. Kidde, Inc., 1974—. Mem. Am. Inst. C.P.A.s, N.Y. State Soc. C.P.A.s. Home: 243 Sunset Ave Ridgewood NJ 07450 Office: Kidde Inc Park 80 West Pla II Saddle Brook NJ 07663

MCBURNEY, THOMAS ROSS, food company executive; b. Mpls., June 16, 1938; s. Lloyd L. and Lorna McB.; m. Barbara L. Dawson; children—Ann, Susan, Megan, Lesley. B.A., Dartmouth U., 1960; M.B.A., Amos Tuck U., 1962; postgrad., Stanford U., 1973. Vice pres., gen. mgr., refrigerated foods Pillsbury Co., Mpls., 1977-80, v.p. gen. mgr. grocery foods, 1980-82, group v.p. frozen and refrigerated foods, 1983-85, pres. U.S. Foods, 1985-86, chmn., 1986-88, exec. v.p., 1987—; bd. dirs. Security Am. Fin. Enterprises, Valspar Corp.; chmn. Internat. Foods, 1988—. Vice chmn. Minn. Pub. Radio, St. Paul; bd. dirs. Freedom from Hunger Found., Davis (Calif.), Minn. Orch., Minn. Council on Founds., Mpls., 1985, UNICEF. Office: Pillsbury Co Pillsbury Ctr 200 S 6th St Minneapolis MN 55402

MCCABE, EDWARD AENEAS, lawyer, financial services corporation executive; b. County Monaghan, Ireland, Mar. 4, 1917; s. Patrick and Alice (McDonnell) McC.; m. Janet Isabel Stevens, Nov. 17, 1951, (dec. Oct. 1981); children: Thomas, Michael, Patrick, Barbara; m. Verna Ann Peterson, June 27, 1985. LL.B., Columbus U., Washington, 1946. Bar: D.C. 1946, U.S. Supreme Ct. 1950. Exec. asst. Joint Congl. Com. Labor Mgmt. Relations, 1947-48; atty. labor relations and trade assn. matters Washington, 1949-52; gen. counsel com. on edn. and labor Ho. of Reps., 1953-55; assoc., White House counsel to Pres. of U.S., 1956-58; adminstrv. asst. President Eisenhower, Washington, 1958-61; ptnr. Hamel, Morgan, Park & Saunders, Washington, 1961-71; ptnr. Hamel, Park, McCabe & Saunders (now Hopkins, Sutter, Hamel & Park), Washington, 1971-82, of counsel, 1982—; dir. First Am. Bank Washington, USA Funds, Inc., Indpls.; chmn. bd. Student Loan Mktg. Assn., 1972-78, 81—, Washington, White House cons. Presdl. transition, 1974-75, advisor, 1980-81; mem. D.C. Criminal Justice Coordinating Bd. Trustee Pub. Defender Service D.C.; bd. govs. USO; trustee Immaculata Coll., Washington, Allentown Coll., Center Valley, Pa.; mem. bd. advisers DeSales Sch. Theology, Washington; bd. dirs. Community Found. Greater Washington; bd. dirs., vice chmn. and Pres. Eisenhower World Affairs Inst., Washington; mem. cardinal's com. laity Archdiocese of Washington, com. for deferred gifts for Archdiocese; mem. exec. cabinet Cath. Charities U.S.A. With U.S. Army, 1941-45. Mem. ABA, Fed., D.C. bar assns., Jud. Conf. D.C. Circuit. Republican. Roman Catholic. Clubs: Capitol Hill, Metropolitan (Washington); Burning Tree (Bethesda, Md.), Kenwood Golf and Country (Bethesda, Md.). Home: 4940 Sentinel Dr Bethesda MD 20816 Office: Hopkins Sutter Hamel & Park 888 16th St NW Washington DC 20006

MCCABE, JOAN YANISH, investment banker; b. Yonkers, N.Y., Aug. 6, 1955; d. Casimir V. and Ruth (Joyce) Yanish; m. Joseph T. McCabe, Jr., May 29, 1982. BA, Yale Coll., 1977; MBA, Harvard U., 1981. V.p. Kidder, Peabody and Co., N.Y.C, 1981-86; 1st v.p. Drexel Burnham, N.Y.C, 1986-87, Paine Webber, N.Y.C, 1987—. Class agt. Yale Coll., New Haven, Conn., 1985—. Mem. Yale Club. Republican. Roman Catholic. Office: Paine Webber 1285 Ave of the Americas New York NY 10019

MCCABE, LINDA KAY, hotel industry executive, sales and marketing executive; b. Greenville, Ohio, Aug. 31, 1945; d. Samuel Orien and Wanda Fern (Wise) McC. BS in Edn., Miami U., Oxford, Ohio, 1968. Exec. sec. Hyatt Hotels Corp., Burlingame, Calif., 1971-74; with catering and conv. service Hyatt Hotels Corp., Monterey, Calif., 1974-77; catering and conv. svcs. mgr. Hyatt Hotels Corp., San Francisco, 1977-81; dir. sales Davre's Inc., Atlanta, 1981-83; dir. sales and mktg. Viscount Hotel, Atlanta, 1983-84, So. Host Hotels, Atlanta, 1984—; mktg. cons., 1984—. Mem. Nat. Tour Assn. Republican. Presbyterian. Office: Southern Host Hotels 3260 Pointe Pkwy Ste 100 Norcross GA 30092

MCCABE, ROBERT P., investment company executive; b. Johnstown, Pa., June 4, 1955; s. Hugh f. and Suzanne (Hipp) McC.; m. Teresa M. Dean, Sept. 10, 1983; children: Michael, Robert Jr. BS in Acctg., U. Md., 1978. Cert. fin. planner. Acct. DeRand Investments, Arlington, Va., 1979-83, investment advisor, rep., 1983—. Mem. Internat. Assn. Fin. Planners, Internat. Bd. Standards and Practice for Cert. Fin. Planners. Republican. Roman Catholic. Home: 1204 N Powhatan St Arlington VA 22205

MCCABE, ST. CLAIR LANDERKIN, publishing executive; b. Toronto, Ont., Can., July 13, 1915; s. Herbert St. Clair and Myrtle (Landerkin) McC.; m. Margaret Letitia Hamilton; children: Mrs. J. Beatson, John Timothy St. Clair. Gen. mgr. Galt Evening Reporter, until 1949; pres. Thomson Newspapers Ltd., Toronto, until 1980; pres., dir. Thomson Newspapers Inc., Toronto, Chew Newspapers of Ohio Inc., Greenville Newspapers Inc., Humboldt Newspapers, Inc., Key West Newspaper Corp., Lock Haven Express Printing Co., Oxnard Pub. Co., The Punta Gorda Herald Inc., Rocky Mount Pub. Co., San Gabriel Valley Tribune, Inc., Thomson Newspaper Pub. Co., Inc., Thomson Pubs. of N.Y. Inc.; pres., dir. Thomson Newspapers Inc., Ala., Fla., Ga., Ill., Ky., Mich., Minn., N.H., Ohio, Pa., Wis.; pres., dir. Thomson Newsprint Inc. Lodge: Masons. Home: 146 Harborage Ct Clearwater FL 33515 Office: Thomson Newspapers Inc 3150 Des Plaines Ave Des Plaines IL 60018 also: Thomson Newspapers Inc 1111 N Westshore Blvd Ste 401 Tampa FL 33607

MCCAFFERTY, MICHAEL GILBERT, financial executive; b. Poteau, Okla., June 26, 1938; s. Rennie Earl and Anna Louise (Pope) McC. B.S., U. Okla., 1960; M.B.A., Stanford U., 1964. Asst. v.p. First Nat. City Bank, N.Y.C., 1964-68; assoc. Thatcher Ptnrs., N.Y.C., 1968-71; with Gt. Western United Corp., Denver, 1971-73, treas., 1972-73; v.p., treas. Kaiser Aetna, Oakland, Calif., 1973-76; asst. treas. Crown Zellerbach Corp., San Francisco, 1976-82, v.p., treas., 1982-85; sr. v.p., treas. Mattel, Inc., Hawthorne, Calif., 1985—. Served with USNR, 1960-62. Club: Univ. (N.Y.C.). Office: Mattel Inc 5150 Rosecrans Ave Hawthorne CA 90250

MCCAFFREY, JUDITH ELIZABETH, lawyer; b. Providence, Apr. 26, 1944; d. Charles V. and Isadore Frances (Langford) McC.; m. Martin D. Minsker, Dec. 31, 1969 (div. May 1981); children: Ethan Hart Minsker, Natasha Langford Minsker. BA, Tufts U., 1966; JD, Boston U., 1970. Bar: Mass. 1970, D.C. 1972. Assoc. Sullivan & Worcester, Washington, 1970-76; atty. FDIC, Washington, 1976-78; assoc. Dechert, Price & Rhoads, Washington, 1978-82; McKenna, Conner & Cuneo, Washington, 1982-83; gen. counsel, corp. sec. Perpetual Savs. Bank, FSB, Alexandria, Va., 1983—. Contbr. articles to profl. jours. Mem. edn. com. Bd. Trade, Washington, 1986—; co-chair Parents Assn. Sch. Without Walls, Washington, 1987. Mem. ABA (chairperson subcom. thrift instns. 1985—), Fed. Bar Assn. (exec. com., banking law com. 1985—), D.C. Bar Assn. (bd. govs. 1981-85), Women's Bar Assn. (pres. 1980-81). Democrat. Episcopalian. Club: Kenwood Country (Chevy Chase, Md.). Office: Perpetual Savs Bank FSB 2034 Eisenhower Ave Alexandria VA 22314

MCCAFFREY, KEVIN JOHN, small business owner; b. Newark, Sept. 6, 1950; s. John Joseph and Ellen (Devery) McC. Student, Spring Hill Coll., 1968-72. Editor, reporter Mobile (Ala.) Press Register, 1972-73; editor news North Dade Jour., North Miami, Fla., 1973-75; asst. mgr. Doubleday Bookshop, New Orleans, 1975-76; mgr. Waldenbooks, New Orleans, 1977-82; asst. mgr. U. New Orleans Bookstore, 1982-87, mgr., 1987-88; owner Children's Hour Books, New Orleans, 1986—; v.p. Booksellers Pub., Inc., N.Y.C., 1988—, also bd. dirs. Contbr. articles to profl. jours. Bd. dirs. Tennessee Williams New Orleans Lit. Festival, 1986—, treas. 1988—. Mem. Am. Booksellers Assn. (bd. dirs. 1986—), New Orleans Booksellers Assn. (charter pres. 1987—), La. Assn. Coll. Stores (bd. dirs. 1987-88), Nat. Assn. Coll. Stores, New Orleans Chess Club (pres. 1977-78). Democrat. Home and Office: 216 Chartres St #3 New Orleans LA 70130

MCCAFFREY, ROBERT HENRY, JR., manufacturing company executive; b. Syracuse, N.Y., Jan. 20, 1927; s. Robert Henry and May Ann (McGuire) McC.; m. Dorothy Anne Evers, Sept. 22, 1956; children: Michael Robert, Kathleen Mary. BS, Syracuse U., 1949. Sales asst. Sealright Corp., Fulton, N.Y., 1949-50; with TEK Hughes div. Johnson & Johnson, Metuchen, N.J., 1950-67, gen. sales mgr., 1958-59, v.p. sales, 1959-62, pres., 1962-67; gen. mgr. med. div. Howmet Corp., N.Y.C., 1967-70; group v.p. Howmedica, Inc., 1970-73, sr. v.p., 1973-74, exec. v.p., also bd. dirs., 1974-76; pres., chief exec. officer C.R. Bard, Inc., Murray Hill, N.J., 1976-78, chmn. bd. dirs., chief exec. officer, 1978-89, chmn. bd., 1989—, also bd. dirs.; bd. dirs. Summit and Elizabeth Trust, Summit Bancorp. Trustee Found. for Univ. Medicine and Dentistry N.J., 1987—; chmn. corp. adv. council Syracuse U., 1974-75, trustee, 1979—. Served with AUS, 1945-46. Mem. Orthopedic Surg. Mfrs. Assn., Health Industry Mfrs. Assn. (dir., chmn. 1982-83), Inst. Medicine, Council on Health Care Tech., N.Y. Sales Execs. Club, Sigma Chi. Clubs: Pinnacle (N.Y.C.); Baltusrol Golf (Springfield, N.J.). Home: 483 Mark Rd Allendale NJ 07401 Office: CR Bard Inc 731 Central Ave Murray Hill NJ 07974

MCCAIG, JOSEPH J., retail food chain executive; b. Bklyn., 1944. B.S., Seton Hall U., 1967. With The Grand Union Co., Elmwood Park, N.J., 1965—; gen. store mgr. The Grand Union Co., 1967-68, resident trainer suburban div., 1968-69, supr. personnel, 1969-70, dist. mgr., 1970-72, supt. stores, 1972-73, asst. to sr. v.p. store ops., 1973-74, v.p. empire div. and v.p. no. region, 1974-78, v.p. no. region, 1978-80, sr. v.p., 1980-81; pres., chief operating officer The Grand Union Co, 1981—. Office: Grand Union Co 201 Willowbrook Blvd Wayne NJ 07470

MCCAIN, H. HARRISON, frozen food products company executive; b. Florenceville, N.B., Can., Nov. 3, 1927; s. A. D. and Laura B. (Perley) McC.; m. Marion M. McNair, Oct. 4, 1952; children: Mark, Peter, Laura, Ann, Gillian. BA, Acadia U.; LLD (hon.), U. N.B., Can., 1986. Chmn. McCain Foods Ltd., Florenceville, N.B., Can.; now chmn. McCain Foods Ltd., Scarborough, Eng.; chmn. bd. McCain Alimentaire S.A.R.L., Harnes, France, McCain Europa bv, Hoofddorp, Netherlands, Day & Ross Inc., Hartland, N.B.; bd. dirs. McCain Espana S.A., Burgos, Spain, McCain Foods Inc. Pty. Ltd., Wendouree, Australia, McCain Foods Inc., U.S.A., McCain Refrigerated Foods Inc., Oakville, Ont., Bilopage Inc., Que., Thomas Equipment Ltd., Centreville, N.B., Britfish Ltd., Hull, Eng., Valley Farms Ltd., McCain Citrus Inc., Chgo., Beau Marais S.A.R.L., Bethune, France, McCain Foods Western, Inc., Othello, Wash., McCain Sunnyland B.V., Turnhout, Belgium, McCain Processing, Inc., Presque Isle, Maine, McCain Foods Ltd., Tokyo, Right-O-Way, Inc., Tustin, Calif.; assoc. McCain Group Cos., Bank of N.S., Petro-Can. Decorated officer Order of Canada; recipient Canadian Bus. Statesman award Harvard Bus. Sch., 1988. Presbyterian. Office: McCain Foods Ltd, Florenceville, NB Canada E0J 1K0

MC CALL, ROBERT R., oil company executive; b. Norman, Okla., June 21, 1926; s. Robert R. and Ida (Smith) McC.; m. Byrdine Grimm, June 12, 1987; children: Claudia, Michael, Melinda, Danny. B.S., U. Okla., 1951, M.S., 1952. With Texaco, Inc., 1952—, gen. mgr. producing Eastern hemisphere, 1972-78; v.p. producing Texaco, Inc., Harrison, N.Y., 1978-80; sr. v.p. Texaco U.S.A., Houston, 1980-83, exec. v.p., 1983—. Bd. dirs. Near East Found. Served with USNR, 1944-46. Mem. Am. Inst. Mech. Engrs., Am. Petroleum Inst., Okla. Profl. Engrs., Pi Epsilon Tau. Republican. Home: 12 S Doe Run The Woodlands TX 77380 Office: Texaco USA 1111 Rusk St Houston TX 77002

MCCALL, WILLIAM CALDER, oil and chemical company executive; b. Hoquiam, Wash., Feb. 1, 1906; s. Dougall Hugh and Hughena (Calder) McC.; m. Marian Hall, Mar. 22, 1946; children—Ernest, Robert. Student U. Oreg., 1924-28. Asst. sales mgr. Anaconda Sales Co., Chgo., 1932-39; chmn. McCall Oil & Chem. Corp., Portland, Oreg., 1939—, Gt. Western Chem. Co., Portland, 1955—, Chemax, Inc., Portland, 1975—; dir. Oreg. Bank, Portland, King Broadcasting Co., Seattle. Pres. Oreg. Art Mus., Portland; trustee Lewis and Clark Coll., Portland; exec. v.p. Oreg. Symphony Soc.; dir. Med. Research Found., Good Samaritan Hosp. Found., Portland. Republican. Episcopalian. Clubs: Eldorado Country (Indian Wells, Calif.) (pres. 1978-79); Arlington (Portland); Pacific-Union (San Francisco); Los Angeles Country, Vintage (Palm Desert, Calif.), Waverley Country, Rainier (Seattle). Office: McCall Family Corp 808 SW 15th Ave Portland OR 97205

MCCALMON, JEFFREY ALAN, banker; b. Kansas City, Mo., Jan. 8, 1955; s. C. Frank and Bonita L. (Maier) McC.; m. michele D. Lange, May 22, 1976; children: Aubrey, Tyler, Reed. BS in Bus., U. Kans., 1976. Lending officer Regional Investment Co., Leawood, Kans., 1976-77, Charles F. Curry Co., Kansas City, 1977-79; v.p. Lomas and Nettleton Co., Dallas, 1979-86; pres. Suburban Fin. Corp., Overland Park, Kans., 1986—; cons. in field; instr. Kans. Real Estate Commn., 1983—, Mo. Real Estate Commn., 1987—. Contbr. articles to profl. jours. Bd. govs. Bacchus Cultural and Ednl. Found., 1980; vice-chmn. Bd. Zoning Appeals, Leawood, 1985-87. Mem. Mortgage Bankers Assn. Greater Kansas City (bd. dirs.), Mo. Mortgage Bankers Assn., U. Kans. Alumni, Alpha Tau Omega. Presbyterian. Home: 12012 Cherokee Ln Leawood KS 66209 Office: Suburban Fin Corp 10300 W 103 St Ste 303 Overland Park KS 66214

MC CAMMON, DAVID NOEL, automobile company executive; b. Topeka, Nov. 6, 1934; s. Noel F. and Freda E. McC.; m. Valerie L. Palliaer, May 18, 1968; children: Jeff, Mark, Scott. B.S. in Bus. Adminstrn, U. Nebr., 1957; M.B.A. (Baker scholar), Harvard U., 1962. With Ford Motor Co., Dearborn, Mich., 1957—; controller Ford div. Ford Motor Co., 1970-71, asst. corp. controller, 1971-77, exec. dir. bus. strategy, 1977-78, v.p. corp. strategy analysis, 1979-84, v.p., controller, 1984-87, v.p. fin., treas., 1987—. Served with U.S. Army, 1957-58. Club: Harvard Bus. Sch. (Detroit). Office: Ford Motor Co World Headquarters The American Rd Dearborn MI 48121

MCCANDLESS, JAMES BRUCE, investment management executive; b. Ravenna, Ohio, Dec. 2, 1945; s. Bruce Anderson and Jane (McCown) McC.; m. Mary Ann McAninch, Aug. 12, 1968; children: William James, Anne. BS in Animal Sci., Okla. State U., 1968. Loan officer Bank of Am., San Francisco, 1968-73; investment officer Conn. Mut. Life Ins. Co., Hartford, 1973-79; v.p. Bell Investment Co., Burlington, Iowa, 1979-83, AgriVest Inc., Glastonbury, Conn., 1983-86; exec. v.p. AgriVest Inc., Glastonbury, 1986—. Contbr. articles to profl. jours. Mem. Am. Soc. Farm Mgrs. and Rural Appraisers. Republican. Presbyterian. Office: AgriVest Inc 500 Winding Brook Dr Glastonbury CT 06033

MCCANDLESS, STEPHEN PORTER, financial executive; b. Denver, Mar. 17, 1941; s. Robert B. and Mary (Porter) McC.; m. Carolyn Keller, Apr. 22, 1972; children: Peter, Deborah. Geol. Engr., Colo. Sch. Mines, 1963; M.B.A., Harvard U., 1969. Geologist Shell Oil Co., Casper, Wyo., 1963-65; securities analyst Kidder Peabody & Co., N.Y.C., 1969-70; fin. analyst Asarco Inc., N.Y.C., 1971-72; asst. to treas. Asarco Inc., 1972-73, asst. treas., 1973-79, treas., 1979—, v.p., 1983—; dir. United Park City Mines Co., 1983-85. Trustee The Town Sch., 1984—. Served with C.E., U.S. Army, 1963-65. Mem. AIME, Tau Beta Pi. Office: Asarco Inc 180 Maiden Ln New York NY 10038

MCCANN, ANTHONY FRANCIS, diversified manufacturing company executive; b. Phila., Apr. 7, 1940; s. Anthony F. and Helen P. (Smith) McC.; m. Sally Ann Peters, Sept. 29, 1962; children: Maureen, Patricia, Anthony. BME, Villanova U., 1962; MBA, Drexel U., 1969. Successively indsl. engr., mfg. engr., mgr. engring., mgr. mfg., pres. splty. div. SKF Industries, Phila., 1962-82; mgr. mfg. Pennwalt Corp., Phila., 1974-76, gen. mgr. Keystone div., 1974-79; group v.p. Inductotherm Industries, Rancocas, N.J., 1982—; bd. dirs. Magnetic Metals, Camden, N.J., Super Products Corp., Milw., Vantage Products Corp., Conyers, Ga., Metl-Saw Systems, Benicia, Calif., W.J. Savage Corp., Knoxville, Tenn. Named Man of Yr., Assn. Registered Ofcls., 1977. Mem. ASME, PA. Interscholastic Athletic Assn., Assn. Registered Conf. Officials, Ea. Assn. Intercoll. Football Officials. Roman Catholic. Home: 75 Skyline Dr Chalfont PA 18914 Office: Inductotherm Industries 10 Indel Ave Rancocas NJ 08073

MCCANN, DAVID DUNCAN, public relations executive; b. Akron, Ohio, Mar. 6, 1955; s. Donald Miles and Margaret Jean (Pfeiffer) McC.; m. Judith Ann Kryah, Feb. 12, 1983; 1 child, Mary Margaret. BA in Social Scis., SUNY, Albany, 1977; postgrad., U. Akron. Asst. dir. Bd. Elections County of Summit, Akron, 1979-80, pub. info. officer, 1981-88; pres. MACOM & Bus. Info Systems Inc., Akron, 1987—; pres. Maccom, Inc., Akron, 1988—; dir. communications Navajo Indian Nation, 1988. Author: (poetry) Dawn's Early Morn, 1977. Mem. Cleve. Orchestra Pub. Relations Adv. Council; bd. dirs. Blick Clinic for Devel. Disabilities. Sgt. U.S. Army, 1974-77. Recipient Outstanding Young Man in Am. award U.S. Jaycees, 1984. Mem. Pub. Relations Soc. (treas. 1987), Sons AM. Revolution, Nat. Assn. Govt. Communicators, Akron Area Council Chs., Rotary Club, Akron City Club. Republican. Roman Catholic. Home: 1600 Sunset Vu W Akron OH 44320 Office: Maccom Inc PO Box 155 Akron OH 44308

MCCANN, DEAN MERTON, lawyer, pharmaceutical company executive; b. Ontario, Calif., Mar. 13, 1927; s. James Arthur and Alma Anis (Hawes) McC.; m. Carol Joan Geissler, Mar. 23, 1957. AA, Chaffey Coll., 1948; BS in Pharmacy, U. So. Calif., 1951; JD, U. Calif., San Francisco, 1954; LLM, NYU, 1955. Bar: Calif. 1955; lic. pharmacist, Calif. Pharmacist San Francisco and Ontario, 1951-54; sole practice law Los Angeles, 1955-60; ptnr. MacBeth, Ford & Brady, Los Angeles, 1960-65, McCann & Berger, Los Angeles, 1965-68; v.p., sec. and gen. counsel Allergan Pharms., Inc., Irvine, Calif., 1968-78; sr. v.p., sec., gen. counsel Allergan, Inc., Irvine, 1978—; instr. pharmacy law U. So. Calif., Los Angeles, 1956-68; exec. v.p. Pharm. Wholesaler Assn., Los Angeles, 1956-68. Mem., past. chmn. bd. counsellors Sch. Pharmacy U. So. Calif., Los Angeles, 1975—, mem., past chmn. QSAD centurion, 1963—. Served with USNR, 1945-46. Fellow Food and Drug Law Inst., 1954-55. Mem. ABA, Calif. Bar Assn., Orange County Bar Assn., Am. Pharm. Assn., Calif. Pharm. Assn., Orange County Pharm. Assn., U. So. Calif. Alumni Assn. (past pres.), Phi Delta Chi. Republican. Clubs: Balboa Bay, Newport Beach (Calif.) Country, Skull and Dagger (Los Angeles). Home: 21 Rockingham Dr Newport Beach CA 92660 Office: Allergan Inc 2525 DuPont Dr Irvine CA 92715

MCCANN, EDWARD, investment banker; b. San Diego, June 22, 1943; s. Edward F. and Anna Marie (McKay) McC.; m. Sara Sheffield Hall, Nov. 15, 1980; children: Sheffield Hall, Henry Howland. BS, U.S. Naval Acad., 1965; MSEE, postgrad., MIT, 1970. Commd. ensign USN, 1965, advanced through grades to lt., res., 1971; program mgmt. exec. Westinghouse Corp. Research Lab., Churchill, Pa., 1971-73; chief planner Chevron Shipping Co., San Francisco, 1973-77, div. mgr., 1977-79; corp. planning and acquisition staff exec. Standard Oil Co. Calif., San Francisco, 1979-83, dir. strategic planning, def. sector Sperry Corp., N.Y.C., 1983-85, merger team, 1986; v.p. corp. fin. Eberstadt Fleming Inc., N.Y.C., 1986-88; sr. v.p. investment banking, dir. aerospace and def. group Robert Fleming Inc., London, N.Y.C., 1988—; bd. dirs. Am. Def. Preparedness Assn., 1988. Mem. long-range planning council United Way, L.I., 1983-86; treas. Oyster Bay Youth and Family Counseling Agy., 1984-86; trustee Oyster Bay Community Found., 1984—. Recipient class prize systems engring. and naval weaponry, S.R. and Daus. of Am. Colonists awards, 1965. Mem. No. Am. Soc. Corp. Planners, Soc. Naval Architects and Marine Engrs., Am. Soc. Naval Engrs., Assn. Old Crows, Am. Def. Preparedness Assn., Navy League, Naval Inst., Assn. Naval Aviators, Naval Acad. Alumni Assn., Am. Def. Preparedness Assn. (bd. dirs. 1988—), Long Island Biol. Assn. (dir. Cold Spring Harbor chpt. 1988—), Bohemian Club (San Francisco), Seawanhaka Corinthian Yacht Club, Beach Club (Cold Spring Harbor). Episcopalian. Home: 191 Oyster Bay Cove Rd Oyster Bay NY 11771 Office: Robert Fleming Inc 2 World Trade Ctr New York NY 10048

MCCANN, JAMES P., manufacturing company executive; b. Feb. 25, 1930; m. Shirley Krebs, Dec. 25, 1952; children: Judy McCann Alton, Patrick A., J. Michael. With Goodyear Tire & Rubber Co., 1951-86; exec. v.p. Bridgestone (USA) Inc., Torrance, Calif., 1986-88; pres., chief exec. officer Bridgestone (USA) Inc., Nashville, 1988—. Home: 165 Charleston Park Nashville TN 37205 Office: Bridgestone Corp USA 100 Briley Corners PO Box 140991 Nashville TN 37214-0991

MCCANN, JOHN FRANCIS, financial services company executive; b. South Orange, N.J., Nov. 30, 1937; s. Frank Charles and Dorothy Marie (Devaney) McC.; m. Mary Ellen Howland, Aug. 4, 1962; children—Sean Francis, Maureen Ellen, Darragh Siobain, Kevin Patrick. Student, LaSalle Mil. Acad., 1951-55, U. Notre Dame, 1955-57, Niagara U., 1959-61, N.J. Nat. Guard, 1959-67, The Wharton Sch., 1984-86. Vice-pres., sales mgr. Imco Container Co., N.Y.C., 1962-68; vice-pres., sales mgr. Eastman Dillon, Union Securities Co., N.Y.C., 1968-72; sr. v.p., sales mgr. Faulkner, Dawkins & Sullivan, N.Y.C., 1972-75; sr. v.p., br. mgr. Faulkner, Dawkins & Sullivan, Chatham, N.J., 1975-77; sr. v.p. Shearson Loeb Rhoades, Chatham, N.J., 1977-83; exec. v.p. Shearson Am. Express, N.Y.C., 1983-84; exec. v.p., dir. Shearson Lehman Bros., N.Y.C., 1984-89; regional dir. Shearson, Lehman, Hutton Philanthropic Found., 1989—. Fund raiser Riverview Hosp. Found., Red Bank, N.J., 1983; regional dir. Am. Express Found., N.Y.C., 1985—, Shearson Lehman Hutton Philanthropic Found. Served to 2d lt. N.J. N.G., 1959-67. Mem. N.Y. Stock Exchange (arbitrator 1982—), Securities Industry Assn., Nat. Assn. Securities Dealers (dist. com. 1988—). Republican. Roman Catholic. Clubs: Navesink Country, Monmouth Beach Bath and Tennis, Beacon Hill. Home: 135 Bingham Ave Rumson NJ 07760 Office: Shearson Lehman Hutton 151 Bodman Pl Red Bank NJ 07701

MCCANN, RAYMOND J., utility company executive; b. N.Y.C., Sept. 28, 1934; married; 4 children. B.S., Fordham U., 1956; M.B.A., CUNY, 1962. Gen. auditor Consol. Edison Co. N.Y., N.Y.C., 1972-74, controller, 1974-76, v.p. acctg., treas., 1976-77, v.p. Manhattan div., 1977-80, exec. v.p. ops., 1980-87, exec. v.p. fin. and law, 1987-89, exec. v.p., chief fin. officer, 1989—. Served to capt. USAR. Office: Consol Edison Co NY Inc 4 Irving Pl New York NY 10003

MCCANN, SANDRA JEAN, accountant; b. Bethesda, Md., Jan. 8, 1963; d. Donald K. and Virginia B. (Blackwell) McKenzie; m. James P. McCann, Feb. 1, 1986. BBA in Acctg., Evangel Coll., 1983. CPA, Va., Md. Accounts payable clk. Tracor Jitco, Inc., Rockville, Md., 1979-80; staff acct. Arthur Young & Co., Oklahoma City, 1984-85; jr. auditor Mustang Fuel Corp., Oklahoma City, 1984-85; staff acct. Stanley L. Simon CPA, Rockville, Md., 1985-87, James L. Tacey CPA, PC, Woodbridge, Va., 1987—. Vol. Med. Ctr. for Fed. Prisoners, Springfield, Mo., 1981-83, Prince William County Juvenile Detention Ctr., Dumfries, Va., 1987—. Mem. Am. Inst. CPAs, Va. Soc. CPAs. Home: 15257 Larkspur Ln Dumfries VA 22026

MCCARD, HAROLD KENNETH, aerospace company executive; b. Corinth, Maine, Dec. 18, 1931; s. Fred Leslie and Ada (Drake) McC.; m. Charlotte Marie Despres, June 29, 1957; children: Robert Fred, Renee Glen. BEE, U. Maine, Orono, 1959; MEE, Northeastern U., 1963; MS in Mgmt., MIT, 1977. Engr. Avco Systems div. Textron, Wilmington, Mass., 1959-60, group leader, 1960-62, section chief, 1962-65, dept. mgr., 1965-72, dir./staff dir., 1972-77, chief engr., 1977-79, v.p. ops., 1979-82, v.p., gen. mgr., 1982-85; pres. Textron Def. Systems (formerly Avco Systems div./ Avco Systems Textron), Wilmington, Mass., 1986—. Mem. Nat. Indsl. Security Assn. (bd. dirs. 1986—), AIAA, Armament Research and Devel. Council, Am. Def. Preparedness Assn. (exec. com.), North Shore C. of C. (bd. dirs. 1986—). Home: 6 Lantern Ln Lynnfield MA 01940 Office: Textron Def Systems 201 Lowell Ave Wilmington MA 01887

MCCARRAGHER, BERNARD JOHN, manufacturing company executive; b. Waukesha, Wis., Sept. 17, 1927; s. Bernard J. and Agnes A. (Brennan) McC.; m. Mary J. Horschak, June 20, 1953; 11 children. BS, Marquette U., 1951. CPA, Wis. Sr. acct. Arthur Andersen & Co., Milw., 1951-57; controller Payne Lumber Co., Oshkosh, Wis., 1957-59; budget mgr. Bergstrom Paper Co., Neenah, Wis., 1959-62; various positions Menasha Corp., Neenah, 1962-81, fin. v.p., 1981-84, sr. v.p., 1984—, also bd. dirs.; bd. dirs. New Eng. Wooden Ware, Gardner, Mass. Served with U.S. Army, 1946-48. Mem. Fin. Execs. Inst. (treas. 1985—). Republican. Roman Catholic. Lodge: Rotary (bd. dirs. Neenah club). Office: Menasha Corp 1645 Bergstrom Rd Neenah WI 54956

MCCARRON, JOHN JERROLD, land development and homebuilding company executive; b. Darby, Pa., Dec. 12, 1949; s. John J. and F. Elizabeth (Elko) McC.; m. Claudia Drennen, Feb 24, 1979; children: Meghan, Alexander, Meredith. Engr. Robert & Co., Atlanta, 1971-72, Kling-Lindquist Co., Phila., 1972-74; project mgr. Georgetown Assocs., Savannah, Ga., 1974-75; owner, mgr. Hatfield, Pa., 1976-79; v.p. Toll Bros. Inc., Huntingdon Valley, Pa., 1979—; prin. Jerrold McCarron Homes, Huntingdon Valley. Home: 733 Willow Run Rd Box 277 Gwynedd Valley PA 19437 Office: Toll Bros Inc 3103 Philmont Ave Huntingdon Valley PA 19437

MC CARTER, THOMAS N., III, investment counseling company executive; b. N.Y.C., Dec. 16, 1929; s. Thomas N., Jr. and Suzanne M. (Pierson) McC.; student Princeton, 1948-51; m. Nancy Kohler Alker, Sept. 23, 1955 (div.); 1 dau., Nancy A.; m. 2d, Renate Bohne von Boyens, June 22, 1976. Sales exec. Mack Trucks, Inc., N.Y.C., 1952-59; partner Kelly, McCarter, D'Arcy Investment Counsel, N.Y.C., 1959-62; v.p., sec., dir. D'Arcy, McCarter & Chew, N.Y.C., 1962-66; v.p., dir. Trainer, Wortham & Co., Inc., N.Y.C., 1967-71, exec. v.p., 1971-75; chmn. bd., dir. Island Security Bank

Ltd., 1976-78; pres. Knottingham Ltd., N.Y.C., 1976—; gen. ptnr. W.P. Miles Timber Properties, New Orleans; exec. v.p., Yorke McCarter Owen & Partels, Inc., N.Y.C., 1986-88, also dir.; pres., dir., Mentor Mgmt. Group, Inc. N.Y.C., 1986—; nat. adv. bd. Fiscal Policy Council; dir. Ramapo Land Co., Onecorp, Sterling & Yorke, Inc. Chmn. bd. trustees Christodora Found., Inc., N.Y., N.Y.C.; charter trustee Dalton Sch., N.Y.C., 1968-76, v.p., 1972-76 ; pres., trustee Civil War Library and Mus., Phila.; chmn. trustee Am. Soc. Prevention Cruelty to Animals; chmn. Loyal Legion Found., N.Y.C.; trustee Children's Aid Soc. N.Y.C., Joffrey Ballet, Found. for Am. Dance, 1973-77; v.p., trustee N.Y.C. Marble Cemetery Assn. Chartered investment counselor. Mem. Loyal Legion U.S. (comdr. N.Y. State 1964-66, nat. comdr. in chief 1977-81). Clubs: Racquet and Tennis, Brook, Links, River, St. Nicholas Soc., Pilgrims of U.S. (N.Y.C.); Meadow (Southampton, N.Y.); Ivy (Princeton, N.J.). Home: 823 Park Ave New York NY 10021 Office: Yorke McCarter Owen & Bartels 825 3rd Ave New York NY 10022

MC CARTHY, DENIS MICHAEL, air cargo company executive; b. Hartford, Conn., Dec. 4, 1942; s. Charles J. and Mary M. (Moynihan) McC.; m. Linda Horn, Aug. 21, 1965; children: Bryan, Kerry, Kevin. B.S., U. Conn., 1964, M.A., 1965. Asst. sec. Mfrs. Hanover Trust Co., N.Y.C., 1965-68; various positions to exec. v.p. Triangle Industries, Inc., Holmdel, N.J., 1968-81; sr. v.p., chief fin. officer Emery Worldwide, Wilton, Conn., 1981-84; sr. v.p. fin. and adminstrn., chief. fin. officer Emery Worldwide, 1984-85, exec. v.p., chief operating officer, 1985-87, pres., chief operating officer, 1987—, also bd. dirs.; mem. fin. adv. bd. Conn. Nat. Bank, Stamford. Home: 120 Prospect Ridge Ridgefield CT 06877 Office: Emery Air Freight Corp Old Danbury Rd Wilton CT 06897

MCCARTHY, EDWARD DAVID, financial planner; b. Providence, Feb. 20, 1955; s. Edward D. and Anna Mary (McDonald) McC.; m. Diane Winkleman, Aug. 18, 1979. BA, U. R.I., 1979; MA, U. S.C., 1981. Account exec. Prudential Bache Securities, Pittsfield, Mass., 1983-84; fin. planner Providence, 1984—; reporter Sta. WJAR-TV, Providence, 1987-88; cons. Goluses & Co., Providence, 1987—; instr. U. R.I., Kingston, 1987—. Contbr. articles on personal fin. to Providence Bus. News, 1987—. Mem. Internat. Assn. Fin. Planning, Inst. Cert. Fin. Planners (chmn., pres. R.I. 1986—). Home: 107 Glenwood Dr Warwick RI 02889 Office: Goluses and Co 310 Reservoir Ave Providence RI 02907

MCCARTHY, FREDERICK WILLIAM, investment banker; b. Boston, Nov. 25, 1941; s. Frederick William and Josephine Leona (Pannier) McC.; children: Daniel Arthur, Frederick William III, Kathryn Elizabeth. BA magna cum laude, Harvard U., 1963, MBA with high distinction, 1967. Mgmt. cons. Booz Allen & Hamilton Inc., Chgo., 1967-70; 1st v.p. investment banking Shearson, Hammill & Co. Inc., N.Y.C., 1970-72, Chgo., 1972-74; mng. dir., bd. dir. Drexel Burnham Lambert Inc., Boston, 1974—; bd. dirs. Am. Capital Corp., Avery, Inc., Banner Industries, Inc., Copelco Lease Receivables Corp., Drexel, Burnham, Lambert, Inc., Seminole Kraft Corp., Stone Forest Industries, Inc., The Westwood Group Inc. Served to 1st lt. U.S. Army, 1963-65. Home: 65 East India Row Unit 28C Boston MA 02110 Office: Drexel Burnham Lambert Inc 1 Federal St Boston MA 02110

MC CARTHY, JOHN MICHAEL, investment company executive; b. Bklyn., Apr. 9, 1927; s. Michael Francis and Catherine (McCarthy) McC.; m. Mary Agnes Hickey, Sept. 8, 1951; children—Stephen J., Neil M., Tara Anne, Laurette E. B.A., St. Francis Coll., 1951; M.B.A., N.Y. U., 1953. Sr. research officer trust dept. Citibank, N.Y.C., 1951-59; sr. research analyst, then dir. research Lord Abbett & Co., N.Y.C., 1960-72; partner Lord Abbett & Co., 1972—; v.p., portfolio mgr., then exec. v.p. Affiliated Fund Inc., N.Y.C., 1972-77, pres., dir., 1977—, sr. ptnr., chief investment officer, 1980—, chmn., 1983—, mng. ptnr., 1983—; pres., dir. Lord Abbett Bond Debenture Fund, Lord Abbett Developing Growth Fund, Lord Abbett Value Appreciation Fund, Lord Abbett Tax-Free Income Fund., Lord Abbett U.S. Govt. Securities Fund, Lord Abbett Cash Reserve Fund, Lord Abbett Fundamental Value fund, Lord Abbett Global Fund. Trustee Winthrop Univ. Hosp. Served with USAAF, 1945-47. Recipient Paper award Investment Bankers Assn., 1962, 63. Mem. N.Y. Soc. Security Analysts, Elec. and Electronic Analysts Group N.Y.C. (past pres.), Hist. Soc. Garden City. Republican. Roman Catholic. Clubs: Downtown Assn., N.Y. Athletic (N.Y.C.); Cherry Valley (Garden City). Office: Affiliated Fund Inc 767 Fifth Ave New York NY 10153

MCCARTHY, JOSEPH HAROLD, retail food company executive; b. Derby, Conn., Dec. 21, 1921; s. Joseph Harold and Kathryn (Feeley) McC.; m. Jean K. Ryan, June 7, 1947; children: Timothy J., Maureen, Barbara, Richard, Joseph Harold. B.S. in Econs., Villanova U., 1944. Sr. v.p. First Nat. Stores Inc., Boston, 1947-76, Grand Union Co., Elmwood Park, N.J., 1976-80; exec. v.p., chief operating officer Great Atlantic and Pacific Tea Co., Inc., Montvale, N.J., 1980—. Served to capt. USMC, 1943-46, PTO; served to capt. USMC, 1951-52, Korea. Home: 558 Taunton Rd Wyckoff NJ 07481 Office: Gt Atlantic & Pacific Tea Co Inc 2 Paragon Dr Montvale NJ 07645

MCCARTHY, KATHLEEN E., marketing executive; b. Mount Vernon, N.Y., Jan. 9, 1951; d. James J. and Kathleen A. (Hart) McCarthy. Student, U. Denver, 1969-73, Denver Inst. Tech., 1973-75. Sales rep. H.R. Meininger Co., Denver, 1974-77, dept. mgr., 1977-80; sr. product mgr. Koh-i-noor Rapidograph, Bloomsbury, N.J., 1980-84; product mktg. mgr. Purolator Courier, Basking Ridge, N.J., 1984-85; product mgr. Nielsen Bainbridge, div. Esselte Letraset, Esselt Pendaflex Corp., Paramus, N.J., 1985-87, v.p. mktg., 1987—. Mem. Am. Mktg. Assn., Am. Mgmt. Assn., Guild Profl. Picture Framers, N.J. Recycling Products Group. Office: Nielsen and Bainbridge 40 Eisenhower Dr Paramus NJ 07652

MCCARTHY, LYNN HAGERMAN, communications company executive; b. Hollywood, Calif., Nov. 2, 1954; d. John C. Hagerman and Isabel La Madrid; m. Thomas J. McCarthy, June 21, 1980; 1 child, Daniel Patrick. BA, U. Calif., Santa Barbara, 1976; MPH, UCLA, 1980. Project coordinator Sch. Pub. Health UCLA, 1978; asst. to dir. health promotion Kaiser Permanente So. Calif., L.A., 1979; health edn. specialist Group Health Coop. Puget Sound, Seattle, 1980-82, project mgr., 1982-84, mgr. patient edn. planning and program devel., 1983-86; dir. safety and health GTE Northwest, Everett, Wash., 1986-88; asst. v.p. safety and health, telephone ops. GTE Northwest, Everett, 1988—; presenter on worksite health promotion, GTE Northwest, 1980—. Bd. dirs. Apple A Day Self Care Ctr., Seattle, 1985; vice chmn. Wash. Gov.'s Council on Health, 1986—. With USPHS, 1979. Fellow Soc. Pub. Health Assn. (treas., chmn. program planning); mem. Am. Pub. Health Assn. (sec. 1987—). Office: GTE Northwest 1800 41st Ave Everett WA 98201

MCCARTHY, RAYMOND MALCOLM, finance company executive; b. Chgo., Feb. 27, 1927; s. Raymond Jerome and Margaret V. (Deady) McC.; m. Mary C. Burns, Oct. 27, 1948; children: Raymond J., John T., Sheila M., Michael J., Timothy P., Kevin P., Kathleen M., Anne T. BBA, Loyola U., Chgo., 1950; AMP, Harvard U., 1980. With GMAC, N.Y.C., 1949—; exec. v.p. ops. GMAC, 1980-85; pres. GMAC, Detroit, 1986—, also dir. Served with USMC, 1944-46. Club: Harvard (N.Y.C.). Office: GMAC 3044 W Grand Blvd Detroit MI 48202

MC CARTHY, WALTER JOHN, JR., utility executive; b. N.Y.C., Apr. 20, 1925; s. Walter John and Irene (Trumbl) McC.; m. Linda Lyon, May 6, 1988; children by previous marriage: Walter, David, Sharon, James, William. B.M.E., Cornell U., 1949; grad., Oak Ridge Sch. Reactor Tech., 1952; D.Eng. (hon.), Lawrence Inst. Tech., 1981; D.Sc. (hon.), Eastern Mich. U., 1983; LHD, Wayne State U., 1984; LLD, Alma (Mich.) Coll., 1985. Engr. Public Service Electric & Gas Co., Newark, 1949-56; sect. head Atomic Power Devel. Assos., Detroit, 1956-61; gen. mgr. Power Reactor Devel. Co., Detroit, 1961-68; with Detroit Edison Co., 1968—, exec. v.p. ops., 1975-77, exec. v.p. divs., 1977-79, pres., chief operating officer, 1979-81, chmn., chief exec. officer, 1981—, also dir.; dir. Perry Drug Stores Inc., Comerica, Inc., Fed. Mogul Corp. Author papers in field. Trustee Edison Inst., Cranbrook Ednl. Community, New Detroit, Harper-Grace Hosps., Rackham Engring. Found.; v.p., dir. Detroit United Fund; bd. dirs. Detroit, Econ. Alliance for Mich., Detroit Renaissance, Detroit Econ. Growth Corp., Inst. Nuclear Power Ops., Detroit Symphony Orch. Hall; co-chmn. NCCJ. Fellow Am. Nuclear Soc., Engring. Soc. Detroit; mem. ASME, Nat. Acad. Engring. Methodist. Clubs: Detroit, Renaissance (Detroit). Office: Detroit Edison Co 2000 2nd Ave Detroit MI 48226

MCCARTY, JOSEPH CHARLES, manufacturing company executive; b. Detroit, June 25, 1942; s. James Leo and Jean Katherine (Meyer) McC.; m. Kathleen Marie Baszuk, May 4, 1968; children: Mary Ann, Joseph Charles Jr. BS, U. Notre Dame, 1964; MBA, U. Mich., 1966. Assoc. Risk mgmt.; CPA, Mich.; CPCU; cert. cash mgr. Auditing staff Coopers & Lybrand, Detroit, 1966-74; div. controller Acme-Cleve. Corp., Cleve., 1974-79, corp. risk mgr., 1979-82, risk and cash mgr., 1982-86, asst. treas., 1986-88, dep. treas., 1988—. Served to 1st lt. U.S. Army, 1968-71. Recipient Disting. Grad. award Ins. Inst. Am., 1982. Mem. Am. Inst. CPA's, Risk and Ins. Mgmt. Soc. (chpt. bd. dirs. 1983—, chpt. sec. 1986, chpt. v.p. 1986-87, chpt. pres. 1987-88, Jim Cristy award 1982), Mich. Assn. CPA's, Soc. CPCU, Cleve. Treas. Club. Republican. Roman Catholic. Office: Acme-Cleve Corp 30195 Chagrin Blvd #300 Cleveland OH 44124

MCCARTY, PHILIP NORMAN, bank holding company executive; b. Indpls., July 1, 1938; s. Estel E. and Catherine J. (McCafferty) McC.; m. Paula B. Boubeau, May 19, 1962; 1 child, Carrie Michel. BBA cum laude, U. Miami, 1960. With Southeast Banking Corp., Miami, 1960-69; asst. v.p. Southeast Banking Corp., 1967-69; sr. v.p., sec., treas., dir. Boatmen's Bancshares, Inc., St. Louis, 1970—; pres., dir. Boatmen's Life Ins. Co., 1976—. Served with U.S. Army, 1961. Mem. Am. Soc. Corp. Secs., Fin. Execs. Inst. Am. Republican. Methodist. Home: 8445 Colonial Ln Ladue MO 63124 Office: Boatmen's Bancshares Inc PO Box 236 Saint Louis MO 63166

MCCASLIN, TERESA EVE, chemical company executive; b. Jersey City, Nov. 22, 1949; d. Felix F. and Ann E. (Golaszewski) Hrynkiewicz; m. Thomas W. McCaslin, Jan. 22, 1972. BA, Marymount Coll., 1971; MBA, L.I. U., 1981. Adminstrv. officer Civil Service Commn., Fed. Republic Germany, 1972-76; personnel dir. Oceanroutes, Inc., Palo Alto, Calif., 1976-78; mgr., coll. relations Continental Grain Co., N.Y.C., 1978-79, corp. personnel mgr., 1979-81, dir. productivity, internal cons., 1981-84; dir., human resources Grow Group, Inc., N.Y.C., 1984-85, v.p. human resources, 1985-86, v.p. adminstrn., 1986—. Career counselor Marymount Coll. Career Ctr., Tarrytown. Recipient Sustained Superior Performance award U.S. Civil Service Commn., Fed. Republic Germany. Mem. Conf. Bd., N.Y. Personnel Mgr.'s Assn., Am. Mgmt. Assn., Human Resources Council. Roman Catholic. Office: Grow Group Inc Pan Am Bldg 200 Park Ave New York NY 10166

MC CAUGHEY, ANDREW GILMOUR, life insurance company executive; b. Montreal, Que., Can., Dec. 8, 1922; s. Andrew Gilmour and Mary Doris (Sheldon) McC.; m. Lorraine Baltera; children: Jennifer H. (Mrs. Kirk Rott), Andrew John, Matthew James. B.Com. with honors in Econs, McGill U., 1949. Auditor Clarkson, Gordon & Co., Montreal, Que., and Toronto, Ont., 1949-53; with Can. Marconi Co., 1953-59, sec.-treas., 1959, exec. v.p. fin. and adminstrn., 1965-67; v.p. fin. Molson Breweries Ltd., 1967; sr. v.p., fin. Molson Cos. Ltd., 1968-70, exec. com., 1970-80; also dir.; dir., pres., chief exec. officer N.Am. Life Assurance Co., Toronto, 1980-87, vice chmn., 1987-88; chmn. Grayrock Shared Ventures, Toronto, 1988—; bd. dirs. Toromont Industries, Ltd. Served as pilot RCAF, 1941-45. Mem. Inst. Chartered Accts. of Que. and Ont., Fin. Execs. Inst. of Toronto (past pres. Montreal chpt.). Conservative. Anglican. Clubs: Univ., Royal Canadian Yacht, Royal Canadian Mil. Inst., Lambton Golf and Country, Goodwood (Toronto); RAF (London). Office: N Am Life Centre, 5650 Yonge St, Willowdale, ON Canada M2M 4G4

MCCAUSLAND, LINDA SHOFF, financial company executive; b. Los Angeles; d. Leonard Wayne Shoff and Mary Ellen (Reiter) Carey; m. Thomas William McCausland, Aug. 22, 1954 (div.). BS, UCLA, 1955. Master tchr. UCLA, Los Angeles city schs., 1955-62; investment counselor Washington, 1962—. Chmn. Aspen (Colo.) Wildflower Beautification Com., 1987; founder Nat. Mus. Women Arts, Washington, 1986—; active Nat. Rep. Senatorial Trust, Washington, 1983—, Nat. Rep. Leadership Council, Washington, 1984—; nat. trustee Washington Opera, 1983—; trustee Corcoran Galllery Art, Washington, 1986—; apptd. by. Pres. Reagan White House Conf. for a Drug-Free Am., 1987, Nat. Parks Found., 1986. Episcopalian. Office: 4200 Massachusetts Ave NW Washington DC 20016

MCCLAIN, LARRY FRENCH, lumber company executive; b. Knoxville, Tenn., Mar. 4, 1937; s. French Charles McClain and Jean (Vineyard) Duff; children: Jennifer, Callie. BA, Baylor U., 1959. V.p. Emmet Vaughn Lumber Co., Knoxville, 1963—. Mem. allocation com. United Way, Knoxville, 1987—; bd. dirs. YMCA Cen., Knoxville, 1975-85, Vol. Helpers Inc., Knoxville, 1987—. With U.S. Army, 1960-62. Mem. Deane Hill Country Club, Rotary (bd. dirs. Knoxville chpt. 1988). Home: 800 Longview Rd #120 Knoxville TN 37919 Office: Emmet Vaughn Lumber Co 3932 Martin Mill Pike Knoxville TN 37920

MCCLANE, ROBERT SANFORD, bank holding company executive; b. Kenedy, Tex., May 5, 1939; s. Norris Robert and Ella Addie (Stockton) McC.; m. Sue Nitschke, Mar. 31, 1968; children: Len Stokes, Norris Robert. BS in Bus. Adminstrn., Trinity U., San Antonio, 1961. With Ford Motor Co., Detroit, 1961-62; with Frost Nat. Bank, San Antonio, 1962—, mem. staff, 1962-68, v.p., 1968-78; exec. v.p. Cullen/Frost Bankers, Inc., 1976—, pres., dir., 1985—; bd. dirs. Frost Nat. Bank, San Antonio, C/F Life Ins. Co., San Antonio, Main Plaza Corp., San Antonio, Daltex Gen. Agy., San Antonio. Crusade chmn. Bexar County chpt. Am. Cancer Soc., 1974; bd. dirs. Bexar County chpt. ARC, 1969-72; sr. warden St. Luke's Episcopal Ch., San Antonio, 1980; trustee Alamo Pub. Telecommunications Council, San Antonio, 1981-88; chmn. San Antonio Econ. Devel. Found., 1987-88, exec. com. 1985; bd. dirs. Plaza Club San Antonio, 1973—. Served with USAR, 1961-62. Mem. Assn. Bank Holding Cos., Greater San Antonio C. of C. (chmn. Leadership San Antonio 1975-76), Trinity U. Alumni Assn. (pres. 1968-69, named Disting. Alumnus 1987). Episcopalian. Clubs: San Antonio German, Order Alamo, Tex. Cavaliers, Argyle, Town. Office: Cullen/Frost Bankers Inc PO Box 1600 San Antonio TX 78296

MCCLARAN, GEORGE JOSEPH, SR., banker; b. Pitts., July 15, 1924; s. Joseph Fred and Adeline Hester (Barnes) McC.; m. Grace Wilma Hunt, May 6, 1950; children: Lynda Ann, Joanne, George Joseph Jr., Richard Hunt. B.A., Ohio Wesleyan U., 1947; postgrad., U. Pitts., 1947-49, Mich. State Normal Coll., 1944. V.p. Pitts. Nat. Bank, 1959-73, sr. v.p., 1973-84, exec. v.p., 1984-85, pres., 1985-88, vice chmn., 1988—, also bd. dirs.; chmn. bd. Forbes Health System, Pitts., Western Pa. Devel. Credit Corp., Pitts.;bd. dirs. Forbes Healthmark, Newcomer Products, Latrobe, Pa., PNC Comml. Corp., Tampa, Fla., PNC Internat. Bank, Pitts., Robroy Industries, Inc., Verona, Pa., Forbes Health Found., Pitts., Landmark Ventures, Inc., Pitts. Served to 1st lt. U.S. Army, 1943-46, 50-52. Mem. Am. Bankers Assn., Pa. Bankers Assn., Assn. Res. City Bankers, Robert Morris Assocs., Greater Pitts. C. of C. Republican. Clubs: Duquesne; Longue Vue (Verona, Pa.) (pres. 1972-74); Bent Tree Country (Sarasota). Lodges: Masons, Shriners, Royal Order Jesters. Home: 70 Holland Rd Pittsburgh PA 15235 Office: Pitts Nat Bank 5th Ave & Wood St Pittsburgh PA 15265

MCCLARY, JIM MARSTON, accountant, executive, consultant; b. Nashville, Feb. 26, 1949; s. Joseph Patrick and Daisy Wynell (Marston) McC.; m. Billie Sue Gwinn, Feb. 27, 1970; children: Traci Gwinn, Matthew Ryan. BSBA with honors, U. Tenn., 1974. CPA, Tenn. Staff acct. Price Waterhouse & Co. CPAs, Nashville, 1974-76; sr. acct. Bradley & Crenshaw, CPAs, Nashville, 1976-77; controller Holder & No. Lumber Sales, Inc., Nashville, 1977-78; pres. Retirement Plans, Inc., Nashville, 1978-80; ptnr. McClary, Yeary & Howell, CPAs, Brentwood, Tenn., 1980-85; cons. Franklin, Tenn., 1985—; pres. Employee Benefit Svcs. Inc., Brentwood, 1985—; ops. prin. Advanced Fin. Planning Securities Corp., Brentwood, 1985—, cons. 1985—. Served with USAF, 1968-69. Mem. AICPA, Tenn. Soc. CPAs, U.S. C. of C. Democrat. Office: Employee Benefit Svcs Inc 5038 Thoroughbred Ln Brentwood TN 37027

MCCLAVE, DONALD SILSBEE, assocation executive; b. Cleve., May 7, 1941; s. Charles Green and Anne Elizabeth (Oakley) McC.; m. Christine Mary Tomkins, Feb. 19, 1966; 1 child, Andrew Green. BA, Denison U., 1963. Mktg. research officer Bank of Calif., San Francisco, 1968-70; v.p. Cen. Nat. Bank, Chgo., 1970-75; v.p. First Interstate Bank, Portland, Oreg., 1975-77, sr. v.p., 1977-79, exec. v.p., 1979-86; pres., chief exec. officer Portland Met. C. of C., 1987—; bd. dirs. Bank Mktg. Assn., Chgo., 1976-79, Consumer Bankers Assn., Washington, 1980-82; instr. Grad. Sch. Mktg. and Strategic Planning, Athens, 1982-84, Pacific Coast Sch. Banking, Seattle, 1976-78. Pres. Oreg. Episcopal Sch. Bd., Portland, 1983-84; pres. Assn. Oreg. Industries Found., Salem, Oreg., 1984-85; co-chmn. Japan-Am. Conf. of Mayors and C. of C., Portland, 1985—. Office: Portland C of C 221 NW 2nd Ave Portland OR 97209

MCCLAY, HARVEY CURTIS, data processing executive; b. Houston, Jan. 2, 1939; s. Clarence and Agnes E. McC.; m. Patricia Lott, Jan. 8, 1961; children: James, John, Susan, Robert. BA in Math., Rice U., 1960. Field engr. Western Electric Co., Marysville, Calif., 1960-62; analyst math. Litton Data Systems Co., Canoga Park, Calif., 1962-63; mgr. programming Lockheed Electronics Co., Houston, 1967-75; systems mgr. City of Houston, 1975-77; project mgr. fin. systems devel. Brown & Root, Houston, 1977-81; mgr. data processing Nat. Supply, Houston, 1981-84; project mgr. Computer Scis. Corp., Houston, 1984—; part-time instr. data processing and mgmt. Houston Community Coll. Address: 2911 Huckleberry St Pasadena TX 77502

MCCLEARY, BENJAMIN WARD, investment banker; b. Washington, July 9, 1944; s. George William and Nancy (Grim) McC.; m. Deirdre Stillman Marsters, May 6, 1967 (div. 1977); children: Benjamin, Katherine; m. Jean Luce Muchmore, Oct. 15, 1983. AB, Princeton U., 1966. Trainee Chem. Bank, N.Y.C., 1969-70, asst. sec., 1970-72, asst. v.p., 1972-74, v.p., 1974-81; sr. v.p. Lehman Bros. Kuhn Loeb, N.Y.C., 1981-84; mng. dir. Shearson Lehman Bros., Inc. (formerly Lehman Bros. Kuhn Loeb), N.Y.C., 1984-87; exec. dir. Shearson Lehman Hutton Internat., London, 1987-88; mng. dir. Shearson Lehman Hutton Inc., N.Y.C., 1988—. Served with USN, 1966-69. Episcopalian. Club: Dunes (Naragansett, R.I.). Office: Shearson Lehman Hutton Inc Am Express Tower World Fin Ctr New York NY 10285-1700

MCCLEARY, PAUL FREDERICK, voluntary agency executive; b. Bradley, Ill., May 2, 1930; s. Hal C. and Pearl (Aeicher) McC.; A.B., Olivet Nazarene U., Kankakee, Ill., 1952; M.Div., Garrett-Evang. Sem., Evanston, Ill., 1956; M.A., Northwestern U., 1972; D.D., MacMurray Coll., Jacksonville, Ill., 1970; m. Rachel Timm, Jan. 26, 1951; children—Leslie Ann, Rachel Mary, John Wesley, Timothy Paul. Ordained to ministry United Methodist Ch., 1956; missionary in Bolivia, 1957-68; exec. sec. structure study commn. United Meth. Ch., 1969-72, asst. gen. sec. to Latin Am., 1972-75; exec. dir. Ch. World Service, N.Y.C., 1975-84; assoc. gen. sec. for research Gen. Council on Ministries, United Meth. Ch., 1984-87; exec. v.p. Save the Children, Westport, Conn., 1987-88; exec. dir. Christian Children's Fund Inc., 1988—; mem., bd. dir. Overseas Devel. Council; mem. adv. com. on economic matters World Council Chs.; mem. com. on African Devel. Strategies; mem. Com. on Dialogue and Devel., Nat. Leadership Commn. on Health Care, Bretton Woods Com.; dep. pres. NGO com. on UNICEF, CODEL, Andean Rural Health Care, Freedom from Hunger Fedn., Christian Century Found. Mem. AAAS, Acad. Polit. Sci., Latin Am. Studies Assn., Masons, Rotary, Alpha Kappa Lambda. Democrat. Author: Global Justice and World Hunger, 1978; co-author: Quality of Life in a Global Society, 1978; contbr. articles to mags. Office: Christian Children's Fund Inc 203 E Cary St Richmond VA 23261

MCCLELLAN, DAVID LAWRENCE, physician, medical facility administrator; b. Burlington, Iowa, Feb. 13, 1930; s. Harold L. and LaVon H. McClellan; divorced; children: David, Steven, Mark, Jeffrey. BA, U. Iowa, 1952, MD, 1955. Intern U.S. Naval Hosp., San Diego, 1955-56; med. officer USS Nereus, 1956-58; pvt. practice Garland Med. Office, Spokane, Wash., 1958-64; pres. DeRe Medica Med. Clinic, Spokane, 1964—; pres., chmn. bd. North Spokane Profl. Bldg., Inc., 1966-86; pres. Inland Health Assocs., Inc., Spokane, 1984—; pres., bd. dirs. Bio-Chem Environ. Svcs., Seattle, 1984; v.p. Forest Resources, 1978-86; pres. Omnex, 1980-86; chief exec. officer, Double N Orchards, 1980-87; mem. staff Holy Family Hosp.; cons. Rotary Marine Engine Industries, Seattle, 1986—. Contbr. articles and papers to med. jours. Lt. USN, 1955-58. Fellow Am. Acad. Family Practice; mem. AMA, Wash. State Med. Soc., Spokane County Med. Soc., Inland Empire Acad. Family Practice, Med. Group Mgmt. Assn. Republican. Roman Catholic. Home: 7151 Audubon Dr Spokane WA 99200 Office: DeRe Medica 99208 N Lidgerwood St Ste 220 Spokane WA 99207

MCCLELLAN, KENT, financial planner; b. Burley, Idaho, Mar. 4, 1953; s. Arthur Dale and Betty Jo (Jensen) McC.; m. Vickie Lyn Smith, May 16, 1975; children: Michael Kent, Corey Ryan, JaNae Lynette, Nathan Dale. AS, Ricks Coll., 1976. Chartered fin. cons. Ins. agt. Farm Bur. Mut., Burley, 1977-78, Lincoln Nat. Life Ins. Co., 1978-81, A.I.M. N.W. Agy., Twin Falls, Idaho, 1981-86; rep. Mut. Service Corp., Detroit, 1986-88; pres., owner Liberty Group, Paul, Idaho, 1986-88; rep. Securities Am. Inc., Omaha, 1988—; v.p. Outreach Assets Mgmt. Ltd., 1988—. Mem. com. Hunsaker for County Commr., Minidoka County, 1986. Mem. Internat. Assn. Fin. Planning, Am. Soc. CLUs and ChFCs. Republican. Mormon.

MCCLELLAN, RICHARD AUGUSTUS, drycleaner, small business owner; b. Gainesville, Fla., Sept. 13, 1930; s. Marion THeodore Sr. and Cornelia (Hampton) McC.; m. Thelma Watson, May 19, 1947 (dec. Mar. 1980); children: Richard A., Wayne Theodore, Viola Patricia, Michael Ray; m. Betty Lee Snow, Dec. 12, 1980; children: Claranell Y., Juanita F., Johnnie C. Diploma, Nat. Inst. Drycleaning, 1975. Drycleaner S & S Cleaners, Gainesville, 1958—. Mem. Am. Soc. Notaries (govt. relations com. 1984, pub. relations com. 1989), Notary Pub. Assn. State Fla., Nat. Notary Assn. Democrat. Methodist. Home and Office: 625 SE 15th St Gainesville FL 32601

MCCLELLAN, STEPHEN TRUE, investment analyst; b. Oak Park, Ill., Nov. 7, 1942; s. Irvin Richard McClellan and Betty (McEwen) Chase; children: Laurel A., Justin A.; m. Judith Hamilton. BA, Syracuse U., 1964; MBA, George Washington U., 1971. Chartered fin. analyst. With U.S. Dept. Commerce, Washington, 1968-71; v.p. Spencer Trask & Co., N.Y.C., 1971-77, Salomon Bros., Inc., N.Y.C., 1977-85; 1st v.p. Merrill Lynch & Co., N.Y.C., 1985—; pres. Software Services Analyst Group, N.Y.C., 1987-88; pres. Computer Industry Analysts, N.Y.C., 1977, 82, 84. Author: The Coming Computer Industry Shakeout, 1984; contbr. articles to profl. jours. Served to lt. USN, 1964-67. Named #1 ranked Security Analyst-Data Services and Software Stocks Instl. Investor mag., 1985-88. Mem. Fin. Analysts Fedn., N.Y. Soc. Security Analysts, Assn. Data Processing Service Orgns. Republican.

MCCLELLAN, WILLIAM MICHAEL, real estate appraiser; b. Stamford, Tex., Oct. 10, 1939; s. William M. and Mary Lou (Waldrip) McC.; m. Nancilu Jackson, Sept. 8, 1963; 1 child, Alison. BBA, Okla. U., 1963. V.p. Toland McClellan, Dallas, 1970-80; pres. McClellan, Massey, Humphries, Naylor & Harmon, Inc., Dallas, 1980—. Served to lt. U.S. Army, 1964-66. Mem. Appraisal Inst. (cert.).

MCCLELLAND, JEFFERY M., advertising and public relations executive, consultant; b. Media, Pa., Apr. 20, 1962; s. John Howard and Elizabeth Mary (Paynter) McC. Student, Goldey Bencom Coll., 1985. Mktg. mgmt. account exec. Shipley Assocs., Wilmington, Del., 1985-86; pres., media dir. Bryan Charles and Assocs., Wilmington, 1986—. Recipient Silver and Merit awards Addes Advt. Club Del., 1987. Mem. Am. Mktg. Assn., Del. Contenders Assn. Home: 1401 Delaware Ave Wilmington DE 19806 Office: Bryan Charles & Assocs 1719 Delaware Ave Wilmington DE 19806

MC CLELLAND, JOHN PETER, winery executive; b. N.Y.C., Aug. 17, 1933; s. Harold Stanley and Helen Lucille (Gardner) McC.; m. Ann Carolyn Campbell, Aug. 27, 1954; children: John, Kristen. Student, UCLA, 1951-53. With Almadén Vineyards, Inc., San Jose, Calif., 1958-83; v.p. sales, then v.p. mktg. Almadén Vineyards, Inc., 1970-76, pres., 1976-83; chmn. bd., chief exec. officer Geyser Peak Winery, 1983—. Served with AUS, 1954-56. Mem. Wine Inst. (chmn. public relations com. 1977—, exec. com. 1979—, chmn. 1986-87), Sonoma County Wine Bd., Internat. Wine and Food Soc.,

Supreme Knight of the Vine, Chaine Des Rotisseurs. Republican. Presbyterian.

MCCLELLAND, W. CLARK, retail company financial executive; b. Detroit, Feb. 6, 1939; s. Fauvia McClelland; m. Marjorie Mele; children: Michael, Troy, Cory, Deborah. Grad., Elizabethtown Coll., 1965. Acct. Coopers and Lybrand, Phila., 1967-70; treas., chief fin. officer Heilig Meyers Corp., Richmond, Va., 1970-74; dir., chief fin. officer Gas Spring Corp., Montgomeryville, Pa., 1974-75; sr. v.p. fin. Hechinger Co., Landover, Md., 1975—; bd. dirs. Bank of Balt. Mem. Am. Inst. CPA's, Nat. Capital Group Fin. Execs. Inst. Office: Hechinger Co 3500 Pennsy Dr Landover MD 20785

MCCLELLAND, WILLIAM CRAIG, paper company executive; b. Orange, N.J., Apr. 21, 1934; s. William N. and Pauline (Lee) McC.; m. Alice Garrett, Dec. 28, 1956; children: Suzanne, Alice Elizabeth, Heather. BS in Econs., Princeton U., 1956; MBA, Harvard U., 1965. Salesman, branch mgr. PPG Industries, Cleve. and Erie, Pa., 1960-63; pres. Watervliet Paper Co. div. Hammermill Paper Co., Mich., 1969-73; product, mktg. mgr. Hammermill Paper Co., Erie, Pa., 1965-69, v.p., 1973-80, sr. v.p., 1980-83, exec. v.p., dir., 1983-85, pres., chief exec. officer, 1985-88, also bd. dirs.; sr. v.p. Internat. Paper Co., 1986-87, exec. v.p., 1987-88, also bd. dirs.; exec. v.p. Union Camp Corp., Wayne, N.J., 1988—; bd. dirs. Quaker State Corp., PNC Fin. Corp., Allegheny Ludlum Corp. Mem. Coun. Fellows, Behrend Coll. of Pa. State U., 1980-88; dir. Pitts. Theol. Seminary, 1988—. Lt. (j.g.) USN, 1956-59. Home: 7 Ridge Crest Rd Saddle River NJ 07458

MCCLEMENTS, ROBERT, JR., oil company executive; b. Phila., Dec. 1, 1928; s. Robert and Emma (Connor) McC.; m. Barbara Joan Rose, Dec. 20, 1952; children: Kathleen, Mary Anne. B.C.E., Drexel U., 1952; Advanced Mgmt. Program, Harvard U., 1977. Project engr. Foster-Wheeler Co., Livingston, N.J., 1952-54; project mgr. Catalytic Construction Co., Phila., 1956-65; plant mgr., v.p. Sun-Great Can. Oil, Ft. McMurray, Alta., Can., 1965-71; dir., materials mgr. Sun Co., Phila., 1971-72, dir. engring., 1972-74; v.p. energy ventures Sun Co., Dallas, 1974-75, pres. Sunoco Energy Devel. Co., 1975-77; exec. v.p. Sun Co., Radnor, Pa., 1977-81, pres., 1981-86, chief exec. officer, 1985—; chmn. bd. Sun Co., Radnor, 1987—; dir. First Pa. Corp., Phila. Bd. trustees, Drexel U., Thomas Jefferson U., Grove City Coll.; pres. adv. council, Ea. Coll.; mem. Assoc. United Ways, Pa., N.J., Greater Phila. First Corp., Pennsylvanians for Effective Govt., Phila. Orch., LISC Phila. policy Bd. Served with U.S. Army, 1954-56. Mem. Am. Petroleum Inst. (bd. dirs.), Am. Productivity Ctr., Greater Phila. C. of C., Nat. Indsl. Adv. Council, Pa. Bus. Roundtable, Urban Affairs Partnership. Clubs: Union League (Phila.); Aronimink Golf (Newtown Square, Pa.). Home: 773 Sugartown Rd Malvern PA 19355 Office: Sun Co Inc 100 Matsonford Rd Radnor PA 19087 *

MC CLENDON, FRED VERNON, rancher, equine consultant; b. Vernon, Tex., Dec. 23, 1924; s. Guy C. and Lexie M. (Johnson) Mc C.; m. Dorothy J. Seibert, June 1943 (div. 1953); children: Cathy, Kent, Tracy; m. Ethel R. Cherry, Sept. 15, 1959; children: Tess, Rob, J.T. Assoc. degree, Hannibal La Grange Coll., 1947; BBA, Baylor U., 1949; MBA, Harvard U., 1951, postgrad.; postgrad., Colo. U., 1951, Denver U., 1952. Asst. cashier U.S. Nat. Bank, Denver, 1951; gen. mgr. Nat. Paper Band Co., Denver, 1952-53; personnel mgr. Houston Fire & Casualty Co., Ft. Worth, 1954-56; gen. sales mgr. City Lincoln/Mercury, Dallas, 1957-58; owner INS-Bank Personnel Agy., Dallas, 1959-61; mng. ptnr. Allen & Mc Clendon Ins., Dallas, 1959-63; owner, broker Mc Clendon Real Estate, Dallas, 1959-63; gen. mgr. Eagle Nest Ranch, Roan Mountain, Tenn., 1963-88, Mile High Ranch, Roan Mt., Tenn., 1988—; cons. Gen. Adjustments Bur., 1981—, Debordieux Corp., 1985—, Wachesaw Corp., 1985—, Hidden Lakes Devel. Corp., various ins. cos. and law firms in U.S. and Can.; lectr. to lodges and assns., 1985—; gen. ptnr. Flexnet Investments, Ltd., Dallas, 1988—; sr. v.p. Vet Kwik, Inc., S.C.; lic. Tenn. ins. agt., 1988—. Contbr. articles to profl. jours. Recipient W.T. Grant fellow Harvard U., 1950-51. Mem. Am. Quarter Horse Assn., Australian Appaloosa Assn., Appaloosa Horse Club (U.S.), Tenn. Permanent Real Estate Broker, Am. Charolais Assn., Am. Charbray Assn., Am. Paint Horse Assn., Am. Soc. Equine Appraisers. Republican. Mem. Seventh Day Adventists. Home: PO Box 190 Roan Mountain TN 37687 Office: Mile High Ranch PO Box #69 Roan Mountain TN 37687

MCCLENDON, IRVIN LEE, SR., data processing executive; b. Waco, Tex., June 12, 1945; s. Irvin Nicholas and Evelyn Lucile (Maycumber) McC.; m. Mary Helen Burrell Swanson, June 26, 1982; 1 son, Richard Lester children by previous marriage: Michael Boyd, Irvin Lee Jr., Laura Ann, Paul Nicholas; stepchildren: Brenda Irene, Kevin Ray, Perry Lee. Student El Camino Coll., 1961-63, U. So. Calif., 1962-66; BA in Math., Calif. State U.-Fullerton, 1970, postgrad. in bus. adminstrn., 1971-76; cert. nat. security mgmt. Indsl. Coll. Armed Forces, 1974; postgrad. in religion Summit Sch. Theology, 1982-84. Engring. lab. asst. Rockwell Internat. Corp., Anaheim, Calif., 1967-68, test data analyst, 1968, assoc. computer programmer, 1968-70, mem. tech. staff, 1970-82; systems programmer A-Auto-trol Tech. Corp., Denver, 1982-84, sr. tech. writer, 1984-86; sr. tech. writer, editor Colo. Data Systems, Inc., Englewood, Colo., 1986-87; engring. writer II CalComp subs. Lockheed Co., Hudson, N.H., 1987; sr. tech. writer CDI Corp., Arvada, Colo., 1987-88; office automation cons. Volt temporary Svcs., 1989, word processing cons., Aurora, Colo., 1989—; staff cons. CAP GEMINI AM., 1989—. Sec. of governing bd. Yorba Linda Libr. Dist., 1972-77; trustee Ch. of God Seventh Day Advent, Bloomington, Calif., 1979-81, treas., 1980-81, mem. Calif. State U. and Coll. Statewide Alumni Coun., 1976-77; 2d v.p. Orange County chpt. Calif. Spl. Dists. Assn., 1976, pres., 1977; mem. Adams County Rep. Cen. Com., 1984—, vice-chmn. 32d House Dist. Vacancy com., 1984-86, chmn., 1986—; dist. capt., mem. exec. com. , 1988—; mem. Luth. Chorale, 1982-85, Colo. Choir, 1988—, Northland Chorale, 1988—. With USAFR, 1967-71. USAF Nat. Merit scholar, 1963-67. Mem. Calif. Assn. Libr. Trustees and Commrs. (exec. bd., So. Calif. rep. 1976-77), Assn. Computing Machinery, Air Force Assn., Nat. Eagle Scout Assn., Calif. State U.-Fullerton Alumni Assn. (dir. 1975-77). Home: 9835 Pennsylvania Dr Thornton CO 80229-2117 Office: 5299 DTC Blvd Ste 610 Englewood CO 80111

MCCLINTIC, GEORGE VANCE, III, petroleum engineer, real estate broker; b. Sayre, Okla., Jan. 27, 1925; s. George Vance and Myrtle Jane (Rogers) M.; m. Margaret Ruth, 1945; m. Betsy Ross, 1969 (dec. 1977); children—Kathern, Michael; m. Judy Prince, 1978 (dec. 1985); m. Caroline Hall, 1986. B.S., Okla. U., 1950. Warehouseman Mid Continent Supply Co., 1950-52, dist. machinery sales mgr., 1952-56; with Sabre Drilling Co., also v.p. 3 Rig Co., 1956-58; Okla. dist. mgr. Republic Supply Co., 1958-59; v.p. Chief Oil Tool Co., Oklahoma City, 1959-62; in real estate, Oklahoma City, 1962—; owner, mgr. McClintic Realty, and Engring. Cos., 1966—; with Jack Callaway Co., 1968-70; pres., engring. officer Geothermal Engring. and Operating Co., Oklahoma City and Carson City, Nev., 1972-76; petroleum engr. SW Mineral Energy Co., Oklahoma City, 1976-79; pres. Flat Tire Caddie Co., Oklahoma City, 1979—. Republican candidate for 5th Dist. Congress, 1976; mayoral candidate for Oklahoma City, 1983. Served with USAAF, 1943-45; ETO. Decorated D.F.C., Air medal with 11 clusters, ETO medal with 5 Campaign bronze stars. Clubs: Oklahoma, Petroleum. Lodge: Masons. Inventor flat tire caddie. Office: Flat Tire Caddie Co 2619 N Harrey #3 Oklahoma City OK 73103

MCCLINTICK, ROBERT ROY, insurance company executive; b. Walnut, Kans., Nov. 19, 1924; s. A.W. and Louella (Burnett) McC.; m. Hazel Jean Wathen, Aug. 12, 1950; children—Suzanne McClintick Dinsmore, Stephanie Owens. B.S., U. Kans., 1949; postgrad. U. Kansas City, 1950-52. CPCU; CLU. With Farmers Ins. Group, Kansas City, 1949-51, Austin, Tex., 1952-55, underwriting mgr., Merced, Calif., 1956-58, gen. underwriting mgr., Los Angeles, 1959-62, dir. underwriting adminstrn. and personal lines, 1963-68, regional mgr. Pacific Northwest, 1969-74, v.p., mgr. Great Lakes region, 1975-76, v.p. claims, Los Angeles, 1977-78, v.p. field ops., 1979-84, sr. v.p. property and casualty ops., 1985—; pres. Fire Underwriters Assn., Los Angeles, 1982—, also dir.; dir. Farmers Underwriters Assn., Truck Underwriters Assn., Mid-Century Ins. Co., A.I.F. Holding Co.; mem. Farmers Ins. Group Safety Found. Investment Com.; v.p., gen. mgr. Farmers Ins. Co. of Wash., 1969-74; pres. Farmers Ins. Co. Oreg., 1969-74, Ill. Farmers Ins. Co., 1974-76; chmn. Oreg. steering com. Western Ins. Info. Service, 1973-74; dir. Oreg. Ins. Guaranty Assn., Assn. Oreg. Industries, Ill. Ins. Info. Service. Mem. U.S. C. of C., C.P.C.U. (Los Angeles chpt.), C.L.U. Office: Farmers Group Inc 4680 Wilshire Blvd Los Angeles CA 90010 also: Fire Ins Exch PO Box 2478 Terminal Annex Los Angeles CA 90051

MCCLINTOCK, DOUGLAS COVE, accounting company executive; b. Detroit, Jan. 26, 1945; s. William George and Norma Lou (Cove) McC.; m. Janet Marie McCarty, Aug. 2, 1969; children: Coleen, William, Margaret. BBA, U. Mich., 1968, MBA, 1969. CPA, Mich. From staff acct. to ptnr. Arthur Andersen & Co., Detroit, 1969-86, audit div. head, 1986-87, mng. ptnr., 1987—. Bd. dirs. Met. Affairs Corp., Detroit, 1987—, Detroit Symphony, 1987—; mem. audit com. Founders Soc. Detroit Inst. of Arts, 1987—. Mem. AICPA, Mich. Assn. CPA's, Detroit Club, Hunters Creek Club, Meadowbrook Country Club, Detroit Athletic Club, Renaissance Club. Office: Arthur Andersen & Co 400 Renaissance Ctr Ste 2500 Detroit MI 48243

MCCLINTON, CURTIS ORR, statisician; b. Birmingham, Ala., Jan. 15, 1937; s. Clarence Paul and Martha Eugenia (Orr) McC.; m. Nancy Margaret Trucks, Aug. 18, 1963 (dec. Apr. 1982); children: Michael and Steven (twins). BS in Indsl. Mgmt., Samford U., 1959; postgrad., U. Ala., Birmingham, 1960-65; spl. tng., Applied Statistics Tng. Inst., 1975-86, Jefferson State Jr. Coll., 1987—. Jr. acct. Stockholm Valves, Birmingham, 1959-60; cost acct. Reynolds Metals Co., Birmingham, 1960-65, Rust Engring., Hunstville (Ala.) and Birmingham, 1965-72; adminstrv. analyst City Council and City Clk. Depts. City of Birmingham, 1972-75; statistician Jefferson County Health Dept., Birmingham, 1975—. Exec. v.p., coach South Roebuck Pony Baseball Little League, Birmingham, 1977-84; bd. dirs. East Side Swim Club, Birmingham, 1981-83; adv. bd. William J. Christian Community Schs., Birmingham, 1986; tchr., deacon, coach Sunday Sch., also supt. fin. com. and Royal Ambassador leader. Mem. Health Workers Assn. (bd. dirs.), Ala. Pub. Health Assn., Assn. Huntsville Area Contractors (bd. dirs. 1968), Toastmasters (local treas. 1960), Lions (chmn. mem. and scholarship com.), Alpha Kappa Psi. Republican. Baptist. Home: 644 Gravlee Ln Birmingham AL 35206 Office: Jefferson County Health Dept PO Box 2646 1400 6th Ave S Birmingham AL 35202

MCCLINTON, EDNA GRACE, real estate broker; b. Windom, Kans., Jan. 2, 1925; d. Ira Francis and Ella Nancy (Joslin) Hites; m. Arthur LeRoy Copeland, Feb. 20, 1943 (div. 1948); children: Clair Arthur, Richard Wade; m. Raymond Arthur McClinton, May 26, 1952 (div.); children: Roxane Dora, Renee Ella, Tamara Yvonne, James Ray, Phillip Lee. Grad. high sch., Albion, Pa. Owner, broker McClinton Real Estate, Meadville, Pa., 1967-70; real estate saleswoman, Meadville, 1967; broker, owner McClinton Co., Meadville, 1971—; beauty tchr. Wel Mar, Meadville, 1983—; owner rooming house, Meadville, 1975—. Mem. Bus. and Profl. Women, Grange. Methodist. Avocations: rebuilding older homes, fishing, travel. Home: 827 Water St Meadville PA 16335 Office: Meadville-McClinton Real Estate and Notary Svc 827 Water St Meadville PA 16335

MCCLISH, C. POLLY, finance executive; b. Lubbock, Tex., May 30, 1933; d. Hershell Lee and Carrie Maude (Johnson) Ward; four children by previous marriage. AA in Bus. Psychology, Amarillo Jr. Coll., Tex., 1966; BS in Acctg., West Tex. State U., 1968, BBA, 1970. Asst. credit mgr., collection mgr. Woolco Inc., Amarillo, Tex., 1968-74; credit mgr. Sakowitz Inc., Amarillo, 1974-79; sales mgr. Med. and Profl. Mgmt. Service, Galveston, Tex., 1979-82, v.p., gen. mgr., 1982-83; pres., bd. dirs. Colelli & Assocs., Galveston, 1983-87; founder, owner MasterCheck of Galveston-Bay Area, 1988—; cons. and lectr. in field. Mem. adv. bd. Tex. Edn. Commn.; mem. aux. U. Tex. Med. Br.; mem., div. chmn. United Fund. Named Outstanding Credit Exec. of Yr., Tex., 1976, to Galveston Women's Hall of Fame for bus. and fin. category. Mem. Internat. Consumer Credit Assn. (legis. adv. council), Am. Collectors Assn. (legis. adv. com., condr. numerous seminars), Asso. Credit Bur., Retail Mchts. Assn. Tex. (pres.), Nat. Assn. Female Execs., Soc. Cert. Consumer Credit Execs., Exec. Career Women, Bus. and Profl. Women (past pres.), C. of C. (pres.'s club, honor guard, Galveston chpt.), Credit Mgmt. Assn. Tex. (past pres.), Credit Women Internat. (past pres. Lone Star council), Am. Collectors Assn. Tex. (pres.), Forgery Investigation Assn. Tex. Club: Propeller (Galveston). Address: PO Box 3189 Galveston TX 77552

MCCLOY, CARTER JAMES, investment banker; b. Cin., Feb. 3, 1931; s. Corneilus James and Mildred Pauline (Carter) McC.; grad. high sch., Batavia, Ohio; m. Martha Dean Gross, June 21, 1958. Pres. C. J. McCloy & Co., Cin., 1961-65; v.p., resident mgr. Prescott Ball & Turben, Cin., 1966-73; pres. McCloy Watterson & Co., Inc., Cin., 1974-79; v.p., mgr. Cowen & Co., Cin., 1979—, now ltd. ptnr. Past pres. Ohio Mcpl. Adv. Coun.; bd. dirs. Clermont Mercy Hosp., Batavia. Mem. Pub. Securities Assn., Queen City Mcpl. Bond Dealers Group (past pres.), Cin. Stock and Bond Club, Nat. Assn. Security Dealers (dist. com.), Coldstream Country Club, Bankers Club. Republican. Home: 440 Bishopsbridge Dr Cincinnati OH 45255 Office: 3 E 4th St Cincinnati OH 45202

MCCLOY, JOHN JAY, II, electronic noise and vibration reduction company executive; b. N.Y.C., Nov. 5, 1937; s. John Jay and Ellen (Zinsser) McC.; m. Laura McGehee, Mar. 7, 1970; children: John Jay III, Rush Middleton. AB, Princeton U., 1959. Mgr. Brown Bros. Harriman & Co., N.Y.C., 1960-76, 80-81; gen. mgr. MFFCA Finanzberatungs G.m.b.H., Munich, 1976-80; pres. J.J. McCloy Inc., N.Y.C., 1981-84; v.p. McConnell & Miller, Inc., Greenwich, Conn., 1984-86; chmn. Noise Cancellation Techs., Inc., N.Y.C., 1986—. Author: A Gift to Germany's Future, 1960. Trustee Am. U. in Cairo, 1968—; chmn. bd. Sound Shore Fund, Greenwich, 1985—. lst lt. U.S. Army, 1960-63. Mem. Live in Coun. on Fgn. Rels., Am. Coun. on Germany, Links Club, Round Hill Club. Republican. Home: 313 Stanwich Rd Greenwich CT 06830 Office: Noise Cancellation Techs 575 8th Ave New York NY 10018

MC CLUNG, JIM HILL, light manufacturing company executive; b. Buena Vista, Ga., Nov. 8, 1936; s. Jim Hill and Marjorie (Oxford) McC.; m. Jo Patrick, July 5, 1958; children—Jim Hill, Karen Mareese. B.A., Emory U., 1958; M.B.A., Harvard U., 1964. With Lithonia Lighting div. Nat. Service Industries, Inc., Conyers, Ga., 1964—; now pres. Lithonia Lighting div. Nat. Service Industries, Inc. Served with USAF, 1958-62. Mem. Illuminating Engring. Soc. N.Am. (vice chmn. lighting research and edn. fund), Nat. Elec. Distbrs. Assn. (mfrs. bd.), Nat. Elec. Mfrs. Assn. (nat. lighting bur.), Intelligent Bldgs. Inst. (bd. dirs.), Lighting Research Inst. (bd. dirs.), Young Pres.'s Orgn. Methodist. Office: Lithonia Lighting Div PO Box A Conyers GA 30207

MCCLUNG, KENNETH AUSTIN, JR., training executive, consultant; b. Decatur, Ga., Apr. 11, 1947; s. Kenneth Austin Sr. and Marianne (Conklin) McC.; m. Christina June Palensar, May 21, 1975. BA, North Ga. Coll., 1969; MS, EdD, U. So. Calif., 1976. Commd. 2d lt. U.S. Army, 1969, advanced through grades to maj., 1980; lt. col. USAR; cons. in field Suffern, N.Y., 1980-81; sr. ptnr. Instructional Design Group, Inc., Morristown, N.J., 1981—; bd. dirs. Nat. Productivity Ctr., Boulder, Colo. Author: Microcomputers for Medical Professionals, 1984, Microcomputers for Legal Professionals, 1984, Microcomputers for Investment Professionals, 1984, Microcomputers for insurance Professionals, 1984, Personal Computers for Executives, 1984, French edit., 1985; co-author: Sales Training Handbook, 1989. Mem. Nat. Soc. for Performance Instruction (pres. N.J. chpt. 1986-88, nat. com. chair. 1988—), Am. Soc. Tng. and Devel., N.J. Sales Tng. Assn., Gourmet Cooking Club (Chester, N.J.) (chmn. 1988—). Office: Instructional Design Group Inc 144 Speedwell Ave Morristown NJ 07960

MCCLURE, DAVID H., utilities company manager; b. Kennesaw, Ga., Apr. 29, 1948; s. Benjamin H. and Katherine E. (Reece) McC.; m. Gail Johnson, Dec. 26, 1968; 1 child, Charissa Diane. B in Indsl. Engring. Tech., So. Coll. Tech., 1976. Assoc. engr. Western Electric Co., Atlanta, 1972-75; jr. acct. Jack McPherson, CPA, Acworth, Ga., 1975-76; div. materials planner Southwire Co., Carrollton, Ga., 1976-78, indsl. engr., 1978-79; process engr. Alcan Cable, Tucker, Ga., 1979-82; rsch. specialist Ga. Power Co., Forest Park, 1982-86, staff rep., 1986-87, staff services engr., 1987—, head of quality assurance sect., 1982—. Chmn. bd. dirs. Am. Diabetes Assn. Ga. Affiliate Inc., Atlanta, 1985-87, nat. bd. dirs., 1988-91, mem. nat. com. on affiliate assocs., 1986-89, vice chair, 1988-89, nat. So. region liaison, 1987-89; chmn. Com. on Pub. Support Devel.mem. quality assurance adv. com. So. Coll. Tech., 1987—, quality ctr. excellence adv. coun, 1987—, chmn., 1989—; chmn. Southeastern Quality Conf. Program, 1989. Served to staff sgt. USAF, 1968-72. Named Vol. of Yr., Am. Diabetes Assn. Ga. Affiliate, Inc., 1983-84, 84-85. Mem. Inst. Indsl. Engrs. (sr. mem.; sec. 1976-77, v.p. seminars 1977-78), Am. Soc. Quality Control (steering com. 1985—, cert. quality engr.), Wire Assn., Nat. Mgmt. Assn. Baptist. Home: 706 Singley Dr Lawrenceville GA 30244

MCCLURE, FLORENCE HELEN, management consultant; b. Chgo., July 21, 1930; d. George and Minnie (LaBarbara) Torre; m. Richard D. McClure, Feb. 16, 1952; children: Kimbert, Brian, Douglas, Ronald. Student Ind. U., 1948-50, Kent State U., 1967-68, Lake Erie Coll., Ohio, 1969-70. Elem. sch. tchr., Geneva, Ohio, 1966-71; coordinator traffic dept. True Temper Corp., Saybrook, Ohio, 1971-72; mktg. dir. Peoples Savs. & Loan, Ashtabula, Ohio, 1973-82; pres. Chem. Seal, Inc., Grand Junction, Colo., 1982-85; mktg./personnel dir. Valley Fed. Savs. & Loan, Grand Junction, 1982-87; with customer rels. Bob Caldwell chrysler/Plymouth, Columbus, Ohio, 1988—; human resource cons., 1985—. Commr., Colo. Housing Authority, Grand Junction, 1985-87; bd. dirs. Alternative Housing Assocs., Grand Junction, 1982-87. Mem. Am. Soc. Personnel Adminstrn., Western Slope Personnel Assocs., Grand Junction C. of C. (pub. relations com. 1985-87, coll. edn. com. 1983-85). Republican. Roman Catholic. Avocations: walking, reading, traveling. Home: 6100 McNaughten Woods Dr Columbus OH 43232

MCCLURE, GARRY L., banker; b. Orange, Tex., May 1, 1954; s. Calvin T. and Nancy (Newby) McC.; m. Ann Hood, Dec. 23, 1978; children: Garry Lee Jr., Thomas Latham. BS in Fin., U. Ala., 1976. Contr. Reisz Engring. Co., Huntsville, Ala., 1976-77; staff auditor First Ala. Bancshares, Huntsville, 1977-79; asst. corp. auditor First Ala. Bancshares, Montgomery, 1982—; sr. fin. analyst Gen. Dynamics Corp., Ft. Worth, 1979-81; audit supr. First United Bancorp., Ft. Worth, 1981-82. Coach Montgomery YMCA, 1986-87; tchr. Trinity Presbyn. Ch., Montgomery, 1986—. Shelby Pleasant Mgmt. scholar, 1972-73, Kazvnas-Douglas scholar, 1974, Alpha Phi scholar, 1975. Mem. Inst. Internat. Auditors (cert., treas. 1983-85, bd. govs. 1983—, chmn. nominating com. 1983-87), Wynlakes Golf and Country Club, Kiwanis. Office: First Ala Bancshares PO Box 204 Montgomery AL 36101

MCCLURE, PAUL THOMAS, stock brokerage executive, educator, stained glass artist; b. Detroit, Feb. 28, 1943; s. Jack Cloer and Helen Maureen (Green) McC.; m. Karen Irene Camp, Sept. 10, 1963 (div. 1977); children: Shauna, Erin, Scott; m. Elizabeth McCullough, Dec. 25, 1979. BS, Calif. Western U., 1964; MPA, U. So. Calif., 1968, PhD, 1972. Cert. fin. planner; registered gen. securities rep., 15 states. Adminstrv. analyst Los Angeles Internat. Airport, 1966-68; policy analyst Rand Corp., Santa Monica, Calif., 1968-73; city mgr. City of Adelanto, Calif., 1973-75; artist/owner Am. Art Glass Co., Adelanto, Calif., 1975-87; stockbroker E.F. Hutton Co., Redlands, Calif., 1982-87; v.p. Paine Webber Co., Hemet, Calif., 1987—; sr. adj. prof. Golden Gate U., San Francisco, 1973—. Mem. Adelanto Sch. Bd., 1973-83, pres., 1976-79; mem. Adelanto Planning Commn., 1973-75, chmn., 1973-75; mem. bd. property and fin. Brookside Free Meth. Ch., 1985—; co-chmn. United Way Campaign, 1986, bd. dirs. Redlands area United Way, 1985—; pres. YMCA Found. Bd. dirs. 1985—. RAND fellow, 1972. TV host bus. profile Inland Empire Illustrated KVCR-TV, PBS, 1984-86; stained glass commns. include: Campus Hill Seventh-day Adventist Ch., Loma Linda, Calif., 10th Ave. Bapt. Ch., Los Angeles, Assembly of God Ch., Hesperia, Calif., Living Waters Chapel, Apple Valley, Calif.; contbr. articles to profl. jours. Mem. Rotary, Masons, Country Footnotes Club. Republican. Avocations: stained glass, country and western dance.

MCCLURE, SUZANNE SHIOUTAKON, accountant; b. Washington, Aug. 2, 1960; d. Thomas Edie and Sandra Leigh (Bowman) Shioutakon; m. Allen Joseph McClure, Apr. 9, 1983. BS in Acctg., U. Md., 1984; MBA in Fin., Am. U., 1988. CPA, Md. Acct. Skigen Assoc., Rockville, Md., 1984, Kirkegaard & Perry Labs., Gaithersburg, Md., 1984-85, Bond, Beebe, Barton & Mucklebauer, Washington, 1985, Greater Potomac Inc., Gaithersburg, 1985-86; asst. mgr. Bell Atlantic, Arlington, Va., 1986-88; controller ARCC, Inc., Bethesda, Md., 1988—; owner, pres. Suzanne S. McClure, CPA, Germantown, 1984—. Mem. Am. Inst. CPAs, Md. Assn. CPAs. Democrat. Roman Catholic. Home: 17302 Seneca Chase Park Rd Poolesville MD 20837 Office: ARCC Inc 4550 Montgomery Ave Suite 620N Bethesda MD 20814

MCCLURE, WILLIAM EARL, investment company executive; b. Tuscaloosa, Ala., Mar. 26, 1946; s. James William and Julie Savanna McC.; m. Alison Todd, Apr. 17, 1971; children: Guerin James, Summer Scripps, Elizabeth Hope, Georgia Ann. Student, U. Ala., 1964-66; BA cum laude, Harvard U., 1970, MBA, 1976. Lending officer Inter-Am. Devel. Bank, Washington, 1971-74; sr. v.p. Royal Trust Bank, Miami, 1976-77; pres. Macdavin Internat., Miami, 1977-78, Synervest Corp., Champaign, Ill., 1978-80; sr. v.p. Roe, Martin & Neiman, Atlanta, 1980-85; pres., chief exec. officer Carnegie Securities Corp., Atlanta, 1985—, McClure Capital Strategies, Atlanta, 1985—. mem. editorial bd. The Wall St. Digest, Princeton, 1985—. Trustee Atlanta Internat. Sch. Served with USAR, 1970-76. Mem. Real Estate Securities and Syndication Inst., Internat. Assn. Fin. Planners, Airplane Owners and Pilots Assn. Clubs: World Trade, Atlanta City, Harvard Bus., Harvard (Atlanta). Home: 3406 Valley Circle NW Atlanta GA 30305 Office: 3495 Piedmont Rd 10 Piedmont Ctr Ste 800 Atlanta GA 30305

MCCLURG, JAMES EDWARD, research laboratory executive; b. Bassett, Nebr., Mar. 23, 1945; s. Warren James and Delia Emma (Allyn) McC. B.S., N.E. Wesleyan U., 1967; Ph.D., U. Nebr., 1973. Instr., U. Nebr. Coll. Medicine, Omaha, 1973-76, research instr., 1973-76, clin. asst. prof. Med. Ctr., 1984—, mem. dean's adv. council Sch. Pharmacy, 1984—; v.p., tech. dir. Harris Labs., Inc., Lincoln, Nebr., 1976-82, exec. v.p., 1982-84, pres., chief exec. officer, 1984—; bd. dirs. Streck Labs., Inc., Omaha, Centennial Industries, Lincoln. Mem. editorial bd. Clin. Research Practices and Drug Regulatory Affairs, 1984. Contbr. articles to profl. jours. Mem. Commn. on Human Rights, Lincoln, 1982-85; com. mem. Nebr. Citizens for Study Higher Edn., Lincoln, 1984. Recipient ann. research award Central Assn. Obstetricians and Gynecologists, 1982. Mem. Am. Assn. Lab. Accreditation (bd. dirs.). Republican. Clubs: Century (pres. Nebr. Wesleyan U. 1983-84), Nebraska (Lincoln). Lodge: Rotary. Avocation: boating. Office: Harris Labs Inc Box 80837 624 Peach St Lincoln NE 68501

MCCLUSKEY, GAYLA JACQUE, safety executive b. Enid, Okla., Apr. 5, 1955; d. Jack and S. Andrea (Matthiesen) McC. BS in Engring. Tech., Okla. State U., 1977; MBA in Engring. Mgmt., U. Dallas, 1984. Diplomate Am. Acad. of Indsl. Hygiene; cert. safety profl. Indsl. hygienist Exxon Nuclear Co., Richland, Wash., 1978-79, OSHA, Dept. Lab., Irving, Tex., 1979-81, United Techs.-Mostek, Carrollton, Tex., 1981-82; cons. risk mgmt. Sun Exploration and Prodn. Co., Dallas, 1982-88; mgr. health, safety & security Interchem Inc., Louisville, 1988—. Chmn., Responsible Citizenship Program, Dallas Women's Coalition, Dallas, 1984-88, Leadership Dallas, 1987-88; Leadership Louisville, 1988—; Louisville Jaycees, co-chair auction; pres., bd. dirs. Women's Ctr. of Dallas; dir. Women in Search of Exec. Responsibilities, 1988. Mem. Am. Mgmt. Assn., Am. Soc. Safety Engrs., Am. Acad. Indsl. Hygiene, Dallas C. of C. (natural resources adv. council), Am. Indsl. Hygiene Assn., Network of Career Women (officer Irving chpt. 1980-88), Leadership Louisville Alumni, Third Century, Soc. of St. Patrick, Tau Iota Epsilon, Omicron Delta Kappa, Sigma Iota Epsilon (officer U. Dallas chpt. 1984-88). Methodist. Home: 3020 Lexington Rd Louisville KY 40206 Office: Interchem 9808 Bluegrass Pkwy Louisville KY 40299

MCCLYMONDS, PAULINE RUTH, brokerage house executive; b. Grove City, Pa., Apr. 14, 1948; d. Paul Russel and Dorothy G. (Gamble) Snyder; m. Kenneth I. McClymonds, Aug. 30, 1968; 1 child, Matthew. EdB, Slippery Rock (Pa.) Coll., 1969. Cert. fin. planner. Tchr. sci. Ellwood City (Pa.) High Sch., 1969-70; coord. congregate dining Luth. Soc. Svcs., Waynesboro, Pa., 1973-75; tchr. sci. Waynesboro High Sch., 1974-76; supr. savs. First Fed. Savs. and Loan, Davenport, Iowa, 1978-83; fin. planner Fin. Planning Group, Bettendorf, Iowa, 1983-84; fin. planner, trust officer N.W. Bank & Trust, Davenport, Iowa, 1984-86; v.p. Cuyahoga Fin. Svcs. Agy., Cleve., 1987—. Contbr. articles to newspapers. Mem. Internat. Assn. Fin. Planning, Inst. Cert. Fin. Planners, Kappa Delta Pi. Republican. Presbyterian. Office: Cuyahoga Fin Svcs Agy One Erieview Pla Cleveland OH 44114

MC COIN, JOHN MACK, social worker; b. Sparta, N.C., Jan. 21, 1931; s. Robert Avery and Ollie (Osborne) McC.; BS, Appalachian State Tchrs. Coll., Boone, N.C., 1957; MS in Social Work, Richmond (Va.) Profl. Inst., 1962; PhD, U. Minn., 1977. Diplomate Acad. Cert. Social Workers, Am. Bd. Examiners in Clin. Social Work. Social svc. worker Broughton State Hosp., Morganton, N.C., 1958-59, John Unstead State Hosp., Butner, N.C., 1960-61; clin. social worker Dorothea Dix State Hosp., Raleigh, N.C., 1962-63; child welfare case worker Wake County Welfare Dept., Raleigh, 1963-64; psychiat. social worker Toledo Mental Hygiene Clinic, 1964-66; sr. psychiat. social worker N.Y. Hosp.-Cornell U. Med. Ctr., 1966-68; social worker VA Hosp., Montrose, N.Y., 1968-73, also vol. mental health worker Westchester County Mental Health Assn. and Mental Health Bd., White Plains, N.Y.; seminar instr. Grad. Sch. Social Work, U. Minn., Mpls., 1973-74; social worker F.D.R. VA Health Care Facility, Montrose, 1975-77; asst. prof. social work U. Wis., Oshkosh, 1977-79, chmn. dept. community liaison com., 1978-79; asso. prof. social work Grand Valley State Colls., Allendale, Mich., 1979-81; social worker VA Med. Ctr. Battle Creek, Mich., 1981-83; supr. social worker VA Med. Ctr., Leavenworth, Kans., 1983—; cons. 44th Gen. Hosp., USAR, Menasha, Wis., 1978-79, 5540th Support Command, USAR, Grand Rapids, Mich., 1979-83; cons. in field; adj. faculty mem. social scis. dept., Kansas City Community Coll., 1985— . Served with USMC, 1948-52; USMCR, 1957-72; lt. col. USAR, 1972—. Recipient Outstanding Performance award VA, 1971, Superior Performance award, 1982, Outstanding Performance award, 1983; grantee NIMH, 1974; cert. social worker, N.Y. Mem. Nat. Assn. Social Workers (social action com. W. Mich. br. 1980-81), Alpha Delta Mu. Democrat. Baptist. Author: Adult Foster Homes, 1983, ; founder (with Human Scis. Press), editor Adult Foster Care Jour., 1987-88, Adult Residential Care Jour., 1989—. Home: 310B Kiowa St Leavenworth KS 66048

MCCOLL, HUGH LEON, JR., banker; b. Bennettsville, S.C., June 18, 1935; s. Hugh Leon and Frances Pratt (Carroll) McC.; m. Jane Bratton Spratt, Oct. 3, 1959; children: Hugh Leon III, John Spratt, Jane Bratton. B.S. in Bus. Adminstrn, U. N.C., 1957. Trainee NCNB Nat. Bank, Charlotte, 1959-61, officer, 1961-65, sr. v.p., 1965-68, sr. v.p., 1968, div. exec., 1969, exec. v.p., 1970-73, vice chmn. bd., 1973-74, pres., 1974-83, chmn. bd., 1983—, also dir.; pres. NCNB Corp., 1981-85, chmn. bd. 1983—; dir. Sonoco Products Inc., Hartsville, S.C., Ruddick Corp., Charlotte. Former trustee Sacred Heart Coll., Belmont, N.C., St. Andrews Presbyn. Coll., Laurinburg, N.C.; bd. dirs. Am. Council on Germany, N.Y.C., 1977-78 ; bd. mgrs. Charlotte Meml. Hosp. and Med. Center, 1975-82; trustee Heineman Found., Charlotte, 1976—, U. S.C. Bus. Sch., Columbia, Queens Coll., Charlotte; chmn. Charlotte Uptown Devel. Corp., 1978-81, 85. Served to 1st lt. USMCR, 1957-59. Mem. Assn. Res. City Bankers, Am. Bankers Assn., N.C. Bankers Assn. (pres. 1974). Democrat. Presbyterian. Office: NCNB Corp 1 NCNB Pla Charlotte NC 28255

MCCOLLUM, ALMEDIA, real estate executive; b. Jamesville, N.C., May 11, 1940; d. Earley and Olivia (James) Whitehurst; m. Leslie McCollum, Dec. 24, 1960; children: Karen, Leslie Jr., Lawrence. Student, Fayetteville State Coll., 1957-60. V.p. Colmedia Corp., N.Y.C., 1978—. Mem. Nat. Assn. Female Execs. Home: 435 E 57th St Brooklyn NY 11203

MCCOLMAN, WILLIAM ERNEST, construction executive; b. Chgo., Oct. 8, 1947; s. William Walter and Irene Laverne (Wildes) McC.; m. Caridad S. Jorajuria, Sept. 19, 1981; children: William Patrick, Scott Mariano. BS in Agrl. Bus., Colo. State U., 1970. Leadman R&D Theil, Chgo., 1972-74; foreman Carpenter Contractors Am., Ft. Lauderdale, Fla., 1974-75; pres. Bamco Constrn., Inc., Pompano Beach, Fla., 1975—, Bamco Homes Fla., Pompano Beach, 1980—, McColman Crane & Equipment Lease, Pompano Beach, 1981—, Bamco Constrn. South Fla., Pompano Beach, 1983—, New Image Homes, Inc., Pompano Beach, 1986—, Cardinal Custom Builders, Pompano Beach, 1988—; bd. dirs. TRNPK Comml. Plaza, Pompano Beach (pres. 1985-86), Tropical Life Style Builders, Inc.; adv. Planning and Zoning Bd., Ocean Ridge, Fla., 1987-88. Editor computer program, 1983. Coach North Lauderdale Little League, 1979-82, Boynton Beach (Fla.) Little League, 1988—; active Margate (Fla.) Girl Scouts, 1982-87, Palm Beach (Fla.) Boy Scouts, 1980—. Recipient Outstanding Service cert. Broward County (Fla.) Girl Scout Council, 1984. Mem. Nat. Small Bus. Assn. (cert. merit, 1977), Fla. Atlantic Builders Assn. (outstanding contbns., 1982, apprenticeship bd. 1979-82), South Fla. Builders Assn. (apprenticeship bd. 1977-78), Nat. Assn. Home Builders, Fla. C. of C. Clubs: Boat/U.S., Royal Holiday, Mexico. Office: Bamco Constrn Inc PO Box 4096 Margate FL 33063

MCCOMAS, MURRAY KNABB, direct mail company executive; b. Warren, Pa., Dec. 3, 1936; s. Donald Emory and Edith Mildred (Knabb) McC.; m. Marie Avanelle Oriole, Nov. 13, 1971; children: Julia Marie, Donald Anthony. BS in Econs., U. Pa., 1958. Asst. exec. sec. Sigma Chi Internat. Frat., Evanston, Ill., 1959-62; advt. prodn. mgr. New Process Co., Warren, 1962-75, v.p. advt., 1975-87, pres., chmn. bd. dirs., 1987—; mem. adv. bd. Marine Bank, Erie, Pa., 1987—. Bd. dirs. Warren County YMCA, 1984—; chmn. United Way Warren County, 1987-88. Mem. Warren County C. of C. (bd. dirs. 1980-84), Sigma Chi (Order of Constantine 1979), Conewango Club (bd. dirs., pres. 1975-86), Elks. Republican. Presbyterian. Home: 321 Bent Twig Rd Warren PA 16365 Office: New Process Co 220 Hickory St Warren PA 16366

MCCOMBS, BOB, accountant; b. Denton, Tex., May 21, 1956; s. Sam Ferguson and Mary Helen (Tillery) McC. BBA, N. Tex. State U., 1976, MBA, 1979, MLS, 1984. CPA, Tex., 1980. Tax counselor Tax Corp. of Am., Denton, 1975-80; asst. bookkeeper City Employees Credit Union, Dallas, 1979-81; pvt. practice tax acct. Denton, 1981—; trustee Tex. Wagon Train Assn., Dallas, 1982; cons. in field. Precinct chmn. Denton County Repub. Party, 1982—. Mem. Tex. Soc. CPAs (treas. 1982-83), Denton Area Assn. CPA's (treas. 1982-83), Dallas Kaypro Users Group (pres. 1984-86), Denton C. of C., Nat. Soc. Pub. Accts, N. Tex. PC Users Group. Home and Office: 1013 N Elm St Denton TX 76201-2938

MCCOMBS, HOWARD LEWIS, JR., manufacturing company executive; b. Mishawaka, Ind., July 19, 1920; s. Howard Lewis and Mabel Elizabeth (Heick) McC.; student public schs., South Bend, Ind.; m. June E. Grubbs, May 14, 1944; 1 child, Linda Sue. Flight and ground sch. instr. Stockert Flying Service, South Bend, 1941-42, 46-48; with Bendix Corp., South Bend, 1948-85, prin. engr. energy controls div., 1982-85; air sci. instr. Ind. U., South Bend, 1960-65. Served with USAF, 1943-46. Decorated Air medal with oak leaf cluster; recipient Innovation Profitability award Bendix Corp., 1948. Republican. Clubs: Bendix Mgmt.; St. Joseph Valley Engrs., Res. Officers Assn. Patentee in field.

MCCOMSEY, ROBERT RONALD, investment company and pension fund executive; b. Lancaster, Pa., Oct. 13, 1944; s. Robert Marvin and Fern Louisa (Dunwoody) McC.; m. Susan Kay Wing, Dec. 23, 1972; children: Michelle Tiffany, Douglas Ryan. BS in Ceramic Engring., Alfred U., 1966; MBA, U. Chgo., 1972. Sr. engr. electronic components div. RCA Corp., Harrison, N.J., 1966-68; sr. tech. mktg. specialist electronic components div. RCA Corp., Chgo., 1968-71; fin. dir. electronic components div. RCA Corp., N.Y.C., 1971-72; pension cons. A.G. Becker & Co., N.Y.C., 1972-74, asst. v.p., 1974-75, v.p., sr. pension cons., 1975-77; exec. v.p. pension mgmt. Neuberger & Berman, N.Y.C., 1977-82, gen. ptnr., 1980—, chief operating officer, pension mgmt., 1982—. Patron Viennese Opera Ball, N.Y.C., 1975—; trustee Alfred U., Alfred, N.Y., 1980—, mem. exec. com., chmn. investment com.; trustee The Hackley Sch., Tarrytown, N.Y., 1982—, mem. exec. com., chmn. investment com.; trustee Briarcliff Manor-Scarborough (N.Y.) Hist. Soc., 1983—; trustee U.S. Mil. Acad., West Point, 1984—, Fifth Ave. Presbyn. Ch., N.Y.C., 1985—; co-chmn. hist. bldgs. and renovations com. U.S. Mil. Acad., West Point, 1985—. Named Cost Reduction Systems Engr. of Yr. RCA Corp., Harrison, N.J., 1968. Mem. Army Athletic Assn. (comdr. in chief A-Club). Republican. Clubs: University (N.Y.C.); Sleepy Hollow (Scarborough). Home: Linden Circle Scarborough-on-Hudson NY 10510 Office: Neuberger & Berman 522 Fifth Ave New York NY 10036

MC CONNAUGHEY, GEORGE CARLTON, JR., lawyer, utility company executive; b. Hillsboro, Ohio, Aug. 9, 1925; s. George Carlton and Nelle (Morse) McC.; m. Carolyn Schlieper, June 16, 1951; children: Elizabeth, Susan, Nancy. B.A., Denison U., 1949; LL.B., Ohio State U., 1951, J.D., 1967. Bar: Ohio 1951. Sole practice Columbus; ptnr. McConnaughey & McConnaughey, 1954-57, McConnaughey, McConnaughey & Stradley, 1957-62, Laylin, McConnaughey & Stradley, 1962-67, George, Greek, King, McMahon & McConnaughey, 1967-79, McConnaughey, Stradley, Mone & Moul, 1979-81, Thompson, Hine & Flory (merger McConnaughey, Stradley, Mone & Moul with Thompson, Hine & Flory), Cleve., Columbus and Washington, 1981—; sec. Alltel Corp., Hudson, Ohio, 1960—; also dir.; bd. dirs. N.Am. Broadcasting Co. (WMNI and WMGG Radio); asst. atty. gen. State of Ohio, 1951-54. Pres. Upper Arlington (Ohio) Bd. Edn., 1967-69, Columbus Town Meeting Assn., 1974-76; chmn. Ohio Young Reps., 1956; U.S. presdl. elector, 1956; trustee Buckeye Boys Ranch, Columbus, 1967-73, 75-81, Ohio Council Econ. Edn.; elder Covenant Presbyn. Ch., Columbus. Served with U.S. Army, 1943-45, ETO. Mem. ABA (council pub. utility law sect.), Ohio Bar Assn., Columbus Bar Assn., Am. Judicature Soc. Clubs: Columbus, Scioto Country, Athletic (Columbus). Lodges: Rotary, Masons. Home: 1969 Andover Rd Columbus OH 43212 Office: Thompson Hine & Flory 100 E Broad St Ste 1700 Columbus OH 43215

MCCONNAUGHEY, JAMES WALTER, telecommunications consultant; b. Washington, May 8, 1951; s. William Eugene and Eunice (Ensor) McC.; m. Rosemarie Fuchs, June 23, 1984. BS with high honors in Econs., U. Md., 1973; MA in Econs., George Washington U., 1979. Industry economist FCC Common Carrier Bur., Washington, 1973-80, sr. economist, 1981-83; sr. assoc. Bolter and Nilsson, Bethesda, Md., 1983; mgr. rsch. studies div. Bethesda Rsch. Inst., 1984—. Author: (with others) Telecommunication Policy for the 1980's: The Transition to Competition, 1984, Telecommunications and the Economics of Public Utility Regulation, 1988, Telecommunications Policy for the 1990's and Beyond Upcoming, 1989. Campaign worker, contbr. nat. and local elections; coach No. Va. Boys' Clubs, Bowie (Md.) Boy's Club; mem. Neighborhood Open Space Com.; worker, contbr. numerous environ. and consumer orgns. Recipient cert. of appreciation for leadership Prince George's County (Va.) Public Sch. System, 1986. Mem. Am. Econ. Assn., Pub. Utilities Group of Am. Econ. Assn., Eastern Econ. Assn., So. Econ. Assn., Soc. Govt. Economists, Indsl. Orgn. Soc., Phi Eta Sigma, Omicron Delta Epsilon, Beta Gamma Sigma, Phi Kappa Phi. Avocations: hiking; reading.

MCCONNELL, CHARLES GOODLOE, gas products company executive; b. Bethany, Mo., Dec. 18, 1943; s. Charles Goodloe and Clara Lorene (Johnson) McC.; m. Barbara Jean Leighty, Mar. 26, 1945; children: Lory, Jennifer, Chris. BS in Chem. Engring., U. Tulsa, 1965; MS in Chem. Engring., U. Tex., Austin, 1967. Project engr. John Zink Co., Tulsa, 1966-69; process engr. Largo Oil & Transp., Aruba, Netherlands Antilles, 1969-71; project engr. Global Engring., Tulsa, 1971-72; mgr. refinery APCO Oil Corp., Cyril, Okla., 1972-78; v.p. Earth Resources Co. Alaska, Fairbanks, 1978-88, MAPCO Inc., Tulsa, 1981-83; pres. MAPCO Gas Products, Inc., Tulsa, 1983—; chmn. dept. chem. engring. U. Tulsa, 1987, mem. indsl. adv. bd., 1986-87. Patentee in field. Bd. dirs. United Way Tanana Valley, Fairbanks, 1979-81, Farthest North council Girl Scouts. U.S., Fairbanks, 1979-81; mem. Alaska Pvt. Industry Council, 1980-81; vice-chmn. Tulsa United Way, 1987; youth soccer coach, 1978-87; fundraiser Boy Scouts Am., Tulsa, 1983. Named Engr. of Yr. U. Tulsa Engring. Club, 1965, Outstanding Alumnus U. Tulsa, 1987. Mem. Nat. Liquified Petroleum Gas Assn., Gas Processors Assn. (bd. dirs. 1983-86). Republican. Presbyterian. Clubs: Oaks Country Golf (Tulsa). Lodge: Rotary (founding sec., pres. 1979-81). Office: MAPCO Gas Products Inc 1717 S Boulder St Room 718 Tulsa OK 74119

MCCONNELL, E. HOY, II, advertising executive; b. Syracuse, N.Y., May 14, 1941; s. E. Hoy and Dorothy R. (Schmitt) McC.; m. Patricia Irwin, June 26, 1965; children: E. Hoy, III, Courtney. B.A. in Am. Studies magna cum laude, Yale U., 1963; M.B.A. in Mktg, Harvard Bus. Sch., 1965. With Foote, Cone & Belding, 1965-76; v.p. account supr. Foote, Cone & Belding, Chgo., 1971-72, 74-76, Phoenix, 1972-74; with D'Arcy-MacManus & Masius, Chgo., 1976-85, sr. v.p., dir. client services, then vice chmn., 1978-80, pres., 1980-84, chmn., 1984-85; mng. dir. D'Arcy Masius Benton & Bowles, Chgo., 1986—; also bd. dirs. D'Arcy Masius Benton, Bowles, Chgo., 1983. Bd. dirs. Evanston (Ill.) United Way, 1980-83; bd. dirs. Evanston Youth Hockey Assn., 1980—, pres., 1981-85; bd. dirs. Off the Street Club, Bus. and Profl. People for Pub. Interest, 1981-83, v.p., 1984—. Served as officer USNR, 1966. Mem. Chgo. Council Am. Assn. Advt. Agys. (gov. at large 1984, sec. 1986, vice chmn. 1987, chmn. 1988—), Better Bus. Bur. Chgo. (mem. advt. rev. bd.). Democrat. Unitarian. Clubs: University, Tavern (Chgo.); Glen View (Ill.) Country; Dairymen's Country. Home: 2703 Colfax Evanston IL 60201 Office: D'Arcy Masius Benton & Bowles Inc 200 E Randolph Dr Chicago IL 60601

MCCONNELL, HILLARD LEE, III, food company executive; b. Atlanta, July 26, 1937; s. H. Lee Jr. and Lula (Brannon) McC.; m. Patricia H. Houston, June 7, 1963; children: Mary Louise, Patricia Elizabeth, Hilary Leigh, H. Lee IV. BA, The Citadel, 1959. Spl. agt. Gt. Am. Ins. Co., Atlanta, 1961-64; ins. agt. So. Fin. Ins. Agy., Augusta, Ga., 1964-66; ins. mgr. Columbia Nitrogen Corp., Augusta, 1966-72; dir. risk mgmt. Hershey (Pa.) Foods Corp., 1972—; v.p. Hershey Ins. Co., Ltd., Hamilton, Bermuda, 1985—; alt. bd. dirs., chmn. underwriting com. GMA Ins. Ltd., Hamilton, 1986—. Chmn. Columbia County Rep. Com., Martinez, Ga., 1970-71; chmn. Londonderry Twp. Planning Commn., Middleton, Pa., 1980-82; vice chmn. Londonderry Twp. Bd. Suprs., 1982. Mem. Risk and Ins. Mgmt. Soc. (pres. cen. Pa. chpt. 1982, bd. dirs. N.Y.C. 1984-87, chmn. industry liaison com. 1987—), Rotary. Mormon. Office: Hershey Foods Corp 14 E Chocolate Ave Hershey PA 17033

MCCONNELL, JACK B., corporate executive, physician; b. Crumpler, W.Va., Feb. 1, 1925; s. Enoch L. and Mattie (Davidson) McC.; m. Mary Ellen Rhodes, NOv. 29, 1958; children: Steven Rhodes, Katherine Marie, Page Samuel. Student, U. Va., 1943-45, U. Miss., 1945-47; MD, U. Tenn., 1949; postgrad., Columbia U., 1963, Harvard U., 1972; DSc, Emory & Henry Coll., 1982. Dir. clin. investigation Lederle Labs., Pearl River, N.Y., 1953-61; v.p. comml. devel. McNeil Labs., Ft. Washington, Pa., 1961-68; corp. dir. advanced tech. Johnson & Johnson, New Brunseick, N.J., 1968—; mem. sci. adv. com. sch. medicine U. Ga., Augusta, 1981—; bd. trustees Morristown (N.J.) Meml. Hosp., 1977-87; bd. dirs. African Med. and Rsch. Found., N.Y.C.; bd. overseers Tufts U., Boston, 1986—. Mem. bd. health, Basking Ridge, N.J., 1972-74; cons. U.S. Senate, Washington, 1987—. With USN, 1943-46. Recipient Disting. Scientist award Tenn. Tech. Found., 1985, Humanitarian award, 1988. Mem. AMA, Royal Instn., Soc. Magnetic Resonance in Medicine, Acad. Med. Dirs, Soc. for Analytical Cytology. Republican. Home: 323 Old Army Rd Basking Ridge NJ 07920 Office: Johnson & Johnson 1 Johnson Pla New Brunswick NJ 08933

MCCONNELL, JOHN HENDERSON, metal and plastic products manufacturing executive; b. New Manchester, W.Va., May 10, 1923; s. Paul Alexander and Mary Louise (Mayhew) McC.; m. Margaret Jane Rardin, Feb. 8, 1946; children—Margaret Louise, John Porter. B.A. in Bus., Mich. State U., 1949; Dr. Law (hon.), Ohio U., 1981. Sales trainee Weirton Steel Co., W.Va., 1950-52; sales mgmt. Shenango-Steel Co., Farrell, Pa., 1952-54; founder, chief exec. officer Worthington Industries, Inc., Columbus, Ohio, 1955—; dir. Alltel Corp., Hudson, Ohio, Anchor Hocking, Lancaster, Ohio, Nat. City Corp., Cleve. Bd. dirs. Children's Hosp., Columbus; trustee Ashland Coll., Ohio. Served with USN, 1943-46. Recipient Ohio Gov.'s award Gov. State of Ohio, 1980; Horatio Alger award Horatio Alger Assn., 1983; named Outstanding Chief Exec. Officer, Fin. World Mag., 1981. Mem. Columbus Area C. of C. (chmn. 1978). Republican. Presbyterian. Clubs: Golf (New Albany, Ohio) (pres. 1983—); Brookside Country (Columbus) (pres. 1964-65). Lodge: Masons. Office: Worthington Industries Inc 1205 Dearborn Dr Columbus OH 43085 •

MCCONNELL, MICHAEL ALFRED, software company executive; b. Nashville, July 4, 1944; s. Laverne Mickey and Alice Emily (Eitel) McC.; m. Marilyn Lundberg, Nov. 12, 1981; children: Ericka, Amy, Emily. BA, Yale U., 1966. V.p. mktg. Computerland Corp., Hayward, Calif., 1972-79; v.p. ops. Computerland Corp., Hayward, 1979-81, exec. v.p., 1981-83, pres. internat. div., 1983-87; v.p. mktg. Gen. Parametrics Corp., Berkeley, Calif., 1987-88; chief exec. officer Chang Labs., Inc., San Jose, Calif., 1988—. Office: Chang Labs Inc 5300 Stevens Creek Blvd San Jose CA 95129

MCCOOL, JOSEPH WILLIAM, infosystems specialist; b. Columbus, Ohio, June 30, 1955; s. Frederick John and Virginia (Pawell) McC.; m. Mary Ann Weis, May 30, 1981; children: Katherine Suzanne, Trevor Joseph. BSBA, Ind. U.Pa., 1979. Pres., chief exec. officer Pyramid Cable Svcs. Inc., Melbourne, Fla., 1981-88, Toledo, 1984—; pres., chief exec. officer Am. Communication Corp., Melbourne, 1988—, McCool Inc., Melbourne, 1988—. Mem. C. of C. (com. mem. South Brevaid area). Home: 219 Neville Circle NE Palm Bay FL 32907 Office: McCool Inc 255 E Dr Ste F Melbourne FL 32904

MCCOOL, RICHARD BUNCH, real estate developer; b. Kokomo, Ind., Jan. 2, 1925; s. James Victor and Margaret (Bunch) M.C.; m. Victoria R. Middleton, Dec. 23, 1977; children: Kathryn, Suzanne, Rick; 1 stepchild, April. AB in Govt., Ind. U., 1950. Chmn., chief exec. officer Holida Corp., Indianapolis, 1950-70, Great Lakes Homes, Indpls., 1970-77, Am. Investment, Indpls., 1971—; bd. dirs. Am. Investment Group, Indpls., Investor Fin. Services, Indpls.; dir., gen. ptnr. Manor Group, Ind., Ky., 1977—; cons. Wickes Corp., 1970-77. Author: Real Estate Investments, 1981; contbr. articles to mags., newspaper column on contract bridge, 1966-74. Pres., chmn. various civic orgns., 1960-77; permanent mem. Nat. Rep. Senate Com., 1984. Recipient Geisenbier award Kokomo Jaycees, 1960; named to the Hon. Order Ky. Col. Served to capt., U.S. Army, 1943-46, PTO. Mem. Am. Contract Bridge League (life master 1972), No. Ind. Bridge Assn. (pres. 1974), Pvt. Pilot Assn. (pres. 1969), Nat. Contractors Assn. (founding pres. 1970, Contractor of Yr. 1974), Apt. Assns., Cert. Mgmt. Group (pres. 1980), Ind. U. Alumni Club, Sigma Nu. Congregationalist. Clubs: Columbia, Skyline (Indpls.). Lodges: Masons, Shriners. Office: 14904 Greyhound Ct Carmel IN 46032

MCCORD, RONALD EUGENE, corporate fitness consultant; b. L.A., July 3, 1955; s. Thomas Josuah and Leatha (Vance) McC.; divorced; 1 child, Ronnie. AA, San Joquin Delta Community Coll., 1979; BA, Calif. State U., Northridge, 1981. Printer Deluxe Check Printers, Chatsworth, Calif., 1979-82; claims rep. Prudential Ins., Woodland Hills, Calif., 1982-84; owner, cons. Fitness Week, Van Nuys, Calif., 1984—. Inventor complete body machine, 1987. Mem. NAACP, Encino C. of C., Los Angeles C. of C. Office: Fitness Week PO BOx 8690 Northridge CA 91327

MC CORKINDALE, DOUGLAS HAMILTON, publishing company executive; b. N.Y.C., June 14, 1939; s. William Douglas and Kathleen (Miles) McC.; children: Laura Ann, Heather Jean. BA, Columbia U., 1961, LLB cum laude (Harlan Fiske Stone scholar), 1964. Bar: N.Y. 1964. Assoc. Thacher Proffitt & Wood, N.Y.C., 1964-70, ptnr., 1970-71; gen. counsel, sec. Gannett Co., Inc., Rochester, N.Y., 1971-72; v.p., gen. counsel, sec. Gannett Co., Inc., Rochester, 1972-77, sr. v.p. fin. and law, 1977-79, sr. v.p., chief fin. officer, 1979—; pres. diversified media div. Gannett Co., Inc., 1980-83, exec. v.p., 1983, vice chmn., chief fin. and adminstrn. officer, 1984—, also dir. all subs. and joint ventures; bd. dirs. Rochester Telephone Corp., Global Govt. Plus Fund, Inc., Global Genesis Fund, Inc., Nat. Resources Fund; trustee Prudential-Bache Mcpl. Bond Fund., Prudential-Bache Flexifund, Prudential-Bache Equity Income Fund. Trustee Gannett Found. Mem. ABA. (chmn. com. Exch. Act of 1934 1971-73), N.Y. State Bar Assn., Am. Newspaper Pubs. Assn. (com. govt. relations), Nat. Press Club. Clubs: Oak Hill Country, Pine Valley Golf, Mid Ocean; Burning Tree. Office: PO Box 7858 Washington DC 20044-7857 Also: Gannett Co Inc PO Box 7858 Washington DC 20044

MCCORMACK, JOHN JOSEPH, JR., insurance executive; b. Morristown, N.J., Aug. 22, 1944; s. John Joseph and Marion Loretta (Smith) McC.; m. Judith Gail Harvey, July 20, 1968; children—Brendan, Matthew, Margaret. B.B.A., St. Bonaventure U., 1966. Group underwriter Tchrs. Ins. and Annuity Assn.-Coll. Retirement Equities Fund, N.Y.C., 1966-71, benefit plan counselor, 1971-72, asst. adv. officer, 1972-73, adv. officer, 1973-74, asst. v.p., 1974-75, 2d v.p., 1975-78, v.p., 1978-80, sr. v.p., 1980-83, exec. v.p., 1983—; trustee Am. Psychol. Assn. Ins. Trust, Washington, 1980—, chmn., 1985-86; trustee Employee Benefit Research Inst., Washington, 1983—, treas., 1986—. Mem. president's council St. Bonaventure U., 1986—, chmn. 1986—, bd. visitors Ctr. for the Study of Future Mgmt., 1987—. Republican. Roman Catholic. Office: Tchrs Ins & Annuity Assn Am 730 3rd Ave New York NY 10017

MCCORMICK, CHARLES PERRY, JR., food products company executive; b. Balt., May 29, 1928; s. Charles P. and Marion (Hinds) McM.; m. Marlene Darby Hicks, July 29, 1950 (div. 1980); children: Charles P. III, William C., Linda M., Gail P.; m. Jimi Helen Faulk, July 1, 1980. Student, Johns Hopkins U., 1946-47, Duke U., 1948-49. V.p. new products McCormick Co., Inc., Hunt Valley, Md., 1962-70, v.p. corp. devel., 1970-81, v.p. packaging group, 1986-87, pres., chief exec. officer, 1987-88, chmn., chief exec. officer, 1988—; chmn., pres. Setco, Inc., Anaheim, Calif., 1981-87, Tubed Products Inc., Easthampton, Mass., 1985-87. Republican. Club: Annapolis Yacht, Hunt Valley Golf Club. Office: McCormick & Co Inc 11350 McCormick Rd Hunt Valley MD 21031

MCCORMICK, JAMES EDWARD, oil company executive; b. Providence, Nov. 5, 1927; s. James Edward and Edna Josephine (Smith) McC.; m. Catherine Sullivan, Aug. 30, 1952. AB in Geology, Brown U., 1952. Engr. trainee Sun Oil Co., Beaumont, Tex., 1953-54; jr. geologist Sun Oil Co., Houston, 1954-67, exploration mgr., 1967-70; regional mgr. geology Sun Oil Co., Dallas, 1970-71, exploration program mgr., 1971-74, div. mgr. strategy planning, 1974-77, v.p. internat. exploration and prodn., 1977-86, pres. exploration and prodn., 1986—; bd. dirs. Suncor, Inc., Toronto, Can., Tex. Research League, Austin. Bd. dirs. United Way Met. Dallas, 1986—; mem. Dallas Citizens Council, 1986—. Served as sgt. USAF, 1945-48. Mem. Am. Assn. Petroleum Geologists, N.Y. Acad. Scis., Nat. Ocean Industries Assn. (bd. dirs. 1986—). Roman Catholic. Clubs: Northwood Country, Las Colinas Country. Office: Sun Energy Partners LP 5656 Blackwell Dallas TX 75231

MCCORMICK, JAMES MICHAEL, management consultant; b. Arlington, Va., Dec. 12, 1947; s. James J. and Emma H. (Fisher) McC.; m. Marsha E. Durham, 1971; 1 child, James M. McCormick Jr. BS with distinction, Cornell U., 1969, M in Engring. and Ops. Research with distinction, 1970. Mem. tech. staff Bell Telephone Labs., Holmdel, N.J., 1968-73; div. head, planning N.Y. Stock Exchange, N.Y.C., 1973-75; engagement mgr. McKinsey & Co., N.Y.C., 1975-77; v.p. ROI Cons., N.Y.C., 1977-80; pres. First Manhattan Cons. Group, N.Y.C., 1980—; cons. various U.S. banks, investment banks and fin. instns., 1975—; speaker various profl. assn. meetings. Club: Larchmont (N.Y.) Yacht. Office: First Manhattan Cons Group 90 Park Ave 19th Floor New York NY 10016

MCCORMICK, JOHN CRIMMINS, agricultural products company executive; b. Binghamton, N.Y., Aug. 17, 1935; s. James L. and Esther (Crimmins) McC. AB, Cornell U., 1957; MBA, Columbia U., 1961. Product mgr. Gen. Foods Corp., White Plains, N.Y., 1961-67, Am. Home Products, N.Y.C., 1967-68; dir. leisure sales Trans World Airlines, N.Y.C., 1968-69; pres. Merchandising Group, N.Y.C., 1970-75; dir. mktg. Am. Maize Products Corp., N.Y.C., 1976-78; pres. J.H. Swisher and Son Inc. div. Am. Maize Products Corp., Jacksonville, Fla., 1978-86, Am. Maize Products Corp., Stamford, Conn., 1986—. Served to lt. (j.g.) USNR, 1957-59. Roman Catholic. Office: Am Maize Products Corp PO Box 10128 Stamford CT 06904 also: Amer Maize Products Co 250 Harbor Dr Stamford CT 06904

MCCORMICK, PETER HAMILTON, retired banker; b. Attleboro, Mass., Apr. 3, 1936; s. Samuel James and Virginia Bradford (Jones) McC.; m. Fair Alice Bullock, July 2, 1960; children: Alexander, Nathaniel, Benjamin. B.A. cum laude, Harvard U., 1959. With New Eng. Mchts. Nat. Bank, Boston, from 1963, sr. v.p., sr. loan officer, head comml. banking div., 1972-78, pres., from 1978; pres. New Eng. Mchts. Co., Inc., 1980; then exec. v.p., dir. New Eng. Mchts. Co., Inc., Boston; now pres. Bank of New Eng. Corp., Boston; chmn., chief exec. officer Bank of New Eng., N.A., Boston, retired, 1988. Trustee Mus. of Sci., Boston, Mass. Gen. Hosp.; mem. Northeastern U., Corp. Woods Hole Oceanographic Inst.; chmn. bd. trustees Jobs for Youth-Boston; bd. dirs., mem. exec. com., treas. United Community Planning Corp.; bd. dirs. Boston Pvt. Industry Council, Greater Boston Arts Fund, Jobs for Mass. Served to lt. (j.g.) USNR, 1959-63. Mem. World Affairs

Council, New Eng. Council, New Eng. Banking Inst. (chmn. sr. adv. council), Boston Com. on Fgn. Relations, Assn. Res. City Bankers (bd. dirs.), Robert Morris Assocs., Catboat Assn. Clubs: Somerset, Commercial, The Country. Office: Bank New Eng Corp 28 State St Boston MA 02109

MCCORMICK, RICHARD DAVID, telecommunications company executive; b. Fort Dodge, Iowa, July 4, 1940; s. Elmo Eugene and Virgilla (Lawler) McC.; m. Mary Patricia Smola, June 29, 1963; children: John Richard, Matthew David, Megan Ann, Katherine Maura. B.S. in Elec. Engring., Iowa State U., 1961. With Bell Telephone Co., 1961-85; v.p., chief exec. officer for N.D. Northwestern Bell Telephone Co., Omaha, 1974-77; asst. v.p. human resources AT&T, Basking Ridge, N.J., 1977-78; sr. v.p. Northwestern Bell, Omaha, 1978-82, pres., chief exec. officer, 1982-85; exec. v.p. U.S. West Inc., Englewood, Colo., 1985-86, pres., chief operating officer, 1986—; dir. Super Valu Stores, Norwest Corp., Prin. Fin. Group. Bd. dirs. Regis Coll. Mem. Phi Gamma Delta. Office: US West Inc 7800 E Orchard Rd Englewood CO 80111 *

MCCORMICK, RICHARD JAMES, marketing company executive, consultant; b. Dallas, July 17, 1948; s. James C. and Barbara (Ostling) McC.; children from previous marriage: Allison, Chad, D'Ann, m. Angela S. Otting, Aug. 20, 1988. BBA, Stephen F. Austin U., 1971. V.p., dir. James Travel Pts. Internat., Boulder, Colo., 1974-85; sr. mgr. mktg. Frontier Airlines, Denver, 1985-86; v.p. mktg. and services Sunworld Internat. Airlines, Las Vegas, Nev., 1986-88; exec. v.p. Volz & McCormick Inc., Las Vegas, Nev., 1988-89, Dallas, 1989—. Vice chmn., chmn. fin. Larimer County Rep. Party, Ft. Collins, Colo.; bd. dirs. Poudre Valley Hosp. Found., Ft. Collins, 1983, Jr. Achievement No. Colo., 1980. Mem. Ft. Collins C. of C. (bd. dirs. 1983). Methodist. Lodge: Lions (pres. 1981-82). Home and Office: 6504 Garlinghouse Ln Dallas TX 75252

MCCORMICK, STEVEN THOMAS, insurance company manager; b. Phila., Dec. 18, 1955; s. Howard C. and Ruth Marion (Stahl) McC.; m. Helene Mary Trommler, Nov. 21, 1981; children: Matthew Thomas, Bria Helene. BBA, U. Ky., 1978; gen. ins cert., Ins. Inst. Am., 1980. Cert. adminstrv. mgr., purchasing mgr., Ky., ins. agt., 1980. Supr. trainee Ky. Farm Bur. Ins. Cos., Louisville, 1978-79, supr. micrographics dept., 1979-83, supr. adminstrv. services, 1983-85, mgr. adminstrv. services, 1985—; dir. Cascade Gardens Condominium Assn. Big brother Big Brothers Am., Lexington, Ky., 1978; den leader Cub Scouts Boy Scouts Am., Lexington, 1979; fund raiser Leukemia Soc., Louisville, 1983, Am. Heart Assn., Louisville, 1985; dir. Cascade Gardens Condo. Assn., 1981-82. Named to Hon. Order Ky. Cols., Outstanding Employee of Yr., Nat. Assn. of Mutual Ins. Cos., 1986, Outstanding Young Man of Am., Outstanding Americans, 1987. Mem. Adminstrv. Mgmt. Soc. (internat. top recruiter 1985, pres. 1988), Acad. Cert. Adminstrv. Mgrs., Louisville Area Telecommunications Assn., Assn. Records Mgrs. and Adminstrs., Nat. Micrographics Assn., U. Ky. Alumni Assn., Sigma Nu. Republican. Club: Toastmasters. Home: 4004 River Oaks Ln Louisville KY 40241 Office: Ky Farm Bur Ins Cos PO Box 7200 Louisville KY 40207-0200

MCCORMICK, WILLIAM EDWARD, business executive, consultant; b. Potters Mills, Pa., Feb. 9, 1912; s. George H. and Nellie (Mingle) McC.; m. Goldie Stover, June 6, 1935; children: John F. (dec.), Kirk W. B.S., Pa. State U., 1933, M.S., 1934. Tchr., Centre Hall (Pa.) High Sch., 1934-37; chemist Willson Products, Inc., Reading, Pa., 1937-43; indsl. hygienist Ga. Dept. Pub. Health, Atlanta, 1946; mgr. indsl. hygiene and toxicology B.F. Goodrich Co., Akron, Ohio, 1946-70; mgr. environ. control B.F. Goodrich Co., 1970-73; mng. dir. Am. Indsl. Hygiene Assn., Akron, 1973-83; exec. sec. Soc. Toxicology, 1976-83; chmn., treas. Envirotox Mgmt., Inc., 1983—; mem. exec. com. rubber sect. Nat. Safety Council, 1955-73; gen. chmn., 1971-72; mem. environ. health com. Chlorine Inst., 1968-73; mem. food, drug and cosmetic chems. com. Mfg. Chemists Assn., 1960-73, chmn., 1967-69, also mem. occupational health com., 1965-73; mem. adv. com. on heat stress U.S. Dept. Labor, 1973; mem. Nat. Adv. Com. Occupational Safety and Health, 1983-85; pres. Am. Indsl. Hygiene Found., 1984, trustee, 1982—. Contbr. articles to profl. jours. Served to capt. USPHS, 1943-46. Mem. Am. Chem. Soc., Soc. Toxicology, AAAS, Am. Indsl. Hygiene Assn. (pres. 1964), Indsl. Hygiene Roundtable, Am. Acad. Indsl. Hygiene. Republican. Episcopalian. Lodges: Masons (33 deg.) Shriner. Home: 419 Dorchester Rd Akron OH 44320 Office: 149 N Prospect St Ravenna OH 44266

MCCORMICK, WILLIAM MALLORY, financial services company executive; b. Hartford, Conn., Aug. 21, 1940; s. Ernest W. and Esther M. McCormick; B.S., Yale U., 1962; M.S., George Washington U., 1967; children—James and Skye (twins). Mgmt. cons. McKinsey & Co., N.Y.C., 1967-72; investment banker Donaldson, Lufkin & Jenrette, N.Y.C., 1972-75; with Am. Express Internat. Banking Corp., 1975-78, sr. v.p. fin., systems and ops., 1977-78; sr. v.p. fin. and planning card div. Am. Express Co., 1978-79, pres. travel div., 1979-80, pres. card div., 1980-81, pres. consumer fin. services group, 1981-82, pres. travel related services, 1982-83; chmn., chief exec. officer Fireman's Fund Ins. Co., 1984—; bd. dirs. Bay Area Council, Ctr. for Excellence in Edn.; mem. adv. council SRI. Served to lt. USNR, 1962-67. Mem. Commonwealth Club of Calif., Calif. Bus. Roundtable. Office: Fireman's Fund Ins Co 777 San Marin Dr Novato CA 94998 also: Fireman's Fund Corp 646 Steamboat Rd Greenwich CT 06830

MCCOUN, GORDON WICKERSHAM, investment advisor; b. Harrisburg, Pa., May 15, 1952; s. Bruce Townsend and Barbara (Wickersham) McC.; m. Kathleen Lynch, Mar. 13, 1982. AB, U. Pa., 1974; MBA, NYU, 1982. Asst. trust officer Bank of N.Y., N.Y.C., 1976-80; asst. v.p. Citibank, NA, N.Y.C., 1980-83; v.p., mng. dir. Pvt. Asset Mgmt. Group, N.Y.C., 1983-86; 2d v.p. Mutual of Am., N.Y.C., 1986-88; mgr. investments Prudential Equity Mgmt. Assocs., Newark, N.J., 1988—. Republican. Episcopalian. Club: University (N.Y.C.). Home: 444 E 52d St Apt 2-B New York NY 10022 Office: Prudential Equity Mgmt Assocs 5 Prudential Pla Newark NJ 07101

MCCOY, GARDNER, heavy engineering company executive; b. Middletown, Ohio, Mar. 2, 1915; s. James W. and Florence (Peterson) McC.; student U. Cin., 1933-38; m. Muriel Marshall, Sept. 25, 1940; children—Kristin, Melissa. With Armco Steel Corp., Middletown, 1933-38, Australia, 1938-56; with firm Gardner L. McCoy and Assos., Australia, 1956-62; mng. dir. McCoy Internat., Sydney, New South Wales, Australia, 1962-85, dir. Bliss Welded Products, Sydney, Australia, 1966-85; dir. Indsl. Ops. Pty. Ltd. Bd. dirs. YMCA, Wollongong. Fellow Inst. Dirs. Australia; asso. mem. Mech. Engrs. Australia; mem. Iron and Steel Engrs. U.S.A. (life), Am. C. of C., Australian Inst. Mgmt., Co. Dirs. Assn. Australia, Metal Trades Industry Assn. Australia. Republican. Home: Highland Park, Mount Pleasant, Balgownie New South Wales, Australia Office: 333 Old South Head Rd, Watsons Bay, Sydney Australia

MCCOY, GREGORY STEWART, financial executive, accountant; b. Wauseon, Ohio, Mar. 26, 1954; s. L. Stewart and Janette (Derocher) McC.; m. Catherine L. Leddon, Aug. 7, 1978; children: Stewart, Daniel, Christen. BA in Econs., Centre Coll., 1976; MBA, Ind. U., 1978. Fin. analyst Chemed Corp., Cin., 1978-79; mgr. fin. planning Dearborn Chem. Co., Lake Zurich, Ill., 1979-82; dir. fin. planning Dearborn div. W.R. Grace, Lake Zurich, 1982-86, v.p. fin., chief fin. officer, 1987—. Home: 715 Fieldstone Circle Lake Zurich IL 60047 Office: WR Grace Dearborn Div 300 Genesee St Lake Zurich IL 60047

MCCOY, JOENNE RAE, psychiatric clinic administrator; b. Detroit, Jan. 26, 1941; d. Harlan and Dorothy (Simpson) Heinmiller; children: Harlan Craig, Cathi-Jo. BA, Mich. State U., 1966; MSW, U. Mich., 1983. Tchr. Owosso and Garden City pub. schs., Mich., 1962-73; psychotherapist, group leader Wayne County Hosp., Mich., 1981-82; psychotherapist East Point, Westland, Mich., 1982-83, Midwest, Dearborn, Mich., 1982-83; owner, dir. Personal Devel. Ctrs., Inc., Plymouth, Mich., 1981—, Co-Dependency Specialists Livonia, Mich., 1988—; bd. dirs. Hospice Suport Services, Inc., Livonia, Mich., 1981—; cons. Westland Convalescent Ctr., Mich., 1983—; supr. grad. students U. Mich., 1986—; cons., facilitator Women-the Emerging Entrepreneurs, Wayne State U. and Small Bus. Assn., 1985—; chmn. Substance Abuse Com., Plymouth Schs., 1982; cons. Salvation Army, Plymouth. Mem. bd. advisors (newsletter) Personal Performance, Balt., 1986—. Mem. steering com. for neighborhood programs YWCA. Soroptimist scholar, 1982. Mem. Internat. Assn. Pediatric Social Workers, Internat. Platform Assn., Mich. Assn. Bereavement Counselors, Families in Crisis: Domestic Violence Inc., Nat. Assn. Social Workers (cert.), Nat. Assn. Female Execs., Am. Entrepreneurs Assn., Women's Network (pres.), Acad. Cert. Soc. Workers. Club: Agora. Avocation: internat. bus. and fin. Home: 37644 N Laurel Park Dr Livonia MI 48152 Office: Personal Devel Ctrs Inc PC 37677 Professional Ctr Dr Ste 130C Livonia MI 48154-1114

MC COY, JOHN BONNET, banker; b. Columbus, Ohio, June 11, 1943; s. John Gardner and Jeanne Newlove (Bonnet) McC.; m. Jane Deborah Taylor, Apr. 21, 1968; children: Tracy Bonnet, Paige Taylor, John Taylor. B.A., Williams Coll., 1965; M.B.A., Stanford U., 1967. With Banc One Corp., Columbus NA, Columbus, Ohio, 1970—, banking officer, 1970-73, v.p., 1973-77, pres., 1977-83; pres., chief operating officer Banc One Corp., Columbus, Ohio, 1983-84, pres., chief exec. officer, 1984-87, chmn., chief exec. officer, 1987—; pres. Bank One Trust Co., 1979-81; bd. dirs. Cardinal Distbn., Inc. Active Boy Scouts Am.; v.p. bd. trustee Kenyon Coll., 1989—, Stanford Univ., Children's Hosp., United Way of Franklin County, Columbus Acad.; pres. Columbus Area Growth Found.; chmn. Capitol South Urban Redevel. Corp. Served to capt. USAF, 1967-70. Mem. Columbus C. of C. (past chmn., trustee), Am. Bankers Assn., Assn. Reserve City Bankers (bd. dirs. 1989—), Assn. Bank Holding Cos., Young Pres.' Orgn. (chmn. Columbus chpt. 1982-83). Episcopalian. Clubs: Columbus, Links (N.Y.C.). Office: Banc One Corp 100 E Broad St Columbus OH 43271-0261

MC COY, LEE BERARD, paint company executive; b. Ipswich, Mass., July 27, 1925; d. Damase Joseph and Robena Myrtle (Bruce) B.; student U. Ala., Mobile, 1958-60; m. Walter Vincent de Paul McCoy, Sept. 27, 1943; children: Bernadette, Raymond, Joan, Richard. Owner, Lee's Letter Shop, Hicksville, L.I., N.Y., 1950-56; mgr. sales adminstrn. Basila Mfg. Co., Mobile, Ala., 1957-61; promotion mgr., buyer Mobile Paint Co., Inc., Theodore, Ala., 1961—. Curator, Shepard Meml. Library, 1972—; bd. dirs. Monterey Tour House, Mobile, 1972-78, Old Dauphin Way Assn., 1977-79, Friends of Mus., Mobile, 1978—, Miss Wheelchair Ala., 1980—; del. Civic Roundtable, 1977-78, bd. dirs., 1980-81, 1st v.p., 1980-81, pres., 1981-82; Pres.'s Com. Employment of Handicapped, 1981—; chmn. Mobile, Nat. Yr. Disabled Persons, 1982; chmn. Mobile, Internat. Decade Disabled Persons, 1983—; mem. Nat. Project Adv. Bd., 1983— Nat. Community Adv. Bd., 1983—, World Com. for Decade of Disabled Persons, 1983—; v.p. Bristol Sister City Soc.; active Mobile Area Retarded Citizens, Am. Heart Assn.; mem. City of Mobile Cultural Enrichment Task Force, 1985—, Mobile United Recreation and Culture Com. Recipient Honor award Civic Roundtable, 1979, 80; Service award Women's Com. of Spain Rehab. Center, State of Ala., 1980; award Nat. Orgn. on Disability, 1983. Mem. Spectromatic Assns., Nat. Paint Distbrs., Hist. Preservation Soc. (color mktg. group), English Speaking Union (v.p.), U.S. C. of C. (local cultural enrichment task force 1986). Methodist. Republican. Clubs: Quota (charter mem. Mobile chpt., dir. 1977—, pres. 1978-80, chmn. numerous coms., recipient Service award Dist. 8, 1979, Internat. award for serving club objectives, 1980, editor Care-Gram, Weekly newsletter for nursing homes 1980—), Bienville; writer 10 books. Home: 1553 Monterey Pl Mobile AL 36604 Office: 4775 Hamilton Blvd Theodore AL 36582

MC COY, WILLIAM DANIEL, manufacturing executive; b. N.Y.C., Nov. 27, 1929; s. William Daniel and Anna Marie (Murphy) McC.; m. Joan Gillette, Nov. 26, 1960; children: Kirk, Kim, Karen. B.S., Fordham U., 1951; M.B.A., Hofstra U., 1958. With IBM Corp., White Plains, N.Y., 1953-69; mgr. basic systems mktg. IBM Corp., 1969-72; pres. Am. Polymers, Inc., Paterson, N.J., 1972-85; with Philip Morris Indsl., Inc., Milw., 1972—; pres., chief exec. officer Philip Morris Indsl., Inc., until 1985; chmn., chief exec. officer Koch Label Co., 1985—; dir. Wis. Tissue Mills, Inc., Plainwell Paper Co., Inc., W.A. Krueger Co., Phoenix, Chesapeake, West Point, Va., Krueger-Ringier, Chgo. Bd. dirs. Wis. Found. Ind. Colls.; bd. dirs. United Performing Arts Fund, Milw. Art Mus.; trustee Ripon Coll.; vice chmn. United Way, 1976, Wis. region NCCJ, 1980-81. Served to capt. USMC, 1951-53. Mem. Am. Paper Inst., Am. Mgmt. Assn., Wis. Assn. Mfrg. and Commerce. Clubs: University, Siwanoy Country (Bronxville, N.Y.). Home: 571 North St Harrison NY 10528 Office: Koch Label Co 60 Arch St Greenwich CT 06830

MCCRACKEN, CHARLES BARRY, financial planning company executive; b. Stafford, Conn., Sept. 8, 1947; s. Charles Beryl and Jean Elizabeth (Herr) McC.; m. Linda Elizabeth McCarthy, Mar. 17, 1972; children: Bethia Lyn, Erin Elizabeth. BA, Dartmouth Coll., 1969. Cert. fin. planner. Underwriter Travelers Ins. Co., Hartford, Conn., 1969-70; psychiat. aide Inst. of Living, Hartford, 1970-72; zone mktg. mgr. Burroughs Corp., New Haven, 1972-78; brokerage cons. CIGNA, Greenwich, Conn., 1978-81; brokerage mgr. CIGNA, Farmington, Conn., 1981-83; assoc. mgr. CNA, Farmington, 1983-84; ptnr. McCracken, Worgaftik & Co., Newington, Conn., 1984—; pres. Total Pension Svcs. Inc., Newington, 1984—, FPC, Inc., Newington, 1984—. Mem. Bethany (Conn.) Republican Town Com., 1985-86; del. Dist. Legis. Conv., 1985. Mem. Am. Soc. Pension Actuaries, Nat. Assn. Life Underwriters, Inst. Cert. Fin. Planners, Conn. Soc. Cert. Fin. Planners (pres. 1986—, chmn. bd. dirs. 1986-88), Hartford Life Underwriters, Dartmouth Club (New Haven). Home: 61 Ralph Rd Bethany CT 06525 Office: McCracken Worgaftik & Co 135 Day St Newington CT 06111

MC CRACKEN, PAUL WINSTON, educator; b. Richland, Iowa, Dec. 29, 1915; s. Sumner and Mary (Coffin) McC.; m. Emily Ruth Siler, May 27, 1942; children—Linda Jo, Paula Jeanne. Student, William Penn Coll., 1937; M.A., Harvard, 1942, Ph.D., 1948. Faculty Found. Sch., Berea Coll., Ky., 1937-40; economist Dept. Commerce, Washington, 1942-43; fin. economist, dir. research Fed. Res. Bank of Mpls., 1943-48; assoc. prof. Sch. Bus. Adminstrn., U. Mich., 1948-50, prof., 1950-66, Edmund Ezra Day Univ. prof. bus. adminstrn., 1966-86, prof. emeritus, 1986—; mem. Council Econ. Advisers, Washington, 1956-59, chmn., 1969-71; mem. Pres.'s Adv. Bd. Econ. Policy, 1981—; bd. dirs. Kmart, Sara Lee. Author: monographs Can Capitalism Survive?; articles on financial, econ. subjects. Fellow Am. Statis. Assn.; mem. Am. Econ. Assn., Am. Finance Assn., Royal Econ. Soc. Presbyn. Clubs: Cosmos (Washington); Harvard (N.Y.C.). Home: 2564 Hawthorn Rd Ann Arbor MI 48104

MCCRAVEN, MARCUS ROLLINS, electrical engineer, utilities executive; b. Des Moines, Dec. 27, 1923; s. Marcus Harry and Buena Vista (Rollins) McC.; m. Marguerite Noel Mills, Sept. 19, 1947; children: Carol J., Stephen A., Paul A. BS in Elec. Engring., Howard U., 1949. Project leader Naval Rsch. Lab., Washington, 1950-56; group leader Lawrence Radiations Lab. U. Calif., Livermore, 1954-64; mgr. engring. Phelps Dodge Communications Co., North Haven, Conn., 1964-69; v.p. environ. engring. United Illuminating Co., North Haven, 1969—; bd. dirs. First Constrn. Bank, New Haven; cons. TRW, L.A.; mem. exec. com. sci adv. bd. EPA, Washington. Patentee high current photomultiplier. Former Commr. City of Menlo Park, Calif.; chmn. Hamden (Conn.) Zoning Commn.; trustee Quinnipiac Coll., Hamden, 1987—; mem. devel. com. Yale Univ. Peabody Mus., 1989—. With U.S. Army, 1942-46. Mem. Edison Electric Inst. (chmn. exec. adv. bd. energy and environ. com. 1987—), Air Pollution Control Assn., Grads. Club Assn. (bd. dirs. 1979—), Sigma Pi Phi, Quinnipiack Club (bd. dirs. 1988—). Republican. Home: 5 Rayzoe Terr Hamden CT 06514 Office: United Illuminating Co 80 Temple St New Haven CT 06510

MCCRAW, LESLIE GLADSTONE, construction and design engineering executive; b. Sandy Springs, S.C., Nov. 3, 1934; s. Leslie Gladstone and Cornelia (Milam) McC.; m. Mary Earle Brown; children: Leslie Gladstone III, James C., John. BSCE, Clemson U., 1956. Registerd profl. engr., Del. Design engr. Gulf Oil Corp., Phila., 1956-57; various engring. and constrn. positions E.I. duPont Co., Wilmington, Del., 1960-75; v.p., mgr. div. Daniel Constrn. Co., Greenville, S.C., 1975-82, pres., 1982-84; pres., chief exec. officer Daniel Internat., Greenville, 1984-86, Fluor Daniel, Greenville and Irvine, Calif., 1986-88; pres. Fluor Daniel, Irvine, 1988—; bd. dirs. Fluor Corp., Irvine, Palmetto Bank, Greenville. Trustee Columbia Coll., S.C., Hampden sydney Coll.; mem. engring. adv. council Clemson U., chmn. pres.' adv. council; bd. dirs. Greenville Tech. Coll. Found. Served to capt. USAF, 1957-60. Mem. Bus. Roundtable (constrn. com., adv. com., contractor), S.C. State C. of C. (bd. dirs.). Republican. Presbyterian. Club: Greenville Country, Commerce (bd. govs.); Vintage Country (Indian Wells, Calif.); Center (Cosa Mesa, Calif.); Pacific (Newport Beach, Calif.). Home: 57 Hillside Dr Newport Beach CA 92660 Office: Fluor Daniel 3333 Michelson Dr Irvine CA 92730 *

MC CRIE, ROBERT DELBERT, editor, publisher; b. Sarnia, Ont., Can., Oct. 8, 1938; s. Robert Newton and Evelyn May (Johnston) McC.; m. Fulvia Madia, Dec. 22, 1965; children: Carla ALexandra, Mara Elizabeth. B.A., Ohio Wesleyan U., 1960; M.S., U. Toledo, 1962; postgrad., U. Chgo., 1962-63. Researcher Connective Tissues Research Lab., Copenhagen, 1963; copywriter numerous advt. agys. 1965-70; pres., editor Security Letter, Inc., N.Y.C., 1970—; editor, pub. HBJ Publs., N.Y.C., 1973-76; pres. Mags. for Medicine, Inc., N.Y.C., 1972-81; faculty John Jay Coll. Criminal Justice, 1985—, asst. prof., 1986—; bd. dirs. numerous cos.; cons. in field; speaker at numerous meetings. Editor: Behavioral Medicine, 1978-81, Security Letter Source Book, 1983—; contbr. books and articles on security. Mem. Newsletter Assn. Am., Am. Correctional Assn., AAUP, Am. Soc. Ind. Security, Alpha Tau Omega, Delta Sigma Rho, Pi Delta Epsilon. Presbyterian (deacon). Clubs: Union League (N.Y.C.); Point O'Woods. Home: 49 E 96th St New York NY 10128 Office: 166 E 96 St New York NY 10128

MCCROSSON, ANDREW JAMES, JR., accountant; b. Atlantic City, Mar. 6, 1951; s. Andrew James McCrosson and Lucetta June (Kline) Sykes; m. Janet Alene Patterson, May 5, 1973; children: Kathryn Anne, Andrea Leigh, Alexis Johanna. AS, Atlantic Community Coll., 1975; BS in Acctg., Villanova U., 1977. CPA, N.J. Jr. acct. Albert N. Gardner & Co. CPAs, Atlantic City, 1978-80; sr. acct. Adams, Swartz & Co. CPAs, Ocean City, N.J., 1980-81; mgr. Maguire, Petlev & Stablini CPAs, Atlantic City, 1981-84; ptnr. Raymond F. Maguire & Co. CPAs, Atlantic City, 1985—; trustee Justice Lodge Scholarship Found., Linwood, N.J., 1985—. Mem. Mcpl. Planning Bd., Upper Township, N.J., 1988; chmn. Mcpl. Zoning Bd. Adjustment, Upper Township, N.J., 1989; elder Community Presbyn. Ch., Brigantine, N.J.; pres. Cape Atlantic Childbirth Edn. Assn., Northfield, N.J. Recipient Albert S. Goodmen award Atlantic City Jaycees, 1980. Fellow N.J. Soc. CPAs; mem. Am. Inst. CPAs, Viking Rowing Club (Ventnor, N.J.), Masons. Republican. Office: Raymond F Maguire & Co 26 S Pennsylvania Ave Atlantic City NJ 08401

MCCUE, MICHAEL, manufacturing executive; b. Denver, Feb. 21, 1951; s. Ethan Roy and Mildred (Haag) McC. AB cum laude, Harvard U., 1973, MBA, 1975. Mgr. brands Brown & Williamson, Louisville, 1975-79; mgr. Northlich Stolley, Inc., Cin., 1979; nat. brand mgr. Brown-Forman Distillers, Louisville, 1980-83; pres. Kangaroo Golf Ltd., Columbus, N.C., 1983—; bd. dirs. Metrex, Inc., Tryon, N.C., 1985—. Pres. Louisville Hist. League, 1977; trustee Polk County Library System Co., Columbus, 1987—. Mem. Harvard Club Ky. (pres. 1980), Water Tower Art Assn. (pres. Louisville 1982), Thermanl Belt C. of C. (pres. 1986), Tryon Country Club, Pendennis Club (Louisville). Democrat. Home: 226 Hogback Mountain Rd Tryon NC 28782 Office: Kangaroo Golf Ltd 108 Mill Spring Rd Columbus NC 28722

MCCUEN, JOHN JOACHIM, defense contractor executive; b. Washington, Mar. 30, 1926; s. Joseph Raymond and Josephine (Joachim) McC.; m. Gloria Joyce Seidel, June 16, 1949; children: John Joachim Jr., Les Seidel. BS, U.S. Mil. Acad., 1948; M of Internatl. Affairs, Columbia U., 1961; grad., U.S. Army War Coll., 1968. Commd. 2d. lt. U.S. Army, 1948, advanced through grades to col.; dir. internal def. and devel. U.S. Army War Coll., Carlisle, Pa., 1969-72; chief U.S. Def. Liaison Group, Jakarta, Indonesia, 1972-74; chief field survey office U.S. Army Tng. and Doctrine Command, Ft. Monroe, Va., 1974-76; ret. U.S. Army, 1976; mgr. tng. Chrysler Def., Center Line, Mich., 1977-82; mgr. modification ctr. Land Systems div. Gen. Dynamics, Sterling Heights, Mich., 1982-83; mgr. field ops. Land Systems div. Gen. Dynamics, Warren, Mich., 1983—; ptnr. East West Connection, Birmingham, Mich.; armor advisor 3d Royal Thai Army, Utaradit, 1957-58; U.S. rep. users' com. NATO Missile Firing Installation Crete, Paris, 1964-66; advisor Vietnamese Nat. Def. Coll., Saigon, 1968-69; speaker on terrorism and counter insurgency. Author: The Art of Counter Revolutionary War-The Strategy of Counter Insurgency, Faber 1966, Stackpole, 1967, Circulo Militar, 1967. Pres. Troy (Mich.) Community Concert Assn., 1985—; v.p. Mich. Oriental Art Soc., Birmingham, 1985—; mem. exec. bd., chmn. bldg. com. Granderview Assn. Sr. Housing and Nursing, Milford, Mich., 1984—; 1st reader First Ch. of Christ Scientist, Birmingham, 1989—. Mem. Soc. Logistics Engrs., Nat. Mgmt. Assn., Assn. U.S. Army. Republican. Home: 32863 Balmoral Birmingham MI 48009 Office: Gen Dynamics Land Systems Div PO Box 527 Warren MI 48090

MCCULLAGH, GRANT GIBSON, architect; b. Cleve., Apr. 18, 1951; s. Robert Ernest and Barbara Louise (Grant) McC.; m. Suzanne Dewar Folds, Sept. 13, 1975; children: Charles Weston Folds, Grant Gibson Jr. BArch, U. Ill., 1973; MArch, U. Pa., 1975; MBA, U. Chgo., 1979. Registered architect, Ill. Project designer Perkins & Will, Chgo., 1975-77; dir. mktg. The Austin Co., Chgo., 1977-83, asst. dist. mgr., 1983-84, dist. mgr., 1984-88, v.p., 1987-88; chmn., chief exec. officer McClier Corp., Chgo., 1988—. Contbr. articles to various indsl. publs. Mem. AIA, Chgo. Architecture Found. (exec. com., trustee, v.p. 1986-87, pres. 1988—), Chgo. Archtl. Found. Aux. Bd. (exec. v.p. 1983-86). Republican. Episcopalian. Clubs: Economics, Chicago, Casino, University; Indian Hill Country. Home: 43 Locust Rd Winnetka IL 60093 Office: McClier Corp 401 E Illinois St Chicago IL 60611

MCCULLOCH, RODERICK ALLISTER, accountant, corporate executive; b. Toronto, Ont., Can., Aug. 8, 1938; s. Allister Hart and Esther Darling (Turnbull) McC.; m. Susan Jane McNeel; children: Scott, Neil, Andrea. B in Commerce, U. Toronto, 1961. Chartered acct. Student mgr. Clarkson Gordon, Toronto, 1961-68; mgr. Clarkson Gordon, Halifax, N.S., Can., 1968-70, mgr. ptnr., 1970-86; exec. v.p. fin. Nat. Sea Products Ltd., Halifax, 1986—. Office: Nat Sea Products Ltd, PO Box 2130, 1959 Upper Water St, Halifax, NS Canada B3H 4K3

MCCULLOUGH, HENRY FREDERICK, aircraft company executive; b. Vancouver, B.C., Can., Sept. 18, 1926 (parents Am. citizens); s. John Andrew and Beatrice Victoria (Warburton) McC.; m. Constance Agnes Van Nes, Jan. 26, 1951; children: Linda, Katherine, Cynthia, John, Pamela, Lucille. Grad. Sch. Mgmt., UCLA. Cert. quality engr., Am. Soc. Quality Control, 1966. Aircraft specialist Boeing of Can., Vancouver, 1943-45; quality control preflight insp. Boeing Co., Seattle, 1945-49, 53—, quality control chief 707-727 system test, 1955-68, quality control mgr. 747 program, from 1968, now ret. Pres., commr. King County Water Dist. #107, 1965; past pres. and bd. dirs. Wash. State Assn. Water/Wastewater dists., chmn. legis. and membership coms.; charter mem. Presdl. Task Force, 1982-86, trustee, 1986; mem. Presdl. Commn., 1986; vol. crime prevention unit precinct III King County Police. With Can. Res. Army, 1939-45; also USAF, 1949-53. Decorated Air medal, Korean Svc. medal; recipient Silver Beaver award Boy Scouts Am., 1978; Golden Acorn, PTA, 1977; cert. Nat. Ct. of Honor for Life Saving, 1974, Recognition award for Vol. Service Water Pollution Abatement in King County. Fellow Am. Soc. Quality Control; mem. Am. Water Works Assn., Water Pollution Control Fedn., Boeing Mgmt. Assn. (life), NRA (life), Meydenbauer Bay Yacht Club, Newport Hills Community Club (past pres., dir.), Renton Fishing and Game Club. Republican. Episcopalian. Home: 6808 128th Ave SE Bellevue WA 98006

MCCULLOUGH, JEFFERSON WALKER, industrial engineering consultant; b. Hartford, Conn., Nov. 2, 1944; s. Sam Walker and Beula (Adamis) McC. Grad. Williston Sch., 1963; student Rutgers U., 1963-69, Greater Hartford Coll., 1979-80. With Textron, Inc., United Technologies, Royal Bus. Machines, Colt Industries, Ill. Tool Works, ALCO Corp., Ingersoll Rand, Combustion Engring., Cooper Industries; cons. indsl. engring. and fin., Rocky Hill, Conn., 1950—; cons. Select Equity Assn. Mem. Wadsworth Atheneum, Hartford, Com. for Def. of Persecuted Orthodox

Christians, Ams. for Legal Reform, Internat. Platform Assn., United Shareholders Assn.; cons. Select Equity Assocs. Avocations: art, music, classical languages. Home: 140 Hayes Rd Rocky Hill CT 06067

MC CULLOUGH, SAMUEL ALEXANDER, banker; b. Pitts., Nov. 10, 1938; s. Alexander and Mary Ruth (Brady) McC.; m. Katharine Graham, Sept. 23, 1967; children: Bonnie McCullough Wideman, Elizabeth McCullough White, Rebecca D., Anne D., Mary D. BBA, U. Pitts., 1960. With Mellon Bank, N.A., Pitts., 1956-75, asst. cashier, 1964-68, asst. v.p., 1968-71, v.p., 1971-75; sr. v.p. corp. banking group Am. Bank and Trust Co. of Pa., Reading, 1975, exec. v.p., 1977, pres., chief exec. officer, 1978-82, chmn., chief exec. officer, 1982—; pres., chief exec. officer Meridian Bancorp., Inc., Reading, 1983-88, chmn., chief exec. officer, 1988—, also bd. dirs.; and bd. dirs. to all prin. subs. cos.; v.p., bd. mem. Fed. Adv. Coun., rep. 3d Fed. Res. Dist.; bd. dirs. Greater Phila. 1st Corp. Bd. dirs. World Affairs Coun. Phila., Pa. Chamber of Bus. and Industry; trustee Albright Coll.; mem. exec. bd. Valley Forge coun. Boy Scouts Am.; bd. dirs., mem. exec. com. N.E. region Boy Scouts of Am.; bd. govs., treas. Pennsylvanians for Effective Govt.; mem. steering com. Bus. Leaders Organized for Cath. Schs.; bd. mem. Commonwealth Found., U. Pitts. Joseph M. Katz Grad. Sch. Bus. Recipient Disting. Pennsylvanian award 1982, Pagoda award for outstanding contbns. to community Berks County Jr. Achievement, 1985, William H. Doran Meml. award, 1987, Bicentennial Medallion U. Pitts., 1988, Ann. Enterprise award Pa. Coun. on Econ. Edn., 1989; named Bus. Person of Yr. award Berks County C. of C. Mem. Am. Inst. Banking, Am. Bankers Assn., Pa. Bankers Assn., Berks County Bankers Assn., Pa. C. of C. (bd. dirs.), Assn. Reserve City Bankers, Assn. Bank Holding Cos. (bd. dirs., mem. legis. policy com.), Internat. Fin. Conf. (bd. dirs., chmn.), Allegheny Country Club, Berkshire Country Club, Moselem Springs Golf Club. Republican. Presbyterian. Office: Meridian Bancorp Inc 35 N 6th St PO Box 1102 Reading PA 19603

MCCULLOUGH, WILLIAM HUNTER, financial executive; b. Wilkinsburg, Pa., Nov. 5, 1934; s. William Thomas and Harriett (Hunter) McC.; m. Betty Davis, Nov. 4, 1968. BBA, Lehigh U., 1957; MBA, NYU, 1965. Cert. fin. planner. Sr. account exec. Merrill Lynch, Pierce, Fenner & Smith, N.Y.C., 1962-76; v.p., fin. cons. Robinson-Humpnrey/Am. Express, Charleston, S.C., 1976—. Capt. USMC, 1958-61. Mem. Inst. Fin. Planners, Greater Charleston Soc. Fin. Planners (sec. 1988—), Charleston Country Club, Carolina Yacht Club. Republican. Presbyterian (elder). Home: 20 Surfsong Rd Johns Island SC 29455 Office: Robinson Humpnrey Am Express 152 E Bay St Charleston SC 29401

MCCURDY, CLAIR EUGENE, manufacturing executive; b. Wellington, Kans., Oct. 15, 1931; s. Harry Clifford and Opal (Howe) McC.; m. Emma Jean Blaney, Aug., 29, 1955; children: Cynthia Diane, Patti Ann, Kristi Lynn, Michael Scott. Student, Southwestern Coll., 1949-50, Wichita State U., 1950-52. With The Coleman Co., Inc., Wichita, Kans., 1950—, dir. credit, 1966-82, asst. sec., 1970-82, v.p corporate services, 1982-83, sr. v.p. corporate services, 1983-87, pres. associated group, 1987-89, sr. v.p. adminstrn., 1989—. Councilman, City of Mulvane, Kans., 1968-74. Served with U.S. Army, 1952-54. Republican. Methodist. Office: Coleman Co Inc 250 N St Francis Ave PO Box 1762 Wichita KS 67201

MCCURTAIN, BRADLEY CHRIS, financial services company executive; b. Portland, Maine, Aug. 12, 1952; s. Francis W. and Anna (Olesen) McC. AA, Northwood Inst., 1970-72; BS, Syracuse U., 1974, postgrad., 1975. Investment broker Burbank & Co., Inc., Portland, 1977-81; prin. Boston Bay Capital, Inc., Portland, 1981-86; pres. Maine Securities Corp., Portland, 1985—. Mem. adv. bd. Salvation Army Greater Portland, 1979—. Mem. Maine Real Estate Devel. Assn. (bd. dirs. 1986—). Club: Cumberland (Portland), Woodfords (Portland). Office: Maine Securities Corp 15 Monument Sq Portland ME 04101

MCCUSKER, JOHN, environmental consultant; b. Bklyn., May 28, 1939; s. John Michael and Helen Frances (Sweeney) McC.; BBA, St. John's U., 1961; m. Brenda Ann Caprio, June 27, 1964; children: John Christian, Joseph Andrew, David Douglas. Sr. acct. Haskins & Sells, N.Y.C., 1961-67; asst. dir. fin. planning Colt Industries, Inc., N.Y.C., 1967-69; dir. fin. planning Shearson Hammill & Co., N.Y.C., 1969-70; dir. fin. analysis The Allen Group, Inc., Melville, N.Y., 1971-73; asst. corporate controller, 1973-76, v.p., controller, 1976-83, v.p. fin., 1983-86, Geraghty & Miller Inc., Plainview, N.Y., 1987—. Vice chmn., bd. dirs., Huntington (N.Y.) Hosp., Family Service League Suffolk County, Huntington, N.Y. Served with U.S. Army, 1963. CPA, N.Y. Mem. Am. Inst. CPAs, N.Y. State Soc. CPAs, Fin. Execs. Inst., Nassau-Suffolk Hosp. Assn. (chmn. bd. dirs.). Republican. Roman Catholic. Home: 4 Harborview Dr Huntington Bay NY 11743 Office: Geraghty & Miller Inc 125 E Bethpage Rd Plainview NY 11803

MCCUTCHAN, GORDON EUGENE, lawyer, insurance company executive; b. Buffalo, Sept. 30, 1935; s. George Lawrence and Mary Esther (De Puy) McC. B.A., Cornell U., 1956, M.B.A., 1958, LL.B., 1959. Bar: N.Y. 1959, Ohio 1964. Pvt. practice Rome, N.Y., 1959-61; atty., advisor SEC, Washington, 1961-64; mem. office of gen. counsel Nationwide Mut. Ins. Co., Columbus, Ohio, 1964—, sr. v.p., gen. counsel, 1982—; sr. v.p., gen. counsel Beaver Pacific Corp., 1985—, Employers Ins. Wausau, a Mut. Co., 1985—; ptnr. McCutchan, Druen, Maynard, Rath & Dietrich, 1964—. Mem. Fed. Bar Assn., Columbus Bar Assn., Ohio Bar Assn., ABA, Am. Corporate Counsel Assn., Assn. Life Ins. Counsel, Fedn. Ins. and Corp. Counsel Assn. Home: 2376 Oxford Rd Columbus OH 43221 Office: Nationwide Mut Ins Co One Nationwide Pla Columbus OH 43216 also: Employers Ins Wausau 2000 Westwood Dr Wausau WI 54401

MC DADE, HERBERT HARDINGE, JR., pharmaceutical company executive; b. Bklyn., Apr. 6, 1927; s. Herbert Hardinge and Mabel L. (Landefeld) McD.; m. Ann Lois Finucane, Oct. 6, 1951; children—Mary Elizabeth, Janice Ann, Mark Daniel, Herbert Hardinge III. B.S., U. Notre Dame, 1949; B. Philosophy, Laval U., Quebec, Can., 1950. With Upjohn Co., 1950-70, product promotion mgr., 1960-62, dir. sales planning and promotion, 1962-68, dir. lab. procedures div., 1968-70; pub. Family Health mag., N.Y.C., 1970-72; pres., chief oper. officer USV Pharm. Corp. subs. Revlon Corp., Tuckahoe, N.Y., 1973-78; pres. Revlon Health Care Internat. Ops., 1978-86; v.p. Revlon, 1983-86; pres. Armour Pharm., Blue Bell, Pa., 1986-87; chmn., chief exec. officer Thoma Corp, White Plains, N.Y., 1987—; chief exec. officer, vice chmn. Chemex Pharms., Inc., Denver; bd. dirs. Nat. Vitamin Found., 1963—, chmn. exec. com., 1964—, chmn. bd., 1966; bd. dirs. Meloy Labs., Cademex Corp., Denver. Formerly co-chmn. indsl. com. Kalamazoo Community Chest; pres. Lansing Diocesan Area Sch. Bd.; mem. Lansing Diocese Bd. Edn.; former bd. dirs. Cath. Social Service Mich.; trustee Thomas Aquinas Coll. Club: Winged Foot Golf. Office: Thoma Corp 50 Main St Ste 1000 White Plains NY 10606

MCDADE, JAMES RUSSELL, management consultant; b. Dallas, Jan. 15, 1925; s. Marion W. and Jeannette (Reneau) McD.; m. Elaine Bushey, Sep. 10, 1955. BSEE, So. Meth. U., Dallas, 1947; MBA, Northwestern U., Evanston, Ill., 1950. Asst. to pres. Davidson Corp., Chgo., 1951-52; asst. to pres. Mergenthaler Linotype Co., Bklyn., 1952-53, comml. works mgr., 1953-56; chief indsl. engr. Tex. Instruments, Inc., Dallas, 1956-57, v.p., 1961-64; chmn. bd. McDade Properties Co., Aspen (Colo.), Denver, Dallas, 1964—; bd. dirs. Pitkin City Bank, Aspen; chmn. bd. dirs. Harley-Davidson Tex., Westec Security of Aspen, Aspen Security, Inc. Founding mem. Aspen Art Mus., 1980; mem. Ballet Aspen, 1980—; pres. club Aspen Valley Hosp., 1984—. Served to 1st lt. USAF, 1943-46. Mem. Rep. Senatorial Inner Circle, Am. Mgmt. Assn., Presidents Assn. Home and Office: 1000 Red Mountain Rd PO Box 9090 Aspen CO 81612

MCDANIEL, RAYMOND LAMAR, retired newspaper editor; b. Natalbany, La., Dec. 15, 1925; s. Franklin Pierce and Mattie (Stilley) McD.; m. Eugenia Hastings, Nov. 10, 1951; 1 son, Raymond Lamar. Student, Southeastern La. U., 1942-43; B.S., La. Tech. U., 1949. State editor Shreveport Times Pub. Co., La., 1950-53; legis. corr. Shreveport Times Pub. Co., 1953-58, city editor, 1958-68, exec. editor, 1968-74, editor, 1974-87. Chmn. bd. dirs. Bapt. Message; bd. dirs. Salvation Army, Teen Challenge. Served with USMCR, 1943-46. Mem. Sigma Delta Chi, Pi Kappa Alpha, Gamma Psi. Baptist (deacon, dir. ch.). Club: Rotarian. Home: 422 Ontario St Shreveport LA 71106 Office: 222 Lake St Shreveport LA 71101

MC DANIEL, RODERICK ROGERS, petroleum engineer; b. High River, Alta., Can., 1926; s. Dorsey Patton and Daisy (Rogers) McD.; m. Marilyn Bouck, Oct. 16, 1948; children: Nancy, Leslie. B.S., U. Okla., 1947. Petroleum reservoir engr. Creole Petroleum Corp., 1947; petroleum reservoir engr. Imperial Oil Ltd., 1948-52, chief reservoir engr., 1952-55; chmn. McDaniel Cons., Calgary, 1955—, PWA Corp, Calgary, 1975—; bd. dirs. Honeywell Can. Ltd., Prudential Steel Ltd., Can. Airlines Internat. Ltd., Wardair Can. Ltd. Hon. dir. Calgary Exhbn. and Stampede. Mem. Assn. Profl. Engrs. Alta. and Sask., Calgary C. of C. (past pres.). Mem. Progressive Conservative Party. Clubs: Calgary Petroleum (past pres.), Calgary Highlanders, Ranchmen's, Calgary Golf and Country; Outrigger (Honolulu). Home: 11 3231 Rideau Ridge Pl SW, Calgary, AB Canada T2S 2T1 Office: PWA Corp, 700 2nd St SW, Calgary, AB Canada T2P 2W2

MCDANIEL, TROY JACKSON, III, accountant; b. Atlanta, July 26, 1953; s. Troy Jackson Jr. and June Virginia (Dyar) McD.; m. Jean Allison Mueller, May 9, 1981. BBA magna cum laude, Valdosta State Coll., 1980; M in Taxation, Ga. State U., 1985. CPA, Ga. Night auditor Days Inn, Lake Park, Ga., 1979-80; staff acct. Draffin & Tucker, Moultrie, Ga., 1980, Robert E. Thigpen & Co., Dublin, Ga., 1980-81; tax acct. Waffle House, Inc., Atlanta, 1981-83; sr. tax acct. Arthur Andersen & Co., Atlanta, 1983-85; tax mgr., head tax dept. Hirsch, Babush, Neiman & Kornman, Atlanta, 1985—; frequent speaker, presenter seminars on taxes. Contbr. articles to profl. jours. Treas. Young Dems. Ga., Atlanta, 1982. Served to sgt. USAF, 1974-78. Named one of Outstanding Young Men of Am. U.S. Jaycees, 1982. Mem. Am. Inst. CPA's (tax div., accounting methods subcom.), Ga. Soc. CPA's (taxation com., com. to revise state tax laws 1986, vice chmn. taxation com.), Tucker (Ga.) Jaycees (v.p. 1982-83). Democrat. Episcopalian. Home: 1352 Mill Lake Circle Stone Mountain GA 30088 Office: Hirsch Babush Neiman & Kornman 3333 Peachtree Rd NE Suite 400 Atlanta GA 30326

MCDANIELS, JOHN FRANCIS, investment banker; b. Manchester, N.H., July 8, 1935; s. John Alexander and Dorothy Moulton (Gosselin) McD.; m. Beverley Cox, Oct. 25, 1958; children: Louise B., Andrea M., Robb A. AB, Brown U., 1957; JSD, Yale U., 1963. Bar: N.Y. 1963. Assoc. Davis Polk & Wardwell, N.Y.C. and Paris, 1963-68; v.p. First Boston Corp., N.Y.C. and London, 1969-73; chmn., mng. dir. Bankers Trust Internat. Ltd., London, 1973-80; sr. v.p. Bankers Trust Co., N.Y.C., 1980-81; mng. dir. Kidder, Peabody & Co. Inc., N.Y.C., 1982—. Lt. (j.g.) USN, 1957-60. Mem. Swiss Soc. N.Y., Belle Haven Club, Swiss Alpine Club (Lausanne, Switzerland), Union Club. Home: 78 Mayo Ave Greenwich CT 06830 Office: Kidder Peabody & Co Inc 10 Hanover Sq New York NY 10005

MC DERMID, RALPH MANEWAL, lawyer; b. Chgo., Feb. 7, 1909; s. Ralph and Lillian (Manewal) McD.; Ph.B., U. Chgo., 1935; J.D., Harvard U., 1938; m. Alice Connell, Nov. 28, 1931; children—Ralph Manewal, Jr., Jane (Mrs. Anders Wiberg), Michael Metcalf, John Fairbanks. Admitted to Ill. bar, 1938, N.Y. bar, 1938, then practiced in N.Y.C.; sr. and mng. partner firm Reid & Priest, N.Y.C., 1942-73; now engaged in practice of law Fed. Cts. Central Fla. Bd. dirs. Morse Gallery of Art Assocs., Friends of Winter Park Library, Loch Haven Art Center; bd. govs. Inst. of Living, Hartford, Conn.; mem. zoning bd. City of Winter Park, Fla. Mem. Am. Arbitration Soc. (Life Time award), Assn. Bar City N.Y., County N.Y. Bar Assn., Phi Delta Phi, English Speaking Union. Episcopalian. Clubs: Harvard (N.Y.C.); Capitol Hill (Washington); Racquet, Stag (pres.), University (v.p., chmn. fin. com.) (Winter Park, Fla.); Harvard of Central Fla. Home: 1445 Granville Dr Winter Park FL 32789

MCDERMOTT, RAYMUND GERALD, pulp and paper manufacturing company executive; b. Seattle, May 23, 1927; m. Phyllis Sanny. BA in Econs. and Bus., U. Wash., 1949. C.P.A., Wash. Jr. acct. Longview Fibre Co., Wash.; 1949-60, chief acct., asst. treas., 1960-67, treas., 1967, v.p. fin., 1975—; sec., 1980—, sr. v.p. finance, 1986—; also bd. dirs. Office: Longview Fibre Co PO Box 639 Longview WA 08632

MCDERMOTT, ROBERT GERARD, financial executive; b. Manhasset, N.Y., Mar. 30, 1963; s. John Francis and Maureen Gertrude (McGloin). BS magna cum laude, St. John's U., 1984; Cert. Fin. Planner, Adelphi U., 1986. News asst. NBC, N.Y.C., 1984, fin. analyst, 1986, ops. supr., 1986-87; exec. compensation and employee benefits analyst Coopers and Lybrand CPAs, N.Y.C., 1987—. Contbr. articles to newspapers. Insp. Nassau County Bd. Elections, N.Y., 1985. Mem. Inst. Cert. Fin. Planners. Republican. Roman Catholic. Home: 77 Adams Rd Central Islip NY 11722 Office: Coppers and Lybrand 1251 Ave of the Americas New York NY 10020

MCDERMOTT, THOMAS CURTIS, health care and consumer products company executive; b. Somerville, Mass., June 25, 1936; s. Thomas Curtis and Kathryn (Vinicomb) McD.; m. Gloria Newmark, June 7, 1958; children—Thomas, Mark, James, Andrew. B.S., Providence Coll. Mgr. corp. security Bristol Myers, N.Y.C., 1965-70; dir. personnel, indsl. relations E.R. Squibb & Son, Princeton, N.J., 1971-78; v.p. human resources Bausch & Lomb, Rochester, N.Y., 1978-80, sr. v.p. human resources, 1981-82, group pres., 1982-85, exec. v.p., pres. U.S. ops., 1985—, pres., chief operating officer, 1986—; v.p. human resources Gen. Cinema, Chestnut Hill, Mass., 1980-81; bd. dirs. Bausch & Lomb, Rochester, Chase Lincoln First Regional Bank. Trustee Rochester Inst. Tech. Served to 1st lt. U.S. Army, 1958-62. Mem. Soc. Former FBI Agts., Rochester C. of C. (bd. dirs.). Roman Catholic. Clubs: Genessee Valley (Rochester), Oak Hill Country. Home: 3465 East Ave Rochester NY 14618 *

MCDERMOTT, WILLIAM THOMAS, accountant, lawyer; b. New Orleans, Jan. 3, 1945; s. William Thomas and Delia Ethel (Belden) McD.; m. Geraldine Dorothy Constantine, Nov. 20, 1965; children: Lisa Anne, Shannon Marie. BSBA, Am. U., 1969, MBA, 1971; JD (with hon.), George Washington U., 1974. Ptnr. in charge tax Ernst & Whinney, Richmond, Va., 1969—; co-chmn. U. Va. Fed. Tax Conf., Charlottesville, 1981—. Contbr. articles to profl. jours. Past chmn. Richmond br. Tuckahoe YMCA bd., 1984; mem. citizens promotion bd. Henrico County Police Dept., Richmond, 1985; bd. dirs. Greater Richmond YMCA, 1983-84, Theater Va., Richmond, 1982—; treas., dir., mem. exec. com. Arts Coun. of Richmond, 1988—. Recipient Cert. Appreciation award Henrico County Police Dept., 1985, Karl B. Wagner Service award Tuckahoe YMCA, 1986. Mem. ABA, Am. Inst. CPA's, Nat. Assn. Accts. (nat. dir. 1987—, prin. Va. council, 1987-88), Va. Soc. CPA's, DC Inst. CPA's. Roman Catholic. Clubs: Hermitage Country; Bull and Bear. Home: 1701 Locust Hill Rd Richmond VA 23233 Office: Ernst & Whinney 901 E Cary St Richmond VA 23219

MCDONAGH, THOMAS JOSEPH, physician; b. N.Y.C., Feb. 29, 1932; s. John and Delia (Lee) McD.; m. Helen Marie Drury, May 18, 1957; children: Kevin T., Eileen D., Thomas J., Brian P., Patricia M. B.S., CCNY; M.D., Columbia U. Diplomate: Am. Bd. Internal Medicine. Intern Bronx Mcpl. Hosp., N.Y., 1957-58, resident, 1958-60; fellow in medicine, trainee in gastroenterology Albert Einstein Coll. Medicine, Bronx, 1960-62; pvt. practice internal medicine Coatesville, Pa., 1962-64; sr. physician Exxon Corp., N.Y.C., 1964-69, asst. med. dir., 1969-79; dir. medicine and environ. health Exxon Chem. Co., Darien, Conn., 1979-80, dir. medicine and environ. affairs, 1980-81; v.p. medicine and environ. health Exxon Corp., N.Y.C., 1981—; dir. medicine and environ. health Exxon Co. Internat., Florham Park, N.J., 1986—; vice chmn. exec. com., bd. dirs. Nat. Assn. Drug Abuse Problems, N.Y.C., 1981—; bd. dirs. Nat. Fund Med. Edn., Boston, 1983—. Contbr. articles in field to med. jours. Chmn. bd. appeals Inc. Village of Bellerose, N.Y., 1977-84, trustee, 1965-77, dep. mayor, 1975-77. Fellow Am. Coll. Occupational Medicine, ACP, Am. Coll. Preventive Medicine; mem. AMA, N.Y. Acad. Scis., N.Y. Acad Medicine. Roman Catholic. Office: Exxon Co Internat 200 Park Ave Florham Park NJ 07932

MCDONALD, CHARLES HARRISON, corporate professional; b. Evanston, Ill., Sept. 12, 1938; s. Grant Harold and Anita Lillian (Hutson) M.; m. Louise Vivian Proctor, Aug. 13, 1960; children: Steven, Cynthia. BS in Bus., Drake U., 1960; MBA, U. Wis., 1961, MA, 1983. Personnel mgr. Meredith Corp., Des Moines, 1965-73; v.p. human resources Allied Group, Des Moines, 1973—; bd. dirs. Allied Group Securities Corp., Des Moines. V.p., bd. dirs. Day Care Services Inc., Des Moines, 1985; bd. dirs. Des Moines Employee Assistance Program, 1986—. 1st lt., USAF, 1961-65; col., USAFR. Mem. Iowa Psychol. Assn. Am. Soc. Personnel Adminstrs. (pres. 1971), Am. Psychol. Assn., Air Force Assn. Republican. Methodist. Clubs: Des Moines Golf and Country (W. Des Moines, Iowa), Bohemian (Des Moines). Office: Allied Group Box 974 701 Fifth Ave Des Moines IA 50304

MCDONALD, CORNELIUS (CON) TRAWICK, investment company executive, consultant; b. Chapel Hill, N.C., Dec. 6, 1955; s. Cornelius (Con) Trawick and Sara (Stacy) McD.; m. Rosemary Irene Anderson, Aug. 4, 1979; 1 child, Thomas Trawick. BSBA, U. N.C., 1979. Registered investment advisor. Acct. Gilliam Coble and Moser, Burlington, N.C., 1979-80; corp. acct. Oakwood Homes Corp., Greensboro, N.C., 1980-84; investment planning The Fin. Group, Inc., Greensboro, N.C., 1984-87; agt. Home Life Ins. Co., Greensboro, N.C., 1984-87; registered rep. Sentra/WS Griffith, Greensboro, N.C., 1984-87, Capital Investment Group, Inc., Raleigh, N.C., 1987—; rep. Capital Investment Counsel, Inc., Raleigh, N.C., 1987—; pres. Planned Fin. Strategies, Inc., Raleigh, N.C., 1987—, Physicians Fin. Svcs., Inc., Raleigh, N.C., 1987—; bd. dirs. Pinehurst (N.C.) Industries, Inc., The Fin. Group, Inc. Editor: (newsletter) Financial Concepts Quarterly, 1986—; writer (editorial) Greensboro Record, 1986; contbr. articles to fin. mags. Fund raiser Boys Club of Wake County, Raleigh, 1988, U. N.C., Greensboro, 1984. Named Hon. Citizen of Tex. State of Tex, Austin, 1978. Mem. Life Underwriters Assn., Brandt Village Assn. (bd. dirs. 1985-87), Nat. Assn. Accts., N.C. CPA Assn. (assoc.), Internat. Assn. Fin. Planners, Nat. Assn. Security Dealers (registered), Toastmasters, Kappa Alpha. Republican. Presbyterian. Office: Physicians Fin Svcs PO Box 32249 Raleigh NC 27622

MCDONALD, DESMOND P., banker; b. Carlow, Ireland, 1927; came to U.S., 1953; Pres., dir. Midlantic Nat. Bank, Newark; dir. Midlantic Corp., K. Hovnanian Enterprises Inc. Office: Midlantic Nat Bank 80 Park Pla Newark NJ 07102

MCDONALD, EUGENE JOHN, healthcare executive; b. Jersey City, N.J., Aug. 25, 1948; s. Eugene John and Mary Rose (Manzo) McD.; m. Darlie Irene Wasicek, June 25, 1983. BS in mktg., Monmouth Coll., 1971; MBA in Mktg., U. New Haven, 1977. Registered account exec. Harris, Upham & Co., Shrewsbury, N.J., 1972-73; hosp. acct. rep. Miles Labs., West Haven, Conn., 1973-75, test market specialist, 1975-77; product mgr. Baxter Travenol Corp., Deerfield, Ill., 1977-78; mgr. new products U.S. Surg. Corp., Norwalk, Conn., 1978-79; mgr. N. Am. Beiersdorf, A.G., Hamburg, Fed. Republic of Germany, 1979-81; v.p. sales and mktg. Beiersdorf, Inc., South Norwalk, Conn., 1981-84; exec. v.p., gen. mgr. Martin U.S.A., Inc., Stamford, Conn., 1984-88; pres. McDonald Mgmt. Cons., Trumbull, Conn., 1988—. Republican. Roman Catholic. Home: 208 Pinewood Trail Trumbull CT 06611 Office: McDonald Mgmt Cons 208 Pinewood Trail Trumbull CT 06611

MC DONALD, HUGH RODERICK, lawyer; b. Brookville, Ont., Can., Mar. 31, 1929; s. Alexander Joseph and Margaret Isobel (McHenry) McD.; B.Comm., U. Ottawa, 1954; Barrister-at-law, Osgoode Hall, 1960; m. Joan Dorothy Gourley, Oct. 6, 1962; 1 son, Patrick Joseph. Called to bar, 1960; asso. firm Low, Honeywell, Murchison, Burns, 1960-70; individual practice law, Nepean, Ont., 1970-78; partner firm McDonald & Landry, Nepean, 1978—. Mem. Nepean Twp. Hydro Commn., 1968-76, chmn., 1971; alderman City of Nepean, 1978-85, police commr., 1984—; sec. Ottawa-Centre Liberal Assn., 1962-79. Served to lt. Royal Can. Navy, 1946-51, 54-56. Mem. Can. Bar Assn., Law Soc. Upper Can., Carleton County Law Assn., Delta Chi. Liberal Party. Roman Catholic. Club: Kiwanis. Home: 5 Tower Rd, Nepean, ON Canada K2G 2E2 Office: 303-1580 Merivale Rd, Nepean, ON Canada K2G 4B5

MCDONALD, JOHN FRANCIS PATRICK, electrical engineering educator; b. Narberth, Pa., Jan. 14, 1942; s. Frank Patrick and Lulu Ann (Hegedus) McD.; m. Karen Marie Knapp, May 26, 1979. B.S.E.E., MIT, 1963; M.S. in Engring., Yale U., 1965, Ph.D., 1969. Instr. Yale U., New Haven, 1968-69, asst. prof., 1969-74; assoc. prof. Rensselaer Poly. Inst., Troy, N.Y., 1974-86, prof., 1986—; founder Rensselaer Ctr. for Integrated Electronics, 1980—. Contbr. articles to profl. publs. Patentee in field. Recipient numerous grants, 1974—. Mem. ACM, IEEE, Optical Soc., Acoustical Soc., Vacuum Soc. Office: Rensselaer Poly Inst Ctr for Integrated Electronics Troy NY 12065

MCDONALD, JOHN GREGORY, finance educator; b. Stockton, Calif., May 21, 1937; s. Earl and Dora (Mitchell) McD.; m. Melody McDonald, June 19, 1973. BS, Stanford U., 1960, MBA, 1962, PhD, 1967. Asst. prof. fin. Stanford U., 1968-71, assoc. prof., 1971-75, prof., 1975-78, Joseph McDonald prof. fin., 1979-87; The Indsl. Bank of Japan Profs., 1987—; bd. dir. Investment Co. Am., New Perspective Fund, EuroPacific Growth Fund, Scholastic, Inc.; mem. adv. bd. InterWest Venture Capital; mem. pension bd. Varian Assocs.; vis. prof. U. Paris, 1972, Columbia U., 1975, Harvard U., 1986. With 25th Inf. Div., U.S. Army, 1962-64. Fulbright fellow, Paris, 1967-68. Mem. Nat. Assn. Security Dealers (bd. govs. 1987—, vice chmn. bd.). Office: Stanford U Grad Sch Bus Stanford CA 94305

MC DONALD, MARSHALL, holding company executive; b. Memphis, Mar. 30, 1918; s. Marshall and Nadine (Hardin) McD.; m. Florence Harris, Jan. 10, 1952 (dec. Nov. 1963); m. Lucille Smoak Collins, May 7, 1965 (dec. Sept. 1980); m. Barbara Hatcher Poole, Dec. 31, 1983; children: Mary Linda Caton, Charles M. Collins, Cynthia Langston, Marshall III, Roger Collins, Davis, James D. B.S. in Bus. Adminstrn, U. Fla., 1939, LL.B., 1941; M.B.A., U. Pa., 1947. Bar: Fla. 1941, Tex. 1949; CPA, Tex. Acct. Houston, 1947-49, atty., 1950-52; treas. Gulf Canal Lines, 1953-54; pres. Investment Co. Houston 1955-58; v.p. Sinclair Oil & Gas Co., Tulsa, 1959-61; v.p., gen. mgr. Oil Recovery Corp., Tulsa, 1962-63; asst. to pres. Pure Oil Co., Palatine, Ill., 1964-65; dir. affiliated cos. Union Oil Co., Los Angeles, 1966-68; pres. Sully-Miller Contracting Co., Los Angeles, 1968-71; pres., chief exec. officer Fla. Power & Light Co., Miami, 1971-79, chmn., chief exec. officer, 1979-83, chmn. bd., 1983-86; pres., chief exec. officer FPL Group, Inc. (parent co.), Juno Beach, Fla., 1984-88, chmn. bd. dirs., 1988—. Served with AUS, 1941-46. Mem. Alpha Tau Omega. Democrat. Presbyterian. Lodge: Masons. Office: FPL Group Inc PO Box 14000 Juno Beach FL 33408

MCDONALD, MARY FARREN, engineering manager; b. Providence, Nov. 24, 1956; d. Roger Patrick and Margaret Theresa (Arkins) Farren; m. William Peter McDonald, May 7, 1983. BS in Environ. Engring., Worcester Poly. Inst., 1979; MS in Indsl. Adminstrn., Union Coll., 1985. Environ. engr. IBM, Poughkeepsie, N.Y., 1979-81, mfg. engr., 1981-85; product assurance engr. IBM, East Fishkill, N.Y., 1985-86; engring mgr. IBM, Hopewell Junction, N.Y., 1986—; chmn. tech. session on packaging reliability, 1987. Contbr. articles to profl. publs. Mem. Internat. Electronics Packaging Soc. (chpt. pres. 1986-88, nat. v.p. 1987—). Office: IBM Rte 52 Box 600 Zip E60 Hopewell Junction NY 12533

MCDONALD, MARY LYNNE, financial executive; b. Indpls., Jan. 22, 1946; d. Marvin Douglas and Helen Elizabeth (Beer) Coates; m. Michael Paul McDonald; Oct. 13, 1970; 1 child by previous marriage, Tammy Sue Stange; children by present marriage: Susan Elizabeth, Michael Paul Jr. Cert. fin. planning, Coll. Fin. Planning, Denver, 1986. Bus. devel. officer Citizens Fed. Savs. & Loan Assn., Tacoma and Seattle, 1978-80; fin. planning officer Citizens Fed. Savs. & Loan Assn., Tacoma and Bellevue, Wash., 1980-82; fin. planner McDonald & Assocs., Tacoma, 1982—; pres., fin. planner Pacific N.W. Fin. Group, Inc., Tacoma, 1985—; tchr. Gig Harbor Sch. Dist., 1985, Tacoma Community Coll., 1985—, Spanaway Sch. Dist., 1988; lectr. Tacoma Women's Conf., 1987. Contbr. articles to profl. jours. Mem. Western Wash. Internat. Assn. Fin. Planning (ethics editor 1983-84, conf. co-chmn. 1985-86), Internat. Assn. Fin. Planning (v.p. edn. 1986-87), Tacoma Pierce County C. of C., Nat. Assn. Accts., Inst. Cert. Fin. Planners, Internat. Assn. Fin. Planning (bd. dirs. 1987—). Republican. Office: Pacific NW Fin Group Inc 700 Market St #500 Tacoma WA 98402

MCDONALD, PAYTON RAY, III, sales executive; b. Birmingham, Ala., Mar. 11, 1953; s. Payton Ray Jr. and Helen Goodall (Blair) McD.; m. Laurie Jean Bickett, July 6, 1974; children: Crystal Lee, James Payton. BS, Rider Coll., 1979. Credit cashier New Ideal, Birmingham, 1974; rsch. technician Personal Products Corp., Milltown, N.J., 1974-75; from cost acctg. clk. to raw materials acct. J&J Products, Inc., Piscataway, N.J., 1975-79; sr. mktg. budget analyst patient care div. J&J Products, Inc., New Brunswick, N.J.,

1979; from sr. brand analyst to sr. fin. coord. J&J Orthopaedic div. J&J Products, Inc., New Brunswick and Boston, 1979-82; mgr. mktg. info. systems J&J Products, Inc., New Brunswick, 1982-83; mgr. mktg. fin. J&J Hosp. Svcs., New Brunswick, 1983-85; contr. Intraocular Lens div. CILCO, Inc., Huntington, W.Va., 1985-86; dir. mktg. and sales fin. CooperVision CILCO, Bellevue, Wash., 1986; dir. sales ops. CooperVision CILCO, Bellevue, 1986—; v.p. mem. rels. Nat. Assn. Accts., Piscataway, 1976-77. Treas. Birchwood Heights Homeowners Assn., Lebanon, N.J., 1984. Mem. Internat. Customer Svc. Assn. Republican. Presbyterian. Home: 2855 220th Pl NE Redmond WA 98053 Office: CooperVision CILCO 3326 160th Ave SE Bellevue WA 98008-5496

MCDONALD, PEGGY ANN STIMMEL, automobile company official; b. Darbyville, Ohio, Aug. 25, 1931; d. Wilbur Smith and Bernice Edna (Hott) Stimmel; missionary diploma with honor Moody Bible Inst., 1952; B.A. cum laude in Econs. (scholar), Ohio Wesleyan U., 1965; M.B.A. with distinction, Xavier U., 1977; m. George R. Stich, Mar. 7, 1953 (dec.); 1 son, Mark Stephen (dec.); m. Joseph F. McDonald, Jr., Feb. 1, 1986. . Missionary in S. Am., Evang. Alliance Mission, 1956-61; cost acct. Western Electric Co., 1965-66; acctg. mgr. Ohio Wesleyan U., 1966-73; fin. specialist NCR Corp., 1973-74, systems analyst, 1974-75, supr. inventory planning, 1975, mgr. material planning and purchasing control, 1976-78; materials mgr. U.S. Elec. Motors Co., 1978; with Gen. Motors Corp., 1978—, shift supt. materials, Lakewood, Ga., 1979-80, gen. ops. supr. material data base mgmt. Central Office, Warren, Mich., 1980, dir. material mgmt. GM Truck and Bus. div., Balt., 1980-87; vis. lectr. Inst. Internat. Trade, Jiao Tong U., Shanghai, China, 1985, Inst. Econs. and Fgn. Trade, Tianjin, China, 1986-87; part time instr. Towson (Md.) State U., 1986-87. Mem. Am. Prodn. and Inventory Control Soc., Am. Soc. Women Accts., AAUW, Balt. Exec. Women's Network, Balt. Council on Fgn. Relations, Baptist. Home: 125 Arbutus Ave Baltimore MD 21228 Office: GM Truck and Bus 2122 Broening Hwy PO Box 148 Baltimore MD 21203

MCDONALD, PETER RICHARD, automobile club executive; b. Winchester, Mass., Feb. 11, 1947; s. John James and Margaret Christine (Flaherty) M.; m. Barbara Ann Fritsch, Aug. 7, 1971; one child, Amy Colleen. BA, Marquette U., 1969; MBA, U. West Fla., 1976. Commd. 2d lt. USMC, 1969, advanced through grades to capt., 1973, resigned, 1977; controller Container Corp. Am., Shelby, N.C., 1977-80; sr. fin. analyst Container Corp. Am., Chgo., 1980-81; regional controller Container Corp. Am., Santa Clara, Calif., 1981-85; dir. fin. controls Auto Club So. Calif., Los Angeles, 1985—. Mem. Fin. Execs. Inst., Inst. Internal Auditors, Nat. Assn. Accts. Office: Automobile Club So Calif 2601 S Figueroa St Los Angeles CA 90007

MCDONALD, PEYTON DEAN, brokerage house executive; b. Kansas City, Kans., Feb. 6, 1936; s. Charles H. and Myra (Miller) McD.; m. Frances B. Beighley, June 14, 1958; children: Peyton D., Todd B. BS, Bucknell U., 1958. Sales rep. Sprout Waldron and Co., Inc., Muncy, Pa., 1958-67; v.p. Blair & Co., Williamsport, Pa., 1967-69; v.p., mgr. Hugh Johnson, Williamsport, 1969-77, E.F. Hutton & Co. Inc., Williamsport, 1977-87; 1st v.p. Shearson Lehman Hutton, Williamsport, 1987—; mem. N.Y. Stock Exchange; pres. Hope Enterprizes. Pres. United Way, Williamsport, 1977-80, Williamsport Coll. Found., 1985-86; campaign chmn. Heinz for Senator, Lycoming County, Pa., 1978. 1st lt. U.S. Army, 1958-59. Republican. Presbyterian. Clubs: Ross (Willamsport), Williamsport Country. Lodge: Masons. Home: 1545 Grampian Blvd Williamsport PA 17701

MCDONALD, RANDAL B., oil production company executive; b. 1930. BBA, U. Tex., 1952. With Arthur Andersen and Co., until 1987; pres., chief operating officer Pennzoil Co., Houston, 1987-88, pres., chief exec. officer, 1988—. Office: Pennzoil Co PO Box 2967 Houston TX 77252 *

MCDONALD, W. R., employee benefits consultant, developer; b. Mt. Vernon, Ill., Nov. 1, 1929; s. Archie R. and Vernadean Pearl (Bailey) McD. BS, Ind. State U., 1953. Pres. Youth, Inc., Terre Haute, Ind., 1947; dist. mgr. New Eng. Life Ins. Co., Sacramento, 1958-62; v.p. Sutter Sq., Inc., Sacramento, 1960-62, Southland Trust Co., Tucson, 1963-65, Am. Equity Group, Inc., Indpls., 1966-68; sr. ptnr. Ins. Investors' Guidance Systems, Mt. Vernon, 1972—; pres. Interstate Investors & Growers Syndicate, Inc., Indpls., 1975—; mng. ptnr. Halia Crest Land Trust, Mt. Vernon, 1977-79; pres. Intermed. Self-Ins. Group, Mt. Vernon, 1979—; sr. gen. ptnr. Interstate Investors Golf and Garden Solar Lodges, 1980—, Investors Strategies Group, St. Louis, 1982-85, Internat. Benefits Adv. Group, St. Louis, 1984; mng. gen. ptnr. Sundowners' Retirement Resorts, 1986—; bd. dirs. Southland Trust Life Ins. Co., Phoenix, 1964; cons. So. Ill. U., Carbondale, 1973, 84—; mktg. cons. Total Health Care, Inc., Centralia, Ill., 1986—. Chmn. United Crusade, Sacramento, 1960; chmn. bd. dirs. Salvation Army, Sacramento, 1961; bd. dirs. USO, 1962. Served with USAF, 1951-57. Recipient Outstanding Flight Officer Achievement cert. USAF, 1957; named Disting. Grad., Aviation Cadets, 1952, U.S. Rookie of Year, New Eng. Life Ins. Co., 1959. Mem. Mt. Vernon C. of C. Republican. Lodge: Civitan (Sacramento Internat. chpt. pres. 1961). Office: PO Box 946 Mount Vernon IL 62864 also: 11 S Meridian Ste 810 Indianapolis IN 46204

MCDONNELL, DENNIS J., securities industry executive; b. Chgo., May 20, 1942; s. Lawrence J. and Eleanor (Lama) McD.; m. Sabina Bielawski, Oct. 16, 1974 (div. Aug. 1979). B.S. in Econs., Loyola U., Chgo., 1965; M.A. in Econs., UCLA, 1969. Vice pres. Continental Bank, Chgo., 1969-83; pres., dir. Van Kampen Merritt Investment Adv Corp. (formerly Am. Portfolio Adv. Svc.), Lisle, Ill., 1983—; sr. v.p. Van Kampen Merritt, Inc., Naperville, Ill., 1983—; dir. McCarthy, Crisanti & Maffei, Inc., N.Y.C., Van Kampen Merritt Life Mktg., Inc., Lisle. Lt. USN, 1965-68. Mem. Mcpl. Analyst Soc. Chgo. (pres. 1978-79), Nat. Fedn. Mcpl. Analysts, Mcpl. Bond Club Chgo., Columbia Yacht Club. Roman Catholic. Office: Am Portfolio Adv Svc 1001 Warrenville Rd Lisle IL 60532 also: Van Kampen Merritt US Govt Fund Inc 1901 N Naper Blvd Naperville IL 60566

MC DONNELL, EDWARD FRANCIS, distillery executive; b. Boston, July 27, 1935; s. John and Margaret (O'Neill) McD.; m. Catherine McNamara, July 18, 1959; children: Edward, Paul, Elizabeth. B.S., Suffolk U., 1959. With Raytheon Co., 1960-64, bus. mgr. radio and TV tube op., 1965-66; with Gen. Foods Corp., 1966-75; fin. ops. mgr. Gen. Foods Internat., 1966-67, asst. to pres., 1968; pres., chief exec. officer Gen. Foods Internat. (Kibin S.P. subs.), Brazil, 1969-75; with Pillsbury Co., Mpls., 1975-81; corp. exec. v.p., pres. Pillsbury Internat., 1978-81; v.p. Pillsbury Internat., Europe, 1977-81; pres. internat. group Seagram's & Sons, N.Y.C., 1981—; now exec. v.p. internat. Joseph E. Seagram and Sons Inc., N.Y.C. Office: Seagram & Son 375 Park Ave New York NY 10152 *

MCDONNELL, EDWARD JOE, business educator; b. Borger, Tex., Mar. 11, 1936; s. Lloyd Clyde and Edlina (Roscoe) McD.; m. Sharon Snyder, Dec. 30, 1958 (div. Jan. 1964); 1 child, Brian Edward. AA, East Los Angeles Coll., 1966; BS, Pepperdine U., 1969; MBA, U. So. Calif., 1970; postgrad., U.S. Internat. U., 1982—. Sales rep. Standard Register Co., Long Beach, Calif., 1960-63; sales rep., contract mgr. Soulé Steel Co., Los Angeles, 1963-67; dist. sales rep., contract mgr. Allison Steel Co., Santa Fe Springs, Calif., 1967-68; mem. faculty Los Angeles City Coll., 1970—, instr., 1970-71; area adminstr. Los Angeles City Coll., Taiwan and Philippines, 1971-72; prof. bus. adminstrn. Los Angeles City Coll., 1972—; lectr. Am. Mgmt. Assn., Calif., 1987&; cons. in bus. adminstrn., Los Angeles, 1980—; advisor Computer Info. Systems Woodbury U., Burbank, Calif., 1987—. Asst. to author H. Igor Angoff in revision of book: Corporate Strategy, 1988. Mem. Acad. Mgmt., Strategic Mgmt. Assn., Calif. Ednl. Computing Consortium, Commerce Assocs. U. So. Calif. Home: 5335 Via San Delarro Los Angeles CA 90022 Office: Los Angeles City Coll 855 N Vermont Los Angeles CA 90029

MCDONNELL, JOHN FINNEY, aerospace and aircraft manufacturing executive; b. Mar. 18, 1938; s. James Smith and Mary Elizabeth (Finney) McD.; m. Anne Marbury, June 16, 1961. BS in Aero. Engring., Princeton U., 1960, MS in Aero. Engring., 1962; postgrad. in bus. adminstrn. Washington U., St. Louis, 1962-66. Strength engr. McDonnell Aircraft Co. (subs. McDonnell Douglas Corp.), St. Louis, 1962, corp. analyst, 1963-65, contract coordinator, adminstr., 1965-68; asst. to v.p. fin. Douglas Aircraft Co. (subs. McDonnell Douglas Corp.), 1968; v.p. McDonnell Douglas Fin. Corp. (subs. McDonnell Douglas Corp.), 1968-71; staff v.p. fiscal McDonnell Douglas Corp., 1971-75, corp. v.p. fin. and devel., 1975-77, corp. exec. v.p., 1977-80, pres., 1980—, mem. exec. com., 1975—, chmn. and chief exec. officer, 1988—, also bd. dirs.; chmn. McDonnell Douglas Computer Systems Co. Mem. Com. Decent Unbiased Campaign Tactics; bd. commrs. St. Louis Sci. Ctr.; trustee KETC, Washington U. Office: McDonnell Douglas Corp PO Box 516 Saint Louis MO 63166 *

MCDONNELL, SANFORD NOYES, aircraft company executive; b. Litte Rock, Oct. 12, 1922; s. William Archie and Carolyn (Cherry) McD.; m. Priscilla Robb, Sept. 3, 1946; children: Robbin McDonnell MacVittie, William Randall. BA in Econs., Princeton U., 1945; BS in Mech. Engring., U. Colo., 1948; MS in Applied Mechanics, Washington U., St. Louis, 1954. With McDonnell Douglas Corp. (formerly McDonnell Aircraft Corp.), St. Louis, 1948—, v.p., 1959-66, pres. McDonnell Aircraft div., 1966-71, corp. exec. v.p., 1971, corp. pres., 1971—, chief exec. officer, 1972—, chmn., 1980-88, chmn. emeritus, 1988—, also bd. dirs.; bd. dirs. Boatmen's Bancorp., St. Louis, Squibb Corp. Active St. Louis United Way; mem. exec. bd. St. Louis and nat. councils Boy Scouts Am.; trustee, elder Presbyn. Ch. Fellow AIAA; mem. Navy League U.S. (life), Tau Beta Pi. Office: McDonnell Douglas Corp PO Box 516 Saint Louis MO 63166

MCDONOUGH, JOHN PATRICK, financial executive; b. Boston, Dec. 10, 1959; s. Colman J. and Beatrice E. (O'Dowd) McD.; m. Lori J. Matuszek, Aug. 19, 1984; 1 child, Christopher. BBA, Stonehill Coll., North Easton, Mass., 1981. CPA, Mass., N.H. Sr. acct. Deloitte Haskins & Sells, Boston, 1981-83; controller Ovation Tech., Norwood, Mass., 1983-85; dir. fin. and adminstrn. Interactive Images, Inc., Woburn, Mass., 1985-86, v.p. fin. and adminstrn., 1986—. Mem. Am. Inst. CPA's, N.H. Soc. CPA's (industry com.), Mass. Soc. CPA's, SBA, Assn. Data Processing Service Orgns. (chief fin. officers' Roundtable). Roman Catholic. Home: 50 Shasta Dr Londonderry NH 03053 Office: Interactive Images Inc 600 West Cummins Park Woburn MA 01801

MC DONOUGH, RICHARD DOYLE, paper company executive; b. St. Stephen, N.B., Can., May 8, 1931; s. Kenneth Paul and Mary (Doyle) McD.; m. Caroline Wilkins, July 7, 1956; children: Elizabeth Wilkins, Richard David, Philip Bradford. AB, Dartmouth Coll., 1952. Mgmt. trainee Gen. Electric Co., Lynn, Mass., 1953-56; various fin. positions lamp div. Gen. Electric Co., Monterrey, Mex., 1956-59; controller Mexican subs. Gen. Electric Co., Mexico City, 1959-63; cost supr. Singer Co., N.Y.C., 1964; fin. dir. Singer Co., Clydesbank, Scotland, 1965-66; controller Eur. div. Singer Co., London, 1967-69; v.p. Singer Co., N.Y.C., 1969-73; pres. mail order div. Singer Co., London, 1973-76, v.p., 1976-79; sr. v.p., chief fin. officer Bowater Co., Darien, Conn., 1979—. Mem. Am. Petroleum Inst. (fin. com. 1908—, steering com. 1987), Fin. Execs. Inst., Nat. Assn. Accts., Morris Country Golf Club, Greenwich Country Club. Republican. Episcopalian. Home: Barons Mead E Point Ln Old Greenwich CT 06870 Office: Bowater Inc 1 Parklands Dr Box 4012 Darien CT 06820

MCDONOUGH, WILLIAM J., banker; b. Chgo., 1934; married. B.S., Coll. of Holy Cross, 1956; M.A., Georgetown U., 1962. Spl. asst. to ambassador to Uruguay, 1961-67, sr. economist Inter-Am. affairs, 1961-67; with 1st Nat. Bank of Chgo., 1967—, asst. v.p. internat. banking dept., 1967-70; v.p., gen. mgr. 1st Nat. Bank of Chgo., Paris, 1970-72; area head, Europe, Middle East and Africa 1st Nat. Bank of Chgo., 1972-73, sr. v.p., head internat. banking dept., 1973-75, exec. v.p., 1975—; chief fin. officer 1st Nat. Bank of Chgo., Chgo., 1982—; chmn. asset and liability mgmt. com. 1st Nat. Bank of Chgo.; vice chmn. 1st Chgo. Corp. and 1st Nat. Bank Chgo., 1986—, also bd. dirs., vice chmn., 1986—. Served to lt. USN, 1956-61. Office: First Chgo Corp 1 First National Pla Chicago IL 60670

MCDOUGALL, GEORGE DOUGLAS, engineering consultant; b. Indpls., July 20, 1930; s. Shirley Alton and Deborah Cleveland (Hall) McD.; student Asbury Coll., 1949-51, Mt. San Antonio Coll., 1960-61, Milw. Sch. Engring., 1977, Calif. State Poly. U., 1978; m. Maria Celia Velasquez, Aug. 4, 1956. Surveyor, Tidelands Exploration Co., Houston, 1954; with Vard, Inc., Pasadena, Calif., 1954-60, Gen. Dynamics, Pomona, Calif., 1960-62; researcher Aerojet Gen. Corp., Azusa, Calif., 1962-68; engr. Davidson Optronics, West Covina, Calif., 1968-69; mfg. mgr. Angeles Metal Systems, L.A., 1969-79; cons. Fremont Gen. Corp., L.A., 1979—; mem. automation rsch. project Inst. Indsl. Relations, U. So. Calif., 1966-68; mem. rsch. team U.S. Govt./U. So. Calif., 1979-81. Adv. bd. Automobile Club So. Calif., 1966-71; bd. dirs. St. Martha's Episcopal Sch., West Covina, 1978-81; lic. lay reader Episcopal Diocese of L.A.; vestryman St. Martha's Episc. Ch., West Covina, 1969-70, 77-79, 81-83; mem. U.S. Congl. Adv. Bd., 1982—; gen. conv. del. Episc. Diocese of L.A., 1970-78; instnl. rep. Boy Scouts Am., 1978-79, coord. San Gabriel Valley council, 1978-79. With JAGC, AUS, 1951-53, Korea. Cert. in mfg. engring., Canadian Council Profl. Cert., 1977; registered profl. engr., Calif. Fellow Internat. Biog. Assn.; mem. Soc. Engrs. (exec. council, sec. 1982; cert.), Computer and Automated Systems Assn. (charter), Nat. Soc. Profl. Engrs., Am. Soc. Safety Engrs., Calif. Soc. Profl. Engrs. (v.p.), Clan MacDougall Soc. U.S. and Can. (life), Highlands Clans and Family Soc. (exec. council 1982), St. Andrews Soc. L.A. (life), 101st Airborne Div. Assn. (life), Am. Legion, SAR, Town Hall of Calif. Club, Masons (life), Shriners. Republican. Home: PO Box 848 Azusa CA 91702 Office: Fremont Gen Corp 9 W 8th St Los Angeles CA 90017

MCDOWELL, CHARLES PATRICK, aerospace company executive; b. Fayetteville, N.C., July 27, 1950; s. Charles Taylor and Mary Frances (Johnson) McD.; m. Louanne Hall, Mar. 4, 1978; children: Charles Caley, Angela Kathleen. BA, U. Tex., Arlington, 1974; MS in Sci., Nat. Execs. Inst., Mendham. N.J., 1976. Exploring exec. Boy Scouts Am., Ft. Worth, 1976-78; program mgr. Menasco Aerosystems div. Colt Industries, Ft. Worth, 1978-82, mktg. mgr., 1982-87, mgr. program devel., 1987—. Campaign chmn. United Way Met. Tarrant Cpounty 1984; mem. exec. bd. Longhorn coun. Boy Scouts Am., Ft. Worth. Mem. Am. Mgmt. Assn., Def. Preparedness Assn., Air Force Assn., Assn. U.S. Army, Nat. Bus. Aircraft Assn., Ducks Unltd., Kiwanis, Pro 35 Club (Arlington, Tex.). Republican. Methodist. Home: 3200 Tranquility St Arlington TX 76016 Office: Colt Industries Menasco Aerosystems Div PO Box 500 Euless TX 76039

MCDOWELL, GEORGE EDWARD, manufacturing executive; b. St. Louis, Feb. 15, 1944; s. Frank and Mary Elizabeth (Neal) McD. BA, Washington U., St. Louis, 1966; MBA, Drury Coll., 1968. CPA, Hawaii. Cost analyst Ford Motor Co., St. Louis, 1968-73; acctg. supr. ITT Grinnell Corp. subs Internat. Telephone and Telegraph Corp., Elmira, N.Y., 1973-74; acctg. mgr. Emerson Electric, St. Louis, 1974-76; data processing mgr. Ethyl Corp., St. Louis, 1976-84; v.p. Clayton Corp., St. Louis, 1984—; instr. Belleville (Ill.) Area Coll., 1982—. Contbr. articles to profl. jours. Served with U.S. Army, 1968-70. Mem. Am. Inst. CPA's, Mo. Soc. CPA's. Home: 657 Craig Woods Dr Kirkwood MO 63122 Office: Clayton Corp 866 Horan Dr Fenton MO 63026

MCDOWELL, JENNIFER, sociologist, playwright, publisher; b. Albuquerque, May 19, 1936; d. Willard A. and Margaret Frances (Garrison) McD.; m. Milton Loventhal, July 2, 1973. BA, U. Calif., 1957, MLS, 1963; MA, San Diego State U., 1958; PhD, U. Oreg., 1973. Tchr. English Abraham Lincoln High Sch., San Jose, Calif., 1960-61; freelance editor Soviet field, Berkeley, Calif., 1961-63; research asst. sociology U. Oreg., Eugene, 1964-66; editor, pub. Merlin Papers, San Jose, 1969—, Merlin Press, San Jose, 1973—; research cons. sociology San Jose, 1973—; music pub. Lipstick and Toy Balloons Pub. Co., San Jose, 1978—; composer Paramount Pictures, 1982-88; tchr. writing workshops; poetry readings, 1969-73; co-producer radio show lit. and culture Sta. KALX, Berkeley, 1971-72. Author: Black Politics: A Study and Annotated Bibliography of the Mississippi Freedom Democratic Party, 1971, Contemporary Women Poets: An Anthology of California Poets, 1977, Ronnie Goose Rhymes for Grown-ups, 1984; co-author (plays off-off Broadway) Betsy and Phyllis, 1986, Mack The Knife Your Friendly Dentist, 1986, The Estrogen Party To End War, 1986, The Oatmeal Party Comes to Order, 1986; contbr. poems, plays, essays, short stories, book revs. to lit. mags. and anthologies; researcher women's autobiog. writings, contemporary writings in poetry, Soviet studies, civil rights movement and George Orwell, 1962—; writer: (songs) Money Makes A Woman Free, 1976, 3 songs featured in Parade of Am. Music; co-creator: musical comedy Russia's Secret Plot to Take Back Alaska, 1988. Recipient 8 awards Am. Song Festival, 1976-79, Bill Casey award in Letters, 1980; AAUW doctoral fellow, 1971-73; grantee Calif. Arts Council, 1976-77. Mem. Am. Sociol. Assn., Soc. Sci. Study of Religion, Soc. Study of Religion under Communism, Poetry Orgn. for Women, Dramatists Guild, Phi Beta Kappa, Sigma Alpha Iota, Beta Phi Mu, Kappa Kappa Gamma. Democrat. Office: care Merlin Press PO Box 5602 San Jose CA 95150

MCDOWELL, MICHAEL DAVID, lawyer, utility executive; b. Lewisburg, Pa., May 10, 1948; s. David Leonard and Mary Ellen (Scallan) McD.; m. Martha LaMantia, Aug. 4, 1973; 1 child, Daniel Joseph. B.S. in Bus. Mgmt., U. Dayton, 1970; J.D., U. Pitts., 1973. Bar: Pa. 1973, U.S. Dist. Ct. (mid. dist.) Pa. 1973, U.S. Tax Ct. 1974, U.S. Ct. Appeals (3d cir.) 1974, U.S. Dist. Ct. (we. dist.) Pa. 1975, U.S. Supreme Ct. 1977, U.S. Ct. Internat. Trade 1981, U.S. Ct. Appeals (fed. cir.) 1982. Asst. U.S. atty. Dept. Justice, Lewisburg, Pa., 1973-75; assoc. Hirsch, Weise & Tillman, Pitts., 1975-76, Plowman & Spiegel, Pitts., 1976-80; counsel Dravo Corp., Pitts., 1980-86, sr. counsel, 1987; attorney West Penn Power Co., Greensburg, Pa., 1987—; mem. panel of arbitrators Am. Arbitration Assn., 1978—, Pa. Bur. Mediation, 1983—, Pa. Labor Relations Bd., 1985—. Contbr. articles to profl. jours. Mem. Union County Child Welfare adv. com., 1974-75; account exec. Southwestern Pa. United Way, Pitts., 1983; bd. govs. Pine Run Homeowners Assn., 1986-87; mem. nat. panel consumer arbitrators Better Bus. Bur., 1986—; mem. supervisory com. ALCOBAR Credit Union, 1986-87. Recipient Dravo Corp. Editorial Achievement awards, 1982, 83, 85, 86; nominated as one of Outstanding Young Men. Am., 1983,84. Fellow Am. Bar Found., Pa. Bar Found.; mem. ABA (Ho. of Dels. 1985—, exec. council sect. labor and employment law 1983-85, exec. council young lawyers div. 1982-84, chmn. YLD Labor Law Com. 1981-83, fellow, 1985—), Pa. Bar Assn. (ho. of dels. 1980—, chmn. special rules subcom. Disciplinary Bd. Study Com. 1983—, com. on legal ethics and profl. responsibility, 1983—, arbitrator lawyer dispute resolution program 1987—, Outstanding Young Lawyer award 1984, Spl. Achievement award 1986), Allegheny County Bar Assn. (profl. ethics com. 1980—, bd. govs. 1979, 85—, asst. sec.-treas. 1979, chmn. young lawyers sect. 1978, council professionalism 1988—, award for outstanding leadership and valuable contbns. to bar 1979), Nat. Constructors Assn. (gen. counsels com. 1983-87), Am. Corp. Counsel Assn., Phi Alpha Delta (justice 1972-73, cert. Outstanding Service 1973). Republican. Roman Catholic. Club: McCandless Swimming (Pitts.) (bd. govs. 1982-85). Office: West Penn Power Co 800 Cabin Hill Rd Greensburg PA 15601

MCDOWELL, ROBERT MICHAEL, management consultant; b. Dubuque, Iowa, Mar. 19, 1961; s. James Patrick and Barbara Jean (Bradley) McD. BS in Indsl. Engring., Iowa State U., 1983. Indsl. engr. 3M Corp., Knoxville, Iowa, 1984-86; chief exec. officer, pres. McDowell Enterprises, Cudahy, Wis., 1986—; pres., chief exec. officer McAid, Ltd., Cudahy, 1986—; cons. McGraw-Edison, Milw., 1987—. Advisor Knoxville Jr. Achievement, 1984, v.p. 1985; active Ams. for Legal Reform. Recipient Citizenship award ABA, 1979. Mem. Inst. Indsl. Engrs. Home and Office: 512 Park Circle Sun Prairie WI 53590

MCDOWELL, ROBERT NEIL, accounting company executive; b. Oakland, Calif., Sept. 20, 1945; s. Kenneth Eugene and Edythe (Bowman) McD.; m. Ruth Edith Bartleson, July 6, 1968; children: Scott, Amy. BA, Juniata Coll., 1967; MA, U. Md., 1974. Mgr. pers. and rehab. Goodwill Industries, Balt., 1967-69; assoc. dir. career planning U. Md., College Park, 1969-74; mgr. pers. Coopers & Lybrand, Chgo., 1974-77; office dir. pers. and adminstrn. Coopers & Lybrand, Phoenix, 1977-80; staff dir. to vice chmn. Coopers & Lybrand, Phila., 1980-83; assoc. nat. dir. pers. Coopers & Lybrand, N.Y.C., 1983-87, staff dir. to chmn. and dep. chmn., 1987-88, nat. dir. personnel, 1988—. Mem. Human Resource Planning Soc., Am. Acctg. Assn., Am. Soc. for Tng. and Devel., Madison Golf Club. Office: Coopers & Lybrand 1251 Ave of the Americas New York NY 10020

MCDUFFIE, DAVID WAYNE, financial planner; b. Buffalo, Feb. 7, 1960; s. Horace Jr. and Fannie (Gibson) McD.; m. Alena Hutchins, Mar. 27, 1982 (div. Oct. 1986); m. Patricia L. Bell, Sept. 9, 1987. BA in Econs., Fredonia (N.Y.) State Coll., 1981. Tchr. Buffalo Pub. Schs., 1981-84; gen. agt. Buffalo Bus. and Estate Planning Corp., 1982-83; tax acct. Control Data Corp., Balt., 1984; fin. mgr. Merrill Lynch, Balt., 1984-88; investment rep. The Chapman Co., Balt., 1988-89; pres. David Alexander Group, Columbia, Md., 1989—; corp. treas. D. Williams, Inc., Balt., Pusch, Inc., Balt.; bd. dirs. Execucorp, Inc., Data Connections, Inc., Balt. Editor Chess Jour., 1981-83. Bd. dirs. Balt. Ctr. for Victims of Sexual Assault, 1985—, NAACP Balt. Br., 1987—, Balt. Urban League, 1988—, Balt. Mus. Art, Joshua Johnson Coun., 1989—; co-founder Friends of Sheila Dixon-Smith, Balt.; mem. Morgan State U. Found., Balt., 1985—; ways and means dir. Young Dems., Balt., 1986-87. Mem. Jaycees (Md. dir. 1986—), U.S. Chess Fedn., N.Y. State Chess Assn. (bd. dirs. 1981-83), Buffalo Inner City Chess Club (mgr. 1981-84). Democrat. Club: Balt. Exchange (founder). Office: David Alexander Group Inc 5289 Rivendell Ln Ste 3 Columbia MD 21044

MCDUFFIE, MICHAEL ANTHONY, investment broker; b. Buffalo, May 1, 1954; s. Horace Jr. and Fran (Gibson) McD.; m. Deborah L. Blann, Mar. 18, 1989. AAS, Canton (N.Y.) Agrl. and Tech. Coll., 1974; BS, SUNY, Geneseo, 1976; cert., Am. Inst. Banking, Buffalo, 1987. Underwriter Aetna Life and Casualty Ins. Co., Buffalo, 1976-77; fin. counselor Bank Am. Corp., Buffalo, 1977-81; soccer, track coach Buffalo State Coll., 1981-85; credit counselor Goldome Fin. Savs. Bank, Buffalo, 1985-86; agent Equitable Fin. Cos., Buffalo, 1986; soccer coach Hilbert Coll., Hamburg, N.Y., 1987—; portfolio investment broker Advest, Inc., 1989—; v.p. David Alexander Group, 1987, Data Connections. 3rd v.p. no. region Black Polit. Caucus, Buffalo, 1987; mem. United Negro Coll. Fund Com., 1987, corp. campaign com. 1989, golf com., bd. dirs. Named one of Outstanding Young Men Am., 1985-86. Mem. Life Underwriter Assn., Buffalo C. of C., U.S. Soccer Fedn., Nat. Soccer Coaches Assn., Buffalo Urban League. Democrat. Baptist. Home: 226 Pershing Ave Buffalo NY 14208

MCEACHRON, STEPHEN BURCHARD, mergers and acquisition consultant; b. Wausau, Wis., Apr. 20, 1940; s. Edgar D. and Elizabeth L. (Burchard) McE.; m. Mary Jane Junker, Dec. 18, 1965; children: Julie, Charlie. BS in Acctg. and Fin., U. Wis., MBA in Mktg. Gen. mgr. GC Plastics, Wausau, 1963-68; venture mgr. Gen. Mills, Mpls., 1969-70; v.p. Northstar Industries, Mpls., 1970-76; pres. Western Cos., Inc., Mpls., 1976—; bd. dirs. Western Cos. Inc., Mpls. Capt. Wis. Air N.G., 1962-66. Office: Western Cos Inc 282 E Wayzata Blvd Wayzata MN 55391

MCELHINNY, WILSON DUNBAR, banker; b. Detroit, July 27, 1929; s. William Dunbar and Elizabeth (Wilson) McE.; m. Barbara Cheney Watkins, June 6, 1952; children: David Ashton, Ward Cheney, Edward Wilson, William Dunbar. BA, Yale U., 1953. With Union and New Haven Trust Co., 1952-63; with Reading Trust Co., Pa., 1963-68, pres., 1968-70; pres. Nat. Central Bank (formerly Reading Trust Co.), Pa., 1970-79, chief exec. officer, 1975-79; chmn. bd. dirs., pres., chief exec. officer Hamilton Bank (formerly Nat. Central Bank), Lancaster, Pa., 1979-81, chmn. bd. dirs., chief exec. officer, 1981-83, chmn. bd. dirs., 1981—; pres. CoreStates Fin. Corp., Phila., 1983-86, vice chmn., 1986—, also bd. dirs.; pres., chief exec. officer, chmn. Hamilton Bank, Lancaster, Pa., 1988—; bd. dirs. Educators Mut. Life Ins. Co., Irex Corp., Pa. Mfrs. Assn. Ins. Co., Phila., Reading Eagle Co., Nuclear Support Services, Inc. Active Lancaster Gen. Hosp.; trustee Franklin and Marshall Coll. Mem. Pa. C. of C. (vice chmn.), Hamilton Club (Lancaster), N.Y. Yacht Club. Home: 1430 Hunsicker Rd Lancaster PA 17601 Office: Hamilton Bank 100 N Queen St Lancaster PA 17604 also: CoreStates Fin Corp NE Corner Broad & Chestnut PO Nox 7618 Philadelphia PA 19107

MCELROY, RANDOLPH WILLIAMS, banker; b. Richmond, Va., Feb. 16, 1935; s. John Lee and Margaret (Williams) McE.; m. Maryanne Harrison Saunders; children: Randolph, Anne Larus, Susan Harrison. BA in Econs., U. Va., 1957. Pres. First and Mchts. Bank, 1974-84, First and Mchts. Corp, 1976-84; vice chmn. Sovran Bank, N.A., 1984-86, Sovran Fin. Corp., 1984—; pres., chief exec. officer Sovran Bank, 1986—; trustee Va. Mus. Fine Arts, Richmond. 1st lt. U.S. Army. Mem. Va. Bankers Assn., Assn. Res. City Bankers, Am. Bankers Assn., Country Club of Va. Episcopalian. Office: Sovran Bank 12th & Main Sts Richmond VA 23219

MCELVAIN, DAVID PLOWMAN, manufacturing company financial executive; b. Chgo., Oct. 16, 1937; s. Carl R. and Ruth P. (Plowman) McE.;

B.B.A., U. Ariz., 1961, M.B.A., 1962; m. Mary Rosalind Hysong, Dec. 20, 1961; children—Jana, Jodi. Consolidation accountant, exec. div. Dresser Industries, Inc., Dallas, 1962-67, corporate fin. controller, 1973-76, dir. fin. services, 1976-78, staff v.p. fin. service and risk mgmt., 1978-82, exec. v.p. fin. services group, 1982-83, pres. fin. services group, 1984-86, v.p. fin., chief exec. officer, 1987—; controller crane, hoist & tower div., Muskegon, Mich., 1967-73. Cert. mgmt. acct. Mem. Nat. Assn. Accts., Beta Gamma Sigma, Phi Delta Theta. Episcopalian. Home: 3806 Beverly Dallas TX 75205 Office: Dresser Industries Inc 1600 Pacific Bldg PO Box 718 Dallas TX 75221

MCEVILY, JOHN VINCENT, JR., mortgage company executive; b. N.Y.C., Dec. 2, 1949; s. John Vincent Jr. and Kathleen Rose (Patrick) M.; m. Denise Laurene Allingham, Sept. 4, 1976; children: Ian, Colin. BA, William Patterson Coll., 1971; postgrad., Villanova U., 1972. V.p., chief ops. officer U.S. Glass Fiber Co., Inc., Little Falls, N.J., 1972—; v.p. comml. property Campbell Corp., Charleston, S.C., 1984-85; chief fin. officer Southsun Properties Corp., Charleston, S.C., 1985; v.p. Comml. Funding Co., Charleston, S.C., 1985—; cons. to various indsl. cos., Conn. and S.C.; bd. dirs. U.S. Glass Fiber Co. Inc., Little Falls, Comml. Funding Co., Charleston. Bd. dirs. Wild Dunes Linkside Assn. Mem. Urban Land Inst., Real Estate Brokers, Mortgage Bankers State of Conn., Am. Mgmt. Assn., Charleston World Trade Ctr. (steering com.), Mortgage Bankers of the Carolinas, Hartford (Conn.) C. of C., Chipanee Country Club, Wild Dunes Club. Roman Catholic. Home: 44 Linkside Dr PO Box 384 Isle of Palms SC 29451 Office: Comml Funding Co PO Box 811 Houston Northcutt Blvd Mount Pleasant SC 29465

MCEVOY, CHARLES LUCIEN, printing company executive; b. Bradford, Pa., Sept. 2, 1917; s. L. Carle and Mary Ellen (McMahon) McE.; m. Rosemary C. Rocca, Sept. 2, 1947. A.B., Xavier U., 1938; postgrad., Georgetown U., 1938-41; J.D., Chgo. Kent Coll. Law, 1950. With Neo Gravure Co. of Chgo., 1947-54, asst. gen. mgr., 1950-52, gen. mgr., 1952-54; v.p. sales The Cuneo Press, Inc., Chgo., 1954-67; exec. v.p. The Cuneo Press, Inc., 1967-73, pres., 1973-88. Served with AUS, 1942-46, PTO. Clubs: Chicago Golf, Chicago Athletic. Home: 3000 Sheridan Rd Chicago IL 60657 Office: 9101 Greenwood Suite 210 Niles IL 60648

MCEVOY, JAMES RICHARD, computer company executive; b. Rochester, N.Y., Nov. 2, 1948; s. Thomas John and Marion (Pfuntner) McE. AS, Rochester Inst. Tech., 1974, BS, 1976, postgrad., 1977-78. Computer systems analyst Mobil Chem. Co., Macedon, N.Y., 1967-76; mgr. computer sect. Rochester (N.Y.) Inst. Tech., 1976-78; mgr. internat. mktg. Wang Labs., Lowell, Mass., 1979-85; dir. internat. mktg. Unisys (formerly Sperry Corp.), Blue Bell, Pa., 1985-88; owner Global Mktg. Services, Boston, 1988—. Served with U.S. Army, 1968-70. Mem. Assn. Systems Mgmt. (hospitality mgr. 1976-77, v.p. 1977-78, recognition award 1977, Member of Yr. 1978), Assn. Data Processing Systems Orgns., World Trade Assn., Small Bus. Assn. New Eng., Boston Computer Soc., Boston Computer Soc. Roman Catholic. Home: 902 W Church Rd Wyncote PA 19095 Office: Global Mktg Services 110 Marlborough St Boston MA 02116

MCEWEN, ROBERT JOSEPH, economist, educator; b. Boston, June 6, 1916; s. Robert John and Mary Ellen (Aherne) McE. A.B., Boston Coll., 1940; Lic. Ph., Weston Sch. Philosophy, 1941; A.M., Fordham U., 1943; S.T.L., Weston Sch. Theology, 1947; Ph.D., Boston Coll., 1957. Instr. mktg. Boston Coll., 1942-43, instr. econs., 1948-51, asst. prof. econs., 1952-56, assoc. prof., chmn. econs., 1957-67, prof., 1968—; vis. prof. Loyola U., L.A., 1963; founder, 1st pres. Consumer Fedn., Washington, 1968-69. Contbr. articles to profl. jours. 1st chmn. Adv. Cons. Council to Atty. Gen., Mass., 1958-63, State Consumers Council, Mass., 1964-65; chmn. Ford Motor-Consumer Appeals Bd., New Eng., 1981-83. Recipient Consumer Tribune award Better Bus. Bur., 1973. Mem. Am. Council on Consumer Interests (pres. 1965-67), Assn. Mass. Consumers (pres. 1971-77), Conf. Cons. Orgns. (vice chmn. 1973-85, chmn. 1985—). Roman Catholic. Club: State (Boston). Avocations: golf; photography. Home: 140 Commonwealth Ave Newton MA 02167 Office: Boston Coll Dept Econs 140 Commonwealth Ave Chestnut Hill MA 02167

MCEWEN, WILLIAM JAMES, advertising executive; b. Montclair, N.J., Aug. 14, 1943; s. Lester Vincent McEwen and Harriet Eleanor (Toner) Mitchell; m. Florence Marie Witkop, Aug. 21, 1965; children: James Garrett, Megan Alicia. BA, St. Anselm Coll., 1965; MA, Mich. State U., 1967, PhD, 1969. Research analyst Leo Burnett Co., Chgo., 1969-70; assoc. prof. U. Conn., Storrs, 1970-76; supr. research Needham Harper & Steers, Chgo., 1975-76; v.p., dir. rsch. and mktg. D'Arcy-MacManus & Masius, San Francisco, 1976-81, pres., 1981-82; dir. product devel. Calif. Milk Adv. Bd., Modesto, 1982-83; sr. v.p., dir. research Foote, Cone & Belding, Chgo., 1983-84; sr. v.p., dir. stategic planning McCann-Erickson, Inc., San Francisco, 1984—; adj. prof. communications Annenberg Sch. Communications U. So. Calif., Los Angeles, 1980-81; cons. Dunlap and Assocs., Darien, Conn., 1973-77, Ctr. for Environment and Man, Hartford, Conn., 1974-77. Author: Communication and Behavior, 1977; contbr. articles to profl. jours. Mem. Coventry (Conn.) Town Council, 1975-76, Dem. Town Com., Coventry, 1975-76; scoutmaster Boy Scouts Am., Barrington, Ill. 1983-84. Mem. Am. Mktg. Assn. (local v.p. programs 1980-81, pres. 1985-87, exec. fellow in residence 1986, Keynoter 1986—). Republican. Roman Catholic. Home: 238 Reed Blvd Mill Valley CA 94941 Office: McCann-Erickson 201 California San Francisco CA 94111

MCFADDEN, BEVERLEE See SIMBOLI, TITO

MCFADDEN, FRANK HAMPTON, former judge, business executive; b. Oxford, Miss., Nov. 20, 1925; s. John Angus and Ruby (Roy) McF.; m. Jane Porter Nabers, Sept. 30, 1960; children—Frank Hampton, Angus Nabers, Jane Porter. B.A., U. Miss., 1950; LL.B., Yale U., 1955. Bar: N.Y. 1956, Ala. 1959. Assoc. firm Lord, Day & Lord, N.Y.C., 1955-58, Bradley, Arant, Rose & White, Birmingham, Ala., 1958-63; partner Bradley, Arant, Rose & White, 1963-69; judge U.S. Dist. Ct. No. Dist. Ala., Birmingham, 1969-73; chief judge U.S. Dist. Ct. No. Dist. Ala., 1973-81; sr. v.p., gen. counsel Blount, Inc., Montgomery, Ala., 1982—; chmn. Blount Energy Resource Corp., Montgomery, 1983-88. Mem. jud. panel Ctr. for Pub. Resources, 1985—. Served from ensign to lt. USNR, 1944-49, 51-53. Mem. Am. Corp. Counsel Assn. (bd. dirs. 1984—, chmn. 1988—). Office: Blount Inc 4520 Executive Park Dr PO Box 949 Montgomery AL 36192-1201

MCFADDEN, JOSEPH PATRICK, insurance company executive; b. Norristown, Pa., Jan. 1, 1939; s. Joseph Patrick and Anna (Brennan) McF.; m. Patricia Ann Burke, Jan. 28, 1961; children: Mary Ann, Linda, Patricia, Joseph, Nancy, Meghan. BA, LaSalle U., 1961. Claim adjuster Allstate Ins. Co., Valley Forge, Pa., 1963-66; various mgmt. positions Valley Forge and Harrison, N.Y., 1966-74; regional claim mgr. Rochester, N.Y., 1974-76, Murray Hill, N.J., 1976-79; zone claim mgr. Bannockburn, Ill., 1979-81; asst. regional mgr. Skokie, Ill., 1981-83; asst. v.p. Northbrook, Ill., 1983-84; regional v.p. Santa Ana, Calif., 1984-86; claim v.p. Northbrook, 1986—. Served to 1st lt. U.S. Army, 1961-63. Mem. Nat. Auto Theft Bur. (bd. govs. 1986), Nat. Assn. Ind. Insurers (claims com. 1986), Ins. Crime Prevention Inst. Roman Catholic. Home: 1005 Ashley Ln Libertyville IL 60048 Office: Allstate Ins Co Allstate Plaza B-7 Northbrook IL 60062

MCFADIN, ROBERT LEE, manufacturing executive; b. Milw., Dec. 16, 1921; s. Charles Lee and Madeline (Hansen) McF.; m. JoAnn Metzger, Sept. 6, 1947; children: Lindsey McFadin Spake, Barbara McFadin Bishop. BS in Mech. Engring., Mich. Tech. U., 1945. Engr. Carrier Corp., N.Y.C., 1945-48; with Marley Co., Mission, Kans., 1948—, exec. v.p. all domestic operating divs., 1968-75, pres., 1975-84, chmn., 1984—, chief exec. officer, 1975-86, also bd. dirs., also bd. dirs. subs.; bd. dirs. Nat. Gypsum Co., Dallas. Past mem. bd. dirs. Heart of Am. United Way; gen. campaign chmn. Kansas City United Way, 1977, pres., 1979, chmn., 1980; trustee Midwest Research Inst.; past bd. dirs. Mid-Am. Coalition on Health Care, Civic Council Kansas City, Greater Kansas City Community Founds. and Affiliated Trusts. Served with USAAF, 1943. Mem. Kansas City C. of C., NAM (past bd. dirs.), Tau Beta Pi. Clubs: Morris County Golf (Convent Station, N.J.); Kansas City Country (Kans.); River (Kansas City, Mo.). Home: 2410 W 63d St Shawnee Mission KS 66208 Office: Marley Co 1900 Shawnee Mission Pkwy Mission Woods KS 66205

MCFARLAND, JAMES WILLIAM, real estate development company executive; b. Montgomery, Ala., Sept. 7, 1948; s. Ward Wharton and Frances Adelia (Morrow) McF.; B.S., U. Ala., 1970; m. Miriam Melinda Webster, Feb. 20, 1971; children—James William, Mimi Morrow. Dir. real estate for Ky., Ind. and Tenn., Winn-Dixie Stores, Inc., Louisville, 1970-72; v.p. Ward McFarland, Inc., Tuscaloosa, Ala., 1972—, also dir. Mem. Council for Devel. of French in La., 1976—, Friends of Library, 1975—; commr. Dept. Mental Health, 1987—; ; Rep. nominee U.S. Congress Ala. 7th Dist., 1986; young churchmen adviser Episcopal Diocese Ala., 1976—, conv. del.; charter investor, chair of real estate U. Ala.; chmn. Ala. Rapid Rail Transit Commn.; vice chmn. La.-Miss.-Ala. Rapid Rail Transit Commn., 1983-84, chmn., 1984—; state advisor Congl. Adv. Com., Am. Security Council; sr. warden Christ Episc. Ch., 1984; bd. dirs. Tuscaloosa Kidney Found.; commr. Dept. Mental Health State of Ala. Named hon. citizen of Mobile and New Orleans, hon. mem. mayor's staff, Mobile. Mem. Nat. Assn. Realtors, Tuscaloosa Bd. Realtors, Nat. Small Bus. Assn., U. Ala. Commerce Execs. Soc., U. Ala. Alumni Assn., Nat. Assn. R.R. Passengers, Ala. Assn. R.R. Passengers (pres. 1982), Delta Sigma Pi. Clubs: North River Yacht; Kiwanis of Greater Tuscaloosa. Home: 4714 7th Ct E Tuscaloosa AL 35405 Office: 325 Skyland Blvd E Tuscaloosa AL 35405

MCFARLAND, JENNIFER LIGHT, accountant; b. Okla. City, Feb. 21, 1958; d. John Wesley and Grace Elise (Harkins) Light; m. Jay Jon McFarland, Aug. 9, 1980; children: Jessica Elise, Jacqueline Jayne, Jacob Jay. BSBA, Okla. State U., 1980. CPA, Tex. Acct. Anadarko Prodn. Co., Houston, 1982-84; prin. Jennifer L. McFarland, CPA, Spring, Tex., 1984-86; supr. internat. acctg. Kerr-McGee Corp., Oklahoma City, 1986—. Mem. Am Inst. CPA's, Okla. Heritage Assn., Okla. 1889er's Soc., P.E.O. Republican. Presbyterian. Home: 3509 Windsor Ave Oklahoma City OK 73122

MCFARLAND, RICHARD M., executive recruiting consultant; b. Portland, Maine, Sept. 10, 1923; s. George Fiske and Phillys C. (Macomber) McF.; BChemE, Rensselaer Poly. Inst., 1944; postgrad. U. Mich., 1946-47; m. Virginia Fitz-Randolph Ripley, Dec. 6, 1947; children: Richard Macomber, Kirk, Jane. Prodn. supr. E. I. duPont, 1947-51; mgr. agrl. chem. market research Brea Chem. (Calif.) subs. Union Oil Co., 1953-55; product mgr. chem. div. FMC Corp., N.Y.C., 1955-59; mgr. mktg. devel. Tex. Butadiene & Chem., N.Y.C., 1959-60; pres. Cumberland Chem. Corp., N.Y.C., 1960-67; gen. mgr. inorganic div. Wyandotte Chem. Co. (Mich.), 1967-69; asso. Heidrick & Struggles, Inc., N.Y.C., 1969-72, v.p., 1972-81; founder, pres. Brissenden, McFarland, Wagoner & Fuccella, Inc. and predecessors, Stamford, Conn., 1981—. Ensign USNR, 1943-46, lt. comdr., 1951-53. Mem. Comml. Devel. Assn., Am. Chem. Soc., Lambda Chi Alpha. Clubs: Landmark, Cedar Point Yacht, Nutmeg Curling. Patentee in field. Home: 16 Clover Ln Westport CT 06880 Office: Brissenden McFarland Wagoner & Fuccella Inc 1 Canterbury Green Stamford CT 06901

MCFARLAND, WANETA JOAN, finance company executive; b. Sheldon, Mo., Dec. 5, 1936; d. Floyd Earl and Gladys Neoma (Cliffman) Holland; m. Thomas Clemson McFarland, Mar. 1, 1958; children: Randall Clayton, Debra Joan, Justin Carroll. Grad. high sch., Bronaugh. Sec. Hallmark Cards, Inc., Kansas City, Mo., 1954-57; exec. sec. First Fin. Co., Nevada, Mo., 1965-67, Thornton Nat. Bank, Nevada, 1972-76, Farm and Home Savs. Assn., Nevada, 1976-78; adminstrv. asst., asst. sec. Farm and Home Savs. Assn., 1978-84, v.p., 1984-86, adminstrv. v.p., 1986—. Mem. Nevada C. of C., Soroptimist Internat. (human rights status of women chmn., budget chmn., budget and fin. sec.), Bushwacker BPW (Nevada, pres.). Home: Rte 1 Box 3 Moundville MO 64771 Office: Farm and Savs Assn 221 W Cherry Nevada MO 64772

MCFARLANE, BETH LUCETTA TROESTER, mayor; b. Osterdock, Iowa, Mar. 9, 1918; d. Francis Charles and Ella Carrie (Moser) Troester; M. George Evert McFarlane, June 20, 1943 (dec. May 1972); children: Douglas, Steven (dec.), Susan, George. BA in Edn., U. No. Iowa, 1962, MA in Edn., 1971. Cert. tchr. Tchr. rural and elem. schs., Iowa, 1936-50, 55-56; elem. tchr. Oelwein Community Schs., Iowa, 1956-64, jr. high reading tchr., 1964-71, reading specialist, 1971-83; mayor of Oelwein, 1982—; evaluator North Cen. Accreditation Assn. for Ednl. Programs; mem. planning team for confs. for Iowa Cities, N.E. Iowa, 1985; v.p. N.E. Iowa Regional Council for Econ. Devel., 1986—; mem. Area Econ. Devel. Com. N.E. Iowa, 1985, Legis. Interim Study Com. on Rural Econ. Devel., 1987-88; mem. policy com. Iowa League Municipalities, 1987-88; bd. dirs. Celwein Indsl. Devel. Corp., 1982—, Oelwein Betterment Corp., 1982—. V.p. Fayette County Tourism Council, 1987-88; Iowa State Steering Com. on Road Use Tax Financing, 1988-89. Named Iowa Reading Tchr. of Yr., Internat. Reading Assn. Iowa, 1978; recipient Outstanding Contbrn. to Reading Council Activities award Internat. Reading Assn. N.E. Iowa, 1978, State of Iowa's Gov.s' Leadership award, 1988. Mem. N.E. Iowa Reading Council (pres. 1975-77), MacDowell Music and Arts Orgn. (pres. 1978-80), Oelwein Bus. and Profl. Women (Woman of Yr. 1983), Oelwein Area C. of C. (bd. dirs. 1986—, Humanitarian award 1987), Delta Kappa Gamma (pres. 1980-82). Republican. Mem. Reorganized Ch. of Jesus Christ of Latter Day Saints. Avocations: bicycling, refinishing antiques, gardening. Home: 512 7th Ave NE Oelwein IA 50662 Office: City of Oelwein 20 2d Ave SW Oelwein IA 50662

MCFARLANE, GERALD JOHN, distribution executive; b. Phila., July 23, 1953; s. Gerald John and Phyllis (Taylor) McF.; m. Susan Benett, Jan. 29, 1977; children: Megan, Patrick. BS, USAF Acad., 1976; MBA, U. Mo., 1979. With Carrier Air Conditioning, 1981—; gen. mgr. distbn. Carrier Air Conditioning, Tampa, Fla., 1988—. Served to capt. USAF, 1971-81. mem. various bldg. assns. Fla. Republican. Home: 510 Forest Park Rd Oldsmar FL 34677 Office: Fla Air Conditioning 13555 44th St N Clearwater FL 34622

MCFARLANE, JOE ROBERT, JR., medical association executive, investor; b. Brownwood, Tex., Aug. 9, 1936; s. Joe Robert and Helen Virginia (Russell) M.; m. Jane Arnot, June 6, 1961; children: Elizabeth Ann, Amy Helen, Joe Robert III. Degree, Stanford U., 1954-57; MD, Baylor U., 1961. Diplomate Am. Bd. Ophthalmology. Practice medicine specializing in ophthalmology San Antonio, 1965-70; v.p. Ophthalmology Assocs. San Antonio, 1970-85, pres., 1986—; mem. practitioner ophthal. adv. faculty Am. Acad. Ophthalmology, San Francisco, 1975-80; clin. prof. U. Tex., San Antonio, 1983-88. Contbr. articles to profl. jours. Pres. high sch. Spirit Group, Alamo Heights, Tex., 1980; treas. Parent Tchr. Student Orgn., Alamo Heights, 1981; mem. bd. control Nix Med. Ctr., San Antonio, 1984-88. Served to maj. USAR, 1962-70. Mem. Am. Acad. Ophthalmology (practitioner adv. faculty, 1975-80, com. interspecialty and allied health edn. 1985-88), Am. Eye Study Club, Am. Bd. Ophthalmology (assoc. examiner 1978-88), Am. Acad. Ophthalmology Council (councillor 1981-88, regional coordinator 1987-88, chmn. com. credentials 1987-88), San Antonio Soc. Ophthalmology (pres. 1975), Tex. Ophthalmology Assn. (councillor 1975-78). Republican. Presbyterian. Clubs: San Antonio Country, Argyle, Giraud. Office: Ophthalmology Assocs 400 Nix Ctr San Antonio TX 78205

MC FEDRIES, ROBERT, JR., chemical industry executive, chemical engineer; b. Chgo., Nov. 11, 1930; s. Robert and Elizabeth (Sharp) McF.; m. Beverly Elaine Carlson, Oct. 25, 1952; children: Randall Robert, Victoria Elaine. BSChemE, Purdue U., 1952, MSChemE, 1956. Devel. engr. Dow Chem. Co., Midland, Mich., 1955-64, research dir., 1964-73, v.p. Dow Chem. Investment and Fin., 1973-75, rsch. dir., 1975-83, dir. mergers and acquisitions, 1983-87, v.p., 1987—; bd. dirs. Magma Power Co., San Diego, Liana Ltd., Midland, Dorinco Reins. Co., Midland, United Agriseeds, Champaign, Ill.; bd. dirs. chmn. bd. Essex Chem. Corp. Patentee multi layer film, 1965. Served to 1st lt. USAF, 1952-54. Mem. Am. Chem. Soc., Am. Inst. Chem. Engring., Assn. Corp. Growth. Republican. Presbyterian. Club: Midland Country (pres. 1977), Fiddlesticks County Club. Home: 5907 Harwood Dr Midland MI 48640 Office: The Dow Chem Co 2030 Willard H Dow Ctr Midland MI 48640

MCGAGH, WILLIAM GILBERT, financial consultant; b. Boston, May 29, 1929; s. Thomas A. and Mary M. (McDonough) McG.; m. Sarah Ann McQuigg, Sept. 23, 1961; children: Margaret Ellen, Sarah Elizabeth. BSBA, Boston Coll., 1950; MBA, Harvard U., 1952; MS, MIT, 1965. Fin. analyst Ford Motor Co., Dearborn, Mich., 1953-55; mem. staff treas. office Chrysler Corp., Detroit, 1955-64; compt., treas. Canadian div. Chrysler Corp., Windsor, 1965-67; staff exec.-fin. Latin Am. ops. Chrysler Corp., Detroit, 1967-68, asst. treas., 1968-75, treas., 1975-76, v.p., treas., 1976-80; sr. v.p. fin. Northrop Corp., Los Angeles, 1980-88; owner McGagh Assocs., Beverly Hills, Calif., 1988—; dir. Pacific Am. Income Shares, Inc. Bd. dirs. Greater Los Angeles Zoo Assn., Ind. Colls. of So. Calif., Sta. KCET-TV, John Tracy Clinic. Served with USAF, 1952-53. Sloan fellow MIT, 1965. Mem. Fin. Execs. Inst. (pres. Detroit chpt. 1979-80). Clubs: Orchard Lake Country; Harvard (N.Y.C. and Boston); Beach (Santa Monica, Calif.); Los Angeles Country, California (Los Angeles), Eastward Ho Country. (Chatham, Mass.). Home: 2189 Century Hill Los Angeles CA 90067 Office: McGagh Assocs 9601 Wilshire Blvd Ste 500A Beverly Hills CA 90210

MC GARR, PAUL ROWLAND, textile company executive; b. Webster County, Miss., Nov. 11, 1933; s. Willie B. and Nina Mae (Rowl) McG.; m. Elizabeth Ann Smith, May 1, 1955; children—Paul Rushton, Lee-anne. B.S., Miss. State U., 1955. C.P.A., Miss. Indsl. engr., cost accountant ITT, Corinth, Miss. and Raleigh, N.C., 1958-62; treas., exec. v.p. So. Gen. Factors, Inc., High Point, N.C., 1962-66; v.p. fin., sec., treas., dir. Guilford Mills, Inc., Greensboro, N.C., 1966—; dir. Arcadian Shores, Inc. Served with USN, 1955-57. Mem. Am. Inst. C.P.A.'s. Republican. Lutheran. Club: Masons. Home: 905 Westminster Dr Greensboro NC 27410 Office: Guilford Mills Inc Drawer U-4 4925 W Market St Greensboro NC 27402

MCGARRY, JOHN PATRICK, JR., advertising agency executive; b. Elizabeth, N.J., Nov. 22, 1939; s. John Patrick and Elizabeth (Weber) McG.; m. Gilda R. Spurio, Oct. 24, 1964; children: Victoria Elizabeth, John Patrick, III. B.S. in Mktg. Econs, Villanova U., 1961. Salesman Exxon Corp., Elizabeth, 1961-64; advt. exec. Young and Rubicam Inc., N.Y.C., 1965-69, sr. v.p., mgmt. supr., 1969-87, pres., mem. ops. com., advt. exec. com., 1987—, also chmn. bd. dirs.; chmn. Client Services Worldwide, N.Y.C., 1987—; bd. dirs. Caramoor. Bd. dirs. New Youth Performing Theatre, Bedford, N.Y., Regional Rev. League, Westchester, N.Y. Louisville Opera Assn., 1981-83, Dominican Coll., Drop-out Prevention Fund; exec. v.p., group dir., dir. mktg., also dir. Young & Rubicam U.S.A.; mng. dir., mem. exec. bd. Young & Rubicam N.Y. Served with U.S. N.G., 1963-69. Democrat. Roman Catholic. Clubs: Bedord (N.Y.); Golf and Tennis. Home: Cantitoe Rd Bedford Village NY 10506 Office: Young & Rubicam Inc 285 Madison Ave New York NY 10017

MCGARY, EDWARD, communications executive; b. Los Angeles, May 26, 1950; s. Edward and Mildred (Dorton) Mc. BS in Bus. Adminstrn., U. So. Calif., 1974; MBA in Fin., St. Francis Coll., Ft. Wayne, Ind., 1980. Fin. assoc. GTE, Santa Monica, Calif., 1974-75, Everett, Wash., 1975; sr. auditor GTE, Ft. Wayne, 1975-77, acctg. mgr. tax, 1977-78, tax acctg. mgr., 1977-78, asst. sec., asst. treas., 1978-79, gen. service mgr., 1979-80; mgr. fin. assoc. devel. program GTE, Stamford, Conn., 1980-84; state dir. budget results GTE, Muskegon, Mich., 1984—. Bd. dirs. West Shore Jr. Achievement, Muskegon, 1986—. Office: Gen Tel North Inc 455 E Ellis Rd Muskegon MI 49443

MCGAW, KENNETH ROY, furniture wholesale company executive; b. Parry Sound, Ont., Can., Aug. 25, 1926; s. Dalton Earnest and Grace (Crockford) McG. Student, Denison U., 1946-48; B.A., Western Res. U., 1949. With Bigelow Carpets, N.Y. and Ohio, 1949-53; representing Frederick Cooper Lamps, Inc., Chgo., 1953—; home furnishing salesman Gates Mills, Ohio, 1958-74, Fort Lauderdale, 1974-77, Dallas, 1978-79; pres. Ken McGaw, Inc., Dallas, 1979—; factory rep. for maj. furniture and furniture accessory mfrs. Bd. dirs. Big Bros. Cleve., 1963-65, Dallas Opera Co., 1981—; v.p. Nat. Council on Alcoholism, Cleve., 1972-74; chmn. fundraising drive Wholesale div. Dallas Industry for Dallas Opera, 1982-83; ruling elder 1st Presbyterian Ch., Dallas, 1981—. Served to 2d lt. U.S. Army, 1944-46. Mem. Greater Dallas Home Furnishings Assn. (bd. dirs. 1985-86), S.W. Homefurnishings Assn., S.W. Roadrunners Assn., Internat. Homefurnishings Reps. Assn. Lodge: Rotary. Home: 5909 Luther Ln The Shelton #1005 Dallas TX 75225 also: 8360 E San Bernardo Ave Scottsdale AZ 85258 Office: Ken McGaw Inc 9010 Dallas World Trade Ctr PO Box 58495 Dallas TX 75258

MCGEE, DOROTHY HORTON, author, historian; b. West Point, N.Y., Nov. 30, 1913; d. Hugh Henry and Dorothy (Brown) McG.; ed. Sch. of St. Mary, 1920-21, Green Vale Sch., 1921-28, Brearley Sch., 1928-29, Fermata Sch., 1929-31. Asst. historian Inc. Village of Roslyn (N.Y.), 1950-58; historian Inc. Village of Matinecock, 1966—. Author: Skipper Sandra, 1950; Sally Townsend, Patriot, 1952; The Boarding School Mystery, 1953; Famous Signers of the Declaration, 1955; Alexander Hamilton—New Yorker, 1957; Herbert Hoover: Engineer, Humanitarian, Statesman, 1959, rev. edit., 1965; The Pearl Pendant Mystery, 1960; Framers of the Constitution, 1968; author booklets, articles hist. and sailing subjects. Chmn., Oyster Bay Am. Bicentennial Revolution Commn., 1971—; historian Town of Oyster Bay, 1982—; mem. Nassau County Am. Revolution Bicentennial Commn.; hon. dir. The Friends of Raynham Hall, Inc.; treas. Family Welfare Assn. Nassau County, Inc., 1956-58; dir. Family Service Assn. Nassau County, 1958-69. Recipient Cert. of award for outstanding contbn. children's lit. N.Y. State Assn. Elem. Sch. Prins., 1959; award Nat. Soc. Children of Am. Revolution, 1960; award N.Y. Assn. Supervision and Curriculum Devel., 1961; hist. award Town of Oyster Bay, 1963; Cert. Theodore Roosevelt Assn., 1976. Fellow Soc. Am. Historians; mem. Soc. Preservation L.I. Antiquities (hon. dir.), Nat. Trust Hist. Preservation, N.Y. Geneal. and Biol. Soc. (dir., trustee), Oyster Bay Hist. Soc. (pres. 1971-75, chmn. 1975-79, trustee), Theodore Roosevelt Assn. (trustee), Townsend Soc. Am. (trustee). Republican. Address: Box 142 Locust Valley NY 11560

MCGEE, ELIZABETH L., manufacturing company executive; b. Worcester, Mass, Aug. 4, 1940; d. Adam M. Louise M. (Callahan) McG. AA, Becker Jr. Coll., 1960; MEd, Antioch U., 1980; Cert. Personnel Adminstrn., Bently Coll. Buyer G. Fox & Co., Hartford, Conn., 1962-64; dept. mgr. Filenes, Boston, 1964-68; personnel mgr. Saphikon div. Tyco Labs, Inc., Waltham, Mass., 1969-79; mgr. office support Dynamics Assocs., Cambridge, Mass., 1980-81; dir. personnel Micro-Dynamics, Inc., Woburn, Mass., 1982—. Mem. Assoc. Industries Mass., Nat. Assn. Mfgs., Survey Group, Human Resource Network. Office: Micro-Dynamics Inc 10 Sonar Dr Woburn MA 02154

MCGEE, KATHLEEN AGNES, pharmaceutical company executive; b. L.A., Mar. 27, 1944; d. William Raymond and Kathleen Elizabeth (Nevin) McG. BS in Pharmacy, Phila. Coll. Pharmacy and Sci., 1968. Registered pharmacist, Pa., Md., Del. Staff pharmacist Wack Apothecary, Wayne, Pa., 1968-71, Paul C. Tigue, Pharmacist, Wilmington, Del., 1970-73; dir. profl. svcs. Nat. Assn. Chain Drug Stores, Alexandria, Va., 1973-76, v.p., 1976-83; exec. dir. Retail Drug Inst., N.Y.C., 1983-84; v.p. Barr Labs., Inc., Pomona, N.Y., 1984—; co-founder Pharmacy Assocs., Inc., Wilmington, 1971. Mem. Am. Pharm. Assn., Am. Soc. Hosp. Pharmacists, Del. Pharm. Soc. (exec. dir. 1970-73), Kappa Epsilon. Republican. Roman Catholic. Office: Barr Labs Inc Two Quaker Rd Pomona NY 10970

MCGEE, WESLEY O., manufacturing executive; b. Rockingham, N.C., Aug. 25, 1942; s. Cleondrus and Hazel (Williams) McG.; m. Judith Ann Williams, Jul. 17, 1965; children: Allison, Jennifer, Lance. BS, N.C. State Coll., 1962; MBA in Fin., Columbia U., 1969. Ptnr. Nathaniel Hill & Assoc., Raleigh, N.C., 1973-76; pres. McGee Assoc., Charlotte, N.C., 1976-83; pres. Va. Packaging Supply Co., Inc., Herndon, 1983—, also bd. dirs.; bd. dirs. Nat. Bank of No. Va., G&L Bldg. Services. Dr. Jr. Achievement Greater Washington, Bethesda, Md., Leadership Fairfax, Vienna, Va. Mem. Soc. Packaging and Handling Engrs. Republican. Episcopal. Club: Washington Golf and Country. Lodge: Rotary. Office: Hedman Co 1158 W Armitage Chicago IL 60195

MC GEHEE, CARDEN COLEMAN, banker; b. Franklin, Va., Aug. 11, 1924; s. Clopton Vivian and Laura (Coleman) McG.; m. Caroline Yarnall Casey, Apr. 21, 1951; children: Carden Coleman, Stephen Yarnall, Margaret Fox Verner. Student, Va. Poly. Inst., 1941-43; B.S., U. Va., 1947; grad., Rutgers U. Grad. Sch. Banking, 1955-58, Harvard U. Advanced Mgmt. Program, 1970. With First & Mchts. Nat. Bank, Richmond, Va., 1948—, asst. trust officer, 1954-56, trust officer, 1956-59, v.p., 1959-62, sr. v.p., 1962, pres., chief adminstrv. officer, 1972-73, chmn. bd., chief exec. officer, dir., 1973-83; chmn. bd., chief exec. officer, dir. First & Mchts. Corp., Richmond, Va., 1974-83; pres. Sovran Fin. Corp., Richmond, Va., 1984-88, chmn. exec.

com., 1988—; chmn. bd. dirs. Sovran Bank N.Am., Richmond, Va., 1986—; dir. Chesapeake and Potomac Telephone Co. Va., Dan River, Inc., RF&P R.R. Co., Visa USA; mem. adv. bd. Eximbank, Washington, 1986-87; instr. evening div. U. Richmond, 1956-62, Va. Commonwealth U., 1958-64. Pres. United Givers Fund, 1971; bd. visitors Va. Commonwealth U., 1968-78; bd. govs. St. Christophers Sch., 1968-74; bd. sponsors Colgate Darden Grad. Sch. Bus. Adminstrn., U. Va., 1980—, Sch. Bus. Adminstrn., Coll. William and Mary, 1974-80; trustee Va. Hist. Soc.; treas. Retreat Hosp. Served with AUS, 1943-46; maj. Va. N.G. until 1966. Mem. Va. Bankers Assn. (pres. 1980-81), C. of C., St. Andrews Soc., Beta Theta Pi, Delta Sigma Rho, Omicron Delta Kappa, Phi Alpha Delta, Beta Gamma Sigma, Omicron Delta Upsilon. Clubs: Rotarian (pres. Richmond 1971-72), Commonwealth, Country of Va; Harvard. Home: 6128 St Andrews Ln Richmond VA 23226 Office: Sovran Bank PO Box 27025 Richmond VA 23261

MCGERVEY, PAUL JOHN, III, management consultant; b. Indpls., Apr. 12, 1947; s. Paul John and Ethel Mae (Shaw) McG.; BS, U. Minn., 1972. Buyer, Daytons Dept. Stores, Mpls., 1970-72; cons. Internat. Mktg. Cons., Devonshire, Bermuda, 1972-74; internal cons. E. F. McDonald Cos., Dayton, Ohio, 1974-76; mgmt. cons., Chgo., 1976-81; v.p. ops. Travel Mgmt. Inc., Chgo., 1981-84; v.p. tech. IVI Travel Inc., Northbrook, Ill., 1984-88, mgmt. cons., Chgo., 1988—; voice and data communication specialist. Served with 101st Airborne Div., U.S. Army, 1967-69; Vietnam. Decorated Bronze Star medal; lic. single and multi engine, land and sea comml. pilot and flight instr. Mem. Am. Mgmt. Assn., Assn. Systems Mgmt. Home: 71 E Division St Chicago IL 60610

MCGETTIGAN, CHARLES CARROLL, JR., investment banker; b. San Francisco, Mar. 28, 1945; s. Charles Carroll McGettigan and Molly (Fay) McGettigan Pedley; m. Katharine Havard King, Nov. 1, 1975 (div. 1981); m. Meriwether Lewis Stovall, Aug. 6, 1983; 1 child, Meriwether Lewis Fay. AB in Govt., Georgetown U., 1966; MBA in Fin., U. Pa., 1969. Assoc., asst. v.p., v.p. Blyth Eastman Dillon, N.Y.C., 1970-75, 1st v.p., 1975-78, sr. v.p., San Francisco, 1978-80; sr. v.p. Dillon Read & Co., San Francisco, 1980-83; gen. ptnr. Woodman Kirkpatrick & Gilbreath, San Francisco, 1983-84; prin. corp. fin. Hambrecht & Quist, Inc., San Francisco, 1984-88, mng. dir, founder McGettigan, Wick & Co., Inc., San Francisco, 1988—; dir. Circadian, Inc., San Jose, Calif., 1980-84, Skouras Pictures, Inc., Hollywood, Calif., 1987—, Sungene Techs., Inc., San Jose, Calif, 1987-88; Raytel Systems Inc, San Jose, 1988—; Shared Techs., Inc., Hartford, Conn., 1988—; adv. dir. Chesapeake Ventures, Balt., 1984—. Trustee St. Francis Meml. Hosp., San Francisco, 1980-86; mem. United San Francisco Rep. fin. com., 1983—, steering com., 1986—; adv. bd. dirs. Leavey Sch. Bus. Adminstrn., Santa Clara U., Calif., 1984—. With USN, 1966. Republican. Roman Catholic. Clubs: Brook, Racquet and Tennis (N.Y.); Pacific Union, Bohemian (San Francisco); Burlingame Country (Hillsborough, Calif.); California (Los Angeles); Boston (New Orleans); Piping Rock (Locust Valley, N.Y.). Home: 3375 Clay St San Francisco CA 94118 Office: McGettigan Wick & Co Inc Pier 9 San Francisco CA 94111

MCGILBERRY, JOE H., food service executive; b. Mobile, Ala., Aug. 6, 1943; s. Thomas Henry and Yvonne (Jorden) McG.; m. Betty Sue Reynolds, Dec. 20, 1964; children: Joe H. Jr., Michele, Brent. BS, Auburn U., 1965; MS, U. Tenn., 1972; PhD, TEx. A&M U., 1978. Gen. plant asst. Gen. Telephone Fla., Tampa, 1966; systems analyst E.I. DuPont de Nemours & Co., Old Hickory, Tenn., 1966-68; research asst. U. Tenn., Knoxville, 1968-69; advanced materials engr. Union Carbide Corp., Texas City, TX, 1969-70; asst. prof. Tenn. Tech. U., Cookeville, 1970-72, 73-75, 76-77; mgr. prodn. support Fleetguard div. Cummins Engine, Cookeville, 1972-73; assoc. research engr. Tex. A&M U., College Station, 1975-76; mgr. food and fiber ctr. Miss. State Coop. Extension Program, 1978—; cons. Dunlap Industries, U. Tenn. at Nashville, Norwalk Furniture Corp., Teledyne-Stillman, Genco Stamping, Inc., Riley Enterprises; lectr. various seminars and presentations, 1978—. Author numerous articles in field. Pres. Starkville (Miss.) High Sch. Athletic Booster Club; coach Starkville Youth Soccer Orgn., Starkville Boys Baseball League; co-organizer Starkville Area Youth Basketball (Leadership award 1969). Mem. Inst. Indsl. Engrs. (sr.), Miss. Indsl. Devel. Council, Order Engrs., Nat. Assn. County Agrl. Agts., Miss. Assn. County Agrl. Agts., Starkville C. of C., Alpha Phi Mu. Office: Food and Fiber Ctr 307 Bost Ctr PO Box 5446 Mississippi State MS 39762

MC GILL, GARY RONALD, consulting engineer; b. Knoxville, Tenn., Apr. 5, 1947; s. Robert Bruce and Maxine (Davis) McG.; BS in Civil Engring., U. Tenn., 1970; cert. in Water Supply Engring., U. N.C., 1977; Design engr. Fla. Power Corp., St. Petersburg, 1970-72; head of engring. Misener Marine Constrn. Co., Inc., St. Petersburg, 1973-74; city engr. Asheville (N.C.), 1974-76; corp. ptnr., officer Butler/McGill Assocs., P.A., Asheville, 1976-84; dir., pres. McGill & Assocs., P.A., Asheville, 1984—. Registered profl. engr., N.C., Tenn., Va., Ky. Mem. Am. Water Works Assn., Water Pollution Control Fedn., Nat. Soc. Profl. Engrs., Nat. Rural Water Assn., Audubon Soc., Nature Conservancy, Nat. Parks and Conservation Assn., Sierra Club, Cousteau Soc., Appalachian Trail Conf. Democrat. Baptist. also: PO Box 2259 Asheville NC 28802 Office: 38 Orange St Asheville NC 28801

MCGILL, JOHN EMMET, JR., trucking manager; b. Paterson, N.J., Apr. 1, 1945; s. J. Emmet Sr. and Elizabeth Catherine (Burns) McG. BA, St. Peters Coll., Jersey City, 1966; MA, Seton Hall U., 1972. Tchr. N.J. Sch. Dist., 1970-75; mgr. McGills Interstate Express, Inc., Paterson, 1976—. With U.S. Army, 1967-69. Mem. KC. Republican. Roman Catholic. Office: McGills Interstate Exp Inc 376 Wabash Ave Paterson NJ 07503

MCGILL, MAURICE LEON, beef processing company executive; b. Malden, Mo., Aug. 22, 1936; s. William Howard and Iris (Phillips) McG.; m. Wanda Coral Wirt, Feb. 2, 1957; children—Melany, Melinda, William Shannon. B.S., U. Mo., 1958, M.A., 1959. C.P.A., Mo., Iowa, Ariz. Mgr. Touche, Ross, Bailey & Smart, Kansas City, Mo., 1959-64; fin. v.p., treas. Iowa Beef Packers, Inc., Dakota City, Nebr., 1964-69; exec. v.p., treas. Spencer Foods, Inc., Iowa, 1969-71, also dir.; sr. v.p. Diamond Reo Trucks, Inc., Lansing, Mich., 1971-72; fin. v.p. Ariz. Colo. Land & Cattle Co., Phoenix, 1972-75; ptnr. Touche Ross & Co., Phoenix, 1975-81; exec. v.p. fin. and adminstrn., treas., bd. dirs. IBP, Inc., Dakota City, Nebr., 1981—. Mem. Am. Inst. C.P.A.s. Club: Sioux City Country. Home: 2505 E Solway Sioux City IA 51104 Office: IBP Inc PO Box 515 Dakota City NE 68731

MC GILL, ROBERT ERNEST, III, manufacturing company executive; b. San Francisco, Apr. 30, 1931; s. Robert Ernest and Madeleine Melanie (Ignace) McG.; m. Daphne Urquhart Driver, Apr. 26, 1958; children: Robert Ernest, Meredith Louise, Christina Elizabeth, James Alexander. B.A., Williams Coll., 1954; M.B.A., Harvard U., 1956. With Morgan Stanley & Co. (investment bankers), N.Y.C., 1956-63; mem. fin. staff Air Products & Chems., Inc., Allentown, Pa., 1963-64; dir. corp. planning and devel. Air Products & Chems., Inc., 1964-68; v.p. Gen. Interiors Corp., N.Y.C., 1968-70; exec. v.p. Gen. Interiors Corp., 1970-73; v.p. fin. Ethan Allen, Inc., Danbury, Conn., 1973-75; v.p. fin., sec. Dexter Corp., Windsor Locks, Conn., 1975-83, sr. v.p. fin. and adminstrn., sec., dir., 1983—; pres. Kettlebrook Ins. Co. Ltd., 1983—, Dexter Credit Corp., 1982-88; dir. Life Techs., Inc., bd. mgrs. Travelers Funds for Variable Annuities. Trustee Greater Hartford Arts Council; bd. dirs. Hartford Symphony Orch.; bd. advisors sch. of bus. U. Conn. Mem. N.Y. Soc. Security Analysts, Fin. Execs. Inst. (pres. Hartford chpt. 1984-85). Office: Dexter Corp 1 Elm St Windsor Locks CT 06096

MC GILLICUDDY, JOHN FRANCIS, banker; b. Harrison, N.Y., Dec. 30, 1930; s. Michael J. and Anna (Munro) McG.; m. Constance Burtis, Sept. 9, 1954; children: Michael Sean, Faith Burtis, Constance Erin Mc Gillicuddy Mills, Brian Munro, John Walsh. A.B., Princeton, 1952; LL.B., Harvard, 1955. With Mfrs. Hanover Trust Co. subs. Mfrs. Hanover Corp., N.Y.C., 1958—, v.p., 1962-66, sr. v.p., 1966-69, exec. v.p., asst. to chmn., 1969-70, vice chmn., dir., 1970, pres., 1971—, chmn., chief exec. officer, 1979—; chmn., chief exec. officer Mfrs. Hanover Corp., N.Y.C.; dir. Kraft Inc., USX Corp., Continental Corp., Allegis Corp., Fed. Reserve Bankof N.Y. Bd. dirs. Nat. Multiple Sclerosis Soc., 1969—; trustee N.Y. Hosp., Princeton U., N.Y. Pub. Library. Served to lt. (j.g.) USNR, 1955-58. Mem. Assn. Res. City Bankers, Bus. Council, Bus. Roundtable. Roman Catholic. Clubs: Westchester Country (Rye, N.Y.); Blind Brook (Port Chester, N.Y.); Princeton (N.Y.C.). Office: Mfrs Hanover Corp 270 Park Ave New York NY 10017 •

MC GIMPSEY, RONALD ALAN, oil company executive; b. Cleve., June 7, 1944; s. John E. and Muriel N. McGimpsey; m. Linda V. Tiffany, Apr. 20, 1974. BS, Case Inst. Tech., 1966; MS, Case Western Res. U., 1974; grad. exec. program, Stanford U., 1987. With BP Am. Inc. (formerly Standard Oil Co.), Ohio, 1966—; treas. BP Am. Inc. (formerly Standard Oil Co.), 1977-81, v.p. fin., 1981-82; sr. v.p. Crude Trading and Transp., 1982-86, Petroleum Products and Refining, Cleve., 1986—. Chmn. bd. trustees Marymount Hosp., Cleve., 1986-88. Office: BP Oil Co 200 Public Sq Cleveland OH 44114 other: BP NAm Petroleum Inc 550 Westlake Pk Blvd Houston TX 77079

MCGINLEY, EDWARD STILLMAN, II, naval officer; b. Allentown, Pa., June 9, 1939; s. Edward Stillman and Dorothy Mae (Kandle) McG.; m. Connie Lee Mayo, July 1, 1962; children: Amanda Lee, Edward Stillman III. BS, U.S. Naval Acad., 1961; SM in Naval Engring., MIT, 1970; MSA, George Washington U., 1972; cert. exec. program, U. Va., 1981. Commd. ensign USN, 1961, advanced through grades to capt., 1982, various positions in submarine engring., 1962-76; repair officer USN, Rota (Spain) and Charleston, S.C., 1976-83; ops. mgr. Mare Island Naval Shipyard, Vallejo, Calif., 1983-87; comdr. Norfolk Naval Shipyard, Portsmouth, Va., 1987—. Contbr. articles to profl. jours. Mem. Am. Soc. Naval Engrs. (sect. chmn. 1980-81), Soc. Naval Architects and Marine Engrs., U.S. Naval Inst., Sigma Xi, Tau Beta Pi. Republican. Baptist. Lodge: Rotary. Home: Qtrs A Norfolk Naval Shipyard Portsmouth VA 23709 Office: Comdr Norfolk Naval Shipyard Portsmouth VA 23709

MCGINN, MARY LYN, real estate company executive; b. New Orleans, Aug. 12, 1949; d. Dan Creedon and Millicent Virginia (White) Midgett; m. Walter Lee McGinn, Mar. 14, 1985. BA, La. State U., 1970, MA, 1972; PhD, U. So. Miss., 1976. Cert. comml.-investment mem., cert. property mgr., master appraiser. Dir., prof. Dillard U., New Orleans, 1972-76, Loyola U., New Orleans, 1976-80; sr. v.p. Equity Investment Services, Inc., New Orleans, 1980-84; pres. Mgmt. Services Group, Inc., New Orleans, 1984-85, Assoc. Investment Services Inc., New Orleans, 1985-87, Northshore Property Mgmt., Inc., New Orleans, 1985-87; asst. v.p. USF&G Realty, Balt., 1987—; br. dirs. Children's Guild, Balt., 1988; cons. colls. and univs., 1976—. Mem. Nat. Assn. Corporate Real Estate Execs., Bldg. Owners and Mgrs. Assn., Comml.-Investment Council, Nat. Assn. Master Appraisers. Office: US Fidelity & Guaranty Co 100 Light St Baltimore MD 21202

MC GINNESS, WILLIAM GEORGE, III, manufacturing company executive; b. Lock Haven, Pa., Apr. 9, 1948; s. William George and Ruby Jean (Cooper) McG., children—Heather Jean, Patrick Robert. B.Chemistry, Lock Haven State U., 1970. Prodn. mgr. Am. Color & Chem. Corp., Lock Haven, Pa., 1969-75; lab. mgr. Novamont/Montedison, Florence, Ky., 1976-79; prodn. mgr. Sun Chem., Cin., 1979-80; v.p. tech. services Natmar, Inc., Cin., 1980-83; pres., chief exec. officer Angstrom Techs., Florence, Ky., 1983—; dir. Natmar, Inc., Sperti Drug Products, Inc., Antex Corp. Mem. Am. Chem. Soc., Soc. Profl. Engrs., Am. Assn. Textile Chemists and Colorists, Soc. Mfg. Engrs., Machine Vision Assn., Robotics Internat., AAAS. Republican. Lutheran. Clubs: Bankers (Cin.); Chemists (N.Y.C.). Home: 2251 Clarkson Dr Union KY 41091 Office: Angstrom Techs Inc 20 Kenton Lands Rd Erlanger KY 41018

MCGINNIS, JAMES ARTHUR, treasurer; b. Milw., May 27, 1947; s. James Mortimer and Lucille Katherine (Kies) McG.; m. Diana Susan Young, Sept. 6, 1969; children: Susan, Michael. BBA in Acctg., U. Wis., Milw., 1970, MBA in Acctg., 1972. CPA, Wis. Sr. auditor Price Waterhouse Co., Milw., 1972-74; budget dir. Mortgage Guaranty Ins. Corp., Milw., 1974-78, dir. internal audit, 1978-80, treas., 1980—; bd. dirs. Comml. Loan Ins. Corp., Milw., WMAC Credit Ins. Corp., Milw. Mem. Am. Inst. CPA's. Republican. Lutheran. Office: Mortgage Guaranty Ins Corp 270 E Kilbourn Ave Milwaukee WI 53202

MCGINNIS, ROBERT WILLIAM, electronics company executive; b. Modesto, Calif., Oct. 31, 1936; s. George Crawford and Lola May (Provis) McG.; B.S. in Elec. Engring. with highest honors, U. Calif., Berkeley, 1962; postgrad. N.Y. U., 1962-63; m. Sondra Elaine Hurley, Mar. 1, 1964; children—Michael Fredrick, Traci Anne, Patrick William. Mem. tech. staff Bell Telephone Labs, Murray Hill, N.J., 1961-63; devel. engr., engring. mgr., product mgr., ops. mgr. Motorola Semiconductor Group, Phoenix, 1963-73, ops. mgr. for hybrid circuits group, communications div., Fort Lauderdale, Fla., 1973-76, solar ops. mgr., 1976-79; v.p., gen. mgr. Photowatt Internat., Inc., Tempe, Ariz., 1979-83; gen. mgr. SAFT Electronic Systems Div., 1983-85, pres., Safe Power Systems, Inc., Tempe, 1985—. Mem. Ariz. Solar Energy Commn., 1977-83; chmn. photovoltaic subcom. Am. Nat. Standards Inst., 1978-83; mem. coordinating council Solar Energy Research Inst. Standards, 1977-82. Served with USNR, 1955-58. Mem. IEEE, Phi Beta Kappa, Tau Beta Pi, Eta Kappa Nu. Republican. Methodist. Contbr. articles in field to profl. jours. Home: 7887 Via Bonita Scottsdale AZ 85282 Office: Safe Power Systems Inc 528 W 21st Tempe AZ 85202

MCGINNIS, SEÁN WILLIAM, financial advisor; b. Wellsville, N.Y., May 5, 1955; s. Frank James and Regina Frances (Ludden) McG. BA, Manhattanville Coll., 1978; MBA in Fin., Fordham U., 1983; JD cum laude, N.Y. Law Sch., 1988. Cert. fin. planner; registered investment advisor. Liaison IBM, Armonk, N.Y., 1979-83; sr. bus. analyst Smith Barney, Harris Upham & Co., N.Y.C., 1983-84; pres. Atlantic Emeritus, Inc., N.Y.C., 1982—; bd. dirs. Medlaw Connections, Inc., N.Y.C.; bd. advisors S.U.N. Internat., Ltd., N.Y.C., 1987—. Lobbyist Ind. Sch. Coalition, Albany, N.Y., 1976-78. Recipient Grand St. Acad. Scholarship, N.Y. Law Sch., N.Y.C., 1985-88, Am. Jurisprudence award Lawyers Coop. Pub., Rochester, N.Y., 1987. Mem. Am. Mgmt. Assn., Nat. Assn. Tax Profls., Mensa. Roman Catholic. Clubs: Ancient Order Hibernians (Bronx, N.Y.). Office: Atlantic Emeritus Inc 663 City Island Ave 2d fl New York NY 10464

MCGIVERIN, DONALD SCOTT, retail company executive; b. Calgary, Alta., Can., Apr. 4, 1924; s. Alfred Chester and Ella (Scott) McG.; m. Margaret-Ann Weld, Sept. 9, 1950 (dec. Nov. 1968); children—Mary Edith, Richard Weld (dec.). B.Comm., U. Man., 1945; M.B.A., Ohio State U., 1946. Mng. dir. retail stores Hudson's Bay Co., Winnipeg, Man., Can., 1969-72, pres., dir., 1972-85, gov., dir., 1982—; bd. dirs. Markborough Properties Ltd., Mfrs. Life Ins. Co., Mfrs. Capital Corp., DuPont Can. Ltd., Noranda Inc. Bd. govs. Wellesley Hosp. Mem. Phi Kappa Pi, Beta Gamma Sigma. Clubs: Lambton Golf and Country, Rosedale Golf, Granite, York, Toronto; LyFord Cay (Nassau, Bahamas); St. Charles Country (Winnipeg); Loxahatchee (Jupiter, Fla.); Mt. Royal (Montreal). Home: 44 Charles St W, Toronto, ON Canada M4Y 1R8 Office: Hudsons Bay Co, 401 Bay St, Toronto, ON Canada M5H 2Y4

MCGLADE, KEITH LYNN, investment and business consultant; b. Zanesville, Ohio, Dec. 8, 1937; s. Kenneth Edward and Dorothy Louise (Archer) McG.; m. Linn Gale McGlade, Aug. 22, 1964; 1 child, Kimberly Ann. BS in Econs., U. Pa., 1959; MBA, U. Mich., 1967. CPA, Mich. With Chevrolet div. Gen. Motors Corp., Detroit, 1959-67; audit supr. Ernst and Ernst, Detroit, 1967-71; treas., controller Detroit Free Press, 1971-77, bus. mgr., treas., 1977; v.p., gen. mgr. Akron (Ohio) Beacon Jour., 1977-80; pub. Hartford (Conn.) Courant, 1980-84; pres. Associated Media Corp., Stamford, Conn., 1984-86; ptnr. Hartford Mgmt. Group, 1986—. Mem. Am. Inst. CPA's, Fin. Execs. Inst. Presbyterian. Home: 75 Orchard Rd West Hartford CT 06117 Office: Hartford Mgmt Group Cityplace 31st Floor Hartford CT 06117

MCGLADE, PETER GERARD, airline exective; b. Newry, Northern Ireland, Aug. 30, 1953; came to U.S., 1954; s. Peter and Josephine (Smyth) McG.; m. Nancy Carol O'Brien, July 23, 1976; children: Sean Peter, Erin Rose, Ryan Patrick. BS in Mgmt., Purdue U., 1975. Prodn. supr. L.D. Sehrieber Cheese Co., Green Bay, Wis., 1975-76; with Northwest Orient Airlines, Mpls., 1976-80; mgr. planning Air Cal, Orange County, Calif., 1980-82; mgr. market planning Pacific Southwest Airlines, San Diego, 1982-83; market planner Southwest Airlines, Dallas, 1983-86; dir. scheduling Southwest Airlines, 1986—. Roman Catholic. Home: 1217 North Slope Carrollton TX 75007 Office: Southwest Airlines PO Box 37611 Dallas TX 75235

MCGLINCHEY, JOSEPH DENNIS, retail corporation executive; b. Lowell, Mass., Mar. 14, 1938; s. Patrick Joseph and Grace E. (Curley) McG.; m. Joan Fitzgerald, Sept. 12, 1964; children: Joseph II, Mark, Christopher, David. BA in Acctg., Bentley Coll., 1965; MBA, Babson Coll., 1971. Internal auditor The Stop and Shop Cos., Inc., Boston, 1962-65, dir. fin. planning and control, 1973-74, corp. controller, 1974-77, v.p., corp. controller, 1977-83, v.p. fin., chief acctg. officer, 1983-86, sr. v.p., treas., chief fin. officer, 1986—; asst. controller Bradlees, Boston, 1967-69, controller, 1972-73; controller Gilchrist Co., Boston, 1969-72. Bd. overseers, mem. fin. com. Harvard Community Health Plan, Brookline, Mass., 1985—; treas. St. Mary's Parish, Randolph, Mass. Served with U.S. Army. Roman Catholic. Home: 359 N Main St Randolph MA 02368 Office: Stop & Shop Cos Inc PO Box 369 Boston MA 02101

MCGONIGLE, JAMES GREGORY, consultant; b. Bklyn., Nov. 17, 1945; s. William John and Helen Bernadette (Dennin) McG.; m. Francine Anne Falango, May 27, 1972; children: Marie Elena, Lauren Anne. AAS in Acctg., CUNY, 1972; BS in Fin. summa cum laude, L.I. U., 1980. Certified Financial Planner. Account exec. Coburn Credit Corp., Rockville Centre, N.Y., 1965-66; asst. credit mgr. UNI-CARD, Greatneck, N.Y., 1966-68; accounts receivable mgr. Granite Leasing Corp., Garden City, N.Y., 1968-73; v.p. Citicorp., N.Y.C., 1973-88; cons. O/E Learning, Inc., Detroit, 1988—. Vol. Family Svc. Assn. Nassau, N.Y., 1981-84, Better Bus. Bur., Farmingdale, N.Y., 1987-88; treas. W. Tresper Clarke Friends of the Arts, 1988—. Mem. Fin. Mgmt. Assn., Internat. Assn. Fin. Planning, Adelphi Soc. Cert. Fin. Planners, Inst. Cert. Fin. Planners (cert. fin. planner), Nat. Assn. Life Underwriters, Nat. Panel of Consumer Arbitrators, Nat. Ctr. for Fin. Edn. (prof. sponsor) (Delta Mu Delta. Republican. Roman Catholic. Home: 2167 Plum Tree Rd N Westbury NY 11590 Office: 33 Willis Ave Mineola NY 11501

MCGONIGLE, JOHN WILLIAM, lawyer, investment company executive; b. Pitts., Oct. 26, 1938; s. Henry J. and Madeline I. (Jones) McG.; m. Mary Ita Smith, July 13, 1963; children: Kevin M., Christine I., Michael J. BS, Duquesne U., Pitts., 1960, LLB, 1965. Bar: Pa. 1965, D.C. 1965. Atty. SEC, Washington, 1965-66; sec., gen. counsel Federated Investors, Inc., Pitts., 1967—; v.p., counsel investment cos. Federated Funds, 1966—; dir. Liberty Bank & Trust,, Gibbsboro,, N.J.; bd. dirs. ICI Mutual Ins. Co.; bd. gov.'s ICI Investment Co. Inst. Editor: Duquesne Law Rev., 1962-65. Mem. Cath. Social Services Bd., Pitts., 1975-78. Served to 1st lt. U.S. Army, 1960-62. Mem. ABA, Pa. Bar Assn. (chmn. com. on corp. law depts. 1979-80), Allegheny County Bar Assn., Am. Soc. Corp. Secs. Clubs: Pitts. Athletic Assn., Duquesne, Rivers, Pitts. Field. Office: Federated Investors Inc Federated Investors Tower Pittsburgh PA 15222-3779

MCGOUGH, EDWARD PATRICK, personnel executive; b. Cresson, Pa., Nov. 10, 1949; s. Charles Edward and Dorothy Louise (Casher) McG.; m. Karen Margaret Langherst, Sept. 20, 1975; 1 child, Erin Langherst. BA, Slippery Rock U., 1971; MA, California U. of Pa., 1978. Inspector safety USX, Clairton, Pa., 1974-75, analyst labor rels., 1975-78, adminstr. labor contract, 1978-82, supr. tng., 1982-83, supr. salary adminstrn., 1983-84, supr. personnel, 1984; supt. personnel svcs. Wheeling-Pitts. Steel, Steubenville, Ohio, 1985; dir. human resources Biodecision Labs., Pitts., 1985—. Mem. Am. Mgmt. Assn. Office: Biodecision Labs 5900 Pennsylvania Ave Pittsburgh PA 15206

MCGOUGH, GEORGE VICTOR, financial company executive; b. N.Y.C., 1940. BS, Mitchell Coll., 1964; MBA, Pace U., 1970. Pres., chief exec. officer Prudential-Bache Securities Can. Ltd., Toronto, Ont., Can., 1986—; bd. dirs. Prudential Mut. Funds Group, Prudential-Bache Securities, Inc., Prudential-Bache Securities Can., Ltd. Mem. steering com. Conf. Bd. Can.; mem. exec. com., mem. patrons' coun. Nat. Ballet Can.; trustee Pace U. With USMC, 1959-64. Office: Prudential-Bache Securities Can Ltd, 33 Yonge St Ste 400, Toronto, ON Canada M5E 1V7

MCGOVERN, E. TOM, real estate investor; b. Racine, Wis., Sept. 11, 1923; s. Edward Thomas and Dorothy (Maibohn) McG.; m. Ruth Ballard, June 5, 1943; children: Jill, Terry, Kay, Lee, Dee, E. Tom III. Student, U. Wis., Madison, 1940-42. Pres. Tom McGovern Assocs., Madison, Wis., 1946-52, McGovern and Co., San Antonio, 1953-62, Empresas y Terrenos de Mex., Mexico City, 1962-63, Edwards Bankers and Co., Houston, 1964-72; chmn. exec. com. Edwards Bankers and Co., St. Petersburg, Fla., 1985—; pres. Energy Research and Devel. Corp., St. Petersburg, Fla., 1972-73, Thomas Equities Corp., St. Petersburg, 1973-85; founding mem. Real Estate Syndication and Securities Inst., Washington, 1970. V.p. fin. Tex. Assn. Mental Health, Dallas, 1960, 61. Mem. Nat. Assn. Homebuilders (bd. dirs. 1945-55), Internat. Found. Timesharing (founding dir. 1981), Inst. Real Estate Mgmt. Republican. Office: Edwards Bankers and Co PO Box 14114 Saint Petersburg FL 33733

MCGOVERN, JOHN FRANCIS, financial executive; b. Port Chester, N.Y., June 4, 1946; s. Charles William and Jeanette Mary (Farrell) McG.; m. Gertrude Anne Mills, June 21, 1969; children—Robert Francis, Sarah Mills. B.S. in Econs., Fordham U., 1968. Asst. treas. Chase Manhattan Bank, N.Y.C., 1973-74, 2d v.p., 1974-76, v.p., 1976-80, v.p. div. treas. forest products, 1980-81; v.p. project fin Ga.-Pacific Corp., Portland, Oreg., 1981-83, v.p., 1983—. Fund raiser Am. Heart Assn., Atlanta, 1985—; adviser Atlanta Ballet, 1985. Served with U.S. Army, 1968-70. Mem. Fin. Execs. Inst. Republican. Roman Catholic. Club: Atlanta Country. Office: Ga-Pacific Corp 133 Peachtree St NE Atlanta GA 30303

MCGOVERN, R(ICHARD) GORDON, food company executive; b. Norristown, Pa., Oct. 22, 1926; s. James Joseph and Marion (Stritzinger) McG.; m. Julia Merrow, June 4, 1955; children: Lucinda, Jennifer, Martha, Douglas. Student, Williams Coll., 1944-45, Coll. Holy Cross, 1945-46; AB, Brown U., 1948; MBA, Harvard U., 1950. With Pepperidge Farm, Inc., 1956-80, pres., 1968-80; dir., v.p. Campbell Soup Co., 1976-80, exec. v.p., 1980, pres., 1980—; bd. dir. North Am. Life Assurance Co., Toronto, Ont., Can., Core States Bank, Smith Kline Beckman. Chmn. The Pa. Orch., N.J. Gov.'s Leadership Commn., United Negro Coll. Fund, N.J. Lt. USNR, 1944-46, 52-54. Mem. Am. Mktg. Assn., Am. Soc. Bakery Engrs., Grocery Mfrs. Assn. (bd. dirs.), Phi Beta Kappa, Sigma Xi, Delta Upsilon. Home: 182 Lounsbury Rd Ridgefield CT 06877 Office: Campbell Soup Co Campbell Pl PO Box 60A Camden NJ 08101 also: Campbell Soup Co Ltd, 60 Birmingham St, Toronto, ON Canada M8V 2B8

MCGOWAN, DANIEL LEONARD, JR., human resources director; b. Geneva, Ala., July 23, 1957; s. Daniel Leonard Sr. and Kathryn (Gilbert) McG.; m. Mellany Carol Enfinger, June 6, 1981; children: Daniel Charles, James Christian. AA in Mgmt., Edison State Coll.; AA, Enterprise State Jr. Coll.; BS in Gen. Bus., NYU; BSBA in Fin. and Mgmt., Edison State Coll. Cert. fin. planner, administrv. mgr. News dir., anchor Sta. WOOF Inc., Dothan, Ala., 1975-79; area mgr. Tom Lipe & Assocs., Dothan, 1979-80; news dir., anchor Woods Communications Corp., Dothan, 1980-84; officer InterFirst Bank Corp., Houston, 1984-86; dir. human resources, registered rep. AMI Investment Corp., Amarillo, Tex., 1986—. Big Bros. of Big Bros. Inc., Abilene, Tex., 1982-84. Mem. Nat. Assn. Securities Dealers (lic. gen. securities prin., fin. ops. prin., registered rep.), Panhandle Personnel Assn. (v.p. 1989—), Personnel Accreditation Inst. (cert.), Kiwanis Club (editor newsletter 1981). Baptist. Home: 7800 Cervin Dr Amarillo TX 79121 Office: 8101 W 34th St Amarillo TX 79121

MCGOWAN, DONALD EDWIN, customer relations manager; b. Monroe, Ga., June 27, 1947; s. John Edwin and Virginia Ann (Breedlove) McG.; m. Marilyn Merrianne Jackson, Oct. 5, 1968 (div. June 1975); 1 child, Tamara Shayne; m. Lisa Ann Byrd, June 4, 1988. BA, U. Ga., 1970, JD, 1972. Bar: Ga. 1972. Assoc. Robert A. DelBello, Atty., Hiawassee, Ga., 1975-76; child abuse counselor Ga. Dept. of Human Resources, Blairsville, Ga., 1977-80; customer relations mgr. Horton Homes Inc., Eatonton, Ga., 1980—. Bd. dirs. Putnam County Assn. for the Performing Arts. Lt. U.S. Army, 1973. Named Disting. Mil. grad. U. Ga., 1970. Mem. State Bar Ga. (mem. ins. law sect. 1986—, corp. counsel 1986—), Ga. Manufactured Housing Assn. (land use planning com.). Baptist. Office: Horton Homes Inc 101 Indsl Blvd Eatonton GA 31024

MCGOWAN, GEORGE VINCENT, public utility executive; b. Balt., Jan. 30, 1928; s. Joseph H. and Ethna M. (Prahl) McG.; m. Carol Murray, Aug. 6, 1977; children by a previous marriage: Gregg Blair, Bradford Kirby. B.S. in M.E., U. Md., 1951. Registered profl. engr., Md. Project engr. nuclear power plant Balt. Gas & Electric Co., 1967-72, chief nuclear engr., 1972-74, pres., chief operating officer, 1980-87, chmn. bd. dirs, 1988—, mgr. corp. staff services, 1974-78, v.p. mgmt. and staff services, 1978-79; dir. Equitable Bancorp., Equitable Bank N.A., Equitable Bank Del. N.A., Balt. Life Ins. Co., McCormick & Co., Life of Md. Inc., Edison Electric Inst., UNC Inc., Orgn. REsources Counselors, Inc. Bd. dirs. Am. Nuclear Energy Council, Washington, 1982—; vice chmn. bd. regents U. Md. System; bd. dirs. U. Md. Med. System; chmn. Gov.'s Vol. Council State of Md.; trustee Walters Art Gallery, Balt., 1982—; bd. dirs. Balt. chpt. ARC, United Way Central Md.; bd. dirs. Balt. Symphony Orch., Greater Balt. Com. Recipient Disting. Alumnus award U. Md. Coll. Engring., 1980, 87. Mem. ASME, Am. Nuclear Soc., U.S. Energy Assn. of the World Energy Conf. (chmn.), Engring. Soc. Balt. (Founders Day award 1988), Md. C. of C.(bd. dirs.). Presbyterian. Clubs: The Center (Balt.); U. Md. M (College Park, Md.); Chartwell Golf & Country (Severna Park, Md.); Annapolis Yacht (Md.); Md. (Balt.). Office: Baltimore Gas & Electric Co PO Box 1475 Baltimore MD 21203

MCGOWAN, TERRY ROBERT, computer industry executive; b. Passaic, N.J., Mar. 24, 1947; m. Cynthia A. Crawford; children: Kelly, Jennifer, Heather, Anne, Lara. BS in Polit. Sci., U. So. Miss., 1969. Account exec. IBM Co., Detroit, 1973-78; regional mgr. Amdahl Corp., Sunnyvale, Calif., 1978-84; pres. KnowledgeWare, Inc., Atlanta, 1984—. Capt. USMC, 1969-73, Vietnam. Mem. Computer Software and Svcs. Industry Assn. Home: 3630 Schooner Ridge Alpharetta GA 30201 Office: KnowledgeWare Inc 3340 Peachtree Rd NE 1100 Atlanta GA 30026

MCGOWAN, THOMAS BERNARD, III, insurance company executive, lawyer; b. Bklyn., Sept. 25, 1945; s. Thomas Bernard and Ruth Margot (Dunne) McG.; m. Holly Fry, Oct. 25, 1969; children: Thomas B., Katherine Megan, Colin Cameron, Alexandra Elise, Eamon Andrew, Neil Patrick. BA, Coll. Holy Cross, 1966; JD, U. Mich., 1969. Assoc. Sweeney, Maher and Vlad, Cleve., 1969-72; v.p. McGowan & Co., Inc., Rocky River, Ohio, 1972—. Contbr. articles to profl. jours. Mem. exec. com. Cleve. Zool. Soc., 1978—; active St. Raphaels Ch. Named Ins. Man Yr., Cleve. Ins. Women. Mem. ABA (various coms.), Ind. Ins. Agts. Assn. (various offices, Ins. Man Yr.), CPCU Soc., St. Ignatious Alumni Assn. (exec. com. 1987—). Roman Catholic. Home: 27000 Bruce Rd Bay Village OH 44140 Office: McGowan & Co Inc 21010 Center Ridge Rd Rocky River OH 44116

MCGRAIN, JONATHAN THOMAS, banker; b. Hyannis, Mass., Nov. 6, 1963; s. Thomas William and Carol Ann (LaFontaine) McG. BA, Columbia U., 1985; postgrad. in bus. admin., NYU. Pres. Colmark, Worcester, Mass., 1983-85; asst. mgr. Citicorp, N.Y.C., 1985-88; asst. sec. Mfrs. Hanover Trust, N.Y.C., 1988, Chem. Bank, N.Y.C., 1988—. Mem. Asia Soc., N.Y.C. Opera Guild, N.Y. Road Runners Club, Kappa Delta Rho. Republican. Roman Catholic. Home: 165 E 89th St Apt 3E New York NY 10128 Office: Chem Bank 52 Broadway New York NY 10004

MCGRATH, CHERYL LYNN, pension fund administrator; b. East Lansing, Mich., Aug. 20, 1956; d. Maurice Wayne and Dorothy Mae (McCarty) Brandt; m. Timothy Jay McGrath, Aug. 19, 1978; children: Kathryn Renee, Kevin Dwight. BA in Bus. Econ., Calvin Coll., Grand Rapids, Mich., 1978; MBA in Mgmt. and Fin., Grand Valley State U., Allendale, Mich., 1986. Systems analyst Gerber Products Co., Fremont, Mich., 1978-83, sr. computer analyst, 1983-85, project leader, 1985-86, bank adminstr., 1986, mgr. benefit plan investments, 1986—; pres. Fremont Growth Investors, 1987-89. Bd. dirs. The Ark Child Care Ctr., Fremont, 1986-88. Mem. Western Mich. Pension Group. Mem. Reformed Ch. Clubs: Rotary (Fremont). Office: Gerber Products Co 445 State St Fremont MI 49412

MCGRATH, DENNIS BRITTON, public relations executive; b. Mpls., Mar. 11, 1937; s. James William and Rosalia Clara (Britton) McG.; m. Susan J. Smith, Apr. 15, 1961 (div. 1972); children: Daniel Scott, Amy Susan; m. Elizabeth Ann Buckley, Sept. 1, 1983; 1 stepson, Felix Buckley Jones. BA in Journalism, U. Minn., 1963. Publs. editor Mut. Service Ins. Co., St. Paul, 1963-65; pub. relations account exec. Kerker, Peterson Advt., Mpls., 1965-69; dir. advt. and pub. relations Dain, Kalman & Quail, Mpls., 1969-70; v.p., dir. pub. relations Carmichael Lynch Advt., Mpls., 1970-75; editor Corp. Report Goldletter Dorn Communications, Mpls., 1975; sr. account supr. Kerker & Assocs., Mpls., 1975-77; v.p. Padilla & Speer Inc., Mpls., 1977-79; v.p. communications Gelco Corp., Mpls., 1979-81; v.p., regional mgr. Doremus & Co., Mpls., 1981-83; pres. Mona, Meyer & McGrath, Mpls., 1983—. Bi-monthly columnist corp. report mag. Communications, 1974-88. Bd. dirs. Cricket Theatre, Mpls., 1985—, Women's Econ. Devel. Corp., St. Paul, 1986-88, Project Pride in Living, Mpls., 1970—, Minn. Hearing Soc., 1986-88, Mpls. Aquatennial Assn., 1988—. Mem. Pub. Rels. Soc. Am. (accredited, bd. dirs. 1988—), Nat. Investor Rels. Inst. (pres. Twin Cities chpt. 1984), Minn. Press Club (chmn., pres. 1980, 81, bd. dirs. 1979-80), Mpls. Aquatemmial Assn. Democrat. Roman Catholic. Club: Mpls. Athletic. Home: 284 Pelham Blvd Saint Paul MN 55104 Office: Mona Meyer & McGrath 701 4th Ave S Minneapolis MN 55415

MCGRATH, EDWARD LEO, bank executive; b. N.Y.C., Apr. 5, 1947; s. Edward Phillip McGrath and Mary Margaret (Kiley) Dennehy. BS, Fordham U., 1969; MBA, Columbia U., 1974. Vol. U.S. Peace Corps, Managua, Nicaragua, 1971-73; sr. fin. analyst Mellon Bank, Pitts., 1974-75; controller Mellon Bank, Tokyo, 1975-78, Hong Kong, 1978-80; dir. internat. fin. Mellon Bank, Pitts., 1980, mgr. internat. credit, 1980-82, internat. controller, 1982-85; rep. Mellon Bank, Mexico City, 1985—; mng. dir. Mellon Overseas Capital, N.V., 1983-87; bd. dirs., mem. fin. com. ABC Hosp., Mex., 1987—; bd. dirs., fin. adv. bd. Francisca Friars Minor, Pitts., 1984-85. Author: The Maquiladora Industry in Nicaragua, 1974. State dir. N.Y. State Young Dems., Nassau County, 1969; mem. Dems. Abroad, Mex., 1985—, chmn. fund raising com. 1988-89, transcriber, exec. com., 1988—. Recipient Cert. Achievement U.S. Govt., 1975. Mem. Airplane Owners and Pilots Assn., Am. C. of C. (viglance com. 1988-89, econ. banking and fin. com. 1985—, vice-chmn. 1987-89), Alpha Kappa Psi (pledgement dir. Chgo. chpt. 1970). Clubs: Club de Golf (Chapultepec, Mex.); Princeton (N.Y.C.); Fgn. Corrs., American (Hong Kong); Bankers' Club (Districo Fed., Mex. chpt.). Office: Mellon Bank NA, Hamburgo 213, Piso 12, 06600 Mexico City Mexico

MCGRATH, JAMES THOMAS, natural gas company executive; b. N.Y.C., Nov. 10, 1942; s. Thomas James and Mary Ita (Finnegan) McG.; 1 child, Tara. BS in Acctg., Providence Coll., 1964. CPA, N.Y. Sr. auditor Coopers & Lybrand, N.Y.C., 1968-72, mgmt. cons., 1972-74; group controller IU Internat. Corp., Phila., 1974-77; v.p. fin. Taylor Enging. Corp. subs. IU Internat., Detroit, 1977-78; controller Pool Co. subs. Enserch Corp., Houston, 1978-85; sr. v.p. fin., treas. Lone Star Gas Co. subs. Enserch Corp., Dallas, 1985—. Served to lt. USN, 1964-68. Mem. Am. Gas Assn. (vice-chmn. adminstrn. sect. 1985—), So. Gas Assn., Am. Inst. CPA's, N.Y. State Soc. CPA's, Am. Mgmt. Assn. Republican. Roman Catholic. Clubs: Dallas Athletic. Office: Lone Star Gas Co 301 S Harwood St Dallas TX 75201

MCGRATH, JOSEPH UPTON, financial planner; b. New Haven, Mar. 31, 1925; s. Joseph A. and Anna E. (Moran) McG.; m. Antoinette Maria Marchese, Dec. 26, 1949; children: Lee U., Paul R. BA, Yale U., 1948; MA, Columbia U., 1951. Cert. fin. planner. Tchr. Locust Valley High Sch., N.Y., 1961-87; fin. planner McGrath Fin. Planning, Huntington, N.Y., 1984-86, Invest Am., Huntington, 1986-87; pres. McGrath Cons., Inc., Huntington, 1987—. With USN, 1943-46. William Coe fellow Stanford U., 1967. Mem. Internat. Assn. Fin. Planning, Inst. Cert. Fin. Planners. Home and Office: 6 Panorama Dr Huntington NY 11743

MCGRATH, KATHRYN BRADLEY, lawyer; b. Norfolk, Va., Sept. 2, 1944; d. James Pierce and Kathryn (Hoyle) Bradley; m. John J. McGrath Jr., June 8, 1968; children: Ian M., James D. AB, Mt. Holyoke Coll., 1966; JD, Georgetown U., 1969. Ptnr. Gardner, Carton & Douglas, Washington, 1979-83; dir. div. investment mgmt. SEC, Washington, 1983—. Named Disting. Exec. Pres. Reagan, 1987. Mem. Fed. Bar Assn. (exec. council securities law com.). Office: SEC Investment Mgmt 450 5th St NW Washington DC 20549

MC GRAW, HAROLD WHITTLESEY, JR., publisher; b. Bklyn., Jan. 10, 1918; s. Harold Whittlesey and Louise (Higgins) McG.; m. Anne PerLee, Nov. 30, 1940; children: Suzanne, Harold Whittlesey III, Thomas Per-Lee, Robert Pearse. Grad., Lawrenceville (N.J.) Sch., 1936; A.B., Princeton U., 1940. With G.M. Basford (advt. agy.), N.Y.C., 1940-41, Brentano's Bookstores, Inc., 1946; with McGraw-Hill Book Co., Inc., N.Y.C., 1947—, successively promotion mgr., dir. co. advt. and trade sales, 1947-55, dir., v.p. charge trade book, indsl. and bus. book depts., co. advt., 1955-61, sr. v.p., 1961-68, pres., chief exec. officer, 1968-74; pres., chief exec. officer McGraw-Hill, Inc., 1974-83, chairman, 1976-88; chairman emeritus 1988—; dir. McGraw Hill, Inc., 1954-88, Schering-Plough. Founder, pres., bd. dirs. Bus. Council Effective Literacy and Bus. Press Ednl. Found. Served as capt. USAAF, 1941-45. Clubs: University (N.Y.C.); Blind Brook (Purchase, N.Y.); Wee Burn (Darien, Conn.). Home: Watch Tower Rd Darien CT 06820 Office: McGraw-Hill Inc 1221 Ave of the Americas New York NY 10020

MCGRAW, LAVINIA MORGAN, retail company executive; b. Detroit, Feb. 26, 1924; d. Will Curtis and Margaret Coulter (Oliphant) McG. AB, Radcliffe Coll., 1945. Sales assoc. The May Dept. Store Corp., Washington, 1977—. Mem. Phi Beta Kappa. Avocation: hiking. Home: 2501 Calvert St NW Washington DC 20008

MCGRAW, LELAND CHESTER, oil company executive; b. Milo, Iowa, Oct. 11, 1924; s. Chester Earl and Edna (Simpson) McG; m. Marilyn Scheib, Mar. 16, 1946; children—Vickie Rae McGraw Sherman, Pamela Sue Hoffman, William Lee. B.S.B.A., Simpson Coll., 1946; M.B.A., Stanford U., 1948; postgrad. Sr. Execs. Program, MIT, 1972. C.P.A., La. 1950. Various fin. assignments ChevronCorp, San Francisco, 1948-65, asst. comptroller, 1965-68, dir. computer services, 1968-76; v.p. fin. Chevron USA, Inc., San Francisco, 1977-85; v.p., info. tech. ChevronCorp, San Francisco, 1985-87, v.p. fin., 1988—. Bd. trustees Simpson Coll., Indianola, Iowa, 1976—. Served to lt. (j.g.), USN, 1943-46; PTO. Recipient Alumni Achievement awrd Simpson Coll., Indianola, 1977. Mem. AICPA, Fin. Execs. Inst., Am. Contract Bridge League (life master), Bankers Club. Republican. Presbyterian. Club: Am. Contract Bridge League (life master). Home: 1350 Hayne Rd Hillsborough CA 94010 Office: Chevron Corp 225 Bush St San Francisco CA 94104

MCGRAW, RICHARD LYLE, public relations executive; b. Montgomery, W.Va., Dec. 27, 1936; s. Henry Paul McGraw and Edythe Lyle (Bagby) Williams; m. Beverly Vaughan, Aug. 4, 1960 (div. Feb. 1964); 1 son, Patrick; m. Barbara A. Callison, May 15, 1964; 1 son, Douglas. Student W.Va., U., 1959-61; BA, Wash. State U., 1964; MA, Mich. State U., 1968. Exec. asst. to sec. U.S. Dept. HUD, Washington, 1973-75, dep. under sec., 1975-77; exec. dir. Alliance to Save Energy, Washington, 1977-79, bd. dirs., 1977—; v.p. G.D. Searle & Co., Skokie, Ill., 1979-83; sr. v.p. Ea. Air Lines, Inc., Miami, Fla., 1983-85; v.p. COMSAT Corp., Washington, 1985—. Contbr. articles to profl. jours. Trustee Skokie Valley Hosp., 1982-83, Fed. City Coun., Washington, 1986—; hon. trustee Arena Stage, Washington, 1986—; bd. dirs. Mailman Ctr., Miami, 1984-85 . Capt. USAF, 1955-59, Vietnam, 61-70, Pentagon. Decorated Bronze Star; recipient Golden Trumpet award Publicity Club Chgo., 1982. Mem. Econ. Club of Washington. Republican. Episcopalian. Avocations: reading, golf, travel. Office: COMSAT Corp 950 L Enfant Pla SW Washington DC 20024

MCGREAL, GARY LIONEL, data processing executive; b. Pulman, Wash., Feb. 16, 1953; s. Robert Dana and Maxine Thelma (Sutfin) McG.; m. Jacqueline Jean Cordray, Apr. 26, 1974; children: Gwendolyn, Conrad. BA in English, Stanford U., 1974. Dir. systems programming Computer Systems Labs., Mountain View, Calif., 1977-78; mgr. digital facilities Stanford Research Inst., Menlo Park, Calif., 1978-81; dir. info. processing U. So. Calif., Marina del Rey, 1981-85; exec. v.p. Complete Systems Inc., Herndon, Va., 1985—, also bd. dirs., 1985—; session chmn. Digital Equipment Corp Users Group, 1979—; mem. ANSI ADA Rev. Group, Washington, 1984; mem. steering com. UNIX 4.2BSD Berkeley, Calif., 1983-85. Author: MSG-Electronic Mail, 1978, USC Research in Computing, 1983, 84, 85. Mem. IEEE, Sun User Group (bd. dirs. 1982-86, service award 1986), Assn. Computing Machinery, Am. Assn. for Artificial Intelligence. Republican. Home: 2874 Spring Chapel Ct Herndon VA 22071 Office: Complete Systems Inc 3206 Wildmere Pl Herndon VA 22071

MCGREGOR, THEODORE ANTHONY, chemical company executive; b. Detroit, Mar. 28, 1944; s. Lorraine Guyeveve Guyette; m. Bonny-Joan Beach, Sept. 14, 1963; children: Todd, Timothy, Amy. Student, Henry Ford Coll., 1961-63. Mem. sales staff Gen. Binding Corp., GBC Sales and Service, Oak Brook, Ill., 1965-69; with indsl. chem. div. Diversey Chem. Corp., Chgo., 1967-69; with Detrex Corp., Detroit, 1969-89, regional mgr. indsl. chem. specialties div., 1975-77, asst. gen. mgr., 1977-81, gen. mgr. indsl. chem. specialties div., 1981-83, 1983-85, corp. v.p., gen. mgr., 1985-89; group v.p. indsl. chem. specialties div. Wayne Chem., RTI, Seibert-Oxidermo, Detroit, 1987-89; also bd. dirs. Wayne Chem., Russell Tech. Inc., Detroit; bd. dirs. Viking Chem. Co. Mem. Wire Inst., Am. Electroplaters Soc., Porcelain Enameling Inst., Detroit Socs. Coating Tech. Home: 3184 Ravinewood E Milford MI 48042

MCGREW, DAVID ROLLIN, manufacturing company executive; b. Uhrichsville, Ohio, July 9, 1936; s. Carl George and Mildred Elizabeth (Hall) McG.; m. Marilyn Dawn Heidt, Aug. 18, 1957 (div. June 1981); children: Michelle, Sean, Kristen. BS, Kent State U., 1958; cert. mktg. research, Columbia U., 1972. Tchr., coach Chardon (Ohio) High Sch., 1958-65; indsl. salesman Mystik Tape div. Borden Co., Columbus, Ohio, 1965-67; sales mgr. Mystik Tape div. Borden Co., Los Angeles, 1967-70; dir. sales, mktg. Mystik Tape div. Borden Co., Chgo., 1970-73; gen. sales mgr. W.H. Brady Co., Milw., 1973-77; owner, pres., chief exec. officer GEM-MAC Industries, Plymouth, Wis., 1977—; gen. ptnr., dir. GEM-MAC Assocs. & Factory Supply, Plymouth, Wis., 1983—. Active Rep. Presdl. Task Force, Washington, 1985—; pres., founder Cedarburg (Wis.) High Sch. Booster Club, 1983. Served with Ohio N.G., 1959-65. Named Coach of Yr., Northeast Ohio High Sch. Athletic Assn., 1963, Tchr. of Yr., Chardon High Sch., 1964, Mgr. of Yr., Borden Co., Los Angeles, 1969. Mem. Northeast Wis. Indsl. Council, Pressure Sensitive Tape Council (vice chmn. market devel. com. 1972-73). Republican. Clubs: Kent State Varsity, Kent State Alumni and Booster. Office: GEM-MAC Industries Inc 2100 Sunset Dr Plymouth WI 53073

MCGUINNESS, BARBARA SUE, food products executive; b. Lansing, Mich., Feb. 8, 1947; d. William Harrison and Gertrude Esther (Parker) Coleman; m. Michael L. Mueller, Aug. 12, 1965 (div. June 1973); children: Meredith Sue, Matthew Parker; m. John McGuinness, Dec. 8, 1978. Student, Meramec Community Coll., 1975-77, Florissant Valley Community Coll., 1984-87. Instr. Lindbergh Sch. Dist., St. Louis, 1975-77; surp. Velvet Freeze Ice Cream Co., St. Louis, 1977-81, v.p., 1981—. Chmn. Fin. Com. Chesterfield (Mo.) Transition Com., 1988—, campaign chmn. Chesterfield Inc. Com., 1988—, chmn. Chesterfield Planning & Zoning Commn., 1988—, chmn. Chesterfield Inaugural Commn., 1988; rep. State Mo. Electoral Coll. U.S., 1988. Recipient Key to City award City Govt. Crestwood, Mo., 1974, Key to City Chesterfield, 1988, Distinguished Service award, 1988, St. Louis County Dem. of Yr. award, 1986. Mem. Area Ice Cream Retailers Assn. (pres. 1979-84), Chesterfield C. of C. (Civic award 1988). Democrat. Baptist. Home: 95 Riverbend Dr Chesterfield MO 63017 Office: Velvet Freeze Ice Cream Co 7355 West Florissant Saint Louis MO 63136

MC GUINNESS, FRANK JOSEPH, construction company executive; b. Trenton, N.J., Aug. 1, 1928; s. Frank J. and Catherine C. (Campbell) McG.; B.S.C.E., Rutgers U., 1953; m. June Atkins; children by previous marriage—Kathleen, Edward, Anne, Mary, Frank. Civil engr. N.J. Hwy. Dept., Trenton, 1951-53; dist. engr. Lehigh Portland Cement Co., Allentown, Pa., 1956-68; exec. v.p. Knott Industries, Balt., 1968-78; pres. The Knott Co., Balt., 1978—; dir. Knott Industries, Inc. Mem. Greater Balt. Com., 1979—. Served to 1st lt., Ordinance Corps, U.S. Army, 1953-56. Registered profl. engr., N.J. Mem. Assn. Builders and Contractors, Nat. Soc. Profl. Engrs., Am. Concrete Inst., Nat. Assn. Office and Indsl. Parks (v.p. 1976-78), Urban Land Inst. Democrat. Roman Catholic. Clubs: Greenspring, Hon. Order of Ky. Cols. Office: 6326 Security Blvd Baltimore MD 21207

MCGUIRE, BRIAN LYLE, health science facility consultant; b. Mobile, Ala., June 13, 1959; s. Frank Ludlow, Jr. and Mary Lyle (Davidson) McG.; m. Jean Ellen Marler, June 18, 1983. BS in Acctg., U. South Ala., 1982, postgrad. in Bus. Adminstrn., 1986—. CPA, Ala. Staff acct. Clements, Sims and Crow, CPA's, Mobile, 1982-83, Smith, Dukes and Buckalew, CPA's, Mobile, 1983-86; corp. acct. So. Med. Health Systems, Mobile, 1986, dir. corp. ops, 1987-88; exec. dir. Med. Arts Clinic, Inc. subs. So. Med. Health Systems, Foley, Ala., 1986-88; mgmt. cons. Med. Mgmt. Consulting Svcs., Inc., Mobile, 1988—. Jr. asst. scoutmaster Boy Scouts Am., Birmingham chpt. Recipient Eagle Scout Order of Arrow Boy Scouts Am., 1977; named one of Outstanding Young Men of Am., 1982. Mem. Nat. Assn. Accts. (bd. dirs. Mobile chpt. 1983-85, v.p. community relations 1985-86, v.p. adminstrn. and fin. 1986-87, pres. 1987-88, Remington Rand Trophy, nat. com. chpt. ops. 1988—), Healthcare Fin. Mgmt. Assn., Ala. Soc. CPA's, Am. Inst. CPA's, Mobile Jaycees (treas. 1983-84, v.p. adminstrn. 1984-85, Presdl. citation 1984), Alumni Assn. U. South Ala., Hist. Mobile Preservation Soc., Pi Kappa Phi. Episcopalian. Clubs: Lake Forest Yacht and Country; Athelstan (Mobile). Office: Med Mgmt and Consulting Svcs PO Box 8143 Mobile AL 33689

MCGUIRE, CHARLES CARROLL, JR., insurance company executive; b. Balt., Jan. 28, 1932; s. Charles Carroll and Mary Catherine (Gunning) McG.; m. Mary Ballman, June 27, 1953; children: Charles, III, Mark T., James M., David M. BS in Acctg., U. Balt., 1955. CPA, Md. Mgt. Ernst & Whinney, Balt., 1957-73; sr. v.p., treas. Mercantile Bankshares Corp., Balt., 1973—; pres., dir. MBC Agy., Inc., Balt., 1979—, Mercantile Life Ins. Co., Balt., 1979—. Contbr. articles to profl. jours. Bd. dirs. YMCA, Catonsville, Md., 1984-85. Served with U.S. Army, 1955-57. Mem. Fin. Execs. Inst., Am. Inst. CPAs, Md. Assn. CPAs, Md. Pub. Fin. Officers Assn. (sec. 1960-70). Democrat. Roman Catholic. Office: Merc Bankshares Corp 2 Hopkins Pla PO Box 1477 Baltimore MD 21203

MCGUIRE, RICHARD ALLEN, insurance company executive; b. Queens, N.Y., June 9, 1946; s. George and Marion R. McGuire; student Armed Forces Inst., 1966-68; B.S. in Engring., U. Md., 1968. Ins. agt. N.Y. Life Ins. Co., N.Y.C., 1969-72; pres., chief exec. officer Richard A. McGuire Assocs., Inc., Bayshore, N.Y., 1972—, Steel & McGuire of N.Y. Inc., 1980—, Suffolk Risk Mgmt. Assocs. Inc., 1980—; ptnr., sr. v.p., John P. Tilden, Ltd., 1986—. chmn. bd., chief exec. officer Harbour Fin. Planning Group, Ltd., Safe Harbour Equities Ltd.; pres. Travelers' Met. Gen. Agts. Counsel; mem. nat. agts. adv. bd. Hanover Ins. Co., exec. v.p., chief operating officer, dir. Nat. Coverage Corp., 1988—; dir., v.p. Nat. Coverage Corp. of Conn., 1988—; dir. Arban Resources, Inc., 1988— ; mem. nat. and regional agts. adv. bd. Utica Mut.; lectr. Sch. Bus., City U. N.Y., 1978-80; speaker nat. and regional life ins. cos., career confs., club confs. and convs.; ins. columnist L.I. Graphic newspaper; exec. dir., founding charter mem. Tax and Ins. Inst., Adelphi U. Chmn. David Levy Meml. Scholarship Fund, Freeport, 1975-77. Served with USAF, 1965-69. Named Man of Yr., N.Y. Life Ins. Co., 1970, 71; recipient Nat. Mgmt. award Gen. Agts. and Mgrs. Assn., 1979, 80, 84. Mem. Nat. Assn. Life Underwriters (nat. quality award 1971-86, nat. sales achievement award 1970-86, nat. health ins. quality award 1972-86, v.p. Nassau chpt. 1974), Nat. Assn. Risk Mgmt., L.I. Gen. Agts. and Mgrs. Assn. (past dir.), Nat. Assn. Fin. Planners, Ind. Ins. Agts. Assn., Profl. Inst. Agts. Assn., Tax and Ins. Inst., Bayshore C. of C. (v.p. 1979-80), Ins. Fire Mark Soc., Travelers Ins. Co. Nat. Leaders Club, Million Dollar Round Table, L.I. Assn. Advancement of Commerce and Industry, Am. Legion, VFW. Clubs: Elks, K.C., Nat. Exchange (past v.p.). Home: 321 Dolphin Ln West Babylon NY 11704 Office: Richard A McGuire Assos Inc 1510 5th Ave Bay Shore NY 11706

MCGUIRK, RONALD CHARLES, banker; b. Balt., Dec. 9, 1938; s. Charles F. and Grace E. (Delcher) McG.; m. Katherine Sauer, Oct. 1, 1960; children: Frank D., Ann E. Student St. John's Coll., Annapolis, Md., 1956-59. Sr. data processing officer 1st Nat. Bank, Balt., 1966-72, v.p. data processing, 1972-76, v.p. mktg., 1976-80, sr. v.p. mktg., 1980—. Bd. dirs. North Arundel Hosp., Glen Burnie, Md., 1974—; mem. adv. bd. Hist. Annapolis, 1982-85, dir., 1985—; chmn. Annapolis Boundary Commn., 1983-84; mem. Anne Arundel County Coun., 1974-82, Anne Arundel County Libr. Bd., 1974-84; pres. Anne Arundel County Scholarship for Scholars/Bd. Edn., 1983-85, treas., 1985-88; mem. Anne Arundel County Charter Commn., Anne Arundel County Govt. Salary Commn.; chmn. Anne Arundel County Impact Fee Study Task Force, 1987-87; pres. Anne Arundel County YMCA, 1987-89, bd. dirs. 1982-87, 89—; mem. Commn. for Ednl. Excellence, 1988—. Mem. Center Club. Democrat. Roman Catholic. Office: 1st Nat Bank Md PO Box 1596 Baltimore MD 21203

MC GURK, JAMES HENRY, cons. co. exec.; b. Phila., July 24, 1936; s. James Henry and Ednah Mae (Kleinsmith) McG.; B.S., Pa. State U., 1957; postgrad. in Econs., Temple U., 1960-62; m. LaVerne M. Kraynek, 1960; children—Heather, Melanye. Cons. mfg., various states, 1968-72; ops. chief mfg. cons. Manatech Internat., Westmont, N.J., 1970-72, A.T. Oxford Inc., N.Y.C., 1972-74; mem. corporate staff mfg. cons. Aspro Inc., Westport, Conn., 1974-77; with LHM, Inc., cons., Rochester, Mich., 1977-79, also dir.; exec. v.p. Morse Hemco Inc., Holland, Mich., 1978-83; pres. Western Spline Gage, 1983—, also dir.; dir. Pegasus Spline, Birmingham, Eng. Served with USAF, 1957-59. Mem. Am. Mgmt. Assn. Republican. Home: 39 Forest Hills Dr Holland MI 49424 Office: 285 James St Holland MI 49423

MCHARG, GERALD BARRON, real estate educator, minister; b. Wichita, Feb. 1, 1932; s. Glen U. and Prudence Elizabeth (Skelton) McH.; m. Willo Lou Lovell, May 27, 1953 (div. Apr. 1978); children: Jeffrey Clay, Kevin Brent, Shannon Leigh; m. Rita S. Daniel, July 28, 1984. BA, Phillips U., 1953; MDiv, Grad. Sem., Enid, Okla., 1956. Ordained Disciples of Christ, 1953. Pastor First Christian Ch., Brawley, Calif., 1956-60, Kearny Mesa Christian Ch., San Diego, 1960-64; dist. pastor Christian Ch. of Pacific S.W. (Disciples of Christ), L.A., 1964-69, assoc. regional pastor, 1969-80; v.p. Real Estate Trainers Inc., Santa Ana, Calif., 1980—; bd. dirs. Universal Tng. Corp., Santa Ana. Author: California Real Estate Agency, 1987. Home: 5514 Greenleaf Ave Whittier CA 90601 Office: Real Estate Trainers Inc 2428-K N Grand Ave Santa Ana CA 90601

MC HENRY, POWELL W., lawyer; b. Cin., May 14, 1926; s. L. Lee McHenry and Marguerite L. (Powell) Heinz; m. Venna Mae Guerrea, Aug. 27, 1948; children: Scott, Marshall, Jody Lee, Gale Lynn. AB, U. Cin., 1949; LLB, Harvard U., 1951, J.D., 1969. Bar: Ohio 1951, U.S. Ct. Appeals (6th cir.) 1964, U.S. Supreme Ct. 1966. Assoc. Dinsmore, Shohl, Sawyer & Dinsmore, Cin., 1951-58; ptnr. Dinsmore, Shohl, Coates & Deupree (and predecessors), Cin., 1958-75; gen. counsel Federated Dept. Stores, Inc., 1971-75; assoc. gen. counsel Procter & Gamble Co., 1975-76, v.p., gen. counsel, 1976-83, sr. v.p., gen. counsel, 1983—; Dir. Republican Club of Hamilton County, Ohio, 1957-58. Mem. com. Hamilton County Pub. Defender, Cin., Cin. Council World Affairs, Def. Research Inst., Cin. With USNR, 1944-46. Recipient award of merit Ohio Legal Center Inst., 1969. Mem. Am. Judicature Soc., ABA, Ohio Bar Assn., Cin. Bar Assn. (pres. 1979-80, pres. exec. com. 1975-81), Harvard Law Sch. Assn. Cin. (pres. 1960-61), Am. Law Inst., Assn. Gen. Counsel (pres. 1986—). Republican. Methodist. Clubs: Harvard, Western Hill Country (dir. 1964-70, sec. 1966-69, 87—, treas. 1969-70), Queen City, Commonwealth. Office: Procter & Gamble Co 2 Procter & Gamble Pla PO Box 599 Cincinnati OH 45202

MCHUGH, JOHN JAMES, financial company consultant; b. Greenwich, Conn., May 14, 1931; s. John and Marie J. (Brady) McH.; m. Clara Louise Canals, Jan. 26, 1939; children: Aletha, John, Edward, Kathleen. B.S., Georgetown U., 1953; LL.B., Fordham U., 1958. Bar: N.Y. 1958. Assoc. firm Cravath, Swaine & Moore, N.Y.C., 1958-62; asst. gen. counsel, asst. sec. Rheem Mfg. Co., N.Y.C., 1962-68; sec. City Investing Co., N.Y.C., 1968-85, v.p., 1974-85; v.p. adminstrn., sec. Home Group, Inc, N.Y.C., 1985-88; cons. in field N.Y.C. and Greenwich, 1988—. Articles editor: Fordham Law Rev., 1957-58. Active fund raising for various orgns. Served to lt. (j.g.) USN, 1953-55. Kennedy scholar, 1957-58. Mem. Am. Soc. Corp. Secs., ABA (assoc.). Republican. Roman Catholic.

MCHUGH, ROBERT EMMETT, association executive; b. Cambridge, Mass., Dec. 6, 1941; s. Joseph Anthony and Marguerite (Smith) McH.; m. Martha "Duffy" Slavin, Jan. 21, 1967; children: Elizabeth, Julie, Marguerite, Mary. BSFS, Georgetown U., 1963; postgrad., U. Pa., 1986, Stanford U., 1987. With Vick Chem. Co., Rochester, N.Y., 1966-69; sales mgr. Vick Chem. Co., Washington, 1969-73; mktg. mgr. Richardson Merrell, N.Y.C., 1973-75, nat. accounts mgr., 1975-77; dir. bus. devel. Richardson-Vicks, Wilton, Conn., 1977-83; v.p. mem. svcs. Nat. Wholesale Druggists' Assn., Alexandria, Va., 1983-88, v.p. ind. affairs, 1988—. Author: 1000 Days and Counting, 1987. Vice-chmn. bd. advisors St. Mary's Acad., Alexandria, 1987—; chmn. centennial St. Mary's Parish, Ridgefield, Conn., 1981. Capt. U.S. Army, 1963-68. Mem. Am. Soc. Assn. Execs., K.C. Republican. Roman Catholic. Home: 8804 Lynnhurst Dr Fairfax VA 22031 Office: NWDA PO Box 238 Alexandria VA 22313

MC ILHANY, STERLING FISHER, publishing company executive; b. San Gabriel, Calif., Apr. 12, 1930; s. William Wallace and Julia (Fisher) M. B.F.A. with high honors, U. Tex., 1953; postgrad. UCLA, 1953-54, 55-57, Universita per Stranieri, Perugia, Italy, 1957, Accademia delle Belle Arti, Rome, 1957-58. Teaching asst., lectr. in art history UCLA, 1953-54, 55-57; art supr. Kamehameha Prep. Sch., Honolulu, 1954-55; instr. Honolulu Acad. Arts, 1955; assoc. editor Am. Artist mag., N.Y.C., 1958-61, editor, 1969-70; host Books and the Artist network series Sta. WRVR, N.Y.C., 1961-62; sr. editor Reinhold Book Corp., N.Y.C., 1962-69; pres. IFOTA Inc., Los Angeles, 1981—; instr. Sch. Visual Arts, N.Y.C., 1961-69. Fellow Christ Coll., Cambridge. Author: Banners and Hangings, 1966; Art as Design—Design as Art, 1970; Wood Inlay, 1972; Simbari, 1975; also articles. Recipient First award tour European art ctrs. Students Internat. Travel Assn., 1952; Rotary fellow Accademia delle Belle Arti, 1957-58. Fellow Internat. Inst. Community Service London; mem. Nat. Soc. Lit. and Arts, Human Resource USA. Roman Catholic. Address: 6376 Yucca St Los Angeles CA 90028

MCILROY, HARRY ALEXANDER (BARON DI NOVARA), merchant banker; b. Belfast, No. Ireland, May 17, 1940; s. Henry and Harriet (Cooke) McI.; m. Winifred McKeown, Sept. 6, 1971; children—Catherine Harriet, Nicholas Henry Christopher. Owner, founder, chmn. bd. dirs. Unico Group Ltd., 1979—; underwriter Lloyd's of London, 1979—; mem. Internat. Fin. Futures Exchange, Bermuda, 1980—. Freeman, City of London. Mem. Worshipful Co. Basketmakers (liveryman), Worshipful Co. Marketors. Clubs: Carlton, East India, City Livery (London). Home: PO Box 1465, Dublin 4, Ireland

MC ILVEEN, WALTER, mechanical engineer; b. Belfast, Ireland, Aug. 12, 1927; s. Walter and Amelia (Thompson) McI.; came to U.S., 1958, naturalized, 1963; M.E., Queens U., Belfast, 1948; H.V.A.C., Borough Polytechnic, London, 1951; m. Margaret Teresa Ruane, Apr. 17, 1949; children—Walter, Adrian, Peter, Anita, Alan. Mech. engr. Davidson & Co., Belfast, 1943-48; sr. contract engr. Keith Blachman Ltd., London, 1948-58; mech. engr. Fred S. Dubin Assos., Hartford, Conn., 1959-64; chief mech. engr. Koton & Donovan, W. Haven, Conn., 1964-66; prin., engr. Walter McIlveen Assos., Avon, Conn., 1966—. Mem. IEEE, Illuminating Engring. Soc., ASME, Hartford Engring. Club, Conn. Engrs. in Pvt. Practice, ASHRAE. Mem. Ch. of Ireland. Home: 3 Valley View Rd Weatogue CT 06089 Office: 195 W Main St Avon CT 06001

MCILWAIN, MAHLON RICHMOND, retail executive; b. Panama City, Fla., Apr. 28, 1943; s. Alton Mahlon and Joanna (Glassell) McI; m. Johnette Hassell, July 1963 (div. 1972); m. Rita Dunkenberger, Sept. 23, 1977; children: Angela, Susan, Courtney. BBA, Tex. Tech. U., 1965. V.p. McIlwaine Cadillac, Inc., Abilene, Tex., 1969-71; v.p. McIlwaine Cadillac, Inc., Metairie, La., 1971-73, pres., 1973—; dealer, council mem. Cadillac Motor Car Div. (mem. zone dealer award); dir. Better Bus. Bur., sec., treas, 1987-88; bd. dirs. Jefferson Guaranty Bank, Metaire. Bd. dirs. New Orleans chpt. Am. Cancer Soc., 1975—; del. White House Conf. Small Bus., 1980. Recipient Quality Dealer award Time Mag., 1985. Mem. Nat. Automobile Dealers Assn. (bd. dirs. 1986—, named Automobile Dealer of Yr. 1984), La. Automobile Dealers Assn. (v.p. region II 1988-90), New Orleans Car Dealers Assn., New Orleans C. of C. (bd. dirs. 1977-79). Republican. Roman Catholic. Club: Metairie Country. Office: McIlwaine Cadillac Inc 3100 Lime St Metairie LA 70006

MCINNES, HAROLD A., manufacturing company executive; b. Groton, Conn., 1927. B.S.M.E., MIT, 1949. With Delco Appliance div. Gen. Motors Corp., 1949-55, Tracerlab, Inc., 1955-60, Reed Rolled Thread Die Co., 1960-62, Dresser Industries, Inc., 1962-65, AMP, Inc., Harrisburg, Pa., 1965—; mfg. mgr. packaging components AMP, Inc., 1966-70, mgr. automach div., 1970-73, group dir. gen. products, 1973-78, v.p. mfg. resources planning, 1978-79, corp. v.p. engring. and tech. resources, 1979, now vice chmn. bd. dirs. Office: AMP Inc 470 Friendship Rd Harrisburg PA 17105

MC INNES, ROBERT MALCOLM, lawyer; b. Pictou, N.S., Can., July 17, 1930; naturalized U.S. citizen, 1964; s. John Logan and Jenny MacKay (Malcolm) McI.; m. June Hughena O'Brien, Apr. 19, 1952; children: Donald, Elizabeth, Susan. B.A., Dalhousie U., Halifax, N.S., 1951, LL.B., 1953; postgrad., Harvard U. Bus. Sch., 1968. Assoc. firm Duquet, MacKay, Weldon & Tetreault, Montreal, Que., Can., 1953-57; with Pickands Mather & Co., Cleve., 1957-69, 71-87; v.p. Pickands Mather & Co., 1971-73, exec. v.p., 1973-83, pres., chief exec. officer, 1983-87; gen. counsel, treas. Diamond Shamrock Corp., 1969-71; group exec. v.p. Cleve. Cliffs Inc., 1987-88; of counsel Arter and Hadden, Cleve., 1988—; bd. dirs. Brush Wellman Inc., Cleveland-Cliffs Inc. Mem. Cleve. Bar Assn., Mayfield Country Club, Cleve. Skating Club, Union Club. Republican. Methodist. Home: 32300 Meadowlark Way Pepper Pike OH 44124 Office: Arter & Hadden 1100 Huntington Bldg Cleveland OH 44115

MCINTOSH, L(ORNE) WILLIAM, marketing executive; b. Kingston, Ont., Can., May 1, 1945; s. Jack Lorne and Lillian (Oaks) McI.; m. Delthyn Lee Johnson, Mar. 11, 1965. BSBA, Lehigh U., 1967, MBA, 1968. Asst. prof. Union Coll., Cranford, N.J., 1968-72; market research analyst Merck, Sharp & Dohme, West Point, Pa., 1972-74, sr. market research analyst, 1974-75, advt. copywriter, 1975-77, product mgr., 1977-79, assoc. dir. advt., 1980-82, dir. licensing and acquisitioning, 1982-83, sr. dir. mktg., 1983-86; exec. v.p. mktg. Medco Containment Svcs., Inc., Fair Lawn, N.J., 1987—. Mem. Am. Econ. Assn., Am. Mktg. Assn., Beta Gamma Sigma, Smoke Rise Club, Antique Automobile Club Am. Home: 174 Hornbeam Ln Kinnelon NJ 07405 Office: Medco Containment Svcs Inc 1900 Pollitt Dr Fair Lawn NJ 07410

MCINTOSH, THOMAS S., energy services holding company executive; b. 1937. B.S., Rice U., 1960; M.B.A., Stanford U., 1964. Mgr. supply and distbn. Tenneco Oil Co., Houston, 1964-73; with Zapata Off-Shore Co., Houston, 1973-87; planning and fin. analyst, v.p. corp. devel. Zapata Off-Shore Co., 1973-74, pres., 1975-87; v.p. offshore mktg. parent Co. Zapata Corp., 1974-77, v.p. offshore drilling, 1977-83; exec. v.p., chief operating officer 1983-87; pres., chief exec. officer Enterra Corp., Houston, 1987—. Office: Enterra Corp PO Box 1535 Houston TX 77251

MCINTYRE, ADELBERT, JR., physicist; b. Providence, Jan. 1, 1929; s. Adelbert and Lucy Forbes (Mackay) McI.; m. Constance Lindberg McIntyre, Feb. 1959 (div. 1985); children: David E. (dec.), Sheryle E., Mark D., Carole A., Marguerite E. Student Ind. U., 1951-52; BS, U. R.I., 1959, postgrad., 1959-61. Scientist Office Aerospace Research, Washington, 1961-63; physicist Air Force Cambridge Research Labs., Hanscom AFB, Mass., 1963-74, program mgr. multispectral measurements program, 1974-83, dir. MSL surveillance tech., 1979-83, chief atmosphere backgrounds br., dep. dir. infrared tech., 1983-86, tech. cons. to Fletcher Com. on post-boost-vehicle observables, 1983, tech. dir. field-widened interferometer rocket measurements program and strategic kill assessment measurements program, 1985, tech dir. stratospheric cryogenic infrared balloon experiment-99, 1985-86; pres., chief scientist, Infratech, Inc., Wayland, Mass., 1986-88; staff scientist Aerojet Electrosystems Co., Azusa, Calif., 1988—. Served to maj. USAF, 1946-50, 51-53, 61-66. Recipient Air Force Sci. Achievement award, 1981, 84. Mem. Internat. Platform Assn., AAAS, AIAA, DAV, VFW, Sigma Xi (exec. com. 1975-78). Avocations: flyfishing, swimming, boating, skeet. Home: 1929 Orangewood Ave Upland CA 91786

MCINTYRE, GEORGE WILLIAM, JR., accountant; b. Worcester, Mass., Nov. 28, 1949; s. George William Sr. and Elda Wren (Clark) McI.; m. Linda Ellen Lamb, Oct. 24, 1970; children: James, Stacey. BA in Psychology, Cornell U., 1971; MBA, Stanford U., 1973. CPA, Calif., Wash., Md., Va. Staff cons. Arthur Andersen & Co., San Francisco, 1973-74; sr. cons. Arthur Andersen & Co., Washington, 1974-76; mgr. fin. Perdue Inc., Salisbury, Md., 1977-78; corp. controller Am. Safety Razor Co., Staunton, Va., 1978-83; chief fin. officer Weinschel Engring. Inc., Gaithersburg, Md., 1983-84; instr. James Madison U., Harrisonburg, Va., 1984-85; mgr. fin. ComSonics Inc., Harrisonburg, 1986—, also dir.; bd. dirs. Carded Graphics Inc., Verona, Va., Shen Ventures Inc., Harrisonburg. Mem. Nat. Assn. Accts. Unitarian. Home: 602 Woodmont Dr Staunton VA 24401 Office: ComSonics Inc 1350 Port Republic Rd PO Box 1106 Harrisonburg VA 22801

MCINTYRE, JOAN CAROL, data processing executive; b. Portchester, N.Y., Mar. 1, 1939; d. John Henry and Molly Elizabeth (Gates) Daugherty; m. Stanley Donald McIntyre, Aug. 24, 1957 (div. Jan. 1986); children—Michael Stanley, David John, Sharon Lynne; m. James Morrow Invy IV, June 1, 1988. Student Northwestern U., 1956-57, U. Ill., 1957-58. Assoc. editor Writer's Digest, Cin., 1966-68; instr. creative writing U. Ala.-Huntsville, 1975; editor Strode Pubs., Huntsville, 1974-75; paralegal Smith, Huckaby & Graves (now Bradley, Arant, Rose & White), Huntsville, 1976-82; exec. v.p. Micro Craft, Inc., Huntsville, 1982-85, pres., 1985—; also dir. and co-owner. Author numerous computer-operating mans. for law office software, 1978-88; co-author: Alabama and Federal Complaint Forms, 1979; Alabama and Federal Motion and Order Forms, 1980; also numerous articles, short stories, poems, 1955-88. Editor: Alabama Law for the Layman, 1975. Bd. dirs. Huntsville Lit. Soc., 1976-77. Hon. scholar Medill Sch. Journalism, Northwestern U., 1956. Republican. Methodist. Office: Micro Craft Inc 688 Discovery Dr Huntsville AL 35806

MCINTYRE, JOHN WILLIAM, banker; b. Valdosta, Ga., Sept. 14, 1930; s. James A. and Julia (Norton) McI.; m. Joan Pruitt, Oct. 8, 1955; children: Anna, John William, Martha, Michael. B.B.A., Emory U., 1951; grad. exec. mgmt. program, Stanford U., 1966. With Citizens & So. Nat. Bank, 1951—; gen. v.p. Citizens & So. Nat. Bank, Atlanta, 1977-79; pres. Citizens & So. Nat. Bank, 1979—, chmn., chief exec. officer, 1986—, also bd. dirs.; chmn., chief exec. officer Citizens and So. Ga. Corp., 1980—, also bd. dirs.; vice-chmn. bd. dirs. Citizens and So. Corp. (parent co.), 1986; dir. Master Card Internat., Inc. Trustee Emory U.; bd. sponsors Atlanta Symphony; trustee Lovett Sch., Atlanta. Served with USAR, 1952-54. Mem. Assn. Res. City Banks, Ga. C. of C. (dir.). Baptist. Clubs: Piedmont Dirving, Cherokee Town and Country, Commerce. Office: Citizens & So Corp 35 Broad St NW Atlanta GA 30303

MCINTYRE, ROBERT MALCOLM, utility company executive; b. Portland, Oreg., Dec. 18, 1923; s. Daniel A. and Bessie W. (Earsley) McI.; m. Marilyn Westcott, Aug. 27, 1949; 1 child, Julie. BA, UCLA, 1950; postgrad., UCLA, U. Soc. Calif., Columbia U. Gen. sales mgr. So. Calif. Gas Co. (subs. Pacific Enterprises), L.A., 1952-70, v.p., 1970-74, sr. v.p., 1974-80, pres., 1980-85, chmn., chief exec. officer, 1985-88, dir., 1988—. Mem. Korean Am. Centennial Commn., Huntington Libr. Soc. Fellows, L.A. Olympic Citizens Adv. Commn.; mem. bus. coun. Newport Harbor Art Mus.; mem. steering com. Orange County Bus. Com. for Arts; mem. ad hoc com. on city fin., L.A.; bd. dirs. NCCJ, Calif. Coun. Environ. and Econ. Balance, Calif. Found. Environment and Economy, L.A. United Way, Hoag Meml. Hosp.; trustee UCLA Found., L.A. Orthopaedic Hosp., mem. exec. com. Lt. USN, 1940-46. Decorated Order of the Rising Sun with Gold Rays and Ribbon (Japan); recipient Outstanding Svc. award Mex. Am. Legal Def. Fund, 1981, Humanitarian award NCCJ, Roy Wilkins award L.A. chpt. NAACP, others. Mem. Pacific Coast Gas Assn. (past dir., 49er Club award 1979), Am. Gas Assn., Inst. Gas Tech. (trustee), U.S.-Mex. C. of C., L.A. C. of C. (past chmn., Medici award), Calif. Club, L.A. Club, Phi Kappa Psi. Republican. Presbyterian. Office: So Calif Gas Co 810 S Flower St Los Angeles CA 90017

MCISAAC, JOHN L., utility executive; b. Chgo., Dec. 12, 1929; s. Leslie A. and Katherine M. (Collins) McI.; m. Patricia A. Tunney, Dec. 2, 1950; children: Michael, Mary, Martin. Student, Fournier Inst., Lemont, Ill., 1945-49. Svc. and sales Peoples Gas Light and Coke Co., Chgo., 1949-59; indsl. sales engr. Wis. gas Co., Milw., 1960, commercial sales mgr., 1961-62, mgr. customer service, 1963-68, mgr. ops., 1969-74, v.p. ops., 1974-84, sr. v.p. ops., 1985—. Recipient Disting. Service award Milw. Fire Dept., 1971, Hon. Membership award, 1985. Mem. Am. Gas. Assn. (service award 1979), Midwest gas Assn. (com. chmn. 1969-73, bd. dirs. 1982-85). Roman Catholic. Club: Milw. Athletic. Office: Wis Gas Co 626 E Wisconsin Ave Milwaukee WI 53202

MCIVER, BRUCE COOLEY, railroad company executive; b. Great Falls, Mont., Dec. 6, 1940; s. Kenneth B. and Genevieve (Cooley) McI.; m. Ann Gregg; children: Elizabeth, Kathryn, Matthew, Melanie, Molly. BA, Columbia U., 1972. Cons. in field 1972-76; staff asst. Mayor's Office, N.Y.C., 1976-79; chief of staff Dep. Mayor for Labor Relations, N.Y.C., 1978-79; dir. labor relations City of N.Y., 1979-83, Met. Transp. Authority, N.Y.C., 1983-85; pres., gen. mgr. L.I. R.R., Jamaica, N.Y., 1985—. Bd. dirs. Hudson Guild, N.Y.C., 1986-87, Greater Jamaica Devel. Corp., 1987. Served with USMC, 1958-61. Mem. Am. Pub. Transit Assn. Democrat. Home: 335 1st St Brooklyn NY 11215 Office: LI RR Jamaica Sta Jamaica NY 11435

MCKAMIE, WILLIAM MICHAEL, lawyer; b. Waco, Tex., Dec. 9, 1950; s. Edgar M. and Lura F. (Snowden) McK.; m. Diane Stafford, Aug. 14, 1976; children: Misty, Zack. BA, U. Tex., 1972; JD, Tex. Tech U., 1978, MPA, 1981. Bar: Tex. 1978, U.S. Dist. Ct. (no. dist.) Tex. 1979, U.S. Dist. Ct. (ea. dist.) Tex. 1985, U.S. Ct. Appeals (5th cir.) 1987. Assoc. Clark, Gorin & McDonald, Greenville, Tex., 1978-79; asst. atty. City of Greenville, 1979-81, 83-87; pvt. practice Lubbock, Tex., 1981-83; assoc. Heard, Goggan, Blair & Williams, Angleton, Tex., 1987-88, Curtis & Paris, Greenville, 1988—; atty. City of Richwood, Tex., 1988. Bd. dirs. Hunt County Tax Appraisal Dist., Greenville, 1986-87; mem. Greenville Chamber Ambassadors, 1986-87. 2d lt. USAR, 1973-75. Mem. ABA, Tex. Bar Assn., Hunt County Bar Assn., Nat. Inst. Mcpl. Law Officers, Tex. City Attys. Assn. (bd. dirs. 1985-87, sec. 1986-87), Rotary, Phi Alpha Alpha, Delta Theta Phi. Democrat. Mem. Ch. of Christ. Office: Curtis & Paris 2708 Washington Greenville TX 75401

MC KAY, DEAN RAYMOND, computer company executive; b. Seattle, Nov. 13, 1921; s. Joseph and Nora (MacDermitt) McK.; m. Jean Davis, Dec. 26, 1942; children: Dean Brian, Bruce Thompson, Robert Joseph. BA, U. Wash., 1944; postgrad., Harvard U., 1955. With IBM Corp., Armonk, N.Y., 1946—, from br. mgr. to dir. pers. div. data processing, 1957-61, v.p. communications, 1961-69, v.p. corp. ops. and services staff, 1969, mem. mgmt. com., 1970, sr. v.p., 1971, sr. v.p., group exec. data processing mktg., 1972—, sr. v.p. corp. ops. and services staffs, also mem. corp. mgmt. com., 1978-82, mem. adv. bd., 1982—, also bd dirs.; bd. dirs. E.I. du Pont de Memours and Co., Wilmington, Del., Marsh & McLennan Cos., Inc., N.Y.C., MCI Communications Corp., Washington. Mem. adv. council Nat. Urban Coalition, Washington; trustee Ford's Theater Soc., Washington. Served to lt. (s.g.) Intelligence Corps USNR, 1942-46. Mem. Phi Beta Kappa. Clubs: Siwanoy (Bronxville, N.Y.); Ekwanok (Manchester, Vt.); Gulf Stream (Delray Beach, Fla.). Office: IBM Corp 2000 Purchase St Purchase NY 10577

MCKAY, DONALD ARTHUR, mechanical contractor; b. Providence, June 10, 1931; s. Benjamin Arthur and Florence (Heeney) McK.; m. Janette Capellaro, Dec. 30, 1978; children by previous marriage: Susan Kelly, Barbara Albury, Laura Lower, Douglas. AB, Harvard U., 1952. Registered profl. engr., Mass. Sales engr. C.P. Blouin, Cambridge, Mass., 1955-60; contract mgr. to v.p. Limbach Co., Boston, 1960-68; exec. v.p. Tougher Heating & Plumbing Co., Albany, N.Y., 1968-74; chmn., chief exec. officer Tougher Industries, Albany, 1986—, pres., 1974-86; bd. dirs. Home and City Savs. Bank; v.p. Spunduct Inc. Pres. Fifty Group of Columbia County, 1972-74; mem. corp. gifts com. Albany Med. Ctr., 1978-84; chmn. 25th reunion fund raising com. of upstate N.Y., Harvard Class '52; mem. curriculum adv. bd. Hudson Valley Community Coll.; chmn. bd. trustees Meml. Hosp. Served with USN, 1951-54. Mem. ASHRAE, Nat. Soc. Profl. Engrs., Mech. Contractors Assn. Am. (pres. capital dist. 1981-82, pres.-elect 1988, pres. 1989-90), Mech. Contractors Assn. N.Y. State (v.p. 1981-82, pres. 1981-82), Aircraft Owners and Pilots Assn., Exptl. Aircraft Assn. Congregationalist. Clubs: Harvard (pres. N.E. N.Y. chpt. 1987—), Ft. Orange (Albany); Masons (Dorchester, Mass.); Wolferts Roost Country. Home: 6 Park Ridge Menands NY 12204 Office: Tougher Industries 175 Broadway PO Box 4067 Albany NY 12204

MC KAY, ROBERT BUDGE, legal educator; b. Wichita, Kans., Aug. 11, 1919; s. John Budge and Ruth Irene (Gelsthorpe) McK.; m. Sara Kate Warmack, Nov. 20, 1954 (dec. Oct. 1986); children: Kathryn Lee, Sara Margaret. BS, U. Kans., 1940; JD, Yale U., 1947; LLD (hon.), Emory U., 1973, Seton Hall U., 1975, U. Tulsa, 1981, John Jay Coll. Criminal Justice, 1983, Pace U., 1981, U. San Diego, 1982, N.Y. Law Sch., 1985, Villanova U., 1989; LHD (hon.), Mt. St. Mary Coll., 1973. Bar: Kans. 1948, D.C. 1948, U.S. Supreme Ct. 1953, N.Y. 1973. With Dept. Justice, 1947-50; asst., then assoc. prof. law Emory U., 1950-53; prof. law NYU, 1953—; dean NYU Sch. Law, 1967-75; bd. dirs. Loews Corp; mem. exec. com. Assn. Am. Law Schs., 1964-65; mem. exec. com. Lawyers Com. for Civil Rights Under Law; chmn. N.Y. State Spl. Commn. on Attica, 1971-72, N.Y.C. Bd. Correction, 1973-74; dir. program on justice, society and individual Aspen Inst. for Humanistic Studies, 1975-80, sr. fellow, 1980—. Author: Reapportionment: The Law and Politics of Equal Representation, 1965; Editor: Annual Survey of American Law, 1953-56, An American Constitutional Law Reader, 1958, Time-Life Family Legal Guide, 1971. Chmn. bd. dirs. Citizens Union, 1971-77; pres. Legal Aid Soc. of N.Y.C., 1975-77; vice chmn. Nat. News Council, 1973-80; dir., bd. dirs. Inst. Jud. Adminstrn., 1980-83; bd. dirs. Am. Arbitration Assn., Mexican-Am. Legal Def. Fund, Revsun Found., Vera Inst. of Justice; v.p. Am. Judicature Soc., 1980-85. Recipient award Am. Friends Hebrew U. Law Sch., 1972, William Nelson Cromwell medal New York County Lawyers Assn., 1973, Arthur T. Vanderbilt medal N.Y. U. Sch. Law, 1974, Albert Gallatin medal N.Y. U., 1975, Disting. Service medal U. Kans., 1983, Justice award Am. Judicature Soc., 1986. Mem. ABA (chmn. commn. on correctional facilities and services 1974-78, sect. legal edn. and admissions to bar 1983-84, action commn. to improve tort liability system 1985-86, bd. govs. 1986-89, ho. of dels. 1985—), N.Y. State Bar Assn. (Gold Medal award 1987), Assn. Bar City N.Y. (chmn. exec. com. 1975-76, v.p. 1976-77, pres. 1984-86, chmn. council criminal justice 1982-84), Delta Upsilon. Presbyterian. Home: 29 Washington Sq W New York NY 10011 Office: NYU Sch of Law 40 Washington Sq S Room 321 New York NY 10012

MC KEE, ALLEN PAGE, investment executive; b. Los Angeles, July 26, 1941; s. Norman C. and Eleanor (Page) McK.; BA in Econs., U. Mich., 1964; MBA, U. Calif.-Berkeley, 1971. Area relations officer internat. div. Bank of Am., San Francisco, 1967-70; investment officer Bamerical Internat. Fin. Corp., San Francisco, 1971-73; v.p. and dir. internat. investments Union Bank, San Francisco, 1973-74; pres. Montgomery Assocs., Inc., San Francisco, 1975—, dir., 1977—; mng. dir. Fal N.V., 1979-87, Willhurst Co. N.V., 1980-86; dir. Hawaiian Plantations, Inc., 1981-83, Dynodata, Inc., 1983—, Analytical Products, Inc., 1984—. Served to lt. USN, 1964-67, Vietnam. Mem. World Affairs Council No. Calif., Western Assn. Venture Capitalists, Soc. Calif. Pioneers, Calif. Bus. Alumni Assn., Delta Kappa Epsilon. Republican. Club: Commonwealth of Calif. Home: 18 Chaucer Ct Mill Valley CA 94941 Office: 555 Montgomery St Ste 1215 PO Box 2230 San Francisco CA 94126

MCKEE, BARBARA JEFFCOTT, accountant; b. Madison, Wis., Jan. 21, 1948; d. William Francis and Florence Ann (Jeffcott) McK.; m. Richard Arthur Rocha, Oct. 1, 1988. BBA, U. Wis., 1968; M in Mgmt., Northwestern U., 1982. CPA, Ill.; cert. internal auditor. Auditor Peat, Marwick, Mitchell & Co., Chgo., 1968-78; cons. Esmark, Inc., Chgo., 1978-79; audit mgr. Deloitte Haskins & Sells, Chgo., 1979-84, controller, 1984-85; v.p. Safeway Stores, Inc., Oakland, Calif., 1985—. Mem. AICPA, Am. Women's Soc. of CPA's, Inst. Internal Auditors. Office: Safeway Stores Inc 430 Jackson St Oakland CA 94660

MCKEE, BOBBY J., pension fund administrator; b. Frankfort, Ky., Feb. 22, 1952; s. Vernie and Katherine (Vice) McK.; m. Connie S. Shirrell, Jan. 7, 1978. BS, Ky State U., 1976. Programmer/analyst Ky. Dept. Transp., Frankfort, 1972-77; systems analyst TVA, Knoxville, 1977, U. Ky., Lexington, 1977-78; investment officer Ky. Retirement Systems, Frankfort, 1978-85, gen. mgr., 1985—; dir. Ky. Deferred Compensation, Frankfort. Mem. Nat. Conf. Pub. Employees Retirement Systems, Nat. Assn. State Retirement Adminstrs., Nat. Assn. State Investment Officers, Govt. Fin. Officers Assn., Elks. Democrat. Office: Ky Retirement Systems 151 Elkhorn Ct Frankfort KY 40601

MC KEE, DONALD DARRELL, real estate broker; b. Highland, Ill., July 20, 1932; s. Earl Michael and Leta Evelyn (Dresch) McK.; grad. high sch.; m. Emma A. Becker, Aug. 28, 1956; children: Dale Michael, Gail Ann. Sales clk. C. Kinne & Co., Highland, 1952-63; salesman Lowenstein Agy., Inc., Highland, 1963-69; owner Don McKee Ins., 1970-77; owner Don McKee Realty, Highland, 1969-73; owner Century 21-McKee Realty, Highland; owner Key Antiques, Key Sales Co; sales mgr. All Seasons Resorts, Inc., Lake Carlyle, Ill. Tchr. real estate So. Ill. U., Edwardsville, 1974-81, Lewis and Clark Community Coll., Godfrey, Ill., Belleville (Ill.) Area Coll.; pres. Real Estate Inst., 1973-79; exec. officer Edwardsville-Collinsville Bd. Realtors, 1975-76; pres. So. Ill. Conf. Real Estate; pres. Coupon Inserts, Inc., Highland, Ill. Mem. So. Ill. Tourism Council, 1969-79; mem. adv. bd. Friends of Lovejoy Library, So. Ill. U.-Edwardsville. Mem. So. Ill. Independent Ins. Agts. (pres. 1974-75), Edwardsville-Collinsville Bd. Realtors (pres. 1974), Nat., Ill. (v.p. dist. 1977) assns. Realtors, Highland C. of C., Highland Hist. Soc. (dir.), Helvetia Sharpshooters Soc., St. Louis Art Mus., Ill. Real Estate Educators, Nat. Real Estate Educators. Club: Highland Country. Contbr. articles to profl. jours. Home: 1403 Pine St Highland IL 62249 Office: 825 Main St Highland IL 62249

MCKEE, EDWARD RAY, small business owner, consultant; b. Ione, Wash., July 19, 1941; s. Lloyd Edward McKee and Gertrud Helen (Daily) Thieman; m. Margaret Alice Kneidel, June 10, 1963 (div. Mar., 1968); children: Robert Ashley, Richard Willard; m. Dianne M. Rush, Apr. 7, 1977; children: Gina Marie. Student, Boise Coll., 1964-66, LaSalle Extension U., Chgo., 1965-67, E.C.P.I., 1969-70, Contra Costa Coll., 1977-78. Coordinator Am. Window Cleaning, Boise, 1964-68; foreman Comml. Bldg. Maintenance, Oakland, Calif., 1968-73; owner, mgr. Busy Bee Svcs., El Cerrito, Calif., 1973-76; asst. dir. to dir. Crothall Hosp. Svc., Berkeley, Calif. and Salem, Oreg., 1976-79; owner, mgr. A-Rems Cert. Cleaning Svc., Salem, 1979—; cons. SBA, Svc. Corps Retired Execs., Active Corps Execs., Salem, 1981—. Served with USAF, 1959-64. Mem. Nat. Fedn. Indep. Bus., Carpet Cleaning Inst. of Northwest, Internat. Inst. Carpet & Upholstery Cleaners Inc. Lodge: Kiwanis. Home: 585 Marino Dr N Keizer OR 97303 Office: A-Rems Cleaning Svc 585 Marino Dr N Keizer OR 97303

MCKEE, ELIZABETH ALEXANDRA, pharmaceutical executive; b. Jersey City, Aug. 16, 1957; d. Frank John and Alice Maureen (Flynn) Niekrasz; m. Philip Winston McKee, Jr., June 16, 1984. BS in Engring with honors, Rutgers U., 1979; MBA in Fin., Loyola Coll., Balt., 1982. Engr. Mobay Chem. Corp., Balt., 1979-80, product mgr., 1980-83; asst. dir. blood services ARC, Washington, 1983-84, dir. plasma ops., 1984-88, gen. mgr. plasma ops., 1988—. Mem. Bravo! Washington Opera, 1986—; mem. com. Bark Ball, Washington Humane Soc., 1988—. Mem. Am. Assn. Blood Banks, Internat. Soc. Blood Transfusion, Rutgers Alumni Assn., Loyola Alumni Assn., Beethoven Soc., Tau Beta Pi. Roman Catholic. Home: 1854 Lindamoor Dr Annapolis MD 21401 Office: ARC 1730 E St NW Washington DC 20006

MCKEE, FRANCIS JOHN, association executive, lawyer; b. Bklyn., Aug. 31, 1943; s. Francis Joseph and Catherine (Giles) McK.; m. Antoinette Mary Sancis; children: Lisa Ann, Francis Dominick, Michael Christopher, Thomas Joseph. AB, Stonehill Coll., 1965; JD, St. John's U., 1970. Bar: N.Y. 1971. Assoc. firm Samuel Weinberg, Esquire, Bklyn., 1970-71, firm Finch & Finch, Esquire, Long Island City, N.Y., 1971-72; staff atty. Med. Soc. of State of

N.Y., Lake Success, 1972-77; exec. dir. Suffolk Physicians Rev. Orgn., East Islip, N.Y., 1977-81, N.Y. State Soc. Surgeons, Inc., New Hartford, 1981—, N.Y. State Soc. Orthopaedic Surgeons, Inc., New Hartford, 1981—, Upstate N.Y. chpt. ACS, Inc., New Hartford, 1981—, N.Y. State Ophthalmol. Soc., 1984—, N.Y. State Soc. Obstetricians and Gynecologists, 1985-86, Orthopac of N.Y., Nat. Commn. Preservation Ortho. Practice, 1968—. Served with U.S. Army, 1966-68. Mem. Oneida County Bar Assn., N.Y. State Bar Assn., Am. Soc. Assn. Execs., Am. Assn. Med. Soc. Execs., Republican. Roman Catholic. Clubs: Engine Eleven, Nightstick (Utica), Skenandoa Club (Clinton). Home: 19 Mulberry St Clinton NY 13323 Office: 210 Clinton Rd New Hartford NY 13413

MC KEE, GEORGE MOFFITT, JR., civil engineer, consultant; b. Valparaiso, Nebr., Mar. 27, 1924; s. George Moffitt and Iva (Santrock) McK.; student Kans. State Coll. Agr. and Applied Sci., 1942-43, Bowling Green State U., 1943; B.S. in Civil Engring., U. Mich., 1947; m. Mary Lee Taylor, Aug. 11, 1945; children—Michael Craig, Thomas Lee, Mary Kathleen, Marsha Coleen, Charlotte Anne. Draftsman, Jackson Constrn. Co., Colby, Kans., 1945-46; asst. engr. Thomas County, Colby, 1946; engr. Sherman County, Goodland, Kans., 1947-51; salesman Oehlert Tractor & Equipment Co., Colby, 1951-52; owner, operator George M. McKee, Jr., cons. engrs., Colby, 1952-72; sr. v.p. engring. Contract Surety Consultants, Wichita, Kans., 1974—. Adv. rep. Kans. State U., Manhattan, 1957-62; mem. adv. com. N.W. Kans. Area Vocat. Tech. Sch., Goodland, 1967-71. Served with USMCR, 1942-45. Registered profl. civil engr., Kans., Okla., registered land Surveyor, Kans. Mem. Kans. Engring. Soc. (pres. N.W. profl. engrs. chpt. 1962-63, treas. cons. engrs. sect. 1961-63), Kansas County Engr's. Assn. (dist. v.p. 1950-51), Northwest Kans. Hwy. Ofcls. Assn. (sec. 1948-49), Nat. Soc. Profl. Engrs., Kans. State U. Alumni Assn. (pres. Thomas County 1956-57), Am. Legion (Goodland 1st vice comdr. 1948-49), Colby C. of C. (v.p. 1963-64), Goodland Jr. C. of C. (pres. 1951-52). Methodist (chmn. ofcl. bd. 1966-67). Mason (32 deg., Shriner); Order Eastern Star. Home: 34 Lakeview Circle Rt 1 Towanda KS 67144 Office: 6500 W Kellogg Wichita KS 67209

MCKEE, JARED REIS, financial executive; b. New Castle, Pa., July 20, 1959; s. Richard Newcombe and Mary Eleanor (Shoaff) McK.; m. Jeanne Legore, June 28, 1986. Student, Coll. of Wooster, Ohio, 1977-81. Systems analyst Advanced Tech., Inc., Reston, Va., 1984; fin. dir. New Eng. Campaign, Hingham, Mass., 1984-86; instl. account exec. Ivy Fin. Svcs., Inc., Hingham, 1986—; class agt. Mercersburg (Pa.) Acad., 1985—. Mem. Plymouth (Mass.) Rep. Town Com., 1988—; mem. fin. com. Old Ship Ch., Hingham, 1986-87. Unitarian. Home: 2046 State Rd Plymouth MA 02360 Office: The Ivy Funds 40 Industrial Pk Hingham MA 02043

MCKEE, KATHRYN DIAN GRANT, banker; b. Los Angeles, Sept. 12, 1937; d. Clifford William and Amelia Rosalia (Shacher) Grant; m. Paul Eugene McKee, June 17, 1961; children: Scott Alexander, Grant Christopher. BA, U. Calif., Santa Barbara, 1959; grad. Sch. Mgmt. Exec. Program, UCLA, 1979. Accredited compensation and benefits. Mgr., Mattel, Inc., Hawthorne, Calif., 1963-74; dir. Twentieth Century Fox Film Corp., Los Angeles, 1975-80; sr. v.p. 1st Interstate Bank, Ltd., Los Angeles, 1980—; treas. Personnel Accreditation Inst., 1983-86, pres., 1986. Contbr. articles to profl. jours. Pres. GEM Theatre Guild, Garden Grove, Calif., 1984-86; bd. dirs. Vis. Nurses Assn., Los Angeles, 1984-88; bd. dirs. ASPA, 1986—, treas., 1988; trustee Garden Grove Assn. for Arts, 1985—, pres., 1988. Recipient Sr. Honor Key, U. Calif., Santa Barbara, 1959; named Outstanding Sr. Woman, 1959. Mem. Internat. Assn. Personnel Women (various offices, past nat. pres., Mem. of Yr. 1986), Orgn. Women Execs., Women in Bus., Am. Compensation Assn. (William Winter award 1986). Club: Los Angeles Athletic. Office: First Interstate Bank 707 Wilshire Blvd Los Angeles CA 90017

MCKEE, SUSAN PARK, meeting planner, writer; b. Ill., Nov. 18, 1945. BA, UCLA, 1968; MS, Ind. U., 1974. Reporter Indpls. Star, 1968-73, fashion editor, 1973-83; meeting planner AGENDA: Indy, Inc., Indpls., 1980—; contbg. editor Indpls. Monthly mag., 1983—; cons. Ind. U. Ctr. on Philanthropy of Ind. U.-Purdue U., Indpls., 1988. Pres. Indpls. Council for Internat. Visitors, 1985—; founder, bd. dirs. Internat. Ctr. Indpls., pres. 1976-77. Mem. Soc. Profl. Journalists. Office: AGENDA: Indy Inc PO Box 68466 Indianapolis IN 46268

MCKEE, TIMOTHY CARLTON, taxation educator; b. South Bend, Ind., Mar. 9, 1944; s. Glenn Richard and Laura Louise (Niven) McK.; m. Linda Sykes Mizelle, Oct. 13, 1984; children: Brandon Richard. BS in Bus. Econs., Ind. U., 1970, MBA in Fin., 1973, JD, 1979; LLM in Taxation, DePaul U., 1980. Bar: Ill. 1980, U.S. Dist. Ct. (no. dist.) Ill. 1980; CPA, Ill., Va. Procedures analyst Assocs. Corp., South Bend, Ind., 1969-71; asst. dir. fin. Ind. U., Bloomington, Ind., 1971-79; sr. tax mgr. Peat Marwick Mitchell & Co., Chgo., Norfolk, Va., 1979-84; corp. counsel K & K Toys, Norfolk, 1984; asst. prof. acctg. Old Dominion U., Norfolk, 1985—; computer coordinator, Peat, Marwick, Mitchell & Co., 1982-84; micro computer cons. Old Dominion U., 1985—. Contbr. articles to profl. jours. Mem. Friends of Music, Bloomington, 1978, Art Inst., Chgo., 1981; loaned exec. United Way, Chgo., 1981; telethon chmn. Va. Orch. Group, Norfolk, 1983. Mem. Am. Acctg. Assn., Am. Tax Assn., Hampton Roads Tax Forum, Inst. Internal Auditors, Beta Alpha Psi. Home: 412 Rio Dr Chesapeake VA 23320-8036 Office: Old Dominion U Hughes Hall 2065 Norfolk VA 23529-0229

MCKENNA, FAY ANN, electrical manufacturing company executive; b. Bennington, Vt., Jan. 7, 1944; d. George Francis and Barbara Mae (Youngangel) Hoag; m. James Dennis McKenna, Sept. 3, 1963 (div. 1983); children: Russell (dec.), Laura, James, Sean, Michael. Student, Mercy Coll. Key punch operator N.Y. State Taxation and Fin. Dept., Albany, 1960-61; receptionist Trine Mfg./Square D Co., Bronx, 1972-76; clk. Square D Co., Bronx, 1976-78, exec. sec., 1978-79, personnel mgr., 1979-86; mgr. mktg. adminstrn. Trine Products Corp., 1986—. Mfg. Fund raiser YMCA, Bronx, 1979—; mem. Community Bd. #9, Bronx, 1984—; Recipient Service to Youth award YMCA, 1985. Mem. Adminstrv. Mgmt. Soc. Republican. Roman Catholic. Avocations: physical fitness, reading, interior decorating. Home: 4100-20 Hutchinson River Pkwy E Bronx NY 10475 Office: Trine Products Corp 1430 Ferris Pl Bronx NY 10461

MCKENNA, JOHN JOSEPH, insurance company executive; b. Evanston, Ill., Dec. 14, 1932; s. Joseph J. and Lorraine C. (Connors) McK. BS in Commerce, Loyola U., Chgo., 1954. CLU, Chartered Fin. Cons.; cert. real estate broker, Ill. Claim adjuster Continental Casualty, Chgo., 1954; gen. mgr. Prudential Ins. and Fin. Svcs., Chgo., 1956—; bd. dirs., sec. Valley Bank Services Corp., St. Charles, Ill.; mem. Chgo. Estate Planning Council, 1976—. Telethon fundraiser United Cerebral Palsy, Chgo. Served to 1st lt. inf. U.S. Army, 1954-56. Mem. Nat. Assn. Life Underwriters (chmn. elections 1984-89), Ill. Life Underwriters Assn. (pres.), Chgo. Assn. Life Underwriters (pres., Disting. Service award 1982), Gen. Agents and Mgrs. Conf. (dir., nat. AMTC chmn. 1987-89, Nat. Mgmt. award 1972-89), Chgo. Gen. Agents and Mgrs. Assn. (pres.), CLUs (chpt. bd. dirs. 1985-87, v.p. edn. 1989), Loyola U. Sch. Bus. Adminstrn. Alumni Bd. Govs. Republican. Roman Catholic. Clubs: Exec. of Chgo., Snow Buddies. Home: 400 E Randolph Chicago IL 60601 Office: Prudential Ins and Fin Svcs 1901 S Meyers Rd Oakbrook Terrace IL 60181

MCKENNA, MICHAEL JOSEPH, manufacturing company executive; b. Phila., Feb. 18, 1935; s. Michael J. and Stella Marie (Gramigna) McK.; B.S., LaSalle Coll., 1962; m. Letitia Ward, Feb. 9, 1957; children—Letita, Carol, Suzanne, Kathleen Jane, Margaret. With Crown Cork & Seal Co., Phila., 1957—, sales rep., 1969, dist. sales mgr., Phila., 1970, regional sales mgr., 1974, v.p. sales and mktg., 1979-86, sr. v.p., 1986—, also bd. dirs. Founding bd. dirs. Northampton Twp. Library, 1967-71; pres. Churchville PTA, 1969-70. Served with U.S. Army, 1955-57. Mem. Can Mfrs. Inst. (standing com. 1980—). Republican. Roman Catholic. Club: Old Guard Soc. Home: 247 Magnolia Dr Churchville PA 18966 Office: Crown Cork & Seal Co Inc 9300 Ashton Rd Philadelphia PA 19136

MCKENNA, QUENTIN CARNEGIE, tool company executive; b. Claremont, Calif., Sept. 2, 1926; s. George Alexander and Lillian Frances (Street) McK.; m. Barbara Louise Williamson, Sept. 12, 1948 (div. 1984); children: Candace, Megan, Carl, Erin. B.A. cum laude, Pomona Coll., 1948; postgrad., Stanford U. (Hewlett Packard fellow), 1948-50, U. So. Calif., 1951-53, UCLA, 1968-69. Mem. tech. staff guided missile div. Hughes Aircraft Co., 1950-52; with Indsl. Electronics, 1952-55; with Hughes Aircraft Co., 1955-78, asst. group exec. missile systems group, 1977-78; pres. Kennametal, Inc., Latrobe, Pa., 1978-79; pres., chief exec. officer Kennametal, Inc., 1979—, chmn. bd., 1986; bd. dirs. Interlake Corp., Pitts. Nat. Bank, PNC Fin. Corp. Patentee in field. Trustee St. Vincent Coll., 1981—. Recipient Eli Whitney Meml. award Soc. Mining Engrs., 1983. Mem. Phi Beta Kappa, Sigma Xi. Episcopalian.

MC KENNA, SIDNEY F., technical company executive; b. Detroit, Nov. 27, 1922; s. Michael James and Elizabeth Josephine McK.; m. Helen Mary Spiroff, Sept. 20, 1944; children—Lynne Marie McKenna Hoss, Dennis Michael, Patrick Conlon, Mary Elizabeth McKenna Raimondi, Maureen T. McKenna Anderson, Christopher John. A.B., U. Mich., Ann Arbor, 1947; M.A., Wayne State U., 1948. With Ward Baking Co., Detroit, 1939-41; prodn. worker Cadillac Motor Co. (div. Gen. Motors Corp.), Detroit, 1941-42; mem. indsl. relations staff Ford Motor Co., Dearborn, Mich., 1942-79, v.p., 1974-79; sr. v.p. human resources United Techs. Corp., Hartford, Conn., 1980-86, sr. v.p. employee and external relations, 1986-87, sr. v.p. pub. affairs, 1987—. Chmn. adv. bd. Providence Hosp., Detroit, 1972-80; bd. dirs. Brighton (Mich.) Hosp., 1976-80, Mercy Coll., Detroit, 1976-80, United Found., 1976-80, St. Francis Hosp., Hartford, Conn., 1983—; bd. dirs. St. Joseph's Coll., 1988—. Served with USN, 1942-46. Mem. Labor Policy Assn. (chmn.), Bus. Roundtable, Orgn. Resources Counselors, Nat. Assn. Mfrs. (bd. dirs. 1988—). Roman Catholic. Clubs: Bloomfield Hills Country (Mich.), Birmingham (Mich.); Athletic; Hartford Golf, K.C. Home: 170 Waterville Rd Farmington CT 06032 Office: United Techs Corp United Techs Bldg Hartford CT 06101

MC KENNA, WILLIAM EDWARD, investment company executive; b. Boston, Aug. 9, 1919; s. Alfred W. and Mary E.C. (Quigley) McK.; children: William P., Kathleen M., Daniel J., Eileen F., Paul V., Mary Ellen; m. Mary N. Smith, Oct. 3, 1968. A.B., Holy Cross Coll., 1947; M.B.A., Harvard, 1949. Diplomate: C.P.A., N.Y., Calif. Staff accountant Touche, Niven, Bailey & Smart, N.Y.C., 1949-52; v.p., controller Monroe Calculating Machine Co., Orange, N.J., 1952-60; also dir.; v.p., treas., controller Litton Industries, Beverly Hills, Calif., 1960-63; sr. v.p. Litton Industries Bus. Equipment Group, Beverly Hills, 1964-67; also dir.; chmn., chief exec., dir. Hunt Foods & Industries, Inc., Fullerton, Calif., 1967-68; chmn., chief exec., dir. Norton Simon, Inc., Fullerton, 1968-69; bus. cons. 1969-70; chmn., dir. Technicolor, Inc., Hollywood, Calif., 1970-76; chmn. bd. Sambo's Restaurants, Inc., Santa Barbara, Calif., 1979-81, Vencap, Inc., Irvine, Calif., 1977-79; dir. Calif. Amplifier, Inc., Safeguard Health Enterprises, Inc., Am. Home Shield Corp., LDB Corp., Calprop Corp., Hydro-Mill Co., WMS Industries, Inc., Drexler Tech., Inc., Midlantic Nat. Bank, Midlantic Corp. Mem. pres.'s council, regent, assoc. trustee Coll. Holy Cross; trustee St. John's Hosp. Found. Mem. Am. Inst. C.P.A.s, Nat. Assn. Accts., Fin. Execs. Inst., Calif. Soc. C.P.A.s, N.Y. Soc. C.P.A.s, N.J. Soc. C.P.A.s, Tailhook Assn., Delta Epsilon. Home and Office: 912 Oxford Way Beverly Hills CA 90210

MCKENNA, WILLIAM JOHN, textile products executive; b. N.Y.C., Oct. 11, 1926; s. William T. and Florence (Valis) McK.; m. Jean T. McNulty, Aug. 27, 1949 (dec. Nov. 1984); children: Kevin, Marybeth, Peter, Dawn; m. Karen Lynne Hilgert, Aug. 6, 1988. B.B.A., Iona Coll., 1949; M.S. (Univ. Store Service scholar), NYU, 1950. V.p. Hat Corp. Am., N.Y.C., 1961-63, v.p. mktg., 1961-63, exec. v.p., 1963-67; pres. Manhattan Shirt Co., N.Y.C., 1967-74, Lee Co., Inc., Shawnee Mission, Kans., 1974-82, also dir.; pres., dir. Kellwood Co., St. Louis, 1982—, chief exec. officer, 1984—, also bd. dirs.; dir. Genovese Drug Stores, Melville, N.Y., United Mo. Bancshares, Kansas City, Mo. Trustee Maryville Col., St. Louis U.; bd. dirs. Boys Hope. Served with USN, 1944-46, PTO. Roman Catholic. Clubs: St. Louis, Town and Country Racquet, Bellerive Country. Office: Kellwood Co 600 Kellwood Pkwy Saint Louis MO 63017

MC KENNEY, WALTER GIBBS, JR., lawyer, publishing company executive; b. Jacobsville, Md., Apr. 22, 1913; s. Walter Gibbs and Mary (Starkey) McK.; m. Florence Roberta Rea, July 17, 1939. Student, Dickinson Sem., 1935-37; Ph.B. Dickinson Coll., 1939; J.D., U. Va., 1942; LL.D., Dickinson Sch. Law, 1964; D.H.L., Lycoming Coll., 1984. Bar: Md. 1942. Practiced in Balt. 1942—; partner McKenney, Thomsen & Burke; partner, gen. mgr., editor Taxes & Estates Pub. Co., Balt., 1946—; chmn. trust com. Equitable Bank, N.A., Balt., 1970-84; dir. Equitable Bancorp., 1960-84; lectr. Southwestern Grad. Sch. Banking, 1966-76. Editor Taxes and Estates, 1946—, Minimizing Taxes, 1946-84, The Educator, 1965—, The Patron, 1968-84. Pres. Kelso Home for Girls; mem. bd. child care Balt. Conf. Meth. Ch., pres., 1961-64; pres. Balt. Estate Planning Council, 1963-64; trustee Goucher Coll., 1968-84, Dickinson Coll., Lycoming Coll., Wesley Theol. Sem., Loyola Coll. at Balt., 1975-83, Franklin Sq. Hosp., Franklin Square Found., Franklin Square Health System, Helix Health System. Served to lt. USNR, 1942-45. Mem. ABA, Md., Balt. bar assns. Republican. Methodist. Home: 102 Estes Rd Baltimore MD 21212 Office: Munsey Bldg Baltimore MD 21202

MCKENNY, JERE WESLEY, geological engineering firm executive; b. Okmulgee, Okla., Feb. 14, 1929; s. Jere Claus and Juanita (Hunter) McK.; m. Anne Ross Stewart, May 4, 1957; children: Jere James, Robert Stewart. BS in Geol. Engring, U. Okla., 1951, MS in Geol. Engring, 1952. With Kerr-McGee Corp., Oklahoma City, 1953—, mgr. oil and gas exploration, 1968-69, v.p. oil and gas, 1969-74, v.p. exploration, 1974-77, vice chmn., 1977—, pres., 1983—, chief operating officer, 1988—; Mem. alumni adv. council sch. Geology and Geophysics U. Okla. Served with U.S. Army, 1953-55. Mem. Am. Assn. Petroleum Geologists, Am. Petroleum Inst. (dir.), Ind. Petroleum Assn. Am. (dir.), Houston Geol. Soc., Oklahoma City Geol. Soc., Sigma Xi, Sigma Gamma Epsilon. Episcopalian. Clubs: Oklahoma City Golf and Country, Whitehall. Home: 2932 Cornwall Pl Oklahoma City OK 73120 Office: Kerr-McGee Corp PO Box 25861 Oklahoma City OK 73125 *

MC KENZIE, HILTON EUGENE, construction company executive; b. Berlin, Pa., Sept. 5, 1921; s. Enoch Joseph and Nellie Savilla (Colefleish) McK.; M.S.C.E. and M.E., M.I.T., 1941; C.E. and B.S.C.E., Va. Poly. Inst., 1939; m. Dorothy Elyea, May 19, 1949; children—Carol, Deborah, Cynthia, Hilton. Sr. cons. Bank Bldg. Corp., St. Louis, 1950-72; sec.-treas. Fin. Bldg. Cons., Atlanta, 1972-75; pres., chmn. Fin. Structures Inc., Atlanta, 1975—; instr. Cornell U., Ithaca, N.Y., 1976. Served to lt. col. U.S. Army, 1940-45. Decorated Bronze Star, Silver Star, Purple Heart. Mem. Nat. Soc. Profl. Engrs., N.C. Soc. Engrs., Soc. Am. Mil. Engrs. Protestant. Club: Elks. Home: Rt 1 Mansfield GA 30255 Office: 2990 Brandywine Rd Atlanta GA 30341

MCKENZIE, JAMES HENRY, executive, corporate chief financial officer; b. Salinas, Calif., July 11, 1950; s. George Durward and Viola Anna (Minnich) McK.; m. Mary Ann Fox, May 18, 1974; children: Michael Christian, Christopher James, Lauren Christine. BS in Commerce, U. Va., 1972. CPA, Va. Auditor, audit sr. Arthur Andersen & Co., Washington, 1972-74; asst. controller Integrated Services, Inc. subs. System Devel. Corp., McLean, Va., 1974-76, controller, dir. bus. ops., 1976-79; asst. corp. controller System Devel. Corp., Santa Monica, Calif., 1979-81; v.p. fin., chief fin. officer Kinetics Tech. Internat. Corp., Pasadena, Calif., 1981-83, Quarterdeck Office Systems, Santa Monica, 1983-85; exec. v.p., chief fin. officer Security Pacific Instl. Services Corp. subs. Security Pacific Corp., Los Angeles, 1985-88, Security Pacific State Trust Co. subs. Security Pacific Corp., Los Angeles, 1987—; also bd. dirs. Security Pacific State Trust Co., Los Angeles; bd. dirs., treas. Security Pacific Employee Benefit Services, Los Angeles, 1985-88. Recipient scholarship Govt. Employees Mut., 1968, U. Va., 1968-69, U.S. Dept. Justice, 1969-72. Mem. AICPA, Calif. Soc. CPAs, Los Angeles Athletic Club. Roman Catholic. Office: Security Pacific State Trust Co 333 S Grand Ave Ste 1700 Los Angeles CA 90071

MCKENZIE, L. RUSSELL, controller, manufacturing executive, contractor; b. Payson, Utah, July 16, 1944; s. Leland S. and Lillian (Russell) McK.; m. Carol Greenhalgh, Dec. 29, 1965; children: Malinda, Laura, Gerald R., Marcinda, Jonathan R., Rahcel, Rebecca, Maria. BA in Econs. and Stats., Brigham Young U., 1969. CPA, Mo., N.Y., Ill., Ky., Pa., Utah. With Gen. Elecric Co., Phoenix and Louisville, 1969-72; corp. auditor Gen. Elecric Co., Schenectady, N.Y., 1972-75; mgr. gen. acctg. indsl. and svc. engring. Gen. Elecric Co., 1975-76; mgr. fin. analysis and adminstrn. Gen. Elecric Co., Oakbrook, Ill., 1976-79; mgr. fin. analysis air conditioning bus. Gen. Elecric Co., Louisville, 1979-81; mgr. fin. apparatus and engring. svcs. Gen. Elecric Co., Phila., 1981-86; v.p., contr. Eaton-Kenway, Salt Lake City, 1986—. Mem. Am. Mgmt. Assn., Elfun Soc. Home: 1256 E 2050 S Bountiful UT 84010 Office: Eaton-Kenway 515 E 100 Salt Lake City UT 84102

MCKEON, ELIZABETH FAIRBANKS, marketing executive; b. Woodstock, Vt., June 16, 1931; d. Dewey Alfred and Margaret Ann (Heavisides) Fairbanks; m. Philip George Goodrow, (div.); children: Craig Alan, William Timothy; m. Henry Arthur McKeon, Oct. 16, 1978. Student, Brown U. Nat. Sch. Savs. Banking, 1974; AA, Quinnipiac Coll., 1983. Clk. Conn. Light and Power, Berlin, 1952-54; mortgage clk. Meriden (Conn.) Savs. Bank, 1954-56; clk., teller Southington (Conn.) Savs. Bank, 1958-68, asst. controller, 1968-75, v.p., 1975-84, sr. v.p., 1984—. Pres. Friends of the Southington Pub. Libr., 1988—, YMCA (sec. 1984-85, pres. 1984-86); sec. United Way Southington. Mem. Southington Pub. Health Assn. (treas. 1970), Sav. Bank Assn. Conn., (pres. forum 1983-84, treas./sec. Group I 1985-86), C. of C. (sec. 1978-80),Arts and Crafts Assn. (past pres.). Club: Arts Crafts Assn. Office: Southington Savs Bank 121 Main St Southington CT 06489

MCKEON, GEORGE A., insurance company executive; b. Orangeburg, N.Y., Jan. 22, 1937; s. Thomas Patrick and Elizabeth Anna McKeon; m. Eileen Ann Connors, June 27, 1959 (dec. Aug. 1977); children: John, Alice, Thomas; m. Fay L. Akins, Aug. 28, 1981. BA, Fairleigh Dickinson U., 1959; LLB, Fordham U., 1963. Bar: N.Y., 1964, Conn., 1967, U.S. Dist. Ct., Conn., 1971. With contracts negotiation Bendix Corp., Teterboro, N.J., 1958-65; div. asst. counsel United Technologies, Windsor Locks, Conn., 1965-69; asst. counsel Travelers Ins. Co., Hartford, Conn., 1969-73, assoc. counsel, 1973-76, counsel, 1976-81; assoc. gen. counsel Travelers Ins. Co., Hartford, 1981-84; gen. counsel Travelers Ins. Co., Hartford, Conn., 1984—; mem. faculty U. Conn. Referee Vol. Pub. Defender Program, Conn. Mem. ABA (chmn. corp. counsel com. tort and ins. practice sect. 1985-87, mem. commn. on Mass. torts 1987-88), N.Y. Bar Assn., Conn. Bar Assn., Hartford County Bar Assn. Roman Catholic. Home: 36 Bradley Brook Dr North Granby CT 06060 Office: The Travelers Corp 1 Tower Sq Hartford CT 06183-1050

MCKEOUGH, WILLIAM DARCY, corporate executive; b. Chatham, Ont., Can., Jan. 31, 1933; s. George Grant and Florence Sewell (Woodward) McK.; m. Margaret Joyce Walker, June 18, 1965; children: Walker Stewart, James Grant. B.A., U. Western Ont., 1954; LL.D. (hon.), 1979, Wilfred Laurier U., 1980. Chmn. Can. Devel. Investment Corp., 1987—; pres., chief exec. officer Redpath Industries Ltd., Toronto, Ont., also bd. dirs.; bd. dirs. Cameco Ltd., Can. Gen. Investments Ltd., Can. Imperial Bank of Commerce, Can. Gen. Tower Ltd., McKeough Sons Co. Ltd., Noranda Mines Ltd., Numac Oil & Gas Ltd., Redpath Industries Ltd., Varity Corp. Inc., Union Enterprises Ltd. Former mem. exec. com. Anglican Diocese of Huron; former mem. Gen. Synod, Anglican Ch., Can.; mem. Chatham City Council, 1960-63; also mem. Planning Bd. and Lower Thames Valley Conservation Authority; former mem. Chatham-Kent adv. bd. Can. Nat. Inst. of the Blind; former bd. dirs. Chatham YMCA, Chatham Little Theatre; chmn. and pres. bd. govs. pres. Ridley Coll.; former bd. govs. Stratford Shakespearian Festival, Wilfrid Laurier U.; former mem. Can. group Trilateral Commn.; mem. Ont. Legislature, 1963-78, minister without portfolio, 1966, minister mcpl. affairs, 1967; treas. and minister of econs., also chmn. Treasury Bd., 1971-72, minister mcpl. affairs, 1972, treas. and minister of econs. and intergovtl. affairs, 1972, parliamentary asst. to premier Ont., 1973, minister of energy, 1973-75, treas. and minister econs. and intergovtl. affairs, 1975-78. Office: Redpath Industries Ltd, The Royal Bank Pla Box 66, Toronto, ON Canada M5J 2J2

MCKEOWN, MARTIN, manufacturing executive; b. Glasgow, Scotland, Sept. 28, 1943; came to U.S., 1968.; s. Martin and Marion (Cameron) M.; m. Anne Campbell, Dec. 30, 1967. Degree in mech. engring., Stow Coll., Glasgow, 1964; BSc, U. Strathclyde, Glasgow, 1966. Cert. mfg. engr. Apprentice Rolls Royce Aero Engine, Glasgow, 1960-66; methods engr. No. Electric, Toronto, Ont., Can., 1966-67; mfg. engr. nuclear fuel div. Westinghouse Electric Corp., Pitts., 1968-72; tool engring. specialist steam turbine div. Westinghouse Electric Corp., Winston-Salem, N.C., 1972-79; mgr. mfg. devel. elevator div. Westinghouse Electric Corp., Randolph, N.J., 1979-81, mgr. mfg. tech. elevator div., 1981-83, mgr. devel. engring. elevator div., 1983-84; mfg. devel. mgr. transp. div. Westinghouse Electric Corp., West Mifflin, Pa., 1984-86, mgr. ops. program mgmt. transp. div., 1986, product line mgr. transp. div., 1986-88; product line mgr. AEG Westinghouse Transp. Systems, Pitts., 1988—. Mem. Inst. Prodn. Engrs., Robotics Internat. Roman Catholic. Office: AEG Westinghouse Transp Systems 1501 Lebanon Church Rd Pittsburgh PA 15236-1431

MCKERNAN, LEO JOSEPH, manufacturing company executive; b. Phila., Feb. 17, 1938; s. Leo Joseph and Mary (Dever) McK.; m. Gail Marie Ryan, Feb. 3, 1962; children: Kim, Jennifer. Student, Iona Coll., 1956-59, NYU, 1961-62, U. Bridgeport, 1962-64. With Eaton Corp., Carol Stream, Ill., 1959-74; mgr. mfg. Controls div. Eaton Corp., Carol Stream, 1974; v.p. gen. mgr. Axle div. Clark Equipment Co., Buchanan, Mich., 1974-77; group v.p. Clark Equipment Co., South Bend, Ind., 1977-83, sr. v.p., then exec. v.p., then chief operating officer, 1983-86, pres., chief exec. officer, 1986—, chmn., 1988—, also bd. dirs.; chmn. supervisory bd. UME Group N.V.; bd. dirs. Sq. D Co., 1st Source Corp. Bd. dirs. South Bend Civic Ctr. Found., Ind., 1978-83; mem. U. Notre Dame Engring. Adv. Coun., 1985—, corp. grants com., 1988—. Mem. Constrn. Ind. Mfrs. Assn., Soc. Automotive Engrs., U.S.-Korea Bus. Coun., Brazil-U.S. Bus. Coun. Office: Clark Equipment Co 100 N Michigan St Box 7008 South Bend IN 46634

MCKIBBIN, JOHN M., III, aluminum company executive; b. Pitts., May 30, 1931; s. John M. Jr. and Eleanor (Kennedy) McK.; m. Katherine Ellison; children: Mary Jane, John, Suzanne, Kelly, Stanton, Margaret, James. BS in Econs., U. Va., 1956. Salesman Alcoa, N.Y.C., 1952-62; asst. mgr. industry Pitts., 1962-66, mgr. industry div., 1966-68, mgr. industry, 1968-70; v.p. sales and mktg. Rolling div. Nat. Aluminum Corp., Danbury, Conn., 1971-79, sr. v.p., 1979-81, pres., 1981-84; exec. v.p. Nat. Aluminum Corp., Pitts., 1984-85, pres., 1986—. Inventor packaging box, 1975. Served as sgt. U.S. Army, 1953-55. Mem. Aluminum Assn. (chmn. packaging 1968-69, div. 1984-86; exec. com. 1986—, bd. dirs. 1986—). Republican. Episcopalian. Clubs: Allegheny Country (Sewickley, Pa.), Edgeworth. Home: Fair Acres Dr Sewickley PA 15143 Office: Nat Aluminum Corp 2 Robinson Pla Ste 300 Pittsburgh PA 15205

MCKIERNAN, THOMAS EUGENE, school administrator; b. Ft. Wayne, Ind., Nov. 26, 1940; s. Thomas and Elizabeth (Kerwin) M.; m. Jean Kallmeyer, Sept. 3, 1970; 1 child: John. AB, Xavier U., Cin., 1963, MBA, 1967; cert. in fin. mgmt., The Wharton Sch., 1981. Tchr. Schs. include Cin. Tech. Coll., Mt. St. Joseph Coll., Seton High Sch., Cin., 1963-70; sch. fin. officer Seton Schs. Archdiocese of Cin., 1970—; trustee Cath. Social Service S.W. Ohio. Active Cin. Hist. Soc. Recipient Greater Cin. award; Cath. Edn. award Today's Cath. Tchr. Mag.; named Knight of the Holy Sepulchre, Elizabeth Seton award, Sister of Charity. Fellow Assn. Sch. Bus. Officers, of U.S. and Can.; mem. Nat. Cath. Edn. Assn., Am. Assn. Sch. Adminstrs. Republican. Roman Catholic. Clubs: Western Hills Country, English Speaking Union. Home: 1075 Overlook Ave Cincinnati OH 45238 Office: Seton Found PO Box 58004 Cincinnati OH 45258

MCKIM, SAMUEL JOHN, III, lawyer; b. Pitts., Dec. 31, 1938; s. Samuel John and Harriet Frieda (Roehl) McK.; children: David Hunt, Andrew John; m. Eugenia A. Leverich. A.A. with distinction, Port Huron Jr. Coll., 1959; B.A. with distinction, U. Mich., 1961, J.D. with distinction, 1964. Bar: Mich. 1965, U.S. Dist. Ct. (so. dist.) Mich. 1965, U.S. Ct. Appeals (6th cir.) 1969. Assoc., Miller, Canfield, Paddock and Stone, Detroit, Bloomfield Hills, Kalamazoo, Lansing, Monroe, Traverse City and Grand Rapids, Mich., Washington, Boca Raton, Fla., 1964-71, ptnr., 1971—, mng. ptnr., 1979-85, chmn., mng. ptnr., 1984-85; mem. tax council State Bar Mich., 1981-84, chmn. state and local tax coms. Real Property sect., 1982—. Trustee, past chmn. Goodwill Industries of Greater Detroit; mem. exec. bd. and asst. counsel Detroit Area Council Boy Scouts Am. Mem. ABA, Mich. Bar Assn., Detroit Bar Assn., Oakland County Bar Assn., Barrister's Soc., Order of Coif, Phi Delta Phi. Presbyterian. Club: Ostego Ski. Assoc. editor Mich. Law Rev. Office: Miller Canfield Paddock & Stone Ste 100 Pinehurst Office Ctr 1400 N Woodward PO Box 2014 Bloomfield Hills MI 48303-2014

MCKINLEY, CHARLES HUGH, aerospace and defense company executive, engineer; b. Overton, Tex., Jan. 18, 1937; s. Hugh Green and Arrie (Beidlman) McK.; m. Clara Jean Dunaway, Jan. 25, 1959; children: Michael Hugh, James Curtis, Wendy Sue. BS in Aero. Engring., Tex. A&M U., 1959; MS in Aero. Engring., U. So. Calif., 1963; MS in Engring. Adminstrn., So. Meth. U., 1966. Registered profl. engr., Tex. Rsch. engr. autonetics div. N.Am. Aviation, Los Angeles, 1959-63; engring. specialist Chance Vought, Dallas, 1963-68; sr. engr. Martin Marietta Corp., Orlando, Fla., 1968-70; project engr. LTV Aerospace and Def. Co., Dallas, 1970-75, v.p., 1979—; dir. land warfare office undersec. of def., rsch. and engring. U.S Govt., Washington and Hunstville, Ala., 1975-79; tech. dir. U.S. Army Missile rsch. and devel. U.S Govt.; mem. army sci. and tech. bd., Nat. Acad. Sci., Washington, 1982-88, naval rsch. adv. com., Naval Weapons Ctr., China Lake, Calif., 1984—, space rsch. and tech. bd., Texas A&M Univ., Coll. Sta., 1985—, tech. dir. U.S. Army Micom 1978-79. Active in adminstrn. Lovers Lane Meth. Ch., Dallas, 1984—. Recipient Meritorious Civilian Service awards, Sec. of Def., 1978, Dept. of Army, 1979. Fellow AIAA (assoc.); mem. Air Force Assn., Assn. U.S. Army, Am. Def. Preparedness Assn., Irving (Tex.) Rep. Club. Republican. Home: 612 Balboa Irving TX 75062 Office: LTV Missiles and Electronics Group PO Box 650003 Mail Stop TH-69 Dallas TX 75265-0003

MCKINLEY, WILLIAM E., banker; b. Clarion, Pa., June 10, 1940; s. Earl Edwin and Dorothy Louise (Callen) McK.; m. Nancy Ann Sigworth, Mar. 14, 1965. Student, Edinboro U. of Pa. Cert. comml. lender. Auditing officer Pennbank, Titusville, Pa., 1975-79, loan rev. officer, 1979-80, asst. v.p., 1980-83, v.p., 1983-84, sr. credit rev. officer, 1984-89; mgr. credit policy dept. Integra Fin. Corp., Titusville, 1989—. chmn. United Fund, Youngsville, Pa., 1973-75; pres. Brokenstraw Valley-Youngsville Mchts. Assn., 1975; chmn. Cornplanter Twp. (Pa.) bd. auditors, 1979—. Served with USN, 1958. Mem. Nat. Assn. Accts. (pres. Keystone Mountain States Coun., 1984-85, nat. committeeman 1980-82, bd. dirs. 1982-83, 83-84, pres. Northwest Keystone Chpt. 1979-80), Am Inst. Banking (instr.), Stuart Cameron McCloud Soc., Robert Morris Assn. (assoc.), Phi Eta Sigma. Republican. Home: 838 Grandview Rd Oil City PA 16301 Office: Pennbank 801 State St Erie PA 16538

MCKINNEY, CHARLES CECIL, advertising executive; b. Newdale, N.C., Nov. 30, 1931; s. Sherbert Day and Florence Van (Hall) McK.; children—Emry Lynn, Robin Ashley, Marc Jason. B.S.B.A., U. N.C.-Chapel Hill, 1957; student, U. Tenn., 1950-52. V.p., creative dir. J.T. Howard Advt., 1957-68; chmn. bd., chief exec. officer McKinney & Silver, Raleigh, N.C., 1968—. Trustee N.C. Symphony, Raleigh, 1983-87; bd. dirs. Bus. Found. of N.C., 1985—; bd. visitors U. N.C. Bus. Sch., Chapel Hill. With U.S. Army, 1952-54. Recipient profl. awards. Mem. Newcomen Soc., Nat. Trust Historic Preservation, N.C. Mus. Art. Republican. Clubs: Sphinx (Raleigh); Figure Eight Yacht (N.C.); Met. (N.Y.). Home: 1021 Cowper Dr Raleigh NC 27608 Office: McKinney & Silver 333 Fayetteville St Raleigh NC 27601

MC KINNEY, DAVID E(WING), information processing products company executive; b. Harriman, Tenn., Nov. 28, 1934; s. David Lloyd and Mattie (Ewing) McK.; children: Mary, John, James, Mark. Student (Founders scholar), Vanderbilt U., 1952-53; B.S. in Mktg. (Gen. Electric scholar), U. Tenn., 1956. With IBM, 1956—; br. mgr. IBM, New Orleans, 1966-68; exec. asst. to chmn. bd. IBM, Armonk, N.Y., 1971-73; pres. info. records div. IBM, Princeton, N.J., 1975-76; v.p. office products div. IBM, Franklin Lakes, N.J., 1976-77; v.p. personnel IBM, Armonk, 1979-80; asst. group exec. IBM Gen. Bus. Group, White Plains, N.Y., 1980—; v.p., asst. group exec. IBM Info. Systems Group, Rye, 1982—; pres. IBM World Trade, Americas/Far East Corp., 1986—, v.p. communications, sr. v.p. corp. ops. staff, mgmt. com., corp. mgmt. bd., 1987-89; pres., dir. gen. IBM Europe, Paris, 1989—. Mem. adv. bd. T. J. Watson Found., Providence; elder First Presbyterian Ch., New Canaan, Conn. Served to lt. U.S. Army, 1957-58. Mem. Internat. Exec. Service Corps (bd. dirs., orgn. resources counselors, trustee internat. house). Clubs: Country of New Canaan;. Office: IBM Corp Old Orchard Rd Armonk NY 10504

MC KINNEY, FRANK EDWARD, JR., banker; b. Indpls., Nov. 3, 1938; s. Frank Edward and Margaret (Warner) McK.; m. Katherine Berry, Aug. 18, 1962; children: Frank Edward, III, Katherine Marie, Margaret Leonard, Madeleine Warner, Robert Warner, Heather Claire. B.S., Ind. U., 1961, M.B.A., 1962; LL.D. (hon.), Butler U., Indpls., 1975. Asst. cashier First Nat. Bank, Chgo., 1964-67; with Am. Fletcher Nat. Bank, Indpls., 1967—; exec. v.p., then pres. Am. Fletcher Nat. Bank, 1970-73; chmn. bd. Am. Fletcher Nat. Bank (now Banc One Corp.), 1973—; chmn. bd. Bank One Corp., 1974—, now also chief exec. officer; dir., vice chmn., mem. exec. com. Allied Bank Internat., N.Y.C.; dir., mem. exec. com. Ind. Bell Telephone Co.; dir. Am. United Life Ins. Co.; dir., mem. exec. com. Indpls. Power & Light Co., IPALCO Enterprises, Inc. Bd. dirs. Indpls. Mus. Art, Exec. Council on Fgn. Diplomats; adv. council Coll. Bus., U. Notre Dame; mem. Ind. State Olympic Com. Served to 1st. lt. AUS, 1962-64. Named to Internat. Swimming Hall Fame, 1975, Ind. U. Acad. Alumni Fellows, 1973, Ind. U. Intercollegiate Athletics Hall of Fame, 1982; recipient Disting. Service award Indpls. Jaycees, 1974. Mem. Assn. Res. City Bankers, Assn. Bank Holding Cos. (dir., vice chmn., exec. com.), Am., Ind. bankers assns., Ind. Soc. Chgo., Internat. Monetary Conf., Penrod Soc., Newcomen Soc. N.Am., Indpls. C. of C., Ind. C. of C., 500 Festival Assocs., Econ. Club Indpls. (pres. 1977), Am. Legion, Sigma Alpha Epsilon. Democrat. Roman Catholic. Clubs: Meridian Hill Country, Indpls. Athletic, Skyline, Notre Dame of Indpls. (Indpls.). Office: Banc One Corp 100 E Broad St Columbus OH 43271-0261 *

MCKINNEY, JANE ELESTINE, auditor; b. Phila., Nov. 25, 1965; d. William Kelson and Halise (Craig) McK. BS in Acctg., Phila. Coll. Textiles and Sci., 1987. Staff auditor Provident Nat. Bank, Phila., 1987-88, auditor, 1989—. Mem. Am. Soc. Women Accts., Nat. Assn. Female Execs. Democrat. Episcopalian. Home: 2008 N 32d St Philadelphia PA 19121 Office: Provident Nat Bank Broad and Chestnut Sts Philadelphia PA 19101

MCKINNEY, JOHN BENJAMIN, steel company executive; b. St. Louis, Nov. 12, 1932; s. Clifford Paul and Mary Adeline (Myers) McK.; m. Margaret Stickney Stark, Oct. 31, 1953; children: Jeffrey Stark, Susan Mary, John Benjamin. BA, U. Va., 1954. With Laclede Steel Co., St. Louis, 1956—, mgr. sales indsl. products, 1967-75, gen. sales mgr., 1975-76, v.p. sales, 1976-81, exec. v.p., 1981, pres., chief exec. officer, 1982—, dir.; bd. dirs. Boatman's Trust. Co. Bd. dirs. John Allen Love Charitable Fund. 1st lt. U.S. Army, 1954-56. Mem. Am. Iron and Steel Inst. (bd. dirs.), St. Louis Country Club, Noonday Club, Stadium Club, Log Cabin Club. Republican. Roman Catholic. Home: 32 Rio Vista Saint Louis MO 63124 Office: Laclede Steel Co Equitable Bldg 10 S Broadway Saint Louis MO 63102

MCKINNEY, JOSEPH F., diversified manufacturing holding company executive; b. Phila., 1931; married. BS, St. Joseph's Coll., 1952; MBA, Harvard U., 1957. Dir. research Warner, Jennings, Mandel & Longstreth, 1957-60; founder, pres. Electro-Sci. Investors, Inc., Richardson, Tex., 1960-63; v.p. Brown, Allen & Co., 1963-64; dir. corp. fin. Ling & Co., 1964-65, Goodbody & Co., 1965-66; pres. Tyler Corp., Dallas, Tex., 1966-83, 1987—, chmn., chief exec. officer, 1972—, also bd. dirs. Office: Tyler Corp 3200 San Jacinto Tower Dallas TX 75201 *

MCKINNEY, MICHAEL DAVID, printing company executive; b. Huntington, W.Va., Dec. 10, 1953; s. Robert Garrett and Erma Larue (Pelfrey) McK.; m. Nancy Lou Cook, Oct. 16, 1972; children: Robert Michael, Ryan Keith. BBA, Marshall U., 1976. Mgr. outlet sales Corbin Ltd., Huntington, 1973-75; indsl. engr. Am. Car and Foundry, Huntington, 1975-76; div. mgr. Chapman Printing Co., Inc., Lexington, Ky., 1976—. Democrat. Baptist. Office: Chapman Printing Co Inc 890 Russell Cave Rd Lexington KY 40505

MC KINNEY, ROBERT SALTER, banking executive; b. N.Y.C., Apr. 24, 1941; s. Elmer Ellsworth and Caroline Elizabeth (Clancy) McK.; B.S. in Mech. Engring., U.S. Mcht. Marine Acad., 1962; M.S. in Mgmt., Columbia U., 1966; postgrad. Advanced Bus. Inst., Harvard U., 1977; m. Carroll Geraldine Driscoll, Aug. 14, 1962; children—Robert S., Richard, James, Glenn. Engr., Moore-McCormack Lines, Inc., 1962-63; engr. Western Electric Co., N.Y.C., 1963-66; mktg. rep. IBM, N.Y.C., 1966-73, account mgr., 1973-76, product mgr., 1976-77; controller bus. services dept. Union Carbide Corp., N.Y.C., 1977-79, dir. mgmt. cons., 1979-83, dir. info. systems and tech., 1983-86, sr. v.p. strategic tech. and research Mfrs. Hanover, N.Y., 1986-87; mng. dir. systems Kidder Peabody, N.Y.C., 1987—. Mem. Assn. Internal Mgmt. Cons., Am. Assn. Artificial Intelligence. Republican. Episcopalian. Club: Columbia. Office: Kidder Peabody 120 Broadway New York NY 10271

MC KINNON, ALAN LEO, banker; b. Boston, Feb. 13, 1928; s. Frederic W. and Helen L. (Cunningham) McK.; m. Eleanor Hannigan, Aug. 13, 1955; children—Alan Leo, Brian, Ian. B.S. in Bus. Adminstrn, Boston U., 1950; student, Bentley Coll., Columbia Grad. Bus. Sch. CPA, Mass. Pub. accountant Alexander, Grant & Co. (formerly Patterson, Teele & Dennis), Boston, 1953-61; tax and ins. mgr. United-Carr, Inc., Boston, 1961-69; exec. v.p. 1st Nat. Bank Boston, 1973-80, 1980—; exec. v.p., chief fin. officer 1st Nat. Boston Corp., 1972-86; bd. dirs. Bank of Boston Internat., Miami, N.Y.C., Boston Overseas Fin. Corp., Bank of Boston Internat., L. A., Mortgage Corp. of the South, FNBC Acceptance Corp., Birmingham, Ala., Caribbean Am. Svc. Investment and Finance Co. Ltd. Bd. dirs. Milton Hosp.; mem. Town Meeting, Milton, 1971—. Served with USNR, 1946-47. Mem. Fin. Execs. Inst., Tax Execs. Inst., Mass. Soc. CPA's, Fed. Club, Milton-Hoosic Club, Milton Town Club, Treasurers Club. Home: 12 Longwood Rd Milton MA 02187 Office: 1st Nat Bank Boston 100 Federal St Boston MA 02110

MCKINNON, ARNOLD BORDEN, transportation company executive; b. Goldsboro, N.C., Aug. 13, 1927; s. Henry Alexander and Margaret (Borden) McK.; m. Oriana McArthur, July 19, 1950; children: Arnold Borden Jr., Colin McArthur, Henry Alexander. AB, Duke U., 1950, LLB, 1951; grad. Advanced Mgmt. Program Harvard U., 1972. Bar: D.C. 1951, N.C. 1966. With Norfolk So. Corp. (formerly So. Ry. System), Norfolk, Va., 1951—, v.p. law, 1971-75, sr. v.p. law and acctg., 1975-77, exec. v.p. law and acctg., 1977-81, exec. v.p. law and fin., 1981-82, exec. v.p. mktg., 1982-86, vice chmn., 1986-87, chmn., pres., chief exec. officer, 1987—; bd. dirs. Sovran Fin. Corp., Atmospheric Fluidized Bed Devel. Corp., Knoxville, Future of Hampton Rhoads, Inc., Children's Health System, Inc., Norfolk, The Pvt. Adjudication Ctr., Inc., Durham, N.C. Bd. visitors Old Dominion U., Norfolk, Fuqua Sch. Bus., Duke U., Durham; mem. Coal Industry adv. bd.; mem. bus. adv. com. Northwestern U. Transp. Ctr.; mem. Mil. Civilian Liaison Group, Nat. Coal Council, N.C. Citizens Business and Industry, Va. Business Council; bd. trustees Boys Clubs Am., Va. Found. for Ind. Colls., Med. Coll. Hampton Roads Found.; elder 1st Presbyn. Ch., Norfolk. Served with U.S. Army, 1946-47. Mem. ABA, N.C. Bar Assn., D.C. Bar Assn., Am. Mgmt. Assn., The Conf. Bd., The House Wednesday Group, Nat. Freight Traffic Assn., Assn. Am. R.R.s, Am. Soc. Transp. Logistics, Bus. Roundtable, Am. Soc. Corp. Execs., Norfolk C. of C., Norfolk Yacht and Country Club, Town Point Club, The Harbor Club, Chevy Chase Club, Metropolitan Club (Washington), The Links Club, The Broad Street Club (N.Y.C.), Laurel Valley Golf Club (Ligonier, Pa.), House Wednesday Group. Home: 1002 Colonial Ave Norfolk VA 23507 Office: Norfolk & Western Ry Co 1 Commercial Pl Norfolk VA 23510-2191

MCKINNON, FLOYD WINGFIELD, textile executive; b. Columbus, Ga., Dec. 1, 1942; s. Malcolm Angus and Sarah C. (Bullock) McK.; m. Barbara Evans Roles, June 18, 1966; children—James Wingfield, Sarah Elizabeth, Robert Kent. A.B., Washington and Lee U., 1964. Exec. v.p. Cotswold Industries, Inc., N.Y.C., 1966—, also bd. dirs.; v.p., corp. sec. Cen. Textiles, Inc., S.C., 1984—, also bd. dirs.; arbitrator Am. Arbitration Assn., 1983—. Pres. Berkley-n-Scarsdale Assn., 1980; admissions rep. Washington and Lee U., 1979—. Mem. St. Andrews Soc. N.Y. Republican. Episcopalian. Clubs: Town (fiscal affairs com. 1974-80) (Scarsdale); Union League (bd. govs. 1974-77, 88—, sec. 1981-83) (N.Y.C.); Scarsdale Golf (bd. govs. 1983—, v.p. 1988—) (Hartsdale, N.Y.); Bras Coupe (exec. com. 1980—) (Maniwaki, Can.). Home: 26 Taunton Rd Scarsdale NY 10583 Office: Cotswold Industries 10 E 40th St New York NY 10016

MCKINNON, JAMES BUCKNER, real estate salesman, writer; b. Tacoma, Dec. 5, 1916; s. James Mitchell and Rochelle Lenore (Buckner) McK.; m. Marylyn Adelle Coote, Mar. 12, 1967 (div. May 1977); children: Michelyn, James H.C. McK.; m. Martha Sackmann, June 12, 1977. BA in Internat. Studies, U. Wash., 1983, H.M. Jackson Sch. Police detective Los Angeles Police Dept., 1946-50; bn. security officer 1st med. bn. 1st Marine div. Fleet Marine Force, 1950-53; owner, operator, mgr., dir. promotional sales The Saucy Dog Drive-In, Venice, Calif., 1953-63; salesman new car sales and leasing Burien Mercury, Seattle, 1963-66; real estate salesman and appraiser various firms Seattle, 1966—; instr., lectr. U.S. Naval Support Activity, Sandpoint, Wash., 1964-74; mem., lectr. NRC 11-8, Naval Postgrad. Sch., Monterey, Calif., 1975-76; Burien Mercury announcer KOMO TV. Published poetry in anthologies; contbr. articles to various newspapers and jours. Served with USN, 1939-53, PTO, Korea. Recipient Wilmer Culver Meml. award Culver Alumni Fictioneers, Seattle, 1979; Occidental Coll. scholar, 1935, Silver Poet award, 1986, Golden Poet award, 1987, 88; named to Honorable Order Ken. Cols., 1976, One of Best New Poets, Am. Poetry Assn., 1988. Mem. U.S. Naval Inst., N.W. Writers Conf., Ret. Officers Assn. (life), Mensa, KP, Masons. Republican. Home: 2312 41st Ave SW Seattle WA 98116

MCKINNON, ROBERT HAROLD, insurance company executive; b. Holtville, Calif., Apr. 4, 1927; s. Harold Arthur and Gladys Irene (Blanchar) McK.; m. Marian Lois Hayes, Dec. 18, 1948; children: Steven Robert, Laurie Ellen, David Martin. BS, Armstrong Coll., 1950, MBA, 1952. Regional sales mgr. Farmers Ins. Group, Austin, Tex., 1961-66, Aurora, Ill., 1966-68; dir. life sales Farmers New World Life, L.A., 1968-75; v.p. mktg. Warner Ins. Group, Chgo., 1975-82; mem. Canners Exchange Dairy Adv. Com., 1977-82; sr. v.p. mktg. The Rural Ins. Cos., Madison, Wis., 1982-89. Scoutmaster Boy Scouts Am., 1971-72. Served with U.S. Army, 1944-45. Fellow Life Underwriters Tng. Coun.; mem. Am. Soc. CLU's, Soc. CPCU's, Internat. Ins. Seminars, Nakoma Golf Club, Rotary. Home: 402 Walnut Grove Dr Madison WI 53717

MCKINSTRY, GREGORY JOHN DUNCAN, retail executive; b. Vancouver, B.C., Can., Sept. 6, 1947; s. F. John B. and Margaret L. McKinstry; m. Nancy M. Crane, June 22, 1974. B of Commerce, U. B.C., 1970, MBA, 1985. Research mgr. Eaton's, Toronto, Can., 1970-72; co-service mgr. Eaton's, Vancouver, 1972-74; sr. mktg. rep. IBM Can. Ltd., Vancouver, 1974-79; research mgr. Woodward's Ltd., Vancouver, 1979-82, co-accounting mgr., 1982-85, treas., 1985-87, sr. v.p. fin., 1987—, also bd. dirs. (and wholly owned subsidiaries). Dir. Vancouver Kidney Found., 1985-86; mem. Vancouver Bd. Trade; bd. dirs. P.A. Woodward Found. Mem. Fin. Exec. Inst., Vancouver Club. Office: Woodward's Ltd, 101 W Hastings St, Vancouver, BC Canada V6B 1H4

MCKITRICK, JAMES THOMAS, retail executive; b. Cin., Sept. 14, 1945; s. Harry J. and L. May (Buck) McK.; m. Margaret J. Haynes, Sept. 6, 1975; children: Angela, Greg, Randal, Paul, Sheri, Richard, Mike. Student, Salem Coll., 1963-64. Dir. mdse. K Mart Corp., Troy, Mich., 1965-84; exec. v.p., gen. mgr. T.G. & Y. Stores, Oklahoma City, 1984-86, exec. v.p. merchandising and mktg., 1986; pres., chief exec. officer Warehouse Club, Skokie, Ill., 1986-87; pres., chief operating officer G.C. Murphy Co. subs. Ames, Rocky Hill, Conn., 1987—; chmn. Zayre Discount, Rocky Hill, 1988—. Republican. Methodist. Home: 16 Pembroke Hill Farmington CT 06032 Office: Ames Dept Stores 2418 Main St Rocky Hill CT 06457

MCKNEW, ROBERT DAVID, banker; b. Washington, Dec. 8, 1947; s. Raymond George and Violet May (Karchem) McK.; m. Doris Ann Hagerty, Aug. 29, 1970; 1 child, Anne Elizabeth. B.A., Dickinson Coll., 1969; M.B.A., Amos Tuck Sch., Dartmouth Coll., 1971. Sr. v.p., treas. Continental Ill. Corp., Chgo., 1982-85; exec. v.p., treas. 1st City Bancorp. of Tex., Houston, 1985-87; sr. v.p., dept. exec. Bank of Boston, 1987—; sect. leader Prochnow Sch. Banking, Madison, Wis., 1976-85. Bd. dirs. Chgo. council Girl Scouts U.S., 1983-85. Mem. Dealer Bank Assn. (bd. dirs. 1981-85, pres. 1984-85), Bond Club Chgo. (trustee 1980-82), Mcpl. Bond Club Chgo. Episcopalian. Clubs: Indian Hill (Winnetka, Ill.); Union League (Chgo.). Home: 1 Amberwood Ln Boxford MA 01921 Office: Bank Boston 100 Federal St Boston MA 02110

MCKNIGHT, SUSAN KAREN, water filtration equipment executive; b. Detroit, Aug. 30, 1954; d. William Ross and Jean Marie Lyda (Thompson) McK. BA cum laude, Eastern Mich. U., 1975, MA in Sociology, 1977. Instr. sociology Henry Ford Community Coll., Dearborn, Mich., 1976-78; adminstr. Lake County, Waukegan, Ill., 1978-81; reseacher, project mgr. No. Ill. U., DeKalb, Ill., 1981-83; prin. Quality Flow, Waukegan, 1983—; prin., v.p. On Tap Premium Quality Water, Wheeling, Ill., 1985-87, Quality Flow Inc., Buffalo Grove, Ill., 1987—. Bd. dirs. Waukegan Crime Stoppers, 1981-82, Lake County Council Against Sexual Assault, 1988—; mem. Lake County Literacy Vols., 1986—; Dem. Committeeman, Lake County, 1986. Recipient NaCo award, Nat. Assn. Counties. Mem. Water Quality Assn., Women in Mgmt. (chair program com.), Achievement Seminars/Franz Bador, Greenpeace, Chgo. Anti-Cruelty Soc. Lutheran.

MC KONE, DON T., manufacturing company executive; b. Jackson, Mich., 1921. Grad., U. Mich., 1947. With Aeroquip Corp. (subs. TRINOVA Corp.), Jackson, Mich., 1949-68; with Libbey-Owens-Ford Co. (name changed to TRINOVA Corp. in 1986) Aeroquip Corp. (subs. TRINOVA Corp.), Toledo, Ohio, 1968—, exec. v.p., 1970-75, pres., chief operating officer, 1975-79, pres., chief exec. officer, 1979-80; chmn. bd., dir. TRINOVA Corp. (formerly Libbey-Owens-Ford Co.), Maumee, Ohio, 1980—, chief exec. officer, 1980-86; chmn. bd., dir. Toledo-Lucas County Port Authority; bd. dirs. NBD Bancorp., Inc., Consumers Power Co., Ashland Oil Co., Champion Spark Plug Co. Office: TRINOVA Corp 1705 Indian Wood Circle Maumee OH 43537

MCLAFFERTY, CHARLES LOWRY, financial executive; b. Evanston, Ill., Apr. 11, 1927; s. Joel Edward and Margaret Eliza (Keifer) McL.; m. Dee Hartmann, Feb. 19, 1949; children: Ardith, Karen McLafferty Foust, Charles L. Jr., Kevin P. BS, U. Nebr., 1949; BS in Bus., Bowling Green U., 1950; MBA, Northwestern U., 1952. CPA, Ill. Sr. acct. Arthur Andersen & Co., Dallas, 1951-54; systems analyst Genesco Inc., Nashville, 1954-59; controller Nat. Pool Equipment Co., Florence, Ala., 1959, Martin Stove and Range Co., Florence, Ala., 1959-60; dir. fin. Alamet div. Universal Oil Products Co., Selma, Ala., 1961-70; pres. Southern Shelter Inc., Selma, Ala., 1970-71; controller Southbridge Plastics div. W.R. Grace and Co., Corinth, Miss., 1971-72; asst. treas. Triangle Corp., Orangeburg, S.C., 1972—; instr. U. Tenn., 1957-59. Treas., USS Alabama Battleship Com., Mobile, Ala., 1963-74; bd. dirs. Nat. Head Injury Found., Southborough, Mass., treas., 1984—; mem. Gov.'s Task Force on Head Injury, 1985-87, S.C. Developmental Disabilities Council, 1988—; gen. chmn. S.C. Festival of Roses, 1975; chmn. bd. trustees John T. Morgan Acad., 1964-66; adv. bd. Vision House, Inc., Andover, Mass.; co-founder, mem., bd. dirs. S.C. Head Injury Assn. With USN, 1944-46. Named Outstanding Citizen City of Selma, 1969. Mem. Fin. Execs. Inst. Lutheran. Home: 1587 Tolly Ganly Cir Orangeburg SC 29115 Office: Triangle Corp Cameron Rd Orangeburg SC 29115

MCLAIN, EDWARD HILL, insurance company executive; b. Arkadelphia, Ark., Aug. 5, 1950; s. John Talbert and Betty Jo (Hill) McL.; children: Marshall Hill, Adam Laurens. BA in Polit. Sci., Ark. State U., 1973, MA in Polit. Sci., 1976. Dist. mktg. mgr. Kemper Group, Dallas, 1977-79, Lubbock, Tex., 1979-82; v.p., ins. agt. Williams-Dwyer Co., Wichita Falls, Tex., 1982—, also bd. dirs.; bd. dirs. Seton Premium Fin. Co. Loan exec. United Way, Wichita Falls, 1984, 85; bd. dirs. Streams and Valleys, Wichita Falls, 1985—, March of Dimes, Wichita Falls, 1985—; chmn. bd. dirs. Leadership Wichita Falls, 1985-87. Recipient Svc. award Bd. Commerce and Industry, 1987. Mem. Ind. Ins. Agts. Wichita Falls, Ind. Ins. Agts. Tex., Lions. Methodist. Home: 4911 Opal St Wichita Falls TX 76310 Office: Williams Dwyer Co PO Drawer 270 Wichita Falls TX 76307

MCLANE, MICHAEL HARROLD, banking software executive; b. Gainesville, Fla., July 17, 1951; s. Roscoe Jr. and Joyce (Hunt) McL.; m. Laura Jean Stewart, Apr. 26, 1987. BA, U. Fla., 1981; MBA, U. Cen. Fla., 1983. Software support cons. Fla. Software Svcs., Altamonte Springs, 1983-85; cons. micro-computer The Maestra Group, Melbourne, Fla., 1985; analyst installations CBS/Newtrend, Winter Park, Fla., 1985-86; mgr. quality assurance CBS/Newtrend, Winter Park, 1986, mgr. product release group, 1986-87; mgr. product devel. Citicorp. Info. Resources, Orlando, Fla., 1987-88; v.p. tech. svcs. APPS div. Mgmt. Decision Systems, Atlanta, 1988—; cons. in field. Served as sgt. U.S. Army, 1971-73. Mem. S.E. Software Assn., Data Processing and Mgmt. Assn., Quality Assurance Inst. Republican. Presbyterian.

MCLANE, ROBERT DRAYTON, JR., food products company executive; b. Cameron, Tex., July 22, 1936; s. Robert Drayton and Gladys (Blaylock) McL.; m. Mary Elizabeth Cockrell, Feb. 2, 1972; children: Robert Drayton III, Denton. BBA, Baylor U., 1958; MS, Mich. State U., 1959. With McLane Co., Inc., Temple, Tex., 1957—, v.p., 1964-74, exec. v.p., sec.-treas., 1974-78, chief exec. officer, pres., 1978—, also bd. dirs.; bd. dirs. First Nat. Bank, Temple, Tex. Pres. United Way Campaign, Temple, 1985—; mem. Tex. State Bd. Mental Health and Mental Retardation, 1985—, exec. bd. Heart O'Tex. Council Boy Scouts Am., 1968—; bd. dirs. Scott and White Meml. Hosp., Temple, 1985—. Recipient Mgmt. Excellence and Achievement award Coll. Bus. Mgmt. U. Ga., 1986; named Entrepreneur of Yr. Arthur Young/Venture, Dallas, 1987. Mem. Nat. Am. Wholesale Grocers Assn. (chmn. 1986-88), Nat. Assn. Convenience Stores, Grocery Mfrs. Am., SW Food Industry Assn. Baptist. Office: McLane Co Inc 2915 Center Street PO Box 6115 Temple TX 76501-6115

MCLARNAN, DONALD EDWARD, banker, corporation executive; b. Nashua, Iowa, Dec. 19, 1906; s. Samuel and Grace (Prudhon) McL.; m. Virginia Rickard, May 5, 1939; children: Marilyn, Marcia, Roxane. A.B., U. So. Calif., 1930; grad., Southwestern U. Law Sch., 1933; postgrad., Cambridge U. Trust appraiser, property mgr. Security-Pacific Nat. Bank, Los Angeles, 1935-54; regional dir. SBA for, So. Calif., Ariz., Nev., 1954-61; area adminstr. SBA for, Alaska, Western U.S., Hawaii, Guam, Samoa, U.S. Trust Terr., 1969-73; pres. Am. MARC, Inc. (offshore oil drillers and mfr. diesel engines), 1961-63, Terminal Drilling & Prodn. Co., Haney & Williams Drilling Co., Western Offshore, 1961-63; v.p., dir. Edgemar Dairy, Santa Monica Dairy Co., 1954-70; founder, pres., chmn. bd. Mission Nat. Bank, 1963-67; pres. Demco Trading Co., Mut. Trading Co.; dir. Coast Fed. Savs. & Loan; cons. numerous corps.; guest lectr. various univs. Contbr. articles on mgmt. and fin. to profl. jours. Chmn. fed. agys. div. Community Chest, 1956; nat. pres. Teachers Day, 1956; bd. councillors U. So. Calif.; founder, chmn., pres. Soc. Care and Protection Injured Innocent; adv. bd. Los Angeles City Coll.; bd. dirs. Calif. Easter Seal Soc.; nat. chmn. U. So. Calif. Drug Abuse Program. Recipient Los Angeles City and County Civic Leadership award, 1959. Mem. Nat. Assn. People with Disabilities (pres.); Mem. Skull and Dagger, Delta Chi. Clubs: Mason (Los Angeles) (K.T., Shriner), Los Angeles (Los Angeles), Jonathan (Los Angeles). Home: 135 S Norton Ave Los Angeles CA 90004 Office: 1111 S Crenshaw Blvd Los Angeles CA 90019

MCLARTY, THOMAS F. (MACK), III, gas company executive; b. Hope, Ark., June 14, 1946; s. Thomas Franklin and Helen (Hesterly) McL.; m. Donna Kay Cochran, June 14, 1969; children—Mark Cochran, Franklin Hesterly. BA, U. Ark., 1968. Founder McLarty Leasing System, Little Rock, 1969-79; pres. McLarty Co., 1979-83, Ark. La. Gas Co., 1983, Arkla, Inc., Little Rock, 1984-88; chmn., chief exec. officer Arkla, Inc., Little Rock and Shreveport (La.), 1985—; now also chmn., chief exec. officer, dir. Arkla Exploration Co. subs. Arkla, Inc., Shreveport. Mem. Ark. Ho. of Reps., 1970-72; chmn. Ark. Democratic Com.; mem. Dem. Nat. Com., 1974-76; treas. David Pryor Gubernatorial Campaign, 1974, Gov. Bill Clinton campaign, 1978; bd. dirs. Hendrix Coll., Conway, Ark.; bd. visitors U. Ark., Little Rock; former chmn. United Negro Coll. Fund Campaign, fund-raising campaign Ark. Symphony. Mem. Greater Little Rock C. of C. (pres. 1983). Office: Arkla Inc PO Box 751 Little Rock AR 72203

MCLAUCHLAN, RODNEY ALAN, bank executive; b. Rio de Janeiro, June 11, 1953; came to U.S., 1976; s. Peter Hugh and Agnieszka (Magdalena) McL. BA, Fed. U. Rio de Janeiro, 1975; MBA, U. Pa., 1978; cert. in taxation, NYU. Assoc. Bankers Trust Co., N.Y.C., 1978-82, v.p., 1982-86, mng. dir., 1986-87; mng. dir., regional dir. Bankers Trust Co., Chgo., 1987—. Bd. dirs. Lyric Opera Chgo., 1988—. Office: Bankers Trust Co 233 S Wacker Ste 5200 Chicago IL 60606

MCLAUGHLIN, ALEXANDER CHARLES JOHN, oil company executive; b. N.Y.C., June 3, 1925; s. Alexander and Margaret (Percival) McL.; m. Joan Kosak, June 10, 1950; 1 child, Jena Hilary. BS, Va. Poly. Inst. and State U., 1946; postgrad. Columbia U., 1947-48. With Standard Vacuum Oil Co., N.Y.C., Shanghai, China, Manila, Saigon, Indochina, Hongkong, Yokohama, Japan, 1946-50; with Trans Arabian Pipeline Co., Turaif, Saudi Arabia, 1951; with Andean Nat. Corp., Cartagena, Colombia, 1952-54; civil engr., N.Y.C., 1954-55; chief project engr. mktg. Am. Oil Co., N.Y.C., chief engr. South, Atlanta, sr. head engr., Chgo., 1955-64; sr. process engr. mfg. and mktg. dept. Amoco Internat. Oil Co., Europe, S.Am., Cen. Am., Asia, Mid. East, Africa, N.Y.C., Chgo., 1969-72; mgr. distbn. Singapore Petroleum Co., 1972-73; constrn. supr. Iran Pan Am. Oil Co., 1973, onshore/offshore and maintenance supr., 1974-75; sr. staff engr. Amoco Internat. Oil Co., Chgo., 1975-78, Amoco Prodn. Co. Internat., Houston, 1978-85, inspection supr. offshore and overseas constrn. dept., 1985-86; cons. oil and gas industry, 1986-88; mgr. projects Hudson Products Corp., 1988—; bd. dirs. Cancun Medicorp. Vol. fireman Long Beach Fire Dept., 1955-63; tng. officer USCG Aux., 1962; Eagle scout, scoutmaster, troop com. mem. Nassau County N.Y. council Boy Scouts Am., 1946-49. Decorated Order White Cloud. Fellow ASCE; mem. NSPE, Nat. Assn. Corrosion Engrs., Omicron Delta Kappa. Republican. Clubs: Pathfinders (London); Columbia Country (Shanghai); Singapore Swim, Singapore Petroleum, Singapore Am.; Tehran Am. Lodge: Moose. Home: 3106 Cedar Knolls Dr Kingwood TX 77339

MCLAUGHLIN, ANN, government consultant; b. Newark, Nov. 16, 1941; d. Edward Joseph and Marie (Koellhoffer) Lauenstein; m. John Joseph McLaughlin, Aug. 23, 1975. B.A., Marymount Coll. Supr. network comml. schedule ABC, N.Y.C., 1963-66; dir. alumnae relations Marymount Coll., Tarrytown, N.Y., 1966-69; account exec. Myers-Infoplan Internat. Inc., N.Y.C., 1969-71; dir. communications Presdl. Election Com., Washington, 1971-72; asst. to chmn. and press sec. Presdl. Inaugural Com., Washington, 1972-73; dir. Office of Pub. Affairs, EPA, Washington, 1973-74; govt. relations and communications exec. Union Carbide Corp., N.Y.C. and Washington, 1974-77; pub. affairs, issues mgmt. counseling McLaughlin & Co., 1977-81; asst. sec. for pub. affairs Treasury Dept., Washington, 1981-84; under sec. Dept. of Interior, Washington, 1984-87; cons. Ctr. Strategic and Internat. Studies, Washington, 1987; Sec. of Labor Dept. of Labor, Washington, 1987-89; vis. fellow Urban Inst., 1989—; mem. Am. Council on Capital Formation, 1976-78; mem. environ. edn. task force HEW, 1976-77; mem. Def. Adv. Com. of Women in the Svcs., 1973-74; bd. dirs. Unocal Corp., Union Camp Corp., Kellogg Co., Pub. Agenda Found. Mem. Washington Woman's Forum, Cosmos Club, Met. Club. Republican. Roman Catholic. Office: Urban Inst 2100 M St NW Washington DC 20037

MCLAUGHLIN, GLEN, financial services company executive; b. Shawnee, Okla., Dec. 21, 1934; s. Champe and Mattie Bet (Jenkins) McL.; m. Ellen Marr Schnake, Aug. 29, 1964; children: Helen Elizabeth, Glen Wallace. B.B.A., U. Okla., 1956; M.B.A., Harvard U., 1964. Asst. treas. Foremost-McKesson, Inc., San Francisco, 1964-69; exec. v.p., dir. MacFarlane's Candies, Oakland, Calif., 1969-70; dir. fin. and adminstrn. Memorex Corp., London, 1970-71; sr. v.p. fin. Four-Phase Systems, Inc., Cupertino, Calif., 1971-82; pres., chmn. Four-Phase Fin., Inc., Cupertino, 1977-82; chmn. bd. Four-Phase Systems, Ltd., Toronto, Ont., Can., 1977-82, Four-Phase Systems Internat., Inc., 1977-82, DeAnza Ins. Co. Ltd., Cayman Islands, 1979-82; gen. ptnr. Matrix Ptnrs., L.P., San Jose and Boston, 1982-86; chmn. bd. Venture Leasing Assocs., 1986—; vice chmn. Cupertino Nat. Bank, Calif.; dir. Phoenix Am. Inc., San Rafael, Calif., Circadian, Inc., San Jose, Calif.; chmn. bd. Calif. Mcpl. Income Fund. Pres. Jr. Achievement Santa Clara County, 1978-79, chmn. bd., 1980-81; chmn. bd. Jr. Achievement Found. Santa Clara County, 1980-87; mem. bus. sch. adv. bd. U. Santa Clara, 1981-84; pres. Boy Scouts Am., Santa Clara County, 1986-87, v.p. adminstrn., 1983-85, mem. exec. council, 1982—, pres. No. Calif. Area, 1988—; mem. pvt. sector investment adv. panel City of San Jose, 1984—. Served to 1st lt. USAF, 1956-62; capt. USAFR, 1964-65. Recipient Silver Leadership award Jr. Achievement, 1981; Silver Beaver award Boy Scouts Am., 1985; Baden-Powell World Fellow, 1986; pub. service citations Calif. State Senate, Calif. State Assembly, Santa Clara County Suprs. Mem. Fin. Execs. Inst., English Speaking Union, Beta Gamma Sigma, Sigma Alpha Epsilon. Clubs: Commonwealth, Harvard U. Bus. Sch. No. Calif. Home: 14016 Camino Barco Saratoga CA 95070

MCLAUGHLIN, JAMES DANIEL, architect; b. Spokane, Wash., Oct. 2, 1947; s. Robert Francis and Patricia (O'Connel) McL.; B.Arch., U. Idaho, 1971; m. Willa Kay Pace, Aug. 19, 1972; children—Jamie Marie, Robert James. Project architect Neil M. Wright, Architect, AIA, Sun Valley, Idaho, 1971-74, McMillan & Hayes, Architects, Sun Valley, 1974-75; now pres., prin. McLaughlin Architects Chartered, Sun Valley. Prin. works include Oakridge Apts., Moscow, Idaho (Excellence in Design award AIA), Walnut Ave. Mall, Ketchum, Idaho (Excellence in Design award AIA, 1987), McMahan Residence, Sun Valley (Excellence in Design award AIA, 1987). Chmn., Ketchum Planning and Zoning Commn., Ketchum Planning Commn., Ketchum Zoning Commn.; vice chmn. Sun Valley Planning and Zoning Commn. Served to 1st lt. U.S. Army. Registered architect, 8 states including Idaho. Mem. AIA , Nat. Council Archtl. Registration Bds., Nat. Home Builders Assn., Ketchum-Sun Valley C. of C. (dir.). Roman Catholic. Club: Rotary. Prin. archtl. works include James West Residence, First Fed. Savs., Fox Bldg. Rehab., Walnut Ave. Mall, First St. Office Bldg. Home: Lot #5 Red Cliffs Subdivision Box 6 Ketchum ID 83340 Office: McLaughlin Architects Chartered PO Box 479 Sun Valley ID 83353

MCLAUGHLIN, JAMES HIGGINS, bank executive; b. Yeadon, Pa., Aug. 15, 1946; s. John James and Frances (Higgins) McL.; m. Suzanne O'Neill; children: Kathleen, Sean. BS, Georgetown U., 1968; cert. in banking, Rutgers U., 1977. V.p. br. ops. Fidelity Bank, Phila., 1969-81; v.p. community banking Standard Fed. Savs. and Loan, Gaithersburg, Md., 1981-84, sr. v.p. br. adminstrn., 1981-84; exec. v.p. community banking, sr. exec. v.p. retail banking, pres. Equibank, Pitts., 1984—, also bd. dirs.; bd. trustees Mercy Hosp. Pres. Legatus, Pitts. chpt.; bd. dirs. Civic Light Opera, Pitts., Jr. Achievement of SW Pa., Pitts., Nat. Conf. of Christians and Jews, Pitts. Partnership Neighborhood Devel.; mem. steering com. Leadership Pitts. Served with USMC, 1969-75. Mem. Pitts. C. of C. Office: Equibank 2 Oliver Pla Pittsburgh PA 15222

MCLAUGHLIN, JOHN GERARD, sales and marketing executive; b. Auburn, N.Y., May 21, 1948; s. T. John and Marie A. (Teahan) McL.; m. Susan Ann Holland, Jan. 1, 1983; children: Meghan Marie, Erin Ann.. BS in Pharmacy, SUNY, Buffalo, 1972. Registered pharmacist, Vt. Salesman Eli Lilly & Co., Fall River, Mass., 1972-78, Beckman Instruments Co., Washington, 1978-81; NW/West Can. sales mgr. Beckman Instruments Co., Seattle, 1981-83; western sales mgr. Boehringer Mannheim Diagnostics, San Francisco, 1983-86; mgr. mktg. program, group mktg., nat. sales Boehringer Mannheim Diagnostics, Indpls., 1983-86; mgr. nat. sales Kallestad Diagnostics, Austin, Tex., 1986-88, dir. sales and mktg. instrument div., 1988—. Roman Catholic. Club: Lost Creek Country (Austin). Office: Kallestad Diagnostics 1120 Capital of Texas Hwy 8 Austin TX 78746

MCLAUGHLIN, JOSEPH MICHAEL, religious order administrator; b. Boston, Aug. 16, 1943; s. Joseph M. and Mary E. (O'Hare) McL. AB, St. Michael's Coll., 1966; MDiv., U. St. Michael's, 1969; AM, St. Michael's Coll. U. Toronto, 1972. Ordained May 16, 1970. Gen. councilor Soc. St. Edmund, Burlington, Vt., 1976-82; treas. gen. Soc. St. Edmund, Winooski, Vt., 1982-86, superior gen., 1986—; dir. sem. St. Basil's Coll., Toronto, 1972-76; asst. prof. St. Michael's Coll., Winooski, 1978—; v.p. Edmundite So. Missions, Inc., Selma, Ala., 1986—. Author: From Pontigny, 1978. Chmn. Prudential Com., Town of Colchester, Vt., 1982-87; clk. Prudential Com., Colchester, 1979-85; mem. Burlington Community Land Trust, 1983—; trustee, sec. St. Michael's Coll., Winooski, 1979—, chmn. bd. trustees, 1986—. Mem. Assn. Gov. Bds., Conf. Major Superiors of Men, Union Superiors Gen. Roman Catholic. Home and Office: Soc St Edmund Fairholt S Prospect St Burlington VT 05401

MCLAUGHLIN, MICHAEL ANGELO, mortgage consultant, author; b. Medford, Mass., Mar. 13, 1950; s. Bernard Thadeus and Rose Francis (Di Stasio) McL.; m. Karen Jean Parker, Nov. 19, 1972 (div. 1985); m. Claudia Chuber, June 29, 1985; 1 child, Camila. BS with honors, Northeastern U., 1975, MPA, 1978. Asst. juvenile supr. Dept. Youth Svcs., Boston, 1972-73; correction officer Dept. Correction, Billerica, Mass., 1974, Dept. Correction-MCI Walpole, Boston, 1974-80; facility mgr. 1st Security Svcs. Corp., Boston, 1980-82; from sales mgr. to owner Solar Resources Internat., Danvers, Mass., 1982-84; acct. exec. New Eng. Rare Coin Galleries, Boston, 1985, Progressive Consumers Fed. Credit Union, 1985, br. mgr., 1988—; lectr. Northeastern U., Boston, 1981; pres. local chpt. Am. Fedn. State, County and Mcpl. Employess, Mass., 1977-79. Candidate, Com. to Elect Mike McLaughlin Sheriff, Middlesex County, Mass., 1980; mem. Spl. Legis. Conf. Com., Boston, 1979, Jt. Labor Mgmt. Com., Boston, 1978. Mem. Am. Correctional Assn., Am. Jail Assn., Master of Pub. Adminstrn. Assn. (activities com. 1982), Sigma Epsilon Rho. Roman Catholic. Avocations: sailing, skiing, pocket billiards, tennis, racquetball. Author: Screw: The Truth about Walpole State Prison by the Gurard Who Lived It, 1989.

MCLAUGHLIN, RICHARD F., III, investment banker; b. Hillsborough, Calif., Sept. 3, 1957; s. Richard F. Jr. and Maryclare F. (Flynn) McL.; m. Peggy Porter, Sept. 17, 1983. BA in Econs., UCLA, 1979; MBA, U. So. Calif., 1982. With Prudential Bache Securities, L.A., 1982-84; 1st v.p. corp. fin. Drexel Burnham Lambert, L.A., 1984—. Republican. Roman Catholic. Office: Drexel Burnham Lambert 131 S Rodeo Dr Beverly Hills CA 90212

MCLAUGHLIN, RICHARD WARREN, insurance company executive; b. Boston, Nov. 25, 1930; m. Marilyn Slye, 1956; children: Kathleen, Richard Warren Jr., Thomas, Judy. B.S., Boston Coll., 1952; grad. Advanced Mgmt. Program, Harvard U., 1979. Trainee Travelers Ins. Co., Hartford, Conn., 1956, asst. sec., 1966-69, sec., 1969-70, 2d. v.p., 1970-73, v.p., 1973-81, sr. v.p., 1981-85, exec. v.p., 1985—; bd. dirs. Travelers of Bermuda, Hamilton, Health Ins. Assn. of Am., Washington; corporator St. Francis Hosp. Served to capt. USAF, 1952-56, Korea. Mem. Am. Pension Conf. Club: Hartford; Eastward Ho (Chatham, Conn.). Home: 20 Duncaster Ln Vernon CT 06066 Office: Travelers Corp 1 Tower Sq Hartford CT 06183

MCLAUGHLIN, WILLIAM FOOTE, land development and property management consultant; b. Chgo., July 16, 1929; s. Frederic and Irene Castle (Foote) McL.; m. Delores Feliu, July 29, 1950 (div. 1961); 1 child, Irene Castle; m. Dorothy Begier, July 3, 1975; 1 child, David Lee. BSBA, Hofstra U., 1951; MBA, U. Ark., 1957, PhD, 1962. V.p., dir. W.F. McLaughlin Co., Chgo., 1957-68; mktg. adminstr. Mid-Western Instruments, Tulsa, 1964; economist, planning analyst Skelly Oil Co., Tulsa, 1968-72; exec. v.p., chief operating officer Main Place Corp., Tulsa, 1972-76; pres. Koppel Devel. Co., Bartlesville, Okla., 1977-78; mgr. corp. facilities and real estate Western Co. N.Am., Ft. Worth, 1979-81; dir. property mgmt. Kiawah Island Co., Charleston (S.C.), 1981-83; pres., chief exec. officer RSVP, Inc., Myrtle Beach, S.C., 1983-84; v.p., dir. property mgmt. Furman Co., Greenville, S.C., 1985-87; instr. econs. and real estate U. Ark., 1957-61, Tulsa Jr. Coll., 1974-78; real estate cons., 1971—. Mem. Mayor's Community Devel. Com., Tulsa, 1972-76. Fellow Co. Mil. Historians; mem. Bldg. Owners and Mgrs. Assn. (Man of Yr. award 1976), Nat. Assn. Corp. Real Estate Execs., Nat. Assn. Realtors (broker S.C., N.C., Ga.), Am. Planning Assn. (assoc.), Nat. Assn. Bus. Economists, Am. Econs. Assn., Nat. Assn. Real Estate Appraisers, Nat. Assn. Rev. Appraisers (sr.), Community Assn. Inst. (profl. community assn. mgr.), Inst. Real Estate Mgmt. (cert. property mgr.), Culver Legion, Sons of Confederacy, Aztec Club, Sigma Chi. Episcopalian. Home: PO Drawer F Aiken SC 29802

MC LAUGHLIN, WILLIAM GAYLORD, metal products manufacturing company executive; b. Marietta, Ohio, Sept. 28, 1936; s. William Russell and Edna Martha (Hiatt) McL.; children: Debora, Cynthia, Leslie, Teresa, Kristin, Jennifer. BS in Mech. Engring., U. Cin., 1959; MBA, Ball State U., 1967. Plant engr. Kroger Co., Marion, Ind., 1959-62; with Honeywell, Inc., Wabash, Ind., 1962-75, mgr. metal products ops., 1971-72, gen. mgr. ops., 1972-75; pres. MarkHon Industries Inc., Wabash, 1975—; mem. N. Cen. Ind. Pvt. Industry Council, 1983-84; mem. bus. adv. bd. Manchester Coll. Patentee design electronic relay rack cabinet. Pres. Wabash Assn. for Retarded Children, 1974-75; gen. chmn. United Fund Drive, 1971; mem. Wabash County Arts Council; pres. Wabash Valley Dance Theater; treas., Young Reps., Wabash, 1968-70; bd. dirs. Youth Service Bur., Sr. Citizens, Jr. Achievement; mem. ofcl. bd. Meth. ch., 1966-71; pres. Meth. men, 1975-77. Recipient Ind. Jefferson award for public service, 1981, Disting. Citizen award Wabash, 1981; named Outstanding Young Man of Year, Wabash Jr. C. of C., 1972. Mem. Indsl. C. of C. (pres. 1973-74), Wabash Area C. of C. (pres. 1976), Precision Metal Forming Assn. (chmn. Ind. dist. 1978, chmn. metal fabrication div.), Ind. Mfg. Assn. (bd. dirs.), Young Pres.'s Orgn. Club: Wabash Country (v.p. 1972-76). Lodges: Rotary (pres. Cincinnatus Soc. 1970-71, dist. youth exchange officer 1974-77, dist. gov. 1979-80), Masons. Home: 141 W Maple St Wabash IN 46992 Office: 200 Bond St Wabash IN 46992

MCLEAN, DAVID LYLE, lawyer; b. Longview, Wash., May 5, 1941; s. David Edward and Helen Margaret (Andrews) McL.; m. Sheila Marsha Avrin, Apr. 27, 1968; children—Alexandra Andrews, David Benjamin Avrin. AB, Princeton U., 1963; LLB, Yale U., 1966. Bar: N.Y. 1967, D.C. 1980, U.S. Dist. Ct. (so. dist.) N.Y. 1968, U.S. Dist. Ct. (ea. dist.) N.Y. 1969, U.S. Ct. Appeals (2d cir.) 1969, U.S. Supreme Ct. 1973. Assoc. Sullivan & Cromwell, N.Y.C., 1967-73; asst. gen. counsel Coopers & Lybrand, N.Y.C., 1973-76, assoc. gen. counsel and prin., 1976—. Treas, Bellamy for State Senate campaigns 1970-76. Served with USMCR, 1966-72. Mem. ABA (com. law and acctg. 1981—), Assn. Bar City N.Y. (com. mil. justice 1971-75, com. corp. law dept's., 1986—), Hemisphere Club. Democrat. Contbr. articles to legal jours. Office: Coopers & Lybrand 1251 Ave of the Americas New York NY 10020

MCLEAN, LAUCHLIN HUIET, lawyer; b. Columbia, S.C., Aug. 28, 1921; s. Samuel Hampton and Ellie (Huiet) McL.; m. Joelle Caroline Hinchman, Sept. 24, 1949; children: Laurie, Andrew, Mary. BA, Ohio State U., 1946; JD, Harvard U., 1949. Ptnr. Payner Hermann, Cleve., 1949-55; v.p. Aetna Life and Casualty, Hartford, 1955—. Dep. mayor, mem. coun. City West Hartford, Conn., 1971-78. Staff sgt. U.S. Army, 1942-45, ETO. Mem. ABA (tax sect.), Am. Coun. Life Ins. (chmn. tax com.), Am. Ins. Assn. (chmn. tax com.). Democrat. Office: Aetna Life and Casualty Co 151 Farmington Ave Hartford CT 06156

MCLEAN, THOMAS EDWARD, accountant, treasurer; b. St. Louis, Feb. 27, 1947; s. Francis Lester and Margaret Helen (Hauser) McL.; m. Rosalie Elaine Wagner, Aug. 12, 1967 (div. Mar. 1987); children: Susan Marie, Patricia Denise, Kelly Kathleen; m. Sarah Elizabeth Phillips, Apr. 16, 1987. BS in Commerce, St. Louis U., 1969. CPA, Mo. Acct., cons. Zielinski and Wolff, St. Louis, 1969-79; chief fin. officer, treas. SCH EnterCorp. Inc., Houston, 1979—; asst. treas. Alliance Nat. Ins. Co., Houston, 1986—; fin. cons. Diocese Austin, Tex., 1979-83; sec., treas. K&M Beverage Co., Houston, 1986—; chief fin. officer Alliance Health Plan Inc., Houston, 1987—; bd. dirs. Port Arthur Surgery Ctr. Treas. civ. assn. Pennyrich Farm Subdiv., St. Louis, 1976; vol. cons. Father Joseph Znotas Scholarship Fund, Austin, 1983. Mem. Mo. Soc. CPAs, Beta Gamma Sigma (hon.). Republican. Roman Catholic. Office: EnterCorp 2600 N Loop W #620 Houston TX 77092

MCLEAVEY, DENNIS WILLIAM, business administration educator, researcher; b. Birkenhead, Eng., Apr. 9, 1946; came to U.S., 1973; s. Dennis Stanfield and Mary Marjorie (Lyons) McL.; m. Janet Adrienne Olexson, Aug. 15, 1970; children: Christine, Andrew. BA in Econs., U. Western Ont., 1968; MBA, Ind. U., 1972, D in Bus. Adminstrn., 1972. Asst. prof. U. Western Ont., London, Can., 1972-73, U. Conn., Storrs, 1973-76; assoc. prof. U. R.I., Kingston, 1976-79, prof., 1980-83, 86—, chmn. dept. bus. adminstrn., 1980-83, assoc. dean, 1983-86; cons., analyst Yorkshire and Humberside, U.K., 1984—; bd. dirs., sr. investment officer White-Hunt Industries, U.K., 1984—. Author: (with others) Production Planning and Inventory Control, 1985, Principles of Operations Research for Management, 1988; contbr. articles to profl. jours. Fellow Fin. Analysts Fedn., Am. Prodn. and Inventory Control Soc.; mem. Am. Econ. Assn., Am. Fin. Assn., Acad. Internat. Bus. Roman Catholic. Home: 121 Estelle Dr West Kingston RI 02892 Office: U RI Coll Bus Adminstrn Kingston RI 02881

MCLENDON, CHRISTOPHER MARTIN, real estate development company executive; b. Darby, Pa., Apr. 12, 1961; s. Walter and Alberta (Petteway) McL. BSBA, BS in Computer Sci., Beaver Coll., 1983; MS in Engring. Sci., Pa. State U., 1986. Software engr. Exxon Office Systems, Princeton, N.J., 1983-84; software engr., systems engr. Intermetrics Inc., Warminster, Pa., 1984-86; realtor assoc. Jewell Realty Co., Phila., 1986—; v.p. Trends II Inc., Phila., 1986—; pres., chief exec. officer Commonwealth Mgmt. Devel. Corp. Inc., Sharon Hill, Pa., 1987—; instr. S.E. Delco High Sch., Sharon Hill, 1987—. Active Rep. Senatorial Inner Circle, Washington, 1988. Recipient Cert. Appreciation Fla. Meml. Coll., Miami, 1987. Mem. Small Bus. Assn. Delaware Valley. Home: PO Box 364 Sharon Hill PA 19079-0364 Office: Commonwealth Mgmt Devel Corp Inc 1107 Jackson St Sharon Hill PA 19079

MCLEOD, WALTON JAMES, JR., lawyer; b. Lynchburg, S.C., Aug. 7, 1906; s. Walton James and Pauline (Mullins) McL.; m. Rhoda Lane Brown, Feb. 2, 1935; children: Walton James III, Peden Brown, William Mullins, Thomas Gordon III. BA, Wofford Coll., 1926, LLD, 1988; LLB, U. S.C., 1930. Bar: S.C. 1930, U.S. Dist. Ct., U.S. Ct. Appeals (4th cir.) 1937, U.S. Supreme Ct. 1936. Ptnr. Jefferies & McLeod, Walterboro, S.C., 1930-40, Jefferies, McLeod & Unger, Walterboro, 1940-54, Jefferies, McLeod, Unger & Fraser, Walterboro, 1954-76, McLeod, Fraser & Unger, Walterboro, 1976-85, McLeod, Fraser & Cone, Walterboro, 1985—; city atty. Walterboro; mem. vice chmn. S.C. Hwy Commn. 1946-50. Mem. nat. exec. com. Young Dems., 1938-42, S.C. Dem. exec. com., 1960-88; Dem. chmn. Colleton County, 1950-60; temporary chmn. state conv., 1976; trustee Walterboro pub. schs., 1936-46, Wofford Coll., 1954-66. Served to lt. comdr. USNR, 1942-46. Recipient Disting. Alumni award Wofford Coll., Durant Disting. Service award S.C. Bar Found.; fellow Am. Bar Found. Mem. Am. Legion (comdr. S.C. 1949-50, mem. nat. exec. com. 1951-52), ABA (ho. of dels. 1950-70, bd. govs. 1964-67, chmn. resolutions com. 1961-62), S.C. (pres. 1969-70), Colleton County Bar Assns. (pres. 1962), Jud. Conf. U.S. Ct. Appeals 4th cir., Am. Coll. Probate Counsel, Am. Law Inst., Am. Judicature Soc., Am. Coll. Trial Lawyers, U. S.C. Law Sch. Assn. (pres., Kappa Alpha, Phi Delta Phi. Methodist. Lodges: Masons, Shriners. Home: 109 Savage St Walterboro SC 29488 Office: 111 E Washington St Walterboro SC 29488

MCLIN, STEPHEN T., investment banker; b. St. Louis, Nov. 11, 1946; s. Leonard Dale and Hazel (Goodlett) McL.; m. Rebecca Missen, Dec. 26, 1965 (div. 1975); children: Cynthia Jeanne, Stephen Dale; m. Catherine Anne Crespi, Oct. 12, 1981; children: Scott Thomas, Stephanie Therese. BSChemE, U. Ill.-Urbana, 1968; MSME, Stanford U., 1970, MBA, 1972. Rch. engr. Atlantic Richfield Corp., Anaheim, Calif., 1968-69; staff officer First Chgo. Corp., 1972-74; asst. v.p. Bank of Am., San Francisco, 1972-75, v.p., 1975-81, sr. v.p., 1979-86, exec. v.p., 1986-87; pres. Am. First Fin. Corp., San Francisco, 1987—; vice chmn., dir. Eureka Fed. Savs., San Francisco, 1988—; profl. lectr. Golden Gate U., San Francisco, 1976-82; bd. dirs. Charles Schwab & Co., San Francisco; vice-chmn. Eureka Fed. Savs., San Carlos, Calif. Bd. regents JFK U., Orinda, Calif., 1977-81. Recipient Disting. Svc. award Golden Gate U., 1982. Mem. Coun. Planning Execs., San Francisco Golf Club, Bankers Club, Conta Costa Country Club. Office: Am First Fin Corp 555 California St #4490 San Francisco CA 94104

MCLORG, TERENCE WYNDHAM, manufacturing company executive; b. Saskatoon, Sask., Can., June 3, 1922; s. Francis Harold and Gladys Angela (Bourke) McL.; m. Marilyn Isobel Meadows, May 14, 1954; children: Colin John, Anthony Barr, Penelope Ann, Wendy Frances. B of Applied Sci., U. B.C., 1944. Asst. to chief engr. Can. Ice Machine Co., Toronto, Ont., 1944-48; sales mgr. air conditioning div. John Inglis Co., Toronto, 1948-56; exec. v.p. Can. Refrigeration and Air Conditioning Assn., Toronto, 1956-67; mktg. mgr. Chrysler Airtemp Can., Bramlea, Ont., 1967-72; mgr. mktg., gen. mgr. div. structures Irvin Industries, Inc., Lexington, Ky., 1972-80; pres. Alpha Structures Inc., Lexington, 1980-87; v.p. Clycan Alpha, Lexington, 1987—; pres. Air-Supported Enclosures Ltd., Lexington, 1987—. Named to Hon. Order Ky. Cols. Mem. ASHRAE, Assn. Profl. Engrs. Ky., Assn. Profl. Engrs. Minn., Assn. Profl. Engrs. Ont. Roman Catholic. Lodge: Rotary. Home: 746 Chinoe Rd Lexington KY 40502 Office: Clycan Alpha 625 E 3d St Lexington KY 40505

MCLOUD, PAULA, paper company executive; b. Trenton, N.J., Feb. 8, 1953; d. Marius Daniel and Philomena (Paul) Bonacci; m. John Austin McLoud, Feb. 9, 1985; children: Charles Edward, Ted Austin, Morgan Ashley. BS in Adminstrn. of Justice, Am. U., 1975. Account mgr. Weyerhaeuser Paper Co., Chgo., 1976-84, Annapolis, Md., 1984—. Home: 596 Wildflower Glade Annapolis MD 21401 Office: Weyerhaeuser Paper Co Plaza One 1511 Governor Ritchie Hwy Arnold MD 21012

MCLOUGHLIN, ROBERT EMMETT, sales and marketing executive; b. White Plains, N.Y., Dec. 17, 1947; s. Robert Emmett and Helen Marie (Cook) McL.; m. Pamela Anne Smith, Aug. 3, 1985; 1 child, Digger. BBA in Mktg., Iona Coll., 1974, MBA in Mktg., 1979. Lic. life and health agt.; cert. mgmt. engring. technician. Fin. mktg. analyst Mitchum-Thayer div. U.S.V. Pharm. Corp., Tuckahoe, N.Y., 1971-74; gen. adminstr. Printex Corp., Ossining, N.Y., 1974-77; dir. mktg. Simuflite, Inc., Dallas, 1977-81; exec. v.p. The Hudson Group, Ghent, N.Y., 1981-83; pres. REM Assocs., Leeds, N.Y., 1981—. Author: Solar Power, The Energy Alternative, 1981. Founder We Care, Washington, 1970; assoc. Greene County Ctr. for Disabled, Catskill, N.Y., 1987. Sgt. USAF, 1967-71. Mem. Am. Mktg. Assn., Am. Mgmt. Assn., Nat. Assn. for Self-Employed. Roman Catholic. Home and Office: Rte 1 PO Box 108 Leeds NY 12451

MCMACKIN, JOHN JAMES, packaging company executive; b. Brockway, Pa., July 29, 1925; s. Bernard Patrick and Gertrude Mechtaldis (Mullany) McM.; m. Helen Marie Schaffner, June 18, 1949; children: Cynthia, Jack, Christopher, Shaun. BEE, Catholic U., 1949; MSEE, Carnegie Inst. Tech., 1950. Registered profl. engr., Pa. Elec. engr. Brockway (Pa.), Inc., 1950-68, v.p. engring., 1968-71, sr. v.p. ops., 1973-74, v.p., gen. mgr. container div., 1974-77, group v.p. packaging, 1977-83; pres., chief operating officer Brockway, Inc., Jacksonville, Fla., 1983—, chmn. bd., chief exec. officer, 1987—, also bd. dirs.; bd. dirs. Consumers Glass Co., Ltd., Toronto, Ont., Can., Brockway Pressed Metals, Keep Am. Beautiful, Inc.; community bd. mem. St. Vincent's Med. Ctr., Jacksonville, Fla.; past chmn., trustee Glass Packaging Inst. Patentee in field. Trustee Jacksonville (Fla.) U. Served to lt. (j.g.) USNR, 1943-53. Mem. Nat. Food Processors Assn. (bd. dirs.). Roman Catholic. Home: 8121 Mar Del Plata Jacksonville FL 32216 Office: Brockway Inc 255 Water St Box 44058 Jacksonville FL 32231-4058 •

MC MAHAN, JOHN WILLIAM, real estate investment advisor; b. San Antonio, Aug. 4, 1937; s. John William and Lena Margaret (Coleman) McM.; A.B., U. So. Calif., 1959; M.B.A., Harvard U., 1961; m. Jacqueline Mary Cardozo, Sept. 22, 1973; children—Cathy, Jason by previous marriage; children—Justin, Vanessa. Dir. feasibility studies Charles Luckman Assos., 1961-63; founder, prin. Devel. Research Assos., Los Angeles, 1963-70; v.p. real estate services Booz, Allen & Hamilton, N.Y.C., 1970-73; mem. faculty Stanford U. Grad. Sch. Bus., 1974—; founder, prin. John McMahan Real Estate Advisors, Inc., San Francisco, 1976—. Mem. Soc. Real Estate Counsellors, Urban Land Inst., Am. Econ. Assn., Am. Inst. Planners, Lambda Alpha, Royal Town Planning Inst. U.K. Clubs: Bankers, Jonathan. Author: Property Development: Effective Decision Making in Uncertain Times, 1989; McGraw Hill Real Estate Pocket Guide, 1979; editor: Ency. of Urban Planning, 1973. Office: 201 California St San Francisco CA 94111

MCMAHON, GARY FRANCIS, accountant; b. Flandreau, S.D., Aug. 31, 1937; s. James McMahon and Eleanora B. (Lemon) McM. Johnson; m. Shirley J. Hahn, Sept. 6, 1958; children—Callae, Michele, Michael. B.S., U. S.D., 1959; M.B.A., U. Wis., 1960. C.P.A., Colo. Acct. Deloitte Haskins & Sells, Denver, 1961-71, ptnr., 1971-77, ptnr.-in-charge, 1977-83, regional mng. ptnr., 1983—. Bd. dirs., treas. Colo. Outward Bound Sch., Denver, 1978-82, trustee, 1982-88; bd. dirs. Boys Clubs Denver, 1980-85, Colo. Council on Econ. Edn., Boulder, 1979-88. Served as lt. U.S. Army, 1960. Named Alumnus of Yr., U. S.D., 1973. Mem. Am. Inst. C.P.A.s, Colo. Soc.

C.P.A.s, Nat. Assn. Accts. Republican. Roman Catholic. Clubs: Denver (pres. 1982-83), Denver Country. Lodge: Rotary (bd. dirs., treas. Denver 1978-83, pres. 1983-84). Home: 3082 Nelson Dr Lakewood CO 80215 Office: Deloitte Haskins & Sells 1560 Broadway Ste 1800 Denver CO 80202

MCMAHON, JOHN A., business consultant; b. N.Y.C., Apr. 5, 1937; s. John and Elizabeth M. (Lall) McM.; B.E.E., Manhattan Coll., 1960; m. Carole I. Taber, Nov. 21, 1959; children—John C., Carole M., Regina M. Bus. systems mgr. C-E-I-R Inc., N.Y.C., 1958-64; exec. v.p. Alphanumeric Inc., N.Y.C., 1964-73; pres. Devoe Lighting Corp, 1979-88, Dyad Corp., Bronxville, N.Y., 1973—, bd. dirs. Harrison-Rye Corp., 1984—. Cert. in data processing Inst. for Cert. of Computer Profls. Club: Westchester Country. Patentee photog. medium scanner. Home and Office: 2 Beechmont Ave Bronxville NY 10708

MCMAHON, NEIL MICHAEL, real estate executive; b. N.Y.C., Oct. 12, 1953; s. Thomas Joseph and Catherine Margaret (Lane) M.; m. Debra Brylawski, Oct. 2, 1982; children: Alexa Lauren, Brendan Patrick. BA, Loyola Coll., Balt., 1975; MBA, U. Notre Dame, 1980. Staff acct. Coopers & Lybrand, Balt., 1975-77; sr. assoc. Korn/Ferry Internat., Chgo., 1980-84; mgr. real estate fin. Prudential Ins. Co., Washington, 1984-87, gen. mgr. real estate devel., 1987-88; mng. dir. Capital Ptnrs. Inc., Washington, 1988—. Bd. dirs. Lawrence Hall Sch. for Boys, Chgo., 1981-84. Named Senatorial Scholar State of Md., 1971-75; named Grad. fellow U. Notre Dame, 1978-80. Mem. Nat. Assn. Indsl. and Office Parks, Real Estate Group, Mortgage Bankers Assn., Notre Dame Club. Republican. Roman Catholic. Home: 3548 Winfield Ln NW Washington DC 20007 Office: Capital Ptnrs Inc 224 E Captiol St Washington DC 20003

MCMAHON, TERESA WISHER, equipment leasing executive; b. Paxton, Ill., Feb. 16, 1958; d. William James Wisher and Ruth Eileen (Carlson) Shull; m. Richard Dana McMahon, June 13, 1981. BS in Acctg., U. Ill., 1980. Audit asst. Touche Ross & Co., Chgo., 1980; audit sr. Peat Marwick Main & Co., Chgo., 1980-83; asst. controller Mediflex Systems subs. HBO & Co., Evanston, Ill., 1983-86; treas. Fin. Investment Assn. subs. Comml. Fed. Savs. and Loan, Northfield, Ill., 1986-87; v.p., treas. Prime Capital Corp., Rolling Meadows, Ill., 1987—. Mem. Am. Inst. CPAs, Ill. CPA Soc., Fin. Exec. Inst.

MCMANNERS, DONALD EDWARD, corporate executive; b. Racine, Wis., May 26, 1930; s. Horace Lesley and Ethle (Doucette) McM. BS, U. Wis., 1958. V.p. personnel Garan, Inc., N.Y.C., 1969-74; pres. eastern region Staub Warmbold, Inc., N.Y.C., 1974-76; mng. dir. Lamalie Assocs., N.Y.C., 1976-80; pres., founder McManners Assocs., Inc., N.Y.C., 1980—. Served as sgt. USAF, 1951-55, Korea. Mem. Nat. Assn. Corp. and Profl. Recruiters, Employment Mgmt. Assn. Club: University (N.Y.C.), Town Tennis (N.Y.C.). Home: 225 E 63d St New York NY 10021 Office: McManners Assocs 555 Madison Ave New York NY 10022

MCMANUS, ARTHUR TERRENCE, JR., treasurer, accountant; b. N.Y.C., Dec. 21, 1937; s. Arthur Terrence Sr. and Ann Theresa (Reilly) McM.; m. terry Mantersteck, Aug. 31, 1963; children: Arthur Terrence III, Patrick R., David E. BS in English Lit., Holy Cross Coll., 1960; MBA in Fin. and Acctg., U. Pa., 1968. CPA, Pa.; cert. mgmt. acct. V.p. 1st Pa. Bank, Phila., 1968-75, Design Store Corp., Gaithersburg, Md., 1975-77; divisional controller Holoman Enterprises Inc., Pennsauken, N.J., 1977-79; dir. planning Ship N Shore div. Gen. Mills Inc., Aston, Pa., 1979-81; chief fin. officer Apparel Affiliates Inc., Quakertown, Pa., 1981—. Bd. dirs. Abington (Pa.) YMCA, 1986—. Capt. USNR, 1960-88. Mem. Inst. Mgmt. Acctg., Pa. Inst. CPAs, Huntingdon Valley Country Club. Home: 307 Fisher Rd Jenkintown PA 19046 Office: Apparel Affiliates Inc Rt 663 Quakertown PA 18951

MCMEEN, ALBERT RALPH, III, writer, lecturer; b. Lewistown, Pa., Oct. 4, 1942; s. Albert Ralph and Margaret McDowell (Parker) McM.; BA in Econs., Williams Coll., 1964; MBA in Fin. (Columbia Internat. Fellows scholar 1964), Columbia U., 1966; m. A. Mary Kelley, June 6, 1965 (div.); children: Albert Ralph, Christopher Benjamin. Asst. v.p. Chem. Bank, N.Y.C., 1966-75; v.p., 1970-75, v.p. mktg. Irving Leasing Co. subs. Irving Trust Co., N.Y.C., 1975-80; v.p. regional ops. USI Capital and Leasing affiliate U.S. Industries, Inc., N.Y.C., 1980-83; pres. Tng. Assocs., Inc., 1986—; assoc. adj. prof. NYU, 1979—; asst. prof. L.I. Univ., 1986—; tng. cons. Citibank, 1986—, Barclay's Bank, 1986—; lectr. Am. Mgmt. Assn., 1986—. Mem. legis. com. Citizens' Union, 1968-75; bd. dirs. Columbia U. Alumni Assn., 1970-75; sec. Gay Fathers Inc. Recipient Columbia Bus. Sch. service award, 1966. Democrat. Author: Treasurers and Controllers New Equipment Leasing Guide, 1984; Techniques of Credit Analysis, 1989. Home: 333 W 88th St New York NY 10024 Office: 333 W 88th St New York NY 10024

MCMELLON, BRUCE ALTON, manufacturing company executive; b. Shreveport, La., May 8, 1946; s. John Alton and Essie Susan (Lange) McM.; 1 child, William Chris. BSME, La. Tech. U., 1970. Project engr. Kast Metals Corp., Shreveport, 1970-71, plant engr., 1971-73; plant engr. Beaird Poulan div. Emerson Elec., Shreveport, 1973-74; dir. mfg. facilities Adirondack Steel Castings Co., Watervliet, N.Y., 1974-76; from tech. mgr. to reg. mgr. BMM Weston Inc., Cleve., 1976-79; v.p. sales BMM Weston Inc., Mpls., Tampa (Fla.), 1979-83; exec. v.p. sales and mktg. Didion Mfg. Co., St. Louis, 1983-84; v.p. Vulcan Engring. Co., Helena, Ala., 1984—. Contbr. articles to profl. jours; inventor in field. Mem. Playhouse Sq. Found., Cleve., 1976. Mem. Am. Foundrymen's Soc., Am. Inst. Plant Engrs., Relay House Club, Heatherwood Golf Club. Republican. Methodist. Home: 453 Saint Annes Dr Birmingham AL 35244 Office: Vulcan Engring Co One Vulcan Dr Helena AL 35080

MCMICHAEL, LARRY RICHARD, manufacturing executive; b. Shelbyville, Ind., Nov. 14, 1947; s. Floyd William and Mary Lucinda (McGrew) McM.; m. Jo Ann Wagner, June 6, 1970; children: Matthew Ryan, Nicole Danielle. BS in Acctg. and Fin., Ind. State U., 1971; MBA, Ind. U., 1978. Dir. fin. planning Majestic div. Am. Standard, Huntington, Ind., 1977-78; dir. bus. planning Majestic div. Am. Standard, Huntington, 1978-83, dir. mktg. & planning, 1983, v.p. fin. & planning, 1983-86; chief fin. officer, sec., treas., bd. dirs. Equus Bldg. Products Inc., Huntington, 1986-88; chief fin. officer, sec., treas. Equus Bldg. Specialties, L.P., Huntington, 1988—; v.p. fin., chief fin. officer Majco Bldg. Specialties, L.P., Huntington, 1988—; dir. EBP Holdings Inc., 1986-88. Office: Majco Bldg Specialties LP 1000 E Market St Huntington IN 46750

MCMILLAN, DAVID ROBERT, business executive; b. Montebello, Calif., Mar. 28, 1957; s. Robert Harold and Olga (Lipinski) McM; m. Patricia J. Jacob, Sept. 21, 1985. BA, U. Calif.-Riverside, 1979. Salesman, Brinkerhoff Realty, Riverside, Calif., 1976-79; account rep. EDP, Burroughs Corp., San Bernardino, Calif., 1979-83; mgr. area mktg. Thor Inc, Riverside, Calif., 1983—. Chmn. parade com. Helping Others Scholarship Orgn., Riverside, 1981. Named one of Outstanding Young Men Am., 1982. Mem. Data Processing Mgmt. Assn., Greater Riverside C. of C. (amb. 1988—), Assn. Info. Systems Profls., Riverside County Pvt. Industry Coun., Palm Springs Jaycees, Calif. Assn. Temporary Svcs. (treas. Inland Empire chpt. 1988-89), Orange County C. of C. Club: Toastmasters (treas. 1982-83). Home: 1621 Toyon Pl Corona CA 91720 Office: Thor Inc 3600 Lime St Ste 128 Riverside CA 92501

MCMILLAN, JAMES ALBERT, electronics engineer, educator; b. Lewellen, Nebr., Feb. 6, 1926; s. William H. and Mina H. (Taylor) McM.; B.S. in Elec. Engring., U. Wash., 1951; M.S. in Mgmt., Rensselaer Poly. Inst., 1965; m. Mary Virginia Garrett, Aug. 12, 1950; children—Michael, James, Yvette, Ramelle, Robert. Commd. 2d lt. U.S. Air Force, 1950, advanced through grades to lt. col., 1970; jet fighter pilot Columbus AFB, Miss., Webb AFB, Tex., 1951-52, Nellis AFB, Nev., 1953, McChord AFB, Wash., 1953-54; electronic maintenance supr. Lowry AFB, Colo., 1954, Forbes AFB, Kans., 1954-56, also in U.K., 1956-59; electronic engr., program dir. Wright-Patterson AFB, Ohio, 1959-64; facilities dir. Air Force Aero Propulsion Lab., Wright-Patterson AFB, 1965-70, ret., 1970; instr., div. chmn. Chesterfield-Marlboro Tech. Coll., S.C., 1971-75; instr., chmn. indsl. div., Maysville (Ky.) Community Coll., 1976—, asst. prof., 1977, assoc. prof., 1980, prof. 1986—; cons. mgmt. and electronic maintenance, 1970—. Served with U.S. Army, 1943-45. Mem. IEEE (sr.), Soc. Mfg. Engrs. (sr.), Nat. Rifle Assn. (life), Sigma Xi (life). Republican. Presbyterian (elder). Clubs: Rotary (Maysville, Ky., pres. 1989—) (Maysville, Ky.), Masons (32 deg.), Shriners. Author: A Management Survey, 1965. Home: 6945 Scoffield Rd Ripley OH 45167

MCMILLAN, JAMES THOMAS, aerospace company executive; b. Alhambra, Calif., Aug. 5, 1925; s. James and Mary W. (O'Hurley) McM.; m. Jean Grunland, June 27, 1953; children: Suzanne, Brian, David, Kathryn, Mary. B in Engring., U. So. Calif., 1951; JD, UCLA, 1954. Engr. freeway system design Calif. State Div. Hwys., Los Angeles, 1951-52; engr. hydraulic studies Calif. State Div. Water Resources, Los Angeles, 1953-54; patent engr. Douglas Aircraft Co., 1954-56, asst. patent counsel, 1956-59, asst. gen. counsel, 1959-67, v.p. fin., 1967-68; pres. McDonnell Douglas Fin. Corp., 1968—, chmn., 1988—, also bd. dirs.; corp. v.p. McDonnell Douglas Corp., 1967-88, sr. v.p.-group exec., 1988—; pres. MCD Realty Co., 1974-78; chmn. bd. dirs. McDonnell Douglas Travel Co., 1986—, McDonnell Douglas Realty Co., 1988—, McDonnell Douglas Truck Services Inc., 1983—, Irish Aerospace Ltd., 1984—; chmn., chief exec. officer McDonnell Douglas Fin. Corp. Ltd., 1981—, also bd. dirs.; pres. McDonnell Douglas-West Personnel Community Service Inc., 1987—, also bd. dirs.; bd. dirs. Pvt. Export Funding Corp., 1988—. Bd. regents Loyola Marymount U., mem. assocs.; past trustee UCLA. Served with USNR, 1943-46. Mem. ABA, Calif. Bar Assn., Los Angeles County Bar Assn., Los Angeles C. of C., Nat. Def. Transp. Assn., Los Angeles World Affairs Council, Order of Coif, Chi Epsilon, Tau Beta Pi. Clubs: Bel-Air Country, California, Los Angeles. Office: McDonnell Douglas Fin Corp 340 Golden Shore Long Beach CA 90802

MCMILLAN, ROBERT ALLAN, chemical company executive; b. Santa Barbara, Calif., Dec. 18, 1942; s. Edward and Thelma (Zuercher) McM.; m. Peggy Sue Damron, Oct. 17, 1964: children: Donald James, Jeffrey Scott; m. Christine Collins, June 17, 1983; children: Michelle Diane Ball, Suzanne Mary Ball. BS in Econs., U. Calif., Santa Barbara, 1968; PhD in Econs., U. Calif., Berkeley, 1972. Cons., economist Bank of Am., San Francisco, 1968-71; economist FRS, Cleve., 1971-74; economist BF Goodrich Co., Akron, Ohio, 1974-75, dir. econ. research, 1975-77, dir. analysis and control, 1977-78, dir. investor relations, 1978-82, exec. dir. planning and devel., 1982-86, v.p., treas., 1986—; mem. bus. adv. council Kent State U. Chmn. Akron Area Joint Econ. Council, 1985. Named Seer of Yr., Harvard U., 1977, 84. Mem. Fin. Execs. Inst., Conf. Bus. Econmists, Nat. Assn. Bus. Economists, Nat. Assn. Corp. Treas. Office: BF Goodrich Co 3925 Embassy Pkwy Akron OH 44313

MCMILLEN, JAMES ELTON, aviation executive; b. Bridgeville, Pa., Aug. 22, 1941; s. Charles P. and Margaret (Gray) McM.; m. Gale McColgan, Mar. 1969 (div. 1974); m. Linda R. Warfield, July 12, 1977; children: Michael, Cassie, James R. B in Aerospace Engring., Pa. State U., 1963; MS, MIT, 1971. Engr. Gen. Electric Corp., Lynn, Mass., 1963-70; mgr. aircraft overhaul Eastern Airlines, Miami, Fla., 1971-74; mgr., sales engr. CFM Internat., Paris, 1974-77; dir. maintenance Pan Am. Airlines, Miami, 1977-81; chmn. Melard Internat., Inc., Miami, 1983-86; pres. Aerothrust Corp., Miami, 1981—, also bd. dirs.; pres. AeroServ Internat., Inc., 1986-88; bd. dirs. AeroServ Internat., Inc., Miami, 1982—, FFV Fin., Inc., Detroit. Contbr. articles to profl. jours. Mem. Internat. Soc. Transport Aircraft Traders, Sigma Tau, Tau Beta Pi, Phi Kappa Phi, Sigma Gamma Tau. Republican. Club: Aviation Exec. (Miami) (v.p. 1986, pres. 1987). Office: Aerothrust Corp PO Box 522236 Miami FL 33152

MCMILLION, CHARLES WAYNE, economist, educator, consultant; b. Ft. Worth, June 20, 1948; s. Charles Wayne and Billie Ruth (Hickman) McM.; m. Marilyn Ruth Saks, Nov. 24, 1982. BA, U. Tex., Arlington, 1970; MA, So. Meth. U., 1972, Rutgers U., 1978; PhD, Rutgers U., 1980. Market rsch., editor Curtis Mathes Sales Co., Dallas, 1970-71; Peace Corps tchr. Imperial Ethiopian Air Force Acad., Debre Zeit, 1972-73; fin. analyst Akin, Gump, Strauss, Hauer & Feld, Dallas, 1973-74; dir. McMillion Assocs., Washington, 1980—; assoc. dir. Inst. for Policy Studies, assoc. prof. Johns Hopkins U., Balt., 1988—; staff dir., chief economist U.S. Senate Dems. Working Group on Competitiveness, 1986; policy dir., chief economist Congl. Econ. Leadership Inst., Washington, 1986-87; assoc. dir. Inst. for Policy Studies, assoc. prof. Johns Hopkins U., Balt., 1988—; econ. cons. Joint Econ. Com. U.S. Congress, Urban Inst. India, Bombay, Pharm. Mfrs. Assn., Washington, Smick-Medley Assocs., Washington. Contbr. articles and reports to econ. lit. Sloan Found. fellow So. Meth. U., 1971; Porte World Peace Found. fellow Rutgers U., 1979-81. Home: 223 F St NE Washington DC 20002 Office: Inst for Policy Studies Johns Hopkins U Baltimore MD 21218

MCMORRIS, GRACE ELIZABETH, banker; b. Malden, Mass., Feb. 6, 1922; d. John Edward and Selma Florence (Swanson) O'Brien; B.A., Boston U., 1944; postgrad. Ariz. State U., 1962; m. William Michael McMorris, May 14, 1944 (dec.); children—Sheila Elizabeth McMorris Christenson, Michael, James, John. Clk., Parlin Meml. Library, Everett, Mass., part-time, 1938-40; clk. student post office Boston U., 1941-42; supr. classified advt. desk The Boston Post, 1942-44; substitute tchr. public schs., Randolph, Mass., 1956-57; with Valley Nat. Bank Ariz., Phoenix, 1960-87, trust adminstr., 1969-73, trust officer, 1973-75, asst. v.p., 1975-78, v.p., 1978-87, corporate trust mgr., 1977-87, ret., 1987. cons. in field, 1988-89. Mem. Am. Soc. Corp. Secs. (treas. Phoenix chpt., v.p.), Pi Lambda Sigma (nat. treas. 1947-48). Roman Catholic. Office: Valley Nat Bank Ariz 241 N Central Ave Phoenix AZ 85004

MCMULLAN, WILLIAM PATRICK, III, investment banker; b. Newton, Miss., Dec. 29, 1952; s. William Patrick Jr. and Rosemary (Lyons) McM.; m. Rachel Smiley McPherson, Oct. 16, 1982. BA, Vanderbilt U., 1974; MBA, U. Pa., 1976. V.p. Lehman Bros. Kuhn Loeb, N.Y.C., 1976-82; assoc. dir. Prudential-Bache Securities, N.Y.C., 1982-85; sr. v.p. Donaldson, Lufkin & Jenrette Securities Corp., N.Y.C., 1985—; dir. Republic Health Corp., Dallas. Clubs: Metropolitan, Doubles (N.Y.C.); Mashomack Fish and Game (Pine Plains). Home: 245 E 72d St New York NY 10021 Office: Donaldson Lufkin & Jenrette Securities 140 Broadway New York NY 10005

MCMULLEN, CYNTHIA DIANE, retail furniture store owner; b. El Paso, Tex., Nov. 23, 1954; d. Everett and Anna Louise (Simnacher) Bishop; m. Ralph Allison McMullen, Feb. 27, 1956; 1 child, Michael Arnett. Student, Dominican Coll., Houston, 1972-74, U. Houston, 1974-78, Delmar Coll., 1979-81. Acct. Everett Bishop, CPA, Houston, 1971-79, Don Ranley, CPA, Corpus Christi, Tex., 1979; owner Expressions in Wood, Corpus Christi, 1979—; acct. Bob Fancher, CPA, Corpus Christi, 1980. Mem. Corpus Christi Beautification Com., 1979-85; active Am. Cancer Soc. Mem. S.W. Homefurnishings Assn., Better Bus. Bur. (bd. dirs.), Corpus Christi C. of C., Corpus Christi 100 Club. Republican. Roman Catholic. Office: Expressions in Wood 3920 S Padre Island Dr Corpus Christi TX 78415

MCMULLEN, JOHN HENRY, JR., manufacturing company executive, educator; b. Phila., Sept. 9, 1944; s. John Henry and Clara (Johnson) McM.; m. Evelyn Corrine Lawson, July 19, 1964; children: Yolanda, John III, Yvette, Yvonne. BS, Tuskegee U., Ala., 1969; MBA, Anna Maria Coll., 1984. Asst. program planner Ingall's Shipbldg., Pascagoula, Miss., 1969-71; indsl. engr. supr. Luken's, Coatesville, Pa., 1971-76; mgr. mfg. engring. Newport News Shipbldg., Va., 1976-78; gen. supr. Polaroid Corp., Cambridge, Mass., 1978-85; mfg. mgr. Keene Corp., East Providence, 1985-86; master scheduler Prime Computer, Natick, Mass., 1987-89; small bus. and small disadvantaged bus. liaison officer GTE Govt. Systems Corp.-C3, Needham Heights, Mass., 1989—; instr. Anna Maria Coll., Paxton, Mass., 1983-86. Ct.-appointed spl. advocate Suffolk County Juvenile Ct., Boston, 1983; bd. dirs. Mattapan Community Health Ctr., Mass., 1983—, treas. 1984-86, pres. 1988—; treas. ADAPT, Inc., Roxbury, Mass., 1986-88, v.p. 1988—. Recipient Vice-Commandants award USAF, 1965; U.S. Dept. Edn. grantee, 1966; NAACP scholar, 1962. Mem. Afro-Am. Cultural Assn. Sharon (founder 1980), Polaroid Found., Inst. Indsl. Engrs., Exec. MBA Assn. of Anna Maria (bd. dirs. 1983-86), Nat. Black MBA Assn. (co-founder, treas. Boston chpt. 1985-87), Alpha Phi Alpha (chpt. pres. 1981-86, Alpha Man of Yr. 1986), Alpha Phi Alpha Edn. Found. (pres., founder 1983—). Club: Tuskegee Alumni (asst. fin. sec. 1988—, Outstanding Alumni award 1988). Lodges: Elks, Shriners. Avocations: bowling; racquetball; jogging; chess; motorcycling. Home: 8 Pine St Sharon MA 02067 Office: 17 A St Needham MA 02194-2892

MC MULLIAN, AMOS RYALS, food company executive; b. Jackson County, Fla., Aug. 28, 1937; s. Andrew Jackson and Willie Ross (Ryals) McM.; m. Jackie Williams, Aug. 27, 1960; children: Amos Ryals, Britton Jackelyn. B.S., Fla. State U., 1962. Successively asst. controller, data processing coordinator, adminstrv. asst. to gen. mgr., asst. plant mgr., plant mgr. Flowers Baking Co., Thomasville, Ga., 1963-70, pres. Atlanta Baking Co. div., 1970-72, regional v.p. parent co., 1972-74, pres., chief operating officer bakery div., 1974-76, chief operating officer industry, 1976-81, pres., 1976-83, dir., 1981—, chief exec. officer, 1983—, co-chmn. exec. com., 1983—, vice chmn. industry and chmn. exec. com., 1984-85, chmn. bd., 1985—. Mem. adv. bd., pres.'s club Fla. State U.; mem. gridiron soc. U. Ga.; past Thomasville C. of C. Served with USMC, 1958-61. Named Outstanding Bus. Alumnus Fla. State U. Mem. Nat. Assn. Mfrs. (bd. dirs.), Am. Bakers Assn. (bd. dirs.), Ind. Bakers Assn. (dir.), Atlanta Bakers Club (past pres.), Atlanta Commerce Club, Thomasville Landmarks Soc. Episcopalian (vestry, sr. warden). Office: Flowers Industries Inc PO Drawer 1338 US Hwy 19 S Thomasville GA 31799

MCMULLIN, RUTH RONEY, publishing company executive; b. N.Y.C., Feb. 9, 1942; d. Richard Thomas and Virginia (Goodwin) Roney; m. Thomas Ryan McMullin, Apr. 27, 1968; 1 child, David Patrick. BA, Conn. Coll., 1963; MS in Pub. and Pvt. Mgmt., Yale U., 1979. Market researcher Aviation Week Mag. McGraw- Hill Co., N.Y.C., 1962-64; assoc. editor, bus. mgr. Doubleday & Co., N.Y.C., 1964-66; mgr. Natural History Press, 1967-70; v.p., treas. Weston (Conn.) Woods, Inc., 1970-71; staff assoc. Gen. Electric Capital Markets Group, Fairfield, Conn., 1979-82; mng. fin. analyst GECC Transp., Stamford, Conn., 1982-84; credit analyst corp. fin. dept. GECC, Stamford, 1984-85; sr. v.p. GECC Capitol Markets Group, Inc., N.Y.C., 1985-87; exec. v.p., chief operating officer John Wiley & Sons, N.Y.C., 1987-89, pres., chief exec. officer, 1989—; bd. dirs. Community Health Care Plan, New Haven, Conn., Bausch & Lomb. Rochester, N.Y. Mem. N.Y. Yacht Club, Stamford Yacht Club. Office: John Wiley & Sons Inc 605 3rd Ave New York NY 10158

MCMURRAY, KAY, government official; b. Oakley, Idaho, Mar. 18, 1918; s. John and Clara Louise (Dahlquist) McM.; m. Roberta Jean Rankin, Sept. 26, 1941; children: Kathleen McMurray Wanger, Julia McMurray Rovins, Mollie. A.B., Stanford U., 1940, postgrad. in Bus. Adminstrn., 1947-48. Exec. adminstr. Airline Pilots Assn. Internat., Washington, 1953-71; cons. govt. affairs United Air Lines, Inc., Washington, 1971-72; mem. Nat. Mediation Bd., Washington, 1972-77, chmn., 1975-77; cons., arbitrator Bethesda, Md., 1977-82; dir. Fed. Mediation and Conciliation Service, Washington, 1982—. Bd. dirs. Joint Action Community Service, Washington, 1974-82. Clubs: Nat. Aviation University (Washington); Hinsdale Golf (Ill.). Office: Fed Mediation & Conciliation Svc 2100 K St NW Washington DC 20427

MCMURTREY, LAWRENCE J., engineer; b. Ririe, Idaho, Mar. 13, 1924; s. Lawrence Jay and Annie Eliza (Forsyth) McM.; m. Dolly L. Hawks, Jan. 28, 1947; children: Glenn J., Kathi, Gary, Luann, David, Jana. BSME, U. Colo., 1944; postgrad., U. Utah, 1949-51, Wichita State U., 1953-56. Registered profl. engr., Wash. Propulsion engr. Boeing co., Seattle, 1946-47; rsch. engr. Boeing co., Wichita, Kans., 1951-56; project mgr. Boeing co., Wichita, 1956-58; new bus. devel. mgr. Boeing co., Seattle, 1958-68, mgr. lunar Rover navigation system, 1971-72; burner II bus. mgr. Boeing Aerospace Co., Seattle, 1972-79; pres. McMurtrey Assocs., Redmond, Wash., 1979—; instr. U. Utah, Salt Lake City, 1947-49. Patentee in field. Pres. Redmond Jr. High PTA, 1965; Rep. precinct committeeman, Redmond, 1968—; mem. Save Our Farms Com., Seattle, 1987; bd. dirs. Master Gardener Found., Seattle, 1981—. Lt. (j.g.) USN, 1943-46, PTO. Mem. Am. Rocket Soc. (pres. Wichita chpt. 1955-56), AIAA, Northwest Small Hydro Assn. (bd. dirs. 1979), Northwest Christmas Tree Assn. (sec. 1987-89). Mormon. Home: 12122 196th NE Redmond WA 98053

MCNABB, FRANK WILLIAM, consumer products company executive; b. Cleve., Apr. 10, 1936; s. Frank L. and Bonita McNabb; m. L. Kay Dixon, Sept. 10, 1959; children: Tom, Mark, Kathy. BME, Ohio State U., 1960; MBA, U. Vt., 1971. Project engr. Union Carbide Corp., Red Oak, Iowa, 1960-64; plant engr. Union Carbide Corp., Charlotte, N.C., 1964-65; gen. foreman prodn. Union Carbide Corp., Bennington, Vt., 1965-66; asst. plant mgr. Union Carbide Corp., St. Albans, Vt., 1966-70; plant mgr. Union Carbide Corp., Wayne, N.J., 1970-76; dir. automotive mfg. Union Carbide Corp., Wayne, 1976-79, dir. home mfg., 1979-80; gen. mgr. prodn. Union Carbide Corp., East Hartford, Conn., 1980-86; v.p., gen. mgr. ops. 1st Brands Corp., Danbury, Conn., 1986—. Roman Catholic. Office: First Brands Corp 39 Old Redgebury Rd Danbury CT 06817

MCNABB, FREDERICK WILLIAM, JR., lawyer; b. Lowell, Mass., Nov. 24, 1932; s. Frederick W. and Katherine (Flanagan) McN.; m. Elizabeth Ann Coleman, May 12, 1956; children: Frederick William III, Mary E. McNabb Bucher, Mark C., Robert O., Patricia A. AB, U. Rochester, 1954; LLB, Yale U., 1959. Bar: N.Y. 1959. Assoc. Nixon, Hargrave, Devans & Doyle, Rochester, N.Y., 1959-64; ptnr. Goldstein, Goldman, Kessler & Underberg, Rochester, 1964-71; v.p., gen. counsel, sec. Continental Investment Corp., Boston, 1971-74, GAF Corp., N.Y.C., 1974-81; sr. v.p., gen. counsel, sec. MacAndrews & Forbes Group, Inc., N.Y.C., 1981—; sr. v.p., sec. Revlon Group Inc., N.Y.C., 1986—, sr. v.p. law Revlon, Inc., N.Y.C., 1986—; adj. lectr. law sch. Cornell U., Ithaca, 1968. Bd. editors Yale Law Jour., 1958-59. 1st lt. USAF, 1955-57. Mem. Am. Corp. Counsel Assn., Am. Soc. Corp. Secs., N.Y. State Bar Assn., ABA, Yale Club, N.Y. Athletic Club, Oak Hill Country Club, Silver Spring Club, Phi Beta Kappa. Home: 578 Valley Rd New Canaan CT 06840 Office: MacAndrews & Forbes Group Inc 21 E 63rd St New York NY 10021

MCNAIR, JOHN FRANKLIN, III, banker; b. Laurinburg, N.C., Apr. 12, 1927; s. John Franklin and Martha (Fairley) McN.; m. Martha Fowler, June 16, 1951; children: John Franklin IV, Elizabeth Fowler. B.S., Davidson Coll., 1949; postgrad., U. N.C., 1954-56. Pres. McNair Automotive Co., Inc., Laurinburg, 1949-66, The State Bank, Laurinburg, 1966-68; sr. v.p. Wachovia Bank & Trust, Laurinburg, 1968-70, Raleigh, N.C., 1970-72; exec. v.p. Wachovia Bank & Trust, Winston-Salem, N.C., 1972-77, vice chmn., 1977-85; vice chmn. The Wachovia Corp., Winston-Salem, N.C., 1977-87; pres., chief exec. officer Wachovia Bank & Trust Co, 1987—, also dir.; exec. v.p. First Wachovia Corp.; bd. dirs. Dixie Guano Co., Laurinburg, Wachovia Corp., Piedmont Natural Gas Co., Park Communications Inc., Fed. Res. Bank of Richmond, Va. Mem. N.C. State Hwy. Commn., Raleigh, 1965-69; chmn. N.C. Bd. Econ. Devel., 1979-85, N.C. Council Econ. Edn., Greensboro, 1980-82; mem. Commn. of Future of N.C., Raleigh, 1981-83; trustee Peace Coll. Raleigh, 1980-89, Winston-Salem Found., 1983—, chmn., 1989—, Davidson Coll., 1985—; chmn. N.C. Citizens for Bus. and Industry, 1988-89; co-chm. gov.'s adv. com. on Superconducting Supercollider Project, 1988. With USN, 1945-46. Recipient Young Man of Yr. award Laurinburg Jaycees, 1962; recipient Silver Beaver award Boy Scouts Am., 1967. Mem. Am. Bankers Assn. (state v.p. 1980-81), Res. City Bankers Assn., N.C. Bankers Assn. (pres. 1976-77). Democrat. Presbyterian. Clubs: Old Town, Piedmont. Lodge: Rotary, St. Andrews Soc. Home: 1215 Tartan Ct Winston-Salem NC 27106 Office: Wachovia Bank & Trust Co PO Box 3099 Winston-Salem NC 27150

MCNALLY, ANDREW, IV, publishing executive; b. Chgo., Nov. 11, 1939; s. Andrew and Margaret C. (MacMillin) McN.; m. Jeanine Sanchez, July 3, 1966; children: Andrew, Carrie, Ward. B.A., U. N.C., 1963; M.B.A., U. Chgo., 1969. Bus. mgr. edn. div. Rand McNally & Co., Chgo., 1967-70; exec. v.p., sec. Rand McNally & Co., 1970-74, pres., 1974—, chief exec. officer, 1978—; bd. dirs. Mercury Fin. Inc., Hubbell Inc., First Ill. Corp., Graphic Arts Tech. Found., Val Pak, Walter Foster Publs., Mercury Fin. Trustee, Hill Sch., Newberry Library; bd. dirs. Childrens Meml. Hosp.; mem. vis. com. of library U. Chgo. With Air Force N.G., 1963-69. Mem. Young Pres. Orgn., Chgo. Map. Soc., Chgo. Club, Saddle and Cycle Club, Commonwealth Club, Glen View Golf Club, Links (N.Y.C.), Commercial Club. Office: Rand McNally & Co 8255 N Central Park Ave Skokie IL 60076

MCNALLY, HARRY JOHN, JR., engineer, construction and real estate executive, consultant, researcher; b. Phila., Nov. 12, 1938; s. Harry John and Jane Sabina (Hub)McN.; m. Lynnette Anne Burley, May 29, 1966 (div. Dec. 1981); children: Megan Kathleen, Harry John III. BA, Lehigh U., 1960; MBA, Columbia U., 1966. Registered profl engr., Pa. Project engr. Turner Constrn. Co., N.Y., 1960-65; devel. engr. Dravo Corp., Pitts., 1966-69; mgr. The Austin Co., Roselle, N.J., 1969-79; sr. mgr. The Lummus Co., Bloomfield, N.J., 1979-82; v.p. The Eagle Group, N.Y., 1983—; cons. in field, N.Y., 1965—. Sec., newsletter editor Cook Sch. Adv. Council, Plainfield, N.J., 1985-86; mem. Nat. Trust Hist. Preservation, Washington, 1985—, Nat. Bldg. Mus., 1986—; treas. Shadyside Young Rep. Club, Pitts., 1966-69; stewardship chmn. Grace Episcopal Ch., Plainfield, 1975-76. Mem. Nat. Soc. Profl. Engrs. (minuteman 1977—), N.J. Soc. Profl. Engrs. (legis. com. 1977—), Lehigh U. Alumni Assn., Omicron Delta Kappa, Alpha Kappa Psi, Chi Psi. Republican. Home: 1757 Watchung Ave Plainfield NJ 07060 Office: Eagle Design & Constrn Group Inc 535 Fifth Ave New York NY 10017 also: EI Assocs 115 Evergreen Pl East Orange NJ 07018

MCNAMARA, ELSA MAE BROESAMLE, sales executive; b. Pitts., June 7, 1958; d. Herman R. and Eva P. (Province) Broesamle; married May 28, 1988. Sales rep. Dardenell Publs., Pitts., 1978-80; sales rep. Advo System, Inc., Houston, 1980-82, sales mgr., 1982-83; dist. mgr. Cleve., 1983-84; regional mgr. Pitts., 1984-85; v.p. Fla. region 1985—. Mem. Am. Mgmt. Assn., Nat. Assn. Female Execs. Office: Advo System Inc 2416 Sand Lake Rd Orlando FL 32809

MCNAMARA, JOHN F., drug company executive; b. 1935. V.p., gen. mgr. McKesson Drug Co., L.A., 1974-78, pres. Value Rite div., 1978-81; with Alco Health Svcs. Corp. Inc., Valley Forge, Pa., 1981—, pres. Kauffman-Lettimer div., 1981-83, v.p., 1983-84, exec. v.p., 1984-85, chief operating officer, exec. v.p., 1985-87, pres., chief operating officer, 1987—, also bd. dirs. Office: Alco Health Svcs Corp 825 Duportail Rd Valley Forge PA 19087 *

MC NAMARA, JOHN J(OSEPH), advertising executive; b. Yonkers, N.Y., Mar. 7, 1934; m. Patricia A. Widmann, Sept. 14, 1963; children: Mary, John. B.S., Yale U., 1956; M.B.A., NYU, 1963. Exec. v.p., eastern regional dir. Young & Rubicam, N.Y.C., 1979; pres. Young & Rubicam U.S.A., from 1982; now pres. McCann Erickson Worldwide, ret., 1988; mayor City of Pelham, N.Y., 1989—. Pres. Pelham United Way, N.Y.; mem. Pelham Manor Zoning Bd.; chmn. Pelham Manor Planning Bd.; trustee City of Pelham Manor. Served to 1st lt. USMC, 1956-58. Clubs: Pelham Country (pres.), Union League, Winged Foot. Home: 71 Cowry Ln Vero Beach FL 32963

MCNAMARA, MARTIN BURR, lawyer, oil and gas company executive; b. Danbury, Conn., Sept. 10, 1947; s. William Joseph and Geraldine Margaret (Young) McN.; m. Anne Rose Hogan, Jan. 15, 1977. BA in English, Providence Coll., 1969; JD, Yale U., 1972. Bar: N.Y. 1973, U.S. Dist. Ct. (so. and ea. dists.) N.Y. 1973, U.S. Ct. Appeals (2d cir.) 1973, Tex. 1980, U.S. Ct. Appeals (5th and 11th cirs.) 1980. Assoc. Shea & Gould, N.Y.C., 1972-76; asst. U.S. atty. (so. dist.) N.Y., N.Y.C., 1976-79; v.p., gen. counsel, sec. Tex. Oil & Gas Corp., Dallas, 1979—; gen. counsel Delhi Gas Pipeline Corp. subs. Tex. Oil & Gas Corp., Dallas; bd. dirs. Ala. Intrastate Gas Corp., Delhi Gas Pipeline Corp., The Nueces Co., Ozark Gas Pipeline Corp., Red River Gas Pipeline Corp., various others. Co-contbr. articles to Yale Law Jour. Mem. exec. com. Yale Law Sch. Assn., 1983-86. Mem. State Bar of Tex. (vice chmn. corp. counsel sect. 1984-86, chmn.-elect 1987-88, chmn. 1988-89), Assn. Bar. City of N.Y., N.Y. State Bar Assn., Fed. Energy Bar Assn. Republican. Roman Catholic. Clubs: Petroleum, Chaparral. Office: Tex Oil & Gas Corp 2600 1st City Ctr 1700 Pacific Dallas TX 75201

MCNAMARA, MICHAEL EDWARD, manufacturing executive; b. Chgo., Oct. 12, 1938; s. Michael Joseph and Ann Josephine (Boyle) McN.; m. Josephine Aquinas Maiden, May 23, 1964; children: Michael, Jennifer, Brian. BSBA, Roosevelt U., 1962. Sr. acct., auditor Peat, Marwick, Mitchell & Co., Chgo., 1962-66; acct. Schwinn Bicycle Co., Chgo., 1966-69, acctg. mgr., credit mgr., 1969-74, asst. treas., 1974-82, treas., 1982—, v.p., 1988—. Served with USMCR, 1962-67. Mem. Nat. Assn. Accts. Roman Catholic. Home: 1432 Oak St Western Springs IL 60558 Office: Schwinn Bicycle Co 217 N Jefferson Ave Chicago IL 60606

MCNAMARA, TOM, scientific consulting corporation executive; b. Battle Creek, Mich., May 23, 1944; s. George P. (stepfather) and Mildred E. Lunt; grad. in Chemistry, Boston U., 1966; M.B.A., Northeastern U., 1970; m. Ellen K. LaRue, Sept. 24, 1977; 1 child, George Lunt. With corp. planning dept. Reynolds Aluminum, Richmond, Va., 1970-72; sr. cons. Technomic Cons., Chgo., 1972-74; founder, pres. NUVENTURES Consultants, Inc., Chgo. and San Diego, 1975—; speaker trade convs. and confs. worldwide. Republican nominee Ill. Gen. Assembly, 1974, 76; mem. various coms. United Fund and Chgo. Assn. Commerce and Industry, 1975-79. Served to 1st lt. Ordnance Corps, U.S. Army, 1966-69. Recipient Presdl. Commendation for heroism, 1974, Chgo. Police Dept. Commendation, 1974; Am.'s Cup advisor, 1988. Mem. Acacia, San Diego Tennis and Racquet., Cortez Racing Assn. Contbr. articles to publs. Office: PO Box 2489 La Jolla CA 92038

MCNAMEE, DANIEL, III, management consultant; b. N.Y.C., Sept. 21, 1944; s. Daniel Vincent McNamee Jr. and Barbara Burroughs (Cooley) Dudley; m. Susan Anderson Thompson, Oct. 21, 1978. BA, Yale U., 1967; post grad., Balliol Coll., Oxford, England. Assoc. pub. MORE mag., N.Y.C., 1973-74; v.p. circulation Downe Communications, Inc., N.Y.C., 1974-77; dir. planning Chartcom, Inc., N.Y.C., 1977-78; v.p. consumer mktg. Charter Pub., N.Y.C., 1978-79; pres. The McNamee Cons. Co., N.Y.C., 1979—; bd. dirs. First Albany (N.Y.) Corp., Silver Eagle Pubs., N.Y.C., Multi-Local Media Corp., Merrick, N.Y. Trustee Assocs. Council Oxford Centre for Mgmt. Studies, 1984—, Ocean Liner Mus., N.Y.C., 1985—, E.N. Huyck Preserve Inc. Served with U.S. Army, 1969-71. Democrat. Clubs: Yale, Manursing Island (Rye, N.Y.). Home: 42 Orchard Ln Rye NY 10580 Office: The McNamee Cons Group 535 Fifth Ave New York NY 10017

MCNAMEE, LOUISE, advertising agency executive. Pres., chief operating officer Della Femina McNamee WCRS Inc., N.Y.C. Office: Della Femina McNamee WCRS 350 Hudson Ave New York NY 10014 *

MCNEAL, KAREN LYNN, management consultant; b. Chgo., Sept. 25, 1947; d. Joseph S. and Camille Marie (Podlesak) Erazmus; m. David G. McNeal, Aug. 1, 1970; 1 child, Karleen Marie. BA, St. Mary of the Woods (Ind.) Coll., 1969; MS, Ind. St. U., 1972; MBA, U. Chgo., 1980. Programmer Aldens Inc., Chgo., 1970, programmer analyst, 1971-72, systems analyst, 1973-74, mgmt. sci. sect. mgr., 1975-78; sr. applications specialist Gen. Electric Info. Svcs., Oak Brook, Ill., 1978-79, project mgr., 1980-81, tech. mgr., 1982-84, sr. cons., 1985—; advisor Am. Nat. Standards Electronic Data Interchange Com., N.Y.C, 1985—; cons. Truck Adv. Group, Detroit, 1987—. Contbr. articles to profl. jours. Bd. dirs. Palos Heights Recreation Bd., 1979—. Mem. Automotive Industry Action Group, Marriage Encounter-Dialogue Group (sec. 1978—). Roman Catholic. Home: 66 Country Squire Rd Palos Heights IL 60463 Office: Gen Electric Info Svcs 2015 Spring Rd Ste 410 Oak Brook IL 60521

MCNEAR, BARBARA BAXTER, communications executive, consultant; b. Chgo., Oct. 9, 1939; d. Carl Henden and Alice Gertrude (Parrish) Baxter; m. Robert Erskine McNear, Apr. 13, 1968 (div. 1981); 1 child, Amanda Baxter; m. Glenn Philip Eisen, June 7, 1987. B.S. in Journalism, Northwestern U., 1961. Editorial asst. Scott Foresman & Co., Chgo., 1961; pub. relations dir. Market Facts Inc., Chgo., 1961-63; acct. supr. Philip Lesly Co., Chgo., 1963-68, 69; acct. exec. Burson-Marsteller, Chgo., 1968; dir. communications CNA Fin. Corp., Chgo., 1969-74; dir. pub. relations Gould Inc., Chgo., 1974; v.p. Harris Bank., Chgo., 1974-80, Fireman's Fund Ins. Co., San Francisco, 1980-83; sr. v.p. First Chgo. Corp., 1983-86; v.p. communications Xerox Fin. Svcs., Inc., Norwalk, Conn., 1987—. Bd. visitors Medill Sch. Journalism Northwestern U., Evanston, Ill. Mem. Pub. Relations Soc. Am., Nat. Investor Relations Inst. (pres. Chgo. chpt. 1974-75, bd. dirs. Chgo. chpt.). Episcopalian. Club: Cliffdwellers. Home: 23 Telva Rd Wilton CT 06897 Office: Xerox Fin Svcs Inc 401 Merritt 7 Norwalk CT 06856

MCNEEL, VAN LOUIS, chemical company executive; b. Laurel, Miss., July 4, 1925; s. George Louis and Pauline (Webb) McN.; m. Betty Tarwater, July 6, 1959 (div. 1966); 1 child, Clayton Webb; m. Diane Kidd, Dec. 30, 1971; 1 child, Ian Edward. Student, Sanford U. (formerly Howard Coll.); LLB, U. Ala., 1949. Project mgr. Reynolds Metals, N.Y.C. and Jacksonville, Fla., 1949-51; div. mgr. Olin Mathieson Chem. Corp., Atlanta, 1951-60, dir. internat. ops., 1960-63; pres. Polymer Internat. Corp., N.Y.C., 1963-64; chmn., chief exec. officer Polymer Internat. Corp., Tampa, Fla., 1964—; pres. Internat. Container Systems, Tampa, 1985—, also bd. dirs.; chmn. Security Tag Systems, St. Petersburg, Fla., 1981—, also bd. dirs.; bd. dirs. SouthTrust Bank of Tampa (formerly Gulf Bay Bank). Trustee U. Tampa, 1955—; bd. dirs. Tampa chpt. ARC.; mem. Golden Triangle Civic Assn., Tampa Bay Area Trade Council Fgn. Relations. Mem. Am. Mgmt. Assn., Soc. Plastic Engrs. Clubs: Palma Ceia Golf and Country, Tampa Yacht and Country, Ctr. Club, University (Tampa). Office: Polymer Internat Corp 5401 W Kennedy Blvd Tampa FL 33609

MCNEELY, WILLIAM MINESS, securities company executive; b. Jasonville, Ind., Nov. 1, 1939; s. William Henry and Ruby Mae (Woods) McN. Student of Engring., GM Inst., Flint, Mich., 1957-60; BSBA, Ind. U., 1966. Adminstrv. trainee Am. Fletcher Nat. Bank, Indpls., 1966-68; registered rep. Shearson, Hammill & Co., Indpls., 1968-70; market rsch. analyst Interthemr-Community Devel. div., Indpls., 1970-71; asst. devel. mgr. Oxford Devel. Corp., Indpls., 1971-73; v.p. Thomson McKinnon Securities, Inc., Indpls., 1973—; tchr. Adult Edn. Div. Continuing Studies, Ind. U.-Purdue U., Indpls, 1983-87. Mem. Kiwanis, Masons. Home: 716 Maple Ln Brownsburg IN 46112 Office: Thomson McKinnon Securities Inc 201 N Illinois Ste 2100 Indianapolis IN 46204

MC NEER, CHARLES SELDEN, utility executive; b. Gilbert, W.Va., Apr. 8, 1926; s. Richard Mason and Bertie May (Sparks) McN.; m. Ann Campbell Bishop, Mar. 20, 1949; children: Charles William, Robert Lee, Thomas Richard. Student, Berea Coll., 1943-44, 46-47, U.S. Mcht. Marine Acad., 1944-46; B.S. in Elec. Engring, Northwestern U., 1950. Registered profl. engr., Wis. With Wis. Electric Power Co., Milw., 1950-61, mgr. elec. engring., 1961-65, engr. Operating Rsch. Bur., 1965-67, asst. v.p., 1967, v.p. adminstrn., 1968, sr. v.p., 1969-73, exec. v.p., 1973-75, pres., 1975—, chmn. bd., chief exec. officer, 1982—; chmn., dir. Wis. Natural Gas Co.; pres., dir. Badger Service; chmn. Am. com. on radwaste disposal, Bradley Ctr. Corp., Assn. Edison Illuminating Cos.; bd. dirs. Fed. Res. Bank. Chgo., Wis. Utilities Assn. Chmn. exec. com. Wis.-Upper Mich. Systems; mem. exec. com. Mid-Am. Interpool Network; bd. dirs. Sinai Samaritan Med. Center, Inc., Forward Wis., Inc., Wis. Electric Utilities Rsch. Found., Milw. Redevel. Corp., Wis. chpt. Nature Conservancy, Greater Milw. Com., YMCA of Met. Milw., Competive Wis., Inc., Milw. Innovation Ctr., Inc., Family Svc. Am.; mem. adv. council U. Wis. Sch. Bus. Adminstrn.; mem. council Med. Coll. Wis.; vice chmn. Met. Milw. Assn. Commerce. With USNR, 1946-47. Mem. Edison Electric Inst. (policy com. environ. affairs) Wis. Soc. Profl. Engrs., Nat. Soc. Profl. Engrs., Kiwanis, Sigma Xi, Eta Kappa Nu, Tau Beta Pi, Sigma Pi Sigma, Pi Mu Epsilon. Home: 1111 N Edison St Milwaukee WI 53202 Office: Wis Energy Power Co 231 W Michigan St Box 2046 Milwaukee WI 53201

MC NEICE, JOHN AMBROSE, JR., investment company executive; b. Quincy, Mass., Sept. 28, 1932; s. John Ambrose and Gladys Lydia (Starratt) McN.; m. Margarete Emma Aust, Apr. 2, 1956; children: Gabriele S., Margarete Anne. B.A. magna cum laude, Boston Coll., 1954; M.B.A., Northeastern U., Boston, 1960. Chartered fin. analyst. With Colonial Mgmt. Assos., Inc. (subsidiary of TCG, Inc.), Boston, 1956—, v.p., 1968-74, exec. v.p., 1974, pres., chief exec. officer, 1975—, chmn., 1982—; chmn., chief exec. officer The Colonial Group, Inc., 1985—. Trustee Boston Coll., St. John's Sem.; mem. Carney Hosp. Found., corp. Northeastern U., Wentworth Inst.; bd. visitors Peter F. Drucker Ctr. Claremont U.; chmn. bd. dirs. Boston Coll. High Sch. Served with AUS, 1954-56. Roman Catholic. Clubs: Union, Algonquin, Wollaston Golf. Home: 47 Green St Canton MA 02021 Office: The Colonial Group Inc 1 Financial Ctr Boston MA 02111

MCNEIL, DAVID JAMES, communications executive, marketing consultant; b. Torrance, Calif., Jan. 20, 1958; s. James Eugene and Nancy Anne (Williams) McN.; m. Sheryl Lillian Stark, Aug. 31, 1980. BA in Bus. Adminstrn. and Mktg., Calif. State U., Northridge, 1982. Pres. McNeil Glass Co., Westlake, Calif., 1978-81; coordinator mktg., pay-per-view Group W., Torrance, 1982-87; mgr. mktg., programming Daniels Cablevision, Arcadia, Calif., 1987, bus. mgr. pay-per-view, 1988; mgr. prodn., pay-per-view United Artists Entertainment, Inc., Glendora, Calif., 1988—; mktg. cons. Cornucopia Mktg. Co., Torrance, 1986—, Golden Rule Mktg. Co., Torrance, 1986—. Mem. Am. Mktg. Assn. (life), So. Calif. Mktg. Coun., Mensa, Torrance C. of C., Simi Valley Jaycees, Torrance Sister City Assn., Delta Sigma Pi (life). Republican. Home: 23930 Los Codona #112 Torrance CA 90505 Office: United Artists Entertainment Southland Complex Cablevision 1041 E Alosta Ave Glendora CA 91740

MCNEIL, JOSEPH MALCOLM, advertising executive; b. Detroit, Oct. 27, 1937; s. Joseph Edgar and Dorothy (Karick) McN.; m. Carol Jean Nave; children: Joseph Paul, Sean Michael, Jennifer Marie. BA in Advt. and English, Mich. State U., 1960. Copywriter D.P. Brother & Co., Detroit, 1962-64; copy group supr. BBD&O, Inc., Detroit, 1964-66; v.p., creative dir. BBD&O, Inc., N.Y.C., 1967-76; group supr. Campbell-Ewald Co., Detroit, 1966-67; exec. v.p., dir. creative svcs. N.W. Ayer, Seattle, 1976-79; sr. v.p., group creative dir. N.W. Ayer, N.Y.C., 1979-80; sr. v.p., creative dir. Campbell-Mithun, Mpls., 1980-83; exec. v.p., exec. creative dir. Creamer, Inc., N.Y.C., 1983-84; sr. v.p., creative dir. McCann-Erickson Inc., N.Y.C., 1984-86, The John Bergin Group/McCann-Erickson Inc., N.Y.C., 1986-87; exec. v.p., exec. creative dir. Ross Roy Communications, Bloomfield Hills, Mich., 1987—. Pfc. U.S. Army. Recipient Gold and Bronze Lions Cannes Film Festival, Spike awards (3) Internat. Broadcasting Assn., Clio awards (8), Effie awards (4), Addy awards (2), Best in the West, Internat. Film Festival awards (3); honored in Smithsonian Instn. Living History sect.; named to Internat. Broadcasting Awards Hall of Fame. Mem. NATAS (Detroit chpt.), Adcraft Club Detroit. Republican. Roman Catholic. Office: Ross Roy Communications 100 Bloomfield Hills Pkwy Bloomfield Hills MI 48013

MCNEIL, STEVEN ARTHUR, food company executive; b. Ft. Thomas, Ky., May 6, 1942; s. Arthur James and Ruby Marie (Lindell) McN.; m. Kathryn Louise Knapp, Aug. 27, 1966; children: Andrew James, Kathryn Marie. BA, Ohio Wesleyan U., 1964; MBA, Dartmouth U., 1966. Mgr. mktg. and devel. Gen. Foods Corp., 1966-80; mgr. mktg. and devel. Campbell Soup Co., Camden, N.J., 1980-81, mgr. Swanson bus. unit, 1981-83, gen. mgr., 1983-84, group gen. mgr., 1984-85, corp. v.p., 1985—; bd. dirs. South Jersey Industries Inc., Folsom, N.J.; vice chmn., mem. exec. com. Frozen Food Inst., McLean, Va.; pres. Mrs. Paul's, 1988—. Trustee West Jersey Health and Hosp. Found. (sec. 1989—), Camden; mem. exec. com. N.J. Sports Authority Kick Off Classic, East Rutherford, N.J.; co-founder The Friends of the Nyacks, Nyack, N.Y., 1972. Served to sgt. USAF, 1967-69. Club: Colony (Medford Lakes, N.J.). Office: Campbell Soup Co Campbell Place Camden NJ 08103

MCNEILL, ALFRED THOMAS, JR., construction executive; b. Elizabeth, N.J., Dec. 21, 1936; s. Alfred T. and Mary Ellen (Byrne) McN.; m. Dorothy J. Keidat, Oct. 4, 1982; children: Mary McNeill Stichter, Gabrielle McNeill Hensley, Matthew, Christopher, Peter, Bartholomew, Elizabeth, Catherine. B.S.C.E., Lehigh U., 1958. Registered profl. engr., Ohio, N.Y. Field engr. Turner Constrn. Co., N.Y.C., 1958, cost engr., 1958-59, asst. project engr., 1959-61, asst. supt., 1961-62; asst. supt. Turner Constrn. Co., Columbus, Ohio, 1962-64; supt. Turner Constrn. Co., Cin., 1964-67; project mgr. Turner Constrn. Co., Toledo, 1967-70; project exec. Turner Constrn. Co., Cin., 1970-73; v.p. corp. ops. Turner Constrn. Co., N.Y.C., 1973-75; v.p., gen. mgr. Turner Constrn. Co., Phila., 1975-80, regional sr. v.p., 1980-85; pres., chief exec. officer Turner Constrn. Co., N.Y.C., 1985—; pres. constrn. Turner Corp., N.Y.C., 1986—, chief operating officer, 1987—, also bd. dirs.; chmn. Ohio Valley Carpenters Dist. Council, Cin., 1970-73; mem. nat. collective bargaining com. Associated Gen. Contractors, 1970-75, nat. dir., 1986—; mem. labor policy com. Gen. Bldg. Contractors Assn., 1975-80, bd. dirs., 1978-84. Co-author: Construction Management for the General Contractor, 1974. Served to 2d lt. U.S. Army, 1959, to capt. USAR, 1959-66. Recipient award St. Louis chpt. Associated Gen. Contrators, 1974; cert. of recognition Harvard Bus. Sch., 1982. Mem. Regional Plan Assn. (bd. dirs.), Econ. Club N.Y. Roman Catholic. Clubs: Union League (Phila.); Aronimink Country (Newtown Square, Pa.); Seaview. Country (Absecon, N.J.); Club 101 (N.Y.C.). Office: Turner Corp 633 3rd Ave New York NY 10017 *

MC NEILL, CARMEN MARY, business broker; b. Charles City, Iowa, July 16; d. Benjamin T. and Mary (Orvis) McN. M.B.A., U. Chgo., 1957. Sec.-treas., Old Rep. Life Ins. Co., 1943-62; cons., officer life cos., 1962-70; broker-finder, owner Am. Cons., Chgo., 1970—. Methodist. Home: 918 Argyle Ave Flossmoor IL 60422 Office: 18118 Martin Ave Ste 1EE Homewood IL 60430

MCNEILL, FREDERICK WALLACE, lawyer, educator, writer, aviation consultant, former military and commercial pilot; b. Chgo., Jan. 4, 1932; s. James Joseph and Irene Gertrude (Stevenson) McN.; m. Judith Carol Austin, Feb. 9, 1957; children: Marjorie, Tamelyn, Kenneth, Patricia, Darcy, Sean, Meghan. BBA, U. Ariz., 1974, JD, 1977. Bar: Ariz. 1977, U.S. Dist. Ct. Ariz., 1977. Served to maj. USAF, 1949-73; ret., 1973; bus. mgr. Engring. & Research Assocs., Inc., Tucson, 1973-74; mng. ptnr. ERA Shopping Ctr., Tucson, 1973-75; chief pilot, spl. agt. Narcotics Strike Force, Ariz., 1975-77; dep. county atty. Pima County, Ariz., 1977-79; atty. Ariz. Drug Control Dist., 1977-79; ptnr. Rees & McNeill, Tucson, 1979-84; writer, 1984—; coordinator legal asst. studies program and adj. prof. Nova U.-Panama Ctr., Republic of Panama, 1987—; sole practice U.S. law, U.S. mil. and PCC installations, 1987—; of counsel Carreira-Pitti P.C. Abogados, Panama, 1987—; sole practice, Panama, 1987—; lectr. air smuggling seminars, organized crime seminars, Ariz., 1977-79. Vice pres. Indian Ridge Homeowners Assn., 1980-82; bd. dirs. Tucson Boys Chorus Bldg. Fund Com., 1972-74. Decorated DFC, Air medal (5), Air Force Commendation medal (2). Mem. ABA, Ariz. Bar Assn., Pima County Bar Assn., Assn. Trial Lawyers Am., Ariz. Trial Lawyers Assn., Lawyer Pilots Bar Assn., Internat. Platform Assn., Ret. Officers Assn., Air Force Assn., DAV, Vietnam Vets. Am., Order of Daedelians, Quiet Birdmen. Office: PSC Box 845 APO Miami FL 34002

MCNEILL, ROBERT PATRICK, investment counselor; b. Chgo., Mar. 17, 1941; s. Donald Thomas and Katherine (Bennett) McN.; m. Martha Stephan, Sept. 12, 1964; children—Jennifer, Donald, Victoria, Stephan, Elizabeth. B.A. summa cum laude (valedictorian), U. Notre Dame, 1963; M.Letters, Oxford U., 1967. Chartered investment counselor. Assoc. Stein Roe & Farnham, Chgo., 1967-72, gen. ptnr., 1972-77, sr. ptnr., 1977-86, exec. v.p., 1986—; underwriting mem. Lloyds of London, 1980—; dir. Comml. Chgo. Corp.; vice chmn. bd. Hill Internat. Prodn. Co., Houston, 1982—; dir., adv. bd. Touche Remnant Investment Counselors, London, 1983—. Voting mem., sec Ill. Rhodes Scholarship Selection Com.; voting mem. Ill. rep. Great Lakes Dist. Rhodes Scholarship Selection Com.; bd. dirs. Kennedy Sch. for Retarded Children, Palos Park, Ill., 1972—, Winnetka United Way, Ill., 1984—, Division St. YMCA, Chgo., 1972—; assoc. Rush-Presbyterian-St. Lukes Med. Ctr., Chgo., 1975—. Rhodes scholar, 1963. Fellow Fin. Analysts Fedn.; mem. Chgo. Council on Fgn. Relations (bd. dirs., vice chmn. 1975—), Inst. European Studies (bd. govs., treas. 1981—), Investment Analysts Soc. Chgo. (chgo. com., com. on fgn. affairs, com. on internat. and domestic issues). Clubs: Sunset Ridge Country (Northfield, Ill.) (bd. dirs. 1983—); Chicago; Econ. of Chgo. Office: Stein Roe & Farnham 1 S Wacker Dr Chicago IL 60606

MCNELIS, THOMAS WILLIAM, vocational rehabilitation facility executive; b. Hazleton, Pa., Aug. 30, 1952; s. William Joseph and Catherine Patricia (Boyle) McN.; m. Patricia Kathleen McAndrew, July 12, 1975; children: Brain Patrick, Terrence Kealy. BA in Psychology, King's Coll., 1974. With Threshold Rehab. Svcs., Reading, Pa., 1974—, prodn. mgr., 1976-77, dir. indsl. ops., 1977—. Mem. Pa. Industries for Blind and Handicapped (dir. 1983—, vice chmn. 1986—), Pa. Assn. Rehab. Facilities, Am. Mgmt. Assn., Rotary (dir. 1985—, pres. 1988—, Rotarian of Yr. 1988). Office: Threshold Rehab Svcs Inc 1000 Lancaster Ave Reading PA 19607

MC NERNEY, WALTER JAMES, health policy educator, consultant; b. New Haven, June 8, 1925; s. Robert Francis and Anna Gertrude (Shanley) McN.; m. Shirley Ann Hamilton, June 26, 1948; children: Walter James, Peter Hamilton, Jennifer Allison, Daniel Martin, Richard Hamilton. B.S., Yale U., 1947; M.H.A., U. Minn., 1950. Research asst. Labor-Mgmt. Center, Yale U., 1947; instr. advanced math. Hopkins Prep. Sch., New Haven, 1947-48; adminstrv. resident R.I. Hosp., Providence, 1949-50; asst. to coordinator Hosp. and Clinics of Med. Center, U. Pitts., 1950-53; also instr., then asst. prof. hosp. adminstrn. at univ., then asst. prof. hosp. and med. adminstrn. Grad. Sch. Pub. Health, U. Pitts., 1953-55; assoc. prof., dir. program hosp. adminstrn. Sch. Bus. Adminstrn., U. Mich., 1955-58; prof., dir. Bur. Hosp. Adminstrn., 1958-61; pres. Blue Cross Assn., Chgo., 1961-77; pres., chief exec. officer Blue Cross and Blue Shield Assns., Chgo., 1977-81; prof. health policy Grad. Sch. Mgmt., Northwestern U., 1982—; cons. in field 1982—; mem. Nat. Coun. on Health Planning and Devel., HEW, 1976-82; mem. bd. dirs. Nat. Health Coun., 1963-77, pres., 1972-73; mem. nat. commn. on cost of med. care AMA, 1977, mem. com. on pvt. philanthropy, 1977-78; past pres. Internat. Fedn. Vol. Health Svc. Funds; mem. devel. com. Yale U.; trustee Nat. Exec. Svc. Corps; chmn. task force on Medicaid and related programs HEW, 1969-70; charter mem. coun. Inst. Medicine-Nat. Acad. Scis., chmn. bd. on health care svcs.; mem. physician payment rev. commn. U.S. Congress; bd dirs. Stanley Works, Knowledge Data, Medicus, Mgmt. Data Communications, Sequel Corp.; chmn. bd. Am. Health Properties Inc. Author: Hospital and Medical Economics, 1962, Regionalization and Rural Health Care, 1962; contbr. articles to profl. jours. Mem. Pres.' Com. on Health Edn., 1972-73; trustee Hosp. Research and Ednl. Fund, Inst. for Future; vis. com. Harvard Med. and Dental Schs. Served to lt. (j.g.) USNR, 1943-46. Named 1 of 100 most important young men and women in U.S. by Life Mag., 1962; recipient Justin Ford Kimball award, 1967; Outstanding Achievement award U. Minn., 1970; sec.'s unit citation HEW, 1970; recipient Yale medal, 1979, award for meritorious service AMA, 1981, award of honor Am. Hosp. Assn., 1982; Nuffield Provincial Hosps. Trust-Kings Fund (Eng.) fellow, 1970. Fellow Am. Pub. Health Assn., Am. Coll. Hosp. Adminstrs. (Silver medal 1978); mem. Am. Mgmt. Assn. (dir., trustee), Royal Soc. Health, Sigma Xi, Delta Sigma Pi. Clubs: Chgo. Commonwealth, Chicago; Yale (N.Y.C.). Office: Northwestern U Grad Sch Mgmt 2001 Sheridan Rd Evanston IL 60208

MCNICHOLAS, DAVID PAUL, automobile rental company executive; b. Youngstown, Ohio, Mar. 1, 1941; s. Paul James and Mary Frances (Dignan) McN.; m. Patricia Marie McAtee; children: Paula, John, Catherine, Tim, Dan. BBA, Youngstown State U., 1962. With Youngstown Sheet and Tube Co. (now subs. LTV), 1964-78, from trainee to dir. data processing; with Avis Inc., N.Y.C., 1978—, sr. v.p., 1985—, also bd. dirs.; bd. dirs. Ohio Franchise Operater Inc. Office: Avis Inc 900 Old Country Rd Garden City NY 11530

MCNICHOLS, GERALD ROBERT, consulting company executive; b. Cleve., Nov. 21, 1943; s. Charles Wellington and June Beatrice (Kalal) McN.; m. Paula Kay Austin, Dec. 26, 1964; children: G. Robert Jr., Kay Lynn, Melissa Sue. BS with honors, Case-Western Res. U., 1965; MS, U. Pa., 1966; ScD, George Washington U., 1976. Cert. cost analyst. Sr. ops. analyst Office of Sec., Dept. of Def., Washington, 1970-76; v.p. GenTech, Inc., Bethesda, Md., 1976-77, J. Watson Noah, Inc., Falls Church, Va., 1977-78; pres. Mgt. Cons. and Rsch., Inc., Falls Church, 1978-87, chmn., chief exec. officer, 1987—. Co-author: Operations Research for Decision Making, 1975; editor Cost Analysis, 1984; contbr. articles to profl. jours. Pres. Rondelay Civic Assn., Fairfax Sta., Va., 1985-87. Capt. USAF, 1966-70. Mem. Inst. Cost Analysis (pres. 1985-88), Nat. Estimating Soc. (regional bd. dirs. 1984-88), Internat. Soc. Parametric Analysts (bd. dirs. 1982-84), Ops. Rsch. Soc. Am. (chmn. mil. applications sect.), Mil. Ops. Rsch. Soc. (sec., treas. 1986-87, v.p. adminstrn. 1987-88, bd. dirs. 1985-88). Home: 8133 Rondelay Ln Fairfax Station VA 22039 Office: Mgmt Cons & Rsch Inc 5113 Leesburg Pike Ste 509 Falls Church VA 22041

MCNULTY, MATTHEW FRANCIS, JR., educator, health care administration educator, university executive, consultant, horse breeder; b. Elizabeth, N.J., Nov. 26, 1914; s. Matthew Francis and Abby Helen (Dwyer) McN.; m.

Mary Nell Johnson, May 4, 1946; children—Matthew Francis, Mary Lauren. BS, St. Peter's Coll., 1938, DHL (hon.), 1978; postgrad., Rutgers U. Law Sch., 1939-41; MHA, Northwestern U., 1949; MPH, U. N.C., 1952; ScD (hon.), U. Ala., 1969, Georgetown U., 1986. Contract writer, mgmt. trainee acturial div. Prudential Life Ins. Co. Am., N.J., 1938-41; dir. med. adminstrn. VA, 1946-49; project officer, adminstr. VA Teaching Hosps., Little Rock, Chgo. and Birmingham, Ala., 1949-54; adminstr. Jefferson-Hillman Hosp., Birmingham, 1954-60; founding gen. dir. U. Ala. Hosps. and Clinics, 1960-66; prof. hosp. adminstrn. U. Ala. Grad. Sch., 1954-69, vis. prof., 1969—, founding dir. grad. program hosp. adminstrn., 1964-69, prof. epidemiology and preventive medicine Sch. Medicine, 1964-69, founding dean Sch. Health Related Professions, 1966-69; pres. Matthew F. McNulty, Jr. & Assocs., 1954—; founding dir. Council Teaching Hosps. and assoc. dir. Assn. Am. Med. Colls., 1966-69; prof. community medicine and internat. health Georgetown U., 1969-86, v.p. med. ctr. affairs, 1969-72, exec. v.p., med. ctr. affairs, 1972-74; chancellor Georgetown U. Med. Ctr., 1974-86; chancellor emeritus Georgetown U., 1986—; chmn. acad. affiars com. bd. trustees Hahnemann U., Phila, 1987—; founding chmn. bd. Univ. D.C. Affiliated Health Plan, Inc., 1974-78; founding chmn. bd. trustees Georgetown U. Community Health Plan, Inc., 1972-80; vis. prof. Cen. U. Venezuela, 1957-61; hosp. cons., 1953—; dir. Kaiser-Georgetown Community Health Plan, Inc., Washington, Kaiser Health Plans and Hosps., Oakland Calif.; mem. VA Spl. Med. Adv. Group, 1978-89, Spl. Higher Edn. Com. on Dental Schs. Curriculum, 1978-79; preceptor hosp. adminstrn. Northwestern U., Washington U., U. Iowa, U. Minn., 1953-69; mem. nat. adv. com. health research projects Ga. Inst. Tech., 1959-65, 73-85; nat. adv. com. health research projects U. Pitts., 1956-60; adv. com. W.K. Kellogg Found., 1960-65; vis. cons., lectr. Venezuelan Ministry Health and Social Welfare, 1967-69; dir. Blue Cross-Blue Shield Ala., 1960-61, 65-68; trustee, mem. exec. com. Blue Cross and Blue Shield Nat. Capital Area, 1973-89, Washington Bd. Trade, 1972-86. Bd. dirs. Greater Birmingham United Appeal, 1960-66; trustee Jefferson County Tb Sanatorium, 1958-64; mem. health services research study sect. NIH, 1963-67; cons. USPHS, 1959-63; mem. White House Conf. on Health, 1965, on Medicare Implementation, 1966, others; trustee Nat. Council Internat. Health, 1975-86; pres. Nat. League Nursing, 1979-81; bd. dirs. Kaiser Found. Health Plans and Hosps., 1980-85. Maj. USAAF, 1941-46, lt. col. USAFR, 1946-55. Recipient Disting. Alumnus award Northwestern U., 1973, Disting. Alumnus award U. N.C., John Benjamin Nichol award Med. Soc. D.C., Mayor and D.C. Coun., Matthew F. McNulty, Jr. Unanimous Recognition Resolution of 1986. Fellow Am. Pub. Health Assn., Am. Coll. Healthcare Execs. (life) (bd. regents and council of regents 1961-67, Disting. Health Sci. Exec. award 1976); mem Am. Hosp. Assn. (life) (Disting. Service award 1984), Ala. Hosp. Assn. (past pres.), Nat. League for Nursing (past pres.), D.C. League Nursing (past dir.), Nat. Forum Health Planning (past pres., Disting. award, 1987), Council Med. Adminstrn., Internat. Hosp. Fedn., Jefferson County Ala. Vis. Nursing Assn. (past pres.; Disting. Service award), Ala. Pub. Health Assn. (past chmn. med. care sect.), Southeastern Hosp. Conf. (past dir.), Birmingham Hosp. Council (past pres.), Hosp. Council Nat. Capital Area (pres. 1985-89), Assn. Univ. Programs in Hosp. Adminstrn. (Disting. award 1971), Greater Birmingham Area C. of C. (Merit award), Washington Acad. of Medicine, Am. Assn. Med. Colls. (chmn. teaching hosp. council 1964-65; Disting. Service Mem.), Royal Soc. Health, Am. Systems Mgmt. Soc. (Disting. award), Orgn. Univ. Health Ctr. Adminstrs., AAAS, Santa Gertrudis Breeders Internat., Bashkir Curley Horse Assn., Omicron Kappa Upsilon. Clubs: University (Ala.); Cosmos, City Tavern, Nat. Press (Washington). Lodge: Knight of Malta. Office: TEOC PENTREF 3100 Phil Davis Dr Off the Old Spanish Trail Ocean Springs MS 39564

MCNULTY, THOMAS PATRICK, marketing executive, consultant; b. Bklyn., Apr. 4, 1955; s. Thomas Daniel and Patricia Elizabeth (Beatty) McN.; m. Nancy Elizabeth Fajen, Oct. 6, 1979; 1 child, Ryan Patrick. AA, Broward Community Coll., 1975; BS, Fla. State U., 1977, MS, 1979. Family therapist Hollywood (Fla.) Pavillion Psychiat. Hosp., 1979-80; clin. supr. Starting Place Inc., Hollywood, 1980-84; dir., mem. provider rels. Internat. Med. Ctrs. Inc., Miami, Fla., 1984-85; dir. mktg. Shari Med. Ctr., North Lauderdale, Fla., 1985-87; v.p. mktg. U.S. Health Svcs. Inc., Tamarac, Fla., 1985-87; dir. mktg. Inst. Med. Spltys., North Miami Beach, Fla., 1987-88; v.p. mktg. Bry-Lin Hosps., Buffalo, 1988—; pres. Success Stories, Inc., mktg. cons., 1988—. Editor newsletter Inst. Insider, 1987—; contbr. to profl. jours. Mem. Am. Mktg. Assn. (bd. dirs. 1987—), Am. Mgmt. Assn., Acad. Health Svcs. Mktg., Am. Soc. for Hosp. Mktg. and Pub. Rels., Am. Soc. for Healthcare Planning and Mktg., N.Y. Fedn. Profl. Health Educators, Fla. Assn. HMO's, K.C., Ancient Order Hibernians. Democrat. Roman Catholic. Home: 78 Old Farm Rd Orchard Park NY 14127 Office: Bry-Lin Hosps 1263 Delaware Ave Buffalo NY 14209

MCNUTT, JACK WRAY, oil company executive; b. Norphlet, Ark., Sept. 7, 1934; s. Fay D. and Mattie E. (Garner) McN.; m. Jordine Chesshir, Aug. 19, 1955; 1 child, Marsha. BS, Harding Coll., 1956; MS, Columbia U., 1957. Acct. Murphy Oil Corp., El Dorado, Ark., 1957-68, exec. mgmt. asst., 1968-69, exec. v.p., 1981-88, chief operating officer, 1986-88, pres., chief exec. officer, 1988—, also bd. dirs.; v.p. planning Murphy Ea. Oil Co., London, 1969-72, pres., 1972-81; bd. dirs. Ocean Drilling & Exploration Co., New Orleans, First Nat. Bank El Dorado, Ark., Murphy Oil Co. Ltd., Calgary, Alta., Can. Mem. Am. Petroleum Inst., Am. Econ. Assn., Nat. Assn. Bus. Economists, 25 Yr. Club of Petroleum Industry, Nat. Petroleum Council. Home: 1705 W Cedar El Dorado AR 71730 Office: Murphy Oil Corp 200 Peach St El Dorado AR 71730

MCPHEE, BONNIE JEAN, computer services executive; b. Kenosha, Wis., Sept. 15, 1936; d. Lester Lawrence and Catherine Chalmers (Marks) Getschman; m. Lawrence Elmer McPhee, Apr. 23, 1959; children: Steven Craig, Laurel Beth McPhee Flynn. BS summa cum laude, Franklin U., 1981; MBA with honors, Capital U., 1985. Cert. systems profl. Asst. to mgr. EDP div. R.L. Polk & Co., Taylor, Mich., 1965-73; planning coordinator Columbus (Ohio) So. Power Co., 1973-77, supr. systems and procedures, 1981-87; systems analyst Celanese Piping Systems, Hilliard, Ohio, 1977-81; pres. Pancom Computer Advs., Columbus, 1987—; adj. prof. Franklin U., Columbus, 1985—. Mem. Assn. Systems Mgmt. (pres. 1987-88). Methodist. Office: Pancom Computer Advs 65 E State St Ste 1000 Columbus OH 43215

MCPHERSON, EDWARD RUSSELL, banker; b. Balt., Sept. 18, 1945; s. Donald Payton and Janet (Russell) McP.; m. Sally Thompson, May 12, 1969; children: Beth, Edward. BA, Williams Coll., Williamstown, Mass., 1967; MS, George Washington U., 1971. Mgmt. cons. Klein & Saks Inc., Washington, 1968, Booz Allen & Hamilton, Washington, 1971-73; v.p. corp. planning and investor relations Republic Bank Dallas, 1973-76; sr. v.p. corp. planning and investor relations RepublicBank Corp., Dallas, 1978-83, sr. v.p., chief fin. officer, 1983-84, exec. v.p., chief fin. officer, 1984-87; exec. v.p., chief fin. officer First RepublicBank Corp., Dallas, 1987—; bd. dirs. Republic Venture Group, Dallas. Trustee Hockaday Sch., Dallas, 1987, Dallas Fiscal Affairs Com., 1983-87. Served to lt. USN, 1968-71. Office: First RepublicBank Corp Pacific & Ervay Sts Dallas TX 75266-0020

MCPHERSON, EUGENE VIRGIL, broadcasting executive; b. Columbus, Ohio, Aug. 29, 1927; s. Arthur Emerson and Emma (Scott) McP.; BA, Ohio State U., 1950; m. Nancy Marie Clark, June 13, 1953; children—Lynne, Scott. Prodn. exec. WBNS-TV, Columbus, 1952-62; exec. producer documentary unit WLWT-TV, Cin., 1962-64; dir. news and spl. projects WLWT-TV, Cin., 1964-66; v.p. news and spl. projects AVCO Broadcasting Co., Cin., 1966-69, v.p. programming, 1969-73; v.p., gen. mgr. WLWI-TV, Indpls., 1973-75; pres. McPherson Media, Inc., 1975-88; owner, operator Stas. WVLN, WSEI, WRBI, KCTE, KGVE, 1975-88; pres. McPherson Prodns., 1988—. With AUS, 1946-47. Recipient Creative Writer Producer award Alfred P. Sloan, 1966, Chris award Columbus Film Festival, 1960, 61, 62, 64, 71, Nat. Assn. TV Execs. Program award, 1968, Ohio State award, 1960, 63, 64, Freedom's Found. award, 1963, Regional Emmy, 1977, Cine Golden Eagle award, 1982, Blue Ribbon, Am. Film Festival, 1985, Silver Apple award, 1987, Genesis award, 1988. Mem. Broadcast Pioneers, Ill. Broadcasters Assn. (pres.). Author: (with Bleum and Cox) Television in the Public Interest, 1961. Writer, producer, dir. films The Last Prom, 1963, Death Driver, 1968, Citizen, 1962, Birth by Appointment, 1960, Diagnostic Countdown, 1962, Veil of Shadows, 1961, Rails in Crisis, 1963, Palm Trees and Ice Bergs, 1977, Tinsel Town and the Big Apple, 1979, Goodbye Carnival Girl, 1980, Atomic Legs, 1981, The Edison Adventures, 1981, The Championship, 1982, Little Arliss, 1984, Umbrella Jack, 1984, Buddies, 1985, That Funny Fat Kid, 1985, Zerk the Jerk, 1985, My First Swedish Bombshell, 1985, Charlie's Christmas Secret, 1985, Just For Kicks, 1986, Nags, 1987, My Father, the Clown, 1987, Charlie's Christmas Project, 1987, Narc, 1987, Pee Wee's Ragtime Band, 1988. Office: 2220 Gilbert Ave Cincinnati OH 45206

MC PHERSON, FRANK ALFRED, corporation executive; b. Stilwell, Okla., Apr. 29, 1933; s. Younce B. and Maurine Frances (Strauss) McP.; m. Nadine Wall, Sept. 10, 1955; 4 children. B.S., Okla. State U., 1957. With Kerr-McGee, 1957—; gen. mgr. Gulf Coast Oil and gas ops., Morgan City, La., 1969-73; pres. Kerr-McGee Coal, 1973-76, Kerr-McGee Nuclear, 1976-77; vice chmn. Kerr-McGee Corp., 1977-80, pres., 1980-83, chmn., chief exec. officer, 1983—. Patentee in field. Bd. dirs. Okla. chpt. Nature Conservancy, U.S. Olympic Com. for Okla., Appeals Rev. Bd. Greater Okla., Leadership Oklahoma City, Bapt. Med. Ctr. of Okla., Okla. State U. Found., United Way of Greater Oklahoma City; mem. Okla. Found. Excellence; mem. adv. council Southwestern Bapt. Theol. Sem.; mem. council on competitiveness Okla. Acad. for State Goals; mem. The Bus. Roundtable. Served to capt. USAF, 1957-60. Mem. Conf. Bd., Soc. Mining Engrs., Am. Mining Congress (dir., exec. com., adv. council), Am. Petroleum Inst. (dir.), Nat. Petroleum Council, 25-Yr. Club of Petroleum Industry Oklahoma City C. of C. (dir.). Republican. Baptist. Office: Kerr-McGee Corp PO Box 25861 Oklahoma City OK 73125 *

MCPHERSON, GAIL, advertising and real estate executive; b. Fort Worth; d. Garland and Daphne McP. Student U. Tex.-Austin; BA, MS, CUNY. Advt. sales exec. Harper's Bazaar mag., N.Y.C., 1974-76; sr. v.p., fashion mktg. dir. L'Officiel/USA mag., N.Y.C., 1976-80; fashion mgr. Town and Country mag., N.Y.C., 1980-82; v.p. advt. and mktg. Ultra mag., Tex. and N.Y.C., 1982-84; fragrance, jewelry and automotive mgr. M. Mag., N.Y.C., 1984-85; sr. real estate sales exec. Fredric M. Reed & Co., Inc., N.Y.C., 1985—. Sponsor Southampton Hosp. Benefit Com., N.Y.; mem. jr. com. Mannes Sch. Music, N.Y.C., Henry St. Settlement, N.Y.C. Mem. Fashion Group N.Y., Advt. Women N.Y., Real Estate Bd. N.Y., U. Tex. Alumni Assn. of N.Y. (v.p.). Republican. Presbyterian. Clubs: Corviglia (St. Moritz, Switzerland), Doubles, El Morocco (mem. jr. com. 1976-77), Le Club (N.Y.C.). Home: 3418 Rutson Dr Amarillo TX 79109 Office: 405 Park Ave New York NY 10022

MCPHERSON, MELVILLE PETER, lawyer, government official; b. Grand Rapids, Mich., Oct. 27, 1940; s. Donald and Ellura E. (Frost) McP.; 1 child, Donald B.; 1 stepchild, Michael D. Kircher. J.D., Am. U., 1969; M.B.A., Western Mich. U., 1967; B.A., Mich. State U., 1963. Bar: D.C. 1977. Peace Corps vol. Peru, 1965-66; with IRS, Washington, 1969-75; spl. asst. to Pres. and dep. dir. Presdl. personnel White House, Washington, 1975-77; mng. ptnr. Vorys, Sater, Seymour & Pease, Washington, 1977-81; acting counsel to Pres. White House, 1981; adminstr. AID, Washington, 1981-87; dep. sec. Dept. Treasury, Washington, 1987—; mem. Bd. for Internat. Food and Agrl. Devel., 1977-80. Mem. D.C. Bar Assn., Mich. Bar Assn. Republican. Methodist. Office: US Dept Treasury 15th & Pennsylvania Ave NW Washington DC 20220 *

MCPHERSON, ROBERT WATSON, diverse industry company executive; b. Trenton, N.J., Sept. 5, 1946; s. Robert Krone and Katherine Chase (Watson) McP.; m. Donna Lynn Collins, Apr. 8, 1972; children: Ian Andrew, Aaron Robert. BS in Chem. Engring., Cornell U., 1969. Tech. rep. FMC Corp., N.Y.C., 1969-71, mgr., distbr. sales, 1973-74, product mgr., 1972-73; product mgr. Continental Oil Co., Houston, 1975-76, bus. mgr., 1977-79; bd. dirs. Haber, Inc., Montville, N.J., 1976—, exec. v.p., 1980-85; chief operating officer Haber, Inc., Montville, 1980-88, vice chmn., 1985-88; bd. dirs. Life Signs, Inc., Boston and Montville, 1980—; pres., exec. dir. Life Signs, Inc., Montville, 1988—; bd. dirs. Silver Tech. Mines, Tombstone, Ariz. Pres. Valhalla Civic Assn., Montville, 1988—. Mem. Licensing Exec. Soc., Cornell Soc. Engrs. Office: Life Signs Inc 437 Main Rd Montville NJ 07082

MCPIKE, MARTIN JOHN, JR., market research analyst; b. Bklyn., June 25, 1946; s. Martin John and Neddy B. (Locco) McP.; B.S. in Mktg. and Econs., Fairfield U., 1969; M.A. in Corp. and Polit. Communications, 1974. Asst. editor R.L. White Co., Inc., Louisville, 1971-72; mortgage officer Conn. Savs. Bank, New Haven, 1972-75; mktg. analyst Internat. Vitamin Co., Union, N.J., 1975-78; dir. mktg. Superior Steel Products, Inc., Cheshire, Conn., 1979-83; market research analyst The Banking Center, Waterbury, Conn., 1983, Harper-Leader Inc., Waterbury, 1984—. Mem. Am. Mktg. Assn., Cheshire C. of C., Fairfield U. Alumni Assn., Phi Kappa Theta. Home: 84 Cedar Ct Cheshire CT 06410-2214 Office: 1046 S Main St Waterbury CT 06720

MCPOYLE, FRANCIS MICHAEL, construction company executive; b. Pottstown, Pa., Jan. 10, 1936; s. Thomas Charles and Katherine Marie (Yensen) McP.; m. Beverly Loretta Imes, Aug. 17, 1937; children: Karen, Kevin, Kirk, Kerry. Student, Villanova U., 1953-55. Laborer Ea. Prestressed Constrn. Corp. Line, Lexington, Pa., 1955-57; sales rep. Atlantic Prestressed Constrn. Corp., Trenton, N.J., 1957-60, Camden (N.J.) Lime Co., 1960-64; sales mgr. Atlas Bldg. Systems, Marlton, N.J., 1964-80; v.p. Atlas Bldg. Systems, Marlton, 1980—. Patentee in field. Mem. MidAtlantic Precast Assn. (pres. 1986-87, dir. 1984-88). Democrat. Roman Catholic. Home: 1340 Arthur Ave Maple Glen PA 19002 Office: Atlas Bldg Systems PO Box 245 Marlton NJ 08053

MC QUADE, LAWRENCE CARROLL, lawyer, corporation executive; b. Yonkers, N.Y., Aug. 12, 1927; s. Edward A. and Thelma (Keefe) McQ.; m. de Rosset Parker Morrissey, Aug. 3, 1968 (dec. Oct. 1978); 1 child, Andrew Parker; m. Margaret Osmer, Mar. 15, 1980. B.A. with distinction, Yale U., 1950; B.A. (Rhodes scholar), Oxford (Eng.) U., 1952, M.A., 1956; LL.B. cum laude, Harvard U., 1954; M.A. (hon.), Colby Coll., 1981. Bar: N.Y. 1955, D.C. 1968. Assoc. firm Sullivan & Cromwell, N.Y.C., 1954-60; spl. asst. to asst. sec. for internat. security affairs Dept. Def., Washington, 1961-63; dep. asst. sec. Dept. Commerce, Washington, 1963-64; asst. to sec. Dept. Commerce, 1965-67, asst. sec., 1967-69; pres. Procon Inc., Des Plaines, Ill., 1969-75; chief exec. officer, dir. Procon Inc., 1969-75; v.p. Universal Oil Products Co., 1972-75, W. R. Grace & Co., N.Y.C., 1975-78; sr. v.p. W. R. Grace & Co., 1978-83, exec. v.p., 1983-87, also bd. dirs.; vice chmn. Prudential Mutual Fund Mgmt., Inc., N.Y.C., 1988—; mng. dir. Prudential-Bache, 1988—; chmn., chief exec. officer Universal Money Ctrs.; bd. dirs. Kaiser Tech, Inc., Crazy Eddie, Prime Cities Broadcasters Corp., and several Prudential-Bache Mutual Funds; expert advisor commn. on transnat. corps. UN, 1989—. Author: (with others) The Ghana Report, 1959; contbr. (with others) articles to profl. jours. Bd. dirs. Fgn. Bondholders Protective Council, N.Y.C., 1978—, The American Forum, 1985—, Am. Council on Germany, 1985—; trustee Colby Coll., 1981—. Served with AUS, 1946-47. Mem. Assn. Am. Rhodes Scholars, Council Fgn. Relations N.Y., Chgo. Council Fgn. Relations (dir. 1969-75), Nat. Fgn. Trade Council (dir. 1979-87), Atlantic Council U.S. (dir. 1969—), Internat. Mgmt. and Devel. Inst. (dir. 1970—), Overseas Devel. Council (dir. 1974-87), Phi Beta Kappa. Clubs: Harvard, Century, Pilgrims (N.Y.C.); Metropolitan (Washington). Office: Prudential Mut Funds Mgmt 1 Seaport Pla New York NY 10292

MCQUADE, TED MICHAEL, finance manager; b. Indpls., May 24, 1954; m. Dora Godio, Mar. 15, 1975. AB in English and Religion, Ind. U., 1976, MBA in Fin., 1983. Asst. controller APD Corp., Indpls., 1976-78; gen. acctg. supr. Burger Chef Systems, Inc., Indpls., 1978-79; controller Mid-Am. Chem. Co., Indpls., 1979-80; analyst Consumer Electronics RCA Corp., Indpls., 1980-83, fin. mgr., 1983-84; mgr. ops. RCA Distbg. Corp., N.Y.C., 1984-85; dir. internat. treasury and ops. analysis RCA Corp., N.Y.C., 1985-86; fin. mgr. GE Fanuc N.A., Inc., Charlottesville, Va., 1986-88; mgr. fin., mfg. div. GE Plastics, Pittsfield, Mass., 1989—. Author: Genesis, 1976 (Bicentennial Essay award). Active Jaycees, Indpls.; exec. com. United Jewish Appeal, N.Y.C., 1985-86. Office: GE Plastics One Plastics Ave Pittsfield MA 01201

MCQUEENEY, THOMAS A., publisher; b. N.Y.C., Aug. 21, 1937; s. Henry J. and Jeannette A. (Beaton) McQ.; m. Ellyn M. Carney, Oct. 11, 1970; children: Kicha Lee, Miya Lyn, Jana Mai. BBA, Northeastern U., 1964. Market analyst Gillette Co., Boston, 1964-65; research analyst Chase Manhattan Bank, N.Y.C., 1965-68; portfolio mgr. Portfolio Planning, Inc., N.Y.C., 1968-71; pub., pres. Money Market Directories, Inc., Charlottesville, Va., 1971—. Editor: Real Estate Investing by Pension Fund Adminstrs., 1975. Mem. Indsl. Devel. Bd. Authority, Albemarle County, 1980—. Served to 1st lt., U.S. Army, 1956-58. Mem. Assn. Investment Mgmt. Sales Execs. Republican. Presbyterian. Lodge: Rotary. Home: 121 Indian Spring Rd Charlottesville VA 22901 Office: Money Market Directories Inc Charlottesville VA 22901

MC QUILLAN, JOSEPH MICHAEL, credit company executive; b. Meridian, Miss., Aug. 9, 1931; s. John Vincent and Florence (Hoban) McQ.; m. Janet Holst, Aug. 30, 1952 (div.); children—Joseph Michael, James Vincent, Ann Marie, Tom Charles, Mary Clare, Tim Sean. B.S., Creighton U., Omaha, 1956. Mgr. Arthur Andersen & Co. (C.P.A.'s), Omaha, Los Angeles, 1956-63; comptroller Cudahy Co., Phoenix, 1963-66; exec. v.p., comptroller Assoc. Corp. N.Am., N.Y.C., 1969—, South Bend, Ind., 1979—. Served with USAF, 1951-55. Mem. Nat. Assn. C.P.A.'s, Financial Execs. Inst., Beta Alpha Pi. Home: 604 Durango Circle S Irving TX 75062 Office: Assoc Corp NAm 250 Carpenter Frwy Dallas TX 75222 *

MC QUILLAN, MARGARET MARY, publishing company executive; b. N.Y.C.; d. John A. and Margaret (Higgins) McQ.; A.B., Coll. New Rochelle, 1945; M.A. Columbia U., 1948. With Harcourt Brace Jovanovich, Inc. (formerly Harcourt, Brace & World), N.Y.C., 1949—; asst. sec., 1960-70, sec., 1971—, v.p. 1975-78, adminstrv. v.p., 1978-80, sr. v.p., 1980—. Home: 125 Crestwood Ave Tuckahoe NY 10707 Office: Harcourt Brace Jovanovich Inc 6277 Sea Harbor Dr Orlando FL 32887

MCQUILLEN, HARRY A., publishing company executive. Formerly with Prentice-Hall; former dir. mktg. services Coll. div. McGraw-Hill; former editor-in-chief Coll. div. CBS Pub., pres. Ednl. and Profl. Pub. div., 1983-87; group v.p. Gen. Pub. Group Macmillan, Inc., N.Y.C., 1987-88, v.p., 1988; pres., gen. pub. group Macmillan Pub., 1988—. Office: Macmillan Inc 866 3rd Ave New York NY 10022 *

MCQUILLEN, JEREMIAH JOSEPH, wallcovering distribution executive; b. Buffalo, Jan. 7, 1941; s. Joseph Bernard and Marca Rita (Ammerman) McQ.; m. Maureen Elaine Brett; children: Michael, Karen, Kathleen. BS, Canisius Coll., 1962. Nat. sales mgr. Birge Wallcoverings, Buffalo, 1973-74, v.p., gen. mgr., 1976-79; v.p. mktg. Reed Decorative Products, Toronto, 1974-76; exec. v.p. Atlanta, 1979-81; exec. v.p. Northeastern Wallcoverings, Boston, 1981-88, pres., 1989—. Served to 1st lt., U.S. Army, 1962-64. Mem. Wallcovering Distbrs. Assn. (sec., treas. 1987—, v.p. 1988, pres. 1989—), Wallcovering Info. Bur. (pres. 1980), Wallcovering Mfg. Assn. (v.p. 1988)., Di Gamma. Republican. Roman Catholic. Home: 3 Nauset St Medfield MA 02052 Office: Northeastern Wallcoverings 300 Summer St Boston MA 02210

MCRAE, HAMILTON EUGENE, III, lawyer; b. Midland, Tex., Oct. 29, 1937; s. Hamilton Eugene and Adrian (Hagaman) McR.; m. Betty Hawkins, Aug. 27, 1960; children: Elizabeth Ann, Stephanie Adrian, Scott Hawkins. BSEE, U. Ariz., 1961; student, USAF Electronics Sch., 1961-62; postgrad., U. Redlands, Calif., 1962-63; JD with honors and distinction, U. Ariz., 1967. Bar: Ariz. 1967, U.S. Supreme Ct. 1979. Elec. engr. Salt River Project, Phoenix, 1961; assoc. Jennings, Strouss & Salmon, Phoenix, 1967-71, ptnr., 1971-85, chmn. real estate dept., 1980-85, mem. policy com., 1982-85, mem. fin. com., 1981-85, chmn. bus. devel. com., 1982-85; ptnr. and co-founder Stuckey & McRae, Phoenix, 1985—; co-founder, chmn. bd. Republic Cos., Phoenix, 1985—; magistrate Paradise Valley, Ariz., 1983-85; juvenile referee Superior Ct., 1983-85; pres., dir. Phoenix Realty & Trust Co., 1970—; officer Indsl. Devel. Corp. Maricopa County, 1972-86; instr. and lectr. in real estate; officer, bd. dirs. other corps. Contbr. articles to profl. jours. Elder Valley Presbyn. Ch., Scottsdale, Ariz., 1973-75, 82-85, corp. pres., 1974-75, 84-85, trustee, 1973-75, 82-85, chmn. exec. com., 1984; trustee Upward Found., Phoenix, 1977-80, Valley Presbyn. Found., 1982-83, Ariz. Acad., 1971—; trustee, mem. exec. com. Phi Gamma Delta Ednl. Found., Washington, 1974-84; trustee Phi Gamma Delta Internat., 1984-86; bd. dirs. Archon, 1986-87; founder, trustee McRae Found.; bd. dirs. Food for Hungry (Internat. Relief), 1985—, exec. com., 1986—, chmn. bd. dirs., 1987—; trustee, mem. exec. com. Ariz. Mus. Sci. and Tech., 1984—, 1st v.p., 1985-86, pres., 1986-88, chmn. bd. dirs., 1988—; Lambda Alpha Internat. Hon. Land Econs. Soc, 1988—; sec.-treas. Ariz. State U. Council for Design Excellence, 1989—, bd. dirs. 1988—, sec.-treas. 1989—; bd. dirs. Crisis Nursery Office of the Chair, 1988—, Maricopa Community Colls. Found., 1988—, Phoenix Community Alliance, 1988—, Interchurch Ctr. Corp., 1987—, Western Art Assocs., 1989—, Phoenix Com. on Fgn. Rels., 1988—, U. Ariz. Pres.'s Club, 1984—, Econ. Club of Phoenix, 1987-88; vol. fund raiser YMCA, Salvation Army, others; mem. Taliesin Council, Frank Lloyd Wright Found., 1985—; mem. fin. com. Kyl for Congress, 1985—; mem. bond com. City of Phoenix, 1987-88; bd. dirs. Food for Hungry (Internat. Relief), 1985—, exec. com., 1986—, chmn. bd. dirs. 1987—; mem. Ariz. State U. Coun. of 100, 1985-89, investment com., 1985—. With USAF, 1961-64. Recipient various mil. awards. Mem. ABA, Ariz. Bar Assn., Maricopa County Bar Assn., AIME, Ariz. Acad., U. Ariz. Alumni Assn., Clan McRae Soc. N.Am., Tau Beta Pi. Republican. Clubs: Phoenix Exec., Phoenix Country, Ariz., Continental Country, Jackson Hole Racquet (Wyo.). Home: 8101 N 47th St Paradise Valley AZ 85253 Office: Republic Cos 5500 N 24th St Phoenix AZ 85016

MCREYNOLDS, ALLEN, JR., investment company executive; b. Carthage, Mo., Dec. 25, 1909; s. Allen and Maude (Clark) McR.; m. Virginia Madeleine Hensley, Jan. 17, 1946; children: Sharron Anne, Amy Elizabeth, Mary Armilda, Allen IV. Student, N.Mex. Mil. Inst., 1926-29, U. Mo., 1929-31. Pres. Joplin (Mo.) Stockyards, Inc., 1945-83; v.p., dir. First Nat. Bank, Monett, Mo., 1943-80; v.p., cashier First Nat. Bank, Golden City, Mo., 1950-56; dir. First Nat. Bancorp, Joplin, 1982-87. Pres. Jasper County Assn. for Soc. Services, 1976-78, Mo. State Southern Coll. Found., Joplin, 1984-85. Democrat. Episcopalian. Home: 1202 Mississippi Joplin MO 64801 Office: 1st Nat Mercantile Bank Bldg Room 408 Joplin MO 64801

MCREYNOLDS, NEIL LAWRENCE, electric utility company executive; b. Seattle, July 27, 1934; s. Dorr E. and Margaret (Gillies) McR.; m. Nancy Joyce Drew, June 21, 1957; children: Christopher, Bonnie. BA in Journalism, U. Wash., 1956. Assoc. editor Bellevue (Wash.) Am., 1956-60, editor, 1960-67; press sec. to Gov. Dan Evans State of Wash., Olympia, 1967-73; N.W. regional mgr. for pub. rels. and pub. affairs ITT Corp., Seattle, 1973-80; v.p. corp. rels. Puget Sound Power & Light, Bellevue, 1980-87, sr. v.p., 1987—; bd. dirs. Contential Savs. Bank, Seattle; chmn. communications adv. com. Electric Power Rsch. Inst., 1989. Bd. dirs. Pub. Affairs Coun., 1981—, Seattle Symphony, 1981—, Ind. Colls. of Wash., 1984—; state chmn. Nature Conservancy, 1989; vice chmn., bd. dirs. Fred Hutchison Cancer Rsch. Ctr. Found., 1987-89; bd. dirs. Corp. Coun. for Arts, 1985—; chmn. bd. dirs. Leadership Tomorrow, Seattle, 1987; pres. Electric Info. Coun., 1988—. Named Citizen of Yr., Bellevue, 1963, One of Wash. State's Three Outstanding Young Men, 1965. Mem. Public Rels. Soc. Am. (accredited), N.W. Electric Light & Power Assn. (pres. 1982-83), Greater Seattle C. of C., LaVics Club (Bellevue), Rainier Club, Overlake Golf & Country Club, Bellevue Athletic Club, Rotary (v.p. Seattle club 1988-89), Sigma Delta Chi. Republican. Episcopalian. Home: 14315 SE 45th St Bellevue WA 98006 Office: Puget Sound Power & Light Co PO Box 97034 Bellevue WA 98009-9734

MCRITCHIE, BRUCE DEAN, advertising agency executive; b. Buffalo, Apr. 12, 1938; s. D.R. and Augusta Louise (Schmidt) McR.; m. Barbara A. Baske, Dec. 8, 1962; children: Marilyn, Scott, John. AB, U. Mich., 1960, MBA, 1961. Media buyer Leo Burnett Inc., Chgo., 1962-64; acct. exec. Leo Burnett Inc., 1964-71; v.p., account supr. Grey Advt., Detroit, 1971-75; sr. v.p., mgmt. supr. Marschalk Co., Cleve., 1975-78, Kenyon & Eckhardt, Detroit, 1979-81; sr. v.p., gen. mgr. Grey Advt., Detroit, 1981-85; sr. v.p., gen. mgr. Grey Advt., Orange County, Calif., 1986-88, exec. v.p., gen. mgr., 1988—. Mem. Adcraft Club Detroit. Office: Grey Advt Inc 6400 W Katella Ave Ste 200 Cypress CA 90630-5208

MCSHEFFERTY, JOHN, research company executive; b. Akron, Ohio, Mar. 14, 1929; s. John and Jean (Conway) McS.; m. Glenna Gloria Childs, Apr. 18, 1959; children: John III, Amy Childs. BSc, U. Glasgow, 1953,

PhD, 1957. Various rsch. positions Sterling Winthrop Rsch. Inst., Rensselaer, N.Y., 1957-62; dir. pharm. devel. Ortho Pharm. Corp. div. Johnson and Johnson, Raritan, N.J., 1962-75; dir. sci. affairs Janssen R & D, Inc., Piscataway, N.J., 1975-77; v.p. R & D family prods. Internat. Playtex, Paramus, N.J., 1977-79; pres. Gillette Rsch. Inst., Gaithersburg, Md., 1979—. Fellow Royal Pharm. Soc. of Great. Britain; mem. Indsl. Rsch. Inst. (bd. dirs. 1988—), Am. Acad. Dermatology, Am. Chem. Soc., Am. Pharm. Assn., Soc. Cosmetic Chemists, Assn. Rsch. Dirs., Sigma Xi. Office: Gillette Rsch Inst 401 Professional Dr Gaithersburg MD 20879

MCSHERRY, JAMES FRANCIS, small business owner, management consultant; b. Chgo., Apr. 18, 1953; s. John Patrick and Evelyn Agatha (Donohue) McS.; m. Peggy Ann Prunty, Oct. 10, 1976; children: Kathleen, Patrick, Meghan, Erin. BS in Bus. Mgmt., John Carroll U., 1975. Mktg. mgr. Union Carbide Corp., Chgo., 1975-77; mgr. ter. sales Union Carbide Corp., Indpls., 1977-79; mgr. regional sales Union Carbide Corp., Milw., 1979-81; v.p. exec. search McSherry & Assocs., Inc., Chgo., 1981-83; prin. exec. search Dieckmann & Assocs., Ltd., Chgo., 1983—. Regional sch. chmn. Joliet (Ill.) Cath. Diocese, 1983—; pres. St. Margaret Mary Parish Coun., Naperville, Ill., 1986—; mem. corp. fundraising com. Mental Health Assn., Chgo., 1984-87. Mem. Am. Mktg. Assn., Human Resource Mgmt. Assn., Employment Mgmt. Assn. Chgo., Univ. Club. Republican. Home: 837 Turnbridge Circle Naperville IL 60540 Office: Dieckmann & Assocs Ltd 75 E Wacker Dr Ste 1800 Chicago IL 60601

MCSHERRY, RICHARD THOMAS, stock brokerage executive; b. N.Y.C., Sept. 7, 1936; s. Richard Thomas and Josephine (McCooey) McS.; m. Ursula Mary Healy, June 4, 1960; children: Jeanne-Marie, Richard Thomas Jr. BBA, St. John's U., 1958. Mktg. exec. IBM, N.Y.C., 1963-81, Chase Bank, N.Y.C., 1981-84; exec. v.p. mktg. and client rels. Abel/Noser Group, N.Y.C., 1984—. Roman Catholic. Office: Abel/Noser Corp 90 Broad St New York NY 10004

MCSWEENY, JOHN EDWARD, defense industry executive; b. San Mateo, Calif., July 19, 1936; s. Edward Joseph and Alice (Barrett) McS.; m. Aug. 26, 1967; children: Sean Edward, Patrick Michael, Erin Marie, Kevin Joseph. BSEE, Loyola U., L.A., 1959; MSEE, U. Colo., 1961. Registered profl. engr., Calif. Electronics engr. Gen. Dynamics Pomona (Calif.) Div., 1961-66, design specialist, 1966-69, sect. head, 1969-70, sr. project engr., 1970-72, dir. phalanx program, 1972-76, v.p., program dir. Navy moderate range tactical weapons, 1976-80, v.p., dep. gen. mgr. programs, 1980-81, v.p., dep. gen mgr. fin. and adminstrn., 1981-82; v.p., gen. mgr. Gen. Dynamics Convair Div., San Diego, 1982—. Mem. Am. Def. Preparedness Assn., Navy League. Roman Catholic. Office: Gen Dynamics/Convair Div PO Box 85357 San Diego CA 92138 also: Gen Dynamics Corp Pierre Laclede Ctr Saint Louis MO 63105

MCSWEENY, WILLIAM FRANCIS, petroleum company executive; b. Haverhill, Mass., Mar. 31, 1929; s. William Francis and Mary Florence (Doyle) McS.; m. Dorothy Pierce, Jan. 20, 1969; children—William Francis III, Cathy Ann, Ethan Madden Maverick, Terrell Pierce. Reporter, columnist, fgn. corr. Hearst Newspapers, 1943-67; dep. chmn., dir. pub. affairs Democratic Nat. Com., 1967-68; spl. asst. to White House Chief of Staff, 1968-69; sr. exec. v.p., bd. dirs. Occidental Internat. Corp., Washington, 1969—, pres., 1976—; exec. v.p. Occidental Petroleum Corp., Washington, 1984—; dir. Fin. Gen. Bankshares Co., Washington, 1978-82, Chevy Chase Savs. and Loan, 1985—; mem. Lloyd's of London. Author: Go Up for Glory, 1965, Violence Every Sunday, 1966, The Impossible Dream, 1967; contbr. articles to profl. jours. Bd. visitors Fletcher Sch. Law and Diplomacy, Tufts U.; bd. advisers Karl F. Landegger Program Internat. Bus. Diplomacy, Sch. Fgn. Service, Georgetown U.; chmn. Meridan House Internat., life trustee; bd. dirs. Washington Soc. Performing Arts, Nat. Arts for Handicapped, Arena Stage, Corcoran Gallery Art, Africare, Fed. City Council, Washington Opera, Folger Shakespeare Theater, USO; bd. dirs., chmn. Ford Theatre, 1988—, Cities in Schs. Nat. Learning Ctr.; v.p. Ct. of the Mary Rose, Portsmouth, Eng.; mem. U.S. Commn. UNESCO; trustee Holton Arms Sch.; chmn. Washington Episcopal Sch.; mem. Presdl. Commn., 1976-80; Pres.'s Rep. to USSR, 1979; mem. Pres.'s Inaugural Com., 1980, 84; Presdl. spl. rep. Oman, 1980; Pres's spl. rep. to Bolivia, 1982; Pres.'s Commn. Korean War Meml., 1987; spl. counsel Speaker of Ho. of Reps., 1971-72; active World Affairs Council; mem. exec. council on fgn. diplomats Dept. of State; bd. dirs. The Atlantic Coun. Served to maj. AUS, 1950-53. Decorated Combat Inf. badge; recipient Outstanding Young Man award Boston Jaycees, 1961, U.S. Disting. Service award, 1968, outstanding service spl. award, 1969, D.C. disting. citizen, 1981, Paul Hill award Kennedy Ctr., 1983, D.C. Cultural Award, 1983; numerous awards for domestic reporting, awards for reporting from Vietnam and Middle East including Best U.S. Reporting, 1963. Mem. Smithsonian Inst. (mem. nat. adv. com. Kellogg Project), Arms Control Assn. Clubs: Cosmos, 1925 F Street, Internat. (Washington). also: Occidental Petroleum Corp 10889 Wilshire Blvd Los Angeles CA 90024

MCTAGUE, JOHN PAUL, automobile manufacturing company executive, chemist; b. Jersey City, Nov. 28, 1938; s. James Aloysius and Teresa Eugenia (Hanley) McT.; m. Carole Frances Reilly, Dec. 30, 1961; children: Kevin W., Catherine E., Margaret A., Maureen E. BS in Chemistry, Georgetown U., 1960; PhD, Brown U., 1965. Mem. tech. staff N.Am. Rockwell Sci. Ctr., Thousand Oaks, Calif., 1964-70; prof. chemistry, mem. Inst. Geophysics and Planetary Physics UCLA, 1970-82; chmn. nat. synchrotron light source dept. Brookhaven Nat. Lab., Upton, N.Y., 1982-83; dep. dir. Office Sci. and Tech. Policy, Exec. Office of Pres., Washington, 1983-86, acting sci. advisor to Pres. Reagan, 1986; v.p. rsch. Ford Motor Co., Dearborn, Mich., 1986—; adj. prof. chemistry Columbia U., 1982-83. Alfred P. Sloan Research fellow, 1971-73; NATO sr. fellow, 1973; John Simon Guggenheim Meml. fellow, 1975-76. Fellow Am. Phys. Soc.; mem. Am. Chem. Soc. (Calif. sect. award 1975), AAAS, Soc. Automotive Engrs., Engring. Soc. Detroit, Sigma Xi, Barton Hills Country Club. Office: Ford Motor Co 20000 Rotunda Dr Sci Rsch Lab Bldg Rm S2106 PO Box 1603 Dearborn MI 48121-1603

MCTEAGUE, BERTRAND LUKE, investment banker; b. Hartford, Conn., Mar. 30, 1935; s. Raymond Wickersham and Katherine (Clary) M.; m. Anneliese Saur, Dec. 8, 1955 (div.); children—Sharon McTeague, Brendan Michael McTeague. BBA Western New Eng. Coll., 1964. Exec. v.p., ptnr. Advest, Inc., Hartford, 1965-71; pres. McTeague & Co., Hartford, 1972—; chmn. Sharbren Devel., Co.; bd. dir. Sage-Allen & Co., Hartford, Lydall, Inc., Manchester, Conn., The Schiavone Corp., New Haven; mem. faculty Practicing Law Inst., 1972-74. Contbg. author: Management Handbook Inc., 1981, also article. Trustee Western New Eng. Coll., Springfield, Mass., 1979; fund raiser St. Peter's Church Restoration, Hartford, 1982; founder F-200 Club, Hartford, 1983. Served to sgt. U.S. Army, 1954-56. Mem. Nat. Assn. Securities Dealers, Hartford Soc. Fin. Analysts (founder), Fin. Analysts Fedn., Conn. Investment Bankers Assn. (pres.), Conn. Venture Group (dir. Central Conn. chpt.). Democrat. Roman Catholic. Clubs: Hartford; Union (Boston). Office: McTeague & Co 241 Main St Hartford CT 06106

MCVAY, MICHAEL ALVIN, radio broadcasting service executive; b. Mount Pleasant, Pa., Sept. 12, 1953; s. Richard Alvin and Wilma Eleanor (Ferguson) M.; m. Doris Elaine Hammond, Dec. 17, 1977; children: Nicole Summer, Jessica Michelle. Grad. high sch., Greensburg, Pa. On-air talent Sta. WMBS Radio, Uniontown, Pa., 1970-72; program dir. Sta. WEIF, Wheeling, W.Va., 1972-73, Sta. WNEU, Wheeling, 1973-76, Sta. WCHS, Charleston, W.Va., 1976-78, Sta. KTNQ, L.A., 1978-79; ops. mgr. Sta. WAKY (formerly Sta. WWWE), Louisville, 1979-81; gen. mgr. Sta. WABB-AM-FM, Mobile, Ala., 1981-82, Sta. WMJI-WBBG, Cleve., 1982-84; pres., chief exec. officer McVay Media, Cleve., 1984—; announcer Sta. WLTF, Cleve., 1988—; cons. Dick Clark Orgn., L.A., 1985—. Columnist Radio At-Work, 1986, Radio Only mag., 1987—; contbr. articles to mags.; creator "Magic" radio format, 1981; patentee Car Tunes, 1988. Advisor Big Bros. Wheeling, 1976-77. Mem. Nat. Assn. Broadcasters, Broadcast Promotion and Mktg. Assn. Democrat. Lutheran. Home: 240 Seaward Way Avon Lake OH 44012 Office: McVay Media 24650 Center Ridge Rd Ste 148 Cleveland OH 44145

MCWALTER, J(OHN) BRYCE, stockbroker, financial planner; b. Seattle, Oct. 28, 1949; s. Jack and Marie C. (Bryce) McW.; m. Maureen B. Pereira, Aug. 11, 1973; children: John Michael, Jaclyn Marie, Jason Bryce. BA, Seattle U., 1972; MBA, Pepperdine U.-Honolulu, 1974. Cert. fin. planner. Account exec. Dean Witter Reynolds, Inc., Seattle, 1976-83, asst. br. mgr., Northgate, Seattle, 1983-86, assoc. v.p. dowtown Seattle office, 1986—; lectr. Chaminade U. Honolulu, 1974-76; instr. U. Puget Sound, 1980-82. Rep. precinct committeeman, King County, Seattle, 1980-84, 1986—; coach Interbay 7-11 Men's Softball Team, 1977-84; chmn. prize com. Cystic Fibrosis Celebrity Golf Tournament, 1986, putting contest, 1987, 88, 89; chmn. Seattle Prep 68 Reunion, 1988; coach Little League, 1989—. Capt. U.S. Army, 1972-76, maj. Res. Mem. Jaycees (pres. treas. Interbay 1977-80, Honolulu Jaycee of Month, 1975, Keyman award 1976), Inst. Fin. Planners, Seattle U. Alumni Assn. (bd. govs.), Res. Officers Assn., Ballard C. of C., U.S. Golf Assn. Roman Catholic. Clubs: College (Seattle), Seattle Downtown Exch. Club. Home: 2621 27th St W Seattle WA 98199 Office: Dean Witter Reynolds Inc 2800 Rainier Bank Tower 1301 5th Ave Seattle WA 98101

MCWHORTER, RALPH CLAYTON, health care company executive; b. Chattanooga, 1933. B.S., Samford U., 1955; postgrad., U. Tenn. Asst. adminstr. Phoebe Putney Meml. Hosp., 1956-65; adminstr. Americus-Sumter County Hosp., 1965-67, City-County Hosp., 1967-70; adminstr. Palmyra Park Hosp. Hosp. Corp. Am., Nashville, 1970-73, div. v.p., 1973-76, sr. v.p. hosp. ops. U.S., 1976-80, exec. v.p. domestic ops., 1980-85, pres., chief operating officer, 1985-87, also bd. dirs.; chmn., chief exec. officer HealthTrust, Inc., Nashville, 1988—. Office: HealthTrust Inc 4525 Harding Rd Nashville TN 37203 *

MEACHAM, JAC DAVID, human resources executive; b. Aurora, Ill., Aug. 9, 1930; s. Ralph Vincent and Gertrude E. (Mortimer) M.; m. Ikuko Akita; children: Jennifer Akita, Stephanie Akita. AA, San Diego City Coll., 1952, BS, 1964; MBA, Pepperdine U., 1974. Dir. personnel devel. Continental Airlines, Los Angeles, 1966-70; dir. personnel resources Flying Tiger Line, Calif., 1970-79; exec. Phototron, San Bernardino, Calif., 1979-83; human resources exec. Lockheel Corp., Saudi Arabia, 1983-85, McDonnell Douglas, Long Beach, Calif., 1985—; cons. Crow Indians, Crow Agy., Mont., 1976-78, Covington Industries, Redlands, Calif., 1978-79. Author: Critical Path, 1986, Corporate Spy, 1986, Crowded Brutal Skies, 1987, Dead-Weight, 1988, Million Dollar Manhunt, 1988. Served as maj. USMC, 1952-57, Korea. Mem. Mystery Writers Am., Nat. Writers Club. Office: McDonnell Douglas 3855 Lakewood 204 34 Long Beach CA 90846

MEAD, GEORGE WILSON, II, paper company executive; b. Milw., Oct. 11, 1927; s. Stanton W. and Dorothy (Williams) M.; m. Helen Patricia Anderson, Sept. 3, 1949; children: Deborah, David, Leslie. B.S., Yale U., 1950; M.S., Inst. Paper Chemistry, Wis., 1952. With Consol. Papers, Inc., Wisconsin Rapids, Wis., 1952—, v.p. ops., 1962-66, pres., chief exec. officer, 1966-71, chmn. bd., chief exec. officer, 1971—, also dir.; pres., dir. Consol. Water Power Co.; chmn. bd. 1st Nat. Bank; bd. dirs. Soo Line R.R., Snap-On Tools Corp. Co-chmn. bldg. fund drive Riverview Hosp., Wisconsin Rapids, 1963-64, mem. bd., 1961-77; bd. dirs. Consol.'s Civic Found.; bd. dirs. Nat. Council for Air and Stream Improvement; trustee Lawrence U., Inst. Paper Chemistry; chmn. bd. trustees Inst. Paper Sci. and Tech., 1988-90. Mem. Am. Paper Inst. (dir. 1967-69, 80—), TAPPI (dir. 1969-72), Wis. Paper Industry Information Service (gen. chmn. 1964-65), Wis. Paper and Pulp Mfrs. Traffic Assn. (exec. com. 1963-75, dir., pres. 1973). Clubs: Milw. Athletic; Chicago. Lodges: Elks (exalted ruler 1958), Rotarian. Office: Consol Papers Inc PO Box 8050 Wisconsin Rapids WI 54495-8050

MEAD, ROBERT L., grocery company executive. Chmn., dir. Assoc. Grocers Inc., Seattle; pres. Mead Foods of Selah (Wash.) Inc. Office: Associated Grocers Inc 3301 S Norfolk St Seattle WA 98118 Office: PO Box 538 Selah WA 98942 *

MEAD, WAYLAND MCCON, insurance holding company executive, lawyer; b. Roxbury, N.Y., Nov. 25, 1931; s. Irvin John and Dorothy (Seablom) M.; m. Barbara Jean Wales, Aug. 24, 1958; children: Michael John, David Scott, Deborah Ellen. B.S., Cornell U., 1953, J.D., 1958. Bar: N.Y. 1958. Assoc. Sage, Gray, Todd & Sims, N.Y.C., 1958-59; atty. Mut. Ins. Rating Bur., N.Y.C., 1959-62, Continental Ins. Co., N.Y.C., 1962-65; atty., then sec., counsel Am. Home Assurance Co., N.Y.C., 1965-75; sec., counsel Nat. Union Fire Ins. Co., N.Y.C., 1968-75; asst. v.p., counsel Am. Internat. Group, Inc., N.Y.C., 1969-75; v.p., gen. counsel Am. Internat. Group, Inc., 1975-82, sr. v.p., gen. counsel, 1982—; dir. Transatlantic Reins. Co., N.Y.C., AIU Ins. Co., N.Y.C., Commerce and Industry Ins. Co., N.Y.C.; chmn. ad hoc com. property and casualty ins. industry, N.Y.C., 1976. Bd. dirs. New Alternatives for Children, 1987—. Served with U.S. Army, 1953-55. Mem. ABA. Home: 22 Lucille Ct Massapequa NY 11758 Office: Am Internat Group Inc 70 Pine St New York NY 10005

MEADE, JAMES GORDON, public relations executive; b. Ionia, Mich., June 22, 1944; s. Henry L Meade and Gladys Marie (Spencer) Covington; m. Nina Rachel Permutt, July 7, 1968; children: Molly Heather, Benjamin Paul, Joshua Michael. BA, Hamilton Coll., 1966; MA, Northwestern U., 1967, PhD, 1971. Instr. Towson (Md.) State U., 1971-72; prof. Maharishi Internat. U., Fairfield, Iowa, 1972-75; writer Cape Cod Times, Hyannis, Mass., 1976-77; lectr. Boston U., 1978-80, Harvard U., Cambridge, Mass., 1978-80; writer Educators Pub. Svcs., Cambridge, Mass., 1977-80; writer, pub. rels. specialist Rath and Strong Systems Products, Lexington, Mass., 1981-82; mktg. specialist Digital Equipment Corp., Merrimack, N.H., 1982-84; founder, pres., chief exec. officer Meade Ink, Fairfield, Iowa, 1984—; cons. Voice Response Inc., Davenport, Iowa, Microsystems Engring., Chgo., Lotus Devel. Corp., Cambridge, MCI Communications, Washington. Author: Rights of Parents, 1978; contbr. articles to profl. jours. Nat. Def. Edn. Act fellow, 1967-70. Mem. Phi Beta Kappa. Home and Office: Meade Ink 608 E Burlington Fairfield IA 52556

MEADE, STEPHEN ALAN, insurance company executive; b. Boston, Nov. 22, 1949; s. Richard Alan and Rosemary (Coakley) M.; m. Donna Marie Dianto, Sept. 12, 1971 (div. Mar. 1981); m. Mary Lou Fountain, Apr. 23, 1983; children: Christine, Michelle. BS, Boston State Coll., 1971. CPCU. Planning dir. Fireman's Fund Ins. Co., San Francisco, 1977-78, sr. project dir., 1978-81; asst. v.p. San Francisco Reins. Co., 1981-85; v.p. Balboa Ins. Group, Irvine, Calif., 1985-86, sr. v.p., 1986-88; pres. Fin. Frontiers, Santa Ana, Calif., 1988—; bd. dirs. Avco Fin. Ins. Group, Irvine, 1986—. Served with USNG, 1970-76. Recipient Acad. Excellence award Ins. Inst. Am., 1981. Episcopalian. Home: 2329 N Linwood Ave Santa Ana CA 92701 Office: Balboa Ins Group 3347 Michelson Dr Ste 400 Irvine CA 92715

MEADER, CRAIG ALAN, banker; b. Plainville, Kans., Oct. 17, 1957; s. Dale A. Meader and Joan B. (Walker) Meader. BBA, Kearney State Coll., 1979. Agt. Security Mut. Life Ins., Kearney, Nebr., 1977-81; exec. v.p. First Nat. Bank, Waverly, Kans., 1981-88, Meader Ins. Agy., Inc., Waverly, 1982—; pres., chief exec. officer, chmn. bd. First Nat. Bank, Waverly, 1988—; bd. dirs. First Nat. Bank, Meader Ins. Agy., Inc., Waverly, Coffey County Bank Shares, Strawn State Bank, Burlington, Kans. Councilman, City of Waverly, 1987-88; bd. dirs. Econ. Devel. Council. Coffey County, Kans.; active Waverly Booster Club. Mem. Kans. Bankers Assn. (edn. com. 1987—), Young Bank Officers Kans., Masons. Office: First Nat Bank PO Box 398 Waverly KS 66871

MEADER, JOHN DANIEL, judge; b. Ballston Spa, N.Y., Oct. 22, 1931; s. Jerome Clement and Doris Luella (Conner) M.; m. Joyce Margaret Cowin, Mar. 2, 1963; children: John Daniel Jr., Julia Rae, Keith Alan. BA, Yale U., 1954; JD, Cornell U., 1962. Bar: N.Y. 1963, U.S. Dist. Ct. (no. dist.) N.Y. 1963, U.S. Ct. Appeals (2d cir.) 1966, U.S. Supreme Ct. 1967, U.S. Ct. Mil. Appeals 1973, Ohio 1978, U.S. Dist. Ct. (no. dist.) Ohio 1979, Fla. 1983. Sales engr. Albany Internat., Inc. (N.Y.), 1954-59; asst. track coach Cornell U., 1959-62; asst. sec., asst. to pres. Albany Internat., Inc., 1962-65; asst. atty. gen. state N.Y., Albany, 1965-68; ops. counsel, attesting sec. Gen. Electric Co., Schenectady, 1968-77; gen. counsel, asst. sec. SCM Corp., Glidden Div., Cleve., 1977-81; chmn. bd., pres. Applied Power Tech. Co., Fernandina Beach, Fla., 1981-84; pres. Applied Energy, Inc., Ballston Spa, N.Y., 1984-88; judge N.Y. State Workers Compensation Bd., Albany, 1988—; dir. Saratoga Mut. Fire Ins. Co. Candidate, U.S. Ho. of Reps., 29th Dist. N.Y., 1964, N.Y. Supreme Ct., 1975, 87. Serving as col. JAGC, USAR, 1968—, dep. staff judge adv. 3d U.S. Army, 1984. Nat. AAU Prep. sch. Track and Field Indoor Championships Outstanding Performer award Melrose Games Assn., 1950; Heptagonal Track 880 Yard Champion 1954; recipient Gardner Mallett award for courage, inspiration and sportsmanship Yale U., 1954. Mem. ABA, N.Y. State Bar Assn., Fla. Bar, Amelia Island Plantation Club (Fernandina Beach), Cyprus Temple Club, Masons (Schenectady), Yale Club of Jacksonville (pres.). Republican. Presbyterian. Author: Labor Law Manual, 1972; Contract Law Manual, 1974. Home: 271 Round Lake Rd Ballston Lake NY 12019 Office: N Y S Workers Compensation Bd 100 Broadway Albany NY 12241

MEADLOCK, JAMES W., computer graphics company executive; b. 1933; married. BSEE, N.C. State U., 1956. Dept. mgr. IBM, 1956-69; pres. Intergraph Corp., Huntsville, Ala., 1969—; also chmn. bd. dirs. Intergraph Corp., Huntsville. Office: Intergraph Corp 1 Madison Industrial Pk Huntsville AL 35807 *

MEADOR, DONALD JASON, manufacturing company executive; b. Atlanta, May 12, 1937; s. James William Meador and Christine (Bobo) Brown; m. Nancy Dunstan, June 4, 1955; children: Christy, Diane, Mark, Carol, Lynda. BSME, Clemson U., 1959. Sales engr. Reynolds Metals Co., Memphis, 1959-62; regional sales mgr. Tex. Instruments Co., Chgo. and Detroit, 1962-69; v.p. sales Ind. Gen., Valparaiso, 1969-71; regional gen. mgr. ITT-Grannell, Providence, R.I., 1971-74; pres. Peninsular Supply Co., Ft. Lauderdale, Fla., 1974-77; exec. v.p. Indsl. Distbn. Am., Atlanta, 1977-79; pres. Titeflex Co. (div. Bundy Corp.), Springfield, Mass., 1979-85; v.p., gen. mgr. Bundy Corp., Springfield, 1985—; dir. NTH-Rolon Co., Japan. Mem. Springfield C. of C. (bd. dirs. 1982-85). Office: Bundy Corp 603 Hendee St Springfield MA 01139

MEADOR, GREG WRAY, advertising and marketing executive; b. Amarillo, Tex., Feb. 4, 1957; s. L. Wray and Yvonne (Whipkey) M.; m. Debra Ann Baldwin, May 16, 1981; children: Jessica Marie, Whitney Suzanne. BS in Advt. and Mktg., Tex. Tech. U., 1980. Advt. account exec. Sta. KGNC-AM-FM, Amarillo, 1980-81; sr. account exec. Smith/Tarter Inc., Amarillo, 1981-85; mktg. dir. Maywood, Inc., Amarillo, 1985-87; ptnr. Meador and Holmes Advt. and Mktg., Amarillo, 1987—. Active Pursuit Ministries, Amarillo, 1987—. Presbyterian. Office: Meador and Holmes Advt 2807 W Sixth St PO Box 10246 Amarillo TX 79106

MEADOWS, JOHN THOMAS, financial consultant; b. Jacksonville, Fla., Apr. 3, 1961; s. John Saffold and Sheila (Jones) M. AA, Miami Dade Jr. Coll., Fla., 1980; BA, U. So. Fla., Tampa, 1983; M in Internat. Mgmt., Am. Grad. Sch. Internat. Mgmt., 1984. Asst. v.p. Am. Mcpl. Mortgage Co., Tampa, 1985-86; systems engr. Electronic Data Sys., Detroit, 1986; fin. cons. Miami, Fla., 1986-87, Met. Mortgage Co., Miami, 1987—. Author: Death of an Englishman, 1988. Mem. exsec. com. Am. Heart Assn., Miami, 1987—. Mem. Am. Mktg. Assn., Coconut Jaycees, Lambda Zeta Kappa. Republican. Jewish. Clubs: Internat. Fin. (chmn. 1984), Agsim Soccer (pres. 1984). Home and Office: 2399 SW 26th Ln Miami FL 33133

MEAGHER, ROBERT JOSEPH, tax and financial planner; b. New Brunswick, N.J., Feb. 21, 1932; s. Edward A. and Helen (Morris) M.; m. Marilyn hayden, Oct. 17, 1953 (dec. Sept. 1978); children: Karen H., Sherrie A.; m. Mary A., July 12, 1980. BS in Acctg., St. Peters Coll., 1958. Cert. fin. planner. Pres. Sci., Inc., Scotch Plains, N.J., 1955-79; Pres. Kasmar, Inc., Tannersville, Pa., 1979—, also bd. dirs. Pres. Jr. Achievement, Monroe County, Pa., 1983-86. With USN, 1951-55. Mem. Inst. Cert. Fin. Planners, Nat. Assn. Tax Practitioners, Nat. Soc. Pub. Accts., Nat. Assn. Enrolled Agts. Roman Catholic. Office: Kasmar Taxkeeping Svc Rt 611 Box 345 Tannersville PA 18372

MEAKEM, CAROLYN S., investment executive; b. Columbus, Ohio, Jan. 11, 1936; d. Junius Dean and Mary Elizabeth (Thomas) Soliday: m. Thomas James Meakem, Aug. 26, 1956; children: Thomas James III, Timothy Dean, Traci Lynn. BS, West Liberty Coll., 1959; MEd., U. Md., 1970. Tchr. Westchester Elem. Sch., Ellicott City, Md., 1956-59, Riverdale (Md.) Elem. Sch., 1959-60, Buckingham Elem. Sch., Willingboro, N.J., 1962-64, Beacon Heights Elem. Sch., Riverdale, 1964-68; dir. Christian edn. Forest Lake Presbyn. Ch., Columbia, S.C., 1961-62; supr. student tchrs U. Md., College Park, 1968-69; tchr. Norwood Sch., Bethesda, Md., 1975-77; with Ferris and Co. Inc., Bethesda, 1978-88, v.p., 1984-86, sr. v.p., 1986-88, also bd. dirs.; sr. v.p. Legg Mason, Inc., Bethesda, 1988—; guest lectr. George Washington U., 1982-83; trustee, tchr. Wharton Sch. Security Industry Inst., Phila., 1986—; tchr., speaker Bus. Inst. for Educators Found., Bethesda, 1987—. Author: Teachers Activity Guide for Dental Health Education, 1973. Trustee, bd. dirs. Holton-Arms Sch., Bethesda, 1985—; mem. com. Nat. Econ. Edn. Found.; mem. leadership, steering com., Montgomery County; hon. mem. bd. Found. for Boys & Girls Homes of Md. Mem. Security Industry Assn. (regional coordinator econ. edn.), Internat. Assn. Fin. Planners. Presbyterian. Home: 10015 Kendale Rd Potomac MD 20854 Office: Legg Mason Wood Walker 6701 Democracy Blvd Ste 100 Bethesda MD 20817

MEANEY, MICHAEL PETER, controller; b. N.Y.C., Oct. 17, 1961; s. Edward F. and Mary B. (Zory) M. Mgr. accounts payable Corp. Printing Co., N.Y.C., 1982-83; asst. contr. Jackson, Lewis, Schnitzler & Krupman, 1983-86, contr., 1986—. Mem. Assn. Legal Adminstrs., Contrs. Exchange, Am. Payroll Assn. Republican. Roman Catholic. Office: Jackson Lewis Schnitzler & Krupman One N Broadway White Plains NY 10601

MEANS, DAVID HAMMOND, advertising executive; b. Lebanon, Pa., Dec. 15, 1928; s. W. Horace and June (Zimmerman) M.; m. Nancy N. Downes, June 21, 1952; children: Elizabeth N., Susan Z., Emily M., David H. B.A., Amherst Coll., 1950. With CIA, 1950-53; with N.W. Ayer Inc., 1953—, exec. v.p., 1976—, also dir.; mng. dir. Ayer U.S.A. and Ayer Enterprises, Inc. Mem. alumni exec. com. Taft Sch., 1967—; trustee Phila. Coll. Textiles and Sci.; bd. dirs. Phila. chpt. Care/Medico. Served to 1st lt. USAF, 1953. Mem. Bus. Profl. Advt. Assn., Psi Upsilon. Episcopalian. Clubs: Merion (Pa.) Golf; Amherst (N.Y.C.); Country of New Canaan (Conn.). Home: Wahackme Ln New Canaan CT 06840 Office: NW Ayer Inc 1345 Ave of the Americas New York NY 10105

MEARS, JOYCE LUND, management consultant; b. Davenport, Iowa, Aug. 20, 1937; d. Hilding Eugene and Thelma (Peitscher) Lund; m. Walter R. Mears, Aug. 4, 1963 (div. Dec. 1983); children: Stephanie Joy, Susan Marie. BFA, Drake U., 1960; postgrad., U. Va., 1984, George Mason Coll., 1985-86. Cert. tchr., Iowa. Travel coordinator Kennedy Summer White House, Hyannis, Mass., 1961; sec. Bank Am., Los Angeles, 1962; quality control Census Bur., Dept. Commerce, No. Va., 1980; owner, mgr. cons. firm J.L. Mears, Inc., McLean, Va., 1981—. Patentee tech cart. Bd. dirs. Deborah's Pl., Washington, 1982, Fairfax County (Va.) PTA, 1978, 84. Grantee Ctr. for Innovative Tech., 1988. Mem. MIT Enterprise Forum Washington/Balt., Mortar Bd., Kappa Kappa Gamma. Lutheran. Home: 1338 Potomac School Rd McLean VA 22101 Office: JL Mears Inc PO Box 8043 McLean VA 22106

MEARS, W. NORVALL, chemical company executive; b. Swartz, La., Oct. 6, 1933; s. Hilton Clifford and Mary Lucretia (Langston) M.; m. Mary Frances Pollard, June 7, 1957; children: William Randall, Laura Elizabeth. BS, U.S. Naval Acad., 1957. Systems analyst Southwestern Bell Telephone Co., Houston and St. Louis, 1962-65; inventory control supr. Tenn. Eastman Co., Kingsport, 1965-67; quality mgr. Dow Chem. U.S.A., Freeport, Tex., 1967—. Chmn. bd. advisers Salvation Army, Freeport, 1986-88; co-chmn. George Bush for U.S. Senate Com., Brazoria County, Tex., 1970; deacon Sharpstown Bapt. Ch., Houston, 1964. Lt. USNR, 1957-62. Mem. Am. Soc. Quality Control (cert.), Nat. Assn. Purchasing Mgmt. (cert.), Brazosport C. of C. (chmn. marine offshore com. 1983-85). Baptist. Home: 1431 McFadden Rd Lake Jackson TX 77566

MEBANE, BARBARA MARGOT, service company executive; b. Sylacauga, Ala., July 21, 1947; d. Audrey Dixon and Mary Ellen (Yaikow) Baxley; m. James Lewis Mebane, Dec. 31, 1971; 1 child, Cieson Brooke. Grad. high sch., Albany, Ga. Line performer J. Taylor Dance Co., Miami, Fla., 1964-65; sales mgr. Dixie Readers Service, Jackson, Miss., 1965-67; regional sales mgr. Robertson Products Co., Texarkana, Tex., 1967-75; owner, pres. Telco Sales, Svc. and Supply, Dallas, 1976—; mem. Dance Masters, Miami, 1975—; cons. Lewisville Ballet, Gallerie Dance Ensemble,

1982; choreographer music videos for pay/cable TV, 1985; co-owner ATS Svcs., Lewisville, Tex.; contract cons. for self-employed women. Author: Paper on Positive Thinking, 1983. Sponsor, St. Jude's Research Hosp., Memphis, Cancer Research Ctr., Dallas; mgr. Dance Connection. Mem. Nat. Fedn. Ind. Businesses, Female and Minority Owned Bus. League, Assoc. Gen. Contractors (assoc.), Female Exec. Club N.Y.C. Avocations: working with children; teaching dance; writing. Home: 3701 Twin Oak Ct Flower Mound TX 75028 Office: Telco Sales Svc and Supply PO Box 29763 Dallas TX 75229

MECKLER, ALAN MARSHALL, publisher, author; b. N.Y.C., July 25, 1945; s. Herman Louis and Lillian (Brodsky) M.; m. Ellen Laurie Finkelstein, Sept. 10, 1969; children—Naomi, Kate, Caroline, John. B.A., Columbia Coll., 1967; M.A., Columbia U., 1968, Ph.D., 1980. Pres., owner Meckler Pub., Westport, Conn., 1970—. Author: The Draft and Its Enemies, 1973; Micropublishing: A History of Scholarly Micropublishing in America, 1938-80, 1982; Complete Guide to Winning Lotteries by Mail, 1985. Served with USAR, 1969-75. Office: 11 Ferry Ln West Westport CT 06880

MEDAGLIA, ELIZABETH MARY HART, computer programmer; b. Birmingham, Eng., July 26, 1952; came to U.S., 1979; d. Eric Gordon Jones and Jean Margaret (Hart) Jones Hurst; m. Frank Anthony Medaglia, Apr. 11, 1982; children: Matthew Frank, Caroline Erica. Student, Sheffield (Eng.) Poly. Inst., 1973-74, Open U., Eng., 1975-77. Programmer, analyst Laycock Engring., Sheffield, Eng., 1974-77, Midland Computer Services, Manchester, Eng., 1977-79; with Mfrs. Hanover Trust Co., N.Y.C., 1979—; now info. systems officer. Mem. New Dorp Cen. Civic Assn. Office: Mfrs Hanover Trust Co 4 New York Pla 21st Fl New York NY 10015

MEDAVOY, MIKE, motion picture company executive; b. Shanghai, China, Jan. 21, 1941; came to U.S., 1957, naturalized, 1962; s. Michael and Dora M.; m. Patricia Duff; 1 child, Brian. B.A., UCLA, 1963. With Casting dept. Universal Studios, 1963; agt. Bill Robinson Assos., Los Angeles, 1963-64; v.p. motion picture dept. GAC/CMA Co., 1965-71, IFA Co., 1971-74; sr. v.p. United Artists Corp., 1974-78; exec. v.p. Orion Pictures Co., Burbank, Calif., 1978-82, Orion Pictures Corp. (formerly Orion Pictures Co.), Burbank, 1982—. Mem. vis. com. Boston Museum Fine Arts.; chmn. Ctr. Internat. Strategic Affairs, UCLA, Com. to Cure Cancer through Immunization UCLA; co-chmn. Olympic Sports Fedn. Com., Music Ctr. Unified Fund Campaign; bd. govs. Sundance Inst., 1980-86; bd. dirs. Calif. Mus. Sci. and Industry, 1984-87. Recipient Academy award for One Flew over the Cuckoo's Nest, Rocky, Annie Hall, Amadeus, Platoon. Mem. Acad. Motion Picture Arts and Scis. (gov. 1977-81), UCLA Found., UCLA Chancellors Assocs. Office: Orion Pictures Corp 1888 Century Pk E 7th Fl Los Angeles CA 90067 also: Orion Pictures Corp 711 Fifth Ave New York NY 10022

MEDFORD, DALE LEON, industrial company executive; b. Dayton, Ohio, May 24, 1950; s. Forest L. and Gertrude M. (Rismiller) M.; m. Karen L. Blair, June 12, 1971; children: Bethany, Kristina. BS in Acctg., Miami U., Oxford, Ohio, 1972. Treas. Reyna Fin. Corp., Dayton, 1981-86, pres., chief exec. officer, 1983-86; treas., asst. sec. The Reynolds and Reynolds Co., Dayton, 1979-81, v.p., treas., 1981-85, v.p. corp. fin., treas., 1985-86, v.p. corp. fin., chief fin. officer, 1986—. Pres. Dayton Opera Assn., 1986-88; trustee Dayton Performing Arts Fund, 1986-88; bd. dirs. Dayton da Vinci, 1987-88. Mem. AICPA, Fin. Execs. Inst. (pres. Dayton chpt. 1988—; officer, bd. dirs. 1984—). Lutheran. Office: Reynolds & Reynolds Co 115 S Ludlow St Dayton OH 45402

MEDHUS, SIGURD DUANE, financial executive; b. Leeds, N.D., Mar. 1, 1929; s. Sigurd and Cora (Nordhougen) M.; m. Dolores Estella Samuelson, Nov. 4, 1949; children—Susan Mary, Mark Steven, Karen Dolores, Eric Sigurd, Nancy Carol, Margaret Joyce, Patricia Louise, Olaf Andrew. BS in Bus. and Tech., Oreg. State U., 1950. With GE (and subs. cos., various locations), 1950—; v.p. fin. Canadian Gen. Elec. Co. Ltd., Toronto, 1971-73; v.p., gen. mgr. consumer financing, bus. dept. Gen. Electric Credit Corp., Stamford, Conn., 1973-76; v.p. fin., treas., dir., mem. exec. com. Hoffmann-LaRoche, Inc., Nutley, N.J., 1976-80; exec. v.p., chief fin. officer Am. Express Co., N.Y.C., 1980-82; exec. v.p., chief fin. officer, dir. U.S. Industries Inc., Stamford, 1982-84; exec. v.p. First City Capital Corp., N.Y.C., 1985; sr. v.p., chief fin. officer Olin Corp., 1986-88; ret. 1989. Bd. dirs. Vis. Nurses Assn., Stamford, 1967-69, Urban Redevel. Commn., Stamford, 1971. Mem. Fin. Execs. Inst., Treasurers Club N.Y.C. Home: 10 Ocean Dr N Stamford CT 06902

MEDINA, ILDEFONSO MIRANDA, computer company executive; b. Pasay, The Philippines, Jan. 23, 1948; came to U.S., 1984; s. Galicano Celestino and Teodorica (Miranda) M.; m. Teresita Matamis Calupitan, June 8, 1974; children: Chris Edward, Ian Charles. BEE, Mapua Inst. Tech., Manila, 1970. Mgr. sales Burroughs Ltd., Manila, 1970-77; v.p. Floro Enterprises, Inc., Manila, 1977-82; pres., gen. mgr. Computerpoint, Inc., Manila, 1982-84; pres. Systems and Encoding Corp., Flushing, N.Y., 1984—. Mem. Info. Industry Assn., N.Y. Personal Computer User Group, Data Entry Mgmt. Assn. (cert. in data mgmt.). Lodge: Rotary.

MEDLEY, SHERRILYN, auditor; b. Oneida, Ky., Sept. 7, 1946; d. Ora E. and Rheba (Allen) Rice; m. James F. Laughlin, Sept. 20, 1966 (div. Apr. 1969); m. James Silas Medley, Jan. 25, 1980. BS in Acctg., U. Ky., 1975; MBA, Xavier U., 1986. Cert. internal auditor, cert. fraud examiner. Tchr. Ky. Bus. Coll., Lexington, 1976-78; claims approver Met. Life Ins. Co., Lexington, 1967-73; staff acct. Jerrico, Inc., Lexington, 1976-77, acctg. supr., 1977-80, sr. auditor, 1980-82, internal audit supr., 1982-86; internal audit mgr., 1986-87; sr. internal. audit mgr., 1988—. Vol. Cen. Bapt. Aux., Lexington, 1984. Mem. Inst. Internal Auditors (chpt. pres. 1985-86), Nat. Assn. Accts., Bluegrass Soc. MBA's, Am. Assn. Female Execs. Beta Alpha Psi. Republican. Home: 2436 Brookshire Circle Lexington KY 40505

MEDLIN, JOHN GRIMES, JR., banker; b. Benson, N.C., Nov. 23, 1933; s. John Grimes and Mabel (Stephenson) M. BS in Bus. Adminstrn., U. N.C., 1956; grad., The Exec. Program, U. Va., 1965. With Wachovia Bank & Trust Co., Winston-Salem, N.C., 1959—, pres., 1974; pres., chief exec. officer Wachovia Bank and Wachovia Corp., Winston-Salem, N.C., 1977, chmn., chief exec. officer, 1985; pres., chief exec. officer First Wachovia Corp., Winston-Salem, N.C., 1985, also bd. dirs., chmn.; bd. dirs. USAir Group, Inc., RJR Nabisco, Inc., First Wachovia Corp., BellSouth Corp., Nat. Service Industries, Inc. Active numerous civic and service orgns.; trustee Wake Forest U., Nat. Urban League; mem. N.C. Bus. Council Mgmt. and Devel.; bd. dirs. Kenan Inst. of Pvt. Enterprise. Served as officer USNR, 1956-59. Mem. Assn. Res. City Bankers (past pres.), Am. Bankers Assn., Order Holy Grail, Order Old Well, Phi Delta Theta. Club: Old Town (Winston-Salem). Lodge: Rotary (pres. Winston-Salem 1973—). Office: 1st Wachovia Corp 301 N Main St PO Box 3099 Winston-Salem NC 27150

MEDNICK, ROBERT, accountant; b. Chgo., Apr. 1, 1940; s. Harry and Nettie (Brenner) M.; m. Susan Lee Levinson, Oct. 28, 1962; children—Michael Jon, Julie Eden, Adam Charles. B.S. in Bus. Adminstrn., Roosevelt U., Chgo., 1962. CPA, Ill. Staff asst. Arthur Andersen & Co., Chgo., 1962-63, sr. acct., 1963-66, mgr., 1966-71, ptnr., 1971—, mng. dir. SEC policies, 1973-76, mng. dir. auditing procedures, 1976-79, vice chmn. profl. standards, 1979-82, chmn. com. profl. standards, 1982—. Contbr. articles to profl. jours. Bd. dirs. Roosevelt U., Chgo., 1980—, vice chmn., 1986—; co-chmn. adv. council Chgo. Action for Soviet Jewry, Highland Park, Ill., 1983-87. Served to sgt. USAFR, 1965-69. Recipient Silver medal Ill. CPA Soc., 1962; named One of Ten Outstanding Young Men in Chgo., Chgo. Jr. C. of C., 1973-74; recipient Rolf A. Weil Disting. Service award, Roosevelt U., Chgo., 1983; Max Block award N.Y. State C.P.A. Soc., 1984; Ann. Literary award Jour. Acctg., 1986, 88. Mem. Am. Inst. CPAs (bd. dirs., 1986-87, numerous coms., Elijah Watt Sells award 1962), Am. Acctg. Assn., Ill. CPA Soc. (acctg. principles com. 1973, legal liability com. 1986—). Jewish. Clubs: Mid-Day, Standard (Chgo.); Elms Swim & Tennis (Highland Park).

MEDVEY, ROBERT EMERY, investment banker; b. Norwalk, Conn., Mar. 18, 1946; s. Emery John and Viola Ann (Sadanos) M.; m. Patricia Ann Antolics, Sept. 3, 1965; children: Cathryn, Robert. BA in Acctg., U. Conn., 1968; MA, Fairfield U., 1980. Corp. banking officer Hartford (Conn.) Nat. Bank & Trust Co., 1968-72; v.p. fin. Largo Adv. Corp., Stamford, Conn., 1972-73; v.p. Conn. Bank and Trust Co., Darien, 1973-81, Daseke & Co., Westport, Conn., 1981-86; pres. Asset Devel., Inc., Stamford, 1986—; bd. dirs. Home Care Corp., Stamford, 1986—, Continue Care, Stamford, 1986—. Dist. vice chmn. Fairfield Rep. Town Com., 1975-76; treas., mem. exec. bd. Jennings Sch. PTA, 1974-76; co-chmn. Fairfield Spl. Olympics, 1975; mem. town of Fairfield Tennis Com., 1974. Mem. Stamford Area Commerce and Industry Assn., Fairfield Jaycees (v.p., bd. dirs.). Republican. Roman Catholic. Clubs: Landmark, Woodway Country, Long Ridge Tennis. Lodge: Rotary (Stamford) (bd. dirs.). Home: 248 Wood House Rd Fairfield CT 06430 Office: Asset Devel Inc 60 Guernsey Ave Stamford CT 06901

MEE, JOHN LAWRENCE, computer company executive; b. Yonkers, N.Y., Jan. 3, 1950; s. Frank Everett and Penelope (Baker) M.; m. Catherine Louise Bennett, Apr. 25, 1986. Student, Wesleyan U. Pres. Lexicon Chandler Corp., Phoenix, 1979—. Patentee in field. Home: 3819 E Camelback Rd Phoenix AZ 85018 Office: Lexicon Chandler Corp 2502 E North Ln Phoenix AZ 85028

MEEDER, LORIN SHIRLEY, credit union executive; b. Denver, July 7, 1936; s. Lorin A. and Gladys E. (Shirley) M.; m. Geraldine L. Torscher, June 18, 1958; children: Barbara L., Kathleen C. BSBA, U. Denver, 1958, MSBA, 1968. With Ford Motor Co., Denver, 1962-68; asst. br. mgr. Fed. Res. Bank, Denver, 1968-73; assoc. dir. Fed. Res. Bd. of Govs., Washington, 1973-83; gen. mgr. U.S. Cen. Credit Union, Overland Park, Kans., 1983—; pres., chmn. bd. Corp. Network Brokerage Svcs., Inc., 1989—. Lt. (j.g.) USN, 1958-62. Republican. Roman Catholic.

MEEHAN, DAVID HOWARD, insurance company executive; b. New Castle, Pa., Nov. 11, 1928; s. Howard Platt and Cienwen (Lewis) M.; m. Nancy M. Kiebort, Sept. 5, 1953; children: Mary Beth, Molly, Martha, David, John. B.A. in Econs., Allegheny Coll., 1950. Supt. USF&G, Pitts., 1953-61; supt. USF&G, Balt., 1961-66, asst. v.p., 1966-72, v.p., 1972-80, sr. v.p., 1980-82, exec. v.p., 1982—; advisor Balt. Local Initiative Support Corp., 1982—. Bd. dirs. Hood Coll., 1981-86. Served with U.S. Army, 1950-52. Office: US Fidelity & Guaranty Co 100 Light St PO Box 1138 Baltimore MD 21202

MEEHAN, JOSEPH GERARD, manufacturing executive; b. Washington, Dec. 27, 1931; s. Michael Joseph and Regina Adele (Lanigan) M.; m. Anne Mary McCue, Sept. 18, 1954; children: Joanne, Patricia, Michael, David. BA in Econs., Georgetown U., 1954. Various fin. mgmt. positions GE, 1956-80; sr. v.p., chief fin. officer Rubbermaid Inc., Wooster, Ohio, 1980—. Co-editor: The CFO's Handbook, 1984. Bd. dirs., treas. Hospice Wayne County, Wooster, 1983-86. 1st lt. USAF, 1954-56. Mem. Fin. Execs. Inst., Wooster Area C. of C. (bd. dirs.), Kiwanis (treas. 1970-73). Republican. Roman Catholic. Home: 581 W Wayne Ave Wooster OH 44691 Office: Rubbermaid Inc 1147 Akron Rd Wooster OH 44691

MEEHAN, ROBERT HENRY, utilities executive, human resources executive, instructor; b. Hakensack, N.J., June 19, 1946; s. Horace Miles and Pauline Jeannette (Pente) M.; m. Ruth Ann Auletta, Sept. 28, 1969; children: Robert Michael, Brian John. BA, Montclair State Coll., 1968; MA magna cum laude, Fairleigh Dickinson U., 1972; postgrad., Pace U., 1985—. Cert. secondary sch. tchr. of social studies, N.J. Job analyst Citicorp, N.Y.C., 1969-70, sr. job analyst, 1970-72, official asst., 1972, project specialist presonnel practices/policy review, 1973, project specialist attitude surveys, 1973-75, personnel officer nat. banking group, 1975-76; asst. dir. personnel N.Y. Power Authority, White Plains, N.Y., 1976-84, dir. compensation, 1984—; instr. Am. Compensation Assn., Scottsdale, Ariz., 1986—. Contbr. articles to profl. jours. Scoutmaster, Boy Scouts Am., Ridgefield Park, N.J., 1968; also scouting coordinator, Maywood, N.J., 1982-83; vestryman, sr. warden St. Martin's Episcopal Ch., Maywood, 1977-84. Mem. Am. Compensation Assn. (cert., instr. 1986—), Am. Soc. for Personnel Adminstrn., Human Resources Planning Soc., N.Y. Human Resources Planners, Doctoral Students Assn. of Pace U., Acad. of Mgmt., Order of DeMolay (master councilor 1962-65, scribe, adv. bd. 1965-68, Meritorious Service award 1965). Episcopalian. Office: NY Power Authority 123 Main St White Plains NY 10601

MEEK, JOHN MARTIN, public relations executive; b. Rocky, Okla., Sept. 4, 1929; s. James Burr and Myrtle May (Hill) M.; m. Reed Whitson Isbell, Jan. 31, 1969 (div.); children: Camilla Jean, David Blake, James Gordon. BA, U. Okla., 1956; MA, Syracuse U., 1958. Reporter, San Angelo (Tex.) Standard-Times, 1956, Syracuse (N.Y.) Post-Standard, 1957-58; mem. staff Syracuse U., 1956-57; mgr. dept. community devel. U.S. Jaycees, 1958-60; press sec. to U.S. Senator Robert S. Kerr, 1961-63; press sec., legis. asst. to U.S. Senator J. Howard Edmondson, 1963-64; press office mgr. Robert F. Kennedy for Senate Campaign, N.Y.C., 1964; asst. press dir. 1965 Presdl. Inaugural Com.; dir. Congressional relations, spl. asst. to chmn. Democratic Nat. Com., 1965-67; coordinator 1968 Dem. Nat. Conv., 1967-68; pres. Edelman Internat. Corp., Washington, 1969-82; exec. v.p. Daniel J. Edelman, Inc.; sr. assoc., Hartz/Carter Assocs., 1982-83; pres., ptnr. Hartz/Meek Internat., Washington, 1983—; adj. prof. internat. public relations Am. U. Bd. dirs. Fairfax Symphony Orchestra. With USN, USMC, Okla. N.G., 1948-55. Mem. NATAS, Country Music Assn., Aviation Writers, U.S. Tennis Assn., Am. Fgn. Svc. Assn. Clubs: Mt. Kenya Safari (Nanyuki, Kenya); George Washington U. Pres.'s. Home: 2737 Devonshire Pl NW Washington DC 20008 Office: Hartz/Meek Internat 806 15th St NW Suite 210 Washington DC 20005

MEEK, LISA LYNN, employment agency executive; b. Bklyn., Jan. 24, 1963; d. Donald Chamberlin and Eunice Mae (Hawkins) M. BA in Econs., U. Md., 1986. Br. mgr. Walton-Thomas Placements, Bethesda, Md., 1986-88; pres. Elite Pers., Inc., Bethesda, 1988—. Precinct chair Connie Morella for Congresswoman, Bethesda, 1986—. Mem. Bethesda/Chevy Chase (Md.) C. of C., Kappa Alpha Theta. Republican. Presbyterian. Home: 6008 Highland Dr Chevy Chase MD 20815 Office: Elite Pers Inc Bethesda Metro Ctr #850 Bethesda MD 20814

MEEK, PAUL DERALD, oil and chemical company executive; b. McAllen, Tex., Aug. 15, 1930; s. William Van and Martha Mary (Sharp) M.; m. Betty Catherine Robertson, Apr. 18, 1954; children: Paula Marie Meek Burford, Kathy Diane Meek Hasemann, Carol Ann Meek Miller, Linda Rae. B.S. in Chem. Engring, U. Tex., Austin, 1953. Mem. tech. dept. Humble Oil & Refining Co., Baytown, Tex., 1953-55; with Cosden Oil & Chem. Co., 1955-76, pres., 1968-76; dir. Am. Petrofina, Inc., Dallas, 1968—, v.p. parent co., 1968-76, pres., chief operating officer, 1976-83, pres., chief exec. officer, 1983-86, chmn. bd., pres., chief exec. officer, 1984-86, chmn. bd., 1986—. Contbg. author: Advances in Petroleum Chemistry and Refining, 1957. Chmn. chem. engring. vis. com. U. Tex., 1975-76; adv. council Coll. Engring. Found., U. Tex., Austin, 1979—; co-chmn. indsl. div. United Way of Met. Dallas, 1981-82; mem. adv. council YWCA of Dallas, 1983-87; trustee Southwest Research Inst.; assoc. bd. visitors U. Tex. M.D. Anderson Cancer Ctr., 1985—. Named Disting. Engring. Grad. U. Tex., Austin, 1969. Mem. Am. Petroleum Inst. (exec., budget, awards and nominations coms. of bd. dirs.), Dallas Wildcat Com. (chmn. exec. com. 1987-88). Office: Am Petrofina Inc 8450 N Central Expwy PO BOx 2159 Dallas TX 75221

MEEK, PHILLIP JOSEPH, newspaper publisher; b. Los Angeles, Nov. 17, 1937; s. Joseph Alcinus and Clara Amy (Phillips) M.; m. Nancy Jean LaPorte, June 25, 1960; children: Katherine Amy, Brian Joseph, Laurie Noel. B.A. cum laude, Ohio Wesleyan U., 1959; M.B.A., Harvard U., 1961. Fin. analyst Ford Motor Co., 1961-63, supr. capacity planning, 1963-66, supr. domestic scheduling, 1966, controller mktg. services, 1966-68; on loan as pres. Econ. Devel. Corp. Greater Detroit, 1968-70; pres., pub. Oakland Press Co., Pontiac, Mich., 1970-77; exec. v.p., gen. mgr. Ft. Worth Star-Telegram, 1977-79, pres., editorial chmn., 1980-82, pres., pub., 1982-86; sr. v.p., pres. pub. group Capital Cities/ABC Inc., N.Y.C., 1986—. Past mem. Pontiac Stadium Bldg. Authority; pres. United Way Pontiac-North Oakland, 1977; pres. Tarrant County United Way, 1982-83, chmn., 1983-84; bd. dirs. Arts Council of Ft. Worth and Tarrant County; chmn. North Tex. Commn., 1983-84; bd. dirs. Tex. Ind. Coll. Fund; trustee Ohio Wesleyan U., 1984—. Mem. Am. Newspaper Pubs. Assn., So. Newspaper Pubs. Assn., Tex. Daily Newspaper Assn. (pres. 1984), Ft. Worth C. of C. (dir. 1980-83); Mem. Phi Beta Kappa, Omicron Delta Kappa, Sigma Delta Chi, Pi Delta Epsilon, Phi Gamma Delta. Methodist. Clubs: Stanwich (Conn.); Crystal Downs (Mich.); Rivercrest (Tex.); Ft. Worth, Petroleum of Ft. Worth. Office: Capital Cities/ABC Inc Pub Group 7 E 12th St New York NY 10003 also: Capital Cities/ABC Inc 77 W 66th St New York NY 10023

MEEK, RICHARD DAVID, computer information scientist; b. Lawton, Okla., July 21, 1952; s. Jack Hayden and Dorothy Louise (Bennet) M.; m. Joan Marie Garcher, Oct. 2, 1987; 1 stepchild, Phillip John Kanjuka. BA in Math with honors, Cameron U., 1978; postgrad, Baldwin-Wallace Coll., 1988. Assoc. engr. Martin Marietta Aerospace, Denver, 1978-79; engr. Woodward Gov. Co., Ft. Collins, Colo., 1979-83; sr. engr. NBI Inc., Boulder, Colo., 1983-85; project mgr. engring. Bailey Controls Co., Wickliffe, Ohio, 1985—. Served as sgt. USAF, 1972-76. Mem. Cleve. Engring. Soc., Instrument Soc. Am., Surface Mt. Tech. Assn. Republican. Home: 4587 Forest Edge Dr Brooklyn OH 44144 Office: Bailey Controls Co 29801 Euclid Ave Wickliffe OH 44092

MEEKER, ARLENE DOROTHY HALLIN (MRS. WILLIAM MAURICE MEEKER), manufacturing company executive; b. Glendale, Calif., June 13, 1935; d. Haddon Eric and Martha (Randow) Hallin; grad. John Muir Jr. Coll., 1953; student L.A. Valley Coll., 1956-58, BA, Whittier Coll., 1973, MBA, 1980; m. William Maurice Meeker, Aug. 19, 66; 1 son, William Michael. Statewide sec. pub. rels. United Reps. Calif., L.A., 1964; personnel specialist Sanford Mgmt. Svcs., Inc., L.A., 1964-66; v.p. personnel Grover Mfg. Corp., Montebello, Calif., 1966-75, pres., 1975—, dir., 1969—, chmn. of bd. 1975—; dir. Brit. Marine Industries, Montebello, 1969-86, chmn. bd. 1986—. Grover Ltd., Bandon, County Cork, Ireland, 1986—, Grover Internat., 1969—. Mem. City of Whittier Transp. and Parking Commn., 1976-84, chmn. commn., 1977-79, vice-chmn., 1982-84; coun. mem. L.A. County Art Mus., 1969-80; chmn. fine arts bd. Hillcrest Congl. Ch., mem. ch. coun., 1977-79; trustee Oxford Prep. Sch., Whittier, Calif., 1981-86; visitors bd. Whittier Coll., 1983—; press chmn. Whittier Rep. Women Federated, 1977-78, 1st v.p., 1981-83; Rep. precinct capt., 1964; active L.A. World Affairs Coun.; pres. Friendly Hills Property Owners Assn, 1982-84. Mem. Docian Soc. (pub. rels. chmn. 1967-68), AAUW, Conglist. Clubs: Newport Harbor Yacht (Newport Beach, Calif.); Friendly Hills Country (Whittier, Calif.), Whittier Lincoln (pres. 1982-84). Home: 9710 Portada Dr Whittier CA 90603 Office: 620 S Vail St Montebello CA 90640

MEEKER, GUY BENTLEY, banker; b. Calcutta, India, Nov. 4, 1945; (parents Am. citizens); s. Lincoln Voght and Fortune Helen (Bentley) M.; m. Lavenia Yale Nelson, Apr. 27, 1967 (div. 1979); children: G. Bentley Jr., Melissa Anne ; m. Marcia Lee Zink, Nov. 4, 1984. BSBA, Georgetown U., 1967; MBA, George Washington U., 1970. Cons. OAS, Washington, 1971-73; v.p. The Deltec Banking Corp., Nassau, Bahamas & N.Y.C., 1973-78, Comml. Credit Internat. Banking Corp., Balt., 1978-82; sr. v.p., gen. mgr. Union Planters Internat. Bank, N.Y.C., 1982-84; exec. v.p., gen. mgr. Worthen Bank Internat., N.Y.C., 1984-86; exec. v.p. Bank Cen. Asia, N.Y.C., 1984—; Mem. corp. council Asia Soc., N.Y.C., 1987—. Contbr. articles, monographs in field. Mem. Inst. Internat. Bankers. Roman Catholic. Club: River, Coffee House, Dutch Treat (N.Y.C.).

MEEKER, MILTON SHY, heavy duty truck manufacturing company executive; b. Knob Noster, Mo., Nov. 9, 1933; s. David and Helen Elizabeth (Kendrick) M.; m. Nancy Orbison, Nov. 27, 1976; 1 child, Sherwin Kendrick. BA, U. Calif., Berkeley, 1955, BS, 1959; MBA, U. Mich., 1963. With Ford Motor Co., 1959-68; dir. purchasing, mktg., rsch. mgr. Paccar, Inc., Seattle, also Newark, Calif., 1968-71; commr. fed. supply svc., commr. automated data and telecommunications, assoc. dep. adminstr. GSA, Washington, 1972-75; dir. purchasing chem. group FMC Corp., Phila., 1975-77, dir. purchasing planning and adminstrn., Chgo., 1977-79; gen. sales mgr. Peterbilt Motors Co. div. Paccar, Newark, Calif., 1979-80, mktg. mgr., 1980-89, dir. dealer devel., 1989—. Chmn., Pres.'s Com. for Purchase of Products from Blind, 1973-74; bd. dirs. Nat. Industries for the Blind, 1976-86. With U.S. Army, 1957-58. Republican. Home: 7900 NE 32d St Bellevue WA 98004 Office: PO Box 1518 Bellevue WA 98009

MEEKINS, EDWARD JOSEPH, banker; b. Oakland, Calif., Sept. 1, 1949; s. Willis Ellsworth and Darlene Ruth (Murphy) M.; m. Mary Lynn Marshall, Nov. 8, 1969; children: Edward Jr., Elizabeth, Michael. Grad. high sch., Mitchell, S.D. Br. mgr. Postal Fin. Co., Sioux City, Iowa, 1970-77; v.p. 1st Union Bank & Trust Co., Winamac, Ind., 1977-80; pres. Mitchell Home Savs. & Loan, 1980-83; v.p. Farmers State Bank & Trust Co., Superior, Nebr., 1983—, also bd. dirs.; bd. dirs. FSB, Inc., Superior. Chmn. Nuckolls County Republican Com., 1986—, mem. Nebr. Rep. State Cen. Com., 1986—; sec. bd. edn. Superior Pub. Schs., 1989—. Mem. K.C. Roman Catholic. Office: Farmers State Bank & Trust PO Box 268 Superior NE 68978

MEEKS, D. MICHAEL, hotel executive; b. Hope, Ark., Mar. 7, 1943; s. Hiram McKinney Meeks and Lula Edna (Frink) Steele; m. Patricia Claudette Sims, 1964; children David Michael, Jonathan McKinney. BS, Lambuth Coll., Jackson, Tenn., 1966; MBA, Memphis State U., 1967; cert. advanced mgmt. program, Harvard U., 1985. Innkeeper Winegardner, Inc., Richmond, Ky., 1969-72; innkeeper Winegardner, Internat., Springfield, Mo., 1973-74, v.p. ops., 1974-75; area mgr. franchise ops. Holiday Inns, Inc., Memphis, 1975-76, regional dir. franchise ops., 1976-79, v.p. system program devel., 1979-80, v.p. product mgmt., 1980-81, v.p. franchise devel., 1981-83, sr. v.p. system devel. east, 1983-84, sr. v.p. system hotels, 1984-85; sr. v.p. hotel devel. Holiday Corp., Memphis, 1985-87, pres. hotel group, 1987—, also bd. dirs.; bd. dirs. Tenn. Restaurant Co., Perkins Mgmt. Co., Perkins Restaurants, Inc., The Orpheum, Friendly Ice Cream Corp. dir. Give Kids the World Bd.; bd. dirs. Memphis Devel. Found. Mem. Nat. Restaurant Assn., Am. Mgmt. Assn., Urban Land Inst. (assoc.), Internat. Franchise Assn. (franchise relations com., ednl com.). Club: Harvard (Boston). Office: Holiday Corp 1023 Cherry Rd Memphis TN 38117

MEEKS, GEORGE OWEN, JR., lumber and building materials company executive; b. Lynchburg, Va., July 20, 1950; s. George Owen and Gwendolyn (Hardy) M.; m. Jean Taylor, Aug. 19, 1974; children: George Owen III, Sarah Campbell, Elizabeth Chesterman. BA in Polit. Sci., Washington and Lee U., 1972. Mktg. researcher Cen. Fidelity Bank, Lynchburg, 1972-74; exec. v.p. Taylor Bros., Inc., Lynchburg, 1974—. Bd. dirs. United Way Cen. Va., 1980-84; chmn. bd. trustees James River Day Sch., Lynchburg, 1983-84; v.p. Cen. Va. Speech and Hearing Assn., 1985. Mem. Homebuilders Assn. Cen. Va. (bd. dirs. 1984-88), Va. Bldg. Material Assn. (bd. dirs. 1989—), Builders Mart Am. (mem. Pres.'s Club). Episcopalian. Office: Taylor Bros Inc 905 Graves Mill Rd Lynchburg VA 24506

MEENDSEN, FRED CHARLES, food company executive; b. Garden City, N.Y., Oct. 28, 1933; s. Frederick Herman and Charlotte Mabel (Reiss) M.; B.A., Colgate U., 1954; M.B.A., Harvard U., 1956; m. Nancy Lou Gross, Nov. 16, 1957; children—Fred Charles, Martha Anne. Mem. mktg. and sales mgmt. dept. Velsicol Chem. Corp., Chgo., 1957-63; with CPC Internat., Inc., N.Y.C., 1963—, pres. subs. Peterson/Puritan, Inc., Danville, Ill., 1977-83, pres. subs. Can. Starch Co., 1983-84, v.p. parent co., 1983—, pres. N.Am. region Corn Wet Milling div., 1984-88, v.p. corp. affairs, 1988—; dir. Can. Starch Co., 1983-88; chmn. Casco Co.; mem. U.S. C. of C. Can. Relations com., 1986—; mem. Sec. Agr. Adv. Comm. on Trade, 1987—. Served to 1st lt. U.S. Army, 1956-59. Author: Atomic Energy and Business Strategy, 1956. Mem. Am. Mgmt. Assn. (gen. mgmt. council 1986—). Home: 63 Oak Rd Saddle River NJ 07458 Office: CPC Internat Inc Internat Pla Englewood Cliffs NJ 07632

MEESE, CELIA EDWARDS, pharmaceutical and nutritional supplement company executive; b. San Diego, May 10; d. Roy Clifford Edwards and Bessie Lucille (Lang) Hill; m. Jed D. Meese, July 6, 1963; 1 son, Scott Edwards. B.A., U. Wis., 1964; B.A. (hon.), U. Taiwan, 1965. Office mgr. Pacific Telephone, San Jose, Calif., 1965-72; pres. Vitaline Corp., Ashland, Oreg., 1972—; v.p. RenalChem, Inc., San Jose, Calif., 1982—, Formulations Tech., Inc., Oakdale, Calif., 1982—; dir. Spectra Diagnostics, San Jose. Bd. dirs. So. Oreg. State Coll. Found.; vol. Tudor Guide. Mem. Pharm. Mfrs. Assn., Am. Soc. Bariatric Physicians, Mensa. Home: PO Box 162 Ashland OR 97520 Office: Vitaline Corp 722 Jefferson Ave Ashland OR 97520

MEHALCHIN, JOHN JOSEPH, entrepreneur, financial executive; b. Hazleton, Pa., Aug. 8, 1937; s. Charles and Susan (Korba) M.; divorced; 1 child, Martin. BS with honors (1st in class), Temple U., 1964; MBA, U. Calif., Berkeley, 1965; PhD, U. Chgo., 1964; Supr. costs Winchester-Western, New Haven, Conn., 1965-67; mgmt. cons. Booz-Allen & Hamilton, N.Y.C., 1967-68; mgr. planning TWA, N.Y.C., 1968-69; officer Smith, Barney, N.Y.C. and Paris, 1970-74; chief fin. officer, pres. leasing co. Storage Tech. Corp., Louisville, Colo. and London, 1974-79; sr. v.p. Heizer Corp., 1979; pres., founder Highline Fin. Svcs., Inc. and fgn. subs., Boulder, Colo., 1979—. With AUS, 1958-61. U. Calif. fellow, Berkeley, 1964; U. Chgo. scholar, 1964. Mem. Fin. Execs. Inst., Am. Assn. Equipment Lessors, Beta Gamma Sigma, Omicron Delta Epsilon. Home and Office: Highline Fin Svcs Inc 1881 Ninth St Ste 320 Canyon Ctr Boulder CO 80302

MEHLENBACHER, DOHN HARLOW, civil engineer; b. Huntington Park, Calif., Nov. 18, 1931; s. Virgil Claude and Helga (Sigfridson) M.; B.S. in Civil Engring., U. Ill., 1953; M.S. in City and Regional Planning Ill. Inst. Tech., 1961; M.B.A., U. Chgo., 1972; m. Nancy Mehlenbacher; children—Dohn Scott, Kimberly Ruth, Mark James, Matthew Lincoln. Structural engr., draftsman Swift & Co., Chgo., 1953-54, 56-57, DeLeuw-Cather Co., Chgo., 1957-59; project engr. Quaker Oats Co., Chgo., 1959-61, mgr. constrn., 1964-70, mgr. real property, 1970-71, mgr. engring. and maintenance, Los Angeles, 1961-64; chief facilities engr. Bell & Howell Co., Chgo., 1972-73; v.p. design Globe Engring. Co., Chgo., 1973-76; project mgr. I.C. Harbour Constrn. Co., Oak Brook, Ill., 1976-78; dir. estimating George A. Fuller Co., Chgo., 1978; pres. Food-Tech Co., Willowbrook, Ill., 1979-80; dir. phys. resources Ill. Inst. Tech., Chgo., 1980—. Served with USAF, 1954-56. Registered profl. engr. and structural engr., Ill. Mem. Am. Mgmt. Assn., ASCE, Constrn. Specifications Inst., Am. Arbitration Assn. Office: IIT Center Chicago IL 60616

MEHLUM, JOHAN ARNT, banker; b. Trondheim, Norway, Nov. 11, 1928; came to U.S., 1950, naturalized, 1955; s. Hans Aage and Olga (Nygaard) M.; diploma Norwegian Bus. Coll., 1946, postgrad. Rutgers U., 1971; m. Ladona Marie Christensen, May 30, 1951 (dec. 1983); children—Ann Marie, Katherine, Susan Jane, Rolf Erik; m. Emel Hekimoglu, Sept. 27, 1986. Clk. Forretningsbanken, Trondheim, 1946-50, First Nat. Bank Oreg., Astoria and Corvallis, 1952-57; cashier, mgr. Bank of Shedd, Brownsville, Oreg., 1958-63; pres., chmn. Siuslaw Valley Bank, Florence, Oreg., 1963—; chmn. bd. Community Bank Creswell (Oreg.), 1970-79; founding dir., pres. Western Banker Svc. Corp., 1983-84; dir. Siuslaw Valley Plaza, Inc., 1966—. Mayor, Dunes City, Oreg., 1973-75. Trustee Lane Community Coll. Found., 1971-78; chmn. bd. dirs. NW Intermediate Banking Sch., Lewis and Clark Coll., Portland, Oreg., 1975-77; trustee, past chmn. Western Lane County Found., 1976-82. With Royal Norwegian Army, 1948-49. Named Jr. First Citizen, Astoria, 1955, First Citizen, Brownsville, 1962; recipient internat. rels. award U.S. Jr. C. of C., 1960; inducted Oreg. Bankers Hall of Fame, 1988. Mem. Western Ind. Bankers (mem. exec. coun. 1970-74), Am. Bankers Assn. (mem. exec. com. community bankers div. 1976-78, governing coun. 1982-84), Oreg. Bankers Assn. (exec. coun. 1977-83, pres. 1981-82), Western States Bankcard Assn. (bd. dir. 1987—), Florence Area C. of C. (pres. 1970), Banking Profession Polit. Action Com. (state chmn. 1973-76), Sons of Norway, Elks, Rotary (pres. 1967-68), Norsemen's League (pres. 1954). Home: PO Box 131 Florence OR 97439 Office: PO Box 280 Florence OR 97439

MEHNER, WILLIAM MICHEL, financial company executive; b. Ada, Okla., Aug. 5, 1943; s. Dors Jenkins and Minnie (Brooks) Snyder; m. Bonnie Lee Hackett, May 31, 1965; children: Bethany Anne, Whitney Alison. BA, Alaska Meth. U., 1965. Mgr. Alaska div. Equitable Fin. Co., Anchorage, 1969—. Contbr. articles to newspapers and mags. Bd. dirs. Western council Boy Scouts Am., Anchorage, 1980-87, Glacier Creek Acad., Girdwood, Alaska, 1985—, Humana Hosp., 1988—, First Fed. Bank, 1988—; pres. Alaska Conservatory Music, Anchorage, 1985-87; del. Anchorage Rep. Com., 1988. 1st lt. U.S. Army, 1965-69. Mem. Alaska Assn. Life Underwriters (pres. 1983-84, bd. dirs.), So. Alaska Life Underwriters (bd. dirs. 1972-85), Internat. Assn. Fin. Planners, Gen. Agts. and Mgrs. Assn. (pres. 1986-87, 89—, 12th yr. Mgmt. award), Soc. CLU, Equitable Regional Mgrs. Assn. (pres. 1985), Rotary. Home: 6641 Roundtree Dr Anchorage AK 99516 Office: Equitable Fin Co 3301 C St Suite 500 Anchorage AK 99503

MEHREN, LAWRENCE LINDSAY, investment company executive; b. Phoenix, May 26, 1944; s. Lawrence and Mary Teresa (Stelzer) M.; B.A., U. Ariz., 1966; M.A., U. Ariz., 1968; m. Lynn Athon McEvers, June 5, 1965; children—Lawrence Lindsay, John Eskridge. Bus. mgr. Rancho Santa Maria, Peoria, Ariz., 1968-69; traffic mgr. Glen-Mar Mfg. Co., Phoenix, 1969-70; account exec. Merrill Lynch, Pierce, Fenner and Smith, Inc., Phoenix, 1970-77, sr. account exec., 1977-78, asst. v.p., 1978-80, v.p., 1980-82; v.p. Harbor Equity Funds, Inc., 1982-84; sr. v.p. Harbor Fin. Group, Inc., Phoenix, 1984-87; pres. Charles and Pierce Asst. Mgmt., Inc., 1987-89; pres. Lawrence Fine Art Inc., Phoenix, 1989—. Chmn. Madison Citizens Adv. Com., 1973-74; mem. Phoenix Art Mus., Phoenix Town Hall; bd. dirs. Planned Parenthood, 1972-75, Brophy Coll. Prep. Sch., 1981-87, Prescott Coll., 1984-85. Recipient award Ariz. Hist. Found., 1968. Mem. Phoenix Stock and Bond Club (bd. dirs. 1979-82), Ariz. Acad. Pub. Affairs, Internat. Wine and Food Soc., Beta Theta Pi. Club: Valley Field Riding and Polo. Home: 515 E Grant Rd #141-318 Tucson AZ 85705 Office: 5515 N 7th St #5107 Phoenix AZ 85016

MEHTA, JAY, controller; b. Varanasi, India, Aug. 16, 1943; came to U.S., 1970; m. Vineeta Mehta, Feb. 20, 1969; children: Nina, Vineet. MBA in Fin., Rutgers U., 1974; MBA in Taxation, Fairleigh Dickenson U., 1983. CPA, N.J.; cert. mgmt. acct. Contract estimator NE region Otis Elevator Co. Subs. United Techs. Inc., Montvale, N.J., 1970-73, sr. contract estimator NE region, 1974-75; corp. staff acct. Otis Elevator Co. Subs. United Techs. Inc., N.Y.C., 1976-77, sr. corp. acct., 1978; div. controller OKI Electric Overseas Corp., Hackensack, N.J., 1979-84; corporate controller OKI Am. Inc., Hackensack, 1984—; trustee OKI Am. Savs. Plan, 1981—; ofcl. grader Inst. Mgmt. Acctg., Montvale, N.J., 1986—. Mem. Am. Mgmt. Assn., N.J. Soc. CPA's. Republican. Office: OKI Am Inc One University Pla Hackensack NJ 07601

MEHTA, NARINDER KUMAR, marketing executive; b. Lahore, Punjab, India, Feb. 18, 1938; s. Puran Chand and Raj Rani Mehta; m. Adele Ackerman, July 25, 1962 (div. May 1970); 1 child, Kiren; m. Salita Yashpaul, Nov. 22, 1971; 1 child, Ravi. Bachelor of Commerce, U. Delhi, India, 1958; MA, U. Minn., 1961. Program dir. All India Mgmt. Assn., New Delhi, India, 1963-67; with Am. Express Co., Chgo., 1968-82; nat. sales dir. Am. Express Co., N.Y.C., 1975-80, v.p. sales, 1980-82; sr. v.p. Shearson Lehman/Am. Express, Boston, 1982-85, Capital Credit Corp., Fairfield, N.J., 1985—; sr. v.p. Temporary Investment Funds, 1982-85, Trust for Short Term Fed. Securities, 1982-85, Mcpl. Fund for Calif. Investors, 1983-85. Contbr. articles to profl. jours. Nat. v.p. Muscular Dystrophy Assn., N.Y.C., 1984-86. Mem. Am. Mgmt. Assn., Tau Kappa Epsilon. Office: Capital Credit Corp 492 Rt 46 East Fairfield NJ 07006

MEHURON, WILLIAM OTTO, electronics company executive; b. Hammond, Ind., Nov. 20, 1937; s. Arthur and Margaret Irene (Soroka) M.; m. Charlotte Anne Nyheim, Aug. 26, 1982; children: Kimberly Anne, Kristine Lynn. BSEE, Purdue U., 1959; MSEE, U. Pa., 1962, PhD, 1966. Tech. staff RCA, Moorestown, N.J., 1959-64, GE, Phila., 1964-68; group leader Mitre Corp., McLean, Va., 1969-74; tech. dir. naval intelligence Dept. Navy, Washington, 1974-81; dir. rsch. and engring. Nat. Security Agy., Ft. Meade, Md., 1981-85; v.p., gen. mgr. data systems div. Ampex Corp. subs. Allied-Signal Co., Redwood City, Calif., 1985-86; sr. v.p. product ops. Daisy Systems Corp., Mountain View, Calif., 1986—. Mem. IEEE, AAAS, Armed Forces Communication and Electronics Assn., Soc. Motion Picture and TV Engrs., Assn. Electronics Warfare, Security Affairs Support Assn. Home: 101 Stockbridge Ave Atherton CA 94025 Office: Daisy Systems Corp 700 E Middlefield Rd Mountain View CA 94039

MEIBURG, CHARLES OWEN, buisness educator; b. Seneca, S.C., Dec. 17, 1931; s. Albert and Gladys Katherine (Burley) M.; m. Elizabeth Rhodes Glenn, June 11, 1955; children: Charles O. Jr., Howard Glenn, Elizabeth Rhodes. BS in Arts and Scis., Clemson U., 1953; MA in Econs., U. Va., 1958, PhD in Econs., 1960. Assoc. prof. U. Va., Charlottesville, 1964-69, prof., 1969—; dir. Taylor Murphy Inst. U. Va., 1967-83; assoc. dean Darden Sch. U. Va., 1983—. Co-author: Cases on Financial Institutions, 1979, Cases in Bank Management, 1986; editor (with others) Loan Officers Handbook, 1986. 1st lt. U.S. Army, 1953-55. Mem. Am. Econ. Assn., Fin. Mgmt. Assn., Assn. for U. and Econ. Rsch. (pres. 1971). Home: 1665 Blackwood Rd Charlottesville VA 22901 Office: U Va Darden Sch Box 6550 Charlottesville VA 22906

MEIJER, ROELF JAN, manufacturing company executive; b. Pekela, Groningen, The Netherlands, Oct. 2, 1919; came to U.S., 1977; s. Ernst and Alberta (Bunt) M.; m. Giny Harmanna Groenwold, Jan. 7, 1947; children: Gerda, Alberta, Ernst. IR, Tech. U. Delft, The Netherlands, 1946, Dr magna cum laude, 1960. Researcher N.V. Philips, Eindhoven, The Netherlands, 1947-53, group leader, 1953-60, sci. advisor, 1960-67, v.p. rsch. lab., 1967-77; cons. Ford Motors Co., Dearborn, Mich., 1977-79; pres., owner Stirling Thermal Motors, Inc., Ann Arbor, Mich., 1979—. Inventor Stirling engine. Presbyterian. Office: Stirling Thermal Motors Inc 2841 Boardwalk Ann Arbor MI 48104

MEILING, GEORGE ROBERT LUCAS, bank holding company executive; b. Columbus, Ohio, Nov. 28, 1942; s. Richard Lewis and Ann Elizabeth (Lucas) M.; m. Margaret Aldena Ludy, May 9, 1970; children: Andrew Edward Ludy, Richardson Lucas. B.A., Yale U., 1964; M.B.A., Harvard U., 1966. With Chem. Bank, N.Y.C., 1966; controller Bank One of Columbus, (Ohio), 1971-73; asst. treas. Banc One Corp., Columbus, 1973-77, treas., 1977—. Mem. alumni bd. Columbus Acad., 1974-78; bd. dirs. Greater Columbus Arts Council, 1986-87, Pro Musica, 1987—, AmeriFlora '92; treas., bd. dirs. Am. Rose Soc., 1987—. Served to capt. USAF, 1966-69. Mem. Corp. Planning Exchange, Nat. Investor Relations Inst., Bank Investors Relations Assn., Assn. Yale Alumni (dir. 1978-80). Republican. Anglican. Clubs: Army and Navy (Washington); Yale (N.Y.C.); Columbus; Yale Cen. Ohio (pres. 1976-78), Columbus Country (Columbus). Home: 274 Revere Rd Columbus OH 43213 Office: Banc One Corp 100 E Broad St Columbus OH 43271-0261

MEINERS, LOUIS MELVIN, JR., accountant, lawyer; b. Louisville, Oct. 4, 1950; s. Louis M. Sr. and Norma J. (Reasor) M.; m. Mary Elizabeth Barefoot, Aug. 20, 1971; children: Kenneth, Suzanne, Laura, Valarie. BS in Commerce and Acctg., U. Louisville, 1971, JD, 1976. CPA, Ky., Ind. Sr. acct. Amick and Helm, Louisville, 1972-73; tax supr. Touche Ross and Co., Louisville, 1974-78; tax mgr. Blue and Co., Indpls., 1978-79, co-owner, dir. tax dept., 1979—. Mem. AICPA, ABA, Ind. CPA Soc. (chmn. taxation com. 1977—), Ind. Bar Assn., Hunting Creek Country Club, Woodland Country Club. Office: Blue and Co 9100 Keystone Crossing Ste 500 Indianapolis IN 46240

MEINERS, PHYLLIS HALL, fund development consultant; b. Boston, Nov. 8, 1940; d. Samuel Henry and Edith (Salvin) Bloom; m. William F. Meiners Jr.; 1 child, Hilary Cynthia Rodriguez. BA, U. Calif., Berkeley, 1962; postgrad., MIT, 1973-74, Rockhurst Coll., 1980-83. Dir. rsch. Harbridge House, Boston, 1964-70; rsch. assoc. MIT, Cambridge, Mass., 1970-71; advvocate planner Urban Planning Aid, Cambridge, 1972-73; program adminstr. U. Hawaii, Honolulu, 1974-79, Mo. div. Community Devel., Kansas City, 1980-82; pres. Corp. Resource Cons., Kansas City, Mo., 1982—. Mem. Nat. Assn. Neighborhood Councils, 49/63 Neighborhood Coalition, South Town Council, Kansas City, 1986—, Friends of Art, Kansas City, 1986—; staff coordinator Mayor Charles B. Wheeler campaign, Kansas City, 1979. Mem. Nat. Soc. Fund Raising Execs. (bd. dirs.), Brush Creek Trolley Barn Assn., Greater Kansas City C. of C. (entrepreneur's coucil), Greater Kansas City Council Philanthropy, NAFE, Brookside Neighborhood Assn., Special Libraries Assn. Democrat. Jewish. Home: 5800 Grand Ave Kansas City MO 64113 Office: 6233 Harrison Kansas City MO 64110

MEINERS, T(HOMAS) SCOTT, hospital administrator; b. Ft. Thomas, Ky., Dec. 8, 1949; s. Thomas Robert Meiners and Helen Marie (Bertke) Jones; m. Sherry A. Hastings, Mar. 4, 1983; 1 child, Jamie L. Christofferson. BS in Indsl. Mgmt., BBA in Quantitative Analysis cum claude, U. Cin., 1972; M. in Hosp. Adminstrn., Xavier U., 1974. Mgmt. cons. Mesa Program, Denver, 1974; project coordinator Blue Cross/Blue Shield, Denver, 1974-76; asst. dir. Cen.-Northeast Colo. Health Systems Agy., Denver, 1977-79; asst. adminstr. Mt. Airy Psychiat. Ctr., Denver, 1979-81, assoc. adminstr., 1981—, chief operating officer, 1983—; dir., chmn. bd. Colo. Health Careers Council, Denver, 1984-87. Trustee, sec., chmn. bd. Denver Better Bus. Bur., 1984—; del. Canyon Area Residents for Environment, 1985. Republican. Home: 28990 Lower Moss Rd Golden CO 80401 Office: Mount Airy Psychiat Ctr 4455 E 12th Ave Denver CO 80220

MEINERT, JOHN RAYMOND, clothing manufacturing executive; b. White Cloud, Mich., Aug. 11, 1927; m. Joyce Macdonell, Nov. 5, 1955; children: Elizabeth Tinsman, Pamela Martin. Student, U. Mich., 1944-45; B.S., Northwestern U., 1949. C.P.A., Ill., 1952. With Hart Schaffner & Marx/Hartmarx Corp., Chgo., 1950—; exec. v.p. Hart Schaffner & Marx, 1975-80, vice chmn., 1981-85, sr. vice chmn., 1985-86, chmn., 1987—, also bd. dirs.; bd. dirs. Amalgamated Life Ins. Co.; trustee Amalgamated Ins. Fund; instr. acctg. Northwestern U., 1949; mem. adv. coun. U. Ill., adv. bd. Northwestern U.; vice chmn. fin. com., bd. dirs. Evanston Hosp., 1987—. Bd. dirs. Better Bus. Bur., Ill. Coun. on Econ. Edn.; mem. conf. bd. Com. Econ. Devel. With AUS, 1945-46. Recipient Alumni Merit award Kellogg Grad. Sch. Northwestern U., 1989. Mem. AICPA (v.p. 1985-86, council mem. 1971—, dir. 1975-78, Gold Medal award 1987), Ill. CPA Soc. (hon. award, dir. 1966-68, pres. 1982-83), Clothing Mfrs. Assn. U.S. (pres., dir. 1982-87, chmn. bd., bd. dirs. 1988—, Apparel Industry Leadership award 1988), Chgo. Assn. Commerce and Industry (treas., bd. dirs.), Univ. Club, Rolling Green Country Club, Rotary (pres., bd. dirs. Chgo. chpt.). Presbyterian (elder). Home: 634 Ironwood Dr Arlington Heights IL 60004 Office: Hartmarx Corp 101 N Wacker Dr 18th Fl Chicago IL 60606

MELCHER, RAYMOND H., JR., banker; b. Reading, Pa., Jan. 7, 1952; s. Raymond H. and Ruth A. (Ormsbee) M.; m. Diane Bricker, May 17, 1975; children: Patrick Michael, Timothy Ryan. BA in Econs., Kutztown State Coll., 1973; BA in Banking and Fin., Alvernia Coll., 1978; MBA, St. Joseph's U., 1987; cert. Consumer Compliance Sch., U. Okla., 1978; cert. Grad. Sch. Consumer Banking, U. Va., 1980. Cert. Consumer Credit Exec. Mktg. rep. Am. Equipment Leasing Co., Reading, 1973-75; mgmt. trainee Conn. Gen. Life Ins. Co., Reading, 1975; retail loan officer Bank of Pa., Reading, 1975-77; exec. v.p. Nat. Bank of Boyertown, Pa., 1977-86; pres. Nat. Penn Life Ins., Penn Mortgage Co. (affiliated Nat. Bank Boyertown), Boyertown, Pa., 1977-86; pres., chief exec. officer Pa. Nat. Bank and Trust Co., Pottsville, 1986-88; exec. v.p. Keystone Fin., Inc. (parent co. Pa. Nat. Bank), Harrisburg, Pa., 1988—; former adj. instr. Alvernia Coll., Am. Inst. Banking; former thesis advisor Grad. Sch. Consumer Banking, U. Va. SME chmn. Boy Scouts Am., Boyertown, 1984—, bd. dirs. Hawk Mountain Council, 1986—; div. chmn. United Way, Reading, 1985; dinner chmn. Kutztown U. Found., 1984, 85; community adv. bd. Reading Phillies, 1983—; bd. dirs. YMCA of Reading and Berks County, 1985-86, Berks Community TV, Reading, 1983-86, Reading Symphony Orch., 1985—, Threshold Rehab. Services, Reading, 1985-86, Jr. Achievement, Reading, 1982-84, Schuylkill County Council for Arts, 1986—, Schuylkill Orch., 1986—, Pottsville Area Devel. Corp., 1986—; trustee St. Joseph Hosp., Reading, 1986; vice chmn. Good Samaritan Hosp. Found., 1986—; bd. dirs. Schuylkill Econ. Devel. Corp., 1986—; chmn. 1988 Cancer Fighters' Dinner for Schuylkill County Unit Am. Cancer Soc. Mem. Pa. Bankers Assn. (active in coms. and as speaker), Am. Inst. Banking (pres. Berks County chpt. 1977-81, named AIB'er of Yr. 1981), Pen-Jer-Del Bank Mktg. Assn., Robert Morris Assn., Ambucs (pres., chmn. bd. Boyertown chpt. 1982-84), Berks County C. of C. (bd. dirs., chmn. bus. and indsl. com.). Republican. Lutheran. Club: Reciprocity (Reading). Lodge: Kiwanis. Home: 1822 Ridgewood Rd Orwigsburg PA 17961 Office: Keystone Fin Inc PO Box 1653 Harrisburg PA 17105

MELEKSON, PAUL, medical products executive; b. Romania, July 20, 1957; came to U.S., 1981; s. Simon and Clara (Volfenson) M.; m. Victoria Cherikover, June 29, 1985. BS, State U., Milan, 1980; AS, YMCA Community Coll., Chgo., 1981. Registered and cert. respiratory therapist. Staff respiratory therapist Columbus Hosp., Chgo., 1981-83; co-founder, v.p., gen. mgr. Simpol Med., Inc., Skokie, Ill., 1982—, Simpol Respiratory and Med. Equipment, Inc., Skokie, 1982—; staff respiratory therapist St. Francis Hosp., Evanston, Ill., 1983-84; ptnr. Svc. Mgmt. and Leasing, Skokie, 1984—, Beta Osteoporosis of Chgo., Skokie, 1985-87, Skokie Wellness Ctr., 1985—; v.p., majority shareholder Express Portable X-Ray, Inc., Evanston, 1986-87, cons., billing mgr., 1986—; co-founder, v.p., gen. mgr. SPS Adult Care, Tucson, 1987—; owner Myron's Health Care & Med. Supply, Inc., Skokie, 1988—; cons. V.R. Distbrs. of Ramm's Food Internat., Wilmette, Ill., 1987-88. Mem. Am. Assn. Respiratory Therapists, Am. Assn. Individual Investors, Skokie C. of C., North Shore Club. Republican. Jewish. Home: 1901 Ivy Way Glenview IL 60025 Office: Simpol Med Inc 3526 W Dempster Skokie IL 60076

MELICAN, JAMES PATRICK, JR., lawyer; b. Worcester, Mass., Sept. 8, 1940; s. James Patrick and Abigail Helen (Donahue) M.; m. Debra A. Burns, Dec. 2, 1978; children: Marlane, James P., David, Molly, Megan. BA, Fordham U., 1962; JD, Harvard U., 1965; MBA, Mich. State U., 1971. Bar: Mich 1966, Calif. 1983. Supervising atty. product liability sect. Gen. Motors Corp., Detroit, 1971-73; atty.-in-charge trade regulation Gen. Motors Corp., 1973-77, atty.-in-charge mktg. and purchasing, 1977-80, asst. gen. counsel, 1980-81; gen. counsel Toyota Motor Sales, U.S.A., Inc., Torrance, Calif., 1981-82, asst. gen. counsel, 1982-84; v.p., gen. counsel Internat. Paper Co., N.Y.C., 1984-87, sr. v.p., gen. counsel, 1987—. Mem. ABA, Am. Law Inst., Assn. of Bar of City of N.Y., N.Y. State Bar Assn. Roman Catholic. Home: 17 Turtleback Ln West New Canaan CT 06840 Office: Internat Paper Co 2 Manhattanville Rd Purchase NY 10577

MELICHER, RONALD WILLIAM, finance educator; b. St. Louis, July 4, 1941; s. William and Lorraine Norma (Mohart) M.; m. Sharon Ann Schlarmann, Aug. 19, 1967; children: Michelle Joy, Thor William, Sean Richard. BSBA, Washington U., St. Louis, 1963; MBA, Washington U., 1965, DBA, 1968. Asst. prof. fin. U. Colo., Boulder, 1969-71, assoc. prof., 1971-76, prof. fin., 1976—, chmn. fin. div., 1978-86; assoc. dir. space law, bus. and policy ctr. U. Colo., 1986-87; research cons. FPC, Washington, 1972-73; cons. NRC, Washington, 1975-76, GAO, Washington, 1981, Ariz. Corp. Commn., 1986-87, IBM Corp., 1985—; dir. annual Exec. Program for Gas Industry, 1975—; instr. annual program Nat. Assn. of Regulatory Utility Commrs. Mich. State U., 1981—. Co-author: Real Estate Finance, 2d edit., 1984, 3d edit., 1989, Finance, 7th edit., 1988, Financial Management, 5th edit., 1982; assoc. editor The Financial Review, 1988-89. Recipient NewsCtr. 4 TV Teaching awards, 1987, MBA/MS Assn. award, 1988; NSF grantee, 1974, 86, NASA grantee, 1986, 87. Mem. Fin. Mgmt. Assn. (membership com. 1974-76, regional dir. 1975-77, assoc. editor 1975-80, v.p. meeting 1985, v.p. program 1987), Am. Fin. Assn., Western Fin. Assn. (bd. dirs. 1974-76), Fin. Execs. Inst., Eastern Fin. Assn., Southwestern Fin. Assn., Midwest Fin. Assn. (bd. dirs. 1978-80), Alpha Kappa Psi, Beta Gamma Sigma. Presbyterian. Home: 5136 Forsythe Pl Boulder CO 80303 Office: U Colo Coll of Bus Campus Box 419 Boulder CO 80309

MELICKIAN, GARY EDWARD, legal services company executive; b. L.A., Apr. 2, 1935; s. Ara Harry Melickian and Virginia Anne (Gargan) Jardine; m. Greta Gail Rasbury, Aug. 20, 1955 (div. 1972); children: Mark Stanley, Lynn Anne. Student, UCLA, 1953-55; EM, Colo. Sch. Mines, 1959; postgrad., U. So. Calif., 1961-67, Calif. Poly. Inst., 1969-71. Lic. geologist, Calif., Alaska, engring. geologist, Calif.; cert. profl. geologist. Geologist Humble Oil & Refining Co., L.A., 1959; civil engr. L.A. County Flood Control Dist., L.A., 1960; staff geophysicist Dames & Moore, L.A., 1961, project geologist, 1962-64, mgr. pers., 1965-66, mgr. pub. rels., 1967-69, ptnr., 1970-84; dir. mining Dames & Moore, Denver, 1970-80; dir. tech. svcs. Dames & Moore, Bethesda, Md., 1980-84; pres., bd. dirs. Consultation Networks, Inc., Washington, 1985—, Expert Witness Network, Washington, 1985—; bd. dirs. Comfac, Inc., La Canada, Calif.; presenter in field. Contbr. articles to profl. jours. Fellow Geol. Soc. Am. (editor Engring. Geology newsletter 1966-67); mem. Am. Inst. Profl. Geologists (pres. Calif. sect. 1971, bd. dirs. 1972-73, sec., treas. 1982, Cert. of Merit 1982, 83), Soc. Mining Engrs. (bd. dirs. 1972-74, chmn. Peele award com., publs. com., program com.), Assn. Engring. Geologists, Am. Assn. Petroleum Geologists, Am. Assn. Cost Engrs., World Future Soc., Human Factors Soc., NSPE, Hist. Earth Sci. Soc. Office: Cons Networks Inc 1608 New Hampshire Ave NW Ste G-100 Washington DC 20009

MELLING, MARK LYNN, accountant executive; b. Cameron, Mo., Oct. 23, 1958; s. Charles and Marjorie Lucille (Kelly) M.; m. Mary Jane Pickering, Sept. 29, 1984. BBA in Acctg. and Mgmt., Cen. Mo. State U., 1981. CPA, Mo. Audit asst. Mo. State Auditor, Jefferson City, 1981-82, semi-sr. auditor, 1982-85; mgr. gen. acctg. services St. Mary's Health Ctr., Jefferson City, 1985-88, controller, 1988—. Republican. Baptist. Home: 1719 Independence Dr Jefferson City MO 65109 Office: St Mary's Health Ctr 100 St Mary's Med Pla Jefferson City MO 65101

MELLMAN, LEONARD, real estate investor and advisor; b. Phila., Mar. 23, 1924; s. Morris and Luba (Levin) M. BA, Temple U., 1949. Owner, mgr. L. Mellman Co., Phila., 1949-84; ret., 1984; owner, mgr. Mellman Investments, 1960—; ptnr. Mellman, Blume Co., 1979—, Cunniff, Mellman Co., 1982—; gen. ptnr. Diamond Acres, Phila., 1981-86, Van Pelt Ct. Ltd. Pres., 1985—, MLC Bd. Settlement Music Sch., Phila., 1983-85, sec. central bd., 1985—. Served with Signal Corps, U.S. Army, 1943-46, ETO, PTO. Pres. arts and sci. alumni bd. Temple U., 1976-78. Mem. Credit Mchts. Assn. (pres. 1970-72, Man of Yr. award 1970), Phila. Bd. Realtors, Temple U. Gen. Alumni Assn. (2nd v.p., Disting. Alumni award 1985), Singing City Choir Bd. (pres.). Democrat. Jewish. Club: Union League. Home and office: 2530 Panama St Philadelphia PA 19103

MELLMAN, NATHAN RON, real estate agent; b. Columbus, Ohio, July 24, 1964; s. Edwin Mark and Florence Hilda (Cooper) M. BS in Fin. and Internat. Bus., NYU, 1986. Strategic analyst ASPID Internat., Columbus, 1986-87; real eatate agt. Cambridge Realty, Columbus, 1987-88, Bickis, Young & Assoc., Inc., Columbus, 1988—. Ohio coordinator Pete duPont for Pres., Columbus, 1988; Franklin County coordinator, Goerge Voinovich for U.S. Senate, Columbus, 1987-88; chmn. Bd. of Lic. Appeals for City of Columbus, 1988—; candidate Ohio State Senate, Columbus, 1986; vol. CSO Picnic with the Pops Concerts, Columbus, 1986—, Columbus Jewish Fedn., Columbus, 1986—. Recipient Cert. of Honor and Recognition, Columbus, 1987. Mem. Columbus Bd. of Realtors, Nat. Assn. Realtors, Alpha Kappa Psi. Republican. Jewish. Home: 52 N Merkle Rd Bexley OH 43209 Office: Bickis Young & Assoc Inc 1535 Brice Rd Reynoldsburg OH 43068

MELLO, JOHN PHILIP, JR., business journal editor; b. Fall River, Mass., June 17, 1950; s. John P. and Beatrice (Medeiros) M. BA, Northeastern U., 1973. Reporter State House News service, Boston, 1973-80; news editor 80 Micro mag., Peterborough, N.H., 1980-82; editor Portable 100 mag., Camden, Maine, 1982-84; mng. editor Boston Bus. Jour., 1985—. Home: 58 Beltran St Malden MA 02148 Office: Boston Bus Jour 451 D St Boston MA 02210

MELLOR, JAMES ROBB, defense company executive; b. Detroit, May 3, 1930; s. Clifford and Gladys (Robb) M.; m. Suzanne Stykos, June 8, 1953; children: James Robb, Diane Elyse, Deborah Lynn. B.S. in Elec. Engring. and Math, U. Mich., 1952, M.S., 1953. Mem. tech. staff Hughes Aircraft Co., Fullerton, Calif., 1955-58; pres. Data Systems div. Litton Industries, Van Nuys, Calif., after 1958; exec. v.p. Litton Industries, Inc., Beverly Hills, Calif.; pres., chief operating officer AM Internat., Inc., Los Angeles, to 1981; exec. v.p., dir. Gen. Dynamics Corp., 1981—; dir. Bergen Brunswig Corp., Kerr. Patentee in fields of storage tubes and display systems; contbr. articles to profl. pubs. Bd. councilors Grad. Sch. Bus. Adminstrn. and Sch. Bus., U. So. Calif.; mem. adv. council Coll. Bus. Adminstrn., Loyola Marymount U.; bd. dirs. Hollywood Presbyterian Med. Center Found. Served to 1st lt., Signal Corps AUS, 1953-55. Mem. IEEE, Am. Mgmt. Assn., Armed Forces Communications and Electronics Assn. (dir.), Computer and Bus. Equipment Mfrs. Assn. (dir.), Sigma Xi, Tau Beta Pi, Eta Kappa Nu, Phi Kappa Phi. Clubs: Los Angeles Country, Old Warson Country, St. Louis, California, Eldorado. Home: 7759 Kingsbury Blvd Saint Louis MO 63105 Office: Gen Dynamics Corp Pierre Laclede Ctr Saint Louis MO 63105

MELLOTT, ROBERT VERNON, b. Dixon, Ill., Jan. 1, 1928; s. Edwin Vernon and Frances Rhoda (Miller) M.; m. Sarah Carolyn Frink, June 11,

1960; children: Lynn Lorraine, Susan Michelle, David Robert. BA, DePauw U., 1950; postgrad. Ind. U., 1950-51, Law Sch., 1959-61, MA, 1983. TV producer, dir. Jefferson Standard Broadcasting Co., Charlotte, N.C., 1951-59; asst. dist. mgr. GM., Flint, Mich., Chgo., 1961-62; TV and radio comml. supr. NW Ayer & Son, Chgo., 1962-65; TV and radio producer Foote, Cone & Belding Advt. Inc., Chgo., 1965-67, mgr. midwest prodn., 1967-69, mgr. comml. coordination, 1969-74, v.p., mgr. comml. svcs., Chgo., 1974—. Mem. media adv. com. Coll. of Dupage, Glen Ellyn, Ill., 1971-82; chmn. Cub Scout Com., Wheaton, Ill., 1978-79; bd. dirs. Chgo. Unltd., 1969-71. Mem. Am. Assn. Advt. Agys. (broadcast adminstrn. policy com., broadcast talent union rels. ANA-AAAA joint policy com.), World Communication Assn., Internat. Platform Assn., Phi Delta Phi, Alpha Tau Omega. Republican. Mem. Evangelical Christian Ch. Clubs: Chgo. Farmers, Ind. U. Alumni. Home: 26 W 130 Tomahawk Dr Wheaton IL 60187 Office: Foote Cone & Belding Advt 101 E Erie St Chicago IL 60611-2897

MELMON, KENNETH LLOYD, physician, biologist, consultant; b. San Francisco, July 20, 1934; s. Abe Irving and Jean (Kahn) M.; m. Elyce Edelman, June 9, 1957; children: Bradley S., Debra W. AB in Biology with honors, Stanford U., 1956; MD, U. Calif. at San Francisco, 1959. Intern, then resident in internal medicine U. Calif. Med. Ctr., San Francisco, 1959-61; clin. assoc., surgeon USPHS, Nat. Heart, Lung and Kidney Inst., NIH, 1961-64; chief resident in medicine U. Wash. Med. Ctr., Seattle, 1964-65; chief div. clin. pharmacology U. Calif. Med. Ctr., 1965-78; chief dept. medicine Stanford U. Med. Ctr., 1978-84, Arthur Bloomfield prof. medicine, prof. pharmacology, 1978—; dir. office new clin. program devel. Stanford U. Hosp., 1986—; mem. sr. staff Cardiovascular Rsch. Inst.; chmn. joint commn. prescription drug use Senate Subcom. on Health, Inst. Medicine and HEW-Pharm. Mfrs. Assn.; mem. Nat. Bd. Med. Examiners, 1987—; pres. Bio 2000, Woodside, Calif., 1983—; founder, Immulogic, Boston, Palo Alto, Calif., 1988; sci. advisor Syntex, Hoffman LaRoche, Recordati, LTI, Cetus, other cons. FDA, 1965-82, Office Tech. Assessment, 1974-75, Senate Subcom. on Health, 1975—; bd. dirs. Pharmatrix, Techno-Genetics, N.Y.C.; cons. to govt. Author articles, chpts. in books, sects. encys.; Editor: Clinical Pharmacology: Basic Principles in Therapeutics, 2d edit, 1978, Cardiovascular Therapeutics, 1974; assoc. editor: The Pharmacological Basis of Therapeutics (Goodman and Gilman), 1984; mem. editorial bd. numerous profl. jours. Surgeon USPHS, 1961-64. Burroughs Wellcome clin. pharmacology scholar, 1966-71; John Simon Guggenheim fellow Weizman Instn., Israel, 1971; NIH fellow, Bethesda, 1972. Fellow AAAS (nat. coun. 1985—); mem. Am. Fedn. Clin. Rsch. (pres. 1973-74), Am. Soc. Clin. Investigation (past pres. 1978-79), Assn. Am. Physicians, Western Assn. Physicians (past pres. 1983-84), Am. Soc. Pharmacology and Exptl. Therapeutics, Inst. Medicine of Nat. Acad. Sci., Am. Physiol. Soc., Calif. Acad. Medicine, Med. Friends of Wine, Phi Beta Kappa. Democrat. Jewish. Home: 51 Cragmont Way Woodside CA 94062 Office: Stanford U Med Ctr Dept Medicine S025 Stanford CA 94305

MELODY, STEPHEN ANTHONY, retail executive; b. Gainesville, Ga., May 13, 1952; s. Giles Lambert and Rose (Moreschi) M.; m. Paula S. Bondurant, May 24, 1975; 1 child, Meredith Elisabeth. Student, U. Ark., 1970-72. Salesman Rings and Things, Fayetteville, Ark., 1970-71; buyer The Dream Merchant, Fayetteville, Ark., 1971-73; asst. mgr. A.J. August, Fayetteville and St. Joseph, Mo., 1973-75; mgr. Morse Shoes, Fayetteville and Canton, Mass., 1975-80; v.p. Cedric's, Inc., Fayetteville, 1980-85, pres., 1985—; pres. Northwest Ark. Mall Merchants Assn., Fayetteville, 1985—, bd. dirs. Northwest Ark. Mall, 1985—. Dir. (TV commls.) Easter Bears, 1986 (ADDY 1987), Christmas Bears, 1986 (ADDY 1987), Ad Campaign, 1986 (ADDY 1987). Co-chmn. United Way, Fayetteville, 1986. Recipient Addy award 1986, TV Advt. Assn. award, 1986. Mem. MacIntosh Users Group. Episcopalian. Home: 450 Assembly Fayetteville AR 72701 Office: Melody's Choices Inc Northwest Ark Mall Fayetteville AR 72703

MELONE, JOHN ANTHONY, financial officer, controller; b. Long Branch, N.J., June 24, 1957; s. Anthony Frank and Nancy (Vinci) M.; m. Maria C., Apr. 10, 1983; children: Jason, Heather. BS in Acctg., Monmouth Coll., 1982; MBA, Fairleigh Dickinson U. CPA, N.J. Sr. fin. analyst Perkin-Elmer, CMD, Ocean Port, N.J., 1979-83; acct. Gentile, Wiener & Penta, Oakhurst, N.J., 1983-84; controller Dorran/3M, Atlantic Highlands, N.J., 1984-88, also bd. dirs., mem. operating com., 1984-88; v.p. fin. and adminstrn., chief fin. officer Verbex Voice Systems, Inc., Edison, N.J., 1988—. Served as cpl. USMC, 1976-79. Fellow Am. Inst. CPA's, N.J. Soc. CPA's.

MELONE, JOSEPH JAMES, insurance company executive; b. Pittston, Pa., July 27, 1931; s. Dominick William and Beatrice Marie (Pignone) M.; m. Marie Jane DeGeorge, Jan. 23, 1960; children—Lisa, Carol. B.S., U. Pa., 1953, M.B.A., 1954, Ph.D. in Econs, 1961. C.L.U., 1963 C.P.C.U., 1964. Asso. prof. ins. U. Pa., 1959-66, mem. pension research council, 1961-66; research dir. Am. Coll. Life Underwriters, 1966-68; v.p. Prudential Ins. Co., Boston, 1969-76; sr. v.p. Prudential Ins. Co., Newark, 1976-81, exec. v.p., 1981-84, pres., 1984—; chmn. bd. dirs. Prudential Property & Casualty Ins. Co., Newark., Pruco Life, Newark; bd. dirs. Foster Wheeler Corp. Author: Collectively Bargained Multi-Employer Pension Plans, 1961; co-author: Risk and Insurance, 1963, Pension Planning, 1966. Bd. trustees Cath. Community Svcs., Newark Mus.; Archbishop's Com. of Laity of Newark Archdiocese, Archdiocesan Bd. Adminstrn., Newark; bd. overseers Wharton Sch. U. Pa. Mem. Am. Risk and Ins. Assn., Am. Soc. CLUs , Am. Coll. (bd. trustees), Am. Inst. Property & Liability Underwriters (bd. trustees), Pa. State U. Internat. Ins. Soc., Internat. Acad. Mgmt., Health Ins. Assn. of Am. (bd. dirs.), Essex Club, Morris County Country Club, Alpha Tau Omega. Home: 281 Hartshorn Dr Short Hills NJ 07078 Office: The Prudential Ins Co Am Prudential Pla Newark NJ 07101

MELSA, JAMES LOUIS, electrical engineer; b. Omaha, July 6, 1938; s. Louis F. and Anne (Pelnar) M.; m. Katherine Smith, June 25, 1960; children: Susan, Elisabeth, Peter, Jon, Jennifer, Mark. BSEE, Iowa State U., 1960; MSEE, U. Ariz., 1962, PhD, 1965. Asst. prof. elec. engring. U. Ariz., Tucson, 1965-67; prof. So. Meth. U., Dallas, 1967-73; prof., chmn. elec. engring. dept. U. Notre Dame, South Bend, Ind., 1973-84; v.p. research and devel. Tellabs, Inc., Lisle, Ill., 1984-89, v.p. strategic planning and advanced tech., 1989—; cons. in field; assoc. mem. tech. staff Radio Corp. Am., Tuscon, 1960-61. Author: Alternatives for Linear Multivariable Control, 1978, (with D.L. Cohn) Decision and Estimation Theory, 1978, A Step by Step Introduction to 8080 Microprocessor Systems, 1977; (with D.G. Schultz) State Functions and Linear Control Systems, 1967, Linear Control Systems, 1969; (with A.P. Sage) Estimation Theory: with Applications to Control and Communications, 1971, System Identification, 1971, Introduction to Probability and Random Process, 1973; (with J.D. Gibson) Nonparametric Detection with Applicaitons, 1975; Computer Programs for Computational Assistance in the Study of Linear Control Theory, 1973; contbr. articles to profl. publs.; mem. editorial bd. Jour. Computers and Elec. Engring., 1972—. Vice chmn. Am. Automatic Control Coun., 1972-74, chmn., 1974-77; bd. dirs. Nat. Engring. Consortium, 1975-79, Ctr. Communications and Signal Processing, N.C. State, 1986—. Fellow IEEE (tech. editor Southwestern conf. 1970, chmn. nat. membership com. Control Systems Soc. 1972-81, v.p. mem. activities 1984-85, v.p. fin. 1984-85, 86, pres. 1988, mem. editorial bd. 1985—); mem. Tau Beta Pi, Pi Mu Epsilon, Eta Kappa Nu, Phi Kappa Phi, Sigma Xi. Home: 2553 Alta Ct Lisle IL 60532 Office: Tellabs Inc 4951 Indiana Ave Lisle IL 60532

MELTON, ANDREW JOSEPH, JR., investment company executive; b. Bay Shore, N.Y., Mar. 4, 1920; s. Andrew J. and Alice (Lonergan) M.; m. Mary Ann Shanks, Sept. 18, 1943; children: Diana, Andrew, Robert, Karen, Marjorie, Sandra, Michaelle, Edward. B.S., Villanova U., 1942. With Smith Barney & Co., N.Y.C., 1946-72; chmn. exec. com. Smith Barney & Co., 1968-72; exec. v.p. Dean Witter & Co., Inc., N.Y.C., 1972—; chmn., chief exec. officer Dean Witter Reynolds, Inc., N.Y.C., 1978-82; chmn. bd. Dean Witter Funds. Served with USMC, 1942-46, 51-53. Mem. Investment Bankers Assn. Am. (pres. 1970), Bond Club of N.Y. (pres. 1982). Clubs: Knickerbocker (N.Y.C.), Links (N.Y.C.), Madison Sq. Garden (N.Y.C.); Jupiter Hills (Fla.), Dorset Field (Vt.), Ekwanok Country (Vt.). Home: 275 Beach Rd Tequesta FL 33469 Office: Dean Witter Funds 5 World Trade Ctr New York NY 10048

MELTZER, JAY H., retail company executive; b. Bklyn., Mar. 30, 1944; s. Solomon G. and Ethel L. (Kraft) M.; m. Bonnie R. Rosenberg, June 27, 1965; children: Wendy, Elizabeth, Jonathan. A.B., Dartmouth Coll., 1964; LL.B., Harvard U., 1967. Bar: N.Y. 1968, Mass. 1978, U.S. Dist. Ct. Mass 1979. Law clk. to U.S. dist. judge, 1967-68; assoc. firm Shearman & Sterling, N.Y.C., 1968-72; with Damon Corp., Needham Heights, Mass., 1972-84; gen. counsel, sec. Damon Corp., 1973-84, v.p., 1977-84; v.p., corp. counsel Zayre Corp., Framingham, Mass., 1984-87, v.p., gen. counsel, sec., 1987—. Mem. ABA, Am. Soc. Corp. Secs., Internat. Wine and Food Soc., New Eng. Corp. Counsel Assn., Phi Beta Kappa. Office: Zayre Corp 770 Cochituate Rd Framingham MA 01701

MELVILLE, JAMES THOMAS, steel company executive; b. Toronto, Ont., Can., May 3, 1951; s. Clinton Hostler and Dorothy (Dure) M.; m. Ann Hollingsworth, Nov. 1, 1986. B.B.A., U. Western Ont., 1974, LL.B., 1977. Bar: Ont. 1979. Various positions Algoma Steel Corp. Ltd., Sault Ste. Marie, Ont., Can., 1979-87, v.p., treas., gen. counsel, 1987—; bd. dirs. Cannelton Industries Huron Steel Products. Bd. dirs. Sault Ste. Marie Econ. Devel. Corp., 1985—. Mem. Can. Bar Assn., Law Soc. Upper Can., Algoma Steel Club (bd. dirs. 1981—), C. of C. (past pres., bd. dirs. 1985—). Home: 65 Alworth Pl, Sault Sainte Marie, ON Canada P6B 5W5 Office: Algoma Steel Corp Ltd, 503 Queen St E, Sault Sainte Marie, ON Canada P6A 5P2

MELZER, HARRY, information systems consultant; b. Nov. 6, 1946; s. Moses and Ida M.; m. Rosalind Grosel, Feb. 11, 1973; children: Marc Aaron, Steven Joshua. BS, CCNY, 1967; MS, Cornell U., 1970. Teaching asst., rsch. assoc. Cornell U., Ithaca, N.Y., 1967-70; mem. staff Fed. Res. Bank N.Y., N.Y.C., 1970-81, mgr. systems devel., 1981-87; v.p. strategic technology Mfrs. Hanover, N.Y.C., 1987—. NDEA fellow, 1967-70. Mem. ACM (chmn. N.Y.C. chpt. Sigmod 1974-76), Phi Beta Kappa. Office: Mfrs Hanover 55 Water St 38F New York NY 10015

MENAKER, FRANK H., JR., lawyer; b. Harrisburg, Pa., Aug. 23, 1940; s. Frank H. and Romaine (Sadler) M.; m. Sharon Ann Lynch, Feb. 21, 1981; children: Denise L., Jamie E.; children by previous marriage: David C., Michelle R. BA, Wilkes Coll., 1962; JD, Am. U., 1965. Bar: D.C. 1966, Md. 1975, U.S. Supreme Ct. 1975. Staff counsel Office Gen. Counsel, GAO, Washington, 1965-67; atty., asst. corp. sec. Dynalectron Corp., Washington, 1968-70; asst. counsel Martin Marietta Aerospace, Balt., 1970-72, gen. counsel, 1977-81; asst. gen. counsel Martin Marietta Corp., 1973-77, dep. gen. counsel, 1981, gen. counsel, 1981—, v.p., 1982—; spl. counsel U.S. Commn. on Govt. Procurement, 1971. Vice pres., dir. Pinemere Camp Assn., Stroudsburg, Pa., 1978—. Mem. ABA, Md. Bar Assn., Am. Corp. Counsel Assn. (bd. dirs. 1987—), Wash. Met. Corp. Counsel Assn. (bd. dirs. 1988—). Office: Martin Marietta Corp 6801 Rockledge Dr Bethesda MD 20817

MENARD, JAYNE BUSH, oil company executive; b. Dover, N.J., Dec. 21, 1946; d. Peter Thomas and Emily Marie (Suk) Bush; m. Michael Paul Menard, Feb. 3, 1979. AB in History, Coll. William and Mary, 1969; postgrad., Fairleigh Dickinson U., 1970-71. With Exxon Corp., Florham Park, N.J., 1970—, mktg. systems coord., 1985-86, planning controls coord., 1986-87; audit systems advisor Exxon Corp., Florham Park, 1987—. Republican. Methodist. Home: PO Box 363 Bernardsville NJ 07924 Office: Exxon Co Internat 200 Park Ave Florham Park NJ 07924

MENCHER, STUART ALAN, sales and marketing executive; b. N.Y.C., Apr. 25, 1939; s. Meyer H. and Mildred B. (Finger) M.; m. Judith Leslie Schneider; children: Jane Lizabeth, Tracy Ellen. B in Mgmt. Engring., Rensselaer Poly. Inst., 1960; MBA, NYU, 1965. Sales rep. Sperry Rand Univac, Albany, N.Y., 1960-62; various sales and mktg. mgmt. positions IBM Corp., Harrison, N.Y., 1965-78; br. mgr. data processing div. IBM Corp., 1978-81; dr. mktg. ops. planning, bus. mktg. dept. AT&T, Basking Ridge, N.J., 1981-83; dir. market planning Morristown, N.J., 1983-84; dir. data systems mktg. AT&T Info. Systems, Morristown, 1984-85, v.p. mktg., large bus. systems div., 1985-87; sr. v.p. sales and mktg. MCI Telecommunications Corp., Washington, 1987—. Pres. Westfield Men's Coll. Scholarship Club, N.J., 1977; coach Westfield Youth Soccer Assn., 1976-81; mem. budget rev. com. United Fund, Westfield, 1983-85. Served to lt. USCGR, 1962-65. Office: MCI Telecommunications Corp 1133 19th St NW Washington DC 20036

MENDELL, GARY MICHAEL, service executive; b. Bridgeport, Conn., Feb. 12, 1957; s. Jerome Harold and Eleanor (Solomon) M.; m. Ellen Jodi Kendall, Mar. 31, 1984; 1 child, Brian Mitchell. BS in Hotel Adminstrn., Cornell U., 1979. Asst. mgr. Ponderosa Systems, Inc., Southington, Conn., 1979; mgr. Ponderosa Systems, Inc., Hartford, Conn., 1979-80; exec. mgr. Ponderosa Systems, Inc., Waterbury, Conn., 1980-81; regional supr. Ponderosa Systems, Inc., Conn., 1981-82; owner, mgr. Duchess Family Restaurant, Fairfield, Conn., 1982-84; pres. Hospitality Equity Investors Inc., Westport, Conn., 1985—; cons. Hospitality Valuation Services, Inc., Mineola, N.Y. Mem. Bldg. Com. B'nai Torah Synagogue, Trumbull, Conn. Mem. Cornell Real Estate Council, Cornell Soc. Hotelmen, Urban Land Inst., Real Estate Securities and Syndication Inst., Sigma Alpha Epsilon (treas. 1976, social chmn. 1977, pres. 1978-79). Republican. Home: 20 Elmstead Rd Trumbull CT 06611 Office: Hospitality Equity Investors Inc 1 Gorham Island Westport CT 06880

MENDELL, OLIVER M., commercial banking officer; b. N.Y.C., Apr. 4, 1925; s. M. Lester and Malvina Mendell; grad. Washington and Lee U., 1950; postgrad. Columbia U. Exec. Course, 1969; m. Shelley R. Disick, Sept. 24, 1962; children—Steven, David. Asst. treas. Bankers Trust Co., N.Y.C., 1950-56; v.p., dir. Queens Nat. Bank, N.Y.C., 1956-58; sr. v.p. Chem. Bank, N.Y.C., 1958—; dir. Cartier, Inc., 1967-69. Pres., Fifth Ave. Assn., 1978-82, chmn., 1982-87; trustee Washington and Lee U. Alumni, vice chmn. alumni fund campaign; bd. dirs. Citizens Budget Commn. N.Y., SSS, 1962-76, JFK Internat. Synagogue, Park 86th Apt. Corp., 1966-71, Joint Distbn. Com.; bd. govs. Sch. Banking and Money Mgmt., Adelphi U., 1975-82; gov. USO World Bd. Govs.; co-treas., bd. dirs. United Jewish Appeal Greater N.Y., Inc.; mem. adv. bd. Regional Emergency Med. Services Council of N.Y.C.; bd. dirs., mem. exec. com. Am. Jewish Com.; trustee Bernard J. Moncharsh Found., Inc., Temple Shaaray Tefila, 1971-74, Fedn. Jewish Philanthropies, B'nai B'rith Banking Lodge; mem. com. legacies and bequests ARC; treas., mem. exec. com. USO, Met. N.Y.; trustee NYU Real Estate Inst.; vice-chmn. steering com., treas. N.Y. Bus. Council for Clean Air, 1966-71; fellow Brandeis U. Served as navigator USAF, 1943-46. Recipient civic awards. Mem. Assn. for Better N.Y. (mem. exec. com.), Phi Epsilon Pi (nat. budget com.), Omicron Delta Kappa. Clubs: Harmonie (N.Y.C.); Rockrimmon Country (Stamford, Conn.). Home: 1040 Park Ave New York NY 10028 Office: Chem Bank 277 Park Ave New York NY 10172

MENDELSON, ALAN MICHAEL, venture capitalist; b. Hartford, Conn., Dec. 20, 1947; s. Morris and Natalie (Ratner) Ziplow; m. Peggy Ann Schloss, Aug. 20, 1970; children: Jason, Jennifer. BA, Trinity Coll., Hartford, 1967; LLB, U. Conn., 1974. Analyst Aetna, Jacobs, and Reeno, Hartford, 1969-74, trust officer, 1974-76, sr. investment officer, 1976-79, asst. v.p., 1979-85, pres., 1985—; cons. DuPont, Wilmington, Del., 1985-88; adv. Battery Ventures, Boston, 1984—, Kimberly, Bronnel, Lehnar, Washington, 1986—; mem. Gov.'s High Tech Adv. Council, 1983—, exec. com. SEC Forum on Small Bus. Capital Formation, Washington. Mem. exec. com. Hartford Jewish Fedn., 1983-88; bd. dirs. synagogue, West Hartford, Conn., 1982-88. Mem. Conn. Venture Group (pres. 1986, chmn. emeritus 1988), Conn. Soc. Fin. Analysts. Democrat. Jewish. Office: Aetna Life City Pl 17th Fl Hartford CT 06156

MENDELSON, LEONARD (MELVIN), lawyer; b. Pitts., May 20, 1923; s. Jacob I. and Anna R. M.; m. Emily Solomon, Dec. 2, 1956; children: Ann, James R., Kathy S. AB, U. Mich., 1947; JD, Yale U., 1950. Bar: Pa. 1951, U.S. Supreme Ct. 1955. Mem., Hollinshead and Mendelson, Pitts., chmn. bd., 1974—; chmn. Lawyer-Realty Joint Com., Pitts., 1971-72. Mem. Pitts. Bd. Pub. Edn., 1975-76. Mem. ABA, Pa. Bar Assn., Allegheny County Bar Assn. Office: 230 Grant Bldg Pittsburgh PA 15219

MENDENHALL, JOHN RYAN, lawyer, transportation executive; b. Des Moines, Jan. 17, 1928; s. Merritt Blake and Elizabeth M. (Ryan) M.; m. Joan Lois Schafer, June 20, 1953; children: Thomas, James, Jane, Julie, Robert, Jennifer. BS, U. Notre Dame, 1950; JD, Harvard U., 1953. Bar: Iowa 1953, U.S. Tax Ct. 1954, D.C. 1975, U.S. Ct. Claims 1975. Mem. tax staff Arthur Andersen & Co., Cleve., 1953-63, ptnr., 1963-66; dir. taxes Arthur Andersen & Co., Chgo., 1966-70; ptnr. Arthur Andersen & Co., Washington, 1970-74, Williams, Connolly & Califano, Washington, 1974-76; gen. tax counsel Union Pacific Corp., N.Y.C., 1977-80, v.p. taxes, 1980—; bd. dirs. Empire Steel Castings, Readinng, Pa. Co-author: Reforming the Tax Structure, 1973; contbr. articles on taxes to various jours. Bd. dirs. Cook County Hosp., Chgo., 1968-71, Inst. Rsch. on Econs. of Taxation, Washington, 1977—; trustee Convent of Sacred Heart, Greenwich, Conn., 1976-80. With U.S. Army, 1946-47, Japan. Mem. ABA (tax sect., chmn. indexing com. 1985-86), Am. Coun. Capital Formation (bd. dirs. 1972--), Bus. Roundtable (tax adv. group), C. of C. U.S. (mem. tax com. 1972--), Am. Law Inst. (tax adv. group), Nat Tax Assn. (pres. 1981-82), Harvard Club (N.Y.C.), Met. Club (Washington), Belle Haven Club (Greenwich, Conn.). Republican. Roman Catholic. Home: 130 Wall St Bethlehem PA 18018 Office: Eighth and Eaton Aves Bethlehem PA 18018

MENDEZ, ALBERT ORLANDO, industrial company executive; b. Bogota, Columbia, Sept. 7, 1935; came to U.S., 1960; naturalized, 1968; s. Angelino Benjamin and Ana Isabel (Gutierre de Cetina) M.; children: Nicole C., Eric A. BS in Nuclear Physics, N.C. State U., 1961, MS in Nuclear Engring., 1963; MBA, U. Hartford, 1970. Physicist, mgr. mfg. Combustion Engring. Co., Windsor, Conn., 1963-67; mgr. corp. devel. and planning Gulf Oil Corp., Pitts., 1967-71; v.p. mktg., controller for Latin Am. Xerox Corp., Stamford, Conn., 1971-76; exec. v.p., chief operating officer, bd. dirs. Ogden Corp., N.Y.C., 1976-84; chmn., chief exec. officer Am. Indstl. Corp., Stamford, 1984-86; chmn., chief exec. officer, prin. Argo-Tech Corp., Aerospace, Cleve., 1986—; bd. dirs. Catalyst Energy Co., N.Y.C., 1st Prin. Corp., N.Y.C.; mng. ptnr. Agnem Ltd. Partnership, New Canaan, Conn., 1984—; pres., chief exec. officer, bd. dirs. Agnem Investment Co., New Canaan, 1983—. Mem. Palm Beach (Fla.) Polo Club. Office: 131 Pequot Ln New Canaan CT 06840

MENDEZ, JOHN FRANK, horticulture company executive, accountant; b. Eureka, Nev., Sept. 12, 1942; s. John George and Neva June (Tognoni) M.; m. Edith Holmes Prentice, Jan. 29, 1966 (div. Dec. 1985); children: Damon, Derek. BA, Golden Gate U., 1968; MBA, Harvard U., 1970. CPA, Calif. V.p. Amfac Distbn., Burlingame, Calif., 1977-78; controller Amfac Electric Supply, Burlingame, 1979-80; asst. v.p. Amfac, Inc., San Francisco, 1980-82; pres. Amfac Garden Products, Burlingame, 1982-83; exec. v.p. Amfac Horticultural, Burlingame, 1983-84; pres. Tri-West, Inc., San Mateo, Calif., 1984—, also chmn. bd. dirs.; instr. Golden Gate U. MBA program, San Francisco, 1972-74. Commr. Am. Youth Soccer, Millbrae, Calif., 1981-85, Millbrae Youth Baseball, 1982. Served with U.S. Army, 1960-63. Mem. Am. Inst. CPA's, Calif. Soc. CPA's. Republican. Office: Tri-West Inc 1875 S Grant Ave Ste 520 San Mateo CA 94402

MENDONSA, ARTHUR ADONEL, city official; b. Wauchula, Fla., Apr. 5, 1928; s. Arthur Abner and Mamie (Swafford) M.; m. Beverly Glover, Sept. 6, 1951; children—Arthur Adonel, George Andrew; m. Suzanne Danzig, Sept. 7, 1980. B.A., Emory U., 1952; M. City Planning, Ga. Inst. Tech., 1954. Planning dir. Gainesville-Hall County (Ga.) Planning Commn., 1954-56, 57-60; sr. planner Charleston (S.C.) County Planning Commn., 1956-57; exec. dir. Savannah-Chatham (Ga.) County Met. Planning Commn., 1960-62; city mgr. Savannah, 1962-67; 71—; dir. field services, asst. prof. Inst. Govt., U. Ga., Athens, 1967-69; exec. asst. to chmn. DeKalb County Bd. Commrs., Decatur, Ga., 1969-71; mem. Coastal Area Planning and Devel. Commn., 1972—, chmn., 1983-85; mem. Ga. Gov.'s Adv. Council on Coastal Zone Mgmt., 1976-78, Ga. Coastal Mgmt. Bd., 1978—. Author: Simplified Financial Management in Local Government, 1967. Recipient All-Pro City Mgmt. Team City and State mags., 1986, 87, 88. Mem. Am. Inst. Planners (bd. examiners), Am. Soc. Pub. Adminstrn., Internat. City Mgrs. Assn. (Outstanding Mgmt. Innovator award 1979), Ga. City-County Mgrs. Assn. (pres. 1974-75), Kiwanis.

MENDOZA, CLAUDIO JUAN, software company executive; b. Havana, Cuba, Nov. 22, 1947; came to U.S., 1960; s. Claudio Jorge and Graciela (Lagomasino) M.; m. Patricia Alvarez, Nov. 1972 (div. 1981); children: Claudette, Annette; m. Ana Maria Diaz, Nov. 26, 1982; 1 child, Cassandra. B in Indsl. Engring., U. Fla., 1970. Engr. Eastern Air Lines, Miami, Fla., 1970-71, sr. engr., 1972-76, mgr., 1976-80; pres. Gen. Systems Mgmt., Miami, 1974-80; exec. v.p. Cybernetics Systems Internat., Miami, 1980-84, pres., 1985—. Writer employee mgmt. and planning systems software. Mem. U.S. C. of C., Am. Inst. Indsl. Engrs., Big Five Club, Doral Club. Republican. Roman Catholic. Home: 8275 SW 53d Ave Miami FL 33143

MENDOZA, ROBERTO G., JR., banker; b. Cuba, 1945. BA, Yale U., 1967; MBA, Harvard U., 1974. With Morgan Guaranty Trust Co., N.Y.C., 1967—, now mng. dir. Office: Morgan Guaranty Trust 23 Wall St New York NY 10015 *

MENEAR, JULIAN FRANCIS, investment banker, high technology consultant; b. Crowborough, Sussex, Eng., Dec. 9, 1956; came to U.S., 1976; s. Gordon Francis and Bernice Elisa (Quant) M.; m. Sharon Elise Oppenheimer, June 21, 1982; children: Ashley Nichole, Kevin Gordon. BA, Boston U., 1979; cert. advanced study, Harvard U., 1980; MBA, Duquesne U., 1982. Registered brokerage rep. Officer Cheverie & Co., Boston, 1982, Peat, Marwick, Mitchell & Co., Boston, 1982-83, A.G. Becker Paribus, Chgo., 1983-84; v.p., supervising analyst Pershing div. Donaldson, Lufkin & Jenrette Securities Corp., Chgo., 1984—; cons. Chgo. Access Corp., 1986. Bd. dirs. MIT U. Enterprise Forum, Chgo., 1985—. Office: Donaldson Lufkin & Jenrette Div 175 W Jackson Blvd Ste A250 Chicago IL 60604

MENEFEE, SAMUEL PYEATT, lawyer; b. Denver, June 8, 1950; s. George Hardiman and Martha Elizabeth (Pyeatt) M. BA, Yale U., 1972; diploma, Oxford (Eng.) U., 1973; BLitt, Oxford U., 1975; JD, Harvard U., 1981; LLM in Oceans, U. Va., 1982. Bar: Ga. 1981, Va.1983, La. 1983, D.C. 1985, Nebr. 1985, Fla. 1985, Me. 1986, Pa. 1986, U.S. Supreme Ct. 1985. Fellow Ctr. for Oceans Law & Policy, Charlottesville, Va., 1982-83, sr. fellow, 1985—; assoc. Phelps, Dunbar, Marks, Claverie & Sims, New Orleans, 1983-85; sr. assoc. Ctr. for Law & Nat. Security, Charlottesville, 1985—; of counsel Barham & Churchill PC, New Orleans, 1985-88; lectr. various nat. and internat. orgns. Author: Wives for Sale: An Ethnographic Study of British Popular Divorce, 1981; co-editor: Materials on Ocean Law, 1982; contbr. numerous articles to profl. jours. Bates traveling fellow, Yale U., 1971; Rhodes scholar, 1972-75; recipient Katharine Briggs prize, 1982. Fellow Royal Anthrop. Inst., Am. Anthrop. Assn.; mem. Southeastern Admiralty Law Inst. (com. mem.), Maritime Law Assn. (proctor, com. mem., chmn. subcom. law of the sea) Marine Tech. Soc., ABA (vice-chmn. marine resources com., mem. Working Group on Terrorism, chmn. law sea com's. subcom. naval warfare, maritime terrorism & piracy), Selden Soc., Am. Soc. Internat. Law, Internat. Law Assn. (rapporteur Am. branch com. EEZ), U.S. Naval Inst., USN League, Folklore Soc., Am. Hist. Soc., Raven Soc., Fence Club, Mory's Club, Elizabethan Club, Leander Club, United Oxford and Cambridge Club, Yale Club, Pendennis Club, Paul Morphy Club, Roundtable Club, Phi Beta Kappa, Omicron Delta Kappa. Republican. Episcopalian. Office: U Va Ctr Law & Nat Security Charlottesville VA 22901

MENGDON, JOSEPH MICHAEL, banker; b. Houston, Sept. 28, 1924; s. H.F. and Amalie (Dittlinger) M.; m. Suzanne Miner, Spet. 30, 1950; children: Anne E., Amanda M., Michael J., Charles L., Melissa M., Mary M. Fitch. PhB, U. Notre Dame, 1949. V.p. Nat. Bank Detroit, 1949-67; exec. v.p., dir. First Mich. Corp., Detroit, 1967—, First Mich. Capital Corp., Detroit, 1967—. Served to 1st lt. USAF. Office: First Mich Capital Corp 100 Renaissance Ctr Detroit MI 48243

MENGEL, MARVIN CALVIN, medical management executive, physician; b. Allentown, Pa., June 20, 1943; s. Marvin and Verna (Sterner) M.; children: Elizabeth, David, Julie. BA, Johns Hopkins U., 1964, MD, 1967. Chief exec. officer Diabetes and Endocrine Ctr. of Orlando, Fla., 1973—; pres. Vision Multimedia, Orlando, 1977-84. Contbr. articles to profl. jours. Maj. USAF, 1969-71. Mem. AMA, Am. Acad. Med. Dirs., Profl. Photographers Am., Christian Med. Soc. (pres. 1986-87). Office: Diabetes Endocrine Ctr of Orlando 1200 E Hillcrest St Orlando FL 32803

MENGES, CARL BRAUN, investment banker; b. N.Y.C., Sept. 17, 1930; s. Hermann and Alice (Braun) M.; m. Cordelia Sykes, Apr. 24, 1965; children: James C., Benjamin W., Samuel G. B.A., Hamilton Coll., 1951; M.B.A., Harvard U., 1953. Salesman Owens Corning Fiberglas Corp., 1954-59, mktg. mgr., 1959-63; with instl. sales dept. Model Roland Co., N.Y.C., 1963-65; with instnl. sales dept., syndicate mgr., dir. internat. Donaldson, Lufkin & Jenrette Inc., N.Y.C., 1965-72; mng. dir. Donaldson, Lufkin & Jenrette Inc., 1972—, chmn. fin. services group, 1984-87, vice chmn. of bd., 1987—; chmn. Wood, Struthers & Winthrop; chmn., bd. dirs. Winthrop Focus Funds, Pine St. Fund; bd. dirs. Neuwirth Fund, Whitbreads, N. Am., Med. Indemnity Assurance Corp. Hosp. for Spl. Surgery, The Greenwal Found. Treas., bd. dirs., trustee Assn. Homemaker Services, N.Y.C., 1971-73; trustee Hosp. for Spl. Surgery, 1977—, Hamilton Coll., Clinton, N.Y., trustee 1985—; v.p., treas., trustee The Allen-Stevenson Sch., N.Y.C., 1979—, Security Industry Assocs. Internat. Com., 1986—; bd. dirs. Boys Club of N.Y. Clubs: Union, Maidstone (gov. 1969--86, pres. 1982-86), National Golf Links America, Madison Square Garden, Devon Yacht, Regency Whist, Doubles, Union, Bond of N.Y. Office: Donaldson Lufkin & Jenrette Inc 140 Broadway New York NY 10005

MENK, CARL WILLIAM, executive search company executive; b. Newark, Oct. 19, 1921; s. Carl William and Catherine Regina (Murray) M.; m. Elizabeth Cullum, May 30, 1947; children: Carl, Elizabeth (dec.), Mary, Paul. B.S.B.A., Seton Hall U., 1943; M.A., Columbia U., 1950. Sr. v.p. P. Ballantine & Sons, Newark, 1946-69; pres. Boyden Assocs., Inc., N.Y.C., 1969-84; chmn. Canny, Bowen, Inc., N.Y.C., 1984—; dir. Howard Savs. Bank; instr. N.J. Inst. Tech. Served as pilot, 2d lt. USAAF, 1943-46. Clubs: Glen Ridge Country, Spring Lake Golf, Montclair Country, Union League of N.Y., John's Island, Knights of Malta. Home: 546 Ridgewood Ave Glen Ridge NJ 07028 Office: 425 Park Ave New York NY 10022

MENKE, WILLIAM CHARLES, lawyer, consultant; b. Cin., Aug. 30, 1939; s. William Garhardt and Margaret Philomena (Mercurio) M.; m. Mary Lou Papan, Jan. 7, 1967; children—William Leo II, Lorelei Louise. B.S., U. Detroit, 1961; M.B.A., Ind. No. U., 1972; J.D., U. Detroit, 1976. Bar: Ohio 1977, U.S. Ct. Appeals (6th cir.) 1977. Sr. engr. Gen. Electric Co., Cin., 1964-67; v.p., gen. mgr. Preventicare Systems, Inc., Dearborn Mich., 1967-71; dir. Comshare, Inc., Ann Arbor, Mich., 1971-76; chief exec. officer William C. Menke & Assocs., Inc., New Richmond, Ohio, 1976—; dir. New Richmond Nat. Bank; city atty. City of New Richmond, 1979-81. Served to lt. (j.g.) USN, 1961-64. Fellow Lawyers in Mensa; mem. ABA, Assn. Trial Lawyers Am., Ohio State Bar. Republican. Roman Catholic. Club: Mensa. Lodge: KC. Home: 1432 Indian Ridge Trail New Richmond OH 45157 Office: William C Menke & Assocs Inc PO Box 10 New Richmond OH 45157

MENNINGER, ROY WRIGHT, medical foundation executive, psychiatrist; b. Topeka, Oct. 27, 1926; s. William Claire and Catharine (Wright) M.; m. Beverly Joan Miller, Mar. 4, 1972; children: Heather, Ariel, Bonar, Eric, Brent, Frederick, Elizabeth. AB, Swarthmore (Pa.) Coll., 1947; MD, Cornell U., 1951; DHL, Ottawa (Kans.) U., 1977; LittD, William Jewell Coll., Liberty Mo., 1985. Diplomate Am. Bd. Psychiatry and Neurology. Intern N.Y. Hosp., 1951-52; resident in psychiatry Boston State Hosp., 1952-53, Boston Psychopathic Hosp., 1953-56; from resident psychiatrist to assoc. med. psychiatrist Peter Bent Brigham Hosp., Boston, 1956-61; teaching and rsch. fellow Harvard U. Med. Sch., Boston, 1956-61; staff psychiatrist Menninger Found., Topeka, 1961-63, dir. dept. preventative psychiatry, 1963-67, pres., 1967—; bd. dirs. Bank IV Topeka N.A., 1974—, CML Corp.; mem. Karl Menninger Sch. Psychiatry, Topeka, 1972—; clin. prof. psychiatry U. Kans. Med. Ctr., Wichita, 1977—; cons. Colmery-O'Neil VA Med. Ctr., Topeka, 1979—; fellow Pacific Rim Coll. Psychiatry. Editor Jour. Medical Aspects Human Sexuality, 1967; editor advisor bd. Parents Mag., 1966—, Clin. Psychiatry News, 1973; reviewer American Jour. Psychiatry, 1980; co-author The Medical Marriage, 1988. Mem. sponsoring com. Inst. Am. Democracy, 1967—; mem. adv. group Horizons '76 Am. Revolution Bicentennial Commn.; adv. bd. Topeka Inst. Urban Affairs, 1967-70, Highland Park-Pierce Neighborhood House, Topeka, 1966-70; bd. dirs. Shawnee council Campfire Girls, Topeka, 1962-79, A.K. Rice Inst., Washington, Sex Info. and Edn. Council U.S., 1970-73, mem. edn. com., long range planning com., 1972-73; bd. dirs. Goals for Topeka, Topeka Inst. Urban Affairs, 1969—, v.p., 1973—; med. adv. com. VA Hosp., 1971—; mem. Gov.'s Com. on Criminal Adminstrn., 1971—; trustee People-to-People, Kansas City, Mo., 1967-69, Baker U., 1968-71, Midwest Research Inst., 1967—, mem. exec. com., 1970—; vis. lectr. Fgn. Service Inst., State Dept., 1963-66; chmn. social issues com. Group Advancement Psychiatry, 1972-82; community adv. bd. Kans. Health Workers Union, 1967-68; adv. com. to bd. dirs. New Eng. Mut. Life Ins. Co., 1967—. With U.S. Army, 1953-55. Recipient Disting. Svs. citation U. Kans., 1985; Pacific Rim Coll. Psychiatry fellow. Fellow Am. Psychiat. Assn. (life, Joint Information Service exec. com.), Am. Coll. Psychiatrists, Am. Orthopsychiat. Assn., Am. Coll. Mental Health Adminstrs.; mem. Northeastern Group Psychotherapy (hon.), AAAS, Physicians Social Responsibility, Kan. Psychiat. Soc., Greater Topeka C. of C. (dir.), Harvard Club (NYC). Episcopalian. Office: Menninger Found 5800 West Sixth Topeka KS 66606

MENOR, MARTA, household products executive; b. Havana, Cuba, Jan. 19; came to U.S., 1961; d. Maximino and Maria Menor. BA in Econs. cum laude, Queens Coll., 1976; postgrad., St. Johns U, N.Y.C., 1977-79. Spl. markets statistics analyst Lever Bros. Co., N.Y.C., 1969-73, fin. analyst, 1973-79, supr., 1979-83, mgr., 1983—. Mem. Omicron Delta Epsilon. Republican. Roman Catholic. Office: Lever Bros Co 390 Park Ave New York NY 10022

MENOUFY, KAIS A. HAMID, high technology company executive; b. Cairo, Oct. 6, 1946; s. Abdul Hamid Ibrahim and Zainab (Mahmoud) M.; m. Anissa Saad Abdul Gawad, Nov. 8, 1972; children—Amira, Karim, Samaah. B.S. in Bus. Adminstrn., Cairo U., 1968; postgrad. Am. U. Cairo, 1969, Ain Shams U., 1971-73, Harvard U., 1977. Comml. rep. Data Gen. M.E., Athens, Greece, 1974-77; mng. dir. Data Gen. OPR, Saudi Arabia, 1977-81; cons. Menoufy Mgmt. Group, Middle East, 1981-82; dep. mng. dir. CBC System, Internat, 1982-83; v.p. internat. ops. Tera Corp., Berkeley, Calif. and Riyadh, Saudi Arabia, 1983-87; pres. Skaks Tech. Co., Foster City, Calif., 1987—; cons. in field. Vice pres. Student Council, Cairo U., 1965-67. Served to capt. Egyptian Army, 1970-74. Decorated Egyptian Golden First Class Mil. Courage medal. Mem. Am. Mgmt. Assn., Hamilton Mgmt. Inst., Harvard Bus. Group. Club: Lawrence Hall of Sci. Avocations: basketball and other sports, theatre, music, reading. Home: PO Box 531 Half Moon Bay CA 94019 Office: 2150 Shattuck Ave Berkeley CA 94704 also: Tera Corp,, PO Box 4615,, Riyadh, Saudi Arabia

MENSCHEL, RICHARD LEE, investment banker; b. N.Y.C., Jan. 6, 1934; s. Benjamin and Helen (Goldsmith) M.; m. Ronay Arlt, Aug. 21, 1974; children: Charis, Sabina, Celene. B.S., Syracuse U., 1955; M.B.A., Harvard U., 1959. Assoc. securities sales adminstr. Goldman, Sachs & Co., N.Y.C., 1959-67; v.p. Goldman. Sachs & Co., N.Y.C., 1967-69; ptnr. securities sales Goldman, Sachs & Co., N.Y.C., 1969-88, mgmt. com., 1980-88, ltd. ptnr., 1988—. Co-chmn. City of N.Y. Transitional Gov. Search Panel, 1977; pres., bd. dirs. Joffrey Ballet Found., 1977-79; bd. dirs. Nat. Corp. Fund. for Dance, 1977-79, Fed. Protestant Welfare Agys., 1978-81, Mcpl. Art Soc., 1980—, Horace W. Goldsmith Found., 1980—; trustee, mem. exec. com. George Eastman House, Rochester, N.Y., 1980—; trustee Nantucket Conservation Found. Inc., Vera Inst. Justice, 1989—; mem. vis. com. Harvard Grad. Sch. Bus. Adminstrn., 1985—; mem. adv. bd. Mus. Modern Art, Oxford, 1987—; trustee The Jewish Mus. Served to lt. USAF, 1955-56. Clubs: Broad Street, Harvard. Home: 880 Fifth Ave New York NY 10021 Office: Goldman Sachs & Co 85 Broad St New York NY 10004

MENSCHER, BARNET GARY, steel company executive; b. Laurelton, N.Y., Sept. 5, 1940; s. Samuel and Louise (Zaimont) M.; student Centenary Coll., 1958-59; B.B.A., U. Tex., 1963; m. Diane Elaine Gachman, June 12, 1966; children—Melissa Denise, Corey Lane, Scott Jay. Vice pres. mktg. Ella Gant Mfg., Shreveport, La., 1964-66; warehouse mgr., dir. material control Gachman Steel Co., Fort Worth, 1966-68, gen. mgr., Houston, 1968-70, v.p., sales mgr. Gulf Coast, 1971-76; pres. Menko Steel Service, Inc., Houston, 1979—; v.p., treas. Gachman Metal Co.; investment cons. D & L Enterprises, 1966—. Mem. solicitation com. United Fund, 1969-76; mem. Nat. Alliance of Businessmen Jobs Program, 1969—. Served with AUS, 1963-65. Mem. Tex. Assn. Steel Importers, Purchasing Agts. Assn. Houston, Credit Assn. Houston, Am. Mgmt. Assn., Assn. Steel Distbrs., Phi Sigma Delta, Alpha Phi Omega. Home: 314 Tealwood Dr Houston TX 77024 Office: PO Box 40296 Houston TX 77040

MENTZ, LAWRENCE, lawyer; b. N.Y.C., Nov. 5, 1946; s. Joseph Walter and Audrey Cecilia (Armstrong) M.; m. Barbara Antonello, Nov. 10, 1973; children: Kathleen Elizabeth, Lawrence Goodwin. BS in Physics, Rensselaer Poly. Inst., 1968; JD, U. Notre Dame, 1973. Bar: N.Y. 1973; Washington 1974. Assoc. Condon & Forsyth, N.Y.C., 1973-80, ptnr., 1981—; speaker Worldwide Airlines Customer Relations Assn. Conf., Singapore, 1983, 2d Cir. Speakers Bur., Com. on BiCentennial of U.S. Constitution, 1987; arbitrator U.S. Dist. Ct. (ea. dist.) Bklyn., 1986—. Served with USNR, 1969-70. Mem. ABA, Fed. Bar Council, N.Y. State Bar Assn. (com. on fed. jud.), Assn. of Bar of City of N.Y. (com. on aeronautics law), Wings Club. Roman Catholic. Office: Condon & Forsyth 1251 Ave of Americas New York NY 10020

MENZER, JOHN BRUCE, financial executive; b. Chgo., Mar. 27, 1951; s. John and Lorraine (Glugla) M. m. Kathleen A. Leahy, Oct. 23, 1976; 1 child, Christine. BBA in Pub. Acctg., Loyola U., 1972, MBA in Fin., 1980. CPA, Ill. Supr. acctg. systems Am. Internat., Mount Prospect, Ill., 1973-75; supr. audit Pannell, Kerr, Forster & Co., Chgo., 1975-77; sr. v.p. Bally Mfg. Corp., 1977-85; exec. v.p. Fox Meyer Corp., Dallas, 1985—. Bd. dirs. Jr. Achievement, Chgo., 1973-75. Mem. Fin. Execs. Inst., Ill. State Soc. CPAs, Nat. Retail Mchts. Assn., Am. Inst. CPAs, Internat. Franchise Assn. (chmn. fin. and tax com., conf. coordinator). Home: 1932 Crescent Ct Hoffman Estates IL 60194

MERAR, ERWIN JEROME, distbg. co. exec.; b. Green Bay, Wis., Jan. 19. 1924; s. Marcus C and Sadye (Rosenberg) M.; student St. Norberts Coll., 1942-43, Bard Coll., 1943-44, U. Wis., 1945-47; m. Emma Lee Stern, Jan. 5, 1952; children—David L., Robert M. Advt. mgr. Humphrey Chevrolet Co., Milw., 1947-49; dir. advt. Samson Appliance Stores, 1949-54; v.p. Standard Electric Supply Co., Milw., 1954-70; pres. Mid-Am. Acceptance Corp., 1960-70, now dir.; pres. Ader Corp., 1962—, Summit Tower Corp., 1958—, Merco Corp., 1970—, CC Refractories, 1980—. Served with AUS, 1942-45. Mem. Am. Legion, Zeta Beta Tau Alumni Club. Mason (32 deg.), Shriner. Club: Wisconsin. Home: 825 Autumn Path Ln Bayside WI 53217 Office: Merco Corp PO Box 12145 4080 N Port Washington Rd Milwaukee WI 53212

MERCADO, PETER NELSON, real estate executive; b. Bklyn., Oct. 9, 1947; s. Roy and Gloria Mercado; m. Anne M. Harrell, Mar. 1, 1974; 1 child, Alexander Peter. AA, Atlantic County Coll., Blackwood, N.J., 1971; BA, Stockton State Coll., Pomona, N.J., 1973; M in Pub. Adminstrn., Cen. Mich. U., 1975; cert. pub. mgr., Rutgers U., 1985. Lic. real estate broker, 1986. Asst. to v.p. for campus programs Stockton State Coll., Pomona, 1975-77, dir. student devel. and services, 1977-81, dean of students, 1981-85, asst. to pres., 1986; pres. Mercado Realty, Pleasantville, N.J., 1986—; Cons., mem. accrediting team Commn. of Higher Edn., New England States Assn., Middle States Assn., mem. legis. and comml. coms. Atlantic City and County Bd. Realtors; chmn. grant evaluating teams HEW; real estate cons. Price Enterprises, 1986, Delta IIne, 1986, Decadon, 1987. Treas. Atlantic County Task Force on Alcohol Abuse, Atlantic City, 1983-84; pres. Absecon (N.J.) City Council, 1985-86; bd. dirs. Atlantic County United Way, Atlantic County ARC, 1987-88, Inst. Human Devel., 1987-88; mem. exec. bd. United Ways of N.J. Served to cpl. USMC, 1967-69, Vietnam. Decorated Bronze Star, Purple Heart (2), D.S.M.; recipient Spl. Innovative Projects award N.J. Dept. Edn. 1975, Outstanding Service to Higher Edn. and Community award Am. Biog. Inst., 1988; named one of Outstanding Young Men of Am., U.S. Jaycees, 1977, 78, 79. Mem. Nat. Assn. Realtors, So. N.J. Tech. Consortium, So. N.J. Devel. Council, Nat. Assn. Student Personnel Adminstrs., Am. Personnel and Guidance Assn., DAV, Am. Legion, VFW. Home: 11 Saddle Ridge Ln McKee City NJ 08232 Office: Mercado Realty 1416 N Main St Pleasantville NJ 08232

MERCER, JOHN BOYD, shipping company executive; b. Melbourne, Australia, Feb. 18, 1939; arrived in Singapore, 1978; s. Leslie Boyd and Joan (Richardson) M.; m. Alicia Ranoschy, Dec. 2, 1963; children: Suzanne, Tina, David Boyd. B of Commerce, U. Melbourne, 1961; diploma, Harvard Bus. Sch., 1978. Chief acct. Conmix Proprietary Ltd., Melbourne, 1961-63, Hall Ham Concrete Ltd., London, 1963-65; sr. cons. Touche Ross and Ptnrs., Melbourne, 1965-67; fin. mgr. Buchan Laird & Buchan Ltd., Melbourne, 1967-69; asst. fin. controller The Australian Estates Ltd., Melbourne, 1969-71; group fin. mgr. TNT Shipping and Devel. Ltd., Sydney, Australia, 1971-78; resident dir. TNT South East Asia, Singapore, 1978—, also bd. dirs.; taxation con. Melbourne, 1961-69. Editor Tip-Off mag., 1960-63, Harvard Bus. Sch. Newsletter, 1982—. Pres. Victorian Intercollegiate Basketball Assn., Melbourne, 1967-73; chmn. Am. Sch. Bd., Singapore, 1984-86. Mem. Australian Soc. Accts. (assoc.). Clubs: Tanglin, Singapore Cricket. Home: 25 Claymore Rd, Apt #03-02, Singapore 0922, Singapore

MERCER, ROBERT E., tire company executive; b. Elizabeth, N.J., 1924; married. Grad., Yale U., 1946. With Goodyear Tire & Rubber Co., Akron, Ohio, 1947—, asst. to pres., 1973-74, pres. Kelly-Springfield Tire Co. (subs.), 1974-76, corp. exec. v.p., pres. tire div., 1976-78, corp. pres., from 1978, chief operating officer, 1980-82, vice chmn., chief exec. officer, 1982-83, chmn., 1983—, chief exec. officer, 1983-88, also dir. Served with USN. Office: Goodyear Tire & Rubber Co 1144 E Market St Akron OH 44316 *

MERCHANT, DONNA RAE, marketing professional; b. Wichita, Kans., Aug. 29, 1948; d. Raymond Houston and Edna Brooks (Waddell) Hobbs; m. Christopher Wayne, Aug. 31, 1968 (div. Aug. 1973); 1 child, Shauna Layne. Student, Wichita State U., 1966-68. Adminstrv. asst. postgrad. edn. U. Kans. Med. Sch., Wichita, 1974-80; activity coord. continuing med. edn. Wesley Med. Ctr., Wichita, 1980-84; mgr. support svcs. 9th dist. Farm Credit Svcs., Wichita, 1984-88; sales and mktg. mgr. Greater Oreg. Travel Inc., Eugene, 1988—; cons. Jr. Leauge Wichita, 1983, Plancon, Inc., Martinsville, N.J., 1987—. Mem. Wichita Conv. and Visitors Bur., 1987, events com. Wichita Festivals, Inc., 1987; mem. Eugene Conv. and Visitors Bur., 1988—. Mem. Am. Mktg. Assn., Adminstrv. Mgmt. Soc., Forum for Exec. Bus. Women, Gt. Plains Bus. Adminstrn. Group, Assn. Travel Execs., Campus Life (bd. dirs.), Eugene C. of C., Delta Gamma Alumni Assn. Republican. Home: 87 E 33rd St Eugene OR 97405 Office: Greater Oreg Travel 205 E 14th Eugene OR 97401

MERCHANT, FRANK S., manufacturing executive; b. Oct. 29, 1948; s. S.H. and A.S. M.; m. S.F. Merchant, June 18, 1977; 2 children. MS in Mech. Engring., U. Wis., 1982. Cert. mfg. engr. Mfg. engr. Sta Rite Industries, Inc., Delavan, Wis., 1973-77, chmn. energy, 1975-77; mfg. engr. Sunstrand Hydro Transmission, Ames, Iowa, 1977-79, supr., mfg. engring. control ctr., 1979-81, supr. process engring., 1981-82; mgr. engring. Huron, Inc., Lexington, Mich., 1983—. Contbr. research in engring. design and mfg. HRH Edn. Found. scholar, 1971. Mem. Soc. Mfg. Engrs. (sr.). Club: St. Patrick's Chess (past pres.). Office: Huron Inc 6554 Lakeshore Rd Lexington MI 48450

MERCHANT, ROLAND SAMUEL, SR., hospital administrator, educator; b. N.Y.C., Apr. 18, 1929; s. Samuel and Eleta (McLymont) M.; m. Audrey Bartley, June 6, 1970; children—Orelia Eleta, Roland Samuel, Huey Bartley. B.A., N.Y.U., 1957, M.A., 1960; M.S., Columbia U., 1963, M.S.H.A., 1974. Asst. statistician N.Y.C. Dept. Health, 1957-60, statistician, 1960-63; statistician N.Y. TB and Health Assn., N.Y.C., 1963-65; biostatistician, adminstrv. coordinator Inst. Surg. Studies, Montefiore Hosp., Bronx, N.Y., 1965-72; resident in adminstrn. Roosevelt Hosp., N.Y.C., 1973-74; dir. health and hosp. mgmt. Dept. Health, City of N.Y., 1974-76; from asst. adminstr. to adminstr. West Adams Community Hosp., Los Angeles, 1976; spl. asst. to assoc. v.p. for med. affairs Stanford U. Hosp., Calif., 1977-82, dir. office mgmt. and strategic planning, 1982-85, dir. mgmt. planning, 1986—; clin. assoc. prof. dept. family, community and preventive medicine Stanford U., 1986-88, dept. health research and policy Stanford U. Med. Sch., 1988—. Served with U.S. Army. 1951-53. USPHS fellow. Fellow Am. Coll. Healthcare Execs., Am. Pub. Health Assn.; mem. Am. Hosp. Assn., Nat. Assn. Health Services Execs., N.Y. Acad. Scis. Home: 953 Cheswick Dr San Jose CA 95121 Office: Stanford U Hosp Stanford CA 94305

MERCIER, JACQUES LOUIS, industrial and commercial promotion company executive; b. Paris, July 7, 1933; s. George Henri and Helene Corneille (Ryckembeush) M.; m. Marie-Annick Therese Ravet, Sept. 14, 1984; 1 child, Marie Helene. Degree in Engring., Fed. Inst. Tech., Zurich, Switzerland, 1958; PhD, U. Wash., Seattle, 1965; D. es-Scis., U. Paris, 1973. Engr. Amman and Whitney, N.Y.C., 1959-61; assoc. research engr. Boeing Co., Seattle, 1961-63; teaching assoc. U. Wash., Seattle, 1963-65; asst. prof. engring. scis. U. Md., College Park, 1965-66; assoc. prof. U. Brazil, Rio de Janeiro, 1966-68; prof. Catholic U., Rio de Janeiro, 1968-73; dir. UP VI Ecole Nat. Sup. des Beaux Arts, Paris, 1973-74; dir., founder Montemer Internat. (substituting MASA Internat.), Rio de Janeiro, 1975—; French fgn. trade counsellor Paris, 1982—; mem. Jury for Candidacy Professorship Cath. U., Rio de Janeiro, 1972-75; counsellor French Fgn. Trade Coun., 1982—. Author: An Introduction to Tensor Calculus, 1971; contbr. articles to engring. publs. Decorated officer French Ordre Nat. du Merite and Brazilian Ordem do Mérito Aeronáutico; recipient Santos Dumont Merit medal Ministry of Aero., Brasilia, 1984; medal Friend of Brazilian Navy, Ministry of Navy, 1985. Mem. French C. of C. (bd. dirs. 1985—), ASME, Council Engrs. and Architects of Rio de Janiero, Swiss Soc. Engrs. and Architects, Sigma Xi. Roman Catholic. Club: Cercle de l'Union Interalliee (Paris). Home: Ave Atlantica 270/1402, 22010 Rio de Janeiro Brazil Office: Ladeira Nossa Senhora 163, 4th Fl, Ed Monteiro Aranha, 22211 Rio de Janeiro Brazil

MERCURI, RIC, food company executive; b. Newark, Feb. 15, 1955; s. Joseph J. and Rose (Marinaro) M.; m. Patricia A. Mascitelli, May 8, 1975. BA in Biology, Montclair State U., 1976; MBA in Indsl. Mgmt., U. Dallas, 1988. Quality control mgr. Red Star Yeast div. Universal Foods Corp., Belleville, N.J., 1976-78, packaging, shipping supt., 1978-82; gen. supt. Red Star Yeast div. Universal Foods Corp., Oakland, Calif., 1982-86; plant mgr. Red Star Yeast div. Universal Foods Corp., Dallas, 1986—. Office: Universal Foods Corp 2306 Motor St Dallas TX 75235

MERDINGER, DONALD JEROME, investment consultant; b. Chgo., Aug. 14, 1928; s. Solomon and Gene (Grossman) M.; m. Jessica Adler, June 6, 1954; children: Phillip, Steven, Michael, Lisa. BS in Acctg., U. Ill., 1950. CPA, Ill. Chief fin. officer Chgo. Food Processors, 1958-80; pres. Sioux-Pac of Iowa Inc., 1981-84; prin., investment advisor Merdinger Fin. Services, Northfield, Ill., 1984—. Capt. USAF, 1950-52, Korea. Mem. Am. Soc. CPA's, Ill. Soc. CPA's, Inst. Cert. Fin. Planners (registered), Internat. Assn. Fin. Planners, Am. Legion, Alpha Epsilon Pi, B'nai Brith. Jewish. Office: Merdinger Fin Svcs Inc 480 Central Ave Northfield IL 60093

MERDINGER, SUSAN, marketing, sales executive; b. Boston, Oct. 5, 1943; d. J. George and Bertha (Lotten) Greenfield; m. Edward Franklin Merdinger, Dec. 21, 1963; children: Mindy Beth, Matthew Joseph. AA, Green Mountain Coll., 1963. Asst. dir. pub. relations Filene's, Boston, 1963; real estate sales, Marlboro, N.J., 1970-78; nat. dir. edn. Network of Homes, Babylon, N.Y., 1978-79; v.p. homefinding Employee Transfer Co., Chgo., 1979-81; dir. mktg. Merrill Lynch Realty, Stamford, Conn., 1981-83, asst. v.p. communications and promotional services, 1983-84, dir. mktg. services, 1984-86; founder, pub. mag. Fine Homes, 1982-87; v.p. Fine Homes Internat., 1986-87; v.p. mktg. services, 1987-88, v.p. internat. mktg., 1988—; lectr. in field. Pres., founder Hadassah, Marlboro, N.J., 1972-75, mem. nat. membership com., 1972-75. Office: Merrill Lynch Realty Assocs 10 Stamford Forum Stamford CT 06901

MEREDITH, DAVID ROBERT, personnel executive; b. Cleve., Apr. 9, 1940; s. Wilbur R. and Lillian B. M.; AB, Colgate U., 1962; PhD (Ford Found. grantee), MIT, 1966; student U.de Cuyo, 1961, U. de Tucuman, 1960; m. Sheila Kay Provost, Dec. 21, 1963; children—Karen, Adam, Alison. Labor cons. W.R. Meredith & Co., Cleve., 1958-65; labor asst. Mountain States Employers Council, Denver, 1965-66; prin. McKinsey & Co., Inc., N.Y.C. and Cleve., 1966-75; pres. Meredith Assocs., Inc., Westport, Conn., 1975-81; chmn., chief exec. Personnel Corp. Am., Norwalk, 1980—; dir. Westport Labs., Gen Data Base Tech., Inc.; chmn. bd. Canberra Industries, 1978—, North Wind Power Co., 1976-78 ; research and teaching asst. M.I.T., 1962-66. Fin. chmn. Weston Community Center, Inc., 1977; mem. Rep. Town Com., Weston, Conn., 1979-81, Weston Transit Study Commn., 1976-78; bd. dirs. Found. for a Greater Weston, Young Audiences of Conn., 1988—; deacon Norfield Ch., 1975-81, fair chmn., 1977, treas., 1981—, trustee, 1981—. NDEA fellow, 1962-65; FTES scholar, 1958-62; Williams scholar, 1960-61; recipient Osborne math. prize, Colgate U., 1962. Clubs: Conn. Golf (exec. com.), Aspetuck Valley Country, Bald Peak, Winged Foot. Contbr. articles to newspapers, bus. and profl. jours. Home: 39 Pheasant Hill Weston CT 06883 Office: 1 Selleck St Shore Point Bldg Norwalk CT 06855

MEREDITH, EDWIN THOMAS, III, media executive; b. Chgo., Feb. 7, 1933; s. Edwin Thomas, Jr. and Anna (Kauffman) M.; m. Katherine Comfort, Sept. 4, 1953; children: Mildred K. (dec.), Dianna M., Edwin Thomas. Student, U. Ariz., 1950-53. With Meredith Corp., Des Moines, 1956—, v.p., 1968-71, pres., chief exec. officer, 1971-73, chmn. bd., 1973-88, chmn. exec. com. bd. dirs., 1988—; bd. dirs., mem. exec. com. Bankers Trust Co., Des Moines; bd. dirs. Mut. of Omaha. Bd. dirs. Nat. Merit Scholarship Corp., Evanston, Ill., Iowa Natural Heritage Found, Des Moines; trustee Iowa Methodist Med. Ctr., Drake U., Des Moines, Iowa 4-H Found., Ames. Served with U.S. Army, 1953-56. Clubs: Chgo; Des Moines, Wakonda (Des Moines). Office: Meredith Corp 1716 Locust St Des Moines IA 50336

MEREDITH, GEORGE (MARLOR), writer association executive; b. Somerville, N.J., Apr. 21, 1923; s. Gilbert Judson and Dorothea (Pope) M.; student Columbia U., 1940-41; m. Elizabeth Jean Moore, Nov. 15, 1955; children: Gilbert Judson III, Scott Arthur. Mng. editor Mast, 1944-47; editor Premium Practice, 1947-55; ptnr., editorial dir. Meredith Assocs., 1955-67, pres. 1967-88, chmn. 1989—; pres. Meredith Rsch. Corp., 1962-74; mng. dir. Meredith & Henry, 1977—; exec. sec. Nat. Premium Sales Execs., 1957-67, exec. dir., 1967-74, pub. rels. dir., 1972—; mng. dir. Eastman Editorial Rsch., 1979-87; exec. sec. Nat. Assn. Food Equipment Mfrs., 1957-59; exec. dir. Nat. Premium Mfrs. Reps., 1963-66, dir. rsch. programs, 1964-67; dir. Mktg. News Bur., 1973—(all Union, N.J.); exec. dir. Trading Stamp Inst. Am., Assn. Retail Mktg. Svcs., 1979—: mng. dir. Mktg. Communications Execs. Internat., 1981-85, exec. dir. N.Y. chpt., 1981-82. Coordinator, moderator Premiums and Incentives Conf., N.Y. U., 1972; public relations dir. Soc. Incentive Travel Execs., 1974-79. Recipient Premium Man of Year award Nat. Premium Mfrs. Reps., 1973; Nat. Premium Sales Execs. Past Pres.'s award, 1966; Disting. Achievement award Premium Advt. Assn. Am., 1963. Mem. Overseas Press Club, Am. Soc. Assn. Execs., Incentive Fedn. (vice chmn. 1984-88, 89—, chmn. 1988-89), Nat. Premium Sales Execs., Premium Merchandising Club N.Y., Lions. Author: Effective Merchandising with Premiums, 1962; Creative Application of Sales Incentive Plans, 1972; (film) The Caine Coil, 1973; Incentives in Marketing, 1977; Something Extra, 1989. Editor: Premiums in Marketing, 1971; exec. editor, research dir. Incentive Marketing Facts, 1968-87; research dir. Incentive Mag., 1988—; editor, pub. Sales Motivation Letter, 1973-74; editor The Register, 1979—, The Communicator, 1982-85. Contbr. articles to profl. publs. Home: 3 Caro Ct Red Bank NJ 07701

MERENBLOOM, ROBERT BARRY, hospital and medical school administrator; b. Balt., July 13, 1947; s. Philip William and Florence Ruth (Surosky) M.; B.A., U. Md., 1969; M.S., Morgan State U., 1973; M.B.A., U. Balt., 1980. Mem. staff Mayor Balt. Office Manpower Resources, 1972-73; assoc. staff mem. Office Dean, U. Md. Med. Sch., 1976-80; adminstrv. officer research and devel. Balt. VA Med. Center, 1974-80; assoc. adminstr. dept. medicine Johns Hopkins U. Sch. Medicine, Balt., 1980-84, adminstr. dept. medicine Johns Hopkins Hosp., 1984-88, assoc. Sch. Hygiene and Pub. Health, 1984-88; lectr. dept. medicine Bowman Gray Sch. Medicine Wake Forest U., 1988—; asst. chmn., Wake Forest U., 1988—; instr. sociology U. Balt., 1973-76; adj. faculty Weekend Coll., Coll. Notre Dame, Balt., 1980—. Exec. dir. J. Paul Sticht Ctr. on Aging. Recipient Hon. Corpsmen Leader award Office Mayor Balt., 1973; Outstanding Performance award Balt. VA Med. Center, 1975, Superior Performance award, 1980. Mem. Am. Gerontology Soc., So. Gerontology Soc., Soc. Research Adminstrs., Nat. Council Univ. Research Adminstrs., Adminstrs. Internal Medicine, Assn. Am. Med. Colls. (group on bus. affairs), Am. Hosp. Assn., Am. Pub. Health Assn., Am. Coll. Healthcare Adminstrs., John Hopkins Club, Piedmont

Club. Home: 2990-P Walnut Forest Ct Winston-Salem NC 27103 Office: 300 S Hawthorne Rd Winston-Salem NC 27103

MERGEL, STEPHANIE ANN, accountant; b. Dover, N.J., June 19, 1964; d. Nicholas John and Joan Rita (Cirincione) M. BS in Acctg. Mgmt. cum laude, U. Scranton, 1986; postgrad., Seton Hall U. Law Sch., 1988—. Interviewer mktg. rsch. Walker Rsch. Inc., Rockaway, N.J., 1980-85; auditor, acct. Arthur Andersen& Co., Roseland, N.J., 1986—. Mem. Big Bros. and Big Sister Club (pres. 1984-86), Alpha Sigma Nu, Delta Mu Delta, Omega Beta Sigma. Home: 216 Perry St Dover NJ 07801 Office: Arthur Andersen & Co 101 Eisenhower Pkwy Roseland NJ 07068

MERGLER, H. KENT, investment counselor; b. Cin., July 1, 1940; s. Wilton Henry and Mildred Amelia (Pulliam) M.; BBA with honors, U. Cin., 1963, MBA, 1964; m. Judith Anne Metzger, Aug. 17, 1963; children: Stephen Kent, Timothy Alan, Kristin Lee. Portfolio mgr. Scudder, Stevens & Clark, Cin., 1964-68, v.p. investments, Chgo., 1970-73; v.p. Gibraltar Research and Mgmt., Ft. Lauderdale, Fla., 1968-70; portfolio mgr., ptnr., exec. v.p., pres., dir. and prin. Stein Roe & Farnham, Inc., Ft. Lauderdale, 1973-84, Chgo., 1984—, also mem. exec. com., arbitrator Nat. Assn. Security Dealers, Inc., 1976-82. Chmn. adminstrv. bd. Christ United Meth. Ch., Ft. Lauderdale, 1981-83; mem. fin. com. Kenilworth Union Ch., 1989—; bd. dirs. Pine Crest Prep. Sch., 1982-84, bd. advisors, 1984-87; bd. dirs. Coral Ridge Little League, 1976-84, pres., 1980-81 . Chartered fin. analyst; chartered investment counselor. Mem. Fin. Analysts Soc. South Fla. (pres. 1975-76, dir. 1974-78), Investment Analysis Soc. of Chgo., Bond Club Ft. Lauderdale (dir. 1978-82), Inst. Chartered Fin. Analysts. Republican. Clubs: Coral Ridge Country (Ft. Lauderdale, Fla.); Metropolitan, La Salle, University (Milw.); Skokie Country; Highlands Country (N.C.). Home: 924 Pine Tree Ln Winnetka IL 60093 Office: 1 S Wacker Dr Chicago IL 60606

MERICO, ANA MARIA, sales executive, educator; b. Buenos Aires, Dec. 8, 1961; came to U.S., 1982; d. Rinaldo and Angela (Martinez) M.; 1 child, Barbara Giselle Osona. Student, Cambridge Inst., 1980; BA in Acctg., Inst. Sagrado Cor, 1980; postgrad., U. Ade, 1982. Exec. bilingual sec. Philip Morris Internat., Buenos Aires, 1981-82; adminstrv. sec. II NCR Corp., Newark, 1983-84; office mgr. Clarion Hotel Cin., 1985-86, mgr. conf. ctr., 1986; mgr. sales Cincinnatian Hotel, Cin., 1986-88, dir. sales, 1986—. Named Hispanic Woman of Yr. Pan Am. Soc. Mem. Hotel Sales and Mktg. Assn., Greater Cin. Trust Council, Exec. Women Internat., Cin. Assn. Execs. Republican. Roman Catholic. Home: 10822 C Lake Thames Dr Cincinnati OH 45242 Office: Cincinnatian Hotel 601 Vine St Cincinnati OH 45202

MERINGOLO, GEORGE J., real estate developer; b. Glen Cove, N.Y., Nov. 14, 1944; s. Salvatore Michael and Angelina (Turano) M.; m. Nicole Carole Minetta, Sept. 17, 1966; children: Denise Danielle, Peter Paul, Jason Jon. BA, St. John's U., Jamaica, N.Y., 1966. Regional mgr. Genovese Drug Stores, Melville, N.Y., 1966-73; gen. mgr. Steinway Ford Hopkins, Chgo., 1973-75; regional v.p. NCH Corp., Dallas, 1975-83; sr. v.p. Icom Mfg. div. Crompton and Knowles, Atlanta, 1983-86; chmn., chief exec. officer Minette Co., Aberdeen, N.J., 1986—; bd. dirs. Aberdeen Marine, Twin Harbour Inc. With U.S. Army, 1965-66. Democrat. Roman Catholic. Home: 84 Elinore Ct Oceanport NJ 07757

MERKEL MONNIN, ANNE INGRAM, management consultant; b. Louisville, June 7, 1952; d. Edward John and Claire (Ingram) M.; m. Mark Lloyd Monnin, June 29, 1985. BA, Ind. U., 1973, cert. in Latin Am. Studies, 1973, MS, 1975, PhD, 1984. Dir. English Lang. and Multicultural Inst., Dayton, 1980-84; exec. mktg. cons. Bernard Haldane Assoc., Cupertino, Calif., 1985-86; personnel adminstr. San Jose (Calif.) State U., 1986; sr. cons. M&M Assocs., Santa Clara, Calif., 1984-87, M and M Communications, Charlotte, N.C., 1987—; mem. Elm Cons. Group, Charlotte, 1988; cons., lectr. in field. Editor: Lifestyle Management, 1986; contbr. articles to profl. jours. Pres. Holdwest, Calif. and N.C., 1987-88. Mem. NAFE, Nat. Assn. Fgn. Student Affairs, Profl. Connections for Women (program chair 1986-87). Mem. Spiritual Unity Ch. Address: M and M Communications 4800 Coronado Dr Charlotte NC 28212

MERKLE, WALTER JOHN, banker; b. Flushing, N.Y., Feb. 10, 1957; s. Walter Joseph and Katherine Mary (Degnan) M.; m. Pegeen Farrell, Oct. 15, 1983; 1 child, Christopher Joseph. BS, Dominican Coll., 1980; diploma, Am. Inst. Banking, 1987, Grad. Sch. Banking, 1987. Asst. mgr. Beneficial Finance Co., Morristown, N.J., 1977-78; asst. sec., mgr. credit ops. United Jersey Bank, Hackensack, N.J., 1978-82; asst. v.p., br. mgr., lending officer New Milford (Conn.) Bank & Trust, 1982-84; asst. treas., bus. devel. officer Conn. Bank & Trust, Hartford, Conn., 1984-86; v.p., comml. loan officer Merchants Bank & Trust, Norwalk, Conn., 1986-88; v.p., bus. devel. officer New Milford Bank & Trust, 1988—; instr. Am. Inst. Banking, Danbury, Conn., 1988—, OMEGA, San Francisco, 1986-88. Named Outstanding Young Man of Am., 1982. Mem. Am. Bankers Assn., Conn. Bankers Assn., Robert Morris Assocs., New Milford 2000, New Milford C. of C., New Milford Downtown Merchants Assn., Greater Norwalk C. of C., Rotary, K.C. Roman Catholic. Office: New Milford Bank & Trust 55 Main St New Milford CT 06776

MERLE, H. ETIENNE, restaurateur; b. N.Y.C., July 8, 1944; s. Pierre and Josephine Merle. BS, Cornell U., 1969. Mgr. food and beverages DiviDivi Beach Hotel, Aruba, Netherlands Antilles, 1969-70; restaurant mgr., chmn. food dept. Tng. Resources for Youth, N.Y.C., 1971; gen. mgr. L'Auberge du Cochon Rouge, Ithaca, N.Y., 1971—; v.p. Pascale Wine Bar and Restaurant, Syracuse, N.Y., 1982—; ops. cons. Merle & Roy Assocs., N.Y.C., 1975—. Mem. Cornell Soc. Hotelmen, Chefs de Cuisine Assn. Am., Société Culinaire Philanthropique, Vatel Club, L'Union Francaise (pres. 1975, 76, 86), N.Y. Athletic Club. Home and Office: 1152 Danby Rd Ithaca NY 14850

MERLINO, GREGORY, financial planning executive; b. Woodbury, N.J., Oct. 20, 1957; s. Frank Joseph Merlino and Gloria Darlene (Koruba) Eck; m. Terri Kelly, May 28. 1983. BS in Commerce, Rider Coll., 1980. Cert. fin. planner. Credit mgr. Norwest Fin. Corp., Houston, 1981-82; fin. planner Fin. Svcs. Ctr., Houston, 1982-86; pres. Ameriway Fin. Corp., Cherry Hill, N.J., 1986—. Treas., campaign for state rep., Delaware County, Pa., 1988. Named to Nat. Honor Soc., Fin. Mgmt. Assn., 1980. Mem. Inst. Cert. Fin. Planners (contbr. study on fin. planning for retired 1987-88), Internat. Assn. Fin. Planning, Cherry Hill C. of C. Roman Catholic. Home: Egret Rd Marlton NJ 08053 Office: Ameriway Fin Svcs 1930 E Rte 70 Ste A-7 Cherry Hill NJ 08003

MERLO, ANDREW EUGENE, real estate developer; b. Jersey City, June 14, 1942; s. John and Rose Merlo; student U. Miami, 1964, N.Y.U., 1968; divorced; 1 dau., Vanessa. Project engr. Wilbur Smith and Assos., 1966-69; corp. real estate rep. Amerada Hess Corp., 1970; mem. sales staff GAC Properties, 1970-71; with U.S. Home Communities Corp., N.J., 1971; v.p. real estate Radice Realty & Constrn. Corp., Ft. Lauderdale, Fla., 1972-78; owner, real estate cons., developer A.E. Merlo Real Estate Cons., Union City, N.J., 1978—; dir. nat. bus. devel. DiScala Assos., Norwalk, Conn., 1980-82. Bd. advs. Creative Music Studio, Woodstock, N.Y., N.Y. Open Ctr., N.Y.C., Childrens Attelier, N.Y.C.; bd. dirs. Found. for Inner-vision. Mem. Nat. Assn. Corp. Real Estate, Indsl. Real Estate Brokers Assn. Buddhist. Home: 314 19th St Union City NJ 07087

MERLO, HARRY ANGELO, forest products executive; b. Stirling City, Calif., Mar. 5, 1925; s. Joseph Angelo and Clotilde (Camussa) M.; 1 son, Harry A. B.S., U. Calif.-Berkeley, 1949, postgrad., 1949. Vice pres. Rockport Redwood Co., Cloverdale, Calif., 1967; v.p. No. Calif. div. Ga.-Pacific Corp., Samoa, Calif., 1967-69; v.p. Western lumber div. Ga.-Pacific Corp., Portland, Oreg., 1969-71, exec. v.p. Western timber, plywood and lumber operations, 1971-73; pres., chmn. bd. La.-Pacific Corp., Portland, 1973—; adv. bd. Sch. Bus. Adminstrn. U. Calif., Berkeley; bd. dirs. World Forestry Ctr., Whitman Industries. Mem. Pres.'s Council, Columbia Pacific council Boy Scouts Am.; former mem. nat. adv. council Salvation Army; trustee Hugh O'Brian Youth Found., Oreg. Mus. Sci. and Industry, Goodwill Industries; past chmn. bd. Am. Acad. Achievement; Western fin. chmn. U.S. Olympic commn.; chmn., adv. bd. Salvation Army, Oreg.; bd. dirs. Marshall U. Soc. Yeager Scholars. Served to lt. USMCR. Named Man of Year Ga.-Pacific Corp., 1969; recipient Golden Plate award Am. Acad. Achievement, 1974; Horatio Alger award, 1980, Gold award for forest products industry The Wall St. Transcript, 1982, 83, Disting. Service award La. Tech. U., 1984, Aubrey Watzek award Lewis and Clark Coll., 1984, Citizen of Merit award Assoc. Builders and Contractors, 1986, Piemontese Del Munde award, 1986, Merit award Calif. Parks & Recreation Soc., 1988. Mem. Calif. Redwood Assn. (past pres., dir.), Am. Paper Inst. (dir.), Knights of the Vine. Clubs: Founders (bd. dirs.), Waverly Country, Arlington, Multnomah Athletic, Ingomar, West Hills Racquet. Office: La-Pacific Corp 111 SW 5th Ave Portland OR 97204

MERLO, PIER ANTONIO, air conditioning company executive; b. Piacenza D'Adige, Padova, Italy, July 12, 1935; s. Luigi-Antonio and Lucia (Sartori) M.; m. Marina Jolanda Vanzina; children: Francesco, Roberto. DEE, Poly. U. Milan, 1960. Engring. trainee Marconi Instruments, St. Albans, Italy, 1961; design engr. Martelli Aerotechnica, Milan, 1962-64; area mgr. Chrysler Airtemp, Dayton, Ohio, 1965-78; exec. v.p. Chrysler Airtemp Italy, Milan, 1976-78; mng. dir. OMR Airtemp Italy, Milan, 1978—; cons. Engring. EQ Services, Milan, 1984, Brightstar, London, 1986—; bd. dirs. Imaco. Milan. Mem. ASCAP, Profl. Engrs. Milan. Home: 3 Senato, 20121 Milan Italy Office: Imaco, 3 Via Pinamonte, da Vimercate, 20121 Milan Italy

MERNER, RICHARD RAYMOND, chemist, management consultant; b. Chgo., Sept. 23, 1918; s. Arthur Frederick and Clara Mary (Moore) M. m. Patricia Ruth Steltz, Apr. 14, 1951; children: Laurie Beth Merner Dillon, Patricia Ann Merner Harris. BS in Chemistry, U. Ill., 1939; postgrad., U. Mo., 1939-40; PhD in Organic Chemistry, Northwestern U., 1949. Research and devel. electrochem. dept. DuPont Co., Niagara Falls, N.Y., 1941-44; reseach and devel. organic chem. dept. DuPont Co., Deepwater, N.J., 1949-55; tech. supr. organic chem. dept. DuPont Co., Deepwater, 1955-67; supr. employee relations DuPont Co., Deepwater and Wilmington, Del., 1967-76, mgr. distbn. C,D. & P dept., 1976-78; mem. faculty bus. adminstrn. U. Del., Newark, 1978-87; pres., cons. Merner Assocs., Avondale, Pa., 1975—. Contbr. articles to profl. jours; patentee in field. Chmn. Avon Grove Chester County Sch. Authority, West Grove, Pa., 1962—. Served to lt. (j.g.) USNR, 1944-46, PTO. Mem. Am. Chem. Soc., AAAS, Sigma Xi. Republican. Presbyterian. Home and Office: RR 2 Box 326 Sullivan Rd Avondale PA 19311

MERO, MARJORIE ANNE, compensation specialist; b. Oregon City, Jan. 17, 1940; d. Richard Nyquist and Julia Annetta (Loy) Schopp; m. Gordon Duane Mero, Feb. 4, 1958; children: Sheryl Ann Mero Burns, Duane Morris. Student, Kinman Bus. U., 1972, Spokane Falls Community Coll., 1974-79. Cert. compensation profl. Dir. M. Smith Childcare Ctr., Kalispell, Mont., 1966-70; clk. Power Co., Spokane, Wash., 1970-71, engr. technician, 1972-75, job analyst, 1975-80; compensation supr. Wash. Water Power Co., Spokane, 1980—; mem. survey steering com. NW Electric and Light, 1984—. Artist watercolor paintings, 1967—. Panel chmn. United Way, Spokane, 1975-79. Mem. Jaycees (officer Kalispell chpt. 1968-70), Spokane Calligraphic Art Soc. Republican. Methodist. Clubs: Extension Homemakers, Rabbit Breeders (Spokane), Scripts and Scribes.

MERRELL, STANLEY WILSON, manufacturing company executive; b. Cin., Jan. 25, 1929; s. Thurston and Helen Theodate (Dresser) M.; m. Lyda Lynn Stuart, June 15, 1956; children: Stanley Wilson III, Caroline Clark, Louise Theodate, Katherine Stuart. A.B., Princeton U., 1951; M.B.A., Harvard U., 1957. With TRW Inc., Cleve., 1957-67, Rockwell Internat., Pitts., 1967-70; v.p. J.P. Morgan & Co. Inc., N.Y.C., 1970-73; v.p. planning and devel. Gen. Instrument Corp., N.Y.C., 1973-76; v.p. corp. devel. Bausch & Lomb Inc., Rochester, N.Y., 1976-81, sr. v.p. adminstrn., 1981—. Bd. govs. Genesee Hosp.; trustee, past pres. Allendale Columbia Sch., Rochester; trustee Ctr. Govt. Research; dir. United Way of Greater Rochester, Rochester Downtown Devel. Corp. Served to lt. (j.g.) USN, 1951-53. Baker scholar Harvard U., 1957. Republican. Episcopalian. Clubs: Country of Rochester, Genesee Valley (Rochester). Home: 3437 Elmwood Ave Rochester NY 14610 Office: Bausch & Lomb Inc 1 Lincoln First Sq Rochester NY 14601

MERRIAM, J. ALEC, maritime company executive; b. Chgo., Apr. 14, 1935; s. John Francis and Lucy Elizabeth (Lamon) M.; m. Gail MacIntosh Angotti, June 10, 1959; 1 dau., Joan Alexander. B.A. magna cum laude, Princeton U., 1957; M.B.A., Harvard U., 1959. Asst. controller No. Natural Gas Co. (now Enron), Omaha, 1959-70; chmn. bd., treas. LOA Corp., Omaha, 1970-71; exec. v.p., dir. Crowley Maritime Corp., San Francisco, 1972-88, dir.; bd. dirs., mem. exec. com. PLM Internat. Inc. Bd. dirs. Omaha Playhouse, 1961-66, pres., 1964-65; bd. dirs., treas. Joslyn Art Mus., Omaha, 1964-71, Omaha Symphony, 1964-71, Nebr. Arts Council, Lincoln, 1969-70. Mem. Wine and Food Soc. San Francisco. Club: Belvedere Tennis.

MERRICK, LEW, mechanical engineer; b. Washington, Oct. 29, 1953; s. Ivan Edward and Barbara Alice (Jones) M.; m. Sharon Ann Bisnett, Apr. 1, 1983; children: Shawna Lynn, Heather Alyse. Registered profl. engr. Engr. The Boeing Co., Seattle, 1978-81; sr. engr. Martin Marietta, New Orleans, 1981-82; consulting engr. Tangent Engring., Lynnwood, Wash., 1982—. Mem. ASME, Am. Soc. Metals, Forth Interest Group, C User's Group, German Machinist's Guild.

MERRICK, PATRICIA RILEY, corporate finance director; b. N.Y.C., Mar. 19, 1942; d. John Francis and Mary Dibble Riley. BA in Polit. Sci., Hunter Coll., 1978; postgrad., Harvard U., 1984. Sec., treas. Charterhouse Group Internat., Inc., N.Y.C., 1973-77, v.p. new bus. devel., 1977-84, sr. v.p., dir. corp. fin., 1984—; bd. dirs. Wundies, Inc., N.Y.C., Charter Power Systems, Inc., Plymouth Meeting, Pa., Steel of W.Va., Huntington, Charterhouse Automotive Group, Fenton, Mich. Bd. mem. The Jericho Project. Mem. Assn. for Corp. Growth (treas. 1986—, internat. dir. N.Y. chpt.), Harvard Club. Office: Charterhouse Group Internat 535 Madison Ave New York NY 10022

MERRIGAN, EUGENE T., financial company executive, marketing specialist; b. Mitchell, Nebr., Nov. 19, 1933; s. William M. and Catherine J. (Farner) M.; m. Joan L. Riha, Sept. 9, 1958; children: Craig, Curtis, Kyle, Kevin. BS in Mktg., U. Nebr., 1958. Various positions in ops. and mktg. Equifax, Inc., Atlanta, 1958-80, pres., gen. mgr. various bus. units, 1980-87, sr. v.p., 1987—, also bd. dirs. Served to cpl. U.S. Army, 1954-56. Republican. Roman Catholic. Lodge: Rotary. Office: Equifax Inc 1600 Peachtree St NW Atlanta GA 30309

MERRILL, DALE MARIE, sales executive; b. Melrose, Mass., Feb. 21, 1954; d. Richard Paul and Rosemarie Reine (Porelle) M. BA in English, U. of Lowell (Mass.), 1976; MA in Am. Studies, Boston Coll., 1983. Sales rep. A-Copy Inc., Natick, Mass., 1976-77; sales mgr. Jan Optical Co., Waltham, Mass., 1977-78; market researcher Decision Research Co., Lexington, Mass., 1979-81; sales rep. Henco Software Co., Waltham, 1981-82; account mgr. Univ. Computing Co., Chgo., 1982-83; regional sales mgr. CompuServe Data Techs. (formerly Software House), Cambridge, Mass., 1983—; bd. dirs. M.T. Corp., Woburn, Mass. Author: How to Buy Software: Avoiding the Traps Salespeople Set, 1989; author, editor: Seeds mag. (Poetry award 1972), 1971-72; contbr. poetry to mags. Organizer 18x72 project, Stoneham, Mass., 1970-71; bd. dirs. Stoneham Hist. Commn., 1976-77. Recipient Top Sales award A-Copy Inc., 1976-77, Interviewer award Decision Research Co., 1981, Triple Crown Sales award, 1985, 86, 87, Million Dollar Sales Club award, 1987, 88. Mem. Nat. Assn. Female Execs., NOW, Digital Equipment Co. User Soc. (DECUS). Democrat. Avocations: skiing, photography, painting, sculpturing, karate. Home: PO Box 2586 Woburn MA 01888 Office: CompuServe Data Techs 1000 Massachusetts Ave Cambridge MA 02138

MERRILL, GEORGE VANDERNETH, lawyer; b. N.Y.C., July 2, 1947; s. James Edward and Claire (Leness) M.; m. Janice Anne Humes, May 11, 1985. AB, Harvard U., 1968, JD, 1972; MBA, Columbia U., 1973. Bar: N.Y. 1973, U.S. Dist. Ct. (so. and ea. dists.) N.Y. 1974, U.S. Ct. Appeals (2d cir.) 1974. Assoc., Cleary, Gottlieb, Steen & Hamilton, N.Y.C., 1974-77, Hawkins, Delafield & Wood, N.Y.C., 1977-79; v.p. Irving Trust Co., N.Y.C., 1980-82; v.p., gen. counsel Listowel Inc., N.Y.C., 1982-84, bd. dirs., exec. v.p., gen. counsel, 1984—, also bd. dirs. Pres. Arell Found., N.Y.C., 1985—, also bd. dirs.; pres. Northfield Charitable Corp., N.Y.C., 1986—; v.p., sec. Brougham Prodn. Co., N.Y.C., 1986—, Marinetics Inc., N.Y.C., 1988—; v.p. Sci. Design and Engring. Co., Inc., N.Y.C., 1987-88, bd. dirs., exec. v.p., 1989—. Recipient Detur award Harvard U., 1968, John Harvard scholar. Mem. ABA, Am. Mgmt. Assn., Assn. of Bar of City of N.Y. Clubs: The Brook, Union, Down Town, Knickerbocker, Racquet and Tennis, Players , Pilgrims of U.S. (all N.Y.C.). Home: 50 Glenbrook Rd Stamford CT 06902 Office: Listowel Inc 2 Park Ave New York NY 10016

MERRILL, HARVIE MARTIN, manufacturing executive; b. Detroit, Apr. 26, 1921; s. Harvie and Helen (Nelson) M.; m. Mardelle Merrill; children—Susan, Linda. B.S. in Chem. Engring, Purdue U., 1942. Devel. engr. Sinclair Refining Co., 1946-47; research and gen. mgr. 3M Co., St. Paul, 1947-65; v.p. fabricated products Plastics div. Stauffer Chem. Co., N.Y.C., 1965-69; with Hexcel Corp., San Francisco, 1969-86, pres., chief exec. officer, 1969-86, chmn. bd., 1976-88; chmn. Nimbus Inc., Rancho Cordova, Calif.; bd. dirs. TIS Mortgage/Investment Co., Corp. Capital Preffered Fund, Fibreboard Corp., Concord, Calif., Fireboard Corp. Trustee Grace Cathedral, San Francisco. Served with USAF, 1942-46. Clubs: Pacific-Union, Bohemian (San Francisco); Links (N.Y.C.). Home: 1170 Sacramento St San Francisco CA 94108 Office: 650 California St Ste 1401 San Francisco CA 94108

MERRILL, J. MARK, financial management executive; b. Memphis, Dec. 6, 1959; s. John F. and Mary Louise (Oakley) M.; m. Ripple Kay Holland, Jan. 7, 1984; 1 child, Sarah Elizabeth. Student, Vanderbilt U., 1977-78; BS in Acctg., Christian Bros. Coll., 1981. CPA, Tenn. Auditor Deloitte Haskins & Sells, Memphis, 1981-82; audit supr. Watkins, Watkins & Keenan, Memphis, 1982-84; fin. mgr. Shelby County, Memphis, 1984-88; chief fin. officer Biotech., Inc., Memphis, 1988—. Mem. AICPA, Tenn. Soc. CPA's, Beta Gamma Sigma. Republican. Evangelical. Home: 1450 Hardwood Trail Cordova TN 38018 Office: Biotech Inc 3035 Directors Row Ste 302 Memphis TN 38131

MERRILL, KENNETH COLEMAN, automobile company executive; b. South Bend, Ind., Feb. 20, 1930; s. Kenneth Griggs and Helen Shapley (Coleman) M.; m. Helen Jean Tagtmeyer, June 10, 1956; children: Barry, Diane, John. B.A., Cornell U., 1953; M.B.A., Ind. U., 1956. With Ford Motor Co., Dearborn, Mich., 1956—; asst. controller Ford Motor Co., Dearborn, 1967-71, gen. asst. controller, 1971-73, controller N.Am. automotive ops., 1973-79, exec. dir. parts ops., 1979-80, exec. dir. bus. planning and trust mgmt., 1980-87; pres. Ford Motor Credit Co., Dearborn, 1987—. Pres. Plymouth (Mich.) Symphony Soc., 1969-70; Vice chmn. bd. dirs. Detroit Inner City Bus. Improvement Forum, 1977-79; pres. Schoolcraft Coll. Found., 1984-86; bd. dirs. Greater Detroit C. of C. Served with AUS, 1953-55. Mem. Fin. Execs. Inst., Detroit Econ. Club, Barton Hills Club, Round Table Club, Beta Gamma Sigma, Psi Upsilon. Episcopalian (treas. 1973-74, 79—). Home: 1450 Maple St Plymouth MI 48170 Office: American Rd Dearborn MI 48121

MERRILL, MARY PETERMANN, financial anaylst; b. Laurium, Mich., Aug. 15, 1937; d. Albert Edward Jr. and Dorothy (Cox) Petermann; m. Alan W. Merrill, June 4, 1960 (div. Jan. 1987); children: Peter, Philip. AB, Cornell U., 1959; MBA, U. Wis., 1982. Cert. fin. planner. Owner, mgr. Fin. Adv. Svc., Madison, Wis., 1981—; asst. v.p. 1st Nat. Bank, Madison, 1986—. Mem. Internat. Assn. fin. Planners, Inst. Cert. Fin. Planners. Home: 306 N Pinckney St Madison WI 53703 Office: PO Box 7900 Madison WI 53707

MERRILL, NEWTON PHELPS STOKES, financial executive; b. Mount Kisco, N.Y., Nov. 14, 1939; s. Edwin Katte Merrill and Helen (Phelps Stokes) Bush; m. Mary DuBois Schwarz, Apr. 30, 1966; children—N. Alexander, Eliot P., Mary S. B.A., Harvard Coll., 1961. Trainee, analyst Bank of N.Y., N.Y.C., 1961-66, investment officer, 1967-69, v.p. nat. div., 1970-75, sr. v.p., 1980-82, exec. v.p. regional banking, 1982-84; exec. v.p. Bank of N.Y. Co. Inc., N.Y.C., 1984-88, sr. exec. v.p., 1988—, also dir. various subs.; sr. exec. v.p. U.S. Comml. Banking, 1984—. Served with USAR, 1962-68. Republican. Episcopalian. Clubs: Harvard, Down Town Assn. (N.Y.C.). Office: Bank NY Co Inc 48 Wall St New York NY 10286

MERRILL, RICHARD THOMAS, publishing executive; b. Chgo., June 26, 1928; s. Thomas William and Mary Ann (Colvin) M.; m. Lisi Y. Snyder, June 7, 1952; children: T. William II, James R., Stephen J. BA, U. Mo., 1950, BJ, 1951. With Commerce Clearing House, Chgo., 1953—, v.p., 1962-76, exec. v.p., 1976-79, pres., chief exec. officer, 1980—, also dir.; bd. dirs. CCH Australia, CCH Can. Ltd., Nat. Quotation Bur., CT Corp. System, Computax, State Capitol Info. Svc., Facts on File, Blvd. Bank, Chgo., Blvd. Bancorp. Inc., Washington Svc. Bur., McDougall, Littell and Co., Fiscal y Laboral (S.A. de C.V.). Capt. USAF, 1951-53. Home: 5 Astor Ct Lake Forest IL 60045 Office: Commerce Clearing House Inc 2700 Lake Cook Rd Riverwoods IL 60015

MERRILL, ROBERT EDWARD, special machinery manufacturing company executive; b. Columbus, Ohio, Oct. 21, 1933; m. Donna Rae Bernstein, Mar. 19, 1967; children—Robert Edward, Aaron Jay, Jonathan Cyrus, Raquel Naomi. MBA, Pepperdine U.; Pres., PSM Corp., San Jose, Calif., 1974—. Served with AUS, 1950-51; Korea. Patentee in pneumatic applications for indsl. press machinery. Home: 858 Fieldwood Ct San Jose CA 95120

MERRIMAN, ILAH COFFEE, financial executive; b. Amarillo, Tex., Mar. 22, 1935; d. Oran and Frances Elizabeth (Rocque) Coffee; children—Pamela, Michael. B.S. in Math., Tex. Tech. U. Cert. secondary tchr., Tex. Pres., chief exec. officer H&R Block Inc., Houston ; pres. H&R Block Inc. Tex.; Trustee, bd. dirs. exec. bd. Tex. Tech U. ex students assn., pres. elect; mem. steering com. Pres.'s Council, bd. dirs. Tex. Tech. Double T Connection, Tex. Tech. Found., Southwest Athletic Conf., Women's Basketball Tournament; mem. enterprize fund Dallas Chpt., Texas Tech. U.; Mem. Dallas Mus. Fine Art, Houston Mus. Fine Art, Dallas Shakespeare Festival, Dallas Theater Ctr., Dallas Symphony Assn., Dallas Hist. Soc., Fort Worth's Kimball Mus., AAUW. Methodist. Office: 8808 Greenville Ave Ste 101 Dallas TX 75243

MERRISS, PHILIP RAMSAY, JR., corporate banker; b. N.Y.C., June 7, 1948; s. Philip Ramsay and Elisabeth (Paine) M.; A.B. magna cum laude in Econs., Lafayette Coll., 1970, M.B.A. (Tuck scholar, Gulf Oil fellow), Dartmouth Coll., 1972; m. Janet Henry Hylan, Oct. 27, 1973. Asso. corp. fin. dept. A.G. Becker and Co. Inc., N.Y.C., 1972-73; fin. analyst corp. banking dept. Chase Manhattan Bank, 1973, asst. treas. N.Y.C. dist., 1974-75, 2d v.p. mining and metals div., 1976-78, 2d v.p. petroleum div., 1978-79, v.p. global petroleum div., 1979-86, client exec., v.p. pub. utilities component, 1986-87, client exec., v.p. global energy component, 1987—. Served to capt. U.S. Army, 1978. Mem. Am. Econ. Assn., Fin Mgmt. Assn., Aircraft Owners and Pilots Assn., N.Y. Road Runners Club, Phi Beta Kappa. Republican. Episcopalian. Clubs: Yale (N.Y.), Westport Athletic, Weston Gun (Conn.). Home: 100 Hills Point Rd Westport CT 06880 Office: Chase Manhattan Bank One Chase Manhattan Pla New York NY 10081

MERRITT, JOHN C., investment banker; b. Glencove, N.Y., May 5, 1940; s. Wilbur M. and Irmgard Merritt; m. Janet H. Blum, July 22, 1961; children—Gregory John, Jacqueline Andrea. B.S. in Bus. Adminstrn., Babson Coll., 1961. Mcpl. bond analyst Drexel & Co., N.Y.C., 1961-64; with Drexel & Co., N.Y.C. and Phila., 1964-72, successively asst. v.p., v.p. and sr. v.p., also bd. dirs.; ptnr. Butcher & Singer Inc., Phila., 1972-79, also bd. dirs.; chmn. bd., chief exec. officer Van Kampen Merritt Inc., Phila., 1979—; former gen. ptnr., bd. dirs. VMS Realty Ptnrs., Chgo., Chgo.-Wheaton Ptnrs. ; chmn., bd. dirs. Van Kampen Merritt U.S. Govt. Fund, Lisle, Ill., Van Kampen Merritt Calif. Insured Tax Free Fund Inc., Lisle, Van Kampen Merritt Tax Free High Income Fund, Lisle, Van Kampen Merritt Insured Tax Free Fund, Lisle, Van Kampen Merritt Corp. High Yield Fund, Lisle, Van Kampen Merritt Pa. Tax Free Income Fund, Lisle, Van Kampen Merritt Growth and Income Fund, Lisle, Van Kampen Merritt Money Market Fund, Lisle, Van Kampen Merritt Tax Free Money Fund, Lisle, Van Kampen Merritt/Xerox Insured MuniFund, Lisle, Van Kampen Merritt Investment Adv. Corp., Lisle, Ind. CashFlow Data Systems Inc., Lisle; ltd. ptnr. Renck, Levy & Co., N.Y.C.; chmn. bd., chief exec. officer Xerox Fin.

Services Life Ins. Co., Lisle, Xerox Fin. Life Ins. Co., Calif.; bd. dirs. VKM Life Mktg. Inc., Lisle, McCarthy, Crisanti & Maffei, Inc., N.Y.C., Xerox Fin. Services, Stamford, Conn. Trustee, bd. dirs. Calvary Luth. Ch., Medford, N.J. Mem. Mcpl. Bond Club Phila. (past pres., bd. govs.). Office: Van Kampen Merritt 2 Pennsylvania Center Pla Ste 1600 Philadelphia PA 19102

MERRITT, WILLIAM ALFRED, JR., lawyer, telecommunications company executive; b. N.Y.C., Aug. 7, 1936; s. William Alfred and Florence Anne (O'Connor) M.; m. Christine Marie Cartnick, Sept. 27, 1969; children—William Tyler, Brian Edward, Elizabeth Cody. BA in Econs., Holy Cross Coll., Worcester, Mass., 1958; LLB, Harvard U., 1964. Bar: N.Y. 1965. Assoc. Olwine, Connelly, Chase, O'Donnell & Weyher, N.Y.C., 1964-68; atty., v.p. ops. and controls Bunge Corp., N.Y.C., 1968-81; exec. v.p. TIE/Communications Inc., Shelton, Conn., 1981—. Served to capt. USNR, 1958-80. Clubs: Tokeneke (Darien); Harvard of N.Y.C. Home: 83 Brookside Rd Darien CT 06820 Office: TIE Communications Inc 8 Progress Dr Shelton CT 06484

MERRIWETHER, DUNCAN, retired manufacturing executive; b. Greenville, Ala., June 9, 1903; s. Jacob and Claudia (Robinson) M.; m. Asenath Kenyon, Feb. 9, 1929; children: Duncan Charles, Virginia Ann (Mrs. L.B. Disharoon), Julia Elizabeth (Mrs. Harris Arnold), Jacob Douglass. B.S., Columbia U., 1928, M.S., 1938. Asst. to mgr. indsl. dept. Peat, Marwick, Mitchell & Co., N.Y.C., 1928-33; various assignments Irving Trust Co., 1933-39; chief accountant Rohm & Haas Co., Phila., 1939-41; asst. treas. Rohm & Haas Co., 1941-43, treas., dir., mem. exec. com., 1943-48, exec. v.p., 1948, vice chmn., 1953-58, past dir., mem. exec. com.; founder Hampshire Nat. Bank, South Hadley, Mass., 1962. Dir. William Penn Found, 1943-70; trustee Mt. Holyoke Coll., 1958-68, chmn. emeritus, 1968—. Mem. Columbia U. Assos. (Distinguished Alumni Service medal 1949), Am. Inst. C.P.A.'s, Alpha Kappa Psi, Beta Gamma Sigma. Episcopalian. Home: 2620 Halfmoon Walk Naples FL 33940

MERSCH, CAROL LINDA, information systems specialist; b. Tulsa, Dec. 13, 1938; d. Forrest Delbert and Betty Clare (Kirk) Baker; m. Paul Grayson Mersch (div. Sept. 1964); 1 child, Teddy Melinda. BSBA, Okla. State U., 1960. Programmer, analyst Rockwell Internat., Tulsa, 1964-68; systems analyst Amoco Prodn. Co., Tulsa, 1968-73; dir., mgr. The Williams Cos., Tulsa, 1973-83; dir. info. svcs. Reading & Bates Corp., Tulsa, 1983—; mem. info. tech. adv. bd. City of Tulsa, 1988—. Author: Systems Development Life Cycle, 1988; contbr. articles to profl. jours. Bd. dirs. United Way Venture Grant, Tulsa, 1987-88. Republican. Christian Scientist. Office: Reading & Bates Corp 3200 Mid-Continent Tower Tulsa OK 74103

MERSEL, CINDA SUE, insurance executive; b. Indpls., Nov. 25, 1954; d. Ivan and Evelyn Elsie (Esteb) Bell; m. Merrill King Mersel, June 30, 1984; 1 child, Matthew King. AA, Miami Dade Coll., 1988; student, Nova Coll., 1989—. Sales rep., mgr. Foremost Ins., Clearwater, Fla., 1977-82; unit mgr. Progressive Ins., Tampa, Fla., 1982; Fla. regional mgr. Progressive Ins., Miami, 1984—; bus. rep. Liberty Mut. Ins., St. Petersburg, Fla., 1983-84. Mem. ORT Club. Democrat. Jewish. Home: PO Box 403503 Miami Beach FL 33140

MERSEL, MARJORIE KATHRYN PEDERSEN, lawyer; b. Manila, Utah, June 17, 1923; d. Leo Henry and Kathryn Anna (Reed) Pedersen; A.B., U. Calif., 1948; LL.B., U. San Francisco, 1948; m. Jules Mersel, Apr. 12, 1950; 1 son, Jonathan. Admitted to D.C. bar, 1952, Calif. bar, 1955; Marjorie Kathryn Pedersen Mersel, atty., Beverly Hills, Calif., 1961-71; staff counsel Dept. Real Estate State of Calif., Los Angeles, 1971—. Mem. Beverly Hills Bar Assn., Trial Lawyers Assn., So. Calif. Women Lawyers Assn. (treas. 1962-63), Beverly Hills C. of C., World Affairs Council. Clubs: Los Angeles Athletic, Sierra. Home: 13007 Hartsook St Sherman Oaks CA 91403 Office: Dept Real Estate 107 S Broadway Los Angeles CA 90012

MERSHON, PAUL JOHNATHAN, financial company executive; b. Wells, Minn., May 31, 1955; s. Robert Gene and Mildred May (Streeter) M.; m. Terry-Lee Mershon, Oct. 11, 1975; children: Brittany Anne, Harrison Bryce. BS, Bus. U. of Minn., 1978. Cert. fin. planner. Fin. cons. North Star Cons., Inc., Mpls., 1978-81; pres., founder Resource Cons., Madison, Wis., 1981—; registered prin., rep. CRI Securities; registered investment advisor rep. Marathon Advisors, Inc. Contbr. articles to profl. jours. Campaign asst. Friends of Jeannie Sealing, Fitchburg, Wis., 1985; stewardship char Madison Reformed Ch., 1985-86, deacon, mem. search com. 1986—. Named Nat. Rookie of Yr. Minn. Mut. Life, 1979, New Assoc. of Yr. North Star Cons., 1979. Mem. Internat. Assn. Fin. Planning (founder Madison chpt. 1985, pres. 1983-85), Nat. Assn. Life Underwriters, Inst. Cert. Fin. Planners, Pro-Trac Fin. Profl. Adv. Panel, Million Dollar Round Table. Republican. Club: Nakoma Country. Home: 5883 Woods Edge Rd Madison WI 53711 Office: Resource Fin Group One Landmark Pl Ste 310 Madison WI 53713

MERTZ, LEN POWELL, rancher, oil and gas executive; b. San Angelo, Tex., Feb. 9, 1955; s. Mortimer Leonard and Madolyn D. (Powell) M.; m. Frances Louise Schneider, Aug. 25, 1979; children: James, Phillip, Louis. BBA, U. Tex., 1976, MA in Pub. Acctg., 1979. CPA, Tex. Rancher operator Mertz 07 and 09 Ranch Cos., San Angleo, 1976—; gen. ptnr. Mayne & Mertz, oil producers, Midland, Tex., 1980—; bd. dirs. Tom Green Nat. Bank, San Angelo, 1987—. Bd. dirs. Cath. Charities, San Angelo, Tex. Diocese, 1987—. Mem. Tex. Soc. CPA's (pres. San Angelo Chpt. 1983-84), Tex. Sheep and Goat Raisers (bd. dirs. 1983—), Tex. and Southwestern Cattle Raisers (com. mem.). Roman Catholic. Home: 3214 Palo Duro San Angelo TX 76904 Office: Len Powell Mertz 502 S Keonigheim 2B San Angelo TX 76903

MERWIN, MARY KAYE, educational association administrator; b. Elkhorn, Wis., Feb. 27, 1942; d. George Reek and Gladys Lucille (Schnitcke) M. BS in Home Econ. Edn., U. Wis. Stout, 1964; MS in Extension Edn. Youth Devel., U. Wis., 1971. 4-H home economist U. Wis. Waukesha County Extension, 1964-67; 4-H youth agt. U. Wis. (Rock County) Extension, 1967-73; area 4-H specialist Tex. A & M U. Systems, Tex. Agr. Extension Svc., College Sta., 1973-75, dist. extension agt. home econ., 1973-75; assoc. dir., edn. program Nat. 4-H Coun., Chevy Chase, Md., 1978-79, dir., program svcs., 1979-81, assoc. adminstr. programs, 1981-84, dir., program div., 1984-86; exec. dir. Cornell Coop. Extension Assn. of Nassau County, Plainview, N.Y., 1987—; bd. dirs. Wis. 4-H Found., Madison; coun. for Advancement of Citizenship, Washington.; cons. Consortum for Internat. Curriculumin Higher Edn., Washington, 1986-87. Elder, clerk of session Gaitherburg (Md.) Presbyn. Ch., 1981-83, Presbyn. Community Ch., Massapequa, N.Y., 1989—. Mem. Am. Home Econ. Assn., N.Y. Econ. Assn. (bd. dirs. 1988—, L.I. bd. 1988—), Am. Soc. Assn. Execs., Nat. Extension 4-H Agts. Assn. (Wis. chpt. pres. 1971-73), Epsilon Sigma Phi (nat. award chmn. 1985), Phi Upsilon Omicron, Order of Eastern Star. Republican. Home: 26 Camp Rd Massapequa NY 11758 Office: Cornell Coop Extension of Nassau County 1425 Old County Rd Bldg J Plainview NY 11803

MERZBACHER, RICHARD WARREN, banker; b. Rockville Centre, N.Y., July 10, 1948; s. Warren and Mary Rita (Wachtel) M.; m. Joyce Eileen Anderson, June 17, 1972; children: Laurene, Kristina, Mark. BA, St. Francis Coll., Bklyn., 1970; MBA, L.I. U., 1974. From credit trainee to asst. cashier Franklin Nat. Bank, 1970-74; from asst. treas. to asst. v.p. Bankers Trust Co., 1974-80; asst. v.p. Chem. Bank, 1980-81; sr. v.p. State Bank L.I., New Hyde Park, N.Y., 1981-87, exec. v.p., 1987—. Chmn. St. Kilian's Sch. Bd., Farmingdale, N.Y., Nassau County ARC, Mineola, N.Y. Mem. Nat. Assn. Accts. (bd. dirs.), Robert Morris Assocs. Office: State Bank LI 1981 Marcus Ave Lake Success NY 11042

MESHOWSKI, FRANK ROBERT, industrial executive; b. Milw., Sept. 10, 1930; s. Frank Louis and Constance (Mockus) M.; m. Olga Skirka, Jan. 26, 1952; children: David, Laurie, Elaine. B in Marine Engring., N.Y. State Maritime Acad., 1951; BS in Mech. Engring., Newark Coll. of Engring., 1954. Project engr., mgr. Curtiss Wright, Inc., Woodridge, N.J., 1952-59; v.p. sales Gulton Industries, Inc., Metuchen, N.J., 1959-68; group v.p., sr. v.p. Nytronics, Inc., Alpha, N.J., 1968-72; v.p. mktg. Gulf & Western Inc., N.Y.C., 1972-79; pres. Unicord div. Gulf & Western Corp., Westbury, N.Y., 1979-86; bus. cons. 1986—; dir. OPT Industries, Phillipsburg, N.J., 1980—. Mem. Am. Mgmt. Assn. Democrat. Roman Catholic. Home: 4 Brandywine Dr East Brunswick NJ 08816 Office: OPT Industries 300 Red Sch Ln Phillipsburg NJ 08865

MESSEMER, GLENN MATTHEW, lawyer; b. Hartford, Conn., Jan. 7, 1947; s. Joseph M. and Mary S. Messemer; BSBA, Georgetown U., 1968; JD, U. Conn., 1971. Bar: Conn. 1972. Staff atty. Kaman Corp., Bloomfield, Conn., 1972-74, asst. sec., 1974-79, asst. v.p., 1979-81, v.p., sec., counsel, 1981—; prof. bus. law Austin Dunham Barney Sch. Bus. Adminstrn., U. Hartford (Conn.), 1974-80; legal counsel Am. Helicopter Soc.; arbitrator Am. Arbitration Assn., 1978-82. Served with M.I., U.S. Army, 1969-75. Mem. Conn. Bar Assn. (founding; exec. com., sec.), ABA, Hartford County Bar Assn. Clubs: Hartford Golf, Hartford, Masons. Office: Kaman Corp Old Windsor Rd Bloomfield CT 06002

MESSERLI, ROBBIN LANCE, employee benefits brokerage-consulting executive; b. Rapid City, S.D., Dec. 2, 1960; s. Robert Vincent and Florence Margaret (Nowack) M.; m. Mary Joellen O'Byrne, Oct. 19, 1985. AA, Ventura Coll., 1981; BA in Psychology and, U. Calif., Davis, 1984. Methods analyst Bus. Men's Assurance Co., Kansas City, Mo., 1985-86; chief fin. officer, ops. mgr. Robert D. O'Byrne & Assocs., Kansas City, 1986—. Republican. Roman Catholic. Office: 1200 Board of Trade Ctr 4900 Main St Kansas City MO 64112

MESSINEO, ANTHONY, library director; b. Rochester, N.Y., Dec. 15, 1933; s. Lewis and Teresa (Leone) M.; m. Violet Totilas, Apr. 15, 1967. BA, U. Miami, Fla., 1960; MLS, Syracuse U., 1962. Librarian Rochester Pub. Library, 1961-64; head adult svcs. Ferguson Library, Stamford, Conn., 1966-68; dir. North Tonawanda (N.Y.) Pub. Library, 1968-73; bldg. cons. Pub. Library of North Tonawanda, 1973-74; dir. Mohawk Valley Library Assn., Schenectady, N.Y., 1977-80; library dir. Greenville (S.C.) County Library, 1980—; vis. lectr. SUNY, Buffalo, 1972. Contbr. articles to porfl. jours. Mem. adv. council N.Y. Senate subcom. on libraries, 1979-81. Mem. ALA, S.C. Library Assn., Southeastern Library Assn., Assn. Pub. Library Adminstrs., Rotary. Home: 36A Tanager Cir Greer SC 29651 Office: Greenville County Library 300 College St Greenville SC 29601

MESSING, CAROL SUE, communications educator; b. Bronx, N.Y.; d. Isidore and Esther Florence (Burtoff) Weinberg; m. Sheldon H. Messing; children: Lauren, Robyn. BA, Bklyn. Coll., 1967, MA, 1970. Tchr. N.Y.C. Bd. Edn., 1967-72; assoc. prof. Lang. arts Northwood Inst., Midland, Mich., 1973—; owner Job Match, Midland, 1983-85; cons. Mich. Credit Union League, Saginaw, 1984-87, Nat. Hotel & Restaurant, Midland, Mich., 1985-86, External Degree program, Continuing Edn. program, Northwood Inst., 1986-87, Dow Chem. Employees' Credit Union, 1988—. Author: (anthology) Symbiosis, 1985, rev. edit., 1987, Controlling Communication, 1987. Mem. Nat. Council Tchrs. English, LWV, Kappa Delta Pi, Delta Mu Delta. Office: Northwood Inst 3225 Cook Rd Midland MI 48640

MESSMORE, THOMAS ELLISON, insurance company executive; b. Monongahela, Pa., June 30, 1945; s. Lindsay Ellison and Margaret (Hoffmann) M.; m. Sharon Weaver, Aug. 19, 1966; children: Lauren, Beth, Benjamin, William. BS in Indsl. Engring., W.Va. U., 1967; MBA, Harvard U., 1969. Chartered fin. analyst. Asst. treas. State Street Bank and Trust Co., Boston, 1969-72; fin. product mgr. Interactive Data Corp., Waltham, Mass., 1972-75; sr. v.p. Keystone Custodian Funds, Inc., Boston, 1975-80; sr. v.p. and chief fin. officer Keystone Mass. Group, Boston, 1981-83; sr. v.p. The Travelers Ins. Co., Hartford, Conn., 1984—. Mem. Inst. Chartered Fin. Analysts. Home: 1090 Prospect Ave Hartford CT 06105 Office: The Travelers Corp 1 Tower Sq Hartford CT 06183-2030

MESSUD, FRANÇIS-MICHEL, manufacturing company executive; b. Toulon, France, June 29, 1931; m. Margaret D. Riches; children: Elizabeth C., Claire D. LLB, LLM, 1956; AM, Harvard U., 1961. With Pechiney Group, France, Greece, Australia, Can. and U.S., 1961-82; pres., chief exec. officer Pechiney World Trade (USA), Inc., Greenwich, Conn., 1982—. Served to lt. French Navy, 1956-59. Clubs: Harvard (N.Y.C.); Am. (Sydney, Australia). Office: Pechiney World Trade (USA) Inc 475 Steamboat Ave Greenwich CT 06830

MESTAD, ORVILLE LAVERNE, bank board chairman; b. Decorah, Iowa, Mar. 22, 1923; s. Clarence Benjamen and Edna Belinda (Larson) M.; m. Shirley Gail Matthews, July 20, 1948; children: Cynthia Mestad Clinton, Ronald Matthew. BS, U. So. Calif., 1949, DDS with honors, 1953. Pvt. practice dentistry Arcadia, Calif., 1953-83; instr. clin. dentistry U. Soc. Calif., Los Angeles, 1953-57; organizer, chmn. Foothill Ind. Bank, Glendora, Calif., 1973—; chmn. Foothill Ind. Bancorp, Glendora, 1986—. Chmn. Foothill Presbyn. Hosp., Glendora, 1972-88; mem. exec. com. Citrus Coll. Found., Glendora, 1982-88. Sgt. U.S. Army, 1943-45, ETO. Decorated Bronze Star. Mem. ADA, Am. Hosp. Assn. (regional policy adv. coun. 1989—), Arcadia Lions Club, Alpha Tau Epsilon. Republican. Presbyterian. Home: 1144 Indian Springs Dr Glendora CA 91740 Office: Foothill Ind Bancorp 510 S Grand Ave Glendora CA 91740

MESZNIK, JOEL R., investment banker; b. Beirut, Lebanon, Oct. 3, 1945; s. Hans and Eugenie (Bagdadi) M.; m. Lynne Mesznik, Mar. 25, 1979; children: Daniel, Jared, Kara. BCE, CCNY, 1967; MBA, Columbia U., 1970. Engr. Ebasco Svcs., N.Y.C., 1967-70; banker Citibank, N.Y.C., 1970-71, Newhouse Capital, N.Y.C., 1971-73, Matthews & Wright, N.Y.C., 1971-76; mng. dir. Drexel Burnham Lambert, N.Y.C., 1976—. Home: 180 East End Ave New York NY 10128 Office: Drexel Burnham Lambert Inc 60 Broad St 4th Fl New York NY 10004

METCALF, ROBERT JOHN ELMER, industrial consultant; b. Glen Ellyn, Ill., June 27, 1919; s. Elmer Simpson and Vida Marie Metcalf; B.S.M.E., U. Pitts., 1947; m. Rosemarie Rusch, Sept. 11, 1947; children—Kathleen, Karen, Patti, Pamela. Asst. staff supr. Westinghouse Electric Co., Buffalo, 1949-52, assoc. engr., 1952-54; assoc. Gemar Assocs., Inc., Greenwich, Conn., 1954-66. v.p., 1966-83; cons., 1983—. Served with U.S. Army, 1943-46. Mem. Am. Arbitration Assn., Am. Inst. Indsl. Engrs. (sr.), Inst. Mgmt. Cons. (founding). Roman Catholic. Home and Office: 300 Woodette Dr Apt 201 Dunedin FL 34698

METCALFE, RANDOLPH C., employee benefits consultant; b. Frederick, Md., July 26, 1954. BA, U. N.C., 1976. Ptnr. M.E. Young Constrn. Co., Frederick, Md., 1976-77; salesman Long Fence Co., Capitol Heights, Md., 1977-78; mktg. dir. H. Chambers Co., Balt., 1978-79; group sales mgr. Home Life Ins. Co., N.Y.C., 1979-87; sr. v.p., dir. Applied Benefits Rsch., Inc., Parsippany, N.J., 1987—. Vol. HALT (nat. org. for legal reform), Washington, 1985, Citizens Against Govt. Waste, N.Y.C., 1985. John Motley Morehead scholar U. N.C., 1976. Democrat. Episcopalian. Home: 16 Beech Ln Morristown NJ 07960 Office: Applied Benefits Rsch 601 Jefferson Rd #201 Parsippany NJ 07054

METIVIER, ROLAND, hospital administrator; b. Lewiston, Maine, May 3, 1944; s. Oscar Joseph and Lucienne (Giguere) M.; m. Yvonne Clark, Aug. 13, 1982; children: Angelique, Aimee. AA, Mitchell Coll., 1964; BA, U. Conn., 1971, MA, 1973; MBA, U. N.Mex., 1987. Asst. adminstr. Bernalillo Mental Health Ctr., Albuquerque, 1978-81; hosp. adminstr. N.Mex. State Hosp., Las Vegas, 1981-83, Vista Sandia Hosp., Albuquerque, 1983-86, Columbine Psychiat. Ctr., Littleton, Colo., 1986—. Sgt. USAF, 1965-68, Vietnam. Mem. Kiwanis Club. Democrat. Roman Catholic. Home: 2617 S Saint Paul St Denver CO 80210 Office: Columbine Psychiat Ctr 8565 S Poplar Way Littleton CO 80126

METRE, RAVI KUMAR, banking executive; b. Amravati, India, Mar. 10, 1944; came to U.S. in 1969; s. Waman Baputi and Shantabai (Akarte), M.; m. Shubha Saklani, Feb. 10, 1987; 1 child, Kanika. BS in Geophysics, Indian Sch. Mines, Dhanbad, India, 1965; MBA in Fin., Indian Inst. Mgmt., Calcutta, India, 1967; MS, U. Pa., 1971. Mgr., cons. Dunlop, Calcutta, India, 1967-69; mgmt. rsch. assoc. Wharton Sch., Phila., 1969-73; dir. Fidelity Bank, Phila., 1973-81; assoc., cons. Booz Allen Hamilton, Dallas, 1981-83; sr. v.p., treas., mgr. planning Barclays Bank Calif., San Francisco, 1984—. Scholar Indian Sch. Mines, 1962-65, Ind. Inst. Mgmt., 1965-67; U. Pa. fellow, 1969-73. Mem. Am. Mgmt. Assn. Home: 1511 Lake St San Francisco CA 94118 Office: Barclays Bank Calif 111 Pine St San Francisco CA 94111

METT, RODERICK MICHAEL, corporate finance executive; b. Milw., Oct. 15, 1939; s. Frederick Paul and Florence (Behling) M.; m. Sylvia Jo McEnery, Dec. 30, 1978; stepchildren: Aaron Thomas, Stewart Miles. AB in history and polit. sci. cum laude, Yale U., 1961; JD, U. Wis., 1968. Bar: Wisc., 1968. Legis. intern Capitol Hill Congl. Office, Washington, 1961; labor relations specialist U.S Post Office Dept., Washington, 1965; gen. counsel, acting commr. Wis. Securities Commn., 1968-71; asst. atty. gen. Dept. Justice State of Wis., 1971-72; sole practice Milw., 1973-80; gen. ptnr. Mett-Garner Assocs., Madison, Wis., 1973-80; pres. Calmont Corp., North Palm Beach, Fla., 1980-85, Coach Investments, Inc. and subs. Internat. Stamp Exchange Corp., Greenwich, Conn. and Miami Beach, Fla., 1985—; qualified expert witness, Wisc., 1972. County commr. Milw. County, 1973-80. Served to lt. comdr. USNR, 1961-65. Mem. Wis. Bar Assn., Am. Philatelic Soc., Phi Gamma Delta. Republican. Presbyterian. Clubs: Madison, Gov.'s. Office: Coach Investments Inc PO Box 1615 West Palm Beach FL 33402 also: 393 Fifth Ave New York NY 10016

METTER, BERTRAM MILTON, advertising agency executive; b. N.Y.C., Aug. 14, 1927; s. Harry W. and Rosella (Fischbein) M.; m. Roslyn H. Reiser, Jan. 11, 1952; children: Joel, Lawrence, Daniel. B.A., Bklyn. Coll., 1949; M.A., Columbia U., 1952; A.M.P., Harvard U., 1980. Copy chief N.Y. Mirror, 1953-56, Newsweek mag., N.Y.C., 1956-59; with J. Walter Thompson Co., N.Y.C., 1959—; v.p. J. Walter Thompson Co., 1965-73, sr. v.p., 1973-78, creative dir., 1974—, exec. v.p., 1978—; vice chmn. J. Walter Thompson, U.S.A., 1984—, chmn. bd. dirs., 1986—. Club: Baliwick (Greenwich, Conn.). Home: 41 Nutmeg Dr Greenwich CT 06831 Office: J Walter Thompson 466 Lexington Ave New York NY 10017

METTLE, VINCENT DOMINICK, accountant; b. Balt., Oct. 9, 1960; s. Joseph Hooper and Rose Marie (Arena) M. BA in Acctg., Loyola Coll., Balt., 1982. CPA, Md. Property acct. Westinghouse Corp., Hunt Valley, Md., 1983; cost acct. Gould Inc., Westminster, Md., 1984; cons. Black & Decker, Hampstead, Md., 1984-85; cost acct. Koppers Corp., Harmans, Md., 1985-88, Solarex, Inc. (div. of Amoco), Rockville, Md., 1988—; fin. analyst Dept. of Def., Ft. Meade, Md., 1988—. Mem. Am. Inst. CPA's, Md. Assn. CPA's, Nat. Assn. Accts., Aircraft Owners and Pilots Assn. Republican. Roman Catholic. Home: 619 Tanglewood Dr Eldersburg MD 21784 Office: Solarex Inc 1335 Piccard Dr Rockville MD 20850

METTLER, RUBEN FREDERICK, electronics and engineering company executive; b. Shafter, Calif., Feb. 23, 1924; s. Henry Frederick and Lydia M.; m. Donna Jean Smith, May 1, 1955; children: Matthew Frederick, Daniel Frederick. Student, Stanford U., 1941; BSEE, Calif. Inst. Tech., 1944, MS, 1947, PhD in Elec. and Aero. Engring, 1949; LHD (hon.), Baldwin-Wallace Coll., 1980; LLD, John Carroll U., 1986. Registered profl. engr., Calif. Assoc. div. dir. systems research and devel. Hughes Aircraft Co., 1949-54; spl. cons. to asst. sec. def. U.S. Dept. Def., 1954-55; asst. gen. mgr. guided missile research div., tech. supr. Atlas, Titan, Thor and Minuteman programs Ramo-Wooldridge Corp., 1955-58; exec. v.p., then pres. TRW Space Tech. Labs. (merger Thompson Products and Ramo-Wooldridge), 1958-65; pres. TRW Systems Group, 1965-68; asst. pres. TRW Inc., 1968-69, pres., chief operating officer, 1969-77, chmn. bd., chief exec. officer, 1977-88, also bd. dirs.; bd. dirs. Bank Am. Corp., Merck & Co., Japan Soc. Inc.; mem. Pres. Reagan's Commn. Exec. Exchange, Adv. Council on Japan-U.S. Econ. Rels., Pres.'s Blue Ribbon Def. Panel, 1969-70; vice chmn. Def. Industry Adv. Council, 1964-70, chmn. Pres.'s Task Force on Sci. Policy, 1969-70; cons. Hughes Aircraft Co., Dept. Def., 1954—. Author: reports on airborne electronic systems; patentee interceptor fire control systems. Nat. campaign chmn. United Negro Coll. Fund, 1980-81; chmn. Nat. Alliance Bus., 1978-79; co-chmn. 1980 UN Day, Washington; chmn. bd. trustees Calif. Inst. Tech.; trustee Com. Econ. Devel., Cleve. Clinic Found.; bd. dirs. Nat. Action Council for Minorities in Engring. Served with USNR, 1942-46. Named one of Outstanding Young Men of Am., U.S. Jr. C. of C., 1955, So. Calif.'s Engr. of Year, 1964; recipient Meritorious Civilian Service award Dept. Def., 1969, Nat. Human Relations award NCCJ, 1979, Excellence in Mgmt. award Industry Week Mag., 1979, Disting. Service award Calif. Inst. Tech., 1966. Fellow IEEE, AIAA; mem. Sci. Research Soc. Am., Bus. Roundtable (chmn. 1982-84), Conf. Bd. (trustee 1982—), Bus. Council (vice chmn. 1981-82, chmn. 1986-87), Nat. Acad. Engring., The Japan Soc. (bd. dirs.), Sigma Xi, Eta Kappa Nu (Nation's Outstanding Young Elec. Engr. 1954), Tau Beta Pi, Theta Xi. Clubs: Cosmos (Washington); Union, 50 (Cleve.). Home and Office: TRW Inc 1900 Richmond Rd Cleveland OH 44124 also: TRW Space & Def Sector 1 Space Park Redondo Beach CA 90278

METZ, FRANK ANDREW, JR., data processing executive; b. Winthrop, Mass., Jan. 28, 1934; s. Frank Andrew and Frances E. (Fallon) M.; married; children: Christopher, Lelia, Amy, Patrick, Joshua, Rebecca; m. Judith Ann Mapes, July 21, 1979. A.B., Bowdoin Coll., 1955. With IBM, 1955—; dir. fin. planning data processing group IBM, Harrison, N.Y., 1969-72; div. v.p. office products IBM, Franklin Lakes, N.J., 1972-75; asst. controller IBM, Armonk, N.Y., 1975-78, controller, 1978-80; v.p., asst. group exec. IBM, White Plains, N.Y., 1980-84, sr. v.p., group exec., 1984-86, sr. v.p., chief fin. officer, 1986—; bd. dirs. Allegheny Power Systems. Trustee St. Luke's Roosevelt Hosp., N.Y.C., 1979—, treas., 1982, vice chmn., 1983; trustee Am. Mus. Natural History, 1986—. Served to 1st lt. Transp. Corps U.S. Army, 1956. Roman Catholic. Office: IBM Corp Old Orchard Rd Armonk NY 10504

METZGER, DIANE HAMILL, paralegal, poet; b. Phila., July 23, 1949; d. David Alexander Sr. and Eunice (Shelton) Hamill; m. Frank Allen Metzger, Aug. 29, 1973; 1 child, Jason Frank. AA in Bus. Adminstrn. magna cum laude, Northampton Coll., 1980; BA in Polit. Sci. magna cum laude, Bloomsburg U., 1987; paralegal cert., Pa. State U., 1988. Statistician Am. Viscose div. FMC Corp., Phila., 1967-72; research asst. Temple U., Phila., 1972-73; clk. II State Correctional Instn. at Muncy, Pa., 1977—; freelance writer and paralegal. Author: (poems) Coralline Ornaments, 1980; lyricist: Come Now, Shepherds, 1979, Sleep Now, My Baby, 1986; poetry pub. in numerous mags., publs. including Gravida, Inside/Out, Working Parents, South Coast Poetry Jour., Pearl. Recipient numerous awards for poetry including 2d place award Phila. Writers Conf., 1969, 1st prize PEN Writing Awards, 1985, 2d prize Carver Prize Essay Competition, 1986; also Citation for Outstanding Achievement Pa. Ho. of Reps., 1988, Citation for Outstanding Achievement Pa. Senate, 1988. Mem. ASCAP, Poetry Soc. Am., Mensa. Democrat. Home: 313 Barker St Ridley Park PA 19078 Office: SCIM #5634-PO Box 180-Rt 405 Muncy PA 17756

METZGER, KATHLEEN ANN, computer systems specialist; b. Orchard Park, N.Y., Aug. 4, 1949; d. Charles Milton and Anna Irene (Matwijow) Wetherby; m. Robert George Metzger, Aug. 29, 1970 (div. June 1988). BS in Edn. cum laude, SUNY Coll., Buffalo, 1970; postgrad., SUNY, Fredonia, 1975. Cert. secondary tchr. Math. tchr. Crestwood High Sch., Mantua, Ohio, 1970-71; sec., bookkeeper Maple Bay Marina, Lakewood, N.Y., 1972; math., bus. tchr. Falconer (N.Y.) High Sch., 1972-76; bookkeeper Darling Jewelers, Lakewood, 1977-78; computer operator Ethan Allen Inc., Jamestown, N.Y., 1978-79, So. Tier Bldg. Trades, Jamestown, 1979; program analyst TRW Bearings Div., Inc., Jamestown, 1980-82, Fla. Power Corp., St. Petersburg, 1982—. campaign advisor United Way, St. Petersburg, 1985. Kappa Delta Pi. Republican. Roman Catholic. Home: 13793 Gull Way N Clearwater FL 34622 Office: Fla Power Corp 3201 34th St S Saint Petersburg FL 33711

METZGER, PAUL S., physician, insurance company executive; b. Westerville, Ohio, Feb. 28, 1925; s. S.C. and Julia (Schrock) M.; m. Mary Anderson, Apr. 18, 1964 (dec. Aug. 1982); m. Lee Metzger, July 15, 1983. MD, Ohio State U., 1948. Diplomate Am. Bd. Internal Medicine. Intern Univ. Hosp., Columbus, Ohio, 1949-50, resident in internal medicine, 1952-55; physician Cen. Ohio Med. Clinic, Columbus, 1956-66; asst. med. dir. Nationwide Ins., Columbus, 1955-66, med. dir., 1966-69, v.p., med. dir., 1969-81, v.p., chief med. dir., 1981—; clin. prof. medicine Ohio State U., Columbus, 1982—. Capt. with USNR, 1943-78. Mem. AMA (del. 1985-88), Assn. Life Ins. Med. Dirs. Am. (pres. 1982), Acad. Medicine (pres. 1979), Am. Soc. Internat. Medicine (trustee 1979-82), Navy League of

Columbus. Lodge: Kiwanis (chmn. CTEE Columbus chpt. 1986—). Home: 4263 Fredericksburg Ave Columbus OH 43228 Office: Nationwide Mut Ins Co One Nationwide Pla Columbus OH 43216

METZGER, ROBERT OWEN, banking consultant, educator, writer; b. N.Y.C., Oct. 22, 1939; s. Homer P. and Catherine Dale (Owen) M.; m. Dorothee Benkenstein, Apr. 25, 1968; 1 child, Joelle Laurence Owen. BS in Econs., U. Md. Overseas Coll., 1963; PMD, Harvard U., 1969; PhD in Bus. Adminstrn., U. Beverly Hills, 1981. Staff exec. IT&T, 1970-72; chief exec. officer Faber Merlin Ltd., Hong Kong, 1973; sr. mgr. McSweeney & Assocs., Newport Beach, Calif., 1974-75; founder, chmn., mag. prin. Metzger & Assocs., Santa Ana, Calif., 1976-88; adj. prof. mgmt. and orgn. Grad. Sch. Bus. Adminstrn. U. So. Calif., Los Angeles, 1984-88; assoc. dir. Ctr. for Ops. Mgmt., Edn. and Tng., 1986-88; sr. v.p. Furash & Co., Washington D.C., 1988—. Author: Organizational Issues to Strategic Planning in the Commercial Banking Industry, 1981, Consulting to Management, 1983, Profitable Consulting: Guiding America's Managers into the Next Century, 1988; editorial rev. bd. and contbr. editor: Fin. Mgrs. Statement Quar., Orgn. and Group Studies, Bankers Monthly; editorial rev. bd.: Jour. Retail Banking, Jour. Mgmt. Cons.; contbr. numerous articles on bank mgmt. to profl. jours. Mem. corp. solicitation com. Nat. Kidney Found. Served with USAF, 1958-62. Mem. Inst. Mgmt. Cons., Acad. Mgmt. (exec. com. mgmt. cons. div.), Hon. Order Ky. Col. Berkshire Sch. Alumni Assn. (founder, pres. So. Calif. chpt.), Astron. Soc. Pacific., Acad. Mgmt. Cons. (managerial div., exec. com.). Club: Harvard Bus. Sch. So. Calif. Home: 3933 Ivy Terrace Ct NW Washington DC 20007

METZGER, VERNON ARTHUR, educator; b. Baldwin Park, Calif., Aug 13, 1918; s. Vernon and Nellie C. (Ross) M.; B.S., U. Calif., Berkeley, 1947, M.B.A., 1948; m. Beth Arlene Metzger, Feb. 19, 1955; children—Susan, Linda, 1 step-son, David. Estimating engr. C. F. Braun & Co., 1949; prof. mgmt. Calif. State U. at Long Beach, 1949—, founder Sch. Bus.; mgmt. cons., 1949—. Mem. Fire Commn. Fountain Valley, Calif., 1959-60; pres. Orange County Democratic League, 1967-68; mem. State Dept. mgmt. task force to promote modern mgmt. in Yugoslavia, 1977; mem. State of Calif. Fair Polit. Practices Commn., Orange County Transit Com. Served with USNR, 1942-45. Recipient Outstanding Citizens award Orange County (Calif.) Bd. Suprs. Fellow Soc. for Advancement of Mgmt. (life; dir.); mem. Acad. Mgmt., Orange County Indsl. Relations Research Assn. (v.p.), Beta Gamma Sigma, Alpha Kappa Psi, Tau Kappa Upsilon. Home: 1938 Balearic Dr Costa Mesa CA 92626 Office: 1250 Bellflower Blvd Long Beach CA 90804

METZLER, YVONNE LEETE, travel agent; b. Bishop, Calif., Jan. 25, 1930; d. Ben Ford and Gladys Edna (Johnson) Leete; student U. Calif., Berkeley, 1949, Empire Coll., 1988—; m. Richard Harvey Metzler, June 2, 1950; children: David Grant, Regan M., Erin E. Student Empire Coll., 1988—. Vocat. instr. Ukiah (Calif.) Jr. Acad., 1962-63; bookkeeper Sid Beamer Volkswagen, Ukiah, 1963-64; acct. Ukiah Convalescent Hosp., 1964, Walter Woodard P.A., Ukiah, 1964-66; asso. dir. Fashion Two Twenty, Ukiah, 1966-67, dir., Santa Rosa, Calif., 1967-71; acct. P.K. Marsh, M.D., Ukiah, 1971-72, Walter Woodard P.A. and Clarence White C.P.A., Ukiah, 1972-74; partner, travel agt. Redwood Travel Agy., Ukiah, 1973-76; owner, mgr. A-1 Travel Planners, Ukiah, 1976—; owner A-1 Travel Planners of Willits, Calif., 1979-88. Commr., Ukiah City Planning Commn., 1979-84, chmn., 1981-83; bd. dirs., rep. Mendocino County Visitors and Conv. Bur., 1988—, Pvt. Industry Council, 1988—; mem. Rep. County Cen. Com., 1978-80. Mem. Ukiah C. of C. (1st v.p. 1980, pres. 1981-82), Mendocino County C. of C. (dir. 1981). Clubs: Soroptimist (pres. 1977-78), Bus. and Profl. Women (treas. 1977-78, named Woman of the 80's). Office: 505 E Perkins St Ukiah CA 95482

MEUGER, STEPHEN JOHN, banker; b. Dover, N.J., Dec. 31, 1949. BA, Seton Hall U., 1971, MBA, 1981; postgrad., Stonier Grad. Sch. Banking, 1984. Asst. comptroller U.S. Savs. Bank, Newark, 1975-77; dep. controller United Jersey Bank, Hackensack, N.J., 1978-81; v.p. planning United Jersey Bank, Hackensack, 1981-83, sr. v.p., treas., 1983—. Bd. dirs., treas., chmn., fin. com. United Way of Bergen Co., Paramus, 1988—; mem. chmn. fin. com. Mine Hill Twp. Bd. Edn., 1982-87. Office: United Jersey Bank 25 E Salem St Hackensack NJ 07601

MEULEMAN, ROBERT JOSEPH, banker; b. South Bend, Ind., May 1, 1939; s. Joseph and Louise (Dutrieux) M.; m. Judith Ann Mc Comb, July 1, 1961; children Joseph, Jennifer, Rachel. BA, U. Notre Dame, 1961; MBA, Mich. State U., 1962. Investment analyst Nat. Bank of Detroit, 1965-68, Heritage Investment Advisors, Milw., 1968-72; sr. investment officer St. Joseph Bank and Trust Co., South Bend, 1972-81; exec. v.p., chief operating officer Amcore Bank N.Am., Rockford, Ill., 1981—. Bd. dirs. Swedish Am. Hosp. Found., Rockford, 1986—, Rockford Pro-Am., 1986—; campaign leader Crusader Clinic, Rockford, 1988. Served to 1st lt. U.S. Army, 1963-65. Mem. Chartered Fin. Analysts, Milw. Fin. Analysts, Rockford C. of C. (bd. dirs. 1985). Republican. Roman Catholic. Club: Rockford Country. Home: 5329 Gingeridge Ln Rockford IL 61111 Office: Amcore Bank NA Rockford 501 7th St Rockford IL 61107

MEUSE, DAVID RUSSELL, investment banker; b. Cairo, Ill., Apr. 20, 1945; s. David L. and Jeanette (Settlemoir) M.; m. Mary Beth Busch, June 21, 1969; children: Lisa Marie, Charles David, Peter Alexander. BA in Polit. Sci., John Carroll U., 1967; postgrad., Cleve. State U., 1968-69. Ptnr. Ball, Burge, Kraus, Cleve., 1967-74, Prescott, Ball & Turben Co., Cleve., 1973-74, McDonald & Co., Columbus, Ohio, 1974-79; pres., chief exec. officer Cranston Securities Co., Columbus, 1979-81; pres. MRC, Inc., Columbus, 1981-86; pres., bd. dirs. Meuse, Rinker, Chapman, Endres & Brooks, Columbus, 1986—; bd. dirs. McDonald & Co. Securities, Cleve., Blue Cross Cen. Benefits Cen. Ohio, Columbus Show Case Co., Vacuform Industries, Inc., Merich Capital, Merich Group, Inc., Merich Gen. Corp., Broad St. Capital, High St. Holding, High St. Capital, MRC Investment, Inc., Brencap Corp. Bd. dirs. Columbus Symphony Orch., Columbus Assn. Performing Arts, Capital Arts Campaign, I Know I Can, Riverside Hosp. Devel. Coun.; bd. dirs., chmn. Childhood League Capital Campaign. Mem. Columbus Area C. of C. (bd. dirs.), Columbus Country Club, Capital Club. Republican. Office: Meuse Rinker Chapman Endres & Brooks 90 N High St Columbus OH 43215

MEYER, CARL SHEAFF, management consultant; b. Mineola, N.Y., Dec. 19, 1932; s. William Herman and Dorothy Gertrude (Anderson) M. BA in Arch., U. Va., 1956. Cert. mgmt. cons. Archtl. specialist, govt. sales coordinator metals div. Olin Corp., 1958-60; sales adminstr., advt. mgr. Gen. Bronze Corp., 1960-61; product mgr. Barrett div. Allied Chem. Corp., 1961-64; cons. Barrington & Co., 1964-68; sr. cons., mng. asso., v.p. Lester B. Knight & Assos., N.Y.C., 1968-77; pres. William H. Meyer & Assos., Manhasset, N.Y., 1977—. Chief Plandome (N.Y.) Fire Dept., 1965-67. Served with USN, 1956-58, capt. Res. ret., 1958-80. Mem. Inst. Mgmt. Cons. (bd. dirs. 1979-84, v.p. 1982-84), Am. Arbitration Assn., Naval Reserve Assn., Theta Chi. Republican. Episcopalian. Clubs: N.Y. Yacht, Manhasset Bay Yacht, Royal Bermuda Yacht, Union League, Meadow Brook Hunt; Coral Beach (Bermuda). Lodges: Masons, Shriners. Office: 29 Park Ave Manhasset NY 11030

MEYER, DANIEL EDWARD, infosystems executive; b. Odenton, Md., July 1, 1956; s. Russell Gordon and Sally Jane (Lovell) M. BS in Zoology, U. Md., 1978. Sr. scientist Tracor Jitco, Rockville, Md., 1980-83; mgr. online devel. ISI, Phila., 1983-87; pres. Advanced Rsch. Techs., Inc., Wayne, Pa., 1988—. Author: Graphic-Based Software for Chemists, 1987, Chemical Structures: The International Language of Chemistry, 1988; co-author, editor: Chemical Structure Software for PCs, 1988; assoc. editor Heldref Publs., Washington, 1978-87; contbr. articles to profl. publs. Mem. Am. Chem. Soc., Chem. Structure Assn., Nat. Fedn. Abstracting and Info. Svcs. Republican. Office: Advanced Rsch Techs Inc PO Box 556 Wayne PA 19087

MEYER, DANIEL JOSEPH, machinery company executive; b. Flint, Mich., May 31, 1936; s. John Michael and Margaret (Meehan) M.; m. Bonnie Harrison, June 22, 1963; children—Daniel P., Jennifer. B.S., Purdue U., 1958; M.B.A., Ind. U., 1963. C.P.A., N.Y. Mgr. Touche, Ross & Co., Detroit, 1964-69; controller Cin. Milacron, Inc., 1969-77, v.p. fin., treas., 1977-83, exec. v.p. fin. and adminstrn., 1983-86, pres., chief operating officer, 1987—, also bd. dirs. Served with U.S. Army, 1959. Mem. Am. Inst. C.P.A.'s. Club: Kenwood Country (Cin.). Home: 8010 Peregrine Ln Cincinnati OH 45243 Office: Cin Milacron Inc 4701 Marburg Ave Cincinnati OH 45209

MEYER, DANIEL PATRICK, paper manufacturing executive; b. Marion, Wis., Dec. 19, 1927; s. Bernard E. and Rena N. (Horn) M.; m. Jeannine Forsmo, Jan. 19, 1952; children: Danielle, Robert, Richard, Christopher, Stephen. BS, U. Wis., 1951. Adminstrv. asst. Consol. Papers, Inc., Wisconsin Rapids, Wis., 1951-56, dir. pub. relations, 1956-74, adminstrv. asst. to pres., 1966-71, adminstrv. asst. to chmn., 1971-74, dir. pub. affairs, 1974—. Bd. dirs. Consol. Papers Found., Inc., 1967—, sec., 1974-77, pres., 1977—; pres., vice chmn., chmn. Mid-State Tech. VTAE Dist. Bd., 1967-84; mem., vice chmn. Mid-State Tech. Found. Bd., 1981—; pres. South Wood County Econ. Devel. Corp., 1982—. Recipient Disting. Service award Wisconsin Rapids Jaycees, 1964, Citizen of Yr. award Wisconsin Rapids Area C. of C., 1974. Mem. Pub. Relations Soc. Am., Assn. Wis. Lobbyists. Republican. Roman Catholic. Club: Madison (Wis.). Lodges: Rotary, Elks (exalted ruler 1956-57, trustee 1957-60). Office: Consol Papers Inc 231 1st Ave N Wisconsin Rapids WI 54494

MEYER, DAVID ANTHONY, savings and loan association executive; b. Indpls., Jan. 13, 1953; s. James Anthony and Mary Ann (Daeger) M.; m. Helen Joyce Chiongson, July 30, 1983; children: Tara Ashley, James Anthony II. BA, Kenyon Coll., 1975; MBA, U. Toledo, 1980. Exec. asst. Mid-Am. Bank, Toledo, 1975-77; mgr. Ohio Citizens Bank, Toledo, 1977-81; asst. v.p., mgr. Security Pacific Bank, San Francisco, 1981-84; asst. v.p. Union Bank, San Francisco, 1984-85; exec. v.p., chief exec. officer City Fed. Savs. & Loan Assn., Oakland, Calif., 1985-89; pres, chief exec. officer Regent Thrift and Loan, San Francisco, 1989—, also bd. dirs. Recipient Disting. Service award Kenyon Coll. Alumni Assn., 1985; named Jaycee of Yr. Toledo Jaycees, 1981. Mem. Lions (pres., dir. San Francisco chpt. 1987-88). Roman Catholic. Office: Regent Thrift and Loan 1351 Powell St San Francisco CA 94131

MEYER, EDWARD HENRY, advertising agency executive; b. N.Y.C., Jan. 8, 1927; s. I.H. and Mildred (Driesen) M.; m. Sandra Raabin, Apr. 26, 1957; children: Margaret Ann, Anthony Edward. B.A. with honors in Econs, Cornell U., 1949. With Bloomingdale's div. Federated Dept Stores, 1949-51, Biow Co. (agy.), 1951-56; with Grey Advt., Inc., N.Y.C., 1956—; exec. v.p. Grey Advt., Inc., 1963-68, pres., chief exec. officer, 1968—, chmn. bd., 1970—; dir. May Dept. Stores Co., Inc., Bowne & Co., Inc., Merrill Lynch Basic Value Fund, Merrill Lynch Capital Fund, Merrill Lynch Equibond I Fund, Merrill Lynch Pacific Fund, Merrill Lynch Spl. Value Fund, Merrill Lynch U.S.A. Govt. Res. Fund, Trans-Lux Corp.; trustee Merrill Lynch Natural Resources Trust, Merrill Lynch Ready Assets Trust. Trustee Assoc. Y's of N.Y.; bd. dirs. USO of Met. N.Y., Found. Children with Learning Disabilities, Am. Film Inst., Am. Mus. Natural History; bd. overseers NYU Schs. Bus., trustee, bd. dirs. NYU Med. Ctr. Served with USCGR, 1945-47. Clubs: University (N.Y.C.), Harmonie (N.Y.C.), Economic (N.Y.C.); Century Country. Office: care Grey Advt Inc 777 3rd Ave New York NY 10017

MEYER, FRED JOSEF, advertising executive; b. Zurich, Switzerland, Jan. 1, 1931; came to U.S., 1959; s. Josef and Claire (Lehmann) M.; m. Beverly Ruth Carter, Apr. 9, 1961 (div. Feb. 1975); children: Fred Jay, Marcus Clinton, Michael Josef; m. Marie-Noelle Vigneron, Oct. 30, 1975. MS, Fed. Inst. Tech., Zurich, 1956; MBA, Harvard U., 1961; LLD (hon.), Sacred Heart U., 1981. Vice pres. planng and adminstrn. Sandoz Inc., Hanover, N.J., 1971-73, exec. v.p., chief fin. officer, 1973-78; pres., chief exec. officer Sandoz U.S., Inc., Greenwich, Conn., 1978-81; mng. dir., chief exec. officer Wander Ltd., Berne, Switzerland, 1981-82; sr. v.p., chief fin. officer CBS Inc., N.Y.C., 1982-88; chief fin. officer, bd. dirs. Omnicom Group, Inc., N.Y.C., 1988—; bd. dirs. SBC Portfolio Mgmt. Internat., N.Y.C., Zurich-Am. Ins. Cos., Ill., AAAA Ins. Co. Mem. Fin. Execs. Inst., Econ. Club, Harvard Club (N.Y.C.), Greenwich Country Club. Republican. Presbyterian. Office: Omnicom Group Inc 437 Madison Ave New York NY 10022

MEYER, FRED WILLIAM, JR., memorial parks executive; b. Fair Haven, Mich., Jan. 7, 1924; s. Fred W. and Gladys (Marshall) M.; m. Jean Hope, Aug. 5, 1946; children—Frederick, Thomas, James, Nancy. AB, Mich. State Coll., 1946. Salesman Chapel Hill Meml. Gardens, Lansing, Mich., 1946-47; mgr. Roselawn Meml. Gardens, Saginaw, Mich., 1947-49; dist. mgr. Sunset Meml. Gardens, Evansville, Ind., 1949-53; pres., dir. Memory Gardens Mgmt. Corp., Indpls., Hamilton Meml. Gardens, Chattanooga, Covington Meml. Gardens, Ft. Wayne, Ind., Chapel Hill Meml. Gardens, Grand Rapids, Mich., Forest Lawn Memory Gardens, Indpls., Lincoln Memory Gardens, Indpls., Sherwood Meml. Gardens, Knoxville, Tenn., Chapel Hill Meml. Gardens, South Bend, Ind., White Chapel Meml. Gardens, Springfield, Mo., Nebo Meml. Park, Martinsville, Ind., Mercury Devel. Corp., Indpls., Quality Marble Imports, Indpls., Quality Printers, Indpls., Am. Bronze Craft, Inc., Judsonia, Ark. Mem. C. of C., A.I.M., Am. Cemetery Assn., Sigma Chi, Phi Kappa Delta. Clubs: Columbia, Meridian Hills Country, Woodland Country. Lodge: Elks. Home: 110 E 111th St Indianapolis IN 46280 Office: 3733 N Meridian St Indianapolis IN 46208

MEYER, HANK, public relations and publicity consultant; b. N.Y.C., Mar. 27, 1920; m. Lenore Mittlemark; 3 daus. BBA, U. Miami, 1942, D (hon.), 1987. Owner, operator public relations agy. Miami, Fla., 1946-49; public relations dir. City of Miami Beach, Fla., 1949-56; pres. Hank Meyer Assocs., Inc., pub. relations cons., Miami, 1956—. Trustee emeritus U. Miami; hon. trustee Biscayne Coll., mem. adv. council Dept. Communication Fla. Internat. U.; founder, trustee U. Miami Symphony Club; sr mem. Orange Bowl Com.; former mem. United Fund Dade County; former mem. bd. govs. Dade Found.; mem. exec. com. to Miami Citizens Against Crime; mem. Greater Miami Coalition, Pillars- United Way of Dade County; mem. steering com. Rediscover Miami Beach; mem. exec. com. Anti-Defamation League Served to chief petty officer USNR, World War II. Named to Fla. Public Relations Hall of Fame, 1966; recipient 1st Outstanding Alumnus award U. Miami; award United Fund; award Papanicolaou Cancer Research Inst.; silver medallion award NCCJ; service award U.S. Jr. C. of C.; ann. award Civic League Miami Beach, 1956; also numerous local, state and nat. service awards and certs. of appreciation. Mem. Am. Mcpl. Public Relations Assn. (v.p. 1950), Govt. Public Relations Assn. (pres. 1956), Public Relations Soc. Am. (pres. Fla. chpt. 1958-59), Fla. Public Relations Assn., Nat. Assn. Travel Orgns., Miami Beach C. of C. (trustee), Greater Miami C. of C. (gov.), Am. Legion, Omicron Delta Kappa, Sigma Delta Chi. Office: Hank Meyer Assocs Inc 2990 Biscayne Blvd Miami FL 33137

MEYER, HAROLD LOUIS, mechanical engineer; b. Chgo., June 25, 1916; s. Norman Robert and Martha (Stoewsand) M.; m. Charlotte Alene Tilberg, June 21, 1941 (dec. 1951); 1 child, John C. Nelson. Student, Armour Inst. Tech., Chgo., 1934-42, U. Akron, 1942-44; BA in Natural Sci., Southwestern Coll., Winfield, Kans., 1951; student, Ill. Inst. Tech., 1955-73. Sales engr. Olsen & Tilgner, Chgo., 1938-39; project engr. Gen. Electric X-Ray, 1939-42, field engr., 1944-46; project engr. Goodyear Aircraft, 1942-44; chief x-ray technologist and therapist William Newton Meml. Hosp., Winfield, 1946-51; sr. design cons. Pollak and Skan, Chgo., 1952-58, cons. design specialist, 1963-68; project engr. Gaertner Scientific Co., Chgo., 1958-63; sr. design specialist Am. Steel Foundries, Chgo., 1969-74; cons. Morgen Design, Milw., 1974-76; proprietor Meyersen Engring., Addison, Ill., 1981—, also bd. dirs.; cons. dir. Miller Paint Equipment, Addison, 1976-87; design cons. R.R. Donnelley, Kraft Foods. Inventor: box sealing sta., 1939, chest X-ray equipment, 1942, G-2 airship, 1944, space program periscope, 1962, reactor test sta. periscope, 1962, beer can filling machine, 1963, atomic waste handling vehicle, 1965, ry. freight car trucks, 1974, hwy. trailer 5th wheels, 1974, motorized precision paint colorant dispensing machines, 1986. Sponsered a family of Cambodian Chinese refugees; mem. Norwood Park (Ill.) Norwegian Old Peoples Home; mem. Family Shelter Svc., Glen Ellyn, Ill. With USNR, 1949-52. Recipient Appreciation award Lioness Club, Glendale Heights, 1985. Mem. AAAS, Chem. Engring. Product Research Panel, Ill. Inst. Tech. Alumni Assn. (new student recruiter 1985-87, Recognition award 1986, 87, honored for 50 yrs. of high standards of profl. activity and citizenship 1988), Am. Registry of X-Ray Techs., Masons, Lions (bd. dirs. 1985-68), Phi Kappa Sigma. Republican. Presbyterian. Office: PO Box 248 Addison IL 60101 also: Meyerson Engring PO Box 248 Addison IL 60101

MEYER, HENRY JOHN, appliance manufacturing executive; b. Amana, Iowa, Jan. 25, 1927; s. Fred Henry and Marie Susanna (Zimmerman) M.; m. Mildred Margaret Ackerman, Oct. 25, 1945; children: Timothy, Cynthia. Buyer Amana Refrigeration, Inc., Iowa, 1946-53, purchasing agt., 1954-64, asst. dir. purchasing, 1965-70, v.p. materials, 1971-75, sr. v.p. materials, 1975-80, exec. v.p., 1980-82, pres., chief exec. officer, 1982-88; chmn., chief exec. officer Amana Refrigeration, Inc., 1988—; chmn. bd. dirs. Speed Queen Co., Ripon, Wis., 1982-86. Mem. Gov.'s Com. for Iowa's Future Growth, 1984, Revitalize Iowa Sound Economy Adv. Com., Iowa Bus. Council, Pres.' Council Iowa State U.; trustee Iowa Natural Heritage, 1984—. Served with U.S. Army, 1945-46. Mem. Cedar Rapids C. of C. (bd. dirs. 1984-87). Republican. Mem. Amana Ch. Office: Amana Refrigeration Inc Amana IA 52204

MEYER, HORST, pharmaceutical company executive; b. Mannheim, Southwest, Germany, Nov. 18, 1942; came to U.S., 1987; s. Kurt and Erna (Bley) M.; m. Gudrun Meissner, Aug. 11, 1973 (div. 1975); m. Brigitte Schuh, Mar. 11, 1977; children: René, Linda. Diploma in chemistry, Heidelberg U., Fed. Republic Germany, 1967, PhD in Chemistry, 1969. Research chemist Bayer AG, Pharm. Div., Wuppertal, Fed. Republic Germany, 1969-75, head sect., 1975-78, dir., 1978-84, v.p., 1984-86; exec. v.p. Miles Inc., Elkhart, Ind., 1987—, also bd. dirs.; pres. Molecular Therapeutics, West Haven, Conn., 1987—; bd. dirs. Molecular Diagnostics, West Haven. Contbr. articles to profl. jours.; patentee in field. Named Hon. Prof. Munster U., Fed. Republic Germany, 1987; BASF AG fellow, 1964-66, Indsl. Chemistry Assn. Germany fellow, 1967-69; grantee U. Heidelberg, 1967. Mem. German Chem. Soc. (bd. dirs. div. medicinal chemistry 1985—). Home: 250 Butternut Lane Stamford CT 06903 Office: Miles Labs Inc 1127 Myrtle St Elkhart IN 46515

MEYER, IRWIN STEPHAN, lawyer, accountant; b. Monticello, N.Y., Nov. 14, 1941; s. Ralph and Janice (Cohen) M.; m. Leslie J. Mazor, July 10, 1977; children: Kimberly B., Joshua A. BS, Rider Coll., 1963; JD, Cornell U., 1966. Bar: N.Y. 1966. Tax mgr. Lybrand Ross Bros. & Montgomery, N.Y.C., 1966-71; mem. firm Ehrenkranz, Ehrenkranz & Schultz, N.Y.C., 1971-74; prin. Irwin S. Meyer, 1974-77, 82—; mem. firm Levine, Honig, Eisenberg & Meyer, 1977-78, Eisenberg, Honig & Meyer, 1978-81, Eisenberg, Honig, Meyer & Fogler, 1981-82. Served with U.S. Army, 1966-71. CPA, N.J. Mem. ABA, N.Y. Bar Assn., Am. Assn. Atty.-CPAs, N.Y. Assn. Atty.-CPAs, Am. Inst. CPAs, N.J. Soc. CPAs. Home: 19 Woodhaven Dr New City NY 10956 Office: 1 Blue Hill Plaza Ste 1006 Box 1663 Pearl River NY 10965 Office: One Blue Hill Plaza Pearl River NY 10956

MEYER, JOHN ROBERT, educator, economist; b. Pasco, Wash., Dec. 6, 1927; s. Philip Conrad and Cora (Kempter) M.; m. Lee Stowell, Dec. 17, 1949; children: Leslie Karen, Ann Elizabeth, Robert Conrad. Student, Pacific U., 1945-46; BA, U. Wash., 1950; PhD (David A. Wells prize), Harvard U., 1955. Jr. fellow Harvard U., 1953-55, asst. prof., 1955-58, assoc. prof., 1958-59, prof. econs., 1959-68, prof. transportation and logistics, 1973-83; prof. Yale U., 1968-73; Harpel prof. capital formation and econ. growth Harvard U., 1983—; dir. Dun & Bradstreet, Rand McNally; vice chmn. Union Pacific Corp., 1982-83, now dir.; trustee Mut. Life. Ins. Co. N.Y. Author: (with others) The Investment Decision-An Empirical Inquiry, 1957, Economics of Competition in the Transportation Industry, 1959, The Urban Transportation Problem, 1965, The Economics of Competition in the Telecommunications Industry, 1980, Autos, Transit and Cities, 1981, Airline Deregulation--The Early Experience, 1981, Deregulation and the New Airline Entrepreneurs, 1984, Deregulation and the Future of Intercity Passenger Travel, 1987, other books; contbr. articles to profl. jours. Mem. Presdl. Task Forces on Transp., 1964, 80, Presdl. Commn. on Population Growth and Am. Future, 1970-72; pres. Nat. Bur. Econ. Research, 1967-77. Served with USNR, 1946-48. Guggenheim fellow, 1958. Fellow Am. Acad. Arts and Scis., Econometric Soc.; mem. Am. Econ. Assn. (mem. exec. com. 1971-73), Council Fgn. Relations, Econ. History Assn. Clubs: Harvard (N.Y.C.); Links. Home: 138 Brattle St Cambridge MA 02138 Office: Harvard U Ctr Bus and Govt 79 Kennedy St Cambridge MA 02138

MEYER, JOSEPH JOHN, insurance executive; b. Somerset, Pa., May 28, 1925; s. Joseph John and Eda Agnes (Lorenz) M.; m. Sidney Elizabeth Donelson, June 5, 1948; children: Christine, Roxanne, Tracy. BA in Bus. Mgmt., U. Hawaii, 1971. Enlisted USN, 1943; commd. ensign USNR, 1945; advanced through grades to capt. USN, ret., 1975; gen. mgr. United Svcs. Automobile Assn., San Diego, 1975-76, asst. v.p., 1976-83; regional v.p. United Svcs. Automobile Assn., San Antonio, 1983-87; sr. v.p. United Svcs. Automobile Assn., Sacramento, 1987—; chmn. bd. dirs., ASTA Corp., Solana Beach, Calif. Bd. dirs. United Way, Sacramento, 1988—, Jr. Achievement, Sacramento, 1988—. Decorated 2 Legion of Merit, Bronze Star. Mem. U.S. Naval Inst., Naval Submarine League, Point West Bus. Assn. (bd. dirs. 1988—). Republican. Roman Catholic. Office: United Svcs Automobile Assn 2241 Harvard St Sacramento CA 95815

MEYER, LASKER MARCEL, retail executive; b. Houston, Jan. 8, 1926; s. Lasker M. and Lucille (Dannenbaum) M.; m. Beverly Jean Goldberg; children: Lynn Meyer Tatar, Susan Meyer Sellinger. Student, Rice U., 1942-43. Pres. Foley's, Houston, 1979, chmn., chief exec. officer, 1982-87; chmn., chief exec. officer Abraham and Straus, Bklyn., 1980-81; bd. dirs. First City Nat. Bank, Houston; chmn. Spoetzl Brewery, Shiner, Tex., Gt. Tex. Brewing Co. Chmn. United Way Tex. Gulf Coast, 1989—; bd. dirs. Harris County Children's Protective Svcs. Jewish. Club: Houston Racquet.

MEYER, LAWRENCE GEORGE, lawyer; b. East Grand Rapids, Mich., Oct. 2, 1940; s. George and Evangeline (Boerma) M.; children from previous marriage: David Lawrence, Jenifer Lynne; m. 2d, Linda Elizabeth Buck, May 31, 1980; children: Elizabeth Tilden, Travis Henley. BA with honors, Mich. State U., 1961; JD with distinction, U. Mich., 1964. Bar: Wis., Ill. 1965, U.S. Supreme Ct. 1968, D.C. 1972. Assoc., Whyte, Hirschboeck, Minahan, Hardin & Harland, Milw., 1964-66; atty. antitrust div. U.S. Dept. Justice, 1966-68; legal counsel U.S. Senator Robert P. Griffin from Mich., 1968-70; dir. policy planning FTC, 1970-72; ptnr. Patton, Boggs & Blow, Washington, 1972-85, Arent, Fox, Kintner, Plotkin & Kahn, Washington, 1985—. Recipient Disting. Service Award, FTC, 1972. Mem. ABA, D.C. Bar Assn. Clubs: U.S. Senate Ex S.O.B.'s, City Tavern, Congl. Country, Pisces (Washington); The Bayhill (Orlando). Contbr. articles on antitrust and trial practice to law jours.; asst. editor. U. Mich. Law Rev., 1960-61. Home: 8777 Belmart Rd Potomac MD 20854 Office: 1050 Connecticut Ave Washington DC 20036

MEYER, MICHAEL C., communications executive; b. Phoenix, Apr. 4, 1956; s. John H. and Lee (Booher) M. BS in Mgmt., Ariz. State U., 1982. Adminstr. bldg. and grounds Internat. Tel. & Tel., Phoenix, 1976-80; bldg. supr. Intel, Albuquerque, 1982-83, mgr. info. systems, 1983-84; ops. mgr. MCM & Assocs., Phoenix, 1984-86; pres., bd. dirs. Facility Ops. Group (FOG), Tempe, Ariz., 1986—, chief exec. officer, 1988—. Mem. Internat. Facility Mgmt. Assn., Telecommunications Assn., Tempe C. of C., Phoenix C. of C., Rotaract. Home: 719 W 13th St Tempe AZ 85282 Office: Facility Ops Group 734 W Alameda Dr Tempe AZ 85282

MEYER, NANCY J., financial executive; b. Iowa; d. Frank Jacob and Marjorie Estelle (Duhme) M.; B.A., Barnard Coll., 1969; Dipl. Supérieur, Alliance Francaise, Paris, 1980; m. Charles Linzner, Nov. 14, 1970. With Krambo Corp., N.Y.C., 1969-76, San Francisco, 1976-77, v.p. and treas., 1973-77, also dir.; 2d v.p., sr. budget officer Chase Manhattan Corp., N.Y.C., 1977, 2d v.p., project mgr. system support, 1980-81, div. exec./ops. fin. planning, 1981-83, v.p., 1982-83; sr. fin. officer Rainier Nat. Bank, Seattle, 1983-85, v.p., 1985; asst. v.p., corp. strategy/acquisitions and divestitures, CIGNA Corp., 1985—. Chartered fin. analyst, 1976; Nat. Merit scholar, 1965-69. Fellow Fin. Analysts Fedn.; mem. Inst. Chartered Fin. Analysts, N.Y. Soc. Security Analysts, The Fin. Analysts of Phila., Corp. Planning 100, The Planning Forum, Barnard Coll. Alumnae Assn. Home: 1515 Rolling Green Rd Yardley PA 19067 Office: 1 Logan Sq 29th Fl Philadelphia PA 19103

MEYER, PAUL JAMES, communications company executive; b. San Mateo, Calif., May 21, 1928; s. August Carl and Isabel (Rutherford) M.; m. Jane Gurley, Nov. 26, 1971; children: Paul James Jr., Larry, Bill, Janna, Leslie. DAviation Edn. (hon.), Embry-Riddle Aero. U., 1956; LHD (hon.), Ft. Lauderdale U., 1957. Mgr. sales Word, Inc., Waco, Tex., 1958-60; founder, chmn. bd. dirs. SMI Internat., Inc., Waco, 1960—. Bd. dirs. Waco Boys Club, 1970—; mem. Nat. Rep. Fin. Com. With airborne U.S. Army, 1946-48. Mem. Am. Mgmt. Assn., Internat. Franchise Assn., Nat. Speakers Bur. Baptist. Office: SMI Internat PO Box 2506 Waco TX 76702

MEYER, PEARL, executive compensation consultant; b. N.Y.C.; d. Allen Charles and Rose (Goldberg) Weissman; m. Ira A. Meyer. BA cum laude, NYU, 1953, postgrad., 1954-59. Statis. specialist, exec. comp. div. Gen. Foods Corp., White Plains, N.Y., 1953-55; exec. v.p. and cons. Handy Assocs., Inc., N.Y.C., 1955—; lectr. on exec. compensation at confs. and seminars. Contbr. numerous articles to profl. jours. Recipient Entrepreneurial Woman award Women Bus. Owners N.Y., 1983. Mem. Am. Mgmt. Assn., Am. Compensation Assn., Am. Soc. Personnel Adminstrs. (cert. accredited personnel diplomate), Women's Econ. Roundtable, Personnel Accreditation Inst., Women's Forum, Inc., Phi Beta Kappa, Pi Mu Epsilon, Kappa Pi Sigma. Clubs: Sedgewood, Bd. Rm., Atrium, Sky. Office: Handy Assocs Inc 250 Park Ave New York NY 10167

MEYER, RANDALL, retired oil company executive; b. Mt. Union, Iowa, Jan. 19, 1923; s. Carl Henry and Edythe (Stuck) M.; m. Barbara Swetman, Nov. 29, 1958; children: Warren, Gretchen, Kirsten. B.S. in Mech. Engring, U. Iowa, 1948; LL.D. (hon.), Iowa Wesleyan Coll., 1977. With Exxon Co. U.S.A. (formerly Humble Oil & Refining Co., div. Exxon Corp.), 1948-88; with tech. and mgmt. depts. Exxon Co. U.S.A., Baton Rouge, Houston, 1948-66; exec. asst. to pres. Exxon Corp., N.Y.C., 1966-67; sr. v.p., dir. Exxon Co. U.S.A., Houston, 1967-72, pres., 1972-88; bd. dirs., exec. com. Greater Houston Partnership;bd. dirs. Houston Industries, Inc. Trustee, mem. exec. com. Kinkaid Sch.; trustee, Am. Enterprise Inst. Pub. Policy Research; pres. Found. for Bus. Politics Economics., bd. dirs. Meth. Hosp., Houston; bd. visitors U. Tex. M.D. Anderson Cancer Ctr. Found.; adv. bd. Inst. Biosciences and Tech., Texas A&M U.; bd.dirs., pres. Greater Houston Community Found. Mem. Am. Petroleum Inst. (bd. dirs.), Tex. Rrsch. League, Forum Club (gov.), Sigma Xi, Tau Beta Pi, Omicron Delta Kappa, Pi Tau Sigma. Methodist. Office: 1100 Milam Ste 4601 Houston TX 77002

MEYER, RICHARD ALAN, auditor; b. Halstead, Kans., Sept. 1, 1939; s. Michael George Meier and Phyllis Eileen (Arrowsmith) Bartunek; m. Karen Louise VanRoyan, Sept. 24, 1965; children: Connie Louise, Chris Alan. BS in Bus. Adminstrn., Kans. State U., 1965. Cert. internal auditor. Internal auditor Rep. Supply Co., Oklahoma City, 1969-79; asst. controller Misco Supply Co., Wichita, Kans., 1979-85; internal auditor The Coleman Co., Inc., Wichita, 1985-86; controller Western Cutlery, Inc., Longmont, Colo., 1986-87; sr. internal auditor The Coleman Co., Inc., Wichita, 1987—. Served with USN, 1965-67. Mem. Inst. Internal Auditors. Republican. Home: 596 W 1 St Valley Center KS 67147 Office: Coleman Co Inc 250 N St Francis Wichita KS 67201

MEYER, ROBERT ALAN, insurance company executive; b. N.Y.C., Mar. 20, 1946; s. Leonard and Mildred M.; m. Gail Rein, Oct. 29, 1967; children: Jonathan, Caroline. BA in Econs., Am. Internat. Coll., 1967; MBA, NYU, 1973. 2nd v.p., mgr. mcpl. bond research Smith Barney Harris Upham and Co., Inc., N.Y.C., 1973-76; 1st v.p., dir. mcpl. bond research E.F. Hutton and Co. Inc., N.Y.C., 1976-82; v.p., mgr. mcpl. bond research Merrill Lynch Pierce Fenner and Smith Inc., N.Y.C., 1982-84; pres. Bond Investors Guaranty Ins. Co., N.Y.C., 1984—. Mem. Soc. Mcpl. Analysts, Mcpl. Analysts Group of N.Y., Mcpl. Fin. Officers Assn., N.Y. Soc. Security Analysts, Mcpl. Forum N.Y., Fin. Analysts Fedn. Home: 20 Stoney Brook Rd Holmdel NJ 07733 Office: Bond Investors Guaranty 70 Pine St New York NY 10270

MEYER, ROBERT LAWRENCE, investment banker; b. Newark, Nov. 7, 1940; s. Abraham Jay and Helen Honig M.; m. Ellen Abby Asch, Mar. 19, 1983; children: David Eric, Jennifer Rachel. BA, Harvard U., 1962, MBA, 1964. Ptnr. H.C. Wainwright & Co., N.Y.C., 1964-77; pres. Wainwright Securities Inc., N.Y.C., 1977-78; mng. dir. Steaua Romana, PLC, London, 1984-87; pres. Orion Resources Inc., N.Y.C., 1978-86; dir. research Fahnestock & Co. Inc., N.Y.C., 1986-88; pres. Convergent Capital Corp., N.Y.C., 1988—. Mem. Inst. Chartered Fin. Analysts. Office: Convergent Capital Corp 810 7th Ave New York NY 10019

MEYER, ROLAND HARRY, manufacturing company executive; b. New Orleans, June 20, 1927; s. Roland Harry and Louise (Wall) M.; m. Eunice Paton, Sept. 4, 1946; children: Stanley Meyer, Carmen Winterschladen, Barbara, Corinne. Student, Tulane U., 1949-52, U. Wash., 1946. Mgr. mfg. Am. Nat. Can Corp. (formerly Nat. Can Co.), Chgo., 1972-74, mgr. MCD ops., 1974, v.p. ops., 1974-77, sr. v.p. MCD ops., 1977-80, sr. v.p. mfg. ops., 1980-83, exec. v.p. mfg. ops., 1983—, vice chmn., bd. dirs., 1986—, chief oper. officer, 1988—; bd. dirs. 1st Comml. Bank Tampa, Allied Van Lines. Chmn. Crusade of Mercy, 1973; chmn. Nat. Can. Corp., 1973; chmn. bd. dirs. United Cerebral Palsy Found. drive, Tampa, Fla., 1972; bd. dirs. United Fund, Auburndale, Fla., 1969, Fla. Prevention of Blindness; founder Keep Fla. Beautiful, 1970, bd. dirs., 1st v.p., 1970. Republican. Roman Catholic. Club: Cress Creek Country (Naperville). Lodge: K.C. (4 degree). Home: 27W 751 Swan Lake Dr Wheaton IL 60187 Office: Am Nat Can Co 8770 W Bryn Mawr Ave Chicago IL 60631

MEYER, RUSSELL WILLIAM, JR., aircraft company executive; b. Davenport, Iowa, July 19, 1932; s. Russell William and Ellen Marie (Matthews) M.; m. Helen Scott Vaughn, Aug. 20, 1960; children: Russell William, III, Elizabeth Ellen, Jeffrey Vaughn, Christopher Matthews, Carolyn Louise. B.A., Yale U., 1954; LL.B., Harvard U., 1961. Bar: Ohio 1961. Mem. firm Arter & Hadden, Cleve., 1961-66; pres., chief exec. officer Grumman Am. Aviation Corp., Cleve., 1966-74; exec. v.p. Cessna Aircraft Co., Wichita, Kans., 1974-75; chmn. bd., chief exec. officer Cessna Aircraft Co., 1975—; bd. dirs. Gen. Dynamics Corp., 4th Nat. Bank, Wichita., Kans. Gas & Electric Co.; presdl. appointee Aviation Safety Commn., 1987—. Bd. dirs. Cleve. Yale Scholarship Com., 1962-74; chmn. bd. trustees 1st Baptist Ch., Cleve., 1972-74; bd. dirs. United Way Wichita and Sedgwick County, Wichita State U. Endowment Assn.; trustee Wesley Hosp. Endowment Assn., Wake Forest U. Served with USAF, 1955-58. Recipient Collier Trophy, 1986. Mem. Am., Ohio, Kans., Cleve. bar assns., Gen. Aviation Mfrs. Assn. (chmn. bd. 1973-74, 81-82), Wichita C. of C. (chmn. 1988—, bd. dirs.). Clubs: Wichita, Wichita Country. Home: 600 Tara Ct Wichita KS 67206 Office: Cessna Aircraft Mktg Div 5800 Pawnee Rd Wichita KS 67218

MEYER, TAMARA ANN, graphics executive; b. Decatur, Ind., Aug. 30, 1957; d. James F. Meyer and Varva Jo (Bishop) Usis. Student, Ind. U., Phoenix Coll., Ariz. State U. Office mgr. Budget Rent A Car, Ft. Wayne, Ind., 1975-79; prodn. mgr. Plaza 21 Printing, Phoenix, 1980-81; v.p., gen. mgr. Ad Design Graphics, Scottsdale, Ariz., 1982-87; owner, pres. TypeCetera, Inc., 1987—; realtor assoc. Ariz. Dept. Real Estate. Mem. Ad II Phoenix, Smithsonian Assns., NAFE, Scottsdale C. of C. Republican. Roman Catholic. Home: 1016 B East Osborn Rd Phoenix AZ 85014

MEYER, WALTER, energy engineer; b. Chgo., Jan. 19, 1932; s. Walter and Ruth (Killoran) M.; m. Jacqueline Miscall, May 8, 1953; children: Kim, Holt, Eric, Leah, Suzannah. B.Chem. Engring., Syracuse U., 1956, M.Chem. Engring., 1957; postgrad. (NSF Sci. Faculty fellow), MIT, 1962; Ph.D. (NSF Sci. Faculty fellow), Oreg. State U., 1964. Registered nuclear engr., Calif. Prin. chem. engr. Battelle Meml. Inst., Columbus, Ohio, 1957-58; instr., then asst. prof. Oreg. State U., 1958-64; rsch. engr. Hanford Atomic Labs., Richland, Wash., 1959-60, Lawrence Radiation Lab., Livermore, Calif., 1964; from asst. prof. to prof. nuclear engring. Kans. State U., Manhattan, 1964-72; prof., chmn. nuclear engring. U. Mo., Columbia, 1972-82; Robert Lee Tatum prof. engring. U. Mo., 1974-82, co-dir. energy systems and resources program, 1974-82; co-founder Energy and Pub. Policy Ctr., 1981-82; 1st holder Niagara Mohawk Energy professorship Syracuse U., 1982—, dir. Inst. for Energy Research, 1984—, prof. pub. adminstrn. Maxwell Sch. Citizenship and Pub. Affairs, 1985—, exec. dir. Indsl. Innovation Extension Svc., Cen. N.Y. Pilot Project, 1988—; dir. summer insts. NSF-AEC, 1969, NSF, 1972; co-dir. summer instr. AEC, 1972, dir. workshop, 1973; dir. (ERDA workshops), 1975-79; mem. Columbia Coal Gasification Task Force, 1977, Gov. Kans. Nuclear Energy Coun., 1971-72; cons. to govt. and industry; exec. dir. Indsl. Innovation Extension Svc. for Cen. N.Y., 1988—. Author; patentee in field. Mem. Manhattan Human Relations Orgn., 1966-72; active local Boy Scouts Am.; co-chmn. No on 11 Com., 1980. Grantee NSF, 1965-67, 73-75, 77-80, AEC, 1969-71, 73-74, Dept. Def., 1969-72, ERDA, 1975, 77—, NRC, 1977-80, Dept. Energy, 1985, Army Rsch. Office, 1987—. Fellow Am. Nuclear Soc. (chmn. pub. info. com. 1975-79, nat. spl. award 1974, outstanding service award 1980, bd. dirs. 1981-84, chmn. univ./industry relations subcom. edn. div. 1980—); mem. Am. Inst. Chem. Engrs. (chmn. nuclear engring. div. 1977-78), Am. Chem. Soc. (touring lectr. 1976-83), Am. Soc. Engring. Edn. (chmn. nuclear div. 1976-77), Am. Wind Soc., N.Y. Acad. Scis., Sigma Xi (v.p., pres. Syracuse sect. 1984-86), Tau Beta Pi. Presbyterian. Home: 17 Horseshoe Ln Chittenango NY 13037 Office: Syracuse U Inst Energy Rsch Link Hall Syracuse NY 13244-4010

MEYER, WILLIAM TRENHOLM, defense consulting company official, real estate executive, former army officer; b. Ancon, C.Z., May 28, 1937; s. Trenholm Jones and Virginia Blanche (Morgan) M.; m. Erna Charlotte Albert, Dec. 14, 1961; children—Cynthia L., Bonnie A., Christopher T., Tori L. B.S., U. Nebr., 1965; grad. U.S. Army Command and Gen. Staff Coll., 1973. Commd. 2d lt. U.S. Army, 1961, advanced through grades to lt. col., 1976, ret., 1981; sr. engr. ManTech Internat. Corp., Sierra Vista, Ariz., 1981-82; mgr. field ops. RCA, Sierra Vista, 1982-88; chief exec. officer MYCO, 1989; gen. ptnr., dir. Southwestern Investment Ltd. Partnership, Sierra Vista, 1983-89; mgr. field ops. GE, 1989—. Sustaining mem. Republican Nat. Com., 1983—. Named to Mil. Intelligence Hall of Fame, 1989. Mem. Assn. Old Crows (regional dir. 1984-87, chpt. pres. 1983-84, Internat. Electronic Warfare-Intelligence medal 1983), Armed Forces Communications and Electronics Assn., Ret. Officers Assn., Assn. U.S. Army. Roman Catholic. Clubs: Kings Tennis (pres. 1980, 87, 88), Aquatic (pres. 1981) (Sierra Vista). Home: 1902 San Diego Circle Sierra Vista AZ 85635 Office: GE 2700 Fry Blvd Ste B-3 Sierra Vista AZ 85635

MEYERROSE, SARAH LOUISE, bank holding company executive; b. Jefferson City, Mo., Nov. 26, 1955; d. William J. and Mary L. (Fricke) Wollenburg; m. Michael J. Meyerrose, Aug. 18, 1978. BA, Vanderbilt U., 1978, MBA, 1987. Chartered fin. analyst. Corp. fin. asst. Commerce Union Corp., Nashville, 1978-80, money market sales rep., 1980-82; asst. treas. First Tenn. Nat. Corp., Memphis, 1982-84, v.p., treas., 1984-88, v.p. sr. fin. officer, 1988—; guest lectr. Vanderbilt U., 1987; instr. Am. Inst. Banking, Memphis, 1985, Tenn. Bankers Assn., Nashville, 1987, 88, 89. Mem. Fin. Analysts Fedn., Econs. Club Memphis. Office: 1st Tenn Nat Corp PO Box 84 Memphis TN 38101

MEYERS, ALAN HAHN, financial planner; b. Phila., Nov. 30, 1940; m. Lois W. Meyers, Mar. 12, 1967; children: Karen, Jessica, Julie. BBA, Boston U., 1962. Cert. fin. planner. V.p. investments Prudential-Bache Securities, Phila., 1965—; mem. external faculty The Am. coll., Bryn Mawr, Pa., 1982; guest lectr. Community Coll., Phila., 1985, U. Pa., 1988, various community orgns., 1977—. Lt. U.S. Army, 1963-65, Korea. Mem. Internat. Assn. Fin. Planners (pres. Del. Valley chpt. 1979-80, chmn. bd. 1980-81), Inst. Cert. Fin. Planners (pres. Del. Valley chpt. 1985-86, chnm. bd. 1986-87), Montgomery County Estate Planning Council. Office: Prudential Bache Securities 1515 Market St Ste 300 Philadelphia PA 19102

MEYERS, GEOFFREY GROMAN, financial executive; b. rochester, Minn., Apr. 5, 1944; s. Ward Carl and Ruth (Groman) M.; m. Molly Ann Murtagh, July 31, 1982. BA, Northwestern U., 1966; MBA, Ohio State U., 1969. With Owens-Ill. Inc., 1970—; mgr. strategic planning glass container div. Owens-Ill. Inc., Toledo, 1980-82, dir. ops. control, 1984-86, dir. fin., asst. treas., 1986-88; exec. v.p. fin./adminstrn. Health Care and Retirement Corp. (subs. Owens-Ill. Inc.), Toledo, 1988—; asst. to chmn. Gerresheimer Glas, Deusseldorf, Fed. Rep. Germany, 1982-84. Mem. Inverness Club. Office: Health Care and Retirement Corp 1 Seagate Toledo OH 43666

MEYERS, GEORGE EDWARD, plastics company executive; b. N.Y.C., June 26, 1928; s. Sol and Ethel (Treppel) M.; student Sampson Coll., 1948-49, Columbia, 1949-50; m. Marianna Jacobson, Dec. 8, 1955; children—Deborah Lynn, Joanne Alyssa. Technician Manhattan Project, 1944; tech. rep. Mearl Corp., 1952-56; student Sampson Coll., Geneva, N.Y., 1948-50, Columbia U., N.Y.C., 1949-50. tech. rep. Mearl Corp., N.Y.C., 1952-56; sales mgr. Rona Labs., Bayonne, N.J.1956-59; v.p. Dimensional Pigments Corp., Bayonne, 1959-60; pres. Plastic Cons. Internat., Inc., Dix Hills, N.Y., 1959—, Tech. Machinery Corp., Plainview, N.Y., 1963-69; pres. Extrudyne, Inc., Amityville, N.Y., 1970-77, also dir.; dir. research and devel. Homeland Industries, Bohemia, N.Y., 1977-80; dir. ops. Aqua-Sol, Inc., Deer Park, N.Y., 1980-85; tchr., staff cons. N.Y.C. Bd. Higher Edn., Bronx Community Coll., 1966-70; lectr. N.Y.U., Technion, Haifa, Israel. Served with CIC, AUS, 1946-48. Mem. Soc. Plastics Engrs. (sr. mem., v.p. N.Y. sect. 1967-68), Soc. Plastics Industry (profl. mem.), Am. Ordnance Assn., Aircraft Owners and Pilots Assn, Nat. Rifle Assn. (life mem.), Am. Chem. Soc., Internat. Assn. Housing Sci. (charter mem.), Internat. Assn. Soilless Culture. Contbr. articles to profl. jours. Patentee in field; lectr.; seminar conductor in plastics and hydroponics and seminar leader Modern Plastics Mag. courses. Avocations: flying, numismatics, pistol shooting, antique collector, technical expert to legal firms and qualified expert witness in state and federal courts. Home and Office: 25 Penn Dr Dix Hills NY 11746

MEYERS, GLENN BARRY, savings and loan executive, accountant; b. Miami, Fla., July 26, 1950; s. Maxime and Martha Meyers; m. Donna Schollman, Aug. 12, 1973; children: Jared, Rachael, Sari. BS in Mgmt. and Mktg., Fla. State U., 1972; BBA in Acctg., Fla. Internat. U., 1973. CPA, Fla. Sr. acct. Laventhol & Horwath, 1973-76; audit supr. Cherry, Bekaert & Holland, Orlando, Fla., 1976-78; treas., cashier Sunset Comml. Bank, Tamarac, Fla., 1978-81, exec. v.p., cashier, 1981-83; exec. v.p., chief fin. officer Ambassador Savs. & Loan, Tamarac, 1983-88, pres., chief exec. officer, 1988—; exec. v.p., chief fin. officer Ambassador Fin. Group, Tamarac, 1983-88, pres., chief exec. officer, 1988—. Mem. Am. Inst. CPAs, Fla. Inst. CPAs, Tamarac C. of C. (bd. dirs. 1988—, v.p. 1988—). Office: Ambassador Savs and Loan 8201 N University Dr Tamarac FL 33321

MEYERS, JUDY YVONNE, wholesale executive; b. Puyallup, Wash., May 22, 1938; d. John Harry and LaVerne (LaBrash) Poolman; m. Victor A. Meyers, Nov. 12, 1978 (dec. June 1981); children: Angela, Donald Jay. Assoc. in Nursing, Bellevue Community Coll., 1970; postgrad. in Adolescent Medicine, U. Wash., 1970-74. RN. Staff RN Echo Glen Children's Ctr., Snoqualmie, Wash., 1970-75; intravenous nurse Swedish Hosp. Med. Ctr., Seattle, 1975-86; exec. v.p. Sweats Unltd. Inc., Kirkland, Wash., 1985-88; owner, pres. Attu Assocs., Kirkland, 1988—. Republican. Roman Catholic. Home: 935 1st St South #2 Kirkland WA 98033 Office: Attu Assocs 935 1 St S Ste 2 Kirkland WA 98033

MEYERS, NICK HARRIS, financial executive; b. Phila., Jan. 30, 1959; s. Harold B. and Reba P. (Greenberg) M.; m. Marci D. Shapiro, Feb. 13, 1988. BSBA, Am. U., 1980; cert., Coll. Fin. Planning, 1987. Cert. fin. planner. Contract negotiator U.S. Navy Aviation Supply Office, Phila., 1980-84; fin. cons. Cigna Individual Fin. Svcs., Cherry Hill, N.J., 1984—. Fellow Estate Planning Council Phila., Nat. Assn. Life Underwriters, N.J. Assn. Life Underwriters, Inst. Cert. Fin. Planners (charter mem. Del. Valley Soc.). Club: Woodcrest Country (Cherry Hill, N.J.). Office: Cigna Individual Fin Svcs 220 Lake Dr E Ste 300 Cherry Hill NJ 08002

MEYERS, RICHARD ALLEN, marketing executive; b. Madison, Wis., Aug. 19, 1940; s. Robert Milton and Josephine Ruth (Small) M.; m. Barbara Buboltz, Aug. 23, 1963 (div. 1967); m. Nancy Ann Weiner, Dec. 30, 1984. BA in History, U. Wis., 1963; MBA in Mktg., Roosevelt U., 1969. Nat. accounts salesman Home Juice Co., Melrose Pk., Ill., 1964-67; product mgr. Swift & Co., Chgo., 1967-68; asst. mgr. mktg., mgr. new products Keebler Co., Elmhurst, Ill., 1968-70; mgr. new products Ekco Products Inc., Wheeling, Ill., 1970-71; mgmt. cons. Peace Corps, Rio de Janeiro, 1971-74; dir. mktg. Helene Curtis Industries Inc., Chgo., 1975-79; v.p. mktg. Ardell Inc., Solon, Ohio, 1979-81; dir. mktg. Schulze & Burch Biscuit Co., Chgo., 1981-87; v.p. mktg. Rice Coun. for Mktg. Devel., Houston, 1987—. Contbr. articles to profl. jours. Methodist. Office: Rice Coun for Market Devel 6699 Rookin St Houston TX 77074

MEYERSON, BRUCE PAUL, real estate executive; b. N.Y.C., Mar. 24, 1955; s. George Joseph and Shirley Harriet (Cohen) M.; m. Francine Jacobs, Nov. 13, 1983; 1 child, Evan Jacobs. BS in Fin., U. Pa., 1976; JD, U. Miami, 1979, LLM, 1979. Bar: N.Y., Pa. Assoc. Cohen, Shapiro, Polisher, Shiekman and Cohen, Phila., 1979-80, Golenbock and Barrel, N.Y.C., 1980-83; real estate exec. Integrated Resources Inc., N.Y.C., 1983—. Mem. N.Y. Bar Assn., Pa. Bar Assn., Mortgage Bankers Assn. (mem. environ. sub.-com. 1988—), Beta Gamma Sigma. Office: Integrated Resources Inc 666 Third Ave New York NY 10017

MIANO, LOUIS STEPHEN, advertising executive; b. N.Y.C., July 28, 1934; s. Louis Clyde and Zefira (Palombo) M. B.A., Dartmouth Coll., 1955; M.A., Columbia U., 1958. Writer Look Mag., N.Y.C., 1960-61; editor Show Mag., N.Y.C., 1961-63, Los Angeles, 1961-63; assoc. producer ABC-TV, Los Angeles, 1963-66, N.Y.C., 1963-66; vice-chmn., dir. creative services AC&R Advt., N.Y.C., 1966—; sec. EEE Theatrical Ventures, N.Y.C., 1974—. Coproducer plays: Design for Living, Corpse, The Seagull, Legends, Inner Voices, 1974-86. Trustee Marymount Manhattan Coll., N.Y.C., 1980—, Cen. Park Hist. Field Trips. Club: N.Y. Athletic. Home: 430 E 57th St New York NY 10022 Office: AC&R 16 E 32nd St New York NY 10016

MICALLEF, JOSEPH VINCENT RAYMOND, business investments executive; b. Catania, Italy, Jan. 10, 1957; came to U.S., 1967; s. John and Maria (Alvano) M.; m. Carla Lee Naylor, June 20, 1987. BS, Lewis & Clark Coll., 1977; MS, MIT, 1979. Dir. strategic planning DAON Devel. Corp., Vancouver, B.C., Can., 1981; pres. Dorchester Capital Corp., Vancouver, 1981-84; pres., chief exec. officer Oreg. Garden Products, Inc., Hillsboro, Oreg., 1984-88; gen. ptnr. Phoenix Ptnrs., Portland, Oreg., 1989—. Author: Between Power and Contradiction: The PCI in Italian Politics, 1979; editor: Country Risk in Brazil, 1981; contbr. articles to profl. jours. Fulbright fellow, 1980-81. Mem. AAAS. Republican. Roman Catholic. Office: Phoenix Ptnrs 401 SW 11th Ave Portland OR 97205

MICETIC, DALE M., contracting company executive, consultant; b. Chgo., Feb. 25, 1953; s. Kenneth A. and Dorothy Jean (Streightenburg) M.; m. W. Sue, May, 30, 1974; children: Kristen, Kimberley, Steven, Jonathan. BS in Biology, Ariz. State U., 1977. Pres. Terrain Systems, Inc., Scottsdale, Ariz. Dir. Salvation Army Youth Bd. Mem. Ariz. Landscape Contractors Assn. (treas. 1981, v.p. 1982, sec. 1983, pres. 1984), Valley Forward, Assn. Scottsdale Leadership, Scottsdale C. of C., Salvation Army Youth Bd., Young Republicans. Home: 5434 E Poinsettia Scottsdale AZ 85253 Office: Terrain Systems Inc 10255 N Scottsdale Rd Scottsdale AZ 85253

MICHAEL, ROSEMARY JANE, computerized training company executive; b. Chgo., Dec. 12, 1947; d. Herbert Dalton and Marianne G. (Krueger) M.; m. Robert W. Wennerholm, Dec. 31, 1973. Student, Phillips U., Fed. Republic Germany, 1967-68; BA, Manchester Coll., 1969; MA, W. Ill. U., 1970; postgrad., U. Ill., 1971; JD, U. Iowa, 1975. Bar: Fla. 1975. Prof. Southeastern Ill. Coll., Harrisburg, 1970-72; assoc. August, Nimkoff & Pohlig, Miami, 1976-80; law clk. to presiding justice U.S. Bankruptcy Ct., Miami, 1980-84; assoc. Paul, Landy, Bailey & Harper PA, Miami, 1984-85; pres. Police Law Inst., Inc., Hollywood, Fla., 1985—; lectr. sch. bus. U. Miami, Coral Gables, Fla., 1976, St. Thomas U., Miami, 1976-77. Editor., pub. newsletter The Pathfollower, 1983—. Mem. Hollywood Lakes (Fla.) Homeowners Assn., 1980—. Grad. fellow Western Ill. U., 1969-70; named to Outstanding Young Women in Am., 1973. Mem. ABA, Fla. Bar Assn., Fla. Assn. Women Lawyers (state treas. 1980-81), S. Fla. Bankruptcy Assn., Nat. Assn. Women Bus. Owners, Sierra Club, Organic Gardening Club, Nature Conservancy Club. Democrat. Mem. Ch. of Brethren. Office: Police Law Inst Inc PO Box 2286 1720 Harrison St #8B Hollywood FL 33022

MICHAELS, FRANK MONTI, treasurer; b. Flushing, N.Y., Nov. 2, 1935; s. Raymond and Enes (Monti) Pastore; BBA, Adelphi U., 1957; postgrad. Pace U., 1965; m. Rosemarie Conti, Feb. 27, 1980; children—Frank Raymond, Andrew Joseph, Vincent Paul. Sr. acct. Coopers & Lybrand, N.Y.C., 1957-63; asst. contr. Stanley Warner Corp., N.Y.C., 1963-67; v.p., treas. Loews Theatres Mgmt. Corp., N.Y.C., 1967—. With U.S. Army, 1958-60, 61-62. C.P.A., N.Y. Mem. N.Y. State Soc. CPA's (faculty, chmn. subcom. motion pictures, entertainment and sports 1982-84, com. chief fin. officers 1984-87), Am. Inst. CPA's, Nat. Assn. Accts., Acctg. Rsch. Assn., Nat. Assn. Accts., Motion Picture Pioneers. Roman Catholic. Club: Variety. Home: 14 Kennedy Ct Middletown NJ 07748 Office: 400 Arcle Dr Secaucus NJ 07094

MICHAELS, GORDON JOSEPH, copper company executive; b. Williamsport, Pa., May 9, 1930; s. Scott Joseph and Gloria Jean M.; m. Cleo Arlene Lela Tietbohl, June 12, 1954; children: Cathryn, Cheryl, Carole. BSEE, Bucknell U., 1959. Tool engr. Ternstedt div. Gen. Motors, Warren, Mich., 1950-59, sr. facilities engr., 1959-65; div. mgr. rectifiers M & T Chem. div. Am. Can Co., Rahway, N.J., 1965-71; v.p. mfg. and engring. Ullrich Copper Co., Kenilworth, N.J., 1971—; pres. Golld Truck Inc., Dorgo Products Inc. Bd. dirs. Tech. Machinery Inst., Union, N.J.; active Jr. Achievement, Elizabeth, N.J.; mem. Nat. Trust Hist. Preservation. Served with AUS, 1954-56. Mem. IEEE, Soc. Mining Engrs., Am. Electroplaters Soc., Soc. Mfg. Engrs., AAAS, Nat. Rifle Assn., Cryogenic Soc. Am., Internat. Platform Assn., Am. Legion, Smithsonian Assn. (assoc.), Nat. Trust for Historic Preservation, Nat. Wildlife Fedn. Republican. Lutheran. Home: Trout Run PA 17771 Office: HC64 PO Box 318 Trout Run PA 17771

MICHAELS, JOHN PATRICK, JR., investment banker, media broker; b. Orlando, Fla., May 28, 1944; s. John Patrick and Mary Elizabeth (Slemons) M.; grad. Jamaica Coll., Kingston, 1961; B.A. magna cum laude, Tulane U., 1966; M.A. in Communications (ABC fellow), U. Pa., 1968; student London Sch. Econs., U. London, 1964; m. Ingeborg D. Theimer, May 2, 1970; 1 dau., Kimberly Lynn. With Times Mirror Co., 1968-72, v.p. mktg. and devel. TM Communications Co., 1968-72; v.p. Cable Funding, N.Y.C., 1973; founder, chmn. Communications Equity Assos., cable TV investment bankers, 1973—; Atlantic Am. Holdings, Tampa, Fla. Tulane scholar, 1962-66; Tulane fellow, 1963-66. Fellow Inst. Dirs. (London); mem. Nat. Cable TV Assn., Internat. Radio and TV Soc., Am. Mktg. Assn., Royal TV Soc. London, Univ. Club, Two Rivers Hounds, Phi Beta Kappa, Phi Eta Sigma. Home: 3024 Villa Rosa Park Tampa FL 33611 Office: 101 E Kennedy Blvd Ste 3300 Tampa FL 33602

MICHAELS, PATRICK FRANCIS, broadcasting company executive; b. Superior, Wis., Nov. 5, 1925; s. Julian and Kathryn Elizabeth (Keating) M.; A.A., U. Melbourne, 1943; B.A., Golden State U., 1954; Ph.D., London U., 1964; m. Paula Naomi Bowen, May 1, 1960; children—Stephanie Michelle, Patricia Erin. War corr. CBS; news editor King Broadcasting, 1945-50; war corr. Mid-East Internat. News Service, 1947-49; war corr. MBS, Korea, 1950-53; news dir. Sta. WDSU-AM-FM-TV, 1953-54; fgn. corr. NBC, S. Am., 1954-56; news dir. Sta. KWIZ, 1956-59; commentator ABC, Los Angeles, 1959-62; fgn. corr. Am. News Services, London, 1962-64; news commentator McFadden Bartell Sta. KCBQ, 1964-68; news commentator ABC, San Francisco, 1968-70; news dir. Sta. KWIZ, Santa Ana, Calif., 1970-74, station mgr., 1974-81; pres. Sta. KWRM, Corona, Calif., Sta. KQLH, San Bernardino, Calif., 1981-88; chmn. Michaels Media, Corona del Mar, Calif., 1988—. Bd. dirs. Econ. Devel. Corp. Mem. Nat. Assn. Broadcasters (bd. dirs.), Calif. Broadcasters Assn. (v.p.), Am. Fedn. TV and Radio Artists, Orange County Broadcasters Assn. (pres.), Sigma Delta Chi (ethics com.). Republican. Clubs: Rotary, Balboa Bay (bd. govs.), South Shore Yacht, Internat. Yachting Fellowship of Rotarians (staff commodore). Home: 4521 Cortland Dr Corona del Mar CA 92625

MICHAELSON, BENJAMIN, JR., lawyer; b. Annapolis, Md., May 30, 1936; s. Benjamin and Naomi Madora (Dill) M.; m. Frances Means Blackwell, Apr. 12, 1986; children: Benjamin, Robert Wendell. BA, U. Va., 1957; JD, U. Md., 1962. Bar: Md. 1962, U.S. Dist. Ct. Md. 1976. Assoc. Goodman, Bloom & Michaelson, Annapolis, 1962-63; pvt. practice, Annapolis, 1963-73; sr. ptnr. Michaelson & Christhilf, P.A., Annapolis, 1973-77, Benjamin Michaelson, Jr., P.A., Annapolis, 1977-81, Michaelson & Simmons, P.A., Annapolis, 1982-86, Michaelson & Newell, P.A., 1987-88, Michaelson, Krause & Ferris, P.A., 1988—; gen. counsel, dir. Annapolis Fed. Savs., 1965—; bd. dirs. Security Title Guarantee Corp. Balt., Md. Svc. Corp.; bd. dirs., gen. counsel Annapolis Bancorp Inc. Counsel Anne Arundel County (Md.) Bd. Edn., 1966-76. Lt. U.S. Army, 1957-59. Named one of Outstanding Young Men Am., Severna Park chpt. U.S. Jaycees, 1965. Fellow Am. Coll. Mortgage Attys.; mem. ABA, Md. Bar Assn. (chmn. real property, planning and zoning sect. council 1982-84, grievance commn. inquiry panel 1976-85, vice-chmn. 1983-85, grievance commn. rev. bd. 1985-88), Anne Arundel County Bar Assn., Jaycees (Md. state legal counsel 1964-65, nat. dir. 1965-66), Sailing of Chesapeake Club (commodore 1982), Annapolis Yacht Club, Rotary (pres. 1975-76, Paul Harris fellow), Delta Theta Phi. Republican. Episcopalian. Home: 3 Southgate Ave Annapolis MD 21401 Office: Michaelson Krause & Ferris PA 80 West St Ste 110 Annapolis MD 21401

MICHAELSON, GERALD ALLEN, marketing consultant; b. Wausau, Wis., Feb. 23, 1929; s. Alexander Knute and Emilie (Schneider) M.; m. Janice Dawn Uekeyt, May 21, 1956; children: Steven, Deanne. BBA, U. Wis., 1951. Field service trainer Maytag Corp., Newton, Iowa, 1951-56; field sales mgr. Magnavox Co., Los Angeles, 1957-65; div. mgr. Magnavox Co., Detroit, 1966-71; v.p. Magnavox Co., N.Y.C., 1971-74, Ft. Wayne, Ind., 1974-80; v.p. N.Am. Philips, Knoxville, Tenn., 1980-84; cons. ABT Assocs., Cambridge, Mass., 1984—; bd. dirs. LaCrosse, Wis. Footwear. Author: Winning the Marketing War, 1987; contbr. articles on sales and mktg. to profl. pubs. 2d lt. U.S. Army, 1952-53, Korea. Mem. Am. Mktg. Assn. (v.p. 1987-88), Univ. Wis. Iron Cross Soc. Home: 201 Inverness Point Knoxville TN 37922

MICHALS, GEORGE FRANCIS, multi-industry company executive; b. Hungary, Sept. 14, 1935; came to Can., 1956, naturalized, 1961; s. Todor and Ilona (Sinkovich) Mihalcsics; m. Patricia Elizabeth Hoffman, June 18, 1971; children: Katherine, Julie, Elizabeth, Georgina. BComm, Sir George Williams U., Montreal, 1961; CA, McGill U., 1963. Chartered acct. McGill U., Montreal, 1963. Acct. Coopers & Lybrand, Montreal, 1963-68; from treas. to exec. v.p. Dominion Textile Co. Ltd., 1969-74; v.p. fin., sr. v.p., then exec. v.p. Genstar Corp., San Francisco, from 1974; now exec. v.p., chief fin. officer Can. Pacific Ltd., Montreal; adv. bd. Ctr. for Real Estate and Urban Econs., Berkeley, Calif. Adv. bd. Ctr. Real Estate Urban Econs., Berkeley, Calif. Mem. Urban Land Inst. Clubs: St. James's (Montreal); Bankers (San Francisco). Home: Can Pacific Ltd, PO Box 6042 Sta A, Montreal, PQ Canada H3C 3E4 Office: Genstar Corp 4 Embarcadero Ctr Ste 3800 San Francisco CA 94111 *

MICHAUD, ALPHEE MARTIAL, retail executive; b. St. Quentin, N.B., Can., Nov. 13, 1938; s. Napoleon and Alpheda (Deschenes) M.; M.D., Laval U., 1965; postgrad. in econs. McGill U., 1973; m. Claudette Gingras, July 4, 1964; children—Harold, Isabelle. Intern, Hotel-Dieu and Hosp. St. Sacrement, Quebec City, Que., 1964-66; resident in internal medicine Hosp. St. Sacrement, Quebec City, 1966-67; gen. practice medicine, Caraquet, N.B., 1968-71; pres., owner Les Pharmacies Populaires Ltd., Caraquet, 1971—; pres. Les Entreprises Ami Ltd., Caraquet, 1972—; pres., sec. Radio-Acadie Ltd., Caraquet, 1976—; pres., owner weekly newspapers; dir. N.B. Devel. Corp., 1973-79. Bd. dirs. Tracadie Assn. Mental Disease, 1973-76, N.B. Indsl. Devel. Bd., 1979—; pres. Le Festival Acadien Caraquet, 1974-76. Mem. Can., N.B. med. assns., Assn. Med. De Langue Francaise, Caraquet Bd. Trade, Atlantic Provinces Bd. Trade (chmn.), Canadian C. of C. (dir. 1980—). Roman Catholic. Med. editor weekly newspaper Le Voilier, 1972-76; pub. weeklies Levoilier/Le Point, 1983—, Week-End, 1983—. Home: PO Box 990, Caraquet, NB Canada E0B 1K0 Office: Place Caraquet, Caraquet, NB Canada E0B 1K0

MICHEL, BENOIT, utilities executive; b. Asbestos, Quebec, Can., June 4, 1940; s. Emile G. and Lucienne (Laroche) M.; m. Monique Lizee, June 29, 1963; children: Nataly, Sylvie. BS in Engring., U. Sherbrooke, 1963; degree in bus. adminstrn., Ecole des Hautes Etudes comerciales, Montréal, 1973. Commissioning engr. Hydro-Québec, Tracy, Can., 1963-65, design engr. nuclear power project, 1965-67; asst. supt. Tracy Generating Station, 1967-74; project mgr. heavy water plant Hydro-Québec, Montréal, Can., 1974-75, project mgr. spl. projects for commn., 1975-77, project dir. Gentilly Nuclear Power Plant, 1977-83; v.p. Mauricie Région Hydro-Québec, Trois-Rivières, Québec, 1983-86; exec. v.p. tech., internat. affaires and IREQ Hydro-Québec, Montrél, 1986-87, exec. v.p. equipment, 1987. Mem. James Bay Energy Soc. (chmn. bd. dirs. 1987), Hydro-Quebec Internat. (1986). Office: Hydro-Quebec, 75 René Lévesque Blvd W, Montreal, PQ Canada H2Z 1A4

MICHEL, GEORGE JOSEPH, JR., manufacturing company executive; b. Bklyn., Sept. 14, 1931; s. George Joseph and Agnes (Shuttleton) M.; m. Pauline Marie Frei, June 20, 1953; children—Katherine, Chrystal, George III. S.B., MIT, 1953. Electro-mech. engr. Nat. Security Agy., Washington, 1953-56; prodn. mgt., asst. plant mgr. Clearing Div. USI, Hamilton, Ohio, 1956-59; v.p. ops. Telecontrol Corp., Old Greenwich, Conn., 1960-67, pres., 1967-70; v.p. Stanadyne Inc., Windsor, Conn., 1970-85, chmn. bd., 1985-88, chmn., chief exec. officer, 1988—; dir. Kuhlman Corp., Birmingham, Mich. Contbr. chpt. to book. Corporator Middlesex Meml. Hosp., Middletown, Conn., 1979—; bd. dirs. Hartford Combined Health Appeal, 1981—, Hartford Jr. Achievement, 1984—. Served to 1st lt. U.S. Army, 1953-56. Recipient Corp. Leadership award MIT, 1980. Republican. Episcopalian. Home: 15 Evans Ln Essex CT 06426 Office: Stanadyne Inc 100 Deerfield Rd Windsor CT 06095

MICHEL, HENRY LUDWIG, civil engineer; b. Frankfurt, Fed. Republic of Germany, June 18, 1924; s. Maximilian Frederick and Loschka (Hepner) M.; m. Mary Elizabeth Strolis, June 5, 1954; children—Eve Musette, Ann Elizabeth. B.S.C.E., Columbia U., 1949. Registered profl. engr., Colo., N.Y., Ohio, Pa., Va., Mass., Conn., N.J., Mont. Chief engr. and gen. mgr. Panero-Weidlinger-Salvadori (cons. engrs.), Rome, 1960-62; pres., chief engr. Engring. Cons., Internat., Rome, 1962-65; partner Parsons Brinckerhoff Quade & Douglas, N.Y.C., 1965—; sr. v.p. Parsons Brinckerhoff Quade & Douglas, 1965-75, pres., 1975—, chief exec. officer, 1975—, dir., 1969—; dir. Parsons Brinckerhoff, Inc.; chmn. Parsons Brinckerhoff Internat.; guest lectr. Grad. Sch. Mgmt., Colo. State U., 1975-76, Cornell U.; advisor Office Tech. Assessment, The White House; chmn. Design Profl. Coalition; instrumental in devel. and mgmt. of maj. transp. and pub. works projects in U.S. and abroad. Contbr. numerous articles on mgmt. and transp. engring. to engring. jours. Fellow ASCE, Soc. Am. Mil. Engrs.; mem. Am. Cons. Engrs. Council , Internat. Road Fedn. (chmn., dir. 1977—), Nat. Assn. Corp. Dirs., N.Y. Soc. Profl. Engrs., Columbia U. Engring. Sch. Alumni Assn. (Egleston medal 1982), Am. Inst. Mgmt. (pres.'s council 1976), Am. European Community Assn. (dir. 1983—), University Club. Home: 35 Sutton Pl New York NY 10022 Office: Parsons Brinckerhoff Inc 250 W 34th St New York NY 10119

MICHEL, PHILIP R., financial consultant; b. Saginaw, Mich., Nov. 28, 1931; s. John and Lydia Bertha (Weirauch) M.; m. Sandra Seaton, July 28, 1956; children: John, David, Timothy, Kristin. BS in Chem. Engring., Mich. Tech. U., 1953. Nat. sales mgr. E.I. Dupont, Wilmington, Del., 1972-74, asst. product mgr., 1974-79; mgr. physical distbn. E.I. Dupont, Wilmington, 1984-85; plant supt. E.I. Dupont, Antioch, Calif., 1979-81; asst. plant mgr. E.I. Dupont, de Lisle, Miss., 1981-84; pres. Spinnaker Fin., Wilmington, 1986—, also bd. dirs.; industry rep. Calif. Mfrs. Assn., 1980-81, No. Calif. Chem. Assn., 1979-80; cons. Portage Assocs., Wilmington, 1985—. Lutheran. Clubs: duPont Country (Wilmington); Bay Waveland Bay Yacht (St. Louis). Office: Spinnaker Fin Inc 2005 Concord Pike Wilmington DE 19803

MICHELSEN, JOHN ERNEST, software services company executive; b. New Brunswick, N.J., May 11, 1946; s. Ernest Arnold and Ursula (Hunter) M.; B.S., Northwestern U., 1969; M.S., Stevens Inst. Tech., 1972; M.B.A. in Fin. with honors, U. Chgo., 1978; m. Ruth Ann Flanders, June 15, 1969; children—Nancy Ellen, Rebecca Ruthann. Real-time programmer Lockheed Electronics Co., Plainfield, N.J., 1969-72; control system designer Fermi Nat. Accelerator Lab., Batavia, Ill., 1972-75; chief system designer Distributed Info. Systems Corp., Chgo., 1975-78, v.p., 1978-79; mgr. M.I.S. adminstrn. FMC Corp., Chgo., 1979-82; pres. Infopro, Inc., 1982—. Mem. Assn. Computing Machinery, Phi Eta Sigma, Tau Beta Pi, Beta Gamma Sigma. Office: 2625 Butterfield Rd Oak Brook IL 60521

MICHELSEN, JOHN LEWIS, resort properties manager; b. Lansing, Mich., Mar. 21, 1945; s. Melvin Leroy and Alice Mae (Hummel) M.; m. Pamela R. Rollins, Oct. 18, 1975; children: Katherine Nell, Nathaniel John, Hunter Herndon. BBA, Mich. State U., 1967. Gen. mgr. Don the Beach Comber, Marina Del Rey, Calif., 1971-72; food and beverage dir. Callaway Gardens, Inc., Pine Mt., Ga., 1972-74; dist. mgr. Bodega Restaurants, Ft. Lauderdale, Fla., 1974-75; asst. gen. mgr., food and beverage dir. Pontchartrain Hotel, New Orleans, 1975-77; corp. dirs. ops. Miracle Mile Resort, Inc., Panama City Beach, Fla., 1977-79; gen. mgr. Pinehurst (N.C.) Hotel and Country Club, 1979-80; ptnr., v.p. ops. Brookstown Mgmt. Assocs., Winston-Salem, N.C., 1980-83; mng. dir. Winthrop Hotels and Resorts (formerly Sherburne Resort Properties), Nantucket, Mass., 1983—; instr. Gulf Coast Community Coll., Panama City, Fla., 1977-78; guest lectr. U. New Orleans, 1976-77, Fla. Internat. U. 1974. Treas. Nantucket Tree Fund, 1984—. Lt. USNR, 1967-70, Vietnam. Mem. Nantucket Lodging Assn. (bd. dirs. 1985, pres. 1988-89), Nantucket Restaurant Assn. (bd. dirs. 1985), Am. Hotel and Motel Assn. (treas. Bay County chpt., Panama City, Fla., 1978-79), Nat. Restaurant Assn., New Eng. Innkeepers Assn. (bd. dirs. 1989—), Nantucket C. of C. (v.p., bd. dirs. 1987-88), New Eng. Civic League (v.p., exec. bd. 1988—), Kiwanis (bd. dirs. Winston-Salem club 1981-83). Republican. Lutheran. Home: 17 Primrose Ln Nantucket Island MA 02554 Office: Winthrop Hotels and Resorts Zero Main St Nantucket MA 02554

MICHELSON, GERTRUDE GERALDINE, retail company executive; b. Jamestown, N.Y., June 3, 1925; d. Thomas and Celia Rosen; m. Horace Michelson, Mar. 28, 1947; children: Martha Ann (dec.), Barbara Jane. B.A., Pa. State U., 1945; LL.B., Columbia U., 1947; LLD with honors, Adelphi U., 1981; DHL with honors, New Rochelle Coll., 1983; LLD with honors, Marymount Manhattan Coll., 1988. With Macy's N.Y., N.Y.C., 1947—; mgmt. trainee Macy's N.Y., 1947-48, various mgmt. positions, v.p. employee personnel, 1963-70, sr. v.p. for labor and consumer relations, 1970-72, sr. v.p. personnel labor and consumer relations, 1972-79, sr. v.p. external affairs, 1979-80; sr. v.p. external affairs R.H. Macy & Co., Inc., 1980—; dir., mem. exec. com. Macy's N.Y., 1970—; bd. dirs. Quaker Oats Co., Chubb Corp., Gen. Electric Co., Stanley Works, Inc., Goodyear Tire & Rubber Co., R.H. Macy and Co., Inc., DCNY, Discount Corp N.Y., Harper & Row Pubs.; trustee Rand Corp.;dep. chmn. N.Y. Fed. Reserve Bank. Bd. dirs. Helena Rubinstein Found., Work in Am. Inst. Inc., Better Bus. Met. N.Y.; trustee Columbia U., Spelman Coll., Interracial Coun. Bus. Opportunity; mem. adv. couns. Columbia U. Grad. Sch. Bus., Catalyst. Recipient Disting. Service medal Pa. State U., 1969. Clubs: Econ. Club N.Y, Women's Forum. Home: 70 E 10th St New York NY 10003 Office: R H Macy & Co Inc 151 W 34th St New York NY 10001

MICHETTI, SUSAN JANE, print media specialist; b. Kenosha, Wis., Dec. 20, 1948. BA cum laude, U. Wis., 1981; Cert. A, B, C for real estate law, appraisal and mktg., Gateway Tech. Inst., Kenosha, 1979; postgrad., Carthage Coll., Kenosha, 1984. Lic. real estate appraiser, Wis. Project dir. Big Bros./Big Sisters of Kenosha County, Wis., 1978-79; tchr. Kenosha Unified Sch. Dist., 1979-84; newspaper editor U. Wis., Parkside, 1980-81; news reporter Milw. Sentinel, 1982-83; news reporter, newscaster WRJN Radio, Racine, Wis., 1982-84; quar. report writer, editor, designer Kenosha Unified Sch. Dist., 1983-84; book editorial and prodn. coord. McDougal, Littel Co., Skokie, Ill., 1985, Scott, Foresman and Co., Glenview, Ill., 1985-88; proprietor Michetti Multi-Media Assocs., Kenosha, 1971—; instr. profl. devel. U. Wis., Parkside, 1988—; mng. editor Nat. News Syndicate, Washington, 1982—; cons. in field. Contbr. articles to profl. jours. Media coord. Tony Earl Gov. campaign, Kenosha, 1982; media cons. Friends of Peter Barca for State Legis., Kenosha, 1985—; art fair asst. Friends of Kenosha Pub. Mus., 1986—; prog. devel. com. Racine Hist. Soc. and Pub. Mus., 1984-85. Scholar, Kenosha Found., 1979-81, Kenneth L. Greenquist, 1980, Vilas, 1968-71, Ida D. Altemus, 1969-70. Mem. NAFE, Am. Soc. Profl. and Exec. Women, Nat. Writers Union, Chgo. Women in Pub., Internat. Soc. Unified Sci., Nat. Assn. Desktop Pubs., Sierra Club (conservation chmn. 1983-86, chmn. water toxics 1988-89).

MICHLES, MARCUS ROBERT, financial executive; b. Fremont, Ohio, Sept. 6, 1935; s. Marcus Joseph and Beatrice (Shlesinger) M.; m. Judy Sharpe; 1 child, Marcus Joseph II. BA, U. Omaha, 1963. Cert. fin. planner. Enlisted U.S. Army, 1956, advanced through grades to maj., retired, 1977; chmn. Roban Inc., Orlando, Fla., 1977-82; exec. dir. athletic dept. U. Cen. Fla., Orlando, 1982-83; assoc. v.p. Dean Witter Reynolds Inc., Orlando, 1983—; pres., bd. dirs. Fotozines Internat. Inc., Windermere, Fla., 1985-87. Bd. dirs. Winter Park Pines Community Assn., Fla., 1983—. Mem. Sertoma Lodge. Office: Dean Witter Reynolds Inc 315 E Robinson St Ste 100 Orlando FL 32801

MIDAS, MICHAEL THOMAS, JR., business educator, executive; b. Lansford, Pa., Apr. 20, 1938; s. Michael Thomas and Martha Midas; m. Agnes Margaret Skrabak, June 11, 1960; children: Michael III, Stephen, Matthew, Mary Rose, Phillip. BS in Engring., U.S. Naval Acad., 1960; MS in Chemistry, Naval Post Grad. Sch., 1969; postgrad., Naval War Coll., 1973. Enlisted USN, 1955, advanced through grades to comdr.; commanding officer U.S.S. Vreeland (FF-1068), 1974-76; exec. asst. to pres. Naval War Coll., Newport, 1976-79; retired USN, 1979; mgr. workmanship excellence Raytheon Corp., Portsmouth, R.I., 1979-80; v.p. Am. Productivity Ctr., Houston, 1980-82; pres. America...1990, New Hartford, N.Y., 1982—; exec. v.p. Hamilton Digital Controls, Utica, N.Y., 1982-83. Advisor Lake Placid (N.Y.) Soccer Ctr., 1985-86; chmn. St. Mary's Hope Appeal Fund Drive, New York Mills, N.Y., 1985-86, The Exec. Com., Atlanta; participant White House Productivity Conf., Pitts. and Washington, 1983. Decorated Bronze Star with Combat V device; Keynote Speaker, Quality Mag., Chgo., 1982; delivered D. Wade Mack Disting. Lecture on Productivity, Utah State U., Salt Lake City, 1982. Mem. U.S. Naval Acad. Alumni Assn., Naval War Coll. Found., Atlantic Salmon Found., U.S. Naval Inst. Roman Catholic. Home: 168 Rockspray Ridge Peachtree City GA 30269

MIDDAUGH, JACK KENDALL, II, management educator; b. Springfield, Ill., Oct. 8, 1949; s. Jack Kendall and Mildred Viola (Davis) M.; m. Maureen Ann Tewey, Aug. 7, 1976; children: Cheryl Lynn, Allison Helen. BBA in Acctg., George Washington U., 1973, MBA, 1975; PhD in Acctg., Ohio State U., 1981. Instr. Ohio State U., Columbus, 1975-80; asst. prof. U. Va., Charlottesville, 1980-87; assoc. prof. Wake Forest U., Winston-Salem, N.C., 1987—; cons. IBM, Armonk, N.Y., 1981—, Amtrak, Washington, 1982-85, U.S. Postal Service, Washington, 1984-85, Ernst & Whinney, Cleve., 1985-87, U.S. Civil Svc. Commn., 1973-76, Digital Equipment Corp., 1985, Armstrong World Industries, 1989—. Contbr. articles to profl. jours. Recipient commendation Ohio Ho. of Reps., 1978; named Outstanding Tchr. of Yr. Pacesetters Ohio State U., 1977, 78. Mem. Am. Acctg. Assn., Decision Sci. Inst., Beta Gamma Sigma. Republican. Methodist. Home: 8016 Kilcash Ct Clemmons NC 27012 Office: Wake Forest U Babcock Grad Sch Mgmt 7659 Reynolda Sta Winston-Salem NC 27109

MIDDLEBERG, VICTOR, management consultant; b. Paris, France, Feb. 27, 1934; s. Robert and Berthe (Liverant) M.; student Temple U., 1959-61; children—Barry, Robert A., Seth. Distbn. mgr. Temple Co., Phila., 1953-59; underwriter Met. Life Ins. Co., Phila., 1960-66; mgmt. cons. Alexander Proudfoot Co., Chgo., 1966-70; v.p. ops., mgmt. cons. KM Consultants, Inc., Upper Saddle River, NJ. Home: 2602 Dudley Dr Bensalem PA 19020

MIDDLEBROOKS, EDDIE JOE, environmental engineer; b. Crawford County, Ga., Oct. 16, 1932; s. Robert Harold and Jewell LaVerne (Dixon) M.; m. Charlotte Linda Hardy, Dec. 6, 1958; 1 child, Linda Tracey. B.C.E., U. Fla., 1956, M.S., 1960; Ph.D., Miss. State U., 1966. Diplomate: Am. Acad. Environmental Engrs.; Registered profl. engr., Ariz., Miss., Utah registered land surveyor, Fla. Asst. san. engr. USPHS, Cin., 1956-58; field engr. T.T. Jones Constrn. Co., Atlanta, 1958-59; grad. teaching asst. U. Fla., 1959-60; research asst. U. Ariz., 1960-61; asst. prof., asso. prof. Miss. State U., 1962-67; research engr., asst. dir. San. Engring. Research Lab., U. Calif.-Berkeley, 1968-70; prof. Utah State U., Logan, 1970-82, dean Coll. Engring., 1974-82; Newman chair natural resources engring. Clemson U., 1982-83; provost, v.p. acad. affairs Tenn. Tech. U., 1983-88; provost, v.p. acad. affairs, prof. chem. engring. U. Tulsa, 1988—; mem. nat. drinking water adv. council EPA, 1981-83; cons. EPA, UN Indsl. Devel. Orgn., Calif. Water Resources Control Bd., also numerous indsl. and engring. firms. Author: Modeling the Eutrophication Process, 1974, Statistical Calculations-How To Solve Statistical Problems, 1976, Biostimulation and Nutrient Assessment, 1976, Water Supply Engineering Design, 1977, Lagoon Information Source Book, 1978, Industrial Pollution Control, Vol. 1: Agro-Industries, 1979, Wastewater Collection and Treatment: Principles and Practices, 1979, Water Reuse, 1982, Wastewater Stabilization Lagoon Design, Performance and Upgrading, 1982, Reverse Osmosis Treatment of Drinking Water, 1986, Pollution Control in the Petrochemicals Industry, 1987, Natural Systems for Waste Management and Treatment, 1988; mem. editorial adv. bd. Lewis Pubs. Inc., Envionment Internat.; contbr. tech. articles to profl. jours. Fellow ASCE; mem. AAAS, Water Pollution Control Fedn. (Eddy medal 1969, dir. 1979-81), Assn. Environ. Engring. Profs. (pres. 1974), Utah Water Pollution Control Assn. (pres. 1976), Internat. Assn. on Water Pollution Research, Am. Soc. Engring. Edn., Am. Soc. Limnology and Oceanography, Sigma Xi, Omicron Delta Kappa, Phi Kappa Phi, Tau Beta Pi, Sigma Tau. Home: 1115 E 20th St Tulsa OK 74120 Office: U Tulsa 600 S College Ave Tulsa OK 74104-3189

MIDDLEKAUFF, ROGER DAVID, lawyer; b. Cleve., May 6, 1935; s. Roger David and Ella Marie (Holan) M.; m. Gail Palmer, Apr. 19, 1963; children: Roger David, Arthur Henry. BChemE, Cornell U., 1957, Cert. Master Engring., 1958; JD cum laude, Northwestern U., 1964. Bar: Ohio 1964, D.C. 1966, U.S. Supreme Ct. 1974; cert. chem. engr. Assoc., Roetzel & Andress, Akron, Ohio, 1964-66, Kirkland, Ellis & Rowe, Washington, 1966-69; assoc. Thompson, and Middlekauff and predecessor firms, Washington, 1969-72, ptnr., 1973-83; ptnr. McKenna, Conner & Cuneo, 1983—; mem. adv. com. extension service project Dept. Agr., 1976; mem. adv. com. solar energy project ERDA, 1975; indsl. observer Codex Alimentarius Commn., FAO/WHO and com. meetings; project rev. group control tech. assessment of fermentation processes, Nat. Inst. Occupational Safety and Health. Co-editor: International Food Regulation Handbook: Policy, Scince, Law, 1989; contbr. articles to legal jours.; editor handbooks, Practising Law Inst.; mem. editorial bd. Jour. Regulatory Pharmacology and Toxicology; co-editor: The Impact of Chemistry on Biotechnology, 1988. Vice chmn. bur. Greater Washington Bd. Trade; trustee Internat. Life Scis. Inst., Nutrition Found., Inc., Risk Sci. Inst.; chmn. Arthur S. Flemming Awards Commn., 1969-70; vol. gen. counsel Episcopal Found. for Drama, 1976-77, Scotland Community Devel. Assn., 1971-73, Congregations United for Shelter, 1971-73, Iona House, 1974-77; sr. warden St. Columbia's Episc. Ch., Washington, 1975-77; sec., bd. dirs. Episc. Ch. Homes, Washington; mem. lawyers' panel Pres. Ford's Com., 1976; chmn. pres.'s cbpt. Nat. Capital Area council Nat. Eagle Scout Assn. Served with USN, 1958-61. Recipient Silver Wreath award local chpt. Boy Scouts Am. Mem. ABA (chmn. subcom. on food and color additives and pesticide residues, food, drug and cosmetic com. 1977-82), Am. Chem. Soc. (chmn. elect div. chem. and law, sec., treas. biotech. secretariat, 1986—, mem. exec. com. chemistry and the law 1985—), Inst. Food Technologists (exec. com. div. toxicology and safety evaluation, 1987—), Order of Coif. Episcopalian. Clubs: Metropolitan, Rotary. Office: McKenna Conner & Cuneo 1575 I St NW Washington DC 20005

MIDDLEMAS, GEORGE MCCLELLAND, venture capitalist; b. Pitts., June 12, 1946; s. George McClelland and Bernice Jean (Hall) M. BA in History and Polit. Sci., Pa. State U., 1968; MA, U. Pitts., 1971; MBA, Harvard U., 1973. CPA, N.Y. Mem. audit staff Arthur Young & Co., N.Y.C., 1973-77; asst. sec. Chem. Bank, N.Y.C., 1975-77; assoc. Kekst & Co., N.Y.C., 1977-79; v.p. Citicorp Venture Capital, N.Y.C., 1979-85; prin., sr. v.p. Inco Venture Capital, N.Y.C., 1985—; dir. Lang. Tech., Inc., Salem, Mass., Security Dynamics Techs., Cambridge, Mass., Tartan Labs., Pitts., Plant Genetics, Inc., Davis Calif., Digital Radio Network, Vienna, Va. Mem. alumni council Pa. State U., 1987—. Mem. Nat. Venture Capital Assn., Am. Electronics Assn., Met. Opera Assn. Presbyterian. Club: Doubles (N.Y.C.). Office: Inco Venture Capital Ltd 1 New York Pla New York NY 10004

MIDDLETON, CAROLE FOSTER, insurance broker, consultant; b. Weymouth, Mass., Dec. 24, 1946; d. David Warren and Hazel Margaret (McRae) Foster; BA, Coll. St. Catherine, 1968; BS, Rutgers U., 1974; MA, Webster U., 1987; m. Finley N. Middleton, II, Mar. 23, 1974. Claims supr. Allstate Ins. Co., 1969-74; asst. account exec. Johnson & Higgins, Brazil, 1974-76; new bus. prodn. mgr. Edward Lumley & Sons, South Africa, 1976-77; asst. v.p. Johnson & Higgins, N.Y.C., 1977-81; asst. v.p. Alexander & Alexander, N.Y.C., 1981-83; pres. Lynmar Internat., Yonkers, N.Y., 1983—, Foxberry Press, Gourmet Internat., Shopping & Mailing Internat., Assn. for Living Abroad (all subs.); adj. faculty mem. Webster U., Leiden campus; speaker on sales techniques, internat. ins., fgn. investment in the U.S., women in ins., women's networking, multinat. corps. Bd. dirs. Bklyn. YWCA, 1980-83, chmn. fin. com., treas., 1982; chair Reps. Abroad-Netherlands, 1987-88. Mem. Nat. Assn. Ins. Women, Am. Mgmt. Assn., Nat. Fedn. Bus. and Profl. Women, Assn. Profl. Ins. Women (adv. bd. 1982-83), Women's Econ. Round Table, Am. Women's Club Denmark (pres. 1986-87). Presbyterian. Clubs: Wall St. Bus. and Profl. Women's (past pres.); Women's Nat. Rep. Columnist Wall St. Woman, 1979-80; editor Chronicle mag., 1984-86; author: Managing Multinational Risk, 1989.

MIDDLETON, ELWYN LINTON, lawyer; b. Pomona, Fla., Oct. 16, 1914; s. William Spencer and Lizzie A. (Williams) M.; m. Annie L. Fielding, Dec. 7, 1942; children—Elwyn Linton, Mary Ann, John David, Phillip Fielding. LL.B., Stetson U., 1939. Bar: Fla. 1939. Assoc., E. Harris Drew, Palm Beach, Fla., 1939-42; ptnr. firm Steel, Hector, Davis, Burns & Middleton (formerly Burns, Middleton, Farrell & Faust), Palm Beach, 1946—; town atty., Palm Beach, 1953-81; dir. Bank of Palm Beach & Trust Co.; mem. adv. bd. First union Bank of Palm Beach, 1988—. Trustee Eckerd Coll., 1958—. Lt. USNR, 1942-46. Mem. ABA, Palm Beach County Bar Assn. (pres. 1951), Fla. Bar (gov. 1954-56), Phi Alpha Delta. Democrat. Presbyterian. Home: 242 Dunbar Rd Palm Beach FL 33480 Office: 440 Royal Palm Way Palm Beach FL 33480

MIDDLETON, MARC STEPHEN, corporate insurance specialist; b. Louisville, Dec. 7, 1950; s. Joseph Scott and Virginia Marie (Schuler) M.; m. Carmen Teresa Fauscette, Feb. 22, 1969; 1 child, Marc Christopher. AA, Dalton Jr. Coll., 1970; BBA, U. Ga., 1972. Sr. risk analyst Deere and Co., Moline, Ill., 1973-78, mgr. corp. claims, 1978-79, mgr. corp. ins. dept., 1980-86; v.p. risk mgmt. services John Deere Ins. Group, Moline, 1987—; v.p., bd. dirs. Tahoe Ins. Co., Reno, 1981-83, Sierra Gen. Life Ins. Co., Reno, 1981-83, Continental Guaranty, Ltd., Hamilton, Bermuda, 1981-83. Mem. Citizen's Adv. Council to East Moline (Ill.) Sch. Bd., 1978-80; coach YMCA Youth Basketball, Moline, 1978. Mem. Risk and Ins. Mgmt. Soc., Risk Mgmt. Council of Machinery and Allied Products Inst., Captive Ins. Cos. Assn., ESIS (Delphi panel 1985—), Internat. Platform Assn. Roman Catholic. Home: 2909 55th St Ct Moline IL 61265 Office: Deere and Co John Deere Rd Moline IL 61265

MIDDLETON, VINCENT FRANCIS, manufacturing company executive; b. N.Y.C., June 24, 1951; s. Vincent Aloysius and Mary Hilda (LeHane) M.; m. Collette Carolyn Peters, July 26, 1986. BSCE cum laude, So. Meth. U., 1974; MBA in Mgmt. summa cum laude, Golden Gate U., 1986. Registered profl. civil engr., Calif. Sr. structural engr. Bechtel, Inc., San Francisco, 1974-77; project mgr. Fisher Devel., Inc., San Francisco, 1977-80; mgr. projects Ecodyne Corp., Santa Rosa, Calif., 1980-81, dir. constrn., 1981-84; mgr. engring. and constrn. Custodis-Ecodyne, Inc., Santa Rosa, 1984-86; mgr. devel. and constrn. Custodis-Ecodyne Inc., Santa Rosa, 1986-87, v.p., gen. mgr., 1987—. Bd. dirs. Jr. Achievement, Sonoma County, Calif., 1986—. Engring. scholar So. Meth. U., Dallas, 1969; Tex. Pub. Works scholar, 1973. Mem. ASCE, Am. Concrete Inst., Nat. Asbestos Coun., Cooling Tower Inst., Mensa. Republican. Roman Catholic. Home: 260 Pacific Heights Dr Santa Rosa CA 95403 Office: Custodis-Ecodyne Inc PO Box 1267 Santa Rosa CA 95402

MIDGLEY, C(HARLES) EDWARD, textile company executive; b. Yonkers, N.Y., Feb. 2, 1937; s. Charles Edward Jr. and Margaret (Hunt) Midgley-Saunders; m. Mary Edie Midgley, June 21, 1958 (div. 1985); children: Ned, David, Susan; m. Laura Parrish, Jan. 12, 1985. BA, Princeton U., 1958; MBA, Harvard U., 1962. Mng. dir. Kidder, Peabody & Co., Inc., N.Y.C., 1962-88; vice chmn. Fieldcrest Cannon, Inc., N.Y.C., 1988—, also bd. dirs.; vice chmn. Amoskeag Co., Boston, 1988—; also bd. dirs.; bd. dirs. A.T.-Walker Corp. Pres. Tarrytown (N.Y.) Sch. Dist., 1979-85. Lt USN, 1958-60. Mem. Union League Club, Sleepy Hollow Country Club (Scarborough, N.Y., bd. govs.), Ardsley Country Club. Republican. Home: Washington Ave Irvington NY 10533 Office: Fieldcrest Cannon Inc 1271 Ave of Americas New York NY 10020

MIDWIG, WILLIAM CARROLL, JR., collection company executive; b. Balt., Apr. 30, 1951; s. William Carroll and Mona Lee (Craig) M., Sr.; m. Karen Ann Adams, Jan. 2, 1971; children—Lisa Ann, Lori Ann. A.A., Essex Coll., 1970; B.S., Towson State U., Md., 1979; M.B.A., Loyola Coll., Balt., 1981. Membership dir. Holiday Spas, Balt., 1970-80; pres. United Barter Service Inc., Shrewsbury, Pa., 1980-84, Nat. Credit Mgmt. Corp., Balt., 1984—. Mem. Am. Guild of Patients Accts. Mgmt., Nat. Assn. Credit Mgmt., Internat. Soc. Consumer Credit Execs. (assoc.). Republican. Episcopalian. Avocation: power boating. Office: Nat Credit Mgmt Corp 300 E Joppa Rd Towson MD 21204

MIELCUSZNY, ALBERT JOHN, wholesale distribution executive; b. Pitts., Oct. 30, 1941; s. Joseph John and Sophie (Krupa) M.; m. Constance Lorraine Snyder, Apr. 25, 1964; children: Alan, William. BS in Acctg., Duquesne U., 1964, MBA in Fin., 1972. CPA, Pa. Mgmt. trainee Jones & Laughlin Steel, Pitts., 1964-65; budget analyst Jones & Laughlin Steel, Aliquippa, Pa., 1967-68; acct. Touche Ross & Co., Pitts., 1968-72; from asst. contr. to sr. v.p. fin. and MIS Servistar Corp. (previously Am. Hardware Supply Co.), Butler, Pa., 1972—; Treas. Butler County CDC, 1974—; bd. advisors Mellon Bank, Butler, 1980-86. Bd. dirs. Salvation Army, Butler, 1981-84. 1st lt. U.S. Army, 1965-67, Vietnam. Republican. Roman Catholic. Office: Servistar Corp PO Box 1510 Butler PA 16001

MIER, PHYLLIS JEAN, program analyst; b. Muncie, Ind., Aug. 9, 1949; d. Philip Wilber and Helen Elizabeth (Moore) M. BA, Ball State U., 1971; postgrad., U. Md. LicensedMd., Va., D.C., Ind. Tchr. Montgomery County Pub. Schs., Rockville, 1971-74; tchr., mgr. Sears, Roebuck and Co., Arlington, Va., 1974-77; cons. Greenhorne and O'Mara, Inc., Riverdale, Md., 1977-78; program analyst Fed. Emergency Mgmt. Agy., Washington, 1978—, sr. program analyst, 1988—; asst. coordinator, driver Sunderland (Md.) Vanpools, 1980—; transportation, tour cons. Calvert Transportation Systems, Sunderland, 1980—; prin. Mier Computer Services, Huntingtown, Md., 1987; owner Vanpools Plus, Inc., Huntingtown, Mo., 1988—. Mem. Nat. Assn. Female Execs. (Who's Who in Female Execs. 1987), Beta Sigma Phi (pres. 1977, 81, 84, 85, council pres. 1977, 84). Home: 1847 Cliff Dr Huntingtown MD 20639 Office: Fed Emergency Mgmt Agy 500 C St SW Washington DC 20472

MIES, JOHN CHARLES, furniture retail executive; b. Peoria, Ill., Aug. 24, 1946; s. Ernest Gregory and Clara Emma (Reese) M.; m. Barbara Larrick; one child, John Charles Jr. BS, Ea. Ill. U., 1968. Tchr. Centennial High Sch., Champaign, Ill., 1969-74; ptnr. The Leather Shop, Champaign, 1974-78, The Waterbed Shop, Champaign, 1978-82; pres., chief exec. officer Mies Corp., Champaign, 1982—. Editor-in-chief The Sleep Connection newsletter. Mem. Nat. Waterbed Retailers Assn. (mem. exec. com., sec.-treas 1988-89), Cen. State Mktg. Group (pres.), Urbana C. of C. (chmn. leadership planning com.), Champaign C. of C. Office: Mies Corp 1102 N Prospect Champaign IL 61820

MIGLIO, DANIEL JOSEPH, telecommunications company executive; b. Phila., June 23, 1940; s. Daniel Joseph and Eleanor (Zucca) M.; m. Tamara Tinker, June, 1963; children: Paige Leslie, Marcus Daniel. BS in Econs., U. Pa., 1962. With So. New Eng. Telephone Co, 1962-84; acct. New Haven, Conn., 1962-67; budget coordinator New Haven, 1967-69; dist. traffic mgr. New London, Conn., 1969-72; gen. acctg. mgr. New Haven, 1972-74; div. ops. mgr. Hartford, Conn., 1974-78; gen. mgr. corp. planning New Haven, 1979-83, v.p. corp. planning and regulatory matters, 1983-84; sr. v.p. fin. and planning So. New Eng. Telecommunications Corp., New Haven, 1984—; bd. dirs., mem. exec. com., audit com. and compensation com. Bank of Boston, Waterbury, Conn., 1984—. Charter mem., bd. dirs. Clinton (Conn.) Jaycees, 1967-68; Chmn. allocations com., bd. dirs. United Way, New Haven, 1973-74; dir., v.p., pres. Gateway Counseling, Essex, Conn., 1975-86; bd. govs. Old Saybrook (Conn.) Hist. Soc., 1979-80; trustee Rector's Concern, Old Saybrook, 1980—; chmn. So. New Eng. Telephone Co. Polit. Action Com., New Haven, 1987—. Mem. U.S. Telephone Assn. (bd. dirs., exec. com. 1984—), Kappa Alpha. Republican. Epsicopalian. Clubs: U. Pa. of Greater Hartford; Univ. of Hartford. Office: So New Eng Telecommunications Corp 227 Church St 15th Fl New Haven CT 06510

MIGNANO, RICHARD ALAN, marketing professional; b. Chgo., Aug. 22, 1948; s. Dominic and Elsie (Ayres) M.; m. Susan O'Malley. BA, Mich. State U., 1970. Ter. mgr. Fort Howard Paper Co., Greenbay, Wis., 1973-77; sr. sales rep. Internat. Paper Co., N.Y.C., 1977; mktg. mgr. Inlander-Steindler Paper Co., Elk Grove Village, Ill., 1977-79, dir. mktg., 1979-82, v.p. sales and mktg., 1982-89, exec. v.p., 1989—; merchant adv. com. Scott Paper Co., Phila., 1987—. Bd. dirs. Timber Creek Homeowners Assn., Lake Zurich, Ill., 1988—. Mem. Nat. Paper Trade Assn. (mem. edn. and tng. com., Great Neck, N.Y., 1983-86), Internat. Sanitary Supply Assn. Republican. Office: 2100 Devon Ave Elk Grove Village IL 60007

MIKA, MURRAY ADAM, financial executive; b. Columbus, Ohio, Oct. 10, 1949; s. Adam Marion and Violet Rosalie (Radcliff) M.; m. Christy Lee Cochran, Oct. 7, 1972; children: Amanda Kathleen, Andrew Nicolas. BS in Acctg., Franklin U., 1972. Staff acct. Touche Ross & Co., Columbus, Ohio, 1972-77; v.p. fin. CBC Cos., Inc., Columbus, 1978—. Mem. Fin. Execs. Inst., Am. Inst. CPA's. Ohio Soc. CPA's (polit. action com. 1986-88). Republican. Methodist. Club: Athletic (Columbus). Office: CBC Cos Inc 175 S Third St Ste 1080 Columbus OH 43215

MIKELBERG, ARNOLD, meat packing company executive; b. N.Y.C., Apr. 28, 1937; s. Nathan and Frances (Levine) M.; m. Judith Pauline Weil, July 5, 1970; children: Hilary, Barrett. B.S., Mich. State U., 1958. Gen. mgr. Hygrade Food Products Corp., Detroit, 1958-70; v.p. South Chgo. Packaging Co., Chgo., 1970-71, Packers Provision Co., Highland Park, Ill., 1971-72, Frederick & Herrud, Detroit, 1972-78; sr. v.p., dir. John Morrell & Co., Northfield, Ill., 1978-88; exec. v.p. Thornapple Valley Inc., Southfield, Mich., 1988—; bd. dirs. Thornapple Valley Inc., Southfield. Mem. Am. Meat Inst. Republican. Office: Thornapple Valley Inc 18700 W Ten Mile Rd Southfield MO 48013

MIKIEWICZ, ANNA DANIELLA, marketing and sales representative; b. Chgo., Dec. 22, 1960; d. Zdislaw and Lucy (Magnusewska) K. BS in Mktg., Elmhurst Coll., 1982; postgrad. Triton Coll. Asst. to Midwestern regional mgr. Meister Pub. Co., Chgo., 1983; sales rep. First Impression, Elk Grove, Ill., 1984; mktg. and customer svcs. rep. Airco Ind. Gases, Broadview and Carol Stream, Ill., 1985, Yamazen USA, Inc., Schaumburg, Ill., 1985-88; mktg. and sales coord. Kitamura Machinery U.S.A, Inc., 1988—. Named Chgo. Polish Queen Polish Am. Culture Club, 1983-84. Mem. NAFE. Republican. Roman Catholic.

MIKLICH, THOMAS ROBERT, paint company executive; b. Cleve., Apr. 17, 1947; s. Joseph Jerome and Josephine (Kmet) M.; m. Patricia A. Perhavec, Oct. 4, 1969; children—Jeffrey, Amy, Christopher, Mary Beth. B.B.A., Cleve. State U., 1969, J.D., 1973. Bar: Ohio bar 1974; C.P.A., Ohio. With Sherwin-Williams Co., Cleve., 1969—; sec., asst. controller Sherwin-Williams Co., 1977-79, treas., 1979-86, sr. v.p. fin., chief fin. officer, 1986—; dir. Van Dorn Co.;. Mem. Am. Inst. C.P.A.'s, Am. Bar Assn., Fin. Execs. Inst., Treasurer's Club, Ohio Soc. C.P.A.'s, Ohio Bar Assn. Republican. Roman Catholic. Office: Sherwin Williams Co 101 Prospect Ave NW Cleveland OH 44115

MIKSIC, BORIS ALEXANDER, chemical company executive; b. Zabreb, Yugoslavia, Oct. 11, 1948; came to U.S., 1974; s. Stephan and Nina (Genrihsen) M.; m. Olga Maria Bonc, Nov. 25, 1972; children: Evonne, Paul. BSME, Zagreb U., 1974. Sr. research engr. No. Instruments Corp., Mpls., 1974-75, v.p. research and devel., 1975-77; founder, pres. The Cortec Corp., St. Paul, 1977-84; pres., chief exec. officer Cortec Corp., St. Paul, 1988—; v.p. Cortec div. Sealed Air Corp., Saddle Brook, N.Y., 1984-88; bd. dirs. Advanced R & D, St. Paul; cons. in field; lectr. in field; condr. symposia. Author: Lay-up and Mothballing of Equipment, 1988; contbr. articles to profl. jours.; patentee in field. Mem. Nat. Assn. Corr. Engrs. (task group chmn. 1976-81). Office: The Cortec Corp 310 Chester St Saint Paul MN 55107

MILAM, JUNE MATTHEWS, life insurance agent; b. Preston, Ga., Mar. 27, 1931; d. Curtis J. and Mary (Doster) Matthews; m. James Cage Lowry, Dec. 20, 1952 (dec.); m. Walker Hinton Milam, Jr., June 15, 1957; children: James L., Melinda K., Lisa W., Matthew W. BA, La. State U., 1952. Agt. N. Y. Life Ins. Co., Metairie, La., 1966—; alderman City of Harahan, La., 1980-86; mayor pro-tem City of Harahan, 1982-84; guest speaker to industry in 22 states, 1968—; charter leader N.Y. Life Ins. Womens' Network, N.Y.C., 1981-83. Contbr. articles to profl. and trade jours. Mem. adv. bd. Battered Women's Program, New Orleans, 1978—, Jefferson Parish Econ. Devel. Commn. Council, 1988—. Named Boss of the Yr., Am. Bus. Womens Assn., Metairie, 1976, Man of Yr., New Orleans Assn. Life Underwriters, 1976. Mem. Nat. Assn. Life Underwriters, La. Assn. Life Underwriters, New Orleans Assn. Life Underwriters, Womens Bus. Owners Assn. (adv. bd. 1984-88), Million Dollar Round Table. Republican. Presbyterian. Office: NY Life Ins Co 3333 W Napoleon Ave Ste 200 Metairie LA 70001

MILAM, WALKER HINTON, JR., insurance underwriter; b. Okalona, Miss., July 9, 1930; s. Walker Hinton Sr. and Mary Lou (Mangum) M.; m. June Matthews, June 15, 1957; children: James L., Melinda K., Lisa W. Milam-Ary, Matthew W. Student, U. Miss., 1948-50, Millsaps Coll., 1950-51; BBA, Miss. Coll., 1955. Agt. Liberty Mut. Ins. Co., New Orleans, 1955; sales rep. Mead Johnson Labs., Baton Rouge, 1955-62; dist. sales mgr. Mead Johnson Labs., New Orleans, 1962-68; agt., registered rep. N.Y. Life Ins. Co., New Orleans, 1968—. Pres. Harahan Playground Boosters Club, 1978, 84; bd. dirs. Harahan (La.) Coun. on Aging, 1984—, chmn. bd., 1986-87. Named Harahan Vol. of Yr., VFW, 1986. Mem. Nat. Assn. Life Underwriters (chmn. long range planning com. 1978-80, Nat. Quality award, 1980, 88, Nat. Sales Achievement award 1987), La. Assn. Life Underwriters (chmn. polit. action com. 1984-85), New Orleans Assn. Life Underwriters (co-chmn. legis. com. 1985-86), Million Dollar Round Table, River Ridge Club (pres. 1981-82), Colonial Country Club (bd. govs. 1989—), Kiwanis (bd. dirs. Harahan chpt. 1978—). Office: NY Life Ins Co 639 Loyola Ave 19th Fl New Orleans LA 70113

MILANESI, DAVID LAURENCE, exploration company executive, accountant; b. San Francisco, Mar. 12, 1947; s. Laurence Leo and Dorothy Elenor (Ahrens) M.; m. Carol Anderson, Dec. 18, 1971. BSBA, Fresno State Coll., 1969; MBA in Fin., Northwestern U., 1972. CPA, Colo. Staff mem. Arthur Anderson and Co., Denver, 1972-77; controller Visa Exploration Co., Denver, 1978-81; chief fin. officer Sheffield Exploration Co., Denver, 1981—. With U.S. Army, 1969-71. Mem. Denver Treas.'s Club. Home: 202 S Dearborn Circle Aurora CO 80012 Office: Sheffield Exploration Co 518 17th St Ste 500 Denver CO 80202

MILANO, DONNA WALL, interior design company executive; b. Amite, La., May 14, 1961; d. Cecil Edward and Linda Faye (Varnado) Wall; m. John Michael Milano, April 26, 1986. AA in Interior Design, Bauder Coll., 1982. Interior designer JC Penney and Co., Baton Rouge, 1983-87; pres. Tones and Textures, Inc., Baton Rouge, 1987—. Republican. Home: 15626 Springwood Ave Baton Rouge LA 70817 Office: Tones and Textures Inc 4733-B Jones Creek Rd Baton Rouge LA 70817

MILAVSKY, HAROLD PHILLIP, real estate executive; b. Limerick, Sask., Can., Jan. 25, 1931; s. Jack and Clara Milavsky. B in Commerce, U. Sask., Saskatoon, Can., 1953. Chief acct., treas., controller Loram Internat. Ltd. div. Mannix Co. Ltd., Calgary, Alta., Can., 1956-65; v.p., chief fin. officer Power Corp. Devels. Ltd., Calgary, Alta., Can., 1965-69; exec. v.p., bd. dirs. Great West Internat. Equities Ltd. (name now Trizec Corp. Ltd.), Calgary, Alta., Can., 1969-76; former pres., now chmn., chief exec. officer, bd. dirs. Trizec Corp. Ltd., Calgary, Alta., Can., 1976—; bd. dirs. Trizec Corp. related cos., Brascan Ltd., Toronto, Can., Carena-Bancorp Inc., Toronto, The Rouse Co., Columbia, Md., Ernest C. Hahn Inc., San Diego, London Life Ins. Co., London, Bramalea Ltd., Toronto, Hees Internat., Toronto, Biotech. Internat. Can. Inc., Calgary, Coscan Devel. Corp., Toronto, Saskatchewan Oil & Gas Corp., Regina Nova Corp. Alberta, Calgary, Amoco Can., Calgary, Internat. Trade Adv. Com., Toronto. Dir. Terry Fox Humanitarian Award Program; past dir. Conf. Bd. Can.; past gov., Acctg. Edn. Found. Alta.; mem. Chancellor's Club, U. Calgary. Fellow Inst. Chartered Accts. Alta.; mem. Inst. Chartered Accts. Sask. and Alta., Can. Inst. Pub. Real Estate Cos. (past pres., bd. dirs.), Can. C. of C. (past chmn.), Internat. Profl. Hockey Alumni (founder). Clubs: Petroleum, Ranchmen's, Glenmore Racquet (Calgary). Office: Trizec Corp Ltd, 700 2nd St SW #3000, Calgary, AB Canada T2P 2W2

MILCH, ROBERT AUSTIN, biotechnology company executive; b. N.Y.C., May 24, 1929; s. Henry and Pearl (Salzberg) M.; m. Margot Wurtzburger, Aug. 14, 1960; children: Pamela Alexandra, Thomas A. AB, Columbia Coll., 1949, MD, 1953; MBA, Loyola Coll., Balt., 1977. Diplomate Am. Bd. of Orthopaedic Surgery. Prof. orthopaedic surgery John Hopkins U., Balt., 1960-66; spl. asst. White House Office of Sci. and Tech., Washington, 1966-68; prin. Peat, Marwick, Mitchell & Co., Washington, 1968-77; prof. mgmt., dean grad. sch. Loyola Coll., Balt., 1977-81; chmn., pres. IGENE Biotechnology, Inc., Columbia, Md., 1981—. Holder over 5 patents; author 5 books; contbr. numerous articles to profl. jours. Office: IGENE Biotechnology Inc 9110 Red Branch Columbia MD 21045

MILES, A. STEVENS, banker; b. Louisville, Nov. 30, 1929; s. Algene Stevens and Edna May (Rietze) M.; m. Ann Berry Houston, Nov. 6, 1954; 1 dau., Elizabeth. B.A., Washington and Lee U., 1951; postgrad., Stonier Grad. Sch. Banking, Rutgers U., 1962-64. With First Nat. Bank, Louisville, 1954—; pres., dir. First Nat. Bank, 1972-81, chief exec. officer, 1975-88, chmn., 1981—; pres., dir. Nat. City Corp., Louisville, 1988—; pres., First Ky. Trust Co., 1973-81 , chief exec. officer, 1975—, chmn., 1981—; pres., First Ky. Nat. Corp., 1974-87; chief exec. officer, 1975-88, chmn. bd. dirs., 1986—. Chmn. Mus. History and Sci. Found., 1984—, Louisville Waterfront Devel. Corp., 1987—; bd. dirs. Louisville Central Area, Inc., 1969—, Ky. Derby Mus., 1986—; exec. bd. Old Ky. Home council Boy Scouts Am., 1973—; bd. dirs. Greater Louisville Fund for Arts, 1974—; trustee Washington and Lee U., 1988— . Served to 2d lt. U.S. Army, 1951-53. Mem. Louisville C. of C. (bd. dirs. 1986). Episcopalian. Clubs: Louisville Country, Pendennis, River Valley. Office: 1st Ky Nat Corp PO Box 36000 Louisville KY 40233

MILES, FRANK CHARLES, newspaper executive; b. Detroit, Jan. 1, 1926; s. Nelson and Ethel Jane (Mennill) M.; m. Catharine Estelle Coleman, Sept. 4, 1948; children—Barbara Ann, Diana Estelle. Student, Westervelt Bus. Coll., 1947-48. With Thomson Newspapers Ltd., Des Plaines, Ill., 1950—, Cambridge, Ont., 1950-52, 54-55; bus. mgr. Sarnia (Ont.) Obs., 1952-54; gen. mgr. Pembroke (Ont.) Obs., 1956-58, Moose Jaw (Sask) Times-Herald, 1958-62; pub. Austin (Minn.) Daily Herald, 1962-66; sr. v.p., gen. mgr. Thomson Newspapers Inc., Des Plaines, Ill., 1966—, also dir. Served with USNR, 1943-46. Mem. Am. Newspaper Pubs. Assn., Inland Daily Press Assn., Sigma Delta Chi. Republican. Mem. Ch. of Christ. Home: 647 Wilton Ct Palatine IL 60067 Office: Thomson Newspapers Inc 3150 Des Plaines Ave Des Plaines IL 60018

MILES, JACKIE DWAIN, electrician, building contractor; b. Soper, Okla., Feb. 16, 1932; s. Audley Odell and Ruby Loraine (LaRue) M.; m. Wilma June Holcomb, Dec. 30, 1952; children: Cynthia Deanne Miles Thompson, Stanley Kevin. Student Solano Coll., 1956-58; A.A., Sacramento State U., 1961. Supr. U.S. Civil Service, Fairfield, Calif., 1956-65; ptnr., dir., contractor B & M Electric, Suisun, Calif., 1965-71; owner, contractor All-Cal Electric, Suisun, 1971—; v.p., dir. developer, builder Casa Grande Homes, Fairfield, 1973—; ptnr., cons., contractor Tri-Co. Electric, Suisun; ptnr., cons., builder Mariah Builders, Fairfield, 1982—; ptnr., cons. Audie Electric Contractors, Fairfield, 1983—, Energy Seal Window Mfrs., Fairfield, 1985—, The Lighting Warehouse, Fairfield, 1985—. Inventor electromech. valve, 1963 (cert. 1964). Served with USAF, 1952-56. Mem. Napa/Solan Builders Exchange. Republican. Club: Exchange (Suisun). Lodges: Elks, Moose. Home: 4319 Green Valley Rd Suisun CA 94585 Office: All-Cal Electric 209 Main St Suisun CA 94585

MILES, JESSE MC LANE, accounting company executive; b. De Funiak Springs, Fla., June 17, 1932; s. Percy Webb and Dora (Pippin) M.; m. Catherine Rita Eugenio, July 18, 1959; children—Jesse Jr., Catherine, Teresa, John, Thomas, Robert. B.S.B.A., U. Fla., 1954. C.P.A., N.Y. Mem. staff, mgr., prin. Arthur Young & Co., N.Y.C., 1954-63, ptnr., 1963—, dep. chmn.-internat., 1985—; chmn. Arthur Young Internat., 1985—. Mem. Am. Inst. C.P.A.s, N.Y. Inst. C.P.A.s, German Am. C. of C. Club: Burning Tree Country (Greenwich, Conn.). Office: Arthur Young & Co 277 Park Ave New York NY 10172

MILES, JOHN ERNEST GEORGE, telecommunications executive; b. Mason City, Iowa, Sept. 23, 1943; s. John Ernest and Beverly Mae (Harris) M.; m. Bärbel B. Brauer, Dec. 16, 1980; children: Lisa, Misty, John. Grad. high sch., Thornton, Iowa. With quality control dept. CSC, McClillan AFB, Calif., 1967-69; mgr. tech. adminstrn. RCA Service Co., San Francisco, 1970-89; tech. support mgr. western region RCA Telephone Systems, Sacramento, Calif., 1989—; Author software Quality Assurance Adminstration, 1981, Telephone Trouble Information System, 1985, Z-Tour (copyright), 1985. Served to sgt. USAF, 1962-66. Republican. Club: Health Users Group (Sacramento). Home: 2538 Los Feliz Way Carmichael CA 95608

MILES, MICHAEL ARNOLD, food company executive; b. Chgo., June 22, 1939; s. Arnold and Alice (Morrissey) M.; m. Pamela L. Miles; children: Michael Arnold Jr., Christopher. BS, Northwestern U., 1961. Various mgmt. positions to v.p., account supr. Leo Burnett Co., Inc., 1961-71; with Heublein, Inc., 1971-82, sr. v.p. mktg. Ky. Fried Chicken, 1971-72, v.p. gen. mgr. grocery products, 1972-75, internat., 1975-77, v.p. group exec. Internat. group, chmn. food svc. and franchise group Ky. Fried Chicken, 1977-81, sr. v.p. foods, Louisville, 1981-82; pres., chief operating officer Kraft Gen. Foods, Glenview, Ill., 1982—; bd. dirs. Capital Holding Corp., Citizens Fidelity Corp. Bd. dirs. Lyric Opera Chgo.; mem. adv. coun. J.L. Kellogg Grad. Sch. Mgmt. Northwestern U., Evanston, Ill. Office: Kraft Gen Foods Kraft Ct Glenview IL 60025

MILGRAM, MORRIS, integrated housing developer; b. N.Y.C., May 29, 1916; s. Benjamin and Fannie (Gladstone) M.; m. Grace B. Smelo, June 26, 1937 (div. Mar. 1969); children: Gene, Elizabeth; m. Jean Babcock Gregg, Apr. 21, 1969 (div. Nov. 1975); m. Lorna Scheide, Dec. 13, 1975 (dec. Aug. 1987); m. Frances Johnson Drevers, June 11, 1988. BA in Econs., Rutgers U., 1939; LHD, Starr-King Sch. for Ministry (Unit.), 1967. Pres. Smelo-Peters-Milgram, Inc., Phila., 1950-53; exec. v.p. Concord Park Homes, Inc./Greenbelt Assocs., Inc., Phila., 1954-57, Princeton (N.J.) Housing Assocs., 1957-59; pres. Modern Community Developers and Planned Communities, Inc., 1958-69; mgr. Mut. Real Estate Investment Trust, N.Y.C., 1965-69; gen. ptnr. Ptnrs. in Housing, Phila., 1969—; pres. Choice Communities Inc., Phila., 1969-77, co-chmn., 1977—; pres. Fund for an Open Soc., Phila., 1975—; bd. dirs. Nat. Housing Conf., Washington. Patentee in field; contbr. articles to profl. jours. Bd. dirs. Rutgers U., New Brunswick, N.J., 1968-74, Rural Advancement Fund, Charlotte, N.C., 1979-87, Bucks County Housing Devel. Corp., Doylestown, Pa., 1987-89; bd. dirs. U.S. Commn. on Civil Rights, Phila., 1985—. Recipient 1st Nat. Human Rights award U.S. Dept. Housing and Urban Devel., 1968, Ernest Siler award Nat. Neighbors, 1984. Mem. Nat. Assn. Home Builders, Nat. Assn. Housing and Redevel. Ofcls., Citizens Housing and Planning Coun. N.Y., Am. Jewish Com., Housing Assn. Del. Valley. Home: 16 Longford St Philadelphia PA 19136 Office: Fund for an Open Soc 311 S Juniper St #400 Philadelphia PA 19107-5804 Office: Choice Communities Inc 1218 Chestnut St #605 Philadelphia PA 19107-4814

MILLAR, JOHN FRANCIS, industrial products company executive; b. Teaneck, N.J., Jan. 23, 1936; m. Doris Connolly, June 2, 1957; children: Michael R., Cynthia A. BS in Fin., Fairleigh Dickinson U., 1961. Sr. auditor Hurdman & Cranston CPAs, NYC, 1961-64; dir. treas. ops. Keuffel & Esser Co., Morristown, N.J., 1964-76; treas., chief fin. officer Bait Bates & Co., Washington, 1976-77, Joseph Dixon Cruciable Co., Jersey City, 1977-83, Dixon Ticonderoga Co., Vero Beach, Fla., 1983-85; exec. v.p. chief ops. officer indsl. products Dixon Ticonderoga Co., Lakehurst, N.J., 1985—; bd. dirs. Dixon Ticonderoga Co., Vera Beach. Served with U.S. Army, 1954-56. Mem. Nat. Assn. Accts. Republican. Roman Catholic. Home: 1780 Rolling Ridge Ln Toms River NJ 08753 Office: Dixon Ticonderoga Co Ridgeway Blvd Lakehurst NJ 08733

MILLARD, JAMES KEMPER, marketing executive; b. Lexington, Ky., Oct. 28, 1948; s. Lyman Clifford and Cora (Carrick) M.; m. Madelyn Hooper, Nov. 26, 1983; children: Lyman Clifford III, Sean Duffy, James Kemper Jr. BA, Transylvania U., Lexington, Ky., 1971. Writer AP, Lexington, 1970-71; asst. news. dir. WLEX-TV, FM, Lexington, 1971-76; producer Ky. Dept. Pub. Info., Frankfort, 1973; dir. rels. Transylvania U., Frankfort, 1973-79; acct. supr. Abbott Advt., Inc., Frankfort, 1979-85; mktg. dir. Steak N' Shake, Inc., Frankfort, 1985; field mktg. mgr. Nutri/System Inc., Willow Grove, Pa., 1985-86, field mktg. dir., 1986-88, v.p. communications, 1988—; bd. dirs. Bluegrass Restaurant Assn., Lexington, 1984-85; mem. acad. adv. com. Ea. Ky. U., Richmond, 1983-87, treas. Bluegrass Integrated Pest Mgmt., Lexington, 1983-85. Author: C&O Streamliners, 1988. Advt. officer Chesapeake & Ohio Ry. Hist. Soc., Alderson, W.Va., 1983—; mem. Hon. Order Ky. Cols. Louisville, 1976—, Kidney found Ind.; deacon Cen. Christian Ch., Lexington, 1984-86; cons. Jr. Achievement Project Bus, Lexington, 1984-85. Recipient Great Menu award Nat. Restaurant Assn., 1982, Key Man award Jerrico Inc., 1981, Silver and Bronze ADDY Awards Lexington Advt. Club, 1982, Gold Award Fla. Restaurant Assn., 1984. Mem. Columbia Club Indpls., Delta Sigma Phi (sec., historian 1961-71). Democrat. Mem. Disciples of Christ. Home: 21 Wetherburn Dr Downingtown PA 19335

MILLER, ALAN JAY, investment company executive; b. Bklyn., July 11, 1936; s. Louis and Claire (Maltz) M.; m. Susan Ruth Morris, Oct. 29, 1961; children—Laurie Ann, Adam Louis. B.A., Cornell U., 1957. Chartered fin. analyst. Pres. Analysis-in-Depth Inc., N.Y.C., 1965-67; mng. editor Value Line Investment Survey, N.Y.C., 1967-68; research dir. Emanuel Deetjen & Co., N.Y.C., 1968-69; exec. v.p., dir. Intersci. Capital Mgmt. Corp., N.Y.C., 1969-71; pres., dir. ICM Equity Fund Inc., N.Y.C., 1970-71, ICM Fin. Fund Inc., N.Y.C., 1970-71; v.p., assoc. research dir. Bache & Co., Inc., N.Y.C., 1972, G.H. Walker & Co., Inc., N.Y.C., 1972-73; 1st v.p., assoc. research dir. Blyth Eastman Dillon & Co. Inc., N.Y.C., 1974-76; dir. research E.F. Hutton & Co., Inc., N.Y.C., 1976-81, sr. v.p., 1976-80, exec. v.p., 1981-88; dir. Hutton Investment Mgmt., 1976-88; mng. dir. SLH Asset Mgmt. Shearson Lehman Hutton, Inc, N.Y.C., 1988—; adj. assoc. prof. Columbia U. Grad. Sch. Bus., 1978-79; mem. faculty N.Y. Inst. Fin., 1977-78; lectr. New Sch. Social Research, 1980. Mem. N.Y. Soc. Security Analysts, Fin. Analysts Fedn., Am. Statis. Assn., Nat. Assn. Bus. Economists, N.Y. Assn. Bus. Economists. Office: Shearson Lehman Hutton Inc 31 W 52nd St New York NY 10019

MILLER, ALLAN ROBERT, stockbroker; b. Wheeling, W.Va., Mar. 20, 1939; s. Robert J. and Mary Magdalen (Schlag) M.; children: Allan Raymond, Beth Ann. BS, Wheeling Coll., 1961. Cert. fin. planner. Stockbroker Legg Mason Wood Walker, Inc., Wheeling, 1961—, v.p. Legg Mason Masten div., 1961—. With U.S. Army, 1961-63. Mem. Internat. Assn. Cert. Fin. Planners, Inst. Cert. Fin. Planners, Wheeling Coll. Alumni Assn. (pres. 1980-81), Civitan (pres. Wheeling 1981-82, lt. gov. 1982-83). Republican. Roman Catholic. Office: Legg Mason Masten Div Bank Plaza Bldg Rm 610 Wheeling WV 26003

MILLER, ALLEN IRWIN, manufacturing executive; b. Bklyn., Oct. 22, 1938; s. Henry Frank and Frieda (Couen) M.; m. Roberta B. Kertcsz, Feb. 26, 1961; children: Deborah, Scott, Michael. CLU, Hofstra U.; BBA, CCNY. Mgr. staff Prudential Ins. Co., Flushing, N.Y., 1962-69; exec. v.p. Eastco Indsl. Safety Corp., Huntington Sta., N.Y., 1969—. Drug counselor Friends of Bridge, Valley Stream, N.Y., 1980-84; various acting roles Jericho Players, 1985-88. Served as pvt. U.S. Army. Mem. Safety Equipment Dist., Am. Soc. Safety Engrs., Nat. Safety Council. Office: Eastco Indsl Safety Corp 130 W 10th St Huntington Station NY 11746-1616

MILLER, ARLYN JAMES, oil company executive; b. LeMars, Iowa, Aug. 31, 1940; s. Clarence Theodore and Irene (DeSmet) M.; m. Loyola E. Valdes, Nov. 11, 1978. BBA, U. Iowa, 1962. CPA, Colo. Staff acct. Peat, Marwick, Mitchell & Co., Denver, 1962-65; acct. Hamilton Brothers Oil Co., Denver, 1965-69, treas., 1969—, v.p., 1978-80, sr. v.p., 1980-81, exec. v.p., chief fin. officer, 1981—; bd. dirs. Health Mgmt., Inc., Wheat Ridge, Colo.,

Tejas Gas Corp., Houston, Luth. Hosp., Wheat Ridge, Colo. Bd. dirs. Luth. Med. Ctr. Found., Wheat Ridge Colo. Mem. Am. Inst. CPA's, Colo. Soc. CPA's. Republican. Roman Catholic. Clubs: Lakewood Country (Colo.), Denver Petroleum. Home: 23765 Currant Dr Golden CO 80401 Office: Hamilton Oil Corp 1560 Broadway Ste 2000 Denver CO 80202

MILLER, BEATRICE E., communications executive; b. Washington, Pa., Oct. 19, 1946; d. I. Roy and Marie (Pratt) M. ABS, Point Park Coll., 1966. Asst. producer Fuller/Smith Ross Advt., Pitts., 1966-69; project assoc. Time-Life, Inc., N.Y.C., 1970; exec. v.p. Communicators/Pitts. Inc., 1971-82; dir. communications svcs. Pet Inc., St. Louis, 1983—. Mem. Bus./Profl. Advt. Assn. (dir. 1988—, chmn. P.A.N. com. 1988—, cert.), Food Mktg. Communicators, Ad Club of St. Louis, Press Club of St. Louis. Home: 4535 Magnolia Ave Saint Louis MO 63110 Office: PET Inc 400 S 4th St Saint Louis MO 63102

MILLER, BRAD THOMAS, finance company executive; b. Feb. 10, 1953; s. Milo Kirk and Genevieve Marie (Gleason) M.; m. Sharon Ann McMurray, Aug. 19, 1978; children: Brad Thomas, Angela Lynn, Ryan Kirk. Student, Emporia State U., 1971-72, Kans. State U., 1973-74. Agt. Penn. Mut. Life Ins. Co., Topeka, 1976-77, dist. mgr., 1977-78; owner, pres. Brad. T. Miller & Assocs., Topeka, 1978—. Author: Easy Way to Financial Independence, 1981; contbr. articles to profl. jours. Bd. dirs. Sch. Future for Abused Children, 1986-88, Capper Found. for Crippled Children, 1988—; active Christian Children's Assn. Mem. Internat. Assn. Fin. Planners, Soc. Fin. Planners, Gen. Agts. and Mgrs. Assn. (past pres.), Planning Forum, Topeka C. of C., Topeka Sizzlers Ambs. (chmn. 1987—). Home: 7623 SW Robin Hood Ct Topeka KS 66614 Office: 2909 SW Maupin Ln Topeka KS 66614

MILLER, BRUCE LOUIS, insurance company executive; b. Covington, Ky., Apr. 6, 1942; s. Wayne D. Miller; m. Susan Backus, Sept. 11, 1965; children: Lisa, Bruce Louis Jr. B.A. in Econs., Cornell U., 1964; M.B.A. in Mktg., U. Pa., 1966. Sr. mgmt cons. McKinsey & Co., Inc., Chgo., 1966-73; dir. bus. devel. dept. Pet, Inc., St. Louis, 1973-75; pres. St. Louis ops. grocery group Pet, Inc., 1975-76; pres. Old El Paso Mexican Foods, Tex., 1976-77; pres., chief exec. officer Glover, Inc., Roswell, N.Mex., 1977-79; exec. v.p. AON Corp., Chgo., 1980-88, also dir.; pres. Union Fidelity Life Ins. Co., Trevose, Pa., 1988—, also bd. dirs.; dir. Harris Bank Glencoe, Ill., Union Fidelity Life Ins. Co., Rollins Burdick Hunter, Chgo., Ryan Ins., Chgo., Combined Ins. Co.; co-founder, co-chmn. planning com. Minority Enterprise Small Bus. Investment Co., Chgo., 1970-71. Contbr.: chpt. to Minority Economic Development: A Resolution for the Seventies, 1973. Episcopalian. Office: Union Fidelity Life Ins Co 4850 Street Rd Trevose PA 19049

MILLER, CAREY BRENT, oil company executive, geologist; b. Chickasha, Okla., Aug. 23, 1949; s. Roy Lee and Wilma LaVelle (Smith) M.; m. Margie Jean Broaddus, June 7, 1969; 1 child, Derrik Brent. BS in Geology, U. Okla., 1978; BS in Math., Okla. Coll. Liberal Arts, 1970. dist. sales rep. United Foam Corp., Shawnee, Okla., 1975-76; researcher Environ. Res. Devel. Assn., U. Okla., Norman, 1976-77; dist. geologist Grace Petroleum Corp., Oklahoma City, 1977-80, Western Pacific Petroleum, Oklahoma City, 1980-82; pres. Hold Exploration Co., Oklahoma City, 1982-85, BriCar Resources, Inc., Oklahoma City, 1982—, also bd. dirs.; bd. dirs. Blue Pine Pottery Corp., Oklahoma City, Park Loan Co., Inc., v.p. 1987—; bd. dirs. Roy-Al Corp., Oklahoma City; v.p., bd. dirs. Am. Oil Change Corp. Served to 1st lt. U.S. Army, 1971-74. Mem. Am. Assn. Petroleum Geologists, Soc. Exploration Geophysicists, Oklahoma City Geol. Soc., Geophys. Soc. Oklahoma City, Oklahoma City C. of C., Phi Gamma Lambda (pres. 1969-70), Sigma Gamma Epsilon. Republican. Baptist. Home: 2511 McGee Norman OK 73072 Office: BriCar Inc 1207 Sovereign Row Oklahoma City OK 73108

MILLER, CARL GEORGE, finance executive; b. Milw., Oct. 3, 1942; s. Carl Conrad and Agnes Frances (Patla) M.; m. Patricia Ann Smith, Apr. 27, 1968; children: Gregory, Brian. BS, St. Louis U., 1964. CPA, Mo. Audit mgr. Ahrens & McKeon, CPAs, St. Louis, 1967-73; supr. internal audit Gen. Dynamics Corp., St. Louis, 1973-75, mgr. fin. analysis, 1975-78, dir. fin. analysis, 1978-80; v.p., controller Quincy (Mass.) Shipbldg. div. Gen. Dynamics Corp., 1980-86; v.p. fin. Cessna Aircraft Co., Wichita, Kans., 1986-88; v.p., contr. Ft. Worth div. Gen. Dynamics Corp., Ft. Worth, 1988—. Bd. dirs. Wichita Jr. Achievement. Named one of Outstanding Young Men Am. Mem. Machinery and Allied Products Inst. (mem. fin. council I), AICPA, Mo. Soc. CPAs, Wichita C. of C., Ridglea Country Club (Ft. Worth), Delta Sigma Pi (pres. 1963-64). Republican. Lutheran. Office: Gen Dynamics Ft Worth Div PO Box 748 Fort Worth TX 76101

MILLER, CHARLES DALY, business executive; b. Hartford, Conn., 1928; (married). Grad., Johns Hopkins U. Sales mgr. Yale & Towne Mfg. Co., 1955-59; assoc. Booz, Allen & Hamilton, 1959-64; with Avery Internat. Corp., Pasadena, Calif., 1964—, group v.p., 1969-72, exec. v.p. ops., 1972-75, pres., 1975-77, chief exec. officer, 1977—, now also chmn., dir. Office: Avery Internat Corp 150 N Orange Grove Blvd Pasadena CA 91103 *

MILLER, CHRISTOPHER LOUIS, manufacturing executive; b. Jackson, Mich., July 26, 1940; s. James Louis and Lucille Isabel (Folk) M.; m. JoAnne Simcox, July 10, 1965; children: Julia Anne, Edward James. BS, Mich. State U., 1967. Pres. J. Miller Co., Homer, Mich., 1977—. Treas. Trojan Found. Edn., Homer, 1985—; v.p. Homer Boosters Assn.; sec. Calhoun County Econ. Devel. Commn., 1984; active Save the Lake Assn. Served with USAF, 1958-62. Mem. Soc. Mfg. Engr., Homer Hist. Soc., Homer Alumni Assn., Mich. State U. Alumni Assn. Lodge: Lions (pres.). Home: 505 Grandview Homer MI 49245

MILLER, CLARK ALVIN, human resource management consultant; b. Akron, Ohio, Oct. 29, 1934; s. Harold J. and Hallie Mary (Coburn) M.; m. Tanya Bellomo, Dec. 29, 1956 (div. 1975); children: Brian, Bruce, Paul, Timothy, David, Joel. BA in Psychology cum laude, U. Buffalo, 1956; grad., Gen. Motors Inst., 1957; MBA, U. Rochester, 1971. Mgr. employment and wage adminstrn. Harrison Radiator div. Gen. Motors, Lockport, N.Y., 1956-64; asst. to pres. U.S. Rubber Reclaiming Corp., Buffalo, 1964-66; div. human resources mgr. Carborundum Co., Niagara Falls, N.Y., 1966-70; group dir. human resources Carborundum Co., Niagara Falls, 1970-78; v.p. human resource Mech. Tech., Inc., Latham, N.Y., 1978-82; v.p. employee relations Coleco Industries, Inc., Amsterdam, N.Y., 1983-85; pres. BSG Mgmt. Cons., Clifton Park, N.Y., 1980—; Bd. dirs. Empire Blue Cross/Blue Shield, N.Y.C., 1980—. Mem. Phi Beta Kappa. Home: 45 Blue Spruce Ln Ballston Lake NY 12019 Office: BSG Mgmt Cons PO Box 788 Clifton Park NY 12065

MILLER, CLIFFORD ALBERT, banker, business consultant; b. Salt Lake City, Aug. 6, 1928; s. Clifford Elmer and LaVeryl (Jensen) M.; m. Judith Auten, Sept. 20, 1976; 1 child, Courtney; children by previous marriage, Clifford, Christin, Stephanie. Student, U. Utah, 1945-50, UCLA, 1956. Staff corp. UP, Salt Lake City, 1949-55; pres. Braun & Co., L.A., 1955-82, chmn., 1982—; exec. v.p. Gt. Western Fin. Corp., Beverly Hills, Calif., 1987—; bd. dirs. Shamrock Holdings, Inc., Burbank, Calif., Gt. Western Savs. Bank, Seattle, Gt. Western Thrift & Loan Assn., Salt Lake City, Gt. Western Fin. Securities, L.A., Gt. Western Fin. Corp., Gt. Western Bank, Burbank, Calif.; cons. to The White House, 1969-74. Trustee Harvey Mudd Coll., Claremont, Calif.; bd. govs. Performing Arts Council, Music Ctr., L.A. Mem. UCLA Chancellor's Assocs., Skull and Bones, Sigma Delta Chi, Pi Kappa Alpha, Lakes Country Club, Calif. Club, L.A. Tennis Club. Office: Gt Western Fin Corp 84844 Wilshire Blvd 10th Fl Beverly Hills CA 90211

MILLER, CROIX TOMPKINS, construction executive, textile consultant; b. Paterson, N.J., Mar. 19, 1947; s. DeForest Croix Tompkins and Beatrice Elenore (Bennett) M.; m. Andrea Perigrin (div.); children: Deanna Marie, DeForest Croix, Andrew John; m. Patricia Ann Wilson, Apr. 10, 1982; 1 child, Ryan Patrick. Student, Sommanset Community Coll., 1981. Lic. gen. contractor, N.C., plumber, N.C., plumbing contractor. Owner, pres. Curtnick Properties Inc., Paterson, 1978-79, Curtnick Corp., Paterson, 1978-79; owner, operator Croix Constrn. Co., Hawthorne, N.J., 1965-79; mgr. plant Como Textile Prints Inc., Paterson, 1966-78; owner Croix Remodeling, Somerset, Ky., 1980-81; supr. Superba Print Works, Mooresville, N.C., 1981, Blue Ridge Textile Paint, Statesville, N.C., 1981-84; foreman So. Constructors, Mooresville, N.C., 1985-86; owner Croix Design and Constrn Co., Statesville, 1983—. Cub master Cub Scouts of Am., 1985-86. Served with U.S. Army, 1965-72. Mem. Home Builders of Statesville and Mooresville (pres. 1987, v.p. 1986, dir. 1989), N.C. Home Builders Assn. (regional v.p. 1988—). Republican. Episcopalian. Home and Office: Croix Constrn Co RR 11 Box 170 H Statesville NC 28677

MILLER, DAVID FRANCIS, retail executive; b. Jacksonville, Fla., June 1, 1929; s. Frank Holten and Verna (Sharp) M.; m. Gloria Parks, June 13, 1952; children—David F., Clara, Elizabeth, Jane. B.S.B.A., U. Fla., 1951. With J.C. Penney Co., Inc., 1953—, mdse. mgr. Dallas regional office, 1964-66, mktg. mgr. women's fashions, 1966-69, dist. mgr., Atlanta, 1969-70, asst. to dir. regional ops., N.Y.C., 1970-72, dir. regional coordination, 1972-74, v.p., 1974-76, regional v.p. Eastern region, 1976-79, sr. v.p., dir., 1980-83; pres. J.C. Penney Stores and Catalog, 1983—, vice chmn., chief operating officer, 1987—. Bd. trustees Jacksonville U., 1987—; bd. dirs. Winn-Dixie, 1987—; mem. adv. com. Women's Prison Assn., 1974-76; mem. adv. council Coll. Bus. Adminstrn., U. Fla.; mem. ofcl. bd. United Meth. Ch., Huntington, N.Y., 1976; chmn. comml. div. United Way, N.Y.C., 1982; chmn. Nat. Minority Supplier Devel. Coun., 1986-88. Served with USAF, 1951-53. Republican. Clubs: Huntington Country, Gleneagles Country. Office: J C Penney Co Inc 14841 N Dallas Pkwy Dallas TX 75240

MILLER, DONALD BRITTON, management consultant; b. Rochester, N.Y., Apr. 10, 1923; s. Alvin Austin and Avis (Britton) M.; m. Alice Ruth Mellgard, Aug. 26, 1950 (dec.); children: Christopher Donald, James Austin; m. Frances Martin Clark, Nov. 21, 1982. BS in Mech. Engring., U. Rochester, 1944; MBA, Columbia U., 1948. Tel. design engr. Stromberg Carlson Co., Rochester, 1943-45; asst. to dean sch. engring. Columbia U., N.Y.C., 1947-52; lab. ops. mgr., dir. personnel, program mgr. human resources IBM, N.Y.C., Poughkeepsie and Harrison, N.Y., San Jose, Calif., 1952-78; mgmt. cons., Saratoga, Calif., 1978—. Author: Personal Vitality, 1977, Personal Vitality Workbook, 1977, Careers, 1980, 81, Working With People, 1979, Managing Professionals in Research and Development, 1986. Pres. Saratoga Sister City Orgn.; trustee Hakone Found. Fellow Soc. Advancement Mgmt. (internat. pres. 1965-66, Human Rels. award 1983, Saratoga Citizen of Yr.); mem. Am. Soc. Engring. Edn. (Disting. Svc. award 1978, Cert. Merit 1986), Am. Soc. Engring. Mgmt., ASME, IEEE, Acad. Mgmt., Assn. Mgmt. Cons., Coll. Firm Prins. Lodge: Rotary. Home: 14600 Wild Oak Way Saratoga CA 95070 Office: 14600 Wild Oak Way Saratoga CA 95070

MILLER, DONALD EDWARD, savings and loan executive; b. Alton, Ill., Sept. 9, 1945; s. Robert G. and Dorothy H. (Mook) M.; m. Suzanne Buescher, Apr. 4, 1943. BS in Bus. Mgmt. and Fin. Planning, So. Ill. U., 1981. Asst. v.p. Roosevelt Fed. Savs. and Loan, St. Louis, 1973-79; dir. underwriting Fed. Home Loan Mortgage Corp., Washington, 1979-81; v.p. Equitable Savs. and Loan, Austin, Tex., 1981, Clover Leaf Savs. and Loan, Edwardsville, Ill., 1983—; pres. Solar and Energy Conservation Mktg., San Francisco, 1982; mem. adv. com. Small House Council U. Ill., 1988. Author: Financial/Lending, 1981; contbr. articles to profl. jours. Bd. dirs. Madison County United Way, 1985-88, 1st v.p., 1987-88; bd. dirs. U. Ill. Extension Edn. Found. Madison County, 1989—; appointee housing planning coun. Southwestern Ill. Area Agency on Aging, 1989. Served to sgt. U.s. Army, 1965-67. Mem. U.S. League Savs. Instns. (com. mem. 1977-79), Inst. Fin. Edn., Home Builders Assn. Madison County (v.p. 1982, state dir., 1st v.p. 1988, pres. 1989). Republican. Club: Metro East Golf. Home: 1313 State St Alton IL 62002 Office: Clover Leaf Savings & Loan 200 E Park St Edwardsville IL 62025

MILLER, DONALD LESESSNE, publishing executive; b. N.Y.C., Jan. 10, 1932; s. John H. and Mamie (Johnson) M.; m. Ann Davie, Aug. 12, 1951 (div. 1981); children: Lynn, Mark; m. Gail Aileen Wallace, June 27, 1981. BA, U. Md., 1967; cert., Harvard Grad. Sch. Bus. Adminstrn., 1969. Enlisted U.S. Army, 1948, advanced through grades to maj., 1966, ret., 1968; spl. asst. to pres., mgr. corp. recruitment Inmont Corp., N.Y.C., 1968-70; v.p. indsl. relations Seatrain Shipbldg. Corp., N.Y.C., 1970-71; dep. asst. sec. def. U.S. Dept. Def., Washington, 1971-73; v.p. personnel mgmt. Columbia U., N.Y.C., 1973-78; dir. personnel devel. and adminstrn. Internat. Paper, N.Y.C., 1978-79; v.p. employee relations Consol. Edison N.Y., N.Y.C., 1979-86, Dow Jones & Co., Inc., N.Y.C., 1986—; bd. dirs. Bank of N.Y. and Bank of N.Y. Co., N.Y.C., Gurney Seed & Nursery Co., Yankton, S.D. Author: An Album of Black Americans in the Armed Forces, 1969. Chmn. bd. Associated Black Charities, N.Y.C., 1982—; bd. dirs. United Way, Jackie Robinson Found., 1981—; trustee Pace U., 1979—. Decorated Legion of Merit; decorated Commendation Medal; recipient Disting. Civilian Service medal Dept. Def., 1973, Disting. Alumnus award U. Md., 1977. Mem. Am. Arbitration Assn. (bd. dirs. 1984—), Alpha Sigma Lambda, Pi Sigma Alpha, Phi Kappa Phi, Alpha Phi Alpha, Sigma Pi Phi. Office: Dow Jones & Co Inc 200 Liberty St New York NY 10281

MILLER, DONALD ROY, financial consultant; b. Hartford, Conn., Apr. 6, 1946; s. Ronald Irvin and J. Beatrice (Smith) M.; m. Veronica June Taylor, May 24, 1969; children: Jonathan Lloyd, Justin Lyle, Jared Lance. AB in Econs., Dickinson Coll., 1968; JD, U. Conn., 1971; postgrad., U. Hartford, 1972-74. Bar: Ohio, Conn.; CLU. Advt. mktg. cons. Phoenix Mut. Life, Hartford, 1971-73; estate and bus. tng. specialist Aetna Life & Casualty, 1973-74; sr. advt. underwriting cons. Home Life, N.Y.C., 1974-76; legal counsel The Planning Group, Inc., Nashville, 1976-77; research dir. Conn. Rep. State Orgn., Hartford, 1977-78; pres. Outlook, Inc., Granby, Conn., 1977-82; qualified plan sales cons. Mass. Mut., Springfield, Mass., 1979-82; fin. svc. cons. Nationwide Life Ins., Columbus, Ohio, 1982—. Commr. Granby Planning and Zoning Commn., 1978-80, 1st selectman, 1981-82; mem. Rep. Town Com., Granby, 1979-82; moderator South Congl. Ch. Granby, 1978-81, Dublin Community Ch., 1987-89. Mem. Life Mgmt. Inst., Am. Coll. Life Underwriters. Home: 2489 Squirewood Ct Dublin OH 43017 Office: Nationwide Life Sales/Fin Svcs One Nationwide Plaza Columbus OH 43216

MILLER, DONALD VINCENT, newspaper publisher; b. Chgo., July 29, 1937; s. Vincent and Marie (Wills) M.; m. Shirley Gene Inman, July 29, 1967; children: Claudine, Laurel. AA, So. Ill. U., 1971; cert. in mgmt. devel., Harvard U., 1973. Gen. mgr. Register Newspapers, Denver, 1960-61; v.p. Express-News Corp., San Antonio, 1961-67; pres., publisher Sedalia (Mo.) Democrat, 1967-73; pres., gen. mgr. Scripps-Howard Bus. Publs., Houston, 1973-76, The Los Angeles Bus. Jour., 1987—. Home: 1007 W Kenneth Glendale CA 91202 Office: Los Angeles Bus Jour 3345 Wilshire Blvd Suite #207 Los Angeles CA 90010

MILLER, DUANE KING, health and beauty care company executive; b. N.Y.C., Mar. 1, 1931; s. Henry Charles and Helen Marion (King) M.; A.B. in Econs. and Fin., NYU, 1951; m. Nancy L. Longley, June 6, 1954; children—Cheryl L., Duane L. Vice pres. mktg. Warner-Chilcott div. Warner Lambert Co., Morris Plains, N.J., 1970-72, pres. div., 1973-77, exec. v.p. Am. Optical div. and pres. Am. Optical Internat. div., Southbridge, Mass., 1978; pres. biol. and proprietary products divs., v.p. Revlon Health Care Group, Revlon Corp., Tuckahoe, N.Y., 1978-80, pres. ethical, proprietary and vision care divs., 1981—, corp. v.p. parent co., 1982, pres. Revlon Health Care Group, 1983—, corp. exec. v.p. parent co., 1984—, pres. Revlon Health Beauty Care and Internat. Group, 1988—; cons. in field. Mem. Republican Nat. Com. Mem. Pharm Mfrs. Assn. (bd. dirs.), Nat. Pharm. Council, Am. Mgmt. Assn., Am. Mktg. Assn. (pres. N.J. chpt. 1967-68), Sales Exec. Club N.Y. Clubs: Princeton N.Y.; Roxiticus (N.J.) Golf; Clubs of Ocean Pines (Md.); Masons, Shriners. Author: (with others) Marketing Planning for Chief Executives and Planners, 1966. Home: PO Box 63 Brookside NJ 07926 Office: Revlon Inc 767 Fifth Ave New York NY 10022

MILLER, EDWARD D., banker; b. 1940; married. Student, Pace U. With Mfrs. Hanover Trust Co., N.Y.C., 1959—, former sr. v.p. consumer credit, sr. v.p., dep. gen. mgr. br. banking group, 1980-82, exec. v.p., head retail banking div., 1982-85, sector exec. v.p. retail banking, 1985-88; sector exec. v.p. retail banking Mfrs. Hanover Corp. (parent), N.Y.C., 1988—; vice-chmn. Mfrs. Hanover Corp and Mfrs. Hanover Trust Co., N.Y.C. Office: Mfrs Hanover Corp 270 Park Ave New York NY 10017

MILLER, EDWARD DAVID, trade association administrator; b. Bradenton, Fla., July 5, 1934; s. Louis and Pauline (Goldman) M.; m. Denise Daniel, Dec. 26, 1973. BA, Fla. So. Coll., 1958; MA, Appalachian State U., 1966; EdS, Cath. U., 1976; EdD, U. Ark., 1988. Cert. tchr., D.C., Fla. Assoc. exec. Nat. Bus. Edn. Assn., Washington, 1969-73; pres., chief exec. officer Future Bus Leaders Am., Washington, 1973—. Chmn. nat. coordinating coun. Vol. Svc. Overseas, Washington, 1980—, Nat. Adv. Coun. for Vocat. Edn., Washington, 1983-86; commr. Nat. Commn. for Employment Policy, Washington, 1983-85. With U.S. Army, 1957-59. Named to Hon. Order Ky. Cols., 1970, Hon. Citizen City of Stateboro, Ga., 1975, One of Outstanding Commrs. Nat. Commn. for Employment Policy, 1983. Mem. Am. Vocat. Assn., Am. Soc. Assn. Execs., Nat. Bus. Edn. Assn., Nat. Assn. State Suprs. Vocat. Edn. Republican. Office: FBLA PBL Inc 1908 Association Dr Reston VA 22091

MILLER, ELLIOTT CAIRNS, banker; b. Cambridge, Mass., May 4, 1934; s. James Wilkinson and Mary Elliott (Cairns) M.; m. Mary Killion, July 2, 1960; children—Jonathan Vaill, Stephen Killion. A.B., Harvard Coll., 1956; J.D., U. Mich., 1961; LL.M., Boston U., 1970. Bar: Conn. 1962. Assoc. Robinson & Cole, Hartford, Conn., 1961-66, ptnr., 1967-72; v.p., counsel Soc. for Savs., Hartford, Conn., 1972-73, sr. v.p., 1973-78, exec. v.p., 1978, pres., chief exec. officer, dir., 1979—; pres., chief exec. officer Soc. for Savs. Bancorp Inc., 1987—, also bd. dirs.; bd. dirs. nat. council Savs. Inst., Washington, 1984—. Trustee, chmn. Kingswood-Oxford Sch., West Hartford, 1977-87; trustee Co-ordinating Council on Founds., 1987—; bd. dirs. Downtown Council, Hartford, 1975—; trustee Greater Hartford Arts Council, 1980—; corporator Hartford Hosp., St. Francis Hosp., Mt. Sinai Hosp., Inst. of Living. Served with AUS, 1956-58. Mem. Conn. Bar Assn. Clubs: Hartford, University. Home: 4 Stratford Rd West Hartford CT 06117 Office: Soc for Savs 31 Pratt St Box 2200 Hartford CT 06145

MILLER, EMERSON WALDO, accountant, tax, financial, business and management consultant; b. Green Island, Jamaica, W.I., Jan. 27, 1920; s. Adolphus Eustace and Catherine Sarah (Dixon) M.; m. Olive Claire Ford, Apr. 10, 1945; children—Cheryll, Hellena, Emerson, Oliver, Donald, Selwyn. Student U. Toronto, (Ont., Can.), 1938-41, U. Calif.-Berkeley, 1950-61. Came to U.S., 1950, naturalized, 1957. Cost accountant Poierier & McLane Corp., N.Y.C., 1941-42; prin. Emerson Miller & Co., Kingston, Jamaica, 1942-49; lectr. accounting and bus. law Jamaica Sch. Commerce, Kingston, 1945-48; tax examiner, conferee Internat. Revenue Service, San Francisco, 1963-64; chief financial and accounting aspects transp. and communications services programs Gen. Services Adminstrn., San Francisco, 1965-70, chief maj. segment financial mgmt. activities, 1970-84; prin. Emerson W. Miller Tax, Fin., Bus. and Mgmt. Services, 1984—; instr. govt. accounting, 1966-69. Fed. Govt. Accountants Assn. rep. mgmt. improvement com. Fed. Exec. Bd., San Francisco, 1973-74. Chmn. credit com. VARO Fed. Credit Union, San Francisco, 1969-81, treas., dir., 1981—. Recipient Disting. Service award Toastmasters Internat., 1968, Commendable Service award Gen. Services Adminstrn., 1968, Spl. Achievement award, 1969; Faithful Service award VARO-SF Fed. Credit Union, 1974. Mem. Am. Accounting Assn., Nat. Assn. Accountants, Fed. Govt. Accountants Assn. (chpt. pres.), Am. Mgmt. Assn., Financial Mgmt. Assn., Brit. Inst. Mgmt., Am. Judicature Soc., Royal Econ. Soc. (Cambridge), U. Calif. Alumni Assn., Internat. Platform Assn., Acad. Polit. and Social Sci., AAAS, N.Y. Acad. Scis. Clubs: Toastmasters Internat. (ednl. v.p.) (San Francisco), No. Calif. Cricket (San Anselmo); Brit. Social and Athletic (Los Angeles). Home: 505 Coventry Rd Kensington CA 94707 Office: PO Box 471 Berkeley CA 94701

MILLER, ERIC JAMES, finance executive; b. Bronxville, N.Y., Aug. 6, 1953; s. Eric Thomas and Eileen (Skillings) M. m. Margaret Solberg; children: Kristin K., James M., Conor S., Eric C., Joseph C. AB, Dartmouth Coll., 1975; MBA, Amos Tuck Sch., 1979. Cert. mgmt. acct. Fin. analyst Internat. Harvester, Chgo., 1979-80; fin. mgr. FMC Corp., Phila., 1980-84; dir. fin. Chilton Pub. Co., Radnor, Pa., 1984-86; chief fin. officer Am. Appraisal Assocs. Inc., Milw., 1986—. Mem. Inst. of Mgmt. Accts. Republican. Club: Milw. Athletic. Office: Am Appraisal Assocs 525 E Michigan St Milwaukee WI 53202

MILLER, EUGENE, financial executive; b. Chgo., Oct. 6, 1925; s. Harry and Fannie (Prosterman) M.; m. Edith Sutker, Sept. 23, 1951 (div. Sept. 1965); children: Ross, Scott, June; m. Thelma Gottlieb, Dec. 22, 1965; stepchildren: Paul Gottlieb, Alan Gottlieb. BS, Ga. Inst. Tech., 1945; AB magna cum laude, Bethany Coll., 1947, LLD, 1969; diploma, Oxford (Eng.) U., 1947; MS in Journalism, Columbia U., 1948; MBA, NYU, 1959; postgrad., Pace U., 1973—. Reporter, then city editor Greensboro (N.C.) Daily News, 1948-52; S.W. bur. chief Bus. Week mag., Houston, 1952-54; asso. mng. editor Bus. Week mag., N.Y.C., 1954-60; dir. pub. affairs and communications McGraw-Hill, Inc., 1960-63, v.p., 1963-68; sr. v.p. pub. rels. and investor rels., exec. com. N.Y. Stock Exch., N.Y.C., 1968-73; sr. v.p. CNA Fin. Corp., Chgo., 1973-75; chmn. Eugene Miller & Assos., Glencoe, Ill., 1975-77; v.p. USG Corp., 1977-82, sr. v.p., 1982-85, mem. mgmt. com., 1982—, exec. v.p., chief fin. officer, 1985-87, elected vice chmn., chief fin. officer, 1987—, mem. exec. com., also bd. dirs.; adj. prof. mgmt. Grad. Sch. Bus. Adminstrn., NYU, 1963-75; prof. bus. adminstrn. Fordham U., N.Y.C., Fordham U. Grad. Sch. Bus. Adminstrn., 1969-75; chmn., prof. fin. Northeastern Ill. U., 1975—; lectr. econs., pub rels. to bus. and sch. groups; bd. dirs. P.O.B. Pub. Co., Wayne, Mich., USG Corp., Chgo., U.S. Gypsum Co., Chgo., USG, Chgo., L&W Supply Co., Chgo., Exch. Nat. Bank, Chgo., Rodman & Renshaw, Inc., Coleman Cable Co., North Chicago, Ill., Merc. Systems, Inc., Chgo.; cons. to Sec. Commerce, 1961—; adv. bd. dirs. Nationwide Acceptance Corp., Chgo. Author syndicated bus. column, 1964—; author: Your Future in Securities, 1974, Barron's Guide to Graduate Business Schools, 1977, 6th edit., 1988; Contbg. editor: Pub. Rels. Handbook, 1971, Boardroom Reports, 1985—. Trustee Bethany Coll.; pres. USG Found., 1979—; mem. alumni bd. Columbia U. Sch. Journalism. Comdr. USNR, World War II. Recipient Outstanding Achievement award Bethany Coll., 1963, 50th Anniversary award Sch. Journalism Columbia U., 1963, Honors award Sch. Journalism Ohio U. , 1964, Disting. Svc. award in invesment edn., 1980, Roalman award Nat. Investor Realtors Inst., 1987. Mem. Am. Econs. Assn., Am. Fin. Assn., Nat. Assn. Bus. Economists, Soc. Am. Bus. Writers (founder), Pub. Rels. Soc. Am., Assn. Corp. Growth, Fin. Execs. Inst., Arthur Page Soc., Newcomen Soc., Sigma Delta Chi, Alpha Sigma Phi. Clubs: River, Mid-Am. (Chgo.); Green Acres Country (Northbrook, Ill.); NYU; Clubs of Inverrary (Ft. Lauderale, Fla.); St. Andrew's Country (Boca Raton, Fla.); Metropolitan (Chgo.). Home: 376 Sunrise Circle Glencoe IL 60022 Office: USG Corp 101 S Wacker Dr Chicago IL 60606 also: 3280 Spanish Moss Terr Lauder Hill FL 33313

MILLER, EUGENE ALBERT, banker. married. B.B.A., Detroit Inst. Tech., 1964; grad., Sch. Bank Adminstrn., Wis., 1968. With Comerica Bank-Detroit (formerly The Detroit Bank, then Detroit Bank & Trust Co.), 1955—, v.p., 1970-71, controller, 1971-74, sr. v.p., 1974-78, exec. v.p., 1978-81, pres., 1981-89, chief exec. officer, 1989—; with parent co. Comerica Inc. (formerly DETROITBANK Corp.), 1973—, treas., 1973-80, pres., 1981—, chief exec. officer, 1989—, also bd. dirs. Office: Comerica Inc 211 W Fort St Detroit MI 48275

MILLER, HAROLD EDWARD, manufacturing conglomerate executive; b. St. Louis, Nov. 23, 1926; s. George Edward and Georgenia Elizabeth (Franklin) M.; m. Lilian Ruth Gantner, Dec. 23, 1949; children—Ellen Susan, Jeffrey Arthur. B.S.B.A., Washington U., St. Louis, 1949. Vice pres. Fulton Iron Works Co., St. Louis, 1968-71; pres. Fulton Iron Works Co., 1971-79, chmn. bd., 1979—; v.p. Katy Industries Inc., Elgin, Ill., 1976-77; exec. v.p. Katy Industries Inc., 1978—, also dir.; dir. W.J. Smith Wood Preserving Co., Mark Andy Inc. Served with U.S. Army, 1945-46. Mem. Sugar Equipment and Service Exporters Assn., Internat. Machine Tool Builders Assn., Cutting Tool Mfrs. Assn. Presbyterian. Clubs: Barrington Tennis, Inverness Golf. Office: Katy Industries Inc 853 Dundee Ave Elgin IL 60120

MILLER, HAROLD T., publishing company executive; b. New Paltz, N.Y., Jan. 5, 1923; s. Harold F. and Grace (Taylor) M.; m. Marcheta Novak, 1947; 1 son, Harold F. B.S., Franklin and Marshall Coll., 1947; M.Ed., Columbia U., 1948. Tchr. high sch. Plainfield, N.J., 1948-50; with Houghton Mifflin Co., 1950—, text book salesman, 1950-57, editor-in-chief test dept., 1957-62, asst. mgr. Midwestern regional office, 1962-65, mgr. Midwestern regional office, 1965-71, v.p. ednl. div., 1971-73, pres., chief exec. officer, 1973-79, pres., chief exec. officer, chmn., 1979—, also bd. dirs.; bd. dirs. Bank of New Eng. Corp., Bank of New Eng., N.A.; trustee Eastern Gas and Fuel Assocs. Active Babson Coll., Simmons Coll.; mem. bd. visitors Ind. U. Sch. Edn., Northeastern U. Coll. Bus. Adminstrn.; trustees' vis. com. Suffolk U. Sch. Mgmt. Mem. Assn. Am. Publishers (dir., chmn. bd. 1977-78), Assoc. Industries Mass. (bd. dirs.), The Conf. Bd. (sr., bd. trustees), Conf. Bd. Can. (bd. dirs.), Am. Antiquarian Soc. (council), Kappa Sigma. Clubs: Union, Algonquin, St. Botolph, Comml. (all Boston).. Office: Houghton Mifflin Co 1 Beacon St Boston MA 02108

MILLER, HARVEY, publishing company executive; b. N.Y.C., Jan. 26, 1942; s. Murry and Minnie (Lieb) M.; m. Elizabeth Eleanor Murphy, Jan. 7, 1967; children Erin Elizabeth, Alyson Dawn, Rachel Maria. BS, Fordham U., 1969, MBA, 1973. CPA, N.Y. Chief acct. Random House, Inc., N.Y.C., 1967-68; sr. acct. Price Waterhouse & Co., N.Y.C., 1968-72; chief fin. officer Parade Publs., Inc., N.Y.C., 1972-75; corp. contr. Warnaco, Inc., Bridgeport, Conn., 1975-79, Salant, Inc., Bridgeport, 1979-80; v.p. fin. and adminstrn. Murjani Internat., 1980-81; v.p. fin. ops. Macmillan Inc., N.Y.C., 1981—. Served with AUS, 1964-66. Mem. AICPA, N.Y. State Soc. CPA's, Nat. Assn. Accts., Inst. Internat. Auditors, Am. Mgmt. Assn. Office: Macmillan Inc 866 3rd Ave New York NY 10022

MILLER, HARVEY STOKES SHIPLEY, medical company executive; b. Phila., Sept. 28, 1948; s. Frank Leroy and Betty Charlotte (Elfont) M. B.A., Swarthmore Coll., 1970; J.D., Harvard U., 1973. Bar: N.Y. 1973. Assoc., Debevoise & Plimpton, N.Y.C., 1973-75; curator and dir. dept. collections and spl. exhbns. Franklin Inst., Phila., 1975-81; v.p. Energy Solutions, Inc., N.Y.C., 1982-84; pres., chief exec. officer, dir. Daltex Med. Scis., Inc., N.Y.C., 1983-86; chief operating officer, vice chmn., 1986—. Author: Milton Avery: Drawings and Paintings, 1976; It's About Time, 1979; author, editor New Spaces: Exploring the Aesthetic Dimensions of Holography, 1979. Mem. vis. com. on photography George Eastman House, Rochester, N.Y., 1976-78; v.p. Milton and Sally Avery Arts Found., N.Y.C., 1983—; assoc. trustee U. Pa., 1981—; trustee Phila. Mus. Art, 1985—; bd. govs. Print Club, Phila., 1976-87; bd. overseers U. Pa. Sch. Nursing, 1981—, Edith C. Blum Art Inst. Bard Coll., 1984-87; bd. dirs., mem. corp. MacDowell Colony, N.Y.C., 1982-85; exec. bd. dirs. Fabric Workshop, Phila., 1976-86; mem. prints and drawings and photographs trustees adv. com. Phila. Mus. Art, 1974—, trustee, 1985—; bd. assocs. Swarthmore Coll. Libraries, Phila., 1978-86 ; treas. Arcadia Found., Norristown, Pa., 1981—; chmn. adv. bd. Inst. Contemporary Art U. Pa., 1982-84; trustee Phila. Coll. Art, 1979-86, Pa. Acad. Fine Arts, 1982—; trustee, vice chmn. Coms. on Instrn.; trustee N.Y. Studio Sch., 1974-80; mem. exec. bd. Citizens for Arts in Pa., 1980, Friends of Moore Coll., 1981-83; bd. dirs. Once Gallery, Inc., 1974-75; chmn. collections and exhibitions commn. Pa. Acad. Fine Arts, 1985-88; mem. Mayor's Cultural Adv. Council, Phila., 1987—. Recipient Noble award Swarthmore Coll., 1968. Mem. ABA, N.Y.C. Bar assn., Athenaeum, Library Co. Phila., Am. Philos. Soc., Hist. Soc. Pa., Phi Sigma Kappa. Republican. Clubs: Harvard, Union League, Rittenhouse (assoc.), Peale. Home: Moorhope Mathers Ln Fort Washington PA 19034 Office: Daltex Medi-Scis Inc 414 Eagle Rock Ave West Orange NJ 07052

MILLER, HERBERT DELL, petroleum engineer; b. Oklahoma City, Sept. 29, 1919; s. Merrill Dell and Susan (Green) M.; B.S. in Petroleum Engring., Okla. U., 1941; m. Rosalind Rebecca Moore, Nov. 23, 1947; children—Rebecca Miller Friedman, Robert Rexford. Field engr. Amerada Petroleum Corp., Houston, 1948-49, Hobbs, N.Mex., 1947-48, dist. engr., Longview, Tex., 1949-57, sr. engr., Tulsa, 1957-62; petroleum engr. Moore & Miller Oil Co., Oklahoma City, 1962-78; owner Herbert D. Miller Co., Oklahoma City, 1978—. Served to maj., F.A., AUS, 1941-47; ETO. Decorated Bronze Star with oak leaf cluster, Purple Heart (U.S.); Croix de Guerre (France). Registered profl. engr., Okla., Tex. Mem. AIME, Petroleum Club. Republican. Episcopalian (pres. Men's Club 1973). Clubs: Oklahoma City Golf, Country. Home: 6708 NW Grand Blvd Oklahoma City OK 73116 Office: 1236 First National Ctr W 120 N Robinson Oklahoma City OK 73102

MILLER, HUGH EDWARD, business executive; b. Franklin, Pa., July 4, 1935; s. Edward L. and Martha (Carr) M.; m. Angela Jones, Mar. 25, 1958; children—Susan D., Michael H., Brian E., Kathryn M. B.A., B.S., Rice U., 1958; postgrad., Internat. Bus. Sch., Harvard U., Vevey, Switzerland, 1974. Salesman Jefferson Chem. Co., Houston, 1957-69; with Atlas Chem. Industry NV, Everberg, Belgium, 1969-79; v.p., gen. mgr. splty. chems. ICI Ams. Inc., Wilmington, Del., 1979-80; pres. Stuart Pharmacy subs. ICI Ams. Inc., Wilmington, 1980-85; sr. v.p. ICI Ams. Inc., Wilmington, 1985—, prin. exec. officer advanced materials and electronics, 1985—; dir. Wilmington Trust Co., Diamond State Telephone Co., Wilmington. Bd. dirs. United Way Del., Wilmington, 1980-85, Med. Ctr. Del., Wilmington, 1981—. Mem. Pharm. Mfrs. Assn. (bd. dirs. 1982-86), Sigma Xi. Republican. Episcopalian. Clubs: Kennett Square Country (bd. dirs. 1983-85) (Pa.); Greenville Country (Wilmington). Office: ICI Ams Inc Concord Pike & New Murphy Wilmington DE 19897

MILLER, JAMES CHRISTOPHER, paper industry information systems specialist; b. Augsburg, Germany, Oct. 20, 1951; came to U.S., 1955, naturalized, 1969; s. William Edwin and Martha (Isele) M.; B.S. in Acctg., Pa. State U., 1973; M.S. in Computer Sci., Rensselaer Poly. Inst., 1975; M.B.A., U. New Haven, 1980; m. Lynette Marie Murri, Aug. 25, 1973; children—Meghan Leigh, Margo Elizabeth. Fin. and EDP auditor United Techs. Corp., Hartford, Conn., 1973-74, fin. systems analyst, 1974-76, asst. mgr. corp. acctg., 1976-77; sr. analyst The Upjohn Co., North Haven, Conn., 1977-79; cons. bus. systems Am. Can Co., Greenwich, Conn., 1980-81, mgr. systems planning, 1981-82, assoc. dir. systems support, 1982; mgr. mgmt. info. systems James River Corp., Richmond, Va., 1983, dir. mgmt. info. systems, 1984-86, v.p. mgmt. info. systems, 1986—; instr. info. systems Conn. Tech. Colls., Waterbury and Thames Valley; instr. bus. adminstrn. Western Conn. State U., Ancell Sch. Bus. Mem. Paper Industry Mgmt. Assn., Grocery Mfrs. Am., Nat. Rifle Assn. Republican. Roman Catholic. Home: 2232 Planters Row Dr Midlothian VA 23113 Office: James River Corp Richmond Plaza 5th floor 110 S 7th St Richmond VA 23219

MILLER, JAMES CLIFFORD, III, economist; b. Atlanta, June 25, 1942; s. James Clifford and Annie (Moseley) M.; m. Demaris Humphries, Dec. 22, 1961; children: Katrina Demaris, John Felix, Sabrina Louise. B.B.A., U. Ga., 1964; Ph.D. in Econs., U. Va., 1969. Asst. prof. Ga. State U., Atlanta, 1968-69; economist U.S. Dept. Transp., Washington, 1969-72; assoc. prof. econs. Tex. A&M U., College Station, 1972-74; economist U.S. Coun. Econ. Advs., Washington, 1974-75; asst. dir. U.S. Council Wage and Price Stability, Washington, 1975-77; resident scholar Am. Enterprise Inst., 1977-81; adminstr. Office Info. and Regulatory Affairs, Office Mgmt. and Budget and exec. dir. Presdl. Task Force on Regulatory Relief, Washington, 1981; chmn. FTC, Washington, 1981-85; dir. Office Mgmt. and Budget, Washington, 1985-88; Disting. fellow, chmn. Citizens for a Sound Economy, 1988—; pres., chmn. bd. Econ. Impact Analysts, Inc., 1978-81. Author: Why the Draft?: The Case for a Volunteer Army, 1968, Economic Regulation of Domestic Air Transport: Theory and Policy, 1974, Perspectives on Federal Transportation Policy, 1975, Benefit-Cost Analyses of Social Regulation: Case Studies from the Council on Wage and Price Stability, 1979, Reforming Regulation, 1980, The Economist as Reformer, 1989. Thomas Jefferson fellow, 1965-66, DuPont fellow, 1966-67, Ford Found. fellow, 1967-68, fellow Found. and Ctr. for Study of Pub. Choice George Mason U., 1988—. Mem. Am. Econ. Assn., Public Choice Soc., So. Econ. Assn. (exec. com. 1980-81), Adminstrv. Conf. U.S. (vice chmn. 1987-88). Republican. Presbyterian. Office: Citizens for a Sound Economy 470 L'Enfant Pla SW Washington DC 20024

MILLER, JAMES DAVIS, engineering company executive. s. John Evans and Margaret Ann (Cheney) M.; m. Barbara Nell Fountain, Sept. 8, 1962; children: Kristina Lane, Brant Davis. BBA, U. Tex., 1964, BSChemE, 1965. Registered profl. engr., Tex. Pres. ESI, Inc., Dallas, 1969-70; staff cons. Indsl. Nucleonics, Inc., Columbus, Ohio, 1971-73; v.p. Mgmt. Computer Svcs., Columbus, Ohio, 1973-78; pres. White Rock Engring., Inc., Dallas, 1978—. Inventer apparatus for dampening pump pressure pulsations. Mem. ASME, Nat. Assn. Corrosive Engrs., Sof. Mfg. Engrs. Office: White Rock Engring Inc PO Box 740095 Dallas TX 75374

MILLER, JEANNE MARIE, manufacturing executive; b. Louisville, Ky., Mar. 28, 1956; d. Paul Edwin and Barbara Jean (Newland) M. BSBA, Calif. State U., Fullerton, 1980. CPA, Calif. Staff acct. Arthur Young and Co., Costa Mesa, Calif., 1980-82; controller Gish Biomed., Inc., Santa Ana, Calif., 1982-86, v.p., chief fin. officer, 1986—. Treas. Sunny Mesa Homeowners Assn., Costa Mesa, 1986—. Mem. Orange County Fin. Soc., Assn. Corp. Growth, Indsl. League of Orange County. Club: Tall Club of Orange County (pres., treas. 1982—). Lodge: Zonta. Office: Gish Biomed 2350 Pullman Santa Ana CA 92705

MILLER, JOEL E., accountant, finance company executive; b. Boston, Mar. 3, 1941; s. Morris I. and Florence (Engleman) M.; m. Irene Mazur, Apr. 12, 1964; children: Jason, Michael, Eric. BA, Rutgers U., 1963, MBA, 1964. CPA, N.Y. Acct. Arthur Andersen & Co., N.Y.C., 1964—, ptnr., 1974-87; chief fin. officer, adminstrv. mng. dir. L.F. Rothschild & Co., Inc., N.Y.C., 1987—. Co-author: (guide) Audit of Brokers and Dealers in Securities. Mem. AICPA (stockbrokerage com. 1983-86, commodities futures com. 1981-82), N.Y. State Soc. CPA's (commodities futures com. 1987)., First Wednesday Group, Securities Industry Assn., Pitts. C. of C. (bd. dirs.). Home: 2 Renee Ct Edison NJ 08820 Office: L F Rothschild & Co Inc 222 Broadway New York NY 10038

MILLER, JOHN ADALBERT, life insurance company executive; b. Wilkes Barre, Pa., June 14, 1927; s. Joseph and Marie (Arenova) M.; m. Margaret Marie Hausler, Aug. 14, 1945; children: Cynthia Joan, Jeffrey Charles, John Joseph, Kristen Marie. A.B., Columbia U., 1948; postgrad., Cornell U. C.L.U., 1954. Asst. adminstrv. personnel mgr. Willys Overland Motors Co., 1948-49; with Aetna Life & Casualty Co., 1948-58; acting gen. agt. Aetna Life & Casualty Co., Seattle, 1957-58; with Life Ins. Agy. Mgmt. Assn., Hartford, Conn., 1958-72; v.p. co. relations Life Ins. Agy. Mgmt. Assn., 1968-72; v.p. sales, then sr. v.p. sales Provident Mut. Life Ins. Co., Phila., 1972-76; pres. Provident Mut. Life Ins. Co., 1976-78, pres., chief exec. officer, 1978-82, chmn., pres., 1982-84, chmn., chief exec. officer, 1984—; bd. dirs. Betz Labs.; bd. dirs., former chmn. bd. Greater Phila. First Corp.; bd. dirs., mem. exec. com. CoreStates Fin. Corp./PNB. Author: What You Should Know About Permanent Life Insurance, 1962, Getting More Out of Life, 1968, others. Elder Bryn Mawr Presbyn. Ch.; bd. dirs. Urban Affairs Ptnrship; former chmn. gen. campaign southeastern Pa. region United Way, 1988—. Served with USMC, 1945-46. Mem. Ins. Fedn. Pa., Inc. (dir., exec. com., chmn. 1981), Greater Phila. C. of C. (bd. dirs. 1977—, exec. com.). Republican. Club: Overbrook Golf. Office: Provident Mut Life Ins Co The Provident Mut Bldg 1600 Market St Philadelphia PA 19101

MILLER, JOHN ANTON, financial and managment consultant; b. Monrovia, Calif., May 18, 1948; s. Anton George and Wilda Joyce (Reed) M.; m. Kathy Little, Dec. 23, 1973; children: Lisa, Michael. BA in Acctg., San Diego State U., 1970. CPA Calif., Tex. Audit mgr. Arthur Andersen & Co., San Diego, 1970-77; chief fin. officer Servco div. Smith Internat., Inc., Gardena, Calif., 1977-79; dir. fin. and ops. planning corp. hdqrs. Smith Internat., Inc., Newport Beach, Calif., 1979-85; v.p. bus. devel. Smith Drilling Systems div. Smith Internat., Houston, 1985—; prin. Miller-Newlin & Co. Bus. Cons., Houston, 1986—. Author mgmt. review and petroleum mgmt. mags. Chmn. accts. sect. United Way, 1976. Mem. Am. Inst. CPA's, Tex. Soc. CPA's, Soc. Petroleum Engrs., Am. Mgmt. Assn., Houston Bankruptcy Forum. Republican. Home: 67 Night Song Ct The Woodlands TX 77381 Office: 12941 I-45 North Ste 606 Houston TX 77060

MILLER, JOHN NELSON, banker; b. Youngstown, Ohio, Sept. 15, 1948; s. W. Frederic and Julia Elizabeth (Lohman) M.; MusB in Cello, Westminster Coll., 1970; MBA in Fin., Wharton Sch. Fin., U. Pa., 1974; m. Lynnette McDonald, May 31, 1974. Asst. br. mgr. Mahoning Nat. Bank, Youngstown, 1970-72; asst. dir. fin. services dept. Mellon Bank N.Am., Pitts., 1974-76; v.p., head cash mgmt. div. Md. Nat. Bank, Balt., 1976-78; v.p., mgr. corp. cash mgmt. div. N.Y. Bank of Am., N.Y.C., 1978-80; dir. cash mgmt., strategic planning, product mgmt. and tng. Bank of Am. S.F., 1980-81; v.p., global account officer for utilities/telecommunications S.E. unit Bank of Am., N.Y.C., 1981-84, team leader, chief fin. officer, corp. payment div. large corp. sales, 1984-87, mgr. credit preparation and analysis unit N.Am. Div., N.Y.C., 1987-88; v.p., eastern region mgr. cash mgmt. div. Wells Fargo Bank N.Y., 1988—; lectr. Wharton Grad. Sch., Am. Mgmt. Assn. cash mgmt. seminars, Bank Adminstrn. Inst., others; speaker Payment Systems Inc., Corp. EFT Seminar, Atlanta; mem. Corp. Payment Task Force, N.Y.C., Corp. EFT Cost-Benefit Task Force. Chmn. ann. giving program Wharton Grad. Sch., 1977-79. Mem. Wharton Grad. Alumni Assn. (pres., local club, rep., nat. dir., mem. exec. com.), Bank Adminstrn. Inst. (mem. subcom. interindustry commn.), Am. Nat. Standards Inst. (sub com. on interindustry optical scan standards), Cash Mgmt. Inst. (dir.), Omicron Delta Kappa. Clubs: Mchts. (Balt.); University (Pitts.); Rotary (N.Y.C.). Office: Wells Fargo Bank 350 Park Ave New York NY 10022

MILLER, JOHN STEWART, III, sociology educator, college administrator; b. Eugene, Oreg., June 21, 1946; s. John Stewart Jr. and F. Sue (Cardwell) M.; m. Linda Mary Bussell, June 19, 1971; children—Michael J., Kevin P. B.A., U. Oreg., 1968, M.A., 1972, Ph.D., 1977. Asst. prof. sociology U. Ark., Little Rock, 1977-81, assoc. prof., 1981-86, chmn. dept., 1981-83, assoc. dean coll. Liberal Arts, 1983-88, assoc. dean acad. affairs Coll. Arts, Humanities and Social Scis., 1988—, prof. 1986— . Author: Sociological Concepts Issues, 1983; editor: State of Black Arkansas, 1987. Served with U.S. Army, 1968-70, Vietnam. Recipient Urban Mission award U. Ark., 1981; NSF grantee, 1980-82; Winthrop Rockefeller Found. grantee, 1984-88. Mem. Am. Sociol. Assn., Soc. for Study Social Problems, S.W. Sociol. Assn., Pacific Sociol. Assn., Ark. Sociol. Assn. (pres. 1984-85). Democrat. Methodist. Lodge: Rotary. Avocations: golf; tennis. Home: 10007 Lemoncrest Little Rock AR 72209 Office: U Ark Coll Arts Humanities and Social Scis 2801 S University Little Rock AR 72204

MILLER, JOHN W., foundation executive; b. Canton, Mo., Aug. 29, 1933; s. Robert Walton and Leona Elizabeth (Bailey) M.; m. Marilyn Jean Peterson, June 26, 1955 (dec. 1982); children: Melanie, Melinda, John II; m. Ruth Kincaid Kitchens, June 4, 1983; stepchildren: Susan, John M., Richard. BS, U.S. Mil. Acad., 1955; postgrad., U.S. Command & Gen. Staff Coll., 1970-71; MPA, U. Mo., Kansas City, 1973. Commd. U.S. Army, 1955-80; inspector gen. U.S. Army, Alaska, Vietnam, 1967-70; advisor German Ministry of Def., Bonn, 1973-76; program dir. Ft. Knox, Ky., 1976-77, multiple program dir., 1977-78, dep. dir. personnel and community activity, 1978-80; exec. dir. Ala. Med. Rev., Inc., Birmingham, 1980-84; chief exec. officer Ala. Quality Assurance Found., Birmingham, 1982—. Contbr. articles to profl. jours. Exec. v.p. Birmingham Civic Opera, 1985-87. Decorated Legion of Merit; recipient Outstanding Scholarship award, U. Mo., 1973. Mem. AMPRA (legis. com. 1985-87), Phi Kappa Phi. Clubs: Green Valley Country, West Point Soc. of Ala. (treas. 1988). Office: 600 Beacon Pkwy W Ste 600 Birmingham AL 35209-3154

MILLER, JON HAMILTON, forest products company executive; b. Des Moines, Jan. 22, 1938; s. Victor George and Virginia Adelaide (Hamilton) M.; m. Sydney Gail Fernald, June 4, 1966; children: Emily, Sara. AB in Econs., Stanford U., 1959, MBA in Mktg. and Fin., 1961. Asst. to pres. Boise (Idaho) Cascade Corp., 1961-62, prodn. service mgr., 1962-65; sr. v.p. bus. products and services and packaging Boise (Idaho) Cascade Corp., Portland, Oreg., 1971-74; exec. v.p. paper and paper products Boise Cascade Corp., Boise, Idaho, 1974-76; exec. v.p. timber/wood products/bldg. materials Boise Cascade Corp., 1976-78, pres. and chief operating officer, 1978—, also dir.; bd. dirs. Northwestern Mut. Life Ins. Co., St. Luke's Regional Med. Ctr., Idaho Power Co. Served with U.S. Army, 1959-60. Recipient Top Mgmt. award Sales & Mktg. Execs. of Boise, 1984; named Idaho Bus Leader of Yr. Alpha Kappa Psi, Idaho State U., 1986. Mem. Greater Boise C. of C. (pres. 1977); Bronco Athletic Assn. (bd. dirs. 1987—). Republican. Methodist. Clubs: Arid (Boise) (bd. dirs. 1987); Multnomah Athletic (Portland). Home: 3330 Mountain View Dr Boise ID 83704 Office: Boise Cascade Corp One Jefferson Sq Boise ID 83728

MILLER, JOSEPH IRWIN, automotive manufacturing company executive; b. Columbus, Ind., May 26, 1909; s. Hugh Thomas and Nettie Irwin (Sweeney) M.; m. Xenia Ruth Simons, Feb. 5, 1943; children: Margaret Irwin, Catherine Gibbs, Elizabeth Ann Garr, Hugh Thomas, II, William Irwin. Grad., Taft Sch., 1927; A.B., Yale U., 1931, M.A. (hon.), 1959, L.H.D. (hon.), 1979; M.A., Oxford (Eng.) U., 1933; LL.D., Bethany Coll., 1956, Tex. Christian U., Ind. U., 1958, Oberlin Coll., Princeton, 1962, Hamilton Coll., 1964, Columbia, 1968, Mich. State U., 1968, Dartmouth, 1971, U. Notre Dame, 1972, Ball State U., 1972, Lynchburg Coll., 1985; L.H.D. (hon.), Case Inst. Tech., 1966, U. Dubuque, 1977; Hum.D., Manchester U., 1973, Moravian Coll., 1976. Asso. Cummins Engine Co., Inc., Columbus, Ind., 1934—; v.p., gen. mgr. Cummins Engine Co., Inc., 1934-42, exec. v.p., 1944-47, pres., 1947-51, chmn. bd., 1951-77, chmn. exec. and fin. com., 1977—; pres. Irwin-Union Bank & Trust Co., 1947-54, dir., 1937—, chmn., 1954-75; chmn. exec. com. Irwin Union Corp., 1976—; mem. Commn. Money and Credit, 1958-61, Pres.'s Com. Postal Reorgn., 1968, Pres.'s Com. Urban Housing, 1968; chmn. Pres.'s Com. on Trade Relations with Soviet Union and Eastern European Nations, 1965, Nat. Adv. Commn. on Health Manpower, 1966; vice chmn. UN Commn. on Multinat. Corps., 1974; adv. council U.S. Dept. Commerce, 1976; mem. Study Commn. on U.S. Policy Toward So. Africa, 1979-81. Pres. Nat. Council Chs. of Christ in U.S.A., 1960-63; trustee Nat. Humanities Ctr.; mem. central and exec. coms. World Council Chs., 1961-68; trustee Ford Found., 1961-79, Yale Corp., 1959-77, Urban Inst., 1966-76, Mayo Found., 1977-82; fellow Branford Coll. Served to lt. USNR, 1942-44. Recipient Rosenberger award U. Chgo., 1977, 1st MacDowell Colony award, 1981; hon. fellow Balliol Coll., Oxford (Eng.) U.; Benjamin Franklin fellow Royal Soc. Arts. Fellow Am. Acad. Arts and Scis.; mem. Am. Philos. Soc., AIA (hon.), Ind. Acad., Bus. Council, Conf. Bd. (sr.), Phi Beta Kappa, Beta Gamma Sigma. Mem. Christian Ch. (Disciples of Christ) (elder). Clubs: Yale, Century, Links (N.Y.C.); Chicago; Indpls. Athletic, Columbia (Indpls.). Office: 301 Washington St Columbus IN 47201

MILLER, JOSEPH PHILLIP, insurance company executive; b. Tappen, N.D., Nov. 30, 1930; s. Benjamin Thomas and Ethel (Barg) M. BS, Colo. U., 1951. CLU; registered pharmacist. Asst. mgr. Liberty Mut. Ins. Co., Chgo. and Dallas, 1956-61; owner Bridge Studio, Dallas, 1961-63; broker Wittow & Co., Denver, 1964-65; pharmacist Retail & Hosp., Denver, 1965-72; programmer City of Lakewood, Colo., 1973-74; pharmacy mgr. Gibson Drugs, Sterling, Colo., 1974-75; programmer Miller Internat., Denver, 1975-76; asst. to pres. Planned Leasing, Tulsa, 1976-79; field underwriter N.Y. Life Ins. Co., Tulsa, 1980—. Mem. Am. Soc. CLU's, Nat. Assn. Life Underwriters, Million Dollar Round Table, Contract Bridge League (life master). Jewish. Office: NY Life Ins Co 5147 S Harvard Suite 116 Tulsa OK 74135

MILLER, KENNETH MICHAEL, electronics executive; b. Chgo., Nov. 20, 1921; s. Matthew and Tillie (Otto) M.; student Ill. Inst. Tech., 1940-41, UCLA, 1961; m. Dolores June Miller, Jan. 16, 1943 (dec. Dec. 1968); children: Barbara Anne Reed, Nancy Jeanne Hathaway, Kenneth Michael, Roger Allan; m. Sally J. Ballingham, June 20, 1970. Electronics engr. Rauland Corp., Chgo., 1941-48; gen. mgr. Lear, Inc., Santa Monica, Calif., 1948-59; v.p., gen. mgr. Motorola Aviation Electronics, Inc., Culver City, Calif., 1959-60; v.p., gen. mgr. Instrument div. Daystrom, Inc., Los Angeles, 1961; gen. mgr. Metrics div. Singer Co., Bridgeport, Conn. and Los Angeles, 1962-65; v.p., gen. mgr. Lear Jet Corp., 1965-66; pres., dir. Infonics Inc., 1967-68; v.p., gen. mgr. Computer Industries, Inc., 1968-69; dir. ops., tech. products group Am. Standard Corp., McLean, Va., also v.p., gen. mgr. Wilcox Electric div., Kansas City, Mo., 1969-71; pres. Wilcox Electric, Inc. subs. Northrop Corp., Kansas City, 1971-72, v.p., dir. World Wide Wilcox, Inc. subs., McLean, Va., 1971-72; pres., chief exec. officer Penril Corp., Rockville, Md., 1973-86, dir. 1973-86, pres. K-M Miller and Assocs., Rockville, Md., 1986—; dir. Palmer Nat. Bank, Washington, Interference Control Techs., Inc., Gainesville, Va. Mem. regional planning council Community Mental Health Services, Bridgeport, 1964; mem. Bridgeport Capital Fund Com.; trustee Park City Hosp.; vice dir. Montgomery County Arts Council; bd. dirs. U. Bridgeport; mem. Md. State Com. High Tech. Recipient Job Makers award Mfrs. Assn. Bridgeport, 1963. Fellow Radio Club Am. (dir., chmn. grants-in-aid com.); mem. Aircraft Owners and Pilots Assn., Am. Inst. Aeros. and Astronautics, Am. Mgmt. Assn., Armed Forces Communications and Electronics Assn. (life), Electronic Industries Assn., IEEE, Instrument Soc. Am. (life), Nat. Aero. Assn., Soc. Non-Destructive Testing, Soc. Automotive Engrs., Air Force Assn., Am. Radio Relay League (life), Amateur Satellite Corp. (life), Am. Def. Preparedness Assn. (life), Aero. Elec. Soc. (life), Nat. Capital DX Assn. (pres. 1987-88), Assn. Old Crows (life), Mfrs. Assn. Bridgeport (dir.), Bridgeport Engring. Inst., Bridgeport C. of C. (pres, 1964), Quarter Century Wireless Assn. (life), Soc. Wireless Pioneers. Clubs: Rolling Hills Country (Wichita); Algonquin (Bridgeport). Mem. adv. bd. Washington Bus. Jour.; contbr. articles to profl. jours. Home and Office: 16904 George Washington Dr Rockville MD 20853-1128

MILLER, KENNETH WILLIAM, holding company executive; b. Albany, N.Y., Sept. 25, 1947; s. Kenneth Carpenter and Rose May (Chatfield) M.; m. Barbara Ann Tortorici, Aug. 5, 1967; children: Justin Carpenter, Jason Chatfield. BBA, SUNY, Albany, 1970. Exec. v.p., chief operating officer Texgas Corp., Houston, 1981-84; chief exec. officer The Edge Cos., Inc., Houston, 1984—, Edge Mgmt. Group, Inc., Houston, 1984—, Superior Energy Group, Ltd., Houston, 1985—, Gulf Butane Co., Houston, 1985-89, Auto-Quip Leasing Co., Houston, 1986—, MetroGas Corp., Mpls., 1986—, MetroGas Supply Corp., Houston, 1986—, TRICO, Inc., Savannah, Ga., 1986—, Tri-County Gas & Appliances Co., Tifton, Ga., 1986—, Delta Storage and Distbg. Co., Hattiesburg, Miss., 1987—, Edge Fin. Group, Inc., Atlanta, N.Y.C. and Houston, 1987—; mem. adv. commn. N.Y. Cotton Exchange, N.Y.C., 1984—; del. to USSR Am. People Amb. Program. Pres. Hidden Dunes Community Assn., Destin. Fla., 1988—. With USAR, 1968-74. Mem. Nat. LP-Gas Assn. (bd. dirs.), Tex. LP-Gas Assn., Ga. LP-Gas Assn. (1st v.p. 1977), University Club (Jacksonville, Fla.), Westlake Club (Houston), Pine Forest Country Club (Houston), Willow Fork Country Club (Houston). Office: The Edge Cos Inc 16225 Park Ten Pl Ste 380 Houston TX 77084

MILLER, L. MARTIN, accountant, financial planning specialist; b. N.Y.C., Sept. 17, 1939; s. Harvey and Julia (Lewis) M.; m. Judith Sklar, Jan. 21, 1962; children—Philip, Marjorie. B.S., Wharton Sch., U. Pa., 1960. C.P.A.; accredited fin. planning specialist. Jr. acct. Deloitte, Haskins & Sells, N.Y.C., 1960-62, sr. acct., Phila., 1962-64; mng. partner Cogen, Sklar, Levick & Co., Phila., 1964—; treas. Coronet Container Co., Inc., Phila., Val Mar Realty Corp., N.Y.C.; dir. Penn Internat. Trading Co., Phila., 1964—; mng. dir. C.P.A. Tax Forum, 1966-69; underwriting mem. Lloyds of London, 1978—; lectr., discussion leader on fin. and taxation; columnist Montgomery and Bucks County Dental News. Mem. Phila. Rep. com., 1963-67; chmn. Lower Merion Twp. scholarship fund, 1975-78; bd. dirs. Penn Valley Civic Assn., 1973-79; mem. Lower Merion Planning Commn., 1978-82; mem. Gov.'s Tax Study Commn.; pres. Mensa Edn. and Research Found., 1984-86 ; mem. SEC Forum on Small Bus. Capital Formation, 1983; apptd. to Pa. State Bd. Accountancy, 1985-89, vice chmn., 1989. Served with U.S. Army, 1961-62. Recipient Outstanding Achievement award Germantown Civic Assn., 1965. Mem. Pa. Inst. C.P.A.s (edn. com. 1975-78, bd. dirs. 1979-81, by-laws chmn. 1980-83), Nat. Assn. State Bds. Accountancy (edn. com. 1987—, nominating com. 1989—), Am. Inst. C.P.A.s (nat. tax commn. 1979-82, exec. com. self regulation div. for C.P.A. firms, acctg. and rev. services com. 1985-88, ethics div. 1985-88), Little 10 Acctg. Assn. (edn. chmn. 1980-84), Mensa (internat. fin. officer 1970-74), Beta Alpha Psi. Clubs: Masons (past master) Plays and Players (treas. 1978-79). Author: Accountants Guide to S.E.C. Filings, 1968; contbr. articles to profl. jours. Home: 204 Dove Ln Haverford PA 19041 Office: Cogen Sklar & Levick 225 City Line Ave Philadelphia PA 19004

MILLER, LANCE RICHARD, state agency administrator; b. Wyckoff, N.J., Nov. 3, 1954; s. William Richard and Charlotte Ann (Traub) M.; m. Denise Ann Buell, Apr. 12, 1980; children: Kyle Richard, Kevin William. BS in Environ. Sci., Rutgers U., 1976. Environ. engr. N.J. Dept. Environ. Protection, Trenton, 1976-80, supr. environ. engr., 1980-83, superfund coordinator, 1983-85, bur. chief, 1985-87, asst. dir., 1987-88, dep. dir. div. hazardous waste mgmt., 1988—. Contbr. articles to profl. publs. Pres. Mercer County Football League, Trenton, 1985—, Ewing (N.J.) Jr. Football Club, 1986—. Mem. N.J. Cert. Pub. Mgr. Soc. Office: NJ Dept Environ Protection CNO28 5th Fl Trenton NJ 08625

MILLER, LANE FRANKLIN, international trade advisor; b. Sept. 22, 1949. B.A. in S.E. Asian Affairs and Biopsychology, Washington U., St.

Louis, 1972; MA in Internat. Rels. John Hopkins U., 1989; cert. in mergers and acquistitions Exec. Programs J.L. Kellogg Grad. Sch. of Mgmt. Northwestern U., 1987. Cons. internat. affairs, Washington and N.Y.C., 1975-80; exec./mgmt. intern internat. banking group Citibank, N.A., N.Y.C., 1978; mem. spl. com. FCC, Washington, 1975-79; acting pvt. sector coordinator, internat. trade investigator Internat. Trade Administrn., U.S. Dept. of Commerce, 1980-82; v.p. internat. banking and export finance Transnational Legal Services, Inc., Washington, 1982-83; prin. internat. investment and venture capital Transnat. Devel. Consortium, Washington, 1982—, exec. dir. Office of Internat. Bus., Govt. of D.C., 1989—; investigator Am. Soc. Internat. Law, Washington, 1975-76. Chmn. del. Peoples Republic of China, Johns Hopkins U. Sch. Advanced Internat. Studies, 1976, now alumni counsel; former mem. adv. bd. D.C. Gen. Hosp.; mem. Cen. Com. D.C. Rep. Party, 1989; presdl. personnel Office of the Pres.-Elect, 1988-89; mem. rapid response and issues Bush/Quayle Campaign, 1988; co-chmn. fin. com. Rep. Com. Primary, Washington, 1988; sr. advisor, contbg. editor internat. econs. and investment policy, 1987-88; co-chmn. Foreign Affairs Adv. Group, chmn. Internat. Econs. and Investment Working Group, Fund for Am.'s Future, 1985-87; with Office of Bus./Corp. Affairs Reagan-Bush, 1984. Mem. Am. Soc. Internat. Law, Soc. Internat. Devel., United Nations Assn. (mem. Econ. Coun.), Washington Internat. Trade Assn., Edwin O. Reischauer Ctr., Scottish Rite Mason (32'), Albert Pike Consistory, U.S./Japan Study Ctr. Home: 2745 29th St NW Ste 216 Washington DC 20008-5518

MILLER, LARRY LYNZELL, foundation administrator, business consultant; b. Columbia County, Fla., May 4, 1950; s. Earl Hubert Miller and Elizabeth (Jackson) Ferrell; m. Jayne Beth Fraizer. Student, Temple U., 1968-73. Jr. acct. Leaseway Transp. Corp., Signal Delivery Service Div., Phila., 1973-77, mgr. transp., 1977-88; dir. fin. Nat. Temple Non-Profit Corp., Phila., 1980—; bus. cons. Lynzell Assocs., Phila.; v.p. Nat. Temple Comml. Devel. Corp., Phila., 1987. Home: 7817 Clyde Stone Dr Elkins Park PA 19117 Office: Nat Temple Non-Profit Corp 1625 W Master St Philadelphia PA 19121

MILLER, LELAND BISHOP, JR., food processing company executive; b. Bloomington, Ill., June 17, 1931; s. Leland Bishop and Nellie (Jolly) M.; m. Alice P. Elder; children: Susan Elizabeth, James Bishop, Steven Robert. B.S. in Chem. Engring, U. Ill., 1954, M.S. in Chem. Engring, 1955, M.B.A., 1978. Research engr. Exxon Research & Engring., Linden, N.J., 1955-58; research asst. Purdue U., 1958-59; with A. E. Staley Mfg. Co., Decatur, Ill., 1959-85; dir. corp. planning A. E. Staley Mfg. Co., 1971-73, asst. treas., 1973-77, corp. treas., 1977-81, v.p., treas., 1981-85; v.p., treas. Staley Continental Inc., Rolling Meadows, Ill., 1985-88; exec. v.p., chief fin. officer MultiFresh Systems, Inc., Hoffman Estates, Ill., 1989—; pres. Indsl. Devel. Research Council, 1973-74. State v.p. United Cerebral Palsy of Ill., 1971-72; pres. United Cerebral Palsy of Macon County, Ill., 1972-73; bd. dirs. Progress Resource, Inc., Decatur. Served to 1st lt. U.S. Army, 1955-57. Mem. Am. Mgmt. Assn. (fin. council), Fin. Mgmt. Assn., Nat. Assn. of Corp. Treas., Alpha Chi Sigma, Phi Lambda Upsilon, Sigma Chi. Office: MultiFresh Systems Inc 2500 W Higgins Rd Hoffman Estates IL 60195

MILLER, LENORE, labor union official; b. Union City, N.J., Mar. 10, 1932; d. Louis Shapiro and Lillian (Bergen) Shapiro; m. Louis Miller, Dec. 25, 1952; 1 child, Jessica. B.A., Rutgers U., 1952; postgrad., Purdue U., 1952-56, New Sch. Social Research, 1957. Sec., asst. to pres. Panel of Ams.; sec., asst. to pres. Retail, Wholesale & Dept. Store Union, AFL-CIO, CLC, N.Y.C., 1958-78, v.p., 1978-80, sec.-treas., 1980-86, pres., 1986—; exec. bd. AFL-CIO Indsl. Union Dept., Washington, 1980-82, AFL-CIO Food & Beverage Trades Dept., Washington, 1980—, Maritime Trades Dept., 1986; vice-chmn. Nat. Trade Union Council for Human Rights, N.Y.C., 1980—; mem. Nat. BD. Workers Def. League, N.Y.C., 1980—; mem. com. Am. Trade Union Council for Histadrut & Afro-Asian Inst., N.Y.C., 1980—; bd. dirs. Health Security Action Council, 1986; trustee RWDSU Welfare and Pension Plan, 1986; mem. labor adv. com. Empire State Coll., N.Y.C., 1980—; vice-chmn. Am. Labor ORT, N.Y.C., 1980—. Mem. adv. com. AFL-CIO Com. on Polit. Edn., Washington, 1978—; mem. adv. com. Frontlash, 1978—; mem. bd. dirs. A. Philip Randolph Ednl. Fund, 1988—, Cen. Labor Rehab. Council N.Y. Named to Acad. of Women Achievers YWCA, 1987. Mem. AFL-CIO (v.p. 1987—, mem. exec. council). Office: Retail Wholesale & Dept Store Union AFL-CIO CLC 30 E 29th St New York NY 10016

MILLER, LEON CAHILL, archivist, small business owner; b. Pine Bluff, Ark., Oct. 12, 1954; s. Janell Sturgis and Angie Lee (Huggins) M. BA, U. Ark., 1977, MA, 1980. Teaching asst. dept. history U. Ark., Fayetteville, 1979-84, tech. asst. III spl. collections univ. libraries, 1984-86, research asst. spl. collections univ. libraries, 1986—; pres. Miller and Assocs., Fayetteville, 1988—. Contbr. articles to profl. jours. Recipient F. Hampton Roy prize Pulaski County Hist. Soc., 1988, Walter L. Brown award, Ark. Hist. Assn., 1989; Mary D. Hudgins grantee U. Ark., 1978, 86. Mem. Soc. Am. Archivists, Soc. S.W. Archivists, Midwestern Archives Conf., Phi Alpha Theta, Phi Mu Alpha.

MILLER, LYNNE MARIE, environmental company executive; b. N.Y.C., Aug. 4, 1951; d. David Jr. and Evelyn (Gulbransen) M. AB, Wellesley Coll., 1973; MS, Rutgers U., 1976. Analyst Franklin Inst., Phila., 1976-78; dir. hazardous waste div. Clement Assocs., Washington, 1978-81; pres. Risk Sci. Internat., Washington, 1981-86, Environ. Strategies Corp., Vienna, Va., 1986—. Editor: Insurance Claims for Environmental Damages, 1989; mng. editor Environ. Claims Jour.; contbr. chpts. to books. Named Ins. Woman of Yr. Assn. Profl. Ins. Women, 1983. Mem. Am. Cons. Engrs. Coun., AAAS, N.Y. Acad. Sci., Washington Wellesley Club. Office: Environ Strategies Corp 8521 Leesburg Pike Ste 650 Vienna VA 22182

MILLER, M. JOY, finance company executive, financial planner, real estate broker; b. Enid, Okla., Dec. 29, 1934; d. H. Lee and M.E. Madge (Hatfield) M.; m. Richard L.D. Berlemann, July 21, 1957 (div. Nov. 1974); children: Richard Louis, Randolph Lee. BSBA, N.Mex. State U., 1956. Cert. fin. planner; grad. Realtors Inst. Tchr. of bus. and mathematics Alamogordo (N.Mex.), Les Cruces (N. Mex.) and Omaha Pub. Schs., 1956-63; tchr., dir. Evelyn Wood Reading Dynamics Southern N.Mex. Inst., 1967-68; registered rep. Westamerica Fin. Corp., Denver, 1968-76, Am. Growth Fund Sponsors, Inc., Denver, 1976—; life ins. agt. Security Benefit Life, Topeka, 1969—, Transport Life, Ft. Worth, 1969—; pres., broker Fin. Design Corp., Las Cruces, 1977—; official goodwill ambassador of U.S. Treasury, U.S. Savs. Bond Div., Washington, 1968-70. Contbr. article to profl. jours. Recipient Top Sales Person award Investment Trust and Assurance, 1976-77. Mem. Internat. Assn. Registered Fin. Planners, Nat. Assn. of Realtors (city-county liason com. Las Cruces Bd. of Realtors 1988-89), Nat. Assn. Homebuilders (Las Cruces Homebuilders Assn.), Nat. Assn. of Life Underwriters (Southwest N.Mex. Assn.), Dona Ana County Rep. Women's Club, Las Cruces City Panhellenic , Altrusa Club, Delta Zeta Alumnae, Order of Eastern Star (chpt. 20). Republican. Methodist. Office: Fin Design Corp PO Box 577 Las Cruces NM 88004-0577

MILLER, MARIAN ESTELLE, financial relations executive; b. Kingston, Ill., July 1, 1936; d. Richard E. and Evelyn I. (Jones) Nottelmann; m. Duane H. Miller, Nov. 29, 1959; children: Robert H., John H., William J. Sec. Horders, Chgo., 1953-55, mgr., 1955-62; payroll mgr. Boise Cascade (acquired Horders), Chgo., 1962-67, exec. sec., 1967-70; sec., payroll mgr. Boise Cascade (acquired Horders), Itasca, Ill., 1976-78; exec. sec. Safety-Kleen Corp., Elgin, Ill., 1978-80; fin. relations coordinator Safety-Kleen Corp., Elgin, 1980-86, asst. sec., 1988—; treas. Horder Employee Credit Union, Chgo., 1957-67; sec. Safety-Kleen Fed. Credit Union, Elgin, 1980-82. Sec. St. Johns Lutheran Sch. PTL, Forest Park, Ill., 1972-74; pres., v.p., sec., treas. Bellwood (Ill.) Youth Baseball, 1972-83; den leader Cub Scout Troop, Forest Park, 1975-82; troop sec., Forest Park Boy Scout Troop, 1976-79. Mem. Nat. Investor Relations Inst. Republican. Office: Safety-Kleen Corp 777 Big Timber Rd Elgin IL 60123

MILLER, MARY JEANNETTE, office management specialist; b. Washington, Sept. 24, 1912; d. John William and David Evengeline (Hill) Sims; m. Cecil Miller, June 17, 1934 (dec.); children—Sylvenia Delores Doby, Ferdi A., Cecil Jr. Student Howard U., 1929-30, U. Ill., 1940-42, Dept. Agr. Grad. Sch., 1957-59, U. Md., 1975; cert. in Vocat. Photography, Prince George's Community Coll., 1986. Chief mail processing unit Bur. Reclamation, Washington, 1940-57; records supr. AID, Manila, Korea, Mali, Guyana, Dominican Republic, Indonesia, Laos, 1957-71; office engr. Bechtel Assos., Washington, 1976-79; real estate asso; tchr. English as 2d lang. Ministry of Edn., Seoul, Korea, 1960-61, Ministry of Fin., Laos, 1968-70; cons. to Ministry of Fin. Royal Lao Govt., 1971-74; cons. AID missions to Yemen, Sudan, Somalia, 1982; records mgmt. cons. AID, Monrovia, Liberia, 1980-81, Sri Lanka, 1984; docent Mus. African Art Smithsonian Inst., Washington, 1986—. Author handbooks on office mgmt. Mem. Mayor's Internat. Adv. Council. Mem. Soc. Am. Archivists, Am. Mgmt. Assn., Montgomery County Bd. Realtors, Am. Fgn. Service Assn., Nat. Trust Hist. Preservation, Zeta Phi Beta. Roman Catholic. Home and Office: 1008 Avery Pl Largo MD 20772

MILLER, MAXWELL PETER, III, publisher, broadcasting company executive; b. Peru, Ill., Dec. 28, 1960; s. M. Peter Jr. and Mary (Lofland) M.; m. Catherine Elizabeth Eberwine, Aug. 28, 1983. BSB, U. Minn., 1983. V.p. LaSalle (Ill.) County Broadcasting, 1983—; also bd. dirs. LaSalle (Ill.) Broadcast Co.; pub. Daily News Tribune, Inc., LaSalle, 1983—, also bd. dirs.; v.p., bd. dirs. Ill. Agri. News Inc., Ind. Agri. News. Inc., v.p. NIIDCO. V.p. No. Ill. Indsl. Devel. Council. Mem. Am. Mgmt. Assn., Am. Newspaper Pubs. Assn., Nat. Newspaper Assn., Inland Daily Press Assn., So. Printing Prodn. Inc., Ill. Valley Area C. of C. Office: News Tribune 426 Second St La Salle IL 61301

MILLER, MELVIN EUGENE, trust company executive; b. Wolf Lake, Ind., June 10, 1949; s. Ralph Monroe Miller and Violet LaVon (Gordon) Steffen; m. Marie Elizabeth Stark, Dec. 18, 1971; children: Adam John, Elaine Kim. BS, Ind. U., 1971; MBA, Ball State U., 1973. Chartered fin. analyst. Prof. Loras Coll., Dubuque, Iowa, 1973-84; chief trust investment officer Dubuque Bank & Trust, 1984—; fin. cons., Iowa, Ill. & Wis., 1977—. Author numerous articles in field. Mem. Fin. Analysts Fedn. (Chgo. chpt.), Rotary. Democrat. Methodist. Home: 800 Clinton St East Dubuque IL 61025 Office: Dubuque Bank & Trust PO Box 747 Dubuque IA 52004-0747

MILLER, MERRILL ANTHONY, JR., oil executive; b. Burlington, Iowa, July 4, 1950; s. Merrill Anthony Sr. and Florence Mae (Douglas) M.; m. Diana Sue Wagner, June 17, 1972; 1 child, Paul. BS in Engring., U.S. Mil. Acad., 1972; MBA, Harvard U., 1980. Team mgr. Procter & Gamble, Mehoopany, Pa., 1977-78; asst. to pres. Helmerick & Payne, Tulsa, 1980-82; v.p. and gen. mgr. no. div. Helmerick & Payne, Okla. City, 1982—; bd. dirs. Internat. Computer Exchange, Inc., Boulder, Colo. Mem. Internat. Assn. Drilling Contractors (bd. dirs. 1985—, chmn. midcontinent chpt. 1986-87). Roman Catholic. Home: 3304 Lytal Ln Edmond OK 73113 Office: Helmerich & Payne Internat Drilling Co PO Box 95969 Oklahoma City OK 73143

MILLER, MICHAEL DARRELL, financial advisor; b. Seattle, Aug. 19, 1959; s. Darrell Dean and Earlene Margaret (Beeson) M.; m. Mary Jane Little, Jan. 16, 1988. Student, Seattle Cen. Community Coll., 1981-82. Cert. fin. planner. V.p. Fin. Profiles, Inc., 1981-83; rep. Pacific West Securities, Renton, Wash., 1981-85; rep., registered prin. Fin. Network Investment Corp., Bellevue, Wash., 1985—; prin. Capital Planning Ins. Services, Bellevue, 1986—; prin., pres. fin. advisor Capitol Planning Corp., Bellevue, 1983—; pres. Barnabas Inc., Bellevue, 1988, also bd. dirs. Counselor, tchr. Calvary Fellowship, Seattle, 1986—. Mem. Internat. Assn. Fin. Planning (pres. 1987), Inst. Cert. Fin. Planners, Fellowship Christian Fin. Advisors (pres. 1986-87). Republican. Office: Capital Planning Corp 3605 132d Ave SE Ste 403 Bellevue WA 98006

MILLER, MICHAEL DAVID, marketing executive; b. Cornwall, N.Y., Oct. 23, 1952; s. Howard P. and Anna (Entwish) M. BS in Indsl. Engring., Lehigh U., 1975; MBA, Loyola Marymouth U., L.A., 1985. Product mgr. mktg. W.S. Shamban & Co., Newbury Park, Calif., 1988—. Mem. Am. Mktg. Assn., Lehigh U. Alumni Club (sec.-treas. 1986—). Home: 285 Country Club Dr Simi Valley CA 93062 Office: WS Shamban & Co 711 Mitchell Rd Newbury Park CA 91320

MILLER, MICHAEL PAUL, toy company executive; b. N.Y.C., Dec. 20, 1938; s. Samuel and Florence (Gordon) M.; m. Susan Arlene Portnoy, June 13, 1964; children—Andrew Laurence, Scott Leigh. B.B.A., Hofstra U., Hempstead, N.Y., 1969. Sr. v.p. real estate Toys R Us, Inc., Paramus, N.J., 1977—. bd. dirs., pres. YMHA-YWHA N.W., 1985—, pres., 1987—, United Jewish Ctrs. With U.S. Army 1956-61. Mem. Internat. Council Shopping Ctrs., Columbia Soc. Real Estate Appraisers. Republican. Jewish. Lodge: Masons.

MILLER, NEIL S., financial executive; b. N.Y.C., July 30, 1958; s. Irving Israel Maltz and Lenore (Goldstein) Miller; m. Karen Joyce Salomon. BS, SUNY, Buffalo, 1980; MBA, SUNY, Binghamton, 1982. CPA, N.Y. Staff auditor Peat Marwick Mitchell & Co., N.Y.C., 1982-83; ops. auditor Gulf & Western Industries, N.Y.C., 1983-84; spl. projects acct. Mickelberry Corp., N.Y.C., 1984-86; sr. v.p. Ptnrs. & Shevack, Inc., N.Y.C., 1986—. Mem. Am. Inst. CPA's, N.Y. State Soc. CPA's. Home: 71 Longview Dr Waldwick NJ 07463 Office: Ptnrs & Shevack Inc 1350 Ave of the Americas New York NY 10019

MILLER, PAUL ALBERT, diversified holding company executive; b. San Francisco, Oct. 30, 1924; s. Robert W. and Elizabeth (Folger) M.; children: Robert L., Charles B., Christian F., Gordon E., Alejandro C., Juan J. BA, Harvard U., 1946. Staff aide So. Calif. Gas Co., Los Angeles, 1948-52; treas., dir. Pacific Enterprises, San Francisco, 1952-58, v.p., treas., 1958-66, exec. v.p., 1966-68, pres., chief exec. officer, 1968-72, chmn. bd., chief exec. officer, 1972—; bd. dirs. Wells Fargo & Co., Wells Fargo Bank, Newhall Mgmt. Corp.; trustee Mut. Life Ins. Co. N.Y. Bd. dirs. Civic Light Opera Assn., Los Angeles World Affairs Council, United Way, Los Angeles, Calif. Bus. Roundtable ; trustee Am. Enterprise Inst., Washington, U. So. Calif.; dir. French Found. for Alzheimer Rsch. Served with U.S. Army, 1943-46. Mem. Calif. C. of C. (bd. dirs.). Clubs: Pacific Union, Bohemian (San Francisco); Brook, Racquet and Tennis (N.Y.C.); The Regency; Regency Whist. London, Portland; White's. Office: Pacific Enterprises 801 S Grand Ave Los Angeles CA 90017

MILLER, PAUL JAMES, coffee company executive; b. San Mateo, Calif., Aug. 23, 1939; s. Paul and Rita M.; m. Patricia Ann Deruette, Aug. 22, 1964; children—Mike, Britt, Brian. B.S. in Bus. Adminstrn. with honors, San Jose (Calif.) State U., 1962; M.B.A. in Mktg, Santa Clara (Calif.) U., 1964. With Hill Bros. Coffee, Inc., San Francisco, 1964—; advt. mgr., then dir. mktg. Hill Bros. Coffee, Inc., 1971-75, pres., 1975-83, chmn. bd., 1983—, also chief exec. officer, dir. Mem. Am. Mgmt. Assn., Grocery Mfrs. Assn. Am., Better Bus. Bur. San Francisco, Conf. Board, U.S. C. of C., Calif. C. of C. Clubs: World Trade, Olympic. Home: 681 Brewer Dr Hillsborough CA 94010 Office: Hill Bros Coffee Inc 2 Harrison St San Francisco CA 94105

MILLER, PAUL LAWRENCE, JR., beverage company executive; b. Starkville, Miss., May 25, 1942; s. Paul Lawrence Sr. and Alma (Boyd) M.; m. Effie Marie Walker, Nov. 9, 1968; children: Paul III, Stephen, Nicole. SB in Acctg., St. Louis U., 1965; postgrad., Stanford U., 1983; MBA, Washington U., 1985. Sub-contract planner McDonnell-Douglas Corp., St. Louis, 1965; v.p. Miller & Sons, Inc., St. Louis, 1968-85; pres. United Svc. Distbrs., St. Louis, 1978-83, P.L. Miller & Assocs., St. Louis, 1980—, Beverage Concepts, St. Louis, 1987—; exec. v.p. LeConte Cosmetics, Inc., L.A., 1974-77; dir. Landmark Bank, St. Louis. Trustee Cen. Bapt. Ch., St. Louis, 1986—; bd. dirs. St. Louis Coun. Boy Scouts Am., 1984—, Goodwill Industries, St. Louis, 1984—. Recipient Entrepreneurship award Sentinel Newspaper, 1983; named Bus. Person of Yr. U.S. Dept. of Commerce, 1984. Mem. Am. Mgmt. Assn., Am. Mktg. Assn. Office: Am Winery Inc Beverage Concepts 4022 W Pine Saint Louis MO 63108

MILLER, RALPH WILLIAM, JR., lawyer; b. Chgo., Mar. 9, 1931; s. Ralph William and Pearl Mae (Bauer) M.; m. Jean Lois Gromer; children: Darlene Miller Martinez, Ralph William, Dean. BS, Northwestern U., 1952, JD, 1955. Bar: Ill. 1956. With firm Taylor, Miller, Magner, Sprowl & Hutchings, 1946-55; pvt. practice, Elgin, Ill., 1957-58, Elmhurst, Ill., 1980-81, Oak Brook, Ill., 1986—; asst. counsel Jewel Cos., Inc., Melrose Park, Ill., 1958-67, ins. atty., 1967-71, sr. atty., 1971-72, gen. atty., 1972-74, v.p. regulatory rsch. and planning Jewel Food Stores div., 1974-80, also gen. counsel, 1975-80; of counsel Law Offices of Francis M. Discipio, 1988—; mem. Indsl. Commn. State of Ill., Chgo., 1981-86. . Mem. Gov.'s Agreed Bill Process Com. for Workers' Compensation in Ill., 1979-81. With U.S. Army, 1955-57. Mem. ABA, Ill. Bar Assn. (chmn. ins. program com. 1971-73), Chgo. Bar Assn. (chmn. food, drug and consumer product safety com. 1975-76), DuPage County Bar Assn., Am. Judicature Soc., Chgo. Assn. of Commerce and Industry, Ill. Self-Insurers Assn., Ill. Def. Counsel, Def. Rsch. Inst., Nat. Conf. Weights and Measures, Assn. Food and Drug Ofcls., Industry Com. Packaging and Labeling (chmn. 1977-79), Food Mktg. Inst. (chmn. metric com. 1978-80), Am. Nat. Metric Council (chmn. retailers sector, vice-chmn. legal adv. com. 1978-80), Ill. State C. of C. (chmn. workers compensation com. 1973-78). Home: 936 Spring Rd Elmhurst IL 60126-4928 Office: 2021 Midwest Rd Oak Brook IL 60521-1342 also: Law Office of Francis M Discipio 35 E Wacker Dr Chicago IL 60601

MILLER, RANDOLPH LATOURETTE, corporate professional; b. Portland, Oreg., Apr. 4, 1947; s. George Manuel and Lucile Clay (Latourette) M.; m. Janet Kay Warner, Sept. 15, 1974; children: Kelsey Anne, Haley Elizabeth, Clayton Randolph, Gregory Warner. BBA, Boston U., 1969; MS in Econs. and Polit. Sci., Portland State U., 1977. V.p. Milcor, Inc./The Moore Co., Portland, 1972-80, pres., 1980—; bd. dirs. Portland Gen. Corp. Contbr. articles to profl. jours. Chmn. Ambassador Program, Portland, 1982—; pres. Portland Arts Festival, 1983. Mem. Am. Social Health Assn. (bd. dirs., v.p. Oreg. 1976—), Sony Nat. Dist. Council (chmn.), Portland C. of C. (chmn.). Episcopalian. Clubs: University, Portland Racquet, Multnomah Athletic. Office: Milcor Inc PO Box 4564 Portland OR 97208

MILLER, RAYMOND F., banker; b. N.Y.C., Apr. 21, 1941; s. Raymond F. and Ann Catherine (Cassidy) M.; children: Christopher Kurt, Gretchen Ann. B.S. in Fin., Lehigh U., 1963. Nat. div. staff mem. Bankers Trust Co., N.Y.C., 1963-71; gen. mgr. Bankers Trust Co., London, 1972-80; sr. v.p. Bankers Trust Co., N.Y.C., 1973—; head Asia Pacific group, 1980-83; head central group world corp. dept. Pacific group, London, 1983-86, mng. dir. investment banking dept., 1986—. Mem. Far East-Am. Council of Commerce and Industry (dir. 1980-83). Congregationalist. Office: Bankers Trust Co 280 Park Ave New York NY 10017

MILLER, RAYMOND HERBERT, manufacturing executive; b. Chgo., Nov. 6, 1948; s. William H. and Adeline A. (Latko) M.; m. Jeanne Louise Halverson, Sept. 6, 1969 (div. Jan. 1987); children: David, Andrew, Jennifer, Steven, Thomas, Grant; m. Christina Ann Wood, Apr. 18, 1987. BA, North Pk. Coll., Chgo., 1969. Asst. mgr. sales Armstrong-Blum Mfg. Co., Chgo., 1976-84; nat. sales mgr. Kysor Machine Tool, Strongsville, Ohio, 1984-85; mgr. U.S. ops. H. Ruhl Machinery, Toronto, Ont., Can., 1985-86; nat. mktg. mgr. Startrite, Inc., Kalamazoo, 1986, v.p., 1986-87, pres., 1987—. Sgt. U.S. Army, 1970-73. Mem. Woodworking Machinery Importers Assn., Mfr.'s Agts. Nat. Assn., Antique Auto Club Am. (Hershey, Pa.), Horseless Carriage Club (L.A.). Republican. Roman Catholic.

MILLER, RICHARD ARTHUR, utility company executive; b. 1927. B.B.A., Case Western Res. U., 1950; LL.B., Harvard U., 1953. With Cleve. Electric Illuminating Co., 1960—, sr. tax acct., 1960-61, prin. tax cons., 1961-62, controller, 1962-69, v.p. fin., 1969-75, v.p. fin. and gen. counsel, 1975-77, exec. v.p., 1977-83, pres., dir., 1983-86; pres. Centerior Energy Corp., Independence, Ohio, 1986-88, chmn., chief exec. officer, 1988—. Served with U.S. Army, 1945-47. Office: Centerior Energy Corp 6200 Oak Tree Blvd Independence OH 44101 *

MILLER, RICHARD C., safety/fire equipment company executive; b. Salt Lake City, Feb. 9, 1954; s. Gordon J. and Velma (Davidson) M.; m. Jenae Porritt, Sept. 29, 1976; children: Jenny, Aaron Richard, Christina, Daniel James. Student, U. Utah. Indsl. salesman Universal Safety & Fire Equipment Co., Salt Lake City, 1980-83; salesmgr. Zee Med., Salt Lake City, 1983-84; indsl. salesman Henry's Safety Supply Co., Salt Lake City, 1984-85, br. mgr., 1985—. Author, editor: Trainsafe Directory, 1983. Mormon.

MILLER, RICHARD GLEN, financial planning executive; b. Plainfield, N.J., Dec. 28, 1949; s. James John and Agnes Margaret (Bergner) M.; m. Bonnie Joy Kunkle, Mar. 6, 1971 (div. 1980); children: Douglas, Daniel; m. Roxanne Louise Wackenhuth, Oct. 14, 1985; 1 child, Mark. BS in Plastics Engring., N.J. Inst. Tech., 1976; MS in Microbiology, U. S.C., 1983, PhD in Biomed. Engring., 1984. Engr. C.R. Bard, Inc., Murray Hill, N.J., 1968-86; fin. planner First Investors Corp., N.Y.C., 1986-88; chief exec. officer Miller Assocs., Internat., West Orange, N.J., 1988—. Appointee N.J. Gov.'s Childcare Legislation Commn.; v.p. bd. dirs. Mount Olive Child Devel. Ctr., Flanders., N.J., chmn. personnel com.; comm. Morris Sussex council Boy Scouts Am.; mem. Morris County Zoning Legislation Bd., N.J. Childcare Advocacy Taskforce, Morris County Childcare Advocacy Taskforce, Citizen's Adv. Com., Twp. of West Orange, N.J. Mem. Soc. Plastics Engrs., Soc. Mfg. Engrs., Soc. Pharm. Engrs., Am. Soc. Microbiology, Theobold Smith Soc., N.J. Mil. Acad. Officer Grads. Assn., Am. Legion, Res. Officers Assn., VFW, Mil. Order Fgn. Wars of U.S., Vet. Corps of Artillery SNY, Randolph Twp. Rep. Club, Order of Arrow, Ends of Earth. Capt. USAR.

MILLER, RICHARD WESLEY, electronics company executive; b. Buffalo, Nov. 22, 1940; s. John Irwin and Rose Mary (Mirco) M.; m. Sharon Ann Betzler, Jan. 28, 1967; children: Barbara Ann, Thomas Andrew. B.B.A., Case Western Res. U., 1967; M.B.A., Harvard U., 1970. With Nat. City Bank, Cleve., 1961-68, credit officer, 1966-68; with Penn Central Corp., N.Y.C., 1970-82; v.p. fin., then exec. v.p. subs. Penn Central Corp. (Arvida Corp.), Boca Raton, Fla., 1972-79, corp. sr. v.p. fin., chief fin. officer, 1979-82; exec. v.p., chief fin. officer RCA Corp., N.Y.C., 1982-85, exec. v.p. consumer products and entertainment, 1985-86; sr. v.p. consumer electronics bus. Gen. Electric Co., 1986-88; pres., chief exec. officer Thomson Consumer Electronics, 1988; ptnr. Am. Indsl. Ptnrs., 1988—; tchr. Interracial Council Bus. Opportunity, N.Y.C., 1971-72. Pres. Econ. Council Palm Beach County, Fla., 1977-78; trustee Fla. Atlantic U., 1977-79, bd. advisors, 1975-79; mem. Gov. Fla. Com. on Energy, 1976; chmn. Housing Adv. Bd. Boca Raton, 1977-78; bd. dirs. South Fla. Coordinating Council, 1977-79; mem. vis. com. Harvard U., 1981-86. Named Bus. Man of Yr. Palm Beach County, 1978. Mem. Urban Land Inst. (chmn. recreational devel. council 1979), Harvard U. Bus. Sch. Assn. (pres. 1980, exec. council), Electronics Industries Assn. (bd. govs. 1987—). Club: Greenwich Country. Home: 27 Normandy Ln Riverside CT 06878 Office: Am Indsl Ptnrs 200 Park Ave Ste 3122 New York NY 10166

MILLER, ROBERT ANTHONY, county official; b. Louisville, Dec. 5, 1949; s. Edward H. and Margaret C. (Keane) M.; m. Elaine Rae Breitenstein, Apr. 16, 1988. BA, Bellarmine Coll., 1971; JD, U. Louisville, 1977. Bar: Ky. 1977. Asst. editor Triumph Mag., Washington, 1971-74; lectr. Bellarmine Coll., Louisville, 1974-79, asst. prof. polit. sci., 1978-79; mgmt. analyst Jefferson County, Louisville, 1979-80, chief budget officer, 1980-82, chief fin. officer, 1982—; pres. Jefferson County Capital Projects Corp., 1983—; commr. Jefferson County Community Improvement Dist., 1983—; treas. Jefferson County Econ. Devel. Corp., 1986—, Jefferson County Community Econ. Devel. Corp., 1987—. Mem. City-County Charter Commn., 1982-83; bd. govs. U. Louisville Hosp., 1981-83. Mem. ABA, Govt. Fin. Officers Assn., Ky. Bar Assn. Democrat. Roman Catholic. Office: Jefferson County Ct 517 Court Pl Louisville KY 40202

MILLER, ROBERT CARL, real estate developer; b. Schenectady, N.Y., June 14, 1943; s. Carl B. and Mary Grace (Messitt) M.; m. Marcia Reilly, Aug. 3, 1968; children: Alison, Robert, Jonathan, Timothy, Geoffrey, Emily. BBA, Siena Coll., 1965; JD, Union U., 1968; LLM, NYU, 1974. Bar: N.Y. 1969, U.S. Tax Ct. 1971. Ptnr. Tate, Tate. Miller & Ruthman, Albany, N.Y., 1970-80; pres. Miller, Seeley & Segel, P.C., Albany, 1980-85, Windsor Devel. Group, Inc., Albany, 1985—. Bd. dirs. Lake George Opera Co., Glens Falls, N.Y., 1986, Schenectady Mus. Art. Com. Roman Catholic. Home: 8 Cardinal Ct Clifton Park NY 12065 Office: Windsor Devel Group Inc 9 Washington Sq Albany NY 12205

MILLER, ROBERT DAVID, insurance company executive, consultant; b. Oak Park, Ill., Jan. 9, 1932; s. David R. and Louise (Reed) M.; BS, Okla.

State U., 1956; MBA, Ill. State U., 1970; m. Sharon Anderson, July 6, 1968; 1 son, Jay-James. Acctg. clk. Country Mut. Ins. Co., Bloomington, Ill., 1956-57, sr. acct., 1957-61, chief acct., 1961-68; controller Country Mut., Country Casualty, Mid-Am., Preferred ins. cos., Bloomington, 1968-79, dir. ops., 1979-83 ; v.p., dir. field ops., bd. dirs. Kramer Capital Cons., Inc., N.Y.C., 1983-89; chief fin. officer Kramer Capital Holding Co.; pres., dir. Nat. Am. Ins. Co. Calif., Long Beach, 1985-88; mgr. ins. cons. Coopers & Lybrand, Chgo., 1989—; sec.-treas., dir. Westminster Village, Bloomington, dir. Ill. Ins. Guaranty Fund.; dir. Great Atlantic Ins. Co.; lectr. in field. Active United Way, 1977-83; sec. bd. trustees 2d. Presbyn. Ch., Bloomington, 1978-81, elder, 1982—. Served with USNR, 1952-54. Recipient Alumni Achievement award Ill. State U., 1980. Mem. McLean County (Ill.) Assn. Commerce and Industry (chmn. tax com. 1977-82), Ins. Acctg. and Systems Assn. (pres. 1979-80, chmn. property/liability ins. acctg. textbook), Fin. Execs. Inst., Nat. Assn. Accts., Nat. Assn. Ind. Insurers (chmn. tax com. 1975-82), Mut. Ins. Com. Fed. Taxation (treas. 1973—), Data Processing Mgmt. Assn. (pres., internat. dir. 1973-75), Nat. Assn. Mut. Ins. Cos. (tax com. chmn. 1972-76, Presdl. award 1973), Adminstrv. Mgmt. Soc., Soc. Ins. Research, Soc. Ins. Accts. Clubs: Bloomington Country. Lodges: Masons, Shriners, Elks. Contbr. articles to profl. jours.

MILLER, ROBERT LEROY, safety and standards engineer, utilities executive; b. Silvercreek, N.Y., Jan. 30, 1930; s. William Roosevelt and Genevieve (Phleuger) M.; m. Doreen Horn, May 26, 1956; children: Christopher Atwood, Adrianne Joy. Cert. in Law and Engring., USAF Inst., Ft. Benning, Ga., 1950. Registered profl. engr., N.Y. Elec. technician Niagara Mohawk Power Corp., Angola, N.Y., 1953—; advisor, vendor Nat. Fuel Gas Corp., Buffalo, 1968-84; advisor U.S. Geol. Obs., Pallisades, N.Y., 1971-72; pres., founder Robert L. Miller Pty., Ltd., Angola, 1984—; instr. (part-time) Lakeshore Cen. High Sch., Angola, 1965-66. Author, editor (brochures) Evans Brant Community, 1981 (Plaque 1982), Evans Guide, 1984 (Plaque 1985); inventor pole erector machine. Chmn. Boy Scouts Am., Angola, 1973-77. With USN, 1948-49; cpl. U.S. Army, 1949-53. Mem. Evans Brant C. of C. (pres. 1980), Evans Jaycees. Roman Catholic. Home and Office: 56 Terrylynn Dr Angola NY 14006

MILLER, ROBERT LYNN, accountant; b. Princeton, Ind., Aug. 29, 1948; s. Cecil L. and Mary Ruth (Willis) M.; m. Mary E. Whitlock, Mar. 1, 1971; 1 child, Angela M. BA in Acctg., U. S.Fla., 1975. CPA, Fla.; cert. fin. planner. Staff acct. Ellis Banking Corp., Bradenton, Fla., 1976-77; tax mgr. Arnold & Co. CPAs, Bradenton, 1977-83, Touche Ross & Co., Bradenton, 1983-85; tax ptnr. Varnadore, Tyler, Miller & Williams, Bradenton, 1985—; instr. Manatee Community Coll., 1979-83. Treas., exec. bd. dirs. Manatee County Council Arts, 1986-88; mem. membership com. Manatee County Econ. Devel. Council, 1986. Served with U.S. Army, 1968-71, Vietnam. Mem. Am. Inst. CPAs, Fla. Inst. CPAs, Inst. Cert. Fin. Planners, Manatee County Estate Planning Council. Democrat. Baptist. Office: Varnadore Tyler Miller & Williams 2424 Manatee Ave W Bradenton FL 34205

MILLER, ROBERT SLADE, accountant; b. Chgo., Jan. 3, 1949; s. James G. and Dagmar Marie (Anderson) M.; A.A., Chgo. City Coll., 1967; B.S., Roosevelt U., 1969, M.S., 1971; divorced; children—Brian Slade, James Geoffery, Sheila Renee, Melinda Anne; m. Deborah A. Hinten, 1987; 1 child, Ashley Ann. Sr. tax acct. S.D. Leidesdorf & Co., Chgo., 1970-74; dir. tax dept. Alberto-Culver Co. & Subs.'s, Melrose Park, Ill., 1974-75; tax partner Favorite, Perry & Miller, C.P.A.'s, South Holland, Ill., 1975-82; treas., dir. Modern Life and Accident Ins. Co., Am. Family Life Ins. Assn., Chgo., 1981-82; pres. Miller & Assocs., Ltd., Chgo., 1982—; bd. dirs. O'Brien of Can.; chmn. acctg. dept. Northwestern U., 1973—, adj. prof. Sch. Law, 1981—; lectr. Medill Sch. Journalism Profl. Grad. Program in Advt., 1986-87. Bd. dirs. United Way, South Holland, 1978-84. C.P.A., Ill. Mem. Am. Inst. C.P.A.'s, Ill. C.P.A. Soc. (pres. Chgo. S. chpt. 1976-77, dir. 1979-82). Republican. Mormon. Office: 6 N Michigan Ave Ste 900 Chicago IL 60602

MILLER, RUSSELL WILLIAM, auditor; b. Phila., Sept. 27, 1925; s. George Russell and Edith Maville (Crowe) M.; m. Jean S. Baur, Oct. 23, 1954; children: Edith Jean Light, Paige Elizabeth. BA in English, Butler U., 1946; MBA in Acctg., U. Richmond, 1957; postgrad., U. Ala., Tuscaloosa, 1965-68. Auditor Peat, Marwick, Mitchell, Richmond, Va., 1956-57, Ernst & Ernst, Richmond, 1957-59; auditor to v.p. Franklin Fed. Savs. and Loan, Richmond, 1959-65; tchr. U. Ala., Tuscaloosa, 1965-68; asst. prof. Va. Commonwealth U., Richmond, 1968-70; exec. v.p. Jarrell Automated Systems, Doswell, Va., 1970-71; sales mgr. Westhamptom Cemetary, Richmond, 1971-72; bus. mgr. to chief internal auditor Va. Dept. Corrections, Richmond, 1973—; adj. tchr. sch. bus. U. Richmond, 1959-65; cons. in franchising, Richmond, 1968-70. Pres. Richmond Full Gospel Businessmen, 1980-84. Served to 1st lt. U.S. Army, 1948-53, ETO. Mem. Inst. Internal Auditors (bd. govs. cen. Va. chpt., 1985-87), Am. Correctional Assn., Am. Legion, Antique Autoclub Am., Delta Tau Delta. Presbyterian. Home: 1809 Murdoch Rd Richmond VA 23229 Office: Va Dept Corrections PO Box 26963 6900 Atmore Dr Richmond VA 23261

MILLER, SAM SCOTT, lawyer; b. Ft. Worth, July 26, 1938; s. Percy Vernon and Mildred Lois (MacDowell) M.; m. Mary Harrison FitzHugh, May 10, 1969. B.A., Mich. State U., 1960; J.D., Tulane U., 1964; LL.M., Yale U., 1965. Bar: La. 1965, N.Y. 1966, Minn. 1969. Assoc. Simpson Thacher & Bartlett, N.Y.C., 1965-68; sr. counsel Investors Diversified Services, Mpls., 1968-73; ptnr. Ireland Gibson Reams & Miller, Memphis, 1973-74; gen. counsel Paine Webber Group, Inc., N.Y.C., 1974-87, sr. v.p., 1976-87; ptnr. Orrick, Herrington & Sutcliffe, N.Y.C., 1987—; adj. prof. NYU Law Sch., 1986—; vis. lectr. Yale Law Sch., 1980-85, Inst. for Internat. Econs. and Trade, Wuhan, China, 1983, U. Calif., 1986; mem. dean's council Tulane U. Law Sch., 1979—; trustee Omni Mut., Inc., 1988—; ombudsman Kidder Peabody Group, 1988—. Contbr. articles to profl. jours.; editor-in-chief: Tulane Law Rev, 1964-65; bd. editors Securities Regulation Law Jour., 1982—. Bd. dirs. Guthrie Theatre Found., Mpls., 1971-74; bd. dirs. Minn. Opera Co., 1971-74, Yale U. Law Sch. Fund, 1981—; bd. govs. Investment Co. Inst., 1980-87. Mem. Assn. Bar City N.Y. (chmn. broker-dealer regulations subcom. 1982-83), ABA (chmn. subcom. broker-dealer matters 1985—), Internat. Bar Assn., Securities Industry Assn. (chmn. fed. regulation com. 1976-78), Order of Coif, Omicron Delta Kappa. Democrat. Baptist. Clubs: Down Town Assn., Knickerbocker. Office: Orrick Herrington & Sutcliffe 599 Lexington Ave 29th Fl New York NY 10022

MILLER, SAMUEL LEE, real estate executive; b. Maywood, Ill., Apr. 22, 1912; s. Samuel Lee and Clarissa (Buck) M.; PhB, U. Chgo., 1935; m. Sally Ann Walton, June 24, 1939 (dec.); 1 child, Sally Ann Roth; m. Irene A. Reed, 1973. Foreman mfg. Am. Can Co., Maywood, 1933-42; adminstrv. mgr. George S. May Co., San Francisco, 1942-47; gen. sales mgr. Hunt Foods and Industries, Fullerton, Calif., 1947-58; with H.M. Parker and Son, wholesale automobile parts co., 1958-68, v.p., gen. mgr., North Hollywood, Calif., 1962-68, bd. dirs., 1959-68; pres. Am. Parts Systems, Inc., North Hollywood, 1968-69, regional sales promotion mgr., 1970-71, gen. mgr., Fairfield, Calif., 1972-76; pres. Roth & Miller Realty, Inc., 1977-85. Mem. Masons, Theta Delta Chi. Republican. Methodist. Home: 248 Cheyenne Dr Vacaville CA 95688

MILLER, SANDRA J., accountant; b. Lewistown, Pa., Sept. 30, 1954; d. Donald G. and Jean M. (Shawver) M. AA, Harrisburg Area Community Coll., 1977; BS, Elizabethtown Coll., 1979. CPA, Pa. Staff acct. to supr. Boyer and Ritter CPA's, Camp Hill, Pa., 1980-84; sole practice Sandra J. Miller CPA, Mifflintown, Pa., 1984-87; ptnr. Sandra J. Miller and Assocs. CPA's, Mifflintown, 1988—. mgr. fin. Lewistown Hosp. Aux. Horse Show, 1983-86. Mem. Am. Inst. CPA's, Pa. Inst. CPA's (chair sole practitioner's com. 1985-86), EDP Auditors Assn., Nat. Fed. Independent Bus., Juniata Valley Area C. of C. (bd. dirs. 1988—, mem. bd. dirs. property com. 1988), Bus. and Profl. Women of Juniata County (sec. 1986-87, 1st v.p. 1987-88, pres. 1988—, mem. nominating com. dist. 4 1988-89), Harrisburg Area Community Coll. Alumni Assn. (life) (liaison vol. for Elizabethtown Coll. 1985-89). Democrat. Lodge: Soroptimist Internat. (chair youth activites com. 1987-88). Home: Washington Ave Mifflintown PA 17059 Office: Sandra J Miller and Assocs CPAs 4 N Sixth St Mifflintown PA 17059

MILLER, SHARYL KAY, insurance company executive; b. Worthington, Minn., Feb. 27, 1945; d. Harold Joseph and Evelyn Marie (Skyberg) Erickson; children: Dennis Dean, Shari Lee; m. John Miller, Dec. 3, 1988. Grad. high sch., Waseca, Minn. Registered psychiat. tech., Minn.; lic. ins. Psychiat. tech. St. Minn., Fairbault, 1966-67; counselor special schs. St. Minn., Owatonna, 1967-72; office mgr. Pepsi-Cola, Taylorville, Ill., 1975-79; sales assoc. Am. Family Life Assurance Co., Columbus, Ga., 1979-80, mgr. dist., 1980-82, mgr. regional, 1982-85, mgr. St. Ill., 1985—; speaker Women's Expo '87, Ea. Ill. U., 1987. Treas. Sr. Baseball League, Taylorville, 1980-82; pres. PTA, Taylorville, 1981-82. Named Bus. Assoc. of Yr. ABWA, 1986-87. Mem. NAFE, Rsch. Inst. Am. Inc. Personal Report, Nat. Women's Econs. Alliance, Jaycees (Named one of Outstanding Young Women in Am. 1975), Owatonna Club. Republican. Methodist. Office: Am Family Life Assurance Co PO Box 1327 Effingham IL 62401

MILLER, SIDNEY, hospital company executive; b. Newark, July 26, 1926; s. Samuel and Nina (Maidonick) M.; m. Constance Bernice Krauss, Apr. 4, 1954; children: Scott Michael, Nancy Beth. B.B.A., CCNY, 1950. With Laventhol, Krekstein & Co., Phila., 1954-60; with Hoffman, Goldfine & Co., Phila., 1960-63; partner Hoffman, Goldfine & Co., 1962-63, Bershad & Co., Phila., 1963-67, Laventhol Krekstein Horwath & Horwath, Phila., 1967-68; v.p. Am. Medicorp, Inc., Bala Cynwyd, Pa., 1968-78; exec. v.p. Universal Health Svcs., Inc., King of Prussia, Pa., 1978—. Served with USNR, 1944-46. Mem. Fin. Execs. Inst., Am., Pa. Insts. CPA's, Hosp. Fin. Mgmt. Assn. Home: 7 Latham Pkwy Melrose Park PA 19126 Office: Universal Health Svcs Inc 367 S Gulph Rd King of Prussia PA 19406

MILLER, SYDELL LOIS, cosmetics executive, marketing professional; b. Cleve., Aug. 10, 1937; d. Jack Harvey Lubin and Evelyne (Saltzman) Brower; m. Arnold Max Miller, Oct. 19, 1958; children: Lauren Beth, Stacie Lynn. Student, U. Miami, 1955-56. Mgr. Hair Salon, Cleve., 1958-60; pres., owner Women's Retail Store, Cleve., 1960-72; exec. v.p. Ardell, Inc., Solon, Ohio, 1972-84; exec. v.p. and owner Matrix Essentials, Inc., Solon, 1980—; pres. Lauren Stacy Mktg., Inc., Solon, 1972—. Editor ednl. books and newsletter, Salons, 1981—. Mem. Mt. Sinai Hosp. Aux., Cleve., 1972—, Beachwood (Ohio) Mus., 1981—, Cleve. Fashion Group. Mem. Am. Beauty Assns. (bd. dirs. 1988—, named Woman of Yr. 1985), Beauty and Barber Supply Inst., Inc., Cosmetic, Toiletry and Fragrance Assn., Inc. Office: Matrix Essentials Inc 30601 Carter St Solon OH 44139

MILLER, TANFIELD CHARLES, accountant; b. Phila., Jan. 25, 1947; s. Richard and Wylma Jane Miller; m. Helen Adams McClennen, Aug. 14, 1977; children: Sophia Adams McClennen, Peter McClennen Miller. BA in History, N.D. State U., 1967; MBA, U. Pa., 1974. CPA, N.J., Fla. Acct. Price, Waterhouse & Co., CPA's, N.Y.C., 1973-77; sr. ptnr. T.C. Miller & Co., CPA's, Ft. Lauderdale, Fla., 1977—; mng. ptnr. Wequassett Inn, Chatham, Mass., 1977—; treas., founder Gold Coast Savs. Bank; vice chmn. Kornhauser & Calene Advt. Inc., N.Y.C., 1986—; bd. dirs. Suncoast Airlines, Best Read Guides, Inc. Contbg. editor profl. jours., 1976-77. Bd. dirs. N.D. State U. Devel. Found., Fargo, 1969—, Broward County Mental Health Assn., 1979-81; trustee Fla. Oaks Sch., 1980-85, Mus. of Art, Ft. Lauderdale, 1987—. Mem. Am. Inst. CPA's, N.J. Soc. CPA's, Fla. Inst. CPA's. Club: Chatham Yacht. Avocation: sailing. Office: TC Miller & Co 1012 E Broward Blvd Fort Lauderdale FL 33301

MILLER, THOMAS WAINWRIGHT, JR., consulting engineer, state official; b. Clearwater, Fla., Nov. 28, 1927; s. Thomas Wainwright and Grace Ellen (Gilbert) M.; B.C.E., Ga. Inst. Tech., 1952, D in Bus. Adminstrn., Carson-Newman Coll., 1988; m. Mavis Stinson, Dec. 25, 1952; 1 son, Thomas Wainwright III. Regional engr. Fla. State Bd. Health, 1952-56; dir. Lee County Mosquito Control Dist., Ft. Myers, Fla., 1956—; engr.-in-charge Lee County Hyacinth Control Dist., 1961—; pres. T.W. Miller & Assos., Inc., 1962—; dir. First Fed. Savs. & Loan Assn. Ft. Myers. Trustee, pres., chief exec. officer Price Found.; trustee Bapt. Found., Palm Beach Atlantic Coll., Edison Community Coll. Endowment Corp.; bd. dirs. Lee Meml. Hosp.; Served with AUS, 1946-47. Registered profl. engr., Fla., La., Mass. Fellow Fla. Engring. Soc., Met. Ft. Myers C. of C. (pres. 1983, dir.); mem. Bus. Devel. Corp. Southwest Fla., Council on Founds. Clubs: Fort Myers Rod and Gun (pres. 1969, now dir.); Royal Palm Yacht. Lodges: Masons, Shriners, Rotary (pres. 1975). Contbr. articles to profl. jours. Office: Lee County Mosquito Control Dist PO Box 06005 Fort Myers FL 33906

MILLER, THORMUND AUBREY, lawyer; b. Pocatello, Idaho, July 14, 1919; s. Roy Edmund and Lillian (Thordarson) M.; m. Hannah A. Flansburgh, Feb. 10, 1946; children: Karen Lynette, Christine Alison. BA, Reed Coll., 1941; LLB, Columbia U., 1948; grad., Advanced Mgmt. Program, Harvard Bus. Sch., 1961. Bar: Calif. 1949, D.C. 1951, U.S. Supreme Ct. 1960. Asso. McCutchen, Thomas, Matthews, Griffiths & Greene, San Francisco, 1948-50; atty. So. Pacific Transp. Co., Washington, 1950-56; asst. gen. atty. So. Pacific Transp. Co., 1956-59, gen. atty., 1959-66; sr. gen. atty. So. Pacific Transp. Co., San Francisco, 1966-75, gen. solicitor, 1975-79, gen. commerce counsel, 1979-83, v.p., gen. counsel, 1983-89; gen. counsel So. Pacific Communications Co., San Francisco, 1970-79; pvt. practice law Atherton, Calif., 1989—; bd. dirs. SP Telecom. Pres. Wood Acres Citizens Assn., Bethesda, Md., 1955-56; mem. exec. com. Holbrook Palmer Recreation Park Found., 1979—, pres., 1982-84; mem. alumni bd. Reed Coll., 1971-72, trustee 1987—. Served with USNR, 1942-46. Mem. ABA, Calif. Bar Assn., Transp. Rsch. Forum, Assn. Transp. Practitioners, World Trade Club. Presbyterian.

MILLER, WALTER RICHARD, JR., banker; b. N.Y.C., Nov. 20, 1934; s. Walter Richard and Ann M. (Phelan) M.; m. Joan M. Groark; children: Kathryn A., Margaret E., Jennifer M., Walter Richard III. AB, Dartmouth Coll., 1955; MBA, Columbia U., 1957; PhD, NYU, 1965. Dir. mktg., v.p. Mellon Nat. Corp., Pitts., 1965-78; sr. v.p. First Atlanta Corp., 1979-81; exec. v.p. Norwest Corp., Mpls., 1981-86; pres., chief exec. officer First Constn. Fin. Corp., New Haven, 1986-87, 1987—, also bd. dirs.; pres., chief exec. officer First Constn. Bank, New Haven, also bd. dirs.; pres. CIRRUS System Inc. Contbr. articles, chpts. to profl. pubs. Bd. dirs. St. Paul Chamber Orch., Minn. Pub. Radio, Sci. Mus. Minn., Quinnipiac Coll., Hamden, Conn., Quinnipiac council Boy Scouts Am., The Mus. of Am. Theatre; pres. Orchestra New England. With USAF, 1958. Teaching fellow NYU, N.Y.C., 1960; Ford Found. fellow NYU, 1962. Mem. Interbank Card Assn. (internat. chmn.), Am. Mktg. Assn. (contbg. editor), Bank Mktg. Assn. (bd. dirs., chmn. mktg. planning council, chmn. mktg. mgmt. council). Clubs: Somerset (St. Paul); New Haven Country, Quinnipiack (New Haven). Home: 2 Marshall Rd Hamden CT 06517 Office: First Constn Fin Corp 80 Elm St New Haven CT 06510

MILLER, WILBUR HOBART, business diversification consultant; b. Boston, Feb. 15, 1915; s. Silas Reuben and Muriel Mae (Greene) M.; B.S., U. N.H., 1936, M.S., 1938; Ph.D. (univ. fellow, 1940-41), Columbia U., 1941; m. Harriett I. Harmon, June 20, 1941; children: Nancy Iber Miller Harray, Warren Harmon, Donna Sewall Miller Davidge. Research chemist Am. Cyanamid Co., Stamford, Conn., 1941-49, Washington tech. rep., 1949-53, dir. food industry devel., 1953-57, tech. dir. products for agr. Cyanamid International, N.Y.C., 1957-60; sr. scientist Dunlap & Assos., Darien, Conn., 1960-63, sr. asso., 1963-66; coordinator new product devel. Celanese Corp., N.Y.C., 1966-67, mgr. comml. research, 1967-68, dir. corp. devel., 1969-84; bus. diversification cons., 1984—; lectr. on bus. and soc. Western Conn. State Coll., 1977-79. Chmn. Stamford Forum for World Affairs, 1954-87, hon. chmn. 1987—; mem. adv. bd. Center for the Study of the Presidency, 1980—; bd. Stamford Symphony, 1974-80, v.p., 1978-80; pres. Council for Continuing Edn., Stamford, 1962, bd., 1960-70; elder United Presbyn. Ch., nominating com., 1960-63; pres. Interfaith Council of Stamford, 1973; internat. fellow U. Bridgeport, 1985—; mem. pres.'s council U. N.H., 1982—. Recipient outstanding achievement award Coll. Tech., U. N.H., 1971, Am. Design award, 1948, Golden Rule Award J.C. Penney & Co., 1986. Fellow AAAS, Am. Inst. Chemists (councillor N.Y. chpt. 1984-85); mem. Am. Chem. Soc. (news service adv. bd., 1948-53), N.Y. Acad. Scis., Société de Chimie Industrielle (v.p. fin. Am. sect. 1980-84, dir. 1984—), Inst. Food Tech., Soc. for Internat. Devel., Am. Acad. Polit. and Social Scis., Sigma Xi. Club: Chemists (treas. 1982-84) (N.Y.C.). Contbr. sci. papers to profl. jours.; patentee in field. Home: 19 Crestview Ave Stamford CT 06907

MILLER, WILLIAM CHARLES, lawyer; b. Jacksonville, Fla., Aug. 6, 1937; s. Charles and Mary Elizabeth (Kiger) M.; m. Hadmut Gisela Larsen, June 10, 1961; children: Monica Lee, Charles Andreas. BA, Washington and Lee U., 1958, LLB, 1961; LLM, N.Y. U., 1963; postgrad., Harvard U., 1978. Bar: Fla. 1961, Calif. 1984, U.S. Supreme Ct. 1968, Ind. 1987. Counsel to electrochem., elastomers and internat. depts. E.I. duPont de Nemours & Co., Wilmington, Del., 1963-66; counsel S. Am. ops. Bristol-Myers Co., N.Y.C., 1967-69; internat. counsel Xerox Corp., Stamford, Conn., 1969-79; assoc. gen. counsel Xerox Corp., Stamford, 1979-80; v.p., gen. counsel, sec. Max Factor & Co., Hollywood, Calif., 1981-85, Boehringer Mannheim Corp., Indpls., 1985—. Bd. dirs. Southwestern Legal Found., 1975-85. Fulbright scholar, 1959-60; Ford Found. fellow, 1961-62; Hague Acad. fellow, 1963; German Govt. grantee, 1962-63; Kappa Sigma scholar, 1959. Mem. Internat. Bar Assn., ABA, Calif. Bar Assn., Fla. Bar Assn., Ind. Bar Assn., Masons, Elks, Phi Beta Kappa, Phi Eta Sigma, Delta Theta Phi. Republican. Mem. Christian Ch. Home: 32 Cool Creek Ct Carmel IN 46032 Office: Boehringer Mannheim Corp 9115 Hague Rd Indianapolis IN 46250

MILLER, WILLIAM DAWES, metals and energy company executive; b. Buffalo, Feb. 14, 1919; s. William S. and Hazel (Sands) M.; m. Celeste M. Fain, Nov. 20, 1943 (dec. 1970); 1 child, Elizabeth F.; m. Anne J. Johnson, Dec. 20, 1972. BS in Mech. Engring., Carnegie Inst. Tech., 1942. Prodn. engr. Wright Aero. Corp., Cin., 1942-44; with AEC, 1944-53, dep. chief Oak Ridge Prodn. div., 1944-49, chief ops. div. Paducah Area, 1949-51, dep. mgr. Paducah Area, 1951-53; v.p., chief engr. Continental Copper & Steel Industries, Inc., N.Y.C., 1953-60; v.p. Consol. Aluminum Corp., Jackson, Tenn., 1960, exec. v.p., 1960-61, pres., chief exec. officer, 1961-69; chmn. bd. AIAG Metals, Inc., Jackson, 1961-69; pres., chief exec. officer Gulf Coast Aluminum Corp., 1967-69, Independence Energy Co., Inc., 1979—, MetVest Inc., 1988—; dir. mfg. planning and devel. Anaconda Co., N.Y.C., 1969-71, v.p., 1971-79; pres. Anaconda Jamaica, 1971-73; v.p. Anaconda Aluminum Co., 1969-73; v.p. Mitsui-Anaconda Corp., 1973-78; bd. dirs. Pioneer Fund, Cooper Life Scis., Inc.; mem. adv. bd. Alexander Proudfoot Co., 1985-88. Clubs: Met. (gov., pres., chief exec. officer 1985—), Doubles, Shinnecock Hills Golf, Meadow Tennis, Southampton (Southampton); Beach, Mayacoo Golf, Old Guard Soc. (Palm Beach, Fla.). Home and Office: 35 E 75th St New York NY 10021

MILLER, WILLIAM FREDERICK, scientist, executive; b. Vincennes, Ind., Nov. 19, 1925; s. William and Elsie M. (Everts) M.; m. Patty J. Smith, June 19, 1949; 1 son, Rodney Wayne. Student, Vincennes U., 1946-47; B.S., Purdue U., 1949, M.S., 1951, Ph.D., 1956; D.Sc., 1972. Mem. staff Argonne Nat. Lab., 1955-64, assoc. physicist, 1956-59, dir. applied math. div., 1959-64; prof. computer sci. Stanford U., Palo Alto, Calif., 1965—; Herbert Hoover prof. pub. and pvt. mgmt. Stanford U., 1979—, assoc. provost for computing, 1968-70, v.p. for research, 1970-71, v.p., provost, 1971-78; mem. Stanford Assocs., 1972—; pres., chief exec. officer SRI Internat., Menlo Park, Calif., 1979—; chmn. bd., chief exec. officer SRI Devel. Co., Menlo Park, David Sarnoff Research Ctr., Inc., Princeton, N.J.; profl. lectr. applied math. U. Chgo., 1962-64; vis. prof. math. Purdue U., 1962-63; vis. scholar Center for Advanced Study in Behavioral Scis., 1976; bd. dirs. Fireman's Fund Ins. Co., Ann. Revs. Inc., Varian Assos. Inc., 1st Interstate Bancorp, 1st Interstate Bank of Calif., Pacific Gas and Electric Co.; mem. computer sci. and engring. bd. Nat. Acad. Sci., 1968-71; mem. Nat. Sci. Bd., 1982-88; mem. corp. com. on computers in edn. Brown U., 1972-79; mem. policy bd. EDUCOM Planning Council on Computing in Edn., 1974-79, chmn., 1974-76; ednl. adv. bd. Guggenheim Meml. Found., 1976-80; com. postdoctoral and doctoral research staff NRC, 1977-80. Assoc. editor: Pattern Recognition Jour, 1968-72, Jour. Computational Physics, 1970-74. Served to 2d lt. F.A. AUS, 1943-46. Fellow IEEE, Am. Acad. Arts and Scis., AAAS; mem. Am. Math. Soc., Am. Phys. Soc., Soc. Indsl. and Applied Math., Assn. Computing Machinery, Nat. Acad. Engring., Sigma Xi. Office: SRI Internat 333 Ravenswood Ave Menlo Park CA 94025

MILLER, WILLIAM ROBERT, pharmaceutical company executive; b. London, 1928; married. B.A., St. Edmund Hall, Oxford (Eng.) U., 1952, M.A., 1955. Various positions including mgr. Central Europe and Africa Pfizer Internat. div. Pfizer Inc., 1952-64; resident mgr. Europe Bristol Labs. Internat. Corp., Bristol-Myers Co., 1964-66; adminstrv. v.p. N.Y. hdqrs. Bristol Labs. Internat. Corp., Bristol-Myers Co., N.Y.C., 1966-67; pres. Bristol Labs. Internat. Corp., Bristol-Myers Co., 1967-68, v.p. internat. div. Europe, Middle East and Africa, 1968-70; exec. v.p. internat. div. Bristol-Myers Co., N.Y.C., 1971-72, corp. v.p. and pres. internat. div., 1972-74, sr. v.p., pres. internat. div., 1974-77, exec. v.p., 1977-85, pres. pharm. and nutritional group, 1981-84, also bd. dirs., vice chmn. bd. dirs., 1985—. Office: Bristol Myers Co 345 Park Ave New York NY 10154

MILLET, BLAINE WILLIAM, management director; b. Salt Lake City, Sept. 9, 1954; s. C. Wayne and Iona Gayle (Jensen) M.; m. Lorrie Adele Slaughter, July 28, 1984; 1 child, Krystal Ashley. BS in Biology cum laude, U. Utah, 1976, MBA in Fin. Mktg., 1979. Ski instr. U. Utah, Salt Lake City, 1973-78; asst. mgr. Millet's Inc., Salt Lake City, 1975-79; bus. mgr. U. Utah Chronicle, Salt Lake City, 1978-79; mktg. rep. IBM Corp., Seattle, 1979-83; mng. dir. Source EDP, Bellevue, Wash., 1983—; pres. Fin. and Personal Cons., Salt Lake City, 1978-79; cons. Millets Inc., 1979-86. Supr. Big Bros. of Am., Salt Lake City, 1978; leader Boys Ranch, Salt Lake City, 1979. Named to Performers Bd., Source Svcs., Mountain View, Calif., 1983, 84, 85, 86, 87. Hundred Percent Club, IBM, Armonk, N.,Y. 1980, 81, 82. Mem. Data Processing Mgmt. Assn., The Million Forum, Hundred Percent Club. Home: 6475 NE 135th Pl Kirkland WA 98034 Office: Source EDP 411 108th Ave NE #1740 Bellevue WA 98004

MILLEY, PATRICIA OWENS, chemical company executive; b. Buffalo, Oct. 25, 1943; d. Thomas J. and Pearl (Stutz) Owens; m. William Milley III, Dec. 31, 1966; children: William, Michael. BS in Chemistry, Daemen Coll., 1965; postgrad., Ohio State U., 1965-66; MBA, SUNY, Buffalo, 1974. Chemist Allied Chem. and Dye, Buffalo, 1966-74; supr. market research Allied Chem. Corp., Morristown, N.J., 1974-77, mgr. fin. planning, 1977-79; product mgr. Allied Corp., Morristown, N.J., 1979-85, mgr. mktg., 1985-87; gen. mgr. Allied Signal Corp., Morristown, N.J., 1987—. Pres. Fairwoods Homeowners Assn., Madison, N.J., 1985-87; advisor to mayor, Citizens Planning for Year 2000, Madison, 1988; analyst, Housing Study Com., Madison, 1986. Mem. Drug Chem. and Allied Trades Assn. Roman Catholic. Home: 8 Ferndale Rd Madison NJ 07940 Office: Allied Signal Corp Columbia Rd Morristown NJ 07960

MILLIAN, KENNETH Y., chemicals company executive; b. Washington, Sept. 29, 1927; s. John Curry and Myrtle (Young) M.; m. Alva Randolph Clarke, Sept. 10, 1949; children: John R., Kenneth Y. Jr., Kathleen M. Gilbert, Elizabeth Walton. BA, U. Md., 1951; MA in Internat. Rels., George Washington U., 1969; Diploma, Nat. War Coll., Washington, 1969; MS in Bus., Columbia U., 1980. Officer U.S. Fgn. Svc., 1951-76; corp. exec. W.R. Grace and Co., N.Y.C., 1976—; corp. v.p., dir. govt. rels. W.R. Grace and Co., Washington, 1982-88; corp. v.p., dir. environmental affairs W.R. Grace and Co., N.Y.C., 1988—; trustee U.S. Council for Internat. Bus., N.Y.C.; mem. exec. com., bd. dirs. Bus.-Govt. Rels., Council, Washington; mem. Nat. Fgn. Trade Council, N.Y.C.; mem. adv. bd. The Parvus Co., Washington; bd. govs. The Found. for the Pres.'s Pvt. Sector Survey on Cost Control, 1986—. Labor columnist Japan Times, 1955-57. Bd. govs. Wesley Sem., Am. U., Washington, 1988. Democrat. Methodist. Office: WR Grace and Co 919 18th St NW Washington DC 20006 also: WR Grace and Co 1114 Ave of the Americas New York NY 10036

MILLIGAN, DAVID KENT, bank executive; b. Vincennes, Ind., Aug. 22, 1955; s. James R. and Jessie S. (Green) M.; m. Sharon A. Frey, Aug. 9, 1975; children: Lori Beth, Melinda Anne. Student, Vincennes U., 1974-75; BS, Ind. U., 1977; cert., Sch. for Bank Adminstrn., Madison, Wis., 1982; postgrad., U. So. Ind., 1987—. Asst. auditor Am. Nat. Bank, Vincennes, 1977-81, chief auditor, 1981-84, adminstrv. asst. to pres., 1984-86, v.p., 1986—; sec. Ambanc Corp., Vincennes, 1983—; dir. banking and fin. adv. com. Vincennes U., 1986—; counselor fin. relationships Krannert Sch. Mgmt., Purdue U., 1984. Dir. Knox County Assn. for Retarded Citizens, Vincennes, 1984—, Children and Family Svcs., Vincennes, 1987—. Named Outstanding Alumni, Vincennes U., 1984; Hoosier scholar State of Ind., 1973. Mem. City of Vincennes Team Tennis Assn. (bd. dirs. 1988—), Elks, Kiwanis. Home: 2804 Old Hwy 41 S Vincennes IN 47591 Office: Am Nat Bank 302 Main St Vincennes IN 47591

MILLIGAN, EDITH, financial services executive; b. Evansville, Ind., Oct. 22, 1958; d. William West and Suzanne (Crimm) M.; m. Paul Alan Delphia, Sept. 1, 1984. BA, Tulane U., 1980. CLU Adminstrv. asst. Bryan Wagner, CLU, New Orleans, 1977-80; sec.-treas. Life Mktg. of La., New Orleans, 1980-81; dist. mgr. Creative Fin. Concepts, Columbus, Ohio, 1981-82; pres. Keeping Track, Inc., Columbus, 1982—. Author: Licensing Study Guide, 1982; Track Records, 1983. Field coordinator Fair and Impartial Redistricting Commn., Columbus, 1981; mem. steering com. Pres. Ford Com., New Orleans, 1976. Mem. Internat. Assn. Fin. Planning, LWV, Mensa. Republican. Office: Keeping Track Inc PO Box 14468 Columbus OH 43214

MILLIGAN, LAWRENCE DRAKE, JR., consumer products executive; b. Lake Forest, Ill., Apr. 6, 1936; s. Lawrence Drake Sr. and Mary Catherine (Cliggit) M.; m. Lucy Shepard, Oct. 20, 1962; children: Michael D., Carolyn S. BA, Williams Coll., 1960. Nat. sales mgr. Bar Soap and Household Cleaning Products div. Procter & Gamble, Cin., 1974-78; gen. mgr. spl. products Procter & Gamble, Cin., 1979-80, gen. mgr. food service and lodging products, 1980-84, v.p. food service and lodging products, 1984, v.p. food products, 1984-87, v.p. sales in Europe, 1987-89, v.p. sales, customer devel. internat., 1989—. Served to sgt. USMC, 1955-58, ETO. Republican. Home: 7475 Old Hickory Ln Cincinnati OH 45243 Office: Procter & Gamble Co One Procter & Gamble Pla Cincinnati OH 45202

MILLIGAN, ROBERT LEE, JR., computer company executive; b. Evanston, Ill., Apr. 4, 1934; s. Robert L. and Alice (Connell) M.; BS, Northwestern U., 1958; m. Susan A. Woodrow, Mar. 23, 1957; children: William, Bonnie, Thomas, Robert III. Account rep. IBM, Chgo., 1957-66; sr. cons. L.B. Knight & Assocs., Chgo., 1966-68; v.p. mktg. Trans Union Systems Corp., Chgo., 1968-73; sr. v.p. sales mktg., sec. Systems Mgmt. Inc., Rosemont, Ill., 1973-87, dir., 1980-87; pres., chief exec. officer, owner Target Data, Inc., Northbrook, Ill., 1987; treas. Systems Mgmt. Inc. Service Corp., 1981-84; dir. Nanofast, Inc., Chgo., 1982—. Div. mgr. N. Suburban YMCA Bldg. Fund, 1967; area chmn. Northfield Twp. Republican Party, 1965-71. Bd. dirs. United Fund, Glenview, Ill., 1967-69, Robert R. McCormick Chgo. Boys Club, 1974—; pres. bd. mgrs. Glenview Amateur Hockey Assn., 1974-79, gen. mgr. Glenbrook South High Sch. Hockey Club, 1973-78. Served with AUS, 1953-55. Mem. Data Processing Mgmt. Assn., Consumer Credit Assn. (dir., sec. 1969-70), Phi Kappa Psi. Presbyterian. Clubs: Northwestern (dir. 1973-75) (Chgo.); Glen View (Ill.). Home: 1450 Lawrence Ln Northbrook IL 60062 Office: Target Data Inc 630 Dundee Rd Ste 125 Northbrook IL 60062

MILLIKEN, KAREN MARIE, foreign service officer, economist; b. Denver, Oct. 19, 1955; d. John Gordon and Marie (Machell) M.; m. Valentino Zardi, June 20, 1982. AB, Mt. Holyoke Coll., 1977; MBA, U. Denver, 1979. Fgn. service office Dept. of State, Milan, Italy, 1979-81, Washington, 1981-83, 85-88, Rome, 1983-85, Mogadishu, Somalia, 1985, Lima, Peru, 1988—. Office: Dept State 2201 C St Washington DC 20526

MILLIKEN, ROGER, textile company executive; b. N.Y.C., Oct. 24, 1915; s. Gerrish and Agnes (Gayley) M.; m. Justine V. R. Hooper, June 5, 1948; children: Justine, Nancy, Roger, David, Weston. Student, Groton Sch., 1929-33; A.B., Yale U., 1937; LL.D. (hon.), Wofford Coll., Rose-Hulman Inst. Tech., Phila. Coll. Textiles and Sci., Brenau Coll., The Citadel; D. Textile Industry (hon.), Clemson U.; D.H.L. (hon.), Converse Coll. Pres. Milliken & Co., N.Y.C., 1947-83, chmn., chief exec. officer, 1983—; bd. dirs. Merc. Stores Co., W.R. Grace & Co.; chmn. bd. Inst. Textile Tech., 1948—; bd. dirs. Am. Textile Mfrs. Inst., S.C. Textile Mfrs. Assn. Chmn. Greenville-Spartanburg Airport Commn.; trustee Wofford Coll., S.C. Found. Ind. Coll. Mem. Bus. Council, Textile Inst. (Eng.) (companion mem.). Clubs: Union League, Links, Augusta Nat. Golf, Yeamans Hall. Office: Milliken & Co Inc PO Box 3167 Spartanburg SC 29304

MILLIMET, STANLEY, armament manufacturing company executive; b. Weehawken, N.J., Mar. 27, 1928; s. Peter and Bertha Lenore Millimet; B.S., Va. Mil. Inst., 1948; M.S. with distinction, Air Force Inst. Tech., 1967; M.S. in Mgmt., Am. Technol. U., 1976; m. Sonia Comora, Sept. 3, 1948; children—Kathi, Beth, Scott. Commd. 2d lt. U.S. Army, 1949, advanced through grades to col., 1971; comdr. tank bn., 1970-71, corps logistician, Vietnam, 1972-73, sr. advisor to Thai army, 1973-74, comptroller research and devel. activity Combined Arms Test Agy., Ft. Hood, Tex., 1975-76, dep. comdr. logistics, Korea, 1976-78, dir. logistics material systems Army Logistics Center, Ft. Lee, Va., 1978-79, ret., 1979; dep. program mgr. Abrams Tank System, Gen. Dynamics Land Systems Div., Warren, Mich., 1979—; prof. mgmt. Am. Technol. U., Killeen, Tex., 1974-76; adj. instr. Macomb Community Coll., 1988—. Pres., Little League Baseball, U.S. Forces Japan, 1964-66; active PTA, 1958-69; mem. Republican Nat. Com., 1980. Decorated Legion of Merit with oak leaf cluster; named Key Logistician, Dept. Army, 1970. Mem. Soc. Logistics Engrs., Am. Def. Preparedness Assn., Assn. U.S. Army, Nat. Mgmt. Assn., Mich. Retired Officers Assn. (pres. 1987—). Jewish. Home: 2667 Pearl Dr Troy MI 48098 Office: Gen Dynamics Land Systems div PO Box 2074 Warren MI 48090

MILLINGTON, CRAIG E., bank executive; b. Flushing, N.Y., June 25, 1942; s. Harry Francis and Audrey (Gardner) M.; m. Joan Loretta Lashier, Dec. 18, 1966; children: Tracey, Harry. BBA, Dowling Coll., 1964. Mgr. maj. accounts Chem. Bank, Jericho, N.Y., 1971-81; asst. v.p., mgr. bank card div. European Am. Bank, Uniondale, N.Y., 1981-84; asst. v.p., mgr. mcht. svcs. Nat. Westminster Bank U.S.A., Melville, N.Y., 1984—. Capt. Melville Vol. Fire Dept., 1977-87; mem. South Huntington (N.Y.) Rep. Club, 1980—. Presbyterian. Home: One Fleetwood Ave Melville NY 11747 Office: Nat Westminster Bank USA 3 Huntington Quadrangle Melville NY 11747

MILLNER, WALLACE B., III, banker; b. Charlotte, N.C., Aug. 1, 1939; s. Wallace B. and Virginia (Reed) M.; m. Nancy Jean Bost, Aug. 25, 1961; children—Wallace Michael, Christopher Bost. A.B., Davidson Coll., N.C., 1961; M.B.A., U. N.C., Chapel Hill, 1962. Asst. v.p., dir. investment research Bank of Va. Co., Richmond, 1971-72, treas., 1973-74, v.p., treas., 1974-76, sr. v.p., treas., 1976-80, chief fin. officer, 1980-85; exec. v.p., chief fin. officer Signet Banking Corp., 1985—. Chmn. bd. dirs. Family and Children's Services, 1984-86. Served to 1st lt. U.S. Army, 1962-64. Decorated Army Commendation medal. Mem. Richmond Soc. Fin. Analysts (pres. 1984-85), Inst. Chartered Fin. Analysts, Fin. Analysts Fedn. (bd. dirs. 1986—). Republican. Presbyterian. Clubs: Westwood Racquet (bd. dirs. 1985—), Country of Va. Home: 111 N Wilton Rd Richmond VA 23226 Office: Signet Banking Corp PO Box 25970 Richmond VA 23260

MILLS, ARMON LEROI, publisher; b. Wichita, Kans., Aug. 4, 1940; s. Armon Mills and Nellie Ann (Holman) Urban; m. Kay Louise Humbert, June 6, 1960 (div. 1973); children: Kathryn K., Marnie A.; m. Sandra Leigh Quist, Sept. 16, 1978; children: Darin L., Trina L. BA in Acctg., Southwestern Coll., Winfield, Kans., 1964. CPA, Kans., Minn., Mo. With Fox & Co., Wichita, 1964-75; ptnr.-in-charge Fox & Co., St. Louis, 1975-77, Kansas City, Mo., 1978-81, Mpls., 1981-84; pres., chief operating officer Am. City Bus. Jours. Inc., Kansas City, 1984-87; owner, pub. The Bus. Jour., Phoenix, 1987—. Mem. fin. com. 1988 Phoenix Citizens Bond Com.; chmn. region II Valley of the Sun United Way; bd. dirs. Phoenix Meml. Hosp. Found., 1987—; Jr. Achievement, 1988—, Salvation Army, 1988—, YMCA, 1988—; bd. trustees Ottawa (Ariz.) U. With USNG, 1957-63. Mem. AICPA, Kans. Soc. CPA's, Minn. Soc. CPA's, Mo. Soc. CPA's, Assn. Area Bus. Publs. (1st v.p., pres. 1988), Decathalon Club, Athletic Club, Olympic Hills Golf Club, Arizona Club. Republican. Lutheran. Office: The Bus Jour 3737 N Seventh St Ste 200 Phoenix AZ 85014

MILLS, BARBARA L., financial firm executive; b. Princeton, N.J., Mar. 20, 1959; d. Bradford and Elizabeth (Leisk) M. BA, Princeton U., 1981; MBA, Columbia U., 1988. Asst. to pres. Bradford Assocs., Princeton, 1982-83, gen. ptnr., 1986—; pres. Bradford Ventures, Princeton, 1984-85; bd. dirs. Cen. Sprinkler Corp., Landsdale, Pa., HWC Distbn. Corp., Houston, OPG Industries, Inc., Toledo. Trustee Mills Found., Princeton, 1980—. Mem. Assn. for Corp. Growth, Sky Club, Princeton Club. Office: Bradford Assocs 22 Chambers St Princeton NJ 08540

MILLS, BRUCE RANDALL, infosystems specialist; b. Warren, Ark., Nov. 2, 1963; s. Fred Adam and Meta Lanette (Calvert) M.; m. Betty Ann Marshall, Mar. 23, 1985; children: Anita, Timothy, Yovonnie. BBA, So. Ark. U., 1985. Programmer Jack Tyler Engrng. Co., Little Rock, Ark., 1986-88, Blue Cross/ Blue Shield, Little Rock, 1988—; auditor Holiday Inns Am., 1985; cons. in field. V.p. Young Reps., 1983. Office: Blue Cross/Blue Shield 6th and Gaines Sts Little Rock AR 72203

MILLS, CAROL MARGARET, trucking company executive; b. Salt Lake City, Aug. 31, 1943; d. Samuel Lawrence and Beth (Neilson) M.; BS magna cum laude, U. Utah, 1965. With W.S. Hatch Co., Woods Cross, Utah, 1965—, corp. sec., 1970—, traffic mgr., 1969—, dir. publicity, 1974—; dir. Hatch Service Corp., Nat. Tank Truck Carriers, Inc., Washington; bd. dirs. Intermountain Tariff Bur. Inc., 1978—, chmn., 1981-82, 1986-87. Fund raiser March of Dimes, Am. Cancer Soc., Am. Heart Assn.; active senatorial campaign, 1976, gubernatorial campaign, 1984, 88, vice chair voting dist., 1988—; witness transp. com. Utah State Legislature, 1984, 85; mem. Pioneer Theater Guild, 1985—; apptd. by gov. to bd. trustee Utah Tech. Fin. Corp. Recipient service awards W. S. Hatch Co., 1971, 80, exec. com., 1988—; gov. apptd. Utah to bd. trustees Utah Tech. Fin. Corp., 1986; mem. Pioneer Theatre Guild, 1985—; capt. Easter Seal Telethon, 1989. Mem. Nat. Tank Truck Carriers, Transp. Club Salt Lake City, Am. Trucking Assn. (public relations council), Utah Motor Transport Assn. (dir. 1982—), Internat. Platform Assn., Beta Gamma Sigma, Phi Kappa Phi, Phi Chi Theta. Home: 77 Edgecombe Dr Salt Lake City UT 84103 Office: W S Hatch Co 643 S 800 W Woods Cross UT 84087

MILLS, EDWARD WARREN, corporation executive, lawyer; b. N.Y.C., Apr. 7, 1941; m. Maria Parascandolo, Sept. 19, 1971; children: Edward Warren, Foy Fitzhugh, Joseph V.O. B.S., Washington and Lee U., 1962; M.B.A., Hofstra U., 1974; J.D., N.Y. Law Sch., 1977. Bar: N.Y. 1978. Acct., Wasserman & Taten, N.Y.C., 1962-69; exec. v.p. L.H. Keller, Inc. and Hugo P. Keller, Inc., N.Y.C., 1969-73; pres. Gen. Ruby & Sapphire Corp., 1973—, Qualistar Corp., 1973—; sole practice, N.Y.C., 1978—. Mem. ABA, N.Y. State Bar Assn., D.C. Bar Assn., N.Y. County Lawyers Assn., Am. Inst. CPAs, N.Y. State Soc. CPAs. Home: 1913 Ingersol Pl New Port Richey FL 34652 Office: 60 E 42d St New York NY 10165

MILLS, ELIZABETH STILZ, communications executive; b. Pitts., July 27, 1925; d. Albert E. Waldfogle and Loretta M. Miller; m. William R. Stilz, 1948 (div. Feb. 1972); children: Fay, Patricia Wingo; m. David E. Mills, May 26, 1979. Grad., Robert Morris Jr. Coll., 1945, Ad Art Studio Sch., Pitts., 1947; postgrad., U. Pitts. Grad. Sch. Bus., 1960-62. Art dir. Bogg's and Buhl Dept. Store, Pitts., 1948-51; publicity and ad dir. Decorator Industries, Pitts., 1956-61; with mktg. and promotion Sta. KDKA-TV, Pitts., 1961-63; dir. promotion Sta. WLWT-TV, Cin., 1963-68; dir. promotion, publicity Cin. Symphony, 1968-73; dir. pub. relations, community svc. Sta. WLWT, Cin., 1973-81; dir. promotion, publicity, advt. Multimedia Program Prodns., Cin., 1981-83; v.p. pub. rels. Multimedia Entertainment, Cin., 1983-85; v.p. corp. communication Multimedia, Inc., Greenville, S.C., 1985—; instr. pub. rels. Xavier U., Cin., 1980. V.p. mktg. United Way Greenville County, 1988-89; bd. drs. Greenville Symphony Assn., Phillis Wheatley Assn.; treas. Goodwill Industries, upper S.C. Recipient Silver medal Am. Advt. Fedn.; named Outstanding Woman in Communications Women in Communications, Inc., 1979, Career Woman of Achievement YWCA. Mem. Pub. Rels. Soc. Am. (pres. Cin. chpt. 1982, outstanding mem. 1980), Commerce Club, City Club (bd. dirs.). Office: Multimedia Inc PO Box 1688 Greenville SC 29602

MILLS, GEORGE MARSHALL, state official, insurance executive; b. Newton, N.J., May 20, 1923; s. J. Marshall and Emma (Scott) M.; m. Dorothy Lovilla Allen, Apr. 21, 1945; children: Dianne (Mrs. Thomas McKay III), Dorothy L.A. (Mrs. Edward Sphatt). BA, Rutgers U., 1943; MA, Columbia U., 1951, profl. cert., 1952. CLU; CPCU; chartered fin. cons. Pres. George M. Mills Inc., North Brunswick, N.J., 1946-75; pres. CORECO, Inc., Newark, 1960-78; risk mgr. N.J. Hwy. Authority, Woodbridge, 1978—; cons. Govs.'s Com. on Bus. Efficiency in Pub. Schs., 1979-80. Bd. dirs. Alpha Chi Rho Ednl. Found.; dir. workshop Easter Seal Soc.; mem. Gov.'s Task Force on Sound Mcpl. Govt., 1981-82; pres. Nat. Interfrat. Conf., 1979-80. Served with USNR, 1943-46. Mem. Am. Coll. Life Underwriters, Am. Coll. Property Liability Underwriters, Internat. Bridge Tunnel and Turnpike Assn. (chmn. risk mgmt. com., mem. bus. ins. risk mgmt. bd. 1988—), New Brunswick Hist. Soc., English Speaking Union, Alpha Chi Rho (nat. councillor 1964-70, nat. pres. 1970-73, nat. treas. 1975-87), Kappa Kappa Psi, Tau Kappa Alpha, Phi Delta Phi. Mem. Reformed Ch. Am. Club: Rutgers U. Alumni-Faculty (New Brunswick, N.J.). Home: 1054 Hoover Dr North Brunswick NJ 08902 Office: US Rte 9 Woodbridge NJ 07095

MILLS, JOSHUA REDMOND, financial executive; b. Lynn, Mass., Aug. 30, 1936: s. Joshua and Adelaide (Redmond) M.; m. Annette Aliferis Perillo, May 29, 1965; children: Carlotta, Anastasia. AB, Harvard U., 1957; postgrad. NYU, 1960-65. Cert. employee benefits specialist. With Chase Manhattan Bank, N.Y.C., 1960-63, Continental Bank Internat., N.Y.C., 1963-66; v.p. Amerconsult Corp., Colombia, Peru, N.Y.C., 1966-74; pres. Joshua Mills & Co., Greenwich, Conn., 1974—, pres. Fin. Counsel Corp., Montvale, N.J., 1984—. Chmn. strategy com., mem. gen. council Presbytery of N.Y.C., 1976-81; rep. to Town Meeting, Greenwich, Conn., 1981-83; mem. steering com. Tri-State Urban Conf., Fairfield County 2000 Task Force (conf.). Republican. Clubs: Harvard (N.Y.C.). Office: PO Box 339 Montvale NJ 07645

MILLS, LAWRENCE, lawyer, trucking company executive; b. Salt Lake City, Aug. 15, 1932; s. Samuel L. and Beth (Neilson) M.; BS, U. Utah, 1955, JD, 1956. Bar: Utah 1956, ICC 1961, U.S. Supreme Ct. 1965. With W.S. Hatch Co. Inc., Woods Cross, Utah, 1947—, gen. mgr., 1963—, v.p., 1970—, also dir.; dir. Nat. Tank Truck Carriers, Inc., Washington, 1963—, pres., 1974-75, chmn. bd., 1975-76; mem. motor carrier adv. com. Utah State Dept. Transp., 1979; keynote speaker Rocky Mountain Safety Supvs. Conf., 1976. Del. to County and State Convs., Utah, 1970-72; v.p. Utah Safety Council, 1979-82, bd. dirs., 1979—, pres., 1983-84; mem. Utah Gov's Adv. Com. on Small Bus.; capt. Easter Seal Telethon, 1989; state vice chmn. High Frontier, 1987—. Recipient Safety Dir., adv. com. Utah State Indsl. Commn., 1988—; award Nat. Tank Carriers Co., 1967, Trophy award W.S. Hatch Co., 1975. Mem. Salt Lake County Bar Assn., Utah Motor Transport Assn. (dir. 1967—, pres. 1974-76), Utah Hwy. Users Assn. (dir. 1981—), Indsl. Relations Council (dir. 1974—), Utah Safety Council (bd. dirs. 1979—), Salt Lake City C. of C., U.S. Jaycees (life Senator 1969—, ambassador 1977—, pres. Utah Senate 1979-80, Henry Giessenbier fellow 1989), Nat. Petroleum Coun., Utah Associated Gen. Contractors (assoc. 1975-77, 88—), Silver Tank Club. Contbr. articles to legal publs. Home: 77 Edgecombe Dr Salt Lake City UT 84103 Office: 643 S 800 West Woods Cross UT 84087

MILLS, LORNA HENRIETTA, banker; b. Long Beach, Calif., Feb. 5, 1916; d. James Herbert and Henrietta (Waller) M. Grad., Johnston's Bus. Inst., 1936. Stenographer, clk. Laguna Fed. Savs., Laguna Beach, Calif., 1936-38, asst. sec., sec.-treas., 1938-57, pres., mgr., 1957-82; pres. Laguna div. (merger Great American First Savs. Bank), Laguna Beach, 1982—; vice chmn. Great Am. First Savs. Bank, San Diego, 1982—, also bd. trustees. Past dir. Laguna Beach C. of C., Orange County C. of C. Mem. Dacowits, DAR. Republican. Reorganized Ch. of Jesus Christ of Latter-day Saints. Club: Soroptomists (Laguna Beach) (past pres.). Office: Gt Am First Savs Bank 260 Ocean Ave PO Box 1047 Laguna Beach CA 92652 also: Gt Am First Savs Bank San Diego Fed Bldg 600 B St San Diego CA 92183

MILLS, MARTIN GENE, food products executive; b. Warrenton, N.C., May 25, 1948; s. Estelle Pauline (Hargrave) M.; m. Deborah Rose Rhoden, June 19, 1971 (div. Nov. 1975); 1 child, Wendy; m. Karen Sue Steele, July 10, 1976; children: Travis, Bradley. Student, Va. Poly. Inst., 1972. Mgr. corp. systems Texfi Industries, Greensboro, N.C., 1972-76; dir. MIS, Mid-Atlantic Coca-Cola, Silver Spring, Md., 1976-81, v.p. MIS and facilities, 1981-85; v.p. MIS and facilities Joyce Beverages, New Rochelle, N.Y., 1985-86; sr. v.p. ops. N.Y. Seven-Up, New Rochelle, 1986—. Mem. Nat. Soft Drink Assn. (key communicator 1986—), N.Y. Soft Drink Assn., N.J. Soft Drink Assn. Republican. Baptist. Office: NY Seven-Up 1 Joyce Rd New Rochelle NY 10802

MILLS, MICHAEL DAVID, transportation executive, management instructor; b. Detroit, Apr. 5, 1963; s. Richard Harland Mills and Mary Elizabeth (Ring) Kelley; m. Sandra Denise Carter, Oct. 18, 1987. BS in Mgmt., Ark. State U., Jonesboro, 1985; MBA, U. Miss., 1987. Asst. mgr. Kettle Restaurants, Inc., Houston, 1980-86; nat. pres. Phi Beta Lambda, Washington, 1986-87; dir. adminstrn. Allegheny Freight Lines, Winchester, Va., 1987—. Lodge: Mason. Office: Allegheny Freight Lines 2929 Valley Ave Winchester VA 22601

MILLS, STANLEY ROBERT, JR., lawyer, corporate executive; b. Middleboro, Mass., Feb. 8, 1929; s. Stanley Robert Sr. and Marguerite Alena (Brown) M.; m. Mary Catherine Plisinski, Sept. 8, 1951; children: Francis Michael, Mary Anne, Mark Damian, Lisa Kayne, Christopher Joseph, Jennifer Alena. BS in Fgn. Svc., Georgetown U., 1952, JD, 1956. Bar: Va. 1956, Mass. 1962, N.Y. 1975, Mich. 1986. Trial atty. antitrust div. U.S. Dept. Justice, Washington, 1956-59; atty. United Brands Co., Boston, 1959-65, 65-67, Johns-Manville Corp., N.Y.C., 1965; exec. v.p. A&W Food Svcs. Can. subs. United Brands Co., Winnipeg, Man., 1967-70; group v.p., gen. mgr. Baskin-Robbins Ice Cream Co. subs. United Brands Co., Southbury, Conn., 1970-74; pvt. practice Brewster, N.Y., 1974-76; v.p., sec., gen. counsel Del. N. Cos. Inc., Buffalo, N.Y., 1976-85; sr. v.p., gen. counsel, sec. Kelly Svcs. Inc., Troy, Mich., 1985—. With USN, 1946-48; also capt. USAFR, 1952-67. Mem. ABA, Am. Soc. Corp. Secs., Mich. Gen. Counsel Assn. Republican. Roman Catholic. Home: 3324 Kenwood Dr Rochester Hills MI 48309 Office: Kelly Svcs Inc 999 W Big Beaver Rd Troy MI 48084

MILLS, WILLIAM RALPH, bank consulting company executive; b. Kansas City, Mo., Oct. 22, 1928; s. William Nuel and Mary Aileene (Arnold) M.; m. Betty Virginia Brus, July 14, 1951; 1 child, Mark William. Student, La. State U., 1972. Asst. cashier Columbia Nat. Bank, Kansas City, 1954-60; cashier Community State Bank, Kansas City, 1961-66; v.p. Boone County Nat. Bank, Columbia, Mo., 1966-72; pres. Mo. State Bank, Sedalia, Mo., 1973-78, County Hill Bank, Lenexa, Kans., 1979-80; sr. assoc. Swords Assoc., Inc., Kansas City, 1981—. Exec. trustee Sch. Banking La. State U., Baton Rouge, 1974-78; bd. dirs. campaign Marshall for Senate, Columbia, 1970; pres. Sedalia Econ. Devel. Corp., 1976-77, United Way, Sedalia, 1977. Served with USAF, 1945-48. Mem. Mo. Bankers Assn. (v.p. 1973-74), Walnut Hills Country Club (pres. 1978), Rotary. Republican. Mem. Christian Ch. (Disciples of Christ). Home: 8100 Bradshaw Lenexa KS 66215 Office: Swords Assoc Inc 2 Brush Creek Blvd Kansas City MO 64112

MILNE, GARTH LEROY, electronics executive; b. St. George, Utah, Aug. 26, 1942; s. Willard M. and Ruth C. (Cottam) M.; m. Kay G. Hanson, Aug. 11, 1965; children: Michelle, Jacqueline, Michael. BS, U. Utah, 1966; MBA, Harvard U., 1968. Asst. treas. internal Chrysler Corp., Highland Park, Mich., 1974-78; v.p. corp. control and devel. Chrysler Fin. Corp., Troy, Mich., 1978-79; asst. treas. Motorola, Inc., Schaumburg, Ill., 1980-83, corp. v.p., treas., 1984—. Author: (chpt.) Chief Financial Officer Handbook, 1985. Dir. Schaumburg Mormon Ch., 1980—; commr., v.p. South Barrington Park Dist., 1987—; exec. bd. Northwest Suburban Council Boy Scouts Am., 1987—. Served with USNG, 1959-66. Mem. B.Y.U. Mgmt. Soc. Chgo. (bd. dirs. 1983-86), Harvard Bus. Sch. Club (bd. dirs. 1984-88), Barrington Swim and Tennis Club, Phi Kappa Phi. Office: Motorola Inc 1303 E Algonquin Rd Schaumburg IL 60196

MILNE, SUSAN BELISLE, banker; b. Pittsfield, Mass., Aug. 28, 1948; d. Alfons and Helena (Kupiec) Bienick; m. Bruce L. Milne, Feb. 14, 1987; 1 child, David. AS with honors, Berkshire Community Coll., Pittsfield, 1984; BS in Acctg. cum laude, North Adams (Mass.) State Coll., 1986; postgrad., U. New Haven. Vice-treas. Berkshire County Savs. Bank, Pittsfield, 1971-84; v.p., comptroller Berkshire Bank and Trust, Pittsfield, 1984-85; asst. v.p. First Fed. Savs. and Loan, Pittsfield, 1985-88; controller Berkshire Armored Car Services, Inc., Pittsfield, 1988-89; acct. City of Pittsfield, 1989—. Mem. Internat. Mgmt. Council (pres. 1984-85), Nat. Assn. Bank Women (membership chmn. 1984-85), Women Savs. Bank Mass. (chmn. 1982-84), Bankers Profl. Network (exec. com. 1982-84), Fin. Mgrs. Office: City of Pittsfield 70 Allen St Pittsfield MA 01201

MILNER, CHARLES FREMONT, JR., manufacturing company executive; b. Durham, N.C., July 21, 1942; s. Charles Fremont and Eloyse (Sargent) M.; B.A., Guilford Coll., 1963; M.B.A., Harvard, 1965; m. Molly Franc Wakefield, Aug. 28, 1965; children—Bernadette Ann, Eloyse Lee. Asst. to comptroller Harvard, 1965-66; instr. Northeastern U., Boston, 1965-66; with Burlington Hosiery Co. div. Burlington Industries (N.C.), 1966-71, asst. v.p., 1970-71; exec. v.p. Parklane Hosiery Co., Inc., New Hyde Park, N.Y., 1971-74, also dir.; pres. Rudin & Roth, Inc. div. NCC Industries, N.Y.C., 1974-75, also dir.; v.p. apparel group M. Lowenstein and Sons, N.Y.C., 1975-76; pres., chief exec. officer BBC Inc. and Camp Industry divs. Genesco Inc., 1976-80, gen. mgr. Johnston and Murphy Shoe Co. div., 1979—, gen. mgr. footwear mktg. and mfg. Genesco Inc., 1980-81, v.p., 1981-82; pres., chief exec. officer Hope Hosiery Mills and C.M. Industries, Inc., Adamstown, PA, 1983—. Trustee, Friends Acad., Locust Valley, N.Y., 1974-79, Guilford Coll., 1982—. Mem. Nat. Assn. Hosiery Mfrs. (dir. 1978-82, 87—). Home: 158 Hamilton Rd Lancaster PA 17603 Office: Box 487 Adamstown PA 19501

MILNER, EARL RUSSELL, manufacturing company executive; b. Baraboo, Wis., Mar. 30, 1926; s. William and Cora (Schultz) M.; m. Marguerite Novak, Aug. 10, 1946; children: Kenneth, Carol. BA, U. Wis., 1950, MBA, 1955. Acct. aero. div. A.O. Smith Corp., Milw., 1950-52, div. controller aero. tools and factory service, 1952-60, mgr. Milw. works, gen. and cost acctg., 1960, mgr. fin. analysis, 1960-66, asst. controller, 1966-81, v.p., controller, 1981—; bd. dirs. AgriStor Credit Corp., Milw., A.O. Smith Harvestore Products Inc., DeKalb, Ill. Bd. mgrs. No. Suburban br. YMCA, Milw., 1965-82. Served with USAAF, 1944-46. Mem. Nat. Assn. Accts., Mgmt. Acctg. Practices, Fin. Execs. Inst., Machinery and Allied Products Inst. (fin. council II). Club: Tripoli Country (Milw.). Home: 7469 N 51st Blvd Milwaukee WI 53223 Office: A O Smith Corp 11270 W Park Pl Milwaukee WI 53224-3690

MILO, TIMOTHY STEVEN, mechanical engineer, small business owner; b. Gary, Ind., Feb. 17, 1955; s. George and Joanne Genevieve (Nicolich) M.; m. Patricia Marie Mainzer, Mar. 21, 1987. BSME, Ill. Inst. Tech., 1985; postgrad., Lake Forest Sch. Mgmt., 1986—. Registered profl. engr., Ill. Plant engr. ITT, Morton Grove, Ill., 1978-83; product design engr. ITT, Chgo., 1985-87, project mgr., 1987-88, new product mgr., 1988—; plant engr. DuPage Die Casting, Niles, Ill., 1983-85; prin. Prism Enring. Co., Hoffman Estates, Ill., 1985—. Mem. ASME, NSPE, Pi Tau Sigma, Tau Beta Pi. Office: ITT 3500 N Spaulding Ave Chicago IL 60618

MILOSEVICH, PAUL ROLAND, real estate investment company executive; b. Urbana, Ill., Apr. 9, 1959; s. Pete Roland and Kathryn Louise (Headlee) M.; m. Heidi Marie Bluthardt, Sept. 26, 1987. BS in Archtl. Studies, U. Ill., 1981; MBA, U. Tex., 1985. Architect Hatfield-Halcomb Archtects, Dallas, 1981-83; mgr. real estate devel. Hunt Properties, Inc., Dallas, 1985-87; real estate investment mgr. The Prudential Property Co., Dallas, 1987—. Mem. YMCA, Dallas, 1987—. Mem. Urban Land Inst., U. Ill. Alumni Assn., Dallas C. of C., CBA Century Club. Office: The Prudential Property Co 901 Main St Ste 4700 Dallas TX 75202

MILOTT, J. EVERETT, computer systems company executive; b. Newton, Mass., Jan. 15, 1943; s. Paul E. and Adrienne M. Milott; B.S.E.E., Tufts U., 1965; M.B.A., Northeastern U., Boston, 1971; m. Carole Levine, Apr. 29, 1967; children—Nicole, Jonathan. Registered profl. engr., Calif. Sr. nuclear test engr. Gen. Dynamics, Conn. and Mass., 1965-67; sr. quality assurance and test engr. Raytheon, Lowell, Mass., 1967-70; project engr. GTE, Boston, 1970-72, mgr. quality assurance systems, 1972-75; dir. quality assurance and labs. GTE Internat., Boston and Sidi-Bel-Abbes, Algeria, 1975-80; dir. quality assurance computer systems div. Gould, Fort Lauderdale, Fla., 1980-83, gen. mgr. computer systems div. P.R. mfg. ops., Humacao, 1983-87; founder, pres. Caribtec, Inc., Sherborn, Mass., 1987—. v.p., gen. mgr. Power Parts, Inc., P.R. and Dominican Republic, 1988—. Mem. Am. Soc. for Quality Control, Elecronic Industries Assn. Office: 67 Greenwood St Sherborn MA 01770

MILSOM, ROBERT CORTLANDT, banker; b. Butler, Pa., Dec. 15, 1924; s. Robert C. and M. Ethel (Leyland) M. B.S., John Carroll U., 1948. With Pitts. Nat. Bank, 1948—, asst. sec., asst. cashier customer relations div., 1953-56, asst. v.p. loan div., 1956-60, v.p. charge comml. loan group, 1960-65, sr. v.p. charge comml. banking div., 1965-68, exec. v.p., 1968-72, pres., 1972-85, chmn., chief exec. officer, 1985—, also dir., 1972—; vice chmn., dir. PNC Fin. Corp; bd. dirs. Visa U.S.A. Inc., Visa Internat. Bd. dirs. Pitts. Mercy Health Corp., Pitts. Ballet Theatre, Regional Indsl. Devel. Corp.; trustee John Carroll U., Cleve. Served to 1st lt. AUS, 1943-46. Mem. Greater Pitts. C. of C. (dir.). Clubs: Pitts. Athletic (Pitts.), Allegheny (Pitts.), Duquesne (Pitts.), Fox Chapel Golf (Pitts.); Laurel Valley Golf, Rolling Rock. Office: PNC Fin Corp 5th Ave & Wood St Pittsburgh PA 15265

MILTON, CHRISTIAN MICHAEL, insurance executive; b. London, Nov. 13, 1947; came to U.S., 1978; s. Frank Harry and Gismonde Marie Susini; m. Rana Nikpour, Mar. 31, 1985. Claims clk. Stewart Smith Co., London, 1966-67; mgr. reins. claims Henry Head & Co., London, 1967-73; asst. v.p. reins. div. Airco, Hamilton, Eng., 1974-78, Nat. Union Fire Ins. Co., Pitts., 1980-81; asst. v.p. reins. div. Am. Internat. Group Inc., N.Y.C., 1978-80, 81-85, v.p. reins. div., 1985—; bd. dirs. Nat. Union Fire Ins. Co., N.Y.C., Am. Home Ins. Co., N.Y.C.; lectr. reins. Ins. Soc. N.Y., 1988—. Office: Am Internat Group Inc 70 Pine St New York NY 10270

MILUNOVICH, STEVEN MARK, securities analyst; b. Milw., Sept. 14, 1960; s. L.G. and Rosemary (Eckert) M. BBA, U. Wis., 1982; M of Mgmt., Northwestern U., 1983. Securities analyst First Boston Corp., N.Y.C., 1983—. Mem. N.Y. Soc. Securities Analysts, Fin. Analysts Fedn. (chartered). Office: First Boston Corp Park Avenue Pla New York NY 10055

MIMAROGLU, SAIT KEMAL, management executive; b. Siirt, Turkey, Aug. 24, 1929; s. Abdullah and Feride Mimaroglu; m. Esma Bilge Calguner, July 8, 1972; children—Feride Idil, Emre Kemal, Cem Kemal. B.S., Faculty Polit. Scis. and Law (Turkey), 1952; LL.D., Faculty of Law (Turkey), 1956. Asst. prof. Faculty Polit. Scis., Ankara, Turkey, 1956-60, assoc. prof., 1960-67, prof., 1967—; chmn., chief exec. officer Tobank, Ankara, 1963-87 ; bd. dirs. Aymar, Istanbul, Turkey, 1978—, Ardem, Istanbul, 1978-87 , Sark, Istanbul, 1978-87; chmn. chief exec. office Mekas, Ankara, 1987—. bd. dirs. Güris, Ankara. Author: Foreigner's Real Estate Ownership in Turkey, 1956; Collective Bargaining in Turkish Law, 1964, Treaty of Business Law, 1967. Active Inst. Internat. de Droit d'Expression Francaise, Paris, R.B.A., Global Econ. Action Inst., N.Y.C. Served to lt. Turkish Army, 1954-56. Named Commendatore dell' Ordine Al Merito della Repulblica Italiana, 1978. Mem. Internat. Bankers Assn. (v.p. 1974-76, exec. com. 1976-78), Tüsiad (Turkish Industrialists and Businessmen's Assn.) Home: Saf Saf Sokak #24 Emirgan, Istanbul Turkey

MIMNA, CURTIS JOHN, financial executive; b. Colorado Springs, Colo., Dec. 7, 1943; s. Curtis T. and Margaret Ann (Witchey) M. B.S. in Econs., Va. Poly. Inst. and State U., 1965; postgrad. George Washington U., 1969-70. Urban land planner Fairfax County Planning Office, 1966-67; mktg. dir. Fairfax County Indsl. Authority, 1968-70; asst. to Fairfax County exec.; dir. market research Shaw Real Estate, Alexandria, Va., 1970-72; v.p. land devel. financing DRG Fin. Corp., Washington, 1972-82; pres. Land Devel. Financing, Inc., Washington, 1982—. Mem. Washington Bd. Realtors, Nat. Assn. Realtors, So. Indsl. Devel. Council. Democrat. Roman Catholic. Clubs: Polo, Army-Navy Country. Home: 1819 Dalmation Dr McLean VA 22101 Office: 7918 Jones Branch Dr Ste 400 McLean VA 22202

MIMS, THOMAS JEROME, insurance executive; b. Sumter County, S.C., Dec. 12, 1899; m. Valma Gillespie, 1926; children: Thomas Jerome Jr., G. Frank. B.A., Furman U., 1921. With Rec. and Statis. Corp. N.Y., 1921-29; asst. mgr. Rec. and Statis. Corp. N.Y., Phila., 1922-25; mgr. Rec. and Statis. Corp. N.Y., Indpls., 1925-27, Boston, 1927-29; ins. spl. agt. State of N.J., 1931-32; mgr. Wm. R. Timmons Agy., Greenville, S.C., 1933—; v.p., sec. Canal Ins. Co., Greenville, 1942-48; pres., dir. Canal Ins. Co., 1948—, Canal Indemnity Co., Greenville; partner Valetep, Greenville, 1975—; mem. Legis. Com. To Study Automobile Liability Ins., 1969-70. Emeritus mem. adv. council Furman U., from 1974; mem. adv. bd. S.C. Safety Council, 1969-84, pres., 1970-75, 81-84; bd. dirs. United Way of Greenville, 1970-88, campaign vice chmn., 1975, chmn., 1976, v.p., 1977, pres., 1978, chmn. bd., 1979, hon. bd. dirs., 1981; bd. dirs. S.C. United Way, 1981-84; mem. fin. com. 1st Bapt. Ch., Greenville, 1971—, past pres. men's Bible class; pres. Rotary Charities, Inc., 1964-65; past mem. bd. dirs. Met. Arts Council; mem. Greenville Little Theatre Council, 1951-85, bus. mgr., 1951-53, 64-66, v.p., 1956-57, 72-73, pres., 1957-58, 73-75; bd. dirs. Greenville Area Mental Health Ctr. Named Boss of Yr., Greenville Jaycees, 1964, Boss of Yr., Greenville Assn. Ins. Women, 1977; S.C. Vol. of Yr., United Way, 1979; Ins. Co. Man of Yr., Ind. Ins. Agts. S.C., 1980; recipient Service award Internat. Ins. Soc., Paris, 1098. Fellow Pres.'s Council AIM; mem. Greenville C. of C. (chmn. community relations com. 1964-69, dir. 1969-74, pres. 1973, pres. Found. 1973), S.C. C. of C., U.S. C. of C. (ins. com. 1959-61, 64-68), Internat. Ins. Soc. (chmn. bd. dirs. 1983-84, bd. electors, registrar 1984-85, past other coms., named to Hall of Fame, Service award 1980), Nat. Assn. Ins. Agts., S.C. Assn. Ins. Agts., Greenville Assn. Ins. Agts. (v.p. 1950-51, pres. 1951-52, chmn. exec. com. 1952-53), Am. Mgmt. Assn., President's Assn., Motor Transp. Assn. (dir. 1973-75, chmn. ins. com. 1951-63), Assn. S.C. Property and Casualty Ins. Cos. (1st v.p. 1961-62, 71-72, pres. 1962-63, 72-73, exec. com. 1961-74), Truck and Heavy Equipment Claims Council (charter mem., chmn. membership com.), Internat. Platform Assn., Newcomen Soc., Conf. Bd. Baptist (former pres. Men's Bible Class, First Baptist Ch., Greenville, mem. fin. com.). Clubs: World Trade (Atlanta); Poinsett (emeritus), Commerce, Greenville Touchdown, (charter, pres. 1963-64), Clemson IPTAY, City, Greenville Touchdown (charter), Furman Paladins (Greenville); Palmetto, Summit (Columbia, S.C.); Short Snout. Lodge: Rotary (pres. Greenville 1963-64, v.p. 1964-65). Office: Canal Ins Co PO Box 7 Greenville SC 29602

MIN, SUNG SIK, accountant; b. Seoul, Republic of Korea, June 30, 1942; came to U.S., 1972.; s. Young Zai and Kyung Hun M.; m. Jane Eunice Yoo; children: Daniel, David, Douglas, John. BA, Korea U., Seoul, 1965, MBA, 1969; MBA, NYU, 1978. CPA, N.Y. Sec., controller Edward A. Viner & Co., Inc., N.Y.C., 1985-88; dir. fin. Intergrated Resources Equity Corp., N.Y.C., 1988—. Mem. Nat. Assn. Securities Dealers (chief fin. officer 1985—). Home: 17 Everett Ave Staten Island NY 10309 Office: Integrated Res Equity Corp 10 E Union Sq New York NY 10003

MINARD, THOMAS MICHAEL, strategic planner, consultant; b. St. Charles, Ill., Dec. 31, 1944; s. Clarence Scott and Ruth L. (Larson) M. Cert., Coll. Advanced Traffic, Chgo., 1964. Gen. mgr. Iowa Terminal R.R. Co., Mason City, 1968-70; mgr. quality control C & NW Ry. Co., Chgo., 1970-73; pres. Great Plains Ry. Co., Seward, Nebr., 1973-76; mgr. railroad sales and procurement L.B. Foster Co., Des Plaines, Ill., 1976-80, project coordinator, 1981-83, transp. cons., Chgo., 1983; co-founder, v.p. Railmode, Inc., Chgo., 1984-85; transp. cons., Chgo., 1986—. Mem. Chgo. Council Fgn. Relations, Coll. Advanced Traffic Alumni Assn., Delta Nu Alpha. Address: 450 W Briar Pl Suite 13F Chicago IL 60657

MINASY, ARTHUR JOHN, aerospace and electronic detection systems executive; b. N.Y.C., July 19, 1925; s. John and Esther (Horvath) M.; B.S. in Adminstrv. Engring., N.Y. U., 1949, M.S. in Indsl. and Mgmt. Engring., 1952; postgrad. Case Inst. Tech., 1953-55; m. Jayne Marion Leary, June 29, 1946; children—Karen Lynn, Keith Leary, Kathy Jayne. Asst. gen. mgr. Def. div. Bulova Watch Co., Maspeth, N.Y., 1950-53; chief indsl. engr. Standard Products Co., Cleve., 1953-55; gen. mgr. ops. Gruen Industries, Cin., 1955-57; mgmt. cons. Booz-Allen and Hamilton, N.Y.C., 1957-60; mfg. mgr. Sperry Gyroscope Co., Great Neck, N.Y., 1960-62; v.p. ops. Belock Instrument Co., College Point, N.Y., 1962-64; pres. Detection Devices, Inc., Woodbury, N.Y., 1963—; pres. KNOGO Corp., Hauppauge, N.Y., 1966—; dir. KNOGO Italia S.r.l., Milan, Italy, KNOGO Internat. Corp., KNOGO Europe Ltd., Brussels, KNOGO SA, Belgium, KNOGO Caribe Inc., Cidra, P.R., KNOGO Australia Party Ltd., Artarmon, KNOGO The Netherlands B.V., KNOGO Switzerland S.A., KNOGO France S.A., KNOGO Denmark APS, KNOGO Deutschland GMBH, KNOGO Scandinavia AB, KNOGO UK Ltd., KNOGO Iberica SA, KNOGO Japan; prin. Arthur J. Minasy Assocs., Mgmt. Cons., 1957-62; adv. bd. Abilities, Inc.; also lectr. in sci. law enforcement and detection systems. Dir., mem. adv. bd. Human Resources Found.; trustee Rehab. Inst. Served with AUS, 1943-46. Recipient Humanitarian of Yr. award Am. Cancer Soc. Mem. Am. Inst. Indsl. Engrs., Am. Ordnance Assn., Am. Mgmt. Assn., Tau Beta Pi, Alpha Pi Mu. Patentee in field. Home: 15 Hunting Hill Rd Woodbury NY 11797 Office: KNOGO Corp 350 Wireless Blvd Hauppauge NY 11788

MINCHIN, MICHAEL M., JR., corporation executive; b. Los Angeles, Sept. 5, 1926; s. Michael M. and Daisy (Salmon) M.; m. Carolyn Brown, June 1, 1961; children: Michael M. III, Montgomery. B.A. cum laude, Stanford U., 1948; postgrad., Sch. Law, 1948-49; M.B.A. cum laude, Harvard U., 1951. Asst. to Sec. of Def., Washington, 1951; asst. to pres. Emporium-Capwell, San Francisco, 1951-53; v.p. Erwin Wasey, Inc., Los Angeles, 1958-65; sr. v.p., gen. mgr. Erwin Wasey, Inc., 1965-73, exec. v.p., also dir., chmn. exec. policy com., 1973-80; v.p. mktg. Collins Foods Internat., Los Angeles, 1973—; exec. v.p. S.R.I., Inc., 1980—; bd. dirs. Sizzler Restaurants Internat. Inc. Home: 15401 Mulholland Dr Los Angeles CA 90077 Office: Collins Foods Internat Inc 4500 Alla Rd Los Angeles CA 90066

MINDEL, LAURENCE BRISKER, restaurateur; b. Toledo, Oct. 27, 1937; s. Seymour Stewart and Eleanor (Brisker) M.; B.A., U. Mich., 1959; m. Deborah Dudley, Oct. 20, 1978; children: Katherine Dudley, Nicolas Laurence; children by previous marriage—Michael Laurence, Laura Beth, Anthony Jay. Gen. mgr. Western Coffee Instants, Inc., Burlingame, Cal., 1962-64, dir., partner, 1964, chmn., chief exec. officer Caswell Coffee Co., San Francisco, 1964-70; pres., chief exec. officer Coffee Instants, Inc., Long Island City, N.Y., 1966-70; v.p. Superior Tea and Coffee Co., 1970-72; chmn., chief exec. officer Spectrum Foods, Inc., 1970-85; pres. Restaurant Group Saga Corp., Menlo Park, Calif., 1985-86; chmn., chief exec. officer Il Fornaio (Am.) Corp., 1987—. Mem. adv. bd. Stanislaus Ptnrs.; mem. exec. com. hospitality mgmt. bd. McLaren Coll. Bus. U. San Francisco; trustee The Branson Sch. Mem. San Francisco Mus. Art, World Bus. Forum. Club: The Concordia-Argonaut (San Francisco). Home: 86 San Carlos Ave Sausalito CA 94965 Office: Il Fornaio Am Corp 725 Greenwich St San Francisco CA 94133

MINEO, RONALD EDWARD, sales executive, marketing consultant; b. N.Y.C., Aug. 22, 1944; s. Thomas G. and Beatrice (Trumontana) M.; m. Peggy Ann Reyes, Jan. 18, 1964; children: Elizabeth, Ronald Edward Jr., Jennifer. AS, N.Y. Inst. Tech., 1968; BS, L.I. U., 1970. Div. mgr. Richardson-Vicks Inc., Wilton, Conn., 1971-81; mgr. nat. mktg. Elgin Internat. Inc., Miami, Fla., 1981-83; mgr. nat. sales Speidel div. Textron Inc., Providence, 1983-84; sr. v.p. Wilkinson Sword Inc., Atlanta, 1984-87; pres. Sales Impact Mgmt. Inc., Norcross, Ga., 1988—. Mem. Nat. Assn. Gen. Mdse. Reps., Nat. Assn. Chain Drug Stores, Nat. Assn. Pers. Cons. Republican. Roman Catholic.

MINER, JOHN BURNHAM, industrial relations educator, writer; b. N.Y.C., July 20, 1926; s. John Lynn and Bess (Burnham) M.; children by previous marriage: Barbara, John, Cynthia, Frances; m. Barbara Allen Williams, June 1, 1979; children: Jennifer, Heather. AB, Princeton U., 1950, PhD, 1955; MA, Clark U., 1952. Lic. psychologist, Ga., N.Y. Research assoc. Columbia U., 1956-57; mgr. psychol. services Atlantic Refining Co., Phila., 1957-60; faculty mem. U. Oreg., Eugene, 1960-68; prof., chmn. dept. organizational sci. U. Md., College Park, 1968-73; research prof. Ga. State U., Atlanta, 1973-87; pres. Organizational Measurement Systems Press, Buffalo, 1976—; prof. Human Resources SUNY, Buffalo, 1987—; cons. McKinsey & Co., N.Y.C., 1966-69; vis. lectr. U. Pa., Phila, 1959-60; vis. prof. U. Calif., Berkeley, 1966-67, U. South Fla., Tampa, 1972; researcher on orgnl. motivation, theories of orgn., human resource utilization, personnel mgmt., bus. policy and strategy, entrepreneurship. Author many books and monographs including Personnel Psychology, 1969; Personnel and Industrial Relations, 1969, 73, 77, 85; The Challenge of Managing, 1975; (with Mary Green Miner) Policy Issues in Personnel and Industrial Relations, 1977; (with George A. Steiner) Management Policy and Strategy, 1977 (James A. Hamilton-Hosp. Adminstrs. Book award 1982, 86) (with M.G. Miner) Employee Selection Within the Law, 1978; Theories of Organizational Behavior, 1980; Theories of Organizational Structure and Process, 1982; People Problems: The Executive Answer Book, 1985; The Practice of Management, 1985; Organizational Behavior: Performance and Productivity, 1988; contbr. numerous articles, papers to profl. jours. Served with AUS, 1944-46, ETO. Decorated Bronze Star, Combat Infantryman's Badge; named Disting. Prof. Ga. State U., 1974. Fellow Acad. Mgmt. (editor Jour. 1973-75, pres. 1977-78), Am. Psychol. Assn., Soc. for Personality Assessment; mem. Indsl. Relations Research Assn. Republican. Club: Princeton (N.Y.C.). Home: 11054 Howe Rd Akron NY 14001 Office: SUNY Dept Orgn & Human Resources Jacobs Mgmt Ctr Buffalo NY 14260

MINES, HERBERT THOMAS, executive recruiter; b. Fall River, Mass., Jan. 30, 1929; s. Abraham and Fanny (Lepes) M.; B.S. in Econs., Babson Coll., 1949; M.S. in Indsl. and Labor Relations, Cornell U., 1954; m. Barbara Goldberg, Oct. 23, 1960; 1 child, Susan. Supr., asst. buyer, employment supr. G. Fox & Co., Hartford, Conn., 1949-52; adminstr. div. tng.-exec. devel. and orgn. planning R.H. Macy & Co., N.Y.C., 1954-66; v.p. personnel Neiman Marcus Co., Dallas, 1966-68, sr. v.p. personnel, 1968-70; v.p. personnel Revlon, Inc., N.Y.C., 1970-73; pres. Bus. Careers, Inc., 1973-78, chmn., 1978-81; pres. Exec. Search and Cons. Div., Wells Mgmt. Corp., 1978-81, Herbert Mines Assocs., Inc., 1981—. Bd. dirs. Fashion Inst. Tech., Am. Jewish Com.Contbr. articles to trade publs. Home: 724 Seney Ave Mamaroneck NY 10543 Office: 780 3d Ave New York NY 10017

MINETTE, DENNIS JEROME, financial computing consultant; b. Columbus, Nebr., May 18, 1937; s. Lawrence Edward and Angela Ellen (Kelley) M.; B.S.E.E., U. Nebr., 1970; M.B.A., Babson Coll., 1978; m. Virginia Rae Jordan, Oct. 27, 1961; children—Jordan Edward, Lawrence Edward II. Brokerage systems designer Honeywell Info. Systems, Mpls. and Wellesly, Mass., 1970-75; devel. mgr. Investment Info., Inc., Cambridge, Mass., 1975-77; product support mgr. Small Bus. Systems div. Data Gen. Corp., Westboro, Mass., 1977-81; pres. Minette Data Systems, Inc., Sarasota, Fla., 1981—. Capital improvement programs committeeman Town of Medway (Mass.), 1978-79, mem. town fin. com., 1979-80. Served with USN, 1956-60, 61-67, served to lt. commdr. res., 1967-87. Mem. IEEE, IEEE Computer Soc., Data Processing Mgmt. Assn. (cert.), Naval Res. Assn. (life), Res. Officers Assn., Am. Legion, U. Nebr. Alumni Assn. (life), Eta Kappa Nu, Sigma Tau. Republican. Roman Catholic. Office: Minette Data Systems Inc PO Drawer 15435 Sarasota FL 34277

MINGER, TERRELL JOHN, management company executive; b. Canton, Ohio, Oct. 7, 1942; s. John Wilson and Margaret Rose M.; BA, Baker U., 1966; MPA, Kans. U., 1969; Urban Exec. Program, M.I.T., 1975; Loeb fellow Harvard U., 1976-77; Exec. Devel. Program, Stanford U., 1979; MBA, U. Colo., 1983; m. Judith R. Arnold, Aug. 7, 1965; 1 child, Gabriella Sophia. Asst. dir. admissions Baker U., 1966-67; asst. city mgr. City of Boulder, Colo., 1968-69; city mgr. City of Vail, Colo., 1969-79; pres., chief exec. officer Whistler Village Land Co., Vancouver, B.C., Can., 1979-81; v.p., gen. mgr. Cumberland S.W. Inc., Denver, 1981-83; exec. asst., dep. chief of staff to Gov. Colo., 1983-87; pres., chief exec. officer Sundance (Utah) Inst. for Resource Mgmt., 1986—; pres., chief exec. officer Sundance Enterprises Ltd., 1988—; adj. prof. grad. sch. pub. affairs U. Colo., 1983—; bd. dirs. Colo. Open Lands, Inc., 1986—. Spl. del. UN Habitat Conf. Human Settlements; founder Vail Symposium; co-founder, bd. dirs. Colo. Park Found., 1985—. Nat. finalist White House Fellowship, 1978; named one of B.C.'s Top Bus. Leaders for the '80's, 1980. Mem. Urban Land Inst., Colo. Acad. Pub. Adminstrn. (charter 1988), Colo. City Mgmt. Assn., Internat. City Mgrs. Assn. (Mgmt. Innovation award 1974-76), Western Gov.'s Assn. (staff coun., chmn. adv. com. 1985-86). Editor: Vail Symposium Papers, 1970-79; author, editor: Growth Alternatives for Rocky Mountain West, 1976; Future of Human Settlements in the West, 1977. Club: Denver Athletic. Home: 785 6th St Boulder CO 80302 Office: Sundance Enterprises RR3 Box A-3 Sundance UT 84604

MINIAWI, AZMI KAMEL, financial executive; b. Cairo, Egypt, July 18, 1940; s. Kamel and Rina Miniawi; m. Violet Michael, Dec. 26, 1964; children: Dina, Shereen. BS, Ein SHAMS U., Cairo, 1964; MBA, Temple U., 1973; advanced studies piano and music theory, Royal Sch. of Music, London, 1967. Sr. auditor Cen. Audit Orgn., Cairo, 1964-68; acctg. supr. World Mut. Ins. Co., King Of Prussia, Pa., 1968-71; controller Nat. Liberty Internat., Valley Forge, Pa., 1971-76; controller, mgr. acctg. Northrop Corp., Hawthorne, Calif., 1976-83; v.p., controller Lavoro Bank, Chgo., 1983-84; dir. internat. bus. planning, offset and countertrade Northrop Corp., Hawthorne, Calif., 1984—; prof. fin. acctg. Eastern Coll., St. Davids, Pa., 1974-76; cons. in field. Author: Introduction to International Music, 1963; composer numerous musical works. Mem. adv. bd. Christian Collegiate Orgn., Phila. 1972-73; pres. Internat. Trade Bur., Phila., 1973-76. Mem. Nat. Assn Accts., Assn. MBA Execs., Am. Acctg. Assn., Inst. Accts. and Auditors (Egypt). Home: PO Box 7221 Huntington Beach CA 92615 Office: Northrop Corp Aircraft Div 1 Northrop Ave Orgn 9351/18 Hawthorne CA 90250-3277

MINICK, STEVEN ALEX, accountant; b. Denton, Tex., Oct. 23, 1954; s. Billy Boyd and Glenda Sheryl (Cox) M.; m. Cynthia Sue Willard, Apr. 12, 1974; children: Stuart Alexander, Catherine Anne. BBA in Acctg., U. North Tex., 1979. CPA, Tex. Mgr. spl. projects The Trident Co., Richardson, Tex., 1973-78; mgr. Price Waterhouse, Dallas, 1979-86, sr. tech. mgr. nat. office real estate industry svcs. group, 1986—; lectr. in field. contbr. articles to profl. jours. Sustaining mem. Rep. Nat. Com., 1983—. Mem. Am. Inst. CPA's, Tex. Soc. CPA's, Nat. Assn. Real Estate Investment Trusts (acctg. and long range planning coms.), Dallas CPA's, Nat. Assn. Real Estate Cos. Lutheran.

MINISH, ROBERT ARTHUR, lawyer; b. Mpls., Dec. 25, 1938; s. William Arthur and Agnes Emilia (Olson) M.; m. Marveen Eleanor Allen, Sept. 16, 1961; 1 children: Roberta Ruth. BA, U. Minn., 1960, JD, 1963. Bar: Minn. 1963. Assoc. Popham, Haik, Schnobrich & Kaufman, Ltd., Mpls., 1963-67, ptnr., 1967—; bd. dirs. Am. Western Corp., Sioux Falls, S.D. Mem. ABA, Minn. Bar Assn. Home: 331 Pearson Way NE Minneapolis MN 55432 Office: Popham Haik Schnobrich & Kaufman Ltd 3300 Piper Jaffray Tower Minneapolis MN 55402

MINIUTTI, JOHN ROBERTS, software services executive; b. Monterey Park, Calif., Feb. 21, 1937; s. Leslie Ezio and Elizabeth May (Roberts) M.; m. Ann Mather Byrne, June 15, 1959; children: Michele Roberts Joubert, John Frederick. BSMechE, MSMechE, Cornell U., 1959; MBA, NYU, 1965. Engr. Worthington Corp., East Orange, N.J., 1962-65; systems engr. IBM Corp., Savannah, Ga., 1965-68; salesman IBM Data Processing Div., Savannah, 1968-71, Chgo., 1971-76; mgr. market devel. Fiat-Allis, Deerfield, Ill., 1976-77, mgr. strategy devel., 1977-78, dir. market planning, 1973-79, mgr. sales planning, 1979-80, dir. sales adminstrn. and bus. planning, 1980-83, dir., ops. mgr., 1979-83; line of bus. mktg. Burroughs Corp. Internat. Group, Detroit, 1983-85; dir. internat. software and systems Burroughs Corp., 1986; dir. software and profl. services Unisys Corp., 1987—. Bd. dirs. The Cove Sch. Devel. Fund, Evanston, Ill., 1975—. Served with USAF, 1959-62. Mem. North Suburban Spl. Recreation Assn. (adv. bd.). Club: Savannah Yacht and Country. Lodge: Lions (dir. 1971). Home: 107 Birches Ln Bryn Mawr PA 19010 Office: Unisys Corp MS B130M Twp Line Rd & Jolly Rd Blue Bell PA 19424

MINK, CHERE MERLE, administrative assistant; b. Burley, Idaho, Sept. 2, 1933; d. Claude Dee and Merle (Booth) Bailey; m. Robert Ray Mink, Nov. 13, 1948; children: Rocky Ray, Rusty Lee. Student, Ea. Oreg. State Coll., 1963-65. Clk., cashier J.C. Penney Co., La Grande, Oreg., 1960-61, window and store decorator, 1961-62, stock room mgr., 1962-63; bookkeeper, salesman Singer Co., La Grande, 1963-65; personal property appraiser, computer operator Union County Assessor's Office, La Grande, 1965-69; adminstrv. asst. and loan specialist Agrl. Stabilization & Conservation Svc., La Grande, 1969—; newsletter editor and publicity chmn. Oreg. Assn. Agrl. Stabilization & Conservation Svc., 1970-74. Newsletter editor and publicity chmn. La Grande Mavericks Inc., 1968-72, recording sec., 1969-76; pres., v.p., treas. Greenwood PTA, La Grande, 1960-64; gate receipts chmn., treas. Blue Mt. Rodeo, La Grande, 1968-76. Mem. Bus. and Profl. Women (sec., treas. 1978-79, v.p., pres. 1980-84), Union County Legal Secs. (recording sec., treas. 1965-67, newsletter editor and publicity chmn. 1967-68), Soroptimist Internat., BMW Owners Am. Democrat. Home: Rte 1 Box 1530 La Grande OR 97850 Office: Union County Agrl Stabilization & Conservation Svc Office La Grande OR 97850

MINK, GARY STUART, investment consultant; b. Rochester, N.Y., June 1, 1953; s. Jack and Louise (Littner) M.; m. Susan Dolan, June 14, 1986. BA in Politics with honors, N.Y.U., 1974. Agt. Mass Mutual Life Ins. Co., Rochester, N.Y., 1974-76; brokerage mgr. Can. Life Ins. Co., Rochester, 1976-78; acct. exec. Fred S. James, Rochester, 1979-82, mgr. employee benefits, 1981-82; pres. Mink Orgn., Rochester, 1982—; advisor Compensation and Benefits Mgmt., N.Y.C., 1984-87. Found chmn. commerce and industry, United Way, 1981. Mem. Rochester Life Underwriters (assoc.), Internat. Assn. Fin. Planners. Democrat. Jewish. Clubs: Midvale Country, Order Ky. Cols. (hon.). Office: Mink Orgn Ltd 815 Sibley Tower Rochester NY 14604

MINK, HELENA JACOBS, foundation administrator; b. Louisville, Mar. 22, 1931; d. Walter Wallace and Dolla May (Carter) Jacobs; m. Albert Ellis Mink, Oct. 24, 1953 (dec. June 1983). BS in Bus. Adminstrn., Berea Coll., 1951. Sec., treas. Louisville Indsl. Found., 1953-86. Asst. sec., treas. The English Speaking Union, Louisville, 1953—; mem. Berea (Ky.) Coll. President's Club, 1983—, Berea Coll. Fin. Planning Com. Mem. Ind. Calligraphy Assn.(treas.), Knight Writers Group (Ind.). Republican. Baptist. Lodge: Masons. (Order of Eastern Star). Home: 2307 Speed Ave Louisville KY 40205 Office: Louisville Indsl Found 833 Starks Bldg Louisville KY 40202

MINKER, STEPHEN JEFFREY, lawyer; b. Reading, Pa., Nov. 16, 1941; s. William and Dorothy (Lasof) M.; m. Barbara Lynn Flook, Aug. 24, 1967. BA, U. Ariz., 1963, JD, 1966. Bar: Ariz. 1966. Prosecutor City of South Tucson, Ariz., 1967-68; sole practice Tucson, 1967—; adj. lectr. U. Ariz., Tucson, 1988. Mem. Ariz. Bar Assn., Pima County Bar Assn. Home: 860 W Ina Rd Tucson AZ 85704

MINNELLA, CORRADO, publishing company executive; b. Rome, Nov. 27, 1943; s. Renato and Hilda Minnella; m. Roberta Ponzi, July, 1976; children: Federica, Gianluca. Degree in Physics, Milan U., 1967; postgrad., Harvard U., 1985. Dep. gen. mgr. Helene Curtis Co., Milan, 1971-80; exec. dir., v.p. S. Paolo-Publiepi, Milan, 1981—. Served to lt. Italian Navy, 1962-66. Home: Via Albani 5, 20149 Milan Italy Office: S Paolo-Publiepi, Via Grotto 36, 20143 Milan Italy

MINNICH, CHARLES JOSEPH, III, medical research company executive; b. Phila., June 17, 1934; s. Charles Joseph Jr. and Catherine Frances (Walsh) M.; m. Jane Marie Hargadon, June 6, 1964; children: Mary Anne, Jane Marie, Charles Joseph IV, Megan Maureen, John Martin. BS, Spring Hill Coll., 1959. Tchr. biology and chemistry St. Joseph's Prep. Sch., Phila., 1959-62; sales rep. Abbott Labs., North Chicago, Ill., 1962-64, liaison med. dept., 1964-66; exec. v.p. Techni-Med Cons., Inc., Wyncote, Pa., 1966—; apptd. rep. Health Systems Agy. of Southwestern Pa., Phila., 1977-83; bd. dirs. Med. Monitors, Inc., Wyncote, Am. MediCtrs., Inc., Wyncote, Physicians Mobile Diagnostic Systems, Inc., Wyncote, TransTel, Inc., Wyncote. Bd. dirs. Home Health Services of Greater Phila., Elkins Park, 1973-87. Mem. AAAS, Assocs. Clin. Pharmacology, N.Y. Acad. Sci. Republican. Roman Catholic. Home: 731 Wyndale Rd Jenkintown PA 19046 Office: Techni-Med Cons Inc Cedarbrook Hill III Wyncote PA 19095

MINNICH, EDWARD ROLLAND, business owner, studio engineer; b. Amherst, Ohio, July 6, 1961; s. Edwarth Milo and Carol Marie (Winkler) M.; m. Vivian Mae Terry, July 7, 1984. Student, Ohio Sch. Broadcast Technique, Cleve., 1982-83. Cert. audio engr. Asst. engr. Cyprus Dragon Recording, Elyria, Ohio, 1981-82; owner, operator On Trak Prodns. Disc Jockey Service, Elyria, 1981—, Track 1 Recording Studio, Elyria, 1983—, Moon Lite Record Pool, Elyria, 1989—; engring cons. Taylor Broadcasting Co., Elyria, 1983. Songwriter numerous music and lyrics, 1982—. Mem. Planetary Soc., Midwest Record Pool, Soc. Engrs. Republican. Lutheran. Home and Office: On Trak Enterprises PO Box 514 Elyria OH 44036

MINNICK, ADRIENNE K., management consultant; b. Evanston, Ill., Dec. 8, 1920; d. Clarence Henry and Elizabeth Victoria (Ashenden) Kavanagh; m. R. Donald Minnick, Mar. 7, 1942 (dec. Mar. 1945); 1 child, Richard Donald. BS, Northwestern U., 1949; MS, U. Mich., 1958, PhD, 1972. Exec. dir. Girl Scouts Bartholomew County, Columbus, Ind., 1945-49, Girl Scouts of Sheboygan, Wis., 1949-51; field supr., dir. research Girl Scouts Met. Detroit, 1951-72; research dir., evaluation analyst Girl Scouts U.S.A., N.Y.C., 1972-85; co-owner Organizational Resource Devel. Cons., Houston, Galveston, Tex., 1986—. Bd. dirs. United Way of Westchester and Putman Counties, N.Y., 1985; tchr. Christian edn. program, St. Helen's Ch., Pearland, Tex., 1988. Mem. Country Place Master Community Assn. (sec. 1986-88, treas. 1988—, bd. dirs., chairperson rules and deed restrictions com.), Assn. Girl Scout Professional Workers. Republican. Roman Catholic. Home: 3338 S Country Meadow Ln Pearland TX 77584 Office: Organizational Resource Devel PO Box 3580-164 Galveston TX 77552-3580

MINOLI, BECKI MARIE, accountant; b. Barre, Vt., May 7, 1958; d. Silvio A. and Gwendolyn M. (George) M. BA, Clarkson U., 1980. CPA. Acct. Gallagher, Flynn and Co., Burlington, Vt., 1980-86; acctg. mgr. U. Health Ctr., Inc., Burlington, Vt., 1986—. Mem. Bus. and Profl. Women's Orgn. (pres. Burlington chpt. 1986-87, various other offices), Vt. Soc. CPAs, Am. Inst. CPAs. Home: 61 Hayes Ave South Burlington VT 05403 Office: Univ Health Ctr Inc 1 S Prospect St Burlington VT 05401

MINOR, EDWARD COLQUITT, paper company executive, lawyer; b. Balt., Dec. 1, 1942; s. Edward Essau and Mary Newell (Schultz) M.; m. Joan Slade, Aug. 29, 1964; 1 child, Elizabeth Colquitt. AB in Econ., Western Md. Coll., 1964; LLB cum Laude, Boston U., 1967. Bar: Md. 1967, Ga. 1972, Va. 1974, U.S. Supreme Ct. Assoc. Semmes Bowen & Semmes, Balt., 1967-68; judge adv. U.S. Army, Savannah and Vietnam, 1968-72; assoc. Connerat Dunn & Hunter, Savannah, 1972-74; sr. atty. Kraft Paper div. Union Camp Corp., Savannah, 1974; asst. gen. counsel, asst. sec. Fine Paper div. Union Camp Corp., Franklin, Ga., 1974-85; assoc. gen. counsel, asst. sec. Fine Paper div. Union Camp Corp., Franklin, 1985—. Bd. dirs. Tidewater Heart Assn., Norfolk, Va., 1980-86, Future of Hampton Roads, Inc.; bd. execs. Gov.'s Commn. Efficiency; chmn. Constitutional Bicentennial Commn., City of Franklin; chmn. bd. dirs. Southampton Acad., Courtland, Va., 1985—; dep. mem. Va. Bus. Council; mem. exec. bd. Diocese of Southeast Va. Episc. Ch., 1985-89, vestry mem. Emmanuel Episc. Ch., Franklin, Va., 1985-87. Served to capt. U.S. Army, 1968-72. Decorated Bronze Star. Mem. Va. Bar Assn., Md. Bar Assn., Ga Bar Assn., Va. Bus. Council, Va. Mfrs. Assn. (chmn. environ. affairs com. 1987). Clubs: Savannah Yacht; Norflok Yacht, Town Point (Norfolk) (founding mem.). Home: 106 Thomas Circle Courtland VA 23837 Office: Union Camp Corp Rte 58 Franklin VA 23851

MINOTT, PHYLLIS WILSON, financial executive; b. Lafayette, Ind., Oct. 9, 1938; m. Paul O. Minott, Aug. 7, 1970. Bs, Ind. U., 1959, MBA, 1960. Various analyst positions Eli Lilly and Co., Indpls., 1960-72, mgr. corp. account devel., 1972-76, internat. treas., 1976-84, gen. auditor, 1984-86, chief account officer, 1986—; bd. dirs. First Ind. Corp., Am. States Ins. Co., Indpls. Hon. dir. Girls Clubs of Greater Indpls., 1984—, bd. dirs. ARC Indpls. chpt., 1985—. Mem. Fin. Execs. Inst., Inst. Internal Auditors. Office: Eli Lilly & Co Lilly Corp Ctr Indianapolis IN 46285-1091

MINSKER, ROBERT STANLEY, consultant, former personnel executive; b. Pitts. Jan. 1, 1911; s. Theodore Kühne and Isabella Lavinia (Trumbor) M.; B.S., U. Ill., 1934; postgrad. Pa. State U., 1938-39; m. Marion Elizabeth Warner, May 29, 1937; children: Norma (Mrs. Leo Jerome Brown II), Robert S., James. D. With Owens-Ill., Inc., Toledo, Ohio, 1934-76, personnel dir. Clarion (Pa.) plant, 1936-40, personnel dir. Columbus (Ohio) plant, 1940-44, mgr. indsl. relations Alton, 1945-72, adminstr. workmen's compensation, safety and health Ill. and pub. affairs Ill. Plants, 1972-76; dir. Germania Fin. Corp., 1963-82, Germania Bank 1953-82, hon. dir., 1982—; assoc. faculty So. Ill. U., 1959-64. Lectr., cons. Chmn. Madison County Savs. Bond Campaign, 1959-61; active Boy Scouts Am.; pres. Piasa Bird Council, 1949-51, mem. exec. bd., 1945—; mem. grievance com. panel State of Ill. Dept. Personnel, 1967-80; vice chmn. Higher Edn. Coordinating Council Met. St. Louis, 1966-70; founder Board Pride, Inc., 1966—. Mem. Bd. Edn., 1957-70, pres. 1961-70. Bd. dirs., treas., sec., exec. com. Alton Meml. Hosp., 1969-88, dir. emeritus 1988—, bd. dirs. Alton Meml. Hosp. Found., 1986——; Jr. Achievement, United Fund.; bd. dirs. Community Chest, v.p., 1949-54, 61-66, gen. chmn., 1949-50; adminstr. Alton Found., sec., 1955—; trustee Lewis and Clark Community Coll., sec. bd., 1970-77; bd. dirs. McKendree Coll., 1981—; mem. pres. council U. Ill. Found. Recipient Silver Beaver award Boy Scouts of Am., 1951; Achievement award U.S. Treasury Dept., 1951; Hall of Fame award Piasa Bird Council, 1969, Alton Citizens' award, 1988; named to Lewis and Clark Hall of Fame, 1977. Mem. Alton C. of C. (chmn. pub. relations 1951-54), U. Ill. Varsity "I" Assn., U. Ill. Alumni Assn., Nature Conservation Assn. (a founder), Acacia, Alpha Phi Omega. Methodist. Clubs: Masons, (32 deg.), K.T., Shriners. Home: 2018 Chapin Pl Alton IL 62002

MINTCHELL, GARY ALAN, computer company executive; b. Sidney, Ohio, Nov. 19, 1947; s. Jacque Eugene and Sandra Irene (Zwiebel) M.; m. Beverly Kay Moseley, June 12, 1970; children: Heather Lorelle, Derek Travis. BA, Ohio Northern U., 1969; postgrad., La. State U., 1970-71. Tchr. Delphos (Ohio) St. John Schs., 1969-70; product mgmt. Airstream div. Beatrice, Jackson Ctr., Ohio, 1971-80; quality assurance mgr. Questor Corp., Piqua, Ohio, 1980-81; mgr. product devel. GLO Internat., Dayton, Ohio, 1981-84; v.p. mktg. Cardinal Tool Corp., Engelwood, Ohio, 1984-88; mgr. Eograph div. Eotron Corp., Dayton, Ohio, 1988—. Mem. Sidney Sch. Bd., 1982—. Mem. Am. Mktg. Assn., The Planning Forum, Sidney Jaycees (Outstanding Community Service Award 1981). Democrat. Methodist. Lodge: Kiwanis (past pres. Sidney). Home: 1227 Colonial Dr Sidney OH 45365 Office: Eotron Corp 121 Westpark Rd Dayton OH 45459

MINTON, DWIGHT CHURCH, manufacturing company executive; b. North Hills, N.Y., Dec. 17, 1934; s. Henry Miller and Helen Dwight (Church) M.; m. Marian Haven Haines, Aug. 4, 1956; children: Valerie Haven, Daphne Forsyth, Henry Brewster. B.A., Yale U., 1959; M.B.A., Stanford U., 1961. With Church & Dwight Co., Inc., Princeton, N.J., 1961—; asst. v.p. Church & Dwight Co., Inc., 1964-66, v.p., 1966-67, pres., 1967-81, chief exec. officer, 1969—, chmn., 1981—, dir., 1966—; dir. Crane Corp. Trustee Atlanta U., 1971—; trustee Morehouse Coll., 1971—. Served with U.S. Army, 1956-57. Mem. Chem. Mfrs. Assn. (bd. dirs. 1980-83), Grocery Mfrs. Am. (dir. 1983-87). Clubs: Seawanhaka Corinthian Yacht, Racquet and Tennis, Yale, Lotos. Office: Church & Dwight Co Inc 469 N Harrison St Princeton NJ 08540

MINTZ, STEPHEN ALLAN, financial services company executive, lawyer; b. N.Y.C., May 21, 1943; s. Irving and Anne (Medwick) M.; m. Dale Leibson, June 19, 1966; children: Eric Michael, Jaclyn Leibson. AB, Cornell U., 1965; JD cum laude, Harvard U., 1968. Bar: N.Y. 1969. Assoc. Proskauer, Rose, Goetz & Mendelsohn, N.Y.C., 1968-76, ptnr., 1976-80; v.p. Integrated Resources, Inc., N.Y.C., 1980-84, 1st. v.p., 1984-86, sr. v.p., 1986-89. exec/ v.p., 1989—; chmn. Resources Hotel Mgmt. Services Div., 1986—. Mem. ABA, N.Y. State Bar Assn., Assn. of Bar of City of N.Y. Democrat. Jewish. Avocation: amateur radio operator. Home: 11 Eve Ln Rye NY 10580 Office: Integrated Resources Inc 666 3d Ave New York NY 10017

MINTZER, LAURENCE ALEXANDER, financial analyst; b. N.Y.C., Sept. 2, 1961; s. Joseph Howard and Serena Maria (Maltese) M. BS in Econs., Wharton Sch., 1983; MBA, Harvard U., 1987. Asst. mgr. HBO Inc., N.Y.C., 1983-85; assoc. Bank New England, Boston, 1986 summer, Goldman, Sachs and Co., N.Y.C., 1987—; fund agt. Harvard Bus. Sch., 1987—; recruiter/advisor secondary sch. com. U. Pa., Phila., 1983—. Mem. County Tennis Club. Democrat. Jewish. Office: Goldman Schs & Co 85 Broad St New York NY 10004

MIRACLE, ROBERT WARREN, banker; b. Casper, Wyo.; m. Maggie Zanoni; children—Mark, John. BS in Law, U. Wyo., 1951; grad. with honors, Pacific Coast Banking Sch., 1960. With Wyo. Nat. Bank (formerly Norwest Bank Casper N.A.), 1954—; exec. v.p. Wyo. Nat. Bank of Casper (formerly Norwest Bank Casper N.A.), 1967, pres., chief exec. officer, 1968-87, chmn., 1983—, also bd. dirs.; pres., chief exec. officer, dir. Wyo. Nat. Bankcorp. (formerly Affiliated Bank Corp. Wyo.), Casper, 1970—; Bd. dirs. Wyo. Nat. Bank East Casper, Wyo. Nat. Bank West Casper, Wyo. Nat.Bank Cheyenne, Wyo. Nat. Bank East Cheyenne, Wyo. Nat. Bank Gillette, Wyo. Nat Bank Kemmerer, Wyo. Nat. Bank Lovell; instr. Bank Mgmt. U. Col., 1971-75. Bd. dirs. United Fund of Natrona County, Wyo., 1963-65, campaign co-chmn., 1973-78; trustee The Myra Fox Skelton Found., 1963—; bd. dirs. Investment in Casper, pres., 1967-70; Wyo. treas. Radio Free Europe, 1967-72; trustee Casper Coll. Found., 1967—, pres. 1973-75, 85—; trustee U. Wyo. Found., 1972-87; chmn. Casper Downtown Improvement Assn., 1974-75; bd. dirs. Central Wyo. Fair Bd., 1974-79, pres. 1977-78. Served to capt. USMC, 1951-53. Recipient James C. Scarboro Meml. award Colo. Sch. Banking., 1977; Disting. Service in Bus. award U. Wyo. Coll. Commerce and Industry, 1980. Mem. Wyo. Bankers Assn. (chmn. legis. com. 1969-80, pres. 1974-75), Am. Bankers Assn. (mem. governing council 1974-75, 81-83), Am. Mgmt. Assn., Rocky Mountain Oil and Gas Assn., Newcomer Soc. in N.Am., Casper C. of C. (pres. 1965-66, Disting. Service award 1981), VFW. Clubs: Casper Petroleum, Casper Country. Lodge: Masons, Lions. Office: Wyo Nat Bancorp PO Box 2799 Casper WY 82602

MIRALIA, LAUREN MARTIN, insurance banking executive; b. New Rochelle, N.Y., July 31, 1940; s. David Theodore and Margaret Marie (Martin) M.; m. Joyce Stephens, Aug. 29, 1964; children: Stephanie Marie, Andrea Martin. AB in Econs., Duke U., 1961; postgrad., George Washington U., NYU. Bond trader, underwriter White Weld & Co., N.Y.C., 1964-67; v.p., mgr. mcpl. bond dept. bank investment securities div. Bank Am., N.Y.C., 1967-70; v.p., dir. N.Y. Securities Co., N.Y.C., 1970-73; exec. v.p. Mcpl. Issuers Svc. Corp., White Plains, N.Y., 1973—; cons. Community Devel. Corp., Hartford, Conn., 1984—. Contbr. articles to profl. jours. Del. N.Y. State Jud. Conv., Albany, 1984-87; pres. Larchmont Hills Civic Assn., Mamaroneck, N.Y., 1983-85, Hommocks Owners Assn., Larchmont, 1986-88. Capt. USNR, 1961-89. Mem. Westchester County Assn. (bd. dirs. 1987-89), Pub. Securities Assn. (chmn. enhancement com. 1984-88), N.Y. Yacht Club, Larchmont Yacht Club, Winged Foot Golf Club (Mamaroneck), Gulfstream Bath and Tennis Club, City Mid-day Club (N.Y.C.). Home: 307 Oliver Rd Bedford NY 10506 Office: Mcpl Issuers Svcs Corp of MBIA Inc 445 Hamilton Ave White Plains NY 10601

MIRANDA, MARK HARLAND, oil company executive, business owner; b. Santa Ana, Calif., Feb. 25, 1960; s. Jesus Leobardo Miranda and Wanda Faye (Thompson) Grinner; m. Iva Rose Taylor,Jan. 23, 1979 (div. Nov. 1985); children: Ernest, Lisa. Mgr. Walt Smith Inc., Corona, Calif., 1980-84; field supr. Prestige Stations Inc., Cerritos, Calif., 1984-85; ops. mgr. Corona Mall Oil Co. Inc., 1985-87, Latta's West, Buena Park, Calif., 1987—; owner Precision Hair Design, Riverside, Calif., 1988; ops. mgr. Calif. K-9 Security, Fullerton, Calif., 1988—. Author numerous poems; editor poetry anthologies. Served with U.S. Army, 1979-80. Recipient Golden Poet award World of Poetry, 1985-88. Republican.

MIRANDA, ROBERT NICHOLAS, publishing company executive; b. Bklyn., July 9, 1934; s. John and Florence Miranda; m. Marilyn H. Pils, May 25, 1958; children—Marilyn, Robert, Susan, Lori, Jennifer. A.A. in Acctg. and Bus. Adminstrn., SUNY-Farmingdale. Pres. Pergamon Press, Inc., Elmsford, N.Y., 1965—, also dir.; dir., exec. v.p., vice chmn. Soc. and Assoc. Service Corp., McLean, Va.; dir. Pergamon Infoline Inc., McLean, Info. on Demand, Berkeley, Calif. Served with USNR, 1954-59. Mem. ALA, Spl. Library Assn., Council Sci. Editors, Fulfillment Mgrs. Assn. Office: Maxwell House Pergamon Press Inc Fairview Pk Elmsford NY 10523

MIRANDO, LOUIS PATRICK, investment company executive; b. Buffalo, N.Y., June 27, 1927; arrived in Can., 1957; s. Pietro and Lucia (Carbone) M.; m. Ada Francescutti, Jan. 15, 1949; children: Martha Louise, Louis Patrick, Victor Joseph, John Anthony, Marianne. Acctg. cert., Jean Summers Bus. Coll., 1948; student, Niagara Coll., 1948-52. Traffic mgr. Detroit Steel Products Co., Buffalo, 1948-50; mgr. Schriebner Trucking Co., Buffalo, 1950-53; sales mgr. Sherks Motor Express Corp., Lancaster, Pa., 1953-55; gen. mgr., mng. dir. Fess Transp. and Harrison Motorways Ltd., Welland, Ont., Can., 1955-63; pres. Uscan Transp., Chippawa, Ont., Can., 1963-65; pres., chmn. bd. Internat. Scanning Devices, Ft. Erie, Ont., Can., 1965-78; sr. ptnr. Columbia Bus. Cons., Buffalo, 1978; pres. Columbia Security and Transfer, Inc., Fr. Erie, 1973—; dir. Columbia Security and Transfer, Inc., 1973—; speaker European Electro-Optics Conf., 1972. Patentee flat T.V., plastic el light sheet. Mem. Repub. Presdl. Task Force, Washington, 1988—; dep. counsul Gen. Can. Affairs Cherokee Nation, Allied Indian Tribes of N.Am., 1988—. Mem. Can. Pilots Assn., 1st Fin. Credit Assn., St. Catherine's (Ont.) Flying Club, U.S. Sen. Club, The 500 P.C. Can. Fund (hon. roll), Delta Nu Alpha. Roman Catholic. Home: 2848 Teresa St, Stevensville, ON Canada L0S 1S0 Office: Columbia Security & Trans, 41 Jarvis St, Fort Erie, ON Canada L2A 5M5

MISCAVICH, RONALD F., real estate broker; b. Hartford, Conn., Aug. 14, 1936; s. Francis and Florida L. (Doyon) M.; m. Charlotte C. Bocwinski, June 6, 1959; children: Mary, Mark. BS in Marine Engring., USCG Acad., 1959. Safety mgr. USCG, Washington, 1955-79; ship supr. Bethleham Steel Sparrows Pt., 1979-80; marine supr. J.J. Henry Co. Inc., 1980-82; sales assoc. W.F. Mann Realty, Md., 1971-76; sales assoc., broker Colquitt-Carruthers, Bowie, Md., 1976-80; assoc. broker Long & Foster Realtors, Crofton, Md., 1980-87; pres., broker Charon Inc., Crofton, Md., 1982—. Served to lt. comdr. USCG. Mem. Nat. Assn. Realtors, Md. Assn. Realtors, Realtors Nat. Mktg. Inst., Womens Council Realtors, Anne Arundel County Bd. Realtors. Republican. Roman Catholic. Club: Disting. Sales Achievement. Home: 2761 Swann Way Davidsonville MD 21035

MISENHEIMER, BARRY KAY, soft drink company executive; b. Durham, N.C., Mar. 25, 1953; s. Kay Moser and Helen Marie (Evans) M. BA, U. N.C., Greensboro, 1976; JD, Woodrow Wilson Coll. of Law, Atlanta, 1982. Bar: Ga. Mfrs. rep. Potpourri Press, Greensboro, 1976-78; legal researcher Greer, Klokik & Daugherty, Atlanta, 1979-80; legal researcher The Coca-Cola Co., Atlanta, 1980-82, personnel regulatory planning coordinator, 1982-83; mgr. of shareholder relations The Coca-Cola Co., 1983-86; asst. sec., dir. shareholder and govtl. relations Coca-Cola Ent., Inc., Atlanta, 1986—; dir. Trees Atlanta, 1985—. Vol. United Way, Atlanta, 1987, Jr. Achievement, Atlanta, 1983, Lawyers for the Arts, Atlanta, 1985—, Legal Aid Soc., Atlanta, 1979—; mem. High Mus. of Art, Atlanta, 1983, Nexus Contemporary Art Ctr., Atlanta, 1987—. Mem. ABA, Ga. Bar Assn., Atlanta Bar Assn., Am. Soc. Corp. Secs., Nat. Investor Relations Inst., Nat. Soft Drink Assn. (adv., mem. govt. affairs adv. com., legal adv. com. and recycling adv. com.). Presbyn. Clubs: Young Lawyers, Young Careers. Office: Coca-Cola Enterprises Inc Coca-Cola Pla Atlanta GA 30313

MISKUS, MICHAEL ANTHONY, electrical engineer, consultant; b. East Chicago, Ind., Dec. 10, 1950; s. Paul and Josephine Miskus; BS, Purdue U., 1972; AAS in Elec. Engring. Tech., Purdue U., Indpls., 1972; cert. mgmt. Ind. U., 1972, Ind. Central Coll., 1974. Cert. plant engr.; m. Jeannie Ellen Dolmanni, Nov. 4, 1972. Service engr. Reliance Electric & Engring. Co., Hammond, Ind., 1972-73; maintenance supr., maintenance mgr. Diamond Chain Co./AMSTED Industries, Indpls., 1973-76; primary and facilities elec. engr. Johnson & Johnson Baby Products Co., Park Forest South, Ill., 1976-81; prin. Miskus Cons., indsl./comml. elec. cons., 1979—; plant and facilities engring. mgr. Sherwin Williams Co., Chgo. Emulsion Plant, Chgo., 1981-85; with Miscon Assocs., Riverside, Calif., 1985—; acting dir. plant and facilities engring. Bourns Inc., 1982—; instr., lectr. EET program Moraine Valley Community Coll., Palos Hills, Ill., 1979; instr. cert. program plant engring. U. Calif.; lectr. energy engring., bldg. automation systems Prairie State Coll., Chicago Heights, Ill., 1980—; mem. adj. faculty, faculty adv. bd. Orange Coast Coll., Costa Mesa, Calif.; commr. Riverside Energy Commn., 1988—; mem. Elec. Industry Evaluation Panel. Mem. faculty adv. bd. Moraine Valley Community Coll., 1980—. Mem. IEEE, Am. Inst. Plant Engrs. (pres. Pomona chpt. 1989—), Assn. Energy Engrs., Assn. Energy Engrs. (sr., So. Calif. chpt.), Illuminating Engring. Soc. N.Am., Internat. Platform Assn., Riverside C. of C. Club: Purdue of Los Angeles. Office: Miscon Assocs PO Box 55353 Riverside CA 92517

MISLEJ, JORGE L., construction company executive; b. Santiago, Chile, Aug. 9, 1949; s. Jorge A. Mislej and Yolanda C. Musalem; m. Maria A. Anania, July 25, 1956; children: Jorge, José Antonio, M. Antonieta, Luis Alberto. MBA, Cath. U. of Santiago, 1972. Asst. to minister Ministry of Econs., Santiago, 1974-77; vice chmn. Lan Chile Airlines, Santiago, 1977-81; dir. Banco Osorno, Santiago, 1981-83, Procesac S.A., Santiago, 1981-84, Banco Concepcion, Santiago, 1983-85; pres. PHS Chile Ltd., Santiago, 1982-86; chmn. Zumasa S.A., Santiago, 1986—; chmn. bd. PHS Internat. Corp., Santiago, 1981—; prof. Cath. U., Santiago, 1972-85, Mil. High Sch., 1976-87; cons. Mislej and Co., Santiago, 1973-87. Bd. dirs. Ski Patrol, Chile, 1969-87, Santiago-Club Aereo, 1986-87, Radio Ham Club Santiago, 1985-87. Mem. Engrs. Assn. Chile. Roman Catholic. Office: Zumasa SA, Vicuña Mackenna 1865, Santiago Chile

MISSAR, RICHARD R., paint and chemical manufacturing company executive; b. Chgo., 1930, student Ill. Inst. Tech., Advanced Mgmt. Program, Harvard U., 1975. With DeSoto Inc., Des Plaines, Ill., 1950—, lab. technician chem. coatings div., 1950-55, salesman, 1955-60, product mgr., 1960-64, regional sales mgr., 1964-69, dir. mktg., 1969-71, gen. mgr., 1971-74, group v.p. chem. coatings div., 1974-75, corp. v.p. corp. mktg. adminstrn., 1975-76, exec. v.p., chief operating officer, 1976-79, pres., chief exec. officer, 1979—, now also chmn. bd., bd. dirs. Served with USMC, 1951-53. Mem. Nat. Paint and Coating Assn. Office: De Soto Inc 1700 S Mount Prospect Rd Des Plaines IL 60017

MISTLER, LINDA CORINNE, banker, teacher; b. Oakland, Calif., Oct. 29, 1946; d. Warren George and Elizabeth Ann (Musgrove) M. BS, Towson U., 1977; M in Adminstrv. Scis., Johns Hopkins U., 1982. Asst. v.p. Maryland Nat. Bank, Balt., 1970-81; asst. treas. U.S. Fidelity and Guaranty Co., Balt., 1981-84; v.p. Maryland Nat. Bank, Balt., 1984-89; v.p. finance com. nat. Equitable Bank NA, Balt., 1989—; instr. Loyola Coll. Md., Balt., 1982-83, MAS program Johns Hopkins U., Balt., 1984—; speaker Career Night Johns Hopkins U., 1983—. bd. dirs. Girl Scouts Cen. Md., Balt., 1984-87, chair fin. com., 1984-87, funds devel., 1985-86. Mem. DAR (vice-regent 1983-85, treas. 1987—).

MITCHAM, JULIUS JEROME, accountant; b. Pine Bluff, Ark., Jan. 2, 1941; s. James Vernon and Bertha Lee (Robertson) M.; m. Janet Claire Berry, Mar. 31, 1970 (div. Sept. 1981); m. Marsha Lee Henderson, Oct. 22, 1983; 1 child, Timothy John. BBA, U. Cen. Ark., 1971. CPA, Ark. Br. mgr. Comml. Nat. Bank, Little Rock, 1961-66; auditor, acctg. supr. Ark. Blue Cross and Blue Shield, Little Rock, 1971-77; controller Riverview Hosp., Little Rock, 1977-81; pvt. practice acctg. Little Rock, 1981-82; controller Henryetta (Okla.) Med. Ctr., 1982-83; fin. report supr. Am. Med. Internat., Inc., Houston, 1983; dir. corp. acctg. Ft. Myers (Fla.) Community Hosp., 1984-86; controller Med. Ctr. of Southeast Okla., Durant, 1986-87; chief fin. officer Gulf Coast Community Hosp./Qualicare of Miss., Inc., 1987-88; asst. adminstr. fin. S.W. Gen. Hosp., San Antonio, 1988—. Served with USN, 1959-61. Mem. Am. Inst. CPA's, Ark. Soc. CPA's, Healthcare Fin. Mgmt. Assn., Lions (sec. 1985-86), Masons. Republican. Baptist. Home: 3438 Butterleigh Dr San Antonio TX 78247

MITCHELL, CHERYL ELAINE, marketing executive; b. Oceanside, N.Y., Dec. 27, 1951; d. Harold Bertram and Doris Meredith (Hose) M. BA in History, Polit. Sci., Hartwick Coll., 1973; postgrad., Syracuse U., 1973-75. Campaign staffer Udall for Pres., N.Y., 1975-76; sr. writer Syracuse (N.Y.) Record, 1976-78; assoc. nat. dir. pub. relations Cushman & Wakefield, Inc., N.Y.C., 1978-81; sr. account exec. JP Lohman Orgn., N.Y.C., 1981-84; v.p. SPGA Group, N.Y.C., 1984-86; pres. Mitchell & Assocs., N.Y.C., 1986—; lectr. in field; press agt. to internat. real estate developers and architects. Contbr. articles to profl. jours; prin. works include numerous corp. and product brochures, advt. and publicity. Recipient ANDY award Art Dirs. N.Y., 1983, Champion award of excellence Graphic Arts Exhbn., 1985, Award of Merit Design and Mktg. Communications, 1986. Mem. Assn. Real Estate Women, Comml. Real Estate Women, NAFE. Democrat. Lutheran. Office: Mitchell & Assocs 36 W 20th St New York NY 10011

MITCHELL, DAVID MILTON, naval officer; b. Chillecothe, Ohio, June 9, 1954; s. Howard Milton and Bette Louise (Bibler) M.; divorced; children: David Milton Jr., Kelly Shawn. BS in Acctg. cum laude, Franklin U., 1978; MS in Fin., Naval Postgrad. Sch., Monterey, Calif., 1985. CPA, Ohio. Staff acct. Coopers & Lybrand, Columbus, Ohio, 1978-79; commd. ensign USN, 1979, advanced through grades to lt., budget officer for comdr., 1984-85; adj. faculty acctg. and fin. Golden Gate U., 1985—. pres. La Mesa Jr. Soccer League, Monterey, 1983-85; scoutmaster Tidewater council Boy Scouts Am., Virginia Beach, 1985-87. Mem. Am. Inst. CPA's, Am. Soc. Mil. Comptrollers, Tidewater Triathlon Club (sec. 1987-88). Republican. Home: 839 Virginia Ct Virginia Beach VA 23451 Office: Comnavairlant Code 031 Norfolk VA 23511

MITCHELL, DAVID T., electronic computing equipment company executive; b. 1942. Prodn. control mgr. Honeywell Inc., Mpls., 1966-69; dir. mfg. planning Memorex Corp., Santa Clara, Calif., 1969-72; dir. materials Fairchild Camera and Instrument Corp., Mountain View, Calif., 1972-75; pres. Castell Inc., Santa Ana, Calif., 1975-77; dir. materials Bendix Corp., San Francisco, 1977-78; gen. mgr. Commodore Bus. Machines Inc., Santa Clara, 1978-80; pres., chief operating officer Seagate Tech., Scotts Valley, Calif., 1980—, also bd. dirs. Capt. USMC, 1963-66. Office: Seagate Tech 920 Disc Dr Scotts Valley CA 95066 *

MITCHELL, DONALD GEORGE, appliance manufacturing executive; b. Aurora, Ill., Nov. 29, 1938; s. Verl S. and Gladys (Brewer) M.; m. Eleanor Spencer (div. 1987); children: Deborah, Amy, Jeffery. BA, U. Evansville, Ind., 1985. With Whirlpool Corp., 1966—; dist. mgr. I Whirlpool Corp., Indpls., 1977-81; dist. mgr. III Whirlpool Corp., Boston, 1981-84; dist. mgr. IV Whirlpool Corp., Deerfield Beach, Fla., 1984—. Republican. Methodist. Office: Whirlpool Corp 350 Fairway Dr Ste 220 Deerfield Beach FL 33441

MITCHELL, DONALD WAYNE, management consultant, investment manager, lawyer, cattle breeder; b. San Bernardino, Calif., Nov. 1, 1946; s. Donald Wardell and Edith Felice (Wood) M.; m. Carol Bruckner, Nov. 11, 1984; children: Donald Weyland, Mark De Saussure, Mandy Sara, Janis Felicia. AB magna cum laude, Harvard U., 1968, JD, 1971. Bar: Mass. 1971. Project mgr. Boston Cons. Group, 1971-74; dir. strategic planning, Heublein, Inc., Farmington, Conn., 1974-77; mng. dir. Mitchell and Co., Weston, Mass., 1977—; pres. Mitchell Investment Mgmt. Co., Inc., Weston, 1981—, DMMJ Cattle Breeding Corp., 1986—, DMMJ Cattle Feeding Corp., 1986—; bd. dirs. Money Tree Prodns. Inc., 1986—. Vice-chmn. law sch. fund Harvard U., Cambridge, 1981-82, chmn. law sch. fund 10th ann. gift campaign, 1980-81, chmn. law sch. class of 1971 15th reunion, 1985-86, co-chmn. class of 1968 20th reunion Harvard U., 1986-88; cons. Greater Hartford Arts Coun., 1975-77; bd. dirs. Newton Soccer Assn., 1985—. Mem. Harvard Alumni Assn. (bd. dirs. 1986-88), Harvard Law Sch. Assn. (mem. centennial com. 1984-86, treas. 1987—). Club: Brae Burn Country (West Newton, Mass.). Office: Mitchell & Co 9 Riverside Rd Weston MA 02193

MITCHELL, GEORGE P., gas and petroleum company executive; b. Galveston, Tex., 1919; married. BS, Tex. A&M Univ., 1940. Exploration engr., geologist Amoco Prodn. Co., 1940-41, cons. geologist, engr., 1946-51; with Mitchell Energy & Devel. Corp., The Woodlands, Tex., 1947—, chmn., pres., 1972—, chief exec. officer, from 1972, also bd. dirs.; pres. George Mitchell & Assocs. Served to maj. U.S. Army, 1942-46. Office: Mitchell Energy & Devel Corp 2001 Timberloch Pl The Woodlands TX 77387 *

MITCHELL, GERALD BENSON, vehicular parts supply executive; b. Goderich, Ont., Can., Aug. 29, 1927; s. Reginald and Mary Elizabeth (Sanders) M.; m. Stephanie Bennett Wood, Oct. 1, 1970; children: Fraser, Jamie, Briar, Michael, Melissa. Student, U. Western Ont. With Hayes Dana Co., Toledo, 1944-67, v.p. mfg., from 1958, pres., 1963-67; exec. v.p. Dana Corp., Toledo, 1967-73, pres., 1973-80, 84-87, chmn. bd., chief exec. officer, 1980—; exec. com. Machinery and Allied Products Inst.; bd. dirs. West Point-Pepperell, Worthington Industries, George Weston Ltd., Can., Mich. Nat. Corp., Direc Spicer Mexico, Hayes-Dana Can. Contbg. author: Chief Executive's Handbook, 1974. Trustee Med. Coll. Ohio at Toledo Found.; trustee Toledo Symphony Orch., Toledo Art Mus. Mem. Western Hwy. Inst. Clubs: Inverness, Renaissance, Anglers, Ocean Reef. Office: Dana Corp PO Box 1000 4500 Dorr St Toledo OH 43697

MITCHELL, JAMES AUSTIN, insurance company executive; b. Cin., Dec. 16, 1941; s. James Austin and Jeannette Louise (Stiles) M.; m. Patricia Ann McNulty, Aug. 12, 1967; 1 child, J. David. A.B., Princeton U., 1963. CLU; chartered fin. cons.; FSA. Various positions Conn. Gen. Life Ins. Co., Hartford, 1963-73, v.p., controller, 1973-77; v.p., chief fin. officer Aetna Ins. Co., Hartford, 1977-82; pres. Cigna RE Corp., Hartford, 1982-84; pres., chief exec. officer IDS Life Ins. Co., Mpls., 1984—; dir. IDS Fin. Services and Affiliated Cos., Mpls. Chmn. Community Initiatives Consortium, 1984—; chmn. Vanguard Div. United Way, Mpls., 1986—. Served with U.S. Army, 1964-70. Fellow Soc. Actuaries; mem. Soc. C.L.U.s. Republican. Presbyterian. Club: Minneapolis. Home: 2685 N Shore Dr Wayzata MN 55391 Office: IDS Life Ins Co 2900 IDS Tower Minneapolis MN 55474

MITCHELL, JAMES ROBERT, insurance agent; b. Oshkosh, Wis., May 5, 1959; s. Jack Brewster and Evelynn Jennifer (Olsen) M.; m. Lori Lee Spiczenski, Feb. 19, 1983; 1 child, Justin. Mgr. United Parcel Service, Oshkosh, 1978-86; sales agt. Oshkosh Ins./Fin. Services, 1986—. Mem. Life Underwriters Assn. Home: 2755 Montclair Pl Oshkosh WI 54904 Office: Oshkosh Ins/Fin Svcs 125 Church Ave Oshkosh WI 54901

MITCHELL, JEROME ROBERT, economic development executive; b. Phila., Mar. 20, 1957; s. Thomas Eugene and Eleanora katie (Davis) M. A in Applied Sci., Community Coll. Phila., 1980; BBA, U. Pa., 1984. Founder, pres. Inner City Income Tax, Phila., 1978-84; auditor Consol. Rail Corp., Phila., 1981-82; mktg. rep. IBM Corp., Reading, Pa., 1984-87; co-founder, pres. Renaissance Devel. Corp., Camden, N.J., 1986-87; group leader Operation Crossroads Africa, Phila., Kajaido (Kenya), 1987; pres., chief exec. officer West Phila. Econ. Devel. Corp., 1987—; mgmt. cons. Phila. Indsl. Devel. Corp., 1987—, Parkside Assn. Phila., 1988—; mktg. cons. West Phila. Credit Union, 1988—. Pub. relations mgr. Chaka Fattah campaign for state legislature, Phila., 1986; area coordinator W. Wilson Goode campaign for mayor Phila., 1987; area field dir. Jesse Jackson for pres. campaign, Phila., 1988; bd. dirs. Local Intiative Support Corp., Prints and Progress, Phila. Bus. and Tech. Ctr. Recipient Outstanding Community Involvement award IBM Corp., Reading, Pa., 1986, Outstanding Alumni Achievement award Pres. Community Coll. Phila. Alumni Council, 1988 Leadership award Leadership Inc. Mem. Am. Mgmt. Assn., Am. Mktg. Assn., West Phila. Leadership Caucus (named Outstanding Young Leader 1987), Council Urban Econ. Devel., Entrepreneurs Club Phila (pres. 1986). Office: West Phila Econ Devel Corp 5070 Parkside Ave Ste 1418 Philadelphia PA 19143

MITCHELL, LEE MARK, communications executive, lawyer; b. Albany, N.Y., Apr. 16, 1943; s. Maurice B. and Mildred (Roth) M.; m. Barbara Lee Anderson, Aug. 27, 1966; children: Mark, Matthew. A.B., Wesleyan U., 1965; J.D., U. Chgo., 1968. Bar: Ill. 1968, D.C. 1969, U.S. Supreme Ct. 1972. Assoc. Leibman, Williams, Bennett, Baird & Minow, Chgo. and Washington, 1968-72; assoc. Sidley & Austin, Washington, 1972-74, ptnr., 1974-84, of counsel, 1984—; exec. v.p. and gen. counsel Field Enterprises, Inc., Chgo., 1981-83, pres. and chief exec. officer, 1983-84; pres., chief exec. officer Field Corp., 1984—; bd. dirs. Manistique Papers, Inc., Field Publs., Muzak, Cabot, Cabot & Forbes Co., Boston, Boulevard Bancorp, Blvd. Bank, Chgo., NOTIS Systems, Inc.; bd. trustees Ravinia Festival Assn. Author: Openly Arrived At, 1974, With the Nation Watching, 1979; co-author: Presidential Television, 1973. Mem. LWV Presdl. Debates adv. com., Washington, 1979-80, 83; U.S. del. Brit. Legislators' Conf. on Govt. and Media, Ditchley Park, Eng., 1974; bd. visitors U. Chgo. Law Sch., 1984-86, Medill Sch. Journalism, Northwestern U., 1984—; pres. Chgo. Met. Planning Council; mem. midwest regional adv. bd. Inst. Internat. Edn., 1987—. Mem. ABA, Fed. Communications Bar Assn., Fed. Bar Assn. Clubs: Econ., Mid-Am., Mid-Day, Chicago (Chgo.); Nat. Press (Washington), Comml. Club Chgo. Home: 135 Maple Hill Rd Glencoe IL 60022 Office: The Field Corp 333 W Wacker Dr Chicago IL 60606

MITCHELL, LINDELL MARVIN, financial planner; b. Hagerman, N.Mex., July 11, 1937; s. Marvin P. and Lillie (Collom) M. m. Wanda L. McFarland, Dec. 7, 1974; children: Lisa A. Purdy, Leah J. Student, N.Mex. State U., 1954-61. Cert. fin. cons. Owner, ins. broker, fin. planner Lindell M. Mitchell & Assocs., Albuquerque, 1971—; registered rep. Gen. Am., Albuquerque, 1971-87, Cardell & Assocs., Inc., Morristown, N.J., 1984-86, T. L. Reed (formerly Source Securities, Inc.), Irving, Tex., 1986—. State chmn. N.Mex. Life Underwriters Polit. Action Com., 1978-82. Mem. Am. Soc. CLUs, Internat. Soc. Fin. Planners, Nat. Assn. Life Underwriters, Registry Fin. Planning Practitioners. Republican. Home: 8800 Osuna NE Albuquerque NM 87111 Office: 5907 Alice NE Ste F Albuquerque NM 87110

MITCHELL, LUCIUS QUINN, financial management consultant, real estate consultant; b. Atlanta, Dec. 12, 1959; s. Lucius R. and Dorothy (Nash) M. Student, Cornell Coll., 1977-78; BA cum laude, Morehouse Coll., 1981. Acct. Equitable Real Estate, Atlanta, 1980-85; intern Equitable Life Ins., N.Y., 1980; appraisal trainee, intern Equitable Life Ins., Atlanta, 1981-82; v.p. Cen. Atlantic Realty Co., Inc., Atlanta, 1985-87; pres. So. Am., Atlanta, 1984—; v.p. Atlantic Assn., Inc., Atlanta, 1985—; vice chmn. Rogers & Logan, Inc., Atlanta, 1986-87; v.p. The Hines Bus Network, Inc., Atlanta, 1987-88; pres. Global Real Estate and Investment Co., Atlanta, 1988—. Co-founder Socius Strata, Inc., Atlanta, 1982—; mem. Historic Oakland Cemetery, Inc., Atlanta, 1984—, Metro Fair Housing, Inc., Decatur, Ga., 1979—. Jr. Acheivement scholar, Atlanta, 1977. Mem. Jr. Enterprenurial Traders Assn. (charter), Jaycees (Outstanding Young Man Am. 1983). Congregationalist. Office: Global Real Estate & Investment Co 252 Northside Dr SW Atlanta GA 30313

MITCHELL, MAURICE CLAYTON, real estate company executive, accountant; b. Sheffield, Ala., Mar. 6, 1952; s. Wylie Clayton and Gladys Paulene (Singleton) M.; m. JoAnn Nunley, Aug. 21, 1970; children—Jeffrey Allen, Sara JoAnn. B.B.A., Augusta Coll., 1977. C.P.A., Tenn. Asst. dept. head Eliza Coffee Meml. Hosp., Florence, Ala., 1972-73; dept. head Doctors Hosp., Augusta, Ga., 1974-76; staff acct. Das A. Borden and Co., Muscle Shoals, Ala., 1977-79, controller, 1980-81, v.p. fin., 1982-87, also bd. dirs.; chief fin. officer Philips Devel. Corp., Englewood, Colo., 1987-88, pres. 1988—. Mem. Am. Inst. C.P.A.s, Aircraft Owners and Pilots Assn. Republican. Baptist. Avocation: golf, flying. Home: 7743 E Kettle Ct Englewood CO 80112 Office: Philips Devel Corp 5575 DTC Pkwy Ste 300 Englewood CO 80111

MITCHELL, MICHAEL KENT, real estate developer; b. Houston, Dec. 27, 1952; s. George Phidias and Cynthia (Woods) M.; m. Ruth Maclay, Aug. 16, 1975 (div. Oct. 1980); m. Donna Lynn Ray, June 7, 1986; 1 child, Michael Aldous. Student, Calif. Western U., 1973-74, U. Tex., 1975-77; MArch., Harvard U., 1981. Designer Huygens & Tappe, Arch., Boston, 1977-78; project designer Synthesis Archs., Wrightsville Beach, N.C., 1981-82; pres., chief exec. officer Bald Head Island (N.C.) Mgmt., Inc., 1983—; bd. dirs. Mitchell Energy & Devel., Houston, 1988—. Councilman Village of Bald Head Island, 1985-88; active Gov. Coastal Resources commn., Raleigh, N.C., 1988—. Office: Bald Head Island Mgmt Inc The Chandler Bldg Bald Head Island NC 28461

MITCHELL, OSCAR ELMER, JR., environmental engineer; b. Birmingham, Ala., June 7, 1948; s. Oscar Elmer and Ruby (Davis) M.; m. Carol Ann Grace, Feb. 12, 1971; children: LaShelle Marie, Nathaniel Bryan. BSChemE, Auburn U., 1970. Chemist Ala. Power Co., Gorgas, 1971-73; chem. engr. Gilbert Assocs., Reading, Pa., 1973; sr. staff engr. Rust Internat. Corp., Birmingham, 1973—. Chmn. com. Birmingham 1st Ch. Nazarene, 1985—; pres. Birmingham Engring. council, 1982-83. Mem. Am. Inst. Chem. Engrs., Am. Water Works Assn., Rust Mgmt. Club. Office: Rust Internat Corp 100 Corporate Pkwy Birmingham AL 35242

MITCHELL, RALPH MELVIN, JR., naval officer; b. Easton, Pa., Oct. 30, 1944; s. Ralph Melvin and Betty (Hummer) M.; m. Shirley Anne Petty, June 11, 1966; children: Amy, Anne, Stephanie. BS, U.S. Naval Acad., 1966; MBA, U. Pa., 1976, MSE in Computer Sci., 1976; advance mgmt. program, Harvard U., 1987. Commd. ensign USN, 1966, supply officer U.S. Naval Ships, 1969-86; personal aide, comdt. 4th Naval Dist. USN, Phila., 1969-71; dir. advance planning Naval Supply Ctr. USN, San Diego, 1976-78; dir. data processing Navy Fin Ctr. USN, Cleve., 1980-82; dir. aircraft engines Aviation Supply Office USN, Phila., 1982-84; dir. navy stock fund Naval Supply Systems Command USN, Washington, 1986-88; exec. asst. to dep. under sec. Dept. Def., Washington, 1988—. Mem. Washington Navy Supply Corps Assn. (chmn. ann. fund drive 1987-88, trustee 1987-88, pres. 1988-89). Republican. Roman Catholic. Home: 8262 Cedar Landing Ct Alexandria VA 22306 Office: Dept Def Office Under Sec Rm 3E1082 Pentagon Washington DC 20301

MITCHELL, RICHARD AUSTIN, lawyer; b. Poughkeepsie, N.Y., Jan. 1, 1949; s. Richard W. and Wanda (Austin) M.; m. Susan H. Hoder, July 1, 1972; children: Lindsay, Brian, Courtney. BA, U. Pa., 1971; JD, Union U., 1974. Bar: N.Y. 1975, U.S. Dist. Ct. (so. and ea. dists.) N.Y. 1975, U.S. Ct. Appeals (2d cir.) 1975, U.S. Dist. Ct. (no. dist.) N.Y. 1980. Assoc. McCabe & Mack, Poughkeepsie, 1974-79, ptnr., 1980—. Bd. dirs. Am. Heart Assn., Poughkeepsie, 1983—, Vassar-Warner Home, Poughkeepsie, 1984—, Area Fund of Dutchess County, 1986—, Bardavon 1869 Opera House, 1987—. Mem. ABA, N.Y. State Bar Assn. (bankruptcy com. 1984—, exec. com. bus. law sect. 1988—), Dutchess County Bar Assn. (pres. young lawyers 1976, chmn. pub. rels. com. 1988—), Fed. Bar Coun., Poughkeepsie Tennis Club (bd. dirs. 1976-81), Amrita Club (Poughkeepsie). Home: 10 Carriage Hill Ln Poughkeepsie NY 12603 Office: McCabe & Mack 63 Washington St Poughkeepsie NY 12602-0509

MITCHELL, RICHARD FRANK, retail company executive; b. Columbus, Ga., Sept. 22, 1931; s. Harry Frank and Esther (Davis) M.; B.S., Auburn U., 1955; grad. exec. program U. Va., 1968; m. Iris Faye Tarvin, Aug. 7, 1955; children—Alison, Bradley. Chief accountant Vulcan Materials Co., Birmingham, Ala., 1958-62, treas., 1965-70; gen. accounting mgr. Bigelow-Sanford Inc., Greenville, S.C., 1962-63; asst. controller Blount Bros. Corp., Montgomery, Ala., 1963-65; exec. v.p. Waddell & Reed, Kansas City, Mo., 1970-74; v.p. fin., treas. Rich's, Inc., Atlanta, 1974—; v.p. fin., treas. Zale Corp., 1976-80, exec. v.p., 1980-84, vice chmn., 1984-87; exec. v.p. Rhodes Inc., Atlanta, 1987—. Past mem. fund raising com. Pembroke County Day Sch., Kansas City, Mo.; mem. bus. adv. council So. Meth. U., Auburn U.; mem. fin. com. Dallas Symphony Assn.; mem adv. bd. Grad. Bus. Sch., U. Tex., Dallas. Served with AUS, 1957. Mem. Fin. Execs. Inst. (sec. Birmingham 1969, past dir. Kansas City chpt., program chmn.), Nat. Assn. Accountants (v.p. Birmingham 1970), Birmingham, Kansas City chambers commerce. Presbyterian. Office: Rhodes Inc 4370 Peachtree Rd Atlanta GA 30319

MITCHELL, ROBERT LEE, III, auditor; b. Smyrna, Tenn., July 31, 1957; s. Robert Lee Jr. and Mary Helen (Lee) M. BA, U. Nebr., Omaha, 1978. Mgr. div. sales J.L. Brandeis, Omaha, 1978-80; asst. mgr. Postal Thrift, Omaha, 1980-82; br. mgr. Security Pacific, Council Bluffs, Iowa, 1982-84; internal auditor Security Pacific Fin. Svcs., San Diego, 1984—. Mem. Am. Mgmt. Assn., Inst. Internal Auditors. Democrat. Home: 5828 Ohio St Omaha NE 68104 Office: Security Pacific Fin Svcs 10089 Willow Creek Rd San Diego CA 92131

MITCHELL, ROBERT R., retired banker; b. 1923; married. Grad., Pacific Coast Sch. Banking, 1960; grad. exec. program, Stanford U., 1972. With U.S. Nat. Bank Oreg., Portland, 1945—, mgr. Lombard-Emerald br., 1959-62, mgr. Hollywood br., 1962-66, mgr. met. br., 1966-68, v.p. mgr. N.W. region, 1968-69, sr. v.p., mgr. orgn. and personnel div., 1969-71, sr. v.p., mgr. br. banking group, 1971-73, exec. v.p. gen. banking, 1973-74, pres., 1974-87, vice chmn., 1987, dir.; vice chmn., dir. U.S. Bancorp; ret. 1988. Office: US Nat Bank Oreg 111 SW 5th Ave PO Box 4412 Portland OR 97208

MITCHELL, ROY DEVOY, industrial engineer; b. Hot Springs, Ark., Sept. 11, 1922; s. Watson W. and Marie (Stewart) M.; m. Jane Caroline Gibson, Feb. 14, 1958; children: Michael, Marilyn, Martha, Stewart, Nancy. BS, Okla. State U., 1948, MS, 1950; B of Indsl. Mgmt., Auburn U., 1960. Registered profl. engr., Ala., Miss. Instr. Odessa (Tex.) Coll., 1953-56; prof. engring. graphics Auburn (Ala.) U., 1956-63; field engr. HHFA, Community Facilities Adminstrn., Atlanta and Jackson, Miss., 1963-71; area engr. Met. Devel. Office, HUD, 1971-72, chief architecture and engring., 1972-75, chief program planning and support br., 1975, dir. archtl. br., Jackson, 1975-77, chief archtl. br. and engring. br., 1977-84, community planning and devel. rep., 1984-88; prin. Mitchell Mgmt. and Engring., 1988—; cons. Army Ballistic Missile Agy., Huntsville, Ala., 1957-58, Auburn Research Found., NASA, 1963; mem. state tech. action panel Coop. Area Manpower Planning System. Mem. Cen. Miss. Fed. Personnel Adv. Council; mem. House and Home mag. adv. panel, 1977; trustee, bd. dirs. Meth. Ch., 1959-60. Served with USNR, 1943-46. Recipient Outstanding Achievement award HUD, Commendation by Sec. HUD. Mem. NSPE, Am. Soc. for Engring. Edn., Miss. Soc. Profl. Engrs., Nat. Assn. Govt. Engrs. (charter mem.), Jackson Fed. Execs. Assn., Cen. Miss. Safety Council, Am. Water Works Assn., Iota Lambda Sigma. Club: River Hills (Jackson). Home and Office: HUD 706 Forest Point Dr Brandon MS 39042

MITCHELL, RYAN DUNNEHOO, JR., construction company executive; b. Belton, S.C., Aug. 1, 1935; s. Ryan Dunnehoo and Laura Haynie (Boyce) M.; m. Barbara Jean Zimmer, Sept. 16, 1954; children: Elizabeth, Pamela, Ryan. BS, Clemson U., 1958; postgrad. Ga. State U., 1965, Manhattan Coll., 1966, U. Okla., 1966. Registered profl. engr., Tex., S.C., Okla., Ark. Engr. Robert M. Angas Assocs., Jacksonville, Fla., 1958-63; mgr. engring. Davco Mfg. Co., Thomasville, Ga., 1963-66; dir. Rhodes Corp., Oklahoma City, 1966-69; pres. Mitchell Engring., Inc., Georgetown, Guyana, South Am., 1969-71; v.p. Lang Engring., Coral Gables, Fla., 1971-72; dir. mktg., v.p. Fluor Daniel Ins. Irvine, Calif. 1972—. Contbr. articles to profl. publs.; patentee in field. Mem. ASCE, ASME, NSPE, Am. Chem. Soc., Soc. Ind. Devel. Council, U.S. C. of C. (internat. policy com., internat. econ. devel. task force), Am. Inst. Plant Engrs., Southeastern Community Devel. Assn. Episcopalian. Clubs: Greenville Country, Pebble Creek Country. Office: Fluor Daniel 411 Hackensack Ave Hackensack NJ 07601

MITCHELL, SAMUEL ROBERT, chamber of commerce executive; b. Milw., Mar. 26, 1938; s. Samuel Robert and Hazel Catherine (McKee) M.; m. Mary Frances Henniger, Feb. 24, 1962; 1 child, Erin Suzanne. Student, Marquette U., 1956-58; B.S., So. Ill. U., 1965. Classified advt. salesman St. Louis Post Dispatch, 1962-65; advt. supr. Allis-Chalmers Mfg. Co., Milw., 1965-68; advt. mgr. Outdoor Power Equipment div. FMC Corp., Port Washington, Wis., 1968-72; dir. advt. Skil Corp., Chgo., 1972-74; exec. dir. Am. Hardware Mfrs. Assn., Palatine, Ill., 1974-80; sr. v.p., pres. nat. hardware show Cahners Expn. Group, N.Y.C., 1980-81; pres. Chgo. Assn. Commerce and Industry, 1981—. Mem. Chgo. Crime Commn., 1981—; mem. adv. council Energy Resources Center, 1981—; bd. dirs. Chgo. Conv. Bur., Ill. Council Econ. Edn., Citizenship Council Met. Chgo.; mem. citizens adv. bd. Chgo. Transit Authority. Served with AUS, 1958-61. Mem. Am. Hardware Mfrs. Assn., Chgo. Soc. Assn. Execs., Ill. Assn. C. of C. Execs., U.S. C. of C. Am. C. of C. Execs. Clubs: Capitol Hill (Washington); Economic Tavern (Chgo.). Office: Chgo Assn C of C 200 N LaSalle St Chicago IL 60601

MITCHELL, STEPHEN MILTON, manufacturing executive; b. Atlanta, Oct. 23, 1943; s. Judge Stephenson and Elizabeth Ruth (Morgan) M.; m. Carolyn Docia Goss, June 29, 1968; children: William Stephenson, Scott Milton, Gregory Stephen. B of Indsl. Engring. with honors, Ga. Inst. Tech., 1965, MS in Indsl. Engring., 1966. Registered profl. engr., Ga. Sr. engr. Lochheed-Ga. Corp., Marietta, 1966-70; mgr. material control Snapper Power Equipment, McDonough, Ga., 1970-73; pres. Atlanta Processing Co., Conley, Ga., 1973-86, Processing Transportation, Inc., Conley, Ga., 1975-85; sr. v.p., gen. mgr. Norcom, Inc., Norcross, Ga., 1986—; chmn. Atlanta Processing B, Inc., 1983—; chmn. Cope Processing Co., Moultrie, Ga., 1981-83, bd. dirs. Atlanta Processing Co., Conley, Ga., Norcom, Inc., Norcross, Ga.; mem. exec. com., treas., bd. dirs. Clairmont Oaks, Inc., 1988—. Deacon First Bapt. Ch. of Decatur, Ga., 1984—. Mem. Young Pres. Orgn., Ga. Tech. Alumni Assn. (trustee 1981-87). Republican. Home: 5268 Browning Way Lilburn GA 30247 Office: Norcom Inc 6866 Jimmy Carter Blvd Norcross GA 30076

MITCHELL, THOMAS EDWARD, financial planner; b. Beaver Falls, Pa., Sept. 15, 1960; s. Leonard L. and Marion B. (Dwyer) M.; m. Dale Elizabeth Anthony, Apr. 4, 1987. BS in Mktg., Pa. State U., 1982. Assoc. Wienken & Assoc., Mut. Benefit Life Ins., State College, Pa., 1982-86; cons. fin. planning Pa. Fin. Group, State College, 1987—. Treas. Am. Heart Assn., Pa., 1982-85, Park Forest Bapt. Ch., State College, 1982—, Pa. Spl. Olympics, Pa., 1987—. Mem. Inst. Cert. Fin. Planners, Assn. Fin. Planners, Phi Beta Lambda (pres. 1980-82), Pa. State Alumni Assn., Toastmasters Internat. Republican. Baptist. Home: PO Box 1025 803-8 Stratford Dr State College PA 16801 Office: Pa Fin Group 270 Walker Dr State College PA 16804

MITCHELL, THOMAS KENT, portfolio manager; b. DeKalb, Ill., May 15, 1956. BA, U. Ill., 1978; M in Internat. Mgmt., Am. Grad. Sch. Internat. Mgmt., Glendale, Ariz., 1980. Investment officer MVenture Corp., Dallas, 1981-84; dir. Stephenson Merchant Banking, Denver, 1985-88; portfolio mgr. U.S. West Fin. Svcs., Denver, 1988—. Mem. Assn. for Corporate Growth (chpt. pres., dir. 1987-88, internat. dir. 1987-88). Episcopalian. Office: US West Fin Svcs 6300 S Syracuse Way Ste 195 Englewood CO 80111

MITCHELL, THOMAS ROBERT, chemical company executive; b. N.Y.C., Mar. 23, 1937; s. Daniel Joseph Mitchell and Dorothy Jane (Simpson) Lubera; m. Ruth Eleanor Daniel (div. 1983); 1 child, Kathleen Jane St. Lawrence; m. Margaret Anne Breen, Aug. 4, 1984. Student, St. John's U., 1954-56, Wagner Coll., 1957-59. Regional mktg. mgr. Reichhold Chems., Inc., White Plains, N.Y., 1959-65, div. mktg. mgr., 1965-80, div. pres., 1980-83, exec. v.p., 1983-88, pres., chief exec. officer, 1988—, also bd. dirs.; chmn. bd. Reichhold A.G., Hausen, Switzerland, Reichhold de Mexico, Mexico City, Synthomer Chemie, Frankfurt, W. Ger.; dir. Doverstrand Ltd., London. Republican. Office: Reichhold Chems Inc 525 N Broadway White Plains NY 10603

MITCHELL, WILLIAM LEROY, mktg. exec.; b. Columbus, Ohio, Nov. 3, 1920; s. Arthur R. and Mary E. (Brown) M.; B.B.A., Ohio State U., 1949; m. Eloise Johnson, Sept. 18, 1953; children—Jacquelyn, Debra, William. Commd. U.S. Army, 1940, advanced through grades to lt. col., 1970; ret., 1970; systems engr. Raytheon Service Co., Colorado Springs, Colo., 1970-71; dir. investment mgmt. Equity Control Corp., El Paso, 1971-72; mktg. v.p. Grupo Bermudez Indsl. Park, Ciudad Juarez, Chihuahua, Mex., 1973—; dir. Vista Hills Bank. Bd. dirs. NCCJ; bd. dirs. Am. Med., Internat., Southwestern Gen. Hosp. Mem. Internat. Mgmt. Assn., Ret. Officers Assn., El Paso C. of C. (dir.), Com. for Production Inc. (v.p. exec. bd.). Home: 1636 Tommy Aaron St El Paso TX 79936 Office: APDO, Postal 424, Juarez City Chihuahua, Mexico

MITCHELSON, THEO KAY, insurance company executive; b. Lake City, Fla., Jan. 21, 1925; s. Kay and Lillian Formie (DeVeau) M.; m. Margaret Marian Barber, Sept. 2, 1950; children: Theo Kay Jr., Laura, Lisa. BS in Indsl. Mgmt., U. Ala., 1950, postgrad., 1950. CPCU; accredited pers. diplomate im employee rels., tng. and devel. Agt. Met. Life Ins. Co., Daytona Beach, Fla., 1950-52; sales rep. Newth-Morris Box Co., Jacksonville, Fla., 1952-53; regional pers. mgr. State Farm Ins. Cos., Jacksonville, 1953-67, div. mgr., 1967-71; exec. asst. to pres. State Farm Ins. Cos., Bloomington, Ill., 1971-78; dep. regional v.p. State Farm Ins. Cos., Monroe, La., 1978—; cons., speaker, writer, seminar leader Leadership Devel. Ctr., Jacksonville and Monroe. Mem. editorial bd. Leaders Digest; contbr. articles to profl. publs. Mem. adv. bd. Salvation Army, Monroe, 1984—; sec., bd. dirs. Crimestoppers Ouachita, Monroe, 1985—; founder, bd. dirs. Jacksonville Episcopal High Sch., 1966; pres. bd. dirs. United Way N.E. La., 1988—; mem. adv. bd. dept. gerontology N.E. La. U., Monroe, 1985—; bd. dirs. Twin Cities YMCA, Monroe, 1987—, Blue Ridge Conf. on Leadership; active numerous other civic orgns. With USAAF, 1943-46, PTO; 1st lt. U.S. Army, 1951-52. Recipient Communications and Leadership award Toastmasters, Bloomington, 1978, Disting. Svc. to Humanity award Twin City Jaycees, 1983. Mem. Am. Soc. Pers. Adminstrn. (life; nat. pres. 1962, Disting. Svc. and Leadership award Jacksonville chpt. 1963), Soc. CPCUs (nat. edn. com. 1970), Nat. Speakers Assn. (charter; cert. profl. speaker), Commerce Execs. Soc. of U. Ala., U. Ala. Alumni Assn., Am. Assn. Ret. Persons, Beta Gamma Sigma, Delta Sigma Pi, Pi Kappa Alpha, Sawgrass Country Club (Ponte Vedra Beach, Fla.), Masons (32d degree), Shriners. Home: 122 Nandina Circle Ponte Vedra Beach FL 32082 Office: State Farm Ins Cos 22 State Farm Dr Monroe LA 71208

MITCHEM, MARY TERESA, publishing company marketing executive; b. Atlanta, Aug. 31, 1944; d. John Reese and Sara Letitia (Marable) Mitchem. BA in History, David Lipscomb Coll., 1966. Sch. and library sales mgr. Chilton Book Co., Phila., 1972-79; dir. market devel. Baker & Taylor Co. div. W.R. Grace, N.Y.C., 1979-81; dir. mktg. R.R. Bowker Co. div. Xerox Corp., N.Y.C, 1981-83, dir. mktg. research, 1983-85; mktg. mgr. W.B. Saunders Co. div. Harcourt, Brace & Jovanovich, Phila., 1985-87; mktg. dir. Congl. Quarterly Inc., Washington, 1987—. Mem. Book Industry Study Group, Inc. (chairperson stats. com. 1984-86), Mktg. Research Assn. Home: 4625 Tilden St NW Washington DC 20016 Office: Congl Quarterly Inc 1414 22nd St NW Washington DC 20037

MITLYNG, ERROL PAUL, financial executive; b. Montevideo, Minn., Oct. 10, 1936; m. Barbara Ann Lundin, Sept. 20, 1938; children: James, Nancy, David. BS, U. Nebr., 1960. CPA, Ill. Audit staff Ernst & Whinney, Chgo., 1960-66; asst. v.p. Wylain Inc., Michigan City, Ind., 1966-72; v.p., controller Wylain Inc., Dallas, 1972-80; sr. v.p. fin., treas. The Marley Co., Mission Woods, Kans., 1980—, also bd. dirs. Bd. dirs. KCPT, Kansas City, Mo., 1986—. Mem. Am. Inst. CPA's, Fin. Execs. Inst. Office: Marley Co 1900 Shawnee Mission Pkwy Mission Woods KS 66205

MITSOCK, MICHAEL JOSEPH, marketing professional; b. Stoneham, Mass., Sept. 11, 1956; s. Edward T. and Lorraine (Collins) M.; m. Lisa M. Dionne, May 6, 1984. BS, MIT, 1978; MS, Northeastern U., 1983; postgrad., Boston U. Engr. Xenergy Inc., Burlington, Mass., 1978-79; cons. engr. 1979-83; product mgr. Cyborg Corp., Newton, Mass., 1983-86; mktg. programs mgr. Lotus Devel. Corp., Cambridge, Mass., 1986-87, mktg. mgr., 1987—; lectr. Boston Archtl. Ctr., 1980-82; cons. engr., Stoneham, Mass. Editor SERI Conf. proceedings, 1979. Recipient Rensselaer medal, Troy, N.Y., 1974. Mem. Am. Mktg. Assn., Assn. Energy Engrs. (pres. 1979-82). Roman Catholic. Club: MIT of Boston. Office: Lotus Develop Corp 55 Cambridge Pkwy Cambridge MA 02142

MITTEL, JOHN J., economist, corporate executive, consultant; b. L.I., N.Y.; s. John and Mary (Leidolf) M.; 1 child, James C.; B.B.A., CUNY. Researcher econs. dept. McGraw Hill & Co., N.Y.C.; mgr., asst. to pres. Indsl. Commodity Corp., J. Carvel Lange Inc. and J. Carvel Lange Internat., Inc., 1956-64, corp. sec., 1958—, v.p., 1964-80, exec. v.p., 1980—; pres. I.C. Investors Corp., 1972—, I.C. Pension Adv., Inc., 1977—; dir. several corps.; plan adminstr., trustee Combined Indsl. Commodity Corp. and J. Carvel Lange Inc. Pension Plan, 1962—, J. Carvel Lange Internat. Inc. Profit Sharing Trust, 1969—, Combined Indsl. Commodity Corp. and J. Carvel Lange Inc. Employees Profit Sharing Plan, 1977—. Mem. grad. adv. bd. Bernard M. Baruch Coll., City U. N.Y., 1971-72. Mem. Conf. Bd., Am. Statis. Assn., Newcomen Soc. N.Am. Club: Union League (N.Y.C.). Co-author: How Good A Sales Profit Are You, 1961; The Role of the Economic Consulting Firm; also numerous market surveys.

MITTENDORF, THEODOR HENRY, paper manufacturing consultant; b. Clay Center, Kans., Jan. 14, 1895; s. Theodor Henry and Antonie (Carls) M.; B.S., Okla. State University, 1917; m. Dorothy E. Solger, May 18, 1919 (dec. Mar. 29, 1979); 1 dau., Laone M. (Mrs. D. R. Hoerl); m. 2d, Marguerite E. McLean, Oct. 3, 1980 Lectr. extension div. Okla. State U., 1917; lectr., free lance writer, 1919-20; dept. supt. Armour & Co., Chgo., 1920-22; sec., dir. sales and advt. Mid-States Gummed Paper Co., Chgo., 1922-38; v.p. charge sales Industrial Training Inst., 1938-39, v.p., gen. mgr. The Gummed Products Co., Troy, Ohio, 1940-48; v.p. charge sales Hudson Pulp and Paper Corp., N.Y.C., 1948-56, exec. v.p., 1956-58, cons., 1958—; pres. Mitt Industries, Inc., Mount Dora, Fla., 1972—; dir. 5 East 71st St. Corp. Dir. Muscular Dystrophy Assn. Served from 2d lt. F.A. to 1st lt. AS, U.S. Army, World War I, AEF. Named to Okla. State U. Alumni Hall of Fame, 1961. Mem. Kraft Paper Assn. (dir., mem. exec. com. 1951-58), Gummed Industries Assn. (pres. 1955-56). Paper Bag Inst. (pres. 1955-56), Paper Club N.Y., Am. Legion, Symposiarchs, Kappa Sigma, Alpha Zeta, Pi Kappa Delta. Republican. Methodist. Clubs: Masons, Order Eastern Star. Mount Dora (Fla.) Golf, Mount Dora Yacht; Ponte Vedra (Fla.); African Safari of Fla., Okla. State U. President's (life), Okla. State U. Henry G. Bennett Soc. (life), Okla. State U. Alumni Assn. (life). Avocation: big game hunting. Home: Box 1138 Mount Dora FL 32757 Office: PO Box 1138 Mount Dora FL 32757

MITTON, LISA J., controller; b. Plainfield, N.J., July 22, 1958; d. Thomas George and Sally Lou (Armstrong) VanderVeer; m. Michael Anthony Mitton, Mar. 7, 1987. BS in Acctg., U. Colo., 1980. Acct. Gulf Mineral Resources Co., Denver, 1980-81; asst. controller PureCycle Corp., Boulder, Colo., 1981-84; controller Anatel Corp., Boulder, Colo., 1984—. Troop leader Girl Scouts Am., Littleton, Colo., 1976. Mem. Nat. Assn. Accts. (mem. Controller's Council), Beta Alpha Psi. Home: 546 Donn Ct Boulder CO 80303 Office: Anatel Corp 2200 Central Ave $S2Ste F Boulder CO 80301

MITTON, MICHAEL ANTHONY, corporate executive; b. Bremen, Germany, Mar. 13, 1947; came to U.S., 1948 (parents Am. citizens); s. Ralph Walter and Aniela (Pilarz) M.; m. Lisa Van der Veer, March 7, 1986. BS, U. Wyo., 1970. Asst. mgr. ops. Moller Steamship Co., N.Y.C., 1970-72; investment analyst Moller Industries, N.Y.C., 1972-73; internal auditor Corning (N.Y.) Glass Works, 1973-75, supr. acctg., 1975-76; dir. acctg. Autotrain Corp., Washington, 1977-78; pres. RMA Ltd., Ft. Collins, Colo., 1978-81; contr. Purecycle Corp., Boulder, Colo., 1981-83; pres., chief exec. officer, treas. Synthetech Inc., Albany, Oreg., 1983—; also bd. dirs. Synthetech Inc., Boulder. Mem. Soaring Soc. Am., Rockies Venture Club (com. 1985—). Home: 546 Donn Ct Boulder CO 80303 Office: Synthetech 1290 Industrial Way Albany OR 97321

MIYAMOTO, CRAIG TOYOKI, advertising and public relations company executive; b. Joliet, Ill., Oct. 14, 1944; s. Robert Mitsuo and Dorothy Toyoko (Okumura) M.; BBA, Woodbury Coll., 1967; MA, U. So. Calif., 1972; m. Diana Chie Ueda, Mar. 24, 1966; children: James Anthony Kazuyuki, Carleton Alan Yasuo. Reporter, Alhambra (Calif.) Post-Advocate, 1968-70; editor Monterey Park Californian, 1970-71; mng. editor So. Calif. Pub. Co., 1971-72; dep. pub. rels. dir. Honolulu Bd. Water Supply, 1972-76, pub. rels. dir., 1976-77; pres. Miyamoto Advt./Pub. Relations, Honolulu, 1977-87; v.p. Profl. Communications, Inc., 1987—; Pineapple Post, Honolulu, 1977—, Aura Publs., Honolulu, 1980-83, instr. pub. rels. U. Hawaii, 1978-80. Pres., Honolulu Jaycees, 1975-76; mem. exec. com. 50th State Fair, 1974-76; dir. pub. rels. Hawaii Jaycees, 1974-75, Monterey Park C. of C., 1970-71; bd. dirs. San Gabriel Valley YMCA, 1971-72, Garfield Community Sch. Bd., 1971-72; mem. Jaycees Internat. Senate, 1976—. Named Man of Yr., Honolulu, 1974; recipient John Armbruster award, 1974, State Svc. award Hawaii Jaycees, 1974. Mem. Am. Advt. Fedn., Pub. Rels. Soc. Am. (accredited, bd. dirs. Hawaii chpt., pres., v.p., sec. Hawaii chpt.), Hawaii Advt. Fedn. (bd. dirs.), Mensa, Am. Philatelic Soc., Am. Topical Assn., Internat. Soc. for Japanese Philately, Bur. Issues Assn., Hawaiian Philatelic Soc., Hawaii Stamp and Coin Dealers Assn. (pres., v.p.). Democrat. Author: How to Earn $2,000 or More Without Hardly Working At All, 1979, The Pineapple Post Catalogue, 1984. Office: 1001 Bishop St Pacific Tower 19th Fl Honolulu HI 96813

MIZEL, LARRY A., housing construction company executive; b. 1942; married. BA, U. Okla., 1964; JD, U. Denver, 1967. Chmn. bd., chmn. exec. com., dir. MDC Holdings Inc., 1972—. Office: MDC Holdings Inc 3600 S Yosemite St Denver CO 80237 *

MIZELL, ANDREW HOOPER, III, concrete company executive; b. Franklin, Tenn., Sept. 26, 1926; s. Andrew Hooper, Jr. and Jennie McEwen (Fleming) M.; B.A., Venderbilt U., 1950; m. Julia Yolanda Mattei, Dec. 20, 1947; children—Andrew Hooper, Julia Fleming. Supt., Wescon Constrn. Co., Nashville, 1950-52; accountant McIntyre & Asso., Nashville, 1952-55; credit mgr. Ingram Oil Co., Nashville, 1955-56, v.p. and dir., 1956-62; v.p., dir. Comml. Sign & Advt. Co., Nashville, 1957-59; v.p. and dir. Gen. Properties Co., New Orleans, 1957-62; v.p. and dir. Minn. Barge & Terminal Co., St. Paul, 1957-62; mgr. real estate and devel. Murphy Corp., El Dorado, Ark., 1962-63, mgr. retail sales, 1962-63; pres. and chmn. bd. Transit Ready Mix, Inc., Nashville, 1963—; pres., Conco, Inc., Apollo Concrete Products, Inc.; ptnr. Mizell Riggs Enterprises. Active United Givers Fund, 1965-66; chmn. Concrete div. Office Emergency Planning, 1965—; mem. Nat. UN Day Com., 1978. Served with USNR, 1944-46. Named Ark. Traveler, 1966, Ky. Col., 1969. Mem. Nat. Ready Mix Concrete Assn. (chmn. membership com. Tenn. sect. 1971—, chmn. marketing com. Tenn. chpt. 1973—), Assn. Gen. Contractors, Tenn. Bldg. Material Assn., Nat. Fedn. Ind. Businessmen, Portland Cement Assn., Nat. Area Bus. and Edn. Radio, Asso. Builders and Contractors, Spl. Indsl. Radio Service Industry, Tenn. Road Builders, Boat Owners Assn. U.S., Nashville C. of C., U.S. C. of C., Am. Concrete Inst. Clubs: Nashville Yacht, Nashville City, Belle Meade Country, The Honors Course, Commodore Yacht (past commodore). Home: 4340 Beekman Dr Nashville TN 37215 Office: Transit Ready Mix Inc Mizell-Riggs Bldg Ward Circle PO Box 1864 Brentwood TN 37027

MIZELLE, ROBERT MITCHELL, investment advisor; b. Richmond, Va., Oct. 21, 1958; s. Joseph Mitchell and Edna Earle (Waters) M.; m. Margaret A. Swanson, Feb. 13, 1988. BS, U. Nebr., 1981. Acct. exec. Paine Webber, Omaha, 1981-84, Smith Barney, Omaha, 1984—. Chmn. Red Cross Spl. Projects, Omaha, 1988. Named Vol. of Yr. Am. Lung Assn. Nebr., Omaha, 1985-86; recipient cert. of completion English Channel Swim Assn., Folkestone, Eng., 1986. Mem. Rotary Club (chmn. 1987—, trustee fin. 1988—, bd. dirs.). Republican. Presbyterian. Office: Smith Barney Harris Upham 366 Regency Pky Omaha NE 68114

MIZER, ROBERT E., sales executive; b. Denver, Jan. 12, 1943; s. Robert E. M.; m. Mary K., Feb. 1, 1969; 1 child, Michael. BS in Bus. and Fin., U. Colo., 1969. Salesman Packaging Corp. Am., Denver, 1969-76; mgr. sales SW Forest Industries, Santa Fe Springs, Calif., 1977-83, Service Container Corp., Compton, Calif., 1983—. Served with USMC, 1961-64. Home: 20272 Adrian Circle Huntington Beach CA 92646 Office: Service Container Corp 301 W Walnut St Compton CA 90220

MLADJENOVIC, PAUL JOSEPH, financial planner; b. San Sego, Croatia, Yugoslavia, Mar. 19, 1959; came to U.S., 1963; s. Milorad and Ana (Bussanich) M. BA, Seton Hall U., 1981. Cert. fin. planner. Officer credit and loans First Jersey Nat. Bank, Jersey City, 1982-84; securities ops. loan dept. Israel Discount Bank of N.Y., N.Y.C., 1984-87; fin. planner, cons., pres., chief exec. officer PM Fin. Svcs., Hoboken, N.J., 1987—; instr. Discovery Ctr., N.Y.C., 1986—; adj. instr. Coll. Fin. Planning, Colo., 1987-88. Author: Small Investment Guide, 1989. Mem. Inst. Cert. Fin. Planners, Toastmasters (treas. 1988, pres. 1989). Republican. Roman Catholic. Office: PM Fin Svcs PO Box 6292 Hoboken NJ 07030

MOBEY, MICHAEL GEORGE, public transportation agency executive; b. Pontiac, Mich., June 1, 1949; s. George Elwin Mobey and Lena Mae (Stevens) Belisle; m. Elizabeth Ann Kerlikowske, June 9, 1973 (div. 1977); 1 child, Kate Elspeth; m. Joanne Grace Willet, Mar. 15, 1980; 1 child, Wesley Robert Kirkey. BA, Cen. Mich. U., 1972, MA, 1974; postgrad., U. Ottawa, 1974-76. With Isabella County Transp. Commn., Mt. Pleasant, Mich., 1978—, gen. mgr., 1983—. Mem. N.E. Transp. Mgrs. Assn. (pres. 1983), Mich. Pub. Transit Assn. (v.p. 1985-87), Mt. Pleasant C. of C. (past officer Energyfest), Soc. Study Indigenous Langs. Ams., Toastmasters, Rotary. Democrat. Roman Catholic. Office: Isabella County Transp Comm 4590 E Pickard St Mount Pleasant MI 48858

MOBLEY, JOHN HOMER, II, lawyer; b. Shreveport, La., Apr. 21, 1930; s. John Hinson and Beulah (Wilson) M.; m. Sue Lawton, Aug. 9, 1958; children—John Lawton, Anne Davant. A.B., U. Ga., 1951, J.D., 1953. Bar: Ga. 1952, U.S. Dist. Ct., D.C. Mem. firm Kelley & Mobley, Atlanta, 1956-63, Gambrell & Mobley, 1963-83; sr. ptnr., Sutherland, Asbill & Brennan, 1983—. Served to capt. JAGC, USAF, 1953-55. Mem. State Bar Ga., ABA, Atlanta Bar Assn., Am. Judicature Soc., Atlanta Lawyers Club, Phi Delta Phi. Clubs: Atlanta Athletic, Atlanta Country, Commerce, Piedmont Driving, Georgian. (Atlanta); N.Y. Athletic, World Trade (N.Y.C.); Metropolitan (Washington). Home: 4348 Sentinel Post Rd Atlanta GA 30327 Office: Sutherland Asbill & Brennan 3100 First Atlanta Tower Atlanta GA 30383

MOBLEY, NORMA MASON GARLAND, real estate corporation officer; b. Rocky Mount, N.C., Sept. 6, 1923; d. Roscoe Gibbs and Elizabeth Estelle (James) Garland; m. Joseph Kinsey Murrill, Jr., Dec. 29, 1942 (div. Oct. 1983); children: Joseph K. III, James B.; m. Leon Jay Mobley; m. May 18, 1984. Student, Va. Intermont Jr. Coll., 1942, Mary Washington U., 1942, Edgecombe Community Coll., 1979, U. N.C., 1980. Lic. real estate broker, N.C.; cert. real estate appraiser. Assoc. broker Charter Assocs., Rocky Mount, 1980-83, Wayne Ferrell Real Estate, Rocky Mount, 1983-84, Gary Mortan and Assocs., Jacksonville, N.C., 1984-85; pres., broker-in-charge Wright Properties, Inc., Jacksonville, 1985—. Officer, bd. dirs. Rocky Mount Jr. Guild, 1953-84; bd. dirs. YWCA, 1961-65. Mem. Jacksonville Bd. Realtors, N.C. Assn. Realtors, Nat. Assn. Realtors, Nat. Assn. Real Estate Appraisers, Nat. Trust Historic Preservation, Nat. Assn. Female Execs. Republican. Methodist. Home: RR 02 Box 109 Beulaville NC 28518 Office: Wright Properties Inc 405 Johnson Blvd Jacksonville NC 28540

MOCCO, CHARLES WILLIAM, credit union executive, priest; b. Green Bay, Wis., Dec. 29, 1930; s. Charles Joseph and Louella Louise (Adrians) M. BA, St. Mary's U., Balt., 1953; Licentiate in Sacred Theology, St. Mary's U., 1957; MBA, Notre Dame U., 1967; MA, So. Ill. U., 1975. Ordained priest Roman Cath. Ch., 1957. Procurator, instr. Sacred Heart Sem., Onedia, Wis., 1958-67; instr. Christian Bros. Coll., Memphis, 1967-70, Silver Lake Coll., Manitowoc, Wis., 1975-80; episcopal vicar Diocese of Green Bay, Newtown, Wis., 1980—; pres., treas. Diocesan Clergy Credit Union, Newtown, 1985—. Chaplain Sharing-Caring Widows Group, Manitowoc, 1986. Mem. Am. Chem. Soc., Assn. Clin. Pastoral Edn., Manitowoc County Clergy Assn. (pres. 1980). Home and Office: 8109 Northeim Rd Newton WI 53063-9630

MOCH, KENNETH IAN, entrepreneur; b. White Plains, N.Y., Sept. 11, 1954; s. Gerald Marvin and Joan Shirley (Kahn) M.; m. Ellen Gray Stolzman, July 27, 1987. AB in Biochemistry, Princeton U., 1976; MBA, Stanford U., 1980. Cons. Channing, Weinberg & Co., Inc., N.Y.C., 1976-78; sr. cons. McKinsey & Co., Inc., Chgo., 1980-82; v.p. Liposome Co., Inc., Princeton, N.J., 1982-88; mng. gen. ptnr. Catalyst Ventures, Ltd., Balt., 1988—; cons. Molecular Genetics Inc., Minnetonka, Minn., 1980-81. Mem. Balt.-Washington Venture Capital Forum (bd. dirs.), Stanford Bus. Sch. Alumni Assn. (v.p. gen. programs N.Y. chpt. 1987—). Office: Catalyst Ventures Ltd 1119 St Paul St Baltimore MD 21202

MOCK, CHARLES NEWMAN, publishing company executive; b. Brunswick, Ga., Feb. 12, 1927; s. Charles Sylvester and Lillie M. (Newman) M.; m. Carolyn L. Cooke; children: Charles Newman Jr., Cynthia Mock Fogarty. LLB, U. Ga., 1951. Bar: Ga., 1950, U.S. Dist. Ct. (so. dist.) Ga., U.S. Ct. Appeals (5th cir.), U.S. Supreme Ct. Spl. agt. Fed. Bur. Investigation, Washington, 1951-59; mgr. labor relations Revlon Inc., Edison, N.J., 1959-61; dir. personnel Foster Grnat Co. Inc., Leominster, Mass., 1961-69; exec. v.p. personnel Providence Jour. Co., 1969—; bd. dirs. Providence Jour. Broadcasting Inc., Communications Properties Inc., greenville, S.C. Bd. dirs. R.I. Lung Assn., Providence, 1985—. Served as sgt. USAAF, 1945-46, PTO. Mem. Newspaper Personnel Relations Assn. (bd. dirs. 1974-79), Soc. Former Spl. Agts. FBI, So. New England Indsl. Relations Council (pres. 1981-83), Am. Newspaper Pub. Assn. (labor human resources com.). Republican. Episcopalian. Clubs: Hope (Providence); Dunes (Narragansett, R.I.). Office: Providence Jour Co 75 Fountain St Providence RI 02902

MOCK, LAWRENCE EDWARD, JR., venture capitalist; b. Louisville, Ky., Apr. 21, 1946; s. Lawrence Edward and Mary Ann (McCoy) M.; m. Beth Grace Butler, Sept 12, 1983; children: Mary Grace, Katherine Lawrence. BA, Harvard Coll., 1968; MS, Fla. State U., 1973; postgrad., London Sch. Econs., 1974. Cons. Booz Allen & Hamilton, Atlanta, 1975-78; ops. mgr. Fuqua Industries, Atlanta, 1978-80; exec. v.p. Hangar One, Inc., Atlanta, 1980-83; prin., ptnr. River Capital, Inc., Atlanta, 1983-86; bd. dirs. Winston Furniture, Inc., Birmingham, chmn. 1985-88, River Capital, Inc., Atlanta; chmn. Roman Internat., 1989—. Served as capt. USMC, 1968-71. Home: 51 Maddox Dr NE Atlanta GA 30309 Office: Two Midtown Pla 1360 Peachtree St NE Ste 1430 Atlanta GA 30309

MOCK, ROBERT CLAUDE, architect; b. Baden, Fed. Republic of Germany, May 3, 1928; came to U.S., 1938, naturalized, 1943; s. Ernest and Charlotte (Geismar) M.; m. Belle Carol Bach, Dec. 23, 1952 (div.); children: John Bach, Nicole Louise; m. Marjorie Reubenfeld, Dec. 20, 1964. B.Arch., Pratt Inst., 1950; M. Arch., Harvard U., 1953. Registered architect, N.Y., Conn., N.J., Nat. Council Archtl. Registration Bds. Architect George C. Marshall Space Center, Huntsville, Ala., 1950-51; archtl. critic Columbia Sch. Architecture, N.Y.C., 1953-54; dir. facility design Am. Airlines, N.Y.C., 1955-60; founder Robert C. Mock & Assocs. (architects and engrs.), N.Y.C., 1960—; Mem. Mayor's Panel of Architects, N.Y.C. Prin. works include: Shine Motor Inn, Queens, N.Y., 1961 (recipient 1st prize motel category Queens C. of C. 1961), temporary terminal bldg. Eastern Air Lines , La Guardia Airport, N.Y.C., 1961, cargo bldgs United Airlines and Trans World Airlines, Kennedy Airport, N.Y.C., Bridgeport (Conn.) Airport, 1961, Eastern Air Lines Med. Ctr., Kennedy Airport, 1962, ticket office Trans World Airlines Fifth Ave., N.Y.C., 1962, terminal bldgs. Eastern Air Lines and Trans World Airlines , La Guardia Airport, N.Y.C., 1963, 7 bldgs. Mfrs. Hanover Trust Co. , 1964-66, kitchen and commissary bldg. Lufthansa German Airlines, 1964, Ambassador Club, La Guardia Airport, 1964, Happyland Sch., N.Y.C., 1965, cargo bldgs. Alitalia and Lufthansa German Airlines, Kennedy Airport, 1965, FAA-Nat. Prototype Air Traffic Control Tower, 1966; Lufthansa German Airlines; Irish Internat. Airlines, El Al Israel Airlines, Varig Brazilian Airlines; passenger terminals Kennedy Airport, 1970; Swiss Air Cargo Terminal, Lufthansa German Airlines, cargo terminals El Al Israel airline cargo terminal, Kennedy Airport, 1972, passenger terminal Aerolineas Argentina, 1974, N.Am. hdqrs. Aerolineas Argentinas, N.Y.C., 1974, corp. hdqrs. Am. Airlines, 1977, N.Am. hdqrs. Varig Brazilian Airlines, N.Y.C., 1977, Norel-Ronel Indsl. Pk., Hollywood, Fla., 1979, N.Am. hdqrs. Irish Internat. Airlines , N.Y.C., 1979, corp. hdqrs. Bankers Trust Co., N.Y.C., 1980, cargo terminal Air India, cargo terminal Flying Tiger, Kennedy Airport, 1982, 2 flight kitchen bldgs. Ogden Food Corp., Kennedy Airport, 1984, 88 and LaGuardia Airport, 1987, Greenwich Assn. Retarded Citizens Sch., 1983, passenger terminal extension Varig Brazilian Airlines , 1985, 3 restaurants La Guardia Airport, 1987. Recipient United Way Vol. of Yr. award, 1984. Mem. Am. Arbitration Assn. Clubs: City, Harvard, Admirals Cove. Office: 185 Byram Shore Rd Greenwich CT 06830

MOCKLER, COLMAN MICHAEL, JR., manufacturing company executive; b. St. Louis, Dec. 29, 1929; s. Colman Michael and Veronica (McKenna) M.; m. Joanna Lois Sperry, Dec. 28, 1957; children: Colman Michael III, Joanna Lois, Emily McKenna, Andrew Sperry. A.B., Harvard U., 1952, M.B.A., 1954. With Gen. Electric Co., 1954-55; mem. faculty Harvard Grad. Sch. Bus., 1955-57; with Gillette Co., Boston, 1957—; treas. Gillette Co., 1965-68, v.p., 1967-68, sr. v.p., 1968-70, exec. v.p., 1970-71, vice chmn. bd., 1971-74, pres., chief operating officer, 1974-76, chief exec. officer, 1975—, chmn. bd., 1976—, dir., 1971—; dir. Bank of Boston Corp., First Nat. Bank Boston, Fabreeka Products Co., John Hancock Mutual Life Ins. Co., Raytheon Co. Chmn. corp. Simmons Coll.; mem. corp. Mus. Sci., Mass. Gen. Hosp. Served with AUS, 1948-49. Fellow Harvard Coll. Club: Harvard (N.Y.C.). Office: Gillette Co Prudential Tower Bldg Boston MA 02199

MOCKLER, EDWARD JOSEPH, financial planner; b. Bklyn., Sept. 3, 1954; s. Earl Jack and Elizabeth (Dalton) M.; m. Margaret M. Morris, July 9, 1977. AAS, SUNY, Farmingdale, 1974, CUNY, Kingsborough, 1982. Cert. fin. planner. Asst. mgr. McLaughlin & Sons, Inc., Bklyn., 1974-78; pres. Edward J. Mockler, Inc., Bklyn., 1978-85; ptnr. Bay Svc. Co., Bklyn., 1978-80; fin. planner Summers & Co., N.Y.C., 1983; v.p. Harbour Fin. Planning Group Ltd., Bay Shore, N.Y., 1983-85, pres., 1985—. Mem. Registry Fin. Planning Practitioners, Inst. Cert. Fin. Planners, Internat. Assn. Fin. Planning, Phi Theta Kappa. Republican. Roman Catholic. Office: Harbour Fin Planning Group Ltd 1510 5th Ave Bay Shore NY 11706

MODAFFERI, ANTHONY KENNETH, III, lawyer; b. N.Y.C., June 29, 1960; s. Anthony Kenneth Jr. and Joanne Marie (Alegretti) M.; m. Jessica Anne Pressler, June 15, 1985; 1 child, Rachael Lyn. BS in Fin. and Econs., Seton Hall U., 1982, JD, 1985. Bar: N.J. 1985, U.S. Dist. Ct. N.J. 1986, U.S. Ct. Appeals (3rd cir.) 1986, U.S. Tax Ct. 1986, U.S. Ct. Appeals (D.C. cir.) 1988, U.S. Claims Ct. 1988, U.S. Supreme Ct., 1989, U.S. Ct. Appeals (fed. cir.) 1989. Counsel Nat. Community Bank, Hasbrouck Heights, N.J., 1986-87; ptnr. Pressler & Modafferi, Hackensack, N.J., 1987—. Chmn. Englewood (N.J.) Rep. Com., 1988; vice-chmn. Englewood Citizens for Fair Taxes, 1988. Mem. ABA (corp. banking and bus. law, tax sect., pub. contracts sect.), D.C. Bar Assn. (administn. law and agy. sect., corp. fin. and securities law sect., govt. contracts and litigation sect.), Fed. Bar Assn., Practising Law Inst., N.J. Bar Assn. (fin. transactions com. banking sect., chmn. new devels. subcom.), Bergen County Bar Assn. Republican. Office: Pressler & Modafferi 20 Mercer St Hackensack NJ 07601

MODERY, RICHARD GILLMAN, marketing and sales executive; b. Chgo., Sept. 20, 1941; s. Richard Gustave Modery and Betty Jane (Gillman) Perok; m. Kay Francis Whitby, July 31, 1966 (div. July 1977); children: Stacey Lynn, Marci Kay; m. Anne-Marie Lucette Arsenault, Feb. 27, 1979. Student, Joliet (Ill.) Jr. Coll., 1959-61, Aurora (Ill.) Coll., 1963-65, Davenport Bus. Coll., Grand Rapids, Mich., 1969-71, Northwestern U., Evanston, Ill., 1987. Mktg. products mgr. Rapistan, Inc., Grand Rapids, 1964-75; mng. estimating, project mgmt., customer service E.W. Buschman Co., Cin., 1975-78; exec. v.p. Metzgar Conveyor Co., Grand Rapids, 1979-84; mng. dir. Metzco Internat (cen. and S.Am.), Grand Rapids, Mich., 1981-84, Transfer Technologies, Inc., Grand Rapids, 1984-87; gen. ptnr., pres., chief exec. officer Nat. Monument Co., Grand Rapids, 1986—; v.p. Translogic Corp., Denver, 1987-88; corp. officer, v.p. mktg., field ops. and sales S.I. Handling Systems, Inc., Easton, Pa., 1988—; speaker and cons. in field. Patentee in field. Commr. City of East Grand Rapids, Mich. Traffic Commn., 1983-86. Served with USNG, 1963-69. Mem. Internat. Material Mgmt. Soc., Am. Mgmt. Assn., Material Handling Inst. (speaker nat. confs.), Conveyor Equipment Mfrs. Assn. Lodge: Masons (32 degree). Home: 3134 Prescott Rd Bethlehem PA 18017 also: PO Box 268 Stockertown PA 18083 Office: SI Handling Systems Inc Kesslersville Rd Easton PA 18042

MODIGLIANI, FRANCO, economics and finance educator; b. Rome, June 18, 1918; came to U.S., 1939, naturalized, 1946; s. Enrico and Olga (Flaschel) M.; m. Serena Calabi, May 22, 1939; children: Andrea, Sergio. D. Jurisprudence, U. Rome, 1939; D. Social Sci., New Sch. Social Rsch., N.Y.C., 1944; LLD ad honorem, U. Chgo., 1967; D. honoris causa, U. Louvain, Belgium, 1974, Istituto Universitario di Bergamo, 1979, Hartford U.; LHD, Bard Coll., 1985, Brandeis U., 1986. Instr. econs. and statistics N.J. Coll. Women, New Brunswick, 1942; instr., then asso. econs. and statistics Bard Coll., Columbia, 1942-44; lectr., asst. prof. math. econs. and econometrics New Sch. Social Rsch., 1943-44, 46-48; rsch. asso., chief statistician Inst. World Affairs, N.Y.C., 1945-48; rsch. cons. Cowles Commn. Rsch. in Econs. U. Chgo., 1949-54; asso. prof., then prof. econs. U. Ill., 1949-52; prof. econs. and indsl. adminstrn. Carnegie Inst. Tech., 1952-60; vis. prof. econs. Harvard U., 1957-58; prof. econs. Northwestern U., 1960-62; vis. prof. econs. MIT, 1960-61, prof. econs. and finance, 1962—, Inst. prof., 1970—; Fellow polit. economy U. Chgo., 1948; Fulbright lectr. U. Rome, also, Palermo, Italy, 1955. Author: The Collected Papers of Franco Modigliani, 3 vols, 1980; co-author: National Incomes and International Trade, 1953, Planning Production, Inventories and Work Forces, 1960, The Role of Anticipations and Plans in Economic Behavior and Their Use in Economic Analysis and Forecasting, 1961, New Mortgage Designs for Stable Housing in an Inflationary Environment, 1975, Mercato del Lavoro, Distribuzione del Reddito e Consumi Privati, 1975, The Debate Over Stabilization Policy, 1986, Il Caso Italia, 1986. Mem. macro econs. policy group Ctr. for European Policy Studies, 1985—. Recipient Nobel prize in econ. sci., 1985, Premio Coltura for Econs. Repubblica Italiana, 1988, Premio APE award, 1988, Graham and Dodd award, 1975, 80, James R. Killian Jr. Faculty Achievement award, 1985. Fellow Econometric Soc. (coun. 1960, v.p. 1961, pres. 1962), Am. Econ. Assn. (v.p. 1975, pres. 1976), Internat. Econ. Assn. (v.p. 1977-83, hon. pres. 1983—), Am. Acad. Arts and Scis.; mem. Nat. Acad. Scis., Am. Fin. Assn. (pres. 1981). Home: 25 Clark St Belmont MA 02178 Office: MIT Sloan Sch Mgmt Cambridge MA 02139

MODLIN, HOWARD S., lawyer; b. N.Y.C., Apr. 10, 1931; s. Martin and Rose Modlin; m. Margot S., Oct. 18, 1956; children—James, Laura, Peter. A.B., Union Coll., Schenectady, 1952; J.D., Columbia U., 1955. Bar: N.Y. 1956, D.C. 1973. Assoc., Weisman, Celler, Spett & Modlin, N.Y.C., 1956-61, ptnr., 1961-76, mng. ptnr., 1976—; sec., dir. Fedders Corp., Peapack, N.J., Gen. DataComm Industries, Inc., Middlebury, Conn.; dir. Trans-Lux Corp., Norwalk, Conn., Fischbach Corp., N.Y.C., Am.-Book-Stratford Press, Inc., N.Y.C. Chmn. bd. dirs. Daus. of Jacob Geriatric Ctr., Bronx, N.Y. Mem. ABA, Assn. Bar City N.Y., D.C. Bar Assn. Office: Weisman Celler Spett & Modlin 320 Park Ave New York NY 10022

MOE, PALMER L., gas company executive; b. Billings, Mont., 1944. BSBA, U. Denver, 1966. Mem. audit staff to mng. ptnr. Arthur Anderson Co., 1965-83; pres., chief operating officer Valero Energy Corp., San Antonio, 1983—; vice chmn., bd. dirs. Valero Transmission Co.; bd. dirs. Valero Natural Gas Co., Valero Storage, Valero Offshore Inc., Valero Offshore Properties Inc., Valero Producing Co. Served with USAR, 1963-69. Office: Valero Energy Corp 530 McCullough St San Antonio TX 78215 *

MOEHRING, FRED ADOLPH, fastener distribution company executive; b. Bklyn., Nov. 4, 1935; s. Fred Henry Christian and Elsa Martha (Klein) M.; m. Marilyn Agnes Rieber, June 7, 1958; 1 child, Donna. Grad. high sch., Jamaica, N.Y. Salesman Miller-Charles and Co., Mineola, N.Y., 1956-63, Century Fasteners Corp., Elmhurst, N.Y., 1963-65; gen. mgr. Stewart Air Industries, Syosset, N.Y., 1965-70; salesman Supreme Lake Mfg. Co., Plantsville, Conn., 1971, Allmetal Screw Products Inc., Garden City, N.Y., 1971-74; cab driver Scull's Angels, Flushing, N.Y., 1972-74; gen. mgr. Empire Fasteners, L.I.C., N.Y., 1974-83, Mar-Lin Sales, Bklyn., 1983—. Mem. ASME, SAE, ASTM, Met. Fastener Distbrs. Assn. (1st v.p. 1987—). Republican. Lutheran. Office: Mar-Lin Sales 208 N 8th St Brooklyn NY 11211-2008

MOELLENBERNDT, KATHY ANN, city government executive; b. Salina, Kans., July 6, 1949; d. N.N. Beck and Evelyn (Yunk) B.; m. Richard Allen Moellenbrandt, May 30, 1977; 1 child, Sarah. BA in Bus., Wichita State U., 1971, MBA in Econs., 1978. Rsch. analyst City of Ft. Worth, 1975-76; budget analyst City of Wichita, Kans., 1976-86; v.p., assoc. dir. econ. devel. Greater Topeka (Kans.) C. of C., 1987—. Author (booklets): Starting a Small Business in Topeka, 1986, Trends, 1982. Named U.S. Small Bus. Advocate of the Year Small Bus. Adminstrn., 1984. Mem. Kans. Indsl. Devel. Assn., Southern Indsl. Devel. Council, Kans. C. of C. Execs., Am. C. of C. Rsch. Assn. (bd. dirs.), Am. Econ. Devel. Council. Office: Greater Topeka C of C 120 E 6th St 3 Townsite Pla Topeka KS 66603

MOELLER, ACHIM FERDINAND GERD, art expert, art dealer; b. Heidelberg, Baden, Germany, July 21, 1942; came to U.S., 1967; s. Friedrich Hermann and Liselotte Gerda Emilie (Kehrer); m. Daniele Poli Ellis, Mar. 24, 1971 (div. 1978); children: Frederic, Beatrice; m. Colette Jeanine Estiveau, Aug. 11, 1986; 1 child, Stephanie. Baccalaureat, Lycée Français, Sarrebruck, Germany, 1961; postgrad. in econs., Hochschule für Wirtschaftswissenschaften, St. Gallen, Switzerland, 1962-64. Asst. mgr. Kunsthaus Lempertz, Cologne, Fed. Republic Germany, 1965-66; researcher Wildenstein & Co., N.Y.C., 1966-67; dir., v.p. Marlborough Gallery, N.Y.C., 1967-71; pres. Achim Moeller Ltd., London, 1971-87, Achim Moeller Fine Art Ltd, N.Y.C., 1983—; dir. Achim Moeller Fine Art Ltd., London, 1987—; curator in chief John C. Whitehead Collection, Washington, 1981—; expert Lyonel Feininger, N.Y.C., 1980—. Editor, author: (exhbn. catalogs) Lyonel Feininger, 1968, 75, 85, 86; (book catalogs) John C. Whitehead Collection, 1987, Julius Bissier, 1987. Mem. Soc. London Art Dealers. Office: 52 E 76th St New York NY 10021

MOELLER, LYNN HARVEY, controller; b. Davenport, Iowa, Aug. 10, 1942; s. Harvey Charles and Evelyn Laura (Krambeck) M.; m. Mary Theresa Marti, Aug. 28, 1964; children: Michael, Stephen. BBA, U. Iowa, 1966, MA, 1967. Sr. auditor Arthur Andersen & Co., Chgo., 1967-71; from acctg. mgr. to asst. contr., contr., sr. v.p. Assocs. Corp. N.Am., Dallas, 1971—. Republican. Lutheran. Office: Assocs Corp N Am PO Box 660237 Dallas TX 75226-0237

MOELLER, PHILIP THEODORE, newspaper business editor; b. Evanston, Ill., Mar. 12, 1946; s. William Graf and Marguerite Laura (DeHaven) M.; m. Cheryl Ann Magazine, Sept. 2, 1979; children: Jonathan, Daniel. AB, Princeton U., 1968; MS in Journalism, Northwestern U., 1970. Bus. writer The Charlotte (N.C.) Observer, 1970-73, The Chgo. Sun-Times, 1973-77; bus. editor The Louisville Courier-Jour., 1977-82, The Balt. Sun, 1982—; instr. journalism Northwestern U.. Evanston, Ill. 1974-76. Recipient John Hancock Excellence award John Hancock Mut. Life Ins. Co. 1977, 80, Mo. Bus. Journalism award U. Mo., 1980, Loeb award UCLA Grad. Sch. Mgmt., 1979; Walter Bagehot fellow Columbia U., 1975. Mem. Soc. Am. Bus. Edn. and Writers (gov. 1983—, pres. 1988-89). Office: The Balt Sun 501 N Calvert St Baltimore MD 21278

MOENCH, ROBERT WILLIAM, utilities executive; b. Albany, Oreg., Jan. 13, 1927; s. Louis Mirle and Gladys Pearl (Monosmith) M.; m. Harriet Thompson, Mar. 23, 1947; children—Libby, Mary, Judy, Nancy. B.S. in Elec. Engring, Oreg. State U., 1951. Registered profl. engr., Oreg. With Pacific Power & Light Co., Portland, Oreg., 1951—; v.p. elec. engring. and constrn. Pacific Power & Light Co., 1977-79, sr. v.p. engring. and power, 1979-81, sr. v.p. planning and ops., 1981-84, exec. v.p., 1984—. Served with USN, 1944-46. Office: Pacificorp 851 SW 6th Ave Portland OR 97204

MOERDLER, CHARLES GERARD, lawyer; b. Paris, Nov. 15, 1934; came to U.S., 1946, naturalized, 1951; s. Herman and Erna Anna (Brandwein) M.; m. Pearl G. Hecht, Dec. 26, 1955; children: Jeffrey Alan, Mark Laurence, Sharon Michele. BA, L.I.U., 1953; JD, Fordham U., 1956. Bar: N.Y. 1956. Asso. firm Cravath, Swaine & Moore, N.Y.C., 1956-65; spl. counsel coms. City of N.Y. and judiciary N.Y. State Assembly, 1960-61; commr. bldgs. City of N.Y., 1966-67; sr. partner, chmn. litigation dept. Stroock & Stroock & Lavan, N.Y.C., 1967—; bd. dirs. N.Y. Post Co. Inc.; cons. housing, urban devel. and real estate to mayor City N.Y., 1967-73; commr. N.Y. State Ins. Fund, 1978—, vice chmn., 1986—. Mem. editorial bd. N.Y. Law Jour., 1985—; assoc. editor Fordham Law Rev., 1956. Asst. dir. Rockefeller nat. presdl. campaign com., 1964; adv. bd. Sch. Internat. Affairs Columbia U., 1977-80; bd. govs. L.I.U., 1966, trustee, 1985—; chmn. Community Planning Bds. 8 and 14, Bronx County, 1977-78; nat. bd. govs. Am. Jewish Congress, 1966; bd. overseers Jewish Theol. Sem. Am., 1983—; trustee St. Barnabas Hosp., Bronx, N.Y., 1985—. Recipient Tristam Walker Metcalf award L.I.U., 1966, cert. N.Y.C. Planning Commn., 1979. Mem. Am. Bar Assn., N.Y. State Bar Assn., N.Y. County Lawyers Assn., Bar Assn. City N.Y. (jud. com.), Free Sons of Israel, World Trade Ctr. Club, Metro. Club. Home: 7 Rivercrest Rd Riverdale NY 10471 Office: Stroock & Stroock & Lavan 7 Hanover Sq New York NY 10004

MOERICKE, DANIEL ELMER, auditor; b. Marion, Wis., Sept. 2, 1956; s. Elmer Arthur and Gladys Martha (Mielke) M.; m. Kay Lorraine Hoffman, Apr. 25, 1981; children: Laura Kay, Steven Daniel. BBA in Acctg. magna cum laude, U. Wis., Milw., 1978. CPA, Wis.; cert. internal auditor. Acct. mut. funds Heritage Investment Advisors, Milw., 1975-78; staff internal auditor Wausau (Wis.) Ins. Co., 1979-80, sr. internal auditor, 1981-84, supr. internal audits, 1985-86, mgr. internal audits, 1986—; chair examining com. Wausau Ins. Co. Employee Credit Union, 1983—; tchr. acctg. North Cen. Tech. Inst., Wausau, 1984, Marathon Ctr., U. Wis., Wausau, 1985. Mem. council Good Shepherd Luth. Ch., Wausau, 1985-87, treas., 1987. Mem. Inst. Internal Auditors (sec. Cen. Wis. chpt. 1980, pres. 1983, cert. of excellence 1981), Wis. Inst. CPA's. Clubs: Wausau Ins. Men's (asst. treas. 1985), Wausau Ins. Men's Golf League (statistician 1986-87). Home: T2238 Hwy WW Wausau WI 54401 Office: Wausau Ins Co 2000 Westwood Dr Wausau WI 54401

MOERINGS, BERT JOSEPH, stockbroker; b. Lobith, Holland, Oct. 11, 1946; came to U.S., 1950; s. Nicolaas A. and Betty J. M.; m. Marsha Rinker, Mar. 15, 1980; children: Nicholas, Lauren. BS in Econs., Spring Hill Coll., 1967. Stockbroker E.F. Hutton, Vero Beach, Fla., 1972-73, Merrill Lynch, Palm Beach, Fla., 1973-79, Alan Bush Brokerage Co., Palm Beach, 1979-86; pres., chief exec. officer CMC Services, Inc., Palm Beach, 1986—; bd. dirs. Money Concepts, Dominick Mgmt. Corp.; so. regional v.p. Dominick and Dominick, Inc. Served to capt. U.S. Army, 1968-71. Decorated Bronze Star. Mem. Palm Beach County Amatuer Golf Assn. (bd. dirs., vice-chmn.). Republican. Home: 2329 Prosperity Bay Ct Palm Beach Gardens FL 33410

MOFFAT, MARYBETH, automotive company executive; b. Pitts., July 25, 1951; d. Herbert Franklin and Florence Grafe (Knerem) M.; m. Brian Francis Soulier, Nov. 30, 1974 (div.). B.A., Carroll Coll., 1973. Indsl. engring. technician Wis. Centrifugal Co., Waukesha, Wis., 1976-77; indsl. engr. Utility Products, Inc., Milw., 1977-79; indsl. engring. mgr. Bear Automotive, Bangor, Pa., 1980—. Group home house parent Headwaters Regional Achievement Ctr., Lake Tomahawk, Wis., 1974. Mem. Am. Inst. Indsl. Engrs., MTM Assn. for Standards Research, Indsl. Mgmt. Soc., Alpha Gamma Delta (standards chmn. 1971-72). Republican. Methodist. Avocations: skiing; horseback riding; swimming; reading. Home: Spring Ridge Apts #P-23 Whitehall PA 18052 Office: Bear Automotive Svc Equipment Co S Main and Werner Sts Bangor PA 18013

MOFFATT, JOHN MYRICK, financial analyst; b. La Mesa, Tex., Dec. 28, 1940; s. John M. and Olene (Stephens) M.; m. Susan S. Moffatt, Sept. 9, 1967 (div. 1987); children: Andrew, Bart. BA, U. Tex., 1964; MS, NYU, 1968. Analyst Citibank, N.Y.C., 1964-67; portfolio mgr. Arnhold and Bleichroeder, N.Y.C., 1967-71; securities analyst Blyth, Eastman, Dillon, N.Y.C., 1971-74; v.p., mng. contr. ADP Network Svcs., Ann Arbor, Mich., 1974-79; pvt. practice Ann Arbor, 1979-81; pres. Analytic Systems Corp., Stamford, Conn., 1981—. Bd. dirs. Greenwich (Conn.) chpt. ARC, 1986-88. Mem. N.Y. Soc. Security Analysts, Elec. Equipment Analysts Group. Republican. Office: Analytic Systems Corp 2001 W Main St Ste 130 Stamford CT 06902

MOFFETT, FRANK CARDWELL, architect, civil engineer, real estate developer; b. Houston, Dec. 9, 1931; s. Ferrell Orlando and Jewell Bernice (Williams) M.; BArch, U. Tex., 1958; m. Annie Doris Thorn, Aug. 1, 1952 (div.); children: David Cardwell (dec.), Douglas Howard; m. Darlene Adele Alm Sayan, June 7, 1985 (div.). Architect with archtl. firms, Seattle, Harmon, Pray & Detrich, Arnold G. Gangnes, Ralf E. Decker, Roland Terry & Assocs., 1958-64; prtnr. Heideman & Moffett, AIA, Seattle, 1964-71; chief architect Wash. State Dept. Hwys., Olympia, 1971-77, Wash. State Dept. Transp., 1977-87; owner The Moffett Co., Olympia, 1974—; founder, treas. TAA, Inc., Olympia, 1987—; advisor Wash. State Bldg. Code Adv. Council, 1975—; instr. civil engring. tech. Olympia Tech. Community Coll., 1975-77; adv. mem. archtl. barriers subcom. Internat. Conf. Building Ofcls.; archtl. works include hdqrs. Gen. Telephone Directory Co., Everett, Wash., 1964; Edmonds Unitarian Ch., 1966; tenant devel. Seattle Hdqrs. Office, Seattle-First Nat. Bank, 1968-70; Wash. State Dept. Transp. Area Hdqrs. Offices, Mt. Vernon, Selah, Raymond, Colfax and Port Orchard 1973-87; Materials Lab., Spokane, Wash., 1974; Olympic Meml. Gardens, Tumwater, Wash., 1988; archtl. barriers cons. State of Alaska, 1978. Chmn. Planning Commn. of Mountlake Terr., Wash., 1963, 64, mem., 1961-67; mem. State of Wash. Gov.'s Task Force on Wilderness, 1972-75, Heritage Park Task Force, Olympia, Wash., 1986—; trustee Cascade Symphony Orch., 1971; incorporating pres. United Singles, Olympia, 1978-79. With USN, 1951-54. Registered architect, Alaska, Calif., Wash., profl. engr., Wash.; cert. Nat. Council Archtl. Registration Bds., U.S. Dept. Def., Fallout Shelter Analysis, environ. engring. Mem. AIA (dir. S.W. Wash. chpt. 1980-82, pres.-elect 1985, pres. 1986, dir. Wash. council 1986, architects in govt. nat. com. 1978-87), Am. Public Works Assn., Inst. Bldgs. and Grounds, ASCE, Constrn. Specifications Inst., Am. Arbitration Assn. (invited panelist), Gen. Soc. Mayflower Descs. (gov. Wash. Soc. 1982-83), Nat. Huguenot Soc. (pres. Wash. Soc. 1981-83, 85-87), Olympia Geneal. Soc. (pres. 1978-80), SAR (state treas. 1984-85), SCV, Sons and Daus. of Pilgrims, (gov. Wash. Soc. 1984), Order of Magna Charta, Rotary (pres. Edmonds, 1969-70), Coll. of Seattle Club, Olympia Yacht Club, Olympia Country and Golf Club. Coauthor: An Illustrated Handbook for Barrier-Free Design, 2d edit., 1984, 3d edit., 1987. Republican. Unitarian. Home: PO Box 2422 Olympia WA 98507 Office: PO Box 2422 Olympia WA 98507

MOFFETT, JAMES ROBERT, oil and gas company executive; b. Houma, La., Aug. 16, 1938; s. Robert E. and Mary G. (Pollack) M.; m. Louise C. Hohmann, June 5, 1960; children: Crystal Louise, James R. B.S., U. Tex., 1961; M.S., Tulane U., 1963. Cons. geologist oil and gas industry New Orleans, 1964-69; v.p. founding ptnr. McMoRan Exploration Co., New Orleans, 1969-74; pres., chief exec. officer McMoRan Oil & Gas Co., New Orleans, 1974-81, 81-85; chmn., chief exec. officer McMoRan Oil & Gas Co., 1985—; dir. McMoRan Oil & Gas Co., New Orleans, 1974—; vice-chmn. Freeport McMoRan Inc., New Orleans, 1981-85; chmn., chief exec. officer Freeport McMoRan Inc., 1985—; dir. Freeport McMoRan Inc., New Orleans, 1981—; bd. dirs. Hibernia Bank, New Orleans, Freeport-McMoRan Inc., McMoRan Oil & Gas Co. Mem. Nat. Petroleum Council, Washington, 1979, Commn. on the Future of South, 1986; bd. dirs. La. Energy Nat. PAC, Metairie, La., 1979, World Trade Ctr., New Orleans, Am. Cancer Soc. Greater New Orleans, Bus. Task Force Edn., Inc.; chmn. bd. La. Coun. Fiscal Reform; chmn. bus. coun. New Orleans and River Region, 1985-87. 2nd lt. U.S. Army, 1961-68, capt. Res. ret. Recipient T award Ex Students Assn. U. Tex., 1960, Hornblower Yr. award Pub. Relations Soc. Am., 1986, Vol. Yr. award Urban League Greater New Orleans, 1987; Minnie Stevens Piper Found. scholar U. Tex., 1960, Jacques E. Yenni, S.J. award Loyola U. of New Orleans for Outstanding Community Svc., Jr. Achievement Bus. Hall of Fame award, 1987, Loyola U. of New Orleans' Integritas Vitae award, 1988; named One of Ten Outstanding Persons of 1985 Inst. for Human Understanding, New Orleans. Mem. All Am. Wildcatters, New Orleans Geol. Soc., Petroleum Club New Orleans, Greater New Orleans Mktg. Com. (exec. com. 1987), Geology Found U. Tex. (adv. council 1972-85), Devel. bd. U. Tex., La. Ind. producers Royalty Owners Assn.. South La. Mid-Continent Oil Gas Assn. (v.p.), Dinner Steering Com. (Disting. Citizen award 1983, 85 Boy Scouts Am. New Orleans div.), Green Wave Club. Republican. Office: Freeport-McMoran Inc 1615 Poydras St New Orleans LA 70112-1217

MOFFITT, DONALD EUGENE, retired transportation and manufacturing company executive; b. Terre Haute, Ind., May 22, 1932; s. James Robert and Margaret Mary (Long) M.; m. Phyllis A. Stepp, Mar. 8, 1953; children: David, Mitchell, Christopher, Michael. B.A., Ind. State U., 1954; postgrad., Ind. U., 1956; grad., Advanced Mgmt. Program, Harvard U., 1972. Accountant Foster Freight Lines, Indpls., 1955-56; with Consol. Freightways Inc., San Francisco, 1956—, v.p. planning, 1969-73; v.p. fin. motor carrier subs. Consol. Freightways Corp. Del. (motor carrier subs.), San Francisco, 1974-75; v.p. fin., treas. parent co. Consol. Freightways Corp. Del., San Francisco, 1976-81; exec. v.p. Consol. Freightways Corp. Del., Palo Alto, Calif., 1981-86; vice chmn. Consol. Freightways, Inc., Palo Alto, 1986-88; dir. TAB Products, Palo Alto. Contbr. articles in field. Leader, mem. bd. Sea Scouts, Stanford Area council Boy Scouts Am.; bd. dirs. Bay Area Jr. Acheivement, Peninsula Conflict Resolution Ctr. Mem. Am. Trucking Assn., Bay Area Commonwealth Club, Fin. Execs. Inst. Club: Islander Yacht. Home: 17304 SE 47th St Issaquah WA 98027

MOFFITT, PETER MIDDLETON, financial consultant; b. New Haven, Apr. 16, 1926; s. John Adams and Virginia Marriott (Hellen) M.; m. Florence F. Beach, June 24, 1962; children: Margaret Moffitt Rahe, Anne, Johanna. BA, Yale U., 1948. Staff Hanover Bank, N.Y.C., 1948-55; mgr. mktg. Conn. Hard Rubber Co., New Haven, 1955-58; exec. v.p. Conn. Devel. Credit Corp., Meriden, 1958-60; assoc. Harriman Ripley & Co., Inc., N.Y.C., 1960-63; ind. cons. N.Y.C., 1963-73; pres. Moffitt and Co., Inc., Southport, Conn., 1973—; bd. dirs. Hussey Mfg. Co., E.A. Sween Co. Trustee Green Farms Acad., 1968-73, Pomfret Sch., 1978—, v.p., 1982—; trustee John Day Jackson 1956 Trust, 1987—; warden St. Timothy's Episcopal Ch., Fairfield, Conn. 1973-76. Mem. Am. Mgmt. Assn. Clubs: Pequot Yacht, Fairfield County Hunt. Home: 3632 Congress St Fairfield CT 06430 Office: PO Box 532 Southport CT 06490

MOGAS, VINCENT LOUIS, manufacturing company executive; b. Laredo, Tex., Sept. 7, 1939; m. Marilyn Lea Palmer, Apr. 19, 1962; children: Valerie, Matthew. BBA, Tex. A&I U., 1963, MS, 1964. Pres., chief exec. officer Mogas Industries, Inc., Houston; dir. MiSeal, Inc., Houston. Office: Mogas Industries Inc 14330 E Hardy Houston TX 77039

MOGUL, EUGENE, executive search consultant; b. N.Y.C., July 27, 1923; s. Samuel and Tillie (Stern) M.; m. Rhoda Marylyn Blate, Sept. 12, 1948; children: Susan, Mark, Samuel, Kim, Jess, Pamela. BS in Engring., Columbia U., 1943. Pres. Comfax Communications Inc., N.Y.C., 1968-71; gen. mgr. service Savin Bus. Machines, Valhalla, N.Y., 1971-73; pres. Mogul Cons., Inc., Jericho, N.Y., 1973—. Mem. IEEE (sr.). Democrat. Jewish. Home: 18 Ridge Rock Ln East Norwich NY 11732 Office: Mogul Cons Inc 380 N Broadway Jericho NY 11753

MOHALLEY, JOHN JOSEPH, financial executive; b. N.Y.C., July 27, 1944; s. William Patrick and Catherine Ann (McShane) M.; m. Carol Joan Thomas, July 19, 1975; children: Jason, Janet. BA, Queens Coll., 1968; postgrad., Redlands U. CPA, N.Y., Calif., Oreg. Audit mgr. Ernst & Whinney, Los Angeles and N.Y.C., 1967-74; v.p. fin. Quantum Sci., Palo Alto, Calif., 1974-76; pvt. practice acctg. San Francisco, 1976-78; mgr. tax and auditing CH2M Hill, Corvallis, Oreg., 1978-83; fiscal coordinator Hosp. Corp. Am., Saudi Arabia, 1983-85; chief fin. officer, treas. Vintage Group, San Rafael, Calif., 1985—; ptnr. Gilbert & Mohalley, CPAs, San Francisco, 1988—. Mem. Nat. Assn. Over-the-Counter Cos. (com. budget and fin.), Am. Inst. CPA's, Calif. Soc. CPA's. Home: 19 Burlwood Dr San Francisco CA 94127 Office: Vintage Group Inc 818 5th Ave San Rafael CA 94901

MOHAMMAD DOKHT MARAGHEH, RAHIM, economist; b. Maragheh, Azarbaijan, Iran, Aug. 10, 1950; came to Holland in 1985.; s. Seifali and Malahat (Azarbaijan) M.; m. Charlotte Elaine Andrews, Apr. 21, 1980; children: Ammar, Tarlan, Ayeh, Nobai. BA, Nat. U., Tehran, Iran, 1974; Grad. studies, U. Tex., Dallas, 1979. Adminstr. Jorjani Hosp., Tehran, Iran, 1970-75; fin. adminstr. consul Red Crescent, Tehran, 1979-80; librarian U. Tex., Dallas, 1975-79; instr. U. Tehran, 1985-86; fin. analyst NIIO, Tehran, 1981-85; investment cons. IPDIC, Tehran, 1985-86; mgr. Osva Alhavi, Tehran, 1980-86, LAL Enterprise, The Hague, Holland, 1986—; cons. D.P., Tehran, 1987—, Inst. Phytotherapy and Drug Design, 1988. Contbr. articles to profl.jours.; editor profl. jours. Islamic.

MOHAN, D. MIKE, transportation company executive; b. Chico, Calif., Apr. 10, 1945; s. Alfred and Velda June (Clark) M.; m. Dixie Watson, June 21, 1969; children—Laurel, Patrick, Christopher. B.A., U. Calif.-Berkeley, 1967, M.B.A., 1968; A.M.P., Harvard U., 1983. With So. Pacific Transp. Co., 1968—; asst. to pres. So. Pacific Transp. Co., San Francisco, 1981-82; v.p.-maintenance So. Pacific Transp. Co., 1982-83, exec. v.p., 1983-88, also dir.; pres., chief operating officer So. Pacific Transp. Co., San Francisco, 1988—. Mem. Nat. Freight Traffic Assn. Office: So Pacific Transp Co 1 Market Pla San Francisco CA 94105

MOHLMAN, LOUIS GERARD, financial planner; b. Logansport, Ind., Jan. 8, 1930; s. Louis Herman and Marie Mohlman; m. Rosemary J. Snider, June 11, 1960; children: Louis G., Anna Marie, Michael, Matthew. Student, Bradley U., Peoria, Ill., 1949. Cert. fin. planner, 1978. Owner Mohlman Jewelers, Logansport, Ind., 1950-73, Lou Mohlman Fin. Svcs., Logansport, 1969-78; cert. fin. planner E.F. Hutton & Co., Inc., Kokomo and Ft. Wayne, Ind., 1978—; cert. fin. planner, v.p. Shearson Lehman Hutton, Ft. Wayne, 1978—; mem. adv. bd. E.F. Hutton & Co., Inc., M.W. Region, 1984. Mem. No. Ind. Soc. Cert. Fin. Planners (pres. 1986-87, chmn. bd. 1987-88), Nat. Inst. Cert. Fin. Planners (dir. 1987—), Internat. Assn. Fin. Planners, Am. Legion, Elks, KC (4th degree). Roman Catholic. Office: Shearson Lehman Hutton Inc 1 Summit Sq 8th Fl Fort Wayne IN 46802

MOHNEY, SHARON EILEEN, marketing management executive; b. Bremerton, Wash., Dec. 7, 1944; d. Forest N. and Jane Ellen (Patnoe) Erlandsen; m. Gayle Alexander Mohney Jr., Dec. 14, 1968. BA, U. Wash., 1971. Mktg. rep. BASF, Williamsburg, Va., 1974-84; mktg. specialist Allied Corp., Petersburg, Va., 1984-85; mktg. mgr. Allied-Signal Corp., Petersburg, 1985—; speaker Nat. Conv. of Assn. Sch. Bus. Ofcls., San Antonio, 1987, ann. conv. Am. Floorcovering Assn., 1989. Contbr. articles to profl. jours. Mem. Am. Soc. Interior Designers, Inst. Bus. Designers, Internat. Facility Mgmt. Assn. (speaker 1987 conv.), Calligraphy Guild. Office: Allied-Signal Inc PO Box 31 Petersburg VA 23804

MOHR, BRIAN JOHN, chemical engineer; b. Lincoln, Nebr., Nov. 20, 1949; s. Kenneth J. and Luetta L. (Hake) M.; m. Wilma Jo Ann Wrigley, June 8, 1974; 1 child, Sarah. BS in ChemE, U. Nebr., 1972, MS in ChemE, 1976. Research engr. Nebr. Dept. Econ. Devel., Lincoln, 1973-74; econ. and scheduling engr. Amoco Oil Co., Sugar Creek, Mo., 1976-77, ops. engr., 1978-79; econ. and scheduling engr. Amoco Oil Co., Whiting, Ind., 1981-84; refinery coordinator Amoco Oil Co., Chgo., 1984-85; econ. and scheduling supt. Amoco Oil Co., Whiting, 1985—; process engring. supr. Energy Coop. Inc., East Chgo., Ind., 1979-81. Rep. NW Ind. Ctr. for Econ. Edn., Hammond, 1985—; mem. prin.'s adv. com. Peifer Elem. Sch., Schererville, Ind., 1987—. Mem. Am. Inst. Chem. Engrs., Tau Beta Phi. Lutheran. Office: Amoco Oil Co 2815 Indianapolis Blvd Whiting IN 46394

MOHR, DONALD R., accountant. Prin., ptnr. Coopers & Lybrand, Chgo. Office: Coopers & Lybrand 203 N LaSalle St Chicago IL 60601 *

MOHR, MILTON ERNST, electronics executive; b. Milw., Apr. 9, 1915; s. Henry O. C. and Agnes (Schellenberg) M.; children—Douglas C., Lawrence H. B.S., U. Nebr., 1938, D.Eng. (hon.), 1959. Communications research Bell Telephone Labs., Inc., N.Y.C., 1938-50; dept. head, radar lab. Hughes Aircraft Co., Culver City, Calif., 1950-54; v.p. Thompson Ramo Wooldridge, Inc., Canoga Park, Calif.; gen. mgr. RW div., Direction of TRW Computers Co., 1954-64; v.p., mgr., indsl. system div. Bunker-Ramo Corp., 1964-65; v.p., gen. mgr. def. systems div. 1965-66, pres., chief exec. officer corp., 1966-70; pres., chief exec. officer Quotron Systems, Inc., 1970—. Recipient hon. mention as outstanding young elec. engr. Eta Kappa Nu, 1948. Fellow IEEE; mem. AIAA Pi Mu Epsilon, Sigma Tau, Eta Kappa Nu. Office: Quotron Systems Inc 5454 Beethoven St Los Angeles CA 90066

MOHR, WILLIAM G., utility company executive; b. Alva, Okla., Jan. 28, 1936; s. Albert Wilhelm and Kathern (Prigmore) M.; m. Sherri Haug, Dec. 18, 1976; children: Christina, Gary. BS, Northwestern Okla. State, 1962. Dir. corp. planning Kans. Gas & Electric Co., Wichita, 1962—. Bd. dirs. Wichita Urban League, 1975-78, Community Action Agy., Wichita, 1977. With USAF, 1956-60. Mem. Edison Electric Inst., Issues Mgmt. Assn., The Planning Forum, Kiwanis (bd. dirs. Wichita club 1977). Republican. Office: Kans Gas & Electric Co 120 E 1st Box 208 Wichita KS 67201

MOHRMANN, ROBERT E., financial executive. With Price Waterhouse and Co., St. Louis, Mallinckrodt Inc., St. Louis. Mem. AICPA, Fin. Execs. Inst., Nat. Assn. Accts. Office: Wetterau Inc 8920 Pershall Rd Hazelwood MO 63042

MOHSENI, MICHAEL, engineer, contractor; b. Tabriz, Iran, Oct. 23, 1932; came to U.S., 1948; m. Beth Crager, 1953 (div. 1969); children—Elizabeth, David, Peter, Charles; m. Maryam Foroughi, Sept. 6, 1973; 1 child, Yasmine. Student Johns Hopkins U., 1950-52; BSCE, Ind. Inst. Tech., 1954. Pres., chief exec. officer Pile Co., Ltd., Tehran, Iran, 1965-77; chief exec. officer Rancho Matilija Corp., Ojai, Calif., 1978—, Mohseni Holding Co., Seattle, 1980—, MWK Internat., Ltd., Seattle, 1980—, Wyatt Engrs., Inc., Seattle, 1980—. Clubs: Rainier (Seattle), Birnam Wood (Santa Barbara, Calif.). Office: Wyatt Engrs Inc 3214 16th Ave SW Seattle WA 98134

MOILANEN, THOMAS ALFRED, construction equipment distributor; b. Hancock, Mich., Sept. 3, 1944; s. A. Edward and Elsie E. (Karkanen) M.; m. Kathleen Ann Maibach, Sept. 18, 1965; children: Todd Alan, Karl Edward. Cert., Wayne State U., 1967. Licensed funeral dir., Mich. Funeral dir. Ross B. Northrop & Son, Inc., Redford, Mich., 1967-68; sales mgr. Cloverdale Equipment Co., Oak Park, Mich., 1971; v.p., gen. mgr. Cloverdale Equipment Co., Oak Park, 1972-78, pres., chief exec. officer, bd. dirs., 1978—; pres., chief exec. officer, bd. dirs. Hasper Equipment Co., Muskegon, Mich., 1980—, SunBelt Crane & Equipment, Sarasota, Fla., 1982—, Armstrong/Cloverdale Equipment Co., Columbia, S.C., 1987—. Treas., bd. dirs. Livonia Hockey Assn., 1981-82. Mem. Associated Equipment Distbrs. Am. (equipment distbn. com. 1984), Mich. Constrn. Equipment Dealers Assn. (pres. 1983, 88), Concrete Improvement Bd. (bd. dirs. 1978-79). Republican. Lodge: Kiwanis (bd. dirs. Redford 1967-69, pres. 1969-70). Home: 18332 Laraugh Northville MI 48167 Office: Cloverdale Equipment Co 13133 Cloverdale Oak Park MI 48237

MOINET, ERIC EMIL, cost accountant; b. Paris, Mar. 17, 1952; s. Emil and Marguerite (Baccon) M.; m. Glynis Carol Moinet, May 6, 1980; children: Danielle Louise, Nicolette Anne. Assoc. in Applied Sci., Queensborough Community Coll., 1982; BBA, Baruch Coll., 1988. Jr. acct. Jason & Berman, CPA's, N.Y.C., 1982-84; sr. asst. internat. tax specialist KPMG, Peat, Marwick, Main & Co., CPAs, N.Y.C., 1984-88; sr. asst. internat. tax specialist KPMG, Peat, Marwick, Main & Co., CPAs, Raleigh, N.C., 1988, tax specialist, 1988-89; cost accountant Dixie Farming & Building Specialties, Inc., Raleigh, N.C., 1989—. Mem. Nat. Assn. Accts., N.Y. State Assn. CPA Candidates, Inc. (chmn. pub. relations, recruiting, and career coms. 1985-87, bd. dirs. 1985-87, v.p. 1986-87), Fin. and Econs. Soc. (rec. sec.), Club for Accts. Seeking Heights (pres., advisor, founding mem.), Queensborough Community Coll. Alumni Assn., Baruch Coll. Acctg. Soc., Baruch Coll. Alumni Assn., Alpha Beta Gamma. Republican. Roman Catholic.

MOIREZ, GUY MAXIME, financial executive; b. Hautmont, France, May 28, 1941; came to U.S., 1967; s. Jean Moirez and J. (Graillet) Rousseau; m. Kathryn A. Hundredmark, Dec. 27, 1969; children: Marc, Eric-John, Lionel. Diploma in Spanish, U. Jose Antonio, Madrid, 1962; undergrad. degree, Lycee Massena, Nice, France; MBA, Essec, Paris, 1985. Officer Marine Midland Bank, N.Y.C., 1967-72; v.p. Am. Express Bank, N.Y.C., 1972-82; dep. exec. mgr. Burgan Bank, Kuwait, 1982-85; mng. dir. Creditcorp International, Inc., N.Y.C., 1985-87, also bd. dirs.; pres. Yankee Pub. FAX Co., Westport, Conn., 1988—. Active Labriola Rep. Campaign for Gov., Weston, Conn., 1986. Mem. India House, Aspetuck Valley Country Club. Office: Yankee Pub FAX Co 325 Post Rd W Westport CT 06880

MOK, CARSON KWOK-CHI, structural engineer; b. Canton, China, Jan. 17, 1932; came to U.S., 1956, naturalized, 1962; s. King and Chi-Big (Lum) M.; B.S. in Civil Engring., Chu Hai U., Hong Kong, 1953; M.C.E., Cath. U. Am., 1968; m. Virginia Wai-Ching Cheng, Sept. 19, 1959. Structural designer Wong Cho Tong, Hong Kong, 1954-56; bridge designer Michael Baker Jr., Inc., College Park, Md., 1957-60; structural engr., chief design engr., asso. Milton A. Gurewitz Assos., Washington, 1961-65; partner Wright & Mok, Silver Spring, Md., 1966-75; owner Carson K.C. Mok, Cons. Engr., Silver Spring, 1976-81, pres., 1982—; facility engring. cons. Washington Met. Area Transit Authority, 1985-86; pres. Transp. Engring. and Mgmt. Assocs., P.C., Washington, 1986—; adj. asst. prof. Howard U., Washington, 1976-79, adj. assoc. prof., 1980-81. Sec., N.Am. bd. trustees, China Grad. Sch. Theology, Wayne, Pa., 1972-74, pres., 1975-83, v.p., 1984—; elder Chinese Bible Ch. Md., Rockville, 1978-80; chmn. Chinese Christian Ch. Greater Washington, 1958-61, 71, elder, 1972-76. Recipient Outstanding Standard of Teaching award Howard U., 1980; registered profl. engr., Md., D.C. Mem. ASCE, ASTM, Constrn. Specification Inst., Nat. Assn. Corrosion Engrs., Concrete Reinforcing Steel Inst., Am. Concrete Inst., Am. Welding Soc., Prestressed Concrete Inst., Post-Tensioning Inst., Soc. Exptl. Mechanics., Internat. Assn. Bridge and Structural Engring. Contbr. articles to profl. jours. Home: 4405 Bestor Dr Rockville MD 20853 Office: 9001 Ottawa Pl Silver Spring MD 20910

MOLINEAUX, CHARLES BORROMEO, lawyer; b. N.Y.C., Sept. 27, 1930; s. Charles Borromeo and Marion Frances (Belter) M.; m. Patricia Leo Devereux, July 2, 1960; children: Charles, Stephen, Christopher, Patricia, Peter, Elizabeth. BS cum laude, Sch. Fgn. Service, Georgetown U., 1950; JD, St. John's U., N.Y.C., 1959. Bar: N.Y. 1959, Mass. 1981, D.C. 1988. Assoc., then ptnr. Nevius, Jarvis & Pilz and successor firms, N.Y.C., 1959-77; ptnr. Gadsby & Hannah, N.Y.C., 1978-80; v.p., gen. counsel Perini Corp., Framingham, Mass., 1980-87; ptnr. Zorc, Rissetto, Weaver & Rosen, Washington, 1987—. Committeeman Republican Party, Nassau County, N.Y., 1965-71, mem. exec. com., 1969. Served to 1st lt. U.S. Army, 1954-56. Mem. ABA, ASCE (chmn. region II pub. contracts sect, vice chmn. model procurement project constrn. and engring. services com.), Fedn. Internationale des Ingenieurs-Conseils (Assoc. Gen. Contractors del. constrn. contract com.), Del. Hist. Soc. Roman Catholic. Home: 7107 Holyrood Dr

McLean VA 22101 Office: Zorc Rissetto Weaver & Rosen 2300 N St NW Washington DC 20037

MOLL, JOHN EDGAR, wholesale grocery company executive; b. Sikeston, Mo., Mar. 25, 1934; s. John A. and Letha A. (McDowell) M.; m. Marjorie Ellison, May 1, 1954; children—John Steven, Lynn Moll Rassieur, Nancy Moll Janeway, Julie Ann. Student Southeast Mo. State Coll., 1952-54, Program Mgmt. Devel. Harvard U., 1964. Office mgr. Malone & Hyde, Inc., Sikeston, 1957-64, div. mgr., 1964-70, div. mgr., Nashville, 1970-72, regional v.p., Nashville, 1972-76, v.p., Memphis, 1976-78, exec. v.p., 1978-88, pres. 1988—, exec. v.p. Fleming Cos. Inc., 1988—; dir. 3d Nat. Bank, Nashville. Bd. advisors Boys Club Memphis. Served with USAF, 1953-57. Republican. Baptist. Office: Malone & Hyde Inc PO Box 1719 Memphis TN 38101

MOLLEGEN, ALBERT THEODORE, JR., engineering company executive; b. Meridian, Miss., Aug. 13, 1937; s. Albert Theodore and Harriette Ione (Rush) M.; m. Glenis Ruth Gralton, Feb. 16, 1962; children: Glenis Ione, Marion Anne. BEE, Yale U., 1961; postgrad. Poly. Inst. Bklyn., 1965-67. Cir. designer Melpar Inc., Falls Church, Va., 1958-59; system engr., group supr. Arma div. AMBAC Industries, N.Y.C., 1961-67; dept. mgr. Mystic Oceanographic Co. (Conn.), 1967-71; v.p., group mgr. Analysis & Tech. Inc., North Stonington, Conn., 1971-76, pres., chief exec. officer, 1976—; bd. dirs. Automation Software, Inc., No. Kingston. R.I., Benthos, Inc., No. Falmouth, Mass., SEATECH, No. Stonington, Ct. Profl. Svcs. Coun., Washington. Inventor towed array rangefinder; writer numerous tech. reports. Chmn. Mystic Area Ecumenical Coun., 1970-72; treas. Seabury deanery Episcopal Diocese Conn., 1974-76, mem. diocesan fin. policy com., 1975, missionary strategy com., 1976-78, chmn. stewardship com., 1982—, del. diocesan conv., 1974—, alt. del. nat. gen. conv., 1982, 85, 88. Mem. Am. Mgmt. Assn., Navy Submarine League (adv. coun.), Acoustical Soc. Am., Nat. Contract Mgmt. Assn., Ops. Rsch. Soc. Am., Inst. Mgmt. Scis., Navy Submarine League U.S. (adv. coun.), Am. Def. Preparedness Assn., IEEE, Am. Soc. Naval Engrs., Surface Navy Assn., The Newcomen Soc. Home: 337 Pleasant St Willimantic CT 06226 Office: Analysis & Tech Inc PO Box 220 North Stonington CT 06359

MOLLEL, PAUL LUCAS, construction company executive; b. Boxzotzarusha, Tanzania, Nov. 5, 1947; s. Lucas and Ruth Mollel; diploma in architecture 1967; Internat. Corr. Schs. Diploma, Inst. Brit. Engrs., 1973. Registered tech. engr., Eng. Archtl. asst. French & Hastings, Brit. Architects, Dar es Salaam, 1968-69; regional archtl. asst. East African Posts and Telegraph Corp., Dar es Salaam, 1970-74; bldg. supt. Williamson Diamond Mine, Mwadui, 1975-77; bldgs. estates mgr. Inst. Devel. Mgmt., Morogoro, 1977-79; sr. project engr. Equator Constrn. Co., Arusha, Tanzania, 1980-84; sr. asst. engr. Wade Adams British Contractors, 1984-88. Mem. Tanzania Inst. Engrs., Archtl. Assn. Tanzania, Inst. Bldgs. Lutheran. Club: Badminton. Office: PO Box 2072, Arusha Tanzania

MOLLER, WILLIAM RICHARD, JR., banker; b. N.Y.C., Mar. 14, 1941; s. William Richard and Inga Elinor (Olsen) M.; m. Molly Ann Tarkington, July 11, 1970; children: William Richard III, Sally McLaughlin, Katherine Tarkington. BA in English, Widener U., 1965; diploma, Am. Inst. Banking, 1976, Rutgers U., 1983, Stonier Grad. Sch. Banking, 1988. Dir. alumni relations Widener U., Chester, Pa., 1970-71; asst. treas. Chemical Bank, N.Y.C., 1971-78; asst. v.p. Putnam Trust Co., Greenwich, Conn., 1978-80; v.p. Putnam Trust Co., Greenwich, 1980-82, v.p., sec., 1982-84, sr. v.p., sec., 1984—. Dir., treas. Greenwich Emergency Med. Service, 1986—; mem. Greenwich Hosp. Bd. Incorporators, 1985—. Served to capt. with U.S. Army, 1965-70, Vietnam. Mem. Am. Soc. Corp. Secs., Nat. Assn. Bus. Ecomonists, Econs. Club Conn., Am. Bankers Assn. (polit. action com. chmn. com. of 52 1983—, adv. com. Stonier grad. sch. bd. 1985—), Conn. Bankers Assn. (chmn. polit. action com. 1985—, legis. com.), Greenwich C. of C. (dir., treas. 1984—). Club: Greenwich Country, Univ. Lodge: Rotary (Greenwich). Home: 12 Hendrie Ave Riverside CT 06878 Office: Putnam Trust Co 10 Mason St Greenwich CT 06830

MOLONEY, EDWARD JOHN, brokerage executive; b. St. Louis, Feb. 20, 1943; s. Thomas O. and Mary Elizabeth (Costigan) M.; m. Susan Kathleen Roth, Feb. 5, 1972; children: Edward John Jr. BBA, Regis Coll., 1966; postgrad., Washington U., 1966-67. Mgr. prodn. and inventory control Colt Industries, Pine Bluff, Ark., 1970-73; account exec. Stifel Nicolaus & Co., Inc., St. Louis, 1973-79, v.p. mut. funds, 1979-82; sr. v.p. product mktg. R. Rowland & Co., Inc., St. Louis, 1982—, sldo bd. dirs.; allied mem. N.Y. Stock Exchange, N.Y.C., 1983-88; sr. v.p. Carnegie Fund Distbrs., Inc., 1988—. Served as staff sgt. U.S. Army, 1968-70. Mem. Internat. Assn. Fin. Planners. Republican. Roman Catholic. Clubs: Greenbriar Hills Country (Kirkwood, Mo.); Town and Country (Mo.) Racquet; Washington U., Media. Home: 18 Devon Rd Glendale MO 63122 Office: LacLede Gas Bldg 720 Olive St Saint Louis MO 63101

MOLONY, MICHAEL JANSSENS, JR., lawyer; b. New Orleans, Sept. 2, 1922; s. Michael Janssens and Marie (Perret) M.; m. Jane Leslie Waguespack, Oct. 21, 1951; children: Michael Janssens III, Leslie, Megan, Kevin, Sara, Brian, Ian, Duncan. JD, Tulane U., 1950. Bar: La. 1950, U.S. Dist. Ct. (ea. and mid. dists.) La. 1951, U.S. Ct. Appeals (5th cir.) 1953, U.S. Supreme Ct. 1972, U.S. Dist Ct. (we. dist.) La. 1978, D.C. 1979, U.S. Ct. Appeals (11th and D.C. cirs.) 1981. Ptnr., Molony & Baldwin, New Orleans, 1950; assoc. Jones, Flanders, Waechter & Walker, 1951-56; ptnr. Jones, Walker, Waechter, Poitevent, Carrere & Denegre, 1956-75, Milling, Benson, Woodward, Hillyer, Pierson & Miller, 1975—; instr., lectr. Med. Sch. and Univ. Coll. Tulane U., 1953-59; mem. Eisenhower Legal Com., 1952. Bd. commrs. Port of New Orleans, 1976-81, pres., 1978, vice-chmn. past pres.'s coun., 1985—; bd. dirs. La. World Expn. Inc., 1974-84; bd. dirs., exec. com. New Orleans Tourist and Conv. Commn., 1971-74, 78, chmn. family attractions com. 1973-75; chmn. La. Gov.'s Task Force on Space Industry, 1971-73; chmn. La. Gov.'s Citizens' Adv. Com. Met. New Orleans Transp. and Planning Program, 1971-77; mem. La. Gov.'s Task Force Natural Gas Requirements, 1971-72; mem. Goals Found. Coun. and ex-officio mem. Goals Found., Met. New Orleans Goals Program, 1969-72, vice chmn. ad hoc planning com. Goals Met. New Orleans, 1969-73; vice chmn. Port of New Orleans Operation Impact, 1969-70, bd. commrs., 1976-81; mem. Met. Area Com., New Orleans, 1970-84; trustee, pres. Pub. Affairs Rsch. Coun. La., 1970-73; pres. bd. dirs., mem. exec. com. Met. Coun. for Lifelong Learning U. New Orleans, 1980—; mem. Mayor's Coun. on Internat. Trade and Econ. Devel., 1978; trustee Gulf South Rsch. Inst., 1980—, Acad. Sacred Heart, Internat. House, 1985—; trustee Loyola U., New Orleans, 1985—, mem. bd. visitors Sch. Bus. Adminstrn., 1981—; mem. Dean's Coun. Tulane U. Law Sch., 1988—; bd. dirs., mem. exec. com. Internat. Trade Mart, chmn. internat. bus. com., 1983-85; chmn. Task Force on Internat. Banking, 1982.Capt. JAGC, USAAF, 1942-46, PTO. Recipient Leadership award AIAA, 1971, Yenni award Loyla U., New Orleans, 1979, New Orleans Times Picayune Loving Cup, 1986. Mem. Fed. Bar Assn., ABA (antitrust law, labor and employment law sects., com. equal opportunity law, subcom. liaison with equal opportunity commn.), D.C. Bar Assn., La. Bar Assn. (past sec.-treas., gov. 1959-60, editor jour. 1957-59, sec. spl. supreme ct. com. on drafting code jud. ethics), New Orleans Bar Assn. (dir. legal aid bur. 1954, vice chmn. standing com. pub. relations 1970-71), Am. Judicature Soc., La. Law Inst. (asst. sec.-treas. 1958-79), Am. Arbitration Assn. (bd. dirs., chmn. La. adv. council), So. Inst. Mgmt. (founder), World Trade Ctr.-New Orleans (bd. dirs. 1978—), AIM, U.S. C. of C. (urban and regional affairs com. 1970-72), La. C. of C. (bd. dirs. 1963-66), New Orleans Area C. of C. (v.p. met. devel. and urban affairs 1969, past chmn. council, bd. dirs. 1970-78, pres.-elect 1970, pres. 1971, exec. com. 1972), Sigma Chi (pres. alumni chpt. 1956). Roman Catholic. Clubs: Internat. House, Plimsoll, So. Yacht, Serra, Lakewood Country, Pickwick, Bienville, City (New Orleans), English Turn Golf and Country. Home: 3039 Hudson Pl New Orleans LA 70131 Office: Milling Benson Woodward Hillyer Pierson & Miller 909 Poydras St Ste 2300 New Orleans LA 70112-1017

MOLSON, ERIC H., beverage company executive; b. Montreal, PQ, Can., Sept. 16, 1937; s. Thomas Henry Pentland and Celia Frances (Cantlie) M.; m. Jane Mitchell, Apr. 16, 1966; 3 children. AB, Princeton U., 1959; postgrad., McGill U., 1962-63. With The Molson Cos. Ltd., Toronto, Ont., Can., now dep. chmn. Office: The Molson Cos Ltd, 2 International Blvd, Toronto, ON Canada M9W 1A2 *

MOLSTER, CHARLES B., JR., healthcare supplies distribution company executive; b. Washington, July 23, 1928; s. Charles B. and Margaret (Jordan) M.; m. Betty Sanford, June 9, 1953; children: Charles, John, Margaret, Jane. BS in Commerce, U. Va., 1952. Supr. C&P Telephone Co., Richmond, Va., 1952-57; credit mgr. Miller & Rhoads, Richmond, 1957-62; contr. Miller & Rhodes, Richmond, 1962-70; v.p. Garfinkel, Brooks Bros., Miller & Rhoads, Inc., Richmond, 1970-83; pres. Molster Barry & Masons, Inc., Richmond, 1983-87; sr. v.p. Owens & Minor, Inc., Richmond, 1987—. Served with U.S. Army, 1946-48. Republican. Episcopalian. Office: Owens & Minor Inc 2727 Enterprise Pkwy Richmond VA 23229

MOLT, CYNTHIA MARYLEE, author, publisher; b. Sierra Madre, Calif., Nov. 1, 1957; d. Lawrence Edward and Evelyn Mary (Novak) Molt. BA in English Lit., Calif. State U., Long Beach, 1980. Mng. editor Assoc. Graphics, Arts and Letters, Monrovia, Calif., 1981-87, pub., sr. and mng. editor, 1987—, authenticator, 1981—; author McFarland and Co., Inc., Pubs., Jefferson, N.C., 1988—. Author: Gone With the Wind: A Complete Reference, 1989; author, editor mag. The Wind, 1981—, Calif. Film, 1987—; spl. corr. Monrovia News-Post, 1985; corr. G.W.T.W. Collector's Club Newsletter, 1979-82, Monrovia Rev., 1975. Vol. adminstrv. asst. student activities Monrovia High Sch., 1976. Mem. Gone with the Wind Soc. (pres. 1985—), Vivien Leigh Fan Club (pres. 1987—), Clark Gable Fan Club (pres. 1987—), Grace Kelly Fan Club (pres. 1987—). Republican. Roman Catholic. Home and Office: 364 N May Ave Monrovia CA 91016

MOMAYEZ-ZADEH, HAMID REZA, manufacturing executive; b. Tehran, Sept. 11, 1955; came to U.S. 1973; s. Abdol Hossein and Azra (Elahi) Momayez-Zadeh. BS in Indsl. Engring., U. Miami, 1978. Rsch. asst. Burger King Corp., Miami, 1978-79; cons. engr. Motorola Corp., Ft. Lauderdale, Fla., 1979-80; fin. cons. Pvt. Practice, Miami, 1980-82; v.p. Intercontinental Properties, Intercontinental Investments, Miami, 1982-83; chmn., pres. Pacific Sun Corp., Miami, 1984-85; chmn., chief exec. officer Equinox Solar, Miami, 1985—. Office: Equinox Solar Inc 3501 NW 60 St Miami FL 33142

MOMTCHILOFF, IVAN NICHOLAS, invester; b. Sofia, Bulgaria, Dec. 14, 1929; came to U.S., 1986; s. Nicholas Ivan and Anna (Sarafova) M.; m. Ann Hartley, Sept. 12, 1959; children: Nicholas Robert, Catherine Hartley. BA in Mech. Sci., Cambridge (Eng.) U., 1953; AM in Engring. Sci., Harvard U., 1958. Project engr. Heat Exchangers Ltd., London, 1958-60; v.p. No. Rsch., London, 1960-68; gen. mgr. Investors in Industry Group, PLC, London, 1968-86, also bd. dirs.; chmn. 3i Corp., Boston, 1986—. Lt. Brit. Army, 1949-50. Decorated Order Brit. Empire. Mem. Inst. Mech. Engrs. (London). Home: 1100 W Roxbury Pkwy Chestnut Hill MA 02167 Office: 3 I Corp 99 High St Boston MA 02110

MONACO, JOSEPH R., metals company executive; b. N.Y.C., June 7, 1945; s. Joseph Mario and Rose (Micelotta) M.; m. Carol Ann Romano, Sept. 7, 1968. BA, Queens Coll., 1965. Traffic mgr. N.J. Zinc, N.Y.C., 1965-70; asst. to pres. Internat. Minerals and Metalsž, N.Y.C., 1970-73; asst. v.p. Brandeis, Goldschmidt & Co., N.Y.C., 1973-76, v.p., 1976-81; sr. v.p. Pechiney World Trade, Secaucus, N.J., 1981—; cons. Habits, Inc., N.Y.C., Sudmetal, Santiago, Chile. Served with U.S. Army, 1965-67. Mem. Minor Metals Assn. Club: Vertical (N.Y.C.). Office: Pechiney World Trade USA Inc 500 Plaza Dr Secaucus NJ 07096

MONAHAN, THOMAS ANDREW, JR., accountant; b. Erie, Pa., Jan. 23, 1920; s. Thomas Andrew and Margaret (McEnery) M.; m. Patricia Tompkins, Sept. 4, 1948 (div. June 1983), m. Rita Fargo, Sept. 3, 1985; children—Kathleen, Thomas P., Kevin, Margaret, Daniel. B.S., U. Pitts., 1942. C.P.A., Pa. Jr. acct. Price Waterhouse & Co., Pitts., 1942-43; sr. acct. Coopers & Lybrand, Phila., 1944-48; lectr. acctg. U. Pitts., 1948-49; pvt. practice acctg., Erie, Pa., 1949—; lectr. Gannon U., Erie, 1965-78. Contbr. articles to C.P.A. jour. Mem. Am. Inst. C.P.A.s (council mem. 1981-83), Pa. Inst. C.P.A.s (v.p. 1971-72, council mem. 1968-71). Club: Kahkwa Country (Erie, Pa.) (treas. 1978-88). Home: 628 Delaware Ave Erie PA 16505 Office: 1202 State St Erie PA 16501

MONASH, CURT ALFRED, venture capitalist; b. Chgo., Jan. 1, 1960; s. Peter Ernest and Anita Kaete (Jonas) M. BS, Ohio State U., Columbus, 1976; AM, Harvard U., 1978, PhD, 1979. Instr. Suffolk U., Boston, 1978; teaching fellow Harvard U., Cambridge, Mass., 1978-79, rsch. fellow, 1979-81; from security analyst to 1st v.p. Paine Webber, Inc., N.Y.C., 1981-87; pres. New World Ventures, N.Y.C., 1987—; dir. DataLink Systems Inc., L.A., 1988—; vis. scholar Cowles Found. Econ. Rsch., Yale U.; pres. New World Investment Advisors, N.Y.C., 1987—. NSF fellow. Mem. Assn. of Data Processing Svc. Orgns. (speaker 1982-85, Disting. Svc. award 1986), Am. Electronics Assn. Democrat. Office: New World Ventures 61 W 62 Ste 10M New York NY 10023

MONBERG, JAY PETER, management consultant; b. N.Y.C., Aug. 19, 1935; s. Carl-Johannes and Maria Anna Sophie (Haugwitz-Hardenberg-Reventlow) Hammerich-Monberg; B.B.A., Northwestern U., 1962, M.B.A., 1968. Corp. controller Furnas Elec. Co., Batavia, Ill., 1966-67; sr. v.p., dir. Logan Mfg. Co., Chgo., 1967-72; exec. v.p. Moser Industries, Inc., Naperville, Ill., after 1972; pres., chief exec. officer, dir. Wickman Machine Tools Inc., Elk Grove Village, Ill., also sector exec. John Brown Co., Ltd., London, 1977-80; internat. mgmt. cons., 1980—. Mem. dean's council Grad. Sch. Mgmt., Northwestern U., 1973—; treas. bd. dirs. We The People Ednl. found. Inc. Fellow Inst. Dirs. of U.K., , Inst. Mktg., British Inst. Mgmt.; mem. European Planning Fedn., Inst. of Mktg., Strategic Planning Soc., Internat. Soc. Planning and Strategic Mgmt., Am. Mgmt. Pres. Assn. Scandinavian-Am. Found., Rebild Nat. Park Soc. (v.p.), Dania Soc., Danish Nat. Com. (trustee), Sheffield Hist. Soc., Danish Am. Lang. Found. (pres.), Danish-Am. C. of C. (v.p., dir.), Chgo. Council on Fgn. Relations, Chgo. Com., Internat. Trade Club of Chgo. Clubs: Execs., Mid-Am., Internat., 100 Club of Cook County, Union League (Chgo.); The Am. Club (London, Eng.), The English Speaking Union (London). Home: 612 Mulford St Evanston IL 60202 also: 1 Passage du Cedre Saint Marceau, 45100 Orleans France Office: 100 Kenilworth Rd, Coventry CV4 7AH, England Office: Lerchenborgvej 1 Vanlose, Copenhagen Denmark

MOND, LAWRENCE A., quality assurance manager; b. N.Y.C., June 23, 1943; s. William T. and Stella M.; m. Sandra Lavin, Jan. 2, 1982; 1 child, William S. BA, Franklin & Marshall Coll., Lancaster, Pa., 1965; MS, U. Conn., 1968. Mgr. programming ITEL Corp., White Plains, N.Y., 1968-76; asst. to v.p. tech. devel. Anstat, Inc., N.Y.C., 1976-82; mgr. design, integration and test TRW, Redondo Beach, Calif., 1983-88; mgr. quality assurance Inference Corp., Los Angeles, 1988—. Mem. Assn. Systems Mgmt. Democrat. Office: Inference Corp 5300 W Century Blvd Los Angeles CA 90045

MONFORT, KENNETH, cattle production and meat processing company executive; b. 1928. Mem. Colo. Ho. of Reps., 1965-69; pres. Monfort of Colo. Inc., Greeley, 1969—, co-chmn., sr. v.p., 1976, pres., chief exec. officer, 1980—, also bd. dirs.; now pres., chief operating officer ConAgra Redmeat Cos. Office: ConAgra Redmeat Cos care Shirley Bernhart 1930 AA St Box G Greeley CO 80632 *

MONGER, TIMOTHY JUSTIN, corporate professional; b. Elkhart, Ind., Oct. 25, 1950; s. Robert Wendell and Angela G. (Thulis) M.; m. Kim Elizabeth Parente; 1 child, Justin R. BS, Purdue U., 1972, MS, 1981. Project coord. Youth Employment Program, Lafayette, Ind., 1972-74; dir. Tippecanoe County Dept. Career Devel., Lafayette, Ind., 1974-78; asst. dir., mgr. local govt. assistance Ctr. Pub. Policy and Pub. Adminstrn. Purdue U., West Lafayette, Ind., 1978-84; exec. asst. econ. devel. to mayor City of Indpls., 1984-85; pres. Indpls. Econ. Devel. Corp., 1986—; bd. dirs. Mid-City Pioneer Corp., Employment and Devel. Systems, Inc.; chmn. Cen. Ind. Econ. Devel. Partnership; mem. dean's adv. com. sch. sci. Purdue U.; v.p. Ind. Area Devel. Coun. Sec. bd. dirs. Greater Indpls. Foreign Trade Zone, Indpls. Pvt. Industry Council; mem. chief's citizens adv. com. Indpls. Police Dept.; Rep. candidate for mayor City of Lafayette, 1983. Mem. Am. Econ. Devel. Council, Mid Am. Econ. Devel. Council. Home: 804 N Audubon Rd Indianapolis IN 46219 Office: Indpls Econ Devel Corp 320 N Meridian St Ste 906 Indianapolis IN 46204

MONICAL, MARY CHRISTINE, biotechnology marketing executive; b. Cin., Apr. 6, 1950; d. Robert Duane and Carol Arnetha (Dean) M. B.S., U. Miami, 1972, postgrad., 1973; postgrad. Butler U., 1980. Tech. specialist Am. Dade div. Am. Hosp. Supply Corp., Miami, Fla., 1976-79; sales rep. Gen. Diagnostics Co., Morris Plains, N.J., 1980-81, microbiology specialist, 1981-83; sales rep. Coulter Immunology, Hialeah, Fla., 1983-85, regional sales mgr., 1985-86, mktg. dir. FAST Systems, Inc., Gaithersburg, Md., 1986—. Recipient best sales tng. performance award Gen. Diagnostics, 1980; named to Pres.'s Club, Outstanding Sales Rep., Coulter Electronics, 1984-85, 85-86. Home: 20415 Sunbright Ln Germantown MD 20874

MONICAL, ROBERT DUANE, consulting structural engineer; b. Morgan County, Ind., Apr. 30, 1925; s. William Blaine and Mary Elizabeth (Lang) M.; m. Carol Arnetha Dean, Aug. 10, 1947 (dec. 1979); children: Mary Christine, Stuart Dean, Dwight Lee; m. Sharon Kelly Eastwood, July 13, 1980; 1 stepson, Jeffrey David Eastwood. B.S.C.E., Purdue U., 1948, M.S.C.E., 1949. Engr. N.Y.C. R.R., Cin., 1949-51, So. Rwy., Cin., 1951; design engr. Pierce & Gruber (Cons. Engrs.), Indpls., 1952-54; founder, partner Monical & Wolverton (Cons. Engrs.), Indpls., 1954-63; founder, partner Monical Assocs., Indpls., 1963—, pres., 1975—; v.p. Zurwelle-Whittaker, Inc. (Engrs. and Land Surveyors), Miami Beach, Fla., 1975—; Mem. Ind. Adminstrv. Bldg. Council, 1969-75; chmn., 1973-75; mem. Meridian St. Preservation Commn., 1971-75, Ind. State Bd. of Registration for Profl. Engrs. and Land Surveyors, 1976-84, chmn., 1979, 83. Served with USNR, 1943-46, USAR, 1948-53. Mem. ASCE (Outstanding Civil Engr. award Ind. sect. 1987), Cons. Engrs. Ind. (pres. 1969, Cons. Recognition award 1986), Am. Cons. Engrs. Council (pres. 1978-79), Ind. Soc. Profl. Engrs. (Engr. of Yr. 1980), Nat. Soc. Profl. Engrs., Constrn. Specifications Inst., Am. Arbitration Assn., Indpls. Sci. and Engring. Found. Mem. Christian Ch. Clubs: Woodland Country, Masons, Shriners. Home: 2922 E 52d St Indianapolis IN 46205 Office: Monical Assocs 5820 Massachusetts Ave Indianapolis IN 46218

MONIN, ROBERT C., finance company executive; b. Niagara Falls, N.Y., Oct. 22, 1948; s. Charles E. and Helen (Juzwiak) M.; m. Sandra G. Maselli, May 4, 1973; children: Matthew M., ChristinaM. AS, Niagara Community Coll., 1969; BS in Mgmt., SUNY, Buffalo, 1971. Asst. mgr. Neisner Bros. Inc., 1971-75, Gold Cir. Stores, Rochester, N.Y., 1975-79; fin. planner Cigna Corp., Buffalo, 1979-86; pres. Progressive Planning Svcs.Inc., Williamsville, N.Y., 1987—, Progressive Planning Agy. Inc., Williamsville, 1987—. Dir. St. Gregory's Men's Golf League, Williamsville, 1985—. Mem. Internat. Assn. Fin. Planning, Inst. Cert. Fin. Planners, St. Gregory's Men's Club (treas. 1988—). Roman Catholic. Home: 1 Auden Ct Williamsville NY 14221 Office: Progressive Planning Svcs Inc 555 International Dr Ste 300 Williamsville NY 14221-5789

MONRO, JAMES ALEXANDER, JR., retail executive; b. Eastlake, Ohio, Sept. 6, 1949; s. James Alexander and Shirley (Geer) M.; m. Susan A. Allison, May 19, 1978; children—Jason Alexander, Jessica Allison. B.A., Bob Jones U., 1972. Buyer, May Co., Cleve., 1971-75, Rike Kumler, Dayton, Ohio, 1975-77; asst. store mgr. Joseph Horne Co., Pitts., 1977-78; div. mdse. mgr. Gold Circle Co., Worthington, Ohio, 1978-79; div. mdse. mgr. Winkelman Stores, Detroit, 1979-80, v.p., div. mdse. mgr., 1980-81, sr. v.p., 1981-83, exec. v.p., 1983-84, pres., 1984—, also dir.; pres., exec. v.p. Fabri-Ctrs. Am. Inc., Beachwood, Ohio, 1986—; dir. Win Spot Ltd. Co., Hong Kong. Mem. Nat. Retail Mchts. Assn., Am. Mgmt. Assn., Mgmt. Horizons. Republican. Presbyterian. Clubs: Renaissance, Detroit, Detroit Athletic (Detroit). Home: 32655 Wintergreen Rd Solonn OH 44139 Office: Fabri Ctrs Am Inc 23550 Commerce Pk Rd Beachwood OH 44122

MONROE, SANDRA LEE, insurance company official; b. Winchester, Conn., July 21, 1955; d. Wilbur Gramaliel and Evelyn Ruth (Leffingwell) Lee; m. William James Monroe, May 22, 1982; 1 child, Matthew James. AA, Manchester Community Coll., 1983. Nurse's aide Valley View Convalescent Hosp., Willimantic, Conn., 1972-74; contract typist Aetna Life & Casualty Co., Hartford, Conn., 1974-75, benefits processor, 1975-77, systems maintenance technician, 1977-79, programmer trainee, 1979-80, programmer analyst, 1980-81, sr. programmer analyst, 1981-83, sr. systems analyst, 1983—. Office: 151 Farmington Ave Hartford CT 06156

MONSKY, MICHAEL DAVID WOLF VON SOMMER, architect, painter; b. N.Y.C., Jan. 6, 1947; s. Leo and Irma Ruth (Reinhold) M.; m. Tina Claire Myers, Jan. 20, 1974; 1 child, Dana Lesley. BA, Northeastern U., 1968; BArch, Cooper Union, 1977; MArch, Yale U., 1979. Registered architect, N.Y. Prin. The Office Michael David Monsky, Architect, N.Y.C., 1980—, MDM Design Prodns., 1988, Galen Med. Design, N.Y.C., 1980—; bd. dir. internship Inst. for Architecture and Urban Studies, N.Y.C., 1981-85. Mem. AIA, N.Y. State Assn. of Architects, Northeastern Alumni Assn., Alumni Assn. of Cooper Union, Nat. Coun. Archtl. Registration Bds. (cert.), Yale U. Club, Yale Alumni Assn. Met. N.Y. Office: 555 Fifth Ave New York NY 10017

MONTAGUE, KEVIN FREDERICK FRANCIS, games manufacturing company executive; b. Santa Monica, Calif., Oct. 9, 1956; s. Patrick Raymond and Patricia (Ryan) M. BA in Communication Arts, Loyola U., Westchester, Calif., 1978. Prodn. foreman entertainment div. Magic Mountain, Valencia, Calif., 1976-79; sales area distbr. Dynique Internat., Woodland Hills, Calif., 1979-80; escrow processor Marshall Plan, Inc., Santa Monica, Calif., 1980; savs. rep. Gibraltar Savs. and Loan, Los Angeles, 1980-83; info. systems processor various employment agys. Los Angeles, 1983-87; pres., bd. dirs. Falcon Games, Unltd., Van Nuys, 1986—; publs. coordinator Sattel Techs., Inc., Van Nuys, Calif., 1987—. Author boardgames. Calif. State scholar, 1974-78. Roman Catholic. Office: Falcon Games Unltd PO Box 102 Van Nuys CA 91408

MONTAGUE, SARAH ANNE, sales and marketing professional, editor; b. N.Y.C., Aug. 18, 1955. BA, Cambridge (Eng.) U., 1973, MA, 1976. Asst. editor Country Life Mag., London, 1977-78; assoc. editor Universe Books, N.Y.C., 1978-83; editor, cons. N.Y.C., 1983-85; editor Simon & Schuster, N.Y.C., 1985-87; dir. publs. Ctr. for Arts Info., N.Y.C., 1987; v.p. sales and mktg. 2PPR Prodns., N.Y.C., 1986—, also bd. dirs. Author: Ballerina, 1979, Pas de Deux, 1981; author, editor N.Y. Calendar, 1982 (award Soc. Illustrators); contbr. numerous articles to profl. jours. Vol. The Names Project, N.Y.C., 1988. Mem. NAFE, Dance Critics Assn., N.Y. Pub. Libr. Office: 2PPR Prodns 34 Gansevoort St New York NY 10014

MONTAMBAULT, LEONCE, communications company executive; b. Quebec City, Que., 1932. B.A., Laval U., 1953, B.S. in Civil Engring., 1957. With Bell Can., 1957—, v.p. provincial area, Quebec City, 1971-76, v.p. Montreal area, 1976-79, v.p. customer services Que. region, 1979, exec. v.p. Que. region, 1979-87, pres., chief exec. officer, 1987—; dir. Bell Can. Techs. Mgmt. Corp., Telesat Can., Memotec Data Inc., Teleglobe Can., Bell-No. Research Ltd., Travelers Can. Bd. dirs. L'Orchestre Symphonique de Montreal, Clin. Research Inst. Montreal; gov. Conseil du Patronat du Que. Mem. Order Engrs. Que., C. of C. Can., la Chambre de Commerce du dist. de Montreal, la Chambre de Commerce du Que. (bd. dirs., exec. com.), la Chambre de Commerce Francaise au Can., Comite Can.-France, l'Association des Anciens de Laval, Bur. Gov. Quebec Diabetes Assn. (pres.), Conseil du Patronat du Quebec (gov.). Clubs: Laval-sur-le-Lac Golf, Saint-Denis, Saint James, Order of St. John (comdr.); Lodge: Sovereign and Mil. Order of Malta. Office: Bell Can, 1050 Beaver Hall Hill, Montreal, PQ Canada H2Z 1S4

MONTAÑA, JORDI, marketing educator; b. Barcelona, Spain, June 20, 1949; s. Francesc and Carmen (Matosas) M.; 1 child, Roger. Grad., E.T.S.I.I.B., Barcelona, 1971; MBA, Escuela Superior Adminstracion y Direc. Empresas, Barcelona, 1976. V.p. CIT Ballve, Textiles, Barcelona, 1971-75; ptnr. Holdstaff, Cons., Barcelona, 1975-78; prof. mktg. Escuela Superior Administracion y Direc. Empresas, 1976—, assoc. dean, 1982-86, chmn. mktg. dept., 1985—; head. tech. dept. B.C.D. Design Ctr., Barcelona, 1978-80; pres. QUOD, Barcelona, 1983—; vis. prof. Ecole Haute Etudes Commerciales, Paris, 1986—, U. Centro Americana, Managua, Nicaragua, 1986—, San Salvador, El Salvador, 1987—; bd. dirs. CODEH, Barcelona, 1985—; expert UN Indsl. Devel. Orgn., Vienna, 1987—; journalist Diari de Barcelona, 1987. Author: Marketing Policy, 1983, The White Book on Design, 1984, Design Policy and Competitive Advantages, 1986, How to

Design a Product, 1988. Active Red Cross Orgn., 1982—. Miro Found. fellow, Barcelona, 1980—. Mem. Colegio Ingenieros Industriales, Am. Mktg. Assn., Acad. Mktg. Sci. (chmn. III world congress 1986), Foment Decorative Arts. Clubs: Centre Excursion, Real Tennis (Barcelona). Office: ESADE, Avenida Pedralbes 60-62, 08034 Barcelona Spain also: QUOD, Carles Mercader n0-9, 08960 Saint Just Desvern Spain

MONTE, SALVATORE JOSEPH, polymer chemicals manufacturing company executive; b. Bklyn., Sept. 18, 1939; s. Michael Salvatore and Antoinette A. (Gentile) M.; B.C.E., Manhattan Coll., 1961; M.S. in Polymeric Materials, Poly. Inst. N.Y., 1969; m. Erika Gertraud Spiegelhalder, Oct. 14, 1961; children—Michelle Marie, Deborah Frances, Denise Christine, Eric Michael. Registered profl. engr., N.Y. State, N.J. Asst. supt. Turner Constrn. Co., N.Y.C., Phila., 1961-64; project mgr. Blaize Constrn. Co., Eastchester, N.Y., 1964-66; v.p. Kenrich Petrochems., Inc., Bayonne, N.J., 1966-69, exec. v.p., 1969-79, pres., 1980—, trustee pension fund, 1976—; mgmt. trustee Oil, Chem. and Atomic Workers Local 8-406 Welfare Fund. Bd. dirs. United Fund, 1970, Jobs of Bayonne, 1980; v.p., sec. South Ganon-Forest Hills Homeowners Assn., 1971-74. Paul Harris Fellow. Mem. Soc. Plastics Engrs. (div. dir. 1980), Soc. Plastics Industries, Am. Chem. Soc. (rubber div.), N.Y. Federated Soc. Coatings Tech., N.Y. (chmn. bd. 1976), Phila., Boston, Blue Ridge, S.E. Ohio rubber groups, Soc. Rheology, Am. Def. Preparedness Assn., AAAS, Bayonne C. of C., Phi Kappa Theta, Chi Epsilon. Republican. Roman Catholic. Clubs: Richmond County Country; Bayonne Rotary (dir. 1974-77, pres. 1981). Contbr. numerous articles to profl. publs. and mags., chpts. to books on interfacial tech. Patentee in U.S. and 22 fgn. countries on monoalkoxy, chelated, coordinated and neoalkoxy titanate and zirconate coupling agts., cumyl phenol derivatives.

MONTEIRO, MANUEL JAMES, manufacturing company executive; b. New Bedford, Mass., 1926; s. Joao and Beatrice (Oliveira) M.; m. Madelyn Wilcox, Dec. 15, 1946; children: Warren James, Mark Alan, Marguerite Ann Monteiro Cavett, Marilyn Jean Monteiro Allen, John Manuel, James Robert, Robert William. BS in Acctg. and Fin., Bryant Coll. With 3M Co., 1950—, cost analyst tape lab., St. Paul, 1950-54, various internat. positions in Colombia, Brazil, 1954-65, mng. dir. 3M Brazil, 1965-71, area dir. Latin Am., 1971-73, div. v.p. Latin Am. and Africa, 1973-75, v.p. European ops., 1975-81, exec. v.p. internat. ops., 1981—; bd. dirs., St. Paul, 1986—. Served with U.S. Army, 1945-46. Recipient Disting. Alumni award Bryant Coll. Presbyterian. Office: Minn Minning & Mfg Co 3M Center Saint Paul MN 55144-1000

MONTGOMERY, ANDREW STUART, financial adviser; b. Decorah, Iowa, May 25, 1960; s. Henry Irving and Barbara Louise (Hook) M. Student bus. adminstrn., Escola Rua de Jardim, Sao Paulo, Brazil, 1978-79; BA in Econs. and Bus. Adminstrn. magna cum laude, Coe Coll., 1983. Cert. fin. planner. Registered rep. 1st Investors Corp., Mpls., 1983-84; fin. adviser Planners Fin. Services, Inc., Mpls., 1984—, asst. to pres., 1984-85, dir. computer dept., 1984-87, investment analyst, 1985—, chairperson investment mgr. selection com., 1986—. Mem. Inst. Cert. Fin. Planners, Internat. Assn. for Fin. Planning, Nat. Assn. Life Underwriters, Mpls. Toastmasters (sec. 1986, treas. 1987), Phi Beta Kappa, Phi Kappa Phi. Office: Planners Fin Svcs Inc 4830 W 77th St Ste C Minneapolis MN 55435

MONTGOMERY, CHARLES HOWARD, retired bank executive; b. Bloomington, Ill., Mar. 23, 1930; s. Dewey H. and Madeline (Wonderlin) M.; m. Diane Dickerson Cohen, Aug. 30, 1978; children: Alison, Douglas. A.B., Ill. Wesleyan U., 1951; M.S., U. Ill., 1960. CPA, Ill. Auditor Lybrand Ross Bros. & Montgomery, Rockford, Ill., 1955-59; with Abbott Labs., North Chicago, Ill., 1959-67; controller Abbott Labs., 1965-67; v.p. finance Anchor Coupling Co., Libertyville, 1967-69; v.p., comptroller First Nat. Bank Chgo., 1969-73, sr. v.p., 1973-75, exec. v.p., 1976-88, comptroller, 1973-88; comptroller First Chgo. Corp.; past chmn. Inter-Assn. Com. Bank Acctg. Served with AUS, 1952-53. Mem. Am. Bankers Assn. (past chmn. Task Force on Accounting), Fin. Execs. Inst., AICPA, Ill. Soc. CPAs, Tau Kappa Epsilon, Phi Kappa Phi. Club: University (Chgo.). Home: 5490 S Shore Dr Chicago IL 60615 Office: First Chgo Corp 1 First National Pla Chicago IL 60670

MONTGOMERY, CLARK TAYLOR, advertising agency executive; b. St. Paul, Jan. 13, 1941; s. Cyrus Alexander and Helen Marie (Hansen) M.; m. Prudence Kappes, Aug. 31, 1963; children: Clark Taylor, Allison. B.A., Princeton U., 1963. Vice-pres., account supr. Norman, Craig & Kummel, N.Y.C., 1963-72; exec. v.p., mgmt. rep. Grey Advt., Inc., N.Y.C., 1972—. Office: Grey Advt Inc 777 3rd Ave New York NY 10017

MONTGOMERY, EDWARD ALEMBERT, JR., retired banker; b. Pitts., July 2, 1934; s. Edward Alembert and Marian (Elder) M.; m. Susan Oliver, June 18, 1938; children—Martha Oliver, Margaret Elder. B.A., Trinity Coll., Conn., 1956; postgrad., Harvard Bus. Sch., Cambridge, 1959. Vice pres. in charge N.Y.C. div. Mellon, N.Y.C., 1970-74; v.p., mgr. Mellon, London, Eng., 1974-77; sr. v.p. Mellon Bank N.A., Pitts., 1977-85; chmn., chief exec. officer Mellon Bank East, Phila., 1985-88, ret., 1988; vice chmn. Mellon Bank Corp., Pitts., 1985-87, also bd. dirs.; chmn. bd. trustees Trinity Coll., Hartford, 1978—; bd. dirs. AP Propane, Inc., Whirlabrater Techniques, Hampton, N.H., 1988—, Acad. Natural Scis., Phila., 1985—, Greater Phila. First Corp., 1985—; vice chmn., dir. Greater Phila. Econ. Devel. Corp., 1985—. Dir. Orchestra Assn.; vice chmn., dir. WHYY, Phila., 1985—; chmn. Ind. Adv. Council Phila. OIC, 1985—; chmn. Phila. Hist. Commn., Am. Music Theater Festival; mem. exec. com. United Way SE Pa.; mem. Com. to Support Phila. Pub. Schs. Served to sgt. U.S. Army, 1956-58. Mem. Pvt. Industry Council Phila. (bd. dirs.), Greater Phila. C. of C. (chmn. 1986—). Republican. Presbyterian. Clubs: Duquesne (Pitts.); Laurel Valley Golf (Ligonier, Pa.). Office: Mellon Bank East Mellon Bank Ctr Philadelphia PA 19102 also: Mellon Bank Corp 1 Mellon Bank Ctr Pittsburgh PA 15258

MONTGOMERY, HAROLD HENCH, company executive; b. Dallas, Sept. 20, 1959; s. Philip and Ruth Ann (Rogers) M. BA, Stanford U., 1982, MBA, 1985. Analyst Wellington Assocs., Dallas, 1985-87; chief exec. officer Videoguard, Dallas, 1987—. Republican. Episcopalian. Office: Videoguard 1819 Firmar Dr Ste 145 Richardson TX 75081

MONTGOMERY, HENRY IRVING, financial planner; b. Decorah, Iowa, Dec. 18, 1924; s. Harry Biggs and Martha Grace (Wilkinson) M.; m. Barbara Louise Hook, Aug. 14, 1948; children—Barbara Ruth, Michael Henry, Kelly Ann, Andrew Stuart. Student U. Iowa, 1942-43, 47-48; B.B.A., Tulane U., 1952, postgrad., 1952; postgrad. U. Minn., 1976. Cert. fin. planner, Colo. Field agt. OSS, SSU, CIG, CIA, Central Europe, 1945-47; pres. Nehi Bottling Co., Decorah, Iowa, 1952-64; prin. Montgomery Assocs., Mktg. Cons., Trieste, Italy and Iowa, 1965-72; pres. Planners Fin. Svcs., Inc., Mpls., 1972—. Author: Race Toward Berlin, 1945. Served with U.S. Army, 1943-46; ETO. Mem. Inst. Cert. Fin. Planners (bd. dirs. 1977-82, pres. 1980-81, chmn. 1981-82, Cert. Fin. Planner of Yr. 1984, chmn. Fin. Products Standards Bd. 1984-88, 88—), Nat. Assn. Securities Dealers Dist. Coms., Internat. Assn. Fin. Planning (internat. dir. 1976-81), Mpls. Estate Planning Coun., Met. Tax Planning Group (pres. 1984-87), Twin City Fin. Planners (pres. 1976-78), Twin Cities Soc. of Inst. Cert. Fin. Planners, Am. Legion, Elks, Beta Gamma Sigma. Avocations: Italian and German langs. Office: Planners Fin Svcs Inc 4830 W 77th St Ste C Minneapolis MN 55435

MONTGOMERY, JAMES FISCHER, savings and loan association executive; b. Topeka, Nov. 30, 1934; s. James Maurice and Frieda Ellen (Fischer) M.; m. Linda Jane Hicks, Aug. 25, 1956; children: Michael James, Jeffrey Allen, Andrew Steven, John Gregory. B.A. in Acctg., UCLA, 1957. With Price, Waterhouse & Co., C.P.A.'s, Los Angeles, 1957-60; controller Conejo Valley Devel. Co., Thousand Oaks, Calif., 1960; asst. to pres. Gt. Western Fin. Corp., Beverly Hills, Calif., 1960-64; fin. v.p., treas. United Fin. Corp., Los Angeles, 1964-69, exec. v.p., 1969-74, pres., 1975; pres. Citizens Savs. & Loan Assn., Los Angeles, 1970-75; chmn., chief exec. officer, dir. Gt. Western Fin. Corp., also Great Western Bank, Beverly Hills, 1975—. Served with AUS, 1958-60. Office: Gt Western Fin Corp 8484 Wilshire Blvd Beverly Hills CA 90211

MONTGOMERY, JOSEPH WILLIAM, investment broker; b. Wytheville, Va., Dec. 23, 1951; s. Ivan Martin and Evelyn Powell (Delp) M; m. Linda Gail Winebarger, Aug. 30, 1980. BBA, William and Mary Coll., 1974. cert. fin. planner. With Wheat, First Securities, Lynchburg and Williamsburg, Va., 1975—; v.p., investment officer Wheat, First Securities, Williamsburg, 1981-82, sr. v.p., investment officer, 1982—, also dirs. circle; bd. dirs. Williamsburg Landing, Inc. Solicitor Salvation Army Bldg. Fund, 1977, United Way campaign, 1978, Lynchburg; team capt. Lynchburg YMCA Fund Drive, 1979; bd. dirs. Peninsula chpt. NCCJ, 1986—; mem. planning com. Kingsmill Community Services Assn., Williamsburg, 1981-82; com. mem. Future of Hampton Roads, Sports Opportunity Group, Norfolk, Va., 1984—, adv. council Peninsula White Sox, 1986; treas. William and Mary Athletic Ednl. Found., Williamsburg, 1980-81, v.p., 1981-83, 1st v.p., 1983-85, pres. 1985-87; fin. planning com. Williamsburg United Meth. Ch., 1985-87; bd. dirs. Williamsburg Community Hosp., mem. fin. and pension coms., 1988, mem. personnel com. 1986-88. Named one of Outstanding Young Men Am., 1983, 84, one of Outstanding College Athletes Am. 1973, 74, Outstanding Broker of 1984 Registered Rep. mag., 1985, William and Mary Athletic Hall of Fame, 1986; elected to Century Club Wheat, First Securities, 1981, Pres.' Club, 1982, Chmn.'s Group 1983, 84, 85; named to Dirs. Circle, 1986, 87; recipient numerous college athletic awards. Mem. Internat. Assn. Fin. Planning, Inst. Cert. Fin. Planners. Methodist. Clubs: Williamsburg German (v.p. 1985-86, pres. 1986-87), Williamsburg Sports (pres. 1981-82). Office: Wheat First Securities Inc PO Box W Williamsburg VA 23187

MONTGOMERY, KAREN SUE, transportation executive; b. Martins Ferry, Ohio, May 17, 1948; d. Robert Courtnay and Edith Margaret (Gardner) M.; m. Patrick A. Barker, Nov. 26, 1966 (div.). Cert., USDA Grad. Sch., Washington, 1975; AS, Coll. of Marin, 1981; BA in Mgmt., St. Mary's Coll., Moraga, Calif., 1984. Adminstrv. asst. U.S. Army Health Clinic, Arlington, Va., 1972-75; research asst. Robertson, Colman, Siebel & Weisel, San Francisco, 1975-79; exec. asst. Booz Allen & Hamilton, San Francisco, 1979-81; asst. land agt. Los Angeles So. Pacific Land Co., San Francisco, 1981-83; adminstrv. mgr. Sutro & Co., Inc., San Francisco, 1983-84; v.p. ops. Brad Peery, Inc., Greenbrae, Calif., 1984-88; property mgr. So. Pacific Transp. Co., San Francisco, 1988—. Grantee Fedn. of Bus. and Profl. Women, 1983; scholar USDA Grad. Sch., 1975. Mem. AAUW, Clan Montgomery Soc. of N.Am., DAR, Union Sq. Bus. and Profl. Womens Club (2d v.p.). Presbyterian. Home: 37 Elizabeth Way San Rafael CA 94901 Office: So Pacific Transp Co One Market Pla Ste 225 San Francisco CA 94105

MONTGOMERY, PARKER GILBERT, merchant banker; b. Norwood, Mass., July 30, 1928; s. Spencer Bishop and Eleanor Carrie (Gilbert) M.; children: Parker Jr., Carol, John B., William W., Kathryn. A.B., Harvard U., 1949, LL.B., 1953. Bar: Mass. 1953, N.Y. 1956. Assoc. Heminway & Barnes, Boston, 1953; assoc. Dewey, Ballantine, Bushby, Palmer & Wood, N.Y.C., 1956; with Baker, Weeks & Co., investment bankers, N.Y.C., 1957; pvt. practice law N.Y.C., Mt. Kisco, 1957-59, 61-63; spl. asst. to sec. state Dept. State, 1959-61; founder Cooper Labs., Inc., Palo Alto, Calif., 1958; chmn. bd., pres. The Cooper Cos., Inc.; chmn. Cooper Devel. Co., Cooper LaserSonics, Inc. Councilman Town of Bedford, 1971-75; vice-chmn. Presdl. Task Force on Internat. Pvt. Enterprise, 1983-84; bd. dirs. Santa Barbara Med. Found. Clinic, Music Acad. West. Lt. USNR, 1945-46, 54-55. Mem. Coun. Fgn. Rels. (N.Y.C.), Econ. Club (N.Y.), Harvard Club (N.Y.C), Pacific Union Club, Metro Club, River Club (N.Y.C.), Royal Thames Yacht Club, Bedford Golf and Tennis Club, The Valley Club of Montecito. Office: Cooper Devel Co 455 Middlefield Rd Mountain View CA 94043

MONTGOMERY, WALTER GEORGE, communications executive, consultant; b. Elmira, N.Y., Aug. 24, 1945; s. Elwood Herbert Montgomery and Eleanor Leila (Manchester) Spiegel; m. Pamela Sue Shaw, June 11, 1966 (div. Oct. 1976); children: Caleb, Kirsten; m. Marian Amy Gruber, Sept. 18, 1977; children: Abigail Lynn, Samuel Edwin. AB, Syracuse U., 1967; MA, Brown U., 1976, PhD, 1979. Lectr. Keene (N.H.) State Coll., 1976-79; assoc. Kekst & Co., N.Y.C., 1979-82, ptnr., 1983; v.p. Am. Express Co., N.Y.C., 1983-85, sr. v.p., 1985-87; ptnr., vice chmn. Robinson, Lake, Lerer & Montgomery, N.Y.C., 1987—; lectr. careers in bus. program NYU, 1979. With U.S. Army, 1970-72. Office: Robinson Lake Lerer & Montgomery 75 Rockefeller Pla New York NY 10019

MONTI, GARY WILLIAM, management consultant; b. Steubenville, Ohio, Nov. 15, 1948; s. Virgil Victor and Nancy Margaret (Sunseri) M.; m. Anita Louise Kalinowski, Mar. 15, 1969; children: Christian Eric, Jill Erin. BA in Chemistry, U. Steubenville, 1970; MS in Pharmacology, Ohio State U., 1975. Asst. editor Chem. Abstract Svc., Columbus, Ohio, 1975-78; project mgr. Stokely-Van Camp, Columbus, 1978-84; program mgr. Advanced Robotics Corp., Columbus, 1984-85; pres. Gary Monti & Assocs., Pickerington, Ohio, 1985—. Mem. Project Mgmt. Inst. (chmn. software survey com. 1987—, cert. project mgmt. profl.). Office: Gary Monti & Assocs PO Box 93 Pickerington OH 43147

MONTIJO, BEN, management consultant; b. San Jose, Calif., Feb. 28, 1940; s. Gabriel and Margaret (Gomez) M.; m. Patricia Lee Martinez, Sept. 8, 1965 (div.) 1981; children: Randy, Kelly. AA in Social Studies, Coll. of the Sequoias, 1961; BS in Sociology, Ariz. State U., 1963; postgrad., Yale U., 1971; MA in Urban Studies, Occidental Coll., 1972; postgrad., Harvard U., 1988. Various personnel and mgmt. cons. positions Calif., Ariz. and Nev.; dep. city mgr. City of Scottsdale, Ariz.; exec. dir. Fresno Housing Authorities, Calif.; mem. State Rental Housing Devel. Loan Com.; exec. dir. San Diego Housing Commn., Calif., 1979-87; mgmt. cons. various fed., state and local orgns., 1965—. Contbr. articles on housing and fin. to local and industry publs. Active Phoenix Manpower Program; chmn. Jobs for Progress, Phoenix. Nat. Urban fellow Ford Found., N.Y.C., 1971-72. Mem. Nat. Assn. Housing and Redevel. Ofcls. (bd. dirs.), Assn. Local Housing Fin. Agys., Internat. City Mgrs. Assn. Democrat. Club: Bonita Valley Tennis. Home: PO Box 37 Bonita CA 92002

MONTIJO, RALPH ELIAS, JR., engineer; b. Tucson, Oct. 26, 1928; m. Guillermina Paredes, Dec. 1947; children: Rafael, Suzanne, Felice. BSEE, U. Ariz., 1952; postgrad. in digital computer engring., U. Pa., 1953-57; postgrad. in mgmt., U. Calif., Los Angeles, 1958-60. Registered profl. engr., Tex. With RCA Corp., 1952-67; design and devel. engr. RCA Corp., Camden, N.J., 1952-55; mgr. West Coast EDP engring. RCA Corp., Los Angeles, 1960-61, mgr. EDP systems engring., 1961-64; mgr. special systems and equipment planning, product div. RCA Corp., Cherry Hill, N.J., 1964-65, mgr. spl. EDP programs, 1966-67; mgr. Calif. Dept. of Motor Vehicles program RCA Corp., Sacramento, Calif., 1965-66; with Planning Research Corp., 1967-72; dep. div. mgr. Eastern and European ops., computer systems div. Planning Research Corp., Washington, 1968; dep. div. mgr. advanced systems planning, reservations systems, computer systems div. Planning Research Corp., Moorestown, N.J., 1968-69; v.p., gen mgr. Internat. Reservations Corp. div. Planning Research Corp., Los Angeles, 1969-70, exec. v.p., 1970-71, pres., 1971-72, also bd. dirs.; v.p. Systems Sci. Devel. Corp. subs. Planning Research Corp., Los Angeles, 1972—; prin., chief exec. officer Omniplan Corp., Santa Monica, Calif. and Houston, 1972—. Contbr. articles to profl. jours.; patentee in field. Mem. IEEE, Am. Mgmt. Assn., Assn. for Computing Machinery, NSPE, U. Ariz. Alumni Assn. (pres. southern Calif. chpt. 1980-81, Alumni Achievement award 1984). Republican. Roman Catholic. Home: 2268 Gemini Ave Houston TX 77058 also: 3651 Beverly Ridge Dr Sherman Oaks CA 91423 Office: Omniplan Corp 17041 El Camino Real Houston TX 77058

MONTLE, PAUL JOSEPH, entrepreneur; b. Medford, Mass., Aug. 28, 1947; s. Joseph Frederick and Frances Elizabeth (Fogarty) M.; m. Elizabeth Anne Rusch, Mar. 3, 1973; children: Alexis Elizabeth, Daphne Caroline. BA in Econs., Tufts U., 1969; postgrad., Boston U., 1969-70. Pres., chief exec. officer Killebrew, Montle & Co. Inc., Boston, 1971-73; v.p. Burgess & Leith, Boston, 1973-75, Hawthorne Securities Corp., 1975-76; founder, pres. First New Eng. Securities Corp., Boston, 1976-80, chmn., 1980-83; founder, pres. The Yankee Cos. Inc., Boston, 1977-88, chmn., chief exec. officer, 1988—; founder, pres. Montle & Co. Internat., Boston and London, 1987—. Editor investment newsletter The Conservative Investor, 1975-78. Trustee, treas. Derby Acad., Hingham, Mass., 1985—; bd. dirs. South Shore Playhouse Assn., Cohasset, Mass., 1987—. Mem. Algonquin Club, Woods Hole Golf Club, Cohasset Golf Club. Avocations: sailing, golf. Office: Yankee Cos Inc 175 Derby St Hingham MA 02043

MONTRONE, PAUL MICHAEL, diversified company executive; b. Scranton, Pa., May 8, 1941; s. Angelo H. and Beatrice M. (Giancini) M.; m. Sandra R. Gaudenzi, May 30, 1963; children: Michele Marie, Angelo Henry, Jerome Lawrence. B.S. in Accounting magna cum laude, U. Scranton, 1962; Ph.D. in Fin., Econs. and Ops. Research, Columbia U., 1965. Ops. analyst Office Sec. Def., Washington, 1965-67; v.p. Penn-Dixie Industries, N.Y.C., 1967-69; exec. v.p., chief fin. officer Wheelabrator-Frye Inc., Hampton, N.H., 1970-83; exec. v.p. Signal Cos., Inc., La Jolla, Calif., 1983-85; pres. Engineered Products Group Signal Cos., Inc., Hampton, N.H., 1983-85; exec. v.p. fin. and adminstrn. Allied-Signal Inc., Morristown, N.J., 1985-86; pres. The Henley Group Inc., LaJolla, Calif., 1986—, also bd. dirs.; pres. Henley Mfg. Corp., Hampton, N.H.; dir. ICI Ams. Inc. Adv. dir. Met. Opera Assn.; mem. dean's adv. council Bus. sch. Columbia U., N.Y.C. Served to capt. U.S. Army, 1965-67. Roman Catholic. Clubs: Brook, University (N.Y.C.); Bald Peak Colony (Melvin Village, N.H.); Lyford Cay (Nassau, Bahamas). Home: Great Hill Hampton Falls NH 03844 Office: The Henley Group Inc 11255 N Torrey Pines Rd La Jolla CA 92073 *

MONTT, DAVID ARTHUR, health physicist, consultant; b. Boston, Mar. 22, 1956; s. David Garcia and Leila Marie (Jensen) M.; m. Lisa Ann Paglia, Sept. 22, 1984; 1 child, Daniel Arthur. BS, Clarkson Coll., 1978; MS, Harvard U., 1982, Yale U., 1988. Loss prevention analyst Liberty Mutual Ins. Co., North Haven, Conn., 1978-80; indsl. hygienist Exxon Chem. Ams., Linden, N.J., 1981; supr. health physics Harvard U., Cambridge, Mass., 1982-84; health physicist Gen. Electric-Knolls Atomic, Windsor, Conn., 1984-88; supr. health physics Gen. Electric-Knolls Atomic, Windsor, 1988—; pvt. practice cons., Boston, 1982-84. Inventor pilot tube bracket, 1987. Vol. sci. instr. Needham Pub. Schs., Mass., 1974. Eastman Meml. scholar, 1974, Clarkson Trustees scholar, 1974, fellow Nat. Inst. Occupational Safety and Health, 1980. Mem. Health Physics Soc., Am. Indsl. Hygiene Assn., AAAS. Republican. Clubs: Harvard (Boston), Mensa (Hartford, Conn.). Lodges: Norfolk, Masons. Home: 586 Poquonock Ave Windsor CT 06095 Office: Gen Electric Knoll Atomic Prospect Hill Rd Windsor CT 06095

MONTY, CHARLES EMBERT, utility company executive; b. Plainfield, Conn., Mar. 9, 1927; s. Arthur Ovila and Mary Louise (Bromley) M.; m. Pauline Violetta Weeman, Feb. 16, 1952; children: Charles E., Mary, Janice, Nathan, Marcia. B.S.E.E., Northeastern U., 1950; M.B.A., U. Maine, 1969. Registered profl. engr., Maine. With Central Maine Power Co., Augusta, 1956—; asst. mgr. prodn. ops. Cental Maine Power Co., Augusta, 1965-71; v.p., mgr. prodn. ops. Central Maine Power Co., Augusta, 1971-76, sr. v.p. engring. and prodn., 1976-84; exec. v.p., chief operating officer Central Maine Power Co., 1984—, dir.; bd. dirs. Maine Yankee Atomic Power Co., 1983-88, chmn. bd. dirs., 1988—; mem. mgmt. com. New Eng. Power Pool, 1982-86; bd. dirs. Electric Council New England. Mem. IEEE, Maine Assn. Engrs. Republican. Mem. United Chs. of Christ. Office: Cen Maine Power Co Edison Dr Augusta ME 04336

MOODY, D. MIKE, banker; b. Cushing, Okla., Oct. 11, 1944; s. Arthur H. and Kate Lou (Jones) M.; m. Cheryl E. Williams, July 3, 1967; children: T. Robb, Thad G. Student, Cen. State U., 1962-65; BBA, U. Okla., 1967; postgrad., So. Meth. U., 1980. Asst. examiner, examiner FDIC, Kansas City, Mo., 1967-71; v.p., dir. Bank of Hydro, Okla., 1971-75, First Nat. Bank, Weatherford, Okla., 1975-78; pres., chief exec. officer First Nat. Bank, Sallisaw, Okla., 1978-81, Community Bank, Bristow, Okla., 1981—; instr. Okla. Intemediate Sch. Banking. Served with U.S. Army, 1967-69. Named Lifetime Future Farmer of Am. Mem. Am. Bankers Assn. (govt. relations com.), Bristow C. of C. (pres.), Okla. Bankers Assn. (bd. dirs.), So. Meth. U. Assn. (bd. dirs.), Rotary (dir.), Lions. Republican. Methodist. Home: PO Box 428 Sallisow OK 74955

MOODY, EVELYN WILIE, consulting geologist; b. Waco, Tex.; d. William Braden and Enid Eva (Holt) Wilie; student Baylor U., 1934-35; B.A. with honors in geology and edn. U. Tex., 1938, M.A. with honors in geology, 1940; children—John D., Melissa L., Jennifer A. Geologist, Ark. Fuel Oil Co., Shreveport, La., New Orleans and Houston, 1942-45; teaching asst. Colo. Sch. Mines, Golden, 1946-47; exploration cons. geologist Gen. Crude Oil Co., Houston, 1975-77; ind. cons. geologist, Houston, 1977—; exploration cons. geologist Shell Oil Co., Houston, 1979-81; faculty dept. continuing edn. Rice U., Houston, 1978. Cert. profl. geologist. Treas., Sipes Found., 1984, pres., 1985, treas., 1984, editor Sipes Bulletin, 1983-1985 . Recipient Sipes Found. Nat. award for Outstanding Service, 1988, Sipes Houston Chpt. Chmn. award for Outstanding Service to Sipes, 1986. Mem. Am. Assn. Petroleum Geologists, Soc. Ind. Profl. Earth Scientists (sec. 1978-79, vice chmn. 1979-80, chpt. chmn. 1980-81, nat. dir. 1982-85), Geol. Soc. Am., Watercolor Soc. Houston, Art Students League N.Y.C., Art Assn., Am. Inst. Profl. Geologists, Houston Geol. Soc., Soc. Econ. Paleontologists and Mineralogists, Pi Beta Phi (nat. officer 1958-60, 66-68), Pi Lambda Theta. Republican. Presbyterian. Contbr. articles to profl. jours.; editor: The Manual for Independence, 1983, The Business of Being a Petroleum Independent (A Road Map for the Self Employed), 1987; co-author: How (To Try) To Find An Oil Field, 1981. Office: 956 The Main Bldg 1212 Main St Houston TX 77002

MOODY, G. WILLIAM, retired aerospace manufacturing company executive; b. Cleveland Heights, Ohio, Nov. 6, 1928; s. John Walter and Anna Barbara (Keck) M.; m. Loisjean Kanouse, Sept. 17, 1955; children: Elizabeth Jean, Cynthia Ann, G. William. Student, Ohio U., 1948-49; BSCE, Mich. State U., 1952; Advanced Mgmt. Program, Harvard Grad. Sch. Bus., 1982. Sales engr. Rich Mfg. Corp., Battle Creek, Mich., 1952-55; chief engr. Air Lift Co., Lansing, Mich., 1955-61; product engr. Aeroquip Corp., Jackson, Mich., 1961-62, chief engr. Barco div., 1962-68, v.p., gen. mgr., 1968-72, v.p., ops. mgr. AMB div., 1972-74, v.p., gen. mgr. aerospace div., 1974-81, group v.p. gen. products, 1981-85, pres., 1985-88; v.p. Trinova Corp., 1986-88; ret. 1988; sr. design engr. Clark Floor Machine Co., Muskegon, Mich., 1962; bd. dirs. Nu-Matic Grinders Inc., Cleve., Aeroquip S.A. Patentee in field. Gen. campaign chmn. Jackson County United Way, 1976, pres., 1980, bd. dirs., 1978-84; mem. Planning Commn. North Barrington, Ill., 1967-72; trustee, chmn. Foote Meml. Hosp., Jackson; chmn. Joint Com. for an Area Hosp., Barrington, 1969-72; trustee, chmn. Physicians Health Plan South Mich.; bd. dirs. United Way Mich., 1978-82. Served with U.S. Army, 1946-48. Mem. Soc. Automotive Engrs., ASME, Am. Polit. Items Coll. Soc., Am. Mgmt. Assn., Am. Philatelic Soc., Fluid Power Soc., Jackson C. of C., Town Club (dir.), Jackson Country Club, Jackson county Sportsman's Club, Psi Upsilon. Lutheran. Home and Office: 2050 Carriage Hill Toledo OH 43606

MOODY, GEORGE FRANKLIN, banker; b. Riverside, Calif., July 28, 1930; s. William Clifford and Mildred R. (Scott) M.; m. Mary Jane Plank, Jan. 19, 1950; children: Jeffrey George, Jane Ellen Moody Fowler, John Franklin, Joseph William. Student, Riverside City Coll., 1948-50; grad. with honors, Pacific Coast Banking Sch., 1963. Bus. officer U. Calif., Riverside, 1950-52; with Security Pacific Nat. Bank, Los Angeles, 1953—, dir. personnel, v.p., 1970-71, sr. v.p. inland div. adminstrn., 1971-73, exec. v.p., 1973-78, vice chmn., 1978-80, pres., chief exec. officer, 1985; pres., chief operating officer Security Pacific Corp., Los Angeles, 1985—, also bd. dirs. Chief prin. officer, mem. nat. bd. govs., ARC, chmn. exec. com. 1979-80; bd. dirs. Found., U.S. Olympic Com., chmn. Western region, 1981-84; trustee Calif. Neighborhood Housing Service Found., Jr. Achievement So. Calif.; trustee, mem. exec. com. Pomona Coll.; pres. Los Angeles area council Boy Scouts Am., 1980—; past bd. dirs. Los Angeles Music Ctr. Operating Co., Los Angeles United Way, Calif. Econ. Devel. Corp.; past. bd. dirs., past v.p. Hollywood Presbyn. Med. Ctr., Calif. Econ. Devel. Corp.; past chmn. Music Ctr. Unified Fund, Invest-In-Am.; past trustee Calif. Mus. Found., Com. for Econ. Devel., Washington; past. mem. bd. govs. Calif. Community Found.; bd. dirs. John Douglas French Found. for Alzheimers Disease; pres. L.A. area C. Of C. Assocs. Mem. Los Angeles C. of C. (past pres.), U.S. C. of C. (bd. dirs.), Colorado River Assn. (pres.), Am. Bankers Assn. (bd. dirs.), Calif. Bankers Assn., Assn. Res. City Bankers, Merchants and Mfrs. Assn. (past chmn.), Performing Arts Council (former gov.), Calif. Club, Los Angeles Country Club, Hacienda Golf Club. Republican. Office: Security Pacific Corp 333 S Hope St Los Angeles CA 90071

MOODY, JOHN STEPHEN, real estate executive; b. Houston, Nov. 11, 1948; s. Dan McMillan and Florence (Hendrick) M.; m. Eileen Arnold, Apr. 10, 1971; children: John, Joe, Dan. BS, Stanford U., 1970; JD, U. Tex., 1973. Ptnr. Wood, Campbell, Moody & Gibbs, Houston, 1973-83; pres. Moody Corp., Houston, 1984-86; 1st v.p. Rotan Mosle, Houston, 1987—; pres., chief exec. officer Paine Webber Properties, N.Y.C., 1987-88. Home: 5 Beechcroft Rd Greenwich CT 06830 Office: Paine Webber Properties 1290 Ave of the Americas Houston TX 10019 also: Paine Webber Inc 1285 Ave of the Americas New York NY 10019

MOODY, LAMON LAMAR, JR., civil engineer; b. Bogalusa, La., Nov. 8, 1924; s. Lamar Lamon and Vida (Seal) M.; B.S. in Civil Engring., U. Southwestern La., 1951; m. Eve Thibodeaux, Sept. 22, 1954; children—Lamon Lamar III, Jennifer Eve, Jeffrey Matthew. Engr., Tex. Co., N.Y.C., 1951-52; project engr. African Petroleum Terminals, West Africa, 1952-56; chief engr. Kaiser Aluminum & Chem. Corp., Baton Rouge, 1956-63; pres., owner Dyer & Moody, Inc., Cons. Engrs., Baker, La., 1963—, also chmn. bd., dir. Chmn., Baker Planning Commn., 1961-63. Trustee La. Council on Econ. Edn., 1987-89. Served with USMCR, 1943-46. Decorated Purple Heart; registered profl. engr., La., Ark., Miss., Tex. Fellow ASCE, Am. Congress Surveying and Mapping (award for excellency 1972); mem. La. Engring. Soc. (dir., v.p. 1980-81, pres. 1982-83, Charles M. Kerr award for public relations 1971, A.B. Patterson medal 1981, Odom award for distinguished service to engring. profession, 1986), Profl. Engrs. in Pvt. Practice (state chmn. 1969-70), La. Land Surveyors Assn. (pres. 1968-69, Land Surveyor of Yr. award 1975), Cons. Engrs. Council, Engrs. Joint Council, Pub. Affairs Research Council of La. (exec. com., trustee 1983-89), Good Roads and Transp. Assn. (bd. dirs. 1984-89), Baker C. of C. (pres. 1977, Bus. Leader of Yr. award 1975), NSPE (nat. dir. 1982-83), Blue Key. Democrat. Baptist. Clubs: Masons (32 deg., K.C.C.H. 1986), Kiwanis (dir. 1964-65). Home: 3811 Charry Dr Baker LA 70714 Office: 2845 Ray Weiland Dr Baker LA 70714

MOON, JAMES VIRGIL, county official; b. Elberton, Ga., Sept. 25, 1950; s. Omer Gordon and Mildred (Bryant) M.; m. Harveda Inglett, Sept. 26, 1980; children: Adam, Angie, Jason. BSBA in Acctg. cum laude, E. Carolina U., 1978. CPA, Ga. Cash mgr. Family Ctr., Inc., Marietta, Ga., 1978-79, corp. acctg. mgr., 1979-81; fin. administr. Cobb County Govt., Marietta, 1981-83, internal audit dir., 1983-85, fin. dir., comptroller, 1985—; chmn. Cir. Defender Adv. Bd., Marietta, 1983; cons. Moon Tax Services, Marietta, 1980—. Program dir., membership chmn., bd. dirs. Marietta Civitans Club; mem. State Ga. Revenue Task Force. Served to sgt. U.S. Army, 1970-72. Mem. Am. Inst. CPAs, Ga. Soc. CPAs (Industry Govt. and Edn. com.), Nat. Assn. Accts., Inst. Internal Audit, Govt. Fin. Officers Assn., Ga. Govt. Fin. Officers Assn. (state treas., Nat. Cash. Mgmt. com.), DAV, Assn. County Commrs. of Ga. (Taxation and Fin. Policy com.), Beta Gamma Sigma. Republican. Presbyterian. Clubs: Chestnut Creek Assn. (treas.), Atlanta Lawn Tennis Assn. Home: 3240 Moss Creek Dr Marietta GA 30062 Office: Cobb County Govt 10 E Park Sq Marietta GA 30090

MOON, JEROME FIRMIN, publishing executive; b. Maryville, Tenn., June 20, 1947; s. Claude F. and Ruby (Myers) M.; m. Deborah Bradford, Aug. 22, 1970; children: Amy, Sarah. BS with high honors, U. Tenn., 1977. Pres., publisher Maryville-Alcoa Newspapers, Inc., 1971—; bd. dirs. First Am. Bank, Knoxville, Tenn. Assocs., Inc., Alcoa, Tenn, Tenn. Press Svc. Bd. dirs. Knoxville Symphony, Knoxville Art Council ; chmn. Blount County Indsl. Devel. Bd.;chmn., n. chancellor's assoc., U. Tenn., Knoxville; chmn. Blount County United Way, 1987—, Pellissippi State Tech. Community Coll. Found.; active Leadership Knoxville, class 1989. With USN, 1965-71. Recipient Disting. Service award Tenn. Vocat. Edn. Council, 1982-83. Mem. Internat. Newspaper Fin. Execs., Inst. Internal Auditors, Tenn. Press Assn. (treas. 1985-88), Blount County C. of C., Phi Kappa Phi (life), Beta Gamma Sigma. Presbyterian. Office: The Daily Times PO Box 568 Maryville TN 37803

MOON, JOHN HENRY, SR., banker; b. Van Buren, Ark., Aug. 19, 1937; s. B.R. and Alma (Witte) M.; A.A., Delmar Coll., Corpus Christi, 1956; B.B.A. cum laude, Tex. A. and I. Coll., 1958; m. Agnes Rose Dickens, Aug. 16, 1958; children—John Henry, Randall Allen. Sr. acct. Tex. Eastern Transp. Co. and subs., 1958-63; exec. v.p., dir. Houston Research Inst., 1963-68; sr. v.p., asst. to chmn. bd., dir. Main Bank, 1968; vice chmn. bd., dir. N.E. Bank, 1969; chief exec. officer, chmn. bd., dir. Pasadena (Tex.) Nat. Bank, 1970-81; gen. partner Moon and Assocs., Ltd., 1977—; chmn. bd., pres. Interservice Life Ins. Corp., Phoenix, Community Bank, Houston, 1975-81, Interstate Bank, Houston, 1977-81; chmn. bd., pres. Community Capital Corp., Houston, 1975—, Ellington Bank Commerce, Houston, 1983—; chmn. bd. Community Nat. Bank, Friendswood, Tex., 1981—; chmn. bd. Peoples Nat. Bank, Pasadena, Tex., 1984—. Past bd. dirs. Pasadena Heart Assn., Salvation Army, Tex. Assn. Prevention of Blindness; past chmn. City of Pasadena Bd. Devel.; past chmn. adv. bd. Pasadena Civic Ctr. Named Outstanding Young Man of Year, Pasadena Jr. C. of C., 1973; named to Pasadena Hall of Fame, 1973. Mem. Pasadena C. of C. (bd. dirs. Southeast Econ. Devel.), Am. Inst. C.P.A.s, Tex. Soc. C.P.A.s, Tex., Ind. bankers assns. Lodge: Rotary. Home: 3914 Peru Circle Pasadena TX 77504 Office: PO Box 34278 Houston TX 77234

MOON, RICHARD DAVID, information systems executive; b. Richland Center, Wis., Feb. 13, 1956; s. Richard Graham and Mary Linda (Hutchins) M.; m. Debra Kay Hoppe, June 12, 1976; children: Sarah Rachel, Benjamin Maurice. BS, Cardinal Stritch Coll., Milw., 1983, MS, 1985; MA, U. Wis., Milw., 1087. Cert. data processor. Sr. computer operator Med. Coll. Wis., Wauwatosa, 1980-8l; systems analyst SST, Inc., Milw., 198l-82; systems and data processing mgr. Tempo Communications, The Jour. Co., Milw., 1982-83; dir. data systems Funway Holidays Funjet, Bayside, Wis., 1983-84, v.p. info. systems, 1984—. With USAF, 1975-79. Mem. Assn. for Computing Machinery, Amnesty Internat., Mensa, Sigma Xi. Mem. Soc. of Friends. Home: 4457 N Prospect Ave Shorewood WI 53211 Office: Funway Holidays Funjet 8907 N Port Washington Rd Bayside WI 53217

MOONEY, J. D., motel executive; b. Kansas City, Mo., Feb. 21, 1932; s. J.L. and Phoebe (Lighton) M.; m. Alayne I. Kohn, June 15, 1958; children: Jo Ann, David Alan. BBA, U. Mich., 1954, MBA, 1957. Cert. hotel adminstr. Mgr. Woolf Bros., Kansas City, 1958-66, asst. to pres., 1967-70; pres. Mission Inn Motel, Inc., Overland Park, Kans., 1970—; bd. dirs. Overland Park Conv. and Visitors Bur., exec. com., 1986—, Hwy. 56 Bus. Dist., 1984-87. Chmn. Hwy. 56 Bus. Dist., 1984-87; vice chmn. Small Properties Adv. Council, 1985-88, chmn., 1988-89, bd. dirs. 1983—; bd. dirs. Johnson County Community Coll. 1982—, chmn. 1986—; bd. dirs. hospitality div. Johnson County Community Coll. , 1982—, chmn, bd., 1986—; bd. dirs. Overland Park (Kans.) Conv. and Vis. Bir., 1983—, Temple Bnai Jehudah, 1972-81; pres., Men's Club, 1972-73, bd. dirs. 1987-89. With U.S. Army, 1954-56. Recipient SPOKE award Kansas City (Mo.) C. of C., 1959. Mem. Chartered Coun. Fin. Cons. (life), Kans. Hotel Motel Assn. (bd. dirs. 1978—, pres. 1987-89), Greater Kansas City Hotel/Motel Assn. (bd. dirs., pres. 1987-893), Kans. Lodging Assn. (bd. dirs. 1984, named Hotel Man of Year 1981, 83, 84), Am. Hotel Assn. (bd. dirs., exec. com., small properties council), Economy Lodging Council (bd. dirs.), Kansas City C. of C. (pres. 1970-72, Hall of Fame 1972), B'Nai Jehudah (bd. dirs., Hall of Fame 1971), Kansas City Athletic Club (treas. 1971-72, bd. dirs. 1969-72). Office: Mission Inn Motel 7508 W 63d St Shawnee Mission KS 66202

MOONEY, JOHN ALLEN, food company executive; b. Amery, Wis., May 17, 1918; s. Harry Edmon and Maybelle (Johnson) M.; m. Nettie O. Hayes, Aug. 29, 1940; children: John Allen, Suzann, Jean, Nancy. Student, U. Wis., River Falls. Salesman Reid Murdock & Co., Chgo., 1940-45; salesman Consol. Foods Corp., Chgo., 1945-69; nat. sales mgr., v.p. M&R Sales Corp., Oak Park, Ill., 1969-78; pres., chief exec. officer, dir. M&R Sales Corp., 1978—; nat. sales mgr., v.p. Western Dressing, Inc., Oak Park, 1970-78; pres., chief exec. officer, dir. Western Dressing, Inc., 1978-89; v.p., dir. Machine Products Co., La Crosse, Wis., also bd. dirs.; bd. dirs. 1st Nat. Bank LaGrange, Ill., Waunakee Alloy Casting Corp., Wis. Festmaster Oktoberfest U.S.A., LaCrosse, 1983; parade marshall Amery (Wis.) Fall Festival, 1962, River Falls (Wis.) Shrine Hosp. Benefit Football Parade, 1962; bd. govs. Shriners Hosp. Crippled Children, Mpls. and St. Paul, 1952-69, now emeritus bd. govs., Chgo., treas., 1983; chmn. Shrine Hosp. Day Shrine Hosp. Crippled Children, Chgo., 1982; assoc. bd. govs. LaGrange Meml. Hosp., 1967; past pres. Gundersen Med. Found., LaCrosse, Wis., trustee; mem. support com. Heritage Club, LaCrosse Lutheran Hosp., 1979; bd. govs. Nat. Fishing Hall of Fame, Hayward, Wis.; exec. bd. Gateway Area council, Boy Scouts Am.; mem. nat. election council Boy Scouts Am., nat. rep. LaCrosse chpt.; mem. corp. LaCrosse Luth. Hosp. Recipient Order of Arrow Boy Scouts Am., Pope John XXIII award, 1984, Community Leadership award LaCrosse Toastmasters, 1984; Named hon. mem. LaCrosse Boys Choir, 1977, Man of Yr. LaCrosse C. of C., 1983, hon. Ky. col.; Mooney Masonic Hall, Amery, established 1979. Mem. Sons of Norway, Rebild Nat. Parks Soc. (Aalborg, Denmark). Clubs: LaCrosse Plugs, LaCrosse Country, The LaCrosse Club. Lodges: Shriners (past potentate Zor Shrine Temple, Madison, Wis., hon. past potentate Medinah Temple, Chgo.), Elks, Moose.

MOOR, MANLY EUGENE, JR., banker; b. Birmingham, Ala., Apr. 28, 1923; s. Manly Eugene and Nell (Pulliam) M.; m. Anne Simms Beddow, Oct. 10, 1944; children: Manly Eugene III, William Tillman, Anne Beddow, John Matthew Bolling. B.S., Auburn U., 1947; grad, Sch. Banking, La. State U., 1956. With Am South Bank N.A. (formerly First Nat. Bank), Birmingham, 1950—; asst. cashier Am South Bank N.A. (formerly First Nat. Bank), 1953-57, mgr. comml. loan dept., 1953-54; mgr. Am South Bank N.A. (formerly First Nat. Bank) (Southside Br.), 1954-57, asst. v.p., 1957-59, v.p., 1959-67, sr. v.p., 1967-68, exec. v.p., 1968-72, pres., 1972-77, vice chmn. bd., 1977—; dir. Matthews Electric Supply Co., Birmingham, AmSouth Fin. Corp., Engel Mortgage Co., Am South Bank Internat. Crusade chmn. Am. Cancer Soc., 1959, Girls Club Birmingham, 1968—, Jefferson County chpt. Am. Cancer Soc., 1962—; mem. adv. bd. Salvation Army, Birmingham, 1963—; gen. treas. YMCA, 1968—; co-chmn. United Appeal, 1966, gen. chmn., 1969; Bd. dirs. Boy Scouts Am., 1960—, Birmingham Downtown Improvement Assn., 1963—; bd. dirs. Blue Cross-Blue Shield of Ala., 1964—, chmn., 1969—. Served with USAAF, 1942-45. Presbyterian. Club: Mountain Brook, Downtown (bd. dirs. 1963—), Redstone (Birmingham); Shoal Creek (pres.). Office: AmSouth Bank PO Box 11007 Birmingham AL 35288

MOORE, ALAN JOHN, construction company executive; b. Aberdeen, Wash., Feb. 4, 1952; s. James Forrestor and Alice Mae (Freed) M.; m. Julie Ann Yzaguirre, Sept. 3, 1977; children: Kaye, Ann. BA, Coll. of Idaho, 1974; MBA, Boise State U., 1985. CPA, Idaho. Various positions Morrison Knudsen Corp., 1974-77; dir. treasury svcs. Morrison Knudsen Corp., Boise, Idaho, 1980—; divisional contr. Beatrice Foods Co., Boise, 1978; asst. treas. Landura Corp., Woodburn, Oreg., 1979; adj. lectr. Coll. of Idaho, Caldwell, 1986—. Econ. cons. Jr. Achievement, Boise, 1985; mem. nat. alumni bd. dirs. Coll. of Idaho, 1987. Mem. AICPA, Idaho Soc. CPA's. Home: 10336 Shadybrook Boise ID 83704 Office: Morrison Knudsen Corp M-K Plaza Boise ID 83707

MOORE, ANDREW TAYLOR, JR., banker; b. Tarboro, N.C., June 17, 1940; s. Andrew Taylor and Mary Dare (Allsbrook) M. BA in History, Duke U., 1962; LLB, U.Va., Charlottesville, 1965. Asst. sec. Signet Banking Corp., Richmond, 1965-71, asst. v.p., corporate sec., 1971-75, v.p., corporate sec., 1975-82, sr. v.p., corporate sec., 1982—. Bd. dirs. Theatre IV, Richmond, Va., 1981, Woodlawn Plantation, Fairfax County, Va., 1983, Va. State YMCA adv. council, Lynchburg, 1988—. Served with U.S. Army, 1967. Mem. Am. Banking Inst., Am. Soc. Corporate Secs. (edn. com.), Assn. Bank Holding Cos. (govt. relations com. 1979—), Am. Bankers Assn. (legis. liason adv. com. 1979—), Va. Bankers Assn. (state legis. com. 1981—), Conf. State Bank Suprs. (state rep., chmn. div. III adv. council 1987-88), Met. Richmond C. of C. (legis. affairs com.), Commonwealth Club. Methodist. Home: 2011 Hanover Ave Richmond VA 23220 Office: Signet Banking Corp 7 N 8th St PO Box 25970 Richmond VA 23260

MOORE, ARCHIE TAYLOR, brick manufacturing company executive; b. Kingsport, Tenn., May 25, 1936; s. Archie Taylor and Helen Rita (Mitchell) M.; m. Gloria Ann Taylor, Apr. 18, 1944; children: Archie Taylor III, Gregory, Melissa. BS, East Tenn. State U., 1973, MBA, 1975. Lab technician Gen. Shale Products Corp., Kingsport, 1959-62, mgr. customer svc., 1962-64; field sales rep. Gen. Shale Products Corp., Indpls., 1964-66; mgr. transp. Gen. Shale Products Corp., Johnson City, Tenn., 1966-76, mgr. market rsch., 1976-79; dist. sales mgr. Gen. Shale Products Corp., Huntsville, Ala., 1979-80; regional sales mgr. Gen. Shale Products Corp., Johnson City, 1980-87, v.p. sales and mktg., 1988—. With USMC, 1956-59. Mem. Brick Inst. Am. (pres. region 5 1983), Appalachian Traffic Club (pres. Kingsport 1969). Baptist. Office: Gen Shale Products Corp PO Box 3547 CRS Johnson City TN 37602

MOORE, BILLIE LEE, transportation executive; b. Denison, Tex., Sept. 15, 1931; s. Emery Wood and Bethel (Jackson) M.; m. Doris Stringer, Nov. 4, 1951; children: Sondra Clare, James Curtis. BBA with honors, U. North Tex. (name formerly North Tex. State U)., 1957, MBA, 1971. Supply officer GSA, Ft. Worth, 1958-62, inventory mgr., 1963-68, mgmt. analyst, 1969-79; traffic mgr. GSA, 1980-84, zone mgr., 1984—; instr. bus. Tarrant County Jr. Coll., Ft. Worth, 1972—; Execs. on Campus speaker North Tex. State U., 1988. Mem. Friends of Weatherford Pub. Library, 1986-89, Nature Conservancy, Austin, Tex., 1986-89. Recipient Community Service award United Fund. Mem. Fed. Bus. Assn. (chmn. pub. affairs 1964, chmn. pub. relations com. 1965, cert. of Achievement, 1964), Fine Arts Assn., Sierra Club, Nat. Wildlife Fedn., Wilderness Soc. Lutheran. Clubs: Whirl-A-Ways (Weatherford) (pres. 1979-80), Toastmasters (Ft. Worth) (v.p. 1974-75).

MOORE, BOB STAHLY, communications executive; b. Pasadena, Calif., July 3, 1936; s. Norman Hastings and Mary Augusta (Stahly) M. Student, U. Mo., 1954-58, MIT, 1958-62. News dir. WPEO, Peoria, Ill., 1958-60, KSST, Davenport, Iowa, 1960-62, WIRE, Indpls., 1962-64, WCFL, Chgo., 1964-67; White House corr. Metromedia, Inc., Washington, 1967-71; news dir. Gateway Communications, Altoona, Pa., 1972-74; Washington Bur. chief MBS, 1974-76; v.p. news MBS, Arlington, Va., 1976-78; White House corr. MBS, 1978-81; dir. communications Fed. Home Loan Bank Bd., Washington, 1981-85; spl. asst. to bd. govs. Fed. Res. System, Washington, 1985—. Active ARC. Served with USAF, 1961-63. Recipient profl. awards Ind. News Broadcasters, 1963, Ill. News Broadcasters, 1965, UPI, 1960, 63, 65, AP, 1956, 58, 61, 65, 67, Mo. News Broadcasters, 1956, 61. Mem. Radio and Television News Dirs. Assn. (Profl. award), White House Corrs. Assn., State Dept. Corrs. Assn., Radio-Television Corrs. Gallery (U.S. Capitol), Chgo. Council on Fgn. Relations, Pub. Relations Soc. Am., Nat., Washington, Chgo. press clubs, U.S. Jr., Mo., Ill. chambers commerce, Sigma Delta Chi. Presbyterian. Home: 817 Crescent Dr Alexandria VA 22302 Office: 20th and Constitution NW Washington DC 20551

MOORE, BRADLEY CLAYSON, controller; b. Payson, Utah, Aug. 4, 1959; m. Carrie Ashton Moore, July 10, 1981; children: Stephen, Camille, Katherine. BS, Brigham Young U., 1983. CPA, Utah, Ariz. Auditor Price Waterhouse, Tucson, 1983-85; sr. auditor Price Waterhouse, Salt Lake City, 1985-86; controller Swire Pacific Holdings, Inc. Bottling Group, Salt Lake City, 1986—. Mem. Am. Inst. CPAs, Ariz Soc. CPAs, Utah Assn. CPAs, Kiwanis INternat. Mormon.

MOORE, BRIAN CLIVE, actuary; b. Everett, Wash., Sept. 7, 1945; s. Frederic E. and Kathleen E. (Miller) M.; m. Lorraine Campbell, Feb. 11, 1946; children: Timothy, Jonathan. BA in Math., Yale U., 1970; MA in Math., U. Calif., 1971. Actuarial assoc. INA, Phila., 1971-73; asst. actuary Reliance Ins. Co., Phila., 1973-77, asst. sec., 1977-78, sec., 1978-80, asst. v.p., 1980-84, v.p., 1984-86, sr. v.p., 1986—. With U.S. Army, 1966-68. Fellow Casualty Actuarial Soc.; mem. Am. Acad. Actuaries. Mem. Unitarian Ch. Office: Reliance Ins Co 4 Penn Ctr Pla Philadelphia PA 19103

MOORE, CHARLES GILBERT, III, venture capitalist; b. Plainfield, N.J., Oct. 23, 1943; s. Charles Gilbert and Dorothy (Johnston) M.; m. Martha Stebbins, June 3, 1967 (div. 1983); children: Jennifer, Nathaniel, Christopher. BA, Dartmouth Coll., 1965; MA, U. Mich., 1968, PhD, 1971. Vis. faculty U. Grenoble, France, 1971-72; asst. prof. Cornell U., Ithaca, N.Y., 1972-75; sr. v.p. ADP Network Services, Ann Arbor, Mich., 1975-81; gen. ptnr. Welsh, Carson, Anderson & Stowe, N.Y.C., 1982—; bd. dirs. Microcom Inc., Norwood, Mass., Relational Tech., Inc., Alameda, Calif. Mem. Assn. Computing Machinery, Downtown Club. Office: Welsh Carson Anderson & Stowe 200 Liberty St Ste 3601 New York NY 10281

MOORE, DALTON, JR., petroleum engineer; b. Snyder, Tex., Mar. 25, 1918; s. Dalton and Anne (Yonge) M. Grad., Tarleton State U., 1938; BS, Tex. Agrl. and Mech. U., 1942; diploma, U.S. Army Command and Gen. Staff Sch., 1945. Field engr. Gulf Oil Corp., 1946; dist. engr. Chgo. Corp., 1947-48, chief reservoir engr., 1949; mgr. Burdell Oil Corp., N.Y.C. and Snyder, Tex., 1950-52; mgr. Wimberly Field Unit, 1953-55; profl. petroleum cons., Abilene, Tex., 1956—; pres. Dalton Moore Engring. Co., 1957-67, First Oil Co., 1960-67, Second Oil Co., 1960-72, Petroleum Engrs. Operating Co., 1967—, Evaluation Engr. for Investment Bankers Corp., 1968—, Investment Bankers Oil Co., Inc., 1968—. Pres. Sweetwater (Tex.) Jr. C. of C., 1938; precinct chmn. Taylor County Dem. Com., 1956-76; bd. dirs. Taylor County chpt. ARC, 1956-62. Served to maj., AUS, 1940-46. Named Eagle Scout, Boy Scouts Am. Mem. AIME (chmn. West Cen. Tex. sect. 1954), Abilene Geol. Soc., VFW. Address: 4065 Waldemar Dr Abilene TX 79605

MOORE, DANIEL HORATIO (BUD), private investment banker; b. El Dorado, Kans., Nov. 7, 1959; s. Daniel Hansford and Julia Lee (Cowan) M.; m. Stacey Jane Harris, Oct. 24, 1981; 1 child, Heather Ann. BBA in Mktg., Tex. A&M U., 1980. Lic. real estate broker, Tex. V.p. D.H. Moore Corp., Dallas, 1980-81, Finch & Moore Assocs., Dallas, 1981—; instr. No. Tex. State U., Dallas, 1985-86. Mem. Tex. Assn. Bus. Brokers (v.p., bd. dirs. 1984—), Internat. Assn. Bus. Brokers, Assn. for Corp. Growth (officer 1988—), Inst. Bus. Appraisers. Roman Catholic. Office: Finch & Moore Assocs 14900 Landmark Blvd Ste 555 Dallas TX 75240

MOORE, DONALD LYNN, county official; b. Kansas City, Mo., Jan. 17, 1947; s. George and Edna Marie (Hockett) Sanders; m. Nellie Mae McKinzy, July 2, 1976; 1 stepchild, Phillip Ray. AA, Kansas City Jr. Coll., 1967; BBA, Wichita State U., 1970; MPA, U. Mo., Kansas City, 1970; postgrad., U.S. Army Res. Grad. Leadership Sch., 1970-76, Rochester Inst. Tech., 1984, U. Okla., 1986. Economist Mid-Am. Regional Coun., Kansas City, 1970-74; mktg. specialist Black Econs. Union, Kansas City, 1974; econ. devel. adminstr. Jackson County Econs. Devel. Commn., Independence, Mo., 1976—. Mem. Gov.'s Gen. Motors Leeds Task Force, Kansas City, 1987-88; mem. Gov.'s CDBG Adv. Coun., Jefferson City, Mo., 1987-88; mem. Hawthorn Found., 1987-88, Ad Hoc Com. on Projections, Jackson County Coalition of Chambers, 1984—. Mem. Mo. Indsl. Devel. Coun. (treas. 1987—, v.p. 1988). Democrat. Methodist. Home: 7325 Lydia St Kansas City MO 64131-1813 Office: Jackson Conty Econs Devel Commn 306 W Kansas Ave Independence MO 64050

MOORE, GEORGE ANDREW, JR., lawyer, former steel company executive; b. Easton, Pa., May 24, 1927; s. George Andrew Moore and Alice Josephine (Speer) Rowe; m. Virginia Lambert, Nov. 29, 1958; children: Jeffrey J., Valerie A. A.B. magna cum laude, Lafayette Coll., 1950; J.D. cum laude, U. Pa., 1953; grad. advanced mgmt. program, Harvard U., 1973. Bar: Pa. 1954, U.S. Dist. Ct. 1958, U.S. Supreme Ct. 1975, N.Y. 1984, D.C. 1984. Assoc. Fackenthal, Teel & Dancer, Easton, Pa., 1953-56; solicitor Pa. R.R., 1956-58; with Bethlehem Steel Co., 1958-83, mgr. indsl. relations, 1965-69, mgr. labor relations, 1970-73, asst. to v.p. indsl relations, 1973-74, asst. v.p. indsl. relations, 1974-78, v.p. indsl. relations, 1978-83; of counsel Gibson, Dunn & Crutcher, N.Y.C., 1984-85; cons. U.S. Postal Service, USX Corp., Washington and Pitts., 1985-87; ptnr. Reed, Smith, Shaw & McClay, Phila., 1987—. Mem. nat. council Lafayette Coll.; past chmn. bd. trustees East Stroudsburg U.; mem. labor relations council U. Pa.; mem. adv. council on benefits curriculum Brandeis U.; bd. dirs. Pa. Med. Care Found.; mem. adv. com. indsl. relations curriculum U. Md.; mem. ch. council St. John's Lutheran Ch. Served with USN, 1945-46. Mem. NAM, Am. Arbitration Assn. (dir.), ABA, Pa. Bar Assn., Northampton County Bar Assn., Am. Iron and Steel Inst., Internat. Iron and Steel Inst., Am. Mining Congress, Bethlehem C. of C., Order of Coif, Phi Beta Kappa. Clubs: Saucon Valley Country; Duquesne (Pitts.); Pomfort (Easton, Pa.). Lodge: Masons. Home: 4017 Freemansburg Ave Easton PA 18042 Office: Reed Smith Shaw & McClay 1600 Ave of the Arts Bldg Broad & Chesnut Sts Philadelphia PA 19107-3426

MOORE, GEORGE EMORY, JR., county official; b. Jamestown, N.Y., Feb. 26, 1949; s. George Emory and Josephine Clara (Trunzo) M.; m. Kathryn Grassi, Sept. 24, 1977; children: Jessica Josephine, George Justin. BA, SUNY, Fredonia, 1972, MA, 1975; postgrad., St. Bonaventure U., 1981—. Cert. elem., secondary tchr., N.Y. Tchr. Jamestown (N.Y.) Pub. Schs., 1971-75; devel. specialist HEW-HHS, N.Y.C., 1976; program dir. Chautauqua County Govt., Mayville, N.Y., 1977-81; asst. adminstrv. dir., sr. coordinator Chautaugua Region Indsl. Devel. Agy., Jamestown, N.Y., 1982—; also bd. dirs. Chautaugua County Indsl. Devel. Agy., Jamestown; indsl. fin. packaging cons., Jamestown, N.Y., 1983—; bd. dirs. New Enterprises Inc., So. Tier West Regional Planning and Devel. Bd. Mem. governing bd. N.Y. State Ednl. Ctr. for Econ. Devel., Lancaster, N.Y., 1984—. Mem. Am. Econ. Devel. Council, N.Y. State Econ., Am. Soc. Personnel Adminstrs., Phi Alpha Theta. Democrat. Roman Catholic. Home: 556 Front St Jamestown NY 14701 Office: Chautauqua County Indsl Devel Agy 200 Harrison St Jamestown NY 14701

MOORE, GEORGE JACKSON, accountant; b. Nashville, June 5, 1930; s. Oren Gary and Retha Inez (McLendon) M.; m. Emajean Ray, June 3, 1956. BS in Acctg. cum laude, Valdosta (Ga.) State Coll., 1972. CPA, Ga. Staff acct. Stewart, Giles & Co. PC, Valdosta, 1969-71, 72-73, dept. mgr., 1974—. Fellow Am. Inst. CPA's, Ga. Soc. CPA's; mem. Alpha Chi, Sigma Alpha Chi. Home: Rte 2 Box 120 Nashville GA 31639 Office: Stewart Giles & Co PC PO Box 1887 Valdosta GA 31603

MOORE, GORDON E., electronics company executive; b. San Francisco, Jan. 3, 1929; s. Walter Harold and Florence Almira (Williamson) M.; m. Betty I. Whittaker, Sept. 9, 1950; children: Kenneth, Steven. B.S. in Chemistry, U. Calif., 1950; Ph.D. in Chemistry and Physics, Calif. Inst. Tech., 1954. Mem. tech. staff Shockley Semicondr. Lab., 1956-57; mgr. engring. Fairchild Camera & Instrument Corp., 1957-59, dir. research and devel., 1959-68; exec. v.p. Intel Corp., Santa Clara, Calif., 1968-75; pres., chief exec. officer Intel Corp., 1975-79, chmn., chief exec. officer, 1979-87, chmn., 1987—; dir. Micro Mask Inc., Varian Assocs. Inc., Transamerica Corp. Fellow IEEE; mem. Nat. Acad. Engring., Am. Phys. Soc. Office: Intel Corp 3065 Bowers Ave Santa Clara CA 95051

MOORE, GREGORY NANCE, food company controller; b. Chgo., Oct. 12, 1949; s. Lester Layne and Margaret Ann (Flood) M.; m. Kathleen Cavanagh, May 26, 1973; children: Megan Kate, Jeffrey David. BBA with honors, U. Tex., 1972; MBA, St. John's U., Queens, N.Y., 1979. CPA, N.Y., Conn. Acct. Union Service Corp., N.Y.C., 1972-73; audit mgr. Arthur Young and Co., Stamford, Conn., 1973-83; controller Pepsico Wines & Spirits Internat., Purchase, N.Y., 1983-86; asst. controller Taco Bell Corp. (div. of Pepsico, Inc.), Irvine, Calif., 1986—. Mem. Am. Inst. CPA's, Conn. Soc. CPA's (industry com., Outstanding Speaker award 1981), N.Y. State Soc. CPA's (industry com.), Beta Gamma Sigma. Republican. Roman Catholic. Office: Taco Bell Corp 17902 Von Karman Irvine CA 92714

MOORE, HENDERSON ALFRED, JR., savings and loan executive, retired; b. Hattiesburg, Miss., May 28, 1912; s. Henderson Alfred and Lucy Alice (Currie) M.; B.A., U. Miss., 1934, LL.B., 1936, J.D., 1968; m. Mary Cleo Barnes, June 16, 1946 (dec. Dec. 1976); children—Betty Barnes Moore McKenzie, H.A., Lucy Currie Moore Pledger; m. 2d, Dot Marie R. Evans, Oct. 24, 1979. Admitted to Miss. bar, 1936; mem. firm Moore and Jones, Hattiesburg, 1961-77, of counsel, 1977—; exec. v.p. First Magnolia (formerly First Fed. Savs. and Loan Assn.), Hattiesburg, 1961-68, pres., 1968-77, chmn. bd., chief exec. officer, 1977-84, chmn. emeritus, 1984—; city pros. atty., 1938-41, 47-49; city judge, 1941-42, city atty., 1949-53. Mem. Forrest County Indsl. Bd., 1965-77; mem. Hattiesburg Redevel. Authority, 1981—, vice chmn., 1984, chmn., 1985. Miss. Econ. Council, 1960-84. Served to lt. USN, 1942-46. Mem. Inst. Fin. Edn., Miss. Bar Found., ABA, South Central Bar Assn., Miss. State Bar, Newcomen Soc. N.Am., Miss. Econ. Council (dir. 1960-84), U.S. League of Savs. Assn. (dir. 1968-71, 74-77), Fed. Home Loan Bank (dir. 1973-74), Miss. Savs. and Loan League (past pres.), Southwestern Savs. and Loan Conf. (dir. 1965-67), Miss. Folklore Soc., Hattiesburg Civic Assn., Soc. War of 1812, SAR, Miss. Hist. Soc., Hattiesburg C. of C., U. So. Miss. Found., U. So. Miss. Alumni Assn., U. Miss. Alumni Assn., Phi Kappa Alpha, Phi Alpha Delta, Phi Kappa Phi. Clubs: Hattiesburg Country; Univ., Capitol City (Jackson). Lodges: Rotary, Elks.

Home: 2312 Carriage Rd Hattiesburg MS 39401 Office: 130 W Front St Hattiesburg MS 39401

MOORE, HERBERTA GRISSOM, small food business executive; b. Knoxville, Tenn., Aug. 30, 1944; d. Herbert Gist and Grace (Gass) Grissom; m. Farris F. Moore Jr., Sept. 17, 1976. Grad. high sch., Nashville. Office mgr., v.p. Mrs. Grissom's Salads, Inc., Nashville, 1964—. Mem. Beta Sigma Phi. Methodist. Office: Mrs Grissoms Salads Inc 2500 Bransford Ave PO Box 40231 Nashville TN 37204

MOORE, HOWARD WOLFE, retail toy store executive; b. Balt., Aug. 18, 1930; s. Charles Dill and Gertrude Melva (Cohen) M.; m. Helene Z. Zayon, June 15, 1952; children: Shelle, Susan, Michael. Ed., Balt. City Coll. Owner, operator Moores Toys, Balt., 1948-66; pres. Toy Town U.S.A., Randallstown, Md., 1966-78; exec. v.p. Lionel Leisure, Phila., 1978-79; exec. v.p., gen. mdse. mgr. Toys R Us, Inc., Paramus, N.J., 1980—; also bd. dirs. Toys R Us, Inc., Rochelle Park, N.J. Served with A.C., USN, 1951-52. Named Brandeis Man of Yr., Brandeis U., 1985. Republican. Jewish. Home: 105 S Woodcrest Ave Long Port NJ 08403 Office: Toys R Us Inc 461 From Rd Paramus NJ 07652

MOORE, JAMES RICHARD, oil and gas company executive; b. Bremerton, Wash., Sept. 27, 1945; s. Lowell William and Velma Lee (Adams) M.; m. Sue Ann Buzzard, Jan. 20, 1968; 1 child, Amy Lee. BBA in Mktg., U. Okla., 1968, MBA in Mgmt., 1969. Various positions Getty Oil Co., Tulsa, 1969-79, mgr. natural gas liquids supply, 1979-80; v.p. Home Petroleum Corp., Houston, 1980-82, Tejas Gas Corp., Houston, 1983-85, Arkla Energy Resources, Shreveport, La., 1985-86; sr. v.p. Arkla Energy Resources, Shreveport, 1986—; exec. v.p. Entex, Houston, 1988—. Served to 1st lt. U.S. Army, 1970-72. Mem. Natural Transp. and Exchange Assn. (charter), Natural Gas Soc. North Tex., Natural Gas Men Houston, Houston Club, Phi Kappa Psi. Republican. Office: Entex 1600 Smith St Houston TX 77002

MOORE, JOHN RONALD, manufacturing executive; b. Pueblo, Colo., July 12, 1935; s. John E. and Anna (Yesberger) M.; m. Judith Russelyn Bauman, Sept. 5, 1959; children: Leland, Roni, Timothy, Elaine. BS, U. Colo., 1959; grad. advanced mgmt. program, Harvard Grad. Sch. Bus., 1981. Mgmt. trainee Montgomery Ward & Co., Denver, 1960-65; distbn. mgr. Midas Internat. Corp., Chgo., 1965-71; v.p., gen. mgr. Midas, Can., Toronto, Ont., 1972-75; pres. Auto Group Midas Internat. Corp., Chgo., 1976-82, pres., chief exec. officer, 1982—, also bd. dirs.; bd. dirs. TI Midas Ltd., London, Midas Australia Pty. Ltd., Melbourne. Served with U.S. Army, 1953-55. Mem. Ill. Mfr.'s Assn., Motor Equipment Mfrs. Assn. (pres.'s council 1982—), Internat. Franchising Assn., Econ. Club of Chgo., Comml. Club Chgo., Harvard Bus. Sch. Alumni Assn., U. Colo. Alumni Assn. Republican. Office: Midas Internat Corp 225 N Michigan Ave Chicago IL 60601

MOORE, JOSEPH, retired lawyer, foundation executive; b. Bluefield, W.Va., May 18, 1920; s. Hugh Paul and Mary Elizabeth (Simpson) M.; m. Barbara Tracy Finkelstein, June 15, 1942; children: Steven, Sandra. JD, Columbia U., 1958, U. Ariz., 1970. Enlisted USN, 1942, advanced through grades to 1st lt., resigned, 1955; assoc. Linscott, Sloan, N.Y.C., 1959-66; sole practice N.Y.C., 1966-77; ptnr. Moore-Henry, Washington, 1977-81; researcher, placement officer Creative Mgmt., Washington, 1981-83; chmn. bd. J&D Meml. Found. Inc., Spencer, W.Va., 1983—; pres., chief exec. officer Creative Prodns. Author: No Time for Tears, 1968, For Fear We Shall Perish, Hold Back the Night, Battered Children; producer Christian films. Mem. White House Conf. on Children; active various programs for homeless; trustee to various bds.; adviser to Christian films. Republican. Jewish. Home: Rte 1 Box 149 Spencer WV 25276 Office: J & D Meml Found Inc PO Box 357 Spencer WV 25276

MOORE, LINDA ELAINE, editor; b. Columbus, Ohio, July 19, 1949. BA in Journalism, Ohio State U., 1973. Prodn. asst. Wanda Kerr Dunbar, Inc., Columbus, 1969-70; newswriter UPI, Columbus, 1972; slot person, copy editor The Balt. Sun, 1973-84; asst. news editor nat. edition The Washington Times, 1984-85; exec. editor ops. Insight, The Washington Times mag., 1985—, Stanford Pub. Course, 1987. Democrat. Home: 6010 Hawthorne St Cheverly MD 20785-3139 Office: Insight Mag 3600 New York Ave NE Washington DC 20002

MOORE, LOUIS LEE, medical instrumentation company executive; b. Cambridge, Md., Mar. 1, 1939; s. Louis Lee and Doris Elizabeth (Kramer) M.; m. Deanna Lynn Whited, Oct. 6, 1979; children: Amy, Laura. BSEE, Swarthmore Coll., 1962; MBA, Harvard U., 1965. Mktg. dir. Harris Intertype, Cleve., 1969-71; exec. v.p. Ohio Nuclear Co., Cleve., 1971-79; pres. Technicare Diagnostic Products Co., Cleve., 1979-82, Johnson & Johnson Ultrasound Co., Independence, Ohio, 1982-87, Moore & Assocs., Cleve., Ohio, 1987—; bd. dirs. Advanced Biomed. Co., Cleve., Prototest Electronics, Chardon, Ohio. Co-author: Automating Newspaper Composition, 1965. Pres. Windward Bound, Cleve., 1982; chmn. service com., bd. dirs. No. Ohio Multiple Sclerosis Soc., Cleve., 1985—, Ohio Gov's. Tech. Task Force, 1982. Mem. Ohio Venture Assn., Edison Biotech. Ctr., Assn. Corp. Growth, Greater Cleve. Growth Assn., Harvard Bus. Sch. Club, Edgewater Yacht Club, Vermilion Yacht Club. Methodist. Home: 23230 Shepards Point Bay Village OH 44140 Office: Moore & Assocs 1991 Crocker Rd Ste 600 Cleveland OH 44140

MOORE, MARY MELISSA, public affairs, government relations official; b. Flint, Mich., Feb. 6, 1957; d. Maurice Malcolm and Marian Adelaide (Zierold) M. B.A. in Govt., Wells Coll., 1979; student Georgetown U., 1977-78. Legis. corr. Sen. Hayakawa, Calif., 1979-80, legis. asst., 1980-82; asst. dir. fed. govt. relations ASME, Washington, 1982-86, dir. pub. affairs devel., 1984-89; ptnr. The Delta Group, Washington; cons. in field. Copyright SDI Co. Reference Guide. Mem. Women in Energy and Environ., Jr. League Washington. Republican. Episcopalian. Avocations: Horseback riding; sailing; snow & water skiing; swimming. Home: 6542 Birchleigh Way Alexandria VA 22310 Office: The Delta Group 1000 Connecticut Ave NW Ste 9 Washington DC 20036

MOORE, MAURICE MALCOLM, investment advisor; b. Mpls., Oct. 16, 1920; s. Maurice Malcolm and Olive (Brown) M.; m. Marian Adelaide Zierold, Aug. 15, 1953; children: Malcolm M., Mary Melissa, Marian Elizabeth Lindblad. BA, Williams Coll., 1942; MBA, Harvard U., 1946. Dir. Flint Aero. Corp., Birmingham, Mich., 1952-54; sales mgr. Lithium Corp. Am., Chgo., 1959-65; sr. account exec. Glore Forgan Corp., Chgo., 1965-70; officer A.G. Becker & Co., Chgo., 1970-80; v.p. Vincent, Chesley & Co., Chgo., 1980-84; stock broker, v.p. Prescott, Ball and Turben, Chgo., 1984—. Served to lt. USNR, 1943-46, 51-52, PTO. Republican. Clubs: Indian Hill (Winnetka, Ill.); Metropolitan (Chgo.). Office: Prescott Ball & Turben 230 W Monroe Chicago IL 60606

MOORE, MICHAEL FREDERICK, lawyer; b. Concord, N.H., Aug. 12, 1957; s. William Burdett and Patricia (Duncan) M.; m. Linda K. Moore, Dec. 29, 1979; children: David, Nancie, Ashley. BA, Albion Coll., 1979; JD, Lewis and Clark U., 1983. Bar: Wis. 1984. Sec. legal counsel KLV Group, Milw., 1984-85; v.p., sec., gen. counsel Koss Corp., Milw., 1988—. Office: Koss Corp 4129 N Port Washington Ave Milwaukee WI 53212

MOORE, MICHAEL KIM, lawyer, foundation executive; b. Kansas City, Mo., June 16, 1949; s. Everett Leroy and Ardis Nadine (Cox) M.; m. Cynthia Ann McDaniel, Sept. 10, 1977; children: Carrie Elizabeth, Michael Todd, Amanda Ann. BA summa cum laude, Southwestern Coll., 1971; JD magna cum laude, Washburn U., 1974. Bar: Kans. 1974. Law clk. U.S. Ct. Appealsfor 10th Circuit, Wichita, Kans., 1974-76; assoc. Foulston, Siefkin, Powers and Eberhardt, Wichita, 1976-81; ptnr. Foulston, Siefkin, Powers and Eberhardt, 1981-87; pres. United Meth. Health Ministry Fund, Hutchinson, Kans., 1987—; bd. dirs. Home State Bank, Longton, Kans. Editor-in-chief Washburn Law Rev., 1973-74. Trustee Southwestern Coll., Winfield, Kans., 1971-87. Mem. Kans. Bar Assn. Republican. Methodist. Lodge: Rotary. Home: 810 Loch Lommond Hutchinson KS 67502 Office: United Meth Health Ministry Fund 335 N Washington St Suite 160 Hutchinson KS 67502

MOORE, MICHAEL THOMAS, natural resource company executive; b. Bklyn., Oct. 10, 1934; s. Michael Joseph and Lucille M. (Wild) M.; m. Beatrice Lorraine Quinto, Sept. 10, 1960; children: Teresa, Stephanie, Jennifer, Elisabeth. BS in Bus., Indiana U. of Pa., 1956; postgrad., U. Pitts., 1959-63, Am. U., 1963-64, NYU, 1964-66. Fin. analyst, supr. U.S. Steel Corp., Duquesne, Pa., 1956-63; plant controller Am.-Standard, Balt., 1963-64; sr. fin. analyst Celanese Corp., N.Y.C., 1964-66; asst. controller to controller Cleve.-Cliffs Inc., 1966-72, v.p. controller, 1972-75, sr. v.p., 1975-83, exec. v.p., chief fin. officer, 1983-86, pres., dir., chief exec. officer, 1987, pres., chief exec. officer, 1987—, chmn., chief exec. officer, 1988—; bd. dirs. MLX Corp., Troy, Mich., Ameritrust. Chmn. bd. trustees Magnificat High Sch., Rocky River, Ohio, 1983—; bd. dirs. Cleve. Tomorrow, 1987—. Served with U.S. Army, 1957-58. Named Outstanding Alumnus Indiana U. of Pa., 1981. Mem. Am. Iron and Steel Inst. (bd. dirs. 1987—), Am. Mining Congress (bd. dirs. 1987—), Bus. Roundtable, Am. Iron Ore Assn. (bd. dirs. 1987—), Greater Cleve. Growth Assn. (bd. dirs. 1989—), Union Club, The Fifty Club, Westwood Country CLub, River Oaks Racquet Club, Pepper Pike Club, Rolling Rock Club. Roman Catholic. Office: Cleve-Cliffs Inc 1100 Superior Ave Cleveland OH 44115

MOORE, NOLAN JOHN, management consultant; b. Cin., July 29, 1938; s. Virgil William and Mary Elizabeth (Sheders) M.; m. Elaine Patricia Burke, June 3, 1972; children: Kathleen, Eric, Michael, Andrew. BS, Xavier U., 1960, MBA, 1963. Asst. to v.p. Western-So. Life Ins., Cin., 1961-69; mgr. Deloitte, Haskins & Sells, Cin., 1969-74; ptnr. Grant Thornton, Cin., 1974-88; mng. dir. The Cambridge Group, Cin., 1988—; personnel chmn. Savs. and Loan League, Cin., 1984-88. Mem. Cin. C. of C., Inst. Mgmt. Cons. Republican. Home: 6256 Twin Willow Ln Cincinnati OH 45247 Office: The Cambridge Group 105 E 4th St Ste 1600 Cincinnati OH 45202

MOORE, PAT HOWARD, engineering and construction company executive; b. Laredo, Tex., Sept. 16, 1930; s. Howard Warren and Odette Evelyn (Bunn) M.; m. Elsie Mae Crossman, Mar. 23, 1954; children: Linda Marie Ford, Margaret Ann, Andrew Patrick. B.A., Rice U., 1952, B.S.C.E., 1953; postgrad., Tulane U., 1956-58. Registered profl. engr., Tex., La. Spl. investigator Army Counter Intelligence Corps., Houston, 1954-56; div. engr. McDermott Inc., Morgan City, La., 1956-58; pres., dir. Navasota Telephone Co., Tex., 1958-63; project mgr. Brown & Root, Inc., Houston, 1963-67; pres., dir. Fluor Ocean Services, Houston, 1968-80; sr. v.p. Raymond Internat., Inc., Houston, 1980-86; pres., dir. Martin Moore Inc., Bellaire, Tex., 1986—; dir. Charter Builders, Inc., Dallas, 1988—; dir. Tex. Commerce Bank-Richmond-Sage, Houston, 1979—. Bd. govs. Rice U., 1984-88. Served with U.S. Army, 1954-56. Fellow ASCE. Lodge: Kiwanis (pres. 1960). Home: 5251 Birdwood St Houston TX 77096 Office: Martin Moore Inc PO Box 1156 Bellaire TX 77401

MOORE, PEGGY SUE, corporation financial executive; b. Wichita, Kans., June 16, 1942; d. George Alvin and Marie Aileene (Hoskinson) M. Student, Wichita State U., 1961-63, Wichita Bus. Coll., 1963-64. Controller Mears Electric Co., Wichita, 1965-69; exec. v.p., sec., treas., chief fin. officer CPI Corp., Wichita, 1969—, also bd. dirs.; Trustee Fringe Benefits Co., Kansas City, Mo., 1984-85. Mem. Rep. Nat. Com., Washington, 1985-86, task force 1986—; bd. dirs. Good Shepherd Luth. Ch., Wichita, 1980-85. Mem. Nat. Assn. Female Execs. Inc, Wichita C. of C., Women's Nat. Bowling Assn. (bd. dirs., pub. com. 1969-76), Internat. Platform Assn., DAR. Office: CPI Corp 816 E Funston Wichita KS 67211

MOORE, PHILIP WALSH, appraisal company executive; b. Burmont, Pa., Aug. 1, 1920; s. Louise J.F. and Florence (Walsh) M.; m. Katherine Shean, Dec. 26, 1967 (div.); children: Jourdan, Thomas, Philip, Edward; m. Marya Phaedra Cocalis; children: Stuart, Kristina. AB, Princeton U., 1942; MBA, NYU, 1950. Security analyst First Boston Corp., N.Y.C., 1946-48, v.p. gen. adminstrn., 1967-70; asst. to pres. Schroder Rockefeller and Co., N.Y.C., 1948-50; pres. First Research Co., Miami, Fla., 1950-67, chmn., chief exec. officer, 1971-84; pres. J&W Seligman Valuations Corp., N.Y.C., 1984—; founder, then bd. dirs. Flagship Banks (now Sun Trust Banks), Miami, 1964. Author: Florida Real Estate, 1960, Branch Banking Strategy, 1964, National Image of Economic South, 1976; author, editor: Internat. Banking Services, 1981. Trustee Ransom Everglades Sch., Miami, 1956-82; mem. adminstrv. com. Lincoln Ctr. Performing Arts, N.Y.C., 1969-75; mem. devel. council U. Hosp., Jacksonville, Fla., 1985—. Served to lt. USN, 1942-46, ETO, PTO. Mem. Inst. Bus. Appraiser, Nat. Assn. Bus. Economists, Am. Soc. Appraisers, Investment Assn. N.Y.C. (pres. 1948-50), So. Assn. Sci. and Industry (trustee, chmn. 1955-72), Overseas Mgmt. Internat. (bd. dirs. 1972-80), Phi Beta Kappa. Republican. Roman Catholic. Clubs: Down Town (N.Y.C.); River (Jacksonville); Ponte Vedra (Fla.). Home: 78 San Juan Dr Ponte Vedra Beach FL 32082 Office: J&W Seligman Valuations Corp 1 Bankers Trust Pla New York NY 10006

MOORE, ROBERT EARL, manufacturing company executive; b. Cleve., Jan. 6, 1938; s. Earl Carlton and Marian (Alexander) M.; m. Diana Moser, Mar. 26, 1958; children: Robert E. Jr., Laurie Ann, Kenneth Edison, Steven Alexander. Student in engring., Ohio State U., 1956-58. Field sales rep. Rep. Coal & Coke Co., Chgo., 1962-75; v.p. McClain Corp., Woodstock, Ill., 1975-80, Koch Carbon, Inc., Wichita, Kans., 1980—; cons. in field. Treas. Crystal Lake (Ill.) Little League, 1969-76. Mem. AIME, Assn. Iron and Steel Engrs., Am. Foundrymen's Soc., Crestview Country Club, Woodstock Country Club. Republican. Methodist. Home: 765 Sandpiper Wichita KS 67230 Office: Koch Carbon Inc PO Box 2219 E 37th St Wichita KS 67201

MOORE, ROBERT FORREST, healthcare holding company executive; b. Cleveland, Tenn., Oct. 27, 1931; s. Forrest R. and Catherine (Baugh) M.; children: Kelly R., Karen A. BS in Fin., U. Mich., 1962. Acct. Gen. Motors Corp., Flint, Mich., 1955-66; controller St. Joseph Hosp., Flint, 1966-71; asst. adminstr. Flint Osteo. Hosp., 1971-72; v.p. fin. St. Vincent's Med. Ctr., Jacksonville, Fla., 1973-84; exec. v.p. corp. services St. Vincent dePaul Community Stewardship Services, Inc., Jacksonville, 1984—; cons. bus. devel. and fiscal mgmt. Daus. Charity Nat. Health System. Contbr. articles to profl. jours. Served to lt. USAF, 1952-55, Europe. Fellow Hosp. Fin. Exec. Assn. (pres. 1966-68); mem. Am. Mgmt. Assn., Am. Hosp. Assn., Fla. Hosp. Assn., Health Care Fin. Mgmt. Assn. Republican. Roman Catholic. Home: 34 Lake Julia Dr S Ponte Vedra Beach FL 32082 Office: St Vincent De Paul 2565 Park St PO Box 40341 Jacksonville FL 32203

MOORE, ROBERT HENRY, JR., coal company executive; b. Bluefield, W.Va., Apr. 17, 1923; s. Robert Henry and Margaret Huston (St. Clair) M.; divorced; children: Diana, Robert Henry III, Turner Cronin. BA, Washington and Lee U., 1944, cert. in commerce, 1947; MBA, Harvard U., 1951; JD, Clev. State U., 1963. Salesman Pitts. Consolidation Coal Co., 1951-54; security analyst, asst. to pres.. sec. asst., treas., dir. Otis and Co., Cleve., 1954-64; with Aquarium of Niagara Falls, Inc., Cleve., 1964-71, chmn. exec. com., dir., 1969-71; with Aquarium Systems, Inc., Eastlake, Ohio, 1964-72, pres., treas., dirs., 1967-72; pres., treas., dir. Mystic Aquarium, Inc., Eastlake, 1971-72; chmn., treas. Aqualife Research Corp., Marathon, Fla., 1975-78; gen. ptnr. Pocahontas Mining Co., 1978—. Exec. dir. Pocahontas Coalfield Centennial Celebration, Inc., Bluefield State Coll. Found.; dir. Nat. Council Coal Lessors, Va. Coal Council, Covenant Fellowship of Presbyterians. Served to lt (j.g.) USNR, 1942-46. Mem. Va. Coal Council (vice chmn., dir.). Republican. Clubs: Union, Cleveland Skating (Cleve.); Army and Navy (Washington); Harvard (N.Y.C.); Bluefield (W.Va.) Country. Home: PO Box 1607 Bluefield WV 24701

MOORE, ROBERT RUSSELL, lodging executive; b. Taft, Calif., Sept. 18, 1937; s. Laurren F. and Marie Julia (Mutchler) M.; m. Linda Jean Neschke, Feb. 2, 1963; children—Gregory, Melissa, Bradley. B.A., Occidental Coll., 1959. Tract loan officer Am. Savs. & Loan, Whittier, Calif., 1965-66; territory mgr. Shell Oil Co., Anaheim, Calif., 1966-73; v.p. devel. Denny's Inc., La Mirada, Calif., 1973-80; exec. v.p., chief devel. officer, dir. La Quinta Motor Inns, San Antonio, 1980—; mem. adv. bd. Barshop Enterprises, Inc., San Antonio, 1985—. Mem., chmn. Planning Commn., La Habra, Calif., 1971-75; mem. Zoning Bd. Adjustment, Hill Country Village, Tex., 1981; mem. Bus. Sch. Adv. Bd. U. Tex., San Antonio, 1982—. Served with U.S. Army, 1960. Mem. Nat. Assn. Corp. Real Estate Execs., Nat. Assn. Office and Indsl. Parks, Internat. Council Shopping Ctrs. Republican.

MOORE, ROBERT WILLIAM, professional organization executive; b. Claysburg, Pa., June 4, 1924; s. Frank B. and Sarah A. (Edelbute) M.; m. Helen Lingenfelter, July 17, 1948; children: Thomas R., Priscilla Jane. B.A., Pa. State U., 1948. With Price Waterhouse & Co., Pitts., 1948-62; mgr. Price Waterhouse & Co., 1955-62; asst. controller Con-Gas Service Corp., Pitts., 1962-65, Consol. Natural Gas Service Co., Inc., Pitts., 1966-72; controller Consol. Natural Gas Service Co., Inc., 1972-78, Consol. Natural Gas Co., Pitts., 1972-78; pres. Fin. Execs. Inst., Morristown, N.J., 1978—; mem. Fin. Acctg. Standards Adv. Council. Bd. dirs. Central Blood Bank, Pitts., 1960-78, treas. corp., 1962-68, chmn. finance com., 1962-68, chmn. bd., 1969-72; mem. exec. bd. Pa. State U. Alumni Council, 1975-83; mem. exec. com. Campaign for Pa. State U.; pres. Pa. State Coll. Bus. Adminstrn. Soc., 1981-83. Served with AUS, 1943-45. Mem. Am., Pa. insts. C.P.A.s, Nat. Assn. Accountants, Fin. Execs. Inst., Pa. State U. Alumni Assn., Pa. Soc., Beta Alpha Psi (nat. forum), Delta Tau Delta. Episcopalian. Clubs: University (dir., pres. 1975-76), Valley Brook Country (dir. 1968-70, v.p. bd. 1970), Duquesne (Pitts.); Board Room, University, Union League (N.Y.C.); Spring Brook Country, Morris County Golf, Morristown (Morristown, N.J.). Home: 928 Bridgewater Dr Pittsburgh PA 15216 Office: Fin Execs Inst 10 Madison Ave PO Box 1938 Morristown NJ 07960

MOORE, STANLEY ALLEN, insurance brokerage executive; b. Denver, July 12, 1949; s. Charles Owens and Virginia (Henderson) M.; m. Kathryn Dell Harrison, Mar. 23, 1974; children: Daniel, Melanie. BA, U. Colo., 1973. Chartered property casualty underwriter, 1985. Underwriter trainee Ins. Co. N.Am., Denver, 1974-75; salesman Transwestern Ins., Denver, 1975-76; v.p. ADCO Gen. Corp., Denver, 1976-80; owner Antero Ins. Svcs., Lakewood, Colo., 1980-81; mgr. brokerage Nat. Farmers Union Ins., Denver, 1981-85; pres. Stan Moore and Assocs., Lakewood, 1986—. Numerous articles in field. Committeeman Rep. Party, Littleton, Colo., 1978-82; dir. Lakehurst Water and Sanitary Dist., Lakewood, 1986-87. Served in U.S. Army, 1970-72, Vietnam. Mem. Am. Inst. Property and Liability Underwriters, Profl. Ins. Agts. of Colo. (legis. com. 1987—), U.S. Naval Inst., Denver Westerners Club. Republican. Home: 17678 Tycoon Ave Morrison CO 80465 Office: Phoenix Enterprises Box 136 Morrison CO 80465

MOORE, STEPHEN RICHARD, financial planner; b. Detroit, Mar. 25, 1945; s. Richard Edwin and Margaret Ellen (O'Brien) M.; m. Susan Mary Petersen, Nov. 1, 1969; children: Jennifer Christine, Molly Elizabeth. BS in Econs., U. Wis., 1969, MBA in Fin., 1976. CLU, chartered financial cons., cert. fin. planner. Br. mgr. The Ziegler Co., Appleton, Wis., 1973-79; fin. planner CIGNA, Dallas, 1979-87, The New Eng., Dallas, 1987—. Columnist fin. planning, 1985-87. Served with USAF, 1969-73. Mem. Internat. Assn. Fin. Planning, Inst. Cert. Fin. Planners, Nat. Assn. Life Underwriters, Tex. Assn. Life Underwriters, Dallas Assn. Life Underwriters, Dallas Soc. Inst. Cert. Fin Planners (v.p. 1986—), Registry Fin. Planning Practioners. Republican. Roman Catholic. Club: Gleneagles Country (Plano, Tex.). Office: New Eng Fin Services 12750 Merit Dr Ste 1210 Dallas TX 75251

MOORE, SUSAN KAY, nuclear industry supply company executive, accountant; b. Atlanta, Apr. 12, 1948; d. Jack Eugene and Alma Louise (Ashley) Ferguson; m. Martin Prell Fisher, Aug. 19, 1972 (div. 1978); 1 child, Susan Ashley; m. Terry Moore, Feb. 15, 1987. BA, Samford U., 1970. CPA, Miss. Tchr. math. Franklin County Bd. of Edn., Rocky Mountain, Va., 1972-74; sr. acct. Koury, Ready & Lefoldt, Jackson, Miss., 1977-79; controller Patterson Enterprises, Ltd., Jackson, 1979-81; v.p. fin. and adminstrn. Fred. S. James of Miss., Jackson, 1981-83; pres., owner The Office Mgr., Jackson, 1983-85; v.p. NSSS, Inc., Jackson, 1985—; also bd. dirs. v.p. NSSS, Inc., Jackson; officer, bd. dirs. Divesco, Inc., Jackson, Wooden Images, Inc., The Holding Co. Bd. dirs. United Cerebral Palsy, Jackson, 1984, Make-a-Wish Found. Miss. Mem. AICPA, Assn. Records Mgrs. and Adminstrs. (pres. 1984-85), Jackson Aquatic Club. Baptist. Home: 27 Bastille St Brandon MS 39042 Office: NSSS Inc 5000 Hwy 80 E Jackson MS 39208

MOORE, THOMAS GALE, economist, educator; b. Washington, Nov. 6, 1930; s. Charles Godwin and Beatrice (McLean) M.; m. Cassandra Chrones, Dec. 28, 1958; children: Charles G., Antonia L. B.A., Geroge Washington U., 1957; M.A., U. Chgo., 1959, Ph.D., 1961. Fgn. research analyst Chase Manhattan Bank, N.Y.C., 1960-61; asst. prof. econs. Carnegie Inst. Tech., 1961-65; assoc. prof., then prof. econs. Mich. State U., East Lansing, 1965-74; sr. staff economist Council Econ. Advisers, 1968-70; hon. research fellow Univ. Coll., London, 1973-74; adj. scholar Am. Enterprise Inst., 1971—, CATO Inst., 1982—; sr. fellow Hoover Inst. on War, Revolution and Peace-Stanford U., 1974—, dir. domestic studies program, 1974-85; mem. Council Econ. Advisers, Washington, 1985-89; mem. Nat. Critical Materials Council, 1985-89; mem. econ. adv. bd. Dept. Commerce, 1971-73; mem. adv. com. RANN, 1975-77, NSF, 1975-77; cons. Dept. Transp., 1973-74, 81-83; mem. adv. panel Synthetic Fuels Corp., 1982; mem. adv. bd. Reason Found., 1982—; dir. Stanford Savs. & Loan, 1979-82, chmn., 1982. Author: The Economics of American Theater, 1968, Freight Transportation Regulation, 1972, Trucking Regulation: Lessons from Europe, 1976, Uranium Enrichment and Public Policy, 1978; co-author: Public Claims on U.S. Output, 1973; contbr. articles to profl. jours. Served with USN, 1951-55, Korea. Fellow Earhart Found., 1958-59; fellow Walgreen Found., 1959-60, Hoover Instn., 1973-74. Mem. Am. Econ. Assn., So. Econ. Assn., Western Econ. Assn., Mont. Pelerin Soc. Club: Chevy Chase. Home: 2141 P St NW #1002 Washington DC 20037 Office: Coun Econ Advisers Old Exec Office Bldg Washington DC 20500

MOORE, VERNON LEE, retired food products company executive; b. Creston, Iowa, Mar. 29, 1928; s. Newton and Eulalia Pearl (Lewis) M.; m. Lorene Shirley Moore, Jan. 29, 1949; children: Dianne, Nancy, Jack. BS in Agr., Iowa State U., 1951. Instr. vocat. agrl. Gowrie (Iowa) Sch. Dist., 1951-55; with Land O'Lakes, Inc., Mpls., 1955-88, sr. v.p., 1988, ret., 1988; cons. in field, Columbia Heights, Minn., 1988—. Bd. dirs., exec. com. Agrl. Coop. Devel. Internat., Washington, 1972—, Am. Inst. Coop., Washington, 1975-88, Minn. 4-H Found., Washington, 1980—; bd. dirs. Vols. in Overseas Coop. Devel., Washington, 1980-88, The Coop. Found., St. Paul, 1978-88; commr. Civil Service Commn., Columbia Heights, Minn., 1975—; mem. U. Minn. Adv. Com., St. Paul, 1984—; various leadership positions Fridley United Meth. Ch., Minn., 1971—. Recipient Internat. Coop. award Coop. Coordinating Group, 1987. Lodges: Rotary, Masons, Shriners.

MOORE, WILLIAM ARTHUR, accountant; b. Roseville, Calif., Dec. 17, 1934; s. Millard P. and Mary June (Wilder) M.; B.A., Fresno State Coll., 1956; m. Dorothy Lee Reece, June 11, 1955; children—Thomas Philip, Robert Kirk, Mari Anne, Lori Anne. Acct., Muncy McPherson & Co., C.P.A.s, San Francisco and Redding, Calif., 1957-65; pvt. practice acctg., Redding, 1965—; Cal Accts'. Mut. Ins. Co. (dir 1986—, chmn. investment com.). Mem. Calif. Soc. CPA's (pres. Sacramento chpt. 1979-80, state dir. 1979-82, 86—, trustee Calif. CPA Found. 1982-86, pres. 1984-86), Redding C. of C. (pres. 1979-80), AICPA (council 1985—, found. 1985—). Republican. Lodge: Masons. Office: 999 Mission de Oro Redding CA 96003

MOORE, WILLIAM GROVER, JR., consultant, former air freight executive, former air force officer; b. Waco, Tex., May 18; s. William Grover and Annie Elizabeth (Pickens) M.; student Kilgore (Tex.) Coll., 1937-39, Sacramento State Coll., 1951, George Washington U., 1962; grad. Air War Coll., Air U., 1957, Nat. War Coll., 1962; m. Marjorie Y. Gardella, Jan. 18, 1943; 1 dau., Allyson. Enlisted U.S. Army Air Force, 1940, commd. 2d lt., 1941, advanced through grades to gen., 1977; comdr. 777th Squadron, 15th AF, Italy, 1944-45, 3535th Maintenance and Supply Group, Mather AFB, Calif., 1951, 3d Bomb Group, Korea, 1952; chief bases and units div. Hdqrs. USAF, 1952-56; asst. dep. chief of staff ops. Hdqrs. USAF Europe, 1957-61; comdr. 314th Troop Carrier Wing, Stewart AFB, Tenn., 1962-63, 839th Air Div., 1963-65; asst. J3 U.S. Strike Command, 1965-66; comdr. 834th Air Div., Vietnam, 1966-67; dir. operational requirements Hdqrs, USAF, 1967-70; comdr. 22d AF, 1970-73, 13th AF, 1973; chief of staff Pacific Command, 1973-76; asst. vice chief of staff Hdqrs. USAF, 1976-77; comdr. in chief Mil. Air Lift Command, 1977-79; ret., 1979; pres., chief operating officer Emery Air Freight Corp., Wilton, Conn., 1981-83; bus. cons., 1983—; pres. Met. Nashville Airport Authority, 1984—. Decorated Def. D.S.M., Air Force D.S.M. with 2 oak leaf clusters, Legion of Merit with 4 oak leaf clusters,

Silver Star, D.F.C. with oak leaf cluster, Air medal with 9 oak leaf clusters, AF Commendation medal with 10 oak leaf clusters (U.S.); Croix de Guerre with palm (France); Armed Forces Honor medal 1st class (Vietnam); Republic of China Cloud and Banner; Legion of Honor (Republic of Philippines); recipient L. Mendel Rivers award of excellence; Jimmy Doolittle fellow in aerospace edn., 1978; named to Minuteman Hall of Fame, 1979. Mem. Air Force Assn., Nat. Def. Transp. Assn., Am. Ordnance Assn. Home: 932 W Main St Franklin TN 37064 Office: Metro Nashville Airport Authority 1 Terminal Dr Ste 501 Nashville TN 37214

MOORHEAD, ROBERT GEORGE CHADBOURNE, financial executive; b. Omaha, Oct. 2, 1937; s. Harley Green and Elizabeth Ward (Speir) M.; A.B., Amherst Coll., 1959; postgrad. Yale Law Sch., 1959-60; M.B.A., N.Y.U., 1968; m. Helen Rudisill Kirkpatrick, Jan. 10, 1970. With Mfrs. Hanover Trust Co., N.Y.C., 1964-74, mem. investment research dept., 1968-70, mem. investment scis. com., 1969-70, head investment scis. group, 1969-70, head budget and planning group personal trust ops., 1970-74; adminstr. pension fund, investment mgr. Chesapeake and Potomac Telephone Co., 1975-77; pension fund mgr. Asarco, Inc., 1977-83; investment counselor RIMCO, 1983-84; portfolio mgr. nuclear decommissioning fund Fla. Power & Light, 1984—. Deacon, elder Fifth Ave. Presbyn. Ch., N.Y.C. Served from ensign to lt. (j.g.), USNR, 1961-64, retired comdr. Res. Named Outstanding Young Man Am., 1973. Mem. N.Y. Soc. Security Analysts, Fin. Analysts Fedn., Am. Statis. Assn., Naval Res. Assn., Navy League, U.S. Naval Inst., Amherst Alumni of N.Y. (bd. dirs.), Amherst Alumni of S. Fla. (asst. treas.). Home: 6855 E Edgewater Dr Coral Gables FL 33133 Office: Fla Power & Light PO Box 029100 Miami FL 33102

MOORHOUSE, DOUGLAS CECIL, engineering consulting company executive; b. Oakland, Calif., Feb. 24, 1926; s. Cecil and Lynda (Roe) M.; BS in Civil Engring., U. Calif., Berkeley, 1950, postgrad., 1961; student Advanced Mgmt. Program, Harvard U., 1973; m. Dorothy Johnson; children: Scott, Jan. Research and resident engr. State of Calif. Div. Hwys., 1950-59; dir. San Diego office Woodward-Clyde & Assos., 1959-62; pres. Woodward-Moorhouse & Assos., 1962-73; pres., chief exec. officer Woodward-Clyde Cons., San Francisco, 1973-87; chief exec. officer, chmn. bd. dirs. Woodward-Clyde Group Inc., 1988—. Trustee, World Coll. West; mem. adv. com., dept. engring. U. Calif. Berkeley. Pres. Hazardous Waste Action Coalition, 1988-89. Served with inf. U.S. Army. Mem. Nat. Acad. Engring., ASCE (Wesley W. Horner award 1979). Office: Woodward-Clyde Group Inc 600 Montgomery St 30th Floor San Francisco CA 94111

MOOSE, SANDRA OHRN, management consultant; b. Boston, Feb. 17, 1942; d. Fritz Andrew and Esther Helen (Bastey) Ohrn. Student U. Vienna, Austria, 1962; BA summa cum laude, Wheaton Coll., 1963; MA, Harvard U., 1965, PhD, 1968. Tutor, Harvard U., Cambridge, Mass., 1964-65; cons. FDIC, Washington, 1966-68; pres. Sandra O. Moose, Inc., Chestnut Hill, Mass., 1981—; v.p., dir. The Boston Cons. Group, Boston, 1968-81, 84—; dir. GTE Corp., Rohm & Haas, New Eng. Life Mut. Funds. Contbr. articles to profl. jours. Trustee, Wheaton Coll., Norton, Mass., 1981—; bd. dirs., treas. Arts Boston, 1976—; mem. Dana Farber Cancer Inst.; corporator New England Deaconess Hosp., Boston, 1981—; trustee Hampshire Coll., 1976-83. Woodrow Wilson fellow, 1963-64; recipient 100th Anniversary award, Wheaton Coll. Alumnae Assn., 1970. Mem. Am. Econs. Assn., Com. of 200. Club: Union. Home: 53 Beverly Rd Chestnut Hill MA 02167 Office: The Boston Cons Group Exchange Pl Boston MA 02109

MOOSS, SAVITHRY V., accountant; b. Kunnamkulam, Kerala, India, Apr. 16, 1948; came to U.S., 1973; d. Narayanan and Priyadetha Naboodiri; m. Vasudevan Mooss. Apr. 24, 1968; children: Sunettha, Susmita, Sujay. BA, U. Kerala, 1985. Pvt. practice accounting and tax svc. Streator, Ill., 1985—; CPA, Ill. Home: 71 Stacy Ave Streator IL 61364

MORA, JUDITH STEVENS, financial institution consultant; b. Oakland, Calif., Dec. 5, 1946; d. Russell Norman and Lorraine C. Stevens; m. Gilbert Mora, Feb. 26, 1977. BA, U. Hawaii, 1969; MA in Mgmt., U. Redlands, 1980. Acting editor ofcl. publ. Navy C.E.C. and Seabees, Pearl Harbor, Hawaii, 1967-70; mgr. pub. relations and advt. Bishop Trust Co., Ltd., Honolulu, 1970-73; mgr. mktg. and promotions Ala Moana Ctr. Dillingham Corp., Honolulu, 1973-75; mus. cons., Hilo, Hawaii, 1975-76; cons. Edward Carpenter & Assocs., Los Angeles, 1976-79; pres., cons. J. Mora & Assocs., Inc., Orange, Calif. and Stafford, Va., 1979—. Contbr. to Hawaii Ency., 1977. Mem. spl. gifts and pub. relations coms. Am. Cancer Soc., 1973-76. Mem. Women in Communications (past chpt. pres.), Bank Adminstrn. Inst. (assoc.), Am. Heart Assn., Ind. Bankers Assn. (assoc.). Office: 2230 W Chapman Ave Ste 222 Orange CA 92668 Office: 1116 Richmond Dr Stafford VA 22554

MORA, KATHLEEN RITA, municipal or county govt. official; b. Atlantic City, Sept. 24, 1948; d. Francis Bernard and Catena Rose (Borzellino) Gribbin; m. Ben P. Mora, June 28, 1969; children: Michael, Brian. AS, Atlantic Community Coll., 1977; BS with program distinction, Stockton State Coll., 1984. Sec. Atlantic City Press, Pleasantville, N.J., 1966-69; personnel adminstr. Atlantic City Press, Pleasantville, 1969-73, adminstrv. asst., 1973-76, fin. asst., 1976-87, acctg. mgr., 1987-89; dir. fin. Superior Ct. Atlantic City, 1989—. Co-hostess annual radio broadcast Miss Am. Pageant; judge Miss Cape County Pageant, 1979; co-hostess TV promotion United Way Program, bd. dirs. Atlantic County, N.J., 1977-78; commentator TV March of Dimes Telethon, 1976-85, N.J.; host weekly radio talk show Healthline. Named Miss Atlantic City Women's Div. C. of C., 1968-69, Miss United Way, Atlantic County, 1975, Outstanding Chairperson, 1987, Outstanding Young Woman Atlantic County Mainland Jr. C. of C., 1978; recipient Contemporary Woman award, McDonald's Corp./Sta. WAYV, 1978, Svc. award 4-Club Coun., 1985. Mem. Nat. Assn. Accts., Internat. Newspaper Fin. Execs., Collier-Jackson Users Group, Atlantic County Personnel Assn. Roman Catholic. Home: 805 N Derby Ave Ventnor NJ 08406 Office: Superior Ct of Atlantic City 1201 Bacharach Blvd Atlantic City NJ 08401

MORAHAN, MATTHEW JOSEPH, investment banker; b. Newark, N.J., Sept. 30, 1949; s. Matthew Joseph and Monica (Maguire) M.; m. Elaine Barrington Roach, Nov. 20, 1948; children: Erin, Megan, Matthew, Caitlin. BS, Villanova U., 1970. V.p. Hornblower Weeks, Hemphill Noyes, N.Y.C., 1971-76; mng. dir. Wertheim Schroder & Co. Inc., N.Y.C., 1976—. Mem. Corp. Bond Traders Club N.Y., Bond Club N.Y., Treasury Securities Luncheon Club, Villanova Fin. Alumni Club. Roman Catholic. Club: Canoe Brook Country (Summit, N.J.). Office: Wertheim Schroder & Co Inc 787 7th Ave New York NY 10019

MORALES, OSVALDO RAMON, insurance company executive; b. Cabaiguan, Cuba, Feb. 28, 1941; came to U.S., 1962; s. Ramon and Lilia (Zaila) M.; m. Marina Gutierrez, Mar. 1, 1960 (dec. 1962); children: Marilyn, Belinda. CLU, Am. Coll., 1969, M of Fin. Svcs., 1981, chartered fin. planner, 1982. Agt. Prudential Ins. Co., Newark, 1965-68; supt. agencies Beneficial Standard Life Ins. Co., Union City, N.J., 1968-76; mgr. gen. agy. Monumental Life Ins. Co., Miami, Fla., 1976-80; mgr. gen. agy. Northwestern Nat. Life Ins. Co., Miami, 1980-83, regional mgr., 1983—; pres., chief exec. officer InsurAm. Corp., Miami, 1979—. Fellow Am. Soc. CLUs (bd. dirs. Miami chpt. 1981-86); mem. Nat. Assn. Life Underwriters, Internat. Assn. Fin. Planners. Roman Catholic. Home: 341 W Park Dr #105 Miami FL 33172 Office: InsurAm Corp 7200 Corporate Center Dr #202 Miami FL 33126

MORAN, HAROLD JOSEPH, retired lawyer; b. N.Y.C., Feb. 21, 1907; s. Thomas J. and Leonore M.F. (Geoghegan) M.; A.B. cum laude, Holy Cross Coll., 1928; LL.B., Fordham U., 1932; J.D., 1968; m. Geraldine D. Starkey, July 12, 1956. Admitted to N.Y. bar, 1934; practiced in N.Y.C., 1934-42, Bklyn., 1949-57, Malverne, N.Y., 1977—; law dept. Title Guarantee & Trust Co., Bklyn., 1945-48; sr. atty. real property bur. N.Y. State Law Dept., Albany, 1957-63, N.Y.C., 1963-77, ret., 1977; spl. dep. atty. gen. election frauds, 1973. Title closer City Title Co., Bklyn., 1949-52; U.S., P.R. mortgage loan examiner Cadwalader, Wickersham & Taft, N.Y.C., 1952-56, 63—, 9th Fed. Savs. & Loan Assn., N.Y.C., 1971—; instr. law St. John's U. Sch. Commerce, Jamaica, N.Y., 1956-57. Served with AUS, 1942-45. Knight Holy Sepulchre. Mem. Am. Bar Assn., Bar Assn. Nassau County, Am. Judicature Soc., N.Y. County Lawyers Assn., Catholic Lawyers Guild. Democrat. Roman Catholic. Club: Southward Ho Country. Home: 407 Hamlet Ave Carolina Beach NC 28428

MORAN, JEFFREY DEAN, financial executive; b. Chgo., Aug. 21, 1958; s. Richard A. and Barbara A. (Pence) M.; m. Lee Ann J. Miller, June 19, 1982. Student, Loras Coll., 1976-78; BS in Acctg., U. Minn., 1981; MBA, Northwestern U., 1989. CPA, Ill. Sr. acct. Arthur Andersen & Co., Chgo., 1981-84; corp. controller Am. Roller Co., Bannockburn, Ill., 1984—. Mem. Am. Inst. CPA's, Ill. CPA Soc. Home: 525 N Halsted St #609 Chicago IL 60622 Office: Am Roller Co 2223 Lakeside Dr Bannockburn IL 60015

MORAN, JENNIFER, lawyer, utility executive; b. Pomona, Calif., Sept. 17, 1949; d. C. John and Ellen (Delano) M.; m. Bruce L. Miller, Aug. 21, 1982. BA, Stanford U., 1971; JD, Cornell U., 1974. Bar: Calif. 1974. Dep. county counsel Los Angeles County, 1974-79; atty. So. Calif. Edison Co., Rosemead, Calif., 1979-84, sr. counsel, 1984-87, sec. corporation, 1987—. Mem. Green and White Select, Girl Scouts USA, Los Angeles, 1988. Fellow Am. Bar Inst.; mem. ABA, Calif. Bar Assn., Orgn. Women Execs., Cap and Gown. Office: So Calif Edison 2244 Walnut Grove Ave Rosemead CA 91770

MORAN, MARTIN JOSEPH, fund raising company executive; b. Bklyn., Nov. 3, 1930; s. Dominick and Mary (Lydon) M.; m. Mary Therese Schofield, June 5, 1954; children: Martin Joseph, John P., Maureen M., Thomas S., Robert P., William M., Maria M. BA, St. John's U., 1952. Profl. fund raising cons., 1956—; founder Martin J. Moran Co., Inc., N.Y.C., 1964, pres., 1964-74, chmn. bd., 1974—. Mem. Cardinal's Com. for Edn., N.Y.C., 1970-79, Cardinal's Com. for Laity Archdiocese N.Y., 1979—, Am. Revolution Bicentennial Commn., Oyster Bay, N.Y.; mem. Massapequa Park (N.Y.) Bd. Zoning Appeals, 1972-84, chmn., 1978-84; mem. Massapequa Park Ethics Commn., 1969-72; trustee Notre Dame Coll., S.I., 1969-72, La Salle Acad., N.Y.C., 1971-87; mem. pres.'s council Cath. U.P.R., Ponce, 1966-71. Served as aviator USNR, 1952-56. Decorated knight Order Holy Sepulchre, Pope Paul VI, 1968, Knight of Malta, Pope Paul VI, 1973; recipient Pietas medal St. John's U., N.Y., 1988. Mem. Navy League, Navy Hist. Assn., St. John's U. Alumni Assn. (pres. 1987—), Am. Assn. Fund Raising Counsel (bd. dirs. 1970—), Friendly Sons of St. Patrick. Roman Catholic. Club: Madison Square Garden (N.Y.C.); Lost Tree Village Golf (North Palm Beach, Fla.). Lodge: KC. Home: 1300 Lake Shore Dr Massapequa Park NY 11762 also: 677 Village Rd North Palm Beach FL 33408 Office: One Penn Pla New York NY 10119

MORCOTT, SOUTHWOOD J., automotive parts manufacturing company executive; b. 1939; married. Student, Davidson Coll.; MBA, U. Mich. Pres. Dana Corp., Toledo, 1963—; sales engineer, plant mgr. Dana Corp., Tyston, Ind., 1963-75; pres. Dana World Trade Corp., 1969; v.p. ops. Hayes Dann Ltd. Dana Corp., 1975-77, exec. v.p., gen. mgr., 1977-78, pres. Hayes-Dana Ltd., 1978-80, group v.p. Dana svc. parts group, 1980-84, pres. N.Am. ops., 1984-86, pres., chief operating officer, 1986—, also bd. dirs. Office: Dana Corp 4500 Dorr St PO Box 1000 Toledo OH 43697 *

MORDO, JEAN HENRI, elevator manufacturing company executive; b. Cairo, Arab Republic of Egypt, Feb. 2, 1945; came to U.S., 1970; s. Henri and Aimee (Arditi) M. m. Nicole Setton, 1966 (div. 1984); children: Candice, Nathaniel; m. Barbara Van Buren, Mar. 31, 1985; 1 child, Janelle. MS in Engring., Ecole Poly., Paris, 1966, MS in Stats., 1969; MBA, Stanford U., 1972. Cons. McKinsey & Co., N.Y.C., 1972-78; dir. planning Otis Elevator Co., West Palm Beach, Fla., 1978-80, dir. fin., 1980-82; v.p. fin. planning Otis Elevator Co., Farmington, Conn., 1982-84, v.p., controller, 1982-85, v.p. fin., 1985—. Home: 8 Somerset Ln Simsbury CT 06070 Office: Otis Elevator Co 10 Farm Springs Rd Farmington CT 06032

MORE, RONALD, investment banking executive; b. London, July 8, 1943; came to U.S., 1961; s. Robert Peter and Thelma Rose (Brooks) M.; m. Eileen M. Farrell Ginger, Sept. 17, 1966; children: Robert, Donna. BS, U. Bridgeport, 1966; MBA in Fin., Boston Coll., 1972. Asst. to pres. Medallic Art Co., Danbury, Conn., 1973-76; v.p. Am. Appraisal Assn., Stamford, Conn., 1976-88, Marigold Enterprises, Inc., Greenwich, Conn., 1988—. Capt. USAF, 1966-71. Home: 300 Banks North Rd Fairfield CT 06430 Office: Marigold Enterprises Inc 32 Field Point Greenwich CT 06830

MOREHEAD, CHARLES RICHARD, insurance company executive; b. Independence, Mo., Jan. 25, 1947; s. Robert E. and Ruth Elizabeth (Taylor) M.; m. Donna Joyce Shores, Feb. 17, 1968 children: Grant, Blaine. BSBA, U. Mo., 1971. CPA, Fla., Mo. Mem. staff Peat, Marwick, Mitchell & Co., Kansas City, Mo., 1972-75; audit mgr. Peat, Marwick, Mitchell & Co., Jacksonville, Fla., 1976-83, audit ptnr., 1983-86; treas. Standard Havens, Inc., Kansas City, 1975-76; sr. v.p., treas. Am. Heritage Life Ins. Co., Jacksonville, Fla., 1986—. Mem. AICPA, Fla. Soc. CPA's. Home: 3947 Hickory Grove Dr Jacksonville FL 32211 Office: Am Heritage Life Ins Co 11 E Forsyth St Jacksonville FL 32202

MORELAND, WILLIAM JOHN, real estate broker; b. Chgo., Feb. 21, 1916; s. James C. and Izora M. (McCabe) M.; A.B., U. Ill., 1938; student Northwestern U., 1937. With James C. Moreland & Son, Inc., real estate and home building, Chgo., 1938—, pres., 1952—; pres. Moreland Realty, Inc., Chgo., 1952-72. Builder, operator Howard Johnson Motor Lodge, Chgo., 1960-72. Helped develop model housing community, El Salvador, Central Am., 1960's. Presidential appointment to commerce com. for Alliance for Progress, 1962-64. Served to lt. USNR, 1941-46. Mem. Home Bldrs. Assn. Chicagoland (pres. 1961-62), Chgo. Assn. Commerce and Industry, Chgo., N.W. Real Estate Bds., N.W. Bldrs. Assn., Nat. Assn. Home Bldrs. (hon. life dir. 1972—), Chi Psi. Republican. Roman Catholic. Office: 5717 Milwaukee Ave Chicago IL 60646

MORELLI, CARMEN, lawyer; b. Hartford, Conn., Oct. 30, 1922; s. Joseph and Helen (Carani) M.; m. Irene Edna Montminy, June 26, 1943; children: Richard A., Mark D., Carl J. BSBA, Boston U., 1949, JD, 1952. Bar: Conn. 1955, U.S. Dist. Ct. Conn. 1958. Sr. ptnr. Morelli & Morelli, Windsor, Conn.; mem. Conn. Ho. of Reps., 1959-61; rep. Capitol Regional Planning Agy., 1965-72; atty. Town of Windsor, 1961; asst. prosecutor Town of Windsor, 1957-58. Mem. Windsor Town Com., 1957-82, chmn. 1964-65, treas., 1960-64, mem. planning and zoning commn., 1965-74, mem. charter revision com., 1963-64, Rep. Presdl. Task Force. Served with USN, 1943-45. Mem. ABA, Conn. Bar Assn., Hartford Bar Assn., Windsor Bar Assn. (pres. 1979), Windsor C. of C. (v.p. 1978), Am. Arbitration Assn. Roman Catholic. Club: Elks, Rotary (sgt. arms, sec. 1989—). Home: 41 Farmstead Ln Windsor CT 06095 Office: 66 Maple Ave Windsor CT 06095

MOREN, NICHOLAS CHARLES, investment and holding company executive; b. Hampton, Va., Sept. 12, 1946; s. Stephen A. and Mary Jane (Dederich) M.; divorced; children: Emily Jane, Alix Evelyn, Benjamin Charles; m. Margaret-Ann Howie, May 14, 1988. B.A., Brown U., 1968; M.B.A., Wharton Sch., 1972. With Trans World Airlines, N.Y.C., 1972-79; asst. controller Transworld Corp., N.Y.C., 1979-81, asst. treas., 1982-83, treas., 1983-85; v.p., treas. TW Services, Inc. (formerly Transworld Corp.), N.Y.C., 1986—. Club: Springdale Golf (Princeton, N.J.). Home: 138 Poe Rd Princeton NJ 08540 Office: TW Svcs Inc 605 3rd Ave New York NY 10158 also: Canteen Corp 1430 Merchandise Mart Chicago IL 60654

MORENO BARBERA, FERNANDO, architect; consultant; b. Ceuta, Spain, June 22, 1913; s. Fernando and Francisca (Barbera Ferrer) Moreno Calderon; m. Margarita von Hartenstein, Feb. 16, 1946 (div.); 1 son, Fernando; m. Carmen Cavengt. Diploma in Architecture, Escuela Superior de Arquitectos, Madrid, 1940; postgrad. Tech. Hochschule, Berlin, 1941, Tech. Hochschule, Stuttgart, 1942; Dr. Architect, Escuela Superior de Arquitectos, Madrid, 1966. Architect Prof. Paul Bonatz, Berlin/Stuttgart, Germany, 1941-43, Ministerio de Educacion, Madrid, 1940-75; exec. pres. M.B. Consultants, Madrid, 1944—; attache Spanish Embassy, Berlin, 1941-43; prof. scenography Escuela Ofcl. de Cinematograffa, Madrid, 1947-49; exec. dir. Empresa Nacional de Turismo, Madrid, 1954-65; prof. Escuela Superior de Arquitectos, Madrid, 1971-72. Restorer and rehabilitator: Hostal Reyes Catolicos, Santiago de Compostela, Spain, 1964, Hostal San Marcos, Leon, Spain, 1956, Palacio Villahermosa, Madrid (Juan de Villanueva award 1979), 1976, Casa del Cordon Burgos (Cert. Engring. Ops. Exec. award 1987); supr. Univ. Laboral de Cheste, Valencia, Spain, 1969, P.P.O. Bldg, Madrid, 1973, Premio Colegio de Arquitectos, 1974, Univ. Campus, Kuwait, 1978. Humbolt Stieftung grantee, 1940; Internat. Coop. Adminstrn. grantee, 1959; recipient Silver Hexagon award Habitation Space Internat., 1979. Fellow Colegio Ofcl. Arquitectos de Madrid, Hermandad de Arquitectos. Roman Catholic. Clubs: Real Puerta de Hierro, de Campo, Real Automovil. Home: El Espinarejo, Manzanares el Real, Madrid Spain Office: M B Cons, Paseo de la Habana 15, 28036 Madrid Spain

MOREY, ROBERT HARDY, communications executive; b. Milw., Sept. 5, 1956; s. Lloyd W. and Ruby C. (McElhaney) M. AA, Ricks Coll., 1978; BA, Brigham Young U., 1983. Program dir. Sta. KABE-FM, Orem, Utah, 1982-83, sales mgr., 1983; nat. mgr. ops. Tiffany Prodns. Internat., Salt Lake City, 1983-84; account exec. Osmond Media Corp., Orem, 1984; corp. sec., bd. dirs. Positive Communications, Inc., Orem, 1984—, chief exec. officer, 1987—; gen. mgr. Sta. KSRR, Orem, 1985—; pres. K-Star Satellite Network, Orem, 1986—; guest lectr. various colls. and univs., 1981—. Chmn. Rep. voting dist., Orem, 1984. Recipient Community Service award Utah Valley Community Coll., 1983; named one of Outstanding Young Men in Am. U.S. Jaycees, 1983. Mem. Rotary. Mormon. Home: 1200 N Terr $S2Apt 228 Provo UT 84604 Office: Sta KSRR 1400 W 400 N Orem UT 84507

MORGAN, BRUCE BLAKE, banker, economist; b. Kansas City, Mo., Feb. 3, 1946; s. Everett Hilger and Dorothy Aletha (Blake) M.; m. Carol Berniese Tempel, Aug. 24, 1968 (div. 1983); children: Bruce Blake, Denise Dawn. BS, Mo. Valley Coll., 1968; MS, U. Mo., Columbia, 1973; MA, U. Mo., Kansas City, 1977, PhD, 1979; diploma in banking U. Wis., 1987. Caseworker, counselor Mo. Dept. Social Services, Jefferson City, 1967-68; community devel. specialist U. Mo. Extension, Columbia, 1968-73; community devel. specialist Midwest Research Inst., Kansas City, 1973-83, also mgr. regional econs., assoc. dir., dir. econs. and social sci., sr. adv. for mgmt.; adj. grad. prof. sch. bus. and pub. adminstrn. U. Mo., Kansas City, 1975—; v.p., exec. v.p. Kansas City Bancshares, 1984-86; dir. fin. services Coopers & Lybrand, 1986-89;pres. Profl. Bank Cons., 1989—; mem. staff Mo. Girls State, 1976—; chmn. Pres's. Adv. Council on Univ. Extension, 1987—. bd. govs. Community Mental Health Ctr. South, 1984—. Mem. Am. Inst. Cert. Planners, Community Devel. Soc. Am. (bd. dirs. 1971-81), Nat. Assn. Bus. Economists. Office: Profl Bank Cons 4210 Shawnee Mission Pkwy Ste 100 Mission KS 66205

MORGAN, CELIA ANN, economics educator; b. Midland, Tex., Jan. 6, 1932; d. Therman Glenn and Cecil Elizabeth (Hill) M. AA, Lamar U., 1951; BBA, U. Tex., 1953; MA in Econs., U. Houston, 1967, PhD in Econs., 1971. Asst. prof. S.W. Tex. State U., San Marcos, 1971-76, assoc. prof., 1976-81, prof. econs., 1981—, chairperson dept. fin. and econs., 1984—; cons. to sec. state Tex., Austin, 1982-86. Contbr. articles to profl. jours; reviewer numerous textbook pubIs. GE fellow, 1982. Mem. Am. Econ. Assn., So. Econ. Assn., Southwestern Soc. Economists (pres. 1979-80), AAUP (pres. S.W. Tex. State U. chpt. 1976-78), LWV (bd. dirs. San Marcos chpt. 1984—). Democrat. Presbyterian. Avocations: hiking, classical music. Home: 819 Hazelton St San Marcos TX 78666 Office: SW Tex State U San Marcos TX 78666

MORGAN, CHARLES DONALD, JR., business executive; b. Ft. Smith, Ark., Feb. 4, 1943; s. Charles Donald Sr. and Betty (Speer) M; m. Jane Dills Morgan, Aug. 20, 1966; children: Caroline Speer, Charles Robert. ME, U. Ark., 1966. Systems engr. IBM, Little Rock, Ark., 1966-71; v.p. Acxiom Corp. (formerly CCX Network, Inc.), Conway, Ark., 1972-75; pres. CCX, Conway, Ark., 1976-82, chief exec. officer, 1983—, also chmn. bd. dirs.; bd. dirs. First State Bank & Trust, Conway. Trustee Hendrix Coll., Conway, 1985—; chmn. bd. dirs. Jobs for Ark. Future, 1986-87, mem. commn. 1988—; mem. Southern Growth Policies Bd., N.C., 1986, Ark. Bus. Council, 1987—. Mem. Third Class Mailers Assn., Pub. Chief Exec. Officers Council. Episcopalian. Home: Rte 5 Box 114-01 Conway AK 72032 Office: ACXiom Corp 301 Industrail Blvd Conway AR 72032

MORGAN, DERRYL DEAN, utilities executive; b. Perryton, Tex., Nov. 10, 1954; s. Arthur Dean and Beverly Rose (Hale) M.; m. Shelly Ann Sikes, Dec. 23, 1976; children: Mindy Jared. AA, York Coll., 1976; BS, Okla. Christian Coll., 1978. CPA, Tex. Sr. acct. Peat, Marwick & Mitchell, Amarillo, Tex., 1978-81; internal control analyst United Gas Pipe Line, Houston, 1981-83, gas acctg. analyst, 1983-84, supr. budgets, 1984-86, supr. billing, 1986, mgr. vol. disbursement and billing, 1986-87, dir. gas acctg., 1987—. Home: 17814 Asphodel Spring TX 77379 Office: United Gas Pipe Line Co PO Box 1478 Houston TX 77251

MORGAN, EVAN CHRISTAL, educational financial administrator; b. Laramie, Wyo., May 28, 1954; s. Newlin D. and Rosa Lee (Christal) M.; m. Elisa Thompson Lee, June 15, 1979; children: Eva Lee, Ethan Thomas. BS, U. Wyo., 1976; MA, Denver Sem., 1985. Cert. fin. planner. Asst. cashier, loan officer Bank of Laramie, 1976-78; mgr. pub. funds First Nat. Bank of Denver, 1979-82; v.p. bus. affairs Denver Sem., 1982—; real estate agt. Renaissance Fin. Services, Denver, 1982—, fin. planner Learned & Co., 1984—. Deacon bd. dirs. Galilee Bapt. Ch., Denver, 1981—; chmn. United Way fund drive, Laramie, 1977. Mem. Internat. Assn. Fin. Planners, Nat. Assn. Coll. and Univ. Bus. Officers, Christian Ministries Mgmt. Assn., Phi Kappa Phi, Beta Gamma Sigma. Republican. Home: 16788 E Prentice Circle Aurora CO 80015 Office: Denver Sem PO Box 10-000 Denver CO 80210

MORGAN, FRANK J., diversified food products company executive; b. 1925; m. Mary Morgan, May 24, 1952; children: Mark, Craig, Kevin, Susan, Karen. BS, Yale U., 1947; postgrad., Harvard U., 1967. With Chance Vought (div. United Techs.), 1947-48; with new departure div. Gen. Motors, 1948-51; with Remington Arms (subs. E.I. Dupont de Nemours), 1951-56; with ARMA (div. Am. bosch Arma Corp.), Garden City, N.Y., 1946-64, mgr. product support dept., 1956-64; with Quaker Oats Co., Chgo., 1964—, mgr. indsl. engring., 1964-68, asst. to group v.p. of mfg. and purchasing, 1968; supt. Quaker Oats Co., Cedar Rapids, Iowa, 1968; prodn. mgr. Quaker Oats Co., Chgo., 1969-70, mgr. orgn. and mgmt. devel., 1970-71, dir. orgn. and mgmt. devel., 1971; gen. mgr. Quaker Oats Co. of Can., Ltd., Peterborough, 1971, pres., chief exec. officer, from 1972; v.p. Quaker Oats Co., Chgo., 1972, v.p. grocery products ops., 1975, group v.p. U.S. grocery products, 1975-76, exec. v.p. internat. grocery products, 1976-79, mem. exec. com., bd. dirs., 1978—, exec. v.p. U.S. and Can. grocery products, 1979-83, pres., chief operating officer, 1983—; bd. dirs. Square D Co., The Molson Cos. Ltd.; guest lectr. U. Ill. Mem. Can.-Am. Com., Chgo. Com., Bd. Sponsors Good Shepherd Hosp. Barrington; chmn. Citizens Bd. of Loyola; trustee Glenwood (Ill.) Sch. for Boys. Served with USN, 1943-46. Mem. Am. Coll. Sports Medicine Found. (bd. dirs.). Club: Chgo. Sunday Evening (bd. dirs.). Office: The Quaker Oats Co Quaker Tower 321 N Clark St Chicago IL 60604 *

MORGAN, GARY, engineering company executive; b. Madrid, Jan. 2, 1955; s. Roy and Mildred (Cantor) M.; m. Katherine Keay, Nov. 24, 1979; 1 child, Andrew Phillip. BA, Va. Poly. Inst. & State U., 1977; MBA, Marymount U., 1984. Planner Paciulli, Simmons & Assocs., Fairfax, Va., 1977-80; fin. analyst Dynamic Systems Inc., McLean, Va., 1980-84; sr. fin. analyst Planning Research Corp./Emhart Corp., McLean, 1984-86; dir. bus. planning Greenhorne & O'Mara Inc., Greenbelt, Md., 1986—; adv. mem. bd. dirs. Gemma Corp., Arlington, Va., Xeta Internat., Indian Head, Md. Contbr. articles to profl. jours. Mem. Tyson's Area Com. Transp., McLean, 1980-82. Mem. Fairfax Police Youth Club Assn., Internat. Soc. Planning and Strategic Mgmt., Nat. Assn. Sci. and Tech., Nat. Assn. Homebuilders, Nat. Comml. Builders Council, Tower Club. Democrat. Unitarian. Home: 9803 Meadow Dale Ct Vienna VA 22180 Office: Greenhorne & O'Mara Inc 9001 Edmonston Rd Greenbelt MD 20770

MORGAN, GLENN JAY, utilities executive; b. Rutland, Vt., May 6, 1932; s. Rufus J. and Nina G. (Gilman) M.; m. Ruth Bechok, June 29, 1964; children: Thomas J., Susan D. Student, Barrington/Gordon Coll., 1950-53, Rutland Bus. Coll., 1958-60. Acct. Cen. Vt. Pub. Service Corp., Rutland, 1960-61, asst. comml. account supr., 1966-68, internal auditor, 1968-73; chief clk. Conn. Valley Electric Co., Claremont, N.H., 1961-66; acct. Vt. Yankee Nuclear Power Corp., Brattleboro, 1973-78, treasury supr., 1978-80, asst. treas., chief acct., 1980-87, asst. treas., sec., 1987—. Served in U.S. Army,

1954-55. Republican. Office: Vt Yankee Nuclear Power Corp Rte 5 Box 169 Ferry Rd Brattleboro VT 05301

MORGAN, GREGORY PAUL, financial planner; b. Cocoa Beach, Fla., Sept. 9, 1958; s. Paul Leo and Mickey Maxine (Cooper) M.; m. Suzanne Pinner, Jan. 14, 1985. BS in Psychology magna cum laude, Pepperdine U., 1980. Fin. analyst Williams & McCombs, Inc., Arlington, Tex., 1980-83; fin. counselor Balanced Fed., Dallas, 1983-86; ptnr. Strategic Fin. Group, Arlington, 1986—; chmn. coun. Lowry Fin. Svcs., West Palm Beach, Fla., 1987—; lectr. numerous profl. orgns. Big Bros. Am. United Way, Dallas, 1986—. Mem. Inst. Cert. Fin. Planners, Internat. Assn. for Fin. Planners, Inst. Chartered Fin. Analysts, Great S.W. Tax and Estate Planning Coun., Dallas Assn. Investment Analysts. Home: 601 Mission Circle Irving TX 75063 Office: PO Box 110655 Arlington TX 76007

MORGAN, GRETNA FAYE, automotive executive; b. Galveston, Ind., Aug. 24, 1927; d. Fred Monroe and Vera Arnetha (Oakley) Goodier; m. Marvin L. Morgan, Mar. 30, 1946; children: Gary Lynn, Vonna Annette, Marvin Richard, Darla Sue, Janice Arnetha. Diploma in cosmetology, Approved U., Indpls., 1946. Sales distributor Kirby Co., Ft. Wayne, Ind., 1955-62; with Dana Corp., Churubusco, Ind., 1962—; plant mgr. Dana Corp., Churubusco, 1981—; mem. adv. bd. Citizens Nat. Bank, Churubusco, 1982-86; bd. dirs. Whitley County Meml. Hosp. Found. Chmn. mayor's com. Employment Handicapped, Athens, Ga., 1980-81; mem. interview bd. selection com. Congressman Dan Coats Mil. Acad., Ft. Wayne, 1985-88, bus. adv. bd. Whitley County Opportunity Ctr., Columbia City, Ind., 1986—, Chem. Dependency Task Force Whitley County, Ind. Gov.'s Task Force on Drunk Driving, budget com. Whitley County United Way; bd. regents Dana U., Toledo, 1978-82; bd. dirs., pres. Whitley County Jr. Achievement, 1977-78. Mem. Clarke County Indsl. Mgmt. Assn. (v.p. 1980-81), Whitley County Mfrs. Assn. (v.p. 1977-78), Power Squadron Club, Order Eastern Star, Churubusco C. of C. (pres. 1975-76). Home: RR 1 Box 96 Albion IN 46701 Office: Dana Corp US 33 PO Box 245 Churubusco IN 46723

MORGAN, HICKS BERNARD, lawyer, treasurer; b. Beaumont, Tex., Sept. 29, 1947; s. Guy H. Sr. and Amy Zella (Hebert) M.; m. Vicki Carol Null, Mar. 27, 1971; children: Hope Layne, Michelle Amy, Heather Elizabeth, Nathan Pollard, Andrew Thomas. AB, Dartmouth Coll., 1970; JD, Georgetown U., 1977. Gen. counsel Morgan Bldgs. & Spas, Dallas, 1977—, sec., 1978—, treas., 1983—; bd. dirs. officer ATMC Investments, Las Vegas, Nev., AM Investment Co. Pres. St. Rita Sch. Bd., Dallas, 1985. Sgt. USAF, 1971-75. Mem. Tex. Bar Assn., Dallas County Bar Assn., Dartmouth Lawyers Assn., St. Rita Men's Club. Roman Catholic. Office: Morgan Bldgs & Spas 2800 McCree Rd Garland TX 75040

MORGAN, HUGH JACKSON, JR., energy company executive; b. Nashville, Aug. 10, 1928; s. Hugh Jackson and Robert Ray (Porter) M.; m. Ann Moulton Ward, Aug. 28, 1954; children—Ann, Grace, Caroline, Hugh. A.B., Princeton U., N.J., 1950; LL.B., Vanderbilt U., Nashville, 1956; A.M.P., Harvard Bus. Sch., 1976. Bar: Tenn. 1956. Practice law Miller & Martin, Chattanooga, 1956-60; atty. So. Natural Gas Co., Birmingham, Ala., 1961-65, gen. atty., 1966-70, v.p., 1971-78, pres., 1982-84, chmn. bd., 1984-87; v.p. Sonat Inc., Birmingham, Ala., 1973-78, sr. v.p., 1979-84, exec. v.p., 1984, vice chmn. bd., 1984-87; vice chmn. Nat. Bank Commerce, Birmingham, Ala., 1987—; also bd. dirs. Nat. Bank Commerce; bd. dirs. AlaTenn Resources, Inc., Ala.-Tenn. Nat. Gas Co., Blue Cross-Blue Shield Ala. Chmn. Birmingham Airport Authority, 1986—; trustee Episcopal High Sch., Alexandria, Va., Vanderbilt U., Nashville; Children's Hosp. Ala., Birmingham, 1974—. Served to lt. (j.g.) USN, 1950-53. Recipient Bennett Douglas Bell Meml. prize Vanderbilt Law Sch., 1956. Mem. Order of the Coif. Clubs: Mountain Brook (pres. 1972), Redstone, (Birmingham); Belle Meade (Nashville); Linville Golf (N.C.). Lodge: Rotary. Home: 3121 Brookwood Rd Birmingham AL 35223 Office: Nat Bank Commerce 1927 First Ave N Birmingham AL 35202

MORGAN, JAMES DURWARD, computer company executive; b. N.Y.C., Sept. 10, 1936; s. Durward Field and Harriet (Airey) M.; m. Ruth Ann Dobson, Jan. 14, 1967; children: Jennifer, Andrew. BEE, Yale U., 1961, MEE, 1962. Systems engr. Calspan Corp., Buffalo, 1962-68; v.p. Comptek Research Inc., Buffalo, 1968-83; v.p. Barrister Info. Systems Corp., Buffalo, 1983—, also bd. dirs.; bd. dirs. Comptek Research Inc., Buffalo. Chmn. adv. council Erie Community Coll., Amherst, N.Y., 1985—; bd. dirs. Yale Alumni Bd., Buffalo, 1987—. Served with USN, 1959-61. Mem. IEEE, Assn. Computing Machinery. Home: 34 Ironwood Ct East Amherst NY 14051 Office: Barrister Info Systems Corp 45 Oak St Buffalo NY 14203

MORGAN, JAMES RICHARD, manufacturing executive; b. Mt. Carmel, Ill., July 3, 1938; s. Gilbert C. and Frances G. (Friedman) M.; m. Nancy L. Lukens, Sept. 12, 1964; children: J. Richard Jr., John G., Matthew K. BS, U. Evansville, 1960. Auditor George S. Olive & Co., Evansville, Ind., 1960-63; contr. Citizens Realty & Ins., Evansville, Ind., 1963-64, Amax Aluminum Co., Evansville, Ind., 1964-66; gen. acctg. mgr. Aeroquip Indsl. Div., Van Wert, Ohio, 1966-70, contr., 1970-81; contr. Aeroquip, Jackson, Mich., 1981-85, v.p. fin., 1986; group v.p. adminstrn. Aeroquip Corp., Maumee, Ohio, 1987—; also bd. dirs. Aeroquip Indsl. Corp., Maumee, Ohio. Active Van Wert Airport Bd. Commn., 1980-81. Sgt. U.S. Army, 1960-65. Mem. Nat. Assn. Accts., Sylvania Country Club. Roman Catholic. Office: Aeroquip Corp 1715 Indian Wood Circle Maumee OH 43537

MORGAN, JO VALENTINE, JR., lawyer; b. Washington, June 26, 1920; s. Jo. V. and Elizabeth Parker (Crenshaw) M.; A.B. magna cum laude, Princeton U., 1942; LL.B., Yale U., 1947; m. Norma Jean Lawrence, May 22, 1943; children—Carol Jo, Jo Lawrence, Susan Leigh. Admitted to D.C. bar, 1948, Md. bar, 1948; mem. firm Whiteford, Hart, Carmody & Wilson, Washington, 1948-85, partner, 1953-76, sr. partner, 1976-85; mem., dir. Jackson & Campbell, P.C., 1985—; dir. Dist. Realty Title Ins. Corp. Chmn. Bethesda USO, 1949-52; pres. Summer Citizens Assn., 1958-61; pres. Westmoreland Citizens Assn., 1956-57. Bd. dirs., gen. counsel Internat. Soc. Protection Animals; gen. counsel Fedn. Am. Socs. Experimental Biology; pres., bd. dirs. Montgomery County Humane Soc.; gen. counsel Fed. Am. Soc. for Experimental Biology. Served from 2d lt. to capt., AUS, 1942-45, ETO. Decorated D.F.C., Purple Heart, Air medals (AAC). Fellow Am. Coll. Trial Lawyers; mem. Am. Bar Assn., Bar Assn. D.C. (bd. dirs. 1958-60, 73-75), D.C. Lawyers Club, Order of Coif, Phi Beta Kappa. Democrat. Episcopalian. Clubs: Chevy Chase, Metropolitan, Princeton, The Barristers; Wesley Heights Community (pres. 1964-67). Home: 5120 Westpath Way Bethesda MD 20816 Office: Jackson & Campbell 1120 20th St NW Ste 300 S Washington DC 20036 also: 200 A Monroe St Rockville MD 20850

MORGAN, JOHN THOMAS, banker; b. N.Y.C., Aug. 17, 1929; s. Samuel Thomas and Addie Marie (Padgett) M.; m. Dorothy Edna Schmalz, Aug. 26, 1951; children—James, Susan, Kathryn. B.S., U. Minn., Mpls., 1951; M.B.A., U. Chgo., 1957; M.P.A., Harvard U., 1963. Fgn. service officer U.S. Dept. State, Washington, 1957-67; state economist Minn. Planning Agy., St. Paul, 1968-69; 1st dep. supt. banks N.Y. State Banking Dept., N.Y.C., 1970-72; chmn., chief exec. officer Am. Savs. Bank, N.Y.C., 1972—; dir. Savs. Banks Trust Co., N.Y.C.; chmn. Nat. Council Savs. Instns., 1987-88, dir., 1988—; mem. adv. council on thrift instns. Fed. Res. Bd., 1984-85; dir. Drayton Co. Ltd. Mem. Thrift Instns. Adv. Panel, Fed. Res. Bank of N.Y. Club: Apawamis (Rye), Harvard (N.Y.C.), University (N.Y.C.). Office: Am Savs Bank 99 Church St White Plains NY 10601

MORGAN, LEON ALFORD, utility executive; b. Washington, Dec. 29, 1934; s. Albert Lewis and Alice Viets (Alford) M.; m. Gwendolyn Eleanor Tullock, Aug. 18, 1978; children: David Richard, Sherry Alice. B.S. in Elec. Engring, Worcester (Mass.) Poly. Inst., 1957. Registered profl. engr., Conn. With United Illuminating Co., New Haven, 1957—; gen. ops. mgr., then v.p. ops. United Illuminating Co., 1973-76, exec. v.p., 1976-83, sr. v.p. fin., 1984—. Bd. dirs. One State St. Condominium, New Haven. Served to 1st lt. C.E. AUS, 1964. Republican. Episcopalian. Club: Quinnipiack (New Haven). Home: 43 Forest Brook Rd Guilford CT 06437 Office: United Illuminating Co 80 Temple St New Haven CT 06506

MORGAN, M. JANE, computer systems consultant; b. Washington, July 21, 1945; d. Edmond John and Roberta (Livingstone) Dolphin; 1 child, Sheena Anne. Student U. Md., 1963-66, Montgomery Coll., 1966-70; BA in Applied Behavioral Sci. with honors; postgrad. Nat. Coll. Edn., 1989—. With HUD, Washington, 1965-84, computer specialist, 1978-84; pres., chief exec. officer Systems and Mgmt. Assocs., 1983-87; dir. systems engring. Advanced Technology Systems, Inc., Vienna, Va., 1984-86; chief tech. staff Tech. and Mgmt. Services, Inc., 1986-89; pres. Advanced Tech. Systems Inc., Vienna, 1989—; mgmt. cons. Mem. Am. Mgmt. Assns. Episcopalian. Club: Order Eastern Star. Office: Care Systems & Mgmt Assocs 10252 Cherry Walk Ct Oakton VA 22124

MORGAN, MICHAEL BREWSTER, publishing company executive; b. L.A., Dec. 30, 1953; s. Brewster Bowen and Eleanor (Boysen) M.; m. Debra Hunter, July 20, 1986. BA, Conn. Coll., 1975. Coll. sales rep. Addison Wesley Pub. Co., Chapel Hill, N.C., 1977-81; sponsoring editor Addison Wesley Pub. Co., Reading, Mass., 1981-84; chief exec. officer Morgan Kaufmann Pubs., San Mateo, Calif., 1984—. Mem. Am. Assn. for Artificial Intelligence, Assn. for Computing Machinery. Office: Morgan Kaufmann Pubs 2929 Campus Dr Ste 260 San Mateo CA 94403

MORGAN, RALPH, manufacturing executive; b. Elkhart, Ind., Feb. 23, 1924; s. Ralph Samuel and Jeanette Rae (Randall) M.; m. Doris Kathleen (Hayward), Sept. 2, 1945 (div. Jan. 1974); children: Christopher Alan, Carol Jane; m. Georgia Lou Teach, Feb. 9, 1975. Student, Wayne State U., 1942-43, 46-47. Apprentice mouthpiece maker J.J. Babbitt Co., Elkhart, 1935-36; profl. woodwind musician various dance bands, Ind., Mich., 1936-52; owner, dir. band Music by Morgan, Detroit, 1943; woodwind technician The Linton Band Instrument Co., Elkhart, 1948-50; woodwind technician The Selmer Co., Elkhart, 1950-52, mgr. SE dist. sales, 1952-68, mgr. nat. band instrument, 1970-74, chief woodwind designer, 1974-80; owner, operator Morgan Music Co., Tampa, 1968-70; prin. Morgan Enterprises, Springfield, Ohio, 1980—; lectr., clinician U. Ky. Music Sch., Louisville, 1986, 87, Clarfest '85 Duquesne U., Pitts., 1985, U. Pitts. Music Dept., 1985, Ind. State U., Terre Haute, 1983. Author, editor Colonial Currency, 1976; patentee in field. Bd. dirs. COMACS, Inc., Champaign, Ill., 1988—. Served to T/sgt. USAF, 1943-45, 45 combat missions. Republican. Lodge: Optimist (v.p. Springfield club 1982-83, pres. 1983-84). Home and Office: 490 Forest Dr Springfield OH 45505

MORGAN, RICHARD THOMAS, publishing executive; b. Herkimer, N.Y., May 19, 1937; s. Roland F. and Eva J. (Butcher) M.; m. Eileen A. Bumbly, Nov. 21, 1966; children: Richard Joseph, Susan Eileen. AB, Hope Coll., 1959; MA, SUNY, Albany, 1960; EdD, Columbia U., 1968. Asst. prof. SUC at Fredonia, N.Y., 1961-64, Fla. Atlantic U., Boca Raton, Fla., 1966-68; sr. v.p., editor-in-chief Ginn & Co,, Lexington, Mass., 1968-79; exec. v.p. Macmillan, Inc., N.Y.C., 1979-83; pres., chief exec. officer Scott, Foresman and Co., Glenview, Ill., 1984-88, also bd. dirs.; pres. Macmillan Ednl. Pub. Co., N.Y.C., 1989—. Bd. dirs. Evanston (Ill.) Hosp., Mindscape Inc., Macmillan. Mem. Exmoor Country Club. Democrat. Roman Catholic.

MORGAN, ROBERT ARTHUR, business consultant; b. Toledo, May 5, 1922; s. Arthur James and Bernice Marie (Farmer) M.; B.S. cum laude in Bus. Adminstrn., Bowling Green (Ohio) State U., 1943; certificate Carnegie Mellon U., 1951; m. Betty Helen Byers, June 19, 1954; children—Todd Byers, Barbara Lee. With Westinghouse Electric Corp., 1947—, mgr. sales devel. indsl. systems div., Buffalo, 1964-66, mktg. mgr. indsl. systems div., 1967-73, mgr. mktg. services indsl. equipment div., 1973-79, mgr. bus. devel. power electronics and drive systems div., 1979-84; ind. cons., instr., lectr., 1984—. Mem. Wilkinsburg (Pa.) City Council, 1961-65, v.p., 1964-65; co-pres. Maple Elem. Sch. PTA, 1966-67; chmn. Citizens Adv. Bd., Williamsville Central Sch. Dist., 1974-77; vestryman Calvary Episcopal Ch., 1979-82. Named Man of Year, Wilkinsburg, 1965; cert. bus. communicator. Mem. Bus./Profl. Advt. Assn. (nat. v.p. 1967-69), Am. Mktg. Assn., Service Corps of Retired Execs., Am. Legion, Civil War Roundtable. Lodges: Masons, Shriners. Contbr. articles on indsl. mktg. to profl. jours. and handbook; editor tng. manuals; columnist local papers. Home: 80 Chaumont Dr Williamsville NY 14221

MORGAN, ROBERT GEORGE, accounting educator, researcher; b. Sanford, Maine, Feb. 20, 1941; s. George Andrew and Katherine (Gray) M.; m. Jacqueline Buhl, Jan. 2, 1965; children—Robert George, Katherine Neva. B.A., Piedmont Coll., Demorest, Ga., 1969; M.Acctg., U. Ga., 1971, Ph.D., 1974. C.P.A., N.C., Tenn. Asst. prof. acctg. U. Wyo., Laramie, 1974-76, Drexel U., Phila., 1976-80; assoc. prof. acctg. U. N.C.-Greensboro, 1980-83; prof. acctg. Loyola Coll., Balt., 1983-85; chmn. dept. acctg. East Tenn. State U., Johnson City, 1985—. Editor Jour. The Mgmt. Rev., 1983-85. Contbr. articles to profl. jours. Treas., Running Brook PTA, Columbia, Md., 1984-85. Mem. Am. Inst. C.P.A.s, Nat. Assn. Accts., Am. Acctg. Assn., Acad. Acctg. Historians, Tenn. Soc. Acctg. Educators (pres. 1987-88), Beta Gamma Sigma, Beta Alpha Psi. Methodist. Avocation: golf. Home: 1 Townview Dr Johnson City TN 37604 Office: E Tenn State U Dept Acctg PO Box 23800-A Johnson City TN 37614-0002

MORGAN, TRAVIS CRUE, insurance company executive; b. New Boston, Tex., Sept. 9, 1929; s. Willialm Henry and Alice Dove (Tutt) M.; m. Jo Ann Harkey, Aug. 4, 1950; children: Linda Kay, Jan, Travis Crue Jr., Pamela, Scott, Kelly. BBA, Tex. A&M U., 1952. V.p., sr. mortgage officer Businessmen's Assurance Co., Kansas City, Mo., 1957—. Bd. dirs. Kansas City Indsl. Found., 1983—. Lt. USAF, 1946-48. Mem. Mortgage Bankers Assn. Am., Kansas City MBA Assn., Kansas City C. of C. Republican. Office: Businessman's Assurance Co 31st St and Southwest Trafficway Kansas City MO 64141

MORGAN, WALTER LEROY, communications executive, consultant; b. Nutley, N.J., Dec. 20, 1930; s. Willard L. and Violet (Miller) M.; m. Emily R., May 7, 1961; 1 child, Edward S. BSEE, Carnegie Mellon U., 1954. Engr. RCA's David Sarnoff Labs., Princeton, N.J., 1954-56; mgr. project RCA Astro Space Div., Princeton, 1956-70; sr. staff scientist COMSAT Labs., Clarksburg, Md., 1970-80; pres. Communications Ctr., Clarksburg, 1980—; cons. to fin., indsl. and communication corp. throughout the U.S., Europe, and Asia. Author: Business Earth Stations for Communications, 1988, Communications Satellite Handbook, 1989. Fellow AIAA (recipient of communications award 1982, chmn. tech. com. communications, mem. standards activity com.), Brit. Interplanetary Soc.; mem. IEEE (sr.), Lions (sec./treas. 1972-79). Methodist. Office: Communications Ctr 2723 Green Valley Rd Clarksburg MD 20871-8599

MORGAN, WILLIAM T., financial services company executive; b. 1928. With Waddell & Reed, Inc., Kansas City, Mo., 1955—, now pres., chief exec. officer. Office: Waddell & Reed Inc 2400 Pershing Rd PO Box 418343 Kansas City MO 64141-9343

MORGENSTEIN, WILLIAM, shoe manufacturing company executive; b. Bklyn., Jan. 11, 1933; s. Samuel and Jeanne Marie (Mittentag) M.; m. Sylvia Dove, June 8, 1952; children: Lee Brian, David Barry. BS in Fin., U. Ala., 1955. Salesman Greenwald Shoe Co., Birmingham, Ala., 1954-56; sr. buyer Melville Shoe Corp., N.Y.C., 1958-67; pres. Kitty Kelly Shoe Co., N.Y.C., 1967-70; exec. v.p. A.S. Beck Shoes, N.Y.C., 1970-71, Sandia Internat., Englewood Cliffs, N.J., 1971-75; pres., chief exec. officer Marquesa Internat. Corp., Englewood, N.J., 1975—; internat. cons. footwear exporting, 1965—. Served with U.S. Army, 1956-58. Mem. Footwear Distbrs. and Retailers Am. (vice chmn., bd. dirs., exec. com.), Internat. Footwear Assn. (chmn. 1989—, vice chmn. 1986—, exec. com. 1986—), 210 Assn. (bd. dirs., Pres.' Circle 1987), Toastmasters (past pres. Teaneck, N.J. chpt.). Republican. Jewish. Office: Marquesa Internat Corp 172 Walkers Ln Englewood NJ 07631

MORGENTHAL, BECKY HOLZ, computer service company owner; b. Altadena, Calif., Aug. 5, 1947; d. E. William and Elizabeth (DeLong) Holz; m. Roger Mark Morgenthal, Aug. 12, 1972. AA, Goldey Beacom Coll., 1967; student, Wilson Coll., 1986—. Clk. Hercules, Inc., Wilmington, Del., 1969-71; acct. Beth Products, Lebanon, Pa., 1971-72; adminstrv. asst. Legal Services, Inc., Carlisle, Pa., 1973-76; office mgr. CEMI Corp., Carlisle, 1976-77; acct. Tressler Luth. Services, Camp Hill, Pa., 1978-79, Benatec Assocs., Inc., Camp Hill, 1979-82; fin. analyst Electronic Data Systems, Camp Hill, 1983-87; owner B.H. Morgenthal Computer Services, Carlisle, 1982—. Pres. Carlisle Jr. Civic Club, 1979-80, v.p., 1978-79; active Diocese of Harrisburg, Pa., 1985—, chmn. pro-life com., 1988—; mem. Council of Cath. Women, Carlisle, 1986—. Republican. Home: 1311 Windsor Ct Carlisle PA 17013-3562

MORGISON, F. EDWARD, investment broker; b. Clay Center, Kans., Oct. 4, 1940; s. Fred and Lena Edna (Chaput) M.; B.A. in Math., Emporia State U., 1963; M.S. in Bus. Adminstrn., U. Mo., Columbia, 1964; M.S. in Acctg. candidate U. Mo., Kansas City, 1981—; m. Karen Lorene Herdman, Nov. 21, 1964; 1 dau., Diana Michelle. Computer programmer U. Mo. Med. Center, Columbia, 1964-65; adminstrv. and budget analyst Urban Renewal Project, Independence, Mo., 1965-66; account exec., bank broker Stifel Nicolaus & Co., Kansas City, Mo., 1966-73; pres., chief exec. officer Will-Mor Investment Systems, Kansas City, Mo., 1973-75; br. mgr. Edward Jones & Co., 1975; editorial and exec. asst. to Morgan Maxfield, candidate for U.S. Congress, Kansas City, 1976; sr. account exec., merger and acquisitions specialist R. Rowland & Co., Kansas City, Mo., 1976-77; chmn. bd., pres., chief exec. officer Mo. Securities Inc., Kansas City, 1977-78; v.p., regional mgr. Charles Schwab & Co., Kansas City, 1978-79; v.p. Profl. Assistance, 1979-81; registered agt. Offerman & Co., Kansas City, 1979-81; chief exec. officer Morgison & Assos., Kansas City, 1979-81; fiscal dir. Housing Authority of Kansas City, 1981; exec. v.p. J. Penner & Assocs., 1981-82; pres. J. Penner & Co., 1982-83; account exec., registered broker Lowell H. Listrom & Co., 1981-84; pres., chief exec. officer First Allen Securities Inc., 1983—; dir., sec. Hubach Group Inc., 1987—; bd. dirs., treas. Skytrader Corp., 1986—, Emergency Systems Services, 1986—; bd. dirs. Internat. Tex. Industries, Inc., San Antonio; chmn. bd., treas. Masters' Mark, Inc., 1986—. Recipient Bausch and Lomb Sci. award, 1959; Sci. award Lambda Delta Lambda, 1962; registered account exec. N.Y. Stock Exchange, Am. Exchange, registered securities agt., Mo., Kans., Ill., gen. securities prin., fin. and ops. prin., mcpl. securities prin. Mem. U. Mo. (life), Emporia State U. (life) alumni assns., Nat. Rifle Assn. (life), U.S. Chess Fedn. (life), Mensa (life). Home: 1000 NE 96th Terr Kansas City MO 64155 Office: First Allen Securities Inc 6506 N Prospect St Ste 101 Gladstone MO 64119

MORHARDT, JOSEF EMIL, IV, environmentalist, engineering company executive; b. Bishop, Calif., Aug. 19, 1942; s. J. Emil III and G.H. Morhardt; m. Sylvia Staehle, Jan. 23, 1965; 1 child, Melissa Camille. BA, Pomona Coll., 1964; PhD, Rice U., 1968. Asst. prof. Wash. U., St. Louis, 1967-75; chief scientist Henningson, Durham & Richardson, Santa Barbara, Calif., 1975-78; v.p., dir. western ops. EA Engring. Sci. & Tech., Inc., Lafayette, Calif., 1978—. Home: 4520 Canyon Rd Lafayette CA 94549 Office: EA Engring Sci & Tech Inc 41A Lafayette Circle Lafayette CA 94549

MORI, KEI, economist, system engineer; b. Kyoto, Japan, Nov. 20, 1932; s. Taikichiro and Hanako (Idogawa) M.; m. Yoko Arisawa, Apr. 2, 1963; children: Mariko, Asuka. B.A., Keio U., Tokyo, 1955, M.A., 1958, Ph.D., 1968. Asst. prof. dept. adminstrn. engring., faculty engring. Keio U., Tokyo, 1958-64, asst. prof., 1964-68, assoc. prof., 1968-73, prof. dept. adminstrn. engring., faculty sci. and tech., Yokohama, 1973—; rsch. assoc. Wharton Sch., U. Pa., 1968-70; inventor, dir. inst. LaForet Engring., Tokyo, 1978—, chmn. bd., 1985—; cons. IBM Japan, Tokyo, 1960-73; organizing engr. life maintenance module of Space Sta., NASA, Tokyo, 1982—; com. chmn. light energy transmission Opto Electronic Industry Devel. Assn., Tokyo, 1982, com. chmn. local area optical network, 1983; counselor Database Promotion Ctr., Japan, 1985—; chmn. bd. dirs. Office Research on Bldgs. & Info. Tech., 1987—; com. mem. The Japan Legal Info. Ctr., Inc., 1987—; mem. steering com. Japan Oceanic Conf.; mem. exec. com. Marine Biotech, planning com. Joint Rsch. & Devel. Hyogo Marine Lab. Inventor solar ray collector and transmission system, 1980, spectrum selection and light emission for biol. applications, 1981; exec. editor Jour. Info. Processing Japan, 1960-67, 73-75. Exec. dir. Assn. Computer Edn. for Pvt. Univs., Tokyo, 1977—; project leader Redevel. Project of ARK Hills in Center City of Tokyo, 1982—. Mem. Econs. and Econometric Soc. Japan, Info. Processing Soc. Japan, Japan Soc. Aero. and Space Scis., Illuminating Engring. Inst. Japan, Japan Rheumatism Assn., Japan Inst. for Macro-Engring, Japan Assn. Simulation & Gaming. Club: Blue Red and Blue (Tokyo). Buddhist. Home: 3-16-3-501 Kaminoge Setagaya-ku, Tokyo Japan Office: La Foret Engring, 2-7-8 Toranomon Minato-ku, Tokyo Japan

MORICE, JAMES LOWRY, management consultant, recruitment company executive; b. Niagara Falls, Sept. 25, 1937; s. John L. and Evelyn (Brown) M.; children by previous marriage: Laura, Diana, Christa, Sharon; m. Patricia E. Burgess, Dec. 1, 1984; children: Jonathan, Jennifer. BS, NYU, 1964. Corp. dir. staffing and manpower planning, dir. pers. and adminstrn. systems dept. Equitable Life Assurance Soc. U.S., N.Y.C., 1964-70; mgr. recruiting and staffing McKinsey & Co. Inc., N.Y.C., 1970-72; cons. Billington Fox & Ellis Inc., N.Y.C., 1972-75; prin. Spencer Stuart & Assocs., N.Y.C., 1976-80; ptnr. William H. Clark Assocs., N.Y.C., 1980-82; founding ptnr. Martin Mirtz Morice Inc., N.Y.C. and Stamford, Conn., 1982—; bd. dirs. Republic N.Y. Corp., N.Y.C., Republic Nat. Bank, N.Y.C., Williamsburgh Savs. Bank, N.Y.C. Bd. dirs. N.Y. Summer Olympics. Office: Martin Mirtz Morice Inc 1 Dock St Ste 304 Stamford CT 06902

MORIN, WOLLASTON GERALD, hotel management company executive, accountant; b. Swansea, Mass., Apr. 9, 1936; s. Arthur William and Eva (Blais) M.; m. Carol Ann Connell, Oct. 12, 1962; children—Lisa Ann, Geoffrey, Elizabeth, Michael. B.S. in B.A., Boston U., 1964. Mgr. bus. analysis United Technologies, Norwalk, Conn., 1966-73; dir. budgets The Sheraton Corp., Boston, 1973-78; sr. v.p., controller Sheraton Mgmt. Corp., Denham, Eng., 1978-81, exec. v.p., 1981-83, pres., dir. ops. Europe, Africa and Middle East, 1983—. Served with USAF, 1954-58. Mem. Nat. Assn. Accts. Republican. Roman Catholic. Home: 103 Shrine Rd Norwell MA 02061 Office: Sheraton Corp 60 State St Boston MA 02109

MORING, STUART ALAN, consulting engineering company executive; b. Evanston, Ill., Sept. 13, 1947; s. James Francis and Julia Aneta (Thompson) M.; m. Manita Gay Council, Dec. 28, 1971. BSCE, U. Ill., 1965; MSCE, M City Planning, Ga. Inst. Tech., 1974. Registered profl. engr., Ky., Ga. Engring. aide Monarch Asphalt Co., Skokie, Ill., 1966-67; engring. technician Ill. Div. Hwys., Chgo., 1968; grad. rsch. asst. Environ. Rsch. Ctr., Ga. Inst. Tech., Atlanta, 1973-75; planning engr. No. Ky. Area Planning Commn., Newport, 1975-77; staff engr. Kenton County Water Dist. 1, Ft. Mitchell, Ky., 1977-79; design engr. City of Albany (Ga.), 1979-85, asst. city engr., 1985-87; regional mgr. BCM Engrs., Inc., Albany, 1987—; chmn. Albany Area Utilities Coordinating Com., 1985-87. Pres. Radium Springs Civic Assn., Albany, 1983, Albany Little Theatre, 1986-88; mem. Leadership Albany, 1986-87. Lt. USN, 1969-72, Vietnam. Mem. ASCE, Am. Pub. Works Assn. (chpt. pres. 1984-85, Svc. award 1985), Kiwanis (bd. dirs. Dougherty County 1983-84). Presbyterian. Home: 207 Hollis Dr Albany GA 31705 Office: BCM Engrs Inc 101 1/2 S Jackson St Ste B Albany GA 31701

MORITZ, CHARLES WORTHINGTON, business information and services company executive; b. Washington, Aug. 22, 1936; s. Sidney Jr. and Ruth Whitman (Smith) M.; m. Susan Prescott Tracy, June 14, 1958; children: Peter W., Tracy W., Margaret Anne. BA, Yale U., 1958. With R.H. Donnelley Corp., 1960—, v.p., gen. mgr. mktg. div., 1972-74, sr. v.p., 1974-76, dir., 1975-85; exec. v.p. Dun & Bradstreet Corp., N.Y.C., 1976-78; vice chmn., dir. Dun & Bradstreet Corp., 1979—, pres., chief operating officer, 1981—, chmn., chief exec. officer, 1985—; bd. dirs. Seamen's Corp., N.Y.C. Served to lt. (j.g.) USNR, 1958-60. Mem. Direct Mktg. Assn. (dir. 1973-76), Am. Mgmt. Assn., Sales Execs. Club, Econ. Club N.Y.. Pine Valley (N.J.) Club, Wee Burn Country Club, Nat. Golf Links Am. Club, John's Island Club, Blind Brook Club, Links Club, Zeta Psi. Republican. Episcopalian. Home: 1 Runkenhage Rd Darien CT 06820

MORITZ, DONALD BROOKS, mechanical engineer, business executive; b. Mpls., June 17, 1927; s. Donald B. and Frances W. (Whalen) M.; m. Joan Claire Betzenderfer, June 17, 1950; children: Craig, Pamela, Brian. B.S. in Mech. Engring., U. Minn., 1950; postgrad., Western Res. U., 1956-58. Registered profl. engr., Ill. Minn., Ohio. Vice pres., gen. mgr. Waco Scaffold Shoring Co., Addison, Ill., 1950-72; group v.p. Bliss and Laughlin Industries, Oak Brook, Ill., 1972-83; sr. v.p. AXIA Inc. (formerly Bliss and Laughlin

Industries, Oak Brook, 1983-84, exec. v.p., chief operating officer, 1984—. Patentee in field. Served with USN, 1945-46. Mem. Scaffold and Shoring Inst. (founder, past pres.), ASME, Mensa. Clubs: Metropolitan (N.Y.C.); Meadow (Ill.). Office: AXIA Inc 122 W 22d St Oak Brook IL 60521

MORITZ, DONALD IRWIN, energy company executive; b. McKeesport, Pa., Oct. 23, 1927; s. Maurice Louis and Rose (Klein) M.; m. Janet Papernick, Nov. 9, 1952; children: Paula, Laurie, J. Kenneth. B.S., U. Pitts., 1948, J.D., 1951. Bar: Pa. 1952. With Equitable Resources, Inc. (and subsidiaries), 1952—; asst. to pres. Equitable Gas Co. (and subsidiaries), 1967-72; exec. v.p. Equitable Gas Co. (and subsidiaries), Pitts., 1972-77; pres. Equitable Gas Co. (and subsidiaries), 1977—, chief exec. officer, 1978—, also dir.; bd. dirs. subsidiaries Equitable Gas-Energy Co., Pitts., Ky-W.Va. Gas Co., Ashland, Ky., Equitable Resources Energy Co., Equitable Energy, Inc., Equitable Resources Exploration Inc., Eastern Ky. Prodn. Co.; bd. dirs. PNC Fin. Corp., Pitts. Nat. Bank. Bd. dirs. Congregation Tree of Life, McKeesport, 1958-78, pres., 1967-69; trustee Montefiore Hosp., Penn's S.W. Assn.; bd. dirs. Pitts. Symphony Soc., United Jewish Fedn. Greater Pitts., Am. Gas Assn. Mem. Pa. Gas Assn. (past pres.), Pa. Bar Assn., Allegheny County Bar Assn., Pitts. C. of C., Pitts. Law Alumni Assn., Order of Coif, Pa. Economy League, Phi Eta Sigma, Beta Gamma Sigma. Republican. Jewish. Clubs: Duquesne (bd. dirs.), Pitts. Athletic Assn; Westmoreland Country, Concordia. Office: Equitable Resources Inc 420 Blvd of Allies Pittsburgh PA 15219

MORITZ, JOHN MATTHEW, JR., sales engineer; b. Phila., Oct. 21, 1962; s. John Matthew and Anna Marie (Cullerton) M.; m. Terri Anne Lee, June 23, 1984; 1 child, Elizabeth Patricia. BSChemE, U. Calif., Santa Barbara, 1984. Asst. mgr. Alltime, Inc., Thousand Oaks, Calif., 1979-80; lab. asst. Litton Guidance & Control, Canoga Park, Calif., 1981; customer service and sales rep. Firestone Co., Thousand Oaks, Calif., 1982; lube plant worker Mobil Oil Corp., Vernon, Calif., 1983; sales engr. Mobil Oil Corp., Dallas, 1984-85, Fairfax, Va., 1985—. Mem. Am. Inst. Chem. Engrs. (mktg. and forest products groups), Internat. Platform Assn., Nat. Amateur Bowlers, Inc. Republican. Roman Catholic. Home and Office: 110 Wythe House Ct Ashland VA 23005-2415

MORITZ, MILTON EDWARD, telephone company executive; b. Reading, Pa., Sept. 5, 1931; s. Edward Raymond and Anna May M.; student U. Md., 1950-51, Fla. State U., 1959-60; m. Elizabeth Ann Walls, June 6, 1952; children: Betsy Ann Moritz Koppenhaver, Stephen Edward, Sandra E. Enlisted in U.S. Army, 1963, served as spl. agt. M.I.; ret., 1970; safety and security dir. Harrisburg (Pa.) Hosp., 1970-72; security mgr. United Telephone Systems, Carlisle, Pa., 1972—; lectr., instr. Harrisburg Area Community Coll. Pres., Greater Harrisburg Crime Clinic, 1974. Decorated Bronze Star with oak leaf cluster. Mem. Am. Soc. Indsl. Security (past pres., chmn. bd. dirs.), Assn. Former Intelligence Officers, Internat. Narcotic Enforcement Officers Assn., Pa. Crime Prevention Assn. (bd. dirs.). Republican. Lutheran. Home: 7723 Avondale Terr Harrisburg PA 17112 Office: 1170 Harrisburg Pike Carlisle PA 17013

MORITZ, TODD JON, controller, food company executive; b. Evanston, Ill., Oct. 7, 1960; s. Jon F. Moritz and Bonnie M. (Smith) Wright; m. Christine Judith Krodel, Apr. 17, 1982. BA in Acctg. and Bus. Adminstrn., Carthage Coll., 1981. CPA, Ill. Trainee fin. Continental Baking Co., Schiller Park, Ill., 1981; supr. acctg. Rochester, Minn., 1981-82; project acct. Hodgkins, Ill., 1982-83; mgr. acctg. Schiler Park, 1983-85, comptroller, 1985-86; controller Kehe Food Distbrs., Inc., Addison, Ill., 1986—, corp. sec., 1987—. Treas. Immanuel Luth. Ch., Palatine, Ill., 1985-87. Mem. Ill. CPA's Soc., AICPA. Republican. Office: Kehe Food Distbrs Inc 333 S Swift Rd Addison IL 60101

MORK, LAURA LUNDE, refrigeration executive; b. Seattle, Dec. 5, 1956; d. Marvin Conrad and Mary Anna (Bowman) Lunde; m. Loren Leslie Mork, Dec. 23, 1980. BS in Chem. Engring., U. Wash., 1980. Engring. intern EPA, Seattle, 1977-78; fuel engr. Bethlehem Steel Corp., Seattle, 1980-85; control engr. Seattle Steel Corp., 1985; utility engr. Lederle Labs., Pearl River, N.Y., 1985-87; head refrigeration dept., 1987—. Rep. precinct committeeman, Seattle, 1980; mem. com. Assn. of Wash. Bus., Olympia, 1983-85. Mem. Assn. Energy Engrs., ASHRAE, Am. Inst. Chem. Engrs., Soc. Women Engrs., Instrument Soc. Am., Nat. Assn. Female Execs.

MORLEY, ALFRED CHARLES, JR., professional organization executive; b. Geneva, Ohio, Jan. 16, 1927; s. Alfred Charles and Hazel Elisa (Patterson) M.; m. Kathryn Ann Black, Aug. 28, 1948; children: Cynthia, William. BSBA, W.Va. U., 1948, MA in Econs., 1949. Chartered fin. analyst. Security analyst Nat. City Bank, Cleve., 1950-52; security analyst Wainwright Orgn., N.Y.C., 1952-56, ptnr., 1961-68, dir. research, 1968-74, mng. ptnr., 1974-78; v.p. Security Trust Co., Miami, Fla., 1978-79; treas. Vanderbilt U., Nashville, 1979-80; exec. v.p. Frank Russell Trust Co., Tacoma, Wash., 1980-81; pres. Frank Russell Investment Co., Tacoma, 1981-84; pres., chief exec. officer Inst. Chartered Fin. Analysts, Charlottesville, Va., 1984—, Fin. Analysts Fedn., Charlottesville, 1986—. Bd. dirs. retirement system ARC, Washington, 1986—. Served as corp. U.S. Army, 1944-47. Mem. Richmond Soc. Fin. Analysts. Republican. Methodist. Office: Inst Chartered Fin Analysts 5 Boar's Head Ln Charlottesville VA 22901

MORLEY, JOHN C., electronic equipment company executive; b. 1931. BA, Yale U., 1954; MBA, U. Mich., 1958. Mng. dir. Esso Pappas Chem. Ae., Greece, 1969-70; pres. Esso Eastern Chems. Inc., N.Y., 1970-71; exec. v.p. Enjay Chem. Co., 1971-74; pres. Exxon Chem. Co. U.S.A., Houston, 1974-78, sr. v.p., 1978-80; pres., chief exec. officer Reliance Electric Co. Inc., Cleve., 1980—, also bd. dirs. Served to lt. (j.g.) USNR, 1954-56. Office: Reliance Electric Co Inc 29325 Chagrin Blvd Cleveland OH 44122 *

MORONEY, ROBERT EMMET, retired stock and bond broker-dealer, investment banker, appraiser of non-marketable securities; b. Dallas, Feb. 15, 1903; s. William Joseph and Lelia (Rodgers) M.; m. Jessie Dew Robinson Coolidge, 1940; children: Linda (Muffie), June. Student, U. Dallas, 1920, Georgetown U., 1921; AB, U. Wis., 1923. With Texpolite Bldg. & Loan Assn., Dallas, 1924, Anchor Savings Bldg. & Loan Assn., Madison, Wis., 1924, Guaranty Co. of N.Y., N.Y.C. and Chgo., 1925-26, Dunn & Carr and successors Carr, Moroney & Co., Moroney & Co., Moroney, Beissner & Co., Inc., Houston, 1927-62; bus. mgr. St. John The Divine Episcopal Ch., Houston, 1963-64; v.p. investments Capital Nat. Bank, Houston, 1965-67; ind. fin. cons. Houston, 1966-68; salesman Moroney, Beissner & Co., Inc., Houston, 1968-74; v.p. valuation Rotan Mosle Inc., Houston, 1974-82, retired, 1982; Co-founder, past nat. committeeman Nat. Security Traders Assn.; co-founder, past gov. Investment Bankers Assn. of Tex.; past chmn., past gov. Tex. group Investment Bankers Assn. of Am. Past bd. dirs. Houston Found. for Ballet, Houston Grand Opera Assn., Soc. for Performing Arts, Diocesan Devel. Bd., Church Found. at Rice U., Sheltering Arms, Intercontinental Airport Inter-faith Chapel, Assn. for Community TV, Retina Research Found.; former vol. driver ARC, Christian Community Service Ctr., Houston Met. Ministries' Meals-on-Wheels. Served with USNR, 1943-45. Recipient Driver #1 award Houston Met. Ministries' Meals-on-Wheels, 1984, Sr. award Houston Met. Ministries' Meals-on-Wheels, 1985. Mem. Houston Soc. Fin. Analysts, Fin. Analysts Fedn., Phi Delta Theta. Episcopalian. Clubs: Houston Stock and Bond (hon. mem. #1), Houston, River Oaks Country. Home: The Hallmark 4718 Hallmark Ln Apt 201 Houston TX 77056

MOROSANI, GEORGE WARRINGTON, real estate developer, realtor; b. Cin., July 20, 1941; s. Remy Edmond and Virginia Caroline (Warrington) M.; m. Judith Clontz, July 3, 1980; children by previous marriage: Katherine Carmichael, Elizabeth Warrington. BA, Rollins Coll., 1964, MBA, 1965. Fin. mgr. Lunar Orbitor and Minuteman Programs, Boeing Co., Cape Canaveral, Fla., 1965-68; controller Equitable Leasing Co., Asheville, N.C., 1968-69; founder, pres., treas. Western Carolina Warehousing Co., Asheville, 1969-87; co-founder, pres. Asheville Jaycee Housing, Inc., 1971-77; founder, pres., treas. A Mini Storage Co., Asheville, N.C., 1976—; co-founder, treas. Accent on Living Co., Asheville, 1978-81; founder, pres., treas. G.M. Leasing, Asheville, N.C. 1986—, The Kingswood Co., Fletcher, N.C., 1986—; gen. partner Pine Needle Apts., Arden, N.C., 1978—, Pine Ridge Apts., Skyland, N.C., 1980—, Morganton Heights Apts., Morganton, N.C., 1981—, Maiden (N.C.) Apts., 1981—, Valley View Shopping Ctr., Candler, N.C., 1982-86, Meadow Garden Apts., Hendersonville, N.C., 1983—, Drexel Apts., N.C., 1983—, Heritage Hill Apts., Marion, N.C., 1983—, Cavalier Arms Apts., Waynesville, N.C., 1986—, Gwenmont Arms Apts., Murphy, N.C., 1986—, Nicol Arms Apts., Sylva, N.C., 1986—, Meadowwood Arms Apts., Gray, Tenn., 1986—, 4 Seasons Apts., Erwin, Tenn., 1986—, M. Realty, Asheville, 1986—, Woods Edge Apts., North Wilksboro, N.C., 1987—, Deer Park Apts., Cleve., N.C., 1987—; ptnr. Laurel Ridge Realty, Litchfield, Conn., 1973—, Laurel Properties, Rochester, Vt., 1978—, Ashland Assocs., Asheville, N.C., 1985-88, Airport Assocs., Asheville, 1986-87; owner George W. Morosani Indsl. Realtor, Fletcher, 1981—; founder, owner George's Rent-All, Asheville, N.C., 1988—. Bd. dirs. Jr. Achievement Greater Asheville Area, 1977—; mem. Regional Housing Adv. Com., Land-of-Sky Regional Council, 1981-86; mem. Council Rural Housing and Devel., 1982—, N.C. Real Estate Licensing Bd., S.C. Real Estate Commn., Tenn. Real Estate Commn., Asheville Multiple Listing Svc., Hendersonville Multiple Listing Svc.; co-founder, treas. N.C. Council Rural Rental Housing, 1985—, sec., 1986—. Named Man of Yr., Asheville Jaycees, 1976. Mem. Sales and Mktg. Execs. Asheville (dir. 1974-76, 1982-84. chmn. membership com. 1976-77), Asheville Realty Investment Assn., Western N.C. Traffic Club (dir. 1973-74, sec.-treas. 1974-76, pres. 1976-77, dir. 1977-79), Asheville Bd. Realtors, Hendersonville Bd. Realtors, Nat. Assn. Realtors, N.C. Assn. Realtors (property mgmt. div.). Mem. Asheville Comml. and Investment Realty Assn. (v.p. programs 1986-87, sec.-treas. 1987—), Nat. Mini-Storage Inst., W.N.C. Exchangers, Greater Asheville Apt. Assn. (chmn. membership com. 1988-89), Council Ind. Bus. Owners, Better Bus. Bur. Asheville/Western N.C. (dir. 1987—), Self-Service Storage Assn., Asheville Area C. of C. (chmn. indsl. relations 1978-79), Assn. Progressive Rental Orgn., Hendersonville C. of C. Episcopalian. Clubs: Biltmore Forest Country, Asheville Downtown City. Lodge: Civitan (dir. 1975-77). Office: Forest Ctr Ste 201 932 Hendersonville Rd Asheville NC 28803

MORPHY, JOHN, manufacturing company executive; b. Rochester, N.Y., Aug. 14, 1947; s. John and Mary (Kelleher) M.; m. Marcia Price, June 5, 1971; children: Jaime, Matthew. BS in Acctg., Le Moyne Coll., Syracuse, N.Y., 1969. CPA, N.Y. Mgr. Arthur Andersen & Co., Rochester, 1969-76; v.p., controller Computer Consoles Inc., Rochester, 1976-85; v.p., chief fin. officer Goulds Pumps Inc., Seneca Falls, N.Y., 1985—. Office: Goulds Pumps Inc 240 Fall St Seneca Falls NY 13148

MORRA, ROBERT, marketing executive, consultant; b. N.Y.C., July 7, 1952; s. Alfred Joseph and Mary (Colletti) M.; m. Linda Marie Russano, Dec. 27, 1980; 1 child, Dominick. BS, U. So. Calif., 1974, MBA, 1984. Account exec. Myers, Bateman, Warnick Advt., L.A., 1974-75; mktg. rep. United Way, L.A., 1975-76; asst. mktg. mgr. Daiwa Corp., Gardena, Calif., 1976-78; owner, mktg. cons. Design Mktg. Cons., Santa Monica, Calif., 1978—; head dept. mktg. Highland Fed. Savs. & Loan, L.A., 1981—. Active Santa Monica YMCA. Home and Office: 1039 Grant St #3 Santa Monica CA 90405

MORRAR, ATEF ISMAIL, communications executive; b. Jerusalem, Sept. 19, 1950; came to U.S., 1967; s. Ismail F. and Nimeh (Hassan) M. BS in Journalism, No. Ill. U., 1977. Ops. mgr. Aim Communications, Chgo., 1981-83, v.p., mng. dir., 1983-84, v.p., dir. account mgmt., 1984-85, v.p., mktg. dir., 1985-86; pres., mktg. dir. Aim Communications Internat., Inc., Chgo., 1986—; speaker numerous advt. and mktg. seminars and internat. events assns., 1985—. Contbr. articles to profl. jours. Mem. Internat. Advt. Assn., Mid Am. Arab C. of C. (bd. dirs. 1985—). Office: Aim Communications Internat 980 N Michigan Ave Suite 1400 PO Box 11623 Chicago IL 60611

MORREL, WILLIAM GRIFFIN, JR., banker; b. Lynchburg, Va., Aug 25, 1933; s. William Griffin and Virginia Louise (Baldwin) M.; m. Sandra Virginia Coats, Jan. 31, 1959; children: William Griffin, John Coats, Elisabeth White, Jere Coleman. BS, Yale U., 1955; postgrad. Rutgers U., 1965-67. With Md. Nat. Bank, Balt., 1955-84, asst. v.p., 1959, v.p., 1964, sr. v.p., 1975-84, mgmt. com. 1979-84, chmn. internat. loan com., others; pres., bd. dirs. Md. Nat. Overseas Investment Corp.; chmn. bd. London Interstate Bank Ltd.; chmn. bd. dirs. Md. Internat. Bank; sr. v.p., chief operating officer Abu Dhabi Internat. Bank, Inc., 1984-86, pres., chief exec. officer Heritage Internat. Bank, 1986—; chief exec. officer, chmn. The Valley Group; consul of the Netherlands at Balt., 1978—. Mem. Balt. Consular Corps, 1978—; chmn. Md. World Trade Efforts Commn., 1983-84; mem. Md. Trade Policy Council, 1985—; vice chmn. Dist. Export Council, 1983—. Contbr. articles to profl. jours. Sr. fellow Ctr. for Internat. Banking Studies, Darden Grad. Bus. Sch. U. Va., 1978—. Served with U.S. Army, 1956-58. Mem. Bankers Assn. for Fgn. Trade (bd. dirs. 1975-78), Robert Morris Assocs. (nat. bd. dirs. 1984—), Internat. Lending Council (bd. dirs., chmn., 1978-80), Md. Hist. Soc. (trustee), Balt. Council Fgn. Relations (trustee), Econ. Devel. Council. Republican. Presbyterian. Clubs: Yale, Farmington Country, Elkridge, Merchants, Ctr. Home: 6 Beechdale Rd Baltimore MD 21210 Office: Heritage Internat Bank 7126 Wisconsin Ave Bethesda MD 20814

MORRELL, CHARLES VINCENT, academic director, consultant; b. Astoria, N.Y., Dec. 22, 1955; s. Richard Gabriel and Marie Ann (Rindone) M.; m. Kathleen Mary Dyer, July 16, 1977; children: Erin Elizabeth, Robert Vincent. AA, Mohegan Community Coll., 1980; BBA, Eastern Conn. State U., 1982. Asst. dir. student activities Mohegan Community Coll., Norwich, Conn., 1980=82, acting athletic dir., 1981-82; asst. dir. ops. U. Conn., Storrs, 1982—. Vol. Conn. Spl. Olympics, Storrs, 1985-86. Served with USN, 1973-78, Vietnam. Mem. Nat. Assn. for Campus Activities (Conn. unit coordinator, 1983-84, chmn. ops. 1983-84, regional treas. 1985-87, site selection chmn. 1985-86, chmn. ops. nat. conf. 1988, mem. regional conf. com. Acadia U., 1989), Assn. for Coll. Unions (internat. region I rep., mem. com. on computer applications 1988-91). Democrat. Roman Catholic. Home: 4 Charlotte Dr Central Village CT 06382 Office: U of Conn 2110 Hillside Rd Storrs CT 06268

MORRILL, ROBERT E., IV, marketing consultant; b. Fredericksburg, Va., May 21, 1943; s. Robert E. and Charlotte (Hanley) M.; m. Genevieve Clare Adams, Aug. 1972; children: Genevieve C., Robert E. BBA, U. Notre Dame, 1966; MBA, Xavier U., Cin., 1967. Instr. U. Portland, Oreg., 1967-70; mgr. mktg. U.S. Pioneer Electronics Corp., various locations, 1972-76; v.p. mktg. and sales Phase Linier div. Pioneer Electronics, Lynnwood, Wash., 1976-80, Electro Voice, Buchanan, Mich., 1980-82; pres., chief exec. officer Remco Mktg., Kirkland, Wash., 1982-85; pres., owner Morrill & Assocs., Buchanan, 1984—; bd. dirs., chmn. bd. Remco Mktg. Mem. Am. Mktg. Assn., Infant Furniture Reps. Assn. Democrat. Roman Catholic. Office: Morrill & Assocs 309 Terre Coupe Buchanan MI 49107

MORRIS, DANIEL T., management services executive; b. Denver, Jan. 28, 1950; s. John J. and Virginia Lee (Quisenberry) M.; m. Kathy Jeanne Duckworth, Sept. 2, 1978; children: Sean Patrick, Aron Michael, Ryan Joseph. BA in Bus. Adminstrn., Western State Coll. Colo., 1972, MA in Bus. Adminstrn., 1973; Assoc. in Risk Mgmt., Ins. Sch. Chgo., 1979. CPCU, 1984. Asst. mgr. K-Mart, Inc., Denver, 1973-74; ins. analyst Walgreen Co., Deerfield, Ill., 1974-77; v.p. risk mgmt. and safety Service-Master Co. L.P., Downers Grove, Ill., 1977—, v.p. risk mgmt. adminstrn., 1985-87; tchr. Ins. Sch. Chgo., 1985—. Mem. Risk and Ins. Mgmt. Soc. (bd. dirs. Chgo. chpt. 1980-84, pres. 1983-84), Soc. CPCU Nat. Safety Council (speaker 1980). Republican. Roman Catholic. Lodge: KC (chancellor) (Bloomingdale, Ill.). Home: 1255 Boa Trail Carol Stream IL 60188 Office: Servicemaster Industries Inc 2300 Warrenville Rd Downers Grove IL 60513

MORRIS, EDWIN BATEMAN, III, banker; b. Washington, July 19, 1939; s. Edwin Bateman and Mary Helen (Chandler) M.; m. Susan Cookman, Sept 14, 1968. B.S., Wharton Sch., U. Pa. Trainee Bank of Boston, 1963, v.p., 1969, sr. v.p., 1973, exec. v.p., 1981, group exec., 1984—. Trustee Radcliffe Coll., Cambridge, Mass., 1980—; assoc. trustee U. Pa., Phila., 1985—. Served with USMC, 1960-61. Mem. Mortgage Bankers Assn. Am. (bd. govs. 1978—). Republican. Clubs: Algonquin, Eastern Yacht (treas. 1981-82). Home: 125 Front St Marblehead MA 01945 Office: Bank of Boston 100 Federal St Boston MA 02110

MORRIS, G. RONALD, automotive executive; b. East St. Louis, Aug. 30, 1936; s. George H. and Mildred C. M.; m. Margaret Heino, June 20, 1959; children: David, Michele, James. B.S. in Metall. Engring, U. Ill., 1959. Metall. engr. Delco-Remy div. Gen. Motors Corp., 1959-60; factory metallurgist Dubuque Tractor Works, John Deere Co., Iowa, 1960-66; with Fed.-Mogul Corp., 1966-79, v.p., group mgr. ball and roller bearing group, 1979; pres. Tenneco Automotive div. Tenneco, Inc., Deerfield, Ill., 1979-82; pres., chief exec. officer PT Components, Inc., Indpls., 1982-88; vice-chmn. Rexnord Corp., Indpls., 1988—; chmn., pres., chief exec officer CTP Holdings Inc., 1986-88; pres., chief exec. officer PT Components Inc.; bd. dirs. Ransburg Corp., Indpls., Mulligan & Assoc., Chgo. Trustee , bd. dirs., exec. com. Indpls. Childrens Mus.; bd. dirs. Econ. Club. Indpls., Jr. Achievement Cen. Ind.; mem. pres.'s council U. Ill. Mem. Am. Soc. Metals, Soc. Automotive Engrs., Engring. Soc. Detroit, Anti-Friction Bearing Mfrs. Assn. (bd. dirs., exec. com.), Indpls. C. of C. (treas., bd. dirs., exec. com.), Meridian Hills C. of C., Exmoor C. of C., Highland Park C. of c., Marshwood C. of C., Landings Savannah (Ga.) Club. Republican. Presbyterian. Club: Consistory, Meridian Hills Country Club (Indpls.), Exmoor Country Club (Highland Park, Ill.), Marshwood Country Club (Savannah, Ga.). Lodges: Elks, Masons. Office: Rexnord Corp 7601 Rockville Rd Box 85 Indianapolis IN 46214

MORRIS, GEORGE BERRIEN, finanical analyst; b. Rome, Ga., July 24, 1937; s. George Franklin and Gladys Elizabeth (Teat) M.; m. Mary Gantt Folline, Apr. 4, 1964; children—Mary Folline, Elizabeth Berrien, George Berrien Jr. BBA, U. Ga., 1959. Statis. rsch. analyst U.S. Dept. Commerce, Washington, 1959; group v.p. 1st Nat. Bank, Atlanta, 1960-74; sr. v.p. Union Trust Co., Balt., 1975-85; treas. Signet Banking Corp., Richmond, Va., 1986—; dir. Union Home Loan Corp., Lutherville, Md., 1981—, Landmark Fin. Services, Silver Spring, Md., 1981—. Treas. Richmond coun. Boy Scouts Am., 1987, Balt. coun., 1980. With WSAF, 1960. Recipient Silver Beaver award Boy Scouts Am., 1985. Mem. Am. Bankers Assn., Am. Inst. Banking, Nat. Investor Rels. Assn., Bank Invextors Rels. Inst., Fin. Execs. Inst., Cherokee Club (Atlata), L'Hirondelle Club (Balt.), Downton Club (Richmond). Democrat. Presbyterian. Home: 8951 Bellefonte Rd Richmond VA 23229 Office: 103 Huckleberry Dr LaPlata MD 20646 also: Signet Banking Corp PO Box 25970 Richmond VA 23260

MORRIS, GEORGE GLENN, JR., financial analyst; b. Bowling Green, Ohio, Aug. 21, 1937; s. George Glenn and Helen (Harvey) M.; m. Carole Marie DeMore, June 23, 1962; children: Lisa Ann, Michelle Marie. BS, Bowling Green State U., 1960; MBA, Case Western Res. U., 1967. Chartered fin. analyst. Trainee Gen. Tire & Rubber Co., Akron, Ohio, 1960-61; works acct. B.P.S. Paint Co., Cleve., 1961-63; purchasing agt. Diamond Shamrock Co., Cleve., 1963-69; securities analyst Saudners, Stiver & Co., Cleve., 1969-70, Prescott, Ball & Turben, Cleve., 1970—. Mem. Cleve. Soc. Security Analysts (pres. 1980-81), Motor Carrier Analysts Group N.Y.C. (pres. 1982-83), Beta Gamma Sigma. Republican. Roman Catholic. Office: Prescott Ball & Turben Co 1331 Euclid Ave Cleveland OH 44115

MORRIS, GORDON JAMES, diversified company executive, financial consultant; b. Mt. Vernon, Ohio, Oct. 6, 1942; s. R. Hugh and Betty Jane (Roberts) M.; m. Janet Ann Swanson, Aug. 28, 1965 (div. 1971); m. Nancy Joan Meyfarth, July 26, 1975; 1 child, Lawrence Hugh; stepchildren: Richard, Gregory. Student, Ohio State U., 1960-61; BA, Otterbein Coll., 1966; postgrad. in law, Capital U., Bexley, Ohio, 1967-68; postgrad., Coll. Fin. Planning, Denver, 1983—. Registered investment adviser. Asst. to pres. Jaeger Machine Co., Columbus, Ohio, 1968-73; rep. Equitable Fin. Services, Sarasota, Fla., 1974-81; pres. Morris & Assocs. P.A., Sarasota, 1981—; chmn. bd. MAP Fin. Group, Inc., Sarasota, 1985—; ptnr. A-plus Ins. Co., Inc., Sarasota, 1985—, 1987—, MAP Connell & Assocs., Inc., Sarasota, 1988—. Past chmn. West Coast chpt. March of Dimes, Bradenton, Fla., bd. dirs., 1986-88; pres. Epilepsy Found. Southwest Fla., Inc., 1986-87, bd. dirs. Mem. Internat. Assn. Fin. Planning, Nat. Assn. Life Underwriters, Million Dollar Roundtable, Nat. Assn. Realtors, Nat. Inst. Fin. Planning. Republican. Methodist. Lodge: Sertoma (pres. local club 1979-80). Office: MAP Fin Group 1950 Landings Blvd Suite 202 Sarasota FL 34231

MORRIS, JAMES MALACHY, lawyer; b. Champaign, Ill., June 5, 1952; s. Walter Michael and Ellen Frances (Solon) M.; m. Mary Delilah Baker, Oct. 17, 1987. Student Oxford U. (Eng.), 1972; B.A., Brown U., 1974; J.D., U. Pa., 1977. Bar: N.Y. 1978, U.S. Dist. Ct. (so. and ea. dists.) N.Y. 1978, Ill. 1980, U.S. Tax Ct. 1982, U.S. Supreme Ct. 1983; admitted to Barristers Chambers, Manchester, Eng., 1987. Assoc., Reid & Priest, N.Y.C., 1977-80; sr. law clk. Supreme Ct. Ill., Springfield, 1980-81; assoc. Carter, Ledyard & Milburn, N.Y.C., 1981-83; sole practice, N.Y.C., 1983-87; counsel FCA, Washington, 1987—; cons. Internat. Awards Found., Zurich, 1981—, Pritzker Architecture Prize Found., N.Y.C., 1981—, Herbert Oppenheimer, Nathan & VanDyck, London, 1985—. Contbr. articles to profl. jours. Mem. ABA, Ill. Bar Assn., N.Y. State Bar Assn., N.Y. County Lawyers Assn., Assn. Bar City N.Y., Brit. Inst. Internat. and Comparative Law. Office: Georgetown Sta PO Box 25723 Washington DC 20007

MORRIS, JOHN STEVEN, marketing professional; b. Columbus, Ohio, Nov. 6, 1947; s. Charles Russell and Arnella Mae (Grove) M.; m. Patricia Ann Kieffer, May 1, 1971; children: Andrew Steven, Molly Ann. BS, Franklin U., 1979; MS, Cen. Mich. U., 1986. Asst. city mgr. City of Westerville, Ohio, 1977-82; city mgr. City of Eaton, Ohio, 1982-86; mng. dir., internat. Asian dept. Woolport Cons., Dayton, Ohio, 1986—; bd. dirs. Miami Valley Health System Coalition, Dayton, 1988. With USAF, 1966-70. Mem. Assn. Internat. Mktg. Execs., Internat. City Mgmt. Assn., Japan Am. Soc., Japan Ohio Internat. Network, VFW, Masons, Engrs. Club Dayton, Browns Run Country Club, Eaton Country Club. Republican. Home: 227 W Main St Eaton OH 45320 Office: Woolport Cons 409 E Monument Ave Dayton OH 45402-1226

MORRIS, J(OSEPH) ANTHONY, public interest organization official; b. nr. Marboro, Md., Sept. 6, 1918; s. Charles Lafayette and Essie (Stokes) M.; B.S., Cath. U. Am., 1940, M.S., 1942, Ph.D., 1947; m. Ruth Savoy, Nov. 1, 1942; children—Carol Ann, Marilyn T., Joseph A., Larry A. Asst. scientist Josiah Macy, Jr. Found., N.Y.C., 1943-44; virologist, Depts. Agr., Interior, Laurel, Md., 1944-47; virologist, chief hepatitis virus research Walter Reed Army Inst. Research, Washington, 1947-56; virologist, asst. chief, dept. virus and rickettsial diseases U.S. Army Med. Command, Japan, 1956-59; virologist chief sect. respiratory viruses, div. biologics standards NIH, Bethesda, Md., 1959—, dir. slow, latent and temperate virus br. FDA, Bethesda, 1972-76; lectr. dept. microbiology U. Md., College Park, 1977-79; vice-chmn. Bell of Atri, Inc., College Park, 1979-82, chmn., 1983; cons. Commn. on Influenza, Armed Forces Epidemiologic Bd., 1960—, Nat. Inst. Neurol. Diseases and Blindness, 1962—. Mem. Soc. Tropical Medicine and Hygiene, Soc. Am. Microbiologists, Soc. Exptl. Biology and Medicine, Am. Assn. Immunologists, N.Y. Acad. Sci. Discoverer of respiratory sycytial virus; research on infectious hepatitis, respiratory diseases of virus etiology and zoonosis. Home: 23-E Ridge Rd Greenbelt MD 20770

MORRIS, LARRY GARNER, transportation company executive; b. New Kensington, Pa., Apr. 1, 1938; s. Fred Chester and Mary Elizabeth (Robinson) M.; m. Janet Louise Moon; children: Blake, Colleen, Kent. BS, Pa. State U., 1960; MBA, U. Pitts., 1964; cert. program for mgmt. devel., Harvard U., 1974. Controller telecommunications ops. Gen. Cable Corp., Greenwich, Conn., 1970-74, v.p. corp. planning, 1974-77, v.p., gen. mgr. power cable, 1977-78; v.p. adminstrn. G.K. Techs., Greenwich, 1978-81; sr. v.p. adminstrn. Penn Cen. Corp. and G.K. Techs., Greenwich, 1981-83; sr. v.p. fin. and adminstrn. electronics telecommunications and def. group Penn Cen., Greenwich, 1983-85; sr. v.p., chief fin. officer Tiger Internat. and Flying Tiger Line, Los Angeles, 1986—. Served to lt. (j.g.) USN, 1960-62. Mem. Fin. Execs. Inst. Assn. Republican. Baptist. Home: 116 Northstar Mall Marina del Rey CA 90292 Office: Tiger Internat 7401 World Way W Los Angeles CA 90009

MORRIS, LAWRETTA GOUDY, land company executive; b. Gold Beach, Oreg., Aug. 9, 1937; d. Lawrence E. and Etta (Owen) Goudy; m. Jon E. Morris, Sept. 9, 1957; children: J. Michael, Daniel. BS, Oreg. State U., 1957; postgrad., Portland State U., 1959-65. Cert. tchr., Oreg. Tchr. David Douglas High Sch., Portland, Oreg., 1958-60, 62-70, Mt. Hood Community Coll., Portland, 1970-76; owner, pres. Goudy Land Co., Portland, 1976—,

Morris Mgmt. Group, Portland, 1987—. Bd. dirs., v.p., sec. Oreg. Mus. Sci. and Industry, Portland, 1981-87, transition dir., 1985; mem. Portland Hist. Landmarks Commn., 1984-86; exec. dir. Oreg. Rep. party, Portland, 1985-86, campaign mgr., 1986; chmn. Portland Planning Commn., 1985—; bd. dirs. Portland Opera Assn., 1988—. Recipient Outstanding Pub. Service award Portland Dept. Pub. Works, 1987. Mem. Am. Planning Assn. Presbyterian. Clubs: Portland City, Portlandia. Lodge: Order Ea. Star. Office: Goudy Land Co 169 N Lotus Beach Dr Portland OR 97217

MORRIS, MIRANDA JANE, outdoor advertising company executive; b. Hinesville, Ga., Sept. 17, 1957; d. Stanley Lewis and Juanita (Brockman) Sexton; divorced; 1 child, Nathaniel Ryan. BA, U. Ky., 1979. Cert. elem. tchr., Ky. Spa technician, asst. mgr. 21st Century Health Spa, Louisville, 1981; staff counselor Physician's Weight Loss Ctr., Middletown, Ohio, 1981; sales rep. Louisville Automobile Club of AAA, 1982; asst. mgr. Lerner Shops, Inc., Louisville, 1982; asst. dir. Fun Skool and Gagel Elem. Sch., Louisville, 1983—; kindergarten tchr. Louisville, 1984; sales rep. Columbia Sussex Corp., Louisville, 1984-86; account exec. Naegele Outdoor Advt., Louisville, 1986—. Active Jullian Carroll for Gov. Campaign, 1987; publicity chmn. Wheeler Sch. PTA, Louisville, 1986-87, 2d v.p., 1987. Named hon. capt. Mayor of Louisville, 1986; named to Hon. Order Ky. Cols. Mem. Nat. Assn. Female Execs. Democrat. Mem. Christian Church (Disciples of Christ). Home: 10801 Cherry Grove Ct Louisville KY 40299 Office: Naegele Outdoor Advt 1501 Lexington Rd Louisville KY 40207

MORRIS, PATRICIA DIANNE, manufacturing executive; b. West Palm Beach, Fla., Nov. 5, 1953; d. John C. and Clara (Gainey) Faulkenberry; m. Dennis Randall Morris, Aug. 30, 1977. BBA, Middle Tenn. State U., 1975; MBA, U. Okla., 1976; postgrad., North Tex. State U., 1982-83, Cornell U., 1988. Fin. analyst Continental Oil Co., Overland Park, Kans., Houston, 1976-77; fin. supr. Singer Corp., Excelsior Springs, Mo., 1977-78; fixed asset acct. PACCAR, Inc., Kenworth Truck Co., Kansas City, Mo., 1979, accounts payable supr., 1979-80; asst. plant controller PACCAR, Inc., Kenworth Truck Co., Seattle, 1985-86; plant controller PACCAR, Inc., Kenworth Truck Co., Chillicothe, Ohio, 1986—; gen. ledger coordinator PACCAR, Inc., Peterbilt Motors Co., Denton, Tex., 1980-81, gen. acctg. supr., 1981-82, cost acctg. mgr., 1982-85. Mem. Am. Mgmt. Assn., Nat. Assn. Accts. Republican.

MORRIS, ROBERT ALAN, aerospace industry executive; b. North Platte, Nebr., Sept. 9, 1934; s. Robert A. and Freda (Zediker) M.; m. Joyce D. Rigg, Dec. 5, 1959; children: Linda K., Laura D., Robert A. BBA, McCook (Nebr.) Jr. Coll., 1954; BS in Journalism, Northwestern U., 1956, MS in Journalism, 1957. Reporter, editor Chgo. Tribune, 1958-60; dir. pub. relations BOAC, Chgo., 1960-64; dir. communications IBM Corp., N.Y.C., 1964-77; v.p. communications Borg-Warner, Chgo., 1977-86, Gen. Dynamics Corp., St. Louis, 1986—; mem. Pub. Rels. Seminar, 1978—, Golden Workshop, N.Y.C., 1981—. Bd. dirs. Family Personal Svc. Ctr., St. Louis, 1986—, Jr. Achievement, Hazelwood, Mo., 1986—, St. Louis Regional Commerce and Growth Assn., 1988—. With USAR, 1957-63. Mem. Aerospace Industries Assn. Am. (communications council 1987—), Pub. Affairs Council (bd. dirs. 1982—), St. Louis Press Club, St. Louis Club, Sigma Delta Chi. Republican. Presbyterian. Office: Gen Dynamics Corp 7733 Forsyth Blvd Pierre Laclede Ctr Saint Louis MO 63105

MORRIS, ROBERT LEE, jewelry designer, gallery administrator; b. Nurnberg, Federal Republic Germany, July 7, 1947; came to U.S., 1947; s. Jack Bret and Sara Ellen (Holloway) M. BA, Beloit Coll., 1969. Pres. Robert Lee Morris/Artwear, N.Y.C., 1977—. Trustee Beloit (Wis.) Coll., 1989—. Recipient Coty award, N.Y.C., 1981, Council Fashion Designers Am. award, 1985, M Spl. award Internat. Gold, N.Y.C., 1986, Disting. Service award Beloit Coll. Alumni Assn., 1988. Home: 28 Howard New York NY 10013 Office: 409 W Broadway New York NY 10012

MORRIS, THOMAS E., retail executive; b. Adrian, Ga., Oct. 9, 1946; s. James Earl and Eloise (Kea) M.; m. Kay Morris, Dec. 17, 1967; children: Scott, Julie. BBA, Ga. So. Coll., 1967. Office: Sears Roebuck & Co Sears Tower Chicago IL 60684

MORRISON, ALAN STUART, lawyer; b. St. Louis, Dec. 24, 1937; s. Marion Stuart and Irene Wilhelmina (Zoss) M.; m. Carolyn Elaine Burgdorf, Sept. 6, 1959; children: Scott Stuart, Kristin Anne. BA, Valparaiso U., 1959, JD, 1962. Bar: Ind. 1962, Mo. 1985, U.S. Supreme Ct. 1976. Asst. counsel Midwestern United Life Ins. Co., Ft. Wayne, Ind., 1962-66; asst. prof. Valparaiso (Ind.) U. Sch. of Law, 1966-69, adj. prof., 1970-85; assoc. Hoeppner, Wagner & Evans, Valparaiso, 1969-73, ptnr., 1973-85; asst. gen. counsel Sverdrup Corp., St. Louis, 1985-86, gen. counsel, sec., 1986—; also bd. dirs. Sverdrup Corp. Mem. Ind. Bar Assn., Mo. Bar Assn., Met. St. Louis Bar Assn., ABA. Lutheran. Home: 12150 Bent Brook Rd Des Peres MO 63122 Office: Sverdrup Corp 801 N 11th Saint Louis MO 63101

MORRISON, DONALD WILLIAM, lawyer, utility executive; b. Portland, Oreg., Mar. 31, 1926; s. Robert Angus and Laura Calista (Hodgson) M.; m. Elizabeth Margaret Perry, July 25, 1953; children: Elizabeth Laura, Carol Margaret. B.S.E.E., U. Wash., 1946; LL.B., Stanford U., 1950. Bar: Oreg. 1950, Calif. 1950, N.Y. 1967, Ill. 1968, Ohio 1974. Assoc. Pendergrass, Spackman, Bullivant & Wright, Portland, 1950-57; ptnr. Pendergrass, Spackman, Bullivant & Wright, 1957-60; gen. atty. Pacific N.W. Bell, Portland, 1960-66; atty. AT&T, N.Y.C., 1966-68; counsel Ill. Bell Telephone Co., Chgo., 1968-74; v.p., gen. counsel Ohio Bell Telephone Co., Cleve., 1974—. Trustee, pres. Govtl. Research Inst.; trustee, vice chmn. Cleve. Inst. Music; vice chair, mem. exec. com. Cleve. Council on World Affairs; mem. adv. com. Cleve. Play House, Garden Ctr. Greater Cleve.; v.p. Health Trustees Inst., Cleve.; mem. vis. com. Cleve. State U. Law Sch. Served with USN, 1943-50. Recipient various bar and civic appreciation awards. Mem. ABA, Ohio State Bar, Bar Assn. Greater Cleve., Oreg. State Bar, State Bar Calif. Clubs: The Country, Clevelander. Office: Ohio Bell Telephone Co 45 Erieview Pla Ste 1600 Cleveland OH 44114

MORRISON, FRED BEVERLY, mortgage banker; b. Gt. Neck, N.Y., May 21, 1927; s. Fred B. and Beverly (Fitzgerald) M.; m. Janet Thornton Johnson, May 22, 1948; children—Jane, Susan, Martha, James, Ann, David. BA, Columbia U., 1948, LLB, 1951. Bar: D.C. 1952. Asst. gen. counsel ARC, Washington, 1951-54; nat. exec. sec., voluntary home mortgage program Housing and Home Fin. Agy., Washington, 1954-57; investment v.p. mortgages Met. Life Ins. Co., N.Y.C., 1957-67; pres. Lomas & Nettleton Co., Dallas, 1967-76, Western Mortgage Corp., L.A., 1976-78; exec. v.p. real estate industries div. Crocker Nat. Bank, L.A., 1978-84; pres. Pearce, Urstadt, Mayer & Greer, N.Y.C., 1984—; bd. dir. Guardian Life Ins. Co., N.Y.C.; chmn. Fed. Nat. Mortgage Assn. Adv. Com., 1981. Mem. Mortgage Bankers Assn. Am. (gov. 1979-84), Union League Club (N.Y.C.). Club: Union League (N.Y.C.). Office: Pearce Urstadt Mayer & Greer 90 Park Ave New York NY 10016

MORRISON, GLEN WARREN, accountant; b. Montgomery, Ala., Sept. 20, 1934; s. Marcus and Gladys (Deavers) M.; m. Joyce Lannom, July 12, 1958; 1 son, Gregg. B.S., U. Ala., 1961; J.D., Jones Law Sch., 1972. CPA, Ala., Ga., Miss., Mo. Staff acct. J. Bradley Haynes & Co., Rome, Ga., 1961-64; sr. acct. Dudley, Hopton-Jones, Sims & Freeman, Birmingham, Ala., 1964-68, ptnr., 1968—, mem. exec. com., 1982—. Mem. AICPA, Ala. Soc. C.P.A.s (audit com. 1975—), Assn. Acctg. Firms Internat. (audit com. 1973—), Inst.Cert. Fin. Planners, Internat. Assn. Fin. Planners, Commerce Exec. Soc. Club: Tip-Off (Birmingham, Ala.). Lodges: Masons, Vestavia Hills Lions (past pres.). Home: 1804 Laurel Rd Birmingham AL 35216 Office: Dudley Hopton-Jones et al 3d Floor 2101 Magnolia Ave S Birmingham AL 35205

MORRISON, GORDON LANGSLOW, data processing consultant; b. Glasgow, Scotland, Jan. 31, 1935; came to U.S., 1950; s. James Breckenbridge and Elizabeth (Langslow) M.; m. Jeanne Clark. Degree in Data Processing, UCLA, 1963. Prin. GLM Cons., Hollister, Calif., 1971—. Served to sgt. USMC, 1952-55. Mem. Data Processing Mgmt. Assn. Home and Office: 285 Morris Dr Hollister CA 95023-9656

MORRISON, GORDON MACKAY, JR., investment company executive; b. Boston, Jan. 18, 1930; s. Gordon Mackay and Alice (Blodgett) M.; m. Barbara J. Lee, June 15, 1954; children: Lee, Leighton, Faith. AB, Harvard U., 1952, MBA, 1954. Regional mgr. Bankers Leasing Corp., Boston, 1965-68; portfolio mgr. Loomis, Sayles and Co., Boston, 1969-71; sr. v.p. Ft. Hill Investors Mgmt., Boston, 1972-75; chmn. bd. Bradford Gordon, Inc., Boston, 1976—; trustee E. Boston Savings Bank, 1961—. Bd. dirs. The New Eng. Hosp., 1961—. Republican. Congl. Club: Harvard. Lodge: Masons. Home: 32 Old Orchard Rd Sherborn MA 01770 Office: Bradford Gordon Inc 50 Congress St Ste 724 Boston MA 02109

MORRISON, HENRY TERRY, JR., entertainment company executive, writer; b. Pleasantville, N.Y., Dec. 21, 1939; s. Henry Terry and Mary (Heffelfinger) M.; children by previous marriage: Jane, Henry, Laura, Alexandra, Catherine, Elizabeth; m. Karen Anne Nelson, Mar. 10, 1979; 1 child, Luke David Dmitri. BA, U. Minn., 1963; MA of Religion, Yale U., 1980; grad., Institut Pour L'Etude des Methodes de L'Entreprise, Lausanne, Switzerland, 1971. Ordained to priesthood Episcopal Ch., 1983. Trainee 1st Banks, Mpls., 1963-66; prodn. mgr. Gen. Mills, Inc., Mpls., 1966-69; v.p. sales Sea Ventures Internat., Nassau, The Bahamas, 1969-71, Pemco, Lausanne, 1971-72; v.p., gen. mgr. Belford Enterprises, Inc., Mpls., 1972-77; priest, freelance author The Episcopal Ch., Ketchum, Idaho, 1978-84; pres., chief exec. officer, mem. bd. dirs. Mill City Entertainment, Inc., Wayzata, Minn., 1985—; bd. dirs. Crocus Entertainment, Inc., Mpls. (chief executive officer 1987—, pres. 1988—). Author: Intercept, 1981, (screenplay) Group Six, 1986. Bd. dirs. Minn. Outward Bound Sch., Mpls., 1967-70, The City, Inc., Mpls., 1973-77. Clubs: White Elephant (London); Lafayette (Mpls.). Lodge: Knights of Malta.

MORRISON, JANE THORNTON, publisher; b. Cranston, R.I., Apr. 9, 1949; d. Fred B. and Janet Thornton (Johnson) M. BA, Mt. Holyoke Coll., 1971, MAT, 1972. Dir. admissions St. Margaret's Sch., Tappahannock, Va., 1972-73, Masters Sch., Dobbs Ferry, N.Y., 1973-75; membership specialist Girl Scouts USA, N.Y.C., 1975-77; with sales ABA Jour., N.Y.C., 1977-80, Bank Systems Mag., L.A., 1980-82; regional mgr. Consumer Electronics Mag., L.A., 1982-84; ad dir. Impresion Mag., L.A., 1984-85; pub. Design Source, San Francisco, 1985-88; home furnishings exec. PFM Mag., Atlanta, 1988—. Mem. Mt. Holyoke Club N.Y. (pres. 1975-77). Episcopalian. Office: Shore Communications 180 Allen Rd #300S Atlanta GA 30328

MORRISON, JOHN JOSEPH, retirement community administrator; b. Indpls., Dec. 4, 1946; s. Lewis Everett and Dorothy Miller (Andrew) M.; m. Cheryl Lee Schinsing, May 25, 1973. BBA, St. Mary's U., San Antonio, 1976; MS, Trinity U., San Antonio, 1978. Asst. unit mgr. Bexar County Hosp. Dist., San Antonio, 1972-74; adminstrv. asst. Brim & Assocs., Portland, Oreg., 1977-79; mgmt. cons. Tex. Hosp. Assn., Austin, 1979-82; asst. v.p. Lafayette Home Hosp., Ind., 1982-85; exec. dir. Westminster Village, W. Lafayette, Ind., 1985—. Loaned exec. United Way, Lafayette, 1983, mem. planning com., 1984-87; teamwalk com. March of Dimes, 1988. Served with U.S. Army, 1967-70. Mem. Ind. Assn. Homes for the Aging (chmn. edn. com. 1987, 1st v.p. 1988, pres. 1989), Lafayette C. of C. (univ. com.). Republican. Baptist. Office: Westminster Village 2741 N Salisbury West Lafayette IN 47906

MORRISON, MICHAEL FRANK, music producer; b. Cedar Rapids, Iowa, June 23, 1951; s. Carl Joseph and Marie Leona Morrison. BA in Speech and Theater, U. No. Iowa, 1973; MA in Theater and Edn., U. No. Colo., 1977. Boat laborer Pacific Yacht Sales, Inc., Seattle, 1985—; musician, singer, songwriter, artist, owner Michael Morrison Prodns., Seattle, 1983—; on-call motion picture actor Lola Hallowell Talent Agy., Seattle, 1980—; substitute tchr. Seattle Pub. Schs., 1980—; freelance drama specialist, 1973—. Active Internat. Theatre for Young People, ALERT, Research Recommendations. Mem. Nat. Inst. Bus. Mgmt., Internat. Bus. Network, Boardroom Classics Inc., Nat. Assn. for Campus Activities, Swap N.W. Office: PO Box 55971 Seattle WA 98155

MORRISON, MICHAEL IAN DONALD, insurance company executive; b. Floriana, Malta, Dec. 22, 1929; came to U.S., 1959; s. Donald Carter and Mabel Margaret (Campbell) M.; m. Eileen Betty Park, July 15, 1963; children: Penelope, Heather, Andrew. Student pvt. schs., Toronto, Ont., Can. and Taunton, Eng. Lloyd's broker Thomas Stephens & Sons Ltd., London, 1953-56; underwriter St. Helens Ins. Co., London, 1956-59; broker N.Y.C., 1959-63; sr. v.p. Am. Internat. Group, N.Y.C., 1964—; vice chmn., dir. Am. Home Assurance Co.; exec. v.p., dir. Nat. Union Fire Ins. Co., Birmingham Fire Ins. Co., Ins. Co. State of Pa.; dir. Commerce & Industry Ins. Co., Commerce & Industry Ins. Co. Can. Served to capt. Brit. Army, 1948-50. Office: Am Internat Group Inc 70 Pine St New York NY 10270

MORRISON, PETER GIFFORD, financial executive; b. Washington, Iowa, Sept. 2, 1948; s. G. Gifford and Sara Lu M.; student Robert Morris Coll., 1967-69; A.B., U. Iowa, 1972, postgrad., 1972. Tax cons. Morrison, Morrison & Morrison, 1966-78; fin. and investment cons. N.W. Bank & Trust Co., Davenport, Iowa, 1974-79; trust officer and affiliate mgr. Iowa-Des Moines Nat. Bank, 1979; specialist computer applications in probate and taxation G. Gifford Morrison, Washington, Iowa, 1980—; specialist computer applications. Mem. Kappa Sigma (Internat. Housing Commr., Dist. Grand Master). Presbyterian. Home: 203 Woodside Dr Iowa City IA 52240 Office: 213 S Marion Washington IA 52353

MORRISON, READ TABER, educational administrator, financial planner, accountant; b. Toronto, Apr. 22, 1951; s. John Taber and Evelyn Alberta (Read) M.; m. Bonnie Jean Diehl, Jan. 3, 1975; children: John Robert, James Read. BA in Bus. Adminstrn., Am. Christian Coll., 1974; cert., Coll. for Fin. Planning, 1987. Personnel asst. Waukesha (Wis.) Engine div. Dresser Industries, 1974-76; bus. mgr. Wis. Voice Christian Youth, Inc., Milw., 1977-80; asst. contr. Grace Schs., Inc., Winona Lake and Warsaw, Ind., 1980-85, asst. dir. devel., 1985-87, contr., 1987—; pres. Morrison Planning Group Fin. Concepts, Warsaw, Ind., 1984—. Chmn. indsl. group Waukesha United Way, 1975; sec. Kosciusko County chpt. ARC, Warsaw, 1986-87, chmn., 1988. Mem. Inst. Cert. Fin. Planners, Nat. Assn. Colls. and Univs. Bus. Ofcls. Republican. Mem. Brethren Ch. Home: 44 Timberline Dr Warsaw IN 46580 Office: Grace Schs Inc 200 Seminary Dr Winona Lake IN 46590

MORRISON, RICHARD CLIFFORD, corporate investments executive; b. Northampton, Mass., June 7, 1940; s. Clifford H. and Viola M. (Morrisette) M.; m. Rebecca A. Broughton, June 23, 1962; children: Susan, Patricia. BA in Econs., W.Va. Wesleyan Coll., 1962; MS in Fin., U. Ariz., 1964. Securities analyst Mass. Mut. Life Ins. Co., Springfield, 1964-67, securities asst., 1967-69, asst. dir. investments, 1969-73, assoc. dir. investments, 1973-76, dir. investments, 1976-82, second v.p. investments, 1982-87, v.p. securities investments, 1987—; v.p. investments Mass. Mut. Corp. Investors, Springfield, 1987—, Mass. Mut. Participation Investors, Springfield, 1988—; bd. dirs. Knapp Shoes, Inc., Brockton, Mass. Chmn. human relations commn. City of Springfield, 1976-82, human services adv. bd., 1982-85; bd. dirs. Community Council of Greater Springfield; treas. Trinity United Meth. Ch., Springfield, 1977-85. Republican. Home: 301 Longhill St Springfield MA 01108 Office: Mass Mut Life Ins Co 1295 State St Springfield MA 01111

MORRISON, ROBERT H., writer, publisher; b. San Bernardino, Calif., Jan. 28, 1938; s. Charles Hugh and Sarah Inez (Morrison-Rutledge) M.; m. Patricia L. Seefried, Apr. 12, 1980; children: Robert Hugh, Jeri L., Donna D., Debra M., James C., Shawn C., Jordan C. AA, Pasadena City Coll., 1958. Various engring. and acctg. positions 1957-61; pres. Fin. Mgmt. Assocs., Inc., Phoenix, 1961-78, Outward Bound, Ltd., Phoenix, 1978—. Author: My Hobby As a Business, 1973, The Fraud Report, 1975, Why S.O.B.'s Succeed and Nice Guys Fail in Small Business, 1976, Contracting Out, The Pawns, The Moneylenders, The Rulemakers, Stalemate, How to Steal a Job, 1977-78, How to Survive and Prosper in the Next American Depression, War or Revolution, 1979, Promoter's Gold, 1979, Divorce Dirty Tricks, 1979, The Greedy Bastard's Business Manual, 1981, Gambler's Gold, 1982, The New Venture Planner, 1982, Tax Navigation, 1983, How to Win, Delay, Reduce or Eliminate Lawsuits for Money Without a Lawyer, 1983, How to Steal a Business, 1983, Getting Money For Your Business, 1983, How to Make Yourself, Your Product, or Your Company Famous, 1983, How to Sell Every Word You Write, 1983, How to Get Blood From a Turnip, 1983, Computer Entrepreneur, 1985, Automatic Income Making System (13 vols.), 1987. Mem. Nat. Assn. Accredited Tax Accts., Honolulu Exec. Assn. Republican. Club: Elks. Office: Morrison Peterson Pub Inc PO Box 25130 Honolulu HI 96734

MORRISON, ROBERT HAYWOOD, real estate developer; b. Hickory, N.C., Mar. 27, 1927; s. Charles Tyson and Rebecca Grace (Tuttle) M. AB, U. N.C., 1947, MA, 1948. Pres. Dialectic Soc., Chapel Hill, N.C., 1945; editor Daily Tar Heel, Chapel Hill, 1945-46; pres. Publs. Bd., Chapel Hill, 1946-47; asst. instr. U. Ill., Urbana, 1948-49; chmn. bus. communication dept. U. Kans., Lawrence, 1949-51; editor Daily News-Enterprise, Newton, N.C., 1952-54; prof. Winthrop Coll., Rock Hill, S.C., 1955-59; pres., gen. ptnr. Morrison and Co., Charlotte, N.C., 1955—; pres. Catawba Captial Corp., Charlotte, 1961—; pres. Investors Corp. S.C., Columbia. Author: A Guide to Bank Correspondence, 1949, Problems and Cases in Business Writing, 1951, Better Letters, 1952, Profit-Making Letters for Hotels and Restaurants, 1959, (with others) Modern Journalism, 1962, Bank Correspondence Handbook, 1964; contbr. articles to profl. jours. Chmn. 1st Rep. precinct, Charlotte, 1970's. Mem. Charlotte Comml. Listing Exchange, Phi Beta Kappa, Delta Sigma Pi. Methodist. Lodge: Rotary (Charlotte) (Paul Harris fellow). Home: 1333 Queens Rd Charlotte NC 28207 Office: Catawba Capital Corp 1373 E Morehead St Ste 2 Charlotte NC 28204

MORRISON, WALTON STEPHEN, lawyer; b. Big Spring, Tex., June 16, 1907; s. Matthew Harmon and Ethel (Jackson) M.; m. Mary Lyon Bell, Dec. 19, 1932. Student Tex. A&M U., 1926-28; J.D., U. Tex., 1932. Bar: Tex. 1932. Asso., Morrison & Morrison, Big Spring, 1932-36, ptnr., 1939, 46; atty. County of Howard, 1937-39, judge, 1941-42, 47-48; atty. City of Big Spring, 1949-58; sole practice, Big Spring, 1953—; lectr. Am. Inst. Banking. Served with USAF, 1942-46. Fellow Tex. Bar Found., Am. Coll. Probate Counsel; mem. Tex. City Attys. Assn. (pres. 1955-56), Am. Judicature Soc., Tex. Bar Assn., ABA. Baptist. Clubs: Rotary (pres. 1949), Masons, Shriner. Home: 1501 E 11th Pl Big Spring TX 79720 Office: 113 E 2d St PO Box 792 Big Spring TX 79720

MORRISSEY, JOHN EDWARD, wholesale grocery company executive; b. N.Y.C., Apr. 21, 1930; s. John Edward and Marilyn Beatrice (Macalis) M.; m. Marilyn Beatrice Macalis, June 6, 1953; children—Michelle, John Edward, Melissa, Dennis. B.S. in Chem. Engring., Villanova U., 1953; M.S. in Nuclear Engring., N.C. State U., 1958; M.B.A., Stanford U., 1969. Asst. dir. Nat. Aero and Space Council Exec. Office of Pres. U.S., Washington, 1969-72, exec. dir. nat. commn. on productivity, 1973-74; sr. v.p. Super Valu Stores, Mpls., 1974—; dir. Malt-o-Meal Corp., Mpls., Ultimap Corp.; Bd. advisers Stanford U. Grad. Sch. Bus., 1983-85. Contbr. articles on productivity in transp. and food distbn. to profl. publs. Served to lt. USNR, 1953-57. Republican. Roman Catholic. Home: 6616 Dovre Dr Edina MN 55436 Office: Super Valu Stores Inc 11840 Valley View Rd Eden Prairie MN 55344

MORRISSEY, THOMAS JEROME, investment banker; b. Racine, Wis.; s. Patrick William and Lillian (Mitchell) M.; PhB, U. Wis., 1940; postgrad. U. Ill., 1942, U.S. Naval Acad., 1942; m. Clovene Marie Nogel, Feb. 21, 1957. Merchandising trainee Vick Chem. div. Richardson-Merrill, Inc., N.Y.C., 1940-41, sales promotion asst., 1941-42, mgr. mil. sales, 1942; pvt. practice mktg. and fin. cons., N.Y.C., 1952-54; dir. mktg. rsch. Pharmacraft Labs. div. Seagrams Distillers, Inc., N.Y.C., 1946-48, mgr. sales promotion, 1948-49, gen. sales mgr., 1949-52; asst. to pres. Turner-Smith Drug Co., N.Y.C., 1954-55, sales mgr., Smithtown, L.I., N.Y., 1955-57; mgr. advt. and sales Denver Chem. Mfg. Co., Stamford, Conn., 1957-58, N.Y.C., 1958-59; v.p., dir. mktg., account exec. Ralph Allum Advt. Agy., N.Y.C., 1959-67; v.p. Community Sci., Inc., 1959-67; account exec. Walston & Co., Inc., N.Y.C., 1967-74, Harris, Upham & Co., Inc., 1974-76; sr. account exec., 2d v.p. Smith Barney Harris Upham & Co., 1976—. Lt. USNR, 1942-46. Decorated Silver Star; knighted Knight of Grace Soverign Orthodox Order of St. John of Jerusalem, Knights Hospitaller. Mem. The Marketeers (pres. 1963-67), Astoria Park Tennis Assn. (pres. 1967-70), Ea. Lawn Tennis Assn. (del. 1967-69), Met. Badminton Assn. (del. 1968- 4), Vet. Corps of Artillery of State of N.Y. (commd. major 1989) Mil. Order of Foreign Wars (bd. govs.), Sigma Chi. Clubs: Dutch Treat (chmn. 1960-61), Army and Navy (pres.), Cen. Badminton (pres. 1971-83), Badminton Club of City of N.Y. (sec. 1985-89), West Side Tennis (Forest Hills). Rsch. in field. Home: 865 UN Pla New York NY 10017 Office: 100 Broadway 23rd Fl New York NY 10005

MORRISSEY, WILLIAM THOMAS, financial planner; b. Vancouver, B.C., Can., Sept. 23, 1950; came to U.S., 1951; s. Gerald Majella and Lucy Marie (dela Giroday) M.; m. Stephanie Kathleen Herbaugh, June 23, 1979; children: Travis, Stephen. Student, Shoreline Community Coll., 1968-69, No. Seattle Community Coll., 1970-74; cert. fin. planner, Coll. Fin. Planning, 1984. Assoc. residential real estate Page & Assocs., Seattle, 1971-74; assoc. comml. real estate Westlake Assocs., Seattle, 1975-76, Schwarz & Scott, Seattle, 1977-78; pres., developer Gerke Morrissey, Inc., Bainbridge Island, Wash., 1978-80; owner, mgr. Islander Lopez (Wash.) Resort, 1980-82; pres., cert. fin. planner Sound Fin. Planning, Inc., Mt. Vernon and Friday Harbor, Wash., 1982—; instr. fin. planning workshop Western Wash. U., Bellingham, 1987—; instr. Small Bus. Resource Ctr., Mt. Vernon, 1988—, Am. Assn. Ret. Persons, Anacortes, Wash., 1988—. Contbg. author: Financial Planning Can Make You Rich, 1986, About Your Future, Financial Planning Will Make the Difference, 1988; columnist Skagit Valley Herald, 1983-85. Vol. firefighter San Juan County Fire Dist., Friday Harbor, 1985—; mem. deferred gifts devel. com. Archdiocese Seattle. Mem. Inst. for Cert. Fin. Planners (pres. 1988-89), Internat. Assn. for Fin. Planning, Registry Fin. Planning Practitioners, N.W. Wash. Estate Planning Coun. (bd. dirs.), Nat. Ctr. for Fin. Edn. (cons., instr. 1986—), Friday Harbor C. of C., Mt. Vernon C. of C. Office: Sound Fin Planning Inc 355 Spring St Friday Harbor WA 98250 also: 1003 Cleveland Mount Vernon WA 98273

MORROW, ANDREW BENNETT, chemical company executive; b. Detroit, Dec. 12, 1938; m. Kathleen Brandt, Aug. 17, 1963; children: Scott, John, Sarah. BA and BS in Bus., U. Mich. Sales rep. Procter and Gamble, Detroit, 1964—; unit mgr. Indpls., 1965-68; mgr. recruiting Cin., 1968-73; div. mgr. Newport Beach, Calif., 1973-83; v.p. sales Fabrilife Chems. Inc., Cin., 1983-87, pres., 1987—. Pres. Harbor View Homeowners, Newport Beach, 1977-78. Mem. Textile Care Allied Trade Assn., Inst. Indsl. Launderers, Textile Rental Svcs. Assn. Am., Newport Beach Water Polo Club, Kenwood Country Club, Leland (Mich.) Country Club. Republican. Episcopalian. Home: 8140 Ravenswalk Cincinnati OH 45243 Office: Fabrilife Chems Inc 4555 Lake Forest Dr Ste 300 Cincinnati OH 45242

MORROW, CHERYL RENE, comptroller; b. Sanford, Fla., Mar. 22, 1960; d. Charles Olden and Christine Georgianne (Mix) M. BBA, Old Dominion U., 1982. CPA, Va. Acct., mgr. Tidewater Beauty and Barber Supply Co., Norfolk, Va., 1983-84; bookkeeper C.F. Hardy Bldg. Corp., Virginia Beach, Va., 1984-86; cost acct. Worthington Pump/Dresser Industries, Chesapeake, Va., 1986-87; comptroller Electronic Inst. Tech., Virginia Beach, 1987—. Mem. Old Dominion U. Black Alumni Assn. (treas. 1988—), Delta Sigma Theta (treas. 1984-87, com. chair 1987-88, mem. adv. coun. for undergrad. chpt. 1986—). Home: 4605 Downeast Ct Apt 202 Virginia Beach VA 23455 Office: Electronic Inst Tech 3133 Magic Hollow Blvd Virginia Beach VA 23455

MORROW, CHERYLLE A., accountant, consultant; b. Sydney, Australia, July 3, 1950; came to U.S., 1973; d. Norman H. and Esther A. E. (Jarrett) Wilson. Student U. Hawaii, 1975; diploma Granville Tech. Coll., Sydney, 1967. Acct., asst. treas. Bus. Investment, Ltd., Honolulu, 1975-77; owner Lanikai Musical Instruments, Honolulu, 1980-86, Cherylle A. Morrow Profl. Svcs., Honolulu, 1981—; fin. managerial cons. E.A. Buck Co., Inc., Honolulu, 1981-84; contr., asst. trustee THC Fin. Corp., Honolulu, 1977-84, bankruptcy trustee, 1984—; panel mem. Chpt. 7 Trustees dist. Hawaii U.S. Depart. Justice, 1988—. Mem. Small Bus. Hawaii PAC, Lanikai Community Assn., Arts Coun. Hawaii, vol., mem. Therapeutic Horsemanship for Handicapped, Small Bus. Adminstrn. (women in bus. com. 1987—). Mem. Australian-Am. C. of C. (bd. dir. 1985—, corp. sec. 1986—, v.p. 1988—), NAFE, Pacific Islands Assn. Women (corp./treas. 1988—). Avocations: reading, music, dancing, sailing, gardening.

MORROW, GEORGE TELFORD, II, health products executive; b. Oakland, Calif., Aug. 25, 1943; s. George Telford and Sterling Elizabeth (Hirschboeck) M.; m. Joan Helen Schieferstein, Apr. 7, 1971. BA with honors, Rutgers U., 1965; MA, Brown U., 1967; JD cum laude, William Mitchell Coll. Law, 1977. Bar: Minn. 1977. Trial lawyer Mpls., 1977-84; gen. counsel Physician's Healthplan, Minnetonka, Minn., 1984-85, pres., chief exec. officer, 1987-88; sec., v.p., gen. counsel United Healthcare Corp., Minnetonka, 1985-87; cons. in field. Contbr. articles to newspapers. Minn. Humanities Commn. grantee, 1978. Mem. ABA, Minn. Bar Assn., Assn. Trial Lawyers Am., Am. Soc. Corp. Secs., KitchiGammi Club, Town and Country Club. Home and Office: 2551 Crescent Ridge Rd Minnetonka MN 55343

MORROW, RICHARD MARTIN, oil company executive; b. Wheeling, W.Va., Feb. 27, 1926; married. B.M.E., Ohio State U., 1948. With Amoco Corp., 1948—; v.p. Amoco Prodn. Co., 1964-66; exec. v.p. Amoco Internat. Oil Co., 1966-70; exec. v.p. Amoco Chem. Corp., 1970-74, pres., 1974-78; pres. Amoco Corp., 1978-83, chmn. chief exec. officer, 1983—; chmn. Am. Petroleum Inst.; bd. dirs. First Chgo. Corp., First Nat. Bank Chgo., Westinghouse Electric Corp. Trustee U. Chgo., Rush-Presbyn.-St. Luke's Med. Ctr. Office: Amoco Corp 200 E Randolph Dr Chicago IL 60601

MORROW, THOMAS CHRISTOPHER, textile design company executive; b. Cambridge, Mass., Sept. 2, 1950; s. Winston Vaughan Jr. and Margaret (Staples) M.; m. Laurie Bogart, Sept. 28, 194; 2 children. BA with honors, Williams Coll., 1973; postgrad. in bus. admin., U. N.H., 1987—. With Hallie Greer Inc., Freedom, N.H., 1987—. Mem. sch. needs com. Freedom Elem. Sch., 1987. Mem. Decorative Fabrics Assn., Industry Found. of Am. Soc. Interior Designers, NRA (life), Custom Gunmakers Guild, Safari Club Internat., Williams Club (N.Y.C.), Bald Peak Colony Club (Melvin Village, N.H.). Republican. Congregationalist. Office: Hallie Greer Inc Cushing Corners Rd Freedom NH 03836

MORROW, THOMAS JARED, newspaper editor, columnist, public relations consultant; b. Centerville, Iowa, Apr. 11, 1939; s. Jared Kennard and Mary Louise (Dowell) M.; m. Kay Murphy, Aug. 24, 1958 (div. Apr. 1972); children: Steven Scott, Shannon Leigh. AA, Phoenix Coll., 1965; BA, Ariz. State U., 1968; PhD in Mktg. Communications, Columbia Pacific U., 1986. Staff writer AP, Phoenix, 1968-69; editor, publisher Valley News and View, Phoenix, 1969-76; columnist, feature writer Times-Advocate, Escondido, Calif., 1978-80; sr. account exec. The Grossman Co., San Diego, 1980-83; v.p. communications Hotel del Coronado, Calif., 1983-85; owner, chief executive officer Cotton-Morrow Communications, San Diego, 1985-88; travel editor, columnist, dir. promotions Daily Vista (Calif.) Press, 1988—; pub. relations cons., instr. Nat. U., San Diego, 1986—; editor spl. pubs. Vista Press. Contbr. articles to profl. jours. Pub. relations cons. Boy Scouts Am., San Diego, 1982—, Air-Space Am. an Interant. Aerospace Expn. Served with USCG, 1977-86. Hon. Dep. Sheriff San Diego County; named Suburban Journalist Suburban Newpapers Am., 1973. Mem. Press Club (pres. 1984-85, bd. dirs.), Paradise Valley C. of C. (pres. 1970-72). Republican. Office: Daily Vista Press PO Box 2168 Vista CA 92083

MORROW, WILLIAM AUBREY, financial planner, educator; b. Oxnard, Calif., July 31, 1945; m. Debbie Foster, Sept. 10, 1978; 1 child, Devin. BS, U. So. Miss., 1968; MBA, Miss. Coll., 1970. Marketer IBM, Detroit, 1973-76, Conn. Gen. Life Ins. Co., San Diego, 1976-80; pres. Fin. Designs Ltd., San Diego, 1980—; prof. fin. planning U. Calif., San Diego, 1985—. Columnist San Diego Bus. Jour.; appeared on nat. and local TV and radio as fin. planning expert; contbr. numerous articles to profl. jours. Chmn. Fin. Independence Week, San Diego, 1988; fund raiser Easter Seal Soc., San Diego, 1986-87. Capt. USMC, 1969-73. Mem. Internat. Assn. Fin. Planning (v.p. pub. relations San Diego chpt. 1984-85, v.p. ways and means 1985-86, v.p. programs 1986-87, pres. 1987-88), Inst. Cert. Fin. Planners (cert., v.p. San Diego chpt. 1986), Kiwanis (pres. San Diego chpt. 1984-85). Office: Fin Designs Ltd 5030 Camino de la Siesta Ste 400 San Diego CA 92108

MORSE, ANDREW RICHARD, fixed income specialist; b. N.Y.C., Jan. 14, 1946; s. Theodore Kane and Elaine (Halpern) M.; m. Iris Graff, June 10, 1971; children: Molly Ann, Elizabeth Graff. B.A., Yale U., 1968. Trader, arbitrage Salomon Bros., N.Y.C., 1969-74; mgr. Salomon Bros. Internat., Ltd., London, 1975-77; sr. corp. v.p. Drexel Burnham Lambert, Inc., N.Y.C., 1978-81; 1st sr. corp. v.p., mgr. fixed income trading Drexel Brunham Lambert, Inc., N.Y.C., 1981—, mgr. internat. dept., 1987—; dir. Ross and Ptnrs., Ltd., London, 1981—, SCF Inc., 1984, Drexel Burnham Lambert, Inc., 1984, Drexel Burnham Lambert Preferred Mgmt. Inc., DBL Espana S.A., DBL Finanz A.G.; mem. corp. bond steering com. Securities Industry Assn., N.Y.C., 1982-83, chmn. fixed income com., 1985; chmn. bd. DBL Securities Ltd., 1988; mem. bd. advisors Trans-Pacific Venture Inc., 1988. Trustee WRT Endowment Trust, Scarsdale, N.Y., 1982—; trustee Westchester Reform Temple, 1983—; mem. investment com. Am. Friends of Weizmann Inst., 1983—, bd. advisors Am. com., 1985, dep. treas., 1987, bd. dirs., co-chmn. investment com.; committeeman Republican Party, Greenburgh, N.Y., 1981—. Club: Bond of N.Y. (elected mem.). Home: 30 Round Hill Rd Scarsdale NY 10583 Office: Drexel Burnham Lambert Inc 60 Broad St New York NY 10004

MORSE, JAMES BUCKNER, health care facility developer; b. St. Louis, July 21, 1930; s. True Delbert and Mary Louise (Hopkins) M.; m. Janet Dorothy Anderson, Dec. 26, 1952 (div. May 1983); children—True, Roger, Stuart. B.S. in Bus. Adminstrn., Washington U., St. Louis, 1952; B.S. in Civil Engring., U. Tex.-Austin, 1957. Engr. Woermann Constrn. Co., St. Louis, 1957-62; engr., mgr. Ralston Purina, St. Louis, 1962-66; mgr. Gallina Blanca Purina, Barcelona, Spain, 1966-68; v.p. Pars Parina, Tehran, Iran, 1968-69; exec. v.p. HBE Corp., St. Louis, 1969-89; pres. J Buckner Morse & Assocs., St. Louis, 1989—. Chmn. Campus YM-YWCA, St. Louis, 1963-66; bd. dirs. Met. YMCA, St. Louis, 1963-66; chmn. Planning Com., Webster Groves, Mo., 1963-65; mem. Mayor's Hosp. Adv. Com., St. Louis, 1980. Served to 1st lt. U.S. Army, 1952-54. Mem. Eliot Soc. of Washington U., Thurtene (hon.), Racquet Club, Chi Epsilon, Tau Beta Pi. Republican. Home and Office: 625 S Skinker Blvd Saint Louis MO 63105

MORSE, JOAN HOLLIS, advertising agency official; b. N.Y.C., July 15, 1951; d. George Joseph and Beatrice (Rubin) Manheimer: m. Joshua Stanford Morse, Feb 6, 1982. Student, U. Grenoble, France, 1969, Italian U. for Foreigners, Perugia, 1970; BA, Rider Coll., 1973. Sec., asst. buyer, media buyer Benton & Bowles, N.Y.C., 1973-76; media buyer Dancer, Fitzgerald, Sample, N.Y.C., 1976-78; media coordinator Pabst Brewing Co., Milw., 1979-80; media supr. W.B. Doner & Co., St. Petersburg, Fla., 1980-82, assoc. media dir., 1982—. Vol. Bayfront Med. Ctr., St. Petersburg, 1986—. Republican. Jewish. Home: 1 Beach Dr Apt 1302 Saint Petersburg FL 33701 Office: WB Doner & Co 9455 Koger Blvd Saint Petersburg FL 33702

MORSE, JOHN ROBERTSON, cable television executive; b. Hackensack, N.J., Mar. 22, 1943; s. James King and Media Gertrude (Robertson) M.; m. Amy Elizabeth Pollock. BA, Occidental Coll., 1965; MPA, Cornell U., 1967; PhD, NYU, 1974. Instr. Bklyn. Coll., 1970-74; program coordinator Empire State Coll., Old Westbury, N.Y., 1974-82, assoc. prof., 1974-84; research supr. ABC, N.Y.C., 1984-86; v.p. research Fin. News Network, N.Y.C., 1986—. Mediator for Nassau County, 1984—. Mem. Am. Mktg. Assn., Am. Assn. Pub. Opinion Researchers, Broadcast Edn. Assn., Sociologists in Bus. Home: 139-15 83d Ave Apt #418 Briarwood NY 11435-1511 Office: Fin News Network 320 Park Ave 3d Floor New York NY 10022

MORSE, KATHLEEN ANN, lawyer; b. Washington, June 23, 1952; d. George Patrick and Margaret Marie (Groeger) M. BA, U. Md., 1976, JD with honors, 1979. Commd. 1lt. U.S. Army, 1982, advance through grades to capt., 1983; assoc. Arent, Fox, Kintner Plotkin & Kahn, Washington, 1979-82; criminal def. counsel (JAG) corps U.S. Army, Nuernberg, Fed. Republic of Germany, 1982-83; criminal trial counsel U.S. Army, Nuernberg, 1983-85; prosecutor, adminstrv. law atty. U.S. Army, Ft. Carson, Colo., 1986-87; asst. atty. gen. Md. State Atty. Gen.'s Office, Balt., 1987—. With USAR, 1982—. Recipient Morris B. Myerowitz Moot Court award. Mem. Md. Bar Assn., Order of the Coif. Roman Catholic. Office: Md State Atty Gen's Office 311 W Saratoga St Ste 1015 Baltimore MD 21201

MORSE, LEON WILLIAM, physical distribution management executive, consultant; b. N.Y.C., Nov. 13, 1912; s. Benjamin and Leah (Shapiro) M.; m. Goldie Kohn, Mar. 30, 1941; children: Jeffrey W., Saul J. BS, NYU, 1935; grad. Acad. Advanced Traffic, 1937, 1954; DBA, Columbia Pacific U., 1979. Registered practitioner ICC, Fed. Maritime Commn. Individual bus., traffic mgmt. cons., Phila., 1950-58; gen. traffic mgr. W.H. Rorer, Inc., Ft. Washington, Pa., 1960-83; adj. prof. econs. of transp., logistics Pa. State U., Ogontz campus, 1960-83; owner Morse Assocs.; course leader seminars in traffic mgmt., phys. distbn. mgmt. and transp. contract negotiations, Am. Mgmt. Assn., others; bd. dirs. Sr. Security Assocs., Inc. Author: Practical Handbook of Industrial Traffic Management, 1980, 87, (manuals) Job of the Traffic Manager, Effective Traffic Management, Fundamentals of Traffic Management, Transportaion Contract Negotiations. Served to capt. transp. corps, AUS, World War II. Recipient Del. Valley Traffic Mgr. of Yr. award, 1963. Mem. Traffic and Transp. Club of Phila., Traffic Club of Phila., Traffic Club of Norristown, Am. Soc. Internat. Execs. (past pres., bd. dirs., sec., cert.), Assn. Transp. Practitioners, Am. Soc. Transp. and Logistics (emeritus), Council Logistics Mgmt., Transp. Research Forum, Drug and Toilet Preparations Traffic Conf. (pres. 1973-75, chmn. bd. 1975-77), Sr. Security Assn., Inc. (bd. dirs.), Mason, Shriner.

MORSE, ROBERT MORETON, construction engineering executive; b. Pasadena, Calif., Dec. 6, 1937; s. Barnard Alexander and Muriel (Moreton) M.; m. Devon Armour Goss, Dec. 29, 1966 (div. 1982); children: Erin Christian, Heather Kirsten, Chelsea Armour, Megan Moreton; m. Karen Lee Zeiders, June 28, 1986; 1 child, Robert Moreton Jr. AA, Pasadena City Coll., 1958; BS, U. So. Calif., 1961. Purchasing agt. Bechtel Group, L.A., 1964-66, sr. engr., 1967-68, mgr. bus. devel., 1969-80; mgr. internat. ops. Bechtel Group, Gaithersburg, Md., 1981-84; regional v.p., gen. mgr. Ebasco Svcs., Inc., Santa Ana, Calif., 1984—; chmn., pres. E&L Techs., Long Beach, Calif., 1984—, also bd. dirs.; pres., bd. dirs. E&L Techs. Inc. (subs. Ebasco Services, Inc.), Long Beach, Calif. Mem. L.A. Town Hall, 1986—, Irvine (Calif.) Indsl. League, 1986—; chief Emerald Bay Fire Dept., Laguna Beach, Calif., 1980-82. Capt. USMC, 1961-64. Mem. ASME, Am. Nuclear Soc., Pacific Coast Elec. Assn., Atomic Indsl. Forum, Archimedes Circle U. So. Calif., L.A. Area C. of C., Pacific Club,El Niguel Country Club, Valley Hunt Club, Center Club, Monarch Bay Beach and Tennis Club, Masons, Beavers, KT. Republican. Episcopalian. Home: 8 Soto Grande Dr Laguna Niguel CA 92677-3880 Office: Ebasco Svcs Inc 3000 W MacArthur Blvd Santa Ana CA 92704

MORSHEIMER, FREDERICK THOMAS, information systems specialist; b. Gloversville, N.Y., Apr. 3, 1948; s. L. Joseph and Emma Elsa (Schrecker) M.; m. Linda L. Liljegren, July 7, 1973; children: Megan Marie, Erin Lynn. BA, Norwich U., 1970; MBA, SUNY, Albany, 1982; MA in Mgmt., Claremont Grad. Sch., 1985. V.p. Grandoe Philippines Inc., Manila, 1976-78; mgr. prodn.Ski Div. Grandoe Corp., Gloversville, N.Y., 1978-79, bus. analyst, 1979-80; regional systems coord. Associated Dry Goods-Western Regional Data Ctr., Culver City, Calif., 1982-84; sr. ops. advisor Associated Dry Goods-Western Regional Data Ctr., Piscataway, N.J., 1984-85; sr. staff cons. Associated Dry Goods, MIS Div., N.Y.C., 1985-86; sr. staff asst. to sr. v.p. May Dept. Stores, St. Louis, 1986-87; v.p., chief info. officer Contempo Casuals, L.A., 1987—. Advisor West Windsor (N.J.) Devel. Commn., 1986—. 1st lt. U.S. Army, 1973. Mem. Assn. for Retail Mgmt. and Info. Systems (bd. dirs. L.A. chpt. 1987-88), Rotary, Beta Gamma Sigma. Office: Contempo Casuals 5433 W Jefferson Blvd Los Angeles CA 90016

MORTENSEN, ARVID LEGRANDE, insurance company executive, lawyer; b. Bremerton, Wash., July 11, 1941; s. George Andrew and Mary Louise (Myers) M.; m. Elaine Marie Mains, Aug. 2, 1968; children: Marie Louise, Anne Catherine, Joseph Duncan. BS in English and Psychology, Brigham Young U., 1965, MBA in Mktg. and Fin., 1967; JD cum laude, Ind. U., 1980. Bar: Ind. 1980, U.S. Supreme Ct. 1983, Mo. 1985, D.C. 1985; CLU. Agt. Conn. Mut. Life Ins. Co., Salt Lake City, 1967-68, agt. and br. mgr., Idaho Falls, Idaho, 1968-74; with Rsch. and Rev. Svc. Am., Inc./ Newkirk Assocs., Inc., Indpls., 1974-83, sr. editor, 1975-79, mgr. advanced products and seminars, 1979-80, sr. mktg. exec., 1980-83; tax and fin. planner, Indpls., 1980-85, St. Louis and Chesterfield, Mo., 1985—. mem. sr. mgmt. com., v.p. Allied Fidelity Corp., 1983-85, Allied Fidelity Ins. Co., 1983-85, Tex. Fire and Casualty Ins. Co., 1983-85; v.p., bd. dirs. Gen. Am. Ins. Co., St. Louis, 1985-86; v.p. Gen. Am. Life Ins. Co., St. Louis, 1985—; pvt. practice, Indpls., 1980-85, St. Louis and Chesterfield, Mo., 1985—; active with Ch. Jesus Christ of Latter-day Saints, Denver, Idaho Falls, Idaho, Indpls, St. Louis. Mem. Assn. Advanced Life Underwriting, Mo. Bar Assn., Bar Assn. Met. St. Louis, D.C. Bar Assn., Ind. Bar Assn., Am. Soc. CLU's, Nat. Assn. Life Underwriters, Mo. Assn. Life Underwriters, St. Louis Assn. Life Underwriters, Internat. Assn. Fin. Planners. Author: Employee Stock Ownership Plans, 1975, Fundamentals of Corporate Qualified Retirement Plans, 1975, 78, 80; Buy-Sell Agreements, 1988; (with Norman H. Tarver) The IRA Manual, 1975-87 edits.; (with Norman H. Tarver) The Keogh Manual, 1975, 77, 78, 80 edits.; (with Norman H. Tarver) The Section 403 (b) Manual, 1975, 77, 78, 80, 84, 85, 87 edits.; (with Leo C. Hodges) The Life Insurance Trust Handbook, 1980, The Key Executive Sale, 1989; contbr. articles to profl. jours.; editor-in-chief various tax and fin. planning courses; bd. editors Ind. Law Rev., 1977-78. Home: 480 Hunters Hill Dr Chesterfield MO 63017 Office: Gen Am Life Ins Co 700 Market St PO Box 396 Saint Louis Mo 63166

MORTENSEN, SUSAN MARIE, manufacturing company executive; b. Portland, Oreg., Jan. 24, 1950; d. Leslie Dean Mortensen and Kathryn Merdell Huff; m. José Garcia Ruiz, Oct. 25, 1986. BA, U. Portland, 1972. Advt. dir. B.A.C. Inc., Portland, 1972-76, v.p., 1976-81; exec. dir. Econ. Devel. Assn. Skagit County, Inc., Mt. Vernon, Wash., 1982-86; mgr. Sugiyo U.S.A., Inc., Anacortes, Wash., 1986-87, exec. dir., 1987—. Active Skagit County Tourism Task Force., Washington, 1984; rep. Team Wash. Asian Mission, Japan, 1986; ambassador Wash. Partnership for Econ. Devel., 1984—. Mem. Japan-Am. Soc., Econ. Devel. Execs. Wash. (bd. dirs. 1985—), Anacortes C. of C. Jansen Found. grantee, 1985, Team Wash. Dept. Trade, 1985, Local Devel. Fund Matching Dept. Com. Devel., Washington, 1986.

MORTENSON, THOMAS THEODORE, medical products executive, management consultant; b. Hallock, Minn., Dec. 18, 1934; s. Theodore William and Esther (Hanson) M.; m. Alice L. Girdvain, June 27, 1958; children: Kim M. Mortenson Zimmerman, Laura Dee. BBA, U. N.D., 1956, postgrad., 1957-58. Sales rep. Johnson & Johnson, Detroit, 1960-66; tng. and product dir. Johnson & Johnson, New Brunswick, N.J., 1967-72; dir. mktg. devel. C.R. Bard, Murray Hill, N.J., 1973-75; gen. mgr. MacBick, Murray Hill, 1976-78; dir. mktg. Bard Med. Systems, Murray Hill, 1979-81, dir. sales, 1982; dir. sales and mktg. Bac-Data Med. Info. Systems, Totowa, N.J., 1983-84; v.p. mktg. and sales United Med. Corp., Haddenfield, N.J., 1985-86; exec. v.p. Daltex Med. Scis., West Orange, N.J., 1987—; guest lectr. Mktg. Scis. Inc., N.Y.C., 1978, Internat. Novel Drug Delivery Techs., Tustin, Calif., 1987. With U.S. Army, 1957-58. Mem. Am. Mgmt. Assn. (instr. 1971), Berkeley Swim Club (Berkeley Heights, N.J.) (pres. 1979-82, bd. dirs. 1974-84). Home: 63 Lawrence Dr Berkeley Heights NJ 07922 Office: Daltex Med Scis 414 Eagle Rock Ave West Orange NJ 07052

MORTH, PAUL ALEXANDER, accountant, medical center executive; b. Valley City, N.D.; s. Herman Isador and Mary Agnes (Schlegel) M.; m. Nancy Marie Hermes, Oct. 28, 1972; children: Megan, Reid. BS in Bus. Edn., Valley City State U., 1971, BBA, 1977. Acct. Mercy Hosp., Valley City, 1971-73, contr., 1973-76, dir. fin. and support svcs., 1976-83, interim adminstr., 1982-83; contr. Medctr. One, Inc., Bismark, N.D., 1983, v.p. fin., 1983—. With N.D. NG, 1967-73. Mem. Healthcare Financial Mgmt. Assn. (pres. N.D. chpt. 1982-83), Nat. Mgmt. Assn. Office: Medctr One Inc 300 N Seventh St PO Box 640 Bismarck ND 58502

MORTON, CLIFFORD A., holding company executive; b. Glasgow, Scotland, May 8, 1936; came to U.S., 1954; s. John Rufus and Jane Dickens (Bowie) M.; m. Katherine Carla; children: Wyant, Stephanie, Christopher. BS, Queen Elizabeth's U., Bristol, Eng., 1952; postgrad. in banking with honors, So. Meth. U., 1968; MBA, Golden Gate U., 1972. V.p. Security Pacific Nat. Bank, Los Angeles, 1954-68; sr. v.p. Bank Calif. N.A., San Francisco, 1968-74; dir. SBA, San Francisco, 1974-75; dir., chmn. audit com. Siliconix Inc., Santa Clara, Calif., 1975-76; v.p. info. services, pres. Clearfield Ins. Boise (Idaho) Cascade, 1976-86; sr. v.p., chief fin. officer Portland (Oreg.) Gen. Corp., 1986—; assoc. prof. Golden Gate U., 1973-74; guest lectr. Stanford U., 1975. Author: Managing Operations in Emerging Companies, 1984. Exec. v.p. Idaho Soccer Assn., 1973-84. Club: Economic (N.Y.). Lodge: Rotary. Office: Portland Gen Corp 121 SW Salmon St Portland OR 97204

MORTON, EDWARD JAMES, insurance company executive; b. Ft. Wayne, Ind., Nov. 8, 1926; s. Clifford Leroy and Clara Marie (Merklein) M.; m. Jean Ann McClernon, Apr. 30, 1949; children: Marcia Lynn, Anne; m. Matthild Schneider, Sept. 19, 1986; 1 child, Katharine. B.A., Yale U., 1949. With John Hancock Mut. Life Ins. Co., Boston, 1949—, v.p., then sr. v.p., 1967-74, exec. v.p., 1974-82, pres., chief operating officer, 1982-86, chmn., chief exec. officer, 1987—. Trustee Boston Plan for Excellence in the Pub. Schs., Mus. Fine Arts; bd. overseers Boston Symphony Orch., Children's Hosp., Mem. Corp., Ctr. for Blood Research, Northeastern U.; active Bd. Jobs for Mass.; dir. New Eng. Council. Served with USAAF, 1945. Fellow Soc. Actuaries; mem. Nat. Assn. Security Dealers (prin.), Actuaries Club Boston, Phi Beta Kappa. Clubs: Comml. (Boston), Algonquin (Boston). Office: John Hancock Mut Life Ins Co PO Box 111 Boston MA 02117

MORTON, GREGG HARRISON, hotel executive; b. Wurzburg, Fed. Republic Germany, Aug. 14, 1955; came to U.S., 1958; s. Paul Stanley and Margaret Jane (Wilson) M.; m. Rosalie Ann Hedegepeth, July 8, 1977; children: Mitchell, Benjamin, Jacob. BA in Psychology, Southwest Mo. U., 1977. Store ops. mgr. Venture Stores Inc., Springfield, Mo., 1974-80; mdse. control mgr. Venture Stores Inc., St. Ann, Mo., 1980-81, mem. staff domestics div., 1981-83; gen. mgr. Drury Inns Inc., Fenton, Mo., 1983-84; city mgr. Drury Inns Inc., St. Ann, 1984-85, regional mgr., 1985—. Bus. chmn. Trinity Episcopal Ch., St. Charles, Mo., 1986—; mem. mission planning com. Christ Ch. Cathedral, St. Louis, 1988. Mem. Am. Mgmt. Assn., Lambda Chi Alpha (alumni adviser 1978-81). Republican. Home: 2805 Kristopher Bend Saint Charles MO 63303-3345

MORTON, HUGHES GREGORY, real estate development executive; b. St. Joseph, Mo., Aug. 11, 1923; s. William Marmaduke and Jeanette (Hughes) M.; B.S., Wharton Sch. U. Pa., 1947; postgrad. UCLA, 1949-50; children: William Marmaduke II, Hughes Gregory, Mary Gladys. Lic. real estate broker Calif. Divisional personnel dir. Carnation Co., Los Angeles, 1950-52; contractors rep. Calif. Portland Cement Co., Los Angeles, 1959-64; v.p. Western Fed. Savs. & Loan Assn., Los Angeles, 1964-70; owner Morton and Assos., Beverly Hills, Calif., 1970—.Served as lt. (j.g.) USNR, 1941-46. Mem. Internat. Assn. Real Estate Appraisers. Office: PO Box 69421 Los Angeles CA 90069

MORTON, JOHN FRANKE, holding company executive; b. Niagara Falls, N.Y., Mar. 26, 1949; s. John B. and Marie Lucille (Franke) M.; m. Barbara Ward Miller, Aug. 14, 1972; 1 child, Kelly Christine. BBA in Acctg., Niagara U., 1972; MBA in Fin., Fairleigh Dickinson U., 1979. Staff acct. Rapid-Am. Corp., N.Y.C., 1972-74, Philip Morris, Inc., N.Y.C., 1974-75; asst. controller Mickelberry Corp., N.Y.C., 1975-79, treas., 1986—; asst. treas. Vornado, Inc., Garfield, N.J., 1979-81, Coca-Cola Bottling Co. of N.Y., Greenwich, Conn., 1981-86. Mem. Fin. Execs. Inst., Risk and Ins. Mgmt. Soc. Office: Mickelberry Corp 405 Park Ave New York NY 10022

MORTON, RICHARD ROLLO, financial planning company executive; b. Clarkdale, Ariz., Nov. 26, 1929; s. Rollo Richard and Thelma (Burkett) N.; m. Patricia Sue Stapley, Aug. 10, 1950; children: Lorel Ann Norton Bayless, Rollo Richard II, Scott Stapley. Student, Phoenix Coll., 1949, Ariz. State U., 1950; diploma in agy. mgmt., Am. Coll. Underwriters, 1960; diploma, Life Ins. Agy. Mgmt. Sch., 1962; cert., Coll. for Fin. Planning, Denver, 1983. CLU; lic. life and disability agt., gen. securities rep., variable contract ins. agt., real estate salesman, gen. securities prin. Agt. Lincoln Nat. Life Ins. Co., Phoenix, 1950-52; gen. agt. Lincoln Nat. Life Ins. Co., San Diego, 1962-70; group sales rep. Aetna Life Ins. Co., Phoenix and Los Angeles, 1962-68; supr. agy. Aetna Life Ins. Co., Los Angeles, 1958-59, asst. gen. mgr. agy., 1959-61, assoc. gen. agt., 1961-62; pres. Norton Fin., Ltd, El Cajon, Calif., 1970—; chmn. 1st Fin. Centre, El Cajon, 1988—, Planners Securities Network Corp., El Cajon, 1988—, Fin. Planners Ins. Svcs. Network, El Cajon, 1988—, Norton Investment Properties, El Cajon, 1988—, Venture Mortgage Co., El Cajon, 1988—, Tax Preparation Svc., El Cajon, 1988—, Fin. Planners Edn. Pub. Co., El Cajon, 1988—; speaker life ins. sales convs. Bd. advisors Nat. Ctr. for Fin. Edn., San Francisco, 1987—; bd. dirs. Jr. Achievement, San Diego, 1987—. Mem. Internat. Assn. Fin. Planners, Inst. Cert. Fin. Planners, Soc. CLU (past pres. San Diego chpt.), San Diego Life Underwriters Assn. (past bd. dirs.), Nat. Speakers Assn. Office: Norton Fin Ltd 266 S Magnolia St Suite 202 El Cajon CA 92020

MORTON, THOMAS JOHN, corporate executive; b. Albany, N.Y., Nov. 5, 1958; s. Robert E. and Eleanor (Huetter) M.; m. Lisa Kelp, Oct. 5, 1985. BS in Mgmt., Mgmt. Info. Systems, Fin. and Econs., Clarkson U., 1981. V.p. Morton Stamp Co., Delmar, N.Y., 1974-84; treas. Sager-Spuck Supply Co. Inc., Albany, N.Y., 1985—. Mem. Am. Philatelic Assn., Nat. Eagle Scout Assn. Office: Sager Spuck Supply Co Inc 432 S Pearl St PO Box 918 Albany NY 12201-0918

MORTON, WILLIAM GILBERT, JR., investment executive; b. Syracuse, New York, Mar. 13, 1937. BA, Dartmouth Coll., 1959; MBA, NYU, 1965. Asst. v.p. Discount Corp. N.Y., 1960-67; co-mgr. trading, sr. v.p., dir. Mitchell Hutchins Inc., 1967-79; mng. stock exchange floors, sr. v.p., dir. Dean Witter Reynolds Inc., 1979-85; chmn., chief exec. officer Boston Stock Exchange Inc., 1985—; chmn. allocation com. N.Y. Stock Exchange, floor official, 1976-81, various working coms. 1970-85; bd. dirs. Tandy Corp., Ft. Worth. Bd. dirs. Vt. Acad., Saxtons River. With USMC, 1959-65. Mem. Field Club Greenwich (Conn., bd. dirs.), Algonquin Club (Boston), Racquet and Tennis Club N.Y.C., N.Y. Stock Exchange Luncheon Club, Manursing Island Club (Rye, N.Y.), Colo. Arlberg Club (Winter Park), Stratton (Vt.) Club. Office: Boston Stock Exch 1 Boston Pl Boston MA 02108

MORTON-SMITH, STEPHEN, passenger cruise line executive; b. Neath, Wales, Apr. 4, 1951; came to U.S., 1985; s. Denzil Morton and Grace Radford (Davies) Smith. Grad., Ealing Coll. Tech., London, 1975. Purser, hotel officer Peninsular & Orient Navigation Co., London, 1972-84; dir. hotel svces. Princess Cruises, LA, 1985-86, v.p., 1987—. Mem. Marine Hotel Catering and Duty Free Assn. (pres. 1988—), Hotel Catering an d Instl. Mgmt. Assn. Office: Princess Cruises 2029 Century Park E Los Angeles CA 90067

MOSBACHER, ROBERT ADAM, secretary of commerce; b. Mt. Vernon, N.Y., Mar. 11, 1927; s. Emil and Gertrude (Schwartz) M.; m. Georgette Paulsin; children—Diane, Robert, Kathryn, Lisa Mosbacher Mears. BS, Washington and Lee U., 1947, LLD (hon.), 1984. Independent oil and gas producer 1948—; sec. Dept. of Commerce, Washington, 1989—; chmn., chief exec. officer Mosbacher Energy Co., Houston; dir. Tex. Commerce Bancshares, Houston, N.Y. Life Ins. Co. Bd. dirs. Choate Sch., Wallingford, Conn.; dir. Aspen Inst., Center for Strategic and Internat. Studies; chmn. bd. visitors M.D. Anderson Hosp.; nat. fin. chmn. George Bush for Pres.; chmn. Pres. Ford Fin. Com.; co-chmn. Republican Nat. Fin. Com.; dir. Tex. Heart Inst. Mem. Mid-Continent Oil and Gas Assn. (past chmn.), Am. Petroleum Inst. (dir., exec. com.), Nat. Petroleum Council (past chmn.), All Am. Wildcatters Assn. (past chmn.), Am. Assn. Petroleum Landmen (past pres.). Presbyterian. Clubs: Petroleum, Bayou, Tejas, River Oaks Country, Tex. Corinthian Yacht, Houston Country, Coronado, N.Y. Yacht, Brook, Royal Bermuda Yacht, Seawanhaka Corinthian Yacht. Office: Dept of Commerce 15th & Constitution Ave NW Washington DC 20230 *

MOSBY, ROBERT ARNOLD, securities company executive; b. Ossining, N.Y., Oct. 11, 1946; s. Arnold M. and Rita Joan (Fitzgerald) M.; m. Margaret Yost, July 2, 1968 (div. 1983); 1 child, John Morgan. AB, Georgetown U., 1972; MA in Philosophy, U. Va., 1975. Stockbroker Wheat First Securities, Richmond, Va., 1978-81; stockbroker, research v.p. Anderson & Strudwick, Richmond, 1981-83; pres. InterMoney, Inc., Richmond, 1983—; bd. dirs. Ragen Corp., North Arlington, N.J., Consumers Automated Referral Service, Richmond, Va. Served to 1st lt. U.S. Army, 1968-71. Decorated Bronze Star, Purple Heart; Gov.'s fellow U. Va., 1972. Roman

Catholic. Home: 1425 Avondale Ave Richmond VA 23227 Office: InterMoney Inc 1719 W Main St PO Box 1554 Richmond VA 23212

MOSCATO, NICHOLAS, JR., business executive; b. Bklyn., Sept. 1, 1942; s. Nicholas and Albina (Donato) M.; diploma Am. Inst. of Banking, 1966; m. Patricia G. Lipski, Apr. 25, 1965; 1 son, Matthew. Clk. internat. div. Chem. Bank, N.Y.C., 1960-65; money mgmt. officer fgn. exchange Marine Midland Bank, N.Y.C., 1965-72; pres. Lasser Bros. Internat., N.Y.C., 1973-75; exec. v.p. Lasser Bros., Inc., N.Y.C., 1972-76; v.p. Berliner Handles und Frankfurter Bank, N.Y.C., 1976-77; sr. v.p. fgn. exch. Garvin GuyButler, N.Y.C., 1977-80; pres. MPI Assocs., 1980—; sr. v.p. MKI Securities, 1980—. 1st lt., USAR. Mem. Fgn. Exch. Assn. N.Am., Stock Loan Assn., Fgn. Exch. Brokers Assn., Republican. Roman Catholic. Club: Friday Night Bond. Home: 71 Strathmore Ln Rockville Centre NY 11570

MOSELEY, EMORY FRANKS, agricultural equipment sales company executive; b. Ebony, Va., Dec. 20, 1928; s. James Branford and Fannie H. (Reid) M.; grad. Indsl. Tng. Inst., 1948; m. Virginia Sunday, Jan. 27, 1950; children—Gary Wayne, Donna Lea, Terri Lynn. Refrigeration engr. Jones, Tompkins & Wright Co., Boydton, Va., 1948-49; with sales and service dept. Gen. Mills, Inc., Richmond, Va., 1950-53; treas. Superior Equipment & Supply Co. Inc., Richmond, Va., 1953—; pres. Dairymen's Supply Co., Inc., Richmond, 1957—, Superior Equipment & Supply Co. Inc., 1979—, Garber & Moseley Inc., 1979—; v.p. Garber & Moseley, Inc., Richmond, 1964—. Served with USN, 1946-47. Baptist. Club: Varina Charles City Sportsman and Ducks Unltd. Home: 8200 Tudor Springs Ln Richmond VA 23231

MOSELEY, JACK, insurance executive; b. Birmingham, Ala., June 21, 1931; s. Rennie and Clariece Ruth (Spinks) M.; m. Patsy Blake, June 21, 1953; children: Jack, Glenn E., Edward B. Student, Huntingdon Coll., 1949-51; B.S., Auburn U., 1953. Casulty trainee U.S. Fidelity and Guaranty Co., Birmingham, Ala., 1953-56, successively casualty asst. supt., asst. to actuary home office actuary dept., v.p.-sr. actuary, until 1971, exec. v.p., 1971-78, pres., 1978-80, chmn. bd., pres., chief exec. officer, 1980—, chief exec. officer, from 1980, also bd. dirs.; bd. dirs. Signet Banking Corp., C&P Telephone Co. of Md., UNC, Inc.; mem. Greater Balt.-Washington Econ. Devel. Council; chmn. Md. Econ. Growth Assocs.; bd. dirs., mem. exec. com. Am. Council Capital Formation; chmn. Balt. Conv. Bur. Bd. dirs. Balt. Symphony Orch.; trustee Goucher Coll., Md. Hist. Soc, Community Found. Greater Balt. Area. Mem. Am. Ins. Assn. (chmn. 1980-82). Republican. Methodist. Clubs: Balt. Country; Maryland (Balt.), Center (Balt.), Burning Tree (Potomac, Md.). Office: US Fidelity & Guaranty Corp 100 Light St PO Box 1138 Baltimore MD 21202

MOSELEY, JAMES FRANCIS, lawyer; b. Charleston, S.C., Dec. 6, 1936; s. John Olin and Kathryn (Moran) M.; m. Anne McGehee, June 10, 1961; children: James Francis Jr., John McGehee. AB, The Citadel, 1958; JD, U. Fla., 1961. Bar: Fla. 1961, U.S. Supreme Ct. 1970. Pres. Taylor, Moseley & Joyner, Jacksonville, Fla., 1963—; chmn. jud. nominating com. 4th Jud. Cir., 1978-80. Assoc. editor: American Maritime Cases; contbr. articles on admiralty, transp. and ins. law to legal jours. Pres. Civic Round Table, Jacksonville, 1974, United Way, 1979, bd. dirs. United Way Fla.; chmn. bd. trustees Jacksonville Pub. Library; bd. trustees Library Found., sec., 1987—; chmn. Southeastern Admiralty Law Inst., 1980; dir. Nat. Young Life Found., 1987—; chmn. Jacksonville Human Svcs. Coalition, 1989—. Fellow Am. Coll. Trial Lawyers, Am. Bar Found.; mem. Jacksonville Bar Assn. (pres. 1975), Fla. Council Bar Pres. (chmn. 1979), Maritime Law Assn. (exec. com. 1978-81, chmn. navigation com. 1981-88), Comite Maritime Internat. on Collision 1984—), Fed. Ins. Corp. Counsel (chmn. maritime law sect.), Internat. Assn. Def. Counsel, Am. Inns. of Ct. (master of bench), Deerwood Club, River Club, Downtown Athletic Club, India House Club, St. John's Diner (pres. 1988). Home: 7780 Hollyridge Rd Jacksonville FL 32217 Office: Taylor Moseley & Joyner 1887 Bldg 501 W Bay St Jacksonville FL 32202

MOSELEY, RICHARD HARLAN, mortgage banker; b. Kansas City, Kans., Nov. 24, 1929; s. Forrest F. and Edna B. (O'Neil) M.; m. Cathy Jean Smith, Jan. 7, 1978; children: Richard H. Jr., Jennifer L. BS, U. Pa., 1952. Pres. Res. Mortgage Corp., Kansas City, Mo., 1962—. Mem. dist. com. Boy Scouts Am., Kansas City, 1985, parade com. Am. Royal, Kansas City, 1985; pres. Big Bros./Big Sisters, Kansas City, 1974, Bishop Spencer Place, Kansas City, 1982. Recipient Outstanding Service award Big Bros./Big Sisters, 1974. Mem. Kansas City Bd. Realtors, Mortgage Bankers Assn. Republican. Episcopalian. Club: Mercury (Kansas City). Home: 2910 W 66th Terr Mission Hills KS 66208 Office: Reserve Mortgage Corp 800 W 47th St Kansas City MO 64112

MOSENSON, DAVID BRUCE, insurance agency executive; b. Phila., Feb. 2, 1957; s. Cecil Mosenson and Joan Gluskin; m. Gayle Michelle Zucker, June 28, 1981; children: Jeffrey, Jonathan. AB in Econs., Lafayette Coll., 1980. Sales rep. Alden-Levine Assoc., Phila., 1979-80, Mayer-Meyer Assoc., N.Y.C., 1980-82; sales exec., cons. J&G Inc., N.Y.C., 1982—; cons. Mut. Benefit Life Ins. Co., Newark, 1987; lectr. in field. Mem. Am. Assn. Life Underwriters, Nat. Assn. Life Underwriters. Home: 7 Castle Dr Woodbury NY 11797

MOSER, ROGER ALDEN, chemical company executive; b. Toledo, June 8, 1929; s. Karl Simon and Dorothy Katherine (Pinkle) M.; m. Marcia Anne Guissinger, Oct. 4, 1952; children: Andrea Jeanette, Kenneth Wayne, Philip Craig. B.S. in Chem. Engring., Purdue U., 1951; postgrad., MIT, 1975. Engr. Ethyl Corp., Baton Rouge, 1951-73; gen. mgr. mktg. Ethyl Corp., Baton Rouge, La., 1973-77, v.p. bus. mgmt., 1977-82, sr. v.p. research and devel., 1982-86; sr. v.p., exec. v.p. chems. ops. Ethyl Corp., 1986—. Served with U.S. Army, 1953-55. Recipient disting. engring. alumnus award Purdue U., 1983. Mem. Am. Inst. Chem. Engrs., Baton Rouge C. of C. (chmn., bd. dirs.). Republican. Methodist. Home: 1707 Applewood Rd Baton Rouge LA 70808 Office: Ethyl Corp 451 Florida Baton Rouge LA 70801

MOSER, RUSSELL ARTHUR, accountant; b. Washington, Aug. 17, 1959; s. Jack Eldon and Margaret Ann (Russell) M.; 1 child, Jaclyn Ann. AA, Ventura Jr. Coll., 1982, AS in Acctg., 1983, Assocs. in Bus. Mgmt., 1983; AA in Music, Brigham Young U., 1984, AA in Genealogy, 1984, BS in Psychology, 1984, BS in Acctg., 1985, MBA, 1987, JD, 1987; D of Bus. Adminstrn., U. Wash., 1988; postgrad. in diplomacy, air and space law, Miquel U., 1989. CPA, Calif. Pres. rAm. Distbg., Ventura, Calif., 1986; computer mktg. rep. Tandy Corp., Ventura, 1987; accountant Soares, Sandall, Bernarchi, Petrovich, Oxnard, Calif., 1988—; dir. transp. VC Student Ctr., Ventura, 1980, 82—. Author: MTC Tng. Guide, 1983, Scripture Marketing System, 1984, Kingdom of God Not in Word but in Power vol. I Book of Mormon, 1985, vol. II, 1986, vol. III Old Testament, 1987, vol. IV New Testament, 1988. Instr. Missionary Tng. Ctr., Provo, Utah, 1983, 85—; ch. rep. Ireland Bublin Mission, 1978-80; active PTA. Recipient Inst. Religion award Ventura Inst. Religion, 1986; named Outstanding Young Man of Am. Mem. Alpha Beta Gamma, Alpha Gamma Sigma, Rotary, Santa Paula Golf Club, Purpont Tennis Club, CAM Flying Club, Nike Ski Club, Appaloosa Horse Club, AKC Shepherd and Collie Assn. Republican. Home: 371 Lynn Dr Ventura CA 93003

MOSES, BRUCE HADLEY, manufacturing company executive; b. Oak Park, Ill., Apr. 20, 1933; s. Donald Phillip and Althea (Hadley) M.; m. Joan Abel, June 30, 1956 (div. 1983); children: Leslie, Mary, Pamela, John, Amy; m. Marilyn Parker, May 31, 1986. BA in Psychology, U. Rochester, 1955. With UARCO Inc., 1955—; sales writer Chgo., 1955-57; sales rep. Tulsa, 1957-63, dist. sales mgr., 1963-65; dist. sales mgr. Kansas City, Mo., 1965-71; region sales mgr. Hartford, Conn., 1971-77, N.Y.C., 1977-81; v.p. sales Barrington, Ill., 1981-86, pres., chief operating officer, 1986—. Trustee coun. U. Rochester, N.Y., 1987—; bd. dirs. Internat. Bus. Forms Industries Inc., 1989—, Internat. Bus. Forms Industries Inc. Club: Meadow (Rolling Meadows, Ill.). Home: 424 S Garfield Hinsdale IL 60521 Office: UARCO Inc W County Line Rd Barrington IL 60010

MOSES, MICHAEL JAMES, insurance company executive; b. Roaring Spring, Pa., Apr. 13, 1956; s. William E. and Carol J. (Berkey) M.; m. Laura L. Bishop, June 7, 1980; 1 child, J'aime Lee. AS, Williamson Trade Sch. Salesman 84 Lumber, Cresson, Pa., 1977-78; area mgr. Nat. Home Life Ins. Co., Valley Forge, Pa., 1978-80; regional v.p. A.L. Williams Agy., Duluth, Ga., 1981—. Republican. Mem. Pentecostal Ch. Office: 1635 E Pleasant Valley Blvd Altoona PA 16602

MOSESON, DARRELL D., agricultural supply company executive; b. Howard, S.D., July 27, 1926; s. Gustav Leonard and Clara Amanda (Arneson) M.; children: Nancy, Joan. B.A. in Econs. cum laude, Augustana Coll., 1950. With Cenex (Farmers Union Central Exchange), St. Paul, 1951—; credit mgr. Cenex (Farmers Union Central Exchange), 1957-62, asst. gen. mgr., 1962-71, sr. v.p. fin., 1971-81, pres., 1981—; chmn. Central Bank for Coops, Denver. Bd. dirs. Luth. Social Service of Minn. Club: Athletic (St. Paul). Office: Farmers Union Cen Exch Inc 5500 Cenex Dr Inver Grove Heights MN 55075 *

MOSIER, FRANK EUGENE, oil company executive; b. Kersey, Pa., July 15, 1930; s. Clarence R. and Helen I. Mosier; m. Julia M. Fife, Sept. 2, 1961; children: Terry F., Patrick E., Kathleen R. BSCE, U. Pitts., 1953. With Standard Oil Co., Cleve., 1953—, mgr. planning and devel. mktg. and refining dept., 1968-71, v.p. supply and distbn., 1972-76, v.p. supply and transp., 1976-77, sr. v.p. mktg. and refining, 1977-78, sr. v.p. supply and transp., 1978-82, sr. v.p. downstream petroleum dept., 1982-85, exec. v.p., 1985-86, pres., chief. operating officer, 1986-88; also bd. dirs; with BP Am. Inc. (1987 merger of Brit. Petroleum and Standard Oil), Cleve., 1987—; pres. BP Am. Inc., Cleve., 1987-88, vice chmn., 1988—, also bd. dirs.; bd. dirs. Soc. Corp., Cleve., Centerior Energy Corp., Cleve. Trustee U. Pitts., John Carroll U., Cleve., Fairview Gen. Hosp., Cleve. With U.S. Army, 1953-55. Mem. Am. Inst. Chem. Engrs., Am. Petroleum Inst., Nat. Petroleum Refiners Assn., Cleve. Yachting Club, Mid-Day Club, Pepper Pike Country Club, Union Club, Westwood Country Club. Roman Catholic. Office: BP Am Inc 200 Public Sq Cleveland OH 44114

MOSKOWITZ, STANLEY ALAN, financial executive; b. N.Y.C., June 8, 1956; s. Sol and Kate (Mermelstein) M.; m. Eve Kronenberger, Sept. 20, 1981; 1 child, Alana. BA, Queens Coll., 1978; MBA in Fin., St. John's U., 1980. Sr. credit analyst Mfrs. Hanover Leasing Corp., N.Y.C., 1979-81; gen. ptnr. Exec. Leasing Co., N.Y.C., 1981-83; pres. Execulease Corp., Elmont, N.Y., 1983—. Mem. Ea. Assn. Equipment Lessors (chmn. pub. rels. 1985-90, bd. dirs. 1988—, Meretorious Svc. award 1986-87), Omicron Delta Epsilon. Republican. Jewish. Office: Execulease Corp 1975 Linden Blvd Elmont NY 11003

MOSLER, JOHN, retired business executive; b. N.Y.C., Sept. 24, 1922; s. Edwin H. and Irma M.; children: Bruce Elliot, John Edwin, Michele Andree. Student, Philips Exeter Acad., 1938-41, Princeton U., 1941-43; L.H.D., Fordham U., 1965; D.C.S., Duquesne U., 1968. With Mosler Safe Co., 1945-67, exec. v.p., 1948-61, pres., 1961-66, chmn., 1966-67; pres., dir. Mosler Lock Co., 1953-67, Mosler de Mexico S.A., 1953-67; exec. v.p., dir. Mosler Research Products, Inc., 1956-67; dir. 1st Caribbean Mainland Capital Co., Inc., 1962-68, chmn. bd., 1963-68, pres., 1966-68; v.p., dir. Am. Standard Inc., 1967-68; chmn. bd., dir., chief exec. officer Holmes Protection, Inc., 1966-73, Holmes Protection Services Corp., 1968-73; chmn. bd. Hidromex, S.A. de C.V., Mexico, 1968—, Mosler N.V., Europe, 1973—; chmn. bd. Internat. Controls Corp., 1973-87, resigned, 1987; past chmn. bd. Royal Bus. Funds Inc.; pres. Mosler Investments. Mem. Mayor's Com. on Judiciary; pres. Am.-Romanian Flood Relief Com.; dir., past pres. N.Y. Guild for Jewish Blind; past dir. Jr. Achievement N.Y.; spl. U.S. ambassador to, Mauritius; to Zambia's Independence ceremony; vice chmn. N.Y. Republican County Com.; trustee, dir. Nat. Urban League; trustee Appeal of Conscience Found.; hon. trustee, past pres. N.Y. Urban League; founder Harlem Prep. Sch.; trustee Linden Hall Sch. Served with CIC AUS, 1943-46. Decorated knight comdr. Ordo Supremus Militaris A. Lilio Regni Navarrae; Sovereign Order Hospitallers St. John of Jerusalem, Knights of Malta; comdt. L'Ordre Senegal; recipient Man of Conscience award Appeal of Conscience Found., 1969. Mem. Young Pres.' Orgn. (past pres.), U.S. C. of C., N.Y. World Bus. Council. Clubs: Bankers of Mexico (Mexico); Princeton; University (N.Y.); Confrerie des Chevaliers du Tastevin, Manhattan; Real Nautico de Barcelona (Spain); Sag Harbor Yacht.

MOSLEY, HENRY WAYNE, food products executive; b. Stephens County, Tex., Apr. 18, 1922; s. Garrett B. and Sarah (Gandy) M.; m. Evelyn Weaver, Sept. 1, 1946; children: Eva, Wayne Jr., Mark, Patrick. Student, Sul Ross State U., Alpine, Tex., 1945-47, Tex. Christian U., 1948. Br. mgr. Banner Dairies, Monahans, Tex., 1949-51; gen. plant mgr. Banner Dairies, Midland, Tex., 1951-53; dist. sales rep. Leaver Bros. Co., Midland, 1953-56; dist. sales mgr. Borden, Inc., Amarillo, Tex., 1956-67; gen. mgr. Borden, Inc., Abilene, Tex., 1967-69, Amarillo, 1969-72; dist. v.p. Borden, Inc., Houston, 1972-81, group v.p., 1981-85, pres. Dairy div., exec. v.p., chmn., 1985—; bd. dirs. Milk Industry Found., Washington, So. Dairy Assn., Raleigh, N.C., pres., 1984, Tex. Dairy Product Inst., Austin, Tex., 1975; mem. vis. com. Office for Info. Tech. Harvard U.; mem. adv. bd. Ctr. Intelligent Control Systems Brown U., Harvard U., MIT. Served as sgt. USMC, 1941-45, PTO. Republican. Baptist. Home: 11622 Normont Houston TX 77070 Office: Borden Inc 16855 Northchase Dr Houston TX 77060-6099

MOSLEY, I(VAN) SIGMUND, JR., computer software executive; b. Jasper, Ga., Sept. 15, 1946; s. Ivan Sigmund and Estelle (Kelley) M.; m. Diana Mosley (div. Jan. 1981); children: Anna Louise, Karen Elizabeth; m. Janet Gayle Barker, July 23, 1983; children: Mark Kent, Lisa Kelley. AA, Oxford Coll., 1966; BBA, Emory U., 1968. Staff acct. Peat, Marwick, Mitchell, Atlanta, 1968-69; staff acct. Mgmt. Sci. Am., Inc., Atlanta, 1969-72, treas., 1972-81, 82—, sec., 1972—, v.p., 1982—; sec./treas., dir. LAS Assocs., Inc. Mem. bd. visitors Emory U., 1986—. Recipient Campbell Acctg. medal Emory U., 1968. Mem. Fin. Execs. Inst., Nat. Credit Mgmt. Assn., Nat. Assn. Accts., Am. Soc. Corp. Secs., Nat. Assn. Treas., Emory Bus. Alumni Assn. (pres. exec. com. 1986-87). Democrat. Baptist. Avocations: college athletics, golf. Office: Mgmt Sci Am Inc 3445 Peachtree Rd NE Atlanta GA 30326

MOSLEY, JAMES NEWTON, financial executive; b. Texarkana, Ark., Oct. 12, 1934; s. James Marian and Nan Gray (Rester) M.; children: Timothy James, Jennifer Ann Mosley Comeau. BS in Math., St. Mary's Coll., Moraga, Calif., 1962; MBA, Santa Clara U., 1966. Supr. program engring. Lockheed Missiles & Space Co., Sunnyvale, Calif., 1962-66; gen. mgr. Western region CTC Computer Corp., Palo Alto, Calif., 1966-69; mktg. mgr. Western region Computer Synetics Inc., Santa Clara, Calif., 1969-72; Western region mgr. TLW Computer Industries Inc., San Jose, Calif., 1972-75; mgr. package leasing Memorex Corp., Santa Clara, 1975-78; mgr. fin. U.S. ops. Amdahl Corp., Sunnyvale, 1978—; bd. dirs. Credit Evaluation Service, San Jose. Editor/author Computer Forum, 1973-75. Served with USAF, 1953-57. Mem. Am. Assn. Equipment Lessors. Republican. Roman Catholic. Office: 2525 Gateway Pl Suite 161 San Jose CA 95110

MOSS, BARBARA BELLANTONI, sales representative; b. Norwalk, Conn., July 27, 1962; d. James Noel and Pauline Anne (Doria) Bellantoni; m. Tony Vernon Moss, Jan. 2, 1988. BS, U. Conn., 1984. Ops. mgr. Itex Total Office Systems, Stamford, Conn., 1984-85; tech. sales rep. health scis. div. Eastman Kodak Co., Atlanta, 1985—. Mem. Am. Soc. Nondestructive Testing, Delta Sigma Pi. Republican. Roman Catholic. Home: 3795 Churchill Dr Marietta GA 30064

MOSS, BILL RALPH, lawyer, publisher; b. Amarillo, Tex., Sept. 27, 1950; s. Ralph Voniver and Virginia May (Atkins) M.; m. Marsha Kelman, Mar. 2, 1985; 1 child, Brandon Price. BS with spl. honors, West Tex. State U., 1972, MA, 1974; JD, Baylor U., 1976; cert. regulatory studies program, Mich. State U., 1981. Bar: Tex. 1976, U.S. Dist. Ct. (no. dist.) 1976, U.S. Tax Ct. 1979, U.S. Ct. Appeals (5th cir.) 1983. Briefing atty. Ct. Appeals 7th Supreme Jud. Dist. Tex., Amarillo, 1976-77; assoc. Culton, Morgan, Britain & White, Amarillo, 1977-80; hearings examiner Pub. Utility Commn. Tex., Austin, 1981-83; asst. gen. counsel State Bar Tex., Austin, 1983-87; founder, owner Price & Co. Publs., Austin, 1987—; instr., lectr. West Tex. State U., Canyon, Ea. N.Mex. U., Portales, 1977-80. Active St. Michael's Epis. Ch. Mem. ABA, Tex. Bar Assn. (speaker profl. devel. programs 1983—), Nat. Orgn. Bar Counsel, Internat. Platform Assn., Alpha Chi, Lambda Chi Alpha, Omicron Delta Epsilon, Sigma Tau Delta, Pi Gamma Mu. Home and Office: 9903 Woodlake Cove Austin TX 78733

MOSS, BRUCE KEVIN, service executive; b. Rockville Centre, N.Y., July 21, 1958; s. Francis W. Jr. and Joan (Powell) M.; m. Lori Ann Carlson, June 7, 1980; 1 child, Lindsey. Student, Ashland Coll., 1976-77; AA, Cen. Piedmont Community Coll., 1979. Asst. gen. mgr. Ramada Inn Coliseum, Charlotte, N.C., 1977-80; gen. mgr. Ramada Inn Cen., Clearwater, Fla., 1980-82; room div. mgr. Airport Hilton, Tampa, Fla., 1982-83; dir. hotel ops. Innisbrook Resort, Tarpon Springs, Fla., 1983-85; v.p. hotel ops. Innisbrook Resort, Tarpon Springs, 1985—; Any additions not made are due to remaining consistent with Marquis style. youth motivator, tutor, Pinellas County Sch. System, Palm Harbor, Fla., 1985—; bd. dirs. Jr. Achievement of Pinellas County, Clearwater, 1987—, treas., 1988-89, pres. 1989—. Named Outstanding Vol. of Yr. Jr. Achievement 1988; recipient Spl. Events award Jr. Achievement, 1986, 88. Mem. Fla. Hotel and Motel Assn. (bd. dirs. 1987—), Am. Hotel and Motel Assn. Edn. Found. (cert.), C. of C. (bd. dirs. 1987—). Office: Innisbrook Resort US Hwy 19 Tarpon Springs FL 34689

MOSS, DAN, JR., stockbroker; b. Greensboro, N.C., Aug. 11, 1948; s. Dan and Caroline (Callaway) M.; m. Gail Summers, Sept. 11, 1976; 1 child, Morgan Callaway. BA, U. N.C., 1970. Mgr. Edison Bros. Stores, Syracuse, N.Y., 1970-72; acct. exec. duPont Walston, Atlanta, 1972-74; v.p. E.F. Hutton & Co., Atlanta, 1974-88, Prudential-Bache Securities, Atlanta, 1988—; adj. instr. Emory U., Atlanta, 1975—. Bd. dirs. Lady Tara Golf Classic, Atlanta, 1981-82. Mem. Internat. Assn. Fin. Planners (cert.), World Trade Club. Lodge: Rotary (local pres. 1981-82, pres. Atlanta Council of Club Pres. 1981-82). Home: 251 W Paces Ferry Rd NW Atlanta GA 30305 Office: Prudential Bache Securities Inc 4 Piedmont Ctr Suite 200 Atlanta GA 30305

MOSS, DEWEY LEE, textile company executive; b. Dalton, Ga., July 1, 1943; s. Denver D. and Lois (Wilson) M.; m. Charlotte A. Adams, May 22, 1968; children: Angela, Amy, Michael, Amanda. BS in Indsl. Mgmt., Ga. Inst. Tech., 1965. Staff cons. Kurt Salmon Assocs., Atlanta, 1968-72; assoc. v.p. mfg. Male Jeans, Atlanta, 1972-75; dir. ops. London Fog Sportswear, Atlanta, 1975-76; pres. D.L.M. & Assocs., Dalton, Ga., 1976-79, Gold Label Carpets, Dalton, 1979—. Served with U.S. Army, 1974-76. Lodges: KC (grand knight 1984-85), Elks. Home: 2217 Rocky Face Cir Dalton GA 30720 Office: Gold Label Carpets PO Box 3876 Dalton GA 30721

MOSS, MICHAEL, economist; b. N.Y.C., Feb. 6, 1943; s. Ed and Rose (Goldstein) M.; m. Sally Schneider, Dec. 12, 1984. Student, Miami Dade Coll., 1961-62, U. Miami, 1963-64. CLU. Div. mgr. Nat. Cash Register, Miami, Fla., 1964-69; asst. gen. agt. Mass Mutual Corp., Miami, 1969-74; mgr. Home Life Ins. Co. of N.Y., Coral Gables, Fla., 1974-80; pres. Moss Group, San Diego, 1982—; v.p. Physicians Planning Service, 1975-81. Author: Snow White Torpedo, 1980. Mem. Young Pres. of Mt. Sinai Hosp., Miami Beach, 1977-82, charter mem. Research Council Scripps Clinic and Research Found., La Jolla, Calif., 1985—, Balboa Park Mus. Art, San Diego, 1986—. Mem. Gen. Agts. and Mgrs. Assn. (pres. 1978-79, Nat. Mgmt. award 1976, 77, 78, Fla. State of Fla. Ram award 1979), Market Technicians Assn., San Diego Computer Soc., Soc. Investigation of Recurring Events, Cinema Soc. San Diego, The Duck Club, Optimist Club Internat. Clubs: Nat. F.M.C.A. (Calif.), Calif. chpt. F.M.C.A., Good Sam (Calif.). Lodges: Masons, Shriners, Order of the Nail (Brotherhood award 1981), Elks. Home: PO Box 90566 San Diego CA 92109

MOSS, RAYMOND LLOYD, lawyer; b. N.Y.C., Apr. 9, 1959. BA in Polit. Sci. cum laude, Bucknell U., 1981; JD, Hofstra U., 1984. Bar: Conn., N.Y., N.J. Atty. Dreyfus Corp., N.Y.C., 1984-85; corp. atty. Kramer, Levin, Nessen, Kamin & Frankel, N.Y.C., 1985-88, Glass, McCullough, Sherill & Harold, Atlanta, 1988—. Author column Conscience, 1983-84. Mem. ABA, N.Y. State Bar Assn., Assn. of Bar of City of N.Y., Ga. State Bar Assn., Phi Eta Sigma. Office: Glass McCullough Sherrill & Harold 1409 Peachtree St NE Atlanta GA 30338

MOSSAFER, SAM ALBERT, retired industrial psychologist; b. Seattle, Nov. 20, 1920; s. David and Serena (Peha) M. BA, U. Oreg., 1946; MA, U. Calif., 1952, PhD, 1955. Pres. Mossafer's of Seattle, 1955-72, Internat. Ltd., Tel Aviv, Israel, 1973-85, Technicom Corp., Bellevue, Wash., 1988—. Author: Golden 20, 1963. Bd. dirs. Overlake Sch., Redmond, Wash., 1965-67, Am. Friends Hebrew U., 1974-88; chmn. fund raising div. Jewish Community Ctr., Mercer Island, Wash., 1970-72; coach LIttle League Football; mem. Dem. Dist. Caucus, Bellevue, 1976-80. Sgt. U.S. Army, 1942-45. Mem. Nat. Med. Soc. (assoc.), Am. Friends of Hebrew U. (bd. dirs. 1974—, bd. dirs. N.W. chpt. 1980-88).

MOSSE, PETER JOHN CHARLES, precious metals company executive; b. Mtarfa, Malta, Sept. 8, 1947; came to U.S., 1977; s. John Herbert Charles and Barbara Haworth (Holden) M. BA, Oxford U., 1969; MBA, U. Pa., 1971, postgrad., 1977—. Bank officer N.M. Rothschild & Sons Ltd., London, 1971-76; spl. projects officer banking Bumiputra Mcht. Bankers Berhad, Kuala Lumpur, Malaysia, 1976-77; v.p., treas., sec. NMR Metals Incorp., N.Y.C., 1977-79, exec. v.p., 1979-83; sr. v.p. Rothschild Inc., N.Y.C., 1983—. Mem. The Gold Inst. (co. rep., bd. dirs. 1985—), The Silver Inst. (co. rep., bd. dirs. 1989—), The Newcomen Soc. U.S., The Copper Club, Soc. Mining Engrs., Can. Inst. Mining and Metallurgy, Prospectors and Developers Assn. Can., Commodity Exch., Inc. Episcopalian. Home: 353 E 72d St 33D New York NY 10021 Office: Rothschild Inc 1 Rockefeller Pla New York NY 10020

MOSSEY, JAMES WILLARD, hydraulics company executive; b. Takoma Pk., Md., Mar. 16, 1944; s. Therlow Willard and Hilda May (Crawford) Busiere M.; m. Pamela Joanne Heinrich, Nov. 25, 1972; children: Laura, Jeffrey, Katy. BS in Indsl. Mgmt., Purdue U., 1967; MBA, U. Notre Dame, 1969. Budget acct. Whirlpool Corp., St. Joseph, Mich., 1969-70; exec. v.p. IMC, Inc., Elkhart, Ind., 1970-77; gen. mgr., owner Elkhart Engring. Corp., 1977-82; gen. mgr. White Hydraulics, Inc., Hopkinsville, Ky., 1982—. Republican. Lutheran. Office: White Hydraulics Inc Bill Bryan Blvd Hopkinsville KY 42240

MOTAMEDI, AHMAD, lawyer; b. Esfahan, Iran, Feb. 6, 1943; s. Mohammad Hassan and Batool (Mazoochian) M.; divorced; 1 child, Setareh; married; 1 child, Salar. BA in Law and Criminology, Tehran (Iran) U., 1967, MA in Law, 1969. Sole practice law Tehran, 1967—; cons. various firms and govt. instns., 1972—; legal commentator Radio Tehran until 1979. Contbr. articles to newspapers, profl. jours. Mem. Internat. Lawyers Union, Internat. Lawyers Congress, Iranian Bar Assn. Moslem. Home: 10 Tir St, Mahmoodieh Ave Shemiran, Tehran Iran Office: 2/4 Pirooz, Bldg #270 Corner of, Mohtasham St and Vali Asr Ave, Tehran Iran

MOTE, JAMES CURTIS, managment consultant; b. San Francisco, May 15, 1945; s. James Emerson and Joan Louise (Apperson) M.; m. Sherrie Lee Jackson, Sept. 6, 1969 (div. Apr. 1971); m. Nancy Stammelback, Jan. 1, 1977. AB in Econs. and Math., Hamilton Coll., 1968; MBA in Acctg., Rutgers U., 1970. Anti-submarine warfare scientist Univac-Sperry Rand, Warminster, Pa., 1968-69; internat. fin. cons. Coopers & Lybrand, N.Y.C., 1970-73; asst. v.p., asst. internat. comptroller Marine Midland Bank, N.Y.C., 1973-75; v.p. taxes, comptroller, treas. Am. Express, N.Y.C., 1975-81; mng. dir., chmn. Grenoble Holdings Ltd., N.Y.C., 1981-87; pvt. cons. Glens Falls, N.Y., 1987—; prof. info. sci. Grad. Sch. Bus., Rutgers U., Newark, 1970-81; prof. computer sci. NYU, N.Y.C., 1977; bd. dirs. Best Pub., N.Y.C., Verflex Chems., Carlstadt, N.J. Contbr. papers to profl. lit. Mem. Intertel, Mensa, Trout Unltd. (nat. bd. dirs. 1983-84), Beta Gamma Sigma. Republican. Home: D-700 Warrensburg NY 12885

MOTLEY, JOHN PAUL, psychiatrist, consultant; b. Carbondale, Pa., July 5, 1927; s. Joseph Adrian and Lillian (McCormick) M.; B.S., Georgetown U., 1951; M.D., Hahnemann Med. Coll., Phila., 1955; m. Barbara Bennett Mitchell, Feb. 1, 1958; children—Marianne, Patricia, Kathleen, John Paul, Elizabeth, Joseph A. III, Grace, Michael. Intern, Hahnemann Med. Coll. Hosp., Phila., 1955-56; resident in psychiatry Inst. of Living, Hartford, Conn., 1956-59; practice medicine specializing in psychiatry, Point Pleasant, N.J., 1961—; mem. staff Jersey Shore Med. Center, 1961-72, chief of psychiatry, 1970-72; mem. staff Point Pleasant Hosp., 1961—, chief of psychiatry, 1961—; exec. v.p., cons. Key Edn. Co., Shrewsbury, N.J., 1981—; cons. Mutual of N.Y.; cons. in forensic psychiatry to various cts. and agys. Trustee

200 Club Monmouth, 1974—. Served with U.S. Army, 1944-46, ETO. Diplomate Am. Bd. Psychiatry and Neurology. Fellow Am. Psychiat. Assn. (pres.); mem. AMA, Royal Coll. Psychiatry, Am. Coll. Psychiatry, N.J. Psychiat. Assn. Clubs: Springlake Golf. Republican. Roman Catholic. Office: 3822 River Rd Point Pleasant NJ 08742

MOTLEY, SUSAN CALLIS, hotel executive; b. Danville, Va., Apr. 7, 1959; d. James Augustine and Mary Royal (Callis) M. BA in History, Coll. William and Mary, 1981. Mem. staff Williamsburg (Va.) Hospitality House, 1979-81; asst. buyer Garfinckel's, Washington, 1981-82; front office supr. Sheraton Washington Hotel, 1982-84; sales mgr. Radisson/Omni, Charlottesville, Va., 1984-86, Boar's Head Inn, Charlottesville, 1986-89; dir. sales and mktg. Sheraton Charlottesville, 1989—. Active Downtown Charlottesville Inc., 1984—; vol. Am. Diabetes Assn., 1987; standing chair publicity, bd. dirs. Four County Players, 1988—. Mem. Hotel Sales and Mktg. Assn. (chpt. bd. dirs. 1987—), Am. Soc. Assn. Execs., Hotel Sales and Mktg. Assn. Internat., Charlottesville/Albemarle Lodging Assn. (sec.-treas.), Greater Washington Soc. Assn. Execs., Charlottesville/Albemarle C. of C., Phi Mu. Presbyterian. Home: 511 N 1st St Charlottesville VA 22901 Office: Sheraton Charlottesville 2350 Seminole Trail Charlottesville VA 22901

MOTLUCK, MARK EDWARD, brokerage house executive; b. Evergreen Park, Ill., Mar. 8, 1957; s. William J. and Elizabeth B. (Chevalier) M.; m. Kelli Sutton, July 29, 1988. BA, Loyola U., Chgo., 1979; JD, U. Miami, 1985. CPA, Fla. Sr. tax acct. Arthur Andersen & Co., Chgo. and Miami, 1979-81; acct. Kwal & Oliva, Coral Gables, Fla., 1982; fin. planner Jannis & Assocs., Coral Gables, 1982-83; pvt. practice acctg. Miami, 1983-85; pres. Global Investor Securities Inc., Miami, 1985—; bd. dirs. Global Investor Securities, Inc., 1986—, Costa Rican Agrl. Inc., Miami, 1987—. Mem. Am. Inst. CPA's, Am. Arbitration Assn. (panel Arbitrators). Republican. Office: Global Investor Securities Inc 2730 SW Third Ave 5th Fl Miami FL 33129

MOTSETT, CHARLES BOURKE, sales and marketing executive; b. Peoria, Ill., Jan. 13, 1949; s. William James and Matilda (Robb) M.; m. Mary T. Werner, Aug. 26, 1972; children: Jon Bourke, Jill Suzanne, Brian Werner. BA in Polit. Sci., U. So. Fla., 1984. Parts and service sales rep. Caterpillar Ams. Co., Mexico City, 1976-79; product support rep. Caterpillar Tractor Co., Vancouver, B.C., Can., 1979-80; leadman remanufactured products Caterpillar Tractor Co., Peoria, Ill., 1981-84; mgr. parts and service sales Caterpillar Tractor Co., Jacksonville, Fla., 1984-85; v.p. sales and mktg. Multi Media Productions of Am., Inc., Jacksonville, 1985-86; v.p. sales and mktg. Consol. Indsl. Skills Corp., Jacksonville, 1987—, corp. officer, 1988—. V.p. Parent tchr. Orgn., Dunlap, Ill., 1981-82; vice chmn. St. Anthony's Ch., Vancouver, 1979-80; chmn. St. Jude Ch., Dunlap, 1982-83, Bishop Kenny High Sch. PTO Polit. Action Com., 1989. Capt. U.S. Army, 1967-70, Vietnam. Decorated Silver Star, Bronze Star with V device, Purple Heart, Air medal with V device., Combat Infantryman's Badge, Vietnemese Jump Wings. Mem. Soc. Automotive Engrs., Am. Soc. Naval Engrs., Soc. Naval Architects Marine Engrs., Propellor Club. Republican. Roman Catholic. Home: 4457 Barrington Oaks Dr Jacksonville FL 32217

MOTT, STEPHEN CRAIG, data processing executive; b. Lake Forest, Ill., July 7, 1949; s. Robert Francis and Frances Louise (Behrend) M.; m. Janie Lynette Saxer, May 25, 1983; 1 child, Kevin Saxer. BA in Journalism and Econs., U. Calif., 1974; MBA, Harvard U., 1979. Publisher, editor-in-chief Daily Californian, Berkeley, 1973-75; staff writer, intern Washington Post, 1975; bus. writer Dallas Times Herald, 1975-77; cons., intern Boston Consulting Group, 1978; engagement mgr. McKinsey & Co., N.Y.C., 1979-82; dir. strategic planning. McGraw-Hill, Inc., N.Y.C., 1982-84; v.p. sales & mktg. MCI Internat., Ryebrook, N.Y., 1984-87; pres. Cognitive Systems, Inc., New Haven, Conn., 1987—; also bd. dirs. Cognitive Systems, Inc.; pres. bd. Gecosys, S.A. Brussels, Belgium, 1987—. Bd. dirs. March of Dimes, 1980-83. Named White House fellow, 1984; Vol. of Yr. March of Dimes, N.Y., 1983. Home: 1386 Long Ridge Rd Stamford CT 06903 Office: Cognitive Systems 234 Church St New Haven CT 06510

MOTT, STEWART RAWLINGS, business executive, political activist; b. Flint, Mich., Dec. 4, 1937; s. Charles Stewart and Ruth (Rawlings) M.; m. Kappy Wells, Oct. 13, 1979. Grad., Deerfield (Mass.) Acad., 1955; B.S. in Bus. Adminstrn, Columbia, 1961, B.A. in Comparative Lit, 1961, postgrad. English lit., 1961-62. Exec. trainee various cos. 1956-63; English instr. Eastern Mich. U., 1963-64; corp. dir. U.S. Sugar Corp., Clewiston, Fla., 1965—; investor various diversified cos., 1968—; dir. Oram Group, Mott Enterprises. Pres., founder Spectemur Agendo, N.Y.C. and Flint, 1965—; bd. dirs. Fund For Peace, N.Y.C., 1967—, S.R. Mott Charitable Trust, 1965—, Nat. Com. for Effective Congress, N.Y.C., 1968—, Planned Parenthood Fedn. Am., 1964—, Am. Commn. on East-West Accord, 1977—, Citizens Research Found., 1977—, Ams. for Dem. Action, 1978—, Friends of Family Planning, 1979-84, Voters for Choice, 1979—; bd. dirs., founder Fund Constl. Govt., 1974—; chmn. Population Action Council, 1978-82. Mem. Phi Beta Kappa. Address: 515 Madison Ave New York NY 10022 *

MOTTEK, CARL T., hotel company executive; b. 1928. With Hilton Hotels Corp., 1951—, dir. food and beverage ops., from 1964, v.p., 1965-68, sr. v.p. food and beverage ops., 1968-73, sr. v.p. so. region, 1973-85, exec. v.p., also pres. div. Hilton Hotels, 1985—, also bd. dirs. Office: Hilton Hotels Corp 9336 Santa Monica Blvd Beverly Hills CA 90210 *

MOUCHLY-WEISS, HARRIET, public relations company executive; b. Bronx, N.Y., Aug. 12, 1940; d. Robert and Anita (Shawmut) Berg; m. Charles Weiss, Sept. 13, 1975; children—Noa, Joey. B.A., Muhlenberg Coll., 1960; M.A., Hebrew U., 1964. Clin. psychologist Hadassah Hosp., Israel, 1962-65; with Ruder Finn and Rotman Ptnrs., Washington, N.Y.C., 1968-86, chmn. 1980-86, sr. v.p. plans, N.Y.C., 1981-84, exec. v.p., 1984-86; pres. GCI Internat., N.Y.C., 1986—; bd. dirs. Sterling, London, Dialogic, Brussels, Chiappe-Bellodi, Rome and Milan, Greco, Paris, Ringpress, Frankfurt, Boetes, Holland. Fellow Am. Surbey Inst.; mem. Greater D.C. Bd. Trade, World Trade Council, Pub. Relations Soc. Am., Internat. Pub. Relations Assn., Com. 200. Office: GCI Internat 777 3rd Ave New York NY 10017 also: Ruder Finn & Rotman Internat Ptnrs 110 E 59th St New York NY 10022

MOULTON, HUGH GEOFFREY, lawyer, business executive; b. Boston, Sept. 18, 1933; s. Robert Selden and Florence (Bracq) M.; m. Catherine Anne Clark, Mar. 24, 1956; children: H. Geoffrey, Cynthia C. Moulton Bassett. B.A., Amherst Coll., 1955; LL.B., Yale U., 1958; postgrad. Advanced Mgmt. Program, Harvard U., 1984. Bar: Pa. 1959. Assoc. Montgomery, McCracken, Walker-Rhoads, Phila., 1958-66, ptnr., 1967-69; v.p., counsel Dolly Madison Industries, Inc., Phila., 1969-70; sec. Alco Standard Corp., Valley Forge, Pa., 1970-72, v.p. law, 1973-79, v.p., sec., gen. counsel, 1979-83, sr. v.p., gen. counsel, 1983—. Pres. Wissahickon Valley Watershed Assn., Ambler, Pa., 1975-78, treas., 1978—; mem. Area Council for Econ. Edn. (bd. dirs. 1985—). Mem. ABA, Phila. Bar Assn., Pa. Bar Assn., Am. Corp. Counsel Assn. (bd. dirs. Delaware Valley chpt. 1984-88, pres. 1986-87). Club: Sunnybrook Golf (Plymouth Meeting, Pa.). Home: 300 Williams Rd Fort Washington PA 19034 Office: Alco Standard Corp PO Box 834 Valley Forge PA 19482

MOULY, EILEEN LOUISE, financial planner; b. Milw., Apr. 18, 1955; d. George Joseph and Gertrude Mary (DuBois) M. BBA in Acctg. summa cum laude, U. Miami, Coral Gables, Fla., 1977, MBA, 1978. CPA, Fla. Acct. Main Hurdman, CPA's, Miami, Fla., 1979-82; Coopers & Lybrand, CPA's, West Palm Beach, Fla., 1982-83, Pannell Kerr Forster CPA's, Miami, 1983-84; cert. fin. planner Consortium Group, Miami, 1984-86; ptnr., fin. planner Evensky & Brown, Miami, 1986—; instr. U. Miami, 1987—, Fla. Internat. U., 1987—; speaker in field. Mem AICPA, Internat. Assn. Fin. Planning, Internat. Assn. Registered Fin. Planners, Inst. Cert. Fin. Planners (cert., v.p. greater Miami chpt. 1987, 88, 89), South Dade C. of C., Jaycees. Office: 14707 S Dixie Hwy Ste 207 Miami FL 33176

MOUNT, JOHN MEREDITH, chemical company executive; b. Dallas, Feb. 27, 1942; s. Almon Howard and Olive Laverne (Breedlove) M.; m. Rosemary Lynch, Nov. 11, 1967; children: John M. Jr., Mary E. BA, Colgate U., 1965; MBA, Xavier U., Cin., 1984. Mgr. mktg. DuBois Indsl., Cin., Amsterdam, 1972-73; sr. mgr. dist. sales DuBois Indsl., Columbia, S.C., 1974; regional mgr. sales DuBois Instnl. div., N.Y.C., 1975-78; v.p. DuBois Instnl. div., Huntington, Conn., 1979; sr. v.p., asst. dir. sales DuBois Instnl. div., Cin., 1979-82, exec. v.p., dir. instnl. sales, 1982-86, pres., 1986; pres. DuBois Co., Cin., 1986—; bd. dirs. Roto-Rooter, Inc., Cin., Omnicare, Nat. Sanitary Supply; bd. dirs., v.p. Chemed, Cin., 1986—. Bd. dirs. Nat. Sanitary Supply, 1988, Omnicare, 1988. Capt. USMC, 1967-72, Vietnam. Mem. Cin. Club, Queen City Club, Banker's Club. Home: 8250 Kroger Farm Ln Cincinnati OH 45243 Office: DuBois Chems Inc 1100 DuBois Tower Cincinnati OH 45202

MOUNTCASTLE, DANIEL JEFFERY, importer; b. Akron, Ohio, Oct. 19, 1949; s. Sidney H. and Alice Ruth (McRae) M.; m. Cindy K. Lookabaugh, June 9, 1971 (div. 1981). BA in Biology and English Lit., Wooster Coll., 1971; MD, Ohio State U., 1974. Clinician Mercy Hosp., Tiffin, Ohio, 1975-76; pres., clinician Jackson County Emergency Physicians, Jackson, Mich., 1976-80; clinician, instr. Tampa (Fla.) Gen. Hosp., 1980-83; cons. Saudi Arabian Nat. Guard, Riyahd, 1983-85; buyer Mountcastle Internat., Ltd., Laos and Burma, 1983-85; pres. Mountcastle Internat., Ltd., Washington and St. Petersburg, Fla., 1985—; cons. Afghan Textiles Devel., Peshawar, Pakistan, 1987—. Author numerous stories on travel. Med. dir. Internat. Rescue Com., Peshawar, 1987. Fellow Am. Coll. Emergency Medicine (Govt. Svc. award 1979). Home: 102 22d Ave Saint Petersburg FL 33706 Office: Mountcastle Internat Ltd 3222 M St NW Washington DC 20007

MOUNTCASTLE, KENNETH FRANKLIN, JR., stockbroker; b. Winston-Salem, N.C., Oct. 8, 1928; s. Kenneth Franklin and May M.; B.S. in Commerce, U. N.C., Chapel Hill, 1950; m. Mary Katharine Babcock, Sept. 1, 1951; children—Mary Babcock, Laura Lewis, Kenneth Franklin, Katharine Reynolds. With Mountcastle Knitting Co., Lexington, N.C., 1952-55, Reynolds & Co., N.Y.C., 1955-71; with Reynolds Securities Inc. (co. name changed to Dean Witter Reynolds 1978), N.Y.C., 1971—, sr. v.p., 1974—. Trustee, New Canaan (Conn.) Country Sch., 1962-68, Ethel Walker Sch., Simsbury, Conn., 1973-74; trustee Coro Found., 1980—, nat. chmn., 1986—; bd. dirs., past pres. Mary Reynolds Babcock Found., Winston-Salem, N.C.; bd. visitors U. N.C., Chapel Hill; bd. dirs. Inform, N.Y.C., Fresh Air Fund, N.Y.C., Sears-Roebuck Found. Served with U.S. Army, 1950-52. Republican. Presbyterian. Clubs: Country of New Canaan; Wee Burn Country (Darien, Conn.); Old Town (Winston-Salem, N.C.); Racquet and Tennis, City Midday, Bond, Stock Exchange Luncheon, Madison Sq. Garden (N.Y.C.). Home: 37 Oenoke Ln New Canaan CT 06840 Office: Dean Witter Reynolds 5 World Trade Ctr New York NY 10048

MOUNTCASTLE, THOMAS LAMAR, data processing executive; b. Baton Rouge, La., Sept. 26, 1953; s. Dean Lamar and Kathryn (Dobyns) M. AS, Va. Commonwealth U., 1974, BS, 1981. Fin. dir. Commonwealth Va., Richmond, 1974-81; planning officer The Computer Co., Richmond, 1981-82, head div. systems devel., 1982-83; dir. info. systems Richmond Meml. Hosp., 1984-86; exec. v.p., gen. mgr. Data Support Systems, Inc., 1987—; adj. prof. J. Sargent Reynolds Community Coll., Richmond, 1983-85; bus. cons. Martinique Sch. of Dance, Richmond, 1979-86. Chmn. bd. trustees Chesterfield Performing Arts Co., Richmond, 1983-87; pres. bd. dirs. Va. Alliance for Art, Chesterfield chpt., Richmond, 1985-87; bd. dirs. Va. State Alliance for the Arts, 1987—. Mem. Assn. Systems Mgmt. (pres. 1986-87, Achievement award 1983-84), Metro C. of C. (bus. support com. 1989—). Republican. Methodist. Home: 2771 Williamswood Rd Richmond VA 23235 Office: Data Support Systems 7318 Impala Dr Richmond VA 23228

MOURSUND, ALBERT WADEL, III, lawyer, rancher; b. Johnson City, Tex., May 23, 1919; s. Albert Wadel and Mary Frances (Stribling) M., Jr.; m. Mary Allen Moore, May 8, 1941; children: Will Stribling, Mary Moore Moursund DesChamps. LLB, U. Tex., 1941. Bar: Tex. 1941. Sole practice, Johnson City, 1946-63; mem. Moursund & Moursund Johnson City, Round Mountain and Llano, Tex., 1963-80; Moursund, Moursund, DesChamps & Moursund, 1980—; county judge Blanco County, Tex., 1953-59; chmn. bd. 1st Llano Bank 1963—, Arrowhead Co., Arrowhead West, Inc., Tex. Am. Moursund Corp., S.W. Moursund Corp., Ranchlander Corp., Cattleman's Nat. Bank, Round Mountain. Mem. Parks and Wildlife Commn., 1963-67, Tex. Ho. reps., 1948-52. Served with USAAF, 1942-46. Mem. ABA, Tex. Bar Assn., Hill County Bar Assn. (past pres.), Blanco County Hist. Soc. (charter), Masons, Woodmen of World. Home: Johnson City TX 78636 Office: Round Mountain TX 78663 Office: PO Box 1 Round Mountain TX 78663

MOUSA, MOUSTAFA WAFEY, business executive; b. Alexandria, Egypt, Feb. 27, 1947; s. Wafey Abdelrahman Mousa and Souad Awad Gamda. LL.B., Faculty of Law. Personel officer Egypt Transport, Alexandria, 1968-73; sole practice, Alexandria, 1974-77; legal counsel Arab Comml. C., Doha-Qatar, 1977-80; dir. personel Hamad Hosp., Doha-Qatar, 1980-82; human resources mgr. Dar Al Maal Al Islami, Geneva, 1982-84; v.p. Kamel Corp., Geneva, 1984—; bd. dirs. Arab Fin. Group, Panama, 1983—; mgmt. cons. Performance Mgmt., Geneva, 1982—. Mem. Egyptian Bar Assn., Mediterranean Congress Young Lawyers, Internat. Commn. Jurists (assoc., sponsor). Home: 52 Pre Gentil, 1242 Satigny Switzerland Office: Kamel Corp SA, PO Box 839, 1200 Geneva Switzerland

MOWELL, JOHN BYARD, investment management executive, high technology company executive; b. Washington, Pa., Oct. 21, 1934; s. Donald H. and Mabel V. (Burdick) M.; m. Sara Sandra Moore, June 15, 1957; children: John Byard Jr., Sarah Anne Mowell Reinhard. BS in Econs., U. Pa., 1956. Asst. v.p. Florindin Co., Tallahassee, 1960-62; ofcl. State of Fla., Tallahassee, 1962-65; owner, mgr. Mowell & Assocs., Tallahassee, 1965-75; v.p. so. ops. Carret & Co., Inc., N.Y.C., 1975-80; pres. Mowell Fin. Group Inc., Tallahassee, 1980—; chmn., chief exec. officer, bd. dirs. Reflectone, Inc., Tampa, Fla.; bd. dirs. Electromagnetic Scis., Inc., Atlanta, Capital City 1st Nat. Bank, Tallahassee. Bd. dirs. Boy Scouts Am., Tallahassee, 1973—; mem. Fla. Econ. Devel. Adv. Counc., 1986—. Comdr. USNR, 1956-60. Mem. Fla. Econs. Club (chmn. emeritus), Rotary. Republican. Methodist. Office: Mowell Fin Group Inc 407 E 6th Ave Tallahassee FL 32303

MOWERY, LYLE EUGENE, financial consultant; b. Fairbury, Ill., July 28, 1947; s. James Russell and Rosella May (Von Bergen) M.; div. Mar. 1979; children: Bret Alan, Leslie Gaye. BS in Bus., Eastern Ill. U., 1969. Sr. mgr. Price Waterhouse, Chgo., 1969-82; controller ednl. ops. Bell & Howell, Chgo., 1982-83; cons. Rath Packing Co., Waterloo, Iowa, 1983-84, chief fin. officer, 1984-85; fin. cons. Mowery Mgmt., Inc., Chgo., 1985-86; chief fin. officer Weinstein Internat. Corp., Mpls., Minn., 1986-88, R.W. Meats, Ltd., Bloomington, Minn., 1986-88; cons. Minn., 1988—. Mem. Am. Inst. CPA's, Ill. Soc. CPA's. Home: 2050 Ridge Dr unit 14 Minneapolis MN 55416 Office: R W Meats Ltd 5001 W 80th St Suite 865 Bloomington MN 55437

MOWREY, TIMOTHY JAMES, telecommunications executive; b. Lewiston, N.Y., Oct. 18, 1958; s. William Ronald and Joan (Cupp) M.; m. Karrie Rae Kaminske, Sept. 9, 1978; children: Christin R., Andrea M., Ryan T. BPS in Mgmt. and Data Processing, SUNY, Buffalo, 1982. Research technician Carborundum Co., Niagara Falls, N.Y., 1978-79; programmer KVS Info. Systems, Kenmore, N.Y., 1979-80; systems analyst Moore Bus. Forms Inc., Niagara Falls, 1980-83; telecommunications project coordinator Marine Midland Bank, N.A., Buffalo, 1983-85; pres., owner Micro-Tec, Niagara Falls, 1982-86; telecommunications specialist Electronic Data Systems, Lockport, N.Y., 1985-86; mng. cons. Computer Task Group Inc., Buffalo, 1986-88, mng. telecommunicatons cons., 1988—. Scholar N.Y. State Bd. of Regents, 1976. Mem. Soc. Mfg. Engrs. Democrat. Roman Catholic. Office: Computer Task Group Inc 800 Delaware Ave Buffalo NY 14209

MOWRY, JOHN L., lawyer; b. Baxter, Iowa, Dec. 15, 1905; s. William and Grace (Conn) M.; B.A., U. Iowa, 1929, J.D., 1930; student Ohio State U., 1926-27; m. Irene E. Lounsberry, June 7, 1941; 1 dau., Madelyn E. (Mrs. Stephen R. Irvine). Admitted to Ia. bar, 1930, N.Y. bar, 1945; spl. agt. F.B.I., 1930-34; mem. staff firm Thomas E. Dewey, N.Y.C., 1935-36; with U.S. Army Air Force, 1941-45; mem. exec. dept. N.Y. State, 1946; pvt. practice law, Marshalltown, Iowa, 1936-41, 47—; owner Evans Abstract Co., also G.M.K. Inc., Marshalltown, 1950—; county atty. Marshall County (Iowa), 1939-41; mayor City of Marshalltown, 1950-55. Mem. Iowa Ho. of Reps., 1956-68, majority floor leader, 1963-65; mem. Iowa Senate 1968-72; del. Republican Nat. Conv., Miami, Fla., 1972. Mem. Soc. Former Spl. Agts. FBI (nat. pres. 1945), Marshall County, Iowa bar assns., Iowa Pioneer Lawmakers Soc., Marshall County Hist. Soc., SAR. Republican. Presbyn. Mason (Shriner), Elk. Home: 503 W Main St Marshalltown IA 50158 Office: Evans Abstract Co 25 N Center St Marshalltown IA 50158

MOXLEY, JOHN HOWARD, III, physician; b. Elizabeth, N.J., Jan. 10, 1935; s. John Howard, Jr. and Cleopatra (Mundy) M.; m. Priscilla Lichty, Aug. 23, 1958; children: John Howard IV, Brook, Mark. BA, Williams Coll., 1957; MD, U. Colo., 1961; DSc (hon.), Sch. Medicine Hannemann U. Bar: Diplomate Am. Bd. Internal Medicine. Intern Peter Bent Brigham Hosp., Boston, 1961-62, resident in internal medicine, 1962-66; with Nat. Cancer Inst., USPHS, 1963-65; asst. to dean, instr. medicine Harvard Med. Sch., Boston, 1966-69; dean Sch. Medicine, U. Md., 1969-73; vice chancellor health scis., dean Med. Sch., U. Calif.-San Diego, 1973-79; asst. sec. for health affairs Dept. Def., Washington, 1979-81; sr. v.p. Am. Med. Internat., Beverly Hills, Calif., 1981-87; pres. MetaMed. Inc., Playa Del Rey, Calif., 1987-89; v.p., ptnr. Torn/Ferry Internat., L.A., 1989—; cons. FDA, NIH (HEW), Instl. Strategy Assos.; dir. Nat. Fund for Med. Edn., 1986—, Henry M. Jachson Found for Adv. Med. Assoc. Coun. on Sci. Affiliates, 1979-88. Contbr. articles to profl. jours. Dir. Polyclinic Health Svcs. Games of XXIII Olympiad. Recipient Gold and Silver award U. Colo. Med. Sch., 1974, award FDA, commr.'s citation for outstanding svc. to over-the-counter drug study, 1977, Dist. Service medal Dept. Def., 1980, Spl. Achievement citation Am. Hosp. Assn., 1983, Sec. of Def. medal for disting. pub. svc., 1981. Fellow ACP, Am. Coll. Physicians Execs.; mem. AMA (chmn. coun. sci. affairs 1985), Calif. Med. Assn. (chmn. sci. bd. 1978-83, councilor), San Diego C. of C., Nat. Acad. Scis. (Inst. of Medicine), Soc. Med. Adminstrs., Am. Hosp. Assn. (trustee 1979-81), Alpha Omega Alpha. Rotary. Office: Torn/Ferry Internat 1800 Century Pk E Ste 900 Los Angeles CA 90067

MOYER, BUDD CLIFTON, JR., publisher; b. Phillipsburg, Pa., Nov. 7, 1944; s. Budd Clifton Sr. and Helen (Klinger) M.; m. Judy McGraw, Aug. 19, 1965 (div. 1970); 1 child, Christina; m. Gale Arlene Gruver, June 11, 1973; children: Joelle, Budd III, Patricia. BA in Bus., U. N.C., 1968. Advt. salesman The Washington Post, 1968-73; nat. sales rep. Suffolk Life Papers, L.I., N.Y., 1973-77; advt. dir. The State News Daily, Dover, Del., 1977-79; advt. mgr. The Ariz. Pennysaver, Phoenix, 1979-80; assoc. pub., gen. mgr. Consumer News Publs., Inc., Cedar Falls, Iowa, 1980-87; lectr., sales trainer state, nat. pubs. groups, 1975—. Contbr. articles to nat. trade jours. V.p. membership Winnebago council Boy Scouts Am., Waterloo, Iowa, 1985-87; chmn. fund raising Cedar Falls area Am. Cancer Soc., 1986. Mem. Shoppers Guides Iowa, Ind. Free Papers Am., Internat. Assn. Printing House Craftsmen, Am. Advt. Club Fedn., Cedar Falls C. of C. (various coms. 1980—), Waterloo C. of C. (bd. dirs. 1985-87), U.S. Chess Fedn. (nat. rating). Methodist. Clubs: Craftsman, Advt./Mktg. (Waterloo). Lodge: Rotary. Home: 621 E Bennett Ave Glendora CA 91740 Office: Azusa Harold Newspaper 234 E Foothill Blvd Azusa CA 91702

MOYER, ERNEST HOWARD, electronics executive; b. Jacksonville, Fla., Nov. 13, 1947; s. John Paul and Faustina (White) M.; m. Paula Jayne Waites, Apr. 4, 1970; children: Meredith Sayres, Megan Elizabeth. AA, North Fla. Jr. Coll., Madison, 1969; BBA, Fla. State U., 1972; postgrad., U. Fla., 1985—. Sr. v.p. Atlantic Banks Fla., Gainesville, 1972-78; v.p., founder Health Physics Systems, Inc., Gainesville, 1978-84; pres. Quadrex-HPS, Inc., Gainesville, 1984-87; v.p., founder Gen. Imaging Corp., Gainesville, 1987—; ptnr. Davis-Moyer Ventures, Gainesville; co-founder GAIN Innovation Network, Gainesville, 1985; bd. dirs. Digital Services Corp., Gainesville, Exit Information Guide, Inc., Gainesville, Citrex Tech., Inc., Gainesville. Contbr. articles to profl. jours. Bd. dirs. United Way of Alachua County, 1977-81; v.p. Gainesville C. of C., 1979; chmn. Gainesville Housing Bd., 1976. Served to cpl. USMC, 1967-69, Vietnam. Mem. Am. Mgmt. Assn., Am. Engring. Assn., Am. Nuclear Soc., Am. Banking Assn., Soc. Profl. Imaging in Electronics. Republican. Episcopalian. Club: Quarterback. Home: 5332 NW 9th Ln Gainesville FL 32605 Office: Gen Imaging Corp 901 NW 8th Ave Gainesville FL 32606

MOYER, JERRY MILLS, financial services company executive; b. Oklahoma City, Mar. 19, 1940; s. Charles and Dorothy Moyer; m. Cecilia L. Clark, Aug. 28, 1960; children: Jerry, James. BS, Okla. State U., 1962. Salesman Jamco, Inc., 1965, Procter & Gamble, 1966; from salesman to credit mgr. B.F. Goodrich Co., 1967-71; with UCC-Communications Systems, Inc., Dallas, 1971-73; mgr. funds control Dr. Pepper Co., Dallas, 1973-80; pres. Cash Cons., Inc., Dallas, 1985—; v.p. InterFirst Services Corp., Houston, 1981-85; v.p. fin. Med. Acceptance Corp., Houston, 1986; pres. Cash Cons. Co., 1986-87; internat. treas. Yemen Hunt Oil Co., 1987—. Contbr. articles to profl. jours. Active United Fund, InterFirst Polit. Action Com. Served with U.S. Army, 1962-65. Decorated Air medal (26), Purple Heart; various profl. awards. Mem. Tex. Cash Mgmt. Assn. (founder, past pres.), Nat. Corp. Cash Mgmt. Assn. (co-founder). Baptist. Lodges: Masons, Shriners, Lions.

MOYER, R. CHARLES, finance educator, consultant; b. Reading, Pa., July 11, 1945; s. Ralph Charles and Jane Anne (Huls) M.; m. Sally Louise Prizer, May 19, 1973; children: Laura Prizer, Craig Prizer. BA in Econs., Howard U., 1967; MBA, U. Pitts., 1968, PhD in Fin., 1971. Asst. prof. fin. U. Houston, 1971-76; fin. economist U.S. Maritime Adminstrn., Washington, 1973-74; assoc. prof. Lehigh U., Bethlehem, Pa., 1976-77; from assoc. prof. to prof. U. N.Mex., Albuquerque, 1977-80; prof., chmn. fin. dept. Tex. Tech U., Lubbock, 1980-87; Integon prof. fin., Babcock Grad. Sch. Wake Forest U., Winston-Salem, N.C., 1988—; pres., founder R.O.E. Cons. Group, Lubbock, 1978; cons. Pub. Svc. Co. N.Mex., 1978—, KN Energy, Denver, 1979—, Gas Co. N.Mex., 1985—, San Diego Gas Electric Co., 1986—; bd. dirs. Inst. Banking Fin. Studies, 1982-86. Author: Contemporary Financial Management, 1989, Managerial Economics, (5th edit.), 1989, Financial Management with Lotus 1-2-3, 1986; contbr. numerous articles to profl. jours. Vice-chmn. Lubbock Gen. Hosp. Found., 1985-88. Capt. U.S. Army, 1969-71. Fed. Res. Bank Cleve. fellow, 1970-71. Mem. Fin. Mgmt. Assn. (bd. dirs., ombudsman 1980-87, v.p. 1988—), Am. Fin. Assn., Am. Econs. Assn., Eastern Fin. Assn., Western Fin. Assn., Phi Beta Kappa, Beta Gamma Sigma. Club: West Tex. Running, Bermuda Run Country, Twin City Track. Office: Wake Forest U Babcock Grad Sch 7659 Reynolda Sta Winston-Salem NC 27109

MOYLAN, JOHN JOSEPH, science administrator; b. Toledo, Sept. 18, 1956; s. James John and Janet (Marilyn) M.; m. Margaret Singley, June 28, 1980; 1 child, Kristin. BS in Chemistry, Bowling Green State U., 1977; MBA, U. So. Calif., 1981. V.p. Delsen Testing Labs., Glendale, Calif., 1980—; bd. dirs. Electronic Component Cert. Bd., Washington. Mem. Am. Chem. Soc., Soc. Advanced Materials and Process Engring. Office: Delsen Testing Labs 1024 Grand Central Ave Glendale CA 91201

MOYLE, BENNETT ISAAC, computer company executive, consultant; b. Columbus, Ohio, Mar. 24, 1946; s. Bennett Oliver and Mary Alice (Lawler) M. BA, U. Minn., 1968. Systems programmer Fed. Reserve Bank, Mpls., 1968-78; owner, mgr. B.I. Moyle Assocs., Inc., Mpls., 1978—. Mem. Minn. DOS Users Group (pres. 1970-72), Ind. Computer Cons. Assn. (dir. 1981-84, 87-88), Am. Arbitration Assn. (arbitrator 1987—). Contbr. articles to profl. jours.

MOYNAHAN, JOHN DANIEL, JR., insurance executive; b. Chgo., Dec. 10, 1935; s. John Daniel and Helen (Hurley) M.; m. Virginia Thomas, Oct. 10, 1959; children: Laura, Mark, Tricia, Kate. B.A. cum laude, U. Notre Dame, 1957. With Met. Life Ins. Co., N.Y.C., 1957—; regional v.p. Met. Life Ins. Co., from 1971, with nat. div. group nat. accounts, 1979-80, sr. v.p. group life and health ops., 1980-86, exec. v.p., 1986—. Office: Met Life Ins Co 1 Madison Ave New York NY 10010

MOYNIHAN, JONATHAN PATRICK, management consultant; b. Cambridge, Eng., June 21, 1948; came to U.S., 1976; s. Noel and Margaret Mary (Lovelace) M.; m. Patricia Mary Underwood, Dec. 20, 1980; 1 stepchild, Vivecca. BA in Philosophy and Psychology, Oxford U., 1970, MA in Philosophy and Psychology, 1971; MS in Stats., London U., 1974; MS in Fin., MIT, 1977. Field adminstr. Save the Children Fund, India, Bangladesh, 1971-72; product mgr. Roche Products, London, 1972-75; cons. McKinsey & Co., Amsterdam, 1977-79; v.p. Strategic Planning Assocs., Washington, 1979-82; mng. v.p. First Manhattan Cons. Group, N.Y.C.,

1982—; bd dirs. Computer Entry Systems, Silver Spring, Md. Mem. Downtown Athletic Club (N.Y.C.), Marylebone Cricket Club (London). Office: First Manhattan Cons Group 90 Park Ave New York NY 10016

MOZZOCHI, DEANNA JEAN, interior designer, business owner; b. North Platte, Nebr., Sept. 30, 1938; d. Francis Whitford and Nancy Elizabeth (Hale) Donnell; m. Michael Joseph Mozzochi, Jr., Sept. 8, 1962; children: Susan Elizabeth, Michael Jospeh III. BA, U. Nebr., 1960; A in Fine Arts, Cotley Coll., 1958; cert. interior design, Paier Coll. Art, 1977. Owner DM Interiors, Clinton, Conn., 1978—. Mem. Am. Assn. Interior Designers (assoc.), Fed. Garden Clubs Conn., Inc., Arbor Garden Club (pres. 1985-88). Home and Office: 16 Shore Rd Clinton CT 06413

MRACKY, RONALD SYDNEY, management consultant; b. Sydney, Australia, Oct. 22, 1932; came to U.s., 1947, naturalized, 1957; s. Joseph and Anna (Janousek) M.; student English Inst., Prague, Czechoslovakia, 1943-47; grad. Parsons Sch. Design, N.Y.C., 1950-53; postgrad. NYU, 1952-53; m. Sylvia Frommer, Jan. 1, 1960; children: Enid Hillevi, Jason Adam. Designer D. Deskey Assocs., N.Y.C., 1953-54; art dir., designer ABC-TV, Hollywood, Calif., 1956-57; creative dir. Neal Advt. Assocs., Los Angeles, 1957-59; pres. Richter & Mracky Design Assocs., Los Angeles, 1959-68; pres., chief exec. officer Richter & Mracky-Bates div. Ted Bates & Co., Los Angeles, 1968-73, pres., chief exec. officer Regency Fin., Internat. Fin. Services, Beverly Hills, Calif., 1974-76; sr. ptnr. Sylron Internat., Los Angeles, 1973—; mgmt. dir. for N.Am. Standard Advt.-Tokyo, Los Angeles, 1978—; chief. exec. officer Standard/Worldwide Cons. Group, Los Angeles and Tokyo, 1981—; cons. in field; exec. dir. Inst. for Internat. Studies and Devel., Los Angeles, 1976-77. Bd. dirs. Dubnoff Ctr. for Child Devel. and Ednl. Therapy, Los Angeles, John Wayne Cancer Clinic/UCLA; bd. dirs., chmn. exec. com. Calif. Chamber Symphony Soc., Los Angeles. Served with U.S. Army, 1954-56. Mem. Am. Mktg. Assn., Los Angeles Publicity Club (com. mem.), Toluca Lake C. of C. Contbr. articles to profl. jours. Recipient nat. and internat. awards design and mktg. Office: 3855 Lankershim Blvd Universal City CA 91604

MRAZEK, KIRK WILLIAM, accountant; b. LaGrange, Ill., Oct. 6, 1956; s. Franklin Charles and Hazel Janet (Maylone) M.; m. Kathleen Ann Brija, July 28, 1979; children: Adam, Brandon. BS in Acctg. and Fin., U. Ill., Chgo., 1979; postgrad., Lewis U. CPA, Ill. Staff acct. Portec Inc., Oak Brook, Ill., 1979-80; staff acct. Evans Food Products Inc., Chgo., 1980-83, sr. staff acct., 1980-85; comptroller Tasty Food Found., Bensenville, Ill., 1985-88; acct. Caldwell, Coren & Co., Downers Grove, Ill., 1988—. Home: 14455 Stately Oaks Cir Lockport IL 60441

MROCZKA, EDWARD JOSEPH, utility company executive; b. Middletown, Conn., Nov. 16, 1940; s. Joseph John and Helen Catherin (Augustyn) M.; m. Frances Monica Pianka, June 22, 1963; children: Matthew, David. B in Chem. Engring., Rensselaer Poly. Inst., 1962, M in Nuclear Sci., 1965; M in Mech. Engring., Rensselaer Poly. U., 1967; MBA, U. New Haven, 1985. Sr. engr. Conn. Advanced Nuclear Engring. Lab., Middletown, Conn., 1962-65, Pratt and Whitney Aircraft Co., East Hartford, Conn., 1965-67; results engr. Middletown Generating Sta., Hartford Electric Light Co., 1967-68; tech. asst. to plant supt. Conn. Yankee Atomic Power Co., Haddam Neck, Conn., 1968-74; sr. engr. Northeast Utilities Svc. Co., Berlin, Conn., 1974-77, nuclear ops. engr., 1976-77, v.p. nuclear ops., 1985-86, sr. v.p. nuclear engring. and ops., 1986—; sta. services supt. Millstone Nuclear Power Sta., Waterford, Conn., 1977-80, sta. supt., 1980-85; bd. dirs. Conn. Light and Power Co., Western Mass. Electric Co., Holyoke Water Power Co., Conn. Yankee Atomic Power Co., Berlin. Mem. adv. coun. Ret. Sr. Vol. Program, Middletown, 1986—; bd. dirs. Newington Childrens Hosp., 1988—. Mem. Electric Power Research Inst. (advisor 1986-88), Inst. Nuclear Power Ops. (advisor 1987-88), Nuclear Utility Mgmt. and Resources Com., Sr. Nuclear Plant Mgmt. Tng. Program (mentor 1987-88), Electric Council New Eng. (advisor 1988—), Tau Beta Pi. Clubs: Hartford Surf Fishing; R.I. Mobile Sports Fishing, Mass. Beach Buggy Assn. Office: NE Utilities PO Box 270 Hartford CT 06141-0270

MRUK, EUGENE ROBERT, marketing professional, urban planner; b. Buffalo, Sept. 12, 1927; s. Stanley and Lucy Ann (Wolanski) M.; m. Florence Helen Guzy, Apr. 15, 1950; children: Linda, Lawrence, Edith, Ginny. AA in Engring., U. Buffalo, 1966, BA in Sociology, 1970, MA in Econs., 1974. Asst. dir. planning City of Buffalo, 1958-70; commr. planning Erie County, N.Y., Buffalo, 1970-74; dir. socioecon. studies Ecology and Environment, Inc., Buffalo, 1974-79, dir. transp. system studies, 1979-81, dir. bus. devel., 1981-86, v.p. sales and mktg., 1986—; pvt. practice planning cons. Buffalo area, 1950-64. Author various mcpl. govt. plans. Coordinator Econ. Devel. Program, Buffalo, 1966; exam. cons. Civil Service Commn. City of Buffalo, 1974; grand marshal Gen. Pulaski Parade com., Buffalo, 1972. Named Man of Yr. in Govt. Am-Pole Eagle newspaper, 1970. Mem. Am. Assn. Cert. Planners, Am. Planning Assn. Democrat. Roman Catholic. Home: 3 Dennis Ln Cheektowaga NY 14227 Office: Ecology and Environment Inc Buffalo Corp Ctr 368 Pleasantview Dr Lancaster NY 14086

MUCCI, ROBERT A., portfolio manager; b. Lexington, Ky., May 30, 1959; m. Billie Lee Mucci, June 19, 1982. BA in Fin., Transylvania U., 1981. Portfolio mgr. Ky. Cen. Life Ins. Co., Lexington, 1981—. Mem. Fin. Analysts Soc. Republican. Office: Ky Cen Life Ins Co Kincaid Towers Lexington KY 40507

MUCCIA, JOSEPH WILLIAM, lawyer; b. N.Y.C., May 31, 1948; s. Joseph Anthony and Charlotte (Mohring) M.; m. Margaret M. Reynolds, June 29, 1985. B.A. magna cum laude, Fordham U., 1970, J.D., 1973. Bar: N.Y. 1974, U.S. Dist. Ct. (so. dist.) N.Y. 1974, U.S. Dist. Ct. (ea. dist.) N.Y. 1980, U.S. Ct. Appeals (2d cir.) 1974, U.S. Ct. Appeals (D.C. cir.) 1980, U.S. Supreme Ct. 1980. Assoc. Cahill Gordon & Reindel, N.Y.C., 1973-82; ptnr. Corbin Silverman & Sanseverino, N.Y.C., 1983—. Assoc. editor Fordham Law Rev., 1972-73. Mem. ABA (litigation sect.), N.Y. County Lawyers Assn., Fed. Bar Council, Phi Beta Kappa, Pi Sigma Alpha. Office: Corbin Silverman & Sanseverino 805 3d Ave New York NY 10022

MUCCIANO, STEPHANIE LYONS, hospitality, travel, and tourism executive; b. Pitts., Jan. 8; d. Ross Cooper and Catherine Dorothy (Perrone) Lyons; m. Richard Francis Mucciano, Apr. 17, 1963 (dec. 1972); 1 child, Stephanie Lynn. Student St. Petersburg Jr. Coll., 1963-64, Alamogordo Bus. Coll., 1970-71. Sales mgr. Bahama Cruise Line, Tampa, Fla., 1978-82; dir. mktg./sales AAA Holidays/St. Petersburg Motor Club, Fla., 1982-84; dir. mktg./sales Travel and Tourism Resources, Inc., St. Petersburg, 1986, prin., pres., 1986—; dir. mktg./sales Island Harbor Resort, Cape Haze, Fla., 1984-86; mgr. Hotel Radisson-Pan-Am. Ocean Hotel, Miami Beach, Fla., 1987—; mktg. cons., bd. dirs., adv. bd. Travel Marketplace, Royal Fiesta Cruises, Clearwater; seminar leader, internat. industry speaker. Mem. Fla. Gulf Coast Symphony Guild, St. Petersburg, 1975—, All Childrens Hosp. Guild, 1975—, Infinity League to Aid Abused Children, 1981—, Pinellas Assn. for Retarded Adults, 1975—, St. Petersburg Internat. Folk Fair Soc.; pres. Tampa Bay Mag., 1982, Pinellas County Leaders Move Recipient Cert. of Recognition, George Greer County Commr., Pinellas, 1986. Mem. Internat. Platform Assn., Pacific Area Travel Assn. (dir.), Sun Coast Travel Industry Assn., Sales & Mktg. Execs. Internat., Travel & Tourism Research Assn., C. of C., Women Execs. in Travel, Fla. Assn. Sales Execs., Hotel Sales and Mktg. Assn., Nat. Assn. Female Execs., Fla. Women's Network, Am. Soc. Travel Agts., Am. Mktg. Assn. Republican. Clubs: Italian-Am.; St. Petersburg Internat. Folk Fair Soc.; S.K.A.L. Avocations: reading, volunteer work. Office: Radisson Pan Am Ocean Hotel 17875 Collins Ave Miami Beach FL 33160

MUCHNICK, STEVEN STANLEY, computer scientist; b. Cambridge, Mass., Dec. 1, 1945; s. Samuel Yaver and Dorothy Helen (Kasdan) M.; m. Nancy Ann Kaplan, June 9, 1968 (div. 1972). AB in Math. with high honors, U. Mich., 1967, AM in Math., 1969; PhD in Computer Sci., Cornell U., 1974. Asst. prof. computer sci. U. Kans., Lawrence, 1974-77, assoc. prof., 1977-81; researcher Hewlett-Packard Labs., Palo Alto, Calif., 1981-83; mgr. programming langs. Sun Microsystems, Mountain View, Calif., 1984-87; disting. engr. Sun Microsystems, Mountain View, 1986—; vis. assoc. prof. U. Calif., Berkeley, 1979-81; vis. lectr. U. Aarhus (Denmark), 1977, 80; cons. IBM Rsch. Lab., San Jose, Calif., 1980. Author: Tempo: Unified Treatment of Binding Times, 1978; author, editor: Program Flow Analysis, 1981; contbr. articles to profl. jours.; patentee in field. Pres., sec. Golden Gate Performing Arts, San Francisco, 1982-83; sec., treas. Homeowners Assn., San Francisco, 1986-87. Rsch. grantee U. Kans., 1974-77, rsch. grantee NSF, 1977-80. Mem. Assn. Computing Machinery (chmn. spl. interest group on programming langs. 1985-87, chmn. 1987—), IEEE Computer Soc., Phi Beta Kappa, Sigma Xi, Phi Kappa Phi. Office: Sun Microsystems Inc 2550 Garcia Ave Mountain View CA 94043

MUCK, GEORGE ARTHUR, food products executive; b. Filmore, Ill., Sept. 28, 1937; s. George O. and Edna M. (Funderburk) M.; m. E. Joanne Inness, June 6, 1959; children: Jane, Dale, Nancy, Lori, Lynn. BS, U. Ill., 1959, MS, 1961, PhD, 1962. With research dept. Dean Foods Co., Rockford, Ill., 1962-67; dir. research Dean Foods Co., Rockford, 1967-70, v.p. research and devel., 1970—. Contbr. articles to profl. jours. Patentee in field. Mem. Am. Dairy Sci. Assn. (pres. 1978-81), Am. Cultured Dairy Products Assn. (pres. 1976). Office: Dean Foods Co 1126 Kilburn Ave Rockford IL 61103

MUCKENFUSS, CANTWELL FAULKNER, III, lawyer; b. Montgomery, Ala., Apr. 25, 1945; s. Cantwell F. and Dorothy (Dauphine) M.; m. A. Angela Lancaster, June 25, 1978; children: Alice Paran Lancaster, Cantwell F. IV. BA, Vanderbilt U., 1967; JD, Yale U., 1971. Bar: N.Y. 1973, D.C. 1976. Law clk. to presiding justice U.S. Ct. Appeals (6th cir.), 1971-72; atty., project developer Bedford Stuyvesant D and S Corp., Bklyn., 1972-73; spl. asst. to the dir. FDIC, Washington, 1974-77, counsel to the chmn., 1977-78; sr. dep. comptroller for policy Office of the Comptroller of the Currency, Washington, 1978-81; ptnr. Gibson, Dunn & Crutcher, Washington, 1981—; mem. editorial adv. bd. Issues in Bank Regulation, Rolling Meadows, Ill., 1977—; mem. bd. advisors Rev. Fin. Regulation, N.Y.C., 1985—; bd. dirs. Fair Tax Edn. Fund, Washington, 1987—. Served with USNG, 1968-70, USAR, 1970-74. Recipient Spl. Achievement award U.S. Dept. Treasury, 1979, Presdl. Rank award U.S. Govt., 1980. Mem. ABA, Fed. Bar Assn. Democrat. Episcopalian. Clubs: Kenwood Country (Bethesda, Md.); Yale (N.Y.C.). Office: Gibson Dunn & Crutcher 1050 Connecticut Ave NW Suite 900 Washington DC 20036 also: Gibson Dunn & Crutcher 200 Park Ave New York NY 10166-0193

MUDD, JOHN PHILIP, lawyer, real estate executive; b. Washington, Aug. 22, 1932; s. Thomas Paul and Frances Mary (Finotti) M.; m. Barbara Eve Sweeney, Aug. 10, 1957; children: Laura, Ellen, Philip, Clare, David. B.S.S., Georgetown U., 1954; J.D., Georgetown Law Center, 1956. Bar: Md. bar 1956, D.C. bar 1963, Fla. bar 1964, Calif. bar 1973. Individual practice law Upper Marlboro, Md., 1956-66; v.p., sec., gen. counsel Deltona Corp., Miami, Fla., 1966-72; sec. Nat. Community Builders, San Diego, 1972-73; gen. counsel Continental Advisers (adviser to Continental Mortgage Investors), 1973-75, sr. v.p., gen. counsel, 1975-80; sr. v.p., gen. counsel Am. Hosp. Mgmt. Corp., Miami, 1980—; pres. Tropic Devel. Corp., 1979—. Former mem. Land Devel. Adv. Com. N.Y. State; chmn student interview com. Georgetown U.; bd. dirs. Lasalle High Sch., Miami; bd. dirs., corporate counsel Com. of Dade County, Fla. Mem. ABA, Fla. Bar Assn., Calif. Bar Assn., Md. Bar Assn., D.C. Bar Assn., Fla. State Bar (exec. com. of corp. counsel com. 1978—). Democrat. Roman Catholic. Home: 1211 Hardee Rd Coral Gables FL 33146 Office: Am Hosp Mgmt Corp 9405 NW 41st St Miami FL 33178

MUDRY, MICHAEL, pension and benefit consultant; b. Lucina, Czechoslovakia, Dec. 5, 1926; (parents Am. citizens); s. John Zaleta and Helen (Molchan) M.; m. Kendall Archer, June 17, 1960; children: F. Goodrich Archer, Benjamin Kendall. BA, U. Conn., 1951. Sr. v.p. Hay/Huggins Co. Inc., Phila., 1956—; actuary Ch. Pensions Conf. Active Com. Gift Annuities, N.Y.C., 1978—. With U.S. Army, 1945-46. Fellow Soc. Actuaries, Conf. Actuaries Pub. Practice; mem. Am. Acad. Actuaries, Internat. Actuarial Assn., Internat. Assn. Cons. Actuaries, Union League Club. Democrat. Home: 749 Mancill Rd Wayne PA 19087 Office: Hay/Huggins Co Inc 229 S 18th St Philadelphia PA 19103

MUEHL, RICHARD ALOYSIUS, financial analyst; b. Faulkton, S.D., Nov. 25, 1948; s. Aloysius Peter and Verna Lois (Davis) M.; m. Diane Ruth Deiter, Apr. 2, 1971 (div. 1976); children: Damon Richard, Andrea Diane; m. Nora Jane Hedstrom, Oct. 14, 1980; 1 child, Miranda Irene. BA, Adams State Coll., 1971. Acct. State of S.D., Pierre, 1971-73; cost acct. Simonsen Mfg. Co., Quimby, Iowa, 1973-77; office mgr. Procon Inc., Chgo., 1977-83; cons. Eilers Constrn. Co., Aberdeen, S.D., 1984-85; acct. Behavioral Health Services, Inc., Yuma, Ariz., 1985-87, fin. analyst, 1988—. Pres. Quimby Booster Club, 1976; coach boys' baseball, Quimby, 1974-75; treas. Big Bros./Big Sisters Yuma, 1988. Republican. Roman Catholic. Office: Behavioral Health Svcs Inc 1073 W 23d St Yuma AZ 85364

MUEHLBAUER, JAMES HERMAN, manufacturing company executive; b. Evansville, Ind., Nov. 13, 1940; s. Herman Joseph and Anna Louise (Overfield) M.; m. Mary Kay Koch, June 26, 1965; children: Stacey, Brad, Glen, Beth, Katy. BSME, Purdue U., 1963, MS in Indsl. Adminstrn., 1964. Registered profl. engr., Ind. Engr. George Koch Sons Inc., Evansville, 1966-67, chief estimator, 1968-72, chief engr., 1973-74, v.p., 1975-81, exec. v.p., 1982—, also bd. dirs.; v.p. Gibbs Die Casting Corp., Henderson, Ky., 1979—, also bd. dirs.; v.p., bd. dirs. Nat. Sealants and Adhesives Inc., Evansville, Ind., 1984—, Uniseal Rubber Products Inc., St. Louis, 1985—; bd. dirs. Citizens Realty and Ins. Co., Evansville, Union Fed. Savs. Bank, Evansville, Red Spot Paint & Varnish Co., Brake Supply Co., Evansville. Author: (with others) Tool and Manufacturing Engineering Handbook, 1976; patentee in field. Past pres., past bd. dirs. Southwest Ind. Easter Seal Soc., 1970-76; bd. dirs., past pres. Evansville Indsl. Found., 1980—, United Way SW Ind. 1988—; bd. dirs. U. So. Ind. Found., 1983—, Deaconess Hosp., Evansville, 1986—; mem. Met. Evansville Devel. Council, 1983-88. Lt. U.S. Army, 1964-66, Vietnam. Recipient Tech. Achievement award Tri-State Council for Sci. and Engring., 1984. Mem. ASME, NSPE, Soc. Mfg. Engrs. (nat. chmn. finishing and coating tech. div., 1971-73), Ind. Soc. Profl. Engrs. (Engr. of Yr. Southwest Ind. chpt., 1983), Evansville Country Club, Evansville Petroleum Club, Evansville Kennel Club. Republican. Roman Catholic. Home: 2300 E Gum St Evansville IN 47714 Office: George Koch Sons Inc 10 S 11th Ave Evansville IN 47744

MUELLER, CHARLES WILLIAM, utility company executive; b. Belleville, Ill., Nov. 29, 1938; s. Charles A. and Clara R. (Jorn) M.; m. Janet Therese Vernier, Oct. 19, 1939; children: Charles R., Michael G., Craig J. BEE, St. Louis U., 1961, MBA, 1966. Registered profl. engr., Mo., Ill. Engr. Union Electric Co., St. Louis, 1961-75, supervisory engr., 1975-77, asst. dir. corp. planning, 1977-78, treas., 1978-83, v.p. fin., 1983-88, sr. v.p. adminstrv. services, 1988—; bd. dirs. Canterbury Enterprises, Inc., Belleville, Union Colliery Co., St. Louis. Mem. IEEE, Soc. Fin. Analysts (assoc.), Fin. Execs. Inst., St. Clair Country Club, Mo. Athletic Club, Oak Hill Tennis Club. Office: Union Electric Co 1901 Gratiot St Saint Louis MO 63103

MUELLER, DONALD DEAN, meat packing executive; b. Columbus, Nebr., Sept. 12, 1937; s. Emil J. and Hulda M. (Cattau) M.; m. JoAnn Ferris, Aug. 17, 1963; children: Bradford Paul, Bartley Brandon. Student U. Nebr., 1956-58, 62-63; BBA, U. Denver, 1965. CPA, Colo. Acct., Ernst & Ernst, Denver, 1965-69; treas. Monfort of Colo., Greeley, 1969-72, v.p. fin. services, 1979-81, group v.p. fin. services and lamb ops., 1982—; v.p. fin. Spencer Foods, Iowa, 1972-79; group v.p. fin. Swift Ind. Packing Co., Greeley, 1987—; bd. dirs. 1st Nat. Bank Greeley. Bd. dirs. Econ. Devel. Action Partnership, Greeley, Weld County, 1984—, pvt. industry council, Greeley, 1985—. Mem. Nat. Assn. Accts., Am. Inst. CPA's, Colo. Soc. CPA's. Republican. Lutheran. Club: Greeley Country. Avocations: church activities, singing, sports. Office: Monfort of Colo Inc PO Box G Greeley CO 80632

MUELLER, PAUL HENRY, corporate director, banker; b. N.Y.C., June 24, 1917; s. Paul Herbert and Helen (Cantwell) M.; m. Jean Bonnel Vreeland, Sept. 10, 1949; 1 child, Donald Vreeland. B.S., NYU, 1940; A.B., Princeton U., 1941; Litt.D. (hon.), Heriot-Watt U., Edinburgh, Scotland. Page Citibank N.A., 1934; on leave 1939-46, asst. cashier, 1947-52, asst. v.p., 1952-58, v.p., 1958-65, sr. v.p., 1965-74, chmn. credit policy com., 1974-82; chmn. bd. Saab-Scania Am. Inc., 1982—; dir. Atlas Copco AB, Stockholm, 1982—; Skandinaviska Enskilda Banken, N.Y.C., 1983—; entered U.S. Fgn. Service, served in Panama, Cairo, Washington, 1941-43; asst. adminstrv. sec. UN Monetary and Fin. Conf., Bretton Woods, N.H., 1944; divisional asst. Dept. State, 1946; sec. West Indian Conf., 2d session, St. Thomas, V.I., 1946; vis. lectr. U. Va., 1980—; founding chmn., sr. fellow Center Internat. Banking Studies. Contbg. author: Offshore Lending by U.S. Commercial Banks, 1975, Bank Credit, 1981, Classics in Commercial Bank Lending, 1981, Vol. II, 1985; author: (with Leif H. Olsen) Credit and the Business Cycle, 1978, Learning from Lending, 1979, Credit Doctrine for Lending Officers, 1976, 81, Credit Endpapers, 1982, Perspective on Credit Risk, 1988. Trustee Bloomfield Coll., N.J., 1983—, vice chmn., 1987-88, chmn. 1988—; treas. Marcus Wallenberg Found., 1984—. Served from 2d lt. to capt. USMCR, 1944-45. Recipient Alumni award Grad. Sch. Credit and Fin. Mgmt., Dartmouth Coll., Disting. Service award Robert Morris Assocs.; decorated Royal Order Polar Star (Sweden). Mem. Bankers Assn. Fgn. Trade (hon., v.p. 1976), Pilgrims, SAR, Beta Gamma Sigma. Republican. Presbyterian. Club: University (N.Y.C.). Home: 75 Rotary Dr Summit NJ 07901 Office: Saab-Scania Am Inc Saab Dr Orange CT 06477

MUELLER, ROY CLEMENT, graphic arts company and direct mail executive; b. Weehawken, N.J., Aug. 15, 1930; s. Adam and Bertha (Le Blanc) M.; m. Patricia Robinson, Sept. 3, 1970; children: Eric, Janet, Deborah, Gregory. Student Rochester Inst. Tech., 1976. Mgr. estimating/billing dept. Editors Press, Hyattsville, Md., 1962-66; v.p., gen. mgr. Peninsula Press div. A.S. Abell Corp., Salisbury, Md., 1967-70; owner, mgr. Crown Decal & Display, Co., Bristol, Tenn., 1972—; pres. chief exec. officer Bristol Screen, Inc., 1977—, Southmark div., 1985—; v.p., gen. mgr. Venture One, Bristol, 1988—. Recipient Ad award Tri-City Advt. Fedn., 1975. Mem. Screen Printing Assn. (internat. exhbn. award 1977), Printing Industry Am., Mail Advt. Service Assn., Internat., Am. Philatelic Soc., Rotary. Republican. Lutheran. Office: 200 Delaware Ave Bristol TN 37620

MUGFORD, ALFRED GEORGE, machine company executive; b. Everett, Mass., Sept. 7, 1928; s. James and Emmie (Boone) M.; m. Martha Black, Nov. 25, 1983; children—Holly Anne Montgomery Nye, Edward du Mee Montgomery, III; children by previous marriage—Janet Anne Sprague, Nancy Anne, George Edward. B.S., Bentley Coll., 1950. With Jerguson Gage & Valve Co., Burlington, Mass., 1947-64; controller Jerguson Gage & Valve Co., 1963-64; treas., controller Sarco Co., Inc., Allentown, Pa., 1964-66; v.p. finance Whitin Machine Works, Whitinsville, Mass., 1966-68; v.p., gen. mgr. Whitin Machine Works, 1967-68, corp. staff, 1968; with White Consol. Industries, Cleve., 1963-87; v.p., corp. staff, group v.p. White Consol. Industries, 1969-76, exec. v.p., 1976-84, sr. exec. v.p., 1984-87; cons. to mfg. industry Bay Village, Ohio, 1987—; v.p., bd. dirs. Alpha Assocs., Inc., Mpls. Chmn. Burlington Finance Bd., 1958-62, New Bldg. and Capital Fund Raising Com., 1960-63. Mem. Burlington Jr. C. of C. (charter mem., v.p. 1956-58), MAPI. Presbyterian (chmn. bd. trustees 1961-63). Clubs: Avon Oaks Country (fin. com. 1974-75, trustee, pres. 1977-78, bd. dirs. 1986—), Duquesne, Lions. Home and Office: 30529 Ednil Dr Bay Village OH 44140

MÜHLANGER, ERICH, ski company executive; b. Liezen, Austria, Aug. 26, 1941; came to U.S., 1971, naturalized, 1975; s. Alois and Maria (Stückelschweiger) M.; m. Gilda V. Oliver, July 13, 1973; 1 child, Erich. Assoc. Engring., Murau Berufsschule Spl. Trade, Austria, 1959; student Inst. Tech. and Engring., Weiler Im Allgau, Germany, 1963-65. Salesman, Olin Ski Co. (Olin-Authier), Switzerland, 1965-67, mem. mktg. dept., 1967-69, service and mfg., 1969-71, quality control insp., Middletown, Conn., 1971-77, supr., 1977-78, gen. foreman, 1978-83, process control mgr., 1983-88; dir. mfg. Entech Corp., 1988—. Charter mem. Presdl. Task Force, trustee; preferred mem. of U.S. Senatorial Club. Served to cpl. Austrian Air Force, 1959-60. Mem. Screenprinting Assn. Am., Am. Mgmt. Assn. Roman Catholic. Club: Mgmt. Home: 13 Clemens Ct Rocky Hill CT 06067 Office: 475 Smith St Simsbury CT 06457

MUHLENBRUCH, CARL W., civil engineer; b. Decatur, Ill., Nov. 21, 1915; s. Carl William and Clara (Theobald) M.; m. Agnes M. Kringel, Nov. 22, 1939; children: Phyllis Elaine (Mrs. Richard B. Wallace), Joan Carol (Mrs. Frederick B. Wenk). BCE, U. Ill., 1937, CE, 1945; MCE, Carnegie Inst. Tech., 1943. Research engineer Aluminum Research Labs., Pitts., 1937-39; cons. engring. 1939-50; mem. faculty Carnegie Inst. Tech., 1939-48; assoc. prof. civil engring. Northwestern U., 1948-54; pres. TEC-SEARCH, Inc. (formerly Ednl. and Tech. Consultants Inc.), 1954-67, chmn. bd., 1967—; Pres. Profl. Centers Bldg. Corp., 1961-77. Author: Experimental Mechanics and Properties of Materials; Contbr. articles engring. publs. Treas., bd. dirs. Concordia Coll. Found.; dir. Mo. Lutheran Synod, 1965-77, vice chmn. 1977-79. Recipient Stanford E. Thompson award, 1945. Mem. Am. Econ. Devel. Council (certified indsl. developer), Am. Soc. Engring. Edn. (editor Educational Aids in Engring.), Nat. Soc. Profl. Engrs., ASCE, Sigma Xi, Tau Beta Phi, Omicron Delta Kappa. Club: University (Evanston). Lodge: Rotary (dist. gov. 1980-81, mem. service projects Ghana and the Bahamas). Office: Tec-Search Inc 1000 Skokie Blvd Wilmette IL 60091

MUI, JIMMY, architect; b. Hong Kong, Sept. 1, 1958; came to U.S., 1971; s. Yuk-on and Kum-Ngor (Yuen) M. BArch, SUNY, Buffalo, 1982, postgrad., 1982-84. Architecture aide City of N.Y. Dept. of Health, 1978; architect, drafter Bradley Corp. Park, Blauvelt, N.Y., 1984-85; asst. architect City of N.Y. Dept. of Housing Preservation and Devel., 1985-87, N.Y.C. Bd. Edn., 1987—. Chmn., bd. dirs. Hong Kong Students Assn. of N.Y. Inc., 1987—, pres. 1986. Recipient N.Y. State Regent Scholarship award, 1977-81, Husted Edward Scholarship award SUNY, 1980. Roman Catholic. Home: 2237 Haviland Ave Bronx NY 10462 Office: NYC BD Edn Div Sch Bldgs 28-11 Queens Plaza N 4th Floor Long Island City NY 11101

MUINO, PHILIP, employee benefits insurance company executive; b. Staten Island, N.Y., Mar. 12, 1955; s. Philip and Barbara Mary (Winkworth) M. BBA, U. South Fla., 1979. Benefit analyst Met. Life Ins. Co., Tampa, Fla., 1979-81; sr. benefit analyst Employee Benefit Svcs., Tampa, Fla., 1981-83; mgr. employee benefit accounts Poe Risk Mgmt. Svcs., Tampa, Fla., 1983-85; v.p., cons. employee benefits Neil L. Bates and Assocs., St. Petersburg, Fla., 1985-88; dir. tech. svcs. Sterling Investors Life Ins. Co., St. Petersburg, Fla., 1988—. Served with USMC, 1973-75. Mem. Nat. Assn. Health Underwriters, Nat. Assn. Life Underwriters, Fla. West Coast Employee Benefits Coun., Self Insured Institute of Am. Republican. Roman Catholic. Home: 6425 Moss Way Tampa FL 33625 Office: Sterling Investors Life Ins Co 150 2d Ave N Saint Petersburg FL 33701

MUIR, BONNIE ANN, management consultant, educator; b. Watertown, N.Y., May 30, 1959; d. Randall Gregor and Elizabeth Augusta (Cuck) M.; m. Greg Jon Welsh, June 28, 1985. BA in Polit. Sci., Am. U., 1982, MS in Tech. Mgmt., 1986. Warehouse mgr. R.G. Muir Distbrs. Inc., Syracuse, N.Y., 1977-79; asst. dir. Georgetown U., Washington, 1979-80; law librarian Pension Benefit Guarantee Corp., Washington, 1980-82; program specialist Am. U., Washington, 1984-87, program mgr., 1984-87, adj. faculty, 1987—; sr. prin. The Oasis Group Inc., Fairfax, Va., 1985—, also bd. dir.s; project & program mgr. ERC Internat., Fairfax, 1987—. Mem. AAUW, Data Processing Mgmt. Assn., Soc. Applied Learning Tech., Higher Edn. Group Washington, D.C. Coll. Personnel Assn., ACLU, LWV. Home: 12622 Glenbrooke Woods Dr Herndon VA 22071-2127 Office: ERC Internat 1725 Jefferson Davis Hwy Ste 300 Arlington VA 22202

MUIR, GLENN PATRICK, high technology venture executive; b. Southbridge, Mass., Feb. 17, 1959; s. William Lawrence and Gabriel Estelle (Audette) M. BBA, U. Mass., 1981; MBA, Harvard U., 1986. CPA, Mass. With Arthur Anderson & Co., Boston, 1981-84; investment assoc. David L. Babson & Co., Boston, 1985; v.p. fin. Mettallon Engineered Materials Corp., Pawtucket, R.I., 1986-88; chief fin. officer, contr. Hologic, Inc., Waltham, Mass., 1988—. Mem. Am. Inst. CPA's, Mass. Soc. CPA's, Beta Alpha Psi. Home: 438 Purgatory Rd Apt E Newport RI 02840 Office: Hologic Inc 200 Prospect St Waltham MA 02158

MUIR, JOHN CARL, investment advisor, securities broker; b. Washington, Mo., Nov. 14, 1954; s. Fred and Muriel Jane (Ringling) M.; m. Teresa Anne Larkin, Aug. 6, 1977; 1 child, John Robert. Student, East Cen. Jr. Coll., 1973-74; BA, Drury Coll., 1977. Mgr. terr. Hyland Diagnostics Inc., Costa Mesa, Calif., 1977-78; cons. U.S. Surgical Corp. Norwalk, Conn., 1978-81; rep. Edward D. Jones & Co., Morris, Ill., 1981-82; br. mgr. Edward D. Jones & Co., Mayfield, Ky., 1982-85; pres. John C. Muir & Co. Fin. Svcs.,

Mayfield, 1985—. Elder 1st Presbyn. Ch., Mayfield, 1986; chmn. drive United Way Mayfield-Graves County, 1985, v.p. bd. dirs., 1984; chmn. bd. dirs. Mayfield-Graves County Sr. Citizens Inc., 1987—. Mem. Internat. Assn. for Fin. Planning, NRA. Office: 316 N 7th St Mayfield KY 42066

MUIR, PAUL MURRAY, trade show producer; b. Glasgow, Scotland, July 4, 1952; came to U.S., 1982; s. Matthew Wilson and Margaret (Murray) M.; m. Linda Marie Hanson, Nov. 28, 1987. BS in Acctg., Glasgow U., 1973. Chartered acct. Watson & Galbraith C.A., Glasgow, 1974-76; exhbn. dir. Reed Exhbns., London, 1976-82; gen. mgr. Convs. and Exhbns., Inc., N.Y.C., 1982-83; dir. project mgmt. The Interface Group, Boston, 1983-87; pres. Nat. Expositions Co., N.Y.C., 1987—. Mem. Nat. Assn. Exhbn. Mgrs. Home: 270 Bronxville Rd Apt A71 Bronxville NY 10708 Office: Nat Expositions Co Inc 15 W 39th St New York NY 10018

MUIRHEAD, ROBERT LLOYD, engineering and gas supply company executive; b. Bartlesville, Okla., Nov. 22, 1924; s. Brian Robert and Ruth (Aller) M.; m. Donna Muirhead, Apr. 27, 1951; children—Jane, Brian, Adair. B.S., Kans. State U., 1949. Registered profl. engr., La. Jr. and asst. engr. Tex. Eastern Transp., 1949-53, engr., rate engr., 1954-65; rate engr. SW Gas Corp., Las Vegas, 1965-73, v.p. rates, 1973-82, sr. v.p. engrng. and gas supply, 1982—. Served to 1st lt. USAF, 1942-46, 51-52, Korea. Republican. Methodist. Office: SW Gas Corp 5241 Spring Mountain Rd Las Vegas NV 89102

MUJICA, MAURO E., architect; b. Antofagasta, Chile, Apr. 20, 1941; came to U.S., 1965, naturalized, 1970; s. Mauro Raul and Graciela (Parodi-Blayfus) M.; m. Barbara Louise Kaminar, Dec. 26, 1966; children: Lillian Louise, Mariana Ximena, Mauro Eduardo Ignacio III. MArch, Columbia U., 1971. Head designer Columbia U. Office Archtl. Planning, N.Y.C., 1966-71; project mgr. Walker, Sander, Ford & Kerr, Architects, Princeton, N.J., 1971-72; prin. Mauro E. Mujica, Architect, N.Y.C., 1972-74; dir. internat. div. Greenhorne & O'Mara, Inc., Riverdale, Md., 1974-78; partner Mujica & Reddy Architects, Washington, 1978-80; prin. Mauro E. Mujica, Architect, Washington, 1980-81; partner Mujica & Berlin Investment Bankers, Washington, 1982-85, Mujica Keppie Henderson Internat., Washington and Glasgow, Scotland, 1981-83, Mujica-Seifert Architects, Washington and London, 1983-87; pres., chief exec. officer The Pace Group, Washington, 1987—. Prin. works include: Tennis Clubhouse, Columbia U., Nat. Hosp., Puerto Barrios, Guatemala, Plaza Hotel interiors, La Paz, Bolivia. Fellow Inst. Dirs. (London); mem. AIA, Columbia U. Archtl. Alumni Assn. Republican. Home: 8807 Fox Hills Tr Potomac MD 20854 Office: The Pace Group 8807 Gallows Rd Dunn Loring VA 22027

MUKA, BETTY LORAINE OAKES, lawyer; b. McAlester, Okla., Jan. 30, 1929; d. Herbert La Fern and Loraine Lillian (Coppedge) Oakes; m. Arthur Allen Muka, Sept. 6, 1952; children: Diane Loraine, Stephen Arthur, Christopher Herbert, Martha Ann, Deborah Susan. Student Monticello Coll., 1946-47; BS, Okla. U., 1950; MS, Cornell U., 1953, MBA, 1970; JD, Syracuse U. 1980. Bar: R.I. 1983, U.S. Dist. Ct. R.I. 1984. Mgr. dining room Anna Maude's Cafeteria, Oklahoma City, 1950-51; faculty dining room mgr. V.P.I., Blacksburg, Va., 1955-56; owner, mgr. The Cottage Restaurant, 1959-60; lectr., lab. instr. foods and organic chemistry Cornell U., 1961; owner, mgr. student housing, 1965-68; jr. acct. Maxfield, Randolph & Carpenter, CPA's, Ithaca, N.Y., 1970-71; income tax cons. H & R Block, Ithaca, 1971-73; atty. pro se, 1972—; hostess-bookkeeper Holiday Inn, Ithaca, 1972-73; salesperson Investors Diversified Services, Ithaca, 1972-73, NASD, 1973; agt. Inventory Control Co., 1975-78; law clk. 1978-79; sole practice, Providence, 1983-85; lectr. in fin. Tompkins Cortland Community Coll. Leader various youth groups, Ithaca, 1964-71. Mem. ABA, N.Y. State Bar Assn., R.I. Bar Assn., R.I. Trial Lawyer's Assn., Assn. Trial Lawyers Am., Mortar Bd., Delta Delta Delta Alumnae (pres. 1974), Phi Delta Phi (bd. dirs. 1980, J. Mark McCarthy award 1980), Sigma Delta Epsilon. Club: Toastmasters. Home and Office: 113 Kay St Ithaca NY 14850

MULARZ, THEODORE LEONARD, architect; b. Chgo., Nov. 6, 1933; s. Stanley A. and Frances (Baycar) M.; m. Ruth L. Larson, Nov. 9, 1963; children: Anne Catherine, Mark Andrew. BArch, U. Ill., 1959. Registered architect Colo., Calif., Utah, Ariz. Assoc., Fredric A. Benedict architect, Aspen, Colo., 1959-63; prin. Theodore L. Mularz, AIA Architects, Aspen, 1963-77; v.p. Benedict-Mularz Assocs. Inc., 1978-81; prin. Theodore L. Mularz & Assocs., Aspen, 1981—. Designer numerous archtl. projects including commercial, indsl., religious, recreational, residential and historic restoration. Active, Music Assocs. of Aspen Fund Drive, 1969-80; vice-chmn. Pitkin County Bd. Appeals, 1972—, City of Aspen Bd. Appeals, 1985—; City of Aspen Planning/Building Dept. adv. com., 1988—; dir. search. com. City of Aspen, Pitkin County, 1989; del. Colo. Democratic Conv., 1972, Colo. Dem. Assembly, 1974; mem. Colo. Bd. Examiners of Architects, 1975-85, pres., 1976-80, v.p., 1978. Served with USCGR, 1953-55. Fellow AIA; mem. Nat. Council Archtl. Registration Bds. (profl. conduct com. 1977-78, procedures and documents com. 1978-82, chmn. edn. com. 1982-83, chmn. procedures and documents com. 1983-84, dir. 1982-84, pres. 1985-86, internat. rels. com. 1984-89, exec. com. 1984-87, mem. interprofl. council on registration 1984-85, pres., 1985, internat. oral exam. com. 1984-89), Colo. Soc. Architects (Community Service award 1975), Aspen Architects Collaborative (chmn. 1973-74), Aspen C. of C. (past dir., past pres., past v.p.), Aspen Hist. Soc. (com. chmn. 1963-64). Roman Catholic. Home: PO Box 166 Aspen CO 81612 Office: Theodore L Mularz & Assocs 406 H Pacific Ave Aspen CO 81611

MULÉ, ANTHONY VINCENT, transportation company executive; b. N.Y.C., July 6, 1943; s. Charles and Constance (Cascio) M.; m. Terri Carter, July 14, 1984; children: Melissa E., Michael A., Matthew C. B in Indsl. Engring., NYU, 1972; D (hon.), Pepperdine U., 1985. Dir. indsl. engring. Am. Airlines, N.Y.C., 1972-77; gen. mgr. Chgo. Am. Airlines, 1977-81; v.p. western div. Am. Airlines, L.A., 1981-85; v.p. southwestern div. Am. Airlines, Dallas/Ft. Worth, 1985-88; sr. v.p. field svcs. and svcs. planning Pan Am. Wold Airways, N.Y.C., 1988—. With USN, 1965-69. Office: Pan Am World Airways Inc 200 Park Ave New York NY 10166

MULFORD, DONALD LEWIS, publisher; b. Montclair, N.J., Apr. 22, 1918; s. Vincent S. and Madeleine (Day) M.; A.B., Princeton, 1940; m. Frances Root, Aug. 9, 1940 (div. Apr. 1954); children—Marcia M., Sally E., Sandra D. (dec.); m. 2d, Josephine M. Abbott Davisson, Apr. 23, 1954 (dec. Mar. 1956); stepchildren—Lee, Joanne, Sue; m. 3d, Emily L. Enbysk, Dec. 29, 1958. With Montclair Times Co., 1940—, exec. v.p., 1950—, asso. pub., 1956-71, pres., co-pub., 1971-79, pres., pub., 1979—; pres., pub. Verona-Cedar Grove Times, 1979—. Mem. N.J. Press Assn. (pres. 1980-81, chmn. bd. 1981-82), Phi Beta Kappa. Rotarian. Clubs: Princeton, Montclair Golf; Nat. Press (Washington); Nassau (Princeton, N.J.). Home: 260 Highland Ave Upper Montclair NJ 07043 Office: 114 Valley Rd Montclair NJ 07042

MULFORD, RAND PERRY, business executive; b. Denver, Sept. 30, 1943; s. Roger Wayne and Ann Louise (Perry) M. B.S.E. cum laude, Princeton U., 1965; M.B.A. with highest distinction (Baker scholar), Harvard U., 1972. Mgmt. cons. McKinsey & Co., Chgo., 1972-80; v.p. planning and control Plastics and Chem. Spltys. Group, Occidental Chem. Co./Occidental Petroleum Inc., Houston, 1980-82; pres. Technivest, Inc., 1982-85; exec. dir. corp. Planning Merck & Co., Inc., 1986-88; dir. Corp. Devel. Marrow Tech., Inc.; dir. Quest Med. Inc., Carrollton, Tex.; adv. bd. L. Karp & Sons, Elk Grove Village, Ill. Served with USN, 1965-70. Club: Princeton (N.Y.C.). Home: 387 Park Slope Mountainside NJ 07092 Office: Marrow-Tech Inc 100 Grass Lands Rd Elmsford NY 10523

MULLALLY, PIERCE HARRY, steel company executive; b. Cleve., Oct. 6, 1918; s. Pierce Harry and Laura (Lynch) M.; student U. Western Ont., 1935; B.S., John Carroll U., 1939; M.D., St. Louis U., 1943; m. Mary Eileen Murphy, Feb. 22, 1943; children—Mary Kathleen, Pierce Harry. Intern, St. Vincent Charity Hosp., Cleve., 1943, resident in surgery, 1944, 47-50, staff surgeon, 1951-62, head peripheral vascular surgery, 1963-76, dir. med. edn., 1967-73, dir. dept. surgery, 1968-75, trustee, 1977-86 ; plant physician Republic Steel Corp., Cleve., 1952-68, med. dir., 1968-76, corp. dir. occupational medicine, 1976-84; cons. LTV Steel Co., 1984-86; med. dir., chmn. med. adv. bd. Ohio Health Choice Plan Inc. Vice-chmn. Cleve. Clinic-Charity Hosp. Com. Surg. Residency Tng., 1970-78; health com. Bituminous Coal Operators Assn.; trustee Wood Hudson Cancer Research Labs., Inc., 1984—; bd. dirs. Phoenix Theatre Ensemble, 1982—. Served to capt. U.S. Army, 1944-46; PTO. Diplomate Am. Bd. Surgery. Fellow ACS, Am. Coll. Angiology; mem. Am. Iron and Steel Inst. (chmn. health com. 1977-79), Am. Acad. Occupational Medicine, Am., Ohio occupational med. assns., Acad. Medicine, Cleve. (dir. 1969-72), Cleve. Surg. Soc., Western Res. Med. Dirs., Soc. Clin. Vascular Surgery. Roman Catholic. Clubs: Cleve. Skating, Cleve. Playhouse, Serra. Home: 2285 Harcourt Dr Cleveland Heights OH 44106

MULLANE, DENIS FRANCIS, insurance executive; b. Astoria, N.Y., Aug. 28, 1930; s. Patrick F. and Margaret (O'Neill) M.; m. Kathryn Mullman, June 28, 1952; children: Gerard, Kevin, Denise. B.S. in Mil. Engring, U.S. Mil. Acad., 1952; LHD (hon.), U. Conn., 1988. C.L.U. With Conn. Mut. Life Ins. Co., Hartford, 1956—, v.p., 1969-72, sr. v.p., 1972-74, exec. v.p., 1974-76, pres., 1977—, chief exec. officer, 1983-85, chmn., chief exec. officer, 1985—; dir. Conn. Natural Gas Co., Conn. Bank & Trust Co., Pitney Bowes Corp., Capitol Properties, Inc., Hartford, Inst. Living. Bd. dirs. St. Francis Hosp., Hartford. Served to 1st lt. C.E. U.S. Army, 1952-56. Recipient John Newton Russell award, 1987, Knight of St. Gregory award, hon. LHD, U. Conn., 1988. Mem. Am. Council Life Ins. (bd. dirs.), Am. Soc. Corp. Execs., Nat. Assn. Life Underwriters, Assn. Grads. U.S. Mil. Acad. (pres.). Republican. Roman Catholic. Office: Conn Mut Life Ins 140 Garden St Hartford CT 06154

MULLANE, ROBERT E., manufacturing company executive; b. Cin., May 27, 1932; s. Robert E. and Marie M.; children: Katherine, Constance, Margaret, Sarah. Grad., Georgetown U., 1954; MBA, Harvard U., 1956. With Automatic Vending Co., 1953-73, Carousel Time, Inc., 1973-74; v.p. Bally Mfg. Corp., Chgo., 1974-79, pres., 1979-89, chmn. bd. dirs., chief exec. officer, 1979—; bd. dirs. Bally's Park Place, Inc. Office: Bally Mfg Corp 8700 W Bryn Mawr Ave Chicago IL 60631 *

MULLANEY, JOSEPH E., lawyer; b. Fall River, Mass., Mar. 22, 1933; s. Joseph E. and Beatrice (Hancock) M.; m. Rosemary Woodman, June 22, 1957; children—Joseph E. III, Sean, Evan. A.B. magna cum laude, Coll. Holy Cross, Worcester, Mass., 1955; LL.B. magna cum laude, Harvard U., 1958. Bar: Ohio bar, D.C. bar, Mass. bar. Partner firm Jones, Day, Cockley & Reavis, Cleve., 1960-70; gen. counsel Office Spl. Rep. Trade Negotiations, Exec. Office Pres., Washington, 1970-71, Cost of Living Council, 1971-72; assoc. gen. counsel Gillette Co., Boston, 1972-77; sr. v.p., gen. counsel Gillette Co., 1977—; dir. Park St. Corp., Greater Boston Legal Services Corp.; mem., dir. Boston Mcpl. Research Bur. Bd. dirs. New Eng. Legal Found. Office: Gillette Co Prudential Tower Bldg Boston MA 02199

MULLARE, T(HOMAS) KENWOOD, JR., publishing company executive, lawyer; b. Milton, Mass., Jan. 19, 1939; s. Thomas Kenwood and Catherine Marie (Leonard) M.; m. Joan Marie O'Donnell, May 27, 1967; children: Jennifer M., Tracy K., Jill M., Joyce M. A.B., Holy Cross Coll., 1961; LL.B., Boston Coll., 1964. Bar: Mass. 1964. Atty. New Eng. Electric System, 1964-71; v.p., gen. counsel, sec. AVX Corp., N.Y.C., 1971-73; v.p., gen. counsel, clk. Tyco Labs., Inc., Exeter, N.H., 1974-77; v.p., gen. counsel, sec. SCA Services, Inc., Boston, 1977-84; v.p., dir. div. bus. software Houghton Mifflin Co., Boston, 1984—. Bd. dirs. Barque Hill Assn., Norwell, Mass., 1980-84, pres., 1981-82; pres. Ch.Hillers, Norwell, Mass., 1983-84. Mem. ABA, Mass. Bar Assn., Boston Bar Assn. Home: 31 Barque Hill Dr Norwell MA 02061 Office: Houghton Mifflin Co 1 Beacon St Boston MA 02108

MULLEIAN, LOLA JEAN, small business owner; b. Chico, Calif., Sept. 4, 1931; d. William and Lola Hester (Huddleson) Clark; m. George Mulleian, May 25, 1954 (dec. 1974); children: Mark W., Douglas C.; m. Warren James Ilsohn, Jan. 27, 1980. Grad. high sch., Chico. Owner, mgr. King of Quality Trucking Co., San Francisco, 1958-76, Fruit Ridge Shopping Ctr., Sacramento, 1978—. Office: Fruit Ridge Shopping Ctr 5657 Stockton Blvd Sacramento CA 95824

MULLEN, DAVID BRUCE, infosystems specialist; b. Hartford, Conn., Oct. 19, 1950; s. Robert Emmett Jr. and Virginia Lee (Johnson) M.; m. Joanne Marie Gass, June 11, 1977; children: Christopher, Andrew. AB, Princeton U., 1972; MBA, U. Pa., 1974. CPA, Ill. Staff acct. Arthur Young & Co., Saddlebrook, N.J. and Chgo., 1974-78; mgr. Arthur Young & Co., Chgo., 1978-82, prin., 1982-83; sr. v.p., chief fin. officer, treas. CCC Info. Svcs., Chgo., 1983-87, exec. v.p., chief fin. officer, 1987-88; chief fin. officer Fin. Protection Svcs. Inc., Chgo., 1988—. Mem. AICPA. Office: Fin Protection Svcs 640 N La Salle St Chicago IL 60610

MULLER, EDWARD ROBERT, lawyer; b. Phila., Mar. 26, 1952; s. Rudolph E. and Elizabeth (Steiner) M.; m. Patricia Eileen Bauer, Sept. 27, 1980; children: Margaret Anne, John Frederick. AB summa cum laude, Dartmouth Coll., 1973; JD, Yale U., 1976. Assoc. Leva, Hawes, Symington, Martin & Oppenheimer, Washington, 1977-83; dir. legal affairs Life Scis. group Whittaker Corp., Arlington, Va., 1983-84; v.p. Whittaker Health Svcs., Arlington, Va., 1984-85; v.p., gen. counsel, sec. Whittaker Corp., L.A., 1985—, chief adminstrv. officer, gen. counsel, sec., 1988—; bd. trustees, treas. Exceptional Children's Found., L.A., 1988—. Office: Whittaker Corp 10880 Wilshire Blvd Los Angeles CA 90024

MULLER, GARY WARD, accountant; b. Albuquerque, Dec. 29, 1960; s. Frank William and Shelby Jean (Malone) M., m. Renae Marie Bednar, Apr. 25, 1987. BA in Bus., Ft. Lewis Coll., 1983. CPA, N.Mex. Accountant Ivener & Demkovich CPAs, Albuquerque, 1983-88; prin. Gary W. Muller CPA, Albuquerque, 1988—. Mem. Am. Inst. CPAs, N.Mex. Soc. CPAs, Assn. Commerce and Industry N.Mex. Republican. Methodist. Office: PO Box 20399 Albuquerque NM 87154

MULLER, PAUL J., human resources consulting principal; b. Amsterdam, North Holland, The Netherlands, Dec. 16, 1944; came to U.S. 1967; s. Jan Willem and Truus Margret (Zomerdijk) M.; m. Joyce Ann McLaughlin, Dec. 13, 1969; children: Marisa Nicole, Mark Paul. Student, Inst. Nijenrode, Breukelen, Holland, 1967; BA, U. Puget Sound, 1968; MBA, U. Wash., 1970. Mgmt. cons. Ernst & Whinney, Indpls., 1970-73; sr. mgmt. cons. A.T. Kearney, Chgo., 1973-77; dir. compensation and orgn. plan Hosp. Corp. Am., Nashville, 1977-80; dir. compensation cons. service div. Runzheimer, Inc., Rochester, Wis., 1980-82; prin., dir. human resources cons. Arthur Young & Co., Chgo., 1982-87; dir. Great Lakes region compensation cons. Ernst & Whinney, Chgo., 1987—; chmn. wage benefits com. Fedn. Am. Hosps., Washington, 1978-79. Invented Runzheimer area differential system, 1981; author: City of Chgo. Shakman Decree Hiring Provisions; contbr. articles to profl. jours. Served to 1st lt. Dutch Army, 1963-65. Recipient Outstanding Service award Indpls. Jaycees, 1972. Mem. Am. Compensation Assn. (workshop condr., Recognition award 1981), Chgo. Compensation Assn., Human Resources Mgmt. Assn. (workshop condr.), Am. Hosp. Assn. Chgo., Netherlands C. of C., Sigma Alpha Epsilon. Club: Dutch Knickerbocker Soc. Chgo. (pres. 1987—). Office: Ernst & Whinney 150 S Wacker Dr Chicago IL 60606

MULLER, PETER, lawyer, entertainment company executive, consultant; b. Teplitz-Sanov, Czechoslovakia, Mar. 4, 1947; came to U.S., 1949; s. Alexander and Elizabeth Rudolpha (Weingarten) M.; m. Irene Smolarski, Nov. 18, 1971 (div. 1973); children: Chloe Aur, Aurora; m. Esther Unterman Meisler, Jan. 4, 1987. BA, NYU, 1968, JD cum laude. Entertainment editor Ambience mag., N.Y.C., 1978-79, Women's Life mag., N.Y.C., 1980-81; sole practice, N.Y.C., 1984—; chief exec. officer Producers Releasing Corp., N.Y. and Nev., 1987-88, pres. entertainment div., 1987-88; pres., founder Muller Entertainment Group, N.Y.C., 1988—; expert Tech. Adv. Service for Attys., Pa., 1987—; lectr. entertainment and communication law to various orgns. Author: Show Business Law; producer: (films) Nancy, The Movie, The Beach of Falesa. Mem. Vol. Lawyers for the Arts, N.Y.C., 1987—. Mem. ABA (forum on entertainment and sports industries, forum on copyright, trademark and patent law), N.Y. State Bar Assn., NYU Alumni Assn. (bd. dirs. 1987—, v.p., bd. dirs. NYU Alumni Assn.). Home: 21 E 66th St New York NY 10021 Office: Muller Entertainment Group 1775 Broadway 7th floor New York NY 10019

MULLETT, JOHN MCLAUGHLIN, marketing representative; b. Pitts., Feb. 21, 1950; s. John Selwyn and Betty June (Nelson) M. B.A. in Psychology, W.Va. Wesleyan Coll., 1972. Sales rep. Philip Morris, USA, 1973-75, mil. mgr., 1975-76, asst. div. mgr., 1976-78, div. mgr., 1978-80, area mgr., 1980-81; mktg. rep. Samsonite Corp., 1981—. Sponsor, Nat. Republican Congressional Com.; mem. Rep. Nat. Com., Walker Art Center. Mem. Am. Mgmt. Assn., Sales and Mktg. Execs. Assn. (bd. dirs.), Lake of Bays Assn., W.Va. Wesleyan Coll. Alumni Assn. Republican. Methodist. Clubs: Southgate Racquet, South Pk. Golf. Home: 1831 Ridge Road Library PA 15129 Home: Fox Point Rd, Dwight Can POA1HO Office: Samsonite Corp 11200 E 45th Ave Denver CO 80239

MULLIGAN, JAMES FRANCIS, business executive, lawyer; b. Attleboro, Mass., Aug. 27, 1925; s. Henry D. and Eleanor R. (Carey) M.; m. Mary Alice Mangels, Aug. 28, 1948; 1 child, Christopher. AB, Tufts U., 1947; JD, Columbia U., 1950. Bar: N.Y. 1950, Pa. 1968, U.S. Supreme Ct. 1986. Gen. atty. Erie-Lackawanna R.R., Cleve. and N.Y.C., 1950-61; gen. counsel Monroe Internat. div. Litton Industries, Orange, N.J., 1961-67; v.p., sec., gen. counsel Lukens Steel Co., Coatesville, Pa., 1967-83; v.p. law and corp. affairs, sec. Lukens, Inc., Coatesville, Pa., 1983-88; ret. Lukens, Inc., Coatesville, 1988. Pres. United Way Chester County, West Chester, Pa., 1980-81. Lt. (j.g.) USNR, 1943-46. Mem. ABA, Pa. Bar Assn., Chester County Bar Assn., Radley Run Country Club, Springhaven Country Club. Home: 1060 Squire Cheney Dr West Chester PA 19382

MULLIGAN, ROBERT J., retail store executive, accountant; b. Bklyn., Oct. 24, 1938; s. William and Alice (Skelly) M.; m. Eileen Chrystal, Oct. 14, 1961; children: Brian, Peter. BBA in Acctg., St. John's U., N.Y.C., 1960. With Peat, Marwick, Mitchell & Co., 1960-65; sr. v.p. fin. and ops. Bonwit Teller, N.Y.C., 1965-71; sr. v.p., treas. Gimbels, N.Y.C., 1971-76; vice chair, chief adminstrv. officer, bd. dirs. Woodward & Lothrop Inc., Washington, 1976—; bd. dirs., asst. treas. Met. Washington Bd. of Trade, 1980—; bd. dirs. Sovran Bank of Md., Bethesda, Sovran Fin. Corp., Richmond, Va. Bd. dirs. Sovereign Mil. Order of Malta, Washington, 1984-87; trustee, vice chair Holy Cross Hosp., 1988, Silver Spring, Md.; chmn. bd. trustees Georgetown Prep. Sch., Washington, 1986—. Recipient Pres.'s award St. John's U., 1985. Mem. St. John's U. D.C. Area Alumni Assn. (pres. 1982-87), Soc. of Friendly Sons of St. Patrick of Washington (pres.). Roman Catholic. Clubs: Congl. (Bethesda); City, Met. (Washington), Econ. (Washington), Gergetown (Washington). Office: Woodward & Lothrop Inc 2800 Eisenhower Ave Alexandria VA 22314

MULLIN, LEO FRANCIS, banker; b. Concord, Mass., Jan. 26, 1943; s. Leo F. and Alice L. (Fearns) M.; m. Leah J. Malmberg, Sept. 10, 1966; children: Jessica, Matthew. AB, Harvard U., 1964, MS, 1965, MBA, 1967. Assoc. McKinsey & Co., Washington, 1967-73; prin. 1973-76; sr. v.p. strategic planning Consol. Rail Corp., Phila., 1976-78, sr. v.p. planning, control and info. systems, 1978-80; sr. v.p. corp. planning First Nat. Bank Chgo., 1981-82; exec. v.p., head The Consumer Bank, Chgo., 1982-87, exec. v.p., head internat. banking group, 1987-88, exec v.p., head North Am. banking group, 1988—. Bd. dirs., treas. Chgo. Urban League, 1981—; trustee Field Mus. Natural History, 1982—, vice chmn., 1987—; bd. dirs. Visa USA, 1982-87, Visa Internat., 1986-87, Chgo. chpt. Juvenile Diabetes, 1985—, Met. Planning Council, 1983—. Mem. Ill Bankers Assn. (regional dirs. 1986-87), Harvard U. Alumni Assn. (bd. dirs. 1987—). Clubs: Chicago, Harvard (Chgo.) (bd. dirs. 1982-87, pres. 1986-87), Economic. Office: First Chgo Corp 1 First National Pla Suite 0089 Chicago IL 60670

MULLINAX, THOMAS EARL, JR., architectural firm executive, consultant; b. Mooresville, N.C., Sept. 16, 1951; s. Thomas Earl Sr. and Peggy Virginia (King) M.; m. Elizabeth Ray, Apr. 25, 1981; children: Thomas Cole, John Zachary.. BA Environ. Design, U. N.C., Charlotte, 1975, BArch, 1976. Architect Sir Basil Spense, London, 1974-75, Snoddy & McCulloch, Charlotte, 1975-78; healthcare architect J.N. Pease Assoc., Charlotte, 1978-80; cons. Healthcare Concepts, Greenville, S.C., 1980-82; pres., architect Flad Mullinax Wash Architects, Gainesville, Fla., 1982—. Mem. Nursing Home Adv. Commn., Charlotte, 1986, Zoning Bd. Adjustments, Charlotte, 1986. Recipient Design award U. N.C. at Charlotte, 1976. Mem. AIA, Am. Assn. Hosp. Planners, Am. Hosp. Assn. Republican. Presbyterian. Home: 3653 Mill Pond Rd Charlotte NC 28226 Office: Flad Mullinax Wash Architects PA 212 S Tryon St Ste 1480 Charlotte NC 28281

MULLINEAUX, RONALD WALTER, data processing executive; b. Chgo., Mar. 7, 1948; s. Walter J. and Betty F. (Ftak) M.; m. Marianne K. Lueth. BS in Acctg., No. Ill. U., 1971; MBA, U. Ill., 1973. CPA, Ill. Mgr. accounts receivable Xerox Corp., Rochester, N.Y., 1973-74; systems analyst Xerox Corp., Rochester, 1974-77, program mgr., 1977-79, mgr. pricing adminstrn., 1979-82; mgr. adminstrv. ops. ctr. Xerox Corp., Greenwich, Conn., 1982-84; mgr. regional adminstrv. planning Xerox Corp., Greenwich, 1984-85; sr. v.p. ops., chief fin. officer Samna Corp., Atlanta, 1985—. Served with USMC, 1966-68, Vietnam. Mem. Am. Inst. CPAs, Beta Alpha Psi. Republican. Lutheran. Home: 3888 Allenhurst Dr Norcross GA 30092 Office: Samna Corp 5600 Glenridge Dr Atlanta GA 30342

MULLINS, JANET WONG, financial executive; b. Shreveport, La., July 17, 1958; d. Joe S. and Mae (Ping) Wong; m. Ronald L. Mullins, Aug. 30, 1980. M in Profl. Accountancy, La. Tech. U., 1981. CPA, La. Staff acct. Wilson, Bratlie and Thomas, Shreveport, La., 1981-83; mgr. tax Touche Ross & Co., Kansas City, Mo., 1983-85, Peat Marwick Main & Co., Shreveport, 1985-88; sr. mgr. Peat Marwick Main & Co., San Francisco, 1988—; tax/fin. commentator KTBS-TV Inc., 1985, 87-88. Contbr. articles to profl. jours. Bd. dirs. First Bapt. Ch., Shreveport, La., 1987—, mem. fin. com., 1987—. Mem. Nat. Assn. Accts. (dir. 1987—), AICPA, Soc. La. CPAs. Republican. Baptist. Lodge: Zonta. Office: Peat Marwick Main & Co 3 Embarcadero Ctr Ste 2100 San Francisco CA 94111

MULQUEEN, KEVIN JAMES, financial planner; b. Montgomery, N.Y., Aug. 5, 1952; s. Michael P. and Mary B. (O'Donovan) M. Cert. fin. planner. V.p. Mulqueen Enterprises Inc., Montgomery, N.Y., 1972-79; prin., owner Mulqueen Agy., Newburgh, 1979—. Chmn. Walden (N.Y.) Indsl. Devel. Agy., 1983-87; pres. Walden Housing Devel. Corp., 1980-87; trustee Village of Walden, 1978-87; bd. dirs. N.Y. Life Underwriters Polit. Action Com., Albany, 1987-89. Mem. Internat. Assn. Fin. Planning, Inst. Cert. Fin. Planners, Nat. Assn. Life Underwriters (Nat. Quality award 1986-87, Nat. Sales Achievement award 1982-87), Orange County Assn. Life Underwriters (pres. 1987088), Million Dollar Round Table, Kiwanis (pres. 1979-80). Home: 451 E 83d St New York NY 10028 Office: Mulqueen Agy PO Box 558 Rt 208 Montgomery NY 12549

MULREADY, THOMAS JAMES, management and training consultant; b. Grand Rapids, Mich., Jan. 24, 1958; s. Thomas James and Alice Marie (Mendendez) M. BBA, Bowling Green State U., 1980. Pres. Mulready Enterprises, Cleve. Author: The Automatic Turnpike, 1985; dir., videographer bus. videotape tng. programs. Office: Mulready Enterprises 1365 Webb Rd Cleveland OH 44107

MULRONEY, JOHN PATRICK, chemical company executive; b. Phila., 1935; married. BS, U. Pa., 1957, MS, 1959. With Rohm & Haas Co., Phila., 1958—, group leader engring. dept., 1962-64, dept. head, 1964-67, asst. dir. research, 1967-71; asst. gen. mgr. Filital, Milan, 1971-74, gen. mgr., 1974-75; bus. mgr. AG Chem., Europe, 1975-78; v.p. polymers, resins, monomers Indsl. Chem., 1978-80, v.p. tech., 1980-82, v.p. corp. bus., from 1982; pres., chief operating officer Rohm & Haas Co., Phila., 1986—, also bd. dirs. Mem. Am. Inst. Chem. Engrs., Am. Chem. Soc. Office: Rohm & Haas Co Independence Mall W Philadelphia PA 19105 *

MULVA, JAMES J., oil company executive; b. Oshkosh, Wis., June 19, 1946; m. Miriam Mulva; 2 children. BBA in Fin., U. Tex., 1968, MBA in Fin., 1969. With. Phillips Petroleum Co., Bartlesville (Okla.) and London, 1974-1985; asst. treas. Phillips Petroleum Co., Bartlesville, 1974, mgr. fgn. exch. and investment, 1976; v.p., treas. Europe/Africa div. Phillips Petroleum Co., London, 1980; mgmt. trainee, treas. Phillips Petroleum Co., Bartlesville, 1983, mgr. corp. and planning, 1984, asst. treas., 1985, treas., 1986, v.p., treas., 1986—. With USN, 1969-73. Roman Catholic. Office: Phillips Petroleum Co Phillips Bldg 4th & Keeler Bartlesville OK 74004

MULVIHILL, TERENCE JOSEPH, investment banking executive; b. Omaha, Feb. 4, 1931; m. Susan F. Bowman, June 21, 1986; children by previous marriage: Mary Louise, Patricia, Kathleen, Joan, Carol, Nancy. B.S. in Econs., Georgetown U., 1952. Sec., treas. Mulvihill Co., Streator, Ill., 1955-64; instl. salesman Goldman, Sachs & Co., Chgo., 1964-71, v.p., 1971-80, asst. regional mgr., 1972-74, regional sales mgr., 1974-80, ptnr., 1980—. Pres. St. Francis Xavier Sch. Bd., Wilmette, Ill., 1971; pres. Regina Dominican High Sch. Parents Assn., 1973; mem. council U. Chgo. Grad. Sch. Bus., 1980—; bd. dirs. Glenkirk Assn for Retarded, Glenview, Ill., 1980-82 ; trustee Regina Dominican High Sch. Charitable Trust, Wilmette, Ill., 1983. Served to 1st lt. US. Army, 1952-54. Mem. Bond Club of Chgo. (dir. 1981-82). Clubs: Metropolitan (Chgo.), Carlton (Chgo.). Office: Goldman Sachs & Co 4900 Sears Tower Chicago IL 60606

MUMFORD, CHRISTOPHER GREENE, corporate financial executive; b. Washington, Oct. 21, 1945; s. Milton C. and Dorothea L. (Greene) M.; B.A., Stanford U., 1968, M.B.A., 1975. Cons., Internat. Tech. Resources Inc., 1974; asst. v.p. Wells Fargo Bank, San Francisco, 1975-78; v.p., treas. Arcata Corp., San Francisco, 1978-82, v.p. fin., 1982—. gen. ptnr. Scarff, Sears & Assocs., San Francisco, 1986—; bd. dirs. Triangle Pacific Corp., Dallas, Norton Enterprises, Inc., Salt Lake City, Community Home Med. Enterprises, Inc., Grass Valley, Calif. Served to lt. USN, 1968-73. Office: Arcata Corp 601 California St San Francisco CA 94108

MUNCASTER, JOSEPH DEAN, merchandising executive; b. Sudbury, Ont., Can., Oct. 23, 1933; s. W. Walter and Beatrice (Vance) M.; m. Grace D. Rodwell, Aug. 27, 1957 (div. Sept. 1975); children: Robert Dean, Bernard Walter; m. Brenda E. Bell, Aug. 9, 1985; 1 child, David A. BA in Bus. Adminstrn., U. Western Ont., 1956; MBA, Northwestern U., 1957; LLD (hon.), Laurentian U., 1975. Fin. analyst Can. Tire Corp. Ltd., Toronto, Ont., 1957-60, retail store mgr., 1960-63; v.p. Can. Tire Corp. Ltd., 1963-66; pres., chief exec. officer Canadian Tire Corp. Ltd., 1966-85; chmn. bd. dirs. Traqson Inc., Toronto; bd. dirs. Corp. Properties Ltd., Emir Oils Ltd., Petromines Ltd., Renaissance Energy Ltd., Royal Ins. Group, Sara Lee Corp., Stelco Inc., Black & Decker Mfg. Co., Royal Ins. Group, Moore Corp. Ltd., Steinberg Inc. Chmn. steering com. Task Force Hydro, 1971-73; mem. adv. com. Sch. Bus. U. Western Ont.; bd. dirs. Robarts Research Inst.; bd. govs. Roy Thomson Hall, Massey Hall; founding mem. Bus. Council on Nat. Issues. Mem. Retail Council Can. (chmn. 1969-71, dir., exec. com. 1968-85), York Club, Granite Club. Office: Traqson Inc, 3080 Yonge St Ste 3000, Toronto, ON Canada M4N 3N1

MUNCH, JENNIFER CLISE, real estate management executive; b. Keyser, W.Va., Oct. 16, 1947; d. James Dale and Jean (Borror) Clise; m. Thomas Lee Munch, Aug. 19, 1967. BS in Acctg. magna cum laude, U. Balt., 1973. CPA, Md. Mgmt. acct. Monumental Properties Inc., Balt., 1972-73, dir. automated rent system, 1973-74, internal auditor, 1974-75, data processing coordinator, then asst. to controller, 1975-77, acctg. mgr., 1977-79; v.p. controller Town and Country Mgmt. Corp., Balt., 1979—. Treas. Carroll County Agrl. Ctr., Westminster, Md., 1979—; mem. allocations com. Balt. United Way, 1983; bd. govs. Carroll County Farm Mus., Westminster, 1985—; chmn. fin. com. Westminster United Meth. Ch., 1985—. Mem. Am. Inst. CPA's, Md. Assn. CPA's, Beta Alpha. Republican. Office: Town & Country Mgmt Corp 100 S Charles St Baltimore MD 21157

MUNDELL, DAVID EDWARD, leasing company executive; b. Montreal, Que., Can., Dec. 27, 1931; s. Charles D.T. and Elise Warden (Dunton) M.; m. Willa Price McReynolds, July 25, 1969; children: David Edward (dec.), Elise Mundell. Diploma, Royal Mil. Coll. Can., 1953; B Engring., McGill U., 1954; MBA, Harvard, 1957. Research and devel. DuPont of Can., 1957-59; pres. Can.-Dominion Leasing Corp., Ltd., Toronto, 1959-65; exec. v.p. U.S. Leasing Corp., 1965-68; pres. U.S. Leasing Internat. Inc., San Francisco, 1968-88, chief exec. officer, 1976—, chmn., 1988—, also bd. dirs.; advisor Orix Corp., Tokyo. Lt. Royal Canadian C.E., 1951-57. Mem. Villa Taverna Club, Pacific-Union Club, Toronto Golf Club. Office: US Leasing Internat Inc 733 Front St San Francisco CA 94111

MUNDEN, ROBIN GHEZZI, manufacturing company executive, lawyer; b. Rome, Italy, May 22, 1947; s. Kenneth White and Lia (Ghezzi) M.; m. Gail J. Schoch, June 2, 1973. BA, U. Denver, 1970; JD cum laude, Northwestern U., 1973. Bar: Ill. 1973, U.S. Dist. Ct. (no. dist.) Ill. 1973. Litigation assoc. McDermott, Will & Emery, Chgo., 1973-79; gen. counsel, sec. King-Seeley Thermos Co., Prospect Heights, Ill., 1979-82; v.p., gen. counsel, sec. Household Mfg. Inc., Prospect Heights, 1982—. Spl. Editor: A Guide to Securities and Exchange Commission Rule 144. Mem. ABA, Chgo. Bar Assn., Pi Gamma Mu. Democrat. Avocation: sailing. Home: 2140 N Bissell St Chicago IL 60614 Office: Household Mfg 2700 Sanders Rd Prospect Heights IL 60070

MUNDINGER, WILLIAM DAVID, engineer; b. Rice Lake, Wis., May 5, 1941; s. Earl Louis and Hildegard A. (Torgerson) M.; m. Karen A. Silfven, June 27, 1964; children: Katrina, Melissa, Sara. BSCE, Mich. Tech. U., 1963. R & D engr. Pullman-Standard, Hammond, Ind., 1963-73; from engr. to pres. Youngstown (Ohio) Steel Door now YSD Industries, 1973—. Lutheran. Office: YSD Industries 3710 Henricks Rd Youngstown OH 44515

MUNDT, RAY B., diversified industry executive; b. Appleton, Wis., Aug. 10, 1928; s. Benjamin J. and Jessie V. (Toft) M.; m. Ruth C. Stanchik, June 15, 1953; children: R. Scott, William C., Robert J., Mary Ruth. BS, U. Wis., Stevens Point, 1953; postgrad., Harvard U., 1969, Syracuse U. Salesman to v.p., gen. sales mgr. Kimberly-Clark Corp., Neenah, Wis., 1953-70; pres. Unisource Corp. (subsidiary Alco Standard Corp.), Valley Forge, Pa., 1970-73; exec. v.p., chief operating officer Alco Standard Corp., Valley Forge, 1973-74; pres., chief operating officer Alco Standard Corp., 1974-80, pres., chief exec. officer, 1980—, chmn., 1986—, also dir. Served with USNR, 1945-49. Clubs: Union League, Phila. Country, Harvard Bus. Sch. of Phila. Lodge: Masons. Office: Alco Health Svcs Corp PO Box 959 Valley Forge PA 19482

MUNDY, MARK J., hospital administrator; b. N.Y.C., July 8, 1942. BS, Murray State U., 1966; MS in Hosp. Adminstrn., Columbia U., 1970. Lic. nursing home adminstr., N.Y. Asst. dir. St. Vincent's Hosp., N.Y.C., 1970-73; assoc. adminstr. Nassau Hosp., Mineola, N.Y., 1973-81; exec. dir. N.Y. Infirmary-Beekman Downtown Hosp., 1981-83; chief exec. officer Quincy (Mass.) City Hosp., 1983—; guest lectr., residency preceptor Columbia U., N.Y.C. Served to capt. U.S. Army, 1966-68. Fellow Am. Coll. Health Care Execs.; mem. Met. Health Adminstrs. Assn. (pres. 1972-73), Columbia U. Sch. Pub. Health Alumni Assn. (pres. 1976-77). Home: 5 Golf View Dr Hingham MA 02043 Office: Quincy City Hosp 114 Whitewell St Quincy MA 02169

MUNFORD, DILLARD, manufacturing company executive; b. Cartersville, Ga., May 13, 1918; s. Robert Sims and Katherine (Aubrey) M.; m. Danne Brokaw; children: Dillard (dec.), Page Shepherd, Mary Aubrey, Robert Davis, Henry Allan. BS in Mech. Engring, Ga. Inst. Tech., 1939. Founder The Munford Co., Atlanta, 1946, Munford Do-It-Yourself Store, Atlanta, 1952; pres., chief exec. officer The Munford Co., Atlanta, 1962; chmn. bd., chief exec. officer Munford Inc. (formerly Atlantic Co.), Atlanta, 1968—, Leewards Creative Crafts subs. Munford Inc., 1985—; dir. Bill Publs., N.Y.C., Blount Inc., Am. Bus. Products, Inc., Garden Services Co., Callaway Gardens and Callaway Found. of Pine Mountains (Ga.), Provident Life Ins. Co., Chatta Tem, United Refrigeration Co.; bd. advisors Assoc. Distributors Inc. Commentator WCNN Radio; columnist Marietta Daily Jour., The Northside Neighbor, 26 other suburban weeklies. Trustee Ida Cason Callaway Found., Atlanta, Morris Brown Coll., LaGrange Coll., Southeastern Legal Found., Gannett Found.; mem. Republican Nat. Finance Com.; dir. Manhattan Inst. for Policy Research; vice-chmn. Unity in Action; bd. govs. 11 Alive Community Service Awards. Served to capt. AUS, 1942-46. Mem. Young Pres.'s Orgn. (past internat. pres.), Chief Execs. Forum (past dir.), NAM (past v.p., dir., mem. exec. com.), Atlanta C. of C. (past dir.), Piedmont Driving Club, Capital City Club, Peachtree Golf Club, Commerce Club, River Club, Annabel's, Wildcat Cliffs Country Club, Homosassa Fishing Club, Sigma Alpha Epsilon. Methodist. Clubs: Rotary, Piedmont Driving, Capital City, Commerce; River (N.Y.C.); Peachtree Golf; Annabels (London); Cartersville Country; Wildcat Cliffs (Highlands, N.C.). Office: Munford Inc PO Box 7701 Station C Atlanta GA 30357

MUNFORD, JOHN DURBURROW, business executive; b. Richmond, Va., Feb. 17, 1928; s. Beverley B. Jr. and Lolita (Cruser) M.; m. Elizabeth Broun, Feb. 15, 1958; children—John Durburrow III, Charles Conway, Elizabeth Page. B.A. in English, U. Va., 1950. With Union Camp Corp., Franklin, Va., 1951—; gen. mgr. Union Camp Corp., 1971-72, v.p., 1972-80, sr. v.p., 1980-84, exec. v.p., 1984—; dir., mem. exec. com. Cadmus Communications, Richmond, Va.; dir. Pulaski Furniture Co., Va., Sovran Bank, Universal Corp; trustee Ctr. for Inovative Tech., Darden Sch. Mgmt. U. Va. Trustee Camp Found., Franklin, Va. Found. Ind. Colls., Richmond, Colgate Darden Grad. Sch. Sponsors U. Va.; dir. Ctr. for Innovative Tech. Served with CIC, U.S. Army, 1951-53. Mem. Va. Mfrs. Assn. (past chmn.), Am. Paper Inst. (past chmn. P-W div.), Va. Bus. Council (past chmn. exec. com.). Republican. Episcopalian. Clubs: Cypress Cove Country (Franklin); Country of Va., Commonwealth (Richmond); Princess Anne Country (Virginia Beach, Va.). Lodge: Rotary. Home: 1009 Clay St Franklin VA 23851 Office: Union Camp Corp Fine Paper Div Rte 58E Franklin VA 23851

MUNHALL, RUTH BEATRICE, business and financial consultant; b. Mendon, Mass., Feb. 8, 1929; d. Lawrence B. and Elsie B. (Gaskill) M. Grad. Salvation Army Officers Coll., Bronx, N.Y., 1951; M.B.A., Calif. Coast U., 1980, Ph.D., D.B.A., 1981. Civilian supr. U.S. Army and VA Hosp., Framingham, Mass., 1946-50; ordained clergywoman; officer Salvation Army centers in Mass., N.Y. and N.J., 1951-64; owner, operator acctg. and real estate firm, N.Y.C., 1964-68; supr. fiduciary and individual taxation Bank of N.Y., N.Y.C., 1968-79; cons. non profit orgns. founder R.M. Scholarship Info. Services, Ark., N.Y., Mass. and Israel, 1981—; pres., chief exec. officer Munhall, Monahan, Chapman Fiduciary Animal Charities, Inc., 1984—; pres. Munhall Research Sci. Corp., 1985—; cons. in field. Recipient 5 Yr. Civil Def. award Gov. N.Y. State. Mem. Am. Mgmt. Assn., DAR, Alumni Assn. Calif. Coast U. Republican.

MUNISTERI, JOSEPH GEORGE, construction executive; b. Rome, Sept. 24, 1930; s. Peter P. and Inez Gertrude (Ziniti) M.; m. Theresa Grasso, June 7, 1952; children: Joanne, Robert, Laura, Stephen, James, Richard. BE, Yale U., 1952. With Bechtel Corp., San Francisco, 1952-59; with The Lummus Co., N.Y.C., London and Houston, 1959-67, gen. mgr., 1964-67; sr. v.p. sales Brown & Root, Inc., Houston, 1967-75, group v.p. power div., 1975-80, group v.p. corp. devel., 1980-81, also bd. dirs.; pres. Enserch Engrs. & Constructors, Inc., Houston, 1981-85; exec. v.p., chmn., pres. Ford, Bacon & Davis, Inc., Dallas, 1985-87; chmn., pres., chief exec. officer Comstock Group, Inc., Danbury, Conn., 1987—; former chmn. bd. Pine-O-Pine. Former mem. Bd. dirs. Atomic Indsl. Forum; Bd. dirs. Am. Nuclear Energy Council. Mem. Atomic Indsl. Forum, Am. Inst. Chem. Engrs., Am. Nuclear Soc., Atomic Indsl. Forum, ASTM, Council Engring. Law, ASCE, Assn. Iron and Steel Engring., Assoc. Builders and Contractors (dir.). Clubs: Yale of N.Y, Yale S.E.T, Houston. Office: Comstock Group Inc 4901 Mandell Unit B-1 Houston TX 77006

MUNN, STEPHEN P., manufacturing company executive. Pres., chief exec. officer Carlisle Cos. Inc., Cin., also bd. dirs.; bd. dirs. Carrier Corp. N.Y. Office: Carlisle Cos Inc 250 E 5th St Cincinnati OH 45202 *

MUÑOZ, CARLOS RAMÓN, banker; b. N.Y.C., Dec. 8, 1935; s. Alejandro and Gladys Helena (Judah) M.; m. Wilhelmina Elaine North, June 8, 1957; children—Carla Christine, Kyle Alexander. B.A., Columbia U., 1957, M.A., 1961. Insp., ofcl. asst. Citibank, N.A., N.Y.C., 1959-64, asst. mgr., then mgr. in Dominican Republic and P.R., 1965-70, asst. v.p., N.Y.C., 1971-72, v.p., dept. head, 1972-78, sr. v.p., regional mgr. and dir. Citicorp. USA, San Francisco, 1978-81, sr. v.p., mem. Credit Policy Com., 1982—. Bd. dirs. Episcopal Mission Soc., N.Y.C., 1974—, vice chmn. exec. com., 1985—; bd. dirs. Inner City Scholarship Fund, 1984—, Corp. for Relief Widows and Orphans of Protestant Episcopal Clergymen in State N.Y., 1974-79. Served as 1st lt. USAR, 1958-64. Recipient Productivity award State Senator Diane Watson, Los Angeles, 1981. Mem. Columbia Coll. Alumni Assn. (bd. dirs. 1983—, treas. 1988—). Republican. Club: Italian Center (Stamford, Conn.). Office: Citibank NA 399 Park Ave 3d Floor Zone 16 New York NY 10043

MUNOZ, MANUEL ANTHONY, finance company executive; b. N.Y.C., June 19, 1945; s. Ralph and Cecilia (Salazar) M.; m. Pauline Scharf, Dec. 30, 1966; children: Melissa Louise, Kyle Bennett. AB, Herbert H. Lehman Coll., 1971, MA, 1974. Tchr., coach Cardinal Spellman High Sch., Bronx, N.Y., 1971-75; asst. football coach Columbia U., 1976-77; with U.S. Mcht. Marine Acad., Kings Point, N.Y., 1977-78; mgr. sales Aetna Life, N.Y.C., 1978-85; v.p. ops. Custom Fin. Planning, N.Y.C., 1985-88; mgr. agy. Monarch Fin. Grp., Englewood Cliffs, N.J., 1988—; bd. advisors Queen (N.Y.) Coll., 1984—, adj. faculty Queens Coll., 1984—. Mem. Internat Assn. Fin. Planners, Internat Bd. Cert. Fin. Planners, Am. Soc. CLU's, Nat. Assn. Life Underwriters, Registry Fin. Planning Practitioners, Coll. for Fin. Planning, Coll. Mt. St. Vincent. Home: 236 Westchester Ave Mount Vernon NY 10552 Office: Monarch Fin Grp 270 Sylvan Ave Englewood Cliffs NJ 08610

MUNRO, J. RICHARD, publishing company executive; b. 1931; (married). B.A., Colgate U., 1957; postgrad., Columbia U., NYU; Litt. D. (hon.), Richmond U., 1983. With Time, Inc., 1957—; pres. Pioneer Press, Inc., subs. Time, 1969; pub. Sports Illus., 1969-71; v.p. Time Inc., 1971-75, group v.p. for video, 1975-79, exec. v.p., 1979-80, pres., 1980-86, chief exec. officer, 1980—, chmn., 1986—, also dir.; dir. IBM Corp. Mem. Pres.' Council on Phys. Fitness and Sport; trustee Experiment in Internat. Living, Brattleboro, Vt., Northfield Mount Hermon Sch., Colgate U.; bd. dirs. Urban League of Southwestern Fairfield County (Conn.), Jr. Achievement, United Negro Coll. Fund; bd. dirs., chmn. edn. com. N.Y.C. Partnership. Served with USMCR., Korea. Decorated Purple Heart with 2 clusters. Clubs: Country of New Canaan (Conn.), River, Winter of New Canaan. Office: Time Inc Time & Life Bldg Rockefeller Ctr New York NY 10020 *

MUNRO, SANFORD STERLING, JR., investment banking company executive; b. Madison, Wis., Mar. 2, 1932; s. Sanford Sterling and Dorothea Irene (Spears) M.; m. Valerie Gene Halbert, Apr. 4, 1956; children—Sanford Sterling, Margaret, Mary, Elizabeth, Peter, Matthew, Andrew. BA, George Washington U., 1957. Mem. profl. staff U.S. Senate, Washington, 1953-61; adminstrv. asst. U.S. Senator Henry M. Jackson, 1961-75; chief of staff Jackson for Pres. Com., 1975-76; govtl. affairs cons. Wenatchee, Wash., 1977; adminstr. Bonneville Power Adminstrn., U.S. Dept. Energy, Portland, Oreg., 1978-81; v.p., nat. dir. pub. power John Nuveen & Co., Inc., Seattle and Chgo., 1981—; bd. dirs. Cen. Wash. Bank, Wenatchee. Bd. dirs. U.S. nat. com. World Energy Conf.; chmn. U.S. Entity for Columbia River Treaty; mem. Pacific N.W. River Basins Commn., 1978-81; trustee Cen. Wash. U., 1977-83, 85—, chmn. bd. 1988—; v.p. Henry M. Jackson Found. With U.S. Army, 1952-53. Mem. Electric Power Rsch. Inst. (vice-chmn. bd. 1978-81), Electric Club Oreg. Democrat. Episcopalian. Clubs: Portland City, Wash. Athletic, Wenatchee Swim and Tennis. Home: 1202 S Hills Dr Wenatchee WA 98801 Office: 3710 Bank of California Ctr Seattle WA 98164

MUNS, MICHAEL CLIFTON, investment company executive; b. Enid, Okla., Sept. 12, 1942; s. Clifton George Muns and Gwendolyn Elsie (Rooker) Cone; m. Veta Iona McDowell, Sept. 15, 1963. Student, Phillips U., 1964, 66, Okla. State U., Enid, 1965; BA in Bus. and Econs., Cen. State U., Edmond, Okla., 1967. Acct. exec. E.F. Hutton, Inc., San Antonio, Tex., 1971-87; v.p. investments Rauscher Pierce Refsnes, San Antonio, 1987—. Mem. Cen. State U. Alumni Assn. (life mem.), San Antonio Leads Exchange (v.p. 1987—), Northside C. of C. Baptist. Office: Rauscher Pierce Refsnes 300 Convent St Ste 1600 San Antonio TX 78205

MUNSCH, KENNETH MICHAEL, telecommunications executive; b. Jacksonville, Fla., June 25, 1947; s. Kenneth R. and Kathleen E. (Meagher) M.; m. Elinor M. Hess, May 20, 1972. BS, Jacksonville U., 1969; MBA, Boston U., 1977. Commd. 2d lt. U.S. Army, 1969, advanced through grades to capt., resigned, 1977; mem. staff telephone svcs. GTE, Durham, N.C., 1977-79; pres. Atcom Inc., Rsch. Triangle Park, N.C., 1979—; chmn. Siemens Gold Seal Coun., Boca Raton, Fla., 1985—; mem. Iwatsu Dealer Coun., Carlstadt, N.J., 1986—. Bd. Dirs. N.C. Better Bus. Bur., Raleigh, 1984-87, Coun. Entrepreneurial Devel., Rsch. Triangle Park, 1987—. Recipient Gov.'s Bus. Excellence award State of N.C., 1985, 86. Mem. N.Am. Telecommunications Assn. Republican. Roman Catholic. Home: 3931 Northampton Rd Durham NC 27707 Office: Atcom Inc 4920 S Alston PO Box 13476 Research Triangle Park NC 27709-3476

MUNSE, SCOTT ROBERT, insurance company executive; b. Chgo., May 10, 1951; s. Robert A. and Erna Gard (Lee) M.; m. Elizabeth Ann Wischmeyer, Mar. 31, 1979; children: Pamela Ann, Allison Ann. BS, Adrian Coll., 1973. Student actuary Ky. Cen. Life, Lexington, 1974-77; assoc. actuary Lone Star Life, Dallas, 1977-81, v.p. actuary, 1981-83, 87—; v.p. actuary Nat. Found. Life, Ft. Worth, 1983-84, sr. v.p., actuary, 1984-87. Mem. Am. Acad. Actuaries, Soc. Actuaries (assoc.). Republican. Roman Catholic. Club: Actuaries of Southwest. Home: 29 Meadowbrook Ln Roanoke TX 76262 Office: Lone Star Life PO Box 35047 Dallas TX 75235

MUNSEE, JOAN ELIZABETH, retail executive; b. Phila., Aug. 8, 1945; d. Harold Raymond and Margaret Evelyn (Marvel) M. BS, Phila. Coll. Textiles and Sci., 1968. Dept. mgr., asst. buyer Macy's, N.Y.C., 1968-70; buyer Lit Brothers, Phila., 1970-73, Gimbels, Phila., 1973-76; div. mdse. mgr. Pomorey's, Levittown, Pa., 1976-81; div. v.p., mdse. mgr. G. Fox, Hartford, Conn., 1981-88; div. mdse. mgr. Catherine's, Memphis, 1988—. Mem. Phila Coll. Textiles and Sci. (pres. 1976-81). Republican. Methodist. Home: 1634 Oaken Breket Dr Memphis TN 38018 Office: Catherine's 1878 Brooks Rd E Memphis TN 38116

MUNSON, ALEXANDER LEE, management consultant; b. Hempstead, N.Y., Aug. 22, 1931; s. Alexander Lawrence and Bertha Louise (Geer) M.; m. Betty Sue Shideler, Dec. 14, 1957 (div. June 1978); children: Eric Lawrence, Genevieve Sue, Anna Lee. B.A., Amherst Coll., 1953; M.B.A., Harvard, 1960. Mgmt. trainee, credit analyst Mellon Nat. Bank & Trust Co., Pitts., 1953-54; asso. Cresap, McCormick & Paget, N.Y.C., mgmt. cons., 1960-62; financial adv. internat. finance Mobil Oil Corp., N.Y.C., 1962-64, Melbourne, Australia, 1964-65; mgr. spl. projects treas. dept. Mobil Internat., N.Y.C., 1965-66, mgr. treasury reports and analysis, 1966-67; treas. Mobil Latin Am. Inc., N.Y.C., 1968-70; v.p.-treas. Fairchild Camera & Instrument Co., Mountain View, Calif., 1971-72, Crown Zellerbach Corp., San Francisco, 1972-82; pres. A.L. Munson & Co., San Francisco, 1982—. Mem. Mayor's Fiscal Adv. Com., 1976—, mem. exec. com., 1982—; mem. San Francisco Civil Service Commn., 1984—, v.p. 1986, pres. 1987-88. Served to lt. USCGR, 1954-64. Recipient SBA Advocate of Yr. award, 1976. Mem. Harvard Bus. Sch. Assn. of No. Calif. , Financial Execs. Inst., Phi Gamma Delta. Republican. Presbyterian. Home and Office: 3369 Jackson St San Francisco CA 94118

MUNSON, LUCILLE MARGUERITE (MRS. ARTHUR E. MUNSON), real estate broker; b. Norwood, Ohio, Mar. 26, 1914; d. Frank and Fairy (Wicks) Wirick; R.N., Lafayette (Ind.) Home Hosp., 1937; A.B., San Diego State U., 1963, student Purdue U., Kans. Wesleyan U.; m. Arthur E. Munson, Dec. 24, 1937; children—Barbara Munson Papke, Judith Munson Andrews, Edmund Arthur. Staff and pvt. nurse Lafayette Home Hosp., 1937-41; indsl. nurse Lakey Foundry & Machine Co., Muskegon, Mich., 1950-51, Continental Motors Corp., Muskegon, 1951-52; nurse Girl Scout Camp, Grand Haven, Mich., 1948-49; owner Munson Realty, San Diego, 1964—. Mem. San Diego County Grand Jury, 1975-76, 80-81, Calif. Grand Jurors Assn. (charter). Home: 5765 Friars Rd Apt 200 San Diego CA 92108 Office: 2999 Mission Blvd # 102 San Diego CA 92109

MUNSON, NANCY KAY, lawyer; b. Huntington, N.Y., June 22, 1936; d. Howard H. and Edna M. (Keenan) Munson. Student, Hofstra U., 1959-62; JD, Bklyn. Law Sch., 1965. Bar: N.Y. 1966, U.S. Supreme Ct. 1970, U.S. Ct. Appeals (2d cir.) 1971, U.S. Dist. Ct. (ea. and so. dists.) N.Y. 1968. Law clk. to E. Merritt Weidner Huntington, 1959-66, sole practice, 1966—; mem. legal adv. bd. Chgo. Title Ins. Co., Riverhead, N.Y., 1981—; bd. dirs., legal officer Thomas Munson Found. Trustee Huntington Fire Dept. Death Benefit Fund; pres., trustee, chmn. bd. Bklyn. Home for Aged Men Found. Mem. ABA, Suffolk County Bar Assn., Bklyn. Bar Assn., N.Y. State Bar Assn., Nat. Rifle Assn. Republican. Christian Scientist. Club: Soroptimist (past pres.). Office: 197 New York Ave Huntington NY 11743

MUNYON, WILLIAM HARRY, JR., architect; b. Panama City, Panama, Feb. 20, 1945 (parents Am. citizens); s. William Harry and Ruth (Hyde) M.; m. Cheryl Lynn Guess, Dec. 31, 1987; B.A., Tulane U., 1967; postgrad. U. Hawaii, 1972-73; B.Arch. with high distinction, U. Ariz., 1978; postgrad. U.S. Naval War Coll., 1984, Armed Forces Staff Coll., 1985. Elec. designer Ohlsen-Mitchell, Inc., New Orleans, 1966-67; research cons. hist. preservation U. Ariz., Tucson, 1974-75; cons. hist. preservation State of Ariz., Phoenix, 1974-75; mktg. dir., programmer, designer Architecture One, Ltd., Tucson, 1975-78; mng. prin. Artistic License II, graphics and design, 1975-86, Aardvark Graphics, 1986—; dir. mktg. Hansen Lind Meyer, P.C., Iowa City and Chgo., 1978-79; v.p. John F. Steffen Assocs., Inc., subs. Turner Constrn., St. Louis, 1979-80; sr. assoc., dir. corp. devel. Rees Assocs., Inc., Oklahoma City, 1980-82; mktg. dir., asst. to pres., dir. planning, dir. interior architecture SHWC, Inc., Dallas, 1982-84; dir. justice facilities program Henningson, Durham & Richardson Inc., Dallas, 1984-87; prin., dir. justice and security facilities Kaplan/McLaughlin/Diaz Architects, San Francisco, 1987—; mktg. cons., 1979—; vice chmn., chief exec. officer Program Mgmt. Assocs. subs. Kaplan/McLaughlin/Diaz, 1987—; mem. adv. bd. Interior Design mag., 1978-79; mem. Bldg. Energy Performance Standards Adv. Panel, 1979-81. Active U. Ariz. Fund for Athletic Devel., 1977—; sponsor Dallas 500; mem. Naval War Coll. Found. Served with USN, 1967-73; capt. Res. Recipient Producer's Coun. prize for design excellence, 1977, Henry Adams award, 1978, Regional Design awards. Mem. AIA (architecture for justice com. 1978—), Nat. Trust Hist. Preservation, Naval Res. Officers Assn., Soc. Archtl. Historians, Am. Planning Assn., Am. Correctional Assn., Am. Jail Assn., Naval Inst., Soc. Mktg. Profl. Services, Res. Officers Assn. U.S., Mensa, Lionel Collectors Club Am., Brit. Model Soldier Soc., Nat. Rifle Assn., Profl. Services Mgmt. Assn., Dallas Mus. Art, Assn. Former Intelligence Officers, Navy League, Tulane U. Alumni Assn., Blue Key, Scabbard and Blade, Phi Kappa Phi (life), Sigma Chi (life). Roman Catholic. Clubs: La Cima, 65 Roses Sports. Founder ann. archtl. history prize U. Ariz., 1979—, ann. mil. leadership award Tulane U., 1985—. Home: 9 Mara Vista Ct Tiburon CA 94920

MUNZ, LARRY MARTIN, educational administrator; b. Prescott, Ariz., May 23, 1940; s. Martin Henry and Dorothy (Draper) M.; m. Carol Jean Blackburn, Jan. 7, 1962 (div. 1984); 1 child, Laurence Blackburn; m. Cynthia Deanne Hardy, Mar. 17, 1984; 1 child, Megal Elise. BS, Oreg. State U., 1962; MA, U. Redlands, 1971. Cert. tchr., adminstr., Calif. Tchr. San Bernardino (Calif.) City Unified Sch. Dist., 1963-64, Redlands (Calif.) Unified Sch. Dist., 1964-71; cons. San Bernardino County Schs., 1971, coordinator, 1974-87; dir. San Jacinto-Moreno Valleys Regional Occupational Program, Hemet, Calif., 1971-72; coordinator Riverside (Calif.) County Schs., 1972-74; supt. Colton-Redlands-Yucaipa Regional Occupational Program, 1987--; asst. prof. Calif. State U.-San Bernardino, 1975-86. Pub., Calif. Jour. Vocat. Edn., 1987-88. Bd. dirs. Redlands Bicycle Classic, 1986-88;mem. membership drive com. Redlands YMCA, 1986-88; chair Redlands Historic and Scenic Preservation Com., 1987--. Mem.Calif. Assn. Vocat. Adminstrs. (pres. 1986-87), Assn. Calif. Sch. Adminstrs. (rep. 1985-86; Outstanding Vocat. Adminstr. 1983), Calif. Assn. Regional Occupational Ctrs.-Programs (So. Calif. rep. 1988-90), Am.Vocat. Assn., Phi Delta Kappa, Kiwanis. Republican. Office: Colton Redlands Yucaipa Regional Occupational Program 105 Tennessee St Redlands CA 92373

MURASKI, ANTHONY AUGUSTUS, lawyer; b. Cohoes, N.Y., July 28, 1946; s. Adam Joseph and Angeline Mary (Vozzy) M.; m. Janice Kay Selberg, Nov. 25, 1978; children: Adam Peter, Emily Jo. BA, MA in Speech/Hearing, Sacramento State Coll., 1970; PhD in Audiology/ Hearing Sci., U. Mich., 1977; JD, Detroit Coll. Law, 1979. Bar: Mich. 1980, U.S. Dist. Ct. (ea. dist.) Mich. 1981, U.S. Ct. Appeals (6th cir.) 1982. Asst. Kresge Hearing Research Inst. U. Mich., Ann Arbor, 1971-77; asst. prof. Wayne State U. Med. Sch., Detroit, 1979-82; assoc. Kitch, Suhrheinrich, Saurbier & Drutchas, Detroit, 1982-83; assoc. prof. Detroit Coll. Law, 1983-85; mng. ptnr. Muraski & Sikorski, Ann Arbor, 1985—; cons. audiology Ministry of Environment, Ont., Can., 1980-81; trustee Deaf, Speech and Hearing Ctr., Detroit, 1981—; legal adv. on air WWJ Radio, Detroit, 1984—; mem. mental health adv. bd. on deafness Dept. Mental Health, 1984, vis. com. U. Mich. Sch. Edn., 1986—. Author: Legal Aspects of

Audiological Practice, 1982, Hearing Conservation in Industry: Licensure, Liability and Forensics, 1985. Mem. ABA, Mich. Bar Assn., Washtenaw County Bar Assn., Am. Speech-Lang.-Hearing Assn. (sci. merit award, 1981), Ann Arbor C. of C. Home: 1603 Westminster Pl Ann Arbor MI 48104 Office: Muraski & Sikorski 300 N Fifth Ave Suite 240 Ann Arbor MI 48104

MURATORE, PETER FREDERICK, securities executive; b. Bklyn., Mar. 18, 1932; s. Fred John and Rose Mary (Muscatello) M.; m. Patricia Margaret Feerick, Jan. 21, 1956; children: John, Robert, Catherine. B.S. in Social Sci., Georgetown U., 1953. Owner, operator St. George Men's Shop, Bklyn., 1955-65; exec. v.p. E.F. Hutton & Co., Inc., N.Y.C., 1965-88; dir. E.F. Hutton & Co., Inc., N.Y.C.; mem. exec. com. N.Y. dist. S.I.A.; guest lectr. Wharton Grad. Sch. Bus. U. Pa., Phila., 1979—; ofcl. Am. Stock Exchange, N.Y.C., 1981-87; sr. exec. v.p. Shearson Lehman Hutton, N.Y.C., 1988—; chmn., Hutton Equipment Mgmt. Co., Hutton Asset Recovery Fund; dir. New Energy Co. Ind., Hutton Aircraft Mgmt., Inc., Employees Pension Service Corp., New Energy Co., Ind. Bd. advisors Fin. Services Rev., 1982. Served to lt. j.g. USNR, 1953-55. Founder Bklyn. Prep. N.Y.C., 1964. Mem. Securities Industry Assn. (chmn. mktg. com. 1979-81), Bond Club. Roman Catholic. Clubs: N.Y. Athletic. Home: Post House Rd Morristown NJ 07960 Office: Shearson Lehman Hutton 2 World Trade Ctr New York NY 10048

MURAWSKI, THOMAS FRANK, telecommunications company executive; b. N.Y.C., Mar. 24, 1945; s. Alexander Stanislaus and Helen Murawski; m. Diane Catherine Dizeo, Oct. 31, 1944; children: Denise, Karen, Thomas. AA, SUNY, 1964; BEE, Polytech. Inst. N.Y., 1973. Engr. ITT World Communications, Inc., N.Y.C., 1964-73, mgr. engring., 1973-76, dir. mktg., 1976-78; v.p., gen. mgr. ITT Domestic Transmissions Systems, N.Y.C., 1978-81; v.p., dir. engring. ITT U.S. Transmissions Systems, N.Y.C., 1981-84; sr. v.p., dir. ITT Communications Svcs., Inc., Secaucus, N.J., 1984-85; exec. v.p., gen. mgr. ITT World Communications, Secaucus, N.J., 1985-87, pres., gen. mgr., 1987-88; exec. v.p. Western Union Corp., Upper Saddle River, N.J., 1988—; pres. Network Svcs. Group, 1988—. Named one of Outstanding Young Men Am., 1975. Mem. Spotswood Jaycees (charter). Office: Western Union Corp 1 Lake St Upper Saddle River NJ 07458

MURCHIE, EDWARD MICHAEL, accountant; b. N.Y.C., Apr. 21, 1947; s. Edward Thomas and Dorothy (Busk) M.; m. Karen M. Raftery, Aug. 26, 1967; children: David, Maureen, Carolyn. B.S., Fordham U., Bronx, N.Y., 1968. C.P.A., N.Y. Staff acct. Price Waterhouse, N.Y.C., 1968-71, sr. auditor, 1971-74, audit mgr., 1974-75; dir. internal audit Eltra Corp., N.Y.C., 1975-78, asst. controller, 1978-79; v.p. fin. Eltra Corp., Morristown, N.J., 1981-82, Converse Rubber, Wilmington, Mass., 1979-81, Allied Corp: Components Co., Morristown, 1982-84; v.p. fin. and control Emery Air Freight Corp., Wilton, Conn., 1984-85, sr. v.p., chief fin. officer, 1985-87; sr. v.p., chief fin. officer Fairchild Industries, Inc., Chantilly, Va., 1987—. Chmn., South Brunswick Rank Levelling Bd., N.J., 1977-78; bd. dirs. Norwalk/Wilton chpt. ARC, 1985. Mem. Am. Inst. C.P.A.s, Fin. Execs. Inst. Republican. Roman Catholic. Office: Fairchild Industries Inc 300 W Service Rd Box 10803 Chantilly VA 22021

MURCHISON, DAVID CLAUDIUS, lawyer; b. N.Y.C., Aug. 19, 1923; s. Claudius Temple and Constance (Waterman) M.; m. June Margaret Guilfoyle, Dec. 19, 1946; children—David Roderick, Brian, Courtney, Bradley, Stacy. Student, U. N.C., 1942-43; A.A., George Washington U., 1947, J.D. with honors, 1949. Bar: D.C. 1949, Supreme Ct. 1955. Asso. Dorr, Hand & Dawson, N.Y.C., 1949-50; partner Howrey, Simon, Baker & Murchison, Washington, 1956—; legal asst. under sec. army, 1949-51; counsel motor vehicle, textile, aircraft, ordnance and shipbldg. divs. Nat. Prodn. Authority, 1951-52; asso. gen. counsel Small Def. Plants Adminstrn., 1952-53; legal adv. and asst. to chmn. FTC, 1953-55. Served with AUS, 1943-45. Mem. ABA (chmn. com. internat. restrictive bus. practices, sect. antitrust law 1954-55, sect. adminstrv. law, sect. litigation), Fed., D.C., N.Y. bar assns., Order of Coif, Phi Delta Phi. Republican. Clubs: Metropolitan, Chevy Chase. Home: 5409 Spangler Ave Bethesda MD 20816 Office: 1730 Pennsylvania Ave NW Washington DC 20006

MURDOCH, ROBERT W., cement and construction materials company executive. Pres. LaFarge Corp., Reston, Va.; chief operating officer LaFarge Corp., Reston, until 1989, chief exec. officer, 1988—. Office: Lafarge Corp 11130 Sunrise Valley Dr PO Box 4600 Ste 300 Reston VA 22090 also: Can Cement LaFarge Ltd, 606 Cathcart, Montreal, PQ Canada H3B 1L7 *

MURDOCH, (KEITH) RUPERT, publisher; b. Melbourne, Australia, Mar. 11, 1931; came to U.S., 1974, naturalized, 1985; s. Keith and Elisabeth Joy (Greene) M.; m. Anna Maria Torv, Apr. 28, 1967; children: Prudence, Elisabeth, Lachlan, James. M.A., Worcester Coll., Oxford, Eng., 1953. Chmn. News Am. Pub. Inc.; chief exec. News Corp. Ltd.; chmn. News Internat.; Ltd. Group, London; chief exec., mng. dir. News, Ltd. Group & Assoc. Cos., Australia; chmn. 20th Century Fox Prodns., 1985—, William Collins PLC, Glasgow, 1989—; owner, pub. numerous newspapers, mags. and TV stas. in Australia, U.K., and U.S. 1983—; dir. News Ltd. Home: 1 Virginia St, London E1 9XN, England Office: News Am Pub Inc 1211 Ave of the Americas 3d Fl New York NY 10022 other: Boston Herald 1 Herald Sq Boston MA 02106 *

MURDOCK, DAVID H., diversified company executive; b. Los Angeles, Apr. 10, 1923. Chmn. Cannon Mills Co., Kannapolis, N.C., 1982-86, chief exec. officer, 1982-84; now sole proprietor, chmn., chief exec. officer Pacific Holding Corp., Los Angeles, Calif.; chmn., chief exec. officer Castle & Cooke, Inc., Los Angeles, 1985—, also bd. dirs. Served with USAAF, 1941-45. Office: Castle & Cooke Inc 10900 Wilshire Blvd Los Angeles CA 90024 also: Pacific Holding Co 10900 Wilshire Blvd Ste 1600 Los Angeles CA 90024 *

MURDOCK, PAMELA ERVILLA, wholesale travel company executive, retail travel company executive; b. Los Angeles, Dec. 3, 1940; d. John James and Chloe Conger (Keefe) M.; children—Cheryl, Kim. BS, U. Colo., 1962. Pres., Dolphin Travel, Denver, 1972-87; owner, pres. Mile Hi Tours, Denver, 1974—, MH Internat., 1987—. Named Wholesaler of Yr., Las Vegas Conv. and Visitors Authority, 1984. Mem. Am. Soc. Travel Agts., Colo. Assn. Commerce and Industry, Nat. Fedn. Independent Businessmen. Republican. Office: Mile Hi Tours Inc 2120 S Birch Denver CO 80222

MURDOCK, PHELPS DUBOIS, JR., marketing and advertising agency executive; b. Kansas City, Mo., May 5, 1944; s. Phelps Dubois and Betty Jane Murdock; student U. Mo., Kansas City, 1962-66; m. Nancy Jane Winfrey, June 7, 1977; children: Susan, Kathleen, Mark, Brooks, Phelps DuBois III, Molly. Sales service mgr. Sta.-KCMO-TV, Kansas City, 1965-66; account exec. Fremerman-Papin Advt., Kansas City, 1966-71, TV prodn. mgr., 1966-70, v.p., 1970-71; mng. ptnr. New Slant Prodns., Kansas City, 1971-73; v.p., creative dir. Travis-Walz-Lane Advt., Kansas City, and Mission, Kans., 1973-76; pres., chief exec. officer Phelps Murdock Mktg. and Advt., Inc., Kansas City, Mo., 1977—; v.p. Scott Guides, Inc., 1988—; guest lectr. colls., univs. Active Heart of Am. United Way, 1966-80, mem. exec. bd., 1976, bd. dirs., 1976-80; active Help Educate Emotionally Disturbed, Inc., Kansas City, Mo., 1968-80, pres. bd. dirs. HEED Found., 1979-80; active Heart of Am. council Boy Scouts Am., 1975-85, bd. govs. Bacchus Ednl. and Cultural Found., Kansas City, 1973-76, found. chmn., 1975; mem. Kansas City Bicentennial Commn., 1975-76; founder, bd. dirs., sec. Kansas City Union Sta. Inc., 1988—; founder, bd. dirs., 1st v.p. Union Sta. Commn., 1987—; bd. dirs. Hist. Kansas City Found., 1989—; mem. issues selection com. Kansas City Consensus, 1988—, mem. strategic planning focus group, 1989—; vol. coach, local youth leagues, 1975-83; cons. Com. for County Progress Campaigns, Charter Campaign, Jackson County, Mo., 1970; Kansas City Magnet Schs., 1986-88, speaker internat. conf., 1988. Recipient various awards including United Way Nat. Communications award, 1975; Effie citation N.Y. Mktg. Assn., 1975; 1st Place Print Ad award and 1st Place Poster award 9th Dist. Addy Awards, 1975, 1st Place Regional-Nat. TV Campaign award, 1976; Omni award, 1980-82, 86, 87; Silver award KCAD, 1981; 1st Place TV Campaign award KCAF Big One Show, 1976; Best-of-Show and Gold medal award Dallas Soc. Visual Communications, 1976; Gold medal Kansas City Litho Craftsmen, 1988; named Mic-O-Say hon. warrior, 1978. Mem. Internat. Platform Assn., Advt. and Sales Execs. Found. Democrat. Author numerous TV, radio commls., film, TV and radio musical compositions; film and television direction; creator "Modulatin' With McCall" NBC, 1976-77; film with Walter Cronkite, Union Station is US., 1988. Home: #1 Chartwell 9505 State Line Rd Kansas City MO 64114 Office: 21 E 29th St Kansas City MO 64108

MURDOCK, SETH, petroleum company executive; b. Detroit, Jan. 13, 1947; s. David Melvin and Mary (Beatty) M.; B.S., Wayne State U., 1979, M.B.A., 1980. Acctg. mgr. J.V. Carr & Son, Inc., Detroit, 1975-80; audit acct. Lockheed Aircraft Corp., Burbank, Calif., 1980-81; chief fin. officer Americal Petroleum, Inc., Ventura, Calif., 1981-83; chmn., chief exec. officer Murdock Industries, Inc., 1983—; dir. Synk Cosmetics, Satellite Internat., Inc., subsidiary Murdock Industries, Inc., Puerto Rico. Active Nat. council Boy Scouts Am. C.P.A., Mich., Calif. Mem. Nat. Assn. Accts., Petroleum Controller League. Republican. Author: Supply Side Economics, 1982. Office: 12440 Moorpark Ave Studio City CA 91604

MURDOCK, WENDY JEAN, management consultant; b. Montreal, Que., Can., Aug. 28, 1952; came to U.S., 1983; d. James David and Bernice Evelyn (Dean) M. BA, McGill U., 1973; MBA, U. Western Ont., 1982. Assoc. McKinsey & Co. Inc., N.Y.C., 1982-87, prin., 1988—. Office: McKinsey & Co Inc 55 E 52d St New York NY 10022

MURDY, WAYNE WILLIAM, oil company executive; b. Los Angeles, July 4, 1944; s. Lee Robert and Louise Marie (Kleinemas) M.; m. Diana Yvonne DeCruse, Nov. 23, 1968; children: Dawn Marie, Christopher John, Joseph William, Elizabeth Anne. A.A., El Camino Coll., 1966; B.S., Calif. State U., Long Beach, 1968. C.P.A., Calif. Adminstrv. assoc. Atlantic Richfield Co., Los Angeles, 1968-69; audit mgr. Arthur Andersen & Co., Los Angeles, 1969-78; gen. auditor Getty Oil Co., Los Angeles, 1978-81; group v.p. Texaco Trading & Transp. Inc., Denver, 1981-87; v.p. fin., chief fin. officer Apache Corp., Denver, 1987—. Mem. Am. Inst. C.P.A.s. Roman Catholic. Clubs: University (Denver); Village (Cherry Hills Village, Colo.). Office: Apache Corp One United Bank Ctr 1700 Lincoln St Denver CO 80203-4519

MURGATROYD, ERIC NEAL, data processing executive; b. Ware, Mass., July 30, 1950; s. Howard E. and Jean Francis (Roberts) M.; m. Pamela Lee Swift, Aug. 14, 1976; 1 child, Lisa Nicole. Student, U. Mass, 1968-70. Computer operator Hammond Organ Co., Chgo., 1972-73; systems analyst Cen. States Health, Welfare and Pension Funds, Chgo., 1973-78; sr. systems analyst Gould-Fluid Components Div., Niles, Ill., 1978-80; project leader mfg. systems Motorola Corp., Schaumburg, Ill., 1980-85; mgr. billing systems Cellular Billing Systems, Inc., Park Ridge, Ill., 1980-85; mgr. data processing Leaf, Inc., Bannockburn, Ill., 1986—. Author computer programs. Mem. Mensa. Office: Leaf Inc 2355 Waukegan Rd Bannockburn IL 60015

MURO, ROY ALFRED, independent media service corporation executive; b. N.Y.C., Sept. 22, 1942; s. Angelo Dominick and Virginia (Guangi) M.; m. Lorraine D. Friedman, July 5, 1968; children: Bradley, Jessica. B.S., Bklyn. Coll., 1964; M.B.A., N.Y. Grad. Sch. Bus., 1966. C.P.A., N.Y. Sr. acct. Price Waterhouse & Co., N.Y.C., 1966-71; comptroller Vitt Media Internat. Inc., N.Y.C., 1979-82, pres., chief operating officer, 1982—; lectr. in field. Mem. Am. Inst. CPA's, N.Y. State Soc. CPA's, Advt. Agy. Fin. Mgmt. Group, Nat. Agrimktg. Assn., Internat Radio and TV Soc., N.Y. Credit and Fin. Mgmt. Assn. (lectr.), Assn. Travel Mktg. Execs. Home: 8 Irene Ct East Brunswick NJ 08816 Office: Vitt Media Internat Inc 1114 Ave of Americas New York NY 10036

MURPHEY, ROBERT STAFFORD, pharmaceutical company executive; b. Littleton, N.C., Oct. 29, 1921; married; 2 children. B.S., U. Richmond, 1942; M.S., U. Va., 1947, Ph.D. in Organic Chemistry, 1949. Research chemist in medicinal chemistry A.H. Robins & Co. Inc., Richmond, Va., 1948-53, dir. chemistry research, 1953-55, assoc. dir., 1955-57, dir. research, 1957-60, dir. internat. research, 1960-66, dir. sci. devel., 1966-82, asst. v.p., 1967-73, dir. sci. devel., v.p., 1973-82, v.p. sci. affairs and corp. devel., 1982-83, sr. v.p. sci. affairs and corp. devel., 1983-87, sr. v.p., dir. new bus. devel., 1983—. Mem. AAAS, Am. Chem. Soc. Office: A H Robins & Co Inc 1407 Cummings Dr PO Box 26609 Richmond VA 23261

MURPHY, AUSTIN DE LA SALLE, economist, educator, banker; b. N.Y.C., Nov. 20, 1917; s. Daniel Joseph and Marie Cornelia (Austin) M.; m. Mary Patricia Halpin, June 12, 1948 (dec. May 1974); children: Austin de la Salle, Owen Gerard; m. Lee Chilton Romero, Dec. 14, 1974; stepchildren: Thomas Romero, Robert Romero. AB, St. Francis Coll., Bklyn., 1938; AM (Hayden fellow 1938-40), Fordham U., 1940, PhD, 1949. Instr. econs. Fordham U., 1938-41; Instr. econs. Georgetown U., 1941-42; asst. statistician, statis. controls Bd. Econ. Warfare, 1942; sr. econs. research editor N.Y. State Dept. Labor, 1947-50; lectr. econs. Fordham U. Sch. Edn., 1946-55; instr. N.Y. U. Sch. Commerce, 1949-51; dean sch. bus. adminstrn. Seton Hall U., South Orange, N.J., 1950-55; Albert O'Neill prof. Am. enterprise, dean sch. bus. adminstrn. Canisius Coll., Buffalo, 1955-62; dir. edn. dept. NAM, 1962-63; exec. v.p. Savs. Banks Assn. N.Y. State, 1963-70; chmn., chief exec. officer East River Savs. Bank, 1970—; trustee Erie County Savs. Bank, 1958-63; charter trustee Savs. Bank Rockland County, 1965-70; chmn. bd., trustee Savs. Bank Life Ins. Fund, 1983-87; chmn. dist I, mem. adv. council Conf. State Bank Suprs.; chmn. bd. Fund Savs. Bank; bd. dir. MSB Fund, Inc., Investors Mortgage Ins. Co., N.Y. Fed. Home Loan Bank. Author: (with Fleming Frasca, and Mannion) Social Studies Review Book, 1946, Leading Problems of New Jersey Manufacturing Industries, (with Bullock and Doerflinger), 1953, Reasons for Relocation, 1955, Forecast of Industrial Expansion in Buffalo and the Niagara Frontier, 1956, Metropolitan Buffalo Perspective, 1958; editor Handbook of New York Labor Statistics, 1950. Mem. Livingston (N.J.) Charter Commn., 1954-55; mem. capital expenditures com., City of Buffalo, 1957-63; trustee Fordham U., 1973-79, N.Y. Med. Coll., 1978-81; bd. dirs. N.Y. council Boy Scouts Am., 1974—, Jr. Achievement of Buffalo, 1958-63, Invest-in-Am. 1st lt. U.S. Army, 1942-46. Named Knight of Malta. Mem. NAM (chmn. ednl. aids com. 1958-63, v.p. 1962-63), Am. Fin. Assn., Nat. Def. Transp. Assn. (life), Nat. Assn. Mut. Savs. Banks (dir., treas. 1976-81), Friendly Sons St. Patrick (chmn. admissions com.), Alpha Kappa Psi, Pi Gamma Mu. Clubs: K.C. (Williamsville, N.Y.), Union League, World Trade (N.Y.C.), Larchmont Yacht, Univ. of Larchmont, Down Town (vice-chmn.), Lower Manhattan Assn. (chmn. Membership and Fin. Com.). Home: 1060 Bay Head Dr Mamaroneck NY 10543 Office: East River Savs Bank 145 Huguenot St New Rochelle NY 10801

MURPHY, CARROL MARIE, municipal housing official; b. Buffalo, N.Y., Aug. 10, 1949; d. Leonard Anthony and Marie Carol (Wilkolaski) Czwojdak; m. Jeffrey Reece Vaughan, Sept. 18, 1970 (div. July, 1978); m. Jim Ray Murphy, May 14, 1982. BA in Psychology, SUNY, Buffalo, 1971. Asst. dir. Optical Recognition Systems, Reston, Va., 1972-74; adminstrv. aide Denney & Co., Pitts., 1975-76; program coord. City of Ashland (Ky.), 1977-79; exec. dir. Appalachian Foothills Housing, Russell, Ky., 1979-87, Statesville Housing Authority, N.C., 1987-89; dir. housing programs San Diego Housing Commn., 1989—; cons. Pvt. Developers, Columbus, Ohio, Appalachian Foothills Housing. Mem. Civitan Club, Statesville, 1988—. Mem. Nat. Assn. Housing & Redevelopement Officials (exec. mgmt. cert.), Nat. Community Devel. Assn., Pub. Housing Authorities Dirs. Assn. Republican. Episcopalian. Office: 1625 Newton Ave San Diego CA 92113

MURPHY, CHARLES HAYWOOD, JR., petroleum company executive; b. El Dorado, Ark., Mar. 6, 1920; s. Charles Haywood and Bertie (Wilson) M.; m. Johnie Walker, Oct. 14, 1939; children: Michael Walker, Martha, Charles Haywood, III, Robert Madison. Ed. pub. schs., Ark.; LLD, U. Ark., 1966. Ind. oil producer 1939-50; chmn. Murphy Oil Corp., El Dorado, Ark., 1972—, also bd. dirs.; chmn. 1st United Bankshares; chmn. exec. com. 1st Comml. Corp., Little Rock. Bd. govs. Oschner Med. Found.; bd. adminstrs. Tulane U.; mem. nat. adv. bd. Smithsonian Instn.; past mem. Ark. Bd. Higher Edn. Served as infantryman World War II. Recipient citation for outstanding individual service in natural resource mgmt. Nat. Wildlife Fedn. Mem. Am. Petroleum Inst. (past exec. com., hon. bd. dirs.), Nat. Petroleum Council (past chmn.), 25 Yr. Club Petroleum Industry (past pres.). Office: Murphy Oil Corp 200 Peach St El Dorado AR 71730

MURPHY, CHARLES JOSEPH, investment banker; b. N.Y.C., Sept. 18, 1947; s. Charles Joseph and Mary V. (Vaughan) M.; m. Karen Lyn Canevari, Aug. 18, 1973; 3 children. B.E.E., Manhattan Coll., 1969; M.B.A., NYU, 1974, A.P.C., 1975. Chartered fin. analyst. Avionics engr. Sikorsky Aircraft, Stratford, Conn., 1969-70; engr., rate analyst Am. Electric Power Co., N.Y.C., 1970-76; equity analyst First Boston Corp., N.Y.C., 1976-78, v.p. capital markets, 1982-84, mng. dir. utilities and telecommunications fin., 1984-87, head investment bankinggroup, 1988—. Mem. N.Y. Soc. Security Analysts (sr.). Roman Catholic. Office: First Boston Corp Park Avenue Pla New York NY 10055

MURPHY, DEBORAH WILSON, financial executive; b. Erie, Pa., Jan. 17, 1950; d. Clair L. and Marion (Latimer) Wilson; m. Douglas S. Murphy, May 26, 1978; children: Mark, Melinda, Ryan. Asst. trust officer Security Peoples Trust Co., Erie, 1968-76; v.p., br. mgr. Paine Webber, Inc., Erie, 1976—; co-owner Miller Travel Svcs., Erie, 1985—. Corporator Hamot Med. Ctr., Erie; bd. dirs. Erie County Hist. Soc., United Way of Erie County; mem. adv. bd. Hamot Women's Resource Ctr., Erie. Named Outstanding Young Woman of Yr., Erie Jaycee's, 1980. Mem. Estate Planning Coun. (pres. 1986-87), Inst. Cert. Fin. Planners (cert.), Nat. Assn. Bank Women (pres. N.W. Pa. group 1975-76), Erie Club. Office: Paine Webber Inc 702 First Nat Bank Bldg Erie PA 16501

MURPHY, EDWARD JEROME, JR, brokerage firm executive; b. Bklyn., Feb. 4, 1938; s. Edward Jerome and Barbara Marie (Shannon) M.; Frances Tripoli, Sept. 10, 1977; Elisabeth, Deborah, Edward, Anmarie, Kristen, Kevin. Grad. high sch., Bklyn. Registered rep., securities broker. Asst. head trader Delafield, Childs, N.Y.C., 1975; trader Cohn, Delaire & Kaufman, N.Y.C., 1975-76; sales trader Mosely, Halgarten & Estabrook, N.Y.C., 1976-77; head trader John Muir & Co., N.Y.C., 1978-79; head inst. trader Fahnestock & Co., N.Y.C., 1979-82; floor broker N.Y. Futures Exchange, N.Y.C., 1982-83; head equity trader Bernard Herold & Co., N.Y.C., 1983-85; sales trader Drexel, Burnham, Lambert, N.Y.C., 1985-86; mgr. trading dept. Newbridge Securities, N.Y.C., 1986. Mem. South St. Seaport Mus., N.Y.C., 1968—, Fraser Civic Assn., Bklyn., 1982-86. Served with USAR, 1956—. Mem. Security Traders Assn. of N.Y., N.Y. Futures Exchange, Non-Commd. Officers Assn. Roman Catholic. KC (Grand Knight 1985-87). Home: 2076 New York Ave Brooklyn NY 11210 Office: Newbridge Securities 120 Wall St New York NY 10005

MURPHY, EDWARD PATRICK, JR., gas utility company executive; b. Syracuse, N.Y., Apr. 28, 1943; s. Edward Patrick and Rosemary Margaret (McCloskey) M.; m. Barbara Lynne Stibitz; children: E. Patrick III, Kevin C., Meghan L. BA in Acctg./Law, Clarkson U., 1965; exec. program, Columbia U., 1984. Mgmt. trainee The Bklyn. Union Gas Co., 1965, various staff and operating positions, 1966-75, budget dir., 1976-81, auditor, 1982-88, asst. v.p., 1988—. Vice chmn. bd. Bklyn. chpt ARC, 1986—; mem. audit com. ARC of Greater N.Y., 1987—. Mem. Inst. Internal Auditors, Am. Gas Assn. (mem. internal auditing com. 1982—, vice chmn. 1985-86, chmn. 1986-87; mem. budgeting and fin. forecasting com. 1974-81, vice chmn. 1977-78, chmn. 1978-79; Outstanding Svc. award 1987). Home: 257 Harvard Ave Rockville Center NY 11570 Office: Bklyn Union Gas Co 195 Montague St Brooklyn NY 11201

MURPHY, EUGENE F., communications and electronics executive; b. Flushing, N.Y., Feb. 24, 1936; s. Eugene P. and Delia M.; m. Mary Margaret Cullen, Feb. 20, 1960; children: Eugene, Terence, Mary Kerry, Colleen, Thomas, John, Timothy, Michael. BA, Queens Coll., 1956; JD, Fordham U., 1959; LLM, Georgetown U., 1964. Bar: N.Y. With RCA Global Communications Inc., N.Y.C., 1964-81, v.p. and gen. counsel, 1969-71, exec. v.p. ops., 1972-75, pres., chief operating officer, 1975-76, pres., chief exec. officer, 1976-81; chmn., chief exec. officer RCA Communications Inc., N.Y.C., 1981-86; sr. v.p. Gen. Electric Co., N.Y.C., 1986—. Served with USMCR, 1959-60. Mem. Armed Forces Communications and Electronics Assn. (past nat. chmn.), ABA, FCC Bar Assn., N.Y. State Bar Assn. Clubs: Marco Polo, Plandome Country, Plandome Field and Marine. Office: GE Co 570 Lexington Ave New York NY 10022

MURPHY, GERALD LEO, commercial property executive, automobile leasing company executive; b. Boston, Dec. 7, 1936; s. John Joseph and Cecelia Ann (Cody) M.; m. Joan Virginia Lautenbach, June 13, 1959; children: Richard, Douglas. BS in Mech. Engring., MIT, 1957; MBA, U. Chgo., 1973. Registered profl. engr., Ind. Assn. exec. 1966-80; dist. mgr. U.S. C. of C., Chgo., 1966-69; exec. v.p. Evanston (Ill.) C. of C., 1969-74; gen. mgr. Potato Growers of Idaho, Blackfoot, Idaho, 1975-80; pres. Levy Venture Mgmt., Inc., Evanston, Ill., 1985—. Inventor impact absorbing steering column for automobile. Mem. exec. com. Ind. Rep. Com., 1966-69; ednl. coun. MIT, 1961-86; bd. dirs. Evanston Salvation Army, 1988—. Named Outstanding State Chmn. Ind. Jaycees, 1964. Mem. Am. Soc. Assn. Execs. (cert., Outstanding Young Man of Yr. 1971), Kiwanis (bd. dirs. Evanston chpt. 1987—). Republican. Presbyterian. Home: 223 Ginger Brook Oak Brook IL 60521 Office: Levy Venture Mgmt Inc 1212 Chicago Ave Evanston IL 60204-5372

MURPHY, GLENN EARL, management consultant; b. Chgo., Dec. 6, 1935; s. Earl and Dorothy (Cranston) M.; m. Carol Louise Holtz; children: Lee, Scott, Michelle, Glenn. AB in Econs., St. Joseph's Coll., 1975. V.p. Corroon & Black Ill., Chgo., 1960-76; mng. prin. G. Murphy & Assocs., Wheaton, Ill., 1976—; bd. dirs. Jet Air Freight, Ft. Wayne, Ind. Bd. dirs. Cen. DuPage Counseling Services, Glen Ellyn, Ill., 1987—, St. James Ch., Glen Ellyn, 1978-81; officer Raintree Homeowners Assn., 1978-80. Sgt. USAF, 1957-63, since with Res. Mem. N.Am. Soc. Employee Assistance, Inst. Cert. Fin. Planners, Economic Club Chgo., Raintree Tennis Club, Wheaton (Ill.) Sports Club. Republican. Roman Catholic. Office: G Murphy & Assocs Inc 2100 Manchester Rd Wheaton IL 60187

MURPHY, HAROLD GEORGE, financial planner; b. L.A., Sept. 11, 1934; s. Harold Robert and Verda Lucille (Christensen) M.; m. Patricia Marilyn Murphy, Nov. 8, 1952; children: Steven, Russell, Jeffrey, Scott, Sheri. Student, Riverside City Coll., 1954-55, U.S. Air Force U., 1962, Washburn U., 1963. Cert. fin. planner. Capt., pilot Continental Airlines, Inc., Denver, 1965-83; assoc. Gekierke/Graham and Assocs., El Paso, Tex., 1984-87; assoc. dir. edn. G.P. Graham and Assocs., El Paso, 1987—. Contbr. articles to profl. jours. Bd. dirs. El Paso Internat. Amigo Air Show, 1986-88. Maj. USAF, 1950-65, Vietnam, mem. Res. (ret.). Decorated D.F.C. Mem. El Paso Estate Planning Coun., El Paso Assn. Life Underwriters, Million Dollar Round Table, Lions. Republican. Office: GP Graham & Assocs 6070 Gateway E 102 El Paso TX 79905

MURPHY, JAMES, diversified communications company executive; b. County Kerry, Ireland, May 22, 1937; came to U.S., 1957; s. Patrick and Mary (Sheahan) M.; m. Elizabeth Mary Kennelly, Aug. 22, 1964; children: Brendan T., Roger W. BBA in Fin., Pace U., 1968, MBA in Mgmt., 1972. Asst. v.p. treasury GTE Corp., Stamford, Conn., 1976-85, v.p., treas., 1986—; v.p. fin. GTE Midwestern Telephone Ops., Westfield, Ind., 1985-86. Served with U.S. Army, 1961-63. Mem. Fin. Execs. Inst., Nat. Assn. Corp. Treas. Roman Catholic. Office: GTE Corp One Stamford Forum Stamford CT 06904

MURPHY, JAMES PATRICK, mechanical engineer; b. St. Paul, July 13, 1943; s. James Edward and Shirley (Peck) M.; m. Susan Mary Ratté, Aug. 13, 1966; 1 child, Sean Patrick. BA, St. Cloud (Minn.) State U., 1968; postgrad., U. Minn., 1969-71. Machinist apprentice Water Gremlin Co., White Bear Lake, Minn., 1968-71; ptnr., mgr. Water Gremlin Co., Ponce, P.R., 1973-76; plant mgr. Schaper Mfg., 1971-73; mgr. Gen. Electric Service Apparatus Shop, Ponce, 1976-78; rotating equipment specialist Gen. Electric Co., Atlanta, 1978-81; mgr. mech. sales Cleve. Electric Co., Atlanta, 1981-84; ptnr., mgr. Murphy Mech. Services, Inc., Lawrenceville, Ga., 1984—. Served with USNR, 1963-68. Mem. Soc. Plant Engrs. Republican. Roman Catholic. Office: Murphy Mech Svcs Inc 396 Sancho Dr Lawrenceville GA 30244

MURPHY, JOAN BARRON, non-profit organization administrator; b. Troy, Ala., Sept. 30, 1935; d. William Gaston and Mary Eunice (Matthews) Barron; m. William Robert Murphy, Dec. 31, 1955; children: Robert

Michael, William Patrick, Pamela Murphy Wright. Student, Troy State Tchrs. Coll., 1952, Mars Hill Coll., 1955, Blue Ridge Tech. Inst., 1980. Sec., bookkeeper City Bd. Edn., Troy, 1952-53; sec. outdoor lighting Gen. Electric Co., Hendersonville, N.C., 1956-57; pub. acct., pub. stenographer Hendersonville, 1957-67; dir. fin. and adminstrn. Western Carolina Community, Hendersonville, 1967—; pub. acct. Barrire's Secretarial Service, Hendersonville, 1965-68; fin. sec. St. James Episcopal Ch., Hendersonville, 1966-68; prin. Church St. 66 Service, Hendersonville, 1984-86; bd. dirs. Quality Tire Co., Inc., Hendersonville; fin. cons. Hendersonville County Workshop, Hendersonville, 1966-69, Council on Aging, Hendersonville, 1967-70, Hands and Fingers, Brevard, N.C., 1970-80; cons. Helping Hand Day Care Ctr., Hendersonville, 1967, Play and Learn Day Care Ctr., Hendersonville, 1968-80. Bd. dirs. Henderson County United Way, Hendersonville, 1968-74; mem. Mayor's Disaster Com., Hendersonville, 1971. Mem. Bus. and Profl. Women's Club (pres. 1968-70). Republican. Baptist. Lodge: Eastern Star (assoc. matron 1985-86). Home: 111 Brightwater Heights Hendersonville NC 28739

MURPHY, JOHN ARTHUR, tobacco and brewing company executive; b. N.Y.C., Dec. 15, 1929; s. John A. and Mary J. (Touhey) M.; m. Carole Ann Paul, June 28, 1952; children: John A., Kevin P., Timothy M., Kellyann, Robert B., Kathleen. B.S., Villanova U., 1951; J.D., Columbia U., 1954. Bar: N.Y. 1954. Since practiced in N.Y.C.; ptnr. firm Conboy, Hewitt O'Brien & Boardman, 1954-62; asst. gen. counsel Philip Morris, Inc., N.Y.C., 1962-66, v.p., 1967-76, exec. v.p., 1976-78, group exec. v.p., 1978-84, pres., 1984—, also bd. dirs.; asst. to pres. Philip Morris Internat., 1966-67, exec. v.p., 1967-71; pres., chief exec. officer Miller Brewing Co., Milw., 1971-78, chmn. bd., chief exec. officer, 1978-84; dir. Nat. Westminster Bank USA. Trustee North Shore Univ. Hosp., Marquette U., Alverno Coll.; dir., mem. exec. com. Keep Am. Beautiful, Inc. Decorated Knight of Malta. Mem. ABA, N.Y. State Bar Assn. Office: Philip Morris Cos Inc 120 Park Ave New York NY 10017

MURPHY, JOHN JOSEPH, manufacturing company executive; b. Olean, N.Y., Nov. 24, 1931; s. John Joseph and Mary M.; m. Louise John; children: Kathleen A. Murphy Bell, Karen L. Murphy Rochelli, Patricia L. Murphy Smith, Michael J. AAS in Mech. Engring., Rochester Inst. Tech., 1952; MBA, So. Meth. U. Engr. Clark div. Dresser Industries, Olean, 1952-67; gen. mgr. roots blower div. Clark div. Connersville, Ind., 1967-69; pres. crane, hoist and tower div. Muskegon, Mich., 1969-70; pres. machinery group Houston, 1970-75; sr. v.p. ops. Dallas, 1980, exec. v.p., 1982, pres., 1982—, chmn. bd., chief exec. officer, 1983—; bd. dirs. PepsiCo, Inc.; mem. Pres.'s Export Council. Chmn. bd. trustees St. Bonaventure (N.Y.) U.; bd. dirs. Tex. Research League. Bus. Served with U.S. Army, 1954-56. Mem. Am. Council for Capital Formation (bd. dirs.), U.S. C. of C. (bd. dirs.), Machinery and Allied Products Inst. (exec. com.). Office: Dresser Industries Inc 1600 Pacific Bldg Box 718 Dallas TX 75221 *

MURPHY, JOHN JOSEPH, JR., investment company executive; b. Elmhurst, N.Y., June 2, 1951; s. John Joseph and Ellen Marie (Ulrich) M.; m. Monica Marie Des Marais, Oct. 10, 1975; children: Abigail, Dylan, Regan. AB, Coll. Holy Cross, 1973; MBA, Dartmouth Coll., 1975. V.p. Citicorp Venture Capital, Ltd., N.Y.C., 1975-83; ptnr. Adler & Shaykin, 1983-87; mng. ptnr. Murphy & Fauver, N.Y.C., 1987—; chmn. bd. Minority Equity Capital Cp., 1979—; bd. dirs. Folger Adam Co., Lemont, Ill., Peterson Outdoor Advt. Corp., Orlando, Fla., Addiction Recovery Corp., Waltham, Mass. Mem. N.Y. Venture Capital Forum (bd. dirs. 1984—), N.Y. Athletic Club. Democrat. Roman Catholic. Home: 3 Stuyvesant Oval 12F New York NY 10009 Office: Murphy & Fauver 30 Rockefeller Ctr 19th Fl New York NY 10020

MURPHY, KATHLEEN JOAN, development company owner; b. N.Y.C., Mar. 24, 1947; d. John Joseph and Frances Lepley (Spates) M.; m. Konstantine W. Tsombikos; children: William Konstantine, John Konstantine. BA, Marymount Manhattan Coll., 1968; MA, NYU, 1971. Cons. McKinsey & Co., Amsterdam, Netherlands, 1971-75, Mexico City, 1975-76, N.Y.C., 1976-82; owner Global Bus. Strategy & Mgmt., N.Y.C., 1982—; adj. prof. Marymount Manhattan Coll., 1984—. Author: Macroproject Development in the Third World, 1983; chmn. adv. bd. TV series Great Projects (in conjunction with Pub. Broadcasting System and Manifold Prodns.), 1985-86; co-founder Tsombikos Contracting, 1985 contbr. articles to profl. jours. Mem. Am. Women's Econ. Devel. Corp. Avocations: swimming, running.

MURPHY, MARY KATHRYN, industrial hygienist; b. Kansas City, Mo., Apr. 16, 1941; d. Arthur Charles and Mary Agnes (Fitzgerald) Wahlstedt; m. Thomas E. Murphy Jr., Aug. 26, 1963; children: Thomas E. III, David W. BA, Avila Coll., Kansas City, 1962; MS, Cen. Mo. State U., 1975. Cert. in comprehensive practice of indsl. hygiene. Indsl. hygienist Kansas City area office Occupational Safety and Health Adminstrn., 1975-78, regional indsl. hygienist, 1979-86; dir. indsl. hygiene Chart Svcs., Shawnee, Kans., 1986-87; dir. indsl. hygiene and hazardous substance control Hall-Kimbrell Environ. Mgmt. and Pollution COntrol, Lawrence, Kans., 1987-88, mgr. dept. indsl. hygiene div. environ. mgmt. and pollution control, 1988-89; dir. indsl. hygiene Hazardous Waste Div. Burns & McDonnell, Engrs., Architects, Kansas City, Mo., 1989—; asst. dir. safety office U. Kans. Med. Ctr., 1978-79. Summer talent fellow Kaw Valley Heart Assn., 1961. Mem. Am. Indsl. Hygiene Assn. (sec.-treas. Mid-Am. sect. 1978-79, bd. dirs. 1981, mem. auditcom.), Am. Chem. Soc., Am. Conf. Govt. Indsl. Hygienists (mem. chem. agts. threshold limit value com.), Am. Acad. Indsl. Hygiene, N.Y. Acad. Scis., AAAS, Internat. Soc. Environ. Toxicology and Cancer, Am. Coll. Toxicology, Am. Conf. on Chem. Labeling. Home: 10616 W 123rd Street Overland Park KS 66213 Office: Burns & McDonnell Engrs Architects & Cons 4800 E 63d Kansas City MO 64130

MURPHY, MARY REYNOLDS, accountant; b. Utica, N.Y., Nov. 15, 1948; m. Desmal Paul Murphy Jr., July 2, 1977. BA, Wash. State U., 1970; MS in Mgmt., Houston Bapt. U., 1987. CPA, Tex; cert. internal auditor. Acct. Verne Engring. Co., Detroit, Houston, 1971-76; auditor ICI Ams., Inc., Bayport, Tex., 1976-78; audit mgr. Aramco Services Co., Houston, 1984—; Pres. PC Users Group Aramco Services Co., Houston, 1985. Mem. Am. Inst. CPA's, Tex. Soc. CPA's (Houston chpt.), Inst. Internal Auditors. Republican. Home: 115 Pine Manor Conroe TX 77385

MURPHY, MICHAEL ALAN, financial analyst, accountant; b. Abington, Mass., Oct. 23, 1956; s. Paul Edward and Lucy Mae (Kozloff) M.; m. Sharon Colleen O'Brien, Sept. 22, 1985. BS, Babson Coll., 1978. CPA,. Contract surety underwriter Safeco Corp., Redmond. Author, editor resource material and tng. manual in fin. analysis for contractors, real estate developers. Mem. Am. Inst. CPA's, Wash. Soc. CPA's, Constrn. Fin. Mgmt. Assn., Am. Mgmt. Assn., Alpha Kappa Psi (treas. 1976-78). Roman Catholic. Clubs: City, Washington Athletic, Harbor (Seattle). Home: 2020 43d Ave E Apt 66 Seattle WA 98112 Office: Safeco Corp Surety 4909 156th Ave NE Redmond WA 98082

MURPHY, MICHAEL EMMETT, food company executive; b. Winchester, Mass., Oct. 16, 1936; s. Michael Cornelius and Bridie (Curran) M.; m. Adele Anne Kasupski, Sept. 12, 1959; children—Leslie Maura, Glenn Stephen, Christopher McNeil. B.S. in Bus. Adminstrn, Boston Coll., 1958; M.B.A., Harvard, 1962. Financial analyst Maxwell House div. Gen. Foods Corp., White Plains, N.Y., 1962-64; cost mgr. Maxwell House div. Gen. Foods Corp., San Leandro, Calif., 1964-65; controller Maxwell House div. Gen. Foods Corp., Jacksonville, Fla., 1965-67, Hoboken, N.J., 1967-68; mgr. fin. planning and analysis Maxwell House div. Gen. Foods Corp., 1968-69; mgr. planning Hanes Corp., Winston-Salem, N.C., 1969-70; corp. controller Hanes Corp., 1970—; v.p. adminstrn. Hanes Corp. (Hanes Knitwear), 1972-74; v.p. finance Ryder System Inc., Miami, Fla., 1974-75; exec. v.p. Ryder System Inc., 1975-79; exec. v.p., dir. Sara Lee Corp., Chgo., 1979—. Jr. Achievement mgmt. adviser, 1965-66; mem. exec. com. Hudson County Tax Research Council, 1967-68; trustee Boston Coll., 1980-88; chmn. Civic Fedn. Chgo., 1984-86; bd. dirs. Jobs for Youth, Chgo., 1983-86, Lyric Opera, 1986—. Served to 1st lt. AUS, 1958-60. Mem. Hoboken, Winston-Salem, Miami chambers commerce, Internat. Platform Assn., Fin. Execs. Inst., UN Assn., Ouimet Scholar Alumni Group, Beta Gamma Sigma. Roman Catholic. Home: 401 Sheridan Rd Winnetka IL 60093 Office: Sara Lee Corp 3 First National Pla Chicago IL 60602

MURPHY, RAMON BIRKETT, financial services company executive; b. Jamaica, Sept. 7, 1935; s. Vincent Hubert and Ruby Mae (Earle) M.; m. Ouida Vivienne Bair, Aug. 18, 1962; children: Juliet A., Donna M., Gordon R., Angela V. Student, U. Toronto, 1968, Coll. Fin. Planning, 1985. Chartered life underwriter, cert. fin. planner. Sales rep. N.Am. Life Assn. Can., Jamaica, 1963-68, tng. mgr., 1968-70; tng. dir. Life of Jamaica, 1970-73, dir. agys., 1973-75, v.p. mktg., 1975-76, sr. v.p. agy., bd. dirs., 1976-78; v.p. sales Lincoln Nat. Miami Fin. Services, Fla., 1983—; v.p., sec., bd. dirs. Advanced Fin. Planning, Miami, 1984—. Fundraiser Miami Children's Hosp., 1986—, March of Dimes, 1980—, Assn. Devel. Exceptional, Miami, 1980—. Mem. Internat. Assn. Fin. Planners, Internat. Bd. Fin. Planners, Inst. Cert. Fin. Planners, Nat. Assn. Life Underwriters, Fla. Assn. Life Underwriters (co-chmn. edn. 1987-88), Miami Assn. Life Underwriters (pres. 1986-87), Million Dollar Roundtable. Republican. Club: Country (Miami). Home: 6329 NW 175th Terr Miami FL 33015 Office: Lincoln Nat Miami Fin Svcs Inc 8390 NW 53d St Suite 200 Miami FL 33166

MURPHY, RANDALL KENT, consultant; b. Laramie, Wyo., Nov. 8, 1943; s. Robert Joseph and Sally (McConnell) M.; student U. Wyo., 1961-65; M.B.A., So. Meth. U., 1983; m. Cynthia Laura Hillhouse, Dec. 29, 1978; children—Caroline, Scott, Emily. Dir. mktg. Wycoa, Inc., Denver, 1967-70; dir. Communications Resource Inst., Dallas, 1971-72; account exec. Xerox Learning Systems, Dallas, 1973-74; regional mgr. Systema Corp., Dallas, 1975; pres. Performance Assocs.; pres., dir. Acclivus Corp., Dallas, 1976—; founder, chmn. Acclivus Inst., 1982—. Active, Dallas Mus. Fine Arts, Dallas Hist. Soc., Dallas Symphony Assn. Served with AUS, 1966. Mem. Am. Soc. Tng. and Devel., Sales and Mktg. Execs. Internat., Inst. Mgmt. Scis., Soc. Applied Learning Tech., Nat. Soc. Performance and Instrn., Assn. M.B.A. Execs., Internat. Platform Assn., Assn. Mgmt. Cons., World Futre Soc., Am. Assn. Higher Edn., World Future Soc., Soc. for Intercultural Edn., Tng. and Research, Internat. Fedn. Tng. and Devel. Orgns., So. Meth. U. Alumni Assn. U. Wyo. Alumni Assn. Roman Catholic. Club: University. Author: Performance Management of the Selling Process, 1979; Coaching and Counseling for Performance, 1980; Managing Development and Performance, 1982; Acclivus Performance Planning System, 1983; (with others) BASE for Sales Performance, 1983, Acclivus Coaching, 1984, Acclivus Sales Negotiation, 1985; BASE for Effective Presentations, 1987, BASE for Strategic Sales Presentations, 1988, The New BASE for Sales Excellence, 1988, Major Account Planning and Strategy, 1989, Strategic Management of the Selling Process, 1989; co-inventor The Randy-Band, multi-purpose apparel accessory, 1968. Home: 6540 Crestpoint Dr Dallas TX 75240

MURPHY, ROBERT BLAIR, management consulting company executive; b. Phila., Jan. 19, 1931; s. William Beverly and Helen Marie (Brennan) M.; B.S., Yale, 1953; m. Elise McBryde, July 10, 1981; children by previous marriage—Stephen, Emily, Julia, David, Catherine. Indsl. engr. Dupont Corp., Aiken, S.C., 1953-55; mgr. sales can div. Reynolds Metals Co., Richmond, Va., 1955-69; gen. mgr. corrugated div. Continental Can Co., N.Y.C., 1969-73; v.p and gen. mgr. beverage div. Am. Can Co., Greenwich, Conn., 1973-75; asso. Heidrick & Struggles, Inc., N.Y.C., 1976-78, v.p., 1978; v.p., mng. dir. Stamford office Spencer Stuart & Assocs., 1978-84, ptnr., 1982-84; co-founder Sullivan-Murphy Assocs., 1984—. Clubs: Round Hill, Riverside Yacht (Greenwich); Yale (N.Y.C.); Merion Cricket (Haverford, Pa.). Home: 11 Indian Mill Rd Cos Cob CT 06807 Office: 6 Landmark Sq Stamford CT 06901

MURPHY, TERESA HODES, nursing service executive; b. Kansas City, Mo., Nov. 28, 1955; d. Richard Erb and Barbara Marie (Altman) Hodes; m. Rick S. Murphy. Apr. 23, 1988. BS in Biology magna cum laude, Regis Coll., 1978; BS in Nursing, U. Colo., Denver, 1980; MBA, U. Phoenix, Denver, 1987. RN. Nurse Denver Gen. Hosp., 1980-82, asst. head nurse, 1982-86; head nurse Rose Med. Ctr., Denver, 1986-87; br. dir. Favorite Nurses, Denver, 1987—. Contbr. papers to nursing jours. Mem. Nat. Orgn. Female Execs., Network for Profl. Devel. Roman Catholic. Home: 840 S Lima Aurora CO 80012 Office: Favorite Nurses 425 S Cherry #100 Denver CO 80222

MURPHY, THOMAS LEE, lawyer; b. Topeka, Kans., Nov. 1, 1945; s. Thomas Jefferson and Barbara Lea (Riley) M.; m. Diane Marcella Jauch, Dec. 18, 1964; children: Steven Thomas, Melissa Anna. BA, Elmhurst Coll., 1967; JD, DePaul U., 1971. Bar: Ill. 1971, U.S. Dist. Ct. (no. dist.) Ill. 1971, U.S. Ct. Appeals (7th cir.) 1974, U.S. Tax Ct. 1981. Claims rep. Traveler's Ins., Chgo., 1967-71; staff atty. Cen. Soya Co., Ft. Wayne, Ind., 1971-74; assoc. Moriarty, Rose & Hultquist Ltd., Chgo., 1974-78; atty. Andrew Corp., Orland Park, Ill., 1978—; asst. sec. Andrew Corp., Orland Park, 1982-84, sec., 1984—; instr. bus. law Keller Grad. Sch., Chgo., 1980-81. Arbitrator Better Bus. Bur., Chgo., 1980—; v.p. church council Christ Luth. Ch., Orland Park; pres. SW cooperative found., Oak Forest, Ill., 1988—, bd. dirs. 1983—. Ill. State Regents scholar, 1963-67. Mem. ABA, Ill. Bar Assn., Chgo. Bar Assn., Am. Corp. Counsel Assn. (v.p., bd. dirs. 1983—, pres. Chgo. chpt. 1988-89), Orland Park Area C. of C. (v.p., bd. dirs. 1983-87, pres. 1988—). Lodge: Rotary. Office: Andrew Corp 10500 W 153d St Orland Park IL 60462

MURPHY, THOMAS S., media company executive; b. Bklyn., May 31, 1925; married. B.S., Cornell U., 1945; M.B.A., Harvard U., 1949. With Kenyon & Eckhardt, 1949-51; with Lever Bros. Co., 1951-54; with Capital Cities ABC, Inc. (formerly Capital Cities Communications, Inc.), N.Y.C., 1954—, exec. v.p., 1961-64, pres., 1964-72, chmn. bd., chief exec. officer, 1966—, also bd. dirs.; dir. Gen. Housewares Corp., Texaco Inc., Johnson & Johnson, Internat. Bus. Machines Corp. Served with USN. Office: Capital Cities ABC Inc 77 W 66th St New York NY 10019

MURPHY, WILLIAM FRANCIS, controller consultant; b. Worcester, Mass., Sept. 3, 1931; s. William Francis and Catherine Frances (Shea) M.; m. Marcia Ann Waters, Sept. 13, 1958; children: Kathryne, Thomas, Nancy, James. BS, Northeastern U., Boston, 1955; student, Boston Coll., 1959-61. Fin. analyst Raytheon Co., Lexington, Mass., 1957-61; acctg. mgr. Raytheon Co., Norwalk, Conn., 1961-62; controller Raytheon Co., Hookset, N.H., 1962-64; v.p. fin. Watts Regulator Co., Lawrence, Mass., 1964-69; pres. Taft Electrosystems, Inc., Princeton, N.J., 1969-75; group controller Johnson & Johnson Internat., New Brunswick, N.J., 1975—. Served as sgt. U.S. Army, 1955-57, Korea. Republican. Roman Catholic. Club: Copper Hill Country (Flemington, N.J.). Home: 8 Wycombe Way Princeton Junction NJ 08550 Office: Johnson & Johnson Internat 1 Johnson & Johnson Pla New Brunswick NJ 08933

MURRAY, ALICE PEARL, data processing company executive; b. Clearfield, Pa., Aug. 4, 1932; d. James Clifford and Leah Mae (Williams) M.; B.S., Pa. State U., 1954. With IBM, 1954—, systems service rep., Pitts., 1954-56, computer test center rep., Endicott, N.Y., 1956-58, edn. devel. coordinator, Endicott, 1958-59, adv. instr., Los Angeles, 1959-63, staff instr., Los Angeles, 1963-68, exec. edn. coordinator, 1968-74, sr. instr. Info. Systems Mgmt. Inst., Los Angeles, 1974-84, sr. edn. rep. IBM Americas Far East Corp., 1984-87; sr. staff mem. customer exec. edn.; coordinator exhibit Calif. State Mus. Sci. and Industry; guest speaker before civic and profl. groups; guest instr. various univs. and colls.; profl. lectr. Recipient Distinguished Educator award IBM, 1974, also Outstanding Professionalism award, 1975; hon. citizen Tex., Alaska. Mem. Los Angeles County Art Mus., Pa. State Alumni Assn., Delta Delta Delta. Republican. Club: Wilshire Country. Home: 514 S Gramercy Pl Los Angeles CA 90020 Office: IBM Ams Far East Corp 355 S Grand Los Angeles CA 90060

MURRAY, ALLEN EDWARD, oil company executive; b. N.Y.C., Mar. 5, 1929; s. Allen and Carla (Jones) M.; m. Patricia Ryan, July 28, 1951; children: Allen, Marilyn, Ellen, Eileen, Allison. B.S. in Bus. Adminstrn, NYU, 1956. Trainee Pub. Nat. Bank & Trust Co., N.Y.C., 1948-49; acct. Gulf Oil Corp., 1949-52; various fin. positions Socony-Vacuum Overseas Supply Co. (Mobil), 1952-56; with Mobil Oil Corp. (subs. Mobil Corp.), 1956—, v.p. planning N.Am. div., 1968-69, v.p. planning, supply and transp. N.Am. div., 1969-74, exec. v.p. N.Am. div., 1974, pres. U.S. mktg. and refining div., exec. v.p., 1975-82, pres. worldwide mktg. and refining, 1979-82, corp. pres., 1983-84, chief operating officer, 1984-86, chief exec. officer, chief operating officer, chmn. exec. com., 1986—, chmn. bd., 1986—, also dir., 1976—; pres., chief operating officer Mobil Corp., N.Y.C., 1984-86, chmn., chief exec. officer, 1986—, dir., 1977—; dir. Met. Life Ins. Co. Mem. adv. council Columbia U. Grad. Sch. Bus.; trustee Presbyn. Hosp., N.Y.C. Served with USNR, 1946-48. Mem. Nat. Fgn. Trade Council (dir.), Am. Petroleum Inst. (dir.), Council on Fgn. Relations. Club: Huntington Country. Office: Mobil Corp 150 E 42nd St New York NY 10017 *

MURRAY, ANITA JEAN, data processing executive, consultant; b. Pitts., May 22, 1943; d. Julius and Nancy (Betza) Czujko; m. Christopher H. Murray, Apr. 6, 1968 (div. 1976). BS in Psychology, U. Pitts., 1964; MS in Stats., Stanford U., 1967. Cert. data processor. Systems analyst Pan Am. World Airways, N.Y.C., 1967-69; asst. controller Bunge Corp., N.Y.C., 1969-79; prin. nat. office Arthur Young & Co., N.Y.C., 1979-82; v.p. mgmt. info. systems Murjani Internat. Ltd., Saddle Brook, N.J., 1982-85; pres. Amston Mgmt., Inc., N.Y.C., 1985—; seminar leader Am. Mgmt. Assn., N.Y.C., 1979-82. Author: Minicomputer Bus. Solutions, 1981. Pres. Married Ams. for Tax Equality, N.Y.C., 1973-76; chmn. office mgmt. com. Community Bd. 1, N.Y.C., 1983. Mem. Data Processing Mgmt. Assn. (speaker 1981-82), Internat. Platform Assn., Am. Women Entrepreneurs. Club: Skating of N.Y. Avocations: photography, design. Office: Amston Mgmt Inc 52 Laight St New York NY 10013

MURRAY, CHARLES COURSEN, footwear manufacturing and retail company executive; b. Oak Park, Ill., Aug. 1, 1933; s. Charles Coursen Murray Sr. and Virginia McDowell (Fair) Hodgkins; m. Amanda Winter, Dec. 5, 1959; children: Marcelyn Amanda, Charles Coursen III, Christopher Winter. BA, Dartmouth Coll., 1956. Pres., chief exec. officer G.H. Bass & Co., Wilton, Maine, 1956-74, Murray Equipment Co., Farmington, Maine, 1975-79; v.p. mktg. Weinbrenner Shoe Co., Merrill, Wis., 1980-82; pres., chief exec. officer Ga. Boot Co., Franklin, Tenn., 1982-85; chmn., chief exec. officer Endicott (N.Y.) Johnson Corp., 1986—; mem. regional adv. bd. Chase-Lincoln 1st Bank, Binghamton, N.Y., 1986—. Mem. adv. com. SUNY Sch. Mgmt., Binghamton, 1986—; bd. dirs. United Way Broome County, Binghamton, 1987, Binghamton Symphony, 1986—. Mem. Footwear Industries Am. (chmn. bd. dirs. 1986—, named Exec. of Yr. 1985). Republican. Presbyterian. Clubs: Megantic Fish and Game (Eustis, Maine); Binghamton, Binghamton Country. Lodge: Masons (high priest 1959). Office: Endicott Johnson Corp 1100 E Main St Endicott NY 13760

MURRAY, CHRISTOPHER CHARLES, III, architect; b. Bklyn., July 6, 1950; s. Christopher Charles and Gertrude Rose (Marr) M.; m. Ann Herring, Nov. 16, 1974. BArch, U. Notre Dame, 1973. Registered architect, N.Y., Md., D.C., Va. Project architect Hibner Architects, Garden City, N.Y., 1973-76; project mgr. BBM Architects, N.Y.C., 1976-79; project dir. Gensler & Assocs., N.Y.C., 1979-84, office dir., v.p., mem. nat. mgmt. com., 1984—. Prin. works include interior design Covington & Burling bldg., 1983, First Am. Bancshares, 1985. Mem. Greater Washington Bd. Trade, 1986. Mem. AIA, N.Y. Soc. Architects, Md. Soc. Architects, N.Y. Bldg. Congress. Roman Catholic. Club: Notre Dame (Washington). Home: 12517 Knightsbridge Ct Potomac MD 20850 Office: Gensler & Assocs 1101 17th St NW Washington DC 20036

MURRAY, FREDERICK FRANKLIN, lawyer; b. Corpus Christi, Tex., Aug. 1, 1950; s. Marvin Frank and Suzanne Louise Murray; m. Susan McKeen. BA, Rice U., 1972; JD, U. Tex., 1974. Bar: Tex. 1975, N.Y. 1987, D.C. 1987, U.S. Dist. Ct. (so. dist.) Tex. 1976, U.S. Dist. Ct. (no. and we. dists.) Tex. 1986, U.S. Ct. Claims 1976, U.S. Tax Ct. 1976, U.S. Ct. Appeals (5th and D.C. cirs.) 1976, U.S. Supreme Ct. 1978, U.S. Ct. Internat. Trade 1985, U.S. Dist. Ct. (ea. dist.) Tex. 1987; CPA, Tex. Ptnr. Chamberlain, Hrdlicka, White, Johnson & Williams, Houston, 1985—; mem. Tax Law Adv. Commn. Tex. Bd. Legal Specialization, 1984—, vice chmn., 1987—; mem. Commn. of Tax Law Examiners, 1984—, vice chmn. 1987—; adj. prof. U. Houston Law Ctr., 1984—, U. Tex. Sch. Law, 1987—; faculty lectr. Rice U. Jones Grad. Sch. Adminstrn., 1987—; speaker various assns. and univs. Author various publs.; mem. bd. advisers Houston Jour. Internat. Law, 1986—, chmn., 1987—. Del. Bishop's Diocesan Pastoral Council, 1979-80; chmn. parish council Sacred Heart Cathedral, Cath. Diocese Galveston-Houston, 1979-81, 89, mem. Red Mass Steering Com., 1986—; mem. exec. com., bd. dirs., 1987—, 89—, chmn. deferred giving com. Houston Symphony Soc., 1984-88, chmn. govt. and pub. affairs com., 1988—; co-trustee Houston Symphony Soc. Endowment Fund, 1987—; mem. fund council Rice U., 1987—, exec. com. 1988—, chmn. Major Gifts Com., 1988—; bd. dirs. com. on fin. and adminstrn. S.E. Tex. chpt. Nat. Multiple Sclerosis Soc. Mem. Am. Arbitration Assn. (panels comml. and internat. arbitrators 1980—), ABA (officer various coms.), Internat. Bar Assn., Houston Bar Assn., State Bar of Tex. (various coms.), N.Y. State Bar Assn., D.C. Bar Assn., Am. Inst. CPA's, Tex. Soc. CPA's, Internat. Tax Forum of Houston (sec. 1981-84, pres. 1984—), Internat. Fiscal Assn., Am. Soc. Internat. Law., Am. Fgn. Law Assn., Union Internationale Des Avocats. Office: Citicorp Ctr 1200 Smith St Ste 1400 Houston TX 77002

MURRAY, JAMES ALAN, municipal official, financial executive; b. Evansville, Ind., Oct. 2, 1942; s. William Dewey and Dorothy Marie (Gleason) M.; B.S., U. N.Mex., 1964; M.B.A., Harvard U., 1969; M.A. (NDEA fellow), U. Oreg., 1971, Ph.D., 1972; m. Amber Lee Tootle; children—Heidi Lynn, Paul Alan, Kendra Leigh. Dir. fin. City of Boulder (Colo.), 1972-73, dir. adminstrv. services, 1973-74; v.p. Briscoe, Maphis, Murray & Lamont, Inc., Boulder, 1974-78, pres., 1978-84, also dir.; dir. fin. City and County of Denver, 1984-86, chief exec. officer, 1986-87, asst. to mayor, 1987—; adj. assoc. prof. Grad. Sch. Public Affairs, U. Colo., Boulder, 1972-80, Denver, 1985—. Mem. open space adv. com. City of Boulder, 1972-74; bd. dirs. Met. Denver Sewage Authority, 1984-85. Mem. Am. Econ. Assn., Western Econ. Assn., Am. Soc. Pub. Adminstrn., Water Pollution Control Fedn., Kappa Mu Epsilon, Pi Alpha Alpha. Home: 99 S Downing #602 Denver CO 80209 Office: 350 City and County Bldg Denver CO 80202

MURRAY, JAMES BRADY, JR., venture capital and investment banking executive; b. N.Y.C., Aug. 30, 1946; s. James Brady and Jean Miller (Brundred) M.; m. Bruce Randolph Murray, Aug. 17, 1968; children: Meghan R., James B. III. BA, U. Va., 1968; JD, Coll. William and Mary, 1974. Bar: Va., U.S. Supreme Ct. Tchr., coach Landon Sch., Washington, 1968-71; ptnr. Richmond & Fishburne, Attys., Charlottesville, Va., 1974-81; mng. ptnr. Comstar Cos., Charlottesville, Va., 1983-87; pres. Brass, Inc., Greenbrier Mgmt., Inc., Charlottesville, Va., 1981—; mng. dir. Schelle, Warner, Murray & Thomas, Inc., Washington, 1987—; bd. dirs. Cellular Tech., Inc., Lubbock, Tex.; chmn. Albemarle County Indsl. Devel. Authority, Charlottesville, 1982—; chmn. exec. com. Napa (Calif.) Cellular Telephone Co., 1987—. Chmn. Charlottesville-Albemarle Community Found., 1983—; trustee, treas. William and Mary Law Sch. Found., 1985—, Home for Aged, 1979—. Recipient Outstanding Alumnus award William and Mary Law Sch. Assn., 1976. Mem. ABA, Va. Bar Assn., Va. Assn. Realtors, Nat. Assn. Realtors, Red Land Club (pres. 1985-86), Boars Head Sports (Charlottesville). Office: Schelle Warner Murray & Thomas Inc "O" Court Square PO Box 1465 Charlottesville VA 22902

MURRAY, JAMES K., JR., insurance executive, information services company executive; b. Elm Grove, W.Va., June 3, 1935; s. James Kirtis and Edith May (Kenyon) M.; m. Sandra Sue High, June 14, 1958; children: Susan, James K. III, Michael. BS, W.Va. U., 1957. Agt. Northwestern Mut. Life Ins. Co., Huntington, W.Va., 1957-62; v.p. mktg. Founders Life, Tampa, Fla., 1962-65; agt. Bankers Life Nebr., Tampa, 1965-70; pres. Plan Services, Inc., Tampa, 1970-81, Dun & Bradstreet Plan Services, Tampa, 1981—; sr. v.p., customer service info. needs Dun & Bradstreet Corp., Tampa and N.Y.C., 1986—. Mem. acctg. adv. com. U. South Fla., Tampa, 1981—; bd. fellows U. Tampa, 1982—; vice chmn. NCCJ, Tampa, 1985; pres. Jesuit High Sch. Found., Tampa, 1984. Mem. Million Dollar Round Table (life), Young Pres.' Orgn., World Bus. Council. Office: Dun & Bradstreet Plan Svcs PO Box 30098 Tampa FL 33630

MURRAY, J(AMES) TERRENCE, banker; b. Woonsocket, R.I., July 11, 1939; s. Joseph W. and Florence (Blackburn) M.; m. Suzanne Young, Jan. 24, 1960; children: Colleen, Paula, Terrence, Christopher, Megan. B.A., Harvard U., 1962. With Fleet Nat. Bank, Providence, from 1962, pres., 1978-86; with Fleet Fin. Group (now Fleet/Norstar Fin. Group), Providence, 1969—, pres., from 1978, chmn., pres., chief exec. officer, 1988—, also bd. dirs.; dir. Fleet Nat. Corp., A. T. Cross Co.; chmn. Fleet Factors Corp., Fleet Real Estate Inc., Fleet Info. Inc., Fleet Mortgage Corp. Bd. dirs.

Providence Found.; bd. dirs. S.E. New Eng. chpt. NCCJ. Office: Fleet Fin Group Inc 50 Kennedy Pla Providence RI 02903 *

MURRAY, JOHN L., food company executive; b. 1927. B.B.A., U. Wis., 1950. C.P.A., Wis. Accountant Touche, Ross, Bailey & Smart (C.P.A.s), prior to 1955; with Universal Foods Corp., Milw., 1955—, v.p., treas., 1966-73, v.p. fin., 1973-76, pres., 1976-84, chief exec. officer, 1979-88, chmn., 1984—, also dir. Office: Universal Foods Corp 433 E Michigan St Box 737 Milwaukee WI 53202 *

MURRAY, JOSEPH WILLIAM, banking executive; b. Alamosa, Colo., July 20, 1944; s. Joseph A. and Virginia (Wood) M.; m. Helen Hoberg, Jan. 20, 1970; children: Brian, Beth, Meghan. BS in Bus. with hon., U. Colo., 1966; MBA with hon., Northwestern U., 1967. Various positions with Continental Ill. Nat. Bank, Chgo., 1967-82; sr. v.p. First Nat. Bank Md., Balt., 1982—; faculty mem. Duke U. Exec. Programs on Cash Mgmt., Durham, N.C., 1982—; lectr. on cash mgmt. Pres. Wakefield Improvement Assn., Timonium, Md., 1987, bd. dirs.; pres. Glen Ellyn (Ill.) Library, 1978-82, trustee; pres. Glen Ellyn Tennis Assn., 1981, bd. dirs.; bd. dirs. Center Stage, 1987—. Recipient Dean's award U. Colo., 1966, Wall St. Jour. award U. Colo., 1966. Mem. Nat. Corp. Cash Mgrs. Assn., Mid-Atlantic Planning Assn., Beta Gamma Sigma. Club: L'Hirondelle (Ruxton, Md.). Office: 1st Nat Bank Md PO Box 1596 Baltimore MD 21203

MURRAY, KATHLEEN ELLEN, editor; b. Chgo., Feb. 23, 1946; d. John Joseph and Marie Agnes (Stoltzman) M.; B.A., Calif. State U., Sacramento, 1973; A.A., Am. River Coll., 1968. File clk. Allstate Ins. Co., Sacramento, 1964-66; clk. typist Calif. Hwy. Patrol, Sacramento, 1968-69; copy editor Sacramento Bee, 1971—; instr. Calif. State U., Sacramento, 1975-76. Newspaper Fund intern, scholar, 1971. Club: Sacramento Press. Home: PO Box 606 Nevada City CA 95959

MURRAY, KENNETH RICHARD, banking executive; b. Phila., Apr. 6, 1938; s. Arthur W. and Rosetta C. M.; m. Marilyn Susan Laird, Aug. 24, 1961. B.A., Princeton U., 1960; M.B.A., NYU, 1967. Vice pres. corp. banking sect. group Chase Mahattan Bank, N.Y.C., 1963-73; sr. v.p. Old Stone Bank, Providence, 1973-76; exec. v.p. corp. banking group Bancohio, Columbus, Ohio, 1976-83, pres. western region, 1977-79, pres. Columbus, 1979-81; exec. v.p. community banking Norwest Corp., Mpls., 1983—. Bd. dirs. St. Catherine Coll., Ctr. of Sci. and Industry. Served to lt USN, 1960-63. Clubs: Mpls. Athletic; Wayzata Country (Minn.); Princeton. Home: 38th Pl N #13005 Plymouth MN 55441 Office: Norwest Corp Norwest Ctr 6th & Marquette Minneapolis MN 55479

MURRAY, LAWRENCE, management consultant; b. N.Y.C., May 10, 1939; s. Gilbert and Edna (Blatt) M.; B.A., Cornell U., 1961; M.B.A., U. Okla., 1966; children—Robert, David, Daniel. Account exec. Merrill Lynch, Paramus, N.J., 1965-69; chmn., pres. Murray, Lind & Co., Inc., Jersey City, 1969-72; dir. investor relations IU Internat. Corp., Phila., 1972-73, dir. spl. projects, 1974-75; dir. fin. communications ARA Services, Inc., Phila., 1975-78; chmn., chief exec. officer Century Mgmt. and affiliated cos., West Chester, Pa., 1976-82; chmn., chief exec. officer Creative Mgmt. Corp., Bala Cynwyd and West Chester, Pa., 1982-87; underwriter Jefferson Standard Life Ins. Co., Greensboro, N.C., 1982-83; chmn., chief exec. officer Fin. Mgmt. Profl. Corp., West Chester, 1983—; v.p. Venture Frontiers Co., Denver, 1984-89; chmn. bd., chief exec. officer Fin. Intelligence Corp., West Chester, 1989—; bd. dirs. Exelaris Corp.; lectr. bus. orgn. and mgmt. Bergen Community Coll., 1971-72. Pres., Congregation Beth Israel, Media, Pa., 1977-78, Parents Without Partners, Valley Forge, Pa., 1982-83; v.p. Cornell U. Class of 1961, 1981-86. Served to 1st lt. arty., U.S. Army, 1963-64. Mem. Nat. Investor Relations Inst. (pres. Phila. chpt. 1976-78), Internat. Council Shopping Centers. Author: The Organized Stockbroker, 1970; A New Era in Mergers and Acquisitions, 1974; Communications: Management's Newest Marketing Skill, 1976; contbr. articles to profl. jours. Home: 924 Hollyview Ln West Chester PA 19380 Office: 924 Hollyview Ln West Chester PA 19380

MURRAY, LESLIE PARK, real estate broker; b. Honolulu, Aug. 24, 1948; s. Theodore Hewitt and Ruth Sinnai (Park) M.; children—Stacia, Ryan. AA, Yakima Valley Coll., 1969. Dir. mktg. Apex Realty, Honolulu, 1980-81; prin. broker Chang Realty, Honolulu, 1981-82; broker in charge Savio Realty, Ltd., Honolulu, 1982-86; pres., prin. broker Royal Hawaiian Properties, Inc., Honolulu, 1986—. Mem. Elks. Home: 1674 Paula Dr Honolulu HI 96816 Office: Royal Hawaiian Properties Inc 33 S King St #401 Honolulu HI 96813

MURRAY, MICHAEL JOSEPH, real estate company executive; b. Castro Valley, Calif., June 23, 1958; s. Daniel Joseph and Sheila Lee (Stribley) Murray-Bethel; m. Catherine Ruth Douat, Dec. 29, 1984. BA, UCLA, 1980; M in Internat. Bus., St. Mary's Coll., 1985. Lic. real estate salesman. Loan officer The Money Lenders, San Francisco; with Highsmith Investments, Burlingame, Calif.; real estate broker Merrill Lynch Comml. Real Estate, San Francisco; ptnr. Park Cen. Investments, Alameda, Calif.; bd. dirs., mem. UCHA, Inc., Los Angeles. Mem. Internat. Sales and Mktg. Execs., San Francisco, 1982-83, Rep. Presdl. Task Force, Washington, 1984—. Mem. Planetary Soc., L-5 Soc., Alameda C. of C. Roman Catholic. Home: 3016 Lincoln Ave Alameda CA 94501 Office: Murray Mgmt Svcs 141A Grand St #100 Alameda CA 94501

MURRAY, NANCY SIEGEL, marketing executive; b. Chelsea, Mass., Nov. 20, 1947; d. Edward Isaac and Bertha (Greenberg) Siegel; m. Ronald Francis Murray, Aug. 8, 1976. B.A., Vassar Coll., 1970; M.Ed., Columbia U., 1975; M.B.A., So. Meth. U., 1980; cert. in COBOL programming, Columbia U., 1983. Cert. rehab. counselor, N.Y. Counseling intern Neurol. Inst., N.Y.C., 1974; supr. counseling Hosp. for Joint Diseases, N.Y.C., 1975-78; market research analyst Acclivus Corp., Dallas, 1980, Suburban Assocs., Ridgewood, N.J., 1981; sr. market research analyst/internat. mktg. Mfrs. Hanover Trust Co., N.Y.C., 1982-84; mktg. officer Marine Midland Bank, N.Y.C., 1984-86, asst. v.p. and market research dir., 1987-88, market research mgr. bus. market group AT&T, Basking Ridge, N.J., 1988—. Mem. Am. Mktg. Assn., Bank Mktg. Assn., Am. Soc. Tng. and Devel., Nat. Rehab. Assn., Vassar Club. Democrat. Home: 183 Lake Rd Morristown NJ 07960

MURRAY, PETER, metallurgist, manufacturing company executive; b. Rotherham, Yorks, Eng., Mar. 13, 1920; came to U.S., 1967, naturalized, 1974; s. Michael and Ann (Hamstead) M.; m. Frances Josephine Glaisher, Sept. 8, 1947; children: Jane, Paul, Alexander. B.Sc. in Chemistry with honors, Sheffield (Eng.) U., 1941, postgrad., 1946-49; Ph.D. in Metallurgy, Brit. Iron and Steel Research Bursar, Sheffield, 1948. Research chemist Steetley Co., Ltd., Worksop, Notts, Eng., 1941-45; with Atomic Energy Research Establishment, Harwell, Eng., 1949-67; head div. metallurgy Atomic Energy Research Establishment, 1960-64, asst. dir., 1964-67; tech. dir., mgr. fuels and materials, advanced reactors div. Westinghouse Electric Corp., Madison, Pa., 1967-74; dir. research Westinghouse Electric Europe (S.A.), Brussels, 1974-75; chief scientist advanced power systems divs. Westinghouse Electric Corp., Madison, Pa., 1975-81; dir. nuclear programs Westinghouse Electric Corp., Washington, 1981—; mem. divisional rev. coms. Argonne Nat. Lab., 1968-73; Mellor Meml. lectr. Inst. Ceramics, 1963. Contbr. numerous articles to profl. jours.; editorial adv. bd.: Jour. Less Common Metals, 1968—. Recipient Holland Meml. Research prize Sheffield U., 1949. Fellow Royal Inst. Chemistry (Newton Chambers Research prize 1954), Inst. Ceramics, Am. Nuclear Soc.; mem. Brit. Ceramics Soc. (pres. 1965), Am. Ceramic Soc., Nat. Acad. Engring. Roman Catholic. Home: 20308 Canby Ct Gaithersburg MD 20879 Office: Westinghouse Electric Corp 1801 K St NW Washington DC 20006

MURRAY, PETER TOM, retail executive; b. St. Paul, Sept. 1, 1941; s. George F. and Audrey E.F. M.; m. Mary Ellen Knedle, July 1, 1967; children: Paul, Jessica, Raul, Lina. BA in Econs., Carleton Coll., 1963; MBA in Fin., U. Pa., 1967. Asst. div. contr. Food Svc./Protein Products div. Gen. Mills Inc., Mpls., 1967-70; mgr. fin. control systems Dayton Hudson Corp., Mpls., 1970-73; expense contr. Joseph Magnin Inc., San Francisco, 1973-75; asst. contr., dir. strategic planning Target Stores, Mpls., 1975-82; dir. corp. planning Federated Dept. Stores, Cin., 1982-86; v.p. corp. planning and devel. Perry Drug Stores, Pontiac, Mich., 1986-87; pres. Auto Works, Pontiac, 1987-88; v.p. adminstrn. ERB Lumber Co., Birmingham, Mich., 1988—. Mgr. campaign United Appeal, Cin., 1982-83; alumni admissions rep. Carleton Coll., Northfield, Minn., 1984-85; fin. advisor to bd. Cin. Pub. Schs., 1983-86; bd. dirs., v.p., pres. Downtown YMCA, Mpls., 1976-82; bd. dirs. Oakland Family Svcs., Pontiac, 1987—.

MURRAY, RALBERN HUGH, utility company exective; b. N.Y.C., Oct. 19, 1929; s. Hugh Gabriel and Rose (Abamont) M.; m. Dorothy Elsie Gil, June 27, 1953; children: Claire, Carol, Diane, Suzanne. B.S. in Chem. Engring., NYU, 1950, M.S. in Indsl. Engring., 1955. Dir. sales and promotion Am. Gas Assn., Arlington, Va., 1950-64; dir. mktg. Consol. Nat. Gas Co., Pitts., 1964-73; v.p., gen. mgr. CNG Energy and CNG Coal, Pitts., 1973-79; sr. v.p. Consol. Gas Transmission Corp., Clarksburg, W. Va., 1979-82; pres. Consol. Gas Transmission Corp., Clarksburg, W.Va., 1982-84; pres., chief operating officer, dir. Consol. Natural Gas Co., Pitts., 1984-85, vice chmn., dir., 1985—; chmn. Group to Advance Total Energy, 1963-68, Distbn. Fed. Power Commn. Nat. Gas Survey, 1972; dir. Empire Nat. Bank, Clarksburg. Mem. com. Coll. Mineral and Energy Resources, Morgantown, W. Va., 1982-84; mem. com. United Hosp. Center, Clarksburg, 1982-84; trustee Carnegie Mellon U., 1986—. Served to 1st lt. USAF, 1951-52. Mem. Am. Inst. Chem. Engrs., Am. Chem. Soc., ASME, Am. Gas Assn. (bd. dirs. 1985—, Hall of Flame 1964, award of honor 1966), Gas Research Inst. (bd. dirs. 1985—, vice chmn. 1989—), W.Va. Oil and Natural Gas Assn. (dir. 1982-84), Interstate Natural Gas Assn. Am. (bd. dirs. 1983-85). Office: Consol Natural Gas Co CNG Tower Pittsburgh PA 15222-3199

MURRAY, ROBERT EUGENE, coal company executive; b. Martins Ferry, Ohio, Jan. 13, 1940; s. Albert Edward and Mildred Etheline (Shepherd) M.; m. Brenda Lou Moore, Aug. 26, 1962; children: Sherri Sue (dec.), Robert Edward, Jonathan Robert, Ryan Michael. B in Engring., Ohio State U., 1962; postgrad. Case Western Res. U., 1968-70, Harvard U. Grad. Sch. Bus. Advanced Mgmt. Program, U. N.D., 1982-83. Registered profl. engr., Ohio. Asst. to mgr. indsl. engring. and coal preparation N.Am. Coal Corp., 1961-63, sect. foreman, plant foreman, gen. mine foreman, Ohio div., 1963-64, asst. supt., 1964-66, supt. 1966-68, asst. to pres., Cleve., 1968-69, v.p. operations, v.p. eastern div., 1969-74, pres. Western div., 1974-83; exec. v.p. and pres. coal ops. N.Am. Coal Corp., 1985-86, pres., chief operating officer, 1986-87, pres., chief exec. officer, 1987—; pres. Coteau Properties Co., Falkirk Mining Co., Western Plains Mining Co., Mo. Valley Properties Co., N. Am. Constrn. and Reclamation Co.; v.p., bd. dirs. Nacco Mining Co.; bd. dirs. Sabine Mining Co. 1987-88; pres., chief exec. officer Ohio Valley Resources Inc., Coal Resources Inc., Am. Coal Sales Co., Ohio Valley Coal Co., Ohio Valley Transloading Co., 1988—; mining engring. departmental asst. Ohio State U., 1960-62; past pres., chmn. bd. N.D. Lignite Council; bd. dirs. Energy Resources, Inc., Energy Transp., Inc. Exec. bd. Greater Cleve. and No. Lights council Boy Scouts Am.; past pres., bd. dirs. United Way of Bismarck; bd. regents U. Mary; trustee, lay speaker, tchr., lay leader Meth. Ch., bd. dirs. Mining Electro-Mech. Assn. (pres. Ohio Valley br. 1967-68), Pitts. Coal Mining Inst. Am., Soc. Mining Engrs. AIME (bd. dirs., exec. com., past chmn. coal div., pres.-elect, Howard N. Evenson award, Disting. Mem. award), Rocky Mountain Coal Mining Inst. (past pres., program chmn., chmn. adv. bd.), Nat. Coal Assn. (past bd. dirs., chmn. acctg. com., exec. com., low rank fuels com.), World Energy Conf., past chmn. ad hoc coalition on internat. electric power trade, research adv. com., generic mineral tech. ctr., Nat. Soc. Profl. Engrs. (pres. east Ohio chpt. 1966-67), Mining Hall Fame (dir.), Am. Mining Congress, Ohio Engrs. in Industry (mem. bd. govs. 1966-67). Republican. Lodges: Masons (32d degree), Shriners. Home: 32 Cotswold Ln Moreland Hills Chagrin Falls OH 44022 Office: Ohio Valley Resources Inc Coal Resources Inc 29525 Chagrin Blvd Suite 111 Pepper Pike OH 44122

MURRAY, ROBERT SANDS, banker; b. Mobile, Ala., Nov. 11, 1955; s. Robert Sands and Margaret (Nicolson) M. BA, Vanderbilt U., 1977, MBA, 1980. Loan rev. analyst First Alabank, Mobile, 1980-82, credit adminstrn. office, 1982—. Account exec. for United Way, Mobile, 1987, 88. Mem. Am. Inst. Banking (instr. 1988), Mobile Country Club, Lakewood Golf Club, Mobile Yacht Club. Home: 16 Lancaster Rd Mobile AL 36608 Office: First Alabank 106 St Francis Mobile AL 36602

MURRAY, RONALD, small business owner; b. N.Y.C., Nov. 21, 1931; s. Adolph and Rhea Evelyn (Wadden) Ansorge; m. Ruth Knecht, June 1951 (div. 1956); children: Robin, Rhea; m. Sallie Susanne Smith, 1970; children: LeeAnn, Lynnette, Todd, Andrew George; 1 stepchild, Jeff Moser. BSBA, Lehigh U., 1953. Analytical reporter Dun & Bradstreet, Allentown, Pa., 1953-56; purchasing agt. R.E. Moyer, Inc., Catasauqua, Pa., 1956-59; salesman United Fund, Allentown, 1959; mgr. mdse. Hess Bros., Allentown, 1959-64; mgr. nat. sales Talens & Son, Union, N.J., 1964-69; ptnr. The Blue Victorian, Allentown, 1970—; mgr., owner Fountain Park & Shop, Allentown, 1970—; owner Gallery Downtown Parking, Allentown, 1988—. Sec. Neighbors in Common Endeavor, Allentown, (pres. 1977-80); v.p. Community Neighborhood Orgn., Allentown, 1980; mem. Housing Rev. Bd., Allentown, 1986—. Mem. Lehigh County Constables Assn. (treas. 1984-88, sec. 1988—). Republican. Lutheran. Home: 945 Walnut St Allentown PA 18102 Office: Fountain Park & Shop 925 Walnut St Allentown PA 18102

MURRAY, WILLIAM D., marketing executive; b. Wilkinsburg, Pa., Aug. 24, 1935; s. Arthur Frederick and Barbara A. (Gilman) M.; m. Barbara Jane Gambrill, June 28, 1958 (div. 1984); children: Gambrill Breton, Barton Gilman; m. Rosalie Wade Reynolds, Aug. 4, 1984. Student, Fresno State U., 1956; BA in English Lit., Lehigh U., 1958, BS in Indsl. Engring., 1958; postgrad., Ohio State U., Dayton, 1959-60. With bus. and tech. personnel tng. group Eastman Kodak, Rochester, N.Y., 1958-59; mgmt. positions Procter & Gamble, Inc., Cin., 1961-65; sr. v.p. Weightman, Inc., Phila., 1965-72; pres. Gen. Ecology, Inc., Lionville, Pa., 1972-75; mng. dir., ptnr. The Mktg. Dept., Villanova, Pa., 1975—; bd. dirs. Lower Merion Counseling Ctr., Ardmore, Pa. Author: (with Rosalie Murray) When ENFP and INFJ Interact, 1987, Opposites, 1988; co-author numerous tng. materials; contbr. articles to profl. jours. Ruling elder Gladwyne Presbyn. Ch., Pa., 1974-80. 1st lt. USAF, 1959-61. Mem. Assn. for Psychol. Type (bd. dirs., sec. Northeast chpt. 1984-86, co-founder, pres. Del. Valley chpt. 1983-87), Alpha Tau Omega. Republican. Office: Mktg Dept PO Box 200 Gladwyne PA 19035-0200

MURRAY, WILLIAM G., museum executive, consultant; b. Cedar Rapids, Iowa, July 15, 1903; s. Frederick Gray and Jeanette Lindsey (Stevenson) M.; m. Mildred Furniss, July 31, 1928 (dec. Aug. 2, 1974); children: David, Jean, John; m. Alice Van Wert, Aug. 9, 1975. BA, Coe Coll., 1924, LHD (hon.), 1956; MA, Harvard U., 1925; PhD, U. Minn., 1932. Asst. agr. economist Washington, 1926-27; asst. prof. Iowa State Coll., Ames, 1927-35; assoc. prof. Iowa State U., Ames, 1931-37, prof., 1937-74, dept. chmn., 1944-55, prof. emeritas, 1974—; chief economist U.S. Farm Credit Adminstrn., Washington, 1935-36; chmn. Living History Farms, Des Moines, 1980—; dir. E.M.C. Group, Inc., Des Moines, 1982—, Coll. Savs. Bank, Ames, 1947-76; rsch. dir. Iowa Taxation Study Com., 1955-56; pres. Am. Farm Econ. Assn., 1948-49, Iowa State Bd. Tax Rev., 1975-81; mem. Iowa Natural Resources Coun., Iowa, 1960-71. Author: Farm Appraisal, 1940; agricultural Finance, 1942, Indian Land Appraisals for U.S. Dept. Justice, 1952-74. Pres. Bd. Edn., Ames, 1941-47; Rep. candidate gov., State Iowa, 1958, 66; trustee Coe Coll., Cedar Rapids, Iowa, 1960-75, pres. 1969-71. Fellow Am. Assn. Agr. Economists, 1984; recipient Disting. Svc. to Agr. award Iowa Farm Bur., 1987; named hon. mem. Nat. Conf. Christians and Jews, Iowa, 1988. Mem. Am. Econ. Assn. Presbyterian. Home: 3207 Oakland St Ames IA 50010

MURRELL, TURNER MEADOWS, finance and insurance company executive, lawyer; b. Greensboro, N.C., Feb. 5, 1923; s. James Robert and Sallie Frances (Page) M.; B.A., Washburn U., 1948, J.D., 1949; m. Patricia L. Shortall, Dec. 4, 1975; children—Gregory S., Leslie Ann, Todd G.; stepchildren—John J., Janis Lynn, Kathleen A., Lisa M. Shortall. Admitted to Kans. bar, 1949, U.S. Supreme Ct. bar, 1950; individual practice law, Topeka, 1949—; ptnr. Baker, Doherty & Murrell, Topeka, 1952-53; judge City of Topeka, 1953-56; ptnr. Meyer, Gault, Marshall, Hawks & Murrell, 1954-61, Murrell, Scott & Quinlan, 1961-69; pres., chmn. Am. Investors Life Ins. Co., Inc., Topeka, 1965—; chmn. Nat. Investment Corp., Inc., 1968—, Internat. Investors Life Ins. Co., Ic., 1969-77; pres. Am. Option and Equity Fund, Inc., 1968-78; dir. Commerce Bank and Trust, Topeka, 1978—; chmn., chief exec. officer Am. Vestors Fin. Corp., 1986—; lectr. Tulane U., New Orleans, 1951-52. Mem. Kans. Ho. of Reps., 1957-61, majority floor leader, 1959-61; trustee Washburn U., 1978—. Served with USN, 1943-46. Recipient Young Man of Yr. award U.S. C. of C., 1957; Disting. Service award City of Topeka, 1957. Mem. ABA, Kans. Bar Assn., Topeka Bar Assn., Delta Theta Phi. Clubs: Topeka Country, Masons, Shriners. Home: 421 Danbury Ln Topeka KS 66606 Office: 415 SW 8th St Topeka KS 66601

MURTAUGH, DANIEL M., financial executive; b. Evanston, Ill., May 8, 1941; s. Lewis Charles and Mary Imelda (Maher) M.; m. Kristen S. Olson, Dec. 28, 1968; children: Charles, Stephen. BA, Holy Cross Coll., 1963; PhD, Yale U., 1967; MBA, Columbia U., 1980. Instr. English Northwestern U., Evanston, Ill., 1965-66; asst. prof. English Boston U., 1967-72, Manhattanville Coll., Purchase, N.Y., 1972-79; fin. analyst W.R. Grace & Co., N.Y.C., 1980-81, mgr. pension fin. adminstrn., 1981-84, dir. pension fin. adminstrn., 1984—. Author: Piers Plowman and the Image of God, 1978; contbr. articles to profl.jours. Bd. dirs. Commonwealth Found., N.Y.C., 1985—; exec. com. Hunter Coll. High Sch. Parents Assn., 1988—. Danforth/Woodrow Wilson Found. fellow, 1963. Democrat. Roman Catholic. Home: 179 E Moshulu Pkwy #3 Bronx NY 10467 Office: WR Grace & Co 1114 Ave of the Americas New York NY 10036

MURTON, WILLIAM NORMAN, II, information systems manager; b. Lakewood, Ohio, Sept. 12, 1944; s. William Norman Sr. and Marica Lydia (Elkins) M.; m. Margaret Ann Cavan, Sept. 9, 1967; children: Margaret Sibley, Amy Elkins, Joshua William, Nathan Douglas, Alexander David. Student, Syracuse U., 1962-64; BSBA, Ohio State U., 1977. Programmer SCOA Industries, Columbus, Ohio, 1969; mgr. systems programming Ohio State U. Hosp. Computer Ctr., 1969-73; sr. systems planner and program mgmt. Horizons Data Systems, 1973-77; mgr. Arthur Andersen & Co., 1977-83; mgr. info. systems Chillicothe (Ohio) Telephone Co., 1983—. Leader Cub Scouts Am., Chillicothe, 1988—; chmn. Boy Scout Troop Advancement com., Chillicothe, 1987-88; chmn. publicity com. Ross County Cen. Ohio Diabetes Assn., 1987-88; v.p. fin. Boy Scouts Am., Chillicothe, 1988— (Dist. Merit award, 1987). Mem. Cen. Ohio Assn. for Systems Mgmt. (pres. 1988—; Pres. award 1988), Assn. for Systems Mgmt. (mem. long range planning com. 1985-88, mem. adv. com. 1988—, Achievement award 1988), Ohio Telephone Assn. (mem. data processing com. 1986—). Republican. Office: Chillicothe Telephone Co 68 E Main St Chillicothe OH 45601

MUSCI, JOHN GREGORY, telecommunications executive; b. Akron, Ohio, June 4, 1956; s. Alfred Veto and Mary Mae (Stalnaker) M.; m. Barbara Lee Ball, Oct. 20, 1983. BSBA, U. Akron, 1978, postgrad. in fin. Mktg. adminstr. Ohio Bell Telephone Co., Cleve., 1978-79, account exec., 1979-80, cert. industry cons., 1980-81; cert. industry cons. Am. Bell, Cleve., 1981, AT&T Info. Systems, Cleve., 1982-84; nat. carrier mgr. Litel Telecommunications, Worthington, Ohio, 1984-85; dir. sales Litel Telecommunications, Cleve., 1985—. Supporting mem. Ohio Ballet, Akron, 1985—, United Way, Akron, 1983—. Mem. Competitive Telecommunications Orgn., Alternative Carrier Transmissions Orgn., U. Akron Coll. Bus. Alumni Assn. (founding). Club: Portage Country (Akron). Home: 445 N Hametown Rd Akron OH 44313 Office: Litel Telecommunications 650 Terminal Tower Cleveland OH 44113

MUSHINSKI, JULIE BERNICE, broadcasting executive; b. Westland, Mich., Apr. 5, 1963; d. Donald Jerome and Shirley Anne (Smith) M. BA, Cen. Mich. U., 1985. Terr. mgr. Continental Cablevision, Dearborn Heights, Mich., 1985-86; account exec. WWCT Radio, Peoria, Ill., 1986, KONO/KITY Radio-Genesis Broadcasting, San Antonio, 1986-88, KTFM Radio-Waterman Broadcasting, San Antonio, 1989—. Mem. NAFE, Am. Women in Radio and TV, San Antonio Radio Advt. Broadcast Execs. Roman Catholic. Office: KTFM Radio PO Box 18128 San Antonio TX 78218

MUSICK, WILLIAM C., bank systems manager; b. Orlando, Fla., Sept. 18, 1954. BS, USAF Acad., 1976; MBA, Stanford U., 1984. Engr. Ford Motor Co., Detroit, 1979-80; project mgr. Gen. Electric Co., San Jose, Calif., 1980-82; intern Citicorp Internat., Miami, Fla., 1983; systems and programming mgr., analyst Wells Fargo Bank, San Francisco, 1984-88, v.p., mgr. systems integration, 1988—. pres. San Francisco AIDS Found., 1985-87; participant Leadership San Francisco, 1986-87. Mem. Golden Gate Bus. Assn. (outstanding community service award 1986). Served to lt. USAF, 1976-78. Home: 3841 19th St San Francisco CA 94114 Office: Wells Fargo Bank 150 Fourth St San Francisco CA 94103

MUSORRAFITI, FRANCESCO ANTONIO, engineering services executive, physicist; b. N.Y.C., Oct. 24, 1929; s. Vincenzo and Antoinette Maria (Calarco) M.; m. Angelina Cecilia Calabrese, Feb. 13, 1955; 1 child, Antoinette Maria. BS in Engring., U.S. Naval Acad., 1953; BS in Nuclear Physics, U.S. Naval Acad., Monterey, Calif., 1964. Commd. ensign USN, 1953, advanced through grades to cmdr., ret., 1974; program mgr. Lulesians Assocs. Inc., Falls Church, Va., 1974-75; dir. navy systems Planning Research Corp., McLean, Va., 1975-78, army mktg. mgr., 1978-79; project mgr. Planning Research Corp., Ft. Monmouth, N.J., 1979-80; dir. mil. systems Planning Research Corp., McLean, 1980-82; pres., chief exec. officer Engring. and Profl. Svcs. Inc., Tinton Falls, N.J., 1984—, also bd. dirs.; bd. dirs. Team Corp., Virginia Beach, Va.; pres. Cirua Corp., Shrewsbury. Author: Analog Computers, 1963. Recruiter for U.S. Naval Acad. Blue and Gold program, 1974—; chmn. bd. dirs. Mariners Cover Horizontal Regional, Annapolis, Md., 1974-78. Mem. Nat. Contracts Mgmt. Assn. (pres. 1986-87), Assn. Old Crows (chmn. 1981-85), Armed Forces Communications Electronics Assn., Navy League U.S. (life), Assn. U.S. Army, Masons. Republican. Office: Engring & Profl Svcs Inc 70 Apple St Tinton Falls NJ 07724

MUSSELWHITE, EDWIN A., management consulting company executive; b. Miami, Fla., Jan. 21, 1940; s. Thomas A. and Edna B. W.; BS, Northwestern U., 1964; m. Linda Silvestrini, 1984; Kenneth, Thomas, Zachary. Mktg. rep. IBM, Chgo., 1964-68, exec. staff asst., 1968, br. sales mgr., Aurora, Ill., 1968-69; dir. profl. personnel Leasco Systems Corp., Oakbrook, Ill. 1969-70; co-founder, exec. v.p. Deltak, Inc., Oakbrook, Ill., 1970-76; pres. Systems Growth Inst., Santa Cruz, Calif., 1976-82; v.p. Zenger-Miller, Inc., Cupertino, Calif., 1982—, also chmn. bd. dirs.; cons. mgmt. to IBM, Gen. Electric Co., Fireman's Fund Ins. Co., Stanford U., TRW, others; guest lectr. at univs.; mem. bd. advs.; Center for Orgn. and Mgmt. Devel., San Jose State U. Served as sgt. U.S. Army, 1964. Mem. Am. Soc. Tng. Devel., Orgn. Devel. Network. Co-author: Toward excellence, 1983, How To Get The Most Training, 1987; contbg. author: Everybody Wins, 1976; Interpersonal Dimensions, 1981; producer over 2000 hours of video-based instrn. in mgmt. devel, data processing and sales skills, 1973—. Office: Zenger-Miller Inc 10201 Torre Ave Cupertino CA 95014

MUSSO, GIANNI LUCA, metal processing executive; b. Turin, Piedmont, Italy, Nov. 9, 1958; s. Giovanni Antonio and Piera Maria (Perinetto) M. Cert. in edn., Royal Charles-Albert Coll., Moncalieri, Italy, 1976; cert. in proficiency and alliance, Lemania Coll., Lausanne, Switzerland, 1978, diploma in commerce, 1980; hautes etudes commerciales, U. of Lausanne, 1982. With Musso Holding, San Gillio Torinese, Italy, 1982—. Author: The Thermoshock Process in the Foundry Industry, 1988. Mem. ASSOFOND Italian Foundries Assn., Indsl. Union of Turin, Italian Assn. Metallurgy, Assn. Technique de Fonderie, Am. Foundrymen Assn. Clubs: Golf Crans s/Sierre-Wallis (Switzerland), Yacht Alassio (Italian Riviera), Montecarlo Yachting (Prin. de Monaco). Office: Musso Holding, 47 Via Valdellatorre, 10040 San Gillio Torinese Italy

MUSTES, PHILLIP GEORGE, manufacturing executive; b. Chgo., Jan. 9, 1949; s. George Joseph and Ayureye (Fotre) M.; m. Joyce Elin Schmidt, Oct. 25, 1975; 1 child, George Walter. BBA, U. Notre Dame, 1971; MBA, Northwestern U., 1979. Acct. rep. Ben Franklin Sav., Oakbrook, Ill., 1972-73; bond assoc. Continental Bank, Chgo., 1973-79; br. contr. Sara Lee Corp., Chgo., 1979-81; v.p. fin. Trane Co-Am. Standard Inc., Hillside, Ill., 1981—. 1st lt. U.S. Army, 1971-72. Mem. Nat. Assn. of Accts. Republican. Roman Catholic. Home: S 633 Cleveland St Winfield IL 60190 Office: Trane Co-Am Standard Inc 235 Fencl Ln Hillside IL 60162

MUSTONE, CAROL LYNCH, small business owner; b. Pitts., Dec. 12, 1956; d. Ralph and Judy (Follansbee) Lynch; m. Paul Dennis Mustone, Sept. 13, 1986. BS, U. Utah, 1979. Paralegal Bingham, Dana & Gould, Boston, 1980-85; sales rep. Yankee Systems, Reading, Mass., 1985-88; pres. Process Forms Group, Boston, 1988—. Mem. Nat. Bus. Forms Assn., Greater Boston C. of C., Small Bus. Assn. New Eng., Boston Athletic Club. Democrat. Presbyterian. Office: Process Forms Group 23 W Broadway Boston MA 02127

MUTCHLER, EDWARD MICHAEL, automobile company executive; b. Akron, Ohio, Mar. 13, 1935; s. Arthur Stephen and Ruth Mary (Doran) M.; m. Dolores Ann Poje, Aug. 4, 1956; children: Jeanne Anne Buehl, Eileen Louise Mazzocco, Alisa Marie Bauer, Bryan John. B in Indsl. Engring., Gen. Motors Inst., 1958. With Gen. Motors Corp., 1953—; various positions Chevrolet Motor div. Ohio and Mich., 1953-81; gen. mfg. mgr. AC Spark Plug div. Flint, Mich., 1981-82; dir. organizational studies Detroit, 1982-83; gen. mgr. Rochester (N.Y.) Products div. 1983-85; v.p., group exec. Detroit, 1986—. Trustee Engring. & Mgmt. Inst. Gen. Motors Inst., 1986—; fundraiser Boy Scouts Am., Rochester, 1984, Detroit, 1987.

MUTH, FREDERICK ANTHONY, JR., lawyer; b. Milw., Oct. 7, 1938; s. Fred Anthony and Jeanne Marie (Hennessey) M.; m. Mary Ellen King, July 15, 1961; children: John Eugene, Daniel Frederick, Maureen Eleanor Katherine. BA, Marquette U., 1960, LLB, 1964. Bar: Wis., 1964, Ariz., 1984. Atty. Whyte & Hirschboeck, S.C., Milw., 1964-84, pres., atty., 1984—; dir., sec. Ph. Orth Co., Milw., 1973—, Modern Machine Works, Inc., Cudahy, Wis., 1985—. Mem. Greater Milw. com., 1986—; vice chmn. Alverno Coll. bd. trustees, Milw., 1987-88. Served to lt. (J.G.) USN, 1960-62. Named Law Alumnus of the Year Marquette U., 1979. Mem. ABA, Wis. Bar Assn., Ariz Bar Assn., Milw. Country Club, University Club. Republican. Roman Catholic. Home: 2135 N 93d St Wauwatosa WI 53226 Office: Whyte & Hirschboeck SC 111 W Wisconsin Ave Milwaukee WI 53202

MUTH, ROBERT JAMES, metal company executive, lawyer; b. Phila., May 13, 1933; s. James H. and Ruth M. (Will) M.; m. Shirley M. Carnes, Jan. 31, 1959; children: Christopher James, Jennifer Augusta. B.A., Lafayette Coll., 1954; postgrad., Yale Div. Sch., 1954-55; LL.B., Columbia U., 1960. Bar: D.C. 1961, N.Y. 1969. Atty. Covington & Burling, Washington, 1960-68; asst. gen. counsel Asarco, Inc., N.Y.C., 1969-71; asso. gen. counsel Asarco, Inc., 1971-77, v.p., 1977—; chmn. Lead Industries Assn., N.Y.C., 1986—; pres. Silver Inst., Washington, 1987-89; vice chmn. Nat. Legal Ctr. for Pub. Interests, Washington, 1986—. Mem. George Sch. Com., Newtown, Pa., 1985—; bd. dirs. No. Lights Inst., Missoula, Mont. Lt. inf. U.S. Army, 1955-57, Korea. Mem. ABA, N.Y. State Bar Assn., Metropolitan Club. Clubs: Metropolitan (Washington); Harvard Bus. Sch. (N.Y.C.); Downtown Assn. (N.Y.C.). Home: 2 Fenwood Pl Yardley PA 19067

MUTHU, FRANCIS SAVARI, county agency administrator; b. Tamil Nadu, India, June 3, 1934; came to U.S., 1969; s. C. Savarimuthu and Nayagammal; m. Regina Roseline Gabriel, May 3, 1967; children: Anna, Sharon. Vidvan, Madras U., India, 1957; B of Oriental Learning, Annamalai U., India, 1962, BEd, 1964; MA, Loyola U., Chgo., 1972, PhD, 1978. Tchr., head Tamil language dept. St. Anns High Sch., Tamil Nadu, 1957-60, St. Bede's High Sch., Tamil Nadu, 1964-69; lectr. Tamil language and literatures Loyola Coll, Madras, India, 1957-59; correctional counselor Cook County Jail, Chgo., 1969-73; counselor, supr. Manpower Cook County office Employment Tng., Chgo., 1973-76, planner Manpower, 1976-80; regional mgr. Cook County office Employment Tng., Maywood, Ill., 1980—; prof. Loyola U., Chgo., 1980-85, adj. prof. of Sociology, Triton Coll., 1987—. Editor: Thozhan, 1958-60; sub-editor Poochendu, 1960-64; editorial bd. Thondan, 1964-69; translator Biblical Commn. of Tamil Nadu, 1964-68. Mem. humanities adv. com. Triton Coll. Arthur J. Schmitt Found. doctoral fellow, Chgo., 1974-75; named Outstanding New Citizen, Citizenship Council Met. Chgo., 1983; recipient Outstanding Citizenship and Americanism award Kiwanis Internat. and The Des Plaines Times, 1984. Mem. Ill. Employment and Tng. Assn. (editorial bd.). Roman Catholic (parish leadership). Club: Chgo. Tamil Sangam (pres. 1983-84). Home: 920 Leahy Circle E Des Plaines IL 60016 Office: Cook County Office Employment Tng 1311 Maybrook Dr Rm 205 Maywood IL 60153

MUTZIGER-BECK, JUDY LYNN, advertising executive; b. Mitchell, S.D., Oct. 7, 1947; d. Leslie Daniel and Rita Rose (Weber) M.; m. Serge Beck, June 4, 1983. Grad. high sch., Etha, S.D.; cert. exec. sec., Nat. Coll. Bus., Rapid City, S.D., 1966. Sec. GTI Corp. Scientific Software, Denver, 1966-68; waitress, ski-bum Red Lion Inn, Vail, Colo., 1968-70, Kulm Hotel, St. Moritz, Switzerland, 1971-73; real estate agt. Paris Placement, France, 1973-75; data bank cons. World Econ. Forum, Geneva, Switzerland, 1976-82; advt. exec. Vert Pomme, Montricher, Switzerland, 1982—.

MUZZIO, CHARLES JOSEPH, financial consultant; b. S.I., N.Y., Apr. 26, 1940; s. Joseph Charles and Elizabeth (Dineen) M.; m. Katherine Rose White, Feb. 3, 1967; children: Lauren, Charles Jr., Kathleen, Elizabeth, Kelly. Student, St. Peter's Coll., 1957-59; AAS, Coll. S.I., 1961. Engr. Western Electric Co., Newark, 1961-70; pres. Charles J. Muzzio Agy. Inc., N.Y.C., 1970-78; investment exec. Bache & Co., Newark, 1978-79; v.p. Shearson Lehman Hutton, Chatham, N.J., 1979—. Pres. Richmondtown Civic Assn., S.I., 1974-78. Mem. Internat. Assn. Fin. Planners, Internat. Bd. Cert. Fin. Planners. Office: Shearson Lehman Hutton 127 Main St Chatham NJ 07928

MYERS, AL, realtor property manager, mayor; b. Oakland, Calif., Aug. 6, 1922; s. Alvi A. and Emma (Thoren) M.; student Oreg. Inst. Tech., 1940-41; m. Viola Doreen Wennermark, Sept. 11, 1954; children: Susan Faye, Pamela Ann, Jason Allen. Supt.'s asst. Aluminum Co. Am., Troutdale, Oreg., 1942-44; asst. mgr. Western Auto Supply Co., Portland, 1944-46; owner, operator Al Myers Auto & Electric, Gresham, Oreg., 1946-53; realtor, broker Al Myers Property Mgmt., 1954—; v.p., sec. Oreg. Country, Inc.; faculty Mt. Hood Community Coll. Chmn., Indsl. and Econ. Devel. Com. for Multonomah County, Oreg. Real Estate Ednl. Program, 1961. Mayor Gresham, Oreg., 1972—. Pres. East Multonomah County Dem. Forum, 1965—, mem. exec. com., 1958—. With AUS, 1943. Mem. Portland Realty Bd., Nat. Assn. Real Estate Bds., Christian Bus. Men's Com. Internat., Internat. Platform Assn., Rho Epsilon Kappa (pres. Oreg.). Mem. Evang. Ch. (trustee, treas.). Home: 935 NW Norman Ave Gresham OR 97030 Office: 995 NE Cleveland Ave Gresham OR 97030

MYERS, CLARA, small business executive; b. Olton, Tex., Sept. 9, 1952; d. Augustine and Magdalena (Solis) Lopez; m. Leslie J. Myers, Feb. 24, 1973; 1 child, Theresa C. Grad., Highland Hills Beauty Acad., Greeley, Colo., 1977. Owner, mgr. New Image Styling Salon of Rockies, Greeley. Baptist. Office: New Image Styling Salon 2530 llth Ave Greeley CO 80631

MYERS, DAVID RICHARD, youth organization financial executive; b. Plainfield, N.J., Oct. 5, 1948; s. George Kelsall and Margaret (Story) M.; m. Loretta Margaret D'Angelo; 1 child, Christina Marie. BS in Bus. Adminstrn., U. Kans., 1971; MBA in Fin., U. Mo., 1981. Check processor No. Trust Bank, Chgo., 1971; officer trainee Commerce Bank Kansas City (Mo.), 1973-74; sales mgr. Sun Life of Can. Ins. Co., Kansas City, 1974-75; with Boy Scouts Am., 1975—; dist. exec. Des Moines, 1975-78, Kansas City, 1978-81; dir. fin. services N.Y.C., 1981-84; dir. fin. and pub. relations Phila., 1984-89; scout exec. Green Mountain Coun. Waterbury, Vt., 1989—; guest lectr. Iowa State U., Ames, 1976-78, Pace U., N.Y.C., 1982-84; tchr. 9 nat./regional meetings Boy Scouts Am., 1977-88, leader 3 overseas trips. Producer 7 in-house booklets, contbr. monthly in-house publs. Boy Scouts Am. Area chmn. United Way Phila., 1986-87; mem. Congl. redistricting com., 1980; bd. dirs. Jaycees, Iowa, Mo., 1972-81. Served to 1st. lt. USMC, 1971-72. Recipient Eagle Scout award Boy Scouts Am., 1962, Medal of Peace Govt. Egypt, 1984; named Man of Yr. Beta Theta chpt. Phi Kappa Tau, 1969, Keyman Kansas City Jaycees, 1974. Mem. Nat. Soc. Fund Raising Execs. (pub. relations com. 1986), Boy Scouts Am. (4 Disting Exec. awards, Good Scout award 1984), U. Kansas Alumni Assn. N.Y. (treas. 1982-84), U. Mo. Kansas City Alumni Assn. Republican. Epsicopalian. Home: 340 Harford Rd Somerdale NJ 08083 Office: Boy Scouts Am Phila Coun Pkwy 22d & Winter Sts Philadelphia PA 19103

MYERS, FREDERICK M., metal products executive; b. 1922; married. Grad., Williams Coll., 1943; LLB, Harvard U., 1948. Assoc. Cravath, Swaine & Moore, N.Y.C., 1948-50, Cain, Hibbard, Myers & Cook, 1951-80; with Lukens, Inc., 1957—, chmn., 1981-88, vice-chmn., 1988—, also bd. dirs. Office: Lukens Inc Coatesville PA 19320 *

MYERS, JACK KAY, financial planner, investment advisor; b. Miami, Fla., May 27, 1946; s. Milton and Elaine (Ehrlich) M.; m. Sandra Cheryl Myers, Dec. 6, 1974; 1 child, Kellie Kaye. Cert. fin. planner; registered investment advisor. Sales rep., mgr. Lincoln Nat. Life Ins. Co., Ft. Lauderdale, Fla. and Columbus, Ga., 1975-79; brokerage rep. CNA, Columbus, 1979-82; pres. Metro South Brokerage Agy. Inc., Columbus, 1983—; Speaker Ala. Optometric Assn., 1983. Capt. U.S. Army, 1968-75. Mem. Internat. Assn. for Fin. Planning, Inst. Cert. Fin. Planners, Columbus Bd. Realtors (assoc.). Republican. Home: 3323 Windermere St Columbus GA 31909 Office: Metro South Brokerage Agy Inc 905 3d Ave Columbus GA 31901

MYERS, JANET LOUISE, management consultant; b. Alliance, Ohio. BS with honors, Kent State U., 1962; MA in Info. Systems, U. Denver, 1968; MBA, Northwestern U., 1974. With First Nat. Bank Chgo., Data Resources, Inc., Omega Cons.; founder, pres. Dearborn Bus. Group, West Lafayette, Ind., 1984—; lectr. in field. Contbr. articles to profl. jours. Office: Dearborn Bus Group 2878 Bridgeway Dr West Lafayette IN 47906

MYERS, LEE EARL, financial and business consultant; b. Chgo., July 20, 1932; s. Earl J. and Dora (Thomas) M.; divorced; children: DeAnna Myers Gibson, Sue Ann Myers Hansford. Chartered fin. cons.; registered fin. planning practitioner. From salesman to corp. officer Mut. N.Y., N.Y.C., 1956-82; owner, mgr. Lee Myers Assocs., Fin. Cons., N.Y.C., 1982-84, New Windsor, N.Y., 1985—; pres. Regent Planning Inc., Monticello, N.Y., 1984-85; lectr. Mt. St. Mary Coll., 1985—, NYU, 1985—, profl. seminars, civic groups, schs., 1985—; former instr. fin. planning Sullivan County Community Coll. Columnist various newspapers, 1985—. Mayor City of Imperial Beach, Calif., 1963-64; chmn. bldg. bond issue South Bay Sch. Dist., Imperial Beach, 1964; bd. dirs. Orange County Mediation Project Inc.; past. chmn. steering com. San Diego Bay Port Authority; bd. dirs. United Meth. Ch., Cornwall, N.Y. With USN, 1952-56. Named Man of Yr. City of Imperial Beach, 1964. Mem. Am. Soc. Chartered Fin. Cons., Internat. Assn. for Fin. Planning (v.p. edn. Westchester-Rockland chpt. 1988—), Mid-Hudson Fin. Planners Forum (pres. 1988—), Estate Planning Coun., Navy League, Toastmasters, Rotary (sec., bd. dirs. New Windsor chpt.), Masons, Shriners, Elks. Office: PO Box 4089 New Windsor NY 12550

MYERS, LOUIS MICHAEL, financial consultant; b. Pitts., July 16, 1930. MA in Internat. Affairs, Columbia U., 1956. Fin. analyst Hammersclag-Kempner, N.Y.C., 1956-59; spl. rep. Am. Express, Paris, 1960-63; v.p. ins. Marrocan Ins. corp., Casablanca, Morroco, 1963-66; internat. v.p. Nat. Torch Corp., Pitts., 1966-71, cons., 1986—; pres. Nat. Torch Can., Toronto, Ont., 1971-86; bd. dirs. Nat. Torch Ltd., London; mem. Lloyds Ins., London, 1985—. Office: Nat Torch Inc 50 Freeport Rd Pittsburgh PA 15215

MYERS, MALCOLM C., manufacturing company executive; b. 1923; married. B.S. in Mech. Engring., Purdue U., 1947. Sales engr. Lukenheimer Co., 1947-50; planning engr. Gen. Electric Co., 1950-52; pres. OPW div. Dover Corp., 1952-70; pres., chief exec. officer Carlisle Corp., Cin., 1970-84, vice-chmn., chief exec. officer, 1984-88, chmn., 1988—, also bd. dirs.; bd. dirs. Union Cen. Life Ins. Co., Sencorp., Cin., Amcast Indsl. Office: Carlisle Cos Inc Carlisle Corp 1600 Columbia Pla 250 E 5th St Cincinnati OH 45202

MYERS, MARILYN VIRGINIA, natural resources executive, importer, financial consultant; b. Tampa, Fla., Jan. 18, 1954; d. Bill Ivan Myers and Rhoda Elizabeth (Edwards) Bean. BA, Auburn U., 1976. Account exec. Merrill Lynch & Co., Atlanta, 1978-82, Stotler and Co., Miami, Fla., 1983-85; chief exec. officer, dir. China Sea Resources, Inc., Vancouver, B.C., Can., 1986-87; pres. Trinity Internat. Trading, Inc., Miami, 1985—; dir., mgr. pub. rels. Supreme Resources, Vancouver, 1987—; fgn. currency cons. Cen. Nat. Bank Mex., Mexico City, 1983-85; chief negotiator, cons. People's Republic of China Aquaculture Joint Venture, Beijing and Hong Kong, 1986—; bd. dirs. Diablo, Denver. Republican. Pentecostal. Office: Trinity Internat Trading Inc 125 Seaview Dr Key Biscayne FL 33149

MYERS, MILLER FRANKLIN, finance company executive, retail executive; b. Aberdeen, S.D., Sept. 26, 1929; s. Burton Franklin and Virginia (Miller) M.; m. Janet Arlene Rylander, June 16, 1951; children: Leslie Ann, Burton F., Claudia Ann, Georgianna. Student, Grinnell Coll., 1947-49; BA, U. Minn., 1951-53, PhD, 1953. From v.p. to pres. Internat. Dairy Queen, Mpls., 1961-65, Dairy Queen of Can., Hamilton, Ont., 1953-70; chmn., chief exec. officer Internat. Dairy Queen, Mpls., 1970-74; pres. Econo-Therm Energy Systems, Mpls., 1975-84; chmn., chief exec. officer Aero Drapery Corp., Mpls., 1984—, Franklin Investments, Inc., Mpls., 1984—; pres., chmn. Dairy Queen Nat. Devel. Corp., St. Louis, 1960-64, Bayview Capital Corp., 1980—; bd. dirs. Northwestern Nat. Bank, Mpls., 1965-69, Northwestern Teleprodns., Mpls., 1969-77. Del. Rep. Conv., St. Paul, 1968; student organizer Stassen for Pres., 1948. Mem. Young Pres. Orgn., 1966-82, World Bus. Counsel, Minn. Execs. Orgn., Mpls. Club, Minikahda Club, Wilderness Country Club, Lafayette Club. Republican. Office: Aero Drapery Corp 5601 Smetana Dr Ste 100 Minnetonka MN 55343

MYERS, NORMAN ALLAN, marketing professional; b. Beeville, Tex., Dec. 10, 1935; s. Floyd Charles and Ruby (Lee) Myers; m. Suzanne Carlile, Oct. 11, 1935; children: Lisa Leigh Myers Nowlin, Matthew Scott. BS in Banking and Fin., Okla. State U., 1958. Salesman Jones and Laughlin Steel Corp., Houston, 1958-64; agt. Acacia Mutual Life Ins., Houston, 1964-69; with Browning-Ferris Industries, Houston, 1969—, exec. v.p., 1976-81, chief mktg. officer, 1981—, vice chmn., 1982—; also bd. dirs.; bd. dirs. Med. Ctr. Bank, Houston. Bd. dirs. My Friends-A Neuenschwander Found. for Children in Crisis. 2nd. lt. U.S. Army, 1958-59. Republican. Clubs: Lakeside Country (Houston); Hills of Lakeway (Austin). Lodges: Shriners, Holland. Office: Browning-Ferris Industries Inc PO Box 3151 757 N Eldrige Houston TX 77253-3151

MYERS, PHILLIP FENTON, business executive; b. Cleve., June 24, 1935; s. Max I. and Rebecca (Rosenbloom) M.; m. Hope Gail Strum, Aug. 13, 1961. B.I.E., Ohio State U., 1958, M.B.A., 1960; D.B.A., Harvard U., 1966. Staff indsl. engr. Procter & Gamble Co., Cin., 1958; sr. cons. Cresap, McCormack & Paget, N.Y.C., 1960-61; staff assoc. Mitre Corp., Bedford, Mass., 1961; cons. Systems Devel. Corp., Santa Monica, Calif., 1963-64; corp. asst. long range planning Electronic Specialty Co., Los Angeles, 1966-68; chmn. Atek Industries, 1968-72; pres. Myers Fin. Corp., 1973—, Steel Fuels Corp., 1976-77; chmn. Amvid Communication Services, Inc., 1975-79, Gen. Hydrogen Corp. Am., 1976-79, Omni Resources Devel. Corp., 1979-83; chmn., pres. Am. Internat. Mining Co., Inc., 1979-83; pres. Whitehall Internat. Mgmt. Co., Inc., 1982—, Global Bond Mktg. Services, Inc., 1987—; gen. ptnr. Pacific Internat. Devel. Co., 1985—; founding dir. Warner Ctr. Bank, 1980-83; lectr. bus. adminstrn. U. So. Calif., Los Angeles, 1967-74; prof. Pepperdine U. Grad. Sch. Bus. Adminstrn., 1974-81. Trustee, treas. Chamber Symphony Soc. Calif., 1971-78; pub. safety commr. City of Hidden Hills, Calif., 1977-83, chmn., 1982-83; co-chmn. budget adv. com. Las Virgenas Sch. Dist., 1983-86; mem. Mayor's Blue Ribbon Fin. Com., 1981-82; mem. dean's select adv. com. Coll. Engring., Ohio State U., 1984—; mem. state exec. com. Calif. Libertarian Party, chmn. region 61. Served to capt. USAF, 1958-60. Ford Found. fellow, 1961-64. Mem. Harvard Bus. Sch. Assn., Ohio State Alumni Assn. Club: Harvard of So. Calif. (bd. dirs. 1970-74, treas. 1971-73). Home and Office: 5819 Fitzpatrick Rd Ste 1000 Calabasas CA 91302

MYERS, RAYMOND SCOTT, metals company executive; b. San Diego, Oct. 2, 1950; s. Raymond W. and Nadine (Peevy) M.; m. Aloma L. Beaver, Aug. 6, 1983; children: Jared, Christine, Jason. AA, Pensacola Jr. Coll., 1970; BA, Fla. State U., 1972. Asst. store mgr. W.T. Grant Co., Milton, Fla., 1973, Brewton, Ala., 1973-75; plant mgr. Reynolds Metals Co., Baton Rouge, 1976-80, Honolulu, 1980-83; regional market mgr. Reynolds Metals Co., Los Angeles, 1983-86; regional bus. mgr. Reynolds Metals Co., Richmond, Va., 1986—. Mem. Pa. Resources Coun. Mem. Am. Mktg. Assn. Republican. Baptist. Home: 1502 Queens Pointe Dr Richmond VA 23233 Office: Reynolds Aluminum Recycling Co 8550 Mayland Dr Ste 203 Richmond VA 23229

MYERS, ROBERT GILBERT, printing company executive; b. Denison, Tex., Nov. 30, 1932; s. Gilbert G. and Jeannette (Richeson) M.; m. Karyl Yates, Sept. 11, 1954; children: Gregory, Karyn, Richard. B.S., Iowa State U., 1954; M.S. (Sloan fellow), Mass. Inst. Tech., 1971. Sales mgr. Glaser Crandell Pickle Co., Chgo., 1957-62; sales mgr. R.R. Donnelley & Sons. Co., Chgo., 1963-70; mgr. operating group R.R. Donnelley & Sons. Co., 1972-73, sr. v.p., 1974-86, group pres., 1986-89. Mem. dean's adv. bd. sch. bus. Iowa State U. Clubs: Shoreacres (Lake Bluff, Ill.); Sky (N.Y.C.). Home: Shoreacres Grounds PO Box 146 Lake Bluff IL 60044

MYERS, ROBERT NORMAN, JR., financial executive; b. Altoona, Pa., July 19, 1949; s. Robert Norman and Elizabeth Ellen (Miller) M.; m. Janet Mae Weaver, Dec. 4, 1971; children: Michael, Patrick. BS in Acctg., Pa. State U., 1971; MBA, Xavier U., 1981. Bus. analyst Dun & Bradstreet, Columbus, Ohio, 1972-74; cost pricing analyst Rockwell Internat., Columbus, 1974-79; fin. analyst Battelle Meml. Inst., Columbus, 1979-81, bus. mgr., 1981-83; mgr. adminstrn. Battelle Meml. Inst., Duxbury, Mass., 1983-85; mgr. fin. and program mgmt. systems Battelle Meml. Inst., Columbus, 1985-87, mgr. fin., 1987—; cons. fin. analysis, Columbus, 1986—. Served to capt. U.S. Army, 1971-80. Republican. Lutheran. Office: Battelle Meml Inst 505 King Ave Columbus OH 43201

MYERS, ROLLAND GRAHAM, investment counselor; b. St. Louis, Aug. 30, 1945; s. Rolland Everett and Lurilien (Graham) M. Diploma, St. Louis Country Day Sch., 1963; AB cum laude in History and Lit., Harvard U., 1966; postgrad. Faculties of Social Scis. and Law, U. Edinburgh, Scotland, 1966-67, Fondation Nationale des Sciences Politiques and Faculte de Lettres et des Sciences Humaines, U. Paris, 1967-68. Trainee global credit dept. The Chase Manhattan Bank, N.A., N.Y.C., 1968-69, mem. 32d spl. devel. program, 1969, strategic planner internat. dept., 1969-70, securities analyst, mktg. coordinator, fiduciary investment dept., 1970; account exec. N.Y. sales dept. Smith, Barney & Co., Inc., N.Y.C., 1971-72, assoc. Smith Barney & Co., Inc., N.Y.C., 1971, account exec. N.Y. sales dept., 1971-72, account exec. N.Y. internat. sales dept., 1972-74, 2nd v.p., stockholder, 1975-76; v.p., stockholder Smith Barney, Harris Upham & Co., Inc. (subs. SBHU Holdings, Inc.), N.Y.C., 1976-78; ltd. ptnr. Croke Patterson Campbell Ltd., Denver, 1975—; prin. W.H. Graham & Sons, 1977—; joint founder, gen. ptnr. Mansion Disbursements, Denver, 1979— ; pres., chmn. exec. com., dir. Fifty-Five Residents Corp., N.Y.C., 1980-84; dir. Fifty-Six Danbury Rd. Assn., Inc., New Milford, Conn. Vestry v.p., vestryman Episcopal Chaplaincy at Harvard and Radcliffe, Cambridge, 1965-66; trustee, mem. corp. Bishop Rhinelander Found., Cambridge, 1973-75; v.p., treas., dir. The Whitehill Graham Found., St. Louis, 1976—; dir., mem. corp. Eliot Pratt Edn. Ctr., Inc., New Milford, Conn., 1987—; treas., bd. dirs., mem. corp. Kent (Conn.) Land Trust Inc., 1989—; project financier Restoration of 1851 Samuel Curtiss Hosford House, Nat. Register Historic Dist., Falls Village, Conn., 1984-86; commr. Housatonic River Commn., Warren, Conn., 1985—, vice chmn. Commn. Conservation, Inland Wetlands and Watercourses commn., Kent, Conn., 1988—. Mem. Cum Laude Soc., St. Louis Country Day Sch. Alumni Assn., Harvard Alumni Assn. Republican. Episcopalian. Clubs: Capitol Hill (Washington), Harvard (N.Y.C.); Hasty Pudding-Inst. of 1770 (Cambridge). Home: Rte 1 PO Box 95 Kent CT 06757 Office: 56 Danbury Rd New Milford CT 06776

MYERS, THEODORE ASH, steel company executive; b. Ellwood City, Pa., Aug. 3, 1930; s. Hiram John and Celia (Emery) M.; m. Katharine Louise Hoy, July 2, 1952 (dec.); children: David, Randall, Mark, Katharine, Scott, Christopher; m. Linda Bromley Moore, Nov. 28, 1986. B.S. in Indsl. Mgmt., Pa. State U., 1952; M.B.A. in Fin., Harvard U., 1966. With indsl. instrument div. Mpls. Honeywell Co., Phila., 1952-56; with Halsey Stuart & Co., N.Y.C., 1957-60, Arnold Malkan & Co., Inc., N.Y.C., 1961-63; mgmt. cons. Belmont, Mass., 1963-66; v.p., treas. Washington Nat. Corp., Evanston, Ill., 1966-74, Whittaker Corp., Los Angeles, 1974-75; asst. v.p. fin. Inland Steel Co., Chgo., 1975-81; v.p. fin. Inland Steel Co., 1981—. Active fund raising YMCA. Mem. Am. Fin. Assn., Am. Iron and Steel Inst., Machinery and Allied Products Inst., Fin. Execs. Inst. Republican. Clubs: Skokie Country (Glencoe, Ill.); Harvard of N.Y.; Harvard Bus. Sch. of Chgo.; Economic, Union League (Chgo.); Ventana Canyon Golf and Racquet (Tucson). Home: 550 Washington St Glencoe IL 60022 Office: Inland Steel Industries Inc 30 W Monroe Chicago IL 60603

MYERS, THOMAS ALDEN, diversified company executive; b. Akron, Ohio, Dec. 1, 1945; s. Minor and Ruth (Libby) M.; m. Lynn Dee Ann Locke, Aug. 24, 1969; children: Emily Michelle, Timothy Alden. BBA, Ohio State U., 1968; MBA, U. Cin., 1970; postgrad. U. Akron, 1974-75. Fin. analyst Mid-Continent Telephone Corp., Hudson, Ohio, 1973-77, supr. fin. results, 1977-78; public relations account exec. Edward Howard & Co., Cleve., 1978-79; mgr. investor relations TRW Inc., Cleve., 1979-81, dir. investor relations, 1982—. Co. photographer Ohio Ballet, Akron, 1976—, trustee, 1979—; founder, dir. The Screamers & Lyric Brass Band, 1986—. Served with U.S. Army, 1970-73. Mem. Nat. Investor Relations Inst. (sec.-treas. Cleve.-Akron chpt. 1981-82, v.p. membership 1982-84), Investor Relations Assn., Ohio State U. Alumni Assn., N.Am. Brass Band Assn. (dir. 1988—), Ohio State U. Marching Band Alumni. Home: 156 N Highland Ave Akron OH 44303 Office: TRW Inc 1900 Richmond Rd Cleveland OH 44124

MYERSON, BERNARD, theatre company executive. m. Muriel Friedman, Nov. 10, 1946; children: Alan, Edward. Formerly exec. Fabian Theatres Co.; exec. v.p. Loew's Corp., 1963—; pres. Loew's Theatres, 1971—, also dir.; pres., chief exec. officer, chmn. bd. Loew's Theatres Mgmt. Corp. subs. Tri-Star Pictures, Inc., 1988—; bd. dirs. Motion Picture Pioneers; mem. exec. com. Bd. Nat. Assn. Theatre Owners. Mem. exec. com. Greater N.Y. chpt. Nat. Found.-March of Dimes.; bd. dirs., hon. chmn. Will Rogers Meml. Fund; trustee Am. Film Inst.; mem. Bd. of Burke Rehab. Ctr. Mem. Nat. Assn. Theatre Owners (dir., exec. com.), Office Motion Picture and TV Devel. (mem. adv. bd. and pvt. sector com. of U.S. Info. Agy.). Clubs: Variety Internat. (bd. dirs.), Friars (mem. fin. com.).

MYHREN, TRYGVE EDWARD, communications company executive; b. Palmerton, Pa., Jan. 3, 1937; s. Arne Johannes and Anita (Blatz) M.; m. Carol Jane Enman, Aug. 8, 1964; children: Erik, Kirsten, Tor; m. 2d Victoria Hamilton, Nov. 14, 1981; 1 stepdau., Paige. B.A. in Philosophy and Polit. Sci., Dartmouth Coll., 1958, M.B.A., 1959. Sales mgr., unit mgr. Procter and Gamble, Cin., 1963-65; sr. cons. Glendinning Cos., Westport, Conn., 1965-69; pres. Auberge Vintners, 1970-73; exec. v.p. Mktg. Continental, Westport, 1969-73; v.p., gen. mgr. CRM, Inc., Del Mar, Calif., 1973-75; v.p. mktg. Am. TV and Communications Corp., Englewood, Colo., 1975-78, sr. v.p. mktg. and programming, 1978-79, exec. v.p., 1980, pres., 1981, chmn. bd., chief exec. officer, 1982-88; pres. Myhren Media, 1989—; v.p. Time Inc., N.Y.C., 1981-86; treas., vice chmn., then chmn. bd., mem. exec com. Nat. Cable TV Assn., Washington, 1982—; mem. FCC Adv. Com. on HDTV, 1987—; bd. dirs. Turner Broadcasting, Atlanta, NovaNet Inc., Englewood, Advanced Mktg. Systems Inc., La Jolla. Vice chmn. Pub. Edn. Coalition; mem. Colo. Forum, 1984—, chmn. higher edn. com., 1986; bd. dirs., founder Colo. Bus. Com. for the Arts, 1985—; mem. exec. council Found. for Commemoration U.S. Constn., 1987—; mem. Nat. GED Task Force, 1987—. Served to lt. (j.g.) USN, 1959-62. Recipient Disting. Leader award Nat. Cable TV Assn., 1988. Mem. Cable TV Adminstrn. and Mktg. Soc. (pres. 1978-79, Grand Tam award 1985), Dartmouth Assn. Gt. Divide (trustee 1982-85), Cable Adv. Bur. (founder 1978). Episcopalian.

MYLES, MARGARET JEAN, hospital supplies buyer, real property appraiser; b. Detroit, Oct. 26, 1952; d. William Thompson and Patricia (Maclean) M. Student, Western Mich. U., 1973, Oakland U., 1974; AA, Coast Line Coll., 1986. Unit sec. Hoag Meml. Hosp., Newport Beach, Calif., 1976-80, buyer, 1981-86; real estate appraiser P.M. Myles & Assocs., Irvine, Calif., 1980—. Mem. Nat. Assn. Purchasing Mgmt., Purchasing Mgmt. Assn. Orange County. Home: 120 A Carriage Dr Santa Ana CA 92707 Office: PM Myles & Assocs 25 Mandrake Way Irvine CA 92715

MYRÉN, PER-OLOF, infosystems specialist, director; b. Stockholm, May 21, 1952; s. Bengt Olof and Ingrid (Wikner) M.; m. Birgitta Korfitsen, June

27, 1980. BEE, Royal Inst. Tech., Stockholm, 1976; MBA, Stockholm Bus. Sch., 1977. Dir., owner Beslutsmodeller AB, Stockholm, 1977—; ptnr. Digitech Computersystem GmBH, Vienna, Austria, 1987, Scala Informatic AG, Zurich, Switzerland, 1988—; com. mem. LKD Computer Supplier Orgn., 1984—. Served as sgt. Swedish Marine Corps, 1978. Office: Beslutsmodeller AB, PO Box 681, S-131 00 Nacka Sweden

MYRICK, CHARLES PIERRE, accountant; b. Washington, July 30, 1955; s. James Hazel and Francoise Marie (Delavant) M. BSBA in Acctg., Georgetown U., 1981. CPA. Acct. Price Waterhouse, Washington, 1981-82, Reznick Fedder & Silverman, Bethesda, Md, 1982-85, Western Devel. Corp., Washington, 1985-87, Charles P. Myrick, CPA, Silver Spring, 1987—. Mem. Am. Inst. CPAs. Office: Charles P Myrick CPA 8401 Colesville Rd Ste132A Silver Spring MD 20910

NABERS, DRAYTON, JR., insurance company executive; b. Birmingham, Ala., Dec. 2, 1940; s. Drayton Sr. and Jane (Porter) N.; m. Fairfax Smathers, Dec. 31, 1965; children: Drayton III, Mary James, Fairfax Virginia. BA, Princeton U., 1962; LLB, Yale U., 1965. Law clk. to justice Hugo Black U.S. Supreme Ct., Washington, 1965-66; assoc. Cabaniss, Johnston, Gardner, Dumas & O'Neal, 1967-71, ptnr., 1971-79; sr. v.p. ops., gen. counsel Protective Life Ins. Co., 1979; pres. Empire Gen. Life Ins. Co., 1980-82; pres., chief operating officer Protective Life Corp./Protective Life Ins. Co., 1982—; bd. dirs. Protective Life Corp., Protective Life Ins. Co., United Founders Life Ins. Co., Am. Found. Life Ins. Co., Energen, Inc., Nat. Bank of Commerce. Mem. steering com. Leadership Birmingham; bd. dirs. Ala. Care Com. Prison Fellowship, Ala. Assn. of Ind. Colls.; pres., bd. dirs. Birmingham Alive. Mem. Birmingham Bar Assn., Ala. Bar Assn., Young Pres's. Orgn. Office: Protective Life Corp PO Box 2606 Birmingham AL 35202

NACHTIGAL, JULIUS HARVEY, cosmetics industry executive; b. N.Y.C., Sept. 17, 1938; s. Elias and Frieda (Laufer) N.; m. Sylvia Renee Heisler, June 24, 1962; children: Sheri Lisa, Lori Jill. BA, Yeshiva Coll., 1959; PhD in Chemistry, Polytech. Inst. Bklyn., 1966. Research chemist Colgate-Palmolive, Piscataway, N.J., 1966-74; group leader Am. Can. Co., Princeton, N.J, 1974-76; dir. research Bonat, Inc., West Paterson, N.J., 1976-78; v.p. research and devel. Conair Corp., Edison, N.J., 1978—. Contbr. articles to profl. jours.; patentee in field. N.Y. Regents scholar, 1955; Rockefeller Found. research fellow, 1961-66. Mem. Soc. Cosmetic Chemists, Am. Chem. Soc. Jewish. Office: Conair Corp 1 Cummings Point Rd Stamford CT 06904

NACOL, MAE, lawyer; b. Beaumont, Tex., June 15, 1944; d. William Samuel and Ethel (Bowman) N.; children: Shawn Alexander Nacol, Catherine Regina Nacol. BA, Rice U., 1965; postgrad., S. Tex. Coll. Law, 1966-68. Bar: Tex. 1969, U.S. Dist. Ct. (so. dist.) Tex. 1969. Diamond buyer/appraiser Nacol's Jewelry, Houston, 1961—; sole practice, Houston, 1969—. Author, editor ednl. materials on multiple sclerosis, 1981-85. Nat. dir. A.R.M.S. of Am. Ltd., Houston, 1984-85. Recipient Mayor's Recognition award City of Houston, 1972; Ford Found. fellow So. Tex. Coll. Law, Houston, 1964. Mem. Houston Bar Assn. (chmn. candidate com. 1970, chmn. membership com. 1971, chmn. lawyers referral com. 1972), Assn. Trial Lawyers Am., Tex. Trial Lawyers Assn., Am. Judicature Soc. (sustaining), Houston Fin. Coun. Women. Presbyterian. Office: 600 Jefferson #690 Houston TX 77002

NADEAU, JOSEPH EUGENE, health care management consultant, information systems consultant; b. Portland, Maine, Sept. 23, 1937; s. Edwin Tustin and Beatrice Margaret (Spiller) N.; m. Mary Lou Prendible, Dec. 2, 1961; children—Laura, Keith, Michael. B.S. in Math., Boston Coll., 1960. Dir. systems devel. Mass. Hosp. Assn., Burlington, 1967-72; S.E. regional mgr. Automatic Data Processing, Miami, Fla., 1972-73; S.E. regional mktg. mgr. Space Age Computer Systems, Louisville, 1973-74; prin. COMPUTERx Cons., Miami, 1974—. Asst. scoutmaster South Fla. council Boy Scouts Am., 1972-81. Served to 1st lt. U.S. Army, 1960-64; Germany. Mem. Am. Hosp. Assn., Soc. Computer Medicine, Data Processing Mgmt. Assn., Hosp. Mgmt Systems Soc., Assn. Systems Mgmt. (pres. 1971-72), Hosp. Fin. Mgmt. Assn. (chmn. data processing com. 1967-84), Am. Arbitration Assn. (arbitrator 1980—). Cert. systems profl. Home: 7750 SW 118th St Miami FL 33156 Office: COMPUTERx Cons 9719 S Dixie Suite 12 Miami FL 33156

NADEL, ELLIOTT, investment firm executive; b. N.Y.C., Nov. 23, 1945; s. Archie and Faye (Braverman) N.; children: Lindsey, Amanda. BBA, Baruch Coll., 1969, MBA, 1971. Portfolio mgr. SwissRe Advisors, N.Y.C., 1973-74; v.p., stockbroker E. F. Hutton, N.Y.C., 1975-84, Shearson Lehman Bros., N.Y.C., 1984-85, Oppenheimer & Co., N.Y.C., 1985, Rooney Pace Inc., N.Y.C., 1986-87, Philips Appel & Walden, N.Y.C., 1987-88; sr. v.p. investments Moore, Schley & Cameron, N.Y.C., 1988—. With U.S. Army, 1969-74. Jewish. Office: 45 Broadway New York NY 10006

NADEL, LEONARD, business executive, management consultant; b. N.Y.C., Aug. 19, 1921; s. Jack and Clare (Hersch) N.; m. Rita Jacqueline Buckner; children: Marilyn Gail Fox, Warren Douglas. BS, NYU, 1942, MBA, 1951; LLD (hon.), Adelphi U., 1981. Personnel mgr. E.R. Squibb & Sons, Bklyn., 1946-53; sr. v.p. Abraham & Straus, Bklyn., 1953-78; exec. v.p. Beldoch Industries, N.Y.C., 1980-87; mgmt. cons. Leonard Nadel Assocs., N.Y.C., 1978-80, Beldoch Industries, N.Y.C., 1987—; adjunct instr. Adelphi U., Garden City, N.Y., NYU, CUNY; trustee Richmond Hill Savs. Bank; chmn. adv. bd. Lab. Inst. of Merchandising. Active speaker to civic and profl. groups; contbr. articles to bus. jours. Mayor Vill. of East Hills, L.I., N.Y.; former mem. Bklyn. Adv. Council State div. Human Rights, Assocs. of C.W. Post Coll.; former mem. bd. zoning appeals Village of East Williston, L.I.; past pres. Bklyn. C. of C., Temple Beth Sholom, Roslyn Heights, L.I.; former mem. exec. bd. Bklyn. council Boy Scouts Am.; bd. dirs. Mcpl. Assistance Corp. for the City of N.Y.; former bd. dirs. Surprise Lake Camp of the Ednl. Alliance and Young Men's Hebrew Assn., Indsl. Home for the Blind; former vice chmn., bd. dirs. Bklyn. Devel. Assocs., Inc.; past chmn. Bklyn. Arts and Culture Assn., Inc., Fulton Mall Improvement Assn., United Fund of Greater N.Y.; former trustee United Fund of L.I.; bd. dirs., former chmn., trustee Adelphi U., chmn. presdl. search com.; trustee, mem. exec. com. L.I. Jewish Hillside Med. Ctr. Recipient Disting. Service Silver Plaque award Nat. Retail Merchants Assn., Bklyn. Hall of Fame award Commerce and Industry, 1973, Community Service and Leadership award Bklyn. div. Council of Chs. of N.Y.C., 1974, Louis C. Wills award for Excellence Indsl. Home for the Blind, 1977; named Man of Yr., C.W. Post Coll., 1972. Mem. Am. Arbitration Assn. (panel of arbitrators). Office: Leonard Nadel Assocs 57 Northern Blvd Greenvale NY 11548

NADERI, JAMIE BENEDICT, owner hazardous waste services brokerage firm; b. New Castle, Pa., Aug. 6, 1951; d. Harold James and June Marilyn (Sipe) Benedict; m. David Lynn Martin, June 25, 1970 (div.); children: Robert Brian, Eric James; m. David James Fanning, Feb. 16, 1980 (div.); m. Bijhan A. Naderi, Sept. 16, 1985. Student, New Castle Bus. Coll., 1967-69, Truckee Meadows Community Coll., 1979-82. Lic. practical nurse, Pa. Nurse Dr. William Stechschulte, Pitts., 1973-76, Dr.'s S & R Ramos, Reno, 1977-81, St. Mary Hosp., Reno, 1979-81; restaurant critic PM Mag., Reno, 1979-81; v.p. BioNova Industries, Irvine, Calif., 1981-83; mgr. Hyatt Regency, Nashville, 1983-84; pres. Moheat, Inc., Houston, 1984—. Treas. Reno Little Theatre, 1979-80, 80-81. Mem. Women in Constrn., Nat. Assn. Female Execs., Physicians Nurses Assn., Nat. Found. of Lic. Practical Nurses. Presbyterian. Office: Moheat Inc 430 Hwy 6 Suite 202 Houston TX 77079

NADHERNY, FERDINAND, executive recruiting company executive. Vice chmn. Russell Reynolds Assocs. Inc., Chgo. Office: Russell Reynolds Assocs Inc 200 S Wacker Dr Suite 3600 Chicago IL 60606

NADKARNI, UDAY P., software company executive; b. Amravati, India, Sept. 21, 1956; came to U.S., 1983; s. Pandharinath S. and Vinita P. (Desai) N. BEE, Indian Inst. Tech., Bombay, 1978. Programmer Tata Unisys Ltd., Bombay, 1978-79; analyst Tata Unisys Ltd., Harrisburg, Pa. and Detroit, 1979-80; project mgr. Tata Unisys Ltd., Hobart, Australia, 1981-82; regional mktg. mgr. Tata Unisys Ltd., Roseland, N.J., 1983-85; assoc. W.L. Gore & Assocs., Newark, 1985-87; pres. Inference Devel. Corp., South Orange, N.J., 1987—. Office: Inference Devel Corp 232 Montague Pl South Orange NJ 07079-2129

NADZICK, JUDITH ANN, accountant; b. Paterson, N.J., Mar. 6, 1948; d. John and Ethel (McDonald) N.; B.B.A. in Acctg., U. Miami (Fla.), 1971. Staff accountant, mgr. Ernst & Whinney, C.P.A.s, N.Y.C., 1971-78; asst. treas. Gulf & Western Industries, Inc., N.Y.C., 1979-83, asst. v.p., 1980-82, v.p., 1982-83; v.p., corp. controller United Mchts. and Mfrs. Inc., N.Y.C., 1983-85, sr. v.p., 1985-86, exec. v.p., chief fin. officer, 1986—, also bd. dirs. 1987—. C.P.A., N.J. Mem. Am. Inst. C.P.A.s, Nat. Assn. Accts., N.Y. State Soc. C.P.A.s, U. Miami Alumni Assn., Delta Delta Delta. Roman Catholic. Home: 2 Lincoln Sq Apt 15G New York NY 10023

NAEGELE, EUGENE LEE, financial counselor; b. Fairview Park, Ohio, Feb. 16, 1926; s. Ray William and Mary (Stephens) N.; m. Irene Blanche Pickering, Aug. 22, 1950; children—Mary Susan Naegele Galvin, Janice Rae. B.S. in Physics, Case Inst. Tech., 1949; postgrad. Northeastern U., 1961-62, Am. U., 1965-68; M.S.E.E., U. Ariz., 1965. Cert. fin. planner. Mgr. Army air def. market research Raytheon Co., Bedford, Mass., 1968-81; v.p. New Eng. Fin. Planning Group, Inc., Burlington, Mass., 1981-87; rep. Investment Mgmt. & Research, Inc., Tucson, 1981-87. Author: Personal Financial Planning, 1981. Vice chmn. Republican Town Com., Boxborough, Mass., 1984-87; chmn., vice chmn. Rep. Town Com., Sudbury, Mass., 1970-83; mem. Com. on Town Adminstrn., Sudbury, 1970-72; Rep. precinct committeeman Dist. 13, Ariz., 1987—; dep. registrar, Pima County, Ariz., 1987—. Served with U.S. Army, 1944-46; to lt. col., 1951-68, ETO, Korea. Mem. Registry Fin. Planning Practitioners, Inst. Cert. Fin. Planners, Internat. Assn. for Fin. Planning, Com. for Monetary Research and Edn., Am. Inst. for Econ. Research (sustaining). Republican. Presbyterian. Avocations: church choir; bridge; fishing. Office: Investment Mgmt & Rsch Inc 1135 N Craycroft Rd Tucson AZ 85712-4914

NAFTALIS, GARY PHILIP, lawyer; b. Newark, Nov. 23, 1941; s. Gilbert and Bertha Beatrice (Gruber) N.; m. Donna Arditi, June 30, 1974; children: Benjamin, Joshua, Daniel, Sarah. AB, Rutgers U., 1963; AM, Brown U., 1965; LLB, Columbia U., 1967. Bar: N.Y. 1967, U.S. Supreme Ct. 1974, U.S. Ct. Appeals (2d cir.) 1968, U.S. Ct. Appeals (3d cir.) 1973, U.S. Dist. Ct. (so. dist.) N.Y. 1969. Law clk. to judge U.S. Dist. Ct. So. Dist. N.Y., 1967-68; asst. U.S. atty. So. Dist. N.Y., 1968-74, asst. chief criminal div., 1972-74; spl. asst. U.S. atty. for V.I., 1972-73; spl. counsel U.S. Senate Subcom. on Long Term Care, 1975; spl. counsel N.Y. State Temp. Commn. on Living Costs and the Economy, 1975; ptnr. Orans, Elsen, Polstein & Naftalis, N.Y.C., 1974-81, Kramer, Levin, Nessen, Kamin & Frankel, N.Y.C., 1981—; lectr. in law Columbia U. Law Sch., 1976-88; vis. lectr. Harvard U. Law Sch., 1979; mem. deptl. disciplinary com. Appellate div. 1st Dept., 1980-86. Author: (with Marvin E. Frankel) The Grand Jury: An Institution on Trial, 1977, Considerations in Representing Attorneys in Civil and Criminal Enforcement Proceedings, 1981, Sentencing: Helping Judges Do Their Jobs, 1986; editor: White Collar Crimes, 1980. Trustee, Boys Brotherhood Republic, 1978—, Blueberry Treatment Center, 1981—. Mem. ABA, N.Y. City Bar Assn. (com. criminal cts. 1980-83, com. judiciary 1984-87, com. on criminal law 1987—, council on criminal justice 1985—), Fed. Bar Council (com. cts. of 2d cir. 1974-77), N.Y. State Bar Assn. (com. state legis. 1974-76). Home: 336 W End Ave Apt 18-C New York NY 10023 Office: Kramer Levin Nessen Kamin & Frankel 919 3rd Ave New York NY 10022

NAGEL, JON ALAN, management consultant; b. Cin., Nov. 8, 1950; s. Arthur R. and Marie Ann (Vollmer) N.; B.A., U. Cin., 1972, M.A., 1975; M.B.A., Columbia U., 1973; postgrad. Emory U. Law Sch., Harvard U., Oxford (Eng.) U.; m. Susan Ellen Nagel, Apr. 28, 1979. Mgmt. cons., Cin. and N.Y.C., 1975—; dir. ARNCO, Inc., 1972—; gen. ptnr. Nagel Ptnrs., 1985—. Dir. The Met. Soc. for the Arts; dir. New Collectors, The New Mus. of Art; dir. Babies Heart Fund Columbia Presbyt. Med. Ctr. Mem. pres.'s council Vis. Nurse Service of N.Y. Mem. Am. Econ. Assn., Am. Fin. Assn., Nat. Council of Am. Ballet Theater, Young Men's Merc. Library Assn. Cin., Phi Alpha Delta. Clubs: Doubles, Jr. Internat., Metropolitan, Met. Opera, St. Bartholomew's (N.Y.C.), 52nd St. Breakfast. Author: World Trade, 1973; Multinational Corporations in World Politics: Ecopolitics and Nation-State Responses, 1975. Home: 2875 Montana Ave Cincinnati OH 45211 Also: One E 60th St New York NY 10022 Office: 644 Linn St Cincinnati OH 45203 Also: 425 E 63d St New York NY 10021

NAGLE, ARTHUR JOSEPH, investment banker; b. Allentown, Pa., Sept. 11, 1938; s. Paul Arthur and Frances Helene (Kline) N.; m. Paige Carlton, Sept. 12, 1970; children: Kathryn Elizabeth, Christopher Paul. BS in Math., Pa. State U., 1961; MBA in Fin., Columbia U., 1967. Systems engr., mktg. rep. IBM, Pitts., 1961-62; trainee to mng. dir. First Boston Corp., N.Y.C., 1967-88; chmn. Vestar Capital Ptnrs., Inc., 1988—; bd. dirs. First Brands Corp., Danbury, Ct., Chart House Restaurants, Solana Beach, Calif., Super D Drugs, Inc., Memphis, Celestial Seasonings, Inc., Boulder, Colo., Triple C Acquisition Corp., Secaucus, N.J. Active Community Fund, Bronxville, N.Y. Served to lt. USN, 1962-66; Vietnam. Office: Vestar Capital Ptnrs Inc 140 E 45th St 35th Fl New York NY 10017

NAGLE, FREDERICK FLOYD, investment counselor; b. Greenwich, Conn., July 10, 1943; s. Smyser Floyd and Vera (Curtis) N.; B.A., Yale, 1966; postgrad. Cornell U. Law Sch., 1969; M.B.A., Fordham U., 1974; m. Susan Nelson, Dec. 10, 1977; children—Curtis Smyser, Kierstin Aurora. Investment reviewer State Nat. Bank Conn., 1967-68; investment officer Citibank, N.Y.C., 1971-78; 2d v.p. Chase Manhattan Bank, N.A., N.Y.C., 1978-79; v.p. J.M. Blewer, Inc., investment counsel, N.Y.C., 1979-86, sr. v.p. investment counsel Fairfield Research Inc., New Canaan, Conn., 1988—. Active alumni schs. com. Yale U., also area chmn.; asst. class agt. Taft Sch. Served to capt., Ordnance Corps, U.S. Army, 1968-71. Mem. N.Y. Soc. Security Analysts (sr. security analyst), Fedn. Fin. Analysts, Assn. Former Intelligence Officers (dir. N.Y. chpt). Republican. Roman Catholic. Club: Field of Greenwich, Coral Beach (Paget, Bermuda). Home: 725 Old Post Rd Bedford NY 10506 Office: Fairfield Rsch Inc New Canaan CT 06840

NAGLE, JUSTINE TERESA, advertising executive; b. N.Y.C., Feb. 3, 1940; d. Nicholas J. and Marguerite P. (Battle) N.; m. Edward Dillon, Sept. 14, 1957 (div. May 1964); children: Justine, Stacy. Student, Pace Coll., 1955-59, Cornell Labor Coll., 1972—, New Sch. Social Research, 1981—. Asst. producer Geyer Advt., 1957-58; coordinator Rose Marie Reid Bathing Suits, 1958-59; dir. advt. Temas Mag., N.Y.C., 1959-63; with Commerce Advt., N.Y.C., 1963—; v.p., account exec. 1969—; owner, pres. Elgan Communications, N.Y.C., 1964—; owner J. Nagle Assocs., 1980—, Kibbe Cab Co., 1979—; owner, pres. Commerce Advt., Inc., 1985—. Vol. The Shelter. Mem. Advt. Womens Club, Conservative Club, Met. Opera Guild, Mus. Natural History, Mus. Art. Republican. Clubs: Belle Harbor Yacht, N.Y. Athlete (assoc.), Atrium. Home: 301 E 47th St New York NY 10017 also: 537 Beach 130 St Belle Harbor NY 11694 Office: 220 E 23d St 8th Floor New York NY 10018

NAGLER, LEON GREGORY, management consultant, business executive; b. Buenos Aires, Argentina, Jan. 29, 1932 (parents Am. citizens); s. Morris and Jennie (Golden) N.; BS cum laude, Boston U., 1953, MBA, 1954; J.D., Cleve. State U., 1961; m. F. Elise Charness, Dec. 20, 1953; children: Jeri Lynn, Sandra Michelle. Bar: Ohio 1961. Tchr. psychology Cameron State Agrl. Jr. Coll., Lawton, Okla., 1956-57; supr. employment and tng. Jones & Laughlin Steel Corp., Cleve., 1957-65; exec. dir. indsl. relations Charles Corp., Cleve., 1965-67; dir. personnel ITT Service Industries Corp., Cleve., 1967-72; v.p. personnel Builder Services Corp., Clearwater, Fla., 1972-73; v.p. adminstrn. Damon Corp., Needham Heights, Mass., 1973-77; pres. Nagler & Co., Wellesley Hills, Mass., 1977—. Mem. Mayfield Heights (Ohio) Planning and Zoning Commn., 1965-67; sec. Mayfield Heights Zoning Bd. Appeals, 1963-65; chmn. Combined Health Fund, Mayfield Heights, 1963; pres. N.E. Ohio region, mem. nat. gov. council Am. Jewish Congress, 1972-73; bd. dirs. New Eng. region Anti-Defamation League, 1977-80; bd. dirs. Jewish Vocat. Service, Boston, 1977—, sec., 1980-83, v.p., 1983-88; bd. dirs. Jewish Community Ctr. Greater Boston, 1988—, Am. Friends Wingate Inst., 1987—, v.p. fin., 1987—; trustee Temple Beth Avodah, Newton, 1978—, v.p., 1979-83, pres., 1983-85; trustee Combined Jewish Philanthropies, Boston, 1985—. Served with AUS, 1955-57. Mem. Ohio, Cleve. bar assns., Am. Soc. Personnel Adminstrn., Nat. Assn. Corp. and Exec. Recruiters, Employment Mgrs. Assn., Boston U. Alumni Assn. (pres. N.E. Ohio 1969-73, nat. council 1973—). Democrat. Lodge: Masons. Office: Nagler & Co Inc 65 William St Wellesley Hills MA 02181

NAGLER, STEWART GORDON, insurance company executive; b. Bklyn., Jan. 30, 1943; s. Henry and Mary N.; m. Bonnie Lawrence, Aug. 9, 1964; children: David, Ellen. B.S. summa cum laude, Poly. U., 1963. With Meteopolitan Life Ins. Co., N.Y.C., 1963—; exec. v.p. Meteopolitan Life Ins. Co., 1978-85, sr. exec. v.p., 1985—. Fellow Soc. Actuaries, Acad. Actuaries. Office: Met Life Ins Co 1 Madison Ave New York NY 10010

NAGURSKI, JAN STEPHEN, controller; b. Long Beach, Calif., Sept. 23, 1944; s. Stephen and Edna Mae (Hart) N.; m. Bernadette Esther Barrett, Apr. 23, 1976; children: Mark, Brian, Kevin. BA in English, Calif. State U., Long Beach, 1967; degree in civilian club mgmt. with honors, Air Force Inst. Tech., Wright-Patterson AFB, Ohio, 1971; MBA, Pepperdine U., 1983. Commd. 2d lt. USAF, 1967, advanced through grades to capt., 1970, resigned, 1975; acct. Sta. WBAP/KSCS, Ft. Worth, 1975-76; mgmt. acct. Adria Ltd., Strabane, Ireland, 1976-78; gen. mgr. Bundoran (Ireland) Holidays, 1978-81; corp. fin. planning mgr. Luxfer USA, Riverside, Calif., 1981-87; controller Superform USA, Inc., Riverside, 1987—; cons., controller Superform USA, Riverside, 1985—; instr. acctg. community colls. Author, editor newsletter Smudgepot, 1984-86. Cubmaster Boy Scouts Am., Canyon Lake, Calif. Recipient Gold Medal Menu award Nat. Restaurant Assn., Ft. Worth, 1973. Mem. Nat. Assn. Accts. (pres. 1985-86), Data Processing Mgmt. Assn., Inst. Adminstrv. Acctg., U.K. Republican. Roman Catholic. Office: Superform USA Inc 6825 Jurupa Ave PO Box 5375 Riverside CA 92517-5375

NAGY, GABRIEL FRANCIS, investment banker; b. Szombathely, Hungary, Oct. 28, 1941; came to U.S., 1949; s. John N. and Helen (Guary) N.; m. Frances P. Roberts, Oct. 7, 1967 (div. Oct. 1981); children: John Estep, Frances Pinkney, Alexander Kennedy; m. Glenna M. Hazeltine, Apr. 5, 1986 (div. Jan. 1989). AB, Princeton U., 1963; LLB, Harvard U., 1966. Bar: Pa. 1968, U.S. Dist. Ct. (ea.) Pa. 1969, U.S. Ct. Appeals (3d cir.) 1969. Assoc. Morgan, Lewis & Bockius, Phila., 1967-75; chief counsel Pa. Securities Commn., Harrisburg, Pa., 1975-77; ptnr., counsel Elkins & Co., Phila., 1977-82; v.p. Prudential-Bache Securities, Phila., 1982-84; ptnr. Howard, Lawson & Co., Phila., 1984—. Columnist: Lawyer's Digest, 1986—. Mem. Nat. Assn. Securities Dealers (gen. securities prin. 1978—), Am.Soc. Appraisers. Clubs: Racquet, Phila Cricket. Office: Howard Lawson & Co 2 Penn Ctr Pla Philadelphia PA 19102

NAGY, MELINDA MCCORKLE, communications executive; b. Seattle, Oct. 2, 1959; d. Richard Dwight and Colleen Constance (Chowning) McC.; m. Andras Miklos Nagy, Sept. 3, 1988. Student, U. Wash., 1978-80, Stirling (Scotland) U., 1981-82; BA in Communications, Wash. State U., Pullman, 1983. Account exec. Jay Rockey Pub. Relations, Seattle, 1983-86; asst. v.p., mgr. corp. communications Wash. Mut. Savs. Bank, Seattle, 1986—. Vol. Children's Hosp., Seattle, 1987—. Mem. Pub. Relations Soc. Am. (2 Totem awards 1985, 1 Totem award 1987). Office: Wash Mut Savs Bank 1101 Second Ave Seattle WA 98101

NAGY, STEPHEN FELSOBUKI, health services company executive; b. Celldomolk, Hungary, June 3, 1944; came to U.S., 1956; s. Michael Felsobuki and Carola (Meliorisz) N.; m. Klara Lukats, July 18, 1981. B.S. in Chemistry, Union Coll., Schenectady, 1967; M.S. in Environ. Health, NYU, 1968; M.S. in Indsl. Mgmt., Columbia U., 1970. Prodn. engr. Consol. Edison Co. N.Y., N.Y.C., 1968-71; various mgmt. positions Booz, Allen & Hamilton, Inc., N.Y.C., 1971-76, v.p., 1976-80; v.p., gen. ptnr. Foster Mgmt. Co., N.Y.C., 1980-82, bd. advisors, 1981-85; pres. Foster Med. Corp., Dedham, Mass., 1982-86, also bd. dirs.; exec. v.p. Avon Products, Inc., N.Y.C., 1985-86; chmn. Greenwich Mgmt. Group Inc., 1987—, Top Labs. Inc., 1987—; bd. dirs. Bloodline Inc., Vein Clinics of Am. Inc. Contbr. articles to profl. jours. Club: N.Y. Athletic. Home: 46 Quail Rd Greenwich CT 06831 Office: Greenwich Mgmt Group Inc 2 Greenwich Pla Ste 100 Greenwich CT 06830 *

NAHIGIAN, ALMA LOUISE, technical documentation manager; b. Peabody, Mass., Sept. 17, 1936; d. Walter Daniel and Alma Edith (Knowles) Higgins; m. Franklin Roosevelt Nahigian, April 30, 1961; children: Ellen Elise, Dana Leigh, Catherine Elizabeth. AA, Boston U., 1956, BS, 1958, MS in Journalism, 1963. Nat. and spl. projects editor Boston U. News Bur., 1959-61; writer, editor Nutrition Found., N.Y.C., 1961-63; writer, editor, cons. Cambridge (Mass.) Communicators, Tech. Edn. Research Ctr., Harvard U., Cambridge, Smart Software, Inc., Belmont, Mass., 1970-82; tech. editor Digital Equipment Corp., Bedford, Mass., 1979-84; prin. tech. writer, editor Wang Labs, Inc., Lowell, Mass., 1984-89, documentation sect. mgr., 1989—; instr. Harvard U., Cambridge, 1988; guest lectr. Northeastern U., Boston, 1979, 88, Radcliffe Coll., Cambridge, 1979. Contbr. numerous articles to profl. pubs. Active, LWV, Arlington, Mass., 1963-73. Mem. Soc. for Tech. Communication (bd. dirs. Boston chpt.). Democrat. Roman Catholic. Home: 30 Venner Rd Arlington MA 02174 Office: Wang Labs Inc One Industrial Ave Lowell MA 01851

NAHIGIAN, ROBERT JOHN, real estate development broker; b. Boston, Feb. 24, 1956; s. John Moses and Theresa (Zeytoundjian) N. BA cum laude, Lehigh U., 1978; MS in Urban Planning, Columbia U., 1980. Property mgr. Auburndale (Mass.) Realty Co., 1972-77; jr. planner Bethlehem (Pa.) Redevel. Authority, 1978; planner, tech. analyst Perkins & Will Archtl. Firm, N.Y.C., 1978-80; city planner, econ. developer City of Bowie, Md., 1980-81; v.p. The Norwood Group, Inc., Burlington, Mass., 1981-88; v.p., dir. The Robbins Group, Cambridge, Mass., 1988—; dir. and lectr. in real estate studies Northeastern U., Boston, 1982—; lectr. in real estate Lehigh U., Harvard Grad. Sch. Design, grad. sch. MIT, assessing dept. City of Boston, N.H. Realtor's C.I. div., NE Constrn. show, So. Calif Constrn. show, Soc. Indsl. and Office Realtors, Mass. Assn. Realtors, profl. orgns., 1984—. Mem. Wang Ctr. for the Performing Arts, Boston, 1985. Recipient cert. of appreciation Northeastern U., 1987, NE Constrn. show, So. Calif. Constrn. show. Mem. Nat. Assn. Realtors, Soc. Indsl. and Office Realtors (cert. profl., ednl. com.), Urban Land Inst., Am. Planning Assn., Nat. Assn. Indsl. Office Parks, Lehigh Club (sr. v.p.), Algonquin Club. Republican. Mem. Armenian Apostolic. Ch. Home: 85 Hosmer St Apt B6 Acton MA 01720 Office: The Robbins Group One Memorial Dr Cambridge MA 02142

NAIL, THOMAS HOUSTON, management consultant; b. Buffalo, Mar. 5, 1952; s. Houston Berry and Evelyn (Rohde) N. BA, U. Buffalo, 1974. Wage and salary mgr. Twin Fair Distbrs. Corp., Buffalo, 1972-76; indsl. relations mgr. Houdaille Industries, Inc., Ft. Lauderdale, 1976-78; pres., prin. Thomas Houston Assoc. Inc., Ft. Lauderdale, 1978—. Contbg. author: EEO Handbook. Mem. Nat. Polit. Affairs Com., Ft. Lauderdale, 1982-83. Mem. Greater Ft. Lauderdale C. of C., Am. Soc. Pers. Adminstrs (mem. nat. EEO com.), Washington Study Group. Republican. Office: 620 Herndon Pkwy Ste 200 Herndon VA 22070

NAIMARK, GEORGE MODELL, advt. agy. and pub. exec.; b. N.Y.C., Feb. 5, 1925; s. Myron S. and Mary (Modell) N.; B.S., Bucknell U., 1947, M.S., 1948; Ph.D., U. Del., 1951; m. Helen Anne Wythes, June 24, 1946; children—Ann, Richard, Jane. Research biochemist Brush Devel. Co., Cleve., 1951; dir. quality control Strong, Cobb & Co., Inc., Cleve., 1951-54; dir. sci. services White Labs., Inc., Kenilworth, N.J., 1954-60; v.p. Burdick Assos., Inc., N.Y.C., 1960-66; pres. Rajah Press, Summit, N.J., 1963—; pres. Naimark and Barba, Inc., N.Y.C., 1966—. Served with USNR, 1944-46. Fellow AAAS, Am. Inst. Chemists; mem. Am. Chem. Soc., N.Y. Acad. Scis., Edinburgh (Scotland) Bibliog. Soc., Am. Mktg. Assn., Pharm. Advt. Council. Author: A Patent Manual for Scientists and Engineers, 1961; Communications on Communication, 1971, 3d edit., 1987. Contbr. articles in profl. jours. Home: 87 Canoe Brook Pkwy Summit NJ 07901 Office: Naimark & Barba Inc 2 Ridgedale Ave Cedar Knolls NJ 07927

NAIMOLI, VINCENT JOSEPH, packaging/consumer products company executive; b. Paterson, N.J., Sept. 16, 1937; s. Ralph A. and Margaret R. (Calabrese) N.; children—Christine, Tory Ann, Alyson, Lindsey. B.S.M.E., U. Notre Dame, 1959; M.S.M.E., N.J. Inst. Tech., 1962; M.B.A., Fairleigh Dickinson U., 1964; grad. Advanced Mgmt. Program, Harvard Bus. Sch.,

1974. With Continental Group, 1965-77, v.p., gen. mgr. ops., 1975-77; pres., chief operating officer Allegheny Beverage Corp., Balt., 1977-78; sr. v.p., group exec. Jim Walter Corp., Tampa, Fla., 1978-81; group v.p. packaging Anchor Hocking Corp., Lancaster, Ohio, 1981—; chmn. bd., pres., chief exec. officer Anchor Glass Container Corp., 1983—. Mem. Glass Packaging Inst. (dir.), The Beer Inst., Nat. Food Processors Assn. (asso. dir.). Roman Catholic. Office: Anchor Glass Container Corp One Anchor Pla 4343 Anchor Pla Pkwy Tampa FL 33634

NAIR, K. M., ceramist; b. Vaikam, India, Jan., 1, 1933; came to U.S., 1962; s. Kumaran and Karthiyani (Amma) N.; m. Xina Nair, Sept. 22, 1970; 1 child, Nathan. B.Sc., U. Kerala, India, 1959, M.Sc., 1961; M.S., Pa. State U., 1964; Ph.D., U. Wash., 1969. Research scientist CGCRI/CSIR, Calcutta, India, 1961-62; research fellow U. Wash., 1970-74; mem. faculty U. Cin., 1974-78; research scientist DuPont Co., Niagara Falls, N.Y., 1978—. Author: Two Dramas in Malayalam, 1957; Processing for Improved Productivity, 1984. Contbr. articles to profl. jours. Patentee in field. Mem. Assoc. Inst. Chemists, Assocs. Royal Inst. Chemistry, Am. Ceramic Soc. (membership chmn. 1978-85, div. publication chmn. 1985—), Am. Ceramic Soc. (membership chmn. 1978—, sec. 1988—), Internat. Soc. Hybrid Microelectronics (mem. electronics div.). Republican. Avocations: reading, writing drama, traveling, music, gardening. Home: 100 Rolling Meadow East Amherst NY 14051 Office: DuPont Co Niagara Falls NY 14302

NAITO, TAKESHI, investment company executive; b. Yakata, Japan, May 17, 1929; s. Shoji and Tsune (Haseba) N.; m. Yasuko Minami, Nov. 22, 1956; children—Naomi, Mary, Walter Akira. B.A., Osaka U. Commerce (Japan), 1953; postgrad. UCLA, 1958. dir. Seibu Securities, Los Angeles, 1962; dir., mng. dir. Yamaichi Securities, Tokyo, 1955-62, chmn., chief exec. officer Yamaichi Internat. (Am.), 1983-88, sr. mng. dir. Yamaichi Investment Trust Mgmt. Co., Ltd., 1988. Mem. Scarsdale Golf (N.Y.), Tokyo Yomiuri Golf, Fgn. Corr. Club (Tokyo), Fuji Lake Side Country (Japan). Home: 1-1 Ogura, Ste D-2104, Sawaiku, Kawasaki 211, Japan Office: Yamaichi Investment Trust Mgmt Co Ltd, 2-3-4 Nihonbashi, Tokyo 103, Japan

NAKAJIMA, ETSUKO, investment company executive; b. Sapporo, Hokkaido, Japan, Dec. 5, 1947; came to U.S., 1980; d. Osamu and Fusako Nakajima. BA, Sophia U., Tokyo, 1970; M in Mgmt., Northwestern U., 1982. Asst. Baker, Weeks & Co., Tokyo, 1972-74, AIU Ins. Co., Tokyo, 1975-79; security analyst Citicorp Scrimgeour Vickers, Tokyo, 1982-84; v.p. Merrill Lynch Asset. Mgmt., Inc., Plainsboro, N.J., 1984—. Co-translator: World's End Is Home, 1977. Home: 105 Claridge Ct Apt 3 Princeton NJ 08540

NAKAMOTO, RONALD HAJIME, financial planner; b. Los Angeles, Jan. 26, 1949; s. Takashi and Sachiko (Sakurai) N.; m. Edna Siu, Sept. 17, 1983. BA, UCLA, 1974; MBA, John F. Kennedy U., 1984. CLU, chartered fin. cons. Instr. communications San Diego State U., 1975-78; mgr. Whittier (Calif.) Florist, Inc., 1978-81, Courthouse Althletic Club, Oakland, Calif., 1981-84; specialist retirement and estate planning The New Eng., San Francisco, 1985—; pres. Ron Nakamoto and Assocs., Hayward, Calif., 1982-88. Bd. dirs. Mesa Verde Homeowners Assn., Hayward, 1985-86. Mem. Internat. Assn. Fin. Planners, Am. Soc. CLU and Chartered Fin. Cons., Nat. Assn. Life Underwriters, San Francisco Estate Planning Council. Republican. Mem. United Ch. Christ. Office: The New Eng 50 California St Ste 3660 San Francisco CA 94111

NAKAOKA, JOHN TATSUYA, sales executive; b. Los Angeles, Nov. 21, 1952; s. Paul T. and Taeko (Kato) N.; m. Joyce Marie Fick, Feb. 25, 1984. BS in Acctg., U. So. Calif., 1976. Sales rep. Xerox Corp., Orange, Calif., 1976-80, supply mgr., 1980-81; mktg. mgr. Xerox Corp., Orange and San Diego, Calif., 1981-82; real estate broker Norris, Beggs & Simpson, Newport Beach, Calif., 1982-83; account exec. Exxon Corp., Costa Mesa, Calif., 1983-84; western regional mgr. Avery/Fasson Div., Irvine, Calif., 1984-86; nat. sales mgr. Avery/Fasson Div., Painesville, Ohio, 1986—. Fin. commr. City of Irvine, 1983-84; transp. commr., 1984-85, bd. edn., v.p., 1979-83; dir. Conv. and Visitors Bur. Newport Beach, 1984-86. Irvine C. of C. (pres., bd. dirs. 1982-85). Republican. Home: 33370 Hiram Tr Moreland Hills OH 44022 Office: Avery Fasson Specialty Div 250 Chester St Mail 4Q Painesville OH 44077

NALEN, CRAIG ANTHONY, government official; b. Montclair, N.J., Apr. 17, 1930; s. Paul Anthony and Mildred A. (Tucker) N.; m. Katherine Andrews, Dec. 30, 1953; children: Katherine M., David A., Peter H. BA, Princeton U., 1952; MBA, Stanford U., 1957. Mktg. exec. Procter & Gamble, Cin., 1957-62, Foremost-McKesson, San Francisco, 1962-64; divisional gen. mgr., corp. v.p. Gen. Mills Inc., Mpls., 1964-72; pres., also bd. dirs. Am. Photograph Corp., Great Neck, N.Y., 1972-75; pres., chmn. bd. dirs. STP Corp., Ft. Lauderdale, Fla., 1975-80; pres. Overseas Pvt. Investment Corp. (govt. agy.), Washington, 1981—, also bd. dirs.; bd. dirs. Firan Corp., Ont., Can., Barry Wright Corp., Newton, Mass. Bd. dirs., founder Children's World, Denver. Served as lt. USNR, 1952-55. Republican. Clubs: Woodhill Country (Wayzata, Minn.); Links, Princeton (N.Y.C.); Chevy Chase ((Md.); Gulf Stream Golf ((Fla.); Ocean (Delray Beach, Fla.). Home: 6880 N Ocean Blvd Ocean Ridge FL 33435 also: 4419 Chalfont Pl Bethesda MD 20816 also: PO Box 2439 Ketchum ID 83340 Office: Overseas Pvt Investment Corp 1615 M St NW Washington DC 20527

NALLE, PETER DEVEREUX, publishing company executive; b. N.Y.C., July 26, 1947; s. Peter Borie and Margaret Graham (Josephs) N.; m. Eleanor Jo Graham, June 14, 1969; 1 child, Graham Devereux. B.A., Brown U., 1969. Salesman and mem. sales mgmt. dept. McGraw-Hill Book Co., N.Y.C., 1970-76, editor, mem. editorial mgmt. dept., 1976-81, mktg. dir., 1981-82, gen. mgr., 1982-84, group v.p., 1984-87; pres., chief exec. officer J.B. Lippincott Co., Phila., 1987—. Bd dirs. Friends of Schuylkill River Park. Mem. Assn. Am. Pubs. (exec. council profl. and scholarly div. 1985-87), Soc. Scholarly Pub., Washington Square Assn. (bd. dirs.), Am. Med. Pubs. Assn. (bd. dirs.), Info. Industry Assn., Friends of Schuylkill River Park (v.p.), Athenaeum of Phila. Club: Brown U. Home: 2113 Delancey St Philadelphia PA 19103 Office: J B Lippincott Co E Washington Sq Philadelphia PA 19105

NALLEY, BLANCHE ALMEDIA (MEDA), real estate development executive, property management director; b. Rocky Mount, N.C., June 26, 1939; d. Walter McDonald, Jr., and Ella Blanche (Phelps) Peacock; m. Richard Kingsman Nalley, Jr., Jan. 16, 1960 (div. 1967); children—Michelle, Karen, Natalie. A.A., U. Fla., 1960. Controller, sta. WPGC, Washington, 1965-68, Trans Continental Industries, Washington, 1968-71, Atlantic Elec. and Bldrs. Hardware, Washington, 1971-74, LBG Distrbrs., Washington, 1974-79; dir. property mgmt., devel. and constrn. Ingersoll & Bloch Chartered, Washington, 1979-89; owner, operator pastry shop, Waynesboro, Pa., 1989—; renovation cons. Nunnery Assocs., Washington, 1983-85, J.C. Assocs., Washington, 1984-89; constrn. cons. P St Assn., Washington, 1985-86; owners rep. 801 Pa. Ave. Assn., Washington, 1985-86; ptnr. Bldg. Services and Maintenance, Inc., Washington, 1986-89. Active design and constrn. hist. structures into office space, 1985-86, renovation hist. landmark bldg., 1985-86. Vol. Alexandria Hosp., Va., 1984; v.p. Elem. Sch. PTA, Hyattsville, Md., 1975, sec. Middle Sch. PTA, 1975. Mem. Property Mgmt. Assn., Apt. Office Bldg. Assn., Multi Housing Assn. Republican. Avocations: running, aerobics, swimming, crocheting, cooking. Home: 15B S Oller Ave Waynesboro PA 17268 Office: 27 E Main St Waynesboro PA 17268

NAMENSON, EDWARD ALAN, hospital administrator; b. Boston, July 15, 1961; s. Gerald Harvey and Shirley (Berman) N.; m. Susan Namenson, Aug. 27, 1988. BBA in Acctg. and Fin., Northeastern U., 1985. Cons. Kenny & McDonald, Sharon, Mass., 1982—; sr. auditor Mass. Rate Setting Commn., Boston, 1982-87; dir. fin. Falmouth (Mass.) Hosp., 1987—; cons. in field. Co-author newsletter Multi-Level Marketing, 1985-86. Mem. Healthcare Fin. Mgmt. Assn. Republican. Jewish. Office: Falmouth Hosp Ter Heun Dr Falmouth MA 02540

NANAVATI, SHISHIR ROMESHCHANDRA, maintenance management company executive; b. Surat, India, Apr. 2, 1943; came to U.S., 1978; s. Romeshchandra Motilal and Vasumati R. (Parekh) N.; m. Mrudula Shishir, Mar. 15, 1969; children: Premal S., Tejal S. BSc in Chemistry, Bombay U., 1965. Sales rep. Alembic Chem. and Pharm. Co., Bombay, 1965-71; area mgr. Schering Corp. U.S.A., Calcutta, India, 1971-75; sales officer Lakhanpal Nat. div. Panasonic Co., Calcutta, 1975-78; sales rep. Pitney Bowes Corp., Milford, Conn., 1979-81, Abbott Labs., Waterbury, Conn., 1981-86; pres. Profl. Maintenance Mgmt. Inc., Conn., 1986—. Mem. Am. Mgmt. Assn., India Assn. Greater Hartford (treas. 1979-80, bd. dirs. 1980-81). Home and Office: 8 Burnt Hollow Ct Cheshire CT 06410

NANCARROW, W(ARREN) GEORGE, oil company executve; b. Texarkana, Tex., Aug. 10, 1923; s. Dorothy Christine (Taylor) N.; m. Hilda Cullom Harkness, Apr. 21, 1947; children: Margie, Mindy, Mark, Matthew. BS, Tex. A&M U., 1947. Engr. Stanolind Oil & Gas Co., Vivian, La., 1947-54; chmn. bd. dirs. DeGolyer and MacNaughton, Dallas, 1954—; bd. dirs. Dresser Industries, Inc., Dallas, lst Bank Las Colinas (Tex.). Mem. Soc. Petroleum Engrs., Am. Petroleum Inst., Dallas Petroleum Club (bd. dirs. 1987-88), Nomads (chmn. 1978). Republican. Home: 7060 Helsem Way Dallas TX 75230 Office: DeGolyer & MacNaughton 400 One Energy Sq Dallas TX 75206

NANCE, CHARLES WAYNE, oil company executive; b. Thornton, Tex., Nov. 28, 1931; s. Louie D. and Bertha (Walker) N.; m. Jane Ann Watson, Sept. 3, 1954; children: Steven Wayne, Scott Edward. BS, U. Tex., 1952, MDP, 1970; postgrad., Harvard U., 1981-82. Petroleum engr. Amoco Prodn. Co., Henderson, Ft. Worth and Midland, Tex., 1952-58; petroleum engr. Tenneco Oil Co., Odessa and Midland, Denver, 1958-79, v.p. Lafayette, 1979-81, sr. v.p. Lafayette and Houston, 1981-82, exec. v.p. exploration and prodn., Houston, 1982-87, pres. Tenneco Oil Exploration and Prodn. Co., Houston, 1987—; mem. adv. council Coll. Engring. Found., U. Tex., Austin, 1984—. Mem. Nat. Ocean Industries Assn. (bd. dirs.), Natural Gas Supply Assn. (mem. exec. com.), Am. Petroleum Inst., Soc. Petroleum Engrs. of AIME. Republican. Mem. Ch. of Christ. Clubs: Petroleum, Raveneaux Country. Avocations: tennis, fishing. Office: Tenneco Oil Co 1100 Milam Bldg Box 2511 15th Fl Houston TX 77252

NANDREA, L. LARRY, sign manufacturing executive; b. Vrsac, Banat, Yugoslavia, Feb. 17, 1934; came to U.S., 1935; s. Michael and Katarina Elizabeth (Levoai) N.; m. Ann E. Teaque, June 19, 1960; children: Lorri, Wendy. BS in Fin., U. Colo., 1964. Draftsman Aeroquip Corp., Burbank, Calif., 1958-59, Stanley Aviation Corp., Aurora, Colo., 1959-60; design and test engr. Martin-Marrietta Corp., Denver, 1960-63; econ. analysis Pub. Svc. Co. Colo., Denver, 1964-72; v.p., gen. mgr. Stonehouse Signs, Inc., Arvada, Colo., 1972—; also bd. dirs. Stonehouse Signs, Inc., Arvada. Bd. dirs. Arvada United Meth. Ch., 1966-68. With U.S. Army, 1953-55, Korea. Mem. Kiwanis (dir. 1974-76). Republican. Office: Stonehouse Signs Inc PO Box 5465 Arvada CO 80001

NANEY, DAVID GLEN, tax consultant; b. Bakersfield, Calif., Apr. 21, 1952; s. Glen Tillman and Olivia Mae N.; children—David Tillman, Michael Christian, Timothy Donovan. AA, Bakersfield Coll., 1972; BA, UCLA, 1974; JD, Loyola U., 1977. Bar: Calif. 1977, U.S. Dist. Ct. (ea. dist.) Calif. 1980, U.S. Dist. Ct. (cen. dirs.) Calif. 1981.Atty. firm Freeman, Freeman & Smiley, L.A., 1978-80; ptv. practice law, Bakersfield, 1980-86; v.p. Cemco Corp.; exec. v.p. Cemland Dev., 1986; v.p. Kern Valley Tank Lines, 1986-87; v.p., corp. sec. legal dept. Lenders Auto Acceptance Corp., 1987-88; asst. v.p. legal dept. Lendco Acceptance Corp.; sr. cons. DuCharme, McMillen and Assocs., Inc., 1988—; former judge pro tempore West Kern Mcpl. Ct. Dist., other Kern County Justice Cts.; prof. law Bakersfield Coll.; legal adviser CAP; instr. in estate planning. Mem. scholarship com. Bakersfield Coll. Mem. UCLA Alumni Assn., Bakersfield Coll. Alumni Assn., Lions, Phi Alpha Delta. Republican. Author (with Douglas K. Freeman): How to Incorporate a Small Business, 1978. Office: DuCharme McMillen & Assocs Inc 5655 Lindero Canyon Rd #222 Westlake Village CA 91362

NANK, LOIS RAE, financial executive; b. Racine, Wis., Jan. 6; d. Walter William August and Lanora Elizabeth (Freymuth) N. BS in Econs., U. Wis., 1962; MS in Profl. Mgmt., Fla. Inst. Tech., 1977. Contract specialist U.S. Naval Ordnance Sta., Forest Park, Ill., 1963-66, U.S. Army Munitions Command, Joliet, Ill., 1966-72; plans/program specialist U.S. Army Munitions Command, Joliet, 1972-73, U.S. Army Armament Command, Rock Island, Ill., 1973-77; chief budget office U.S. Army Auto Log Mgmt. System Act, St. Louis, 1977-81; sr. budget analyst U.S. Army Materiel Command, Alexandria, Va., 1981-87, Def. Mapping Agy., McLean, Va., 1987—. Council mem. Bread of Life Luth. Ch., Springfield, Va., 1986—, chair person; bd. dirs. Cedar Wood Homeowners' Assn., 1975-77, Oak Homeowners' Assn. 1980-81. Mem. NAFE, Am. Soc. Mil. Comptrollers, Va. Assn. Female Execs., Order of Ea. Star. Home: 7812 O'Dell St Springfield VA 22153 Office: Def Mapping Agy McLean VA 22102

NANNEN, GERALD WILLIAM, real estate syndicator, financial planner; b. White Plains, N.Y., Nov. 27, 1946; s. Howard Woodrow and Alice Henriette (Johnson) N.; m. Cynthia A. Hughes, Feb. 15, 1969 (div. Oct. 1977); m. Antoinette Ann Spinelli, Oct. 28, 1978; children: Matthew S., Angela C.S., Stefanie S. BA, Davis and Elkins (W.Va.) Coll., 1968. Chartered life underwriter, fin. cons. Mgmt. trainee Fireman's Fund Ins. Co., Boston, 1968-69; real estate assoc. Springfield, Mass., 1969-70; mgr., ins. agt. John Hancock Life Ins. Co., Springfield, Mass., 1970-72; ins. agt. Mass. Mut. Life, Springfield, Mass., 1973-75; gen. ins. agt. Nannen Co., Springfield, Mass., 1975-76; co-owner Capital Planning, Inc., Springfield, Mass., 1976-77; gen., agt, real estate assoc. Nannen Internat., Springfield, Mass., 1978-85; chmn. The Bottom Line Group, Inc., Springfield, Mass., 1985—; registered investment advisor Bottom Line Advisors, Inc., Springfield, 1985—; prin. Bottom Line Securities, Inc., Springfield, 1985—; cons. real estate Am. Oil Change Corp., Springfield, 1986—. Mem. com. YMCA, Springfield, 1975-80. Mem. Nat. Assn. Life Underwriters (bd. dirs. 1976-80), Internat. Assn. for Fin. Planning, Hampden County Estate Planning Coun., Real Estate Securities Syndication Inst., Nat. Assn. Securities Dealers, Nat. Assn. Realtors, Rotary. Home: 75 Marci Ave East Longmeadow MA 01028

NAPIER, AUSTIN, physicist, educator; b. Jenkins, Ky., Aug. 18, 1947; s. Carl and Lena Thelma (Sergent) N.; m. Linda Elizabeth Cerveny, Dec. 6, 1972. BS in Physics, MIT, 1969, PhD in Physics, 1979. Rsch. assoc. high-energy physics Tufts U., Medford, Mass., 1979-80, asst. prof. physics, 1980-86, assoc. prof., 1986—; guest scientist Fermi Nat. Accelerator Lab., 1988-89. Contbr. articles to physics jours. Served with U.S. Army, 1971-73. NDEA fellow, 1973-76. Mem. Am. Phys. Soc., Div. of Particles and Fields of Am. Phys. Soc., Computer Soc. of IEEE, Sigma Xi. Home: 11 Curtis Ave Somerville MA 02144 Office: Tufts U Dept Physics 530 Boston Ave Medford MA 02155

NAPOLITANO, PAT, former union official; b. N.Y.C., Feb. 1, 1916; s. Giuseppe and Anna (Liquori) N.; m. Beatrice G. Gagliardo, Apr. 25, 1959. Student Fordham U., 1944-47. With tech. facilities dept. Western Union, 1943-81, now ret.; former mem. exec. bd. Comml. Telegraphers Union, AFL; sec.-treas. local 1177 Communications Workers Am. AFL-CIO, 1966-69, del. L.I. Fedn. Labor, AFL-CIO, 1966-76; freelance writer. Mem. N.Y. Police Coordinating Councils, 1940-55, N.Y. Civilian Def., 1943-55; sch. visitor N.Y. Adult Edn. Council, Inc., 1945-55; active Boy Scouts Am., 1938-55. Mem. Nassau County (N.Y.) Dem. Com., 1960-75; pres. New Hyde Park Dem. Club, 1969-70; trustee, Ch. Most Precious Blood, 1942-59; lector, usher, extraordinary minister of eucharist Cath. Ch. Named Citizen of Month, Beverly Hills Visitor, Fla., May 1984. Mem. Assn. Cath. Trade Unionists, Ams. of Italian Descent, Father Drumgoole Alumni Assn. (pres. 1965-73, chmn. bd. officers 1974-84), Nat. Council Cath. Men, Holy Name Soc., Third Order St. Francis, Order Sons of Italy in Am. (charter mem.). Democrat. Clubs: Italian-Am. Social (Beverly Hills, Fla.) (pres. 1981-83), KC (Grand Knight 1983-84, Family of Month, June 1984). Address: 221 S Harrison St Beverly Hills FL 32665

NARANG, HARBIR SINGH, real estate management executive; b. Rawalpindi, India, May 20, 1946; s. Sewa Ram and Satwant (Chabra) N.; m. Sushil Kaur Gambhir, Mar. 24, 1973; children: Enisha, Sonia, Sunny. B Commerce, Dayal S Coll., 1969; MBA, Woodbury Coll. Pres., chief exec. officer First Columbia Conominium Mgmt., Inc., Granada Hills, Calif., 1987—. Club: Toastmaster 412 (pres. Los Angeles chpt., area A gov.). Office: FCCM I of J L Moyer Co 15650 Devonshire St #103 Granada Hills CA 91344

NARDIN, THEODORE CELESTE, publisher; b. Weehawken, N.J., July 28, 1948; s. Anthony Q. and Gioia (Lucca) N.; m. Elizabeth Higgins, Feb. 12, 1972; children: Katherine, Thomas. BA in History, Holy Cross Coll., 1970. Asst. editor Communications Channels, N.Y.C., 1972-74; book editor Prentice-Hall Pubs., Englewood Cliffs, N.J., 1974-79, mktg. mgr., 1979-81, product mgr., 1982-87, editor-in-chief, v.p., 1987—. Mem. Am. Assn. Pubs. (profl. and sci. pub. div.), Profl. Publishers Mktg. Group. Home: 460 Second Ave New York NY 10016 Office: Prentice-Hall Pub Sylvan Ave Englewood Cliffs NJ 07632

NARDONE, DON D., financial planner; b. N.Y.C., Feb. 10, 1924; s. Sebastian and Mary (Genero) N.; BS in Econs. and Fin., CCNY, 1948; m. Mary-alice Clark, Feb. 5, 1955; children: Karin, Michael, Nora. Account exec. Charles Plohn & Co., N.Y.C., 1962-70; v.p. Thomson McKinnon Securities, Inc., N.Y.C., 1970-89; v.p. investments Dean Witter Reynolds, Inc., Garden City, N.Y., 1989—; lectr. on fin. products, 1963—. 1st lt. inf. U.S. Army, 1943-46. Club: Shelter Rock Tennis (Manhasset, N.Y.). Contbr. articles to profl. jours. Home: 34 Shrub Hollow Rd Roslyn NY 11576 Office: Dean Witter Reynolds Inc 1225 Franklin Ave Garden City NY 11530

NARINS, CHARLES SEYMOUR, lawyer, instrument co. exec., hosp. ofcl.; b. Bklyn., Mar. 12, 1909; s. Joshua and Sarah E. (Levy) N.; LL.B., Yale U., 1932; B.S., N.Y. U., 1929; m. Frances D. Kross; children—Lyn Ross, Joyce Hedda. Admitted to N.Y. bar, 1933, Mass. bar, 1955; atty. Curtin & Glynn, N.Y.C., 1932-34, Glynn, Smith & Narins, 1934-37, Probst & Probst, 1937-47; pres., dir., counsel C. L. Berger & Sons, Inc., 1947-68; div. chmn. Berger Instruments div. High Voltage Engring. Corp., Boston, 1968-74; dir., chmn. med. planning New Eng. Sinai Hosp., Stoughton, Mass., 1974—. Trustee Boston Ballet Co., Boston Opera; bd. dirs. Boston Civic Symphony, 1975-76; bd. dirs., 1st v.p. Greater Palm Beach Symphony; mem. corp. Norfolk House, Boston. Mem. Am., N.Y., Mass., Boston bar assns., Assn. Bar City N.Y., N.Y. County Lawyers Assn., Am. Congress Surveying and Mapping, Am. Judicature Soc., Boston C. of C., Assn. Yale Alumni (law sch. rep.), Internat. Cultural Soc., Pi Lambda Phi. Clubs: Univ., Yale (Boston); Boston Yacht (Marblehead, Mass.); Yale, Poinciana (Palm Beach); Yale, N.Y. U. (N.Y.C.); Kernwood Country (Salem, Mass.); Palm Beach (Fla.) Country (bd. govs., sec.). Home: 150 Bradley Pl Palm Beach FL 33480 Summer: 24 Skinners Path Marblehead MA 01945

NARRIN, ROBERTA PETRONELLA, financial consultant; b. Providence, Oct. 11, 1939; d. Anthony and Maria G. (Barra) Petronella; m. Sidney Narrin, April 22, 1961 (div. Nov. 1971); children: Christine E. De Pari, Anthony F. Student, Bryant Coll., 1959; cert., Nat. Assn. Securities Dealers, 1978. CLU, Pa. Exec. sec., adminstrv. asst. Allied Adjustment Svcs., Providence, 1967-71; account exec. Advertisers Workshop, East Providence, R.I., 1971-75; pres. Roberta Narrin Assocs., Providence, 1975-77, A Chris Corp., Providence, 1980—; fin. cons. Phoenix Mut. Life Ins., One-120 Assocs. MBF, Inc., Providence, 1977—. Pres. PTA, No. Providence, 1969; v.p. R.I. Assn. Brain Injured, No. Providence, 1968; sec. The Learning Ctr., Providence, 1977-79, R.I. Assn. Retarded Children, 1970—; mem. West Bay Residential Human Rights Commn., Cranston Chpt. Retarded Citizens March of Dimes, R.I. Estate Planning Coun. Mem. NAFE, R.I. Assn. Life Underwriters (Nat. Quality award 1981—, pub. rels., editor Life Notes), R.I. Chpt. CLU's (R.I. Chpt., pub. rels.), Million Dollar Round Table. Office: Phoenix Mutual Life Ins One-120-Assocs MBF Inc 2 Richmond Sq Providence RI 02906

NASH, CHARLES EDWARD, financial consultant; b. Nashville, Oct. 4, 1959; s. Charles Maxwell and Mary Loretta (Tidwell) N.; m. Deborah Ann Kish, Sept. 12, 1981; 1 child, Lauren Alicia. AS in Acctg., Nashville State U., 1980. Cert. LUTCF. Agt., mgr. Liberty Nat. Life Ins. Co., Nashville, 1981-83; agt. Vol. State Life Ins. Co., Nashville, 1983-84, Conn. Mut. Life Ins. Co., Nashville, 1984-85; fin. cons. Wall & Assocs., Nashville, 1985-88, Burton Tally Agy., Nashville, 1988—. Mem. Nat. Assn. Life Underwriters, Internat. Assn. for Fin. Planning, Inst. Cert. Fin. Planners, Am. Soc. CLU and CLFC, Chartered Fin. Cons. Republican. Home: 1104 White Mountain Ln Antioch TN 37031 Office: Burton Tally Agy 1707 Division St Ste 202 Nashville TN 37013

NASH, HAROLD RONALD, financial executive; b. Atlanta, Apr. 18, 1949; s. Harold Ronald and Mary Anne (Jessee) N.; m. Eleanor Randolph Land, Nov. 27, 1971 (div.); 1 child, David Ronald; m. Susan Cadenhead, Dec. 12, 1987; 1 child, Stacey Leigh. BS in Indsl. Engring., Ga. Inst. Tech., 1970; MS in Fin., U. Tex., Dallas, 1979. Registered profl. engr., Tex. Bus. mgr. Electronic Data Systems Corp., Dallas, 1973-79; pres. Rubicon Corp., Richardson, Tex., 1979-84, Teleci, Inc., Irving, Tex., 1984-85; pres. Advanced Telemktg. Corp., Irving, 1985—, also bd. dirs. Mem. exec. com., trustee Greenhill Sch., Dallas, 1987—. Sgt. U.S. Army, 1971-72. Mem. Inst. Indsl. Engrs. (sr.), Tex. Soc. Indsl. Engrs., Nat. Soc. Profl. Engrs., Ga. Inst. Tech. Alumni Assn., U. Tex. at Dallas Alumni Assn. (chmn. 1983-87), Chandlers Landing Yacht Club, Alpha Phi Mu. Republican. Home: 5835 Del Roy Dr Dallas TX 75230 Office: Advanced Telemktg Corp 8001 Bent Branch Dr Irving TX 75063

NASH, RANDY H., business owner, marketing executive, accountant; b. Albany, N.Y., Apr. 16, 1956; s. Mort and Barbara (Schecter) N. BS in Acctg., Case Western Res. U., 1978. CPA, Ohio, N.C. Staff acct. Barnes, Wendling & Cook, Cleve., 1978-80; tax sr. Touche Ross & Co., Chapel Hill, N.C., 1981-82; audit-in-charge Coopers & Lybrand, Raleigh, N.C., 1982-84; dir. mktg. Fin. Audit Systems, Inc. (acquired by Prentice Hall 1989), Raleigh, 1984—. Mem. Am. Inst. CPA's, N.C. Soc. CPA's. Home: 7204 Woods Edge Ct Raleigh NC 27615

NASH, STEPHEN MICHAEL, chemist, hazardous materials compliance representative; b. Spencer, Ind., Jan. 24, 1947; s. William Christian Nash and Juanita (Brown) Foley; m. Deanna Faye Wood, Mar. 29, 1983; children: Christopher Jon and Brian Michael (twins). BS in Chemistry, Ind. U., 1969; MS in Chemistry, Purdue U., Indpls., 1972. Tech. assoc. Lilly Research Labs., Indpls., 1968-69, assoc. organic chemist, 1969-73, organic chemist, 1973-78, asst. sr. organic chemist, 1978-80; hazardous materials compliance rep. Eli Lilly & Co., Indpls., 1980—; advisor Chemtrec, Washington, 1985—; bd. dirs. Hazardous Materials Adv. Coun., Washington, 1986—. Contbr. articles to profl. jours.; patentee in field. Mem. nat. adv. bd. Findlay U., 1988—; del. to United Nations Com. of Experts on the Transport of Dangerous Goods, Geneva, Switzerland, 1988. Fellow Am. Inst. Chemists; mem. AAAS, Am. Chem. Soc., Internat. Union Pure and Applied Chemistry (affiliate), Internat. Platform Assn., N.Y. Acad. Scis., Ind. U. Alumni Assn., Marion County Hazardous Materials Planning Com. (appointee). Club: Royal Oak Country. Office: Eli Lilly & Co Lilly Corp Ctr Indianapolis IN 46285

NASH, SYLVIA D., religious organization executive, consultant; b. Montevedio, Minn., Apr. 25, 1945; d. Owen Donald and Selma A. (Tollefson) Dotseth; divorced; 1 child, Elizabeth Louise; m. Thomas L. Nash, Dec. 20, 1986. Grad., Calif. Luth. Bible Sch., 1965. Office mgr. First Congl. Ch., Pasadena, Calif., 1968-75; adminstrv. asst. Pasadena Presbyn. Ch., 1975-78; dir. adminstrv. svcs. Fuller Theol. Sem., Pasadena, 1978-81; chief exec. officer Christian Ministries Mgmt. Assn., Diamond Bar, Calif., 1981—; bd. dirs. Evang. Council Fin. Accountability, Washington, Gospel Lit. Internat., Rosemead, Calif.; mem. adv. com. Christian Mgmt. Rev., Chgo., 1986—; cons. various orgns., 1985—. Editor: The Clarion, 1975-78, The Christian Mgmt. Report, 1981-86; contbr. articles to profl. jours. Chmn. bd. Lamb's Players, National City, Calif., 1985—. Mem. Nat. Assn. Ch. Adminstrs. (sec. 1979-81), NAFE, Am. Soc. Assn. Execs. Office: Christian Ministries Mgmt Assn PO Box 4638 Diamond Bar CA 91765

NASHMAN, ALVIN E., computer company executive; b. N.Y.C., Dec. 16, 1926; s. Joseph and Fay (Portnoy) N.; m. Honey Weinstein, May 29, 1960; children—Jessica Rachel, Pamela Wynne, Stephanie Paige. B.E.E., CUNY, 1948; M.E.E., NYU, 1951; Sc.D. (hon.), Pacific U., 1968, George Washington U., 1986. With Ketay Mfg. Corp., N.Y.C., 1951-52; sr. project engr., exec. engr., assoc. lab. dir., lab. dir. ITT Fed. Labs., Nutley, N.J., 1952-62;

dir. ops. ITT Intelcom, Inc., Falls Church, Va., 1962-65; pres. System Scis. Corp., Falls Church, 1965-67; with Communications & Systems, Inc., Falls Church, 1967-69; pres. Systems div., corp. v.p. Computer Scis. Corp., Falls Church, 1969-77; pres. Systems Group, corp. v.p., 1977—, also dir. Patentee in field; contbr. articles to profl. jours. Served with U.S. Navy, 1944-46. Fellow IEEE; mem. Armed Forces Communications and Electronics Assn. (dir., internat. v.p. 1976-79, chpt. pres. 1979-80, exec. com. 1980-84, chmn. bd. 1984-86), AIAA, Nat. Space Club, Nat. Security Indsl. Assn., Tau Beta Pi, Eta Kappa Nu. Republican. Jewish. Home: 3609 Ridgeway Terr Falls Church VA 22044 Office: Computer Scis Group 6565 Arlington Blvd Falls Church VA 22046 also: Computer Sciences Corp 2100 E Grand Ave El Segundo CA 90245

NASHMAN, JIM ALLAN, investment consultant; b. Calgary, Alta., Can., Dec. 24, 1955; came to U.S., 1981; s. Samuel James and Ivy Elaine (Meger) N.; m. Tammy Lynne Hampton, Aug. 8, 1981; 1 child, Meagan Lauren. BBA, U. Calgary, 1977. Mgr. div. Profl. Interiors Ltd., St. Louis, 1981-85; comml. broker Turley Martin Co., St. Louis, 1985—. Mem. Cert. Comml. Investment Mgrs., Bldg. Owners Mgmt. Assn., Chesterfield C. of C. Home: 11322 Meadowside Dr Saint Louis MO 63146

NASSAU, ROBERT HAMILL, manufacturing company executive; b. Plainfield, N.J., Nov. 30, 1941; s. Charles Francis and Helen (Hudson) N.; m. AnnRae Falicki, July 13, 1968; children: Aimee, Robbie, Rebecca. A.B., Dartmouth Coll., 1963, M.B.A., 1964. Fin. analyst Ford Motor World Hdqrs., Dearborn, Mich., 1964-67; with (Ford Tractor), Troy, Mich., 1967-72; mgr. market and product analysis (Ford Tractor), 1971-72; asst. controller N.Am. truck ops. Ford Motor Co., Dearborn, 1972-73; agrl. product planning mgr. Ford Tractor, Troy, 1973-76; gen. sales mgr. overseas direct markets Ford Tractor, 1976-78; gen. mgr. Ford Tractor Intercontinental Ops., 1979-80; sr. v.p. mktg. and corp. planning J.I. Case Co., Racine, Wis., 1980-82, exec. v.p. worldwide agrl. ops., 1982; pres., chief exec. officer AMDURA Corp. (formerly Am. Hoist & Derrick Co.), St. Paul, 1982—; also dir. Am. Hoist & Derrick Co., St. Paul; bd. dirs. First Bank Systems Met. Bd., The Toro Co. Mem. Young Pres.'s Orgn. Republican. Congregationalist. Clubs: Minnesota, St. Paul Athletic, Minikahda Country. Home: 1913 Montane Dr E Golden CO 80401 Office: AMDURA Corp 1800 Landmark Towers 345 St Peter St Saint Paul MN 55102

NATCHER, STANLEY RONALD, nuclear research and development company executive; b. Downton, Eng., Aug. 20, 1932; arrived in Can., 1954; s. Reginald and Nellie Evelyn (Weekes) H.; m. Gladys Mary Robinson, Sept. 17, 1955; children: Adrian, Kevin, Michael, David. BS with honors, U. Birmingham, Eng., 1953, MS with honors, 1954; PhD in Chem. Engring., U. Toronto, 1958. Head process tech. group Bruce Heavy Water Plant, 1973-74; researcher in reactor chem. and process systems Atomic Energy Can. Ltd., 1958-63, head chem. engring. sect., head chem. tech. branch, 1963-68, liason officer at U.K. Atomic Energy Authority, 1968-69, dir. applied sci. div., 1974-77, asst. to exec. v.p. rsch. and devel., 1977-78; v.p., gen. mgr. Atomic Energy Can. Ltd., Manitoba, 1978-81; v.p. mktg. and sales Atomic Energy Can. Ltd. CANDU Ops., 1981-86; pres. Atomic Energy Can. Ltd. Rsch. Co., 1986—. Fellow Chem. Inst. Can.; mem. Am. Nuclear Soc. (bd. dirs. 1986-88, planning com. 1986—), Can. Nuclear Assn., Can. Nuclear Soc., Can. Soc. for Chem. Engring., Assn. Profl. Engrs. Ont. Home: RR 1, Terra Cotta, ON Canada L0P 1N0 Office: Atomic Energy Can Ltd, 275 Slater St 17th Fl, Ottawa, ON Canada K1A 0S4

NATHANSON, LINDA SUE, technical writer, software training specialist, systems analyst; b. Washington, Aug. 11, 1946; d. Nat and Edith (Weinstein) N.; m. James F. Barrett. BS, U. Md., 1969; MA, UCLA, 1970, PhD, 1975. Tng. dir. Rockland Research Inst., Orangeburg, N.Y., 1975-77; asst. prof. psychology SUNY, 1978-79; pres. Cabri Prodns., Inc., Ft. Lee, N.J., 1979-81; research supr. Darcy, McManus & Masius, St. Louis, 1981-83; mgr. software tng., documentation On-Line Software Internat., Ft. Lee, 1983-85; pvt. practice cons. Ft. Lee, 1985-87; founder, exec. dir. The Edin. Group, Inc., Gillette, N.J., 1987—. Author: (with others) Psychological Testing: An Introduction to Tests and Measurement, 1988; contbr. articles to mags. and profl. jours. Recipient Research Service award 1978; Albert Einstein Coll. Medicine Research fellow, 1978-79. Mem. Ind. Computing Cons.'s Assn. (editor Interface newsletter of N.Y./N.J. chpt.). Jewish. Home and Office: 102 Sunrise Dr Gillette NJ 07933

NAU, H. GENE, retail department store company executive. Pres. The Higbee Co, Cleve. Office: Higbee Co 100 Public Sq Cleveland OH 44113

NAUGHTON, PAUL FRANCIS, financial executive; b. Port Monmouth, N.J., Sept. 1, 1942; s. John Paul and Gertrude (Sheehan) N.; BS, LaSalle U., 1964; MBA, St. John's U., 1969; m. Jean Connell, Sept. 18, 1965; children: Thomas, Brian, Jacqueline Ann. Sr. analyst Dean Witter & Co., N.Y.C., 1968-70; partner, sr. analyst F.S. Smithers & Co., N.Y.C., 1970-72; v.p. 1st Boston Corp., N.Y.C., 1972-75; treas. Am. Natural Service Co., Detroit, 1975-79; v.p. Dean Witter Reynolds Inc., 1979-81; v.p. fin. Mich. Consol. Gas Co., Detroit, 1981-84, also dir.; sr. v.p. chief fin. officer Primark Corp., McLean, Va.; pres., chief exec. officer Primark Fin. Services, Inc., McLean, 1984-86; mng. ptnr. Fin. Resource Enterprises, 1986-87; sr. v.p., chief fin. officer Potomac Capital Investment Corp., 1987—. Mem. Fin. Execs. Inst., Fairfax C. of C., N.Y. Soc. Security Analysts, Delta Sigma Pi. Club: Hidden Creek Country (Va.). Home: 1058 Harriman St Great Falls VA 22066

NAUGHTON, WILLIAM ALOYSIUS, publishing company executive; b. Jersey City, Nov. 22, 1930; s. Martin and Margaret (Horgan) N.; m. Josephine Ann Gallagher, Oct. 15, 1955; children: Marybeth, William, Joanne, Jeaneen, Matthew. BS, St. Peter's Coll., Jersey City, 1952; MBA, Rutgers U., 1959. CPA, N.J. Sr. tax acct. Peat Marwick Mitchell & Co., Newark, 1954-60; instr. St. Peter's Coll., Jersey City, 1960-65; ptnr. Kelly Collins & Moran, Jersey City, 1963-65; audit mgr. Champion Internat., N.Y.C., 1965-70; v.p., controller Diamondhead Corp., Mountainside, N.J., 1970-75; v.p. Macmillan Inc., N.Y.C., 1975—. Served with U.S. Army, 1952-54, Korea. Mem. Am. Inst. C.P.A.s. Roman Catholic. Lodge: KC. Office: Macmillan Inc 866 3rd Ave New York NY 10022

NAUGLE, THOMAS EARL, investment company executive; b. Garber, Okla., Feb. 12, 1939; s. Earl Henry and Amber Jewel (Dunlavy) N.; m. Barbara Ann Pigman, Oct. 4, 1980; children: Kimberly Dawn, Rodney Bo. BS in Chem. Engring., Okla. State U., 1961; MBA, Harvard U., 1967. V.p. planning Cooper Industries, Houston, 1972-74; pres. Cooper Energy Services Div., Mt. Vernon, Ohio, 1974-79; sr. v.p. Cooper Industries, Houston, 1979-80; pres., chief exec. officer Cooper Mfg. Co., Tulsa, 1980-82; pres. Naugle & Co., Tulsa, 1982—; chmn. Barrett Trailers, Inc., Oklahoma City, 1984—, Tulsa Winch, Inc., 1986—; rancher Sallisaw, Okla. Mem. Tulsa Club, So. Hills Country Club. Republican. Office: Naugle & Co PO Box 471617 Tulsa OK 74147

NAUMAN, EDWARD FRANKLIN, electronics manufacturing company executive; b. Kansas City, Mo., May 1, 1915; s. Edward Augustus and Lida (Stevens) N.; m. Elizabeth Wiles, Feb. 6, 1943 (dec. 1962); m. 2d, Jeanne Gardner, Nov. 1963 (div. 1970); children: Edward Bruce, Kent Jerome, Mark Robert; m. 3d, Eleanor Conley, Jan. 18, 1973. B in Chem. Engring., Kansas City Jr. Coll., 1935; postgrad. in chemistry, U. Kansas City, 1939-40. Chem. engr. explosives research Remington Arms Co., Independence, Mo., 1941-45; tech. dir. J.A. Folger & Co., Kansas City, 1945-54; gen. mgr. Thiokol Chem. Corp., Marshall, Tex., 1954-60; gen. mgr. Thiokol Chem. Corp., Brigham City, Utah, 1960-65, v.p., 1963-65; sr. exec. research and devel., v.p., dir. U.S. Plywood-Champion Papers, Inc., Chgo., 1965=71; pres. Disposal Systems, Inc., Chgo., 1971-73, Nauman Electronics Co., Chgo., 1975—; chmn. bd. Disposal Tech., Inc. Inventor in field of extraction, heat transfer, materials handling, pigments and organic chems., electronic devices. Chmn. Airport Adv. Bd. Harrison County (Tex.), 1958-60; active United Fund, 1951—. Mem. Am. Inst. Chem. Engrs. (v.p. E.Tex. chpt. 1959-60), C. of C. (dir. 1958-60), Am. Ordnance Assn. (v.p. Shreveport post 1959-60), Am. Rocket Soc., Am. Chem. Soc., AAAS, Assn. U.S. Army, N.Y. Acad. Scis. Clubs: Rotary, Marshall Country, Chemists of N.Y.; Union League (Chgo.). Home: 508 Highland Blvd Brigham City UT 84302

NAUMANN, WILLIAM CARL, food equipment manufacturing company executive; b. Peoria, Ill., Mar. 25, 1938; s. William Louis and Emma (Bottin) N.; m. Polly Naumann, May 20, 1962 (div. 1980); children: Jeff, Heather, Derek; m. Kathryn Bickerman, June 20, 1983. BSCE, Purdue U., 1960; MBA, U. Chgo., 1975. With Inland Steel Co., Chgo., 1960-74, N.Y. dist. mgr., 1968-70, div. gen. mgr., 1971-74; group v.p., bd. dirs. Inryco, Melrose Park, Ill., 1974-81; asst. chief engr. Inland Steel Co., Chgo., Ind., 1981-82, asst. gen. mgr. corp. planning, 1982-83, asst. gen. mgr. sales, 1983-86, gen. mgr. sales and mktg., 1986-87; exec. v.p. internat. ops. Hussman Corp., Bridgeton, Mo., 1987, exec. v.p. mktg., 1987, group pres., 1987—. Mem. U. Chgo. Exec. Program Club (pres. 1980-81), U. Chgo. Alumni Assn. (exec. coun.), Hinsdale (Ill.) Golf Club, Beta Gamma Sigma, U. Chgo. Club Met. Chgo. (pres. 1986-87). Home: 53 Brook Mill Town and Country MO 63017 Office: Hussmann Corp 12999 St Charles Rock Rd Bridgeton MO 63044

NAUTA, ROGER LEE, sales executive; b. Oak Park, Ill., Nov. 26, 1937; s. Henry W. and Jean (Tolsma) N.; m. Janice C. Lachowicz, Jan. 1, 1953; children: Beth A., Lisa T., Heather L. BA, Elmhurst Coll., 1961. Sales rep. Armstrong World Industries, Lancaster, Pa., 1961-64; regional dir. Kaiser Ind., Oakland, Calif., 1964-74; nat. sales mgr. Herman Miller, Inc., Zeeland, Mich., 1974-75, Olin Kraft, Inc., Louisville, 1975-77; v.p. sales., dir. ODL, Inc., Zeeland, 1977—; pres., owner Profls. Inc., Grand Rapids, 1985—; chief exec. officer Janlee Assocs., Kentwood, Mich., 1985—. Mem. Am. Mgmt. Assn., Nat. Sash and Door Jobbers, Nat. Home Builders Assn., Nat Bld. Materials Distbrs., Nat. Assn. Remodelers. Republican. Mem. Reformed Ch. of Am. Home: 2297 Whispercove SE Kentoowd MI 49508 Office: ODL Inc 215 Roosevelt Ave Zeeland MI 49464

NAVARRO, SAMUEL ENRIQUE, investment research executive; b. Matagalpa, Nicaragua, Dec. 27, 1955; came to U.S., 1973, naturalized, 1986; s. Ernesto Navarro and Perla Amador. BS, U. Tex., 1976; MS, Stanford U., 1978; MBA, U. Pa., 1983. Registered profl. engr., Calif. Assoc engr. URS/John A. Blume Assoc., San Francisco, 1978-80; sr. engr. Chemplant Designs, N.Y.C., 1980-81; jr. analyst Equity Research Assocs., N.Y.C., 1982, sr. analyst, 1983-84; mng. dir., ptnr. Ladenburg, Thalmann & Co., N.Y.C., 1984—; sr. v.p. Ladenburg, Thalmann Asset Mgmt., N.Y.C., 1984-86, chmn., chief investment officer, 1986—. Sustaining mem. Nat. Rep. Com., Washington, 1983—. Mem. Investment Assn. N.Y. Roman Catholic. Clubs: Wharton Sch. (N.Y.C.); Stanford U. Office: Ladenburg Thalmann & Co Inc 540 Madison Ave New York NY 10022

NAVIA, HERNAN ALFREDO, financial and investment consultant; b. Bogota, Colombia, Apr. 18, 1958; s. Hernan and Gloria M. (Medina) N.; m. Sylvia Gastelbondo, Aug. 21, 1981; children: Andres H., Daniel A. BA in Indsl. Engring., Javeriana U., Bogota, 1981; MS in Indsl. Mgmt., SUNY, Stony Brook, 1982; cert., Coll. for Fin. Planning, Denver, 1987. Investigator Inst. Technol. Rsch., Bogota, 1981; sr. fin. planner Paul S. Fredericks and Co., Miami, Fla., 1983-85; fin. cons., cert. fin. planner Mfrs. Fin. Group, Coral Gables, Fla., 1985-88, coord. study investment group, 1984—; mng. dir., ptnr. Integrated Capital Fin. Group, Miami, 1988—; mng. exec. Integrated Resources Equity Corp., Coral Gables, 1988—; cons. fin. seminars, Miami, 1984—. Mem. Inst. Cert. Fin. Planners (cert.), Colombian-Am. C. of C. Greater Miami (1st v.p.). Office: Integrated Capital Fin Group 800 Brickell Ave 6th Fl Miami FL 33131

NAYLOR, FRANK WESLEY, JR., financial executive; b. Mulvane, Kans., Feb. 7, 1939; s. Frank Wesley Sr. and Hildred Ethel (Reed) N.; m. Marilyn Everest, May 16, 1987; children: Mary Allison, Frank Wesley III, Erin Mark. BA, U. Kans., Lawrence, 1961; postgrad., Rockhurst Coll., Kansas City, Mo., 1966-68. Staff mgr. Met. Life Ins. Co., Grand, Kans., 1965-69; dep. mgr. Fed. Crop Ins. Corp., USDA, Washington, 1969-72; exec. asst. to adminstr. VA, Washington, 1972-74; assoc. adminstr. Farmers Home Adminstrn., USDA, Washington, 1974-77; sr. v.p. Farm Credit Banks, Sacramento, 1977-81; under sec. USDA, Washington, 1981-86; chmn. Farm Credit Adminstrn., Washington, 1986-88; pres., chief exec. officer U.S. Adricredit Inc., Washington, 1988—. Mem. Community Services Dist. Bd., Shingle Springs, Calif., chmn. Eldorado County Fin. Com., Shingle Springs; bd. dirs. Sacramento C. of C., 1977; active Presdl. campaigns, Washington, 1968, 72. Mem. Kansas City (Kans.) Jr. C. of C. Republican. Home: 2 Clapham Ct Sterling VA 22170 Office: US Agricredit Inc 1025 Thomas Jefferson St NW Ste 301-W Washington DC 20007

NAYLOR, GEORGE LEROY, lawyer, railroad executive; b. Bountiful, Utah, May 11, 1915; s. Joseph Francis and Josephine Chase (Wood) N.; student U. Utah, 1934-36; student George Washington U., 1937; J.D. (Bancroft Whitney scholar), U. San Francisco, 1953; m. Maxine Elizabeth Lewis, Jan. 18, 1941; children—Georgia Naylor Price, RoseMaree Naylor Hammer, George LeRoy II. Admitted to Calif. bar, 1954, Ill. bar, 1968; v.p., sec., legis. rep. Internat. Union of Mine, Mill & Smelter Workers, CIO, Dist. Union 2, Utah-Nevada, 1942-44; examiner So. Pacific Co., San Francisco, 1949-54, chief examiner, 1955, asst. mgr., 1956-61; carrier mem. Nat. R.R. Adjustment Bd., Chgo., 1961-77, chmn., 1970-77; atty. Village of Fox River Valley Gardens, Ill., 1974-77; practice law, legal cons., Ill. and Calif., 1977—; gen. counsel for Can-Veyor, Inc., Mountain View, Calif., 1959-64; adj. instr. dept. mgmt. U. West Fla., 1981. Served with AUS, World War II. Mem. ABA, Ill. Bar Assn., Calif. Bar Assn., Chgo. Bar Assn., San Francisco Bar Assn. Mormon. Author: Defending Carriers Before the NRAB and Public Law Boards, 1969, Choice Morsels in Tax and Property Law, 1966, Underground at Bingham Canyon, 1944; National Railroad Adjustment Board Practice Manual, 1978. Office: Round Barn Sta PO Box 6323 Champaign IL 61826-6323

NAYLOR, JEAN ANN, accountant; b. Pomona, Calif., Oct. 21, 1948; d. Paul Woodrow and Urdelle Cecile (Sparlin) Waters; 1 child, Tamara LeAron. AA in Legal Sec., Shasta Coll., Redding, Calif., 1976; AA in Computer Acctg., Reno Bus. Coll., 1985, BA in Acctg., 1986. Cert. instr. acctg., Nev. Stunt rider King's Motordome, San Jose, Calif., 1968-74; owner, mgr. House of Wigs, Redding, 1974-81; bookkeeper, counselor Shasta County Women's Refuge, Redding, 1981-83; revenue auditor Reno Hilton, 1983-85; instr. Reno Bus. Coll., 1986—; acct. Western Village, Reno, 1985—; acctg. mgr. Eddie's Fabulous 50's, 1986; controller The Gold Club, 1987; sr. acct. Karl's Silver Club, Sparks, Nev., 1988—; cons. in acctg., Las Vegas, Nev., 1985-86. Peer counselor Shasta County Women's Refuge, Redding, 1983; campaign dir. Jon Lyons for County Auditor, Redding, 1982. Mem. Nat. Acctg. Assn., Showfolks of Am. Club: Toastmasters. Office: Karl's Silver Club PO Box 3567 Sparks NV 89432-3567

NEAFSEY, JOHN PATRICK, oil company executive; b. Woodside, N.Y., Aug. 4, 1939; s. James F. and Mary C. (Burns) N.; B.S. in Mech. Engring. (Sloan scholar), Cornell U., 1962, M.B.A. in Fin. (univ. bus. sholar), 1963; m. Marilla Bowman, Sept. 2, 1962; children—John Patrick, Terence E., William C. Fin. analyst Esso Research & Engring. Co., 1963-65; planning coordinator Standard Oil Co. (N.J.), 1965-67; with Sun Oil Co., Inc., 1967—, v.p. fin. services, Radnor, Pa., 1975-78, sr. v.p. fin., 1978-86, exec. v.p., 1987—, also bd. dirs.; bd. dirs. Sun Co., Inc., Suncor, Ltd., Toronto, Ont., Can.; bd. dirs. Provident Mutual Life Ins. Co. of Phila., The West Co. Bd. dirs. Crozer-Chester Med. Ctr., Chester, Pa, Crozer-Chester Med. Ctr. Health Systems, Chester, Phila. Drama Guild, Greenwich (Conn.) Capital Markets, Mgmt. Policy Council; mem. adv. council Cornell U. Johnson Grad. Sch. of Mgmt.; bd. trustees Cornell U. Mem. Am. Petroleum Inst., Pi Tau Sigma. Office: Sun Co Inc 100 Matsonford Rd Radnor PA 19087

NEAL, JERRY EUGENE, controller; b. Columbus, Ohio, Nov. 17, 1941; s. Levert and Anna (Weaver) N.; m. Judith Ann Lehnert; children: Brian, Jeffrey, Timothy. BS, Ohio State U., 1965. Controller Mattel Toys Inc., Hawthorne, Calif., 1979—. Home: 6788 Alta Vista Dr Rancho Palos Verdes CA 90274 Office: Mattel Toys Inc 5150 Rosecrans Ave Hawthorne CA 90250-6692

NEAL, LARRY CLYDE, property manager; b. Tacoma, Oct. 15, 1941; s. Raymond Jackson Neal and Dorothy Hermina (Reynolds) Stevens; m. Marilyn Ann Bottoms, Dec. 26, 1963 (div. June 1966); m. Vickie Lynn Neal, Sept. 30, 1984; children: Tamera Annette, Keith James. BS in Psychology, Wash. State U., 1963; MS in Clin. Psychology, Stanford U., 1971; ABA in Apt. Mgmt., U. Nev., Las Vegas, 1974; cert. in apt. mgmt., Clover Park Vocat. Sch., 1988. Asst. mgr. Golden West of Calif., Santa Barbara, 1972-76; apt. mgr. Armstrong Properties, Olympia, Wash., 1976-79, N.W. Properties, Inc., Tacoma, 1979-82, Wintergreen Properties, Bellevue, Wash., 1982-84, Gt. N.W. Mgmt., Beaverton, Oreg., 1984-87; property mgr. Neal Mgmt., Tacoma, 1989—; cons. Valley Village Apts. Auburn, Wash., 1987—. Mem. Apt. Assn. Seattle-King County, Apt. Assn. Pierce County, Wash. Apt. Assn. (lobbyist 1977), Portland Multi-Housing Coun., Eagle (pres. 1966-68). Home and Office: Neal Property Mgmt 2219 D St SE Auburn WA 98002

NEAL, PHILIP MARK, JR., specialty chemical company financial executive; b. San Diego, Aug. 28, 1940; s. Philip Mark and Florence Elizabeth (Anderson) N.; m. Linda Reardon, Aug. 2, 1962; children: Brian, Kevin. B.A., Pomona Coll., 1962; M.B.A., Stanford U., 1964. Mgr. financial planning and analysis CBS, Hollywood, 1964-66; cons. McKinsey & Co., Los Angeles, 1966-73; v.p., controller Avery Internat. Corp., Los Angeles, 1974-78; sr. v.p. fin. Avery Internat. Corp., Pasadena, 1979-88, group v.p. materials group, 1988—. Mem. Fin. Execs. Inst., University Club. Republican. Episcopalian. Office: Avery Internat Corp 150 N Orange Grove Blvd Pasadena CA 91103

NEAL, RICHARD LEE, accountant; b. Mt. Vernon, Ill., May 10, 1956; s. E. Earl and Mary E. (Vaught) N. BS in Acctg., So. Ill. U., 1978; MBA, U. Ariz., 1979. CPA. Staff/sr. auditor Laventhol and Horway, Las Vegas, 1980-82; controller Caesars Tahoe Hotel and Casino, Reno, 1983, Peppermill Hotel and Casino, Reno, 1984; supr. audit Laventhol and Horwath, Phoenix, 1985—. Mem. Am. Inst. CPA's, Ariz. Soc. CPA's, Internat. Assn. Hospitality Accts. (bd. dirs. 1987—), Sierra. Democrat. Home: 10002 N 7th St 1145 Phoenix AZ 85020 Office: Laventhol & Horwath 3200 N Central 16th Floor Phoenix AZ 85012

NEALE, F. BRENT, V, investment banker; b. N.Y.C., Aug. 28, 1919; s. G. Brent and Sophie Hill (Hamilton) N.; student N.Y. Inst. Fin., 1938-41, St. Peter's Coll., 1950, NYU Grad. Sch. Bus., 1954-58, Coll. Fin. Planning, 1978-80; m. Elizabeth M. Rowan, Apr. 25, 1953. Asst. syndicate mgr. Loeb Rhoades Co., N.Y.C., 1945-54; syndicate mgr. Parrish & Co., N.Y.C., 1954-58; salesman Lehman Bros., N.Y.C., 1958-62; sales mgr. and v.p. Blair Granbery Marache & Co., N.Y.C., 1962-64; assoc. mem. N.Y. Stock Exchange, 1962-64; asst. v.p. sales E.F. Hutton Co., N.Y.C., 1965-71; instl. salesman Riter Pyne Kendall & Hollister, Inc., N.Y.C., 1971-72; instl. sales Hayden Stone Co., N.Y.C., 1972-74; investment banking and instl. sales Hoppin Watson Inc., N.Y.C., 1974-76; salesman Smith Barney, Harris Upham & Co., Inc., Tinton Falls, N.J., 1976-79; investment adv., fin. planner, ins. agt.; mgr. Sands Point South Condominium, Monmouth Beach, N.J., 1980-81; dir. Pkwy. Plastics Co., Piscataway, N.J., 1960—, Neale Assocs., 1978—, AGCO Sales, Inc., Union City, N.J., 1984—; mgr. tobacco farm, 1945-54. Chmn. Monmouth (N.J.) Ocean Damage Control Bd., 1958-64; chmn. Central Rd.-Seaview Ave.-Monmouth Beach Project, 1975-81; mem. planning bd. Boro of Monmouth Beach, 1976-77, 78-81, commr. revenue and fin., 1977-78, mayor, 1978-81; campaign mgr. Monmouth County Republican primary candidates, 1958, 62; mem. Monmouth County Mayor's Beach Erosion Com., 1978-81, chmn., 1981; trustee Ch. of Precious Blood, Monmouth Beach; spl. Eucharist Minister Bishop Trenton. Served with AUS, 1941-45. Decorated Purple Heart, Bronze Star, Combat Infantryman's Badge with 7 battle stars; recipient citations Fairleigh Dickinson U., 1954, 56, Kiwanis Internat., 1950, Internat. Lions Clubs, 1951; Cath. Action medal, 1950. Registered investment adviser. Mem. Internat. Assn. Fin. Planning (treas., dir. Central N.J. chpt. 1982-84, Cert. of Appreciation 1984). Md. Soc., N.Y. Soc. (pres. 1951-54, 70-74, pres. emeritus 1983—), So. Soc. (trustee 1970-74), Wall Streeters (pres. 1958-76), SAR, Order Magna Charta (baron), Order Descs. Charlemagne, Sovereign Order Temple Jerusalem (Knight Immacula), Manor Lords Md., Channel Club, Money Marketeers, Soc. 1st Div., Cath. War Vets. (N.J. trustee 1948-50, comdr. Hudson County 1949-50), Monmouth Beach Bus. Men's Club. Clubs: K.C., Monmouth Beach Bath and Tennis (trustee 1972-75). Home: 94 Ocean Ave Monmouth Beach NJ 07750 Office: PO Box 215 Monmouth Beach NJ 07750-0215

NEARY, FREDERICK RICHARD, insurance company executive; b. Dallas, Nov. 4, 1937; s. William Herrmann and Peggy (McLarry) N.; m. Mary Louise Brown, June 9, 1962 (div. Feb. 1967); 1 child, Kelly Allene; m. Ravelle Rainey, July 25, 1971 (div. Dec. 1985); children: Heather Elizabeth, Channing Colleen. Ba in English, So. Meth. U., 1960, BBA, 1961. Cert. fin. planner; registered securities prin.; lic. real estate broker, ins. agt. V.p. Southwestern Life Ins. Co., Dallas, 1961-81, FTS Life Ins. Agy., Inc., Dallas, 1985—; real estate investor Dallas, 1981-82; exec. v.p. Balanced Fin. Corp., Dallas, 1982-85. Bd. dirs. Family Guidance Ctr., Dallas, 1979-85; crisis counselor Suicide and Crisis Ctr., Dallas, 1985-86. Fellow Life Mgmt. Inst.; mem. Inst. Cert. Fin. Planners, Internat. Assn. For Fin. Planning. Presbyterian. Home: 2973 County Place Cir Carrollton TX 75006 Office: FTS Life Ins Agy Inc 14951 Dallas Pkwy Ste 105 Dallas TX 75240

NEAS, JOHN THEODORE, petroleum company executive; b. Tulsa, May 1, 1940; s. George and Lillian J. (Kasper) N.; BS, Okla. State U., 1967, MS, 1968; m. Sally Jane McPherson, June 10, 1966; children: Stephen, Gregory, Matthew. CPA, Okla. With acctg. dept. Rockwell Internat., 1965; with controller's dept. Amoco Prodn. Co., 1966-67; mem. audit and tax staff Deloitte, Haskins & Sells, 1968-75; pres. Nat. Petroleum Sales, Inc., Tulsa, 1975—, Port City Bulk Terminal, Inc., Tulsa, 1976—, McPherson Fuels & Asphalts, Inc., 1981—, John Neas Tank Lines, Inc., 1986—, BSC Tulsa, Inc., 1986—, Triple T Services, Inc., 1986—; asst. instr. U. Tulsa, 1974; bd. dirs. waterways bd. Okla. Dept. Commerce. Mem. AICPA, Nat. Assn. Accts. (v.p. membership 1976-77), Okla. Soc. CPA's, Am. Petroleum Inst., McClellan-Kerr Arkansas River Navigation System Hist. Soc. Republican. Lutheran. Clubs: Petroleum, Oil Marketers, Transportation (Tulsa); Propeller, Oaks Country, Okla. State U. President's, Okla. State U. Bus. Adminstrn. Assocs., Golf (Okla.). Home: 2943 E 69th St Tulsa OK 74136 Office: Triple T Svcs Inc 5401 S Harvard Ste 200 Tulsa OK 74135

NEBERGALL, DONALD CHARLES, investment executive; b. Davenport, Iowa, Aug. 12, 1928; s. Ellis W. and Hilda (Bruhn) N.; m. Shirley Elaine Williams, Apr. 12, 1952; children: Robert W., Nancy L. Nebergall Bosma. BS, Iowa State U., 1951. With Poweshiek County Nat. Bank, 1958-72, sr. v.p., to 1972; founding pres. Brenton Bank and Trust Co., Cedar Rapids, Iowa, 1972-82, chmn. bd., 1982-86; v.p. Chapman Co., 1986-88; bd. dirs. Telephone & Data Systems, Inc., Guaranty Bank and Trust, vice-chmn., bd. dirs. ITS, Inc. (subs. Iowa Bankers Assn.). V.p., bd. dirs. Iowa 4-H Found., 1972-76; div. campaign chmn. United Way; founding dir. Iowa Masonic Libr. Found.; bd. dirs. ARC, Boy Scouts Am.; bd. dirs., treas., past pres. Methwick Manor Retirement Home; founding trustee Cedar Rapids Community Sch. Dist. Found. Served with AUS, 1946-48. Recipient Ptnr. in 4-H award Iowa 4-H, 1983. Mem. Cedar Rapids Greater Downtown Assn. (pres., bd. dirs.), Rotary, Alpha Zeta, Gamma Sigma Delta, Delta Upsilon. Republican. Methodist. Office: 2919 Applewood Pl NE Cedar Rapids IA 52401

NECKERMANN, PETER JOSEF, insurance company executive; b. Wuertzburg, Germany, Oct. 26, 1935; came to U.S., 1977; s. Josef and Annemarie (Brueckner) N.; m. Jutta Voelk, Feb. 10, 1960; children: Susanne, Christian. Grad., J.W. Goethe U., Frankfurt, W.Ger.; M.A., J.W. Goethe U., 1962. Pres. Neckermann Versand KGaA, Frankfurt, W.Ger., 1962-77; dir. econ. analysis and systems Nationwide Ins. Cos., Columbus, Ohio, 1977-79, v.p. econ. and investment services, 1979—. Pres. Columbus Council on World Affairs, 1983-85. Home: 1261 Fountaine Dr Columbus OH 43221 Office: Nationwide Mut Ins Co One Nationwide Pla Columbus OH 43216

NEDERVELD, RUTH ELIZABETH, real estate executive; b. Hudsonville, Mich., Oct. 29, 1933; d. Ralph and Hattie (Ploeg) Schut; m. Terrill Lee Nederveld, June 6, 1952; children: Courtland Lee, Valerie Lynn Nederveld Heisey, Darwin Frederic. Degree in Real Estate, U. Mich., 1979; student, Pa. State U., Centre Hall, 1973, Aquinas Coll., Grand Rapids, Mich., 1974; degree, Grad. Realtors Inst., 1979. Cert. residential specialist; registered securities agt. With sales dept. Field Enterprises, Lancaster, Pa., 1962-72; sales assoc. E. James Hogan, Lancaster, 1972-74, C-21 Packard, Grand Rapids, Mich., 1974-80; assoc. broker comml. div. Markland Devel., Inc., Grand Rapids, 1980-86, Am. Acquest Realty, Inc., Grand Rapids, 1986-89; broker, owner R.E. Nederveld Realtors, 1989—. Pres. Civic Nucomers of Grand Rapids, 1978; trustee, elder Forest Hills Presbyn. Ch., Cascade,

Mich., 1983-86. Mem. Nat. Assn. Realtors (mem. comml. dept. 1973—), Mich. Assn. Realtors, Grand Rapids Real Estate Bd., Woman's Council Realtors (corr. sec. 1986-87), Nat. Assn. Female Execs., Assn. Sales and Mktg. Execs. (exec. dir. internat. chpt. 1977-84, pres. Grand Rapids chpt. 1986-87). Republican. Lodge: Order of Eastern Star. Office: Am Acquest Inc 5958 Tahoe SE Grand Rapids MI 49506

NEEDHAM, NANCY JEAN, management consultant; b. Chgo., July 21, 1941; d. Robert Leonard and Grace Irene (Bennett) N.; children: Thomas, Charles, Catharine, Jessica. BA, Wellesley Coll., 1964; MBA, Harvard U., 1972, DBA, 1977. Pubs. specialist MIT, Cambridge, Mass., 1964-65; editor SRA, Chgo., 1966; sr. editor Ency. Britannica, Chgo., 1967; cons. ABT Assocs., Cambridge, 1968; program mgr. Am. Sci. & Engring., Boston, 1969; faculty Harvard Bus. Sch., Cambridge, 1973-75; cons. CRI, Cambridge, 1977-78; prof. mgmt. Poly. U. N.Y., N.Y.C., 1986—; assoc. dir. Ctr. for Advanced Tech. in Telecommunications, N.Y.C., 1986—; pres. ICGS Inc., Boston, 1978—. Contbr. articles to profl. jours. Mem. Am. Soc. Macro Engring. (bd. dirs. 1984—), C.G. Jung Found. (bd. dirs. 1988—), Phi Beta Kappa. Presbyterian. Home: 14 E 4th St New York NY 10012 Office: ICGS c/o W Roy Inc 105 Beach St Boston MA 02111

NEEL, HOLMES, agricultural supply company executive. Formerly vice chmn. Gold Kist Inc., Atlanta, now chmn., also bd. dirs. Office: Gold Kist Inc 244 Perimeter Ctr Pkwy NE Atlanta GA 30346 *

NEELANKAVIL, JAMES PAUL, marketing educator, consultant, researcher; b. Anjoor, India, May 29, 1940; came to U.S., 1973, naturalized, 1985; s. Paul V. and Mary (Velara) N.; m. Salvacion Querol Pena, July 15, 1973; children—Angel Mary, Prince Jacques. BS, St. Thomas Coll., India, 1961; MBA, Asian Inst. Mgmt., Philippines, 1972; PhD, NYU, 1976. Asst. prof. N.Y. Inst., 1976-78; assoc. prof. Montclair State Coll., N.J., 1978-80; asst. prof. NYU, 1980-84; chmn. mktg. and internat. bus. dept. Hofstra U., Hempstead, N.Y., 1984-86, assoc. dean sch. bus., 1986—; supr. Firestone, Bombay, India, 1961-70; cons. Internat. Advt. Assn., N.Y.C., 1979—, GTE Inc., Stamford, Conn., 1980—, Healthchem Inc., N.Y.C., 1980-83. Author: Self-Regulation, 1980, Agency Compensation, 1982, Advertising Regulation, 1985; also articles. Mem. Internat. Advt. Assn., Am. Mktg. Assn., Acad. Internat. Bus., Advt. Research Found. (council mem. 1983—). Avocations: reading, tennis, travel.

NEELY, EARL FISHER, manufacturing company executive; b. Lamartine, Pa., Aug. 5, 1927; s. Lawrence Lester and Mildred Earla (Fisher) N.; m. Helen Marie Webb, June 10, 1950; children—Michael, Pamela, Bruce, Melinda. B.S., Grove City Coll., 1950. Controller Knox Glass Inc., Pa., 1950-61; v.p. finance Richards Musical Instrument Co., Elkhart, Ind., 1962-64; exec. v.p. Angelica Corp., St. Louis, 1964-84, pres., chief operating officer, dir., 1984-88, ret., 1988. Served with USMCR, 1945-46. Home: 715 Timber Trail Dr Frontenac MO 63131

NEERHOUT, JOHN, JR., business executive; b. 1931. BSME, U. Calif., 1953. With Bechtel Petroleum, Inc. (now Bechtel, Inc.), San Francisco, 1966—; pres. Bechtel Petroleum, Inc. (now Bechtel, Inc.), 1983-86, also dir. Bechtel Group, Inc. Office: Bechtel Inc PO Box 3965 San Francisco CA 94119

NEFF, FRED LEONARD, lawyer; b. St. Paul, Nov. 1, 1948; s. Elliott Ira and Mollie (Poboisk) N. BS with high distinction, U. Minn., 1970; JD, William Mitchell Coll. Law, 1976. Bar: Minn. 1976, U.S. Dist. Ct. Minn. 1977, Wis. 1986, U.S. Ct. Appeals (8th cir.) 1985, U.S. Supreme Ct. 1985, Wis. Supreme Ct. 1986. Tchr. Hopkins (Minn.) Pub. Schs., 1970-72; instr. Inver Hills Community Coll., St. Paul, 1973-76, U. Minn., Mpls., 1974-76; sole practice, Mpls., 1976-79; asst. county atty. Sibley County, Gaylord, Minn., 1979-80; mng. atty. Hyatt Legal Services, St. Paul, 1981-83, regional ptnr., 1983-85, profl. devel. ptnr., 1985-86; pres. Neff Law Firm, P.A., Mpls., 1986—; counsel Am. Tool Supply Co., St. Paul, 1976-78; cons. Nat. Detective Agy., Inc., St. Paul, 1980-83; lectr., guest instr. U. Wis., River Falls, 1976-77; spl. instr. Hamline U., St. Paul, 1977; vis. lectr. Coll. Saint Scholastica, Duluth, Minn., 1977; bd. dirs. Acceptance Ins. Holdings, Inc., Omaha, 1988—. Author: Fred Neff's Self-Defense Library, 1976, Everybody's Self-Defense Book, 1978, Karate Is for Me, 1980, Running Is for Me, 1980, Lessons from the Samurai, 1986, Lessons from the Art of Kempo, 1986, Lessons from the Western Warriors, 1986, Lessons from the Fighting Commandos, 1989, Lessons from Ancient Japanese Masters of Self-Defense, 1989, Lessons from the Eastern Warriors, 1989; co-host TV series Great Unsolved Crimes, Minn. Advisor to bd. Sibley County Commrs., 1979-80; speaker civic groups, 1976-82; mem. Hennepin County Juvenile Justice Panel, 1980-82, Hennepin County (Minn.) Pub. Def. Conflict Panel, 1980-82, 86—, Hennepin Bar Assn. Advice Panel Law Day, 1987, Panel Union Privilege Legal Svcs. div. AFL-CIO, 1986—, Montgomery Wards Legal Svcs. Panel, 1986—, Edina Hist. Soc.; charter mem. Commn. for the Battle of Normandy Mus.; founding sponsor Civil Justice Found., 1986—. Recipient St. Paul Citizen of Month award, Citizens Group, 1975, Student Appreciation U. Minn. award, 1978, Commendation award Sibley County Attys. Office, 1980, Leadership award Hyatt Legal Services, 1984, Mgn. Attys. Guidance award 1985, Justice award 1986, Creative Thinker award regional staff 1986, Good Neighbor award WCCO Radio, 1985, Lamp of Knowledge award Twin Cities Lawyers Guild, 1986, numerous other awards and honors. Fellow Roscoe Pound Found., Nat. Dist. Attys. Assn.; mem. ABA, Assn. Trial Lawyers Am., Minn. Bar Assn., Hennepin County Bar Assn., Wis. Bar. Assn., Ramsey County Bar Assn., Am. Judicature Soc., Internat. Platform Assn., Minn. Martial Arts Assn. (pres. 1974-78 Outstanding Instr. award 1973), Nippon Kobudo Rengokai (bd. dirs. North Cen. States 1972-76), Edina C. of C., Masons, Kiwanis, Sigma Alpha Mu. Avocations: reading, far ea. and oriental studies, civic activities, phys. conditioning, gardening. Home: 4515 Andover Rd Edina MN 55435 Office: 701 4th Ave S Ste 500 Minneapolis MN 55415 also: 345 St Peter St Ste 800 Saint Paul MN 55102 also: 5930 Brooklyn Blvd Ste 100 Brooklyn Center MN 55429 also: 7380 France Ave S Ste 100 Edina MN 55435 also: 1611 W County Rd B Ste 110 Roseville MN 55113

NEFF, JAMES DENNIS, manufacturing company executive, consultant; b. Ft. Wayne, Ind., Aug. 24, 1937; s. James Marion and Margaret Ann (Lynch) N.; m. Jeanette Ann Day, Apr. 8, 1966; children: Bryan James, Julie Ann, Sarah Lynn. Student, Purdue U., 1955-57; BSME, U. Ill., 1959; MBA, Ind. U., 1963. Sr. mktg. analyst Allison div. Gen. Motors Corp., Indpls., 1963-67; mgr. Merwins Internat. Harvestor Truck Dealership, St. Croix, V.I., 1967-68; sr. v.p. Hexcel Corp., Dublin, Calif., 1968—; coll. instr. V.I., 1967-68. Served with U.S. Army, 1960. Mem. Aerospace Industries Assn., Am. Def. Preparedness Assn. (bd. dirs. 1975), Soc. Advancement of Material and Process Engring. (presenter). Office: Hexcel Corp 11555 Dublin Blvd Dublin CA 94568

NEFF, RAY QUINN, electric power consultant; b. Houston, Apr. 29, 1928; s. Noah Grant and Alma Ray (Smith) N.; m. Elizabeth McDougald, Sept. 4, 1982. Degree in Steam Engring., Houston Vocat. Tech., 1957; BSME, Kennedy Western U., 1986. Various positions Houston Lighting & Power Co., 1945-60, plant supr., 1960-70, plant supt. asst., 1970-80, tech. supr., 1980-85, tng. supr., 1985-87; owner, operator Neff Enterprises, Bedias, Tex., 1987—; cons. Houston Industries, 1987-88. Author: Power Plant Operation, 1975, Power Operator Training, 1985, Power Foreman Training, 1986. Judge Internat. Sci. and Engring. Fair, Houston, 1982, Sci. Engring. Fair Houston, 1987. Mem. ASME, Assn. Chief Operating Engrs. Republican. Methodist. Lodge: Masons. Home: 946 W 31st St Houston TX 77018 Office: Neff Enterprises Hwy 90 Rt 2 Box 193-A Bedias TX 77831

NEFF, THOMAS JOSEPH, executive search firm executive; b. Easton, Pa., Oct. 2, 1937; s. John Wallace and Elizabeth Ann (Dougherty) N.; m. Susan Culver Paull, Nov. 26, 1971 (dec.); children: David Andrew, Mark Gregory, Scott Dougherty; m. Sarah Brown Hallingby, Jan. 20, 1989; stepchildren: Brooke, Bailey. BS in Indsl. Engring., Lafayette Coll., 1959; MBA, Lehigh U., 1961. Assoc. McKinsey & Co., Inc., N.Y.C. and Australia, 1963-66; dir. mktg. planning Trans-World Airlines, N.Y.C., 1966-69; pres. Hosp. Data Scis., Inc., N.Y.C., 1969-74; prin. Booz, Allen & Hamilton, Inc., N.Y.C., 1974-76; regional ptnr. N.Am.; bd. dirs. Spencer Stuart & Assos., N.Y.C., 1976-79; pres., bd. dirs. Spencer Stuart & Assocs., N.Y.C., 1979—; bd. dirs. Macmillan, Inc., Lord Abbett & Co. Mut. Funds, Affiliated Fund. Served with U.S. Army, 1961-63. Republican. Roman Catholic. Clubs: Links, Yale, Sky, Racquet and Tennis; Blind Brook; Quogue (N.Y.) Beach, Quogue Field; Round Hill; Field. Home: 25 Midwood Rd Greenwich CT 06830 Office: Spencer Stuart & Assocs Park Ave Pla 55 E 52d St New York NY 10055

NEHER, TIMOTHY PYPER, cable company executive; b. Jersey City, Sept. 9, 1947; s. Harry Paul and Alice (Pyper) N.; m. Mary Ann King, June 13, 1970; children: Amy, Victoria. BA in Math., Cornell U., 1969; MBA in Fin., Boston U., 1971. Loan officer Bank New Eng., Boston, 1971-74; regional mgr. Continental Cablevision, Boston, 1974-77, v.p., gen. mgr., 1977-80, v.p., treas., 1980-82, exec. v.p., 1982-85, pres., chief operating officer, 1985—, also bd. dirs.; bd. dirs. Turner Broadcasting Inc., Atlanta, Pay-Per-View Network Inc., N.Y.C., Tolerate, Inc., N.Y.C. Republican. Clubs: Weston (Mass.) Golf; Boston Racquet; Old Marsh Golf, Lost Tree Golf (North Palm Beach, Fla.). Office: Continental Cablevision Inc The Pilot House Lewis Wharf Boston MA 02110

NEHRLING, ARNO HERBERT, JR., chemical company executive; b. Richmond, Ind., Mar. 5, 1928; s. Arno Herbert and Irene Thelma (Dahlberg) N.; m. Mary Helen Mudd, Jan. 11, 1958; children: Amy Irene Nehrling Belz, Dorothy Louise. BA, Cornell U., 1950; MBA, HArvard U., 1955. Various supervisory and mgmt. positions E.I. Du Pont de Nemours & Co., Wilmington, Del., 1955-64; dir. fin. E.I. Du Pont de Nemours & Co., Dusseldorf, Fed. Republic Germany and Mexico City, 1965-71; asst. mgr. credit div., asst. mgr. treasury div., asst. mgr. fgn. and banking div. E.I. Du Pont de Nemours & Co., Wilmington, 1972-76, asst. treas., dir. employee compensation and benefits, 1977—. Mem. Fin. Execs. Inst. (past chmn. employee benefits com., chmn. com. on other post employment benefits), Assn. Pvt. Pension and Welfare Plans (bd. dirs., exec. com.), ERISA Industry Com. (bd. dirs.). Home: 612 Berwick Rd Wilmington DE 19803 Office: EI Du Pont de Nemours & Co Nemours Bldg Rm 10510 Wilmington DE 19898

NEILL, ROLFE, newspaperman; b. Mount Airy, N.C., Dec. 4, 1932; s. Kenneth A. and Carmen (Goforth) N.; m. Rosemary Clifford Boney, July 20, 1952 (div.); children: Clifford Randolph, Sabrina Ashley, Dana Catlin, Jessica Rosemary Ingrid, Quentin Roark Robinson; m. Ann Marshall Snider, Sept. 24, 1988. A.B. in History, U. N.C., 1954. Reporter Franklin (N.C.) Press, 1956-57; reporter Charlotte (N.C.) Observer, 1957-58, bus. editor, 1958-61; editor, pub. Coral Gables (Fla.) Times and The Guide, 1961-63, Miami Beach (Fla.) Daily Sun, 1963-65; asst. to pub. N.Y. Daily News, 1965-67, suburban editor, 1967-68, asst. mng. editor, 1968-70; editor Phila. Daily News, 1970-75; v.p., dir. Phila. Newspapers Inc., 1970-75; chmn., pub. Charlotte (N.C.) Observer, 1975—. Served with AUS, 1954-56. Office: Knight Pub Co 600 S Tyron St PO Box 32188 Charlotte NC 28232

NEILLY, ANDREW HUTCHINSON, JR., publisher; b. Balt., 1923; m. Janet Dayton, 1949; children: Susan, Thomas, Sarah. Grad., U. Rochester, 1947. Coll. sales rep. John Wiley & Sons, Inc., N.Y.C., 1947-51, asst. sales mgr., 1951-57, asst. v.p. domestic sales and promotion, 1957-61, v.p. mktg. div., 1961-67, exec. v.p., chief operating officer, 1967-71, pres., chief operating officer, 1971-79, pres., chief exec. officer, 1979-89, vice chmn., 1989—, also bd. dirs. Trustee U. Rochester, Columbia U. Press. Mem. Internat. Pubs. Assn. (pres. 1988-92), Internat. Group STM Pubs. (exec. com.). Club: Century Assn. Office: John Wiley & Sons Inc 605 3rd Ave New York NY 10158

NEILSON, JOHN WILBERT TENNANT, research company executive, consultant, educator; b. Oakland, Calif., May 9, 1944; s. Donald Wilbert Tennant and Mary Vera (Peart) N.; divorced; children—Sean Wilbert Tennant, Kimberly Mary. B.S. in Edn., So. Oreg. State Coll., 1969, M.S. in Gen. Studies, 1972. Registered sanitarian trainee Oreg. State Dept. Health, 1973. Dept. chmn. Days Creek (Oreg.) High Sch., 1969-70; chmn. biology dept. South Umpqua High Sch., Myrtle Creek, Oreg., 1970-75; microbiologist, chemist Umpqua Research Co., Myrtle Creek, Oreg., 1973-76, field rep., 1976-78; prof. sci. Lane Community Coll., Eugene, Oreg., 1976-78; salesman Jewett Office Supply, Medford, Oreg., 1978-80, Truscott Office Products, Medford, 1978-82, chief exec. officer pres. Neilson Research Medford, 1976—; lab. analyst, cons. drinking water. Served with U.S. Army, 1962-65, USAR, 1976—. Mem. Am. Soc. Microbiology, Am. Water Works Assn., Assn. Ofcl. Analytical Chemists, Water Pollution Control Fedn. Republican. Episcopalian. Club: Rotary. Author: Northwestern CB Log Book, 1976. Office: 446 Highland Dr Medford OR 97504

NEIMAN, ROBERT LEROY, management consultant; b. Chgo., Feb. 9, 1930; s. Maurice and Shirley (Albin) N.; B.S. in Communications with honors, U. Ill., 1951, M.A. in Social and Behavioral Scis., 1952; m. Marlene Kaufman (dec. Mar. 1972); m. Barbara Milkes (dec. Mar. 1983); 1 dau., Debra Bea. Asst. to pres. Utility Plastic Packaging Co., Chgo., 1953-54; from dept. mgr. to v.p. Castle and Assos., Chgo., 1954-73; v.p. Mendheim Co., Chgo., 1973-77, sr. v.p., 1977-86, pres. Neiman & Assocs, 1986— ; guest radio speaker on cancer research fund raising, 1984. Chmn. Marlene K. Neiman Meml. Found. of Am. Cancer Soc., 1972-75, chmn. Barbara J. Neiman Meml. Found. for Lung Cancer, 1983; bd. dirs. Morton Grove, Ill. unit Am. Cancer Soc. Served as 1st lt. USAF, 1951-53. Recipient Presdl. citation; Joggers award Lehmann Sports Club. Mem. Am. Personnel and Guidance Assn., Am. Inst. Indsl. Engrs., Soc. Mfg. Engrs., Am. Mgmt. Assn., Nat. Assn. Corp. and Profl. Recruiters, Air Force Assn., North Shore Assn. for Retarded, Sigma Delta Chi, Sigma Delta Pi. Club: Skokie Valley Kiwanis (program chmn.). Author articles in field. Home: 9401 Natchez Ave Morton Grove IL 60053 Office: 9401 N Natchez Morton Grove IL 60053

NEIMARK, PHILIP JOHN, financial consultant, editor; b. Chgo., Sept. 13, 1939; s. Mortimer William and Hortense (Peters) N.; m. Vassa Lynn; children: Tanya Lee, Joshua Daniel. Student U. Chgo., 1956-58, Northwestern U., 1958-59; D in Bus. Mgmt. (hon.), Ricker Coll., Houlton, Maine, 1976. Mem. Chgo. Mercantile Exchange, 1968-74; owner Josephson Neimark Trading Co., Chgo., 1972-73; ptnr. Rosenthal & Co., Chgo., 1973-77; owner, prin. Philip J. Neimark Investments, Miami, Fla., 1977-79, Chgo., 1979—; pres. Neimark Fin. Pub. Co., 1985—; pres., Croesus Assocs., 1988—; dir. mktg., Callard, Madden & Assocs.; editor, pub. Philip J. Neimark Viewpoint, N.Y.C., 1976-85, editor Pro Trade, 1984—, Low Priced Stock Edit., 1984—; fin. editor Money Maker mag., 1979-85; mem. Internat. Monetary Market, 1971-74, N.Y. Mercantile Exchange, 1973-74, Chgo. Bd. of Options Exchange, 1973-75; editor, Low Priced Stock Edition, 1984—, Pro Trade, 1985—. Author: How to Be Lucky, 1975; contbg. editor Consumers Digest mag., 1977-85. Bd. dirs. Luth. Gen. Med. Found., Principal Vassa Group. Mem. Fla. Exec. Planning Assn., South Fla. Fin. Planners Assn., Investment Co. Inst., Nat. Paso Fino Assn. (founder). Office: 224 E Ontario Chicago IL 60611

NEINER, A(NDREW) JOSEPH, financial executive; b. Ft. Scott, Kans., Feb. 15, 1950; s. Andrew W. and Celeste H. (Beck) N.; m. Linda M. Koening, Aug. 21, 1969; children: Carrie L., Christine M., Joseph M., Elizabeth A. BSBA, U. Mo., St. Louis, 1972; MBA, St. Louis U., 1976. Fin. analyst Chrysler Corp., Fenton, Mo., 1972-75; fin. mgr. Gen. Cable Corp., St. Louis, 1975-79; corp contr. Consolidated Aluminum Corp., St. Louis, 1985, dir. corp. planning, 1986, v.p. fin. and planning, 1986—, bd. dirs.; conducted fin. workshops Interlaken, SW for Alusuisse Ltd., Zurich SW, 1985; instr. St. Louis Jr. Coll., 1978-80, U. Mo., St. Louis, 1987; bd. dirs. Electro Savs. Credit Union. Recipient Disting. Leadership award Am. Biog. Inst., 1987-88, Disting. Am., 1987. Mem. Am. Mgmt. Assn., Fin. Execs. Inst. Roman Catholic. Home: 15104 Appalachian Trail Chesterfield MO 63017 Office: Consolidated Aluminum Corp 11960 Westline Industrial Dr Saint Louis MO 63146

NEIRA, THELMA, lawyer; b. Buenos Aires, Oct. 28, 1958; came to U.S., 1963, naturalized, 1969; d. Oscar Benito and Ageles Estella Neira. BA in Criminal Justice summa cum laude, L.I. U., 1980; JD, Union U., Albany, N.Y., 1983. Bar: N.Y. 1984. Law clk. Office N.Y. State Atty. Gen., Albany, 1982; assoc. Zinman and Chetkof P.C., Jericho, N.Y., 1983-84, Robert D. Frankfort, Deer Park, N.Y., 1984—. Active local polit. campaigns. Mem. N.Y. State Bar Assn., Suffolk County Bar Assn. Democrat. Roman Catholic. Home: 120 Eastwood Ave Deer Park NY 11729 Office: Robert D Frankfort 2061 Deer Park Ave Deer Park NY 11729

NEIS, ARNOLD HAYWARD, pharmaceutical company executive; b. N.Y.C., Feb. 13, 1938; s. Harry Hayward and Ruth (Bishop) N.; B.S. cum laude, Columbia U., 1959; M.B.A., N.Y.U., 1967; children—Nancy R., Robert C. With Scott Chem. Co., 1959-64; v.p. mktg., then v.p. Odell, Inc., N.Y.C., 1964-71, pres. Knomark div., 1969-71; pres., chief exec. officer, E.T. Browne Drug Co., Inc., Englewood Cliffs, N.J., 1971—; dir. Esquire A.B. Stockholm, Knomark Can. Ltd., E.T. Browne Internat. Fellow Royal Soc. Chemists, N.Y. Acad. Scis.; mem. Am. Chem. Soc., Am. Pharm. Assn., AAAS, Explorers Club, Chemists Club. Unitarian. Club: Lotos. Home: 898 Park Ave New York NY 10021 Office: 140 Sylvan Ave PO Box 1613 Englewood Cliffs NJ 07632

NEIS, ARTHUR VERAL, real estate development constuction company executive; b. Lawrence, Kans., May 30, 1940; s. Veral Herbert and Louise (Schlegel) N.; m. Fleeta Weigel, Apr. 12, 1969; children: Frederich Arthur, Benjamin Jason, Sarah Louise. BS in Bus., U. Kans., 1962, MS in Acctg., 1963. CPA, Kans., Iowa. Mgmt. cons. Arthur Andersen & Co., Kansas City, Mo. and Mpls., 1963-74; chief corp. acctg. Carlson Co., Mpls., 1974-76; controller The Fullerton Cos., Mpls., 1976-78; asst. treas. Fru-Con Corp., St. Louis, 1978-80, asst. controller, 1981, controller, 1982-86; corporate controller The Weitz Corp., Des Moines, 1986-87, treas., 1987—; treas. Weitz Properties, Des Moines, 1987—, Life Care Services Corp., Des Moines, 1987—. Bd. dirs. Inst. Humane Studies George Mason U., Fairfax, Va., 1973—, exec. com., 1975-83, chmn., 1978-83; bd. dirs. Lake Country Sch., Mpls., 1973-78, treas., 1974-78, bd. dirs. Found. Advance Studies in Liberty, Wichita, Kans., 1979-83; Villa di Maria Montessori Sch., St. Louis, 1982-86, chmn. fund raising, 1980-81, 83-84, chmn. Parenting fair activities, 1984; trustee Crossroads Sch., St. Louis, 1984-86, exec. com. bd., 1984-86; chmn. fund raising, Crossroads Sch. Parent Resource Orgn., 1983-85; active Bus. for Peace, 1988. Mem. Am. Inst. CPA's, Kans. Soc. CPA's, Iowa Soc. CPA's, Fin. Execs. Inst. (bd. dirs. 1986, 88, sec. 1988), Bus. for Peace. Club: Des Moines Golf & Country. Home: 1575 NW 106th Des Moines IA 50322 Office: The Weitz Corp 800 Second Ave Des Moines IA 50309

NEISER, RICHARD WILLIAM, utility executive; b. Covington, Ky., June 16, 1938; s. Richard William Neiser Sr. and Elizabeth Mildred (Marz) Raible; m. Joy Lee, Aug. 27, 1960; children: David, Linda, Mary Beth. BA, Centre Coll., 1960; JD, Stetson Coll. Law, 1963. Trust rep., trust officer Barnett Bank & Trust Co., St. Petersburg, Fla., 1963-64; sole practice, St. Petersburg, 1965; staff atty. Fla. Power Corp., St. Petersburg, 1966-68, asst. counsel, 1968-74, asst. gen. counsel, 1974-76, asst. v.p., asst. gen. counsel, 1976-78, v.p., asst. gen. counsel, 1978-83, sr. v.p., gen. counsel, 1983-87, sr. v.p. corporate services, 1987—. Mem. Leadership St. Petersburg Alumni Assn. Mem. ABA, Fla. Bar Assn., St. Petersburg Bar Assn., Am. Judicature Soc., Fla. C. of C., St. Petersburg C. of C., Edison Electric Inst. Legal Com. Republican. Club: Suncoast Tiger Bay (St. Petersburg). Office: Fla Power Corp 3201 34th St S Saint Petersburg FL 33711

NEISH, FRANCIS EDWARD, advertising agency executive; b. McKeesport, Pa., Feb. 24, 1925; s. Francis Edward and Florence (Peterson) N.; B.A., Pa. State U., 1947. Mem. advt. dept. Daily News, McKeesport, 1947-59; pres. Frank Neish Advt., McKeesport, 1959—. Pres., McKeesport Hosp. Found., 1977-89; pres. adv. bd. McKeesport Campus, Pa. State U., 1984—; trustee E.R. Crawford Found., 1975—; bd. dirs. McKeesport Hosp., 1974-89, McKeesport Versailles Cemetery, 1988—. V.p. Mon Yough Chamber Found., 1988—, McKeesport Symphony; chmn. adv. bd. Salvation Army, 1982. Served to lt. (j.g.) USNR, 1943-47, PTO. Mem. Pitts. Advt. Club, Pitts. Radio and TV Club, Mon-Yough C. of C. (past pres., bd. dirs.) Club: Toastmasters. Lodges: Rotary (pres. 1973-74), Masons, Shriners. Avocations: music; reading. Office: 1614 Lysle Blvd McKeesport PA 15132

NEITERMAN, LARRY JAY, management consultant; b. Boston, Apr. 15, 1958; s. Norman and Louise (Bernson) N.; m. Elin Williams, June 22, 1986. AB in Econs. and Orgnl. Behavior, Brown U., 1980; MBA in Fin. and Strategic Planning, Dartmouth Coll., 1982. Mgr. Touche Ross, Boston, 1982—. Mem. Healthcare Fin. Mgmt. Assn., Group Health Assn. Am. Office: Touche Ross 1 Federal St Boston MA 02110

NELLA, ALFRED LAWRENCE, accountant; b. Petaluma, Calif., July 6, 1928; s. Lawrence and Clelia Alice (Spolini) N.; BS, U. San Francisco, 1951. Ptnr. Samuel Mendelson & Co., CPA's, San Francisco, 1954-73, Nella & Getz, CPA's, San Francisco, 1973-76; propr. Alfred L. Nella, CPA's, San Francisco, 1976—; chief exec. officer Alan J. Blair Personnel Svcs., Inc.; bd. dir. G-W Tank Lines, Inc., Pacific Blue, Inc., Berkeley Warehouse and Drayage Co., Inc., Berkeley Truck Leasing, Inc., Club Turkish, Inc., Groskopf-Weider Trucking Co., Dart Personnel Agy., Inc. Bd. dirs., v.p. Fin. of Pride Found.; bd. dir., treas. San Francisco Concert Opera Assn., Stop AIDS Project. CPA, Calif. Mem. Am. Inst. CPA's, Calif. Soc. CPA's, Golden Gate Bus. Assn. (dir., treas.). Republican. Roman Catholic. Home: 77 Fair Oaks St San Francisco CA 94110 Office: 1390 Market St Ste 1004 San Francisco CA 94102

NELLI, DONALD JAMES, business school executive, accountant; b. Seneca Falls, N.Y., Feb. 19, 1917; s. Thomas and Vita N.; m. Victoria Margaret Serino, Aug. 31, 1941 (dec. May 1980); children: Thomas, Diane, Joseph, John; m. 2d, Carmel L. Dowd, Sept. 19, 1981; BS, Syracuse U., 1948. CPA, N.Y. Staff acct. Seidman & Seidman, N.Y.C., 1948-49, Stover, Butler & Murphy, Syracuse, N.Y., 1949-55; instr. Syracuse U., 1953; instr. acctg. Central City Bus. Inst., Syracuse, 1955-58, pres., 1958—, also pvt. practice acctg., Syracuse. Served with USNR, 1943-46. CPA, N.Y. Mem. Am. Inst. CPAs, N.Y. State Soc. CPAs, Am. Acctg. Assn., AAUP. Roman Catholic. Clubs: Lakeshore Yacht and Country (Clay, N.Y.), Italian Am. Athletic (Syracuse). Home: 7929 Boxford Rd Clay NY 13041 Office: Cen City Bus Inst 953 James St Syracuse NY 13203

NELLIGAN, MICHAEL PATRICK, accountant; b. Greenville, S.C., July 18, 1954; s. Owen Buckley and Dorothy Elizabeth (Anderson) N.; m. Eva Helen Hanson; children: Gustav Patrick, Victor Bernhard. BBA cum laude, U. Miami, Coral Gables, Fla., 1974; postgrad., Stonier Grad. Sch. Banking, 1987—. CPA, Fla., Md., D.C. With Price Waterhouse, 1975—; mgr. Price Waterhouse-Europe Price Waterhouse, Sweden and The Netherlands, 1980-83; sr. mgr. Price Waterhouse, Washington, 1984-86, ptnr., 1987—. Active Bus. Execs. Roundtable, Am. Embassy, Stockholm, 1980-81. Mem. AICPA, Am. Assn. Accts., Nat. Assn. Accts., Inst. Internal Auditors, U. Miami Alumni Assn., Swedish-Am. Cultural Union, Am. Scandinavian Assn. Washington, Swedish-Am. C. of C., Kenwood Golf and Country Club, City Club of Washington, Beta Alpha Psi. Office: Price Waterhouse 1801 K St NW Washington DC 20006

NELLIS, BARBARA BROOKS, trust company executive; b. Akron, Ohio, Mar. 16, 1935; d. Frank and Alice (Woodhall) Brooks; m. William J. Waltenbaugh, Oct. 31, 1953 (div. 1965); children: Bonnie, Becky, Brooks; m. Robert E. Nellis, June 25, 1971; children: Cheryl, Jack Lori, Kathryn, Robert. Student, Kent State U., 1964, Akron U., 1965, Purdue U., 1977, Malone Coll., 1978-88. Sec. Goodyear Tire and Rubber Co., Akron, 1952-62; exec. sec. Morgan Adhesives Co., Stow, Ohio, 1969-71; mgmt. cons. Brouse McDowell Hunsicker and Assocs. Law Firm, Akron, 1971-88; real estate agt. Kallstrom Realty, Akron; pres. TMI and D Co. Inc., Akron, 1978-88, T.M. Investment and DUP'T, Akron, 1978-88; real estate agt. Marting Realty, Akron, 1982, McInnis Realty, Akron, 1987; sales mgr. McInnis Coldwell Banker. Recipient Presdl. citation, 1988. Fellow Akron Area Com., Nat. Assn. Realtors, Ohio Assn. Realtors. Democrat. Home: 664 Pebble Beach Dr Akron OH 44313 Office: TMI & D Co Inc 2331 E Market St Apt 519 Akron OH 44312

NELSEN, DAVID JONATHAN, engineer, corporate executive; b. Champaign, Ill., May 19, 1956; s. David Daniel and Marilyn Phyllis (Nett) N. BSCE, U. Kans., 1978. Registered profl. engr., Kans., Colo. N.Mex., Miss. Engr. Norton & Schmidt Cons. Engrs., Kansas City, Mo., 1978-80, v.p., 1980—. Mem. ASCE, Am. Concrete Inst., Greater Kansas City C. of C. (chmn. metro affairs). Club: Kansas City Businessmen's (pres. 1987). Office: Norton & Schmidt 1009 Baltimore Ave #800 Kansas City MO 64105

NELSON, ALBERT LOUIS, III, finance executive; b. St. Louis, Apr. 29, 1938; s. Albert Louis and Mildred Mary (Bischoff) N.; m. Pamela Eakins, Mar. 14, 1970; children: Holly Reid, Amy Bischoff. BS in Mech. Engring., Washington U., St. Louis, 1960, MBA, 1962; LLB, George Washington U., 1964. Exec. v.p. Equity Research Assocs., Inc., N.Y.C., 1967-69; pres. The Westwood Group, Inc., Los Angeles, 1969-73; dir. chem. plastics Gen. Tire & Rubber Co., Akron, Ohio, 1973-75; sr. v.p., dir. corp. service dept. Prescott, Ball & Turben, Cleve., 1975-86; pres. Albert Nelson Investment Co., Inc., Fairlawn, Ohio, 1986—. Served with U.S. Army, 1964-66. Clubs: N.Y. Stock Exchange Lunch; Portage Country.

NELSON, ARTHUR HUNT, real estate company executive; b. Kansas City, Mo., May 21, 1923; s. Carl Ferdinand and Hearty (Brown) N.; AB, U. Kans., 1943; JD, Harvard, 1949; m. Eleanor Thomas, Dec. 27, 1954; children: Carl F., Frances, Pamela. Staff radiation lab. Mass. Inst. Tech., 1943-44; sr. engr., cons. Raytheon Mfg. Co., Boston, 1948-52; admitted to Mass. bar, 1949, practiced in Boston; v.p., treas., dir. Gen. Electronic Labs., Inc., Cambridge, Mass., 1951-64, chmn. bd., 1959-63; treas., dir. Sci. Electronics, Inc., Cambridge, 1955-64; treas., dir. Assocs. for Internat. Research, Inc., 1954—, pres., 1968—; treas., dir. Victor Realty Devel., Inc., 1959-76, pres., 1972-76, gen. ptnr., 1976—; gen. ptnr. Prospect Hill Exec. Office Park, 1977—; dir. Internat. Data Group, Inc. Pres., trustee Tech. Edn. Research Centers, Inc., 1965—; trustee Winsor Sch., Boston, 1978—, treas., 1978-82; bd. dirs. Charles River Mus. Industry, Boston, 1986—. Served to lt. USNR, 1944-46. Mem. Am., Mass., Boston Bar Assn., Boston Computer Soc. (bd. dirs. 1985—), Greater Boston C. of C., Harvard Club (Boston), Beta Theta Pi, Phi Beta Kappa, Sigma Xi. Home: 75 Robin Rd Weston MA 02193 Office: Internat Rsch Inc 200 5th Ave Waltham MA 02154

NELSON, BARBARA MAE, bank executive; b. Milw., Nov. 23, 1934; d. Edwin Raymond and Agnes Josephine (Bethke) N. BS, Marquette U., 1956; grad. Bank Adminstrn. Inst., U. Wis., 1984. With First Wis. Nat. Bank, Milw., 1956-78, acctg. officer, 1975-78; sr. auditor First Wis. Corp., Milw., 1979-82, audit officer, 1983-84; asst. v.p. bank auditing Firstar Corp. (formerly First Wis. Corp.), Milw., 1984—. Mem. Nat. Assn. Bank Women, Nat. Assn. Chartered Bank Auditors, Nat. Assn. Cert. Trust Auditors. Roman Catholic. Office: Firstar Corp 777 E Wisconsin Ave Milwaukee WI 53202

NELSON, BRUCE SHERMAN, advertising agency executive; b. Lansing, Mich., Nov. 3, 1951; s. Max and Blanche (Sherman) N.; m. Minette Raskin; 1 child, Henry Reed. AB, UCLA, 1973. Sr. copywriter Ogilvy & Mather, Los Angeles, 1977-78, Young & Rubicam, N.Y.C., 1978-79; assoc. creative dir. McCann Erickson, Inc., N.Y.C., 1979-80, v.p., 1980-81, sr. v.p., 1981-83, exec. v.p., creative dir., 1983-86, sr. v.p. worldwide, dir. strategic creative devel., 1987—; founder, chief exec. officer Ira Madris, Bruce Nelson & Colleagues, 1986-87. Office: McCann-Erickson Worldwide 750 3d Ave New York NY 10017

NELSON, CHARLES ROBERT, financial planner; b. Philippines, Jan. 14, 1930; m. Beverly Ann Nelson, May 17, 1980. V.p., mgr. Paine Webber Jackson and Curtis, Newport Beach, Calif., 1972-73, Bache Halsey Stuart, Tucson, 1973-77; owner, mgr. King Of The North, Irvine, Calif., 1978-84; owner, mgr. Nelson Fin., Laguna Hills, Calif., 1983-84; gen. mgr. First Liberty Securities, Carlsbad, Calif., 1984-86; sr. ptnr. Nelson Fin. Assocs., Laguna Niguel, Calif., 1986—. Mem. planning adv. com. Orange County Hosp., 1979; bd. dirs., v.p. Palm Desert Resort Country Club Homeowner's Assn., 1982-83; mem. bd. mgrs. South Coast YMCA, 1988; vol. bus editor Dana Point/Laguna Niguel News. Mem. Internat. Assn. Fin. Planners, Alpha Delta Phi. Club: Marbella Country (San Juan Capistrano, Calif.). Lodge: Rotary. Office: Nelson Fin Assocs 27782 El Lazo Ste B Laguna Niguel CA 92677

NELSON, DAVID CHARLES, department store executive; b. St. Cloud, Minn., July 25, 1949; s. Rudolph B. and Ethel J. (Mattson) N.; m. Lori Ann Johnson, June 19, 1982; children: Matthew, Berit Elaine. BA, Macalaster Coll., 1971; MBA, Columbia U., 1975. Product devel. analyst Ford Motor Co., Dearborn, Mich., 1975-77; fin. analyst Dayton Hudson Corp., Mpls., 1977-78, dir. credit analysis, 1983-84, dir. fin. planning, 1984—; mgr. gross margin control Hudson's Dept. Store Co., Detroit, 1979, dir. fin. planning, 1980, gen. mgr. credit, 1981, div. v.p. Broadway Dept. Stores, L.A., 1981-83. Mem. Twin Cities Treas. Assn. Served to 1st lt. U.S. Army, 1971-74. Republican. Mem. Congregationalist Ch. Home: 5613 Heather Ln Edina MN 55436 Office: Dayton Hudson Corp 777 Nicollet Mall Minneapolis MN 55402

NELSON, DAVID LEONARD, process management systems company executive; b. Omaha, May 8, 1930; s. Leonard A. and Cecelia (Steinert) N.; m. Jacqueline J. Zerbe, Dec. 26, 1952; children: David John (dec.), Nancy Jo. BS, Iowa State U., 1952. Mktg. adminstr. Ingersoll Rand, Chgo., 1954-56; with Accuray Corp., Columbus, Ohio, 1956—, exec. v.p., gen. mgr., 1967, pres., 1967-87, chief exec. officer, 1970-87; pres. process automation bus. unit Combustion Engring., Inc., Columbus, 1987—; bd. dirs. Herman Miller Inc. Patentee in field. Bd. dirs. Cardinal Fund, Columbus, Cardinal Govt. Securities Trust, Columbus, Cardinal Tax Exempt Money Trust, Columbus, Cardinal Govt. Guaranteed Fund, Columbus. Served to capt. USMCR, 1952-54. Mem. IEEE, Instrument Soc. Am., Newcomen Soc. N.Am., Tau Beta Pi, Phi Kappa Phi, Phi Eta Sigma, Delta Upsilon. Office: Combustion Engring Inc 650 Ackerman Rd PO Box 02248 Columbus OH 43202

NELSON, DAVID WILLIAM, industrial executive; b. Jackson, Mich., Dec. 24, 1949; s. William Arnum and Jananne Adele (Moss) N.; m. Carolyn Guiver, Aug. 13, 1977; children: Michelle Ann, Michael Ray, Keri Jo. BS in Indsl. Engring., U. Mich., 1972. Engr., mgr. Envirotech Corp., Salt Lake City, 1973-79; mgr. engring. Eaton-Kenway, Salt Lake City, 1979-83, product mgr., 1983-84; v.p. Barrett Electronics Corp., Northbrook, Ill., 1984-85, Mannesmann Demag Corp., Grand Rapids, Mich., 1985—; cons., Salt Lake City, 1976-83. Contbr. articles to profl. jours. Fellow Am. Prodn. and Inventory Control Soc. (chpt. pres. 1980-81); mem. Inst. Indsl. Engrs., Am. Mgmt. Assn., Material Handling Inst. (subcom. chmn. 1987—), Green Ridge Club (Grand Rapids). Mormon. Office: Mannesmann Demag Corp 2660 28th St SE Grand Rapids MI 49512

NELSON, GARRETT R., retail food company executive. Sr. v.p., chief fin. officer The Vons Cos. Inc., until 1987, exec. v.p. retail support group, 1987—. Office: Vons Grocery Co 10150 Lower Azusa Rd El Monte CA 91731 *

NELSON, GORDON LEIGH, chemist, educator; b. Palo Alto, Calif., May 27, 1943; s. Nels Folke and Alice Virginia (Fredrickson) N. BS in Chemistry, U. Nev., 1965; MS, Yale U., 1967, PhD, 1970. Staff research chemist corp. research and devel. Gen. Electric Co., Schenectady, N.Y., 1970-74; mgr. combustibility tech. plastics div. Gen. Electric Co., Pittsfield, Mass., 1974-79, mgr. environ. protection plastics div., 1979-82; v.p. materials sci. and tech. Springborn Labs. Inc., Enfield, Conn., 1982-83; prof., chmn. dept. polymer sci. U. So. Miss., Hattiesburg, 1983—; cons. in field. Author: Carbon-13 Nuclear Magnetic Resonance For Organic Chemists, 1972; editor books on coatings sci. tech.; contbr. articles to profl. jours. Mem. Am. Inst. of Chemists, Soc. Plastics Engrs., Am. Chem. Soc. (pres. 1988, bd. dirs. 1977-85, 87-89, Henry Hill award 1986), Computer and Bus. Equipment Mfrs. Assn. (chmn. Plastics Task Group), ASTM (E5 cert. of appreciation 1985), So. Soc. for Coatings Technology, Nat. Fire Protection Assn., IEC (U.S. tech. adv. group on info. processing equipment), Structural Plastics div. Soc. of the Plastics Industry (mem. exec. com., chmn. combustibility com., Man of Yr. 1979), Miss. Acad. Scis., Yale Chemists Assn. (pres. 1981—), Nev. Hist. Soc., Sigma Xi. Republican. Presbyterian. Office: U So Miss Dept Polymer Sci Southern Station Box 10063 Hattiesburg MS 39406-0063

NELSON, HEDWIG POTOK, financial executive; b. Detroit, Oct. 6, 1954; m. Richard Alan Nelson. BA with honors, U. Mich., 1976; MBA, Am. U., 1980. Fin. asst. antitrust div. U.S. Dept. Justice, Washington, 1979-80; fin. analyst corp. treasury Martin Marietta Corp., Bethesda, Md., 1980-81, fin. adminstr. aggregates div., 1981-83, sr. fin. adminstr. bus. devel. data systems div., 1983, mgr. fin. planning and analysis, 1983-85; mgr. mergers and acquistions M/A-COM Devel. Corp., Rockville, Md., 1985-87; fin. and investment advisor, small bus. cons. Fulton, Lauroesch and Assocs., Bethesda, 1987-88; sr. analyst group fin. Marriott Corp., Bethesda, 1988-89, mgr. fin. planning, 1989—. Mem. Internat. Assn. Fin. Planners, Nat. Assn. Female Execs. (treas. Montgomery County chpt. 1987-88), Nat. Women's Econ. Alliance, Bethesda/Chevy Chase C. of C. Home: 4601 N Park Ave #319 Chevy Chase MD 20815 Office: Marriott Corp One Marriott Dr Washington DC 20058

NELSON, JOHN MARSHALL, publishing executive; b. Madison, Wis., Oct. 28, 1941; s. Russell Arthur and Dorothea (Smith) N.; m. Linda Taylor, Oct. 13, 1962 (div. June 1968); children: Ann, David; m. Katherine Dianne Hoagland, Sept. 24, 1972; children: James, George. AB, Harvard U., 1963; MD, Case Western Reserve U., 1967; MBA, U. Chgo., 1983. Diplomate Am. Bd. Internal Medicine. Staff assoc. NIH, Bethesda, Md., 1968-71; rsch. assoc., asst. prof. medicinePromis Lab. Med. Sch. Univ. Vt., 1973-76; med. dir. Madison Gen. Hosp., 1976-84; assoc. clin. prof. Med. Sch. U. Wis., 1976-84; v.p. corp. med. affairs Gen. Health Mgmt. Co., Madison, 1984-86; dir. med. and ednl. affairs Washington Hosp. Ctr., 1986-87; pres. Nelson Info. Systems, Bethesda, Md., 1987—; cons. Med. Sch. U. Utah, Salt Lake City, 1985-86. Contbr. articles to profl. jour. Coach youth soccer, 1984-85; merit badge counselor Boy Scouts Am., 1987; mem. Harvard Schs. Com., Md., 1988—; vestry St. John's Episcopal Ch., Bethesda, 1988—. Harvard Hon. Nat. Scholar, 1959-62; recipient Stewer Meml. award Case Western Reserve U., Cleve., 1967. Fellow Am. Coll. Physicians, Am. Coll. Physician Execs.; mem. AMA, Am. Hosp. Assn., Rotary (Washington, polio plus com.), Univ. Club Chgo., Alpha Omega Alpha. Republican. Episcopalian. Home and Office: 6616 Millwood Rd Bethesda MD 20817

NELSON, JOHN MARTIN, corporate executive; b. N.Y.C., Aug. 9, 1931; s. Martin H. and Margaret (Larkin) N.; divorced; children: Murrey E., Christopher L. A.B., Wesleyan U., 1953; M.B.A., Harvard U., 1959. With Norton Co., Worcester, Mass., 1959—, v.p. abrasive ops., 1971-78; pres., chief exec. officer Norton Christensen Inc. subs. Norton Co., Salt Lake City, 1978-86; pres., chief operating officer Norton Co., Worcester, 1986-87, chmn., chief exec. officer, 1988—; dir. Brown & Sharpe Mfg. Co., North Kingstown, R.I., Cambridge BioScience, Worcester, Mass. Trustee Wesleyan U., 1978-81, Worcester Poly. Inst., 1986—, Worcester Art Mus., 1989—. Lt. (j.g.) USN, 1953-56. Home: 727 Salisbury St #424 Worcester MA 01609 Office: Norton Co 120 Front St Ste 800 Worcester MA 01608

NELSON, JOHN MICHAEL, entrepreneur; b. Rice Lake, Wis., Jan. 29, 1941; s. Lloyd Franklin and Maxine Rae (Petersen) N.; m. Natalie Sheryll Fornell, June 5, 1965; children: Laura, Karl, Heather, Susana, Claudinei, Claudia, Adriano, Alessandra. BS in Tech. Agr., Wis. State U., Platteville, 1970; MS in Audio-Visual Communication, Wis. State U., Menomonie, 1976. Started or bought and re-organized 15 bus. since 1966, currently mng. 3. Mem. adminstrn. com. Oak Hills Fellowship and Coll.; bd. dirs. Masters Mgmt. Services. Served with USN, 1962-66, Mediterranean. Mem. AIM (bd. dirs.). Republican. Mem. Evangelical Ch. Office: Specialty Contracting Rte 1 PO Box 204 Guthrie MN 56461

NELSON, JOHN P., accountant, consultant; b. Ogden, Utah, June 1, 1932; s. John W. and Fern Pardoe N.; m. Shirley M. Parker, May 18, 1952 (div. 1984); m. Alice M. Rindlisbacher, Setp. 13, 1986; children: Julie Ann Owens, Daivd Bradley. MS in Mgmt., Am. Coll., 1986. Staff acct. William E. Mickey, CPA, Bakersfield, Calif., 1955-57; asst. chief acct. Kern County Land Co., Bakersfield, 1957-64; contr. Transonic, Inc., Bakersfield, 1964; office mgr. Carnation Co., Bakersfield, 1964-69; sr. acct. Contel Svc. Corp., Bakersfield, 1970-78; project mgr. Contel Svc. Corp., 1978-80, sr. tax acct., 1980-84, tax mgr., 1984—. Precinct worker Rep. Cen. Com. Bakersfield, 1970. With U.S. Army, 1952-54, Korea. Mem. Na.t Soc. of Pub. Accts., Nat. Assn. of Accts. (pres. 1977-78, bd. dirs. 1974-88, Most Valuable Mem. 1978), Accreditation Coun. for Accountancy. Republican. Mormon. Home: 11350 Foothill Blvd #5 Lakeview Terrace CA 91342

NELSON, JOHN WALTER, JR., diversified company executive; b. N.Y.C., Sept. 29, 1923; s. John Walter and Anna Victoria (Hanson) N.; B.Ch.E., Bklyn. Poly. Inst., 1950; m. Marie J. Hornberger, Nov. 25, 1950; children—Nancy Ann, John Walter III. Mfg. engr. Nat. Starch Co., N.Y.C., 1948-54; div. engring. head Liberty Products, Farmingdale, N.Y., 1954-57; sr. product engr. Sonotone Corp., Cold Spring, N.Y., 1957-63; asst. v.p. Chemprene div. Chem. Rubber Products, Beacon, N.Y., 1963-65; dir. pub. works, Poughkeepsie, N.Y., 1965-72; dir. Richard Solomon Assos., Wappinger Falls, N.Y., 1972-79; cons. in engring. and mgmt., 1977—. Committeeman, counselor, treas., dist. commr., dist. chmn., exec. com., mem. exec. bd. Dutchess County council Boy Scouts Am., 1971—; cons. Girl Scouts Dutchess County, N.Y., 1969-71; bd. dirs. Stony Kill Found., 1980—. Served with USNR, 1942-46. Recipient Nat. Leadership award Am. City Mag., 1966. Mem. Forest Products Research Soc., Am. Pub. Works Assn. (exec. com. 1965—, Dutchess County Water Operators (bd. dirs.), dir. sch. edn. 1970—, pres. Mid Hudson br. 1972—), Hist. Soc. Stony Creek. Lutheran (pres., founder, trustee). Clubs: Chelsea (N.Y.) Yacht (trustee); Stonycreek (N.Y.) Rod and Gun. Editor Polytechnic Reporter, Bklyn., 1941-43; edit. writer Naval Bur. Personnel Mag., 1943-48; contbr. Forest Products Research Publ., 1948-54. Contbr. articles Am. City Mag., 1965—. Home and Office: Sky Top Dr Chelsea NY 12512

NELSON, JONATHAN BRENT, investment executive; b. Ridgewood, N.J., May 6, 1966; s. David Allen and Patricia Ann (Larson) N. Student, Parkland Coll., 1983-86, Wartburg Coll., 1987—. Pres. Nelson Fin. Services, Champaign, Ill., 1981-86; chmn., pres. Nelson Investments, Champaign, 1986-87; pres. First Realty Capital, Waverly, Iowa, 1988—. Charter mem. Rep. Presdl. Task Force, Washington, 1984; mem. Rep. Nat. Com., Washington, 1984, U.S. Senatorial Club, Washington, 1985. Mem. Urban Land Inst., Assn. Collegiate Entrepreneurs. Republican. Lutheran. Office: 203 Brown Ln Waverly IA 50677

NELSON, JULIUS, publisher; b. Minsk, Russia, Aug. 15, 1910; s. Abraham and Temme Dolores (Solow) N.; B.S., Indiana U. of Pa., 1932; M.A., Columbia U., 1940; m. Goldie Goldstein, Aug. 1, 1942; children—Temma Nelson Rubin, Abra Nelson Goldfarb. Tchr., Windber (Pa.) High Sch., 1932-42; field tax investigator IRS, 1943-47; instr. bus. edn. N.J. State Tchrs. Coll., Paterson, 1947-49, U. Balt., 1949-52; specialist in higher edn. U.S. Office Edn., Washington, 1953-54; pres., chmn. bd. Artistic Typing Hdqtrs. Inc., Balt., 1972—; lectr. in field; fin. analyst Growth Assocs., 1987—. Bd. dirs. Hebrew Sunday Schs., Windber, 1932-41; v.p. Randallstown (Md.) Synagogue Center, 1963-64, bd. dirs. synagogues, 1961—; sponsor Nat. Typing Championships, 1963—. Recipient Outstanding achievement award Md. Vocat. Assn., 1970; charter mem. Exec. and Profl. Hall of Fame; named to Windber Hall of Fame, 1980. Mem. Eastern, Nat. bus. tchrs. assns., Nat. Profl. Secs. Assn. (co-founder 1951), Alpha Phi Gamma, Gamma Rho Tau, Phi Delta Kappa, Pi Omega Pi. Jewish. Mason. Author numerous books on typewriting, including keyboard instruction, accuracy building, speed building, and ornamentation; designer instructional aids to develop proficiency in shorthand and accounting; appeared in film Unusual Occupations, 1941. Home and Office: 3200 Southgreen Rd Baltimore MD 21207

NELSON, LEONARD EARL, investment executive; b. Duluth, Minn., Mar. 6, 1944; s. Bernard Julius and Anne Mae (Brozic) N. Student, U. Minn., 1963-67, Acad. Vocal Arts, Phila., 1969-72, NYU, 1975. V.p. Jageson Assocs., N.Y.C., 1974-81; stockbroker WH Newbold's Son & Co. Inc., Phila., 1981-83; asst. v.p. Butcher & Singer, Phila., 1983-86; v.p. 1st of Phila. Investment Group, 1986—. Soloist 1st Presbyn. Ch., Germantown, Pa., 1981-88; mem. 1st Presbyn. Ch. Phila. Mem. Phila. Securities Assn., Stone Harbor Country Club, Northland Country Club, Old York Rd. Country Club, Lulu Country Club. Republican. Home: 1504 The Kenilworth 2979 School House Ln Philadelphia PA 19144 Office: First Phila Investment Group 2009 Chestnut St Philadelphia PA 19103

NELSON, MAGNUS CHARLES, accountant, former bank executive; b. Richfield, Utah, Dec. 23, 1938; s. Duane Miller and Naomi (Horne) N.; m. Marilyn Kaye Haynie, Mar. 17, 1962; children: Michael D., Thea T., Kristin Nelson Strobelt, Camilla T. Nelson Entote, John D. BS in Acctg., U. Utah, 1962. CPA, Utah; chartered bank auditor. Ptnr. Ernst & Whinney, Winston-Salem, N.C., 1963-84, 86—; sr. v.p., dir. control services BankAm. Corp., San Francisco, 1984-86. Co-author: Implementing Mergers and Acquisitions in the Financial Services Industry, 1985. Treas., bd. dirs. Southeastern Ctr. for Contemporary Art, 1986—; regional chmn. Young Reps., Anchorage, 1966; scoutmaster Boy Scouts Am., 1977-78. Served with USAR, 1960-61. Mem. Am. Inst. CPAs (banking com. 1980-83), Utah Assn. CPAs, Bank Adminstrn. Inst. (CPA advisor audit commn. 1976-79, bd. regents 1982-85). Mormon. Club: Piedmont (Winston-Salem). Office: 2000 Wachovia Bldg Winston-Salem NC 27111

NELSON, MARVIN RAY, life insurance company executive; b. Thornton, Iowa, Aug. 29, 1926; s. Clarence Anton and Rose Bessie (Nicolet) N.; m. Juanita Mae Brown, May 26, 1951; children: Nancy, Kenneth. BS, Drake U, 1951. Actuary Security Mut. Life Ins. Co., Lincoln, Nebr., 1951-58; assoc. actuary Life Ins. Co. N.Am., Phila., 1958-59; group actuary Bankers Life of Nebr., Lincoln, 1959-66; actuary Mut. Service Life Ins. Co., St. Paul, 1966-68; sr. v.p. Horace Mann Educators Corp., Springfield, Ill., 1968-77; sr. v.p. Security Life of Denver, 1977-83, exec. v.p., 1988—; pres., chief oper. officer, dir., mem. investment com. Midwestern United Life Ins. Co., Denver, 1983—. Bd. dirs., treas. Ft. Wayne Urban League, 1983-87; bd. dirs. Taxpayers Research Assn., Ft. Wayne, 1984-88. Served with U.S. Army, 1946-47. Fellow Soc. Actuaries; mem. Am. Acad. Actuaries, Phi Kappa Phi. Home: 7636 Windford Parker CO 80134 Office: Security Life of Denver Ins Co 1290 Broadway Denver CO 80203

NELSON, MERLIN EDWARD, international business consultant, company director; b. Fargo, N.D., Jan. 30, 1922; s. Theodore G. and Eva C. (Hultgren) N.; m. Nancy Ellen Craig, June 1952 (div. June 1962); children: Craig Edward, Brian Anthony; m. Janet April Pope, Aug. 30, 1963; children: Claudia Jane, Rolf Merlin. BS in Polit. Sci., U. Oreg., 1943; postgrad., Fordham U., 1943-44; JD, Yale U., 1948. Bar: Oreg. 1948, N.Y. 1954, U.S. Dist. Ct. D.C. 1954. Atty. Office Gen. Counsel, ECA, Washington and Paris, 1949-52; assoc. Davis, Polk, Wardwell, Sunderland & Kiendl, 1952-59; exec. asst. to v.p. AMF, Inc., N.Y.C., 1960-62; chmn., mng. dir. AMF Internat., Ltd., London, 1962-63; v.p., group exec. AMF, Inc., 1963-70, exec. v.p., vice chmn., 1970-84, now cons., 1984—; ret. 1984; dir. Avon Products, Inc., Indsl. Bank of Japan Trust Co., Am. Crown Life Ins. Co., Derby Internat. Corp., S.A.; cons. Wyndham Estate Wines Ltd., Australia, Byvest Mgmt. Buyout Group, Sydney, Australia, Mitsui & Co. (USA) Inc. Bd. dirs. AIESEC/USA; mem. Council Fgn. Relations, Overseas Devel. Council. Served with U.S. Army, 1943-45, ETO. Decorated Purple Heart. Home and Office: 215 E 72d St New York NY 10021

NELSON, PAUL JAMES, educator; b. Porter, Ind., Dec. 1, 1932; s. Forrest Ross and Bessie Marie (Kline) N.; m. Judith Ann Benda, Feb. 14, 1956; children: Douglas Ross, Paula Ann, Daniel Forrest. Grad. high sch., Chesterton, Ind. Lic. comml. pilot; cert. tchr., Ind. With U.S. Steel Co., Gary, Ind., 1951-54, 59-83; pilot, instr. Phillips Airlines, Michigan City, Ind., 1983-85; tchr. Gary Community Sch. Corp., 1985—. Author: (text book) Machinist Study Guides, 1980. Trustee Town of Pines, 1970; pres. Pines Planning Commn., Ind., 1973, Pines Bd. Zoning Appeals, 1978; mem. Ind. Dunes Nat. Lakeshore Task Forces, 1980, Gary Regional Airport Task Force, 1988; cert., airlift vol. Am. Cancer Soc., 1981. With USAF, 1954-56. Democrat. Home: 1545 Ash St The Pines Michigan City IN 46360 Office: Gary Career Ctr 1800 E 35th Ave Gary IN 46409

NELSON, PETER ALAN, marketing executive; b. Oak Park, Ill., July 11, 1932; s. Theodore Martin and Katharine (Child) N.; m. Peggy Ann Amaden, June 24, 1960; 1 child, Charles. AB, Monmouth Coll., 1954. With Needham, Harper & Steer, Chgo., 1956-84, exec. v.p., 1976-82, fin. and adminstrv. officer, 1980-82, also bd. dirs., pres., chief operating officer, 1982-84; sr. v.p. McDonald's Corp., 1984—; bd. dirs. Del E. Webb Corp. Served with U.S. Army, 1954-56. Mem. Barrington Hills Country Club, Lake Zurich Golf Club. Republican. Methodist. Home: 823 Dormy Ln Barrington IL 60010 Office: McDonald's Corp Kroc Dr Oak Brook IL 60521

NELSON, RICHARD BURTON, patent consultant; b. Powell, Wyo., Dec. 10, 1911; s. Severt A. and Sedona Lenora (Fesenbeck) N.; m. Maxine Caroline George, Feb. 25, 1950 (div. June 1963); 1 child, Anna Afton Ghandour; m. Pauline Wright, Dec. 29, 1969. Student, San Diego State Coll., 1930-32; BS in Physics with honors, Calif. Inst. Tech., 1935; PhD, MIT, 1938. Registered patent agt. Physicist R.C.A. Mfg. Co., Harrison, N.J., 1938-41, Nat. Research Council, Ottawa, Ont., Can., 1941-42; research assoc. G.E. Research Lab., Schenectady, 1942-50; div. mgr. Varian Assocs., Palo Alto, Calif., 1960-63, chief engr., 1963-74, patent agt., 1974-77, cons., 1977—; bd. dirs. 1st Nat. Bank, Powell, Lovell (Wyo.) Nat. Bank, 1st Co., Powell. Author of numerous tech. papers; patentee in field. Fellow IEEE; mem. N.W. Wyo. Community Coll. Assocs. Club: Los Altos Golf and Country. Home and Office: 27040 Dezahara Way Los Altos Hills CA 94022

NELSON, RICHARD HENRY, manufacturing company executive; b. Norfolk, Va., May 24, 1939; s. Irvin Joseph and Ethel Blair (Levy) N.; m. Carole Ellen Rosen, Mar. 12, 1966; children: Christopher, Karin. BA, Princeton U., 1961; postgrad., Georgetown U. Sch. Law, 1962-63. Spl. asst. to dir. Peace Corps, Washington, 1961-62; mil. aide to v.p. Office of U.S. V.p., Washington, 1962-63; asst. to U.S. Pres. White House, Washington, 1963-66; spl. asst. to sec. HUD, Washington, 1966-68; v.p. Am. Internat. Bank, N.Y.C., 1968-70, Studebaker-Worthington, N.Y.C., 1970-73; pres. Sartex Corp., N.Y.C., 1973-80; pres., chief exec. officer Cogenic, Inc., N.Y.C., 1980—; bd. dirs. Nelco Corp., Laurel, Md.; pres. 910 Park Ave, Inc., N.Y.C., 1980—; chmn. bd. Utility Systems Corp., N.Y.C., 1983—, Powersave Inc., N.Y.C., 1984—. Bd. dirs. Nat. Hypertension Assn., N.Y.C., 1982—; exec. com. Southampton Assn., N.Y., 1983—; advisor to mayor Historic Preservation Com., Southampton, 1986—; prin. Ctr. Excellence in Govt., Washington, 1987—. Served to 1st lt. U.S. Army, 1962-64. Recipient Presdl. Medal Office of Pres. of U.S., 1965. Mem. Internat. Cogeneration Assn., Am. Gas Assn., Am. Cogeneration Coalition, Ind. Power Producers. Democrat. Clubs: Princeton, Doubles (N.Y.C.). Home: 910 Park Ave New York NY 10021 Office: Cogenic Inc 76 Madison Ave New York NY 10016

NELSON, RICHARD HENRY, manufacturing executive; b. Medford, Wis., Feb. 7, 1952; s. Charles Henry and Ruth Ann (Blake) N. BS in Elec. amd Computer Engring. with honors, U. Wis., 1974. Design engr. Tracor No., Madison, Wis., 1974-78; application engr. Nicolet Instrument, Madison, 1978-82; product mgr. Nicolet Biomedical, Madison, 1982-83, internat. tech. support mgr., 1983-87, internat. mgr., 1987—. Mem. IEEE, Madison Internat. Trade Assn., Eta Kappa Nu (v.p. Madison chpt. 1973-74). Republican. Roman Catholic. Home: PO Box 9908 Madison WI 53713 Office: Nicolet Biomedical 5225 Verona Rd Madison WI 53711

NELSON, ROBERT EARL, JR., financial services company executive; b. Mobile, Ala., May 15, 1938; s. Robert Earl Sr. and Frances Lucille (Till) N.; m. Sandra Anne Berry, Aug. 3, 1964; children: Robin Lynne, Robert Earl III, Patricia Anne. BS in Indsl. Mgmt., Ga. Inst. Tech., 1960; MBA, U. Ala., 1963. CPA, Ga., N.Y. Gen. mgmt. trainee Borg Warner Corp., Chgo., 1963-65; mgr., mgmt. cons. Peat, Marwick, & Mitchell, Atlanta, 1965-71; corp. controller VF Corp., Reading, Pa., 1971-73; ptnr., mgmt. services Arthur Young & Co., N.Y.C., 1973-81; sr. v.p. Cable Am. Inc., Atlanta, 1981-84; exec. v.p., chief ops. officer Kroh Bros. Devel. Co., Kansas City, Mo., 1984-87; chief exec. officer Nelson & Co., Atlanta, 1987—. Contbr. articles to profl. jours. Served to 1st lt. USMC, 1960-62. Mem. Am. Inst. CPA's, Am. Inst. Indsl. Engrs., Fin. Execs. Inst., Whitney Mus. (mem. Whitney Cir., 1989). Republican. Episcopalian. Clubs: Union League (N.Y.C.); New Canaan Field (bd. govs. 1979-81); Carriage (Kansas City). Home: 5100 Jett Forest Trail NW Atlanta GA 30327 Office: Nelson & Co 100 Galleria Pkwy Ste 400 Atlanta GA 30339

NELSON, ROBERT JOHN, publisher; b. Cumberland, Wis., Apr. 5, 1926; s. Arthur N. and Alma O. (Johnson) N.; m. Constance Joan Wollan, Sept. 24, 1955 (div. 1970); children: Kevin, Pamela, Cynthia. BA cum laude, U. Minn., 1949. Section mgr. Powers Dept. Store, Mpls., 1950-51; agt. Res. Life Ins. Co., Mpls., 1951-52; rep., editor James C. Fifield Co., Mpls., 1952-67; founder, owner The Nelson Co., Hopkins, Minn., 1967—. Editor, publisher: Nelson's Law Office Directory, 1967—. Served with USAAF, 1944-

45. Republican. Lutheran. Home: 5300 Vernon Ave Edina MN 55436 Office: The Nelson Co PO Box 309 Hopkins MN 55343

NELSON, ROGER DUANE, management specialist; b. Stockton, Calif., July 5, 1957; s. Bruce Ellis and Barbara Jean (Ellis) N. Security specialist, supr. various cos., 1979-85; ops. supr. Sun Microsystems, Mountain View, Calif., 1986—. Office: Sun Microsystems 2550 Garcia Ave Ste M2-39 Mountain View CA 94043

NELSON, VITA JOY, editor, publisher; b. N.Y.C., Dec. 9, 1937; d. Leon Abraham and Bertha (Sher) Reiner; m. Lester Nelson, Aug. 27, 1961; children: Lee Reiner, Clifford Samuel, Cara Ritchie. BA, Boston U., 1959. Promotion copywriter Street & Smith, N.Y.C., 1958-59; asst. to mng. editor Mademoiselle Mag., N.Y.C., 1959-60; mcpl. bond trader Granger & Co., N.Y.C., 1960-63; founder, editor, publisher Westchester Mag., Mamaroneck, N.Y., 1968-80, L.I. Mag., 1973-78, Moneypaper, Larchmont, N.Y., 1981—. Bd. dirs. Westchester Tourism Council, Westchester County, N.Y., 1974-75, Sackerpath council Girl Scouts U.S.A., White Plains, N.Y., 1976-79; bd. govs. v.p. Am. Jewish Com., Westchester, N.Y., 1979—. Recipient citation Council Arts, 1972; Media award Pub. Relations Soc. Am., 1974. Mem. Women in Communications (Outstanding Communicator award 1983), Sigma Delta Chi. Democrat. Home: Pleasant Ridge Rd Harrison NY 10528 Office: Temper of the Times Communications 930 Mamaroneck Ave Mamaroneck NY 10543

NELSON, WANDA LOUISE KOESTER, controller, consultant; b. Cin., Oct. 8, 1949; d. Louis Charles and Bertha O'Delle (St. Clair) Chretien; m. John Wesley Nelson Jr., Jan. 23, 1971 (div. Apr. 1979). AA in Acctg., Coll. of DuPage, Glen Ellyn, Ill., 1976; BA in Acctg., Aurora (Ill.) U., 1980, MS in Bus. Mgmt., 1983. Statis. clk. David J. Joseph Co., Cin., 1968-71; acctg. clk. Vulcan Materials, Countryside, Ill., 1971-72; supr. accounts payable C.G. Conn, Ltd., Oak Brook, Ill., 1972-77; mgr. acctg. office Authentic Furniture Products, Aurora, 1977; acct. Wil-Fred's, Inc., Naperville, Ill., 1977-78, supr. acctg., 1978-80; cost acct. Alcan Ingot & Powders, Joliet, Ill., 1981-83; controller Ingersoll-Rand, Naperville, 1983-87, Carol Stream, Ill., 1987—; computer cons. Kupco Constrn. Co., Houston and Miami, Fla., 1983—. Treas. Pebblewood Home Owners Assn., Naperville, 1974-75, bd. dirs., 1973-74. Named one of Outstanding Young Women of Am., 1982. Mem. Nat. Assn. Female Execs., NOW. Democrat. Methodist. Home: 9 Pebblewood Tr Naperville IL 60540 Office: Ingersoll-Rand Co 125 Tubeway Dr Carol Stream IL 60188

NELSON, WARREN BRYANT, commodity brokerage executive; b. Manhattan, Kans., Sept. 29, 1922; s. Oscar William and Eda Caroline (Hokanson) N.; BS cum laude in Agrl. Econs., Kans. State U., 1942, postgrad., 1950; postgrad. Am. U., 1947; m. Betty Lou Wiley, Dec. 24, 1944; children—Barbara Ann, David William, Marcia Lynn, Robert Warren. Statistician agrl. div. Bur. Census, U.S. Dept. Commerce, Washington, 1945-48, Statis. Reporting Svc., U.S. Dept. Agr., Topeka, 1948-50; price analyst Longstreet Abbott & Co., St. Louis, 1951-59, ptnr., 1959-69; sec. Clayton Brokerage Co., St. Louis, 1959-69, exec. v.p., 1969-72, pres., 1972-77, vice-chmn. bd., 1977-86, chmn. bd. 1986—. Lt. USAAF, 1942-45. Decorated D.F.C. with 2 oak leaf clusters. Republican. Club: St. Louis. Home: 839 Elm Tree Ln Kirkwood MO 63122 Office: 77 W Port Pla Ste 459 Saint Louis MO 63146

NELSON, WILLIAM BRUCE, newspaper company executive; b. Mpls., July 13, 1950; s. William Harry and Marian (Anderson) N.; m. Sherry Graham, Dec. 28, 1974; children—Timothy, Jeffrey, Michael. B.S. in Indsl. Engring., Northwestern U., M.B.A. in Mgmt. Loan rep. 1st Nat. Bank Chgo., 1975-77; fin. analyst Tribune Co., 1977-78, mgr. fin. planning, 1978-79; dir. fin. planning Chgo. Tribune Co., 1979-82, v.p., chief fin. officer, 1982—. Mem. Inst. Newspaper Fin. Execs. Office: Chgo Tribune Co 435 N Michigan Ave Chicago IL 60611

NELSON, WILLIAM CURTIS, banker; b. Cin., Apr. 17, 1937; s. Curtis Clinton and Mary Elizabeth (Sloan) N.; m. Barbara Ann Koval, Aug. 12, 1972; children—Christopher Curtis, Jonathan Graham, David Sloan. B.A., Yale U., 1959; postgrad., U. Pitts. Grad. Sch. Bus., 1961-63. Vice-pres., gen. mgr. Mellon Bank, London, 1971-75; v.p. Internat. Mellon Bank, Pitts., 1975-80; sr. v.p. community banking Mellon Bank, Pitts., 1980-83; exec. v.p. personal fin. services InterFirst Bank, Dallas, 1983-87; exec. dir. gen. banking First Republic Bank Corp. (formerly InterFirst Bank Dallas and RepublicBank Dallas), 1987-88; pres. Boatmen's First Nat. Bank Kansas City, 1988—, also bd. dirs.; dir. Boatmen's Bank of Del., 1988; chmn. Am. Banks Assn., London, 1974; bd. dirs. Rsch. Med. Ctr., Mo. Repertory Theatre, Boatmen's Trust Co. Kansas City, Rsch. Med. Ctr., Mo. Repertory Theatre, Boatmen's Trust Co. of Kansas City; pres., chief exec. officer Boatmen's First Nat. Bank Kansas City, 1989. Chmn. Woolworth Soc. City of London, 1973; pres. Children's Mus., Pitts., 1982-83, Pitts. Dance Council, 1983; trustee Dallas Ballet, 1984—; mem. bus. adv. council U. Tex.-Arlington, 1984—. Served with U.S. Army, 1959-65. Mem. Am. Bankers Assn. (exec. com. 1984—), Consumer Bankers Assn. (bd. dirs. 1986—, edn. com. 1984—), Bus. Adv. Council U. Tex.-Dallas, Indian Hills Country Club, Kansas City Club, Duquesne Club, Pitts. Golf Club. Home: 6521 Wenonga Terr Mission Hills KS 66208 Office: Boatmen's 1st Nat Bank 14 W 10th St Kansas City MO 64105

NELSON, WILLIAM EDWARD, oil company executive; b. Kerens, Tex., Sept. 10, 1929; s. Joe Bailey and Vennie Aldora (Tramel) N.; m. Geraldine Lillian Sloier, July 19, 1954; children: Michael Edward, David Andrew. Student, Kilgore Jr. Coll., 1946-47; BSME, Tex. A&M U., 1951. Maintenance engr. Pan Am. Refining, Texas City, 1954-56; indsl. engr. Am. Oil Co., Texas City, 1956-61, supr. maintenance planning, 1961-65; supr. shop Amoco Oil Co., Texas City, 1965-71, mgr. materials, 1971-72, mgr. engring. services, 1972-73, mgr. maintenance services, 1973—. Contbr. articles to profl. jours.; patentee in field. Mem. adv. bd. Tex. A&M U. Turbomachinery Symposium, 1971-88, Tex. A&M U. Internat. Pump Users Symposium, College Station, 1982-83; commr., asst. scoutmaster Boy Scouts Am., Dickinson, Tex., 1962-76. Served to lt. USN, 1951-54. Mem. ASME (commendations 1979, 83, 84, 85, 86), Internat. Maintenance Inst. (commendation 1976), Vibration Inst. (commendations 1985, 87). Republican. Methodist. Home: 1201 Plantation Dr Dickinson TX 77539 Office: Amoco Oil Co 2401 5th Ave S Texas City TX 77590

NEMECEK, RICHARD THOMAS, sales executive; b. Cleve., Dec. 12, 1948; s. Fredrick F. and Elizabeth Helen (Novak) N.; m. Pauline Carmigiano, Aug. 21, 1971; children: Monica Elizabeth, Nicholas Richard. Student, U. Cin., 1967-68; BS, Ohio State U., 1972, postgrad., 1972-74. Meat mgr. Fisher Foods, Inc., Bedford Heights, Ohio, 1969-76; meat supr. S.M. Flickinger Co., Inc., Columbus, Ohio, 1976-78; ops. specialist Hannaford Bros. Co., Inc., Portland, Maine, 1978-82; cons. Mid-Atlantic div. Iowa Beef Processors Svc. Ctr., Fairfax, Va., 1982-85; pres. East Cent. div. Iowa Beef Processors Svc. Ctr., Columbus, 1985—. Republican. Roman Catholic. Office: IBP Svc Ctr Corp 304 Cramer Creek Ct Dublin OH 43017

NEMSHICK, RICHARD GEORGE, insurance company executive; b. Washington, Nov. 18, 1953; s. Joseph Richard and Josephine Agnes (White) N.; m. Mary Elaine Wornson, Feb. 13, 1982; 1 stepchild, Greg W. Steiner. BS in Quantitative Bus. Analysis, Pa. State U., 1975; postgrad., Boston U., 1976-77; cert. in gen. ins., Ins. Inst. Am., 1981. Office adminstrn. trainee Hartford Ins. Co., Cleve., 1977-78; asst. office adminstrv. mgr. Hartford Ins. Co., Omaha, 1978-79, Des Moines, 1979-80; systems analyst Hartford Ins. Co., Hartford, Conn., 1980-81; adminstrn. mgr. Transam., Hartford, 1981-83, Orion Group, West Hartford, Conn., 1983-84, Hanover Ins. Co., Kenner, La., 1984—. Vol. La. Spl. Olympics, 1987. With U.S. Army, 1975-77. Mem. Adminstrv. Mgmt. Soc. (pres. New Orleans chpt. 1987-88, merit award 1987), Ormond Civic Assn. Democrat. Office: Hanover Ins Co 2400 Veterans Blvd Ste 400 PO Box 1758 Kenner LA 70063

NERMAN, JEROME STANLEY, truck sales executive; b. Kansas City, Mo., Feb. 26, 1920; s. Gilbert and Esther (Jacobson) N.; m. Margaret Ann Rubin, Aug. 8, 1941; 1 son, Lewis E. Chmn. bd. Arrow Truck Sales Inc., Kansas City, 1950—; chmn. bd. dirs. Cen. Bank Kansas City; advisor Truck Blue Book, Chgo., 1979-84; v.p. Nationwide Auctions, Inc. Chmn. fund raising Kansas City Heart Assn., 1979-81; mem. exec. com. Kehilath Israel Synagogue, Kansas City, 1984; pres. Used Truck Sales Network, Chgo., 1988—; bd. dirs. Shalom Group, 1985—, Jewish Community Ctr., Kansas City, 1984-87, v.p. exec. bd., 1985-87; treas. Friends of Shalom Plaza, 1983, bd. dirs., 1986-87; active Contemporary Art Soc., Kansas City, 1984—; pres. Saddlewood Homes Assn., 1988—. Mem. Mo. Bus and Truck, Kansas City C. of C. (transp. com. 1984-88). Democrat. Clubs: Oakwood Country (Kansas City). Lodge: Shriners. Office: Arrow Truck Sales Inc 3200 Manchester Kansas City MO 64129

NERONI, PETER JOSEPH, retired business executive; b. Cleve., Dec. 21, 1932; s. Decenzio and Maria (Calasena) N.; m. Barbara Baldwin, Sept. 10, 1960; children—Barbara, Michael, Mark, Timothy. B.S., John Carroll U., 1956. Sales mgr. Dayco Corp., Dayton, Ohio, 1971, v.p. plastics div., 1971-73, exec. v.p. Dayflex div., 1973-74, pres. Dayflex div., 1974-76, corp. group v.p., 1976-82, exec. v.p., 1982-88. Patentee plastic hoses. Served with U.S. Navy, 1955-57. Republican. Roman Catholic. Office: Day Internat Corp 333 W 1st St Dayton OH 45402

NESBIT, KIRK RONIN, data processing executive; b. Quincy, Ill., Apr. 29, 1962; s. James Kenneth and Constance Jean (Kirsch) N.; m. Kelly J. Bryan, Aug. 5, 1983; 1 child, Keegan. BS in Computer Sci., Quincy Coll., 1983; MS in Computer Sci., Western Ill. U., 1985. Programmer, analyst Gardner-Denver/Cooper Industry, Quincy, 1981-83; Programmer, analyst Moorman Mfg., Quincy, 1985-86, sr. systems programmer, 1986-87, data processing mgr., 1987—; cons. Forbes Cons., Quincy, 1986—; asst prof. Quincy Coll., 1987. Guest speaker Quincy Notre Dame High Sch., 1985-86, Quincy Sr. High Sch., 1985-86; advisor Jr. Achievement. Mem. Spring Lake Country Club. Republican. Roman Catholic. Home: 4 Deveron Cir Quincy IL 62301 Office: Moorman Mfg 1000 N 30th Quincy IL 62301

NESBIT, LEROY, JR., automotive management professional; b. Memphis, Aug. 20, 1947; s. Leroy Sr. and Celia (Finley) N.; m. Gwendolyn Anita Nesbit, Dec. 21, 1974; 1 child, Jacqueline L. AA, Baker Bus. Coll., 1968; BBA, Ferris State U., 1975. With GM, Flint, Mich., 1973-87; supr. material handling systems GM, Flint, 1987—; bd. dirs., treas. Dort Fed. Credit Union, Flint, 1975—. Canvass coord. Am. Cancer Soc., Flint, 1977, 78; chmn. bd. dirs. Flint Area Conv. Vis. Bur., 1986; v.p. Coun. GM Credit Unions, 1984—; Mich. travel commr. Dept. Commerce Travel Bur., Lansing, Mich., 1987—; chmn. Mich. Credit Union League, Southfield, 1988; legis. rep. 1983-86. Recipient Svc. award, 1985, Leadership award, 1985. Mem. Kappa Alpha Psi. Democrat. Baptist. Home: 12093 Riverbend Dr Grand Blanc MI 48439 Office: AC Spark Plug 1300 N Dort Hwy Flint MI 48506

NESBITT, JOHN ALFRED DREAN, investment banking exec.; b. Belfast, No. Ireland, May 18, 1945; s. John and Blanche Elizabeth Margaret (Drean) N.; BA, Oxford (Eng.) U., 1967; MBA, U. Pa., 1969. Econ. asst. H.M. Treasury, London, 1967-68; asso. Eastman Dillon Union Securities & Co., N.Y.C., 1969, 1st v.p. Blyth Eastman Dillon & Co. Inc., 1974, sr. v.p., 1976, mng. dir. Blyth Eastman Paine Webber Inc., 1980-84, Paine Webber Inc., 1984-86; ptnr. Trilby Auckland & Co., 1987—. Clubs: Downtown Assn., Racquet and Tennis, Links, Stanwich, Royal Belfast Golf. Home: 500 E 77th St New York NY 10162 Office: Trilby Auckland & Co PO Box 366 Palisades Park NJ 07650

NESBITT, LEROY EDWARD, inventor, design specialist; b. Phila., Sept. 14, 1925; s. Lonnie Reynolds and Josephine Elvira N.; student Temple U., 1965-69; m. Vivian Elizabeth Lee, June 27, 1952; 1 son, Warren Eric. Founder, pres. Incentives, Inc., Wilmington, Del., 1975—; design specialist Sperry Corp., Blue Bell, Pa. Served with U.S. Army, 1943-46. Decorated Bronze Star (4). Home and Office: 6213 Gardenia St Philadelphia PA 19144

NESLER, TIMOTHY HAROLD, oil and gasoline company executive; b. Findlay, Ohio, June 11, 1956; s. Edgar Franklin and Patricia Ann (Alexander) N.; m. Melinda Kay Miller, Dec. 12, 1980; children: Miranda, Audra. BS, Findlay Coll., 1977. CPA. Auditor Ernst and Ernst, Toledo, 1977-78, Marathon Oil Co., Findlay, 1978-80; controller, asst. treas. P.V. Commodity Systems subs. Marathon Oil Co., Calgary, Alta., Can., 1980-81; fin. analyst spl. projects Marathon Internat. Oil Co., Findlay, 1981-82; advance fin. analyst acctg. research Marathon Oil Co., Findlay, 1982-83; supr. subs. acctg. Marathon Petroleum Co., Findlay, 1983-86, mgr. consolidation and subs. acctg., 1986-87, mgr. acctg. policy and fin. forecasting, 1987—. Mem. fin. com., trustee Winebrenner Haven; mem. fin. com. St. Michaels Parish, Findlay. Mem. Am. Inst. CPA's, Ohio Soc. CPA's. Republican. Roman Catholic.

NESSEN, WARD HENRY, typographer, lawyer; b. Empire, Mich., Nov. 29, 1909; s. Henry L. and Louise (Stecher) N.; m. Jane Randall, Apr. 4, 1959. AB, U. Mich., 1931; JD, John Marshall Law Sch., Chgo., 1937; course in acctg. Northwestern U. Grad. Sch., 1946. Bar: Ill. 1937. With trust dept. No. Trust Co., Chgo., 1934-41; sales planning Am. Home Products, 1946-51; sales exec. Permacel Tape Corp., 1951-55; pres. The Highton Co., Newark, 1955-75; sr. v.p. Arrow Typographers, Newark, 1975-84; chmn. Coll. Communications Seminar, 1973. Mem. Civic Clubs Council Greater Newark Area, 1957-59, Bd. Comml. Arbitration N.Y.C., 1982-86; chmn. selection com. Advt. Hall of Fame of N.J., 1983. Served from 2d lt. to lt. col. AUS, 1941-46, ETO, assigned SOS. Decorated Bronze Star with oak leaf cluster, Army Commendation medal; recipient Elmer G. Voigt award, 1975. Mem. Typographers Internat. Assn. (pres. 1970-71), N.J. Typographers Assn. (pres. 1957-59), Printing Industries N.J. (pres. 1967-69), Printing Industries N.Y. (bd. govs. 1967-69), Order of John Marshall, Sigma Phi. Republican. Episcopalian. Clubs: Type Dirs.; Advt. N.J. (bd. govs 1972-84). Home: 11 Euclid Ave Summit NJ 07901

NETHERTON, GEORGE BECKLEY, IV, beverage company executive; b. N.Y.C., Nov. 25, 1948; s. George Beckley III and Dorothy Elizabeth (Fontana) N.; m. Pamela Jean Eberhardt, July 29, 1972; children: Tara Inger, Kate Elizabeth. BBA, Coll. Ins., N.Y.C., 1980; MBA, Fordham U., 1983. CPCU. Account exec. with various brokerage firms, N.Y.C., 1972-78, AIG Risk Mgmt., Inc., N.Y.C., 1978-79; corp. ins. specialist Sperry Corp., N.Y.C., 1979-80, asst. mgr. internat. ins., 1980-82, asst. mgr. corp. ins., 1982-83; entertainment risk mgr. Coca-Cola Co., Atlanta, 1983-85, asst. dir. risk mgmt., 1985-86, dir. corp. risk mgmt., 1986—; adj. asst. prof. Coll. Ins., N.Y.C., 1983, Ga. State U., Atlanta, 1987—; bd. dirs. Gm of A Ins. Co., Ltd., 1986—. Com. mem. Rep. party, Huntington, N.Y., 1982, 83; trustee Edn. Found., Inc., 1988—. Mem. Risk and Ins. Mgmt. Soc. (edn. conf. chmn. Atlanta chpt. 1988, treas. Atlanta chpt. 1988—, Jim Cristy award 1980) CPCU Soc. Roman Catholic. Home: 4500 Exmoor Dr Marietta GA 30067 Office: The Coca-Cola Co PO Drawer 1734 Atlanta GA 30301

NETHERTON, JANE, bank executive; b. Boston, Dec. 5, 1945. With Crocker Nat. Bank, 1967-74; with Harbor Bank, 1974-86, former sr. v.p., chief fin. officer; pres., chief exec. officer Internat. City Bank NA, Long Beach, Calif., 1986—; mem. adv. bd. Office of Extended Edn., Sch. Bus. Calif State U., Long Beach. Mem. adv. bd. Sch. of Bus., Calif. State U., Long Beach, Children's Mus., Long Beach. Mem. Long Beach C. of C. (treas., mem. exec. com.), Bank Adminstrn. Inst. (regional dir., nat. bd. dirs.), Calif. Bankers Assn. (vice chair ops. com., co-chair sr. ops. mgmt. conf. 1985-86, chmn. ops. com. 1987-88), Conservation Corp. of Long Beach (chmn.). Mailing Address: Internat City Bank NA 780 Atlantic Ave Long Beach CA 90813

NETTELS, GEORGE EDWARD, JR., engineering company executive; b. Pittsburg, Kans., Oct. 20, 1927; s. George Edward and Mathilde A. (Wulke) N.; m. Mary Joanne Myers, July 19, 1952; children: Christopher Bryan, Margaret Anne, Katherine Anne, Rebecca Jane. B.S. in Civil Engring, U. Kans., Lawrence, 1950. With Black & Veatch Engrs., Kansas City, Mo., 1950-51, Spencer Chem. Co., Kansas City, Mo., 1951-55, Freeto Constrn. Co., Pittsburg, 1955-57; pres. Midwest Minerals, Inc., Pittsburg, 1957—; chmn. bd. McNally Pittsburg Mfg. Corp., 1970-76, pres., chief exec. officer, 1976-87; ret. McNally Pitts. Inc., 1987; dir. Bank IV, Pittsburg, First Fed. Savs. & Loan Assn., Pittsburg, Kansas City Power & Light Co.; past chmn. bd. Nat. Limestone Inst.; bd. advisers Kans. U. Sch. Engring., Center Bus. and Econ. Devel. of Pittsburg State U.; bd. dirs. Pittsburg Indsl. Devel. Com. Bd. advisers Kans. U. Endowment Assn.; mem. Kans. U. Chancellor's Club, Kans., Inc.; past pres. Bd. Edn. 250, Pittsburg; past chmn. bd. trustees Mt. Carmel Hosp.; past mem. Kans. Commn. Civil Rights; chmn. Kans. Republican Com., 1966-68; Kans. del. Rep. Nat. Conv., 1968, Kans. Bus. and Industry Com. for Re-election of the President, 1972. Served with AUS, 1946-47. Recipient Disting. Service citation U. Kans., 1980, Disting. Engring. citation U. Kans., 1985; named Kansan of Yr., 1986. Mem. ASCE, NAM (past. dir.), Kans. C. of C. and Industry (dir., chmn. 1983-84), Kans. Right to Work (dir.), Pittsburg C. of C. (past dir.), Kans. U. Alumni Assn. (pres. 1977), Kans. Leadership Com., Tau Beta Pi, Omicron Delta Kappa, Beta Theta Pi. Presbyterian. Clubs: Crestwood Country (Pittsburg); Wolf Creek Golf (Olathe). Office: Midwest Minerals Inc PO Box 412 Pittsburg KS 66762

NETTER, CORNELIA ANN, real estate broker; b. N.Y.C., July 11, 1933; d. Frank H. and Mary (MacFadyen) N.; divorced: 1 child, Cornelia Jr. Student, U. Denver, 1951-53, C.W. Post Coll., 1958-60; BS, N.Y. State Regents, 1972. Sec. Newsday Bus. Office, Garden City, N.Y., 1959-61; adminstrv. asst. to U.S. Senator J. K. Javits N.Y., 1961-66; spl. asst. to Gov. Nelson A. Rockefeller Office of Gov., N.Y.C., 1966-69; pub. affairs dir. N.Y. State Health Planning Commn., 1969-72; dir. Office of Planning Services N.Y. State Human Resources Planning Commn., Albany and N.Y.C., 1972-76; pres. Netter Communications, N.Y.C., 1976-83, Netter Real Estate, N.Y.C., 1982—, Independent Brokers Network, 1988—. Founding mem. N.Y. State Women's Polit. Caucus, Albany, 1971; mem. N.Y. State Del. Appilachian Regional Commn., 1973-75, Rep. Family Com., N.Y.C., 1986—; mem. steering com. Breakthru Found., N.Y.C., 1983-85; bd. dirs. N.Y. Citiworks, 1987—; dept. campaign mgr. Rockefeller Gubernatorial, N.Y.C., 1966, dir. spl. groups, 1970; co-campaign mgr. N.Y. Nixon Presdl., 1968, dir. ethnic and spl. groups, 1972; candidate N.Y. State Assembly, 1974. Mem. Nat. Assn. Realtors, Nat. Assn. Real Estate Appraisers (CREA designation 1986), Real Estate Bd. of N.Y., Greenwich Village C. of C. (bd. dirs. 1988—). Republican. Office: Netter Real Estate 853 Broadway #1007 New York NY 10003

NETTER, KURT FRED, building products company executive; b. Mannheim, Germany, Dec. 3, 1919; came to U.S., 1941, naturalized, 1944; s. Arthur and Kate (Gruenfeld) N.; m. Alice Dreyfus, May 26, 1942; children: Nadine, Ronald, Alfred. Student, Swiss Inst. Tech., 1938-39, U. Toronto, 1939-41; BS, Columbia U., 1942. Ptnr. Interstate Engring. and Machinery Co., N.Y.C., 1942-44; officer, dir. Supradur Cos., Inc., 1946—, pres., chief exec. officer, 1953—, also bd. dirs.; chief exec. officer subs. Supradur Mfg. Corp., Wind Gap, Pa., Suprawall Corp., Rye, N.Y., The Triton Co. Inc., Rye, Precision Fabricators Inc., Garden City Park, N.Y., Twin City Tool Inc., Olathe, Kans. Bd. dirs. Selfhelp Community Services, Inc., treas. 1970-85, pres. 1985—. Served with AUS, 1944-46. Home: 203 Griffen Ave Scarsdale NY 10583 Office: Supradur Cos Inc 411 Theodore Fremd Ave Rye NY 10580

NETTIE, ROGER ALLEN, insurance company executive; b. Milw., June 12, 1961; s. Elmer Jack and JoAnne Carol (Zuehls) N.; m. Karen Vogel, July 30, 1983; children: Sarah, Rebecca. BBA, U. Wis., 1983. CPA, Wis. Acct. Baillies, Denson, Erickson & Smith, Madison, Wis., 1984-85, Luttig & Anunson, Madison, 1985-87, Morton, Nehls & Tierney, Madison, 1987-88; acct. CUNA Mut. Ins. Soc., Madison, 1985-87, research specialist, 1987-88, technology services cons., 1988—. Treas. Grace Luth. Ch., Madison, 1984—. Mem. Am. Inst. CPA's, Nat. Assn. Accts., Wis. Inst. CPA's, Beta Alpha Psi. Home: 1709 Main St Cross Plains WI 53528 Office: CUNA Mut Ins Soc 5910 Mineral Point Rd Madison WI 53705

NETZEL, PAUL ARTHUR, fund raising management executive, consultant; b. Tacoma, Sept. 11, 1941; s. Marden Arthur and Audrey Rose (Jones) N.; BS in Group Work Edn., George Williams Coll., 1963; m. Diane Viscount, Mar. 21, 1963; children: Paul M., Shari Ann. Program dir. S. Pasadena-San Marino (Calif.) YMCA, 1963-66; exec. dir. camp and youth programs Wenatchee (Wash.) YMCA, 1966-67; exec. dir. Culver-Palms Family YMCA, Culver City, Calif., 1967-73; v.p. met. fin. devel. YMCA Met. Los Angeles, 1973-78, exec. v.p. devel., 1979-85; pres. bd. dirs. YMCA Employees Credit Union, 1977-80; chmn. N.Am. Fellowship of YMCA Devel. Officers, 1980-83; adj. faculty U. So. Calif. Coll. Continuing Edn., 1983-86, Loyola Marymount U., Los Angeles, 1986—; chairman, chief exec. officer Netzel/Steinhaus and Assocs., Inc., 1985—; pvt. practice cons., fund raiser. Pres. bd. Culver City Guidance Clinic, 1971-74; mem. Culver City Bd. Edn., 1975-79, pres., 1977-78; mem. Culver City Edn. Found., 1982—; bd. dirs. Los Angeles Psychiat. Service; mem. Culver City Council, 1980-88, vice-mayor, 1980-82, 84-85, mayor, 1982-83, 86-87; mem. Culver City Redevel. Agy., 1980-88, chmn., 1983-84, 87-88, vice chmn, 1985-86; bd. dirs. Los Angeles County Sanitation Dists., 1982-83, 85-87, Region IV United Way, 1986—, chmn. 1987—; vice-chmn. bd. dirs. Calif. Youth Model Legislature, 1986-87. Recipient Man of Year award Culver City C. of C., 1972; trustee Washington Med. Ctr. 1988—. Mem. Nat. Soc. Fund Raising Execs. (nat. bd. dirs. 1989—, vice-pres. bd. dirs. Greater Los Angeles chpt. 1986-88, pres. bd. dirs. 1989—, Profl. of Yr. 1983). Roman Catholic. Clubs: Los Angeles Athletic, Rotary (bd. dirs. Los Angeles chpt.), Mountain Gate Country. Address: Netzel Steinhaus & Assocs 9696 Culver Blvd Ste 204 Culver City CA 90232

NEUBAUER, JOSEPH, business executive; b. Oct. 19, 1941; s. Max and Herta (Kahn) N.; m. Antonia R. Brody, May 21, 1965; children: Lawrence, Melissa. B.S. in Chem. Engring, Tufts U., 1963; M.B.A. in Fin, U. Chgo., 1965. Asst. treas. Chase Manhattan Bank, 1965-68, asst. v.p., 1968-70, v.p., 1970-71; asst. treas. Pepsico Inc., Purchase, N.Y., 1971-72; treas. Pepsico Inc., 1972-73, v.p., 1973-76; v.p. fin. and control Wilson Sporting Goods Co., River Grove, Ill., 1976-77, sr. v.p., gen. mgr. team sports div., 1977-79; exec. v.p. fin. and devel., chief fin. officer, dir. ARA Services, Inc., Phila., 1979-81, pres., chief operating officer, dir., 1981-83, pres., chief exec. officer, 1983-84, chmn., pres., 1984—; bd. dirs. First Fidelity Bancorp., Bell of Pa.; trustee Penn Mut. Life Ins. Co. Bd. dirs. Phila. Orch. Assn., Mann Music Ctr.; chmn. Inroads/Phila., Inc.; trustee Hahnemann U., Tufts U., Mus. Am. Jewish History, Univ. of the Arts, Bus. Council Pa., Greater Phila. First Corp., Com. for Econ. Devel.; bd. govs. Joseph H. Lauder, Inst. Mgmt. and Internat. Studies, U. Pa. Mem. Phila. C. of C. (bd. dirs.). Clubs: Union League, Locust, Philadelphia. Office: ARA Svcs Inc ARA Tower 1101 Market St Philadelphia PA 19107

NEUBERG, SUSAN ELLEN, lawyer; b. Bklyn., June 7, 1958; d. Jerry J. and Helen (Lipshitz) Doulman; m. Phillip W. Neuberg, Sept. 1, 1985. BA, Harpur Coll., 1979; MA, Stanford U., 1980; JD, Yeshiva U., 1983. Bar: N.Y. 1984, U.S. Ct. Appeals (10th cir.) 1984. Law clk. to presiding justice U.S. Ct. Appeals (10th cir.), Salt Lake City, 1983-84; assoc. Proskauer, Rose, Goetz & Mendelsohn, N.Y.C., 1984-86; v.p., counsel Home Life Ins. Co., N.Y.C., 1986—; vis. prof. Utah, Salt Lake City, 1984. Mem. Cardozo Sch. Law Rev., 1981-83. Mem. ABA, N.Y. State Bar Assn., Fed. Bar Assn., Am. Coun. Life Ins., Phi Beta Kappa. Home: 115 E 9th St Apt 17E New York NY 10003 Office: Home Life Ins Co 75 Wall St New York NY 10005

NEUENSCHWANDER, FREDERICK PHILLIP, management professional; b. Akron, Ohio, Mar. 19, 1924; s. Willis Lee and Esther (Mayer) N.; student Franklin and Marshall Coll., 1942-43, U. Akron, 1946-48; m. Mary Jane Porter, Mar. 19, 1948 (dec.); children: Carol, Frederick Philip, Lynn, Dean, Richard. Chief insp. Retail Credit Co., Akron, 1948-55; exec. v.p. Wadsworth (Ohio) C. of C., 1955-62, Wadsworth Devel. Corp., 1955-62, Wooster (Ohio) C. of C., 1962-63, Wooster Expansion, Inc., 1962-63; dir. devel. dept. State of Ohio, Columbus, 1963-71; exec. v.p. James A. Rhodes & Assos., Columbus, 1971-74; prin. F.P. Neuenschwander & Assos., Worthington, Ohio, 1975—. Mem. adv. council SBA, Ohio Scenic Rivers Commn.; exec. dir. Wadsworth United Fund, Inc., 1956-62; pres. Templed Hills, Inc.; pres. Central Ohio exec. bd. Boy Scouts Am.; vice-chmn. Ohio Water Commn., Ohio Expns. Commn.; chmn. Ohio Water and Sewer Rotary Fund Commn.; mem., past chmn. Midwest Gov.'s Adv. Council; sec. Ohio Devel. Council, Ohio Devel. Finance Commn. Adv. council Rio Grande Coll.; 1st chmn. bd. trustees Ohio Transp. Research Center; trustee Eden Theological Seminary; bd. dirs. League Against Child Abuse, United Ch. Bd. for World Ministries, Am. Schs. in Turkey. Served with AUS, 1943-46. Named Outstanding Young Man of Year, Wadsworth Jr. C. of C., 1958; recipient SIR award for directing outstanding state indsl. devel. program N. Am., 1966,

68, Ohio Gov.'s award 1967. Mem. Am., Gt. Lakes Indsl. Devel. Councils, C. of C. Execs. of Ohio, Huguenot Soc. Am., Am. Legion, Ohio Soc. N.Y. (res. v.p.). Mem. United Ch. of Christ (property mgmt. com. Ohio Conf.). Club: Worthington Hills Country. Home: 5614 Chapman Rd Delaware OH 43015-9203 Office: 7870 Olentangy River Rd Worthington OH 43235

NEUHARTH, ALLEN HAROLD, newspaper publisher; b. Eureka, S.D., Mar. 22, 1924; s. Daniel J. and Christina (Neuharth) N.; m. Loretta Fay Helgeland, June 16, 1946 (div. 1972); children: Daniel J. II, Jan; m. Lori Wilson, Dec. 31, 1973 (div. 1982). BA cum laude, U. S.D., 1950. Reporter Rapid City (S.D.) Jour., 1948; sports writer Mitchell (S.D.) Daily Republic, 1949; staff writer AP, Sioux Falls, S.D., 1950-52; editor, pub. SoDak Sports, Sioux Falls, 1952-54; with Miami (Fla.) Herald, 1954-60, asst. mng. editor, 1958-60; asst. exec. editor Detroit Free Press, 1960-63; gen. mgr. Times-Union and Democrat and Chronicle, Rochester, N.Y., 1963-66; exec. v.p. Gannett Co., Inc., Washington, 1966-70, pres., chief operating officer, 1970-73, pres., chief exec. officer, 1973-79, chmn., chief exec. officer, 1979-86, chmn., 1986—; founder, chmn. USA Today, 1982; bd. dirs. Gannett New Service, Inc. and other subs., Marine Midland Banks, Inc. Trustee Gannett Found.; bd. dirs. Nat. Council Better Bus. Burs., Inc. Served with inf. AUS, 1943-46, ETO, PTO. Decorated Bronze Star; recipient Horatio Alger award, 1975; named Outstanding Chief Exec. of Yr. in Pub. and Printing Industry for 3 consecutive yrs. Mem. Am. Newspaper Pubs. Assn. (bd. dirs. 1968-82, chmn., pres. 1979-80), Sigma Delta Chi (past nat. region I dir.). Clubs: Carlton (Chgo.); Genesee Valley (Rochester); Jockey (Miami); Ocean Reef (Key Largo, Fla.); Sky (N.Y.C.); Marco Polo (N.Y.C.). also: Gannett Co Box 7858 Washington DC 20044

NEUMAN, RICHARD FRANK, sales executive; b. St. James, Minn., Feb. 23, 1944; s. Frank Albert and Ann Marie (Suess) N.; m. Margaret Mary Fischer, Dec. 20, 1969 (div. Mar. 1986). BA, U. Minn., 1972; MS in Bus. Adminstrn., Ind. U., South Bend, 1977. Analyst Univac div. Sperry Rand, Roseville, Minn., 1970-72; svc. engr. No. Trust Co., Chgo., 1972-73; materials mgr. South Bend Range Corp., 1973-77, plant supt., 1977-78; dir. mfg. Roper Appliance, Kankakee, Ill., 1978-81; v.p. ops. Gen. Radiator-Chromalloy, Mt. Vernon, Ill., 1981; dir. Mpls. ops. Gen. Radiator-Chromalloy, Litton, 1981-85, dir. pvt. brand sales, 1985-86; v.p. sales Litton Microwave Cooking Products, Memphis, 1986—. Treas. Dan Manion for State Senate, South Bend, 1978. 1st lt. U.S. Army, 1965-69, Vietnam. Fellow nat. Assn. Food Svc. Mfrs., Stone Bridge Country Club (Cordova, Tenn.). Republican. Roman Catholic. Home: 7960 Tennis Ct Dr #4 Cordova TN 38018 Office: Litton Microwave 4450 Mendenhall Rd S Memphis TN 38101-1976

NEUMANN, ARIE ZODOK, computer software executive, educator; b. Boston, Aug. 1, 1961; s. Helmut David and Johanna Jutta (Gerechter) N. BBA in Fin. and Computer Info. Systems, U. Mich., 1987. Adminstr. U. Mich., Ann Arbor, 1986-87; instr. office automation Essential Resources, Inc., N.Y.C., 1987-88, regional sales mgr., 1988—. Co-author: Marketing: Advertising Plan for the City of Denver, Colorado, Real Estate: Student Housing Proposal, Marketing: Children and Television Advertising, Real Estate: Day Care Center Proposal, Finance: World Copier Industry-1987. A Strategic Analysis. Speaker Hillel B'nai B'rith Found., Ann Arbor, 1984; mem. Judith Wood Probate Judge, Ann Arbor, 1985. With Israel Navy, 1979-82. Mem. Digital Equipment Computer Users Soc., U. Mich. Alumni Assn., Animal League Assn. Jewish. Home: 83 33 118th St Kew Gardens NY 11415 Office: Essential Resources Inc 462 Broadway New York NY 10013

NEUMANN, RANDY, financial planner; b. Englewood, N.J., July 21, 1948; s. Robert Henry and Maria Nancy (Beck) N.; m. Kathleen Thatcher, Apr. 8, 1984; children: Randy Brooke, Dylan Daniel. BS, Fairleigh Dickinson U., 1975. Cert. fin. planner. Prize fighter 1969-75; asst. v.p. Garden State Nat. Bank, Cliffside Park, N.J., 1978-79; agt. Jack Alter Assocs., Lyndhurst, N.J., 1979-82; owner, mgr. Randy Neumann CFP & Assocs., Paramus, N.J., 1982—. Weekly fin. columnist, 1987; contbr. articles to profl. publs. Mem. Internat. Assn. for Fin. Planning, Inst. Cert. Fin. Planners, Registry Fin. Planning Practitioners, Kiwanis (pres. Cliffside Park 1978-79). Home: 150 Overlook Ave Hackensack NJ 07601 Office: 80 Rte 4 E Ste 400 Paramus NJ 07652

NEUMANN, ROBERT WILLIAM, engineer; b. Plainfield, N.J., Feb. 21, 1952; s. Robert Thomas and Lucille Francis (Perry) N. BS in Engring., Lafayette Coll., 1974; MS in Mgmt., Stevens Inst., 1984. Cert. plant engr. Marine tech. Larry Smith Electronics, Absecon, N.J., 1974; plant mgr. Neumann Sheet Metal, Plainfield, N.J., 1974-75; plant engr. Allison Corp., Garwood, N.J., 1976-77; engr. Midland Ross Corp., Somerset, N.J., 1977-81; plant engr. Container Corp. of Am., Matawan, N.J., 1981-85, Eastern Steel Barrel, Piscataway, N.J., 1985—. Pres., treas. South Plainfield (N.J.) Jaycees, 1975— (outstanding citizen 1982-83); v.p. N.J. Jaycees, 1977— (keyman 1982-83, 85); sec., treas. N.J. J.C.I. Senate, 1984—; pres. N.J. Leadership Seminars, 1986-87. Mem. Inst. Elec. and Electronic Engrs., Inst. Industrial Engrs., Am. Inst. Plant Engrs. Home: 1507 Central Ave South Plainfield NJ 07080 Office: Eastern Steel Barrel 4100 New Brunswick Ave Piscataway NJ 08855-1323

NEUNUEBEL, DAVID F., brokerage house executive; b. Chgo., June 8, 1947; s. Robert F. Neunuebel; m. Judy Van Horn, Jan. 26, 1980. BA, U. Calif., Santa Barbara, 1977. Chartered fin. planner, chartered fin. cons., CLU. Agt. Prudential Ins. Co. Am., Santa Barbara, 1978-82; account exec., 1st v.p. investments Dean Witter Reynolds, Santa Barbara, 1982—; instr. high sch. fin. planning program Coll. for Fin. Planning, 1988. Instr. Sunday sch. El Monticito Presbyn. Ch., Santa Barbara, 1987-88. With U.S. Army, 1966-68. Mem. Nat. Assn. Life Underwriters, Soc. CLUs, Internat. Assn. Fin. Planning. Republican. Home: 1015 Roble Ln Santa Barbara CA 93103 Office: Dean Witter Reynolds 118 E Cambrillo St Santa Barbara CA 93101

NEVILLE, JAMES MORTON, food company executive; b. Mpls., May 28, 1939; s. Philip and Maurene (Morton) N.; m. Judie Martha Proctor, Sept. 9, 1961; children: Stephen Warren, Martha Maurene. BA, U. Minn., JD magna cum laude, 1964. Bar: Minn. 1964, Mo. 1984. Assoc. firm Neville, Johnson & Thompson, Mpls., 1964-69, ptnr., 1969-70; assoc. counsel Gen. Mills, Inc., Mpls., 1970-77, sr. assoc. counsel, 1977-83, corp. sec., 1976-83; v.p., sec., asst. gen. counsel Ralston Purina Co., St. Louis, 1983-84, v.p., gen. counsel, 1984—; lectr. bus. law. U. Minn., 1967-71. Named Man of Yr. Edina Jaycees, 1967. Mem. ABA, Minn. Bar Assn., Hennepin County Bar Assn., Mo. Bar Assn., St. Louis Bar Assn., U. Minn. Law Alumni Assn., Am. Soc. Corp. Secs., Order of Coif, Phi Delta Phi, Psi Upsilon, Mo. Athletic Club. Episcopalian. Home: 11565 New London Dr Creve Coeur MO 63141 Office: Ralston Purina Co Checkerboard Sq Saint Louis MO 63164

NEVIN, JOHN JOSEPH, tire and rubber manufacturing executive; b. Jersey City, Feb. 13, 1927; s. Edward Vincent and Anna (Burns) N.; m. Anna Filice, June 16, 1951; children: Stanley James, John Joseph, Richard Charles, Paul Edward, Gerald Patrick, Mary Anne. B.S., U. Calif., 1950; M.B.A., Harvard U., 1952. Various positions fin., product planning and mktg. Ford Motor Co., Dearborn, Mich., 1954-71; v.p. mktg. Ford Motor Co., 1969-71; pres. Zenith Radio Corp., Chgo., 1971-76; chmn. Zenith Radio Corp., 1976-79; pres. Firestone Tire & Rubber Co., Akron, Ohio, 1979-82, chief exec. officer, 1980—, chmn., 1981—. Gen. chmn. Summit County United Way, 1983. Served with USNR, 1945-46. Office: Firestone Tire & Rubber Co 205 N Michigan Ave Ste 3800 Chicago IL 60601

NEVIN, ROBERT CHARLES, information systems executive; b. Dayton, Ohio, Nov. 4, 1940; s. Robert Steely and Virginia (Boehme) N.; m. Linda Sharon Fox, Apr. 16, 1966; children: Heather, Andrew. B.A., Williams Coll., 1962; M.B.A., U. Pa., 1970. Fin. planning mgr. Huffy Corp., Dayton, Ohio, 1971-72, asst. treas., 1972-73, treas., 1973-75, v.p. fin., 1975-79, exec. v.p., 1982-85; pres., gen. mgr. Frabill Sporting Good, Milw., 1979-82; exec. v.p. Reynolds & Reynolds, Dayton, Ohio, 1985-88, pres. bus. forms div., 1988—; bd. dirs. Reynolds & Reynolds. Bd. dirs. Camp Fire Girls, Dayton, 1975; bd. dirs. ARC, 1977; participant, then trustee Leadership Dayton, 1978; trustee Miami Valley Hosp., Dayton; trustee, treas. Victory Theater Assn., Dayton Mus. Natural History. Served to lt. USN, 1962-70. Mem. Beta Gamma Sigma. Republican. Episcopalian. Clubs: Racquet (Dayton), Dayton Country, Dayton Bicycle. Office: Reynolds & Reynolds 115 S Ludlow St Dayton OH 45402

NEVINS, DAVID HOWARD, marketing executive; b. N.Y.C., Oct. 13, 1954; s. Frederick and Joan N. BS, Towson State U., 1975; MS, John Hopkins U., 1977. Asst. to. v.p. Towson State U., Balt., 1976-79, dir. mktg., 1979-82; dir. mktg. Balt. Symphony Orch., 1982-84; pres. Nevins & Assocs., Balt., 1984—; prof. mktg. Johns Hopkins U., Balt., 1984—. Columnist Balt. Bus. Jour., 1988. Mem. Pub. Relations Soc. Am., Towson State U. Alumni Assn., Towson Bus. Assn. (pres. 1982). Home and Office: 3719 Michelle Way Pikesville MD 21208

NEVINS, ROBERT CHARLES, insurance broker; b. N.Y.C., Dec. 19, 1933; m. C. Ann Nevins; children: Beth, Mary, Tom. BS, Miami U., Oxford, Ohio, 1955, AA in Risk Mgmt., 1974. Asst. mgr. INA, San Francisco, 1955-64; pres., mng. ptnr. Dinner Nevins, San Francisco, 1964-83; chmn., pres. Fred S. James of Calif., 1983-84, exec. v.p., chief operating officer, 1984-86; exec. v.p. mktg. The Home Ins. Co., N.Y.C., 1986-88; vice chmn. Alexander & Alexander of Calif., Inc., San Francisco, 1989—. Mem. Nat. Soc. CPCU (past pres.), Soc. Ins. Brokers (past chmn. 1975), Ins. Ednl. Assn. (chmn. 1984-85), Ins. Forum, Risk Mgmt. Forum, Ins. Inst. Am. (bd. dirs.), Western Assn. Ins. Brokers, CNA Agts. Group (chmn. 1973), NASCA, San Francisco C. of C. (bd. dirs.), Am Inst. Property and Liability. Home: 3355 McGraw Ln Lafayette CA 94549 Office: Alexander & Alexander Calif Inc 2 Embarcadero Ctr Ste 1400 San Francisco CA 94111

NEW, EUGENE RUFUS, utilities executive; b. Sylacauga, Ala., June 19, 1936; s. Samuel Bernice and Mamie (Tillery) N., m. Joy L. Dull, Nov. 16, 1957; children: Larry C., Terry S. BS, U. Ala., 1972; Masters in Mil. Sci., U.S. Army Command and Gen. Staff Coll., 1975; MA, Appalachian State Coll., 1976. Commd. 2nd lt. U.S. Army, 1955, advanced through grades to major, 1975, ret., 1981; mgr. tng. Lummus Crest Inc., Bloomfield, N.J., 1981-84; supr. ops. support tng. Houston Lighting and Power Co., Bay City, Tex., 1984—. Contbr. articles to profl. jours. Explorer Post Advisor Boy Scouts, Tuscaloosa, Ala., 1972-74. Decorated two silver stars, two purple hearts, four bronze stars. Mem. Ret. Officer Assn., Am. Assn. of Retired People. Republican. Home: 3924 Wickersham Bay City TX 77414

NEWALL, JAMES EDWARD MALCOLM, manufacturing company executive; b. Holden, Alta., Can., Aug. 20, 1935; 1959; 3 children. B.Comm., U. Sask. With Du Pont Can., Inc., 1958—; v.p. mktg. Du Pont Can., Inc., Montreal, Que., 1975; exec. v.p. Du Pont Can., Inc., 1975-78, dir., 1976-78, pres., chief exec. officer, 1978—, chmn. bd., 1979—; bd. dirs. Alcan Aluminium Ltd., Can. Packers Inc., Molson Cos. Ltd., Pratt & Whitney Can. Inc., Royal Bank Can. Chmn. adv. com. on bus./govt. exec. exchange to Prime Minister. Clubs: Forest and Stream, Mt. Royal (Montreal); Toronto. Office: Du Pont Can Inc, PO Box 2200, Streetsville, ON Canada L5M 2H3

NEWBERG, WILLIAM CHARLES, stock broker, real estate broker, automotive engineer; b. Seattle, Dec. 17, 1910; s. Charles John and Anna Elizabeth (Anderson) N.; B.S. in Mech. Engring., U. Wash., 1933; M. in Mech. Engring., Chrysler Inst. Engring., 1935; LL.B. (hon.), Parsons Coll., 1958; m. Dorothy Beck, Nov. 3, 1939; children—Judith N. Newberg Bookwalter, Robert Charles, James William, William Charles. Salesman, Am. Auto Co., Seattle, 1932-33; student engr. Chrysler Corp., Detroit, 1933-35, exptl. engr., 1935-42, chief engr. Chgo. plant, 1942-45, mem. subs. ops. staff, Detroit, 1945-47, pres. airtemp. div., Dayton, Ohio, 1947-50, v.p., dir. Dodge div., Detroit, 1950-51, pres. Dodge div., 1951-56, group v.p., Detroit, 1956-58, exec. v.p., 1958-60, pres., 1960; corp. dir. Detroit Bank & Trust, Detroit, 1955-60; corp. cons., Detroit, 1960-76; realtor Myers Realty, Inc., Reno, 1976-79; owner Bill Newberg Realty, 1979—; account exec. Allied Capital Corp., Reno, 1980—; chmn. Newberg Corp., 1982. Elder, St. John's Presbyterian Ch., Reno, 1976—; exec. bd. Detroit Area council Boy Scouts Am., 1955-74, Nev. Area council Boy Scouts Am., 1976—; Mich. state chmn. March of Dimes, 1967-68. Mem. Soc. Automotive Engrs., Am. Def. Preparedness Assn. (life), Automotive Orgn. Team (life), U. Wash. Alumni Assn. (life), Newcomen Soc., Franklin Inst., Alpha Tau Omega. Clubs: Bluecoats of No. Nevada, Prospectors, Harley Owners Group, Goldwing Road Riders, Rider Motorcycle Touring, Internat. Retreads. Lodge: Elks. Home: 2000 Dant Blvd Reno NV 89509

NEWBERRY, ELIZABETH CARTER, owner greenhouse and floral company; b. Blackwell, Tex., Nov. 25, 1921; m. Weldon Omar Newberry, Sept. 24, 1950 (dec. Nov. 1984); 1 child. Student Hardin Simmons U., 1938-39. Office mgr. F. W. Woolworth, Abilene, Tex., 1939-50; acct. Western Devel. & Investment Corp., Englewood, Colo., 1968-72; owner, operator Newberry Bros. Greenhouse and Florist, Denver, 1972—; bd. dirs. Western Devel. and Investment Corp. Englewood, Colo., 1979-87. Pres. Ellsworth Elem. Sch. PTA, Denver, 1961-62; v.p. Hill Jr. High Sch. PTA, Denver. Home: 201 Monroe Denver CO 80206 Office: Newberry Bros Greenhouse 201 Garfield Denver CO 80206

NEWBERRY, RICHARD ALAN, financial executive; b. Franklin, Ind., Oct. 19, 1954; s. Charles Edward and Rema Dixie (Jong) N.; m. Jo Kay Tweed, July 10, 1976. BS in Acctg. cum laude, Ind. Cen. U., 1976; MS in Taxation (hon.), DePaul U., 1980. CPA, Ill.; cert. mgmt. acct.; cert. fin. planner. Acct. Ryder & Ford, Indpls., 1975; tax mgr. Coopers & Lybrand, Chgo., 1976-77, 78-81; asst. controller Playboy Enterprises, Inc., Chgo., 1977; chief fin. officer NWT Natural Resources Co., Chgo., 1981-85; chief fin. officer John H. Hill & Assocs., Dallas, 1985-88; v.p., chief fin. officer L. R. Newson Copr., Peoria, 1988—. Mem. AICPA, Nat. Assn. Accts., Inst. Mgmt. Acctg., Fin. Execs. Inst., Phi Beta Alpha (Outstanding Bus. Mgmt. award 1975). Clubs: Las Colinas Sports, Pres.' Health. Home: 618 Ravinswood Dr Peoria IL 61615

NEWBERRY, TIM RUSSELL, manufacturing executive; b. Ogden, Utah, May 20, 1959; s. John Thomas and Ethel Geraldine (Chapman) N. Student, So. Utah State Coll., Cedar City, 1975, Utah Tech. Coll., Provo, 1980, Weber State Coll., Ogden, 1984-85. Owner, operator T&R Carpets, Ogden, 1976-85; pres. Fun Time Tables, Inc., Clearfield, Utah, 1986—. Patentee in field. Mem. Nat. Spa & Pool Inst. Republican. Office: Fun Time Tables Inc PO Box 1524 Bldg E-6 Clearfield UT 84016

NEWCOMB, ROBERT BATEMAN, investor, former banker; b. Buffalo, Aug. 17, 1916; s. Walter Cattell and Alice Murray (Rann) N. B.A., Denver U., 1947; B.S.B.A., U. Buffalo, 1951, M.B.A., 1961, pre-standard, standard, grad. cert. Am. Inst. Banking. Messenger, Marine Midland Western Bank, Buffalo, 1938-39, br. clk., 1939-42, br. auditor, 1947-48, utility clk., trust dept., 1948-49, charge trust cage, 1950-51, trust and estate adminstr., 1952-62, fiduciary income tax cons., 1962-80, trust officer, 1964; pvt. investor, real estate mgr., 1980—; instr., radio-TV appearances on investments. Served with inf., AUS, 1942-46. Cert. Am. Inst. Banking. Mem. Audubon Soc., Buffalo Archeol. Soc. (pres. 1976-80), Buffalo Council Fgn. Affairs, Soc. Colonial Wars (pres. Western sect.), Buffalo Fine Arts, SAR (trustee Empire State Soc., v.p. gen. North Atlantic dist. 1977-79, nat. bd. trustees 1975, state pres. 1973-74), Internat. Platform Assn., Western N.Y. Geneal. Soc., Inc. Club: Automobile of Western N.Y. Lodges: Masons, Ancient Landmarks (past jr. deacon). Address: 825 Richmond Ave Buffalo NY 14222

NEWELL, RICHARD NELSON, banker; b. Toledo, June 2, 1932; s. James Reed and Florence Newell; m. Judith Dewey, July 30, 1960; children: Richard Nelson, Phillip, Elizabeth. BS in Econs., U. Pa., 1955. Account exec. Merrill Lynch, Pierce, Fenner & Smith, Inc., Toledo, 1958-68; investment officer First Nat. Bank of Toledo, 1968-71, v.p. trust investments, 1971-76, v.p. bank investments, 1976-87, v.p. 1987—; fin. trustee Med. Coll. Ohio at Toledo Found., 1973—. Treas. St. Michael's In-the-Hills Episcopal Ch., Toledo, 1977-85; chmn. fin. sect. employees div. United Way, Toledo, 1978-81, vice chmn. employees div., 1983-85, chmn. employees div. 1985-86, mem. allocations com., 1981-85, chmn. health allocations com., 1985-87; mem. fund mgmt. com. Luth. Social Services NW Ohio, 1982-84; mem. endowment devel. com. Toledo Mus. Art, 1982-87; mem. fin. com. Boys & Girls Clubs, Toledo, 1988—; mem. investment adv. com. City of Toledo, 1989—. Recipient Disting. Guest Speaker award U. Toledo Coll. Bus. Adminstrn., 1978. Mem. Econ. Club of Detroit, Fin. Analysts Soc. Toledo (pres. 1978-79), Ohio Bankers Assn. (funds mgmt. div. 1984-86, 88—) Wharton Alumni Assn. Mich. Home: 3436 Brookside Rd Toledo OH 43606 Office: First Nat Bank Toledo PO Box 1868 Toledo OH 43603

NEWELL, ROBERT LINCOLN, retired banker; b. Hartford, Conn., Dec. 2, 1922; s. Robert B. and Helen C. (Lincoln) N.; m. Sally C. Erdman, July 28, 1944; children: Sally N. Huss, Helen N. Douglas, Robert Lincoln, Katharine Erdman, William Henry II. Student, Wesleyan U., Middletown, Conn. With Conn. Nat. Bank, Hartford, 1946-88, exec. v.p., 1967-72, 1st exec. v.p., 1972-75, pres., 1975-78, chmn., 1978-87, ret., 1987; bd. dirs. Kaman Corp., N.Am. Philips Corp.; former chmn. Hartford Nat. Corp. Corporator Hartford Hosp., Mt. Sinai Hosp., Hartford Sem. Found.; bd. dirs., corporator St. Francis Hosp.; trustee St. Joseph Coll., Mystic Seaport Mus. Served to lt. USNR, 1943-46. Mem. Greater Hartford C. of C. (dir.). Home: 42 Mountain View Dr West Hartford CT 06117

NEWHALL, CHARLES WATSON, III, venture capitalist; b. Washington, Nov. 18, 1944; s. Charles Watson Jr. and Gladys (Brantley) N.; m. Mary W. Newhall, Oct. 14, 1967 (dec. 1982); children: Charles Ashton, Adair Brantley; m. Amy Louise Liebno, June 4, 1983. BA in English with honors, U. Pa., 1967; MBA, Harvard U., 1971. Investment analyst T. Rowe Price Assocs., Balt., 1971-73, asst. v.p., 1973-74; v.p. New Horizons Fund, Balt., 1974-77; co-founder New Enterprise Assocs., Balt., 1978—; bd. dirs. Am. Health Capital Ventures, Brentwood, Tenn., Communication Systems Tech., Columbia, Md., Crop Genetics Internat., Dorsey, Md., Dallas Biomed. Corp., Enzytech, Concord, Mass., Healthsouth Rehab. Corp., Birmingham, Ala., Integrated Health Services, Hunt Valley, Md., Queue Sstems, Inc., North Branch, N.H., Russ Pharms., Birmingham, Ala., Sepracor, Inc., Marlborough, Mass., Zymark Corp., Hopkinton, Mass. Trustee Balt. Mus. Art; mem. gallery com. Md. Hist. Soc., Balt. 1st lt. U.S. Army, 1967-69, Vietnam. Decorated Silver Star, Bronze Star, Purple Heart, Air medal. Mem. Balt.-Washington Venture Capital Group (pres.), Somerset Club, Rolling Rock Club, Greenspring Valley Hunt Club. Office: New Enterprises Assocs 1119 Saint Paul Baltimore MD 21202

NEWHARD, HARRY WALLACE, investment banking executive; b. St. Louis, Aug. 19, 1930; s. Chapin Slater and Anne Kennard (Wallace) N.; divorced; children: Jean Mortimer, Pennock H. BA, Brown U., 1953. Ptnr. Newhard, Cook and Co., St. Louis, 1956-71, pres., bd. chmn., 1971—; sec., treas. Miss. Valley Group, I.B.A., 1968, vice chmn., 1969, chmn., 1970, exec. com., 1971. Served to lt (j.g.) USN, 1953-56. Clubs: St. Louis Country, Round Table. Home: #2 Pebble Creek Rd Saint Louis MO 63124 Office: Newhard Cook & Co Inc 1600 S Brentwood Blvd PO Box 6717 Saint Louis MO 63144-0717

NEWHOUSE, STEPHAN F., securities company executive. Mng. dir. Morgan Stanley & Co. Inc., N.Y.C. Office: Morgan Stanley & Co Inc 1251 Ave of the Americas New York NY 10020 *

NEWILL, JAMES WAGNER, accounting executive; b. Greensburg, Pa., Dec. 22, 1934; s. James Meyers and Ruth Elizabeth (Wagner) N.; m. Helene Margaret Dolibois, Feb. 18, 1957; 1 child, J. Eric. BBA, St. Vincent Coll., Latrobe, Pa., 1962. CPA, Pa., Ohio, Fla. Staff acct. George Conti and Co., CPA, Greensburg, 1962-65; internal auditor Duquesne Light Co., Pitts., 1965-67; supr. accounts payable and gen. ledger Kennametal, Inc., Latrobe, 1967-71; asst. controller Glosser Stores, Inc., Johnstown, Pa., 1971-73; controller, asst. treas. Meriadian Plastics, Inc., Byesville, Ohio, 1973-76; regional controller Friendly Ice Cream Corp., Wilbraham, Mass., 1976-79; pres. J.W. Newill Co., Troy, Ohio, 1979—; bd. dirs. Southwest Nat. Bank, Greensburg. pres. bd. dirs. Troy-Hayner Cultural Ctr., 1982-85. Served to staff sgt. USAF, 1954-58. Mem. Am. Inst. CPA's, Pa. Inst. CPA's, Ohio Soc. CPA's, Fla. Inst. CPA's, Nat. Assn. Accts. Republican. Methodist. Lodge: Rotary (chmn. com., Paul Harris fellow), Elks. Home: 1111 Hillcrest Dr Troy OH 45373 Office: 16 S Short St Troy OH 45373

NEWKIRK, JOHN BURT, biomaterials engineer, administrator; b. Mpls., Mar. 24, 1920; s. Burt Leroy and Mary Louise (Leavenworth) N.; m. Carolyn Mae Jordan, Aug. 4, 1951; children: Jeffrey Burt (dec.), John Jordan, Victoria Louise Lierheimer, Christina Brooks. B. Metall. Engring, Rensselaer Poly. Inst., Troy, N.Y., 1941; M.S., Carnegie Inst. Tech., 1947, Sc.D., 1950. Registered profl. engr., Colo. Metall. investigator Bethlehem Steel Co., Pa., 1941-42; Fulbright postdoctoral fellow Cambridge (Eng.) U., 1950-51; research metallurgist research lab. Gen. Electric Co., Schenectady, 1951-59; prof. Cornell U., 1959-65; Phillipson prof. U. Denver, 1965-74, prof. phys. chemistry, 1975-84, Phillipson prof. emeritus, 1984—; pres. Colo. Biomed., Inc., 1969—. Editor Rews. on High Temperature Materials, 1973-78; 16 ann. volumes Advances in X-Ray Analysis; contbr. articles profl. jours. Served with USNR, 1942-46. Fellow Am. Soc. Metals (life mem.); mem. Sigma Xi, Tau Beta Pi, Phi Kappa Phi, Alpha Sigma Mu. Republican. Presbyterian. Office: Colo Biomedical Inc 6851 Hwy 73 Evergreen CO 80439

NEWLIN, TERENCE WILLIAM, financial consultant, accountant; b. Portland, Oreg., Mar. 19, 1947; s. Nicholas Paul and Iris Marie (Gibbs) N.; m. Linda R. Small, June 22, 1968; children: Jason Andrew, Tracy Day, Deborah Anne. Student, U. Wash., 1966-68; BS in Acctg., Calif. State U., Long Beach, 1970. CPA, Calif., Tex. Audit mgr. Arthur Andersen & Co., Orange County, Calif., 1970-75, Houston, 1975-78; treas., controller Shelton Ranch Corp., Kerrville, Tex., 1978-81; controller Servco div. Smith Internat., Carson, Calif., 1982-83; v.p. fin., chief fin. officer Smith Drilling Systems, Houston, 1983-86; founder, ptnr. Miller-Newlin & Co., Houston, 1986—. Contbr. articles to profl. jours. Treas. McCullough High Sch. Basketball Assn., 1988. Mem. AICPA, Tex. Soc. CPAs (com. chmn. 1987-89), C. of C., Riverhill Club, Greenspoint Club, Kiwanis. Office: Miller-Newlin & Co 12941 I-45 N Ste 606 Houston TX 77060

NEWLIN, WILLIAM RANKIN, lawyer; b. Pitts., Dec. 1, 1940; s. Theodore F. Newlin and Elizabeth Crooks; m. Ann Kleinschmidt, Aug. 25, 1962; children: Steffler Ann, Shelley Kay, William Rankin II. BA, Princeton U., 1962; JD, U. Pitts., 1965. Bar: Pa. 1965. Assoc. Buchanan Ingersoll, Pitts., 1965-71, ptnr., 1971—, mng. dir., 1980—; mng. gen. ptnr., chief exec. officer Ventre Fund, Pitts., 1985—; bd. dirs. Kennametal, Inc., Latrobe, Pa., Electronic Control Systems, Inc., Fairmont, W.Va., Union Nat. Bank Pitts., Black Box Corp., Pitts. Editor in chief U. Pitts. Law Rev., 1963; contbr. articles to profl. jours. Chmn., Gov. Thornburgh's Corp. Adv. Com., 1980-82; bd. dirs. Mfr. Studies Bd. Nat. Rsch. Coun., Washington, 1988—, Pitts. High Tech. Coun., 1982—. Fellow Am. Bar Found., Pa. Bar Found.; mem. ABA (corp. banking, bus. law sect., internat. law sect.), Pa. Bar Assn. (mem. coun. corp. banking and bus. law sect. 1973-82, chmn. sect. 1979-81, Spl. Achievement award 1982), Allegheny County Bar Assn., Am. Law Inst., Assn. of Bar of City of N.Y., Nat. Assn. Svc. Dealers (arbitrator), Duquesne Club (dir. 1982-85), Rivers Club (bd. dirs. 1983—), Laurel Valley Golf Club, Allegheny Country Club (bd. dirs. 1988—). Office: Buchanan Ingersoll 600 Grant St 58th Fl Pittsburgh PA 15219

NEWMAN, ANDREW EDISON, retail executive; b. St. Louis, Aug. 14, 1944; s. Eric Pfeiffer and Evelyn Frances (Edison) N.; m. Peggy Gregory, Feb. 14, 1984; children: Daniel Mark, Anthony Edison. BA, Harvard U., 1966, MBA, 1968. With Office of Sec. Def., Washington, 1968-70; with Edison Bros. Stores, Inc., St. Louis, 1970—, v.p. ops. and adminstrn., 1975-80, dir., 1978—; exec. v.p. Edison Bros. Stores, Inc., 1980-86, chmn., 1986—; bd. dirs. Washington U., St. Louis, Boatmen's Bank, N.A., St Louis. Bd. dirs., commr. Children's Hosp., Downtown St. Louis; Wash. U. Med. Ctr., St. Louis Sci. Ctr., vice-chmn.; pres. John Burroughs Sch. Office: Edison Bros Stores Inc 501 N Broadway Saint Louis MO 63102

NEWMAN, BARRY INGALLS, banker; b. N.Y.C., Mar. 19, 1932; s. M.A. and T.C. (Weitman) N.; BA, Alfred U., 1952; JD, N.Y. U., 1955; m. Jean Short, Mar. 6, 1965; children: Suzanne, Cathy, David. Admitted to N.Y. State Bar, 1957, Ohio bar, 1957, U.S. Supreme Ct. bar, 1967; practiced in N.Y.C., 1957; partner firm Shapiro Persky Marken & Newman, Cleve., 1957-63; asst. v.p. Meinhard & Co. (now Meinhard Comml. Corp.), N.Y.C., 1963-65; v.p. Amsterdam Overseas Corp., N.Y.C., 1966-68; pres. No. Fin. Corp., Los Angeles, 1968-72; sr. v.p. Aetna Bus. Credit, Inc., Hartford, Conn.,

1972-78; exec. v.p. Security Pacific Fin. Group, San Diego, 1978-81, chmn., pres., chief exec. officer, 1981-82; sr. exec. v.p. Gt. Am. First Savs. Bank, 1982-88; ret. 1988; chmn. bd. dirs. San Diego County Capital Asset Leasing Corp. Served with U.S. Army, 1955-57. Recipient Distinguished Service award Cleve. Jr. C. of C., 1961. Mem. ABA, N.Y. State Bar Assn., Ohio Bar Assn., San Diego Bar Assn., San Diego Taxpayers Assn. (bd. dirs.). Republican. Club: Fairbanks Ranch Country; Univ. Club of San Diego (pres.). Lodge: Masons. Home: 3308 Avenida Sierra Escondido CA 92025

NEWMAN, CHARLES WILLIAM, holding company executive, controller; b. Miami, Fla., Nov. 19, 1949; s. Charles Frederich Newman and Vera Ann (O'Rourke) Shepitka; divorced; 1 child, Charles Joseph; m. Diane Anderson; children: Marc Adam, Lauren Perii. BBA in Acctg., Fla. Internat. U., 1974. CPA, Fla.; chartered bank auditor. Sr. acct. Ernst & Ernst, Miami, 1974-77; v.p., EDP auditor Flagship Banks Inc., Tampa, Fla., 1977-81; v.p., controller Flagship Banks Inc., Miami, 1981-83; v.p., dep. controller Barnett Banks Fla. Inc., Jacksonville, 1983-85, sr. v.p., dep. controller, 1985-87, sr. v.p., controller, 1987-88, exec. v.p., controller, 1988—. Capt. United Way, Jacksonville, 1985; founding mem. Amyotrophic Lateral Sclerosis orgn. Dade County chpt., Miami, 1982-83, bd. dirs. Fla. chpt., Miami, 1983. With USCG, 1967-71. Mem. AICPA, Fla. Inst. CPAs. Republican. Presbyterian. Office: Barnett Banks Inc 100 Laura St PO Box 40789 Jacksonville FL 32203-0789

NEWMAN, EDWIN STANLEY, lawyer, publishing company executive; b. N.Y.C., Apr. 26, 1922; s. Gordon H. and Rosalind (Zieph) N.; m. Evaline Ada Lipp, Sept. 2, 1945; children: Scott D., Linda S. Newman Perl. BA summa cum laude, CCNY, 1940; LLB, Columbia U., 1943. Admitted to N.Y. State bar, 1943, U.S. Ct. Internat. Trade. Asst. to pres. Am. Jewish Com., 1946—; ins. co. exec., 1960-69; v.p., gen. counsel Oceana Publs., Inc., Dobbs Ferry, N.Y., 1969—, also dir.; past lectr. New Sch. Social Research. Author: Freedom Reader, 1963, Hate Reader, 1964, Law of Philanthropy, 1955, Fundraising Made Easy, 1954, Law of Civil Liberty and Civil Rights, 7th edit., 1987; editor: U.S. Internat. Trade Reports, 1981—. Chmn. bd. Elmont Jewish Ctr., 1953-57. Served with U.S. Army, 1943-46, 51-52. Mem. Internat. Bar Assn., Columbia Law Sch. Alumni Assn., Internat. Assn. Jurists (Italian-Am. sect.), Phi Beta Kappa. Home and Office: 75 Main St Dobbs Ferry NY 10522

NEWMAN, FRANK NEIL, financial executive; b. Quincy, Mass., Apr. 20, 1942; s. Robert David and Ethel F. N.; m. Mo Newman, June 16, 1966; 1 child, Daniel. B.A. in Econs. magna cum laude, Harvard U., 1963. Exec. v.p., chief fin. officer Wells Fargo & Co. and Wells Fargo Bank, San Francisco, 1980-86; vice chmn., chief fin. officer Bank Am. Corp, Bank of Am., San Francisco, 1986—; dir. various subsidiaries. Bd. dirs. Japan Soc. of Calif. Club: Harvard (San Francisco). Office: BankAm Corp Bank America Ctr San Francisco CA 94104

NEWMAN, GERALD, restaurant franchise company executive; b. Chgo., May 26, 1931; s. Morris and Sara (Glaser) N.; m. Bobbi F. Greenblatt, Dec. 18, 1955 (div.); children: Marc, Jeffrey; m. Lisa Broh. Student, Chgo. City Jr. Colls., 1949-51, U. Ill., 1949, Roosevelt U., 1957. Bookkeeper Evans Fur Co., Chgo., 1951; controller Stacy Constrn. Co., Chgo., 1951-59; co-owner, accountant Met. Roofing Co., Chgo., 1959-61; with McDonald's Corp., Oak Brook, Ill., 1961—; v.p., controller McDonald's Corp., 1969-72, exec. v.p., 1972-80, sr. exec. v.p., 1980—, also dir.; bd. dirs. Family Foods of Holland; former chmn. bd. Golden Arches of Eng. Adv. bd. dirs. DePaul U. Sch. Acctg.; pres., chief exec. officer Ronald McDonald Children's Charities, 1984; past bd. trustees Spertus Coll. Mem. Am. Inst. Corp. Controllers. Jewish. Office: McDonald's Corp 1 McDonald's Pla Oak Brook IL 60521

NEWMAN, GORDON HAROLD, lawyer, food company executive; b. Sioux City, Iowa, Mar. 31, 1933; s. George I. and Esther (Goldman) N.; m. Toby M. Dunitz, Dec. 26, 1955; children: Debra Susan, Stacy Fae, Eric Scott. B.S.C., U. Iowa, 1955, J.D. with distinction, 1961. Bar: Iowa 1961, Ill. 1963. Assoc. Gamble, Riepe, Martin & Webster, Des Moines, 1961-62; asst. counsel, asst. sec. Bell & Howell Co., 1962-67; assoc. gen. counsel, asst sec. Sara Lee Corp., Chgo., Ill., 1967-70, v.p., assoc. gen. counsel, sec., 1971-75, v.p., gen. counsel, sec., 1975-78, sr. v.p., gen. counsel, 1978—. Served to 1st lt. USAF, 1955-58. Mem. ABA, Northwestern Univ. Assocs., Ill. Bar Assn., Chgo. Bar Assn., Am. Soc. Corp. Secs. Club: Standard (Chgo.). Home: 58 Sheridan Rd Highland Park IL 60035 Office: Sara Lee Corp 3 First National Pla Chicago IL 60602

NEWMAN, JEANNE LOUISE, association executive; b. Boston, June 29, 1946; d. William Collyer and Barbara (Bailey) Smith; m. Harry Stephen Newman, June 9, 1968 (div. 1977); children: Michael Stephen, Catherine Louise. BSBA, Am. U., 1968. Bookkeeper Am. Pharm. Assn., Washington, 1968-69; bus. mgr. Soc. Photog. Scientists and Engrs., Washington, 1969-73; controller Nat. Ctr. for Vol. Action, Washington, 1973-75; fin. officer Bur. Rehab., Washington, 1975-79; acting dir. bus. affairs Assn. Am. Med. Colls., Washington, 1979-88, dir. fin. services, 1988—. Treas. Potomac Valley Civic Assn., 1975-77; pres. Franconia Commons Homeowners Assn., Alexandria, Va., 1982—. Mem. Nat. Assn. Female Execs., Am. Soc. of Assn. Execs. Office: Assn Am Med Colls 1 DuPont Cir NW Washington DC 20036

NEWMAN, JERROLD MITCHELL, investment firm executive; b. N.Y.C., June 15, 1954; s. George and Frances (Rudolph) N. BS, Cornell U., 1976; MBA, Dartmouth Coll., 1980. CPA, N.Y. Mem. exec. tng. program Abraham & Straus, Bklyn., 1976-78; staff acct. Price Waterhouse, N.Y., 1980-82; cons. Booz, Allen & Hamilton, N.Y., 1982-83; v.p., treas. Cofinam Inc., N.Y., 1983—. Mem. Am. Inst. CPA's, Assn. Corp. Growth (treas. N.Y. chpt. 1987—), The Asia Soc., Japan Soc. Clubs: Yale (N.Y.C.), Miramar. Home: 145 W 55th St Apt 6F New York NY 10019 Office: Cofinam Inc 125 E 56th St New York NY 10022

NEWMAN, LARRY BRUCE, corporate professional; b. N.Y.C., May 24, 1949; s. Bernard and Beverly (Nathanson) N.; m. Marianne Scopelliti, May 30, 1971; children: Peter D., Jonathan W. BS, St. John's U., N.Y.C., 1971. Audit supr. Coopers & Lybrand, N.Y.C. and West Palm Beach (Fla.), 1971-77; treas. Cadillac Fairview, Boynton Beach, Fla., 1977-80; controller Context Industries, Inc. subs., Miami, 1980-81; v.p., treas. Context Industries, Inc., Miami, 1981-84, exec. v.p., treas., chief operating officer, 1984-86, pres. all subs., 1987—, also bd. dirs.; bd. dirs. Allied Health Care Corp. Coauthor: Audit of CETA Grants, 1976. Mem. St. John's U. Alumni (pres. Ft. Lauderdale chpt.). Democrat. Jewish. Home: 13503 Brixham St Wellington FL 33414 Office: 5350 10th Ave N Suite 8 Lake Worth FL 33463

NEWMAN, LAWRENCE WALKER, lawyer; b. Boston, July 1, 1935; s. Leon Bettoney and Hazel W. (Walker) N.; m. Cecilia Isette Santos, Nov. 29, 1975; children: Reynaldo W., Timothy D., Virginia I.S., Isabel B., Thomas H. A.B., Harvard U., 1957, LL.B., 1960. Bar: D.C. 1961, N.Y. 1965. Atty. U.S. Dept. Justice, 1960-61, Spl. Study of Securities Markets and Office Spl. Counsel on Investment Co. Act Matters, U.S. SEC, 1961-64; asst. U.S. atty. So. Dist. N.Y., 1964-69; assoc. Baker & McKenzie, N.Y.C., 1969-71, ptnr., 1971—; mem. internat. adv. coun. World Arbitration Inst., 1984-87 ; mem. adv. com. Asia Pacific Ctr. for Resolution of Internat. Trade Disputes, Litigation, 1987—; columnist N.Y. Law Jour. Columnist N.E. Internat. Bus. jour.; contbr. to profl. jours. Mem. ABA (com. internat. litigation, com. internat. arbitration), Internat. Bar Assn. (com. dispute resolution, com. constrn. litigation), Inter-Am. Bar Assn., Fed. Bar Council, Am. Fgn. Law Assn., Maritime Law Assn. U.S., Assn. of Bar of City of N.Y. (mem. com. on arbitration 1977-79, mem. com. on fgn. and comparative law 1987—), Am. Arbitration Assn. (corp. counsel com. 1987—), U.S. Council Internat. Bus. Home: 1001 Park Ave New York NY 10028 Office: Baker & McKenzie 805 3d Ave New York NY 10022

NEWMAN, LAWRENCE WILLIAM, financial executive; b. Chgo., Jan. 14, 1939; s. Eskil William and Adele Diane (Lawnicki) N.; m. Christine Harriet Jaronski, Sept. 22, 1962; children: Paul, Scott, Ron. BBS, U. Ill., 1965; MBA, Northwestern U., 1970. CPA, Ill. Controller ECM Corp., Schaumburg, Ill., 1966-70; controller Nachman Corp., Des Plaines, Ill., 1970-76, v.p., treas., controller, 1976-79; v.p. fin. P & S Mgmt. Inc., Schiller Park, Ill., 1979-83; controller Underwriters Labs., Northbrook, Ill., 1983-85, asst. treas., 1985—. Mem. Fin. Execs. Inst., Am. Inst. CPA's. Club: Exec. of Chgo. Office: Underwriters Labs 333 Pfingsten Rd Northbrook IL 60062

NEWMAN, LEONARD JAY, retail jewel merchant, gemologist; b. Milw., Oct. 25, 1927; s. David and Pia Goldie (Smith) N.; m. Louise Shainberg, Jan. 14, 1951; children—Shelley, Marty, Alan, Heidi, Dee. BS, Purdue U.; postgrad. Washington U., St. Louis. Owner, mgr. Newman's Diamond Ctr., Jasper, Ind., 1951—; tchr. The Jasper Ctr., Ind., 1970-80. Bd. dirs. VUJC Found., State Bd. Health Systems Agy., sub area Health Systems Agy.; 1st v.p. Vincennes Univ. Found.; past pres. Jasper Community Arts Commn.; pres. Friends of Arts; commnr. Boy Scouts Am.; mem. Dubois County Mental Health Assn., lay adv. bd. Convent Immaculate Conception Sisters of St. Benedict, Ferdinand, Ind., Jasper Hist. Soc., German Club, Young Abe Lincoln Soc.; bd. dirs. Dubois County Crippled Children's Soc., Bloomington (Ind.) Symphony, Patoka Valley Vocat. Coop.; pres. Jasper Edn. Fund; bd. dirs. Patoka Valley Rehab. Ctr; mem., chmn. nominee com. Raintree Coun. Girl Scouts U.S.A., bd. dirs. Recipient Outstanding Citizenship award Purdue U. Alumni Assn., 1980 Outstanding Alumni award Jasper High Sch. Mem. Nat. Assn. Jewelry Appraisers (sr.), Ind. Jewelers Orgn. Am., Retail Jewelers Am., Jasper C. of C., Jaycees (Rooster, past pres., past nat. bd. dirs., Disting. Svc. award 1957), Purdue Agrl. Alumni Assn. (hon.), Skull and Crescent (hon.), Hadassah, Sigma Alpha Mu, Alpha Phi Omega. Lodges: Lions, Masons, Shriners (past pres.), B'nai Brith. Home: 923 McArthur Jasper IN 47546 Office: Newman's Diamond Ctr 3D Pla Jasper IN 47546

NEWMAN, PETER KENNETH, economist, educator; b. Mitcham, Eng., Oct. 5, 1928; came to U.S., 1961, naturalized, 1970; s. Charles Francis and Harriet Anne (Newbold) N.; m. Jennifer Mary Hugh-Jones Steed, Sept. 30, 1974; children by previous marriage: Jean Ellen, John Lincoln, Kenneth Richard, Alan Peter. B.Sc. in Econs, Univ. Coll. U. London, Eng., 1949, M.Sc. in Econs, 1951, D.Sc. in Econs, 1962. Lectr. U. West Indies, Jamaica, 1957-59, sr. lectr., 1959-61; prof. econs. U. Mich., Ann Arbor, 1961-63, Johns Hopkins, 1964-65, 66—; sr. asso. Robert R. Nathan Assos., Washington, 1965-66. Author: British Guiana, 1964, Malaria Eradication and Population Growth, 1965, Theory of Exchange, 1965; editor: (with others) The New Palgrave: A Dictionary of Economics, 4 vols., 1987. Home: 3410 Guilford Terr Baltimore MD 21218 Office: Johns Hopkins U Dept Econs Baltimore MD 21218

NEWMAN, RAYMOND HOWARD, transportation executive; b. Jersey City, Sept. 12, 1936; m. Carolyn Ann Dally, Dec. 7, 1963; children: Lesley, Scott, Karen. BS in Engring., U. Mich., 1959; postgrad., NYU, 1969-77. Naval architect George C. Sharp, Inc., N.Y.C., 1961-63, sr. systems analyst, ptnr., 1964-70; port planner Port of N.Y. Authority, 1963; mgr. marine planning Esso S.Am. Petrolera, Buenos Aires, 1970-71; sr. marine econ. cons. John J. McMullen Assoc., N.Y.C., 1973-76; dir. transport sci. John J. McMullen Assocs., N.Y.C., 1976-77; with New Eng. Petroleum, 1977—; pres. Charter Marine Transp. Co. div. New Eng. Petroleum, Jacksonville, Fla., 1988—; founding pres. Martifacts, Inc. Lt. (j.g.) USN, 1959-61. Mem. Harbor Waterway Assn. (founder, treas. 1984—), Soc. Naval Architects and Marine Engrs., USN Inst., Propeller Club, St. Augustine Yacht Club, Downtown Athletic Club. Republican. Home: 11517 Portside Dr Jacksonville FL 32225 Office: Charter Marine Transp Co PO Box 19105 Jacksonville FL 32245 also: New Eng Petroleum Corp 4655 Salisbury Rd Ste 220 Jacksonville FL 32256

NEWMAN, SCOTT DAVID, lawyer; b. N.Y.C., Nov. 5, 1947; s. Edwin Stanley and Evaline Ada (Lipp) N.; m. Judy Lynn Monchik, June 24, 1972; 1 child, Eric. B.A. magna cum laude, Yale U., 1969; J.D., Harvard U., 1973, M.B.A., 1973; LL.M. in Taxation, NYU, 1977. Bar: N.Y. 1974, U.S. Dist. Ct. (so. and ea. dists.) N.Y. 1975, U.S. Ct. Appeals (2d cir.) 1975, U.S. Ct. Claims 1976, U.S. Tax Ct. 1979. Assoc. Dewey, Ballantine, Bushby, Palmer & Wood, N.Y.C., 1973-76, Stroock & Stroock & Lavan, N.Y.C., 1976-78; assoc., ptnr. Zimet, Haines, Moss & Friedman, N.Y.C., 1978-81; tax counsel Phibro-Salomon Inc., N.Y.C., 1981-84; ptnr. Baer, Marks & Upham, N.Y.C., 1984-87; ptnr. Wiener, Zuckerbrot, Weiss & Newman, N.Y.C., 1987—. Coauthor tape cassettes: New Tax Reform Act of 1976, Tax Reform '78, 1978. Tax Reform Act of 1984, 1986, Tax Reform Act of 1986, 1986; contbr. article to profl. jour. Mem. Phi Beta Kappa. Home: 21 Kipp St Chappaqua NY 10514 Office: Wiener Zuckerbrot Weiss & Newman 260 Madison Ave New York NY 10016

NEWMAN, SHELDON OSCAR, computer company executive; b. N.Y.C., June 25, 1923; s. Morris and Anna (Schlanger) N.; m. Miriam Jasphy, July 30, 1950; children—Barry Marc, Amy Stacy, Andrew Eric. B.S.E.E., CUNY, 1944. Project engr. NASA, Sunnyvale, Calif., 1946-47; gen. mgr. info. and communications div. Sperry Corp., Gt. Neck, N.Y., 1947-67; chmn. bd., chief exec. officer Algorex Corp., Hauppauge, N.Y., 1968—. Chmn. bd. trustees Orthopaedic Inst., Hosp. for Joint Diseases, N.Y.C.; bd. dirs. HJD Research and Devel. Found.; pres. Pine Lake Park Coop. Assn., Peekskill, N.Y. Patentee in field. Served to lt. (j.g.), USN, 1944-46. Mem. IEEE, Archaeol. Inst. Am. (pres.), L.I. Soc., Masons, Tau Beta Pi, Eta Kappa Nu.

NEWMAN, TILLMAN EUGENE, JR., food company executive; b. Greenwood, Ark., Feb. 13, 1938; s. Tillman Eugene and Theresa Christine (Simmons) N.; m. Linda Gail Childers, Feb. 13, 1983; children—James Barton Langley, Robert, John, Michael, Kristen Newman. B.S. in Chem. Engring., U. Ark., 1963. Registered profl. engr., Ark., Iowa, Mo. Plant mgr. Ralston Purina, St. Louis, 1963-67, project mgr., 1967-71; v.p. Huxtable-Hammond, Kansas City, Mo., 1971-79; dir. engring. Tyson Foods, Russellville, Ark., 1979—; bd. dirs. Mech. Controllers of Iowa, 1976-78; mem. Ark. Allied Industries, Little Rock, 1980—. Bd. dirs. Ark. Fedn. Water and Air, 1984—. Served to sgt. USNG, 1956-65. Mem. Nat. Soc. Profl. Engrs., Am. Inst. Chem. Engrs., Am. Soc. Mech. Engrs., Russellville C. of C. Baptist. Avocations: fishing; boating. Office: Tyson Foods 2210 Oaklawn Springdale AR 72764

NEWSTADT, DAVID ROLAND, food company executive; b. N.Y.C., Mar. 19, 1930; s. Herbert Morris and Evelyn (Bleckerman) N.; m. Millicent R. Brown, Nov. 23, 1952; children—A. Todd, Tracy Heather. A.B. magna cum laude, Syracuse U., 1951; M.B.A., NYU, 1957. With Johnson & Johnson, 1955-58, 61-73, various product mgmt. positions to dir. mktg., 1961-69, gen. mgr. dental div., domestic operating co., 1969-71, v.p., mem. mgmt. bd. domestic operating co., 1971-72; pres. Johnson & Johnson Dental Products Co., 1972-73; asst. account exec. Compton Advt., 1958-59, account exec., 1959-61; with CPC Internat. Inc., 1974-85; pres., chief exec. officer Sun-Diamond Growers Calif., Pleasanton, 1986-87; chmn., pres., chief exec. officer S.B. Thomas, Inc. affiliate CPC N.Am., 1974-78; pres. Consumer Devel. unit CPC N.Am., 1978-81; v.p. CPC Internat. Inc., 1978-85; pres. Best Foods U.S. unit CPC N.Am., 1981-84; exec. v.p. Best Foods N.Am. div. CPC Internat. Inc., Englewood Cliffs, N.J., 1984-85; bd. dirs. GoodMark Foods Inc., Raleigh, N.C., Internat. Food and Beverages, Irvine, Calif. Served to lt. (j.g.) USNR, 1951-55. Mem. Am. Mgmt. Assn. (pres. assn.), NYU Grad. Sch. Bus. Alumni Assn. (bd. dirs. 1977—, past pres.), Phi Beta Kappa, Psi Chi. Republican. Jewish. Office: Sun-Diamond Growers Calif 1050 S Diamond St Stockton CA 95201

NEWTON, BOBBY LEX, industrial supply company executive; b. Burlington, N.C., Nov. 11, 1943; s. Charles Clyde Sr. and Pearl Irene (Roberson) N.; m. Betty Louise Greeson, Apr. 28, 1963; children: Susan Michelle, Dana Lynn. Student, Tech. Sch. Alamance, 1968, Pa. State U., 1977. Supply room supr. Kayser-Roth Hosiery Co., Inc., Graham, N.C., 1962-64; lab. supr. Kayser-Roth Hosiery Co., Inc., Graham, 1964-66; electrician Dandridge Electric Co., Burlington, 1966-68; sales rep. Levin Bros. Plumbing Co., Burlington, 1968-69; warehouse mgr. Blue Ridge Hardware and Supply Co., Burlington, 1969-73; owner, ptnr. Alco Electric Service, Burlington, 1973-75; warehouse mgr. L.A. Benson Co., Inc., Greensboro, N.C., 1975-77; gen. mgr. L.A. Benson Co., Inc., Greensboro, 1977—; mem. distbr. adv. bd. Robert Bosch Power Tool Co., New Bern, N.C., 1988. Mem. So. Indsl. Distbrs. Assn., Greensboro Jaycees (hon. life mem.). Home: 2329 Venie St Burlington NC 27215 Office: LA Benson Co Inc 2704 Patterson St Greensboro NC 27407

NEWTON, FREDERICK CARTER, drilling contracting company executive; b. Rockdale, Tex., Sept. 11, 1924; s. James Oscar and Anne Boswell (Rumpel) N.; m. Patricia Rae McBride, June 3, 1945; children: Frederick Carter Jr., Stephen Barrett, Kimberly Leigh. BS, USAF Inst. Tech., 1951; MBA, TempleU., 1964. Commd. 2d lt. USAF, 1943, advanced through grades to col., pilot, navigator, 1943-74, ret., 1974; v.p. Global Marine, Inc., L.A., 1974-77; sr. v.p. Global Marine Drilling Co., Houston, 1977—. Mem. Am. Petroleum Inst., Nat. Ocean Industries Assn., Internat. Assn. Drilling Contractors, Petroleum Club, Westlake Club (Houston). Republican. Episcopalian. Home: 807 Silvergate Dr Houston TX 77079 Office: Global Marine Drilling Co 777 N Elridge Rd PO Box 4379 Houston TX 77210

NEWTON, GALE JOANN, financial consultant; b. Mich., Nov. 23, 1954; d. Gilbert Allen Sr. and Marjorie J. (Lockard) N. Student, Grand Valley State U., Allendale, Mich., 1978; cert., Life Underwriter Tng. Coun., 1983, 85, 87, 88—. Registered rep. Investors Diversified Svcs., Grand Rapids, Mich., 1980-83; acct. exec. Primus Fin. Svcs. Inc., Grand Rapids, 1983-87; cons. Stifel, Nicolaus & Co., Grand Rapids, 1987—; v.p. bd. Attitudinal Healing Ctr. Grand Rapids. Pres. Midwest Mich. Herb Assn., 1989-90; bd. dirs. Attitudinal Healing Ctr. of Grand Gapids. Grant Taggart scholar Am. Coll., 1985. Mem. Nat. Assn. Profl. Sales Women, Mich. Profl. Sales Women, NAFE, Nat. Assn. Life Underwriters, Mich. and Grand Rapids Life Underwriters. Office: Stifel Nicolaus Inc 4450 Cascade Rd SE Grand Rapids MI 49506

NEWTON, GEORGE ADDISON, investment banker, lawyer; b. Denver, Apr. 2, 1911; s. George Addison and Gertrude (Manderson) N.; m. Mary Virginia Powell, Sept. 18, 1937; children: George Addison IV, Nancy Ella, Virginia Powell. A.B., U. Colo., 1933; LL.B., Harvard U., 1936. Bar: Ill. 1937, Mo. 1946. Asso. firm Scott, MacLeish & Falk, Chgo., 1936-42; partner G.H. Walker & Co., St. Louis, 1946-62; mng. partner G.H. Walker & Co., 1962-72; chmn. bd. Stifel Nicolaus & Co., Inc., St. Louis, 1972-82, chmn. emeritus, 1982—; chief exec. officer Stifel Nicolaus & Co., Inc., 1974-78. Bd. govs. Greater St. Louis Community Chest; mem. Council on Civic Needs; bd. dirs. Episcopal Home for Children, St. Luke's Hosp.; bd. dirs. Goodwill Industries, 1963—, chmn. bd., 1980-82; bd. dirs. U. Colo. Improvement Corp., U. Colo. Found., St. Louis Conservatory Music; dir. devel. fund U. Colo., 1954-55, chmn., 1955; trustee Fontbonne Coll., 1972-80, chmn., 1974-77; trustee Govtl. Research Inst.; trustee, Whitfield Sch., 1978—, pres. 1986-88. Served to maj. USAAF, 1942-45. Recipient C. Fobb award U. Colo., 1955, alumni recognition award, 1958; named to C Club Hall Fame, 1968; silver ann. All Am. award Sports Illustrated, 1957; Norlin award U. Colo., 1968; U. Colo. medal, 1984. Mem. Investment Bankers Assn. Am. (pres. 1961), Nat. Assn. Securities Dealers (gov. 1954-56, vice chmn. 1956), Assn. Stock Exchange Firms (gov. 1969-72), Sales Execs. Assn. (dir. 1955-60), U. Colo. Assn. Alumni (dir. 1965-67), Japan-Am. Soc. St. Louis (dir. 1980—, pres. 1982-85), Phi Beta Kappa, Phi Gamma Delta. Episcopalian (treas. diocese of Mo., 1958-69; sr. warden; trustee diocesan investment trust). Clubs: Racquet (St. Louis), Noonday (St. Louis), St. Louis (St. Louis), Bellerive Country (St. Louis); Denver Country; Legal (Chgo.); Boulder (Colo.) Country; Links (N.Y.C.). Home: 6428 Cecil Ave Saint Louis MO 63105 Office: Stifel Nicolaus & Co Inc 500 N Broadway Saint Louis MO 63102

NEWTON, MARTHA LOUISE, company executive; b. Suffern, N.Y., Mar. 21, 1949; d. Albert Beresford and Dorothy Ruth (Wittmann) N.; m. Jeffrey James Skelley, July 4, 1985. BA, Wagner Coll., 1971; MBA, Fairleigh Dickinson U., 1977. Acct. analyst Western Union Telegraph Co., Upper Saddle River, N.J., 1973; budget analyst Am. Cyanamid Co., Wayne, N.J., 1973-75; circulation analyst Ziff-Davis Pub. Co., N.Y.C., 1975-76; fin. analyst Warner-Lambert Co., Morris Plains, N.J., 1976-78; asst. product mgr. Warner-Lambert Co., Morris Plains, 1978-79; product mgr. Cooper Labs., Inc., Fairfield, N.J., 1979-81; mgr. acquisitions and internat. bus. devel. Johnson and Johnson Ortho. Pharm. Corp., Raritan, N.J, 1981-82; product dir. Johnson and Johnson Ortho. Pharm. Corp., Raritan, 1982-84; pres. Three Bears, Inc., Newport, R.I., 1985—. Episcopalian. Home and Office: 208 Coggeshall Ave PO Box 447 Newport RI 02840

NEWTON, WALLACE BERKELEY, bank executive; b. Newport News, Va., Jan. 31, 1949; s. Willie Berkeley and Susan Alice (Fell) N.; m. Linda Lee Jones, Apr. 25, 1950; children: Wallace Berkeley Jr., Andrew Lee. BS, Va. Tech., 1971, MBA, 1972; cert. bank investments and mcpl. securities, So. Meth. U., 1977; cert. bank lending, U. Okla., 1983. Assoc. fin. analyst Newport News Shipyard, 1972-73; v.p. Bank of Va., Richmond, 1973-84; sr. v.p. PanAm. Bank, Miami, Fla., 1984-86; sr. v.p., chief fin. officer, treas., dir. Heritage Fin. Corp., Richmond, 1986—; adj. faculty J. SArgeant Reynolds Community Coll., Richmond, 1979—, Va. Union U., Richmond, 1981, U. Richmond, 1982—. Pres. Huntington Civic Assn., Richmond, 1974-77; bd. dirs., vol. Trinity United Meth. Ch., Richmond, 1975—; tchr. Jr. Achievement, Richmond, 1980—. Mem. Soc. Fin. Analysts, Fin. Execs. Inst., Am. Inst. Banking (treas., bd. dirs. Richmond chpt. 1980), Richmond Jaycees (pres. 1978-79), Richmond C. of C. (bd. dirs. inter club council 1978-80), Am. Bankers Assn. (reviewer, speaker 1981—), Pine Run Civic Assn. (pres. 1987-88), Va. Tech. MBA Alumni Assn. (bd. dirs. 1988—), Fin. Mgrs. Soc., Theta Xi, Beta Gamma Sigma, Phi Kappa Phi. Republican. Home: 12204 Lateefa Ct Richmond VA 23233 Office: Heritage Fin Corp 500 Forest Ave Richmond VA 23229

NEY, EDWARD NOONAN, investment company executive; b. St. Paul, May 26, 1925; s. John Joseph and Marie (Noonan) N.; m. Suzanne Hayes, 1950 (div. 1974); children: Nicholas, Hilary, Michelle; m. Judith I. Lasky, May 24, 1974. B.A. (Lord Jeffrey Amherst scholar 1942), Amherst Coll., 1947. With Young & Rubicam, Inc., N.Y.C., 1951-86, pres., chief exec. officer, chmn., 1970-77; chmn., chief exec. officer Young & Rubicam, Inc., 1977-85, chmn., 1985-86; chmn. Young & Rubicam Ventures, N.Y.C., 1989—, Paine Webber/Young & Rubicam Ventures, N.Y.C., 1986-89; vice-chmn. Paine Webber, Inc., N.Y.C., 1986-89; bd. dirs. Ctr. for Communication, 1986—. Trustee Nat. Urban League, 1974—, Amherst Coll., 1979—, NYU Med. Center, 1979—, Mus. of Broadcasting, 1982—; bd. govs. Fgn. Policy Assn., 1980—; mem. adv. council Columbia Grad. Sch. of Bus., 1979—; mem. adv. bd. Ctr. for Strategic and Internat. Studies, 1986—; mem. Council on Fgn. Relations. Served to lt. (j.g.) USNR, 1943-46. Mem. Bd. Internat. Broadcasting Ad Coun. (bd. dirs. 1973—, chmn. 1987-88, hon. chmn. 1988—). Office: Young & Rubicam Ventures 540 Madison Ave New York NY 10022

NGUYEN, CHARLES CUONG, engineering educator, researcher; b. Danang, Vietnam, Jan. 1, 1956; came to U.S., 1978, naturalized, 1984; s. Buoi and Tinh Thi Nguyen. Diplom Ing. Konstanz U., Fed. Republic Germany, 1978; M.S. with distinction, George Washington U., 1980, D.Sc. with superior performance, 1982. Engr. Siemens Corp., Erlangen, Fed. Republic Germany, 1977-78; lectr. George Washington U., Washington, 1978-82; asst. prof. engring. Cath. U. Am., Washington, 1982-87, assoc. prof. elec. engring., 1987—; dir. Ctr. for Artificial Intelligence and Robotics, 1985—. Contbr. numerous papers IEEE Transaction of Automatic Control, Internatl Jour of Control. NASA and Am. Soc. Elec. Engrs. fellowship, 1985, 86; recipient Research Initiation award Engring. Found., 1985. Mem. IEEE (v.p. Washington chpt.), Internat. Soc. Mini- and Microcomputers, Am. Biographical Inst., Internat. Biographical Ctr. (rsch. bd. advisors), Sigma Xi, Tau Beta Pi. Roman Catholic. Avocations: guitar, singing, tennis, skiing, ping pong.

NICANDROS, CONSTANTINE STAVROS, oil company executive; b. Port Said, Egypt, Aug. 2, 1933; came to U.S., 1955, naturalized, 1963; s. Stavros Constantine and Helen (Lianakis) N.; m. Tassie Boozalis, May 24, 1959; children: Steve Constantine, Vicky Ellen. Diplome, HEC Ecole des Hautes Etudes Commerciales, 1954; license en droit, Law Sch. U. Paris, 1954, doctorate in economic sci, 1955; M.B.A., Harvard U., 1957. With planning dept. Conoco Inc., Houston, 1957-61; With planning dept. Conoco Inc., N.Y.C., 1961-64, land acquisition internat. exploration-prodn. dept., 1964-65, dir. planning eastern hemisphere, 1966-71, gen. mgr. supply and transp., eastern hemisphere, 1971-72, v.p. supply and transp. eastern hemisphere, 1972-74, exec. v.p. eastern hemisphere refining, mktg. and supply and transp., 1974-75; exec. v.p. worldwide supply and transp. Conoco Inc., Stamford, Conn., 1975-78; group exec. v.p. petroleum products Conoco Inc., Houston, 1978-83, pres. petroleum ops., 1983-87, pres., chief exec. officer, 1987—, also bd. dirs.; dir. and exec. v.p., mem. exec. com. E.I. duPont de Nemours & Co.; bd. dirs. Tex. Commerce Bancshares, Inc., Tex. Commerce

Bank-Houston. Gov. bd. Houston Symphony Soc.; bd. dirs. Am. Heart Assn.; trustee Houston Ballet Found., Mus. Fine Arts-Houston, United Way of Tex. Gulf Coast (1988-89 campaign chmn.), Houston Grand Opera, Baylor Coll. Medicine; chmn. Tex chpt. of Am. Com. on French Revolution Bicentennial. Mem. Am. Petroleum Inst. (bd. dirs.), Tex. Rsch. League (bd. dirs.), Inst. Internat. Edn. (so. regional adv. bd.), Internat. Inst. for Strategic Studies, Ctr. Strategic and Internat. Studies (adv. bd.), The Forum Club (bd. govs. 1983-89), Tex. Ctr. for Superconductivity at U. Houston (adv. bd.), Nat. Petroleum Coun. Greek Orthodox. Office: Conoco Inc PO Box 2197 Houston TX 77252

NICE, DURWARD GALE, JR., city official; b. Independence, Kans., Aug. 11, 1939; s. Durward Gale Sr. and Elizabeth Fern (Parks) N.; m. Barbara Ann Hephner, Mar. 31, 1962; children: Gary Alan, Marvin Gale, Jeffrey Lynn, Steven Wayne. BA in Bus. Adminstrn., Wichita (Kans.) State U., 1963. Entrepreneur Jayhawk Accts. Inc., Wichita, 1969-79; tax acct. Beech Aircraft Inc., Wichita, 1979-80; mgr. taxes Santa Fe Industries Inc., Wichita, 1980-81; entrepreneur Nice & Assocs., Wichita, 1981-85; city adminstr. City of Girard, Kans., 1985-87; fin. dir. City of Colby (Kans.), Kans., 1987—; cons. Unified Sch. Dist. 411, Goessel, Kans., 1983-84, Tymshare Inc., Wichita, Kans., 1984-85; bd. dirs. Mcpl. Energy Agy., McPherson, Kans., 1985-87. Bd. dirs. East Branch YMCA, Wichita, 1981-83, Camp Wood YMCA, Elmdale, Kans., 1981-85. Served to maj. USAF, 1963-85. Mem. Internat. City Mgmt. Assn., Govt. Fin. Officers Assn., City Clks. and Mcpl. Fin. Officers Assn. Kans., Internat. Inst. Mcpl. Clks., Kans. Assn. City Mgmt., Am. Soc. Pub. Adminstrn., Kiwanis (pres. Andover, Kans. chpt. 1967-68, Optimists (sec.-treas. Wichita S.E. chpt. 1977-79). Lodges: Kiwanis (pres. Andover, Kans. chpt. 1967-68), Optimists (sec.-Treas. Wichita SE chpt. 1977-79). Home: 1220 Lue Dr Colby KS 67701-2814 Office: City of Colby 585 N Franklin St Colby KS 67701-2399

NICHOLAS, JOHN RICHARDS, financial administrator; b. N.Y.C., Oct. 3, 1945; s. John Richards and Elizabeth (Morris) N.; m. Nancy Engelhardt, Sept. 10, 1966; children: Suzanne, Diana. AB, Coll. William and Mary, 1969; MBA, Thomas Coll., 1988. Product distbn. specialist Cadillac Motorcar div. Gen. Motors Corp., Teaneck, N.J., 1969-72; employment counselor Me. Dept. Personnel, Augusta, 1973-74; budget analyst Me. bur. budget Me. Gov.'s Office, Augusta, 1974-78; dir. adminstrv. svcs. Me. Dept. Pub. Safety, Augusta, 1978-86; dir. fin., adminstrn. Me. Vocat.-Tech. Inst. System, Augusta, 1986—. Chmn. budget com. Town of Litchfield, Me., 1979. Recipient Gov.'s Disting. Svc. award, Me., 1974. Mem. Inst. Internal Auditors, Nat. Assn. Coll. and Univ. Bus. Officers, Masons, Rotary. Democrat. Episcopalian. Office: Me Vocat Tech Inst System 323 State St Sta 131 Augusta ME 04333

NICHOLAS, LAWRENCE BRUCE, import company executive; b. Dallas, Nov. 9, 1945; s. J. W. and Helen Elouise (Whiteacre) N.; B.B.A., So. Meth. U., 1968; m. Virginia Pearl Farmer, Aug. 5, 1967; children—Helen Brooke, John Lawrence, Alexis Bradlee. Mem. sales staff Nicholas Machinery Co., Dallas, 1963-69; sales mgr. Indsl. and Comml. Research Corp., Dallas, 1969-74; v.p. Precision Concepts Corp., Dallas, 1974-76, gen. mgr., 1976-78, pres., Addison, Tex., 1978-86, dir., 1974-86 ; pres. INCOR Inc., Addison, 1974—, dir., 1972—; pres. INCOR Internat., Dallas, 1981—; pres., dir. Multiple Axis Machine Corp., 1986—. Served as officer Ordnance Corps, U.S. Army, 1968, N.G., 1968-74. Mem. Nat. Sporting Goods Assn., Nat. Assn. Diecutters and Diemakers, Nat. Rifle Assn., Nat. Shooting Sports Found., Safari Club Internat, Game Conservation Internat., Dallas Council on World Affairs (dir.), Internat. Trade Assn. of Dallas. Club: Bent Tree Country. Office: INCOR Inc PO Box 918 Addison TX 75001

NICHOLAS, NICHOLAS JOHN, JR., communications company executive; b. Portsmouth, N.H., Sept. 3, 1939; s. Nicholas John N.; B.A. magna cum laude, Princeton U., 1962; M.B.A., Harvard U., 1964; m. Llewellyn Jones, May 27, 1972; children: Charlotte, John, Hilary, Alexander, Alexandra. Dir. fin. analysis Time Inc., N.Y.C., 1964-69, asst. to pres., 1970, asst. treas., 1971-73, v.p., from 1975, now pres., chief operating officer, 1986—, dir.; pres. Manhattan Cable TV, 1973-76; pres. Home Box Office, N.Y.C., 1976-80, chmn., 1979-81, chief fin. officer, 1982—. Office: Time Inc Time & Life Bldg New York NY 10020 *

NICHOLAS, ROBERT B., insurance executive; b. 1929; married. BA, Denison U., 1950; MS, Columbia U., 1954. With Mobile Oil Corp., 1956-60; mgr. corp. planning Atlantic Richfield Co., 1960-71; v.p. corp. planning Aetna Casualty & Surety Co., Hartford, Conn., 1971-76, v.p. fin. and planning, 1976-86, sr. v.p. corp. planning and devel., 1986—. 1st lt. U.S. Army, 1951-53. Office: Aetna Casualty & Surety Co 151 Farmington Ave Hartford CT 06156 *

NICHOLS, C. WALTER, III, banker; b. N.Y.C., Aug. 25, 1937; s. Charles Walter and Marjorie (Jones) N.; B.A., U. Va., 1959; m. Anne Sharp, Aug. 8, 1959; children—Blair, Sandra, Walter, Hope. Vice pres. Citibank, N.Y.C., 1962-78, Morgan Guaranty Trust Co. N.Y., N.Y.C., 1979—. Bd. dirs. Nichols Found., Inc., 1969—, pres. 1988—; Choate Rosemary Hall, 1972-77, 82-89, Greenwich House, 1972—, pres., 1984—, Lower Hudson (N.Y.) chpt. Nature Conservancy, 1978-87, hon. trustee, 1988—, John Jay Homestead, 1980—, Nat. Audubon Soc., 1983-87, pres. council, 1988—; mem. adv. bd. N.Y. Zool. Soc. (Bronx Zoo), 1987—. Served to 1st lt. U.S. Army, 1960-62. Decorated Army Commendation medal. Mem. Am. Sunbathing Assn., Naturist Soc. Clubs: Bedford (N.Y.) Golf and Tennis, Pilgrims of U.S. Office: Morgan Guaranty Trust Co NY 9 W 57th St New York NY 10019

NICHOLS, CHARLES LEE, professional services executive; b. Seminole, Okla., Nov. 1, 1941; s. Calvin Eugene Nichols and Irene Frances (Newport) Christopher; m. Ofelia Luna, Nov. 27, 1967 (div. Oct. 1986); 1 child, William C. BA in English, Tex. A&M U., 1963; LLB, U. Tex., 1966. Bar: Tex. 1966, Calif. 1971. Sr. v.p. Sci. Applications Internat. Corp., San Diego, 1970—. Bd. dirs. Profl. Services Council, Washington, 1985. Capt. USAF, 1966-70. Mem. Calif. Bar Assn., Tex. Bar Assn. Club: San Diego Yacht. Home: 6455 La Jolla Blvd #146 La Jolla CA 92037 Office: Sci Applications Internat Corp 10260 Campus Point Dr San Diego CA 92121

NICHOLS, DUANE RAY, federal law enforcement officer; b. St. Louis, Feb. 9, 1943; s. Ray Smith and Evelyn Ann (Carpenter) N.; m. Sue Anne Barbarick, Mar. 22, 1965; children: Evelyn Anne, Eric Allen. BA, Cen. Mo. State U., 1968. Agy. rep. Justice Dept. Strike Force, Kansas City, 1974, Republican Conv., 1976, Kansas City Arson Com., 1981-82, Organized Crime Drug Task Force, 1986—; spl. agt. Bur. Alcohol, Tobacco and Firearms U.S. Dept. Treasury, Kansas City, Mo., 1988—. Vol., asst. coach Lee's Summit (Mo.) Little League basketball, soccer, baseball, 1980-86. Served with USMC, 1961-64. Recipient Agy. award Honor for Outstanding Accomplishment Narcotic Law Enforcement Internat. Narcotic Enforcement Officers Assn., 1988. Mem. Mo. Conservation Fedn., Mo. Hist. Soc. Presbyterian. Home: 211 SE Westwind Dr Lee's Summit MO 64063 Office: BATF US Treasury 811 Grand Ave Room 106 US Courthouse Kansas City MO 64106

NICHOLS, HAROLD NEIL, pipeline company executive; b. Digby, N.S., Can., June 15, 1937; s. Harold A. and Lillian (Nielsen) N.; m. Doris E. Outhouse, Mar. 2, 1957; children—Michael, Dale, Sherri, Susan, Lori. G-rad. high sch. Cert. Mgmt. Acct. Various financial positions TransCan. PipeLines Ltd., Toronto, Ont., 1956-73; treas. TransCan. PipeLines Ltd., 1973-77, v.p., treas., 1977-80, v.p. fin., treas., 1980-81, sr. v.p. fin., 1982-83, sr. v.p., chief fin. officer, 1983-87, exec. v.p., 1988—; bd. dirs. Union Bank Switzerland (Can.), Temcell Inc., Trans Quebec. and Maritime Pipeline Inc., TCPL Nederland B.V., Western Gas Mktg., Cyprus Anvil Mining Corp., TransCanada Pipelines (USA); pres. Sable Gas Systems Ltd.; mem. Fin. Execs. Inst., Bd. of Trade Metro Toronto. Home: 7 Blackwell Ct, Unionville, ON Canada Office: TransCan Pipelines Ltd, Commerce Ct W PO Box 54, Toronto, ON Canada M5L 1C2

NICHOLS, HENRY ELIOT, lawyer, savings and loan executive; b. N.Y.C., Jan. 3, 1924; s. William and Elizabeth (Lisse) N.; m. Frances Griffin Morrison, Aug. 12, 1950 (dec. July 1978); children: Clyde Whitney, Diane Spencer; m. Mary Ann Wall, May 31, 1987. B.A., Yale U., 1946; J.D., U. Va., 1948. Bar: D.C. 1950, U.S. Dist. Ct. 1950, U.S. Ct. Appeals 1952, U.S. Supreme Ct. 1969. Assoc. Frederick W. Berens, Washington, 1950-52; sole practice, Washington, 1952—; real estate columnist Washington Star, 1966-81; pres., gen. counsel Hamilton Fed. Savs. & Loan Assn., 1971-74; vice chmn. bd. Columbia 1st Fed. Savs. & Loan Assn., Washington, 1974—; pres. Century Fin. Corp., 1971—; regional v.p. Preview, Inc., 1972-78; dir., exec. com. Columbia Real Estate Title Ins. Co., Washington, 1968-78; dir. Greater Met. Bd. Trade, 1974-78, Dist. Realty Title Ins. Co., 1978-86. Nat. adv. bd. Harker Prep. Sch., 1975-80; exec. com. Father Walter E. Schmitz Meml. Fund, Cath. U., 1982=83; bd. dirs. Vincent T. Lombardi Cancer Research Ctr., 1979-84; del. Pres. Johnson's Conf. Law and Poverty, 1967; vice chmn. Mayor's Ad Hoc Com. Housing Code Problems, Washington, 1968-71; mem. Commn. Landlord-Tenant Affairs Washington City Council, 1970-71; vice chmn. Washington Area Realtors Council, 1970; exec. com., dir. Downtown Progress, 1970; bd. dirs. Washington Mental Health Assn., 1973, Washington Med Ctr., 1975. Served to capt. USAAF, 1942-46. Mem. Am. Land Devel. Assn., Nat. Assn. Realtors, Nat. Assn. Real Estate Editors, Washington Bd. Realtors (pres. 1970, Realtor of Yr. 1970, Martin Isen award 1981), Greater Met. Washington Bd. Trade (bd. dirs. 1974-80), U.S. League Savs. Assns. (attys. com. 1971-80), Washington Savs. and Loan League, ABA, D.C. Bar Assn., Internat. Real Estate Fedn., Omega Tau Rho. Episcopalian. Clubs: Yale, Cosmos, Rolls Royce, Antique Auto, St. Elmo. Patentee med. inventions; contbr. articles profl. jours. Address: 1 Kittery Ct Bethesda MD 20817 Office: 1122 Connecticut Ave NW Washington DC 20036

NICHOLS, JAMES PHILLIP, insurance agency executive; b. Kenosha, Wis., Jan. 14, 1944; s. Oswald R. and Emily B. (Kowski) N.; student public schs., Kenosha; m. Linda Bedlyon, May 19, 1973; 1 son, Jeremy James. Sales agt. Phoenix Mut. Life, Chgo., 1968-69, office mgr., Phila., 1969-79, sales mgr., 1979—, v.p. corp. fin. services, 1979—. Served with U.S. Army, 1965-67. Mem. Internat. Assn. Registered Fin. Planners, Am. Soc. C.L.U.s, Phila. Assn. Life Underwriters, Phila. Gen. Agts. and Mgrs. Assn. Nat. Assn. Securities Dealers (registered rep.). Home: 109 Round Hill Rd Voorhees Township NJ 08043 Office: Phoenix Mutual Life The Bellevue 4th Fl Philadelphia PA 19102

NICHOLS, JAMES RICHARD, trust company executive; b. Newton, Mass., Apr. 19, 1938; s. Richard M. and Ruth J. (Killian) N.; m. Elizabeth Dunn, Sept. 7, 1963; children: Jennifer, Richard. BA, Dartmouth Coll., 1960; LLB, Harvard U., 1963. Bar: Mass. 1963; chartered fin. analyst. Assoc. Herrick & Smith, Boston, 1964-69; assoc. Goodwin, Procter & Hoar, Boston, 1969-77; ptnr. Nichols & Pratt, family trustee office, Boston, 1977—; dir. Foxboro Co., Middle South Utilities, Inc. Commr. trust funds Town of Weston, Mass., 1976—; chmn., trustee Mus. of Sci., Boston. Mem. Boston Bar Assn., Boston Security Analysts Soc., Union Club (Boston). Home: 23 Wellesley St Weston MA 02193 Office: Nichols & Pratt 50 Congress St Boston MA 02109

NICHOLS, JOHN D., diversified manufacturing corporation executive; b. Shanghai, China, 1930; m. Alexandra M. Curran, Dec. 4, 1971; children: Kendra E., John D. III. B.A., Harvard U., 1953, M.B.A., 1955. Various operating positions Ford Motor Corp., 1958-68; dir. fin. controls ITT Corp., 1968-69; exec. v.p., chief operating officer Aerojet-Gen. Corp., 1969-79; exec. v.p. Ill. Tool Works Inc., Chgo., 1980-81; pres. Ill. Tool Works Inc., 1981—, chief operating officer, 1981-82, chief exec. officer, dir., 1982—, chmn., 1986—; bd. dirs. Household Internat., Rockwell Internat., NICOR, Stone Container Corp. Trustee U. Chgo., Argonne Nat. Lab., Chgo. Symphony Orch., Lyric Opera Chgo., Mus. Sci. and Industry, Jr. Achievement Chgo. Served to lt. AUS, 1955-58. Clubs: Harvard (Chgo.); Indian Hill (Winnetka, Ill.); Olympic (San Francisco), Chgo., Comml., Econ. Club Chgo. Office: Ill Tool Works Inc 8501 W Higgins Rd Chicago IL 60631

NICHOLS, JOSEPH, implant technology executive; b. N.Y.C., July 9, 1917; s. Nathan and Minnie (Minken) N.; m. Sylvia Dickler, July 13, 1951; children: Peter, Robert. BS, CCNY, 1938, MS, 1942; PhD, U. Minn., 1943; postgrad., Fed. Inst. Tech., Zurich, Switzerland, 1950-51. Sr. chemist Interchen. Corp., N.Y.C., 1943-49; from chief organic chemistry to dir. rsch. Ethicon, Inc., New Brunswick, N.J., 1951-68; pres. Princeton (N.J.) Biomedix Inc., 1968-76, Helitrex Inc., Princeton, 1976-85; v.p. rsch. and devel. Am. Biomaterials Corp., Plainsboro, N.J., 1985-86; pres. Prodex Inc., Princeton, 1986—. Patentee in field; contbr. articles to profl. jours. Recipient Johnson medal, Johnson & Johnson Co., 1965. Mem. Am. Chem. Soc., AAAS, Soc. Biomaterials, Am. Assn. Artificial Internal Organs, N.Y. Acad. Scis. Home: 28 Longview Dr Princeton NJ 08540 Office: Prodex Inc 3490 US 1 Princeton NJ 08540

NICHOLS, MARILYN JACKSON, financial planner; b. New Brunswick, N.J., Mar. 29, 1938; d. Wilfrid James and Mabel (Mott) Jackson; m. David C. Nichols, Feb. 21, 1962; 1 child, Deborah Kay Hannan. BA, Oberlin Coll., 1959. Cert. fin. planner. Asst. young adult program dir. YWCA, Flint, Mich., 1959-60; group mgr. Gimbel's, Phila., 1960-62; rep. All Am. Mgmt., Springfield, Ill., 1969-83; pres. Money Matters, Inc., Champaign, Ill., 1975—; corp. sec. IAA, Ill., Inc., Savoy, 1968—. Author: The Woman's Guide to Financial Planning, 1978, The Teacher's Manual for the Woman's Guide, 1979; developer cassette tapes, course materials in field. Mem. adv. bd. women's program Parkland Coll., Champaign, 1974, 75; mem. endowment com. YWCA, Campaign, 1986—; adviser Parents Without Ptnrs., Champaign, 1976—. Mem. Internat. Assn. Fin. Planning, Inst. Cert. Planners, AAUW. Office: Money Matters Inc Devonshire Corp Centre 510 Devonshire Dr Ste A1 Champaign IL 61820

NICHOLS, ROBERT LEE, food company executive; b. Clarksburg, W.Va., Nov. 4, 1924; s. Clarence Garfield and Reatha Maude (Berry) N.; m. Vianne Hope Demaray, Oct. 21, 1973; children: Donna Beth, Michael Alan, Jeffrey Mark. Student, Bus. Coll., 1944, U. Detroit, 1959. Sales rep. Kellogg Sales Co., Battle Creek, Mich., 1944-50; dist. mgr. Kellogg Sales Co., 1950-61, asst. div. mgr., 1961-64, sales promotion dir., 1964-69, exec. v.p., gen. sales mgr., 1969-71, pres., 1976-78; pres. Fearn Internat., 1971-76, dir., 1971-82; group exec. v.p. Kellogg Co., Battle Creek, 1979-82, dir., 1977—, vice chmn., 1983—; pres., dir. Mrs. Smith's Frozen Foods Co., 1979-82, McCamly Square Corp., 1983—; dir., pres. Battle Creek Unltd., 1985-87; bd. dirs. Cereal Inst., 1976-79, Am. Frozen Food Inst., 1979-82, Battle Creek Gas Co., 1986—, Mich. Nat. Bank, 1986—, Cereal City Devel. Corp., 1986; bd. govs. Acad. Food Mktg., St. Joseph U., 1976-79. Exec. v.p., bd. dirs. Jr. Achievement, Battle Creek, 1970-71; trustee Mich. Colls. Found., 1985—, Thomas Jeferson Found., Lakeview Schs., 1987—, Mich. Biotechnology Inst., 1985—, Citizens Research Council of Mich, 1985—; mem., bd. dirs. United Way of Greater Battle Creek Area, 1984—, campaign chmn. 1985; pres. Battle Creek Unltd., 1985-87; vice chmn. Battle Creek Airport Adv. Com., 1984—; mem. Nat. Corp. Council Interlochen Ctr. for the Arts, 1986—. Mem. Battle Creek Area C. of C. Clubs: Battle Creek Country, Masons. Office: Kellogg Co 1 Kellogg Sq PO Box 3599 Battle Creek MI 49016-3599

NICHOLS, ROBERT WAYNE, financial company executive; b. Houston, June 28, 1938; s. Edward Wallace and Frankie (Nelson) Reed; m. Pamela Lee Williams, Dec. 18, 1965 (div. 1972); m. Jacqueline Roberta Pyne, Sept. 22, 1980; children: Lauren Ashley, Shannon Hillary, Reed Chandler. MBA, Pepperdine U., 1980; MA in Mgmt., Claremont Grad. Sch., 1983; MBA in Fin., Claremont Coll., 1984, postgrad., 1984—. Pres. RNC Capital Mgmt. Co., Los Angeles, 1971—, also bd. dirs.; pres. Roley, Nichols Capital Group, Los Angeles, 1971—, also bd. dirs.; chmn. Westwind, Regency, Income, Liquid assets, Convertible RNC Short/Internat. Govt Bond Fund, RNC Mutual Fund Group, 1971—; bd. dirs. IMC Asset Mgmt. Co., L.A.; staff writer Modern Maturity Mag., Wilson County News. Gen.-chmn. USMC Scholarship Found., Los Angeles, 1986; bd. advisors Salvation Army; trustee USMC Command and Staff Coll. Found.; bd. dirs. L.A. Unified Sch. Dist. Pension Fund. Capt. USMC, 1963-67, Vietnam. Decorated 9 Air medals, Purple Heart. Mem. Ironwood Country Club, Bel Air Country Club, Bel Air Bay Club. Republican. Office: Roley Nichols Capital Group Inc 11601 Wilshire Blvd Penthouse Los Angeles CA 90025

NICHOLS, THOMAS EDWARD, welding inspector; b. Brownfield, Miss., Nov. 30, 1947; s. E. V. and Vildean (Welch) N.; m. Debra Kay Mannon, Sept. 11, 1978; children: Stacy, Angela, Justin, Danny. Student, Ark. State U., 1966-69. Quality control inspector Taylor Machine Works, West Memphis, Ark., 1975-78; quality control mgr. Taylor Machine Works, West Memphis, 1978-79; quality control inspector Plant Service Corp., Memphis, 1979—. Sgt. U.S. Army, 1970-72. Mem. Stage Park Neighborhood Assn., Am. Welding Soc. (co-chmn. hospitality com. 1988), So. Investment Group (pres. 1987—), VFW. Republican. Baptist. Office: Plant Maintenance Svc Corp 3000 Fite Rd Memphis TN 38168

NICHOLSON, CHARLES WILLIAM, finance company executive; b. Balt., Sept. 25, 1929; s. Walter James and Ada Flavia (Jubb) N.; m. Fay Ann, Aug. 25, 1985. AA, U. Balt., 1948. Collector G.E. Credit Corp., Balt., 1957-60; credit mgr. Washington, 1960-61; mgr. Harrisburg, Pa., 1962-67; dist. mgr. Balt., 1968-74, Atlanta, 1974-76; region mgr. Danbury, Conn., 1976-80; territory mgr. Danbury, 1981-84; v.p. Stamford, Conn., 1984-86; v.p. div. G.E. Capitol Corp., Stamford, 1986—; chmn., bd. dirs. GECC Leasing, P.R., 1980, IGE Credit, London, 1986, Navistar Credit Corp., Burlington, Ont., 1986; mem. GFC, Hawaii, 1987. chmn. bd. dirs. GECC Leasing, Puerto Rico, 1980—, IGE Credit, London, 1986, Navistar Credit Corp., Burlington, Ont., Can., 1986. Active United Way, Stamford, 1986—. Sgt. U.S. Army, 1951-54. Mem. Am. Assn. Equipment Lessors (com. govt. relations 1987—), Am. Trucking Assn. (bd. dirs.). Home: 136 Roberton Crossing Fairfield CT 06430 Office: GE Capital Corp 260 Long Ridge Rd Stamford CT 06902

NICHOLSON, HUBERT EDWIN, architect; b. Wichita Falls, Tex., Aug. 27, 1924; s. Oran and Beulah Elizabeth (Cooper) N.; m. Bobbie Joyce McNeese Nicholson, June 9, 1946; children: Kay Joyce Greehaw, Gary Edwin. Student, Hardin Jr. Coll., 1942; BS in Archtl. Engring., U. Tex., 1949, BArch, 1950, postgrad., 1976. Cert. architect, Tex., profl. engr., Tex. Draftsman Walsh & Hazlewood, Amarillo, Tex., 1946-48; teaching fellow U. Tex., Austin, 1948; structural designer Wilson & Cuttingham, Engrs., Austin, 1948-50; architect Malcolm G. Simons, San Antonio, 1950-51; pvt. practice San Antonio, 1952-59; pres., dir. Ed Nicholson Assocs., Inc., San Antonio, 1960—; architect Community Savs. and Loan Home Offices, 1964, Frito-Lay Distbn. Ctr. Network, 1978-83; v.p., bd. dirs. Bowlerlarama of Tex., San Antonio, 1980—. Pres. McArthur Band Parents Assn., San Antonio, 1967; architect Hispanic Bapt. Theol. Sem., 1960—, David Thrift Meml. Chapel, 1956. With U.S. Army, 1943-46, ETO. Mem. Nat. Coun. Architects, AIA, Tex. Soc. Architects, Alzafar Shrine Club, San Antonio Club, Scottish Rite. Baptist. Home: 8802 Pineridge San Antonio TX 78217 Office: 8523 Tee Cee Ln San Antonio TX 78217

NICHOLSON, LELAND ROSS, retired utilities company executive, energy consultant; b. Carrington, N.D., Feb. 21, 1924; s. Malcom and Lena May (Kerlin) N.; m. Virginia E. Blair, Mar. 16, 1946; children: Heather Lee Nicholson Studebaker, Leland B., Holly Kay. Student, Northwestern U., 1940-41; BSEE, U. N.D., 1949; postgrad. in utility mgmt., U. Minn., 1952. Planning and mktg. engr. Minkota Power Coop., Grand Forks, N.D., 1949-54; dir. new bus. Kans. Power & Light Co., Topeka, 1954-64, v.p. mktg., 1964-76, sr. v.p., 1976-80, exec. v.p., 1980-83, also bd. dirs.; pres. Kans. Power & Light Gas Service, Topeka, 1985-88, ret., 1988; pres., chief operating officer The Gas Service Co., Kansas City, Mo., 1983-85; pres. Indsl. Devel. Corp., Topeka; chmn. Kans. Council on Electricity and Environment; exec. com. Kansas City Labor Mgmt. Council, 1986-89; mem. Mktg. Execs. Conf.; bd. dirs. Gas Service Energy Corp., Kansas City, Merchants Nat. Bank, Topeka. Idea innovator heat pump water heater, photo cell controlled yard light, electric grill. Bd. dirs., area relations com. Kansas City (Mo.) Area Econ. Devel. Council, 1983-89; bd. dirs. Kansas City Pvt. Industry Council, 1986-89, Kansas City Downtown Council; trustee U. Mo., Kansas City, 1984—; mktg. chmn. Kansas City Full Employment Council; past chmn., mem. Topeka-Shawnee County Planning Commn.; adult adv. com. Sea Scouts. Served to master sgt. USMC, 1942-46. Mem. Am. Gas Assn., Midwest Gas Assn. (bd. dirs. 1985-89), Mo. Valley Electric Assn. (chmn. 1979-81), Edison Electric Inst. (mktg. chmn. 1978-80), Assoc. Industries of Mo., Kans. Assn. Commerce and Industry, Greater Kansas City (Mo.) C. of C. (bd. dirs. 1983-89), Top of First Club (bd. dirs. 1979-82), Shawnee Yacht Club (Topeka, commodore 1972-74), Kansas City Club, Rotary. Republican. Congregationalist.

NICHOLSON, LUTHER BEAL, financial consultant; b. Sulphur Springs, Tex., Dec. 15, 1921; s. Stephen Edward and Elma (McCracken) N.; B.B.A., So. Meth. U., 1942, postgrad., 1946-47, Tex. U., 1947-48; diploma Southwestern Grad. Sch. Banking, 1967; m. Ruth Wimbish, May 29, 1952; children—Penelope Elizabeth, Stephen David. Controller, Varo, Inc., Garland, Tex., 1946-55, dir., 1947-72, v.p. fin., 1955-66, sr. v.p., 1966-67, exec. v.p., 1967-70, pres., 1970-71, chmn. bd., 1971-72, cons. to bd. dirs., 1972-75; gen. mgr. Challenger Lock Co., Los Angeles, 1956-58; dir. Varo Inc. Electrokinetics div., Varo Optical, Inc., Biometrics Instrument Corp., Varo Atlas GmbH, Micropac Industries, Inc., Gt. No. Corp., Garland Bank & Trust Co. Bd. dirs., exec. v.p. Harriett Stanton-Edna Murray Found. Served with AUS, 1942-46. Mem. Fin. Execs. Inst. (past pres.), Am. Inst. C.P.A.'s, AIM, Am. Mgmt. Assn., NAM. Home: 1917 Melody Ln Garland TX 75042 Office: 610 Main Garland TX 75040

NICHOLSON, PHILIP EARL, marketing communications official; b. Cleve., June 4, 1947; s. Burton Albert and Ruth (Wilks) N.; A.S. Engring., Cuyahoga Community Coll., 1968; m. Claire Lois Beaumier, Dec. 21, 1969; children—Jennifer Ruth, Laura Ann, Stephen Owen, Cheryl Lynn, Amy Renée. Draftsman, Tylok Internat., Euclid, Ohio, 1963-65; illustrator, draftsman Preformed Line Products Co., Cleve., 1965-69; illustrator, technician Preformed Line Products Co., Cleve., 1972-73; communications mgr. Stock Equipment Co., Cleve., 1973-84; communications mgr. automotive aftermarket div. Sherwin-Williams Co., 1984-88, store mgr. Radio Shack div. Tandy Corp., 1988—. Mem. Boy Scouts Am. Alumni. With USN, 1969-72. Republican. Presbyterian.

NICHOLSON, STUART ADAMS, lawyer, ecologist and environmental scientist; b. Albany, N.Y., May 24, 1941; s. Kenneth Gerald and Gladyce (Wenz) N.; children: Laura Ellice, Paul Michael. BS in Biology, SUNY-Albany, 1964, MS in Biology, 1965; PhD in Botany, U. Ga., 1970; JD, U. N.D., 1983. Bar: N.D. 1983, Minn. 1984. Research assoc. atomospheric sci. SUNY-Albany, 1970-71; asst. prof. biology State U. Coll., Fredonia, N.Y., 1971-75; ecologist Environment Cons. Inc., Mayville, N.Y., 1975-76; lectr. biology U. So. Pacific, Suva, Fiji, 1976-78; sr. research analyst St. Lawrence-Eastern Ont. Commn., Watertown, N.Y., 1979-80; sr. research scientist U. N.D., Grand Forks, 1980-82, assoc. dir., 1982-83, program dir., 1983-84; atty. various law firms, Mpls., 1984—; cons. firms, corps., 1973-79; sr. practitioner Legal Aid Assn. N.D., Grand Forks, 1982-83; mem. Voluntary Income Tax Assistance, Grand Forks, 1981; tchr. U. Ga., State U. Coll., Fredonia, U. South Pacific, Empire State Coll., 1965-67, 71-79; advisor govtl. orgns., 1972-84; ecology resource advisor N.Y. State Dept. Environ. Conservation, Albany, 1973; bd. dirs. Chautauqua County Environ. Def. Council, Jamestown, 1973-75, Grand Forks Food Coop., 1984; organizer Chautauqua Lake Biology Symposium, 1974. Contbr. articles to profl. jours.; reviewer Bull. of Torrey Bot. Club, 1974, 83. Grantee U. South Pacific, 1976-78, NSF grantee, 1974; State U. Coll. fellow, 1972-75; N.D. Pub. Service Commn. research contract 1983, Office Surface Mining research contract, 1982. Mem. ABA, Minn. State Bar Assn., State Bar Assn. N.D., Ecol. Soc. Am., Brit. Ecol. Soc., Sigma Xi, Phi Sigma, Beta Beta Beta. Home: Box 201312 Bloomington MN 55420

NICKEL, ALBERT GEORGE, advertising agency executive; b. Pitts., July 12, 1943; s. Frank George and Dorothy (Wiefling) N.; m. Margery Flanders, May 31, 1968; children: Melissa, Mark. AB, Washington and Jefferson Coll., 1965; MBA, Ind. U., 1967. Mktg. research analyst Pfizer, Inc., N.Y.C., 1967, profl. service rep., 1967-68, mktg. research mgr., 1968-69, product mgr., 1969-70; product mgr. USV Internat., Tuckahoe, N.Y., 1970-71; account exec. J. Walter Thompson (Deltakos), N.Y.C., 1971-72, account supr., 1972-73; account supr. Sudler & Hennessey, N.Y.C., 1973-77; sr. v.p. mgmt. group supr. Young and Rubicam, N.Y.C., 1977-79; exec. v.p./dir. ops. Dorritie & Lyons, Inc., N.Y.C., 1979—. Trustee Wilton YMCA; bd. dirs., exec. com. Wilton LaCrosse Assn., Wilton High Sch. Long Range Planning Team. Served to capt. USAF, 1969. Mem. Pharm. Advt. Council, Mkdwest Pharm. Adv. Council. Club: Wilton Riding (pres.), Shore and Country, Silver Spring Country. Home: 97 Keelers Ridge Rd Wilton CT 06897 Office: Dorritie & Lyons Inc 655 3d Ave 21st Fl New York NY 10017

NICKEL, SUSAN EARLENE, physical education educator, financial analyst; b. Fort Madison, Iowa, June 27, 1951; d. Earl Dean and Irma Ellen (Ivins) N. BE, Northeast Mo. State U., 1973. Phys. edn. tchr. Ft. Madison (Iowa) Sr. High. Sch., 1974-79; phys. edn. specialist Los Angeles Unified Schs., 1979—; fin. planner, then mgr. Martin Fin. Services, Marina Del Rey, Calif., 1986—. Bd. dirs. Connexxus Womens' Ctr., Los Angeles, 1985-87, profl. women's facilitator, 1984—; vol. facilitator Los Angeles Womens' Ctr., 1981-84; vol. Spl. Olympics, U.S. Assn. for Blind Athletes, Exceptional Games, Women's Wheelchair Basketball Assn., all Los Angeles. Mem. Los Angeles Adapted Phys. Edn. Assn. (bd. dirs.), Calif. Assn. Health, Phys. Edn., Recreation and Dance, Bus. and Profl. Alliance, Nat. Assn. Female Execs. Office: Martin Fin Svcs 13160 Mindanao Way Marina del Rey CA 90292

NICKELS, ROBERT EDWARD, plastic manufacturing company executive; b. Detroit, Jan. 23, 1943; s. William Edward and Winifred June (Hocking) N.; m. Carol Lee Johnson, Jan. 26, 1963; children: Tracy Lee, Robbie Lynn. BS in Mech. Engring., Mich. State U., 1966, MBA, 1967; postgrad., Stanford U., 1978. With Procter & Gamble, Chgo., 1967-69; prodn. mgr. Roper Lawn Products, Newark, Ohio, 1969-71; v.p., gen. mgr. Roper Lawn Products, Savannah, Ga., 1971-77; v.p. mfg. Roper Outdoor Products, Bradley, Ill., 1977-79, exec. v.p., 1979-81, pres., 1981-83; v.p. mfg. Sewell Plastics, Inc., Atlanta, 1983-84, exec. v.p., 1984-85, pres., chief exec. officer, 1985—; adv. bd. Allendale Ins., Johnson, R.I., 1986—. Mem. Nat. Assn. for Plastic Container Recovery (chmn. 1987—), Flying Rebel Club. Republican. Presbyterian. Home: 646 Gunby Rd SE Marietta GA 30067 Office: Sewell Plastics Inc 5375 Drake Dr Atlanta GA 30336

NICKELSON, DONALD EUGENE, brokerage house executive; b. Emporia, Kans., Dec. 9, 1932; s. Harry and Mildred B. (Nicholson) N.; m. Barbara Ruth Fronterhouse, Jan. 7, 1950; children: Marta, Nancy, Donny, Dana, Harry, Margaret, Elizabeth, James, Douglas. Mgr. Bache & Co., Beverly Hills, Calif., 1956-64; partner A.G. Edwards & Sons, St. Louis, 1964-66; sr. v.p., dir. Paine Webber Jackson & Curtis, Los Angeles, 1967-80; exec. v.p., dir. Paine Webber Jackson & Curtis, 1980-81, pres., chief exec. officer, 1981—; pres. consumer mkts. Paine Webber Inc., 1986-88; pres. Paine Webber Group, 1988—; former chmn. Pacific Stock Exchange; chmn. Pacific Depository Trust.; dir. Chgo. Bd. Options Exchange; bd. dirs. Work Wear Corp., Inc., Fletcher Jones Found., Wyndham Baking Co., Inc., Hoover Group, Inc., Motor Wheel, Corp., Braniff, Peebles, Inc., Harbour Group, Ltd. Chmn. Harris County (Tex.) March of Dimes, 1968. Mem. Securities Industry Assn. (dir.), Jonathon Club, Stock Exchange Club, N.Y. Athletic Club, Recess Club, Ramada Club, L.A. Bond Club, Econ. Club of N.Y., N.Y. Bond Club, Petroleum Club, University Club. Republican. Lutheran. Office: Paine Webber Group 1285 Ave of the Americas New York NY 10019

NICKEY, KARYL KRISTINE, accountant; b. Elmhurst, Ill., Oct. 1, 1950; d. Edward Albert and Verna Eulalia (Bergdahl) N.; student Western Ill. U., 1968-69; B.A. in Acctg. (Farmers Ins. Group scholar), B.A. in Psychology, North Central Coll., 1977. Billing and accounts payable clk. NBC, 1972-75; acct. Oak Brook Devel. Co., 1976-77; acctg. mgmt. trainee A.C. Nielsen Co., Northbrook Ill., 1977-78, supr. payroll and payroll taxation, 1978-80; corp. payroll mgr. Brunswick Corp., Skokie, Ill., 1980—. Tchr. swimming to handicapped ARC; founder, coach Villa Park Swim Team, 1967-69; asst. coach Oak Brook Bath and Tennis Club, 1969-71, swimming instr., 1968-73; asst. instr. Horseback Riding for the Handicapped, 1976-77; vol. Good Shepherd Hosp., Barrington, Ill., unit co-chmn. vols. for orthopedics and obstets., 1980-82; mem. Horsemasters Drill Team; appeared in film Managing Your Emotions. Mem. Nat. Assn. Accts. (asso. dir. meetings Chgo. chpt. 1979-80, dir. meetings 1980-81, program dir. 1981-82), Am. Payroll Assn. Mem. First Ch. of Oak Brook. Club: Riding (Barrington Hills, Ill.), Oak Brook Bath and Tennis.

NICKLAS, JAMES BISHOP, manufacturing company executive; b. Chambersburg, Pa., Oct. 18, 1949; s. Reginald Bishop and Margaret Ann (Kirkpatrick) N.; m. Rebecca Ann Dickson, June 3, 1972; children: Peter, James, Laura, John. BS, Pa. State U., 1971; MBA, Shippensburg U., 1984. Prodn. supt. Grove Mfg., Shady Grove, Pa., 1974-76; prodn. mgr. Hennessy Products, Chambersburg, 1976-78, v.p. mfg., 1978-84, v.p. fin., 1984—, also bd. dirs. v.p., bd. dirs. Children's Aid Soc., Chambersburg, 1978-84; active local Little League. Served to 1st lt. USMC, 1972-74. Mem. Am. Mgmt. Assn., Nat. Corp. Cash Mgmt., Greater Chambersburg C. of C. (chmn. bd. 1988). Republican. Plymouth Brethren Lodge: Rotary (pres. bd. dirs. 1987-88). Home: 135 Riddle Rd Chambersburg PA 17201 Office: Hennessy Products Inc 910 Progress Rd Chambersburg PA 17201

NICKLE, DENNIS EDWIN, electronics engineer; b. Sioux City, Iowa, Jan. 30, 1936; s. Harold Bateman and Helen Cecilia (Killackey) N. BS in Math., Fla. State U., 1961. Reliability mathematician Pratt & Whitney Aircraft Co., W. Palm Beach, Fla., 1961-63; br. supr. Melpar Inc., Falls Church, Va., 1963-66; prin. mem. tech. staff Xerox Data Systems, Rockville, Md., 1966-70; sr. tech. officer WHO, Washington, 1970-76; software quality assurance mgr. Melpar div. E-Systems Corp., Falls Church, 1976—; ordained deacon Roman Catholic Ch., 1979. Chief judge for computers Fairfax County Regional Sci. Fair, 1964-88 ; mem. Am. Security Council; scoutmaster, commr. Boy Scouts Am., 1957—; youth custodian Fairfax County Juvenile Ct., 1973-87; chaplain No. Va. Regional Juvenile Detention Home, 1978-88 ; moderator Nocturnal Adoration Soc. Served with U.S. Army, 1958-60. Recipient Eagle award, Silver award, Silver Beaver award, other awards Boy Scouts Am.; Ad Altare Dei, St. George Emblem, Diocese of Richmond. Mem. Assn. Computing Machinery, Old Crows Assn., Rolm Mil-Spec Computer Users Group (internat. pres.), Nat. Security Indsl. Assn. (convention com. 1985—, software quality assurance subcom., regional membership chmn. 1981—), IEEE (sr.)(mem. standards working group in computers 1983—), Computer Soc., Hewlett Packard Users Group, Smithsonian Assn., Internat. Platform Assn., Nat. Rifle Assn. (life), Alpha Phi Omega (life), Sigma Phi Epsilon. Club: KC (4 deg.). Co-author: Handbook for Handling Non-Productive Stress in Adolescence. Office: 7700 Arlington Blvd Falls Church VA 22046

NICOLAI, EUGENE RALPH, investments consultant; b. Renton, Wash., June 26, 1911; s. Eugene George and Josephine (Heidinger) N.; student U. Wash., 1929, Whitman Coll., 1929-30; B.A., U. Wash., 1934; postgrad. Am. U., 1942; M.A., George Washington U., 1965; m. Helen Margaret Manogue, June 5, 1935; 1 son, Paul Eugene. Editor, U. Wash. Daily, Seattle, 1934; asst. city editor, writer, nat. def. editor Seattle Times, 1934-41; writer Sta. KJR, Seattle, 1937-39; writer, editor, safety edn. officer Bur. Mines, Washington, 1941-45; news dir. Grand Coulee Dam and Columbia Basin Project, Washington, 1945-50; regional info. dir. Bur. Mines, Denver and Pitts., 1950-55, asst. chief mineral reports, Washington, 1955-61, news dir. office of oil and gas, 1956-57; sr. info. officer, later sr. public info. officer Office Sec. Interior, Washington, 1961-71, staff White House Nat. Conf. on Natural Beauty, spl. detail to White House, 1971, ret.; now public relations cons., tech. editor, writer. Formerly safety policy adviser Interior Dept.; com. mem. Internat. Cooperation Year, State Dept., 1971. With George Washington U. Alumni Found.; founder, mng. dir. Josephine Nature Preserve; pres. Media Assocs. Bd. dirs. Wash. State Council on Alcoholism; adviser Pierce Transit Authority, Pierce County Growth Mgmt., Pierce County Ethics Commn. Named Disting. Alumnus, recipient Penrose award, both Whitman Coll., 1979. Mem. Nature Conservancy, Wash. Environ. Council, Nat. Audubon Soc. (Am. Belgian Tervuren dist. rep.), Crook County (Oreg.) Hist. Soc., Washington State Hist. Soc., Emerald Shores Assn, Sigma Delta Chi, Pi Kappa Alpha. Presbyn. Clubs: George Washington U., Purdy (pres.). Lodge: Masons. Author: The Middle East Emergency Committee; editor: Fed. Conservation Yearbooks. Home: North 9809 Seminole Dr Spokane WA 99208

NICOLAS, GEORGES SPIRIDON, computer service company executive, consultant; b. Koura Dist., Lebanon, Feb. 18, 1952; came to U.S., 1970; s. Spiridon Georges and Selwa Nahme (Harb) N.; m. Maureen Ellen O'Day, Apr. 9, 1983; children: Samira Selwa, Elyse Cathryn. B of Engring. summa cum laude, Villanova U., 1973, M of Engring., 1974; DSc, Washington U., St. Louis, 1979. Systems analyst Burroughs Corp., Paoli, Pa., 1974; rsch. asst. Barnes Med. Ctr., St. Louis, 1974-75; system designer Sherwood Med. Industries, St. Louis, 1976; sr. systems analyst McDonnell Douglas Corp., St. Louis, 1977-78; mgr. system devel. Interface Tech., Inc., St. Louis, 1979; project mgr. MITRE Corp., McLean, Va., 1980-81; dept. mgr. Fed. Home Loan Mortgage Corp., Washington, 1981-82; pres. COMSYS Corp., Arlington, Va., 1982-87; bus. cons. Nicolas Enterprises, Inc., Falls Church, Va., 1986—; pres. Megasource Corp., McLean, 1988—; NIH rsch. fellow Washington U., 1974-75; asst. prof. George Washington U., Washington, 1980-83. Nat. sec. Am. Lebanese League, 1980-82; chmn. Am. Lebanese Freedom Alliance, 1988—. Ford Found. scholar, 1976. Mem. IEEE (chmn. St. Louis chpt. 1976), Assn. for Computing Machinery, Tau Beta Pi, Eta Kappa Nu. Greek Orthodox. Home: 7738 Marshall Heights Ct Falls Church VA 22043 Office: Nicolas Enterprises Inc PO Box 9270 McLean VA 22102-0270

NICOLAY, JOHN EDWARD, JR., computer store executive; b. Denver, June 28, 1969; s. John Edward Sr. and Anges (Wangen) N.; m. Janis Rae Minkler, Aug. 9, 1969. BA, U. Minn., 1978, MBA, 1985. Store mgr. Modern Merchandising Co., Minnetonka, Minn., 1971-76; regional mgr. Modern Merchandising Co., 1976-79; dir. employee relations Norwest Bank, N.I.S., Mpls., 1979-82; dir. strategic planning Norwest Bank, N.I.S., 1982-83; gen. mgr. MicroAge, Minnetonka, 1986—; mem. adj. faculty dept. mgmt. scis. U. Minn., Mpls., 1987; pres. Lotus Lake Homeowners Assn., Chanhassen, Minn., 1982; active Big Bros., Mpls. With USMC, 1963-66. Mem. Minnetonka C. of C., Wayzata (Minn.) Yacht Club. Home: 608 Pleasant View Rd Chanhassen MN 55317 Office: 5153 W 98th St Minneapolis MN 55437

NICOLELLA, MICHAEL BERNARD, mortgage banker; b. Washington, Pa., Feb. 18, 1947; s. Carmen and Mary M. (Odato) N.; m. Nancy Lynn Crede, May 18, 1974; children: M. Gabriel, Lacy Elizabeth. Account exec. Investors Mortgage Ins. Co., Pitts., 1977-80; br. mgr. Cen. Mortgage Co., Pitts., 1980-84; asst. v.p. Chase Home Mortgage Corp., Pitts., 1984—; real estate broker State of Pa., 1980—; pres. Realtest Cons., Bridgeville, Pa., 1981—. Mem. Mortgage Bankers Assn. Pitts. (pres. 1986, Mortgage Banker of Yr. 1987). Republican. Home: 1284 Manor Dr Upper Saint Clair PA 15241 Office: Chase Home Mortgage Two Chatham Ctr Suite 1410 Pittsburgh PA 15219

NICOLETTI, FRANCOIS-XAVIER, banker; b. San Giovanni in Fiore, Italy, Nov. 30, 1936; s. Giovanni and Angela (Mangone) X.; m. Annick Rouez, Sept. 22, 1962; 1 son, Laurent. B.A., Columbia Pacific U., 1981, M.B.A, 1982, Ph.D. in Internat. Bus. Adminstrn., 1984. Area acct. Borini Prono Nigeria Ltd., Lagos, 1960-64; asst. adminstrn. mgr. Sté . Francaise Dragages Travaux Publics (Paris), Beira, Mozambique, 1965-67, fin. acct., Kitwe, Zambia, 1967-68; acct. Finacor, Paris, France, 1968-69; adminstrn. mgr. Kefinco Ltd., Nairobi, Kenya, 1969-70; asst. mgr. fgn. exchange and internat. dept. Banque Europeenne de Financement, Paris, 1970-72; mgr. fonde de pouvoirs internat. dept. Banque Canadienne Nationale (Europe), Paris, 1972-73; with Am. Express Internat. Banking Corp., 1973-79, dir. gen. adjoint Paris br., 1977-79, dir. Amex Bank Ltd., London, 1977-78, v.p., N.Y.C., 1978-79; dir. internat. fin. dept. Midland Bank France S.A., Paris, 1979-81; adminstr.-dir. gen. Overland Trust Fin. S.A., Geneva, 1981-87; dir. internat. fin. ops. Finorsud S.A., Geneva, 1987—. Author: Professional Work: Financing Exports With Promissory Notes, 1977 Recipient Silver medal Arts, Sciences et Lettres, 1976. Mem. Am. Mgmt. Assn. Internat., Club des Directeurs de Banques (Paris), Maxim's Bus. (Paris), Cercle Interallié (Paris). Roman Catholic. Home: 52 Route de Florissant, 1206 Geneva Switzerland Office: Finorsud SA, 1 place du Port, 1204 Geneva Switzerland

NICOLETTI, JOSEPH DANIEL, manufacturing executive; b. Detroit, Feb. 18, 1930; s. Donato Liberato and Florence Loreta (Iannitelli) N.; m. Jeanne Marie Bates, Nov. 11, 1961; children: Jodi Jeanne, Joseph Daniel II. Tool and die apprentice, Henry Ford Trade Sch., Dearborn, Mich.; student, U. Detroit, 1948-53; LLB, Detroit Coll. Law, 1961. Bar: Mich 1961. Sole practice Mt. Clemens, Mich., 1961-76; pres. Broaches, Inc., Roseville, Mich., 1976—. Inventor external helical pot broach, 1976. Served as cpl. U.S. Army, 1953-55. Mem. Cutting Tool Mfrs., Macomb County Bar Assn. Republican. Roman Catholic. Lodge: San Pancrazio (sec. 1955-61). Home: 37898 E Horseshoe Dr Mount Clemens MI 48043 Office: Broaches Inc of Mich 16600 Eastland Roseville MI 48066

NICOTRA, KATHY SUE, construction company executive; b. Albany, Ky., Jan. 20, 1950; d. Agnes Lucille (Gillentine) Rodgers; m. Glen Stuart Nicotra, Sept. 29, 1984; 1 child, Stephanie Eran. Student, U. Ga., 1968-70; BS with honors, Ga. State U., 1978. Cert. and lic. bldg. contractor. Constrn. mgr. Fredericks Devel. Corp., Atlanta, 1971-76; project mgr. Calibre Co. Ga., Atlanta, 1979-83; v.p. Calibre Co. Va., Fairfax, 1983-85, Calibre Co. Fla., Boca Raton, 1985-87; div. mgr. Coscan Fla., Inc., Boca Raton, 1987—; cons. in hist. restoration, West Palm Beach, Fla., 1987—. Organizer Just Say No campaign, West Palm Beach, 1988—. Named Woman of Yr. County Govt., Washington, 1984. Mem. Fla. Builders Assn., Nat. Hist. Soc., NOW. Republican. Baptist. Home: 3417 Washington Rd West Palm Beach FL 33405

NICULESCU, DEBBIE EIDE, personnel management consultant; b. Owensboro, Ky., Sept. 19, 1956; d. Harry Stur and Jane Annabelle (Willis) Eid; m. Alexander George Niculescu, Aug. 24, 1985; children: Yori Alexander, Danielle Marianna. BA in Psychology, Calif. State U., 1986. Research asst. Essex County Youth Services, Belleville, N.J., 1980-81; evaluator Merritt Personnafax, Montclair, N.J., 1981-82; staff asst. Archdiocese of Newark, 1982-84; assoc. Plotkin & Assocs., San Bernardino, Calif., 1984—. Mem. Exec. Women's Internat., Am. Soc. Tng. and Devel., West End Exec. Assn., Exec. Assn. San Bernardino, No. Calif. Human Resources Coun. Methodist. Lodge: Zonta. Office: Plotkin & Assocs 1255 E Highland Ave Suite 209 San Bernardino CA 92404

NIDADAVOLU, ACHYUTA SIVA, accountant; b. Rajahmundry, Andhra Pradesh, India, June 30, 1957; came to U.S., 1985; s. Venkata Rao and Annapurna (Vamaraju) N.; m. Vani Kasinadhuni, June 21, 1988. Bachelor of Commerce, Anidhra U., 1977; Profl. Communications (hon.), Indian Inst. Sci., 1984. CPA. Sr. acct. Sen & Ray Co, Chartered Accts., Calcutta, India, 1977-83; sr. fin. analyst Canara Bank-H.Q., Bangalore, India, 1983-85; asst. to controller Newsbank Inc., New Canaan, Conn., 1985-86; acct. KMG Main Hurdman, CPA's, Stamford, Conn., 1986-87; sr. acct. Milton H. Freidberg, Smith & Co., Stamford, Conn., 1987—; cons. Community Acctg. Aid and Services Inc., Conn., 1988—. Contbr. critiques of works in field. Mem. Inst. chartered Accts. India (assoc.). Home: 12 Fairweather Dr Norwalk CT 06851

NIEBLING, CHRISTOPHER RAY, fire department captian; b. Morristown, N.J., May 10, 1954; s. Walter L. and Gene S. Niebling; m. Lisa Cook Niebling, Aug. 2, 1980. Cert. in Fire Sci., Broward Community Coll., 1987. Firefighter City of Lighthouse Point, Fla., 1973-76; cpt. City of Sunrise Fire Rescue, Fla., 1977—; pres. Firetech, Inc., Davie, Fla., 1987—; instr. Broward County Sch. Bd., Fort Lauderdale, Fla., 1982—. Active Orange Bowl Festival Staging Com., Miami, 1986—. Named Firefighter of Yr. Sunrise Jaycees, 1982. Mem. Internat. Assn. Fire Service Instrs., Internat. Assn. Firefighters, Masons, MAHI Shrine. Democrat. Methodist. Office: Firetech Inc PO Box 291372 Davie FL 33329

NIEFELD, JAYE SUTTER, advertising executive; b. Mpls., May 27, 1924; s. Julius and Sophia (Rosenfeld) N.; m. Piri Elizabeth Von Zabrana-Szilagy, July 5, 1947; 1 child, Peter Wendell. Cert., London U., 1945; B.A., U. Minn., 1948; B.S., Georgetown U., 1949; Ph.D., U. Vienna, 1951. Project dir. Bur. Social Sci. Research, Washington, 1952-54; research dir. McCann-Erickson, Inc., Chgo., N.Y.C., 1954-57; dir. marketing Keyes, Madden & Jones, Chgo., 1957-60; pres., dir. Niefeld, Paley & Kuhn, Inc., Chgo., 1961-71; exec. v.p. Bozell, Jacobs, Kenyon & Eckhardt, Inc., Chgo., 1971—; chmn. Ctr. Advanced Communications Research; pres. Glencoe Angus Farms, J & J Enterprises; dir. Mktg. Decisions, Inc.; Cons. U.S. depts. State, Commerce, HEW, also; Intertel, Inc.; lectr. Columbia U., U. Chgo., Northwestern U. Author: (with others) Marketing's Role in Scientific Management, 1957, Advertising and Marketing to Young People, 1965, The Making of an Advertising Campaign, 1988; also articles. Mem. adv. bd. Glencoe Family Service.; bd. dirs. Big Bros. Met. Chgo.; exec. v.p. City of Hope, Am. Film Inst. Served to 1st lt. AUS, 1942-46. Decorated Bronze Star. Mem. Am. Assn. Pub. Opinion Research, Am. Marketing Assn., Am. Sociol. Assn., Am. Film Inst., Smithsonian Instn. Home: 1011 Bluff Rd Glencoe IL 60022 Office: Bozell Jacobs Kenyon & Eckhardt Inc 625 N Michigan Ave Chicago IL 60611

NIEHAUS, ROBERT JAMES, electrical contracting company executive; b. Ann Arbor, Mich., Jan. 6, 1930; s. Julius Herman and Mary Johanna (Koch) N.; m. Jacqueline C. Mallier, Aug. 5, 1982. BBA, U. Mich., 1951; MBA, U. Detroit, 1958. Asst. sr. buyer Ford Motor Co., Dearborn, Mich., 1954-58; gen. purchasing agt. Hercules Motors Co., Canton, Ohio, 1959-60; v.p. procurement Schwitzer Corp., Indpls., 1960-66; sr. v.p. Wallace Murray Corp., N.Y.C., 1966-82; v.p. spl. projects Fischbach Corp., N.Y.C., 1983-84, sr. v.p., 1985-87; chief exec. officer, vice chmn. Fischbach & Moore, Inc., Dallas, 1987—. Served to lt. USN, 1951-54. Mem. Am. Mgmt. Assn. (gen. mgmt. council 1982—). Clubs: Union League (N.Y.C.); Greenwich (Conn.) Country. Home: 95 Rowayton Woods Dr Norwalk CT 06854

NIEHENKE, JOHN JOSEPH, investment banker; b. Phila., Dec. 29, 1944; s. John Joseph Jr. and Eleanor Marie (Utzy) N.; m. Kathleen Marie Nice, Nov. 7, 1970; children: J. Michael, William J., Jennifer Ann. BS cum laude, St. Joseph's Coll., Phila., 1970; postgrad., Temple U., 1971-73. V.p. Girard Bank, Phila., 1968-76, sr. v.p., 1978-84; spl. asst. to Sec. U.S. Treasury Dept., Washington, 1976-78; dep. asst. sec. U.S. Treas. Dept., Washington, 1984-86; sr. v.p. Nomura Securities Internat. Inc., N.Y.C., 1986—. Councilman Burough of Lansdowne (Pa.), 1980-84; asst. treas. Lansdowne Boys' Club, 1982-86. Republican. Roman Catholic. Home: 6 Arbor Way Convent Station NJ 07961 Office: Nomura Securities Internat Inc 180 Maiden Ln 38th Fl New York NY 10038

NIEHOFF, K. RICHARD B., financial executive; b. Cin., May 11, 1943; s. Karl George and Jean (Besuden) N.; children—K. Richard B. Jr., Kelly B. B.A., U. Cin., 1967. Corp. trust officer 5th-3d Union Trust, Cin., 1968-74; v.p., sec. Weil, Roth & Irving, Cin., 1974-76; mcpl. fin. dept. Thomson McKinnon Securities, Cin., 1976-79; chmn. bd. trustees Cin. Stock Exchange, 1978-79, pres., 1979—; Exchange rep. Consol. Quote, Consol. Tape and Inter-Market Operating Coms., 1979—. Trustee, sec. Contemporary Arts Ctr., 1975-83; mem. devel. com. Tangeman Gallery of Art, 1981-82. Mem. Cin. Stock and Bond Club (past 1st v.p.), Queen City Mcpl. Bond Club (trustee 1974-79), Cleve. Security Traders Assn., Cin. Area C. of C. (devel. and small bus. fin. coms. 1975-78), Phi Alpha Theta. Clubs: University, Miami (Cin.); Keenland Assn. (Lexington, Ky.). Office: Cin Stock Exch 205 Dixie Terminal Bldg Cincinnati OH 45202

NIEHOUSE, OLIVER LESLIE, management consultant; b. St. Louis, July 25, 1920; s. Oliver Lewis and Edythe Mae (Burch) N.; m. Ellen Verdell Sims, Apr. 1, 1945; 1 child, Daniel Lee (dec.). BS, Sir George Williams U., Montreal, 1957; MBA, U. Chgo., 1963; postgrad. NYU, 1968-78; MS, Calif. Am. U., 1979. With Olin Industries Inc., East Alton, Ill., 1941-51, research and devel. supr., 1947-51, mgr. tech. sales, N.Y.C., 1951-55; mgr. advt. and sales devel. TCF of Can., Ltd., Montreal, P.Q., 1955-58; dir. sales Yardley of London Ltd., Toronto, Ont., 1958-60; gen. mgr. Sunbeam Corp., Chgo., 1960-65; v.p., dir. Sunbeam A.G., Zug, Switzerland, 1965-67; mng. dir. Sunbeam Electric Ltd., East Kilbride, Scotland, and London, 1965-67; v.p., gen. mgr. Pantasote Co. of N.Y., N.Y.C., 1967-70; pres. subsidiaries, exec. v.p. Polypump Ltd., Toronto, Ont., 1970-71; asst. prof. Hofstra U., Hempstead, N.Y., 1971-78; pres. Niehouse & Assocs. Inc., Forest Hills, N.Y., 1971—; vis. assoc. prof. Mktg. NYU, 1988—; dir. ctr. for mgmt. devel., disting. lectr. in mgmt. Coll. of Bus., Rochester Inst. Tech., 1986-87. Patentee in field. Editorial bd. Management Solutions jour.; contbr. articles to profl. jours. Recipient Disting. Teaching award Hofstra U., 1975. Mem. Nat. Speakers Assn., Acad. of Mgmt., Am. Mktg. Assn., Am. Soc. for Tng. and Devel., Am. Chem. Soc. Home: 175 Kellogg Dr Wilton CT 06897 Office: Niehouse & Assocs Inc 109-23 71st Rd Forest Hills NY 11375

NIEKAMP, ALBERT, publishing company auditing director; b. Brummen, Netherlands, Sept. 5, 1930; s. Egbertus and Hendrika Johanna (Harmsen) N.; m. Jacoba Bertha Verschleuss, Nov. 9, 1963; children—Egbert Gerrit, Gerard Esse. Registered acct. Netherland Inst. Registered Accts. Asst. auditor Moret & Starke, Rotterdam, 1952-54; asst. auditor KLM, Amsterdam, also N.Y.C., 1959-62; sr. auditor Arthur Andersen & Co., The Hague, 1962-67; internal auditor Holland-Amerika Line, Rotterdam, 1967-70, S.H.V., Utrecht, 1970-79; dir. auditing Elsevier nv, Amsterdam, 1979—; expert-examiner auditing Free U., Amsterdam, 1979—. Contbr. articles to profl. jours. Mem. editorial bd. Corp. Crime and Security Bull.-Oxford, 1980. Bd. dirs. Nat. Mus. Mus. Clocks and Street Organs, Utrecht, 1974. Served with Dutch Royal Air Force, 1950-52. Fellow Nat. Inst. Register accountants, Inst. Internal Auditors, Inst. EDP auditors, Nat. Assn. Accountants. Christian Democrat. Dutch Reformed. Club: Bunnik Lawn Tennis. Home: Camminghalaan 5, Bunnik, Utrecht 3981 GD The Netherlands Office: Elsevier, PO Box 470, 1000 AL, Amsterdam The Netherlands

NIELSEN, MARK JOSEPH, communications chief executive officer; b. Chgo., Apr. 5, 1959; s. Torben Harold and Nancy Ann (Ingraffia) N. BS, Northwestern U., 1980. Legal asst. Louis G. Davidson & Assocs., Chgo., 1980-83; telecommunications cons. Nielsen & Assocs., Chgo., 1978-84; cable TV contract negotiator City of Chgo., 1983-84; sales, mktg. dir. Cellular Bus. Systems, Inc. div. Cin. Bell Info. Systems, Inc., Chgo., 1984-88; pres. Subscriber Computing Inc., Irvine, Calif., 1988—; faculty mem. dept. engring. profl. devel. U. Wis., Madison, 1985, Nat. Communications Forum, 1987—, Nat. Engring. Consortium, 1988—; pres. Subscriber Computing, Inc., Irvine, 1988—; adv. bd. Nat. Telmarketing Found., 1985—; exec. producer (cons.) ABA, 1981-82; legis. cons. ACLU, Chgo., 1982-84; incorporator, bd. dirs. Chgo. Access Corp., 1983—; bd. dirs. Jazz Inst. Chgo. 1987—, Ednl. Overseers Council, Nat. Engring. Consortium, 1987—. Mem. Chgo. Forum, 1982-84; co-convenor, moderator Midwest Conf. on Communications Issues, Chgo., 1979; presbytor, com. chmn. Presbytery of Chgo., 1980-83; bd. dirs., com. chmn. Ch. Fedn. Greater Chgo., 1977-84. Recipient Churchmanship-Can-Be-Creative award Chgo. Sun-Times, 1982; Arthur Baer fellow Chgo. Lit. Club, 1979; named one of Outstanding Young Men in Am., 1987. Mem. Am. Marketing Assn., Am. Mgmt. Assn., Internat. Platform Assn., Chgo. Cable Club, Chgo. Forum, Telocator Network of Am., Cellular Telecommunications Industry Assn. Democrat. Presbyterian. Club: Chgo. Literary. Home: 33521 Via De Agua San Juan Capistrano CA 60626 Office: Subscriber Computing Inc 18 Technology Dr #210 Suite 601 Irvine CA 92718

NIELSEN, ROGER PAUL, computer company executive; b. Racine, Wis., Oct. 16, 1942; s. Paul J. and Carol Louise (Mannering) N.; m. Sandra Lee Bupp, Jan. 20, 1968; children: Erik Paul, Alexander. BS in Elect. Engring., U. Wis., 1967; MS, U. So. Calif., 1970; MBA, UCLA, 1975. Project mgr. Hughes Aircraft Co., Culver City, Calif., 1971-73; mgr. fed. mktg. Data Gen. Corp., Washington, 1973-80; dir. original equipment mfr. mktg. div. NCR Corp., Dayton, Ohio, 1980-82; v.p. mktg. and sales Raster Techs., Inc., North Billerica, Mass., 1982-86; pres., chief exec. officer Monitronix Corp., Westerville, Ohio, 1986—. With USAF, 1963-71. USAF scholar, 1965-67. Mem. Am. Mktg. Assn., Am. Mgmt. Assn., IEEE, Rotary, Eta Kappa Nu. Episcopalian. Home: 325 Meditation Ln Worthington OH 43238-4601 Office: Monitronix Inc 929 Eastwind Dr. #220 Westerville OH 43081-3329

NIELSEN, WILLIAM EDWARD, manufacturing executive; b. Summit, N.J., Aug. 8, 1957; s. Edward George and Margaret E. (Sterner) N. BS in Applied Math., Carnegie-Mellon U., 1979, MSME, 1981; MBA, U. Chgo., 1983. Cons. engr. Swanson Engring. Assoc. Corp., McMurray, Pa., 1979-81; assoc. Booz, Allen & Hamilton, Chgo., 1982, The MAC Group, Chgo., 1983-86; mgr. planning Masonite Corp., Chgo., 1986—; cons. Bus. Vols. for the Arts, Chgo., 1984—, Chgo. Architectural Found., 1985—. Mem. The Planning Forum (dir. 1987-88), ASME. Home: 1115 S Plymouth Ct Apt 610 Chicago IL 60605 Office: Masonite Corp 1 South Wacker Dr 36th Fl Chicago IL 60606

NIEMAN, JAMES MICHAEL, marine engineer; b. Annapolis, Md., July 18, 1951; s. Kenneth Rogers and Elizabeth Jeanne Neiman. Registered profl. engr. Waterman Chesapeake Bay, Shadyside, Md., 1966—; ind. scuba instr. Profl. Assn. Diving Instrs., Santa Ana, Calif., 1978—; marine engr. U.S. Mcht. Marine, Balt., 1980—; pres. Chesapeake Underwater Sports, Shadyside, 1987—. Sgt. USAF, 1971-75. Mem. Profl. Assn. Diving Instrs. (1978—), Marine Engrs. Beneficial Assn., Capital Divers Assn. Democrat. Roman Catholic. Home: 309 Beach Dr Annapolis MD 21403 Office: Chesapeake Underwater Sports 1464 Snug Harbor Rd Shadyside MD 20764

NIEMANN, JOHN PAUL, controller; b. Chgo., Oct. 1, 1936; s. Herbert P. and Evelyn (Hedges) N.; m. Rubinette Miller, Apr. 16, 1966; children: Elizabeth L., John W. AB, Kenyon Coll., 1958; MBA, Columbia U., N.Y.C., 1960. Fin. trainee indsl. products div. Corning (N.Y.) Glass Works, 1962-63; asst. plant and systems controller dairy products div. Corning (N.Y.) Glass Works, Blacksburg, Va., 1963-66; plant controller indsl. products div. Corning (N.Y.) Glass Works, Danville, Va., 1966-68; sr. fin. analyst TV div. Corning (N.Y.) Glass Works, Corning, 1968-75; div. controller fine wire Copperweld Corp., Oswego, N.Y., 1975-79; dir. fin. Lawrence Industries, Burlington, N.C., 1979-85; controller Bristol (Va.) ops. U.S. Mfg. Electrolux Corp., 1985—. Capt. USAF, 1960-63. Mem. Nat. Assn. Accts., Nat. Assn. Credit Mgrs., Kiwanis (1st v.p. 1974-75, bd. dirs. 1980-85). Republican. Methodist. Home: 106 Triple Crown Dr Abingdon VA 24210 Office: Electrolux Corp PO Box 191 Bristol VA 24201-0191

NIEMOLLER, ARTHUR B., engineer; b. Wakefield, Kans., Oct. 4, 1912; s. Benjamin Henry and Minnie Christine (Carlson) N.; m. Ann Sochor, May 29, 1937 (dec. June 1982); children: Joanna Matteson, Arthur D. BSEE, Kans. State U., 1933. Registered profl. engr., N.Y., N.J., Pa., Ill., Ohio. Engr. Westinghouse, Newark, Hillside, N.J., 1937-59, Chgo., 1959-61, Pitts., 1961-65, Cin., 1965-77; pvt. practice engr. Montgomery, Ohio, 1977—. Patentee in field. Served with USN, 1933-37. Mem. IEEE, NSPE. Republican. Presbyterian. Home and Office: 7888 Mitchell Farm Ln Cincinnati OH 45242

NIENABER, CAROL HELEN, financial planner; b. Harvard, Ill., Apr. 3, 1959; d. T. William and Helene Kerr (McFadden) N. BS in Fin., No. Ill. U., 1983. Cert. fin. planner. Stock broker Olde Discount Stock Brokers, Detroit, 1983-85; fin. planner, stock broker Integrated Resources Equity Corp., Crystal Lake, Ill., 1985-87, Crown Fin. Planners & Crown Investments, Ltd., Barrington Hills, Ill., 1987—. Treas. Human Devel. Corp., McHenry County, 1988—; bd. dirs. McHenry County Family Svcs., 1987—. Mem. Internat. Assn. for Fin. Planning (bd. dirs. 1986—), Inst. Cert. Fin. Planners, Leads, Toastmasters. Republican. Episcopalian. Home: 1606 N Rosefarm Rd Woodstock IL 60098

NIENBURG, GEORGE FRANK, security professional; b. N.Y.C., Feb. 14, 1938; s. Carl George and Louise Elizabeth (Baum) N. Grad., Ctr. for Media Arts German Sch. Photography, 1989. Veterinarian asst. Stamen Animal Hosp., New Rochelle, N.Y., 1966-70; trainer guard dogs Paradise Guard Dog Service, N.Y.C., 1970-71; animal care technician, pres. Am. Soc. for Prevention Cruelty to Animals, N.Y.C., 1971-82; security guard Cen. Nat. Investigation agy., New Rochelle, 1983-88. Active Rep. Nat. Com., Washington, 1983—, sustaining mem., 1986—; mem. nat. leadership coalition Campaign Am., Washington, 1987—; mem. Nat. Rep. Senatorial Com., 1989—; sustaining sponsor Ronald Reagan Found., Washington, 1987—; chartered founder Presdl. Trust Fund.; charter mem., supporter Battle Normandy Mus., 1988—; sponsor Nat. Rep. Congl. Com., Washington, 1983; life mem. Rep. Presdl. Task Force, Washington, 1988; charter founder Ronald Reagan Ctr., 1988—; mem. St. Luke's Ch., 1974—. Mem. Washington Legal Found (patron), U.S. Senatorial Club, Masons (master 1986—), Nat. Trust for Hist. Preservation, Am. Space Frontier Com. (sustaining mem.), Citizens for Am. (insider mem.), Nat. Flag Found. (standard bearer 1987—). Home: 22 Edgewood Park PO Box 511 New Rochelle NY 10802-0511

NIEUWSMA, MILTON JOHN, newspaper syndicate executive; b. Sioux Falls, S.D., Sept. 5, 1941; s. John and Jean (Potter) N.; BA, Hope Coll., Holland, Mich., 1963; postgrad. Wayne State U., 1963-65; MA, Sangamon State U., 1978; m. Marilee Gordon, Feb. 1, 1964; children: Jonathan, Gregory, Elizabeth. Public info. officer Wayne State U., Detroit, 1963-69; public relations dir. Sinai Hosp., Detroit, 1969-72; dir. div. officer services Am. Hosp. Assn., Chgo., 1972-73; asst. prof. journalism Wayne State U., Detroit, 1974; dir. public relations and devel. Meml. Med. Center, Springfield, Ill., 1975-79; v.p. for public affairs Grant Hosp., Chgo., 1979-87; v.p. devel., 1987-88; pres. Trans Am. Syndicate, Inc., Riverside, Ill., 1988—. governing mem. Chgo. Zool. Soc., 1981—. Bd. dirs. Springfield (Ill.) Boys Clubs, 1979-80, Sangamon County Heart Assn., 1978-80, Riverside Community Fund (Ill.), 1986; pub. relations chmn. Sangamon County Heart Fund Campaign, 1978; pres. Ford Com., 1975-76; bd. dirs. United Meth. Housing Corp., Detroit, 1968-70, Riverside-Brookfield Edn. Found., 1987—; chmn. Sch. Dist. 205 Caucus, 1983—; mem. exec. com. Village Riverside, 1986— . Mem. Public Relations Soc. Am., Lincoln Park C. of C. (bd. dirs.). Republican. Presbyterian. Contbr. articles in field to profl. jours. Home: 322 Scottswood Rd Riverside IL 60546 Office: 365 S Wabash Ave Ste 700 Chicago IL 60603

NIGITO, DANIEL GREGORY, financial executive; b. Elizabeth, N.J., May 9, 1956; s. Dominic and Margaret (Gallo) N.; m. Joanne T. Marman, Oct. 25, 1980; children: Natalie, Dominic, Vincent. BA, Moravian Coll., 1978. Cert. fin. planner. Ins. cons. Provident Mut. Life Ins. Co., Allentown, Pa., 1978-80; v.p., sr. fin. planner Shearson Lehman Bros., Allentown, Pa., 1980-86; chmn., chief exec. officer Profl. Services Group Am. Inc., Allentown, Pa., 1986—; bd. dirs. Barnabee's Ltd., Poughkeepsie, N.Y. Mem. Internat. Assn. Fin. Planners, Nat. Assn. Life Underwriters, Internat. Bd. Cert. Fin. Planners, Allentown C. of C. (govt. affairs com. 1987—). Republican. Roman Catholic. Office: Profl Services Group Am Inc 1251 S Cedar Crest Ste 102A Allentown PA 18103

NIHART, ROBERT WILLIAM, communications executive; b. Wabasha, Minn., Nov. 2, 1960; s. Robert W. and Marlene (Karsted) N.; m. Cynthia M. Travis, Apr. 25, 1987. BS in Bus., Mankato State U., 1984; postgrad., St. Mary's Coll., Mpls. Tel. data optic cabling supr. P&T Communication Profls., Mpls., 1984—. Mem. Soc. Mech. Engrs., Elks. Office: P&T Communication Profls 4011 W Broadway Minneapolis MN 55422

NIKOLAI, JAMES A., insurance executive. V.p. Farmers Group Inc., L.A., Farmers Ins. Cos. Office: Farmers Ins Group Cos 4680 Wilshire Blvd Los Angeles CA 90010 *

NIL, GÜVEN, finance company executive, banking advisor; b. Istanbul, May 20, 1944; s. Mehmet and Hayriye (Colakoğlu) N.; m. Vicdan Alaybek, Sept. 19, 1970; children: Eren, Emir. BSc, Robert Coll., Istanbul, 1967; MBA, Robert Coll., 1969. Gen. mgr. Vigi AS, Istanbul, 1973-79; pres. Erem Ltd., Istanbul, 1980—; rep. Petrabank, Jordan, 1984—. Mem. Istanbul C. of C. Home: Kisikli CAD 118, Camlica, Istanbul Turkey Office: Erem Ltd, Ortaklar CAD 2/16 Mecidiyekoy, 80290 Istanbul Turkey

NILSEN, LLOYD RAYMOND, mining company executive; b. Kelvington, Sask., Can., Apr. 20, 1932; s. Olaf Nicolas and Eva Ragna (Evenson) N.; m. Norma Joan Warrington, Apr. 22, 1959; children: Mark Franklin, Kristin Laura, Erik Norman, Joel Matthew, Heidi Leigh. BS, U. Sask., 1955. Engr. Hudson Bay Mining & Smelting Co. Ltd., Flin Flon and Snow Lake, Man., Can., 1959-67, mine supt., 1967-75, mgr. plant services, 1975-76, mgr. of mines, 1976-78, mgr. long range planning, 1978-81; v.p., gen. mgr. Hudson Bay Mining & Smelting Co. Ltd., Flin Flon and Snow Lake, Man., 1983-86, pres., chief operating officer, 1986—; v.p. ops. Tantalum Mining Corp. Can. Ltd., Lac du Bonnet, Man., 1981-83. Mem. Can. Inst. Mining and Metallurgy, Mining Assn. Man. (v.p. 1987-88, pres. 1984-85), Profl. Engrs. Man. Club: Royal Can. Legion (Flin Flon) (hon.). Lodge: Rotary (hon. mem. Flin Flon club). Home: Company Cottage #2, Flin Flon, MB Canada R8A 1M3 Office: H Bay Mining & Smelting Co, Toronto-Dominion Ctr Box 28, Toronto, ON Canada M5K 1B8

NILSSON, NIC, union executive; b. Lund, Sweden, Nov. 1, 1933; s. Jons Olof and Hanna Linnea (Nilsdotter) N.; m. Aina Ingrid Andersson, June 10, 1955 (div. 1972); 1 child, Sven Niclas; m. Ulla Ingegerd Carlson, Mar. 27, 1976. Student, Scandinavian Sch., Geneva, 1967, Brit.-Nordic Sch., Manchester, Eng., 1971. Policeman Molndals, Sweden, 1955-60; ombudsman Stockholm SSU Dist., 1960-63, Swedish Tenants Union, Stockholm, 1963—; gen. sec. Internat. Tenants Union, Stockholm, 1985—. Author: Space for Play, 1969, Play for All, 1975, Together in the Block, 1978, Play Everywhere, 1987; contbr. articles to various publs. Mem. Stockholm Leisure Bd., 1967-88, Swedish Play Council, 1971—; pres. Internat. Falcon Movement, socialist edn., Brussels, 1979-88. Served with Swedish Army, 1950-55. Authors Soc. grantee, 1981. Mem. Internat. Assn. for Child's Right to Play (pres. 1981—), European Leisure and Recreation Assn. (council 1972—), Internat. Fedn. Park and Recreation Assn. (bd. dirs. 1985-88). Home: Norrtullsgatan 12B X, S-11327 Stockholm Sweden Office: Internat Union Tenants, PO Box 7514, S-10392 Stockholm Sweden

NIMMO, HERBERT LEE, engineer; b. Kansas City, Kans., Oct. 8, 1934; s. Forrest Herbert and Velma Irene (Barker) N.; m. F. Elizabeth Turner, June 7, 1963; 1 child, Martha Ann. BSME, Finlay Engring. Coll., 1959. Cert. mfg. engr.; registered profl. engr., Mo. Design engr. United Mfg. & Engring. Corp., Independence, Mo., 1960-61; sr. design engr. George W. Johnson Mfg., Kansas City, Mo., 1961-62; sr. process engr. Remington Arms Co., Inc., Lake City Plant, Independence, 1962-69, area process engr., 1969-83, chief supr. quality assurance, 1983-84, chief process engr., 1984-85; mgr. mfg. engring. def. systems group Olin Corp., Independence, 1985-87; supr. mfg. engring. Winchester Div. Olin Def. Systems Group L.C.A.A.P., Independence, 1987—; co-chmn. tech. adv. bd. Cen. Mo. State U., Warrensburg, Mo., 1984—. Contbr. articles to profl. jours. With U.S. Army, 1954-57. Recipient Pub. Svc. award Am. Radio Relay League, Inc., 1977. Mem. Soc. Mfg. Engrs. (chpt. chmn. 1986-87, Achievement award 1982-83, scholarship chmn. region V zone 3 1986—), Mo. Soc. Profl. Engrs. (chmn. profl. engrs. in industry 1982-83), Am. Soc. Metals (chmn. pub. rels. 1984-85), Am. Soc. Quality Control, Soc. Am. Mil. Engrs., Am. Legion, NRA. Clubs: Independence FM Amateur Radio, Soc. for Preservation of Blue Grass Music in Am., Am. Radio Relay League. Avocations: amateur radio, blue grass music, personal computing. Home: Rte 1 PO Box 121 Higginsville MO 64037 Office: Olin Def Systems Group Lake City Plant Independence MO 64050

NINKE, ARTHUR ALBERT, accountant, management consultant; b. Coloma, Mich., Aug. 20, 1909; s. Paul F. and Theresa Grace (Warskow) N.; m. Claudia Wagner, Sept. 13, 1930; children: Doris Ninke Hart, Donald, Marion, George, Arthur Albert, Thomas, Mark, Albert. Student acctg. Internat. Bus. Coll., 1928; diploma commerce Northwestern U., 1932. Auditor, Arthur Andersen & Co., CPA's, Chgo., 1929-36, St. Louis, 1950-55, Midwest Stock Exchange, 1936-41, SEC, 1942-45; expense controller Butler Bros., Chgo., 1946-49; office mgr. Hargis Electronics, 1956-59; auditor HUD, Detroit, 1960-64; owner Urban Tech. Staff Assoc., cons. urban renewal projects and housing devel., Detroit, 1965-81; pres. Simplified Systems & Computer Sales, 1978—; exec. dir. Urban Mgmt. Services 1984—, Urban Computerized Services, Inc., 1984-88, Computer Mgmt. Services, 1985—, Complete Bus. Service, Dallas, 1979-82, Loving Shepherd Nursing Home, Warren, Mich., 1975-83; sec. Gideons Detroit North Woodward, 1981-83, treas., 1986-87. Author: Family Bible Studies; Computer Networking; dir. Family Bible Hour Club, 1986—. Developer simulated machine bookkeeping system; trade mark holder Record-Checks-Systems, 1981—. Controller, Lake Superior R&D Inst., Munising, Mich., 1973-76; lay minister Redford Luth. Ch., 1988—; pres. Luth. Friendship Homes, Inc., 1975-85; lay evangelist Faith Lut. Ch., 1986-88, treas., 1985-86; mng. dir. Family Evangelism Found., 1977—; controller S.E. Mich. Billy Graham Crusade, 1976-77; pres. Project Compassion Met. Detroit, Inc., 1982—; bd. dirs. Lutheran Credit Union Greater Detroit, 1982-88; mem. Nat. Council on Aging. Recipient tribute Mich. State Legislature, 1982, tribute City of Warren, 1982. Mem. Nat. Soc. Pub. Accts., Nat. Assn. Housing and Redevel. Ofcls. (treas. Mich. 1973-75), Luth. Center Assn. (treas. 1975-81, dir. 1975-81), Internat. Luth. Laymen's League (treas. S.E. Mich. 1971-75, dir. 1976-81), Am. Mgmt. Assn., Fairlane Club of Dearborn. Home: 22405 Riverdale Dr Southfield MI 48034 Office: 17600 Northland Park Ct Southfield MI 48075

NIOSI, JAMES PETER, banker; b. Boston, July 6, 1935; s. James Anthony and Lillian (DeNatale) N.; m. Mary Elizabeth Gallagher, Apr. 22, 1961; children—Marybeth, Carolyn, Peter, Paula, Marc. Sr. fgn. exchange officer Bank of Boston, 1967-72; v.p. State St. Bank & Trust Co., Boston, 1972-79; sr. v.p. Shawmut Bank N.A., 1979—; dir. Forex Assn. of U.S., N.Y.C., 1977-82; East Coast rep. Fed. Res. Bank of N.Y., Fgn. Exchange Com., 1983-86; advisor Brandeis U. Career Devel., Waltham, Mass., 1984-85. Author: International Banking U.S. Laws and Regulations, 1984. Pres., bd. dirs. Stoughton Assn. for Exceptional Citizens, Mass., 1977-83; actor, dir. Stoughton Little Theatre, 1969-80; football coach Stoughton Youth Athletic Assn., 1969-83. Served with USAF, 1961-62. Mem. Assn. Cambiste Internat. Paris. Democrat. Roman Catholic. Lodge: K.C. Office: Shawmut Bank NA 1 Federal St Boston MA 02110

NISHIDA, KOHZO, business administration researcher, educator; b. Nagoya, Japan, Nov. 1, 1938; s. Norihiro and Toki (Utani) N.; m. Junko Murase, Nov. 3, 1968; children: Kazuhiko, Kimito. PhD in Bus. Adminstrn., Kobe U., Japan, 1971. With Matsushita Electric Indsl. Co., Ltd., Osaka, Japan, 1961-63; asst. prof. Aichi U., Toyohashi, Japan, 1968-71; prof. Nagoya City U., Japan, 1971—; vis. prof. Internat. Inst. for Studies and Tng., Fuzinomiya, Japan, 1971-82. Author 14 books; editor 2 books; contbr. articles to profl. jours. Home: 3-2 Nekogohora-dori, 464 Nagoya Japan Office: Nagoya City U Faculty Econs, 1 Yamanohata Mizuho-cho, 467 Nagoya Japan

NISHIMURA, JOSEPH YO, retail executive, accountant; b. Berkeley, Calif., Nov. 4, 1933; s. Masamoto and Kimiko (Ishihara) N.; m. Joyce Toshiye Mori, Sept. 1, 1956; children: Brenda Joyce, Stephen Lloyd. AB cum laude, Princeton U., 1956; MBA, Stanford U., 1961. CPA, Calif., N.Y.; cert. Employee Benefit Specialist. Audit supr. Touche Ross & Co., San Francisco, 1961-66; contr. Scott Co. of Calif., Oakland, 1966-67, Purity Stores, Inc., Burlingame, Calif., 1967-69; pres. Cubit Systems Corp., Burlingame, 1969-72; sr. v.p. Golden West Fin. Corp., Oakland, 1972-73; exec. v.p. Victory Markets, Inc., Norwich, N.Y., 1973—, dir., 1976—; dir. Carl's Drug Co., Rome, N.Y., 1988—. v.p., bd. dirs. Chenango Meml. Hosp., Norwich, 1981-87. Bd. dirs. United Fund, Norwich, 1984—, Binghamton (N.Y.) Symphony Orch, 1988—. Served to lt. (j.g.) USN, 1956-59; Japan. Mem. AICPA, N.Y. State Soc. CPA's, Calif. Soc. CPA's, N.Y. State Food Mcht. Assn. (bd. dirs. 1988—). Democrat. Presbyterian. Club: Princeton (N.Y.C.). Office: Victory Markets Inc 54 E Main St Norwich NY 13815

NISSEN, JUDY KAY, college administrator; b. George, Iowa, Mar. 24, 1942; d. Theodore and Marie Myrtle (Ackerman) Harms; m. Gordon Lee Elzenga, June 13, 1964 (dec.); m. James Gould Kerr, Aug. 15, 1973 (div. Jan. 1982); children: Jodi (dec.), Jana (dec.); m. Robert Eugene Nissen, Sept. 24, 1983; stepchildren: Melinda Duffy, Kathy Howell, Matt, Mary Riley, Jennifer Sagar. BA in Vocat. Home Econs. Edn., U. No. Iowa, 1963; MA in Higher Edn., Northeast Mo. State U., 1987; postgrad., Iowa State U., 1988—. Tchr. vocat. home econs. Tyler (Minn.) Community Sch., 1963-66, Le Mars (Iowa) Community Schs., 1968-78; tchr. home econs. Ft. Dodge (Iowa) Community Sch., 1966-67, Sioux City (Iowa) Cen. Sch., 1967-68; substitute tchr. U.S. Dept. Def. Sch., Seoul, Republic of Korea, 1978-80; trainer, retail salesperson Stretch & Sew Fabrics, Colorado Springs, Colo., 1980-81; coordinator bus. and home econs. adult edn. Iowa Valley Community Coll., Marshalltown, Iowa, 1981-86; dir. bus. devel. ctr Iowa Valley Community Coll., Marshalltown, 1986—, cons., 1986-88; trainer Fisher Controls, Marshalltown, 1987-88; presenter workshops Iowa Community Coll., 1986-88. Vol. ACE/SCORE, Marshalltown, 1984—. Named Woman of Yr. Marshalltown chpt. Am. Bus. Women's Assn., 1985; nominated to Women of Achievement YMCA, 1985. Mem. Am. Soc. Tng. and Devel., Iowa Assn. Lifelong Learning (treas. 1987—, Disting. Service award 1984), Am. Home Econs. Assn., Am. Vocat. Assn., Mo. Valley Edn. Assn., Marshalltown C. of C., Grinnell (Iowa) C. of C., Iowa Falls (Iowa) C. of C., TTT (chpt. pres. 1985-86), Phi Kappa Phi, Alpha Delta Kappa (corr. sec. 1986-88). Home: 1914 S 5th Ave Marshalltown IA 50158 Office: Iowa Valley Community Coll 3700 S Ctr St Marshalltown IA 50158

NITCHKE, HOWARD DEAN, president of executive search firm; b. New Haven, Jan. 26, 1949; s. Wilbur Dean and Martha Anne (Proctor) N.; m. Teresa Karen Maloney, Oct. 22, 1978; children: Ginette Katherine, James Howard. BA in Criminal Justice, U. Hartford, 1986, BS in Organizational Behavior, 1988. Cons., mgr. Rita Personnel, New Britain, Conn., 1973-75; gen. mgr. Rita Personnel, Boston, 1975, Execudex, Hartford, Conn., 1975-78; pres. Deane, Howard & Simon, Hartford, 1978—. Host "Issues in the Business Interests" TV program. Bd. dirs. Hartford Ballet, 1984—; campaign chmn. State House seat. Mem. Nat. Assn. Corp. and Profl. Recruiters (bd. dirs.), Conn. Bus. & Industry Assn. (small bus. adv. council 1982-85), Hartford C. of C. (gov. affairs com. 1981-85), West Hartford C. of C. (chmn. 1982-85). Republican. Congregationalist. Home: 20 Sunny Reach Dr West Hartford CT 06117

NITENSON, SHELDON, corporation executive; b. Boston, Mar. 1, 1927; s. Irving and Pauline (Gershman) N.; children: Lee Maxine, Janis Faye, Charles Harvey, Nancy Carol, Stacey. BChemE, Northeastern U., 1952. Registered profl. engr. Engr. Raytheon Mfg. Co., Waltham, Mass., 1952-63; founder, owner Crown Kennels, Inc., Sharon, Mass., 1960-75, All-Temp Engring., Inc., Needham, Mass., 1963-72, Sharon Machinery Co., Quincy, Mass., 1964-77, Vacuum Tube Industries, Inc., Brockton, Mass., 1965—. Office: Vacuum Tube Industries Inc PO Box 2009 Brockton MA 02403-2009

NIX, DENNIS WARREN, waste disposal service executive; b. St. Louis, Nov. 12, 1945; s. Frank Wilmore and Geneva Louise (Edwards) N.; m. Hee Yon (lee), Aug. 16, 1983 ; children: Shauna Lee, Robert Warren. Student, So. Ill. U., Edwardsville, 1978. Contractor various construction cos., Ill. and Mo., 1976-80; cons. toxic waste Kans. and Mo., 1980-83; founder, chmn., pres. AmerEco Environ. Services (formerly PCB Disposal Systems), Kingsville, Mo., 1983—; owner Holden Rev. Newspaper, Kingsville, 1988—; owner Holden Review newspaper. Inventor PCB Processing. Served with USAF, 1983-87. Mem. Air Pollution Control Assn. Republican. Baptist. Club: Optimist. Office: AmerEco Environ Svcs Inc Rt 1 Box 159 Kingsville MO 64061

NIX, HAROLD MANSON, accounting educator; b. Ft. Collins, Colo., June 18, 1931; s. Benjamin Manson and Eva Mae (Sampson) N.; m. Myrna Lee Miller, Dec. 15, 1969; children: Kristi Ann, John Benjamin. BA, Western State Coll., Gunnison, Colo., 1967, MA, 1969; PhD, Okla. State U., 1973. CPA, Colo., Alaska, Idaho; cert. mgmt. acct. Owner, operator Nix Lumber Co., Colorado Springs, Colo., 1949-65; assoc. prof., chmn. dept. acctg. Boise (Idaho) State U., 1973-78; prof., chmn. dept. acctg. U. Alaska, Anchorage, 1978-86; prof. acctg. Bradley U., Peoria, Ill., 1986—; cons., advisor, SBA, Anchorage, 1978-86. Contbr. articles to profl. jours. Mem. Anchorage Mcpl. Budget Adv. Commn., 1982-85. Mem. Am. Inst. CPA's, Nat. Assn. Accts., Fin. Execs. Inst. Home: Rt 1 Dunlap IL 61525 Office: Bradley U Dept Acctg Peoria IL 61625

NIXON, PETER MARLBOROUGH, steel company executive; b. Sault Ste. Marie, Ont., Can., Dec. 25, 1929; s. George E. and Isobel N.; m. Dorothy O. Herbst, 1953; children: Carol Ann, Ian James. B.Sc. in Mining Engring., Queen's U., 1953. Mine supt. Dominion Steel and Coal Corp., 1955-59; with Algoma Ore div. Algoma Steel Corp., 1959-68; now pres., chief exec. officer Algoma Steel Corp.; also bd. dirs.; mem. adv. bd. on Can. Ingersoll-Rand. Mem. Assn. Profl. Engrs. Ont., Am. Iron & Steel Inst. (bd. dirs.), Internat. Iron & Steel Inst. (bd. dirs.), Can. Steel Producers Assn. (chmn.), Can. Steel & Employment Congress (bd. dirs.). Office: Algoma Steel Corp, 503 Queen St E, Sault Sainte Marie, ON Canada P6A 5P2

NIXON, PHILIP ANDREWS, diversified company executive; b. Bklyn., Nov. 23, 1938; s. Philip A. and Hilda (Weidman) N.; m. Brooke Nichols, June 9, 1963; children: Lucia, Rachel, Eliot, Oliver, Preya, Malini. B.A., Yale U., 1960. Vol. Peace Corps, Sierra Leone, Africa, 1965-67; aide to gov. State of Maine, Augusta, 1967-70; asst. to chmn. Dead River Co., Bangor, Maine, 1970-71, v.p., 1971-73, exec. v.p., 1973, pres., chief exec. officer, 1974—; pres., chief exec. officer Dead River Group of Cos., Bangor, Maine, 1974-85; chnm. bd. Dead River Group of Cos., 1985—; dir. Fleet/Norstar Bank Maine, Forster Mfg. Co., Wilton, Maine. Sec. Maine Pulp & Paper Found., 1976-86; bd. dirs. New Eng. Council, 1978-86, Maine Community Found.; trustee Kenduskeag Found., Bangor, 1979—, Portland Sch. Art, 1983—. Served with USN, 1961-65. Mem. C. of C. of U.S., Conf. Bd. Democrat. Clubs: Union (Boston); University (N.Y.C.). Home: 71 Federal St Brunswick ME 04011 Office: Dead River Co 1 Dana St Portland ME 04101

NIXON, TAMARA FRIEDMAN, economist; b. Cleve., June 3, 1938; d. Victor and Eva J. (Osteryoung) Friedman; B.A. with honors in econs. (Wellesley scholar), Wellesley Coll., 1959; M.B.A. (fellow), U. Pitts., 1961; m. Daniel D. Nixon, June 14, 1959; children—Asa Joel, Naomi Devorah, Victoria Eve. Asst. economist Fed. Res. Bank, N.Y.C., 1959-60, 61-62; economist R.P. Wolff Econ. Research, Miami, Fla., 1972-75; econ. cons., Miami, 1975-79; sr. v.p. Washington Savs. & Loan Assn., Miami Beach, Fla., 1979-81; pres. T.F. Nixon Econ. Cons. Inc., 1982—; sr. v.p. CenTrust Savs. Bank, 1984—; real estate feasibility cons.; investment adminstr. Land use chmn. Dade County chpt. LWV, 1975-76. Mem. Econ. Soc. S. Fla. (v.p. programs, dir.), Am. Econ. Assn. Office: CenTrust Savs Bank One CenTrust Fin Ctr Miami FL 33131

NOALL, ROGER, bank executive; b. Brigham City, Utah, Apr. 1, 1935; s. Albert Edward Noall and Mabel Clayton; m. Judith Ann Stelter, Mar. 16, 1962 (div.); children: Brennan, Tyler; m. Colleen Henrietta Mannion. BS, U. Utah, 1955; LLB, Harvard U., 1958; LLM, NYU, 1959. Legal asst. Donavan, Leisure, Newton & Irvine, N.Y.C., 1959-61; assoc. Olwine, Connelly, Chase, O'Donnell & Weyher, N.Y.C., 1961-65, ptnr., 1965-67; with Bunge Corp., N.Y.C., 1967-85, exec. v.p., 1975-83; exec. v.p., chief fin. officer Centran Corp., Cleve., 1985-85; vice chmn., chief adminstrv. officer Soc. Corp., Cleve., 1985—; bd. dirs. The Shelby Ins. Co. Served in USNG, 1959. Office: Soc Corp 800 Superior Ave Cleveland OH 44114

NOBBS, KENNETH JOHN, camera company executive; b. Norfolk Island, South Pacific, Apr. 10, 1938; s. Charles Hebblethwaite Hasty and Sylvia Esther (Robinson) N.; m. Pamela Vicary, Oct. 15, 1960; children: Debbie Norma, Roy Anthony. Diploma in accountancy, Longburn Coll., New Zealand, 1955. Clk. Alex Harvey & Sons Pty. Ltd., Auckland, New Zealand, 1956-58; postmaster Posts and Telegraphs, Madang and Mt. Hagen, Papua New Guinea, 1958-64; salesman K.A. Prentice & Co., Norfolk Island, 1965-67; propr. Cameralines Ltd., Norfolk Island, 1967-70, mng. dir., 1970—; exec. dir. South Pacific Shipping Co. (N.I.) Ltd. Mem. Soc. Descendants Pitcairn Settlers. Lodge: Rotary (pres. 1980-81). Home: Peters Hwy, Norfolk Island Australia Office: Cameralines Ltd, PO Box 29 Burnt Pine, Norfolk Island Australia

NOBLE, JAMES KENDRICK, JR., investment firm executive; b. N.Y.C., Oct. 6, 1928; s. James Kendrick and Orrel Tennant (Baldwin) N.; m. Norma Jean Rowell, June 16, 1951; children: Anne Rowell, James Kendrick III. Student, Princeton U., 1945-46; B.S., U.S. Naval Acad., 1950; M.B.A., NYU, 1961; postgrad., Sch. Edn., 1962-68. Commd. ensign USN, 1950; transferred to USNR 1957; advanced through grades to capt. USNR, 1973; asst. gunnery officer in U.S.S. Thomas E. Fraser 1950-51; student naval aviator USNR, 1951-52, pilot asst. ops. officer, 1952-55; student USN Gen. Line Sch., 1955-56; instr. U.S. Naval Acad., 1956-57, Officer Candidate Sch., Newport, R.I., 1958; asst. to pres. Noble & Noble, Pub., Inc., N.Y.C., 1957-60; dir. spl. projects Noble & Noble, Pub., Inc., 1960-62, v.p., 1962-65, exec. v.p., 1965-66, dir., 1957-65; dir., v.p. Translation Pub. Co., N.Y.C., 1958-65; cons. Translation Pub. Co., 1965-66; v.p., dir. Elbon Realty Corp., Bronxville, N.Y., 1960-65; cons. Elbon Realty Corp., 1965-66; comdg. officer NAIRU R2, 1968-70; staff NARS W2, 1970-71, NRID 3-1, 1971-74; comdg. officer NRCSG 302, 1974-76; sr. analyst F. Eberstadt & Co., 1966-69; sr. analyst Auerbach, Pollak & Richardson, 1969-75, v.p., 1972-75, mgr. spl. research projects, 1973-75, dir., 1975; v.p. research Paine, Webber, Jackson & Curtis, Inc., 1975-77, assoc. dir. research, 1976-77; v.p. Paine Webber, N.Y.C., 1977-79; 1st v.p. Paine Webber, 1979—; dir. Curriculum Info. Center, Inc., Denver, 1972-78; instl. investor All Am. Research Team, 1972—. Author: Ploob, 1949, rev., 1956; editor pub.: The Years Between, 1966; also articles in various kinds publs. Vice pres. Bolton Gardens Assn., 1959-61; mem. Bronxville Bd. Edn., 1968-74, pres., 1970-72; Republican coleader 21st Dist., Eastchester, N.Y., 1961-65; Dir. Merit; cons., dir. Space and Sci. Train, 1962-63; trustee St. John's Hosp., Yonkers, N.Y., 1972—, com. chmn., 1980—. Fellow AAAS; mem. Info. Industry Assn. (disting. profl. mem.), Nat. Inst. Social Scis., N.Y. Soc. Security Analysts (mem. com. 1971—, dir. 1975-84, v.p. 1977-81, exec. v.p. 1981-82, pres. 1982-83), Am. Textbook Pub. Inst. (com. chmn. 1964-66), AIAA (mem. com. 1957-61), Media and Entertainment Analysts Assn. (pres. 1969-71), Fin. Analysts Fedn. (dir. 1984-87), Chartered Fin. Analyst, Naval Res. Assn. (v.p. N.Y. Navy chpt. 1968-76), others. Mem. Reformed Ch. Clubs: Wings (N.Y.C.);

Siwanoy Country (Bronxville, N.Y.). Home: 45 Edgewood Ln Bronxville NY 10708 Office: Paine Webber Inc 1285 Ave of the Americas New York NY 10019

NOBLE, PHILLIP R., radio station owner, manager; b. Anna, Ill., Sept. 12, 1945; s. Loyde N. and Frances (Owen) N.; m. Lynn Birleffi, Apr. 25, 1987. BA in Tech. Journalism, Colo. State U., 1974. Reporter Sta. KYCU-TV, Cheyenne, Wyo., 1974-76; dir. news Sta. KRAE-Radio, Cheyenne, 1976-77; capitol correspondent Sta. KTWO-TV/Radio, Cheyenne, 1977-80; cons. mktg. Sta. KTAG-Radio, Cody, Wyo., 1981; cons. media Wyo. Dept. Health and Social Services, Cheyenne, 1983; owner/mgr. Blue Sky Broadcasting Inc., Cheyenne, 1983—; cons. media for various polit. candidates, Cheyenne, 1982—; participant Atlantic Exchange Program, Rotterdam, Holland, 1987. Mgr. campaign Gov. Ed Herschler Re-election Campaign, Cheyenne, 1982; chmn. Laramie County Tourism Bd., 1987-88; pres. Cheyenne Civic Ctr. Golden Star Bd., 1986-87; mem. Newcomer Soc., 1987-88. Served with U.S. Navy, 1963-66. Mem. Cheyenne C. of C. (pres. 1989), Nat. Fedn. Independent Bus. (Guardian), Wyo. Assn. Broadcasting (dir.), Sigma Delta Chi. Democrat. Home: 1018 W Pershing Blvd Cheyenne WY 82001 Office: Sta KLEN-FM 1416 Bradley Ave Cheyenne WY 82001

NOBLE, THOMAS PAUL, automobile leasing executive; b. Boston, June 26, 1958; s. George D. Jr. and Ruth (Raftrey) N.; m. Margie Levine Noble, May 31, 1987. BS in Mgmt., Providence Coll., 1980. Sr. account rep. Wallace Computer Svcs., Inc., Boston, 1980-83; sr. dist. sales mgr. Hertz-U.S. Fleet Leasing, Inc., Boston, 1983—. Roman Catholic. Home: 11 Bailey Ct Canton MA 02021 Office: Hertz-US Fleet Leasing Inc 470 Totten Pond Rd Waltham MA 02154

NODVIN, MARVIN PHILLIP, lawyer; b. N.Y.C., Nov. 30, 1928; s. Morris M. and Hattie (Cohen) N.; m. Sondra D. Hagen, Sept. 27, 1974; children: Stephen C., Neal L., Jeffrey M., Margaux S., Hillary C. BA, U. Ga., 1949; JD, Emory U., 1951. Bar: Ga. 1951, U.S. Dist. Ct. (no. dist.) Ga., U.S. Ct. Appeals (5th and 11th cir.), U.S. Supreme Ct., Ga. Ct. Appeals, Ga. Supreme Ct. Atty. The Nodvin Firm, Atlanta, 1951—. Pres. Atlanta Men's Chpt. Am. Orgn. Rehab. Through Tng. Fedn., 1987—. Fellow Ga. Bar Assn. (com.), Atlanta Bar Assn.; mem. ABA. Office: The Nodvin Firm 100 Galleria Pkwy NW Suite 1180 Atlanta GA 30339

NOEL, MICHAEL LEE, utility executive; b. Rapid City, S.D., Apr. 5, 1941; s. Milton George and Merel Lyreen (Roth) N.; children—Christy Carole, Craig Arnold. B.S. in Finance cum laude, Calif. State U., Long Beach, 1964; M.B.A. summa cum laude, U. So. Calif., 1973. With So. Calif. Edison Co., Rosemead, 1964—, mgr. corp. planning, 1974-75, asst. treas., 1975-76, treas., 1976—, v.p., 1980—; guest lectr. U. So. Calif., Fullerton, Calif. State U., Long Beach; bd dirs. Current Income Shares, Inc., Hancock Savs. and Loan Assn. Chmn., bd. dirs. Los Angeles Jr. C. of C. Mem. L.A. Soc. Fin. Analysts, Pacific Coast Elec. Assn., L.A. Treas., Seacliff Tennis Club. Club: Seacliff Racquet. Home: 353 Ultimo Ave Long Beach CA 90814 Office: So Calif Edison Co 2244 Walnut Grove Ave Rosemead CA 91770

NOETZEL, ARTHUR JEROME, business administration educator, management consultant; b. East Cleveland, Ohio, July 2, 1916; s. Arthur John and Margaret (Weinfurtner) N.; m. Dorothy Elizabeth McKeon, Oct. 23, 1945 (dec. March 1988); children: Catherine Ellen Noetzel Levitt, Gretchen Marie Noetzel Walsh. BSBA, John Carroll U., 1938; MBA, Northwestern U., 1940; PhD, U. Mich., 1955; LittD (hon.), John Carroll U., 1985. Instr. John Carroll U., Cleve., 1941-42, asst. prof., 1942-46, prof. bus. adminstrn., 1955—; asst. dean Sch. Bus. John Carroll U., Cleve., 1945-56, dean, 1956-70, academic v.p., 1970-84; bd. dirs. Ctr. for Family Bus., Cleve., Ohio Coll. Podiatric Medicine, Cleve. Contbr. articles and book reviews to profl. jours. Bd. dirs. St. Vincent Charity Hosp., Cleve., 1970-82, Borromeo Coll., Wickliffe, 1978-84; chmn. Communication and Devel. Commn., Univ. Heights, Ohio, 1980—. Named Citizen of Yr., City of Univ. Heights, Ohio, 1983; recipient Alumni award John Carroll U., 1984, Cert. of Merit, Minority Developers Council, Cleve., 1985; Danforth Found. fellow, 1956. Roman Catholic. Home: 2405 Fenwood Rd University Heights OH 44118 Office: John Carroll University University Heights Cleveland OH 44118

NOFELT, ULF, banker; b. Malmo, Sweden, Oct. 26, 1949; came to U.S., 1967; s. Sune and Inge N.; m. Else Clausen; 1 child, Peter. BA, Calif. State U., Fullerton, 1974; postgrad., Maximilian U., Munich, Fed. Republic Germany, 1974; MA, Am. Grad.Sch. Internat. Mgmt., 1975. With Bank of Am., Copenhagen, 1976-79; asst. v.p. Bank of Am., London, 1979-84; rep. Privatbanken, Los Angeles, 1984-88; v.p., mgr. fin. Privatbanken, N.Y.C., 1988—; established UN Cons. fin. and mktg. cons. co. Mem. Fgn. Bankers Assn., Danish Am. C. of C. Home: 120 Potter Rd Scarsdale NY 10583 Office: Privatbanken AS 13-15 W 54th St New York NY 10019

NOFSINGER, WILLIAM MORRIS, engineering executive; b. Orange, N.J., Sept. 11, 1932; s. Charles William and Grace Elizabeth (Morris) N.; m. Bonnie Jean Haisler, Nov. 6, 1965; children: Barry Jean, Betsy Jayne. BS in Chem. Engring., U. Kans., 1955. Registered profl. engr. With The C.W. Nofsinger Co., Kansas City, Mo., various positions to v.p., 1959-78, pres., 1978—. Lt. USAF, 1955-58, capt. Res. Fellow Am. Inst. Chem. Engrs.; mem. NSPE, Am. Chem. Soc., Mo. Soc. Profl. Engrs., Kans. Engring. Soc. Republican. Lodge: Rotary (v.p. 1983-84, pres. elect 1984-85, pres. 1985-86). Home: 6645 Brookside Rd Kansas City MO 64113 Office: The CW Nofsinger Co 4600 E 63d St Box 419173 Kansas City MO 64141-0173

NOGG, DONALD IRWIN, paper distribution executive, population researcher; b. Omaha, Feb. 17, 1930; s. Nathan L. and Ruth (Brown) N.; m. Ozzie Katz, Aug. 22, 1954; children: Kathy, Marsha, Rachel, Anthony. Student, U. Colo., 1947-51. Pres., chief exec. officer Nogg Bros. Paper Co., Omaha, 1980—; chmn. Hudson Pulp Adv. Com., N.Y.C., 1975-77; chmn. bd. Network Assoc. Inc., 1984-86. Pres. Chanticleer Theatre, Council Bluffs, Iowa, 1966-68, Met. Actors Guild, Omaha, 1968-70, Beth El Synagogue, Omaha, 1979-81. Fellow Am. Geog. Soc.; Population Assn. Am., Am. Names Soc. Jewish. Home: 9719 Frederick St Omaha NE 68124 Office: Nogg Bros Paper Co PO Box 3728 Omaha NE 68103

NOGUCHI, HIDEO, insurance agency executive; b. Kyoto, Japan, Jan. 17, 1945; s. Tasao and Ishiko (Tsujii) N.; m. Eleanor Kazuko Horii, May 7, 1970; children—Mark H.Y., Mitchell H.Y. B.B.A., U. Hawaii, 1969. Buyer RCA Purchasing Co., Tokyo, 1969-73; ins. specialist Continental Ins. Agy., Honolulu, 1973-82; pres. Noguchi & Assocs., Inc., Honolulu, 1983—; cons. Recipient Nat. New Agt. Leadership award CNA Corp., 1974, Agt. of Yr. award Continental Ins. Agy., annually 1973-81, Key Club award CNA Co., 1975, 79-81. Mem. Nat. Assn. Life Underwriters, Honolulu Assn. Life Underwriters, Million Dollar Round Table. Lodge: Elks. Home: 3678 Woodlawn Terrace Pl Honolulu HI 96822 Office: 1314 S King St Suite 560 Honolulu HI 96814

NOIA, ALAN JAMES, utility company executive; b. Selbitz, Germany, Feb. 18, 1947; came to U.S., 1949; s. Fiore and Anneliese (Gossler) N.; m. Cynthia Dee Rathman. B.S. in Elec. Engring., U. Va., Charlottesville, 1969. Engr. Allegheny Power System, Hagerstown, Md., 1962-72; supr. tech. services Allegheny Power System, Greensburg, Pa., 1972-75; staff asst. Allegheny Power System, N.Y.C., 1975-79, asst. v.p., 1979-80, treas., 1980-82, v.p., 1983—, chief fin. officer, 1987—; bd. dirs. Monongahela Power Co., Potomac Edison Co., West Penn Power Co. Trustee East Central Nuclear Group, N.Y.C. 1979—; mem. elec. engring. indsl. adv. bd. U. Va. Mem. Phi Eta Sigma, Eta Kappa Nu, Tau Beta Pi. Republican. Roman Catholic. Home: Deer Trail Clarksburg NJ 08510 Office: Allegheny Power System 320 Park Ave New York NY 10022

NOLAN, PATRICK JOSEPH, furniture company executive; b. Glendale, N.Y., July 17, 1938; s. Daniel Patrick and Anne Margaret (Krautter) N.; m. Carol Mirabel, Nov. 14, 1964; children—Daniel, Peter, Brian, Patrick. B.S. in Accounting, Fordham U., 1964; postgrad., Pace Coll., 1968. Fin. analyst W.R. Grace & Co., N.Y.C., 1964-68; asst. to v.p.-fin. Holly Sugar Corp., N.Y.C., 1968-70; sr. v.p., treas. Levitz Furniture Corp., Boca Raton, Fla., 1970—; dir. Coral Savs. and Loan, Coral Springs, Fla., Covenant House, Fla. Mem. Fin. Execs. Inst., Palm Beach County Econ. Coun., Frenchman's Creek Club, Palm Beach Club, Palm Beach Yacht Club. Republican. Roman Catholic. Home: 13744 Le Bateau Ln North Palm Beach FL 33410 Office: Levitz Furniture Corp 6111 Broken Sound Pkwy NW Boca Raton FL 33487

NOLAND, LLOYD U., III, wholesale utility supplies company executive; b. Balt., 1943; married. BA, U. Va., 1966; MBA, U. Pa., 1968. Sales trainee Noland Co., Newport News, Va., 1968-69, salesman, 1969-71, mgr. Durham (N.C.) br., 1971-73, mgr. Nashville br., 1973-77, mgr. merchandising, plumbing and heating South div., 1977-80, mgr. merchandising, plumbing and heating, 1980-81, v.p. merchandising, plumbing and heating, 1981, now chmn., chief exec. officer, also bd. dirs.; bd. dirs. Cen. Fidelity Bank, N.A., So. Wholesalers Assn. Mem. Am. Supply Assn. (bd. dirs.), Innovative Tech. Authority (bd. dirs.), So. Wholesalers Assn. (pres.). Office: Noland Co 2700 Warwick Blvd Newport News VA 23607

NOLAND, ROBERT LEROY, manufacturing company executive; b. Lawrence, Kans., Sept. 7, 1918; s. Harry L. and Angela (Scola) N.; m. Delpha Mae Mierndorf, June 16, 1962; children: Gary, Fabra Jeanine, Derice Elizabeth. B.S. in Mech. Engring, Calif. Inst. Tech., 1941. Design and devel. rocket propelled devices Calif. Inst. Tech., 1941-45; supr. propulsions Naval Ordnance Test Sta., China Lake, Calif., 1945-46; asst. chief engr. Aerojet Gen. Corp., 1946-52; cons. engr. plastic components, rockets and missiles 1952-54; exec. v.p. Rienhold Engring. and Plastics Co., 1954-57, pres., 1957-59; exec. v.p. Haveg Industries, Wilmington, Del., 1959-66; exec. v.p. Ametek, Inc., Paoli, Pa., 1966-68, pres., bd. dirs., 1968-88; pres., chief exec. officer, dir. Ketema Inc., Bensalem, Pa., 1988—. Home: PO Box 109 Glenbrook NV 89413 Office: Ketema Inc 2233 State Rd Bensalem PA 19020

NOLEN, TRULY WILLIAM, retail executive; b. Miami, Fla., Sept. 2, 1951; s. Truly D. and Pat (Morrow) N.; 1 child, Winter. Student, Cen. Ariz. Coll., 1969-72, U. Ariz., 1972-74, 76, U. So. Calif. Salesperson Pest Control, Los Angeles, 1965-78; mgr. Pest Control, San Marcus, Calif., 1978-79; mgr. los control Pest Control, Tucson, 1979—. Office: PO Box 43550 Tucson AZ 85733

NOLTE, GEORGE WASHINGTON, former investment company executive; b. nr. Woodbury, N.J., Apr. 2, 1904; s. Harry Kircher and Anna (Porch) N. BS, U. Pa., 1924. CPA, Pa. Acct. Lybrand, Ross Bros. & Montgomery, Phila., 1924-32; comptroller Atwater Kent Mfg. Co., Phila., Wilmington, Del., 1932-49, v.p., 1949-67, pres., 1972-81; v.p. Kent Co., Wilmington, 1972-81; treas. Kent Elec. Mfg. Corp., 1949-71; bd. dirs. Atwater Kent Mfg. Co. Cons. parks, recreation com. Bd. Chosen Freeholders, Gloucester County, N.J., 1965-66; pres., trustee Gloucester County Conservancy, Etlon Found. Served to comdr. USNR, 1942-46. Recipient Disting. Service award for outstanding community service Woodbury Jr. C. of C., 1965. Mem. Am. Inst. CPA's. Home: 801 Lake Shore Dr #517 Lake Park FL 33403 Office: 3411 Silverside Rd Wilmington DE 19810

NOLTE, HENRY R., JR., automobile company executive, lawyer; b. N.Y.C., Mar. 3, 1924; s. Henry R. and Emily A. (Eisele) N.; m. Frances Messner, May 19, 1951; children: Gwynne Conn, Henry Reed III, Jennifer, Suzanne. BA, Duke U., 1947; LLB, U. Pa., 1949. Bar: N.Y. 1950, Mich. 1967. Assoc. Cravath, Swaine & Moore, N.Y.C., 1951-61; assoc. counsel Ford Motor Co., Dearborn, Mich., 1961, asst. gen. counsel, 1964-71, assoc. gen. counsel, 1971-74, v.p., gen. counsel, 1974-89; v.p., gen. counsel Philco-Ford Corp., Phila., 1961-64; v.p., gen. counsel, sec. Ford of Europe Inc., Warley, Essex, Eng., 1967-69; gen. counsel fin. and ins. subs. Ford Motor Co., 1974-89; sr. ptnr., chmn. Miller, Canfield, Paddock & Stone, Detroit, 1989—; bd. dirs. First Fed. of Mich. Trustee Cranbrook Ednl. Community; mem. Internat. and Comparative Law Ctr. of Southwestern Legal Found. Served to lt. USNR, 1943-46, PTO. Mem. ABA (past chmn. com. corp. law depts.), Mich. Bar Assn., Assn. Bar City of N.Y., Assn. Gen. Counsel. Episcopalian. Clubs: Orchard Lake Country; Bloomfield Hills Country (Mich.); Detroit; The Everglades (Fla.). Office: Miller Canfield Paddock and Stone 1400 N Woodwind Ave Bloomfield Hills MI 48303-2014

NOMELAND, LESLIE CORNELL, lawyer; b. Taunton, Minn., May 28, 1936; s. Carl T. and Beatrice J. (Knutson) N.; m. LaVonne E. Kolflat, Mar. 28, 1959; children: Richard, Melinda, Lisa, Stacy. BA, St. Cloud State Coll., 1960; JD, William Mitchell Coll. Law, St. Paul, 1972. Bar: Minn. 1972. Adminstrv. mgr. Hartford Ins. CO., Mpls., 1961-64, Great Am. Ins. Co., Mpls., 1964-72; corp. counsel Great Am. Ins. Co., Cin., 1972-78, Am. Fin. Corp., Cin., 1978-80; gen. counsel Provident Bancorp Inc., Cin., 1980—. With USAF, 1955-58. Mem. ABA, Minn. Bar Assn., Cin. Bar Assn. Republican. Unitarian.

NOONAN, PETER EDWARD, JR., insurance executive; b. Albany, N.Y., Apr. 22, 1936; s. Peter Edward and Dorothea (McLean) N.; m. Mary Anne Dyer, Feb. 16, 1963; children: Mary A. Noonan Stafford, Peter Edward III. BA, Union Coll., Schenectady, N.Y., 1957. Underwriter Glens Falls Ins. Co., N.Y., 1957-59; with Aurora, Inc., Albany, N.Y., 1959—, pres., 1965, chmn. bd., 1967—; pres. Metroland Execs., Albany, 1978-80. Contbr. articles to profl. jours. Trustee Albany Coll. Pharmacy, 1980—, Leukemia Soc., 1984—, Nat. Found. for Ileitis & Colitis, 1987—; bd. dirs. Capital Dist. Basketball Corp., Albany, 1983—. Mem. Albany Area C. of C. (pres. 1980-81), Ins. Agts. of Albany Co. (pres. 1978-79), Am. Arbitration Assn. (mediator 1984—), Sigma Chi. Democrat. Roman Catholic. Club: Wolferts Roost Country (dir. 1980-83). Lodge: Elks. Office: Aurora Inc 41 State St Albany NY 12207

NOPAR, ALAN SCOTT, lawyer; b. Chgo., Nov. 14, 1951; s. Myron E. and Evelyn R. (Millman) N. BS, U. Ill., 1976; JD, Stanford U., 1979. Bar: Ariz. 1979, U.S. Dist. Ct. Ariz. 1980, U.S. Ct. Appeals (9th cir.) 1980, U.S. Supreme Ct. 1982; CPA, Ill. Assoc. O'Connor, Cavanagh, Anderson, Westover, Killingsworth & Beshears P.A., Phoenix, 1979-85, ptnr., 1985-87; of counsel Tower, Byrne & Beaugureau, Phoenix, 1987-88, Minutillo & Gorman, San Jose, Calif., 1989—. Mem. Ariz. Rep. Caucus, Phoenix, 1984-88. Mem. ABA (bus. law sect., pub. contract law sect., forum com. on franchising), Ariz. Bar Assn. (corp. banking and bus. law sect.), Maricopa County Bar Assn. (corp. banking and bus. law sect.), Am. Inst. CPA's. Office: Minutillo & Gorman 55 S Market St Ste 1100 San Jose CA 95113

NORBERG, ERIC ANTHONY, financial executive; b. Denver, May 21, 1954; s. James Arthur and Shirley Lou (Walstrom) N.; m. Catherine Ann Baker, Mar. 8, 1980; children: Bridget M., Heather A. BS, U. Md., 1977; postgrad., Franklin U., 1978-79. CPA, D.C.; CLU; chartered fin. cons.; cert. fin. planner. Comptroller DeFranceaux Realty Group Inc., Washington, 1978-83; pres. Fin. Svc. Ctr., Vienna, Va., 1983-87; v.p. fin. planning Montgomery Fin. Corp., Rockville, Md., 1987-88; tax specialist Cooper & Lybrand, Washington, 1989—. Mem. Internat. Assn. Fin. Planning (treas. local chpt. 1987-88), Am. Inst. CPAs, Am. Soc. CLU, Chartered Fin. Cons., Washington Soc. Security Analysts (affiliate), D.C. Inst. CPAs. Office: Montgomery Advisors Inc 6290 Montrose Rd Rockville MD 20852

NORD, HAROLD EMIL, JR., small business owner, consultant; b. Manistee, Mich., Dec. 28, 1928; s. Harold Emil Nord and Anna Margaret (Simmons) Chase; m. Dolores Lillian Matistic, Apr. 26, 1952; children: Harold Emil III, Karen. BS in Hotel Adminstrn., Mich. State U., 1950. Cert. air transport pilot. Capt. Eastern Airlines, Miami, Fla., 1957-88; owner, operator Golden Gate Cottages, Laconia, N.H., 1969-73, Seaplane Services, INc., Laconia, 1969-73; pres. Aviation Mgmt. Advisors, Inc., West Palm Beach, Fla., 1978—. Mem. U.S. Rep. Senatorial Club, Washington, 1977—, Futures Group of Palm Beach, 1984, Pundits of Palm Beach, 1983. Served to capt. USAF, 1950-57, major USAFR, 1957-64. Named Master Bush Pilot, Ladd Air Force Base, Fairbanks, Alaska, 1955. Mem. Airline Pilots Assn., Internat. Fellowship Flying Rotarians, Mich.State Alunmi (Atlanta chpt. pres. 1959-61), Retired Eastern Pilots Assn., Nat. Seaplane Pilots Assn., Rotary, Quiet Birdmen. Home and Office: Aviation Mgmt Advisors Inc 41 South Rd Rye Beach NH 03871 also: 5200 N Dixie #2101 West Palm Beach FL 33407

NORDDAHL, BIRGIR VALSON, physicist, researcher; b. Reykjavik, Iceland, Feb. 11, 1947; s. Valur Gudmundsson and Karin Marie (Jensen) N.; m. Helle Bodil Damslund; children: Mette Maj, Jon Asger, Martin Halldor. BSc in Chemistry, U. Aathus, Denmark, 1971, MSc in Physics, 1974. Research fellow CERN, Geneva, 1972-74, Niels Bohr Inst., Copenhagen, 1974; faculty Midtfyn Mcpl. Coll., Ringe, Denmark, 1974-83, Svendborg (Denmark) Nursing Coll., 1975-77; researcher in chemistry and physics Roulunds Fabriker, Odense, Denmark, 1983-84, mgr. power transmission research and devel., testing and documentation, 1985-88; mgr. Dansk Miljo Tecnic Ltd., 1988—; project engr. Samfundsteknik, Odense, 1984; dir. Rudme Coop. Bank. Contbr. articles to profl. jours. Mem. Danish Physics Tchrs. Assn. (chmn. 1980-82), Danish Assn. Rubber Tech., Am. Assn. Physics Tchrs., Danish Assn. Academics. Home: Rudmevej 38, 5750 Ringe Denmark Office: Danish Bioprotein/Miljoteknik, Stenhuggervej 7-9, Odense Denmark

NORDELL, EUGENE CARL, research company executive; b. Dunkirk, N.Y., Dec. 30, 1925; s. Carl Evar and Jennie (Naslund) N.; children: Karen Jayne, Melinda Anne. Diploma in TV Engring., DeVry Tech. Inst., 1950; student, SUNY, Syracuse, 1951-52, U. Tex., El Paso, 1975-76; B in Profl. Studies, Empire State Coll., 1979. With Gen. Electric Co., Syracuse and Phila., 1951-70; ops. mgr. El Paso br. Syracuse U. Rsch. Corp., 1971-74; owner, operator Avert-A-Ray, El Paso, 1975-76; program mgr. site ops. Rome Rsch. Corp., Verona, N.Y., 1976-77; v.p. test and instrumentation div. Rome Rsch. Corp., Verona, 1978-83; pres. Rome Rsch. Corp., New Hartford, N.Y., 1983-88; also chmn. bd. dirs. Rome Rsch. Corp., New Hartford. Patentee radar signal processing techniques; contbr. articles to various publs. Vol. Bryn Mawr, Pa. Republican campaigns, 1967-69. With USN, 1943-47, 47-48. Mem. Electronic Industries Assn., Gen. Electric Engrs. Assn., Foreman's Assn., Antenna Measurements Tech. Assn., Rsch. Engring. Soc. Am., Assn. Old Crows (bd. dirs. local chpt. 1987), Sigma Xi. Unitarian. Lodge: Assn. Old Crows (v.p. 1989—). Club: Verona Golf. Home: 112 Kimry Moor Fayetteville NY 13066 Office: Rome Rsch Corp Par Technology Park New Hartford NY 13413

NORDEN, K. ELIS, management consultant; b. Stockholm, Feb. 27, 1921; s. Daniel Henrik and Ella Amanda (Larsson) N.; m. Astrid Margaretha Lethin, June 24, 1946; children: Jan-Henrik, Gunilla, Carl-Magnus. BEE, Royal Inst. Tech., Stockholm, 1954. Devel. engr. Swedish Radio AB, 1940-44; chief radar devel dept. Royal Swedish Air Bd., 1944-54; founder, pres. Elenik Automation AB, Stockholm, 1955-64, Norden Automation Systems AG, Zurich, Switzerland, 1964-79, NAS Austria, Vienna, 1966-79, NAS Holland, Woudenberg, 1968-79; mgmt. cons. to airlines, iron, steel and chem. industry, specialist in motion wieghing, computer controlled material handling, Norden Cons. Internat. Ltd., Zug, Switzerland, 1987—; course dir. modern electronic weighing Ctr. Profl. Advancement, East Brunswick, N.J.; tchr. Royal Swedish Air Force High Sch., 1955-64. Author: The Inventors Book, 1963, Pulp and Paper, 1968, Aufbereitungstechn, 1972, Electronic Weighing in Industrial Processes, 1984; patentee in field. Mem. Swedish Inst. Tech., Swedish Assn. Elec. Engrs., Assn. Instrument Tech., Verein Deutscher Eisen. Club: Sallskapet (Sweden); Nueva Andalucia Golf and Country (v.p.) (Spain). Home: Spitzackerstrasse 2, 7310 Bad Ragaz Switzerland also: P34 Calle 11D, Brisas del Golf Nueva, Andalucia, Marbella Spain Office: Alpenstrasse 2, PO Box 4535, CH-6304 Zug Switzerland

NORDLING, BERNARD ERICK, lawyer; b. Nekoma, Kans., June 14, 1921; d. Carl Ruben Ebben and Edith Elveda (Freeburg) N.; m. Barbara Ann Burkholder, Mar. 26, 1949. Student, George Washington U., 1941-43; AB, McPherson Coll., 1947; JD, U. Kans., 1949. Bar: Kans. 1949, U.S. Dist. Ct. Kans. 1949, U.S. Ct. Appeals (10th cir.) 1970. Pvt. practice law Hugoton, Kans., 1949—; ptnr. Kramer & Nordling, 1950-65, Kramer, Nordling, Nordling & Tate, 1966—; city atty. City of Hugoton, 1951-87; county atty. Stevens County (Kans.), 1957-63; Kans. mem. legal com. Interstate Oil Compact Commn., 1969—; mem. supply tech. adv. com. nat. gas survey FPC, 1975-77. Editor U. Kans. Law Rev., 1949. Mem. Hugoton Sch. Bds., 1954-68, pres. grade sch. bd., 1957-63; trustee McPherson Coll., 1971-81, mem. exec. com., 1975-81; ken. Kans. Energy Adv. Coun., 1975-78, mem. exec. com., 1976-78; bd. govs. U. Kans. Law Soc., 1984—. With AUS, 1944-46. Mem. ABA, Kans. Bar Assn., S.W. Kans. Bar Assn., Am. Judicature Soc., City Attys. Assn. Kans. (exec. com. 1975-83, pres. 1982-83), Nat. Assn. Royalty Owners (bd. govs. 1980—), S.W. Kans. Royalty Owners Assn. (exec. sec. 1968—), Nat. Honor Soc., Order of Coif, Phi Alpha Delta. Home: 218 N Jackson St Hugoton KS 67951 Office: 209 E 6th St PO Box 250 Hugoton KS 67951

NORDLUND, DONALD ELMER, manufacturing company executive; b. Stromsburg, Nebr., Mar. 1, 1922; s. E.C. and Edith O. (Peterson) N.; m. Mary Jane Houston, June 5, 1948; children: Donald Craig, William Chalmers, Sarah, James. A.B., Midland Coll., 1943; J.D., U. Mich., 1948. Bar: Ill. 1949. With Stevenson, Conaghan, Hackbert, Rooks and Pitts, Chgo., 1948-55, A.E. Staley Mfg. Co., Decatur, Ill., 1956-85; v.p., dir., mem. exec. com. A.E. Staley Mfg. Co., 1958-65, pres., chief operating officer, 1965-80, dir., mem. exec. com., 1965-85, also chmn., 1975-85; chief exec. officer Staley Continental, Inc., Rolling Meadows, Ill., 1985-88, chmn. and chief exec. officer, 1985-88; dir. Ill. Bell Telephone Co., Amsted Industries, Inc., Sentry Ins., Sundstrand Corp., Midwest Fin. Group, Inc.; adv. council Kellogg Grad. Sch. Mgmt. Northwestern U., Evanston, Ill. Past chmn. bd. trustees Millikin U., now hon. trustee; trustee Vanderbilt U., Mus. Sci. Industry, Chgo., Rush-Presby. St. Lukes Med. Ctr.; bd. dirs. Lyric Opera Chgo.; mem. grad. dirs. council Decatur Meml. Hosp., Ill. Gov.'s Commn. on Sci. and High Tech., Nat. Citizens Commn. on Alcoholism. 1st lt. AUS, 1943-46, 51-52. Mem. ABA, Chgo. Bar Assn., Corn Refiners. Assn. (bd. dirs., past chmn., now hon. dir.), The Lincoln Acad. of Ill., Legal Club, Commercial Club, Chgo. Club, Tavern Club, Barrington Hills Club, Phi Alpha Delta.

NORDMANN, GARY ARNOLD, corporate executive; b. Berwyn, Ill., Jan. 29, 1942; s. Arnold Friedrich and Mildred Ellen (Forslund) N.; m. Nancy Olivia House, June 9, 1966 (div. Sept. 1982); 1 child, Leila Olivia; m. Caroline C. Brune, Feb. 20, 1988. BS in Indsl. Mgmt., Purdue U., 1964; MBA, Harvard U., 1970. Asst. to v.p. fin. S.C. Johnson & Sons, Inc., Racine, Wis., 1970-72; controller Wilson Sporting Goods Co., River Grove, Ill., 1972-77; v.p. corp. devel. Mattel, Inc., Hawthorne, Calif., 1977-81; v.p. fin. Marriott Corp., Inc., Gurnee, Ill., 1981-83; exec. v.p. Whitbread N.Am., Inc., Lake Success, N.Y., 1983—; instr. U. Wis., Parkside, 1970-73. Lt. USN, 1965-68. Mem. Nat. Assn. Accts., Cold Spring Harbor Beach. Office: Whitbread N Am Inc One Hollow Ln Lake Success NY 11042

NORDQUIST, STEPHEN GLOS, lawyer; b. Mpls., May 13, 1936; s. Oscar Alvin Nordquist and Georgiana (Glos) Ruplin; m. Cynthia Alexandra Turner, Aug. 16, 1958 (div. Aug. 1967); children: Darcy Alden, Timothy Turner; m. Regina Frances Stanton, Nov. 1, 1969; 1 child, Nicholas Alden. BA cum laude, U. Minn., 1958, LL.B cum laude, 1961. Bar: Minn. 1961, N.Y. 1962. Assoc. Dewey, Ballantine, Bushby, Palmer & Wood, N.Y.C., 1961-69, ptnr., 1969-85; sr. v.p. W.P. Carey & Co., Inc., N.Y.C., 1985-86, exec v.p., sec., 1986-87; ptnr. Cole & Deitz, N.Y.C., 1988—; pres., bd. dirs. Carey Corp. Property, Inc., Carey-Longmont Inc., Carey-Longmont Real Property, Inc., N.Y.C., 1985-87, 520 East 86th Street, Inc. 1st v.p., dir. Seaview Assn. Fire Island (N.Y.), Inc. Republican. Congregationalist. Clubs: Knickerbocker (house com.), Club at World Trade Ctr. Home: 520 E 86th St Apt 3B New York NY 10028 Office: Cole & Deitz 175 Water St New York NY 10038-4981

NORDQVIST, ERIK ASKBO, shipping company executive; b. Copenhagen, Aug. 8, 1943; s. Joergen and Lissie (Moeller) A.; ed. Danish Comml. Coll. Commerce, London, 1963-64, U. S.C., 1964-65; m. Kirsten Vibeke Kenholt, Sept. 17, 1970; children—Ken-Martin, Alexander. Vice pres. Import Center W.S., Los Angeles, 1964-65; mgr. Denning Freight Forwarders Ltd., Toronto, Ont., Can., 1965-66; sales dir. overseas Samson Transp. Co., Copenhagen, 1967-68; mng. dir., pres. Seair AS, Copenhagen, 1969-71, Nordbird Group, Vedback, Denmark, 1971—, Nordbird AS, 1971—, also Nordbird Oil, Nordbird Fin., Copenhagen, Nordbird Internat. Financing Ltd., Toronto, Ont.; v.p. N. Sea Products Inc., High Point, N.C., 1980—; dir. Frano Aps, Copenhagen, 1979-80, Fino Travel, Odense, Denmark, 1979—, Annex Furniture Galleries, 1980—, Olsen & Nordqvist Holding, Holbaek, Denmark, 1984—, pres., 1986—, NQ-Byg Aps, Holbaek, 1986—, Auto Dan-Am., Holbaek, 1986—, Autotel Internat., Roskilde, 1987—, On Holding APS, Vedbaek Dansk-Fransk Osters Aps, 3 Danish Open, U.S., Great Britain, Japan, 1988—, Tins and Cans, Denmark, 1988—; cons.

Frederikshavns. Skibsvaerf AS. Recipient Devel. honor for shipping City of Le Havre, France, 1971. Mem. Det Udenrigspolitiske Selskab, Funen Soc. (founder, past pres.). Conservative. Lutheran. Office: 11 Rammetoften, 2950 Vedbaek Denmark

NOREM, GLENN ALLEN, venture capitalist; b. Chgo., Sept. 7, 1952; s. Martin W. and Barbara S. (Morgan) N.; divorced; 1 child, Stefanie L. BEE, So. Ill. U., 1978; MBA, U. Chgo., 1983. Registered profl. engr., N.Y. Devel. engr. IBM Systems Communications Lab., Kingston, N.Y., 1978-81; bus. devel. mgr. Tex. Instruments, Dallas, 1983-84; gen. ptnr. Berry Cash Southwest Ptnrs., Dallas, 1984—, InterWest Ptnrs., Dallas, 1985—; dir. Telinq Systems Corp., Dallas, Intratec Systems Corp., Dallas, Proteon, Inc., Westborough, Mass.; speaker, lectr. in field. Editor tech. publs. Served with U.S. Army, 1972-74. Named Outstanding Elec. Engr., St. Louis Elec. Bd. Trade, 1978; recipient Service award So. Ill. U., Carbondale, 1978. Mem. IEEE, Dallas Venture Capital Assn. (bd. dirs. 1985—), Am. Mgmt. Assn., Am. Electronics Assn., Nat. Venture Capital Assn., U. Chgo. Alumni Club Dallas, Los Colinas Sports Club. Republican. Methodist. Home: 3750 Duchess Trail Dallas TX 75229 Office: Interwest Ptnrs 1 Galleria Tower Suite 1375 Dallas TX 75240

NORKUNAS, JOHN JOSEPH, mechanical engineer; b. Wilkes Barre, Pa., May 2, 1947; s. John Joseph and Adele (Vosilius) N.; m. Elyse Melanie Dunn, Nov. 26, 1970; children: Jeffrey, Mark, Tricia, Kevin. BSME, N.J. Inst. Tech., 1973. Registered profl. engr., Va. Project engr. Allied Fibers and Plastics, Petersburg, Va., 1983-86; assoc. cons. Internat. Plastics Cons. Corp., Richmond, Va., 1986-87; supr. project engring. ICI Ams., Fayetteville, N.C., 1987-88; sr. engr. Franklin Co., Richmond, 1988—. Mem. ASME, ASHRAE, Soc. Plastics Engrs., Jaycees. Republican. Roman Catholic. Home: 5327J Huntmaster Dr Midlothian VA 23113 Office: Franklin Co 10825 Midlothian Turnpike Richmond VA 23235

NORMAN, ANDREW LEE, investment trader; b. Washington, Sept. 29, 1940; s. Andrew Jackson and Blanche Virginia Browning (Lee) N.; m. Lin Osgood, Sept. 3, 1960; children: Randal Osgood, Sandra Lin Pine, Christopher Scott, Kelly Lin, Marisol Frances. Student, U. Md., 1960, 68-70; AA in Fin. Adminstrn., Strayer Coll., 1961. With Geico Corp. and subs. cos., Washington, 1962—, asst. v.p., 1980-84, investment officer, 1984—. Trustee, deacon Calverton Bapt. Ch., Silver Spring, Md., 1967—; bd. dirs. No. Prince Georges YMCA, Beltsville, Md., 1970-72; v.p., bd. dirs. F.I.S.H. of Beltsville, 1986—. Named Foster Parent of Yr., Prince Georges County Dept. Social Svcs., 1977; recipient Spl. Recognition award Md.-Del. Conf. for Deaf, 1987, Muriel Hollen award for svc. to deaf, 1985. Mem. Washington Assn. Money Mgrs., Fin. Forum Washington. Democrat. Baptist. Home: 13019 Flint Rock Dr Beltsville MD 20705 Office: Geico Corp Geico Pla Washington DC 20076

NORMAN, DENNIS PAUL, real estate company executive; b. St. Louis, Mar. 26, 1961; s. Bobby Lee and Dorothy Lee (Miller) N.; m. Kim K. Kiss, Dec. 29, 1979. V.p. Saaman Corp., St. Louis, 1985-89, pres., 1989—; pres. Dennis Norman Realty, Inc., St. Louis, 1985—. Mem. Nat. Assn. Realtors, Mo. Assn. Realtors, Real Estate Bd. Met. St. Louis, Masons. Home: 10535 Tate St Saint Louis MO 63136 Office: Saaman Corp 8604 Olive St Olivette MO 63132

NORMAN, GEOFFREY ROBERT, financial executive; b. Orpington, Kent, Eng., Jan. 31, 1944; came to U.S., 1968, naturalized, 1974; s. Leonard Robert and Minnie Rose (Carter) N.; m. Christina Norman, June 8, 1968; children—Catarina, Camilla. B.A., St. Catharine's Coll., Cambridge, Eng., 1966, M.A., 1968. Corp. auditor Gen. Electric Co., Schenectady, 1971-74, comptroller GE Española, Bilbao, Spain, 1974-78, cons. corp. fin., Fairfield, Conn., 1978-81, mgr. fin., Bridgeport, Conn., 1981-83; v.p., treas. Gen. Electric Fin. Services, Inc. and Gen. Electric Credit Corp., N.Y.C., 1983-85, Stamford, Conn., 1985-88; exec. v.p. Gen. Elec. Investment Mgmt. Inc., 1988—; State scholar Govt U.K., 1962; Open Exhbn. scholar St. Catharine's Coll., 1962. Office: Gen Electric Investment Mgmt Inc 3003 Summer St Stamford CT 06905

NORMAN, STEPHEN PECKHAM, financial services company executive; b. Norwich, Conn., May 20, 1942; s. Richard Leonard and Mary Ellen (Carr) N.; m. Jacqueline Mary Batten, June 29, 1968; children—Adrian Gates, Hilary Batten, Philip Douglas, Matthew Jeremy Mitchell. B.A., Yale U., 1964; J.D., U. Pa., 1967. Bar: Conn. 1967, N.Y. 1972. Atty. Am. Express Co., N.Y.C., 1970-78, v.p. corp. office, 1978-82, sec., 1982—. Served to sgt. U.S. Army, 1968-70; Vietnam. Mem. Conn. Bar Assn., N.Y. Bar Assn., Am. Soc. Corp. Secs. Republican. Episcopalian. Club: Am. Yacht (Rye). Home: 6 Highland Park Pl Rye NY 10580 Office: Am Express Co 200 Vesey St World Fin Ctr New York NY 10285

NORMAN, STEVEN CRAIG, investment broker; b. Woodward, Okla., June 8, 1963; s. Bobby Ray and Zelda Jean (Story) N. BS, Okla. State U., 1985. Investment rep. Edward D. Jones & Co., Vinita, Okla., 1985—. Mem. Vinita C. of C., Delta Sigma Pi. Republican. Methodist. Lodge: Lions. Home: 601 S Foreman Vinita OK 74301 Office: Edward D Jones & Co PO Box 883 Vinita OK 74301

NORMAN, WALLACE, pipe company executive; b. Houlka, Miss., Feb. 5, 1926; s. Leland Fleming and Alma Lucile (Brown) N.; student East Central Jr. Coll. 1942, U. Miss., 1946, Millsaps Coll., 1946; B.S., Oklahoma City U., 1948; m. Maurene Collums, Dec. 26, 1950; children—Wallace, Karen Jean, Emily June, Lauren Beth, John Crocker. Owner, operator Wallace Norman Ins. Agy., Houston, Miss., 1949—; pres. Norman Oil Co., Houston, 1956—, Nat. Leasing Co., Houston, 1969—, U.S. Plastics, Inc., Houston, 1969—, Calhoun Nat. Co., 1974—, Norman Trucking Co., 1975—, Plastics Am., Inc., 1982—. Chmn. Running Bear dist. Boy Scouts Am., 1971-73. Served with USNR, World War II. Mem. Miss. Econ. Council, Miss. Assn. Ins. Agts., Miss. Mfrs. Assn., Am. Waterworks Assn., DAV, VFW, Am. Legion. Methodist. Clubs: Gideons, Exchange. Address: Plastics Am Inc PO Box 208 Houston MS 38851

NORMAN, WILLIAM STANLEY, transportation company executive; b. Roper, N.C., Apr. 27, 1938; s. James Colbitt and Josephine Cleo (Woods) N.; m. Elizabeth Patricia Patterson, May 31, 1959; children: Lisa Renée, William Stanley II. BS, West Va. Wesleyan U., 1960; MA, Am. U., 1967; exec. program, Stanford U., 1976. Math. tchr. Washington High Sch., Norfolk, 1961; commd. USN, 1962; advanced through grades to comdr. 1973; naval flight officer Airborne Early Warning Squadron Eleven, 1962-65; asst. combat info. ctr. officer U.S.S. Constellation, 1965; staff officer air weapons systems analysis Office Chief Naval Ops., Pentagon, Washington, 1965-66; history and fgn. affairs instr. U.S. Naval Acad., 1967-69; social aide The White House, 1967-69; carrier div. staff officer SE Asia 1969-70, spl. asst. to Chief Naval Ops. for Minority Affairs, 1970-72, asst. to Chief Naval Ops. for Spl. Projects, 1972-73; dir. corp. action Cummins Engine Co. Inc., Columbus, Ind., 1973-74, exec. dir. corp. responsibility, 1974-76, exec. dir. distbn. mktg., 1976-78; v.p. ea. div. N.Y.C., 1978-79; v.p. sales and mktg. AMTRAK, Washington, 1979-81, group v.p., 1981-84, exec. v.p., 1984—; mem. adv. coun. on travel and tourism industry U.S. Senate Com. on Commerce, Sci. and Transp. Bd. dirs. U.S. Navy Meml. Found., Washington, 1980—, Travelers Aid Soc., Washington, 1986—, Travelers Aid Internat., Washington, 1988—; trustee Phelps-Stokes Fund, N.Y.C., 1983—. Capt. USNR. Mem. Travel Industry Assn. Am. (bd. dirs. 1980—, chmn. bd. 1987—), UN Assn. of U.S. (bd. dirs. 1983—, bd. govs. 1985—), Council on Fgn. Relations, Inst. Cert. Travel Agts., Am. Mgmt. Assn., Bretton Woods Com., Travel and Tourism Govt. Affairs Coun. (bd. dirs. 1988—). Democrat. Episcopalian. Home: 1308 Timberly Ln McLean VA 22102 Office: AMTRAK 60 Massachusetts Ave NE Washington DC 20001

NORMAN, WYATT THOMAS, III, landman, consultant; b. Austin, Tex., Dec. 30, 1952; s. Wyatt Thomas Jr. and Frances Claire (Bliss) N. BS in Agronomy, Tex. A&M U., 1975. Cert. profl. landman. Mgr. farm and ranch Bennett Bros., Inc., Pearsall, Tex., 1975-78; landman Corpus Christi, Tex., 1978—. Mem. Flour Bluff (Tex.) Vol. Fire Dept. Mem. Am. Assn. Petroleum Landmen, Corpus Christi Assn. Petroleum Landmen, Mich. Assn. Petroleum Landmen, Assn. Former Students, Padre Isles Property Owners Assn., Internat. Game Fish Assn. Republican. Presbyterian. Home: 15229 Cruiser St Corpus Christi TX 78418 Office: Oil Industries Bldg 723 North Upper Broadway Ste 407 Corpus Christi TX 78403

NORMAND, ROBERT, utility industry executive; b. Montreal, Que., Can., Jan. 9, 1940; s. Albert and Germaine (Levesque) N.; m. Pauline Ross, July 14, 1962; children—Patrice, Isabelle. Bus. cert., U. Montreal, 1966. Chartered acct., Can. External auditor Richter Usher Vineberg, Montreal, 1962-65, Coopers & Lybrand, Montreal, 1966-67; chief acct. Tioxide of Can., Tracy, 1967-68; comptroller Scott Lasalle Ltd., Montreal, 1969-71; v.p. Gaz Metropolitain Inc., Montreal, 1972—; dir. Soc. Investissement Desjardins, Montreal, Tremplin 2000, Montreal, Daubois Inc., Montreal, Celliers du Monde, Montreal. Mem. Can. Gas Assn. (fin. mag. com. 1982-88), Fin. Execs. Inst. (bd. dirs. 1980-82, 1987-89), Order of Chartered Accts. Roman Catholic. Home: 177 Grande Cote, Rosemere, PQ Canada J7A 1H5

NORRIE, K. PETER, manufacturing executive; b. Madison, Wis., Mar. 7, 1939; s. Kenneth Peter and Clara Frances (Storey) N.; m. Susan Kelliher, Sept. 6, 1960 (dec. 1975); children: Peter Clark, David Doherty, Charles Kelliher; m. Betty Buzard, Oct. 14, 1978 (div. Apr. 1989). BCE, Gonzaga U., 1961; MBA, Harvard U., 1964. Estimator H. Halvorsen Contractors, Spokane, Wash., 1961-62; gen. mgr. Boise (Idaho) Cascade Corp., 1964-70, mgr. gen. sales, 1970-72, v.p., 1972-76, sr. v.p., 1976—, also bd. dirs. Trustee UCLA Found. With USMCR, 1956-62. Recipient Disting. Alumni Merit award Gonzaga U., 1987. Republican. Roman Catholic. Office: Boise Cascade Corp 1 Jefferson Sq Boise ID 83728

NORRIS, DARELL FOREST, insurance company executive; b. Pontiac, Mich., Oct. 19, 1928; s. Forest Ellis and Mabel Marie (Smith) N.; m. Thordis Marie Johansen, Aug. 21, 1955; children—Dara Lee, Jennifer, Lisa, Nancy. BS, U. Kans., 1950. CLU, chartered fin. cons. Reporter, sports staff Kansas City Star, Mo., 1950-51; pilot TWA, 1955-56; div. agy. mgr. Merced region Farmers Group, Inc., Calif., 1959, sales rep., Colorado Springs region, 1962, regional agy. mgr., Aurora, Ill., 1964, regional sales mgr., Santa Ana, Calif., 1966, mgmt. tng. program staff, dir. agys., L.A., 1969, regional mgr., Austin, Tex., 1971, v.p. sales, L.A., 1973, v.p. field ops. midwestern zone, 1976, v.p. field ops., western zone, 1979—; pres. Farmers New World Mgmt. Co., 1977-81, v.p. staff ops., 1981-85, sr. v.p. life co. ops. and staff support svcs., 1985—. Chmn. bd. deacons First Baptist Ch., Granada Hills, Calif., 1977-89; sustaining mem. Rep. Nat. Com. Capt. USAF, 1951-55. Mem. Am. Soc. CLUs, Chartered Fin. Cons. (San Fernando Valley chpt.), Ins. Edn. Assn. (trustee), Sigma Delta Chi Profl. Journalism Soc. Office: Farmers Ins Group Cos 4680 Wilshire Blvd Los Angeles CA 90010

NORRIS, DAVID STUART, financial executive; b. Balt., May 17, 1938; s. Norman W. and June (Aler) N.; m. Ann King, July 6, 1967; children: Virginia A., Robert S. BS in Acctg., Va. Commonwealth U., 1963. Acct. A.M. Pullen, Richmond, Va., 1962-65; tax mgr. Ernst and Whinney, Richmond, 1966-72; v.p. Sovran, Richmond, 1973; exec. v.p., controller Signet Banking Corp., Richmond, 1974—. Sr. warden Ch. Redeemer Episc. Ch., Richmond, 1981. Served with USAF, 1961-62. Fellow Am. Inst. CPA's, Va. Soc. CPA's, Fin. Execs. Inst. (pres. 1987-88 cen. Va. chpt.); mem. Va. Commonwealth U. Alumni Assn. (bd. dirs. 1985—), Assn. Bank Holding Cos. Clubs: Bull and Bear, Willow Oaks Country (Richmond). Office: Signet Banking Corp 7 N 8th St Richmond VA 23219

NORRIS, HUGH JONES, JR., banker, lawyer; b. Richmond, Va., Sept. 25, 1943; s. Hugh Jones and Mary Miller (Noblett) N.; m. Linda Jane Chandler, Aug. 15, 1970; children: Salem Chandler, James Derek. BS, Campbell U., 1965; MBA, U. Pa., 1973; JD, Wake Forest U., 1970. Bar: N.C.; CPA, N.C. Instr. bus. Campbell U., Buies Creek, N.C., 1970-74; acct. Coopers & Lybrand, Lynchburg, Va., 1974-76; v.p., contr. 1st Nat. Bank, Bluefield, W.Va., 1976-81; treas. Planters Corp., Rocky Mount, N.C., 1981-88, v.p. fin., 1988—; v.p. fin. Planters Nat. Bank, Rocky Mount, 1988—, also contr. subs., 1981-88; mem. adj. faculty Bluefield State Coll., 1978-80, W.Va. Coll. Grad. Studies, Charleston, 1979-80, Campbell U., 1982—. Bd. dirs. Christian Fellowship Homes, Rocky Mount, 1983-86. Mem. ABA, N.C. State Bar Assn., AICPA, N.C. Soc. CPA's, Nat. Assn. Accts., Rotary. Episcopalian. Home: PO Box 175 Rocky Mount NC 27802 Office: Planters Nat Bank 131 N Church St Rocky Mount NC 27804

NORRIS, JOHN ANTHONY, business executive, federal official, lawyer, editor, professor; b. Buffalo, Dec. 27, 1946; s. Joseph D. and Maria L. (Suite) N.; m. Kathleen E. Mullen, July 13, 1969; children: Patricia Marie, John Anthony II, Joseph Mullen, Mary Kathleen, Elizabeth Mary. BA, U. Rochester, 1968; JD, MBA with honors, Cornell U., 1973; cert., Harvard U. Sch. Govt., 1986. Bar: Mass. 1973. Assoc. Peabody, Brown, Boston, 1973-75; assoc. Powers Hall, Boston, 1975-76, ptnr., mem. exec. com., 1976-80, v.p., dir., 1979-80, chmn. adminstrv. com., 1976-79, chmn. hiring com., 1979-80; chmn. bd., pres., chief exec. officer, founder Norris & Norris, Boston, 1980-85; dep. commr. and chief operating officer FDA, Washington, 1985-88, chmn. action planning and cap coms., 1985-88, chmn. reye syndrome com., 1985-87, chmn. trade legis. com., 1987-88; corporate exec. v.p. Hill and Knowlton, Inc., N.Y.C., 1988—; worldwide dir. Health Scis. Consulting Group Hill and Knowlton, Inc., Boston, 1988—; mem. faculty Tufts Dental Sch., 1974-79, Boston Coll. Law Sch., 1976-80, Boston U. Law Sch., 1979-83, Harvard U. Public Health Sch., 1988—; mem. bd. editors FDA Drug Bulletin and FDA Consumer Report, 1985-88. Founder, faculty editor-in-chief Am. Jour. Law and Medicine, 1973-81, emeritus 1981—; editor-in-chief Cornell Internat. Law Jour., 1971-73; reviewer New Eng. Jour. Medicine Law-Medicine Notes, 1980-81; assoc. editor Medicolegal News, 1973-75. Mem. U.S. Del. to Japan (chmn.), Austria, Saudi Arabia, 1987, mem., chmn. Finland, Denmark, Italy, 1986; chmn. Mass. Statuatory Adv. Com. on Regulation of Clin. Labs., 1977-83; chmn. Boston Alumni and Scholarship Com., U. Rochester, 1979-85; mem. trustees council U. Rochester, 1979-85; mem. exec. com. Cornell Law Sch. Assn., 1982-85; mem. Mass. Gov.'s Blue Ribbon Task Force on DON, 1979-80, bd. trustees Jordan Hosp., 1978-80, mem. exec. com., 1979-80, chmn., chief exec. officer search com., 1980; chmn. Joseph D. Norris Health, Law and Pub. Policy Fund, 1979—; chmn. bd. Boston Holiday Project, 1981-83; mem. U.S. Pres. Chernobyl Task Force, 1986, vice-chmn. health affects sub-com.; mem. U.S. Intra-Govtl. AIDS Task Force, 1987; mem. IOM Drug Devel. Forum, 1986—, co-chmn. end points sub-com., 1987-88, Fed. Pain Commn., 1984-85. Served with U.S. Army, 1972-73, with res. Fed. Comprehensive Health Planning fellow, 1970-73; recipient Kansas City Hon. Key award, 1988, Nat. Health Fraud Conf. award, 1988, TOYL award, 1982, FDA Award of Merit, 1987, 88, PHS award, 1987, HHS Sec. award, 1988. Mem. ABA (vice chmn. medicine and law com. 1977-80), Mass. Bar Assn., Am. Soc. Hosp. Attys., Nat. Health Lawyers, Am. Soc. Law and Medicine (1st v.p. 1975-80, chmn. bd. 1981-84, life mem. award 1981), Soc. Computer Applications to Med. Care (mem. bd. 1984-85), Phi Kappa Phi. Home: 531 W Washington St Hanson MA 02341 Office: Hill & Knowlton Inc Health Scis Cons Group 30 Rowes Wharf Boston MA 02110

NORRIS, LISA ANN, retail executive; b. Albany, N.Y., Sept. 20, 1960; d. Benjamin F. and Mary C. (Gabriel) N. BS, Russell Sage Coll., Troy, N.Y., 1982. Asst. mgr. Lerner Shops, Schenectady, 1982-84, Barbara Moss, Albany, 1984; mgr. Barbara Moss, Holyoke, Mass., 1984-85, Clifton Park, N.Y., 1985-87; dist. mgr. Barbara Moss, Albany, 1986-87, Petite Sophisticate, Albany, 1987—. Mem. Nat. Assn. Female Execs. Roman Catholic. Home: 3 Denny Rd Guilderland NY 12084 Office: Petite Sophisticate 210 Colonie Ctr Albany NY 12205

NORRIS, RANDY LEE, marketing professional; b. Battle Creek, Mich., May 24, 1957; s. Russell and Sandra Kay (Bailey) Norris Skinner; m. Michele Lee Marcil, Aug. 26, 1979; 1 child, Alexander Lee. AA, U. South Fla., 1977, BA, 1979. Mgr. terr. Milliken and Co., Hickory, N.C., 1980-83, Tampa, Fla., 1983-84; sales supr. Avery Internat., Tampa, Fla., 1984-87; dir. mktg. Serigraphic Arts, Inc., Tampa, Fla., 1987—. Vol. Big Bros. and Big Sisters, 1986, 87. Named Outstanding Young Man Am., 1986. Home: 14163 Fennsbury Dr Tampa FL 33624

NORRIS, SUSAN FETNER, bank examiner; b. Lansing, Mich., Feb. 3, 1949; d. R. Scott Sr. and Joann (Louckes) Fetner; m. Robert B. Norris, Sept. 26, 1987. BA, Mich. State U., 1971. Teller Mich. Nat. Bank, Lansing, 1971-74; supr. new accounts Grand Rapids (Mich.) Bank N.Am., 1974-75; bank examiner Office of the Comptroller of the Currency, Nat. Bank Examiners Bd., Kalamazoo, Mich., 1975-82; policy analyst Office of the Comptroller of the Currency, Nat. Bank Examiners Bd., Washington, 1982-86; asst. field office dir. Office of the Comptroller of the Currency, Nat. Bank Examiners Bd., Kansas City, Mo., 1986-87; mgr. examination support Office of the Comptroller of the Currency, Nat. Bank Examiners Bd., Dallas, 1988—. Contbg. author: The Banker's Handbook, 1988. Home: 7015 Brookshire Dr Dallas TX 75230 Office: Comptroller of the Currency 500 N Akard 1600 Lincoln Plaza Dallas TX 75201-3394

NORSWORTHY, JOHN RANDOLPH, economist; b. Norfolk, Va., Aug. 26, 1939; s. John Tignor and Annie Vivian (Smith) N.; m. Elizabeth Krassovsky, June 24, 1961 (div. 1962); 1 child, Leonid. Alexander; m. Susan Foster, Aug. 15, 1964 (div. 1971); 1 child, Ann Randolph. BA with distinction, U. Va., 1961; PhD in Econs., U. Va., 1966. NDEA fellow, U. Va., 1961-65; postdoctoral fellow econs. U. Chgo., 1965-66; asst. prof. econs. U. Ill.-Chgo., 1966-68; asst., then assoc. prof. Temple U., Phila., 1968-71; chief applied econs. div. Office of Emergency Preparedness, Exec. Office Pres., Washington, 1971-73; chief productivity research div. Bur. Labor Stats., Washington, 1973-82; chief ctr. for econ. studies Bur. Census, U.S. Dept. Commerce, Washington, 1982-85; cons. economist, 1985-86; prof. econ. and mgmt. Rensselaer Poly. Inst., 1986—; mem. Brookings Panel on Econ. Activity, 1979. Contbr. articles to profl. jours. Recipient Disting. Achievement Award for Rsch., U.S. Dept. Labor, 1980, Lawrence R. Gordon award for Grad. Teaching and Rsch. in Econs. Rensselaer Poly. Inst., 1988. Mem. Am. Econ. Assn., Am. Statis. Assn., Conf. on Rsch. in Income and Wealth (exec. com. 1981-85), Phi Beta Kappa, Phi Eta Sigma, Tau Kappa Epsilon.

NORTH, KENNETH E(ARL), lawyer; b. Chgo., Nov. 18, 1945; s. Earl and Marion (Temple) N.; m. Susan C. Gutzmer, June 6, 1970; children: Krista, Kari. AA with high honors, Coll. of DuPage, Glen Ellyn, Ill., 1970; BA with high honors, No. Ill. U., 1971; JD, Duke U., 1974. Bar: Ill. 1974, U.S. Dist. Ct. (no. dist.) Ill. 1974, Guam 1978, U.S. Tax Ct., 1975, U.S. Ct. Appeals (7th cir.), 1978, U.S. Supreme Ct., 1978, U.S. Ct. Internat. Trade 1978, U.S. Ct. Appeals (9th cir.) 1979. Div. chief DuPage County State's Attys. Office, Wheaton, 1976-78; spl. asst. U.S. atty. Terr. of Guam, Agana, 1978-79, atty. gen., 1979-80; prin. Law Offices Kenneth E. North & Assocs.; pres., editor North Pub. Co.; adj. prof. law John Marshall Law Sch., Chgo., 1985—, Keller Grad. Sch. Mgmt. Northwestern U.; instr. Northwestern U. Traffic Inst., 1985—; cons. Terr. of Guam, 1980-81; lectr., cons. regarding computer-aided litigation support, 1985—; counsel to various fin. instns. and domestic corps. Co-author: Criminal and Civil Tax Fraud, 1986; bd. editors Attorneys' Computer Report, 1986—; contbr. articles to legal publs. Trustee, mem. adv. bd. Ams. for Effective Law Enforcement, 1986—; v.p. Glen Ellyn Manor Civic Assn., 1981-84, pres., 1984—; police commr. Village of Glen Ellyn, 1982—. Mem. Assn. Trial Lawyers Am. (sec. criminal sect. 1986-87, 2d vice chair 1987—), ABA, Ill. Bar Assn., World Bar Assn., Chgo. Bar Assn., Chgo. Duke Bar Assn. (pres. 1986-87), Chgo. Council Fgn. Relations, Internat. Platform Assn., Mensa. Republican. Pioneer use of computer in ct. Office: 1200 E Roosevelt Rd Ste 305 Glen Ellyn IL 60137

NORTHROP, STUART JOHNSTON, manufacturing company executive; b. New Haven, Oct. 22, 1925; s. Filmer Stuart Cuckow and Christine (Johnston) N.; m. Cynthia Stafford Daniell, Feb. 23, 1946; children: Christine Daniell, Richard Rockwell Stafford. B.A. in Physics, Yale U., 1948. Indsl. engr. U.S. Rubber Co., Naugatuck, Conn., 1948-51; head indsl. engring. dept. Am. Cyanamid Co., Wallingford, Conn., 1951-54; mfg. mgr. Linear, Inc., Phila., 1954-57; mgr. quality control and mfg. Westinghouse Electric Co., Pitts., 1957-58; mfg. supt. SKF Industries, Phila., 1958-61; v.p. mfg. Am. Meter Co., Phila., 1961-69; founder, v.p., gen. mgr. water resources div. Singer Co., Phila.; pres., dir. Buffalo Meter Co., Four Layne Cos.; dir. Gen. Filter Co., 1969-72; chmn., chief exec. officer Huffy Corp., Dayton, Ohio, 1972-85, chmn. exec. com., 1985—; bd. dirs. Lukens, Inc., Coatesville, Pa., Fischer & Porter, Phila., Union Corp., N.Y.C.; former dir. DPL (formerly Dayton Power & Light Co.), Duriron, Bank One Dayton, Danis Constrn., Carlisle Retailers. County fin. chmn. George Bush Presdl. campaign, 1980; presdl. appointee Pres.'s Commn. on Ams. Outdoors, 1985-86; chmn. nat. hwy. safety adv. com. Dept. Transp., 1986—. Served with USAAF, 1944-45. Named Chief Exec. Officer of Yr. for leisure industry Wall Street Transcript, 1980. Mem. Del. Valley Investors (past pres.), Interlocutors, Elihu, Am. Bus. Conf. (founding), Fin. Commn. of Fund Ams. Future, Merion Cricket Club (Haverford, Pa.), Delta Kappa Epsilon, KOA Soc. Home: 226 Cheswold Ln Haverford PA 19041 Office: Huffy Corp 7701 Byers Rd Miamisburg OH 45342

NORTON, BARRY AMOS, oil company executive; b. Wilmington, Del., Feb. 20, 1940; s. W. Amos and Mary Amelia (Brown) N.; m. Barbara Ann Daisey, Nov. 29, 1969 (div. 1980); 1 child, Joanna; m. Constance Ann Smith, July 16, 1980. B.S., U. Del., 1967. Mktg. rep. Amoco Oil Co., Chgo., 1967-72; pres. Norton Petroleum Corp., Newark, Del., 1972—. Served with USAF, 1962-68. Mem. Am. Soc. Lubricant Engrs., Nat. Lubricating Grease Inst., Ind. Lubricant Mfrs. Assn., Pa. Petroleum Assn. Republican. Methodist. Club: Newark Country (Del.); Kennett Square Country (Pa.); Rodney Sq. (Wilmington). Office: Norton Petroleum Corp 290 Possum Park Rd Newark DE 19711

NORTON, D. KENT, real estate corporation executive; b. Ogden, Utah, Jan. 24, 1951; s. Darrel K. and Gladys (Kinghorn) N.; m. Jane Marie Ashton, June 25, 1974; children: Amy, Susan, Kristen, David. BS, U. Utah, 1975; JD, Brigham Young U., 1978. Bar: U.S. Supreme Ct. 1987. Assoc. Backman, Clark & Marsh, Salt Lake City, 1978-83; pres. Crestmark Corp. (formerly Consol. Capital Corp.), Salt Lake City, 1983—; exec. v.p. Sterling Med. Systems, Inc., Salt Lake City, 1983—; weather announcer Sta. KSL-TV, Salt Lake City, 1973—. Chmn. state crusade Utah div. Am. Cancer Soc., 1981; trustee Osmond Found. Children's Miracle Network Telethon, 1980-83. Mem. Utah Bar Assn. Club: Exchange (Holladay, Utah). Office: Crestmark Corp 4600 Holladay Blvd Salt Lake City UT 84117

NORTON, DAVID PHILLIP, bank executive; b. Noccalula Falls, Ala., Sept. 16, 1950; s. William Curtis and Hilda Dean (Williams) N.; m. Lydia Carter Cheney, May 5, 1973 (div. July 2, 1984). AB, Birmingham-So. U., 1972; MS, Masters of City Planning, Ga. Tech. Inst., 1975. Export coord. Huntsville (Ala.) C. of C., 1976-79; internat. officer AmSouth Bancorporation, Mobile, Ala., 1979-81, 1st Wachovia Corp., Winston-Salem, N.C., 1981-85; asst. v.p. Standard Chartered Bank, London, 1985-86; v.p. Security Pacific Corp., N.Y.C., 1987, The Dai-Ichi Kangyo Bank, Ltd., Tokyo, 1988; prin. Inter-Am. Mortgage Corp., Atlanta, 1988—. Vol. United Way Campaign Atlanta; vol., aux. mem. Shepherd Spinal Clinic; sponsoring patron High Mus. Art, Atlanta; donor Atlanta Arts Alliance/Woodruff Ctr.; mem. Atlanta Hist. Soc., Atlanta Botanical Gardens, Clan Johnstone In Am., Garden Hills (Buckhead) Neighborhood Civic Assns., Internat. House. Named Spl. Friend Carter Presdl. Cen. and Libr. Mem. Am. Inst. Bankers (Atlanta chpt.), Southeastern Internat. Bankers Assn., St. Andrews Soc. Atlanta, Ga. Tech. Athletic Assn., Kappa Alpha order (No. 1, Phi chpt.). Episcopalian. Home: 542 E Wesley Rd NE Atlanta GA 30305 Office: 225 Peachtree St NE Ste 2000 South Tower Atlanta GA 30303 also: Rte 2 Box 274 6175 Nisbet Lake Rd Jacksonville AL 36265

NORTON, DOUGLAS RAY, auditor general; b. Portales, N.Mex., Mar. 23, 1933; s. Clayton G. and Lillian W. (Powers) N.; m. Wanda Jones, May 23, 1951 (div. July 1979); children: Debbie Norton Goodman, Vicki Norton Hulet, Denise Norton Jolley; m. Patricia M. Zins, July 21, 1982. BS, U. Ariz., 1963. CPA, Ariz. Staff acct., audit supr. Ernst & Ernst, Tucson, Ariz., 1963-67; ptnr. Baker, Price & Norton, Prescott, Ariz., 1968-75, Lester Witte & Co., Prescott, Ariz., 1975-76; auditor gen. State of Ariz., Phoenix, 1976—; mem. Profl. Adv. Bd. Sch. Acctg., Ariz. State U., Tempe, 1984—. Pres. Prescott Bd. Edn., 1976. Served with U.S. Army, 1953-55. Mem. Am. Inst. CPA's, Ariz. Soc. CPA's, Nat. Assn. State Auditors, Comptrollers and Treasurers, Nat. State Auditors Assn. (pres. 1982-83), Nat. Intergovtl. Audit Forum (chmn. 1979-83, mem. 1983—). Lodge: Lions (pres. Prescott chpt. 1973-74). Home: PO Box 12147 Phoenix AZ 85002-2147 Office: Office Ariz Auditor Gen 2700 N Central Suite 700 Phoenix AZ 85004

NORTON, H. GAITHER, food company executive; b. Bklyn., Aug. 16, 1918; s. Dwight Fanning and Jessie (Gaither) N.; m. Ann Lou Allen, Mar. 23, 1941; children: Priscilla Ann, Lou Elaine; m. Laura Louise Smith, July 26, 1950; children: Craig Gaither, Laura Marjorie, Scott Clark, Ellen

Louise. Student Middlebury Coll., 1936-37, NYU, 1939-40, Lafayette Coll., 1938-39, Stevens Inst. Tech., 1941; AB in Econs. with hons., UCLA, 1952. With Continental Can Co., 1937-41, sales trainee, 1939-41; employment interviewer, Grumman Aircraft Corp., 1941-43; USMC personnel classification and rehab. interviewer, counsellor, 1943-46; F.W. Boltz Corp., L.A., 1947-48, nat. sales mgr., 1948-50; asst. div. mgr. Northeast div. Welch's Grape Juice Co., N.Y.C., 1952-54; pres. H.G. Norton Co., Inc., New Milford, Conn., 1954—. Bd. dirs. Weantinoge Heritage Land Trust, Inc., New Milford, 1965-76, hon. bd. dirs., 1976-82, 1st v.p., 1966-76, 82-88; mem. zoning bd. appeals, New Milford, 1970, planning commn. to set up Com. on Aging, New Milford, 1972, panel to examine town police needs, 1980; sec., bd. dirs. Sunny Valley Found., 1978-79; mem. New Milford Conservation Commn., 1981—, Rep. Town Com., New Milford, 1982-86, Econ. Devel. Commn., 1984—. With USMC, 1943-46. Mem. Nat. Assn. Specialty Food Trade (pres., 1962-63), Nat. Assn. Splty. Food and Confection Brokers (pres. 1972-74, chmn. Internat. Fancy Food and Confection Show 1969), Nat. Food Distbrs. Assn. (dir. mfrs. council 1974-75, 88—, conv. com., 1975), Phi Beta Kappa, Pi Gamma Mu. Home: Sprucegate Farm West Meeting House New Milford CT 06776 Office: PO Drawer 269 New Milford CT 06776

NORTON, HERBERT STEVEN, hotel and casino executive; b. Jacksonville, Fla., Feb. 6, 1934; s. Herbert Willfred and Thelma (Lassiter) N.; m. Lillian May Bobson, Mar. 1963; children—Ronald Stephen, Mark Bradley, Catherine Kimberly, Caron Elizabeth, Robert Jeffrey, Wendy Victoria. B.S. in Bus., Davidson Coll., 1956. Exec. v.p. Resorts Internat., Inc., Atlantic City, N.J., 1979—. Bd. govs. Atlantic City Med. Ctr. Mem. Casino Assn. N.J., (vice chmn.), Atlantic City Conv. Bur. (chmn.), N.J. Hotel and Motel Assn. (bd. dirs., chmn.), N.J. C. of C. (bd. dirs.), Am. Hotel Motel Assn. (bd. dirs.). Republican. Presbyterian. Club: Friars. Lodge: Rotary (pres.). Office: Resorts Internat Inc 915 NE 125th St North Miami FL 33161

NORTON, JAMES J., union official; b. Boston, June 9, 1930; s. Patrick P. and Annie (Flaherty) N.; m. Patricia A. Tuley, Sept. 19, 1953; children: James, Ann Marie, Robert, Thomas, Donald, David, Brian. Treas. Boston Photo Engravers Union, 1957-60, pres., 1960-62; internat. rep. Graphic Arts Union, Boston, 1962-78; sec. treas. Graphic Arts Union, Washington, 1979-83; rec. and fin. sec. Graphic Communications Internat. Union, 1983-85, pres., 1983—. Coach Peewee-Bantum level Dorchester Youth Hockey Program, Boston, 1958-79; coach Midget level Fairfax Hockey Program, Va., 1980-81. Mem. Monclair C. of C. Dumfries, Va. Roman Catholic. Lodge: K.C. Office: Graphicommunicator Internat Union 1900 L St NW Washington DC 20036

NORTON, JANE ANNETTE, advertising and public relations executive; b. Annapolis, Md., Aug. 28, 1947; d. Ervin Thompson and Ruth (Sherwood) N. BS, Tenn. State U., 1968; postgrad., Ind. U. Customer service rep. Sherwood Med., St. Louis, 1970-71, copywriter, 1971-75, sales promotion coordinator, 1976-77, mktg. services coordinator, 1977; advt. mgr. Zimmer Inc., Warsaw, Ind., 1977-79, dir. mktg. services, 1979-86, dir. communications, 1986-88, dir. pub. rels., 1988—; speaker Nat. Assn. Orthopedic Nurses, Pitman, N.J., 1984. Pres. Woodbridge Homeowners Assn., South Bend, Ind, 1982-84. Mem. Sales and Advt. Exec. Club. Office: Zimmer Inc PO Box 708 Warsaw IN 46580

NORTON, JOHN WILLIAM, lawyer, investment advisory firm executive; b. St. Paul, Sept. 30, 1941; s. John William Jr. and Dorothy (Sheridan) N.; m. Kathleen L. Smith, Aug. 19, 1967 (div.); children: Tiffany, Sean. BA in Bus. Adminstrn., Marquette U., 1964; JD, Stetson U., 1968. Bar: Fla. 1968, Minn. 1968. Atty. Minn. Mut. Life Ins. Co., St. Paul, 1968-73; asst. counsel IDS Life Ins. Co., Mpls., 1973; atty., adviser fin. SEC, Washington, 1973-78; v.p., gen. counsel, sec. AMEV Advisers, Inc., AMEV Investors, Inc., St. Paul, 1978—; v.p. eight investment cos. including AMEV Securities, Inc., AMEV Capital Fund, Inc., AMEV Fiduciary Fund, Inc.; v.p. gen. counsel investment products Western Life Ins. Co., 1988—; Mem. ABA, Minn. Bar Assn., Fla. Bar Assn. Home: 8285 Ingleside Ave Cottage Grove MN 55016

NORTON, JOHN WILLIAM, management consultant; b. Queens County, N.Y., June 12, 1954; s. Michael Vincent and Dorothy Winifred (Ragl) N.; m. Louise Rita Elefante; 1 child, Louise Elizabeth. Student, Nassau Coll., 1973; BBA, SUNY. Asst. mgr. sales and mktg. Sun Life Assn. Co., Can., Phila. and Cherry Hills, N.J., 1976-77; mgr. ops. circulation dist. Phila. Inquirer, 1977-78; pres. Internat. Executive Reports, Blackwood and Marlton, N.J., 1978-84, chief exec. officer, 1978—; pres., mgmt. cons. Norton Group (formerly Norton Industries), Lake Ariel, Pa., 1984—; pres. Cheridel, Inc., Norton Stamets & Leone, PC, Cherry Ridge Airport, BAO/Am. Maid, 1987—. Editor: The Strategist, 1982; contbr. articles to profl. jours. Inventor electric power transfer device. Recipient Outstanding Sales and Mktg. award Sun Life Co., 1977. Mem. Ind. Cons. Am., Internat. Mgmt. Council, Am. Mgmt. Assn. Republican. Roman Catholic. Lodge: K.C. Home: 2626 Boulder Rd Lake Ariel PA 18436 Office: PO Box 73 Lake Ariel PA 18436

NORTON, NATHANIEL GOODWIN, marketing executive; b. Chgo., Jan. 7, 1948; s. Wilbur H. and Eva (Geneen) N.; m. Ariel Taylor, Nov. 15, 1980 (div. July 1987). BA, U. N.C., 1969. Mktg. mgr. Canteen Corp., Chgo., 1971-74; sr. v.p. Mathieu, Gerfen & Bresner, N.Y.C., 1974-83; pres. Rand Pub. Relations, N.Y.C., 1983—. Office: Rand Pub Rels 149 Fifth Ave New York NY 10010

NORTON, PETER BOWES, publishing company executive; b. London, May 4, 1929; came to U.S., 1969; s. James Peter and Margaret (Bowes) N.; m. Heather Pearch, Jan. 16, 1954; children: Jan Heather, Fiona Mary. Student, S.E. Essex Tech. Coll., 1942-45, Royal Naval Colls., 1949-54. Commd. officer Royal Navy, 1945, advanced through grades to lt., 1954, ret., 1960; personnel officer United Dominions Trust, London, 1960-63; jr. exec. to mng. dir. Ency. Britannica, London, 1963-68, mng. dir., 1968-69; v.p. internat. div. Ency. Britannica, Chgo., 1969-70; pres. Ency. Britannica Can., 1970-73, Ency. Britannica U.S.A., Chgo., 1974-85, Ency. Britannica Inc., 1986—; bd. dir. Ency. Universalis (Paris); chmn., bd. dirs. Ency. Britannica Ednl. Corp., Chgo., 1988—; Am. Learning Corp., 1988—. Bd. dirs. William Benton Found. Fellow Chartered Inst. Secs. (Eng.), Chartered Inst. Adminstrs. U.K., Chartered Inst. Dirs. U.K.; mem. Japan Am. Soc. of Chgo., Inc. (bd. dirs.), Internat. Edn. (adv. bd.), Chgo. Club. Mem. Ch. of Eng. Clubs: Royal Automobile (London); Chgo., Carlton. Home: 180 E Pearson St #3401 Chicago IL 60611 Office: Ency Brit Inc 310 S Michigan Ave Chicago IL 60604

NORTON, RICKIE EDWARD, retail executive; b. Little Rock, Oct. 17, 1956; s. Alvin Lee and Mildred Christine (Dobbs) N.; m. Jennifer Ann Ross, May 21, 1977; children: Rebecca Ann, Kendra Lee, Krystal Michelle. BS, Ariz. State U., 1977. Inventroy control specialist Circle K Corp., Phoenix, 1978-79; mgr. All Seasons Pool and Patio, Phoenix, 1979-80; pres. Tines Leisure, Inc. doing bus. as All Seasons Pool and Patio, Phoenix, 1980—; dir. Silica Source Technology, Tempe, Ariz. Patentee, pool cleaners. Republican. Baptist. Office: All Seasons Pool & Patio 3539 W Dunlap Ave Phoenix AZ 85051

NORTON, ROBERT LEO, SR., mechanical engineering educator, researcher; b. Boston, May 5, 1939; s. Harry Joseph and Kathryn (Warren) N.; m. Nancy Auclair, Feb. 27, 1960; children: Robert L., Jr., MaryKay, Thomas J. BS, Northeastern U., 1967; MS, Tufts U., 1970. Registered profl. engr., Mass, R.I., N.H. Engr. Polaroid Corp., Cambridge, Mass., 1959-67; project engr. Jet Spray Cooler, Inc., Waltham, Mass, 1967-69; research assoc. N.E. Med. Ctr., Boston, 1969-74; prof. Tufts U., Medford, Mass., 1974-79; sr. engr. Polaroid Corp., Waltham, 1979-81; prof. mech. engring., Worcester Poly., Mass., 1981—; pres. Norton Assocs., Norfolk, Worcester, 1970—. Patentee (13) in field; contbr. articles to profl. jours. Mem. ASME, Am. Soc. Engring. Edn. (J.F. Curtis award 1984, Merle Miller award 1987), Inst. Elec. Engrs., Pi Tau Sigma, Sigma Xi. Democrat. Avocations: sailing, computers. Office: Norton Assocs WPI 100 Institute Rd Worcester MA 01609

NORVILLE, CRAIG HUBERT, lawyer; b. N.Y.C., June 10, 1944; s. Hubert G. and Harriett (Johnson) N.; 1 child, Margaret Amelia. AB, Harvard U., 1966; LLB, U. Va., 1969. Bar: N.Y. 1971, Pa. 1979, Tenn. 1985. Instr. law U. Mich., 1969-70; assoc. Cravath, Swaine & Moore, N.Y.C., 1970-76; sr. atty. Bethlehem (Pa.) Steel Corp., 1976-80; v.p., assoc. gen. counsel Holiday Corp., Memphis, 1980-84, v.p., gen. counsel, 1984-86, sr. v.p., gen. counsel, 1986—. Articles editor U. Va. Law Rev. Mem. Raven Soc., Hasty Pudding Inst. of 1770, Order of Coif. Club: Harvard Varsity (Cambridge, Mass.). Office: Holiday Corp 1023 Cherry Rd Memphis TN 38117

NORWOOD, JANET LIPPE, government official; b. Newark, Dec. 11, 1923; d. M. Turner and Thelma (Levinson) Lippe; m. Bernard Norwood, June 25, 1943; children—Stephen Harlan, Peter Carlton. BA, Douglass Coll., 1945; MA, Tufts U., 1946; PhD, Fletcher Sch. Law and Diplomacy, 1949; LLD (hon.), Fla. Internat. U., 1979; LL.D. (hon.), Carnegie Mellon U., 1984. Instr. Wellesley Coll., 1948-49; economist William L. Clayton Ctr. Tuft U., 1953-58; with bur. labor stats. Dept. Labor, Washington, 1963—; dep. commr., then acting commr. bur. labor stats. Dept. Labor, 1975-79, commr. labor stats. bur. labor stats., 1979—. Author papers, reports in field. Recipient Disting. Achievement award Dept. Labor, 1972, Spl. Commendation award, 1977, Philip Arnow award, 1979, Elmer Staats award, 1982, Pub. Svc. award, 1984; named to Alumni Hall of Fame, Rutgers U., 1987; recipient Presdl. Disting. Exec. rank, 1988. Fellow Am. Statis. Assn. (pres.), AAAS, Royal Statis. Soc., Nat. Assn. Bus. Economists; mem. Am. Econ. Assn., Indsl. Rels. Rsch. Assn., Royal Statis. Soc., Women's Caucus in Stats., Com. Status Women Econs. Profession, Internat. Statis. Inst., Internat. Assn. Ofcls. Stats., Nat. Acad. Pub. Adminstrn., Soc. Disting. Achievement, Am. Statis. Assn. (pres. elect 1988). Home: 6409 Marjory Ln Bethesda MD 20817 Office: Labor Dept Labor Stats Bur 441 G St NW Washington DC 20212

NORWOOD, SAMUEL WILKINS, III, corporate planning and development executive; b. Chgo., Apr. 6, 1941; s. Samuel Wilkins and Miriam Lois (Cary) N.; m. Julianne Parker Jones, Jun. 15, 1962 (div. Sept. 1981); children: Samuel Parker, Elizabeth Cary. Student, Vanderbilt U., 1959-61; BA, Tulane U., 1964; MBA, U. Chgo., 1965. Supr. spl. studies Allied Corp., N.Y.C., 1965-67; mgr. analysis and planning ITT Semiconductors Corp., West Palm Beach, Fla., 1967-69; dir. fin. planning Fuqua Industries, Atlanta, 1969-73, v.p. planning, 1976-81, v.p. corp devel., exec. asst. to chmn., 1981-89; v.p. fin. Williams Svc. Group, Inc., Stone Mountain, Ga., 1989—; adv. bd. The Planning Rev. mag.; cons., Atlanta, 1973-76. Founder N. Atlanta Mediation Ctr., 1972. Mem. Planning Execs. Inst. (bd. dirs. 1979-85, chmn. 1984-85, pres. Atlanta chpt. 1976-77), The Planning Forum (bd. dirs. 1985-87).), Atlanta Yacht Club (bd. Govs. 1984-87, commodore 1989), Allatobna Canoe and Sailing Club (commodore 1988-89). Home: 110 Palisades Rd NE Atlanta GA 30309 Office: Williams Svc Group Inc 2076 W Park Pl Stone Mountain GA 30087

NOTCH, JAMES STEPHEN, structural engineering executive, consultant; b. Mpls., Aug. 24, 1950; s. Edwin Henry and Mary Adele (Heinz) N.; m. Sandra Jean Johnson, Apr. 28, 1973; children: Kristin Rachelle, Ryan Christopher, Kelly Marie. BSCE summa cum laude with highest honors, Marquette U., 1973; MSCE with honors, Lehigh U., 1974; Murray Buxton diploma, Inst. Structural Engring., London, 1987. Registered profl. engr., Ala., Calif., Ind., Fla., Colo., La., Minn., Miss., Tex., Wis., N.Y., Ga., Mich., N.C., Okla., Pa., N.J., Ohio, Va., Md., Ariz., Mo., Mass., Conn. Mgr. constrn. project Rauenhorst (Opus) Corp., Mpls., 1970-73; project engr. Ellisor Engrs., Inc., Houston, 1974-76; project mgr. Ellisor & Tanner, Inc., Houston, 1976-81; v.p., dir. Ellisor & Tanner, Inc., Houston and Dallas, 1981-86; pres., mng. ptnr. Datum/Moore Partnership, Irving, Tex. and Washington, 1986-88; pres. Notch & Assocs, Arlington, Tex., 1988—; pres. JSN Enterprises, Inc., Irving, 1986—. Prin. works include (structural designs) Four Allen Ctr., Houston, Citicorp Ctr., LL&E Tower, New Orleans, NASA Mission Control Bldg., others; contbr. numerous articles to profl. jours. Chmn. Hurricane Alicia Code Rev. Commn. Constrn. Industry Council Houston, 1983; spokesman Sta-KPRC, Sta-KTRK, Houston, 1983. Lehigh U. research fellow, 1973-74; recipient Grand award Am. Consulting Engrs. Council, 1984; also others. Mem. Am. Concrete Inst. (chmn. various coms.), ASCE (nat. chmn. tall bldgs. com., mem. various coms.), Post-Tensioning Inst., Am. Inst. Steel Constrn., Research Council Structural Connections of Engring. Found., Internat. Council Tall Bldgs. & Urban Habitat, Internat. Assn. Bridge & Structural Engrs., Structural Engrs. Assn. Tex., Profl. Engrs. in Pvt. Practice, NSPE (chmn. edn. com., Houston Young Engr. of Yr., San Jacinto chpt. 1984), Tex. Soc. Profl. Engrs. (Tex. Young Engr. of Yr. 1984), Prestressed Concrete Inst. Nat. Acad. Forensic Engrs., Cons. Engrs. Coun. Dallas Com. on High Rise Bldgs. Roman Catholic. Lodge: KC. Office: Notch & Assocs 2603 Cypress Hills Ct Ste 200 Arlington TX 76006-4006

NOTHMANN, RUDOLF S., legal researcher; b. Hamburg, W.Ger., Feb. 4, 1907; came to U.S., 1941, naturalized, 1943; s. Nathan and Henrietta G. (Heymann) N. Referendar, U. Hamburg, 1929, Ph.D. in Law, 1932; postgrad. U. Liverpool Law Sch. (Eng.), 1931-32. Law clk. Hamburg Cts., 1929-33; export, legal adviser, adviser ocean marine ins. various firms, Ger., Eng., Sweden, Calif., 1933-43, 46-47; instr. fgn. exchange, fgn. trade Extension div. UCLA, 1947-48, vis. assoc. prof. UCLA, 1951; asst. prof. econs. Whittier Coll., 1948-50, assoc. prof., 1950-51; contract work U.S. Air Force, U.S. Navy, 1953-59; contract negotiator space projects, space and missile systems orgn. U.S. Air Force, Los Angeles, 1959-77; pvt. researcher in internat. comml. law, Pacific Palisades, Calif., 1977—. Served with U.S. Army, 1943-45; ETO. Recipient Gold Tape award Air Force Systems Command, 1970. Mem. Internat. Bar Assn. (vice chmn. internat. sales and related comml. trans. com. 1977-82), Am. Econ. Assn., Calif. Bar Assn. (internat. law sect.), Am. Soc. Internat. Law. Author: The Insurance Certificate in International Ocean Marine Insurance and Foreign Trade, 1932; The Oldest Corporation in the World: Six Hundred Years of Economic Evolution, 1949. Club: Uebersee (Hamburg). Home: PO Box 32 Pacific Palisades CA 90272

NOTOWIDIGDO, MUSINGGIH HARTOKO, information systems executive; b. Indonesia, Dec. 9, 1938; s. Moekarto and Martaniah (Brodjonegoro) N.; m. Sihar P. Tambunan, Oct. 1, 1966 (dec. Nov. 1976); m. Joanne S. Gutter, June 3, 1979; children: Matthew Joseph, Jonathan Paul. BME, George Washington U., 1961; MS, NYU, 1966, postgrad., 1970. Cons. Dollar Blitz & Assocs., Washington, 1962-64; ops. research analyst Am. Can Co., N.Y.C., 1966-69; prin. analyst Borden Inc., Columbus, Ohio, 1969-70, mgr. ops. research, 1970-71, mgr. ops. analysis and research, 1972-74, asst. gen. controller, officer, 1974-77, corp. dir. info. systems/econ. analysis, officer, 1977-83; v.p. info. systems Wendy's Internat., 1983—; adj. lectr. Grad. Sch. Adminstrn. Capital U. Contbr. articles to profl. jours. Mem. Fin Execs. Inst. (chmn. MIS com.), Ops. Research Soc., Inst. Mgmt. Sci., Am. Mgmt. Assn., Nat. Assn. Bus. Economists, Long Range Planning Soc., Am. Statis. Assn., AAAS, World Future Soc., Data Processing Mgmt. Assn., Soc. Info. Mgmt., N.Y. Acad. Scis. Republican. Clubs: Capital, Racquet. Home: 1965 Brandywine Dr Upper Arlington OH 43220 Office: Wendy's Internat 4288 W Dublin-Granville Rd Dublin OH 43017

NOVACK, JOHN MORGAN, controller; b. Arlington, Va., Dec. 22, 1951; s. John Arnold and Gertrude May (Morgan) N.; m. Susan Barbara Copley, June 15, 1974; children: Karen, Mark. BBA, Coll. William and Mary, 1973. CPA, Va. Audit mgr. Arthur Andersen & Co., Washington, 1973-81; v.p., controller Woodward & Lathrop, Alexandria, Va., 1981—. Office: Woodward & Lothrop 2800 Eisenhower Ave Alexandria VA 22314

NOVAK, ALBERT JOHN WITTMAYER, electronic systems and parts manufacturing company executive; b. Grand Rapids, Mich., Mar. 30, 1921; s. Albert Joseph and B. Joan (Wittmayer) N.; A.B. magna cum laude in Physics, Harvard U., 1941; postgrad. M.I.T., 1944, Case Inst. Tech., 1946-48; m. Patricia M. Henline, Mar. 25, 1950 (div. Oct. 22, 1980); children—Patricia Joan, Albert John Wittmayer, David Bruce, Loren Lee; m. Suzanne Stover Basye, Apr. 30, 1984. Indsl. engr. RCA, Camden, N.J., 1941-42; sales mgr. Brush Instruments div. Clevite Corp., Cleve., 1946-53, gen. mgr. Tex. div., Houston, 1955-57; mgr. sales and engring. Ansonia Wire & Cable Co., Ashton, R.I., 1957-59; gen. mgr. Electronics div. Hoover Co., Balt. and Pompano Beach, Fla., 1959-65; founder, pres., chmn. bd. Novatronics Group, Inc., Novatronics, Inc., Pompano Beach, 1965-85, Novatronics of Can., Ltd., Stratford, Ont., Novatronics South, Inc., Delray Beach, Fla.; cons., bd. dirs. Nedax Inc., 1985—; adv. bd. Barnett Banks. Chmn., Broward Indsl. Bd., 1967, 75, Broward County Community Relations Commn., 1974, South Fla. Dist. Adv. Council, SBA, 1978; pres. Ft. Lauderdale Symphony Assn., 1970-72; v.p. Opera Guild, 1985-86; bd. dirs. South Fla. Edn. Center, 1963—, pres., 1970—; bd. dirs. United Way Broward County, 1975—, v.p., 1977—; mem. Gov.'s Mgmt. Adv. Council for Health and Rehab. Services, 1977—, chmn. Dist. X Health and Rehab. Services Adv. Council, 1977; trustee Mus. of Art; bd. dirs. Center for Pastoral Counseling and Human Devel., 1973—, pres., 1977-79. Served to lt. comdr. USNR, 1942-46. Named Industrialist of Yr., Pompano Beach, 1966-67, 75-76; recipient Outstanding Service award Nat. Elec. Mfrs. Assn., 1967. Mem. Broward Mfrs. Assn. (pres. 1966-67), Am. Electronics Assn. (bd. dirs.), Greater Ft. Lauderdale C. of C. (dir. 1973-74), Phi Beta Kappa. Club: Harvard (pres. 1976-78) (Broward County). Home & Office: PO Box 858 Clinton WA 98236

NOVAK, DAVID EDWARD, restaurant executive; b. Chgo., Nov. 10, 1956; s. Richard Edward and Vilma (Stepanek) N.; m. Cynthia L. Leslie, July 19, 1980; 1 child, Ashley Linn. BS, Kent (Ohio) State U., 1980. Mktg. dir. Edward J. DeBartolo Corp., Akron, Ohio, 1980-81; gen. mgr. Edward J. DeBartolo Corp., Balt., 1981-83, regional mgr., 1983-84; asst. v.p. The Macerich Co., Dover, Del., 1984-85; pres. South Harbor Restaurant Corp., Annapolis, Md., 1985—. Office: South Harbor Restaurant Corp PO Box 748 Severna Park MD 21401

NOVAK, DEBORAH GAYLE, healthcare executive; b. Ft. Worth, Apr. 2, 1950; d. Lloyd and Frances (Graves) Jones; m. Paul John Novak Jr., Aug. 7, 1970 (div. 1981). BS in Psychology, English, Stephen F. Austin State U., Nacogdoches, Tex., 1972; MEd, Stephen F. Austin State U., 1973; MA in Ednl. Psychology, U. Tex., 1976, PhD in Ednl. Psychology, 1979. From ednl. program coordinator to asst. v.p. Tex. Hosp. Assn., Austin, 1974-80; health care cons. Meml Hosp. System, Houston, 1980-84; v.p. VHA Enterprises Cons. Svcs., Tampa, Fla., 1984-85; v.p. corp. ops. devel. Vol. Hosp. Am., Inc., Irving, Tex., 1986—; sr. cons. Jones Bright Internat., The Woodlands, Tex., 1977-85; speaker in field. Author: Cheaper by the Dozen? 1977, Alcoholism Ins. Coverage, 1975 (reprinted 1976); co-author: Alcoholism: Gen. Hosp. Issues, 1976. Mem. Tex. Hosp. Assn. (past dir.). Roman Catholic. Office: Vol Hosps Am Inc 5215 N O'Connor 12th Fl Irving TX 75039

NOVAK, TIMOTHY VIRGIL, accountant; b. Minot, N.D., July 22, 1955; s. Virgil William and Esther Faye (Rittenbach) N.; m. Janet Rae Hoffmann, June 6, 1976; 1 child, Erin Elisabeth. BBA, Union Coll., Lincoln, Nebr., 1977. CPA, N.C. Acct. Hansen Johnson & Assocs., Hendersonville, N.C., 1977-85, owner, 1985—. Mem. Am. Inst. CPAs, N.C. Assn. CPAs., Kiwanis (sec. Hendersonville club 1984-87). Office: Hansen Johnson & Assocs 1620 Asheville Hwy Hendersonville NC 28739

NOVEK, GREGG RICHARD, securities analyst; b. White Plains, N.Y., Feb. 28, 1961; s. Elliot and Constance Joyce (Beck) N. BS, Lehigh U., 1983; postgrad., Seton Hall U. Fin. analyst The Ayco/Am. Express Co., Albany, N.Y., 1983-85; assoc. dir. rsch. Ryan, Beck & Co., West Orange, N.J., 1985-88; bank analyst Fox-Pitt, Kelton, Inc., N.Y.C., 1998—. Mem. Bank and Fin. Analysts Soc., Phi Eta Sigma, Omicron Delta Kappa, Phi Alpha Theta. Home: 50 Euclid Ave Apt 3C Hackensack NJ 07601

NOVELLO, LEONARD P., lawyer; b. Bklyn., Dec. 5, 1940; s. Leonard G. and Vivian T. (DiStefano) N.; m. Joanna C. Guastella, Aug. 8, 1971; 1 child, Kathyrn A. BA, Coll. Holy Cross, 1961; JD, Fordham U., 1964. Law clk. to presiding judge U.S. Dist. Ct. (so. dist.) N.Y., N.Y.C., 1964-65; assoc. Cravath, Swaine & Moore, N.Y.C., 1969-75; assoc. gen. counsel Peat, Marwick, Mitchell & Co., N.Y.C., 1975-86; gen. counsel Peat Marwick Main & Co., N.Y.C., 1986—; bd. dirs. Pail/Padva, Bermuda. Contbr. articles to New York Law Jour. Mem. planning bd. Hastings-on-Hudson, N.Y. Capt. USAF, 1965-68. Mem. ABA (various coms.), N.Y. State Bar Assn., Assn. Bar City of N.Y., Am. Corp. Counsel Assn., Univ. Club, Ardsley Country Club. Republican. Roman Catholic. Office: Peat Marwick Main & Co Park Avenue Pla 55 E 52nd St New York NY 10055

NOVELLO, ROBERT J., manufacturing executive; b. Malden, Mass., 1938. Grad., Northeastern U., 1968; postgrad., Babson Coll., 1973. Pres. Branson Group, Danbury, Conn.; group v.p. Emerson Electric Corp.; v.p. Copeland Corp., Sidney, Ohio. Office: Copeland Corp 1675 Campbell Rd Sidney OH 45365 *

NOVEMESTKY, FREDERICK, investment executive, electrical engineer; b. N.Y.C., Aug. 8, 1946; s. Bernard and Elva (Nazavio) N.; m. Deborah Yanofsky, July 4, 1971; children: Laurie, Clifford, Philip, Sandi. BSEE, U. P.R., Mayaguez, 1969; MSEE, Polytech. U., 1971, PhD, 1982. Registered profl. engr., N.Y. With tech. staff Bell Telephone Labs., Whippany, N.J., 1969-73; investment officer Chase Manhattan Bank, N.Y.C., 1973-85; mgr. investments Chase Investors Mgmt. Corp., N.Y.C., 1985—. Mem. N.A. Soc. Corp. Planners, Tau Beta Pi. Home: 41 Eastover Dr East Northport NY 11731 Office: Chase Investment Mgmt Corp 1211 Avenue of the Americas 37th Fl New York NY 10036

NOVIELLO, FRANK, sales agency executive; b. Bklyn., June 9, 1947; s. Joseph and Anna (Conner) N.; m. Rosemary Posillico, June 14, 1969; children: Kristine, Stephen. BA in Econs., Queens Coll., 1974. Mem. sales staff Meyers & Merl Assocs., Inc., Elmont, N.Y., 1970-72, sales mgr., 1972-74, v.p., gen. mgr., 1974-87, pres., 1987—; bd. dirs. Approved Lightning Protection, Inc., Elmont. Sgt. U.S. Army, 1967-69. Mem. ASHRAE, Nat. Elec. Mfrs. Reps. Assn., West Birchwood Civic Assn., Sons of Italy. Roman Catholic. Office: Meyers & Merl Assocs Inc 439 Meacham Ave Elmont NY 11003

NOVITCH, MARK, physician, pharmaceutical company executive; b. New London, Conn., Apr. 23, 1932; s. Charles Weinger and Mary (Margolick) N.; m. Katherine Louise Henderson, Oct. 9, 1971; 1 dau., Julia Drummond. A.B., Yale U., 1954; M.D., N.Y. Med. Coll., 1958. Intern, asst. resident in medicine Boston City Hosp., 1958-60; research fellow Harvard Med. Sch., 1960-62, asst. in medicine, 1962-64, instr. medicine, 1964-67; mem. med. staff Peter Bent Brigham Hosp., Boston, 1962-67; asst. physician Univ. Health Services, Harvard U., 1961-67; asst. to dep. asst. sec. for health and sci. affairs HEW, Washington, 1967-71; dep. asso. commr. for med. affairs FDA, Washington, 1971-78; asso. commr. for health affairs FDA, 1978-81; dep. commr. food and drugs Dept. Health and Human Services, 1981-85; corporate v.p. The Upjohn Co., Kalamazoo, 1985-86, sr. v.p. sci. adminstrn., 1986-88, exec. v.p., 1989—; bd. dirs. Nat. Health Council, N.Y.C., The Upjohn Co.; del.-at-large U.S. Pharmacopeial Conv., Inc.; prin. Ctr. Excellence in Govt., Washington. Mem. adv. neighborhood commn. 3F, D.C., 1976-78; bd. dirs. Nat. Fund Med. Health, Boston. USPHS fellow, 1960-62; Brookings Instn. fed. exec. fellow, 1970-71. Mem. AMA, Mass. Med. Soc., Am. Public Health Assn. Home: 7204 Glade Trail Kalamazoo MI 49009 Office: Upjohn Co 7000 Portage Rd Kalamazoo MI 49001

NOVOTNY, DEBORAH ANN, financial executive; b. Oak Lawn, Ill., Sept. 23, 1964; d. Russell Anthony and Barbara J. (Doran) N. BA in Econs., Northwestern U., 1986. Mgr. lab., cons. Northwestern U., Evanston, Ill., 1983-86; asst. mgr. microcomputer services Sara Lee Corp., Chgo., 1986; sr. cons. Lante Corp., Chgo., 1987-88; fin. exec. IDS Fin. Svcs., Inc., Mpls., 1988—. Active teen retreat team St. Michael's Ch., Orland Park, Ill., 1982—. Ill. State scholar. Mem. Macintosh Users Group, Chi Omega Rho (charter, chmn. housing assn. 1986—). Home: 14424 West Ave Orland Park IL 60462 Office: IDS Fin Svcs Inc IDS Tower 10 Minneapolis MN 55440

NOWATZKI, DONALD JACK, hazardous waste company executive; b. Watertown, Wis., Dec. 1, 1930; s. Bernhard Carl and Dorothy Florence (Biefeld) N.; m. Jean Ann Wetzel, June 21, 1953; children: Debra, Kim, Jack. BBA, U. Wis., 1953; MBA, Long Beach State U., 1959. CPA. Acctg. supr. Shell Chem. Co., Martinez, Calif., 1956-63; controller Rogers Foods Inc., Idaho Falls, Idaho, 1963-75; v.p. Rogers Foods Inc., Idaho Falls, 1976-79, Energy Inc., Idaho Falls, 1979-85, Waste-Tech Svcs. Inc., Golden, Colo., 1985—. Lt. U.S. Army, 1954-56. Republican. Lutheran. Home: 2006 S Parfet Dr Lakewood CO 80227 Office: Waste Tech Svcs Inc 18400 W 10th Ave Golden CO 80401

NOWICKI, PAUL ANTHONY, municipal government official; b. Adams, Mass., Jan. 11, 1959; s. Stephen W. and Mary F. (Skubel) N.; m. Linda M. Michaels, Oct. 9, 1982; children: Matthew P., Carrie L. BSBA cum laude, N. Adams State Coll., 1980. Audit analyst Office of Mass. State Auditor, Boston, 1979-80; payroll ckl. R.L. Polk and Co., Boston, 1980-81; acct. Berkshire Chem. Co., Adams, 1981-82; treas./collector Town of Adams, 1983—; acct. Internat. TV Trading Corp., South Egremont, Mass., 1982-83, East Hoosac Athletic Assn., South Egremont, Mass., 1988—; fin. cons. Author Auditor's Statistics Course. Mem. Collector's and Treasurers' Assn. (mem. exec. com. 1988), Adams Gebirgs Verein (treas. 1982-87), St. Stanislaus Kostka Soc. (fin. sec. 1988—), Elks. Democrat. Roman Catholic. Home: Upper E Hoosac St Adams MA 01220 Office: Town of Adams 65 Park St Adams MA 01220

NOWIK, HENRY IAN, marketing executive, consultant; b. Posen, Poland, Feb. 3, 1917; came to U.S., 1979; s. Alexander Joseph and Elizabeth Augusta (von Kuhn) N.; m. Evelyn Phyllis Barnard, Sept. 17, 1949. BS in Econs., London U., 1949; PhD, U. Lyon, 1948. Student advisor U. London, 1948-52; export mktg. exec. Parke Davis Ltd., Eng., 1952-54; mgr. market rsch. Mather & Crowther, Eng., 1954-56; mgr. new products Hoover Ltd., Eng., 1956-58; mgr. market rsch. Petfoods Ltd. div. Mars, Inc., Eng., 1958-64; v.p. mktg., sales Uncle Ben's, Australia, 1964-68, gen. mgr., mng. dir., 1968-78; v.p. mktg. Mars, Inc., U.S., 1979-80, group pres., 1980-84; cons. mktg. 1984—; sr. cons. Food System Assocs., Washington, 1985—; prof., lectr. Georgetown U., Washington, 1984—. Author: Disciplined Entrepreneur, 1976, Research in Marketing, 1964, (with others) Product and Process Development in the Food Industry, 1985; contbr. articles to profl. jours. Justice of Peace, Sydney, Australia, 1973; bd. dirs. Australian Ballet Found., Melbourne, 1975; trustee World Wildlife Fund, Australia, 1976; chmn. Decentralization Adv. Bd., Canberra, Australia, 1977-78. Served with RAF, 1936-45. Decorated Officer of Most Excellent Order Brit. Empire, Officer of Order of Australia, Comdr. with Star of Polonia Restituta, Polish Gold Cross of Merit, Knight Supreme Mil. Order Temple Jerusalem. Fellow Royal Statis. Soc., Brit. Inst. Mgmt., Australian Inst. Mgmt., Advt. Inst. Australia, Inst. Dirs. Australia; mem. Internat. Law Assn., Acad. Polit. Sci. (life), Lloyds of London (underwriting), Market Rsch. Soc., Inst. Mktg. and Sales Mgmt., Am. Mgmt. Assn., N.Y. Acad. Sci., London Reform Club, Georgetown Club (Washington), Royal Yacht Squadron Club. Roman Catholic. Office: Georgetown U Sch Fgn Svc Washington DC 20057

NOWLAN, JOHN EDWARD, JR., sales executive; b. Boston, Jan. 4, 1949; s. John Edward and M. Claire (Dacey) N.; m. Karen Louise Fain, Sept. 16, 1978; 1 child, Elizabeth Colleen. BS, Rochester Inst. Tech., 1970; MBA, Loyola Marymount U., L.A., 1983. Tech. sales rep. Eastman Kodak Co., Whittier, Calif., 1970-82; nat. accounts dir. Eastman Kodak Co., Rochester, N.Y., 1982-84; dist. sales mgr. Eastman Kodak Co., Dallas, 1984-86; zone mgr. western zone, govt. markets Eastman Kodak Co., Whittier, 1986—. Mem. Am. Assn. Clin. Chemistry, Town Hall of Calif. Roman Catholic. Club: Palos Verdes Yacht (commodore 1978-79). Office: Eastman Kodak Co 12100 Rivera Rd Whittier CA 90606

NOYCE, ROBERT NORTON, electronics company executive; b. Burlington, Iowa, Dec. 12, 1927; s. Ralph B. and Harriet (Norton) N.; m. Ann S. Bowers; children: William B., Pendred, Priscilla, Margaret. BA, Grinnell Coll., 1949; PhD, MIT, 1953. Rsch. engr. Philco Corp., Phila., 1953-56, Shockley Semicondr. Lab., Mountain View, Calif., 1956-57; founder, dir. rsch. Fairchild Semicondr., Mountain View, 1957-59; v.p., gen. mgr. Fairchild Semicondr., 1959-65; group v.p. Fairchild Camera & Instrument, Mountain View, 1965-68; founder, pres. Intel Corp., Santa Clara, Calif., 1968-75; chmn. Intel Corp., 1968-75, vice chmn., 1979—; pres., chief exec. officer Sematech, Austin, Tex., 1988—. Patentee in field. Trustee Grinnell Coll., 1962—. Recipient Stuart Ballentine award Franklin Inst., 1967, Harry Goode award AFIPS, 1978, Nat. Medal of Sci., 1979, Nat. Medal of Tech. Pres. of U.S., 1987, Harold Pender award U. Pa., 1980, John Fritz medal, 1989; named to Nat. Bus. Hall of Fame, 1989. Fellow IEEE (Cledo Brunetti award 1978, medal of honor 1978, Faraday medal 1979); mem. Nat. Acad. Engring., AAAS, Nat. Acad. Sci. Office: Sematech 2706 Montopolis Dr Austin TX 78741

NOYES, JAMES W., insurance executive; b. Swarthmore, Pa., Apr. 29, 1939; s. Edward Lee and Jean (Walton) N.; m. Susan Williams; children: Kelley, Jillian, Julie. BA in English, Amherst Coll., Mass., 1961. Pres. Noyes Svcs., Media, Pa., 1961—; bd. dirs., mem. exec. com. Freedom Valley Bankshares, Ltd.; bd. dirs. PAR, Ltd.; mem. adv. group PMA, Home Ins. Co. Mem. adv. bd. Swarthmore Coll. Friends of Athletics; past dir. Riddle Meml. Hosp.; chmn. selection com. Div. III Men's Lacrosse All Am. With U.S. Army, 1961-67. Mem. Young Pres.'s Orgn., Del. County C. of C. (psat chmn., Disting. Bus. Man of Yr. 1981), Soc. Friends, Rotary (past dir.). Home: 1650 Ridley Creek Rd Media PA 19063 Office: Noyes Svcs 300 W State St Media PA 19063

NUCCITELLI, SAUL ARNOLD, civil engineer, consultant; b. Yonkers, N.Y., Apr. 25, 1928; s. Agostino and Antoinette (D'Amicis) N.; m. Concetta Orlandi, Dec. 23, 1969; 1 child, Saul A. BS, NYU, 1949, MCE, 1954; DCE, MIT, 1960. Registered profl. engr., N.Y., Mo., Colo., Conn., Mass.; lic. land surveyor, Mo., Colo., Conn., Mass. Asst. civil engr. Westchester County Engrs., N.Y.C., 1949-51, 53-54; project engr. H.B. Bolas Enterprises, Denver, 1954-55; asst. prof., research engr., U. Denver, 1955-58; mem. staff MIT, 1958-60; asst. prof. engring. Cooper Union Coll., N.Y.C., 1960-62; pvt. practice cons. engring., Springfield, Mo., 1962—; organizer Met. Nat. Bank, Springfield; adviser, dir. Farm & Home Savs. and Loan Assn. Contbr. articles to profl. jours. Chmn. Adv. Council on Mo. Pub. Drinking Water; bd. dirs. Community Found. Greene County, Mus. of Ozarks; past chmn. Bd. City Utilities, Springfield; past pres. Downtown Springfield Assn. Served with U.S. Army, 1951-53. Recipient Cert. of Appreciation, Mo. Mcpl. League, 1981; named Mo. Cons. Engr. of Yr., 1973. Fellow ASCE; mem. Nat. Soc. Profl. Engrs., Mo. Soc. Profl. Engrs. (past pres. Ozark chpt.), Boston Soc. Civil Engrs., Am. Concrete Inst., Am. Inst. Steel Constrn., Am. Welding Soc., ASTM, Am. Soc. Mil. Engrs., Springfield C. of C. (past v.p.). Home: 2919 Brentmoor Ave Springfield MO 65804 Office: 122 Park Central Sq Springfield MO 65806

NUGENT, DANIEL EUGENE, business executive; b. Chgo., Dec. 18, 1927; s. Daniel Edward and Pearl A. (Trieger) N.; m. Bonnie Lynn Weidman, July 1, 1950; children: Cynthia Lynn, Mark Alan, Dale Alan. BSME, Northwestern U., 1951. With U.S. Gypsum Co., Chgo., 1951-71, dir. corp. devel., to 1971; pres. Am. Louver Co., Chgo., 1971-72; v.p. ops. ITT Corp., Cleve., 1972-74, exec. v.p., St. Paul, 1974-75; pres., chief exec. officer Pentair, Inc., St. Paul, 1975-86, chmn., chief operating officer, 1986—, also bd. dirs.; bd. dirs. Niagara of Wis. Paper Corp., Cross Point Paper Corp., Porter-Cable Corp., Delta Internat. Machinery Corp., McNeil Ohio Corp., Fed.-Hoffman, Inc. Vice chmn. local planning commn., 1968-72; vice chmn., trustee Harper Coll., Palatine, 1970-73, trustee Dunwoody Inst.; mem. exec. com. Indianhead Council Boy Scouts Am. Served with AUS, 1946-47. Mem. ASME, Am. Mgmt. Assn. Republican. Presbyterian. Club: North Oaks Golf. Office: Pentair Inc 1700 W Hwy 36 Suite 700 Saint Paul MN 55113

NULL, EARL EUGENE, financial services company executive; b. South Bend, Ind., Jan. 13, 1936; s. Glenn Cecil and Alberta (Bosler) N.; children—Laura, Debra, Pamela; m. Orpha Cecelia Stepniak, Sept. 16, 1961. B.S. in Bus. Adminstrn., U. Notre Dame, 1957. Adminstrv. mgr. Assocs. Corp., South Bend, 1956-67; gen. mgr. Gen. Elec. Co., Stamford, Conn., 1967-78; exec. v.p. ITT Fin. Corp., N.Y.C., 1978-87; pres., dir. ITT Diversified Fin. Corp., St. Louis, 1987—; Vice chmn. Newport Balboa Savs. & Loan, Newport Beach, Calif., ITT Mortgage Corp., Sherman Oaks, Calif.; chmn. ITT Small Bus. Fin., Mpls. Served with U.S. Army, 1958-60. Home: 13529 Weston Park Dr Town and Country MO 63131 Office: ITT Diversified Fin Corp 11885 Lackland Rd Saint Louis MO 63146

NULTY, GEORGE P., food products company executive; b. Somerville, N.J., May 19, 1942; s. Maurice R. and Margaret (Beggan) N.; m. Maureen E. Sullivan, June 30, 1966; children: Sean, Erin, Megan, Caitlin. BS, St. Peter's Coll., 1964. Buyer Campbell Soup Co., Camden, N.J., 1967-68; asst. purchasing agt. Campbell Soup Co., Salisbury, Md., 1970-73, purchasing agt., 1973-77; procurement agt. Campbell Soup Co., Omaha, 1977-78; mgr. purchasing Campbell Soup Co., Camden, 1978-79, dir. ops., ingredient dir., 1980-81, dir. agr., 1981-82, dir. procurement, 1982-83, v.p. procurement, 1983—. Lt. USN, 1964-67. Mem. Nat. Food Products Assn., Am. Inst. Food Distbrs., Nat. Assn. Purchasing Mgmt. Roman Catholic. Office: Campbell Soup Co Campbell Pl Camden NJ 08101

NUMATA, NOBUO, software company executive, consultant, engineer; b. Ashiya, Hyogo, Japan, Mar. 5, 1954; came to U.S., 1964; s. Jack Tetsuya and Tomoko (Noguchi) N. BEE, Princeton U., 1976; M in Computer Sci., Columbia U., 1979. Registered profl. engr., Japan. Analyst Impex (Japan) Ltd., Tokyo, 1976-78, mgr., 1978-80, v.p., 1980-82, pres., 1982—; pres. Tecnopac Inc., N.Y.C., 1988—; v.p. Am. Tech. Group, Palo Alto, Calif., 1984-86. Contbr. articles to profl. jours. Trustee Princeton-in-Asia, 1979—. Clubs: Princeton (N.Y.C.); Tokyo Am., Fgn. Corrs. Japan, Tokyo Lawn and Tennis, Internat. House Japan, Princeton (Tokyo), Univ. Club (N.Y.C). Home: 870 United Nations Pla Apt 15B New York NY 10017 Office: Tecnopac Inc 767 Fifth Ave #2700 New York NY 10153

NUNEMAKER, RICHARD A., manufacturing executive; b. Chgo., July 31, 1948; s. Clifford E. and Vivian R. N.; m. Jane F. Nunemaker, Jan. 30, 1971; chldren: Bradley, Scott. BS in Acctg., U. Ill., 1970, MS in Acctg., 1974. CPA, Ill. Audit supr. Touche, Ross and Co., Chgo., 1971-76; various acctg. positions Esmark, Inc., Chgo., 1976-80, asst. controller, 1980-84, v.p., controller, 1984-86; v.p., controller Diversifoods, Inc., Varlen Corp., Naperville, Ill., 1986—. Mem. Am. Inst. CPA's, Ill. Soc. CPA's, Fin. Execs. Inst. Office: Varlen Corp 305 E Shuman Blvd Suite 500 Naperville IL 60566

NUNEZ-LAWTON, MIGUEL GUILLERMO, international finance specialist; b. Havana, Cuba, Feb. 8, 1949; came to U.S., 1964; s. Miguel Nunez-Portuondo and Silvia Lawton-Alfonso. BBA, Georgetown U., 1971, postgrad. in Econs., 1973. Asst. treas. Deltec Securities Corp., N.Y.C., 1971; external debt specialist debt and internat. fin. div. World Bank, Washington, 1973—, treas., 1987—; chief adviser to Ministry of France in debt mgmt., UNCTAD project, Manila, Philippines, 1989—. Bd. dirs. Friends of Latin-Am. Mus. Modern Art OAS, Washington. Roman Catholic. Home: 2844 Wisconsin Ave NW Washington DC 20007 Office: World Bank 1818 H St NW Washington DC 20433

NUNEZ-PORTUONDO, RICARDO, investment company executive; b. N.Y.C., June 9, 1933; s. Emilio and Maria (Garcia) N-P.; m. Dolores Maldonado, Sept. 7, 1963; children—Ricardo Jose, Emilio Manuel, Eduardo Javier. LL.D., U. Havana, Cuba; postdoctoral in law, U. Fla., 1975. Bar: Cuba, Fla. Editor Latin Am. div. USIA, Miami, Fla., 1961-71; editor Latin Am. div. USIA, Washington, 1961-71; nat. dir. Cuban Refugee Program, Washington, 1975-77; pres. Internat. Mktg. Realty, Miami, 1977—, Central Investment Trust, Coral Gables, Fla., 1977—; chmn. bd. Interstate Bank of Commerce, Miami, 1986—. Author: The Other Image of Cuba, 1965; A Critique on the Linowitz Report, 1975. dir. Nat. Hispanic Scholarship Fund, San Francisco, 1978—; dir. COSSMHO, Washington, 1980—; trustee emeritus Fla. Internat. U., 1984—; pres. Mercy Hosp. Found., Miami, 1985—; bd. dirs. ARC, Greater Miami. Recipient numerous awards for civic contbns. including day named in honor Ricardo Nunez Day, Miami, 1975. Mem. Cuban Lawyers Assn., Cuban Acad. History, Metro. Club, Lyford Cay Club, Ocean Reef Club, Key Biscayne Yacht Club, Big Five Club, 200 Club. Republican. Roman Catholic. Home: 675 Solano Prado Coral Gables FL 33156 Office: PO Box 141720 Coral Gables FL 33114

NUNIS, RICHARD ARLEN, amusement parks executive; b. Cedartown, Ga., May 30, 1932; s. Doyce Blackman and Winnie E. (Morris) N.; 1 child, Richard Dean. B.S. in Edn, U. So. Calif., 1954. With The Walt Disney Co., 1955—; dir. ops. Disneyland, Calif., 1961-68; chmn. park ops. com. Disneyland, 1968-74; corp. v.p. Disneyland Ops., 1968—, Walt Disney World, Orlando, Fla., 1971—; exec. v.p., then pres. Walt Disney Attractions and Disneyland Internat., 1972—; mem. exec. com. Walt Disney Co.; dir. Sun Bank Inc., Orlando, Fla. Mem. exec. com. Pres.'s Council for Internat. Youth Exchange; bd. dirs. Give the Kids the World; co-chmn. Orange County Com. on Children. Named first acad. All-Am., U. So. Calif., 1952. Mem. Fla. C. of C. (bd. dirs.), Fla. Coun. of 100. Republican. Office: 1313 Harbor Blvd Anaheim CA 92803 also: 1675 Buena Vista Dr Lake Buena Vista FL 32830

NUNLEY, DONALD BRITTON, advertising and promotion company executive, art director; b. Glendale, Calif., Mar. 5, 1939; s. Willard O. and Dorothy H. (Flecher) N.; m. Joyce Carman Coleman, Sept. 12, 1959 (div. 1971); children: Dayna Lynn, Debora Kay, Lisa Ann. AA, Pierce Coll., Los Angeles, 1959. Propman Internat. Alliance of Theatrical Stage Employees, Hollywood, Calif., 1959-63; propmaster IATSE No. 44, Hollywood, Calif., 1963-70; prodn. designer ind. film producers Hollywood, 1970-79; pres., chief exec. officer Unique Product Placement, North Hollywood, Calif., 1979—. Mem. Motion Picture Acad. Arts and Scis., North Hollywood C. of C. Office: Unique Product Placement 10865 Burbank Blvd North Hollywood CA 91501

NUNLEY, STEPHEN NOEL, employment management executive; b. Okla., Sept. 27, 1956; s. Loftus Noel and Lois Geneva (Banks) N.; m. Marcia Joy Sampson, Jan. 11, 1986. BS, East Tex. State U., 1978. First line supr. Tex. Instruments, Inc., Sherman, Tex., 1979-81; ops. prodn. mgr. The Pillsbury Co., Denison, Tex., 1981-86; daily ops. coordinator Texoma Regional Planning Commn., 1986—; tng. officer Job Tng. Ptnrship. Act Denison, 1986—. v.p. Sherman Adult Literacy Team, 1986—; mem. choir 1st Bapt. Ch., 1986—; mem. engring. adv. com. Grayson Community Coll., 1985-86, vocat. nursing adv. com., 1980-81, 87-88. Named one of Outstanding Young Men of Am., 1985. Mem. Soc. Mfg. Engrs., Aircraft Owners and Pilots Assn. Republican. Baptist. Home: 2601 Arapaho Cove Denison TX 75020 Office: Texoma Regional Planning Commn 10000 Grayson Dr Denison TX 75020

NUNN, PHILIP CLARK, III, management scientist; b. Cin., Apr. 4, 1933; s. Philip Clark and Frances Kay (Patton) N.; student Kenyon Coll., 1951-53; B.A., Aquinas Coll., 1969; M.S., Western Mich. U., 1983; m. Hildegarde Loretta Bauer, Jan. 17, 1953; children—Annette, Catherine, Margaret, Christopher. Cert. Project Mgmt. Profl., 1984. With Lear Siegler, Inc., Grand Rapids, Mich., 1957-70, devel. project coordinator, 1962-70; mgr. environ. systems devel. Nat. Sanitation Found., Ann Arbor, Mich., 1970-74; dir. urban and environ. studies inst. Grand Valley State Colls., Allendale, Mich., 1974-80; internat. coordinator research and devel. Amway Corp., Ada, Mich., 1980-83 ; engring. and research mgmt. cons., Comstock Park, Mich., prof. masters degree progam Project Mgmt, Devry Inst. Tech., 1986-88, acad. dean, 1988—; adj. prof. F.E. Seidman Grad. Coll. Bus. and Adminstrn., 1976-81. Health dir. Cin. area Boy Scout Camp, 1952; regular panel mem. Soundings weekly radio program WOOD-AM and FM, Grand Rapids, Mich., 1973-80; vice chmn. community health planning sect. W. Mich. Health Systems Agy., 1976-80; mem. central planning com. W. Mich. Comprehensive Health Planning Unit, 1973-76; chmn. environ. simulation sect. Summer Computer Simulation Conf., 1972; bd. dirs. Kent County Conservation League, 1964-65. Served with USAF, 1953-57. Kenyon Coll. scholar, 1951. Mem. Soc. Gen. Systems Research (chmn. orgn. and mgmt. studies 1970-74), Soc. Computer Simulation, Project Mgmt. Inst., Am. Mgmt. Assn., Alpha Delta Phi. Episcopalian. Contbr. articles to profl. jours. Home and Office: 201 Netherfield St Comstock Park MI 49321

NUNOI, KEIJIRO, management consultant; b. Nagasaki, Japan, Mar. 21, 1930; s. Yasujiro and Raku Nunoi; divorced; children: Haruto, Keiko, Fred, Masako, Sumiko. Student, Fgn. Services Inst., 1959. Shipping clk. Jardine, Matheson and Co. Ltd., Kobe, Japan, 1954-58; consuler staff Am. Embassy, Tokyo, 1958-63; pres. Overseas Research Inst., Inc., Tokyo, 1964-77; owner Nunoi Adminstrv. Scrivners Office, Tokyo, 1977-83; chmn. Nunoi Internat. Bus. Cons. Group, Inc., Tokyo, 1983—; cons. Small Bus. Corp., Japanese Govt., Tokyo, 1986—. Author: U.S. Immigration and Nationality Act, 1958. Chmn. bd. dirs. Nunoi Found., 1987—; regular mem. Am. C. of C. in Japan, 1988—. Recipient Dark Blue Ribbon medal Japanese Emperor, 1986. Mem. Am. Japan Soc., Internat. House of Japan, Tokyo Adminstrv. Scrivners Assn. (bd. dirs. 1978-80). Club: Izu Nirayama Country (Japan). Home: Keijiro Nunoi, Hyness Azabu Toriizaka 301, 5-11-38 Roppongi Minato-ku, Tokyo Japan Office: Nunoi Internat Office, Chiyoda Bldg, 2-9-4 Aakasaka Minato-ku, Tokyo Japan

NURNBERGER, THOMAS SALISBURY, JR., utility company executive; b. Coleman, Mich., May 27, 1918; s. Thomas S. and Edith Marie (Bellinger) N.; m. Alice Jeanette Engstrom, Aug. 30, 1940; children—Nancy Ann, Janet Alice, Thomas Albert. B.S., U. Mich, 1939; LL.D. (hon.), U. Nebr.-Omaha. Pres. Ind., Bell Telephone Co., Indpls., 1968-70; pres. Northwestern Bell Telephone Co., Omaha, 1970-75; exec. v.p. AT&T, N.Y.C., 1975-78; Edison Sault Electric Co., Sault Ste. Marie, Mich., dir., 1978-80, chmn., 1980—; bd. dirs. Principal Fin. Group, Des Moines. Served to lt. col. C.E., U.S. Army, 1939-48. Republican. Congregationalist. Clubs: Omaha. Office: 100 S 19th St Omaha NE 68102

NUROCK, ROBERT JAY, investment analysis company executive; b. Phila., May 25, 1937; s. Abe and Sid (Smokler) N.; m. Doris L. Whitliff, Oct. 19, 1974 (div.); m. 2d, Bridget A. McManus, June 16, 1984; children: Megan, Andrew. BA, Pa. State U., 1958. Owner, pres. Md. Brake Alignment Service, Balt., 1959-67; v.p. investor support Merrill Lynch & Co., Inc., N.Y.C., 1967-79; 1st v.p. market strategy Butcher & Singer, Inc., Phila., 1979-82; pres., market strategist Investor's Analysis, Inc., Paoli, Pa., 1982—; lectr. various ednl. and fin. orgns., 1973—. Panelist program Wall St. Week, Pub. Broadcasting System TV, 1970—; author, pub. The Astute Investor, Paoli, Pa., 1979—; contbg. editor The Hume Moneyletter, Atlanta, 1982—. Mem. Market Technicians Assn. (v.p. 1977-78), N.Y. Soc. Security Analysis, Analysts Club (pres. 1979). Republican. Office: Investors Analysis Inc PO Box 988 Paoli PA 19301

NUSSBAUM, LUTHER JAMES, computer company executive; b. Decatur, Ind., Jan. 13, 1947; s. Leo Lester and Janet Nell (Gladfelter) N.; m. Ginger Mae McCown, Aug. 24, 1968; children: Kari, Kris. BA, Rhodes Coll., 1968; MBA, Stanford U., 1972. Dir. compensation Cummins Engine Co., Columbus, Ind., 1974-75, v.p. distbn. cos., 1977-79, v.p. parts bus., 1979-82, v.p. strategic planning, 1982-83; gen. mgr. Mex. region Cummins Engine Co., Mexico City, 1975-77; v.p. field ops. Businessland, San Jose, Calif., 1983-84, v.p. ops., 1984-85, sr. v.p. mktg., ops., 1985-86; pres., chief operating officer Ashton-Tate, Torrance, Calif., 1986—; bd. dirs. Interbase, Bedford. Mem. Dem. Nat. Fin. Council, 1986—, Dem. Nat. Bus. Council, 1987—. Mem. Young Pres's. Orgn., Phi Beta Kappa. Home: 6110 Armaga Springs Rd Rancho Palos Verdes CA 90274 Office: Ashton-Tate Co 20101 Hamilton Ave Torrance CA 90502

NUSSBAUM, MARK STEPHEN, securities trader; b. Greenwich, Conn., Oct. 4, 1952; s. Philip Kaufman and Doris Elaine (Gross) N.; m. Patricia Ann Richardson, June 12, 1976; children: Stephen, Peter, Brian. Diploma, Ecole Hoteliere, Lausanne, Switzerland, 1975; BA in Econs. magna cum laude, Amherst Coll., 1976; MBA in Fin. with distinction, NYU, 1982. Trader Bankers Trust Co., N.Y.C., 1976-82; trading mgr., treas. Bankers Trust Co., Hong Kong, 1982-84; funding and risk mgr. Bankers Trust Co., N.Y.C., 1984-86, mem. staff global risk mgmt., 1986-87; mgr. propriety trading Paine Webber, Inc., N.Y.C., 1987-88, chief fin. officer, co-head fixed income div., 1988—. Mem. Forex. Office: PaineWebber Group Inc 1285 Ave of the Americas New York NY 10019

NUSSBAUM, THEODORE JAY, consultant; b. N.Y.C., Feb. 9, 1953; s. Norman Bernard and Theresa Ray (Schary) N.; m. Oraine Sophia Dallas, Jan. 5, 1954; children: Ross Dallas, Gregory Dallas. BA, CUNY, Queens, 1978; MPA, N.Y. U., 1980; MS, Pace U., 1986. Cons. Program Planners Inc., N.Y.C., 1973-80; sr. cons. Coopers and Lybrand, N.Y.C., 1980-86, ptnr., 1987. Contbr. articles to profl. jours. Democrat. Jewish. Office: Coopers & Lybrand 1250 Ave of the Americas New York NY 10020

NUZUM, JOHN M., JR., bank executive; b. Milw., Dec. 22, 1939; s. John M. and Helen (Ollis) N.; m. Margaret Bolway, Feb. 25, 1967; children: Kimberly, Courtney, Leah, Jonathan. AB, Princeton U., 1962; MBA, U. Pa., 1964. Sr. v.p. Chase Manhattan Bank, N.Y.C., 1965—. V.p., bd. dirs. Project Reach Youth, Bklyn., 1977-87; treas., bd. dirs. Park Slope Family Ctr., Bklyn., 1984-86. Clubs: Montauk (bd. dirs. 1985—), Hieghts Casino (Bklyn.); Princeton (N.Y.C.). Office: Chase Manhattan Bank 1 Chase Manhattan Pla New York NY 10081

NYBERG, CHARLES D., corporate executive, lawyer; b. 1930; married. B.S.L., U. Minn., J.D., 1959. Atty. George A. Hormel & Co., Austin, Minn., 1959—, asst. sec., 1968-69, sec., dir. pub. relations, 1969-81, sec., gen. counsel, 1981—, v.p., 1984-86, gen. counsel, sec. human resources, 1986, sr. v.p., bd. dirs. 1987—; bd. dirs. Hormel Found., 1987—. Served with USAF, 1947-52. Office: George A Hormel & Co 501 16th Ave NE PO Box 800 Austin MN 55912

NYE, ERLE ALLEN, utilities executive, lawyer; b. Ft. Worth, June 23, 1937; s. Ira Benjamen N.; m. Alice Ann Grove, June 5, 1959; children: Elizabeth Nye Kirkham, Pamela Nye Schneider, Erle Allen Jr., Edward Kyle, Johnson Scott. BEE, Tex. A&M U., 1959; JD, So. Meth. U., 1965. With Dallas Power & Light Co., 1960-75, v.p., 1975-80; exec. v.p. Tex. Utilities Co., Dallas, 1980-87, pres., 1987—. Bd. dirs. Dallas Bar Found., 1980-83, Dallas Cen. Bus. Plan Com., 1980-83, Inroads/Dallas-Ft. Worth, Inc., 1984—; trustee Baylor Dental Coll., Dallas, 1985—. Served to 2d lt. U.S. Army, 1959-60. Mem. ABA, Dallas Bar Assn., Tex. State Bar Assn. Methodist. Clubs: Engineers (pres. 1982-83), Northwood (Dallas). Home: 6924 Desco Dallas TX 75225 Office: Tex Utilities Co 2001 Bryan Tower Dallas TX 75201

NYGREN, STEVEN E., marketing professional; b. Abington, Va., Apr. 19, 1961; s. E. Herbert and Louise Nygren; m. Marsha Brinson, Apr. 21, 1984. BS, Taylor U., 1983; MS, Aurora U., 1987, postgrad., 1987—. Programmer, analyst Nalco Chem. Co., Naperville, Ill., 1983-84, systems analyst, 1984-87, mktg. specialist, 1987—. Mem. Am. Chem. Soc. Home: 30 W 177th Allister Ln Naperville IL 60540 Office: Nalco Chem Co One Nalco Ctr Naperville IL 60566

NYKIEL, JOSEPH JEROME, controller; b. Elmira, N.Y., May 11, 1952; s. Joseph Leo and Elizabeth Teresa (Tinkler) N. BS in Econs., Niagara U., 1974; MBA in Fin., U. Pa., 1976. Asst. program mgr. MBI, Inc., Norwalk, Conn., 1976-78; dir. fin. and adminstrn. Sunmaster Corp., Corning, N.Y., 1979-83; contr. RKB Enterprises, Elmira, 1984-85, Artistic Greetings, Elmira, 1985-88. Bd. dirs. So. Tier Assn. of the Blind, Elmira, 1986—. Mem. Nat. Assn. Accts. (bd. mem. 1986-87), Hiberians Club. Democrat. Roman Catholic. Home: Strouse Rd PO Box 217 Pine City NY 14871 Office: Artistic Greetings 409 William St Elmira NY 14901

NYTKO, DIANA GAY, real estate appraising company executive; b. N.Y.C., Sept. 30, 1942; m. Donald E. Nytko, Feb. 1961; children: David, Steven. BA in Bus., CCNY, 1963; postgrad. in residential and comml. appraisal and bus. law, U. New Haven, 1981-85. Owner, broker Diana Nytko Realty, Milford, Conn., 1965—; owner, sr. appraiser Conn. Property Appraisers, Milford, 1976—. Chmn., dir. Ann. Milford Oyster Festival, 1975-79; treas., past pres. Milford Progress Inc., 1978—. Mem. Nat. Assn. Mortgage Rev. Appraisers (sr.), Nat. Assn. Real Property Appraisers (sr. real property appraiser), Nat. Assn. Realtors, Soc. Real Estate Appraisers (candidate), New Haven Bd. Realtors, Bridgeport Bd. Realtors, New Haven Home Builders Assn., Milford C. of C. (1st v.p., bd. dirs. 1974-84, Lifetime Vol. award 1985). Office: Conn Property Appraisers 49-53 River St Milford CT 06460

NZEGWU, LOUIS IFEANYI, finance and marketing educator, consultant; b. Onitsha, Nigeria, Aug. 28, 1953; m. Mary Chiazor Mbanugo, Dec. 2, 1985; children: Christian, Devine. BS, Alcorn State U., 1979; MBA, Morgan State U., 1981; MEd, U. So. Miss. Fin. analyst Sunbelt Agrl. Industry, Pattison, Miss., 1978-85; instr. Alcorn State U., Lorman, Miss., 1981—; pres. Louis and Lincs Assocs., Lorman, 1984—. Mem. Am. Mktg. Assn., SW Fedn. Adminstrv. Disciplines, So. Mktg. Assn., Southwestern Mktg. Assn., Port Gibson C. of C., Alpha Phi Alpha. Home: 305 Village Sq Blvd Natchez MS 39096 Office: Alcorn State U Dept Bus Adminstrn Box 1207 Lorman MS 39096

OAKES, ROBERT GIBSON, retired electronics company executive, management consultant; b. Oyster Bay, N.Y., Mar. 20, 1918; s. George Nettleton and Sarah (Thornton) O.; m. Delores Marie Cook, June 12, 1954

(div. Oct. 1962); 1 child, Robert Jr. BBA, Manhattan Coll., 1941; postgrad., Harvard U., 1942-43; MBA, NYU, 1954; cert. in profl. contracts mgmt., UCLA, 1969. Cert. profl. contracts mgr. Enlisted USN, 1943, advanced through grades to comdr.; asst. naval attache USN, Rome, 1949-50; retired USN, 1965; adminstrv. buyer N. Am. Aviation Co., Downey, Calif., 1966-68; subcontract mgr. Rockwell Internat. Corp., Downey, 1968-72; head cost analysis group Hughes Aircraft Co., El Segundo, Calif., 1973-80, mgr. cost analysis, 1980-85, procurement mgr., spl. projects (Hughes-Gen. Motors), 1986-88; mgmt. cons. 1988—. Fellow Nat. Contract Mgmt. Assn.; mem. Hughes Mgmt. Club. Republican. Roman Catholic. Club: Navy Yacht (Long Beach, Calif.). Home: 15153 Otsego St Sherman Oaks CA 91403

OAKES, ROBERT ROY, financial management consultant; b. Evergreen Park, Ill., Sept. 28, 1951; s. Roy Ellsworth and Delores Catherine (Reisenauer) O.; m. Patricia Lynn Marose, Dec. 9, 1972 (div. Sept. 1985); children: Christopher Robert, Jonathan Carl. AA, Moraine Valley Community Coll., 1972; BS in Acctg., U. Ill., Chgo., 1974; M in Mgmt., Northwestern U., 1987; M in Accountancy with distinction, DePaul U., 1988. CPA, Ill.; lic. pub. acct., Ill.; cert. internal auditor, Inst. of Internal Auditors; accredited acctg. practioner, Nat. Soc. of Pub. Accts. Staff auditor Wolf and Co., CPA's, Chgo., 1974-75; audit sr. Alexander Grant and Co., CPA's, Chgo., 1975-79; propr. Robert Oakes and Co., Fin. Svcs., Oak Forest, Ill., 1979-82; audit supr. Friedman, Eisenstein, Raemer & Schwartz, CPA's, Chgo., 1982-83; fin. dir. Access Living, Chgo., 1984-86; chief fin. officer ChildServ, Park Ridge, Ill., 1987—. Editor The Glacier (coll. newspaper), 1971-72. Commr. Village Planning Commn., Matteson, Ill., 1979-80; trustee Rich Twp. Sch. Trustees, Olympia Fields, Ill., 1979-80; treas., bd. dirs., co-founder Fox River Valley Ctr. for Ind. Living, Elgin, Ill., 1985-87; chmn., bd. dirs., founder Progress Ctr. for Ind. Living, Oak Park, Ill.1986—; vol. speaker on disability-related issues. Mem. AICPA, Ill. CPA Soc., Fin. Mgmt. Assn., Beta Gamma Sigma, Delta Mu Delta (named scholar 1988, Golden Medallion award 1988), Beta Alpha Psi, Omicron Delta Epsilon. Home: 9801 S Karlov Ave Oak Lawn IL 60453 Office: ChildServ 1580 N Northwest Hwy Park Ridge IL 60068

OAKLEY, ROBERT ALAN, insurance executive; b. Columbus, Ohio, Nov. 1, 1946; s. Bernard Harmon and Mary Evelyn (Mosier) O.; m. Ann Lucille Liesenhoff, Aug. 3, 1968; children: Jeff, David. BS in Aero. Engring., Purdue U., 1968; MBA, Ohio State U., 1969, PhD in Fin., 1973. Mgr. fin. projects Nationwide Mut. Ins. Co., Columbus, 1976-79, regional controller, 1979-82, dir. ops. controls, 1982-83, v.p., corp. controller, 1983—. Author: Insurance Informations Systems, 1985. Capt. USAF, 1972-76. Mem. Fin. Mgmt. Assn., Fin. Execs. Inst., Am. Soc. CLU's. Office: Nationwide Mut Ins Co One Nationwide Pla Columbus OH 43216

OBATA, GYO, architect; b. San Francisco, Feb. 28, 1923; s. Chiura and Haruko (Kohaski) O.; m. Majel Chance, 1947 (div. 1971); children: Kiku, Nori, Gen; m. Courtney Bean, Nov. 28, 1984; 1 child, Max. BArch, Washington U., St. Louis, 1945; MArch in Urban Design, Cranbrook Acad. Art, 1946. Registered architect 37 states, D.C., Singapore. Sr. designer Skidmore, Owings, & Merrill, Chgo., 1947-51; designer Helmuth, Yamasaki & Leinweber, Detroit, 1951-55; pres., chmn. bd. dirs. Hellmuth, Obata & Kassabaum, Inc., St. Louis, 1951—; affiliate prof. Washington U., 1971; frequent lectr. design and urban environment; serves on competition juries on design throughout country. Projects include Nat. Air & Space Mus., King Saud U., Riyadh, Saudi Arabia, Dalls and Houston Gallerias, King Khaled Airport, Riyadh, hdqrs. Kellogg Co., hdqrs. BPAmerica, World Bank, Washington, St. Louis Union Station Metropolitan Square, Dallas-Ft. Worth Airport, E.R. Squibb Research Ctr., Lawrenceville, N.J., numerous others. Fellow AIA. Clubs: Log Cabin, Noonday, St. Louis. Office: Hellmuth Obata & Kassabaum Inc 1831 Chestnut Saint Louis MO 63103

OBER, STUART ALAN, investment consultant, book publisher; b. N.Y.C., Oct. 2, 1946; s. Paul and Gertrude E. (Stollerman) O.; m. Joanne Michaels, Sept. 20, 1981; 1 son, Erik Kenneth. BA, Wesleyan U., Middletown, Conn., 1968; postgrad., U. Sorbonne, Paris, 1970, CUNY, 1976. Pres., editor-in-chief, chmn. bd. Beekman Pubs. Inc., N.Y.C., 1972—; investment cons. 1972—; tax shelter specialist Loeb, Rhoades & Co., 1976-77; div. dir. tax investment dept. Josephthal & Co., Inc., 1977; mgr. tax-shelter dept. Bruns, Nordeman, Rea & Co., 1978-80; pres. Ober Tax Shelter Cons., 1980—, Securities Investigations, Inc., 1981—; sr. v.p. Cash Franchise Mgmt., Inc., 1988—. Author: Everybody's Guide to Tax Shelters; editor-in-chief: Ober Income Letter, 1983-88; pub.: Tax Shelter Blue Book, 1983—. Chmn. Woodstock Arts and Cultural Com., 1988; bd. dirs., pres. Woodstock Playhouse Assn., 1985-87. Mem. Inst. Cert. Fin. Planners (fin. standards product bd. 1986—, treas. 1988—, bd. dirs.). Office: PO Box 888 Mill Hill Rd Woodstock NY 12498

OBERHAUSEN, JOYCE ANN WYNN, aircraft company executive, artist; b. Plain Dealing, La., Nov. 12, 1941; d. George Dewey and Jettie Cleo (Farrington) Wynn; m. James J. Oberhausen, Oct. 15, 1966; 1 dau., Georgann; m. Dale Estein, Sept. 15, 1958 (div. 1960); children: Darla Renee Estein Oberhausen Minor, Dale Henry Estein Oberhausen. Student Ayers Bus. Sch., Shreveport, 1962-63, U. Ala., 1964-65. Stenographer, sec. Lincoln Nat. Life Co., Shreveport, 1965-66; sec. Baifield Industries, Shreveport, 1975-86; internat. art tchr., Huntsville, Ala., 1974—; v.p., co-owner Precision Splty. Co., Huntsville, 1966—, Mil. Aircraft, Huntsville, 1979—; pres., owner Wynnson Enterprises, Huntsville, 1983—; owner, artist, designer Wynnson Galleries Pvt. Collections, Florist, Meridianville, 1987; owner North Ala. Whole Flowers, 1988—. Mgr. basketball team Meridianville, 1985-86; founder Nat. Mus. Women in Arts; active Nat. Mus. Women in Arts. Mem. NAFE, Internat. Porcelain Guild, People to People, Porcelain Portrait Soc., United Artists Assn., Am. Soc. of Profl. and Executive Women Hist. Soc., Nat. Trust Hist. Preservation, Internat. Platform Assn., Met. Mus. Art, Smithsonian Assn., Assn. Community Artists, Rep. Senatorial Inner Circle, Ala. Sheriffs Assn., C. of C., Better Bus. Bur., Huntsville Art League and Mus. Assocs., Avocations: oil painting, antiques, handcrafts, gourmet cooking, horseback riding. Home: 156 Spencer Dr Meridianville AL 35759 Office: Precision Splty Corp 150 Wells Rd Meridianville AL 35759

OBERHOLTZER, JAY ROY, retail executive; b. Manheim, Pa., Sept. 9, 1930; s. Harry B. and Martha P. (Snagrey) O.; m. Rhoda Stauffer, May 3, 1952; children: Donovan, Gregory, Steven. Grad. high sch., Manheim. Treas., exec. Stauffer of Kissel Hill, Lititz, Pa., 1959—; pres. S.K.H. Mgmt. Co., Lititz, 1983—, chmn. bd. dirs.; mem. adv. bd. Commonwealth Nat. Bank, Lancaster, Pa., 1968, 85. Bd. dirs. Lititz Springs Park, 1968-80; treas. Heartsease Home Inc., N.Y.C.; treas., deacon Little Mennonite Ch., Lititz, Pa., 1978—. Republican. Home: 807 Lititz Park Lititz PA 17543 Office: SKH Mgmt Co PO Box 1500 Lititz PA 17543

OBERLIES, JOHN WILLIAM, utilities company executive; b. Rochester, N.Y., June 9, 1939; s. Hubert H. and Martha (Voght) O.; m. Mary Theresa Sundholm, Sept. 29, 1962; children: Katie, Daniel. BCE, Villanova U., 1961; MBA, U. Rochester, 1978. From surveyor to purchasing agt. Rochester Gas & Electric Co., 1959-79, gen. mgr., 1979-82, v.p., 1982-87, sr. v.p., 1988—. Trustee Aquinas Inst., Rochester; chmn. bd. Preferred Care, Inc., Rochester, 1986—; trustee Cath. Charities, Rochester, bd. dirs. 1984-85; mem. Diocesan Pastoral Council; bd. dirs. Rochester Area Found., 1984-85, Highland Hosp. Served with U.S. Army, 1961-62. Mem. Rochester C. of C. (chmn. polit. action com. 1987). Republican. Home: 242 Shoreham Dr Rochester NY 14618 Office: Rochester Gas & Electric Corp 89 East Ave Rochester NY 14649

OBERLIN, EARL CLIFFORD, III, securities brokerage company executive; b. Bryan, Ohio, Dec. 10, 1956; s. Earl Clifford II and Pauline Lois (Weber) O. BS in Acctg. and Fin., Miami U., Oxford, Ohio, 1979; MS, Cin. Coll., 1980. Cert. fin. planner, gen. securities prin., mcpl. bond prin., registered options prin. V.p. Mut. Funds Investors Corp., Bryan, 1977-80, treas., 1980-84; pres., chief exec. officer, vice chmn. Mut. Funds Investors Corp., Toledo (Ohio) and Bryan, 1984—; v.p. Merit Co., Bryan, 1979-87, pres., chief exec. officer, 1988—; v.p. Oberlin and Ford, Inc., Bryan, 1979-87, vice-chmn., 1979—, pres., chief exec. officer, 1988—; pres., chief exec. officer Quality Care Med. Equipment, Bryan, 1980-85; pres., chief exec. officer, vice chmn. MFI Advisors, Inc., Bryan and Toledo, 1987—. Bi-weekly columnist Personal Investing for Women, 1987. Bd. dirs. Jr. Achievement N.W. Ohio Inc., 1989—; pres., bd. dirs. Jr. Achievement, Bryan, 1989—. Jr. Achievement NW Ohio scholar, 1975. Mem. Inst. Cert. Fin. Planners, Internat. Assn. for Fin. Planning (broker/dealer com.), Toledo Club, Rotary, Eagles, Moose. Republican. Methodist. Home: 208 N Lynn St Bryan OH 43506 Office: MFI Investments Corp 126 N Main St Bryan OH 43506

OBERMANN, RICHARD MICHAEL, technology and policy analyst; b. May 21, 1949; s. Baird J. and Phyllis L. (Weber) O. BS of Engring. in Aerospace and Mech. Scis. cum laude, Princeton U., 1971, PhD in Engring., Aerospace and Mech. Scis., 1977; MS of Engring. in Astronautics and Aeros., Stanford U., 1972; postgrad., Va. Poly. Inst. and State U., Am. U. With MITRE Corp., McLean, Va., 1977-88, engr. transp. systems analysis, transp. energy analysis, telecommunications, project leader, mem. tech. staff in communications and system design; sr. staff officer aeros. and space engring. bd. NRC, Washington, 1988—, study dir. and analyst technol. and policy issues. Author techn. papers and presentations. Fellow Brit. Interplanetary Soc., AIAA (assoc.); mem. NAS (telecommunications adv. group U.S.-Indonesian Sci. and Tech. Symposium), IEEE, Internat. Inst. Communications, Japan-Am. Soc., Asia Soc., Am. Astronautical Soc., Nat. Space Club, Pacific Telecommunications Council.

OBERMAYER, HERMAN JOSEPH, newspaper publisher; b. Phila., Sept. 19, 1924; s. Leon J. and Julia (Sinsheimer) O.; student U. Geneva (Switzerland), 1946; A.B. cum laude, Dartmouth, 1948; m. Betty Nan Levy, June 28, 1955; children—Helen Julia, Veronica O. Atnipp, Adele Beatrice, Elizabeth Rose. Reporter, L.I. Daily Press, Jamaica, N.Y., 1950-53; classified advt. mgr. New Orleans Item, 1953-55; asst. to publisher Standard-Times, New Bedford, Mass., 1955-57; editor, pub. Long Branch (N.J.) Daily Record, 1957-71, No. Va. Sun, Arlington, 1963—; dir. Moleculon Research Corp., Cambridge, Mass.; Pulitzer Prize juror, 1983, 84. Bd. dirs. Monmouth Med. Center, 1958-71; mem. exec. council Monmouth Boy Scouts Am., 1958-71, mem. exec. com. Nat. Capital council, 1971-79, v.p., 1974-77; mem. Va. Legis. Alcohol Beverage Control Study Commn., 1972-74; bd. dirs. Monmouth Mus., 1968-71, No. Va. Jr. League, 1981-86; trustee Arlington (Va.) Bicentennial Commn., Am. Jewish Com., 1984—, v.p. Washington chpt. (Community Service Award 1986). Served with AUS, 1943-46; ETO. Rhineland Campaign; recipient Friends of Scouting Award, 1966, Silver Beaver, 1977. Mem. Am. Soc. Newspaper Editors, Am. Newspaper Pubs. Assn., So. Newspapers Pubs. Assn. (dir. 1981-84), White House Corrs. Assn., Soc. Profl. Journalists, Sigma Chi. Jewish. Rotarian. Clubs: Nat. Press (Washington); Washington Golf and Country (Arlington, Va.); Dartmouth (N.Y.C.). Contbr. column Editor's Viewpoint to No. Va. Sun; articles to Sat. Eve. Post, This Week, Japan Economic Jour., Pageant, Travel, Ebony, Mag. Digest, Everybody's Digest, others. Home: 4114 N Ridgeview Rd Arlington VA 22207 Office: No Va Sun 1227 N Ivy St Arlington VA 22201

OBERMAYER, MARY CULLUM, accountant, consultant; b. Jersey City, N.J., Oct. 10, 1955; d. Francis Joseph and Lois Ann (Peter) C.; m. William Charles Obermayer, June 22, 1985. BS, Boston Coll., 1977; MPA, NYU, 1981. CPA. Acctg. asst. Jennison Assocs., N.Y.C., 1977-78, statistical asst., 1978-79; acct. NYU Med. Ctr., N.Y.C., 1979-81, 1981-82; asst. acct. Arthur Andersen and Co., N.Y.C., 1982-85, sr. acct., 1985—. Vol. N.Y. Women's Homeless Shelter, N.Y.C., 1985—. Mem. Assn. Ind. CPA's, N.Y. State Soc. CPA's. Republican. Roman Catholic. Home: 400 E 85th Apt 21F New York NY 10028 Office: Arthur Andersen and Co 1345 Ave of the Americas New York NY 10105

OBERREIT, WALTER WILLIAM, lawyer; b. Paterson, N.J., Oct. 7, 1928; s. William and Gertrud (Limpert) O.; m. Anne-Marie Gohier, July 6, 1955; children: Stephan, Alexis, Jerome. BA, U. Mich., 1951; diploma, U. Paris Inst. Polit. Studies, 1955; JD, Yale U., 1958. Bar: N.Y. Assoc. Cleary, Gottlieb, Steen & Hamilton, N.Y.C., 1958-62, Paris, 1962-66; assoc. Cleary, Gottlieb, Steen & Hamilton, Brussels, 1966-67, ptnr., 1967—. Contbr. articles to profl. jours., chpts. to books. Lt. (j.g.) USN, 1953-55. Mem. ABA, Assn. of Bar of City of N.Y. (co-chmn. com. on relations with European Bars 1981—), Am. Arbitration Assn., Internat. Fiscal Assn., Ctr. European Policy Studies, Inst. Royal Relations Internat., Am. Soc. Internat. Law, Union Internat. Des Avocats. Clubs: Cercle Royal Gaulois, Cercle Nations, Am. Common Market (Brussels). Home: Ave Geo Bernier 7, 1050 Brussels Belgium Office: Cleary Gottlieb Steen Hamilton, rue de la Loi 23, 1040 Brussels Belgium

OBERST, ROBERT JOHN, financial analyst; b. Hackensack, N.J., Aug. 20, 1929; s. Bernard and Elsie (Schneider) O.; m. Ingrid Heilbut, Oct. 6, 1956; children: Jeanne, Robert John, Carl Edward. PhD in Fin. Mgmt., Columbia Pacific U., 1984. Cert. fin. planner, registered health underwriter. Spl. agt., mgr. Prudential Ins. Co. Am., Asbury Park, N.J., 1958-68; pres. Robert J. Oberst, Sr. & Assocs., Red Bank, N.J., 1969—; chmn. bd. regents Coll. Fin. Planning, Denver, 1978-82. Author newspaper column Fin. Planning, 1986-87; producer, host TV show Fin. Planning Today, 1983—; contbr. articles to profl. jours. Pres. Monmouth/Ocean Devel. Council, Manasquan, N.J., 1981-83; bd. dirs. Monmouth County Council Boy Scouts Am., Ocean, N.J., 1986-88; trustee Brookdale Coll. Found., Middletown, N.J., 1986—. Served with USN, 1946-50. Recipient Silver Gull Service award Monmouth/Ocean Devel. Council, 1984. Mem. Inst. Cert. Fin. Planners (Cert. Fin. Planner of Yr. 1979), Internat. Assn. Fin. Planning (bd. dirs. 1986—), Estate Planning Council (pres. 1971-72), Million Dollar Round Table (life), Nat. Assn. Life Underwriters, Red Bank C. of C. (bd. dirs.), Registry Fin. Planning Practitioners (chmn. 1987—), N.J. State Assn. Life Underwriters (state pres. 1969-70). Republican. Home: 15 Mulberry Ln Colts Neck NJ 07722 Office: Robert J Oberst Sr & Assocs 218 Broad St Red Bank NJ 07701

OBERT, CHARLES FRANK, banker; b. Cleve., Apr. 28, 1937; s. Carl William and Irene Frances (Urban) O.; m. Linda Marie Thoss, June 3, 1961; children—Lisa Marie, Charles David. Student, Ohio State U., 1955-57. With Ameritrust Corp., Cleve., 1958—, sr. v.p. affiliate bank div., 1975-80, sr. v.p. corp. service div., 1980-87, sr. v.p. br. adminstrn., 1987—. Mem. Solon (Ohio) Recreation Commn., 1978—, Solon Bd. Edn., 1986. Mem. Am. Inst. Banking, Am. Bankers Assn., Nat. Corporate Cash Mgmt. Assn., Ohio Bankers Assn., Bank Adminstrn. Inst., Internat. Assn. Laryngectomees, Cleve. Hearing and Speech Ctr., Greater Cleve. Growth Assn. Club: Cleve. Athletic. Home: 6498 Creekside Trail Solon OH 44139 Office: Ameritrust Corp 900 Euclid Ave Cleveland OH 44115

OBERT, PAUL RICHARD, manufacturing company executive, lawyer; b. Pitts., Aug. 24, 1928; s. Edgar F. and Elizabeth T. (Buchele) O. B.S., Georgetown U., 1950; J.D., U. Pitts., 1953. Bar: Pa. 1954, D.C. 1956, Ohio 1972, Ill. 1974, U.S. Supreme Ct. 1970. Sole practice Pitts., 1954-60; asst. counsel H.K. Porter Co., Inc., Pitts., 1960-62, sec., gen. counsel, 1962-71; sec., gen. counsel Addressograph-Multigraph Corp., Cleve., 1972-74; v.p. law Marshall Field & Co., Chgo., 1974-82, sec., 1976-82; v.p., gen. counsel, sec. CF Industries, Inc., Long Grove, Ill., 1982—, also officer, dir. various subs. Served to lt. col. USAF. Mem. ABA (corp. law dept. com.), Pa. Bar Assn., Allegheny County Bar Assn., Ill. Bar Assn., Chgo. Bar Assn., Am. Soc. Corp. Secs., Am. Retail Fedn. (dir. 1977-80), Georgetown U. Alumni Assn. (bd. govs.), Delta Theta Phi. Clubs: Pitts. Athletic Assn; Univ. (Chgo.). Office: CF Industries Inc Salem Lake Dr Long Grove IL 60047

OBERWAGER, WASHBURN SCOVILL, portfolio manager; b. N.Y.C., Feb. 6, 1947; s. Edwin Richard and Elizabeth (Scovill) O.; m. Susan Mathes, Nov. 15, 1980; children: Bradford Scovill, Jane Washburn, Andrew Whiting, Edward Hamilton Mathes. BSEE, Syracuse U., 1968; MBA, U. Pa., 1970. Founder, pres. Scovill Holdings Inc., Phila., 1970—, Scovill Group, Phila., 1983—; bd. dirs. Western Sky Industries Inc., Hayward, Calif. Trustee, dir. Internat. House of Phila., 1988. Lt. USAF, 1968-70. Mem. Young Pres.'s Orgn. (officer 1984-85, 86—). Home: 712 Righters Mill Rd Penn Valley PA 19072 Office: Scovill Holdings Inc 1700 Market St Philadelphia PA 19103

O'BLOCK, ROBERT PAUL, management consultant; b. Pitts., Mar. 9, 1943; s. Paul Joseph and Mary Elizabeth (Galicic) O'B.; m. Megan Marie. B.S.M.E., Purdue U., 1965; M.B.A. (Research fellow), Harvard U., 1967. Research and teaching fellow in fin., econs. and urban mgmt., Harvard U., 1967-70; assoc. in real estate mgmt. and fin. McKinsey & Co., Inc., N.Y.C., 1969-78, prin., 1979-84, dir., 1984— ; gen. and mng. partner Freeport Center, Clearfield, Utah, 1971—; vis. lectr. urban econs. Yale Law Sch., Princeton U.; cons. Mass., N.J. housing fin. agys., Rockefeller Assn., HUD, 1968-76; chmn. mgmt. com. Snowbird Lodge (Utah), 1974-86. Mem. nat. adv. bd. Snowbird Arts Inst., 1977-83; mem. budget com. N.Y. Public Library, 1977-79; mem. adv. bd. Internat. Tennis Hall of Fame, 1986—; mem. bd. overseers Boston Symphony Orch., 1988—. Roman Catholic. Clubs: River (N.Y.C.); Devon Yacht, Maidstone (East Hampton, N.Y.); Nat. Golf Links Am. (Southampton, N.Y.); Alta (Salt Lake City); Algonquin, Badmitton and Tennis (Boston); Ogden (Utah) Golf; The Country (Brookline, Mass.). Contbr. articles to profl. jours. Office: 277 Dartmouth St Boston MA 02116

O'BRIEN, CHARLES O., chemical company executive; b. Albany, N.Y., Dec. 11, 1929; s. John E. and Ann (Drew) O'B.; m. Maureen T. Kenny, June 2, 1951; children: Ellen, Kenneth, Charles, Christopher, Gail, Deirdre, Gregory. B.S. magna cum laude, Fordham U., 1955, LL.B. with honors, 1959. Atty. CIBA-GEIGY Corp., Ardsley, N.Y., 1962-66, v.p. mktg. agrl. div., 1966-70; pres. agr. div. CIBA-GEIGY Corp., Greensboro, N.C., 1970-82; pres. pharms. div. CIBA-GEIGY Corp., Summit, N.J., 1982-86; exec. v.p., chief operating officer CIBA-GEIGY Corp., Ardsley, 1986—; bd. dirs. Summit and Elizabeth Trust. Bd. dirs. United Way, Greensboro, N.C. Mem. Pharms. Mfrs. Assn. (bd. dirs. 1982), Greensboro C. of C. Roman Catholic. Office: CIBA-GEIGY Corp 444 Saw Mill River Rd Ardsley NY 10502

O'BRIEN, DANIEL WILLIAM, lawyer, corporation executive; b. St. Paul, Jan. 6, 1926; s. Daniel W. and Kathryn (Zenk) O'B.; m. Sarah Ward Stoltze, June 20, 1952; children: Bridget Ann, Daniel William, Kevin Charles, Timothy John. Student, U. Dubuque, 1943, Ill. State U., 1944; B.S.L., U. Minn., 1948, LL.B., 1949. Bar: Minn. 1949. Practice in St. Paul, 1950—; partner Randall, Smith & Blomquist, 1955-65; of counsel Doherty, Rumble & Butler, 1965—; pres. F.H. Stoltze Land & Lumber Co., 1964—, Maple Island, Inc., 1968—; dir. Villaume Industries, Inc. Served to ensign USNR, 1943-46. Mem. Minn., Ramsey County bar assns., World Bus. Council, Chief Execs. Orgn. Home: 685 Linwood Ave Saint Paul MN 55105 Office: 219 N Main St Stillwater MN 55082

O'BRIEN, G. DENNIS, information systems executive, economist; b. Yonkers, N.Y., Aug. 24, 1943; s. George Walter and Eleanor Cecilia (Arnold) O'B.; m. Mary Schneller, Sept. 12, 1970; children: Terrence Michael, Bridget Mary. BA, Manhattan Coll., 1966; MA, Fordham U., 1968; postgrad., SUNY, Albany, 1967-70. Economist Union Carbide Corp., N.Y.C., 1969-71; dir. indsl. econs. Data Resources, Inc., Lexington, Mass., 1971-73, v.p. mktg., 1973-76, sr. v.p. mktg. and prodn. devel., 1976-79; exec. v.p. Ziff Davis Pub. Co., N.Y.C., 1979-81; chmn. bd. O'Brien Browne Assocs., Boxford, Mass., 1981-83; exec. v.p. Office of Pres. Dun & Bradstreet Tech. Econ. Svcs., Cambridge, Mass., 1983-86; group v.p. mktg. and planning TRW Info. Systems Group, Long Beach, Calif., 1986—. Mem. Info. Industry Assn. (program chmn. spring conf. 1988, chmn. 1989), Omicron Delta Epsilon. Republican. Roman Catholic. Office: TRW Info Systems Group 200 Oceangate Suite 1200 Long Beach CA 90802

O'BRIEN, HELENE JEANNETTE, manufacturing company official; b. Rochester, N.H., July 29, 1946; d. Raymond Sylvio and Lucie E. (Fortier) LeHoullier; divorced; children: Christine Lynn, Lisa Marie, Patricia Anne. AA, No. Essex Community Coll., 1977; B in Gen. Studies, U. N.H., 1978. Ednl. asst. Hampton (N.H.) Acad., 1974-77; acting dean students N.H. Vocat.-Tech. Coll., Portsmouth, 1977-79; cons. Portsmouth, 1979-80; adminstrv. mgr. Kingston Warren Corp., Newfields, N.H., 1980-83; planning mgr. Wang Labs Inc., Tewksbury, Miss., 1983-86; materials/ops. specialist Pratt Whitney Co., United Techs., North Berwick, Maine and Columbus, Ga., 1986—; speaker profl. confs. and meetings. Author: Paraprofessionals in Education, 1977; contbr. articles to profl. jours. Mem. Am. Prodn. and Inventory Control Soc. (nat. instr.). Home: 13 Pine Meadows Dr Exeter NH 03833 Office: Pratt & Whitney Co Macon Rd Columbus GA 31908

O'BRIEN, JOHN, aerospace company executive. Grad., SUNY, 1951; MBA, MIT, 1966. With Grumman Corp., Bethpage, N.Y., 1954—; from flight test engr. to pres. Grumman Data Systems, 1958-86; pres., chief operating officer Grumman Corp., Bethpage, N.Y., 1986—, chmn., chief exec. officer, 1988—. Served to 1st lt. U.S. Army, 1951-54. Office: Grumman Corp 1111 Stewart Ave Bethpage NY 11714 *

O'BRIEN, JOHN EDWARD, market executive; b. St. Louis, May 30, 1929; s. Edward Joseph and Norma Mary (Yaw) O'B.; m. Marilyn Jean, Aug. 15, 1953; children—Mary Pat, Cathryn Jean, Lynn Marie. A.B., N. Notre Dame, 1952. Assoc. advt. mgr. paper div. Procter & Gamble, 1954-67; v.p., dir. Campbell-Mithun Advt. Agy., Chgo., 1967-72; v.p. mktg., dir. Calgon Consumer Products, Pitts., 1972-77; pres. NoNonsense Fashions, Inc., Greensboro, N.C., 1977-82, chmn. of bd. Rexall Corp., St. Louis, 1982-84; exec. v.p. J.H. Filbert Co., Balt., 1985; pres., owner Visu-Com, Balt., 1986—. Served with USNR, 1952-54. Republican. Roman Catholic.

O'BRIEN, JOHN M., savings and loan executive; b. Phila., Sept. 29, 1930; s. James W. and Julia A. (Doyle) O'B.; m. Mary Ellen Thompson, Oct. 8, 1955; children: James, Maureen, Michael, Denise, MaryEllen, Kevin. BS, Temple U., 1955. Corp. sec., mortgage officer North Phila. Savs. & Loan Assn., 1949-66; pres. Cen. Pa. Savs. Assn., Shamokin, 1966—, Cen. Pa. Fin. Corp., Shamokin, 1986—; past vice chmn. Fed. Home Loan Bank Pitts.; bd. dirs. Ctr. for Fin. Studies. Bd. dirs. Boy Scouts Am.; active United Way. Recipient cert. of appreciation Pa. Savs. and Loan League, 1974-75, Laredo Achievement award 1972; named Man of Yr., Phila. Soc. Savs. and Loan Mortgage Officers, 1972. Mem. U.S. League Savs. Instns. (bd. dirs., pres. 1973-74), Nat. Coun. Savs. Instns. (bd. dirs.), Pa. Assn. Savs. Instns. (legis. chmn.), Shamokin C. of C., Indian Hills Golf and Tennis Club, Susquehanna Valley Country Club, Moose, Elks, Kiwanis (past lt. gov., Outstanding Leader award). Democrat. Roman Catholic. Home: RD 2 Terrace at Orchard Shamokin PA 17872 Office: Cen Pa Savs Assn 100 W Independence St Shamokin PA 17872

O'BRIEN, JOHN RUSCH, health insurance marketing executive; b. Chgo., July 17, 1935; s. John Roger O'Brien and Helen M. (Rusch) Mallen; m. Marguerite J. Kopfer, Aug. 17, 1957; children: Sean, Erin, Kerry, Holly. BA in Bus., Muhlenburg Coll., 1957. Underwriter Am. Casualty Co., Reading, Pa., 1958-64; sales rep. Am. Casualty Co., Chgo., 1964-65; asst. v.p. mktg. Reliance Life Ins. Co., Schaumburg, Ill., 1965-67, v.p. sales, 1967-70; mktg. health officer Kemper Group, Long Grove, Ill., 1970-87; v.p. mktg. Nat. Casualty Co., St. Louis, 1987—. Mem. Nat. Assn. Health Underwriters (commr. register health underwriter 1982-86), Health Ins. Assn. Am. (nat. com. corp. ins. 1980-84), Am. Assn. Ins. Profl. Group Adminstrs., Chgo. Health Underwriters, Profl. Ins. Massmktg. Assn. Home: 2184 Wide Oak Ct Chesterfield MO 63017 Office: Nat Casualty Co One City Center Saint Louis MO 63101-1877

O'BRIEN, JOHN WILLIAM, JR., investment management company executive; b. Bronx, N.Y., Jan. 1, 1937; s. John William and Ruth Catherine (Timon) O'B.; B.S., MIT, 1958; M.S., UCLA, 1964; m. Jane Bower Nippert, Feb. 2, 1963; children—Christine, Andrea, Michael, John William III, Kevin Robert. Sr. asso. Planning Research Corp., Los Angeles, 1962-67; dir. fin. systems group Synergetic Scis., Inc., Tarzana, Calif., 1967-70; dir. analytical services div. James H. Oliphant & Co., Los Angeles, 1970-72; chmn. bd., chief exec. officer, pres. O'Brien Assos., Inc., Santa Monica, Calif., 1972-77; v.p. A.G. Becker Inc., 1977-81; chmn., chief exec. officer Leland O'Brien Rubinstein Assos., 1981—. Served to 1st lt. USAF, 1958-62. Recipient Graham and Dodd award Fin. Analysts Fedn., 1970. Mem. Delta Upsilon. Home: Box 3159 Blue Jay CA 92317 Office: Leland O'Brien Rubenstein Assocs 523 W 6th St Suite 220 Los Angeles CA 90014

O'BRIEN, JOSEPH PATRICK, JR., turbine manufacturing company executive; b. Haverhill, Mass., May 25, 1940; s. Joseph P. and Helen M. (Atwood) O'B.; m. Gail E. Harris, May 19, 1962 (div. Apr. 1981); children: Michael, Pamela, Matthew, Amy; m. Phyllis L. Corso, July 12, 1981; children: Alicia, Jack. B.S.B.A., Northeastern U., Boston, 1963. C.P.A., N.J. Auditor Ernst & Ernst, N.Y.C., 1962-65; acctg. mgr. Austenal div. Howmet Corp., Dover, N.J., 1965-68, controller Alloy div., 1969-71, budget dir., 1972-75; controller Pechiney Ugine Kuhlmann Co., Greenwich, 1976-80; v.p. fin. Howmet Corp., Greenwich, 1980—. Mem. Am. Isnt. C.P.A.'s, Nat. Assn. Accts., Fin. Execs. Inst., Nat. Assn. Bus. Economists. Home: 66

Coachlamp Lane Stamford CT 06902 Office: Howmet Corp 475 Steamboat Rd Greenwich CT 06830

O'BRIEN, KENNETH ROBERT, life insurance company executive; b. Bklyn., June 18, 1937; s. Emmett Robert and Anna (Kelly) O'B.; m. Eileen M. Halligan, July 1, 1961; children: Joan Marie, Margaret Mary, Kathy Ann. B.S. in Bus. Adminstrn, Coll. Holy Cross, Worcester, Mass., 1959. With N.Y. Life Ins. Co., N.Y.C., 1962—; 2d v.p. N.Y. Life Ins. Co., 1973-77, v.p. investments, 1977-82, sr. v.p. pensions, 1982-87, sr. v.p. individual products, 1987—. Active Cath. Youth Orgn. Served to 1st lt. USAF, 1959-62. Mem. Nat. Consumer Fin. Assn., Fin. Forum, N.Y. Soc. Security Analysts. Home: 165 E Loines Ave Merrick NY 11566 Office: NY Life Ins Co 51 Madison Ave New York NY 10010

O'BRIEN, MARY DEVON, communications executive, consultant; b. Buenos Aires, Argentina, Feb. 13, 1944; came to U.S., 1949, naturalized, 1962; d. George Earle and Margaret Frances (Richards) Owen; m. Gordon Covert O'Brien, Feb. 16, 1962 (div. Aug. 1982); children: Christopher Covert, Devon Elizabeth; m. Christopher Gerard Smith, May 28, 1983. BS, Rutgers U., 1975, MBA, 1976. Controller manpower Def. Communications div. ITT, Nutley, N.J., 1977-80, adminstr. program, 1977-78, mgr. cost, schedule control, 1978-79, voice processing project, 1979-80; mgr. project Avionics div. ITT, Nutley, 1980-81, sr. mgr. projects, 1981—; cons. strategic planning, N.J., 1983—; lectr. in field. Author: Pace: System Manual, 1979, Voices, 1982; contbr. articles to profl. jours. Chmn. Citizens Budget Adv. Com., Maplewood, N.J., 1984-87, chmn. recreation, library, pub. services, 1982-83, chmn. pub. safety, emergency services, 1983-84, chmn. schs. and edn., 1984-85; bd. dirs., officer Civic Assn., Maplewood, 1984—; bd. trustees United Way Essex and West Hudson Community Svc. Council, 1988—; first v.p. Maplewood Civic Assn., 1987-89, pres., 1989—; chmn. Maple Leaf Svc. award Com., 1987-89, Community Svc. Council of Oranges and Maplewood Homelessness, Affordable Housing, Shelter Com. 1988—; nat. chmn. Project Mgmt. Jour. Survey; mem. Maplewood Zoning Bd., 1983—; officer, mem. exec. bd. N.J. Project Mgmt. Inst., 1985—, pres., 1987-88.; chmn. bd. dirs. Performance Mgmt. Assn. Charter Com.; chmn. region III Internat. Project Mgmt. Inst. Jour. and Membership survey, 1986-87, mktg. com., 1986—, long range planning and steering com., 1987—; bd. dirs. C&P Interaction Com., 1986—, Internat. Project Mgmt. Inst.; adv. bd. Project Mgmt. Jour., 1987—, N.J. PMI Ednl., 1987—; mem. MCA/N.J. Blood Bank Drive; trustee community svc. council and edn. program United Way Essex and West Hudson, 1988—;v.p. Internat. Project Mgmt. Inst. Region II.. Recipient spl. commendation for community svc. Twp. Maplewood, 1987, Anti-Shoplifting Program award Distributive Edn. Club Am., 1981, N.J. Fedn. of Women's Clubs, 1981, 82, Retail Mchts. Assn., 1981, 82; Commendation and Merit awards Air Force Inst. Tech., 1981; Pres.'s Safety award ITT, 1983; State award N.J. Fedn. of Women's Clubs Garden Show, 1982, Outstanding Pres. award Internat. Project Mgmt. Inst., 1988, Outstanding Svc. and Contbrn. award 1986-87; Cert. Spl. Merit award N.J. Fedn. of Women's Clubs, 1982. Mem. Internat. Platform Speakers Assn., Grand Jury Assn., Telecommunications Group and Aerospace Industries Assn., Women's Career Network Assn., Nat. Security Indsl. Assn., Assn. for Info. and Image Mgmt., ITT Mgmt. Assn., Nat. Assn. Female Execs., Rutger's Grad. Sch. Bus. Mgmt. Alumni Assn., LWV, Maplewood Women's Evening Membership Div. (pres. 1980-82). Home: 594 Valley St Maplewood NJ 07040 Office: ITT Avionics 417 River Rd Nutley NJ 07110

O'BRIEN, PAUL CHARLES, telephone company executive; b. N.Y.C., May 12, 1939; s. Charles Edward and Clare Mary (Becker) O'B.; m. Marie P. Moane, Dec. 30, 1961; children: Carolyn M., Deirdre M., Barbara M., Erin M. BEE, Manhattan Coll., 1960; MBA, NYU, 1968. Supervising engr. N.Y. Telephone Co., N.Y.C., 1964-67, div. engr., 1967-72, gen. staff supr., 1972-75, gen. planning engr., 1975-77, asst. v.p., 1977-83, pres. N.Y. New Eng. Exchange Enterprises, 1973-85, v.p. customer service, 1985-86; exec. v.p., chief exec. officer New Eng. Telephone Co., Boston, 1987-88, pres., chief exec. officer, 1988—; bd. dirs. N.Y. New Eng. Exchange Systems Mktg. Co., N.Y.C., N.Y. New Eng. Exhange Info. Resources Co., Lynn, Mass., N.Y. New Eng. Exchange Service Co., White Plains, N.Y. Bd. dirs. YMCA, N.Y.C., 1986, Greater Boston Adult Literacy Fund, 1988, Jobs for Mass., Boston, 1988; assoc. chmn. United Way Ea. New Eng., 1988. Capt. USAF, 1961-64. Mem. AFCA, IEEE. Roman Catholic. Office: New Eng Tel & Tel Co 185 Franklin St Boston MA 02107

O'BRIEN, RAYMOND FRANCIS, transportation executive; b. Atchison, Kans., May 31, 1922; s. James C. and Anna M. (Wagner) O'B.; m. Mary Ann Baugher, Sept. 3, 1947; children: James B., William T., Kathleen A., Christopher R. B.S. in Bus. Adminstrn, U. Mo., 1948; grad., Advanced Mgmt. Program, Harvard, 1966. Accountant-auditor Peat, Marwick, Mitchell & Co., Kansas City, Mo., 1948-52; controller-treas. Riss & Co., Kansas City, Mo., 1952-58; regional controller Consol. Freightways Corp. of Del., Indpls., also, Akron, Ohio, 1958-61; with Consol. Freightways, Inc., San Francisco, 1961—; controller-treas. Consol. Freightways, Inc., 1962-63, v.p., treas., 1963-67, v.p. finance, 1967-69, exec. v.p., 1969-75, pres., 1975—, chief exec., 1977, chmn., chief exec. officer, 1979, also dir., pres. motor carrier subs., 1973-75; dir. Consol. Freightways Corp. of Del., CF Data Services, Inc., CF Land Services, Inc., Canadian Freightways Ltd., Canadian Freightways Eastern Ltd., CF Air Freight Inc., Transam. Corp., Union Bank, Watkins-Johnson, Inc., CF Ocean Services; past chmn., now dir. Western Hwy. Inst. Former mem. bus. adv. bd. Northwestern U., U. Calif., Berkeley; chmn. bd. trustees St. Mary's Coll.; bd. dirs. Charles Armstrong Sch. Served to 1st lt. USAAF, 1942-45. Mem. Am. Trucking Assn. Clubs: Pacific Union, World Trade, Commonwealth (San Francisco); Palo Alto Hills Golf and Country, Burning Tree Country, Menlo Country, Congressional Country, Firestone Country. Home: 26347 Esperanza Dr Los Altos Hills CA 94022 Office: Consol Freightways Inc PO Box 10340 Palo Alto CA 94303

O'BRIEN, RAYMOND VINCENT, JR., banker; b. Bronx, N.Y., Sept. 23, 1927; s. Raymond Vincent and Blanche (Harper) O'B.; m. Theresa Sweeney, Mar. 29, 1952 (dec. June 15, 1981); children: Susan, Raymond, Christopher, Sean, Carol, Nancy.; m. Ellen Boyle, July 24, 1982. A.B., Fordham U., 1951, J.D., 1958; postgrad., Advanced Mgmt. Program, Harvard U., 1969. With Chase Manhattan Bank (N.A.), N.Y.C., 1953-74; chmn., chief exec. officer Emigrant Savs. Bank, N.Y.C.; dir. Todd Shipyards Corp., Internat. Shipholding Corp., Savs. Bank Trust Co., Community Preservation Corp. Trustee Fordham U.; chmn. bd. trustees Regis High Sch. Served with AUS, 1946-47, 51-53. Mem. ABA, N.Y. State Bar Assn., Guild Catholic Lawyers. Republican. Roman Catholic. Clubs: Sky, Economic, Madison Square Garden (N.Y.C.); Navesink Country (Middletown, N.J.); Sawgrass Country (Ponte Vedra, Fla.). Lodges: Knights of Malta, Friendly Sons St. Patrick. Home: 4 Mt Vernon Ct Colts Neck NJ 07722 Office: Emigrant Savs Bank 5 E 42nd St New York NY 10017

O'BRIEN, RICHARD FRANCIS, advertising agency executive; b. Everett, Mass., Aug. 3, 1942; s. James Raymond and Gertrude Lucille O'B.; m. Clare Lynch, Apr. 7, 1973; children: Catherine Lynch, Miles Edward. A.B. magna cum laude, Boston Coll., 1964; M.A., Ind. U., 1965; M.B.A., Columbia U., 1967. With Grey Advt. Inc., N.Y.C., 1967-83; v.p., mgmt. supr. Grey Advt. Inc., 1973-77, sr. v.p., mgmt. rep., 1977-80, exec. v.p., mgmt. rep., 1980-83; exec. v.p., mgmt. dir. Dancer Fitzgerald Sample, Inc. (name changed to Saatchi & Saatchi Advt.), N.Y.C., 1983-88; vice chmn. Dancer Fitzgerald Sample, Inc. (became Saatchi & Saatchi Advt.), N.Y.C., 1988—. Bd. dirs. Spl. Olympics, Inc., 1983—. Office: Saatchi & Saatchi Advt 375 Hudson St New York NY 10014

O'BRIEN, RICHARD STEPHEN, assistant treasurer; b. Chgo., Apr. 29, 1949; s. Stephen Richard and Alberta (Ambrzas) O'Br. BS, No. Ill. U., 1971; MBA, Loyola U., 1975. Staff acct. Brunswick Corp., Skokie, Ill., 1971-72, acct. cash control, 1972-73, acct. fin. analysis, 1973-75, regional mgr. fin. services, 1975-79, mgr. fin. planning, 1979-82, dir. corp. fin., 1982-83, asst. treas., 1983—. Mem. Nat. Assn. Corp. Treas. (bd. dirs. 1988). Home: 1359 S Highland Arlington Heights IL 60005 Office: Brunswick Corp One Brunswick Pla Skokie IL 60077

O'BRIEN, ROBERT DAVID, finance company executive; b. Salem, Mass., Apr. 20, 1958; s. David Gerard and Alice Barbara (Jagiello) O'B. BBA, U. Wis., 1980. Div. mgr. Coll. Craft Enterprises, Wheaton, Ill., 1977-83; account exec. Blunt, Ellis & Loewi Inc., Oak Brook, Ill., 1983-84; v.p. Smith, Barney, Harris, Upham & Co., Inc., Oak Brook, 1984—. Mem. Ill. Govt. Fin. Office Assn. Republican. Roman Catholic. Office: Smith Barney Harris Upham & Co Inc One Tower Ln Suite 2200 Oakbrook Terrace IL 60181

O'BRIEN, ROBERT THOMAS, investment executive; b. Phila., Oct. 7, 1941; s. James Francis Sr. and Mildred Anita (Gomez); m. Aurora Carol Forsthoffer, Nov. 7, 1964; 1 child, Michael Joseph. Cert., N.Y. Inst. Fin., 1963; BS, St. Joseph's U., 1971. Securities trader Brown Bros. Harriman, Phila., 1964-69, portfolio mgr., 1969-77, investment officer, 1977-80, asst. mgr., investment adv., 1980-83; v.p. Newbold's Asset Mgmt., Phila., 1983-85, sr. v.p., 1985—. Bd. dirs. Cath. Philopatrian Literary Inst., 1973-76. Served with USAF and Pa. Air N.G., 1960-67, Vietnam. Mem. Phila. Securities Assn., Air Force Assn. Republican. Roman Catholic. Clubs: Racquet of Phila., Sailing Assn. (commodore 1980-82); Lewes Yacht, Miles River Yacht, Aronimink Golf, Idle Hour Tennis. Home: 665 Dodds Ln Gladwyne PA 19035 Office: Newbolds Asset Mgmt Inc 937 Hverford Rd Bryn Mawr PA 19102

O'BRIEN, THOMAS HENRY, bank holding company executive; b. Pitts., Jan. 16, 1937; s. J. Vick and Georgia (Bower) O'B.; m. Maureen Sheedy; children—Thomas Henry, Lauren C., Timothy B. BS in Commerce, U. Notre Dame, 1958; MBA, Harvard U., 1962. With Pitts. Nat. Bank, 1962—, v.p., 1967-73, sr. v.p., 1973-80, exec. v.p., 1980-83, vice chmn., 1983-84; pres., bd. dirs., chief exec. officer PNC Fin. Corp., 1984—; also chmn. PNC Fin. Corp., Pitts., 1988—; bd. dirs. Hilb, Rogal & Hamilton Co., Aristech Chem. Corp., Bell Atlantic Corp., Pvt. Export Funding Corp., Fed. Adv. Council, Internat. Monetary Conf. Bd. dirs. United Way Southwest Pa., Pitts. Symphony Soc., Children's Hosp., Pitts., Allegheny Trails council Boy Scouts Am., Pitts. Allegheny Conf. Community Devel., U. Pitts., World Affairs Council Pitts., Carnegie Inst. Res. City Bankers. Named Man of Yr. in fin. Vectors, Pitts., 1985. Mem. Assn. Res. City Bankers, Pa. Bankers Assn. Roman Catholic. Clubs: Duquesne, Allegheny (bd. dirs.), Pitts. Field, Rolling Rock, Laurel Valley Golf. Office: PNC Fin Corp 5th Ave & Wood St Pittsburgh PA 15222

O'BRIEN, THOMAS HENRY, JR., banker; b. Middletown, Conn., Feb. 18, 1943; s. Thomas Henry and Maryanne (Kachinski) O'B.; m. Monica Mayer, July 26, 1969 (div. Oct. 1983); children: Kelly Ann, Timothy William; m. Sally May Saabye, June 27, 1987. BS in Edn., Villanova U., 1965. V.p., team leader, account officer corp. banking Chem. Bank, N.Y.C., 1979-80, v.p., chief credit officer fin. inst. group, 1980-83, sr. v.p., group head worldwide commodities, agribusiness and ship fin., 1983-86, mng. dir., chief credit officer capital markets, 1986-87, sr. v.p., sr. credit policy officer consumer banking group, 1987—. Contbr. to profl. jour. Chmn. Cranford (N.J.) Planning Bd., 1980-82, Downtown Mgmt. Corp., Cranford, 1985-87; trustee Cath. Community Services, Newark, 1984-87. 1st lt. N.Y. Nat. Guard, 1966-74. Recipient Community Service award C. of C., Cranford, 1987. Mem. Robert Morris Assocs.

O'BRIEN, WILLIAM P., real estate developer; b. Dallas, Dec. 20, 1946; s. Robert David O'Brien and Frances (Buster) Gould. BArch., U. Tex.-Arlington, 1970; MArch., U. Pa., 1977, M. in City Planning, 1977. Dir. devel. Good Fin. Corp., Dallas, 1971-73; real estate cons., Dallas, 1974-75; sr. project mgr. Trammel Crow Co., Chgo., 1977-81; v.p., regional mgr. Coldwell Banker, Chgo., 1981-85; pres. Rescorp Devel. Co., Chgo., 1985-86; real estate cons., Chgo., 1987-88, pres. Briar Investment Group, Chgo., 1989—. Mem. Nat. Assn. Indsl. and Office Parks, Am. Planning Assn., Nat. Realty Com., Urban Land Inst., Alpha Rho Chi (Nat. Gold medal 1970).

OCCHIPINTI, VINCENT MICHAEL, electronics and computer company executive; b. Cheyenne, Wyo., Jan. 4, 1940; s. Saverio and Lillian R. Occhipinti; m. Karen Hart Ganahl, Nov. 28, 1981; children: Mari, Cynthia, John, Michael. Student, U. Calif.-Berkeley, 1961-62; BA in Econs. with honors, Stanford U., 1963. With various CPA firms Oakland, Calif., 1958-63; gen. agt. Fidelity Union Life Ins. Co., Oakland, Calif., 1963-65; product dir. mgr. Levi Strauss Co., San Francisco, 1965-68; v.p. mktg. Mobility Systems Inc., Santa Clara, Calif., 1968-74; prin. founder, pres., chief exec. officer Logisticon Inc., Sunnyvale, Calif., 1974-80; gen. ptnr. Fund & Woodside (Calif.) II, Mgmt. Corp., 1980—; pres., chief exec. officer Woodside Village Sch., 1980—; chmn. bd. dirs. Alis Tech.; bd. dirs. Sundale Beverages, Veneer Tech., Telassist. Contbr. articles to profl. jours. Trustee, Woodside Village Sch., 1973-79. Mem. Am. Electronics Assn., Stanford Alumni Assn. Home and Office: 850 Woodside Dr Woodside CA 94062

OCCHIUZZO, LUCIA RAJSZEL, restaurant executive; b. Casablanca, Morocco, Nov. 5, 1951; came to U.S., 1958, naturalized, 1973; d. Tadeusz Joseph and Irmina Elizabeth (Wacholska) Rajszel; m. Joel Occhiuzzo, Dec. 9, 1976. BA, Montclair U., 1974. Owner, pres. Mr. O's, Dallas, 1977-83, L n J's Restaurant & Club, Richardson, Tex., 1984—. Guest star Sta. Telecable TV, 1985; L n J's Restaurant subject of TV program, 1986; contbr. articles to newspapers. Recipient Restaurant of Month award Dallas Times Herald, 1978. Mem. Richardson C. of C., ASCAP. Republican. Roman Catholic. Avocations: music, photography, writing. Home: 156 Hidden Cir Richardson TX 75080 Office: L 'n J's Restaurant & Club 2475 Promenade Ctr Richardson TX 75080

OCHOA MEJIA, JOSE, banker; b. Cali, Colombia, Dec. 24, 1940; s. Jose and Victoria (Mejia) O.; B.Mech. Engr. (Dean's scholar), Cornell U., 1965; M.B.A., 1967; m. Jennifer C. Lowe, Aug. 4, 1973; children—Alexis David, Lucas Sebastian. Fin. analyst Celanese Corp., N.Y.C., 1967-69; project mgr. Internat. Life Ins. Co. Ltd., London, 1969-73; mgr. Rothschild Intercontinental Bank Ltd., London, 1973-77; sr. mgr. Libra Bank Ltd., London, 1977; asst. gen. mng. Scandinavian Bank, London, 1978-80, sr. v.p., rep., N.Y.C., 1980-83, gen. mgr., London, 84; mng. dir. Corporacion Privada de Inversiones de Centroamerica S.A., San Jose, Costa Rica, 1985; v.p. Citibank N.A., London, 1986—. Mem. Cornell U. Council. Clubs: Bentley Drivers. Home: Rectory Cottage, Woodmancote, Henfield BN5 9SR, England Office: Citibank NA, 41 Berkeley Sq, London WIX 6NA, England

OCHSENREITER, DONALD CHRISTOPHER, management consultant, investment banker; b. Walterboro, S.C., Oct. 7, 1957; s. Donald Clarence and Martha (Smoak) O.; m. Kelly Leigh Wood, May 25, 1985; 1 child, Lindsey Leigh. BA, U. N.C., 1979, BS, 1979; MBA, U. Tex., 1981. Cons. McKinsey & Co., Inc., Dallas, 1980-83, Houston, 1983-85; dir. market devel. Fleming Cos., Inc., Oklahoma City, 1985-87; v.p. Chandler, Leigh & Co., Atlanta, 1987—; assoc. instr. U. Tex., Austin, 1979-81, So. Meth. U., U. Tex., North Tex. State U., Dallas, 1984-85. Mem. Am. Inst. Cons., Planning Forum, U. N.C. Alumni Assn. (pres. Oklahoma City chpt. 1985-87), Grad. Bus. Sch. Club of Austin, Druid Hills Golf Club (Atlanta), Club of Buckhead, Rotary, Phi Beta Kappa, Phi Eta Sigma. Republican. Methodist. Home: 4505 Hampton Woods Dr Marietta GA 30068

OCKERBLOOM, RICHARD C., newspaper executive; b. Medford, Mass., Dec. 19, 1929; s. Carl F. and Helen C. (Haraden) O.; m. Anne Joan Torpey, Sept. 17, 1955; children: Catherine, Carl, Gail, Mark, John, Peter. B.S. in Bus. Adminstrn, Northeastern U., 1952. With Boston Globe, 1948—, salesman, 1955-63, asst. nat. advt. mgr., 1963-70, nat. advt. mgr., 1970-72, asst. advt. dir., 1972-73, advt. dir., 1973-77, v.p. mktg. and sales, 1977-81, exec. v.p., 1981—, gen. mgr., chief operating officer, 1984-86, pres., chief operating officer, 1986—; dir. Met. Sunday Newspapers. Vice-chmn. Greater Boston Conv. and Visitors Bur.; bd. overseers Northeastern U.; bd. dirs. Winchester Hosp., Northeastern U., United Way Mass. Bay. Served with U.S. Army, 1952-54, Europe. Mem. Advt. Club Greater Boston (dir.), Nat. Assn. Coop. Edn. (trustee 1985—). Clubs: Algonquin, Winchester Country. Home: 40 Mayflower Rd Winchester MA 01890 Office: Globe Newspaper Co 135 Morrissey Blvd Boston MA 02107

O'CONNELL, BRIAN CHARLES, financial planner; b. Bitburg (USAFB), Fed. Republic of Germany, Jan. 6, 1958; s. Ronald L. and Patirica L. (Carson) O'C. AA, St. Petersburg Jr. Coll., 1978; BS, Fla. State U., 1980. Cert. fin. planner; lic. realtor, Fla. Account exec. Stockton, Whatley, Davin & Co., Tampa, 1980-82, Raymond James & Assocs., Crystal River, Fla., 1982-84; co-owner O'Connell Fin., Crystal River, 1984—. Mem. Inst. Cert. Fin. Planners, Internat. Assn. Fin. Planners, Suncoast Better Bus. Assn., Crystal River C. of C., Citrus County Bd. Realtors, Kiwanias (pres. 1985, chartered). Roman Catholic. Home and Office: O'Connel Fin 547 W Ft Island Trail Crystal River FL 32629

O'CONNELL, CARMELA DIGRISTINA, executive, consultant; b. Johnstown, Pa., Nov. 8, 1925; d. Salvatore and Josephine (Riggio) Digristina; m. Maurice F. O'Connell, Sept. 21, 1974 (dec. Feb. 1984); children: Geraldine, John, Bernard. Diploma, Eastern Secretarial Sch., N.Y.C., Sch. Interior Design, N.Y.C. From typist to sec.-treas. Philip P. Masterson Co., N.Y.C., 1942-72; exec. v.p., bd. dirs. Masterson & O'Connell Inc., N.Y.C., 1972-80, cons., 1981—; founder, pres. N.Y. Appraisal Corp., N.Y.C., 1971-80; co-founder, pres. Park Ave. Appraisal, N.Y.C., 1981—. Mem. N.Y. Rep. Com., 1974—, Met. Opera Guild, N.Y.C., 1986; chmn. Ch. of Our Saviour, N.Y.C., 1986. Recipient Amita award for Bus. Woman of Yr., 1977. Mem. Nat. Fedn. Bus. and Profl. Women's Clubs Inc. (2d v.p. 1964, 1st v.p. 1966). Roman Catholic. Home: 80 Park Ave New York NY 10016

O'CONNELL, DANIEL STEPHEN, banker, private investor; b. N.Y.C., Feb. 7, 1954; s. Daniel R. and Josephine (Morris) O'C.; m. Gloria Perri, Nov. 26, 1976; children: Carly, Evan, Jared. AB, Brown U., 1976; M in Pub. and Pvt. Mgmt., Yale U., 1980. Assoc. Dillon, Read & Co., Inc., N.Y.C., 1980-82; assoc. The First Boston Corp., N.Y.C., 1982-84, v.p., 1984-87, pres., 1986-88, mng. dir., 1987-88; also bd. dirs. First Boston LBO, Inc., N.Y.C.; founding ptnr., pres. Vestar Capital Ptnrs., Inc., N.Y.C., 1988—; bd. dirs. The Chart House, Solana Beach, Calif., First Brands Corp., Danbury, Conn., Dunlop Tire Corp., Buffalo, Interstate Bakeries, Kansas City, Mo., Big V Supermarkets, Inc., Florida, N.Y., Super D Drugs, Inc., Memphis, Celestial Seasonings, Inc., Boulder, Colo. Mem. Yale Univ. Club. Roman Catholic. Club: Field (Greenwich, Conn.). Home: 4 Meadow Rd Riverside CT 06878 Office: Vestar Capital Ptnrs Inc 140 E 45th St 35th Fl New York NY 10017

O'CONNELL, DANIEL WALTER, investment company executive; b. Chgo., July 31, 1946; s. David Walter and Gertrude Ann (Schmidt) O'C.; m. Paula Marie Williams, Sept. 26, 1981. BS in Chemistry with high honors, U. Ill., 1968; MBA, Harvard U., 1974; MSA with distinction, DePaul U., Chgo., 1983. Research chemist U.S. Gypsum, Des Plaines, Ill., 1968-69; fin. analyst 1st Chgo. Corp., 1974-75, ltd. market advisor, trust officer, asst. v.p., 1975-79, v.p., mgr. instl. venture capital fund, 1979-84; mng. ptnr. Alpha Capital Venture Ptnrs., Chgo., 1984—; advisor R.W. Allsop & Assocs., Cedar Rapids, 1981—; bd. dirs. Channel One Communications, Clayton, Mo., CarCare Enterprises, Chgo. Served as lt. (j.g.) USN, 1969-72. Mem. Nat. Assn. Small Bus. Investment Cos., Chgo. High Tech. Assn. Club: Harvard U. Bus. Sch. Chgo. (v.p. 1979-83). Office: 3 First Nat Plaza Suite 1400 Chicago IL 60670

O'CONNELL, DAVID H., marketing professional; b. Marlboro, Mass., July 9, 1936; s. Charles J. and Dorothy F. (Keaney) O'C.; m. Carol M. Van Pietersom, June 24, 1961; children: Daniel C., Jody A., Kathleen M. BS, Holy Cross Coll., 1958. With Tecumseh Products Co., Grafton, Wis., 1960—; v.p. mktg. and sales Tecumseh Products Co., Grafton, 1986—. Lt. j.g. U.S. Navy, 1958-60. Office: Tecumseh Products Co 900 North St Grafton WI 53024

O'CONNELL, FRANCIS V(INCENT), textile printing company executive; b. Norwich, Conn., July 8, 1903; s. Thomas Francis and Isabelle (Gelino) O.'C.; LL.B., Blackstone Coll. Law, 1932, J.D., 1940, LL.M., 1942; m. Marie Louise Lemoine, Nov. 7, 1940. Textile screen printer U.S. Finishing Co. Norwich, 1921-30; foreman Ahern Textile Print Co., Norwich, 1930-36; pres., owner Hand Craft Textile Print Co., Plainfield, Conn., 1936—. Roman Catholic. Home: 25 14th St Norwich CT 06360 Office: Bishop's Crossing Plainfield CT 06374

O'CONNELL, FRANK JOSEPH, apparel company executive; b. Ithaca, N.Y., May 11, 1943; s. Daniel Michael and Virginia (Davidson) O'C.; m. Gail Young, 1961 (div. 1971); children: Lauren Beth, Kimberly; m. Barbara Jean Smith, Dec. 6, 1974; children: Shaun, Thomas. BS in Econs., Cornell U., 1965, MBA, 1966. Product mgr. Carnation Co., Los Angeles, 1966-71, Hunt-Wesson Foods, Fullerton, Calif., 1971-72; mktg. mgr. Archon Pure Products Co., Beverly Hills, Calif., 1972-73; dir. mktg. Oroweat Foods Co. div. Continental Grain Corp., San Francisco, 1973-80; gen. mgr., v.p. mktg. Arnold Baking Co. Seattle, Denver and Greenwich, Conn., 1980; sr. v.p. sales and mtkg. Mattel Toys, Hawthorne, Calif., 1980-82; pres., chief exec. officer Fox Video Games, San Jose, Calif., 1982-84, Optionware, Inc., Bloomfield, Conn., 1984-85, HBO Video, N.Y.C., 1986-88; pres. Reebok Brands and Apparel, Canton, Mass., 1988—. Mem. com. United Jewish Appeal, N.Y.C., 1986-87, People for the American Way, 1986-87. Roman Catholic. Home: 815 Park Ave New York NY 10021 Office: Reebok 150 Royall St Canton MA 02021

O'CONNELL, HENRY FRANCIS, lawyer; b. Winthrop, Mass., Jan. 4, 1922; s. Henry F. and Anna (Cunning) O'C. B.A., Boston Coll., 1943, J.D., 1948. Bar: Mass. 1948, U.S. Supreme Ct. 1956. House counsel electronics div. Am. Machine & Foundry Co., Boston, 1951-54; sole practice, Boston, 1954-60; assoc. Glynn & Dempsey, Boston, 1960-70, Avery, Dooley, Post & Avery, 1970-88; asst. atty. gen. mcpls. affairs State of Mass., 1969-88. Mem. Winthrop Bd. Selectmen, 1958-64, 68-72, chmn. 1960-61, 68-69, 71-72. Served to lt. USCGR, World War II. Mem. Mass. Bar Assn., Nat. Boating Fedn. (past pres.), Mass. Selectmen's Assn., Mass. Bay Yachts Clubs Assn. (past commodore). Home: 20 Belcher St Winthrop MA 02152

O'CONNELL, JEANNE, financial planner, insurance broker; b. Stoneham, Mass., Dec. 9, 1951; d. Kenneth Edward and Frances Evelyn (Matulewicz) O'C. Student U. Oreg., 1971-72; BFA cum laude, U. Mass.-Amherst, 1974; U. Calif.-Sacramento, summer 1973; postgrad. Northeastern U., 1975; Suffolk U., MBA, 1984. CPCU, CLU, Chartered fin. cons.; assoc. in underwriting. Ins. clk. S.B. Swaim & Co., Boston, 1969-72, Hollis Perrin & Co., Boston, 1972; underwriting asst. Pub. Service Mut. Ins. Co., Newton, Mass., 1974-77; personal lines analyst Comml. Union Ins. Co., Boston, 1977-80, sr. personal lines analyst, 1980-83, tech. specialist, 1983-88; pvt. practice fin. cons., brokerage Boston, 1988—; lic. ins. agt. Mut. of N.Y.; registered rep. Mony Securities; ind. tax preparer; founder, dir. Red Dragon Arts Coop., Boston, 1983; potter, artist Radcliffe Pottery Studio, Boston, 1980-85. Mem. exec. student adv. bd. Suffolk U., 1982-83, student liason mem. between Exec. MBA Program and regular MBA Program and dean's adv. bd., coordinator Exec. MBA Program Policy Seminar Weekend, 1983. Mem. Internat. Assn. Fin. Planners, Nat. Assn. Life Underwriters, NAFE, Soc. CPCUs (bd. dirs. Boston chpt., joint adv. bd. Mass. Ins. Commr.), Soc. Chartered Fin. Cons., Delta Mu Delta. Avocations: reading sci. fiction, photography. Home and Office: 41 Atkins St Boston MA 02135

O'CONNELL, PHILIP RAYMOND, paper company executive, lawyer; b. N.Y.C., June 2, 1928; s. Michael Joseph and Ann (Blaney) O'C.; m. Joyce McCabe, July 6, 1957; children: Michael, Kathleen, Jennifer, David. A.B., Manhattan Coll., 1949; LL.B., Columbia U., 1956; grad., Advanced Mgmt. Program, Harvard U., 1967. Bar: N.Y. State 1956, U.S. Supreme Ct. 1961, Conn. 1988. Assoc. Dewey, Ballantine, Bushby, Palmer & Wood, N.Y.C., 1956-61, 62-64; gen. counsel, sec. Laurentide Finance Corp., San Francisco, 1961-62; gen. counsel Wallace-Murray Corp., 1964-66, div. mgr., 1966-70; pres., chief exec. officer, dir. Universal Papertech Corp., Hatfield, Pa., 1970-71; sec. Champion Internat. Corp., Stamford, Conn., 1972—, v.p., 1979-81, sr. v.p., 1981—; mem. legal adv. com. N.Y. Stock Exchange, 1985-88; chmn. lawyers steering com. corp. responsibility task force The Bus. Roundtable, 1981-87. Trustee Champion Internat. Found., 1979—; bd. visitors Fairfield U. Sch. Bus., 1981—, chmn., 1983—; bd. dirs. Kearney-Nat. Corp., 1975-78. Served with USNR, 1951-54. Mem. Am. Law Inst., ABA, Am. Soc. Corp. Secs. (chmn. 1988—). Office: Champion Internat Corp 1 Champion Pla Stamford CT 06921

O'CONNOR, BERNARD JAMES, marketing professional, art director, writer; b. N.Y.C., July 21, 1953; s. Bernard James and Josephine V. (Scherer) O'C.; m. Cathleen Christine Christy, Oct. 14, 1978. Student, H.S. of Art and Design, N.Y.C., 1971-74. Asst. art dir. J.M. Mathes, N.Y.C., 1971-73; art dir. Darcy-Macmanus-Masius, N.Y.C., 1973-75; editor Countrywide

Publs., N.Y.C., 1976-77; exec. art dir. Macmillan Publs., N.Y.C., 1977-78; assoc. creative dir. MCA Advt., N.Y.C., 1978-83; creative dir. Alley Mktg., N.Y.C., 1986-88; sr. art dir. COMART Assocs., N.Y.C., 1988-89; assoc. creative art dir. Am. Consulting Corp., N.Y.C., 1989—; instr. Sch. Visual Arts, 1987—. Author: How to Investigate UFO's, 1979; dir. documentary How to Choose a Therapist, 1983-84 (Director's award Am. Film Festival 1985). Administrv. dir. Assn. for the Advancement and Practice of Psychotherapy, Bklyn., 1983—. Home: 90 Lexington Ave New York NY 10016 Office: Am Consulting Corp 55 Fifth Ave New York NY 10003

O'CONNOR, EDWARD GERARD, jewelry sales executive; b. Newark, Jan. 20, 1952; s. Gerard Joseph and Bernardine A. (Washeleski) O'C.; m. Linda C. Massey, Mar. 18, 1989. BSBA, Montclair State Coll., 1973. Sales rep. Monet Jewelers, N.Y.C., 1974-79, multi-line rep., 1979; v.p., regional sales mgr. Riviera Trading Corp., N.Y.C., 1979-81; v.p., sales mgr. Lorenzo de Medici, N.Y.C., 1981-82; ind. sales rep. Pacific Jewelry Mfg. Co., Inc. and Christian Dior Bijoux/Gnosse Jewels and Oromeccanica Inc., 1982-83; regional sales mgr. Strike Gold Internat., also sales rep. Sutton Ltd., Anne Klein Watches, 1984; pres. SGI Internat. Inc., 1985—; regional sales mgr. Sutton Time Ltd., Anne Klein, Mr. G. Watches, 1984-85; chief exec. officer E&S Jewelry Inc., 1985-87; regional sales mgr. Gemini Trading Co. rep. Sutton Time Ltd. and ALWilliams Assocs., N.Y.C., 1987—. Home: 7147 La BoiTeaux Ave North College Hill OH 45231

O'CONNOR, JAMES JOHN, utility company executive; b. Chgo., Mar. 15, 1937; s. Fred James and Helen Elizabeth (Reilly) O'C.; m. Ellen Louise Lawlor, Nov. 24, 1960; children: Fred, John (dec.), James, Helen Elizabeth. BS, Holy Cross Coll., 1958; MBA, Harvard U., 1960; JD, Georgetown U., 1963. Bar: Ill. 1963. With Commonwealth Edison Co., Chgo., 1963—, asst. to chmn. exec. com., 1964-65, comml. mgr., 1966, asst. v.p., 1967-70, v.p., 1970-73, exec. v.p., 1973-77, pres., 1977-87, chmn., 1980—, chief exec. officer, also bd. dirs.; bd. dirs. Corning Glass Works, Midwest Stock Exchange, Tribune Co., First Chgo. Corp., 1st Nat. Bank of Chgo., United Air Lines, Scotsman Industries, Scotsman Industries. Mem. Ill. com. United Negro Coll. Fund, Statue of Liberty-Ellis Island Centennial Commn., Christopher Columbus Quincentenary Jubilee Commn.; bd. dirs. Assocs. Harvard U. Grad. Sch. Bus. Adminstrn., Leadership Council for Met. Open Communities, Lyric Opera, Mus. Sci. and Industry, St. Xavier Coll., Reading Is Fundamental, Helen Brach Found., Leadership Greater Chgo.; campaign chmn., dir. United Way Crusade Mercy, Chgo.; dir. Chgo. Cen. Area Com.; chmn. Citizenship Council of Met. Chgo., 1976—; past pres. Cath. Charities Chgo., 1986—; past chmn. Inst. Nuclear Power Ops., Met. Savs. Bond Campaign; trustee Adler Planetarium, Michael Reese Med. Ctr., Northwestern U., Coll. Holy Cross; bd. dirs., past chmn. Chgo. Urban League; bd. advisors Mercy Hosp. and Med. Ctr.; past chmn. bd. trustees Field Mus. Natural History; trustee Mus. Sci. and Industry; mem. vis. com. Sch. Social Svc. Adminstrn. U. Chgo., exec. bd. Chgo. Area coun. Boy Scouts Am.; chmn. Cardinal Bernardin's Big Shoulders Fund.; exec. v.p. The Hundred Club Cook County; mem. citizens bd. U. Chgo. With USAF, 1960-63; civilian aide to Sec. Army 1978-80. Mem. Am., Ill., Chgo. bar assns., Chgo. Assn. Commerce and Industry (dir.), Casino Club. Roman Catholic. Clubs: Comml., Econ., Chgo., Chgo. Commonwealth, Met. (Chgo.). Home: 9549 Monticello Ave Evanston IL 60203 Office: Commonwealth Edison Co 1 First Nat Pla PO Box 767 Chicago IL 60690

O'CONNOR, LEONARD ALBERT, utilities executive; b. Springfield, Mass., Nov. 19, 1926; s. James W. and Eva (Tatro) O'C.; children: Anita M., Charles F., Stephen J., Thomas J. B.A., U. Mass., 1950; M.A., U. N.C., 1951; J.D., U. Conn. Law Sch., 1973. Utilities analyst SEC, Washington, 1951-52; various exec. positions to tax accountant Conn. Light & Power Co., 1952-66; tax mgr. N.E. Utilities, Hartford, Conn., 1966-70; treas. N.E. Utilities, 1970-89; v.p., chief fin. officer Yankee Energy System, Rocky Hill, Conn., 1989—; bd. dirs. Bay Bank Conn. Served with USNR, World War II. Mem. Am., Conn., County bar assns., Am. Econ. Assn., Edison Electric Inst., Tax Execs. Inst. Home: 130 Mill St Wethersfield CT 06109 Office: Yankee Energy System PO Box 4002 Rocky Hill CT 06067

O'CONNOR, MARY ALICE, investor; b. Pitts., Feb. 8, 1942; d. Francis Joseph and Alice (Klein) O'C. BA, Carlow Coll., 1963; MLS, U. Pitts., 1964; PhD, Fla. State U., 1978. Libr. Edinboro (Pa.) State coll., 1970-72; dir. libr. Flagler Coll., St. Augustine, Fla., 1972-75; pvt. practice investor Fla., 1975—; pres., chief exec. officer "Wall St.", Naples, Fla., 1980—.

O'CONNOR, RALPH STURGES, investment company executive; b. Pasadena, Calif., Aug. 27, 1926; s. Thomas Ireland and Edith Masury (Sturges) O'C.; m. Alice Maconda Brown, Apr. 28, 1950; children—George Rufus, Thomas Ireland III, Nancy Isabel, John Herman. B.A., Johns Hopkins, 1951. With Highland Resources, Inc., Houston, 1951—, exec. v.p., 1961-64; pres. Highland Resources, Inc., 1964-87; pres., chief exec. officer Ralph S. O'Connor and Assocs., 1987—; dir. Tex. Eastern Transmission Corp., Houston, First City Nat. Bank, Houston, Westheimer Transfer & Storage, Houston, Waste Recovery, Inc., Dallas. Bd. dirs. Am. Petroleum Inst.; bd. govs. Rice U., Houston; mem. vis. com. Harvard Bus. Sch.; bd. chmn., trustee Hermann Hosp. Estate, Houston. Served with USAAF, 1943-46. Mem. Am. Assn. Petroleum Landmen. Clubs: Bayou (Houston), Ramada (Houston), River Oaks Country (Houston). Home: 3335 Chevy Chase Houston TX 77019 Office: Ralph S Connor & Assocs 4422 First City Tower Houston TX 77002-6708

O'CONNOR, RICHARD DONALD, advertising company executive; b. Nyack, N.Y., Dec. 29, 1931; s. James Patrick and Sophie Kathryn (Hensel) O'C.; m. Lucille Hartigan, Jan. 25, 1958 (div. 1986); children: Richard D., Kathryn Helen, Timothy Joseph, Meghan Mary, John Patrick. B.A., U. Mich., 1954. With Lintas: Campbell-Ewald Co., Detroit, 1956—, exec. v.p., chief operating officer, 1975-76, pres., 1976-79, vice chmn., chief exec. officer, 1979-82; chief exec. officer, vice chmn. Marschalk/Campbell-Ewald Worldwide, 1982-86, chmn., chief exec. officer, 1984-85; chmn., chief exec. officer Campbell-Ewald Co., N.Y.C. and Warren, Mich., 1985—; bd. dirs. Interpub. Group Cos., Lintas: U.S.A. Past trustee Walsh Coll., Troy, Mich., 1976-77; promotion chmn. United Found. Torch Drive, 1976; mem. adv. com. Mich. Cancer Found., 1976-77; mem. exec. com. Detroit Better Bus. Bur., 1977—; trustee Detroit Country Day Sch.; mem. Boys Clubs Am., past trustee; trustee Bus./Edn. Alliance Southeastern Mich., Northwood Inst.; dir. Boys and Girls Clubs Southeastern Mich.; fellow Pierpont Morgan Library; active Boys Clubs N.Y., past trustee Boys Club Am. Served with U.S. Army, 1954-56. Recipient Robert E. Healy award Interpub. Group Cos., 1974. Mem. Adcraft Club Detroit (past pres.), Detroit Advt. Assn., Am. Assn. Advt. Agys. (bd. dirs.), Am. Advt. Fedn. (bd. dirs. 1987—), Advt. Council (bd. dirs. 1987—), Advt. Ednl. Found. (bd. dirs.), Advt. Club N.Y. (v.p. 1985-86, pres. 1987—), Am. Ireland Fund (bd. dirs. 1985—), U. Mich. Alumni Assn. Republican. Roman Catholic. Clubs: Recess (pres. 1981), Bloomfield Hills; Detroit Athletic, Econ. of Detroit (bd. dirs.); Grosse Point (Mich.); Duquesne; Econ. of N.Y.C, Hundred, Racquet, Le Club, Links, The Friars, The Old (Mich.). Office: Lintas: Campbell-Ewald Co 30400 Van Dyke Ave Warren MI 48093 also: Lintas Campbell-Ewald Co 1 Dag Hammarskjold Pla New York NY 10017

O'CONNOR, ROBERT JEROME, power company executive; b. Uniontown, Wash., Aug. 23, 1927; s. Eugene Joseph and Kathryn (Lunders) O'C.; m. Margaret Jean Carter, Aug. 27, 1950; children: Mary Sue, John Carter. B.S. in Elec. Engring., U. Idaho, 1951. With GE, Schenectady, N.Y., 1951-52; with Idaho Power Co., Boise, 1952—, various positions, 1952-70, vice pres., asst. to pres., 1970-72, sr. v.p. adminstrn., 1972-76, exec. v.p. ops., 1976-81, pres., chief operating officer, 1981-85, pres., chief exec. officer, 1985-87, chmn., chief exec. officer, 1987—, also bd. dirs.; bd. dirs. Key Bank Idaho, Boise. Mem. Boise Planning and Zoning Commn., 1963-67; bd. dirs. St. Lukes's Regional Med. Ctr.; exec. com. Idaho Council on Econ. Edn., 1983—. Served with U.S. Army, 1946-48. Mem. Idaho Assn. Commerce and Industry (chmn. bus. week 1979), Boise C. of C. (exec. com.). Republican. Roman Catholic. Lodge: Rotary. Home: 710 Ranch Rd Boise ID 83702 Office: Idaho Power Co 1220 Idaho St PO Box 70 Boise ID 83707

O'CONNOR, RUTH ELKINTON, real estate executive, consultant; b. Oakland, Calif., May 19, 1927; d. Alfred Cope and Anna (Lydia) Elkinton; m. Roger Edward O'Connor, Oct. 12, 1950; children: Bruce E., Colleen, Lynn, Michael, John E. AA, U. Calif., 1949. Salesman Ruth Hendrickson, Realtor, Honolulu, 1966-68; salesman, broker John D. McCurry, Realtor, Honolulu, 1968-76; prin. broker O'Connor Realty, Honolulu, 1976-80; owner, pres. R.E.O. Inc., Honolulu, 1980—; owner Ga. Manor Nursing Home, Amarillo, Tex., 1981—; pres. Farm and Land Brokers, Honolulu, 1972; mem. profl. standards com. Grievance Honor Bd., Honolulu, 1983-85. Editor: Friends of Samoa, 1979. Recipient Exchangor of the Yr. award The Investment Group, Realtors, 1968, Councelor of the Yr. award The Investment Group, Realtors, 1969, Arts Council award Govt. of Am. Samoa, 1980. Mem. Honolulu Bd. Realtors (dir. 1970-72), Hawaii Bd. Realtors, Nat. Assn. of Realtors (real estate aviation chpt.), Internat. Real Estate Fedn., Nat. Assn. Female Execs., Pan Pacific S.E. Asian Women (life), Arts Council (dir. 1976-79), The Ninety-Nines (Hawaii del. 1985), Profl. Assn. Diving Instrs., Tex. Nursing Home Assn., Am. Nursing Home Assn., Am. Health Care Assn., Berkeley City Club, Outrigger Canoe, Berkeley City Club, Alpha Omicron Pi. Mem. Soc. of Friends. Club: Outrigger Canoe. Office: REO Inc 417 Kanekapolei St Ste 103 Honolulu HI 96815

ODEAL, ERWIN JOSEPH, civil engineer; b. Cleve., Nov. 3, 1944; s. Erwin and Marjorie (Looman) O.; m. Kathleen Bryske, Sept. 2, 1968; children: Laurel, Brian. BCE, Cleve. State U., 1967; MCE, U. Akron, 1973. Dist. engr. Ohio Dept of Health, Cuyuhuga Falls, 1967-71, Three Rivers Watershed Dist., Cleve., 1971-74; mgr. planning N.E. Ohio Regional Sewer Dept., Cleve., 1974-79, dep. dir., 1979-83, exec. dir., 1983—; v.p. Assn. Metro. Sewerage Agy., Washington, 1986—, pres., 1988—; bd. dirs. Instrument Testing Services, Washington, 1987—. Bd. dirs. Midtown Corridor, Cleve., 1988, HELP/Six Chimneys, Cleve., 1988; alumnus Leadership Cleve., 1985. Mem. ASCE (named Civil Engr. Year 1987), Am. Mgmt. Assn., Water Pollution Control Fed., Am. Pub. Works Assn., Nat. Environ. Trainers Assn. Office: NE Ohio Regional Sewer Dist 3826 Euclid Ave Cleveland OH 44115

ODELL, FRANK HAROLD, banker; b. Hobart, N.Y., May 17, 1922; s. Harold E. and Naomi (Cole) O.; m. Elizabeth J. Hetherington, Dec. 29, 1946; children—Thomas A., Nancy E., Susan. A.B., U. Ala., 1943; M.B.A., Harvard U., 1949; postgrad., Stonier Grad. Sch. Banking, Rutgers U., 1958. With State Bank of Albany, N.Y., 1949-71; v.p. State Bank of Albany, 1963-69, sr. v.p. in charge bank's loan portfolio, 1969-71; exec. v.p. Norstar Bancorp Inc., Albany, 1971-72; also vice chmn. Norstar Bancorp Inc.; chmn., chief exec. officer Norstar Bank of Upstate N.Y., 1972-87, also bd. dirs.; bd. dirs. Norstar Trust, Fleet/Norstar Fin. Group. Chmn. bd. trustees YMCA, past bd. dirs.; bd. dirs. Albany Inst. History and Art, Robert Morris Assn., Capital Region Tech. Devel. Council, Mayor's Downtown Adv. Com., N.Y. State Banking Bd., Albany Med. Ctr., Albany chpt. ARC, United Way, Russell Sage Coll., Sta. WMHT-TV. Capt. C.E., AUS, 1943. Mem. Albany C. of C., Harvard Club (N.Y.C.), Fort Orange Club (past pres.)., Wyndemere C.C., Masons. Republican. Methodist. also: 33 Darwley Greene Delmar NY 12054 Office: Norstar Bank Upstate NY 69 State St Albany NY 12201

ODESCALCHI, EDMOND PÉRY, financial and management executive, consultant; b. Budapest, Hungary, Oct. 11, 1928; came to U.S., 1950; s. Prince Béla and Princess Charlotte (De Bay) O.; m. Esther De Kando, Sept. 30, 1961; children: Daniel, Dominic. Student, Cornell U., 1951, U. Pa., 1956-57; MS in Econs., St. Andrews U., Scotland, 1959. Adminstrv. asst. French Govt., Baden, Fed. Republic Germany, 1948-50; world trade specialist IBM Corp., Poughkeepsie, N.Y., 1952-60, project mgr., 1960-74; devel. mgr. IBM Corp., East Fishkill, N.Y., 1974; pres. Global Tech., Inc., N.Y.C., 1975—; Internat. fin. cons. Author: The Global Arena, 1973, Faces of Reality, 1975; contbr. articles to profl. jours. Mem. Rep. Nat. Com., 1984—. Mem. Bus. Cons. Assn., Am. Mus. Natural History (assoc.), Internat. Platform Assn. Home: 6 Freedom Rd Pleasant Valley NY 12569 Office: Global Tech Inc 5 31 50th Ave Long Island City NY 11101

ODOM, JIMMY LANE, computer systems executive; b. Cleveland, Tenn., Sept. 2, 1934; s. James Washington and Geneva Adell (Goins) O.; m. Marilyn Brombach, Apr. 8, 1961 (div. Feb. 1972); 1 child, Jimmy Lane Jr.; m. Nickie Kaye Cassidy, Aug. 27, 1972; children: Shana Leigh, Heath Cassidy. BSBA, Tenn. Tech. U., 1959. Mgmt. trainee U.S. Steel Corp., Birmingham, Ala., 1959-63; project mgr. adminstrv. computer systems NASA, Huntsville, Ala., 1963-87; supervisory computer specialist GE, Huntsville, 1967-68; exec. ADP mgmt. Safeguard Systems Command, Huntsville, 1968-73, Forces Command, Atlanta, 1973-74, Automated Logistics Mgmt. Systems Command, St. Louis, 1974-88; v.p. pub. and mktg. CEC Inc., St. Louis, 1982—. Bd. dirs. Ctr. for Study Data Processing Washington U., St. Louis, 1984—. With U.S. Army, 1954-57. Recipient Meritorious Civil Svc. award Dept. Army, 1983, Comdr.'s award, U.S. Army, 1980. Republican. Presbyterian. Home: 1528 Candish Ln Chesterfield MO 63017 Office: CEC Inc PO Box 186 Chesterfield MO 63006

O'DONNELL, CHRISTOPHER JOHN, commercial banking executive; b. Detroit, Jan. 3, 1940; s. Dayton H. and Marguerite (Barthel) O.; m. Patricia Halliwell, July 16, 1977; children: Erin E., Meghan A., Kelly C. BS, Regis Coll., 1961; MA, Marquette U., 1963. Cert. fin. planner. Asst. mgr. air cargo Am. Airlines, Chgo., 1966; v.p. Continental Bank, Chgo., 1966-74, v.p., div. mgr., 1978—; v.p. Builders Capital Limited, Toronto, Can., 1974-78; vis. lectr. Am. Bankers Assn., Washington, 1985—. Chmn. CCD Com. Sacred Heart Ch., 1987—. 2d lt., USMC, 1963-65, col. res. ret. Mem. Internat. Assn. of Cert. Fin. Planners, Am. Bankers Assn. Roman Catholic. Office: Continental Bank 231 S LaSalle St Chicago IL 60697

O'DONNELL, DAVID DANIEL, educational services company executive; b. Washington, Aug. 31, 1941; s. Ferd D. and Angelina O'Donnell; m. Carol Knackstaedt, June 14, 1965 (div. 1969); 1 son, David Sean; m. Kay Boughner, Oct. 27, 1970; children: Daniel Joseph, Richard Robert. Student East Carolina U., 1964, Am. U., 1965-66; BA, Colo. Tech. Coll., 1988. Ops. mgr. Record Sales, Washington, 1956-61; v.p. sales Capitol Sewing Machine Co., Washington, 1967-70; cons. Macro Systems, Silver Spring, Md., 1970-71; sales mgr. Control Data Corp., Miami, 1971-73; key accounts mgr. Sealy, Miami, 1973-75; dir. mktg. ITT-ITT Ednl. Services, Inc., Indpls., 1975—; gen. mgr., v.p. ITT Employment and Tng. Systems, Inc., Indpls., 1985-86; pres., chmn. bd. Colo. Tech. Coll., 1986—; guest speaker, lectr., cons. Served with USMCR, 1961-65. Republican. Home: 13920 Wyandott Dr Colorado Springs CO 80908 Office: Colo Tech Coll 4435 N Chestnut St Colorado Springs CO 80907

O'DONNELL, F. SCOTT, banker; b. Brownsville, Pa., Sept. 20, 1940; s. Francis Horner and Rebecca (Warren) O'D.; m. Ann Bukmir, Dec. 30, 1976. BA, Grove City (Pa.) Coll., 1962; postgrad., U. Wis. Grad. Sch. Banking, 1970, Internat. Sch. Banking, U. Colo., 1972. Nat. bank examiner Comptroller of Currrency State of Ohio, Cleve., 1965-71; supt. of banks State of Ohio, Columbus, 1975-77; sr. v.p. First Nat. Bank, Steubenville, Ohio, 1971-75; exec. v.p. Heritage Bancorp, Steubenville, 1977-80; v.p. Society Corp., Cleve., 1980-86, sr. v.p., 1986—; mem. state banking bd. Div. of Banks, Columbus, 1979-85, govt. affairs com. Ohio Bankers Assn., 1982-84. Served with USCG, 1963-69. Clubs: Lakewood Country; Univ. (Pitts.). Lodge: Elks. Home: 31830 Lake Rd Avon Lake OH 44012 Office: Soc Corp 800 Superior Ave Cleveland OH 44114

O'DONNELL, JOSEPH MICHAEL, electronics executive; b. Rochester, N.Y., May 9, 1946; s. Robert Lawrance O'Donnell and Josephine Marie (Schickler) Vosper; m. Barbara Lee Hasselmann, Feb. 27, 1977; children: Shannon, Lindsey, Colleen. BS, U. Tenn., 1968, MBA, 1970. Sales mgr. telecommunications ITT, Chgo., 1973-75; dir. mktg. communication ITT, Hartford, Conn., 1975-77; dir. mktg. Gen. Instrument Corp., N.Y.C., 1977-81; gen. mgr. Gen. Instrument Corp., Post Falls, Idaho, 1981-84; v.p. Conrac Corp., Stamford, Conn., 1984-87; pres. OD & S Ventures, Stamford, 1987-88; v.p. Handy & Harman, N.Y.C., 1988—. Mem. Am. Mktg. Assn. Republican. Congregationalist. Clubs: Landmark, Landmark Athletic (Stamford); Aspetuck Country. Home: 587 Shrub Oak Ln Fairfield CT 06430 Office: Handy & Harman 850 Third Ave New York NY 10022

O'DONNELL, MICHAEL, sales and marketing executive; b. Cleve., Mar. 18, 1954; s. John C. and Rebecca (Atchley) O'D.; m. Melinda Kay Osbun, Dec. 3, 1982. Student, Ohio State U., 1972, 72-73; AS in Indsl. Tech., Ohio U., 1975; BS in Indsl. Mgmt., Franklin U., Columbus, 1978. With Trico Mfg., Mansfield, Ohio, 1969-72, Ruff Mfg. Co., Mansfield, Ohio, 1972-73; indsl. engr. Babcock & Wilcox, Lancaster, Ohio, 1973-75, McGraw Edison Corp., Columbus, Ohio, 1975-76; indsl. engr./supr. Magic Chef Corp., Columbus, 1976-77; sales engr. Atlas Butler Inc., Columbus, 1977-82; gen. mgr. Park Ave. Mktg., Mansfield, 1982-86; mgr. sales, mktg. Weiss Ind., Mansfield, 1986—; v.p., gen. ptnr., Ultraliner, Mansfield, 1985—; instr. Columbus C. of C. in sales, 1979, 80, Mansfield Bus. Coll., 1984. Co-author: Basic Sales Theory, 1979; contbr. articles to profl. jours. Pres. North Cen. Ohio Bus. Devel. Orgn., 1984; bd. dirs. Richland Cts. Bd. of MR and DD, 1985-87. Served with USCGR, 1973-75. Recipient award for Outstanding Achievement Columbus Jaycees, 1981, Exchange Club, 1988. Mem. C. of C., Huron Yacht Club, RNO Internat. Club, Exchange Club. Republican. Roman Catholic. Home: 206 Taylor Rd Mansfield OH 44903 Office: Weiss Industries 2480 N Main St Mansfield OH 44903

O'DONNELL, PETER, sales executive; b. Phila., Dec. 17, 1940; s. John T. and Thelma (Woodruff) O'D.; children: Tracey, Katharine. BS, LaSalle U., 1976. Sr. sales exec. Pitney Bowes, Phila., 1973—. Served with U.S. Army, 1959-63. Republican. Roman Catholic. Home: 369 Hilltop Dr King of Prussia PA 19406

O'DONNELL, RICHARD WALTER, lawyer, accountant, brokerage company executive; b. Newark, Oct. 17, 1945; s. James Richard and Alice (Drep) O'D. BA, Rutgers U., 1967, MBA in Fin., 1969, MBA in Acctg., 1972, JD, 1985. Bar: N.J. 1985; CPA, N.J. Fin. analyst Allied Chem. Corp., Morristown, N.J., 1969-72; sr. audit mgr. Peat, Marwick, Mitchell & Co., Newark, 1972-80; asst. controller Crane Co., N.Y.C., 1980-81, controller, 1981-83; treas. Lehman Bros. Kuhn Loeb, Inc., N.Y.C., 1983-84; sr. v.p. Shearson Lehman Bros., Inc., N.Y.C., 1984-85; mng. dir. Kidder, Peabody & Co., Inc., N.Y.C., 1985—. Mem. Am. Inst. CPA's, N.J. Soc. CPA's (chmn. community svcs. com. 1978-80), Nat. Assn. Accts., N.J. Bar Assn., Wayne C. of C. (treas. 1979-80), Beta Gamma Sigma. Home: 12 Perrin Dr Wayne NJ 07470 Office: Kidder Peabody & Co Inc 2 Broadway 7th Fl New York NY 10004

O'DONNELL, THOMAS MITCHELL, brokerage firm executive; b. Cleve., Apr. 9, 1936; s. John Michael and Mary L. (Hayes) O'D.; m. Nancy A. Dugan, Feb. 4, 1961; children—Christopher, Colleen, Julie. BBA, U. Notre Dame, 1959; MBA, U. Pa., 1960. Cert. Chartered Fin. Analyst. Fin. analyst Saunders Stiver & Co., Cleve., 1960-65; rsch. dir. McDonald & Co., Cleve., 1965-66, exec. v.p. corp. fin., 1967-83, gen. ptnr., 1968-83; pres. McDonald & Co. Securities, Cleve., 1983-88, chmn., chief exec. officer, 1988—; bd. dirs. (subs.) MCD Agy., Inc., MCD Oil and Gas Co., Inc., (also chmn.), MCD Real Estate Inc.; chmn. bd. dirs. McDonald & Co. Venture Capital, Inc.; bd. dirs. McDonald Fin. Services, Inc., Hauserman Inc., Seaway Food Town. Author: The Why and How of Mergers, 1968. Trustee Cath. Charities, Cleve. Mem. Cleve. Soc. Security Analysts (cert.). Roman Catholic. Clubs: Mid-Day, Union, Westwood Country, Sharon Golf, 50 Club of Cleve., The Tavern. Home: 1325 Timberlea Westlake OH 44145 Office: McDonald & Co Securities Inc 2100 Soc Bldg Cleveland OH 44114

O'DONNELL, WILLIAM DAVID, construction firm executive; b. Brockton, Mass., Aug. 21, 1926; s. John Frank and Agnes Teresa (Flanagan) O'D.; m. Dixie Lou Anderson, Jan. 31, 1951; children—Craig Patrick, Ginger Lynn. BS, U. N.Mex., 1953. Registered profl. engr., Ill., 1958. Engr., State of Ill., 1953-59; with Gregory-Anderson Co., Rockford, Ill., 1959—, gen. mgr., 1960-61, sec., 1961-81, pres., 1981—; dir. 1st Nat. Bank & Trust Co. of Rockford, 1st Community Bancorp, Inc., Growth Enterprise, Starvision, Inc. Dir. St. Anthony Med. Ctr., Starvision, Inc.; bd. dirs. Rockford YMCA, pres., 1984. Served with USN, 1943-47. Recipient Friend of the Boy award Optimist Club, 1966, Excalibur award for community service Rockford Register Star, 1971; named Titan of Yr., Boylan High Sch., 1974. Fellow ASCE, Nat. Soc. Profl. Engrs.; mem. No. Ill. Bldg. Contractors, Aircraft Owners and Pilots Assn., Balloon Fedn. Am., Sigma Tau, Chi Epsilon, Tau Beta Pi. Clubs: Forest Hills Country (Rockford); Adventurers (Chgo.). Lodges: Elks, Rotary (Service Above Self award 1972; v.p. Rockford chpt. 1983, pres. 1984). Home: 2004 Bradley Rd Rockford IL 61107 Office: Gregory Anderson Co 2525 Huffman Blvd Rockford IL 61103

O'DONNELL, WILLIAM THOMAS, radar systems marketing executive; b. Latrobe, Pa., Feb. 22, 1939; s. William Regis and Kathryn Ann (Coneff) O'D.; m. Judith Koetke, Oct. 1, 1965; children: William Thomas, William Patrick, Allison Rose, Kevin Raymond. Student Eastern N.Mex. U., 1958-61; student in mktg. John Carroll U., 1961-65, Ill. Inst. Tech., 1965-66; BSBA, U. Phoenix, 1982, MBA with distinction, 1984. Various sales positions Hickok Elec. Instrument Co., Cleve., 1961-65, Fairchild Semicondr., Mpls., 1965-67; Transitron Semicondr., Mpls., 1967-69; Burroughs Corp., Plainfield, N.J., 1967-71; mktg. mgr. Owens-Ill. Co., 1972-73, v.p. mktg. Pantek Co., subs. Owens-Ill. Co., Lewistown, Pa., 1973-75, v.p. mktg., nat. sales mgr., Toledo, 1975-76; mktg. mgr., nat. sales mgr. Govt. Electronics div. group Motorola Co., Scottsdale, Ariz., 1976-80, U.S. mktg. mgr. radar positioning systems Motorola Govt. Electronics Group, 1981—; gen. mgr. J.K. Internat., Scottsdale, 1980-81; mgmt. cons. Pres. Cambridge Group, 1987—; adj. prof. Union Grad. Sch.; guest lectr. U. Mich. Grad. Sch. Bus. Adminstrn.; instr., chair strategic mgmt. U. Phoenix, 1988, Scottsdale Community Coll., Paradise Valley Community Coll.; area chair-gen. mgmt. Union Grad. Sch. Maricopa Community Coll., U. Phoenix. Chmn., Rep. Precinct, Burnsville, Minn., 1968-70; city fin. chmn., Burnsville; dir. community devel. U.S. Jaycees, Mpls., 1968-69; mem. Scottsdale 2000 Com. Served with USAF, 1957-61. Recipient Outstanding Performance award Maricopa Community Coll. System, 1987, Faciliation award, Maricopa Community Coll., Citation for Faciliation Ability U. Phoenix, 1986; named Hon. Citizen, Donaldsville, La., 1978; others. Mem. Phoenix Execs. Club, Am. Mktg. Assn., U. Phoenix Faculty Club (pres. 1988-89, recipient Presdl. Designation award, officer, pres. 1988-89), North Cape Yacht Club, Scottsdale Racquet Club, Toftnees Country Club. Roman Catholic. Home: 8432 E Belgian Trail Scottsdale AZ 85258

O'DRUDY, LEO KEARNEY, JR., lawyer, title insurance company counsel; b. N.Y.C., June 12, 1933; s. Leo Kearney and Cecile (Lean) Drury; m. Caitríona Ní Néill, Mar. 11, 1972; children: Leo Kearney III, Caoilfhionn Caitlín, Éadaoin Eibhlín. BA magna cum laude, Mount St. Mary's Coll., Emmitsburg, Md., 1955; JD, Villanova U., 1958; LLM with highest honors, George Washington U., 1975. Bar: Pa. 1959, Calif. 1963, Va. 1983, U.S. Ct. Mil. Appeals, U.S. Navy-Marine Corps Ct. Mil. Review, U.S. Supreme Ct. 1970. Commd. 2d lt. USMC, 1958, advanced through grades to lt. col., ret., 1982; assoc. Cranwell & O'Connell, Arlington, Va., 1984-86; counsel Coldwell Banker Settlement & Title Co., Vienna, Va., 1986-87; underwriting counsel Commonwealth Land Title Ins. Co., Washington, 1987—; adj. prof. Comml. Law Far East div. U. Md., Japan, 1978-81, U. Va., Falls Ch., 1986—; instr. real property law Nat. Inst. Real Estate, Vienna, Va., 1985—. Mem. editorial staff Villanova Law Rev., 1956-58. Named Dougherty fellow Villanova U., 1955-58. Mem. Va. State Bar Assn., Calif. State Bar Assn., Am. Land Title Assn., D.C. Land Title Assn., Md. Land Title Assn. Roman Catholic. Home: 2419 Newton St Vienna VA 22181-4053 Office: Commonwealth Land Title Ins Co 1828 L St NW Ste 301 Washington DC 20036-5150

OEFFINGER, JOHN CLAYTON, research foundation executive, educator; b. Ft. Sill, Okla., Oct. 30, 1952; s. Jack Clayton and Sally Josephine (Lehman) O.; m. Kathryn Gayle Pourteau, May 11, 1975; 1 child, John Clayton II. BA, Tex. A&M U., 1976, postgrad. in pol. sci., 1976-77. Mgr. congl. campaign T. Chet Edwards, Duncanville, Tex., 1977-78; congl. campaign asst. Congressman James Mattox, Dallas, 1978, dist. rep., 1979-80, mgr. congl. campaign, 1980, dist. rep., 1980-81; dir. office of grants mgmt. Baylor U. Med. Ctr., Dallas, 1981-82; v.p. Baylor U. Med. Ctr. Found., Dallas, 1982; founder, v.p. Baylor U. Rsch. Found., Dallas, 1982-88; also bd. dirs. Baylor Research Found., Dallas; sr. v.p., chief exec. officer Tex. Hosp. Edn. and Rsch. Found., sec., treas., bd. dirs.; co-chmn., co-founder Internat. Informatics Access, Dallas, 1986-87; internat. cons. UN Indsl. Devel. Orgn., 1987—; cons. Pan Am. Health Orgn., Washington, 1986-88; editorial adv. bd. Telematics & Informatics, Pergamon Press, 1988—; adv. bd. MEDNET Telecommunication Project Heath Sci. Ctr. Tex. Tech. U., 1989—. Founding mem., bd. dirs. MSC Enrichment Fund, 1979-84; campaign coord. dist. 7 Dallas Area Rapid Transit Bond Election, Dallas, 1984, councilman John Evans, 1985, 87, Opportunity Dallas, fall 1987. Grantee Apple Corp., 1984—; named one of Outstanding Young Men of Am. U.S. Jaycees, 1983.

Mem. AAAS, Nat. Coun. Univ. Rsch. Adminstrs., Tex. Tech. Transfer Assn. (bd. dirs.), Dallas C. of C. (internat. com.). Democrat. Roman Catholic. Lodge: Rotary (dir. internat. service Fair Park club Dallas, 1987—). Office: Tex Hosp Edn & Rsch Found PO Box 15587 Austin TX 78761-5587

OEHMLER, GEORGE COURTLAND, corporate executive; b. Pitts., May 6, 1926; s. Rudolph Christian and Virgia Sylvia (Stark) O.; B.S. in Indsl. Engring, Pa. State U., 1950; m. Martha Jane Swagler, July 3, 1954; children—Wendy Lynn, Christy Ann, Geoffrey Colin. Indsl. engr. Allegheny Ludlum Steel Corp., Pitts., 1953-54, salesman, 1954-60, mgr. export sales, 1960-67, mgr. flat rolled products, 1967-68, asst. to chmn., 1968-73, v.p. internat., 1973-75, v.p. internat. Allegheny Internat., Inc., Pitts., 1975-81, v.p. public and internat. affairs, 1981-86 ; pres., chief operating officer World Affairs Council, Pitts., 1987—; dir. Mathews Internat. Corp. Mem. exec. bd. Pa. State U. Alumni Council, 1976-82; bd. dirs. United Way Allegheny County, 1982-84, Pitts. Ballet, 1982—, Pitts. Pub. Theater, 1986—, Mendelssohn Choir of Pitts., 1987—. Served with U.S. Army, 1944-46, 51-52. Mem. Am. Iron and Steel Inst., Assn. Iron and Steel Engrs., Machinery and Allied Products Inst. (internat. and pub. affairs councils), World Affairs Council Pitts. (pres. 1980-82, dir.), Pitts. Council for Internat. Visitors (dir. 1975-87, pres. 1976-78), Greater Pitts. C. of C. Republican. Presbyterian. Clubs: Duquesne, Longue Vue (gov. 1982-84). Home: 321 Braddsley Dr Pittsburgh PA 15235 Office: World Affairs Coun Pitts 100 5th Ave Pittsburgh PA 15222

OELBAUM, HAROLD, lawyer, corporate executive; b. Bklyn., Jan. 9, 1931; s. Max and Betty (Molomet) O.; m. Nancy Rothkopf, June 28, 1968; children—Louise, Andrew, Jennifer. A.B., Franklin and Marshall Coll., 1952; J.D., Harvard, 1955; LL.M., N.Y. U., 1959. Bar: N.Y. 1955, Mass. 1960. Atty. Hellerstein & Rosier, Esqs., N.Y.C., 1955-59; gen. atty. Raytheon Co., Lexington, Mass., 1959-68; sr. atty. Revlon, Inc., N.Y.C., 1968-72; exec. v.p., dir., mem. exec. com. Kane-Miller Corp., Tarrytown, N.Y., 1972—. Home: 77 Chestnut Ridge Rd Mount Kisco NY 10549 Office: Kane-Miller Corp 555 White Plains Rd Tarrytown NY 10591

OERTLI-CAJACOB, PETER, management consultant; b. Höri, Zürich, Switzerland, May 29, 1941; s. Fritz Maximilian and Liselotte (Haedenkamp) O.; m. Cilla Cajacob, Sept. 2, 1972; children: Thomas, Adrian, Matthias. MSc, Swiss Fed. Inst. Tech., Zürich, 1968, DSc, 1975. Control engr. Brown Boveri & Cie AG, Baden, Switzerland, 1968-70; sci. asst. Inst. Mgmt. Sci. Swiss Fed. Inst. Tech., Zurich, 1970-72; mgmt. systems mgr. Hilti AG Fastening Systems, Schaan, Principality of Liechtenstein, 1972-75; tech. dir. Hilti Equipment Ltd., Manchester, Eng., 1976; v.p. mktg. Maag Gear Wheel Co., Zürich, 1977-82; group mgmt. cons. Knight Wendling AG, Zürich, 1983-87; ptnr. SCG St. Gallen Cons., Zürich, 1988—; pres. bd. Eltrans AG, Zürich, 1986—. Author: Cybernetics of Economic Systems, 1977, translation in Russian, 1983, Innovation staff Resignation, 35 Perspektiren für eine neue Zeit, 1989; contbr. articles in econs., cybernetics, mgmt., mktg., and logistics to profl. jour. Bd. dirs. Tech. Soc., Zürich, 1987—. Mem. Swiss Soc. Mgmt., Swiss Group Artificial Intelligence and Cognitive Sci., Swiss Soc. Engrs. and Architects, Swiss Soc. Info. Tech. Free Democrats. Club: Efficiency (Zürich). Office: SCG St Gallen Cons Group, Airport Business Center, Schaffhauserstr 134, CH-8152 Zurich Glattbrugg, Switzerland

OETKEN, STANLEY GENE, insurance company executive; b. Longmont, Colo., Oct. 5, 1948; s. Lawrence Martin and Henrietta June (Bens) O.; m. Elaine Joyce Longseth, Sept. 4, 1969; children: Colin, Kirk, Kristin. BS, Wake Forest U., 1970. Underwriter Ins. Co. N.AM., Denver, 1972-76; cons. Crump, Warren & Sommer, Denver, 1976-83, v.p., 1983-85; asst. v.p. Profl. Liability Underwriting Mgrs. Inc., Eden Prairie, Minn., 1985—. Mem. Soc. Chartered Property Casualty Underwriters. Republican. Mem. Evangelical Free Ch. Home: 10630 34th Ave N Plymouth MN 55441 Office: Profl Liability Underwriting Mgrs 11095 Viking Dr Suite 480 Eden Prairie MN 55344

OFFERMAN, CHRISTIANE TOENNE, marketing consultant; b. Hannover, Germany, Apr. 30, 1947; came to U.S., 1977; d. Adolf and Eva (Kretzschmar) Toenne; m. Louis Offerman, May 15, 1983; children: Anna, Elena. MBA, U. Hamburg, Fed. Republic Germany, 1972; postgrad. Clark U., 1977-78. Project dir. GFM, Hamburg, 1973-74, Makrotest, Dusseldorf, Fed. Republic Germany, 1974-75, Delphi Marktforschung, Dusseldorf, 1975-80; ptnr. Delphi Sales Cons., Inc., Lexington, Mass. and Chatham, N.J., 1980-84, Oasis Consulting, Inc., N.Y.C., 1984—. Pub. relations coordinator Amnesty Internat., Dusseldorf, 1975-77, group leader, Worcester, Mass., 1977-78. Mem. Smaller Bus. Assn., Nat. Assn. Female Execs. Lutheran. Office: Oasis Cons Inc 230 W 13th St New York NY 10011

OFFERMAN, LOUIS, marketing professional, management consultant; b. Long Beach, N.Y., June 21, 1959; s. Bernard and Sally (Malvon) O.; m. Christiane Anna Toenne, May 15, 1983; children: Anna Leonore, Elena Rose. Student, Clark U., 1977-80. Interviewer, analyst Delphi Marktforschung GmbH, Lexington, Mass., 1980-82; project dir. Delphi Sales Cons., Inc., Chatham, N.J., 1982-83, jr. ptnr., 1983-84; co-founder, pres. Oasis Cons., Inc., N.Y.C., 1984—. Mem. Amnesty Internat. (regional membership coordinator New Eng. 1979-81, N.Y.C. 1981-82). Jewish. Office: Oasis Cons Inc 230 W 13th St New York NY 10011

OFNER, WILLIAM BERNARD, lawyer; b. Los Angeles, Aug. 24, 1929; s. Harry D. and Gertrude (Skoss) Offner; m. Florence Ila Maxwell, Apr. 13, 1953 (div. 1956). AA, Los Angeles City Coll., 1949; BA, Calif. State U., Los Angeles, 1953; LLB, Loyola U., Los Angeles, 1965; postgrad. Sorbonne, 1951, cert. de Langue Francaise, 1987; postgrad. U. So. Calif., 1966, Glendale Community Coll., 1986-89. Bar: Calif. 1966, U.S. Dist. Ct. Calif. 1966, U.S. Supreme Ct. 1972. Assoc., Thomas Moore and Assocs., Los Angeles, 1967-69; sole practice, Los Angeles, 1969-70, 74—; assoc. Peter Lam, Los Angeles, 1981-87; assoc. C.M. Coronel, 1986-87, Jack D. Janofsky, 1987—; pres., fund mgr. DT Mktg. Inc.; lectr. Van Norman U., 1975. Served with USNR, 1947-54. Mem. Inst. Gen. Semantics, Inst. for Antiquity and Christianity, Soc. Judgement, Shakespeare Soc. (bd. dirs. 1987). Democrat. Jewish. Clubs: Los Angeles Athletic, Toastmasters. Avocations: water color painting, photography, linguistics. Office: 1102 Brand N Blvd #24 Glendale CA 91202

ÖFVERHOLM, STEFAN, electrical engineer; b. Ludvika, Sweden, Nov. 21, 1936; s. Håkan and Ragnhild Gudrun (Andersson) O.; m. Eva Guy Tiselius, Sept. 9, 1966 (div. 1971); m. Ulrika Mathilda Marie Skaar, Oct. 10, 1975; children: Harald, Ingegerd. MSEE, Chalmers U. Tech., Gothenburg, Sweden, 1963. Engr. microwave systems devel. Ericsson AB, Mölndal, Sweden, 1963-66; mgr. microwave lab. Trelleborgplast AB, Ljungby, Sweden, 1966-67; mgr. process and prodn. control projects Ericsson AB, Stockholm, Sweden, 1967-71; head computer devel. dept. Ericsson AB, Mölndal, Sweden, 1974-77; head testing methods and tech. Ericsson AB, Stockholm, Sweden, 1977-81; mgr. design and devel. Asea Lme Automation AB, Västerås, Sweden, 1971-74; v.p., gen. mgr. hybrid div. Rifa AB, Stockholm, Sweden, 1981-85; gen. mgr. controls div. Tour & Andersson AB, Västerhaninge, Sweden, 1985-89; mktg. mgr. U.S./Can.mobile telephone systems div. Ericsson Radio Systems AB, Stockholm, 1989—. Home: Erik Dahlbergsallen 11, S-11524 Stockholm Sweden Office: Tour & Andersson AB, Fabriksvagen 1, S-13737 Vasterhaninge Sweden

OGAWA, OSAMU, manufacturing executive; b. Kanda, Miyako, Fukuoka, Japan, Apr. 5, 1945; s. Hisamitu and Tamayo Ogawa; m. Eiko Inomoto, May 18, 1972. B, Kyusyu Inst. Tech., Kitakyusyu, Japan, 1968. Registered profl. engr., architect, Tokyo. Researcher Tokyo Rope Mfg. Co., Ltd., Tokyo, 1968-84, mgr., cons., 1984—. Inventor in field. Mem. Japan Soc. Civil Engrs., Soc. Naval Architects Japan. Home: Miyawada 531-2-712, 300-15 Fujishiro-Machi Kitasouma, Ibaragi Japan Office: Tokyo Rope Mfg Co Ltd, Chuouku Nihonbashi 2-5-11, 103 Tokyo Japan

OGBURN, CHARLES HARRIS, investment banker, lawyer; b. Guatemala City, Guatemala, May 26, 1955; came to U.S., 1962; s. William H. and Charlotte (Shepherd) O.; m. Lisa Demartini, Aug. 9, 1986. AB, Duke U., 1977; JD, Vanderbilt U., 1980. Bar: Ga. 1980. Assoc. King & Spalding, Atlanta, 1980-85; v.p. The Robinson-Humphrey Co., Atlanta, 1985—; bd. dirs. Crawford Post Prodn., Inc., Atlanta. Mem. Ga. Bar Assn. Office: Robinson Humphrey Co 3333 Peachtree Rd Atlanta GA 30326

OGDEN, JOANNE, real estate executive; b. Cumming, Ga., Apr. 9, 1941; d. Crafton Kemp Sr. and Mary Evelyn (Willis) Brooks; m. William Rush Williams, Jan. 3, 1961 (div. 1966); 1 child, Paul Rush Williams; m. Cecil Leavern Ogden, Sr.; stepchildren: Cecil Laverne Jr., Michael Vann. Grad. high sch., Cumming. Prin. Ogden & Ogden, Milledgeville, Ga., 1966—. Candidate Baldwin County Commnr., Milledgeville, 1984. Republican. Methodist. Club: 700 (Virginia Beach). Home: 402 Allen Memorial Dr SW Milledgeville GA 31061 Office: Ogden & Ogden 2600 Irwinton Rd Milledgeville GA 31061

OGDEN, SYLVESTER O., coal company executive; b. Paris, Mo., Oct. 29, 1935; s. Lester and Anastasia Ogden; m. Martha Jane Peterman, Feb. 15, 1964; children: Stasia, John. AA, Hannibal (Mo.) LaGrange Coll., 1957; BSChemE, U. Mo., 1961; MSChemE, U. Mo., Rolla, 1964; MBA, Cen. Mich. U., 1971. Various positions Dow Chem., Midland, Mich., 1964-71; v.p. planning and devel. Youghiogheny & Ohio, Cleve., 1971-75; pres., chief exec. officer Colorado Westermoreland; v.p. Westmoreland Coal, Colorado Springs, Colo., 1975-78, Panhandle Eastern Corp., 1978-81; pres., chief exec. officer Sunedco Co., Denver, 1981-84; v.p. Occidental Petrol, Lexington, Ky., 1984—; also chmn. bd., chief exec. officer Island Creek Coal Corp.; dir. Nat. Coal Council, Washington, Island Creek of China Coal, Ltd.; mem. joint cen. com. An Tai Bao Surface Mine, People's Republic China, 1986—. Founding chmn., dir. Alliance Clean Energy, Washington, 1983—. Mem. Nat. Coal Assn. (dir. 1978—), Ohio Mining and Reclamation Assn. (dir. 1978-81), Ky. Coal Assn. (dir. 1984—).

OGG, WILSON REID, poet, curator, publisher, lawyer, educator; b. Alhambra, Calif., Feb. 26, 1928; s. James Brooks and Mary (Wilson) O. Student Pasadena Jr. Coll., 1946; A.B., U. Calif. at Berkeley, 1949, J.D., 1952; Cultural D in Philosophy of Law, World Univ. Roundtable, 1983. Assoc. trust Dept. Wells Fargo Bank, San Francisco, 1954-55; admitted to Calif. bar; pvt. practice law, Berkeley, 1955-78; real estate broker, cons., 1974-78; curator-in-residence Pinebrook, 1964—; owner Pinebrook Press, Berkeley, Calif., 1988—; research atty., legal editor dept. of continuing edn. of bar U. Calif. Extension, 1958-63; psychology instr. 25th Sta. Hosp., Taegu, Korea, 1954; English instr. Taegu English Lang. Inst., Taegu, 1954. Trustee World U., 1976-80; dir. admissions Internat. Soc. for Phil. Enquiry, 1981-84; dep. dir. gen. Internat. Biographical Centre, Eng., 1986—; dep. gov. Am. Biographical Inst. Research Assn., 1986—. Served with AUS, 1952-54. Cert. community coll. instr. Recipient 5th Prize for poem "My Cat and I" Am. Poetry Assn., 1987. Fellow Internat. Acad. Law and Sci.; mem. ABA, State Bar Calif., San Francisco Bar Assn., Am. Arbitration Assn. (nat. panel arbitrators), World Univ. Round Table, World Future Soc. (profl. mem.), AAAS, Am. Assn. Fin. Profls., Am. Soc. Psychical Research, Calif. Soc. Psychical Study (pres., chmn. bd. 1963-65), Soc. for Phys. Research (London), Parapsychol. Assn. (asso.), 999 Soc., Internat. Soc. Unified Sci., Worldwide Acad. Scholars, Am. Acad. Polit. and Social Sci., World Acad. Arts and Culture, Inc., Artists Embassy Internat., Internat. Platform Assn., Intertel, Ina Coolbrith Circle, Cincinnatus Soc., Minerva Soc., Am. Legion, VFW, Mensa, Lawyers in Mensa, Psychic Sci. Spl. Interest Group, Am. Legion, VFW. Unitarian. Mason, Elk. Clubs: Faculty (U. Calif.), City Commons (Berkeley); Press (San Francisco); Commonwealth of Calif.; Town Hall Calif. Author, illustrator: My Escaping Self, 1988, Suns Without End, 1988; author: Love's Cradle, 1988, We Hatch Our Embryo, 1988; editor: Legal Aspects of Doing Business under Government Contracts and Subcontracts, 1958, Basic California Practice Handbook, 1959; contbr. numerous articles profl. jours; contbr. poetry to various mags. including American Poetry Anthology Vol. VI Number 5, Hearts on Fire: A Treasury of Poems on Love, Vol. IV, 1987, New Voices in American Poetry, 1987, The Poetry of Life A Treasury of Moments An. Poetry Anthology, Vol. VII, 1988. Home: 1104 Keith Ave Berkeley CA 94708-1607 Office: Eight Bret Harte Way Berkeley CA 94708-1611

OGLESBY, JOHN NORMAN, data processing, distribution, oil exploration and development executive; b. Dublin, Ga., Aug. 29, 1948; s. Theodore Nathaniel and Ruth (Moncrief) O.; m. Jansie Marie Bennett, June 4, 1966; children: John Norman, Julia Elizabeth. B in Aerospace Engring., Ga. Inst. Tech., 1971, M in Indsl. Mgmt., 1973. Data processing cons. First Computer Services Trust, Charlotte, N.C., 1973-76; securities analyst First Union Nat. Bank, Charlotte, 1977-79; pres. Oglesby Assocs., Charlotte, 1978-82, Memphis, 1983—; mgr. First Tenn. Nat. Bank Info. Ctr., 1982—; pres. Hercules Investor Services, 1983-84; pres. Am. Petroleum Devel., 1985—, Info. Processing Assocs., 1985—; gen. ptnr. Diamond Oil Co.; cons. data processing, bus. and fin.; internat. lectr. Designer, author Q.E.S. System, 1977, QESVAL, 1977, APT (productivity tool), 1983, CGS (county govt. system), 1984, IC-SCRAM (co-founder 1983, pres. 1985-87). Active Rep. Nat. Com., sponsor victory fund, 1981; mem. Citizens Choice. Acad. scholar Ga. Inst. Tech., 1966-71; Ga. Inst. Tech. Research and Teaching fellow, 1973. Mem. AIAA (v.p. 1970), Ambassador's Internat., Soc. Info. Mgmt. (pres. 1986-87, sec./treas. 1987, v.p. programs 1988), Amway Distbrs. Assn. Mem. Assembly of God. Home and Office: 7927 Woodleaf Memphis TN 38138-7150

OGOREK, JAMES JOHN, real estate and finance executive; b. Chgo., Apr. 24, 1945; s. Frank John and Elvera Delores (Krantz) O.; m. Helen Strotshuk, Jan. 27, 1968; children: Jennifer Ann, Paul James. BS, U. Ill., 1967. CPA, Fla., Ill. Staff acct. Ernst & Ernst, Chgo., 1967, in-charge acct. to sr. mgr., 1970-79; v.p. fin. Gould Fla., Inc., West Palm Beach, 1979-81, v.p. fin. and ops., 1981-85; chief operating officer Mershon, Sawyer, Johnston, Dunwody & Cole, Miami, Fla., 1985-88; v.p., chief fin. officer MIG Realty Advisors, Inc., West Palm Beach, 1988—; dir. R.O. Investors, Inc., Oger Inc., Roni Buns, Inc. Coach T-Ball, Little League and soccer West Palm Beach, 1979-83. Served with AUS, 1968-70. Mem. Am. Inst. CPA's (real estate com.), Fla. Inst. CPA's, Ill. Inst. CPA's, West Palm Beach C. of C., Palm Beach Polo and Country Club, Wellington Golf and Tennis Club, Gov.'s, Univ., Greenview Cove Golf Club. Republican. Roman Catholic. Home: 12706 Headwater Cir Wellington FL 33414 Office: MIG Realty Advisors Inc 1645 Palm Beach Lakes Blvd Ste 600 West Palm Beach FL 33401

OGOREK, RICHARD ALAN, financial executive; b. Wilmington, Del., Mar. 20, 1951; s. Alexander Joseph and Nancy Mary (O'Neal) O.; m. Diane Jane Hynson, Dec. 21, 1976; children: Justin, Lauren, Adam, Jillian. Student, U. Del., 1970-73; BBA in Acctg., Wilmington Coll. cum laude, 1976. CPA, Pa., Del. Acct. Touche Ross & Co., Phila., 1977-82, Belfint, Lyons & Shuman, Wilmington, 1982-83; sr. audit mgr. Alco Standard Corp., Valley Forge, Pa., 1983-84, mgr. corp. fin. planning, 1984-86; v.p., group controller Alco Packaging Co. div. Alco Standard Corp., Valley Forge, Pa., 1986-88; v.p. fin., chief fin. officer Jet Plastica Industries, Inc., Hatfield, Pa., 1988—; v.p. Delaware Valley Acctg. and Fin. council, Phila., 1978-79, pres., 1979-80. Mem. Am. Inst. CPA's, Pa. INst. CPA's, Kennett Sq. Golf and Country Club. Republican. Roman Catholic. Home: 1108 Woodstock Ln West Chester PA 19382

OGRIZOVICH, JOHN JAY, public utility executive; b. Kansas City, Mo., Aug. 14, 1945; s. Pete Ogrizovich and Adrienne (Flaspohler) Layton; m. Patricia Ann Lesniak, Nov. 5, 1966; children: Lara Suzanne, Julie Lynn. AA, Metro Community Coll., 1970; BA in Econs., U. Mo., Kansas City, 1972; MBA, U. Mo., 1976. Various position Sears, Roebuck & Co., Kansas City, 1963-70; programmer, analyst United Telecom, Shawnee Mission, Kans., 1970-72, staff acct., 1972-74, mgr. data ops., 1974-77, mgr. programming services, 1977-79, dir. data services, 1979-81; v.p. data services Lone Star Gas Co., Dallas, 1981-84, sr. v.p. adminstrn., 1984—. Chmn. budget panel United Way, Dallas, 1982—; chmn. Dallas Mayor's Com. for Employment Disabled, 1986—; mem. Bus. Adv. Council, Dallas, 1986—. Mem. Am. Gas Assn., So. Gas Assn., Soc. for Info. Mgmt., Independence Jaycees (bd. dirs. 1976-80, Key Man of Yr. award 1979). Office: Lone Star Gas Co 301 S Harwood St Dallas TX 75201

OH, MAY BUONG YU LAU, lawyer; b. Singapore, May 20, 1940; d. Pai Hu Liu Lau and Uk Cung Liu Hu; m. Siew Leong Oh, May 22, 1965; children—Su Lin, Siang Peng. Student Anglo Chinese Jr. Coll., Singapore, 1958-59; Barrister-at-Law, Lincoln's Inn (London), 1964. Called to bar of Eng., 1965; called to bar of Singapore, 1967; Adv., solicitor Supreme Ct. Singapore, 1967. Cert. Am. and internat. bus. law and transactions, acctg., taxation. Legal asst. firm Lee & Lee, Singapore, 1966-67; legal officer Housing and Devel. Bd., 1967; mgmt. asst. Mobil Oil Malaysia Sdn. Bhd., 1967, apptd. co. sec., 1968; legal counsel Mobil East, N.Y.C., 1970, Mobil Europe, London, 1970; apptd. gen. counsel Mobil Oil Singapore Pte Ltd., 1970, apptd. exec. dir. bd. dirs., 1971 (first Asian appointee), assigned primary responsibilities for govt. affairs, Singapore, 1973, dir. legal/govt. affairs Mobil Oil Singapore Pte Ltd. with regional responsibilities for Singapore, Malaysia and Thailand, 1973-84; dir. Mobil Asia Pte Ltd., 1974-84; ptnr. May Oh & Co., 1984—; sr. ptnr. May Oh & Wee Advocates & Solicitors, 1985—; mem. adv. bd. Internat. Comparative Law Ctr., Dallas; participant, speaker profl. internat. confs., Singapore, U.S., Europe. Contbr. articles to publs. Chmn. organizing com. Pvt. Investment in Asia and the Pacific, 1973; bd. govs. Methodist Girls' Sch., 1978—; pres. Meth. Girls' Sch. Alumnae Assn., 1981—. chmn. Internat. Energy Conf., Singapore and Jakarta, 1984, 85. Conf. fellow Acad. Am. and Internat. Lat, 1970. Mem. Am. Inst. Mgmt. (council fellow 1981—), Singapore Law Soc., Singapore Econ. Soc., Internat. and Comparative Law Center (U.S.), Singapore Am. Bus. Council, Internat. Bar Assn. (conf. host planning com. 1982), Law Assn. for Asia and Western Pacific (chmn. energy sect.). Methodist. Clubs: Singapore Island Country, Jurong Country, Tanglin. Home: 27 Ewart Park, Singapore 1027, Singapore Office: May Oh & Wee, 21 Collyer Quay #14-02, Hong Kong Bank Bldg, Singapore 0104, Singapore

OH, TAI KEUN, business educator; b. Seoul, Korea, Mar. 25, 1934; s. Chin Young and Eui Kyung (Yun) O.; came to U.S., 1958, naturalized, 1969; B.A., Seijo U., 1957; M.A., No. Ill. U., 1961; M.L.S., U. Wis., 1965, Ph.D., 1970; m. Gretchen Brenneke, Dec. 26, 1964; children—Erica, Elizabeth, Emily. Asst. prof. mgmt. Roosevelt U., Chgo., 1969-73; assoc. prof. Calif. State U., Fullerton, 1973-76, prof. mgmt., 1976—; vis. prof. U. Hawaii, 1983-84, 86; advisor Pacific Asian Mgmt. Inst., U. Hawaii; cons. Calty Design Research, Inc. subs. Toyota Motor Corp. Merchants and Mfrs. Assn.; seminar leader and speaker. Named Outstanding Prof., Sch. Bus. Adminstrn. and Econs., Calif. State U., Fullerton, 1976, 78. NSF grantee, 1968-69, recipient Exceptional Merit Service award Calif. State U., 1984, Meritorious Performance and Profl. Promise award Calif. State U., 1987. Mem. Acad. Mgmt., Indsl. Relations Research Assn., Acad. Internat. Bus. Editorial bd. Acad. Mgmt. Rev., 1978-81; contbg. author: Ency. Profl. Mgmt., 1978, Handbook of Management 1985; contbr. articles to profl. jours. Home: 2044 E Eucalyptus Ln Brea CA 92621 Office: Calif State U Fullerton CA 92634

O'HARA, ALFRED PECK, lawyer; b. Patterson, N.Y., Apr. 27, 1919; s. Peter and Anna L. (Peck) O'H.; m. Muriel A. Sandberg, Aug. 30, 1940 (dec.); children: Jane Ann O'Hara Toth, Margaret Kathleen O'Hara Duff, Peter James, John Edward; m. 2d Thelma deVries (div.); m. 3d Martha Stein, June 22, 1984. B.A., Syracuse U., 1940; LL.B., Fordham U., 1942. Bar: N.Y. bar 1942, U.S. Supreme Ct 1956. Sec. to U.S. Dist. Ct., 1942-43; partner firm McLaughlin & Stickles, 1946-52; asst. U.S. atty., chief civil div. So. Dist. N.Y., 1953-56; cons. to atty. gen. N.Y. State, 1956; sr. ptnr. firm Rogers Hoge & Hills, N.Y.C., 1958-86; of counsel Kelley, Drye & Warren, N.Y.C., 1986—; counsel U.S. Trademark Assn., 1967-70; chmn. bd. Bacardi Corp., 1982-87, chmn. fin. com.; bd. dirs. Sogrape U.S.A., Bacardi Capital Ltd., Shippan Internat. Ins. Co. Mem. Assn. Bar City of N.Y., N.Y. State Bar Assn., Am. Bar Assn., NAM (bd. dirs. 1978—), Fed. Bar Council, Am. Law Inst. (life), Internat. Patent and Trademark Assn. Clubs: Williams, Bankers of P.R, Quaker Hill. Home: RR 4 Box 55 Birch Hill Rd Patterson NY 12563 Office: Kelley Drye & Warren 101 Park Ave New York NY 10178 also: Bacardi Corp PO Box G3549 San Juan PR 00960

O'HARA, MARY MARGARET, advertising specialty company, owner; b. Corning, N.Y., July 27, 1950; d. William Desmond and Mary Margaret (Fleming) O'H. BA in Sociology, St. Mary's Coll., Notre Dame, Ind., 1972. Adminstrv. asst. Corning (N.Y.) Urban Renewal Agy., 1972-73; office mgr. Quality Specialty Co., Corning, 1973-79, ptnr., owner, 1979-87, owner, 1987—. V.p. Corning Hosp. Chpt. D, 1979, pres., 1980, sec. chapts. coun., 1981-84. Mem. Corning Country Women's Golf Assn. (chmn. 1984, treas. 1985—). Democrat. Roman Catholic.

O'HARE, DEAN RAYMOND, insurance company executive; b. Jersey City, June 21, 1942; s. Francis and Ann O'H.; m. Kathleen T. Walliser, Dec. 2, 1967; Dean, Jason. B.S., NYU, 1963; M.B.A., Pace U., 1968. Trainee Chubb Corp., N.Y.C., 1963-64, tax advisor, 1964-67, asst. v.p., mgr. corp. fin. devel., 1968-72, sr. v.p., mgr. corp. fin. devel. dept., 1979—, chief fin. officer, 1979—, pres., 1986-88, chmn., chief exec. officer, 1988—; chmn. Chubb Life Ins. Co. Am., 1981—; chmn., pres. Fed. Ins. Co., 1988—, Vigilant Ins. Co., 1988—; chmn., dir. Bellemead Devel. Corp., 1973—; chmn. Colonial Life Ins. Co. Am., 1980—, United Life & Accident Ins. Co., 1980—; dir. Chubb Ins. Co. Can., Fed. Ins. Co., Vigilant Ins. Co. Mem. Urban Land Inst. Clubs: India House, Hanover Square; Halifax (Daytona Beach, Fla.). Home: Lake Rd Far Hills NJ 07931 Office: Chubb Corp 15 Mountain View Rd Warren NJ 07061 also: 15 Mountain View Rd Warren NJ 07061-1615

O'HARE, DON R., corporate executive; b. Joliet, Ill., 1922; married. B.S., U. Minn., 1943. Plant engr. Western Electric Co., 1946-47; sales engr. Wallace & Tiernan Co., 1947-50; sales trainee Falk Corp., Milw., 1950-51, sales engr., 1951-55, dist. office mgr., 1955-72, v.p., sales mgr., 1972-74, pres., 1974-76; with Sundstrand Corp., Rockford, Ill., 1976—, v.p., 1976-77, group v.p., 1977-79, exec. v.p., 1980-88, vice chmn., 1989—, also bd. dirs.; dir. M & I Corp., Modine Mfg. Corp. Served with USN, 1943-46. Office: Sundstrand Corp 4949 Harrison Ave Box 7003 Rockford IL 61125-7003 *

O'HARE, JAMES RAYMOND, energy company executive; b. Evergreen Park, Ill., July 20, 1938; s. Raymond Clarence and Helen (Nickel) O'H.; m. Nan Jane Raleigh, Sept. 18, 1965; children: Joan, Daniel, Colleen, Patrick. B.S., Marquette U., 1960; M.B.A., U. Calif. at Los Angeles, 1961. C.P.A., Ind., Ill., Ky., Calif., Tex. Mgr. Peat, Marwick, Mitchell & Co., Chgo., 1961-68, South Bend, Ind., 1968-69; controller Essex Internat., Inc., Fort Wayne, Ind., 1969-76, Am. Air Filter Co., Inc., Louisville, 1976-80; fin. v.p. and treas. Petrolane Inc., Long Beach, Calif., 1980-85; treas. Tex. Eastern Corp., Houston, 1985-87, v.p., treas., 1987-88; sr. v.p. fin. and adminstrn. Texas Eastern Gas Pipeline Co., Houston, 1988—. Served with USNR, 1962-68. Mem. Evans Scholars, Am. Inst. C.P.A.s, Fin. Execs. Inst., Beta Gamma Sigma. Clubs: Houston, Houston Center; Pine Forest Country. Office: Tex Ea Corp 1221 McKinney St Houston TX 77010

OHGREN, DEBI MICHELLE, construction company executive; b. Colorado Springs, Colo., Mar. 30, 1956; d. Melvin O. and Mary Jewitt (Bokowski) Nielsen; m. Gunnar A. Ohgren, Dec. 20, 1975 (div. Sept. 1981). Student, Colo. State U., 1974. Teller with bookkeeping, open accounts, drafts Acad. Blvd. Bank, Colorado Springs, 1974-75; asst. mgr. Applegates Landing, Del Rio, Tex., 1978-79; substitute tchr. Uvalde (Tex.) Ind. Sch. Dist., 1980; asst. mgr. Kalino's, Del Rio, 1981-82; gen. mgr. Jay Miller Constrn. Co., Inc., Del Rio, 1983-88, pres., 1988—. Office: Jay Miller Constrn PO Box 420006 Del Rio TX 78842

OHLFS, MARY IRENE, community volunteer; b. Oxnard, Calif., May 18, 1923; d. Michael Gustav and Elizabeth Theresa (Godde) Vujovich; m. Fabian Henry Ohlfs, June 20, 1960; 1 child, Michael Jeffrey. BA, Mt. St. Mary's Coll., L.A., 1946. Teen-age recreation, playground dir. Oxnard Recreation Dept., 1946-48; field dir. Girl Scouts U.S., Ventura County, Calif., 1949-54; social worker Ventura County Welfare Dept., 1954-60. Vol. West Valley Rep. Women, Saratoga, Calif., 1965—, Santa Clara County Girl Scouts, 1965—, Boy Scouts Am., 1965—. Recipient Marillac Svc. award Santa Clara County Cath. Social Svcs. Aux., 1979, Alumnae Svc. award Mt. St. Mary's Coll., 1972. Mem. AAUW, Mt. St. Mary's Coll. Alumni Assn., Native Daus. of Golden West, Young Ladies Inst., Santa Clara Univ. Catala Club. Roman Catholic. Home: 13923 Malcolm Ave Saratoga CA 95070

OHLMAN, CHARLES EDWARD, utilities company executive; b. Peru, Ind., Dec. 11, 1926; s. Walter Edward and Mabel M. (Nicely) O.; m. Lillian Delores DePasquale, Oct. 24, 1953; children: Diane, Mark. B.S.E.E., Purdue U., 1951. Registered profl. engr., Ind. Engr. Indpls. Power & Light Co., 1954-71, chief planning engr., 1971-77, asst. v.p. engring. and constrn., 1977-78, v.p. power supply, 1978-79, sr. v.p. consumer services, 1979—. Served to 1st lt. U.S. Army, 1945-46, ETO. Mem. IEEE (sr.), Am. Mgmt. Assn., Indpls. Sci. and Engirng. Found., Newcomen Soc. Clubs: Indpls. Athletic, Columbia, Hillcrest Country; Optimist (Indpls.). Lodge: Masons. Home:

9678 Decatur Dr Indianapolis IN 46256 Office: Indpls Power & Light Co PO Box 1595 B Indianapolis IN 46204

OHLMAN, DOUGLAS RONALD, lawyer, investment consultant; b. Rockville Centre, N.Y., Mar. 25, 1949; s. Maxwell and Miriam (Frucht) O.; m. Elat Menashe, Dec. 4, 1983. B.A., Columbia Coll., 1971; J.D., Hofstra U., 1974. Bar: N.Y. 1975, U.S. Dist. Ct. (so. and ea. dists.) N.Y. 1976, (no. and we. dists.) N.Y. 1978, U.S. Tax Ct. 1978, U.S. Supreme Ct. 1978, U.S. Ct. Claims 1978, U.S. Customs Ct. 1978. Vice pres. Info. & Research Services, Inc., Roslyn, N.Y., 1975-81; assoc. Baer & Marks, N.Y.C., 1974-75, Rains, Pogrebin & Scher, Mineola, N.Y., 1975-76, Weisman, Celler, Spett, Modlin & Wertheimer, N.Y.C., 1976-79, Hoffberg, Gordon, Rabin & Engler, N.Y.C., 1979-80, Bergner & Bergner, Blum & Ruditz, N.Y.C., 1980-81; gen. counsel Greenfield Ptnrs., N.Y.C., 1981-86, gen. ptnr., 1982-86, dep. mng. ptnr., 1984-86, chief operating officer, sr. v.p., sec., dir. V.W. Investors, Inc., J.L. Investors, Inc., N.Y.C., 1985-88, dir. Track Data Corp., N.Y.C., 1983-87; allied mem. N.Y. Stock Exchange, Inc., 1982-88. Mem. radio news team WKCR-FM, N.Y.C. (Writers Guild award, Peabody nomination 1968); notes and comments editor Hofstra Law Rev., 1973-74. Communications dir., dep. radiol. officer Nassau County Civil Def., Town of Roslyn, N.Y., 1964-74; mem. com. Nassau County Liberal Party, 1982. Mem. ABA, N.Y. State Bar Assn., N.Y. County Lawyers Assn., Assn. Bar City N.Y. Home: 6751 Via Regina Boca Raton FL 33433

O'HOP, PAUL ALBERT, SR., director business program; b. Avoca, Pa., June 26, 1939; s. William and Estelle (Cofferan) O'H.; m. Florentine Wrobleski, Nov. 29, 1958; children: Lynne O'Hop Feeney, Paul Jr., Suzanne. Cert. in Health Care Mgmt., Naval Sch. Hosp. Adminstrn., 1969; BS, George Washington U., 1969, MBA, 1973. Enlisted USAF, 1955, advanced through grades to major, 1973, ret., 1976; v.p. Libra Tech., Rockville, Md., 1976-78; mgmt. analyst VA Med. Ctr., Wilkes-Barre, Pa., 1978-79; asst. prof. Marywood Coll., Scranton, Pa., 1979-85; assoc. prof. Wilkes Coll., Wilkes-Barre, 1985—, v.p. bus. affairs/aux. enterprises, 1986—; bd. dirs. Pa. Internat. Trade Congress, Easter Pa.-Bahia (Brazil) Com. Bd. dirs. United Way, Lackawanna County, Pa.; co-chmn. Reagan-Bush Com., 1984; mem. Pa. Milk Mktg. Bd. Mem. Acad. Mgmt., Soc. for Gen. Systems Research, Assn. of Pa. Economists, Am. Coll. Hosp. Care Execs., Advt. Club of N.E. Pa., Nat. Fedn. Independent Businessmen, Am. Legion, Am. Vets. Republican. Roman Catholic. Lodge: Elks. Home: Janette Cir Moscow PA 18444 Office: Wilkes Coll 170 S Franklin St Wilkes-Barre PA 18766

OHRSTROM, RICARD RIGGS, financial executive; b. Tarrytown, N.Y., Aug. 1, 1922; s. George Lewis and Emma (Riggs) O.; m. Mary Elizabeth Murchison, Mar. 16, 1949 (div. Mar. 1966); m. Elizabeth Rinehart, Dec. 26, 1968 (div. 1977); m. Jane Hoyt, May 19, 1978 (div. 1984); m. Allen Dunnington, Sept. 3, 1985; children: Ricard Riggs, Kenneth, George L. II, Christopher, Barnaby, Mark. AB cum laude in Public Affairs, Princeton U., 1944; LLB, U. Va., 1949. Bar: Va. 1949. Assoc., G.L. Ohrstrom & Co., N.Y.C., 1949-50; atty. civil div. Chief Counsel's Office, Bur. Internal Revenue, Washington, 1950-52; with W.C. Norris, Tulsa, 1952-54; partner G.L. Ohrstrom & Co., N.Y.C., 1954-55, mng. partner, 1955-69, semi-active gen. partner, 1970—; dir. Carlisle Corp., 1955—, Dover Corp. 1955—, Leach Corp., Los Angeles, 1953-55, chmn. bd., 1955-74; dir. Leigh Corp., 1962-79, Round Hill Devels., Ltd., 1968-85, chmn. bd., 1977-84, others. Bd. dirs. Middleburg (Va.) Community Center, 1956—, chmn. bd. 1972-77; bd. dirs. Hill Sch., 1971-76, Sun Valley Ctr. for Arts, 1980—, chmn., 1982—; pres. The Catesby Found.; del. Va. State Rep. Conv., 1980. Served with USMC, 1943-46. Home: Old Whitewood The Plains VA 22171 Office: PO Box 325 Middleburg VA 22117

OKAMOTO, RODNEY JIN, health care agency executive, pharmacist; b. Lodi, Calif., Jan. 1, 1954; s. Jin J. and Yoshiko Josie (Shintaku) O.; m. Paula Roberta Cancino, Feb. 12, 1978; children: Travis, Jason, Haley. BS in Pharmacy, U. Pacific, Stockton, Calif., 1977. Staff pharmacist Merced (Calif.) Med. Ctr., 1977-78; clin. pharmacist U. Calif. Med. Ctr., Davis, 1978-83; owner Maps Pharmacy, Sacramento, 1979-83; mgr. Maps Pharmacy subs. DELMED, Inc., Sacramento, 1983-87, Maps Pharmacy subs. NMC Homecare, Inc., Sacramento, 1987—. Co-pub.: Home Care mag., 1986. Mem. Elk Grove (Calif.) PTA, 1987—. Mem. Calif. Pharmacist Assn., Am. Soc. Parenteral and Enteral Nutrition, No. Calif. Soc. Parenteral and Enteral Nutrition. Democrat. Office: NMC Homecare Inc 65 G Quinta Ct Sacramento CA 95823

O'KEEFE, GERALD JAMES, plastics office accessories manufacturing company; b. Springfield, Mass., Dec. 11, 1937; s. Gerald Edward and Mildred Brown O'K; m. Susan M. Lyons, June 20, 1970; children: John Ryan, William Neil. Student, Bridgewater State Coll., 1955-57; BA, U. Mass., 1957-59. Sales rep. Calif. Chem. div. Standard Oil Calif., 1961-66; sales rep. Mercedes Benz Co., 1966-70; European del cons. Lowery Corp., Hartford, Conn., 1970-71; sales rep. Papermate div. Gillette Co., New Eng., N.Y.C., 1971-75, Gates Paper div. SCM Corp., Marion, Ind., 1975-77; sales mgr. for east coast Eldon Office Products Co., Glastonbury, Conn., 1977-80; gen. mgr. Arlac Werk, Hamburg, Fed. Rep. Germany, Branford, Conn., 1980-82; pres. Alexander & O'Keefe, Inc., 1982—. Active Glastonbury Service Club. Mem. Nat. Office Products Assn. Home: 47 Delmar Rd Glastonbury CT 06403

O'KEEFFE, JOHN JOSEPH, JR., lawyer, holding company executive; b. Norwalk, Conn., Dec. 21, 1941; s. John Joseph Sr. and Mary Ellen (Snee) O'K.; m. Valerie Anne Moore, Sept. 2, 1967; children: Anna Gould, John Moore. BA, Fairfield U., 1965; JD, George Washington U., 1968. Bar: N.Y. 1969. Atty. Pan Am. World Airways, Inc., N.Y.C., 1968-72; atty. TWA, N.Y.C., 1972-77, corp. sec., asst. gen. counsel, 1977-83; asst. gen. counsel Transworld Corp., N.Y.C., 1979-83; v.p, gen. counsel Transworld Corp., 1983-86, gen. counsel, 1986, gen. counsel, corp. sec., 1986-87; sr. v.p., gen. counsel, corp. sec. TW Svcs. Inc., 1987—. Mem. N.Y. State Bar Assn., Larchmont Yacht Club. Republican. Roman Catholic. Home: 11 Dante St Larchmont NY 10538 Office: TW Svcs Inc PO Box 904 Paramus NJ 07653-0904

O'KELLEY, CHARLES PATRICK, accountant; b. El Paso, Tex., Mar. 1, 1954; s. William Charles and Ruby Jane (Moody) O'K.; m. Carla Deidre Jones, May 1977 (div. 1985); m. Barbara Ann Alexander, Apr. 25, 1987. BBA in Fin., Tex. A&M U., 1976; MS in Acctg., U. Houston, 1985. CPA, Tex.; Cert. Mgmt. Acct. Customer service rep. C.I.T. Fin. Co., Houston, 1976-77; jr. credit person Northwest Acceptance Corp., Houston, 1977-79; credit rep. Nat. Steel Products Co., Houston, 1979-80; v.p., treas. Mesbic Fin. Corp., Houston, 1980—. Mem. Nat. Assn. Accts. (bd. dirs. 1986—), Tex. Assn. Single Sailors (assoc.). Club: Toastmasters. Office: Mesbic Fin Corp 811 Rust St Ste 201 Houston TX 77002

O'KON, JAMES ALEXANDER, engineering executive; b. Buffalo, Aug. 8, 1937; s. A.C. and Rita (McGaugh) O'K.; m. Carol Ann Smith, 1987; children: Sean Fitzgerald, Katherine Shannon. BCE, Ga. Inst. Tech., 1961; MCE, NYU, 1970. Registered profl. engr. Tenn., N.Y., Ill., Fla., Tex., Miss., Calif., Ga., Mass., La., N.J., S.C., Ala., Ky., Va., N.C., Kans., Colo. Hwy. engr. Ga. Hwy. Dept., Atlanta, 1960-62; structural engr. Robert & Co., Atlanta, 1962-64; project coordinator So. Design, Spartanburg, S.C., 1964-67; project engr. Crawford-Russell, Stamford, Conn., 1967-68, Faraks Barron Ptnr., N.Y.C., 1968-69; v.p. Lev Zetlin Assocs., N.Y.C., Atlanta, 1969-77; pres. O'Kon and Co. (formerly Lev Aetlin Assocs.), Atlanta, 1977—; bd. dirs. Superior Demolition Co., Atlanta; chmn. bd. Five Star Travel, Inc. Author: Floating Factory to Produce Precast Concrete Components, 1973, Energy Conservation Noise and Vibration Control in Construction of Offshore Power Plants, 1975, Guidelines for Investigative Engineering, 1987, Methodology For The Life Prediction of Buildings, 1989. Dir. United Urban Community, N.Y.C., 1970-73, Urban Village Works, Atlanta, 1984—; Interdisciplinary Council, N.Y.C., 1970-73; pres. Skyview Tenants Assn., N.Y.C., 1970-73; mem. Jimmy Carter Peanut Brigade, New Hampshire, Ga., 1976; chmn. United Way Fund, Atlanta, 1978; dir. Com. to elect Andrew Young for Mayor, Atlanta, 1981, 85. Recipient Grand award Builder's Mag., 1983, Archtl. Excellence award Am. Inst. Steel Constructors, 1984, Engring. Excellence award Am. Consulting Engrs. Council Ga., 1983, 88, Grand Award for Engring. Excellence Am. Cons. Engrs. Council, 1988, 89. Mem. ASCE (com. to develop guidelines for failure investigation, tech. coun. for forensic engring.), Am. Inst. Archaeology, Am. Cons. Engr.'s Coun., Smithsonian Inst., Atlanta Preservation Soc. (mem. Preservation Profls. Group), Am. Arbitration Assn. (panel of arbitrators), Internat. Platform Assn. Democrat. Roman Catholic. Home: 26104 Plantation Dr NE Atlanta GA 30324 Office: Okon & Co 1375 Peachtree St NE Ste 400 Atlanta GA 30309

OKUN, RICHARD ALLEN, pension fund administrator; b. N.Y.C., Mar. 29, 1952; s. Phillip and Florence (DuVal) Popper; m. Kim Jenell Carr, Mar 3, 1981. BS, BA, Syracuse U., 1974. Mgr. Computerland Fairfield, Conn., 1982-83; v.p. MicroFunding Inc., Wallingford, Conn., 1983—, Rush Computers, 1985, Svc. Inc., 1988, Comprehend, 1988—. Capt. USAF, 1974-82. Mem. Rotary (award 1974). Jewish. Home: 37 Miller Rd Bethany CT 06525 Office: MicroFunding Inc 135 N Plains Industry Rd Wallingford CT 06492

OKWUMABUA, BENJAMIN NKEM, corporate executive; b. Issele-Uku, Nigeria, June 20, 1939; came to U.S., 1963; naturalized, 1978; s. Daniel Ikeduba and Nwaonogwu Emily O.; m. Constance Lee, Mar. 16, 1968; children: Benjamin Nkem, Oblamaka Patricia, Richard Ikeduba, Daniel Ikeduba. BS, Cen. State U., 1967; MBA, Mich. State U., 1969, M in Labor and Indsl. Relations, 1971, PhD, 1974. Prof. Saginaw (Mich.) Valley State Coll., 1971-75, dept. chmn., 1971-75; sales mgr. Oldsmobile div. Gen. Motors Corp., Buffalo, 1975-78; pres., chief exec. officer AFRO-LECON, Inc., Jamestown, N.Y., 1978—. Mem. gov.'s adv. council on minority bus. devel. State of N.Y., council on western N.Y. econ. devel. Researcher in field. Mem. Acad. Mgmt., Am. Mgmt. Assn., Am. Mktg. Assn., Indsl. Relations Research Assn., Beta Gammas Sigma, Sigma Iota. Democrat. Baptist. Lodge: Rotary. Home: 505 Chautauqua Ave Jamestown NY 14701 Office: AFRO-LECON Inc 335 Harrison St Jamestown NY 14701

OLANDER, RAY GUNNAR, lawyer; b. Buhl, Minn., May 15, 1926; s. Olof Gunnar and Margaret Esther (Meisner) O.; m. Audrey Joan Greenlaw, Aug. 1, 1959; children—Paul Robert, Mary Beth. B.E.E. with distinction, U. Minn., 1949, B.B.A. with distinction, 1949; J.D. cum laude, Harvard U., 1959. Bar: Minn. 1959, Wis. 1962, U.S. Patent Office 1968. Elec. engr. M. A. Hanna Co., Hibbing, Minn., 1950-56; assoc. Leonard, Street & Deinard, Mpls., 1959-61; comml. atty. Bucyrus-Erie Co., South Milwaukee, Wis., 1961-70, dir. contracts, 1970-76, v.p. comml., 1976-88, gen. atty., 1978-80, corp. sec., 1978-88, gen. counsel, 1980-88; vice chmn. Bucyrus-Erie Co., South Milwaukee, 1988—; bd. dirs. Bucyrus-Erie Co., B-E Holdings Inc., Bucyrus Internat., Inc., Bucyrus (Africa) (Proprietary) Ltd., Bucyrus (Australia) Proprietary, Ltd., Wis. Holdings Proprietary Ltd., Equipment Assurance Ltd., Minserco Inc., Western Gear Machinery Co. Bd. dirs. Ballet Found. Milw., Inc., 1978—, Pub. Expenditure Research Found., Inc., Madison, Wis., 1978—, Pub. Expenditure Survey Wis., Madison, 1978-82. Served with USN, 1944-46. Mem. ABA, Wis. Bar Assn., Wis. Intellectual Property Law Assn., Am. Soc. Corp. Secs., Inc., Am. Corp. Counsel Assn., VFW, Eta Kappa Nu, Tau Beta Pi, Beta Gamma Sigma. Republican. Roman Catholic. Clubs: Harvard (N.Y.C.), Harvard of Wis., University (Milw.), Tuckaway Country (Franklin, Wis.). Lodges: Masons, Shriners. Home: 5881 Fleming Ct Greendale WI 53129 Office: Bucyrus-Erie Co 1100 Milwaukee Ave South Milwaukee WI 53172

OLBRECHTS, GUY ROBERT, electrical engineer, consultant; b. Mechelen, Belgium, May 22, 1935; came to U.S., 1967, naturalized, 1978; s. Alphonse and Blanche (Van Coolput) O.; m. Andree Julia Van Nes, Oct. 19, 1961; children: Philippe, Ingrid, Dominique. Ingenieur civil electricien Catholic U. Leuven, Belgium, 1960; MBA, Seattle U., 1976. Lead engr. Ctr. D'Etudes Nucleaires, Mol, Belgium, 1962-65; quality control mgr., chief engr. for magnetics Sprague Electromag., Ronse, Belgium, 1965-67; sr. engr. Boeing Co., Seattle, 1967-79; sect. mgr. data systems engring. and product support Sundstrand Data Control Corp., Redmond, Wash., 1979-88; project engr. memory systems Sundstrand Data Control; propr., cons., designer Gentronics, Bellevue, Wash., 1970—. Patentee gyro wheel speed modulator, 1981, integrated strapdown/airdata sensor system, 1981, slow-acting phase-locked loop, 1983. Served as cpl. Belgian Army, 1961-62. Recipient inventor award Boeing Co., 1978. Republican. Roman Catholic. Home: 4809 116th Ave SE Bellevue WA 98006 Office: Sundstrand Data Control Corp 15001 NE 36th Stark Redmond WA 98073-9701

OLDHAM, MAXINE JERNIGAN, real estate broker; b. Whittier, Calif., Oct. 13, 1923; d. John K. and Lela Hessie (Mears) Jernigan; m. Laurance Montgomery Oldham, Oct. 28, 1941; 1 child, John Laurence. AA, San Diego City Coll., 1973; student Western State U. Law, San Diego, 1976-77, LaSalle U., 1977-78; grad. Realtors Inst., Sacramento, 1978. Mgr. Edin Harig Realty, LaMesa, Calif., 1966-70; tchr. Bd. Edn., San Diego, 1959-66; mgr. Julia Cave Real Estate, San Diego, 1970-73; salesman Computer Realty, San Diego, 1973-74; owner Shelter Island Realty, San Diego, 1974—. Author: Jernigan History, 1982, Mears Geneology, 1985, Fustons of Colonial America, 1988. Mem. Civil Service Commn., San Diego, 1957-58. Mem. Nat. Assn. Realtors, Calif. Assn. Realtors, San Diego Bd. Realtors, San Diego Apt. Assn., Internationale des Professions Immobilieres (internat. platform speaker), DAR, Colonial Dames 17th Century, Internat. Fedn. Univ. Women. Republican. Roman Catholic. Avocations: music, theater, painting, geneology, continuing edn. Home: 3348 Lowell St San Diego CA 92106 Office: Shelter Island Realty 2810 Lytton St San Diego CA 92110

OLDS, JOHN THEODORE, banker; b. N.Y.C., Dec. 24, 1943; s. Richard J. and Barbara (Moses) O.; m. Candace Rose; children—Richard W., Samantha. Grad. Hill Sch., 1961; B.A., U. Pa., 1965. With Morgan Guaranty Trust Co. N.Y., N.Y.C., 1973—, sr. v.p., 1982—, exec. v.p., head securities group for Middle East, Asia and Africa, 1983-86, exec. v.p. Asia-Pacific Sector, 1986, J.P. Morgan & Co., 1986—. Episcopalian. Clubs: University (N.Y.C.); Bedford (N.Y.) Golf and Tennis; Mid-Ocean (Bermuda). Home: Plateau Ln Bedford NY 10506 Office: Morgan Guaranty Trust Co 23 Wall St New York NY 10015

OLDSHUE, JAMES Y., manufacturing company executive; b. Chgo., Apr. 18, 1925; s. James and Louise (Young) O.; m. Betty Ann Wiersema, June 14, 1947; children: Paul, Richard, Robert. B.S. in Chem. Engring., Ill. Inst. Tech., 1947, M.S., 1949, Ph.D. in Chem. Engring., 1951. Registered engr., N.Y. With Mixing Equipment Co., Rochester, N.Y., 1950—; dir. research Mixing Equipment Co., 1960-63, tech. dir., 1963-70, v.p. mixing tech., 1970—. Author: Fluid Mixing Technology, 1983; contbr. chpts. and articles to books and jours. Chmn. budget com. Internat. div. YMCA; bd. dirs. Rochester YMCA. Served with AUS, 1945-47. Recipient 1st Disting. Service award NE YMCA Internat. Com., 1979; Victor Marquez award Interam. Confedn. Chem. Engrs., 1983; named Rochester Engr. of Yr., 1980. Fellow Am. Inst. Chem. Engrs. (pres. 1979, treas. 1983-89, Eminent Chem. Engr., 1983, Founders award 1981); mem. Am. Assn. Engring. Socs. (chmn. 1985, K.A. Roe award 1987), Am. Chem. Soc., Internat. Platform Assn., Nat. Acad. Engring. (adv. com. internat. activities), World Congress Chem. Engrs. (v.p. 1986), Sigma Xi. Mem. Reformed Ch. in Am. (gen. program council). Club: Travelers Century. Lodge: Rotary. Home: 141 Tyringham Rd Rochester NY 14617 Office: 135 Mt Read Blvd Rochester NY 14611

OLDSHUE, MARY HOLL, real estate development company executive; b. Utica, N.Y., Oct. 15, 1951; d. Oscar and Rosemary (Goetz) Holl; m. Paul F. Oldshue, July 12, 1975; children: Emily, Andrew, Abigail. AB, Vassar Coll., 1973; postgrad., NYU, 1977. Asst. sec. Chem. Bank, N.Y.C., 1973-78; asst. v.p. 1st Interstate Bank, Portland, Oreg., 1978-79; dir. fin. adminstrn. NERCO, Inc. sub. PacifiCorp, Portland, 1980-81, mgr. fin. adminstrn., 1981-82, treas., 1982-87; v.p., chief fin. officer Pacific Devel. Inc. (subs. PacifiCorp.), Portland, 1987—. Pres. Aux. Emmanuel Hosp. and Med. Ctr. Mem. Fin. Execs. Inst., Met. Mus. Art, Oreg. Mus. Sci. & Industry. Clubs: Vassar of N.Y. and Oreg. Office: Pacific Devel Inc 825 NE Multnomah St Portland OR 97232

OLDSHUE, PAUL FREDERICK, financial executive; b. Chgo., Nov. 4, 1949; s. James Young and Betty Ann (Wiersema) O.; m. Mary Elizabeth Holl, July 12, 1975; children: Emily Jane, Andrew Armstrong. Abigail Anne. BA, Williams Coll., Williamstown, Mass., 1971; MBA, NYU, 1978. With Chem. Bank, N.Y.C., 1973-78, asst. sec., 1976-78; with Orbanco Fin. Svc. Corp., 1978-84, v.p., treas., 1980-83; exec. v.p. Oreg. Bank, Portland, 1984-88; v.p. syndications & participations PacifiCorp Fin. Inc., 1988—. Mem. Fin. Execs. Inst. Republican. Club: Founders (Portland).

O'LEARY, PATRICK J., research microbiologist; b. Corvallis, Oreg., Nov. 30, 1951; s. John E. and Margaret Ruth (Johnson) O'L.; m. Jill Johnson, June 6, 1981. BS, Oreg. State U., 1974, MS, 1977, PhD, 1980; postgrad., U. Ill., 1978. Instr. Baylor Coll. Medicine, Houston, 1980-83; sr. scientist Becton Dickinson, Balt., 1983-85; mgr. immunology Baxter Micro Scan, West Sacramento, Calif., 1985-86, dir. research, 1986-88; dir. infectious disease Ortho Diagnostic Systems, Inc., Raritan, N.J., 1988—; cons. in field. Contbr. articles to profl. jours. Recipient Tartar award State Oreg., 1978. Mem. AAAS, Am. Soc. Microbiologists. Republican. Roman Catholic. Office: Ortho Diagnostic Systems Inc Rt 202 Raritan NJ 08869

OLEN, GARY, marketing company executive; b. Milw., Mar. 29, 1942; s. Norbert John and Irene (Rydlewicz) O.; m. Maryann Wozniak (div. May 1988); children: Wendy, Jeff. Grad. high sch., Milw. Rebuyer catalog div. J.C. Penney Co., Milw., 1960-67; buyer C&H Distbrs., Milw., 1967-70; mktg. dir. Fidelity Products, Mpls., 1970-77; owner, mgr. Sportsman's Guide, Mpls., 1977-89, exec. v.p., prin., 1989—. Republican. Roman Catholic. Home: 40 Jewel Ln Plymouth MN 55447 Office: Sportsmans Guide 965 Decatur Ave N Minneapolis MN 55427

OLENDORF, WILLIAM CARR, JR., small business owner; b. Albany, N.Y., Oct. 3, 1945; s. William Carr Sr. and Mary Zilpha (Gillies) O.; m. Barbara Kay Cowan, Aug. 14, 1966; children: Mark, Julie, Jennifer. Student, Columbia Coll., 1964-65, So. Ill. U., 1965-66. Radio announcer Sta. WERX, Wyoming, Mich., 1967-68; sales rep. Sta. WCFL, Chgo., 1968-70, Sta. WJJD-FM, Chgo., 1970-72; v.p. Promotion Network, Chgo., 1972-74; account exec. AVCO-TV, Chgo., 1974-76, Peters, Griffin & Woodward, Chgo., 1976-82, Petry TV, Chgo., 1982-83; owner Point South KOA Resort, Yemassee, S.C., 1983—. Commr. Point S. Pub. Service Dist.; mem. tax adv. bd. Jasper County, 1985—. S.C. Campground Owners Assn. (v.p. 1985-87, pres. 1987—), S.C. Campground Assn. (pres. 1987-88). Republican. Episcopalian. Home and Office: Rte 1 Yemassee SC 29945

OLESEN, DOUGLAS EUGENE, research institute executive; b. Tonasket, Wash., Jan. 12, 1939; s. Magnus and Esther Rae (Myers) O.; m. Michaele Ann Engdahl, Nov. 18, 1964; children: Douglas Eugene, Stephen Christian. B.S., U. Wash., 1962, M.S., 1963, postgrad., 1965-67, Ph.D., 1972. Research engr. space research div. Boeing Aircraft Co., Seattle, 1963-64; with Battelle Meml. Inst., Pacific NW Labs., Richland, Wash., 1967-84, mgr. water resources systems sect., water and land resources dept., 1970-71, mgr. dept., 1971-75, dep. dir. research labs., 1975, dir. research, 1975-79, v.p. inst., dir. NW div., 1979-84; exec. v.p., chief operating officer Battelle Meml. Inst., Columbus, Ohio, 1984-87, pres., chief exec. officer, 1987—. Patentee process and system for treating wast water. Trustees Capital Univ., Columbus Mus. of Art, Riverside Hosp., Columbus Zoo, INROADS/Columbus Inc., Franklin County United Way, Columbus 1992 Commn., Columbus Symphony Orch.; mem. Columbus Capital Corp. for Civic Improvement; bd. dirs. Ohio State U. Found. Mem. Ohio C. of C. (trustee), Columbus Area C. of C. (exec. com., bd. dirs.). Office: Battelle Meml Inst 505 King Ave Columbus OH 43201

OLFMAN, LORNE, information systems analyst, educator; b. Calgary, Alta., Can., Nov. 29, 1948; came to U.S., 1983; s. Hymie and Sara Frances (Martin) O.; m. Darlene May Puhach, Dec. 30, 1981. BSC in Computing Sci., U. Calgary, 1970, MA in Econs., 1980; MBA, Ind. U., 1986, PhD in Bus. Mgmt. Info. Systems, 1987. Computer programmer Bercov Computer Cons. Ltd., Calgary, 1969-71; teaching asst. Dept. Econs. U. Calgary, 1973-74; economist Transport Can. Air Adminstrn., Edmonton, Ottawa and Toronto, Alta. and Ont., Can., 1973-80; planning analyst B.C. (Can.) Telephone Co., Vancouver, 1981-83; instr. Sch. Bus. Ind. U., Bloomington, 1983-86; research assoc. Devel. Tng. Ctr., Bloomington, 1986-87; asst. prof. Info. Sci. Dept. Claremont (Calif.) Grad. Sch., 1987—. Assoc. editor: Jour. Bus. and Econs. Perspectives, 1988—; contbr. articles to profl. jours. Ind. U. fellow, 1983-86, IBM fellow, 1985, Richard D. Irwin fellow, 1986-87. Mem. Assn. Computing Machinery, Inst. Mgmt. Scis., IEEE Computer Soc., Decision Scis. Inst. Office: Claremont Grad Sch Info Sci Dept Claremont CA 91711-6190

OLINGER, GLENN SLOCUM, manufacturing company executive, entrepreneur; b. New Castle, Ind., May 3, 1929; s. Glenn Arthur and Eva Lucille (Slocum) O.; m. Phyllis Lucile Roper, July 6, 1949 (div. Oct. 1981); children—Deborah Sue, Glenn Alan, Craig William, Gwen Gay; m. Diana Sue Hurst, Oct. 2, 1982. B.S., U. Chattanooga, 1952; M.B.A., Northwestern U., 1955. Various sales and gen. mgmt. positions Gen. Electric, Louisville, 1955-75; pres. Speed Queen Corp., Ripon, Wis, 1975-79; gen. mgr. Major Appliance Internat. div. Gen. Electric, Louisville, 1979-82; pres. Kitchen Aid Inc., Troy, Ohio, 1982-87; v.p. Whirlpool Corp., Benton Harbor, Mich., 1986-87; v.p. MII Inc., pres. Lundia Div., 1987—. Trustee Ripon Coll., 1976-79; trustee Dayton Art Inst., 1984-85. Served with USN, 1946-49, 52-53. Northwestern U. scholar, 1954. Mem. Am. Mgmt. Assn., Jacksonville C. of C., Mensa. Republican. Presbyterian. Lodges: Masons, Rotary. Home: 19 Book Ln Jacksonville IL 62650

OLIVA, RALPH ANGELO, marketing executive; b. Tarrytown, N.Y., July 1, 1946; s. I. Ralph and Raechel O.; m. Kathryn Kaye Stembridge. BS in Physics, Fordham U., 1966; MS and PhD in Physics, Rensselaer Poly. Inst., 1973. Mem. tech. staff Tex. Instruments Inc., Dallas, 1973-76, merchandising mgr., 1976-77, dir. learning ctr., 1977-79, mgr. merchandising strategy, 1979-81, dir. external edn., 1981-83, mgr. ednl. mktg., 1983-85, mgr. worldwide mktg. communications, 1985-89, v.p. market communications, 1989—. Co-author: Sourcebook for Programmable Calculations, 1979, Math on Keys, 1980, Calculating Better Decisions, 1981, Laboratory Physics, 1985. Mem. Am. Assn. Artificial Intelligence, Am. Assn. Physics Tchrs. Roman Catholic. Office: Tex Instruments Inc 8360 LBJ Freeway Dallas TX 75243

OLIVELLA, BARRY JAMES, financial executive; b. Can., 1947. BA, York U., Toronto, Ont., Can., 1968. Chartered acct., Ont. Ptnr. Arthur Young Clarkson Gordon, Toronto, 1968-87; v.p. corp. devel. Bombardier, Inc., Montreal, Que., Can., 1987—. Pres. Uxbridge (Ont.) C. of C., 1986-87; chmn. Indsl. Adv. Com., Uxbridge, 1979. Mem. Inst. Chartered Accts. Ont., Nat. Club. Office: Bombardier Inc, 800 Rene-Levesque Blvd W, Ste 1700, Montreal, PQ Canada H3B 1Y8

OLIVER, DANIEL, government official; b. N.Y.C., Apr. 10, 1939; s. Andrew and Ruth (Blake) O.; m. Anna Louise Vietor, Sept. 16, 1967; children: Anna Louise, Andrew II, Daniel Jr., Susan F., Peter A. BA, Harvard Coll., 1964; LLB, Fordham U., 1967. Bar: N.Y. 1967. Assoc. Hawkins, Delafield & Wood, N.Y.C., 1967-70; editorial asst. Nat. Rev. mag., N.Y.C., 1970-71, exec. editor, 1973-76; assoc. Alexander & Green, N.Y.C., 1971-73, 76-79; pvt. cons. 1980-81; gen. counsel U.S. Dept. Edn., Washington, 1981-83, U.S. Dept. Agr., Washington, 1983-86; chmn. FTC, Washington, 1986—; coun. Adminstrv. Conf. U.S., 1983-89. Active Christ Ch., Greenwich, Conn., mem. vestry, 1972-75; mem. vestry St. Andrews Ch., Edgartown, Mass., 1985-87; bd. dirs. Am. Conservative Union, Washington, 1974-86, N.Y. State Polit. Action Co., 1976-79. Mem. Federalist Soc. Law Pub. Policy Studies (v.p. 1984, 86), Phila. Soc., Mont Pelerin Soc. Republican. Episcopalian. Home: 3105 Woodley Rd NW Washington DC 20008 Office: Fed Trade Commn 6th & Pennsylvania Ave NW Washington DC 20580 *

OLIVER, EDWARD CARL, investment executive; b. St. Paul, May 31, 1930; s. Charles Edmund and Esther Marie (Bjugstad) O.; m. Charlotte Severson, Sept. 15, 1956; children—Charles E., Andrew T., Peter A. B.A., U. Minn., 1955. Sales rep. Armstrong Cork Co., N.Y.C., 1955; registered rep. Piper, Jaffray & Hopwood, Mpls., 1958; mgr. Mut. Funds, Inc. subs. Dayton's, Mpls., 1964; mgr. NWNL Mgmt. Corp. subs. Northwestern Nat. Life Ins. Co., Mpls., 1968-72, v.p., 1972-81, pres., dir., 1981—; v.p. Select Cash Mgmt. Fund, Inc., Select Capital Growth Fund, Inc., Wash. Sq. Cash Fund, Inc., Northwestern Cash Fund, Inc. Bd. dirs. Hennepin County United Way, 1963; mem. Minn. Republican Party State Central Com., 1972-75. Served to sgt. USAF, 1951-52. Mem. Life Ins. Mktg. and Research Assn. (fin. products mktg. com.), Internat. Assn. Fin. Planners (past pres. Twin City chpt., mem. nat. governing com.), Psi Upsilon. Presbyterian (elder). Club: Mpls. Athletic. Home: 20230 Cottagewood Rd Deephaven MN 55331 Office: NWNL Mgmt Corp 20 Washington Ave S Minneapolis MN 55401

OLIVER, JOYCE ANNE, journalist, editorial consultant; b. Coral Gables, Fla., Sept. 19, 1958; d. John Joseph and Rosalie Cecile (Mack) O. BA in Communications, Calif. State U., Fullerton, 1980, postgrad. sch. mgmt., 1988. Corp. editor Norris Industries Inc., Huntington Beach, Calif., 1979-82; pres. J.A. Oliver Assocs., La Habra Heights, Calif., 1982—; corp. editorial cons. Norris Industries, 1982, Better Methods Cons., Huntington Harbour, Calif., 1982-83, Summit Group, Orange, Calif., 1982-83, UDS, Encinitas, Calif., 1983-84, ALS Corp., Anaheim, Calif., 1985, Gen. Power Systems, Anaheim, 1985, MacroMarketing, Costa Mesa, Calif., 1985-86, PM Software, Huntington Beach, Calif., 1985-86, CompuQuote, Canoga Park, Calif., 1985-86, Nat. Semicondr. Can. Ltd., Mississauga, Ont., Can., 1986, Frame Inc., Fullerton, Calif., 1987-88, The Johnson-Layton Co., Los Angeles, 1988-89, Corp. Research Inc., Chgo., 1988; mem. Research Council of Scripps Clinic and Research Found., 1987-88. Contbr.: Cleve. Inst. Electronics publ. The Electron, spl. feature editor, 1988—; contbg. editor Reseller Management mag. (formerly Computer Dealer mag.), 1987-88; also contbr. to Can. Electronics Engring. Mag., PC Week, The NOMDA Spokesman, Entrepreneur, Adminstrv. Mgmt., High-Tech Selling, Video Systems, Tech. Photography, Computing Canada, Stores. Mem. Internat. Platform Assn., IEEE, Soc. Photo-Optical Instrumentation Engrs., Inst. Mgmt. Scis., Nat. Writers Club (profl.), Internat. Mktg. Assn., Sigma Delta Chi/Soc. Profl. Journalists. Republican. Roman Catholic. Office: JA Oliver Assocs 2045 Fullerton Rd La Habra Heights CA 90631

OLIVER, LEANN MICHELLE, government financial officer; b. Eureka, Calif., Nov. 15, 1955; d. George L. and Laura Maxine (Jennings) O. BS, Willamette U., 1977; MPA, SUNY-Albany, 1980; cert. Nat. Comml. Lending Sch. of Am. Bankers Assn., 1982. Mgmt. trainee U.S. GAO, Albany, N.Y., 1979-80; presdl. mgmt. intern U.S. SBA, Washington, 1980-83, fin. analyst, policy and program devel., 1983—; bd. dirs. Lafayette Fed. Credit Union, Washington, asst. treas., 1986—. Mem. Internat. Platform Assn. Roman Catholic. Office: SBA 1441 L St NW Rm 720 Washington DC 20416

OLIVER, MARK, computer software specialist, consultant; b. Eldorado, Kans., July 3, 1957; s. Walter and Reba Naomi (Watt) O.; m. Cathleen Ann Campbell, June 19, 1982 (div. Mar. 1985). AA, Butler County Jr. Coll., 1977; postgrad., Emporia State U., 1979-84. With IBP Inc., Emporia, Kans., 1977-81, prodn. supr., 1981-84, computer programmer, 1984-87, programmer, analyst, 1987-88, systems analyst, 1988—; pvt. practice programming cons., Emporia, 1979-84. Author: Yield System User's Manual, 1984; co-author tech. manual. Republican. Home: RR 1 PO Box 180F South Sioux City NE 68776 Office: IBP Inc Hwy 35 Dakota City NE 68731

OLIVER, NEIL EDWARD, SR., naval architect; b. Washington, Nov. 4, 1921; s. Edward James and Sarah Mildred (Cravens) O.; m. Marjorie Flo Bridges, June 2, 1951; children: Joy Lynn, Neil Edward Jr., Carol Ann. AME, Cath. U. Am., 1948; cert. in advanced electronic engring., Capital Radio Engring. Inst., 1959. Engring. technician David Taylor Naval Ship Research and Devel. Ctr., Bethesda, Md., 1951-65; naval architect technician David Taylor Naval Ship Research and Devel. Ctr., Bethesda, 1965-72, naval architect, 1972-77; assoc. tchr. Knoxville (Tenn.) Sch. System, 1977-86; sr. engring. technician CDI Marine Co., Portsmouth, Va., 1986—. Contbr. articles to profl. jours. Served with U.S. Army, 1941-44. Mem. Soc. Naval Architects and Marine Engrs., Kiwanis. Methodist. Home: 3762A Towne Point Rd Portsmouth VA 23703 Office: CDI Marine Co 301 Queen St Portsmouth VA 23704

OLIVER, ROBERT BRUCE, investment company executive; b. Brockton, Mass., Aug. 1, 1931; s. Stanley Thomas and Helen (Sabine) O.; m. Sylvia E. Bell, Feb. 17, 1954; children: Susan Pamela, Robert Bruce. A.B., Harvard U., 1953; postgrad., Bus. Sch., 1971, Boston U. Law Sch., 1955-57; M.A., Mich. State U., 1958. Chmn., pres. John Hancock Income Securities Trust, Boston, 1973—; chmn., pres. John Hancock Investors Trust, John Hancock Bond Trust, John Hancock Growth Trust, John Hancock Tax Exempt Cash Mgmt. Trust, John Hancock Govt. Securities Trust, John Hancock Tax Exempt Income Trust, John Hancock Cash Mgmt. Trust, John Hancock Spl. Equities Trust, John Hancock Global Trust, John Hancock World Trust, John Hancock High Income Trust, John Hancock Tax Exempt Series Trust; dir. John Hancock Distbrs.; vice chmn., chief exec. officer John Hancock Advisers, Inc.; chmn., mng. dir. John Hancock Advisers Internat. Ltd. Served to 1st lt. USMCR, 1953-55. Mem. Investment Co. Inst. (gov.), Harvard Bus. Sch. Assn. Boston. Clubs: St. Botolph, Harvard of Boston, Harvard of Quincy (Mass.), Blue Hill Tennis, Boston Econ. Office: John Hancock Advisers Inc 101 Huntington Ave 7th Fl Boston MA 02199 also: John Hancock Investors Trust John Hancock Pl Boston MA 02117

OLIVERA, HERBERT ERNEST, educator, retired dean, accountant, consultant; b. N.Y.C., Apr. 6, 1923; s. James Phillip and Francella (Haylett) O.; m. Jewell Hackett, July 4, 1956; children: Herbert Ernest Jr., Angela Dawn; m. Elizabeth Bacon, Dec. 21, 1969. BS, Ky. State U., 1950; MA, NYU, 1953; MBA, U. Oreg., 1961; M in Acctg., U. Ariz., 1969, PhD, 1973. CPA, Ky., Ariz., Ill., Ala., Md. Assoc. prof. Ky. State U., Frankfort, 1955-68; rsch. asst. U. Ariz., Tucson, 1968-70; assoc. prof. Pima (Ariz.) Coll., 1970-73; chmn. acctg. Gov.'s State U., Park Forest, Ill., 1973-77; dean Sch. Bus., Ala. A&M U., Huntsville, 1977-81, Sch. Bus., Morgan State U., Balt., 1981-88; prof. Sch. Bus., Towson (Md.) U., 1988—; prin. Herbert Olivera & Assocs., Park Forest, 1973-79; cons., co-owner Olivera-Bashty Buckenmeyer, Park Forest, 1975-79. Mem. Pima County Health Planning Commn., Tucson, 1970-73; pres. SCORG/ACE, Huntsville; mem. Xiamen Sister City Com.; mem., chmn. fin. and tax com. Village of Park Forest, 1974-78. Served with USMC, 1944-46. Named Outstanding Tchr., Ky. State U., 1965. Mem. Am. Acctg. Assn., Balt. Engring. Club, Fin. Execs. Inst., Govtl. Acctg. Assn., Am. Taxation Assn., HUB Club (chmn. econ. devel. com. 1984—), Alpha Kappa Mu, Beta Alpha Psi, Beta Gamma Sigma. Democrat. Episcopalian. Home: 1200 Griffith Pl Riverside MD 21017

OLIVIER, JON PAUL, data processing executive; b. Franklin, La., May 1, 1962; s. Daniel Joseph and Louise Anna (Guidry) O.; m. Susan Marie Smith, Oct. 21, 1983. AS, Nicholls State U., 1983, BS in Computer Sci., 1983. Computer programmer Service Machine Group, Inc., Morgan City, La., 1983-84; computer system mgr. Nicholls State U., Thibodaux, La., 1984-86; dir. computer ops. Gulf South Engrs., Inc., Houma, La., 1986—; v.p., dir. D.J.O., Inc. INvestments, Thibodaux, 1977—; owner Jon Paul Olivier Cons., 1985—. Mem. Digital Equip. Corp. Users Soc., La. Engring. Soc., Urban and Regional Info. Systems Assn. Democrat. Roman Catholic. Home: 705 Funderburk Ave Houma LA 70364 Office: Gulf South Engrs 1700 Grand Callou Rd Houma LA 70363

OLLOR, WALTER GBUTE, economist; b. Eleme, Rivers, Nigeria, Dec. 20, 1950; s. Jonah Ollor and Cecilia Lale (Ngesia) Ollornta; m. Helen Yorowa Osarollor, Jan. 3, 1978; children: Nyimeawia, Ntefomi, Nkaatoaan. BSc, U. Ife, 1975; PhD, Iowa State U., 1980. Research asst. Iowa State U., Ames, 1977-80; lectr. U. Port Harcurt, Nigeria, 1980-85, sr. lectr., 1985—; cons. Econometric and Acctg. Assocs., Port Harcourt, 1980—; chmn. bd. dirs. Internat. Mcht. Bank, Lagos, Nigeria; chmn. Fedn. Accounts Com. Sec. Acad. Staff Union of Univs., U. Port Harcourt, 1983-84; chmn. Eleme Devel. Union, 1986—; mem. Constituent Assemble Abuja, 1988-89. Mem. Am. Econ. Assn., Econometric Soc., Nigerian Econ. Soc. Clubs: Eleme Social (pres. 1984-85); The Rivers Soc. (Port Harcourt) (sec. gen. 1984-86). Office: Internat Mcht Bank, 1 Akin Adesola St, Victoria Island Lagos Nigeria

OLMAN, MARYELLEN, human resources administrator; b. Grand Rapids, Mich., Dec. 24, 1946; d. Norman Adolph and Mary Irene (McCarthy) Olman; m. Richard Isaac Fine, Nov. 25, 1982; 1 child, Victoria Elizabeth. B.A. in Community Service, Mich. State U., 1968. Legis. researcher Hon. Gerald R. Ford, U.S. Ho. of Reps., 1969-71; spl. asst. Hon. Jack F. Kemp, U.S. Ho. of Reps., 1971-74; personnel analyst Los Angeles City Housing Authority, 1975-78; profl. placement rep. Gen. Telephone of Calif., Santa Monica, 1978-81, mgmt. staffing adminstr., 1981-84. Mem. Los Angeles Internat. Visitors Assn., 1982—; mem. founders circle Los Angeles Music Ctr. Mem. Am. Soc. Personnel Adminstrs., Coll. Placement Council, Western Coll. Placement Assn., Personnel and Indsl. Relations Assn. Republican. Home: 5331 Horizon Dr Malibu CA 90265

OLMEDO, ALFREDO PHILLIPS, banker; b. Matamoros, Tamaulipas, Mex., Sept. 2, 1935; s. Howard Phillips and Dolores Olmedo; m. Maureen Greene de Phillips; children: Alfredo, Ricardo, Adriana. B, U. Nacional Autónoma de Mex.; postgrad. degree, U. London, U. Cambridge, Eng., George Washington U., Am. U. Loan officer Interam. Devel. Bank, 1965-66; exec. dir. Internat. Monetary Fund, 1966-70; mgr. internat. and econ. affairs Banco de Mex., Mexico City, 1971-75, dep. dir. internat. affairs, 1975-82; gen. dir. Banco Nacional de Comercio Exterior SNC, Mexico City, 1982—; chief dept. economy and fiscal progress Ministry Fin., Washington, dep. chief dept. banks and investments; pres. of deps. Group Twentyfour I.M.F., Washington; treas. Latin Am. Export Bank; profl. bus. U. Iberoamericana, Mex. Contbr. articles to profl. jours. Advisor, fin. rep. Gov. Tamaulipa, Mex.; coord. fin. devel., mem. cons. bd. IEPES PRI, Mex. Lt. Army Mex. Decorated Cruzeiro du Sul Brazil, El Sol del Peru; recipient Francisco Miranda award Venezuela. Mem. Club Nautico (Valle de Bravo), Club Raqueta (Lomas). Home: Monte Antuco 510, Lomas Barrilaco 11000, Mexico Office: Banco Nacional de Comercio Exterior, Camino Santa Teresa 1679, Mexico City 1900, Mexico

OLMEN, ROBERT WILLIAM, college administrator; b. Duluth, Minn., Aug. 16, 1926; s. Daniel Norman and Anna (Christensen) O.; m. Catherine Lee Hodges, May 2, 1953; children: Timothy Andrew, Julie Ann. BS in Physics, U. Minn., 1949; postgrad., U. Chgo., 1949-50; MBA, U. Minn., 1964. Specification writing technologist U.S. Govt. Gen. Svcs. Adminstrn., Washington, 1950-52; owner, mgr. Audibel Co., Mpls., 1956-60, Aquatoy Mfg. Co., St. Paul, 1952-65; physicist, staff physicist, supervisory physicist, mgr., group mgr., staff scientist Sperry-Rand Univac DSD, St. Paul, 1952-72; owner, mgr. Camper's World-Resort, Panasoffkee, Fla., 1972-78; dir. career svcs., asst. prof. bus. adminstrn. Greenville (Ill.) Coll., 1979—; cons. Small Bus. Inst., U.S. SBA, Greenville, 1981-84. Patentee in field. Active Higher Edn. Coun., St. Louis; chmn. St. Louis Coop. Edn. Coun., 1980-82. Cpl. U.S. Army, 1945-46. Grantee Household Internat., Greenville, 1983, U.S. Dept. Edn., 1982-88. Mem. Am. Mktg. Assn., Ill. Coop. Edn. Assn. (dir. So. Ill. 1983-84), Nat. Coop. Edn. Assn., Nat. Coll. Placement Assn., Midwest Coop. Edn. Assn. Republican. Methodist. Home: 833 E College Ave Greenville IL 62246 Office: Greenville Coll 315 E Coll Ave Greenville IL 62246

OLMSTEAD, FRANCIS HENRY, JR., electronics industry executive; b. Corning, N.Y., June 21, 1938; s. Francis Henry and Josephine (Andolino) O.; B.S., Detroit U., 1960; M.S., Purdue U., 1962; postgrad. program for mgmt. devel. Harvard, 1976; m. Mary Helen Nelson, Sept. 2, 1961; children—Kathleen, Ann, John. Foreman, Corning Glass Works, 1962, sect. foreman, 1963-64, dept. foreman, 1965-66, prodn. supt., 1967-69, plant mgr., 1970-71, mgr. mktg., 1972-73, gen. sales and mktg. mgr., 1973-75, bus. mgr. lighting products, 1976-79, bus. mgr. TV products, 1979-80, v.p., gen. mgr. TV products, 1981—, gen. mgr. elec. products div., 1982-83 ; exec. v.p. N.Am. Philips Lighting Corp., Bloomfield, N.J., 1984-86; exec. v.p., gen. mgr., Somerset, N.J., 1986-88, pres., chief operating officer Anchor Advanced Products, Inc., Morristown, Tenn., 1988—; instr. bus. adminstrn. Elmira Coll., 1972-73; vis. lectr. Purdue U., 1973. Mem. exec. bd. Steuben area council Boy Scouts Am., 1975—, v.p. fin., 1977-79, pres. Steuben Area council, 1979-84, bd. dirs. N.E. region, 1984-88, pres. N.J. Area, 1985-88, pres., bd. dirs. S. Region Bd. Boy Scouts Am., 1988—; mem. dean's adv. coun. Krannert Sch. Purdue U., Coll. Engring. U. Detroit.. Served to capt. U.S. Army, 1961-62. Recipient Silver Beaver award Boy Scouts Am., Disting. Alumni award Purdue U. Mem. ASME, Illuminating Engring. Soc., Nat. Assn. Elect. Distbrs., Corning C. of C., Krannert Sch. Alumni Assn. Purdue U. (pres.), Tau Beta Pi, Pi Tau Sigma. Republican. Roman Catholic. Club: Corning Country. Home: 7328 Misty Meadow Pl Knoxville TN 37919 Office: Anchor Brush Co 209 E Desoto Morristown TN 37814

OLOFSON, TOM WILLIAM, business executive; b. Oak Park, Ill., Oct. 10, 1941; s. Ragnar V. and Ingrid E. Olofson; BBA, U. Pitts., 1963; m. Jeanne Hamilton, Aug. 20, 1960; children: Christopher, Scott. Various mgmt. positions Bell Telephone Co. of Pa., Pitts., 1963-67; sales mgr. Xerox Corp., Detroit, 1967-68, nat. account mgr., Rochester, N.Y., 1968, mgr. govt. planning, Rochester, 1969, mgr. Kansas City (Mo.) br., 1969-74; corp. v.p. health products group Marion Labs., Inc., Kansas City, Mo., 1974-78, sr. v.p., 1978-80; exec. v.p., dir. Electronic Realty Assn., Inc., 1980-83; chmn. bd., chief exec. officer ETL Corp., 1983-88, Emblem Graphic Systems, Inc., 1983-88; chief exec. officer Electronic Processing, Inc., 1988—, also chmn. bd. dirs.; chmn. bd. dirs. DemoGraFX; dir. Optico Industries, Kalo Labs., Am. Stair-Glide, Marion Health and Safety, Marion Sci., Marion Internat., Bank of Kansas City, Kansas City Bank & Trust Co., ASG Corp., ICP, Inc., Calix Corp. Mem. Menninger Found.; trustee Barstow Sch.; chmn. bd. trustees Village United Presbyn. Ch.; bd. dirs. Kansas City Better Bus. Bur., Mid. Am. Immunotherapy and Surg. Research Found., Inc. Mem. Omicron Delta Kappa, Sigma Chi. Republican. Presbyterian. Club: Kansas City. Home: 4808 W 87th St Prairie Village KS 66207 Office: Electronic Processing Inc 501 Kansas Ave Kansas City KS 66105

O'LOUGHLIN, JOHN KIRBY, insurance executive; b. Bklyn., Mar. 31, 1929; s. John Francis and Anne (Kirby) O'L.; m. Janet R. Tag, July 5, 1952; children: Robert K., Steven M., Patricia A., John A. BA in Econs., St. Lawrence U., Canton, N.Y., 1951. State agt. Royal Globe Ins. Group, 1953-58; with Allstate Ins. Co., 1958—, mktg. v.p., group v.p., then exec. v.p., 1972—; pres. Allstate Life Ins. Co., 1977—; chmn. bd. Allstate Ins. Co. and Life Co. Can., 1976—, sr. exec. v.p. corp. mktg. devel., planning, systems info. and adminstrv. ops., 1980—; bd. dirs. all cos. in Allstate Ins. Group and Allstate Enterprises, Inc.; pres. Allstate Enterprises, Inc., Allstate Motor Club, Mature Outlook, Inc., Enterprises Publ. and Direct Mktg. Ctr., Inc. Trustee St. Lawrence U., U.S. Marine Staff and Command Coll. Found. Bd.; mem. bd. govs. ATO Found., Inc.; bd. dirs. Lake Symphony, Council of Ind. Colls.; chmn. No. Suburban Chgo. United Way; elder First United Presbyn. Ch., Lake Forest, Ill.; bd. dirs. Project Invest. Served to capt. USMCR, 1951-53. Mem. Sales and Mktg. Execs. Internat. (dir.), Alpha Tau Omega (chmn. bd. govs. found.). Clubs: Met. (Chgo.); Knollwood (Lake Forest); Lahinch (Ireland). Office: Allstate Ins Co Allstate Plaza Bldg F-8 Northbrook IL 60062

OLPIN, GLEN W., credit union executive and chief economist; b. Ogden, Utah, Aug. 20, 1950; s. Lawrence Dee and Cynthia (Larsen) O.; m. Joy Taylor, Mar. 8, 1974; children: Adam, Chad, Shannon, Natalie, Tyler. BA in Econs., Weber State Coll., 1975; cert., Western CUNA Mgmt. Sch., 1986. Acct. Fed. Employees Credit Union, Ogden, 1976-77, internal auditor, 1977-79, fin. and acctg. mgr., 1979-80, controller, 1980-82; treas. Am. First Credit Union, Ogden, 1982-87, v.p., chief economist, 1987—; mem. Wasatch Front Econ. Forum. Mem. Nat. Assn. Accts., Inst. Chartered Fin. Analysts, Nat. Credit Union Inst. Club: Utah Bond. Home: 519 Madison Ave Ogden UT 84404 Office: Am First Credit Union 1344 W 4675 S PO Box 9199 Ogden UT 84409

OLSEN, JOHN ROBERT, insurance company executive; b. Portland, Oreg., Nov. 24, 1928; s. John and Katherine Elizabeth (Shepard) O.; m. Lorna Lee, Aug. 29, 1947; children: Mark, Julie, Pam, Kelley. BBA, U. Oreg., 1950. Asst. mgr. mortgage loan dept. Standard Ins. Co., Portland, Oreg., 1960-65; mgr. real estate dept. Standard Ins. Co., 1965-70, asst. v.p. investments, mgr. real estate, 1970-71, v.p. investments, 1972-84, sr. v.p. investments, 1984—. Trustee, mem. exec. com. Oreg. 4-H Club Found.; chmn. bd. dirs., mem. exec. com. Holladay Park Med. Ctr.; bd. dirs. HealthLink; trustee, chmn. investment com. Herbert A. Templeton Found.; chmn. investment adv. com. Oreg. Arts Heritage Endowment Fund; chmn. fin. com., fin. adv. com. Oreg. Community Found.; chmn. Oreg. Bd. Maritime Pilots; bd. advisers Oreg. Downtown Devel. Assn.; bd. dirs., v.p. found. Oreg. Sch. Arts and Crafts Found.; bd. dirs. Oreg. Bus. Com. for Arts. Republican. Clubs: University, Columbia Edgewater, Founders (Portland). Office: Standard Ins Co 1100 SW 6th Ave Portland OR 97404

OLSEN, KENNETH HARRY, manufacturing company executive; b. Bridgeport, Conn., Feb. 20, 1926; s. Oswald and Svea (Nordling) O.; m. Eeva-Liisa Aulikki Valve, Dec. 12, 1950. B.S. in Elec. Engring, MIT, 1950, M.S., 1952. Elec. engr. Lincoln Lab., MIT, 1950-57; founder Digital Equipment Corp., Maynard, Mass., 1957, now pres., dir.; dir. Polaroid Corp., Shawnut Corp., Ford Motor Co. Patentee magnetic devices. Mem. Pres.'s Sci. Adv. Com., 1971-73; trustee, v.p. Joslin Diabetes Found.; mem. corp. Wentworth Inst., Boston, MIT, Cambridge; trustee Gordon Coll., Wenham, Mass. Served with USNR, 1944-46. Named Young Elec. Engr. of Year Eta Kappa Nu, 1960. Mem. Nat. Acad. Engring. Home: Weston Rd Lincoln MA 01773 Office: Digital Equipment Corp 111 Powdermill Rd Maynard MA 01754 *

OLSEN, KENNETH MICHAEL, manufacturing and distributing company executive; b. Coeur D'Alene, Idaho, Apr. 15, 1948; s. Howard George and Irma Dean (Harris) O.; m. Dixie Kathleen McCowan, Dec. 28, 1968; children—Glenn Michael, Kerri Michelle. B.A. in Bus. Adminstrn. with high honors, U. Wash., 1970, M.B.A., 1971. C.P.A., Wash., Idaho. Staff auditor Arthur Andersen & Co., Seattle, 1971-73, sr. auditor, Boise, Idaho, 1973-75, audit mgr., 1975-80; treas., chief fin. officer Futura Corp., Boise, 1980-83, v.p., 1981-83; controller Southwest Forest Industries, Inc., Phoenix, 1983-86; v.p., chief fin. officer ISC Systems, Inc., Spokane, Wash., 1986—, v.p. treas., 1987—; spl. lectr. acctg. Boise State U., 1976; mem. bus. adv. com. Coll. Bus. and Econs., Wash. State U., 1987—. Mem. Am. Inst. C.P.A.s, Idaho Soc. C.P.A.s, Am. Acctg. Assn., Inst. Internal Auditors, Fin. Execs. Inst., Am. Mgmt. Assn. Republican. Home: 10621 E 46th Spokane WA 99201 Office: ISC Systems Inc PO Box TAF-C8 Spokane WA 99220

OLSEN, KIRSTEN, stockbroker; b. Copenhagen, Nov. 5, 1942; came to U.S., 1948, naturalized, 1956; d. Jens Peder and Else Emilie (Jorgensen) Jensen; student Coll. San Mateo, 1964; Stanford U., 1976; m. Thomas A. Skornia, May 22, 1976 (div. 1987); 1 child, Erika Skornia-Olsen. Asst. to pres., mgr. pub. relations Drexler Tech., Mountain View, Calif., 1968-73; investment broker Merrill Lynch, Palo Alto, Calif., 1974-77, Paine Webber Jackson & Curtis, Palo Alto, 1977-80, Smith Barney Harris Upham, Menlo Park, Calif., 1980-82; ptnr. Triangle Ventures, Menlo Park, 1982-86; pres. Kirsten Olsen & Co., Inc., Investment Bankers, (now London Zurich Securities), Menlo Park, 1984—; mem. adv. bd. Silicon Valley Bank, Santa Clara, Calif., 1984—; bd. dirs. San Jose (Calif.) Cleve. Ballet, Calif. Music Ctr., Morgan Hill; trustee San Jose-Cleve. Ballet; Democratic Party nominee U.S. Congress, 1978-80. Republican. Lutheran. Mem. Peninsula Stock and Bond Club (past pres.), Am. Electronics Assn. Home: 1601 Stone Pine Ln Menlo Park CA 94025 Office: Kirsten Olsen & Co Inc 642 Santa Cruz Ave Menlo Park CA 94025

OLSEN, NIELS-ERIK, accountant; b. Copenhagen, Dec. 15, 1948; s. Børge Thomas and Else Johanne (Andersen) O.; m. Debra Lynn Wagstaff, Dec. 23, 1983; children: Anne Leigh, Elizabeth Lynn. BS in Econs., Copenhagen Sch. Econ. and Bus. Adminstrn., 1972, MS in Econs., 1974. CPA, Calif.; authorized pub. acct., Denmark. Audit mgr. Coopers and Lybrand, CPA's, Copenhagen, 1974-80; audit supr. Coopers and Lybrand, CPA's, Los Angeles, 1980-83; asst. controller Ashton Tate, Inc., Los Angeles, 1983-84; ptnr. Real Estate Ptnrship, Copenhagen, 1984-85; corp. controller The East Asiatic Co., Ltd. A/S, Copenhagen, 1985—. Served to pvt. Danish Army, 1968-69. Mem. Danish Inst. State Authorized Pub. Accts. Office: The East Asiatic Co Ltd A/S, Holbersgade 2, DK-1099 Copenhagen Denmark

OLSEN, NORMAN OSCAR, merger-acquisition search company executive; b. Wilmington, Del., Mar. 25, 1930; s. Oscar Emanualson and Viola (Pace) O.; m. Joan Beach (div.); children: Karin, Andrea, Roderick, Mimi; m. Dorothy Olsen (dec.); children: Kirstin, Freya; m. Gail L. Fiene, Dec. 8, 1988. Grad. high sch., Jenkintown, Pa. Product mgr. AMP, Inc., Harrisburg, Pa., 1953-64; regional mgr. Photocircuts Corp., Glen Cove, N.Y., 1964-68; ptnr. Winmill Jones Walker, N.Y.C., 1968-69; freelance cons. Chgo., 1969-73; pres. The Mgmt. Meeting Co., Clearwater, Fla., 1973—. Pres. Clearwater Olympic Yachting Com., 1878-88. Mem. Clearwater Yacht Club (commodore 1986). Office: The Mgmt Meeting Co 600 Ponce DeLeon Blvd Clearwater FL 33416

OLSEN, ROBERT ARTHUR, finance educator; b. Pittsfield, Mass., June 30, 1943; s. Arthur Anton and Virginia O.; B.B.A., U. Mass., 1966, M.B.A., 1967; Ph.D., U. Oreg., 1974; m. Maureen . Joan Carmell, Aug. 21, 1965. Security analyst Am. Inst. Counselors, 1967-68; research assoc. Center for Capital Market Research, U. Oreg., 1972-74; asst. prof. fin. U. Mass., 1974-75; prof. fin. Calif. State U., Chico, 1975—; cons. bus. feasibility studies for Stinson, Isom Assocs. & Career Assocs., Calif. State U., Chico, Endowment Fund, U.S. Forest Service. Stonier Banking fellow, 1971-72; Nat. Assn. Mut. Savs. Banks fellow, 1975-76; scholar Stanford U., Decision Research, Inc., 1986. Recipient Research award Calif. State U.-Chico, 1983, 86, Profl. Achievement award, 1985. Mem. Am. Fin. Assn., Fin. Execs. Inst., Western Fin. Assn. (Trefftzs award 1974), Southwestern Fin. Assn., Fin. Mgmt. Assn., Eastern Fin. Assn., Sierra Club. Contbr. articles to profl. jours. Office: Calif State U Sch Bus Chico CA 95929

OLSEN, ROBERT JOHN, savings and loan association executive; b. N.Y.C., July 8, 1928; s. Christian Marinius and Agnes Geraldine (Jensen) O.; m. Eleanor Marion Peters, June 19, 1981; 1 child, Philip John. BS Strayer Coll., 1956. Supervisory agt. Fed. Home Loan Bank Bd., N.Y.C., 1956-65; pres., dir. Keystone Savs. & Loan Assn., Asbury Park, N.J., 1965-82; chmn. bd., pres. Rapid Money Services, Inc., Deal, N.J., 1977-82; chmn. bd., pres. Elmora Savs. and Loan Assn., Elizabeth, N.J., 1982-88; pres. Ramsey (N.J.) Savs. and Loan Assn., 1988—, also bd. dirs.; pres. 2d Century Corp., Asbury Park, 1980-82; dir. Central Corp. of Savs. & Loans, Newark, 1976-82, Fed. Home Loan Bank N.Y., 1974-77. Councilman, Borough of Oceanport, N.J., 1971-73, 77-80, council pres., 1979; police commr. Oceanport, N.J., 1972-80; v.p. Econ. Devel. Corp., Asbury Park, N.J., 1972-81, Oceanport, N.J., 1974-77; mem. Zoning Bd. of Adjustment, Oceanport, 1969-70; mem. Citizens Adv. Council, Oceanport, 1975-76; dir. Monmouth and Ocean Devel. Council, Eatontown, N.J., 1974-82; trustee Savs. and Loan Found. of Washington, 1978-82; chmn. N.J. Electronic Funds Transfer Com., 1971-82; mem. Monmouth County Fair Housing Task Force, 1980-82, Monmouth County Vocat. Sch. Bd., 1981-83; pres. Paulinskill Lake Assn., 1987—. Served with USMC, 1946-48, 1950-56. Mem. N.J. Savs. League (pres. chpt. 1966-67), U.S. Savs. League (vice chmn. com. on internal ops., chmn. remote service unit com.), Nat. Assn. Review Appraisers and Mortgage Undewriters, Fin. Mgrs. Soc. (adv. council), Nat. Assn. Savs. and Loan Suprs., Nat. Soc. Fin. Examiners, Monmouth County, Eastern Union County Realtors Assn., Sussex County Realtors Assn., Internat. Union Bldg. Socs. and Savs. Assns., Navy League, Assn. U.S. Army. Clubs: World Trade (N.Y.C.); Channel (Monmouth Beach, N.J.); Provost Marshals Guild (Ft. Monmouth, N.J.); Wheelman's (Asbury Park, N.J.). Home: RD 6 Box 508 Newton NJ 07860 Office: Ramsey Savs & Loan Assn 121 Broad St Elizabeth NJ 07201

OLSHAN, KENNETH S., advertising agency executive; b. Evansville, Ind., July 15, 1932; s. Harry and Ethel (Hamburg) O.; m. Patricia E. Shane, Aug. 25, 1954; children: Margot E., Mathew S., John K. BA, Ind. U., 1954; postgrad., Grad. Sch. Bus. Washington U., 1955. Trainee, TV-radio buyer Batten Barton Durstine & Osborn (Advt.), N.Y.C., 1958-60; v.p., account exec. Doherty, Clifford, Steers & Shenfield, N.Y.C., 1960-64; v.p., account mgmt. supr. McCaffrey & McCall, N.Y.C., 1964-67; pres. Olshan, Smith & Gould, N.Y.C., 1967-69, Doherty, Mann & Olshan, N.Y.C., 1969-76; exec. v.p. Wells, Rich, Greene, N.Y.C., 1976-80; pres. Wells, Rich, Greene/East, 1980-81; chmn. Wells, Rich, Greene/USA, 1981-82, also dir.; chmn. Wells, Rich, Greene/World Wide, 1982—; lectr. journalism Miriam Meloy Sturgeon Ind. U., 1981; mem. dean's adv. coun. Ind. U. Sch. Bus., 1988—. Chmn. Communication Arts Lunch-O-Ree, N.Y. council Boy Scouts Am., 1974; v.p., dir. Inter-Community Camp, 1974-78; mem. Democratic Town Com., Westport, Conn., 1973-80; mem. dean's adv. coun. Ind. U. Sch. Bus, 1988—; trustee, v.p. Westport Pub. Library, 1976-83, v.p., 1980-81; vice chmn. Jr. Achievement of Greater N.Y., 1980-84; bd. dirs. Nat. Multiple Sclerosis Found., 1984—, Poly. U., 1988—. Served with U.S. Army, 1954-56. Mem. Blue Key, Sigma Alpha Mu. Office: Wells Rich Greene Worldwide 9 W 57th St New York NY 10019

OLSHEN, ABRAHAM CHARLES, actuary, insurance company executive; b. Portland, Oreg., Apr. 20, 1913; s. Ben and Rebecca (Greenstein) O.; m. Dorothy Olds, June 21, 1934; children—Richard Allen, Beverly Ann Olshen Jacobs. BA, Reed Coll., 1933; MSc, U. Iowa, 1935, PhD, 1937. Chief statistician City Planning Commn., Portland, 1933-34; research asst. math. and biometrics U. Iowa, 1934-37; actuary, chief examiner Oreg. Ins. Dept., 1937-42, 45-46; actuary, sr. v.p. West Coast Life Ins. Co., San Francisco, 1946-48, also dir.; pres. Olshen & Assocs., San Francisco, 1978—; pvt. practice actuarial and ins. mgmt. cons., 1968—; vice chmn., dir. Home Fed. Savs. and

Loan Assn. San Francisco, 1972-85. Served with U.S. Navy, 1942-45. Fellow AAAS, Conf. of Actuaries in Pub. Practice; mem. Actuarial Club of Pacific States (pres. 1954), Actuarial Club San Francisco (pres. 1963), Am. Acad. Actuaries, Am. Risk and Ins. Assn., Internat. Assn. Cons. Actuaries, Internat. Congress Actuaries (U.S. del.), Ops. Research Soc., Soc. Indsl. and Applied Math., Inst. Math. Stats., Sigma Xi. Clubs: Press, Commonwealth (San Francisco). Home: 2800 Hillside Dr Burlingame CA 94010 Office: 760 Market St Ste 739 San Francisco CA 94102

OLSON, CLIFFORD LARRY, management consultant, entrepreneur; b. Karlstad, Minn., Oct. 11, 1946; s. Wallace B. and Lucille I (Pederson) O.; m. B.A. Blue Blodgett, March 18, 1967; children: Derek, Erin. B in Chemical Engrng., U. Minn., 1969, B in Physics, 1969; MBA, U. Chgo., 1972; Licence en Sciences Economiques, U. de Louvain, Brussels, 1972. CPA, Cert. mgmt. cons. Project engr. Procter & Gamble, Chgo., 1969-71; engagement mgr. McKinsey & Co., Chgo., 1972-75; ptnr., midwest regional dir. mgmt. consulting Peat, Marwick, Mitchell, St. Louis, 1976-87; chmn. Casson Industries Inc., St. Louis, 1987—; bd. dirs. Mo. Venture Forum, St Louis. Bd. dirs.Opera Theatre of St. Louis, 1981—, Mo. State Pub. Defender Commn. Mem. Am. Inst. CPA's, Inst. Mgmt. Cons., The Planning Forum, Washington U. Elliot Soc. Episcopal. Clubs: St. Louis; Tavern Club (Chgo.); Noonday. Office: Casson Industries Inc 200 S Bemiston Ste 106 Saint Louis MO 63105

OLSON, EUGENE RUDOLPH, printing company executive; b. St. Paul, Apr. 9, 1926; s. Rudolph and Martha E. (Karlson) O.; m. Leona F. Solie, June 28, 1952; children: Kathleen, Wayne, Brian. With Deluxe Check Printers Inc., St. Paul, 1944—, mgr. related products div., 1964-70, nat. dir. market research, 1970-72, v.p., 1972-76, pres., 1976—, chief exec. officer, 1977-86, chmn., 1981—, also dir.; dir. Minn. Mutual Ins. Co., 1st Trust Co., St. Paul. Bd. dirs. Bapt. Hosp. Fund; mem. World Trade Ctr. Adv. Council. Mem. Bank Stationers Assn. (dir.). Baptist. Clubs: Mpls., Midland Hills Country. Home: 2024 Evergreen Ct Saint Paul MN 55113 Office: De Luxe Check Printers Inc 1080 W County Rd F Saint Paul MN 55112 •

OLSON, FRANK ALBERT, airline company executive; b. San Francisco, July 19, 1932; s. Alfred and Edith Mary (Hazeldine) O.; m. Sarah Jean Blakely, Oct. 19, 1957; children—Kimberly, Blake, Christopher. AA, City Coll. San Francisco, 1954. Gen. mgr. Barrett Transp. Co., San Francisco, 1950-64; gen. mgr. Valcar Co. subs. Hertz Corp., San Francisco, 1964-68; with Hertz Corp. sub. Allegis Corp. (formerly United Air Lines), N.Y.C., 1968-87, mgr. mktg. N.Y. zone, 1968-69, v.p., mgr. eastern region, 1969-70, v.p., gen. mgr. rent-a-car div., 1970-73, exec. v.p. corp. rent-a-car div., 1973-77, pres., chief exec. officer, 1977-80, chmn. bd., 1980, also dir., chief exec. officer, from 1982; chmn., pres., chief exec. officer Allegis Corp., 1987; pres., chief exec. officer United Airlines, 1987; chmn., chief exec. officer, chief operating officer Hertz Corp., N.Y.C., from 1987; formerly chmn., pres., chief exec. officer Hertz Corp., now chmn., chief exec. officer; bd. dirs. UAL Corp., United Air Lines Inc.;. Trustee Nat. Commn. Against Drunk Driving; bd. dirs. Nat. Multiple Sclerosis Soc.; mem. adv. bd. for Religion in Am. Life; pres. San Francisco Jr. C. of C., 1960. Served to 1st lt. U.S. Army, 1957-63. Mem. Sales Execs. Club N.Y.C. Republican. Roman Catholic. Clubs: Arcola Country (Paramus, N.J.); Prouts Neck Country (Scarburgh, Maine); Metropolitan (N.Y.C.). Office: The Hertz Corp 225 Brae Blvd Park Ridge NJ 07656

OLSON, LAWRENCE WAYNE, software company executive; b. Evanston, Ill., Nov. 23, 1945; s. Raymond G. and Arvilla N. (Bergstrom) O.; m. Dolores Ann McGovern, Feb. 19, 1966; children: Scott, Kelly, Eric. Student, Wright Coll., 1963-65, 67, Harper Jr. Coll., Palatine, Ill., 1968-70, Ill. Inst. Tech., 1970-71, Northeastern Ill. U., 1974, Harvard U., 1988—. Cert. in data processing, computer programming. Systems programmer Walgreen Co., Deerfield, Ill., 1967-70; product mgr. Pansophic Inc., Oak Brook, Ill., 1970-73; v.p. info. services Vend-Tronics, Inc., Roselle, Ill., 1973-78; pres. Performance Programming, Schaumburg, Ill., 1978-80; chmn. bd. Performance Programming, Schaumburg, 1977-80; v.p. research devel. LPC, Inc., Lombard, Ill., 1980-83; pres. LPC, Inc., Glen Ellyn, Ill., 1983—; bd. dirs. Inteliquest, Inc., Schaumburg; mem. Ill. Indsl. Liaison Com. Co-author numerous software products. Served with USMC, 1965-67. Mem. Assn. Data Processing Service Orgn., Ill. Inventors Council, Young Pres. Orgn., Schaumburg Athletic Assn. (coach), Mensa. Home: 15 Ambrose Ln South Barrington IL 60010 Office: LPC Inc 1200 Roosevelt Rd Glen Ellyn IL 60137

OLSON, ROBERT WYRICK, lawyer; b. Madison, Wis., Dec. 19, 1945; s. John Arthur and Mary Katherine (Wyrick) O.; m. Carol Jean Duane, June 12, 1971; children: John Hagan, Mary Catherine Duane. BA, Williams Coll., 1967; JD, U. Va., 1970. Assoc. Cravath, Swaine & Moore, N.Y.C., 1970-79; asst. gen. counsel Penn Cen. Corp., Cin., 1979-80, assoc. gen. counsel, 1980-82, v.p., dep. gen. counsel, 1982-87, sr. v.p., gen. counsel, sec., 1987—. Mem. ABA. Office: Penn Cen Corp 1 E 4th St Cincinnati OH 45202

OLSON, RUSSEL EINAR, utility company executive; b. Seattle, Apr. 20, 1931; s. Olaf Einar and Margot Marie O.; m. Betty Virginia Rygg, Apr. 21, 1951; children: Charlene, David, Steven. B.A. in Acctg., U. Wash., 1959; postgrad., Exec. Devel. Program, 1968; M.B.A., Pacific Lutheran U., 1982. With Puget Sound Power & Light Co., Bellevue, Wash., 1959-61; auditor Coopers & Lybrand, Seattle, 1961-62; spl. acct. Puget Sound Power & Light Co., 1962-65, Puget Western, Inc., Renton, Wash., 1965-68; asst. v.p. Puget Western, Inc., 1968-69; budget supr. Puget Sound Power & Light Co., 1969-70, fin. planning supr., 1970-72, mgr. fin. planning, 1972-74, asst. treas., 1974-77, treas., 1977-80, v.p., treas., 1980—; tchr. adult edn.; dir. Interwest Savs. Bank. Mem. fin. bd. visitors Pacific Lutheran U.; elder Overlake Christian Ch. Served in USCG, 1950-53. Mem. Fin. Execs. Inst. (chpt. officer dir.), Electric League Pacific N.W., N.W. Electric Light and Power Assn., Providence Found. (bd. dirs.). Club: Rainier, Bellevue Athletic. Office: Puget Sound Power & Light Co 411-108th Ave NE OBC 15 Bellevue WA 98004-5515

OLSON, RUSSELL L., pension fund administrator; b. Elizabeth, N.J., Jan. 3, 1933; s. Harold B. and Edythe M. (Roberts) O.; m. Jeanette A. Sanderson, Aug. 9, 1958; children: Tracy, Stephen, Heather. BA, Rutgers U., 1954; MBA, Harvard U., 1971. Trainee Eastman Kodak Co., Rochester, N.Y., 1954-56, with pub. rels. dept., 1957-69, coordinator internt. info. svcs., 1964-69, treas. staff, 1971-74; adminstrv. asst. pension investments Eastman Kodak Co., Rochester, 1974-82, dir. pension investments, 1982—. With USAF, 1954-56. Presbyterian. Office: Eastman Kodak Co 343 State St Rochester NY 14650

OLSON, SANDRA L., accountant; b. Bridgeport, Conn., Mar. 14, 1963; d. Richard H. and Edith L.(McBurnie) O. BS, Sacred Heart U., 1985. Acct. Arthur Young & Co., Stamford, Conn., 1985-88; sr. ptnr. Diversified Fin. Concepts, 1988—. Mem. Nat. Soc. Pub. Accts.

OLSON, SIGMUND LARS, corporate finance executive; b. Green Bay, Wis., Feb. 7, 1935; s. Edwin Louis and Marjorie Magdelene (Miller) O.; m. Diana Lynn Armentrout, Mar. 15, 1961 (div. 1974); children: Eric L., Lafe S., Britta C., Gunnar A.; m. Linda Marie Larson, Sept. 25, 1974. BS, Calif. State U., Long Beach, 1963; MBA, U. Iowa, 1964. With fin. staff Ford Motor Co., Detroit, 1964-69; with mgmt. staff Mattel, Inc., Los Angeles, 1969-72, Allen Group, Los Angeles, 1972-77; dir. planning Internat. Harvester Co., Chgo., 1977-78, dir. fin. German div., Düsseldorf, 1978-79, v.p. fin. European div., Paris, 1979-82, asst. controller, Chgo., 1982-84, asst. treas., 1984-85; v.p. treas. Ecolab, Inc., St. Paul, 1985-86, v.p., controller, 1986-88, v.p. fin., 1988—. Bd. dirs., asst. treas YMCA, St. Paul, 1986-89. Served to cpl. USMA, 1957-60. Mem. Fin. Execs. Inst., Planning Execs. Inst., Am. Mgmt. Assn., Nat. Assn. Corp. Treas. Lutheran. Club: Univ. (St. Paul). Office: Ecolab Inc Ecolab Ctr Saint Paul MN 55102

OLSON, STEPHEN EDWARD, manufacturing executive; b. Glendale, Calif., Dec. 5, 1941; s. Victer Alfred and Peggy Irene (Wheeler) O.; m. Joan Peterson, June 14, 1961; children: Scott, Todd. BA, U. Redlands, 1967; MBA, Pepperdine U., 1973. Asst. to pres. Bowes Pacific Co., Riverside, Calif., 1961-65; v.p. Dean Witter & Co., Los Angeles, 1967-75; chmn., chief exec. officer Signet Scientific Co., El Monte, Calif., 1975—, also bd. dirs.; chmn. TGFT Piping Systems Group Am.; founder, dir. Pacific Home Industries, Asusa, Calif.; bd. dirs. Transdynamics Inc., El Monte, Plastics Systems Inc., Tustin, Calif., COM Systems, Van Nuys, Calif. Author: San Bernardino County, A Political Profile, 1967; contbr. articles on marine instrumentation and indsl. instrumentation to profl. jours. Fund raiser Los Angeles County Art Mus., 1980—, Long Beach Art Mus., 1980—, Los Angeles Mission, 1984—; bd. advisors Grad. Sch. Bus. Pepperdine U. Mem. Young Pres.'s Orgn. (edn. chmn. Golden West chpt.; mem. pres.' forum 1984-86), Instrument Soc. Am., Water Standards Industry Assn., Boating Industry Assn., Los Angeles Children's Home Soc., Pepperdine U. Assocs. (named Outstanding Alumni of Yr. 1984). Republican. Club: Long Beach Yacht. Lodge: Masons.

OLSON, STEPHEN HOWARD, manufacturing representative; b. Akron, Ohio, Mar. 16, 1942; s. Irving J. and Ruth (Bogen) O.; m. Elizabeth Victoria Stewart, Sept. 8, 1963 (div. 1974); children: Francine Miller, Mark; m. Kay Blitzer, June 26, 1976; children: Emily, Benjamin. BS in Econs., U. Pa., 1963. Store mgr. Olson Electronics, Mayfield Heights, Ohio, 1964-68; pres. Olson Sales, Foster City, Calif., 1968-77, Steve Olson Assocs., Foster City, 1977—. Bd. dirs. Suicide Prevention and Crisis Ctr. San Mateo County, Burlingame, Calif., 1974-87, v.p., 1977-78, pres., 1979-81; mem. local bd. Selective Svc. System, San Mateo, 1982—. Mem. Electronic Reps. Assn. No. Calif. (sr. v.p. 1988—). Jewish. Home: 207 Loon Ct Foster City CA 94404 Office: Steve Olson Assocs 1157 Chess Dr Ste C Foster City CA 94404

OLSON, TODD JACK, designer, artist; b. New Ulm, Minn., Aug. 22, 1961; s. Kenneth Orvis O. and Irene (Larson) Hendrickson; m. Christine Clare Arnoldy, June 22, 1985; 1 child, Emma Irene. BS in Art cum laude, U. Wis., Stout, 1983. Indsl. designer Debrey Design, Mpls., 1983-85; product designer Tonka Corp., Minnetonka, Minn., 1985-88, Fisher-Price Co., East Aurora, N.Y., 1988—. Designer home safety device. Mem. Indsl. Designers Soc. Am. (sec.-treas. Minn. chpt. 1986-88). Roman Catholic. Home: 203 King St East Aurora NY 14052 Office: Fisher Price Co 636 Girard Ave East Aurora NY 14052

OLSTOWSKI, FRANCISZEK, chemical engineer, consultant; b. N.Y.C., Apr. 23, 1927; s. Franciszek and Marguerite (Stewart) O.; A.A., Monmouth Coll., 1950; B.S. in Chem. Engrng., Tex. A. and I. U., 1954; m. Rosemary Sole, May 19, 1952; children—Marguerita Antonina, Anna Rosa, Franciszek, Anton, Henryk Alexander. Research and devel. engr. Dow Chem. Co., Freeport, Tex., 1954-56, project leader, 1956-65, sr. research engr., 1965-72, research specialist, 1972-79, research leader, 1979-87; dir. Tech. Cons. Services, Freeport, 1987—. Lectr. phys. scis. elementary and intermediate schs., Freeport, 1961-85. Vice chmn. Freeport Traffic Commn., 1974-76, chmn., 1976-79, vice chmn. 1987—. Served with USNR, 1944-46. Fellow Am. Inst. Chemist; mem. Electrochem. Soc. (sec. treas. South Tex. sect. 1963-64, vice chmn. 1964-65, chmn. 1965-67, councillor 1967-70), AAAS, Am. Chem. Soc., N.Y. Acad. Sci. Patentee in synthesis of fluorocarbons, natural graphite products, electrolytic prodn. magnesium metal and polyurethane tech.

O'MALLEY, EDWARD JOSEPH, JR., criminal justice adminstr.; b. Flushing, N.Y., Jan. 4, 1942; s. Edward Joseph and Elsie Anne (Ende) O'M.; B.S., Widener Coll., 1963; M.B.A., St. Johns U., Jamaica, N.Y., 1976; m. Iris Theresa Hill, Aug. 10, 1975. Ins. agt. Liberty Mut. Ins. Co., N.Y.C., 1966-67; supr. group home Children's Village, Bayside, N.Y., 1967-69; unit head N.Y. Narcotic Addiction Control Commn., N.Y.C., 1970-71; exec. dir., sch. dist. drug and alcohol abuse program, Howard Beach, N.Y., 1971-81; spl. asst. to Kings County dist. atty., 1982-85, adminstrv. asst., spl. advisor, 1986—. Past chmn., sec. N.Y.C. Coalition Sch. Based Drug Prevention Programs; past vice chmn. Comprehensive Health Planning Agy., Queens, N.Y.; mem. Queens Community Planning Bd.; past v.p. Flushing (N.Y.) Boys Club; past chmn. bd. dirs. Regular Democratic Club, Rockaway, N.Y.; mem. N.Y. State Dem. Com.; mem. Parish Council St. Camillus Ch.; mem. Chancellor N.Y.C. Bd. Edn. Task Force on Drug Abuse; bd. dirs. Queens chpt. ARC, N.Y.C. Health Systems Agy., Rockaway Task Force on Arts, Far Rockaway chpt. NAACP; chmn. Anti-Redlining Com. of Rockaways; vice chmn. Com. for Casino Gambling in Rockaways, Surfside Housing Assn. for Tenants; mem. N.Y. State Urban Coalition Task Force Drug Abuse. Mem. Emerald Assn. L. I. Beta Gamma Sigma. Club: Rockaway Kiwanis (past pres.). Home: 110 Ocean Pkwy Brooklyn NY 11218 Office: Kings County Dist Atty's Office Mcpl Bldg Brooklyn NY 11201

O'MALLEY, EUGENE FRANCIS, investment banker; b. Boston, Mar. 27, 1950; s. Charles Desloge and Mary Louise (Drew) O'M.; m. Kathleen Marie Sullivan, July 10, 1982; children: Charles, Allison. BS in Fin., Boston Coll., 1972; MBA, Fordham U., 1979. Cons. Theodore Barry & Assocs., N.Y.C., 1979-82; sr. cons. Touche Ross & Co., Boston, 1982-83; pres. Commerx., Ltd., Boston, 1983-85, Faneuil Hall Capital Group, Boston, 1985-87, Mercant, Inc., Boston, 1988—; ind. cons. Arthur D. Little, Cambridge, Mass., 1988—; incorporator, bd. dirs. Wainwright Bank & Trust, Boston. Mem. N.Y. Athletic Club. Roman Catholic. Home: 32 Pine Ridge Rd Wellesley MA 02181 Office: Arthur D Little Acorn Park Cambridge MA 02140

OMAN, DENNIS OLIVER, real estate broker; b. Portland, Oreg., July 30, 1942; s. Oliver Fredrick and Esther (Nau) O.; m. Marion McVeigh Raney, Apr. 9, 1983. AA, Grays Harbor Coll., 1962; BA in Econs., Western Wash. U., 1966; postgrad., U. Hawaii, 1965; MA, Eastern Wash. U., 1970. Tchr., coach Mabton (Wash.) High Sch., 1966-67, Grand Coulee (Wash.) High Sch., 1967-71; prin., tchr. coach Toutle (Wash.) Lake High Sch., 1971-76; prin. Dennis Oman Realty, Long Beach, Wash., 1982—. Contbr. articles to profl. jours. Pres. Washington Coaches Assn. (Coach of Yr. 1975), Jaycees (chartered), Pa. Booster Club (pres. 1980), Elks. Democrat. Office: Long Beach Realty PO Box 741 Long Beach WA 98631

OMANOFF, DENNIS, electronics company manager; b. N.Y.C., Apr. 30, 1955; s. Michael and Julia (Privato) O.; m. Elaine Ann Marino, Sept. 8, 1984; children: Lauren, Eric. BA, Fordham U., 1977; MBA, Hofstra U., 1978. Mfg. engrng. supr. Tex. Instruments, Dallas, 1978-82, mgr. factory planning and automation, 1985—; gen. foreman Martin Marietta Aerospace Co., Orlando, Fla., 1983—; prodn. mgr. Storage Tech., Louisville, Colo., 1983-85. Mem. Am. Soc. Quality Control (cert.), Am. Prodn. and Inventory Control Soc. (cert.). Roman Catholic. Home: 3420 Santana Ln Plano TX 75023 Office: Tex Instruments 13500 N Central Expy Dallas TX 75243

O'MARA, THOMAS PATRICK, manufacturing company executive; b. St. Catharine's, Ont., Can., Jan. 17, 1937; s. Joseph Thomas and Rosanna Patricia (Riordan) O'M.; m. Nancy Irene Rosevear, Aug. 10, 1968; children: Patricia Catharine, Tracy Irene, Sara Megan. B.S., Allegheny Coll., 1958; M.S., Carnegie Inst. Tech., 1960. Mktg. analyst U.S. Steel Corp., Pitts., 1960-65; dir. info. systems Screw & Bolt Corp., Pitts., 1965-68; v.p., gen. mgr. Toy div. Samsonite Corp., Denver, 1968-73; regional mgr. Mountain Zone, Hertz Corp., Denver, 1973-75; asst. to chmn. Allen Group, Melville, N.Y., 1975-76; group exec. v.p. fin. and adminstrn. Bell & Howell Co., Chgo., 1976-77; controller Bell & Howell Co., 1977-78, corp. v.p., 1978-85, pres. visual communications, 1978-85; pres., chief operating officer, dir. Bridge Product Inc., Northbrook, Ill., 1985-87; chmn., chief exec. officer Micro Metl Corp., Indpls., 1987—. Served with USAR, 1961-66. Mem. Econs. Club Chgo., Fin. Execs. Inst., Newcomen Soc. U.S., Sigma Alpha Epsilon. Club: Knollwood. Home: 1350 Inverlieth Lake Forest IL 60045 Office: Micro Metl Corp 3419 Roosevelt Ave Indianapolis IN 46210

OMHOLT, BRUCE DONALD, product designer, mechanical engineer, consultant; b. Salem, Oreg., Mar. 27, 1943; s. Donald Carl and Violet Mae (Buck) O.; m. Mavis Aronow, Aug. 18, 1963 (div. July 1972); children—Madison, Natalie; m. 2d, Darla Kay Faber, Oct. 27, 1972; 1 son, Cassidy. B.S.M.E., Heald Coll. Engring., San Francisco, 1964. Real estate salesman R. Lea Ward and Assocs., San Francisco, 1962-64; sales engr. Repco Engrng., Montebello, Calif., 1964; in various mfg. engrng. and mgmt. positions Ford Motor Co., Rawsonville, Saline, Owosso and Ypsilanti, Mich., 1964-75; chief engr. E. F. Hauserman Co., Cleve., 1975-77; dir. design and engrng. Am. Seating Co., Grand Rapids, Mich., 1977-80; pres. Trinity Engrng., Grand Rapids, Mich., 1980-81, Rohnert Park, Calif., 1981—; 1986 U.S. Patent For Vertical Mitre Machine; cons. mfg. U.S., fgn. patentee carrier rack apparatus, motorcycle improvements, panels.

O'NEIL, ALAN WADE, health science facility administrator; b. Grand Forks, N.D., Dec. 21, 1955; s. Jack Leland and Lona Merle (Sample) O'N.; m. Mary Jane Bjornstad, May 29, 1982; children: Joel, Leigh Ann. BA, Mayville State U., 1979. Installation coordinator Luth. Hosps. and Homes Soc. Am., Fargo, N.D., 1983—; dir. fiscal affairs Fairbanks (Alaska) Meml. Hosp. div. Luth. Hosps. and Homes Soc. Am., 1985—. Mem. HealthCare Fin. Mgmt. Assn.

O'NEIL, JOHN MICHAEL, meat packing company executive; b. Middletown, N.Y., Dec. 12, 1956; s. Robert Joseph and Helen (Haus) O'N.; m. Lisa Ann Lotrecchiano, Aug. 21, 1982; 1 child, Joseph Miles. BA, SUNY, Plattsburgh, 1982. Ptnr. O'Neil Packing Co., Plattsburgh, N.Y., 1968—. Mem. Nat. Assn. Meat Purveyors. Roman Catholic. Home: RD #1 Box 213 Plattsburgh NY 12901 Office: O'Neil Packing Co 73 Bridge St Plattsburgh NY 12901

O'NEILL, DONALD EDMUND, pharmaceutical company executive; b. Port Angeles, Wash., Feb. 10, 1926; s. Edward I. and Christine (Williamson) O'N.; m. Violet Elizabeth Oman, June 12, 1948; children: Shelly O'Neill Lane, Erin O'Neill Kennedy, Shawn O'Neill Hoffman. B.S., U. Wash., 1949. With G.D. Searle & Co., 1950-71, regional sales dir., 1962-64, dir. med. service, 1964-68, dir. mktg., 1968-71; with Warner-Lambert Co., 1971—, v.p., 1974-77, exec. v.p. pharm. group, 1977, now exec. v.p.; pres. Internat. profl. group, 1974-76, Parke-Davis & Co., 1976-78; pres., exec. dir. Warner-Lambert/Parke Davis Research Div., 1978, pres. Health Care Group, 1978-81; pres. Parke-Davis Group, 1981, Health Techs., 1982, Internat.; bd. dirs. NJ Resources Corp. Bd. trustees Morristown Meml. Hosp. Served with USAF, 1944-46. Club: John's Island (Fla.) Golf and Country, Morris County Golf (Convent Station, N.J.). Office: Warner-Lambert Co 201 Tabor Rd Morris Plains NJ 07950

O'NEILL, FRANK R., JR., real estate executive; b. Danbury, Conn., Apr. 3, 1947; s. Frank R. Sr. and Elizabeth (Farley) O'N.; m. Joyce Hartell, Jan. 22, 1977; children: Jennifer, Meghan, Andrew, Daniel. BS in Fin., Northeastern U., 1970. Pres. Tom Collins Appraisers, Inc., Danbury, 1986—. Mem. Am. Assn. Cert. Appraisers, Nat. Assn. Indep. Fee Appraisers. Lodge: Lions.

O'NEILL, JAMES JOHN, lawyer, entrepreneur; b. N.Y.C., Feb. 9, 1938; s. Walter John and Catherine Christina (Koerner) O'N.; m. Anne Marie Loretta Regin, June 19, 1965; children: Jennifer Anne, Jane Courtney, James John Jr., Colin Regin. BA, St. Francis Coll., N.Y.C., 1959; LLB, St. John's U., 1962; postgrad., NYU, 1966-68. Bar: N.Y. Assoc. in trusts Comptroller of Currency U.S. Treasury, N.Y.C., 1963-66; asst. v.p. Am. Stock Exchange, N.Y.C., 1966-74; exec. dir., gen. counsel Com. Publicly Owned Cos., N.Y.C., 1974-86; v.p. Rothschild Inc., N.Y.C., 1986—; bd. dirs. Biotech. Investments, Inc., N.Y.C., Shared Communications Services, N.Y.C.; bd. dirs. N.Y. Inst. Fin. Law Ctr., N.Y.C., 1969-72; pres. Ctr. for U.S. Capital Markets, N.Y.C., 1974—. Chmn. U.S. Youth Council, 1962-64; mem. advance staff Presdl. Campaign Robert F. Kennedy, 1968; civic dir. Fund for Am. Studies, 1974-83, bd. visitors, 1983—; bd. dirs. Am. Council Young Polit. Leaders, 1975-83, Nazareth Regional High Sch., N.Y.C., 1976-84, St. Francis de Sales Sch. for Deaf, N.Y.C., 1980—. Named one of Outstanding Young Men Am., Jaycees, Chgo., 1970. Mem. Fgn. Policy Assn. (bd. dirs. 1974-80, bd. visitors 1983—), Delta Phi Delta. Roman Catholic. Clubs: Larchmont Yacht (N.Y.); University (N.Y.C.). Office: Rothschild Inc One Rockefeller Pla New York NY 10020

O'NEILL, JOSEPH PATRICK, retail association executive; b. Boston, July 18, 1947; s. John Matthew and Mary Elisabeth (Connolly) O'N.; m. Linda Ann Quelle, Nov. 3, 1948; children: Susannah, Patrick, Kathleen. AB in Internat. Relations cum laude, Harvard U., 1969; M in Pub. Affairs, U. Tex., 1973. Planner City of Dallas, 1971-73; econ. cons. NASA, Houston, 1973; exec. asst. to Sen. Lloyd Bentsen, Austin, 1973-80; adminstrv. asst. to Sen. Lloyd Bentsen, Washington, 1980-84; pres. Am. Retail Fedn., Washington, 1985—; instr. LBJ Sch. U. Tex., Austin, 1974-75; advisor on U.S. cleared trade to Multilateral Trade Negotiations, Washington, 1986-87; dir. Retail Industry Trade Action Coalition, Washington, 1985-87; bd. dirs. Cranston Bank, Washington; chief of staff for v.p. campaign Sen. Lloyd Bentsen, summer 1988. Editor: Social Services in Texas, 1973. Mem. Bus. Roundtable Dem. Senatorial Campaign com., 1987; bd. dirs. Am. Retail Edn. Found., 1985-87; chief of staff vice-presdl. campaign Senator Lloyd Bentsen, 1988. Roman Catholic. Club: Harvard (Washington) (Austin) (treas. 1977-78), Avenel (Potomac, Md.), Army-Navy (Washington). Office: Am Retail Fedn 1616 H St NW Washington DC 20005

O'NEILL, PAUL HENRY, aluminum company executive; b. St. Louis, Dec. 4, 1935; s. John Paul and Gaynald Elsie (Irvin) O'N.; m. Nancy Jo Wolfe, Sept. 4, 1955; children—Patricia, Margaret, Julie, Paul Henry. A.B., Fresno State Coll., 1960; Haynes Found. fellow, Claremont Grad. Sch., 1960-61; postgrad., George Washington U., 1962-65; M.P.A., Ind. U., 1966. Site engr. Morrison-Knudsen, Inc., Anchorage, 1955-57; systems analyst VA, Washington, 1961-66; budget examiner Bur. of Budget, Washington, 1967-69; chief human resources program div. U.S. Govt. Office of Mgmt. and Budget, Washington, 1969-70; asst. dir. U.S. Govt. Office of Mgmt. and Budget, 1971-72, assoc. dir., 1973-74, dep. dir., 1975-77; v.p. Internat. Paper Co., N.Y.C., 1977-81, sr. v.p., 1981-85, pres., dir., 1985-87; chmn., chief exec. officer Aluminum Co. Am., Pitts., 1987—, also bd. dirs.; mem. adv. com. Fin. Acctg. Standards Bd., 1982-86; bd. dirs. Nat. Westminster Bank. Chmn. health and welfare com. Fairfax Fedn. Civic Assns., 1967; mem. JFK bd. visitors Harvard U., 1977-82, mem. adv. com, 1982—; bd. dirs. Gerald R. Ford Found., 1981—; mem. Manpower Devel. Research Corp., 1981—, Pres.'s Nat. Commn. on Productivity, 1981-83. Recipient Nat. Inst. Pub. Affairs Career Edn. award, 1965, William A. Jump Meritorious award, 1971; Fellow Nat. Inst. Pub. Affairs, 1966. Methodist. Home: 3 Von Lent Pl Pittsburgh PA 15232 Office: Aluminum Co Am 1501 Alcoa Bldg Pittsburgh PA 15219 •

O'NEILL, PETER MICHAEL, lawyer; b. Summit, N.J., Nov. 22, 1946; s. Peter Eugene and Mary Patricia (O'Neill) O'N.; m. Ann Howard Conley, Aug. 28, 1971; children: Kathleen, Sarah, Michael. AB, Colgate U., 1968; JD, Boston U., 1971. Bar: N.J. 1971, Conn. 1972, U.S. Supreme Ct. 1982. Jud. clk. to Francis W. Hayden Newark, 1971-72; asst. prosecutor Essex County Prosecutor's Office, Newark, 1972-73; assoc. Kraft and Hughes, Newark, 1973-76, William C. Baggitt, Princeton, N.J., 1976-77; ptnr. Wills and O'Neill, and precedessor Strauss, Wills and O'Neill, Princeton, 1977—; mem. adv. coun. The Trust Co. of Princeton, 1988—. Trustee, treas. Community Guidance Ctr., Princeton, 1976-80; bd. dirs. Stony Brook Millstone Watershed Assn., Hopewell, N.J., 1981-86, pres., 1982-85, treas., 1985-86; trustee Princeton Community Tennis Program, 1985—. Mem. Princeton Bar Assn. (treas. 1978-80). Club: Bedens Brook (Skillman, N.J.). Home: 470 Riverside Dr Princeton NJ 08540 Office: Wills & O'Neill 10 Nassau St Princeton NJ 08542

O'NEILL, W. P(AUL), chemical company executive; b. Toronto, Can., 1938; m. Marilyn O'Neill; 2 children. BA, U. Toronto, 1960; Chartered Acct., Inst. Chartered Accts. Ontario, 1964. V.p. fin. Atomic Energy Can. Ltd., Kanata, Ont., 1978-82; corp. exec. v.p., chief fin. officer Atomic Energy Can. Ltd., Ottawa, Ont., 1982-85; pres. Radiochem. Co. div. Atomic Energy Can. Ltd., Kanata, 1985-88; pres., chief exec. officer Nordion Internat. Inc. (successor to Radiochem. Co.), Kanata, 1988—. Office: Nordion Internat Inc, 447 March Rd, PO Box 13500, Kanata, ON Canada K2K 1X8

O'NEILL, WILLIAM FRANCIS, financial executive; b. Cambridge, Mass., Oct. 30, 1929; s. George Francis and Alice L. (Denehy) O'N.; m. Gloria T. Blouin, Aug. 18, 1951; children: Marcia E., Carol A., William W. BBA, Boston U., 1962; AMP, Harvard U., 1979. Staff analyst Exxon Corp., Boston, 1953-63; acting mgr. Arthur D. Little, Inc., Cambridge, Mass., 1963-74; fin. project mgr. Arthur D. Little, Inc., Rio de Janeiro, 1974-77; internat. controller Arthur D. Little, Inc., Cambridge, 1977-81, controller, 1981-85, sr. v.p., chief fin. officer, 1985—; bd. dirs. Cambridge Cons. Ltd., U.K., Opinion Research Corp., Princeton, N.J. Incorporator Winchester (Mass.) Hosp. Served with USAF, 1951-53. Mem. Fin. Exec. Inst. (profl. devel. com.). Clubs: Harvard, Treas.' (Boston). Home: 105 Ridge St Winchester MA 01890 Office: Arthur D Little Inc Acorn Park Cambridge MA 02140

ONG, JOHN DOYLE, rubber products company executive; b. Uhrichsville, Ohio, Sept. 29, 1933; s. Louis Brosee and Mary Ellen (Liggett) O.; m. Mary Lee Schupp, July 20, 1957; children: John Francis Harlan, Richard Penn Blackburn, Mary Katherine Caine. BA, Ohio State U., 1954, MA, 1954; LLB, Harvard, 1957; LHD, Kent State U., 1982. Bar: Ohio 1958. Asst. counsel B.F. Goodrich Co., Akron, 1961-66; group v.p. B.F. Goodrich Co., 1972-73, exec. v.p., 1973-74, vice chmn., 1974-75, pres., dir., 1975-77, pres., chief operating officer, dir., 1978-79, chmn. bd., pres., chief exec. officer, 1979-84, chmn. bd., chief exec. officer, 1984—; asst. to pres. Internat. B.F. Goodrich Co., Akron, 1966-69, v.p., 1969-70, pres., 1970-72; dir. Cooper Industries, Am. Info. Technologies Corp., The Kroger Co. Vice-pres. exploring Great Trail council Boy Scouts Am., 1974-77; bd. dirs. Nat. Alliance for Bus.; trustee Mus. Arts Assn., Cleve., Bexley Hall Sem., 1974-81, Case Western Res. U., 1980—, Kenyon Coll., 1983-85; trustee Hudson (Ohio) Library and Hist. Soc., pres., 1971-72; trustee Western Res. Acad., Hudson, 1975—, pres. bd. trustees, 1977—; nat. trustee Nat. Symphony Orch., 1975-83; mem. bus. adv. com. Transp. Center, Northwestern U., 1975-78, Carnegie-Mellon U. Grad. Sch. Indsl. Adminstrn., 1978-83; mem. adv. bd. Blossom Music Center. Served with JAGC AUS, 1957-61. Mem. Ohio Bar Assn. (bd. govs. corp. counsel sect. 1962-74, chmn. 1970), Rubber Mfrs. Assn. (dir. 1974-84), Conf. Bd., Bus. Roundtable, Chem. Mfrs. Assn. (bd. dirs. 1988—), Phi Beta Kappa, Phi Alpha Theta. Episcopalian. Clubs: Portage Country, Akron City; Union (Cleve.); Links (N.Y.C.), Union League (N.Y.C.); Ottawa Shooting; Met. (Washington); Rolling Rock (Ligonier, Pa.); Castalia Trout. Home: 230 Aurora St Hudson OH 44236 Office: The B F Goodrich Co 3925 Embassy Pkwy Akron OH 44313

ONOFREY, DEBRA ANNE CATHERINE, accounting administrator; b. Lakewood, Ohio, Jan. 18, 1956; d. John Martin and Dolores Marlene (Sefcovic) O. Student, Tex. Luth. Coll., 1974-76, John Cabot Internat. Coll., Rome, 1977. Bookkeeper, clk. Ress Realty Co., Cleve., 1978-80; acctg. clk. U. Tex. SW Med. Ctr., Dallas, 1981-83, sect. coordinator, 1983-86, mgr., 1986—. Co-editor Med. Service Research and Devel. plan Monarch newsletter, 1984. Mem. Nat. Assn. Female Execs., Smithsonian Inst.. Roman Catholic. Home: 4005 N Beltline #526 Irving TX 75038

ONSTEAD, CHARLES EDWARD, industrial engineer, consultant; b. Jonesboro, Ark., Jan. 9, 1941; s. Paul Edward and Rosa Lee (Carter) O.; m. Lavita Mae Gartman, June 7, 1958 (dec. Apr. 1983); children: Sheila Kay Onstead Dunlap, David Alan; m. Anna Mae Woods, May 5, 1984. Student, Ark. State U., 1965. Standards engr. Crane Co., Jonesboro, Ark., 1965-68, product engr., 1968-78, engring. mgr., 1979-80; process engr. Lincoln, Jonesboro, 1978-79; sales engr. GTE-Valeron Corp., Troy, Mich., 1981—; indsl. cons. Mfg. Tech. Service, Jonesboro, 1981—; pres. OMNI Tool & Mfg., Jonesboro, 1985—. Served to sgt. U.S. Army, 1958-61. Mem. Soc. Mfg. Engrs. (sr., bulletin editor 1979-83, advt. chmn. 1982-86, presdl. award 1985). Democrat. Lodge: Elks. Home: 607 Oakhollow PO Box 2217 Jonesboro AR 72402 Office: GTE Valeron Corp 750 Stephenson Hwy Troy MI 48007-3750

OOSTEN, ROGER LESTER, medical manufacturing executive; b. Rock Valley, Iowa, Sept. 21, 1937; s. Henry and Martha (Kersbergen) O.; m. Patricia Nan Hanlon, Oct. 21, 1961; children: Kimberly Kay, Kurtis James, Jan Hendrik. BSEE, U. Iowa, 1967. Engr. Ball Bros. Research Corp., Boulder, Colo., 1967-73; pres. Mgmt. Bus. Machines, Inc., Denver, 1973-76; dir. research and devel. Neomed, Inc., Boulder, 1976-78; v.p. research and devel. Concept, Inc., Clearwater, Fla., 1978-81; v.p. surg. div. Birtcher Corp., El Monte, Calif., 1982-85; founder, pres. Bergen Mfg., Fla., 1985—. Patentee in field. Served with USN, 1956-60. Named Man of Yr., NASA, 1974. Mem. Assn. Advancement Med. Instrumentation. Home: 5461 DeCubellis Rd New Port Richey FL 34654

OPASKS, WALTER PETER, accountant; b. Pitts., Mar. 1, 1950; s. Peter and Rita (Drundy) O.; m. Christine Mary Voke, Apr. 29, 1972; children: Wally, Brain, Stacey. BA in Polit. Sci., U. Pitts., 1972; BS in Acctg., Point Park Coll., 1976. CPA, N.J., N.C. Examiner U.S. Postal Svc., Pitts., 1977; insp. U.S. Postal Svc., Bellmawr, N.J., 1978-82, Phila., 1982-84; computer security officer U.S. Postal Svc., Raleigh, N.C., 1984—; pvt. practice acctg. Raleigh, 1985—. Fellow N.C. Soc. CPA's; mem. Am. Inst. CPA's, Digital Equipment Co. Users Soc. Home: 917 Pebblebrook Dr Raleigh NC 27609-6001 Office: US Postal Svc 4921 Prof Ct Raleigh NC 27609

OPEKA, JOHN FRANK, utility executive, electrical engineer; b. Forest City, Pa., Nov. 9, 1940; s. Frank Carl and Albina (Chodorwski) O.; m. Jacqueline Marie Fiorillo, Oct. 25, 1969; children—Jennifer, Janel. B.S.E.E., Pa. State U., 1962; M.B.A., Rensselaer Poly. Inst., 1982; P.M.D., Harvard Bus. Sch., 1984. Project engr. Combustion Engring., Windsor, Conn., 1967-70; asst. sta. supt. Millstone Point, Northeast Utilities, Waterford, Conn., 1977-78, sta. supt., 1978-80, systems supt. nuclear ops. Northeast Utilities, Berlin, Conn., 1980-81, v.p. nuclear ops., 1981-85, sr. v.p. nuclear engring and ops., 1985-86, exec. v.p. engring ops., 1986— ; chmn. NEIL Engring. Adv. Commn., Bermuda, 1984-86; chmn. Analysis and Engring. Industry Rev. Group, Inst. Nuclear Power Ops., Atlanta, 1984-86 . Bd. dirs. Thames Sci. Ctr., New London, Conn., 1984—, pres. bd. 1988—, Opportunities Industrialization Ctr., New London, 1984. Mem. Am. Nuclear Soc. Served to lt. USN, 1962-67. Republican. Roman Catholic. Club: Christ the King Men's (Old Lyme, Conn.). Office: NE Utilities PO Box 270 Hartford CT 06141

OPEL, JOHN R., business machines company executive; b. Kansas City, Mo., Jan. 5, 1925; s. Norman J. and Esther (Roberts) O.; m. Julia Carole Stout, Dec. 28, 1953; children: Robert, Nancy, Julia, Mary, John. A.B., Westminster Coll., 1948; M.B.A., U. Chgo., 1949. With IBM Corp., Armonk, N.Y., 1949—, salesman, various mgmt. positions, 1949-66, v.p., 1966-68, mem. mgmt. com., 1967, v.p. corp. finance and planning, 1968-69, sr. v.p. finance and planning, 1969-72, group exec. data processing group, 1972-74, dir., 1972—, pres., 1974-83, chief exec. officer, 1981-86, chmn., 1983-86, chmn. exec. com., 1986—; bd dirs. Pfizer, Inc., Time Inc., Prudential Ins. Co. Am. Trustee U. Chgo., Westminster Coll. Served with U.S. Army, 1943-45. Mem. Bus. Council, Council on Fgn. Relations. Office: IBM Corp 590 Madison Ave New York NY 10022

OPITZ, BERNARD FRANCIS, JR., postal service administrator; b. Springfield, Mass., Dec. 9, 1947; s. Bernard Francis and Bertha Margaret (Diamond) O.; m. Elena Louise Cotti, Oct. 10, 1970 (div. 1979); children: Bernard Francis III, Douglas Richard; m. Patricia Ann Menzer, Feb. 29, 1980; 1 stepchild, Karyn Renee Beaty. AAS, Springfield Tech. Inst., 1968. Sr. detail draftsman Combustion Engring., Windsor, Conn., 1968-71; distbn. clk. U.S. Post Office, 1966-68; with U.S. Postal Svc., Springfield, 1971—, supr. prodn. planning, 1978-80, customer requirements specialist, 1980—. Mem. Am. Mgmt. Assn., Springfield Indsl. Assn. (exec. bd. 1985—), Sacred Heart Alumni Assn., Springfield Tech. Alumni Assn., Rotary. Roman Catholic. Office: US Postal Svc 190 Fiberloid St Springfield MA 01152-9601

OPOTOWSKY, STUART BERGER, holding company executive; b. N.Y.C., Feb. 23, 1935; s. Rubin S. and Rebecca (Sapolin) O.; m. Enid Berk, June 27, 1959 (div. Apr. 1972); children: Peter, Catherine; m. Barbara Berger, Aug. 3, 1972; 1 child, Sasha. BBA, Wayne State U., 1957, LLB, 1962. Bar: Mich. 1963, Calif. 1965, N.Y. 1972; CPA, Mich. Gen. tax counsel Norton Simon Inc., N.Y.C., 1964-76; ptnr. Phillips Nizer Benjamin Krim & Ballon, N.Y.C., 1976-80; gen. tax counsel The Penn Cen. Corp., N.Y.C., 1980-82; ptnr. Feit & Ahrens, N.Y.C., 1982-87; v.p. tax Loews Corp., N.Y.C., 1987—; adj. prof. law NYU, N.Y.C., 1975—. Mem. N.Y. State Bar Assn. Office: Loews Corp 667 Madison Ave New York NY 10021-8087

OPP, WILLIS REUBEN, investment banker; b. Leola, S.D., Sept. 12, 1939; s. Reuben J. and Freda (Feickert) O.; m. Patricia Pinkston, Apr. 3, 1965; children: David S., Michael J., Kevin L., John D. AB in Russian, Syracuse U., 1965. Tech. sales rep. food products div. Union Carbide, Columbus, Ga., 1965-67; account exec. Merrill Lynch Co., Inc., Denver, 1967-72; sr. v.p., sales mgr. Kirchner, Moore & Co., Denver, 1972—. Coach Jefferson (Colo.) County Little League Football and Basketball, 1969—. Served with USAF, 1961-65. . Republican. Presbyterian. Clubs: Rolling Hills Country (Golden, Colo.) (treas. 1984-86, pres. 1986-87, ex-officio 1987—); Regis High Sch. Parents Club (Denver) (pres. 1985-88, ex-officio 1988—). Home: 15096 W Maple Ave Golden CO 80401 Office: Kirchner Moore & Co 717 17th St Ste 2500 Denver CO 80202

OPPENHEIM, ROBERT, beauty industry executive; b. N.Y.C., May 21, 1925; s. Hyman and Hannah (Lieberman) O.; BS cum laude, Syracuse U., 1950; m. Ruth Wigler, Feb. 7, 1954; children: Nancy Ellen, David Paul, Howard P. Product sales specialist McKesson & Robbins, Yonkers, N.Y., 1950-55; asst. sales mgr. Clairol, Inc., N.Y.C., 1955-60; dir. marketing Haircolor div. Revlon, Inc., N.Y.C., 1960-68, dir. marketing and sales Salon div., 1968-70; exec. v.p. Milton R. Barrie Co., Inc., 1970-71; mgmt. cons., 1971-76; pub. Beauty Salon Newsletter, N.Y.C., 1971-83; pres. Salon div. Clairol, Inc., N.Y.C., 1988—, chmn. Profl. Products div., 1983-87; pres. Oppenheim Communications, N.Y.C., 1988—; pub. Salon Update, 1987—, The Oppenheim Letter, 1988—, mgmt. cons., 1988—. Served with AUS, 1942-44; ETO. Mem. Nat. Beauty and Barber Assn. (pres. 1984-85), Am. Beauty Assn. (pres. 1985-86). Mason. Home: 241 Sickletown Rd West Nyack NY 10994 Office: Oppenheim Communications 153 E 57th St New York NY 10022

OPPENHEIMER, FRANZ MARTIN, lawyer; b. Mainz, Germany, Sept. 7, 1919; s. Arnold and Johanna (Mayer) O.; m. Margaret Spencer Foote, June 17, 1944; children: Martin Foote, Roxana Foote, Edward Arnold. B.S., U. Chgo., 1942; student, U. Grenoble, France, 1938-39; LL.B. cum laude (note editor Law Jour. 1945), Yale U., 1945. Bar: N.Y. 1946, D.C. 1955. Rsch. asst. com. human devel. U. Chgo., 1942-43; law clk. to Judge Swan, U.S. Circuit Ct. of Appeals, N.Y., 1945-46; assoc. atty. Chadbourne, Wallace, Parke & Whiteside, N.Y.C., 1946-47; atty. IBRD, Washington, 1947-57; individual practice law 1958-59; ptnr. firm Leva, Hawes, Symington, Martin & Oppenheimer, 1959-83, Fort & Schlefer, Washington, 1984—; bd. dirs. Commerzbank U.S. Fin., Inc.; presdl. apptd. mem. Panel of Arbitrators of Internat. Centre for Settlement of Investment Disputes; bd. dirs. Commerzbank U.S. Fin., Inc. Contbr. articles to profl. and other jours. Bd. dirs. Internat. Student House; founding mem. Company of Christian Jews; trustee Inst. Empirical Econ. Research, Berlin, West Germany; hon. trustee Com. 100 on Fed. City, Washington. Decorated officer's cross Order of Merit (Fed. Republic Germany). Mem. Am. Psychol. Assn., Am., Fed. bar assns., Am. Soc. Internat. Law (treas. 1964-76), Council Fgn. Rels. Episcopalian. Clubs: Yale, Century (N.Y.C.); City Tavern, Metropolitan (Washington). Home: 3248 O St NW Washington DC 20007 Office: Fort & Schlefer 1401 New York Ave NW Washington DC 20005

OPPENHEIMER, TOM L., advertising executive; b. N.Y.C., Jan. 26, 1943; s. Theodore Daniel and Hetty H. (Stern) O.; m. Fran Cora Fahrer, Aug. 22, 1965 (div. Aug. 1987); children: Kim T., Kevin S. BA, NYU, 1965. V.p. Topp Studio Inc., N.Y.C., 1967-74, pres., 1974—; pres. Oppenheimer Advt. Inc., N.Y.C., 1977—; bd. dirs. 225 Fifth Ave. Assn. N.Y.C., 1980, also sec. 1982—. Bd. dirs. 225 Fifth Ave. Assn., 1980—, sec., 1982—. Served to cpl. U.S. Army, 1966-67. Mem. Alpha Epsilon Pi. Office: Oppenheimer Advt 21 E 26th St New York NY 10010

OPPENLANDER, ROBERT, airline executive; b. N.Y.C., May 20, 1923; s. Robert and Lillian (Ahrens) O.; m. Jessie I. Major, Sept. 30, 1950; children—Kris (Mrs. John Paul Austin, Jr.), Robert Kirk, Tenley. B.S., MIT, 1944; M.B.A., Harvard U., 1948. With Metals & Controls Corp., Attleboro, Mass., 1948-53; prin. Cresap, McCormick & Paget, N.Y.C., 1953-58; comptroller, treas. Delta Air Lines, Inc., Atlanta, 1958-88; v.p. fin. Delta Air Lines, Inc., 1964-67, sr. v.p. fin., treas., 1967-78, sr. v.p. fin., 1978-83, vice chmn. bd., chief fin. officer, 1983-88, ret., 1988, also dir.; dir. C&S Investment Advisors, Inc. Served to lt. USNR, 1944-46. Club: Capital City. Home: 3944 Powers Ferry Rd NW Atlanta GA 30342 Office: Delta Air Lines Inc Hartsfield Atlanta Internat Airport Atlanta GA 30320

OPPENLANDER, ROBERT KIRK, management information systems specialist; b. Providence, Oct. 15, 1952; s. Robert and Jessica Isabelle (Major) O. AB in Psychology and Econs., Duke U., 1974; postgrad., Emory Law Sch., 1977-78; MBA in Internat. Bus., Ga. State U., 1982. With mktg. dept. IBM Corp., Atlanta, 1975-77, Nimslo Corp., Atlanta, 1981-82; with fin. control orgn. AT&T, Parsippany, N.J., 1983; with corp. contract mgmt. AT&T, Morristown, N.J., 1983-85, with bus. devel. orgn., 1985-86; dir. mktg. with advanced decision support systems AT&T, Whippany, N.J., 1986—. AT&T coordinator United Way campaign, Morristown, 1983-85. Club: Capital City (Atlanta). Home: 7 Harrow Ln Bedminster NJ 07921 Office: AT&T-Advanced Decision Support Systems div 100 S Jefferson Rd Whippany NJ 07981

ORAZIO, JOAN POLITI, financial planning company executive; b. N.Y.C., Mar. 24, 1930; d. Joseph and Anna B. Politi; B.S., Mercy Coll., 1975; cert. fin. planner Coll. Fin. Planning, 1979; m. Dr. Louis D. Orazio, Aug. 24, 1952; children—Louise Orazio Mason, Joanne Orazio Tonkin, Paul, Phyllis Orazio Kearsing. Exec. v.p. Gary Goldberg & Co., Suffern, N.Y., 1977—; instr. Rockland Community Coll., 1977-84 ; workshop leader, seminar speaker various colls., corps. community orgns., 1970—. Trustee Rockland Community Coll. Mem. Internat. Assn. Fin. Planners, Inst. Cert. Fin. Planners, Nat. Orgn. Italian Am. Women, Nat. Assn. Female Execs., Rockland County Bus. and Profl. Women. Roman Catholic. Lodge: Kiwanis. Home: 17 Wilder Rd Suffern NY 10901 Office: Gary Goldberg & Co Inc 75 Montebello Rd Suffern NY 10901

ORAZIO, PAUL VINCENT, financial planner; b. Flushing, N.Y., July 9, 1957; s. Louis D. and Joan (Politi) O.; m. PattiAnn DeMarzo, May 1, 1982; children: Louis D. II, Christina M. BS in Bus., Fordham U., 1979; cert. fin. planning, Coll. for Fin. Planning, 1987. Cert. fin. planner. Acct. exec. Levi Strauss & Co., Inc., San Francisco, 1979-83; sr. fin. planner Gary Goldberg & Co., Inc., Suffern, N.Y., 1983—; bd. dirs. Vol. Counseling Service, New City, N.Y., 1985—. Mem. Internat. Assn. of Fin. Planners, Internat. Bd. Standards and Practices for Cert. Fin. Planners, Inst. of Cert. Fin. Planners, Kiwanis. Roman Catholic. Home: 43 Lorna Ln Suffern NY 10901 Office: Gary Goldberg & Co Inc 75 Montebello Rd Suffern NY 10901

ORBE, LAWRENCE FRANCIS, III, investment banker, lawyer; b. Paterson, N.J., Sept. 20, 1938; s. Lawrence Francis, Jr., and Vera Mary (Scola) O.; B.S., Lafayette Coll., 1960; M.B.A., Harvard U., 1962; postgrad. U. Pa., 1980; J.D., Fla. State U., 1983; children: Lance, William, Robert. Ptnr. Glore Forgan & Co., 1962-68, v.p. corp. fin., 1965-68; owner, operator L.F. Orbe & Co., Investment Bankers, Gulf Breeze, Fla., 1968-83; assoc. Donovan, Leisure, Newton & Irvine, N.Y.C., 1983-85, Ruffa & Hanover, N.Y.C., 1986-88, Adler Hindy Turner & Glaser, N.Y.C., 1988—; dir. various corps.; cons. govt. agys. and ofcls.; internat. lectr. Contbr. numerous articles to law revs. and profl. jours. Republican. Roman Catholic. Home: Box 71 Ponte Vedra FL 32082 Office: Adler Hindy Turner & Glaser 440 Park Blvd S 16th Fl New York NY 10016

ORBEN, JACK RICHARD, investment company executive; b. Bklyn., June 16, 1938; s. Stanley Souza and Helena Emily (Hall) O.; A.A., Valley Forge, 1956; B.A., Tufts U., 1960; m. Patricia Wells, Dec. 17, 1960; children—Stacey Souza, Stephanie Anne, Bradford Richard. Sales mgr. nat. accounts N.Y. Telephone Co., 1960-66; founder, exec. v.p. Facts, Inc., 1966-69; with Orben Assocs., Inc., N.Y.C., 1970—, pres., 1982—; chmn., chief exec. officer Fiduciary Counsel, Inc., Estate Mgmt., Inc., Econ. Analysts, Inc., Starwood Corp.; pres. Venturevest, Inc.; dir. Kinderhill Corp., A.E. Beer & Co., Inc.; chmn. Seward, Groves, Richard & Wells. Past pres. White Plains Child Day Care Assn., Thomas Slater Ctr.; chmn., bd. dirs. White Plains YMCA. Served with N.G., 1960-66. Clubs: Larchmont Yacht, Union League, Windemere Island, University (dir.), Taconic Hunt, St. James, Wall St. Home: 177 Soundview Ave White Plains NY 10606 Office: Assoc Family Services 40 Wall St New York NY 10005

ORBEN, ROBERT ALLEN, engine company executive; b. Bklyn., Aug. 18, 1936; s. Stanley Souza and Helena Emily (Hall) O.; m. Mary West Foster, May 7, 1960; children: Christopher Riis, Janet Hyde, Virginia Hamilton, William Robert. BA in Fin., Lehigh U., 1958; MBA in Acctg., Rutgers U., 1960. CPA, N.Y. Audit mgr. Price Waterhouse & Co., N.Y.C., 1958-73; asst. controller NCR Corp., Dayton, Ohio, 1973-74, corp. controller, 1974-76; v.p., controller Cummins Engine Co., Columbus, Ind., 1976—; bd. dirs. Fin. Execs. Inst., Morristown, NJ; adv. council Payton Acctg. Ctr., Ann Arbor, 1982-86; pres. Fin. Execs. Research Found., Morristown, 1985-86. Treas. Bartholomew Consol. Sch. Found., Columbus, 1986-87; adv. council Beta Alpha Psi; bd. dirs. Sans Souci, Inc., Columbus, 1985-86. Served to 1st lt. U.S. Army, 1960-62. Mem. Am. Inst. CPA's, Fin. Execs. Inst. (bd. dirs., pres. com. corp. reporting 1985-86), Am. Inst. CPAs, Ohio State Acctg. Hall Fame (mem. adv. com.). Presbyterian. Clubs: Harrison Lake Country (Columbus). Home: 4390 N Riverside Dr Columbus IN 47203 Office: Cummins Engine Co PO Box 3005 Columbus IN 47202-3005

ORDWAY, JOHN DANTON, pension administrator, lawyer, accountant; b. Mpls., Mar. 19, 1928; s. John Dunreath Ordway and Inez Adelaide (Stahl) Larson; m. Mary E. Bateman, June 16, 1951(div. 1978); 1 child, David. BBA, Am. U., 1963, JD, 1965. Bar: U.S. Dist. Ct. D.C. 1966; CPA, Minn. Dir. ins. Nat. Automobile Dealers Assn., Washington, 1957-69; v.p. Edward H. Friend and Co., Washington, 1969-74; exec. v.p. Pension Bds. United Ch. of Christ, N.Y.C., 1974—. Alt. mem. Planning Bd., Stamford, Conn., 1982-86. With U.S. Army, 1946-47. Mem. AICPAs. Republican. Mem. United Ch. of Christ. Club: Westwood Country (Vienna, Va.); Quail Run Golf Club (Naples, Fla.). Lodge: Kena Temple. Home: 9 Tamarac Rd Westport CT 06880

OREFFICE, PAUL FAUSTO, chemical company executive; b. Venice, Italy, Nov. 29, 1927; came to U.S., 1945, naturalized, 1951; s. Max and Elena (Friedenberg) O.; m. Franca Giuseppina Ruffini, May 26, 1956; children: Laura Emma, Andrew T. B.S. in Chem. Engring., Purdue U., 1949. With Dow Chem. Co., various internat. locations, 1953—; assigned to Switzerland, Italy, Brazil and Spain to 1969; pres. Dow Chem. Latin Am., Coral Gables, Fla., 1966-70; corporate fin. v.p. Dow Chem. Co., Midland, Mich., 1970-75, pres. Dow Chem. U.S.A., 1975-78, pres., chief exec. officer, 1978-86, chmn., pres., chief exec. officer, 1986-87, chmn. bd., 1987—; bd. dirs. Morgan Stanley Group Inc., Inc., CIGNA Corp., No. Telecom Ltd., Coca Cola Co. Trustee Am. Enterprise Inst. Served with AUS, 1951-53. Decorated Encomienda del Merito Civil Spain, 1966. Mem. Chem. Mfrs. Assn., Bus. Council, Conf. Bd. Office: The Dow Chem Co 2030 Willard H Dow Ctr Midland MI 48674

O'REILLY, ANTHONY JOHN FRANCIS, food company executive; b. Dublin, Ireland, May 7, 1936; s. John Patrick and Aileen (O'Connor) O'R.; m. Susan Cameron, May 5, 1962; children: Susan, Cameron, Justine, Gavin, Caroline, Tony. Student, Belvedere Coll., Dublin, Univ. Coll., Dublin, Wharton Bus. Sch. Overseas, 1965; B.C.L.; D.C.L. (hon.), Ind. State U.; Ph.D. in Agrl. Mktg, U. Bradford, Eng.; LL.D. (hon.), Wheeling Coll., Trinity Coll., Dublin, Rollins U. Indsl. cons. Weston Evans, 1958-62; personal asst. to chmn. Suttons Ltd., Cork, 1960-62; lectr. dept. applied psychology Univ. Coll., Cork, 1960-62; dir. Robert McCowen & Sons Ltd., Tralee, 1961-62; gen. mgr. An Bord Bainne/Irish Dairy Bd., 1962-66; dir. Agrl. Credit Corp. Ltd., 1965-66, Nitrigin Eireann Teoranta, 1965-66; mng. dir., chief exec. officer Comhlucht Siuicre Eireann Teo. and Erin Foods Ltd., 1966-69; joint mng. dir. Heinz-Erin Ltd., 1967-70; dir. Allied Irish Investment Bank Ltd., 1968-71; mng. dir. H.J. Heinz Co. Ltd., U.K., 1969-71; sr. v.p. N.Am. and Pacific H.J. Heinz Co., 1971-72; exec. v.p., chief operating officer H.J. Heinz Co., Pitts., 1972-73, pres., chief operating officer, 1973-79, pres., chief exec. officer, 1979—, chmn., 1987—; chmn. Atlantic Resources, Dublin, Ind. Newspapers Ltd., Dublin, Fitzwilton Ltd., Dublin, Ireland Fund; ptnr. Cawley Sheerin Wynne and Co., Dublin; chmn. Fitzwilton Ltd., Dublin, Atlantic Resources, Dublin, Ind. Newspapers Ltd., Dublin; bd. dirs. Mobil Oil Corp., Bankers Trust N.Y. Corp., Bankers Trust Co., N.Y., Washington Post Co., London Tablet Found.; bd. trustees U. Pitts.; bd. dirs. and mem. exec. com. Pitts. Opera. Author: Prospect, 1962, Developing Creative Management, 1970, The Conservative Consumer, 1971, Food for Thought, 1972. Bd. govs. Hugh O'Brian Found., Los Angeles; mem. council Rockefeller U., N.Y.C.; bd. dirs. Assocs. Grad. Sch. Bus. Adminstrn. of Harvard U., Cambridge, Mass.; sr. bd. dirs. The Conf. Bd.; trustee U. Pitts., Com. for Econ. Devel.; mem. Nat. Com. Whitney Mus. Am. Art. Fellow Brit. Inst. Mgmt., Royal Soc. Arts; mem. Inst. Dirs., Inc., Law Soc. Ireland (treas.), Grocery Mfrs. Am. (sec., bd. dirs.), Am. Irish Found., Internat. Life Scis. Inst. Nutrition Found. (chmn., chief exec. officer council), Irish Mgmt. Inst. (council), Exec. Council Fgn. Diplomats (bd. dirs.). Clubs: St. Stephens Green, Kildare St., University (Dublin); Annabels, Les Ambassadeurs (London); Union League (N.Y.C.); Duquesne, Allegheny, Pitts. Golf, Fox Chapel Golf (Pitts.); Rolling Rock (Ligonier) (bd. govs.); Lyford Cay (Bahamas). Office: H J Heinz Co 600 Grant St PO Box 57 Pittsburgh PA 15219 also: Mobil Corp 150 E 42d St New York NY 10017

O'REILLY, JAMES JOSEPH, computer specialist; b. Chgo., June 24, 1937; s. Thomas Patrick and Ruth Anne (Flannery) O'R.; m. Rhonda Jean Garrett, Sept. 23, 1978; children: Kathleen A., James J. BS in English, Loyola U., Chgo., 1963, MBA in Fin., 1972. Account rep. Honeywell Corp., Chgo., 1963-68; computer cons. Peat Marwick & Main, Chgo., 1968-75; head computer services Sargent & Lundy, Chgo., 1975—; v.p. AMIPM Computing, Inc., Roselle, Ill., 1984—. Committeeman Village of Schaumburg, Ill., 1977; pres. Apple Canyon Lake (Ill.) Homeowners Assn., 1983, bd. dirs., 1981-82; mem. Rep. Senatorial Inner Circle, Washington, 1988. Mem. Assn. Computing Machinery, University Club. Roman Catholic. Office: Sargent & Lundy 55 E Monroe St Chicago IL 60603

O'REILLY, JAMES THOMAS, lawyer, educator, author; b. N.Y.C., Nov. 15, 1947; s. Matthew Richard and Regina (Casey) O'R.; m. Rosann Tagliaferro, Aug. 26, 1972; children: Jean, Ann. BA cum laude, Boston Coll., 1969; JD, U. Va., 1974. Bar: Va. 1974, Ohio, 1974, U.S. Supreme Ct. 1979, U.S. Ct. Appeals (6th cir.) 1980. Atty. Procter & Gamble Co., Cin., 1974-76, counsel, 1976-79, sr. counsel for food, drug and product safety, 1979-85, corp. counsel, 1985—; adj. prof. in adminstrv. law U. Cin., 1980—; cons. Adminstrv. Conf. U.S., 1981-82; arbitrator State Employee Relations Bd.; mem. Ohio Bishops Adv. Council, Mayor's Infrastructure Commn. Author: Federal Information Disclosure, 1977, Food and Drug Administration Regulatory Manual, 1979, Unions' Rights to Company Information, 1980, Federal Regulation of the Chemical Industry, 1980, Administrative Rulemaking, 1983, Ohio Public Employee Collective Bargaining, 1984, Protecting Workplace Secrets, 1985, Emergency Response to Chemical Accidents, 1986, Product Defects and Hazards, 1987, Toxic Torts Strategy Deskbook, 1989; Protecting Trade Secrets Under SARA, 1988, Complying With Canada's New Labeling Law, 1989, Canada's New Labeling Requirements, 1989; contbr. articles to profl. jours.; editorial bd. Food and Drug Cosmetic Law Jour. Mem. Hamilton County Dem. Central Com. Served with U.S. Army, 1970-72. Mem. Food and Drug Law Inst., ABA (chmn. com. on food, drug and cosmetic law, com. on consumer product regulation), Fed. Bar Assn., Leadership Cin. Democrat. Roman Catholic. Office: Procter & Gamble Co PO Box 599 Cincinnati OH 45201

OREM, CHARLES ANNISTONE, retired military officer, nuclear engineer, marine and hydraulic products company executive; b. Bryn Mawr, Pa., Apr. 1, 1929; s. Howard Emery and Elizabeth Clements (Stone) O.; B.S. in Engring., U.S. Naval Acad., 1950; postgrad. George Washington U., 1968-69; M.E.E., U.S. Navy Postgrad. Sch., 1960; m. Gerry Morgan Wellborn, June 15, 1951; children—Nancy Elizabeth, Catherine Stone, Sarah Annistone. Commd. ensign U.S. Navy, 1950, advanced through grades to comdr.; commd. U.S.S. Seawolf, 1957; navigator U.S.S. Abraham Lincoln; exec. officer U.S.S. Thomas Jefferson; comdr. U.S.S. Simon Bolivar, 1965-68; submarine specialist Office of Chief of Naval Ops., 1968-70; ret., 1970; various mgmt. positions Babcock & Wilcox Co., Barberton, Ohio, 1970-77, dir. corp. planning and devel., N.Y.C., 1977-79; exec. v.p. Bird-Johnson Co., Walpole, Mass., 1979-80, pres., chief exec. officer, 1980—; lectr. mgmt. prins. Am. Mgmt. Assn. Bd. dirs. New Eng. Coun., Bay Bank. Recipient 6 Polaris Patrol award U.S. Navy, 1968; recipient Meritorious Service medal USN, 1970. Mem. IEEE, Soc. Naval Architects and Marine Engrs., Am. Soc. Naval Engrs., AIAA, Machinery and Allied Products Inst. (mktg. coun. 1979—), Am. Assn. Indsl. Mgmt. (bd. dirs.), Shipbuilders Coun. Am., Navy League, Ret. Officers Assn., Sigma Xi (assoc.). Republican. Clubs: Wellesley Country, Metropolitan (D.C.), Army-Navy Country. Home: 25 Saddlebrook Rd Sherborn MA 01770 Office: Bird-Johnson Co 110 Norfolk St Walpole MA 02081

OREM, SANDRA ELIZABETH, health systems administrator; b. Balt., Sept. 26, 1940; d. Ira Julius and Mabel Ruth (Peeples) O. Diploma, Ch. Home and Hosp. Sch. Nursing, 1962; BS with honors, The Johns Hopkins

U., 1968; MS, U. Md., 1972. Staff, charge nurse Ch. Home and Hosp., Balt., 1962-63; asst. instr. Ch. Home and Hosp. Sch. Nursing, Balt., 1963-64, instr., 1964-70; clin. nurse specialist Johns Hopkins Hosp., Balt., 1972-77, asst. dir. nursing, 1977-79, dir. nursing, 1979-87; clin. assoc. faculty The Johns Hopkins U. Sch. of Nursing, 1984-87; program dir., instr. intermediate massage course Balt. Holistic Health Cr., 1987—; pres. Nursing Edn. and Cons. Service, Inc., Balt., 1976-78, Oasis Health Systems, Inc., Balt., 1987—. Contbr. articles to profl. publs. Vol. Office on Aging, Balt., 1982-83, Boy Scouts Am., Balt., 1984-85. Mem. Am. Holistic Nurses Assn., Ch. Home and Hosp. Sch. Nursing Alumni Assn. (treas. 1970-72, pres.-elect 1975-76), Nat. Assn. Female Execs., NOW, Balt.-Am. Massage Therapy Assn., Md. Assn. Massage Practitioners, Johns Hopkins U. Alumnae Assn., Sigma Theta Tau. Democrat. Episcopalian.

ORENT, GERARD M., information company executive; b. Bklyn., Jan. 28, 1931; s. Nathan and Sylvia Lenore (Hackett) O.; m. Sally Elaine Cardon, Sept. 6, 1953; children: Andrew Mark, Eric Scott. B.B.A., Hofstra U., 1954. Systems analyst Met. Life Ins. Co., N.Y.C., 1956-60; sr. systems analyst McGraw-Hill Book Co., N.Y.C., 1960-65; project dir. editorial devel. McGraw-Hill Book Co., 1965-66, mgr. inventory control, 1966-67, gen. mgr. inventory control, 1967-68, dir. inventory mgmt., 1968-71, v.p. mfg. and inventory mgmt., 1971-80; v.p. resource mgmt. McGraw-Hill, Inc., N.Y.C., 1980-81; sr. v.p. operating services McGraw-Hill, Inc., 1981—. Bd. dirs. Babylon (N.Y.) Public Library, 1978-80. Served to 1st lt. U.S. Army, 1954-56. Office: McGraw-Hill Inc 1221 Ave of the Americas New York NY 10020

ORKAND, DONALD SAUL, management consultant; b. N.Y.C., Mar. 2, 1936; s. Harold and Sylvia (Wagner) O.; B.S. summa cum laude, N.Y.U., 1956, M.B.A., 1957, Ph.D., 1963; children—Dara Sue, Katarina Day. Statistician, Western Electric Co., N.Y.C., 1956-58; group v.p. Ops. Research, Inc., Silver Spring, Md., 1960-69; pres. Ops. Research Industries, Ltd., Ottawa, Ont., Can., 1968-69; pres., chief exec. officer The Orkand Corp., Silver Spring, 1970—. Served with Ordnance Corps, U.S. Army, 1958-60. Mem. Am. Econs. Assn., Am. Statis. Assn., Ops. Research Soc. Am. Contbr. articles to profl. jours. Home: 5225 Pooks Hill Rd 204-N Bethesda MD 20814 Office: 8484 Georgia Ave Silver Spring MD 20910

ORLOFF, ROGER BARTON, investment banker; b. Bklyn., Jan. 17, 1940; s. Edward Malcolm and Sally (Robin) O.; m. Barbara Feinberg, June 10, 1962 (div. 1980); children: Eric Michael, Meredith Susan; m. Barbara Jane Ditchik, Aug. 30, 1980. B. Mgmt. Engring., Rensselaer Poly. Inst., 1960; MBA with distinction, Harvard U., 1963. Mgr. mktg. planning and research Diamond Alkali Co., Cleve., 1963-67; dir. corp. planning Amerace Corp., N.Y.C., 1967-69; dir. corp. devel. Indian Head Inc., N.Y.C., 1969-71; asst. to chmn. Eltra Corp., N.Y.C., 1971-73; v.p. adminstrn. Reed Paper Ltd., Toronto, Can., 1973-77; v.p. Wood Gundy Ltd., Toronto, Can., 1977-81; v.p. merger and acquisition services div. Mellon Bank Corp. Fin. Group, Phila., 1981—. Mem. Planning Forum (pres. 1972-73), Assn. Corp. Growth (v.p. 1984-87), Delaware Valley Venture Group, Bankers Assn. Corp. Finance, Rensselaer Alumni Assn. (v.p. 1988—, Dir.'s award 1985), Harvard Bus. Sch. club Phila. (chmn. 1986-87), Rensselaer Club Delaware Valley (pres. 1983-87). Clubs: Racquet (Phila.); Racquet (Mt. Laurel, N.J.). Home: 2 Independence Pl Philadelphia PA 19106 Office: Mellon Bank 3 Mellon Bank Ctr Philadelphia PA 19102

ORME, DENIS ARTHUR, management consultant; b. Auckland, New Zealand, Jan. 24, 1946; came to U.S., 1981; BA in Mgmt. and Econs., Victoria U., 1975; BA in Organizational Devel., Massey U., 1976. Insp. mgmt. svcs. New Zealand Police Dept., Wellington, 1963-77; bus. mgr. Russell McVeagh et al, Auckland, 1977-79; chief exec. officer, receiver Comml. Svcs., Inc., Auckland, 1979-81; mgr., cons. Price Waterhouse, Houston, 1981-82; pres., mgmt. cons. Orme Assocs. Inc. and Med. Bus. Systems, Inc., Houston, 1982—. Contbr. articles to profl. jours. Mem. tech. adv. com. Tex. Healthcare Found., 1987-88. Mem. Am. Abritation Assn., Health Svcs. Mktg. Soc. (bd. dirs., treas. 1986), ABA (strategic planning for mktg. com. 1987, 88) Houston C. of C. (chmn. bus. group 1985-86), Tex. Bar Assn. (peer com.), Kiwanis (chmn. internat. com. 1986-87, vice chmn. internat. com. 1987-88). Anglican. Home: 10311 Covey Ct Houston TX 77099 Office: Orme Assocs Inc 1200 Smith St Citicorp Ctr Houston TX 77002

ORONA, ERNEST JOSEPH, real estate and construction company executive; b. Belen, N.Mex., Oct. 5, 1942; s. Joseph B. and Melinda (Sanchez) O.; B.A. in Latin Am. Affairs and Spanish, U. N.Mex., 1968; m. Margaret M. Guinan, Aug. 22, 1964; children—Mary Melinda, Marie-Jeanne. Vol. community devel. Peace Corps, Colombia, S. Am., 1962-64; instr. Peace Corps tng. U. Mo., Kansas City, summer 1964, Baylor U., Waco, Tex., summer 1965, also U. Ariz., N.Mex. State U., Las Cruces, 1966, U. N.Mex., Albuquerque, 1966; exec. dir. Mid-Rio Grande Community Action Project, Los Lunas, N.Mex., 1965-66; community devel. cons. Center for Community Action Services, Albuquerque, 1967-68; project dir. Peace Corps Tng. Center, San Diego State U., Escondido, Calif., 1968-70; propr., developer GO Realty and Constrn. Co., Albuquerque, 1970—; pres. La Zarzuela de Alburquerque; pres. Benchmark Real Estate InvestmentInc. Mem. Albuquerque Sister Cities. Mem. Nat. Bd. Realtors, Albuquerque Bd. Realtors, Albuquerque C. of C., Albuquerque Com. on Fgn. Relations. Roman Catholic. Home: 908 Sierra Dr SE Albuquerque NM 87108 Office: GO Realty & Constrn Co 10601 Lomas NE Ste 112 Albuquerque NM 87112

OROPEZA, MARK, airport director; b. Tallahassee, Fla., Dec. 29, 1955; s. Oscar and Dorothy Ann (Miller) O.; m. Terry Lee Bradford, Feb. 14, 1981; children: Christopher, Andrew. AS in Aviation Adminstrn., Miami (Fla.) Dade Community Coll., 1975; B of Aviation Mgmt., Auburn U., 1978. Cert. flight instr. Flight instr. Flightsafety Internat., Vero Beach, Fla., 1978; asst. dir. Dekalb Peachtree Airport, Atlanta, 1979-86; dir. Columbus (Ga.) Metro Airport, 1986—; instr. aviation Dekalb Community Coll., Atlanta, 1984. Active Leadership Columbus, 1988-89. Mem. Southeastern Airport Mgrs. Assn. (program com. 1985-88), Am. Assn. Airport Execs., Kiwanis. Methodist. Office: Columbus Metro Airport 1000 Airport Thruway Columbus GA 31909

O'ROURKE, DENNIS, lawyer; b. Whiteclay, Nebr., Oct. 31, 1914; s. Frank L. and Jerene (Rebbeck) O'R.; m. Ruth Rouss, Jan. 21, 1940; children: Susan, Kathleen, Brian, Dennis, Ruth, Dolores. A.B. cum laude, Nebr. Tchrs. Coll., 1935; J.D. with distinction, George Washington U., 1939. Bar: D.C. 1939, U.S. Supreme Ct 1945, Colo. 1946. Typist, auditor GAO, Washington, 1935-39; lawyer solicitor's office U.S. Dept. Agr., Washington, 1939-45; chief basic commodity div. U.S. Dept. Agr., 1945; gen. counsel Group Health Assn., Washington, 1943, Holly Sugar Corp., Colorado Springs, Colo., 1945; v.p. Holly Sugar Corp., Colorado Springs, 1953-63, pres., 1963-67, chmn. bd., 1967-69, dir., 1983-88; vice chmn. bd., mem. exec. com. Holly Sugar Co. (merged with Imperial Sugar Co.), Colorado Springs, 1986-88; v.p., gen. counsel Holly Oil Co., 1955-63; sr. ptnr. Rouss & O'Rourke, Colorado Springs and Washington; U.S. counsel Union Nacional de Productores de Azucar, Mexico, 1970-82; pres. Man Exec., Inc., Colorado Springs and Washington; dir. 1st Nat. Bank Colorado Springs, 1963-84, chmn. examining com., 1983-84. Contbr. articles financial and bus. jours. Bd. dirs. Colo. Pub. Expenditure Coun., vice chmn., exec. com., 1986-76; dir. Nat. C. of C. of the U.S., 1968-70; trustee, pres. Colorado Springs Fine Arts Center, 1961-62, 68-71, 73, chmn. adv. coun., 1981-84, hon. trustee, 1988; founder, 1st chmn. Colo. Com. (now Coun.) on Arts and Humanities, 1963; Mem. Bus. and Industry Adv. Com. OECD, Paris, France, 1969-71; adviser U.S. dels. Internat. Sugar Confs., Geneva, 1965, Mexico City, 1959; chmn. Colorado Springs-El Paso County Citizens' Task Force on Local Govt. Reorgn., 1976-77. Mem. Newcomen Soc., Am. Soc. Sugar Beet Technologists, Internat. Soc. Sugar Cane Technologists, ABA, Fed. Bar Assn., Colo. Bar Assn., El Paso County Bar Assn, Order of Coif, Cheyenne Mountain Country Club, El Paso Club, Garden of Gods Club, Sugar Club, Met. Club, Rotary, Phi Delta Phi. Home: 8 Heather Dr Broadmoor Colorado Springs CO 80906 Office: PO Box 572 Colorado Springs CO 80901 also: 1614 20th St NW Washington DC 20009

O'ROURKE, INNIS, JR., concrete company executive, consultant; b. Kings Point, N.Y., Sept. 22, 1921; s. Innis O'Rourke and Augusta (Linherr) Travers; m. Louise Olympe Fraser, Mar. 4, 1950; children: Innis III, Colleen. BA, Yale u., 1942. Jr. exec. Transit Mix Concrete Corp., N.Y.C., 1946-50; pres. PreCast Inc., N.Y.C., 1950-78, Concrete Conduit Corp., N.Y.C., 1950-78; chmn. bd. Prefabricated Concrete Inc., N.Y.C., 1969-77; dir. JWP Inc., Purchase, N.Y., 1985—; adv. bd. MHT Co., N.Y.C., 1962-87; arbitrator N.Y. Stock Exchange, 1965—; trustee Green point Savs. Bank, 1966—. Trustee Upper Brookville Village, N.Y., 1968—. Served to lt. USN, 1942-46, PTO. Clubs: Creek (sec. 1977) (Locust Valley, N.Y.), (bd. govs. 1957—), Yale (N.Y.C.). Office: PO Box 539 Locust Valley NY 11771

O'ROURKE, PATRICK GORMAN, controller; b. Houston, June 4, 1949; s. Daniel Alfred and Christine (Doyal) O'R. BBA, Stephen F. Austin U., 1972; MBA, U. Houston, 1981. CPA, Tex. Internal audit supr. Stewart & Stevenson Svcs., Inc., Houston, 1973-74; tax mgr. Stewart & Stevenson Svcs., Inc., 1974-76, corp. acctg. mgr., 1976-79, contr. engine ops., 1979-82, corp. contr., 1983—. Mem. Nat. Assn. Accts., Tex. State Soc. CPA's, Houston Soc. CPA's, Am. Inst. CPA's, Am. Prodn. and Inventory Control Soc., Inst. Cert. Mgmt. Accts. Roman Catholic. Home: 5616 Flack St Houston TX 77081 Office: Stewart & Stevenson Svcs Inc 2707 N Loop W Ste 800 Houston TX 77251

ORR, THERESA J. CASTELLANA, university official; b. Waltham, Mass., Dec. 5, 1941; d. Angelo and Josephine (Vaccarello) C.; divorced; children: Lisa M., Allison J. BA, Brandeis U., 1963; MEd, Northeastern U., 1976. Tchr. Waltham Pub. Schs., 1963-71; asst. dir. fin. aid Brandeis U., Watham, 1971-77; dir. fin. aid Sch. Medicine Tufts U. Sch. Medicine, Boston, 1977-80, Harvard U., Boston, 1980—; chmn. Loan Counseling Task Force Mass., 1983-88; rec. sec. 13 Med. Sch. Consortium, 1984-87; mem. faculty Nat. Assn. Coll. and Univ. Bus. Officers, 1986—; cons. U. Iowa Med. Sch., 1987; lectr., conf. presenter. Contbr. articles to profl. pubis. Chmn. parent's council Merrimack Coll., North Andover, Mass., 1985-88; faculty coordinator Harvard U. Program for Persons with Disabilities, 1988—. Recipient spl. ann. award Mass. Higher Edn. Assistance Corp., 1988. Mem. Am. Assn. Med. Colls. (fin. aid com. northeast group student affairs 1982-86), Nat. Assn. Student Fin. Aid Adminstrs., Mass. Assn. Student Fin. Aid ADminstrs., Harvard Fin. Aid Officers Council (chmn. 1984-85), Cath. Alumni Club (Boston). Office: Harvard U Med Sch 25 Shattuck St Boston MA 02115

ORTALDA, ROBERT ANSELM, JR., accountant; b. Ventura, Calif., Jan. 25, 1951; s. Robert Anselm Sr. and Jeanne Marie (Georges) O.; m. Mary Michele La Vaun, Sept. 5, 1981; children: Michelle Tregae, Michael Robert. BSC, U. Santa Clara, 1973. CPA, Calif. Reporter Anchorage Daily Times, 1968-72; cons. pub. rels. Standard Oil Co. Calif., San Francisco, 1972; acct. Hurdman, Cranstoun, Penney & Co., San Francisco, 1973-75, Polly & Scatena, Burlingame, Calif., 1978-81, Schulman/Ortalda Inc., Oakland, Calif., 1981-83; writer San Francisco, 1976; pvt. practice acctg. San Mateo, Calif., 1981, San Francisco, 1983-85, Redwood City, Calif., 1985—. Author: Financial Sanity, 1989. Treas., bd. dirs. Rudolph Schaeffer Sch. Design, San Francisco. Mem. AICPA, Calif. Soc. CPAs, Software Entrepreneurs Forum. Libertarian. Roman Catholic. Home and Office: 1506 Hopkins Ave Redwood City CA 94062

ORTEGA, ILDEFONSO B., accountant; b. Havana, Cuba, Feb. 3, 1935; came to U.S., 1967; s. Ildefonso and Pilar (Santamaria) O.; m. Caridad C. Student, Vilanova U., Havana, 1958-61; BBA, U. Havana, 1963, U. Miami, Fla., 1973. CPA, Fla. Sr. acct. Manuel Zaiac, CPA, Miami, 1972-81; pvt. practice acctg. Miami, 1982—. Mem. Am. Inst. CPA's, Fla. Inst. CPA's (chmn. new mem. com. 1986-87, mem. exec. com., pres. South Dade chpt. 1985-86, past sec., treas., v.p, regional v.p. region VI 1986-87, mem.-at-large of bd. govs. 1987-88), Cuban Am. CPA's Assn. (continuing edn. chmn. 1981-83, v.p. 1982-83, pres. 1983-84), Beta Alpha Psi.

ORTEGA, KATHERINE D., treasurer of U.S.; b. July 16, 1934. B.A., Eastern N.Mex. U., 1957. Tax supr. Peat, Marwick, Mitchell & Co., 1969-72; v.p., cashier Pan Am. Nat. Bank, 1972-75; pres. Santa Ana (Calif.) State Bank, 1975-77, Copyright Royalty Tribunal, 1982-83; Treas. U.S. Washington, 1983—. Office: US Dept Treasury 15th & Pennsylvania Ave NW Washington DC 20220 *

ORTENBERG, ELISABETH CLAIBORNE See CLAIBORNE, LIZ

ÖRTENGREN, JOHN, marketing and financial consultant; b. Stockholm, Sept. 27, 1931; s. Helmer and Amparo Maria Del Carmen (Carreras) Ö; B.B.A., Stockholm Grad. Sch. Advt., 1954; M.B.A., Syracuse U., 1955, Ph.D., 1961; m. Lena Cedrenius, Apr. 13, 1957; children—Henrik, Anders, Torsten. Pub. relations cons. Dr. Axel Wenner-Gren, 1954-55; mktg. dir. Young & Rubicam, Stockholm, 1955-62; pres., prin. owner AB Marknadsforskning, Sollentuna, Sweden, 1962—, Marknadsföring AB John Örtengren, Sollentuna, 1972—; chmn. Sibe Group Cos., 1975—, Sams-företagen AB, 1981—, Tureberg Garden i Sollentuna AB, 1988— ; dir. AB Femco, Dantherm Trading AB, LBC Tureberg AB; head instr. advt. Grad. Sch. Advt., Stockholm, 1956-60. Served to capt. Swedish Antiaircraft Corps, 1964-67. Mem. Assn. Market Researchers in Sweden, European Mktg. Assn., European Soc. for Opinion and Mktg. Research, Swedish Mktg. Research Inst. Assn., Swedish Mktg. Fedn. (auditor, 1984—), Alumni Assn. Grad. Sch. Advt. (chmn. 1962-67), Internat. Advt. Assn. (chmn. Stockholm chpt. 1967-71), Swedish Forum for Market Econs. (chmn. 1981—), Swedish Soc. Hist. Certs. (vice chmn. 1986—). Clubs: Rotary (past pres., Paul Harris fellow, Sollentuna-Tureberg chpt., GSE chmn. dist. 235 coun.). Author: Market and Consumer Legislation in Sweden, 1977, 2d edit., 1980; co-author: Management 83/84. Home: Alvagen 17B, 19143 Sollentuna Sweden Office: PO Box 4, 19121 Sollentuna Sweden

ORTINO, LEONARD JAMES, manufacturing company executive; b. Seneca Falls, N.Y., May 31, 1919; s. Michael Vito and Florence (Campeggio) O.; m. Evangeline Canellos, Apr. 1, 1945; children: Evangeline Edlund, Stephanie Kittleson. BS MechE, Carnegie-Mellon U., 1945; MBA, U. Mich., 1967. Registered profl. engr., Pa. Design group leader Westinghouse Electric Co., Pitts., 1940-50; engring. mgr. IBM Corp., Poughkeepsie, N.Y., 1950-55; chief mech. engr. Beckman Instruments, Fullerton, Calif., 1955-60; chief. mech. engr. Magnavox, Ft. Wayne, Ind., 1960-66; pres. Indsl. Mgmt. Council, Morris Plains, N.J., 1966—; pres., chief exec. officer Mich. Dynamics Inc., Garden City, 1973—. Author: Optical Instruments, 1953; also articles. pres. Forest Hills (Pa.) Civic Assn., 1948-49; scoutmaster Boy Scouts Am., Seneca Falls, N.Y., 1937-40, dist. chmn., Fullerton, Calif., 1956-60. Served to 1st lt. U.S. Army, 1944-47. Mem. ASME (dist. chmn. 1952-54), Filtration Soc. (pres. 1984-86), Am. Mfg. Assn., Instrument Soc. Am. (dist. chmn. 1957-59), Mich. Mfg. Assn., Theta Kappa Phi (Disting. Service award 1947), Phi Kappa Phi. Republican. Roman Catholic. Lodges: Rotary, Elks. Home: 9443 Hidden Lake Ct Dexter MI 48130 Office: Mich Dynamics Inc 32400 Ford Rd Garden City MI 48135

ORTIZ, ANTONIO IGNACIO, public relations executive; b. Mexico City, Feb. 22, 1961; s. Antonio and Sylvia (Vega) O.; m. Socorro Chinolla, June 12, 1982. B in Bus., Baja State U., Tijuana, Baja Calif. Norte, 1984. With acctg. dept. Bank of the Atlantic, Tijuana, 1979-83; mgr. Aldaco, Tijuana, 1983-84; dir. pub. relations Oh! Laser Club, Tijuana, 1984-88, Iguanas, Tijuana, 1988—; cons. DDBSA Corp., Chula Vista, Calif., Calif. Alson, Ltd., San Diego, Exim Trading Co., San Diego, Aldaco, Tijuana. Home: PO Box 1859 San Ysidro CA 92073 Office: Exim Trading Corp PO Box 5108 San Ysidro CA 92073

ORTIZ-PATINO, JAIME, business executive; b. Paris, June 20, 1930; s. Jorge and Graziella (Patiño) Ortiz-Linares; m. Uta Krebber, Mar. 28, 1970; children by previous marriage—Carlos and Felipe (twins). Pres., chief exec. officer Patiño Investments Ltd., 1982—; dir. John Labatt Ltd., London, Ont., 1980; consul gen. of Costa Rica in Geneva, 1976—, pres. Valderrama S.A., Spain; Sotoalto S.A., Spain. Trustee Simon I. Patiño Found., Geneva, 1965, Lahey Clinic Found., Burlington, Mass., 1984, Mem. World Bridge Fedn. (pres. emeritus). Home and office: 56 route de Vandoeuvres Ch-1253, Geneva Switzerland

ORTNER, ROBERT, economist; b. N.J., Oct. 19, 1927; s. Josef and Bella O.; m. Evelyn Jacobs, May 21, 1947; children: Peter, Nicole. B.S., U. Pa., 1949; M.S., Columbia U., 1955, Ph.D., 1960. Lectr. U. Pa., 1955-62; economist Carl M. Loeb, Rhoades & Co., N.Y.C., 1962-64; sr. v.p., chief economist Bank of N.Y., 1965-81; chief economist U.S. Dept. of Commerce, Washington, 1981-86, under sec. econ. affairs, 1986—; dir. N.Am. Reins. Corp., N.Y.C., 1973-81; ops. research cons. Air Force. Contbr. articles to profl. jours. Fellow Ford Found., 1956-57. Mem. Am. Econ. Assn., Am. Econometric Soc., Am. Statis. Assn., Nat. Assn. Bus. Economists, Beta Gamma Sigma. Office: Undersec Econ Affairs Commerce Dept Rm 4850 Washington DC 20230

ORVANANOS, ALEJO, manufacturing executive; b. Mexico City, July 21, 1941; s. Alejo and Carmen (Altamirano) O.; m. Angeles Rodriguez, Jan. 11, 1969; children: Alejo, Gerardo, Maria. BSBA, U. Ibero Americana, 1965; MBA, Fla. Atlantic U., 1979; MA in Communication Rsch., Stanford U., 1982. Mgr. advt. Kodak Mexicana, Mexico City, 1965-70, v.p. mktg., 1987—; v.p. corp. communications Grupo Hylsa, Mexico City, 1970-78, Grupo Alfa, Monterrey, Mex., 1978-82; chmn. Antar Publicidad, Mexico City, 1983—. Mem. Mut. Advt. Agy. Network, Mexican Assn. Pub. Rels. Profls. (v.p. 1974), University Club (Mexico City, treas. 1977-78). Home: Fuego 861, 01900 Mexico City Mexico

ORWOLL, GREGG S. K., lawyer; b. Austin, Minn., Mar. 23, 1926; s. Gilbert M. and Kleonora (Kleven) O.; m. Laverne M. Flentie, Sept. 15, 1951; children—Kimball G., Kent A., Vikki A., Tristen A., Erik G. B.S., Northwestern U., 1950; J.D., U. Minn., 1953. Bar: Minn. 1953, U.S. Supreme Ct. 1973. Assoc. Dorsey, Owen, Marquart, Windhorst and West, Mpls., 1953-59; ptnr. Dorsey, Owen, Marquart, Windhorst and West, 1959-60; assoc. counsel Mayo Clinic, Rochester, Minn., 1960-63; gen. counsel Mayo Clinic, 1963-87, sr. legal counsel, 1987—; gen. counsel, dir. Rochester Airport Co., 1962-84, sec., 1962-81, v.p., 1981-84; gen. counsel Mayo Med. Svcs., Ltd., 1972—; bd. dirs. Edn. and Rsch., 1984—; gen. counsel Mid-Am. Orthopedic Soc., 1982—, Minn. Orthopedic Soc., 1985—; asst. sec. Mayo Found., Rochester, 1972-76, 82-86 , sec., 1976-82, 86—; bd. dirs. Charter House, 1986—; dir. Travelure Motel Corp., 1968-86, sec., 1972-83, 86, v.p., 1983-86; adj. prof. William Mitchell Coll. Law, St. Paul, 1978-84. Contbr. articles and chpts. to legal and medico-legal publs.; bd. editors HealthSpan, 1984—; editorial bd. Minn. Law Rev., 1952-53. Trustee Minn. Council on Founds., 1977-82, Mayo Found., 1982-86, William Mitchell Coll. Law, 1982-88, pres. 1989—; pres. Rochester Council Chs., 1968-69; mem. bd. advisers Rochester YWCA, 1966-72; bd. dirs. Rochester Med. Ctr. Ministry, Inc., 1975-81; bd. dirs. Zumbro Luth. Ch., 1962-64, 77-79, pres., 1964-65; bd. dirs. Rochester YMCA, 1966-70; trustee Courage Found., 1974-80, YMCA-YWCA Bldg. Corp., 1966-73 ; bd. visitors U. Minn. Law Sch., 1974-76, 1985—; mem. U. Minn. Regents Selection Adv. Council, 1988—. Served with USAAF, 1944-45. Mem. Am. Acad. Hosp. Attys., Minn. Soc. Hosp. Attys. (dir. 1981-86), Minn. State Bar Assn. (chmn. legal med. com. 1977-81), ABA, Olmsted County Bar Assn. (v.p. 1977-78, pres. 1978-79), Rochester C. of C., AMA (affiliate), U. Minn. Law Alumni Assn. (bd. dirs. 1973-76, 85—), Phi Delta Theta, Phi Delta Phi. Republican. Club: Rochester University (pres. 1977). Home: 2233 5th Ave NE Rochester MN 55904 Office: Mayo Clinic 200 1st St SW Rochester MN 55905

OSBORN, GUY A., food products company executive; b. 1936. BSBA, Northwestern U., 1958. Group mktg. mgr. Pillsbury Co., Mpls., 1958-65; with Universal Foods Corp., Milw., 1971—, dir. mktg., 1971-73, v.p. spl. products, 1973-78, group v.p., 1978-82, exec. v.p., 1982-84, pres., 1984—, chief operating officer, 1984-88, chief exec. officer, 1988—. Office: Universal Foods Corp 433 E Michigan Ave Milwaukee WI 53202 *

OSBORN, JANET LYNN, information systems executive; b. Berea, Ohio, Dec. 25, 1952; d. Walter Martin and Mary Alice O. BS in Systems Analysis, Miami U., Ohio, 1975; MBA, U. Mich., 1984; postgrad., Universidad de las Americas, Puebla, Mex., 1974. Cons. mgmt. info. systems Arthur Andersen and Co., Cinn., 1975-77; systems analyst Consumers Power Co., Jackson, Mich., 1977-79; sr. systems analyst Consumers Power Co., Jackson, 1979-81; supr. analyst Consumer Power Co., Jackson, 1982, mgr. corp. systems, 1983-85, mgr. litigation systems, 1985-87, mgr. quality assurance and data adminstrn., 1988-89, mgr. info. and tech. planning and quality assurance, 1989—. Solicitor United Way, Jackson, 1983-84. Mem. Women's Info. Network, NAFE, Pi Mu Epsilon, Phi Kappa Phi, Delta Delta Delta. Office: Consumers Power Co 1945 W Parnall Rd Jackson MI 49201

OSBORNE, GAYLA MARLENE, sales executive; b. Owenton, Ky., Aug. 9, 1956; d. Frederick Clay and Helen Beatrice (Mason) O. AAS, No. Ky. U., 1982, BS, 1986; cert. in Chinese Mandarin, Def. Lang. Inst., 1975. Personnel clk. Dept. Edn. State Ky., Frankfort, 1974; sec. Dept. Health, Edn., Welfare Nat. Inst. Occupational Safety Health, Cin., 1977-79; specialist sales promotion U.S. Postal Svc., Cin., 1980, coord. customer liaison, task force pub. image, account rep., 1986-87; reservation sale agt. Delta Airlines, 1987—. Councilmember Florence City Coun., Ky. 1984-87; vol. Children's Home, Covington, 1982, 87. With USAF, 1974-76. Named to Hon. Order Ky. Cols. Mem. Disabled Am. Veterans, No. Ky. U. Alumni Assn., Nat. Assn. Postmasters U.S., Boone County Fraternal Order Police, Ky. Assn. Realtors, Nat. Bd. Realtors. Democrat. Baptist. Club: Fraternal Order Police. Home: 8395 Juniper Ln Florence KY 41042

OSBORNE, RICHARD COGSWELL, manufacturing company executive; b. Buffalo, Feb. 13, 1944; s. Henry Watson and Anita Marie (Krause) O.; m. Katherine Sue Lang; children: Sean, Todd, Amy. AS, Erie Community Coll., Buffalo, 1964; BS, U. Buffalo, 1969; MA, Sangamon State U., 1973. Engr. Chevrolet div. Gen. Motors, Tonawanda, N.Y., 1963-67; dir. mfg. Pillsbury Co., Mpls., 1967-79; exec. v.p. Household Mfg. Inc., Prospect Heights, Ill., 1979—. Office: Household Mfg Inc 2700 Sanders Rd Prospect Heights IL 60070

OSBORNE, RICHARD DE JONGH, refining company executive; b. Bronxville, N.Y., Mar. 19, 1934; s. Stanley de Jongh and M. Elizabeth (Ide) O.; m. Cheryl Anne Archibald, Dec. 14, 1957; children: Leslie Anne, Lindsay Ide, Nicholas de J., Stanley de J. A.B. in Econs., Princeton U., 1956. With Cuno Engring. Corp., Meriden, Conn., 1956-60; fin., planning and mktg. exec. IBM Corp., Armonk, N.Y., 1960-69; investment adviser Sherman M. Fairchild, N.Y.C., 1969-70; exec. v.p. fin. and bus. devel., dir. Fairchild Camera & Instrument Corp., Mountain View, Calif., 1970-74; v.p. fin. ASARCO Inc. (formerly Am. Smelting & Refining Co.), N.Y.C., 1975-77, exec. v.p., 1977-81, pres., 1981-85, chmn., pres., chief exec. officer, 1985—, also bd. dirs.; bd. dirs. Schering-Plough Corp., Mex. Desarrollo Indsl. Minero (S.A.), E.T. & H.K. Ide, Inc., So. Peru Copper Corp., Copper Devel. Assn. Trustee Com. Econ. Devel. Mem. AIME, NAM (dir.), Council Fgn. Relations, Council Ams. (dir.), Internat. Copper Assn. (chmn.), Am. Australian Assn. (v.p., dir.). Clubs: Down Town Assn., Economic, River, Brook, City Midday; Bedens Brook; Sakonnet Golf. Home: 167 Edgerstoune Rd Princeton NJ 08540 Office: Asarco Inc 180 Maiden Ln New York NY 10038

OSBORNE, RICHARD JAY, electric utility company executive; b. N.Y.C., Feb. 16, 1951; s. Victor and Evelyn Celia (Sweetbaum) O. B.A., Tufts U., 1973; M.B.A., U. N.C., 1975. Fin. analyst Duke Power Co., Charlotte, N.C., 1975-78, sr. fin. analyst, 1978-80, mgr. fin. rels., 1980-81, mgr. treasury activities, 1981, treas., 1981-88, v.p. fin., 1988—; bd. dirs. NCM Capital Mgmt. Group Inc. Exec. com. Mecklenburg County Council Boy Scouts Am., 1987; bd. dirs. Planned Parenthood of Greater Charlotte; pres. Historic Elizabeth Neighborhood Found. Mem. Fin. Execs. Inst., Southeastern Electric Exchange (fin. sect.). Democrat. Jewish. Lodge: Rotary. Office: Duke Power Co 422 S Church St Charlotte NC 28242

OSBORNE, RICHARD L., utilities executive; b. New Castle, Ind., Nov. 5, 1942; s. Paul and June (Lawless) O.; m. Deborah Dunn, Oct. 10, 1979 (div. Mar., 1984); 1 child, John Paul. BA, Ind. U., 1965, MBA, 1967. Sales rep. Xerox Corp., Indpls., 1967-69; adminstrv. mgr. Borg-Warner Corp., Chgo., 1969-72, mgr. trucking svc., 1972-74, mgr. strategic planning, 1974-77; dir. corp. planning and develop. Krause Milling, Milw., 1977-81, v.p., cons., 1981-82; v.p. Wis. Gas Co., Milw., 1982-85, v.p. mktg. svcs., pub. affairs, 198588, v.p. mkt. svcs., gas supply, 1988—; advisor dept. bus. econs. Cardinal Stritch Coll., 1983-84; mem. exec. bd. dirs. Wis. Pub. Utility Inst., Forward Wis. Mem. exec. bd. dirs. Big Bros./Big Sisters, 1987—. With U.S. Army 1967-69, Vietnam. Home: 12543 N Woodberry Dr Mequon WI 53092 Office: WI Gas Co 626 E Wisconsin Ave Milwaukee WI 53202

OSBORNE, RONALD DRAKE, health services management executive; b. Wheeling, W.Va., Mar. 20, 1941; s. William Thornton and Earnestine V. (Drake) O.; m. Linda Kay Bach, Jan. 4, 1964; children: Keri Lin, Keith Evan. BA, Ohio State U., 1963. Personnel devel. asst. Gen. Tel. Calif., Santa Monica, 1970-72, manpower planning adminstr., 1972-73; mgr. personnel devel. Blue Cross of So. Calif., Hollywood, 1973-75; coord. nat. health ins., v.p. corp. planning Blue Cross Assn., Chgo., 1975-81; v.p. cost containment Blue Cross-Blue Shield Ill., Chgo., 1982-84; v.p. contracting St. Joseph Health System, Orange, Calif., 1984-87; pres. Medworth Futures Inc., Brea, Calif., 1987; chief operating officer Beech St. Inc., Irvine, Calif., 1987-89; chief exec. officer Nat. Specialty Networks, Inc., 1989—. Bd. dirs. Pilgrimage Family Therapy Ctr., Orange, 1986—, Opportunity Internat., Inc., Oakbrook Ill., 1989; elder United Presbyn. Ch. Lt. Comdr. USN, 1964-70. Home: 106 S Flower Hill Brea CA 92621 Office: Beech Street Inc #3 Ada Irvine CA 92718

OSBORNE, RONALD ROSS, university administrator; b. South Kingstown, R.I., Sept. 12, 1945; s. Carleton Walter and Elizabeth Evelyn (Ross) O.; m. Sharon Marie Underwood, Aug. 1, 1970; children: Heather, Amy. BS, U. R.I., 1970. CPA, R.I. Auditor Arthur Young & Co., Providence, 1970-72; chief div. auditor ITT Royal Electric, Pawtucket, R.I., 1972-74; asst. controller Univ. R.I., Kingston, 1974-76, controller, treas., 1976—; bd. dirs. U. R.I. Research Corp., Kingston; supervisory com. Pettaquamscutt Credit Union, Kingstown, 1972-76. Treas. South Kingstown PTA, 1975-76. Mem. Am. Inst. CPA's, R.I. Inst. CPA's, Nat. Assn. Coll. and Univ. Bus. Officers, Eastern Assn. Coll. and Univ. Bus. Officers, Nat. Acctg. Assn., Nat. Controllers Council, Acctg. Research Assn., South Kingstown Jaycees. Home: Enterprise Terr Kingston RI 02881 Office: U RI 110 Administration Bldg Kingston RI 02881

OSBORNE, THERESA JO, investment administrator; b. Seattle, Aug. 22, 1945; d. Stanley and Jean (Strazdas) Pospichal; m. Herbert L. Osborne Jr., June 3, 1967 (div. Feb. 1987); children: Amanda Jennifer, Maxwell Joseph. BFA in Art Printmaking, U. Nebr., Omaha, 1967; MFA in Arts Mgmt., Bklyn. Coll., 1982. Supr. art Burlington (N.J.) Twp., 1967-68, Harpswell Schs., Topsham, Maine, 1968-70; dir. spl. projects Borough of Queens City of N.Y.C., 1979-81, project coordinator Bklyn. Bridge Centennial, 1981-82, dir. cultural affairs Borough of Queens, 1982-85; community coordinator Bklyn. Acad. Music, 1980; exec. mgr., corp. sec. Live Oak Realty Corp., N.Y.C., 1985—. Trustee Old Stone House Gowanus, Bklyn., 1978, Flushing Meadows-Corona Park Corp., Queens, 1987—. Mem. N.Y.C. Jr. League (bd. mgrs. 1984-85), N.Y. Drama League, Chi Omega. Democrat. Roman Catholic. Club: Women's City (N.Y.C.). Home: 19 Ingram St Forest Hills Gardens NY 11375 Office: Live Oak Realty Corp 40 E 75th St Ste 1-A New York NY 10021

OSBORNE, THOMAS CRAMER, metals company executive; b. Winnipeg, Man., Can., Mar. 21, 1927; s. Claude H. and Marguerite S. (Cramer) O.; m. Geraldine Smith, May 9, 1950; children—James, Michael. B.S. with honors, U. Man., 1948, M.S., 1949; postgrad., U. Ariz., 1949-50. Geologist Internat. Nickel Co., Copper Cliff, Can., 1949-52, 60-62; geologist Asarco Mexican Mining Dept., Taxco, Parral, Santa Barbara, 1952-56, 60-62; geologist, asst. dir. exploration, dir., v.p. exploration Asarco Inc., Tucson, Can., N.Y.C., 1964-80; exec. v.p. Asarco Inc., 1980—, dir. various Asarco subsidiaries; pres. Federated Metals Corp.; chmn. Capco Pipe Co. Mem. Can. Inst. Mining and Metallurgy, AIME. Home: 1150 Cushing Rd Plainfield NJ 07062 Office: Asarco Inc 180 Maiden Ln New York NY 10038

OSER, ROMAN BERNARD, manufacturing company executive; b. Huntingburg, Ind., June 16, 1930; s. Roman N. and Alene J. (Sumner) O.; m. Barbara Brown, May 28, 1960; children: Debra, Nancy, Mary. Student, Ind. U., 1954, Lockyears Coll., 1956. Credit mgr. Austin Powder Co., 1956-59; comptroller Kimball Internat. Inc., Jasper, Ind., 1959-64, exec. v.p. raw materials div., 1965—. Served with U.S. Army, 1952-53. Mem. Forest Products Research Soc., Am. Mgmt. Assns., Am. Forestry Assn., Nat. Hardwood Lumber Assn., Am. Legion, Jasper C. of C. Roman Catholic. Home: Rte 4 PO Box 56 Jasper IN 47546 Office: Kimball Internat Inc 1600 Royal St Jasper IN 47546

OSGOOD, LAWRENCE WALTER, managed accounts program executive, financial planner; b. Buffalo, Mar. 29, 1946; s. C.W. Osgood and Elizabeth Ann (Cudmore) Wallace; m. Kathleen Howard, Aug. 1968 (div. June 1970); m. Julia Katherine Wright, Aug. 23, 1980. BFA, U. Okla., 1973. Mgr. Ridgway Co., Dallas, 1975-77; salesman Barton Co., Grand Prairie, Tex., 1977-80; securities broker Paine Webber, Dallas, 1980-84, Rauscher Pierce Refsnes, Inc., Dallas, 1984—. Mem. Inst. Cert. Fin. Planners (chmn. speakers bur., 1986—), Dallas Audubon Soc., Ducks Unltd., North Tex. Astronomy Club. Home: 742 Finland Grand Prairie TX 75050 Office: Rauscher Pierce Refsnes Inc Plaza Americas 2500 RPR Tower Dallas TX 75201

O'SHEA, JOHN, lawyer, accountant; b. N.Y.C., May 3, 1928; s. William and Margaret (Heffron) O'S.; BS, NYU, 1952; LLM, 1966; JD, St. John's U., 1955; m. Mary Ward, May 25, 1963. Admitted to N.Y. State bar, 1955, U.S. Supreme Ct. bar, 1964; mem. audit staff Haskins & Sells, 1955-58, Lopez, Edwards Co., 1958, S.D. Leidesdorf & Co., 1958; tax specialist J.K. Lasser & Co., 1958-65; tax. supr. Ernst & Ernst, 1965-68, Hurdman & Cranstoun, 1968-72; tax mgr. Louis Sternbach & Co., 1972-74, Sperduto, Priskie Co., 1974, George F. Sheehan & Co., 1947-77, Price, Waterhouse & Co., 1977-80, Kaufman, Nachbar & Co., 1980-83, Faculty Bank, Found. Acctg. Edn.; sole practice tax atty., acct. John O'Shea & Co., 1984—; lectr. in field. Candidate for Democratic nomination U.S. Ho. of Reps. from 3d N.Y. dist., 1982. Served with USMC, 1946-48. CPA, N.Y. State. Mem. New York County Lawyers Assn., Am. Inst. CPAs, N.Y. State Soc. CPAs, Am. Assn. Atty.-CPAs. Roman Catholic. Contbr. articles to profl. jours. Home: 305 Mill Spring Rd Manhasset NY 11030

O'SHIELDS, RICHARD LEE, natural gas company executive; b. Ozark, Ark., Aug. 12, 1926; s. Fay and Anna (Johnson) O'S.; m. Shirley Isabelle Washington, Nov. 8, 1947; children: Sharon Isabelle O'Shields Boles, Carolyn Jean O'Shields, Richard Lee. B.S. in Mech. Engring, U. Okla., 1949; M.S. in Petroleum Engring, La. State U., 1951. Registered profl. engr., Kans., Tex. Instr. petroleum engring. La. State U., 1949-51; prodn. engr. Pure Oil Co., 1951-53; sales engr., chief engr., v.p. Salt Water Control, Inc., Ft. Worth, 1953-59; cons. engr. Ralph H. Cummins Co., Ft. Worth, 1959-60; with Anadarko Prodn. Co. and parent co. Panhandle Eastern Pipe Line Co., 1960—; pres. Anadarko Prodn. Co., 1966-68; exec. v.p. Panhandle Eastern Pipe Line Co., 1968-70, pres., chief exec. officer, 1970-79, chmn., chief exec. officer, 1979-83, chmn., 1983-88; pres., chief exec. officer Trunkline Gas Co., 1970-79, chmn., chief exec. officer, 1979-83, chmn., 1983-88 ; dir. Daniel Industries. Bd. dirs. Tex. Research League. Served with USAAF, 1945. Mem. Am. Petroleum Inst. (dir.), Soc. Petroleum Engrs., Mid Continent Oil and Gas Assn. (dir.), Ind. Natural Gas Assn. Am. (dir.), Am. Gas Assn. (dir.), Gas Research Inst. (dir.), Ind. Petroleum Assn. Am. (dir.), So. Gas Assn., Tau Beta Pi. Republican. Baptist. Lodge: Masons. Home: 10 S Briar Hollow Ln #95 Houston TX 77027 Office: Panhandle Eastern Pipe Line Co PO Box 1642 Houston TX 77001

OSHMAN, M(ALIN) KENNETH, electrical engineer; b. Kansas City, Mo., July 9, 1940. AB, Rice U., 1962, BSc, 1963; MSc, Stanford U., 1965, PhD, 1967. Mem. tech. staff Sylvania Elec. Products, 1963-69; formerly pres. Rolm Corp., Santa Clara, Calif.; pres., chief exec. officer Echelon, 1988—. Mem. IEEE, Nat. Acad. Engring. Office: Echelon 727 University Ave Los Gatos CA 95030 *

OSIAS, RICHARD ALLEN, international financier and investor, real estate investment executive; b. N.Y.C., Nov. 13, 1938; s. Harry L. and Leah (Schenk) O.; m. Judy D. Bradford, Oct. 26, 1985; children: A. Kimberly, Alexandra Elizabeth. Student, Columbia U., 1951-63. Founder, chmn., chief exec. officer Osias Orgn., Inc., N.Y.C., Ft. Lauderdale, Fla., St. Clair, Mich., San Juan, P.R., 1953—. Prin. works include city devel., residential and apt. units, founder City N. Lauderdale, Fla., complete residential housing communities, shopping centers, country clubs, golf courses, hotel chains, comprehensive housing communities. Mem. North Lauderdale City Council, 1967—, mayor, 1968—, police commr., 1967—; mem. Gold Circle, Atlanta Ballet, Red Gables Soc. of Ensworth Sch., Nashville; benefactor Atlanta Symphony Soc.; patron High Mus. Art, Alliance Theatre Co.; active Boys Clubs Broward County, Tower council Pine Crest Prep. Sch., Ft. Lauderdale; mem. condr.'s circle Nashville Symphony; mem. Ensworth Sch. Red Gables Soc.. Served with USAF, 1953. Recipient Am. House award Am. Home mag., 1962, Westinghouse award, 1968; named Builder of Yr. Sunshine State Info. Bur. and Sunshine State Sr. Citizen, 1967-69; profiles on network TV, internat. and nat. media. Mem. Ft. Lauderdale Better Bus. Bur., Offshore Power Boat Racing Assn., Fraternal Order Police Assn. (pres.), Fla. C. of C., Margate C. of C., Ft. Lauderdale C. of C., Smithsonian Instn., Soc. Founders of U. Miami, Tower Council and Columns Soc. Pinecrest. Clubs: Bankers Top of First (San Juan); Quarter Deck (Galveston, Tex.); Boca Raton Yacht and Country (Fla.); Maunalua Bay (Honolulu); Leonist Country Club; Tryall Golf and Country; Bankers (Miami, Fla.); Top of the Home (Puerto Rico); Service Plus (France); Cannes Yacht; Cariary Islands Yacht. Home: 5353 Hillsboro Rd Nashville TN 37215 also: Kimberly Plantations Sparta GA 31087

OSIGWEH, CHIMEZIE ANTHONY BAYLON-PASCAL, management educator; b. Ejemekwuru, Owerri, Nigeria, Nov. 11, 1955; s. Joseph A.A. and Lucy Mgbokwere (Ogbonna) O.; m. Brenda Jean Jolley, Apr. 21, 1981; children: Amarachi N., Nkechinyere, Ndidi M. BS in Spl. Edn. and Polit. Sci., East Tenn. State U., 1976-78; MA in Internat. Relations, Ohio State U., 1980, M in Labor Relations and Human Resource Mgmt., 1981, PhD in Labor Relations, Human Resource Mgmt. and Internat. Relations, 1982. Asst. dean of studies Presentation Secondary Sch., Ogbaku-Owerri, Nigeria, 1975-76; asst. instr. Ohio State U., Columbus, 1979-80, instr., 1981; research assoc. Mershon Ctr. for Research, Columbus, 1979, 82; asst. prof. NE Mo. State U., Kirksville, 1982-85, mem. grad. council, 1984-85; prof. mgmt. Norfolk (Va.) State U., 1985—, mem. faculty senate, 1986—; chmn. Nat. Conf. on Communicating Employee Responsibilities, Kirksville, 1984-85. Editor in chief: Employee Responsibilities and Rights Jour., 1988—; author: The Divided Organization, 1990, Professional Management, 1985, Communicating Employee Responsibilities and Rights, 1987, Organizational Science Abroad, 1989, Managing Employee Rights and Responsibilities, 1989, Improving Problem-Solving Participation, 1983, (poems) Petals of Fire, 1984. Recipient Outstanding Virginian Faculty award State of Va., 1989. Mem. Acad. Mgmt., Acad. Internat. Bus., Am. Inst. for Decision Scis. (SE region), Internat. Studies Assn., So. Mgmt. Assn., Council on Employee Responsibilities and Rights (pres. 1985—, chmn. ann. programs 1986-87). Home: 4000 Topaz Ln Virginia Beach VA 23456 Office: Norfolk State U Mgmt Dept Norfolk VA 23504

OSLER, GORDON PETER, utility company executive; b. Winnipeg, Man., Can., June 19, 1922; s. Hugh Farquarson and Kathleen (Harty) O.; m. Nancy A. Riley, Aug. 20, 1948; children: Sanford L., Susan Osler Matthews, Gillian Osler Fortier. Student, Queen's U., Kingston, Ont., Can., 1940-41. Pres. Osler, Hammond & Nanton Ltd., Winnipeg, 1952-64, UNAS Investments Ltd., Toronto, Ont., Can., 1964-72; chmn. Slater Steel Industries, Toronto, Ont., Can., 1972-86, N.Am. Life Assurance Co., Hamilton, Ont., 1986—; chmn. TransCan. Pipelines, Toronto, 1983-89, ret., 1989, dir.; bd. dir. Toronto-Dominion Bank, Toronto, Household Internat., Prospect Heights, Ill., Maclean Hunter Ltd., Toronto, IPSCO Inc., Regina, Sask., MICC Investments Ltd., Toronto, Co-Steel Inc., Toronto. Bd. dirs. Can. Hearing Soc., 1983—. Served to lt. Can. Army, 1942-45; ETO. Clubs: Toronto, York (Toronto); Everglades (Palm Beach, Fla.). Home: 112 Dunvegan Rd, Toronto, ON Canada M4V 2R1 Office: TransCan Pipelines, Commerce Ct W, 36th Fl, PO Box 54, Toronto, ON Canada M5L 1C2

OSLICK, MARLENE TANNENBAUM, accountant, educator; b. Phila., Apr. 13, 1939; d. Harry and Clara Sarah (Sperling) Tannenbaum; m. Harold Oslick, June 14, 1959; children: Marci Lynn, Rochelle, Harvey Raymond, Jeffrey Sheldon. Diploma in teaching, Gratz Coll., 1958; BS in Edn., Temple U., 1960; MBA, Fairleigh Dickinson U., 1985. Cert. secondary, math. and physical sci. tchr., N.J. Tchr. B'nai Aaron, Phila., 1958-59, Temple Beth El, West Hartford, Conn., 1960-63, Temple Beth Hillel, Bloomfield, Conn., 1963-68; co-owner, mgr. Park Crescent, Plainfield, N.J., 1977-78; supr. field ops., instr. bur. census U.S. Dept. Commerce, Elizabeth, N.J., 1980; with bus. and fin. communications Regisgard, Ltd. div. W.E. Connor, Seoul, Republic of Korea, 1983-84; controller Leonard Engring., Inc., Cranford, N.J., 1986-87; sr. staff acct. Alan Grassano & Co., CPAs, Fairfield, N.J, 1987-88, Lerman & Co. CPAs, Springfield, N.J., 1988—; sec. Plainfield Bd. Jewish Edn., 1972-74. Author (mag.) Outlook, 1986; editor (mag.) Bus. Korea, 1984. Leader Girl Scouts U.S., Westfield, N.J., 1968-72; den mother Cub Scouts Boy Scouts Am., Westfield, 1973-74, 78. Mem. Nat. Soc. Tax Practitioners, Women's League for Conservative Judaism (nat. social action com.), Seoul Internat. Women's Assn., Nat. Council Jewish Women, Hadassah Club (Westfield)(v.p. fundraising 1978-80), Cedar Mar Yacht, Sigma Pi Sigma. Democrat. Home: 847 Nancy Way Westfield NJ 07090 Office: Lerman & Co 99 Morris Ave Springfield NJ 07081

OSSIP, JEROME J., restaurateur consultant; b. N.Y.C., Mar. 15, 1920; s. Harry A. and Fannie O.; B.S., U. Ill., 1940; M.B.A., N.Y. U., 1949; m. Audrey A. Herman, May 30, 1949; children—Dale Ava, Brad Henry, Michael Ian. Pres. Bards Systems, Inc., N.Y.C., 1950-73; pres. Churchills Enterprises, Inc., N.Y.C., 1953-58; Cambridge Inns, Inc., Paramus, N.J., 1960-72, Greentree Restaurants, Inc., N.Y.C., 1974-83; chmn. Guardian Food Service Corp., N.Y.C., 1974-86; chmn. Ossip Cons., Inc. Editor: 509th Composite Group, 1946. Former pres. Nat. Democratic Club. Served to capt. USAF, 1943-46. Mem. N.Y. Restaurant Assn., Nat. Restaurant Assn., N.Y. Vis. Conv. Bur. Clubs: Sixty East, Delaire Golf, Braeburn Country. Office: Ossip Cons Inc 275 Madison Ave New York NY 10016

OSTBERG, HENRY DEAN, company executive; b. Bocholt, Germany, July 21, 1928; came to U.S., 1939, naturalized, 1945; s. Fred and Lotte (Hertz) O.; m. Sydelle Burns, Dec. 13, 1987; 1 child, Neal; stepchildren: Elysa Bari, Brent Adam, Ross Jay. LLB, N.Y. Law Sch., 1950; MBA, Ohio State U., 1953, PhD, 1957. Pres. H.D. Ostberg Assos., N.Y.C., 1950—; chmn. bd. Admar Research Co., Inc., N.Y.C., 1960; dir. Self-Instructional Devel. Corp., Amherst Group, Porter Industries, Inc.; pres. Eastman Enterprises, Inc.; assoc. prof. mktg. NYU, 1954-63. Trustee Ostberg Found. Capt. USAF, 1950-53. Mem. Inst. Mgmt. Scis., Am. Mktg. Assn. Jewish. Contbr. articles to profl. jours. Home: 278 Fountain Rd Englewood NJ 07631 Office: Admar Rsch Inc 304 Park Ave S New York NY 10010

OSTER, MICHAEL CROLY, insurance executive; b. Los Angeles, Nov. 1, 1944; s. Otto and Irene Evelyn (Croly) O.; m. Linell Ruth Rynkiewicz, Oct. 1, 1985. BS with honors, Calif. State U., Long Beach, 1969; cert. ins., Orange Coast Coll., Costa Mesa, Calif., 1975. CLU, Cert. Ins. Cons. Engring. cost data analyst McDonnell-Douglas Aircraft Corp., Long Beach, 1966-70; mktg. rep. Continental Can Co., Los Angeles, 1970-72; v.p. mktg. Calif. Casualty Mgmt. Co., San Mateo, 1972-79; exec. v.p. Frank B. Hall & Co., San Francisco, 1979—. Contbr. articles to profl. jours. Mem. Bay Area Council. Staff sgt. USAFR, 1966-72. Recipient Gov.'s Commendation Medal, State of Calif., 1967. Mem. Commonwealth Club, Lahaina Yacht Club (Maui, Hawaii), Grand Banks Cruising Club, San Francisco Bay Club, Olympic Club, South Beach Yacht Club. Office: Frank B Hall & Co 1 Market Pla Ste 2100 San Francisco CA 94105

OSTERHOFF, JAMES MARVIN, computer company executive; b. Lafayette, Ind., May 18, 1936; s. Abel Lyman and Mildred Paulene (Post) O.; m. Marilyn Ann Morrison, Aug. 24, 1958; children—Anne Michelle, Amy Louise, Susan Marie. B.S.M.E., Purdue U., 1958; M.B.A., Stanford U., 1963. Staff asst. FMC Corp., San Jose, Calif., 1963-64; with Ford Motor Co., Dearborn, Mich., 1964-84; v.p. fin. Ford Motor Credit Co., Dearborn, 1973-75; controller car ops. N. Am. Automotive Ops., Ford Motor Co., Dearborn, 1975-76; asst. controller N. Am. Automotive Ops., Ford Motor Co., 1976-79; controller tractor ops. Ford Motor Co., Troy, Mich., 1979-84; v.p. fin. Digital Equipment Corp., Maynard, Mass., 1985—; bd. dirs. Arkwright Mut. Ins. Co.; bd. dirs. mem. chief fin. officer task force Pvt. Sector Council; mem. Conf. Bd. Fin. Council. Served to lt. (j.g.) USN, 1958-61. Mem. Fin. Execs. Inst. Office: Digital Equipment Corp 146 Main St Maynard MA 01754

OSTERMAN, JOHN THEODORE, financial consultant; b. Streator, Ill., Aug. 13, 1943; s. Theodore W. and Edyth C. (Hakes) O.; m. Anne Peterson, Aug. 14, 1965; children: Kimberly, David, Erin. BA in Math, Culver-Stockton Coll., 1965; MBA, Ill. State U., 1968. CLU, chartered fin. cons. Factory rep. Caterpillar Tractor Co., Peoria, Ill., 1968-72; gen. mgr. Braden Machinery Co., Yuma, Ariz., 1972-79; owner, pres. Osterman Fin. Group, Yuma, Ariz., 1979—. Pres. Boy's Club, Yuma, 1984, Yuma Sch. Dist. Trust, 1987—; chmn. Yuma Econ. Devel. Com., 1987. Mem. Nat. Assn. Life Underwriters, Top of Table, Yuma C. of C. (bd. dirs. 1985). Home: 1406 Camino Real Yuma AZ 85364 Office: Osterman Fin Group 1763 W 24th St Ste 100 Yuma AZ 85364

OSTERMAN-OLSON, KAREN, securities sales and financial consultant; b. Newark, Nov. 20, 1951; d. David and Harriet (Hirschoff) Rosenstein; m. Walter S. Olson, Apr. 9, 1984. BBA, Kent (Ohio) State U., 1972; MBA, No. Ill. U., 1981. Acct. Alexander Grant & Co., Chgo., 1973-74; tax acct. Interstate United Corp., 1974-77; asst. tax mgr. Chamberlain Mfg. Corp., Elmhurst, Ill., 1977-81; mgr. tax systems Data-Tax, Inc., Naperville, Ill., 1981-85; v.p., gen. mgr. IMD, Inc., 1985-86; fin. cons. Lisle, Ill., 1986—. Mem. Internat. Assn. for Fin. Planning. Republican.

OSTFELD, LEONARD S., computer company executive; b. Passaic, N.J., Oct. 1, 1942; s. Edward and Anne (Grossman) O.; m. Barbara Molen, Aug. 22, 1965; children: Robert, Scott. BS in Acctg., NYU, 1964; MBA, Fairleigh Dickinson U., 1968. Sr. acct. Coopers & Lybrand, Newark, 1965-68, Ward Foods, N.Y.C., 1968-69; mgr. acctg. Reliance Group Inc., N.Y.C., 1969-78; v.p. acctg., treas. Ampal Am. Israel Corp., N.Y.C., 1978-81; v.p., controller CGA Computer Assocs., Holmdel, N.J., 1982-84; v.p., chief fin. officer AGS Computers Inc., Mountainside, N.J., 1985—. Mem. Am. Inst. CPAs, N.J. Soc. CPAs, Fin. Execs. Inst. Office: AGS Computers Inc 1139 Spruce Dr Mountainside NJ 07092

OSTLER, DAVID SORENSON, small business owner, state legislator; b. Nephi, Utah, June 17, 1931; s. LeRoy Taylor and Anna Marie (Grace) O.; m. Sharon Scott, Aug. 24, 1955; children: David V., Cynthia Shipley, Suzanne Shippen, Randall S., Emily Glasheen, Christopher T. BA, Brigham Young U., 1956; MBA, Harvard U., 1958. Salesman Pride Co., North Hollywood, Calif., 1958-59, Given Machinery Co., Los Angeles, 1959-60; sales mgr. Ariel Davis Mfg. Co., Salt Lake City, 1960-64; gen. mgr. The Williamsen Cos., Salt Lake City, 1964-69; pres. Med. Devel. Corp., Salt Lake City, 1969-70; treas. Intermountain Labs., Salt Lake City, 1969-73; pres. Medlab Computer Services, Salt Lake City, 1973-76, O.J. Industries, Salt Lake City, 1976-79; prin. Davo Leasing & Investments, Salt Lake City, 1976—; mem. Utah Ho. of Reps., 1986—; pres. The Bus. Brokerage, Inc., Salt Lake City, 1980—, ImmunoMed Corp., Tampa, Fla., 1983-85, also chmn. bd. dirs.; bd. dirs. Animed, Inc., Roslyn, N.Y., Cordin Co., Salt Lake City, I.E. Sensors, Salt Lake City. Patentee fluid collection systems, 1972-74. Bd. trustees St. Mark's Hosp. With U.S. Army, 1950-52, Korea. Phi Kappa Phi. Mormon. Republican. Club: Harvard (Utah). Home: 2666 Hillsden Dr Salt Lake City UT 84117 Office: Davo Leasing & Investments PO Box 17844 Salt Lake City UT 84117

OSTLING, PAUL JAMES, lawyer; b. Jamaica, N.Y., Sept. 22, 1948; s. John Carl and Margaret Ruth (Reilly) O.; m. Jane B. Mahler, June 1, 1974 (div. 1980); m. Julie Eileen Boyum, Feb. 20, 1982 (div. 1988). BS in Math. and Philosophy, Fordham U., 1969, JD, 1973. Bar: N.Y. 1974, U.S. Dist. Ct. (so. and ea. dists.) N.Y. 1974, U.S. Ct. Appeals (2d cir.) 1974, U.S. Ct. Appeals (4th, 5th, 9th, 10th, 11th cirs.) 1978. Assoc. Chadbourne Parke, N.Y.C., 1973-77; asst. gen. counsel Authur Young & Co., N.Y.C., 1977-79, assoc. gen. counsel, 1979-82, ptnr., assoc. gen. counsel, 1982, nat. dir. human resources, 1985—. Office: Arthur Young & Co Nat Office 277 Park Ave New York NY 10172

OSTROM, FRANCIS L., III, banker, trust company executive; b. Syracuse, N.Y., Jan. 11, 1958; s. Francis L. and Barbara J. (Kelleher) O.; m. Elizabeth M. Fahy, June 4, 1983; 1 child, Clare F. BBA in Fin., St. Bonaventure U., 1980. Cert. fin. planner. Trust adminstr. The Nat. Bank of Washington, 1980-84; v.p. bus. devel. Norstar Trust Co./Northstar Fin. Svcs., Rochester, N.Y., 1984—; instr. St. John Fisher Coll., Rochester, 1987—. Sec.-treas. Rochester Area Crime Stoppers Program, 1985—. Mem. Estate Planning Council, Internat. Assn. Fin. Planners, Inst. Cert. Fin. Planners, Rochester Profl. Sales Assn., Univ. Club. Home: 180 Clovercrest Dr Rochester NY 14618

OSTROM, JOHN SIBLEY, university offical; b. Atlantic City, Oct. 17, 1929; s. Selden W. and Constance (Murdock) O.; m. Mary Elizabeth Weaver, Apr. 19, 1952; children: Kathryn Ann, Janet Louise, John Selden, Donald Murdock. BA, Cornell U., 1951. CPA, N.Y., N.J. Assoc. dir. budget Princeton (N.J.) U., 1966-73, assoc. controller; dir. fin. systems devel. Cornell U., Ithaca, N.Y., 1973-77, controller, 1977—. Mem. Nat. Assn. Coll. and Univ. Bus. Officers (cons., tchr. 1979—). Republican. Presbyterian. Office: Cornell U 437 Day Hall Ithaca NY 14853-2801

OSTROUT, PAUL WAYNE, retail executive; b. Hartford, Conn., May 2, 1952; s. Robert Ensign and Frances Geraldine (McLean) O.; m. Marie Terese Flieger, June 16, 1973; children: James, Michael, Jason. Student, Cen. Conn. State Coll., 1971-72. Supply clerk, store planning staff D&L Venture Corp., New Britain, Conn., 1971-74, asst. distbn. ctr. mgr., 1974-76, distbn. ctr. mgr., 1976-81, dir. distbn., 1981—; bd. dirs. Frederick Atkins Distbn. Group, N.Y.C.; corporator Constructive Workshop, New Britain, 1987—. V.p. Holmes Sch. PTA, New Britain, 1983-85, pres. 1986—; corporator YMCA, New Britain, 1986; mem. program facility and planning commn. City of New Britain. Mem. Nat. Retail Mfrs. Assn. (bd. dirs. transp. com. 1984—), Delta Nu Alpha Frat., Cen. Conn. Traffic Assn. Democrat. Roman Catholic. Home: 2180 Stanley St New Britain CT 06053 Office: D&L Venture Corp 227 Main St New Britain CT 06050

OSTROW, JOSEPH W., advertising executive; b. N.Y.C., Feb. 22, 1933; s. Meyer H. and Helen (Small) O.; m. Francine Lee Goldberg, Sept. 4, 1955; children: Elizabeth Sara, Peter Mathew, William Nathan. B.S. in Mktg., NYU, 1955. Researcher W.R. Simmons, N.Y.C., 1954-55; with Young & Rubicam, N.Y.C., 1955-87; sr. v.p., dir. communication planning Young & Rubicam, 1972-73, exec. v.p., dir. communications services, 1973-87, mem. N.Y. exec. com., U.S.A. bd. dirs.; pres., chief operating officer worldwide Direct Mktg. Group of Cos., 1983-84; exec. v.p., dir. media worldwide Foote, Cone & Belding Co., N.Y.C., 1987—; media dir. FCB/Leber Katz Ptnrs., 1987—; lectr. in field; past chmn. Traffic Audit Bur.; dir. Audit Bur. Circulations.; bd. dirs., past mem. exec. com. Advt. Info. Services, Advt. Research Found.; bd. dirs. FCB/LKP, Am. U. Rome. Mktg. columnist Media Decisions mag. Mem. parents com. on edn. NYU and Cornell U. fund-raising, UN Adv. Coun. to Dept. Pub. Info.; fund-raiser Flm. Cancer Soc., Taft Sch.; assn. dir. Faculty/Industry Seminar and Coll. Conf. Mem. Media Dirs. Council (past pres.), Am. Assn. Advt. Agys. (past vice chmn. media policy com.), Internat. Radio and TV Soc., Internat. Radio and TV Found. (bd. dirs.). Office: Foote Cone Belding Communications Inc 767 Fifth Ave New York NY 10153

OSTROW, SAMUEL DAVID, public relations executive; b. Chgo., Nov. 6, 1945; s. Herbert Harold and Rose (Brown) O.; m. Toby Michelle Gurewitz, Mar. 23, 1969 (div. May 1976); m. Judith Ann Platt, May 11, 1980; children: Adam, Rachel. AB, Dartmouth Coll., 1967; JD with honors, John Marshall Law Sch., 1975. Bar: Ill. 1975, U.S. Dist. Ct. (no. dist.) Ill. 1975. V.p. Pub. Communications, Inc., Chgo., 1971-76; sr. v.p. Manning, Selvage & Lee, N.Y.C., 1977-84; exec. v.p. Rowland Co. Worldwide (formerly The Rowland Co.), N.Y.C., 1984—, gen. mgr. internat. div., 1988—. Contbr. articles to profl. jours. Sec. Pound Ridge (N.Y.) Assn., Inc., 1986, trustee, 1985-87, pres., 1988—; trustee Harold Parmington Found., Hanover, N.H., 1970—. Mem. Nat. Investor Rel. Inst. (pres. Chgo. chpt. 1975-76, v.p. programs, bd. dirs. N.Y.C. chpt. 1988—). Office: Rowland Co Worldwide 415 Madison Ave New York NY 10017

OSTROWSKI, STEPHEN, data processing executive; b. N.Y.C., Mar. 1, 1938; m. Carolyn Clare Metzger, June 17, 1961; children: Mark, Mike. Computer operator Bulova Watch Co., N.Y.C., 1960-64; programmer Chem. Bank, N.Y.C., 1964-67; sys. analyst Ideal Toy Co., N.Y.C., 1967-69; mgr. project First Atlanta Bank, 1969-83; v.p. Magnum Communications, Atlanta, 1983-85; owner Otek Cons. Group, Atlanta, 1985—; cons. in field. Contbr. articles to profl. jours. Served with USAF, 1955-58. Mem. Assn. of

Personal Computer Users, Turbo Technix. Republican. Roman Catholic. Home and Office: Otek Cons Group 2839 Bayberry Dr Marietta GA 30060

OSTRUSZKA, WAYNE DEVERE, data processing executive; b. Chgo., June 5, 1947; s. Leo Edwin and Stephine Lillian (Mazur) O.; m. Kathleen Michele Zelek, July 26, 1969; children: Katherine, Leo. BS in Mgmt., DePaul U., 1969. Sr. systems analyst Bell & Howell Corp., Chgo., 1974-75; data processing cons. Systems and Programming Resources, Chgo., 1975-78; project coordinator Cap Gemini Am., Milw., 1978-82, mktg. rep., 1983-87; mktg. mgr. Cap Gemini Am., 1987, mgr. Milw. fin. branch, 1988—; cons. Data Processing Milw., 1982-83. Dir. Crystal Lake (Ill.) Jaycees, 1975. Named Number 1 Mktg. Rep. Cap Gemini Am., 1984, 85. Mem. Assn. for Systems Mgmt., Data Processing Mgmt. Assn. Republican. Roman Catholic. Home: 2101 Harris Highland Dr Waukesha WI 53188 Office: CAP Gemini Am 10150 W National Ave Suite #200 Milwaukee WI 53227

OSUMI, MASATO, utility company executive; b. Osaka, Japan, Aug. 20, 1942; s. Masahiro and Sachiko Osumi; m. Masako Nakajima, Apr. 21, 1968; children: Masanori, Koji, Yuko. BS, Yokohama Nat. U., 1966; MS, NYU, 1971; D in Engring., Kyoto U., 1978. Engr. Sanyo Elec. Co.Ltd., Hirakata, Osaka, 1966-71; engr. Tokyo Sanyo Elec. Co. Ltd., Hirakata, Osaka, 1971-73, chief researcher rsch. ctr., 1978-85, mgr., 1985-86, mgr. cen. systems rsch. ctr., 1987-89, div. mgr., 1989—. Contbr. articles to profl. jours. Mem. Japanese Soc. Mech. Engrs. (bd. dirs. 1986-87), Japanese Soc. Precision Engrs. Home: 3-33 Takiimotomachi, Moriguchi, Osaka 570, Japan Office: Sanyo Elec Co Ltd 1-18-13, Hashiridani, Hirakata, Osaka 573, Japan

OSUNDE, JOHN IRIOWEN, trading company executive; b. Benin City, Nigeria, Sept. 28, 1939; s. Peter Oduwa and Ayanon Evbima (Ovbiogbe) O.; LL.B., Blackstone Sch. Law, 1967; D.D. (hon.), Christ Sch. Theology, 1975; m. Victoria King, Dec. 28; children—Patrick, Paul. Edn. officer, Benin City, 1956-57, Nigerian Civil Service, 1958-61; mem. UN Peace Mission to Congo Republic, 1961-62; pres. Manson Overseas Trade Corp., Lagos, 1976—. Rehab. coordinator Nigeria Civil War, 1969-70; founder, 1970, since pres. Gen. Internat. Helpless Children Soc. Recipient Nigerian Ind. medal, 1960, UN God medal, 1962. Mem. Internat. Trade Orgn., Chambers Inst. Mgmt., Internat. Fundamental Human Rights Assn. Democrat. Clubs: African Golf (pres.), Masons (Lagos). Author poems. Home: 62 Lawanson Rd, Surulere, Lagos Nigeria Office: 45 Tejuosho St, Surulere PO Box 1485, Marina, Lagos Nigeria

OSWALD, JAMES MARLIN, educator; b. Plainview, Tex., Aug. 17, 1935; s. James Buchanan and Eula Bea (Marlin) O.; BS, West Tex. State Coll., 1957, MA, 1958; EdD, Stanford U., 1970; m. Dorothy Anne Veigel, Dec. 27, 1956; children: Richard, Ramona, Roberta. Tchr., supr. Salt Lake City pub. schs., 1958-66; curriculum specialist Am. Insts. Research, 1966-68; staff asso. Nat. Council Social Studies, 1968-69; asst. prof. social studies and social sci. edn. Syracuse (N.Y.) U., 1969-72; researcher-writer, dir. global cultural studies edn. projects Am. Univs. Field Staff, 1972-75; asst. supt. instrn. East Penn Sch. Dist., Emmaus, Pa., 1975-78; field coordinator Pa., Del. and N.J. citizen edn., Research for Better Schs., Phila., 1978-80; instrnl. development specialist Community Coll. Phila., 1980—; propr. Energy Cons. and Main Line Stoves, 1978—; curriculum instrn. and tng. specialist; edn. and energy cons.; research analyst; speaker; pres. N.Y. State Council Social Studies, 1971-72. Served with AUS, 1957-58. Recipient Sertoma Service to Mankind award Salt Lake City, 1966; grantee NSF, U.S. Office Edn., Inst. Internat. Studies, Henry Newell fellow, 1966-68, Fulbright-Hays SEAsia U. Singapore Study Program fellow, 1967. Mem. Am. Ednl. Research Assn., Nat. Soc. for Performance and Instrn., Social Sci. Edn. Consortium, Tex. Panhandle-Plains Hist. Soc., Utah Hist. Soc., N.Am. Vegetarian Soc., India-U.S. Found., Pa. Forestry Assn., Phi Delta Kappa. Author: The Monroe Doctrine: Does It Survive?, 1969; Research in Social Studies and Social Science Education, 1972; co-author, Earthship, 1974; Planet Earth, 1976; Our Home, the Earth, 1980; contbr. articles to profl. jours.. Home: 333 Bryn Mawr Ave Bala-Cynwyd PA 19004

OSWALD, SCOTT F., health products company executive; b. Seattle, June 19, 1953; s. Hugo Edmond Jr. and Olive (Davis) O.; m. Phyllis Kamps, Dec. 17, 1977; children: Brooke Anne, Forrest Guy, Spencer Miles. BA in Econs. with honors, Stanford U., 1976; MBA, U. Wash., 1979. Bus. planning supr. Simpson Timber Co., Seattle, 1979-82; gen. mgr. Nutricare div. Advanced Healthcare subs. Avadyne, Inc., Monterey, Calif., 1982—; cons. in field. Chmn. Tomorrow's Leaders, Eugene, Oreg., 1981-82. Republican. Club: Washington Athletic. Home: 5 Forest Vale Pl Monterey CA 93940 Office: Advanced Healthcare 2801 Salinas Hwy Bldg F Monterey CA 93940

OSWALD, WILLIAM JACK, financial investor; b. Chgo., Feb. 10, 1927; s. Jeho and Maria Jeanette (Van Calcar) O.; student Ill. Inst. Tech., 1943-44, U. Wis., 1944-45; B.S., Barry Coll., 1978, MBA, Barry U., 1986; m. Delores Jean Kipple, Dec. 6, 1958; 1 son, William Randolph. Pres. Star Corps., Chgo., 1953-74, chmn. bd., 1964-74; pres. Interam. Car Rental, Inc., 1976-81, Am. Autolet Corp., 1977-81; chmn. bd. Capital & Devel. Control Corp., Ft. Lauderdale, Fla., 1975—; pres. Star Nat. Enterprises, Inc.; pres. Williams Investment Realty, Inc., 1984—; chmn. Advanced Computeronics, Inc., 1984—; dir. Ostar, Inc., Williams & Co. Inc. Served with USAAF, 1945-46. Cert. employment cons. Am. Inst. Employment Counseling. Home: 6662 Boca del Mar Dr Boca Raton FL 33433 Office: 1515 N Federal Hwy Boca Raton FL 33432

OTA, AKIRA, small business owner; b. Hagi, Yamaguchi, Japan, July 8, 1933; s. Kanemitsu and Kumayo (Suizu) O.; m. Chieko Mogi, May 12, 1961; children: Takashi, Kazumi. Chmn. Fujitsu-kiden Labor Union, Tokyo, 1961-63, cons., 1963-66; pres. Clever Industry Corp., Tokyo, 1986—. Mem. Japan Skin Esthetic Assn. Home: 2-9-1 Masugata, Tama Devision, Kawasaki, Kanagawa 214, Japan Office: Clever Industry Corp, 3-6-17 Osaki, Shinagawa, Tokyo 141, Japan

OTHERSEN, CHERYL LEE, insurance broker, realtor; b. Bay City, Mich., Aug. 17, 1948; d. Andrew Julius and Ruth Emma (Jacoby) Houthoofd; m. Wayne Korte Othersen, Sept. 5, 1964; 1 child, Angela. Lic. ins., Mich. State U., 1980, lic. realtor, 1981. Owner, operator Glad Rags Boutique, Unionville, Mich., 1976-79; dept. mgr. Gantos, Saginaw, Mich., 1979-80; agt., bookkeeper Othersen Ins. Agy., Inc., Unionville, 1979-81, v.p., 1981—; realtor Osentoski Realty Corp., Unionville, 1981—. Active Mich. chpt. Nat. Head Injury Found., Mich. chpt. Nat. Found. for Ileitis and Colitis, Nat. Mus. In The Arts, Nat. Trust for Hist. Preservation; vol. local Rep. campaigns, 1982, 84, 86. Fellow (hon.) John F. Kennedy Libr. Found.; mem. Profl. Ins. Agts., Unionville Bus. Assn., Nat. Mus. Women in the Arts (charter). Mem. Moravian Ch. Club: Sherwood-on-the-Hill Country (Gagetown, Mich.). Home: 4483 S Unionville Rd Unionville MI 48767 Office: Othersen Ins Agy Inc 6639 Center St Unionville MI 48767

OTHMAN, TALAT MOHAMAD, financial consultant, investment banker; b. Betunia, Palestine, Apr. 27, 1936; came to U.S., 1947, naturalized, 1954; s. Mohamad Racheed and Damelize (Ahmed) O.; m. Souheir Eldefrawy, Nov. 1957; children—Joseph, Suad, Jamil, Rashid. Student Northwestern U. With Harris Bank, Chgo., 1956-78, v.p., div. head, 1974-78; gen. mgr., chief exec. officer Saudi Arab Fin. Corp., S.A., Paris, 1978-83; pres. Dearborn Financial, Inc., Arlington Hts., Ill., 1983—; bd. dirs. Bank One Wis. Corp., Milw., Harken Oil and Gas Co., Dallas, Ellsworth Fin., Inc., Phoenix; chmn. Dansk Internat. Designs, Inc., Mt. Kisko, N.Y., 1985—, Goodson Polymer, Inc., Troy, Ohio, 1987-88. Contbr. chpts. to Technique of Foreign Exchange Trading, 1975; also articles and booklets. Bd. dirs. Inst. World Affairs, Milw., 1986-89, Khail Gibran Meml. com., Washington, D.C., 1987-89. Mem. Arab Bankers Assn. (pres. 1985-87, bd. dirs. 1984-89, recipient plaque of Appreciation), Forex Assn. of N.Am. (chmn., founding pres. Chgo. chpt. 1976, recipient plaque of Appreciation), Mid Am. Arab C. of C. (bd. dirs. 1974-78, 84—, founding pres. 1977, recipient plaque of Appreciation). Moslem. Clubs: Chicago, Attic (Chgo.); LaSalle (Chgo.). Avocations: tennis, racquetball, reading.

OTHMER, DONALD FREDERICK, chemical engineer, educator; b. Omaha, May 11, 1904; s. Frederick George and Fredericka Darling (Snyder) O.; m. Mildred Jane Topp, Nov. 18, 1950. Student, Ill. Inst. Tech., Chgo., 1921-23; B.S., U. Nebr., 1924, D.Eng. (hon.), 1962; M.S., U. Mich., 1925, Ph.D., 1927; D.Eng. (hon.), Poly. U., Bklyn., 1977, N.J. Inst. Tech., 1978. Registered profl. engr., N.Y., N.J., Ohio, Pa. Devel. engr. Eastman Kodak Co. and Tenn. Eastman Corp., 1927-31; prof. Poly. U., Bklyn., 1933; disting. prof. Poly. U., 1961—, sec. grad. faculty, 1948-58; head dept. chem. engring. 1937-61; hon. prof. U. Conception, Chile, 1951; cons. chem. engr., licensor of process patents to numerous cos., govtl. depts., and countries, 1931—; developer program for chem. industry of Burma, 1951-54; cons. UN, UNIDO, WHO, Dept. Energy, Office Saline Water of U.S. Dept. Interior, Chem. Corps. and Ordnance Dept. U.S. Army, USN, WPB, Dept. State, HEW, Nat. Materials Advisory Bd., NRC Sci. Adv. Bd., U.S. Army Munitions Command; mem. Panel Energy Advisers to Congress, also other U.S. and fgn. govt. depts.; sr. gas officer Bklyn. Citizens Def. Corps.; lectr. Am. Swiss Found. Sci. Relations, 1950, Chem. Inst. Can., 1944-52, Am. Chem. Soc., U.S. Army War Coll., 1964, Shri RAM Inst., India, 1980, Royal Mil. Coll. Can., 1981; plenary lectr. Peoples Republic of China; hon. del. Engring. Congresses, Japan, 1983; plenary lectr., hon. del. Fed. Republic of Germany, Greece, Mex., Czechoslovakia, Yugoslavia, Poland, P.R., France, Can., Argentina, India, Turkey, Spain, Rumania, Kuwait, Iran, Iraq, Algeria, China, United Arab Emirates; designer chem. plants and processes for numerous corps., U.S., fgn. countries. Holder over 150 U.S. and fgn. patents on methods, processes and engring. equipment in mfg. of pharms., sugar, salt, acetic acid, acetylene, fuel-methanol, synthetic rubber, petro-chems., pigments, zinc, aluminum, titanium, also wood pulping, refrigeration, solar and other energy conversion, water desalination, sewage treatment, peat utilization, coal desulfurization, pipeline heating, etc.; contbr. over 350 articles on chem. engring., chem. mfg., synthetic fuels and thermodynamics to tech. jours.; co-founder/co-editor: Kirk-Othmer Ency. Chem. Tech., 17 vols, 1947-60, 24 vols., 2d edit., 1963-71, 26 vols., 3d edit., 1976-84, Spanish edit., 16 vols., 1960-66; editor: Fluidization, 1956; co-author: Fluidization and Fluid Particle Systems, 1960; mem. adv. bd.: Perry's Chem. Engr.'s Handbook; tech. editor: UN Report, Technology of Water Desalination, 1964. Bd. regents L.I. Coll. Hosp., bd. dirs. numerous ednl. and philanthropic instns., engring. and indsl. corps. Recipient Golden Jubilee award, Ill. Inst. Tech., 1975, Profl. Achievement award, Ill. Inst. Tech., 1978, Award of Honor for Sci. and Tech. Mayor of N.Y.C., 1987; named to Hall of Fame, Ill. Inst. Tech., 1981. Fellow AAAS, Am. Inst. Cons. Engrs., Am. Inst. Chemists (Honor Scroll 1970, Chem. Pioneer award 1977), ASME (hon. life, chmn. chem. processes div. 1948-49), N.Y. Acad. Scis. (hon. life, chmn. engring. sect. 1972-73), Instn. Chem. Engrs. (London) (hon. life), Am. Inst. Chem. Engrs. (Tyler award 1958, chmn. N.Y. sect. 1944, dir. 1956-59); mem. Am. Chem. Soc. (council 1945-47, E.V. Murphree-Exxon award 1978, hon. life mem.), Soc. Chem. Industry (Perkin medal 1978), Am. Soc. Engring. Edn. (Barber Coleman award 1958), Engrs. Joint Council (dir. 1957-59), Societe de Chimie Industrielle (pres. 1973-74), Chemurgic Council (dir.), Japan Soc. Chem. Engrs., Assn. Cons. Chemists and Chem. Engrs. (award of Merit 1975), Newcomen Soc., Am. Arbitration Assn. (panel mem. or sole arbitrator numerous cases), Sigma Xi (citation disting. research 1983), Tau Beta Pi, Phi Lambda Upsilon, Iota Alpha, Alpha Chi Sigma, Lambda Chi Alpha; hon. life mem. Deutsche Gesellschaft für Cheme. Apparatewesen. Clubs: Norwegian (Bklyn.), Chemists (N.Y.C.) (pres. 1974-75), Rembrandt (Bklyn.). Home: 140 Columbia Heights Brooklyn NY 11201 Office: Poly U 333 Jay St Brooklyn NY 11201

OTIS, JOHN JAMES, civil engineer; b. Syracuse, N.Y., Aug. 5, 1922; s. John Joseph and Anna (Dey) O.; m. Dorothy Fuller Otis, June 21, 1958; children: Mary Eileen, John Leon Jr. B of Chem. Engring., Syracuse U., 1943, MBA, 1950, postgrad., 1951-55. Registered profl. engr., Ala., Tex. Jr. process engr. Gen. Motors Corp., Syracuse, 1951-53, prodn. engr., 1954-58, process control engr., 1958-59, process engr., 1960-61; engr., writer Gen. Electric Co., Syracuse, 1961-63; configuration control engr. Gen. Electric Co., Phila., 1969; assoc. research engr. Boeing Co., Huntsville, Ala., 1963-65; assoc. Planning Research Corp., Huntsville, Ala., 1965-67; prin. engr. Brown Engring. Co. subs. Teledyne Co., Huntsville, Ala., 1967-69; mech. designer Drever Co., Beth Ayres, Pa., 1970-71; civil engr. U.S. Army Corps. Engrs., Mobile, Ala., 1971-74, Galveston, Tex., 1974—. Lector, lay minister Roman Cath. Ch. Served with USNR, 1944-46. Mem. Am. Inst. Indsl. Engrs. (past v.p. Syracuse and Hunstville chpts.), Tex. Soc. Profl. Engrs. (dir. Galveston County chpt. 1976-79, sec.-treas. 1979-80, v.p. 1980-81, pres. 1982-83), Tau Beta Pi, Phi Kappa Tau, Alpha Chi Sigma, Chi Eta Sigma. Home: 2114 Yorktown Ct N League City TX 77573 Office: US Army Corps Engrs 444 Barracuda St Galveston TX 77550

OTIS, KIRK JAMES, certified public accountant, financial executive; b. Midland, Mich., Apr. 15, 1960; s. James Leonard and Barbara Lou (Alward) O.; m. Adrienne DeForest, Jan. 18, 1986; 1 child, Jacqueline Nichole. BS, Bowling Green State U., 1982; MBA, So. Meth. U., 1988. CPA, Ohio. Auditor Price Waterhouse, Columbus, Ohio, 1982-84; internal auditor The LTV Corp., Dallas, 1985, fin. analyst, 1985-86, sr. analyst corp. fin., 1986-88; asst. treas., contr. LTV-SMI Electro-Galvanizing Co., Cleve., 1988—. Mem. Am. Soc. CPA's, Tex. Soc. CPA's, Ohio Soc. CPA's. Republican. Office: LTV-SMI Electro-Galvanizing 3100 E 45th St Cleveland OH 44127

O'TOOLE, AUSTIN MARTIN, lawyer; b. New Bedford, Mass., Oct. 5, 1935; s. John Brian, Jr. and Helen Veronica O'T.; m. Kay Murphy, Nov. 27, 1982; children: Erin Ann, Austin Martin 2d. B.S. in Bus. Adminstrn., Coll. Holy Cross, 1957; J.D., Georgetown U., 1963. Bar: N.Y. 1965, D.C. 1963, Tex. 1975. Law clk. to judge U.S. Ct. Appeals, Washington, 1962-63; assoc. White & Case, N.Y.C., 1963-74; sr. v.p., dep. gen. counsel, sec. Coastal Corp., Houston, 1974—. Bd. editors Georgetown Law Jour., 1962-63. Bd. dirs. Houston Council on Alcoholism and Drug Abuse, Houston, 1986—; com. mem. Houston-Tenneco Marathon. Served as officer USMCR, 1957-60. Mem. Am. Soc. Corporate Secs. (bd. dirs. 1982-85), ABA, Tex. Bar Assn. (com. securities and investment banking), Houston Bar Assn. (past chmn. corp. counsel sect. 1979-80). Home: 2008 Timberlane Houston TX 77027 Office: Coastal Corp 9 Greenway Pla E Houston TX 77046

O'TOOLE, JOHN E., advertising executive; b. Chgo., Jan. 17, 1929; m. Phyllis Treadway, 1955; children: Sally, Ellen. BJ, Northwestern U., 1951. With Batten, Barton, Durstine & Osborn, 1953-54, Foote, Cone & Belding, 1954-85; successively copy writer, copy supr., v.p., creative dir. Foote, Cone & Belding, L.A. and Chgo.; pres. Foote, Cone & Belding, N.Y.C., 1969; pres. Foote, Cone & Belding Communications, Inc., N.Y.C., 1970-81, chmn., 1981-85; dir. Am. Assn. Advt. Agys., Washington, 1986-88, pres., 1988—; dir. Nat. Advt. Rev. Coun.; bd. dirs. Knapp Comm'ins Corp. Author: The Trouble with Advertising, 1981. Served with USMCR, 1951-53; ret. Res. 1956. Home: Greenwich CT Office: Am Assn Advt Agys 666 Third Ave New York NY 10017

O'TOOLE, ROBERT JOSEPH, manufacturing company executive; b. Chgo., Feb. 22, 1941; s. Francis John O'Toole; children: William, Patricia, Timothy, Kathleen, John. BS in Acctg., Loyola U., Chgo., 1961. Fin. analyst A.O. Smith Corp., Milw., 1963-66, mgr. corp. fin. analysis and planning, 1966-68; controller electric motor div. A.O. Smith Corp., Tipp City, Ohio, 1968-71; mng. dir. Bull Motors, Ipswich, Eng., 1971-74; gen. plant mgr. electric motor div. A.O. Smith Corp., Tipp City, 1974-79, v.p., gen. mgr., 1979-83; sr. v.p. A.O. Smith Corp., Milw., 1984-85, pres., 1986-89, pres., chief exec. officer, 1989—, also bd. dirs.; bd. dirs. 1st Wis. Nat. Bank, Milw.; mem. The Exec. Com. TEC XIV, Milw., Wis. Mfrs. and Commerce, Madison, Aspin/Met. Milw. Assn. Commerce Def. Procurement Program, Milw.; mem. exec. com. Machinery and Allied Products Inst. Mem. Greater Milw. Com. Clubs: Univ., Tripoli Country (Milw.). Office: A O Smith Corp 1 Park Pla 11270 W Park Pl Milwaukee WI 53224-3690

OTT, GILBERT RUSSELL, JR., lawyer; b. Bklyn., Apr. 15, 1943; s. Gilbert Russell Sr. and Bettina Rose (Ferrel) O.; m. Lisa S. Weatherford, Apr. 12, 1986; 1 child, Gilbert R. III. BA, Yale U., 1965; JD, Columbia U., 1969, MBA, 1969. Admitted to N.Y. State bar, 1970; assoc. firm Chadbourne, Parke, Whiteside & Wolff, N.Y.C., 1969-72, LeBoeuf, Lamb, Leiby & MacRae, N.Y.C., 1972-78; asso. gen. counsel, asst. sec. Kidder, Peabody & Co., Inc., N.Y.C., 1978—, asst. v.p., 1978-79, v.p., 1979-86, mng. dir., 1986—; v.p. Webster Cash Res. Fund, Inc., 1980—, gen. counsel, sec., 1982—, bd. dirs., 1985—; v.p., gen. counsel, sec. Kidder, Peabody Premium Account Fund, 1982—, trustee, 1985—; v.p., gen. counsel, sec. Kidder, Peabody Govt. Money Fund, Inc., 1983—; dir., 1985—; v.p. Kidder, Peabody Group, Inc., 1989—. Mem. Assn. Bar City N.Y. Clubs: Piping Rock, Down Town, University (N.Y.C.). Home: 260 Highwood Cir Oyster Bay NY 11771-3205 Office: 20 Exchange Pl New York NY 10005

OTTAWAY, JAMES HALLER, JR., newspaper publisher; b. Binghamton, N.Y., Mar. 24, 1938; s. James Haller and Ruth Blackburne (Hart) O.; m. Mary Warren Hyde, June 19, 1959; children—Alexandra, Christopher, Jay. Grad., Phillips Exeter Acad., 1955; B.A., Yale U., 1960; D.Journalism (hon.), Suffolk U., Boston, 1970; D.B.A. (hon.), Southeastern Mass. U., 1984. Reporter, mgmt. trainee New-Times, Danbury, Conn., 1960-62, Times Herald-Record, Middletown, N.Y., 1962-63; editor Pocono Record, Stroudsburg, Pa., 1963-65; publisher New Bedford (Mass.) Standard-Times, 1965-70; pres. Ottaway Newspapers, Inc., Campbell Hall, N.Y., 1970-85, chief exec. officer, 1976-88, chmn. bd., 1979—; v.p. Dow Jones & Co., 1980-86 sr. v.p. Dow Jones & Co., 1986—, also bd. dirs.; dir. Associated Press, 1982—. Past v.p. bd. trustees Phillips Exeter Acad.; trustee Am. Sch. Classical Studies at Athens, StormKing Art Ctr., Cornwall, N.Y.; past pres., bd. dirs. Arden Hill Hosp. Found., Goshen, N.Y. Mem. Am. Newspaper Pubs. Assn., Am. Soc. Newspaper Editors. Episcopalian. Office: PO Box 401 Campbell Hall NY 10916

OTTKE, ROBERT CRITTENDEN, small business owner; b. Louisville, Jan. 23, 1922; s. Robert Lee and Alma (Eastin) O.; m. Helen Grant Eddy, Oct. 23, 1943 (div. 1958); children: Robert R., Marcia G.; m. Jane Minniear, Nov. 8, 1958; children: Susan H., Peter E. BS, Yale U., 1948, PhD, 1953. Postdoctoral fellow Stanford U., Palo Alto, Calif., 1950-51; with Pfizer Inc., N.Y.C., 1951-57; pres. Caribe Chem. Corp., San Juan, P.R., 1957-58; tech. dir. internat. Baxter Travenol, N.Y.C., Chgo., 1958-63; pres. Parke-Davis, S.A., Madrid, Spain, 1964-69; v.p. Boyden Assocs., Madrid, San Francisco, 1969-76; pres. Robert Ottke Assocs., Newport Beach, Calif., 1976—; dir. Luther Med. Products Inc., Tustin, Calif., 1985—, sec., 1989— . Capt. USAAF, 1942-46. Mem. Am. Chem. Soc., Sigma Xi. Republican. Home: 2939 Perla St Newport Beach CA 92660 Office: Robert Ottke Assocs PO Box 7553 Newport Beach CA 92660

OTTO, INGOLF HELGI ELFRIED, institute fellow; b. Duesseldorf, Fed. Republic of Germany, May 7, 1920; s. Frederick C. and Josephine (Zisenis) O.; m. Carlyle Miller, 1943 (div. 1960); children—George Vincent Edward, Richard Arthur Frederick. A.B., U. Cin., 1941; M.A., George Washington U., 1950, Ph.D., 1959. CPCU. Assoc. prof. fin. NYU, N.Y.C., 1960-62; prof. fin. U. Nuevo Leon, Monterrey, Mexico, 1962-65, U. So. Miss., Hattiesburg, 1965-67, U. So. Ala., Mobile, 1967-81; sr. fellow Inst. Banking and Fin., Mexico City, 1981—. Contbr. articles on fin. to profl. jours. Served to col. U.S. Army, 1941-46. Decorated Legion of Merit, Meritorious Service medal, Purple Heart. Mem. Am. Econ. Assn., N.Am. Econ. and Fin. Assn.

OTTO, WILLIAM STUART, infosystem executive; b. Mpls., Oct. 21, 1945; s. Lyle Clifford and Edna Victoria (Gumboldt) O.; m. Mary Rae Melchert, Dec. 16, 1967; children: Rachel, Elizabeth. Student, U. Minn., 1963-65. Test equipment designer Control Data Corp., St. Paul, 1965-72; lead programmer Fed. Intermediate Credit Bank, St. Paul, 1972-74; systems mgr. T.C.S.I., St. Paul, 1974-76; dir. mgmt. info. staff Twin City Freight Inc., St. Paul, 1976-77; mgr. info. system Transp. Computer System, St. Paul, 1977-81, exec. v.p., 1981—. Sgt. USAR, 1965-71. Mem. Am. Trucking Assn., Data Processing Mgmt. Assn. Lutheran. Office: TCSI 80 E Little Canada Rd Little Canada MN 55117

OTU, JEAN BURFORD, communications executive; b. Washington, Jan. 26, 1964; d. Theodore Harrison and Sally Frances (Coleman) Burford; m. Didonis Chris Otu, Apr. 9, 1986; 1 child, Christine Bessomo. BA in Psychology, George Washington U., 1985. Mktg. rep. Md. Blood Ctr., Upper Marlboro, 1985-86; br. adminstr. Philips Info. Systems, Arlington, Va., 1986-87; br. adminstr., mgr. TDX Systems/Cable and Wireless Communications, Rosslyn, Va., 1987-88; mgr. customer svc. Nat. Inst. Bus. Mgmt., Old Towne Alexandria, Va., 1988—. Editor: Tipics Connection in Georgetown, 1986-87. Fund raiser Planned Parenthood Orgn., 1986-87. Mem. NAFE, Nat. Assn. Am. Blood Banks. Democrat. Roman Catholic. Home: 14729 Winding Loop Woodbridge VA 22191

OULTON, RICHARD JAMES, lawyer, healthcare educator; b. Peekskill, N.Y., Jan. 8, 1945; s. John and Martha (Smith) O.; m. Ava Liu, July 4, 1986; 1 child, John Lawrence. BA, SUNY, Buffalo, 1970, JD, 1973; MBA, CUNY, N.Y.C., 1976. Asst. adminstr., atty. Roosevelt Hosp., N.Y.C., 1973-77, N.Y. Med. Coll., N.Y.C., 1977-78; 2d v.p. Va. Ins. Reciprocal, Richmond, 1978-87, v.p., 1987-88; pres. Oulton Assocs. Inc., Glen Allen, Va., 1988—, Affliated Atty P.C., Richmond, 1989—; mem. Adv. Bd. on Edn. and Pub's., 1984—; mem. adv. bd. Joint Commn. on Accreditation of Hosps., Chgo.; asst. prof. dept. health care adminstrn. Va. Commonwealth U., Richmond, 1982-87, assoc. prof., 1987—;speaker numerous seminars. Editor: quality assurance risk mgmt. newsletter; mem. editorial adv. com. Quality Rev. Bull., 1984—; contbr. articles to profl. jours. With USN/USMC, 1964-67, Vietnam. Decorated Purple Heart. Mem. ABA, Va. Bar Assn., Am. Coll. Health Care Execs., Am. Acad. Hosp. Attys., Nat. Health Lawyers Assn., Am. Soc. for Hosp. Risk Mgmt., Nat. Assn. Quality Assurance Profls. Home: 2403 Islandview Ct Richmond VA 23233 Office: Oulton Assocs Inc 10831 W Broad St Glen Allen VA 23060

OUNJIAN, MARILYN J., employment and training company executive; b. Harrisburg, Pa., Oct. 24, 1947; d. Stanley Wolf and Rebecca (Darrow) Freeman; m. Irving Henry Schwartz, Aug. 24, 1974 (dec. May 1975); 1 child, Jennifer; m. George Edward Ounjian, July 31, 1982; children: Jonathan, Kori. Student, U. Md. Pres. Today's People, Phila., 1973-81; chmn., founder, chief exec. officer Careers USA, Phila., 1981—; pres., chief exec. officer The Career Inst., Phila., 1981—. Mem. Rep. Senatorial Inner Circle; bd. dirs. Phila. Econ. Devel. Coalition. Mem. Cen. City Proprietors Assn., Nat. Assn. Female Execs. Inc., Nat. Assn. Women Bus. Owners, Greater Phila. C. of C., Pa. C. of C., Assn. Venture Founders. Club: Gov.'s Del. Office: Careers USA 1825 JF Kennedy Blvd Philadelphia PA 19103

OURANT, ROBERT HUGH, insurance company executive; b. Bowerston, Ohio, July 22, 1923; s. Lyle and Geneva Ann (Hugh) O.; m. Gladys I. Wilson, May 8, 1948; children: Kimberly, Kay. B.A. in Acctg., Columbus Bus. U., 1947; cert. Exec. Program, Columbia U., 1966. CLU, Am. Coll. Life Underwriters. Underwriter Nationwide Ins. Cos., Columbus, Ohio, 1947-52, adminstrv. mgr., 1952-62; regional v.p. Nationwide Ins. Cos., Memphis, 1963-72; v.p. Medicare Nationwide Ins. Cos., Columbus, Ohio, 1972-74; v.p. field ops. Nationwide Ins. Cos., Columbia, Ohio, 1974-81; sr. v.p. corp. svcs. Nationwide Ins. Cos., Columbus, Ohio, 1981-88; ret.; dir. Employers of Wausau, Nat. Assn. Mut. Ins. Cos. Pres. Vision Ctr. of Central Ohio, Columbus, 1971, hon. dir., 1972; bd. dirs. Met. YMCA, Columbus, 1982—. Served to staff sgt. USAF, 1943-45, ETO. Mem. Assn. CLUs (cert.), Conf. Casualty Ins. Cos. (dir. 1980-83, pres. 1983-84), Golden Key Soc., Nat. Assn. Mut. Ins. Cos. (bd. dirs. 1985-87). Republican. Presbyterian. Lodges: Lions, Masons, Shriners. Home: 4295 Stratton Rd Columbus OH 43216

OUSSANI, JAMES JOHN, stapling company executive; b. Bklyn., Jan. 3, 1920; s. John Thomas and Clara (Tager) O.; B.M.E., Pratt Inst., 1938-42; m. Lorraine G. Tutundgy, Apr. 25, 1954; children—James J., Gregory P., Rita C. Dir. research, mfg. Supertronic Co., N.Y.C., 1943-46; sr. partner Perl-Oussani Machine Mfg. Co., N.Y.C., 1946-49; founder The Staplex Co., Bklyn., 1949, pres., 1949—; exec. dir. Lourdes Realty Corp.; dir. Junios Corp., Gregrita Realty Corp.; producer air sampling equipment for radioactive fallout AEC, 1951—. Mem. Bur. Research Air Pollution Control, Pres.'s Council on Youth Opportunity, Cardinal's Com. for Edn.; trustee Ch. of Virgin Mary; founder, bd. dirs. Oussani Found.; mem. cardinal's com. of laity, bishop's com. of laity; mem. council St. John's U.; mem. Coll. of Boca Raton Aux. Recipient Blue Ribbon Mining award, Sch. Mgmt. award, Aerospace Pride Achievement award. Mem. Adminstrv. Mgmt. Soc., Office Adminstrn. Assn., Nat. Stationery and Office Equipment Assn., Office Execs. Assn., Nat. Office Machine Mfg. Assn., Nat. Office Machine Dealers Assn., Nat. Office Products Assn., Bus. Equipment Mfrs. Assn., Our Lady Perpetual Help Holy Name Soc., Knights of Holy Sepulchre, Knights of St. Gregory, Knights of Malta. Clubs: Rotary, Salaam (N.Y.C.); Mahopac Golf (Lake Mahopac, N.Y.); Boca Raton Hotel. Inventor automatic electric stapling machine. Patentee in field. Office: 777 5th Ave Brooklyn NY 11232

OUTLAW, ARTHUR ROBERT, mayor; b. Mobile, Ala., Sept. 8, 1926; s. George Cabell and Mayme Lily (Ricks) O.; m. Dorothy Turner Smith; children: Karen Ann Outlaw Fendcey, Arthur R. Jr., Mary Gaye. BA, Spring Hill Coll., Mobile, Ala., 1950. Acct. Holliman, Childree and Ramsey, Mobile, 1949-52; asst. auditor Morrison, Inc., Mobile, 1952; sec., treas., vice chmn. bd. various orgns.; city mayor City of Mobile, 1985—; bd. dirs. Morrison, Inc., Mobile, Amsouth Bank, N.A., Birmingham, Outlaw Baking Co., Inc., Mobile. City commr. City of Mobile, 1965-69. Served with USAF, 1945-47. Republican. Roman Catholic. Office: City Hall PO Box 1827 Mobile AL 36633 other: Morrison Inc PO Box 160266 Mobile AL 36625

OUZTS, WILLIAM TRUMAN, oil company executive; b. Devol, Okla., Sept. 1, 1933; s. John William and Mildred Opal (england) O.; m. Barbara Joan McKinney, Nov. 3, 1953; 1 child, Stephanie Sue Ouzts Davage. BS in Engring. Physics, U. Tulsa, 1960. With Shell Oil Co., various locations, 1960-74; mgr. engring Shell Oil Co., Houston, 1974-79, mgr. purchasing, 1979-81; exec. v.p. Damson Oil Corp., Houston, 1981—; also bd. dirs. Damson Oil Corp., N.Y.C. Pres. Del Lago Property Owners Assn., Montgomery, Tex., 1986—, Del Lago Utility Co., Houston, 1987—. With U.S. Army, 1953-55. Mem. Am. Petroleum Inst., Soc. Petroleum Engrs., Del Lago Country Club. Republican. Methodist. Home: 18 La Jolla Circle Montgomery TX 77356 Office: Damson Oil Corp PO Box 4391 Houston TX 77210

OVERBECK, GENE EDWARD, airline executive, lawyer; b. St. Louis, June 16, 1929; s. Harry C. and Edna (Kessler) O.; m. Patricia June Bay, Oct. 5, 1957; children: Richard, Thomas, Elizabeth, Katherine. B.A., U. Mich., 1951, J.D., 1953. Bar: Mich. 1953, Mo. 1954, N.Y. 1958, Tex. 1980. Asso. firm Sullivan & Cromwell, N.Y.C., 1957-59; gen. atty. Am. Airlines, 1959-67, v.p., gen. counsel, 1967-72, sr. v.p., 1972—. Served with AUS, 1954-57. Club: Larchmont Yacht. Home: 4634 Charleston Terr NW Washington DC 20007 Office: Am Airlines Inc 1101 17th St NW Washington DC 20036 Other: Am Airlines Inc PO Box 619616 Dallas/Ft Worth Airport Dallas TX 75261

OVERCASH, REECE A., JR., financial company executive; b. Charlotte, N.C., June 15, 1926; s. Reece A. and Mary Louise (Daniel) O.; m. Christa Lee Anderson; children—Susan Kay, Mary Ann Overcash Austin, Sarah Lee, Alex. B.B.A., U. N.C., 1946. With Am. Credit Corp., Charlotte, 1952-75, pres., 1970-75; pres. Assocs. Corp. N.Am., Dallas, 1975-81, chmn., chief exec. officer, 1978—; dir. Assocs. Corp. N.Am. (now The Associates), Dallas; chmn. Assocs. First Capital Corp.; sr. exec. v.p. Gulf & Western Inc., N.Y.C., 1983-87; pres. Gulf & Western Fin. Services Group, N.Y.C., 1987—; bd. dirs. Duke Power Co., Charlotte, Belo Corp., Dallas, Aancor Holdings, Dallas. Mem. North Tex. Commn.; bd. dirs. Dallas Citizens Council, 1986—; campaign chmn.United Way Met. Dallas, 1979, exec. com., from 1979, pres. exec. com., 1981, bd. dirs. 1986—; v.p. Met. Dallas, 1980-81, pres., from 1981, bd. dirs., 1978—; bd. dirs. Dallas County Community Coll. Dist. Found., 1977—, vice chmn., 1978-79, chmn., 1979-81; mem. consumer adv. council Fed. Res. Bd., 1976-78; bd. trustees Dallas Baptist U., 1986—; bd. dirs. Circle Ten Council Boy Scouts Am., 1978-86, North Tex. Commn., 1977-85, Better Bus. Bur. Met. Dallas, 1979—, Community Council Greater Dallas, 1981; mem. devel. council U. Dallas Campaign, 1980; vice chmn. patron gifts com. Dallas Mus. Fine Arts, 1980; adv. council Credit Research Ctr., Purdue U., 1980; bd. overseers Wingate Coll., Charlotte, 1979—; bd. dirs. Dallas County chpt. ARC, 1982—; mem. bus. devel. com. So. Meth. U., 1985; mem. strategic planning com. United Way Am., 1985; chmn. bd. Dallas United Adv. Council, 1986—; bd. trustees Dallas Bapt. U., 1988—; exec. bd. Cox Sch. Bus. of So. Meth. U., 1983—; adv. com. Dallas County Treasurer's Office, 1987. Served with inf., AUS, World War II. Named Man of Yr., Charlotte, 1972; recipient Disting. Bus. Leadership award U. Tex., 1988. Mem. Dallas C. of C. (bd. dirs. 1977-80, 86—, chmn. adv. com. Leadership Dallas program 1979-80, 86), Tex. Research League (bd. dirs. 1977—), Am. Fin. Services Assn. (bd. dirs., exec. com. 1966-83, Distinguished Service award, 1973). Baptist. Clubs: Myers Park Country, City (Charlotte); Brookhollow Country, Petroleum (Dallas). Office: Assocs Corp N Am 250 Carpenter Frwy Irving TX 75062

OVERHOLT, MILES HARVARD, cable television consultant; b. Glendale, Calif., Sept. 30, 1921; s. Miles Harvard and Alma Overholt; A.B., Harvard Coll., 1943; m. Jessie Foster, Sept. 18, 1947; children—Miles Harvard, Keith Foster. Mktg. analyst Dun & Bradstreet, Phila., 1947-48; collection mgr. Standard Oil of Calif., Los Angeles, 1948-53; br. mgr. RCA Service Co., Phila., 1953-63, ops. mgr. Classified Aerospace project RCA, Riverton, N.J., 1963; pres. CPS, Inc., Paoli, Pa., 1964-67; mem. pres.'s exec. com. Gen. Time Corp., Mesa, Ariz., 1970-78; gen. mgr., dir. service Talley Industries, Mesa, 1967-78; v.p., gen. mgr. Northwest Entertainment Network, Inc., Seattle, 1979-81; mcpl. cable cons., 1981—. Served with USMCR, 1943-46. Decorated Bronze Star, Purple Heart (two). Mem. Assn. Home Appliance Mfrs., Nat. Assn. Microwave Distbn. Service Cos. Editor, publisher Mcpl. Cable Regulation Newsletter. Club: Harvard (N.Y.C.). Home: 8320 Frederick Pl Edmonds WA 98020 Office: NW Entertainment Network 4517 California Ave SW Ste B Seattle WA 98116

OVERMAN, DEAN LEE, lawyer, investor, author, real estate developer; b. Harvey, Ill., Oct. 9, 1943; s. Harold Levon and Violet Claire (True) O.; m. Linda Jane Olsen, Sept. 6, 1969; children: Elisabeth True, Christiana Hart. BA, Hope Coll., 1965; student, Princeton (N.J.) Sem., 1965-66; JD, U. Calif., Berkeley, 1969; postgrad. in bus., U. Chgo., 1974, U. Calif. Bar: Ill. 1969, D.C. 1977. Assoc. to ptnr. D'Ancona, Pflaum et al., Chgo., 1970-75; white house fellow Washington, 1975-76; assoc. dir. Domestic Council The White House, Washington, 1976-77; sr. ptnr. Winston-Strawn, Washington, 1977—; cons. The White House; spl. counsel to Gov. James Thompson, Springfield, Ill.; adj. faculty in secured financing U. Va. Law Sch., Charlottesville; vice chmn. J.F. Forstmann Co. Author: Toward a National Policy on State and Local Government Finance, 1976, Effective Writing Tecniques, 1980, (with others) Financing Equipment, 1973, Sales and Financing Under the Revised UCC, 1975; monthly newspaper column Chgo. Daily Law Bull.; contbr. articles to profl. jours. Commencement speaker Hope Coll., Holland, Mich., 1978. Mem. ABA, Ill. Bar Assn., D.C. Bar Assn., Chgo. Bar Assn. Office: Winston & Strawn 2550 M St NW Suite 500 Washington DC 20037

OVERMYER, JOHN EUGENE, manufacturing company executive; b. Ft. Wayne, Ind., Mar. 16, 1933; s. Arthur N. and Glady M. (Fry) O.; m. Shirley A. Johnson, Dec. 27, 1956; children: Patrick T., Michael E., Kathleen M., Andrew V., Thomas V., John J., Anne I., Maureen R., Marie. BS, Ind. U., 1957. Mem. acctg. dept., speciality budget tax and spl. projects Gen. Tel., Ft. Wayne, 1957-62; sales planning Magnavox, Ft. Wayne, 1962; budget dir. Tokheim Corp., Ft. Wayne, 1962-68, contr., 1968-74, treas., 1974-79, v.p., treas., 1979-86, pres., 1986—; also bd. dirs. Tokheim Corp.; chmn. bd. Tokheim Corp., Ft. Wayne, 1988—; bd. dirs. Nat. Controls Corp., West Chicago, Ill., Tokheim B.V., Leiderdorp, Netherlands, Tokheim Investment Corp., Houston, Tokheim Ltd., Glenrothes, Scotland, Tokheim South Africa Pty, Ltd., Johannesburg. Treas., bd. dirs. United Way Allen County, Ft. Wayne, 1976-87, chmn. 1987-88, pres., 1987-88; active fin. commn. Ancilla Systems, Chgo.; trustee St. Francis Coll., Ft. Wayne, 1984-87. Cpl. U.S. Army, 1953-55. Named to Acad. Alumni Fellows Sch. Bus. Ind. U., 1988. Mem. Fin. Execs. Inst. (v.p. 1972, pres. 1987), Nat. Assn. Accts. (v.p. 1964, pres. 1976, bd. dirs., Stuart Cameron McClead Soc. award 1975), Nat. Assn. Mfrs. (bd. dirs.), Ind. Mfrs. Assn. (bd. dirs.), Nat. Assn. of Mfrs. and Ind. Mfrs. Assn. (bd. dirs.), Lions (pres Leo, Ind. 1970). Republican. Roman Catholic. Office: Tokheim Corp PO Box 360 Fort Wayne IN 46801

OVERTON, GEORGE WASHINGTON, lawyer; b. Hinsdale, Ill., Jan. 25, 1918; s. George Washington and Florence Mary (Darlington) O.; m. Jane Vincent Harper, Sept. 1, 1941; children—Samuel Harper, Peter Darlington, Ann Vincent. A.B., Harvard U., 1940; J.D., U. Chgo., 1946. Bar: Ill. 1947, U.S. Dist. Ct. (no. dist.) Ill. 1947, U.S. Supreme Ct. 1951. Assoc.l Pope & Ballard, Chgo., 1946-48; ptnr. Overton & Babcock, Chgo., 1948-51, Taylor, Miller, Busch & Magner, Chgo., 1951-60; pvt. practice Chgo., 1960; ptnr. Overton, Schwartz & Fritts and predecessor cos., Chgo., 1960-81; of counsel Wildman Harrold Allen & Dixon, Chgo., 1981—; bd. dirs. Ill. Inst. Continuing Legal Edn., 1974-81, chmn. 1980-81. Contbr. articles to profl. jours. Bd. dirs. Open Lands Project, 1961—, pres., 1978-81; bd. dirs. Upper Ill. Valley Assn., 1981—, chmn., 1981-84; mem. com. on profl. responsibility of Ill. Supreme Ct., 1986—. 1st lt. U.S. Army, 1942-45. Mem. ABA (mem. com. on counsel responsibility 1985—), Ill. Bar Assn., Chgo. Bar Assn. (bd. mgrs. 1981-83), Assn. Bar City N.Y., University Club, Tavern Club. Home: 5648 Dorchester Ave Chicago IL 60637 Office: 1 IBM Plaza Chicago IL 60611

OVERTON, ROSILYN GAY HOFFMAN, financial services executive; b. Corsicana, Tex., July 10, 1942; d. Billy Clarence and Ima Elise (Gay) Hoffman; m. Aaron Lewis Overton, Jr., July 2, 1960 (div. Mar. 1975); children: Aaron Lewis III, Adam Jerome. BS in Math., Wright State U., Dayton, Ohio, 1972, MS in Applied Econs. (fellow), 1973; postgrad. N.Y. U. Grad. Sch. Bus., 1974-76; Cert. Coll. Fin. Planning, 1987. Research analyst Nat. Security Agy., Dept. Def., 1962-67; bus. reporter Dayton Jour.-Herald, 1973-74; economist First Nat. City Bank, N.Y.C., 1974, A.T. & T. Co., 1974-75; broker Merrill Lynch, N.Y.C., 1975-80; asst. v.p. E.F. Hutton & Co., N.Y.C., 1980-84; v.p., nat. mktg. dir. investment products Manhattan Nat. Corp., 1984-86; pres. R.H. Overton Co., N.Y.C., 1986—; ptnr. Brown & Overton Fin. Svcs., 1987—. Named Businesswoman of Yr., N.Y.C., 1976. Mem. Nat., N.Y. Assns. Bus. Economists, Nat. Fedn. Bus. and Profl. Women, Internat. Assn. Fin. Planners, Women's Econ. Roundtable, Gotham Bus. and Profl. Womens Club, Wright State U. Alumni Assn., Mensa, Zonta. Methodist. Office: 20 Exchange Pl New York NY 10005

OWCZA, JURGEN, hotel corporation executive. Mng. dir. SRS Hotels, N.Y.C. Office: Steigenberger Hotels Corp 40 E 49th St 7th Floor New York NY 10017 *

OWEN, DANIEL BRUCE, building products company executive; b. Waterloo, Iowa, Apr. 5, 1950; s. Emlyn and Gladys Alyda (Wangen) O.; m. Suzy Williams, Aug. 5, 1972; children: Carolyn Ann, Thomas Alexander. BS, Eastern Ill. U., 1972; MBA, Central Mich. U., 1975. Internal auditor Amoco Corp., Chgo., 1975-77, sr. internal auditor, 1977-78; operational auditor Abbott Labs., North Chicago, Ill., 1978-80; sr. mfg. cost analyst Abbot Labs., North Chicago, Ill., 1980-81; controller Bulldog Jordan Co. div. Newell Co., Ft. Lauderdale, Fla., 1981-84, v.p., controller, 1984-85; corp. controller Miller Industries Inc., Miami, Fla., 1985, dir., sec.-treas., corp. controller, 1985-86, dir., pres., chief exec. officer, 1986—. Bd. dirs. New Century Town Condo Assn., Vernon Hills, Ill., 1979; pres. bd. dirs. New Century Town Homeowner's Assn., Vernon Hills, 1980. Mem. Pres.' Assn., Sigma Iota Epsilon. Republican. Presbyterian. Home: 721 NW 67th Ave Fort Lauderdale FL 33317 Office: Miller Industries Inc 16295 NW 13th Ave Miami FL 33169

OWEN, H. MARTYN, lawyer; b. Decatur, Ill., Oct. 23, 1929; s. Honore Martyn and Virginia (Hunt) O.; m. Candace Catlin Benjamin, June 21, 1952; children—Leslie W., Peter H., Douglas P. A.B., Princeton U., 1951; LL.B., Harvard U., 1954. Bar: Conn. 1954. Assoc. Shipman & Goodwin, Hartford, Conn., 1958-61, ptnr., 1961—. Mem. Simsbury (Conn.) Zoning Bd. Appeals, 1961-67, Simsbury Zoning Commn., 1967-79; sec. Capitol Region Planning Agy., 1965-66; bd. dirs. Symphony Soc. Greater Hartford, 1967-73; trustee Renbrook Sch., West Hartford, Conn., 1963-72, treas., 1964-68, pres., 1968-72, hon. life trustee, 1972—; trustee Simsbury Free Library, 1970-84; pres. Hartford Grammar Sch., 1987—, trustee; corporator Hartford Hosp., Inst. Living, Hartford. Lt. USNR, 1954-57. Mem. ABA, Conn. Bar Assn., Hartford County Bar Assn., Am. Law Inst. Republican. Episcopalian. Clubs: Hartford; Princeton (N.Y.C.); Ivy (Princeton, N.J.); Dauntless (Essex, Conn.). Home: 44 Pinnacle Mountain Rd Simsbury CT 06070 Office: 799 Main St Hartford CT 06103

OWEN, HERBERT RODNEY, data processing executive; b. Bremerton, Wash., Oct. 10, 1935; s. Herbert Harry Owen and Maude Winona (Byington) Garner; children: Jeffrey Rod, Perry Jay. BSCE, Walla Walla Coll., 1962; BS in Phys. Scis., Wash. State U., 1973; M in Internat. Mgmt., Am. Grad. Sch. Internat. Mgmt., 1974. ADP intern Mgmt. Engring. Tng. Agy., Rock Island, Ill., 1963-64; ADP dir. Naval Sta., Keflavik, Iceland, 1968-70; ADP project mgr. Naval Ships System Command, Bremerton, 1970-74; supr. systems analyst Naval Supply Depot, Subic Bay, Philippines, 1975-79; ADP coordinator Far East Engring. Dist., Seoul, Republic of Korea, 1981-83; ADP security officer Trident Tng. Facility, Bangor, Wash., 1979-81, 83-85; ADP dir. Commdr. Fleet Activities, Okinawa, Japan, 1985-89; dir. mgmt. info. systems Fort Ord, Calif., 1989—. Bus. mgr. Northwest Chess Mag. Mem. U.S. Chess Fedn. (sr. tournament dir.), Wash. Chess Fedn. (bd. dirs.), Am. Bowling Assn. (regional pres.). Republican. Clubs: Flying (Keflavik), Toastmasters. Office: Navy Air Facility Kadena ADP Commdr Fleet Activities Okinawa Seattle WA 98770-1150

OWEN, JOHN LAVERTY, human resources executive; b. Mayfield, Ky., July 28, 1923; s. John Clarence and Lydia (Laverty) O.; m. Marjory Clara Wallace, June 29, 1946; children: John Wallace, David William, Jeffrey Daniel. BA magna cum laude, Westminster (Mo.) Coll., 1944; postgrad. Purdue U., 1945; MS in Psychology, Pa. State U., 1951. With Hamilton Watch Co., Lancaster, Pa., 1946-70, staff personnel services dir., 1963-70, corporate employee relations dir. HMW Industries, Inc., Lancaster, 1970-77, dir. human resources Hamilton Tech., Inc., Lancaster, 1977-80, v.p. human resources and public relations, 1980-84, sec., v.p. human resources and pub. relations, 1984-85; v.p. human resources Gen. Def. Corp., York, Pa., 1985-88; pres. Performance Systems Internat., cons., Lancaster, 1984—; v.p., cons. Greenfield Assocs. Ltd., Lancaster, 1988—. Bd. dirs. Lancaster County United Way, 1972-78, 84-86, Lancaster chpt. Nat. Urban League, 1972-81, Assos. in Downtown Lancaster, 1981-86, Lancaster YMCA, 1984-86, Lancaster Area Arts Council, 1987—; bd. dirs. Lancaster Guidance Clinic, 1959-63, pres., 1961-63. Lic. psychologist, Pa. Mem. Am., Eastern, Pa. psychol. assns., Am. Mgmt. Assn., Am. Soc. for Personnel Adminstrn. (accredited exec.), Am. Soc. Tng. and Devel., Lancaster Chamber Commerce and Industry, Omicron Delta Kappa, Psi Chi, Phi Kappa Phi, Delta Tau Delta. Republican. Presbyn. Office: Greenfield Assocs Ltd 1853 William Penn Way Lancaster PA 17605

OWEN, KAREN CORDELIA, estate planner; b. Whittier, Calif., Sept. 11, 1943; d. Ralph and Janet Elaine (Benito) O.; m. William Robert Ives, July 24, 1963 (div. Aug. 1976); children: Janet Ellen Ives, JoAnn Elaine Ives. Grad. high sch., Yucaipa, Calif. Owner, operator Ives Electric Cars, Romoland, Calif., 1968-72; cost acct., office mgr. Harvill Machine Co., Perris, Calif., 1972-74; owner LaGrange (Wyo.) Bar, 1974-81; planner, cons. ARCO Securities, Inc., Cheyenne, Wyo., 1982-88; br. mgr. Chatfield Investment Co., Cheyenne, 1988—; mem. arbitration bd. Better Bus. Bur., Ft. Collins, Colo., 1985. Committeewoman Rep. Party, LaGrange, 1981. Mem. Nat. Assn. Securities Dealers (fin. ops. prin. 1985, registered rep. 1983, supr. prin. 1983), Calif. Scholastic Fedn. (life). Baptist. Office: ARCO Securities Inc PO Box 6343 Cheyenne WY 82001

OWEN, MARTIN FREDERICK, oil company executive, lawyer; b. Houston, June 26, 1932; s. William Franklin and May Elizabeth (Spraul) O.; m. Nancy Elizabeth Harwell, Aug. 31, 1957; children: Scott Martin, Melissa Kay, Steven Harwell. BBA, U. Tex., 1958, JD, 1959. Bar: Tex. 1959. Of counsel Humble Oil and Refining Co., Houston, 1959-66; of counsel Duval Corp., Houston, 1966-69, v.p. legal, 1969-81, sr. v.p., 1981-84; gen. counsel Pennzoil Co., Houston, 1984—. Served to sgt. USMC, 1952-54. Mem. ABA, Tex. Bar Assn., Houston Bar Assn., Internat. Bar Assn., Internat. and Comparative Law Ctr. (bd. dirs. SW Legal Found. 1986—), Middle East Inst. (dir.). Presbyterian. Office: Pennzoil Co 700 Milam Houston TX 77002

OWEN, PATRICIA ROSE, investment company executive; b. Chattanooga, Feb. 13, 1955; d. David G. and Elsie E. (Newman) Owen; m. Joseph Edward Thompson, May 2, 1987. AA, Broward Community Coll., 1974; BA, U. South Fla., 1976; MBA, Nova U., 1985. Cert. USCG ocean operator, 1983. Tchr. Dade County Sch. System, Miami, 1976-78; v.p. Securities Rsch. and Mgmt., Inc., Ft. Lauderdale, Fla., 1977-82, exec. v.p., 1982-84, dir., 1984—, pres., chief exec. officer, 1986—. Author numerous poems. Episcopalian. Clubs: Coconut Grove Sailing (Miami, Fla.); Seven Seas Cruising Assn. (Ft. Lauderdale, Fla.), Cruising Assn. (London). Office: Securities Rsch & Mgmt Inc 800 Corporate Dr Ste 602 Fort Lauderdale FL 33334

OWEN, ROBERT RANDOLPH, accountant; b. Ardmore, Okla., June 24, 1939; s. Buford Randolph and Ruth Marie (Cleeton) O.; m. Patra Malinda Randolph, June 20, 1958; children: Stacy Malinda Owen Hodges, Mindy Carol Owen Long. BBA with high honors, So. Meth. U., 1961; postgrad., Harvard U., 1985. CPA, Tex. Various positions Alford, Meroney & Co., Dallas, 1961-67, mgr., 1967-69, ptnr., 1969-73, mng. ptnr. Dallas office, 1975-78, firm mng. ptnr., 1978-80; dep. regional mng. ptnr. S.W. region Arthur Young & Co., Dallas, 1980-83, ptnr., nat. dir. entrepreneurial svcs., 1983-86, ptnr., nat. dir. indsl. specialization, 1986—. Author, editor: The Arthur Young Guide to Financing for Growth, 1986. Capt. USAF, 1961-64. Mem. Tex. Soc. CPAs (pres. Dallas chpt. 1988—, bd. dirs. 1986—), AICPA. Baptist. Office: Arthur Young & co 2121 San Jacinto Ste 300 Dallas TX 75201

OWEN, THOMAS JOHN, banker; b. Washington, Nov. 27, 1934; s. Thornton Washington and Collette (Radlebeck) O.; m. Louise Daniel, Aug. 27, 1960; children—Elizabeth W., Jeannette T. BA, Williams Coll., 1957. Real estate appraiser Thomas J. Owen & Sons, Washington, 1959-76, pres., chmn., 1965-76; pres. Perpetual Fed. Savs. and Loan, Washington, 1976-79;, chmn., chief exec. officer Perpetual Savs. Bank, 1979—; trustee Washington Mut. Investors Fund., 1982—. Trustee George Washington U., 1985—; bd. regents Md. Univ. System, 1988—; pres. greater Washington Bd. of Trade, 1983; trustee Fed. City Council, 1975—. Served with USMC, 1957-59. Recipient Outstanding Community Service award United Black Fund, Washington, 1983, Service award Assn. for Renewal in Edn., Inc., Washington, 1983, Leadership award Housing Counseling Service, Inc., Washington, 1983. Mem. Soc. Real Estate Appraisers (bd. dirs., officer), Am. Inst. Real Estate Appraisers (bd. dirs.). Clubs: Metropolitan (Washington); Chevy Chase (Md.). Office: Perpetual Savs Bank 2034 Eisenhower Ave Alexandria VA 22314

OWEN, THOMAS LLEWELLYN, senior investment executive; b. Patchogue, N.Y., June 24, 1928; s. Griffith Robert and Jeanette Roberts (Hatfield) O.; A.B. in Econs., Coll. William and Mary, 1951; postgrad. Columbia U., 1952, N.Y. Inst. Fin., 1960-62; M.B.A., N.Y. U., 1966. Exec. trainee Shell Oil Co., N.Y.C. and Indpls., 1951-59, supr., 1958-59; petroleum and chem. investment analyst Paine, Webber, Jackson & Curtis, N.Y.C., 1959-62; sr. oil investment analyst DuPont Investment Interests, Wilmington, Del., N.Y.C., 1962-66, asst. dir. research, 1964-66; v.p., sr. investment officer, mem. policy, investment coms. Nat. Securities and Research Corp., N.Y.C., 1966-75; sr. investment exec., v.p., portfolio mgr. F. Eberstadt & Co. and Eberstadt Asset Mgmt., Inc., N.Y.C., 1975—, mem. policy com., 1979—, also dir. portfolio rev. com. Mem. N.Y. Soc. Security Analysts, Oil Analysts Group N.Y., Am. Econ. Assn., Investment Assn. N.Y., Am. Petroleum Inst., Nat. Assn. Petroleum Investment Analysts, Internat. Assn. Energy Economists. Contbr. chpt. "Oil and Gas Industries" to Financial Analysts Handbook, 1975. Home: 251 E 32d St New York NY 10016 Office: Eberstadt Asset Mgmt Inc 61 Broadway New York NY 10006

OWEN, WARREN HERBERT, utility executive; b. Rock Hill, S.C., Jan. 8, 1927; s. Warren Herbert and Margaret Elizabeth (White) O.; m. Virginia Lea Boulware, Oct. 22, 49; children: Virginia Ann, Carol Elizabeth, Susan Laine. B.M.E., Clemson (S.C.) U., 1947; JD (hon.), Clemson U., 1988. With Duke Power Co., 1948—; prin. mech. engr., design engring. dept. Duke Power Co., Charlotte, 1966-71; v.p. design engring. Duke Power Co., 1971-78, sr. v.p. engring. and constrn., 1978-82, exec. v.p. engring. and constrn., 1982-84, exec. v.p. engring., constrn. and prodn., 1988—, also dir. Recipient Robinson award Duke Power Co., 1965, Philip T. Sprague award Instrument Soc. Am., 1970. Fellow ASME (James L. Landis medal 1987); Mem. Am. Nuclear Soc., Atomic Indsl. Forum (Clyde Lilly award 1981), N.C. Soc. Engrs. (Engr. of Yr. award 1984), Profl. Engrs. N.C., Charlotte Engrs. Club (Disting. Service award 1981), Nat. Acad. Engring. Episcopalian. Lodge: Rotary. Home: 2131 Valencia Terr Charlotte NC 28226 Office: Duke Power Co 422 S Church St Charlotte NC 28242

OWENS, ROGER L., electrical engineer; b. Abilene, Tex., July 9, 1943; s. Lewis E. and Audrey (Dillenger) O.; m. Rosemary Donald, May 22, 1962 (div. 1977); children: Deborah, Michele; m. Patricial Williford, June 9, 1978; children: Jessica, Samantha. BSEE, N.C. State U., 1968, MSEE, 1969, postgrad., 1974-75. Enlisted USN, 1961, advanced through grades to cmmdr., 1961-81, ret., 1981; sr. engr. Travelers Ins., Charlotte, N.C., 1981-83; v.p. Furmanite Am., Inc., Virginia Beach, Va., 1983-86; prin. McDowell Owens Engring., Kingwood, Tex., 1986—; assoc. prof. George Washington U., Washington D.C., 1972; prof. engring. U. N.C., Raleigh, 1983, U. Va., Richmond, U. Tex., Austin, 1986. Contbr. articles to various. jours. Named Sci. scholar USN, 1965. Mem. Nat. Soc. Prof. Engrs., IEEE, N.C. Soc. of Boiler Inspectors, Tex. Soc. Profl. Engrs. Republican. Roman Catholic. Office: McDowell Owens Engring Inc Tex Commerce Bank Bldg 1075 Kingwood Dr Ste 100 Kingwood TX 77339

OWENS, WILLIAM ROBERT, utilities company executive; b. Syracuse, N.Y., May 12, 1932; s. William James and Florence Elizabeth (Haar) O.; m. Lois Ruth Gumprecht, Apr. 7, 1956; children: William Michael, Robert Joseph, Steven Patrick. BBA, Lemoyne Coll., 1953; MS in Edn., Syracuse U., 1985. Cert. flight and ground sch. instr. Svc. technician Carrier Corp., Syracuse, 1953, Porter-Cable Power Tool Co. div. Rockwell Mfg. Co., Syracuse, 1955-61; mgr. corp. systems devel. Crouse-Hinds Co., Syracuse, 1961-80, dir. corp. mgmt. systems, 1980-82; mgr. systems devel. Niagara Mohawk Power Corp., Syracuse, 1982—; founder, chief exec. officer Mgmt. Solutions, Inc., Syracuse, 1985—; instr. systems and data processing Auburn (N.Y.) Community Coll., 1967—, cons. data processing adv. com. 1969-75; guest lectr. Syracuse U. Sch. Mgmt., 1977. Author booklet on aviation, 1978. With U.S. Army, 1953-55. Mem. Assn. Systems Mgmt. (pres. Cen. N.Y. chpt. 1968-69, Merit award 1970, Nat. Achievement award 1971), CAP (asst. squadron comdr. 1975-76), Cen. N.Y. Pilots Assn. (pres. 1973-74), Syracuse Systems Execs. Assn. (co-founder 1971). Home: 4062 Pawnee Dr Liverpool NY 13090 Office: Niagara Mohawk Power Corp 300 Erie Blvd W Syracuse NY 13202

OWENSBY, BRENDA GAIL EARL, credit union executive, educator; b. Knoxville, Tenn., Oct. 1, 1950; d. Eulas Everette Earl and Maxine (Wyrick) Rorex; m. Robbie L. Owensby, Oct. 20, 1973. BS, U. Tenn., 1972, PhD, 1985; MS, Augusta Coll., 1978. Lic. psychologist. Grad. teaching asst., counseling psychology intern U. Tenn, Knoxville, 1978-82; assoc. dir. Appalachian Adolescent Health and Edn. Project, Morristown, Tenn., 1982-85; dir. human resources ORNL Fed. Credit Union, Oak Ridge, Tenn., 1985-89; v.p. ORNL Fed. Credit Union, Oak Ridge, 1989—; mem. adj. faculty Tusculum Coll., Greeneville, Tenn., 1985—. With U.S. Army, 1971-78, maj. res. Mem. Am. Soc. Tng. and Devel., Credit Union Execs. Soc. (chmn. com. human resources Tenn. chpt. 1987—), Tenn. Valley Personnel Assn., , Phi Delta Kappa. Presbyterian. Office: ORNL Fed Credit Union 221 S Rutgers St Oak Ridge TN 37830

OWEN-TROWBRIDGE, MARGARET JOSEFA, small business consultant; b. Clark AFB, Philippines, Dec. 14, 1954; d. Charles Austin and Marina (Gomez) Owen; m. David Michael Begin, May 10, 1975 (div. 1982); m. Douglas Wayne Trowbridge, Sept. 29, 1985; 1 child, Whitney Lorraine. AA, San Bernardino Valley Coll., 1982. Bookkeeper Kingsway Services, Riverside, Calif., 1981-82, Howard M. Leff and Assocs., Riverside, 1982, Riverside Vis. and Conv. Ctr., 1982-83; office mgr. Atlantic Services, Wichita, Kans., 1983-85; owner, mgr. Owen-Trowbridge and Assocs., Towanda, Kans., 1985—; cons. Small Bus. Devel. Ctr., Wichita, 1986—. Home and Office: 556 N 8th St Towanda KS 67144

OWINGS, JOHN STEVEN, maintenance executive; b. Chester, S.C., Feb. 10, 1957; s. John Luther and Valeria (Phillips) O.; m. Cynthia Ellen Barwick, Oct. 1, 1983; 1 child, Amelia Revay. Student, York Tech. Coll., 1987—. With maintenance dept. Springs Mills, Inc., Lancaster, S.C., 1982-85; technician Millwright Glass Fiber Techs., Chester, S.C., 1985-86; maintenance specialist Duracell U.S.A., Lancaster, 1986—. With USMC, 1977-82. Mem. Bass Masters Club. Democrat. Baptist. Home: 300 Duke St Great Falls SC 29055 Office: Duracell Inc Lancaster Ave Lancaster SC 29720

OWNBEY, LENORE F. DALY, real estate investment specialist; b. Fremont, Nebr., Feb. 24; d. Joseph E. and Anna R. (Godel) Daly; m. Amos

B. Ownbey, June 18, 1948; children: Kenton, Stephen. BBA, U. Nebr. Cert. comml. investment mem. Real estate and comml. investment specialist Denver, 1976—; lectr. in field. Writer, speaker Investment, Business and Personal Skills, Motivational and Inspirational. Mem. Nat. Speakers Assn., Colo. Chpt. Nat. Speakers Assn., Internat. Platform Assn., Denver Bd. Realtors, Colo. Assn. Realtors, Nat. Assn. Realtors, Realtors Nat. Mktg. Inst. (Cert. Comml. Investment Mem. Colo.-Wyo. chpt. #6), Real Estate Educators Assn., Colo. Real Estate Educators Assn., Am. Real Estate Soc.

OWOC, VICTOR A., utility executive; b. New Castle, Pa., Mar. 24, 1924; s. Aloysius J. and Hedwig B. (Mateja) O.; m. Clara J. Pilch, June 7, 1947; children: Kathryn, Diane, Richard, Kimberly. B.S. in Elec. Engring, U. Pitts., 1948; M.S. in Physics, John Carroll U., Cleve., 1956; D.Sc. (hon.), Alliance Coll., Cambridge Springs, Pa., 1979. Sr. engr. tech. studies dept. Cleve. Elec. Illuminating Co., 1948-51; sr. analyst fin. and rate research dept. Gilbert Assos., N.Y.C., 1952-60; with Ohio Edison Co., 1960—, v.p., 1967-68, dir., chief fin. officer, 1968-78, sr. v.p., chief fin. officer, 1978-79, exec. v.p., chief fin. officer, 1979—; dir. Pa. Power Co., Bank One Akron. Dir. Summit County chpt. ARC, 1982. Served with USAAF, 1942-45. Republican. Roman Catholic. Clubs: Fairlawn Country, Cascade, Sharon Golf. Office: Ohio Edison Co 76 S Main St Akron OH 44308

OXFORD, MICHAEL EDWARD, data processing executive, consultant; b. Gilmer, Tex., Feb. 1, 1947; s. Wilton Edward and Dorothy (Carpenter) O.; m. Valerie Titus (div. Jan. 1987); 1 child, Kirk Edward. BA, Tex. Luth. Coll., 1972; MA, Ball State U., 1974. Enlisted USAF, 1965, advanced through ranks to staff sgt., 1972, resigned, 1976; systems analyst NCR, Dallas, 1976-79; mgr. data processing Moncrief Oil/Montex Drilling, Ft. Worth, 1979—; owner, cons. Am. Nat. Computer cons., Ft. Worth, 1981-85; cons. Northwood Inst., Cedar Hill, Tex., 1985-88; lectr. External Degree Program, 1987. Chmn. Vote Bond Issue, North Richland Hills, Tex., 1986; vice chmn. library bd., North Richland Hills, 1986-88; bd. dirs. Casa R. Chacon Shelter, Ft. Worth, 1987—. Mem. Data Processing Mgmt. Assn. (v.p. 1984), SW NCR User Group (pres. 1985-86), Fedn. NCR User Groups (bd. dirs. 1988—, info. and publs. com. 1988—). Democrat. Unitarian. Home: 6913 Briardale Fort Worth TX 76180 Office: Moncrief Oil 9th and Commerce Fort Worth TX 76102

OXLEY, PHILIP, oil company executive; b. Utica, N.Y., Feb. 1, 1922; s. Chester Jay and Beatrice (Heller) O.; m. Dafna Ronn-Oxley; children by previous marriage: Christopher, Jonathan, Timothy, Philip, Patricia. BA, Denison U., 1943; MA, Columbia U., 1948, PhD, 1952. Instr., asst. prof. geology Hamilton Coll., Clinton, N.Y., 1948-53; geologist Standard Oil Co. Calif., 1953-57; dist. geologist, also div. exploration mgr. Tenn. Gas Transmission Co., 1957-61; exploration mgr., v.p. domestic exploration Signal Oil & Gas Co., Los Angeles, 1961-69; exec. v.p. Tex. Crude Oil Co., Houston, 1969-71; geol. mgr., exec. v.p., pres. Tenneco Oil Exploration and Prodn. Co., Houston, 1971-87; chmn. Tenneco Europe Ltd., London, 1987-89; prof., dir. minerals and energy rsch. ctr. U. Colo., Boulder, 1989—. Former trustee Denison U.; former chmn. so. regional bd. Inst. Internat. Edn.; former pres. Stavanger-Houston Sister City Soc. Served to lt. (j.g.) USNR, 1943-46. Fellow Geol. Soc. Am.; mem. Assn. Am. Petroleum Geologists, Nat. Ocean Industries Assn. (bd. dirs.), Houston Geol. Soc., Geology Found. U. Houston (past chmn. bd.), Sigma Xi, Phi Delta Theta. Republican. Office: U Colo Boulder Dept Geol Scis Campus Box 250 Boulder CO 80309-0250

OXNER, GLENN RUCKMAN, financial executive; b. Greenville, S.C., July 10, 1938; s. G. Dewey and Frances Oxner. Student Duke U., 1956-57; B.S., U.S.C., 1961. Trainee stock bd. broker Alester G. Furman Co., Greenville, S.C., 1961, v.p., 1964-67, exec. v.p., 1967-75; pres. S.C. Securities Co., 1975-77; sr. v.p. Interstate Securities, Charlotte, N.C., 1977-82, exec. v.p., 1982-85; chmn. First Tryon Securities, Charlotte, N.C., 1986-89; mng. dir. NCNB Investment Banking Co., Charlotte, 1989—. Served with U.S. Army, 1957. Mem. Nat. Assn. Security Dealers (com. chmn. dist. 7 1974, gov. 1981-84), Security Industry Assn. (gov. 1974), Security Dealers Carolinas (pres. 1977). Home: 203 Perrin Pl Charlotte NC 28207 Office: First Tryon Securities Inc 2550 NCNB Plaza Charlotte NC 28280

OYLER, WILLIAM KENNETT, III, manufacturing company executive; b. Lafayette, Ind., Apr. 15, 1958; s. William K. and Beverly (Taylor) O.; m. Katherine Wyatt, Apr. 13, 1983; 1 child, Elizabeth. Student, U. Colo., 1976-79; BS in Mktg., U. Louisville, 1980, MBA, 1982. Cash mgmt. officer Citizens Fidelity Bank, Louisville, 1980-82; asst. treas. Henry Vogt Machine Co., Louisville, 1982-84, treas., chief fin. officer, 1984-89, v.p. fin., chief fin. officer, 1989—; speaker in field. Mem. edit. bd. Cashflow Mag., Atlanta, 1985—; contbr. articles to profl. jours. Mgr. Henry Vogt Found., 1984—; treas. Jr. Achievement of Kentuckiana, Louisville, 1985—; vice chmn. fin. Nat. Safe Place YMCA Ctr. for Youth Alternative, Louisville, 1985—. Mem. Kentuckiana Cash Mgmt. Assn. (founder, treas.), Leadership Louisville. Republican. Presbyterian. Office: Henry Vogt Machine Co 1000 W Ormsby Louisville KY 40210

OZAG, DAVID, accountant, controller; b. Connellsville, Pa., Apr. 16, 1962; s. Joseph and Barbara Lee (Brady) O. BS, U. Md., 1984, postgrad., 1985; MBA, Mt. St. Mary's Coll., Md., 1987. CPA. Acct. Aronson Greene Fisher and Co., Bethesda, Md., 1984-86, Keller, Zanger and Co., Frederick, 1986-87; controller Grove Hill Enterprises Inc., Frederick, Md., 1985-88; div. mgr. Standard Fed. Savs. and Loan, Gaithersburg, Md., 1988—; basketball coach Gov. Thomas Johnson High Sch., Frederick, 1987—. Mem. Am. Inst. CPA's, Md. Assn. CPA's, U. Md. Alumni Assn. Republican. Roman Catholic. Home: 148 Willowdale Dr #33 Frederick MD 21701 Office: Standard Fed Savs & Loan 5280 Corporate Dr Frederick MD 21701

OZAKI, ROBERT H., food products executive; b. Jan. 8, 1947; s. Kenneth and Maye O. Student, Hamline U., 1964-66; BA, U. Hawaii, 1969, postgrad., 1969-71. Dir. pub. relations and community resources Am. Lung Assn. Hawaii, Honolulu, 1976-79; account supr., exec. Stryker Weiner Assocs., Honolulu, 1979-81; mgr. corp. communications Amfac Inc., Honolulu, 1981-83, asst. v.p., 1983, v.p., 1984-86, exec. v.p., 1988—; sr. v.p. Amfac Hawaii Inc., Honolulu, 1986-88, chmn., 1988—. Mem. Hawaii Council on Econ. Edn. Recipient Silver Anvil award, Pub. Relations Soc. Am., Koa Anvil award, Pub. Relations Soc. Am., 1983, 84, Pub. Relations Casebook award for Crisis Communications, Pub. Relations Casebook award for Community Relations, Community Partnership award Community Relations Report, Pele award for Newsletter Design Honolulu Advt. Fedn. Mem. Internat. Inst. Edn., Urban Land Inst., Pacific Asian Affairs Council, Nature Conservancy, Japan-Am. Soc. Hawaii. Office: AMFAC Hawaii Inc 700 Bishop St Honolulu HI 96813 Also: Amfac Inc Box 3230 Honolulu HI 96801

OZANNE, JAMES HERBERT, credit company executive; b. Oak Park, Ill., Aug. 23, 1943; m. Susan Shennan; children: Timothy, Jill, Jeanne Marie, William. BS, DePaul U., Chgo., 1967. Pres. North American Car Corp., Chgo., 1975-83, Gen. Electric Railcar Services Corp., Chgo., 1983-84; v.p., gen. mgr. Gen. Electric Credit Corp., Stamford, Conn., 1984-86, exec. v.p., 1986—; bd. dirs. BMW Credit Corp., Kidder, Peabody & Assoc., N.Y.C., Polaris Aircraft Leasing Corp., San Francisco. Office: GE Credit Corp 260 Long Ridge Rd Stamford CT 06902

OZOLS, SANDRA LEE, lawyer; b. Casper, Wyo., June 24, 1957; d. Virgil Carr and Doris Louise (Conklin) McC.; m. Ojars Herberts Ozols, Sept. 2, 1978 (div.); children: Michael Ojars, Sara Ann, Brian Christopher. BA with distinction, U. Colo., 1978; JD magna cum laude, Boston U., 1982. Bar: Colo. 1982, U.S. Dist. Ct. Colo. 1985. Assoc. Cohen, Brame & Smith, Denver, 1983-84, Parcel, Meyer, Schwartz, Ruttum & Mauro, Denver, 1984-85, Mayer, Brown & Platt, Denver, 1985-87; counsel western ops. GE Capital Corp., Lincolnshire, Ill., 1987—. Mem. Phi Beta Kappa, Phi Delta Phi. Republican. Mem. Ch. of Christ. Home: 917 Crestfield Ave Libertyville IL 60048 Office: GE Capital Corp 100 Tri-State Internat Ste 200 Lincolnshire IL 60015

PABARCIUS, ALGIS, investment executive; b. Telsiai, Lithuania, May 1, 1932; came to U.S., 1950, naturalized, 1956; s. Vacius and Brone (Ziuryte) P.; B.S., U. Ill., 1955; M.S., Ill. Inst. Tech., 1958, Ph.D., 1964; postgrad. Technische Hochschule Muenchen, Germany, 1962; m. Eleanor A. Rakovic, Aug. 18, 1956; children—Nina, Lisa, Algis. Engr., Esso Research & Engring. Co., Linden, N.J., 1955-56; instr. U. Ill., Chgo., 1956-59, asst. prof., 1959-64; partner Zubkus, Zemaitis & Assocs., Architects and Engrs., Chgo., Washington, 1959-67; v.p. Garden Hotels Investment Co. and Whitecliff Corp., Lanham, Md., 1967-75; pres. Aras Investment Corp., 1975-79, Colony Funding Corp., Washington, 1979—. Registered profl. engr. Ill., D.C.; structural engr. Ill.; Danforth Found. grantee, 1960-61; NSF faculty fellow, 1961-62. Mem. ASCE, Sigma Xi, Tau Beta Pi, Sigma Tau, Chi Epsilon, Phi Kappa Phi. Home: 3251 Prospect St NW Washington DC 20007 Office: Colony Funding Corp 3062 M St NW Washington DC 20007

PABST, THOMAS EDWARD, accountant; b. Chgo., Aug. 25, 1958; s. Walter J. and Mary E. (Smit) P.; m. Suzanne H. Ziolo, Aug. 1, 1981; children: Robert, Laura. BA, U. Ill., 1980. CPA, Ill. Staff auditor Coopers & Lybrand, Chgo., 1980-85; contr. JG Industries, Chgo., 1985—; chief fin. officer Goldblatt's Dept. Store, Inc., 1985—. Mem. Chgo. Retail Exec. Assn. (bd. dirs. 1987—, treas. 1988), Am. Inst. CPA's, Ill. CPA Soc. Office: JG Industries Inc 919 N Michigan Ave Ste 1401 Chicago IL 60611

PACE, CAROLINA JOLLIFF, communications executive; b. Dallas, Apr. 12, 1938; d. Lindsay Gafford and Carolina (Juden) Jolliff; student Holton-Arms Jr. Coll., 1956-57: BA in Comparative Lit., So. Meth. U., 1960; m. John McIver Pace, Oct. 7, 1961. Promotional advisor, dir. season ticket sales Dallas Theatre Center, 1960-61; exec. sec. Dallas Book and Author Luncheon, 1959-63; promotional and instl. cons. Henry Regnery-Reilly & Lee Pub. Co., Chgo., 1962-65; pub. trade rep. various cos., instl. rep. Don R. Phillips Co., Southeastern area, 1965-67; Southwestern rep. Ednl. Reading Service, Inc.-Troll Assocs., Mahwah, N.J., 1967-72; v.p., dir. multimedia div. Melton Book Co., Dallas, 1972-79; v.p. mktg. Webster's Internat., Inc., Nashville, 1980-82; pres. Carolina Pace, Inc., 1982—; mem. adv. bd. Nat. Info. Center of Spl. Edn. Materials; mem. materials rev. panel Nat. Media Center for Materials of Severely-Profoundly Handicapped, 1981; mem. mktg. product rev. bd. LINC Resources, 1982, 83, 84, mktg. task force, 1983, adv. bd., 1987; reviewer spl. edn. U.S. Dept. Edn., 1975-79, 85; rev. cons. Health and Humas Svcs., 1982, 83, 84, 86; product rev. task force CEC, 1984, 85, 86; cons. Ednl. Cable Consortium, Summit, N.J. Mem. adv. council Grad. Sch. Library and Info. Sci. Found., U. Tex. Mem. Women's Nat. Book Assn., Nat. Audio Visual Assn. (conf. speaker), Internat. Communications Industries Assn., Assn. Ednl. and Communications Tech., Assn. Spl. Edn. Tech. (nat. dir., v.p. publicity 1980-82), Women in Communications, Dallas Founders, Friends of the West End (pres. 1988—), West End Assn. Dallas (chmn. subcom. on traffic and parking 1986-87, com. demographic study 1987-88), Pub. Relations Soc. Am., Council Exceptional Children (dir. exhibitors com., chmn. publ. com. 1979 conf., conf. speaker 1981), DAR (Jane Douglas chpt.), Dallas Zool. Soc., Dallas Mus. of Art, ALA, Dallas Southern Meml. Tex. Parking Assn., Kimball Art Mus., Press Club of Dallas, Alpha Delta Pi. Presbyterian. Producer ednl. videos; contbr. articles to profl. jours. Home: 4524 Lorraine Ave Dallas TX 75205

PACE, JAMES GARVEY, lawyer, realtor; b. Shelbyville, Ky., Jan. 8, 1912; s. Virgil and Mary (Garvey) P. LLB, Jefferson Sch. Law, 1934; JD (hon.), U. Louisville, 1968. Bar: Ky. 1934, Fla. 1936. Acct., estimator H. Bornstein Constrn. Co., Louisville, 1931-33; pvt. practice Miami, Fla., 1936—; owner, mgr. James G. Pace & Assocs., realtors, Miami, 1956—. With AUS, 1940-45, ETO, NATOUSA. Mem. Nat. Assn. Realtors, Internat. Assn. Realtors, Fla. Assn. Realtors, Miami Assn. Realtors, Internat. Real Estate Inst., Fla. Bar Assn., Miami Bar Assn., Flying Lawyers Bar Assn. (v.p. Fla. 1958—), Real Estate Flyers Assn. (pres., bd. dirs. 1962, 68). Democrat. Office: James G Pace & Assocs 15180 Biscayne Blvd North Miami Beach FL 33160

PACE, STANLEY CARTER, aeronautical engineer; b. Waterview, Ky., Sept. 14, 1921; s. Stanley Dan and Pearl Eagle (Carter) P.; m. Elaine Marilyn Cutchall, Aug. 21, 1945; children: Stanley Dan, Lawrence Timothy, Richard Yost. Student, U. Ky., 1939-40; B.S., U.S. Mil. Acad., 1943; M.S. in Aero. Engring., Calif. Inst. Tech., 1949; LLD (hon.), Maryville Coll., 1987. Commd. 2d lt. USAAF, 1943, advanced through grades to col., 1953; pilot, flight leader B-24 Group, 15th Air Force 1943-44; chief power plant br., procurement div. Hdqrs. Air Materiel Command Wright-Patterson AFB, Ohio, 1945-48; assignments, procurement div. Hdqrs. Air Materiel Command 1949-53, dep. chief prodn. Hdqrs. Air Materiel Command, 1952-53, resigned, 1954; with TRW, Inc., Cleve., 1954-85, successively sales mgr., asst. mgr., mgr. West Coast plant; mgr. jet div. Tapco plant, Cleve.; asst. mgr. Tapco group, 1954-58, v.p., gen. mgr., 1958-65, exec. v.p. co., 1965-77, pres., 1977-85, vice chmn., 1985, dir., 1965-85; vice chmn., dir. Gen. Dynamics Corp., St. Louis, 1985, chmn., chief exec. officer, 1985—, also bd. dirs.; dir. Consol. Natural Gas Co. Head United Way drive, Cleve., 1984; former council commr., pres. Great Cleve. Council Boy Scouts Am.; former trustee Nat. Jr. Achievement, Denison U., Judson Park; former chmn. Greater Cleve. Roundtable, Cleve. Found. Distbn. Com., Nat. Assn. Mfrs.; trustee Washington U. Decorated Air medal with oak leaf clusters. Mem. AIAA, Soc. Automotive Engrs., Delta Tau Delta. Clubs: Union Country, Pepper Pike, Eldorado, Rolling Rock, Log Cabin, St. Louis, St. Louis Country. Home: 2 Chatfield Rd Saint Louis MO 63141 Office: Gen Dynamics Corp Pierre Laclede Ctr Saint Louis MO 63105

PACK, ALLEN S., coal company executive; b. Bramwell, W.Va., Dec. 11, 1930; s. Paul Meador and Mable Blanche (Hale) P.; m. Glenna Rae Christian, June 21, 1952; children: Allen Scott Jr., David Christian, Mark Frederick, Andrew Ray. B.S., W.Va. U., 1952. Gen. mgr. Island Coal Co., Holden, W.Va., 1969-70, pres., 1970-73; v.p. adminstrn. Island Coal Co., Lexington, Ky., 1973-75; exec. v.p. Cannelton Holding Co., Charleston, W.Va., 1975-77, pres., chief ops. officer, 1977-80, pres., chief exec. officer, 1980—; dir. Tilden Iron Ore Co., Cleve., 1980—, Algoma Tube Corp., Houston, 1977—, Maple Meadow Mining Co., Charleston, 1976—. Bd. dirs. Buchskin council Boy Scouts Am., Charleston, 1976—, pres. Buckskin council, 1980; bd. dirs. W.Va. Univ. Found., Morgantown, 1978—; trustee Davis and Elkins Coll., 1981. Served to capt. USMC, 1952-54. Recipient Silver Beaver award Boy Scouts Am., 1981. Mem. W.Va. Coal Assn. (dir., past chmn.), Nat. Coal Assn. (dir.), Bituminous Coal Operators Assn. (dir., chmn. bd.), Kanawha Coal Operators Assn. (dir.). Presbyterian. Office: Cannelton Industries 315 70th St Charleston WV 25304

PACK, DONNA MARIE, finance executive; b. Cleve., May 23, 1960; d. Bernard Adam and Joanne (McCoy) P.; m. Robert Wapperer, June 21, 1986. BBA in Finance, Cleve. State U., 1986; postgrad., Case Western Reserve U., 1988. Cert. cash mgr. Coordinator/cash acctg. The Sherwin-Williams Co., Cleve., 1980-82, administr. of cash and investment, 1982-84; cash mgr. Cole Nat. Corp., Cleve., 1984-86, mgr. fin., 1986—. Pres. Dover West Condominium Unit Owner's Assn., Westlake, Ohio, 1988—. Mem. Northeastern Ohio Cash Mgmt. Assn., (bd. dirs., 1988—). Roman Catholic. Home: 28646 Lynhaven Dr North Olmsted OH 44070 Office: Cole Nat Corp 5915 Landerbrook Dr Cleveland OH 44124

PACKARD, DAVID, manufacturing company executive, electrical engineer; b. Pueblo, Colo., Sept. 7, 1912; s. Sperry Sidney and Ella Lorna (Graber) P.; m. Lucile Salter, Apr. 8, 1938 (dec., 1987); children: David Woodley, Nancy Ann Packard Burnett, Susan Packard Orr, Julie Elizabeth Stephens. B.A., Stanford U., 1934, M.E.E., 1939; LLD (hon.), U. Calif., Santa Cruz, 1966, Catholic U., 1970, Pepperdine U., 1972; DSc (hon.), Colo. Coll., 1964; LittD (hon.), So. Colo. State Coll., 1973; D in Eng. (hon.), U. Notre Dame, 1974. With vacuum tube engring. dept. Gen. Electric Co., Schenectady, 1936-38; co-founder, ptnr. Hewlett-Packard Co., Palo Alto, Calif., 1939-47, pres., 1947-64, chief exec. officer, 1964-68, chmn. bd., 1964-68, 72—; U.S. dep. sec. defense Washington, 1969-71; dir. Genetech, Inc., 1981—; bd. dirs. Caterpillar Tractor Co., 1972-83, Chevron, 1972-85; chmn. Presdl. Commn. on Def. Mgmt., 1985-86; mem. White House Sci. Council. Mem. President's Commn. Personnel Interchange, 1972-74, Trilateral Commn., 1973-81, Dirs. Council Exploratorium, 1987; pres. bd. regents Uniformed Services U. of Health Scis., 1975-82; mem. U.S.-USSR Trade and Econ. Council, 1975-82; trustee The Ronald Reagan Presdl. Found., 1986—; mem. bd. overseers Hoover Instn., 1972—; bd. dirs. Nat. Merit Scholarship Corp., 1963-69; dir. Found. for Study of Presdl. and Congl. Terms, 1978—, Alliance to Save Energy, 1977-87, Atlantic Council, 1972-83, (vice chmn. 1972-80), Am. Enterprise Inst. for Public Policy Research, 1978—, Nat. Fish and Wildlife Found., 1985-87, Hitachi Found. Adv. Council, 1986—; trustee Herbert Hoover Found., 1974—, dir. Wolf Trap Found.; vice chmn. The Calif. Nature Conservancy, 1983—; trustee Stanford U., 1954-69, (pres. bd. trustees 1958-60), Hoover Instn., The Herbert Hoover Found.; mem. Dir.'s Council Exploratium, 1987. Decorated Grand Cross of Merit Fed. Republic of Germany, 1972, Medal Honor Electronic Industries, 1974; numerous other awards including Silver Helmet Def. award AMVETS, 1973, Washington award Western Soc. Engrs., 1975, Hoover medal ASME, 1975, Gold Medal award Nat. Football Found. and Hall of Fame, 1975, Good Scout award Boy Scouts Am., 1975, Vermilye medal Franklin Inst., 1976, Internat. Achievement award World Trade Club of San Francisco, 1976, Merit award Am. Cons. Engrs. Council Fellows, 1977, Achievement in Life award Ency. Britannica, 1977, Engring. Award of Distinction San Jose State U., 1980, Thomas D. White Nat. Def. award USAF Acad., 1981, Disting. Info. Scis. award Data Processing Mgmt. Assn., 1981, Sylvanus Thayer award U.S. Mil. Acad., 1982, Environ. Leadership award Natural Resources Def. Council, 1983, Dollar award Nat. Fgn. Trade Council, 1985, Presdl. MEdal of Freedom, 1988. Fellow IEEE (Founders medal 1973); mem. Nat. Acad. Engring. (Founders award 1979), Instrument Soc. Am. (hon. lifetime mem.), Wilson Council, The Bus. Roundtable, Bus. Council, Am. Ordnance Assn. (Crozier Gold medal 1970, Henry M. Jackson award 1988, Nat. Medal Tech. 1988, Presdl. Medal of Freedom 1988), Sigma Xi, Phi Beta Kappa, Tau Beta Pi, Alpha Delta Phi (Disting. Alumnus of Yr. 1970). Clubs: Bohemian, Commonwealth, Pacific Union, World Trade, Engrs. (San Francisco); The Links (N.Y.C.); Alfalfa, Capitol Hill (Washington). Office: Hewlett-Packard Co 1501 Page Mill Rd Palo Alto CA 94304

PACKARD, PETER KIM, diversified products company executive; b. Rome, N.Y., Dec. 23, 1938; s. Walter E. and Gretchen (Kauth) P.; m. Evelyn A. Stumphauzer, Apr. 28, 1962; children: Laurel A. Springer, David J., Brian K. BSEE, Pa. State U., 1960; MS in Mgmt., MIT, 1971. With GT Sylvania, 1960-80; various mktg. and sales positions 1960-71; ops. mgr. picture tubes Seneca Falls, N.Y., 1971-72; gen. mgr. Cable TV div. El Paso, Tex., 1972-74; v.p. Western Switch Gear div. Los Angeles, 1974-77; v.p. Engineered Products div. St. Louis, 1977-80; v.p., group exec. Warner & Swasey div. Bendix Corp., Cleve., 1980-82, pres., 1984-85; v.p., group exec. Allied/Bendix, Cleve., 1982-84; pres., chief operating office Hobart Bros. Co., Troy, Ohio, 1985—. Exec. com. Labor Mgmt. Forum Greater Cleve. Roundtable, 1984-85; adv. bd. Ohio State U. Coll. Engring., 1987-89; various offices United Way Cleve., 1980-84; bd. trustees Dayton Performing Arts Fund, Dayton C. of C.; active Roman Cath. Ch. parish activities. Sloan fellow MIT, 1970-71; named one of Outstanding Young Men Am., 1972. Mem. IEEE, Nat. Electrical Mfrs. Assn. (bd. govs. 1986—, chmn. indsl. automation div. 1987-88), Nat. Machine Tool Builders Assn., Am. Welding Soc., Dayton C. of C. Home: 5409 Spice Bush Centerville OH 45429 Office: Hobart Bros Co 600 W Main St Hobart Sq Troy OH 45373

PACKER, RUSSELL HOWARD, beverage company executive; b. Santa Fe, Sept. 8, 1951; s. Russell Howard Thorwaldsen and Florence (Bullis) Bryant; m. Melanie Lea Martell, Aug. 31. 1974; children: Lindsey Anne, Andrew Thomas. BS, U. So. Calif., 1973, MBA, 1975. Research analyst Automobile Club of So. Calif., Los Angeles, 1973-75, sr. fin. analyst, 1975-81, mgr. fin. and investment analysis, 1982-83; dir. planning and devel. Coca Cola Bottling Co. of Los Angeles, 1983-87; v.p. planning, adminstrn. Coca Cola Bottling Co. of San Diego, 1987-88; contr. Sunroad Capital Corp., Dan Diego, 1988-89; v.p., dir., contr. Sunroad Enterprises, Dan Diego, 1989—; lectr. fin. Calif. State U., Los Angeles, 1977-87, San Diego State U., 1988—. Mem. Am. Fin. Assn., Assn. MBA Execs., Beta Gamma Sigma. Republican. Home: 12519 Shropshire Ln Rancho Bernardo CA 92128-1016 Office: Sunroad Enterprises 1455 Frazee Rd San Diego CA 92108

PACKO, JOSEPH JOHN, industrialist; b. Toledo, Mar. 9, 1925; s. Joseph Steve and Mary (Toth) P.; student thermodynamics engring. John Carroll U., U. N.C., 1943-44; B.S. in Physics, Math., Bus. Adminstrn., Fin., Bowling Green State U., 1948; postgrad. in nuclear chemistry Toledo U., 1950; D.Sc. in Comml. Sci., Southeastern Mass. U., 1969; m. Bette Throne, July 10, 1948; children—Jo Anne, Mark. With Packo Industries, Ft. Lauderdale, Fla., 1953—; pres. J.J. Packo Mortgage Corp., 1954-69; pres. Packo Enterprises, 1955—, S. Fla. Asphalt Co., 1956-65; pres., chmn. Am. Dynamics Internat., Inc. 1967-73, Packo Internat., 1978—; chmn. bd., chief exec. officer Cryo-Chem Internat. Inc., 1982—. Mem. Trade Mission, West Berlin, 1965; adv. panel Dept. Army, 1974-78. Bd. dirs. Fla. chpt. Nat. Soc. Prevention Blindness, Holy Cross Hosp., Nova U. Alumnae Assn., A.R.C. Served with USNR, 1943-45. Mem. Opera Guild Ft. Lauderdale, Young Presidents Orgn. (vice-chmn., sec.-treas. Fla. chpt.), Am. Mgmt. Assn., AAAS, Symphony Soc., Asphalt Inst., Nat. Bd. Realtors, Nat. Mortgage Bankers Assn., Nat. Bituminous Assn., Bowling Green U. Alumni, Southeastern Mass. U. Alumni, Navy League, Sigma Xi. Clubs: Lago Mar Country, Capitol Hill; Onion Creek Country (Austin, Tex.). Patentee in field. Home: 119 Colonial Dr Saint Simons Island GA 31522

PADDOCK, BENJAMIN HENRY, III, banker; b. Detroit, Feb. 8, 1928; s. Benjamin Henry and Mary (Bulkley) P.; m. Anne Sherer, Aug. 23, 1958; children—Benjamin Henry, Anthony, Matthew, Ann. B.A., Trinity Coll., 1950; M.B.A., U. Mich., 1952. Asst. v.p., loan officer Nat. Bank Detroit, 1956-65; exec. v.p. City Nat. Bank, Detroit, 1968-70, pres., chief exec. officer, 1970-77; pres. No. States Bancorp, Detroit, 1973-77; pres. B.H. Paddock & Assocs., Detroit, 1977-80; exec. v.p. AmeriTrust Co., N.A., Cleve., 1980-84, sr. exec. v.p., 1984-87, vice-chmn., dir., 1987—; pres./dir. Minbanc Capital Corp., 1976—; dir. Gt. Lakes Constrn. Co., 1985—. Bd. dirs. Soc. for Crippled Children, Cleve., 1983, Gt. Lakes Shakespeare Festival, Cleve., 1984; mem. steering com. YMCA, Cleve., 1984. Served to lt. USN, 1952-56. Mem. Assn. Res. City Bankers, Robert Morris Assocs., Am. Inst. Banking. Episcopalian. Clubs: Country, Yondotega (Detroit); Kirtland Country (Ohio); Union, Clevelander (Cleve.), Queen City (Cin.), Cin. Country, Pepper Pike. Home: 11 Hill & Hollow St Cincinnati OH 45208 Office: AmeriTrust Corp 525 Vine St Cincinnati OH 45202

PADDOCK, PAUL BRADLEY, marketing executive; b. Glendale, Calif., Nov. 16, 1942; s. Bill and Pauline P.; m. Carolyn Morgan, July 9, 1981; children: Laurel Elizabeth, Kira Dawn. BBA, U. Ala., 1970, MA in Promotion and Advt., 1972. Promotional mgr. Simon and Assocs., Bessemer, Ala. amd Lafayette, Ind., 1972-75; sales mgr. Holiday Inns Inc., Nashville, Columbus Ga. and Montgomery, Ala., 1975-78; market analyst, expansion planning Holiday Inns Inc., Memphis, 1978-79, sr. evaluator, food and beverage, 1979-80, supr. field mktg., 1980-81, supr. nat. promotion and merchandising, 1981-83; mktg. mgr. PSI Process Systems Inc., Memphis, 1983-85; corp. mktg. dir. Wilson Hotel Mgmt. Co. Inc., Memphis, 1985—; mem. adv. bd. Hotel & Restaurant, Northwest Community Coll. Vol. Memphis-in-May, 1979—. Served with USAF, 1960-64. Mem. Am. Mktg. Assn. (pres. Memphis chpt. 1986-87), Am. Mgmt. Assn., Pub. Relations Soc. Am., Hotel Sales and Mktg. Assn. Internat. Republican. Episcopalian. Office: Wilson Hotel Mgmt Co Inc 1629 Winchester Rd Memphis TN 38116

PADILLA, LORRAINE MARIE, insurance company executive; b. Bklyn., Mar. 24, 1952; d. Amerigo L. and Helen M. (Mosca) Muratore; m. Samuel P. Padilla, Aug. 21, 1971; 1 child, Adam L. BS in Math., NYU, 1973. CLU., chartered fin. cons. Contract's actuarial specialist N.Am. Reassurance Co., N.Y.C., 1973-75; regional mgr. pension sales The Phoenix, N.Y.C., 1975—; instr. pension retirement planning and employee benefits Nat. Inst. Fin., N.J., 1980-85. Mem. Snug Harbor Cultural Ctr., N.Y. Mus. Natural History. Nat. Merit and Regents scholar, 1969. Mem. Gen. Agts. and Mgrs. Assn., Nat. Life Underwriters, Women Life Underwriters, Chartered Life Underwriters. Republican. Roman Catholic. Home: 40 Mallow St Staten Island NY 10309 Office: The Phoenix 888 7th Ave 44th Fl New York NY 10106

PAGANO, CELESTE ANN, realtor; b. Bridgeport, Conn., Apr. 12, 1950; d. Peter Angelo and Carmella Marie (Carrafiello) P. Student, U. Bridgeport, 1974-81; AAS in Broadcast Journalism, Grahm Jr. Coll., Boston, 1970. Lic. realtor, Conn. Editorial asst. Nat. Underwriter Co., N.Y.C., 1970-71; asst. prodn. mgr. Conover-Mast Pub. Co., Stamford, Conn., 1971-73; account exec. K&S Advt. Agy., Bridgeport, 1973-75, Ansonia, Conn., 1977-83; rep. display advt. Stamford Adv. newspaper, 1975-77; sales mgr. Johnson Pub. Co., Loveland, Colo., 1983-85; realtor Toth & Formato Real Estate, Bridgeport, 1985-89; pvt. practice real estate investor Conn., 1989—; guest speaker Conn. Realtors Conv., Hartford, 1987. Organizer donation drives for various orgns., Bridgeport, 1987. Recipient Outstanding Fair Housing Action award Bridgeport Fair Housing, 1986. Mem. Nat. Assn. Realtors, Conn. Assn. Realtors, Greater Bridgeport. Bd. Realtors (chairperson equal opportunity com. 1988), Fairfield Bd. Realtors, Conn. Comml. Investment. Democrat. Roman Catholic. Home and Office: 91 Beachview Ave Bridgeport CT 06605

PAGANUCCI, PAUL DONNELLY, corporate executive, lawyer, college official emeritus; b. Waterville, Maine, Apr. 18, 1931; s. Romeo J. and Martha (Donnelly) P.; m. Marilyn McLean, Sept. 10, 1966; children: Thomas Donnelly, Elizabeth Mary. A.B., Dartmouth Coll., 1953; M.B.A., Amos Tuck Sch. Bus. Adminstrn., 1954; J.D., Harvard U., 1957. Bar: N.Y. 1958, N.H. 1972. Staff asst. to pres. W.R. Grace & Co., N.Y.C., 1958-61, vice chmn., dir., 1986—; bd. dirs. W.R. Grace & Co. Found., N.Y.C.; pres., treas., dir. Lombard, Vitalis, Paganucci & Nelson, Inc., N.Y.C., 1961-72; prof. bus. adminstrn. Amos Tuck Sch. Dartmouth Coll., Hanover, N.H., 1972-77, assoc. dean, 1972-76, sr. investment officer, 1976-77, v.p., 1977-84, v.p. and treas., 1984-85; chmn. bd. Computer Property Corp., N.Y.C.; bd. dirs. The Home Ins. Co., Home Group Inc., State Mut. Securities, Nat. Med. Care, Fairfield Communities, Inc., HRE Properties; allied mem. N.Y. Stock Exchange, 1961-72. Chmn. bd. trustees Dartmouth Cath. Student Ctr., 1973-85, overseer, 1973—; trustee Colby Coll., 1975-85, 87—, Coll. Mt. St. Vincent, Casque and Gauntlet; mem. Pres.'s Pvt. Sector Survey on Cost Control; bd. dirs. Hands Across N.Y. Served with AUS, 1956-62. Mem. Inst. Chartered Fin. Analysts. Clubs: Dartmouth of N.Y. (dir., v.p., pres.); Union (Boston); Knights of Malta. Home: 33 Rope Ferry Rd Hanover NH 03755 Office: W R Grace & Co 1114 Ave of the Americas New York NY 10036

PAGE, DAVID KEITH, lawyer, supermarket executive; b. Detroit, Aug. 23, 1933; s. Milton Walter and Hilda (Schoenfield) P.; m. Andrea Burdick, July 6, 1954; children: Mark Daniel, Jason William, Sarah Leslie. A.B. summa cum laude, Dartmouth, 1955; LL.B. magna cum laude (editor law rev. 1958), Harvard, 1958; Fulbright scholar, London (Eng.) Sch. Econs., 1959. Bar: Mich. 1959. Ptnr. Honigman, Miller, Schwartz & Cohn, Detroit, 1959—; sec. Allied Supermarkets, Detroit, 1963-85, chmn., chief exec. officer, 1985-87, also bd. dirs.; chief exec. officer Meadowdale Foods Inc., 1987—; bd. dirs. Highland Superstores Inc. Pres., bd. dirs. Detroit Men's Ort chpt.; trustee, chmn. audit com., mem. exec. com. Children's Hosp. Mich., 1973—, chmn. bd., 1982—; trustee, vice chmn. grants com. Community Found. for Southeastern Mich., 1984—; mem. Detroit Area council Boy Scouts Am., 1972—; trustee Marygrove Coll., 1977-83; v.p., bd. dirs. United Found., 1986—; bd. dirs., mem. exec. com. Detroit Med. Ctr., 1982—; bd. govs. Detroit Jewish Welfare Fedn., 1977—, v.p., 1983—. Mem. ABA, Detroit Bar Assn., Phi Beta Kappa. Jewish religion (trustee, pres. temple 1976-77). Clubs: Detroit, Knollwood Country. Home: 2661 Indian Mound S Birmingham MI 48010 Office: Meadowdale Foods Inc 8711 Meadowdale Detroit MI 48228 Also: Honigman Miller Schwartz & Cohn 2290 1st National Bldg Detroit MI 48226

PAGE, EARL MICHAEL, management specialist; b. Providence, Sept. 5, 1950; s. Earl Gee and Joan V. (Moran) P.; m. Marilyn Martin Wagner, Nov. 30, 1984; children: Keri Wagner, Mike Wagner; 1 child from previous marriage, Michael. BA, Boston Coll., 1972; MEd., Northeastern U., 1977; MBA, Fla. Atlantic U., 1986. Program coordinator Mass. Gen. Hosp., Boston, 1972-76; unit dir. Chandler St. Ctr., Worcester, Mass., 1977-80; pres. Page Three, Inc., North Palm Beach, Fla., 1981-83, Palm Beach Mgmt. Cons., Pompano Beach, Fla., 1983—; mgr. tng. and devel. AAA East Fla., Miami, 1986-87; dir. human resources Waterbed City, 1987—; prof. Coll. Bus. and Pub. Adminstrn. Fla. Atlantic U., Boca Raton, Fla. Mem. Bus. Inc. of Palm Beaches, 1981-85. Mem. Am. Assn. Counseling & Devel., Am. Soc. for Tng. & Devel., Am. Soc. Personnel Adminstrn., Phi Kappa Phi, Beta Gamma Sigma. Republican. Roman Catholic. Home: 8 SE 7th Ave Deerfield Beach FL 33441 Office: 1001 W McNab Rd Pompano Beach FL 33069

PAGE, EDDEE ELIZABETH, banker; b. Salisbury, N.C., Dec. 8, 1942; d. James Richard and Aline (Houston) Giles; m. Russell M. Page, Oct. 2, 1961 (dec. May 1980); children—Judith, Russell M., Nathan, James. A.S. in Gen. Bus. with honors, Norwalk Community Coll., 1985; student U. Conn. From teller to head teller State Nat. Bank, Darien, Conn., 1969-75, adminstrv. asst., 1975-79; asst. br. mgr. Citytrust Bank, Bridgeport, Conn., 1979-81, loan workout officer, 1981-83, asst. v.p., corp. fin. services sales officer, 1988—; fin. sec. Conn. Minority Bankers, New Haven, 1980-82. Treas. St. Joseph's Home/Sch. Assn., Norwalk, Conn., 1978-82; trustee Faith Tabernacle Ch., Stamford, Conn., 1979-86, mem. credit com. Faith Tabernacle Fed. Credit Union, 1981-85. Democrat. Baptist. Home: 71 Marlin Dr Norwalk CT 06854 Office: Citytrust Bank 961 Main St Bridgeport CT 06601

PAGE, JEANETTE GENEVIEVE, nursing administrator; b. Pottsville, Pa., Aug. 11, 1941; d. F. C. and G. V. Smith. Registered nurse Harrisburg Polyclinic Hosp. Sch. Nursing, 1962; B.A. in Human Resources, Pacific Western U., 1975, M.A. in Human Resources, 1977. Cert. registered nurse anesthetist, cert. nurse adminstr. Asst. dir. nursing Oxnard Community Hosp., Calif., 1975-78; dir. nursing service Belair Convalasarium, Balt., 1979; office nurse Dr. M. Diamond, D.D.S., Pottsville, Pa., 1979-80; dir. nursing service Tigua Gen. Hosp., El Paso, Tex., 1982-84, Parkview Hosp., Midland, Tex., 1984-85; dir. patient care services Physicians & Surgeons Hosp., Midland, 1985—; mem. adv. bd. El Paso Community Coll. R.N./L.V.N. Program, El Paso, 1982-84; com. chmn. Transcultural Council, El Paso, 1984, bd. dirs., 1985; guest lectr. U. Tex.-El Paso Coll. Nursing, 1983; mem. speakers forum Hospice of El Paso, 1982-84; mem. adv. bd. RN program Midland Coll., Tex., 1984-86. Mem. Am. Assn. Nurse Anesthetists, Am. Hosp. Assn. (Nursing Service Adminstrs. Soc.), Tex. Hosp. Assn. (com. chmn. Soc. Nursing Adminstrs. 1983-84, bd. dirs. 1985-87), West Tex. Dir. Nurses' Council, Polyclinic Sch. Nursing Alumni Assn. Lodge: Order Eastern Star. Avocations: play bagpipe; traveling; needlecrafts; ceramics.

PAGE, JOHN DAVID, real estate development; b. Tacoma, Mar. 18, 1950; s. W.D. and Patricia Ann McDonald (Madonald) P. BA in Econs., Harvard U., 1972; postgrad., U. Wash., 1974-75. Field supr. Cambridge (Mass.) Survey Rsch., 1972-73; real estate broker Norris, Beggs & Simpson, Tacoma, 1973-75; prin., real estate syndicator Rainier Brokers, Inc., Tacoma, 1975—; prin., real estate developer Dominion Developments, Inc., Tacoma, 1983—; bd. dirs. CKT Technologies, Newbury Park, Calif. Mem. fin. com. congressman Norm Dicks, Tacoma, 1978—; mem. civil service Bd., Pierce County, Wash., 1982—; mem. steering com. Gov. Booth Gardner, Seattle, 1983—; bd. dirs. Tacoma Art Mus., 1986—, Pantages Performing Art Ctr., Tacoma, 1985—. Mem. Homebuilders Assn., Builder 100. Democrat. Home: 8101 N Thorne Ln SW Tacoma WA 98498 Office: Dominion Developments Inc 5911 Orchard St W Tacoma WA 98467

PAGE, THOMAS ALEXANDER, utility executive; b. Niagara Falls, N.Y., Mar. 24, 1933; m. Evelyn Rainnie, July 16, 1960; children: Christopher, Catherine. B.S. in Civil Engring, Purdue U., 1955, M.S. in Indsl. Adminstrn, 1963. Registered profl. engr., N.Y. C.P.A., Wis., Tex. Comptroller, treas. Wis. Power & Light Co., Madison, 1970-73; treas. Gulf States Utilities Co., Beaumont, Tex., 1973-75, sr. v.p. fin., 1975, exec. v.p., 1975-78, also bd. dirs.; exec. v.p., chief operating officer San Diego Gas & Electric Co., 1978-81, pres., chief exec. officer, 1981—, chmn., 1983—, also bd. dirs., 1979—. Mem. Dane County Bd. Suprs., Wis., 1968-72. Served to capt. USAF, 1955-57. Home: 1904 Hidden Crest Dr El Cajon CA 92020 Office: San Diego Gas & Electric Co 101 Ash St San Diego CA 92101

PAGE, THOMAS CRAMER, management educator; b. Martinsville, Ohio, Mar. 28, 1920; s. Earl S. and Elizabeth Jane (Cramer) P.; m. Jessie Morris, Sept. 11, 1944; children: Patricia Page Hugus, Thomas Morris, Susan Page. BBA, Miami U., Oxford, Ohio, 1942; MBA, Harvard U., 1947. Indsl. engr. Eastman Kodak Co., Rochester, N.Y., 1947-51; with mktg. planning, gen. mgmt. Ford Motor Co., Dearborn, Mich., 1952-69, group v.p., 1975-78; v.p. Ford Latin Am. Ford Motor Co., 1978-79, v.p. diversified products ops., 1979-81, exec. v.p., 1981-85, ret., 1985; prof. mgmt. Miami U., 1985—; bd. dirs. Firestone Tire & Rubber Co., Akron, Ohio; chmn. bd. Ford Aerospace and Communications Corp.; v.p. Ford Mktg. Corp., Dearborn, 1970-71; pres. Philco-Ford Corp., Dearborn, 1971-75. Vice chmn. Detroit United Fund, 1970-71. Served to maj. USAAF, 1943-46, USAF, 1970-71. Mem. Pres. Assn., Phila C. of C. (bd. dirs. 1972-73), Delta, Sigma Pi. Home: 581 Golf Crest Dr Dearborn MI 48124

PAGET, ALLEN MAXWELL, investment company executive; b. Karuizawa, Nagano Prefecture, Japan, Sept. 12, 1919 (parents Am. citizens); s. Allen Maxwell and Mary (Baum) P.; m. Dorothy A. Lord, Dec. 22, 1941. BSBA, Lehigh U., 1941. With C. L. Emmert & Co., 1955-58; with Waddell & Reed, Inc., 1958-68, investment mgr., distbr. united group of mutual funds, 1958-68, regional mgr., resident v.p., Harrisburg, Pa., 1961-68; v.p. Mark Securities, Inc., Camp Hill, Pa., 1968—; chmn. bd. dirs., pres., treas. Penn-Ben, Inc., 1969-83; chmn. bd. dirs., pres., treas. Paget-San Enterprises, Inc. (Benihana of Tokyo), 1973-83; gen. ptnr. Penn-Ben Ltd. Partnership, 1983—; v.p. Gamma Lambda Corp., 1973-78. Served to comdr. Supply Corps, USN, 1941-55, capt. Res., ret. 1972. Named Eagle Scout, Boy Scouts Am., 1936. Mem. Am. Philatelic Soc. (life), Navy League U.S., Res. Officers Assn. (pres. Cent. Pa. chpt. 1972-73), Mil. Order World Wars (comdr. Central Pa. chpt. 1979-82, comdr. Region III 1982-88, staff officer 1988—), The Retired Officers Assn., Internat. Assn. Fin. Counselors (charter), Navy Supply Corps Sch. Alumni Assn. (founding mem.), Mid Atlantic Shrine Clowns Assn., Internat. Shrine Clown Assn., Capital Region and West Shore Area C. of C., Nat. Sojourners (1st v.p. Cen. Pa. chpt. No. 76, 1987, pres. 1988-89), Heros of '76, Brown Key Soc., Lambda Mu Sigma (hon., founder Lehigh U. 1940), Pi Kappa Alpha (treas.), Alpha Phi Omega, Pi Delta Epsilon, Cen. Pa. Lehigh Alumni (pres. 1966), Cen. Pa. Execs. (bd. dirs. 1985-88), Antique and Classic Car Unit (founder), Rotary (bd. dirs., Paul Harris fellow), Masons (master 1968, lodge treas. 1984—), KT, Shriners (potentate Zembo temple 1978), pres. Pa. Shrine Assn. 1978-79, v.p. Mid Atlantic A. 1980-82, pres. 1982-83, Shrine Clowns of Zembo Temple, all Shrine clubs of Zembo Temple), Tall Cedars Lebanon, Legion of Honor (organizer 1975), Grand Sword Bearer of Grand Lodge Pa., 1988-89. Republican. Presbyterian. Home: Keiseian 308 Lamp Post Ln Pine Brook Camp Hill PA 17011

PAGNOTTA, PASQUALE ANTHONY, interior designer; b. Bklyn., Dec. 18, 1939; s. Anthony and Frances P.; B.F.A., Pratt Inst., 1961. Designer, Ariston Interior Designers, N.Y.C., 1963-71; partner, owner L.I.T. Assocs., Inc., N.Y.C., 1972-87; partner, designer Design Mates, Inc., N.Y.C., 1973—; work featured in Interior Design, The Designer, Contract, Great Ideas sect. Family Circle, cover of Home Entertainment. Mem. The Springs Improvement Soc., 1969—, Nat. Trust Hist. Preservation, 1975—. Mem. Am. Soc. Interior Designers, Inst. Bus. Designers, Guild Hall East Hampton, Mus. City N.Y., Whitney Mus. Republican. Roman Catholic. Club: Amagansett Tennis. Office: Design Mates Inc 71 W 35th St New York NY 10001

PAIGE, MICHAEL REID, electrical engineer; b. Worcester, Mass., Jan. 11, 1946; s. Harold William and Harriet Bernice (Comen) P.; m. Cathy Ellen Croucher, Aug. 18, 1978; children: Margot Noel, Nathan Tyler. BSEE, Worcester Polytech., 1968; MS, U. Ill., 1969, PhD, 1971; MBA, Boston U., 1982. Registered profl. engr., Conn. Tech. staff Gen. Rsch. Corp., Santa Barbara, Calif., 1971-74; project mgr. Sperry Rand Rsch. Ctr., Sudbury, Mass., 1974-75; tech. dir. Sci. Applications, Inc., San Francisco, 1975-77; mgr. The Analytic Scis. Corp., Reading, Mass., 1977-80, Wang Labs., Lowell, Mass., 1980-84; v.p. engring. Gerber Sci. Instruments, Inc., South Windsor, Conn., 1984—. Contbr. articles to profl. jours. U. fellow U. Ill., 1968-69. Mem. IEEE, Sigma Xi, Tau Beta Pi, Alpha Psi Omega, Pi Mu Epsilon, Eta Kappa Nu. Home: 75 Millstone Rd Glastonbury CT 06033 Office: Gerber Sci Instruments Inc 83 Gerber Rd W South Windsor CT 06074

PAILEY, WILLIAM JOHN, JR., business planning and services company executive; b. Boston, May 5, 1940; s. William John and Ruth E. Pailey; A.B., Brown U., 1962; M.B.A., Columbia U., 1964; m. Maryann Brahos, Nov. 24, 1973; children—Joann Ruth, Julie Ann. Sr. cost analyst Bruning div. Adresssograph Co., 1964, sr. market analyst, 1965, econ. planner, 1966; cons. A.T. Kearney & Co., Chgo., 1966-70; v.p., treas. Memory Gardens Cemetery Inc., Arlington Heights, Ill., 1970—; pres. Pailey Computer Specialties, Inc., Arlington Heights, 1974—, pres. CEM Planning, Inc., Arlington Heights, 1981—. Treas. Village of Kildeer (Ill.), 1981-87, village trustee, 1987—; dir. Lake County Solid Waste Planning Agy., 1988—. Mem. MICRU Internat. of Microdata Users Group (founding mem., dir., treas.), Am. Cemetery Assn., Ill. Cemetery Assn. (bd. dirs., sec.), Met. Chgo. Cemetery Ofcls. Office: 2501 E Euclid Ave Arlington Heights IL 60004

PAINE, BRUCE EDWIN, financial consultant; b. Amsterdam, N.Y., Dec. 4, 1933; s. Richard Candee and Gladys (Van Vranken) P.; m. Fredericka Ione Zimpel, Feb. 19, 1959 (div. 1968); children: Kevin Bruce, Richard Stephen; m. Charlotte Flanagan, June 15, 1971 (div. 1978); m. Natalie Thompson, May 28, 1983. MusB, Yale U., 1955; student, NYU, 1959-63, U. Pa., 1979-80. Corp. trust adminstr. Morgan Guaranty Trust Co., N.Y.C., 1958-60; asst. to pres., editor Prentice Hall, Inc., Englewood Cliffs, N.J., 1960-62; asst. dir. fl. dept. N.Y. Stock Exch., N.Y.C., 1962-66; corp. v.p. Paine Webber, Inc., N.Y.C., 1966-88; pres. Bruce E. Paine Retirement Planning Assocs., Inc., 1988—, Buck Cons., N.Y.C., 1988—; lectr. found. acctg. edn. Berkshire Community Coll., N.Y. Inst. Finance; arbitrator N.Y. Stock Exch. Author numerous articles in field. Mem. Internat. Assn. Fin. Planners, Internat. Soc. Pre-Retirement Planners, Found. for Acctg. Edn., N.Y. Inst. Fin., Yale Club N.Y.C., Columbia County Golf Club. Episcopalian. Home: 99 Overlook Terr Leonia NJ 07605 Office: PO Box 312 Leonia NJ 07605 also: PO Box 751 Philmont NY 12565

PAINE, GLEN HUNTER, private investor; b. West Palm Beach, Fla., Nov. 9, 1926; s. Robert Glen and Frances Wilard (Headspeth) P.; m. Annette Deck, June 18, 1948; children: Robert, Sandra. Student, U. Palm Beach, 1947-49; AA, Sinclair Coll., Dayton, Ohio, 1956, BBA, 1957. Credit supr. Chrysler Airtemp Corp., Dayton, 1953-61; credit mgr. Allied Egry, Dayton, 1961-64; asst. gen. credit mgr. Fyr Fyter Inc., Dayton, 1964-67; credit mgr. Dayco Corp., Dayton, 1967-85; pvt. practice fin. investing Dayton, 1980—; mem. credit exec. com. Motor and Equipment Mfrs. Assn., Teaneck, N.J., 1982-84. V.p. Harrison Twp. Rep. Club, Dayton. Served with USMC, 1945-46, CBI. Named to Hon. Order of Ky. Cols. Fellow Nat. Inst. Credit; mem. Am. Legion. Republican. Lodge: Optimist. Home: 5325 Brendonwood Ln Dayton OH 45415

PAINTER, JOHN WILLIAM, diversified company executive; b. Herrin, Ill., July 24, 1929; s. Charles F. and Helen A. (Anderson) P.; m. Dorothy E. Woodward, Feb. 1, 1952; children: John W., Thomas A., Andrew W. B.S. in Bus. Adminstrn, U. Ill., 1950. Gen. sales mgr. Hupp Aviation Co., Chgo., 1950-60; marketing mgr. Lord Mfg. Co., Erie, Pa., 1960-64; pres. Ohio Rubber Co. div. Eagle-Picher Industries, Willoughby, Ohio, 1964-73; group v.p. parent co. Eagle-Picher Industries, Cin., 1974-76; exec. v.p. Eagle-Picher Industries, 1977, pres., 1977—, exec. v.p., 1980-89, pres., chief exec. officer, 1989—, also dir.; dir. Central Trust Bank, Cin., Central Bancorp., Cin., Kuhlman Corp., Birmingham, Mich. Bd. dirs. Boys' Clubs of Greater Cin. Mem. Alpha Chi Rho, Sigma Iota Epsilon. Clubs: Kenwood Country (Cin.), Commonwealth (Cin.), Bankers (Cin.), Queen City (Cin.). Home: 5475 Graydon Meadow Ln Cincinnati OH 45243 Office: Eagle-Picher Industries Inc 580 Walnut St PO Box 779 Cincinnati OH 45201

PAINTON, RUSSELL ELLIOTT, lawyer, mechanical engineer; b. Port Arthur, Tex., Dec. 5, 1940; s. Clifford Elliott and Edith Virginia (McCutheon) P.; m. Elizabeth Ann Mullins, Aug. 13, 1969 (div. Dec. 1977); 1 child, Todd Elliott; m. Mary Lynn Weber, May 5, 1981. BS in Mech. Engring., U. Tex.-Austin, 1963, JD, 1972. Bar: Tex. 1972; registered profl. engr., Tex. Engr. Gulf States Utilities, Beaumont, Tex., 1963-66, Tracor, Inc., Austin, Tex., 1966-70; corp. counsel Tracor, Inc., Austin, 1973-83, v.p., gen. counsel, 1983—; lawyer Brown, Maroney, Rose, Baker & Barber, Austin, 1972-73, Childs, Fortenbach, Bech & Guyton, Houston, 1973; bd. dirs. Electrosource, Inc., 1987—. Gen. counsel Paramount Theatre for Performing Arts, 1977-83, 2d vice chmn., 1978-80, 1st vice chmn., 1980-82, chmn. bd., 1982-84, retiring chmn., 1984-85; active Centex chpt. ARC, 1976-87; bd. dirs. Austin Sci. Acad., 1985-88, Austin Transp., 1985-88, mem. adv. bd.; bd. dirs. Tex. Industries for the Blind and Handicapped, 1988—. Named Boss of Yr. Austin Legal Secs. Assn., 1981. Mem. ABA, Tex. Bar Assn. (vice chmn., treas. corp. counsel sect. 1982-83), Travis County Bar Assn., Nat. Chamber Litigation Ctr., Better Bus. Bur. (arbitrator 1983—), Am. Electronics Assn. (chmn. Austin coun. 1985-86), Delta Theta Phi, Austin Yacht Club (race comdr. 1968-69, treas. 1970-71, sec. 1972, 75, vice commodore 1980, commododre 1981—, fleet comdr. 1986—), Order Blue Gavel. Republican. Episcopalian. Office: Tracor Inc 6500 Tracor Ln Austin TX 78725

PAIVA, JOSEPH MOURA, biotechnology company executive; b. Rahway, N.J., Aug. 18, 1955; s. Joseph A. and Lucille S. (Moura) P.; m. Madeline A. Makoski, Sept. 9, 1978. BS in Acctg., Fairleigh Dickinson U., 1977; MBA, Rutgers U., 1982. CPA, N.J. Sr. acct. Peat, Marwick, Mitchell & Co., Hacksensack, N.J., 1977-80; controller T.J. McGlone & Co., Inc., Edison, N.J., 1980-83; fin. controller, asst. sec. Cytogen Corp., Princeton, N.J., 1983—; bd. dirs., first v.p. So. N.J. Venture Capital Group, Mt. Holly, N.J., 1985-87; fin. cons., Howell, N.J., 1984-87. Mem. AICPA, N.J. Soc. CPAs, Mensa, Phi Zeta Kappa, Phi Omega Epsilon. Roman Catholic. Home: 43 Heritage Dr Howell NJ 07731 Office: Cytogen Corp 201 College Rd E Princeton NJ 08540

PAJDA, JACQUELINE KAY, human resourses director; b. Omaha, June 25, 1942; d. Benjamin Joseph and Cecilia M. (Koke) McCord; m. Donald Stephen Pajda, July 6, 1985; 1 child, Christopher. BA, Coll. Notre Dame, Calif., 1973; MEd, Ft. Wright Coll., 1979; PhD in Ministry, Jesuit Sch. Theology, 1980. Specialist human resources devel. Calif. Credit Union League, Pomona, 1985—; bd. dirs. Exec. Leadership Co., Portland, Oreg. Mem. Assn. Tng. & Devel. Democrat. Roman Catholic. Office: Calif Credit Union League 2350 S Garey Ave Pomona CA 91766

PALANGE, VALENTINA HELENA, pharmaceutical executive; b. Lewiston, Maine, May 25, 1958; d. Vincent John and Helen Blanc (Mardos) P.; 1 child, Nicole Marie. BSBA cum laude, BA in Speech Communicaitons cum laude, U. Maine, 1980. Coating and printing supr. McNeil CPC, Fort Washington, Pa., 1986-87; project leader McNeil CPC, Ft. Washington, Pa., 1987-88, product leader mfg., 1988—. Capt. U.S. Army, 1980-86. Republican. Roman Catholic. Office: McNeil CPC Camp Hill Rd Fort Washington PA 19034

PALAZZI, JOSEPH L(AZARRO), manufacturing executive; b. New Haven, July 5, 1947; s. Joseph Anthony and Helen (Volosevich) P.; m. Lorna May Mickiewicz, May 27, 1978. BS, Quinnipiac Coll., 1969; MBA, U. New Haven, 1973. Mgr. budgets The Stanley Works, New Britian, Conn., 1972-76; mgr. planning Bangor Punta Corp., Greenwich, Conn., 1976-79; asst. corp. controller Pepperidge Farm, Norwalk, Conn., 1979-81, dir. fin. services, 1981-82, group controller, 1982-83; corp. controller Plessey, Inc., White Plains, N.Y., 1983-84, v.p. finance, 1984-86, chief fin. officer, 1986—. Mem. Rep. Town. Com., Newtown, Conn., 1981; bd. dirs. Danbury Hosp., 1987—. Served with U.S. Army, 1969-76. Mem. Am. Inst. CPA's, Nat. Assn. Accts. Episcopalian. Club: Quasapuag Yacht (Middlebury, Conn.). Home: 24 Huntingtown Rd Newtown CT 06470 Office: Plessey Inc 925 Westchester Ave White Plains NY 10604

PALECKE, PETER VACLAY, real estate developer, management consultant; b. Prague, Bohemia, Czechoslovakia, Apr. 28, 1940; came to U.S., 1969; s. Vaclav and Anna (Zemkova) P.; m. Hana Kazdova, Nov. 15, 1968; children: David, Michael, Thomas. MS, Czechoslovak Inst. Tech., 1965; MBA, Stanford U., 1971. Field engr. indsl. Automation Co., Prague, 1965-69; assoc. dir. Philip Morris Internat., Lausanne, Switzerland, 1971-74; mktg. analyst Peterbilt Motors, Newark, Calif., 1976-77; sr. mgmt. cons. SRI Internat., Menlo Park, Calif., 1977-87; sr. v.p. mktg. Landbank Investments, Redwood City, Calif., 1987—; asst. to pres. Krofta Engring., Lenox, Mass., 1984-86. Exec. dir. World Freedom Found., Redwood City, 1984-87; pres. Ski Found., 1985-86; patroller Nat. Ski Patrol, 1976—. 1st lt. Czechoslovak Army, 1965. Mem. Urban Land Inst., Alpine Meadows Club (Calif.). Republican. Roman Catholic. Home: 68 Mesa Ct Atherton CA 94025 Office: Landbank Investments 2221 Broadway St Redwood City CA 94063

PALERMO, NICHOLAS J., banker; b. Jersey City, Feb. 9, 1937; s. Joseph Anthony and Agostina (Tosto) P.; m. Josephine Davino, Apr. 30, 1960; children: Jennifer Lee, Cristina Nicole. B.A. in Polit. Sci., Rutgers U., 1958; M.B.A. in Bus. Mgmt., Fairleigh Dickinson U., 1967. V.p. personnel ops. Citibank, N.Y.C., 1973-75; v.p. div. exec. ops. Europe Chase Manhattan Bank, N.Y.C., 1975-76, v.p. internat. ops. and systems, 1976-78, sr. v.p., group exec. customer services, 1978-81, sr. v.p., group exec. human resources and customer services, 1981-82, sr. v.p., group exec. internat. ops. and systems, 1982-88; with Amalgamated Bank N.Y., 1988, pres., chief exec. officer, 1989—; dir. Chase Bank Internat., Newark, Del., 1979—. Disting lectr.: oral thesis The Management Process, 1979—. Commr. recreation Borough of Oradell Mcpl. Govt., N.JH., 1980—; founder, past pres. Oradell chpt. Unico Nat., 1981—. Served to 1st lt. U.S. Army, 1958-61; maj. USAR, ret., 1979. Named Mgr. of Yr. Fla. A&M U., Tallahassee, 1982. Mem. Am. Bankers Assn. (chmn. automation subcom. 1971-73), Com. on Internat. Banking, Columbus Citizens Found., Rutgers U. Alumni Assn., Fairleigh Dickinson Univ. Grad. Sch. Alumni Assn., Delta Mu Delta. Republican. Roman Catholic. Home: 385 Chapin Ct Oradell NJ 07549 Office: Amalgamated Bank NY 11-15 Union Sq New York NY 10003

PALERMO, PETER M., JR, photography equipment company executive; b. Rochester, N.Y., Aug. 21, 1941; s. Peter M. and Adeline M. (Bruno) P.; m. Marcia G. Hendershott, Aug. 25, 1962; children; Peter M., Lisa M., Michelle A. B.A., Bowling Green U., 1963; M.B.A., U. Rochester, 1973. Mgr. mktg. Kodak Caribbean, Ltd., San Juan, P.R., 1976-79; gen. mgr. Kodak Philippines Ltd., Manila, 1979-81; gen. mgr. Mexican Ops. Eastman Kodak Co. Internat. Photo div., Mexico City, 1983-84; corp. v.p., gen. mgr. Eastman Kodak Co. Health Scis. div., Rochester, N.Y., 1984-86; corp. v.p., gen. mgr. consumer products div. Eastman Kodak Co., Rochester, 1986—; adj. faculty mem. Rochester Inst. of Tech., 1965-69. Contbr. articles to profl. jours. Dir. Am. C. of C., Manila, 1979-81. Recipient Catholic Media award Pope John Paul II, Manila, 1981; named one of Outstanding Young Men of Am., 1973. Fellow Profl. Photog. Soc. of Philippines; mem. Health Industry Mfrs. Assn. (corp. mem.), Internat. Mgmt. Assn. (corp. mem.), Photo Mktg. Assn. Internat. (corp.mem.), Assn. Photog. Mfrs. Mex. Republican. Roman Catholic. Clubs: Manila Polo, Dorado Beach Country P.R. Lodge: Rotary (dir. Manila, 1979-81). Office: Eastman Kodak Co 343 State St Rochester NY 14650

PALEY, RICHARD THOMAS, real estate developer, consultant; b. N.Y.C., Sept. 5, 1936; s. Jack and Kate (Tuman) P. Student Rensselaer Poly. Inst., 1954-57. Chmn. The Palinger Corp., N.Y.C., 1981—; chmn. internat. adv. bd. Inst. Specialized Plastic and Reconstructive Surgery, Norfolk, Va., 1984—. Contbr. articles to profl. jours. Bd. dirs. Har-You Act Corp., N.Y.C., 1969-70, Omega Inst., Rhinebeck, N.Y., 1982—, Western Wind Ensemble, N.Y.C., 1983—. Avocations: astronomy; music; writing. Office: The Palinger Corp 20th E 35th St Ste 1B New York NY 10010

PALEY, WILLIAM S., broadcasting executive; b. Chgo., Sept. 28, 1901; s. Samuel and Goldie (Drell) P.; m. Dorothy Hart Hearst, May 11, 1932; children: Jeffrey, Hilary; m. Barbara Cushing Mortimer, July 28, 1947; children: William Cushing, Kate Cushing. Grad., Western Mil. Acad., Alton, Ill., 1918; student, U. Chgo., 1918-19; B.S., U. Pa., 1922; LL.D., Adelphi U., 1957, Bates Coll., 1963, U. Pa., 1968, Columbia U., 1975, Brown U., 1975, Pratt Inst., 1977, Dartmouth Coll., 1979; L.H.D., Ithaca Coll., 1978, U. So. Calif., 1985, Rutgers U., 1986, L.I. U., Southampton, 1987. Vice-pres., sec. Congress Cigar Co., Phila., 1922-28; pres. CBS, Inc., N.Y.C., 1928-46, chmn. bd., 1946-83, founder chmn., 1983-86, acting chmn., 1986-87, chmn., 1987—, also dir.; ptnr. Whitcom Investment Co., 1982—; founder, bd. dirs. Genetics Inst., 1980—, Thinking Machines Corp., 1983—; co-chmn. Internat. Herald Tribune, 1983—. Trustee Mus. Modern Art, from 1937, pres., 1968-72, chmn., 1972-85, chmn. emeritus, 1985—; life trustee Columbia U., 1950-73, trustee emeritus, 1973—, bd. dirs. W. Averell Harriman Inst. for Advanced Study of Soviet Union, Columbia U.; mem. Com. for White House Conf. on Edn., 1954-56; chmn. Pres.'s Materials Policy Commn. which produced report "Resources for Freedom, 1951-52; mem. exec. com. Resources for the Future, 1952-69, chmn., 1966-69, hon. bd. dirs., from 1969; chmn. N.Y.C. Task Force on Urban Design which prepared the report The Threatened City, 1967, Urban Design Council City N.Y., 1968-71; pres., dir. William S. Paley Found., Greenpark Found., Inc.; trustee North Shore Univ., Hosp., 1949-73, co-chmn. bd. trustees, 1954-73; founding mem. Bedford-Stuyvesant

D and S Corp., dir., 1967-72; founder, chmn. bd. Mus. of Broadcasting, from 1976; mem. Commn. on Critical Choices for Am., 1973-77, Commn. for Cultural Affairs, N.Y.C., 1975-78; life trustee Fedn. Jewish Philanthropies of N.Y. Served as col. AUS, World War II; dep. chief psychol. warfare div. SHAEF; dep. chief info. control div. USGCC. Decorated Legion of Merit; Medal for Merit; officer Legion of Honor France; Croix de Guerre with Palm France; comdr. Order of Merit Italy; assoc. comdr. Order of St. John of Jerusalem; recipient Gold Achievement medal Poor Richard Club; Keynote award Nat. Assn. Broadcasters; George Foster Peabody award citation, 1958, 1961; spl. award Broadcast Pioneers; award Concert Artist Guild, 1965; Skowhegan Gertrude Vanderbilt Whitney award; gold medal award Nat. Planning Assn., David Sarnoff award U. Ariz., 1979, gold medallion Soc. of Family of Man, 1982, Joseph Wharton award Wharton Sch. Club N.Y., 1983, Life Achievement award TV Guide, 1984, award Ctr. for Communications, 1985; co-recipient Walter Cronkite award Ariz. State U., 1984; Medallion of Honor City of N.Y.; First Amendment Freedoms award Anti-Defamation League B'nai B'rith; Robert Eunson Distinguished Service award Assn. Press Broadcasters; named to Jr. Achievement Nat. Bus. Hall of Fame, 1984. Mem. Council Fgn. Relations, France Am. Soc., Acad. Polit. Scis., Nat. Inst. Social Scis., Royal Soc. Arts (fellow). Clubs: River, Century Assn; The Metropolitan (Washington); Turf and Field, Nat. Golf, Meadowbrook; Economic (N.Y.); Lyford Cay (Nassau); Bucks (London). Office: Mus Broadcasting 1 E 35th St New York NY 10022 also: CBS Inc 51 W 52nd St New York NY 10019

PALINKAS, JAMES THOMAS, accountant, financial executive; b. Winburne, Pa., Apr. 30, 1945; s. Thomas Philip and Sophie Mae (Biggins) P.; m. Patricia Ann Bruggeman, Apr. 15, 1972. AS in Acctg., York Coll., 1973, BS %, 1977; MBA in Fin., Loyola Coll., 1982. CPA, Pa., Md. Acct. Fecor Industries, York, Pa., 1969-70, Wickes Industries, Mt. Wolf, Pa., 1970-72, Record Club Am., Manchester, Pa., 1972-73; chief acct. Graham Engring.Corp., York, 1973-80; contr. Graham Container Corp., York, 1980-83; contr. Poly Seal Corp., Balt., 1983-86, v.p. fin., 1986—. Bd. dirs. YMCA, Balt., 1986-87. Sgt. USAF, 1965-69. Mem. Md. Assn. CPA's. Republican. Lutheran. Home: 514 Haverball Rd Joppa MD 21085 Office: Poly Seal Corp 8303 Pulaski Hwy Baltimore MD 21237

PALITZ, BERNARD G., financial service company executive; b. N.Y.C., Aug. 21, 1924; s. Clarence Y. and Ruth (Krummas) P.; m. Louise Beringer; children—Bernard G.Jr., Anne L. BS, MIT, 1947. Chmn. bd. Comml. Alliance Corp., N.Y.C., 1963—, Credit Alliance Corp., N.Y.C., 1963—, Leasing Svc. Corp., N.Y.C., 1963—, Fin. Guaranty Ins. Co., Wilmington, Del., 1975—, Colonial Surety Co., Pitts., 1976—. Trustee Coun. for Arts, MIT, 1979—, Haverford Coll., Pa., 1979-82, Rockefeller U. Coun. Mem. Harmonie Club (N.Y.C.), Quaker Ridge Club (Scarsdale, N.Y.), Beach Point Club (Mamaroneck, N.Y.). Home: PO Box 287 221 E 70 St New York NY 10021

PALITZ, CLARENCE YALE, JR., commercial finance executive; b. N.Y.C., Jan. 21, 1931; s. Clarence Yale and Ruth (Krumnes) P.; children: Michael, Suzanne. B.A., Dartmouth Coll., 1952; M.B.A., NYU, 1953. With Bankers Trust Co., N.Y.C., 1952-53; v.p., dir. Credit Am. Corp., N.Y.C., 1956-58; asst. sec. James Talcott, Inc., N.Y.C., 1958-60; v.p., mng. dir. Shopper's Park-Westmount, Ltd., Edmonton, Alta., Can., 1958-74; pres., dir. 140 E 72d St. Corp., N.Y.C., 1962-65, Comml. Alliance Corp., N.Y.C., 1963—, Credit Alliance Corp., N.Y.C., 1963—, Leasing Service Corp., N.Y.C., 1963—, Colonial Surety Co., Pitts., 1976—, Fin. Guaranty Ins. Co., Wilmington, Del., 1976—, Kidde Credit Corp., N.Y.C., 1976-80, First Interstate Comml. Alliance Corp., 1984-88, Fin. Fed. Corp., N.Y.C., 1989—; pres. Am. Rediscount Corp., N.Y.C., 1988—; pres., chmn. bd. dirs. First Land Devel. Inc., Allamuchy, N.J., 1987—; chmn. bd. Fin. Fed. Credit Corp., Houston; bd. dirs. City & Suburban Fin. Corp. Served to lt. (j.g.) USN, 1953-56. Office: Comml Alliance Corp 745 Fifth Ave New York NY 10021

PALIZZI, ANTHONY N., lawyer, retail corporation executive; b. Wyandotte, Mich., Oct. 27, 1942; s. Vincenzo and Nunziata (Dagostini) P.; m. Bonnie Marie Kirkwood, Mar. 11, 1966; children—A. Michael, Nicholas A. Ph.B., Wayne State U., 1964, J.D., 1966; LL.M., Yale U., 1967. Bar: Mich. 1967. Prof. law Fla. State U., Tallahassee, 1967-69; prof. law Tex. Tech U., Lubbock, 1969-71; atty. Kmart Corp., Troy, Mich., 1971-74, asst. sec., 1974-77, asst. gen. counsel, 1977-85, v.p., assoc. gen. counsel, 1985—. Editor law rev. Wayne State U., 1964-66. Chmn. Brandon Police and Fire Bd., Mich., 1982-87. Mem. ABA, State Bar Assn. Mich., Am. Soc. Corporate Secs. Roman Catholic.

PALKOWITSH, MARCUS STEVE, real estate developer and investor; b. Great Bend, Kans., Oct. 7, 1946; s. Anton Lawrence and Armina (Graf) P.; m. Margaret Mary Sheehan, Feb. 7, 1980. BS in Econs., Regis Coll., 1968. Owner MSP Cos., Denver, 1972—; bd. dirs. Jefferson Bank & Trust Co., Denver. Mem. Urban Land Inst., Nat. Home Builders Assn., Ducks Unltd. Republican. Roman Catholic. Office: MSP Cos 650 S Cherry St Suite 1050 Denver CO 80222

PALLONE, JOSEPH ANDREW, financial executive; b. Bridgeport, Conn., May 20, 1947; s. Andrew Daniel and Mary (Totora) P.; student Fairfield U., 1965-67; B.S. in Mgmt., Sacred Heart U., 1976, M.B.A., 1985; m. Leslie Gina Klein, Dec. 16, 1979; 1 son, Benjamin Joseph. With Litton Industries Credit Corp., 1972-76; dir. fin. services DPF Inc., Hartsdale, N.Y., 1976-81; v.p. fin. Somerset Investment Services, Westport, Conn., 1981-84; pres. Amerigroup Leasing, Inc., Conn., 1984-87; pres. AmeriGroup, Inc., Conn., 1986-87; pvt. fin. and real estate investment cons., Longwood, Fla., 1987—; adj. instr. Orlando Coll., 1989. Served with USAF, 1967-71. Recipient cert. of accomplishment Nat. Credit Office. Home: 414 Twisting Pine Cir Longwood FL 32779 Office: PO Box 916281 Longwood FL 32791-6281

PALM, LOU LAVANCE, clothing company executive; b. Fairfield, Iowa, Jan. 28, 1937; s. Paul LaVance and Ercel I. (Keller) P.; m. Janice Elaine Smith, Nov. 23, 1958; children: Paula, Steven. BA, Parsons Coll., 1959. Asst. mgr. Perry Clothing, Fairfield, 1954-65; owner, operator Palm Clothing, Creston, Iowa, 1965—. Bd. dirs. Creston Devel., 1978-88. Mem. Iowa Retail Clothing Assn. (bd. dirs. 1978-81). Roman Catholic. Lodges: KC, Elks. Home: RR Rt 4 Country Club Creston IA 50801 Office: Palm Clothing 110-112 N Maple Creston IA 50801

PALM, NANCY CLEONE, medical center administrator, radiography technologist; b. Portland, Oreg., July 8, 1939; d. Oscar Emanuel and Hallie Vernice (Thurber) Palm. Student U. Oreg. Sch. Radiology, 1957; grad. Hosp. Corpswave, Hosp. Corps Sch., Great Lakes (Ill. Naval Base, 1958; grad. X-ray Tech., Sch. Radiology, Bremerton, Wash. Naval Base, 1961. Lic. radiography technologist, Oreg. Chief radiography technologist New Lincoln Hosp., Toledo, Oreg., 1961-63; sr. radiography technologist Gresham (Oreg.) Gen. Hosp., 1963-65; chief radiography technologist Neurol. Clinic, Portland, Oreg., 1965-79; head bookkeeper Rinehart Clinic, Wheeler, Oreg., 1979-80; owner, gen. mgr. San Dune Motel, Manzanita, Oreg., 1971-83; bus. agt. Rinehart Found., Inc., Manzanita, 1983—; owner Sears & Roebuck Catalog Store, Nehalem, Oreg., 1979-81; adminstrn. mgr. Rinehart Found., Inc. (Nehalem Bay Med. Ctr.), Manzanita and Garibaldi, Oreg., 1980—. Sponsor Willamette council Campfire Girls, Inc., 1982-84. Served with USN, 1958-61. Fellow Nat. Coll. Radiography Technologists; mem. Oreg. Med. Group Mgmt. Assn., Nat. Assn. Female Execs., Am. Registry Clin. Radiography Technologists (nat. dir. 1970-76, trustee 1972-74, sec. 71-72, pres. 72-74; Citation award 1970, Disting. Service award 1971, 73, Order of Golden Ray 1974, founder Margaret Harris Award Competition 1973). Republican. Presbyterian. Home: 423 Dorcas Lane PO Box 262 Manzanita OR 97130 Office: PO Box 580 Manzanita OR 97130

PALME, LENNART ALEXANDER, JR., commodity trading consultant; b. Port Chester, N.Y., Sept. 30, 1935; s. Lennart A. and Jessica Burt (Colvin) P.; student U. Calif., Santa Barbara, 1952-53; B.A., Stanford U., 1956, M.B.A., 1958; m. Virginia Ann Fisher, Dec. 23, 1977; children by previous marriage—Theodore Colvin, Pamela Esterly Koenig, Christopher Alexander. Supr. agrl. mktg. Kern County Land Co., Bakersfield, Calif., 1958-64; agrl. economist Armour & Co., Chgo., 1964-67; livestock economist Hayden Stone Co., Chgo., 1967-70; mgr. Clayton Brokerage Co., Santa Barbara, Calif., 1971-76; mgr. livestock mktg. Allied Mills, Inc., Chgo., 1976-78; mgr. agrl. research Chgo. Merc. Exchange, 1978-83; v.p., cons. assoc. Robert H. Meier & Assocs., Chgo., 1983-84; mgr. commodity trading Geldermann Inc., 1985-86; account exec., trade advisor Stotler & Co., Chgo., 1987-88; rsch. dir., tchr. Market Logic Sch., 1989—; instr. Santa Barbara Coll., 1973-74. Regional v.p. Calif. Young Republicans, Bakersfield, 1964; chmn. Kern County (Calif.) Goldwater for Pres., Bakersfield, 1964; campaign mgr. Crane for Congress, Northbrook, Ill., 1969. Mem. Livestock Merchandising Inst. (trustee), Chgo. Agrl. Economists Club (past pres.), Stanford Alumni Assn., Phila. Soc. Republican. Christian Scientist. Contbg. author The Feedlot, 1972, Trading Strategies, 1984; contbr. articles to profl. jours. Home: 739 Forest Glen Oak Brook IL 60521 Office: Market Logic Sch 401 S LaSalle St 1101 Chicago IL 60605

PALMER, CURTIS HOWARD, diversified company executive, lawyer; b. Oakland, Calif., 1908; s. Howard H. and Catherine May (Larkin) P.; m. Helen Hayes, Apr. 8, 1936. LL.B., U. Calif., 1932. Sole practice 1932-35; tax counsel Calif. Bd. of Equalization, 1935-43; gen. counsel Alfred Hart, Los Angeles, 1943-60; exec. officer City Nat. Bank, Beverly Hills, Calif., 1960-75, chmn. bd., 1975; chmn. bd. Arden Group, Inc., Beverly Hills, 1976—; dir. Internat. Aluminum Corp.; chmn. bd. dirs. Arden Group Inc. Office: Arden Group Inc 9595 Wilshire Blvd Ste 411 Beverly Hills CA 90012

PALMER, DAISY ANN, marketing coordinator; b. Burkburnett, Tex.; d. Leroy Evans and Christine Cleo (Givens) Walker; children: Christy Ann Yazdi, Cyndi Ann Thornhill. Cert. in Human Relations, Oreg. Coll. Edn., 1976, BA cum laude in Liberal Studies, Edwards U., Tex., 1983. Cert. interpreter for hearing impaired, Tex. and U.S. Mgr., R.R. Realty/Ins., Wichita Falls, Tex., 1973-75; cons. state agys., 1975-85; asst. coordinator Travis County Services for Deaf, Austin, 1979-81; adminstr. Tex. Assn. Deaf, Austin, 1981-85; promotion dir. McGregor Studios, Austin, 1981—; mktg. coordinator Tex. Mcpl. League, Austin, 1985—; interpreter, legis. communicator VISTA, 1981-82. Editor: Tex. Assn. Deaf Directory of Services, 1984; researcher and author of statis. studies; interpreter for first Japan-U.S. Conf., 1985. Chmn. Gov.'s Communication Barriers Council, 1984; vice chair Austin St. Sch. Adv. Council, 1984-86. Recipient Golden Hand award Nat. Assn. Deaf, Toastmasters Internat. Communication Leadership award, 1976. Mem. Nat. Registry Interpreters, Tex. Assn. Deaf (Golden Hand award for legis. activities 1983), Austin Bus. League. Home: 7301 Ferndale Cove Austin TX 78745 Office: Tex Mcpl League 211 E 7th Ste 1020 Austin TX 78701

PALMER, DAVID WILLIAM, broadcast executive, operator; b. Columbus, Ohio, Nov. 25, 1949; s. Fred Alden and Miriam Francis Palmer; m. Barbara Jean Wince, June 1971 (div. Aug., 1986); children: Jacquelin Rain, Nicholas Marshall; m. Patricia Bair- Bresnahan, Oct. 1987. Student, Sheridan Coll., 1967-69, Ohio State U., 1969-70, U. Hawaii, 1972-73; exec. computer mgmt. course, IBM; broadcast exec. mgmt. course, Harvard U. Pres. Sta. WATH/WXTQ, Athens, Ohio, 1973—, Target Broadcast Group Inc., Norfolk, Va., 1987—, Sta. WRAP, Norfolk, Va., 1987—. Regional dir. Emergency Broadcast System, 1975—; mem. Ohio U. Trustees Acad., 1973—; bd. dirs. Athens Community Improvements Corp., 1984—, Friends of the Orch., 1984—, Ohio Valley Summer Theater, 1981-84; chmn. pub. mission com. Ohio U. Sch. Music, 1981-83; advisor dept. indsl. tech. Ohio U., 1979—; founder United Srs. of Athens Inc., 1979-81; v.p. Housing for Athens Sr. Residents Inc., 1977-84; mem. Ohio U. Learning Alternatives Task Force, 1977-78; bd. dirs. Athens County Heart Fund, 1976-78; advisor Hocking Tech. Coll., 1974-88; bd. dirs. Dairy Barn Cultural Arts Ctr., 1978-82; treas. Athens County United Appeal, 1973-80; bd. dirs. Athens Hist. Downtown Revitalization Project, 1977—; pres. Athens City Council, 1979-88; treas. First Presbyn. Ch., 1983-85. Served with U.S. Army, 1970-73. Decorated Joint Service Commendation medal; recipient Emergency Broadcast Systems award 1978. Mem. Nat. Assn. Broadcasters, (bd. dirs. 1983—), Daytime Broadcasters (chmn. 1984—), Radio Advt. Bur. N.Y.C., Ohio Assn. Broadcasters, Soc. Broadcast Engrs. N.Y.C., Audio Engring. Soc. N.Y.C., Athens C. of C. (chmn. 1983-84, meritorious service award 1985), Tidewater C. of C. (sales and mktg. execs.), Athens Jaycees (v.p. 1973-76, DSA 1978), Ohio C. of C., Ohio U. Assocs., VFW, Am. Fedn. Musicians, Percussion Arts Soc., Nat. Assn. Rudimental Drummers. Club: Ohio U. Green & White (v.p. 1974-76). Lodges: Kiwanis (community service award 1969), Rotary (v.p. Athens club 1985—). Home: 200 82nd St Virginia Beach VA 23451 Office: WRAP Radio 3850 Broadway Portsmouth VA 23703

PALMER, JAMES ROBERT, electronics executive, consultant; b. Elm Creek, Nebr., Dec. 13, 1923; s. Charles Andrew and Margaret Eleanor (Mitchell) P.; m. Barbara M. Raeder, Aug. 21, 1948; children: Janet Palmer Lipcon, David, Charles. BS, Iowa State U. 1944; postgrad. U.S. Naval Officers PreRadar and Radar Schs., Bowdoin Coll., Mass. Inst. Tech.; postgrad. advanced engring. program Gen. Electric Co. 1947. Registered profl. engr., Pa. Project engr. Gen. Electric Co., Phila. 1946-51; elec. engr. United Engrs. and Constructors, Inc., Phila., 1951-53; project engr. Haller, Raymond and Brown, Inc., State College, Pa. 1953-56; pres. Centre Video and subs., State College, 1956-72; pres. C-COR Electronics, State College, 1956-83, chmn., chief exec. officer, 1983-85; pres. Pa. Ctr. Stage, Caribbean Descramblers Co.; bd. dirs. Broadband Networks, Inc., Diamond Materials Inst., Inc., Allegheny Ednl. Broadcast Council, 1966-74; mem. profl. adv. com. for radio, TV and film Pa. State U., 1983-85; mem. elec. engring. adv. council Iowa State U., 1984—. Patentee in field. Mem. Nat. Cable TV Assn. (bd. dirs. 1965-68, chmn. various coms.), Pa. Community Antenna Assn. (pres. 1966-67, bd. dirs. 1960-66), Pa. Cable TV Hall of Fame, IEEE (sr. mem.; vice-chmn. communication and info. policy com. 1983-84), Soc. Cable TV Engrs. (sr.), Tau Beta Pi, Eta Kappa Nu, Phi Kappa Phi. Presbyterian (elder).

PALMER, JAMES RUSSWORTH, theoretical physicist, high energy laser optics researcher; b. Madera, Calif., Oct. 12, 1936; s. James Russworth Palmer and Georgella (Bartmann) Palmer Irelan; m. Norma Elizabeth Boyer (div. 1974); children: Susan Lynn, Debra Ann, Martin Daniel; m. Bonnie Elizabeth Shields, Aug. 7, 1977 (div. 1986); m. Nancy Diane Byrne, Jan. 21, 1988. BSChemE, Calif. State U., 1963, MSChemE, 1966; PhD, UCLA, 1973. Project scientist Aerospace Controls, Los Angeles, 1963-66; project engr. Electroptical Systems, Pasadena, Calif., 1966-70; pres.-cons. Doc Jim Enterprises, Orange, Calif., 1970—; chief scientist Comarco, Inc., Ridgecrest, Calif., 1983-87; adj. sr. research scientist U. Ala. Ctr. for Applied Optics, Huntsville, 1987—; cons. Seven Engring., Santa Monica, Calif., 1980—. Author: Laser Damage in Optical Thin Films, 1985; also numerous articles, 1963—. Served to lt. (j.g.) USN, 1955-59. Mem. Optical Soc. Am., Am. Inst. Physics, N.Y. Acad. Scis., Internat. Soc. Optical Engring. (Rudolf Kingslake Silver medal 1984), Sigma Xi.

PALMER, JUDSON LEE, JR., lawyer, real estate developer; b. Kansas City, Mo., Dec. 21, 1944; s. Judson Lee and Jane (Simrall) P.; m. Linda Rowland, Mar. 21, 1970; 1 child, Judson Lee III. BS, U. Mo., 1966, JD, 1969. Bar: Okla. 1969, Mo. 1970. Jr. ptnr. Stinson Mag Law Firm, Kansas City, 1970-78; sr. ptnr. Gaar & Bell Law Firm, Kansas City, 1978-86; mng. dir. Bingham & Co., Kansas City, 1986—. Served to lt. USAR, 1969-75. Mem. ABA, Okla. Bar Assn., Mo. Bar Assn., Nat. Assn. Bond Attys. Democrat. Methodist. Clubs: Kansas City, Clayview Country (Liberty, Mo.), Liberty Hills Country. Lodge: Lions. Home: 317 Camelot Dr Liberty MO 64068 Office: Bingham & Co 1044 Main St Ste 560 Kansas City MO 64105

PALMER, PAUL EDWIN, JR., financial planner; b. Lake Charles, La., Feb. 24, 1958; s. Paul Edwin and Yolande Marie (McLin) P.; m. Heather Harland Gill, Aug. 31, 1958. BSBA, La. State U., 1980; cert., Coll. for Fin. Planning, Denver, 1986. Acct. Mobil Oil Corp., Dallas, 1980-82; comml. lender Nat. Bank Commerce-Houston, 1983-84; fin. planner CIGNA Individual Fin. Svcs. Co., Houston, 1984—. Mem. Inst. for Cert. Fin. Planners, Internat. Assn. for Fin. Planning. Republican. Episcopalian. Home: 11223 Hambleton Way Houston TX 77065 Office: CIGNA Individual Fin Svcs Co 1360 Post Oak Blvd Suite 2500 Houston TX 77056

PALMER, PHILIP RONALD, electrical engineer; b. Wolverhampton, Eng., Oct. 2, 1956; came to U.S., 1981; s. Ronald Frederick and Wendy Ann (Parry) P.; m. Sally Ann Saunders, July 26, 1986. BS in Electronics and Physics with honors, North Wales U., Eng., 1978. Engr. Brit. Aerospace, Warton, Eng., 1978-81; with GTE Products, Westboro, Mass., 1981-82; mgr. Simmonds Precision Co., Vergennes, Vt., 1982—. Mem. IEEE, Inst. Elec. Engrs. London, Bentley Owners Eng. Republican. Home: 9 Davis Ave Shelburne VT 05482 Office: Simmonds Precision Panton Rd Vergennes VT 05491

PALMER, ROBERT TOWNE, lawyer; b. Chgo., May 25, 1947; s. Adrian Bernhardt and Gladys (Towne) P.; BA, Colgate U., 1969; JD, U. Notre Dame, 1974; m. Ann Therese Darin, Nov. 9, 1974; children: Justin Darin, Christian Darin. Bar: Ill. 1974, D.C. 1978, U.S. Supreme Ct. 1978. Law clk. Hon. Walter V. Schaefer, Ill. Supreme Ct., 1974-75; assoc. McDermott, Will & Emery, Chgo., 1975-81, ptnr., 1982-86; ptnr. Chadwell & Kayser, Ltd., 1987-88; Connelly, Mustes and Palmer, 1988—; mem. adj. faculty Chgo. Kent Law Sch., 1975-77, Loyola U., 1976-78; mem. adv. com. Fed. Home Loan Mortgage Corp., 1988—. Mem. ABA, Ill. State Bar Assn. (Lincoln award 1983), Ill. Assn. Def. Trial Counsel, Chgo. Bar Assn., D.C. Bar Assn., Internat. Assn. Def. Counsel, Chgo. Club, Univ. Club, Dairymen's Club, North Shore Country Club, Lambda Alpha. Republican. Episcopalian. Contbr. articles to legal jours. and textbooks. Office: Connelly Mustes & Palmer 208 S LaSalle St Ste 1800 Chicago IL 60604

PALMER, RUSSELL EUGENE, accountant, dean of faculty; b. Jackson, Mich., Aug. 13, 1934; s. Russell E. and Margarite M. (Briles) P.; m. Phyllis Anne Hartung, Sept. 8, 1956; children: Bradley Carl, Stephen Russell, Russell Eugene, III, Karen Jean. BA with honors, Mich. State U., 1956; D in Comml. Sci. (hon.), Drexel U., 1980; MA (hon.), U. Pa., 1984; PhD (hon.), Chulalongkorn U., 1988. With Touche Ross & Co., N.Y.C., 1956-83, mng. ptnr., chief exec. officer, 1972-82, also bd. dirs., exec. coms.; mng. dir., chief exec. officer Touche Ross Internat., 1974-83; dean, Reliance prof. mgmt. and pvt. enterprise Wharton Sch. U. Pa., 1983—; bd. dirs. GTE Corp., The May Dept. Stores Co., Bankers Trust Co., Allied-Signal, Inc. Mem. pub. bds. Dirs. & Bds., Mergers & Aquisitions. Pres. Fin. Acctg. Found., 1979-82; trustee Acctg. Hall of Fame; bd. dirs. Joint Council Econ. Edn., 1978-83, United Fund Greater N.Y., 1980-83, UN Assn. USA; mem. Bus. Com. Arts, 1977-83; mem. Pres.'s Mgmt. Improvement Council, 1979-80; mem. N.Y. adv. bd. Salvation Army; former mem. adv. council Columbia U. Sch. Internat. and Pub. Affairs, Stanford U. Grad. Sch. Bus., Womens Way; mem. Assocs. Council Bus. Sch., Oxford U.; former mem. nat. adv. bd. Salvation Army; adv. panel Comptroller Gen. U.S.; mem. U.S. Sec. Labor's Commn. on Workforce Quality and Labor Market Efficiency. Recipient Gavin Meml. award Beta Theta Pi, 1956, Disting. Community Service award Brandeis U., 1974, Outstanding Alumnus award Mich. State U., 1978, LEAD Bus. award, 1984, Good Scout award Phila. Council Boy Scouts Am., 1987. Mem. Dirs. Table (bd. govs.), Beta Gamma Sigma (bd. govs.), Conf. Bd. (bd. dirs.). Presbyterian. Clubs: Links (N.Y.), Union League (N.Y.); The Courts of Phila.; Merion Cricket, Field of Greenwich, Round Hill; Lost Tree Country (Palm Beach, Fla.). Office: U Pa Wharton Sch 3620 Locust Walk Ste 1000 Philadelphia PA 19104-6364

PALMESE, RICHARD DOMINICK, music company executive; b. Bklyn., Oct. 21, 1947; s. Dominick Arthur and Teresa Gertrude (Buonagura) P.; m. Lana Dee Beery, Oct. 20, 1951; 1 child, Richard Andrew. BA, St. Louis U., 1969; postgrad., Mission Fathers Sem., St. Louis, 1971-73. Disc jockey Sta. KSHE, St. Louis, 1966-70; sales mgr. Hartford (Conn.) Times, 1970-71; Midwest mgr. Buddah Records, N.Y.C., 1974-75; sr. v.p. Arista Records, N.Y.C., 1975-83; exec. v.p., gen. mgr. MCA Records, Los Angeles, 1983—. Named Promotion Exec. of Yr., Poe Pop Music Awards, 1979, 82, Exec. of Yr., Poe Pop Music Awards, 1983, 86. Democrat. Roman Catholic. Office: MCA Records Inc 70 Universal City Pla Universal City CA 91608

PALMIERI, VICTOR HENRY, lawyer, business executive; b. Chgo., Feb. 16, 1930; s. Mario and Maria (Losacco) P.; m. Martha Cooley, Dec. 27, 1951 (div. 1980); children: Victor Henry, Matthew B., John W.; m. Rhonda K. Martyn, Oct. 10, 1981 (div. 1987). AB in History, Stanford U., 1951, JD, 1954. Bar: Calif. 1954. Assoc. O'Melveny & Myers, L.A., 1955-59; exec. v.p. Janss Investment Corp., L.A., 1959-63, pres., 1963-68; chmn. Pa. Co. and its subs. Great S.W. Corp., 1969-77; chmn. bd. Palmieri Co., N.Y.C., 1969—; chmn. bd. PHL Corp. Inc., Phila. 1983-87—, Pa. Co. and subs. Great Southwest Corps., 1969-77. Chmn. Am. Learning Corp., 1970-85; dep., exec. dir. Nat. Adv. Commn. on Civil Disorders, 1967-68; ambassador-at-large, U.S. Coordinator Refugee Affairs, Dept. State, 1979-81; trustee Rockefeller Found., 1979-89; pres., bd. dirs. Lincoln Ctr. Theater; chmn. Overseas Devel. Coun. Office: Palmieri Co 237 Park Ave 11th Fl New York NY 10017

PALMS, PETER JOHN, IV, venture capitalist; b. Rijswijk, The Netherlands, Apr. 27, 1934; came to U.S., 1951; s. Peter John III and Mimi Adele (De Jong) P.; children: Bart Douglas, Valerie Grace.douglos. BS, Rutgers U., 1957; PhD in Econs., U. Oxford, Eng., 1986. V.p. R.J. Reynolds Co., Miami, Fla., 1968-71; pres. Palms & Co., Redmond, Wash., 1968—; pres. enterprises div. Yakima (Wash.) Indian Nation, 1978-80, Lummin Indian Community Devel. Corp., Bellingham, Wash., 1980, Pacific NW Venture Fund, Redmond, 1984—; v.p., dir. Asian Yukon Gold Mines, Ltd., Can., 1988—; v.p. Pacific NW Enterprises, Bremerton, Wash., 1988—; chmn. bd. dirs. Internat. Payphones, Inc., Redmond, 1988—; dir. Minority Bus. Devel. Ctr., Seattle Minority Bus. Devel. Agy., U.S. Dept. Commerce. Roman Catholic. Office: Palms & Co 6702 139th Ave NE Suite 760 Redmond WA 98052

PALOMBO, JAN ALMA, jewelry manufacturing executive, designer; b. Lynn, Mass., Apr. 24, 1943; d. Carl Albert and Alma Clara (Wilson) Palombo; children: Sarah Brothers, Flora Ann Brothers. Student, Boston Mus. Sch., 1963, 65; BA, Jackson Coll., Medford, Mass., 1964. Tchr. Lynnfield (Mass.) High Sch., 1964-65; archeology asst. U. Ala., Merida and Yucatan, Mex., 1965-66; tchr. Algiers (La.) High Sch., 1967; chief exec. officer, designer Gt. Falls Metalworks, Paterson, N.J., 1968—. Home: 71 Norwood Ave Glen Rock NJ 07452

PALSHO, DOROTHEA COCCOLI, publishing executive; b. Phila., June 9, 1947; d. John Charles and Dorothy Lucille (Decker) C.; m. Edward Robert Palsho; children: Christopher, Ryan, Erica (stepchild). BS, Villanova U., 1976; MBA, Temple U., 1977. With Dow Jones & Co., Princeton, N.J., 1977—. Named one of Class of Women Achievers YWCA Acad. of Women Achievers, 1985. Office: Dow Jones & Co Inc PO Box 300 Princeton NJ 08543

PALUBIAK, RICHARD CRAIG, marketing professional, educator; b. St. Louis, Nov. 30, 1954; s. Charles and Francis (Zenthoefer) P.; m. Gail Simpson, Dec. 27, 1979; children: Kelly Michelle, Steven Guy. BS in Mktg., U. Mo., 1977; MBA, No. Ill. U., 1979. Sales rep. Metco, Inc., Westbury, N.Y., 1979-83; sales rep. Enterprise Fleets, Inc., St. Louis, 1983-85, nat. mgr., 1985-86, v.p. sales and mktg., 1986—; prof. Webster U., St. Louis, 1985—. Republican. Roman Catholic. Home: 2044 Oak Dr Saint Louis MO 63131 Office: Enterprise Fleets Inc #7 Hunter Ave Saint Louis MO 63124

PALUCH, BRIAN MICHAEL, controller; b. Chgo., Nov. 6, 1956; s. Stanley G. and Helen (Sulich) P.; m. Caroline E. Dittert, June 6, 1981; children: Matthew Brian, Emily Catherine. BS, Marquette U., Milw., 1978. Corp. auditor Allis Chalmers, Milw., 1978-80; sr. auditor Phillip Morris Cos., Milw., 1980-83; sr. fin. analyst Phillip Morris Cos., N.Y.C., 1983-85; corp. acct. mgr. Phillip Morris Cos., 1985-87; controller Cobro Corp., St. Louis, 1987—. Recipient Evans scholarship Western Golf (Ill.) Assn., 1974. Mem. Am. Inst. CPA's, Am. Mgmt. Assn. Home: 15585 Highcroft Chesterfield MO 63017

PALUMBO, JAMES FREDRICK, financial insurance company executive; b. Everett, Mass., Nov. 30, 1950; s. Bruno James and Lillian Elizabeth (Picardi) P.; m. Nancy Laurie Richards, July 24, 1976; children: Elizabeth Richards, Andrew Reid, Alexander Thomas. BA, Lake Forest Coll., 1973; MBA, Washington U., 1975. Market surveillance analyst Nat. Assn. of Securities Dealers, Washington, 1975-76, asst. treas., 1976-78; regional rep. Student Loan Mktg. Assn., Washington, 1978-79, mgr., 1979-81, dir., 1981-82, asst. v.p., 1982-83, v.p., 1983-87; sr. v.p. Sallie Mae Mgmt. Services Corp., Coll. Constrn. Loan Ins. Assn., Washington, 1987—; participant Govt.-Univ.-Inudstry Research Roundtable, Washington, 1986. Actor popular and children's theater, 1973-76. Chmn. sports announcers com.,

D.C. Spl. Olympics, Washington, 1986, 87, D.C. Regional Counsel, Lake Forest Coll., Washington, 1976-80; mem. Elliott Soc. mem. com. Washington U., 1986—, Great Falls (Va.) Hist. Soc.; bd. govs. Lake Forest Coll., 1978-82. Mem. Soc. Coll. and Univ. Planners, Great Falls Swim and Tennis Club (bd. dirs.), Alpha Psi Omega. Office: Coll Constrn Loan Ins Assn 2445 M NW Ste 450 Washington DC 20036

PAMPEL, ROLAND D., computer company executive; b. Mystic, Conn., Nov. 16, 1934; s. Alban and Doris (Denison) P.; m. Carol Patricia Clay, Apr. 5, 1958; children: Lynne Pampel Albertini, Jean Pampel Losier, Sandra. BSEE, U. Conn., 1956. Product mgr., then gen. mgr. IBM Corp., 1960-81; gen. mgr., lab dir. IBM Corp., Kingston, N.Y., until 1981; v.p. research and devel. Prime Computer, Natick, Mass., 1981-84; sr. v.p. mktg. and devel. AT&T Computer Div., Morristown, N.J., 1985; pres., chief operating officer Apollo Computer Inc., Chelmsford, Mass., 1986-88; pres., chief exec. officer Honeywell Bull Inc., Billerica, Mass., 1988—; also bd. dirs. Honeywell Bull Inc. Lt. USN, 1956-59. Mem. Nat. Computer Graphics Assn. (vice chmn. 1988—), Braeburn Country Club (Newton, Mass.). Office: Honeywell Bull Inc 300 Concord Rd Billerica MA 01821

PAMPLIN, ROBERT BOISSEAU, JR., agricultural company executive, minister, writer; b. Augusta, Ga., Sept. 3, 1941; s. Robert Boisseau and Mary Katherine (Reese) P.; m. Marilyn Joan Hooper; children: Amy Louise, Anne Boisseau. Student in bus. adminstrn. Va. Poly. Inst., 1960-62; BSBA, Lewis and Clark Coll., 1964, BS in Acctg., 1965, BS in Econs., 1966, MBA, U. Portland, 1968, MEd, 1975, LLD (hon.), 1972; MCL, Western Conservative Bapt. Sem., 1978, DMin, 1982, PhD, Calif. Coast U., DHL (hon.), Warner Pacific Coll., 1988; cert. in wholesale mgmt. Ohio State U., 1970; cert. in labor mgmt., U. Portland, 1972; cert. in advanced mgmt., U. Hawaii, 1975; DD (hon.), Judson Baptist Coll., 1984; DBA (hon.), Marquis Giuseppe Scicluna Internat. U. Found., 1986; LittD (hon.), Va. Tech. Inst. and State U., 1987, LHD (hon.), Warner Pacific Coll., 1988. Pres. R.B. Pamplin Corp., Portland, Oreg., 1964—; chmn. bd. Columbia Empire Farms, Inc., Lake Oswego, Oreg., 1976—; pres. Twelve Oaks Farms, Inc., Lake Oswego, 1977—; dir. Mt. Vernon Mill Inc.; lectr. bus. adminstrn. Lewis and Clark Coll., 1968-69; adj. asst. prof. bus. adminstrn., U. Portland, 1973-76; pastor Christ Community Ch., Lake Oswego, Oreg. lectr. in bus. adminstrn. and economics, U. Costa Rica, 1968, Va. Tech. Found., 1986, dir. R.B. Pamplin Corp., Ross Island Sand & Gravel Co. Author: Everything is Just Great, 1985, The Gift, 1986, Another Virginian: A Study of the Life and Beliefs of Robert Boisseau Pamplin, 1986, (with others): A Portrait of Colorado, 1976, Three in One, 1974, The Storybook Primer on Managing, 1974, One Who Believed, 1988; editor Oreg. Mus. Sci. and Industry Press, 1973, trustee, 1971, 74—; editor Portrait of Oregon, 1973, (with others) Oregon Underfoot, 1975. Mem. Nat. Adv. Council on Vocat. Edn., 1975—; mem. Western Interstate Comm. for Higher Edn., 1981-84; co-chmn. Va. Tech. $50 million Campaign for Excellence, 1984-87, Va. Tech. Found., 1986—, Albert Einstein Acad. Bronze medal, 1986, Va. 0 Oreg. State Scholarship Commn., 1974—, chmn., 1976-78; mem. Portland dist. adv. council SBA, 1973-77; mem. Rewards Review Com., City Portland, 1973-78, chmn., 1973-78; mem. bd. regents U. Portland, 1971-79, chmn. bd., 1975-79, regent emeritus, 1979—; trustee Lewis and Clark Coll., 1980-84, 85, Oreg. Epis. Schs., 1979. Named disting. alumnus, Lewis and Clark Coll., 1974; recipient Air Force ROTC Disting. Service award, USAF, 1974, Albert Einstein Acad. Bronze medal, 1986; Va. Tech Coll. of Bus. Adminstrn. renamed R.B. Pamplin Coll. of Bus. Adminstrn. in his honor; Western Conservative Bapt. Sem. Lay Inst. for Leadership, Edn., Devel. and Research named for R.B. Pamplin, Jr., 1988. Mem. Acad. Mgmt., Delta Epsilon Sigma, Beta Gamma Sigma, Sigma Phi Epsilon, Waverley Country Club, Arlington, Multnomah Athletic Club, Capitol Hill Club, Rotary. Republican. Episcopalian.

PANARETOS, JOHN, mathematics and statistics educator; b. Kythera, Lianianika, Greece, Feb. 23, 1948; s. Victor and Fotini (Kominu) P.; m. Evdokia Xekalaki; 1 child, Victor. First degree, U. Athens, 1972; MSc, U. Sheffield, Eng., 1974; PhD, U. Bradford, Eng., 1977. Lectr. U. Dublin, Ireland, 1979-80; asst. prof. U. Mo., Columbia, U.S, 1980-82; assoc. prof. U. Iowa, Iowa City, U.S., 1982-83, U. Crete, Iraklio, Greece, 1983-84; assoc. prof. div. applied math., Sch. Engring. U. Patras, Greece, 1984—, assoc. dean sch. engring., 1986-87; vice-rector U. Patras, 1988—; chmn. div. applied math. U. Patras, 1986-87; sec.-gen. Ministry Edn. and Religious Affairs, Greece. Contbr. articles to profl. jours. Active Sci. Counsil of Greek Parliament, 1987—. Mem. Am. Statis. Assn., Inst. Math. Statistics, Bernoulli Soc. for Probability and Math. Statistics, Greek Math. Soc., Greek Statis. Inst., Scientific Council Greek Parliament, Internat. Statis. Inst. Home: 18 Spetson St, 153 42 A Paraskevi, Athens Greece Office: U Patras Sch Engring, PO Box 1325, 26110 Patras Greece

PANASCI, HENRY ANTHONY, JR., retail drug chain executive; b. Rome, N.Y., June 7, 1928; s. Henry and Nellie (Cimini) P.; m. Faye B. Kocher, Sept. 3, 1955; children: Beth Ann, David H. BA in Sci., U. Buffalo, 1948, BS in Pharmacy, 1952; DSc (hon.), Union U., 1984, L.I. U., 1985. V.p. Carls Drug Co. Inc., Rome, N.Y., 1952-55; sales mgr. Brown Jones Drug Co., Erie, Pa., 1955-57; co-founder Fay's Drug Co., Inc., Liverpool, N.Y., 1958—; chmn. bd. Fay's Drug Co., Inc., 1976—; bd. dirs. Continental Info. Systems, Inc., Oneida Ltd., Unity Mut. Life Ins. Co., Onondaga Venture Capital Fund, Inc., Niagara Mohawk Power Corp. Chmn. Syracuse Symphony Orchestra, 1977-79, 84-88; pres. Arthritis Found. Central N.Y., 1980-81; trustee Syracuse U. Named Business Man of Year Syracuse Herald Jour., 1978. Mem. Nat. Assn. Chain Drug Stores (chmn. 1983-84), Syracuse C. of C. (chmn. 1981). Clubs: Century of Syracuse, Bellevue Country (Syracuse). Home: 3000 Howlett Hill Rd Camillus NY 13031 Office: Fays Drug Co 7245 Henry Clay Blvd Liverpool NY 13088

PANDO, ALAN OSCAR, advertising company executive; b. Iowa City, Nov. 13, 1931; s. Oscar Benjamin and Eva Marie (Schillig) P.; m. Elizabeth Harlow, June 22, 1956; children: Karen, Scott, Robert; m. Stacie Hunt, Oct. 17, 1981. B.S., U. Notre Dame, 1953. Product mgmt. cons. Chesebrough Ponds, N.Y.C., 1956-60; v.p. Benton & Bowles, N.Y.C., 1960-66; sr. v.p. Kenyon & Eckhirdt, N.Y.C., 1966-68; group sr. v.p. Doyle Dane Bernbach, N.Y.C., 1968-82; pres. Della Femina Travisano & Ptnrs., Los Angeles, 1982-85, DDB Needham West, Los Angeles, 1986—. Served to lt. (j.g.) USN, 1953-56. Office: DDB Needham West 5900 Wilshire Blvd Los Angeles CA 90036

PANFILE, ORLANDO ERNEST, aviation company executive; b. Little Ferry, N.J., May 20, 1928; s. Sante Panfile and Madeline Aiello; married; children: Esther, John. BS in Mgmt., Seton Hall U., 1951; MS in Statistics, Rutgers U., 1964. Cert. engr. Quality control mgr. Tung-Sol Elec., Bloomfield, N.J., 1951-64; v.p. Ampac, Inc., Jersey City, N.J., 1964-72; pres. Aero Services, Teterboro, N.J., 1972—; with Aviation Svcs. Group, Inc., Chgo. Author: Truncation and Its Effect on Average and Standard Deviation, 1963. Mayor Upper Saddle River, N.J., 1980-84. Mem. Rep. Club (pres. 1982—). Home: 96 Buckhaven Hill Upper Saddle River NJ 07458 Office: Aviation Svcs Group 5320 W 63rd St Chicago IL 60638

PANG, JOSHUA KEUN-UK, trade company executive; b. Chinnampo, Korea, Sept. 17, 1924; s. Ne-Too and Soon-Hei (Kim) P.; came to U.S., 1951, naturalized, 1968; B.S., Roosevelt U., 1959; m. He-Young Yoon, May 30, 1963; children—Ruth, Pauline, Grace. Chemist, Realemon Co. Am., Chgo., 1957-61; chief-chemist chem. div. Bell & Gossett Co., Chgo., 1961-63, Fatty Acid Inc., div. Ziegler Chem. & Mineral Corp., Chgo., 1963-64; sr. chemist-supr. Gen. Mills Chems. Inc., Kankakee, Ill., 1964-70; pres., owner UJU Industries Inc., Broadview, Ill., 1971—, also dir. Bd. dirs. Dist. 92, Lindop Sch., Broadview, 1976-87; chmn. Proviso Area Sch. Bd. Assn., Proviso Twp., Cook County, Ill., 1976-77; bd. dirs. Korean Am. Community Services, Chgo., 1979-80; mem. governing bd. Proviso Area Exceptional Children, Spl. Edn. Joint Agreement, 1981-84, 85-87; alumni bd. govs. Roosevelt U., 1983—. Mem. Am. Chem. Soc., Am. Inst. Parliamentarians (region 2 treas. 1979-81, region 2 gov. 1981-82), Internat. Platform Assn., Ill. Sch. Bd. Assn., Chgo. Area Parliamentarians, Parliamentary Leaders in Action (pres. 1980-81), Nat. Speakers Assn. (dir. Ill. chpt. 1981-82, nat. parliamentarian 1982-84, 2d v.p. chpt. 1983-84). Club: Toastmasters (dist. gov. 1969-1970), DADS Assn. U. Ill. (chmn. Cook County 1985—, bd. dirs. 1987—). Home: 2532 S 9th Ave Broadview IL 60153-4804 Office: JU Industries Inc PO Box 6351 Broadview IL 60153-6351

PANGERAPAN, BOB GEORGE, import-export and freight forwarding companies executive; b. Manado, Indonesia, Jan. 24, 1938; s. Timothius Simon T. Pangerapan and Welhelmina P. Lumingkewas; m. Ivonne Poluan, Nov. 29, 1962; children—Irene, Shirley, Debbie, Daisy. Ed. Faculty Econs., Indonesia U., Jakarta, 1961; PhD in Comml. and Indsl. Econ., WP U., L.A., 1988. Cert. internat. trade lectr. Ministry Trade Republic Indonesia. Import mgr. trading co., Jakarta, 1958-59; br. mgr. shipping co., Jakarta and Surabaya, 1959-63; pres., dir. import export Co., Jakarta, 1964—; ops. dir. stevedoring and transp. co., Jakarta, 1975-80; pres., dir. internat. freight-forwarding co., Jakarta, 1980—, PT. Roda Pelita Angkasa Internat. Freight Forwarding, Jakarta, 1980—, PT. Opedamy Ltd., Jakarta, 1980—, PT. Royal Perintis Abadi Corp., Jakarta, 1981—; chmn. PT. Pettor Indoversco, Jakarta, 1981—; pres. Indonesian Contract Bridge Jakarta, 1986. Sponsor, treas. Bohusami Found., Jakarta, 1983—; sponsor, v.p. Maesa Sport Assn., Jakarta, 1983—; sponsor, advisor student sport activities of various univs., Indonesia, 1979—, Jakarta Capital City Labour Found., 1980—. Sponsor, officer, team mgr. local, nat. and internat. contract bridge orgns., 1978—. Winner more than 20 1st prize cups in bridge competitions, numerous other prizes and certs. Mem. Indonesian Freight Forwarders Assn. (cert.)(chmn. bd. dirs. 1987), Internat. Freight Forwarders Assn., Indonesian C. of C. and Industry, Indonesian Custom Brokerage and Warehousing Assn., Indonesian Contract Bridge Assn. (v.p. 1986). Roman Catholic. Clubs: Frequent Bus. Travellers (Hong Kong); Sheraton Internat. (U.S.A.); Hilton Exec. (Indonesia); Six Continents (U.S.A.). Lodge: Kawanua (mem. bd. 1973—). Avocations: playing bridge; hunting; reading. Home: Jln Layur 39, East Jakarta 13220, Indonesia

PANGIA, ROBERT ANTHONY, banker; b. Greenwich, Conn., Sept. 16, 1952; s. Anthony and Mary Josephine (Barlow) P.; m. Deborah Susan Ariotti, Nov. 1, 1986. BS magna cum laude, U. Conn., 1980, MBA, 1983. Fin. analyst Mfrs. Hanover Trust Co., N.Y.C., 1980-85; product profitability analyst Citytrust Bancorp, Inc., Bridgeport, Conn., 1985-86; asst. v.p. cost acctg. First Fidelity Bank, N.A., Newark, 1986—. Mem. First United Meth. Ch., Stamford, Conn., 1984. Mem Nat. Assn. Bank Cost Analysts. Republican. Home: 44A Watertown Ct Princeton NJ 08540 Office: First Fidelity Bank NA 550 Broad St Newark NJ 07102

PANICCIA, MARIO DOMENIC, architect; b. Torrice, Italy, May 13, 1948; s. Sebastiano and Clara (Mancini) P.; B.Arch., Cooper Union, 1972. With William F. Griffin & Assocs., Milford, Conn., summers 1968-72; designer Raffone, Elovitz & Fischer, Architects & Engrs., Bridgeport, Conn., 1972-75; prin. Paniccia Assocs., Architects & Planners, Bridgeport, 1975-86, Paniccia Architects and Engrs. Inc., 1987—. Nat. Council Archtl. Registration Bds.; registered architect, Conn., N.Y., Tex., Minn., N.J., Idaho, S.C., Ala., W.Va., Ga., Tenn., Ind., Mich., Mo., Fla., La., Md., Ma., N.C., Ohio, Pa., Iowa, Va., Calif. Commr. Monroe Conservation & Water Resources and Inland Wetland Commn. Mem. Conn. Soc. Architects (dir. 1979-80, commr. chpt. affairs 1979, commr. community affairs 1980, commr. profl. practice, 1985-86), Bridgeport Assn. Architects (dir. 1979, v.p. 1980, 83, pres. 1981), AIA (nat. housing com. 1988-89, commr. conservation com. 1980—), Nat. Trust Hist. Preservation, Inst. Urban Design, Bridgeport C. of C. Roman Catholic. Clubs: Elks (Fairfield, Conn.); K.C. (3d deg.); Exchange (Monroe, Conn.). Home: 25 Easton Rd Monroe CT 06468 Office: Paniccia Architects & Engrs Inc 4270 Main St Bridgeport CT 06606

PANKIN, JAYSON DARRYL, entrepreneur, biotechnologist, venture capitalist; b. Newark, N.J., June 2, 1957; s. Harvey A. and Edythe R. (Simons) P. BBA in Acctg., George Washington U., 1979, MBA in Internat. Bus., 1980. Chmn., pres. PolyCell, Inc., Detroit, 1983—; pres. Growth Funding Ltd., Detroit, 1983—, also bd. dirs., v.p.; v.p. Venture Funding Ltd., Detroit, 1983—, also bd. dirs.; treas., v.p. U. Sci. Ptnrs., Inc., Detroit, 1984-85; pres., sec. Quest Blood Substitute, Detroit, 1986—, also bd. dirs.; bd. dirs., v.p. Quest Biotech., Inc., Growth Funding Ltd; bd. dirs. Quest Am., Inc. Home: 200 Riverfront Park Dr Ste #20-J Detroit MI 48226 Office: Venture Funding Ltd 321 Fisher Bldg Detroit MI 48202

PANOSSIAN, HAGOP VARTEVAR, aerospace engineer; b. Anjar, Lebanon, June 8, 1946; came to U.S., 1973; s. Vartevar Sarkis and Satenig B. (Injeyan) P.; m. Ani Kochakjian, Aug. 31, 1975; children: Lorig, Baruir, Armen. BSc, Am. U. Beirut, 1969; MSc, U. S.C., 1974; Engr. degree, UCLA, 1979, PhD, 1981. Dept. head. C. Gulbenkian Coll., Anjar, 1969-73; grad. teaching asst. U. S.C., Columbia, 1973-74; post grad. research engr. UCLA, 1975-80; sr. engr. HR Textron, Valencia, Calif., 1980-85, engring. supr., 1986-87; sr. specialist Rockwell Internat., Rocketdyne div., Canoga Park, Calif., 1987—. Contbr. articles to profl. jours., chpts. to books; inventor in field. Fulbright Exchange Scientist, 1987. Mem. AAAS, IEEE (sr.), AIAA, Armenian Engrs. & Scientists Am. (past pres., founder). Republican. Orthodox. Home: 18106 Miranda St Tarzana CA 91356

PANTAZELOS, PETER GEORGE, financial executive; b. Cambridge, Mass., Dec. 8, 1930; s. George P. and Marion (Nichols) P.; m. Hytho Haseotes, May 26, 1963; children—George, Marion. BSEE, Northeastern U., 1953; MSEE, MIT, 1955; Acctg. Cert., Bentley Corp., Waltham, Mass., 1975. Mgr. engring. dept. Thermo Electron Engring. Corp., Waltham, Mass., 1960-68; v.p. corp. planning Thermo Electron Corp., Waltham, Mass., 1968-72, v.p. ops. fin., 1972-80, exec. v.p., 1980—. Mem. IEEE, Am. Mgmt. Assn., Fin. Execs. Inst., Eta Kappa Nu, Tau Beta Pi, Sigma Xi. Mem. Greek Orthodox Ch. Club: Brae Burn (Newton, Mass.). Office: Thermo Electron Corp 101 1st Ave Waltham MA 02254

PANTIN, LESLIE PEDRO, insurance executive; b. Havana, Cuba, May 10, 1922; came to U.S., 1960, naturalized, 1966; s. Leslie V. and Ondina I. (De Armas) P.; m. Rosario Kindelan, Nov. 20, 1947 (div. 1979); children: Leslie V., Victor M., Maria del Rosario; m. Maria Elena Diaz Rousselot Torano, Sept. 28, 1980. LLD, U. Havana, 1946. CPCU Vice pres. Leslie Pantin & Sons, S.A., Havana, 1950-60; pres. LaGarantia, Compania de Seguros, S.A., Havana, 1957-60; chmn. bd. AmerInsurance (formerly Pantin Ins. Agy.), Miami, 1965—, mem. nat. adv. council Adolph Coors Co. Chmn. Little Havana Devel. Authority, Miami, 1979, Fla. State Commn. for Hispanic Affairs, Tallahassee, 1980, Fla. 1992 Columbus Exposition, Inc., Miami, 1980-82, Fla. Columbus Hemispheric Trade Commn.; chmn. City Miami Parking Authority. Mem. Soc. Property and Casualty Underwriters, Fla. C. of C. (bd. dirs.), Greater Miami C. of C. (vice chmn. 1976), InterAm. Businessmen's Assn. (pres. 1968-70). Democrat. Roman Catholic. Clubs: Miami, Big Five, City Club. Avocations: non-elective political activities. Home: 150 SE 25 Rd #14-M Miami FL 33129 Office: AmerInsurance 9485 Sunset Dr Miami FL 33173-3248

PAOLINO, VINCENT ANTHONY, sales executive; b. Providence, May 14, 1943; s. Vincent and Assunta (DiGennaro) P.; m. Sue Kimbal, July 30, 1982(div.); children: Patricia, Nancy, Vincent Jr. Student, R.I. Sch. Design, 1961-66. System integration engr. Raytheon Corp., Wayland, Mass., 1964-70; owner, mgr. various bus. ventures, R.I., 1970-77; field sales mgr. Astro-Med, Inc., West Warwick, R.I., 1977-82; regional mgr. Astro-Med, Inc., West Warwick, 1982-86, internat. sales mgr., 1986—. Mem. Internat. Soc. Designers (co-chmn. R.I. chpt. 1964-65). Home: 889 Halifax Ct Warwick RI 02856 Office: Astro Med Inc 600 E Greenwich Ave West Warwick RI 02893

PAPADIMITRIOU, DIMITRI BASIL, economist, college administrator; b. Salonica, Greece, June 9, 1946; came to U.S., 1965, naturalized, 1974; s. Basil John and Ellen (Tacas) P.; BA, Columbia U., 1970; PhD, New Sch. Social Research, 1974; m. Viki Fokas, Aug. 26, 1967; children—Jennifer E., Elizabeth R. Vice pres., asst. sec. ITT Life Ins. Co. N.Y., N.Y.C., 1970-73; exec. v.p., sec., treas. William Penn Life Ins. Co. N.Y., N.Y.C., 1973-78, also dir.; exec. v.p., provost Bard Coll., 1978—, exec. dir. Bard Coll. Ctr., Jerome Levy Econs. Inst., 1980—; adj. lectr. econs. New Sch. Social Research, 1975-76; prof. Bard Coll., 1978—; fellow Ctr. for Advanced Econ. Studies, 1983; dir. William Penn Life Ins. Co. N.Y.; pres. and bd. dirs. Catskill Ballet Theatre, Hudsonia, Inc., mem. adv. com.; bd. overseers Simon's Rock of Bard Coll.; bd. govs. Jerome Levy Econs. Inst., 1986—. Bd. dirs. Dutchess County Council for Arts. Mem. Am. Econ. Assn., Royal Econ. Soc., Am. Fin. Assn., Atlantic Econ. Soc., Econ. Sci. Chamber of Greece. Home and Office: Bard Coll Annandale-on-Hudson NY 12504

PAPALEO, LOUIS ANTHONY, accountant; b. N.Y.C., Sept. 15, 1953; s. Domenico Vincent and Antoinette (Pica) P.; m. Kathy Maehlenbrock, June 23, 1971; children: Leigh, Domenic, Adriana. BS in Acctg., Iona Coll., 1975, MBA, 1986. Staff acct. Papaleo & Co., New Rochelle, N.Y., 1975-80, v.p., 1980-84, pres., 1984—. Chmn. Downtown Businessman's and Merchants Assn., New Rochelle, 1984. Mem. Nat. Acctg. Assn., N.Y. State Acct. Assn., Nat. Soc. Public Accts. Republican. Roman Catholic. Lodge: Masons. Office: Papaleo & Co 557 Main St New Rochelle NY 10801

PAPALEO, ROBERT THOMAS, securities trader; b. Mineola, N.Y., July 6, 1961; s. Robert Thomas and Adele Ann (Ciofalo) P.; m. Gertrude Mary Amato, Jan. 10, 1987. BA in English, Dowling Coll., 1984. Fin. cons. Merrill Lynch, Pierce, Fenner & Smith, Melville, N.Y., 1985—. Mem. Huntington N.Y. C. of C. Roman Catholic. Office: Merrill Lynch 200 Broadhollow Rd Melville NY 11747

PAPAY, LAWRENCE T., engineer; b. Weehawken, N.J., Oct. 3, 1936; s. Joseph Adam and Elizabeth Ethel (Corse) P.; m. Carol Diana Hornby, Dec. 31, 1960; children: Lisa, Gregory, Diane. BS, Fordham U., 1958; MS, MIT, 1965, DSc, 1969. Registered profl. engr., Calif. Sr. shift supr. MIT, Cambridge, 1965-68; rsch. fellow Euraton Rsch. Ctr., Ispra, Italy, 1968-70; dir. rsch. So. Calif. Edison, Rosemead, 1970-78, gen. supt., 1978-79, v.p., 1980-83, sr. v.p., 1983—; pres., bd. dirs. Energy Services, Inc., Rosemead, 1981—. Mem. energy rsch. adv. bd. U.S. Dept. Energy, 1984—; chmn. Planning Commn., City of Arcadia, Calif., 1986—; bd. dirs. San Gabriel Valley Coun. Boy Scouts Am., Pasadena, Calif., 1985—, San Gabriel Region United Way, Arcadia, 1988—. Lt. USN, 1959-63. NATO postdoctoral fellow U.S. Govt., 1968; Euraton fellow European Econ. Community, 1969; recipient Extraordinary Pub. Service award, U.S. Dept. Energy, 1988. Mem. NAE, Am. Nuclear Soc. Republican. Roman Catholic. Office: So Calif Edison Co 2244 Walnut Grove Ave Rosemead CA 91770

PAPAZISSIS, MICHAEL GEORGE, lawyer; b Serres, Macedonia, Greece, Jan. 2, 1935; s. George and Zoe (Katsaridou) P.; m. Athena Vogassari, Oct. 25, 1959; children: Byron, Joan, Georgia, Natalie. LLB, U. Thessaloniki (Greece), 1961, Postgrad. Diploma Law, 1967; LLM, U. Montreal, 1968. Bar: Thessaloniki 1965, Athens 1980, Supreme Ct. Athens 1969. Pvt. practice, Athens, 1980—; legal advisor Citibank N.Y., 1969—, Credit Commercial de France, Athens, 1981-82, B.I.A.O. of Paris, Athens, 1982-85, Bank of Macedonia and Thrace, 1984—. Ford Found. scholar, U. Montreal, 1968-69, medal Youth for Understanding, Student Exchange Program, Ann Arbor, Mich., 1974. Mem. Youth for Understanding Student Exchange Program (nat. chmn. Hellenic com. 1970—). Greek Orthodox. Home: 83 Naiadon St, Paleo Faliro, Athens Greece Office: 17 Voulis St, 10563 Athens Greece

PAPE, BARBARA HARRIS, lawyer; b. Casper, Wyo., Aug. 12, 1936; d. Herbert Garfield and Leah Jean (Case) Harris; m. William Martin Pape, June 28, 1969; children: Kyri Dannan, Kirsten Tara. AA in Theatre, Stephens Coll., 1956; BJ, BA, U. Mo., 1960, MA, 1966, BS in Edn., 1968, PhD, JD, 1980. Bar: Mo. 1981, U.S. Dist. Ct. (we. dist.) Mo. 1981, U.S. Supreme Ct., 1986. Mem. faculty U. Mo., Columbia, 1966-74; daily TV show hostess Triton Prodns., Inc., Columbia, 1973-76; realtor Tara Realty, Columbia, 1977-81; sole practice, Columbia, 1981-82; ptnr. Cronan, Robinson, Lampton & Pape, Columbia, 1982-85, Barbara Harris Pape & Assocs, P.C., Columbia, 1986—. Assoc. editor Litigation mag., 1983-85; contbr. articles to mags. Bd. dirs. Columbia Resource Ctr., Inc., 1981—; pres. adv. bd. YWCA, YMCA, Columbia, 1977-78; pres. bd. trustees Coll. Arts and Scis. U. Mo., Columbia, 1986-88; alumni bd. dirs. Stephens Coll., 1977-80. Recipient Roscoe Anderson award. Mem. ABA, Mo. Bar Assn., Boone County Bar Assn., Am. Assn. Trial Lawyers (vice chairperson publs. 1985-87, chairperson 1987—, pub. bd. Everyday Law 1988—, faculty Nat. Coll. Advocacy), Mo. Assn. Trial Lawyers, Mo. Criminal Def. Lawyers, Internat. Order Barristers, U. Mo. Alumni Orgn. (bd. dirs. 1986—), Kappa Tau Alpha, Delta Theta Phi. Democrat. Home: 3301 Westcreek Cir Columbia MO 65201 Office: Barbara Harris Pape & Assocs PC 16 N 8th St Columbia MO 65201

PAPES, THEODORE CONSTANTINE, JR., computer company executive; b. Gary, Ind., Jan. 31, 1928; s. Theodore Constantine and Mary E. (DiPaolo) P.; m. Centes Marie Morrill, July 17, 1954; children: Matthew, Thaddeus, Daniel, Karin. B.A., U. Mich., 1952. With IBM, Armonk, N.Y., 1969—, v.p., 1969-72, pres. div., 1972-78; dir. gen. IBM Europe, Paris, 1979-82; pres., chief exec. officer Prodigy Services Co., White Plains, N.Y., 1984—. Mem. vis. com. U. Mich. Bus. Sch., 1980-86; co-chmn. Campaign for Mich., 1983-88. Served with USN, 1946-48. Mem. Phi Beta Kappa. Office: Prodigy Svcs Co 445 Hamilton Ave White Plains NY 10601

PAPITTO, RALPH RAYMOND, manufacturing company executive; b. Providence, Nov. 1, 1926; s. John and Maria (David) P.; m. Norma J. Ewart, June 10, 1943 (div.); children: Andrea (Mrs. Harry Crump), Aurelia, David John; m. Barbara Auger, Apr. 1982. BS in Finance, Bryant Coll., Providence, 1947, DSc Bus. Adminstrn. (hon.), 1987; student, Boston U. Law Sch., 1948-49; DSc Bus. Adminstrn. (hon.), Roger Williams Coll., 1985; LLD (hon.), New Eng. Inst. Tech., 1985, Suffolk U., 1986, New England Inst. Tech. Exec. v.p. fin. Ritz Products, Inc., Providence, 1951-56; pres. Glass-Tite Industries, Inc., Providence, 1956-63, chmn. bd., 1963—, also bd. dirs.; chmn., bd. dirs. Nortek, Inc., Providence; bd. dirs. Hi-G, Inc., The LVI Group Inc., N.Y.C. Fin. dir., Town Johnston, R.I., 1955-59; trustee Roger Williams Coll., Bristol, R.I., now chmn. bd. trustees; bd. dirs. Meeting St. Sch. Retarded; mem. Gov.'s Blue Ribbon Commn., Roger Williams Hosp. Home: 6 Water Valley Rd Scituate RI 02831 Office: Nortek Inc 50 Kennedy Pla Providence RI 02903

PAPP, LASZLO GEORGE, architect; b. Debrecen, Hungary, Apr. 28, 1929; came to U.S., 1956; m. Judith Liptak, Apr. 12, 1952; children: Andrea, Laszlo-Mark (dec. 1978). Archtl. Engr., Poly. U. Budapest, 1955; MArch, Pratt Inst., 1960. Designer Harrison & Abramovitz, Architects, N.Y.C., 1958-63; ptnr. Whiteside & Papp, Architects, White Plains, N.Y., 1963-67; pres. Papp Architects, P.C., White Plains, N.Y., 1967—. Mem. Pres.'s Adv. Com. on Pvt. Sector Initiatives; mem. adv. com. Westchester Community Coll., 1971—, Iona Coll., New Rochelle, N.Y., 1982—, Norwalk State Tech. Coll., 1983—; bd. dirs. Clearview Sch., 1985—, Builders Inst., 1982—. Fellow AIA (regional dir. 1983-85); mem. Internat. Union Architects (rep. Habitat com. 1986—), N.Y. State Assn. Architects (v.p. 1977-80, pres. 1981), Am.-Hungarian Engrs. Assn. (dir. 1978-86), Hungarian Univ. Assn. (pres. 1958-60), White Plains C. of C. (dir. 1968-71, vice chmn. bd. for area devel. 1983-89, chmn. bd. dirs. 1989—). Home: 1197 Valley Rd New Canaan CT 06840 Office: Papp Architects PC 7-11 S Broadway White Plains NY 10601

PAPPANO, ROBERT DANIEL, corporate treasurer; b. Chgo., Apr. 8, 1942; s. John Robert and Lucille Carmelita (Metallo) P.; m. Karen Marie Muellner, July 2, 1966; children: John, Kim, Bob, Bill. BS in Commerce, DePaul U., Chgo., 1964; MBA, Roosevelt U., Chgo., 1982. CPA, Ill. Audit supr. Alexander Grant & Co., Chgo., 1964-73; with W.W. Grainger, Inc., Skokie, Ill., 1973—, asst. to contr., 1973-75, contr., corp. acct., 1975-78, contr., asst. treas., 1978-84, v.p., contr., asst. treas., 1984-85, v.p., treas., asst. sec., 1985—; treas. Grainger FSC, Inc., Skokie, 1985—; treas., asst. sec. WWG Internat., Inc., Skokie, 1985—; treas. Dayton Electric Mfg. Co., Chgo., 1985—. 1st lt. U.S. Army, 1965-67, Vietnam. Mem. AICPA, Ill. CPA Soc., Fin. Execs. Inst. Roman Catholic. Office: WW Grainger Inc 5500 W Howard St Skokie IL 60077

PAPPAS, NICHOLAS, chemical company executive; b. Kearny, N.J., Sept. 22, 1930; s. Christ and Evangeline (Pappastilou) P.; m. Dorothy Demont, June 14, 1953; children: Thalia, Christopher D., Gregory N., Nikki. B.S. in Chemistry, Yale U., 1952; Ph.D. in Organic Chemistry, Brown U., 1956. Mgr. corp. planning E.I. du Pont de Nemours, Wilmington, Del., 1976-77, dir. automotive mktg. devel., 1977-78, gen. mgr. fabrics and finishes dept., 1978-81, v.p. fabrics and finishes, 1981-82, v.p. polymer products, 1982-83, group v.p., 1983-88, exec. v.p., 1988—. State campaign chmn. United Way of Del., 1982; chmn. bd. dirs. United Way Del., 1985-86. Mem. Am. Chem. Soc., Soc. Chem. Industry. Office: E I du Pont de Nemours & Co 1007 Market St Wilmington DE 19898

PAQUETTE, JOSEPH F., JR., utility company executive; b. Norwood, Miss., Aug. 24, 1934; married. BS in Civil Engring., Yale U., 1956. Pres. CMS Energy Corp., until 1988; now chmn., pres., chief exec. officer Phila. Electric Co., 1956-86, 88—; chief fin. officer, exec. v.p. Consumer Power Co., 1986-87, vice chmn., chief fin. officer, 1987—. Office: Phila Electric Co 2301 Market St Philadelphia PA 19101 *

PAQUETTE, ROLAND JOSEPH, JR., utility company executive; b. Manchester, N.H., Sept. 20, 1949; s. Roland Joseph and Gemma Marie (DesJardins) P.; m. Elizabeth Elsa Bloch, May 27, 1972; children: Kristina, Roland. BSBA, U. N.H., 1974; MBA, Ariz. State U., 1975. Instr. N.H. Coll., Manchester, 1976-79, U. N.Mex., Albuquerque, 1979—; programmer, analyst United Life & Accident, Concord, N.H., 1975-80; mgmt. cons. Pub. Svc. Co. of N.Mex., Albuquerque, 1980-82, dir. treasury system, 1982—. With U.S. Army, 1970-72. Mem. Nat. Corp. Cash Mgmt. Assn. (bd. dirs. 1988—). Office: Pub Svc Co NMex Alvarado Sq Albuquerque NM 87158

PAQUIN, PAUL PETER, mortgage finance executive; b. Marlboro, Mass., Aug. 20, 1943; s. Adolph Phileous and Hazel Ann (Duplessis) P.; m. Lorraine Theresa Belliveau, June 24, 1965; children: Renée, Michele, Kenneth, Raymond. BSBA, Clark U., 1968, MBA, 1971; PhD, ABD, Cath. U., 1982. Fin. analyst Honeywell Inc., Framingham, Mass., 1963-67, Sprague Electric Co., Worcester, Mass., 1969-72; sr. analyst Fed. Nat. Mortgage Assn., Washington, 1972-76, dir. investor relations, 1976-85, v.p. investor relations, 1985—. Mem. Nat. Investor Relations Inst. (pres. capitol area chpt., 1979, officer 1978-80). Office: Fed Nat Mortgage Assn 3900 Wisconsin Ave NW Washington DC 20016

PARADICE, SAMMY IRWIN, real estate investor; b. Beaumont, Tex., May 26, 1952; s. Alfred E. and Timmia E. (Holder) P. Student, Lamar U., 1970, Okla. State U., 1970, U. Tulsa, 1971. Lic. real estate broker, Tex. Page U.S. House of Reps., Washington, 1969-70; owner Southwestern Mktg. Systems, Beaumont, 1972-75; owner, mgr. First Realty, Sam Paradice & Assocs., Vidor, Tex., 1976—. Author: (books) Arab Money Hotline, 1985, Real Estate Counterattack, 1984, (cassette study course) How To Be A Business Tycoon. Methodist. Club: Toastmasters. Office: 935 N Main Vidor TX 77662

PARAN, MARK LLOYD, lawyer; b. Cleve., Feb. 1, 1953; s. Edward Walter and Margaret Gertrude (Ebert) P. AB cum laude in Sociology, Harvard U., 1977, JD, 1980. Bar: Ill. 1980, Mass. 1986. Assoc. Wilson & McIlvaine, Chgo., 1980-83, Lurie Sklar & Simon, Ltd., Chgo., 1983-85, Sullivan & Worcester, Boston, 1985—. Mem. ABA, Mass. Bar Assn. Avocations: tornado hunting, observation of severe thunderstorms, photography. Home: 84 Gainsborough St #106W Boston MA 02115 Office: Sullivan & Worcester One Post Office Sq Boston MA 02109

PARANJPE, ASHA VERNEKAR, marketing executive; b. Bombay, Jan. 13, 1946; came to U.S., 1967; d. Vinayak Shankar and Suhasini (Potdar) Vernekar; m. Arvind Gangadhar Paranjpe, June 7, 1968; children: Kiran, Anjelika. BA with honors, St. Xavier's Coll., Bombay, 1966; MA, Cornell U., 1968; PhD, NYU, 1974. Asst. prof. Fairleigh Dickinson U., Teaneck, N.J., 1974-79; rsch. assoc. Rutgers U., New Brunswick, N.J., 1979-82; rsch. dir. Louis Harris and Assocs., N.Y.C., 1983-84; asst. v.p. MONY Fin. svcs., Purchase, N.Y., 1985-87; v.p. Beacon Corp. Benefit Svcs., Stamford, Conn., 1987—. Contbr. articles to profl. jours. Walter A. Anderson fellow NYU, 1968-70. Mem. Am. Mktg. Assn., Bus. Coun. Southwestern Conn. Home: 60 Sturbridge Hill New Canaan CT 06840 Office: Beacon Corp Benefit Svcs 6 Stamford Forum Stamford CT 06901

PARASCOS, EDWARD THEMISTOCLES, utilities executive; b. N.Y.C., Oct. 20, 1931; s. Christos and Nina (Demitrovich) P.; BSME, CCNY, 1956, MSME, 1958; postgrad. ops. rsch. N.Y.U., 1964; m. Jenny Morris, July 14, 1978; children: Jennifer Melissa, Edward Themistocles. Design engr. Ford Instrument, 1957-61; reliability engring. supr. Kearfott div. Gen. Precision Inc., 1961-63; staff cons. Am. Power Jet, 1963-64; reliability mgr. Perkin Elmer Corp., 1964-66; dir. system effectiveness CBS Labs., Stamford, Conn., 1966-72; pres. Dipar Cons. Svcs. Ltd., East Elmhurst, N.Y., Lapa Trading Corp.; gen. mgr. power generation svcs. Consol. Edison Co., N.Y.C., 1972—; pres., chmn. bd. RAM Cons. Assocs.; pres., 1978-80. vice chmn. Reliability Div., 1968-72; chmn. 1st Reliability Engring. Conf. Electric Power Industry, 1974, also 4th conf.; lectr. in field. Registered profl. engr., Calif. Fellow Am. Soc. Quality Control (vice chmn. 1968-70, sr. mem.); mem. Am. Mgmt. Assn., ASME, Am. Statis. Assn., Inst. Environ. Scis., Soc. Reliabilty Engrs., Edison Engring. Soc. Home: 30-02 83d St Jackson Heights NY 11370 Office: 4 Irving Pl New York NY 10003

PARASKAKIS, MICHAEL EMANUEL, insurance company executive; b. Crete, Greece, Apr. 18, 1930; s. Emanuel and Calliopi (Hatzakis) P.; m. Georgia-Maria Etta Zoides, June 4, 1960; 1 child, Emanuel. Diploma, Athens Sch. Econ. and Comml. Scis., 1955. Internat. purchase agreements Ministry Agr., Athens, 1951-56; personnel asst. Mobil Oil Greece, Athens, 1958-62; mng. prin. Legal and Gen. Assurance Soc., Agy. for Greece, 1962—; mng. dir. Pegasus Ins. Co., Athens, 1974-82, chmn., mng. dir., 1983—; dir. Horizon Ins. Co., Athens, 1970-83; vice chmn. bd. Ras Hellas S.A., 1986—; chmn. Greek Insurers European Com., Athens, 1983-88, sec. gen. 1989. Contbr. articles to profl. jours. Cpl. Greek Army, 1953-54. Mem. Assn. Ins. Cos. (chmn. 1977-81, bd. mem. 1981—), Internat. Ins. Soc. (charter mem.), Com. Européen des Assurances (mem. presdl. coun. 1988—), Brit. Hellenic Chamber, Athens (hon.), Internat. Motor Insurers Bureau (chmn. 1986—, green card). Greek Orthodox. Home: 21 Lykavittou St, 10672 Athens Greece Office: Pegasus Ins Co, 5 Stadiou St, 10562 Athens Greece

PARCHMAN, TODD LIDDELL, portfolio manager, investment banker; b. Chgo., Aug. 16, 1954; s. Liddell Jackson and Marguerite June (Anderson) P; m. Bryn Bjella, Oct. 30, 1982; children: Liddell Jackson III, Andrew Arley. BA, U. N.C., 1975; MBA, U. Chgo., 1978. Corp. banking officer 1st Nat. Bank Chgo., 1975-79; sr. v.p. Norwest Bank, Mpls., 1979-84; prin. Parchman & Co., Mpls., 1984-85; sr. mng. dir. Signet Investment Banking Co., Richmond, Va., 1985—. Mem. Minn. Gov.'s Energy Coun., 1981-83; trustee Culver Ednl. Found., 1983-85. Morehead Found. scholar, 1972-75. Mem. Culver Legion (pres. 1983-85), Capital Club (founding bd. govs. 1987—, Richmond). Office: Signet Investment Banking Co 801 E Main St Ste 1100 Richmond VA 23219

PARCO, SALVADOR ABONAL, marketing consultant; b. Nabua, Camarines Sur, Philippines, Jan. 3, 1934; came to U.S., 1967; s. Eulogio Almazan and Anacleta Dorozan (Abonal) P.; m. Alicia Tan Uy, Dec. 22, 1957; children: Marilou, Farolito, Maria Stella, Salvador Jr., William. AB, Ateneo de Naga, Philippines, 1955; MS, Cornell U., 1963; PhD, Pa. State U., 1973. Presdl. asst. Office of the Pres., Manila, 1956-64; assoc. prof. sociology and anthropology Ateneo de Manila U., 1964-67; grad. asst. sociology Pa. State U., University Park, 1967-70; asst. prof. Pa. State U., Erie, 1970-77; machinist, assembler,welder, union steward Gen. Electric Co., Erie, 1977-79; assoc. indsl. engr. Am. Sterilizer Co., Erie, 1980-82, tech. tng. instr., 1982-86; account exec. Transworld Systems, Inc., Erie, 1986-87; registered rep. Waddell & Reed, Inc., Erie, 1987-88; registered rep. Forth Fin. Network, Erie, 1988, mktg. cons., 1988—; lectr. Gannon U., Erie, 1977-79, Villa Maria Coll., Erie, 1980—; cons. Peace Corps, Philippine Rural Reconstructive Movement, 1964-67, Ops. Brotherhood Internat., Philippines, Nat. Land Reform Council, Inst. Social Order, Philippine Nat. Bank Exec. Devel. Acad.; bd. dirs. Internat. Inst., Erie. Editor jour. Philippine Sociological Review, 1966; contbr. articles to profl. jours.; newspaper columnist Bicol Examiner, 1952-56. Vol. Students for Magsaysay for Pres. Movement, Philippines, 1953. 2d lt. Philippine Army, 1955-57. Fellow Agy. for Internat. Devel., Nat. Econ. Council, U.S., India, 1962-63; grantee The Asia Found., Kabul, Afghanistan, 1967. Mem. Toastmasters Internat. (AMSCO pres. 1983-84, Area 7 Gov. 1984-86), Alpha Kappa Delta, Gamma Sigma Delta. Home: 655 E 41st St Erie PA 16504 Office: Forth Fin Network 2005 W 8th St Ste 102 Erie PA 16505

PARDEE, SCOTT EDWARD, securities dealer; b. New Haven, Oct. 11, 1936; s. William Durley and Catherine (Eames) P.; m. Aida Milagros Fuentes Tavarez, Jan. 29, 1966; children: Alan Alexander, Cynthia Lynn. B.A., Dartmouth Coll., 1958; Ph.D., MIT, 1962. Research asst. Fed. Res. Bank, Boston, 1959-62; teaching asst. in econs. MIT, Cambridge, Mass., 1961-62; research economist Fed. Res. Bank N.Y., N.Y.C., 1962-66, mgr. fgn. dept., 1967-70, asst. v.p. fgn. dept., 1970-74, v.p. fgn. dept., 1974-79; tchr. banking and fin. NYU, 1965-67, Am. Inst. Banking, 1969-72; adj. prof. Grad. Sch. Bus. Columbia U., N.Y.C., 1972-75; dep. mgr. fgn. ops. Fed. Res. System Open Market Account, 1975-79, mgr. fgn. ops., 1979-81; exec. v.p. Discount Corp. N.Y., N.Y.C., 1981-86; vice chmn. Yamaichi Internat. Am. Inc., N.Y.C., 1986-88, chmn., 1988—. Author: A Study of Inter-City Wage Differentials, 1962. Woodrow Wilson fellow MIT, 1958-59; recipient Dr. Louis M. Spadaro award Fordham U., 1980. Mem. Phi Beta Kappa. Club: Forex of N.Am. (mem. exec. com. 1974-81). Home: 250 S End Ave New York NY 10280 Office: Yamaichi Internat Am Inc 2 World Trade Ctr Ste 9650 New York NY 10048

PARDINI, SHARON KAY BROWN, architectural and interior designer; b. Grand Junction, Iowa, Apr. 15, 1938; d. Loyal Melvin Blanshan and Frances Mildred (Brown) Manen; m. Frederick Brown, Oct. 19, 1957 (div. Apr. 1963); 1 child Randal Alan; m. Joseph Leslie Pardini, Nov. 11, 1975; 1 child, Tiana Margaret. BA in Cosmetology, Lee Ann Acad., 1957; AA, U. Calif., Berkeley, 1966; BBA, U. Calif. Owner Sharon's Hair Fashions Salons, Oakland, Calif., 1958-80; v.p., sec., treas. Western Container Transp. Inc.i, 1978—; pres. Par-West Inc. Design Firm, 1983—; adv. bd. mem. Bd. Cosmetology, Oakland., 1965-69; owner The Collection Designer Gallery, Lafayette, Calif., 1987—. Task force mem. Republicans, Washington, 1981—; mem. service league Santa catalina Sch., Monterey, Calif., 1986. Mem. Calif. Cosmetologist Assn. (v.p. 1973-75, bd. dirs. 1970-77). Club: Mission Hills Country. Office: Par-West Designs Inc 3190 Old Tunnel Rd Lafayette CA 94549

PARDUE, DWIGHT EDWARD, building supply retail company executive; b. North Wilkesboro, N.C., Aug. 3, 1928; s. Gilbert F. and Nina (Glass) P.; m. Annie Eller, Mar. 24, 1951; children: Richard S., Dwight E. Cert., Clevenger Bus. Coll., 1956. Dir. warehousing Lowe's Co., Inc., North Wilkesboro, 1956-57; store mgr. Lowe's Co., Inc., Sparta, N.C., 1957-59, Richmond, Va., 1959-70; regional v.p. Lowe's Co., Inc., North Wilkesboro, 1970-75, sr. v.p. store ops., 1975-78, exec. v.p. sales and store ops., 1978-86, sr. exec. v.p., 1986—; mem. steering com. Home Ctr. Leadership Council, Nat. Home Ctr. Home Improvement Congress and Exposition, 1983-86. Served with U.S. Army, 1950-52. Mem. Nat. Assn. Home Builders, N.C. Assn. Home Builders. Club: Oakwoods Country (Wilkesboro). Lodge: Masons. Office: Lowe's Co Inc PO Box 1111 North Wilkesboro NC 28656

PARDUS, DONALD GENE, utility executive; b. Stafford Springs, Conn., Aug. 1, 1940; s. William L. and Marion (Wondrasck) P.; m. Marilyn L. Riquier, June 10, 1961; children: David J., Susan L., Linda M. B.S. in Bus. Adminstrn, U. Hartford, Conn., 1966; grad., Program Mgmt. Devel., Harvard U., 1977. Internal auditor Conn. Light and Power Co., Berlin, 1958-67; fin. asst., then asst. treas. N.E. Utilities Service Co., Berlin, 1967-79; v.p., chief fin. officer, treas., trustee Eastern Utilities, Boston, 1979-85; pres., chief fin. officer Eastern Utilities, 1985-87, pres., chief operating officer, trustee, 1987-89, pres., chief exec. officer, 1989—; vice chmn., dir. Blackstone Valley Electric Co., Eastern Edison Co.; pres., dir. Montaup Electric Co.; pres., dir. EUA Service Corp., EUA Investment Corp., EUA Ocean State Corp., Eastern Unicord Corp.; vice chmn., dir. EUA Cogenex Corp.; pres., bd. dirs. EUA Power Corp. Mem. Electric Council New Eng., New Eng. Power Pool, Boston Pub. Utility Analysts Assn. Office: Ea Utilities Assocs 1 Liberty Sq PO Box 2333 Boston MA 02107

PARELL, MARY LITTLE, banking commissioner, lawyer; b. Fond du Lac, Wis., Aug. 13, 1946; d. Ashley Jewell and Gertrude (McCoy) Little; m. John Francis Parell, May 28, 1972; children: Christie, Morgan, Shawn, John Brady. AB in Polit. Sci. cum laude, Bryn Mawr Coll., 1968; JD, Villanova U., 1972; LLD (hon.), Georgian Ct. Coll., 1987. Bar: N.J. 1972. Assoc. McCarter & English, Newark, 1972-80, ptnr., 1980-84; commr. N.J. Dept. Banking, Trenton, 1984—; chmn. bd. Pinelands Devel. Credt Bank. Bd. trustees Exec. Commn. Ethical Standards, Trenton, 1984—, Corp. Bus. Assistance, Trenton, 1984—, N.J. Housing & Mortgage Fin. Agy., Trenton, 1984—, N.J. Cemetery Bd. Assn., 1984—, N.J. Hist. Soc., 1976-79., YMCA of Greater Newark, 1973-76, Diocesan Investment; mem. Supreme Ct. N.J. Civil Practice Com., 1982-84, Supreme Ct. N.J. Dist. Ethics Com., 1982-84; lay assesor Ecclesiastical Ct. Episc. Diocese Newark, 1980-84; active Jr. League Monmouth County; chairperson Task Force Emergency Room Hosp. Facilities, Newark Emergency Services for Families, 1979-81. Mem. ABA, N.J. Bar Assn., Monmouth Bar Assn. Home: 8 Sycamore Ln Rumson NJ 07760 Office: NJ Dept Banking 20 W State St Trenton NJ 08625

PARENT, DAVID CHARLES, transportation executive; b. McIvor, Mich., Aug. 25, 1930; s. Harold Anthony and Ardith (Jordan) P.; m. Patricia Felske, July 26, 1952 (div. June 1982); children: Debbie, Brian, Tami, Bruce, Dru; m. Grace Welcher. Grad. high sch., Tawas City, Mich.; student, Mich. State U., 1948-50. Ind. truck driver McIvor, 1948-60; owner grocery store, McIvor, 1960-63; truck owner, lic. carrier Seven-Up Bottling Co. of Flint (Mich.), 1964-76; owner, prin. Parent Trucking, Inc., National City, Mich., 1977—. Roman Catholic. Lodge: K.C. Home and Office: 3222 S Sand Lake Rd National City MI 48748

PARHAM, JASON SCOTT, contract administrator; b. Boynton Beach, Fla., Jan. 18, 1963; s. Rebeckah Claudette (Miller) P. BSBA, Tampa Coll., 1987. Wallpaper installer Largo, Fla., 1981-87; with accounts receivable dept. Goodwill Industries, St. Petersburg, Fla., 1987; contract adminstr. Greiner Engring. Inc., Tampa, Fla., 1987—. Home: 8ll Gershwin Dr Largo FL 34641 Office: Greiner Enging Inc 5601 Mariner St Tampa FL 33609

PARIKH, JEKISHAN RATILAL, chemical company executive; b. Bombay, Dec. 21, 1922; came to U.S., 1948; s. Ratilal B. and Ruxmani (Parikh) P.; m. Jean Audrey Fuller, May 1, 1959; children: Jane, Anne, Lynn. BS with honors, U. Bombay, 1943; MS, U. Calif., Berkeley, 1950; PhD, U. Calif., 1953. Rsch. officer U. Va., Charlottesville, 1953-55; postdoctoral rsch. asst. Nat. Inst. Health, Bethesda, Md., 1955-58; rsch. officer Glaxo, U.K., 1958-60; exec. officer India div. Glaxo, Bombay, 1959-64; with UpJohn Co., Kalamazoo, 1964—; dir. UpJohn Co., 1980—. Mem. Am. Chem. Soc. Democrat. Home: 2614 Russet Dr Kalamazoo MI 49008 Office: UpJohn Co Kalamazoo MI 49008

PARIS, STEVEN MARK, software engineer; b. Boston, May 26, 1956; s. Julius Louis and Frances (Keleishik) P. BS, Rensselaer Poly. Inst., 1978; MS, Boston U., 1980, postgrad., 1980-84. Sr. software engr. Prime Computer Inc., Framingham, Mass., 1978-82; sr. analyst Computervision Corp., Bedford, Mass., 1982-84, prin. engr. Lotus Devel., Inc., Cambridge, Mass., 1984-88; pres. Tri-Millennium Corp., 1988—. Lt. Mass. Civil Def. Recipient Boston Sci. Fair 1st prize, 1973, 74; State of Mass. Sci. Fair 3d prize, 1973; 2d prize, 1974. Mem. Assn. for Computing Machinery, IEEE, Boston Computer Soc., Planetary Soc. Jewish. Home: 27 Colwell Ave Brighton MA 02135 Office: Tri-Millennium Corp 31 Page Rd Bedford MA 01730

PARISER, RUDOLPH, chemical company executive; b. Harbin, China, Dec. 8, 1923; came to U.S., 1941, naturalized, 1944; s. Ludwig Jacob and Lia (Rubinstein) P.; m. Margaret Louise Marsh, July 31, 1972. BS in Chemistry, U. Calif., Berkeley, 1944; PhD in Phys. Chemistry, U. Minn., 1950. With E.I. du Pont de Nemours & Co., Wilmington, Del., 1950—, with elastomer chems. dept., 1967-79, dir. pioneering rsch., 1974-79, rsch. dir. polymer products dept., 1980-81, dir. polymer sci. cen. R & D dept., 1981-86, dir. advanced materials sci. cen. R & D dept., 1986-89; cons., pres. R. Pariser & Co., Inc., Wilmington, 1989—; mem. materials rsch. adv. com. Nat. Sci. Found., 1986-89. Assoc. editor Jour. Chem. Physics, 1966-69, Chem. Physics Letters, 1967-70, Du Pont Innovation, 1969-75; adv. bd. Jour. Polymer Sci., 1980-89; editorial bd. New Polymeric Materials, 1985—; patentee in field; contbr. articles to sci. jours. With U.S. Army, 1944-46. Mem. Am. Chem. Soc., Soc. Rheology, AAAS, N.Y. Acad. Sci., Am. Phys. Soc., Internat. Union Pure and Applied Chemistry, Phila. Interlocutors (pres. 1972-76), Sigma Xi, Phi Lambda Upsilon, Du Pont Country Club, Rodney Sq. Club, Univ. and Whist Club Wilmington. Office: EI du Pont de Nemours & Co PO Box 80328 Wilmington DE 19880-0328

PARISH, ALBERT EUGENE, JR., educator, columnist, media consultant; b. Charleston, S.C., Aug. 23, 1957; s. Albert Eugene and Thelma Kathleen (Jenkins) P. BS, Coll. Charleston, 1979; PhD in Math. Econs., U. N.C., 1987. Lectr. math. and econs. U. N.C., Chapel Hill, 1979-82; asst. prof. Coll. Charleston, 1982—; econs. columnist Charleston News-Courier, 1983—; ind. cons. in field; cons. Sta. WCIV-TV, Mt. Pleasant, S.C., 1983—; ptnr. Parish-O'Leary Investor Adv. Service, 1987—. Author (with Niles): Computer Aid to Calculus, 1987. Speaker Charleston Speakers Bur., 1983—. Mem. Am. Math. Soc., Math. Assn. Am., Planetary Soc. (charter), Am. Econs. Assn., Soc. Indsl. and Applied Maths., Pi Mu Epsilon, Phi Kappa Phi, Omicron Delta Kappa, Omicron Delta Epsilon. Home: 610 Citadel Haven Dr A3 Charleston SC 29414 Office: Coll of Charleston Dept of Math Charleston SC 29424

PARISOTTE, HENRY SAMUEL, JR., chemical company executive, real estate investor; b. St. Louis, May 3, 1949; s. Henry Samuel and Angeline (Azzoline) P.; m. Mary Lue Nordquist, Aug. 18, 1972; children: Heather, Shannon. BS, U Mo., 1973; MBA, St. Louis U., 1976; cert. in fin. futures mgmt., Northwestern U., 1983. Cert. mgmt. acct., cash mgr. Mgmt. trainee Mark Twain Banks, St. Louis, 1971-72, officer, 1972-73, asst. mgr. bank 21, 1973-74; sr. auditor dept. internat audit Monsanto Co., St. Louis, 1974-76, fin. analyst dept. internat. treasury, 1976-77, sr. fin. analyst, 1977-78, mgr. fin. for Latin Am.-Can. dept. treasury, 1978-79, mgr. fin. for Asia/Pacific, 1979-81, mgr. banking and investments, 1981-84, mgr. corp. real estate, 1984-87, dir. risk mgmt. and real estate, 1987—; bd. dirs. Clay Oak Condominiums, St. Louis; bd. dirs. Profl. Home Health Care, Tulsa. Mem. fin. com. Full Gospel Evang. Ch., St. Louis, 1982-88, bd. dirs., 1984-85. With U.S. Army, 1968-70. Fellow Am. Inst. Corp. Asset Mgmt.; mem. Indsl. Devel. Rsch. Coun., Inst. Cert. Mgmt. Accts., Ducks Unltd., Mo. Wildlife Fedn., Ozark Fly Fisherman Club. Republican. Office: Monsanto Co 800 N Lindbergh Blvd Saint Louis MO 63167

PARISSE, ANTHONY JOHN, cosmetics executive; b. Bklyn., Oct. 25, 1936; s. Albert (stepfather) and Teresa (Patti) Dirjish; m. Virginia Grace Keil, Nov. 7, 1959; children: Andrea Grace, Erika Anne. BS in Chemistry, St. John's U., N.Y.C., 1958; MBA in Mgmt., Rutgers U., 1973. Quality control chemist Am. Pharm. Co., N.Y.C., 1958; analytical chemist Whitehall Labs., Hammonton, N.J., 1959-61; research chemist Johnson & Johnson, New Brunswick, N.J., 1961-65; dir. product evaluation Carter-Wallace, Cranbury, N.J., 1965—. Contbr. articles to profl. jours. Treas. Young Rep. Club, Metuchen and Edison, N.J., 1962-70; Rep. committeeman, Edison, 1984—. Served with U.S. Army, 1958-64. Mem. Am. Chem. Soc., Am. Pharm. Assn., Am. Acad. Sci., Soc. Cosmetic Chemists, Dermal Clin. Evaluation Soc. Roman Catholic. Home: 60 Oliver Ave Edison NJ 08820 Office: Carter Wallace Half Acre Rd Cranbury NJ 08512

PARIZEK, RICHARD ANDREW, savings and loan association executive; b. Grinnel, Iowa, Nov. 4, 1958; s. Arthur Keith and Marilyn Gwen (Martin) P.; m. Jan Marie Honeycutt, Aug. 21, 1982; 1 child, Marion Elizabeth. BBA, Baylor U., 1981, MBA, 1982. Credit analyst InterFirst Bank, Dallas, 1982-84; loan officer Western Savs. and Loan, Phoenix, 1984-85, mgr. comml. real estate, 1985—; mem. adv. com. Ariz. Mortgage Banker's Assn., Phoenix, 1987—. Team mem. Ariz Mountaineering Club Rescue Team, Phoenix, 1975-78. Republican. Clubs: S.W. Outdoor (Tempe, Ariz.), Ariz. Mountaineering (Phoenix). Office: Western Savs & Loan 6001 N 24th St Phoenix AZ 85016-2018

PARK, ANNE, retail executive; b. Seoul, Korea, Feb. 11, 1958; arrived in U.S., 1970; d. Joong Ho and Choong Shik (Mihn) P. BFA in fashion design, Pratt Inst., Bklyn., 1980. Asst. designer Charles James Esquire, N.Y.C., 1977-79; sales rep. Diane Pernet, N.Y.C., 1979-80; talent mgr. La Rocka Modeling Agy., N.Y.C., 1980; buyer Burghard's, N.Y.C., 1980-82; v.p. sales OLA Designs, N.Y.C., 1982-85; v.p. merchandising Et Vous, N.Y.C., 1985—. Grantee scholarship Connell Rice and Sugar Co., N.J., 1976-80.

PARK, CHARLES DONALD, SR., financial executive; b. N.Y.C., Aug. 1, 1945; s. Charles and Madeline (Springer) P.; m. Pauline De Meo; children: Paula, Madeline. BA, Pace U., 1968, MBA, 1970. Coord. fin. reports Gen. Telephone & Electronics, N.Y.C., 1968-70; mgr. fin. analysis Mobil Corp., N.Y.C., 1970-73; mgr. corp. bus. planning and analysis Gen. Instrument, N.Y.C., 1973-74; controller Microelectronics Group Gen. Instrument, Hicksville, N.Y., 1974-77, chief fin. officer, 1977-81; corp. dir., fin. analysis Bendix, Southfield, Mich., 1981-82; v.p. fin. and adminstrn. MCI Internat., Inc., Rye Brook, N.Y., 1982-86; sr. v.p. fin. Sprague Techs., Inc., Stamford, Conn., 1987—. Office: Sprague Techs Inc 4 Stamford Forum Stamford CT 06901

PARK, JA IN, chemical company executive; b. Kwang Joo, Korea, Oct. 15, 1948; came to U.S., 1978; s. Taei Seun and Yun Yae (Yang) P.; m. Yun Chu Kim, May 31, 1975; children: Elizabeth, Marion, Linda. BS, U. Hamburg, Fed. Republic Germany, 1972, MS, 1973, PhD, 1976. Postdoctoral fellow U. Alta., Edmonton, Can., 1976-78; group leader Lee Pharmaceuticals, El Monte, Calif., 1978-80; dir. research and devel. Applied Plastics Co. Inc., El Segundo, Calif., 1980-85; cons. Hexcel Corp., Chatsworth, Calif., 1985; pres. Imperial Polychemicals Corp., Irwindale, Calif., 1983—. Pres. Korean Assn., Los Angeles, 1985. Scholar, Gesellschaft der Deutschen Chemiker, 1973. Mem. Am. Chem. Soc., Soc. Advanced Material and Process Engrs., Soc. Plastics Engrs., Los Angeles Soc. Coatings and Tech. Office: Imperial Polychemicals Corp 5380 N 3d St Irwindale CA 91706

PARK, QUE TE, optical industry executive; b. Pohang City, Republic of Korea, Dec. 5, 1946; came to U.S., 1982; s. In K. and K.R. (Yang) P.; m. Jung J. Kim, June 2, 1974; children: Charles S., James S., Nina S. BA, Hankuk U. Fgn. Studies, Republic of Korea, 1973, MBA, 1981; exec. program, Northwestern U. Kellogg Grad. Sch. Bus., 1984. Pres. Sambo Optical Co., Ltd., Masan, Republic of Korea, 1977-78; exec. dir. Tongkook Corp., Seoul, Republic of Korea, 1978-81; pres. Tongkook Am., Inc., Elk Grove Village, Ill., 1982-86, Quetée Inc., Elk Grove Village, 1983—, S.Y. Optical, Inc., Elk Grove Village, 1986—. Mem. Northwest Internat. Traders Club. Mem. Assembly of God. Office: S Y Optical Inc 1157 Pagni Dr Elk Grove Village IL 60007

PARK, SANGIL, electrical engineering researcher; b. Seoul, Republic of Korea, Nov. 17, 1954; came to U.S., 1981; s. Dong-yoon and Kyu-soon (Lee) P.; m. Hearan Rose Kimm, Nov. 16, 1985; 1 child, Andrew Youngbin. BS, Yonsei U., Seoul, 1977; MS, Kans. State U., 1983; PhD, U. N.Mex., 1987. Broadcast engr. Yonsei Broadcasting, Seoul, 1973-77; software engr. Gold-Star R&D Labs., Anyang, Republic of Korea, 1979-81; research asst. Kans. State U., Manhattan, 1981-83; research asst., instr. U. N.Mex., Albuquerque, 1983-87; asst. prof. U. Pitts., 1987-88; with tech. staff DSP ops. Motorola Inc., Austin, Tex., 1988—. Mem. IEEE, Korean Sci. and Engring. Assn., Sigma Xi, Phi Kappa Phi, Tau Beta Pi, Eta Kappa Nu. Republican. Presbyterian. Home: 212 Hurst Creek Rd Austin TX 78734 Office: Motorola Inc DSP Ops 6501 William Cannon Dr W Austin TX 78735

PARKER, BARRY JAMES CHARLES, retail executive; b. St. Louis, Sept. 9, 1947; s. James M.C. and Ruth E. (Cummings) P.; m. Donna Nardin, June 19, 1970; children: Thomas J.J., Michael B.B. BA, Washington U., St. Louis, 1969; MBA, U. Pa., 1971. Buyer, dist. merchandise mgr. F & R Lazarus & Co., Columbus, Ohio, 1971-75; v.p. and gen. merchandise mgr., sr. v.p. The Children's Place, Pinebrook, N.J., 1975-85; pres. County Seat Stores Inc., Dallas, 1985—. Mem. Nat. Retail Merchants Assn., Internat. Council Shopping Ctrs. Roman Catholic. Office: County Seat Stores Inc 17950 Preston Rd Ste 1000 Dallas TX 75252

PARKER, CLARISSA HARRISON JONES, marketing executive; b. Washington, Oct. 27, 1941; d. Joseph Marion and Sarah (Harrison) Jones; m. Christopher John Parker, June 12, 1965 (div. 1979); 1 child, Katherine Harrison Hersey Parker. BA, Oberlin Coll., 1964. Head tchr. U. Iowa Lab. Sch., Iowa City, 1965-75; adminstrv. asst. Sat. Rev., N.Y.C., 1977-78; asst. office mgr. Rolling Stone mag., N.Y.C., 1978-80; office mgr. Design Communications, Inc., Washington, 1980-84; dir. client svcs. Walter Dorwin Teague Assocs., Inc., N.Y.C. and Washington, 1984—. Contbr. articles to profl. jours. Office: Walter Dorwin Teague Assocs Inc 733 15th St NW Washington DC 20016

PARKER, DANIEL LOUIS, lawyer; b. Smithfield, N.C., Sept. 2, 1924; s. James Daniel and Agnes Augusta (Toussaint) P.; m. Mae Comer Osborne, Aug. 2, 1958. AB, U. N.C., 1947, LLB, 1950. Bar: N.C. 1950. With escrow sect. mortgage loan dept. Pilot Life Ins. Co., Greensboro, N.C., 1950-53, with trust dept. N.C. Nat. Bank, Greensboro, 1953-62; investment counsel Pilot Life Ins. Co., 1962-71, counsel 71-77, 2d v.p., 1977-84; 2nd v.p., asst. gen. counsel Jefferson Standard Life Ins. Co. (now Jefferson-Pilot Life Ins. Co.), Greensboro, 1984—. With U.S. Army, 1944-46. Mem. N.C. Bar Assn., Assn. Life Ins. Counsel, Greensboro Bar Assn., Greensboro Jr. C. of C., Phi Beta Kappa. Republican. Roman Catholic. Home: 308 W Greenway S Greensboro NC 27403 Office: Jefferson-Pilot Life Ins Co 101 N Elm St Greensboro NC 27401

PARKER, DAVID RAYMOND, services industry executive; b. Corpus Christi, Tex., July 6, 1943; s. Jesse Raymond P. and Mary Jane (Valentine) Arrington; m. Judith Evans, Aug. 2, 1969. B.S. in Engring., U. Tex., 1966; M.B.A., Harvard Grad. Sch. Bus., 1972. Dist. ops. mgr. AT&T Long Lines div., Dallas, 1968-70; mgr. Boston Cons. Group, 1972-76; v.p. strategic planning Am. Can Co., Greenwich, Conn., 1976-78, sr. v.p. metal container packaging, 1978-81, sr. v.p.and sector exec. metal container packaging, 1981-83, exec. v.p. packaging, 1983-84; sr. exec. v.p., chief operating officer Bus. Services Group Ryder System, Inc., Miami, Fla., 1984—; dir. Am. Can of Can., Am. Can (UK) Ltd., Envases Venezolanos, 1983—; bd. dirs. Can. Mfrs. Inst., 1981—, Sun Bank, Miami. Active Nat. Planning Assn., Washington, 1982; active Internat. Mgmt. and Devel., 1982, U.S. Council Internat. Bus., N.Y.C., 1982; bd. dirs. Exec. Council on Fgn. Diplomats, Armonk, N.Y.; chmn. bd. dirs. The Beacon Council, Miami, Inst. for Ednl. Leadership, Inc., Washington. Served with USAR, 1968-74. Harvard U. Fredrich Sheldon fellow, 1972; Baker scholar Harvard U., 1972. Episcopalian. Clubs: Harvard Faculty, Harvard Bus. Office: Ryder System Inc 3600 NW 82nd Ave Miami FL 33166

PARKER, DONALD LARUE, management consultant; b. Birmingham, Ala., Jan. 13, 1935; s. Ernest Jefferson and Dorothy Whitfield (McGee) P.; m. Alice Limperis, June 3, 1966; 1 child, Allison Cay. BA, Rhodes Coll., 1957; M Div., Yale U., 1960; diploma, U. Geneva, Switzerland, 1964. Min. First Presbyn. Ch., Old Hickory, Tenn., 1960-63; program rep. USPHS, Detroit, 1964-66; mgmt. tng. specialist GM, Detroit, 1966-68; area supr. GM, Flint, Mich., 1968-70; sr. v.p. Playboy Enterprises, Chgo., L.A., 1974-82; pres. Parker Cons., Santa Monica, Calif., 1982-84, Southport, Conn., 1988—; sr. dir. tng. and devel. Pan Am. World Airways, N.Y.C., 1970-74, sr. v.p., 1984-88; pres. Parker Cons., Southport, Conn., 1988-89; chmn. Parker and Bonnell Inc., 1989—. Mem. nat. corp. council Interlochen (Mich.) Arts Acad., 1986—; bd. dirs. Los Angeles Master Chorale, 1981-84, 87—; citizen's adv. com. Los Angeles Olympics, 1983-84. Presbyterian. Office: Parker & Bonnell Inc 272 Post Rd E Westport CT 06490

PARKER, EARLE LEROY, medical products executive; b. Manhattan, Kans., Sept. 13, 1943; s. Earle L. Parker and Dorothy J. (Weber) Ackenback; m. Alice Braden, June 8, 1966; children: Anne, John, Brad. BS, U.S. Mil. Acad., 1966; MS, Boston U., 1970. Commd. 2d lt. U.S. Army, 1966, advanced through grades to capt., arty./fin. corp., 1968, res., 1970; v.p., contr. U.S. Catheter and Instruments div. C.R. Bard, Inc., Billerica, Mass., 1979—. Mem. Nat. Acctg. Assn., Contrs. Coun., Inst. Managerial Accts., Strategic Planning Bd., fin. Execs. Inst. Republican. Methodist.

PARKER, ELLIS JACKSON, III, lawyer, broadcaster; b. Haleyville, Ala., Oct. 2, 1932; s. Ellis J. and Elizabeth (Funderburg) P.; m. Nancy Elizabeth Bealer; children: Francis Hill, Ellis Stuart. Student, U.S. Mil. Acad., West Point, N.Y., 1953-57; AB, U. Ala., 1958, LLB, 1960, JD, 1961; diplome de droit, U. Compare, Luxembourg, 1959; cert., Acad. Internat. Law, Hague, The Netherlands, 1960. Bar: Ala. 1960, D.C. 1972, Md. Ct. Appeals 1973, U.S. Tax Ct. 1960, U.S. Supreme Ct. 1966. Adminstrv. asst. to U.S. Congressman Grant Washington, 1961-62; legis. atty. IRS, Washington, 1963-64; pvt. practice Birmingham, Ala., 1964—; spl. asst. to Pres. Richard Nixon White House, Washington, 1968-69; v.p., counsel Birmingham Broadcasting Co., 1964-83; ptnr. Taylor, Smith & Parker Law Office, Washington, 1970—; v.p., sec. C.C.C. Devel. Corp., Upper Marlboro, Md., 1968-72; pres. Washington-Ala. News Reports, Washington, 1980—; pres. Sta. WNPT, Tuscaloosa, Ala.; v.p. Sta. WLPH, Birmingham, Ala., Linder Radio, Parker Real Estate, Birmingham, N. Haase Real Estate, Washington; founder Women's Nat. Bank, Washington. Mem. steering com. Rep. Party, Balt., 1972; chmn. bd. trustees Prince George's Hist. and Cultural Trust, Upper Marlboro, 1974; chmn. bd. advisors Prince George's Equestrian Ctr., Upper Marlboro, 1980; bd. dirs. Hospice of Prince George's County, Upper Marlboro, 1982; mem. Upper Marlboro Devel. Com. Mem. ABA, Fed. Communications Bar Assn., Fed. Bar Assn., Inter-Am. Bar Assn., IEEE, Chevy Chase Club, MD Club, Metro. Club, Pi Kappa Alpha, Scabbard and Slade. Home: 11133 Stephalee Ln Rockville MD 20852 also: 1504 S 17th Ave Birmingham AL 35205 Office: WANR Inc 229 3d St North Port AL 35476

PARKER, GEORGE ANTHONY, computer leasing company executive; b. Norfolk, Va., Jan. 29, 1952; s. Milton Andrew Parker and Lillian Beatrice (Davis) Carr; m. Michele Annette Fleuranges, Aug. 16, 1980; 1 child, Jenifer Ann. BS, Wake Forest U., 1974; MBA, U. N.C., 1976. 2d v.p. Continental Ill. Nat. Bank, Chgo., 1976-82; v.p., treas. DPF Computer Leasing Corp., Hartsdale, N.Y., 1982-84; dir., v.p., chief fin. officer Leasing Techs. Internat., Inc., Darien, Conn., 1984—, also bd. dirs.; pres., chmn. bd. Atlantic Computer Funding Corp., Darien, 1984—; bd. dirs. Conn. Bancorp, Inc., Norwalk; v.p. Urban Bankers Forum, 1981-82. Active mem. Glenwood Lake Assn., New Rochelle, 1983—; mem. YMCA, Nat. Urban League. Fellow Consortium for Grad. Studies, St. Louis, 1974-75. Mem. Eastern Assn. Equipment Lessors, Black MBA Assn., U. N.C. Alumni Assn. Democrat. Baptist.

PARKER, GORDON RAE, natural resource company executive; b. Cape Town, South Africa, Dec. 2, 1935; came to U.S., 1981; s. David Rae and Gwen Elizabeth (Armstrong) P.; m. Pamela Margaret Pearce, Sept. 1, 1962; children: Gillian Rae, David Rae. BS, Mont. Coll. Mineral Sci. and Tech., 1958, MS, 1959; MBA, U. Cape Town, 1966. Mng. dir. Tsumeb Corp., Namibia, South Africa, 1975-81; mng. dir. O'okiep Copper Co., Cape, South Africa, 1975-81; v.p. Newmont Mining Corp., N.Y.C., 1981-84, pres., 1984-86, chief exec. officer, 1985-86, chmn., pres. and chief exec. officer, 1986—, also bd. dirs.; bd. dirs. Consol. Gold Fields, PLC, London, The Williams Cos., Inc., Newmont Gold Co., Newmont Australia Ltd., Peabody Holding Co. Inc.; chmn. World Gold Council, 1986—; trustee Western Regional Council, 1987—. Fellow Instn. Mining and Metallurgy (London), South African Inst. Mining and Metallurgy; mem. AIME, British North Am. Com. Clubs: Mining, Sky, Union League (N.Y.C.); Blind Brook (Purchase, N.Y.); Silver Spring Country (Ridgefield, Conn.), Mid Ocean, Hamilton, Bermuda. Home: 13 Sunset Dr Englewood CO 80110 Office: Newmont Mining Corp 1700 Lincoln St Denver CO 80203

PARKER, JAMES JOHN, electrical engineering administrator; b. Oak Park, Ill., June 16, 1947; s. John J. and Marjorie (Grohmann) P.; m. Mary P. Nash, Oct. 21, 1972; children: Elizabeth Ann, John James, Patricia Mary. BS in Elec. Engring., Marquette U., 1971; BSBA, Elmhurst Coll., 1981; MBA, U. Chgo., 1987. Student engr. Motorola Consumer Products, Franklin Park, Ill., 1968-70, engring. assoc., 1972-74; co-op engr. Warwick Electronics, Niles, Ill., 1971-72; sr. engr. research and devel. Quasar Electronics, Inc., Franklin Park, 1974-76; sr. project engr. Motorola Data Products, Carol Stream, Ill., 1976-79; sr. project engr. Zenith Electronics Co., Glenview, Ill., 1979-82, market research mgr., 1982-85, sect. mgr., 1985—; part-time faculty Wright Jr. Coll., Chgo., 1975-80. Editorial adv. bd. Electronic Products Mag., 1976-77. Adviser Jr. Achievement, Chgo., 72-78. Mem. IEEE Midcon. (vice-chmn. pub. relations, 1979, chmn. spec. exhibits, 1981, vice-chmn. spec. exhibits, 1983), Delta Mu Delta. Home: 421 Berkley Ave Elmhurst IL 60126 Office: Zenith Electronics Corp 1000 Milwaukee Ave Glenview IL 60025

PARKER, JAMES WILLIAM, food company executive; b. Dallas, Apr. 5, 1938; s. William B. and Irma Jo (Shettlesworth) P.; m. Linda DeAnn Creech, June 6, 1963; children—Laura D., Kari L. Student, Abilene Christian U., 1957-59; B.A., North Tex. State U., 1963. Cons. P.M.D. Inc., Barrington, Ill., 1968-70; div. mgr. The Southland Corp., Dallas, 1974-80, v.p., 1980-82, exec. v.p., 1982-88; chmn. bd., chief exec. officer Morningstar Foods Inc., Dallas, 1988—; bd. dirs. Milk Industry Found., Washington, 1970—; chmn. bd., chief exec. officer Moringstar Foods, Inc., 1988—. Served with U.S. Army, 1959-61. Mem. Charles County C. of C. (bd. dirs. 1975-78), So. Assn. Food Mfrs. (pres. 1980-81). Republian. Lodge: Rotary (bd. dirs. local club 1967-68). Office: Morningstar Foods Inc 3988 N Central Expwy Dallas TX 75204

PARKER, JOHN MALCOLM, management and financial consultant; b. Halifax, N.S., Can., June 13, 1920; s. Charles Fisher and Mabel (Hennigar) P.; came to U.S., 1936, naturalized, 1942; m. Irene Wilson Davis, Oct. 11, 1942 (dec. Nov. 1987); 1 child, Elane Parker Jones. With Standard Oil Co. N.J., Charlotte, N.C., 1941, Duke Power Co., Charlotte, 1941-42, So. Bell Tel. & Tel. Co., Charlotte, 1946-50, Atlanta, 1950-68, with South Central Bell Telephone Co., Birmingham, Ala., 1968-83, asst. v.p., gen. internal auditor, 1981-83; pres. Omega Assocs., Inc., 1983—. Served with AUS, 1942-46. Certified internal auditor. Mem. Nat. Assn. Accountants (pres. chpt. 1972-73, dir.), Am. Mgmt. Assn., Inst. Internal Auditors (pres. chpt. 1978-79, dist. dir. 1979-81, regional dir. 1981-83, internat. vice chmn. 1983-84, internat. bd. dirs. 1979-87, v.p. found. 1984-85). Internat. Platform Assn. Republican. Presbyn. (commr. gen. assembly Presbyn. Ch. of U.S. 1968, 81). Home: 3520 Belle Meade Ln Birmingham AL 35223 Office: Omega Assocs Inc PO Box 7352-A Birmingham AL 35253

PARKER, JOSEPH MAYON, printing and publishing executive; b. Washington, N.C., Oct. 11, 1931; s. James Mayon and Mildred (Poe) P.; m. Lauretta Owen Dyer, Mar. 23, 1957; children: Katherine Suzanne, Joseph Wilbur. Student, Davidson Coll., 1949-51; BA, U. N.C., 1953; postgrad., Carnegie Inst. Tech., 1955-56. Mgr. print div. Parker Bros., Inc., Ahoskie, N.C., 1956-71, chief editorialist, 1961-77, gen. mgr., 1971-77, pres., chief exec. officer, 1977—; treas. Chowan Graphic Arts Found., Murfreesboro, N.C., 1971-88, v.p., 1988—. Editor, columnist five community newspapers, N.C.; panelist: (TV talk show) North Carolina This Week, 1986—. Mem. Ind. Devel. Commn., 1974—; vice chmn. N.C. Goals and Policy Bd., Raleigh, 1977-84; trustee Pitts. County Meml. Hosp., 1980—; pres. Com. of 100, Winton, N.C., 1984—; chmn. Northeastern N.C. Tomorrow, Elizabeth City, 1981-84, sec. 1984—; del. Dem. Nat. Conv., N.Y.C., 1980, platform com. 1988; dist chmn. N.C. Dem. Party, 1980-82. Served with U.S. Army, 1953-54, col. Res., 1954—. Mem. Soc. Profl. Journalists, East N.C. Press Assn. (past pres.), N.C. Press Assn., Nat. Newspaper Assn. (state chmn. 1976-83), Roanoke Island Hist. Assn. (vice chmn. 1987—), Rotary. Democrat. Methodist. Home: 310 S Colony Ave Ahoskie NC 27910 Office: Parker Bros Inc 116-120 N McGlohon St Ahoskie NC 27910

PARKER, JOSEPHUS DERWARD, corporation executive; b. Elm City, N.C., Nov. 16, 1906; s. Josephus and Elizabeth (Edwards) P.; A.B., U. of South, 1928; postgrad. Tulane U., 1928-29, U. N.C., 1929-30, Wake Forest Med. Coll., 1930-31; m. Mary Wright, Jan. 15, 1934 (dec. Dec. 1937); children—Mary Wright (Mrs. Mallory A. Pittman, Jr.), Josephus Derward; m. 2d, Helen Hodges Hackney, Jan. 24, 1940; children—Thomas Hackney, Alton Person, Derward Hodges, Sarah Helen. Founder, chmn. bd. J.D. Parker & Sons, Inc., Elm City, 1955—, Parker Tree Farms, Inc., 1956—; founder, pres. Invader, Inc., 1961-63; pres. dir. Brady Lumber Co., Inc., 1957-62; v.p., dir. Atlantic Limestone, Inc., Elm City, 1970—; owner, operator Parker Airport, Eagle Springs, N.C., 1940-62. Served to capt. USAF, 1944-47. Episcopalian. Clubs: Moose, Lions; Wilson (N.C.) Country. Home: PO Box 905 Elm City NC 27822-0905

PARKER, KELLY LYNN, natural gas, marketing and tranportation company executive, accountant; b. Lubbock, Tex., Mar. 26, 1958; s. Walton Shea and Neva (Wise) P. BBA, Tex. Tech U., 1980; postgrad., So. Meth. U. CPA, Tex. Sr. auditor Arthur Young and Co., Dallas, 1980-82; sr. tax specialist Peat Marwick, Main & Co., Midland, Tex., 1982-84; controller Citigas Corp., Midland, 1984-86, v.p. fin., 1986—, also bd. dirs.; bd. dirs. Citigas Corp., 1987—; sec.-treas. N.Mex. Gas Co., Midland, 1985-87. Mem. Rep. Task Force, Midland, 1984—. Named Most Outstanding Mem., Sigma Nu Frat.,1980, one of Outstanding Young Men in Am., 1985. Mem. Am. Inst. CPA's., Tex. Soc. CPA's, Am. Mgmt. Assn., Sigma Nu. Republican. Baptist. Lodge: Lions.

PARKER, MARILYN MORRIS, business executive; b. St. Louis, Jan. 2, 1935; d. Walter Louis and R. Viola (Morris) Priebe; B.B.A., Washington U., 1954, M.B.A., 1955; m. H. Virgil Parker, Mar. 11, 1971. With IBM Corp., various locations, 1957—, mgr. IBM Aids, Los Angeles, 1971-75, mgr. performance evaluation, San Jose, Calif., 1976-79, tech. asst. to mgr. performance and tech., 1979-80, mgr. IBM Los Angeles Sci. Center, 1981—; v.p. Cherokee Creek Enterprises, Los Angeles and San Jose, 1973—. Cofounder, pres. Am. Indian Scholarship Fund, 1971-76, No. Calif. regional dir., 1977-80, exec. dir., 1981—; Author: Information Economics, 1988; mem. Santa Clara County Alcoholism Adv. Bd., 1977; bd. dirs. Try Found., 1977-78. Named KNX Newsradio Citizen of the Week, Feb. 1974; recipient City of Los Angeles Cert. of Merit, 1976, others. Mem. Cherokee Confederacy, Am. Indian Edn. Assn., Washington U. Alumni Council, Am. Harp Soc. Lutheran.

PARKER, MAYNARD MICHAEL, journalist, magazine executive; b. Los Angeles, July 28, 1940; s. Clarence Newton and Virginia Esther (Boyce) P.; m. Judith Karen Seaborg, Dec. 11, 1965 (div.); 1 child, Francesca Lynn; m. Susan Fraker, Sept. 15, 1985; 1 child, Nicholas Maynard. B.A., Stanford U., 1962; M.A., Columbia U., 1963. Reporter Life mag., 1963-64, corr. Hong Kong Bur., 1966-67; corr. Hong Kong Bur. Newsweek, 1967-69; Saigon bur. chief Newsweek, Vietnam, 1969-70; chief Hong Kong Bur. Newsweek, 1969-73, sr. nat. affairs editor, 1975-77, asst. mng. editor, 1977-80, exec. editor, 1980-82, editor, 1982—; mng. editor Newsweek Internat. Newsweek, N.Y.C., 1973-75. Contbr. articles to Fgn. Affairs, Fgn. Policy, Reporter, Atlantic. Served to 1st lt. inf. U.S. Army, 1964-66. Mem. Council on Fgn. Relations, Am. Soc. Mag. Editors. Episcopalian. Office: Newsweek Mag 444 Madison Ave New York NY 10022-6999

PARKER, PATRICK STREETER, manufacturing executive; b. Cleve., 1929. B.A., Williams Coll., 1951; M.B.A., Harvard U., 1953. With Parker-Hannifin Corp. and predecessor, Cleve., 1953—, sales mgr. fittings div., 1957-63, mgr. aerospace products div., 1963-65, pres. Parker Seal Co. div., 1965-67, corp. v.p., 1967-69, pres., 1969-71, pres. and chief exec. officer, 1971-77, chmn. bd. and chief exec. officer, 1977-84, chmn. bd., 1984—, pres., 1982-84, also dir. Pres. and trustee Woodruff Hosp. of Cleve. Bd. trustee Case Western Res. U.; trustee Woodruff Found. Served with USN, 1954-57. Office: Parker Hannifin Corp 17325 Euclid Ave Cleveland OH 44112 *

PARKER, STEPHEN, financial services company executive; b. Melrose, Mass., July 7, 1934; s. Henry Stephen and Olga Hilda (Palmgren) P.; m. Bernice Dowe, June 1957 (div. 1977); children: Susan, Matthew, Sarah; m. Patricia Barbara Valente, May 27, 1983; children: Jeffrey, Katherine. BA in Econs., Harvard U., 1957. Investment broker Moseley Hallgarten, Boston, 1957-67, br. mgr., 1967-73; nat. sales mgr. Moseley Hallgarten, Boston and N.Y.C., 1973-84, pres., chief exec. officer, 1984-87; pres., chief exec. officer Interact Mgmt., Inc., Boston, 1987-89; chmn., chief exec. officer Freedom Capitol Mgmt. Corp., Boston, 1989—. Capt. U.S. Army, 1958-59. Mem. Securities Industry Assn. (bd. dirs., chmn. sales and mktg. com., S.I.I. trustee), Harvard Club, Winchester Country Club (Mass.), Mid-Ocean Club (Bermuda). Office: Freedom Capitol Mgmt Corp 1 Beacon St Boston MA 02108

PARKER, THEODORE CLIFFORD, electronics engineer; b. Dallas, Oreg., Sept. 25, 1929; s. Theodore Clifford and Virginia Bernice (Rumsey) P.; B.S.E.E. magna cum laude, U. So. Calif., 1960; m. Jannet Ruby Barnes, Nov. 28, 1970; children—Sally Odette, Peggy Claudette. Vice pres. engring. Telemetrics, Inc., Gardena, Calif., 1963-65; chief info. systems Northrop-Nortronics, Anaheim, Calif., 1966-70; pres. AVTEL Corp., Covina, Calif., 1970-74, Aragon, Inc., Sunnyvale, Calif., 1975-78; v.p. Teledyne McCormick Selph, Hollister, Calif., 1978-82; sr. staff engr. FMC Corp., San Jose, Calif., 1982-85; pres. Power One Switching Products, Camarillo, Calif., 1985-86; pres. Condor D.C. Power Supplies, Inc., 1987-88, pres. Intelligence Power Tech. Inc., Camarillo, 1988—. Mem. IEEE (chmn. autotestcon '87), Am. Prodn. and Inventory Control Soc., Am. Def. Preparedness Assn., Armed Forces Communications and Electronics Assn., Nat. Rifle Assn. (life), Tau Beta Pi, Eta Kappa Nu. Home: 1290 Saturn Ave Camarillo CA 93010 Office: Intelligence Power Tech Inc 829 Flynn Rd Camarillo CA 93010

PARKER, TRUMAN (TED), financial planner; b. Houlton, Maine, July 18, 1938; s. Truman and Phyllis (Cunningham) P.; m. Carletta Ann Brandt, Dec. 28, 1960; 1 child, Barry Dean. BA in Math., Tex. A&M U., 1960, MS in Meteorology, 1967, MS in Computer Sci., 1968; BS in Meteorology, U. Wash., 1961. Cert. fin. planner. Enlisted USAF, 1960, advanced through grades to col., ret., 1984; assoc. Key Fin. Planning Corp., Jacksonville, Fla., 1984-87; pres. Benoit, Parker, Driscoll & LeMaistre, Jacksonville, 1987—, also bd. dirs. Active Am. Cancer Soc., Jacksonville. Col. USAF, 1960-84. Decorated Bronze Star, Legion of Merit, Meritorious Svc. medal with 2 oak leaf clusters. Mem. Inst. Cert. Fin. Planners (treas. Jacksonville br. 1988—), Internat. Assn. Fin. Planners, Registry of Fin. Planning Practitioners, Jacksonville Soc. of Inst. for Cert. Fin. Planners (treas. 1988—), Kiwanis (bd. dirs. Jacksonville 1987—). Republican. Presbyterian. Office: Benoit Parker Driscoll & LeMaistre 4417 Beach Blvd Ste 101 Jacksonville FL 32207

PARKHURST, CHARLES LLOYD, electronics company executive; b. Nashville, Aug. 13, 1943; s. Charles Albert Parkhurst and Dorothy Elizabeth (Ballou) Parkhurst Crutchfield; m. Dolores Ann Oakley, June 6, 1970; children: Charles Thomas, Deborah Lynn, Jere Loy. Student, Hume-Fogg Tech. Coll., 1959-61; AA, Mesa Community Coll., 1973; student, Ariz. State U., 1973-76. Mem. design staff Tex. Instruments, Dallas, 1967-68; mgr. design Motorola, Inc., Phoenix, 1968-76; pres. LSI Cons., Inc., Tempe, Ariz., 1976-85, LSI Photomasks, Inc., Tempe, 1985—. Mem. Rep. Congl. Leadership Council, Washington, 1988. Served as cpl. USMC, 1961-64. Mem. Bay Area Chrome Users Soc., Nat. Trust Hist. Preservation. Baptist. Office: LSI Photomasks Inc 406 S Price Rd Ste 5 Tempe AZ 85281

PARKINSON, HOWARD EVANS, insurance company executive; b. Logan, Utah, Nov. 3, 1936; s. Howard Maughan and Valeria Arlene (Evans) P.; B.S., Brigham Young U., 1961; M.B.A., U. Utah, 1963; m. Lucy Kay Bowen, Sept. 2, 1960; children—Blake, Gregory, Dwight, Lisa, David, Rebecca. Mgmt. intern AEC, Richland, Wash., 1963-65; v.p. Belstar, Inc., Rexburg, Idaho, 1965-71, dir., 1966-76, pres., 1971-76; v.p., dir. Grand Targhee Resort, Inc., Rexburg, 1967-69; v.p. Fargo-Wilson-Wells Co., Pocatello, Idaho, 1974-76; equity qualified agt. Equitable Life Assurance So. U.S., Idaho Falls, Idaho, 1977-80, mem. nat. council sales group, 1978; dist. mgr. Mass. Mut. Life Ins. Co., Idaho Falls, 1980—; fin. cons. small bus. Bd. dirs. Little League Baseball, 1974-75; coach Little League Basketball, 1975-76; high councilman Rexburg Stake, Ch. of Jesus Christ of Latter-day Saints, 1976-77, bishop, 1977—. Recipient Bronze award Mass. Mut. Life Ins. Co.; C.L.U. Mem. Million Dollar Roundtable. Republican. Club: Toastmasters (past pres.). Office: Mass Mut Life Ins Co 720 N Holmes Idaho Falls ID 83401

PARKINSON, JAMES THOMAS, III, investment consultant; b. Richmond, Va., July 10, 1940; s. James Thomas and Elizabeth (Hopkins) P.; m. Molly O Owens, June 16, 1962; children: James Thomas, Glenn Walser. BA, U. Va., 1962; MBA, U. Pa., 1964. Trainee Chem. Bank, N.Y.C., 1964-66; assoc., corp. fin. dept. Blyth & Co., Inc., N.Y.C., 1968-69; v.p., corp. fin. dept. Clark Dodge & Co., Inc., N.Y.C., 1969-74; pvt. practice investment mgmt., N.Y.C., 1974-85, 87—; v.p. Pleasantville Advisors, Inc., N.Y.C., 1986-87; bd. mgrs. Am. Bible Soc., N.Y.C.; instr. corp. fin. Ind. U., 1966-68. Sr. warden Ch. of Holy Trinity, N.Y.C., 1978-79; trustee Cancer Care Inc., Nat. Cancer Care Found. Inc. With AUS, 1966-68. Republican. Episcopalian. Clubs: Univ., Ch. (N.Y.C.); Va. Country (Richmond). Office: 575 Madison Ave Ste 1006 New York NY 10022

PARKINSON, JOHN DAVID, electrical and electronic manufacturing company executive; b. Phila., Nov. 26, 1929; s. Granville and Dorothy (Crooks) P.; m. Sally Ann Brokaw, Nov. 10, 1956; children: David Gregory, Rex Granville, Leanne. B.S., Rutgers U., 1951. With Thomas & Betts Corp., Elizabeth, N.J., 1954—; various sales mgmt. positions Thomas & Betts Corp., Syracuse, 1954-67; v.p. mktg. Thomas & Betts Corp., 1968, v.p., gen. mgr., 1969, pres. div., 1969, v.p. corp., 1971, exec. v.p., 1971-74, pres., chief exec. officer, 1974-84, chmn. bd., 1975—, also dir., 1968—; dir. Perkin-Elmer Corp. Mem. Nat. Elec. Mfrs. Assn. (bd. govs., chmn.), Elec. Mfrs. Club. Club: Union League (N.Y.C.). Office: Thomas & Betts Corp 1001 Frontier Rd Bridgewater NJ 08807

PARKINSON, THOMAS IGNATIUS, JR., lawyer; b. N.Y.C., Jan. 27, 1914; s. Thomas I. and Georgia (Weed) P.; A.B., Harvard U., 1934; LL.B., U. Pa., 1937; m. Geralda E. Moore, Sept. 23, 1937; children—Thomas Ignatius III, Geoffrey Moore, Cynthia Moore. Admitted to N.Y. bar, 1938, since practiced in N.Y.C.; assoc. Milbank, Tweed, Hope & Hadley, 1937-47, partner, 1947-56; pres. Mar Ltd., 1951—; pres. Breecom Corp., 1972-80, chmn. bd., 1980—; dir., exec. com. Pine St. Fund, Inc., N.Y.C., 1949-83, Trustee State Communities Aid Assn., 1949-83; dir. Fgn. Policy Assn., 1949-53; bd. dirs., exec. com. Milbank Meml. Fund, 1948-84. Mem. Am. Bar Assn., Assn. Bar City N.Y., Pilgrims U.S.A., Brit. War Relief Soc. (officer), Met. Unit Found., Phi Beta Kappa. Clubs: Down Town Assn., Knickerbocker, Union. Office: Breecom Corp 780 Third Ave 25th Fl New York NY 10017

PARKS, ED HORACE, III, lawyer; b. Tulsa, Apr. 11, 1948; s. Ed H. Jr. and Nancy D. (Dickson) P. BS in Philosophy, Okla. State U., 1972; JD, U. Tulsa, 1975. Bar: Okla. 1975, U.S. Dist. Ct. (no. and we. dists.) Okla. 1975, U.S. Ct. Appeals (10th cir.) 1975, U.S. Supreme Ct. 1980. Assoc. Boyd & Parks, Tulsa, 1975-79; ptnr. Parks & Buck, Tulsa, 1980—. Bd. dirs. Okla. Health Systems Agy., Oklahoma City, 1978-86, vice chmn., 1986. Served with Okla. N.G., 1969-75. Mem. ABA, Okla. Bar Assn., Tulsa County Bar Assn. (grievances com.), Assn. Trial Lawyers Am., Okla. Trial Lawyers Assn., Phi Alph Delta (pres. 1973). Democrat. Baptist. Club: Utica Sq. Lodge: Lions (pres. Tulsa 1976). Home: 1333 E 60th St Tulsa OK 74105 Office: Parks & Buck 1146 E 61st St Tulsa OK 74136

PARKS, FLOYD MASON, accounting firm consultant; b. Phila., Dec. 9, 1952; s. Kenneth Earl and Twila Elene (Tomlin) P.; m. Melanie Ann Leonard, Feb. 17, 1979. AAS in Data Processing with distinction, U. So. Colo., 1976, BBA with distinction, 1978; MBA, U. Utah, 1982. Cert. systems profl.; cert. info. systems auditor. Dir. residence hall U. So. Colo., Pueblo, 1978; dir. student family housing U. Utah, Salt Lake City, 1978-79, staff specialist, 1979-82; mgr. Deloitte Haskins & Sells, Denver, 1982—. Rep. precinct chmn., Salt Lake City, 1981-82. Served with USNR, 1971-79, USAR, 1979-82, Vietnam. Mem. Am. Mgmt. Assn., Assn. MBA Execs., Internat. Platform Assn., Mensa. Baptist. Office: Deloitte Haskins & Sells 1560 Broadway Ste 1800 Denver CO 80202

PARKS, JAMES THOMAS, financial company executive; b. Enid, Okla., Feb. 14, 1947; s. Harold Johnson and Olive Berneise (Sheets) P.; m. Karen G. Parks, June 14, 1969; children: Jennifer T., Heidi R. BS, Okla. State U., 1969; M of Accountancy, U. Okla., 1973. CPA. Sr. mgr. Peat Marwick Main and Co., Oklahoma City, N.Y.C., 1973-83; v.p. fin. standards and corp. taxes Fed. Nat. Mortgage Assn., Washington, 1983—. With U.S. Army, 1969-71. Mem. Am. Inst. CPA's, Fin. Execs. Inst. Republican. Methodist. Home: 11 Dairyfield Ct Rockville MD 20852 Office: Fed Nat Mortgage Assn 3900 Wisconsin Ave NW Washington DC 20016

PARKS, MICHAEL JAMES, publisher, editor; b. Spokane, Wash., June 3, 1944; s. Floyd Lewis and C. Marie (McHugh) P.; m. Janet K. Holter, Aug. 12, 1967; children: Michael J., Gregory F., Sarah M. BA, Seattle U., 1966. Reporter The Seattle Times, 1966-74, fin. editor, 1974-77; pub., editor Marple's Bus. Newsletter, Seattle, 1977—. Bd. govs. Seattle U. Alumni Assn.; trustee Seattle Rotary Service Found. Fellow Am. Press Inst., N.Y.C., 1973. Roman Catholic. Lodge: Rotary. Office: Marples Bus Newsletter 911 Western Ave Ste 509 Seattle WA 98104-1031

PARMA, ROBERT, technical school administrator; b. Chgo., Sept. 23, 1925; s. Frank and Anna A. (Zeman) P.; m. Dorrell A. Beaumont, Jan. 22, 1960; children: Dorothy Jeanne Kolentus, Cathy Anne Parma Kimoto. BS, U. So. Calif., Los Angeles, 1954, MBA, 1970. Asst. buyer Aldens, Inc., Chgo., 1947-48; dir. consumer relations Admiral Corp., Chgo., 1948-49; exec. asst. Dunlaps, Inc., San Pedro, Calif., 1954; mgr. Air Reduction Inc.,

Burbank, Calif., 1955-60; mktg. dir. Robert Morton Co., Glendale, Calif., 1960-63; pres. Nat. Tech. Schs., Los Angeles, 1963—, also bd. dirs.; sec. West Coast Corp., Los Angeles, 1976—, Pacific Coast Corp., Los Angeles, 1976—; v.p. United Edn. and Software, Encino, Calif., 1986—. Mem. Nat. Assn. Trade and Tech. Schs., Nat. Home Study Council (pres. 1986-88), Corr. Accredited Sch. Assn. (pres. 1985), Western Council Proprietary Schs. (bd. dirs., treas. 1987). Democrat. Club: Pasadena (Calif.). Office: Nat Tech Schs 4000 S Figueroa St Los Angeles CA 90037

PARMELEE, CHARLES DAVID, management company executive; b. Ottawa, Ont., Can., Nov. 13, 1932; s. Wilfrid Alexander and Lillas (Stitt) P.; widower. Cert. in aero. engring., RCAF Aero. Engring. Sch., 1952; grad. diploma in mech. engring., Royal Mil. Coll., Kingston, Ont., 1954; B.Engring. Mechanics, McGill U., Montreal, Que., Can., 1955; Grad. Diploma in Mgmt. and Bus. Adminstrn., McGill U., 1959; M.B.A., U. Western Ont., London, 1960. Registered profl. engr., Ont. Exec. asst. to chmn. Denison Mines Ltd., Toronto, Ont., 1968-72, v.p. corp. affairs, 1974-81, exec. v.p. corp. affairs, 1981-82, exec. v.p., 1982—, also dir.; v.p. Lake Ontario Cement, Toronto, 1972-74; pres., chief operating officer, dir. Roman Corp., 1985—; dir. Quintette Coal Ltd., Tumbler Ridge, B.C., Can.; dir., vice chmn. Lawson Mardon Group Ltd., Toronto; pres., dir. Parlake Resources Ltd., Toronto; dir., v.p. Concord Fin. Corp. Ltd. Mem. Can. Mediterranean Inst. Ottawa (trustee), Can. and Keswick Power Squadrons, Can.-Taiwan Bus. Assn. (dir.), Ont. Bus. Adv. Council, The Corp. Fin. Inst., Pulp and Paper Assn. Progressive Conservative. Anglican. Club: Royal Can. Yacht (former commodore), Toronto Bd. of Trade, Royal Mil. Coll. of Can., Toronto. Home: Kings Landing, 480 Queens Quay W Ste 806W, Toronto, ON Canada M5V 2Y5 Office: Roman Corp & Denison Mines Ltd, Royal Bank Pla PO Box 40, Toronto, ON Canada M5J 2K2

PARNELL, DONALD RAY, chemical company executive; b. Grafton, N.D., Aug. 27, 1942; s. Donald James and Ruth Page (Flett) P.; m. Lynda Jo Porter, Aug. 5, 1964; children: Coralie Ann, Derek Ray, Ryan Edward, Mark Lawrence. BS in Chemistry, U. N.D., 1964, PhD, 1972. Sr. rsch. chemist Corning (N.Y.) Glass Works, 1973-77; supr. chem. tech. Am. Can Co., Neenah, Wis., 1977-81; tech. dir. Akrosil, Menasha, Wis., 1981—; gen. sec. 3d Internat. Organosilicon Symposium, Madison, 1972. Contbr. articles to profl. jours. Capt. U.S. Army, 1968-71. Mem. Am. Chem. Soc., Thilmany Mgmt. Assn. (bd. dirs. 1988—), Pacesetters Running Club (treas. Menasha chpt. 1983-85, pres. 1986-87). Office: Akrosil 206 Garfield Ave Menasha WI 54952-8001

PARNES, STEVEN JONATHAN, retail corporation executive; b. Bklyn., June 17, 1957; s. Stanley and Frances (Meyers) P.; m. Nancy L. Spector, July 31, 1983; 1 child, Michelle Allison. BS in Acctg., Syracuse U., 1978. CPA, N.Y. Staff acct. Mann Judd Landau CPAs, N.Y.C., 1978-80; sr. acct. Edward Isaacs & Co. CPAs, N.Y.C., 1980-83; asst. v.p., controller Barney's Inc., N.Y.C., 1983-88; controller Century 21 Dept. Stores, N.Y.C., 1988—. Mem. Am. Inst. CPAs, N.Y. State Soc. CPAs.

PARNOW, ROBERT JESS, flour milling company executive; b. Thief River Falls, Minn., Oct. 19, 1950; s. Robert Otto and Adeline Irene (Kulseth) P.; m. Gayle Clarise McDonald, Aug. 12, 1972. BS, U. Minn., 1972; MBA, Coll. of St. Thomas, St. Paul, 1979. Data analyst Pillsbury Co., Mpls., 1971-72, tech. analyst, 1972-73; environ. tech. North Star Rsch. Labs., Mpls., 1973-75; quality systems coord. Peavey Co., Chaska, Minn., 1975-77; schedule coord. Peavey Co. Flour Mills, Hastings, Minn., 1977-79; mgr. ops. adminstrn. Peavey Co. Flour Mills, Mpls., 1979-80; prodn. mgr. Peavey Co. Flour Mills, Alton, Ill., 1980-82, plant mgr., 1982-83; v.p., gen. mgr. Dixie Portland Flour Mills, Inc., Chgo., 1983—. Bd. dirs. River Bend United Way, Alton, 1982-83, Boy Scouts Am., Wood River, Ill., 1982-83. Mem. Bakers Courtesy Club Chgo. (1st v.p. 1987—), Bakers Club Chgo., Chgo. Bakery Prodn. Club, Southwestern Ill. Indsl. Assn. (bd. dirs. 1982-83), Riverside Golf Club. Republican. Presbyterian. Home: 1036 Superior St Oak Park IL 60302 Office: Dixie Portland Flour Mills 1300 W Carroll Ave Chicago IL 60607

PARR, DORIS ANN, financial institution executive, consultant; b. Fergus Falls, Minn., July 10, 1933; d. Henry Fritzolf and Esther Marie (Ahlgren) Peterson; m. Mark Hoffman, 1949 (div. 1960); children: Cynthia Lee Davis, David Alan Hoffman; m. Harold R. Parr, 1961 (div. 1974). Student Am. Savs. and Loan Inst., 1965-66, Pioneer Nat. Title Ins. Co., 1969, Menlo Coll., 1975. Comml. loan officer Savbank Service Corp., Seattle, 1975-77; exec. v.p., mgr. Sound Savs. & Loan, Seattle, 1976-78; v.p. Queen City Savs. & Loan, Seattle, 1978-82; v.p., mgr. State Savs. & Loan Assn., Dallas, 1983-84; pres. Nat. Real Estate Mortgage Services Inc., Dallas, 1984—; instr. real estate law San Francisco City Coll., 1975. Recipient 1st Pl. Speech trophy Am. Savs. & Loan Inst., 1964. Mem. Assn. Profl. Mortgage Women (program chmn. Seattle chpt. 1969-70, program chmn. San Jose chpt. 1973-74, pres. 1975-76, Woman of Yr. 1979), U.S. Savs. and Loan League (consumer affairs and secondary market com.), Nat. Assn. Females Execs., Fed. Home Loan Bank Bd. (maj. comml. loan underwriter). Organized and managed 1st U.S. minority savs. and loan assn. Home: 2208 Canyon Valley Trail Plano TX 75023

PARR, HARRY EDWARD, JR., financial executive; b. Dayton, Ohio, Sept. 2, 1928; s. Harry Edward and Naomi Theresa (Oesbeck) P.; m. Suzanne Johnson, Oct. 3, 1953; children: Constance, Cynthia, Claudia, Brian, Patrick. BSBA, U. Dayton, 1951. With Chrysler Corp., Detroit, 1953-66; v.p., controller Diebold, Inc., Canton, Ohio, 1966-78, v.p., treas., 1978-82, sr. v.p. fin., treas., 1982—, also bd. dirs. Bd. dirs. Jr. Achievement Stark County, Canton United Way; trustee Walsh Coll., Canton, Canton Cultural Ctr. for Arts; trustee, mem. devel. bd. Stark County; bd. dirs. Aultman Hosp. Served to 1st lt. U.S. Army, 1951-53. Mem. Fin. Execs. Inst., Nat. Assn. Accts., Planning Execs. Inst., Canton C. of C. (former trustee). Club: Brookside Country (Canton). Office: Diebold Inc 5995 Mayfair Rd North Canton OH 44720

PARR, RICHARD ARNOLD, II, lawyer; b. Edmond, Okla., July 26, 1958; s. Jack Ramsey and Martha (Suttle) P.; m. Becky Fay Stapp, Feb. 28, 1987. BA cum laude, Vanderbilt U., 1979; JD, Cornell U., 1982. Bar: Okla. 1982, Tex. 1983. Law clk. to chief justice U.S. Ct. Appeals, Oklahoma City, 1982-83; assoc. Johnson & Swanson, Dallas, 1983-85, Gardner, Carton & Douglas, Dallas, 1986-88; sr. atty. Valero Energy Corp., San Antonio, 1988—; bd. dirs. AmeriVenture Corp., San Antonio, Paragon Home Care Corp., San Antonio. Sr. editor Cornell Law Rev., 1981-82, contbr., 1983. Mem. ABA, State Bar Tex., Okla. Bar Assn. Republican. Episcopalian. Home: PO Box 120004 San Antonio TX 78212-9204 Office: Valero Energy Corp 530 McCullough Ave San Antonio TX 78292

PARR, THOMAS CHARLES, retail executive; b. Mansfield, Ohio, May 29, 1942; s. Robert Fredrick and Dorothy Pauline (Hassinger) P.; student public schs. Columbus, Ohio; m. Jane Elaine Kropp, Feb. 17, 1963; children—Connie Sue, Thomas Andrew. Dept. mgr. IGA, Columbus, Ohio, 1958-66; firefighter Upper Arlington Fire Div., Columbus, Ohio, 1966-81, paramedic coordinator, 1979-81; pres. Parr Emergency Product Sales, Inc., Galloway, Ohio, 1974—. Recipient World Champion 1st Aid Competition team award, 1973; named Franklin County Fireman of Yr., 1974, Central Ohio Heart Assn. Vol. of Yr., 1974. Mem. Ohio Assn. Emergency Med. Services (pres. 1975-79), Nat. Assn. Emergency Med. Technicians. Lutheran. Home and Office: 6106 Bausch Rd Galloway OH 43119

PARRIS, GREGORY AUGUSTO, accountant, auditor; b. Panama City, Panama, Aug. 31, 1959; came to U.S., 1962; s. Leslie A. and Doris (Bell) P.; m. Kimberly Davis, May 25, 1985; children: Vanessa, Kristin. BS, NYU, 1981. CPA, N.Y.; cert. info. systems auditor. Jr. auditor Mfr.'s Hanover Trust Co, N.Y.C., 1981-83; sr. auditor Chase Manhattan Bank, N.Y.C., 1983, 2d v.p., mgr. debt arbitrage, 1988—; sr. auditor Kidder Peabody, N.Y.C., 1983-85; supervisory auditor Salomon Bros., N.Y.C., 1985-87; fin. contr. Stewart Devel. Co., Waterbury, Conn., 1987-88. Mem. Nat. Assn. Black Accts. (bd. dirs. N.Y.C. 1986-87). Republican. Roman Catholic. Office: Chase Manhattan Bank New York NY 10081

PARRISH, ROBERT RAY, communications supervisor; b. Cave City, Ky., Jan. 6, 1938; s. Roy A. and Bernice (Boyd) F., m. Judith Rae Howell, June 26, 1959; children: Ronold Lee, Christopher Rodney. Grad. high sch., Louisville. With Louisville Gas and Electric Co., 1957, tech. service supr., 1963—. Mem. Utilities Communications Council, Assn. Cert. Technicians. Home: 3106 Schneider Ave Louisville KY 40215 Office: Louisville Gas & Electric Co 731 W Ormsby Ave Louisville KY 40203

PARROTT, JORGE ERNEST, financial advisor, small business owner; b. Jacksonville, Ill., Aug. 10, 1954; s. John William Sr. and Isabel Gabriella (Place) P.; m. Luanne Marie Lemphier, Apr. 15, 1978; children: Orion W., Matthew A., Jonathan E. BA, Ill. Coll., 1976; cert. in systems analysis, Harvard U., 1978. Dist. mgr. Combined Ins. Co., Brookline, Mass., 1982-85; sales rep. John Hancock Ins., Boston, 1985-87; owner Parrott Fin. Advisors, Yarmouth, Maine, 1987—, Employee Benefit & Pension Design Co., Yarmouth, Maine, 1988—; past bd. dirs. Resource Strategies, Inc., Athol, Mass.; tchr. fin. planning Life Underwriters, Portland, Maine, 1982—. Editor, owner newspaper Albatross, 1969-73. Coordinator Open Space Adv. Com., Yarmouth, Maine, 1986—. Mem. Internat. Assn. for Fin. Planners (mem. steering com. 1987—), Nat. Assn. Life Underwriters, Internat. Assn. Registered Fin. Planners (chartered; pres. 1987—), U.S. C. of C. (territory mgr. insured plans 1988—. Democrat. Clubs: Key (Jacksonville, Ill.) (pres. 1971-72); Modern Woodmen (sec. 1987—). Home: 136 Portand St Yarmouth ME 04096 Office: Parrott Fin Advisors Inc 136A Portland St Yarmouth ME 04096

PARROTT, WILLIAM W., retirement planner; b. N.Y.C., Oct. 10, 1927; s. Wilburt L. and Mary J. (Hardy) P.; m. Aileen B. Cotter; children: Geraldine, John, Theresa, Joseph, Mary, Regina, Mark. M in Pub. Adminstrn., NYU, 1954; MS in Fin. Services, Am. Coll., Bryn Mawr, Pa., 1983. City mgr. Village of Patchogue, N.Y., 1950-58; life underwriter Equitable Life Ins. Co., Hempstead, N.Y., 1958-68, N.Y.C., 1968-80; estate planner Fred S. James Co., N.Y.C., 1980-82; fin. planner Merrill Lynch & Co., N.Y.C., 1982-88; retirement planning company executive Creative Retirement Planning, Inc., N.Y.C., 1988—. Pres. Dems. for New Politics, Bayside, N.Y., 1975-77, Cath.-Jewish Relations Com. Northeast Queens, N.Y., 1985-88; lay theologian Roman Cath. Ch., San Francisco, 1963-68. Served with USN, 1945-47. Mem. N.Y.C. Estate Planners Council, Internat. Assn. Fin. Planners. Club: North Shore Tennis (Bayside) (trustee 1978-80). Office: Creative Retirement Planning 30 Rockefeller Plaza New York NY 10020

PARRY, CAROL JACQUELINE, banker; b. Chgo., Apr. 12, 1941; d. Ralph G. and Estelle (Hoffman) Newman. B.A., Tufts U., 1964; M.S.W., U. Conn., 1969; postgrad., Harvard U., 1984. Dir. program planning N.Y.C. Agy. for Child Develop., N.Y.C., 1971-72; cons. McKinsey & Co., N.Y.C., 1972-74; asst. commr. Spl. Svcs. for Children, N.Y.C., 1974-77; v.p., dist. head Chem. Bank, N.Y.C., 1978-80, sr. v.p., div. head, 1981-86, sr. v.p. nat. expansion program, 1985, sr. v.p. comml. sector, chmn. regional bank, 1985-87, head private banking, 1987-89; ptnr. Personnel Corp. of Am., N.Y.C., 1989—. Bd. dirs. N.Y. Urban Coalition, Nat. Child Labor Com. Channel 13 adv. bd., N.Y. Landmarks Conservancy; chmn. N.Y. State Juvenile Justice Bd. Recipient Big WEAL award Women's Equity Action League, 1984. Home: 60 E 8th St New York NY 10003 Office: Chem Bank 277 Park Ave New York NY 10172

PARSLEY, STEVEN DWAYNE, title company executive; b. Monrovia, Calif., Dec. 31, 1959. BBA magna cum laude, U. Albuquerque, 1985. Lic. agt. to issue title ins., N.Mex. Data processing asst. The Orion Corp., Albuquerque, 1978-79; title searcher N.Mex. Title, Albuquerque, 1979; v.p., mgr. title ops. Rio Grande Title Co., Albuquerque, 1979—, also bd. dirs. Recipient Presdl. scholarship U. N.Mex., Albuquerque, 1978, Superior Service award Rio Grande Title Co., Albuquerque, 1983, 85. Mem. N.Mex. Land Title Assn. (edn. com.), Albuquerque Bd. Realtors (affiliate rels. subcom.). Home: 9702 Mcknight NE Albuquerque NM 87112 Office: Rio Grande Title Co 6400 Indian School NE Albuquerque NM 87110

PARSONS, ANDREW JOHN, management consultant; b. Kingston, Surrey, Eng., July 22, 1943; came to U.S., 1968; s. S. John and Hylda P. (Wili) P.; m. Carol Ann Iannucci, June 6, 1970; children: Alexandra, Katherine. BA, MA, Oxford U., 1965; MBA, Harvard U., 1970. Account exec. Leo Burnett, London, 1965-68; from strategic planning dir. to v.p. mktg. Prestige Group Ltd. div. Am. Home Products, N.Y.C. and London, 1970-76; v.p. mktg. Kurzweil Computer Products div. Xerox Corp., Cambridge, Mass., 1979-80; assoc. McKinsey & Co., Inc., N.Y.C., 1976-82, prin., 1982-88, dir. consumer goods sector, mktg. ctr., 1988—; underwriting mem. Lloyds of London, 1986—. Contbr. articles to profl. jours. Vice-chmn. adv. bd. Salvation Army, N.Y.C., 1983—; bd. dirs. United Way, N.Y.C., 1988—. Baker scholar Harvard Bus. Sch., 1970. Mem. Siwanoy Country Club. Home: 50 Highland Circle Bronxville NY 10708 Office: McKinsey & Co Inc 55 E 52d St New York NY 10022

PARSONS, BEN G., electronic banking consultant; b. Detroit, Sept. 23, 1944; s. Charles H. and Mary Elizabeth (Cosgrove) Fletcher. Student U. Colo., 1962-65; BA, U. Pitts., 1970; MBA, Golden Gate U., 1977. Evening supr. charge services div. Mellon Bank, Pitts., 1967-70; v.p., mgr. ops. control and advanced planning credit card dept. Crocker Bank, San Francisco, 1970-75, v.p., mgr. electronic banking products, 1975-77; prin. Parsons Cons. Group, San Rafael, Calif., 1972—; bd. dirs. Support Systems Internat. Corp., Richmond, Calif., 1976—, Federated Employers of Bay Area; lectr. Dominican Coll., San Rafael, 1972—. Pub.: EFT Execs.' Directory, Guide to Home Banking Activities, Home Banking Highlights, Pub. Access Highlights, Electronic Banking Contacts. Bd. dirs. Community Assn., ARC. Mem. Ind. Computer Cons. Assn., Assn. Data Communications Users, IEEE, Am. Electronics Assn., Environ. and Occupational Health Com., Am. Electronics Assn. Home and Office: 201 Irwin St San Rafael CA 94901

PARSONS, JOHN RUSSELL, retail company executive; b. Birmingham, Mich., Jan. 12, 1931; s. John Russell and G. Lola (Dubey) R.; m. Carol Butcher; children: Joanne, Julia, Jeff, Janee. BS, Mich. State U. Nat. mgr. home fashion accessories Sears, Roebuck and Co., Chgo., 1969-72, nat. mgr. linens and domestics, 1972-76, nat. mgr. furniture, 1976-77, v.p. womens accessory group, 1977-81, v.p. home improvement group, 1981—. Episcopalian. Office: Sears Roebuck & Co Sears Tower Chicago IL 60684

PARSONS, ROBERT EUGENE, university research administrator; b. Cin., Apr. 19, 1931; s. Charles Eugene and Samantha Ellen (Snider) P.; m. Beverly Greenhalgh, Dec. 30, 1949; children: Brian Scott, Barry Lawrence, Robert Stephen, Kimberly Ann. ME, U. Cinn., 1954; MSME, Drexel Inst. Tech., 1959. Registered profl. engr., Calif., Nev., Md., Ohio. Asst. project engr. The Martin Co., Balt., 1956-62, sect. mgr., 1962-64; dep. dir. Supersonic Transp. Office FAA, Washington, 1964-71; dir. rsch. and devel. plans U.S. Dept. Transp., Washington, 1971; assoc. adminstr. Fed. RR Adminstrn., Washington, 1975-80; dir. ctr. field methods Nat. Bur. Standards, Gaithersburg, Md., 1980-81; dir. RR rsch. and devel. program U. Calif., Berkeley, 1981—; cons. Walnut Creek, Calif., 1984-89; dir. program on advanced technology for hwy. U. Calif. Berkeley, 1986—; cons. Assn. Am. RRs, Washington, 1983-85. Contbr. articles to profl. jours. Com. chmn. Transp. Res. Bd., Washington, 1981-82. Mem. Commonwealth Club. Methodist. Home: 3130 Sugarberry Ct Walnut Creek CA 94598

PARSONS, RUTH CONNORS, insurance executive; b. Savannah, Ga., May 2, 1948; d. John Manson Jr. and Louise Frances (Wallace) Owens; m. Alden A. Connors, Sept. 28, 1968 (div. Jan. 1981); children: Sean Alden, Erin Rebecca; m. Michael Robert Parsons, Feb. 14, 1987. BA in History, Mt. St. Agnes Coll., 1970. Lic. ins. agt., Ga.; CLU, chartered fin. cons. Tchr. Secondary and adult edn., 1970-81; claims adjuster Nationwide Ins. Co., Gainesville, Fla., 1981-82; comml. ins. underwriter Nationwide Ins. Co., Gainesville, 1982-83, sr. comml. underwriter, agt., spl. agt., 1983-84; agy mgr. Nationwide Ins. Co., Atlanta, 1985-89; mgr. sales adminstrn. Nationwide Ins. Co., Wallingford, Conn., 1989—. Mem. Nat. Assn. Life Underwriters, Am. Soc. CLU's and CHFC's. Home: 510 Church St Wallingford CT 06492 Office: Nationwide Ins Co 2751 Dixwell Ave Hamden CT 06492

PARSONS, VINSON ADAIR, computer software company executive; b. Frankfort, Ky., Oct. 22, 1932; s. Richard Adair and Nina (Mefford) P.; m. Elizabeth Ann Peltier, June 2, 1956. A.S., Mitchell Coll., 1959; B.S., U. Conn., 1960; AMP, Harvard U., 1985. Auditor, Price Waterhouse & Co. (C.P.A.s), Hartford, Conn., 1960-65; controller Pervel Industries Inc., Plainfield, Conn., 1965-70; v.p., controller Akzo Am. Inc., Asheville, N.C., 1970-71, 73-83, v.p., chief fin. officer, 1983-86; v.p., chief fin. officer System Software Assocs. Inc., Chgo., 1986—, also bd. dirs.; dir. Am. Tape Co., BRIntec Co., Control Tech. Corp. Served with USN, 1953-57. Mem. Am. Mgmt. Assn., Fin. Execs. Inst., Nat. Assn. Accts. (pres. local chpt. 1969-70). Clubs: Asheville Country, Asheville City; University (N.Y.C.); Lake Barrington Shores Country. Home: 1512 Guthrie Dr Inverness IL 60010 Office: System Software Assocs Inc 500 W Madison St Chicago IL 60606

PARTIPILO, WILLIAM CARL, service executive; b. Chgo., Dec. 24, 1938; s. Vito and Theresa (Russo) P.; m. Electra Lee Norka, Jan. 27, 1962; children: Cindy, Cheryl, William Jr. BS, Purdue U., 1963. Dir. info. services Johnson & Johnson, New Brunswick, N.J., 1963-85; v.p. info. services Coca-Cola Corp., Atlanta, 1985-87; corp. v.p. info. services Kloster Cruise Ltd., Miami, 1988—; lectr. tng. sch. IBM, Poughkeepsie, N.Y., 1983. Vol. exec. United Way, New Brunswick, 1984; treas. Houston Pops Orch., 1986-87. Mem. Data Processing Mgrs. Assn., Distbn. Mgrs. Assn., System Mgrs. Assn. Republican. Roman Catholic. Club: Kingwood (Tex.). Lodge: Elks (v.p. East Brunswick, N.J. club 1984-85). Home: 131 NW 127th Ave Plantation FL 33325 Office: Kloster Cruises Ltd 2 Alhambra Pla Coral Gables FL 33134

PARTLOW, DAVID FRANCIS, financial planner; b. Dayton, Ohio, May 7, 1934; s. James Arthur and Irene (Clemens) P.; m. Patricia Flanagan, Oct. 30, 1939; children: Thomas D., Pamela, Patricia, Suzanne, Michael. BSBA, U. Dayton, 1959. Cert. fin. planner. V.p. Johnson & Higgins Ill., Chgo., 1961-77, Johnson & Higgins Oreg., Portland, 1977-83; v.p., sec. Interwest Fin. Group, Portland, 1983—. Trustee Meridian Park Med. Found., Tulatin, Oreg., 1987-88; mem. adminstrv. counc. St. Clare's Ch., Portland, 1987-88. Mem. Internat. Assn. Fin. Planning, Inst. Cert. Fin. Planners. Office: Interwest Fin Group 4640 SW Macadam Ste 250 Portland OR 97201

PARTRIDGE, BRUCE JAMES, lawyer, mining company executive; b. June 4, 1926, Syracuse, N.Y.; came to Can., 1969; s. Bert James and Lida Marian (Rice) P.; m. Mary Janice Smith, June 13, 1948 (dec. 1986); children: Heather Leigh, Eric James, Brian Lloyd, Bonnie Joyce; m. May S. Archer, May 28, 1988. AB cum laude, Oberlin Coll., Ohio, 1946; LLB, Blackstone Coll., Chgo., 1950, JD, 1952; LLB, U. B.C., 1974. Called to B.C. bar, 1976, N.W.T. bar, 1980. Research physicist Am. Gas Assn., Cleve., 1946-48; bus. adminstr. Rochester Inst. Tech., N.Y., 1953-58, Baldwin-Wallace Coll., Berea, Ohio, 1951-53, Cazenovia (N.Y.) Coll., 1948-51; v.p. bus. and mgmt., U. Del., Newark, Del., 1958-63; v.p. adminstrn. Johns Hopkins U., Balt., 1963-69; pres. U. Victoria, B.C., Can., 1969-72; assoc. Clark, Wilson & Co., Vancouver, B.C., 1975-78; successively solicitor, mng. solicitor, gen. solicitor, v.p. law and gen. counsel, 1978-86, v.p., gen. counsel, sec. Cominco Ltd., Vancouver, 1978-88; exec. dir. Baker & McKenzie, Hong Kong, 1988—. Coauthor: College and University Business Administration, 1968. Chmn. editorial com. Purchasing for Higher Education, 1962. Contbr. numerous articles to profl. jours. Chmn. commn. on adminstrv. affairs Am. Council on Edn., Washington, 1966-69; mem. Pres.'s Com. on Employment of Handicapped, Washington, 1967-69; mem. adv. council Ctr. for Resource Studies, Queen's U.; bd. dirs. L'Arche in the Americas; mem. adv. council Westwater Research Centre, U. B.C. Mem. Law Soc. B.C., Law Soc. of N.W. Ters., Assn. Can. Gen. Counsel, Fedn. Ins. and Corp. Counsel, Def. Research Inst. (product liability com.), Am. Corp. Counsel Assn. Club: Vancouver. Office: care Baker & McKenzie, 10 Harcourt Rd 14th Fl, Hutchinson House, Hong Kong Hong Kong

PASAKARNIS, PAMELA ANN, worldwide diagnostics company executive; b. Pittsfield, Mass., May 11, 1949; d. Richard W. and Regina (Piskorski) Turner; m. Donald L. Pasakarnis, May 25, 1974; children: Seth M., Casey L. BA, Northeastern U., 1972; M.T., New Eng. Deaconess Hosp., Boston, 1973. Staff med. technologist New Eng. Deaconess Hosp., 1972-75, supr. clin. chemistry, 1975-77; tech. product supr. Corning Med. Co., Medfield, Mass., 1977-83, product mgr. clin. instrumentation, 1983-85; mgr. mktg. communications CIBA Corning Diagnostics Corp., Medfield, 1985-88, mgr. mktg. ops., 1988—. Mem. Am. Assn. Clin. Chemists, Clin. Lab. Mgrs. Assn., Biomed. Mktg. Assn., Am. Mgmt. Assn. Republican. Avocations: winemaking; fashion design; interior decorating; needlework. Home: 3 Partridge Ln Walpole MA 02081

PASCAL, HAROLD SAUNDERS, health care executive; b. Coffeyville, Kans., Mar. 16, 1934; s. Michael William and Jacqueline V. P.; B.S., So. Meth. U., 1956; M.B.A., Ga. So. U., 1973; m. Dinah L. Filkins, Aug. 13, 1955; children—Lee Ann, Tracey Michele. Commd. 2d lt. U.S. Army, 1957, advanced through grades to maj., 1967; served med. service dept.; asso. exec. dir. Gen. Hosp., Humana Inc., Ft. Walton Beach, Fla., 1974-75, adminstr. Sarasota (Fla.) Palms Hosp., 1975-76, exec. dir. Llano (N.Mex.) Estacado Med. Center, 1976-77; pres. Americana Hosp. Co. (Cenco Inc.), Monticello, Ill., 1977-80, Continental Health Care Ltd., 1980-87, World Health Service, Ltd., 1987—. Pres. PTA, San Antonio, 1969-70; bd. dirs. NE Sch. Dist., San Antonio, 1968-69; dir. community blood drive, San Francisco, 1964-65. Decorated Bronze Star, Air Medal, Purple Heart, Cross of Gallantry, Combat Med. Badge. Fellow Am. Acad. Med. Adminstrs. (diplomate); Am. Hosp. Assn., Am. Coll. Healthcare Execs. Adminstrs., Am. Soc. Hosp. Engrs., Ill. Hosp. Assn., Fla. Hosp. Assn., Fedn. Am. Healthsystems (dir.), Psi Chi. Presbyterian. Clubs: Hunter Riding (pres., 1972-73), Rotary, Toastmasters. Author: Plight of the Migrant Worker, 1974; Installation Supply Procedures, 1968; programmed text on Supply Procedures, 1969; Dictionary of Supply Terms, 1969. Home: 10 S 321 Jaime Ln Hinsdale IL 60521 Office: World Health Svc Ltd 20 N Wacker Chicago IL 60611

PASCUAL, ROSA MONICA, banker; b. Miami, Fla., Oct. 15, 1961; d. Ignacio Dimas and Rosalin F. (De Paz) P. AS in Mktg. Mgmt., Broward Community Coll., Fla., 1982; BS in Profl. Studies, Barry U., 1988. Cert. profl. photographer N.Y. Inst. Photography, 1986. Clk.-typist Landmark Bank, Plantation, Fla., 1980-82, Spanish sec. I, 1982-83, new accounts rep. III, 1983-84, customer svc. rep. III, 1984-86; sr. customer svc. rep. C&S Nat. Bank, Ft. Lauderdale, Fla., 1986-87; ops. mgr. C&S Nat. Bank, Pompano, Fla., 1987; adminstrv. asst. Gold Coast Savs. Bank, Plantation, 1987, br. mgr., 1987-88, br. adminstr., 1988—. Fla. Bankers Assn. scholar, 1982. Mem. Am. Inst. Banking (charter Tallahassee chpt.; ofcl. photographer 1985—, bd. dirs. Davie, Fla. 1986—, asst. mktg. dir. 1986—, edn. com. 1986—), Nat. Assn. Bank Women, Assn. Photographers Internat., Photog. Soc. Am., Plantation C. of C., Smithsonian Inst. Assocs., Nat.Trust for Historic Preservation. Democrat. Roman Catholic. Office: Gold Coast Savs Bank 1801 N Pine Island Rd Plantation FL 33323

PASMAN, JAMES S., JR., aluminum company executive; b. East Orange, N.J., 1930. Grad., Upsala Coll., 1956, NYU, 1962. Now pres., chief exec. officer Kaisertech Ltd., Oakland, Calif.; also chmn., chief exec. officer Kaiser Aluminum subs. KaiserTech Ltd., Oakland; also bd. dirs. Chem. Corp. subs. KaiserTech Ltd., Oakland. Office: Kaiser Aluminum & Chem Corp 300 Lakeside Dr Oakland CA 94643

PASQUALE, FRANK ANTHONY, engineering administrator; b. Jersey City, Oct. 27, 1954; s. Frank F. and Josephine (Marano) P.; m. Elaine J. Rinaldi; children: Frank A. II, Phillip, Marielle. BSME, Fairleigh Dickinson U., 1976; postgrad., U. Mich., 1977. Registered profl. engr., N.J. Supr. chassis engr. Ford Co., Dearborn, Mich., 1976-80; engr. mgr. Bavarian Motor Works of N.Am., Montvale, N.J., 1980-82; mgr. engring. dept. Purolator Products Inc, Rahway, N.J., 1982-85; dir. ops. Inverness Inc., Fairlawn, N.J., 1985-87; dir. engring. and quality control Transworld Inc., East Rutherford, N.J., 1987—; cons. Marine-Tech. Corp., Wood-Ridge, N.J., 1985—; bd. dirs. Custom Craft Corp. Forked River, N.J., Spin-Tech. Corp., Hoboken, N.J., Internat. Offshore Tackle, Inc., Montville, N.J. Patentee in field. Mem. ASME, Soc. Plastic Engrs., Soc. Automotive Engrs., Soc. Mfg. Engring. Home: 6 Jean Dr Towaco NJ 07082

PASQUARELLI, JOSEPH J., real estate, engineering and construction executive; b. N.Y.C., Mar. 5, 1927; s. Joseph and Helen (Casabona) P.; B.C.E. cum laude, Manhattan Coll., 1949; m. JoAnne Brienza, June 20, 1964; children—Ronald, Richard, June, Joy. Engr., Madigan-Hyland, N.Y.C. and Burns & Roe Inc., N.Y.C., 1949-56; sr. engr., asst. to exec. dir.

Office of Sch. Bldgs., N.Y.C. Bd. Edn., 1956-67; dir. design and constrn. mgmt. City U. N.Y., 1967-72; dir. constrn. mgmt. Morse/Diesel Inc., N.Y.C., 1972-76; dir. projects and proposals Burns & Roe Indsl. Services Corp., Oradell, N.J., 1976-80, dir. facilities and infrastructure, 1980-86; dir. constrn. Xerox Realty Corp., Stamford, Ct., 1986—; instr. Mechs. Inst., N.Y.C. Community Coll. Applied Arts, Sci., 1955-58. Chmn. United Fund R. for Morse/Diesel Inc., 1973-75; mem. Cardinal's Com. of Laity for Roman Catholic Charities of N.Y.C., 1967-77; mem. North Caldwell (N.J.) Skating Pond Com. Served with U.S. Army, 1944-46. Licensed profl. engr., N.Y., N.J. Fellow ASCE; mem. N.Y. Bldg. Congress (past gov., chmn. legis. com.), Nat. Soc. Profl. Engrs., Mcpl. Engrs., Am. Arbitration Assn. (panel of arbitrators), Chi Epsilon. Club: Essex Fells Country. Contbr. articles to profl. jours. Home: 38 Oak Pl North Caldwell NJ 07006 Office: Xerox Realty Corp 800 Long Ridge Rd Stamford CT 06904

PASSINO-KUHLMANN, BARBARA JOYCE, marketing executive; b. Jersey City, May 22, 1947; d. Herbert J. and Frances (Schuettler) Passino; m. John A. Kuhlmann, Feb. 9, 1978. BS, Mt. Holyoke Coll., 1969; postgrad., Dartmouth Coll., 1970-72. Registered rep. N.Y. Stock exchange. Mgr. Irving Trust Co., N.Y.C., 1977-79; v.p., mgr. ops. rev. and planning Dean Witter, N.Y.C., 1979-82; 1st v.p. account svcs. mktg. Dean Witter Reynolds, N.Y.C., 1982-85; sr. v.p., dir. mktg. Pilgrim Group, L.A., 1985—. Contbr. articles to profl. jours. Mem. Investment Co. Inst. (seminar speaker, direct mktg. com., sales force mktg. com.), Direct Mktg. Assn., L.A. Advt. Club. Office: Pilgrim Group 10100 Santa Monica Blvd Los Angeles CA 90067

PASSMAN, ROGER, building materials company executive; b. Chgo., June 2, 1943; s. Peter and Jeanette (Melnick) P.; m. Elizabeth Shwachman, Apr. 24, 1969 (div. Apr. 1984); children: Benjamin, Leah Rebecca; m. Susan Kriesman, Nov. 23, 1986. BS in History, Bradley U., 1966. Pres. Malkov Lumber Co., Chgo., 1987—, also bd. dirs. Bd. dirs. Human Growth Found., Mpls., 1976-80; cons. Assn. for Jewish Blind, Chgo., 1987-88. Mem. Nat. Retail Hardware Assn., Ill. Bldg. Material Dealers, Hoo-Hoo. Office: Malkov Lumber Co 1201 S Campbell Ave Chicago IL 60608

PASSODELIS, CHRISTOPHER, insurance consultant, real estate developer, restaurant owner; b. Pa., Apr. 1, 1932; s. William and Molly P.; m. Catherine Vlahos, Aug. 1957; children: William C., Michael Z., Christopher Jr., Constantine. BA in Law, Wabash Coll., 1955. CLU. Agt. Pa. Mut. Life Ins., 1956—; owner, operator Christopher's Restaurant, Pitts., 1973—, Mahoney's Restaurant, Pitts., 1968—, Odyssey Apts., Coraopolis, Pa., 1970—; pres. C.P. Fin. Cons., Inc.; sr. ptnr. Gateway Fin. Group. Chmn. bd. dirs. Pan-Icarian Fund, Pitts.; bd. dirs. UNICEF, Pitts., Pitts. Opera, Western Pa. Olympic Com.; bd. dirs., co-chmn. YMCA, Dapper Dan, Multiple Sclerosis, Pitts., Holy Cross Greek Orthodox Ch., Pitts.; trustee Wabash Coll. Named Man of Yr., YMCA, Pitts., 1976, Man of Yr., Nat. Mulitple Sclerosis Soc., Pitts., 1979, Man of Yr. City of Hope 1989, Man of Yr. Western Pa. Assn. of Wabash Men 1989. Mem. Million Dollar Round Table, Am. Soc. CLU's. Democrat. Office: Two Northshore Ctr 3d Fl Pittsburgh PA 15212

PATAKY, MARIE ANN, accountant; b. Wilkensburg, Pa.; d. John Andrew and Elizabeth Ann (Koczka) P.; BS in BA, Robert Morris Coll., 1974; AS in Data Processing, Community Coll. Allegheny County, Pitts., 1970. CPA, Pa., N.J.; cert. fin. planner. Auditor, Peat, Marwick, Mitchell & Co., Pitts., 1974-76; tax acct. G.L. Roteman & Assos., Pitts., 1976-77; acctg. cons. Career & Life Planning Inst., Pitts., 1977-78; tax acct. Westinghouse Electric, Pitts., 1978-80; internal auditor Johnson & Johnson, New Brunswick, N.J., 1980-81; tax supr. Interpublic Group of Cos., Inc., N.Y.C., 1981—; fin. cons., bd. dir. Contrarian Investment Inst., Princeton, N.J., 1981—; pres. Princeton Fin. Plans, 1985—. Treas., Children's Hosp. Fund., 1979-80. C.P.A., Pa., cert. fin. planner, Pa.; Robert Morris scholar, 1972-74. Mem. Am. Inst. CPA's, Pa. Inst. CPA's, Nat. Assn. Accts., Assn. MBA Execs., Am. Women's Soc. CPA's, Inst. Cert. Fin. Planners, Internat. Inst. Fin. Planning, Toastmistress Club (treas. 1979-80). Office: PO Box 1442 Palmer Sq Princeton NJ 08542

PATANO, PATRICIA ANN, health and fitness professional, marketing and public relations specialist; b. Chgo., June 14, 1960; d. Thomas Vincent and Gladys Estelle (Olejniczak) P. Student, Los Angeles Pierce Coll., 1968-70, UCLA, 1974-84. Pub. relations mgr. Motel 6, Inc., Century City, Calif., 1974-77; mgr. corp. communications 1st Travel Corp., Van Nuys, Calif., 1977-79; mktg. pub. relations mgr. Unitours, Inc., Los Angeles, 1979-81; asst. v.p. pub. relations Los Angeles Olympic Com., 1981-84; pres., co-owner PaVage Fitness Innovations, Playa del Rey, Calif., 1984-88; dir. spl. projects J.D. Power and Assocs., Agoura Hills, Calif., 1988—; trustee Nat. Injury Prevention Found., San Diego, 1983—; cons. Dick Clark Productions, Burbank, Calif., 1985, Reebok USA Ltd., Boston, 1983—. Co-author: MuscleAerobics, 1985; contbr. articles to profl. jours. Vol. Motion Picture Hosp., Woodland Hills, Calif., 1968-70; bd. dirs. Los Angeles Boys and Girls Club, 1984—; mem. council San Fernando Natural History Mus., 1987—; big sister Pride House, Van Nuys, 1987—; active juvenile delinquent program Pride House. Recipient Corp. award Pres.'s Council Phys. Fitness, 1983. Mem. Los Angeles Advt. Club, Nat. Injury Prevention Found. (bd. trustees 1984—). Republican. Presbyterian. Clubs: Mid Valley Athletic (Reseda, Calif.); Marina City (Marina del Rey, Calif.). Office: JD Power & Assocs 30401 Agoura Rd Agoura Hills CA 91301

PATE, JACQUELINE HAIL, data processing company manager; b. Amarillo, Tex., Apr. 7, 1930; d. Ewen and Virginia Smith (Crosland) Hail; student Southwestern U., Georgetown, Tex., 1947-48; children—Charles (dec.), John Durst, Virginia Pate Edgecomb, Christopher. Exec. sec. Western Gear Corp., Houston, 1974-76; adminstr., treas., dir. Aberrant Behavior Ctr., Personality Profiles, Inc., Corp. Procedures, Inc., Dallas, 1976-79; dist. adminstrn. mgr. Digital Equipment Corp., Dallas, 1979—. Active PTA, Dallas, 1958-73. Mem. Internat. Assn. Facility Mgrs., Daus. Republic Tex. Methodist. Home: 3519 Casa Verde #268 Dallas TX 75234 Office: Digital Equipment Corp 14131 Midway Rd Ste 800 Dallas TX 75244-3608

PATE, JAMES LEONARD, economist, oil company executive; b. Mt. Sterling, Ill., Sept. 6, 1935; s. Virgil Leonard and Mammie Elizabeth (Taylor) P.; student U. Md., 1957-58; A.B., Monmouth Coll., 1963; M.B.A., U. Ind., 1965, J.D., 1968; m. Donna Charlene Pate, Oct. 23, 1955; children—David Charles, Gary Leonard, Jennifer Elizabeth. Prof. econs. Monmouth (Ill.) Coll., 1965-68; sr. economist Fed. Res. Bank Cleve., 1968-72; chief economist B.F. Goodrich Co., Akron, Ohio, 1972-74; asst. sec. Dept. Commerce, Washington, 1974-76; spl. adviser to White House, Washington, 1976; sr. v.p. fin. Pennzoil Co., Houston, 1976—. Fellow Royal Econ. Soc.; mem. Am. Econ. Assn., Soc. Social Polit. Scientists, Nat. Assn. Bus. Economists, Pi Gamma Mu. Republican. Contbr. articles to profl. jours. and text books. Home: 5346 Longmont Dr Houston TX 77056 Office: Pennzoil Co PO Box 2967 Houston TX 77252

PATERNOTTE, WILLIAM LESLIE, brokerage house executive; b. Phila., Apr. 26, 1945; s. Alexander Leslie Parenotte and Mary (Harris) Waterbury; m. Nancy Brewster, June 15, 1968; children: Nancy Moffett, William Brooks, Christopher Brewster. AB, Princeton U., 1967; MBA, U. Pa., 1969. Fin. analyst Alex Brown & Sons, Balt., 1969-79, dir. research, 1979—; bd. dirs. JB's Restaurants, Inc., Salt Lake City, Vie de France Corp., Vienna Va. Trustee Gilman Sch., Balt., 1986—, Adirondack Mountain Res., St. Huberts, N.Y., 1987—; pres. bd. dirs. Bryn Mawr Sch., Balt., 1981-84. Mem. Balt. Security Analyst Soc. (pres. 1978-79), Fin. Analyst Fedn., Inst. Chartered Fin. Analysts., Md. Club, Elkridge Club, Ausable Club. Republican. Episcopalian. Office: Alex Brown & Sons Inc 135 E Baltimore St Baltimore MD 21202

PATERSON, RICHARD DENIS, financial executive; b. Ottawa, Ont., Can., Oct. 13, 1942; m. Antoinette; children: Christopher, Russell. B.Commerce, Concordia U., Montreal, Que., Can., 1964. Auditor Coopers & Lybrand, Montreal, 1964-67; acct. Genstar Corp., Montreal, 1967-69; dir. fin. and adminstrn. Indussa Corp. (subs. Genstar Corp.), N.Y.C., 1969-73; v.p., comptroller Genstar Corp., Montreal and San Francisco, 1973-83; sr. v.p., chief fin. officer Genstar Corp., San Francisco, 1983-87; exec. v.p. Genstar Investment Corp., San Francisco, 1987—. Mem. Fin. Execs. Inst., Order Chartered Accts. Que. Office: Genstar Investment Corp 801 Montgomery St Ste 500 San Francisco CA 94133

PATIL, SAKHARAM K., chemical executive; b. Shahada Dhulia, Maharashtra, India, Apr. 1, 1942; came to U.S., 1968; s. Karsan and Kahsibai Patil; m. Pramila S. Patil, May 11, 1968; children: Deepak, Ravi. BS in Chemistry, Poona U., 1965; MS in Food Tech., Mysore U., 1967; PhD in Cereal Chemistry, Kans. State U., 1972. Research asst. Kans. State U., Manhattan, 1968-72; chief chemist Continental Milling, Curaçao, Netherlands Antilles, 1973-74; lab. dir. N.Am. Plant Breeders, Brookston, Ind., 1975-78; mgr. quality control labs. Am. Maize ProductsCo., Hammond, Ind., 1979-80; mgr. quality control dept. Am. Maize ProductsCo., Hammond, 1980-82, dir. quality and tech. service, 1983-87, dir. comml. devel., 1987—. Contbr. articles to profl. jours. Scholar Food and Agriculture Orgn. UN, Mysore, India, 1966-67, H.E.H. Nizam Hyderabad India scholar, Manhattan, 1968-69. Mem. Am. Assn. Cereal Chemists, Inst. Food Tech., Investment Club. Home: 1939 Sir Richard Rd Schererville IN 46375 Office: Am Maize Products Co 1100 Indianapolis Blvd Hammond IN 46320

PATON, N. E., JR., marketing, public relations and advertising counselor; b. Kansas City, Mo., Sept. 18, 1931; s. N. Emerson and Ruth L. (Britt) P.; children: Russell E., Neal E. AA, Kansas City Jr. Coll., 1951; BA, U. Mo., 1953. With news and prodn. staff Sta. KCMO-TV, Kansas City, Mo., 1953-56; owner, chief exec. officer pub. relations, mktg. and advt. Paton Assocs., Inc., Kansas City, 1956—. Home: 3704 W 119th Terr Leawood KS 66209 Office: Paton & Assocs Inc PO Box 7350 Leawood KS 66207

PATONAI, STEVEN D., health facility administrator; b. Akron, Ohio, Apr. 19, 1956; s. Dezo and Vera P.; m. Elana Patonai, Apr. 24, 1981; 1 child, Ben. BS in Pharmacology, Ohio No. U., Ada, 1979; M in Hosp. and Health Adminstrn., U. Ala., Birmingham, 1986; postgrad., Fla. State U., 1988—. Dir pharmacy Lodi (Ohio) Community Hosp., 1979-80; pharmacy supr. Ft. Myers (Fla.) Community Hosp., 1980-83; pharmist West Fla. Hosp., Pensacola, 1983-84; v.p. Tallahassee (Fla.) Regional Med. Ctr., 1986-87; adminstr. Gadsden Mem. Hosp., Quincy, Fa., 1987—. Mem. Hosp. Fin. Mgmt. Assn., Phi Eta Sigmn, Omicron Theta Kappa, Phi Kappa Phi. Lodge: Rotary. Office: Gadsden Meml Hosp PO Box 819 Hwy 90E Quincy IL 32351

PATRICK, DENNIS ROY, government official; b. Glendale, Calif., June 1, 1951; s. Gene O. and June E. Patrick. AB, Occidental Coll., 1973; JD, UCLA, 1976. Bar: Calif. 1976, D.C. 1985. Assoc. Adam, Duque & Hazeltine, L.A., 1976-81; assoc. dir. legal and regulatory agencies Office of Presdl. Personnel The White House, Washington, 1981-83; commr. FCC, Washington, 1983-87, chmn., 1987—; assoc. dir. for legal and regulatory agys. Office Presdl. Pers., The White House, 1989—. Contbr. articles to profl. jours. Mem. D.C. Bar Assn. Republican. Office: FCC 1919 M St NW Washington DC 20554

PATRICK, JANE AUSTIN, association executive; b. Memphis, May 27, 1930; d. Wilfred Jack and Evelyn Eudora (Branch) Austin; m. William Thomas Spencer, Sept. 11, 1952 (div. Apr. 1970); children: Anthony Duke, Tonilee Candice Spencer Hughes; m. George Milton Patrick, Oct. 1, 1971. Student Memphis State U., 1946-47; BSBA, Ohio State U., 1979. Service rep. So. Bell Telephone and Telegraph, Memphis, 1947-52; placement dir. Mgmt. Personnel, Memphis, 1965-66; personnel asst. to exec. v.p. E & E Ins. Co., Columbus, Ohio, 1966-69; Ohio exec. dir. Nat. Soc. for Prevention of Blindness, Columbus, 1969-73; regional dir. Ohio and Ky. CARE and MEDICO, Columbus, 1979-87; lectr., cons. in field. Mem. choir 1st Community Ch., Columbus, Ohio State Univ. Hosp.'s Service Bd.; bd. dirs. Columbus Council on World Affairs, 1981—, sec., 1983—, chmn. devel. com.; devel. dir. Hunger Task Force, 1989—. Recipient commendations Nat. Soc. Prevention Blindness and Central Ohio Lions Eye Bank, 1973, Nat. Soc. Fund-Raising Execs., 1984, 85, Plaques for Service award Upper Arlington Pub. Schs., 1986. Mem. Non-Profit Orgn. Mgmt. Inst. (pres.), Nat. Soc. Fund-Raising Execs. (cert., nat. dir.), Pub. Relations Soc. Am. (cert., membership com. chairperson), Ins. Inst. Am. (cert.), Mensa Internat., Columbus Dental Soc. Aux., Alpha Gamma Delta, Epsilon Sigma Alpha. Home: 2511 Onandaga Dr Columbus OH 43221

PATRICK, JOHN BOOTH, institutional selling analyst; b. Cornwall, N.Y., June 15, 1924; s. James Hunter and Annie (Booth) P.; m. Elizabeth Ann Bean, June 10, 1950 (div. 1964); children: Ann L. Patrick Degener, Alexander B.; m. Barbara Ann Schoenlein, July 24, 1964; children: Iam M.H., Jennifer B. BA, Amherst Coll., 1945. Wool trader Balfour Guthrie and Co. Ltd., N.Y.C., 1945-57; ptnr. firm Coggeshall and Hicks, N.Y.C., 1957-62, Richard J. Buck and Co., N.Y.C., 1963-65, W.E. Burnet and Co., N.Y.C., 1965-75; instl. selling analyst Adams and Peck, N.Y.C., 1976-79, Bacon, Whipple and Co., N.Y.C., 1979-83, Herzog, Heine, Geduld Inc., N.Y.C., 1983—; fruit farmer Lamont Landing Farm, Esopus, N.Y. With U.S. Army, 1943-44. Mem. Caledonian Club, India House Club. Republican. Episcopalian. Home: Lamont Landing Farm Esopus NY 12429 Office: Herzog Heine Geduld 26 Broadway New York NY 10004

PATRICK, ROBERT SCOTT, controller; b. Ft. Wayne, Ind., Jan. 9, 1958; s. Glen Robert and Ruth Amelia (Henline) P. BS in Bus., Ind. U., 1980. CPA, Ind. Acct. Park Ctr., Inc., Ft. Wayne, 1980-83; acct. Ft. Wayne Newspapers, Inc., 1983, budget mgr., 1983-84, acctg. mgr., 1984-86, controller, 1986—; bd. dirs. Profl. Fed. Credit Union, Ft. Wayne. Mem. Internat. Newspaper Fin. Execs., Am. Inst. CPAs, Ind. CPA soc. Methodist. Club: Toastmasters. Office: Ft Wayne Newspapers Inc 600 W Main St Fort Wayne IN 46802

PATRIKIS, ERNEST T., lawyer, banker; b. Lynn, Mass., Dec. 1, 1943; s. Theodore A. and Ethel (Stasinopolous) P.; m. Emily Herrick Trueblood, Mar. 18, 1972. BA, U. Mass., 1965; JD, Cornell U., 1968. Bar: N.Y. 1969. Exec. v.p., gen. counsel Fed. Res. Bank N.Y., 1968—; dep. gen. counsel Fed. Open Market Com., 1988—. Contbr. articles to legal jours. Mem. Assn. of Bar of City of N.Y. (banking law com. 1982-84, futures regulation com. 1986—); N.Y. State Bar Assn. (chmn. com. internat. banking, securities and fin. transaction 1987—, banking law com. 1986—), ABA (subcom. on gen. banking matters 1986). Home: 20 E 9th St New York NY 10003-5944 Office: Fed Res Bank NY 33 Liberty St New York NY 10045

PATTERSON, BEVERLEY, accountant; b. London, Feb. 6, 1956; came to U.S., 1975; d. Ernest Charles and Barbara (Wiseman) Patterson; children: Tamara, Russell, Stuart. AAS with honors, Tacoma Community Coll., 1978; BBA with honors, U. Puget Sound, 1980. CPA, Wash. Accounts payable clk. Hillhaven Corp., Tacoma, 1975-76, staff acct., 1980-83, acquisition analyst, 1984-86; contr., chief fin. officer Tacoma Luth. Home and Retirement Community, 1987—; cons. in field, 1984—. Vol. Make a Wish, Tacoma. Mem. Nat. Assn. Accts., Wash. Soc. CPA's, Am. Soc. Women Accts. Home: 4007 31st Ave NW Gig Harbor WA 98335 Office: Tacoma Luth Home & Retirement Community 1301 Highland Pkwy Tacoma WA 98406

PATTERSON, DANNY MAURICE, data processing executive; b. Talledega, Ala., Aug. 30, 1951; s. William Arvil Patterson and Frankie Joan (Wilson) Woodruff; m. Blanche Babette Baggett, Nov. 3, 1978. AA, Jefferson State Coll., 1972; cert. real estate, Samford U., Birmingham, Ala., 1973; BS, Calif. Western U., 1985. Owner Continental Food Stores, Florence, Ala., 1978-80; profl. relations cons. Block Drug Co., Birmingham, 1980-82; polit. dir. Ala. Rep. Party, Birmingham, 1982-83; systems cons. CARS Dyatron, Inc., Memphis, 1984-86; nat. field tng. dir. CARS Dyatron, Inc., Birmingham, 1986—. Author: Selling Techniques, 1980; editor: How to Run for Local Office, 1982, Running A Successful Campaign, 1982. Chmn. Ala. Rep. Com., Birmingham, 1980-82; rep. Jefferson County Rep. Com., Ala., 1980-83; mem. Shelby County Reps., Memphis, 1985—, Presdl. Task Force, Tenn., 1984—. Named one of Outstanding Young Men in Am., U.S. Jaycees, 1982. Mem. U.S. C. of C. Episcopalian. Home: 3108 Wood Bridge Dr Birmingham AL 35243

PATTERSON, DAVID CHARLES, safety administrator; b. Glasgow, Mont., Mar. 11, 1949; s. Harville Hamilton and Lillyan Mae (Blair) P; m. Barbara Ann Gibbs, Dec. 20, 1969. BS in Biology and Chemistry, Belmont Coll., 1971; safety engring. cert. U. Tenn., 1982; MS in Safety Mgmt., Mid. Tenn. State U., 1988. Cert. Am. Coll. Sports Medicine; cert. Aerobics Inst., Dallas. Tchr. Castle Heights, Lebanon, Tenn., 1971-76; environmentalist Metro Govt. of Nashville, 1976-80, safety engr., 1980-82; loss control cons. Hosp. Corp. of Am., Nashville, 1982-84; health and safety promotion mgr. TryUMPH for Health, United Meth. Pub. House, Nashville, 1984-86; loss control mgr. Maryland Casualty Co., 1986—; lectr. in field; contbr. articles to profl. jours. Mem. Mayor's Task Force on Wellness, Nashville 1984; exec. com. Tenn. Safety Congress, 1986-87, steering com. Tenn. Hwy. Safety Conf., 1985-87; mem. Mayor's Safety Adv. Bd., Nashville, sec., 1985—. Recipient Outstanding Coach, 1973, Century award YMCA, 1982, Outstanding Corp. Fitness Dir. award Calif.'s Cost Care, Inc., 1985; named to Top 10 Industry Leaders in Health Promotion, Corp. Fitness and Recreation, 1986; recipient Gov.'s award for Outstanding Worksite Wellness (TryUMPH), 1986. Mem. Am. Soc. of Safety Engrs. (pres. 1985-87, regional chpt. achievement award 1987, Tenn. Hwy. Safety award 1987), Tenn. Health and Safety Assn. (treas. 1982), Am. Coll. of Sports Medicine, Assn. Fitness in Bus. (nominated Achievement award 1985, Tenn. state rep. 1985-86). Subject of articles Bus. and Health, Risk Management mags. Avocations: running, biking, swimming, marathons, triathlons. Home: 916 Harpeth Trace Dr Nashville TN 37221 Office: Maryland Casualty Co 1375 American General Ctr Nashville TN 37205

PATTERSON, EUGENE CORBETT, retired editor, publisher; b. Valdosta, Ga., Oct. 15, 1923; s. William C. and Annabel (Corbett) P.; m. Mary Sue Carter, Aug. 19, 1950; 1 child, Mary Patterson Fausch. Student, North Ga. Coll., Dahlonega, 1940-42; A.B. in Journalism, U. Ga., 1943; LL.D., Tusculum Coll., 1965, Harvard U., 1969, Duke U., 1978, Stetson U., 1984; Litt.D., Emory U., 1966, Oglethorpe Coll., 1966, Tuskegee Inst., 1966, Roanoke Coll., 1968, Mercer U., 1968, Eckerd Coll., 1977, U. South Fla., 1986. Reporter Temple (Tex.) Daily Telegram and Macon (Ga.) Telegraph, 1947-48; mgr. for S.C. United Press, 1948-49; night bur. mgr. United Press, N.Y.C., 1949-53; mgr. London bur. United Press, also chief corr. U.K., 1953-56; v.p., exec. editor Atlanta Journal-Constitution, 1956-60; editor Atlanta Constitution, 1960-68; mng. editor Washington Post, 1968-71; prof. polit. sci. Duke U., 1971-72; editor, pres. St. Petersburg (Fla.) Times, 1972-84, chmn., chief exec. officer, 1978-88, editor emeritus, 1988—; editor, pres. Congl. Quar., Washington, 1972-86; chmn., chief exec. officer Congl. Quar., 1978-88; chmn. bd., chief exec. officer Fla. Trend mag., 1980-88, Ga. Trend mag., 1984-88, Ariz. Trend mag., 1986-88, Governing mag., 1987-88, Modern Graphic Arts, Inc., 1978-88, Poynter Inst. Media Studies, 1978-88, Poynter Fund, 1978-88. Vice chmn. U.S. Civil Rights Commn., 1964-68; mem. Pulitzer Prize Bd., 1973-84; trustee ASNE Found., 1981-84, U. Ga. Found., 1982-88, Am. Press Inst., Reston, Va., 1983-88, Duke U., 1988—. Served to capt. U.S. Army, 1943-47. Decorated Silver Star, Bronze Star with oak leaf cluster in 10th Armored Div., Gen. Patton's 3rd Army; recipient Pulitzer prize for editorial writing, 1966; fellow Soc. Profl. Journalists, 1978; William Allen White nat. citation, 1980. Mem. Am. Soc. Newspaper Editors (pres. 1977-78), Am. Newspaper Publishers Assn., Internat. Press Inst. Clubs: St Petersburg Yacht, St. Petersburg President's, Nat. Press, Federal City. Home: 1967 Brightwaters Blvd NE Snell Isle Saint Petersburg FL 33704 Office: 233 3rd St N Saint Petersburg FL 33701

PATTERSON, GARY WAYNE, real estate developer; b. Rosedale, Miss., July 15, 1947; s. C.B. and Genevieve (O'Connel) P.; m. Katherine Helen Patterson; children: Denise, Gary Jr. BBA, U. Miss., 1969; MBA, Stanford U., 1971. CPA, Miss., Tex., Fla. Asst. to audit supr. Peat, Marwick, Mitchell & Co., Houston, 1971-78; sec., treas. Builders Interests Group, Houston, 1978-86; pres. Hammerly Mgmt. Services, Houston, 1986—; ptnr. Columbia Capitol Group, Houston, 1987-88; bd. dirs. Tex. Cons. Constrn.; exec. v.p., chief fin. officer Restaurant Devel. Group, Ft. Lauderdale, Fla., 1988—. Contbr. articles to profl. jours. Pres., co-founder Houston chpt. Stanford Grad. Sch. Bus., 1974-75; vol. personal solicitation program, 1975-85; regional chmn., 1983-88; bd. dirs. Spring Shadows (Tex.) Civic Assn., 1977-79, pres., 1978; mem. Spring br. ind. sch. Friends of Edn., 1981-88; treas. Terr. Elem. PTA, Houston, 1981; precinct del. Dem. Dist. Conv., Houston, 1980. Mem. Am. Inst. CPA's, Tex. Soc. CPA's (instr. 1979), Miss. CPA Soc. (silver medal 1969), Tex. Assn. Realtors. Home: 11196 NW 5th Manor Coral Springs FL 33071 Office: Hammerly Mgmt Svcs 10105 Hammerly Blvd Ste 112 Houston TX 77080

PATTERSON, HARLAN RAY, finance educator; b. Camden, Ohio, June 27, 1931; s. Ernest Newton and Beulah Irene (Hedrick) P.; m. Carol Lee Reighard, Aug. 31, 1970; children by previous marriage: Kristan Lee, Elizabeth Jane; children: Leslie, Nolan Gene. BS, Miami U., Oxford, Ohio, 1953, MBA, 1959; PhD, Mich. State U., 1963. Asst. prof. fin. U. Ill., Champaign-Urbana, 1962-66; mem. faculty Ohio U., Athens, 1966—; prof. fin. Ohio U., 1977—; vis. prof., fellow Chgo. Merc. Exchange, 1971; fin. cons., researcher projects for industry. Contbr. articles to acad. and profl. jours. Chmn. City of Athens Adv. Bd., 1972-77; state chmn. scholarship com. for Ohio Rainbow Girls, 1975-87. Served as commd. officer USN, 1953-56. Won competitive appointment U.S. Naval Acad., 1950. Stonier fellow, 1961; Found. Econ. Edn. fellow, 1965, 67, 69, 71; Chgo. Bd. Trade summer intern, 1983. Mem. Masons (32nd deg.), Shriners, Order of Eastern Star (Worthy Patron 1989), Phi Beta Kappa, Beta Gamma Sigma (faculty advisor), Phi Eta Sigma, Omicron Delta Epsilon, Pi Kappa Alpha, Alpha Kappa Psi, Delta Sigma Pi, Sigma Tau Alpha (advisor). Republican. Home: 17 La Mar Dr Athens OH 45701

PATTERSON, JOSEPH CROMWELL, financial company executive; b. Detroit, Nov. 21, 1928; s. Walter Rodney and Mildred Lona (Cromwell) P.; student Ohio State U., 1953; B.A., Ohio Wesleyan U., 1954; m. Anne Elizabeth Ferrall, Jan. 19, 1952; children—J. Sean, Kevin B., Michael B., Mary A., Kathleen M., Julia M., Susan E., Margaret A., Patrick D., Jane M. Pres., Med. Mgmt. Inc., Dayton, Ohio, 1954-60; exec. staff Research Inst. Am., N.Y.C., 1960-62, 62-64; cons. E.F. MacDonald Co., Dayton, 6 mos.; pres. Fin. Mgmt. Inst., Dayton, 1964-72, Fiscal Concepts Inc., Newport Beach, Calif., 1972—; cons. in field. Served with USAAF, 1946-49, 51-52. Mem. Am. Mgmt. Assn., Am. Soc. Mgmt. Cons., Am. Profl. Practice Assn. (editor ofcl. jour. 1966-68), Internat. Assn. Fin. Planners. Republican. Roman Catholic. Editorial adviser Med. Econs. mag., 1956-60. Office: Fiscal Concepts Inc 2000 Dove St Newport Beach CA 92660

PATTERSON, LYDIA ROSS, industrial relations specialist, consulting company executive; b. Carrabelle, Fla., Sept. 3, 1936; d. Richard D. Ross and Johnnie Mae (Thomas) Kelley; m. Edgar A. Corley, Aug. 1, 1964 (div.); 1 child, Derek Kelley; m. Berman W. Patterson, Dec. 18, 1981. BA, Hunter Coll., 1958. Indsl. relations specialist U.S. Dept. Energy, N.Y.C., 1966-68; regional dir./mgr. Div. Human Rights State of N.Y., N.Y.C., 1962-66, 68-76; v.p. Bankers Trust Co., N.Y.C., 1976-87; pres., chief exec. officer Extend Cons. Services, N.Y.C., 1985—; v.p., mgr. Merrill Lynch and Co. Inc., N.Y.C., 1987—; seminar speaker Columbia U., Wharton Sch. Bus., Harvard U., Duke U., Cornell U., 1976-85; mem. Bus. Policy Rev. Council, Exec. Leadership Council. Bd. dirs. Project Discovery Columbia U., 1988. Mem. Am. Soc. Personnel Adminstrn., N.Y. and Nat. Urban League, Employment Mgrs. Assn., Fin. Women's Assn. (govt./community affairs com. 1986-87), Women's Ctr. Edn. Advancement (bd. dirs. 1978—), Employment Dissemination of Information Group Awareness Edn. Solving of Problems (bd. dirs. 1979—). Office: Merrill Lynch & Co Inc World Fin Ctr South Tower New York NY 10080-6111

PATTERSON, MICHAEL ELLMORE, bank executive; b. N.Y.C., Mar. 18, 1942; s. Ellmore Clark and Anne Hyde (Choate) P.; m. Elena Carrillo, June 18, 1964; chidren: Elena, Anne, Michael Jr. BA, Harvard U., 1964; LLB, Columbia U., 1967. With J.P. Morgan & Co., Inc., N.Y.C. Mem. Links Club, Fishers Island Country Club. Office: Debevoise & Plimpton 875 3rd Ave New York NY 10022 also: J P Morgan & Co Inc 23 Wall St New York NY 10015

PATTERSON, RICHARD BROWN, manufacturing company executive; b. Detroit, Jan. 12, 1937; s. William M. and Laura E. (Brown) P.; m. Helen L. Kroesing, Sept. 17, 1960; children: Janice, Robert. BBA, U. Detroit, 1960; MBA, U. Newhaven, 1987. Corp. controller Echlin, Inc., Branford, Conn., 1980-85, v.p. fin., 1985-88; v.p. fin., chief fin. officer CTS Corp., Elkhart, Ind., 1988—. Served with USAR, 1954-65. Mem. Fin. Execs. Inst., Nat. Assn. Accts. Home: 16830 Barrington Ct Granger IN 46530 Office: CTS Corp 905 W Boulevard N Elkhart IN 46514

PATTERSON, ROBERT EUGENE, insurance company executive; b. Lancaster, Pa., June 13, 1932; s. Blanchard S. and Lydia L. (Wert) P.; m. Dorothy J. Shenk, May 26, 1951; children: Craig Robert, Tracy Ann. BS in Econs. magna cum laude, Franklin and Marshall Coll., 1959; postgrad., Temple U., 1960, Harvard U., 1977. CPA, D.C. With Armstrong World Industries, Lancaster, 1950-69, Hamilton Watch Co., Lancaster, 1969-71; v.p. fin., treas. K-D Mfg. Co., Lancaster, 1971-76, dir., officer and dir. subs., 1972-76; sr. v.p. fin. and legal services Blue Shield, Camp Hill, 1976—; treas. Camp Hill Ins. Co., 1981—, also dir.; bd. dirs. Keystone Health Plans Inc., Automated Med. Systems Inc., Keystone Technologies Inc.; treas., bd. dirs. Keystone Health Plan East, Inc.; bd. dirs. Keystone Health Plan Cen., Inc.; sec., bd. dirs. Keystone Health Plan West, Inc., KHP Services, Inc.; adj. faculty Franklin and Marshall Coll.; sec./treas. Health Benefits Mgmt., Inc.; v.p. Keystone Ventures Inc.;. Sec., treas. Health Care Cost Containment Council of Pa.. Served with U.S. Army, 1952-54. Mem. Fin. Execs. Inst. (chpt. pres., area dir., nat. v.p.), Nat. Assn. Accts., Am. Inst. CPAs, Pa. Soc. CPAs, Lancaster C. of C., Pa. C. of C. Episcopalian. Club: Hamilton. Office: 1800 Center St Camp Hill PA 17011

PATTERSON, ROBERT LYNN, petroleum engineer; b. San Antonio, Nov. 12, 1939; s. Benjamin Franklin Jr. and Sarah Penelope (Robert) P.; m. Rosemary Cherry, Feb. 22, 1963; children: Robert L. Jr., John A., Patrick B., Michael C. BS in Petroleum Engring., U. Tex., 1963, MS in Petroleum Engring., 1964. Registered profl. engr. Tex. Area engr. Union Oil Co. Calif., Abbeville (La.), Tyler and Houston (Tex.), 1966-69; dist. engr. Union Oil Co. Calif., Lafayette, La., 1969-74; mgr. prodn. Argonaut Energy Corp., Amarillo, Tex., 1974; v.p. prodn. Argonaut Energy Corp., Amarillo, 1975-78; pres., chief exec. officer Medallion Equipment Corp., Amarillo, 1978-81, 85-88; pvt. practice cons. Amarillo, 1981-85, 88—; bd. dirs. Tex. Vanguard Oil Co. Trustee Amarillo Mental Health/Mental Retardation Bd., Amarillo, 1975-84, Amarillo Ind. Sch. Dist., 1984-89; bd. dirs. Canadian River Mcpl. Water Authority, Sanford, Tex., 1974-89. Mem. Soc. Petroleum Engrs., Tex. Profl. Engrs., E. Tex. Engring. Com., Cotton Valley Operators Com., Kiwanis, Phi Kappa Psi. Democrat. Mem. Disciples of Christ. Home: 6907 Dogwood Hollow Austin TX 78750 Office: 13706 Research Blvd Ste 205 PO Box 26296 Austin TX 78755

PATTERSON, RONALD R(OY), healthcare company executive; b. Baton Rouge, Mar. 4, 1942. BS, U. Houston, 1965; MS, Trinity U., San Antonio, 1973. Asst. adminstr. Med. Br. Tex. U., Galveston, 1972-75; asst. v.p. Hosp. Affiliates Internat., Nashville, 1975-81; chief oper. officer Affiliated Hosp. Systems, Houston, 1981-82; sr. v.p. Republic Health Corp., Dallas, 1982-88; pres. Miller Patterson Inc., Plano, Tex., 1989—. Fellow Am. Coll. Healthcare Execs.; mem. Tex. Hosp. Assn. (vice chmn. multi-hosp. constituency 1987), Fedn. Am. Health Systems. Clubs: Willow Bend Polo and Hunt (Dallas), Univ. (Dallas). Office: Miller Patterson Inc 3100 Independence Pkwy Ste 311 Plano TX 75075

PATTERSON, SOLON P., investment counselor; b. Atlanta, Nov. 11, 1935; s. Pete George and Frances (Marinos) P.; m. Marianna Reynolds, Oct. 29, 1960; children: John Solon, Joseph Peter. BBA, Emory U., 1957, MBA, 1958. Chartered fin. analyst, chartered investment counselor. Security analyst, portfolio mgr. Piedmont Adv. Corp., N.Y.C., 1958-62; investment counselor Montag & Caldwell, Atlanta, 1962-73, pres., chief exec. officer, 1973-84, also chmn., 1977—; trustee, chmn. fin. com. Gammon Theol. Sem., Atlanta. Mem. Emory U. Mgmt. Conf. Bd., 1976—, Regional Bd. Nat. Conf. of Christians and Jews; bd. visitors Wake Forest (N.C.) Babcock Grad. Sch. Mgmt.; bd. dirs. Atlanta Coll. Art. Named Atlanta's Outstanding Young Man of Yr. in Bus., Atlanta Jr. C. of C., 1968. Mem. Bus. Council of Ga. (bd. dirs.), Nat. Assn. Bus. Economists, Atlanta Econs. Club (pres. 1974-75), Atlanta Soc. Fin. Analysts (pres. 1968-69), Fin. Analysts Fedn. (chmn. 1977-78), Soc. Internat. Bus. Fellows. Republican. Greek Orthodox. Clubs: Commerce, Piedmont Driving (Atlanta). Lodge: Rotary. Home: 1360 Barron Court NE Atlanta GA 30327 Office: Montag & Caldwell Inc 3565 Piedmont Rd NE Two Piedmont Ctr Suite 500 Atlanta GA 30363

PATTON, DANIEL CRAIG, business executive; b. Ft. Wayne, Ind., Feb. 7, 1952; s. Lynn James and Phyllis Ilene (Brown) P.; B.S., Ind. U., 1974; M.S., St. Francis Coll., 1982; m. Linda Lorell Montoney, Sept. 10, 1982 (div. Dec. 1988). Plant acct. Weatherhead Corp., Antwerp, Ohio, 1974-77; plant acct. United Technologies-Essex-MWI div., Ft. Wayne, Ind., 1977-79, div. acctg. supr., 1979-80, supr. gen. acctg., 1980-81, acctg. systems specialist, 1981-82, controller U.S. Samica Corp. div. United Technologies, Ft. Wayne, Ind., 1982-83, MWI inventory control and insulation acctg. mgr., 1984-86, sr. internal auditor, 1986—. Bd. dirs. Essex Credit Union, 1979-82, 85-86, supervisory com., chmn. audit, 1980-81, treas., legis. dir., 1986; mem. fin. com. Vt. Rev. Bd., 1982. Mem. Ind. U. Alumni Assn., Allen County Hist. Soc., Ft. Wayne Fine Arts Found., Ft. Wayne Zool. Soc., N.E. Ind. P.C. Users Group. Republican. Presbyterian. Home: 8518 Bull Rapids Rd Woodburn IN 46797 Office: United Technologies 1601 Wall St Fort Wayne IN 46804

PATTON, GEORGE THOMAS, JR., credit agency executive; b. Birmingham, Ala., Sept. 22, 1929; s. George Thomas and Jewell Inez (Garner) P.; m. Hope Kirby, Dec. 20, 1953; children—Thomas Kirby, Neal Garner. B.A., Birmingham-So. Coll., 1949. With Gen. Motors Acceptance Corp., Detroit, 1949—, treas., 1970-72, v.p., 1972-78, exec. v.p., 1978—, dir., 1974—. Chmn. Municipal Planning Bd., Norwood, N.J., 1967-72; Trustee Pascack Valley Hosp., Westwood, N.J., 1975-81; chmn. planning commn. Village of Bingham Farms, Mich., 1983—. Mem. Sigma Alpha Epsilon, Omicron Delta Kappa. Presbyn. (elder). Office: GMAC 3044 W Grand Blvd Detroit MI 48202

PATTON, JAMES LEELAND, chemical company executive; b. Mt. Vernon, Ohio, Apr. 1, 1932; s. Harold Smith and Beatrice Evelyn (Sloan) P.; m. Deborah Craig, July 3, 1982; children: James Leeland, Hugh Crawford, Eleanor Stuart. BS, U. Tenn., 1954, MS, 1955. Rsch. engr. E.I. duPont de Nemours & Co., Wilmington, Del., 1955-64; sr. rsch. engr. E.I. duPont de Nemours & Co., Wilmington, 1964-66, sr. supr., 1966-82, planning mgr., 1982-88, sr. cons., 1988—. Patentee in field. Committeeman Boy Scouts Am., Wilmington, 1964-72. Mem. Am. Inst. Chem Engrs., Wilmington Country Club, Tau Beta Pi. Republican. Episcopalian. Home: 2409 Delaware Ave Wilmington DE 19806

PATTON, RAY BAKER, financial executive; b. Enid, Okla., Jan. 24, 1932; s. Dwight Lyman Moody and Opal (Hembre) P.; BA, U. Okla., 1955, MRCP, 1960, MAPA, 1969. m. Gloria Ruth Chambers, June 6, 1954; children: David Baker, Dayna Erin. Asst. dir. planning San Joaquin, Calif., 1959-61; dir. planning City of Norman (Okla.) and planning cons. U. Okla., Norman, 1961-65; dir. planning Oklahoma City, 1965-67; dir. planning St. Louis County, Mo., 1967-71; pres. Creative Environs., Inc., Clayton, Mo., 1972-74; chmn. Creative Cons., Inc., Clayton, 1972-75; v.p. Land Dynamics, Inc., 1973-74; pres. Patton Real Estate, Inc., Success Power, Inc., St. Louis; prin. Raymond B. Patton & Assocs., Ballwin, Mo., 1975-81; dir. pub. works and planning, health commr., zoning enforcement officer City of Des Peres, Mo., 1977-79; zone mgr. Investors Diversified Svc.s, Chesterfield, Mo., 1980-81; investment broker, fin. planner A.G. Edwards & Sons, Inc., Clayton, 1981-83; fin. planning coord., dir. seminars E.F. Hutton & Co., Inc., St. Louis, 1983-84; securities prin. The Patton Fin. Group, Inc., Westport Fin. Group, Inc., St. Louis, 1984-86; securities products coord., agy. edn. coord., fin. planner, chmn. compliance com., asst. agy. mgr. The Equitable Fin. Cos., St. Louis; also motivational speaker; chmn. bd., chief exec. officer Success Power, Body Works, St. Louis, 1989—; mem. faculty Nat. Inst. Farm and Land Brokers, 1971-76. Scoutmaster, St. Louis Area coun. Boy Scouts Am., 1976-80, vice chmn. adult tng., 1977-83; mem. Christian Bus. Men's Com., Chesterfield, Mo. Served with USMC, 1955-58. Named Outstanding Mcpl. Employee, State of Okla., 1963; recipient IDS Mercury award, 1980; A.G. Edwards & sons Crest award, 1982; Outstanding Exec. award E.F. Hutton, 1983, Blue Chip award, 1983; designated profl. fin. advisor 1984. Mem. Am. Inst. Cert. Planners, Am. Inst. Planners (pres. elect Mo., Kans., Okla. chpt. 1967, co-founder St. Louis Metro sect. 1969), Inst. Cert. Fin. Planners, Internat. Platform Assn., Internat. Assn. Fin. Planners, Eagle Scout Assn. (life), Fellowship Christian Fin. Advisors, Lambda Chi Alpha (pres. 1953-54). Methodist (minister of music, Ballwin 1978-83, choir dir. E. Free Ch., Ladue, Mo. 1986-87). Contbr. articles to profl. jours. Home: 904 Chestnut Ridge Rd Saint Louis MO 63021 Office: Equitable Bldg Ste 1600 10 S Broadway Saint Louis MO 63102

PATTON, RICHARD BOLLING, food company executive; b. Pitts., Jan. 8, 1929; s. Melvin Gerald and Anne (King) P.; m. Mary Ann Bickford, June 8, 1963; children—Pamela Watson, Edward Bickford, Richard Randolph, Jennifer Bolling. B.A., Yale U., 1952; M.B.A., Harvard U., 1954. Product mgr. Heinz U.S.A., Pitts., 1958-62; gen. mgr. mktg. Heinz-Australia, 1964-66; asst. v.p. Ogden Corp., N.Y.C., 1966-68; v.p. passenger sales and services TWA, N.Y.C., 1968-70; pres. N. Am. Cunard Line, Ltd., N.Y.C.; also dir. Cunard Line, Ltd., Cunard Steamship Co., Ltd., Cunard Trafalgar Hotels, Ltd., 1970-73; v.p. mktg. and sales, then v.p. tomato products and condiments div. Heinz U.S.A., 1973-76, pres., 1976-80; area dir. H.J. Heinz Co., Pitts., 1980-82, sr. v.p., dir., 1982—; dir. Weight Watchers Internat., Heinz-Can., Olivine Holdings (Pvt.) Ltd. Bd. dirs. Pa. Economy League, African-Am. Inst.; mem. adv. council African Devel. Found. Served to 1st lt. USMCR, 1954-57. Clubs: Pitts. Golf, Duquesne (Pitts.); Fox Chapel Golf; Yale, The Brook (N.Y.C.); John's Island (Fla.). Lodge: Knights of Malta. Home: 109 Royston Rd Pittsburgh PA 15238 Office: H J Heinz Co 600 Grant St Pittsburgh PA 15219

PATTON, RICHARD CONNELL, restaurant executive, investment company executive; b. Ft. Worth, Aug. 4, 1961; s. Richard Earl Patton and Ann Ellen (Connell) Penn. BS, Vanderbilt U., 1984. Pres. San Antonio Taco Co., Nashville, 1984—; sec. Patton Delmer Interests, Nashville, 1985—. Fund raiser Bush for Pres., Nashville, 1988; mem. jr. bd. Friends St. Thomas Hosp., 1988—. Republican. Episcopalian. Home: 200 Kenner Nashville TN 37205 Office: Patton Delmer 2200 Hillsboro #310 Nashville TN 37212

PATTON, ROBERT EARL, financial executive; b. Canton, Ohio, May 31, 1936; s. Jesse Earl and Ruth Ann (Robson) P.; B.S., Kent State U., 1958; m. Alice Schuck, June 28, 1959; children—Pamela Alice, Kimberly Ann. Sr. staff acct. Hall, Kistler & Co., Canton, 1960-65; sr. internal auditor Hoover Co., North Canton, Ohio, 1965-68; corp. staff acct. Teledyne, Inc., Los Angeles, 1968-69; asst. controller Beverly Enterprises, Pasadena, Calif., 1969-73; dir. internal audit Santa Anita Consol., Inc., Los Angeles, 1973-76; corp. controller USA Petroleum Corp., Santa Monica, Calif., 1976-77, chief fin. officer Ronson Realty Investments, Inc., Fullerton, Calif., 1977-82; v.p., chief fin. officer ITI Fin. Corp., 1982-86, v.p., chief fin. officer Gen. Aluminum Forgings, Inc., 1986—. Mem. budget com. Sierra Bonita Community Assn. Served with USAF, 1959-65. C.P.A., Calif. Mem. Nat. Assn. Accts. Republican. Clubs: Rancho San Joaquin, Athletic. Home: 19461 Sierra Santo Rd Irvine CA 92715 Office: Gen Aluminum Forgings Inc 2111 S Anne St Santa Ana CA 92715

PATULOT, JUN J. R., insurance company executive; b. Manila, Oct. 30, 1947; came to U.S., 1975; s. Silvino M. and Sotera P. P.; m. Connie Castro Patulot, Sept. 2, 1950; children: Patrick, Aires. BS in Fgn. Svc., Lyceum of Philippines, Manila, 1968; postgrad., Seattle Community Coll., 1980. Fgn. svc. staff officer Ministry of Fgn. Affairs, Manila, 1970-74, Philippine Consulate Gen., Seattle, 1975-84; spl. supr. Gt. Am. Res. Ins. Co., Seattle, 1985-87; exec. sales dir. Surety Life Ins. Co., Seattle, 1987—; pvt. practice ins. brokerage, Seattle, 1987—. Recipient Nat. Sales Achievement award, Nat. Quality award. Mem. Million Dollar Round Table. Home: 15325 SE 183rd Dr Renton WA 98058 Office: Surety Life Ins Co PO Box 30030 Salt Lake City UT 84130-9981

PATURIS, E(MMANUEL) MICHAEL, lawyer; b. Akron, Ohio, July 12, 1933; s. Michael George and Sophia M. (Manos) P.; m. Mary Ann, Feb. 28, 1965; 1 child, Sophia E. BS in Bus., U. N.C., 1954, JD with honors, 1959, postgrad. in acctg., 1959-60. Bar: N.C. 1959, D.C. 1969, Va. 1973; CPA, N.C. With acctg. firms, Charlotte and Wilmington, N.C., 1960-63; assoc. Poyner, Geraghty, Hartsfield & Townsend, Raleigh, N.C., 1963-64; atty. Chief Counsel's Office, IRS, Richmond, Va. and Washington, 1964-69; ptnr. Reasoner, Davis & Vinson, Washington, 1969-78; pvt. practice, Alexandria, Va., 1978—; instr. bus. law, econs. and acctg. Bd. editors U. N.C. Law Rev. Served with U.S. Army, 1954-56. Recipient Block award U. N.C. Law Sch. Mem. ABA, D.C. Bar Assn., Va. Bar Assn., Am. Assn. Attys.-CPAs (past pres. Potomac chpt.), Phi Beta Kappa, Beta Gamma Sigma. Republican. Greek Orthodox. Club: Washington Golf and Country (Arlington, Va.). Lodge: Rotary. Home: 6326 Stoneham Ln McLean VA 22101 Office: 431 N Lee St Alexandria VA 22314-2350

PATZKE, RICHARD JOSEPH, energy company executive; b. Chgo., July 20, 1941; s. Robert Kirk and Mary Catherine (Foran) P.; m. Kathleen Gallagher, Aug. 10, 1968; children—Ann, Susan, Michael, Kerry, Eileen. B.A., St. John's U., 1963; M.B.A., U. Chgo., 1965. C.P.A., Ala., Ill. Mgr. Arthur Andersen & Co., Chgo., 1965-78; exec. v.p., also bd. dirs. Energen Corp., Birmingham, Ala., 1978—, also bd. dirs.; dir. Am. Combustion Inc., Atlanta. Bd. dirs. ARC, Birmingham, 1979—. Mem. Fin. Execs. Inst. (pres. Birmingham chpt. 1984—), Am. Inst. C.P.A.s. Roman Catholic. Club: Vestavia Country (Birmingham).

PAUKEN, THOMAS WEIR, venture capital executive; b. Victoria, Tex., Jan. 11, 1944; s. Thomas N. and Patricia (Weir) P.; m. Ida Ayala; children: Thomas II, Michelle, Angela, Elizabeth, Daniel, Victoria, Monica. AB in Polit. Sci., Georgetown U., 1965, postgrad., 1966-67; JD, So. Meth. U., 1973. Bar: Tex., 1975. Staff asst., dep. dir. White Ho. fellows Washington, 1970-71; pvt. practice atty. Dallas, 1974-80; dir. ACTION, Washington, 1981-85; pres. Sta. KRZI-Radio, Waco, Tex., 1985-86; v.p., corp. counsel Garvon, Inc., Dallas, 1986—, also bd. dirs., 1987—; bd. dirs. 50-Off, Inc., San Antonio; pres. Stellar Group, Inc., Dallas. Author: (with others) Steering the Elephant, 1987. Contbr. articles to popular jours. Rep. candidate for U.S. Congress, Dallas, 1978, 80; mem. Reagan transition team Counsel's office, Washington, 1980-81. Served to first lt. U.S. Army, 1967-70, Vietnam. Recipient Drug Edn. Leadership award PRIDE, 1985, Dir.'s award U.S. Office of Personnel Mgmt., 1985; Weaver fellow 1965. Roman Catholic. Office: Garvon Inc 900 Meadows Bldg Dallas TX 75206

PAUL, AMY SUE, medical devices company marketing executive; b. Detroit, Nov. 5, 1951; d. C. Craig Paul and Thelma M. (Hill) Stearns; m. William T. Henry, 1981. BA cum laude, Boston U., 1973, MBA with honors, 1978. Project mgr. GTE Sylvania, Needham, Mass., 1973-77; saleswoman Kendall Co., Boston, 1978-80, product mgr., 1980-82; sr. product mgr., mktg. mgr. Davol subs. CR Bard Co., Cranston, R.I., 1982-88; dir. mktg. Bard Cardiopulmonary, Billerica, Mass., 1988—. Office: Bard Cardiopulmonary Box M Billerica MA 01821

PAUL, ANDREW MITCHELL, venture capitalist; b. N.Y.C., Feb. 10, 1956; s. John William and Bobba Lorraine (Ice) P.; m. Margaret Rae Batchelor, Sept. 19, 1987. BA, Cornell U., 1978; MBA, Harvard U., 1983. Mktg. rep. IBM Corp., N.Y.C., 1978-81; assoc. Hambrecht & Quist Venture Capital Co., San Francisco, 1983-84; gen. ptnr. Welsh, Carson, Anderson & Stowe, N.Y.C., 1984—; bd. dirs. Dealer Info. Systems, Bellingham, Wash., GMD Systems, Atlanta, Trinet, Inc,. Parsippany, N.J., Ross Data, Inc., Palo Alto, Calif., Carefirst, Inc., Balt., Source Telecomputing, McLean, Va., Mobile Tech., L.A. Mem. Info. Industry Assn. (chmn. new bus. com. 1987—), Nat. Venture Capital Assn., N.Y. Venture Capital Assn., Lupus Found (chmn. fin. com.), Bronxville Field Club, Siwanoy Country Club. Home: 313 Central Pkwy Mount Vernon NY 10552 Office: Welsh Carson Anderson & Stowe One World Fin Ctr Ste 3601 New York NY 10281

PAUL, CHRISTIAN THOMAS, insurance company executive; b. Southington, Conn., Feb. 11, 1926; s. Scott E. and Magdeline E. (Zwick) P.; m. Shirley Welch, Dec. 27, 1952; children: Colleen Paul Quinn, Cynthia Paul Newman, David, Christine. BS, Yale U., 1948. With The Travelers Ins. Co., Hartford, Conn., Kansas City, Mo., and Cin., 1948—; 2d v.p. The Travelers Ins. Co., Hartford, 1968-71, v.p., 1971-85, sr. v.p., 1985-88; chmn. bd. dirs. Ctr. for Corp. Health Promotion, Reston, Va., Travelers Plan Adminstrs., Inc., Hartford, Travelers Health Network, Inc.; bd. dirs. Resource Info. Mgmt. Systems, Inc., Oakbrook, Ill., Constitution State Service Co., Hartford. Served as naval aviation cadet USN, 1943-45. Mem. Life Ins. Mktg. Research Assn., Health Ins. Assn. Am. Home: 50 Metacomet Rd Farmington CT 06032 Office: The Travelers Corp 1 Tower Sq Hartford CT 06183

PAUL, DAVID LEWIS, real estate developer, financial executive; b. N.Y.C., May 1, 1939; s. Isadore and Ruth (Goldstein) P.; m. Sandra Rosenzweig; children: David J., Michael M., Deanna M. BS in Econ., U. Pa., 1961; JD, Columbia U., 1969, Columbia U., 1967. Chmn., chief exec. officer CenTrust Savs. Bank, 1983—, CenTrust Trust (formerly Westport Co.), 1983—; bd. dirs. CenTrust Mortgage Corp., Calvin Klein Industries, Weintraub Entertainment Group. Author: The effect of the AFL-CIO Merger on Centralization, 1961, Progressive Architecture, 1967. Mem. policy adv. bd. Ctr. for Real Estate and Urban Econs. U. Calif. Berkeley; bd. dirs. St. Thomas U. Sch. of Law, Pub. Health Trust, Jackson Meml. Hosp., Miami, Am. Symphony Orch. League; trustee Temple Emanu-El, Miami, NCCJ, Miami, Nat. Found. for Advancement of Arts; chmn. New World Symphony Miami; mem. steering com. Greater Miami Jewish Fedn.; bd. dirs., former governing mem. Lincoln Ctr. Repertory Theatre; bd. govs. Philharmonic Orch. of Fla.; nat. chmn. majority trust Dem. Senatorial Campaign Com.; bd. dirs., trustee Garn Inst. Fin. U. Utah; trustee Barry U., Miami. Clubs: Standard, Mid-America (Chgo.); City Club, Brickell, Fisher Island (Miami); Ocean Reef, Key Largo and Cat Cay, Chubb Cay.

PAUL, DOUGLAS ALLAN, insurance executive; b. Chgo., Feb. 9, 1949; s. Eugene Frank and Flo Sinclair (Broomhead) P.; m. Pamela DeGroot, Oct. 20, 1984. BS, Rensselaer Polytechnic Inst., Troy, N.Y., 1971; MBA, U. Pa., 1976. Asst. dir. admissions and alumni affairs Rensselaer Polytechnic Inst., 1971-74; sr. mgr. McKinsey and Co. Inc., N.Y.C., 1977-82; v.p. strategic planning Am. Internat. Group, N.Y.C., 1983—; bd. dirs. Bond Investors Group, N.Y.C., 1984—. Mem. Wall St. Planning Group (exec. dir. 1984—). Home: 284 W 11th St New York NY 10014 Office: Am Internat Group Inc 70 Pine St New York NY 10270

PAUL, HERBERT MORTON, lawyer, accountant, taxation educator; b. N.Y.C.; s. Julius and Gussie Paul; married; children—Leslie Beth, Andrea Lynn. BBA, Baruch Coll.; MBA, NYU, LLM; JD, Harvard U. Ptnr. Touche Ross & Co., N.Y.C., 1957-82; assoc. dir.-tax Touche Ross & Co., dir. fin counseling; mng. ptnr. Herbert Paul, P.C., N.Y.C., 1982-88, Mahoney, Cohen, Paul & Co., P.C., N.Y.C., 1988—; dir. N.Y. Estate Planning Council; prof. taxation, trustee NYU. Author: Ordinary and Necessary Expenses; editor: Taxation of Banks; adv. tax editor The Practical Accountant; mem. adv. bd. Financial and Estate Planning, Tax Shelter Insider, Financial Planning Strategist, Tax Shelter Litigation Report; bd. dirs. Partnership Strategist, The Business Strategist; cons. Professional Practice Management Mag.; mem. panel The Hot Line; advisor The Partnership Letter, The Wealth Formula; cons. The Insider's Report for Physicians; mem. tax bd. Business Profit Digest; cons. editor physician's Tax Advisor; bd. fin. cons. Tax Strategies for Physicians; tax and bus. advisor Prentice Hall; contbg. editor. Jour. of Accountancy. Mem. bd. overseers Grad. Sch. Bus., NYU; mem. com. on trusts and estates Rockefeller U.; trustee Alvin Ailey Am. Dance Theatre, Associated Y's of N.Y.; bd. dirs. Alumni Fedn. of NYU; co-chmn. accts. div. Fedn. Philantropies. Served with U.S. Army, 1954-56. Mem. Inst. Fed. Taxation (adv. com. chmn.), Internat. Inst. on Tax and Bus. Planning (adv. bd.), Assn. of Bar of City of N.Y., NYU Tax Soc. (pres., chmn. com. on tax shelters), Bur. Nat. Affairs-Tax Mgmt. (adv. com. on exec. compensation), Am. Inst. CPAs (com. on corp. taxation), Tax Study Group, ABA (tax sect.), N.Y. County Lawyer's Assn., N.Y. State Soc. CPAs (chmn. tax div. com. on fed. taxation, gen. tax com., furtherance com., com. on relations with IRS, bd. dirs.), Nat. Assn. Accts., Assn. of Bar of City of N.Y., Accts. Club of Am., Pension Club, Nat. Assn. Estate Planners (bd. dirs.), N.Y. C. of C. (tax com.), Grad. Soc. Bus. of NYU Alumni Assn. (pres.), Pres. Council (NYU). Clubs: Wall St., City Athletic (N.Y.C.), Inwood Country.

PAUL, HERMAN LOUIS, JR., valve manufacturing company executive; b. N.Y.C., Dec. 30, 1912; s. Herman Louis and Louise Emilie (Markert) P.; student Duke, 1931-32, Lehigh U., 1932-33; m. Janath Powers; children—Robert E., Charles Thomas, Herman Louis III. Power plant engr. Paul's Machine Shop, N.Y.C., 1935-43; pres., chief engr. Paul's Machine Shop, N.Y.C., 1943-48; v.p., chief engr. Paul Valve Corp., East Orange, N.J., 1948-54; pres., chief engr. P-K Industries, Inc., North Arlington, N.J., 1954-59; v.p., dir. research Gen. Kinetics, Englewood, N.J., 1959-62; engring. cons., N.Y.C., 1962-65; v.p., dir. Hydromatics, Inc., Bloomfield, N.J., 1965-67; with P.J. Hydraulics, Inc., Myerstown, Pa., 1967—, pres., chief engr., 1968-80, dir. and stockholder, 1980-81; pres. Flomega Industries, Inc., Cornwall, Pa., 1982—; cons. to Metal Industries Devel. Center, Taiwan, 1979; engring. cons. valves and complimentary equipment, 1980—; valve cons. Continental Disc Corp., Kansas City, Mo., 1980—. Vice chmn. Nat. UN Day Com., 1977, 78, 79, 80. Mem. ASME, Instrument Soc. Am., Am. Soc. Naval Engrs., Internat. Platform Assn., Nat. Contract Mgmt. Assn., AAAS, The Navy League, The Naval Inst. Club: Heidelberg Country (Bernville, Pa.), Quentin (Pa.) Riding. Patentee in field. Home: 370 Dogwood Ln RD 5 Lebanon PA 17042

PAUL, JAMES ROBERT, energy company executive; b. Wichita, Kans., Sept. 10, 1934; s. Harold Robert and Zona Belle (Marlatt) P.; B.S., Wichita State U., 1956; m. Julia Ann Haigh, Aug. 14, 1955; children: John Robert, Jeffrey James, Julie Renee. With Boeing Co., Wichita, 1956-67; mgmt. cons. Peat, Marwick, Mitchell & Co., Houston, 1967-70; v.p. fin. and adminstrn. Robertson Distbn. Systems, Inc., Houston, 1970-73; treas. Colo. Interstate Gas Co., Colorado Springs, 1973-74; treas. The Coastal Corp., Houston, 1974-75, v.p. fin., 1975-78, sr. v.p. fin., 1978-81, chief fin. officer, from 1981, sr. exec. v.p., from 1981, now pres., chief operating officer, dir. Mem. Am. Petroleum Inst., Fin. Execs. Inst. Republican. Methodist. Office: Coastal Corp 9 Greenway Pla E Houston TX 77046 *

PAUL, ROBERT, lawyer; b. N.Y.C., Nov. 22, 1931; s. Gregory and Sonia (Rijock) P.; m. Christa Holz, Apr. 6, 1975; 1 child, Gina. BA, NYU, 1953; JD, Columbia U., 1958. Bar: Fla. 1958, N.Y. 1959. From assoc. to ptnr. Paul, Landy, Beiley & Harper, P.A., Miami, 1964—; counsel Republic Nat. Bank Miami, 1967—. Past pres. Fla. Philharm., Inc., 1978-79; trustee U. Miami. Mem. ABA, N.Y. Bar Assn., Fla. Bar Assn., Inter-Am. Bar Assn., French-Am. C. of C. of Miami (pres. 1986-87). Home: 700 Alhambra Cir Coral Gables FL 33134 Office: Paul Landy Beiley & Harper PA 200 SE 1st St Miami FL 33131

PAUL, ROBERT ARTHUR, steel company executive; b. N.Y.C., Oct. 28, 1937; s. Isadore and Ruth (Goldstein) P.; m. Donna Rae Berkman, July 29, 1962; children: Laurence Edward, Stephen Eric, Karen Rachel. AB, Cornell U., 1959; JD, Harvard U., 1962, MBA, 1964. With Ampco-Pitts. Corp. (formerly Screw & Bolt Corp. Am.), 1964—, v.p., 1969-71, exec. v.p., 1972-79, pres., 1979—, treas., 1973—, dir., 1969—; v.p., asst. sec., asst. treas., dir. Parkersburg Steel Corp., Louis Berkman Co., Follansbee Steel Corp., Louis Berkman Realty Co.; dir. 1st Nat. Bank of Washington, Pa., Intergr Fin. Corp., U.S. Biochem. Corp., N.W. Steel and Wire; gen. partner Romar Trading Co.; Instr. Grad. Sch. Indsl. Adminstrn., Carnegie Mellon U., 1966-69; trustee Montefiore Hosp., pres. bd. 1982-85. Trustee H.L. and Louis Berkman Found.; trustee, treas. Ampco-Pitts. Found. Mem. ABA, Mass. Bar Assn., Soc. Security Analysts, Harvard Club, Concordia Club, Harvard-Yale-Princeton Club, Pitts. Athletic Club, Duquesne Club. Republican. Jewish. Office: AMPCO-Pitts Corp 600 Grant St Pittsburgh PA 15219

PAUL, ROBERT JOHN, financial planner, accountant; b. Mandan, N.D., Apr. 25, 1948; s. Joseph J. and Monica (Eckroth) P.; m. Peggy Jean Hohbein, Aug. 3, 1968; children: Tamara, Teri, Scott. AA, Bismarck (N.D.) Jr. Coll., 1969; BBA in Acctg., U. N.D., 1971. LPA, N.D. Co-owner Puklich & Paul Acctg. Svc., Bismarck, 1971-73; fin. planner N.D. State Hwy. Dept., Bismarck, 1973-78; project controller Basin Electric Power Coop., Bismarck, 1978-80, bus. analyst, 1980-82, fin. coordinator, 1982-84, mgr. debt and fin. planning, 1984—; owner Paul's Acctg. Svc., Mandan; lectr. in field. Developed computerized system, mktg. innovation. Bd. dirs. St. Joseph's Sch. Bd., Mandan, 1974-76, St. Joseph's Ch. Fin. Com., Mandan, 1979-84; pres. Park Bd., Mandan, 1978-82; cubmaster Boy Scouts Am., Mandan, 1984. Mem. N.D. LPA's, Basin Electric Employee Assn., Jaycees (pres. 1975, Outstanding Jaycee of Yr. 1972, Key Man, 1973, Disting. Svc. award 1979). Roman Catholic. Lodge: K.C. (fin. cons. 1979-87, dep. grand knight 1977, grand knight 1978, Knight of Yr. 1980). Office: Basin Electric Power Coop 1717 E Interstate Ave Bismarck ND 58501

PAUL, WILLIAM GEORGE, lawyer; b. Pauls Valley, Okla., Nov. 25, 1930; s. Homer and Helen (Lafferty) P.; m. Barbara Elaine Brite, Sept. 27, 1963; children—George Lynn, Alison Elise, Laura Elaine, William Stephen. B.A., U. Okla., 1952, LL.B., 1956. Bar: Okla. bar 1956. Practiced in Norman, 1956, Oklahoma City, 1957-84; partner Crowe & Dunlevy, 1962-84; sr. v.p., gen. counsel Phillips Petroleum Co., Bartlesville, Okla., 1984—; assoc. prof. law Oklahoma City U., 1964-68. Author: (with Earl Sneed) Vernon's Oklahoma Practice, 1965. Served to 1st lt. USMCR, 1952-54. Named Outstanding Young Man Oklahoma City, 1965, Outstanding Young Oklahoman, 1966. Fellow Am. Bar Found., Am. Coll. Trial Lawyers; mem. ABA, Okla. Bar Assn. (pres. 1976), Oklahoma County Bar Assn. (past pres.), Nat. Conf. Bar Pres. (pres. 1986), U. Okla. Alumni Assn. (pres. 1973), Phi Beta Kappa, Order of Coif, Phi Delta Phi, Delta Sigma Rho. Democrat. Presbyn. Home: 1800 Country Club Rd Bartlesville OK 74006 Office: Phillips Petroleum Co Phillips Bldg 18th Floor Bartlesville OK 74004

PAULEY, RHODA ANNE, communications and mktg. exec.; b. Elizabeth, N.J., Nov. 26, 1939; d. Isadore and Jean Litin Manheim. BA magna cum laude, Smith Coll., 1961; postgrad. in Am. lit. Stanford U., 1961-63. Editorial asst. Edn. and World Affairs, N.Y.C., 1963-65; tech. writer Data Processing div. U.S. Life Ins. Corp., N.Y.C., 1965-67; dir. publs. and mktg. Diebold Group, Inc., N.Y.C., 1967-72; gen. mgr. Direct Mail/Mktg. Assn., Inc., N.Y.C., 1972-75; cons. on new bus. and orgn. devel., 1975-76; v.p. communications and clearinghouse Work Am. Inst., Scarsdale, N.Y., 1976-81; dir. communications svcs. Girl Scouts U.S., 1981—; chmn. Com. for Liaison on Advt. and Sales Promotion, 1974. Chmn., Task Force on Employee-Mgmt. Rels. and Quality of Working Life, Transp. Rsch. Bd./NRC, 1979-82. Editor: The Student in Higher Education, 1968. Mem. Women in Communications. Home: 233 E 69th St New York NY 10021 Office: Girl Scouts US 830 3rd Ave New York NY 10022

PAULEY, RICHARD HEIM, real estate counselor; b. Cleve., Dec. 14, 1932; s. Kenneth H. and Romaine (Heim) P.; m. Jan E. Minnick, Oct. 26, 1957; children—Tyler Kent, Elysa Pauley Del Guercio. BA in Polit. Sci., Stanford U., 1954; postgrad. U. So. Calif., 1956-57. Sr. cons. Coldwell Banker & Co., Newport Beach, Calif., 1963-77; owner Richard H. Pauley Co., Investment Realtors, Newport Beach, Beverly Hills and Tustin, Calif., 1977—; sr. mktg. exec. The Seeley Co., Irvine, Calif., 1986—; registered prin. Titan Capital Corp., Tustin, 1988—; ins. rep. Mission Viejo (Calif.) Ins. Svcs., Inc., 1988—. Bd. dirs. Orange Coast YMCA, 1973-78. Capt. USAFR, 1965. Recipient Cert. of Appreciation City of Newport Beach, 1975-76; Disting. Svc. award Rehab. Inst. Orange County, 1973. Mem. Am. Soc. Real Estate Counselors (chmn. internat. activities com.), Internat. Real Estate Fedn., Calif. Assn. Realtors, Nat. Assn. Realtors, SAR, Beta Theta Pi, Phi Delta Phi; Stanford Club of Orange County (past pres.). Republican. Club: Center (Costa Mesa, Calif.). Home: 22 Morning Sun Irvine CA 92715

PAULICK, ERNEST ERICH, bank executive; b. Detroit, June 13, 1946; s. Franz Erich and Elizabeth Duthie (McWatt) P. BSBA, Cen. Mich. U., 1969. Nat. bank examiner Office of the Controller of Currency, Detroit, 1969-77; regional dir. human resources Office of the Controller of Currency, Chgo., 1978-84; exec. v.p. First Nat. Bank of Bad Axe (Mich.), 1984—; v.p. State Bank Fraser, Mich., 1978-84; bd. dirs. First Huron Corp., Bad Axe. Food product patentee. Drum major Mich. Scottish Pipes and Drums, Detroit, 1980—. Home: 140 S Verona Rd Bad Axe MI 48413 Office: First Nat Bank Bad Axe 1 E Huron Bad Axe MI 48413

PAULIN, MICHAEL VINCENT, resort development executive; b. Los Angeles, July 10, 1941; s. Clarence Harold and Barbara and Louisa (Geraldi) P.; m. Rosemarie Kathe Anne Haase, Dec. 15, 1972; 1 child by previous marriage: Derek Michael; children by present marriage: Annemarie, Maya. BS, U. So. Calif., 1963. Pres. Worldwide Living, Inc., Los Angeles, 1964-68; v.p. sales Colony Hotes, Los Angeles, 1968-71; regional v.p. for Pacific Colony Hotes, Honolulu, 1971-78; sr. v.p. Aston Hotels & Resorts, Honolulu, 1978-87; pres. Paulin Pacific Group, Ltd., Honolulu, 1987—; bd. dirs. Pacific Asia Travel Assocs., San Francisco, 1987—. Pres. Festival of Pacific, Honolulu, 1983-86; bd. dirs. Hawaii Visitors Bur., Honolulu, 1977-78. Mem. Pacific Asia Travel Assocs., Hawaii Hotel Assn., Kappa Alpha (pres. 1962-63, 67-68). Republican. Lutheran. Club: Outrigger Canoe. Office: Paulin Pacific Group Ltd 2155 Kalakaua Ave Ste 710 Honolulu HI 96815-2351

PAULSEN, BORGE REGNAR, agricultural cooperative executive; b. San Francisco, July 26, 1915; s. Anton and Christa (Regnar) P.; m. Beverly Ann Gephart, July 3, 1942; children: Lee Ann Paulsen Hanna, R. Anthony, Eric Dana, Carol Louise Paulsen Thomsen. Student Stanford, 1933-35; BS, U. Calif., Berkeley, 1937. Sec., Agrl. Adjustment Adminstrn., Yolo County, Calif., 1937-41; owner, operator Sunset Rice Dryer, Inc., Woodland, Calif., 1946—; pres. Demeter Corp. Woodland, Agrivest Corp., Woodland; pres. Crane & Cross Books, Inc., Sacramento; dir. emeritus Wells Fargo Bank, 1986—; dir. Wells Fargo & Co.; farmer, rice grower, 1937—; mem. rice research and mktg. com. U.S. Dept. Agr., others; chmn. adv. bd. Berkeley Bank for Coops., 1976. Bd. dirs., v.p. Calif. Rice Research Found., Yuba City, Woodland Meml. Hosp., also former pres.; former pres. Sutter (Calif.) Mut. Water Co.; bd. dirs. Robert Louis Stevenson Sch., Pebble Beach, Calif., Agrl. Council Calif.; adv. bd. Calif. State U., Sacramento. Served with U.S. Army, 1941-46. Recipient Distinguished Service award Calif. Farm Bur., 1974, Outstanding Service award Woodland Meml. Hosp., 1976, Calif. Rice Industry Man of Year award, 1978; named Agribus. Man of Yr., Yolo County Calif. Mem. Rice Research and Mktg. Bd. Calif. (v.p.), Rice Growers Assn. Calif. (pres., chmn. bd. 1968-70), Bean Growers Assn. Calif. (past pres.), Delta Kappa Epsilon. Republican. Episcopalian. Clubs: Commonwealth, Bankers (San Francisco); Rotary Woodland (former pres.); Sutter, Yolo Fliers Country, El Macero Country; Alderbrook Golf and Yacht (Union, Wash.). Home: 202 Rancho Way St Woodland CA 95695 Office: 1021 Lincoln Ave Woodland CA 95695

PAULSEN, JOSEPH CHARLES, V, publishing company executive; b. N.Y.C., Nov. 30, 1925; s. Frank J. and Mary (Weaffer) P.; m. Ann D. Moore, Sept. 17, 1949; children: Brad, Joann, Nancy, Amy. Student, Birmingham So. Coll., 1943-44, St. John's U., 1945-48, CCNY, 1949. Researcher Hearst Advt. Service, 1949; advt. salesman N.Y. Jour.-Am., 1949-51; account exec. Robert Bories Co., 1951-52; v.p. Austin LeStrange Co., N.Y.C., 1952-57; Ea. mgr. Okla. Pub. Co., N.Y.C., 1957-65, dir. advt., Oklahoma City, 1965; pres. J. Paulsen, Inc., N.Y.C., 1967—; chmn., chief exec. officer Paulsen Pub. Inc., N.Y.C. and St. Paul, 1984—; cons. to mag. pubs.; guest speaker Nat. Assn. Radio-TV Farm Dirs.; dir. Agr. Pub. Reports. Contbr. articles to mags. Active Hartsdale Rep. Club; v.p. Hartsdale Civic Assn.; v.p., past chmn. Community Chest. Mem. Farm Pub. Men N.Y. (past pres.), Agrl. Pubs. Assn. (past bd. dirs.), State Farm Paper Bur. (bd. dirs.), Nat. Agrl. Mktg. Assn. (v.p. S.W. chpt.), Mensa. Roman Catholic. Club: Orient Yacht (commodore). Lodge: K.C. Home: 499 C Heritage Hills Somers NY 10589 Office: 420 Lexington Ave New York NY 10170

PAULSON, SANDRA L., real estate executive; b. Helena, Mont., May 14, 1946; d. Jack and Lucille A. (Tooker) Stambaugh Bourquin; m. Wallace Paulson, Aug. 31, 1961 (div. 1977); 1 child, Jacquie. BS, U. Mont., 1973. Data processor Am. State Bank, Williston, N.D., 1965-67; clk. Williams County Ct., Williston, 1967-69; tchr. Sch. Dist. #1, Missoula, Mont., 1974-75; salesperson Lambros Realty, Missoula, 1976-84, gen. mgr., 1984—; pres. Hartman Investments, Missoula, 1976—. Contbr. article to profl. jour. Named Miss Williston, Bus. Profl. Women, 1968. Mem. Nat. Assn. Female Execs (network dir. 1984-86), Nat. Assn. Realtors, Missoula County Realtors (com. 1986), Mont. Assn. Realtors (state and county dir. 1980-81, v.p. 1980-81, pres. elect 1987, state chairperson listing com. 1988), Missoula Bd. Realtors (pres. 1988—, Realtor of Yr. 1988). Avocations: piano, guitar, skiing, backpacking. Office: Lambros Realty 1001 S Higgins Missoula MT 59801

PAULUS, ERWIN FERDINAND, JR., forestry company executive; b. Warren, Ark., May 23, 1921; s. Erwin F. and Blanche (Cahill) P.; m. Olive Wise, Sept. 3, 1946; children: Lee Paulus Leming, Tom, Michael. BSBA, U. Ark., 1948. V.p., mgr. Warren Cotton Oil Co., 1948-59; sales mgr. Wilson Oak Flooring Co., Warren, 1960-69; land agt. So. div. Potlatch Corp., Warren, 1970—. Mem. nat. devel. coun. U. Ark., Fayetteville, 1986—; mayor City of Warren, 1960-64; bd. dirs. S.E. Ark. Concert Assn., 1978—, U. Ark. Found., 1985—. Mem. Ark. Forestry Assn. (bd. dirs. 1973—, Pres.'s award 1981), Warren Country Club (v.p. 1968), Masons, Rotary (past pres. Warren chpt.), Sigma Alpha Epsilon. Democrat. Presbyterian. Home: 211 E Chruch St Warren AR 71671 Office: Potlatch Corp PO Box 390 Warren AR 71671

PAVEK, CHARLES CHRISTOPHER, information scientist; b. Torrington, Conn., Jan. 15, 1955; s. Charles Hansen and Veronica (Donder) P.; m. Bryn Carpenter, Dec. 17, 1977. Cert de la Civilisation Française, U. Paris, 1977; BA, U. So. Calif., 1978. Asst. archivist U.S. Senate Staff, Washington, 1978-81; sr. researcher Fulbright & Jaworski, Washington, 1981-86; owner, operator Data Base Data, Washington, 1986-87; sr. libr. Nat. Econ. Rsch. Assocs., Washington, 1987—. With USN, 1974-75. Mem. Am. Assn. Law Libraries, Spl. Libraries Assn., Law Librs. Soc. D.C. (v.p. 1982-85). Democrat. Roman Catholic.

PAVELKA, SUSAN, internal auditor; b. Irvington, N.J., July 8, 1964; d. Joseph and Dolores (Vinesky) P. BS in Acctg., U. Bridgeport, 1986. Acct. Texaco, Inc., White Plains, N.J., 1986-88; internal auditor ADT Inc., Parsippany, N.J., 1989—. Vol. Papermill Playhouse Guild, Millburn, 1983—, Union Twp. (N.J.) Hist. Soc., 1981—. Mem. Inst. Internal Auditors, Am. Soc. Women Accts., Phi Kappa Phi, Beta Gamma Sigma. Roman Catholic.

PAVELSKI, RICHARD R., agricultural products supplier; b. Stevens Point, Wis., Aug. 8, 1949; s. Albert Myron and Irene (Ciesewski) P.; m. Barbara J. Walenski, Nov. 13, 1974; children: Michelle, Andria, Jeremie. Grad. high sch., Stevens Point. V.p. A.M. Pavelski and Sons Inc., Stevens Point, 1967-77; pres. Pavelski Enterprises Inc., Amherst Junction, Wis., 1977—; owner, sec. Portage County Bancshares Inc., 1987—; owner, v.p. Pavelski Farms Inc., 1984—. Pres. Wis. Agri-Bus. Council, Madison, 1988; pres. Village of Amherst Junction, 1985—. Recipient Businessman of the Yr. award Waussau (Wis.) Daily Herald, 1987, Outstanding Contribution to Agriculture award City of Stevens Point, 1985. Mem. Wis. Potato and Vegetable Growers Assn. (pres. 1985). Office: Pavelski Enterprises 3895 Crop Care Ct Amherst Junction WI 54407

PAVONY, WILLIAM H., retail sales executive; b. Bklyn., Mar. 1, 1940; s. Harry and Mollie (Leibell) P.; m. Geraldine Rice, June 10, 1961; 1 child, Sheryl. BBA cum laude, Hofstra U., 1960. CPA, N.Y., Tex. Mgr. Arthur Andersen & Co. Inc., N.Y.C., 1960-73; group sr. v.p. Purolator Services Inc., New Hyde Park, N.Y., 1973-75; v.p., controller Purolator Inc., Piscataway, N.J., 1975-78; sr. v.p. Zale Corp., Dallas, 1978-85; sr. v.p. fin., chief fin. officer Alexander's Inc., N.Y.C., 1985-88, exec. v.p., chief fin officer, 1988-89; exec. v.p. adminstrn. The Kobacker Co., Columbus, Ohio, 1989—. Treas., bd. dirs. Tex. Vis. Nurses Assn., Dallas, 1984-85. Mem. Fin. Execs. Inst. (former dir. North Tex. chpt), Am. Inst. CPA's, N.Y. Soc. CPA's, Met. Retail Fin. Execs. Inst., Nat. Assn. Accts. Home: 6445 Quarry Ln Dublin OH 43017 Office: The Kobacker Co 6606 Tussing Rd Columbus OH 43216

PAVSEK, DANIEL ALLAN, banker, educator; b. Cleve., Jan. 18, 1945; s. Daniel L. and Helen A. (Femec) P.; m. M. Ellen Canfield, Apr. 11, 1980 and July 26, 1985 (div. Sept. 1981). A.B., Maryknoll Coll., Glen Ellyn, Ill., 1966; M.A., Maryknoll Sch. Theology, Ossining, N.Y., 1971, Cleve. State U., 1972; Ph.D., Case Western Res. U., 1981. Pres. Council Richmond Heights, Ohio, 1972-75; lectr. econs. Cleve. State U., 1972-75; asst. prof. Baldwin-Wallace Coll., Berea, Ohio, 1975-81; v.p., economist Ameritrust Co., Cleve., 1981—; adj. prof. bus. adminstrn. Baldwin-Wallace Coll., Berea, Ohio, 1981—. Mem. Am. Econ. Assn., Nat. Tax Assn., Pub. Choice Soc., Nat. Assn. Bus. Econs. Democrat. Home: 2110 Lester Rd Valley City OH 44280 Office: Ameritrust Co 900 Euclid Ave Cleveland OH 44101

PAWELEC, WILLIAM JOHN, retired electronics company executive; b. Hammond, Ind., Feb. 15, 1917; s. John and Julia (Durnas) P.; B.S. in Acctg., Ind. U., 1939; m. Alice E. Brown, May 30, 1941 (dec. Dec. 1970); children—William John, Betty Jane Pawelec Conover; m. 2d, June A. Shepard, Nov. 27, 1976 (div. June 1980). Statistician, Ind. State Bd. Accounts, 1939-41; with RCA, 1941—, mgr. acctg. and budgets internat. div., 1957-61, controller internat. div., 1961-68, corp. mgr. internat. fin. ops. and controls, 1968-75, mgr. corp. acctg., 1975-77, dir. internat. acctg., 1977-81, ret., 1981; controller RCA Internat., Ltd., Electron Ins. Co., 1977, RCA Credit Corp., 1979; ret., 1981. Active, Westfield United Fund, 1967—. Mem. Nat. Assn. Accts. (past nat. v.p.), Watchung Power Squadron, N.J. State C. of C., Commerce and Industry Assn. N.Y., Stuart Cameron McLeod Soc., Ind. U. Alumni Assn. (pres. N.J. chpt.), Beta Gamma Sigma, Sigma Epsilon Theta. Club: Echo Lake Country. Home: 86 New England Ave Summit NJ 07901

PAXSON, LOWELL WHITE, home shopping network executive; b. Rochester, N.Y., Apr. 17, 1935; s. Donald Earl and Maybelle L. (White) P.; m. Jean Louise Blauvelt, May 2, 1961 (div. Apr. 1977); children: Todd L., Devon W., Julie; m. Barbara Ann Chapman, Nov. 19, 1977; children: Thomas, Jennifer. BA, Syracuse U., 1956. Pres., owner Sta. WACK-AM, Newark, N.Y., 1957-61, Sta. WKSN-AM/FM, Jamestown, N.Y., 1961-68, Sta. WNYP-TV, Jamestown, 1966-68, Sta. WTBY-AM, Waterbury, Conn., 1968-70, Sta. WYND-AM, Sarasota, Fla., 1968-74, Sta. WAVS-AM, Ft. Lauderdale, Fla., 1973-77, Sta. WWQT-AM, Clearwater, Fla., 1977-83, Sta. WHBS-FM, Holiday, Fla., 1977-83; pres. Full Circle Mktg., Fla., 1968-77; pres., owner, chief operating officer Home Shopping Network Inc., St. Petersburg and Clearwater, 1981—, also bd. dirs. Trustee Milligan Coll., Tenn., 1987—; bd. dirs. Broadcap, Washington, 1986—; mem. Council of 100 of Pinellas County, St. Petersburg, 1985—; chmn. City of Sarasota Planning & Zoning Commn., 1970-74. Capt. U.S. Army, 1956-57. Mem. Nat. Assn. Broadcasters, Nat. Cable TV Assn., Direct Mktg. Assn. Am., Roebling Soc. Republican. Home: 700 Spottis Woode Ln Clearwater FL 33616 Office: Home Shopping Network 12000 25th Ct N Saint Petersburg FL 33716

PAXTON, JOHN WESLEY, electronics company executive; b. Camden, N.J., Jan. 9, 1937; s. John Irving and Francis Rose (Jones) P.; m. Janet Rose Croteau, Nov. 4, 1975; children—David R., William A., John Wesley, Jacqueline R., Thomas W., Scott A. B.S., NYU, 1970; postgrad. in mfg. tech. U. Mich., 1976; postgrad. Rivier Coll., 1979, Calif. Western U., 1980. Registered profl. engr., Calif. With RCA, Camden, Hightstown, N.J. and Burlington, Mass., 1959-75, mgr. quality assurance, 1972-75; dir. mfg. Kollsman Instrument Co. div. Sun Chem. Corp., Merrimack, N.H., 1975-80; dir., plant mgr. Ocala ops. Martin Marietta Corp. (Fla.), 1980-83, dir. product ops., Orlando, Fla., 1983-84; pres. Intermec Corp., Lynnwood, Wash., 1986-88, pres., chief exec. officer, chmn. bd., 1988—. With USN, 1955-59. Mem. Nat. Soc. Profl. Engrs., Am. Soc. Quality Control, Am. Soc. Mfg. Engrs. Republican. Presbyterian. Lodges: Lions, Masons.

PAYNE, DEBORAH ANNE, medical company officer; b. Norristown, Pa., Sept. 22, 1952; d. Kenneth Nathan Moser and Joan (Reese) Dewhurst; m. Randall Barry Payne, Mar. 8, 1975. AA, Northeastern Christian Jr. Coll., 1972; B in Music Edn., Va. Commonwealth U., 1979. Driver, social asst. Children's Aid Soc., Norristown, Pa., 1972-73; mgr. Boddie-Noell Enterprises, Richmond, Va., 1974-79; retail food saleswoman Hardee's Food Systems, Inc., Phila., 1979-81; supr., with tech. tng. and testing and computer depts. Cardiac Datacorp., Phila., 1981—. Mem. Nat. Assn. Female Execs., Delta Omicron (pres. Alpha Xi chpt. 1978-79, pres. Epsilon province 1980-85, chmn. Ea. Pa. alumni div. 1986—, Star award 1979), Am. Soc. Profl. and Exec. Women. Republican. Office: Cardiac Datacorp 1429 Walnut St 2d Floor Philadelphia PA 19102

PAYNE, E. PALMER, newscaster; b. Cin., July 13, 1930; s. Elmer Curry and Agnes Isabella (Palmer) P.; children: John, Thomas, Palmer Jr. (dec.), Jennifer. BA, Boston U., 1952. News dir. Sta. WFEA-WGIR, Manchester, N.H., 1955-60, Sta. WPTR, Albany, N.Y., 1960-61, Sta. WCOP, Boston, 1961-63; anchorman Sta. WNAC-TV 7, Boston, 1963-65; news reporter The Yankee Network, Boston, 1963-68, WCBS-TV, N.Y.C., 1968-79; anchorman Sta. WLIW-TV, Plainview, N.Y., 1987-88; newsman Sta. WINS-AM, ABC News, Sta. WABC-TV, N.Y.C., 1979—. Mem. prin.'s adv. com. Carle Place (N.Y.) High Sch., 1982-86, Anti-Crime Com., Carle Place Civic Assn., 1987-88. Sgt. U.S. Army, 1948-52, Korea. Recipient Tom Phillips award UPI Broadcasters Assn. Mass., 1961. Unitarian. Home: 349 Rushmore Ave Carle Place NY 11514

PAYNE, JAMES WILLIAM, III, food products executive, data processing executive; b. Monroe, Mich., Dec. 4, 1937; s. James William and Mary Elizabeth (Harrington) P.; m. Mary Grace Boff, Dec. 26, 1961; children: Michele, Colette, Noelle. BS in Physics, Holy Cross Coll., 1959; MBA, Mich. State U., 1978. Field engr. Gen. Electric Co., Utica and Bethpage, N.Y., 1962-64; application engr. Gen. Electric Co., Detroit, 1964-67; programming mgr. Chrysler Corp., Detroit, 1964-67; systems mgr. Chrysler Corp., 1970-71, sales info. processing ctr. mgr., 1971-80; v.p. mgmt. info. systems Jostens Inc., Mpls., 1980-82; dir. systems and programming Super Valu, Mpls., 1982—; cons. Regina High Sch., Mpls., 1983-86, St. Edwards Parish Programs, Mpls., 1986-88. Pres. State Scholasticas Parish Coun., Detroit, 1973; chmn. Adminstv. Com. Epiphany, Detroit, 1968; chmn. Com. Fund Raising Devel. Raffle, Mpls., 1984. Lt. USN, 1959-62. USN ROTC scholar, 1955-59; grantee Chrysler Corp., 1976-78. Mem. Am. Legion. Roman Catholic. Home: 6108 W 101st St Bloomington MN 55438 Office: Super Valu Stores Inc PO Box 990 Minneapolis MN 55440

PAYNE, JOHN W., communications executive; b. Washington, Mar. 29, 1946; s. John W. and Frances (Eberstadt) P.; m. Gail S. Payne, June 1, 1970; children: Jocelyn W., Brandt. BA in History, U. of South, 1969; MBA, Columbia U., 1977. Assoc. F. Eberstadt Co., N.Y.C., 1970-75; pres. Payne Broadcasting, Safford, Ariz., 1977-83, Celutel, Inc., Tucson, 1983—. Bd. dirs. Eberstadt Found., 1970—. With USNR, 1970-73. Mem. Univ. Club. Office: Celutel Inc 1994 N Kolb Rd Tucson AZ 85715

PAYNE, PAUL PATTON, personnel service company executive; b. Beckley, W.Va., July 4, 1934; s. Paul Patton and Orva (DePue) P.; m. Nancy Louise Howell, Aug. 10, 1957 (div. May 1969); children: Stephen Paul, Marshall Creel, Katherine Howell ; m. Ingrid Marie Payne, June 9, 1972. BSBA, U. N.C., 1956. Mgr. Purity Baking Co., Beckley, 1959-63; pres. DuPay Enterprises, Inc. dba ASOSA Pers., Tucson, 1964—; pres., dir. HSP Enterprises, Inc., Phoenix, 1967—; exec. v.p. dir. A Sus Ordenes, Mexico City, Mex., 1969—, Servi Temporal, 1976—; dir. Empire Bank, Tucson, 1988—, Kivona Corp., Tucson, 1972—; mem. employment adv. coun. State of Ariz., Phoenix, 1989—. Dir. Better Bus. Bur., So. Ariz., 1983-88; v.p. dir. Tucson Country Club Estates, Tucson, 1981-82; pres. San Rafael Neighborhood Assn., Tucson, 1967, 68; elder Christ Presbyn. Ch., Tucson, 1981-84. Lt. (j.g.), USN, 1956-59. Mem. Ariz. Assn. Pers. Consultants (pres. 1971, 77, 84), Nat. Assn. Pers. Consultants (cert., dir. 1971-73), Tucson Pers. Assn. (sec. 1965-66), VIP Club, Tucson Country Club, Rotary, Elks. Office: ASOSA Pers 1016 E Broadway Tucson AZ 85719

PAYNE, WILLIAM TAYLOR, JR., word processing and technical publications consultant; b. Bradshaw, W.Va. ; s. William Taylor and Clara Mae (Horn) P.; m. Joan M. Reinhardt ; children: Susan C., William Taylor III, Karen L. Student various USAF tech. courses, Keio U., Sch. Electronics, Balt., Comml. Radio Inst., Balt. Publs. engr. Westinghouse Electric Corp., Balt., Collins Radio Co., Cedar Rapids, Iowa; supr. tech. publs. Gen. Dynamics Corp., Rochester, N.Y.; supr. engring. writing Curtiss Wright Corp., East Patterson, N.J.; mgr. tech. publs. ACF Industries, Riverdale, Md.; services mgr. tech. publs. Bechtel Power Corp., Gaithersburg, Md. Contbr. articles to profl. jours. Served with USAF, Japan. Mem. Internat. Word Processing Assn., Research Inst. Am., Internat. Assn. Tech. Communication for Co. Communicators, Nat. Assn. Govt. Communicators, Soc. Tech. Communication. Home: PO Box 486 Lanham MD 20706

PAYTON, ROBERT DONALD See PROUD, ROBERT DONALD

PAYTON, ROGER EDWARD, president and chief executive officer; b. Aberfeldy, Scotland, Jan. 19, 1956; came to U.S., 1983; s. James Edward Allan and Ruth Millicent (Wiseman) P.; m. Debra Lyn Edwards, Nov. 8, 1986; children: Randi, Rian, Rikki. Grad. high sch. Various positions to dir. Pickfords Removals, Ltd., Enfield, Middlesex, UK, 1972-84; pres. Mchts. Home Delivery Scv., Oxnard, Calif., 1984-88; pres., chief exec. officer Allied Van Lines, Inc., Naperville, Ill., 1988—. Mem. Rep. Nat. Com., Calif., 1986-87. Recipient Profl. Competence award, Dept. Transport, UK. Mem. Rep. Nat. Com., Calif., 1986-87. Office: Allied Van Lines Inc 300 Park Pla Naperville IL 60540

PAYTON, THOMAS WILLIAM, corporate professional; b. Toronto, Ont., Can., Sept. 7, 1946. With Can. Imperial Bank of Commerce, Toronto; dir. Bramalea Ltd., Toronto, 1981-82, v.p., 1982-88, sr. v.p., 1988—; bd. dirs. Can.'s Wonderland, Coseka Resources Ltd. Office: Bramalea Ltd, 1867 Yonge St, Toronto, ON Canada M4S 1Y5

PEABODY, ALAN DOUGLAS, venture capitalist, entrepreneur, lawyer; b. Chelsea, Mass., June 29, 1952; s. Malburne Jewett and Anne Margaret (Harp) P. BA in History cum laude, Dartmouth Coll., 1974; postgrad., Vanderbilt U., 1974-75; JD, U. Va., 1977; MBA, U. Pa., 1982. Bar: Pa. 1977. Assoc. Ballard, Spahr, Andrews & Ingersoll, Phila., 1977-80; cons. Inco Venture Capital Mgmt. Co., N.Y.C., 1981-82; investment mgr. Inco Venture Capital Mgmt., N.Y.C., 1982-83; v.p. Inco Venture Capital Mgmt. Co., N.Y.C., 1983-84, sr. v.p., 1984—, prin., 1986—; bd. dirs. TVSM Acquisition Co., Inc. (Cable Guide), N.Y.C., Houston Biotech., Inc., The Woodlands, Tex., Quantum Computer Services, Inc., Vienna, Va., Dytel Corp., Schaumburg, Ill., Lang. Processors, Inc., Framingham, Mass.; bd. dirs., co-chmn. Hippocrates, Inc, Sausalito, Calif., 1986—. Mem. Nat. Venture Capital Assn., N.Y. Venture Capital Forum. Office: Inco Venture Capital Mgmt One New York Pla 37th Fl New York NY 10004

PEACE, H. W., II, oil company executive; b. Clinton, Okla., May 21, 1935; s. Herman Wilbern and Bernice (Mitchell) P.; m. Norma June Williams; children: Hugh William, Susannah Lee. BS in Geology, U. Okla., 1959, MS in Geology, 1964; postgrad., U. Southwest La., 1968. Jr. geologist Union Oil Co. Calif., Houston, 1964-65; area geologist Union Oil Co. Calif., Lafayette, La., 1965-70; geologist dist. exploration Union Oil Co. Calif., Oklahoma City, 1970-77; mgr. Rocky Mountain exploration Union Oil Co. Calif., Casper, Wyo., 1977-80; mgr. div. exploration Cotton Petroleum Corp., Tulsa, 1980-83; v.p. exploration Hadson Petroleum Corp., Oklahoma City, 1983-85, exec. v.p., chief operating officer, 1985-88, also bd. dirs.; exec. v.p., chief ops. officer Mosswood Oil and Gas Co., Oklahoma City, 1985-88; exec. v.p., chief ops. officer Anadarko Supply Co., Oklahoma City, 1986-88, also bd. dirs.; mng. ptnr. EXAD, Oklahoma City, 1988—. Dir. sch. geology adv. com. U. Oklahoma, Norman, 1984—, vice chmn., 1988-89, chmn. 1989—. Served to lt. (j.g.) USN, 1959-63, as capt. USNR, 1963-82, retired. Mem. Am. Assn. Petroleum Geology (rep. del. 1984—), Soc. Exploration Geophysicists, Soc. Econ. Paleontologists and Mineralogists, Wyo. Oil and Gas Assn., Tulsa Geol. Soc., Oklahoma City Geol. Soc. (chmn. profl. affairs 1976-77), Naval Res. Assn., Cherokee Hills Homeowners Assn. (pres. 1971-73), Fieldstone Homeowners Assn. (pres. 1983), Navy League. Republican. Lodge: Civitan. Office: EXAD 6161 N May Ave Ste 263 Oklahoma City OK 73112

PEACOCK, A(LVIN) WARD, textile company executive; b. Durham, N.C., June 17, 1929; s. Erle Ewart and Vera Louise (Ward) P.; m. Barbara Sheppard White, July 2, 1955; children: Alvin Ward, Stephen White, Nancy Lay. B.S. in Commerce, U. N.C., 1950; M.B.A., Harvard U., 1952. Asst. to v.p. Erwin Mills, Inc., Durham, 1953-55, sec., 1957-62, sec.-treas., 1962-64; v.p. Dixie Yarns, Inc., Chattanooga, 1964-76, sr. v.p., 1976-81; sr. v.p. Springs Industries, Fort Mill, S.C., 1981-86; exec. v.p. Springs Industries, Fort Mill, 1986—; bd. dirs. Am. Mfg. Co., Chattanooga; regional dir. First Wachovia Corp., Charlotte, N.C. Trustee Holston Conf. Colls., Tenn., 1968-79; dir. Chattanooga Meml. Hosp., 1979-81; chmn. Hamilton County chpt., ARC, 1975-77; dir. Allied Arts Fund, 1978-81; mem. Chattanooga Wastewater Regulation Bd., 1978-81. Served to 1st lt. USAF, 1955-57. Mem. Tenn. Mfrs. Assn. (chmn. bd. 1980-81), Chattanooga Mfrs. Assn. (pres. 1968-69), Am. Textile Mfrs. Inst., University Club, Mountain City Club, River Hills Club, Phi Beta Kappa, Alpha Kappa Psi, Sigma Nu. Republican. Methodist. Home: 22 Wood Hollow Rd Lake Wylie SC 29710 Office: Springs Industries Inc 205 N White St Fort Mill SC 29715

PEAPPLES, GEORGE ALAN, automotive executive; b. Benton Harbor, Mich., Nov. 6, 1940; s. Arthur L. and Kathleen C. (Peters) P.; m. Rebecca

Dean Sowers, June 27, 1962; children: Lucia Christine, Sarah Bouton. BA in Econs., U. Mich., 1962, MBA in Fin., 1963. Fin. analyst Gen. Motors Corp., Detroit, 1964-68; dir. capital analysis and investment N.Y.C., 1968-73; asst. div. comptroller Delco Moraine div. Dayton, Ohio, 1973-75; asst. treas. bank relations Detroit, 1975-77, asst. comptroller, 1980-82; group dir. strategic bus. planning Chevrolet-Pontiac-Canada group Warren, Mich., 1984-86; v.p. Detroit, 1986—; v.p., fin. mgr. Gen. Motors of Can., Ltd., Oshawa, Ont., 1982-84, pres., gen. mgr., 1986—; asst. sec. of Navy U.S. Dept. Def., 1977-80; mem. Bus. Council on Nat. Issues, Can.-Am. Com., Premier's Council on Tech. Innovation; mem. adv. com. U. Western Ont. Bd. of govs. Jr. Achievement of Can. Recipient Disting. Pub. Service award, Washington, 1980. Office: GM/Can Ltd, 215 William St E, Oshawa, ON Canada L1G 1K7 also: GM Gen Motors Bldg Detroit MI 48202

PEARCE, BETTY MCMURRAY, manufacturing company executive; b. Hastings, Nebr., Oct. 11, 1926; d. Frank Madry and Scereta (Mudd) McMurray; B.S. in Aerospace, U. Tex., Austin, 1949; 1 dau., Karen A. Harsley. Draftsman, Koch & Fowler, Civil Engrs., Dallas, 1945-47; with LTV-APG-AMSD Corp., Dallas, 1949—, project engr., 1955-77, engring. project mgr., 1977-83, dir. engring., 1983—; dir. LTV Fed. Credit Union, v.p. LTV Mgmt. Club; cons. Active Aux. St. Joseph's Hosp.; pres., St. Andrews Catholic Ch. Council, Fort Worth, 1977-78; mem. Bishop's Adv. Council Fort Worth Diocese, 1980-87, chmn. service com., 1980-81, pres., 1981-82, 84-85; mem. Allied Communities of Tarrant, 1982—. Mem. AIAA, Tech. Mktg. Soc. Am. Home: 4205 Galway Ave Fort Worth TX 76109 Office: PO Box 225907 Dallas TX 75265

PEARCE, HARRY JONATHAN, lawyer; b. Bismarck, N.D., Aug. 20, 1942; s. William R. and Jean Katherine (Murray) P.; m. Katherine B. Bruk, June 19, 1967; children: Shannon P., Susan J., Harry M. BS, USAF Acad., Colorado Springs, Colo., 1964; JD, Northwestern U., 1967. Bar: N.D. 1967, Mich. 1986. Mcpl. judge City of Bismarck, 1970-76, U.S. magistrate, 1970-77, police commr., 1976-80; sr. ptnr. Pearce & Durick, Bismarck, 1970-85; assoc. gen. counsel GM, Detroit, 1985-87, v.p., gen. counsel, 1987—. Mem. vis. com. sch. law Northwestern U. Capt. USAF, 1964-70. Hardy scholar Northwestern U., Chgo., 1964-67. Fellow Am. Coll. Trial Lawyers, Internat. Soc. Barristers; mem. Am. Law Inst., Mich. Gen. Counsels Assn. Office: GM 3031 W Grand Blvd PO Box 33122 Detroit MI 48232

PEARCE, PAUL KIRBY, banking executive; b. Childress, Tex., Mar. 22, 1955; s. F. Archie and Peggy Jo (Kirby) P.; m. Sherri Elaine Riddle, May 5, 1979; children: Seth, Adam. BBA, Okla. State U., 1977; MBA with honors, Okla. City U., 1982. Customer account rep. Ford Motor Credit Co., Okla. City, 1977-80; asst. v.p. Security Nat. Bank, Duncan, Okla., 1980-83; v.p. Am. Nat. Bank, Duncan, 1983-87, exec. v.p., 1987—; instr. banking Red River Vo-Tech, Duncan, 1981-83, acctg. Cameron U., Lawton, Okla., 1985, bus. law U. Arts and Scis., Chickasha, Okla., 1986—. Pres. Duncan United Way, 1986; dr. chmn. 1985. Mem. Duncan C. of C. (small bus. chmn. 1984, retail trade chmn. 1986, Leadership award 1983), Duncan Jaycees (bd. dirs. 1983, v.p. 1984, Officer of Yr. 1983, 84). Democrat. Mem. Christian Ch. Home: 2609 Virginia Duncan OK 73533 Office: Am Nat Bank PO Box 750010 Duncan OK 73575

PEARCE, THEODORE DELANEY, insurance company executive; b. Vigus, Mo., Jan. 30, 1934; s. James McMellon and Serena (Williams) P.; m. Mary Yvonne Leis, Feb. 12, 1966; children: James, Trudy. BA, U. Mo., 1959. Chartered property and casualty underwriter, CLU. Casualty spl. agt. Ins. Co. N.Am., Dallas, 1963-65; agt. Great Am. Res., Longview, Tex., 1965-66; agt. Employers Ins. of Tex., Ft. Worth, 1966-69, dist. sales mgr., 1969-71; adminstrv. mgr. Employers ins. of Tex., Dallas, 1971-73; dist. mgr. Employers Ins. of Tex., Midland, 1973-84, Dallas, 1974—; rancher Callahan County, Tex.; pres. Greenwood Water Supply Corp., Midland, 1981-82. Mem. Greenwood Ind. Sch. Bd., Midland, 1982-83; mem. curriculum com. Red Oak (Tex.) Ind. Sch. Dist.; alderman City of Pecan Hill, Tex., 1987—; bd. dirs. Red Oak Creek Civic Assn., 1987—. Paul Harris fellow Midland Rotary Club, 1981. Mem. Charter Property and Casualty Underwriters (treas. Lubbock, Tex. 1975-76). Republican. Baptist. Club: Oak Cliff (Tex.) Country. Lodge: Rotary. Home: Rte 2 PO Box 195E Waxahachie TX 75165 Office: Employers Ins Tex PO Box 152009 Irving TX 75015-2009

PEARCE, TOM FINLEY, finance planning company executive; b. Victoria, Tex., Nov. 4, 1941; s. Hailds Robert and Sue Finley Pearce; m. Janet Ann, Mar. 21, 1981; children: Greg, Jennifer. BBA in Acctg., North Tex. State U., 1965. Project mgr. Vought Corp., Dallas, 1970-77, mgr. applications, 1974-77; systems cons. Arco Oil & Gas Co., Dallas, 1977-81, dir. fin., 1981-86; pres. Pearce Capital Mgmt., 1986—. Pres. Plano (Tex.) Homeowners Assn., 1985-86. Recipient Outstanding Achievement award Vought Corp., 1972, Exceptional Contbn. award Arco Oil & Gas Co., 1986. Mem. Am. Mgmt. Assn., Data Processing Mgmt. Assn., Dallas Tennis Assn. (bd. dirs. 1977-78), Los Rios Tennis Assn. (bd. dirs. 1983-84). Home: 2600 Skipwith Plano TX 75023

PEARL, CARLETON DAY, fast food chain executive; b. N.Y.C.; s. G. Carleton and Margaret (Scheuer) P.; m. Judith A. Weatherston, 1969. BA, Colgate U., 1965; MBA, NYU, 1967. V.p. Bankers Trust Co., N.Y.C., 1968-75; v.p., gen. mgr. Bankers Trust Internat. (Midwest), Chgo., 1974-77; dir. internat. fin. McDonald's, 1978, assist. v.p., mng. dir. internat. fin., 1981, v.p. fin., 1981, v.p. pres., treas., 1987—. Served to lt. comdr.USCGR, 1967-71. Democrat. Episcopalian. Office: McDonald's Corp McDonald's Plaza Oak Brook IL 60521

PEARLMAN, JERRY KENT, electronics company executive; b. Des Moines, Mar. 27, 1939; s. Leo R. Pearlman; married; children: Gregory, Neal. B.A., Princeton U., 1960; M.B.A., Harvard U., 1962. With Ford Motor Co., 1962-70; v.p. fin. dir. Behring Corp., 1970-71; controller Zenith Electronics Corp., Glenview, Ill., 1971-74, v.p., 1972-74, v.p. fin., 1974-78, sr. v.p. fin., 1978-81, sr. v.p. fin., group exec., 1981-83, pres., chief exec. officer, 1983—, chmn., 1984—, also dir.; dir. Stone Container Corp., First Chgo. Corp. Dir. Evanston (Ill.) Hosp.; trustee Mus. Sci. and Industry, Northwestern U. Office: Zenith Electronics Corp 1000 Milwaukee Ave Glenview IL 60025 *

PEARLMAN, LOUIS JAY, aviation and advertising company executive; b. Flushing, N.Y., June 19, 1954; s. Herman and Reenie (Nevler) P. BA, Queens Coll., 1976; MBA, Century U., 1980; Degree in Sales Mgmt., SUNY, Buffalo, 1980; PhD in Bus. Adminstrn., Centruy U., 1983. Pres. Commuter Helicopter Corp., N.Y.C., 1974-75; pres., chief operating officer Trans Continental Airlines, Inc., N.Y.C., 1975—; gen. mgr. U.S. Westdeutsche Luftwerbung GmbH, N.Y.C., 1976-85; chmn., pres., chief exec. officer Airship Internat. Ltd., N.Y.C., 1982—, bd. dirs., 1985—; cons. Queens Coll., CUNY, 1977—; bd. dirs. Fed. Airlines Corp., N.Y.C. Author: Survey and Analysis of the Airline Industry, 1983; song writer. Active Mitchell-Linden Civic Assn., Flushing, 1980-82, Kissimmee (Fla.) Mcpl. Airport, 1985—. Mem. U.S. Power Squadron, Wings Club (disting., recipient Lighter-than-Air award 1987), Lighter-than-Air Soc. (hon.), Young Entrepreneurs Am., Young Millionaires Club, Internat. Air Transport Assn., Blimp Port U.S.A. (pres. 1987—). Home: One Bay Club Dr PH-V Bayside NY 11360 Office: Airship Internat Ltd/ Trans Continental Airlines Inc 500 Fifth Ave Ste 2505 New York NY 10110

PEARLSTINE, NORMAN, newspaper editor; b. Phila., Oct. 4, 1942; s. Raymond and Gladys (Cohen) P.; m. Nancy Colbert Friday, 1988. A.B., Haverford Coll., 1964; LL.B., U. Pa., 1967. Staff reporter Wall Street Jour., Dallas, Detroit, Los Angeles, 1968-73; Tokyo bur. chief Wall Street Jour., 1973-76; mng. editor Asian Wall Street Jour., Hong Kong, 1976-78; exec. editor Forbes Mag., Los Angeles, 1978-80; nat. news editor Wall Street Jour., N.Y.C., 1980-82; editor, pub. Wall St. Jour./Europe, Brussels, 1982-83; mng. editor, v.p. Wall Street Jour., N.Y.C., 1983—. Mem. ABA, D.C. Bar Assn., N.Y. Hist. Soc. (chmn. and trustee), Council on Fgn. Relations, Haverford Coll. (bd. mgrs.), Am. Soc. Newspaper Editors. Office: Wall St Jour World Fin Ctr 200 Liberty St New York NY 10281

PEARSALL, ROSELLEN DEE, insurance executive; b. Ft. Dix, N.J., Aug. 15, 1945; d. Raymond Donald and Rosemary (Dannenberg) P. BS in Nursing, U. Ky., 1967. RN U. Ky. Med. Ctr., Lexington, 1967-68; RN Cardiac Care Unit Cedars of Lebanon Hosp., Los Angeles, 1968-69; rehab. nurse cons. Employers Ins. of Wausau, Los Angeles, 1969-76; asst. v.p. rehab. services Fremont Compensation Ins. Co., Los Angeles, 1976—; ins. adv. bd. Casa Colina Inc., Pomona, Calif., 1984—. Recipient Cert. Achievement in Bus. and Industry Los Angeles YWCAs, 1978, 80. Mem. Nat. Assn. Rehab. Profls. in the Pvt. Sector (legis. chair Calif.), Nat. Rehab. Assn. (pres. So. Calif. chpt. 1979-80, Outstanding Achievement award 1981), Rehab. Nurses Soc. (founding pres. 1972-74, Outstanding Services award 1980, Greatest Support award 1984-85), Ins. Rehab. Study Group. Club: Los Angeles Athletic. Office: Fremont Compensation Ins Co 1709 W 8th St Los Angeles CA 90017

PEARSON, G(EORGE) BURTON, JR., retired trust company executive; b. Middletown, Del., Aug. 8, 1905; s. George Burton and Mary Estelle (Cochran) P.; m. Mary Isbella Turner, June 27, 1941 (dec. Nov. 1962); children: Isabella Turner Pearson Ryan, Margaret Cochran Pearson; m. Edith duPont Riegel, Jan. 4, 1968. AB magna cum laude, Princeton U., 1927; JD, U. Pa., 1931; LLD (hon.), U. Del., 1988. Bar: Del., 1931, U.S. Supreme Ct. 1936. Law clk. Hon. Victor B. Woolley, U.S. Ct. Appeals (3d cir.), 1930-31; assoc. atty. Law Office Hugh M. Morris, Wilmington, Del., 1931-39; vice chancellor State of Del., 1939-46; assoc. judge including Del. Supreme Ct., 1946-50; sr. v.p., dir., chmn. trust com. Wilmington Trust Co., Del., 1950-70, assoc. dir., mem. trust com., 1970—; mem. adv. bd. Del. Bank, 1959-69. Trustee U. Del., Newark, 1951—, Tower Hill Sch., Wilmington, 1962-73; mem. Newark Spl. Sch. Dist., 1933-41; trustee, now pres. Unidel Found., Inc., Wilmington. Mem. Del. Bar Assn., ABA, Am. Law Inst., SAR, Soc. Colonial Wars, Soc. of Cin., Chevalier du Tastevin, Alliance Francaise. Clubs: Wilmington (past bd. dirs.), Wilmington Country, Greenville Country, Fishers Island Country, Fishers Island Yacht, Mill Reef. Avocations: travel, foreign languages, education. Home: PO Box 68 Montchanin DE 19710

PEARSON, LOUISE MARY, retired manufacturing company executive; b. Inverness, Scotland, Dec. 14, 1919 (parents Am. citizens); d. Louis Houston and Jessie M. (McKenzie) Lenox; grad. high sch.; m. Nels Kenneth Pearson, June 28, 1941; children—Lorine Pearson Walters, Karla. Dir. Wauconda Tool & Engring. Co., Inc., Algonquin, Ill., 1950-86; reporter Oak Leaflet, Crystal Lake, Ill., 1944-47, Sidelights, Wilmette, Ill., 1969-72, 79-82. Active Girl Scouts U.S.A., 1955-65. Recipient award for appreciation work with Girl Scouts, 1965. Clubs: Antique Automobile of Am. (Hershey, Pa.); Veteran Motor Car (Boston); Classic Car of Am. (Madison, N.J.). Home: 125 Dole Ave Crystal Lake IL 60014

PEARSON, NATHAN WILLIAMS, investment management executive; b. N.Y.C., Nov. 26, 1911; s. James A. and Elizabeth (Williams) P.; m. Kathleen P. McMurtry, Apr. 9, 1947; children: James S. (dec.), Nathan Williams. A.B., Dartmouth Coll., 1932; M.B.A., Harvard, 1934; LL.D., Thiel Coll., 1972. With U.S. Steel Corp., 1939-42; mgr. research Matson Navigation Co., 1946-47; controller Carborundum Co., 1947-48; with T. Mellon and Sons, Pitts., 1948-70; v.p., gov. T. Mellon and Sons, 1957-70; fin. exec. for Paul Mellon, 1948—; dir. Chgo. Dock and Canal Trust, State St. Growth Fund, State St. Investment Corp, State Exchange Fund; chmn., chief exec. officer Mellon Nat. Corp. and Mellon Bank (N.A.), 1987, now chmn. emeritus. Served from lt. (j.g.) to comdr. USNR, 1942-46. Republican. Presbyterian. Clubs: Duquesne, Allegheny Country, Edgeworth, Harvard-Yale-Princeton (Pitts.); Racquet and Tennis (N.Y.C.); Laurel Valley Golf, Rolling Rock (Ligonier, Pa). Home: 10 Woodland Rd Sewickley PA 15143 Office: Mellon Bank Corp 525 William Penn Pl Pittsburgh PA 15230

PEARSON, NORMAN, planning consultant, writer; b. Stanley, County Durham, Eng., Oct. 24, 1928; arrived in Can., 1954. Joseph and Mary (Pearson) P., m. Gerda Maria Josefine Reidl, July 25, 1972. BA with honors in Town and Country Planning, U. Durham (Eng.), 1951; PhD in Land Economy, Internat. Inst. Advanced Studies, 1979; MBA, Pacific Western U., Colo., 1980, DBA, 1982; PhD In Mgmt. Calif. U. for Advanced Studies, 1986—. Cons. to Stanley Urban Dist. Council, U.K., 1946-47; planning asst. Accrington Town Plan and Bedford County Planning Survey, U. Durham Planning Team, 1947-49; planning asst. to Allen and Mattocks, cons. planners and landscape designers, Newcastle upon Tyne, U.K., 1949-51; adminstrv. asst. Scottish Div., Nat. Coal Bd., Scotland, 1951-52; planning asst. London County Council, U.K., 1953-54; planner Central Mortgage and Housing Corp., Ottawa, Ont., Can., 1954-55; planning analyst City of Toronto Planning Bd., 1955-56; dir. of planning Hamilton Wentworth Planning Area Bd., Hamilton, Ont., Can., 1956-59; dir. planning for Burlington (Ont.) and Suburban Area Planning Bd., 1959-62, also commr. planning, 1959-62; pres. Tanfield Enterprises Ltd., London, Ont., Can., 1962—, Norman Pearson & Assocs. Ltd., Can., 1962—, Internat. Planning Mgmt. Cons.; cons. in urban, rural and regional planning, 1962—; life mem. U.S. Com. for Monetary Research and Edn., 1976—; spl. lectr. in planning McMaster U., Hamilton, 1956-64, Waterloo (Ont.) Luth. U., 1961-63; asst. prof. geography and planning U. Waterloo (Ont.), 1963-67; assoc. prof. geography U. Guelph (Ont.), 1967-72, chmn., dir. Ctr. for Resource Devel.; prof. polit. sci. U. Western Ont., London, 1972-77; adj. prof. of ecological planning and land econs. Internat. Inst. for Advanced Studies, Clayton, Mo., 1980—; core faculty Doctoral Program in Mgmt. Walden U., Mpls., 1986—, chair adminstrn.-mgmt., 1989—; mem. bd. regents Calif. U. for Advanced Studies, Petaluma, 1987; mem. Social Scis., Econ. and Legal Aspects Com. of Research Adv. Bd. Internat. Joint Commn., 1972-76; cons. to City of Waterloo, 1973-76, Province of Ont., 1969-70; adviser to Georgian Bay Regional Devel. Council, 1968-72; real estate appraiser, province of Ont., 1976—; pres., chmn. bd. govs. Pacific Western U., Canada, 1983-84; with faculty adminstn./mgmt. dept., PhD program Walden U., Mpls., 1985—. Pres. Unitarian Ch. of Hamilton, 1960-61. Served with RAF, 1951-53. Knight of Grace, Sovereign Order St. John of Jerusalem. Fellow Royal Town Planning Inst. (Bronze medal award 1957), Royal Econ. Soc.; mem. Internat. Soc. City and Regional Planners, Am., Canadian insts. planners, Canadian Polit. Sci. Assn. L'Association Internationale des Ingenieurs et des Docteurs ès Sciences Appliquées à l'Industrie. Clubs: Empire; Ontario; University (London). Author: (with others) An Inventory of Joint Programmes and Agreements Affecting Canada's Renewable Resources, 1964. Editor, coauthor (with others) Regional and Resource Planning in Canada, 1963, rev. edit., 1970; editor (with others) The Pollution Reader, 1968. Contbr. numerous articles on town planning to profl. jours. and chpts. in field to books. Office: PO Box 5362, Station A, London, ON Canada N6A 4L6

PEARSON, P. A. (LEE), marine consultant; b. Phoenix, June 23, 1939; d. David Samuel and Margaret (Holtzman) Hamburger; divorced; 1 child, Stuart Deene. Student, Glendale Coll., 1963-64, Yacht Design Inst., 1975-76. Surveyor, cons. Lenders Yacht Mfrs. Ins. Co., 1974—; prin. Pearson Enterprises, Seabrook, Tex., 1974-79, 1982—. Instr. USCG Aux. Mem. Soc. Naval Architects/Marine Engrs., Soc. Small Craft Designers, Am. Boat and Yacht Coun., Mensa (Most Outstanding Art award), Boat U.S. Tech. Exch., Soc. Accredited Marine Surveyors. Democrat. Office: Pearson Enterprises PO Box 580547 Houston TX 77258

PEARSON, RICHARD JARVIS, diversified manufacturing company executive; b. Chgo., June 3, 1925; s. Andrall E. and Dorothy M. (MacDonald) P.; m. Janice Lee Pope, Mar. 2, 1951; 1 child, Douglas R. BA, U. So. Calif., 1946; MBA, Harvard U., 1947. Dir. mktg. Bireley's, Hollywood, Calif., 1947-55; dir. mktg. Forest Lawn Meml. Park, Glendale, Calif., 1955-57, Revell, Inc., Venice, Calif., 1957-60; dir. mktg. Avery Label Co., Monrovia, Calif., 1960-64, v.p., gen. mgr., 1964-70; group v.p. Avery Internat., San Marino, Calif., 1970-76, exec. v.p., 1976-81; exec. v.p., chief operating officer Avery Internat., Pasadena, Calif., 1981-83, pres., chief operating officer, 1983—; bd. dirs. Ameron, Inc., Monterey Park, Calif., Ducommun, Inc., Los Angeles. Chmn. United Way, 1982-83; bd. dirs. Boy Scouts Am., 1983-84; bd. dirs. Am. Heart Assn., 1986—; trustee Ponoma Coll., 1988—. Served to lt. (j.g.) USN, 1946. Mem. Merchants and Mfrs. Assn. (bd. dirs. 1986—). Republican. Presbyterian. Clubs: Annandale, Calif., PGA West. Home: 1046 Oak Grove Pl San Marino CA 91108 Office: Avery Corp 150 N Orange Grove Blvd Box 7090 Pasadena CA 91103

PEARSON, WILLIAM JAMES, finance company executive; b. Ogdensburg, N.Y., Jan. 31, 1938; s. John A. and Mary (McDonald) P.; m. Deborah A. DeOrsey, Dec. 30, 1983. BA in History and English, Hamilton Coll., 1960. Various positions N.Y. Telephone, Kingston, 1960-66, comml. mgr., 1966-70; mgr. personnel adminstrn. Paul Revere Ins. Group, Worcester, Mass., 1970-72; mgr. personnel Paul Revere Ins. Group, Worcester, 1972-74, 2nd v.p., dir. personnel, 1974-79, v.p. human resources, 1979-87; sr. v.p. human resources Avco Fin. Services, Irvine, Calif., 1987—. Mem. Am. Soc. Personnel Adminstrn. (nat. govt. affairs com. 1979-83, nat. chmn. 1987), Personnel Mgmt. Assn. (exec. com. 1987). Home: 21 Terraza Del Mar Dana Point CA 92629 Office: Avco Fin Svcs Inc 3349 Michelson Dr Irvine CA 92715

PEASBACK, DAVID R., recruiting company executive. 1 child, Jennifer. B.A., Colgate U., 1955; LL.B., U. Va., 1961. Mgmt. trainee Proctor & Gamble, N.Y.C., 1955-56; assoc. Covington & Burling, Washington, 1961-64; litigation counsel Litton Industries, Inc., Beverly Hills, Calif., 1965-67; v.p. Bangor Punta Ops., Greenwich, Conn., 1968-71; assoc. Heidrick and Struggles, N.Y.C., 1972-76, ptnr., 1976-88, pres., chief exec. officer, 1983-87; pres., chief exec. officer Canny, Bowen, Inc. (exec. recruiting firm), N.Y.C., 1988—. Served as sgt. USMC, 1956-58. Office: Canny Bowen Inc 425 Park Ave New York NY 10022

PEASE, LEROY THAYER, JR., credit company executive; b. Summit, N.J., Aug. 5, 1924; m. Dorothy A. Ahern, Feb. 15, 1947. BS, U. Pa., 1949. Sr. v.p., dir. Sears Roebuck Acceptance Corp., Greenville, Del., 1980—. Mem. Fin. Execs. Inst. (chpt. v.p. 1984-85, bd. dirs. 1982-85). Lodge: Rotary. Office: Sears Roebuck Acceptance Corp PO Box 4680 Greenville DE 19807

PEASE, WALTER LEON, technology company executive; b. Corning, N.Y., Oct. 9, 1950; s. Gerald A. and Helen L (Manning) P.; m. Joan Elizabeth Rickert, Aug. 4, 1973; children: Joel L., Matthew S. BS in Engring., Bucknell U., 1972; MBA, U. Pitts., 1973; MS in Econs., Lehigh U., 1981. Engr. Consol. Natural Gas Corp., Pitts., 1973-76; fin. analyst Carpenter Tech. Corp., Reading, Pa., 1976-80, mgr. cash mgmt., 1980—. Councilman, Wyomissing Hills Borough Coun., Pa., 1987—. Republican. Home: 55 Downing Dr Wyomissing Hills PA 19610 Office: Carpenter Tech Corp 101 W Bern St Reading PA 19603

PEASLAND, BRUCE RANDALL, financial executive; b. Buffalo, N.Y., Mar. 24, 1945; s. Kenneth Arthur and Edith Grace (Bristow) P.; m. Debra Myers Peasland, June 13, 1981; children: Michael John, Timothy Scott, Amanda Jean. BBA, U. So. Calif., 1971, MBA in Fin., 1978; JD, Western St. U., 1983. Price and cost analyst McDonnell Douglas Corp., Long Beach, Calif., 1966-70; mgr. cost accountant The Gillette Co., Santa Monica, Calif., 1971-78; controller Lear Siegler Inc., Santa Ana, Calif., 1978-85, British Petroleum, Hitco, Newport Beach, Calif., 1986-87; v.p. fin., dir. Control Components Inc., Rancho Santa Margarita, Calif., 1987—; dir., sec. Koson B.V., The Hague, Netherlands, 1987—. Youth advisor YMCA, Dana Point, Calif., 1985—. With USMC, 1963-69. Recipient of Mgr. of Yr. award Nat. Mgmt. Assn., 1984. Fellow U. So. Calif. MBA Assn.; mem. Nat. Assn. of Accts., Nat. Mgmt. Assn. (dir. 1978-85), U. So. Calif. Trojan Club, U. So. Calif. Alumni Club. Republican. Episcopalian. Home: 25211 Yacht Dr Dana Point CA 92629 Office: Control Components Inc 22591 Avenida Empresa Rancho Santa Margarita CA 92688

PEATROSS, WILLIAM CAMPBELL, title company executive; b. Shreveport, La., Sept. 15, 1943; s. Sydney Kerley and Margaret (Brinkmann) P.; m. Farron Francis Goodell, Aug. 23, 1968; children: Scott Brinkmann, Nelson Kellerman. BA, La. State U., 1965, JD, 1968. V.p. Caddo Abstract & Title Co., Inc., Shreveport, 1968-74, pres., 1974—; bd. dirs. Comml. Nat. Bank, Comml. Nat. Corp. Past chmn. Downtown Devel. Authority, Shreveport, 1987; vice chmn. Shreveport Airport Authority, 1988—; past pres. Biomed. Rsch. Found., Shreveport, 1988—; chmn. State of La. Econ. Devel. Corp. Named one of Outstanding Young Men in Am., Shreveport Jaycees, 1980. Fellow Am. Coll. Mortgage Attys.; mem. ABA, Am. Land Title Assn. Democrat. Presbyterian. Home: 554 Longleaf Shreveport LA 71106 Office: Caddo Abstract & Title Co Inc PO Box 126 Shreveport LA 71120

PEAVY, HOMER LOUIS, JR., real estate executive, accountant; b. Okmulgee, Okla., Sept. 4, 1924; s. Homer Louis and Hattie Lee (Walker) P.; children: Homer Martin, Daryl Mark. Student Kent State U., 1944-49; grad. Hammel-Actual Coll., 1962. Sales supr. Kirby Sales, Akron, Ohio, 1948-49; sales mgr. Williams-Kirby Co., Detroit, 1949-50; area distributor Peavy-Kirby Co., Phila., 1953-54; salesman James L. Peavy Realty Co., Akron, 1954-65; owner Homer Louis Peavy, Jr., Real Estate Broker, Akron, 1965—; pvt. practice acctg., Akron, 1962—; fin. aid officer Buckeye Coll., Akron, 1982. Author: Watt Watts, 1969; poet: Magic of the Muse, 1978, P.S. I Love You, 1982; contbr. poetry to Am. Poetry Anthology, 1983, New Worlds Unlimited, 1984, Treasures of the Precious Moments, 1985, Our World's Most Cherished Poems, 1985; songs: Sh...Sh, Sheree, Sheree, 1976, In Akron O, 1979; teleplay: Revenge, 1980. Bd. dirs. Internat. Elvis Gold Soc., 1978—; charter mem. Statue of Liberty-Ellis Island Found., 1984, Nat. Mus. of Women in Arts, 1986; mem. Nat. Trust for Hist. Preservation. Recipient Am. Film Inst. Cert. Recognition, 1982, Award of Merit cert. World of Poetry 10th ann. contest, 1985, Golden Poet award World of Poetry, 1985, 87, 88. Mem. Ohioana Library Assn., Internat. Black Writers Conf., Acad. Am. Poets, Manuscript Club Akron, Internat. Platform Assn., Ohio Theatre Alliance, Kent State U. Alumni Assn. Democrat. Home and Office: 1160 Cadillac Blvd Akron OH 44320

PECHERSKY, PAUL N., infosystems executive; b. Pitts.; s. Louis and Mildred Pechersky; m. Diane, May 25, 1968; children: Marc, Bryan. BS, Duquesne U., 1964; MS, Am. U., 1977. Fin. mgr. Sears, Roebuck & Co., Phila., 1964-68, programmer, analyst, 1968-70; supr. analyst Temple U., Phila., 1970-71; asst. dir. info. systems Georgetown U., Washington, 1972-77; dir. MIS, Harris Corp., Dallas, 1977-81; corp. dir MIS, E-Systems Inc., Dallas, 1981—; mem. CALS steering com. Nat. Security Indsl. Assn., Washington, 1986—; info. tech. com. Aerospace Industries Assn., Washington, 1988—. mem. exec. systems planning com. Am. Heart Assn., Dallas, 1986—; industry adv. bd. U. No. Tex., Denton, chmn. 1988—. Mem. Dallas Soc. for Info. Mgmt. (founding, chmn. 1988—). Office: E-Systems Inc PO Box 660248 Dallas TX 75266-0248

PECHMAN, JOSEPH AARON, economist; b. N.Y.C., Apr. 2, 1918; s. Gershon and Lena (Pechman) P.; m. Sylvia Massow, Sept. 29, 1943; children: Ellen Massow, Jane Elizabeth. B.S., CCNY, 1937; M.A., U. Wis., 1938, Ph.D., 1942, LL.D. (hon.), 1978. Statistician Nat. Research Project, Phila., 1937; research asst. econs. U. Wis., 1937-38, research assoc., 1939-41; asst. dir. Wis. income tax study Wis. Tax. Commn., 1938-39; economist OPA, 1941-42; tax adv. staff Treasury Dept., 1946-53; assoc. prof. finance Sch. Indsl. Mgmt., M.I.T., 1953-54; economist Council Econ. Advisers, 1954-56, Com. Econ. Devel., 1956-60; exec. dir. studies govt. finance Brookings Instn., 1960-69, sr. fellow, 1960-88, dir. econ. studies, 1962-83, sr. fellow emeritus, 1988—; Arnold Bernhard vis. prof. Williams Coll., 1988; Irving Fisher research prof. Yale, 1965-66; cons. Council Econ. Advisers, Treasury Dept., 1961-68; fellow Center for Advanced Study in Behavioral Scis., 1975-76. Author: Federal Tax Policy, 5th edit., 1987, (with Henry Aaron and Michael Tausig) Social Security: Perspectives for Reform, 1968, (with Benjamin Okner) Who Bears the Tax Burden?, 1974, (with George Break) Federal Tax Reform: The Impossible Dream?, 1975, Who Paid the Taxes, 1966-85, 1985, Tax Reform, The Rich and the Poor, 1989; contbr. numerous articles, reports in field. Served with AUS, 1942-45. Fellow Am. Econ. Assn. (bd. editors 1960-63, exec. com. 1972-74, v.p. 1978, pres. 1989, Disting. Fellow 1985); mem. Am. Acad. Arts and Scis., Phi Beta Kappa. Home: 7112 Wilson Ln Bethesda MD 20817 Office: Brookings Instn 1775 Massachusetts Ave NW Washington DC 20036

PECHTER, RICHARD S., finance company executive. Mng. dir. Donaldson, Lufkin & Jenrette, Inc., N.Y.C., also chmn. fin. svcs. group. Office: Donaldson Lufkin & Jenrette Inc 120 Broadway New York NY 10271 *

PECK, ANNE ELLIOTT ROBERTS, estates and trust specialist; b. N.Y.C., Dec. 17, 1935; d. James Ragan and Jane Ziegler (Elliott) Roberts; m. George Linn Davis, May 29, 1955 (div. Aug. 1967); children: James Roberts, Elliott Britton, George Linn Jr., William Vaughn (dec.); m. Robert Gray Peck III, Oct. 24, 1969; children: Andrew Adams, Matthew Canfield

Roberts. BA in English with honors, Wellesley Coll., 1957; MA with honors in Comparative Lit., Columbia U., 1966; postgrad. Villanova U., 1978-80, U. Bridgeport, 1988 Bus. Law and Corp. Fin. diploma, The Phila. Inst., 1988. Contbg. editor "Newsfront" mag., 1960-63; English tchr. The Masters Sch., Dobbs Ferry, N.Y., 1963-65; sports feature writer Westchester-Rockland newspapers, Gannett chain, White Plains, N.Y., 1969-70; corr., weekly column Knickerbocker News-Union Star, Capital Newspapers, Hearst chain, Albany, N.Y., 1971-73; public and exec. tax preparer H & R Block, Inc., Wayne, Pa., 1976-79; sr. estate planning trust officer Provident Nat. Bank-Trust div. PNC Fin. Corp., Phila., 1981-86; asst. v.p., new bus. devel. div., trusts and investments dept. Mellon Bank East N.A., 1986-87; asst v.p., trust officer People's Bank, Stamford, Conn., 1987-88; estates legal asst. estates dept. Pepper, Hamilton and Scheetz, Berwyn, Pa., 1988; pres., ptnr. ChoirMaster, Inc., 1988—. Mem. Mus. Art and Sci., Schenectady, N.Y., 1960-68; asst. producer Poetry, Channel 25-TV, N.Y.C.; bd. dirs., legis. chmn. Greenacres Sch. PTA, 1967-69; public relations chmn. Planned Parenthood League, Schenectady; sec., parliamentarian N.Y. State Legis. Forum, 1971-73; pres. The Career Group, Phila., 1983-85; editor directory St. David's Ch., 1976, mem. exec. com. every-member canvass, 1977; ann. fair gates-keeper Episcopal Diocese Phila., 1974-80, rep. Merion Deanery; on-screen TV panel moderator Access, Channel 17, Albany-Schenectady-Troy, N.Y.; maj. gift solicitor Planned Parenthood Southeastern Pa., 1975-76; mem. plant sale exec. com. Haverford Sch., 1976, 77; Republican pollchecker Tredyffrin Twp., 1978, 79; majority insp. of elections Tredyffrin Twp. E-2, 1980—. Recipient prize Coll. Bd. Contest Mademoiselle mag., 1954; Prix de Paris, Vogue mag., 1957. Mem. DAR (bd. mgrs.-pub. relations Phila. chpt., treas. 1983, Phila. Bicentennial Celebration com. 1987, Jeptha Abbott Chap Club), AAUW (dir. Schenectady 1971-73, legis. chmn. Valley Forge br., Albany-Schenectady br.), N.Y. State Womens Club (Capital dist. br.), Jr. League Phila. (sustaining, edn. com., child abuse center com., bicentennial cookbook com., Waterworks Restoration com., 1984, bd. dirs. 1960-61), Schenectady Curling Club, Valley Forge Council Repub. Women, Mohawk Golf Club (Schenectady), Shenorock Shore Club (Rye, N.Y.), Merion Cricket Club (Haverford, Pa.), Acorn (Phila.), Little Acorns Investment, Career Group (founder, chair 1983-85), Wellesley Alumnae (Phila.), Little Egg Harbor Yacht Club (Beach Haven, N.J.), Jr. League of Phila. (sustainer, Waterworks restoration com.). Republican. Episcopalian. Home: PO Box 356 100 Steeplechase Rd Devon PA 19333 Office: Pepper Hamilton & Scheetz 3000 Two Logan Sq 18th and Arch Sts Philadelphia PA 19103

PECK, CHARLES EDWARD, construction company executive; b. Newark, Dec. 1, 1925; s. Hubert Raymond and Helen (White) P.; m. Delphine Murphy, Oct. 15, 1949; children—Margaret, Charles Edward, Katherine, Perry Anne. Grad., Phillips Acad., 1943; B.S., U. Pa., 1949; student, MIT, 1943-44. With Owens-Corning Fiberglas Corp., various locations, 1949-61; sales mgr. home bldg. products Owens-Corning Fiberglas Corp., Toledo, 1961-66; v.p. home bldg. products mktg. div. Owens-Corning Fiberglas Corp., 1966-68, v.p. constrn. group, 1968-75, v.p. bldg. materials group, 1976-78, exec. v.p., 1978-81, also dir.; co-chmn. The Ryland Group, Columbia, Md., 1981-82, chmn., 1982—; also dir. The Ryland Group; dir., v.p. Producers Coun., Washington, 1974-77; mem. statutory vis. com. U.S. Nat. Bur. Standards, 1972-77; mem. adv. com. Fed. Nat. Mortgage Adminstrn., 1977-78, 85-86; vis. com. Mass. Inst. Tech.-Harvard Joint Center for Urban Studies; chmn. Producers Adv. Forum, 1977-81; bd. dirs. Sanborn, Steketee, Otis & Evans (SSOE), Inc., Toledo. Mem. vis. com. Harvard U. Grad. Sch. Design, 1981-86; chmn. Howard County United Way Campaign, Md., 1987; bd. dirs. Nat. Inst. for Urban Wildlife, 1986—, United Way Cen. Md., 1987—, Howard County Gen. Hosp., 1988—, Columbia Festival, Inc.; adv. bd. continuing edn. Johns Hopkins U., 1988—, Columbia Arts Festival, Inc.; chmn. chancellor's adv. com. U. Md., 1988—. 2d lt. USAAF, 1944-46. Mem. U.S. C. of C. (dir. 1975-81), Ohio C. of C. (dir. 1975-81), Depression and Related Affective Disorders Assn. (pres. 1986-89, bd. dirs. 1986—), Belmont Country Club (Perrysburg, Ohio), Toledo Club, Capitol Hill Club (Washington), Metropolitan Club (Chgo.), Talbot Country Club (Md.), City Club (Washington), Center Club (Balt.), Phi Gamma Delta. Home: 7649 Woodstream Way Laurel MD 20707 Office: Ryland Group Inc 10221 Wincopin Circle Columbia MD 21044

PECK, FRED NEIL, economist, educator; b. Bklyn., Oct. 17, 1945; s. Abraham Lincoln and Beatrice (Pikholtz) P.; m. Jean Claire Ginsberg, Aug. 14, 1971; children: Ron Evan, Jordan Shefer, Ethan David. BA, SUNY, Binghamton, 1966; MA, SUNY, Albany, 1969; MPhil, NYU, 1984; PhD, Pacific Western U., 1984. Lectr. SUNY, Albany, 1969-70; research asst. N.Y. State Legislature, Albany, 1970; sales and research staff Pan Am. Trade Devel. Corp., N.Y.C., 1971; v.p., economist The First Boston Corp., N.Y.C., 1971-88; mng. dir. Sharpe's Capital Mkt. Assocs. Inc., N.Y.C., 1988—; adj. prof. Hofstra U., Hempstead, N.Y., 1975; lectr. NYU, 1982; mem. faculty New Sch. for Social Research, N.Y.C., 1974—. Author, editor: (biennial publ.) Handbook of Securities of U.S. Government, 1972-86. Mem. Am. Econ. Assn., Eastern Econ. Assn., Econometric Soc., Nat. Assn. Bus. Economists, Am. Statis. Assn. Democrat. Jewish. Lodges: Knights Pythias, Knights Khorassan. Office: Sharpe's Capital Mkt Assocs Inc 78 Christopher St New York NY 10014

PECK, SUSAN, data processing executive; b. Bklyn., Aug. 31, 1948; d. Cornelius Lawrence and Loretta Agnes (Freligh) Cleary; m. Richard Carl Peck, Mar. 7, 1972; 1 child, Mary Catherine. BS in Speech, St. John's U., 1970. Lic. real estate salesman, N.Y. Speech therapist, dept. chair, tchr. Christ the King Elem. Sch., Commack, N.Y., 1970-72; supr. purchase planning Estee Lauder, Inc., Melville, N.Y., 1973-78; staff analyst Gen. Instrument Corp., Hicksville, N.Y., 1978-83; systems analyst ADP, Melville, 1983-85; mgr. info. systems R. A. Rodriguez, Inc., Garden City, N.Y., 1985-87; dir. personal computer ops., liaison healthforce Career Employment Services, Inc., East Meadow, N.Y., 1987; dir. data processing svcs., law clk. McSherry and Flynn Attys. at Law, Huntington, N.Y., 1989—; v.p. Richard Peck Ltd., Shirley, N.Y., 1982—. Lector, extraordinary minister of eucharist St. Joseph the Worker Roman Cath. Ch., East Patchogue, N.Y., 1980-82; vol. Brookhaven (N.Y.) County Task Force, 1987. Touro Coll. Law Scholar, 1987—. Mem. Nat. Assn. for Female Execs., Mensa. Republican. Office: McSherry & Flynn 453 New York Ave Huntington NY 11743

PECKENPAUGH, ROBERT EARL, investment adviser; b. Potomac, Ill., July 17, 1926; s. Hilery and Zella (Stodgel) P.; m. Margaret J. Dixon, Sept. 21, 1945; children—Nancy Lynn, Carol Sue, David Robert, Daniel Mark, Jeanne Beth, Douglas John. Student, Ind. U., 1946-47; B.S., Northwestern U., 1949, M.B.A. with distinction, 1952. Chartered fin. analyst. with First Nat. Bank Chgo., 1949-52; pres. Security Suprs., Inc., Chgo., 1952-73; v.p. Chgo. Title & Trust Co., 1973-77; pres. Hotchkiss & Peckenpaugh, Inc., Chgo., 1977-84; investment mgr. Morgan Stanley Asset Mgmt. Inc., 1984-86; v.p. Morgan Stanley & Co., Inc., Chgo., 1986— . Chmn., Evang. Covenant Ch. of Hinsdale, 1981-84. Served with USNR, 1944-46. Mem. Investment Analyst Soc. Chgo. (pres. 1963-64). Clubs: Chgo., Mid-Day, Chgo. Athletic, Economic (Chgo.), Hinsdale Golf. Home: 429 S County Line Rd Hinsdale IL 60521 Office: Morgan Stanley & Co Inc 440 S LaSalle St Chicago IL 60605

PECKER, KEVEN HOWARD, retail executive; b. N.Y.C.; s. Jacob and Esther (Pross) P.; m. Helene Bentman, dec. 19, 1981. BBA, Baruch Coll., 1978. Liaison H.L.C. Imports Corp., N.Y.C., 1976-84; treas. The Jasm Corp., N.Y.C., 1984—; pres. The Color Merchants Inc., N.Y.C., 1987—; bd. dirs. Mid-Eastern Coops. Inc., N.Y.C. Chmn. Environment Action Com., N.Y.C., 1971-76. Mem. Mfg. Jewelers and Silversmiths, Jewelers' Bd. Trade, Baychester Consumer Soc. (pres. N.Y.C. 1984-86). Office: The Jasm Corp 6 E 45th St New York NY 10017

PECOT, CHARLES MATTHEW, insurance company executive; b. Baton Rouge, Oct. 21, 1934; s. Alice M. Gauthier; m. Nancy Mary McMahon, June 18, 1960; children: C. Matthew, Julie Ann, Ellen Louise, Jonathan Michael. BS, La. State U., 1956. Spl. agt. Fidelity & Deposit Co. of Md., New Orleans, 1959-66, asst. mgr., 1966-67; asst. mgr. Fidelity & Deposit Co. of Md., Balt., 1967-69, mgr., 1969-75, v.p., 1975—. Lt. (j.g.) USN, 1956-59. Mem. Casualty and Surety Club Balt. (pres. 1977). Democrat. Roman Catholic. Club: Oriole Advs. (treas. Balt. chpt. 1980-86). Home: PO Box 1227 Baltimore MD 21203 Office: Fidelity & Deposit Co of Md 510 Fidelity Bldg Baltimore MD 21201

PECZE, DAVID EMERY, marketing analyst; b. South Bend, Ind., Mar. 19, 1958; s. Geza David and Yolanda Joan (Batiz) P. BA in Telecommunications, Ind. U., 1980; BS in Bus. Mktg., Ind. U., South Bend, 1984. Sales mgr. LaPorte County Broadcasting, Ind., 1980-82; mktg. analyst St. Joseph Bank & Trust Corp., South Bend, 1984-85; campaign assoc. United Way St. Joseph County, South Bend, 1985-88; mktg. analyst CTS Corp., Elkhart, Ind., 1988—. Mem. LaPorte Jaycees (dir. 1981-82, Rookie Yr. award 1981), Adams Alumni, Image Club, Masons, Kiwanis (bd. dirs. 1986-88). Home: 710 Clarinet Blvd W Elkhart IN 46516 Office: CTS Corp 905 W Blvd N Elkhart IN 46514

PEDERSEN, RICK ALAN, lawyer, real estate executive; b. Denver, Oct. 5, 1952; s. Waldon A. and Forence E. (Lewis) P. BSBA, U. Denver, 1974, MBA, 1977, JD, 1977. Bar: Colo. 1977. Assoc. Harbridge House Inc., Boston, 1978-82; sr. v.p. Frederick Ross Co., Denver, 1982—; bd. dirs. Colo. Mech. Systems Inc., Denver. Mem. Colo. Gov.'s Revenue Estimating Adv. Com., 1985—, Denver Capital Devel. Adv. Com., 1986—, Denver Planning Bd., 1987—, Denver Downtown Transit Adv. Com., 1987—. Mem. Nat. Assn. Corp. Real Estate Execs., Urban Land Inst., Am. Arbitration Assn., Denver Club, Denver Athletic Club, Beta Gamma Sigma. Office: Frederick Ross Co 707 17th St Ste 2700 Denver CO 80202

PEDERSEN, WESLEY NIELS, public relations and public affairs executive; b. South Sioux City, Nebr., July 10, 1922; s. Peter Westergaard and Marie Gertrude (Sorensen) P.; m. Angela Kathryn Vavra, Oct. 17, 1948; 1 son, Eric Wesley. Student, Tri-State Coll., Sioux City, Iowa, 1940-41; B.A. summa cum laude, Upper Iowa U.; postgrad., George Washington U., 1958-59. Editor, writer Sioux City Jour., 1941-50; corr. N.Y. Times, Life, Time, Fortune, 1948-50; editor Dept. State, 1950-53; fgn. service officer Dept. State, Hong Kong, 1960-63; fgn. affairs columnist, roving corr., counselor summit meetings and fgn. ministers confs. USIA, 1953-60, chief, worldwide spl. publs. and graphics programs, 1963-69; chief Office Spl. Projects, Washington, 1969-78, Office Spl. Projects, Internat. Communication Agy., 1978-79; v.p. Fraser Assocs., pub. relations, Washington, 1979-80; dir. communications and pub. relations Public Affairs Council, Washington, 1980—; lectr. creative communications Upper Iowa U., 1975; chmn., Europe, Ambassadorial Internat. Affairs Seminar, Fgn. Service Inst., 1975; lectr. internat. public relations Pub. Relations Inst., Am. U., 1976; lectr. bus. and mgmt. div. N.Y. U., 1976, 77, 78; cons. pub. relations, editorial and design; del. founding sessions 1st Amendment Congress, Phila. and Williamsburg, Va., 1980, exec. com., 1980. Columnist: Public Relations Jour., 1980-85; author: Legacy of a President, 1964, American Heroes of Asian Wars, 1969; co-author: Effective Government Public Affairs, 1981; editor: Escape At Midnight and Other Stories (Pearl S. Buck), 1962, Exodus From China (Harry Redl), 1962, Education in China (K.E. Priestley), 1962, The Peasant and the Communes (Henry Lethbridge), 1962, China's Men of Letters (K.E. Priestley), 1963, Children of China (Pearl S. Buck and Margaret Wylie), 1963, Macao (Richard Hughes), 1963, The Americans and the Arts (Howard Taubman), 1969, The Dance in America (Agnes de Mille), 1969, Getting the Most from Grassroots Public Affairs Programs, 1980, Cost-Effective Management for Today's Public Affairs, 1987, Making Community Relations Pay Off: Tools and Strategies, 1988, Winning at the Grassroots: How to Succeed in the Legislative Arena by Mobilizing Employees and Other Allies, 1989, Public Affairs Rev. mag, 1980-86, Impact, newsletter on nat. and internat. pub. affairs, 1980—; contbr. to: The Commissar, 1972, Political Action for Business, 1981, Informing the People: A Public Affairs Handbook, 1981, The Practice of Public Relations, 1984; mem. editorial bd.: Public Relations Quar, 1975—, Fgn. Service Jour., 1975-81; contbr. articles to profl. jours. Founding chmn. bd. dirs. Nat. Inst. for Govt. Public Info. Research, Am. U., 1977-80. Served with USAAF, 1943-46. Recipient 2 awards A.P. Mng. Editors Assn., Iowa, 1949, Meritorious Service award USIA, 1963, 1st prizes Fed. Editors Assn., 1970, 74-75, 1st prizes Soc. Tech. Communication, 1974, 75-76, Gold award Internat. Newsletter Conf., 1982, Silver award, 1985, Eddi award for design excellence Editor's Workshop, 1983, Gold Circle award for outstanding communications, Am. Soc. Assn. Execs., 1983-88, Editors' Forum award, 1988; named Most Outstanding Info. Ofcl. in Exec. Br. Govt. Govt. Info. Orgn., 1975, named Ky. Col. and Adm. Nebr. Navy, 1984. Mem. Am. Fgn. Service Assn., Internat. Assn. Bus. Communicators (vice chmn. govt. relations com. 1976-77, chmn. nat. capital dist. conf. 1977, dir. Washington chpt. 1977-78, Communicator of Yr. Washington chpt. 1978, various awards 1973, 76-78, 84), Nat. Assn. Govt. Communicators (pres. 1978-79, Communicator of Yr. 1977, Disting. Service award 1978), Pub. Relations Soc. Am. (mem. Counselor's Acad. 1980—, chmn. 1st Amendment task force 1980-81, co-recipient Thoth award 1980, co-recipient award 1981). Episcopalian. Clubs: Fgn. Service, Nat. Press (Washington); Overseas Press (N.Y.C.). Home: 5214 Sangamore Rd Bethesda MD 20816 Office: Pub Affairs Coun 1255 23d St NW Ste 750 Washington DC 20037

PEDIGO, ROBERT EUGENE, venture capitalist; b. French Lick, Ind., Oct. 23, 1932; s. Albert Leon and Bessie Opal (Hagan) P.; m. Masako Miyoshi, Sept. 26, 1960; children: Sheree, Jeffrey, David. BA, U. Calif., Berkeley, 1954; MS, George Washington U., 1971. Commd. ensign USN, 1954, advanced through grades to comdr., 1968, ret., 1974; v.p. W.R. Grace & Co., N.Y.C., 1974-78, Chemed Corp., Cin., 1978-81; pres. Dearborn Utilities, Cin., 1981-83; exec. v.p. Grace Ventures Corp., Cupertino, Calif., 1983—; bd. dirs. Marine Culture Enterprises, Honolulu, BioCare Inc., Campbell, Calif. Mem. Nat. Venture Capital Assn., Western Venture Capital Assn., Am. Electronics Assn. Republican. Office: Grace Ventures Corp 20300 Stevens Creek Blvd Ste 330 Cupertino CA 95014

PEDUTO, JAMES R., lawyer, marketing executive; b. Johnson City, N.Y., May 3, 1961; s. Ross Joseph and Carole (Castaldi) P. BA, Bucknell U., 1983; JD, Villanova U., 1986. Assoc. Levene, Gouldin & Thompson, Binghamton, N.Y., 1987—; mgr. mktg. G.B. Roberts Maintenance and Supply, Inc., Johnson City, 1987—. Mem. ABA, N.Y. State Bar Assn., Broome County Bar Assn., Internat. Sanitary Supply Assn. Republican. Roman Catholic. Club: Triple Cities Ski (Binghamton). Home: 3715 Kirk Rd Endwell NY 13760 Office: GB Roberts Maintenance & Supply 19 Ave D Johnson City NY 13790

PEELER, STUART THORNE, lawyer, petroleum industry consultant; b. Los Angeles, Oct. 28, 1929; s. Joseph David and Elizabeth Fiske (Boggess) P.; m. Sylvia Frances Townley, Nov. 5, 1985. B.A., Stanford U., 1950, J.D., 1953. Bar: Calif. 1953. Ptnr. Musick, Peeler & Garrett, Los Angeles, 1958-73; with Santa Fe Internat. Corp., Orange, Calif., 1973-81; v.p., sec., assoc. gen. counsel Santa Fe Internat. Corp., 1973-74, sr. v.p., gen. counsel, dir., 1975-81; vice-chmn. bd., chmn. exec. com. Supron Energy Corp., 1978-82; chmn. bd., chief exec. officer Statex Petroleum, Inc., 1982-89; cons. 1989—; bd. dirs. Cal Mat Co., Stateline Drilling Co., Homestake Mining Co., Homestake Gold of Australia Ltd., Chieftain Internat. Inc. Trustee J. Paul Getty Trust; mem. U.S. Tuna Team, 1957-67, capt., 1966. Served with U.S. Army, 1953-55. Decorated Army Commendation medal. Mem. State Bar Calif., Am. Judicature Soc., AIME, Theta Chi, Phi Delta Phi. Republican. Congregationalist. Clubs: Dallas Petroleum, Tucson Country. Office: PO Box 35852 Tucson AZ 85740

PEENEY, JAMES DOYLE, executive search consultant; b. Trenton, N.J., Feb. 28, 1933; s. William C. and Emily (Courtney) P.; m. Dorothy Shestko, Aug. 3, 1957; children: Timothy J., Jennifer L., Thomas D. BA, U. Pa., 1955; postgrad., Temple U., 1955-56, U. Mich., 1962-65; MBA, Seton Hall, 1968. Trainee Ford Motor Co., Dearborn, Mich., 1962-65; recruiting mgr. Merck & Co., Rahway, N.J., 1965-68; assoc. Boyden Assocs., N.Y.C., 1968-72; v.p. pers. Mfrs. Hanover Trust, N.Y.C., 1973-74; v.p. Drake Beam Morin, N.Y.C., 1974-78, Goodrich & Sherwood, N.Y.C., 1978-80; pres. Peeney Assocs. Inc., Fanwood, N.J., 1980—. Dist. chmn. Watchung area coun. Boy Scouts Am., Mountainside, N.J., 1976—. Named One of Fifty Leading Retainer Search Firms U.S. Exec. Recruiter News, Ritzwilliam, N.H., 1986-88. Mem. Nat. Assn. Corp. and Profl. Recruiters, Princeton Club (N.Y.C.), Renaissance Club (Detroit). Office: Peeney Assoc Inc 141 South Ave Fanwood NJ 07023

PEERY, WILLIAM WHITLEY, II, infosystems specialist; b. Oak Ridge, Tenn., Sept. 17, 1952; s. William Whitley and Joan Hildegard (Hampton) P.; m. Deborah Anne Curtis, Dec. 15, 1973; children: Jennifer Ryan, Clinton Curtis,. BS in Indsl. Mgmt., Ga. Inst. Tech., 1973; MBA, U. Cen. Fla., 1976. Consumer services rep. Fla. Power & Light Co., Cocoa, 1973-77, power services rep., 1978; mgmt. analyst Fla. Power & Light Co., Miami, 1979-80; consumer services supr. Fla. Power & Light Co., Pompano Beach, 1981; service planning supr. Fla. Power & Light Co., Delray Beach, 1982-84, systems coordinator, 1985; systems mgr. Fla. Power & Light Co., Miami, 1986—. Chmn. internal audit com., City of Delray Beach, 1984. Named Eagle Scout, Boy Scouts Am., 1966. Mem. Sigma Alpha Epsilon (Ga. Phi chpt.). Methodist. Office: Fla Power & Light Co PO Box 029100 Miami FL 33102

PEEVEY, MICHAEL R., electric utility executive; b. N.Y.C., Feb. 8, 1938; s. Willard Michael Bliss and Miriam Gardiner (Cooke) Bliss Peevey; m. Lauretta Ann Peevey, Mar. 17, 1961 (div. 1976); children—Darcie Ann, Maria Beth; m. Carole Jean Liu, May 27, 1978; 1 child, Jared Liu. B.A. in Econs., U. Calif.-Berkeley, 1959, M.A. in Econs., 1961. Economist U.S. Dept. Labor, Washington, 1961-65; coordinator community programs Inst. Indsl. Relations, U. Calif.-Berkeley, 1969-70; dir. research Calif. Labor Fedn., AFL-CIO, 1971-73, 65-69; pres. Calif. Council for Environmental/Economic Balance, San Francisco, 1973-84; v.p. So. Calif. Edison Co., Rosemead, 1984—, sr. v.p., 1985—, exec. v.p., 1986—. Bd. dirs. Calif. Housing Fin. Agy., Sacramento, 1984-86; mem. Commn. to Rev. the Master Plan for Higher Edn., Calif., 1985—; trustee Calif. State U. and Colls., 1977-85, Joint Council on Econ. Edn., N.Y., 1969-85; mem. Gov.'s Infrastructure Rev. Task Force, Sacramento, 1983-84; bd. govs. Econ. Literacy Council of Calif., 1982—; bd. visitors Calif. Maritime Acad., 1980-83; mem. steering com. State Solid Waste Mgmt. Bd., 1980-83; commr. Nat. Commn. on State Workmen's Compensation Laws, Washington, 1971-72; bd. dirs. Consumer Fedn. Calif., 1972-78; co-chmn. Citizens for Adequate Energy, 1979-82. Mem. Indsl. Relations Research Assn., World Trade Club (San Francisco), Sutter Club (Sacramento), Calif. Club (L.A.). Democrat. Episcopalian. Office: So Calif Edison Co 2244 Walnut Grove Ave Rosemead CA 91770

PEIFFER, ELIZABETH ANNE, computer systems consultant, auditor; b. Syracuse, N.Y., Dec. 5, 1954; d. Robert Victor and Marion Alice (Jagelle) P.; m. Gerald Lee Brickey, June 9, 1978. BA in Econs., Acctg. and Psychology Magna Cum Laude, Coll. Holy Cross, 1976. CPA, Oreg., Ill.; cert. info. systems auditor. Mem. audit staff Arthur Young & Co., Chgo., 1976-78; sr. auditor, computer auditor Arthur Young & Co., Portland, Oreg., 1978-80; corp. auditor EDP Orbanco Fin. Services Corp., Portland, Oreg., 1980-82, systems audit mgr., 1982-83, asst. v.p., asst. dir. auditing, 1983-84; computer audit mgr. Coopers & Lybrand, Portland, 1984-88, computer auditor, cons. mgr., 1988—; instr. Concordia Coll., Portland, 1986-87; cons. 1000 Friends of Oreg., Portland, 1981; lectr. in field. Developer, editor EDP ednl. materials. Econ. adviser Portland Energy Commn., 1980; fundraiser Northwest Artists Workshop, Portland, 1984; adviser St. Mary's Acad., Portland, 1986—. Mem. Am. Inst. CPA's, Inst. Internal Auditors (bd. dirs. 1988—), Oreg. Soc. CPA's (chair 1987-88, bd. dirs. 1988—), EDP Auditors Assn. (chpt. pres. 1985-86, regional asst. v.p. 1986-88, regional v.p. 1988—), Phi Beta Kappa. Office: Coopers & Lybrand 2700 1st Interstate Tower Portland OR 97201

PEIRCE, KENNETH B., JR., retail company executive, lawyer; b. Holland, Mich., June 19, 1943; s. Kenneth B. Sr. and Margaret P.; m. Jill Bolhous, June 16, 1978; children: Tracey, Chris, Drew. BA, Notre Dame U., 1965; JD, St. Louis U., 1968. Asst. city counselor City of St. Louis, 1968-72; corp. atty Wolverine World Wide, Rockford, Mich., 1972-74; corp. atty Gerber Products Co., Fremont, Mich., 1974-80, assoc. gen. counsel, 1980-83, sec., gen. counsel, 1983-85, v.p., gen. counsel, 1985-86, exec. v.p., gen. counsel, gen. mgr. apparel group, 1986-88; exec. v.p., gen. mgr. apparel group Gerber Products Co., Fremont, 1988—; pres. Fremont Area Found., Mich., 1985—. Mem. ABA, Mich. Bar Assn., Newaygo County Bar Assn., Am. Apparel Mfgs. Assn. (bd. dirs.), Am. Mgmt. Assn., Nat. Assn. Mfg., Food and Drug Law Inst. (bd. dirs., trustee 1986). Office: Gerber Products Co 445 State St Fremont MI 49412

PEISER, ROBERT ALAN, financial executive; b. N.Y.C., Apr. 17, 1948; s. Donald Edward and Natalie Audrey (Phillips) P.; m. Kathleen Lorraine Reilly, Jan. 11, 1970; children: Karyn, Brian, Craig, Scott. BA, U. Pa., 1969; MBA, Harvard U., 1972. Dir. corp. fin. Trans World Airlines, N.Y.C., 1972-77, sr. v.p. fin., chief fin. officer, 1983-86; treas. Hertz Corp., N.Y.C., 1977-80; staff v.p., treas. ops. RCA Corp., N.Y.C., 1980-81; v.p., treas., Trans World Corp., N.Y.C., 1982-83; sr. v.p., chief fin. officer ALC Communications Corp., Birmingham, Mich., 1986-88; sr. v.p. fin., chief fin. officer Borman's Inc., Detroit, 1988—. Mem. Fin. Execs. Inst., Nat. Assn. Corp. Treasurers. Club: Nassau Country (Glen Cove, N.Y.). Home: 326 Lakewood Dr Bloomfield Hills MI 48013 Office: Borman's Inc 18718 Borman Ave Detroit MI 48232

PELCZAR, OTTO, electrical engineer; b. Vienna, Austria, Aug. 9, 1934; moved to Australia, 1950; s. Joseph Franz and Brigitte (Von Witkowski) P.; m. Amy Margueritte Ludovici, May 9, 1959; children—Suzanne Patricia, Vicki Josephine, Michelle Amy, Paul Daniel. Diploma Elec. Engring., Perth Tech. Coll., W. Australia, 1967; B.Applied Sci., Inst. Tech., Perth, 1978; M.B.A., U. Western Australia, Perth, 1982. Labourer, welder Roads Bd., Maylands, 1950-56; chief draughtsman Westate Elec. Ind., Perth, 1956-70; dist. engr. Pub. Works Dept., 1970-72; comdg. officer Her Majesty's Australian Ship Acute, 1973-78; engr. Pub. Works Dept., Perth, 1972-85; lectr. Tech. Coll., Subiaco, 1979—; mng. dir. Opex Pty. Ltd., W. Perth, 1982—. Convener, West Coast Secession Movement, Perth, 1981, v.p. 1989—; nominee W. Australian Parliament, 1983. Served to comdr. Royal Australian Naval Res., 1956—. Australian Commonwealth scholar, 1967. Fellow Inst. Engrs.; mem. Royal United Services Inst. (v.p. 1983—), Inst. Draughtsmen, Australian Inst. Internat. Affairs. Club: Old Austria (life mem.). Lodge: Rotary (program dir. 1984—). Avocations: chess; tennis; yachting. Home: PO Box 50, Mount Lawley 6050 Australia Office: 59 Malcolm St, Ste 93, West Perth 6005, Australia

PELL, ARTHUR ROBERT, personnel consultant, author; b. N.Y.C., Jan. 22, 1920; s. Harry and Rae (Meyers) P.; m. Erica Frost, May 19, 1946; children—Douglas, Hilary. AB, NYU, 1939, MA, 1944; PhD, Calif. Coast U., 1977; profl. diploma, Cornell U., 1943. Personnel dir. Eagle-Electric Mfg. Co., Long Island City, N.Y., 1946-50, North Atlantic Constructors, N.Y.C., 1950-53; v.p. Harper Assos., Inc. (personnel consultants), N.Y.C., 1953-75; cons. Human Resources Mgmt., 1975—; adj. asso. prof. mgmt. Sch. Continuing Edn., NYU, 1962-84; lectr. Baruch Sch. Bus. and Pub. Adminstrn. Coll. City N.Y., 1948-67; adj. asso. prof. mgmt. Coll. Bus. Adminstrn., St. John's U., 1971-76. Author: (with W.B. Patterson) Fire Officer's Guide to Leadership, rev. edit, 1963, Placing Salesmen, 1963, Placing Executives, 1964, Police Leadership, 1967, How to Get the Job You Want After 40, 1967, Recruiting and Selecting Personnel, 1969, (with M. Harper) Starting and Managing an Employment Agency, 1970, Recruiting, Training and Motivating Volunteer Workers, 1972, Be A Better Employment Interviewer, 1972, rev., 1978, 86, The College Graduate Guide to Job Finding, 1973, (with Wilma Rogalin) Women's Guide to Executive Positions, 1975, (with Albert Furbay) College Student's Guide to Career Planning, 1975, (with Dale Carnegie Assocs.) Managing Through People, 1975, rev., 1978, rev., 1987, Choosing a College Major: Business, 1978, Enrich Your Life: The Dale Carnegie Way, 1979, The Part Time Job Book, 1984, Making the Most of Medicare, 1987, (with George Sadek) Resumes for Engineers, 1982, Resumes for Computer Professionals, 1984; editorial cons. for revision Dale Carnegie's How To Win Friends and Influence People, 1981, How to Sell Yourself on an Interview, 1982, The Job Finders Kit, 1989; also articles. Served with AUS, 1942-46. Mem. Am. Soc. Personnel Adminstrn., Am. Soc. Tng. and Devel., Nat. Assn. Personnel Cons. Office: 111 Dietz St Hempstead NY 11550

PELLETIER, CLAUDE HENRI, biomedical engineer; b. Riviere-Ouelle, Can., Que., Dec. 15, 1941; s. Lucien Pelletier and Ernestine Michaud. Immatriculation sr., Coll. Universitaire U. Sherbrooke, 1961; B.Sc.A., U. Sherbrooke, 1966; M.Sc.A., Ecole Poly technique, U. Montreal, 1972. Project engr. Alcan, Alma, Can., 1966-69; mgr. computer ctr. in physiology dept. faculty medicine U. Montreal, 1972-73; biomed. engr. Sacre-Coeur Hosp., Montreal, 1973-75; chief engr. biomed. engring. dept. Montreal Heart Inst., 1975—; lectr. faculty of medicine U. Montreal, 1972-74, research asst. faculty of medicine, 1973-75; cons. Montreal Heart Inst., 1975—. Contbr. articles to profl. jours. Mem. Order of Engrs. Que., IEEE, Assn. Advancement Med.

Instrumentation, Assn. Des Physiciens Et Ingenieurs Biomedicaux Du Que. Roman Catholic. Avocations: swimming; tennis. Home: 5732 Plantagenet, Montreal, PQ Canada H3S 2K3

PELLETT, THOMAS LAWRENCE, II, commercial banking executive; b. Mpls., Apr. 7, 1958; s. Thomas Rowand and Anne (Iffert) P.; m. Laurie Sue Lodes, May 4, 1984. BBA, So. Meth. U., 1980; MBA, So. Ill. U., 1988. Comml. loan officer Centerre Bank, NA, St. Louis, Mo., 1980-84; dist. mgr. Mfrs. Hanover, The CIT Group Corp. Fin., Inc., St. Louis, Mo., 1984—. Home: 525 Selma Ave Webster Groves MO 63119-4141 Office: Mfrs Hanover/The CIT Group 7733 Forsyth Blvd Suite 1280 Saint Louis MO 63105

PELTIER, RONALD JAMES, real estate corporation officer; b. St. Paul, Mar. 18, 1949; s. George Anthony and Shirley (Peterson) P.; m. Arlyce Corrine Brink, Feb. 15, 1970; children: Jean Paul, Janeē. BA with honors, U. Minn., 1971; MA, St. Thomas U., 1974. Tchr. Annoka Hennepin Schs., Blaine, Minn., 1974-77; salesman Edina Realty, Mpls., 1977-78, br. mgr., 1979-80; regional mgr. Edina Realty, St. Paul, 1980-83; gen. mgr. Edina Realty& Fin., Inc., First Realty Iowa, Mpls., St. Paul, 1983—; pres. Peltier Devel. Corp., Dellwood, Minn., 1985—, White Bear (Minn.) Lake Hotel, 1987—; owner Peltier Homes Contracting, 1982—, ptnr. J.R. Farms, Inc., 1988. Coach Community Receation Programs, White Bear; bd. dirs. U. Minn., 1984-86, St. Andrews Lutheran Ch., Mahtomedi, Minn., 1986-87. Mem. Nat. Assn. Realtors, Minn. Assn. Realtors, St. Paul Bd. Realtors, Mpls. Bd. Realtors, Anoka County Bd. Realtors, Rotary Club. Home: 77 Apple Orchard Rd Dellwood MN 55110 Office: Edina Realty Inc 4015 W 65th Edina MN 55435

PELTON, JOAN ELIXABETH MASON, wholesale company executive; b. Bristol, Pa., Feb. 15, 1932; d. William and Mary-Scott (Ryder) Mason; m. Clifford L. Pelton, Feb. 29, 1952 (div. 1977); children: William, Seth, Jesse, Aaron. BA, Pomona Coll., Claremont, Calif., 1953. Owner, chief exec. officer Silo Inc./Alcazar Inc., Waterbury, Vt., 1977—; cons. in field. Musician recording The Hammered Dulcimer, 1972; producer records Kitchen Junket, 1977-81, others. Founder Waterbury Alive, Vt., 1984; bd. dirs. Champlain Valley Folk Festival. Mem. Nat. Assn. Ind. Record Distbrs. (bd. dirs. 1984-88), Women Bus. Owners of Vt. Office: Silo Inc/ Alcazar Prodns Inc PO Box 429 S Main St Waterbury VT 05676

PELTON, VIRGINIA LUE, small business owner; b. Utica, Kans., Apr. 15, 1928; d. Forrest Selby and Nellie (Simmons) Meier; m. Theodore Trower King Jr., Oct. 27, 1956 (div.); m. Harold Marcel Pelton, July 11, 1970; children: Mary Virginia Joyner, Diana Jean. Student, Kans. State U., 1946-47, Ft. Hays U., 1947-48, Washington U., St. Louis, 1950-51. Instr. Patricia Stevens Modeling Sch., Kansas City, Mo., 1948-50; model various cos., Calif. and N.Y., 1951-53; fashion cons. Giorgio, Beverly Hills, Calif., 1967-68, Charles Gallay, Beverly Hills, 1975-77, Dorso's, Beverly Hills, 1977-79; buyer, mgr. giftware Slavick's, Laguna Hills, Calif., 1980-83; owner P.J. Secretarial Svcs., Laguna Hills, 1980—; v.p. H.P. Fin. Inc., Laguna Hills, 1983—. Editor Profl. Network newsletter, 1980—. Sec. Leukemia Soc. Am., Santa Ana, 1985—; mem. Laguna Beach Art Mus., 1986—. Mem. Profl. Network Assn. (sec. 1986—), Market Plus The Consumer Network, Saddleback C. of C., Laguna Hills Club, Kappa Delta. Republican. Methodist. Home: 24942 Georgia Sue Dr Laguna Hills CA 92653

PELTON, WILLIAM HARVEY, geophysicist, company executive; b. New Westminister, B.C., Can., July 21, 1946; came to U.S.; s. Ralph Charles and Ethel Lilly (Moe) P.; BS in Engring. Physics, U.B.C., 1969; Ph.D., U. Utah, 1977. Geophysicist, McPhar Geophysics, Toronto, Ont., Can., 1969-71; v.p., gen. mgr. McPhar Philippines, Manila, 1971-73; v.p. Phoenix Geophysics, Toronto, 1977-85, pres., Denver, 1982-85; founder, chmn. Phoenix Geosci., Denver, 1987— ; mem. trade mission to Peking, 1972; cons. UN Devel. Program, India, 1978, 80; dir. spectral ip research program for 11 mining cos., 1978-81; dir. hydrocarbon research for 14 oil cos., 1981. Recipient Best Paper award Geophysics Mag., 1978. Mem. Soc. Exploration Geophysicists (award 1977). European Assn. Exploration Geophysicists, Can. Inst. Mining and Metallurgy, AIME. Developer spectral induced polarization method and equipment, 1979; supr. design of magnetotelluric equipment, 1981. Home: 1625 Larimer St #1005 Denver CO 80202 Office: Phoenix Geosci Inc 555 17th St #2570 Denver CO 80202

PELTZ, NELSON, manufacturing company executive; b. 1943; married. MBA, U. Pa. With A. Peltz & Sons, Inc., N.Y.C., 1963-70; with Trafalgar Industries, Inc., 1970—, now chmn., chief exec. officer, dir.; pres. Triangle Industries, Inc., N.Y.C., 1983-84, chief exec. officer, 1983—, chmn. bd., chief exec. officer, 1984—, also bd. dirs. Office: Triangle Industries Inc 900 3rd Ave New York NY 10022 *

PELTZER, DOUGLAS LEA, semiconductor device manufacturing company executive; b. Clinton, Ia., July 2, 1938; s. Albert and Mary Ardelle (Messer) P.; B.A., Knox Coll., 1960; M.S., N.M. State U., 1964; m. Nancy Jane Strickler, Dec. 22, 1959; children—Katharine, Eric, Kimberly. Research engr. Gen. Electric Co., Advanced Computer Lab., Sunnyvale, Calif., 1964-67; large scale integrated circuit engr. Fairchild Camera & Instrument, Research & Devel. Lab., Palo Alto, Calif., 1967-70, supervisory engr. bipolar memory devel., Mountain View, Calif., 1970-73, process engring. mgr., bipolar memories div., 1973-83, tech. dir., 1977-83; v.p. tech. ops. Trilogy Systems Corp., Cupertino, Calif., 1983-85 ; pres. Tactical Fabs, Inc., 1985-89; dir. process devel. Chips and Techs. Inc., 1989—. NSF fellow, 1962-63; recipient Sherman Fairchild award for tech. excellence, 1980, Semiconductor Equipment and Materials Inst. award, 1988; Inventor of Yr. award Peninsula Patent Law Assn., 1982. Mem. AAAS, IEEE, Sigma Pi Sigma. Inventor in field; patentee in field. Home: 10358 Bonny Dr Cupertino CA 95014 Office: Tactical Fabs Inc 270 E Brokaw Rd San Jose CA 95112

PELUSI, PHILIP PAUL, cosmetologist, adminstrator; b. Pitts., Jan. 14, 1939; s. Philip Gabriel and Evelyn (Constestable) P.; m. Jacqueline Fine, Sept. 20, 1965; 1 child, Marta Eva. Diploma, Pitts. Beauty Acad., 1963. Lic. cosmetologist, Pa. Sheet metal worker Pitts., 1959-63; owner, pres. Philip Pelusi Salons Inc., Pitts., 1963—; creative dir. Internat. Design Team, Pitts., 1970—; cons. presdl. haircolorists council Clairol Inc., N.Y.C., 1984—; educator N.Y. Hair Group, Japan, 1984. Named Top Hair Designer, Lo Zeffiro mag., Milan, 1983, Am. Salon mag., 1984, The World; recipient Magnum Opus award, Phila., Fashionplate award Fashion Group Inc., Pitts., 1986. Mem. Nat. Beauty Salon Chain Assn., Internat. Color Exchange. Office: Philip Pelusi Salons Inc 5725 Forward Ave Pittsburgh PA 15217

PEMBERTON, ERNEST HUGH, manufacturing company executive; b. Marion, Ind., Nov. 28, 1943; s. Ernest Harm and Beatrice Ann (Wilson) P.; m. Judith Kay Cox, Aug. 3l, 1963; children: Anthony Hugh, Shawn Edward. Student, U. Cin., 196l-62; BSME, Purdue U., 1966; postgrad., Toledo U., 1970-7l; MBA, Bowling Green State U., 1982. With Owens-Ill., 1966-84; finish product mgr. glass container div. Owens-Ill., Toledo, 1975-82, mgr. applied process rsch., 1982-84; pres. Powers Mfg. div. Emhart's Glass Machinery Group, Elmira, N.Y., 1984—; bd. dirs. Capabilities, Inc., Elmira. Patentee in field. Mem. Clemeens Ctr. for Performing Arts, Elmira, 1984—. Mem. ASME, Chemung County C. of C. (govt. affairs coun. 1988), Arnot Art Mus., Purdue U. Alumni Assn., Bowling Green State U. Alumni Assn., Masons, Tau Beta Pi, Pi Tau Sigma. Republican. Presbyterian. Office: Powers Mfg Co ll40 Sullivan St Elmira NY 14901

PEMBERTON, NANCY JOYCE, financial executive; b. Dayton, Ohio, Feb. 23, 1953; d. Stephen Edward and Geneva (White) Fedop; m. Thomas Garry Pemberton, Nov. 24, 1985; 1 child, Christina Elizabeth. Student, St. Nicholas Coll., Sussex, Eng., 1981; BS, Ohio State U., 1982; postgrad., U. N.C., Charlotte, 1986. Teller Crocker Nat. Bank-Wells Fargo, Pomona and Twin Peaks, Calif., 1975-81; tchr. Montessori Presch., Newark, Ohio, 1973-75; asst. br. mgr. Metrolina Nat. Bank, Charlotte, 1982-83; tng. mgr. First Union Nat. Bank, Charlotte, 1983—. Editor newsletter Notes of Interest, 1985-87. Violin player Queens Coll. Community Orch., Charlotte, 1984-86, Claremont Coll. Community Orch., Calif., 1978-79. Office: First Union Nat Bank 301 S Tryon St CCO-3 Charlotte NC 28288

PEMBERTON, RONALD RAY, city official, financial company executive; b. Chgo., Oct. 14, 1950; s. Oral F. and Charlotte M. (Station) P.; m. Beverly S. Smith, Nov. 13, 1974; children: Amy, Kelly. AS in Gen. Studies, Drury Coll., 1980, BS in Sociology and Criminal Justice, 1985. Budget analyst engring and housing City of Ft. Leonard Wood, Mo., 1979-80, utility sales officer, 1980—; prin. Pemberton Fin. Svcs., Richland, Mo.; utility sales officer Energy, Mgmt., Engring. and Housing, Ft. Leonard Wood. Tchr. Sunday Sch., Beulah Bapt. Ch., Richland, 1983—, song leader, 1984—. With USN, 1968-72. Mem. Masons. Democrat. Home: PO Box 573 Richland MO 65556 Office: Energy Mgmt Fort Leonard Wood MO 65473

PEMBERTON, WILLIAM THOMAS, purchasing manager, pharmacist; b. McLeansboro, Ill., Oct. 12, 1946; s. Russell Harper and Lula Mae (Elder) P.; m. Judith Rose Hawn, Aug. 8, 1970; children: Steven, Jill. AA, Rend Lake Coll., 1974; BS in Pharmacy, St. Louis Coll., 1977. Pharmacist Walgreen Co., Maryland Heights, Mo., 1977-81; chief pharmacist Walgreen Co., Florissant, Mo., 1981-87; purchasing mgr. Correctional Med. Systems, St. Louis, 1987—. Served with USN, 1966-70, Vietnam. Mem. Am. Correctional Assn. Office: Correctional Med Systems 999 Executive Pkwy Saint Louis MO 63141

PEÑA, JORGE FELIPE, manufacturing executive; b. Acuna, Coahuila, Mex., Dec. 7, 1940; came to U.S., 1976; s. Felipe E. and Maria Concepcion (Sanchez) P.; m. Karen F. Cromack, May 18, 1968; children: Karen Patricia, Jorge Kermit. BBA, U. Tex., 1966; MBA, U. IberoAmerican, Mex. City, 1972. Cert. acct., Mex. Asst. treas. AHMSA, Monclova, Mex., 1966-69; dir. budgeting Fundidora Monterrey, Mexico City, 1969-71; v.p. fin. Industrias Franco, Mexico City, 1971-73; cons. Arthur D. Little, Inc., Mexico City, 1974-76; v.p. Tex. Commerce Bank, Brownsville, 1976-79; pres. Frontier Techs., Brownsville, 1980-86; controller, treas., adminstrv. mgr. Trico Techs., Brownsville, 1986—. Mem. Maquiladora Assn. (labor com.), Planning Execs. Inst. Mexico City, Indsl. Relations Inst. Mexico City, Rotary. Republican. Roman Catholic. Home: 1432 Robinhood Brownsville TX 78520 Office: Trico Techs Inc 1995 Billy Mitchell Brownsville TX 78520

PENCE, JERROLD BLAIR, II, real estate developer; b. Inglewood, Calif., Dec. 29, 1958; s. Jerrold Blair and Mildred Diane (Bultman) P.; m. Mary Patricia Anderson, July 24, 1982. BBA, U. So. Calif., 1981; Cert. Real Estate Fin., UCLA, 1983. Lic. real estate broker, Calif., gen. contractor, Calif. Analyst Lea Assocs., Inc., L.A., 1980-81; indsl. broker Grubb & Ellis Co., L.A., 1981-82; v.p. LeRoy Owen Co., L.A., 1982-84; pres. Pence Investment Corp., L.A., 1984—; corp. sec. Pence Fine Art, Inc., cba Pence Gallery, Santa Monica, Calif., 1986—. V.p. U. So. Calif. Friends of Fine Art, L.A., 1988-89; gov. Goodwill Industries of So. Calif., 1985—; trustee Wilshire United Meth. Ch., L.A., 1984-86; founder L.A. Mus. Contemporary Art, 1983. Mem. Am. Indsl. Real Estate Assn., Nat. Assn. Realtors, Self-Svc. Storage Assn., L.A. Bd. Realtors (pres. 1989), Calif. Assn. Realtors (bd. dir. 1986, 88, 89), Jonathan Club, L.A. Tennis Club. Republican. Methodist. Office: Pence Investment Corp 10201 S La Cienega Blvd Los Angeles CA 90045

PENCE, LARRY MICHAEL, marketing executive; b. Denver, Feb. 26, 1951; s. LeRoy Francis and Flora L. (Battochio) P.; m. Barbara J. Cuthbertson, Aug. 10, 1974. BS, Colo. State U., 1973. Agt. Mutual of Omaha Ins. Co., Denver, 1974-76, dist. mgr., 1976-83; gen. mgr. mktg. Mutual of Omaha Fund Mgmt. Co., Inc., Omaha, 1987—; cons. joint mktg. staff Mutual of Omaha Cos., 1987—. V.p. Homeowners Assn., Omaha, 1988. Mem. Investment Co. Inst., Gen. Agts. and Mgrs. Assn., Nat Assn. Life Underwriters. Repubilcan. Roman Catholic. Office: Mutual of Omaha Fund Mgmt Co 10235 Regency Circle Omaha NE 68114

PENDER, MICHAEL ROGER, engineering consultant, professional society administrator; b. Bklyn., Feb. 18, 1926; s. Horace Gibson and Lilian Frances (Higgins) P.; m. Francina Joan Krosschell, June 4, 1949; children: Michael Roger, Jr., William J., Robin Jane, Richard A., John A. AB, Dartmouth Coll., 1949, MS in Civil Engring., 1950. Registered profl. engr., Fla., N.Y., N.H.; diplomate Am. Acad. Environ. Engrs. Project engr. Madigan-Hyland, Inc., L.I., 1950-60; dir. state exhibits N.Y. World's Fair, Flushing, 1960-65; commr. pub. works, Town of Hempstead (N.Y.), 1966-77, Nassau County, Mineola, N.Y., 1978-82; supt. pub. works Village of Valley Stream (N.Y.), 1982-85; tech. advisor N.Y. State Assembly, Albany, 1985-86; cons. engr. Boyle Engring. Corp., Sarasota, Fla., 1986—; exec. dir. World's Fair Collectors Soc., 1968—; mem. Sarasota County Pub. Utilities Adv. Bd., 1986-87. Contbr. articles to profl. jours. Treas. Town of Hempstead Local Devel. Corp., 1967-86, Town of Hempstead Ind. Devel. Agy., 1973-86, Nassau County Local Devel. Corp., 1978-83; pres. Univ. Club of L.I., Hempstead, 1987-88; mem. Mote Marine Lab., Sarasota, 1987—. Sgt. U.S. Army, 1945-46. Named Profl. Engring. Mgr. of Yr., N.Y. State Soc. Profl. Engrs., 1979. Fellow ASCE, Inst. Transp. Engrs. (life); mem. NSPE (v.p. 1982-84), Fla. Engring. Soc., Am. Pub. Works Assn. (life; pres. 1984-85; one of Top Ten Pub. Works Ofcls. in U.S. 1973); Com. of 100, S.W. Br. Am. Pub. Works Assn., Sarasota County C. of C., Dartmouth Club of Sarasota (v.p.). Republican. Episcopalian. Lodge: Rotary. Avocations: photographing railroad depots. Home: 6639 Waterford Ln Sarasota FL 34238-2639 Office: World's Fair Collectors Soc PO Box 20806 Sarasota FL 34238-3806

PENDERGAST, PAULA BROWN, personnel consultant; b. Cin., Nov. 17, 1943; d. Everett Raymond and Gayle (Hosutt) Brown; m. Michael Stewart Colvin, July 1962 (div. Aug. 1972); children: Kimberly Elaine, Barbara Gayle; m. Joseph Barry Pendergast, Apr. 1975; 1 child, Patrick Alexander. Student, SUNY, Hartsdale, 1988—. Office adminstr. Eastman Kodak, Washington, 1961-63; pers. cons. Weatherby Assocs., Stamford, Conn., 1972-76; pres. Human Resources, Inc., Stamford, 1980—. Mem. Internat. Assn. for Pers. Women (v.p. publs. com. 1986-87, bd. dirs. Conn. chpt.), Nat. Assn. Temp. Svcs. (1st Pl. award for temp. employment newsletter), Nat. Assn. Pers. Cons., Profl. Collective. Republican. Congregationalist. Office: Human Resources Inc 1911 Summer St Stamford CT 06905

PENDLETON, OTHNIEL ALSOP, fund raiser, clergyman; b. Washington, Aug. 22, 1911; s. Othniel Alsop and Ingeborg (Berg) P.; m. Flordora Mellquist, May 15, 1935; children: John, James (dec.), Thomas, Ann, Susan. AB, Union Coll., Schenectady, N.Y., 1933; BD, Eastern Bapt. Theol. Sem., 1936; MA, U. Pa., 1936, PhD, 1945; postgrad., Columbia U., 1937-38. Ordained to ministry Bapt. Ch., 1936. Pastor chs. Jersey City, 1935-39, Phila., 1939-43; dean Sioux Falls Coll., S.D., 1943-45; fund raiser Am. Bapt. Ch., N.Y.C., 1945-47; fund-raiser Mass. Bapt. Ch., Boston, 1947-54; fund-raiser Seattle, Chgo., Boston, Washington, N.Y.C. and Paris, France, 1955-64, Westwood, Mass., 1971-84; staff mem. Marts & Lundy, Inc., N.Y.C., 1964-71; lectr. Andover-Newton Sem., Newton, Mass., 1958, Boston U. Sch. Theology, 1958, Harvard U., Cambridge, Mass., 1977-84. Author: New Techniques for Church Fund Raising, 1955, Fund Raising: A Guide to Non-Profit Organizations, 1981; contbr. articles in field to profl. jours. Address: 529 Berkeley Ave Claremont CA 91711

PENG, LIANG-CHUAN, mechanical engineer; b. Taiwan, Feb. 6, 1936; came to U.S., 1965, naturalized, 1973; s. Mu-Sui and Wang-Su (Yang) P.; diploma Taipei Inst. Tech., 1960; M.S., Kans. State U., 1967; m. Wen-Fong Kao, Nov. 18, 1962; children—Tsen-Loong, Tsen-Hsin, Lina, Linda. Project engr. Taiwan Power Co., 1960-65; asst. engr. Carlson & Sweatt, N.Y.C., 1966-67; asst. engr. Pioneer Engrs., Chgo., 1967-68; mech. engr. Bechtel, San Francisco, 1969-71; sr. specialist Nuclear Services Co., San Jose, Calif., 1971-75; sr. engr. Brown & Root, Houston, 1975; stress engr. Foster Wheeler, Houston, 1976; staff engr. AAA Technologists, Houston, 1977; prin. engr. M.W. Kellogg, Houston, 1978-82; pres., owner Peng Engring., Houston, 1982—; instr. U. Houston. Chmn., South Bay Area Formosan Assn., 1974, No. Calif. Formosan Fedn., 1975. Registered profl. engr., Tex., Calif. Developer: (computer progarams) SIMFLEX. Mem. ASME, Nat. Soc. Profl. Engrs. Confucian. Home: 3010 Manila Ln Houston TX 77043

PENGLASE, FRANK DENNIS, publishing company executive; b. Sherman, Tex., July 20, 1940; s. William Oliver and Martha Elizabeth (Keese) P.; m. Hilary Janet Hoffman, June 20, 1964; children: R. Benjamin, Martha D., Amy E. BA, Stanford U., 1962; MBA, Columbia U., 1966. Various exec. positions Exxon Corp., 1966-76; chief fin. and planning officer Esso Brazil (Exxon), Rio de Janeiro, 1976-81; asst. treas. Esso Europe (Exxon), London, 1981-86; sr. v.p., treas. McGraw-Hill, Inc., N.Y.C., 1986—; v.p., treas. McGraw-Hill Found., N.Y.C., 1987—. Past bd. pres. Am. Sch. Rio de Janeiro, 1979-80; v.p. alumni bd. Sch. Bus. Columbia U., 1987-88; bd. dirs. Westminister House Owners, Inc., N.Y.C., 1987—. Served to lt. (j.g.) USN, 1962-64. Mem. Fin. Execs. Inst., N.Y. Treas. Group (pres. 1987-88), Nat. Assn. Corp. Treas. Republican. Methodist. Club: Am. of London. Office: McGraw-Hill Inc 1221 Ave of the Americas New York NY 10020

PENHALLEGON, ROBERT DAY, transportation engineer; b. Evanston, Ill., Dec. 15, 1941; s. James Sherman and Virginia (Day) P.; m. Rosalia Ann Penhallegon, Dec. 5, 1970; children: William, Douglas. BS in Indsl. Engring., Lehigh U., 1964. Asst. indsl. engr. Balt. and Ohio R.R., Balt., 1966-69; indsl. engr. Chessie System R.R., Balt., 1969-74, mgr. indsl. engring., 1974-77; project mgr. Chessie System R.R., Cin., 1977-81, asst. supt. ops., 1981-82; mgr. mech. planning Chessie System R.R., Huntington, W.Va., 1982-83; dir. mech. planning Chessie System R.R., Huntington, 1983-86; dir. facility planning CSX Transp., Balt., 1986—. Mem. Am. Inst. Indsl. Engrs., Am. Railway Engring. Assn. Home: 14216 Sawmill Ct Phoenix MD 21131

PENICNAK, A. JOHN, manufacturing company executive; b. Chgo., Sept. 14, 1938; s. Clyde A. and Helen J. P.; Fern E. Penicnak; children: Deke, Christine, Adrianna. AB, Ripon Coll., 1960; MA, U. S.D., 1961; PhD, U. Mass., 1965. With Pfizer, Inc., N.Y.C., 1965-76; sr. v.p. Cosmair, Inc., N.Y.C., 1976—. Contbr. articles to profl. jours.; patentee in field. Fellow Am. Inst. Chemists, Soc. Cosmetic Chemists; mem. Am. Acad. Dermatology, N.Y. Acad. Sci., Rockaway River Country Club. Home: 151 Lookout Rd Mountain Lakes NJ 07046 Office: Cosmair Inc 575 Fifth Ave New York NY 10017

PENISTEN, GARY DEAN, pharmaceutical company executive; b. Lincoln, Nebr., May 14, 1931; s. Martin C. and Jayne (O'Dell) P.; m. Nancy Margaret Golding, June 3, 1951; children: Kris D., Janet L., Carol E., Noel M. B.S. in Bus. Adminstrn., U. Nebr., Omaha, 1953. With Gen. Electric Co., 1953-74; mgr. group fin. ops. power generation group Gen. Electric Co., N.Y.C., 1973-74; asst. sec. navy fin. mgmt. 1974-77; sr. v.p. fin., chief fin. officer, dir. Sterling Drug Inc., N.Y.C., 1977—. Bd. dirs. Goodwill Industries Greater N.Y., Goodwill Industries Am.; bd. govs. Lawrence Hosp., Bronxville, N.Y. Recipient Disting. Public Service award Navy Dept., 1977; Alumni Achievement citation U. Nebr., Omaha, 1975. Mem. Fin. Execs. Inst., Navy League U.S. Republican. Unitarian. Clubs: Union League, Econs. (N.Y.C.); Siwanoy Country. Home: 10 Fordal Rd Bronxville NY 10708 Office: Sterling Drug Inc 90 Park Ave New York NY 10016

PENNEY, CHARLES RAND, lawyer, civic worker; b. Buffalo, July 26, 1923; s. Charles Patterson and Gretchen (R) P. B.A., Yale U., 1945; J.D., U. Va., 1951. Bar: Md. 1952, N.Y. 1958, U.S. Supreme Ct. 1958. Law sec. to U.S. Dist. Ct. Judge W.C. Coleman, Balt., 1951-52; dir. devel. office Children's Hosp., Buffalo, 1952-54; sales mgr. Amherst Mfg. Corp., Williamsville, N.Y., 1954-56, also; Delevan Electronics Corp., East Aurora, N.Y.; mem. firm Penney & Penney, Buffalo, 1958-61; practiced in Niagara County, N.Y., 1961—. Mem. Lockport Meml. Hosp. Served to 2d lt. AUS, 1943-46. Recipient disting. service to culture award SUNY-Potsdam Coll. Arts and Scis., 1983. Mem. Albright-Knox Art Gallery Buffalo (life), Buffalo Mus. Sci. (life), Buffalo and Erie County Hist. Soc. (life), Niagara County Hist. Soc. (life), Old Ft. Niagara (life), Buffalo Soc. Artists (hon. trustee), Hist. Lockport (life), Landmark Soc. of Western N.Y. (life), Nat. Trust Hist. Preservation, Am. Ceramic Circle, Rochester Mus. and Sci. Center, Historic Lewiston (life), Friends of U. Rochester Libraries (life); mem. Meml. Art Gallery U. Rochester (dir.'s circle, hon. bd. mgrs.), Smithsonian Instn., Rochester Hist. Soc. (life); Mus. Am. Folk Art; mem. Whitney Mus. Am. Art, Am. Craft Council, Am. Fedn. Arts, Archives Am. Art, Margaret Woodbury Strong Mus. (charter), Met. Mus. Art, Mus. Modern Art, Mark Twain Soc. (hon.), U. Rochester's Pres.'s Soc. (hon. life), U. Iowa's Pres.'s Club (hon. life), Internat. Mus. Photography, George Eastman House, Va. Law Found., Roland Gibson Art Gallery, SUNY Coll. of Arts and Sci., Genesee Country Mus., numerous other art assns. and museums, Am. Assn. Ret. Persons, Roycrofters-at-Large Assn., Ctr. African Studies, Nat. Geog. Soc. (life), Roy Crofters-at-Large Assn., Internat. Sculpture Ctr., Soc. of Archtl. Historians, Nat. Acad. of Design, Chi Psi, Phi Alpha Delta. Clubs: Automobile (Lockport); Zwicker Aquatic, Niagara County Antiques (hon.); Rochester Art (hon. life), Plaza Athletic (Rochester). Office: 538 Bewley Bldg Lockport NY 14094

PENNIMAN, NICHOLAS GRIFFITH, IV, newspaper publisher; b. Balt., Mar. 7, 1938; s. Nicholas Griffith Penniman and Esther Cox Lony (Wight) Keeney; m. Linda Jane Simmons, Feb. 4, 1967; children: Rebecca Helmle, Nicholas G. V. AB, Princeton U., 1960. Asst. bus. mgr. Ill. State Jour. Register, Springfield, 1964-69, bus. mgr., 1969-75; asst. gen. mgr. St. Louis Post-Dispatch, 1975-84, gen. mgr., 1984-86, pub., 1986—. Chmn. Downtown St. Louis, Inc., 1988—; chmn. Mo. Health and Ednl. Facilities Adminstrn., St. Louis, 1982-85; chmn. Ill. State Fair Bd., Springfield, 1973-75; trustee St. Louis Country Day Sch., 1983-86; bd. dirs. St. Louis Arts and Edn. Council, St. Louis Area Council Boys Scouts Am., 1987—, First St. Forum, Washington U. Library Nat. Council, Regional Commerce and Growth Assn., 1988; chmn. Caring Found. for Children, 1988—. Served with U.S. Army, 1962-67. Clubs: St. Louis Country, Noonday. Home: 1240 Lay Rd Saint Louis MO 63124 Office: St Louis Post Dispatch 900 N Tucker Blvd Saint Louis MO 63101

PENNINGTON, BRUCE CARTER, corporate communications consultant; b. Kansas City, Mo., Oct. 22, 1932; s. Dwight Hillis and Esther Helena (Carter) P.; m. Gloria Artinian, July 1, 1960(div. 1985); children: Bruce Carter, Juliet Jean, Adam Dwight; m. Sigrid Helga Schley, July 22, 1987. BA, Kenyon Coll., 1953; postgrad., U. So. Calif., 1957. Feature writer, book reviewer Kansas City Star, 1947-62; brakeman Santa Fe R.R., 1952; TV story editor Universal Studios, Four Star Studios, L.A., 1956-59; writer Time Mag., Beverly Hills, Calif., 1959; feature writer Sta. CBS-TV, Los Angeles, 1960-63; free-lance writer, producer Beverly Hills, 1963-65; dir. new TV programs Benton & Bowles, Los Angeles, 1964-65; dir TV program devel. Grey Advt., N.Y.C., 1966-67; dir. TV spls. BBDO, N.Y.C., 1967-68; 1st producer Sesame St., 1969; mgr. TV program Needham, Harper & Steers, N.Y.C., 1969-70; communications cons., producer Nat. Assn. Mfrs., Washington, 1971-73; communications cons., producer office of edn. HEW, Washington, 1973-74; cons., dir. mgmt. communications Am. Can Co., Greenwich, Conn., 1974-76; founder, v.p., mng. dir. corp. communications div. Young & Rubicam, N.Y.C., 1976-77; ptnr., v.p. Chester Burger & Co., N.Y.C., 1978-81; dir. communications, cons. Hay Assocs., N.Y.C., 1981-83; pres. Pennington/Wilke Assocs., Ltd., N.Y.C., 1983-85; prin. Bruce Pennington Assocs., Inc., N.Y.C., 1985—; lectr. Columbia U. Grad. Sch. Bus. U. Mo., 1980—; also other Univs. Officer Hastings-on-Hudson Vol. Fire Dept. With U.S. Army, 1953-55. Recipient award U.S. Indsl. Film Festival, 1977, Freedoms Found., 1954. Fellow Cambridge Inst. Applied Rsch.; mem. Pub. Rels. Soc. Am., Mensa, Beta Theta Pi. Episcopalian. Home: 456 W 25th St New York NY 10001 Office: Bruce Pennington Assocs Inc 1180 Ave of Americas New York NY 10036

PENNINGTON, LEE DOYAL, financial planner; b. Oklahoma City, Oct. 3, 1930; s. Lee and Fannie Etta (Clary) P.; m. Andrea Scott (div. 1955); children: Michael Scott (adopted), Diantha Lee Pennington Roberts; m. Beth Lee Feather, June 5, 1960; 1 child, Penni Lynn. Student, Connors State A&M U., 1950, Okla. U., 1954-55; student Inst. Ins. Mktg., So. Meth. U., 1958. Cert. fin. planner. Life ins. salesman Acacia Mut. Ins. Co., Okla., 1953-55; mgr. First Pyramid Life Ins. Co., Ark. and Okla., 1955-60, Tex. Life Ins. Co., Lubbock, 1960-68; fin. planner Fin. Service Corp., Lubbock, 1968-74; owner, fin. planner, chief exec. officer, chmn. bd. dirs. Pennington, Bass & Assocs., Inc., Lubbock, 1975—; grad. Coll. Fin. Planning, Denver, 1974. Contbr. articles to trade jours., mags., newspapers. Pres. Lubbock Theater Ctr., 1971-72; mem. human rels. commn. City of Lubbock, 1972-76; cons. Family Service Assn., Lubbock, 1975-76; bd. dirs. Am. Heart Assn., Lubbock, 1971-73; mem. dean's adv. coun. for devel. coll. home econs. Tex. Tech U., 1987—. Served with USMC, 1950-53, Korea. Mem. Internat. Assn. for Fin. Planning (nat. bd. dirs. 1981-83, frequent speaker at conferences, founder West Tex. chpt.), Inst. Cert. Fin. Planners (named planner of yr. so. region 1985), Found. for Fin. Planning (trustee 1986-87), Internat. Bd. Standards and Practices (nat. bd. dirs. 1986-88), Million Dollar Round Table (life). Baptist. Office: Pennington/Bass Cos 1001 Main Ste 100 Lubbock TX 79401

PENNISTEN, JOHN WILLIAM, actuary, computer scientist; b. Buffalo, Jan. 25, 1939; s. George William and Lucy Josephine (Gates) P. AB with hons. in math. and chem., Hamilton Coll., 1960; NSF fellow in math. Harvard U., 1960-61; postgrad. U.S. Army Lang. Sch., 1962-63; MS in Computer Sci. with hons., N.Y. Inst. Tech., 1987; cert. in taxation, NYU, 1982; cert. in profl. banking Am. Inst. of Banking of Am. Bankers Assn., 1988. Actuarial asst. New Eng. Mut. Life Ins. Co., Boston, 1965-66; asst. actuary Mass. Gen. Life Ins. Co., Boston, 1966-68; actuarial assoc. John Hancock Mut. Life Ins. Co., Boston, 1968-71; asst. actuary George B. Buck Cons. Actuaries, Inc., N.Y.C., 1971-75, Martin E. Segal Co., N.Y.C., 1975-80; cons. actuary Laiken Siegel & Co., N.Y.C., 1980; cons. Bklyn., 1981—; timesharing and database analyst Chem. Bank N.Y.C. banklink corp. cash mgmt. div. 1983-85; programmer analyst Empire Blue Cross and Blue Shield, N.Y.C., 1986—; enrolled actuary U.S. Fed. Pension Legis. Bklyn., 1976—. Contbr. articles to profl. jours. Served with U.S. Army, 1961-64. Mem. AAAS, Soc. Actuaries (fellow), Am. Acad. Actuaries, Practising Law Inst., Am. Mgmt. Assn., Assn. Computing Machinery, IEEE Computer Soc., Am. Assn. Artificial Intelligence, Linguistic Soc. Am., Assn. Computational Linguistics, Am. Math. Soc., Math. Assn. Am., Nat. Model R.R. Assn. (life), Nat. Ry. Hist. Soc., Ry. and Locomotive Hist. Soc. (life), N.Y.C. Opera Guild, Met. Opera Guild, Am. Friends of Covent Garden, Harvard Gra. Soc., Am. Legion, Phi Beta Kappa, others. Home: 135 Willow St Brooklyn NY 11201

PENNOCK, DONALD WILLIAM, mechanical engineer; b. Ludlow, Ky., Aug. 8, 1915; s. Donald and Melvin (Evans) P.; B.S. in M.E., U. Ky., 1940, M.E., 1948; m. Vivian C. Kern, Aug. 11, 1951; 1 son, Douglas. Stationary engring., constrn. and maintenance Schenley Corp., 1935-39; mech. equipment design engr. mech. lab. U. of Ky., 1939; exptl. test engr. Wright Aero. Corp., Paterson, N.J., 1940, 1941, investigative and adv. engr. to personnel div., 1941-43; indsl. engr. Eastern Aircraft, div. Gen. Motors, Linden, N.J., 1943-45; factory engr. Carrier Corp., Syracuse, N.Y., 1945-58, sr. facilities engr., 1958-60, corporate material handling engr., 1960-63, mgr. facilities engring. dept., 1963-66, mgr. archtl. engring., 1966-68, mgr. facilities engring. dept., 1968-78. Staff, Indsl. Mgmt. Center, 1962, midwest work course U. Kan., 1959-67. Mem. munitions bd. SHIAC, 1950-52; trustee Primitive Hall Found., 1985—. Elected to Exec. and Profl. Hall of Fame, 1966. Registered profl. engr., Ky., N.J., D.C. Fellow Soc. Advancement Mgmt. (life mem., nat. v.p. material handling div. 1953-54); mem. ASME, Am. Material Handling Soc. (dir. 1950-57, chmn. bd., pres. 1950-52), Am. Soc. Mil. Engrs., Nat. Soc. Profl. Engrs., Am. Mgmt. Assn. (men. packaging council 1950-55, life mem. planning council), Nat. Material Handling Conf. (exec. com. 1951), Found. N.Am. Wild Sheep (life), Internat. Platform Assn., Tau Beta Pi. Protestant. Mng. editor Materials Handling Engring. (mag. sect.), 1949-50; mem. editorial adv. bd. Modern Materials Handling (mag.), 1949-52. Contbr. articles to tech. jours. Contbg., cons. editor: Materials Handling Handbook, 1958. Home: 24 Pebble Hill Rd De Witt NY 13214

PENNOYER, RUSSELL PARSONS, oil company executive; b. N.Y.C., June 7, 1951; s. Robert Morgan and Victoria Lee (Parsons) P.; m. Helen Bearn, Sept. 30, 1978; children: Gordon Slocum, Robert Morgan II, Margaret Elliot. BA, Harvard U., 1974; JD, Columbia U., 1982. Bar: N.Y. 1983. Banker Morgan Guaranty Trust, N.Y.C., 1974-79; assoc. Davis Polk & Wardwell, N.Y.C., 1982-84; v.p., gen. counsel Am. Exploration Co., N.Y.C., 1984-86, v.p. fin., gen. counsel sec., 1986-87, sr. v.p., gen. counsel, 1988—. Trustee Bodman Found., Achelis Found. Mem. ABA, Assn.of Bar of N.Y.C. Republican. Presbyterian. Home: 145 E 74th St New York NY 10021 Office: Am Exploration Co Ste 2500 885 3rd Ave New York NY 10022

PENNY, ROGER PRATT, metallurgical engineer; b. Buffalo, July 13, 1936; s. George Albert and Louise (Mings) P.; m. Judith Stevens, Aug. 25, 1957; children: David, Sarah, Julia. BS in Adminstrv. Engring., Union Coll., 1958. Registered profl. engr., N.Y., Ind., Pa. From supt. to sr. mgr. Bethlehem Steel Corp., Lackawanna, N.Y., 1958-83; gen. mgr. Bethlehem Steel Corp., Burns Harbor, Ind., 1983-87; sr. v.p. Bethlehem (Pa.) Steel Corp., 1987—. Mem. United Way, Buffalo, 1960-82; chmn. campaign United Way Porter County, Valparaiso, Ill., 1986; councilman Orchard Park Town Council, 1970-82; mem. adv. bd. Purdue U., Lafayette, Ind., 1985-86, bus. sch. Valparaiso U., 1986; bd. dirs. Minsi Trails Council Boy Scouts Am., Lehigh Valley, Pa., 1988—. Mem. Am. Iron & Steel Inst., Assn. Iron & Steel Engrs., Valparaiso C. of C. (dir. 1985-86), Orchard Park C. of C., Buffalo C. of C., Sand Creek Club (pres. 1983-86), Bethlehem Mgmt. Club (pres. 1962-82), Buffalo Soccer Club (pres. 1960-75), Saucon Valley Country Club. Republican. Episcopalian. Office: Bethlehem Steel Corp Martin Tower Rm 2018 701 E 3rd St Bethlehem PA 18106

PENROSE, CYNTHIA C., health plan administrator, consultant; b. Manila, Philippines, Nov. 24, 1939; came to U.S., 1940; d. Douglas Lee Lipscomb Cordiner and Jane (Sturgeon) Edises; m. Douglas Francis Penrose, July 11, 1959 (div. 1981); children—Vicki Lynn, Lee Douglas; m. Alan Harrison Magazine, Aug. 30, 1984. B.A., U. Calif.-Berkeley, 1963; M.B.A., U. Santa Clara, 1977. Cert. social services. Vice pres and dir. employment Resource Ctr. for Women, Palo Alto, Calif., 1973-78; bus. planner Raychem Corp., Menlo Park, Calif., 1979; adminstrv. mgr. Electric Power Research Inst., Palo Alto, 1979-83; dir. ops. Utility Data Inst., Washington, 1984-85; dir. ops. Randmark, Inc., 1986-87; coordinator mkt. devel. for Mid-Atlantic States Kaiser Foundation Health Plan, Washington, 1987-88, asst. to Assoc. regional mgr., 1988—; sr. ptnr. MB Assocs., Washington, 1983-88; bd. dirs. and treas. Unique Enterprises, Washington, 1985-87; sec. Wesley Property Mgmt. Co., 1987—; bd. dirs. Wesley Housing Devel. Corp., 1988—. Bd. dirs., v.p. LWV, Berkeley and Palo Alto, 1966-73; chmn. program adv. council Resource Ctr. for Women, Palo Alto, 1980-83; mem. Affirmative Action Adv. Com. Palo Alto, 1975-76. Mem. Exec. Women's Roundtable (Washington, founder), Peninsula Profl. Women's Network (v.p. 1981-82), Women in Energy, Am. Soc. Assn. Execs., Wed. Group U. Calif. Alumni Assn., AAUW (Bicentennial br. sec. 1986-88, bd. dirs. Washington div. 1988—), Am. Soc. on Aging, United Srs. Health Coop., LWV. Democrat. Episcopalian. Avocations: swimming; nutrition and health; reading. Home: 1302 Chancel Pl Alexandria VA 22314 Office: Kaiser-Permanente 4200 Wisconsin Ave Washington DC 20016

PENTHENY, LAURA EDNA, construction executive; b. Framingham, Mass., Oct. 28, 1948; d. Harold Otis Pentheny and Hedwig Edna (Zaleski) Ramsey; m. Robert W. Perry, Oct. 23, 1976. Student, Dade jr. Coll., 1966-68, Cole Constrn. Coll., 1974-76. Cert. gen. contractor, Fla.; comml. contractor, Tenn.; bldg. contractor, La.; gen. contractor, S.C. Estimator Hammer Constrn. Corp., Miami, Fla., 1971-73; sec.-treas. P.D. Ray Constrn. Corp., Miami, Fla., 1973-76, Bob Perry Constrn. Corp., Miami, 1976—; pres. B.P.C. Corp., Miami, 1981—. Mem. Assn. Gen. Contractors (S. Fla. chpt.), Everglades Recreation and Protection Soc. Republican. Congregationalist. Office: BPC Corp 8350 NW 70th St Miami FL 33166

PENTIMAKI, ISAAC RALPH, information systems specialist; b. Grand Rapids, Mich., Aug. 4, 1958; s. Oliver Adolph and Gertrude Martha (Frederick) P. BS in Computer Scis., U. Wis., 1981. Pres., chief exec. officer R.R. Software, Inc., Madison, Wis., 1981—. Mem. Assn. for Computer Machinery. Office: R R Software Inc PO Box 1512 Madison WI 53701

PEPER, CHRISTIAN BAIRD, lawyer; b. St. Louis, Dec. 5, 1910; s. Clarence F. and Christine (Baird) P.; m. Ethel C. Kingsland, June 5, 1935; children: Catherine K. Peper Larson, Anne Peper Perkins, Christian B. A.B. cum laude, Harvard, 1932; LL.B., Washington U., 1935; LL.M. (Sterling fellow), Yale, 1937. Bar: Mo. bar 1934. Since practiced in St. Louis; of counsel Peper, Martin, Jensen, Maichel & Hetlage.; Lectr. various subjects Washington U. Law Sch., St. Louis, 1943-61; partner A.G. Edwards & Sons, 1945-67; pres. St. Charles Gas Corp., 1953-72; dir. St. Louis Steel Casting Inc., Hydraulic Press Brick Co.; pres. Tricor Drilling Co. Editor: An Historian's Conscience: The Correspondence of Arnold J. Toynbee and Columba Cary-Elwes, 1986. Contbr. articles to profl. jours. Mem. vis. com. Harvard Div. Sch., 1964-70; counsel St. Louis Art Mus.; bd. dirs. Chatham House Found. Mem. Am., Mo., St. Louis bar assns., Order of Coif, Phi Delta Phi. Roman Catholic. Clubs: Noonday, University, Harvard (St. Louis); East India (London). Home: 1454 Mason Rd Saint Louis MO 63131 Office: 720 Olive St Saint Louis MO 63101

PEPPER, LOUIS HENRY, financial executive, lawyer; b. Libertyville, Ill., July 21, 1924; s. Louis Henry and Dora Anna (Sievers) P.; m. Mollie Venables, Apr. 25, 1953; children: Louis S., Margaret E. Pepper Glessner, Elizabeth A., Catherine A. BA, U. Wis., 1950, JD, 1951; Sr. ptnr. Foster Pepper Riviera, Seattle, 1952-81; pres., chief exec. officer Wash. Mut. Savs. Bank, Seattle, 1981-82, chmn., chief exec. officer, 1982—; chmn. Joint House Fin. Inst. Commn., Wash. State Legis., Olympia, 1984-85; mem. thrift instn. adv. council Fed., Res. Bd., Washington, 1988. Regent Wash. State U., Pullman, 1986—; bd. dirs. Downtown Seattle Assn., 1985—, Washington Savs. League, 1988, Fed. Home Loan Bank of Seattle, 1988; chmn. Seattle Sch. Levy campaign, 1986, 88, Seattle-King County Econ. Devel. Council, 1987-88. Served to 1st lt. USAAF, 1943-46, PTO. Named one of top 20 banking attys. in U.S. Nat. Law Jour., 1983. Mem. ABA (com. chmn. 1977-82), Wash. Bar Assn., Am. Coll. Real Estate Lawyers, Anglo-Am. Real Property Inst., Assn. Mut. Savings Banks (gen. counsel 1954-80), Nat. Coun. Savs. Instns. (bd. dirs. 1986—, chmn. com. legis., regulatory policy 1982-84), Greater Seattle C. of C. (bd. dirs. 1984—), Rainier Club, Univ. Club, Seattle Tennis Club (pres. 1972-74), Rotary. Avocations: skiing, writing. Office: Wash Mut Savs Bank 1101 2nd Ave PO Box 834 Seattle WA 98111

PEPPER, MARY JANICE, educational consultant; b. Pearsall, Tex., Oct. 1, 1942; d. Muriel Newton and Jane (Harbour) Moore; m. Clifton Gail Pepper, Feb. 19, 1961; children: John David, James Newton, Jeffery Michael. Student, U. Tex., 1960, 65, 76. Bus. mgr. Natalia (Tex.) Independent Sch. Dist., 1967-71; statistician Tex. Edn. Agy., Austin, 1971-72; mgr. bookkeeping div. Tex. Ednl. Cons. Service Inc., Austin, 1972-76, adminstrv. v.p., 1976-82, v.p., chief operating officer, 1982—; team tchr. edn. program. U. Tex., Austin, 1985; lectr. Tex. Assn. Secondary Sch. Prins., Austin, 1988. Editor: Sch. Fin. Newsletter, Update for Sch. Adminstrs. Sec. Community Indsl. Found., Natalia, 1969-71, Medina County Water Control and Improvement, Natalia, 1970-71; mem. adv. com. Tex. Edn. Agy. Mem. Tex. Assn. Sch. Bus. Ofcls. (instr. 1987-88), Mended Hearts. Baptist. Home: 1311 Quail Park Dr Austin TX 78758 Office: Tex Ednl Consultative Svcs Inc 1005 E Saint Elmo Rd Austin TX 78745

PEPPET, RUSSELL FREDERICK, accountant; b. Chgo., Oct. 3, 1939; s. George Russell and Elizabeth (Foster) P.; m. Rosemary Meyer, June 18, 1960; children—Cynthia, Jeffrey, Scott. B.S. in Math, Mich. State U., 1960; M.B.A., Northwestern U., 1963. C.P.A., Ill., Minn. Cons. Peat, Marwick, Mitchell & Co., Chgo., 1961-68; head mgmt. cons. dept. Peat, Marwick, Mitchell & Co., Mpls., 1968-72; partner Peat, Marwick, Mitchell & Co., 1969-88; sr. cons. partner for Continental Europe, Paris, 1972-78, partner-in-charge mgmt. cons. dept., N.Y. office, 1978-81, vice chmn. mgmt. cons., 1981-86; mng. ptnr. San Jose Bus. Unit, 1986-88; v.p. internat. devel. Towers Perrin, N.Y.C., 1989—. Bd. dirs. Exec. Council on Fgn. Diplomats. Served with U.S. Army, 1962-64. Mem. Am. Inst. C.P.A.'s. Club: Sky (N.Y.C.). Home: 150 E 69th St #18G New York NY 10021 Office: Towers Perrin 245 Park Ave New York NY 10167-0128

PEPPLES, ERNEST, tobacco company executive; b. Louisville, Feb. 13, 1935; s. Ernest Clifton and Goldie Mae (Byington) P.; m. Martha Scott Norman; children: J. Craig, Eleanor Evans, Cindy. AB, Yale U., 1957; LLB, U. Va., 1963. Bar: Ky., 1963. Ptnr. Wyatt, Graton & Sloss (name changed to Wyatt, Tarrant & Combs), Louisville, 1963-75; v.p., gen. counsel Brown & Williamson Tobacco Corp., Louisville, 1975-80, sr. v.p., 1980—, also bd. dirs.; bd. dirs. Tobacco Inst., Washington, Council for Tobacco Research Inc., N.Y., Ky. Tobacco Research Bd., Lexington. Pres. Louisville and Jefferson County Health and Welfare Council, 1972-73, Neighborhood Housing Services Inc., Louisville, 1986-87. Served to 1st lt. U.S. Army, 1957-60. Mem. ABA, Ky. Bar Assn., Tobacco Mchts. Assn. (bd. dirs. 1975—). Democrat. Mem. Christian Ch. Clubs: Louisville Country, Pendennis, Tavern. Home: 2420 Longest Ave Louisville KY 40204 Office: Brown & Williamson Tobacco Corp 1500 Brown & Williamson Tower Louisville KY 40202

PERATIS, MERLE, ceramics wholesaler; b. Rigby, Idaho, Feb. 18, 1919; d. Delos Clark Waters and Hannah Leona (Ossmen) Waters Buchmiller; m. Tom John Peratis, Apr. 8, 1944; children: Jeri Peratis Warner, Janelle Peratis Cushing. BS, Brigham Young U., 1940. Prin. Merle's Ceramic Studio, St. George, Utah, 1949-50; owner, mgr. Capital Ceramics, Salt Lake City, 1950-69; corp. officer Capital Ceramics, Inc., Salt Lake City, 1969—. Author: Wonderful Business of Ceramics, 1967; contbr. articles to Popular Ceramics mag., Ceramic Scope mag. Mem. Ceramic Arts Assn. Utah, Nat. Ceramic Assn., Ceramic Bus. Assn., Ceramic Distbrs. Am., Ceramic Arts Fedn. Am., Ceramic Arts Fedn. Internat. Office: Capital Ceramics Inc 2174 S Main St Salt Lake City UT 84115

PERDUE, FRANKLIN P., poultry and farm products company executive. m. Mitzi Henderson Ayala, July 1980. Chmn. bd. Perdue Farms Inc., Salisbury, Md.; also chmn. bd. Perdue Inc. subs. Perdue Farms Inc., Salisbury. Office: Perdue Farms Inc PO Box 1537 Salisbury MD 21801 *

PERELLA, JOSEPH ROBERT, investment banker; b. Newark, Sept. 20, 1941; s. Dominic A. and Agnes P.; m. Amy Gralnick, Jan. 20, 1974. B.S., Lehigh U., 1964; M.B.A., Harvard U., 1972. C.P.A., N.Y. Pub. acct. Haskins & Sells, N.Y.C., 1964-70; cons. Internat. Bank for Reconstruction & Devel., Washington, 1971; assoc. The First Boston Corp., N.Y.C., 1972-74, asst. v.p., 1974-75, v.p., 1975-78, mng. dir., 1978-88; chmn. Wasserstein, Perella & Co., N.Y.C., 1988—. Office: Wasserstein Perella & Co 31 W 52d St New York NY 10019

PERELMAN, DALE R., retail company executive; b. New Castle, Pa., Jan. 12, 1942; s. Lawrence and Janice (Sandusky) P.; m. Michele Gail Keyes, July 28, 1963; children: Sean Loren, Robyn Anne. BA, Brown U., 1963; MBA, U. Pa., 1965; grad., Gemological Inst. Am., 1985. Dir. mktg. Campus Sportswear, Cleve., 1965-81; v.p. King's Jewelry, New Castle, 1972-81, pres., 1981—; bd. dirs. 1st Fed. Savs. & Loan, New Castle. Author: Mountain of Light, 1985. Pres. New Castle Playhouse, 1980, Temple Israel, 1982-83; bd. dirs. United Way, 1986—, Lawrence County Hist. Soc., 1986—. Named Honoree of Yr. State of Israel Bonds, New Castle, 1988. Mem. Am. Soc. Appraisers, Nat. Assn. Jewelry Appraisers, Am. Soc. Appraisers (v.p. Pitts. chpt. 1986—, bd. dirs.), Diamond Council Am. (guild gemologist, v.p. 1984-87, pres. 1988—, bd. dirs.), Jewelers of Am., Pa. Jewelers Assn., (bd. dirs. 1986—), Greater New Castle C. of C. Republican. Jewish. Clubs: New Castle Country, Lawrence. Lodges: Masons, B'nai Brith, Rotary (bd. dirs. 1987—). Office: King's Jewelry PO Box 630 New Castle PA 16103

PERELMAN, LEON JOSEPH, paper manufacturing executive, university president; b. Phila., Aug. 28, 1911; s. Morris and Jennie (Davis) P.; m. Beverly Waxman, Jan. 27, 1945 (div. Apr. 1960); children: Cynthia, David. B.A., LaSalle Coll., 1933, LL.D., 1978; postgrad., U. Pa. Law Sch., 1933-35; L.H.D. (hon.), Dropsie U., 1976. Ptnr., Am. Paper Products Co. (later Am. Paper Products Inc.), Phila., 1935-42; pres. Am. Paper Products Co. (later Am. Paper Products Inc.), 1943—, Am. Cone & Tube Co. Inc., 1953—, United Ammunition Container Inc., 1961—, Ajax Paper Tube Co., 1962—; vice chmn. bd. Belmont Industries, 1963—; pres. Dropsie U., 1978—. Author: Perelman Antique Toy Mus., 1972. Fin. chmn. Valley Forge council Boy Scouts Am., 1968; founder, bd. dirs. Perelman Antique Toy Mus., Phila., 1969; pres. West Park Hosp., 1975-78, 81—; trustee La Salle U., Balch Inst. Ethnic Studies. Served to 1st lt. USAAF, 1942-45. Recipient citation Jewish Theol. Sem., 1965; Beth Jacob award, 1966; award Pop Warner Little Scholars Inc., 1972; Cyrus Adler award Jewish Theol. Sem., 1976. Mem. AAUP, Jewish Publ. Soc. Am. (treas. 1983), Franklin Inst., Am. Assn. Mus. Republican. Jewish. Clubs: Union League (Phila.); Masons, Shriners. Office: 2113-41 E Rush St Philadelphia PA 19134

PERELMAN, MELVIN, pharmaceutical company executive; b. Omaha, Oct. 12, 1930; s. Benjamin and Sarah (Fox) P.; m. Jill Louise Stott, Aug. 1, 1953; children: Steven Eric, Wendy Lynn, Kent Bryan. BS, Northwestern U., 1952; PhD, Rice U., 1956; postdoctoral research, Fed. Inst. Tech., Zurich, 1956-57. Organic chemist Eli Lilly and Co., Indpls., 1957-58, sr. organic chemist, 1958-62, corp. trainee, 1962-64, staff asst. to exec. dir. control, 1964, mng. dir. rsch. activities in Eng., 1964-70, elected v.p. Eli Lilly Internat., 1969, exec. dir. facilities planning, 1970-72, v.p. devel. rsch., 1972-74, v.p. facilities planning, 1974-76, pres. Eli Lilly Internat. Corp, 1976-86, exec. v.p. and pres. Lilly Rsch. Labs., 1986—, also bd. dirs.; exec. v.p., pres. Lilly Rsch. Labs., 1986—. Contbr. articles to profl. jours., 1954-64; patentee in field. Chmn. founder bd. Indpls. Zool. Soc., 1986—; bd. dirs. Pub. Svc. Ind., Plainfield, 1980—. Home: 3030 W 116th St Carmel IN 46032 Office: Eli Lilly & Co Lilly Corporate Ctr Indianapolis IN 46285

PERELMAN, RONALD OWEN, diversified holding company executive; b. Greensboro, N.C., 1943; s. Raymond and Ruth (Caplan) P.; m. Claudia Cohen; 4 children. BA, U. Pa., 1964; MBA, Wharton Sch. Fin., 1966. With Belmont Industries Inc., 1966-78; chmn., chief exec. officer, dir. MacAndrews & Forbes Holdings, Inc., Wilmington, Del., 1983—; chmn., chief exec. officer MacAndrews & Forbes Group, Inc. (subs.), N.Y.C., 1978—; chmn., chief exec. officer, dir. Revlon Group, Inc., N.Y.C., 1985—; chmn., chief exec. officer Revlon, Inc. (subs.), N.Y.C., 1985—; also chmn. Nat. Health Labs., Inc., 1985—, Andrews Group, Inc., 1985—; bd. dirs. Four Star Internat. Inc., Compact Video Inc. Jewish. Office: Revlon Inc 767 Fifth Ave New York NY 10022 also: MacAndrews & Forbes Group Inc 36 E 63rd St New York NY 10021

PERERA, CHARITH, marketing executive; b. Moratuwa, Sri Lanka, Oct. 6, 1957; came to U.S., 1981; parents John Eardley Russel and Rita Shirley Vennetia (Fernando) P. BS with honors, U. Colombo, Sri Lanka, 1979; MS in Mgmt., MIT, 1983. Cost analyst Mikechris Group, Colombo, Sri Lanka, 1979-80, fin. analyst, 1980-81, stragic planner, 1982; market analyst CSX Transp., Jacksonville, Fla., 1983-84, market mgr., 1984-85; dir. mktg. CSX Transp., Balt., 1985—. Mem. Chartered Inst. Mgmt. Accts. Office: CSX Transp 100 N Charles St Baltimore MD 21230

PEREZ, DANIEL LUJAN, banker; b. Agana, Guam, Jan. 25, 1954; s. Ignacio B. and Trinidad C. (Lujan) P.; m. Priscilla N. Peredo, Oct. 9, 1976; children: Philip, Patrick, Peter, Preston. BBA, U. Guam, Agana, 1977; cert. in banking, U. Wash., 1986. V.p., mgr. Bank of Guam, Agana, 1986-88, v.p., gen. auditor, 1988—. Named one of Outstanding Young Men of Am., 1984. Mem. Calif. Bankers Assn., San Francisco C. of C. Office: Bank Guam PO Box BW Agana GU 96910

PEREZ, GERARD VINCENT, art publishing company executive; b. LeMans, France, Oct. 5, 1946; came to U.S., 1971; s. Georges and Marie-Laurence (Anziani) P.; m. Nancy J. Rudin, Apr. 23, 1976; children: Samantha, Amanda. BA, B. Franklin Coll., Orleans, France, 1966; MBA, ESCAE Marseille, France, 1970; postgrad., Am. Grad. Sch. Internat. Mgmt., Glendale, Ariz., 1973. Owner, mgr. Mariettes Unltd., St. Tropez, France, 1967-69; sales engr. Paper Converting Machine Co., Inc., Green Bay, Wis., 1973-75; mgr. sales J.D. Marshall Internat., Skokie, Ill., 1975-77; pres. Fine Art Resources, Inc., Chgo., 1977-86, London Contemporary Art, Prospect Heights, Ill., 1986—; also bd. dirs. London Contemporary Art, Deerfield, Ill. Served with French Armed Forces, 1970-71. Home: 335 Babcock St Palatine IL 60067

PERILMAN, STUART HENRY, accountant; b. Pitts., June 10, 1942; s. Saul I. and Florence (Bennett) P.; m. Wendy Lupovitz, June 21, 1964; children: Mark Lyle, Staci Vanessa. BA, Duquesne U., 1964. Staff acct. McKeever, Swartz & Co., Pitts., 1963-66; audit mgr. Alexander Grant & Co., Washington and Pitts., 1968-75; pvt. practice Stuart H. Perilman, CPA, Pitts., 1975—; pres. Banksville Cleaners, Inc.; treas. Equity Holdings, Inc. Pres. B'nai B'rith Lodge, 1975-77; membership chmn. Pitts. Council B'nai B'rith, 1977-78, treas. 1979-82, 2d v.p. Western region youth orgn., 1978; asst. fin. sec., 1980-82. v.p., 1982-86, pres. 1986-88; mem. Bethel Congregation of South Hills, 1985-87. 2d lt. U.S. Army, 1976-78. Decorated Bronze Star, Vietnam Service medal. Mem. Am. Inst. CPA's, Pa. Inst. CPA's.

PERINI, JOSEPH R., corporate executive; b. Framingham, Mass., Sept. 7, 1930; m. Rosemarie P.; 5 children. B.S. in Engring., Va. Polytech. Inst., 1952; postgrad. U. Hawaii, 1954-55, Boston U., 1957; LL.D., St. Anselem's Coll., 1980. Sr. v.p., chmn. exec. com., bd. dirs., vice chmn., pres. Perini Internat. Corp., Framingham. Bd. dirs., chmn. Family Counseling and Guidance Ctrs. Inc., 1970-73; active Algonquin council Boy Scouts Am., Named Disting. Citizen of Yr., Algonquin council Boy Scouts Am., 1979. Mem. Am. Road and transp. Builders Assn. (bd. dirs., nat. chmn. 1983-84), Constrn. Industries Mass. (1st pres., past bd. dirs.), ASCE, Am. Soc. Mil. Engrs., Assn. Profl. Engrs. (Can.), Moles. Lodges: Knights of Don Orione (gen. chmn., named Don Orione Home Man of Yr. 1976); Knights of Malta. Office: Perini Corp 73 Mt Wayte Ave Framingham MA 01701

PERKINS, CARROLL MASON, utility financial official; b. Green Creek, Ohio, Mar. 11, 1929; s. James Montgomery and Marian (Lund) P.; m. Maxine Joan Corrington, June 24, 1952; children: Michael J., Sherrill L., Timothy C., Jeffrey S. BS, U. Calif.-Berkeley, 1950; MS, Ariz. State U., 1963, D.B.A., 1975. Agr. statistician USDA, 1951-56; rate analyst, supr. rates, mgr., power service dir., planning, asst. gen. mgr. fin. services, treas. Salt River Project, Phoenix, 1956-85; treas. Salt River Project, 1980—, assoc. gen. mgr., fin. and info. services, chief fin. officer, 1985—; mem. Mcpl. Securities Rulemaking Bd. Past bd. dirs. NW YMCA., Heritage Sq. Found.; pres. Ariz. Lung Assn., Phoenix, 1983—; mem. Council of 100, Ariz. State U. Coll. of Bus. Served with USN, 1951-53. Mem. Ariz. Reclamation Assn., Am. Public Power Assn. (chmn. rate com. 1971, treas. 1984—), Ariz. Tax Research Assn. (past bd. dirs.), Ariz. Electric League (bd. dirs. 1974-75). Republican. Methodist. Lodge: Phoenix Kiwanis (bd. dirs. 1979-80). Office: Salt River Project 1521 Project Dr Tempe AZ 85072

PERKINS, DAVID MILES, SR., die casting company executive; b. Racine, Wis., Feb. 11, 1949; s. Charles E. and Barbara (Miles) P.; m. Catherine Cann, May 26, 1972; children: Charles William, Daivd Miles Jr. BA in Econs., DePaul U., 1971; MBA, Marquette U., 1974. Purchasing agt. Acme Die Casting Co., Racine, 1972-73; contr. Acme Die Casting Co., 1973-76, v.p. fin., treas., 1975—, sec., 1980—, bd. dirs.; bd. dirs. Racine Federated, Inc. Mem. Racine Planning Coun., 1981-86; bd. dirs. Family Planning Coun., 1984—, St. Luke's Meml. Hosp., Racine, 1987—. Mem. Racine Country Club (bd. dirs. 1981-86, pres. 1985), Rotary. Home: 300 Lake Crest Dr Racine WI 53402 Office: Acme Die Casting co 5626 21st St Racine WI 53406

PERKINS, GEORGE WILLIAM, II, financial services executive, film producer; b. Salem, Mass., Sept. 10, 1926; s. George William and Daisy A. (Chase) P.; m. Mildred Boyle, Oct. 6, 1951; children: George William III, Clifton Alfred Dow, Mark Paige. Student, Northeastern U., 1944-49; B.Sc., Curry Coll., 1952; postgrad., Eastern Sch. Photography, Boston U.; Cert., Coll. Financial Planning, Denver, 1974. Registered investment advisor. Travel lectr., color cinematographer 1946—; in charge road testing Renault auto, Alcan Hwy., Alaska, 1949; pres. Neily Film Prodns., Inc., 1953-55; Eastern regional v.p. Western Res. Life Assurance Co., Ohio, 1973-75; pres., chmn. bd. Fin. Mktg. Systems, Inc., Nashua, N.H., 1976—; chmn. Holmes Travel Orgn., 1978—; chmn. bd., v.p. Fin. Cons. Group for Women, Inc., 1981—; registered prin. Fin. Cons., Inc., Stoneham, Mass., 1975—; div. mgr. Calif. Pacific Ins. Services Inc., 1977-80; pres. Fin. Benefits Planning Corp., 1983—; sr. v.p. Penn Distbn. Co, Inc., 1983—, Penn RE Life Ins. Co., 1984-88; v.p. Polymer Balloon Corp., 1984-88; dir., treas. Linsco Ins. Agy., Inc., 1987—; dir. Fin. Cons. Mgmt. Corp., Sonolite Corp., Contrex Co.; speaker on sales and service motivation; assoc. prof. bus. adminstrn. Curry Coll., until 1963, also sr. mem. bd. trustees, mem. coll. corp., also chmn. reorgn., 1963; pvt. trustee and executor, 1972—. Narrator, film producer: Burton Holmes travelogues, 1950-70; appearances at Carnegie Hall, N.Y. Music Hall, Phila. Symphony Hall, Boston Symphony Hall, Nat. Geog. Soc., Washington, numerous other cities, U.S., Mexico and Can.; designer world's largest portable cinemascope motion picture screen; contbg. editor: monthly newsletter Fin. Strategies and Money Mgmt. for Women; contbr. articles on ins. and sales to various publ., also photographic and cinematographic publs. Served with USNR, World War II, PTO. Recipient Nat. Quality award Nat. Assn. Life Underwriters. Mem. Merrimack Valley Life Underwriters Assn. (v.p., dir. 1968-69), Boston Life Underwriters Assn., Advt. Club Greater Boston, Internat. Assn. Fin. Planners (charter pres. No. Mass. chpt.), Nat. Assn. Security Dealers (prin.), Northeastern U., Curry Coll. alumni assns., Mass. Brokers Assn., Inst. Cert. Fin. Planners, Ins. Conf.

Planners Assn., Am. Soc. Assn. Execs. Clubs: Mason, Rotarian (charter pres. Chelmsford, Mass. 1967-68). Home: 278 Lowell St Lynnfield MA 01940 Office: 33 Main St Ste 201 Nashua NH 03060 also: 100 Corp Pl I 95 Ste 304 Peabody NH 01960

PERKINS, HENRY LEE, mortgage company executive; b. Oakland, Calif., Aug. 30, 1958; s. Henry J. and Mattie Louise (Coleman) P.; m. Patricia Ann Sheppard-Perkins, Mar. 6, 1982; children: Enree Havier, Enjoli Gabrielle. AA in Bus. Adminstrn., Coll. Alameda, Calif., 1981; student, Golden State Sch. Theology. Lic. real estate agent, Calif. Loan clk. Wells Fargo Bank, Oakland, Calif., 1979-82; loan analyst Transam. Mortgage Co., San Francisco, 1982-83; loan processor Great Western Savs., San Francisco, 1983-84; br. mgr. Greater Suburban Mortgage Co., Alameda, 1984-88; v.p., mortgage banker Am. Suburban Mortgage, Oakland, 1988—; dir. music Pleasant Grove Bapt. Ch., 1976-84, associated minister, 1984—. Mem. Nat. Assn. Estate Brokers, Calif. Assn. Real Estate Brokers, Oakland Bd. Realtors, Associated Real Property Brokers (pres. 1989), Calif. State Young AdultConv. (2d v.p. 1987, 1st v.p. 1988, Outstanding Young Man of Yr. 1980, Outstanding Youth of Yr. 1979). Democrat. Home: 4150 Maynard Ave Oakland CA 94605 Office: Am Suburban Mortgage Inc 7700 Edgewater Dr Ste 600 Oakland CA 94621

PERKINS, MARIETTA L., trust examiner; b. Sioux Falls, S.D., Sept. 11, 1955; d. James Russell and Shirley Mae (Lemonds) Perkins. BA, Concordia Coll., Minn., 1976; MBA, U. S.D., 1980. Asst. nat. trust examiner Comptroller of the Currency, Kansas City, Mo., 1978-81; sub-regional supr. NTE, Austin, Tex., 1981-83; tech. edn. specialist tng. and devel. Comptroller of the Currency, Washington, 1983-86, policy analyst NTE EDP Activities div., 1986— . Author: IRA Investments, 1986. Mem. Women in Housing and Fin., Nat. Assn. Female Execs. Democrat. Avocations: tennis, photography, biking. Home: 3533 Valley Dr Alexandria VA 22302 Office: Comptroller of the Currency 490 L'Enfant Pla Washington DC 20219

PERKINS, ROBERT AUSTIN, automotive company executive; b. Springfield, Mass., Apr. 2, 1934; s. Harold Robert and Marjorie (Pinney) Potter; m. Jane Hukill Perkins, Aug. 11, 1959; children: Deborah, Kimberly. B.A., Dartmouth Coll., 1955; M.B.A., U. Pa., 1957. Dir. Japan ops. Chrysler Corp., Tokyo, 1976-78, dir. Far East, 1978-80, dir. internat. liaison, 1980-81, v.p. Far East, 1981-83; v.p. Chrysler Corp., Washington, 1983—. Office: Chrysler Corp 1100 Connecticut Ave NW Washington DC 20036

PERKINS, THOMAS JAMES, venture capital company executive; b. Oak Park, Ill., Jan. 7, 1932; s. Harry H. and Elizabeth P.; m. Gerd Thune-Ellefsen, Dec. 9, 1961; children: Tor Kristian, Elizabeth Siri. B.S.E.E., M.I.T., 1953; M.B.A., Harvard U., 1957. Gen. mgr. computer div. Hewlett Packard Co., Cupertino, Calif., 1965-70, dir. corp. devel., 1970-72; gen. partner Kleiner & Perkins, San Francisco, 1972-80; sr. partner Kleiner Perkins Caufield & Byers, San Francisco, from 1980; chmn. bd. Tandem Computers, Genentech; dir. Spectra Physics., Corning Glass Works, Collagen Corp., LSI Logic Corp., Hybritech Inc., Econics Corp., Vitalink Communications Corp. Author: Classic Supercharged Sports Cars, 1984. Trustee San Francisco Ballet, 1980—. Mem. Nat. Venture Capital Assn. (chmn. 1981-82, pres. 1980-81). Clubs: N.Y. Yacht, Links, Am. Bugatti (pres. 1983—). Office: Tandem Computers Inc 10435 N Tantau Ave Cupertino CA 95014-3548 also: Genentech Inc 460 Point San Bruno San Francisco CA 94080 *

PERKINS-CARPENTER, BETTY LOU, service executive; b. Rochester N.Y., Jan. 22, 1931; d. Edward C. and Bertha M. (Loeser) Kalmn; m. Floyd F. Perkins, Jan. 31, 1951 (div. 1979); children: Cheryl Lee, F. Scott; m. Marcellus Chipman Carpenter, Oct. 10, 1981. BS in Phys. Edn. Adminstrn., Empire State Coll., N.Y., 1979; MS in Early Childhood Edn. Adminstrn., Nova U., 1983. Tchr., coach Rochester YWCA, 1954-59, Perkins Swimming Sch., Penfield, N.Y., 1959-64; pres. Perkins Swim Club, Inc., Rochester, 1964—, Perkins Fit By Five, Inc., Rochester, 1969—, Child Fitness Prodns., Inc. d/b/a Sr. Fitness Prodns., Rochester, 1983—, Fit By Five Franchise Corp., Rochester, 1984—; diving coach Olympic Games, Montreal, 1976; mem. adv. com. N.Y. State Task Force Phys. Fitness and Sports, 1978-82; bd. dirs. U.S. Olympic Diving Com., 1976-80; cons. European sports facilities, 1969-83, Pres.'s Council on Phys. Fitness and Sports, 1986—; mem. adv. com. Community Savs. Bank, Rochester, 1976-79; mem. adv. bd. O.A.S.I.S. Author: The Fun of Fitness-A Handbook for the Senior Class, 1988; Am. editor: Teaching Babies to Swim, 1979; contbr. articles to profl. jours. Exec. producer audio-visual instructional materials. Served with USAF, 1948-51. Recipient Gold medal Inst. Achievement of Human Potential, Brazil, 1973; Mike Malone Meml. Diving award, 1977; Cady Diving award, 1977; named to Monroe County Athletes Hall of Fame, Rochester, 1979; named Sports Woman of Yr., U.S. Olympic Diving Commn., 1979, Citizen of Yr. Rotary, 1988. Mem. U.S. Diving Assn. (life, numerous offices), Rochester Assn. Edn. of Young Children, Nova U. Alumnae Assn., Genesee Valley Sports Medicine Coun., Oak Hill Country Club, Order Eastern Star (life). Republican. Avocations: swimming, cross-country skiing, reading, travel. Office: Perkins Swim Club 1606 Penfield Rd Rochester NY 14625

PERKINSON, DIANA AGNES ZOUZELKA, import company executive; b. Prostejov, Czechoslovakia, June 27, 1943; came to U.S., 1962; d. John Charles and Agnes Diana (Sincl) Zouzelka; m. David Francis Perkinson, Mar. 6, 1965; children: Dana Leissa, David. BA, U. Lausanne (Switzerland), 1960; MA, U. Madrid, 1961; MBA, Case Western Res. U., 1963; cert. internat. mktg. Oxford (Eng.) U., 1962. Assoc. Allen Hartman & Schreiber, Cleve., 1963-64; interpreter Tower Internat. Inc., Cleve., 1964-66; pres. Oriental Rug Importers Ltd., Cleve., 1979—; pres. Oriental Rug Designers, Inc., Cleve., 1980—; pres. Oriental Rug Cons., Inc., Cleve., 1980—; chmn. Foxworthy's Inc. subs. Oriental Rug Importers Ft. Myers, Naples, Sanibel, Fla.; dir. Beckwith & Assocs., Inc., Cleve., Secura Inc., Dallas, Dix-Bur Investments, Ltd. Trustee, Cleve. Ballet, 1979, exec. com., 1981; mem. Cleve. Mayor's Adv. Com.; trustee Diabetes Assn. Greater Cleve.; chmn. grantsmanship Jr. League of Cleve., 1982; mem. mem. Cleve. Found.-Women in Philanthropy, 1982; trustee Diabetes Assn. Greater Cleve. Mem. Women Bus. Owners Assn., Oriental Rug Retailers Am. (dir. 1983), Cleve. Racquet Club, Recreation League, Hillbrook Club. Republican. Roman Catholic. Home: Ravencrest 14681 County Line Rd Cleveland OH 44022 also: Stratford at Pelican Bay Crayton Rd Naples FL 33940 Office: Oriental Rug Importers Ltd Inc 23533 Mercantile Rd Beachwood OH 44122

PERLIS, MICHAEL FREDRICK, lawyer; b. N.Y.C., June 3, 1947; s. Leo and Betty F. (Gantz) P.; children—Amy Hannah, David Matthew; m. Angela M. Rinaldi, Dec. 23, 1988. B.S. in Fgn. Service, Georgetown U., 1968, J.D., 1971. Bar: D.C. 1971, U.S. Dist. Ct. D.C. 1971, U.S. Ct. Appeals 1971, D.C. Ct. Appeals 1971, Calif. 1980, U.S. Dist. Ct. (no. dist.) Calif. 1980, U.S Dist. Ct. (cen. dist.) Calif. 1985, U.S. Ct. Appeals (9th cir.) 1980, U.S. Supreme Ct., 1980. Law clerk D.C. Ct. Appeals, Washington, 1971-72; asst. corp. counsel D.C., Washington, 1972-74; counsel U.S. SEC, div. enforcement, Washington, 1974-75, br. chief, 1975-77, asst. dir., 1977-80; ptnr. Pettit & Martin, San Francisco, 1980-89; ptnr. Stroock & Stroock & Lavan, L.A., 1989—. adj. prof. Cath. U. Am., 1979-80. Mem. ABA (co-chmn. subcom. securities and commodities litigation 1982-83), D.C. Bar Assn., Calif. State Bar Assn., San Francisco Bar Assn. Office: Stroock & Stroock & Lavan 2029 Century Pk E Los Angeles CA 90067

PERLMAN, LAWRENCE, business executive, lawyer; b. St. Paul, Apr. 8, 1938; s. Irving and Ruth (Mirsky) P.; m. Medora Scoll, June 18, 1961; children: David, Sara. B.A., Carleton Coll., 1960; J.D., Harvard U., 1963. Bar: Minn. 1963. Law. clk. for fed. judge 1963; ptnr. Fredrikson, Byron, Colborn, Bisbee, Hansen & Perlman, Mpls., 1964-75; gen. counsel, exec. v.p. U.S. pacing ops. Medtronic, Inc., Mpls., 1975-78; sr. ptnr. Oppenheimer, Wolff & Donnelly, Mpls., 1978-80; sec., gen. counsel, v.p. corp. services Control Data Corp., Mpls., 1980-83; pres., chief op. officer, dir. Comml. Credit Co., 1984-85; pres. Data Storage Products Group, 1985-88, exec. v.p., 1986-88, pres., chief op. officer, 1988—; bd. dirs. Control Data Corp., Bio-Medicus Corp., Inter-Regional Fin. Group, Inc., Micro-Electronics and Computer Tech. Corp.; adj. prof. Law Sch., U. Minn., 1974-76, 79-80. Chmn. Mpls. Municipal Fin. Commn., 1978-79; bd. dirs. Walker Art Center, Minn. Orchestral Assn.; trustee Carleton Coll. Mem. Phi Beta Kappa. Club: Mpls. Home: 2366 W Lake of the Isles Pkwy Minneapolis MN 55405 Office: Control Data Corp 8100 34th Ave S Minneapolis MN 55420

PERLMUTH, WILLIAM ALAN, lawyer; b. N.Y.C., Nov. 21, 1929; s. Charles and Roe (Schneider) P.; m. Loretta Kaufman, Mar. 14, 1951; children: Carolyn, Diane. AB, Wilkes Coll., 1951; LLB, Columbia U., 1953. Bar: N.Y. 1954. Assoc. Cravath, Swaine & Moore, N.Y.C., 1955-61; ptnr. Stroock & Stroock & Lavan, N.Y.C., 1962—; bd. dirs. Knogo Corp., Hicksville, N.Y. Editor Columbia U. Law Rev., 1952-53. Trustee Aeroflex Found., N.Y.C., 1965—, Harkness Founds. for Dance, N.Y.C., 1976—, Wilkes Coll., Wilkes-Barre, Pa., 1980—, Hosp. for Joint Diseases Orthopaedic Inst., N.Y.C., 1980—, Weininger Found., 1985—. Served to sgt. U.S. Army, 1953-55. Mem. N.Y. State Bar Assn., Assn. of Bar of City of N.Y. Jewish. Clubs: The Downtown Assn., The Wall St. (N.Y.C.). Home: 880 Fifth Ave New York NY 10021 Office: Stroock & Stroock & Lavan 7 Hanover Sq New York NY 10004-2594

PERLMUTTER, DIANE F., communications executive; b. N.Y.C., Aug. 31, 1945; d. Bert H. and Frances (Smith) P. Student, NYU, 1969-70; AB in English, Miami U., Oxford, Ohio, 1967. Writer sales promotion Equitable Life Assurance, N.Y.C., 1967-68; adminstrv. asst. de Garmo, Inc., N.Y.C., 1968-69, asst. account exec., 1969-70, account exec., 1970-74, v.p., account supr., 1974-76; mgr. corp. advt. Avon Products, Inc., N.Y.C., 1976-79, dir. communications Latin Am., Spain, Can., 1979-80, dir. brochures, 1980-81, dir. category merchandising, 1981-82, group dir. motivational communications, 1982-83, group dir. sales promotion, 1983-84, v.p. sales promotion, 1984, v.p. internat. bus. devel., 1984-85, area v.p. Latin Am., 1985, v.p. advtg. and campaign mktg., 1985-87, v.p. U.S. operational planning, 1987; cons. N.Y.C., 1987-88; sr. v.p. Burson-Marsteller, N.Y.C., 1988—; chairperson ann. meeting Direct Selling Assn., Washington, 1982; v.p. Nat. Home Fashions League, N.Y.C., 1975-76; bd. dirs. Double L.P. Industries, Inc., 1988—. Founding bd. mem. Am. Red Magen David for Israel, N.Y.C., 1970-75; mem. adv. coun. Miami Sch. Bus., 1986—, Miami Sch. Applied Scis., 1978-81. Mem. Advt. Women of N.Y., Women in Communications, Miami U. Alumni Assn. (pres., chair 1986), Atrium club (N.Y.C.), Beta Gamma Sigma. Office: Burson-Marsteller 230 Park Ave S New York NY 10003

PERLMUTTER, HOWARD VICTOR, international management educator; b. Framingham, Mass., Nov. 4, 1925; s. David and Anna (Patrick) P.; m. Foulie Psalidas; 1 child, David Dimitri. BSME, MIT, 1946; PhD in Psychology, Kans. U., 1952; MA (hon.), U. Pa., 1971. Research dir. Ctr. Internat. Studies, MIT, Cambridge, Mass., 1952-58; lectr. Menninger Sch. Psychiatry, Topeka, Kans., 1958-61; prof. Imede, U. Lausanne, Switzerland, 1962-67; vis. prof. Stockholm Sch. Econs., Sweden, 1974-82; dir. Worldwide Instns. Research Project, Phila., 1968-85; prof. Wharton Sch., U. Pa., Phila., 1968—; bd. dirs. Pharmacia, Inc., Piscataway, N.J.; adv. bd. Alfa Laval, Inc., Ft. Lee, N.J. Author: Social Architecture, 1965, Multinational Organizational Development, 1978, An Indefinite Reprieve, 1985; author, editor: International Technology Trasfer (3 vols.), 1981; mem. editorial bd. Human Relations, 1970—. Bd. dirs. Greater Phila. Internat. Network, 1977—, Phila. Export Network, 1980—, Global Interdependence Ctr., Phila., 1980—; chmn. mulitnat. unit. Wharton Sch., 1971-78; mem. pres.'s com. on long range internat. planning , U. Pa., 1983—, internal adv. bd. U. Pa. Ctr. for Internat. Studies, 1983—. Served to lt. (j.g.) USN, 1943-46. Fulbright scholar The Sorbonne, U. Paris, 1949. Mem. Acad. of Scis. of Phila., Fulbright Alumni, Phila. Assn. for Clin. Trials (bd. dirs. 1987—), IICS. Mem. Club of Rome (Washington). Home: 773 Millbrook Ln Haverford PA 19041 Office: U Pa Whalton Sch Philadelphia PA 19104

PERLMUTTER, LEONARD MICHAEL, concrete construction company executive; b. Denver, Oct. 16, 1925; s. Philip Permutter and Belle (Perlmutter); m. Alice Love Bristow, Nov. 17, 1951; children: Edwin George, Joseph Kent, Cassandra Love. B.A., U. Colo., 1948, postgrad., 1948-50. Ptnr. Perlmutter & Sons, Denver, 1947-58; v.p. Prestressed Concrete of Colo., Denver, 1952-60; pres. Stanley Structures, Inc., Denver, 1960-83; chmn. bd. Stanley Structures, Inc., 1983-87; dir. Colo. Nat. Bankshares, Inc.; chief exec. officer Econ. Devel. Gov.'s Office State of Colo., 1987-88; chmn. bd. Colo. Open Lands, 1989—. Chmn. bd. U. Colo. Found., Boulder, 1979-81; dir. Santa Fe Opera Assn., N.Mex., 1976-85; v.p. Santa Fe Fedn., 1979-87; chmn. bd. Nat. Jewish Hosp.-Nat. Asthma Ctr., Denver, 1983-86; pres. Denver Symphony Assn., 1983-84, chmn. bd., 1985. Recipient Humanitarian Am. Jewish Com., 1981. Mem. Am. Concrete Inst., Prestressed Concrete Inst. (pres. 1977, dir. 1973-74). Club: Rolling Hills Country (Golden) (pres. 1966-68). Home: 15125 Foothill Rd Golden CO 80401 Office: LAP Inc 1515 Arapahoe Three Park Cen Ste 222 Denver CO 80202

PERLMUTTER, NATHAN MARTIN, insurance company executive; b. Bklyn., Aug. 14, 1947; s. Joseph Meyer and Molly (Alderoty) P.; m. Rosalyn Taffet, Oct. 31, 1970; children: Jacqueline, Andrea, David. BBA, Pace U., 1971. CLU; chartered fin. cons. Sales rep., sales mgr., dist. mgr. Met. Life Ins. Co., N.Y.C., 1972-80; gen. agt. Guardian Life, Elmhurst, N.Y., 1980—; pres. NMP Planning, Elmhurst, 1980—, Forest Hills (N.Y.) Fin. Group, 1985—, Holly View Devel. Corp., Monroeville, N.J., 1986—; chmn. bd. Holly View Farms, Monroeville, 1986—, Perl Brokerage, Forest Hills, 1988—; vice chmn. bd. Parker Brokerage Co. Inc., 1988—; cons. Nyles Tiecher Assocs., Gt. Neck, N.Y., 1985—, Sutton & Edwards, Inc., Lake Success, N.Y., 1986—. Contbr. articles to profl. jours. Bd. dirs. Temple Beth Am Brotherhood, Merrick, N.Y., 1985-87. Mem. Gen. Agts. and Mgrs. Assn. (br. pres. 1979-80, Nat. Mgmt. award 1983-87), N.Y.C. Assn. Health Underwriters (co-founder, v.p. 1984—), Atlantic Agy. Mgrs. Assn. (pres. 1982-83), Million Dollar Round Table, N.Y.C. Life Underwriters Assn. (pres. 1988-89), Pace U. Alumni Assn. (pres. 1987-89). Home: 1951 Helen Ct Merrick NY 11566 Office: Forest Hills Fin Group Inc 108-14 72d Ave Forest Hills NY 11375

PERLOWITZ, BRUCE HOWELL, controller; b. Massapequa Park, N.Y., June 12, 1956; s. Murray and Eunice (Prager) P.; m. Karen Jean Strohlein, Jan. 12, 1980; children: Daniel, Kevin. BBA, Pace U., 1980. CPA, N.Y. Tax preparer, cons. Baer Bus., Bklyn., 1972-78; acct. Slater & Co., Malverne, N.Y., 1978-79; sr. acct. Greller & Co. PC, Tarrytown, N.Y., 1980-81; supr. tax dept. Ernst & Whinney, White Plains, N.Y., 1981-85; controller Crystal Techs., Elmsford, N.Y., 1985-87; controller, gen. administr. Soudronic Ltd., Briarcliff Manor, N.Y., 1987—. Vol. Arthritis Found., N.Y., 1979-86; treas., head coach football Dads Club, Pleasantville, N.Y. 1985-88, dir. football ops., 1988, officer/treas., 1986-88. Mem. Am. Inst. CPA's, N.Y.C. Soc. CPA's. Democrat. Jewish. Home: 260 Mountain Rd Pleasantville NY 10570 Office: Soudronic Ltd 465 North State Rd Briarcliff Manor NY 10510

PERMAR, MARY ELIZABETH, real estate investor; b. Augusta, Ga., Mar. 18, 1956; d. Philip Howard and Doris (Maxwell) P. BS in Architecture, Clemson U., 1978; MArch, U. Ill., 1981, MBA, 1982. V.p., sec., treas. Assn. Student Chpts., AIA, Washington, 1978-79; with The Prudential Realty Group, 1982—; investment mgr. The Prudential Realty Group, Chgo., 1982-85; dir. acquisitions and sales The Prudential Realty Group, Newark, 1985-87; dir. acquisitions The Prudential Realty Group, Chgo., 1988—. Mng. editor CRIT The Archtl. Student Jour., 1978-79. Tutor Program for Underprivileged Children, Chgo., 1982-85; trustee Chgo. Acad. of Sci. Charles G. Rummel fellow U. Ill. Sch. Architecture, 1979-82. Mem. Nat. Assn. Indsl. and Office Pks., Execs. Club Chgo., Western Soc. Engrs. Republican. Presbyterian.

PERMUT, STEVEN ELI, marketing consulting company executive; b. Denver, May 29, 1946; s. George Gordon and Frieda (Replin) P.; m. Joanna Baumer; 1 child, Lisa Le Van. BA, U. Colo., 1969; MS, U. Ill., 1970, PhD, 1975; postgrad., Yale U., 1972. Instr. mktg. U. Ill., Urbana, 1970-73, Yale U., New Haven, 1973-74; asst. prof. Sch. Mgmt. Yale U., New Haven, 1976-79, assoc. prof., 1979-86, lectr., 1986—; asst. prof. Sch. Mgmt. Boston U., Boston, Brussels, 1974-76; pres. Mktg. Scis., Inc., New Haven, 1978—; cons., expert witness to bd. govs. FRS, 1976-77; chmn. nat. adv. com. U.S. Consumer Product Safety commn., 1977-78; tech. com. Tech. Investment Fund, New Haven, 1985—; bd. dirs. New Haven Ind., 1987—. Editor: Government Marketing, 1981; gen. editor Marketing the Arts, 1980, Marketing Ideas and Issues, 1982, Political Marketing, 1983, Marketing Public Transit, 1987, A Theory of Political Choice Behavior, 1987; mem. editorial bd. Jour. Mktg., 1978-85, Jour. Consumer Mktg., 1984—, Jour. Forecasting, 1984—, Jr. Bus. and Indsl. Mktg., 1986— and others. Bd. dirs. Shubert Theatre, New Haven, 1986—. Recipient Elm and Ivy award Yale U., 1984; postdoctoral fellow Yale U., 1973. Mem. Nat. Acad. Scis., Am. Mktg. Assn., Conn. Venture Group (bd. dirs. New Haven chpt., Lawn Club, Mory's Assn., Sigma Xi, Phi Kappa Phi, Kappa Tau Alpha. Office: Mktg Scis Inc 2 Whitney Ave New Haven CT 06510

PERMUTTER, NATHAN MARTIN, insurance executive; b. Bklyn., Aug. 14, 1947; s. Joseph Meyer and Molly (Alderoty) P.; m. Rosalyn Taffet, Oct. 31, 1970; children: Jacqueline, Andrea, David. BBA, Pace U., 1971. CLU, 1978; chartered fin. cons. Sales rep. Met. Life Ins. Co., N.Y.C., 1972-80; gen. agt. Guardian Life, Elmhurst, N.Y., 1980—; pres. NMP Planning, Elmhurst, 1980—, Forest Hills Fin. Group, N.Y.C., 1985—, Holly View Devel. Corp., Monroeville, N.J., 1986—, Perl Brokerage, Forest Hills., 1988—; vice chmn. Parker Brokerage Co., Inc., N.Y.; cons. Nyles Teicher Assocs., Great Neck, N.Y., 1985—, Sutton & Edwards, Inc., Lake Success, 1986—. Contbr. articles to profl. jours. Bd. dirs. Temple Beth Am Brotherhood, Merrick, 1985-87. With USNR, 1974-79. Mem. Pace U. Alumni Assn. (pres. 1987-89), N.Y.C. Assn. Health Underwriters (co-founder, v.p. 1984—), Atlantic Agy. Mgrs. Assn. (pres. 1982-83), Gen. Agts. Mgrs. Assn (br. pres. 1979-80, Nat. Mgmt. award 1983-87), Million Dollar Round Table (life), N.Y.C. Life Underwriters Assn. (pres. 1988-89). Home: 1951 Helen Ct Merrick NY 11566 Office: Forest Hills Fin Group Inc 108-14 72d Ave Forest Hills NY 11375

PERNA, FRANK, JR., manufacturing company executive; b. Detroit, Jan. 15, 1938; s. Frank and Mary (Cataldo) P.; m. Monika Doering, May 10, 1960; children: Laura, Reneé, Christopher. BSME, Gen. Motors Inst., 1960; MSEE, Wayne State U., 1966; MBA in Mgmt. (Sloan fellow), MIT, 1970. Asst. to dir. reliability Gen. Motors Corp., Detroit, 1955-70; v.p., dir. engring. Sun Electric Corp., Crystal Lake, Ill., 1971-77, exec. v.p. ops., 1977-78, pres., chief exec. officer, 1978-81; v.p., group exec. Whittaker Corp., Los Angeles, 1983-85; pres. MagneTek, Inc., Los Angeles, 1985—; bd. dirs. 1st State Bank and Trust, Hanover Park, Ill., 1st Nat. Bank of Hoffman Estates, Ill. Named one of Outstanding Young Man of Am., 1968. Mem. Bd. Profl. Engrs. Office: MagneTek Inc 11111 Santa Monica Blvd Los Angeles CA 90025

PERNSTEINER, CAROL ANN, hotel executive; Mar. 16, Medford, Wis.; d. Alvin Anton and Lillian Therese (Spreen) P. BA, Marquette U., 1969. With The Sheraton Corp., 1971—, front office mgr. Sheraton Washington, D.C., 1979-81, resident mgr. Sheraton Hotel, St. Louis, 1981-88, gen. mgr., 1988—. Capt. Op. Brightside, St. Louis, 1984-86. Recipient Pres.'s award The Sheraton Corp., Washington, 1979, Divisional Pres.'s award, St. Louis, 1985. Mem. Hotel and Motel Assn. Greater St. Louis, Mo. Hotel and Motel Assn., Mo. Athletic Club, Downtown St. Louis Inc. (bd. dirs.). Republican. Avocations: violin, piano. Home: 428 Carswold Dr Clayton MO 63105 Office: Sheraton St Louis Hotel 910 N 7th St Saint Louis MO 63101

PERO, JOSEPH JOHN, insurance company executive; b. N.Y.C., Nov. 5, 1939; s. Joseph John and Grace Margaret (Picchione) P.; m. Margaret Ann Carey, July 11, 1964; children: Ann Marie, Christopher. B.S., Manhattan Coll., 1961; M.B.A., NYU, 1967. With Gen. Motors Corp., 1963—; dir. profit and investment analysis Gen. Motors Corp., N.Y.C., 1973-76; asst. treas., sec. to exec. com. Gen. Motors Corp., Detroit, 1976-79, N.Y.C., 1980-81; exec. v.p.-fin. Motors Ins. Corp. (subs. Gen. Motors Corp.), Detroit, 1981-87, pres., 1987—; dir. Blue Cross & Blue Shield of Mich., Detroit, 1978-80; bd. dirs. Gen. Motors Acceptance Corp., Detroit. Bd. dirs. Inner City Bus. Improvement Forum, Detroit, 1978-79; trustee Mt. Elliot Cemetery Assn., 1978-79. Served with Army N.G., 1963-69. Mem. Nat. Assn. Ind. Insurers (bd. govs.), Forest Lake Country Club, Detroit Athletic Club. Home: 4097 Waterwheel Ln Bloomfield Hills MI 48013 Office: Motors Ins Corp 3044 W Grand Blvd Detroit MI 48202

PEROT, H. ROSS, investments and real estate group executive, data processing services company executive; b. 1930; married. Ed., U.S. Naval Acad. Data processing salesman IBM Corp., 1957-62; founder Electronic Data Systems Corp., Dallas, 1962, chmn., chief exec. officer, also dir., to 1986; now with The Perot Group, Dallas; founder Perot Systems Corp., Washington, 1988—. Served with USN, 1953-57. Recip. Internat. Disting. Entrepreneur Award, U. Man., 1988. Office: The Perot Group 12377 Merit Dr Ste 1700 Dallas TX 75251 *

PEROTTI, ROSE NORMA, lawyer; b. St. Louis, Aug. 10, 1930; d. Joseph and Dorothy Mary (Roleski) Perotti. B.A., Fontbonne Coll., St. Louis, 1952; J.D., St. Louis U., 1957. Bar: Mo. 1958. Trademark atty. Sutherland, Polster & Taylor, St. Louis, 1958-63, Sutherland Law Office, 1964-70; trademark atty. Monsanto Co., St. Louis, 1971-85, sr. trademark atty., 1985—. Honored with dedication of faculty office in her name, St. Louis U. Sch. Law, 1980. Mem. Mo. Bar Assn., Bar Assn. Met. St. Louis, ABA, Am. Judicature Soc., Smithsonian Assocs., Friends St. Louis Art Museum, Mo. Bot. Garden. Office: Monsanto Co 800 N Lindbergh Blvd Saint Louis MO 63167

PERRAULT, DOROTHY ANN JACQUES, small business owner, nurse; b. New Orleans, Aug. 25, 1937; d. Alvin Joseph and Dorothy (Angelety) Jacques; m. Harry Joseph Perrault Jr., Oct. 24, 1959; children: Harry J. Perrault III, TroyLynne Ahmed, Sabrina. BSN, Dillard U., 1960. RN. Head nurse Sara Mayo Hosp., New Orleans, 1960; supr. Flint Goodridge Hosp., New Orleans, 1960-64; relief supr. Charity Hosp., New Orleans, 1964-69, nursing instr., 1969-70, supr., 1970-71, 1971-77, asst. dir., 1969-77; owner, pres. Perrault Kiddy Kollege, Inc., New Orleans, 1972—; pres. Deli Deluxe Catering Service, The Fashion Korner, New Orleans; bd. dirs. Coalition Child Care, New Orleans, Nat. Assn. for Edn. Children, New Orleans, La. Fedn. Child Care, New Orleans; 1st v.p. Bayou Fed. Savs. & Loan Assn., 1980-87; mem. adv. bd. First Fed. Bank of New Orleans. Editor, chief of yearbooks and many orgnl. souvenir booklets; composer, dir., producer, stage mgr. children's theatrical plays. Bd. dirs. Am. Security Coun., New Orleans, 1979—, Pvt. Industry Coun., New Orleans, United Negro Coll. Fund, New Orleans, 1986—; mem. exec. com. La. League Good Govt., New Orleans, 1979; past pres. Nurses' Fedn. Charity Hosp.; 2 mayoral appointments Pvt. Industry Coun. and Bldg. Commn., 1984-88. Recipient Thomas Jefferson award Am. Inst. for Pub. Svc., 1978, Achievement in Child Care Mayor of New Orleans, 1987, La. Gov.'s award, 1983, 86, numerous others; named Disting. Alumni Dillard U., 1985, one of Outstanding Bus. Women of Yr. Nat. Coun. of Negro Women, 1988. recipient awards from. Sec. of State, La. 1985, Sec. of Commerce, La., 1985; awards for participation in the Headstart Program of Total Community Action. Mem. NAACP, Nat. Assn. Univ. Women, Dillard U. Profl. Orgn. Nurses (pres. 1988), Dillard U. Nat. Alumni Assn. (pres. 1981-83, (founder of Perpetual scholarship friends, friends of Amistad), NAFE, Nat. Assn. Mgrs., New Orleans C. of C., Nat. Black Bus. League, Nat. Assn. Negro Bus. and Profl. Women Club (Bus. Women of Yr. for Excellence in Bus., 1988.), Zeta Phi Beta. Democrat. Roman Catholic. Club: Estelle Hubbard. Lodge: Knights of Peter Claver. Office: Perrault Kiddy Kollege Perrault Pla 6201 Chef Menteur Hwy New Orleans LA 70126

PERREAULT, MARK PHILIP, insurance company executive; b. Gardner, Mass., June 6, 1958; s. Alvin Philip and Louise (Cole) P. BBA, Marquette U., 1980; MBA, Babson Coll., 1982. lic. real estate agt. Fin. analyst Simplex Time Recorder Co., Gardner, 1980-82; staff acct. Carlin Ins. div. Consolidated Resources Corp., Natick, Mass., 1982-83, comptroller, 1983-86, treas., dir., 1986-88; pres., dir. Carlin Leasing, Inc., Natick, 1988—; ptnr., trustee Stejon Assocs, Natick, 1982—, Clearwater Realty Trust, Natick, 1984—, North Main St. Realty Trust, Natick, 1984—. Mem. Sales and Mktg. Execs. of Greater Boston. Republican. Roman Catholic. Home: 25 N Main St Natick MA 01760 Office: Carlin Leasing Inc 233 W Central St Natick MA 01760

PERRELLA, ANTHONY JOSEPH, electronics engineer; b. Boulder, Colo., Sept. 16, 1942; s. Anthony Vincent and Mary Domenica (Forte) P.; B.S., U. Wyo., 1964, postgrad., 1965; postgrad. U. Calif. at San Diego, 1966-67, U. Calif. at Irvine, 1968-70; m. Pamela Smith, July 19, 1980. Flight engr. U.S. Naval Tng. Devices Center, San Diego, 1965-67; research engr. Collins div. Rockwell Internat. (formerly Collins Radio Co.), Newport Beach, Calif., 1967-69, electromagnetic interference and TEMPEST group head, 1969-74, supr., 1974-75, mgr., 1975-77, mgr. systems integration, 1977, mgr. space communication systems, 1977-78; sr. mem. tech. staff ARGOSystems Inc., Sunnyvale, Calif., 1978—, program mgr., 1978-81, dep. dept. mgr. EW Systems, 1980-83, div. EW staff engr., 1983-84, dept. mgr., 1984-87 , Sun Microsystems Inc., Mountain View, 1987—; v.p. research and devel. Things Unlimited, Inc., Laramie, Wyo., 1965-72, pres., 1972-75. Mem. Am. Mgmt. Assn., IEEE, AAAS, N.Y. Acad. Scis., Assn. Old Crows, Tau Kappa Epsilon. Roman Catholic. Home: 931 Brookgrove Ln Cupertino CA 95014 Office: 2550 Garcia Ave Mountain View CA 94043

PERRELLA, JAMES ELBERT, manufacturing company executive; b. Gloversville, N.Y., May 30, 1935; s. James E. and A. Irene (Ferguson) P.; m. Diane F. Campesi; 1 child, Joy. B.S.M.E., Purdue U., 1960, M.S.I.M., 1961. Gen. mgr. Centac div. Ingersoll-Rand Co., Mayfield, Ky., 1972-75; gen. mgr. Air Compressor Group Ingersoll-Rand Co., Woodcliff Lake, N.J., 1975-77, corp. v.p., pres. Air Compressor Group, 1977-82, exec. v.p., 1982—. Named Disting. Alumnus Sch. Mech. Engring., Purdue U., 1982; named Disting. Alumnus Krannert Mgmt. Sch., Purdue U., 1982. Office: Ingersoll-Rand Co 200 Chestnut Ridge Rd Woodcliff Lake NJ 07675 *

PERRETTE, JEAN RENE, banker; b. Dinan, France, May 24, 1931; s. Rene Jean and Marie Cecile (Ollivier) P.; came to U.S., 1961; HEC Bus. Sch. Paris, 1953; LL.D., U. Paris, 1955; Ph.D. in Econs., 1959; m. Virginia Moore Schott, Sept. 8, 1962; children—Virginie-Alvine, Clarisse, Jean-Briac, Julien-Yannick. Asst. to gen. mgmt. Worms CMC, Paris, 1959-61, U.S. rep. N.Y.C., 1961-65; U.S. rep. Banque Worms, N.Y.C., 1965-86 ; pres. Worms & Co. Inc. and Permal Mgmt. Services, Inc., U.S. reps. Messrs. Worms & Cie., Paris, other European cos., N.Y.C., 1965-86, Services, Inc.; dir. several cos.; cons. French pub. group, 1967-71. Served with French Navy, 1956-59. Mem. HEC Bus. Sch. U.S. Alumni Assn. (pres. 1975-76), French C. of C. in U.S. (exec. com. 1975-82). Club: Union (N.Y.C.). Home: 14 E 90th St New York NY 10128 Office: 900 3d Ave New York NY 10022

PERRY, ALBERT JOSEPH, III, financial consultant; b. Balt., Feb. 8, 1948; s. Albert Joseph and Mary Lee (Galbraith) P.; m. Stephanie Barbara Sadusk, Sept. 10, 1971; children: Katherine Young, William Andrew. BA in Polit. Sci., Emory U., 1970; JD, U. Fla., 1972. Bar: Fla. 1973, Md. 1978; cert. fin. planner. V.p. Mercantile Safe Deposit & Trust Co., Balt., 1974-82, Broventure Co., Inc, Balt., 1982-83; pres. A.J. Perry & Co., Balt., 1983—. Bd. dirs., com. chmn. Balt. Ballet, 1984-86; bd. dirs. St. Luke's Health Ministries, Balt., 1986-88. Capt. USAF, 1973. Non-resident scholar U. Fla., 1971. Mem. Inst. Cert. Fin. Planners, Internat. Assn. Fin. Planning, ABA, Fla. Bar Assn., Md. Bar Assn., Balt. Estate Planning Coun., L'Hirondelle Club (Ruxton, Md.). Republican. Episcopalian. Office: AJ Perry & Co Inc 14 W Mount Vernon Pl Baltimore MD 21201

PERRY, BERNARD JOHN, management executive, engineer; b. St. Louis, Nov. 27, 1945; s. Bernard Aloysius and Ruth May (Carr) P.; m. Rosemary Frances Reed, Nov. 7, 1975; children: Keith Joseph, Christopher John, Brian Jeffrey. BS in Aerospace Engring., Parks Coll., 1967. Mfg. engr. McDonnell Douglas Corp., St. Louis, 1966-69; mech. engr. U.S. Naval Ordnance Sta., Louisville, 1970-78, engr. supr., 1978-80; sr. v.p. QCI Internat., Red Bluff, Calif., 1980—. Author: Introduction to Quality Circles for Potential Members, 1983, Dynamics of Quality Circles: Orientation Volume, 1983; contbr. articles to profl. jours. Mem. Assn. Quality and Participation (founder, bd. dirs. 1979, cert. 1979), Philippine Soc. Quality Control (hon.). Home: 2706 Bishop Rd Jeffersonville IN 47130 Office: QCI Internat 1425 Vista Way Red Bluff CA 96080

PERRY, BERYL HENRY, JR., government official, accountant; b. Windsor, Va., Apr. 19, 1956; s. Beryl Henry Sr. and Georgia (Nurney) P.; m. Mary Lovette Vinson, Oct. 20, 1979; children: Beryl Henry III, Nicholas Lloyd. BBA, Christopher Newport Coll., 1978. CPA, Va. Acct. ITT Gwaltney, Inc., Smithfield, Va., 1978-79, A. Lee Rawling's CPA's, Smithfield, 1979-82; comptroller V.H. Monette, Inc., Smithfield, 1982-84; treas. County of Isle of Wight, Va., 1984—. Mem. Am. Inst. CPA's, Va. Soc. CPA's, Treas. Assn. Va., Va. Assn. Locally Elected Constl. Officers (officer), Peanut Growers Assn., Va. Farm Bur., Tidewater Treas. Assn. (officer), Jaycees. Democrat. Baptist. Lodges: Ruritan (past pres., dist. gov.), Masons, Kiwanis. Home: Rte 3 PO Box 108 Windsor VA 23487 Office: Office of Treas Courthouse Isle of Wight VA 23397

PERRY, DAVID, lawyer, insurance executive, real estate consultant; b. Phila., Nov. 13, 1940; s. Harry J. and Alice M. (Heller) P.; B.A. in English Lit., Carleton Coll., 1962; LL.B., U. Pa., 1965, M.A. in Econs., 1972, Ph.D. in Econs., 1974; m. Sherryl Frances Rosenbaum, June 24, 1962. Bar: Pa. 1965. Law clk. firm Freedman, Borowsky and Lorry, Phila., 1964-65; atty. HUD, Phila., 1965-67; sole practice law, Phila., 1967-72; sr. fin. and planning analyst INA Corp., Phila., 1972-74; exec. asst. to pres. Certain-Teed Products Corp., Valley Forge, Pa., 1974; dir. capital budgeting INA Corp., Phila., 1974-75, asst. treas., 1975-78, v.p., 1979-82, pres. Phila. Investment Corp. subs. INA Corp., 1980-82; partner, real estate cons. Ironwood Assocs., 1982-83; ptnr. law firm Perry, Goldstein, Fialkowski and Perry, 1983—. Brookings Inst. research fellow, 1968-69. Mem. Phila. Bar Assn., Am. Econ. Assn. Club: Union League of Phila. Home: 431 Boxwood Rd Rosemont PA 19010 Office: Ironwood Assocs Two Mellon Bank Ctr Ste 2400 Philadelphia PA 19102

PERRY, DAVID LEWIS, lawyer, manufacturing company executive; b. Boston, July 13, 1940; s. George Bangs and Ruth (Gordon) P. B.A., Amherst Coll., 1963; J.D., U. Calif.-Berkeley, 1966. Bar: Calif. 1967, Mass. 1967. Gen. atty. FTC, Washington, 1967-69; atty. Kaiser Aluminum & Chem. Corp., Oakland, Calif., 1969-73; gen. atty. Kaiser Aluminum & Chem. Corp., 1973-83, asst. gen. counsel, 1983-84, v.p., gen. counsel, 1984—. Mem. ABA, San Francisco Bar Assn. Office: Kaiser Aluminum & Chem Corp 300 Lakeside Dr Oakland CA 94643

PERRY, EVELYN REIS, communications company executive; b. N.Y.C., Mar. 9; d. Lou L. and Bertl (Wolf) Reis; m. Charles G. Perry III, Jan. 7, 1968; children: Charles G. IV, David Reis. BA, Univ. Wis., 1963; student Am. Acad. Dramatic Arts, 1958-59, Univ. N.Mex., 1963-64. Lic. real estate broker, N.C. Vol. ETV project Peace Corps, 1963-65; program officer-radio/tv Peace Corps, Washington, 1965-68; dir. Vols. in Svc. to Am. (VISTA), Raleigh, N.C., 1977-80; exec. dir. CETA Program for Displaced Homemakers, Raleigh, 1980-81; cons. exec. dir. to Recycle Raleigh for Food and Fuel, Theater in the Park, 1981-83, Artspace, Inc., Raleigh, 1983-84; pres., chief exec. officer Carolina Sound Communications, MUZAK, Charleston, S.C., 1984—; pub. rels. account exec. various cos., Washington, Syracuse, N.Y., 1969-71; cons. pub. rels. and orgn. Olympic Organizing Com., Mexico City, 1968; cons. pub. rels., fundraising, arts mgmt. pub. speaking, Ill., Pa., N.C., 1971-77; organizational and pub. speaking cons. Perry & Assocs., Raleigh, 1980—. Mem. adv. bd. Gov.'s Office Citizen Affairs, Raleigh, 1981-85; mem. Involvement Coun. of Wake County, N.C., Raleigh, 1981-84; mem. Adv. Coun. to Vols. in Svc. to Am., Raleigh, 1980-84; mem. Pres.'s adv. bd. Peace Corps, Washington, 1980-82; v.p., bd. dirs. Voluntary Action Ctr., Raleigh, 1980-84, bd. dirs., Charleston, 1988—; sec. bd. dirs. Temple Kahil Kadosh Beth Elohim, 1987-89, sec. fin. com., 1989—; bd. dirs. Chopstik Theater, Charleston, 1989— . Mem. N.C. Coun. of Women's Orgns. (pres., v.p. 1982-84), Charleston Hotel and Motel Assn., N.C. Assn. Vol. Adminstrs. (bd. dirs. 1980-84), Internat. Planned Music Assn. (bd. dirs. 1986—, newsletter editor), NAFE, Nat. Fedn. Ind. Businesses (mem. adv. bd. 1987—), Internat. Platform Assn., Charleston Assn. Female Execs. Office: Carolina Sound Communicatins Inc 1023 Wappoo Rd Ste B-27 Charleston SC 29407

PERRY, GEORGE LEWIS, research economist, consultant; b. N.Y.C., Jan. 23, 1934; s. Lewis G. and Helen L. (Couloumbis) P.; m. Jean Marion West, 1956 (div. 1987); children: Elizabeth, Lewis G., George A.; m. Dina Needleman, 1987. BS, MIT, 1954, PhD, 1961. Sr. economist Pres.'s Council Econ. Advisers, Washington, 1961-63; prof. econs. U. Minn., Mpls., 1963-69; sr. fellow Brookings Instn., Washington, 1969—; dir. Brookings panel on Econ. Activity; bd. dirs. State Farm Mut. Automobile Ins. Co., Bloomington, Ill., Dreyfus Mut. Funds, N.Y.C. Columnist Los Angeles Times, 1981—; author: Unemployment, Money Wage Rates and Inflation, 1966; editor: Curing Chronic Inflation, 1978, Brookings Papers on Econ. Activity, 1970—; contbr. articles to profl. jours. Served to capt. USAF, 1955-57. Mem. Am. Econs. Assn. Office: Brookings Instn 1775 Massachusetts Ave NW Washington DC 20036

PERRY, JAMES BENN, casino and hotel executive; b. New Castle, Pa., Jan. 15, 1950; s. Samuel Wesley Jr. and Grace Elizabeth (Brumbaugh) P.; m. Cathy Ann Jackson, Dec. 27, 1982; children: James Benn Jr., Lauren Elizabeth, Julie Ann. BA in History, Ohio Wesleyan U., 1972; postgrad., Ariz. State U., 1975-76; student, Tulane U., 1968-70. CPA, N.J. Internal auditor Ramada Inns, Phoenix, 1976-78, regional controller, 1978-79; asst. controller Tropicana Hotel & Casino, Las Vegas, Nev., 1979-80; controller Tropicana Hotel & Casino, Atlantic City, 1980-82, v.p. fin., 1982-85, sr. v.p., casino ops., 1987—; v.p., controller Ramada Inns, Phoenix, 1985-87, sr. v.p., 1987. Mem. N.J. Soc. CPA's (chmn. gaming conf. com. 1985-86), Am. Inst. CPA's. Office: Tropicana Hotel & Casino Iowa Ave & Boardwalk Atlantic City NJ 08401

PERRY, JESSE LAURENCE, JR., investment manager, financier; b. Nashville, Oct. 15, 1919; s. Jesse Laurence and Mamie Lucretia (White) P.; m. Susan Taylor White, Nov. 5, 1949 (dec. Mar. 1972); children: Robert Laurance, Judith Foulds; m. 2d Sarah Kinkead Stockell, Apr. 6, 1974. BA magna cum laude, Vanderbilt U., 1941; MBA, Harvard U., 1943; postgrad. in edn. retarded children George Peabody Coll., summer 1953. Treas., J.L. Perry Co., Nashville, 1947-4°; v.p., 1949-54, pres., 1954-73, also dir.; pres., chmn. bd. Perry Enterprises, Nashville, 1973-80, Naples, 1980, 1st So. Savs. & Loan, Inc., 1973-80; pres. PortersField, Inc., Nashville, 1973-80, The Jelpee Co., Naples, Fla. Pres., Police Assistance League, 1973-74; hon. col., Staff Gov. Tenn., 1962-74; 1st v.p. Tenn. Assn. for Retarded Children, 1954-62; mem. Tenn. Mental Retardation Adv. Council, 1966-72; bd. advisers Salvation Army, 1958-72; founder, sec. Tenn. Bot. Garden and Fine Arts Ctr., 1958—; chmn. 5th dist. Republican Exec. Com., 1950-54; vice chmn. Tenn. Rep. Exec. Com., 1950-54; Middle Tenn. Campaign mgr., 1956, 60, 66; state mgr. Pub. Service Com. Campaign, 1964; mem. spl. com. on urban devel. Rep. Nat. Exec. Com., 1962; del. Rep. Nat. Exec. Com., 1960, vice chmn. Tenn. del., 1960, alt. del., 1968; dist. mem. Rep. State Exec. Com., 1954-75; state chmn. Rep. Capitol Club, 1971-73; state Rep. committeeman, 1956-74; bd. govs. U. South, Sewanee Acad., 1968-74. Served to capt. AUS, 1943-46. Decorated knight Hospitaller Order St. John Jerusalem, chevalier Ordo Constantini Magni knight (comdr.) Order Temple of Jerusalem. Mem. Episc. Churchmen Tenn. (v.p. 1956), Am. Ch. Union (v.p. 1958), SAR (chpt. pres. 1977-79), U.S. C. of C., Nat. Office Mgmt. Assn. (pres. Nashville chpt. 1958-59), Am. Legion, English Speaking Union, Magna Charta Barons, Baronial Order Magna Charta, Gen. Soc. Colonial Wars, Ams. of Royal Descent, Plantagenet Soc., Order Crown Charlemagne, Order of Three Crusades, Phi Beta Kappa, Omicron Delta Gamma, Pi Kappa Alpha. Clubs: Nashville Exchange, Nashville Sewanee, Nashville City, Capitol Hill (Washington), Naples Harvard, Royal Poinciana Golf (Naples), Naples Yacht. Home: Colonial Club 1275 Gulf Shore Blvd N Naples FL 33940 Office: Tenn Bot Garden & Fine Arts Ctr PO Box 915 Naples FL 33939

PERRY, JOSEPH QUENTON, JR., accountant; b. Greenwich, Conn., Aug. 12, 1942; s. Joseph and Kathryn (Reider) P.; B. Acctg., U. Conn., 1964; M. Econs., Pace Coll., 1966; m. Lucille Stafanelli, Aug. 13, 1966; 1 dau., Heather Lynn. Trust officer Morgan Guaranty Trust Co., N.Y.C., 1966-71; sr. acct. Whitman & Ransom, 1971-76; pres. Fiduciary Services, Old Greenwich, Conn., 1976—; dir. Wharton Gord Orch., Inc., Rogers Bus. Service, Claude Heroux Prodns. Inc., Whitaker Prodns. Inc., Tri-Media Inc. Mem. N.Y. State Tax Com., 1967-71. Mem. Am. Inst. C.P.A.s. Republican. Roman Catholic. Club: Burning Tree Country. Home: 64 Circle Dr Greenwich CT 06830 Office: Fiduciary Svcs 79 E Putnam Ave Greenwich CT 06830

PERRY, KENNETH WALTER, integrated oil company executive; b. Shamrock, Tex., Feb. 24, 1932; s. Charles Bowman and Sunshine Virginia (Grady) P.; m. Mary Dean Sudderth, Aug. 28, 1953; children: Mary Martha Perry Mitchell, Kathryn Virginia Perry Foster. BSME, U. Okla., 1954. Sales engr. Mid-Continent Oil Well Supply Co., 1954-55; with Cosden Oil & Chem. Co., Big Spring, Tex., from 1957, jr. engr., 1957-59, project engr., 1959-60, chem. salesman, 1960-64, chem. products mgr., 1964-65, mktg. mgr., then v.p. mktg., 1965-69, v.p. chems., 1969-72, sr. v.p., 1972076, pres., 1976—; group v.p. Am. Petrofina, Inc., Dallas, 1976-85, sr. v.p., 1985-86, pres., chief exec. officer, 1986-88, also bd. dirs., vice chmn., bd. dirs., 1989—; chmn. bd. dirs. United Commerce Bank, Highland Village, Tex., 1989—. Mem. bd. govs. Dallas Symphony Orch., 1987—; bd. dirs. Dallas Coun. World Affairs, 1980; mem. engring com. U. Okla. Aerospace, Nuclear, 1982; bd. dirs. Colo. Mcpl. Water Dist., 1972. 1st lt. USASC, 1955-57. Mem. Am. Petroleum Inst. (bd. dirs. 1986—); Nat. Petroleum Coun., Nat. Petroleum Refiners Assn. (chmn. petrochemical com. 1984-87), Ctr. Strategic and Internat. Studies, 25-yr. Clubs, Petroleum Industry Club, Petrochemical Industry Club, Northwood Club, Energy Club, Petroleum Club. Office: Am Petrofina Inc 8350 N Central Expwy PO Box 2159 Dallas TX 75221

PERRY, LEE ROWAN, lawyer; b. Chgo., Sept. 23, 1933; s. Watson Bishop and Helen (Rowan) P.; m. Barbara Ashcraft Mitchell, July 2, 1955; children: Christopher, Constance, Geoffrey. B.A., U. Ariz., 1955, LL.B., 1961. Bar: Ariz. 1961. Since practiced in Phoenix; clk. Udall & Udall, Tucson, 1960-61; mem. firm Carson, Messinger, Elliott, Laughlin & Ragan, 1961—. Mem. law rev. staff, U. Ariz., 1959-61. Mem. bd. edn. Paradise Valley Elementary and High Sch. Dists., Phoenix, 1964-68, pres., 1968; treas. troop Boy Scouts Am., 1970-72; mem. Ariz. adv. bd. Girl Scouts U.S.A., 1972-74, mem. nominating bd., 1978-79; bd. dirs. Florence Crittenton Services Ariz., 1967-72, pres., 1970-72; bd. dirs. U. Ariz. Alumni, Phoenix, 1968-72, pres., 1969-70; bd. dirs. Family Service Phoenix, 1974-75; bd. dirs. Travelers Aid Assn. Am., 1985—; bd. dirs. Vol. Bur. Maricopa County, 1975-81, 83-86, pres., 1984-85; bd. dirs. Ariz. div. Am. Cancer Soc., 1978-80, Florence Crittenton div. Child Welfare League Am., 1976-81; bd. dirs. Crisis Nursery for Prevention of Child Abuse, 1978-81, pres., 1978-80. Served to 1st lt. USAF, 1955-58. Mem. State Bar Ariz. (conv. chmn. 1972), Am., Maricopa County bar assns., Phi Delta Phi, Phi Delta Theta (pres. 1954). Republican (precinct capt. 1970, chmn. Reps. for Senator De Concini 1976, 82, 88, precinct committeeman 1983-84). Episcopalian (sr. warden 1968-72). Clubs: Rotary (dir. 1971-77, pres. 1975-76), Plaza, Ariz. Office: Citibank Tower PO Box 33907 Phoenix AZ 85067

PERRY, MERVYN FRANCIS, investment company executive; b. Brockton, Mass., Feb. 20, 1923; s. Mervyn Elsworth and Marie (Therrien) P.; m. Marian D. Sprong, June 9, 1949 (div. 1979); children: Richard Caverhill, Cynthia Perry Parr, Susan Perry Diette, Janet Perry Horton; m. Gayle A. Lenihan, Sept. 17, 1980. AB, Boston U., 1950, JD, 1951. Mgr. Conn. Gen. Life Ins. Co., Cleve., 1956-62; v.p., dir. Mass. Gen. Life Ins. Co., Boston, 1962-65; pres., chief exec. officer, dir. Mass. Co. Distbr., Inc., Boston, 1965-69; pres., chmn. bd., chief exec. officer Mass. Fund for Income, 1973-78; pres., chief exec. officer, dir. Mass. Co., Inc., 1969-77; chmn. bd., pres., chief exec. officer, dir. Freedom Fund, Inc.; pres., dir., chmn. bd. Massco Investment Mgmt. Corp., 1969-78; pres., chief exec. officer Ready Reserves Trust, 1975-78; chmn. bd., chief exec. officer Investment Mgmt. Assocs., Inc., Denver, 1978—. With USNR, 1942-45, PTO, with USAAF, 1946-48. Mem. Union Club (Boston), Univ. Club (Boston), Met. Club (Denver), Beaver Creek Club. Republican. Episcopalian. Home: 1934 Five Iron Dr Castle Rock CO 80104 Office: Investment Mgmt Assn Inc One Denver Tech Ctr 5251 Denver Tech Ctr Pkwy Ste 1210 Englewood CO 80111

PERRY, NANCY JEAN, business journalist; b. San Antonio, Aug. 14, 1955; d. William Kurtz Perry and Dorothy Elizabeth (Weeks) McManus. BS in Psychology and Spanish magna cum laude, Va. Poly. Tech., 1977. Mktg. rep. IBM Corp., Moline, Ill., 1977-79; mktg. officer Citibank, N.A., N.Y.C., 1979-81; free-lance writer N.Y.C., 1981-83; reporter Fortune Mag. (Time Inc.), N.Y.C., 1983-87, writer, assoc. editor, 1987—. Columnist: Follow-Up, 1984-85, Fortune People, 1987-88; sr. researcher pilot TV show Business Briefing, 1984; contbr. articles to major publs. Vol. UNICEF, N.Y.C., 1984—; mem. Citizen Exchange Council, N.Y.C., 1984—. Mem. LWV (co-chmn. internat. relations com. 1984—), United Nations Assn., Phi Beta Kappa, Phi Kappa Phi. Republican. Roman Catholic. Office: Fortune Mag-Time Inc 1271 Ave of the Americas New York NY 10020

PERRY, ROBERT JOSEPH, telecommunications executive; b. Kingston, N.Y., Aug. 14, 1934; s. Robert J. and Mary (Nacarato) P.; m. Marilyn Johnson, Dec. 28, 1957; children: Kathleen Ann, Robert Andrew, Debra Ann, Joseph Robert. BBA, Siena Coll., 1956. Controller IBM Corp., Bethesda, Md., 1956-78; v.p. fin. and adminstrn. Satellite Bus. Systems, McLean, Va., 1978-86; chief fin. officer Communications Satellite Corp., Washington, 1986—. Bd. dirs. Bullis, Potomac, Md., 1983-87. Served with U.S. Army, 1958-62. Clubs: Norbeck (Rockville, Md.); Avenel (Potomac, Md.). Office: Communications Satellite Corp 950 L'Enfant Pla SW Washington DC 20024 also: Satellite Bus Systems 8283 Greensboro Dr McLean VA 22102

PERRY, STEPHEN CLAYTON, manufacturing executive; b. Atlanta, Feb. 9, 1942; s. Clayton Henry and Elizabeth Hill (Staples) P.; m. Bonnie Janet Bentley, Nov. 27, 1965; 1 child, Beverly Elizabeth. B in Indsl. Engring., Ga. Inst. Tech., 1964; MBA, Harvard U., 1968. Indsl. engr. Union Carbide Corp., Columbia, Tenn., 1964; systems analyst metals and controls div. Tex. Instruments, Attleboro, Mass., 1967; with Exxon Corp., 1968-86, gen. mgr. Toledo Scale Corp. subs. Reliance Electric Co., Worthington, Ohio, 1984-89; pres. Toledo Scale Corp. (subs Ciba-Giegy), 1989—. Bd. dirs. Ctr. Sci. and Industry, Columbus, Ohio, 1984—; mem. Berkeley Heights Twp. (N.J.) Com; 1977-79, dep. mayor, police commr., 1978, mayor, 1979. Served to capt., inf., AUS, 1964-66. Ethyl Corp. scholar, 1964; Pillsbury fellow, 1968. Mem. Scale Mfrs. Assn. (pres. 1987-89). Republican. Baptist. Home: 396 Delegate Dr Worthington OH 43235 Office: 350 W Wilson Bridge Rd Worthington OH 43085

PERRY, THOMAS BERNARD, engineering and construction company executive, accountant; b. Roanoke, Ala., June 26, 1948; s. Thomas Bernard Perry and Mary (Benefield) Woody; m. Vernell Stewart, Dec. 23, 1967; children: Thomas Bernard III, Heather Michele. BS, U. Ala.-Tuscaloosa, 1970. CPA Sr. auditor Arthur Andersen & Co., Birmingham, Ala., 1972-77; v.p. fin. Rust Internat. Corp., Birmingham, 1977—. Cub master Birmingham area Council Boy Scouts Am., Birmingham, 1977-80, asst. scout master, 1983, dist. commr., 1979; dir. Jefferson-Shelby March of Dimes, 1986-88, chmn., 1988—; elder Trinity Presbyterian Ch., 1983-86, treas. 1983-88; trustee Ala. Ballet, 1986—. Mem. profl. adv. bd., U. Ala. Sch. Acctcy., 1987—. Served to 1st lt. U.S. Army, 1970-72, to Capt. USAR, 1972-77. Mem. Am. Inst. CPAs, Ala. Soc. CPAs, Nat. Assn. Accts. (dir. 1979-81, 84-85, v.p. 85-87, pres. 87-88), Constrn. Fin. Mgmt. Assn., Fin. Execs. Inst., Rust Mgmt. Assn. (dir. 1983-84, v.p. 1985 -86). Office: Rust Internat Corp 100 Corporate Pkwy Box 101 Birmingham AL 35201

PERSAVICH, WARREN DALE, diversified manufacturing company executive; b. Cleve., Dec. 15, 1952; s. Nick and Sophie (Makris) P.; m. Anita Geraldine Zeleznik, Oct. 12, 1974; children: Nicholas, Katherine. BBA, Kent State U., 1975. CPA, Ohio. Staff acct. Price Water House, Cleve., 1975-76; asst. controller Banner Industries Inc., Cleve., 1976-79, controller, 1979-86, treas., 1986-88, v.p., 1988—. Mem. Am. Inst. CPA's, Ohio Soc. CPA's. Republican. Office: Banner Industries Inc 25700 Science Park Dr Cleveland OH 44122

PERSKY, STEWART ALAN, accountant; b. St. Louis, Sept. 26, 1952; s. Julius Edward Persky and Selma (Gross) Garon; m. Gail Madeliene Perry, June 23, 1974; children: Jason, Nicole, Jessica. B in Journalism, U. Mo., 1974, MBA with honors, 1977. CPA. Staff acct. Lester Witte and Co., Clayton, Mo., 1977-79; mgr. tax and healthcare Stone Carlie, Clayton, 1979-84; mgr. tax Brown, Smith and Co., Clayton, 1984-85; pvt. practice acctg. Creve Coeur and Clayton, Mo., 1985—; dir. tax and healthcare services Tiger Fireside Stone Carlie CPA's, St. Louis, 1981-84; radio personality, pub. speaker on tax, fin. and healthcare planning, various orgns. Active PTA, St. Louis. Mem. AICPA, Mo. Soc. CPAs, Mo. Healthcare Assn., Olivette Athletic Assn., Creve Coeur Athletic Assn. Home: 803 Somerton Ridge Saint Louis MO 63141 Office: 222 S Central Suite 902 Clayton MO 63105

PERSUITTI, PETER ANTHONY, electronics information technology sales; b. Hudson Falls, N.Y., Aug. 18, 1953; s. Albert A. and Barbara J. (Landry) P.; m. Mary Louise Johnson, Aug. 22, 1981; 1 child, Justin. BA in Classics, U. Scranton, 1975; MA in Classics, Ohio State U., 1976. Dir. student activities Portsmouth Abbey Sch., R.I., 1975-78; dir., founder Classical Travel/Academic Program in Greece, Athens, summers 1980-85; dir. admissions and fin. aid Choate Rosemary Hall, Wallingford, Conn., 1981-86; retail sales exec. Electronic Data Systems, Morristown, N.J., 1986—; ind. ednl. cons., Lawrenceville, N.J., 1986—; state chmn. R.I. Jr. Classical League, 1978-81. Mem. Sacra Musica choir Resurrection Roman Catholic Ch., Wallingford, 1981-86. Mem. Nat. Retail Mchts. Assn., Assn. Secondary Schs. for Internat. Students , Alpha Sigma Nu, Eta Sigma Phi (fellow Am. Acad. for Classical Studies, Rome 1979). Home: 98 Irwin Pl Lawrenceville NJ 08648 Office: Electronic Data Systems 95 Madison Ave Morristown NJ 07960

PERUN, JOHN JOSEPH, JR., finance professional; b. Danbury, Conn., July 3, 1963; s. John Joseph Sr. and Georgina Diack (Lawler) P. BS in Mgmt., Rensselaer Poly. Inst., 1985; postgrad., Pace U., 1986—. Staff acct. Barden Corp., Danbury, Conn., 1985-86; fin. systems analyst James River Corp., Norwalk, Conn., 1986-88; mfg. cost coord. Easton, Pa., 1988—. Mem. Rep. Nat. Com., Washington, 1985—. Mem. Assn. MBA Execs., NRA, Sigma Phi Epsilon (alumni bd. dirs. 1986—). Roman Catholic. Home: 3 Apple Blossom Ln New Fairfield CT 06812 Office: James River Corp Dixie Products 605 Kuebler Rd Easton PA 18042

PERUTZ, GERALD ERIC ALEXANDAR, manufacturing company executive; b. Vienna, Austria, Sept. 8, 1929; came to U.S., 1977; s. Georg Perutz and Helen Traill; m. Dinah Fyffe, Sept. 19, 1953; children: Sandra Fyffe, Simon G.A., Timothy P.G. Diploma, Loughborough (Eng.) U., 1950. Jr. engr. Harbour & Gen. Works Ltd., London, 1951-53; engr. Foster Wheeler Ltd., London, 1953-57; exec. The Rank Orgn., London, 1957-63; chief exec. officer Europe Bell & Howell, London, 1963-77; corp. exec., v.p., bd. dirs. Bell & Howell, Chgo., 1977-83; chmn. bd. dirs. Nimlok Co., Niles, Ill., 1983—; bd. dirs. Nimlok Ltd., London, Micro Metal Co., Indpls. Fellow Inst. of Dirs., Soc. Motion Pictures and TV, England (hon.). Home: 223 Melrose Ave Kenilworth IL 60043 Office: Nimlok Co 6019 W Howard Niles IL 60648

PERUZZO, ALBERT LOUIS, actuary, accountant; b. Chgo., Dec. 27, 1951; s. Anthony L. and Annette (Gentile) P. BS in Math., No. Ill. U., 1973, BS in Accountancy, 1974, MBA, 1975. CPA, Ill. Auditor Deloitte, Haskins & Sells, CPA's, Chgo., 1976-79; mgr. valuation compliance CNA Ins., Chgo., 1979—. Treas., bd. dirs. Dignity/Chgo., 1982-84, Integrity, Chgo., 1988—; dep. vol. Voter's Registrar Bd. Elections, Chgo., 1984-86. Recipient Ill. Silver medal Nat. Hon. Mention, 1975. Mem. Am. Acad. Actuaries, Soc. Actuaries (assoc.), Am. Inst. CPA's, Ill. CPA Soc. Democrat. Roman Catholic.

PESCHMANN, KRISTIAN RALF, physicist; b. Hamburg, Germany, Dec. 11, 1940; came to U.S., 1980; s. Erich Peschmann and Kathe Lucy (Bliesath) Schwartz; m. Hanna E. Orlowski (div. 1978); children: Kristin, Konrad. Diploma in physics, U. Kiel, 1967, Dr. Rer. Nat., 1969. Asst. prof. U. Kiel, Fed. Republic Germany, 1969; scientist Philips Research Labs., Aachen, Fed. Republic Germany, 1970-80; assoc. prof. radiology U. Calif., San Francisco, 1980—; v.p. Imatron, Inc., South San Francisco, 1982—; researcher Nat. Inst. Health & Welfare, 1980-83; prin. investigator U.S. Army Med. Research and Devel. Command, 1987—. Author: (with others) Radiology of the Skull and Brain, 1981, New Developments in Imaging, 1986; contbr. articles to profl. jours. Mem. Am. Assn. Physicists in Medicine, Internat. Soc. Optical Engring. Office: Imatron Inc 380 Oyster Point Blvd South San Francisco CA 94080

PESHKIN, SAMUEL DAVID, lawyer; b. Des Moines, Oct. 6, 1925; s. Louis and Mary (Grund) P.; m. Shirley R. Isenberg, Aug. 17, 1947; children—Lawrence Allen, Linda Ann. B.A., State U. Iowa, 1948, J.D., 1951. Bar: Iowa bar 1951. Since practiced in Des Moines; partner firm Bridges & Peshkin, 1953-66, Peshkin & Robinson, 1966—; Mem. Iowa Bd. Law Examiners, 1970—. Bd. dirs. State U. Iowa Found., 1957—, Old Gold Devel. Fund, 1956—, Sch. Religion U. Iowa, 1966—. Fellow Am. Bar Found., Internat. Soc. Barristers; mem. ABA (chmn. standing com. membership 1959—, ho. of dels. 1968—, bd. govs. 1973—), Iowa Bar Assn. (bd. govs. 1958—, pres. jr. bar sect. 1958-59, award of merit 1974), Inter-Am. Bar

Assn., Internat. Bar Assn., Am. Judicature Soc., State U. Iowa Alumni Assn. (dir., pres. 1957). Home: 505 36th St Apt 302 Des Moines IA 50312 Office: Peshkin & Robinson 1010 Fleming Bldg Des Moines IA 50309

PESKIN, KENNETH, retail executive. Postgrad., Harvard U. Pres., chief oper. officer Pathmark div. Supermarkets Gen., N.J., 1984-86, pres., chief exec. officer, 1986-87; chmn., chief exec. officer Supermarkets Gen. Holdings Corp., N.J., 1987—. Office: Supermarkets Gen Corp 200 Milik St Carteret NJ 07008 *

PESKIN, STEPHEN TODD, accountant; b. Springfield, Mass., Jan. 24, 1959; s. Robert J. and Marilyn C. (Raine) P.; m. Nancy Hazen, May 20, 1984. BBA, U. Mass., 1981. CPA, Mass. Staff acct. Meyers Bros., Handelsman & Adelesti, Springfield, 1981-84; controller, v.p. Paysaver Catalog. Showrooms, Inc., Holyoke, Mass., 1984-88; asst. controller Atlantic Maritime Svcs., Inc., Springfield, 1988—; ptnr. Car Gallery of Springfield; bd. dirs. Paysaver Catalog Showrooms. Mem. AICPA, Nat. Acct. Assn. Home: 43 Colony Dr East Longmeadow MA 01028 Office: Atlantic Maritime Svcs Inc 55 State St Springfield MA 01103

PESKY, ALAN DONALD, publishing executive; b. N.Y.C., Dec. 17, 1933; s. Louis I. and Belle (Silverstein) P.; m. Wendy Stern, Mar. 30, 1961; children: Heidi, Lee, Greg. A.B., Lafayette Coll., 1956; M.B.A., Dartmouth Coll., 1960. Product mgr. Standard Brands, N.Y.C., 1960-63; account supr. Papert, Koenig, Lois, Inc. (Advt. Agency), N.Y.C., 1963-67; founding ptnr., vice-chmn., chief operating officer Scali, McCabe, Sloves, internat. advt. agency, N.Y.C., 1967-87; gen. ptnr. Rock Flower Assocs., 1987—; chmn. Peak Media Inc.; adv. bd. Present Tense Mag. Trustee Lafayette Coll.; bd. overseers Amos Tuck Sch., Dartmouth Coll.; chmn. Coalition to Free Soviet Jews; exec. com. Everyman's U. Served to lt. U.S. Army, 1956-58. Mem. Am. Assn. Advt. Agys. Clubs: City Athletic; Pound Ridge Tennis; Am. Alpine. Home: 874 Rockrimmon Rd Stamford CT 06903

PESOLA, WILLIAM ERNEST, cable television company executive; b. Marquette, Mich., May 2, 1945; s. Ernest Ensio and Janice Mary (LeDuc) P.; m. Kathleen Mary Deschaine, July 9, 1966; children: Christie Lynn, Laurie Anne. BS, No. Mich. U., 1968, MS, 1971. Route driver Coca Cola Co., Marquette, 1963-68; tchr. Gwinn (Mich.) Schs., 1968-78; pub. Sch. News, 1969; pres. Pesola Mgmt., Marquette, 1974—; pres. Humboldt Ridge, Marquette, 1977—; treas. Elite Bar, Inc., Marquette, 1978—; v.p. Marquette Cablevision, 1981-85, also dir.; cons. cable TV, 1985—, Bresnan Communications, 1984—. Pres. Gwinn Edn. Assn., 1975-77; regional pres. Upper Peninsula Edn. Assn., 1977-78; mem. Marquette City Commn., 1977-81. Mem. NEA, Mich. Edn. Assn. Roman Catholic. Lodge: Rotary. Home: 1026 N Front St Marquette MI 49855

PESSES, PAUL D., real estate and investment management company executive; b. Davenport, Iowa, Oct. 4, 1955; s. Marvin and Elaine (Katz) P.; m. Kim Meisel, Aug. 19, 1978. BA in Econs. summa cum laude, Ohio State U., 1977; MBA, Harvard U., 1980. Bus. analyst engineered products group Cabot Corp., Boston, 1979-80; v.p., treas., dir. Metcoa, Inc., Solon, Ohio, 1980-82, Columbia Alloys Co., Twinsburg, Ohio, 1980-82; adminstrv. mgr. splty. metals and alloys Ashland Chem. Co. div. Ashland Oil, Inc., Cleve., 1983; pres. Stonestreet Mgmt. Co., Beachwood, Ohio, 1983—, also dir. Trustee Cleve. com. UNICEF; vol. Cleve. Playhouse, Kidney Found. Ohio, United Way campaign; big bro., trustee Big Bros.; treas. Pesses Charitable Found. Mem. Phi Eta Sigma, Phi Kappa Phi. Clubs: Northeast Yacht., Harvard Bus. Sch. (officer) (Cleve.), Oakwood Country.

PESTILLO, PETER JOHN, lawyer, automotive executive; b. Bristol, Conn., Mar. 22, 1938; s. Peter and Ruth (Hayes) P.; m. BettyAnn Barraclough, Aug. 29, 1959; children: Kathleen, Karen, Kerry. BSS, Fairfield (Conn.) U., 1960; LLB, Georgetown U., 1963. Bar: D.C. 1964. Mgr. union relations planning Gen. Electric Co., N.Y.C., 1968-74; v.p. employee relations B.F. Goodrich Co., Akron, Ohio, 1974-80; v.p. labor relations Ford Motor Co., Dearborn, Mich., 1980-85; v.p. employee relations Ford Motor Co., 1985-86, v.p. employee and external affairs, 1986—. Mem. adv. bd. United Found., Detroit. Mem. Am. Arbitration Assn. (dir.), U.S. C. of C. (labor relation com.), D.C. Bar, Bus. Roundtable, Labor Policy Assn., Nat. Assn. Mfgs., UBA. Home: 338 Provencal Grosse Pointe Farms MI 48236

PETER, LILY, plantation operator, writer; b. Marvell, Ark.; d. William Oliver and Florence (Mowbrey) P. B.S., Memphis State U., 1927; M.A., Vanderbilt U., 1938; postgrad. U. Chgo., 1930, Columbia U., 1935-36; L.H.D., Moravian Coll., Bethlehem, Pa., 1965, Hendrix Coll., Conway, Ark., 1983; LL.D., U. Ark., 1975. Owner, operator plantations, Marvell and Ratio, Ark.; writer poetry, feature articles pub. in S.W. Quar., Delta Rev., Cyclo Flame, Etude, Am. Weave, others; mem. staff S.W. Writers Conf., Corpus Christi, Tex., 1954—, sponsor Ark. Writers' Conf. Chmn., Poetry Day in Ark., 1953—; chmn., sponsor music Ark. Territorial Sesquicentennial, 1969. Author: The Green Linen of Summer, 1964; The Great Riding, 1966; The Sea Dream of the Mississippi, 1973; In the Beginning, 1983. Bd. dirs. Ark. Arts Festival, Little Rock, Grand Prairie Festival Arts; chmn. bd. Phillips County Community Center, 1969-73; hon. trustee Moravian Music Found. Recipient Moramus award Friends of Moravian Music, 1964, Disting. Alumni award Vanderbilt U., 1964, Gov.'s award as Ark. Conservationist of Year, Ark. Wildlife Fedn., 1975, Whooping Crane award Nat. Wildlife Fedn., 1976; named Poet Laureate Ark., 1971, Democrat Woman of Year, 1971, 1st Citizen of Phillips County, 1st Citizen of Phillips County C. of C., 1985, Most Disting. Woman of Ark., Ark. C. of C., 1985. Mem. DAR, (hon. state regent), Nat. League Am. Pen Women, Ark. Authors and Composers Soc., Poets' Roundtable Ark., poetry socs. of Tenn., Tex., Ga., Met. Opera Assn., So. Cotton Ginners Assn. (dir. 1971—), Big Creek Protective Assn. (chmn. 1974—), Sigma Alpha Iota (hon.). Republican. Episcopalian. Clubs: Pacaha (Helena, Ark.); Woman's City (Little Rock). Home: Route 2 Box 69 Marvell AR 72366

PETER, PHILLIPS SMITH, lawyer; b. Washington, Jan. 24, 1932; s. Edward Compston and Anita Phillips (Smith) P.; m. Jania Jayne Hutchins, Apr. 8, 1961; children: Phillips Smith Peter Jr., Jania Jayne Hutchins. BA, U. Va., 1954, JD, 1959. Bar: Calif. 1959. Assoc. McCutchen, Doyle, Brown, Enerson, San Francisco, 1959-63; with GE (and subs.), various locations, 1963—; v.p. corp. bus. devel. GE (and subs.), 1973-76; v.p. GE (and subs.), Washington, 1976-79, v.p. corp. govtl. rels., 1980—; bd. dirs. Inst. for Rsch. on Econs. of Taxation. Mem. editorial bd. Va. Law Rev., 1957-59. Trustee Howard U.; v.p. Federal City Coun., Washington, 1979-85; bd. dirs. Carlton. Served with Transp. Corps, U.S. Army, 1954-56. Mem. Calif. Bar Assn., Order of Coif, Wee Burn Club, Ea. Yacht Club, Farmington Country Club, Ponte Vedra Club, Lago Mar Club, Landmark Club, Congl. Country Club, Georgetown Club, Chevy Chase Club, Pisces Club, F Street Club, Coral Beach and Tennis Club, John's Island Club, Omicron Delta Kappa. Episcopalian. Home: 10805 Tara Rd Potomac MD 20854 also: 1000 Beach Rd John's Island Vero Beach FL 32963 Office: GE 1331 Pennsylvania Ave Ste 800 S Washington DC 20004 also: 690 Ocean Rd John's Island Vero Beach FL 32963

PETERNELL, BEN CLAYTON, hospitality company executive; b. Ft. Wayne, Ind., Nov. 5, 1945; s. Frank and Marabelle (Kigar) P.; m. Pamela S. Lorman, Dec. 28, 1968; children: Andrew, Mark. BA in Psychology, Hanover Coll., 1968; MBA in Mgmt. and Devel. Behavior, Ind. U., 1970. Various mgmt. positions Firestone Tire & Rubber Co., Akron, Ohio, 1970-73; group v.p., personnel Am. Hosp. Supply Co., Evanston, Ill., 1973-85; sr. v.p human resources Holiday Corp., Memphis, 1985—. Active Germantown (Tenn.) Youth Scoccer Club, 1986—; mem. commn. on 21st century Rhodes Coll.; bd. dirs. Sta. WKNO pub. Radio-TV, 1987—. Mem. Conf. Personnel Officers. Presbyterian. Home: 2313 Dogwood Meadows Cove Germantown TN 38138 Office: Holiday Corp 1023 Cherry Rd Memphis TN 38117

PETERS, CHARLES D., design draftsman; b. St. Johns, Antigua, West Indies, Dec. 8, 1945; s. Gerald William and Amy H. (Brown) P.; m. Bernice H. Martin, May 28, 1972 (div. 1982); children: Charline, Andrea, Devan, Aletha. Student, No. Am. Sch. Drafting, 1971-74, grad. (hon.), 1979. Residential constrn. Milton Jackson Constrn. Co., Antigua, 1965-67; project supr. Seventh Day Advantist New Ch., Antigua, 1967-69; carpenter foreman Estate Welcome, Inc., St. Croix, U.S. Virgin Islands, 1973-76; sr. archtl. draftsman Rolling Nielsen Architect & Urban Planner, St. Croix, U.S. Virgin Island, 1976-83, Richard E. Baringer F.A.I.A. & John R. Rollings A.I.A., St. Croix, U.S. Virgin Island, 1983-85; project supr. Pate/Martin Architects A.I.A., Ft. Lauderdale, Fla., 1986; pres. Caribbean Drywall & Acoustic Inc., Annapolis, Md., 1987—. Mem. AIA, Choice Caribbean Constrn. Enterprises, Am. Inst. Design and Drafting, Constrn. Specifications Inst., So. Bldg. Code Congress Internat. Home: 607 Harbor Dr Annapolis MD 21403 Office: Caribbean Dry Wall & Acoustic PO Box 6267 Annapolis MD 21403

PETERS, DAVID LOUIS, food company executive; b. Mt. Pleasant, Pa., Oct. 12, 1945; s. William O. and Mary (Maciupa) P.; m. Barbara J. Kelanic, Oct. 18, 1968; children: Marian, Michael. BA, California (Pa.) State U., 1971; MA, Cen. Mich. U., 1977. Area mgr. Hormel Co., Austin, Minn., 1971-76; v.p. sales Holsum Co., Waukesha, Wis., 1976-80; v.p. sales and mktg. PVO Internat., St. Louis, 1981; sr. v.p. Doskocil Foods Group, Jefferson, Wis., 1982-88; v.p. sales/mktg. Pocino, Inc., City of Industry, Calif., 1988—. Pres. Time-Out, Inc., 1983-85. Served with USMC, 1963-67. Mem. Am. Mgmt. Assn., Am. Legion. Republican. Mem. Ch. Brethren. Club: Kettle Moraine Soccer (pres. 1987—). Home: Franklin Rd Upper Saint Clair PA 53183 Office: Pocino Inc 14250 Lomitas Ave City of Industry CA 91746

PETERS, GARRY LOWELL, wholesale grocery executive; b. Gary, Ind., Oct. 1, 1952; s. Lowell Arwin and Geraldine Rose (Garner) P.; m. Patricia Louise Thursby, Dec. 28, 1974; children: Eric Matthew, Blake Jordan, Joel Ryan. BA, Taylor U., 1975. Route salesman Pepsi-Cola Bottling Co., Indpls., 1975-76, merchandiser, 1977, dist. mgr., 1978; merchandising mgr. Pepsi-Cola Bottling Group, Indpls., 1979-80, sales mgr., 1981-83; area v.p. Pepsi-Cola Bottling Group, Austin, Tex., 1984-86; pres. McMahan-Leib Frozen World, Inc. div. Allied Co., Indpls., 1987-88; exec. v.p. Allied Grocers Ind. div. Allied Co., Indpls., 1988—. Home: 105 Cherokee Ln Noblesville IN 46060 Office: Allied Grocers Ind Inc 55 S State Ave Indianapolis IN 46201

PETERS, JAMES ELLIOT, marketing executive; b. Bethlehem, Pa., Oct. 8, 1960; s. Elliot James and Elizabeth (Kripper) P.; m. Carol Ann Hoppes, July 7, 1984. BSChemE, U. Va., 1982; MBA, U. Pa., 1986. Project engr. Borg-Warner Chem. Inc., Parkersburg, W.Va., 1982-83; project mgr. Borg-Warner Chem. Inc., Parkersburg, 1983-84; research assoc. U. Pa., Phila., 1984-88; labor relations cons. 1984-86; cons. fin. mktg. Strategic Mgmt. Group, Phila., 1986-87, dir. curriculum, 1987, dir. mktg., 1987-89; advisor planning Arco Chem. Corp., Newtown Square, 1989—; bd. dirs. Applied Telematics Inc., cons., 1986—, Devon, Pa., Strategic Technical Solutions, Phila.; cons. in field.,. Mktg. cons. Oncology Nursing Soc., Phila., 1987. Recipient Labor Relations award Master Printers Am., 1985. Mem. Am. Mktg. Assn., Am. Inst. Chem. Engrs. (chpt. v.p. 1981-2), Am. Assn. MBA Exec. Republican. Lutheran. Office: Arco Chem Corp 3801 Westchester Pike Newtown Square PA 19073

PETERS, JOHN BASIL, electronic company executive; b. Vancouver, B.C., Can., Nov. 3, 1952; s. James John and Una Lois (Timms) P. Tech. diplomas with hon., B.C.I.T., Burnaby, B.C., 1973; BSEE with hon., U. B.C., 1977, PhDEE, 1982. Registered profl. engr., B.C. Chmn., chief exec. officer Nexus Engring. Corp., Burnaby, 1982—; research and devel. cons. RMS Indsl. Controls, Port Coquitlan, B.C., 1980-82, Channel One Video, Vancouver, 1979-81; project coordinator U. B.C. Electric Vehicle Project, Vancouver, 1974-77; bd. dirs. Infostat Telecommunications Ltd.; adj. prof. Engring. Simon Fraser U., Burnaby, 1986—. Bd. govs. U. B.C., Vancouver, 1976-79, B.C. Inst. Tech., Burnaby, 1987—, chmn bd. fin., adminstrn., pers. Recipient Alumni Achievement award B.C. Inst. Tech., 1986, Bus. Leader of Yr. award Vancouver Bd. Trade, 1989, B.C. Sci. and Engring. Gold Medal, 1988, Can. Award for Excellence, 1987, Cert. of Merit in Enterpreneurship, 1988; named B.C. Hydro and Power Authority scholar, 1973, Sherwood Lett Meml. scholar, 1977-79, Hector J. MacLeod scholar, IEEE, 1971-81, Nat. Scis. and Engring. Research Council scholar, 1977-81, C.A. and J.C.A. Banks Found. scholar, 1974-77. Mem. Assn. Profl. Engrs. of the Province of B.C. (prize 1977), Young Presidents Orgn., Sci. Council B.C. (electonics and communications com. 1987—, post-doctoral fellow, 1982-84).

PETERS, JOHN GRAYBILL, JR., security company executive; b. Lancaster, Pa., Dec. 13, 1951; s. John Graybill and Mabel Lucercia (Johnson) P.; m. Wendy Jean Hershey, Aug. 20, 1972 (div. Mar. 1983); m. Laurie A. Leupold, July 17, 1983; children: Jason William, Geoffrey Michael. AA, No. Va. Community Coll., 1972; BS in Criminal Justice, U. Balt., 1975; MS in Pub. Relations, Boston U., 1976; MBA, Babson Coll., 1978; postgrad., Gonzaga Law Sch., 1984, Suffolk U., 1978. Clk. FBI, Washington, 1969-72; dep. sheriff York County (Pa.) Sheriff's Dept., 1972-77; staff exec. Braintree (Mass.) Police Dept., 1977-78; sr. researcher Pub. Systems Evaluation, Cambridge, Mass., 1978-79; chmn. bd. Reliapon Police Products, Albuquerque, 1983—; pres. Defensive Tactics Inst., Inc., Albuquerque, 1979—; v.p. mktg. Impact Prodns., Albuquerque, 1987—; adj. prof. No. Essex Community Coll., Haverhill, Mass., 1977-80. Author: Official Kubotan Techniques, 1980, Realistic Defensive Tactics, 1981, Afraid of the Dark, 1985; exec. producer (video manuals) Defensive Tactics with Flashlights, 1982, Tactical Handcuffing. Mem. Braintree Fin. Com., 1980-82, fin. com. Joe Mercer for Gov. Campaign, Albuquerque, 1986, town meeting Town of Braintree, 1979-83. Named Hon. Citizen Louisville. Mem. Am. Soc. Indsl. Soc., U.S. Secret Service Defensive Tactics Adv. Panel. Republican. Baptist. Office: Defensive Tactics Inst Inc 608 7th St SW Albuquerque NM 87102

PETERS, KATHRYN HUCKABEE, compliance officer; b. Durham, N.C., Mar. 3, 1958; d. James Gaston Jr. and Kathryn (Cole) Huckabee; m. Jay Lytton Peters. BA in Econs., Duke U., 1980. Registrations adminstr. Fin. Service Corp., Atlanta, 1981-83, sr. compliance adminstr., 1983-85, supr. investment adv. compliance, 1985-87; pres. Advisors Compliance, Inc., Atlanta, 1987—; gen. securities prin., registered options prin., mcpl. securities prin. FSC Securities Corp., Atlanta, 1982—. Author: (manual) Supervisory Procedures for Financial Planners/Registered Investment Advisers, 1985. Mem. Jr. League of Atlanta, Inc., 1981—. Home: 3046-G Clairmont Rd NE Atlanta GA 30329 Office: Advisors Compliance Inc 3490 Piedmont Rd NE Ste 1500 Atlanta GA 30305

PETERS, MAX, oil and gas producer, author; b. N.Y.C., May 12, 1949; s. Jerry Peters and Evelyne (Budofsky) Cornell; m. Ruth Lynette Grimstad, June 10, 1973; children: Alexis-Anne, Eliot, Dwight, Galina. Grad. high sch., Norwalk, Conn. Asst. dir. drug rehab. ctr. Luth. Social Svcs., L.A., 1971-74; asst. brokerage mgr. Transamerica Corp., Sacramento, 1975-79; editor Ecology Digest, Sacramento, 1979-82; chief exec. officer TRA Energy Corp., Sacramento, 1982—. Author: A Less Troubled God, 1987. Mem. Ohio Oil and Gas Assn., The Nature Conservancy. Office: TRA Energy Corp 1779 Tribute Rd Ste D Sacramento CA 95815

PETERS, RALPH FREW, investment banker; b. Mineola, N.Y., Mar. 21, 1929; s. Ralph and Helen Louise (Frew) P.; m. Diana Joyce Clayton, Dec. 19, 1969; children: Louise Frew, Jean Reid, Ralph Frew, Melvyn T., Richard Clayton. B.A., Princeton U., 1951; postgrad., Stonier Grad. Sch. Banking, Rutgers U., 1962. With Corn Exchange Bank & Trust Co., 1947-52; chmn. exec. com., dir. Discount Corp. N.Y., N.Y.C., 1955—; dir. Internat. Investors Inc., Sun Life Ins. & Annuity. Served with USNR, 1948-55. Mem. Public Securities Assn. (gov.). Episcopalian. Clubs: Anglers, Leash, Links, North Woods, Down Town Assn. Office: DCNY Corp 58 Pine St New York NY 10005

PETERSEN, BRUCE EDWARD, controller; b. Omaha, June 8, 1962; s. Robert Edward and Martha (Bodlak) P.; m. Lisa Jean Pencek, Mar. 1, 1986. BBA, U. Nebr., 1985. Installer, technician Carl Jarl Security Systems, Omaha, 1978-81, Security Internat., Omaha, 1981-83, NECO Alarm Systems, Lincoln, Nebr., 1983-86; controller Electronic Contracting Co., Lincoln, 1986—. Recipient U. Nebr. Regents scholarship, 1980-82. Republican. Presbyterian. Office: Electronic Contracting Co 2630 N 27th St Lincoln NE 68521

PETERSEN, DAVID LEE, insurance agent; b. Louisville, Dec. 17, 1943; s. Clifford Warren and Martha Lee (Schmidt) P.; m. Edwina Marie Stiles, June 22, 1968; children—Christopher Lee, Jennifer Wood, Joshua Kulk. B.S. in Bus. Adminstrn., Marquette U., 1966; M.B.A., U. Utah., 1971. Commd. 2d lt. U.S. Air Force, 1967; advanced through grades to maj., 1979; chief maintenance 601st Tactical Control Maintenance Squadron, Sembach AFB, Germany; navigator 437 Mil. Airlift Wing, Charleston AFB, S.C., 1972-73; instr. navigator 374 Tactical Airlift Wing, Clark AB, Philippines, 1973-74; navigator flight examiner 314 Tactical Airlift Wing, Little Rock AFB, Ark., 1974-76; chief ops. programs 61 Mil. Airlift Support Wing, Hickam AFB, Hawaii, 1976-79; asst. chief inspections 317 Tactical Airlift Wing, Pope AFB, N.C., 1979-83; chief plans and policy HQ Tactical Air Command Info. Systems, Langley AFB, Va., 1983-87; retired from USAF, 1987; ins. agt. Met. Life Ins. Co., Newport News, Va., 1987—. Vice pres. Wendwood Assn., Newport News, Va., 1984-85, pres., 1985-86, newsletter editor 1987-88. Decorated 2 Air Force Meritorious Svc. medals, 3 Air medals, 2 Humanitarian Svc. medals. Mem. Internat. Platform Assn., Retired Officers Assn., Kiwanis (bd. dirs., charter pres. Oyster Pt. chpt. 1988-89). Republican. Roman Catholic. Avocations: woodworking, antique and art collecting, consumer advocate, stamp collecting. Home: 335 Wendwood Dr Newport News VA 23602 Office: Met Life Ins Co 827 Diligence Dr Ste 106 Newport News VA 23606

PETERSEN, DONALD E(UGENE), automobile company executive; b. Pipestone, Minn., Sept. 4, 1926; s. William L. and Mae (Pederson) P.; m. Jo Anne Leonard, Sept. 12, 1948; children: Leslie Carolyn, Donald Leonard. BSME, U. Wash., 1946; MBA, Stanford U., 1949; DSc (hon.), U. Detroit, 1986; LHD (hon.), Art Ctr. Coll., Pasadena, 1986. With Ford Motor Co., Dearborn, 1949—, v.p. car planning and rsch., 1969-71, v.p. truck ops., 1971-75, exec. v.p. diversified products ops., 1975-76, exec. v.p. internat. automotive ops., 1977-80, pres., 1980-85, chmn. bd. dirs., chief exec. officer, 1985—, also bd. dirs. Trustee Cranbrook Inst. Sci., Bloomfield, Mich., 1973—, Citizens Rsch. Coun. of Mich., Safety Coun. for S.E. Mich., Detroit Inst. Arts, Mich. Cancer Found., Corp. Found. for Aid to Edn., TARGET; mem. adv. bd. U. Wash. Grad. Sch. Bus. Adminstrn.; bd. overseers Oreg. Health Sci. Univ.; mem. New Detroit, Inc., Detroit Renaissance, Inc.; bd. dirs. Hewlett-Packard Co., Dow Jones & Co., Inc., Detroit Strategic Planning Project, Mich. Commn. Sch. Fin. Served with USMC, 1946-47, 51-52. Recipient Disting. Alumnus award U. Wash., 1981, Arbuckle award Stanford U. Bus. Sch. Alumni Assn., 1985, 1st Am. Achievement award Brookgreen Gardens, 1986, Bus. Statesman award Harvard Bus Sch. Club Detroit, Good Neighbor award U.S. Mex. C. of C., Man of Yr. award Motor Trend Mag., 1987, Nat. Humanitarian award Nat. Jewish Ctr. Immunology and Respiratory Medicine; Disting. Svc. citation Automotive Hall of Fame, Humanitarian award Burden Ctr. for Aging, Freedom of Human Spirit Internat. Ctr. for Disabled, Svc. to Democracy award Columbia U. Am. Assembly, Bus. Leadership award U. Mich. Sch. of Bus., Quarterback of Industry award The Quarterback Club, Semper Fidelis award Marine Corps Scholarship Found, others. Mem. The Bus. Coun., Bus. Roundtable (mem. policy com., mem. U.S.-Japan bus. council, mem. adv. com. for trade negotiations, mem. emergency com. for Am. trad), Bus.-Higher Edn. Forum, Soc. Automotive Engrs., Engring. Soc. Detroit, Mensa, Motor Vehicle Mfrs. Assn., Soc. Mech. Engrings. (hon. mem. 1989), Nat. Acad. Engring., Detroit Club, Bloomfield Hills Country Club, Bloomfield Open Hunt Club, Ostego Ski Club, Detroit Econ. Club, Phi Beta Kappa, Sigma Xi, Tau Beta Pi. Episcopalian. Office: Ford Motor Co The American Rd Dearborn MI 48121

PETERSEN, GAYLE ANNA, director clinical education; b. Moline, Ill., Aug. 11, 1961; d. LeRoy Francis and Barbara Jean (Korb) P. AS, Black Hawk Coll., 1981; BS, Coll. St. Francis, Joliet, Ill., 1987. Cert. respiratory therapy technician, pulmonary function technologist; registered respiratory therapist. Respiratory therapist Luth. Hosp., Moline, Ill., 1981-84; dir. clin. edn. respiratory care programs Ill. Cen. Coll., East Peoria, 1984—; item writer Nat. Bd. for Respiratory Care, Shawnee Mission, Kans., 1985; instr. CPR, advanced cardiac life support provider Am. Heart Assn., 1985—. Mem. Am. Assn. Respiratory Care, Ill. Soc. for Respiratory Care (chmn. local chpt. 1984-86), Lambda Beta. Home: 6516 N University Apt 112 Peoria IL 61614 Office: Ill Cen Coll Allied Health East Peoria IL 61635

PETERSEN, NORMAN WILLIAM, naval officer, engineering facility administrator; b. Highland Park, Ill., Aug. 26, 1933; s. Jens Edlef and Marie (Wenderling) P.; m. Ann Nevin, Aug. 24, 1956; children: Richard Nevin, Robert William, Thomas Marshall, Anita, David Arthur. BEE, U. N.Mex., 1956; MEE with distinction, Naval Postgrad. Sch., Monterey, Calif., 1962; postgrad., Harvard Bus. Sch., 1982. Registered profl. engr., Mass., Calif. Shops engr. Naval Station, Key West, Fla., 1956-59; personnel dir. Bur. Yards and Docks, Washington, 1959-60; pub. works officer Fleet Anti-Air Warfare Ctr., Dam Neck, Va., 1962-64; engring. coord. Southwest div. Naval Facilities Engring. Command, San Diego, 1964-66; exec. officer Amphibious Constrn. Battalion 1, San Diego, 1966-67; force civil engr. Comdr. Naval Air Force Pacific, San Diego, 1967-70; pub. works officer Naval Air Sta. Miramar, San Diego, 1970-73; exec. officer Pub. Works Ctr., Great Lakes, Ill., 1973-75; comdg. officer Navy Civil Engring. Rsch. Lab., Port Hueneme, Calif., 1975-78, Pub. Works Ctr. San Francisco Bay Area, Oakland, Calif., 1978-80; comptroller, programs dir. Naval Facilities Engring. Command, Washington, 1980-84; pub. works officer Pacific Missile Test Ctr., Point Mugu, Calif., 1984-86; deputy assoc. dir. for plant engring. Lawrence Livermore (Calif.) Nat. Lab., 1986—. Contbr. articles to profl. jours. Bd. dirs. CBC Fed. Credit Union, Port Hueneme, 1984-86, Ventura County United Way, Oxnard, Calif., 1976-78, strategic planning com., Camarillo, Calif., 1984-86; guest mem. Ventura County Assn. Govts., 1984-86. Decorated (twice) Legion of Merit; Gallantry Cross (Republic Vietnam). Mem. Am. Soc. Mil. Comptrollers, Soc. Am. Mil. Engrs., Assn. Phys. Plant Adminstrs. (affiliate), Navy League, Oxnard Gem and Mineral Soc. (2d v.p.), Sigma Xi, Lambda Chi Alpha. Office: Lawrence Livermore Nat Lab PO Box 808 L-657 Livermore CA 94550

PETERSEN, THOMAS ROBERT, marketing executive, management consultant; b. Indpls., Oct. 29, 1962; s. W. Harold and M. Jacqulyn (O'Meara) P.; m. Kathleen Baker, Aug. 12, 1984. BS, Calif. State U., Northridge, 1985. Photog. technician Petersen Lithograh Corp., Santa Monica, Calif., 1973-78; computer programmer Mass Benefit Corp., L.A., 1978-80; from instr. to dive operator to dir. rescue tng. Internat. Sport Dives, L.A., 1980-85; with sales and mktg. dept. Petersen Mktg. & Mgmt. Corp., L.A., 1985-86, v.p. mktg., dir. health products, 1986—; moderator Disability Fin. Planning. Svcs., L.A. Author: Disability Sales, 1987; contbr. articles to profl. jours. Instr. CPR L.A. chpt. Am. Heart Assn., 1985—. Recipient LAAHU-Paladin award for excellence, 1989. Mem. Nat. Assn. Life Underwriters, Calif. Assn. Life Underwriters, L.A. Life Underwriters, Nat. Assn. Health Underwriters, L.A. Health Underwriters, ISD Dive Club (pres. 1986—), Calif. Yacht Club (Marina del Ray). Office: Petersen Mktg 11704 Wilshire Blvd Ste 210 Los Angeles CA 90025

PETERSEN-FREY, ROLAND, manufacturing executive; b. Hamburg, Fed. Republic Germany, Aug. 17, 1937; came to U.S., 1958; s. Georg and Erna (Coltzau) P.-F.; m. Christa Caroline Ufer, Nov. 25, 1961; children: Martin, Anya. BA in Fin., CUNY, 1967, MA in Fin., 1970. Asst. v.p. Mfrs. Hanover, N.Y.C., 1961-70; v.p. gen. mgr. Rusch Inc., N.Y.C., 1970-75; chief exec. officer Inmed Corp., Atlanta, 1975—, chmn. bd.; bd. dirs. Inmed U.K. Ltd., Worthing, Eng., Inmed Sinderian. Berhad, Penang, Malaysia. Served with U.S. Army, 1959-61. Fellow Inst. Dirs. Republican. Club: WCT Peachtree Tennis (Atlanta). Home: 5000 Morton St Alpharetta GA 30201 Office: Inmed Corp 100 Technology Dr Alpharetta GA 30201

PETERSON, ALLEN, management company executive; b. L.A., Sept. 5, 1944; s. Edward S. and Doris Ann (Christensen) P.; m. Norma J. Mitchell, Aug. 24, 1968 (div. 1985); children: Jacob Andrew, Mitchell Paul. BA in Psychology, U. Calif., Berkeley, 1971. Owner, mgr. wholesale antiques, 1971-76; mgr. The Insulation Co., 1976-78; cons. Ritchie & Assocs., Beverly Hills, Calif., 1979-84; founder, pres. Abear Mgmt. Systems Inc., Paso Robles, Calif., 1984—; cons. Iowa Beef Processors, Dakota City, 1982, Purolator Courier, Toronto, Ont., Can., 1983; cons., advisor Ctr. for Mgmt. and Productivity, Port au Prince, Haiti, 1988. Inventor videographic system. Welfare sec. Salvation Army, Paso Robles, 1987—; bd. dirs. Food Bank Coalition San Luis Obisbo. With U.S. Army, 1966-68. Football scholar UCLA, 1963. Mem. Am. Mgmt. Assn., Inst. for Indsl. Engrs., Internat. Interactive Communications Soc., Silicon Valley Computer Soc., U. Calif.-Berkeley Alumni Club, Beta Theta Pi. Methodist. Office: Abear Mgmt Systems Inc 810 12th St Ste 201 Paso Robles CA 93446

PETERSON, ARTHUR JACK, finance company executive; b. San Francisco, Aug. 31, 1941; s. Arthur Wallace and Lyyli (Tuomala) P.; m. Joanne Maria Sacco, June 28, 1946 (div. July 1987); 1 child, Michelle Marie. BS in Math., Mich. Technol. U., 1963; MBA, UCLA, 1971. Ops. rsch. analyst McDonnell Aircraft, St. Louis, 1963-66, N.Am. Rockwell, El Segundo, Calif., 1966-67, Lockheed Missile and Space, Sunnyvale, Calif., 1967-69; sales rep. Burroughs Corp., Oakland, Calif., 1971-72; various positions Fireman's Fund Ins., San Francisco, 1972-81; v.p. fin. and adminstrn. Agy. Automation, San Francisco, 1981-83; sr. v.p. corp. devel. Avco Fin. Svcs., Irvine, Calif., 1983—. Mem. Assn. Corp. Growth, Newport Beach (Calif.) Country Club. Republican. Lutheran. Home: 251 Lower Cliff Dr #8 Laguna Beach CA 92651 Office: Avco Fin Svcs Inc 3349 Michelson Dr Irvine CA 92715

PETERSON, BRUCE EDWARD, collection company executive; b. Charleston, W.Va., Oct. 29, 1947; s. Vernon Leslie and Anna Jane (lecher) P.; m. Mary Eloise Hougland, Aug. 15, 1970; 1 child, Jocelyn Jane. BA, Wash. State U., 1969. Asst. mgr. Household Fin. Corp., Tacoma, 1972-74; collection supr. Wash. State Employees Credit Union, Olympia, 1974-79; collection mgr. Horizon Fed. Credit Union, Spokane, Wash., 1979-84; ind. fin. cons. Spokane, 1984—. Served to 1st lt. U.S. Army, 1970-72. Mem. Spokane Chpt. Credit Unions (pres. 1980-83), Wash. Credit Union Collectors Assn. (pres., v.p. 1981-84), Res. Officers Assn. (life), Nat. Rifle Assn. (life). Republican. Episcopalian. Lodge: Elks. Office: PO Box 943 Veradale WA 94037

PETERSON, DEBRA ANN, accountant; b. Austin, Tex., Apr. 12, 1961; d. Henry William Anderson and Barbara Marie (Lunt) Miller; m. Joseph L. Peterson, Nov. 19, 1986. BS in Acctg., U. Tex., 1983. CPA. Staff acct. Price Waterhouse, Dallas, 1983-85, sr. acct., 1985—. Mem. Dallas 2001; fundraiser Dallas Symphony Orch. Mem. AICPA, Tex. Soc. CPA's, DAR. Home: Werik Apts 5635 Yale Blvd 1st fl Dallas TX 75206

PETERSON, DONALD CURTIS, life care executive, consultant; b. Seattle, Feb. 27, 1931; s. Arthur O. and Agnes V. (Erickson) P.; m. Marilyn Jane, June 21, 1952; children: Bruce D., Mark A., Daryl R., Debra L., Joseph J. AA, North Park Coll., 1950; cert. in mgmt., Am. Mgmt. Assn., 1965. With fgn. ops. staff Internat. Harvester Co., Chgo., 1950-54; mktg. exec. UARCO, Inc., Barrington, Ill., 1954-67; group v.p. Victor Comptometer, Lincoln, Nebr., 1967-68; pres. Nationwide Data, Wheeling, Ill., 1968-71, Nationwide Bus. Farms, Wheeling, 1968-71, Ins. Producers Bulletin, Wheeling, 1968-71, Alpha Internat., Sawyer, Mich., 1971-83; exec. dir. Freedom Sq. U.S.A., Seminole, Fla., 1983—; mktg. cons. Balt. Bus. Forms., Hunt Valley, Md., 1974-76. Supr., chmn. water bd., sanitary bd. Chikaming Twp., Lakeside, Mich., 1972-76. Served with U.S. Army, 1952-57. Republican. Baptist. Home: 7603 Ulmerton Rd 28-C Largo FL 34641 Office: Freedom Square USA 7800 Liberty Ln Seminole FL 34642

PETERSON, ERLEND JAMES, financial planner; b. Sheboygan, Wis., Sept. 9, 1930; s. Emory and Ina Marguerite (Carley) P.; children: Erlend Jr., Christopher, Mary, Kathryn, Robert, Susie; m. Joan Hawthone Matthews, Aug. 26, 1988. BS, U. Wis., 1957. Registered rep. Investors Diversified Svcs., Pasadena, Calif., 1973-75, Westam. Fin., L.A., 1975-81; registered prin., registered investment advisor, cert. fin. planner Titan Capital Corp., L.A., 1981—; assoc. Renaissance Bus. Assocs., L.A., 1984-88. Mem. Internat. Assn. Fin. Planning (v.p., dir.), Inst. Cert. Fin. Planners (v.p., bd. dirs. 1986—), Am. Fin. Advisors (founder, pres. 1983—). Mem. Emissaries Ch. Office: 2930 Westwood Blvd Los Angeles CA 90064

PETERSON, GEORGE EMANUEL, JR., lawyer, business executive; b. Mt. Vernon, N.Y., Mar. 8, 1931; s. George E. and Lydia Evelyn (Peterson) P.; m. Barbara Ritter, Aug. 30, 1957; children—Lisa Manvel, George Emanuel III. B.A., Yale, 1953; LL.B., U. Va., 1958. Bar: N.Y. State 1959, Conn. 1974. Assoc. firm Reid & Priest, N.Y.C., 1958-68, ptnr., 1968-70; v.p., gen. counsel Insilco Corp., Meriden, Conn., 1970-72, v.p. fin., 1972-76, v.p., sec., 1976-79, v.p., gen. counsel, 1976-89; pvt. practice North Haven, Conn., 1989—. Served to lt. USNR, 1953-55. Mem. ABA, N.Y. State Bar Assn. Office: PO Box 2034 North Haven CT 06473

PETERSON, LARRY DALE, trust company executive; b. Sharon, Pa., Apr. 23, 1948; s. Milton Harold and Berdeen Elza (Floch) P.; m. Linda Ann Deason, Aug. 2, 1969; children: Amy Elizabeth, Susan Jane. BS, Pa. State U., 1970; M in Banking, Ruters U., 1980. Sr. v.p., mgr. nat. div. Ameritrust Co. N.A., Cleve., 1984-85, sr. v.p., mgr. consumer banking div., 1985-87, pres. Cin. region, 1987—. Republican. Methodist. Club: Bankers (Cin.). Office: Ameritrust Co NA 525 Vine St Cincinnati OH 45202

PETERSON, MICHAEL ALDEN, construction executive; b. Indpls., Sept. 12, 1949; s. Morris A. and Roma E. (Whippo) P.; m. Paula J. Adams; children: Mark, Nicholas. BS in Bus. and Acctg., Butler U., 1971. CPA, Ind.; cert. mgmt. acctg. Audit mgr. Ernst & Whinney, Indpls., 1971-81; v.p. The Demars Corp., Indpls., 1981—. Bd. dirs Am. Cancer Soc., Indpls., 1977-82, Better Bus. Bur., Indpls., 1985—, Indpls. Speech and Hearing Inst., 1986—, treas. 1988—; treas. Fishers United Meth. Ch., 1986—. Mem. Nat. Assn. Accts. (pres. 1986—), Fin. Execs. Inst., Am. Inst. CPA's, Ind. Soc. CPA's, Inst. Mgmt. Accts. Republican. Clubs: Indpls. Athletic, Hillcrest Country (Indpls.). Lodge: Masons (chpt. master 1980). Office: 1919 N Meridian Indianapolis IN 46206

PETERSON, NAD A., lawyer, corporate executive; b. Mt. Pleasant, Utah, 1926; m. Martha Peterson, 1948; children—Anne Carroll (Mrs. Stanford P. Darger, Jr.), Christian, Elizabeth (Mrs. Henry G. Ingersoll), Robert and Lane (twins). A.B., George Washington U., 1950, J.D., 1953. Bar: D.C. 1953, Calif. 1960, U.S. Supreme Ct. 1958. With firm Pierson, Ball & Dowd, Washington, 1953-60; sec., asst. gen. counsel Dart Industries, Los Angeles, 1960-67; chief counsel Fluor Corp., Irvine, Calif., 1967-73; gen. counsel Fluor Corp., 1973-79, v.p. law, 1979-82, sr. v.p. law, 1983-84, sr. v.p., 1984—. Mem. Am., Orange County bar assns., State Bar of Calif., George Washington Law Rev., Phi Delta Phi. Clubs: Big Canyon Country (Newport Beach, Calif.), Back Bay (Newport Beach, Calif.). Office: Flour Corp 3333 Michelson Dr Irvine CA 92730

PETERSON, NANCY ANN, real estate broker; b. Fargo, N.D., Sept. 18, 1947; d. Simar Kristian and Rhoda Alice (Anderson) Nelson; m. John William Peterson, Oct. 20, 1967 (dec. Aug. 1979); 1 child, Dauvin John. BS, Moorhead State U., 1979; student Real Conservatorio, Madrid, Spain, 1981. Cert. comml. investment mgr. Owner, pres. Circle Realtors Inc., Fargo, 1971—; bd. dirs. Town & Country Realty; Honorarium prof. Classical Guitar Moorhead State U. Bd. dirs. Plains Art Mus., Moorhead, Minn., 1983—, pres., 1987—; mem. devel. council Moorhead State U., 1987; treas. O'Rourke-Plains Mus., Moorhead, 1984-85, v.p., 1986-87; pres. O'Rourke-Plains Arts Assn., 1987-88; pres. Plains Art Mus., 1987-88. Mem. Nat. Assn. Realtors, Fargo-Moorhead Bd. Realtors, Women's Council Realtors (pres. 1977), Fargo-Moorhead Home Builders, Linden Assoc., Fargo-Moorehead Black History Orgn. (com. dir. 1989). Lodge: Zonta. Avocations: classical guitar, fishing, scuba diving, skiing. Office: Cir Realtors Inc 1220 Main Ave Fargo ND 58103

PETERSON, NANCY CAROL, employee benefits company executive; b. Evergreen Park, Ill., Aug. 6, 1953; d. Ernest Irwin and Frances Ruth (Dubnicek) P. Student, Ill. Benedictine Coll., 1971-73; BS in Acctg. summa cum laude, DePaul U., 1975. CPA, Ill. Audit mgr. Lester Witte & Co., CPAs, Chgo., 1974-82; controller Rogan Corp., Northbrook, Ill., 1982-87; v.p. fin. Datalogics, Inc., Chgo., 1987-88; chief fin. officer EPACO, 1988—. Mem. Am. Inst. CPAs, Ill. Soc. CPAs, Chgo. Soc. Women CPAs (pres. 1987-88). Office: EPACO 135 S LaSalle Chicago IL 60603

PETERSON, RICHARD CARSON, financial management company executive, healthcare consultant; b. Wilmington, N.C., Sept. 15, 1953; s. Graham Howard and Lillie Truman (Johnson) P.; m. Karen Zurn, Feb. 14, 1982. B.A. in Econs., Duke U., 1975, M.H.A. (Equitable Assurance Soc. U.S. Scholar), 1977. Adminstrv. resident The Duke Endowment, Charlotte, N.C., 1977; adminstrv. asst. N.C. Baptist Hosps., Inc., Winston-Salem, N.C., 1977-78;ptnr. Andersen Consulting div. Arthur Andersen & Co., St. Louis, 1978—. Mem. Am. Coll. Healthcare Execs., Healthcare Fin. Mgmt. Assn., Healthcare Info. Mgmt. System Soc., Duke U. Alumni Assn. Republican. Episcopalian. Home: 14645 Brittania Dr Chesterfield MO 63017 Office: Arthur Andersen & Co 1010 Market St Saint Louis MO 63101

PETERSON, RICHARD STANE, economist; b. Seattle, July 18, 1930; s. William Stane and Mabel (Bock) P.; m. Geraldine Pease, children: Kristen Marie, Suzanne. B.A., Wash. State U., 1953; postgrad., U. Cailf.-Berkeley, 1955-59. Economist Bank of Am., San Francisco, 1959-69; sr. v.p. Continental Bank, Chgo., 1969—, editor Continental Comment. Treas. Lake Bluff Park Bd., (Ill.), 1974-76. Served with U.S. Army, 1953-55. Mem. Nat. Assn. Bus. Economists, Am. Econ. Assn., Econ. Club Chgo. Home: 1550 Everett Rd Lake Forest IL 60645 Office: Continental Ill Nat Bank 231 S LaSalle St Chicago IL 60697

PETERSON, ROBERT AUSTIN, mower manufacturing company executive; b. Sioux City, Iowa, July 5, 1925; s. Austen W. and Marie (Mueller) P.; m. Carol May Hudy, May 19, 1925; children: Roberta, Richard, Thomas, Bruce. B.S., U. Minn., 1946, B.B.A., 1947. Credit mgr. New Holland Machine div. Sperry Rand Corp., Mpls., 1952-61; credit mgr. Toro Co., Mpls., 1961-68; treas. Toro Co., 1968-70, v.p. and treas. of internat. fin., 1970-83; v.p. fin., pres. Toro Credit Co., 1983—; bd. dirs. State Bond & Mortgage Co., State Bond Ins. Co., New Ulm, Tesco, South Miami, Fla., Duke Equipment Co., Sacramento, Toro Australia. Chmn. Prior Lake Spring Lake Watershed Dist., 1970-80; Chmn., mem. bd. dirs. Prior Lake Bd. Edn., 1965-71; chmn. Scott County Republican Party, 1969-70; Bd. dirs. Scott Carver Mental Health Center, 1969-73, Minn. Watershed Assn., 1972-76. Served to ensign USNR, 1943-46. Mem. Fin. Execs. Inst. Clubs: Prior Lake Yacht (bd. dirs.); Decathlon Athletic (Mpls.); St. Petersburg Yacht. Home: 14956 Pixie Point Circle SE Prior Lake MN 55372 Office: Toro Co 8111 Lyndale Ave S Minneapolis MN 55420

PETERSON, ROBERT BYRON, petroleum company executive; b. Regina, Sask., Can.. BSc in Chem. Engring., Queen's U., Kingston, Ont., Can., 1959, MSc in Chem. Engring., 1961. Various prodn. positions Imperial Oil Ltd. and affiliates, Can. and U.S., 1960-82; pres., chief exec. officer Esso Resources Can. Ltd., Calgary, Alta., Can., 1982-85; dir. Imperial Oil Ltd., Toronto, Ont., Can., 1984—; exec. v.p., chief operating officer Imperial Oil Ltd., Toronto, 1985-88, pres., chief operating officer, 1988—; exec. v.p., chief operating officer, dir. Imperial Oil Ltd., 1985-88, pres., chief operating officer, 1988—; bd. dirs. Interhome Energy Inc., Calgary, 1983—. Mem. adv. council Sch. Bus. Queen's U.; mem. policy analysis com. C.D. Howe Inst., Toronto; bd. govs. U. Western Ont. Mem. Assn. Profl. Engrs. Geologists and Geophysicists of Alta. Office: Imperial Oil Ltd, 111 St Clair Ave W, Toronto, ON Canada M5W 1K3

PETERSON, ROBERT L., meat processing executive; b. Nebr., July 14, 1932; married; children: Mark R., Susan P. Student, U. Nebr., 1950. With Wilson & Co., Jim Boyle Order Buying Co.; cattle buyer R&C Packing Co., 1956-61; cattle buyer, plant mgr., v.p. carcass prodn. Iowa Beef Processors, 1961-69; exec. v.p. ops. Spencer Foods, 1969-71; founder, pres., chmn., chief exec. officer Madison (Nebr.) Foods, 1971-76; group v.p. carcass div. Iowa Beef Processors, Inc. (name now IBP, Inc.) div. Occidental Petroleum Corp., Dakota City, Nebr., 1976-77, pres., chief operating officer, 1977-80, chief exec. officer, 1980-81, co-chmn. bd. dirs., 1981-82, chmn., chief exec. officer, pres., 1981—; exec. v.p., dir. Occidental Petroleum Corp., Los Angeles, 1982-87. Served with Q.M.C. U.S. Army, 1952-54. Mem. Sioux City Country Club. Office: IBP Inc Box 515 Dakota City NE 68731

PETERSON, ROGER ERIC, hardware wholesale company executive; b. Chgo., Dec. 14, 1937; s. Erick Herman and Greta (Moren) P.; m. Joyce Marlene Holtz, Aug. 22, 1959; children: Stephen, Cindy, Linda, Kristin, Kathrin, Scott. BBA, U. Miami, 1960. Indsl. engring. supr. Montgomery Ward, Chgo., 1960-63; area mgr. J.C. Penney, Wauwatosa, Wis., 1963-67; dist. devel. mgr. Ben Franklin div. City Products, Des Plaines, Ill., 1967-72; exec. v.p. C.P. Products Corp., Elkhart, Ind., 1972-76; nat. distbn. mgr. Ace Hardware Corp., Oak Brook, Ill., 1976-82, v.p. ops., 1982-85, exec. v.p., 1985-86, pres., 1986—; Mem. Midwest adv. bd. Allendale Ins. Co., Providence, 1986—. Bd. dirs. Center Inst., 1989. Club: Elgin (Ill.) Country. Office: ACE Hardware Corp 2200 Kensington Ct Oak Brook IL 60521

PETERSON, ROLAND OSCAR, electronics company executive; b. Bklyn., Jan. 18, 1932; s. Oscar Gustaf and Klara Ingegerd (Lindau) P.; m. Agnes Frances Walsh, Sept. 12, 1953; children: Joan, Lauren, Paul, Michael. BEE, Poly. Inst. N.Y., 1953, MEE, 1954. Registered profl. engr., N.Y. Research fellow Microwave Research Inst., Bklyn., 1953-54; sr. engr. Sperry Gyroscope Co., Great Neck, N.Y., 1956-60; with Litton Industries Inc., Woodland Hills, Calif., 1961—; v.p. advanced systems engring. Guidance and Control Systems div., Litton Industries Inc., Woodland Hills, Calif., 1973-76, v.p. bus. devel., 1976-77, pres., 1977-83; v.p. Litton Industries Inc., 1979-83; sr. v.p., group exec. Litton Industries Inc., Beverly Hills, Calif., 1983-88, pres., chief operating officer, 1988—. Regional chmn. Los Angeles United Way campaign , 1985-86. Served to 1st lt. U.S. Army, 1954-56. Recipient Disting. Alumni award Poly. Inst. N.Y., 1986. Mem. Am. Electronics Assn., Inst. Navigation (western regional v.p. 1975-76, Hays award 1982). Roman Catholic.

PETERSON, TOM LOOMIS, lawyer, corporate executive; b. Lincoln, Nebr., Aug. 17, 1932; s. Martin Severin and Wilma M. (Loomis) P.; A.B., Harvard U., 1954, LL.B., 1960; m. Arlayne Hedderly-Smith, Aug. 27, 1954; children—Eric Severin, Mark Loomis, Anne Elizabeth. Bar: Hawaii 1961, Mass. 1967, N.H.; assoc. Carlsmith, Carlsmith, Wichman & Case, Honolulu, 1960-65; dep. atty. gen. State of Hawaii, Honolulu, 1965-67; corp. counsel United-Carr Inc., Boston, 1967-70; sec. Standex Internat. Corp., Salem, N.H., 1987—; ptnr. Gaston & Snow, Boston, 1970-75; sr. counsel TRW Inc., Burlington, Mass., 1975-82; gen. counsel Wyman-Gordon Co., Worcester, Mass., 1982-86; counsel Warner & Stackpole, Boston, 1986-87. Mem. Am. Arbitration Assn. (arbitrator 1970—), New Eng. Corp. Counsel Assn. (bd. dirs. 1986), Boston Bar Assn. (chmn. com. corp. counsel 1977-80). Home: 12 Turning Mill Rd Lexington MA 02173 Office: Standex Internat Corp 6 Manor Pwy Salem NH 03079

PETILLO, JAMES THOMAS, diversified utility company executive; b. Magnolia, Ark., Aug. 13, 1944; s. Thomas Evans and Reba (Polk) P.; m. Nancy Elizabeth Moody, Apr. 15, 1967; children: Deanna Elizabeth, Thomas Evans. BS, U.S. Naval Acad., 1966; MBA, Fla. State U., 1972; PMD 44, Harvard U., 1982. Commd. ensign USN, 1966, advanced through grades to lt., resigned, 1971; adminstrv. asst. Fla. Power & Light Co., Miami, 1973-74, sr. planning analyst, 1974-75, pub. affairs coordinator, 1976; dist. mgr. Fla. Power & Light Co., Delray Beach, 1976-80; dir. mktg. and energy conservation Fla. Power & Light Co., Miami, 1980-84; v.p. Fla. Power & Light Co., Sarasota, 1984-86, Miami, 1986-87; v.p. Fla. Power & Light Group, Inc., North Palm Beach, 1987—; chmn. residential com. Electric Power Research Inst., Palo Alto, Calif., 1982-84. Mem. Fla. C. of C. (regional chmn. 1985-86). Republican. Methodist. Office: Fla Power Light Group Inc PO Box 08801 North Palm Beach FL 33408

PETITT, GERALD WILLIAM, hotel executive; b. Denver, Nov. 6, 1945; s. Claude William and Mable Irene (Hanson) P.; m. Kathleen Overby, May 13, 1972; children: Eric, Mark, Jess. AB, Dartmouth Coll., 1967, B in English, MBA, 1969. Sales trainee IBM, Denver, 1969; dir. mktg. Am. Express, N.Y.C., 1969-74; v.p. ops. Best Western Internat., Phoenix, 1974-81; exec. v.p. Quality Inns Internat., Washington, 1981—, also bd. dirs.; bd. dirs. Quality Hotels Ltd., London, Hotels Calindas, Mexico City; chmn. bd. dirs. Quality Inn India, New Delhi. Office: Quality Inns Internat 10750 Columbia Pike Silver Spring MD 20901

PETKEVICH, JOHN MISHA, banker, venture capitalist; b. Mpls., Mar. 3, 1949; s. Frank Michael and Delphine Marie (Proulx) P.; m. Mary Elizabeth Burns, Aug. 25, 1984; children: Michelle Ann, Lisa Christine, Jonathan Worthington. AB cum laude, Harvard U., 1973; PhD, Oxford U., 1978. Figure skating color commentator Sta. CBS TV, 1977, 84-87, Sta. NBC TV, 1981-84, Sta. ESPN, 1985-88; biotech. research analyst Hambrecht & Quist, N.Y.C., 1983-86, prin. corp. fin., 1987—, gen. ptnr., 1988—; bd. dirs. Tellos Pharms., La Jolla, Calif., Ann Arbor (Mich.) Stromal, Protense Inhibitor Rsch. Co., Phila. Author: The Skater's Handbook, 1984, Sports Illustrated's Figure Skating, 1988; composer chamber music. Founder Evening with Champions, Children's Cancer Research Found., Cambridge, 1969—. Scholar Rhodes Trust, 1973; mem. U.S. Olympic Team, 1968, 72; U.S. men's figure skating champion, 1971, N.Am. men's figure skating champion, 1971, World U. Games champion, 1972. Club: A.D. (Cambridge); Knickerbocker (N.Y.C.). Office: Hambrecht & Quist One Bush St 18th Floor San Francisco CA 94104

PETRIE, JEFFREY WAYNE, engineer; b. Riverside, Calif., July 4, 1962; s. H. Wayne and Joyce R. (Scales) P.; m. Karen Marie Lavan, July 9, 1988. BS, U. Calif., Riverside, 1984. Programmer Indsl. Mktg. Cons. Corp., Riverside, 1983; programmer analyst USDA Forest Service Fire Lab., Riverside, 1983-84; software engr. Aerojet Electro Systems Co., Azusa, Calif., 1984—. Co-author: Simulator for the AOSP Distributed Network, 1987. Democrat. Presbyterian. Home: 7487 Mt Vernon St Riverside CA 92504 Office: Aerojet Electro Systems Co PO Box 296 Bldg 1 Dept 8552 Azusa CA 91702

PETRILLI, JOHN ANTHONY, aerospace engineer; b. Pitts., May 4, 1949; s. Edmund Stephen and Ann Gloria (Swick) P. BS, U. Pitts., 1971; MA, Pa. State U., 1973. Cert. profl. estimator. Grad. asst. Pa. State U., University Park, 1971-73; indsl. engring. trainee Jones & Laughlin Steel Corp., Pitts., 1974-75, indsl. engr., 1975-76, sr. indsl. engr., 1976-80; sr. indsl. engr. McDonnell Douglas Helicopter Co., Culver City, Calif., 1981-82, supr. indsl. engring., 1982-85; mgr. indsl. engring. McDonnell Douglas Helicopter Co., Culver City, 1985-86; mgr. program planning, Mesa, Ariz., 1986—. Mem. Nat. Estimating Soc., Mensa, McDonnell Douglas Helicopter Co. Mgmt. Club, McDonnell Douglas Helicopter Co. Gun Club, Phi Beta Kappa. Republican. Roman Catholic. Home: 6127 E Saddleback St Mesa AZ 85205 Office: McDonnell Douglas Helicopter Co 5000 E McDowell Rd Mesa AZ 85205

PETRINA, ANTHONY J., mining executive. Formerly sr. v.p., chief oper. officer Placer Devel. Ltd., Vancouver, B.C., Can., exec. v.p., chief oper. officer, until 1988, now pres., chief exec. officer, 1988—. Office: Placer Dome Inc, 1600-1055 Dunsmuir St, PO Box 49330 Bentall Postal Sta, Vancouver, BC Canada V7X 1P1 *

PETROCCO, WILLIAM PATRICK, retail executive; b. Jersey City, Apr. 21, 1946; s. Michael and Sarah (LoDico) P.; m. Linda Lamb, May 9, 1970; children: Billy, Alison, Christopher. BSBA, Fairleigh Dickinson U., 1968; postgrad., N.Y. Inst. Tech., 1971-72. Asst. buyer housewares J.C. Penney Co., N.Y.C., 1968-71; mdse. mgr. Shop Rite Supermarkets, Wakefern Food Corp., Elizabeth, N.J., 1971-84; sr. v.p. gen. mdse., corp. officer Peter J. Schmitt Co., Inc., West Seneca, N.Y., 1984—. Mem. Nat. Assn. Food Wholesalers, Food Mktg. Inst., Gen. Mdse. Distbrs. Council, Buffalo C. of C. Republican. Roman Catholic. Office: Peter J Schmitt Co Inc 355 Harlem Rd Buffalo NY 14240

PETRY, ROBYN ERICA, librarian; b. Buffalo, Aug. 2, 1949; d. Yale Goldstein and Ruth (Cohen) Winer; m. Frank C. Petry, May 25, 1980. BA in Sociology, SUNY, Buffalo, 1975; MLS, SUNY, Albany, 1977. Libr. of the libr. of health scis. U. Ill. Med. Ctr., Chgo., 1977-80; libr. region 5 U.S. EPA, Chgo., 1980-81; asst. libr. Akzo Chem. Inc. (formerly Akzo Chemie Am.), McCook, Ill., 1980-81; head libr. Akzo Chem. Inc. (formerly Akzo Chemie Am.), 1981—. Mem. Spl. Librs. Assn. Home: 4305 N Central Park Chigago IL 60618 Office: Akzo Chem Inc 8401 W 47th St McCook IL 60526

PETRY, THOMAS EDWIN, manufacturing company executive; b. Cin., Nov. 20, 1939; s. Edwin Nicholas and Leonora Amelia (Zimpelman) P.; m. Mary Helen Gardner, Aug. 25, 1962; children: Thomas Richard, Stephen Nicholas, Daniel Gardner, Michael David. B.S., U. Cin., 1962; M.B.A., Harvard, 1964. Group v.p., treas. Eagle-Picher Industries, Inc., Cin., 1968-81; pres. Eagle-Picher Industries, Inc., 1981—, chief operating officer, from 1981, chief exec. officer, dir., 1982—. Republican. Clubs: Queen City, Terrace Park (Ohio) Country, Cin. Country. Office: Eagle-Picher Industries Inc 580 Walnut St Cincinnati OH 45202 *

PETTERSEN, KJELL WILL, retired stockbroker; b. Oslo, Norway, June 19, 1927; came to U.S., 1946, naturalized, 1957; s. Jens Will and Ragna O. (Wickstrom) P.; m. Marilyn Ann Stevens, Aug. 16, 1952; children: Thomas W., Maureen, Kevin W., Maryann, Kathleen. Student, Zion Theol. Sch., 1945-49, N.Y. Inst. Finance, 1955-56. Mgr. A.M. Kidder & Co., N.Y.C., 1954-64; sr. v.p., sec., dir. Halle & Stieglitz, Fillor Bullard Co., Inc., 1964-73; sr. v.p., dir. mktg. Parrish Securities, Inc., N.Y.C., 1973-74; cons. Loeb, Rhoades & Co., N.Y.C., 1974-79; mng. dir. Prudential Bache Securities,, N.Y.C., 1979-81; ret. 1981; dir. Ski for Light Inc., Mpls., Creative Arts Rehab. Ctr. Inc., N.Y.C.; Allied mem. N.Y. Stock Exchange, Am. Stock Exchange, Chgo. Bd. Trade.; Dir. Norwegian affairs N.Y. World Fair, 1964-65. Democratic candidate N.Y. State Assembly, Nassau County, 1962. Served with U.S. Army, 1949-53. Mem. N.Y. C. of C., Security Industry Assn., Nat. Assn. Security Dealers, Scandinavian Found., Bankers Club of Am., Norwegian-Am. C. of C. (dir.). Club: Norwegian (N.Y.C.). Home: 420 N Collier Blvd Marco Island FL 33937

PETTIBONE, PETER JOHN, lawyer; b. Schenectady, N.Y., Dec. 11, 1939; s. George Howard and Caryl Grey (Ketchum) P.; m. Jean Kellogg, Apr. 23, 1966; children: Stephen, Victoria. AB summa cum laude, Princeton U., 1961; JD, Harvard U., 1964; LLM, NYU, 1971. Bar: Pa. 1965, D.C. 1965, N.Y. 1968, U.S. Supreme Ct. 1974. Assoc. Cravath, Swaine & Moore, N.Y.C., 1967-74, Lord Day & Lord, Barrett Smith, N.Y.C., 1974-76; ptnr. Lord Day & Lord, Barrett Smith, N.Y.C. and Washington, 1976—; bd. dirs., vice chmn. N.Y. State Facilities Devel. Corp., N.Y.C., 1983—. Trustee Civitas, N.Y.C., 1984—. Served to capt. U.S. Army, 1965-67. Mem. ABA, Assn. of Bar of City of N.Y., U.S.- USSR Trade and Econ. Council, Inc., (U.S. co-chmn. legal com. 1980—), Phi Beta Kappa. Episcopalian. Clubs: Anglers (N.Y.C.), Shelter Island (N.Y.) Yacht, Soc. of Cin. Home: 1158 Fifth Ave New York NY 10029 also: 1201 Pennsylvania Ave NW Washington DC 20004

PETTIETTE, ALISON YVONNE, lawyer; b. Brockton, Mass., Aug. 16, 1952; d. David and Loretta (LeClair) Waters; Student Sorbonne, Paris, 1971-72; BA, Sophie Newcomb Coll., 1972; MA, Rice U., 1974; JD, Bates Coll., 1978. Bar: Tex. 1979, U.S. Dist. Ct. (so. dist.) Tex. 1980, U.S. Ct. Appeals (5th cir.) 1981. Ptnr. Harvill & Hardy, Houston, 1979-83; pvt. practice, Houston, 1983-84; assoc. O'Quinn & Hagans, Houston, 1984-86, Jones & Granger, Houston, 1986-88; pvt. practice, Houston, 1988—. Editor Houston Law Rev. U. Houston, 1976-78. Exercise instr. YWCA, Houston, 1976-81, U. St. Thomas, Houston, 1982—. NDEA fellow Rice U., Houston, 1972-74; Woodrow Wilson scholar, Tulane U., New Orleans, 1972. Mem. ABA, Assn. Trial Lawyers Am., Tex. Trial Lawyers Assn., Houston Trial Lawyers Assn., Phi Delta Phi, Phi Beta Kappa.

PETTINELLA, NICHOLAS ANTHONY, financial executive; b. Little Falls, N.Y., Sept. 9, 1942; s. Nicholas and Rose (Zuccaro) P.; m. Nancy C. Whitehouse, Oct. 28, 1978; children: Albert J., Michael A. BS, Bentley Coll., 1968; MBA, Babson Coll., 1975; postgrad. Harvard U., 1979, Stanford U., 1983. CPA, Mass. Auditor, Coopers & Lybrand, Boston, 1970-76; treas. Courier Corp., Lowell, Mass., 1976-80; controller corp. ops. Digital Equipment Corp., Maynard, Mass., 1980-81; dir. fin. Intermetrics, Inc., Cambridge, Mass., 1981-83; v.p. fin., chief fin. officer, treas., 1983—; bd. dirs. The Computer Mus., Boston, 1986—, treas. 1988—. Chmn. fin. com. Town of Ashland, Mass., 1980-82. Served with U.S. Army, 1964-66. Mem. Fin. Execs. Inst., AICPA, Nat. Assn. Accts., Mass. Soc. CPAs, Treas. Club Boston. Roman Catholic. Home: 141 South St Ashland MA 01721 Office: Intermetrics Inc 733 Concord Ave Cambridge MA 02138

PETTIT, DALE ALEXANDER, retail company executive; b. Brantford, Ont., Can., Aug. 28, 1940; s. Donald Leroy and Ada Elizabeth (Morrison) P.; m. Patrcia Carrol Barker, Aug. 15, 1964; children: Erin Kathleen, Andrew Donald, Michael Lloyd. BA, U. Western Ont., 1964. Chartered acct. Various positions Clarkson Gordon, London, Ont., Can., 1964-75; controller Silcorp Ltd., Mississauga, Ont., Can., 1975-80; treas. Silcorp Ltd., Mississauga, 1980-85, chief fin. officer, 1985—; pres., dir. Silcorp Employee Holdings Ltd., 1986—; sec./treas./dir. Execsil Corp., 1981—. Mem. United

Church. Home: 60 Hampton Cres, London, ON Canada N6H 2N9 Office: Silcorp Ltd, 6205 Airport Rd, Mississauga, ON Canada L4V 1E1

PETTIT, WENDY JEAN, advertising agency executive; b. Gary, Ind., Oct. 6, 1945; d. Wendell E. and Ethel (Binkley) Pettit. B.A., MacMurray Coll., 1967; M.S.B.A., Ind. U., 1978. Acctg. clk. J. Walter Thompson USA, Chgo., 1967-68, adminstrv. asst., 1968-72, personnel asst., 1973-74, fin. analyst, 1974-78, office services asst., 1978-79, acctg. dept. mgr., 1979—. Bd. dirs. Miller Citizens Corp., Gary, 1979-86, treas., 1979-82. Named Career Woman of the Year, Bus. and Profl. Women, Gary, 1967. Mem. Nat. Assn. Female Execs., Am. Mgmt. Assn., LWV. Methodist. Avocations: singing; piano; cooking. Home: 8000 Oak Ave Gary IN 46403 Office: J Walter Thompson USA Inc 900 N Michigan Ave Chicago IL 60611

PETTY, GEORGE KIBBE, communications executive; b. Albuquerque, Nov. 26, 1941; s. George Kibbe and Annabelle (Deeter) P.; m. Margaret Catherine Pobar, Feb. 6, 1965; children: Jennifer, Lisa. BSEE, N.Mex. State U., 1965. With AT&T, San Francisco, 1969—, v.p. bus. mktg. group, 1986—; bd. dirs. Ctr. for Telecommunications Mgmt., L.A., Calif. Econ. Devel. Corp., Sacramento. Mem. Mayor of San Francisco Blue Ribbon Com., 1987—; bd. dirs. Chester Twp. Sch. Bd., Va., 1984-85. Capt. USAF, 1965-69. Mem. Moraga (Calif.) Country Club. Republican. Presbyterian. Office: AT&T 795 Folsom St Ste 600 San Francisco CA 94107

PETTY, LARRY DEAN, financial executive; b. Olney, Ill., Apr. 19, 1941; s. Burl E. and Opal A. (Richey) P.; m. Karen J. Henrickson, July 14, 1975. BA, Lee Coll., 1964; MS, Am. Coll., 1982, postgrad., 1978-82. Cert. fin. planner. Mgr. Met. Life Ins. Co., Rockford, Ill., 1974-79, New Eng. Life Ins. Co., Rockford, 1979-81; v.p. Herrling and Schmitt, Inc., Rockford, 1981—; dean Christian Life Bible Coll., Rockford. Mem. Rockford Assn. Life Underwriters (pres. 1982-83), Chartered Life Underwriters (pres. No. Ill. chpt. 1983-84), Internat. Assn. Fin. Planning (pres. Rockford chpt. 1984-85), Employee Benefits Assn. No. Ill., Ill Life Underwriters Assn. (bd. dirs. 1986—). Republican. Mem. Assembly of God Ch. Office: Herrling & Schmitt Inc 419 N Mulford Rockford IL 61107

PETTY, RONALD FRANKLIN, public relations executive; b. Trenton, Mar. 17, 1947; s. Warren Herman Lee and Geraldine Frances (Roberts) P.; m. Cynthia Ann Hoover, Sept. 16, 1967 (div. 1987); children: Scott Eric, Christopher Lee. BA in Advt., Syracuse U., 1969, BA in Econs., 1972. Asst. sales promotion mgr. Cambridge Filter Corp., Liverpool, N.Y., 1969-72; advt. mgr. Am. Challenger, Fulton, N.Y., 1972, mgr. communications, 1973; advt./pub. relations account exec. Barlow/Johnson Advt., Fayetteville and Latham, N.Y., 1973-75; advt./pub. relations account exec. Nowak-Voss Advt., Syracuse, N.Y., 1975-77, dir. pub. relations, 1976-77; pub. relations dir. U.S Pioneer Electronics Corp., Moonachie, N.J., 1977-81, gen. mgr. communications, 1981-82; dir. communications Pioneer Video, Inc., 1982-84; dir. mktg. services SONY Broadcast Products Co., 1984-86; dir. mktg. broadcast and profl. audio products SONY Communications Products Co., 1986-87; dir. corp. communications SONY Corp. of Am., 1987—; pub. relations cons. to artist Peter Max; cons. in field. Mem. com. for redistricting, Liverpool (N.Y.) Sch. Bd., 1976; mem. Rockaway Boro Citizens Adv. Com., 1981-82, mem. planning bd., 1982-85, chmn. planning bd., 1983, councilman, 1983-87, chmn. ordinance com., 1984-85, chmn. personnel com., 1986-87, mem. pub. safety com., 1984, 86, 87, mem. pub. works com., 1985-87; del. N.J. State Dem. Conv., 1983; mem. Rockaway Boro Shade Tree Commn., 1983-84; benefactor, patron Met. Opera Assn., 1981-84; sustaining mem. Republican Nat. Com., 1980-83, 86. Recipient citation for community service United Way of Central N.Y., 1976; dir. Project-of-the-Yr. award, Syracuse Jr. C. of C., 1977. Mem. Assn. of Indsl. Advertisers, Public Relations Soc. Am., Electronic Industry Assn. (chmn. show adv. com. 1982). Contbr. articles to profl. jours. Office: Sony Dr Park Ridge NJ 07656

PETTY, WILLIAM CALVIN, III, investment counselor; b. Port Chester, N.Y., Nov. 24, 1940; s. William Calvin and Helen L. (Lathrop) P.; B.A., Yale U., 1963; m. Nancy Claire Dowling, Nov. 28, 1970; children—Jonathan Calvin, Timothy Dowling. With Dominick & Dominick, Inc., N.Y.C., 1967-69, Estabrook & Co., Inc., N.Y.C., 1969-72, Drexel Burnham, N.Y.C., 1972-73; v.p., nat. sales mgr. Mfrs. Hanover Investment Corp., N.Y.C., 1973-85; prin. Estabrook Capital Mgmt. Inc., 1985—. Pres. Cedar Knolls Colony, Yonkers, N.Y., 1981-82. Served with U.S. Navy, 1963-66. Mem. Assn. Investment Mgmt. Sales Execs. (pres 1985-86), Kent Sch. (chmn. alumni fund), Fedn. Fin. Analysts. Republican. Episcopalian. Club: Yale of N.Y.C., Lawrence Beach. Office: Estabrook Capital Mgmt 430 Park Ave New York NY 10022

PEVEHOUSE, BYRON CONE, neurosurgeon, company official; b. Lubbock, Tex., Apr. 5, 1927; s. William Monrow and Myrtle Elizabeth (Cone) P.; m. Maxine E. Smith, June 16, 1951 (dec. July 1978); children: Deann Pevehouse Frietag, Carol Pevehouse Palato, Lesa; m. Lucille Seguin, Jan. 30, 1981. BS, Baylor U., 1948; MD, Baylor Coll. Med., 1952; MSc, McGill U., 1960. Diplomate Am. Bd. Neurosurgery. Intern Colo. Gen. Hosp., Denver, 1952-53; resident in gen. surgery U. Oreg. and V.A. Hosps., Portland, 1953-54; resident in neurol. surgery U. Calif. Med. Ctr., San Francisco, 1954-58; prof. neurosurgery U. Calif., San Francisco, 1960—; practice medicine specializing in neurosurgery San Francisco, 1960—; pres. Pevehouse Devel. Co., Lubbock, Tex., 1972—. Trustee Pacific Presbyn. Med. Ctr., San Francisco, 1983—. NSF fellow Montreal (P.Q., Can.) Neurol. Inst., 1958-59, Spl. Postdoctoral fellow in neurology and neurophysiology USPHS, Inst. Neurology, Queen Sq., London, 1959-60. Mem. Am. Assn. Neurol. Surgeons (pres. 1983-84), Neurosurgical Assocs. Med. Group (pres.), Olympic Club . Office: Neurosurg Assocs 2351 Clay St San Francisco CA 94115

PEW, GEORGE THOMPSON, JR., investment banker; b. Bryn Mawr, Pa., Mar. 25, 1942; s. George Thompson and Constance (Clarke) P.; student Yale U., 1965, U. Pa., 1971; m. Sandra Kennedy, Oct. 23, 1982; children: George Thompson III, Alexis Clarke, Jameson E. Delk. Chief exe. officer, pres. Nat. Ry. Mgmt. Corp., Villanova, Pa., 1979—, also bd. dirs.; prin. Phila. Investment Banking Co., 1983—, also bd. dirs. bd. dirs. Glenmede Fund, Inc., Crusader Savings & Loan; registered rep. N.Y. Stock Exch., Am. Stock Exch., NASD, Butcher & Singer, Inc., 1971-84, Sun Co., Phila, 1963-64. Bd. dirs., v.p. Phila Charity Ball, 1976—; dir. exec. com. Opera Co. Phila.; bd. mgrs. Saunders House. With U.S. Army, 1966-69. Mem. Assn. MBA Execs., Corinthian Yachts Club (trustee, treas.), Union League, Racquet Club, Rittenhouse Club, Merion Cricket Club, The Cts. Club, Bay Head Yacht Club, St. Elmo Club, Radnor Hunt Club.

PEYROUX, ROBERT ALBERT, accounting company executive; b. New Orleans, Dec. 10, 1930; s. John Alexander and Alma Marie (Guidry) P.; m. Terry Lynn DeJaive, July 27, 1951 (div. 1968); children: Dale, Gina, Donna, Neil; m. Salle Markely, May 2, 1969; 1 child, Jill. BBA, Tulane U., 1951. Staff acct. J.K. Byrne & Co., New Orleans, 1953-65, ptnr., 1965-75, mng. ptnr., 1975-85; mng. ptnr. Touche Ross, New Orleans, 1985—; bd. dirs. Inroads, Inc., New Orleans. Past pres. Vis. Nurses Assn., New Orleans, City Park, New Orleans Mus. Art.; pres. Metairie Endowment Fund, New Orleans, 1985—. Mem. Am. Inst. CPA's (council 1980, 85), La. Soc. CPA's (pres. 1975-76, Disting. Service award 1985, pres. New Orleans chpt. 1967-68, Outstanding service award 1976), Metairie C. of C. (pres. 1985-86), Rotary. Office: Touche Ross & Co 4100 Pl St Charles New Orleans LA 70170-4100

PEYTON, PRESTON CARLTON, marketing consulting company executive; b. Asheville, N.C., July 28, 1952; s. Preston Carlton and Ruth Geraldine (Robinson) P. BS, Appalachian State U., 1974; MBA, U. Houston, 1986. Br. mgr. Gen. Binding Corp., Houston, 1977-83; dist. mgr. NCR Corp., Houston, 1983-86; v.p. mktg. TSI div. Bell Atlantic Corp., Houston, 1986-87; v.p., bd. dirs. Bristol Mgmt. Corp., Houston, 1987-88; pres. Bristol Telemarketing div. Bristol Mgmt. Corp., Houston, 1988—; also bd. dirs. Bristol Market Rsch., Houston. Mem. Am. Mgmt. Assn., Houston Direct Mktg. Assn. Republican. Episcopalian. Home: 5292 Memorial Ln Houston TX 77007

PFAFF, DAVID NOEL, bank executive; b. Des Moines, Dec. 25, 1934; s. William Wendell and Adele Clara (Keeline) P.; m. Dorothy Sue Jenkins, DEc. 29, 1956 (div. 1975); 1 child, Susan Elizabeth Rojas; m. Daphne Margaret Harrison, Dec. 3, 1976; children: Carolyn Schmidt, Lisa Eichenlaub, Charles Page. BA, U. Notre Dame, 1956. Staff announcer WRBL Radio, Columbus, Ga., 1948-51, WDAK Radio, Columbus, 1951-52; staff dir. WSBT-TV, South Bend, Ind., 1954-56; news dir., asst. mgr. WNOG Radio, Naples, Fla., 1956-60; corr. Ft. Myers (Fla.) News Press, 1957-60; pres., prin. The David Co., Inc., Naples, 1969—; ptnr., gen. mgr. Collier Broadcasting Co., Naples, 1971-74; v.p., dir. mktg. Citizens and So. Nat. Bank, Naples, 1979-86, Sun Bank/Naples, N.Am., 1986—; adv. coms. Edison Community Coll., Ft. Myers, 1973-83, adj. instr. 1981—; instr. Fla. Sch. Banking, U. Fla., 1987; bd. advisors Fla. Mental Health Inst. of U. So. Fla., Tampa, 1985—, chmn. 1987—; bd. dirs. David Lawrence Mental Health Ctr., Inc., Naples, 1987—. Bd. dirs. Naples Safety Council, 1965, Cath. Service Bur., Naples, 1970-71, Aqualane Shores Property Owners Assn., Naples, 1980-85, ABUSE of Naples, Inc., 1981, Econ. Devel. Council Collier County, 1974, mem. edn. com. 1978-80, mem. film promotion com. 1987, United Way of Collier County, 1958-62, 70-72, vice-chmn. 1961, campaign chmn. 1970, Sunrise Acad. for the Learning Disabled, Naples, 1982-85, Naples/Marco Island Philharmonic Guild, 1986-87; charter pres. Moorings Property Owners Assn., Naples, 1961-63; mem. coordinating com. Southwest Fla. Symphony, 1981-83, Southeast Area council Am. Jr. Red Cross, 1952, Collier County Sch. Bd. adv. coms., 1968-70, Collier County adv. com. U. Miami, 1974-78; pres. Collier County Hist. Soc., 1970; treas. Symphony Guild, 1984-86; trustee Collier Cultural Ctr., 1980—, vice-chmn., 1983—; co-chair Naples YMCA devel. Campaign, 1972. Recipient Gov. Farris Bryant Tourism Promotion award, 1964, Certificate of Merit Naples Jaycees, 1957. Mem. Bank Mktg. Assn. (charter, bd. dirs. Fla. chpt. 1981-87, sec. 1984, v.p. 1985, pres. 1986), Aircraft Owners and Pilots Assn., Mental Health Assn. Fla. (bd. dirs. 1983-86, v.p. and mem. exec. com. 1985-86, chmn. orgn. com. 1985-86), Collier County Mental Health Assn. (bd. dirs. 1957-58, 79-85, pres. 1983-84), Naples C. of C. (chair and mem. of several committees), Southwest Fla. Notre Dame Alumni Club. Republican. Club: Naples Sailing and Yacht. Lodge: Rotary (mem. numerous coms., pres. 1973-74, Paul Harris fellow). Home: 696 16th Ave S Naples FL 33940 Office: Sun Bank/Naples NAm 801 Laurel Oak Dr Naples FL 33963

PFAHL, JOHN K., management consultant; b. Akron, Ohio, Jan. 17, 1927; s. Charles A. and Hazel (Kerch) P.; m. Floradelle Atwater, June 19, 1948; children: Jay Charles, John Christopher, Susan K. BA, Pa. State U., 1947; MBA, Ohio State U., 1949, PhD, 1953. Prof. fin. Ohio State U., Columbus, 1953-71, chmn. fin. faculty, 1968-71; exec. v.p. Mgmt. Horizons Inc., Columbus, 1971-76; pres. John K. Pfahl, Columbus, 1976—; bd. dirs. Columbia Gas Ohio, The Ltd. Inc., Nationwide Corp., Ohio Art Co., Simpson Industries Inc., M/I Schottenstein Homes Inc., Rax Restaurants Inc., Midwest Grain Products Inc. Author: Personal Finance, 1975; Corporate Finance, 1971. Mem. nat. fin. com. United Cerebral Palsy Assns. Inc., N.Y.C., 1964-71; pres. Ranch Hands, Columbus, 1978-81; chmn. budget United Way, Columbus, 1966-72; treas. Columbus Symphony, 1980-86. Served to ensign USN, 1945-46. Named Outstanding Young Man Columbus Jaycees, 1959; recipient Disting. Service award Investor Edn. Inst., N.Y.C., 1965, Founder's award Phi Sigma Kappa, Indpls., 1960. Mem. Soc. Fin. Analysts, Fin. Execs. Inst. (pres. 1972), Fin. Mgmt. Assn. (pres. 1973, Founder's award 1973), Midwest Fin. Assn. (pres. 1969). Republican. Lutheran. Club: Scioto Country (Upper Arlington, Ohio). Home: 2610 Charing Rd Columbus OH 43221 Office: John K Pfahl 1685 Fishinger Rd Columbus OH 43220

PFEFFER, PHILIP MAURICE, distribution company executive; b. St. Louis, Jan. 20, 1945; s. Philip McRae and Jeanne (Kaufman) P.; m. Pamela Jean Korte, Aug. 28, 1965; children: John-Lindell Philip, James Howard, David Maurice. B.A. in Math. and Chemistry, So. Ill. U., 1965, M.A. in Econs., 1966; postgrad., Vanderbilt U., 1966-68. Economist Genesco, Inc., Nashville, 1968, mgr. internat. fin., 1969; pres. Genesco Export Co., Nashville, 1970-75; dir. fin. planning Ingram Distribution Group, Inc., Nashville, 1976-77, v.p. fin. and adminstrn., 1977-78, exec. v.p., 1978, pres. and chief exec. officer, 1978-81, chmn. bd. and chief exec. officer, 1981—, dir., 1978—; exec. v.p. Ingram Industries, Inc., Nashville, 1981—, dir., 1981—; bd. dirs. Tenn. Ins. Co.; instr. fin. and econs. U. Tenn., Nashville, 1968-77; lectr. corp. fin. Vanderbilt U., 1972-77. Mem. exec. bd. dir. Boy Scouts Am., Nashville, 1978—, mem. nat. exploring com., Dallas, 1982—; mem. community planning com. United Way of Nashville and Middle Tenn.; bd. assocs. Owen Grad. Sch. Mgmt. Vanderbilt U., Nashville, 1981—; bd. dirs. So. Ill. U. Found., 1982—, YMCA. Served with USCG, 1962-63. Recipient Long Rifle and Silver Beaver award Boy Scouts Am., Nashville, 1981; recipient Benjamin Gomez award for Disting. Contbns. to the Art of Book Pub. Mem. Fin. Execs. Inst. (pres. 1978-79), Nat. Eagle Scout Assn. (bd. dirs., Silver Wreath award), Nashville Area C. of C. (aviation com.), Am. Wholesale Booksellers Assn. (past v.p., trustee), So. Ill. U. Alumni Assn. (past bd. dirs.). Club: Percy Priest Yacht (Nashville). Lodge: Rotary (Nashville). Office: Ingram Distbn Group Inc 347 Reedwood Dr Nashville TN 37217

PFEIFFER, ASTRID ELIZABETH, utility executive; b. N.Y.C., Nov. 15, 1934; d. Ernest and Alice (Strobel) P.; m. Edmund Lee Gettier, III, May 28, 1956 (div. 1966); children: Evan Ernest, Elizabeth Lee, Edmund Lee, Sheila Anne Astrid, David Brian. BA, Cornell U., 1955; JD cum laude, Wayne State U., Detroit, 1967; grad. exec. program bus. adminstrn., Columbia U., 1976. Bar: Mich. 1968, N.Y. 1969, Fla. 1975. Mng. editor Detroit Inst. Arts, 1962-67; atty. J.P. Mattimoe, Detroit, 1967-68, Chubb & Son, N.Y.C., 1969-70, Cadwalader, Wickersham & Taft, N.Y.C., 1971-73; corp. sec. Fla. Power & Light Co., Miami, 1974—, FPL Group, Inc., 1984—; lectr. in field. Mem. ABA, Fla. Bar Assn., Am. Soc. Corp. Secs. (pres. S.E. region 1979-80, nat. dir. 1981-85), Fla. Assn. Women Lawyers. Home: 5810 W Waterford Dr Davie FL 33331 Office: FPL Group Inc 9250 W Flagler St PO Box 029100 Miami FL 33102

PFEIFFER, JOHN WILLIAM, publisher, management consultant; b. Wallace, Idaho, July 10, 1937; s. John William and Mary Loretta (Schmidt) P.; m. Sandra Lou Withee, 1964 (div. 1973); 1 child, Heidi Erika; m. Judith Ann Cook, Dec. 14, 1973; 1 child, Charles Wilson. B.A., U. Md., 1962; Ph.D. (fellow), U. Iowa, 1968; J.D., Western State U., 1982; DABS (hon.), Calif. Am. U., Escondido, 1980. Instr. U. Md., 1965-67; dir. adult edn. Kirkwood (Iowa) Community Coll., 1967-69; dir. ednl. resources Ind. Higher Edn. Telecommunications Systems, Indpls., 1969-72; pres. Univ. Assocs., San Diego, 1972—; adj. tchr. Ind. U., 1969-72, Purdue U., 1971-72. Author: Instrumentation in Human Relations Training, 1973, 2d edit., 1976, Reference Guide to Handbooks and Annuals, 1975, 2d edit., 1977, 3d edit., 1981, (with Goodstein and Nolan) Applied Strategic Planning, 1986; editor: A Handbook of Structured Experiences for Human Relations Training, 10 vols, 1969-85, The Annual Handbook for Group Facilitators, 10 vols, 1972-81, Group and Orgns. Studies Internat. Jour. for Group Facilitators, 1976-79, The Annual for Facilitators, Trainers and Consultants, 1982-89, Strategic Planning: Selected Readings, 1986, The Instrumentation Kit, 1988, Shaping Strategic Planning, 1988, Training Technology, 7 vols, 1988. Served with U.S. Army, 1958-62. Office: Univ Assocs Inc 8517 Production Ave San Diego CA 92121

PFEIFFER, RALPH ALOYSIUS, JR., retired manufacturing company executive; b. Fordyce, Ark., Mar. 19, 1927; s. Ralph Aloysius and Catherine (Winter) P.; m. Maryruth Price, Sept. 3, 1949 (div. Mar. 1974); children: Mary Ellen, Karen, Christine, JoAnne, Ralph Aloysius III, Elizabeth, John, William, Nancy, Thomas E.; m. Jane Pennington Cahill, June 3, 1975. B.B.A., John Carroll U., 1950; postgrad., John Marshall Law Sch., 1951-52. With IBM, 1949-87, data processing div. v.p., regional mgr. for govt.-edn.-med. region, 1963-69, corp. dir. mktg., 1969-70, corp. v.p. ops. staff, 1970, pres. data processing div., 1970-74, corp. sr. v.p., chmn., chief exec. officer IBM W.T. Ams./Far East Corp., 1974-86; dir. Smith Kline Beckman Corp., Royal Bank Can., MacKay Shields MainStay Family of Funds, Arthur D. Little Inc., IBM World Trade, Asia Pacific Group, Alexander Proudfoot Co., Campbell Soup Co. Gov., exec. com. Fgn. Policy Assn.; ; nat. bd. dirs. Covenant House; dir. Japan Soc., Internat. Rescue Com., Technoserve, Americas Council; adv. council J.L. Kellogg Grad. Sch. Mgmt. Northwestern U.; adv. bd. Ctr. for Strategic and Internat. Studies, U. S.C.; trustee U.S. Council for Internat. Bus.; mem. Council on Foreign Relations, Inter-Am. Dialogue. Served with USNR, 1945-46. Mem. Internat. C. of C. (former chmn. U.S. council for internat. bus., mem. exec. bd.), Internat. Club, Congl. Country Club, F Street Club, Econ. Club, Apawamis Country Club, Belle Haven Club, Stanwich Club, Mid-Ocean Club, Isle of Palms Beach and Racquet Club, Kiawah Golf and Tennis Club, Ekwanok Country Club. Home: 90 Field Point Circle Greenwich CT 06830

PFEIFFER, ROBERT JOHN, business executive; b. Suva, Fiji Islands, Mar. 7, 1920; came to U.S., 1921, naturalized, 1927; s. William Albert and Nina (MacDonald) P.; m. Mary Elizabeth Worts, Nov. 29, 1945; children—Elizabeth Pfeiffer Tumbas, Margaret Pfeiffer Hughes, George, Kathleen. Grad. high sch., Honolulu, 1937; DSc (hon.), Maine Maritime Acad.; HHD (hon.), U. Hawaii; DHL (hon.), Hawaii Loa Coll. With Inter-Island Steam Navigation Co., Ltd., Honolulu, (re-organized to Overseas Terminal Ltd. 1950); With (merged into Oahu Ry. & Land Co. 1954), 1937-55, v.p., gen. mgr., 1950-54, mgr. ship agy. dept., 1954-55; v.p., gen. mgr. Pacific Cut Stone & Granite Co., Inc., Alhambra, Calif., 1955-56, Matcinal Corp., Alameda, Calif., 1956-58; mgr. div. Pacific Far East Line, Inc., San Francisco, 1958-60; with Matson Nav. Co., San Francisco, 1960—; v.p. Matson Nav. Co., 1966-70, sr. v.p., 1970-71, exec. v.p., 1971-73, pres., 1973-79, chmn. bd., chief exec. officer, 1979-84, 85-89, chmn. bd., pres., chief exec. officer, 1984, chmn. bd. dirs., 1989—; v.p. The Matson Co., San Francisco, 1968-70; pres. The Matson Co., 1970-82; v.p., gen. mgr. Matson Terminals, Inc., San Francisco, 1960-62; pres. Matson Terminals, Inc., 1962-70, chmn. bd., 1970-79; chmn. bd. Matson Services Co., 1973-79, Matson Agys., Inc., 1973-78; sr. v.p. Alexander & Baldwin, Inc., Honolulu, 1973-77; exec. v.p. Alexander & Baldwin, Inc., 1977-79, pres., 1979-80, chmn., pres., chief exec. officer, 1980-84, 89—, chmn., chief exec. officer, 1985-89, also dir.; chmn. bd., pres., dir. A&B-Hawaii, Inc., 1988-89, chmn. bd., 1989—; bd. dirs. A&B Devel. Co. (Calif.), Inc., A&B Properties, Inc., McBryde Sugar Co. Ltd., First Hawaiian Inc., First Hawaiian Bank, Calif. and Hawaiian Sugar Co., WDCI, Inc., also pres.; mem. adv. bd. Pacific Resources, Inc.; mem. Gov.'s comm. on exec. salaries State of Hawaii, com. on jud. salaries. Past chmn. maritime transp. research bd. Nat. Acad. Sci.; former mem. select com. for Am. Mcht. Marine Seamanship Trophy Award, commn. sociotech. systems NRC.; Mem. adv. com. Joint Maritime Congress; trustee Pacific Tropical Bot. Garden, Bishop Mus., Pacific Aerospace Mus., also bd. dirs.; mem. Japan-Hawaii Econ. Council, Army Civilian Adv. Group; vice-chmn. Hawaii Maritime Ctr.; chmn. A Commitee on Excellence (ACE), Hawaii; mem. adv. council Girl Scouts U.S. Council of the Pacific; bd. govs. Hugh O'Brian Youth Found.; mem. exec. com. Research Round Table Alameda County chpt. Am. Heart Assn.; bd. govs. Japanese Cultural Ctr. Hawaii; mem. bd. nominators Am. Inst. for Pub. Svc.; Govs. Commn. Exec. Salaries, State Hawaii, Com. Jud. Salaries, Veterans Foreign Wars U.S. Served to lt. USNR, World War II; comdr. Res. ret. Mem. Am. Inst. Pub. Svc., Nat. Assn. Stevedores (past pres.), Internat. Cargo Handling Coordination Assn. (past pres. U.S. nat. com.), Propeller Club U.S. (past pres. Honolulu), Nat. Def. Transp. Assn., Conf. Bd., 200 Club, Long Beach C. of C., Portland C. of C., Oakland C. of C., Richmond (Calif.) C. of C., Seattle C. of C., Kauai C. of C., Los Angeles C. of C., San Francisco C. of C., Hawaii Island C. of C., Hawaii C. of C., Maui C. of C., Am. Bur. Shipping (bd. mgrs.), Aircraft Owners and Pilots Assn., VFW (life). Republican. Clubs: Pacific, Outrigger, Oahu Country (Honolulu); Maui (Hawaii) Country, U. Hawaii, Pacific Union, Bohemian, World Trade (San Francisco). Lodges: Masons, Shriners. Home: 535 Miner Rd Orinda CA 94563 Office: Alexander & Baldwin Inc 822 Bishop St Honolulu HI 96813

PFEIL, DON CURTIS, real estate executive; b. Wausa, Nebr., Dec. 4, 1923; s. Leonard W. and Katherine A. (Peterson) P.; m. Jane Cole Magee, Sept. 14, 1946; children: Bruce, Mark, Joan. Grad. high sch., Wausa. Farmer Wausa, 1946-64; pres. Don C. Pfeil & Assoc., Inc., Wausa, 1964—. Bd. dirs., sec. Cedar-Knox Pub. Power Dist., Hartington, Nebr., 1962—; chmn. governing bd. N.E. Community Coll., Norfolk, Nebr., 1972—; mem. Nebr. Council on Vocat. Edn., Lincoln, 1983—; bd. dirs. Osmond (Nebr.) Gen. Hosp., 1970-77. Sgt. AC U.S. Army, 1943-46. Mem. Realtors Land Inst., Am. Soc. Farm Mgrs. and Rural Appraisers, Lewis and Clark Bd. Realtors (pres. 1970), Grad Realtors Inst. (dean 1978-83). Democrat. Lutheran. Home: RR 1 PO Box 114 Wausa NE 68786 Office: Don C Pfeil & AssocsInc PO Box 220 Wausa NE 68786

PFISTER, GAIL WILLIAMS, economics educator; b. Seattle, May 6, 1936; d. Randall Smallwood Jr. and Jean (Miller) Williams; m. John S. Williams, Aug. 23, 1958 (div. 1979); children: Eric, Lori; m. Cloyd Harry Pfister, Apr. 24, 1982; stepchildren: Gaby, Cathy, Michael, Romi. AA, Marymount Coll., Rome, 1955; BA in Econs., Oberlin Coll., 1957; MA in History, Fairleigh Dickinson U., 1968; MA in Econs., NYU, 1976. Rsch. assoc., then lectr. Fairleigh Dickinson U., Teaneck, N.J., 1973-79; asst. prof. George Mason U., Fairfax, Va., 1979-82; lectr. U. Md., Heidelberg, Fed. Republic of Germany, 1982-84, U. Ariz., Tucson, 1984-86, U. South Fla., Tampa, 1986—, Echerd Coll., St. Petersburg, Fla., 1986—. Author: Multinational Corporations: Problems and Prospects, 1975, Transborder Data Flows and Multinational Enterprise, 1988. Home: 8007 W Riverchase Dr Tampa FL 33637

PFISTER, JAMES JOSEPH, publishing company executive; b. N.Y.C., Oct. 29, 1946; s. Stanley George and Rosemary Ann (Cullen) P.; m. Kendra Elaine Nelson, Mar. 23, 1974; 1 child, Charles Joseph. BS, Northwestern U., 1970. Mktg. supr. Nat. Register Pub. Co., Wilmette, Ill., 1970-73, dist. sales mgr., 1973-76, nat. sales mgr., 1976-80, pub., 1980-85, pres., 1985—; pres. Marquis Who's Who, Wilmette, Ill., 1985—, Macmillan Directory Div., Wilmette, Ill., 1985—, Creative Black Book, N.Y.C., 1987—. Sec. Libertyville (Ill.) Homeowners Assn., 1981-83, pres., 1983-85; mem. Com. to Re-elect Ronald Reagan, 1984. Served with U.S. Army, 1967-69, Vietnam. Decorated Bronze Star with V device, Bronze Star with oak leaf cluster, Air medal, Purple Heart. Mem. Chgo. Advt. Club, Am. Assn. Mus. (cons. 1978—). Republican. Office: Nat Register Pub Co 3004 Glenview Rd Wilmette IL 60091 *

PFLUGER, RANDALL CHARLES, mechanical engineer; b. Batesville, Ind., Jan. 25, 1956; s. Elmer Carl and Eileen (Kichta) P.; m. Jamie Elizabeth Query, Jan. 22, 1983; 1 child, Heather Elyse. BSME, Rose-Hulman Inst. Tech., Terre Haute, Ind., 1978. Field engr., contract coordinator Bechtel Power Corp., San Francisco, 1978-79; project engr. Olin Corp., Stamford, Conn., 1979-85; sr. project mgr. Frito-Lay, Inc., Dallas, 1985—; ptnr., cons. Estrella Ventures Group, Phoenix, 1986—; prin. McIntosh Select Classics, 1988—. Bd. dirs. Big Bros. Program, Ashtabula, Ohio, 1980-81; chief advisor Jr. Achievement Program, Ashtabula, Ohio, 1980-81; mem. First Bapt. Ch., Carrollton, Tex., 1988—. Recipient of Outstanding Young Man of Am. awards U.S. Jaycees, 1980, 81. Mem. Soc. of Automotive Engrs., ASME, Rose-Hulman Alumni Assn., Alpha Tau Omega Alumni. Republican. Home: 4207 Spurwood Dr Carrollton TX 75007 Office: Frito-Lay Inc 7701 Legacy Dr Plano TX 75024

PFOUTS, RALPH WILLIAM, economist, consultant; b. Atchison, Kans., Sept. 9, 1920; s. Ralph Ulysses and Alice (Oldham) P.; m. Jane Hoyer, Jan. 31, 1945 (dec. Nov. 1982); children: James William, Susan Jane (Mrs. Osher Portman), Thomas Robert (dec.), Elizabeth Ann (Mrs. Charles Klenowski); m. Lois Bateson, Dec. 21, 1984. B.A., U. Kans., 1942, M.A., 1947; Ph.D., U. N.C., 1952. Rsch. asst., instr. econs. U. Kans., Lawrence, 1946-47; instr. U. N.C., Chapel Hill, 1947-50, lectr. econs., 1950-52, assoc. prof., 1952-58, prof., 1958-87, chmn. grad. studies dept. econs. Sch. Bus. Adminstrn., 1957-62, chmn. dept. econs. Sch. Bus. Adminstrn., 1962-68; cons. econs. Chapel Hill, 1987—; vis. prof. U. Leeds, 1983; vis. research scholar Internat. Inst. for Applied Systems Analysis, 1983. Author: Elementary Economics-A Mathematical Approach, 1972; editor: So. Econ. Jour, 1955-75; editor, contbr.: Techniques of Urban Economic Analysis, 1960, Essays in Economics and Econometrics, 1960; editorial bd.: Metroeconomica, 1961-80, Atlantic Econ. Jour, 1973—; contbr. articles to profl. jours. Served as deck officer USNR, 1943-46. Social Sci. Research Council fellow U. Cambridge, 1953-54; Ford Found. Faculty Research fellow, 1962-63. Mem. AAAS, Am. Statis. Assn., N.C. Statis. Assn. (past pres.), Am. Econ. Assn., So. Econ. Assn. (past pres.), Atlantic Econ. Soc. (v.p. 1973-76, pres. 1977-78), Population Assn. Am., Econometric Soc., Phi Beta Kappa, Pi Sigma Alpha, Alpha Kappa Psi, Omicron Delta Epsilon.

PFUND, EDWARD THEODORE, JR., electronics co. exec.; b. Methuen, Mass., Dec. 10, 1923; s. Edward Theodore and Mary Elizabeth (Banning) P.; B.S. magna cum laude, Tufts Coll., 1950; postgrad U. So. Calif., 1950, Columbia U., 1953, U. Calif., Los Angeles, 1956, 58; m. Marga Emmi

Andre, Nov. 10, 1954 (div. 1978); children—Angela M., Gloria I., Edward Theodore III; m. Ann Lorenne Dille, Jan. 10, 1988. Radio engr., WLAW, Lawrence-Boston, 1942-50; fgn. service staff officer Voice of Am., Tangier, Munich, 1950-54; project. engr. Crusade for Freedom, Munich, Ger., 1955; project mgr., materials specialist United Electrodynamics Inc., Pasadena, Calif., 1956-59; cons. H.I. Thompson Fiber Glass Co., Los Angeles, Andrew Corp., Chgo., 1959, Satellite Broadcast Assocs., Encino, Calif., 1982; teaching staff Pasadena City Coll. (Calif.), 1959; dir. engring., chief engr. Electronics Specialty Co., Los Angeles and Thomaston, Conn., 1959-61; with Hughes Aircraft Co., various locations, 1955, 61—, mgr. Middle East programs, also Far East, Latin Am. and African market devel., Los Angeles, 1971—, dir. internat. programs devel., Hughes Communications Internat., 1985—. Served with AUS, 1942-46. Mem. Phi Beta Kappa, Am. Inst. Aeros. and Astronautics, Sigma Pi Sigma. Contbr. articles to profl. jours. Home: 25 Silver Saddle Ln Rolling Hills Estates CA 90274 Office: PO Box 92919 Airport Station Los Angeles CA 90009

PHALON, PHILIP ANTHONY, marketing executive; b. Paterson, N.J., Apr. 18, 1929; s. John J. and Agnes (Maher) P.; m. Anna M. Moran. B.S., Boston Coll., 1950. Vice-pres. internat. Whittaker Corp., Los Angeles, 1972-73; v.p. internat. affairs Raytheon Co., Lexington, Mass., 1973-83; sr. v.p. corp. mktg. Raytheon Co., 1983—; dir. New Japan Radio Co., Tokyo. Bd. dirs. World Affairs Council Boston, Emerson Hosp., Concord, Mass., 1981—. Served with U.S. Army, 1950-53. Roman Catholic. Office: Raytheon Co 141 Spring St Lexington MA 02173

PHAM, HAI QUANG, chemical engineer; b. Da Nang, Vietnam, Sept. 30, 1956; came to U.S., 1974; s. Houng Q. Pham and Kim Chi (Thi) Nguyen. BS in Chem. Engring., U. Wis., Madison, 1979. Process engr. Texaco Chem. Co., Port Arthur, Tex., 1980-83; sr. process engr. Texaco Chem. Co., Port Arthur, 1983-84, area engr., 1984-88; control engr. Profimatics Inc., Thousand Oaks, Calif., 1988—. Mem. Am. Inst. Chem. Engrs. Home: 617 N Las Posas Apt 104 Camarillo CA 93010 Office: Profimatics Inc 77 Rolling Oaks Thousand Oaks CA 91361

PHAM, KINH DINH, electrical engineer, educator, administrator; b. Saigon, Republic of Vietnam, Oct. 6, 1956; came to U.S., 1974; s. Nhuong D. and Phuong T. (Tran) P.; m. Ngan-Lien T. Nguyen, May 27, 1985. BS with honors, Portland State U., 1979; MSEE, U. Portland, 1982. Registered profl. engr., Oreg., Calif. Elec. engr. Irvington-Moore, Tigard, Oreg., 1979-80; elec. engr. Elcon Assocs., Inc., Beaverton, Oreg., 1980-87, sr. elec. engr., assoc. ptnr., 1987—; adj. prof. Portland (Oreg.) Community Coll., 1982—. Contbr. articles to profl. jours. Recipient Cert. Appreciation Am. Pub. Transit Assn. and Transit Industry, 1987. Mem. IEEE. Buddhist. Office: Elcon Assocs Inc 12670 NW Barnes Rd Portland OR 97229

PHANG, YVONNE MARIA, insurance executive; b. Kingston, Jamaica, Aug. 28, 1952; came to U.S., 1971; d. William and Saak Yin (Chai) P.; m. Mahmoud Hatami, Mar. 21, 1988. BA in Spanish, U. Houston, 1974; MBA, Concordia U., Montreal, Ont., Can., 1977. CPA, Tex.; registered representative NASD. Acct. B.B. Watkins, CPA, Houston, 1977-79, Pacesetter Industries, N.Y.C., 1979-80; sr. corp. auditor F.W. Woolworth Co., N.Y.C., 1980-82; v.p. Chase Manhattan Bank, N.Y.C., 1982-88; sales agt. Murphy Realty, Jersey city, 1988; acct. rep. Met. Life, Bayonne, N.J., 1988—. Mem. AICPA, Tex. Bd. Accountancy. Home: 818 Jefferson St#3A Hoboken NJ 07030 Office: Met Life 564 Broadway Bayonne NJ 07002

PHEIFF, ROBERT FRANK, infosystems educator; b. Bethlehem, Pa., July 3, 1930; s. Andrew O. and Grace (Pinter) P.; m. Anna Dolores Rich, June 11, 1955; children: Loretta Anne, Suzanne. BS, U.S. Mil. Acad., 1955; MBA, George Washington U., 1970. Commd. 2d. lt. USAF, 1955, advanced through grades to lt. col., 1978, various flying assignments, 1956-73; commanding officer 22d squadron USAF Acad., Colo., 1964-65; instr. mil. tng. USAF, 1965-66; instr. pilo 12 Air Command Squadron USAF, Socialist Republic of Vietnam, 1967-68; programmer, systems analyst USAF, HQ Europe, 1971-74; project mgr. tactical air control ctr. USAF, Langley AFB, Va., 1975-76; dep. commdr. mission support USAF, Tinker AFB, Okla., 1976-78; instr. computer sci. Cen. State U., Edmond, Okla., 1978—. Author, editor USAF Military Training for Freshmen, 1965. Decorated 2 Silver Stars, 2 DFCs, Vietnamese Cross of Gallantry. Mem. Assn. Retired Tchrs. Retired Officers' Assn., Air Force Assn., Elks. Republican. Home: 1400 Ridgcrest Rd Edmond OK 73013 Office: Cen State U Dept Computer Sci MCS Bldg Room 124 Edmond OK 73060-0124

PHELAN, JOHN J., JR., stock exchange executive; b. N.Y.C., May 7, 1931. BBA magna cum laude, Adelphi U., 1970, LLD (hon.), 1987; LLD (hon.), Hamilton Coll., 1980, Niagara U., 1985; hon. doctorate, U. Notre Dame, 1986. Ptnr. Nash & Co., N.Y.C., 1955-57; mng. dir. Phelan & Co., N.Y.C., 1957-62; mem. NY Stock Exchange, N.Y.C., 1957-80; bd. govs. N.Y. Stock Exchange, N.Y.C., 1971-72, bd. dirs., 1974-80, vice chmn., 1975-79, pres., chief oper. officer, 1980-84, chmn., chief exec. officer, 1984—; sr. ptnr. Phelan, Silver, Vesce, Barry & Co., N.Y.C., 1962-72; chmn. N.Y. Futures Exchange, 1979-85, Presdl. Bd. Advisors on Pvt. Sector Initiatives, 1986—; bd. dirs. Met. Life Ins. Co., Fed. Hall Meml. Assocs., Eastman Kodak Co.; bd. dirs. Bus. Coun. N.Y. State, vice chair bd., chmn. fin. com., 1988—; trustee Com. for Econ. Devel., 1985—; mem. N.Y. State Temporary Com. on Banking, Ins., and Fin. Services, 1983-84; leader del. to symposium N.Y. Stock Exchange/Peoples Bank China, Beijing, 1986. Mem. cardinal's com. of laity Archdiocese N.Y., 1968—, mem. fin. coun., 1986—; chmn. Wall St. div. NCCJ, 1973, 76; bd. dirs. Mercy Hosp., Rockville Centre, N.Y., 1976-81, N.Y. Heart Assn., 1979-84; chmn. campaigns N.Y.C. Heart Fund, 1982-83; trustee Adelphi Coll., 1980-86, chmn. bd. trustees, 1981-85, trustee emeirtus, 1986—; trustee Tulane U., 1981-84, trustee emeritus, 1984—; mem. bd. advisors Boston U. Ctr. for Banking Law Studies, 1981—; trustee N.Y. Med. Coll., 1984—, Com. for Econ. Devel., 1985—, Cath. Charities, 1985—, Asia Soc., 1987—; chmn. fin. svcs. div. United Way N.Y., 1985-86, trustee United Way Am., 1988—; mem. bd. councillors Holy Sepulcher, 1985—; mem. adv. bd. Bus. Higher Edn. Forum, 1985—. With USMC, 1951-54. Decorated knight Sovereign Mil. Order of Malta, knight Holy Sepulchre of Jerusalem; Medal of Arts and Letters (France); recipient Brotherhood award NCCJ, 1974, Disting. Alumni award Adelphi U., 1979, Nat. Youth Services award B'nai B'rith Found., Wall St. Man of Yr. award B'nai B'rith, 1980, Stephen S. Wise award Am. Jewish Congress, 1981, Good Scout award Greater N.Y. coun. Boy Scouts Am., 1983, Man of Yr. award Nat. Found. for Ileities and Colitis, 1985, Chancellor's Medal award Molloy Coll., 1987, Disting. Service award Investment Edn. Inst., 1987, award of merit for disting. entrepreneurship The Wharton Sch., U. Pa., 1987, Silver Ambrosiana award Commune of Milan, 1987, Lion of Venice award City of Venice, 1987, Medal of Veneto Veneto region Govt. of Italy, 1987, Albert Schweitzer Leadership award Hugh O'Brien Youth Found., 1987, Torch of Learning award NYU Ctr. for Ednl. Rsch., 1987, others. Mem. Fedn. Internat. Bourses de Valeurs (v.p.). Office: NY Stock Exch Inc 11 Wall St New York NY 10005

PHELPS, GEORGE ELMER, financial company executive; b. Fond du Lac County, Wis., Sept. 19, 1897; s. Elmer Nathaniel and Permelia Augusta (Banker) P.; m. Marion Genevieve Grinder, Aug. 21, 1925 (div. 1950); children: Gayle Marion Wood (dec.), Bonita Banker Jones (dec.); m. Georgia Fadler, June 15, 1950 (dec. 1982). BS in Elec. Engring., Marquette U., 1923. Rate analyst Milw. Electric Ry. & Light Co., 1923-25; investment analyst, br. head 1st Wis. Co., Milw., 1925-32; co-founder, mgr. Duff and Phelps, Chgo., 1932-40, fin. cons., 1940-42, 47-51; mfg. exec. Phelps Mfg. Co., Los Angeles, 1951-67; analyst, investment advisor Lester, Ryons Co., Los Angeles, 1967-68; investment cons. Francis I. Du Pont Co., N.Y.C., 1968-69; pres., fin. and investment cons. George E. Phelps Co., Los Angeles, 1969—. Contbr. articles to profl. jours. Served to col. Signal Corps, U.S. Army, 1942-47. Decorated Legion of Merit; named Disting. Engring. Alumnus Marquette U., 1986. Mem. Tau Beta Pi. Republican. Mem. Dutch Ref. Ch. Home: 340 Magpie Ln Fountain Valley CA 92708

PHELPS, MICHAEL EVERETT JOSEPH, energy company executive; b. Montreal, Que., Can., June 27, 1947; s. Arthur A. and Hendrina (Von De Roer) P.; m. Joy Slimmon, Aug. 8, 1970; children: Erica, Julia, Lindsay. BA, U. Manitoba, 1967, LLB, 1970; LLM, London Sch. Econs., 1971. Crown atty. Province of Man., Winnipeg, 1971-73; ptnr. Christie, Degraves, Winnipeg, 1973-76; counsel Dept. Justice, Ottawa, Ont., 1976-78; exec. asst. Minister of Justice, Ottawa, 1978-79, Minister of Energy, Mines & Resources, Ottawa, 1980-82; sr. advisor to pres. & chief exec. officer Westcoast Transmission Co. Ltd., Vancouver, B.C., 1982-83; v.p. strategic planning Westcoast Transmission Co. Ltd., Vancouver, 1983-87, sr. v.p., 1987, exec. v.p., chief fin. officer, 1987-88; pres., chief exec. officer Westcoast Energy, Inc. (formerly Westcoast Transmission Co Ltd.), Vancouver, 1988—, also bd. dirs.; bd. dirs. Saratoga Processing Co. Ltd.; chmn. bd. Westcoast Petroleum Co. Ltd., chmn. bd. dirs. Can. Roxy Petroleum Ltd., vice-chmn., bd. dirs. Foothills Pipe Lines (Yukon) Ltd. Mem. Interstate Natural Gas Assn. Am. (bd. dirs.), Can. Petroleum Assn. (bd. dirs.), Bus. coun. British Columbia, The Vancouver, Hollyburn Country, Terminal City (Vancouver), Vancouver Club, Hollyburn Golf & Country Club, Terminal City Ckub. Office: Westcoast Energy Inc, 1333 W Georgia St, Vancouver, BC Canada V6E 3K9

PHELPS, RICHARD GEORGE, JR., printing company executive; b. White Plains, N.Y., Nov. 27, 1950; s. Richard George and Bernice Joan (Malloy) P.; m. Lynne Margaret Bommer, July 20, 1974; children: Richard G. III, Courtney L. BS in Bus. Adminstrn., Davis and Elkins Coll., 1972. Tech. svc. mgr. Allen-Bailey Tag and Label Inc., Caledonia, N.Y., 1975-77, plant mgr., 1977-79, gen. mgr., 1979—; mem. Livingston County Adv. Bd. Chase Lincoln Bank N.A., Caledonia, 1986—. Active Zoning Bd. Appeals, Caledonia, 1987—, PTA, Caledonia, 1987—; pres. coun. Atonement Luth. Ch., Rochester, N.Y., 1987—. With U.S. Army, 1972-75. Recipient Meritorious Svc. medal White House Communications Agy., Washington, 1975, Presdl. Svc. badge, 1975. Mem. Flexographic Tech. Assn., Screen Printing Assn. Internat. Republican. Home: 21 Stoney Oak Circle Caledonia NY 14423 Office: Allen-Bailey Tag & Label Inc 3177 Lehigh St Caledonia NY 14423

PHILIP, THOMAS PETER, mining executive; b. Bellville, Cape, Republic South Africa, Feb. 5, 1933; came to U.S., 1984; s. David Henderson and Nora (VanWyk) P.; m. Adriana van Schalkwyk, Dec. 3, 1954 (div. 1982); children: Wayne, Lorinda, Lynette, Debra. BSMetE, U. Ariz., 1958. Asst. gen. mgr. Tsumeb Corp., Namibia, 1970-74; gen. mgr. O'okiep Copper Co., Nababeep, Republic South Africa, 1975-84; chief exec. officer O'okiep Copper Co., Nababeep, 1981-84, also bd. dirs.; exec. v.p., gen. mgr. Carlin (Nev.) Gold Mining Co., 1984-85; pres. Newmont Gold Co., Carlin, 1985—, also bd. dirs.; sr. v.p. Newmont Mining Corp., N.Y.C., 1986—; bd. dirs. Newmont Autstralia, Ltd., Melbourne. Fellow South Africa Inst. Mining and Metallurgy; mem. Soc. Mining Engring., Denver Club, Namutoni Club (master 1971). Home: 5403 S Fulton Cr Englewood CO 80111 Office: Newmont Mining Corp 1700 Lincoln St Denver CO 80203

PHILIP, WILLIAM WARREN, banker; b. Tacoma, Oct. 26, 1926; s. Warren F. and Lillian (Lehman) P.; m. Dorothy Mary Mitchell, Oct. 14, 1954; children: Cynthia Ann, Susan Kelly. Student, U. Wash., 1946-47; grad., Pacific Coast Banking Sch., 1961; postgrad., Pacific Luth. U., 1987. With Puget Sound Nat. Bank, Tacoma, 1951—; pres. Puget Sound Nat. Bank, 1971—, chmn., 1979—; bd. dirs. Fed. Res. Bd. San Francisco; chmn. Pierce County, Savs. Bond div. Treasury Dept. Bd. dirs. Lakewood Water Dist., Tacoma Pierce County Econ. Devel.; chmn. Multicare Hosp. Tacoma; chmn. bus. adv. bd. Pacific Luth. U.; past chmn. bd. Mary Bridge Children's Hosp. Mem. Wash. Roundtable, Tacoma Golf and County Club, Rainier Club, Columbia Tower Club. Office: Puget Sound Nat Bank 1119 Pacific Ave Tacoma WA 98402

PHILIPPBAR, DEBORAH DEBARR, retail executive, financial consultant; b. Grafton, W.Va., Dec. 18, 1951; d. Perry J. DeBarr and Mary Angela (Bevilocke) Stephenson; m. Mark Davies Philippbar, Feb. 28, 1986; 1 child, Kristan Angela. Student, Blue Ridge Coll., 1970-71, SUNY, Binghamton, 1981-83. Cert. fin. cons., ins. broker, N.Y., Conn., Va., Md., D.C. Fin., ins. cons. Binghamton, 1978-81; owner Faces and Things, Binghamton, 1980-82, Twice But Nice, Binghamton, 1980-82; fin. cons. Pat Ryan and Assocs., Chgo., 1983-86; bus. mgr. Tony March Buick, Hartford, Conn., 1986—; dir. tng. F&I Alternatives, Inc., Springfield, Mass., 1988—; credit cons., Hartford, 1986—. Nat. Assn. Female Execs., Nat. Orgn. Fin. and Ins. Specialists. Republican. Baptist.

PHILIPS, GEORGE, publishing company executive; b. N.Y.C., Feb. 1, 1931; s. Phillip and Antonina (Richko) P.; m. Barbara Joan Unger, Nov. 1, 1952; children: Andrea, Gregory, Elisabeth. BS in Civil Engring., Cooper Union, 1952; MS in Indsl. Mgmt., MIT, 1954. Pres. Corplan Assocs., Chgo., 1956-66; exec. v.p. Tootsie Roll Industries, Chgo., 1966-69; pres. Foto Fair, Internat., Dayton, Ohio, 1969-70; v.p. Cadence Industries, West Caldwell, N.J., 1970-80; sr. v.p. AAMCO, Phila., 1980-81; group v.p. Macmillan Inc., N.Y.C., 1981—. Author, editor: Economic Impact of Technology Upon Chicago, 1978. Trustee Patterson Gen. Hosp., N.J., 1968, Katherine Gibbs Sch., Mountclair, N.J., 1984. Served with U.S. Army, 1955-56. Home: 285 Manor Rd Ridgewood NJ 07450 Office: Macmillan Inc 866 3rd Ave New York NY 10022

PHILIPS, JESSE, manufacturing company executive; b. N.Y.C., Oct. 23, 1914; s. Simon and Sara (Berkowitz) P.; m. Carol Jane Frank, Dec. 23, 1945 (div. 1971); children: Ellen Jane, Thomas Edwin; m. Caryl Ann Dombrosky, Sept. 11, 1978. AB magna cum laude, Oberlin Coll., 1937; MBA, Harvard U., 1939; DBA (hon.), Hillsdale Coll., 1985; HLD (hon.), U. Dayton, 1986; DH (hon.), Oberlin Coll., 1988. Pres. Philips Industries Inc., Dayton, Ohio, 1957-68, chmn. bd., chief exec. officer, 1968-89, chmn. bd. dirs.; dir. Soc. Corp., Cleve. Author: International Stabilization of Currencies, 1936, British Rationalization, 1937; contbg. author: Chief Executive Handbook. Chmn. Dayton Found. Ind. Colls., Dayton Jewish Community Devel. Coun.; asso. chmn. Dayton Community Chest drive.; Bd. dirs. Good Samaritan Hosp., Dayton, Dayton Jr. Achievement, Dayton Better Bus. Bur., Miami Valley coun. Boy Scouts Am., Dayton coun. Salvation Army, Jewish Community Council; trustee Oberlin Coll., U. Dayton, Ohio Found. Ind. Colls., Arthritis Found., Wright State U. Found., Sinclair Coll. Found.; mem. exec. com. President's Council on youth Exchange, Sister Cities Internat.; vis. com. Harvard U. Grad. Sch. Bus. Adminstrn. Mem. Conn. N.G., 1930-33. Served with USAAF, 1942-43. Decorated comdr. Ordre Souvenain de Chypre; recipient Free Enterprise award, 1965; Disting. Svc. award Harvard Bus. Sch.; Exec. of Yr. award Dayton Exec. Club, 1983; Spirit of Am. Free Enterprise award Jr. Achievement and Free Enterprise Found., 1983; Big Bros. and Big Sisters award, 1983; award U. Dayton chpt. Beta Gamma Sigma; recognition award NCCJ; CEO bronze award Fin. World, 1985, 86; Nat. On Behalf of Youth award Camp Fire, 1985; Nat. Trustee of Yr. award Assn. Governing Bds. Univs. and Colls., 1986; Internat. Ambassador's award U.S. Dept. State-Sister Cities Internat., 1986; Jesse Philips Day in Dayton proclaimed Sept. 10, 1978; named Ohio gov. for a day, 1982; Andrew Wellington Cordier fellow Columbia U. Mem. Dayton C. of C. (dir.), Dayton Retail Mchts. Assn. (dir.), Nat. Retail Dry Goods Assn., Joint Distbn. Com., Columbia Yacht Club, Meadowbrook Country Club, Cavendish Bridge Club, St. Moritz Toboganning Club, Motor Yacht Club of Cote D'Azur. Office: Philips Industries Inc 4801 Springfield St Dayton OH 45401

PHILLIPPI, ELMER JOSEPH, JR., data communications analyst; b. Canton, Ohio, May 31, 1944; s. Elmer Joseph and Rita M. (Tillitski) P.; m. Susan Mary Schrader, July 10, 1971; 1 child, Nathan Audie. AB, Cornell U., 1966; MA, Rice U., 1970. Cert. energy auditor. Tchr. Brackenridge High Sch., San Antonio, 1970-71; asst. prof. engring. tech. Muskingum Tech. Coll., Zanesville, Ohio, 1971-80, sec., treas. AAUP chpt; data communications analyst Chem. Abstracts Services, Columbus, Ohio, 1980-87; sr. software engr. Control Data Corp., Dayton, Ohio, 1987-89, analyst computing Boeing Computer Svcs., Huntsville, Ala., 1989—; communications cons. Ala. Supercomputer Network; designer, devel. Tech. Order Tracking System USAF, 1988; part-time instr. physics Ohio U. Editorial referee Am. Jour. Physics, 1975-85; network design cons. Aeronautical Systems div. USAF. NSF grantee, 1979. Mem. Assn. Computing Machinery (treas. Central Ohio chpt., mem. symposium com.), N.Y. Acad. Scis., Air Force Assn., Rice U. Alumni, Cornell Club Southwestern Ohio, Sigma Xi. Republican. Avocations: ham radio, music, bicycling. Home: 8041 Navios Dr Huntsville AL 35802 Office: Boeing Computer Svcs 686 Discovery Dr Huntsville AL 35806

PHILLIPS, CARLTON VERNON, banker; b. Dartmouth, Mass., July 19, 1924; s. Robert Henry and Helen Estelle P.; A.B. in Econs., Brown U., 1957; grad. U.S. Army Command and Staff Coll., 1972, U.S. Air Force War Coll., 1976; M.A. in Mgmt., St. Mary's Coll. of Calif., 1979; m. Gladys Marie Lynch, Apr. 23, 1949; children—Carlton Vernon, John, Maura, Sally, Sheila, Regina, Nathan. Resident mgr. Mitchum Jones & Templeton, Phoenix, 1966-70, Quinn and Co., Phoenix, 1970-71; sr. v.p., pres. Continental Am. Securities, Inc., 1971-84; chmn. and chief exec. officer Century Pacific Corp., 1984-88; dir. Ad Tech Microwave, First Cen. Bank of Ariz., States West Airline. Served with U.S. Army, 1942-54, served to col. AUS. Decorated D.F.C., Air Medal with 3 oak leaf clusters. Republican. Roman Catholic. Clubs: Brown U. (Ariz. chpt., Phoenix), U.S. Army Assn. (Scottsdale), KC (Scottsdale). Home: 5112 N Wilkinson Rd Paradise Valley AZ 85253 Office: 3200 E Camelback Phoenix AZ 85018

PHILLIPS, DERWYN FRASER, manufacturing company executive; b. St. Catharines, Ont., Can., Aug. 31, 1930; came to U.S., 1975; s. John Arthur and Margaret (Cameron) P.; m. Janice Irene Hunt, Sept. 24, 1955; children: John Timothy, Laurie Cameron, Jay Derwyn. B.A., U. Western Ont., London, 1954. V.p. mkgt. Rexall Drug Co., Ont., 1966-68; v.p., dir. mktg. Gillette-Can., Montreal, Que., 1969-71; pres. Gillette-Can., 1971-75; pres. toiletries div. Gillette Co., Boston, 1975-77; pres. personal care div. Gillette Co., 1977-81, exec. v.p., 1981-87, vice chmn., 1987—; dir. Can. Tire Corp., Toronto, 1984-86. Trustee New Eng. Colls. Fund, Boston, 1982—. Mem. Greater Boston C. of C. (dir. 1982—), Cosmetic Toiletry and Fragrance Assn. (dir. 1981-83). Office: Gillette Co 3900 Prodential Tower Boston MA 02199

PHILLIPS, DONALD JOHN, mining and industrial company executive; b. Ebbw Vale, Wales, Jan. 8, 1930; s. Archie Thomas and Ruth Emma (Thorne) P.; m. Susan Elizabeth Haire, Feb. 28, 1986; children by previous marriage: Simon Hugh, Janet Katherine. BSc, U. Wales, 1951. Lectr. in chemistry Portsmouth (Eng.) U., 1954-56; tech. officer Inco Europe, London, 1956-67; sales mgr. Internat. Nickel Co. Can., 1967-69, gen. mktg. mgr., 1969-70, mng. dir., 1971-72, chmn., chief exec. officer European ops., 1972-77; pres. Inco Metals Co., Toronto, Ont., Can., 1977-80; pres. Inco Ltd., Toronto, 1980-82, pres., chief operating officer, 1982-87, chmn., pres., chief exec. officer, 1987—; bd. dirs. Toronto-Dominion Bank, Enserch Corp.; mem. Bus. Council on Nat. Issues; Ont. Bus. Adv. Bd. Mem. Hosps. of Ont. Investments Com. Served with RAF, 1952-54. Fellow Instn. Mining and Metallurgy; mem. Internat. Copper Research Assn. (bd. dirs.), Council Can. Unity (bd. dirs.), Brit. Inst. Mgmt. (companion). Mem. Ch. of England. Clubs: Nat., Canadian, Hurlingham, Toronto. Home: 65 Harbour Sq Apt 401, Toronto, ON Canada M5J 2L4 Office: Inco Ltd, Royal Trust Tower Box 44, Toronto, ON Canada M5K 1N4

PHILLIPS, EARL NORFLEET, JR., financial services executive; b. High Point, N.C., May 5, 1940; s. Earl Norfleet Phillips and Lillian Jordan; m. Sarah Boyle, Oct. 19, 1971; children—Courtney Dorsett, Jordan Norfleet. BS in Bus. Adminstrn., U. N.C., 1962; MBA, Harvard U., 1965. Security analyst Wertheim & Co., N.Y.C., 1965-67; exec. v.p. Factors Inc., High Point, N.C., 1967-71, exec. v.p. First Factors Corp., High Point, 1972-81, pres., 1982—; chmn., bd. dirs. Oakdale Cotton Mills; dir. Styrex, Inc. Trustee U. N.C., Chapel Hill, 1983—, bd. dirs. N.C. Bus. Found.; mem. N.C. Econ. Devel. Bd., Raleigh, N.C., 1984—. Named Young Man of Yr., High Point Jaycees, 1971; named One of Five Outstanding Young Men, N.C. Jaycees, 1971. Mem. Nat. Comml. Fin. Assn. (bd. dirs.). Clubs: The Brook (N.Y.C.); Country of N.C. (Pinehurst); Willow Creek, String and Splinter (High Point). Lodge: Gorgons Head. Office: 1st Factors Corp PO Box 2730 High Point NC 27261

PHILLIPS, EDWARD DAVID, investment research consultant; b. Lancaster, Ohio, Jan. 9, 1938; s. Frank and Lula Irene (Tiller) P.; m. Ada Dorthea Hunsbedt, Dec. 15, 1976; children: Pamela, Valerie. BA summa cum laude, Park Coll., Parkville, Mo., 1973; MA, Ball State U., 1976; PhD, Ohio U., 1981. Enlisted USAF, 1957, advanced through ranks to master sgt., 1977, Vietnam service, 1965, 69-70; dir. measurement program Bell Aerospace, Buffalo, 1981-83; economist NCR Comten., St. Paul, 1984-86; research cons. Hartford (Conn.) Ins. Group, 1987—; pres. No. States Research Group, Mpls., 1983-84, U.S. Research Group, Farmington, Conn., 1986—. Contbr. articles to profl. jours. Recipient George Washington Honor medal Freedom's Found., 1971, Presdl. scholar Park Coll., 1973. Mem. Ind. Research Assn. (pres. Mpls. chpt. 1983-84), Ops. Research Soc. Am., Nat. Assn. Bus. Economists, Hartford Area Bus. Econs. Home: 5C Talcott Glen Rd Farmington CT 06032 Office: 690 Asylum Ave Hartford CT 06115

PHILLIPS, EDWARD EVERETT, insurance company executive; b. Orange, N.J., Sept. 14, 1927; s. Edward Everett, Jr. and Margaret (Jaffray) P., Jr.; m. Margaret Whitney, Sept. 7, 1952; children: John Whitney, Margaret Jaffray, Nancy Osborne. BA cum laude, Amherst Coll., 1952; LLB, Harvard U., 1955. Bar: Mass. 1955. With Mirick, O'Connell, De Mallie & Lougee, Worcester, Mass., 1955-57, John Hancock Mut. Life Ins. Co., Boston, 1957-69; v.p. agy. dept. John Hancock Mut. Life Ins. Co., 1965-69; with New Eng. Mut. Life Ins. Co., Boston, 1969—, v.p., sec., 1969-72, exec. v.p., 1972-74, pres., 1974-81, chmn., chief exec. officer, 1978—, also dir., 1973—; bd. dirs. NYNEX Corp. Past trustee New Eng. Aquarium, Boston Plan for Excellence in the Pub. Schs.; trustee emeritus Amherst Coll.; chmn. New England Conservatory, Greater Boston Arts Stabilization Fund, ACCESS; bd. dirs. United Way of Am. Mem. Am. Coun. Life Ins. (past dir., chmn. 1985), Mass. Bus. Roundtable (past chmn.). Office: New Eng Mut Life Ins Co 501 Boylston St Boston MA 02117

PHILLIPS, EDWIN WILLIAM, concrete, materials supply company executive; b. Jersey City, Jan. 26, 1904; s. Edward E. and Elizabeth (Pansing) P.; Litt.B., Rutgers U., 1927; m. Margaret Underhill Alpers, Sept. 12, 1931 (dec. 1981); children—Adelaide Elizabeth (Mrs. Calvin T. Bull), Kenneth Edwin. Office sales, mgmt. Harrison Supply Co., East Newark, 1927-32, pres., 1948-83, chmn. bd., 1983—; mgmt., pres., treas. Concrete Carriers, Inc., Hillsborough, N.J., 1937-69, v.p., dir., 1981—; exec. v.p., dir. F.F. Phillips, Inc., New Brunswick, N.J.; chmn. bd., chief exec. officer, dir. Phillips Concrete Inc., Hillsborough, N.J.; officer, dir. Mascot Savs. and Loan Assn., Newark, 1954-64, Essential Savs. and Loan Assn., Verona, N.J., 1964-74; Lacrosse coach, 1936-41. Past mem. N.J. Citizens Hwy. Com. Trustee, bd. dirs., past chmn. bd. Boys' Clubs of Newark; trustee Essex County Coll. Found., 1976-81; mem. Circus Saints and Sinners, 1960-81; spl. power vessel insp. State of N.J., 1955-66. Recipient Man of Year Community Service award Boys' Clubs Newark, 1973. Mem. N.J. Concrete Assn. (dir., past pres.; gen. chmn. 1st Ann. Awards Dinner cosponsored with N.J. chpt. Am. Concrete Inst. 1964, 65, 66), Am. Concrete Inst., ASTM, Navy League U.S., Circus Saints and Sinners (dir. N.J. tent), N.Y. Athletic Club, Essex Club, Baltusrol Golf Club, Beta Theta Pi. Home: Folly Rd2 Green Pond NJ 07435 Office: 800 Passaic Ave East Newark NJ 07029

PHILLIPS, ELWOOD HUDSON, bookstore executive, real estate executive; b. Ludlow, Ky., May 30, 1914; s. Clarence Bell and Hallie Josephine (Hudson) P.; m. Edna Mae Johnson, May 20, 1934; children—Janet Carolyn, Martha Lee. Student U. Cin., 1933, Anderson Coll., 1952-54. Foreman, supt. sales, service mgr., packaging engr. Container Corp. Am., Cin. and Rock Island, Ill., 1932-47; owner, mgr. Phillips Book Store, Springfield, Ohio, 1947—; mgr. bookstore Anderson Coll., Ind., 1950-68; owner, mgr. Phillips Real Estate, Anderson, 1956—. Pres. Madison County (Ind.) Hist. Soc., 1985-87, chmn. bd. dirs. 1988; v.p. Anderson East Side Community Club, 1987-88, pres. 1988—. Mem. Nat. Bd. Realtors, Ind. Assn. Realtors, Am. Booksellers Assn., Anderson Bd. Realtors, Christian Booksellers Assn. Democrat. Mem. Ch. of God. Avocation: geneology. Home: 807 Nursery Rd Anderson IN 46012 Office: Phillips Book Store 32 E Washington St Springfield OH 45502

PHILLIPS, HARRY JOHNSON, SR., waste management company executive; b. Memphis, Jan. 19, 1930; s. Joseph Hunter and Mildred Bell (Johnson) P.; m. Louise Bondurant, Apr. 1; children—Harry Johnson, Julian B., Howard H., Clifton B., Percy P. Ed., U. Miss. Founder, owner, operator refuse collection and disposal service Memphis & later Houston San Juan, Jackson & Biloxi, Miss., 1955-70; pres., chief operating officer Browning-Ferris Industries, Inc., Houston, 1970-77; pres. Browning-Ferris

Industries, Inc., 1977-80, chief exec. officer, 1977—, chmn. bd., 1980—; dir. Nat. Commerce Bancorp. Trustee Rhodes Coll., Memphis U. Sch. Mem. Nat. Solid Waste Mgmt. Assn. (dir.), Am. Productivity Ctr. Episcopalian. Clubs: Memphis Country, Memphis Hunt and Polo, Memphis Petroleum. Office: Browning-Ferris Industries Inc 14701 Saint Mary's Ln Houston TX 77079 *

PHILLIPS, JOHN BURTON, food company executive; b. Stockton, Calif., Oct. 20, 1935; s. John and Betty (Lucy) P.; m. Dee Ann Raymond, June 6, 1958; children: Jeffrey, Stacy, Dean. B.S., Utah State U., 1958. With Campbell Soup Co., Camden, N.J., 1958-80; v.p., gen. mgr. Swanson Frozen Foods div., 1979; pres. Swanson Frozen Foods, 1979-80; pres., chief operating officer Banquet Foods Corp., St. Louis, 1981-82; v.p. ConAgra, Inc., Omaha, 1981-82; pres., chief operating officer ConAgra Prepared Food Cos., Omaha, 1982-86, asst. to chmn. bd., 1986—; bd. dirs. Bishop-Clarkson Hosp., Swanson Ctr. Nutrition, Omaha C. of C., Nebr. Futures, Inc., Henry Doorly Zoo, Omaha Food Bank. Bd. dirs. NCCJ. Mem. Am. Frozen Food Inst. (dir.), Frozen Food Action Communications Team (dir.), Am. Meat Inst. (bd. dirs.), Grocery Mfrs. Am. Office: ConAgra Inc One Central Park Plaza Omaha NE 68102

PHILLIPS, JOHN DAVID, communications executive; b. Charlotte, N.C., Nov. 27, 1942; s. Louis and A. Viola (Pack) P.; m. Cheryl Helen Rudd; children: Hunter, Scott, Andrew, Lauren. Student, U. Va., 1962-63. Pres. RMS Distbg., Frankfurt, West Germany, 1965-66, NGK Spark Plugs, Atlanta, 1967-82; pres., chief exec. officer Advanced Telecommunication, Atlanta, 1982—, also bd. dirs.; owner Specialized Hauling Trucking Co., 1987—; bd. dirs. Pub. Utility Trucking, Forest Pk., Ga., 1985—. Served to capt. USMC, 1963-64. Republican. Methodist.

PHILLIPS, JOSEPH DOUGLAS, corporate executive, consultant; b. Prescott, Ariz., Aug. 12, 1938; s. Thomas Alexander and Gertrude Bernadet (Zilles) P.; m. Judith Ann Fuller, Aug. 26, 1961 (div. Aug. 1983): children: Scott, Shana; m. Elizabeth Susanne Williams, Sept. 22, 1985; 1 child, Tara. AA, Mt. San Antonio Coll., 1962; BS in Mktg., Calif. Poly., 1964; MBA in Mgmt., Golden Gate U., 1967. Market research analyst Standard Oil Co. of Calif., San Francisco, 1964-67; market research analyst Merck, Sharp & Dohme, West Point, Pa., 1967-70, supr. market research, 1970-72, product mgr., 1972-75; dir. mktg. and planning Merck, Sharp & Dohme Internat., Rahway, N.J., 1975-79; dir. human resources Merck & Co., Inc., Rahway, 1979-84, dir. corp. planning, 1984-87, sr. dir. corp. planning, 1987—; mem. adv. bd. Nat. Home and Sch. Inst., Washington, 1983—; chmn. World Congress on Human Aspects Automation, Long Beach, Calif., 1986; bd. dirs. Healthways Found., Woodcliff Lakes, N.J., Inst. for Am. Values, N.Y.C. Author, editor: The HR Scanner, 1982. Commr. police, supr. Montgomery Twp., Pa., 1970-73; chmn., mayor Montgomery Twp., 1972-73. Served with USN, 1957-61. Veri Christee fellow West Coll. Placement Assn., 1966; named one of Outstanding Citizens, Montgomery Mchts., 1973; recipient Merit award Ctrs. for Disease Control, 1973, Letter of Commendation Pres. Richard M. Nixon, 1973, Douglass medal Douglass Coll., 1986. Mem. Planning Forum. Republican. Roman Catholic. Office: Merck & Co Inc 126 E Lincoln Ave Rahway NJ 07065

PHILLIPS, KATHLEEN JOAN, lawyer; b. Jersey City, Apr. 14, 1946; d. Irving S. and Frances (Dunberg) P. BA, U. Rochester, 1968; MA, Boston Coll., 1974; JD, Boston U., 1978. Bar: Mass. 1978. From asst. counsel to assoc. counsel Bank of Boston, 1978-84; sr. counsel Computervision, Bedford, Mass., 1984-88; v.p., gen. counsel, sec. Harris Graphics Corp. subs. Heidelberger Druckmaschineu, Dover, N.H., 1988—; bd. dirs. New Eng. Loan Mktg. Corp., Braintree, Mass. Mem. ABA, Mass. Bar Assn., Nat. Assn. Corp. Counsel. Home: 364 Main St North Andover MA 01845 Office: Harris Graphics 121 Broadway Dover NH 03820-1289

PHILLIPS, KENNETH L., telecommunications executive; b. N.Y.C., Mar. 31, 1948; s. Jack Phillips and Jacqueline (Kasper) Ehrman. MA, N.Y. Sch. Social Reserach, N.Y.C., 1974; MS, CUNY, 1977; PhD, Columbia U., 1983. Dir. telecommunications Honeywell Corp., N.Y.C., 1968-72; co-dir. Castalia Seminars Harvard U., Lugano, Switzerland, 1971-74; chmn. Datagram Systems Group, White Plains, N.Y., 1974-76; v.p. telecommunications policy Citicorp, N.A., N.Y.C., 1976—; prof. Tisch Grad. Sch. N.Y.U., 1980—; chmn. Corp. Communication-Telecommunications Users, N.Y.C., 1982—; ptnr. Hargadon, Phillips & Solomon, N.Y.C., 1987—. Author: Studies, NonDeterministic Psychology, 1980; contbr. articles to numerous jours. Mem. N.Y. State AGLP (dir. legal affairs, pres. 1985), Soc. of N.S.W. Australia. Democrat. Clubs: Cosmos (Washington D.C.), Pemling. Home: 41 Fifth Ave New York NY 10003 Office: 399 Park Ave New York NY 10043

PHILLIPS, LARRY DUANE, gemologist, appraiser; b. Silver City, N.Mex., Nov. 19, 1948; s. Fredric Duane and Bernice Larry (Dannelley) P.; m. Ellen Catherine Keaveny, May 6, 1972; 1 child, Tamara Lynn. Student, N.Mex. State U., 1966-70, Ind. U., 1986—; grad. in gemology, Gemological Inst. Am. Cert. gemologist and appraiser. Jeweler, designer Larry Phillips Studios, Albuquerque, 1971-73; jewelry mfr. The Cloud Gatherer, Albuquerque, 1973-78; custom jeweler, gemologist The Jewelry Works, Albuquerque, 1978-82; gemologist, appraiser Butterfield Jewelers, Albuquerque, 1982—. Musician, entertainer Larry Phillips Studios, Albuquerque, 1971—; entertainment dir. Four Hills Country Club, Albuquerque, 1984-85. Mem. Internat. Soc. Appraiser (designated, gem and jewelry com. 1987-88), Am. Soc. Appraisers (v.p. N.Mex. chpt. 1987-88), Am. Gem. Soc. (appraisal com. 1987-88), Nat. Jewelers Assn., N.Mex. Jewelers Assn. (treas. 1984), Accredited Gemologists Assn. Club: Albuquerque Musicians Co-op (pres. 1977-78). Home: 801 Marie Park NE Albuquerque NM 87123

PHILLIPS, LARRY EDWARD, lawyer; b. Pitts., July 5, 1942; s. Jack F. and Jean H. (Houghtelin) P.; m. Karla Ann Hennings, June 5, 1976; 1 son, Andrew H.; 1 stepson, John W. Dean IV. B.A., Hamilton Coll., 1964; J.D., U. Mich., 1967. Bars: Pa. 1967, U.S. Dist. Ct. (we. dist.) Pa. 1967, U.S. Tax Ct. 1969. Assoc. Buchanan, Ingersoll, Rodewald, Kyle & Buerger, P.C. (now Buchanan Ingersoll P.C.), Pitts., 1967-73, mem., 1973—. Bd. dirs. Psychol. Service of Pitts., 1972—, pres., 1985-87. Mem. Am. Coll. Tax Counsel, Tax Mgmt. Inc. (adv. bd.), Pitts. Tax Club, ABA (sect. taxation, com. on corp. tax and sect. real property, probate and trust law), Allegheny County Bar Assn., Pa. Bar Assn. Republican. Presbyterian. Clubs: Duquesne, St. Clair County. Contbr. articles to profl. jours. Office: Buchanan Ingersoll 600 Grant St 57th Fl Pittsburgh PA 15219

PHILLIPS, LEO HAROLD, JR., lawyer; b. Detroit, Jan. 10, 1945; s. Leo Harold and Martha C. (Oberg) P.; m. Patricia Margaret Halcomb, Sept. 3, 1983. BA summa cum laude, Hillsdale Coll., 1967; MA, U. Mich., 1968; JD cum laude, 1973; LLM magna cum laude, Free Univ. of Brussels, 1974. Bar: Mich. 1974, N.Y. 1975, U.S. Supreme Ct. 1977, D.C. 1979. Fgn. lectr. Pusan Nat. U. (Korea), 1969-70; assoc. Alexander & Green, N.Y.C., 1974-77; counsel Overseas Pvt. Investment Corp., Washington, 1977-80, sr. counsel, 1980-82, asst. gen. counsel, 1982-85; asst. gen. counsel Manor Care, Inc., Silver Spring, Md., 1985—, asst. sec. 1988—; vol. Peace Corps, Pusan, 1968-71; mem. program for sr. mgrs. in govt. Harvard U., Cambridge, Mass., 1982. Contbr. articles to legal jours. Chmn. legal affairs com. Essex Condominium Assn., Washington, 1979-81; deacon Chevy Chase Presbyn. Ch., Washington, 1984-87, moderator, 1985-87, supt. ch. sch., elder, trustee, 1987—, pres., 1988—. Recipient Alumni Achievement award Hillsdale Coll., 1981; Meritorious Honor award Overseas Pvt. Investment Corp., 1981, Superior Achievement award, 1984. Mem. ABA (internat. fin. transactions com., vice chmn. com. internat. ins. law), Am. Soc. Internat. Law (Jessup Internat. Law moot ct. judge semi-final rounds 1978-83), Internat. Law Assn. (Am. br.; com. sec. 1982), D.C. Bar, N.Y. State Bar Assn., Royal Asiatic Soc. (Korea br.), State Bar Mich., Washington Fgn. Law Soc. (sec.-treas. 1980-81, bd. dirs., program coordinator 1981-82, v.p. 1982-83, pres.-elect 1983-84, pres. 1984-85, chmn. nominating com. 1986, 88), Washington Internat. Trade Assn. (bd. dirs. 1984-87), Assn. Bar City N.Y., Hillsdale Coll. Alumni Assn. (co-chmn. Washington area 1977—). Club: University (N.Y.C.). Home: 4740 Connecticut Ave NW Apt 702 Washington DC 20008 Office: Manor Care Inc 10750 Columbia Pike Silver Spring MD 20901

PHILLIPS, MICHAEL JOHN, financial consultant; b. Istanbul, Turkey, Jan. 20, 1948; came to U.S., 1985; s. Leslie Roy and Yolanda (Minutelli) P.; m. Wendy Patricia Moore, Nov. 14, 1970; children: Katherine Anne, Elizabeth Rose. LLB, U. London, 1970. Investment officer Barclays Investment Mgmt., London, 1971-75, asst. fund mgr., 1975-77, fund mgr., 1977-81; mng. dir. designate Frank Russell Internat., London, 1981-83, mng. dir., 1983-85; dir. internat. cons. Frank Russell Co., Tacoma, 1985-88, dir. cons., 1988—. Contbr. articles to jours., chpts. to books. Mem. London Soc. Investment Analysts, Seattle Soc. Investment Analysts, Tacoma Club. Office: Frank Russell Co PO Box 1616 Tacoma WA 98401

PHILLIPS, PAMELA KIM, lawyer; b. San Diego, Feb. 23, 1958; d. John Gerald and Nancy Kimiko (Tabuchi) P. BA, The Am. U., 1978; JD, Georgetown U., 1982. Bar: N.Y. 1983, U.S. Dist. Ct. (so. dist.) N.Y. Assoc. atty. Curtis, Mallet-Prevost, Colt & Mosle, N.Y.C., 1982-84; assoc. LeBoeuf, Lamb, Leiby & MacRae, N.Y.C., 1984—. Mng. editor The Tax Lawyer, Georgetown U. Law Sch., Washington, 1980-81. Halloween Benefit com. mem. The Fresh Air Fund, N.Y.C., 1988-89. Am. Univ. scholar, Washington, 1976-78. Mem. ABA (mem. exec. com. young lawyer div. Young Lawyer Devel. Com.), Women's Bar Assn., Assn. of Bar of City of N.Y. (sec. Young Lawyers com. 1987-89, chmn. 1989—), Georgetown Club (N.Y.C.). Home: 107 E 36th St #3 New York NY 10016 Office: LeBoeuf Lamb Leiby & MacRae 520 Madison Ave New York NY 10022

PHILLIPS, PHILIP KAY, stained glass manufacturing and retail company executive; b. Kansas City, Mo., Jan. 3, 1933; s. Ernest Lloyd and Mildred Blanche (Moser) P.; B.A., Bob Jones U., Greenville, S.C., 1958; postgrad. Central Mo. State U., 1977-78, 81-83; m. Constance Diana Lucas, June 12, 1955; children—John Allen, David Lee, Stephen Philip, Daniel Paul, Joy Christine. Ordained minister Baptist Ch., 1959; pastor Mt. Moriah Baptist Ch., Clarksburg, Mo. 1958-59; security officer Mo. Dept. Corrections, Jefferson City, Mo., 1959-64; field mgr. office Darby Corp. and Piping Contractors Inc., Kansas City, Kans., 1965-72, safety and security dir. Darby Corp. and Leavenworth Steel Inc., Kansas City, 1972-84; with Stained Glass Creations, North Kansas City, Mo., 1984—. Mem. planning com. Kans. Gov.'s Indsl. Safety and Health Conf., 1977-78, chmn. mfg. sect., 1978. Mem. Nat. Safety Mgmt. Soc., Am. Soc. Safety Engrs. (chpt. exec. com. 1980-81, treas. chpt. 1981-82, sec. chpt. 1982-83, 2d v.p. chpt. 1983-84, 1st v.p. 1984-85, chpt. pres. 1985-86), Kans. Safety Assn. (v.p., mem. exec. com. 1979-80), North Kansas City Mchts. Assn. (pres. 1986-87, bd. dirs. 1988-89, treas. 1989—). Home: 3205 NE 66th St Gladstone MO 64119 Office: Stained Glass Creations 316 Armour Rd North Kansas City MO 64116

PHILLIPS, RICHARD LEE, health insurance financial executive; b. Phila., Apr. 30, 1941; s. Alexander and Dorothea (Rathgeber) P.; m. E. Katherine Peoples, Nov. 23, 1963; children: Pamela B., Kristen A. BA, Wesleyan U., 1963; MBA, Drexel U., 1973. Trust adminstrn. trainee First Pa. Bank, Phila., 1963-65; mgr. auto ins. acctg. Ins. Co. N.Am., Phila., 1965-67; mgr. adminstrn. and research services Sun Oil Co., Phila., 1967-71; orgn. and systems devel. cons. Sun Oil Co., Radnor, Pa., 1971-73, corp. budget coord., 1973-75; chief fin. officer P.R. Sun Oil Co., San Juan, P.R., 1975-78; controller Pa. Blue Shield, Camp Hill, 1978-82, v.p. fin., 1982—; bd. dirs. Health Info. Reporting Co., Chgo., sec.-treas. 1986—; treas. Pro-Forma Enterprises, Ltd., Boiling Springs, 1988—. Mem. Fin. Execs. Inst., Ins. Acctg. and Systems Assn., Cen. Pa. Investment Mgrs. Assn. Republican. Lutheran. Home: 779 Dogwood Terr Boiling Springs PA 17007 Office: Pa Blue Shield 1800 Center St Camp Hill PA 17011

PHILLIPS, ROBERT MAYFIELD, consumer products executive; b. Glen Ridge, N.J., July 15, 1938; s. John and Margaret (Ballou) P.; m. Patricia Cole, Dec. 4, 1965; children: Graham E., Lora B. B.A., Dartmouth Coll., 1960; M.B.A., Columbia U., 1961. Vice pres. mktg. health and beauty div. Chesebrough-Ponds Inc., Westport, Conn., 1974-76; pres. div. Chesebrough-Ponds Inc., 1976-79, exec. v.p., 1985-86, pres., chief operating officer, 1986—, also dir.; pres. G.E.C. div. Nabisco, East Hanover, N.J., 1979-81; exec. v.p. Clairol, N.Y.C., 1981-84; pres. Clairol, 1984-85. Trustee King Sch., Stamford, Conn., 1984—; bd. dirs. Stamford Symphony, 1978—. Served to 1st lt. U.S. Army, 1961-63. Clubs: University (N.Y.C.); Stamford Yacht; Madison Beach (Conn.). Home: 291 Ocean Dr E Stamford CT 06902 *

PHILLIPS, ROBERT WESLEY, university administrator; b. East St. Louis, Ill., Mar. 3, 1946; s. Everett Wesley and Margaret Marie (Wells) P. BS in Acctg., So. Ill. U., 1973; MBA in Mgmt., Golden Gate U., 1978. Auditor Mo. br. U.S. Army Audit Agy., St. Louis, 1974; acct. funds controller's office Stanford (Calif.) U., 1974-77, mgr. gen. acctg. controller's office, 1977-79, mgr. aux. and service ctr. acctg., 1979-80, mgr. fund's controller's office, 1980, dir. fin. info. tech. services, 1980—; prin. Systems Cons. Consortium Inc., Palo Alto, Calif., 1987—; cons. Input, Inc., Mountain View, Calif., 1980—; teaching asst. So. Ill. U., 1973. Served with U.S. Army, 1966-68, Vietnam. Office: Chief Fin Officer Systems Cons Consortium Inc Palo Alto CA also: Stanford U Stanford Data Ctr Stanford CA 94999-0305

PHILLIPS, ROGER, steel company executive; b. Ottawa, Ont., Can., Dec. 17, 1939; s. Norman William Frederick and Elizabeth (Marshall) P.; m. Katherine Ann Wilson, June 9, 1962; 1 child, Andrée Claire. B.Sc., McGill U., Montreal, 1960. Vice pres. mill products Alcan Can. Products Ltd., Toronto, Ont., Can., 1969-70, exec. v.p., 1971-75; pres. Alcan Smelters and Chems. Ltd., Montreal, Que., Can., 1976-79; v.p. tech. Alcan Aluminum Ltd., Montreal, Que., Can., 1980-81; pres. Alcan Internat. Ltd., Montreal, Que., Can., 1980-81; pres., chief exec. officer IPSCO Inc., Regina, Sask., Can., 1982—; bd. dirs. Royal Trustco Ltd.; sr. mem. Conf. Bd. Inc., N.Y., 1987—. Chmn. Council for Can. Unity, Montreal, 1987—; bd. dirs. Conf. Bd. Inc., N.Y.C., 1984-87, Inst. for Polit. Involvement, Toronto, 1982-88. Mem. Can. Assn. Physicists, Bus. Council on Nat. Issues, Am. Iron and Steel Inst. (bd. dirs. 1984—), Saskatchewan C. of C. (bd. dirs. 1984—), Que. C. of C. (pres. 1981), Inst. for Saskatchewan Enterprise (pres.), Pub. Policy Forum (bd. dirs.). Clubs: Assiniboia (Regina); St. Denis, University (Montreal). Home: 3220 Albert St, Regina, SK Canada S4S 3N9 Office: IPSCO Inc, PO Box 1670, Regina, SK Canada S4P 3C7

PHILLIPS, RORY STEVEN, commercial banker; b. San Francisco, May 5, 1952; s. Russell Parr and Olive Marie (Sharp) P.; m. Mary Elizabeth Zehender, May 28, 1978; children: Melissa, Ryan, Sean. BA, U. Calif., Davis, 1974; MA, Fletcher Sch. Law and Diplomacy, Medford, Mass., 1975. Asst. treas. Chem. Bank, N.Y.C., 1975-79; v.p. Marine Midland Bank, N.Y.C., 1979-84, Credit Lyonnais, N.Y.C., 1984-85; v.p., mgr. corp. banking Kansallis-Osake-Pankki, N.Y.C., 1985—. Office: Kansallis-Osake-Pankki 575 Fifth Ave New York NY 10017

PHILLIPS, SCOTT DOUGLAS, financial advisor; b. Los Angeles, Dec. 11, 1946; s. Douglas Clifford and Marian (Smith) P.; m. Jeanne Williams, May 12, 1976; children: Adam, Nicole, Alexis, Clark. BS, Brigham Young U., 1971; postgrad., U. Pa., 1987, Am. Coll. Chartered fin. cons., CLU, cert. fin. planner. Fin. adivsor Pacific Fin. Cons. Corp., Salt Lake City, 1975-84; advanced investment cons. Forsight Fin. Group, Salt Lake City, 1984—; prin., registered investment advisors Fullmer & Phillips, Salt Lake City, 1984—; pres. Petro Ventures Inc., 1981-88; registered rep., mng. exec. Integrated Resources Equity Corp., 1984—; lectr. CPA Utah Annual Conv., 1986, several seminars; speaker CPA Assn., 1986-87. Mem. Internat. Assn. Cert. Fin. Planners, Soc. CLU & ChFC, Nat. Assn. Life Underwriters, Toastmaster (sgt.-at-arms 1985-86). Republican. Mormon. Office: Fullmer & Phillips 4460 S Highland Dr Suite 300 Salt Lake City UT 84124

PHILLIPS, THOMAS L., corporate executive; b. Istanbul, Turkey, May 2, 1924. BSEE, Va. Poly. Inst., 1947, MSEE, 1948; hon. doctorates, Stonehill Coll., 1968, Northeastern U., 1968, Lowell U., 1970, Gordon Coll., 1970, Boston Coll., 1974, Babson Coll., 1981, Suffolk U., 1986. With Raytheon Co., Lexington, Mass., 1948—, exec. v.p., 1961-64, chief operating officer, 1964-68, pres., 1964-75, chief exec. officer, 1968—, chmn. bd., 1975—; bd. dirs. John Hancock Mut. Life Ins. Co., State St. Investment Corp., Knight-Ridder, Inc. Trustee Gordon Coll., Northeastern U.; mem. corp. Joslin Diabetes Ctr., Mus. Sci., Boston. Recipient Meritorious Pub. Service award for work in Sparrow III missile system, U.S. Navy, 1958. Mem. Nat. Acad. Engring., Bus. Council, Bus. Roundtable. Office: Raytheon Co 141 Spring St Lexington MA 02173

PHILLIPS, WARREN HENRY, newspaperman; b. June 28, 1926; s. Abraham and Juliette (Rosenberg) P.; m. Barbara Anne Thomas, June 16, 1951; children: Lisa, Leslie, Nina. AB, Queens Coll., 1947, LHD (hon.), 1987; JD (hon.), U. Portland, 1973; LHD (hon.), Pace U., 1982, L.I. U., 1987; DHL, Queen's (N.Y.) Coll. Copyreader Wall St. Jour., 1947-48; fgn. corr. Wall St. Jour., Germany, 1949-50; chief London Bur., 1950-51, fgn. editor, 1951-53, news editor, 1953-54, mng. editor Midwest edit., 1954-57, mng. editor, 1957-65; exec. editor Dow Jones & Co., 1965-70, v.p., gen. mgr., 1970-71, editorial dir., 1971—, exec. v.p., 1972, pres., 1972-79, chief exec. officer, 1975—; pub. Wall Street Journal, 1975-88; chmn. bd. Dow Jones & Co., 1978—, also dir.; copyreader Stars & Stripes European edit., 1949; Pres. Am. Council Edn. for Journalism, 1971-73; mem. Pulitzer Prizes Bd., 1976-87. Author: (with Robert Keatley) China: Behind the Mask, 1973. Trustee Columbia U., 1980—; mem. vis. com. Kennedy Sch. Govt. Harvard U., 1984—; mem. corp. adv. bd. Queens Coll. Served with AUS, 1943-45. Named one of Ten Outstanding Young Men in U.S. U.S. Jaycees, 1958; inducted into the Info. Industry Assn's. Hall of Fame, 1984. Mem. Am. Newspaper Pubs. Assn. (dir. 1976-84), Am. Soc. Newspaper Editors (pres. 1975-76), Bridgehamton (N.Y.) Club, River Club. Office: Dow Jones & Co Inc 200 Liberty St New York NY 10281

PHILLIPS, WILLIAM EUGENE, advertising agency executive; b. Chgo., Jan. 7, 1930; s. William E. and Alice P.; children: Michael, Tom, Sarah. B.S., Cornell U., 1951; M.B.A., Northwestern U., 1955. Brand mgr. Procter & Gamble, Cin., 1955-59; with Ogilvy & Mather, N.Y.C., 1959—; chief exec. officer Ogilvy Group, 1981-88, chmn., mem. exec. com., 1988—; dir. Ogilvy Group. Trustee Outward Bound, Cornell U., City Vol. Corps, N.Y.C.; mem. bus. adv. bd. Mus. Modern Art, Cornell's Sapsucker Woods; dirs. Am. Women's Econ. Devel. Council. Served to lt. (j.g.) USN, 1951-54, Korea. Mem. Am. Assn. Advt. Agys. (bd. dirs.). Clubs: Old Lyme Country, Am. Alpine. Home: 200 North Cove Rd Old Saybrook CT 06475 Office: The Ogilvy Group Inc 2 E 48th St New York NY 10017

PHILP, FRANCIS HIGGINSON, banker; b. N.Y.C., Aug. 21, 1930; s. Leonard Jerome and Louise Genevieve (Fellows) P.; A.B. cum laude, Princeton, 1952; postgrad. Harvard Law Sch., 1952-54, 56-58. Asso. law firm Dunnington, Bartholow & Miller, 1958-59, Dominick & Dominick, 1960-63 (both N.Y.C.); asst. treas. Empire Trust Co. (merged into Bank N.Y. 1967), N.Y.C., 1963-66, asst. v.p., 1968-72; v.p. Fiduciary Trust Co. N.Y., N.Y.C., 1972-88, sr. v.p., 1988—. Trustee N.Y. Infirmary-Beekman Downtown Hosp., Big Bros. N.Y., Clarion Music Soc., Council Arts Westchester, Clear Pool Camp, Carmel, N.Y., Princeton Library, N.Y.C.; pres. bd. trustees Fund for Blind; mem. Alumni Council, Phillips Exeter Acad. Mem. N.Y. Soc. Security Analysts, SAR, SR, Soc. Colonial Wars, Pilgrims of U.S. Republican. Episcopalian. Clubs: Union, Brook, Down Town Assn. (N.Y.C.); Larchmont (N.Y.) Yacht. Home: 25 Rocky Rd Larchmont NY 10538 Office: Fiduciary Trust Co NY 2 World Trade Ctr 94th Fl New York NY 10048

PHINIZY, ROBERT BURCHALL, electronics executive; b. Ben Hill, Ga., June 30, 1926; B.S., U. Ariz., 1951; postgrad. U. So. Calif., 1952-55, UCLA, 1956-62; children—Robert B., William, David. Pres., LB Products, Santa Monica, Calif., 1954-68, IMC Magnetics Western, South Gate, Calif., 1968-69, Am. Electronics, Fullerton, Calif., 1969-71; gen. mgr. electronics div. Eaton Co., Anaheim, Calif., 1971-82; pres., chief exec. officer Genisco Tech. Corp., Compton, Calif., 1972-83; chmn. bd., chief exec. officer Genisco Computers Corp., Costa Mesa, Calif., 1983—; chmn., chief exec. officerTrans Tech. Alliances, Calif., 1986— . Bd. dirs. U. Calif., Dominguez Hills; mem. Los Angeles Town Hall; bd. chmn. Calif. State U. Found., 1986. Served to capt. USN, 1943-47, USNR, 1947-80. Fellow Coll. Engrs. Los Angeles; mem. IEEE, Communication and Computers Indsl. Assn. Electronics Assn. Calif. (treas. 1986). Democrat. Contbr. articles to tech. jours.; patentee in field. Home: PO Box 151 Yorba Linda CA 92686 Office: 3365 E Miraloma Ave Anaheim CA 92806

PHIPPS, ALLEN MAYHEW, management consultant; b. Seattle, Oct. 3, 1938; s. Donald Mayhew and Virginia (McGinn) P.; B.A. in Econs., U. Calif., Berkeley, 1961; M.B.A. with honors, Stanford U., 1969; m. Joyce Elisabeth 00060; Aug. 21, 1971; children—Ramsey Mayhew, Justin Beckwith. Security analyst Morgan Guaranty Trust Co., 1968; with Boston Cons. Group, Inc., 1969—, mgr. 1971-74, mem. sr. team, Calif., 1974-77, corp. v.p., dir., 1975—; mgr. Boston Cons. Group, G.mb.H, Munich. W. Ger., 1978-82, partner-in-charge West Coast client devel., Menlo Park, Calif., 1982-84; pres. Techno Digital Systems, Inc., 1984—; pres., chief exec. officer, Techno Digital System (Sellectek, Inc.), 1984-85; exec. v.p., Regis McKenna Inc., Palo Alto, Calif., 1985-87; pvt. practice mgmt. cons., Menlo Pk., 1987—. Served to capt. U.S. Army, 1961-67. Decorated Bronze Star, Army Commendation medal with 2 oak leaf clusters. Mem. Alpha Delta Phi. Republican. Presbyterian. Clubs: Bohemian (San Francisco); Stanford (Calif.) Golf; Univ. (Palo Alto). Home: 33 Prado Secoya Atherton CA 94025 Office: Allen M Phipps Mgmt Cons 800 Menlo Ave Ste 120 Menlo Park CA 94025

PHIPPS, ARTHUR RAYMOND, manufacturing company executive; b. Waltham, Mass., Aug. 28, 1931; s. David Raymond and Florence (MacPhee) P.; m. Lenore Bolling, June 3, 1953; children: Lenore E., Amy S. BS in Engring., U.S. Mil. Acad., 1953; MS in Electonics, U. Rochester, 1962. Commd. 2d lt. USAF, 1953, advanced through grades to lt., 1953, resigned, 1957; engr., mgr. Gen. Dynamics, Rochester, N.Y., 1957-62; chief engr. Xerox Corp., Rochester, 1964, v.p. duplicator devel., v.p., mgr. world wide services, v.p., gen. mgr. copier strategic bus. unit, 1970-86, v.p., mgr. U.S. service op.; pres. Lifeline Systems Inc., Watertown, Mass., 1987—. Mem. Westpoint Soc. New Eng., Harvard's Pres.'s Club. Office: Lifeline Systems Inc One Market Place Watertown MA 02172

PHIPPS, C(ORNELIUS) MARK, plastics specialities company executive; b. LaCross, Wis., Apr. 22, 1921; s. C.H. and Grace (Hart) P.; m. Jean D. Ecklor, Feb. 9, 1946; children: Cornelius Jr., Hal A. BS, U. Wis., 1949. Product developer Marathon Corp., Menasha, Wis., 1950-54; salesman Fed. Paper Co., Chgo., 1954-59; v.p. Plastifilm, Inc., Wheaton, Ill., 1959-84; pres. Plastic Specialties, Inc., Carol Stream, Ill., 1965—. Inventor power source for balloon catheter, others. Sgt. U.S. Army, 1942-45, ETO. Home: 1001 Crescent St Glen Ellyn IL 60137

PHOCAS, GEORGE JOHN, international lawyer, business executive; b. N.Y.C., Dec. 1, 1927; m. Katrin Gorny, Feb. 26, 1966; 1 child, George Alexander. A.B., U. Chgo., 1950, J.D., 1953. Bar: N.Y. 1955, U.S. Supreme Ct. 1962. Assoc. Sullivan & Cromwell, N.Y.C., 1953-56; counsel Creole Petroleum Corp., Caracas, Venezuela, 1956-60; internat. negotiator Standard Oil Co. N.J. (Exxon), 1960-63; sr. ptnr. Casey, Lane & Mittendorf, London, 1963-72, counsel, 1972—; exec. v.p. Occidental Petroleumm Corp., Los Angeles, 1972-74; adv., U.S. del. UN, ECAFE, Teheran, 1963. Trustee Assn. Naval Aviation, Washington, Owl's Head Aviation Mus., Maine; mem. vis. bd. U. Chgo. Law Sch.; bd. visitors U. Chgo. Law Sch. Served to capt. U.S. Army. Mem. Law Soc. London, Brit. Inst. Comparative Law, Am. Soc. Internat. Law, ABA, Assn. Bar City N.Y. Clubs: Boodles (London); Metropolitan (N.Y.C.); Sleepy Hollow. Home: 28 Aubrey Walk, London England W8 also: 5020 Goodridge Ave Riverdale NY 10471

PHYPERS, DEAN PINNEY, retired computer company executive; b. Cleve., Jan. 13, 1929; s. Fordham S. and Grace Ellen (Pinney) P.; children: Dean A., Toni T., William C., Jonathan W., Katharine L. B.A. in Physics, Harvard U., 1950; postgrad., U. Mich. Sch. Bus., 1952. With IBM, 1955-87; v.p. bus. plans IBM, Armonk, N.Y., 1972-74; v.p. fin. and planning IBM, 1974-79, sr. v.p. fin. and planning, dir., 1979-82, sr. v.p., dir., 1982-87; bd. dirs. Bethlehem Steel, Am. Internat. Group, Church & Dwight Co., Inc., N.Y.C., Cytogen Corp., Cambrex Inc. Trustee Com. for Econ. Devel. Served with USNR, 1952-55. Mem. Am. Planning Assn. (trustee). Home: 831 Oenoke Ridge Rd New Canaan CT 06840 Office: IBM Corp Old Orchard Rd Ormonk NY 10504

PIAZZA, MARIE THERESA, business educator; b. N.Y.C., May 26, 1928; d. Anthony and Marie Theresa (Capri) P. BS in Acctg., Fairleigh Dickinson U., 1972. Cert. tchr., N.J. Acctg. clk. N.Y. Life Ins. Co., N.Y.C., 1946-49; stenographer Civil Aeronautics Adminstrn., Kennedy Airport, N.Y., 1949-50; adminstrv. asst. Nipkow & Kobelt, Inc., N.Y.C., 1950-54; sec. to v.p. Schwab Bros. Corp., N.Y.C., 1954-61, adminstrv. asst., 1963-70; sec. to dir.

engring. Wellington Electronics, Inc., Englewood, N.J., 1961-62; exec. sec. York Radio Corp., South Hackensack, N.J., 1970-72; bus. tchr. Cresskill (N.J.) High Sch., 1972—. Named Tchr. of the Year and recipient grant Gov. Kean's Tchr. Recognition Program, 1986. Mem. Am. Soc. Women Accts. (dir. 1985—), NEA, N.J. Bus. Edn. Assn., Cresskill Edn. Assn., Phi Zeta Kappa, Phi Omega Epsilon. Home: 274 Baldwin Ave New Milford NJ 07646 Office: Cresskill High Sch Lincoln Dr Cresskill NJ 07626

PICARD, HOWARD RICHARD, data processing executive; b. Albany, N.Y., Nov. 9, 1939; s. William Henry and Mary Elizabeth (Van O'Linda) P.; m. Ann Priscilla Marino, Nov. 26, 1960; children: Lori, James, Joseph, Michael, Amy. Diploma, Albany Bus. Coll., 1959. With adminstrn. and sales IBM Corp., Albany, 1963-74; mgr. data processing Sweet Assocs., Schenectady, N.Y., 1974-77; mgr. info. processing Schenectady Chems., Inc., 1977—. With USN, 1959-63. Roman Catholic.

PICARD, LAURENT, management educator, administrator, consultant; b. Quebec, Que., Can., Oct. 27, 1927; s. Edouard and Alice (Gingras) P.; m. Therese Picard; children: Andre, Marc, Robert, Denys, Jean-Louis. BA, Laval U., Quebec, 1947, BS, 1954; DBA, Harvard U., 1964. Prof. U. Montreal, Que., Can., 1962-68, dir. bus. adminstrn. dept., 1964-68; exec. v.p. Can. Broadcasting Corp., Ottawa, Ont., 1968-72, pres., chief exec. officer, 1972-75; joint prof. McGill U. and U. Montreal, 1977-78; dean faculty mgmt. McGill U., Montreal, 1978-86, prof., 1986—; mem. Royal Commn. on Newspapers, Royal Commn. on Econ. Union and Devel. Prospects for Can.; conciliation commr. Maritime Employers Assn., Port of Montreal; bd. dirs. Astral Bellevue Pathe, Lombard-Odier Trust Co., Cablevision Ltd., Jean Coutu Group, Télémetropole, Inc., Farmico, Canagex Placements, Inc., Videotron, Fondation des diplomés de Polytechnique; cons. to industry; guest speaker internat. meetings. Contbr. articles to profl. jours. Chmn. Nat. Book Festival, 1978-79; chmn. jury Prix Gerin Lajoie, Ministry Cultural Affairs, 1982. Decorated companion Order of Can., 1977. Mem. Commonwealth Broadcasting Assn. (1st pres.). Home: 5602 Wilderton Ave, Montreal, PQ Canada H3T 1R9 Office: McGill U Faculty Mgmt, 1001 Sherbrooke St W, Montreal, PQ Canada H3A 1G5

PICARD, THOMAS JOSEPH, JR., manufacturers representative; b. Boston, Dec. 7, 1933; s. Thomas Joseph and Bertha Mildred (Brightman) P.; B.S. in Mech. Engring., U. Mass., 1959; M.B.A., Rollins Coll., 1985; m. Renee E. Coulmas, Aug. 20, 1977; children by previous marriage: T. Gerald, Pamela P. Mfg. engr. Gen. Electric Co., 1959-60; application and sales engr. Masoneilan Div., McGraw Edison Co., 1960-65; v.p. M.D. Duncan & Assocs., Inc., Orlando, Fla., 1965-74, pres., 1974—. Pres., Brookshire Sch. PTA, Winter Park, Fla., 1969-71, Glenridge Jr. High Sch. PTA, Winter Park, 1972-73; v.p. Winter Park Little League, 1968; mem. Orange County Republican Exec. Com., 1973; mem. 35th Internat. Sympsium Com., 1988—. Served with AUS, 1953-55. Named Exec. of Month, Orlando Area, Sta. WDBO, June 1977; profl. tennis umpire. Mem. Instrument Soc. Am. (sr.; chmn. 1980, dist. v.p. 1981-83, nominating com., chmn. dist. honors and awards com. 1987—, mem. nat. edn. com., profl. cert. com., parliamentarian 1984-86, dir. edn. dept. 1985—, v.p. 1989—, pres's. adv. com. Aerospace Industries div.1988—), U.S. Tennis Assn. Conglist. Clubs: Rotary Orange County East (charter mem., pres. 1972-73), Masons.

PICCHIONE, NICHOLAS EVERETT, accountant, publishing company executive; b. Providence, July 9, 1928; s. Nicholas and Lillian Lucille (Baldoni) P.; m. Ann Marie Orr, Nov. 11, 1951; children: Deborah A., Nicholas II, Nancy O., Mary E., Helen L. BS, U. R.I., 1950; postgrad., Bentley Coll., 1955. CPA, R.I. Ptnr. Nicholas Picchione & Co., Providence, 1956-83; pvt. practice acctg. Warwick, R.I., 1983—; treas., John J. Orr & Son, Inc., Providence, 1956—, also bd. dirs.; treas. Dome Pub. Co., Inc., Warwick, 1950-66, pres., 1966-88, chmn., 1988—, Data Binding, Inc., Warwick, 1985-66, pres., 1966-88, chmn., 1988—; trustee Dome Enterprises Trust, Warwick, 1972—. Co-author: Dome Tax Tip, 11982; author: Dome Tip Income Record, 1986, Dome Travel Expense Record and Mileage Log, Dome Travel and Entertainment Record. Mem. bd. govs. Gordon Sch., East Providence, 1959-65, treas. 1962-65; bd. dirs. , treas. R.I. Arts Festival, Providence, 1958-70, Moses Brown Sch. Alumni Assn. 1975-76; commr. Providence Mayor's Task Force, 1975; trustee Nicholas Picchione Dome Found., Warwick, 1960—. Mem. Am. Inst. CPA's, (council mem. 1979-81), R.I. Soc. CPA's (pres. 1978-79), Am. Acctg. Assn., Nat. Assn. Acctg., Nat. Assn. State Bds. Accountancy, R.I. Bd. Accountancy (chmn. 1985-86), Wholesale Stationers Assn. (audit com. 1974—), Estate Planning Council. Clubs: Point Judith Country (Narragansett, R.I.) (treas. 1987—); University (Providence), Turnberry Isle Yacht & Country (North Miami, Fla.). Lodge: Masons (32 degree). Home: 546 Angell St Unit 3 Providence RI 02906 Office: 10 New England Way Warwick RI 02886

PICCIANO, THOMAS BERNARD, finance and administration executive; b. Greensburg, Pa., June 6, 1948; s. Camille A. and Margaret R. (Gallagher) P.; m. Judy M. Ebers; children: David, Eric. CPA, Ohio, Wash. Supervising tax specialist Coopers & Lybrand, Dayton, Ohio, 1970-75; instr. taxation and acctg. Wright State U., Dayton, 1975-77; controller St. Lukes Gen. Hosp., Bellingham, Wash., 1977; acct. Metcalf, Hodges & Co., Bellingham, 1977-79; controller, adminstrv. mgr. Snelson-Anvil Inc., Anacortes, Wash., 1979-84; v.p. fin. and adminstrn. Call U.S. Inc., Portland, Oreg., 1984—. Contbr. articles to various publs. Co-presentor proposal Corp. Pub. Broadcasting, Washington, 1976. Served with USAR, 1970-76. Recipient best short article award Nat. Assn. Accts., 1976. Mem. Exec. Fin. Mgrs. Assn. (charter, pres. 1988—), Dayton Tax (pres., v.p., sec.-treas. 1971-74), Beta Alpha Psi, Beta Gamma Sigma. Home: 7036 SW 10th Portland OR 97219 Office: Call US Inc 921 SW Washington Suite 600 Portland OR 97201

PICHLER, JOSEPH ANTON, food products executive; b. St. Louis, Oct. 3, 1939; s. Anton Dominick and Anita Marie (Hughes) P.; m. Susan Ellen Eyerly, Dec. 27, 1962; children: Gretchen, Christopher, Rebecca, Josh. BBA, U. Notre Dame, 1961; MBA, U. Chgo., 1963, PhD; PhD, 1966. Asst. prof. bus. U. Kans., 1964-68, assoc. prof., 1968-73, prof., 1973-80; dean U. Kans. (Sch. Bus.), 1974-80; exec. v.p. Dillon Cos. Inc., 1980-82, pres., 1982-86; exec. v.p. Kroger Co., 1985-86, pres., chief operating officer, 1986—, also bd. dirs.; Spl. asst. to asst. sec. for manpower U.S. Dept. Labor, 1968-70; chmn. Kans. Manpower Services Council, 1974-78; bd. dirs. Frank Paxton Co., Johnson Co. Nat. Bank, Cities Service Corp., B.F. Goodrich Co.; indsl. cons. Author: (with Joseph McGuire) Inequality: The Poor and the Rich in America, 1969; contbg. author: Creativity and Innovation in Manpower Research and Action Programs, 1970, Contemporary Management: Issues and Viewpoints, 1973, Institutional Issues in Public Accounting, 1974, Co-Creation and Capitalism: John Paul II's Laborem Exercens, 1983; Co-editor, contbg. author: Ethics, Free Enterprise, and Public Policy, 1978; Contbr. articles to profl. jours. Bd. dirs. Kans. Charities, 1973-75, Benedictine Coll., Atchison, Kans., 1979-83, Cin. Opera; nat. bd. dirs. Boys Hope, 1983—, Tougaloo Coll., 1986—; mem. nat. bd. Nat. Alliance of Bus.; bd. advisors U. Cin. Coll. Bus. Adminstrn. Recipient Performance award U.S. Dept. Labor Manpower Adminstrn., 1969; Woodrow Wilson fellow, Ford Found. fellow, Standard Oil Indsl. Relations fellow, 1966. Mem. Kans. Assn. Commerce and Industry. Clubs: Queen City, Comml. (Cin.). Office: The Kroger Co 1014 Vine St Cincinnati OH 45202

PICKARD, WILLIAM FRANK, plastics company executive; b. LaGrange, Ga., Jan. 28, 1941; s. William H. and Victoria (Woodward) P. AS, Mott Community Coll., 1962; BS, Western Mich. U., 1964; MSW, U. Mich., 1965; PhD, Ohio State U., 1971; PhD in Bus. Adminstrn. (hon.), Cleary Coll., 1980. Dir. employment and edn. Urban League Cleve., 1965-67; exec. dir. NAACP, Cleve., 1967-69; assoc. dir. dept. urban studies Cleve. State U., 1971-72; assoc. prof. Wayne State U., Detroit, 1972-74; owner, operator McDonald's Restaurants, Detroit, 1971—; chmn., chief exec. officer Regal Plastics, Roseville, Mich., 1985—; vis. lectr. Cleve. State U., U. Chgo., Hiram Coll., U. Toledo, U. Mich., Case Western Res. U., Ohio State U., Wayne County Community Coll., McDonald's Hamburger U.; participant mgmt. seminar Case Western Res. U., Greater Cleve. Associated Found. and Rockefeller Found., 1968; chmn. Gov.'s adv. com. on minority bus., pres. 1976; bd. dirs. First Ind. Nat. Bank, Mich. Nat. Bank Corp. Mem. Pres.-elect Ronald Reagan's transition team to SBA; chmn. econ. devel. com. Nat. Black Rep. Council, 1978, bd. dirs. com. to elect Gov. Ronald Reagan Pres., 1980, chmn. congl. liaison com., 1982; chmn. Mich. Reps. Urban Campaign to elect Gov. Reagan Pres., 1980; vice chmn. Mich. Rep. State Com., 1981; bd. control Grand Valley State Coll., Allendale, Mich.; bd. dirs. Oakwood Hosp., Kirkwood Gen. Hosp., Detroit, Detroit Black Causes, Detroit Econ. Devel. Corp., 1977, Nat. Minority Purchasing Council, Washington, Detroit Urban League, vice chmn.; appointed by Pres. Ronald Regan, and confirmed by U.S. Senate Chmn. of African Devel. Found., 1983. Named one of Ten Outstanding Young Men Cleve., Jaycees, 1969; Alice W. Gault schlor, 1962-63; Nat. Urban League fellow, 1964. Mem. Booker T. Washington Bus. Assn., NAACP, Jaycees, Alpha Phi Alpha. Home: 335 Pine Ridge Dr Bloomfield Hills MI 48013 Office: 2990 W Grand Blvd M-15 Detroit MI 48202

PICKEN, JOSEPH CLARKE, III, financial executive; b. Ames, Iowa, July 10, 1943; s. Joseph Clarke Jr. and Dorothy (Parrish) P.; m. Mary D. Marsh, Mar. 9, 1968; children: David, Matthew, Anna, Christopher. AB in Econs., Dartmouth Coll., 1965, MBA, 1966. V.p., treas. Creare, Inc., Hanover, N.H., 1970-73; fin. mgr. Xerox Corp., Dallas, 1973-78; corp. controller Trailways, Inc., Dallas, 1978-79; v.p. fin. and planning Cooper Mining and Constrn., Dallas, 1980-82; v.p. fin. Kentron Internat., Dallas, 1982-83; exec. v.p., treas. The Flight Internat. Group, Atlanta, 1983-87; pres. Joseph C. Picken & Assocs., McKinney, Tex., 1987—. Mem. Civic Commn. McKinney Tex., 1981-88. Served with USN, 1966-70. Mem. McKinney C. of C., Fin. Execs. Inst., Rotary. Republican. Roman Catholic. Home: 401 W Lamar McKinney TX 75069 Office: Joseph C Picken & Assocs 708 S College Ste 207 McKinney TX 75069

PICKENS, THOMAS BOONE, JR., oil company executive; b. Holdenville, Okla., May 22, 1928; s. Thomas Boone and Grace Molonson P.; m. Beatrice Louise Carr, Apr. 21, 1972. BS in Geology, Okla. State U., 1951. Geologist Phillips Petroleum Co., 1951-55; founder, pres., chmn. bd. Mesa Petroleum Co., Amarillo, Tex.; gen. ptnr. Mesa Ltd. Partnership, Amarillo; mem. Nat. Petroleum Council, 1970—; founder, chmn. United Shareholders Assn., Washington. Author: Boone, 1987. Advisor Nat. Campaign for a Drug Free Am. Home: Woodstone One Amarillo TX 79106 Office: Mesa Ltd Partnership Box 2009 Amarillo TX 79189

PICKERING, ROBERT EARL, JR., airline executive; b. Ft. Riley, Kans., Jan. 10, 1952; s. Robert Earl and Elenore (Grossman) P.; m. Linda O. Pickering, Oct. 5, 1974 (div. May 1985); children: Robert Earl III, Lindsay Wave; m. Mary Neill, March 5, 1988; 1 child, David Neill. BBA, Baylor U., 1972, MBA, 1974. Ptnr. Arthur Andersen & Co., Houston, 1974-85; exec. v.p. First City Bancorporation, Houston, 1985-88; v.p. tech. Continental Airlines, Houston, 1988—. Mem. dean's adv. bd. Baylor Bus. Sch.; vice chmn. adminstrv. bd. Foundry United Meth. Ch., Houston, 1983, trustee, 1983. Office: Continental Airlines 2929 Allen Pkwy Ste 1900 Houston TX 77019

PICKERING, ROBERT HARVEY, financial consultant; b. N.Y.C., May 12, 1937; s. Harvey Pickering and Rose S. (Sekeres) Stohr; children: Shari, Sally, Katherine; m. Nell H. Hartwick, June 30, 1984; stepchildren, Terri, Jerry. BS, Northwestern U., 1959. CLU. V.p. John M. Shannon & Assoc., Inc., Chgo., 1964-72; pres. Robert H. Pickering & Assoc. Ltd., Denver, 1972—; radio show commentator Money Talks Sta. KNUS-AM, Denver, 1981-84, Sta. KOA-AM, Denver, 1986—. Contbr. articles to profl. jours.; inventor anchor bolt. Mem. Sch. Bd., Deerfield, Ill., Arapahoe County (Colo.) Retirement Bd., 1980—, vice chmn., 1986—; treas. Suburban Community Service Council, Englewood, Colo., 1978, chmn. 1979-81. Served with USAR, 1960-66. Recipient Service award Regional Social Security Adminstrn., 1985. Mem. Nat. Assn. Life Underwriters, Internat. Assn. Fin. Planners (mem. The Registry), Denver Assn. Life Underwriters, Rocky Mountan Chpt. Fin. Planners, Nat. Assn. Securities Dealers. Republican. Episcopalian. Clubs: Columbine Country (Littleton, Colo.); Ocean Reef (Key Largo, Fla.). Office: Robert H Pickering Assocs Ltd 3773 Cherry Creek Dr N Suite 1000 Denver CO 80209

PICKETT, FLOYD CARL, insurance company executive, consultant; b. Des Moines, Sept. 21, 1905; s. William Carl and Barbara (Kronmueller) P.; student public schs., Des Moines; m. Luella C. Peterson, Aug. 1, 1928; children—Barbara Lue, David Floyd. Clerical and claims examiner So. Surety Co., Des Moines, 1922-28, St. Louis, 1928-30, bond claims examiner, N.Y.C., 1930-32; claims examiner liquidation bur. N.Y. State Ins. Dept., N.Y.C., 1932-37; dept. mgr. Home Ins. Co., N.Y.C., 1937-65; v.p. Excel Mortgage Ins. Corp., Bettendorf, Iowa, 1965-74; cons. ins. regulations, Davenport, Iowa, 1974—; 2d v.p. Sovereign Life Ins. Co., Santa Barbara, Calif., 1979—. Mem. Nat. Assn. Life Cos., Ins. Soc. N.Y., Soc. Fin. Examiners, Life Insurers Conf. Presbyterian. Clubs: Hon. Order Blue Goose, Hon. Order Ky. Cols. Contbr. articles to profl. jours. Home and office: 2501 Jersey Ridge Rd Davenport IA 52803

PICKETT, THOMAS WILLIAM, financial services company executive; b. Detroit, Mar. 24, 1957; s. Kermit A. and Frances (Narkun) P.; m. Lynne Beachum, Sept. 7, 1986; children: Thomas W. Jr., John Christopher. BA, Ripon Coll., Wis., 1978; MBA, Emory U., 1980. CPA, Tex. Acct. Laventhol & Horwath, Atlanta, 1980-81; sr. acct. Peat, Marwick & Co., Midland, Tex., 1981-82; asst. controller Natural Resource Mgmt. Corp., Dallas, 1982-85, v.p., treas. corp., 1985—. Mem. Am. Inst. CPA's. Home: 3108 Bellflower Carrollton TX 75007 Office: Natural Resource Mgmt Corp 2121 San Jacinto Suite 2600 Dallas TX 75201

PICKETT, WILLIAM WALTER, real estate development company executive; b. Houston, Mar. 2, 1952; s. Walter Marion and Kathleen Lloyd P.; student S.W. Tex. State U., 1970-71; BS, U. Ark., 1974; m. Lucinda Hunt, Apr. 4, 1980; children: Christina Kathleen, Eric Kilion, Jennifer Elizabeth. Pres. Horseshoe Devel. Group, Inc., Houston, 1974—. Mem. Kappa Sigma. Republican. Episcopalian. Club: The Houston.

PICKLE, ROBERT DOUGLAS, lawyer; b. Knoxville, Tenn., May 22, 1937; s. Robert Lee and Beatrice Jewel (Douglas) P.; m. Rosemary Elaine Noser, May 9, 1964. AA, Schreiner Mil. Coll., Kerrville, Tex., 1957; BSBA, U. Tenn., 1959, JD, 1961; honor grad. seminar, Nat. Def. U., 1979. Bar: Tenn. 1961, Mo. 1964, U.S. Ct. Mil. Appeals 1962, U.S. Supreme Ct. 1970. Atty. Brown Shoe Co., Inc., St. Louis, 1963-69, asst. sec., atty., 1969-74; sec., gen. counsel Brown Group, Inc., St. Louis, 1974-85, v.p., gen. counsel, corp. sec., 1985—; indiv. mobilization augmentee, asst. army judge adv. gen. civil law The Pentagon, Washington, 1984—. Provisional judge Municipal Ct., Clayton, Mo., summer 1972; chmn. Clayton Region attys. sect., profl. div. United Fund Greater St. Louis Campaign, 1972-73, team capt., 1974—; chmn. City of Clayton Parks and Recreation Commn., 1985—; liaison admissions officer, regional and state coordinator U.S. Mil. Acad., 1980—. Col. JAGC, U.S. Army, 1961-63. Fellow Harry S. Truman Meml. Library; mem. ABA, Tenn. Bar Assn., Mo. Bar Assn., St. Louis County Bar Assn., Bar Assn. Met. St. Louis, St. Louis Bar Found. (bd. dirs. 1979-81), Am. Corp. Counsel Assn., Am. Soc. Corp. Secs. (treas. St. Louis regional group 1976-77, sec. 1977-78, v.p. 1978-79, pres. 1979-80), U. Tenn. Gen. Alumni Assn. (pres., bd. dirs. St. Louis chpt. 1974-76, 80—, bd. govs. 1982—), U.S. Trademark Assn. (bd. dirs. 1978-82), Tenn. Soc. St. Louis (bd. dirs. 1980—, treas., sec., v.p. 1984—, pres. 1987—), Smithsonian Nat. Assocs., Am. Legion, University Club (v.p., sec. St. Louis chpt. 1971-81, bd. dirs. 1976—), Stadium Club, Scabbard and Blade, Kappa Sigma, Phi Delta Phi, Phi Theta Kappa, Beta Gamma Sigma, Phi Kappa Phi. Republican. Presbyterian. Home: 214 Topton Way Saint Louis MO 63105-3638 Office: Brown Group Inc 8400 Maryland Ave Saint Louis MO 61105-3647

PICKLES, MARLON WILLIAM, banker, consultant; b. Sanford, Maine, June 25, 1931; s. William and Hazel Mae (Weston) P.; m. Patricia Ann Wacker, Jan. 26, 1956; 1 child, Marlon William. BS, Johns Hopkins U., 1953. V.p. Capital Mortgage Corp., Chevy Chase, Md., 1975-79; pres. Potomac Svc. Corp., Chevy Chase, 1979—; corp. v.p. Nat. Coop. Bank, Washington, 1985—; mgr. spl. assets Heritage Internat. Bank, Bethesda, Md. Life mem. Md. PTA, Balt., 1969. With U.S. Army, 1950, Korea. Mem. Nat. Assn. Credit Mgmt. (v.p. 1986-88). Republican. Unitarian. Office: Nat Coop Bank 1630 Connecticut Ave NW Washington DC 20009

PIEKOS, STANLEY DWIGHT, controller; b. Springfield, Mass., Nov. 17, 1947; s. Stanley John and Wanda M. (Lazarz) P.; m. Patricia E. Gilfillan, June 6, 1970 (div. Aug. 1983); children: Brian J., David M. BS with honors in Fin., Northeastern U., 1970; postgrad., U. Chgo., 1971-73; MBA, Babson Coll., 1978. Staff acct. Dewey & Almy div. W. R. Grace & Co., Cambridge, Mass., 1970-71; mgr. acctg. W.R. Grace Polyfibron Div., Chgo., 1971-73; bus. mgr. W.R. Grace Polyfibron Div., Columbia, Md., 1973-75; product mgr. W.R. Grace Polyfibron Div., Lexington, Mass., 1975-78; product mgr. indsl. photopolymers W.R. Grace Polyfibron Div., Columbia, 1978-79; treas. W.R. Grace Polyfibron Div., Lexington, 1979-85; controller Helix Tech. Corp., Waltham, Mass., 1985-87, v.p., controller, 1987-89, v.p., treas., controller, 1989—; bd. dirs. Ulvac Cryogenics, Inc., Chigasaki, Japan, CII-Cryogenics Inc., London. Adminstr. Westford (Mass.) Youth Basketball, 1982-87.With USAR, 1970-84. Mem. Fin. Execs. Inst., Phi Kappa Phi, Beta Gamma Sigma, Phi Kappa Tau (Scholastic Achievement award 1970). Roman Catholic. Home: 22 Bradley Lane Westford MA 01886 Office: Helix Tech Corp 204 2nd Ave Waltham MA 02254

PIEPER, JAY BROOKS, hospital executive; b. Atlantic, Iowa, Sept. 11, 1943; s. Elmer Paul and Leona Bertha (Knop) P.; m. Beverly Jeanne Schultz, Aug. 12, 1967; 1 child, Cynthia Marie. BA, Cornell Coll., 1965; MBA, Washington U., St. Louis, 1967. Staff acct. Pabst Brewing Co., Milw., 1967-69, corp. fin. mgr., 1969-72, treas., 1972-81, asst. to pres., 1976-79, v.p. corp. devel., 1979-81; v.p., treas., sec. Midland Glass Co., Inc., Cliffwood, N.J., 1981-84; asst. prof. fin. Monmouth Coll., Long Branch, N.J., 1985-86; sr. v.p., chief fin. officer Brigham Med. Ctr., Inc., Boston, 1986—, Brigham and Women's Hosp., Boston, 1986—; ptnr. PRS Fin., Inc., Little Silver, N.J., 1985—; treas. Bioscis. Rsch. Found., Inc., 1986—. Mem. Fin. Execs. Inst. Lutheran. Home: 48 Draper Rd Wayland MA 01778 Office: Brigham Med Ctr Inc 75 Francis St Boston MA 02115

PIEPER, RAYMOND FRANCIS, construction company executive; b. St. Louis, Mar. 3, 1926; s. Frank Henry and Rose Elizabeth (Wessels) P.; m. Elizabeth May Strubhart, Oct. 14, 1950; children: Joan, Diane, Kathryn, Stephen. BSCE, Washington U., 1949. With J.S. Alberici Constrn. Co., St. Louis, 1949—, v.p., corp. sec., 1962-69, exec. v.p., 1969-76, treas., v.p., 1975-76, pres., 1976—; bd. dirs., past pres. Mark Twain Banks, St. Louis. Past bd. dirs. Mo. Transp. and Devel. Council; bd. dirs. Cystic Fibrosis Found., St. Louis, Boys Hope, St. Louis. Served with USN, 1943-46. Mem. Associated Gen. Contractors, Associated Gen. Contractors of St. Louis (chmn. of yr. 1969, community service award 1977), NSPE, ASCE, Mo. Soc. Profl. Engrs., Nat. Erectors Assn. (bd. dirs.), Engrs. Club St. Louis (trustee endowment fund, past pres.). Club: Bellerive Country (St. Louis). Office: J S Alberici Constrn Co Inc 2150 Kienlen Ave Saint Louis MO 63121

PIER, JEROME ROLAND, railroad supply executive; b. Mt. Jewett, Pa., June 25, 1926; s. Jerome Warner and Gladys LeJune (Eshbaugh) P.; B.S.M.E., Pa. State U., 1950; m. Betty Ann Simpson, Nov. 7, 1953; children—Bruce, Donald, Clifford, LeJune. Engr. WABCO, Wilmerding, Pa., 1950-64, mass transit engring. mgr., 1964-69, propulsion systems sales mgr., 1969-73; mgr. spl. projects Rohr Industries, Chula Vista, Calif., 1973, program mgr., turboliner div., 1974-76, engring. mgr., rail div., 1976-77; mgr. passenger/transit mktg. Westinghouse Air Brake, Wilmerding, 1977-79, mgr. bus. and product planning, 1979—, v.p and gen. mgr. WABCO div. WABCO Standard, Hamilton, Ont., Can., 1980-86; pres. J.R. Pier and Assocs., 1986—; transp. cons. Sec., Sch. Bldg. Authority, Trafford, Pa., 1961-66. Served with U.S. Army, 1944-46. Mem. ASME, IEEE (land transp. com. 1973-76), Am. Public Transit Assn., Hamilton and Dist. C. of C. Republican. Presbyterian. Clubs: Toronto Ry. (dir.), Masons, Shriners. Contbr. articles to profl. jours.; patentee in pneumatic and elec. fields. Home: 238 Glenafton Dr, Burlington, ON Canada L7L 1G9 Office: 238 Glen Afton Dr, Burlington, ON Canada L7N 1G9

PIERCE, FRANCIS CASIMIR, civil engineer; b. Warren, R.I., May 19, 1924; s. Frank J. and Eva (Soltys) Pierce; student U. Conn., 1943-44; B.S., U. R.I., 1948; M.S., Harvard U., 1950; postgrad. Northeastern U., 1951-52; m. Helen Lynette Steinouer, Apr. 24, 1954; children—Paul F., Kenneth J., Nancy L., Karen H., Charles E. Instr. civil engring. U. R.I., Kingston, 1948-49, U. Conn., Storrs, 1950-51; design engr. Praeger-Maguire & Ole Singstad, Boston, 1951-52; chief found. engr. C.A. Maguire & Assocs., Providence, 1952-59, assoc., 1959-69, v.p., 1969-72; sr. v.p. C.E. Maguire, Inc., 1972-76, officer-in-charge Honolulu office, 1976-78, exec. v.p., corp. dir. ops., 1975-87; dir. The Maguire Group, Inc., 1979—, gen. mgr. East Atlantic Casualty Co., Ltd., 1987-88; also dir.; pres. Magma, Inc., tech. ops. service co., 1986—; lectr. found. engring. U. R.I., 1968-69, trustee, 1987—; mem. Coll. Engring. adv. council, 1986—, U.S. com. Internat. Commn. on Large Dams. Vice chmn. Planning Bd. East Providence, R.I., 1960-73; bd. dirs. R.I. Civic Chorale and Orch., 1986—. Served with AUS, 1942-46. Recipient Chester H. Kirk Disting. Engr. award U. R.I. Coll. Engring., 1987. Mem. ASCE (chpt. past pres., dir.), R.I. Soc. Profl. Engrs. (nat. dir., engr. of year award 1973), Am. Soc. Engring. Edn., Soc. Am. Mil. Engrs., ASTM, Soc. Marine Engrs. and Naval Architects, Am. Soc. Planning Ofcls., Harvard Soc. Engrs., Scientists, Providence Engrs. Soc., R.I. Soc. Planning Agys. (past pres.). Contbr. articles to profl. jours. Recipient USCG Meritorious Pub. Service award, 1987. Home: 156 Barney St Rumford RI 02916 Office: One Davol Sq Providence RI 02903

PIERCE, GRETCHEN NATALIE, investment company executive; b. Eugene, Oreg., July 7, 1945; d. Nils Bernard and Jewel (Bauman) Hult; m. Howard Walter Pierce, Dec. 26, 1970; children: Eric Nils, Hailey Lynn, . BA, U. Oreg., 1966. Research analyst Boise (Idaho) Cascade Corp., 1966-68, mgr. divs., 1968-84, dir. info. adminstrn., 1984-86; gen. mgr. Hult & Assocs., Eugene, 1986—; bd. dirs. Siuslaw Valley Bank, Florence, Oreg., Nat. Printing Corp., Seattle. Trustee U. Oreg., 1986, Sacred Heart Hosp., 1987, YMCA Endowment Fund, 1987. Mem. Profl. Women's Network, Oreg. Women's Forum, U. Oreg. Alumni (Disting. Alumni award 1984). Republican. Lutheran. Lodge: Rotary. Office: Hult & Assocs 401 E 10th St Ste 500 Eugene OR 97401

PIERCE, JAMES D(ENNIS), tax practitioner; b. L.A., Sept. 17, 1923; s. Dennis L. and Edna M. (James) P. AA, UCLA, 1947. Freelance writer Glendale, Calif., 1948-50; account exec. T.E. Parkhouse Advt., Glendale, 1951-54; investor, freelance writer Glendale, 1955-80, enrolled tax practitioner, fin. cons., 1981—; instr. Tax Counseling for the Elderly, Glendale, 1981—. Author: Adventures of Davy West, 1964, Shackle, 1965; contbr. articles to mags. Sgt. U.S. Army, 1942-45. Mem. Nat. Assn. Enrolled Agts., Calif. Soc. Enrolled Agts., Authors Guild of Authors League Am., Am. Legion. Republican. Office: 530 W Stocker St Glendale CA 91202

PIERCE, JAMES FRANKLIN, data systems consultant; b. Seaford, N.Y., Aug. 24, 1950; s. James Franklin and Marion April (Augustine) P.; m. Kit Lan Lee, July 4, 1980; 1 child, James Franklin. AAS, Olympic Coll., 1970; BSBA, U. Phoenix, 1984; BS, SUNY, 1984; MBA, U. Phoenix, 1986. Cert. systems profl. Cons. GTE-Informatics Co., N.Y.C., 1974-75, Frito-Lay Co., Dallas, 1976-77, Occidental Petroleum Co., Houston, 1977-78, Lockheed Missiles & Space Co., Sunnyvale, Calif., 1978-79; cons., owner Intel Corp., San Jose, Calif., 1979—. Mem. Republican Task Force. Mem. Assn. Systems Mgmt., ACM. Home and Office: 32807 Orick St Union City CA 94587

PIERCE, MARIANNE LOUISE, financier, venture management executive, real estate developer, consultant; b. Atchison, Kans., Apr. 22, 1949; d. James Arthur and Marian Louise (Patton) P.; m. Woodrow Theodore Lewis Jr., June 23, 1973 (div. June 1981). Student, Barnard Coll.; AB, Columbia U., 1970, MBA, 1975. Dep. dir. N.Y. Model Cities, N.Y.C., 1971-73; assoc. corp. fin. Citibank Mcht. Banking, N.Y.C., 1975-77; sr. assoc. Booz Allen Hamilton, N.Y.C., 1977-82; dep. biotechnology dir. Ciba Geigy A.G., Basel, Switzerland, 1982-85; pres. Life Scis. Assocs., Ltd., N.Y.C.; Conn.; Basel; Adelaide, Australia, 1985-88; pres., mng. dir. Patton, Pierce, Brandon & Co., 1986—; bd. dirs. Patton, Pierce & Brandon, EPCO, Inc., Woodbury, Conn. Author: (pamphlet) Developing Biotechnology Strategies for Multinational Corporations, 1985. Mem. Brit. Biotech. Assn., Comml. Devel. Assn.

PIERCE, MARK HERBERT, television station executive; b. Worcester, Mass., Sept. 29, 1942; s. Herbert Chester and Gertrude Florence (DeCouteau) P.; m. Dolce Jo Alviani, Aug. 8, 1964; 1 child, Todd Douglas. Student, Leland Powers Sch. Radio, TV and Theater, Boston, 1961-63. News dir. WPBT-TV, Miami, Fla., 1974-76, WCSC-TV, Charleston, S.C., 1976-79; news dir. WTVN-TV, Columbus, Ohio, 1979-80, Indpls., 1980-82; exec. v.p., gen. mgr. WCSC-TV, Charleston, 1982—. Exec.

producer: (TV documentary) Klan, 1981 (Nat. Emmy award, Nat. Scripps Howard award, Nat. Ohio State award, N.Y. Internat. Film Festival award 1981). Mem. S.C. Broadcasting Assn. (bd. dirs. 1985—), S.C. Broadcasting Assn. Ednl. Found. (bd. dirs. 1986—), Nat. Assn. Broadcasters, Nat. Assn. TV Program Dirs., Nat. TV Bur. of Advt. Charleston C. of C. Episcopalian. Office: Sta WCSC-TV 485 E Bay St Charleston SC 29402

PIERCE, ROBERT L., petrochemical, oil and gas company executive. Chmn. and chief exec. officer Foothills Pipe Lines (Yukon) Ltd., Calgary, Alta., Can.; chmn. Pan-Alta. Gas.; bd. dirs. NOVA Corp. of Alta., Novacor Chemicals Ltd., Bank of N.S., Husky Oil Ltd. Mem. Can. C. of C. (bd. dirs.). Office: NOVA Corp Alta, 801 7th Ave SW PO Box 2535, Calgary, AB Canada T2P 2N6

PIERCE, SAMUEL RILEY, JR., lawyer, government official; b. Glen Cove, L.I., N.Y., Sept. 8, 1922; s. Samuel R. and Hettie E. (Armstrong) P.; m. Barbara Penn Wright, Apr. 1, 1948; 1 dau., Victoria Wright. A.B. with honors, Cornell U., 1947, J.D., 1949; postgrad. (Ford Found. fellow), Yale Law Sch., 1957-58; LL.M. in Taxation, NYU, 1952, LL.D., 1972; various other hon. degrees including LL.D., L.H.D., D.C.L., Litt.D. Bar: N.Y. 1949, Supreme Ct. 1956. Asst. dist. atty. County N.Y., 1949-53; asst. U.S. atty. So. Dist. N.Y. 1953-55; asst. to under sec. Dept. Labor, Washington, 1955-56; asso. counsel, counsel Jud. Subcom. on Antitrust, U.S. Ho. Reps., 1956-57; pvt. practice law 1957-59, 61-70, 73-81; sec. Housing and Urban Devel., 1981-89; faculty N.Y. U. Sch. Law, 1958-70; guest speaker colls., univs.; judge N.Y. Ct. Gen. Sessions, 1959-61; gen. counsel, head legal div. U.S. Treasury, Washington, 1970-73; Cons. Fund Internat. Social and Econ. Edn., 1961-67; chmn. impartial disciplinary rev. bd. N.Y.C. Transit System, 1968-81; Chmn. N.Y. State Minimum Wage Bd. Hotel Industry, 1961; mem. N.Y. State Banking Bd., 1961-70, N.Y.C. Bd. Edn., 1961, Adminstrv. Conf. U.S., 1968-70, Battery Park City Corp. Authority, 1968-70, N.Y.C. Spl. Commn. Inquiry into Energy Failures, 1977; mem. nat. adv. com. comptroller of currency, 1975-80; adv. group commr. IRS, 1974-76; mem. Nat. Wiretapping Commn., 1973-76; Dir. N.Y. 1964-65 World's Fair Corp.; former Dir. Prudential Ins. Co., U.S. Industries, Inc., Gen. Electric Co., Rand Corp., 1st Nat. Boston Corp., 1st Nat. Bank of Boston, Pub. Service Electric and Gas Co.; dir. Internat. Paper Co., Turner Corp.; gov. Am. Stock Exchange, 1977-80. Contbr. articles to profl. jours. Trustee Inst. Civil Justice, Mt. Holyoke Coll., 1965-75, Hampton Inst., Inst. Internat. Edn., Cornell U., Howard U., 1976-81; bd. dirs. Tax Found. U.S. del. Conf. on Coops., Georgetown, Brit. Guiana, 1956; mem. panel symposium Mil.-Indsl. Conf. on Atomic Energy, Chgo., 1956; fraternal del. All-African People's Conf., Accra, Ghana, 1958; mem. Nat. Def. Exec. Res., 1957-70; mem. nat. exec. bd. Boy Scouts Am., 1969-75; mem. N.Y.C. U.S.O. Com., 1959-61; mem. panel arbitrators Am. Arbitration Assn. and Fed. Mediation and Conciliation Service, 1957—; Bd. dirs. Louis T. Wright Meml. Fund, Inc., Nat. Parkinson Found., Inc., 1959-61; sec., dir. YMCA Greater N.Y., 1960-70; Mem. N.Y. State Republican Campaign Hdqrs. Staff, 1952, 58; gov. N.Y. Young Rep. Club, 1951-53. Served with AUS, 1943-46; as 1st lt. J.A.G.C. Res., 1950-52. Recipient N.Y.C. Jr. C. of C. Ann. Distinguished Service award, 1958, Alexander Hamilton award Treasury Dept., 1973, Disting. Alumnus award Cornell Law Sch., 1988, Disting. Service Medallion Nassau County Bar Assn., 1988, Reagan Revolution Medal of Honor, 1989, Presdl. Citizens medal, 1989, Salute to Greatness award Martin Luther King Jr. Ctr., 1989. Fellow Am. Coll. Trial Lawyers; mem. Cornell Assn. Class Secs., Telluride Assn. Alumni, Cornell U. Amumni Assn. N.Y.C. (gov.), C.I.D. Agts. Assn. (gov.), Am. Bar Assn., Assn. N.Y.C. Bar, N.Y. County Lawyers Assn., Inst. Jud. Adminstrn., Phi Beta Kappa, Phi Kappa Phi, Alpha Phi Alpha, Alpha Phi Omega. Methodist (former mem. commn. on interjurisdictional relations United Meth. Ch.). Office: 280 Park Ave New York NY 10017

PIERCE, WILLIAM COBB, commercial banker; b. Madison, N.J., June 14, 1940; s. William Edward and Constance (Cobb) P.; m. Elizabeth Williams, Oct. 7, 1967; children: William Edward, Kemper Winn. B.A., Dartmouth Coll., 1962; M.B.A., NYU, 1967. Mgmt. trainee Chem. Bank, N.Y.C., 1962-66, asst. mgr., 1966-68, asst. sec., 1968-69, asst. v.p., 1969, 71, v.p., 1971-76, sr. v.p., 1976-83, exec. v.p., 1983—, mng. dir., chief credit officer banking and corp. fin. group, 1987—, chief credit officer, vice chmn. credit policy, 1988—; bd. dirs. Chem. USA Inc.; bd. dirs., trustee Buckeye Mgmt. Co.; vice-chmn. Chem. Bankin Corp. Credit Policy, 1988, mem. mgmt. com.; dir., vice-chmn. Chem. Internat. Fin. Ltd., and Chemco Internat. Inc.; mem. Lending/Fin. div. Council of Robert Morris Assocs. Mem. Fin. Com. Bklyn. Mus., Council on Environ., N.Y.C.; bd. dirs. Bklyn. Hist. Soc. Mem. fin. com. Bklyn. Mus., mem. Council on Environ. of N.Y.C. Mem. Am. Gas Assn., Bklyn. Hist. Soc. (dir.). Club: Heights Casino Bklyn.). Home: 86 Joralemon St Brooklyn Heights NY 11201 Office: Chem Bank 277 Park Ave New York NY 10172

PIERCY, JOAN MARY, management consultant; b. Eau Claire, Wis., Nov. 23, 1944; d. Gerald S. and Alice (Erpenback) P. BA in Bus. Adminstrn., U. Wis., 1967. Underwriter Hartford (Conn.) Ins. Group, 1967-74, cons., 1974-76; asst. sec. —, 1976-79, div. dir., corp. sec., 1979-83, v.p. bus. mgmt. group, 1983-85; v.p. Hartford Integrated Techs. Inc., 1985-86; mgr. ins. cons. Deloitte Haskins & Sells, Hartford, 1986—. Co-chmn. Women's Exec. Conf., Hartford, 1988; pres. Leadership Greater Hartford Alumni Assn., 1984-85; bd. dirs. Leadership Greater Hartford, 1988-89. Recipient Women in Leadership recognition award YWCA, Hartford, 1980. Mem. Improvement Inst., Univ. Club. Roman Catholic. Office: Deloitte Haskins & Sells City Place Hartford CT 06103

PIERREPONT, RUTHERFURD STUYVESANT, III, oil company executive; b. N.Y.C., Apr. 15, 1954; s. Rutherfurd Stuyvesant Pierrepont and Mary Dugan Shriver; m. Virginia Lake Crawford, 1986; 1 child, Ailsa Hamilton. BBA, U. Miami, 1977. Credit analyst trainee Bankers Trust Co., N.Y.C., 1977-78; asst. bond trader Roosevelt & Cross, N.Y.C., 1978-79; ptnr. The Diversified Cos., N.Y.C., 1979-82; sr. v.p. Triumph Oil & Gas Corp., N.Y.C., 1982-89, dir., 1989—; v.p. fin. Strata Corp., N.Y.C., 1988—, also bd. dirs.; cons. In-Flight Shopping, N.Y.C., 1984—, various venture capital projects; dir. B.T. Investment Corp.; founder Einstein Automation Systems, Inc., N.Y.C., 1986. Mem. Nat. Assn. Securities Dealers, Racquet and Tennis Club, Piping Rock Club, Mashomack Fish and Game Club, Turkey Hollow Club, Anglers Club. Office: Triumph Oil & Gas Corp 1270 Ave of the Americas New York NY 10020

PIERSANTE, DENISE, marketing executive; b. Detroit, Jan. 9, 1954; d. Joseph Lawrence and Virginia (Grunwald) P.; m. Wilfred Lewis Was II, June 7, 1975 (div. 1981). BA in Communications, Mich. State U., 1978. Tchr. Northwestern Ohio Community Action Commn., Defiance, 1979-80, counselor, 1980-82, job developer, 1982-83; job developer Pvt. Industry Council, Defiance, 1983, job developer coordinator, 1983-84, dir. pub. relations and job devel., 1984-86; market master North Market, Columbus, Ohio, 1986-87; dir. mktg. Richard S. Zimmerman Jr., Columbus, 1987—; cons. Small Bus. Mgmt., Archbold, Ohio, 1985-87; promotion dir. Miss N.W. Ohio Pageant, Defiance, 1985-87; promotion dir. Gallery Jazz Series, 1988, organizer, Prism Awards Competition, 1987; scholarship auction, 1988; pub. relations coordinator Defiance County Social Service Agys., 1981-86; author of various grants. Editor Job Tng. Partnership Act newsletter, 1984-86, (newsletter) North Market Soc., 1986-87. Defiance County Social Service Agys. newsletter, 1981-86; Value/Style Community News, 1987—. Organizer Auglaize River Race, Defiance, 1985. Nat. Merit scholar, 1972; recipient Am. Legion Citizenship award, 1969, 72. Mem. Pub. Relations Soc. Am., Nat. Assn. Female Execs., Am. Mktg. Assn., Jaycees (Jaycee of Month 1985). Club: Bus. and Profl. Women (Defiance); Corps de Ballet (Columbus); Conductors (Columbus); Operation Operatics (Columbus). Home: 1010 Annagladys Worthington OH 43085 Office: 100 S 3d St Suite 414 Columbus OH 43215

PIERSON, JEAN-LOUIS PIERRE, banker; b. Dombasle, France, May 9, 1947; came to U.S., 1969; s. Charles Rene and Genevieve (Masson) P.; m. Deborah E. Bennett, Dec. 6, 1986. Dipl Ing Comm, U. Nancy, 1969; MBA, Columbia U., 1970. Trainee Mfrs. Hanover Trust, N.Y.C., 1972-74; asst. v.p., credit mgr. Fuji Bank & Trust Co., N.Y.C., 1974-81, Irving Leasing Corp., N.Y.C., 1981-85; v.p., credit mgr. Comml. Bank Kuwait, N.Y.C., 1985-88; regional credit mgr. Household Comml. Fin. Svcs., Inc., Trumbull, Conn., 1988—. Mem. Robert Morris Assocs. Republican. Presbyterian. Home: 16 Devon Rd Darien CT 06820 Office: Household Comml Fin Svcs Inc 120 Hawley Ln Trumbull CT 06611

PIERSON, ROBERT DAVID, banker; b. Orange, N.J., Mar. 5, 1935; s. Carleton Wellington and Muriel Browning (Potter) P.; BA, Lehigh U., 1957; m. Virginia Duncan Knight, Apr. 30, 1960; children—Lisa Duncan, Alexandra Beach, Robert Wellington. Exec. asst. 1st Nat. City Bank N.Y., N.Y.C., 1958-61; asst. to pres. Cooper Labs. Inc., N.Y.C., 1961-65; dir. mktg. svcs. Arbrook div. Johnson & Johnson, Somerville, N.J., 1965-69; v.p. Klemtner Advt. Inc., N.Y.C., 1969-71; sr. v.p. Bowery Savs. Bank, N.Y.C., 1972-80; vice chmn., dir. Carteret Bancorp, Inc. Wilmington, Del., 1980—, Carteret Savs. Bank, F.A., Morristown, N.J., 1980—. With USCG, 1958-59. Republican. Presbyterian. Clubs: Morris County Golf, Morristown. Home: Green Hills Rd Mendham NJ 07945 Office: Carteret Savs Bank FA 200 South St Morristown NJ 07960

PIESCIK, JOHN BERNARD, systems analyst, management consultant; b. Miami, Fla., May 29, 1957; s. John Bernard and Natalie Elaine (Sullivan) P.; m. Martha Marie Maturi, June 9, 1984; 1 child, Rachel Marie. AB in Govt., Georgetown U., 1979; M in Pub. and Pvt. Mgmt., Yale U., 1981. Mgmt. analyst U.S. Dept. Navy, Washington, 1980; prin., dir. fed. marketing Am. Mgmt. Systems, Inc., Arlington, Va., 1986—; cons. USN, 1981-82, GSA, Washington, 1982—, EPA, Washingotn, 1986—, Commodity Futures Trading Commn., Washington, 1984, 88. Founding editor Student Press Service, 1978; co-founder Youth Policy mag., 1979. Organizer Ctr. Environ. Studies, West Palm Beach, Fla., 1973-75. Robert F. Kennedy Meml. found. fellow, 1976-79. Mem. Assn. computing Machinery, Data Adminstrn. Mgmt. Assn., Assn. Fed. Info. Resources Mgmt., Guide Internat. Democrat. Roman Catholic. Home: 1701 Abbey Oak Dr Vienna VA 22182 Office: Am Mgmt Systems Inc 1777 N Kent St Arlington VA 22209

PIETRANTONI, JOSEPH GEORGE, academic administrator; b. Syracuse, N.Y., July 22, 1938; s. Gene A. and Jennie (Cianfrocca) P.; m. Marilyn J. Kalode, Apr. 19, 1958; children: Joseph Jr., Mary Ann, John. Student, Rollins Coll. Sr. material controller Gen. Electric Co., Cape Kennedy, Fla., 1961-64, specialist program adminstrn., 1964-67, ops. mgr., 1967-70; program mgr. Duke U., Durham, N.C., 1970-72, assoc. dir., phys. plant, 1972-76, dir. campus services, 1976-80, asst. bus. mgr., 1980-87, asst. v.p., auxiliary services, 1987—. Contbr. articles to profl. publs.; numerous presentations. Coach, YMCA Youth Basketball, 1973-77, YMCA Youth Football, 9175-76; chmn. Red Cross Blood Drive for Duke U., 1970-74; dir. United Fund, 1967-68. Recipient Award for Excellence in Journalism, 1987, Rauch Disting. Service Award for Creative Mgmt., 1983, Vol. Service award, 1980, YMCA Youth Basketball Coach of Yr. Mem. Nat. Assn. Coll. Auxiliary Services, Jaycees. Democrat. Roman Catholic. Club: Broken Anchor Boat. Home: 5302 Pelham Rd Durham NC 27713

PIETRUSKI, JOHN MICHAEL, JR., retired pharmaceutical company executive; b. Sayreville, N.J., Mar. 12, 1933; m. Roberta Jeanne Talbot, July 3, 1954; children: Glenn David, Clifford John, Susan Jane. B.S. with honors, Rutgers U., 1954. With Proctor and Gamble Co., 1954-63; pres. med. products div. C.R. Bard, Inc., 1963-77; with Sterling Drug, Inc., N.Y.C., 1977-88; pres. Pharm. Group, N.Y.C., 1977-81, corp. exec. v.p., 1981-83; pres., chief operating officer Sterling Drug Inc., N.Y.C., 1983-85, chmn., chief exec. officer, 1985-88, ret., 1988; bd. dirs. Hershey Foods Corp., Gen. Pub. Utilities Corp., Lincoln Corp. Past bd. dirs. Council Better Bus. Burs., Rutgers U. Found. 1st lt. U.S. Army, 1955-57. Mem. Phi Beta Kappa. Club: Union League (N.Y.C.). Home: 3 Bruce Ct Edison NJ 08820

PIGOTT, CHARLES MCGEE, transportation equipment manufacturer; b. Seattle, Apr. 21, 1929; s. Paul and Theiline (McGee) P.; m. Yvonne Flood, Apr. 18, 1953. B.S., Stanford U., 1951. With PACCAR Inc, Seattle, 1959—, exec. v.p., 1962-65, pres., 1965-86, chmn., pres., 1986-87, chmn., chief exec. officer, 1987—, also bd. dirs.; dir. Boeing Co., Citibank/Citicorp, Chevron Corp. Pres. Nat. Boy Scouts Am., 1986-88, mem. exec. bd. Mem. Bus. Council. Office: PACCAR Inc 777 106th Ave NE PO Box 1518 Bellevue WA 98004 *

PIGOTT, JAMES CALVIN, management consultant; b. Seattle, Aug. 5, 1936; s. Paul Pigott and Theilene (McGee) Pigott McCone; m. Gaye Titcomb, Apr. 23, 1960; children: Paul, Lisa, Sara, Julie. BCE, Stanford U., 1959; MBA, Harvard U., 1963. Asst. gen. mgr. Structural Steel div. PACCAR, Renton, Wash., 1963-68; pres., chief exec. officer Sicard, Inc. div., Montreal, Can., 1969-72; asst. gen. mgr. Kenworth Truck div., Renton, 1972-75; pres. Stetson-Ross Inc., Kent, Wash., 1976-83, Pigott Enterprises, Inc., Bellevue, Wash., 1983—, Mgmt. Reports and Svcs., Inc. doing bus. as Marcoin Bus. Svcs., Seattle, 1986—; bd. dirs. Mgmt. Reports and Svcs., Inc.; bd. dirs. No. Life Ins., Seattle, Americold Corp., Portland, Oreg.. Chmn., trustee Seattle U.; trustee Norcliffe Found. Lt. (j.g.) USN, 1959-61. Mem. Bohemian Club, Rainer Club. Republican. Roman Catholic. Home: 1500 52nd Ave E Seattle WA 98112 Office: Mgmt Reports and Svcs doing bus as Marcoin Bus Svcs Westin Bldg Ste 2501 Seattle WA 98121

PIGOTT, RICHARD J., food company executive; b. 1940; married. B.B.A., U. Notre Dame, 1961; J.D., U. Wis., 1966. Law ptnr. Winston & Strawn, 1966-77; with Beatrice Foods Co., Chgo., 1977—, sr. v.p., gen. counsel, 1977-80, exec. v.p., gen. counsel, chief adminstrv. officer, 1980-81, exec. v.p., chief adminstrv. officer, 1981-88; mng. dir. Delano and Kopperl, Chgo., 1988—. Served with U.S. Army, 1961-63. Office: Delano and Kopperl 2 N LaSalle St Ste 2010 Chicago IL 60602 *

PIKE, ALLEN W., supermarket company executive. Student, Carleton Coll.; grad., Harvard U., 1932. With Kroger Co., Cin., 1932-35; with Piggly-Wiggly Corp., Atlanta, 1935-41; with Almac's Inc., East Providents, R.I., 1941—, now chmn. bd., chief exec. officer, dir. Office: Almac's Inc 1 Noyes St East Providence RI 02916

PIKE, ROBERT WILLIAM, communication consulting company executive; b. Chgo., Apr. 22, 1947; s. Louis Gustav and Patricia May (Svenson) P.; m. Karen J. McGinnes, Apr. 9, 1988; children by previous marriage; Elizabeth, Sara, Rebecca, Robert, Andrew, John. B.A. in Pastoral Tng., Moody Bible Inst., Chgo., 1970. Licensed to preach, 1970; asst. pastor Indian Hill Chapel, Ingleside, Ill., 1967-70; sr. v.p. Master Edn. Industries, Denver, 1970-73; v.p. Personal Dynamics, Inc., Mpls., 1974-79; adminstr. U. LaVerne (Calif.), 1975-79; pres. Profl. Edn. Inst., Mpls., 1979—; condr. leadership devel. programs for businesses, instns., colls. and univs., 1974—; prin. Communication Cons., 1979-83; pres. Resources for Orgns., Inc., Eden Prairie, Minn., 1982—; dir. profl. edn. programs Coll. St. Scholastica, Duluth, Minn., 1979-80; dir. Cardinal Health Systems. Exec. editor Brain & Strategy Newsletter, 1984-85, Creative Tng. Techniques Newsletter, 1985—; adv. bd. mem. The Tng. Dirs. Forum; prin. speaker The Jaycess Internat. Leadership Acad., Okinawa, Japan, 1988. Mem. adv. bd. Christian Berets, 1977—; trustee Chapel Hill (Minn.) Acad., 1977-80. Served with USNR, 1965-72. Recipient numerous service awards. Mem. Am. Soc. Tng. and Devel. (chmn. tng. with religious assn. spl. interest group 1977, 79, nat. dir. 1980-81), Salesman With A Purpose (1st v.p. S.E. Denver chpt. 1974), Am. Personnel and Guidance Assn., Nat. Assn. Evangelicals. Club: Calhoun Beach. Author: The Creating Training Techniques, 1988, 10 Lessons I've Learned About Classroom Delivery, 1988, Sales Training and the Lecture Method, 1989, The Psychology of Selling; The Psychology of Management; author seminar texts on leadership, attitudes, motivation, tng. techniques, others; contbr. articles to profl. publs. Home: 13320 Pepperwood Ln Minnetonka MN 55343-6835 Office: 6440 Flying Cloud Dr Ste 130 Eden Prairie MN 55344

PIKE, ROBERT WILLIAM, insurance company executive, lawyer; b. Lorain, Ohio, July 25, 1941; s. Edward and Catherine (Stack) P.; m. Linda L. Feitz, Dec. 26, 1964; children: Catherine, Robert, Richard. BA, Bowling Green State U., 1963; JD, U. Toledo, 1966. Bar: Ohio 1966, Ill. 1973. Ptnr. Cubbon & Rice Law Firm, Toledo, 1968-72; asst. counsel Allstate Ins. Co., Northbrook, Ill., 1972-74, assoc. counsel, 1974-76, asst. sec., asst. gen. counsel, 1976-77, asst. v.p., asst. gen. counsel, 1977-78, v.p., asst. gen. counsel, 1978-86, sr. v.p., sec., gen. counsel, 1987—, also bd. dirs.; bd. dirs. Allstate subs., including the Northbrook Group of Cos. Bd. dirs., exec. com. Assn. Calif. Ins. Cos., Nat. Assn. Ind. Insurers. Served to capt. inf. U.S. Army, 1966-68. Mem. ABA, Ill. Bar Assn., Ohio Bar Assn. Roman Catholic. Clubs: Thorngate Country (Deerfield, Ill.); The Metropolitan (Chgo.). Home: 510 Brierhill Rd Deerfield IL 60015 Office: Allstate Ins Co Allstate Pla Northbrook IL 60062

PIKE, WILLIAM EDWARD, banker; b. Ft. Collins, Colo., Jan. 25, 1929; s. Harry H. and Alice Francis (Swinscoe) P.; m. Catherine Broward Crawford, June 26, 1965; children: Elizabeth Catherine, Robert Crawford, Daniel William. Student, U. Colo., 1947-48; B.S., U.S. Naval Acad., 1952; M.B.A., Harvard, 1960. Commd. ensign USN, 1952, advanced through grades to lt., 1958; ret. 1958; asst. treas. Morgan Guaranty Trust Co., N.Y.C., 1962-64; asst. v.p. Morgan Guaranty Trust Co., 1964-66, v.p., 1966-71, sr. v.p., 1971-74, chmn. credit policy com., 1974-86; exec. v.p. J.P. Morgan & Co. Inc., 1986—; bd. dirs. VF Corp., Am. States Ins. Co. Episcopalian. Club: Country (New Canaan, Conn.). Home: 4 Carriage Rd Greenville DE 19807 Office: J P Morgan & Co Inc 23 Wall St New York NY 10015

PIKEY, RICHARD ALLAN, quality assurance engineer; b. St. Louis, Sept. 20, 1961; s. Ruben Franklin and Ruby Jewel (Thacker) P.; m. Patricia Ellen Kunza, Aug. 14, 1982; children: Robert Allan, Bradley Allan. Cert. Drafting & Design, NE Mo. State U., Kirksville, 1981; BS in Indsl. Tech., SE Mo. State U., Cape Girardeau, 1983. Quality control inspector Diagraph Corp., Herrin, Ill., 1983-85; layout insp. Westloff Tool & Die, Crestwood, Mo., 1985; quality assurance mgr. Wainwright Industries, Inc., St. Peters, Mo., 1985—. Webelos Scout leader Boy Scouts Am., 1987. Mem. Am. Soc. Quality Control, Brighm Young U. Mgmt. Soc. Republican. Mormon. Home: 18 River Bluff Dr Saint Peters MO 63376 Office: Wainwright Industries Inc 17 Cermak Blvd Saint Peters MO 63376

PIKLO, CHARLENE LORRAINE, retail professional; b. Camden, N.J., Sept. 21, 1954; d. John Alfred and Loretta H. (Vogt) P. BS, U. Tampa, 1975. Mgr. trainee Roses Stores Inc., Macon, Ga., 1975-76; asst. mgr. Roses Stores Inc., Onley, Va., 1976; sr. asst. mgr. Roses Stores Inc., Burlington, N.C., 1976-77; merchandiser Roses Stores Inc., Henderson, N.C., 1977-78; asst. buyer Roses Stores Inc., N.Y.C., 1978-79; buyer Roses Stores Inc., Henderson, 1979-83, div. mgr. mdse., 1983-86; gen. mgr. mdse. Conston Corp., Phila., 1986—. Recipient Torch of Liberty Anti Defamation League, 1988—. Mem. NAFE, Profl. Bus. Sorority, Phi Gamma Nu. Roman Catholic. Office: Conston Corp 3250 S 76th St Philadelphia PA 19153

PILAT, JOANNE MARIE, telecommunications company executive. BA cum laude, Siena Heights Coll., 1969; MSW, Cath. U. Am., 1974; M of Mgmt., Northwestern U., 1988. Tchr., organizer community services various orgns., Mich., Ill., 1961-72; family therapist Oak Park (Ill.) Family Service and Mental Health Ctr., 1974-75; patient therapist Luth. Ctr. for Substance Abuse, Park Ridge, Ill., 1975-80, dir. social services, 1980-81; dir. med. social services Luth. Gen. Hosp., Park Ridge, 1981-82, dir. clin. social services, 1982-84; mgr., regional mgr. employee assistance program AT&T, Chgo., 1984-88, cons. orgn. devel., 1988—; co-chair bus. and industry Internat. Council Alcohol and Addictions, Lausanne, Switzerland, 1980-84, co-chair. social work, 1984—; mem. subcom. White House. Conf. for Drug-Free Am., 1987—; instr. Ctr. Family Studies, Northwestern U., 1980—, Grad. Sch. Social Work, Loyola U., Chgo., 1980—; chair edn. and tng. Ill. Gov.'s Adv. Council Alcoholism, 1980; mem. Ill. Alcoholism Counselors' Cert. Bd.; speakerin field U.S. and abroad. Contbr. chpt. to book, articles to profl. jours. Bd. dirs. Alcohol, Drug Dependence Luth. Social Services, Chgo., 1987—; mem. studies bd. Northwestern U. Inst. Psychiatry, 1984—. Mem. Assn. Labor/Mgmt. Adminstrs. Cons. (nat. bd. dirs.), Alcoholism, Northwestern U. Mgmt. Club, Women in Mgmt., Alumni Assn. Ctr. for Family (membership chair 1984-87). Office: AT&T 1 S Wacker Dr 13th fl Chicago IL 60606

PILATO, MICHAEL JOHN, accountant; b. N.Y.C., May 27, 1958; s. Michael A. and Angela M. (Casale) P. BS, Fairfield U., 1981; MBA, Pace U., 1985. CPA, Conn. Acct. GE Credit Corp., Stamford, 1981-82; acctg. mgr. Masotti & Masotti, Stamford, 1982-87; owner, mgr. Norwalk (Conn.) Lock and Safe Co., 1987—. Roman Catholic. Home: 235 Red Oak Ln Bridgeport CT 06606 Office: Norwalk Lock & Safe Co 167 Main St Norwalk CT 06851

PILCHER, WALTER HAROLD, apparel company executive; b. Washington, Oct. 21, 1941; s. Milton Alfred and Elizabeth (Haywood) P.; m. Carol Ann Beebe, July 17, 1965; children—Walter Todd, Jennifer Beebe, Carolyn Elizabeth. B.A., Wesleyan U., 1963; M.B.A., Stanford U., 1966. Product mgr. L'Eggs Products, Winston-Salem, N.C., 1969-73, v.p. mktg., 1979-83, pres., 1983-87; v.p. mktg. Hanes Knitwear, Winston-Salem, 1973-75; mktg. mgr. Wix Corp., Gastonia, N.C., 1975-77; v.p. mktg. L'Erin Cosmetics, Winston-Salem, 1977-79; pres., chief operating officer Sara Lee Hosiery, Sara Lee Corp., Winston-Salem, 1987-88; pres., chief exec. officer Kayser Roth Hosiery, Inc., Greensboro, N.C., 1989—. Mem. allocations com. Forsyth United Way, Winston-Salem, 1978; mem. pres.'s council of advisors Christian Broadcasting Network U., 1986—. 1st lt. USAR, 1963-70. Republican. Presbyterian. Avocations: creative writing, photography. Office: Kayser-Roth Hosiery Inc 2303 W Meadowview Rd Greensboro NC 17407

PILGRIM, RAYMOND WINFRED, manufacturing company executive; b. Trion, Ga., June 14, 1936; s. Thomas Grady and Donnie May (Tate) P.; m. Katheryn Loraine Hegwood, Dec. 22, 1956; children—Jeffrey Kyle, Anthony Warren. B.S. in Indsl. Mgmt., Ga. Inst. Tech., 1959, M.S., 1962. Vice Pres., adminstr. Oxford Industries, Atlanta, 1962-69; gen. mgr. mktg. Diversified Products, Opelika, Ala., 1969-70, exec. v.p., dir., 1978—; exec. v.p., dir. Bayly Corp., Denver, 1970-78; exec. v.p. Diversified Products Corp., 1978-86; pres., chief exec. officer Daisy Mfg. Co., Inc., Rogers, Ark., 1987-88; chief exec. officer Tuscarora Mktg. Group, Cahpin, S.C., 1988—; chmn. exec. com. SGMA Govt. Relations, ISAC-4; rep. Sporting Goods Industry.versified Products Can., 1985-86. Mem. Citizen Adv. Com., Montgomery, Ala., 1982. Served to 1st lt. U.S. Army, 1960-62. Mem. Ark. Dist. Export Council, Ark. World Trade Assn., U.S. C. of C., Am. C. of C., Rogers C. of C., Sporting Goods Mfrs. Assn. Republican. Lodges: Elks, Lions (v.p. 1974-75). Office: Tuscarora Mktg Group PO Drawer G Chapin SC 29036

PILGRIM, RICHARD M., utilities executive; b. Poteet, Tex., Aug. 27, 1943; s. Wilson H. Pilgrim and Alma V. (Nash) Smith; m. Martha E. Pilgrim, July 16, 1965; children: Roxanne, Lori Kay. BS, Tex. A & I U., Kingsville, 1969. With sales dept. Chgo. Pneumatic Tool Co., Alice, Tex., 1965-68; pres. South Tex. Fire & Safety, Alice, 1968-72; tchr., coach Alice-Kenedy (Tex.) High Schs., 1972-77; contracts mgr. then v.p. ops. Ensco Operating Co., Alice, Houston, 1977-88; pres. Blocker Services Co., Alice, Houston, 1988—. Mem. Am. Petroleum Inst., Internat. Assn. Drilling Contractors. Democrat. Baptist. Lodges: Lions, Rotary (Alice chpt.). Office: Blocker Svcs Co PO Box 3410 Alice TX 78333-3410

PILLA, FELIX MARIO, hospital administrator; b. Phila., Sept. 22, 1932; s. Domenick and Carmela (DiPalma) P.; m. Sally Irene Bixler, Oct. 2, 1953; children: Mark, Beth Ann, Michael, Matthew. Diploma profl. nursing, Pa. Hosp. Sch. Nursing, 1956; B.S. in Bus. Adminstrn, LaSalle Coll., Phila., 1959; M.S. in Hosp. Adminstrn, Columbia U., 1961. Mgr. central supply dept. Jefferson Med. Coll. Hosp., Phila., 1957-59; asst. adminstr. Hackensack (N.J.) Hosp., 1961-64; mgr. hosp. relations Md. Blue Cross, Balt., 1964-66; asst. dir. Hosp. Planning Assn. Allegheny County, Pitts.; assoc. dir. Presbyn.-Univ. Hosp., Pitts., 1966-67; asst. dir. planning Med. Ctr. Bklyn. and Queens, N.Y.C., 1967-69; assoc. adminstr. Monmouth Med. Ctr., Long Branch, N.J., 1969-70; exec. dir. Monmouth Med. Center, 1970-80; adminstrv. dir. U. Ariz. Health Scis. Center, Tucson, 1980-82; pres. Newton-Wellesley Hosp., Newton, Mass., 1982-85, Abington Meml. Hosp., Pa., 1985—; chmn. N.J. State Health Planning Council, 1976-77. USPHS tng. grantee, 1961. Fellow Am. Pub. Health Assn.; mem. Am. Hosp. Assn., N.J. Hosp. Assn. (chmn. 1979-80), Am. Coll. Hosp. Adminstrs., Hosp. Assn. of Pa. (trustee 1988—), Del. Valley Hosp. Council (trustee 1986—). Office: 1200 York Rd Abington PA 19001

PILLA, GEORGE JOSEPH, financial executive; b. Waltham, Mass., Mar. 29, 1951. BS in Acctg., Boston Coll., 1973; MBA, Harvard U., 1982. CPA, Mass. Audit profl. Coopers & Lybrand, Boston, 1973-80; v.p. fin. and adminstrn. Polymer Tech. Corp., Wilmington, Mass., 1982-84, Steinbrecher

Corp., Woburn, Mass., 1984—. Fellow AICPA, Mass. Soc. CPA's. Roman Catholic. Office: Steinbrecher Corp 185 New Boston St Woburn MA 01801

PILLING, DANIEL GORDON, electronics company executive; b. Detroit, Nov. 27, 1962; s. Arnold Remington and Patricia Leslie (Marks) P.; m. Sue Bandelean, Sept. 20, 1987. BA in Bus., Mich. State U., 1984. Cert. purchasing mgr. Intern Am. Motors Corp., Detroit, 1984; sr. buyer Magnavox Electronic Systems Co., Ft. Wayne, Ind., 1985—. Troop adviser Ft. Wayne Area Boy Scouts Am., 1985; project bus. cons. Ft. Wayne Jr. Achievement, 1985-88. Mem. Nat. Assn. Purchasing Mgmt. (asst. treas., chmn. reservation Ft. Wayne chpt. 1985—), Ft. Wayne Track Club, Delta Chi. Home: 2719 N Haven Ct Fort Wayne IN 46825

PILLSBURY, LELAND CLARK, service executive; b. Rochester, N.Y., Feb. 12, 1947; s. Donald Clark and Mildred (Van Zandt) C.; m. Mary Milne, Dec. 27, 1969. BS in Hotel Adminstrn., Cornell U., 1969; MBA, Northwestern U., 1982. Gen. mgr. Marriott Hotels div. Marriott Corp., Washington, 1978-82; v.p. market devel. product planning Marriott Hotels div. Marriott Corp., 1982-83, v.p. and corp. officer, strategic planning, 1983-85; sr. v.p., gen. mgr. and corp. officer Fairfield Inns div., 1985-87; exec. v.p., gen. mgr. and corp. officer Residence Inns div., 1987-88; pres., prin. Hist. Inns Am., 5 Inns Midatlantic Region, Annapolis, Md., 1988—. Mem. Am. Mktg. Assn., J.L. Kellogg Grad. Sch. Alumni Assn. (bd. dirs.), Cornell Soc. of Hotelmen. Clubs: Annapolis Yacht Club (Annapolis, Md.), Ferrari of Am. Home: 345 Sherwood Trail Annapolis MD 21401 Office: Hist Inns Am 16 Church Cir Annapolis MD 21401

PILSON, ROGER LLOYD, sales management professional; b. Bklyn., Dec. 28, 1950; s. Frank Martin and Pauline (Levy) P.; m. Lorraine Nancy Sadlock, June 5, 1971; children: Christine, Heather. BS, William Paterson Coll., 1980, MPH, 1984. Sales rep. Smith Kline Clin. Lab., N.Y.C., 1978-83; dist. sales mgr. Smith Kline Bio-Sci. Lab., N.Y.C., Phila., 1983—. Contbr. articles to profl. jours. Served as sgt. USAF, 1971-81, Vietnam. Decorated Bronze Star. Mem. Clin. Lab. Mgrs. Assn. (cert.). Republican. Home: 62 Theresa Ct Toms River NJ 08753

PILUN-OWAD, CHAIYUT, financial and securities company executive; b. Nakornratchasima, Thailand, Jan. 1, 1949; s. Bugyong and Teing P.-O.; m. Orawan Lophansri; children: On-Anong, On-Narumol, Chaichat, Chaivichit. BBA in Acctg., Thammasat U., Bangkok, 1971; MBA in Mgmt., NYU, 1974, PhD in Fin. and Econs., 1977. CPA, Thailand. V.p. corp. fin. and planning dept. Asia Credit Ltd., Bangkok, 1977-78; exec. v.p. Union Asia Fin. Ltd., Bangkok, 1979-86, pres., 1987—; researcher customs dept. Ministry Fin., Bangkok, 1977-78; lectr. fin. Thammasat U., Nat. Inst. Devel. Adminstrn., Bangkok, 1977-81. Mem. Assn. Fin. Cos. in Thailand (bd. dirs.), Assn. Mems. Securities Exchange in Thailand (bd. dirs.). Clubs: Heritage, Royal Bangkok Sport. Home: 204 25 Pasuk Village, Bangkok 10250, Thailand Office: Union Asia Fin Ltd, 132 Silom Rd, Bangkok 10500, Thailand

PINA, JON JOSEPH, plant safety administrator; b. Indiana, Pa., July 31, 1950; s. Joseph Albert and Helen Virginia (Dyer) P.; m. Isabel Margie Silveri, Aug. 17, 1974; 1 child, Melanie Marie. BS in Geosci. Edn., Indiana U. of Pa., 1972, MS in Geology, 1978, MS in Safety Mgmt., 1989. Cert. tchr., Pa. Tchr. earth and space sci. Westmont (Pa.) Hilltop Jr. High Sch., 1972-76; chem. operating technician Stearns-Roger, Inc., Homer City, Pa., 1976-81; plant operator Kaiser Engrs., Homer City, 1981-88, dir. safety, emergency med. technician, 1984—; tech. adviser County Emergency Planning Commn., Am. Trauma Soc., 1987—; guest lectr. Indiana U. of Pa., 1983-84. Bd. dirs. Trout Unltd. Stream Improvement, Indiana, 1976-77. Mem. Am. Soc. Safety Engrs., Investment Club, Nat. Rifle Assn. Roman Catholic. Home: RD 6 Box 25 Indiana PA 15701 Office: Kaiser Engrs PO Box 98 Power Plant Rd Homer City PA 15748

PINAMONTI, VALERIE LYNN, purchasing manager, consultant; b. Harvey, Ill., Sept. 7, 1953; d. Marion Lenard and Dorothy Olive (Busby) P. BBA, Calif. State U., Fullerton, 1984. Cert. purchasing mgmt. Purchasing agt. Conversion Equipment, Anaheim, Calif., 1978-80; purchasing supr. ATC/Comdial, El Monte, Calif., 1980-85; purchasing mgr. Datapower, Inc., Santa Ana, Calif., 1985; materials mgr. Informer, Inc., Garden Grove, Calif., 1985-86; sales rep. Cal-Abco, Costa Mesa, Calif., 1986-87; sales mgr. Golden West Tech., Fullerton, Calif., 1987—; v.p. Performance Cons. Group, Placentia, Calif., 1971—. Mem. Purchasing Mgmt. Assn., Am. Prodn. and Inventory Control Soc., Women in Sales. Republican. Methodist.

PINARD, RAYMOND R., pulp and paper company executive; b. Trois-Rivieres, Que., Can., May 13, 1930; s. Albert and Mariette (Dufresne) P.; m. Estelle Frechette, Nov. 5, 1965; children: Robert, Andree. B.A., U. Laval, (Que., Can.), 1951; B.Eng., McGill U., Montreal, 1955. Registered profl. engr., Que. Process engrng. plant mgr. Domtar Inc., East Augus, Que., 1955-68; gen. mgr. Domtar Kraft & Bd. Domtar Inc., Montreal, 1968-73, v.p., gen. mgr. Domtar Newspring & Pulp, 1974-79, pres. Domtar Pulp & Paper, 1979-81, exec. v.p., chief operating officer, 1981—, also dir.; dir. Sidbec, Montreal. Bd. dirs., past chmn. PPRIC, U. Que. à Montreal; bd. dirs. Fondation de l'Universite' du Que. à, Montreal, 1979—, United Auto Parts, Nat. Adv. Council Sci and Tech. Mem. Can. Pulp and Paper Assn. (chmn. 1982), TAPPI, C.D. Howe Inst., Corp. Profl. Engrs. Que., Engrng. Inst. Can., Can. Mfrs. Assn. (chmn. 1988-89). Club: Club Saint-Denis (Montreal). Office: Domtar Inc, 395 de Maisonneuve Blvd W, Montreal, PQ Canada H3A 1L6

PINDERA, JERZY TADEUSZ, mechanical and aeronautical engineer; b. Czchow, Poland, Dec. 4, 1914; immigrated to Can., 1965, naturalized, 1975; s. Jan Stanislaw and Natalia Lucia (Knapik) P.; m. Aleksandra-Anna Szal, Oct. 29, 1949; children: Marek Jerzy, Maciej Zenon. BS in Mech. Engring, Tech. U., Warsaw, 1936; MS in Aero. Engring, Tech. U., Warsaw and Lodz, 1947; D in Applied Scis., Polish Acad. Scis., 1959; DS in Applied Mechanics, Tech. U., Cracow, 1962. Registered profl. engr., Ont. Asst. Lot Polish Airlines, Warsaw, 1947; head lab. Aero. Inst., Warsaw, 1947-52, Inst. Metallography, Warsaw, 1952-54; dep. prof., head lab. Polish Acad. Scis., 1954-59; head lab. Bldg. Research Inst., Warsaw, 1959-62; vis. prof. mechanics Mich. State U., East Lansing, 1963-65; prof. mechanics U. Waterloo (Ont. Can.), 1965-83, adj. prof., 1983-86, prof. emeritus, 1987—; pres. J.T. Pindera & Sons Engring. Services, Inc., Waterloo, 1980—; chmn. Internat. Symposium Exptl. Mechanics, U. Waterloo, 1972, dir. Inst. for Exptl. Mechanics, 1983-86; chmn. 10th Can. Fracture Conf., 1983; hon. adv. prof. Chongging (Sichuan, China) U., 1988—; hon. prof. Shanghai (China) Coll. Archtl. and Mcpl. Engring., 1988—; hon. chmn. Internat. Conf. on Advanced Exptl. Mechanics, U. Tianjin, People's Republic of China, 1988; vis. prof. in France and Fed. Republic Germany; cons. in field. Mem. editorial adv. bd. Mechanics Research Communications, 1974—; mem. bd. editors Theoretical and Applied Fracture Mechanics, 1984—; patentee in field; contbr. tech. books, articles and chpts. in books. Served with Polish Army, 1939. Fellow Soc. Exptl. Mechanics (M.M. Frocht award 1978); mem. Gesellschaft Angewandte Mathematik und Mechanik, N.Y. Acad. Scis., Soc. Engring. Sci., ASME, Assn. Profl. Engrs. Ont. Home: 310 Grant Crescent, Waterloo, ON Canada N2K 2A2 Office: U Waterloo Dept Civil Engring, 200 University Ave, Waterloo, ON Canada N2L 3G1

PINES, WAYNE LLOYD, public relations counselor; b. Washington, Dec. 31, 1943; s. Jerome Martin and Ethel (Schnall) P.; B.A., Rutgers U., 1965; postgrad. George Washington U., 1969-71; m. Nancy Freitag, Apr. 16, 1966; children—Noah Morris, Jesse Mireth. Reporter, city editor Middletown (N.Y.) Times Herald-Record, 1965-68; copy editor Reuters News, 1968-69; asso. editor FDC Reports, Washington, 1969-72; chief Consumer Edn. and Info., FDA, also editor FDA Consumer, 1972-74; exec. editor Product Safety Letter and Devices and Diagnostics Letter, Washington, 1974-75; dep. asst. commr. for pub. affairs, chief press relations FDA, Rockville, Md., 1975-78, assoc. commr. public affairs, 1978-82; adj. prof. Washington Public Affairs Center, U. So. Calif., 1980-81; instr. N.Y.U. Sch. Continuing Edn., 1982-84; spl. asst. to dir. NIMH, 1982-83; sr. v.p., sr. counselor Burson-Marsteller, 1983-87 ; exec. v.p., 1987—; instr. Profl. Devel. Inst., 1983-85; columnist Med. Advt. News. Contbr. numerous articles in field to profl. jours. Home: 5821 Nevada Ave NW Washington DC 20015 Office: Burson-Marsteller 1850 M St NW Washington DC 20036

PING, ALBERT, manufacturing executive; b. Shanghai, Republic of China, Sept. 1, 1940; came to U.S., 1965; s. Wallace and Helen (Lo) P.; m. Ling Tam, Nov. 24, 1977; children: Mary, Jenny. V.p. china trade C. Itoh Am., Inc., N.Y.C., 1975—. Republican. Methodist. Office: C Itoh & Co (Am) Inc 335 Madison Ave New York NY 10017

PINGEL, JOHN SPENCER, advertising executive; b. Mt. Clemens, Mich., Nov. 6, 1916; s. George F. and Margaret (Dalby) P.; m. Isabel Hardy, Dec. 12, 1939; children—John S., Roy Hardy. Student, U.S. Mil. Acad., 1936; B.A., Mich. State U., 1939. Asst. dir. truck merchandising Dodge div. Chrysler Corp., 1940-41, fleet sales rep., 1949; adminstrv. asst. Mich. State U., 1945-46; dir. advt. Reo Motors, Inc., 1947-48; with mdsg. dept. Brooke, Smith, French & Dorrance, Inc., 1949-55, v.p., account supr., 1955-57, v.p., asst. to pres., 1957-60, exec. v.p., 1960; exec. v.p. Ross Roy-BSF & D, Inc., Detroit, 1960-62; exec. v.p. Ross Roy, Inc., 1962-64, pres., 1964—. Exec. bd., pres., chmn. orgn. and extension com. Detroit area council Boy Scouts Am; pres. Inst. for Econ. Edn., 1971; mem. adv. bd. United Found., 1970-71; mem. Pres.'s Council on Phys. Fitness and Sports, 1975—; Trustee Alma Coll., New Detroit, Inc., Grace Hosp., Oakland U. Found.; mem. exec. com. Grosse Pointe U. Sch., 1957-58, trustee, 1959—; bd. dirs. Boys Republic, Inc., Greater Met. Detroit Project Hope, Greater Mich. Found.; trustee emeritus Mich. State U. Served from 2d lt. to lt. col. 95th Inf. Div. AUS, 1941-45. Decorated Bronze Star, Purple Heart; named to Nat. Football Hall of Fame, 1968, to Mich. Sports Hall of Fame, 1973. Mem. Detroit Sales Execs. Club (v.p. 1951), Am. Assn. Advt. Agys. (chmn. Mich. 1960, nat. chmn. 1978-79), Mich. C. of C. (dir.), Greater Detroit C. of C. (dir. 1970-71, chmn. 1977-78). Presbyterian (elder). Clubs: Detroit Athletic, Country of Detroit, Adcraft (pres. 1960-61), Detroit, Economic, Yondotega (Detroit); Seminole Golf, Everglades (Palm Beach, Fla.); Jupiter Hills. Home: 582 Peach Tree Ln Grosse Pointe Woods MI 48236 also: 80 Celestial Way Juno Beach FL 33408 Office: Ross Roy Inc 100 Bloomfield Hills Pkwy Bloomfield MI 48013

PINGS, ANTHONY CLAUDE, architect; b. Fresno, Calif., Dec. 16, 1951; s. Clarence Hubert and Mary (Murray) P.; m. Carole Clements, June 25, 1983. AA, Fresno City Coll., 1972; BArch, Calif. Poly. State U., San Luis Obispo, 1976. Lic. architect, Calif.; cert. Nat. Council Archtl. Registration Bds. Architect Aubrey Moore Jr., Fresno, 1976-81; architect, prin. Anthony C. Pings, AIA, Fresno, 1981-83, 86—, Pings-Taylor Assocs., Fresno, 1983-85. Prin. works include Gollaher Profl. Office (Masonry Merit award 1985, Best Office Bldg. award 1986), Fresno Imaging Ctr. (Best Institutional Project award 1986, Nat. Healthcare award Modern Health Care mag. 1986), Orthopedic Facility (award of honor Masonry Inst. 1987, award of merit San Joaquin chpt. AIA 1987). Mem. Calif. Indsl. Tech. Edn. Consortium Calif. State Dept. Edn., 1983, 84. Mem. AIA (bd. dirs. Calif. chpt. 1983-84, v.p. San Joaquin chpt. 1982, pres. 1983, Calif. Council evaluation team 1983, team leader Coalinga Emergency Design Assistance team). Democrat. Home: 4350 N Safford Ave Fresno CA 93704 Office: Anthony C Pings AIA 1640 W Shaw Ste 107 Fresno CA 93711

PINKELMAN, FRANKLIN CHARLES, auditor; b. Toledo, May 2, 1932; s. Theodore B. and Henrietta M. (King) P.; m. Elizabeth Jean Kirwan, Apr. 30, 1960; children: Franklin, James, Nancy, Michael, Brian, Catherine. BS in Acctg., U. Detroit, 1957, MBA, 1963. Auditor Marvin Polewach, CPA, Birmingham, Mich., 1957-59, Miller Bailey & Co., CPA, Detroit, 1959-61, Nat. Bank Wyandotte, Taylor, Mich., 1961-64; asst. prof. U. Detroit, Mich., 1964-66; dep. auditor gen. Office Auditor Gen., Lansing, Mich., 1966-82; auditor gen. Office Auditor Gen., Lansing, 1982-89; v.p., gen. auditor Blue Cross Blue Shield of Mich., Detroit, 1989—; past chmn. Govt. Acctg. Standards Adv. Coun.; adj. prof. grad. program Wayne State U., Detroit. Contbr. articles to profl. jour. Bd. dirs. Northville Little League Baseball, 1977, 78, St. Francis Home for Boys, Detroit, 1987-89; mem. Ad Hoc Com. on Code for Student Behavior; mem. adv. council Cen. Mich. U. Dean of Bus. Sch. Served to cpl. U.S. Army, 1953-55. Mem. AICPA, Mich. Assn. CPA's, Nat. Assn. State Auditors, Compts., and Treas. (exec. com.), Nat. State Auditors Assn. (pres. 1986), Detroit Chpt. Inst. Internal Auditors (pres. 1986-87), Govt. Fin. Officers Assn. (com. on acctg.). Office: Blue Cross Blue Shield of Mich 600 Lafayette Ste 2009 Detroit MI 48226

PINKERTON, JAMES DONALD, diversified corporation executive; b. Chgo., May 28, 1940; s. R. Donald and Naomi (Rettke) P.; m. Cynthia W. Willis, Nov. 26, 1960; children—Brian, Tom, Jay. B.S. in Law, Northwestern U., 1961, J.D., 1963. Bar: Ill 1963. Atty. Swift and Co., Chgo., 1963-66; atty. Household Fin. Corp., Chgo., 1966-68, asst. sec., 1968-72, sec., 1972-74, sec., asst. gen. counsel, 1974-78; v.p. adminstrn., sec. Household Fin. Corp., Prospect Heights, Ill., 1978-80, sr. v.p. adminstrn., sec., 1980-81; sr. v.p. adminstrn., sec. Household Internat. Inc., Prospect Heights, 1981—. Mem. Am. Soc. Corp. Secs., ABA, Ill. State Bar Assn., Am. Soc. for Personnel Adminstrn., Chgo. Bar Assn., Chgo. Council on Fgn. Relations, Com. Fgn. Affairs. Office: Household Internat Inc 2700 Sanders Rd Prospect Heights IL 60070

PINKERTON, ROBERT BRUCE, mechanical engineer; b. Detroit, Feb. 10, 1941; s. George Fulwell and Janet Lois (Hedke) P.; student MIT, 1959-61; m. Barbara Ann Bandfield, Aug. 13, 1966; 1 child, Robert Brent. BS in Mech. Engrng., Detroit Inst. Tech., 1965; MAE, Chrysler Inst. Engrng., 1967; JD, Wayne State U., 1976. From mech. engr. to emissions and fuel economy planning specialist Chrysler Engrng. Office, Chrysler Corp., Highland Park, Mich., 1967-80; dir. engrng. Replacement div. TRW, Inc., Cleve., 1980-83, v.p. engrng. TRW Automotive Aftermarket Group, 1983-86; v.p. engrng. and research Blackstone Corp., Jamestown, N.Y., 1986-89, pres., 1989—; pres. Chautauqua Co. Fund for Arts. Mem. Soc. Automotive Engrs. (chmn maintenance div.), Am. Soc. Mech. Engrs. Presbyterian. Clubs: Moon Brook Country, Chautauqua Lake Yacht. Home: 5 Ridgley Terr Jamestown NY 14701

PINNELL, GARY RAY, juridicial consultant, lawyer; b. San Antonio, Oct. 2, 1951; s. Raymond A., Jr., and Mary Ruth (Waller) P. BBA, U. Tex.-Austin, 1973, postgrad., 1976-77; JD, St. Mary's U., San Antonio, 1976. Bar: Tex. 1976, U.S. Supreme Ct. 1982, U.S. Ct. Appeals (all cirs.), U.S. Tax Ct. 1976, U.S. Ct. Claims 1977, U.S. Ct. Customs and Patent Appeals 1978. Sole practice, Austin, Tex., 1976-77, San Antonio, 1977-88; juridicial cons., 1988—; legis. asst. to Rep. Danny E. Hill, 1977; instr. U. Tex.-Austin, 1976-77. Bd. govs. Soc. Colonial Wars, Tex., 1978-88, gov., 1987-88. Decorated officer Order St. John, Queen Elizabeth II, 1977, comdr., 1985; officer Order Polonia Restituta (Poland), 1982, comdr. with star, 1984, grand cross, 1986; knight Teutonic Order (Vatican), 1979, Order Constantine St. George, Italy, 1979, numerous others. Mem. Internat. Bar Assn., Mexican Acad. Internat. Law, Tex. Soc. S.R., Tex. Soc. SAR, Soc. of War 1812, Omicron Delta Kappa, Delta Sigma Pi, Phi Alpha Delta. Republican. Roman Catholic. Club: St. John's (London). Contbr. articles legal jours. Home: 118 Rio Bravo San Antonio TX 78232

PINOLA, JOSEPH JOHN, banker; b. Pittston, Pa., May 13, 1925; m. Doris Jean Walker; children: Mary, James. B.A. in Econs, Bucknell U., 1949; postgrad., Dartmouth Coll., 1960; A.M.P., Harvard U., 1971; H.L.D., Wilkes Coll., 1978. With Bank of Am., 1953-76, sr. v.p., 1970-74, exec. v.p. N.Am. div., 1974-76; pres., dir. United Calif. Bank, 1976-77; dir. First Interstate Bancorp. (formerly Western Bancorp.), L.A., 1977—; chmn., chief exec. officer First Interstate Bancorp. (formerly Western Bancorp.), 1978—; bd. dirs. First Interstate Bank Wash., First Interstate Bank Calif., Lockheed Corp., SCEcorp, SCEcorp, So. Calif. Edison Co. Mem. adv. bd. Salvation Army, Los Angeles; campaign chmn. L.A. Area United Way, 1981-82; chmn. bd. govs. Music Ctr. L.A. County. With USNR. Mem. Assn. Res. City Bankers, Calif. Club, L.A. Country Club. Office: First Interstate Bancorp 707 Wilshire Blvd Los Angeles CA 90017

PINZ, JOSEPH JOHN, accountant; b. Queens, N.Y.C., Jan. 30, 1955; s. Joseph John and Mary Elizabeth (Walsh) P. AA in Liberal Arts, SUNY, Farmingdale, 1975; BS in Acctg., St. John's U., 1977; MBAin Fin., Fordham U., 1985. CPA, N.Y. Jr. acct. 1st Boston Group, N.Y.C., 1978-79; acct. Transatlantic Reins. Co., N.Y.C., 1979-82, Schlumberger, Ltd., N.Y.C., 1982-84, Izod Lacoste, N.Y.C., 1984-86; jr. auditor Sperduto, Spector & Co. CPAs, N.Y.C., 1986-87; sr. corp. acct. Aegon Reins. Co. Am., N.Y.C., 1987—. Mem. AICPAs. Home: 76-11 45th Ave Elmhurst NY 11373 Office: Aegon Reins Co 127 John St New York NY 10038

PIOTROWSKI, CRAIG L., vocational college official; b. Kansas City, Mo., Oct. 26, 1945; s. Stanley and Betty (Hartwell) P.; m. Beverly Ann Boelter, June 19, 1945; children: James Craig, David William. AA in Acctg., Fox Valley Tech. Coll., 1966; BA, U. Wis., Oshkosh, 1972; MBA, U. Wis., Milw., 1981. CPA, Wis. Data processing mgr. Universal Foundry, Oshkosh, 1965-70; tax acct. Williams & Guiles, Oshkosh, 1971-72; staff acct. Deloitte Haskins and Sells, Milw., 1972-73; comml. auditor Arthur Andersen and Co., Milw., 1973-78; v.p. Waukesha County Tech. Coll., Pewaukee, Wis., 1978—; past chmn. fin. acctg. com. Wis. Tech. Coll. System; past mem. policies and procedures coordinating com. Wis. Vocat. Tech. and Adult Edn.; mem. govt. acctg. standards adv. coun. Contbr. articles to profl. publs. Elder Beautiful Savior Luth. Ch., Waukesha, Wis., 1986—. Mem. Nat. Assn. Coll. and Univ. Officers (past chmn.), AICPA, Wis. Inst. CPA's (chmn. acctg. careers com. 1975), Assn. Sch. Bus. Ofcls. (chmn. acctg. resch. 1978), Govt. Fin. Officers Assn., Nat. Coun. Community Coll. Bus. Ofcls., Internat. Assn. Bus. Sch. Ofcls. (certs. excellence in fin. reporting), Govt. Acctg. Standards Adv. Coun., Beta Gamma Sigma. Republican. Office: Waukesha County Tech Coll 800 Main St Pewaukee WI 53072

PIOTROWSKI, JOHN ALFRED, food company executive; b. Phila., July 26, 1954; s. J. Alfred and Lucille Mary (Ferrante) P.; m. Joan Eleanor McBeth, Oct. 1, 1977; children: Kristen, Kathleen. BS, Drexel U., 1976; MBA, Wharton Sch. U. Pa., 1980. CPA, Pa. Acct. Deloitte Haskins & Sells, Phila., 1976-78; exec. trainee Anheuser-Busch Cos., Inc., St. Louis, 1980-81, analyst, 1981-82, mgr. diversification planning, 1982-83; dir. planning Campbell Taggart sub. Anheuser-Busch Cos., Inc., Dallas, 1983, v.p. planning, devel., 1983—, also bd. dirs. Office: Campbell Taggart Inc 6211 Lemmon Ave Dallas TX 75209

PIPER, ADDISON LEWIS, securities executive; b. Mpls., Oct. 10, 1946; s. Harry Cushing and Virginia (Lewis) P.; m. Louise Wakefield (div.); children: Gretchen, Tad, William; m. Cynthia Schuneman, Nov. 14, 1979; children: Elisabeth LaBelle, Richard LaBelle. BA in Econs., Williams Coll., 1968; MBA, Stanford U., 1972. Mktg. cons. Earl Savage and Co., Mpls., 1968-69; mem. capital market dept. Piper, Jaffray and Hopwood, Mpls., 1969-70, asst. syndicate mgr., 1972-73, v.p., 1973-79, dir. trading, 1973-77, dir. sales, 1977-79, exec. v.p., dir. mktg., 1979-83, chief exec. officer, chmn. mgmt. com., 1983—, chmn. bd. dirs., 1988—; adv. com. N.Y. Stock Exchange, 1986—. Fin. chmn. Senator Durenberger Fin. Com., Mpls., 1980—; bd. dirs. Minn. Pub. Radio, Mpls., 1986—, Minn. Bus. Partnership, Spring Hill Conf. Ctr., Wayzata, Minn., 1986—, Guthrie Theater, Mpls., Abbott NW Hosp., Mpls., Washburn Child Guidance Ctr., Mpls., Stanford Bus. Sch.; bd. dirs., exec. com. Mpls. Downtown Council, 1986—. Mem. Securities Industry Assn. (bd. govs. 1986—). Republican. Episcopalian. Clubs: Woodhill Country (Wayzata); Minneapolis. Office: Piper Jaffray & Hopwood Inc 222 S 9th St PO Box 28 Minneapolis MN 55440

PIPER, GEORGE EARLE, retailing design and services company executive; b. Greenfield, Mass., Jan. 31, 1932; s. George B. and Elizabeth J. (Jones) P.; B.E., Keene State Coll., 1959, postgrad., 1959-60; postgrad. U. Mass., 1959-60, Boston U., 1960-61; Harvard, 1984; m. Barbara Ann Piper; children: Sherri, Terri, Luanne, Mark. Cert. Store Profl. Dir. aux. services Keene (N.H.) State Coll., 1959-61; dir. purchasing and aux. enterprises U. Vt., Burlington, 1961-64; dir. state univ. store system U. Maine, Orono, 1964-68; pres. Store Ops. Services, Inc. and Creative Design Concepts, Franklin, Mass., 1968—; tchr. U. Maine, Orono, 1966-67; chmn. various profl. workshops, 1965-83; mem. various nat. merchandising coms. 1959-61, 69-71. Mem. sch. bd. Winchester, N.H., 1959-61. Served with A.C., USN, 1951-55. Recipient 4 nat. merchandising awards, 1961-66, service awards Nat. Assn. Coll. Stores, 1969-70, Nat. Assn. Coll. Aux. Services, 1974-75; 2 week nat. tour award Nat. Assn. Aux. Enterprises, 1976. Mem. Inst. Store Planners, Am. Soc. Interior Designers, Boston Soc. Architects, Nat. Assn. Coll. Stores, Coll. Stores of New Eng. (pres. 1967-69), Mid-Atlantic Coll. Stores, Mass. Businessmen's Assn., Kappa Delta Phi. Clubs: Masons, Shriners. Designer more than 490 coll. univ. aux. service areas of stores; contbr. to profl. jours.; columnist for prof. jours. Home: 8 Smith Hollow Dr Edgartown MA 02359 Office: 5 Main St Franklin MA 02038

PIPKIN, ALVA (CLAUDE), beverage company executive; b. Mulberry, Fla., Mar. 16, 1931; s. Edgar Holmes and Cleo Judson (Limeberger) P.; m. Lois Rhodes, Oct. 14, 1961; children: Stephen Rhodes, Amy Lois. BS in Acctg. and Econs. magna cum laude, Fla. So. U., 1953. Acct./supr. Chemstrand Corp., Pensacola, Fla., 1953-60; sr. auditor N.Y.C., 1960-65; audit mgr. Monsanto Co., St. Louis, 1965-68, systems mgr., 1968-72; asst. controller Iowa Beef Processors, Inc., Dakota City, Nebr., 1972-75, asst. v.p., asst. controller, 1975-78, asst. v.p., ops. controller, 1978-81; v.p., controller Adolph Coors Co., Golden, Colo., 1981—; bd. advisors Faulkner & Gray's Corp. Controller. Bd. dirs. Tech. Assistance Ctr., Denver, 1986—; mem. adv. bd. Computer Sci. and Tech. Info. Systems, Regis Coll., Denver, 1988; mem. adv. bd. Bus. Alumni U. Colo., 1986—. Mem. Planning Forum, Fin. Execs. Internat., Nat. Assn. Accts., Controllers Council, Fin. Mgmt. Assn., Sigma Iota Epsilon (Businessman of Yr. 1987). Methodist. Home: 142 S Devinney St Golden CO 80401 Office: Adolph Coors Co 12th & Ford Golden CO 80401-1295

PIRET, MARGUERITE ALICE, investment banker; b. St. Paul, May 10, 1948; d. E.L. and Alice Piret; m. Richard H. Rosen, Dec. 23, 1970; children: Andrew, Anne. AB, Radcliffe Coll., 1969; MBA, Harvard U., 1974. Comml. loan officer Bank New Eng., Boston, 1974-79; mng. dir. Kridel Securities Corp., N.Y.C., 1979-81; pres., founder Newbury, Piret & Co., Boston, 1981—, also bd. dirs.; trustee, mem. audit com. Pioneer Fund, Pioneer II Fund, Pioneer Three Fund, Pioneer Bond Fund, Pioneer Mcpl. Bond Fund, Pioneer Money Market Fund. Mem. visitors' com. Am. Decorative Arts and Sculpture at Mus. Fine Arts, Boston, 1982—; mem. overseer candidates nominating com. Harvard U., bd. dirs. nominating com. Harvard Alumni Assn., 1983-86, adv. com. on shareholder responsibility, 1986-87; trustee, exec. com. Univ. Hosp., 1980—; trustee Boston Ballet Sch. Mem. Mass. Hosp. Assn. (trustee 1983-86). Clubs: City, Harvard. Office: Newbury Piret & Co One State St 12th Fl Boston MA 02109

PIRIE, ROBERT S., security dealer, lawyer; b. Chgo., 1934; m. Deirdre Pirie. A.B., Harvard U., 1956, LL.B., 1962. Bar: Mass. 1962. Law clk. to chief justice Mass. Supreme Ct., 1962-63; formerly counsel Gaston, Snow, Motley & Holt, Boston; ptnr., then sr. ptnr. Skaddeu, Arps, Slate, Meagher & Flom, Boston; pres., chief exec. officer Rothschild, Inc., N.Y.C., 1982—; chmn. Rothschild Asset Mgmt., Inc., N.Y.C., 1982—. Mem. Brook Club. Office: Rothschild Inc 1 Rockefeller Pla New York NY 10020 *

PISATURO, RONALD JOSEPH, entrepreneur; b. N.Y.C., Dec. 18, 1954. BS in Applied Math., MIT, 1976. Mgr. Citicorp, N.Y.C., 1976-79; pres., founder Am. Renaissance Schs. Inc., White Plains, N.Y., 1979—; cons. Crocker Nat. Bank, San Francisco, 1980, AT&T, Piscataway, N.J., 1983, Citicorp, N.Y.C., 1983. Contbr. articles to profl. jours. Office: Am Renaissance Sch 468 Rosedale Ave White Plains NY 10605

PISER, DONALD HARRIS, construction company executive; b. N.Y.C., July 4, 1941; B.S.C.E., Villanova U., 1962. Formerly with Bethlehem Steel Corp.; with Morse/Diesel, Inc., N.Y.C., v.p., 1970, sr. v.p. Western Region, 1976, pres., 1979—, chief exec. officer, chmn. bd., 1980—. Office: Morse/ Diesel Inc 1515 Broadway New York NY 10036 *

PISNEY, RAYMOND FRANK, consulting services executive; b. Lime Springs, Iowa, June 2, 1940; s. Frank A. and Cora H. P. BA, Loras Coll., 1963; postgrad., Cath. U. Am., 1963; MA, U. Del., 1965. Asst. adminstrn. and rsch. Mt. Vernon, Va., 1965-69; historic sites adminstr. N.C. Archives and Hist. Dept., Raleigh, 1969; asst. adminstr. div. historic sites and museums N.C. Dept. Art, Culture and History, Raleigh, 1969-72; cons. Cannon Mills Co., Kannapolis, N.C., 1972-73; exec. dir. Woodrow Wilson Birthplace Found., Staunton, Va., 1973-78, Mo. Hist. Soc., St. Louis, 1978-87; v.p. cons. svcs. Exec. Transitions Inc., Washington, 1987—; pres. Va. History and Museums Fedn., 1977-78; pres. Mo. Museums Assoc., 1982-84. Author: Historical Markers: A Bibliography, 1977, Historic Markers: Planning Local Programs, 1978, A Preview to Historical Marking, 1976, Old Buildings: New Resources for Work and Play, 1976; editor: Virginians Remember Woodrow Wilson, 1978, Woodrow Wilson in Retrospect, 1978, Woodrow Wilson: Idealism and Realty, 1977, Historic Preservation and

Public Policy in Virginia, 1978. Mem. internat. com. Charles A. Lindbergh Anniversary, 1987. Recipient Bertha Black Rhoda award NAACP, 1985; Hagley fellow U. Del., 1963-65; Seminar for Hist. Adminstrs. fellow, 1965. Mem. Am. Assn. Museums, Nat. Trust Historic Preservation U.S., Am. Assn. State and local History, Can. Museums Assn., Brit. Museums Assn., Internat. Council Monuments and Sites, Internat. Council Museums, Phi Alpha Theta. Roman Catholic. Office: 1655 N Fort Myer Dr Ste 1150 Arlington/Rosslyn VA 22209

PISTNER, STEPHEN LAWRENCE, retail chain executive; b. St. Paul, Mar. 14, 1932; s. Leopold and Prudence Charlette (Selcer) P.; children: Paul David, John Alan, Betsy Ann. B.S.B.A., U. Minn., 1953. Pres., chief exec. officer Target Stores, Inc., Mpls., 1973-76, chmn., chief exec. officer, 1976; exec. v.p. Dayton Hudson Corp., Mpls., 1976-77, pres., chief operating officer, 1977-81, also dir.; pres., chief exec. officer Montgomery Ward & Co., Inc., Chgo., 1981-85; chmn. bd., chief exec. officer McCrory Corp., 1985-88; exec. v.p. Rapid-Am. Corp., N.Y.C., 1985-88. Bd. dirs. Lyric Opera Chgo., Sundance Inst., Utah; trustee Chgo. Symphony Orch., Orchestral Assn. Chgo.; mem. council U. Chgo. Grad. Sch. Mem. Nat. Retail Mchts. Assn. (bd. dirs., exec. com.), Am. Retail Fedn. (bd. dirs.). Office: 1021 Rhodes Villa Ln Delray Beach FL 33483

PISTOR, CHARLES HERMAN, JR., banker; b. St. Louis, Aug. 26, 1930; s. Charles Herman and Virginia (Brown) P.; m. Regina Prikryl, Sept. 20, 1952; children: Lori Ellen, Charles Herman III, Jeffrey Glenn. BBA, U. Tex., 1952; MBA, Harvard U., 1956, So. Meth. U., 1961. Chmn., chief exec. officer First RepublicBank Dallas, 1980-88, also bd. dirs.; chief exec. officer Northpark Nat. Bank, Dallas, 1988—, also chmn. bd. dirs.; bd. dirs. Am. Brands, AMR, Centex Corp., Sun E&P. Trustee So. Meth. U., Dallas; elder Presbyn. Ch. Served to lt. USNR, 1952-54. Mem. Am. Bankers Assn. (pres., bd. dirs.). Club: Dallas Country. Home: 4200 Belclaire Dallas TX 75205 Office: Northpark Nat Bank PO Box 12206 Dallas TX 75225

PITCHER, MAX GROW, exploration company executive, geologist; b. Calgary, Alta., Can., Apr. 22, 1935; s. Morgan Hinman and Favorite (Grow) P.; m. Diana Nutter, Feb. 12, 1960; children—Stephen, Shauna, Thomas, Andrea, Marcia. B.S. in Geology, Brigham Young U., 1959, M.S. in Geology, 1960; Ph.D. in Geology, Columbia U., 1964. Cert. petroleum geologist, Can. Research scientist Conoco Inc., Ponca City, Okla., 1963-65, dir. geologic research, 1965-68; asst. to v.p. Conoco Inc., Houston, 1968-69, dir. geology Western hemisphere, 1973-76; Rocky Mountain div. geologist Conoco Inc., Denver, 1969-73; v.p., gen. mgr. N.Am. exploration Conoco Inc., Houston, 1976-86, v.p. internat. exploration, 1986—. Contbr. articles to profl. jours. Vice pres. Sandalwood Civic Assn., Houston, 1978-79, pres., 1979-80. Mem. Houston Geologic Soc., Am. Assn. Petroleum Geologists (grantee 1981-85, subcom. chmn., research com. chmn. 1984-86, mem. selection com. future petroleum geologists 1985-86), Am. Petroleum Inst. (gen. com. exploration affairs 1984-86), Worldwide Exploration (exec. v.p. 1988). Republican. Mem. Ch. of Jesus Christ of Latter-day Saints. Office: Conoco Inc 600 N Dairy Ashford St Houston TX 77079

PITEGOFF, PETER ROBERT, lawyer, educator; b. N.Y.C., Mar. 6, 1953; s. Joseph and Libbie (Shapiro) P.; m. Ann Casady, Mar. 22, 1986; 1 child, Maxwell Jacob. AB, Brown U., 1975; JD, NYU, 1981. Bar: Mass 1981, N.Y. 1988; cert. tchr., R.I. Tchr. Hope High Sch., Providence, 1974-75; community organizer Nat. Assn. for So. Poor, Petersburg, Va., 1975-76, Citizens Action League, Oakland, Calif., 1977-78; gen. counsel Indsl. Coop. Assn., Somerville, Mass., 1981-88; ptnr. Arrington & Pitegoff, Somerville, 1986-88; assoc. prof. law SUNY, Buffalo, 1988—; guest instr. law Harvard U., Cambridge, Mass., 1986; adj. asst. prof. law NYU, 1986-88; cons. in field, 1978—; legal counsel community devel. worker purchases of bus. and plant shut-down responses. Contbr. to profl. publs. Root-Tilden scholarship NYU, 1978; grantee Pub. Interest Law Found., N.Y.C., 1981. Democrat. Jewish. Office: SUNY Faculty Law John Lord O'Brien Hall Buffalo NY 14260

PITKOWSKY, MURRAY, financial executive; b. N.Y.C., June 25, 1931; s. Aaron and Celia (Zaft) P.; m. Peggy Wilsker, June 19, 1954; children: Lisa Joy, Fayne Leslie, Daniel Jay, Erica Lynn. BA, CCNY, 1952; MBA, U. Pa., 1954. Plant controller Corning (N.Y.) Glass Works, 1956-58; asst. div. controller Raytheon Co., Newton, Mass., 1958-61; group controller tech. products The Singer Co., N.Y.C., 1961-67; v.p. fin. Anken Industries, Morristown, N.J., 1967-71; v.p. controller Crompton & Knowles Corp., Parsippany, N.J., 1972-83; v.p. fin. Petroferm, Inc., Fenandina Beach, Fla., 1983-86; v.p. fin., treas. Datascope Corp., Paramus, N.J., 1986—; bd. dirs. Petroferm, Inc. Served with U.S. Army, 1954-56. Mem. Nat. Assn. Accts. (v.p.), Fin. Exec. Inst. Office: Datascope Corp 580 Winters Ave Paramus NJ 07653-0005

PITT, EARLE WILLIAM, manufacturing company executive; b. Bklyn., June 4, 1923; s. Earle D. and Catherine T. (O'Neil) P.; B.S. in Mech. Engring., So. Meth. U., 1948; m. Alice M. Altman, Oct. 23, 1946; children—Linda, Karen, Earle, Alice Susan, Margaret. Gen. mgr. Foxboro Co. (Mass.), 1965-68, exec. v.p., 1968-70, pres., 1970-81, chief exec. officer, 1973-88, chmn., 1977—, also dir.; dir. Bank of New England, N.A., Boston, Wyman-Gordon, Worcester, Mass., GenRad, Concord, Mass., Liberty Mut. Ins. Co., Boston, Liberty Mut. Fire Ins. Co., Boston. Bd. dirs., v.p. Neponset Valley Found., Norwood, Mass.; trustee St. Michael's Coll., Winooski, Vt.; trustee, past mem. exec. com. New Eng. Coll. Fund. Served with AC, U.S. Army, 1942-46. Mem. Sci. Apparatus Makers Assn., Elec. Mfrs. Club, Instrument Soc. Am. Office: The Foxboro Co Bristol Park 38 Neponset Ave Foxboro MA 02035

PITT, GAVIN ALEXANDER, management consultant; b. Berkeley, Calif., Aug. 4, 1915; s. David Alexander and Maude Elizabeth (Hanna) P.; m. Eleanore Whiting, Sept. 2, 1939; children: Gavin Alexander, Gaele Whiting, Judson Hamilton. AB, Brown U., 1938; MEd, Johns Hopkins U., 1959. Asst. dean Brown U., Providence, 1938-42; mgr. exec. tng. Macy's, N.Y.C., 1942-43; dir. personnel Hazeltine Electronics Corp., N.Y.C., 1943-45; asst. indsl. adminstr. AMF, Inc., N.Y.C., 1945-49; assoc. Booz, Allen & Hamilton, N.Y.C., 1949-55; dir. personnel services Gen. Dynamics Corp., N.Y.C., 1955-57; v.p. Johns Hopkins U. and Hosp., Balt., 1957-60; pres. Presbyn.-St. Lukes Hosp., Chgo., 1960-63; pvt. practice cons. 1963-66, 70-74; pres. St. John's Mil. Acad., Delafield, Wis., 1966-70; adminstrv. officer Antioch Coll. and U. Yellow Springs, Ohio, 1974-79; devel. officer Wright State U., Dayton, Ohio, 1981-86; pres. Gavin Pitt Assocs., Inc., Chgo., Denver and Calif., 1986—, Water Tower Pub. House, Chgo., 1989—; lectr. CCNY, 1948-57; exec. dir. Inst. Medicine of Chgo., 1963-66; bd. dirs. Balt. Life Ins. Co. Author: The Twenty Minute Lifetime, 1959. Sec., bd. dirs. Am. Assn. Gifted Children, N.Y.C, 1985-86, v.p. Chgo. area council Boy Scouts Am., 1961-66, mem. nat. council, 1966-68; trustee Latin Sch. Chgo., 1962-64; bd. corporators The Peddie Sch., Hightstown, N.J. Mem. Am. Mgmt. Assn. (personnel div. adv. council), Assn. Military Schs. and Colls., Nat. Council Chs. (gen. personnel com.), Brown U. Alumni Assn. (Brown Bear Disting. Alumnus 1961), Omicron Delta Kappa, Newcomen Soc. Club: Dayton Racquet, Engineers; Saddle and Cycle (Chgo.). Office: 625 N Michigan Ave Chicago IL 60611

PITT, GEORGE, lawyer; b. Chgo., July 21, 1938; s. Cornelius George and Anastasia (Geocaris) P.; m. Barbara Lynn Goodrich, Dec. 21, 1963; children: Elizabeth Nanette, Margaret Leigh. BA, Northwestern U., 1960, JD, 1963. Bar: Ill. 1963. Assoc. Chapman and Cutler, Chgo., 1963-67; ptnr. Borge and Pitt, and predecessor, 1968-87; ptnr. Katten Muchin & Zavis, Chgo., 1987—. Served to 1st lt. AUS, 1964. Mem. ABA, Ill. State Bar Assn., Chgo. Bar Assn., Eta Sigma Phi, Phi Delta Phi, Phi Gamma Delta. Home: 600 N McClurg Ct Chicago IL 60611 Office: Katten Muchin & Zavis 525 W Monroe St Ste 1600 Chicago IL 60606

PITTI, DONALD ROBERT, financial service company executive; b. N.Y.C., Sept. 15, 1929; s. August and Mary (Vitaglione) P.; m. Grace Allen Curtis, Aug. 14, 1954; children: Gail, Robert. BJ, NYU, 1959; postgrad., Adelphi U., 1963-65. Asst. v.p. Standard & Poor's Corp., N.Y.C., 1959-65; v.p. Quotron, Inc., N.Y.C., 1965-67; pres. Wiesenberger & Co., N.Y.C., 1967-76; v.p. John Nuveen & Co., Inc., N.Y.C., 1976-87; pres. Monarch Resources, Inc., N.Y.C., 1987-88; chmn., chief exec. officer Monarch Fin. Svcs., Inc., N.Y.C., 1988—; trustee Found. Fin. Planning, Atlanta, 1986—. Editor: Handbook of Financial Planning, 1988; contbr. articles to profl. publs. With USN, 1948-49, 50-52. Mem. Internat. Assn. Fin. Planning (pres.), Union League, Manhasset Bay Yacht Club. Home: 169 Kensett Rd Manhasset NY 11030 Office: Monarch Fin Svcs 780 3d Ave New York NY 10017

PITTMAN, CRAIG SORRELL, SR., lawyer; b. Enterprise, Ala., Sept. 6, 1956; s. John Edwin and Marjorie (Brunson) P.; m. Kathleen P. Perrott, May 19, 1979 (div. Mar. 1987); children: Craig Sorrell Jr., Jennifer Leigh. BA, Middlebury (Vt.) Coll., 1978; JD, Samford U., 1981. Bar: Ala. 1981, Fla. 1982. Law clk. to sr. judge U.S. Dist. Ct. (so. dist.) Ala., Mobile, 1981-83; assoc. Hamilton, Butler, Riddick, Tarlton & Sullivan, Mobile, 1983-87; pvt. practice Mobile, 1987—. Mem. Ala. Bar Assn., Fla. Bar Assn., Mobile Bar Assn., Maritime Law Assn., Southeastern Admiralty Law Inst. Republican. Methodist. Home: 210 S Georgia Ave Mobile AL 36604 Office: 1905 Government St PO Box 66733 Mobile AL 36660-1733

PITTMAN, EDGAR LAWTON, JR., manufacturing company executive; b. Jackson, Miss., Aug. 6, 1940; s. Edgar Lawton and Beaulah (Shaw) P.; divorced; 1 child, Angela Kaye; m. Sue Hicks, Oct. 29, 1977. BBA, U. Tex., Arlington, 1965. CPA, Tex. Acct. Fox & Jacobs Constrn. Co., Dallas, 1962-67; supr. Ernst & Whinney, Raleigh, N.C., 1967-72; sr. v.p., chief fin. officer AMIC Corp., Raleigh, 1972-83; pres. Microwave Labs., Inc., Raleigh, 1983—. Mem. steering com. Wake County Republican Com., 1987—. Mem. AICPA, N.C. Assn. CPA's, Tex. Soc. CPA's, Airplane Owners and Pilots Assn. Baptist. Office: Microwave Labs Inc 8917 Glenwood Ave Raleigh NC 27612

PITTOCK, EDWIN JOSEPH, securities trading company executive; b. Colorado Springs, Colo., June 6, 1943; s. Carl L. and Lois M. (Hansen) P.; m. Pamela M. Martin, Apr. 16, 1965; children: Troy, Casey. BA in Bus. Adminstrn., U. No. Colo., 1965; advanced degree in Fin., N.Y. Inst. Fin., 1966. Account exec. Bosworth, Sullivan & Co., Greeley, Colo., 1967-72; account exec., pres. Barton & Co., Greeley, Colo., 1972-74; chmn. bd. dirs. E.J. Pittock & Co., Inc., Greeley, Colo., 1974-86; chmn. bd. Continental Heritage Mut. Funds, Denver, Colo., 1986—; chmn. RAFCO, Denver, Colo., 1986—; instr. investment courses U. No. Colo., Greeley, 1969-79. Bd. dirs. Greeley Philharmonic, 1977, U. No. Colo. Found., 1981—; active No. Colo. Med. Ctr. Found. fund drive, 1981-82; chmn. fund drive Weld County United Way, 1977—; bus. chmn. Cancer Crusade, 1974; nat. astham com. Greeley Concert Assn., 1980-81. Recipient Outstanding Bus. Achievement award Anchor Corp., 1978, Greeley Jaycees Disting. Service award, 1977; named Greeley Bus. Person of Yr. award, 1977. Mem. Young Pres.'s Orgn., Nat. Assn. Securities Dealers (chmn. 1977-81), Sigma Phi Epsilon. Republican. Congregationalist. Clubs: Greeley Country (pres. 1977-80), Greeley Quarterback (pres. 1968-71), Totem; Glenmoor Country. Lodges: Lions, Elks. Home: 100 Humboldt St Denver CO 80218 Office: Continental Heritage Mut Funds 535 16th St Ste 900 Denver CO 80202

PITTS, DON DUANE, telecommunications company executive; b. North Little Rock, Ark., May 22, 1931; s. James Elmer and Mary Elizabeth (Rexroad) P.; m. Janice March Hewgley, Feb. 4, 1950; children—Richard William, Walter Gregory. Little Rock U., 1962-64. C.P.A., Mo. Audit mgr. Arthur Andersen & Co., St. Louis, 1964-69; div. controller Continental Telephone Co., St. Louis, 1969-71; v.p. Continental Telephone Co., Bakersfield, Calif., 1971-76; controller Continental Telephone Co., Atlanta, 1976-82; v.p., treas. Contel Corp. (formerly Continental Telecom, Inc.), Atlanta, 1982—. Recipient Student Achievement award Wall St. Jour., 1964. Mem. Am. Inst. C.P.A.s. Office: Contel Corp 245 Perimeter Center Pkwy Atlanta GA 30348

PITTS, GARY, health products company executive; b. Auburn, Ala., Aug. 17, 1945; s. Robert Giles and Ruby (Miniard) P.; m. Leslie Eisenberg, Apr. 15, 1984; 1 child, Robert Geoffrey. BS, Auburn U., 1967, MS, 1969; PhD, La. State U., 1971; JD, Rutgers U., 1982. Bar: N.J. 1983. Research fellow NIH, 1971-72; scientist Warner-Lambert Co., Morris Plains, N.J., 1972-77, mgr. chem. and biol. research, 1977-78, dir. biol. research, 1978-83; mgr. applied research Unilever NV, Edgewater, N.J., 1983-85; v.p. biol. Schering-Plough Labs., Memphis, 1985-86; v.p. Oral-B Labs., Redwood City, Calif., 1986—; pvt. practice law Morris Plains, 1983-85; bd. dirs. U.S. Biothane, Atlanta. Mem. ABA, Am. Chem. Soc., Internat. Assn. Dental Research, Am. Soc. Microbiology, N.Y. Acad. Scis., Sports Car Club Am. (pres. local chpt. 1983), Ferrari Owners Club. Republican. Office: Oral B Labs 1 Lagoon Dr Redwood City CA 94065

PITTS, JOE W., III, lawyer, law educator; b. Baton Rouge, Nov. 24, 1960; s. Joe Wise Pitts Jr. and Bobbie (Chachere) Edwards. Cert., Cambridge (Eng.) U., 1980; spl. diploma, Oxford (Eng.) U., 1981; BA, Tulane U., 1982; JD, Stanford U., 1985. Bar: Tex. 1986. Mgr. Leopold Price & Rolle, Houston, 1977-78; prodn. mgr. Tulane U. Theatre, New Orleans, 1978-79; legal assoc. Exxon Co. USA, Houston, 1983, Andrews & Kurth, Houston, 1983, Liddell Sapp, Houston, 1984; legal assoc. Carrington Coleman Sloman & Blumenthal, Dallas, 1984-85, assoc., 1985-88; assoc. Legal Resources Ctr., Johannesburg, Republic South Africa, 1984; vis. asst. prof. law So. Meth U., Dallas, 1988—; cons. Internat. House Publs., Dallas, 1987—; del. UN Commn. on Human Rights, Geneva, 1989. Author numerous articles in field. Bd. dirs. Shakespeare Festival Dallas, 1987—, Proyecto Adelante 1988—; chmn. pub. awareness effort, Dallas Young Lawyers Constitutional Bicentennial Program, 1985-87, bd. dirs., 1987—; vol. Cath. Charities Dallas, 1987—, North Cen. Tex. Legal Services, 1985— (cert. recognition 1985-87). Recipient Cert. of Appreciation Lawyers Against Domestic Violence, Dallas, 1985-87. Mem. ABA (vice chmn. sect. of bus. law, young lawyers div. 1986-88, editor corp. civil and comml. law practice notes, Barrister Mag. 1988—), Dallas Bar Assn. (Disting. Pro Bono Service award, 1987, coord. immigration amnesty appeals com. 1987-88, chair, minority participation com. 1988—), Tex. Assn. Young Lawyers (internat. law, editorial coms. 1985-88, treas. 1989—), Dallas Assn. Young Lawyers (chair, membership com. 1987-88, chair, bill of rights com. 1988—, treas. 1988—) , Tex. Accts. and Lawyers for Arts, Dallas Com. Fgn. Relations (gen. counsel 1987—), Council on Fgn. Relations N.Y. (term mem.), Plaza Athletic Club, Crescent Spa Club, Phi Beta Kappa, Pi Sigma Alpha, Omicron Delta Kappa. Democrat. Unitarian. Office: So Meth U Law Sch 3315 Daniel Dallas TX 75275-0116

PITTS, KEVIN C., management consultant; b. Bklyn., Dec. 20, 1957; s. Robert and Carloyn (Cuffee) P.; m. Tammy Elizabeth Anderson, July 16, 1983. BA in Philosophy, Colgate U., 1978, MBA, 1987. Account exec., valuation specialist Mut. of N.Y., N.Y.C. and Chgo., 1978-84; sr. account exec. HealthChicago, Oakbrook, Ill., 1984-85, Phenix Mut., Chgo., 1985; rsch. analyst Conning & Co. Venture Capital, Hartford, Conn., 1987; mgmt. cons. United Rsch. Co., Morristown, N.Y., 1988—. Baptist. Home: 405 Linden Ln #1A Media PA 19063

PITZELE, DOUGLAS H., electronics technician; b. Mpls., Mar. 6, 1936; s. Marion Blinderman and Fern (Greenberg) Pitzele; m. Sandra Hoffman, May 7, 1955 (div. May 1968); children: Katherine, Lisa, Julie, Eric; m. Lois K. Pitzele, May 25, 1969; 1 child, Anne. Student, U. Minn. Electronics technician Sherburne Communications Ctr., Elk River, Minn.; pres., chief exec. officer Dousan Electronics Inc., Elk River, 1957—. Active work with handicapped children MS Soc.; precinct chmn. Democratic Farm Labor party, Livonia, 1988. Recipient Vol. of Yr. award North Star chpt MS Soc., Mpls., 1987. Jewish. Clubs: Anoka Shrine, Zurah Shrine. Lodge: Elks. Home: PO Box 156 Zimmerman MN 55398 Office: Sherburne Communication Ctr 920 W Hwy 10 Elk River MN 55330

PIVIK, ROBERT WILLIAM, accounting executive; b. Renton, Pa., Oct. 29, 1937; s. George and Amelia (Kern) P.; m. Yvonne C. Pivik, Aug. 6, 1960; children: Keith, Sharon, Tracey. BS, Pa. State U., 1959. CPA, D.C. Staff acct. Deloitte Haskins & Sells, Pitts., 1959-67; mgr. Deloitte Haskins & Sells, N.Y.C., 1967-72, ptnr., 1972, various positions, 1967-83; ptnr.-in-charge Deloitte Haskins & Sells, Washington, 1983-86; area mng. ptnr. Deloitte Haskins & Sells, Md., Va. and Washington, 1986—; also bd. dirs. Deloitte Haskins & Sells. Mem. Greater Washington Bd. Trade, 1983, tax policy task force, 1985; mem. legacy com. Am. Cancer Soc., Md. div., Silver Spring, 1984; adv. com. DeSales Sch. Theology, Washington, 1986. Mem. AICPA, Columbia Inst. CPA's, Wash., Balt. Regional Assn. (bd. dirs.), Tournament Players Club (Avenel), Univ. Club, The City Club, Beta Gamma Sigma, Phi Kappa Phi, Alpha Psi. Republican. Roman Catholic. Office: Deloitte Haskins & Sells 1001 Pennsylvania Ave NW Ste 350 Washington DC 20004-2505

PIXLEY, JOHN SHERMAN, SR., research company executive; b. Detroit, Aug. 24, 1929; s. Rex Arthur and Louise (Sherman) P.; B.A., U. Va., 1951; postgrad. Pa. State U., 1958-59; m. Peggy Marie Payne, Oct. 16, 1949; children—John Sherman, Steven, Lou Ann. Asst. cashier Old Dominion Bank, Arlington, Va., 1953-56; tech. dir. John I. Thompson & Co., research and engring. firm, Bellefonte, Pa., 1956-65; co-founder, exec. v.p. Potomac Research Inc., Alexandria, Va., 1965-80; v.p. Gov. Svcs. Div. Electronic Data Systems, 1980-81; co-founder, pres. Potomac Research Inc. Inc., Alexandria, Va., 1981—. Owner Edgeworth Farm, Orlean, Va. Mem. Fairfax County Republican Com., Annandale, Va., 1964-72; mem. fin. com. for U.S. Rep. Joel T. Broyhill, Republican, Va., 1970-72. Served to 1st lt. AUS 1952-53; maj. Res. ret. Decorated Army Commendation medal. Mem. IEEE, Am. Radio Relay League, Sleepy Hollow Woods Civic Assn. (v.p., pres. 1969-71). Episcopalian. Club: Quantico (Va.) Flying (charter mem.). Home: 3711 Sleepy Hollow Rd Falls Church VA 22041 Office: Potomac Rsch Inc 6121 Lincolnia Rd Alexandria VA 22312

PIZIAK, THOMAS EDWARD, financial analyst; b. Milw., July 15, 1956. BA, Marquette U., 1978; MBA, U. Wis., 1983. Corp. fin. analyst Manpower Inc.

PIZZANO, JOSEPH MATTHEW, health care facility developer; b. Newark, Nov. 16, 1926; s. Sylvester and Phyllis (Merendino) P.; m. A. Ramona Cortese, June 11, 1950: children: Robert, Gregory, Denise, Linda. BSBA, Rutgers U., 1955; postgrad., Seton Hall Law Sch., 1961. Mgr. field sales Alcoa Aluminum, Newark, 1946-50; planning analyst research and devel. Burns & Roe, N.Y.C., 1956-58; dir. contract mgmt. ITT Corp., N.J., Minn., Fla., 1958-76; program exec. Europe, Nigeria ITT Corp., N.Y.C., 1976-82; organizer, gen. ptnr. Care Properties of Montville, N.J., 1980—; founder, pres. Change Bridge Inn, Inc., Montville, 1981—. Served to sgt. USAF, 1945-46, 50-51. Fellow Nat. Contract Mgmt. Assn. (founder, pres. North Jersey chpt. 1970-71, chpt. dir. 1972-73), Delta Sigma Pi (pres. 1953-54). Republican. Lodge: Kiwanis. Home: Meadowbrook Rd RR5 Boonton Township NJ 07005 Office: Change Bridge Inn Inc 165 Change Bridge Rd Montville NJ 07045

PIZZELANTI, ANTHONY F., publishing company executive. V.p. info. systems Macmillan Inc., N.Y.C. Office: Macmillan Inc 866 3rd Ave New York NY 10022 *

PIZZELLA, ANTHONY NICOLA, accountant, realty executive, catering company executive; b. N.Y.C., Oct. 16, 1957; s. Pete and Josephine (Cinotti) P.; m. Cindy Ann Ocera, Mar. 20, 1982; children: Jaclyn Marie, Jeannie Michelle. BBA, Hofstra U., 1978, MBA, 1979. CPA, N.Y.; notary pub. N.Y.; lic. real estate salesman, N.Y. Pvt. practice acctg. Merrick, N.Y., 1979—; sec.-treas. C.O.F. Realty Corp., Massapequa, N.Y., 1981—; owner, sec.-treas. Manor East Caterers, Massapequa, 1981—; acct., co-owner S.I. (N.Y.) & L.I. Devel. Corp., 1986—; staff tax acct. Arthur Anderson & Co., N.Y.C., 1980-81. Mem. Am. Inst. CPA's, L.I. Bd. Realtors, N.Y., State Assn. Realtors, Advancement for Commerce and Industry Club, Beta Gamma Sigma, Beta Alpha Psi. Republican. Roman Catholic. Office: Manor East Caterers 201 Jerusalem Ave Massapequa NY 11758

PLACE, GEOFFREY, consumer goods manufacturing company executive; b. Accrington, Eng., Mar. 11, 1931; came to U.S., 1968; s. Harry and Edith (Salthouse) P.; m. Margaret Janice Entwistle, Aug. 9, 1955; children: Fiona, Andrew, Nicholas, Susan. BA, Kings Coll., Cambridge, Eng., 1953, MA, 1958. With Procter & Gamble Co., 1954—, v.p. research and devel., 1977—; mem. acad. corp. liaison program adv. com. Nat. Acad. Scis. Trustee, chmn. research com. Children's Hosp. Med. Ctr., Children's Hosp., 1979—; trustee Internat. Child Health Found. Served to maj. Brit. Army. Mem. Indsl. Research Inst. Inc. (past pres.), Dirs. Indsl. Research. Episcopalian. Clubs: Queen City, Cowan Lake Sailing Assn. Office: Procter & Gamble Co PO Box 599 Cincinnati OH 45201

PLAGA, ERICH H., mortgage company executive; b. Kassel, Germany, Feb. 21, 1935; came to U.S., 1961; s. Otto Plaga; m. Pamela M. Corke, Apr. 3, 1958; children: Barry, John. BS, Calif. State U., 1965. Chief fin. officer Unionamerica Inc., 1970-78; pres. Genstar Mortgage Corp., Glendale, Calif., 1978—; chmn. Stategic Mortgage Investments, Glendale, 1984—. Office: Genstar Mortgage Co 700 N Central Ave Glendale CA 91203

PLAISS, LINDA CAROL, insurance company executive; b. Highland Park, Mich.; d. Arvil Leo and Mary Beatrice (Barr) Becht; divorced; children: Christopher, Robert. A Computer Sci., Ind. U. S.E., New Albany, 1982. Bookkeeper Bierman Bulldozing, Floyd Knos, Ind., 1962-63; cost acctg. clk. Louisville Bedding, 1963-65; clk. County Clk.'s Office, New Albany, 1967-73; acctg. clk., programmer Mid Continent Carton subs. Ky. Fried Chicken, Louisville, 1973-76; programamer Ky. Fried Chicken, Louisville, 1976-77; asst. v.p. acctg. Ky. Farm Bur. Ins. Co., Louisville, 1977—. Asst. leader Brownies, Girl Scouts U.S.A., Floyd Knobs, 1962; coach local ch. girls' softball league, 1963-65; co-chmn. Mothers' March on Birth Defects, March of Dimes, New Albany, 1972-76. Recipient award for acad. excellence Alliance Am. Insurers, 1988. Mem. Ins. Inst. Am. (assoc. in ins. acctg. and fin.). Roman Catholic. Home: RR 1 Floy Knobs IN 47119 Office: Ky Farm Bur Mut Ins Co 120 S Hubbard Ln Louisville KY 40207

PLAJA, ROBERTO, portfolio executive; b. Palermo, Italy, July 11, 1954; came to U.S., 1973; s. Eugenio and Elena (Pagliarello) P.; m. Dorothea Tantillo, Apr. 23, 1983; children: Eugenio, Umberto. BA in Econs., Cornell U., 1976; MBA, Harvard U., 1979. V.p. Bankers Trust Co., N.Y.C., 1979-84; v.p., internat. investments CIC Asset Mgmt. Corp., N.Y.C., 1984—. Home: 105 Fifth Ave New York NY 10003 Office: CIC Asset Mgmt Corp 108 Maiden Ln 6th Fl New York NY 10038

PLAMAN, MICHAEL ANTHONY, chiropractor; b. Milw., Sept. 3, 1952; s. Lester Bechlin and Joan (Siever) Rechlin; m. Jill Kosinski, June 3, 1978; children: Collin Eric, Christopher Ryan. Student, U. Wis., Milw., 1970-73; D of Chiropractic, Northwestern Coll. Chiropractic, Mpls., 1977. Owner, chiropractor Caremore Chiropractic Ctrs., Albuquerque, 1978—. Mem. N.Mex. Chiropractic Assn., Bernalillo County Chiropractic Assn. Home: 3316 Vista Del Sur NW Albuquerque NM 87120 Office: Caremore Chiropractic Ctr 3100 Coors Rd NW Albuquerque NM 87120

PLANCHER, ROBERT LAWRENCE, manufacturing company executive; b. N.Y.C., Feb. 21, 1932; s. Murray Leon and Pearl P.; m. Ellen Roslyn, Feb. 14, 1954; children: Kevin, Daryn. B.B.A., CCNY, 1954. With American Brands, Inc., N.Y.C., 1963—; asst. tax dir. American Brands, Inc., 1967, tax dir., 1971, controller, 1978, dir., v.p., controller, 1981-86, sr. v.p., chief acctg. officer, 1986—, also bd. dirs.; dir. Acushnet Co., Acme Visible Records Inc., Acushnet Co., Am. Tobacco Internat. Corp., Jim Beam Brands Co., James B. Beam Distilling Co., Franklin Life Ins. Co., Franklin United Life Ins. Co., Golden Belt Mfg. Co., Gallaher Ltd., Andrew Jergens Co., Masterbrand Ind., Inc., Corp. Officers and Dirs. Assurance Ltd., 1700 Ins. Co., Am. Franklin Co., Master Lock Co., MCM Products Inc., Sunshine Biscuits Inc., Swingline Inc., Wilson Jones Co., Am. Brands Internat.Corp., Am. Brands, Inc., The Am. Tobacco Co., Pinkerton's, Inc., Corp. Officers and Dirs. Assurance Ltd., Acco World Corp., Southland Life Ins. Co., Acme Visible Records, Inc.; pres. 1700 Ins. Co. Ltd.; mem. met. adv. bd. Arkwright Mut. Ins. Co. Served with U.S. Army, 1954-56. Mem. Tax Execs. Inst., Fin. Execs. Inst., Am. Inst. Corp. Controllers, Nat. Assn. of Mfgs., Nat. Assn. of Accts. Office: Am Brands Inc 1700 E Putnam Ave PO Box 819 Old Greenwich CT 06870-0819

PLANT, MARETTA MOORE, public relations executive; b. Washington, Sept. 4, 1937; d. Henry Edwards and Lucy (Connell) Moore; m. William Voorhees Plant, June 14, 1959; children—Scott Voorhees, Craig Culver, Suzannah Holliday. B.S. in Bus. Adminstrn., U. Ark., 1959. Owner, mgr. Handcrafts by Maretta, Westfield, N.J., 1966-73; photographer M-R Pictures, Inc., Allendale, N.J., 1973-77; communications asst. United Way-

Union County, Elizabeth, N.J., 1977-79; pub. relations cons. Creative Arts Workshop, Westfield, 1977-81, Coll. Adv. Cons., 1983—; community relations coordinator Raritan Bay Health Services Corp., Perth Amboy, N.J., 1979-81; dir. pub. relations St. Elizabeth Hosp., Elizabeth, 1981-86; dir. mkgt./communications Somerset Med. Ctr., Somerville, N.J., 1986—. Trustee Bridgeway House, Elizabeth, 1982-86; mem. pub. relations com. N.J. Hosp. Assn., Princeton, 1982-83, council auxs. 1988—; committeewoman Union County Republican Com., Westfield, 1983-85. Mem. Pub. Relations Soc. Am., Nat. Fedn. Press Women, N.J. Press Women, Nat. Assn. Female Execs., Am. Soc. Hosp. Mktg. and Pub. Relations (council mem. Region II, membership com.), N.J. Hosp. Mktg. and Pub. Relations Assn. (corr. sec. 1984-86, pres. 1986-88), Internat. Platform Assn., U. Ark. Alumni Assn., Summit-Westfield Assn., Delta Gamma. Clubs: Coll. Women's (Westfield); Soroptomists Internat. (charter). Home: 118 Effingham Pl Westfield NJ 07090 Office: Somerset Med Ctr Rehill AVe Somerville NJ 08876

PLANTES, MARY KAY, marketing executive; b. Youngstown, Ohio, Dec. 15, 1951; d. William Joseph and Bernadette (McGinley) P.; m. Roy M. Christianson, May 25, 1980. BS, Pa. State U., 1973; PhD in Econs., MIT, 1979. Analyst Congrl. Budget Office, Washington, 1977-78; asst. prof. econs. U. Wis., Madison, 1979-81; adminstr. dept. of devel. State of Wis., Madison, 1981-83; with Ohmeda, Murray Hill, N.J., 1984—, dir. bus. devel., 1988—. Bd. advisors Madison Community Craft, 1985-87, Dane County Employment Project, 1987—. MIT fellow, 1973-76. Mem. Mortar Bd., Beta Gamma Sigma. Roman Catholic. Office: Ohmeda 575 Mountain Ave Murray Hill NJ 07974

PLASKETT, THOMAS G., transportation company executive; b. Raytown, Mo., Dec. 24, 1943; s. Warren E. and Frances S. (Winegar) P.; m. Linda Lee Maxey, June 8, 1968; children—Kimberly, Keith. B.I.E., Gen. Motors Inst.; M.B.A., Harvard U. Supr. indsl. engring. Gen. Motors, Flint, Mich., 1968, supt. indsl. engring., 1969-73; sr. staff asst., treas Gen. Motors, N.Y.C., 1973; asst. controller Am. Airlines, N.Y.C., 1974, v.p. mktg. adminstrn., 1975-76, sr. v.p. fin., 1976-80; sr. v.p. mktg. Am. Airlines, Dallas, from 1980; pres., chief exec. officer Continental Airlines Inc., Houston, Tex., until 1988; chmn., chief exec. officer, pres. Pan Am Corp., N.Y.C., 1988—; dir. Mary Kay Cosmetics, Dallas, Interfirst Bank, Fort Worth. Bd. dirs. Dallas Symphony, 1984—, Goodwill Industries, Dallas, 1983—. Office: Pan Am Corp 200 Park Ave New York NY 10166 •

PLAT, RICHARD VERTIN, corporate finance executive; b. San Jose, Calif., July 14, 1929; s. Gaston and Frances (Vertin) P.; widowed; children: Julie, Carl, Marsha. BEE, U. Santa Clara, 1951; MBA, Washington U., St. Louis, 1957. Sr. ind. econ. Stanford Rsch. Inst., Menlo Park, Calif., 1959-65; dir. planning Litton Industries, Inc., Beverly Hills, Calif., 1965-70; v.p. Waltham Industries, N.Y.C., 1970-71, Computer Machinery Corp., L.A., 1971-77; sr. v.p. Pacific Scientific Co., Newport Beach, Calif., 1978—; bd. dirs. IMEC Corp., Boston, HTL Industries, Duarte, Calif., Sigma Instruments, Inc., Weymouth, Mass., HTL Caribe Inc., P.R., Sigma De P.R., Pacific Scientific Ltd., Eng., Pacific Scientific S.A.R.L., France, Pacific Scientific GmbH, Fed. Republic of Germany, Pacific Scientific Internat. Inc, U.S., Virgin Islands. 1st lt. U.S. Army, 1951-54. Mem. Fin. Execs. Inst. (bd. dirs., v.p. 1984—). Republican. Club: Jonathan (L.A.), Balboa Bay (Newport Beach, Calif.). Home: 1315 Bayside Dr Corona del Mar CA 92625 Office: Pacific Scientific Co 620 Newport Center Dr Newport Beach CA 92660

PLATEK, RICHARD ALAN, research firm executive, mathematics educator; b. N.Y.C., Sept. 27, 1940; s. Jonas and Pearl (Kiviat) P.; m. Sandra Jane Shindell, Nov. 1, 1960 (div. Jan. 1968); children: Barbara, Brenda; m. Evelyn Janet Bloom, Nov. 30, 1968; 1 child, Jessica. BS, MIT, 1961; PhD, Stanford U., 1966. Instr. dept. math. MIT, Cambridge, 1966-67; asst. prof. dept. math. Cornell U., Ithaca, N.Y., 1967-69, assoc. prof., 1969—; pres. Odyssey Research Assocs., Ithaca, 1982—; cons. Inst. for Def. Analyses, Alexandria, Va., 1986—. Contbr. articles to scholarly jours. Chmn. Sch. of Finger Lakes, Ithaca, 1987-88; tchr. Wisdom's Goldenrod, Valois, N.Y., 1970-80. Mem. IEEE, Am. Math. Soc., Assn. for Symbolic Logic, Assn. for Computing Machinery (chair SIGAda/formal methods com. 1986-87). Office: Odyssey Rsch Assocs 301 A Dates Dr Ithaca NY 14850

PLATT, DAVID RICHARD, automotive executive; b. Pitts., Oct. 29, 1927; s. Adam P. and Magdalen M. (Wasel) P.; m. Mary Grace Metford, June 12, 1954; children: Susan Kay, Cindy Ellen, Michael Adam. B.A., Pa. State U., 1950; M.B.A., Harvard U., 1955. Purchasing dir. PAACAR, Inc., Seattle, 1966-68; pres. Sicard, Inc., Montreal, Que, Can., 1968-71; procurement exec. Ford Motor Co., Detroit, 1971-80; v.p. Chrysler Corp., Detroit, 1980—. Bd. dirs. Detroit Jr. Achievement, 1982—; bd. dirs. Consortium for Human Devel., Troy, Mich., 1982—. Served to cpl. U.S. Army, 1945-47. Republican. Roman Catholic. Clubs: Meadowbrook Country (Northville, Mich.); Detroit Athletic. Office: Chrysler Motors Corp 12000 Chrysler Dr Highland Park MI 48288-2866

PLATT, LEWIS EMMETT, electronics company executive; b. Johnson City, N.Y., Apr. 11, 1941; s. Norval Lewis and Margaret Dora (Williams) P.; m. Joan Ellen Redmund, Jan. 15, 1983; children: Caryn, Laura, Amanda, Hillary. BME, Cornell U., 1964; MBA, U. Pa., 1966. With Hewlett Packard, Waltham, Mass., 1966-73, engring. mgr., 1973-76, ops. mgr., 1976-77, div. gen. mgr., 1977-80, group gen. mgr., Palo Alto, Calif., 1980—, v.p., 1983—; exec. v.p., 1987—; dir. Molex Inc., Lisle, Ill. Trustee Waltham Hosp., 1978-80; bd. dirs. Palo Alto Area YMCA, 1980-86. Mem. IEEE, Sci. Apparatus Mfg. Assn. (dir. 1978-80). Office: Hewlett Packard Co 3000 Hanover St Palo Alto CA 94304

PLATTEN, DONALD CAMPBELL, banker; b. N.Y.C., Sept. 18, 1918; s. John Homer and Katherine Campbell (Viele) P.; BA, Princeton U., 1940; grad. Advanced Mgmt. Program, Harvard U., 1966; m. Margaret Leslie Wyckoff, June 24, 1940; children: Katherine L. Platten Naylor, Peter W., Alison C. Platten Vanderbilt. With Chem. Bank N.Y.C., 1940—, sr. v.p., 1964-67. exec. v.p., 1967-70, 1st v.p., 1970-72, pres., 1972-73, chmn. bd., 1973-83; chmn. bd. Chem. N.Y. Corp., 1973-83, chmn. exec. com., 1983—; Reader's Digest Assn. Inc., Thomson Newspapers, Inc., Consol. Edison Co. N.Y., Cleve.-Cliffs, Inc. Bd. dirs. Goodwill Industries Greater N.Y., Charles A. Dana Found.; trustee Collegiate Sch., N.Y.C., Presbyn. Hosp., Am. Mus. Natural History, Am. U. Beirut, United Student Aid Funds; emeritus trustee Princeton U.; mem. Pres. Carter's Commn. on Nat. Agenda for 80s. Served to 1st lt. AUS, 1944-46. Mem. . Council Fgn. Relations. Clubs: Univ., Blind Brook. Office: Chem Bank 30 Rockefeller Pla New York NY 10112

PLATTHY, JENO, cultural association executive; b. Dunapataj, Hungary, Aug. 13, 1920; s. Joseph K. and Maria (Dobor) P.; m. Carol Louise Abell, Sept. 25, 1976. Diploma, Peter Pazmany U., Budapest, Hungary, 1942; PhD, Ferencz J. U., Kolozsvar, Hungary, 1944; MS, Cath. U., 1965; PhD (hon.), Yangmingshan U., Taiwan, 1975; DLitt (hon.), U. Libre Asie, Philippines, 1977. Lectr. various univs. 1956-59; sec. Internat. Inst. Boston, 1959-62; adminstrv. asst. Trustees of Harvard U., Washington, 1962-85; exec. dir. Fedn. Internat. Poetry Assns., UNESCO, 1976—; pub. New Muses Quar., 1976—. Author: Winter Tunes, 1974, Ch'u Yüan, His Life and Works, 1975; Springtide, 1976, (opera) Bamboo, Collected Poems, 1981, The Poems of Jesus, 1982, Holiness in a Worldly Garment, 1984, Ut Pictures Poeta, 1984, European Odes, 1985, The Mythical Poets of Greece, 1985, Book of Dithyrambs, 1986, Asian Elegies, 1987, Space Eclogues, 1988, Cosmograms, 1988, Nova Comoedia, 1988, Bartök: A Critical Biography, 1988, Celebration of Life, 1989, Nova Comoedia Part Two, 1989, Celebration of Life, 1989, Nova Comoedia Part Two, 1989, Plato: A Critical Biography, 1990, numerous others, translations; editor-in-chief Monumenta Classica Perennia, 1967-84. Named poet laureate 2d World Congress of Poets, 1973; recipient Confucius award Chinese Poetry Soc., 1974. Mem. Internat. Soc. Lit., PEN, Die Literarische Union, ASCAP, Internat. Poetry Soc., Melbourne Shakespeare Soc., 3d Internat. Congress Poets (pres. 1976, poet laureate 1976). Office: Fedn Internat Poetry Assns UNESCO PO Box 579 Santa Claus IN 47579

PLATZ, KATHLEEN LOUISE, accountant; b. Chgo., July 2, 1955; d. Jack Allen and Patricia Ann (Johnson) Schwartz; m. Mark W. Platz, Feb. 4, 1978; 1 child, Christopher Mark. BS, Calif. State U., Sacramento, 1981; MS, Golden Gate U.; cert. Advanced Personal Fin. Planning. CPA, Calif. Staff acct. Harris, Schwartz & Young CPA, Sacramento, 1972-78; controller Western Fairs Assn., Sacramento, 1978-80; staff acct. Schwartz, Winkler & Platz CPA, Sacramento, 1980-82; ptnr. Schwartz & Winkler CPA, Sacramento, 1982—; mem. tech. rev. com. Calif. State Bd. Accountancy, Sacramento, 1984—. Chairperson speakers bur. LWV, Sacramento, 1985-86; team capt. YMCA Fundraiser, Sacramento, 1986. Mem. Calif. Soc. CPA's, Soc. CPA Fin. Planners, Sacramento C. of C. Office: Schwartz Winkler & Platz CPA 2024 J St Sacramento CA 95814

PLAVOUKOS, SPENCER, advertising executive; b. N.Y.C., May 30, 1936; s. George and Elva (Murzi) P.; m. Harriet Phylis Gladstone, Jan. 9, 1964; children: Stacy, Matthew. B.S., Syracuse U., 1961. Account exec. SSC&B, Inc., N.Y.C., 1961-64; account exec. Grey Advt., 1964-67; exec. v.p., dir. account service Manoff Advt., N.Y.C., 1967-79; exec. v.p. SSC&B, N.Y.C., 1979; now chmn., chief exec. officer Lintas:N.Y. (formerly SSC&B), N.Y.C.; vice chmn. Lintas:USA. Clubs: Country of New Canaan, Marco Polo (N.Y.C.), St. James (London). Office: Lintas:NY 1 Dag Hammarskjold Pla New York NY 10017

PLAYER, WANDA HOPE, accountant; b. Hampton, Va., Oct. 2, 1955; d. Clyde Louis and Mary Janet (Gulledge) P.; m. James G. Pappas, Jr., July 27, 1985. BSBA, U. S.C., 1977. CPA, Va.; cert. fin. planner. Sr. acct. Peat Marwick, Mitchell & Co., Charlotte, N.C., 1977-80; internal audit mgr. 1st Va. Banks, Inc., Roanoke, Va., 1980-81; dist. mgr. Automatic Data Processing, 1981-82; mgr. Young & Prickett, P.C. CPAs, 1982-87; prin. W. Hope Player CPA, Roanoke, 1987—. Grad. Leadership Roanoke Valley, 1987-88, mem. curriculum com. 1988—; vol. Roanoke Festival in Park, 1987-88; adv. bd. Women's Ctr. Hollins Coll., 1988—; bd. dirs. Voice of Blue Ridge, 1988—. Named one of Outstanding Young Women of Am., 1987. Mem. Nat. Assn, Accts. (bd. dirs. 1981—, v.p. 1987-88), Roanoke Regional C. of C. (com. mem., small bus. coun. com., bd. dirs. 1989—), Am. Inst. CPAs, Inst. Cert. Fin. Planners, Va. Soc. CPAs, Porsche Club (treas. 1988—). Presbyterian. Home: 1915 Bluemont Ave SW Roanoke VA 24015 Office: 316 Mountain Ave SW PO Box 781 Roanoke VA 24004-0781

PLEAK, RUTH ELAINE, insurance company executive; b. Council Bluffs, Iowa, Feb. 19, 1952; d. Strauther Van and Esther Evaline (Liebers) P.; m. Clifford John Frank, June 16, 1973; children: Flona, Dawson. BS in Stats., Iowa State U., 1973; MS in Acctg., Drake U., 1977. CPA, Iowa. Pvt. practice statis. cons. Medfield, Mass., 1973-74; product testing analyst The Gillette Co., South Boston, Mass., 1974; research asst. Iowa State U., Ames, 1975-76; sr. acct. Ernst & Whinney, Des Moines, 1976-80; tax acct. Touche Ross & Co., Omaha, 1980-83; v.p., asst. sec. World Ins. Co., Omaha, 1983—. Contbr. articles to profl. jours. Mem. Douglas County Republican Cen. Com., Omaha, 1983-84; treas. Omaha Republican. Bus. and Profl. Women's Club, 1982-84, bd. dirs. 1984-85. Fellow Life Mgmt. Inst., Life Mgmt. Soc. of Nebr. (charter) (treas. 1983-84); mem. Am. Inst. CPA's, Nebr. Tax Forum (treas. 1982-84), Nebr. Soc. CPA's, Iowa Soc. CPA's. Republican. Presbyterian. Office: World Ins Co 1000 World Pla North Park Omaha NE 68164

PLECHY, CHRIS JOHN, tax consultant; b. Paterson, N.J., June 5, 1963; s. Joseph Nicholaus and Barbara (Szima) P. BS in Fin., Pa. State U., 1985; postgrad., Fairleigh Dickinson U., 1988—. Fin. cons. Ayco Corp., Morristown, N.J., 1986; tax cons. Fenzel & Co., Inc., Morristown, 1986—. Mem. Optimists. Office: Fenzel & Co 15 Mount Kemble Ave Morristown NJ 07960

PLESKOW, ERIC ROY, motion picture company executive; b. Vienna, Austria; came to U.S., 1939; Film officer U.S. War Dept., 1946-48; asst. gen. mgr. Motion Picture Export Assn., Germany, 1948-50; continental rep. for Sol Lesser Prodns., 1950-51; with United Artists Corp., 1951—, Far Eastern sales mgr., 1951-52, South African mgr., 1952-53, German mgr., 1953-58, exec. asst. to continental mgr., 1958-59, asst. continental mgr., 1959-60, continental mgr., 1960-62, v.p. in charge fgn. distbn., 1962, exec. v.p., chief operating officer, 1973, pres., chief exec. officer, 1973-78; pres., chief exec. officer Orion Pictures Co., N.Y.C., 1978-82, Orion Pictures Corp., N.Y.C., 1982—. Office: Orion Pictures Co 711 Fifth Ave New York NY 10022

PLEWES, STEVEN ARTHUR, financial consultant; b. Suffolk, Va., July 27, 1954; s. Benjamin Arthur and Leah (Gillette) P.; m. Janet Marie Furton, Sept. 16, 1978; children: Stephanie Lynn, Michelle Marie. Student, Elon Coll., 1972-74; student, U. Md., 1979-80; chartered fin. cons., Am. Coll., 1986, CLU, 1987. Pvt. practice local sports mgmt. Silver Spring, Md., 1977-80; account mgr. The Acacia Group, Rockville, Md., 1980-86; fin. cons. Potomac Fin. Group, Rockville, Md., 1986-89, v.p., 1989—; mem. Million Dollar Roundtable, 1985—. Chmn. Citizens Adv. Com. to Planning Commn., Gaithersburg, Md., 1985—; chmn. Archtl. Com. Homeowners Assn. for Montgomery Meadows, Gaithersburg, Md., 1985—. Named one of Outstanding Young Men Am., 1986; named mem. Honor Council The Acacia Group, Washington, 1985. Mem. Internat. Assn. Fin. Planning, Am. Soc. CLUs, Estate Planning Council Suburban Md., Nat. Assn. Life Underwriters (Nat. Sales award 1981-87, Nat. Quality award 1981-87), Suburban Md. Life Underwriters (bd. dirs. 1988—, chair awards com. 1987—, field practices com. 1987—, chmn. pub. relations com. 1988, treas. 1989), Nat. Assn. Securities Dealers. Republican. Baptist. Home: 3 Thorburn Rd Gaithersburg MD 20878 Office: Potomac Fin Group 15200 Shady Grove Rd Ste 460 Rockville MD 20850

PLEXICO, JON LINDSEY, manufacturing executive; b. Detroit, Feb. 18, 1938; s. Robert Spratt and Marian (Jefferson) P.; m. Virginia Penn, Aug. 22, 1964; children: Anne Lindsey, Jon Mabrey. BSME, Princeton U., 1959; MBA, Harvard U., 1964. Pres. Plastic Omnium, Inc., Canton, Mass., 1977-84, dir., 1977—, also bd. dirs.; v.p. Tecogen, Inc., Waltham, Mass., 1984—. Trustee Joslin Diabetes Ctr., Boston, 1979—. Served to 1st lt. U.S. Army, 1960-62. Office: Tecogen Inc 45 1st Ave Waltham MA 02254

PLICHTA, THOMAS FRANCIS, b. Wyandotte, Mich., Apr. 10, 1952; s. Frank R. and Wanda (Latta) P.; m. Marlene Kovacs, June 14, 1975; children—Brandon Travis, Thomas Francis Jr., Drew Robert. B.A. with honors, Mich. State U., 1974; M.B.A., Wayne State U., 1978. C.P.A., Mich., Tex. Mgr. Deloitte Haskins & Sells, Inc., Detroit, 1974-79; v.p., treas. Condo Marine Properties, Detroit, 1980-81, Paul Bosco & Sons, Dallas, 1982; exec. v.p., chief operating officer, chief fin. officer Barge Assocs., Inc., Dallas, 1982-85, also dir.; pres. Assoc. Prime Equities, Inc., Dallas, 1984-85; pres. Prime Devel., Inc., Dallas, 1985—; vice chmn. dir. Med. Bldg. Corp., Dallas, 1985-86. Recipient Disting. Advisor of Yr. award Jr. Achievement Assn. Southeastern Mich., 1977, Disting. Alumni award Taylor Ctr. High Sch., 1988. Mem. Am. Inst. C.P.A.s, Mich. Assn. C.P.A.s, Tex. Soc. C.P.A.s, Beta Alpha Psi. Roman Catholic. Home: 205 Coyote Ct Lewisville TX 75067 Office: Prime Devel Inc PO Box 1713 Lewisville TX 75067

PLIER, ROBERT EDWIN, financial company executive; b. Port Washington, Wis., Apr. 8, 1947; s. Emil T. and Edna Plier; m. Carol L. Plier. B.B.A., U. Wis., Whitewater, 1969; postgrad. Bradley U., 1977, 78. Sr. staff accountant Clifton, Gunderson & Co., C.P.A.'s, Peoria, Ill., 1969-74; treas. Peoria Disposal Co., 1974-83; pres. Robert E. Plier & Assocs., Ltd., 1983—. Bd. dirs. Boys Club Peoria, 1977-78. Mem. Am. Mgmt. Assn., U.S. Jaycees (treas. 1978-79, senator 1981—), Ill. Jaycees (state chaplain 1975-76, dir. children's camp, 1977-79, ambassador, 1976—), Am. Inst. C.P.A.s, Nat. Assn. Accountants, Ill. Soc. C.P.A.s. Club: Kennel Lake Sportsmen's. Home: 1049 E Jefferson St Morton IL 61550 Office: 508 N Jefferson St Peoria IL 61603

PLITT, ARTHUR M., financial services company; b. N.Y.C., Sept. 14, 1940; s. George and Rose Plitt; m. Miriam Plitt; children: Hugh, Seth. BS, St. Lawrence U., 1962; MBA, Columbia, 1963. CLU; chartered fin. cons. Assoc. Mass. Mut. Life Ins. Co., Providence, 1978-84; pres. PFA, Providence, 1984-85; sr. v.p. First Am. Fin., Providence, 1987-88, Fin. Resources & Strategies, Inc., Providence, 1988—; prof. Bryant Coll., Smithfield, R.I., 1988—; pres. Four Winds Assocs., Pawtucket, 1975—; v.p. Ocean Group, Ltd., Wilmington, Del., 1985—. Chmn. charitable gifts R.I. Heart Assn., 1987-88. Fellow Inst. Cert. Fin. Planners; mem. Internat. Assn. Registered Fin. Planners (cons. nat. speaker 1987), Internat. Assn. Fin. Planning (exec. v.p. 1987-88, 89), R.I. Jaycees (pres. 1976-77), Striders Club (pres.), Elks (scout com.). Home: 44 Cooke St Pawtucket RI 02860 Office: Ocean Group Ltd Box 28383 Providence RI 02908

PLOESER, WALTER CHRISTIAN, business consultant, former ambassador; b. St. Louis, Jan. 7, 1907; s. Christian D. and Maud Elizabeth (Parr) P.; m. Dorothy Annette Mohrig, Aug. 17, 1928; children: Ann Ploeser Burgan, Sally Ploeser Chapel. Student, City Coll. of Law and Finance, St. Louis; LL.D. (hon.), Norwich U., 1948; Dr. hon. causa, Nat. U. Asuncion, Paraguay. In ins. business St. Louis, 1922—; founded firm Ploeser, Watts & Co., 1933; organized subsidiary Marine Underwriters Corp., 1935; former pres., dir. Boatmen's Bank; founder Ins. Inst. Mo., 1938, pres., 1938-40; past pres. Grant, Ploeser & Assocs., Inc., nat. and internat. pub. relations; U.S. ambassador to Republic of Paraguay, 1957-59; to Costa Rica, 1970-72; Mem. Mo. Legislature, 1931-32; chmn. 5th dist. com. finance and budget Rep. Nat. Program Com., 1937-39; mem. 77th-80th congresses from 12th Mo. Dist.; mem. appropriations com., Rep. steering com., chmn. select com. on small business, chmn. subcom. on govt. corps.; mem. econ. adv. com. U.S. Senate com. on banking and currency, 1953-54; Rep. nat. committeeman for, Mo., 1964-66. Mem. emeritus St. Louis unit Shriners Hosp. for Crippled Children; bd. dirs. Scottish Rite Found. Mo.; chmn. bd. Salvation Army St. Louis, 1967-70; mem. pres.'s council Sch. of Ozarks. Recipient Freedoms Found. award, 1949; decorated Grand Cross Republic of Paraguay, 1959. Mem. Miss. Valley Assn. (chmn. bd. 1956, pres.), DeMolay Legion of Honor, Ins. Bd. of St. Louis, St. Louis C. of C. (chmn. nat. affairs com. 1964-66). , ubs: Mo. Athletic, Triple A Golf and Tennis. Lodges: Masons (33 deg.) Shriners (sovereign grand insp. gen. Mo. Scottish Rite 1967, emeritus 1967-88), Order of De Molay (Supreme council exec., grand master internat. 1952, Hall of Fame 1986), K.T. (Cross of Honor 1983). Home: 275 Union Blvd Saint Louis MO 63108 Office: Scottish Rite Cathedral 3633 Lindell Blvd Saint Louis MO 63108

PLOTKIN, IRVING H(ERMAN), economist, consultant; b. Bklyn., July 19, 1941; s. Samuel H. and Dorothy (Falick) P.; BS in Econs., U. Pa., 1963; PhD in Math. Econs., Mass. Inst. Tech., 1968; m. Janet V. Bufe, July 26, 1969; children—Aaron Jacob, Joshua Benjamin. Corp. planning analyst Mobil Oil Co., N.Y.C., 1962-63, Mobil Oil Italiana, Genoa, Italy, 1965; ind. cons. econs. and ops. rsch. to banks, mut. funds, ins. cos. govt. agys., Cambridge, Mass., 1965-68; sr. economist Arthur D. Little, Inc., Cambridge, 1968—; bd. dir. regulation and econs., 1974—, v.p., 1979—; bd. dir. Arthur D. Little Valuation, Inc., 1980—; trustee Arthur D. Little, Inc., ESOP, 1988—; instr. fin. and computer scis. Mass. Inst. Tech., 1965-68; lectr. maj. univs. U.S. and abroad; expert witness U.S. Ho. of Reps. and Senate coms., U.S. Ct. Claims, U.S. Tax Ct. I.C.C., FTC, Fed. Maritime Commn., Fed. Dist. Cts., Fed. Res. Bd., other fed. and state govt. agys., 1967—. NASA fellow, 1963-66, NSF fellow, 1967, Am. Bankers Assn. fellow, 1968. Mem. Am. Econ. Assn., Econometric Soc., Am. Fin. Assn., Beta Gamma Sigma, Pi Gamma Mu, Tau Delta Phi (chpt. pres. 1962-63). Editorial reviewer Jour. Am. Statis. Assn., 1968, Jour. Indsl. Econs., 1968—, Jour. Risk and Ins., 1980—; author: Prices and Profits in the Property and Liability Insurance Industry, 1967, The Consequences of Industrial Regulation on Profitability, Risk Taking, and Innovation, 1969, National Policy, Technology, and Economic Forces Affecting the Industrial Organization of Marine Transportation, 1970, Government Regulation of the Air Freight Industry, 1971, The Private Mortgage Insurance Industry, 1975, On The Theory and Practice of Rate Review and Profit Measurement in Title Insurance, 1978, Torrens in the United States, 1978, Total Rate of Return and the Regulation of Insurance Profits, 1979, Studies on the Impact of Sophisticated Manufacturing Industries on the Economic Development of Puerto Rico, 1981, The Economic Consequences of Controlled Business in the Real Estate Industry, 1981, On the Nature of Captive Insurance, 1984, Economic Foundations of Limited Liability for Nuclear Reactor Accidents, 1985, Transfer Prices, Royalties, and Adam Smith, 1987; contbr. numerous articles to profl. jours. Home: 55 Baskin Rd Lexington MA 02173 Office: 35 Acorn Park Cambridge MA 02140

PLOVNICK, MARK STEPHEN, business educator; b. N.Y.C., June 8, 1946. s. Jacob and Dorothy Edith (Berger) P.; m. Daisy Shulan Chan, Mar. 13, 1982. BS in Mech. Engring., Union Coll., 1968, BA in Econs., 1968; MS in Mgmt., Mass. Inst. Tech., 1970, PhD in Mgmt., 1975. Instr., researcher Mass. Inst. Tech., Cambridge, 1970-76; asst. prof. Clark Univ., Worcester, Mass., 1976-79; assoc. prof., 1979-89; prof., dean Sch. Bus. & Pub. Adminstrn. U. Pacific, Stockton, Calif., 1989—. chmn. dept. mgmt., 1979-82, assoc. dean Grad. Sch. Mgmt., 1982—; cons. to various orgns., 1970—; dir. Devel. Research Assocs., Reston, Va., 1979-82; adj. assoc. prof. U. Mass. Med. Sch., Worcester, Mass., 1982-89; adj. asst. prof. Boston Univ. Sch. Medicine, 1974-75; clin. instr. Harvard Med. Sch., Boston, 1977-78. Author 5 books. Contbr. numerous articles to profl. jours. Trustee Art Inst. Boston, 1983—, Worcester Vis. Nurse Assn., 1985—. Mem. Acad. Mgmt., Assn. Info. and Decision Scis., Orgn. Devel. Inst. Home: 92 New Bridge Rd Sudbury MA 01776 Office: U Pacific Sch Bus & Pub Adminstrn Stockton CA 95211

PLUMBRIDGE, ROBIN ALLAN, mining company executive; b. Republic South Africa, Apr. 6, 1935; s. Charles Owen and Marjorie Aileen (Bevan) P.; m. Celia Anne Millar, Nov. 18, 1959; twin sons. Grad., St. Andrew's Coll., Republic South Africa; MA, Oxford (Eng.) U. Statistician Goldfields of S. Africa Ltd., 1957-62, asst. mgr., 1962-65, mgr., 1965-69, exec. dir., 1969-74, dep. chair, 1974-80, chair, 1980—, also chair mining house; chair Driefontein Consolidated Ltd., Gold Fields Mining and Devel. Ltd., Gold Fields S. Africa Holdings Ltd., Vellefontein Tin Mining Co. Ltd., Waterval (Rustenburg) Platinum Mining Co. Ltd., West Driefontein Gold Mining Co., Ltd.; bd. dirs. Black Mountain Mineral Devel. Co. (Pvt.) Ltd., Consolidated Gold Fields PLC, Deelkraal Gold Mining Co. Ltd., Kloof Gold Mining Co. Ltd., O'Okiep Copper Co. Ltd., Devel. Bank of S.A., Newmont Mining Corp., Std. Bank Investment Corp. Ltd., Tsumeb Corp. Ltd. Trustee S.A. Found., S.A. Nature Found.; mem. Council for Sci. and Indsl. Research St. Andrew's Coll.; bd. govs. Rhodes U.; mem. Econ. Adv. Council State Pres. Decorated for Meritorious Service, S. African govt., 1982. Mem. Witwatersrand Agr. Soc. (life v.p.). Club: Rand. Office: Gold Fields S Africa Ltd, 75 Fox St, Johannesburg 2001, Republic of South Africa

PLUMMER, DANIEL CLARENCE, III, insurance company executive; b. Chgo., Apr. 30, 1927; s. Daniel C. and Ida May (Hayden) P.; m. Margaret Louise Marshall, Apr. 30, 1955; children—Daniel C., Judith Ann, David Marshall. B.S., Northwestern U., 1950. C.P.A., Ill. Sales rep. Sunbeam Corp., Chgo. and Phila., 1950-51; sr. acct. Touche Ross & Co., Chgo., 1952-56; adminstrv. mgr. Consol. Foundries & Mfg. Corp., Rockford, Ill., 1956-59; dir. internal audit Continental Casualty Co., Chgo., 1959-63; sec.-treas. Moline Malleable Iron Co., St. Charles, Ill., 1963-64; v.p. Allstate Ins. Cos., Northbrook, Ill., 1964—. Co-author: Property-Liability Insurance Accounting, 1986. Bd. dirs. Chgo. council Boy Scouts Am., 1979-87, mem. fin. com., 1979-87, chmn. audit com., 1983-87, mem. exec. com., 1979-81, asst. treas., 1979-81, chmn. ins. com. 1986, adv. bd., 1987—. Served with USN, 1945-46. Mem. Nat. Assn. Ind. Insurers (chmn. acctg. com. 1984-85), Nat. Assn. Ins. Commrs. (acctg. prins. adv. com. 1983-85, emerging issues com. 1985—, chmn. data systems adv. com. 1986—), Ill. Soc. C.P.A.s (chmn. ins. industry com. 1976-77), Ins. Acctg. and Systems Assn. Club: Torch Lake Yacht (Mich.). Office: Allstate Ins Co Allstate Pla Northbrook IL 60062

PLUMMER, MICHAEL KENNETH, financial consultant; b. Jacksonville, Fla., Apr. 24, 1954; s. Kenneth Albert and Edith Lorraine (O'Brien) P. BBA in Econs., U. North Fla., 1976. Econ. analyst Barnett Banks of Fla., Jacksonville, 1976-78; exec. v.p. Home Owners Warranty Corp., Jacksonville, 1978-80; market analyst Plantec Corp., Jacksonville, 1980-81; assoc. Laventhol & Horwath, Miami, 1981-84; sr. mgr., dir. real estate cons. Peat, Marwick, Main & Co., Atlanta, 1984—. Mem. Gov's. Econ. Adv. Com., Fla., 1982-84. Fla. Bankers Assn. scholar; named Eagle Scout Boy Scouts Am., 1972. Mem. Urban Land Inst., Nat. Assn. Corp. Real Estate Execs., Fed. Fin. Analysts. Republican. Methodist. Office: Peat Marwick Main & Co 245 Peachtree Ctr Ste 1900 Atlanta GA 30043

PLUMMER, PAUL JAMES, telephone company executive; b. Scottsbluff, Nebr., Aug. 3, 1946; s. Virgil Frank and Helen Louise (Hultberg) P.; B.A., U. Nebr., 1968; postgrad. Platte Coll., 1974-75; M.B.A., U. Iowa, 1982; m. Pamela Lee Purdom, June 26, 1976; 1 child, Brittany Lane. With Gen. Telephone Co. of the Midwest, 1968-82, div. traffic supr., Columbus, Nebr.,

1969-75, div. traffic mgr., Columbia, Mo., 1975-78, labor relations adminstr., Grinnell, Iowa, 1978-79, labor relations mgr., 1979-82, Compensation and services mgr., 1982; staff specialist customer service GTE, Stamford, Conn., 1982-83, group specialist customer service, 1983-84, customer services mgr., 1984-87, ops. support planning mgr., 1987-89, mgr. strategic planning telephone ops., Irving, Tex., 1989—. Active Boy Scouts Am. Mem. Am. Assn. Personnel Adminstrn., Personnel Mgmt. Assn. Columbia (exec. bd. dirs., 1st v.p. 1975-78). Episcopalian. Clubs: Optimist (past pres. Columbus, Nebr., lt. gov. Nebr. 1973-74), Elks. Home: 2808 Meadowview Dr Colleyville TX 76034 Office: 5205 N O'Connor Blvd Irving TX 75039

PLUNKETT, LARRY NEIL, electrical engineer; b. Hannibal, Mo., Dec. 15, 1945; s. Russell Neil and Marjorie Elaine (Steffen) P.; m. Linda Lee Mitchell, Sept. 6, 1964 (div. 1983); children: Jeffrey, Jeremy; m. Nancy Jonell Jarvis, Feb. 22, 1985; 1 stepchild, Heather Hidritch. BS in Elec. Engring., U. Mo., 1969. Registered profl. engr., Mo., Kans. Asst. project engr. Sachs Electric Co., St. Louis, 1969-72, project engr., 1972-73, v.p. Kansas City div., 1973-77, sr. v.p., 1977-80, exec. v.p., 1980-82, pres., 1982—. Mem. Civic Entrepreneurs Orgn., St. Louis, 1986—. Fellow Acad. Elec. Contracting; mem. Young Pres.'s Orgn., Nat. Elec. Contractors Assn. (pres. St. Louis chpt. 1985-87, co-rep. 1974—, v.p. exec. nat. com. 1988—), Engrs. Club. Republican. Baptist. Office: Sachs Electric Co 16300 Justus Post Rd Chesterfield MO 63017

PLUNKETT, MICHAEL STEWART, manufacturing company executive; b. Moline, Ill., Oct. 2, 1937; s. Stewart Vincent and Lois Charlotte (Hughes) P.; m. Carolyn Louise Billiet, Aug. 22, 1959; children: Timothy Stewart, Todd Louis, Douglas Michael. B.A. in Math., Augustana Coll., 1968. Various indsl. engring. positions Deere & Co., Moline, Ill., 1958-70; mgr. indsl. engring. John Deere Foundry, East Moline, Ill., 1970-72, mgr. mfg. and plant engring., 1972-74, works mgr., 1974-75, gen. mgr., 1975-77; dir. health care Deere & Co., Moline, 1977-80, v.p. indsl. relations and personnel, 1980-83; also bd. dirs. Deere & Co., sr. v.p. engring., tech. and human resources, 1983—; dir. 1st Nat. Bank Moline, HON Industries, Muscatine, Iowa; trustee St. Ambrose Coll., Davenport, Iowa, 1982—. Bd. dirs. Quad Cities Area Inc. Jr. Achievement, Davenport, 1974—, pres., 1982; pres. Upper Rock Island County Family YMCA, Moline, 1985; bd. dirs. Quad City Health Plan, Davenport, 1981-86, pres., 1981-82; bd. dirs. Quad-City Devel. Group, 1985—, United Way, Quad City, 1986-88. Mem. Machinery and Applied Products Inst. (chmn. human resources council II 1983-85). Republican. Roman Catholic. Office: Deere & Co John Deere Rd Moline IL 61265

PLUTCHOK, JONATHAN L., financial writer; b. Glen Ridge, N.J., June 30, 1953; s. George N. and Sylvia (Dardik) P.; m. Ziva Babayoff, June 23, 1974; children: Orli, Daniella, Michael. BA, U. Pa., 1974; JD, Washington U., 1977. Bar: Mo. 1977, N.Y. 1981. Assoc. Chused, Strauss, Chorlins, et. al., St. Louis, 1979-80; editor Prentice-Hall, Inc., Englewood Cliffs, N.J., 1980; editor-in-chief Atrium Pub. Corp., Manhasset, N.Y., 1981-83; v.p. mktg., mng. editor Integrated Resources, Inc., N.Y.C., 1984-88; writer, editor, cons. Jonathan Pluchok Bus. and Fin. Communications, Syosset, N.Y., 1982—. Contbg. editor and contbr. articles to profl. jours. Mem. ABA, Internat. Assn. Fin. Planning. Home and Office: 4 Drury Ln Syosset NY 11791

POBLETE, CONRADO NAZARENO, entrepreneur; b. Naic, Cavite, Philippines, Mar. 13, 1951; came to U.S., 1980; s. Cecilio Vasquez and Salud (Nazareno) P.; 1 child, Sally Jane Siazon. BSBA, DeLasalle Coll., Manila, Philippines, 1971, BS in Acctg., 1972. Pres. Sally Jane Enterprises, Trenton, N.J., 1983—. Mem. Nat. Rifle Assn. Club: Ft. Dix (N.J.) Rod and Gun. Office: SJ Enterprises Inc 850 Hamilton Ave Trenton NJ 08629

POCHICK, FRANCIS EDWARD, financial consultant; b. Metuchen, N.J., May 28, 1931; s. Frank Stephen and Bertha Barbara P.; student Rutgers U., 1949-50, 54-55; m. Shirley Ann Elliott, Feb. 16, 1957; children—Bonnie Lynn, Keith Francis. Agt., New Eng. Mut. Life Ins. Co., Newark and New Brunswick, N.J., 1958-61; agt. Lambert M. Huppeler Co., Inc., N.Y.C., 1962-64, cons., 1964, sr. cons. employee benefits, 1968—. Mem. adv. bd. Mercer Fund, Community Found. N.J., 1986—. Served with USMC, 1951-54. Mem. Am. Soc. Pension Actuaries, Nat. Assn. Life Underwriters, Internat. Assn. Fin. Planners, Estate Planning Council. Home: 118 Orchard Ave Hightstown NJ 08520 Office: PO Box 804 Hightstown NJ 08520 also: No Jersey Br 30 Two Bridges Rd Fairfield NJ 07006

POCHTER, ALAN IRA, controller, accountant; b. Bklyn., May 8, 1958; s. Morris and Estelle (Verby) P. BS, Bklyn. Coll., 1979. Gen. acctg. mgr. Gimbel Bros., Inc., N.Y.C., 1979-81; controller, v.p. Infotech Mgmt., Inc., Long Island City, N.Y., 1981-87; corp. controller Beanstalk Group of Cos., Rockville Centre, N.Y., 1987—. Bd. dirs. Park Stoner Apts., Inc., Great Neck, N.Y., 1987-88. Home: 14 Stoner Ave Great Neck NY 11021 Office: Beanstalk Group of Cos 1221 Ave of Americas New York NY 10020

POCRASS, RICHARD DALE, management consultant; b. Meadville, Pa., Mar. 7, 1940; s. Irving F. and Roslyn (Sperber) P.; m. Rena Levy, Feb. 3, 1968; children—Michael B., S. Douglas. B.S. in Math., U. Pitts., 1962; M.B.A. in Fin., 1964. EDP sales mgr. NCR Corp., Pitts., 1962-67, retail mktg, mgr., Los Angeles, 1972-74; v.p., dir. Nanoseconds Systems, Fairfield, Conn., 1967-69, dir. 1968-72; v.p. gen. mgr. Hart Jewelry Co., Warren, Ohio, 1969-71, dir. 1981—; mktg. mgr. Data Source Corps subs. Hercules, Inc., El Segundo, 1974-75; pres. Webster-Pocrass & O'Neil (name changed to Pocrass Assocs. 1981), Los Angeles, 1976—, Health Tech. Inc. Pub., author: The Recruitment Letter; author (with Maronde) Drug Abuse Study for Hoffman LaRoche, 1980. Bd. dirs. West Valley Little League. Mem. Los Angeles Speakers Bur., Am. Soc. Personnel Adminstrs., Woodland Hills C. of C., Am. Mktg. Assn., Bank Mktg. Assn., Retail Controllers Assn., Calif. Exec. Recruiters Assn., Personnel and Indsl. Relation Assn., Internat. Platform Assn., Personnel and Indsl. Relations Assn. Republican. Jewish. Lodge: Rotary. Home: 18815 Paseo Nuevo Dr Tarzana CA 91356 Office: 16760 Stagg St #218 Van Nuys CA 91406

POCSI, LAURIE L., accountant; b. Paterson, N.J., Nov. 17, 1955; d. Lawrence R. Sr. and Anita (Ballini) Biggs; m. Richard Pocsi, Nov. 20, 1976; children: Adrian, Alexis, Lauren, Richard Jr. Student, Rutgers U., 1973-74; BA, William Paterson coll., 1983. CPA, N.J. Controller Adrian Motor, Carlstadt, N.J., 1979-83; staff acct. Richard C. Fleischer, CAPA, Pompton Lakes, N.J., 1984-86; owner Laurie L. Pocsi CPA, Wayne, N.J., 1986—. Fellow N.J. Soc. CPA's; mem. AICPA. Office: 41 Marlton Dr Wayne NJ 07470

PODOJIL, LAWRENCE ROBERT, JR., rubber company executive; b. Moorehead City, N.C., May 29, 1949; s. Lawrence Robert and Evelyn (Lomond) P.; m. Connie Marie Larsen, Feb. 1, 1969; children: Bradley Christopher, Leslie Anne. BS in Edn., U. Nebr., 1971. Sales rep. Hilti Fastening Systems, Tulsa, 1973-75, regional mktg. mgr., 1975-76, sales mgr., 1976-79; regional export slaes rep. ITT Phillips Drill Co., Michigan City, Ind., 1979-82; export mgr. ITT Phillips Drill Co., Michigan City, 1982-83, gen. export mgr., 1984-85; nat. sales mgr. indsl. Am. Rubber Corp., La Porte, Ind., 1986—; mem. sr. mgmt. com. Am. Rubber Corp., LaPorte, Ind., 1988; lectr. in field; dir. Gemco, Inc., LaPorte. Dir. communications Ind. Pvt. Sch., Michigan City, 1986. Mem. Phi Epsilon Kappa (treas. 1969-71). Office: Am Rubber Corp 315 Brighton La Porte IN 46350

PODUSKA, HOWARD J., retired banker, consultant, director; b. Union City, N.J., Mar. 16, 1920; s. Frank and Louise (Zeman) P.; m. Margaret R. Jerman, June 12, 1943. BS, NYU, 1946; advanced mgmt. program, Harvard U., 1962. Page boy to vice chmn. and pres. The Bank of N.Y., N.Y.C., 1938-79, ret., 1979; bd. dirs. Sterling Bancorp., N.Y.C., Sterling Nat. Bank, N.Y.C., Glenview State Bank, Ill., Cummins Allison Corp., Mt. Prospect, Ill., Cummins Allison Corp., Ind., Cummins Am. Corp., Mt. Prospect, Turnberry Savs. & Loan, North Miami Beach. Home: 6300 Mariner Sands Dr Stuart FL 34997

POEHNER, RAYMOND GLENN, banker; b. Cleve., Oct. 1, 1923; s. Raymond Frank and Winifred (Kirchbaum) P.; student pub. schs., Chgo. and Cleve.; m. Frances E. Dunaway Gillespie, Jan. 4, 1958; children: R. David, Jacquline Diane, Leslie Marie, Jon Anthony, Rebecca Glen; stepchildren: Bruce Gillespie, Tony Gillespie. Enlisted U.S. Navy, 1941, advanced through grades to chief petty officer, 1957, ret., 1965; with Security Pacific Nat. Bank, San Diego, 1966—, loan officer, 1971-74, credit card officer, 1975—81, asst. br. mgr., 1974-81, asst. mgr., 1981—. Mem. U.S. Naval Inst., VFW, Nat. Hist. Soc., Fla. Sheriff's Assn., Am. Biog. Soc. (nat. bd. advisors), Nat. Preservation of Hist. Trust, R.I. Research (cert. assoc.), Fleet Res. Assn., Smithsonian Assocs., Nat. Geographic Soc. Republican. Club: Optimist (dir. 1978). Lodge: Fraternal Order Police (booster Fla. chpt.) Home: 6674 Water St Gulf Breeze FL 32561 Office: 4144 El Cajon Blvd San Diego CA 92105

POETKER, FRANCES LOUISE, florist; b. Cin., Apr. 16, 1912; d. Charles Benjamin and Louise (Johnston) Jones; BA, Vassar Coll., 1933; MA, U. Cin., 1934; m. Joseph G. Poetker, Aug. 10, 1937. Buyer Mabley & Carew Dept. Store, Cin., 1933-35; former owner Jones the Florist, Cin., 1942-85, cons., 1985-87; lectr. in field; dir. Cin. Bell Telephone Co.; co-chmn. flower decorations Winter Olympics, 1980 (silver medal); hostess Nat. Gov.'s Conf., Cin.; dir. profl. flower shows, N.Y. and France, commentator wedding shows; mem. Nat. Eisenhauer People to People expedition to China, 1987; cons. Cin. Zool. Botanical Gardens 1st flower and plant show. Mem. spl. dirs. com. Cin. Park Bd.; Appeared in Cin. Enquirer Bicentennial Flashback, Images Gallery Bicentennial Show; designer numerous floral settings for period mus. including U. Cin., Taft Mus.; designer Internat. Flower Show Peabody Mus., Salem, Mass.; lectr. Cooking With Flowers, 1987-88, mus. instruments; hostess rev. of Tall Stacks Riverboat Reunion, Cin., 1988; mem. honors com. U. Cin.; founding mem. Nat. Mus. Women in the Arts, 1986, charter mem.; mem. Friends of Taft Mus., Cin. Mus. Natural History; friend of Nat. Arboretum Wildlife Protection Inst. Am.; mem. program com. Cin. Hist. Soc.; pres.'s com. Xavier U., Cin.; exec. com. Cin. Opera; Coll. Club of Cin. (hon mem.1986); v.p. Air Pollution Control League Cin.; adv. bd. Civic Garden Ctr.; bd. dirs. Bethesda Hosp., Cin.; mem. Cin. Beautiful Com. Recipient award of appreciation Dept. Agr., 1962, Sylvia award floral excellence, 1976; Belle Skinner Clark fellow, 1930; named Woman of Year, Cin. Enquirer, 1978; named to Floricultural Hall of Fame, 1967; Author: Symbolism ofPlant Materials in Porcelain Collection Taft Mus. Cin., 1988. Mem. Am. Hort. Soc. (dir., chmn. 1982 conv., chmn. decorations N.Y.C. nat. meeting, Frances Jones Poetker award named for, 1988), Soc. Am. Florists (1st Century award 1982), Florists Transworld Delivery Assn. (commentator 1942), Am. Acad. Florists (dir. emeritus), Allied Florists Assn. Cin., Profl. Florist Commentators Internat. (Tommy Bright award 1982), MacDowall Soc., McMicken Soc., N.C. Florists Assn. (mem. nat. com. on capital formation and estate taxation), Hillside Trust, Nature Conservency, Am. Music Scholarship Assn. (bd. dirs. 1987), English Speaking Union (Cin. chpt.). Lutheran. Clubs: Travel (pres., dir.), Women's, Symphony (lectr.), Banker's (Cin.); Garden of Am. (mem.-at-large), Town. Co-author: Wild Wealth, 1971; co-author (articles) The Herbalist; newspaper columnist Fun With Flowers, 1941—; contbr. articles to mags.; designer food, fashion and floral illustrations for trade publs.; panelist weekly TV program Sunday Soul; actress, designer 3 syndicated movie shorts for Soc. Am. Florists; designer Florists Transworld Delivery and 3 florist shops, subject of various mag. articles. Home and Office: 1059 Celestial St Cincinnati OH 45202

POFFEL, JAMES, marketing professional; b. Balt., July 3, 1946; s. Robert E. and Edea (DeCarlintanio) P.; m. Marjorie Cunningham, Nov. 29, 1974; children: Michael, Marne. Student, U. Balt., 1969-74, 75-76. Account exec. Friden, Balt., 1969-72; sales mgr. Friden, Washington, 1972-74; dist. sales mgr. Singer/Friden, Cin., 1974-77; gen. mgr. sales Southern Bus. Machines, Balt., 1977-78; dist. sales mgr. Royal/Pertec, Washington, 1979-81; account exec. Hewlett Packard, Balt., 1981-84; mktg. mgr. Hewlett Packard, Rockville, Md., 1984-89; fed. market bus. devel. mgr. Hewlett Packard, Arlington, Va., 1989—. Mem. Exchange Club (pres. 1978-79). Office: Hewlett Packard 1550 Wilson Blvd Arlington VA 22209

POGGE, HORST, turf implement company executive; b. Meklenburg, Germany, Mar. 6, 1926; came to U.S., 1952; s. Karl W. and Gertrude (Poel) P.; m. Irena B. Kant, Sept. 13, 1948; children: Karin, Hans J., Kirk H. Degree in Agronomy, Schwerin Holzminden U. Farm mgr. Fed. Republic Germany, 1948-52; chief exec. officer Grassland Equipment and Irrigation Corp., Latham, N.Y., 1961—. 2d v.p., trustee Pruyn House Hist. Site, Town of Colonie, N.Y., 1987—; trustee Albany Rural Cemetery Assn., 1988. Mem. Albany C. of C. (bd. dirs. 1980-86), Latham C. of C. (bd. dirs. 1986—), Graeter Loudonville Assn. (bd. dirs. 1983—). Office: Grassland Equipment & Irrigation Corp 892-898 Troy Schenectady Rd Latham NY 12110

POGUE, DONALD ERIC, tobacco company executive; b. Southampton, N.Y., Feb. 12, 1949; s. Issiah P. and Virginia (Mines) P.; m. J. Marie Biggers, Aug. 21, 1982; 1 child, Eric Spencer. BS in Psychology, Heidelberg Coll., 1970; MA in Pers., Bowling Green State U., 1971. Asst. dir. acad. support Case Western Res. U., Cleve., 1971-72, instr., 1972-74; staff devel. trainer Cleve. State U., 1972-76; sr. compensation analyst Diamond Shamrock Corp., Cleve., 1976-78, supr. compensation adminstrn., 1978-79; mgr. employee rels. Diamond Shamrock Corp., Dallas, 1979-80; mgr. human resources Diamond Shamrock Corp., Painesville, Ohio, 1980-82; v.p. human resources Reichhold Chems., Inc., White Plains, N.Y., 1982-87, sr. v.p., 1987-88; staff v.p. pers. Philip Morris Cos., Inc., N.Y.C., 1988—; cons. U.S. CSC, 1973-75, Ohio Intergovtl. Pers., 1973-75; adj. prof. Cuyahoga Community Coll., Cleve., 1977-79. Advisor Jr. Achievement, Cleve., 1977; div. mgr. United Way Greater Cleve., 1979. Mem. Am. Mgmt. Assn., Am. Soc. for Pers. Adminstrn., Human Resource Planning Soc., Westchester-Conn. Pers. Roundtable (program chmn. 1987), Town Club. Democrat. Presbyterian. Home: 1 Brookby Rd Scarsdale NY 10583 Office: Philip Morris Cos Inc 120 Park Ave New York NY 10017

POGUE, THOMAS FRANKLIN, economics educator, consultant; b. Roswell, N.Mex., Dec. 28, 1935; s. Talmadge Franklin and Lela (Cox) P.; m. Colette Marie LaFortune, June 3, 1961; children—Michael Frederick, Robert Franklin. B.S., N.Mex. State U., 1957; M.S., Okla. State U., 1962; Ph.D., Yale U., 1968. Asst. prof. econs. U. Iowa, Iowa City, 1965-69, assoc. prof., 1970-75, prof., 1975—, chmn. dept., 1983-84; vis. prof. Tex. Tech. U., Lubbock, 1975-76, U. Adelaide, Australia, 1985. Author: Government and Economic Choice, 1978. Contbr. articles to profl. jours. Author, researcher Gov.'s Tax Study, State of Iowa, Des Moines, 1967, Minn. Tax Study Commn., St. Paul, 1984, Iowa Econ. Devel. Policy Study, 1986-87, Iowa Econ. Devel. Plan, Des Moines, 1987. Served to capt. USAF, 1957-60. Grantee Nat. Inst. Justice, Washington, 1978-79, Consumers Research Group, Washington, 1970, HUD, 1970. Mem. Am. Econ. Assn., Nat. Tax Assn. Democrat. Presbyterian. Avocation: tennis. Home: 3 Wellesley Way Iowa City IA 52245 Office: U Iowa Phillips Hall Dept Econs Iowa City IA 52242

POGUE, WILLIAM ALEXANDER, diversified company executive; b. Birmingham, Ala., July 1, 1927. B.S., U.S. Mil. Acad., 1950. Various depts. engring., mfg., field constrn. Chgo. Bridge & Iron Co., 1954-57, sales engr. N.Y. Sales Office, 1957-64, sales mgr., 1964-68, mgr. Houston ops., 1968-71, v.p., mgr. So. area ops., 1971-76, sr. v.p., mgr. ops., 1976-79, exec. v.p., dir., 1979—; sr. v.p. CBI Industries Inc., Hinsdale, Ill., 1979-81, pres., 1981-82, chmn. bd., chief exec. officer, 1982—; dir. No. Trust Co., Nalco Chem. Co. Served to capt. U.S. Army, 1945-54; served with USN. Office: CBI Industries Inc 800 Jorie Blvd Oak Brook IL 60522-7001 *

POINDEXTER, JOHN BRUCE, venture capitalist; b. Houston, Oct. 7, 1944; s. George Emerson and Rose Ellen (McDowell) P.; B.S.B.A. with honors, U. Ark., 1966; M.B.A., N.Y. U., 1971, Ph.D. in Econs. and Fin., 1976. Assoc., Salomon Bros., N.Y.C., 1971-72; v.p. Lombard, Nelson & McKenna, N.Y.C., 1972-76; v.p., registered prin. Dominick & Dominick, Inc., N.Y.C., 1973-76; sr. v.p. Smith Barney Venture Corp., N.Y.C., 1976-83; gen. partner First Century Partnership, N.Y.C., 1980-83; mng. partner KD/P Equities, ptnr. Kellner, DiLeo & Co., N.Y.C., 1983-85; mng. ptnr., J.B. Poindexter and Co., 1985—; chmn. bd. dirs. Carolina Steel Corp., EFP Corp., Nat. Steel Service Ctr., Leer, Inc.; adj. assoc. prof. L.I. U. Served to capt. U.S. Army, 1966-70; Vietnam. Decorated Silver Star, Bronze Star (2), Purple Heart (2), Air medal, others. Mem. Beta Gamma Sigma, Alpha Kappa Psi. Club: Metropolitan. also: 1100 Lousiana Houston TX 77002

POINSETTE, DONALD EUGENE, business executive, value management consultant; b. Fort Wayne, Ind., Aug. 17, 1914; s. Eugene Joseph and Julia Anna (Wyss) P.; student Purdue U., 1934, Ind. U., 1935-37, 64; m. Anne Katherine Farrell, Apr. 15, 1939; children—Donald J., Eugene J., Leo J., Sharon Poinsette Smith, Irene Poinsette Snyder, Cynthia Poinsette West, Maryanne Poinsette Stohler, Philip J. With Gen. Electric Corp., RCA, Stewart Warner Corp., 1937-39; metall. research and field sales cons. P.R. Mallory Corp., 1939-49; dist. sales mgr. Derringer Metall. Corp., Chgo., 1949-50; plant engr. Cornell-Dubilier Electric Corp., Indpls., 1950-53; with Jenn-Air Corp., Indpls., 1953-74, purchasing dir., 1953-71, mgr. value engring. and quality control, 1969-74; bus. mgmt. cons. Mays and Assocs., Indpls., 1974-76; Recipient Testimonial Golden Anniversary award Purdue U., 1987; named to U.S. Finder's List, Nat. Engrs. Register, 1956. Pres., Marian Coll. Parents Club, Indpls., 1969-70; com. mem. Boy Scouts Am. Nat trustee Xavier U., 1972-73, Dad's Club, Cin. Mem. Nat. Assn. Purchasing Mgmt., Indpls. Purchasing Mgmt. Assn., Soc. Am. Value Engrs. (certified value specialist; sec.-treas. Central Ind. chpt. 1972-73), Soc. Ret. Execs. Indpls., Ind. U., Purdue U. alumni assns., Columbian (pres. 1972-73), Triad choral groups, Internat. Platform Assn., Tau Kappa Epsilon. Club: K.C. (4 deg.). Home: 5760 Susan Dr E Indianapolis IN 46250

POIRIER, RICHARD OVEILA, talent agent, personal manager, motion picture investment company executive; b. Boston, Dec. 10, 1947; s. Oveila A. and Evelyn G. (Sullivan) P. Student, George Washington U., 1968; diploma in Law, City of London Coll., 1969; BS summa cum laude, Boston U., 1976. Exec. producer Kaleidescope Records, Boston, 1979-81; acct., law office mgr. William R. Dickerson & Assocs., Los Angeles, 1981; artist royalty supr. Capitol and EMI Am. Records, Hollywood, Calif., 1981-83; dir. royalties Warner/Elektra/Atlantic Internat. Records, Warner Home Video, Burbank, Calif., 1983-86; pres. Richard Poirier and Assocs., Los Angeles, 1986—; cons. in field.; guest speaker various functions. Contbr. articles to Boston U. Pubs., The Daily Free Press, 1975-76. Mem. Ford Hall Forum, Boston, 1974-79, Boston Mus. Fine Art, 1973-79. With U.S. Army, 1967-69. Mem. Nat. Acad. Rec. Arts and Scis., Nat. Acad. Video Arts and Scis., Beverly Hills Bar Assn. (entertainment law sect., legis. com.), Music Industry Network, Hollywood C. of C., 5% Club of L.A., Mondrian Models and Photographers Club, The Actors Ctr., Club de L'Ermitage. Home: 11701 Oxnard St #1 North Hollywood CA 91606 Office: Richard Poirier & Assocs 3575 Cahuenga Blvd W #254 Los Angeles CA 90068

POIRIER, VICTOR LUCIEN, electronics and mechanical executive, researcher, engineer; b. Lowell, Mass., July 3, 1941; s. Joseph N. and Beatrice A. (Lajeunesse) P.; m. Carmel C. Baron, June 29, 1941; children: Donna M., Nicolle M. AEME, U. Lowell, 1965; BSME, Northeastern U., 1970, MBA, 1981. Designer Thermo Electron Corp., Waltham, Mass., 1961-69, engr., 1969-79, dept. mgr., 1979-83; sr. v.p. Thermedics, Inc., Woburn, Mass., 1983—; exec. v.p. Thermo Cardiosystems, Inc., Woburn, Mass., 1988—; asst. prof. surgery Tufts U. Sch. of Medicine, Boston, 1980—. patentee in field. Leader Boy Scouts Am. Lowell chpt., 1975-80. Mem. Am. Soc. Artificial Organs (program com. 1988—), Assn. Advancement Med. Inst., Internat. Soc. Artificial Organs. Office: Thermedics Inc 470 Wildwood St Woburn MA 01801

POIROT, JAMES WESLEY, engineering company executive; b. Douglas, Wyo., 1931; m. Raeda Poirot. BCE, Oreg. State U., 1953. With various constrn. firms, Alaska and Oreg.; with CH2M Hill Inc., 1953—, v.p., Seattle and Atlanta, from 1967, chmn. bd., Englewood, Colo., 1983—; former chmn. CEO Western Regional Council, Design Profls. Coalition. Named ENR Constrn. Man of Yr., 1988. Fellow ASCE (chmn. steering com. quality manual from 1985, bd. dirs.); mem. Am. Cons. Engrs. Coun. (pres. 1989—). Office: CH2M Hill Inc 6060 S Willow Dr Englewood CO 80111

POIS, JOSEPH, lawyer, educator; b. N.Y.C., Dec. 25, 1905; s. Adolph and Augusta (Lesser) P.; m. Rose Tomarkin, June 24, 1928 (dec. May 1981); children: Richard Adolph (dec.), Robert August, Marc Howard.; m. Ruth Livingston, Nov. 27, 1983 (div. 1984). A.B., U. Wis., 1926; M.A., U. Chgo., 1927, Ph.D., 1929; J.D., Chgo.-Kent Coll. Law, 1934. Bar: Ill. 1934, Pa. 1978. Staff mem. J.L. Jacobs & Co., Chgo., 1929-35; jr. partner J.L. Jacobs & Co., 1946-47; gen. field supr. Pub. Adminstrn. Service, Chgo., 1935-38; chief adminstrv. studies sect. U.S. Bur. Old Age and Survivors Ins., 1938-39; chief adminstrv. and fiscal reorgn. sect. U.S. Bur. Budget Exec. Office of Pres., 1939-42; dir. finance State of Ill., 1951-53; counsel, asst. to pres., v.p., treas., dir. Signode Corp., 1947-61; prof. U. Pitts., 1961-76, emeritus, 1976—, chmn. dept. pub. adminstrn., 1961-71, asso. dean, 1973-75; dir. Vision Service Plan of Pa., 1984-85; cons. ECA, 1948, Dept. State, 1949, 62-65, U.S. Dept. Def., 1954, Brookings Instn., 1962-63, AID, 1965, Indian Inst. Pub. Adminstrn., 1972, Commn. on Operation Senate, 1976, Pitts. Citizens' Task Force on Refuse Disposal, 1976-78; mem. cons. panel Comptroller Gen. of U.S., 1967-75. Author: The School Board Crisis: a Chicago Case Study, 1964, Financial Administration in the Michigan State Government, 1938, Kentucky Handbook of Financial Administration, 1937, Public Personnel Administration in the City of Cincinnati, 1936, (with Edward M. Martin and Lyman S. Moore) The Merit System in Illinois, 1935, Watchdog on the Potomac, 1979; contbg. author: the New Political Economy, 1975, Eric Louis Kohler, Accounting's Man of Principles, 1979, State Audit-Developments in Public Accountability, 1981; contbr. articles to profl. jours. Mem. Chgo. Bd. Edn., 1956-61; pres. Chgo. Met. Housing and Planning Council, 1956-57, Immigrants Service League, Chgo., 1960-61; dir. Pitts. Council Pub. Edn., 1965-67; mem. citizens bd. U. Chgo., 1958-78; mem. Pitts. Bd. Pub. Edn., 1973-76; bd. dirs. Pitts. Center for Arts, 1977-85, World Federalist Assn. Pitts., 1984—, Pitts. dist. Zionist Orgn. Am., 1979-81, mem. Hunger Action Coalition, Pitts., 1985-86; mem. Allegheny County Bd. Assistance, 1981—, chmn. 1981-87. Served from comdr. to capt. USCGR, 1942-46. Decorated Navy Commendation medal; recipient alumni citation for pub. service U. Chgo., 1960; award for pub. service U.S. Gen. Accounting Office, 1971. Mem. ABA, Am. Accounting Assn., Chgo. Bar Assn., Fed. Bar Assn., Allegheny County Bar Assns., Am. Polit. Sci. Assn., Am. Soc. Pub. Adminstrn.(award for pub. service Pitts. Area chpt., 1985), Center Study Presidency, Govt. Fin. Officers Assn., Fin. Execs. Inst., Nat. Assn. Accountants, Royal Inst. Pub. Adminstrn. (Britain), Phi Beta Kappa, Pi Lambda Phi, Phi Delta Phi. Clubs: Army and Navy (Washington); U. Chgo. Alumni (Pitts.) (pres. 1981-84). Home: 825 Morewood Ave Pittsburgh PA 15213

POITRAS, PIERRE, leisure and transportation products company executive; b. Quebec, Que., Can., July 8, 1934; s. Adrien and Simone (Talbot) P.; m. Micheline Gagnon, Oct. 25, 1958; children—Richard, Lucie, Guy, Denis. M.C.S., Laval U., 1957; M.B.A., Am. U., 1958. Vice pres., treas. Bombardier Inc., Montreal, Que., 1964-68; dir. fin. Bombardier Ltd., 1968-71, v.p. fin., 1971—; past pres. Creditel of Can. Ltd. Mem. Can. Chartered Accountants Inst., Fin. Execs. Inst. Club: K.C. Home: 231 Third Concession, Noyan, PQ Canada JOJ 1B0 Office: Bombardier Inc Ste 1700, 800 Dorchester Blvd W, Montreal, PQ Canada H3B 1Y8

POLAND, RICHARD DAVID, accountant, state official; b. Wheeling, W.Va., Jan. 14, 1957; s. Harry Lee and Eleanor Jean (Henning) P. BSBA, Youngstown State U., 1982. CPA, Ohio. Acct. Anthony Amatore PA, Youngstown, Ohio, 1985; state examiner III Ohio State Auditor's Office, Youngstown, 1986—. Home: 4812 State Rte 45 Bristolville OH 44402 Office: Ohio State Auditor's Office 4822 Market St Youngstown OH 44512

POLDRACK, CARL HERMAN, III, manufacturing company executive; b. Taylor, Tex., Mar. 24, 1961; s. Carl Herman Jr. and Faye Ellen (Loosier) P.; m. Melinda Lou Jones, Aug. 31, 1985. AA, South Plains Coll., 1983. Mgr. outside services Hoesch Tubular Products Co. Inc., Baytown, Tex., 1983-84, mgr. forging and heat-treating, 1984—. Mem. Saltwater Angler's League Tex., Phi Theta Kappa. Republican. Club: Am. Kennel (N.Y.C.). Office: Hoesch Tubular Products Co Inc 2600 Spur 55 Baytown TX 77520

POLEMITOU, OLGA ANDREA, accountant; b. Nicosia, Cyprus, June 28, 1950; d. Takis and Georgia (Nicolaou) Chrysanthou. BA with honors, U. London, 1971; PhD, Ind. U.-Bloomington, 1981. CPA, Ind. Asst. productivity officer Internat. Labor Office/Cyprus Productivity Ctr., Nicosia, 1971-74; cons. Arthur Young & Co., N.Y.C., 1981; mgr. Coopers & Lybrand, Newark, 1981-83; mgr. Bell Atlantic, Phila., 1983—; chairperson adv. council Extended Day Care Community Edn., West Windsor Plainsboro,

1987-88. Contbr. articles to profl. jours. Bus. cons. project bus. Jr. Achievement, Indpls., 1984-85; chairperson adv. council Community Edn., West Windsor, Plainsboro, N.J., 1987-88. Mem. Nat. Assn. Female Execs., Nat. Trust for Hist. Preservation, Ind. CPA Soc., N.J. CPA Soc., AICPAs., Princeton Network of Profl. Women (program dir.). Avocations: water skiing, tennis. Home: PO Box 401 Princeton Junction NJ 08550 Office: Bell Atlantic 1880 John F Kennedy Blvd 4th Floor Philadelphia PA 19103

POLEN, DAVID MARTIN, financial executive; b. Bklyn., July 31, 1943; s. Sol and Estelle (Kimmel) P.; m. Rosa Polen; children: Carra, Solomon. BA, Bklyn. Coll., 1965. With Walston & Co., N.Y.C., 1967-70, Oppenheimer & Co., N.Y.C., 1971-72, Hornblower & Weeks, N.Y.C., 1972-73, Goldberg Polen & Co., N.Y.C., 1973-79; owner, pres., chmn. bd. Polen Capital Mgmt. Corp., N.Y.C., 1979—. Served with USMC, 1967-72. Cert. fin. planner; registered fin. prin. Mem. Internat. Assn. Fin. Planners (dir. N.Y.C. chpt. 1978-82). Jewish. Clubs: Lone Star Boat. Home: 500 E 77th St New York NY 10162 Office: Polen Capital Mgmt Corp 100 Wall St 29th Fl New York NY 10005

POLEN, GEORGE RAYMOND, electronic engineer, engineering company executive; b. Royal Oak, Mich., Apr. 20, 1931; s. Norman N. and Jessie (Smith) P.; m. Elizabeth A. Perry, Jan. 11, 1969; children: Nancy, Thomas. BSEE, Worcester Poly. Inst., 1953. Engr. ITT Fed. Labs., Nutley, N.J., 1953-60; sect. mgr. Hewlett Packard Co., Rockaway, N.J., 1960-68; program mgr. Microstate, New Providence, N.J., 1968-70; with Boonton Electronics Corp., Randolph, N.J., 1970—, v.p., 1973—; mem. County Coll. of Morris Indsl. Adv. com., Randolph, 1973—, v.p., 1984—. With U.S. Army, 1953-55. Mem. IEEE (sr.), N.J. RF/Microwave Industries Assn., Soc. Am. Magicians (trustee Morris County 1978—). Home: 6 Stafford Terr Parsippany NJ 07054 Office: Boonton Electronics Corp 791 Rt 10 Randolph NJ 07869

POLEN-DORN, LINDA FRANCES, communications executive; b. Cleve., Mar. 23, 1945; d. Stanley and Mildred (Kain) Neuger; m. Samuel O. Dorn; children: Lanelle, Brian, Adam, Dawn. BA cum laude, U. Miami, 1967. Reporter Miami (Fla.) News, 1966-67; writer Miamian Mag., 1967-68; dir. pub. rels. Muscular Dystrophy Assn., Miami, 1968-72; cons., adv. and pub. rels. Ft. Lauderdale, 1974-77; pub. rels. writer J. Cory and Assocs., Ft. Lauderdale, Fla., 1978-79; account supr. Maizner & Franklin, Fla., 1979-86; v.p., communications mgr. Glendale Fed. Savs. & Loan, Fla., 1986—. Sustaining mem. Mus. Art., Ft. Lauderdale, 1986—, Philharmonic Soc., Ft. Lauderdale, 1987—. Mem. Internat. Assn. Bus. Communicators, Pub. Rels. Soc. Am., Women in Communications, Broward C. of C. (vice chmn. govt. affairs 1984-85). Office: Glendale Fed Savs & Loan 301 E Las Olas Blvd Fort Lauderdale FL 33301

POLETTE, PAUL LEROY, publishing company executive; b. Herculaneum, Mo., Jan. 15, 1928; s. Ferdinand and Fanny Marie (Justin) P.; m. Nancy Jane McCaleb, Dec. 23, 1950; children: Paula Jane, Keith Paul, Marsha Ellen. BS in Indsl. Mgmt., Washington U., St. Louis, 1969; MBA in Mgmt., St. Louis U., 1974. Supr. McDonnell-Douglas Corp., St. Louis, 1952-82; pres. Book Lures, Inc., O'Fallon, Mo., 1979—; instr. bus. St. Mary's Coll., O'Fallon, 1970-85. Photographer: Exploring Science Fiction, 1983, Supernatural, 1983, others. Mem. O'Fallon Planning Zoning Subcom., 1975, O'Fallon Bicentennial Com., 1976, St. Charles County Com. for Jr. Coll. Dist., 1984-86. Served as sgt. USAF, 1948-52. Mem. St. Charles City C. of C. Republican. Roman Catholic. Avocations: fishing, photography, travel.

POLICH, RICHARD ALBERT, engineer; b. Detroit, Aug. 5, 1955; s. Donald Joseph and Barbara Ann (Dana) P.; m. Jill Mills, June 17, 1978; children: Megan, Anne. BS in Nuclear and Mech. Engring., U. Mich., 1979, MBA, 1985. Registered profl. engr., Mich. With Consumer Power Co., Jackson, Mich., 1979—, sr. engr. corp. mktg. services, 1987—; engr. Midland (Mich.) Nuclear Project, 1980-86; sr. engr. Midland Cogeneration Venture, 1986-87; speaker in field. Vol. Jackson Big Brothers/Big Sisters, 1979-84; ofcl. U.S. Cycling Fedn., Mich., 1987—; mem. Jackson Metroplex Com., 1988. Mem. NSPE (awards chair, Young Engr. Yr. 1987), Assn. Energy Engrs., Am. Gas Assn. (mem. cogeneration com., natural gas vehicle com.), Ann Arbor Velo Club (pres. 1984-86), Cascades Cycle Club. Office: Consumers Power Co 212 W Michigan Jackson MI 49201

POLIFKA, FRANK JACOB FREDERICK, insurance executive; b. El Paso, Tex., Feb. 6, 1952; s. Frank J.F. and Zetta Marie P.; m. Carol Ann Seeley, Jan. 18, 1975; 1 child, Matthew J.F., Stefanie J. AA, San Joaquin Delta Coll., 1972; BA, Calif. State U., Stanislaus, 1974; postgrad., Calif. State U., Fresno, 1975-77. Agt. Farmers Group, Inc., Fresno, 1977—; dist. mgr. trainee Farmers Group, Inc., Merced, Calif., 1984; expert witness for ins. suits The Frank Polifka Agy., Clovis, Calif., 1980; cons. numerous firms, Calif., 1985—. Republican. Mormon. Home: 8376 N First St Fresno CA 93710 Office: The Frank Polifka Agy 3097 Willow Ave Ste 17 Clovis CA 93612

POLINER, RANDALL EDWARD, electronics executive; b. Seattle, Dec. 30, 1955; s. Saul and Mary (With) P.; m. Kathleen Elizabeth Graham, Apr. 22, 1978; children: Graham Edward, Caitlin Joy. BSEE, Ga. Inst. Tech., 1977; MSEE, Carnegie-Mellon U., 1980; MBA, Harvard U., 1983. Project mgr. Westinghouse Electric Corp., Pitts., 1978-82; v.p., chief operating officer Macrodyne Inc., Boston, 1982-84; spl. asst. to pres. Scientific Systems Services, Melbourne, Fla., 1984-85; v.p. ops. Scientific Systems Services, Melbourne, 1985-86, v.p. mktg. and sales, 1986-88, v.p. Computer Task Group, 1988-89; v.p. South Atlantic Capital, Tampa, Fla., 1989—. Mem. IEEE, Soc. Mfg. Engrs. (sr.). Office: South Atlantic Venture Ptnrs 614 W Bay St Ste 200 Tampa FL 33606

POLING, HAROLD ARTHUR, automobile company executive; b. Troy, Mich., Oct. 14, 1925; s. Plesant Arthur and Laura Elizabeth (Thompson) P.; m. Marian Sarita Lee, 1957; children—Pamela Lee, Kathryn Lynn, Douglas Lee. BA, Monmouth (Ill.) Coll., 1949; MBA, Ind. U., 1951; LHD (hon.), Monmouth Coll., 1981, Hofstra U., 1986. With Ford Motor Co., Dearborn, Mich., 1951-59, 60—, asst. controller transmissions and chassis div., 1964-66, controller transmission and chasis div., 1966-67, controller engine and foundry div., 1967-68; controller product devel. group Ford Motor Co., 1968-72; v.p. finance Ford of Europe, 1972-75; pres. Ford of Europe, Inc., Brentwood, Eng., 1975-77; chmn. bd. Ford of Europe, Inc., from 1977; exec. v.p. Ford Motor Co., Dearborn, Mich., 1979, exec. v.p. N.Am. automotive ops., 1980-85, mem. office of chief exec., 1984, pres., chief operating officer, 1985-87, vice chmn., chief operating officer, 1987—, also dir.; bd. dirs. NCR Corp. bd. dirs. The Monmouth (Ill.) Coll. Senate; mem. dean's adv. Council Ind. U. Sch. Bus., chmn. univ. ann. giving program; chmn. Nat. 4-H Council; bd. visitors Sch. Econs. and Mgmt. Oakland U., Mich., Grad. Sch. Bus. U. Pitts.; conf. bd., v.p. Boys and Girls Club Southeast Mich.; conf. bd. Bus.-Higher Edn. Forum, U.S. Korea Bus. Council. Served with USNR, 1943-45. Recipient Disting. Service Citation award Automotive Hall Fame, 1986, Leadership award Engring. Soc. Detroit, 1986. Mem. The Bus.-Higher Edn. Forum, U.S. Korea Bus. Council. Office: Ford Motor Co The American Rd Rm 118 Dearborn MI 48121

POLINSKY, DAVID BRAM, lawyer, corporate secretary; b. Englewood, N.J., Nov. 3, 1946; s. Eugene and Mary Margaret (Post) P.; m. Susan Lynn Lecin, June 18, 1972; children: Daniel Benjamin, Lauren Lecin. BSEE, Purdue U., 1968; JD, Rutgers U., 1976. Bar: N.J. 1976, U.S. Dist. Ct. N.J. 1976, N.Y. 1977, N.C. 1978, U.S. Dist. Ct. (mid. dist.) N.C. 1978. Electronics engr. Space Craft, Inc., Huntsville, Ala., 1968-69; long range planning engr. N.J. Bell Telephone Co., Newark, 1969-71; outside plant engr. N.J. Bell Telephone Co., Midland Park, 1971-72; computer systems adminstr. N.J. Bell Telephone Co., Newark, 1973; computer systems specialist Rapidata, Inc., West Caldwell, N.J., 1974-75; atty. AT&T Techs., Inc. (formerly Western Electric Co.), Greensboro, N.C., 1976—; corp. sec. Airways Facilities Engring. Co., Vienna, Va., 1987—. Contbr. articles to profl. jours.; editor: Rutgers U. Law Rev. Treas. Brotherhood Temple Emanuel, Greensboro, 1987—, religious sch. parent ctr., 1987—. Served with USAF, 1969. Mem. ABA (sect. pub. contract law, sect. law, sci. and tech.), Armed Forces Communications and Electronics Assn., Western Electric N.C. (pres. 1982-84), Starmount Forest Country Club, WENOCA Club (pres. Greensboro chpt. 1982-84). Democrat. Jewish. Home: 3702 Watauga Dr Greensboro NC 27410-4622 Office: AT&T Techs Inc PO Box 25000 Greensboro NC 27420

POLIQUIN, BRUCE LEE, investment manager; b. Waterville, Maine, Nov. 1, 1953; s. Lionel Joseph and Esther Louise (Cyr) P. BA in Econs., Harvard U., 1976. Mktg. rep. Harris Trust and Savs. Bank, Chgo., 1976-77; dir. mktg. Evaluation Assocs. Inc., Norwalk, Conn., 1978-80; v.p., dir. mktg. and prin. Avatar Assocs., N.Y.C., 1981—. Contbr. articles to profl. jours. Recruiter Phillips Acad., Andover, Mass., 1976—. Mem. Assn. Investment Mgmt. Sales Execs., Polit. Club for Econs. Growth. Republican. Roman Catholic. Home: 73 Emery St 2d Fl Portland ME 04102 Office: Avatar Assocs 900 Third Ave New York NY 10022

POLITZINER, NORMAN JAY, financial planner, insurance and pension consultant; b. New Brunswick, N.J., Oct. 30, 1942; s. Seymour and Ethel (Watkin) P.; m. Dorothy Miriam Strauss, Oct. 19, 1968; children: Deborah, Amanda. BS, NYU, 1964; MBA, Rutgers U., 1966. Cert. fin. planner. Mgr. carpet dept. Bloomingdales, N.Y.C., 1967-68; asst. buyer Sears Roebuck & Co., N.Y.C., 1969; v.p. ops. Diamond Supply Co., New Brunswick, N.J., 1969-77; fin. cons. Modern Estate Planning, Edison, N.J., 1978—; cons. retail trade. Past pres. B'nai Tikvan, North Brunswick. Served with AUS, 1968-72. Recipient Nat. Sales award, Nat. Health award, Nat. QUality award. Mem. Nat. Assn. LIfe Underwriters, Raritan Valley Assn. Life Underwriters (pres. emeritus), Million Dollar Round Table, Internat. Assn. for Fin. Planning (exec. v.p. Princeton, West N.J. chpt.), Inst. Cert. Fin. Planners, Pres.'s Club of Nat. Life Ins. Co. Vt. (life). Lodge: Kiwanis. Home: 1505 N Indian Pl North Brunswick NJ 08902 Office: Modern Estate Planning 2015 Lincoln Hwy Edison NJ 08817

POLIVKA, G. MARKUS, insurance agency executive; b. Bamberg, Fed. Republic Germany, June 9, 1949; came to U.S., 1953, naturalized, 1974; s. Karl J. and Elsbeth E. (Geisel) P.; m. Melinda Lani Wight, Dec. 21, 1974; 1 child, Eric Kamuela. Student, U. Nebr., 1967-70, Chaminade U., 1972-73. Underwriter Theo. Davies, Inc., Honolulu, 1971-72, Indsl. Indemnity, Honolulu, 1972-75; v.p., account exec. Alexander of Hawaii, Honolulu, 1975-81; pres. Monarch Ins. Co., Honolulu, 1981—. Pres. Bishop Mus. Assn., Honolulu; treas. Friends of Iolani Palace, Honolulu; dir. Hawaii Easter Seal Soc. Mem. Hawaii Underwriters Assn. Clubs: Oahu Country, Outrigger Canoe, Blue Goose, Honolulu. Home: 2167 Halakau St Honolulu HI 96821 Office: Monarch Ins Svcs 846 S Hotel St 305 Honolulu HI 96813

POLK, JOHN GEORGE, company executive; b. Vienna, Austria, June 30, 1932; came to U.S., 1941; s. Eric and Joan (Hahn) P.; m. Barbara Frank, June 21, 1959; children: Michael, Suzanne. B.S. in Chem. Engring., MIT, 1953, M.S. in Chem. Engring., 1954. Various engring. and fin. positions M&T Chems. Inc., Rahway, N.J., 1956-75; with Am. Can Co., Greenwich, Conn., 1975-86; sr. v.p., controller Am. Can Co., 1981, sr. v.p. ops. control, 1981-84, exec. v.p., sector exec. packaging, 1984-86, pres. Am. Can Packaging Sector, 1986; sr. v.p. Triangle Industries, Inc., N.Y.C., 1986-87; sr. v.p. Primerica Corp., Greenwich, Conn., 1987-88, ret., 1988. Bd. Overseers Dartmouth Inst., 1986-88; bd. dirs. Keep Am. Beautiful, Inc., 1980—, Food Research and Action Com., 1985—. 1st lt. Signal Corps U.S. Army, 1954-56.

POLK, LEE THOMAS, lawyer; b. Chgo., Feb. 25, 1945; s. Lee Anthony and Mary Josephine (Lane) P.; m. Susan Luzader, Mar. 21, 1975; children: Adam, Angela. AB, Coe Coll., 1967; JD, U. Chgo., 1970. Bar: Ill. 1970, U.S. Dist. Ct. (no. dist.) Ill. 1970, U.S. Ct. Mil. Appeals 1972, U.S. Dist. Ct. (we. dist.) Mich. 1983, U.S. Claims Ct. 1983, U.S. Ct. Appeals (7th cir.) 1984, U.S. Ct. Appeals (6th cir.) 1987, U.S. Tax Ct. 1987, U.S. Ct. Appeals (3d cir.) 1989. Assoc. firm Vedder, Price, Kaufman & Kammholz, Chgo., 1970-72, 75-77, ptnr. 1977-86; ptnr. Murphy, Smith & Polk, 1986—. Contbr. articles on employee benefits and health law to profl. jours. Served to capt. JAGC, U.S. Army, 1972-75. Mem. ABA (sects. on tax, employee benefits, pub. contracts and bus.), Ill. Bar Assn., Chgo. Bar Assn. (chmn. employee benefits com. 1987-88), Midwest Pension Conf. (chmn. Chgo. chpt. 1986), Nat. Contract Mgmt. Assn., Nat. Health Lawyers Assn., Phi Beta Kappa, Phi Kappa Phi. Roman Catholic. Club: Union League (Chgo.). Home: 820 Sheridan Rd Evanston IL 60202 Office: Murphy Smith & Polk Two First National Pla 24th Fl Chicago IL 60603

POLLACK, FLORENCE ZAKS, management consultant; b. Washington, Pa.; d. Charles and Ruth (Isaacson) Zaks; divorced; children—Melissa, Stephanie. BA, Flora Stone Mather Coll., Western Res. U., 1961. Pres., treas. Exec. Arrangements, Inc., Cleve., 1978—. Lobbyist Ohio Citizens Com. for Arts, Columbus, 1975-83; mem. Leadership Cleve., 1978-79; trustee Jr. Com., Cleve. Orch., Great Lakes Theatre Festival, 1989; pub. relations adv. com., Cleve. Ballet, Dance Cleve., Jr. Com. of No. Ohio Opera Assn., Cleve. Opera, Shakers Lakes Regional Nature Ctr., Cleve. Music Sch. Settlement, Playhouse Sq. Cabinet, Cleve. Ctr. Econ. Edn., Cleve. Conv. and Visitors Bur., domed stadium adv. com. Named Idea Woman of Yr., Cleve. Plain Dealer, 1975; named to Au Courrant list Cleve. Mag., 1979, named to Cleve.'s 100 Most Influential Women, 1985, named one of 1988 Trendsetters Cleveland Woman mag. Mem. Cleve. Area Meeting Planning. Clubs: Skating, University, Women's City, Playhouse. Avocations: arts, travel, reading. Office: Exec Arrangements Inc 13221 Shaker Sq Cleveland OH 44120

POLLACK, GERALD J., financial executive; b. N.Y.C., Jan. 20, 1942; s. Charles and Reba P.; m. Diane Pollack, Aug. 30, 1964; children: Suzanne, Jenifer, John. BS in Physics, Rensselaer Poly Inst., 1963; MBA, Dartmouth Coll., 1965. Comptroller trainee Exxon Corp., N.Y.C., 1965-67; asst. ops. comptroller Amerada Hess, Woodbridge, N.J., 1967-68; mgr. customer svc. Arthur Young & Co., N.Y.C., 1969-73; dir. mgmt. svc. Arthur Young & Co., Stamford, Conn., 1973-74; v.p., controller Avis Inc., Garden City, L.I., 1975-81; v.p., chief fin. officer ITT Rayonier, Stamford, 1982—. Mem. Southwestern Area & Commerce Industry Assn. (steering com. 1988), Fin. Exec. Inst. Office: ITT Rayonier Inc 1177 Summer St Stamford CT 06904

POLLACK, JEFFREY LEE, restaurateur; b. San Francisco, May 1, 1945; s. Albert and Loretta (Popper) P.; m. Patricia Bowdle Connell, Feb. 20, 1983; children: Lizebeth Ann, Hilary Margaret, Nicholas Albert. BA, San Jose State U. Owner, surety underwriter North Beach Bonding Co., San Francisco, 1968-75; proprietor Old Waldorf, San Francisco, 1974-80, Julius' Castle, San Francisco, 1980—, New Joe's, San Francisco, 1984—, Shadows, San Francisco, 1985—, Iron Horse, 1986—; pres. Pollack Group, San Francisco, 1985—. Mem. Downtown Assn. (bd. dirs. 1987—), Union Sq. Assn. Democrat. Home: 302 Greenwich St San Francisco CA 94133 Office: Pollack Group Ltd 347 Geary St San Francisco CA 94102

POLLACK, MARY LOUISE, hotel executive; b. Phila., Nov. 15, 1949; d. Edward Latshaw and Mary Louise (Dempsey) Gruber; m. Stephen J. Pollack, May 15, 1977 (div. 1981). BA in English, Duke U., 1971; postgrad. Hotel Sch., Cornell U. Cert. tchr., Pa. Travel agt. G & O Travel, N.Y.C., 1977-80; sales mgr. Halloran House, N.Y.C., 1980-81; regional dir. Halloran Hotels, N.Y.C., 1981-83, nat. dir. sales, 1983-84; assoc. dir. mktg. Treadway Hotels and Resorts, Saddle Brook, N.J., 1984-85, dir. mktg., 1985-86, v.p. mktg., 1986-87, also bd. dirs.; dir sales, mktg. Eastern region Prime Mgmt., Fairfield, N.J., 1987—; dir. Somerset Hotels, N.J., Treadway Inns Corp. Mem. Hotel Sales Mgrs. Assn. Internat., U.S. Tour Operators Assn., Am. Bus Assn., Meeting Planners Internat., Nat. Passenger Traffic Assn. (hotel com. 1986), Am. Soc. Travel Agts., Travel Industry Assn. Am. (planning com. 1983-84), Nat. Tour Assn. (conv. com. 1982-84, membership com. 1984, cert. com. 1986, mktg. com. 1987), Pa. Travel Council (program chmn. for 1st Gov.'s Conf. on Travel 1983, mem. mktg. com. 1983).

POLLAK, EDWARD BARRY, chemical manufacturing company executive; b. N.Y.C., Sept. 6, 1934; s. Ben N. and Harriet E. (Springer) P.; m. Marianne E. Modi, Feb. 27, 1960; children—David, Anne, Kari. B.Chem. Eng., Cornell U., 1956, M.B.A., 1957. With Olin Corp., 1957—; bus. mgr. specialty and consumer products Olin Corp., Stamford, Conn., 1970-72; v.p. Olin Corp. (internat. Chems. Group), 1973-76, v.p., gen. mgr. designed products dept., 1976-80, corp. v.p., internat., 1980-86; pres., chief exec. officer Olin Hunt Specialty Products, Inc., 1986—; dir. Etoxyl C.A., Venezuela, Asahi-Olin Ltd., Japan; mem. internat. bd. dirs. Union Trust Co., Stamford; mem. steering com. internat. affairs group Chem. Mfrs. Assn. and Synthetic Organic Chem. Mfrs. Assn., 1979-81. Mem. Synthetic Organic Chem. Mfrs. Assn. (gov. 1977-81, v.p. 1978, pres. 1979-80), Internat. Isocyanate Inst. (dir. 1979-81), Cornell Soc. Engrs. (dir. 1967-72, v.p. 1971-72). Club: Cornell of Fairfield County. Office: Olin Corp 120 Long Ridge Rd Stamford CT 06904

POLLAK, TIM, advertising agency executive. Exec. v.p. Young & Rubicam N.Y., to 1987; pres., chief exec. officer DYR Worldwide (now HDM Wordwide), 1987—; also corp. chief exec. officer HDM Worldwide; corp. chief exec. officer, HDM USA, 1988—. Mem. Internat. Advt. Assn. (pres. N.Y. chpt.). Office: HDM 810 Seventh Ave New York NY 10019

POLLAN, STEPHEN MICHAEL, lawyer, author; b. N.Y.C., May 19, 1929; s. Robert and Harriet (Morganstern) P.; m. Corrine Staller, July 18, 1954; children: Michael, Lori, Tracy, Dana. BBS, L.I. U., 1985; LLB, Bklyn. Law Sch., 1951. Bar: N.Y. 1951. Asst. prof., Marymount Coll., 1960-70; pres. Royal Bus. Funds (AMEX), 1970-76; sr. real estate cons. Nat. Westminster Bank, 1976-78; asst. prof. fin. C.W. Post Coll., Sch. Bus. L.I. U.; dir. Credit Inst. Vice chmn. UN Com. for UN Day, 1971-72; advisor Pres.'s Commn. Small Bus., 1974; pres. Gay Head Community Coun., 1975. Mem. Nat. Assn. Small Bus. Investment Cos. (regional pres. 1975; bd. govs.; cert of apprecation). Co-author: How to Borrow Money, Field Guide to Home Buyers, Field Guide to Starting a Business in America; regular contbr. articles to profl. jours.; guest expert Good Morning America TV Show, The Today Show, other TV shows; frequent guest Nightly Bus. Report; segment holst CNBC Cable TV. Home: 1095 Park Ave New York NY 10028 also: Gay Head Martha's Vineyard MA 02535 Office: 404 E 79th St New York NY 10021

POLLAND, REBECCA ROBBINS, foundation executive; b. Phila., Jan. 11, 1922; d. Louis Aron Jonah and Edith Frances (Kapnek) Robbins; B.A., Bryn Mawr Coll., 1942; M.A., U. Calif., Berkeley, 1957, Ph.D., 1971; m. Harry L. Polland, July 14, 1946 (div. 1979); children—Louise, Margaret, Jonathan. Analyst, cons., commisson mem., local and nat. govt., 1942-82; cons. U.S. Dept. Agr., 1977; lectr. Polit. sci. Sacramento State U., 1975-76; asst. prof. Sonoma State U. (Calif.), 1976-78; asst. prof. Rutgers U., Camden, N.J., 1978-86. Chmn. bd. Frogmore Tobacco Estates Ltd., Zimbabwe; Presdl. appointee Bd. Internat. Food and Agrl. Devel., 1979-82. Exec. trustee J.F. Kapnek Charitable Trust, Phila., 1980—, also pres. 1988— ; mem. Berkeley City Commn. on Recreation and Parks, 1970-75; v.p.; mem. White House Conf. Food, Nutrition, Health, 1969, World Food Conf., Rome, 1974. Mem. Am. Polit. Sci. Assn., AAUP, Am. Soc. Public Adminstrn., Am. Soc. Tropical Medicine and Hygiene, Assn. Dirs. Internat. Agrl. Programs Assn. Women in Devel. (founding). Contbr. articles to profl. jours. Home: 220 Locust St Apt 30A Philadelphia PA 19106 Office: 10 Hendrikz Way, Emerald Hill, Harare Zimbabwe

POLLARD, CHARLES WILLIAM, health care services executive; b. Chgo., June 8, 1938; s. Charles W. and Ruth Ann (Humphrey) P.; m. Judith Ann, June 8, 1959; children: Julie Ann, Charles W., Brian, Amy. A.B., Wheaton Coll., 1960; J.D., Northwestern U., 1963. Bar: Ill. 1963. Mem. firm Wilson and McIlvaine, 1963-67, Vescelus, Perry & Pollard, Wheaton, Ill., 1968-72; prof., v.p. fin. Wheaton Coll., 1972-77; sr. v.p. ServiceMaster Industries, Downers Grove, Ill., 1977-80, exec. v.p., 1980-81, pres., 1981-83; pres., chief operating officer ServiceMaster Industries, 1981-83; pres., chief exec. officer ServiceMaster Co., Downers Grove, Ill., 1983—; bd. dirs. Gary-Wheaton Bank, Wheaton Coll., Herman Miller Inc. Office: Service Master Co 2300 Warrenville Rd Downers Grove IL 60515 *

POLLARD, JOSEPH AUGUSTINE, retail marketing executive; b. N.Y.C., June 22, 1924; s. Joseph Michael and Mary Theresa (Sheerin) P.; m. Helen Frances O'Neill, Jan. 18, 1947 (dec.); children: Christopher (dec.), Kenneth, Eugene, Daniel, Theresa, Michael; m. 2d, Lee Sharon Rivkins, Jan. 1, 1981. Student Pratt Inst., 1946-50. Advt. mgr. Boston Store, Utica, N.Y., 1951-53; sales promotion dir. Interstate Stores, N.Y., 1954-60, 67-70; v.p. sales Community Discount Stores, Chgo., 1960-63; dir. sales S. Klein, N.Y., 1964-66; v.p. advt. and pub. relations Peoples Drug Stores, Alexandria, Va., 1970—; bd. dirs. Seasons Savs. Bank, Richmond, Va. Trustee D.C. div. Am. Cancer Soc., pres. 1985-86; pres. Modern Retailers Ill., 1962. Served with USAF, 1943-46, 50-51. Recipient Am. Advt. Fedn. Silver medal award, 1982, St. George's medal Am. Cancer Soc., 1984. Mem. Advt. Club Met. Washington (pres. 1975-76). Club: Country of Fairfax (Va.). Home: 5848 Kara Pl Burke VA 22015 Office: Peoples Drug Stores Inc 6315 Bren Mar Dr Alexandria VA 22312

POLLARD, JOSEPH WARREN, data processing executive; b. Honolulu, Sept. 17, 1956; s. Jack Gordon and Ellen (Warren) P.; m. Kathy Ann Fogg, Dec. 14, 1979; children: Amanda Ellen, Joseph Warren. BSET in Computer Systems, Memphis State U., 1979. Mfg. engr. Honeywell, Richardson, Tex., 1979-81; sales rep. Digital Equip. Corp., Dallas, 1981-83; nat. account mgr. Apollo Computer, Dallas, 1983—. Recipient Golden Ring Apollo Computer, 1985, 87. Mem. Sigma Chi. Methodist. Home: 2206 High Country Dr Carrollton TX 75007 Office: Apollo Computer 1215 N O'Connor Irving TX 75039

POLLARD, THERON ASBURY, specialty advertising distributer; b. Emmett, Idaho, Feb. 5, 1932; s. Frank George Pollard and Ella Armelda (Asbury) P.; m. LaMelva Jean Peterson, June 1, 1953; children: David, Debra, Donald, Dee Diann, Destry. Student, U. Utah, 1951-52, Idaho State U., 1958-61. Owner, operator Tee Pee Avtg. Co., Phoenix, 1953-56, Tee Pee Advt. Co., Pocatella, Idaho, 1958—. With USAF, 1952-56. Mem. Dallas Specialty Advtg. Assn. Internat., Utah and Idaho Specialty Advtg. Assn. (v.p. 1983-84, pres. 1988—), Civitan Club, Lions. Republican. Home: 153 Taft Pocatello ID 83201 Office: Tee Pee Advt Co 155 Taft Pocatello ID 83201

POLLEY, DAVID E., textile manufacturing executive; b. Bklyn., May 3, 1934; s. Henry M. and Mildred (Brown) P.; m. Nancy Sind, May 2, 1965 (div. Aug. 1985); children: Douglas Mark, Diana Hope; m. Virginia Lucile Cobb Spangler, Mar. 29, 1986; 1 child, Frank Henry Spangler. BS in Econs., U. Pa., 1955; MS, Columbia U., 1956. Buyer Abraham & Straus, Bklyn., 1956-66; div. mgr. Korvettes, N.Y.C., 1966-69; exec. v.p. Stephen Leedom, N.Y.C., 1969-72; chmn. David Industries, Dalton, Ga., 1972-81; pres. Lees Carpets (div. Burlington Industries), N.Y.C., 1981-86, Burlington Residential Carpet Group, Valley Forge, Pa., 1986—. Office: Lees & Burlington House Carpets Valley Forge Corp Ctr King of Prussia PA 19406

POLLEY, MALCOLM EMERSON, financial analyst; b. Berkeley, Calif., Nov. 10, 1962; s. George Warren Polley and Judith Maxine (Yarger) Hull; m. Lora Kay Drenth, Dec. 21, 1985. BBA, Iowa State U., 1985. Chargeback mgr. First Data Services, Inc., Plymouth, Minn., 1986-87; fin. planner Brink Fin. Services, Prior Lake, Minn., 1987—; chargeback cons. Bank One Columbus, NA, Plymouth, 1987. Mem. Am. Assn. Individual Investors, Am. Entrepreneurs Assn. Democrat. Mem. Reformed Ch. Home: 3828 Scott Ave N Robbinsdale MN 55422 Office: Brink Fin Svcs 16817 Duluth Ave SE Prior Lake MN 55372

POLO, RICHARD JOSEPH, engineering executive; b. Barranquilla, Colombia, Oct. 14, 1936; s. Pedro Pastor and Clotilde (Verano) P.; m. Ana Isabel Cepeda, Feb. 1, 1958; children: Richard J. Jr., James Alan. BCE, NYU, 1957; MS in Structural Engring., Iowa State U., 1963, PhD in Structural and Nuclear Engring., 1971; disting. grad., Command and Gen. Staff Coll., Ft. Leavenworth, Kans., 1970; grad., Inter-Am. Def. Coll., Ft. McNair, Washington, 1977; MBA, Marymount U., 1986. Registered profl. engr., Md., Iowa, Fla., Pa., Conn. Commd. 2d lt. U.S. Army, 1957, advanced through grades to col., 1979, various positions, 1957-79; asst. dir. civil works Pacific U.S. Army Office Chief of Engrs., 1979-80; corps engr., engr. brigade comdr. U.S. Army, Ludwigsburg, Fed. Republic Germany, 1980-83; dep. study dir. U.S. Army Office Chief of Staff, Washington, 1984-85; ret. U.S. Army, 1985; v.p. constrn. Kidde Cons. Inc., Balt., 1985, sr. v.p. constrn., 1986—, exec. v.p., 1986-88, corp. sec., 1988—, also bd. dirs.; bd. dirs. KCI Holdings, 1988—. Contbr. articles on mil. and structural engring. to profl. jours. Inventor arcuate space frame. Community comdr. and sr. U.S. rep. Ludwigsburg Mil. Community, 1980-83—. Decorated Legion of

Merit with bronze oak leaf cluster, Bronze Star, others; Brookings Institution Fed. Exec. fellow, 1983. Mem. ASCE, NSPE, Soc. Am. Mil. Engrs. (bd. dirs. El Paso, Tex. chpt. 1967-68, pres. Stuttgart chpt. Fed. Republic Germany, 1980-82), Md. Soc. Profl. Engrs., Va. Soc. Profl. Engrs. (dir. no. Va. chpt., 1985—, pres. elect 1988—), Assn. U.S. Army (pres. Ludwigsburg chpt. 1980-83), Sigma Xi, Phi Kappa Phi, Tau Beta Pi, Chi Epsilon, Psi Upsilon (pres. local chpt. 1956-57). Republican. Roman Catholic. Home: 8201 Pettit Ct McLean VA 22102 Office: Kidde Cons Inc 1020 Cromwell Bridge Rd Baltimore MD 21204

POLON, MARTIN ISHIAH, science and technology consultant; b. Chgo., May 18, 1942; s. Solomon I. and Bernice V. Polon; m. Janine Petit, Feb. 11, 1984. BA, UCLA, 1964, MA in TV, 1968, postgrad., 1970. Dir. audio-visual services UCLA, 1970-80; founder Computer Merchandising and Software Merchandising Mags., 1980-83; prin. Polon Research Internat., Boston, 1983—; lectr. U. Lowell, Mass.; assoc. prof. U. Colo., Denver; forecaster of consumer acceptance of high tech. Speaker various conventions and profl. orgns.; v.p., mem. bd. review Audio Engring. Soc. Jour.; contbr. over 200 articles to mags. and profl. jours., including: Video Mag., Audio Mag. and Billboard, TV Broadcast Mag., Sight and Sound (U.K.), Studio Sound (U.K.), One to One (U.K.), Broadcast Systems Engring. (U.K.). Mem. Audio Engring. Soc. (gov., chmn. edn. com. 1985—, govs. award for service in edn.), Soc. Motion Picture and TV Engrs. (participating mem. com. on audio), Soc. Profl. Audio Recording Studios, Assn. Profl. Rec. Studios (U.K.), Japan Soc. Boston, Sapphire Audio Group, U.S. Naval Inst. Democrat. Jewish.

POLOS, JAMES, investment company executive; b. N.Y.C., Oct. 3, 1944; s. James and Eileen Rita (Hamlin) P.; m. Susan Louise Horton, Sept. 22, 1984; children: Louisa Eileen, Thomas James; child from previous marriage, Alyssa Ann. BA, St. Lawrence U., 1966; postgrad., Adelphi U., 1969. Cert. fin. planner. Personal risks underwriter Liberty Mut. Ins., Lynbrook, N.Y., 1966-67; account exec. Prudential-Bache, N.Y.C., 1970-79; v.p. sales Smith Barney Harris Upham, N.Y.C., 1979—; mem. adj. faculty Coll. for Fin. Planning, Denver, 1980-83, New Sch. for Social Research, N.Y.C., 1984—. Trustee St. Lawrence U. Alumni Fund, Canton, N.Y., 1985—. Served as lt., U.S. Army, 1967-69. Recipient Cert. of Appreciation, Coll. Fin. Planning, 1981, 82. Home: 2 Ashby Pl Katonah NY 10561 Office: Smith Barney 1345 Avenue of the Americas Retail Sales Fl 21 New York NY 10022

POLOWITZ, STEVEN H(OWARD), lawyer; b. Boston, Jan. 7, 1951; s. David and Shirley (Goolst) P.; m. Candace L. Caprow, June 27, 1982; children: Jasyn I., Marisa R. BA, SUNY, Buffalo, 1973, JD, 1978. Bar: N.Y. 1980, Fla. 1981. Ptnr. Abbate & Polowitz, Buffalo, 1980-84; pvt. practice law Buffalo, 1984—; bd. dirs., sec. 1st N.Y. Funding Corp., Buffalo, 1985-87; mem. Housing Ct. Adv. Council City of Buffalo, 1986—. Bd. dirs. West-Side Neighborhood Housing Svcs., Inc., Buffalo, 1981—; bd. dirs., past pres. Buffalo Neighborhood Housing Svcs., Inc., 1983-87; trustee Kadimah Sch. Buffalo. Mem. Fla. Bar Assn., Erie County Bar Assn. (mem. profl. ethics com.), Phi Beta Kappa. Democrat. Office: 120 Delaware Ave Ste 200 Buffalo NY 14202

POLSKY, NORMAN, furniture company executive; b. Kansas City, Mo., Jan. 31, 1924; s. Isadore and Rachel (Rosenblatt) P.; m. Elaine Broudy, July 4, 1946; children: Karen, Larry, Joel, Steven. BS, UCLA, 1947; postgrad., Purdue U., 1943-44; student, Kansas City Jr. Coll., 1941-42. Pres., founder Fixtures Furniture, Kansas City, Mo., 1947—. Contbr. articles to profl. jours. Mem. Multi-Assn. Action Com. for Product Liability, Washington, 1977; chmn. Jr. Achievement, 1972-74; mem. bus. council Nelson Atkins Mus. Art, Kansas City, 1985—. Served to 2d lt. USMC, 1942-46. Named Dir. of Yr., Jr. Achievement, 1972; recipient Bronze Leadership award, 1987, Best of Competition award, 1981, 1983. Mem. Am. Soc. Interior Designers, Inst. Bus. Designers (Pres.'s award 1987), Internat. Facility Mgrs. Assn., Found. for INterior Design Edn. Research, Bus. and Industry Furniture Mfrs. (bd. dirs. 1978-86), Young Pres.'s Orgn., World Bus. Council, C. of C. of Washington. Republican. Jewish. Clubs: Colo. Outward Bound Ice Axe. Lodges: Rotary, B'nai B'rith. Home: 2009 W 70th St Mission Hills KS 66208 Office: Fixtures Furniture 1642 Crystal Kansas City MO 64126

POLYDOROS, NICK JAMES, finance company executive, accountant; b. Chgo., Dec. 30, 1957; s. Nicholas and Loretta Polydoros; m. Pamela Gayle, June 20, 1982; 1 child, Nicolette. BS in Acctg. cum laude, No. Ill. U., 1978, MS in Acctg., 1979. Staff acct. Deloitte Haskins & Sells, Chgo., 1979-80; sr. acct. Rome & Co., Chgo., 1980-82, Shepard, Schwartz & Harris, Chgo., 1982-83; account exec. Merrill Lynch, Chgo., 1983-84; fin. cons. Northbrook, Ill., 1984-86; account v.p. Paine Webber, Inc., Northbrook, 1986—; guest commentator on stock market TV sta., Chgo., 1986-88. Office: Paine Webber Inc 707 Skokie Blvd Northbrook IL 60062

POLZER, ECKHARD FRANZ, medical equipment company executive; b. Dittersdorf, Germany, Dec. 25, 1943; came to U.S., 1979.; s. Franz and Olga (Nather) P.; m. Susan Rae Weinstock, May 15, 1972; children: Tara Y., Elena G. Degree in Mech. Engring., Rudolf-Diesel Polytechnicum, Augsburg, Fed. Republic of Germany, 1965; degree engring. aerospace, Tech. U., Munich, 1972; postgrad., Georgetown U., 1982. Design engr. Siemens AG, Munich, 1965-66; program mgr. Siemans AG, Munich, 1973-77; program mgr. Dornier GmbH, Friedrichshafen, Fed. Republic of Germany, 1977-79, exec. asst., 1982-84; co. rep. Dornier GmbH, Washington, 1979-82; pres. Dornier Med. Systems Inc., Atlanta, 1984—. Office: Dornier Med Systems Inc 824 Livingston Ct Marietta GA 30067

POMERANTZ, JOHN J., manufacturing executive; b. N.Y.C., July 4, 1933; s. Fred P. and Greta (Grainsky) P.; m. Laura H. Herman; children: Andrea, Susan, Marnie. BS in Econs., U. Pa., 1955. With Leslie Fay Cos., Inc., N.Y.C., 1955—, exec. v.p., 1968-71, pres., 1971-87, chmn., chief exec. officer, 1987—; bd. trustees Fashion Inst. Tech., pres. edni. found. F.I.T. Bd. dirs. Am. Com. for Shenkar Coll. Textile Tech. and Fashion in Israel, Inc.; founder Albert Einstein Coll. Medicine, N.Y.C., Nat. Jewish Hosp. and Research Ctr., Denver, Israel Bonds Century Club; fundraising com. Am. Cancer Soc.; past chmn. Greater N.Y. Council Boy Scouts Am. Receipient award of Merit, Jack Martin Fund, Champion of Youth award Internat. Officers of B'nai B'rith, Humanitarian award Albert Einstein Coll. Medicine. Clubs: Quaker Ridge (Scarsdale, N.Y.); Palm Beach (Fla.) Country. Office: Leslie Fay Cos 1400 Broadway New York NY 10018

POMERANZ, FELIX, accounting educator; b. Vienna, Austria, Mar. 28, 1926; s. Joseph and Irene (Meninger) P.; m. Rita Lewin, June 14, 1953; children: Jeffrey Arthur, Andrew Joseph. BBA, CCNY, 1948; MS, Columbia U., 1949. CPA, N.Y., Va., La., N.C.; cert. systems profl.; cert. fraud examiner. Audit staff Coopers & Lybrand, CPAs, N.Y.C., 1949-56, dir. operational auditing, 1966-68, ptnr., 1968-85; disting. lectr. and dir. Ctr. for Acctg., Auditing and Tax Studies, Fla. Internat. U., Miami, 1985—; mgr. Marks, Grey & Shron (now Kenneth Leventhal & Co.), CPAs, N.Y.C., 1956-58; asst. chief auditor Am.-Standard, N.Y.C., 1958-62; mgr. systems Westvaco Corp., N.Y.C., 1962-66; founding shareholder Audit Com. Support Network. Co-author: Pensions-An Accounting and Management Guide, 1976; Auditing in the Public Sector: Efficiency, Economy, and Program Results, 1976, Comparative International Auditing Standards, 1985; author: Managing Capital Budget Projects, 1984; contbr. articles to profl. jours. Emeritus trustee Nat. Center for Automated Info. Retrieval. Served to 1st lt. AUS, 1944-46, 51-52. Spear Safer Harmon faculty fellow. Mem. Am. Inst. CPA's, N.Y. State Soc. CPA's, Assn. Systems Mgmt., Acad. Acctg. Historians, Assn. Govt. Accts., N.Y. Acad. Scis., Am. Acctg. Assn. (adv. com. internat. sect.), Inter-Am. Acctg. Assn. (audit commn.), Beta Gamma Sigma, Beta Alpha Psi. Home: 90 Edgewater Dr Coral Gables FL 33133 Office: Sch Acctg Fla Internat U University Park Miami FL 33199

POMEROY, HORACE BURTON, III, accountant, corporate executive; b. Bronxville, N.Y., July 11, 1937; s. Horace Burton Jr. and Juhn (McCalla) P.; m. Margarita Maria Benavidez, July 14, 1973; children: Josephine, Emily. BS in Bus Administrn., U. Ariz., 1964; MBA, Boise State U., 1982. Comml. bank officer Continental Bank, Chgo., 1964-67; cons. Morgan Olmstead Kennedy Gardner, L.A., 1967-74; mgr. cash and banking Morrison Knudsen Corp., Boise, Idaho, 1974—; rep. Idaho State Legistature Dist. 16, 1988—. With U.S. Army, 1959-60. Mem. Nat. Assn. Accts., Nat. Corp. Cash Mgrs. Assn., Nat. Philatelic Assn., Masons, Elks. Republican. Episcopalian. Home: 6822 Kingsdale Dr Boise ID 83704 Office: Morrison Knudsen Corp 1 MK Pla Boise ID 83729

POMEROY, ROBERT LEE, food distribution executive; b. Lakewood, Ohio, Dec. 25, 1938; s. Robert Chester and Helen (Paddock) P.; m. Mary V. Sitera, Mar. 3, 1984; children: Jane, Jim, Robert. BS, U. Okla., 1960, MBA, 1961. Mktg. engr. IBM Corp., Houston, 1962-67; v.p. distbn. Uniroyal Corp., Houston, 1967-72; sr. v.p. store ops W.E. Walker Stores, Jackson, Miss., 1972-77; sr. v.p. distbn. Wetterau Inc., St. Louis, 1977—. Contbr. articles to profl. jours. Home: 14535 Amstel Ct Chesterfield MO 63017 Office: Wetterau Inc 8920 Pershall Rd Hazelwood MO 63042

POMMER, FRANCES MIRIAM, insurance company representative; b. Balt.. BA, Moore Inst., Phila.; BS, MA. CPCU. Mgr. producer relations Zurich & Md. Casualty Co., Phila.; agt. Wohlreich & Anderson, N.Y.C., A.W. Topkis & C., Bala Cynwyd, Pa., E.C.B.M., Bala Cynwyd, Pa.; co. rep. EDS, Phila., 1978—; instr., adj. faculty Rutgers U., Camden, 1968-83; nat. faculty CIC, 1978—. Contbr. to CPCU textbooks. Mem. CPCU Nat. Assn., N.Y. CPCU's, Pa. CPCU's, N.J. CPCU's, Profl. Ins. Agts. Assn., NAFE. Office: EDS 522 DuBois Ave Barrington NJ 08007

POMPAN, JACK MAURICE, management consultant; b. N.Y.C., Jan. 23, 1926; s. Maurice A. and Helen (Schmidt) P.; B.S. in Indsl. Mgmt., Ga. Inst. Tech., 1948; M.B.A. with distinction, N.Y. U., 1973, advanced profl. certificate, 1978; m. Esther Scharaga, July 4, 1958; children—Neil Charles, Lori Beth. Trainee to budget mgr. Redmond Co., Owosso, Mich., 1948-55; mgmt. cons. Coopers and Lybrand, N.Y.C., 1955-60; controller Hazel Bishop Inc., N.Y.C., 1960-61; treas. Floyds Stores Inc., Valley Stream, N.Y., 1961-66; pres. Farmers Pantry Inc., Mamaroneck, N.Y., 1966-68; v.p. pub. div. Intext, Inc., N.Y.C., 1968-74; prin. Baxter, Pompan & Storr, Mgmt. Cons., and predecessors, Greenwich, Conn. and N.Y.C., 1974-83, Jack M. Pompan, Mgmt. Cons., Rockville Centre, N.Y., 1983— ; adj. prof. Hofstra U., 1977, Roth Grad. Sch. Bus. Adminstrn., C. W. Post Center, L.I. U., 1974-79, NYU, 1982—. Trustee, edn. chmn., v.p. Central Synogogue, Rockville Centre, N.Y., 1983-86, pres. 1986-88. Served to lt. USNR, 1943-46, 51-53. Mem. Am. Fin. Assn., NYU Bus. Forum, Nat. Assn. Accts. (cert. of merit 1953), Regional Plan Assn., Am. Prodn. and Inventory Control Soc. Clubs: NYU, Ga. Tech. (N.Y.C.). Bus. and econs. editor Info. Please Almanac, 1978-82. Office: 389 Raymond St Rockville Centre NY 11570

POND, BYRON O., manufacturing company executive; b. 1936. BSBA, Wayne State U. With Fed. Mogul Corp., Detroit, 1958-68; with Maremont Corp., Chgo., 1968—, dir. sales exhaust systems div., 1970-74, corp. v.p., 1974-76, sr. v.p. nat. accounts, 1976-78, exec. v.p., 1978-79, pres., chief exec. officer, from 1979, now pres., chmn. bd. dirs., chief exec. officer. Office: Maremont Corp 250 E Kehoe Blvd Carol Stream IL 60188

POND, DALE CLAUDE, retail executive; b. Spokane, Wash., Apr. 7, 1946; m. Susan Irwig; 1 child, Ashli. BBA, Washburn U., 1969. Account exec. to v.p. mktg. services Bernstein/Rein Advt., Inc., Denver, 1972-81; v.p. mktg. Payless Cashways, Inc., Kansas City, Mo., 1981-86; sr. v.p. mktg. Payless Cashways, Inc., Kansas City, 1986-87, sr. v.p. mktg. and merchandising, 1987—. V.p. bd. dirs. Do-It-Yourself Research Inst.; v.p. State Ballet of Mo.; active Kansas City Tomorrow Leadership Program. Office: Payless Cashways Inc 2 Pershing Sq Box 419466 Kansas City MO 64141-0466

POND, NORMAN H., electronic instrument manufacturing company executive; b. 1938; married. BS, U. Mo., Rolla, 1959; MS, UCLA, 1961. Project mgr. Hughes Aircraft Co., 1959-62; project engr. GT&E Sylvania, 1962-65; engring. mgr., then exec. v.p., then pres. Teledyne MEC, 1965-83; group exec. Teledyne, 1983-84; with Varian Assocs. Inc., Palo Alto, Calif., 1984—, pres. electron device group, 1984-86, exec. v.p., pres. electron device group, 1986-87, pres., chief operating officer, 1987—, also bd. dirs. Office: Varian Assocs 611 Hansen Way Palo Alto CA 94303 *

POND, WILLIAM ADAMS, accountant, controller; b. Orange, N.J., Aug. 14, 1943; s. William Adams and Ruth (Hertzschuch) P.; m. Patricia Reed; children: Brian W., Jeffrey T. BS in Fin., Lehigh U., 1965. CPA, Conn. Auditor corp. audit staff Gen. Electric Co., Schenectady, N.Y., 1970-75, audit adminstr. corp. audit staff, 1975-78; mgr. fin. sect. wiring device bus. dept. Gen. Electric Co., Providence, 1978-81; mgr. distbn. fin. ops. gen. electric supply co. bus. div. Gen. Electric Co., Bridgeport, Conn., 1981-84; v.p., corp. controller Rockefeller Group, Inc., N.Y.C., 1984—. Served to capt. U.S. Army, 1966-68. Mem. Am. Inst. CPA's, N.Y. Soc. CPA's, Fin. Execs. Inst.

PONDER, KENT, financial research company executive; b. San Diego, Feb. 7, 1932; s. Charles Elmer and Zelpha (Gledhill) P.; m. Vasaloloa Taualii, Aug. 29, 1955; children: Lynnae Tasi, Charlene, Susanne Tilo, Michelle Sina, Bruce, Craig, Lisa. BA with honors, Brigham Young U., 1960; MA with honors, Middlebury Grad. Sch., 1962; PhD with honors, Georgetown U., 1973. Chmn. fgn. langs. dept. Keystone Coll., La Plume, Pa., 1963-64; instr. linguistics Iona Coll., New Rochelle, N.Y., 1964; asst. prof. lang. dept. U.S. Naval Acad., Annapolis, Md., 1965-66; chmn. dept. Middle East/African langs. U.S. Def. Lang. Inst./ Crowell Collier, Washington and Arlington, Va., 1968-69; assoc. prof. langs. linguistics SUNY, Oneonta, 1970-76; pres., founder Achievement Research & Verification Systems, Inc., Albuquerque, 1976—; pres., owner Hawaii Diet Plan Inc., Honolulu, 1983-86; lectr. mktg. communications, Upjohn Pharm. Sales, Marina del Rey, Calif., 1988; mktg. cons., Supernutrition Inc., San Francisco, 1987-88. Author: (books) Fire Your Boss, 1982, Quick Start, 1982, Ultimate Insider Manual, 1983; editor, pub. (newsletter) Netword Hotline, 1987—. Served with USAF, 1951-55. Republican. Mormon. Office: AR&VS Inc 1650 Univ NE Ste 200 Albuquerque NM 87102

PONKA, LAWRENCE JOHN, automotive executive; b. Detroit, Sept. 1, 1949; s. Maximillian John and Leona May (Knobloch) P.; m. Nancy Kathleen McNamara, Feb. 20, 1988. AA, Macomb County Community Coll., 1974; BS in Indsl. Mgmt., Lawrence Inst. Tech., 1978; MA in Indsl. Mgmt., Cen. Mich. U., 1983. Engr.'s asst. Army Tank Automotive Command, 1967-68; with Sperry & Hutchinson Co., Southfield, Mich., 1973, Chrysler Corp., Detroit, 1973; with Gen. Motors Corp., Warren, Mich., 1973-82, engring. systems coordinator engring. staff, 1976-82, current product engring. until 1982; mfg. engr. Buick-Oldsmobile-Cadillac Group, Gen. Motors Assembly Div.-Orion Pontiac, Mich., 1982-84, sr. analyst advanced vehicle engring. Chevrolet-Pontiac-Can. group Engring. Ctr., Warren, 1985-86; mfg. planning adminstr. Detroit-Hamtramck Assembly Ctr., Cadillac Motor Car Co., Allanté, 1986—. cons. internal; mfg. planning administr./human resource advisor. Served with USAF, 1968-72, Vietnam. Decorated Air Force Commendation medal. Mem. Soc. Automotive Engrs., Am. Legion, Vietnam, Japan, Okinawa DAV, NRA. Roman Catholic. Home: PO Box 732 Plymouth MI 48170-0732 Office: GM 2500 E General Motors Blvd Detroit MI 48211-2002

PONNÉ, NANCI TERESA, publisher; b. Chgo., May 10, 1958; d. Joseph Anthony and Irene Theresa (Nasadowski) P. BA, DePaul U., 1980. Actress, model Chgo., 1978—; pub. Chgo. Talent Directory, 1985—; speaker in field. Vol. Dems. to Re-elect Mayor Washington, 1987. Named Miss Chgo., recipient Spl. Judges award Miss America Scholarship Pageant, 1981-82. Mem. Women in Film, Women's Advt. Club of Chgo., Chgo. Advt. Club, New Chgo. Coalition, Theatre Chgo. Affiliates, Entrepreneurs Assn., Nat. Assn. Female Execs. Roman Catholic. Home: 2215 E 83d St Chicago IL 60617 Office: Chgo Talent Directory 230 N Michigan Ave Chicago IL 60601

PONS, JOHN M., oil company executive; b. N.Y.C., June 20, 1948; William F. and Martha (Schott) P.; m. Marsh B. Baggott, Aug. 15, 1981. BS in Acctg., St. John's U., 1969. CPA, N.Y., Tex. Auditor Arthur Young and Co., N.Y.C., 1969-72; asst. controller Arlen Realty and Devel., N.Y.C., 1972-75; various acctg. positions with Aminoil Inc., Houston, 1975-85; acctg. mgr. Phillips Petroleum, Denver, 1985-88; controller Columbus Energy Co., Denver, 1988—; bd. dirs. Phillips 66 Credit Union. Served as SP5 U.S. Army, 1967-72. Mem. Am. Inst. CPAs, Tex. Soc. CPAs, Colo. Soc. CPAs, Petroleum Accts. Soc. (chmn. Computer User com. 1987—). Republican. Home: 7554 S Cook Way Littleton CO 80122 Office: Columbus Energy Corp 1860 Lincoln St Denver CO 80295

PONTIKES, KENNETH NICHOLAS, computer leasing company executive; b. Chgo., Mar. 15, 1940; m. Lynne M. Weston, June 21, 1980. BS, So. Ill. U., 1962. With Internat. Bus. Machines, 1961-67; sales dept. OEI Sales Corp., 1967; sales rep. Officer Eletrs Inc., Chgo., 1967-68; mgr. brokerage ops. Data Power Inc., Chgo., 1968-69; pres. Comdisco, Inc., Des Plaines, Ill., 1969-76; chmn. bd., pres., chief exec. officer Comdisco, Inc., 1976—. With USAR, 1963-69. Office: Comdisco Inc 6111 N River Rd Rosemont IL 60018

PONTIOUS, JAMES CARL, marketing professional; b. Toledo, Sept. 4, 1938; s. Richard C. and Evelyn (Hughes) P.; married Jan. 20, 1966; children: Deborah, Karen, James Jr. BBA, U. Minn., 1961; postgrad., NYU, 1965-66; cert. in mgmt., Northwestern U., 1973. Service engr. Pullman Standard Co., Birmingham, Ala., 1961-64; sales rep. Pullman Standard Co., N.Y.C., 1964-66; mktg. mgr. Pullman Standard Co., Chgo., 1966-71; asst. to pres. Pullman Standard Co., Washington, 1971-74; asst. gen. mgr. passenger unit Pullman Standard Co., Chgo., 1974-75; program mgr. Amtrak superliners Pullman Standard Co., Hammond, Ind., 1975-76; v.p. mktg. N.Y. Air Brake Co., Watertown, N.Y., 1977—; trustee Watertown Savs. Bank, 1979—. Chmn. bd. trustees Watertown YMCA, 1980—. Served with USMCR, 1956-64. Mem. Nat. Defense Transp. Assn. (life, v.p. 1969-70), R.R. Progress Inst. (chmn. passenger transp. com. 1969-75), Am. R.R. Found., Kappa Sigma. Republican. Presbyterian. Club: Black River Valley (Watertown). Home: 1444 Holcomb St Watertown NY 13601 Office: New York Air Brake Co Starbuck Ave Watertown NY 13601

PONZER, JOHN LEWIS, engineering executive; b. Brinkley, Ark., Feb. 20, 1913; s. Karl Lewis and Grace (Short) P.; m. Willetta Woody, Nov. 26, 1945; children: Grace Stratton, Janet Lee. BSEE, N.C. State U., 1935. Supt. REA, Wilson, N.C., 1935-37; jr. indsl. engr. Carolina Power & Light Co., Asheville, N.C., 1937-41; sr. indsl. engr. Carolina Power & Light Co., Southern Pines, N.C., 1946-66; lighting specialist Carolina Power & Light Co., Raleigh, N.C., 1966-78; pres., chief exec. Energy Assocs., Southern Pines, 1978—; tech. cons. N.C. Dept. Labor, Raleigh, 1963-70; lighting chmn. N.Y.C. Edison Electric Inst. Electrification Council, 1968-70; keynote speaker All-Industry Conv., Myrtle Beach, S.C., 1968; conceived, co-developed Research Triangle Park, Durham, N.C., 1953; created Total Environ. Program Nat. Elec. Contractors Assn., 1967; lectr., speaker numerous colls., assns. Contbr. numerous articles to profl. jours. Chmn. Southern Pines Indsl. Com., 1958; exec. bd. N.C. Cong. PTA's, 1964-65; dir. engring. sect. Civil Def.; chmn. fund drive ARC, 1960; lay reader Emmanuel Episc. Ch., Southern Pines, 1959-66. Served to col. U.S. Army, 1941-46, ETO, grad. Command and Gen. Staff Sch. Decorated four battle stars; recipient Outstanding Scouter award Boy Scouts Am., Southern Pines, 1954, Elec. Man of Yr. award Nat. Elec. Contractors Assn., 1970; named Eagle Scout, Boy Scouts Am. Mem. IEEE (chmn. nat. textile com., 1957, chmn. indsl. com. 1962, Outstanding Service award 1961), Illuminating Engring. Soc. (dir. 1958-60, section pres. 1968-69, Disting. Service award 1969), N.C. Engring. Soc., Nat. Assn. Lighting Maintenance, N.C. State U. Alumni Assn. (pres. 1953), Phi Eta Sigma, Sigma Phi Epsilon. Clubs: Mens' Garden (Southern Pines) (pres.); Cotillion (Asheville); City (Raleigh); Southern Pines Country; North Ridge Country; Biltmore Forest Country. Lodges: Royal Brigade Guards, Kiwanis (pres. Southern Pines club 1955-56, Lt. gov. Carolinas dist. 1957, Disting. Service award 1962), Elks, Masons, Brotherhood St. Andrews (pres. 1958). Home: 295 Hillside Rd Southern Pines NC 28387 Office: Energy Assocs PO Box 345 Southern Pines NC 28387

POOLE, EARLE GOWER, clothing manufacturing company executive; b. Dundalk, Ont., Can., Dec. 1, 1929; s. Lawrence Gower and Ethel Virginia (LeGarrie) P.; m. Fern McFarlane, Mar. 21, 1951; children: Leslie, Lorraine. Supr. Gulf Oil, Toronto, 1950-62; mgr. systems and EDP Work Wear Corp. Can., Toronto, 1962-67, controller, 1967-70, gen. mgr. adminstrv. services, 1970-74, group gen. mgr., 1974-81, exec. v.p., chief operating officer Rental div., 1981-84, pres., chief exec. officer, 1984—, chmn. bd., 1986—; pres., chief exec. officer Work Wear Corp. Inc., Cleve., 1986—; lectr. Ryerson Poly. Inst., Toronto, York U., Humber Coll. Active mem. Variety Village Tent 28, Toronto. Mem. Toronto Bd. Trade. Office: Work Wear Corp Inc 1768 E 25th St Cleveland OH 44114

POOLE, JILLIAN HANBURY, cultural center administrator, educator; b. London, Aug. 11, 1930; came to U.S., 1943; d. Anthony Henry Robert Culling and Una (Rawnsley) Hanbury; m. Richard Armstrong Poole, Nov. 2, 1957; children: Anthony Hanbury, Colin Rawnsley. AB, George Washington U., 1952; MA, George Mason U., 1984. Research asst. to bur. chief Ridder Newspapers, 1958-60; adminstr. Nat. Planning Assn., 1953-57; exec. sec. Nat. Cathedral Assn., Washington, 1960-64; dir. Nat. Cathedral Fund, Washington, 1966-69; mgr. devel. Corcoran Gallery Art, Washington, 1969-71; dir. devel. John F. Kennedy Ctr. Performing Arts, Washington, 1972—, asst to chmn., 1987—. Trustee N.C. Sch. Arts Found., 1980-84, The Acting Co., N.Y.C., 1981—, Nat. Bldg. Mus., Washington, 1985—, George Mason U. Found., 1984—. Office: John F Kennedy Ctr Performing Arts Washington DC 20566

POOLE, PEGGY ELAINE, savings and loan executive; b. Wilmington, Ohio, Oct. 19, 1953; d. Andrew Arthur Stanforth and Mildred May (Berkley) Crone; m. Carl Samuel Poole III, Mar. 10, 1974; 1 child, Lori Ann. Grad. high sch., Ft. Myers, Fla. V.p. First Fed. Savs. and Loan Assn. Ft. Myers, 1971—. Mem. exec. bd. S.W. Fla. Postal Customer Coun. Mem. Profl. Secs. Assn. (past pres.). Democrat. Home: 8601 Henderson Grade North Fort Myers FL 33917 Office: First Fed Savs & Loan PO Box 940 2201 Second St Fort Myers FL 33902

POOLE, RICHARD WARREN, data processing consultant; b. N.Y.C., Oct. 8, 1948; s. Joseph Russell and Rose (Montenegro) P.; m. Caroline Brock, Sept. 2, 1972 (div. Oct. 1974); m. Marti Fernald Allen, Dec. 31, 1977; children: Christopher Warren, Rosanna Kimberly. BS, Bates Coll., 1969; postgrad., Fairleigh Dickinson Coll., 1970-74. Systems programmer Chubb & Sons, Short Hills, N.J., 1969-73; sr. systems programmer Beneficial Fin., Morristown, N.J., 1973-74; mgr. Blue Cross N.Y., N.Y.C., 1974-77; v.p. Citicorp, N.Y.C., 1977-81; sr. v.p. Baker and Taylor, Bridgewater, N.J., 1981-87; pres. Poole Cons., Summit, N.J., 1987—; sr. assoc. Booz-Allen & Hamilton, N.Y.C., 1988—. Chmn. Substandard Housing Bd., Summit, 1976-81; active on Summit Rent Commn., 1974-76, Summit Zoning Bd., 1981-86; chmn. local Reps., 1973-80. Mem. Mayflower Soc., Sons Am. Revolution. Presbyterian. Lodge: Optomist (pres. 1984-85). Home: 84 Mountain Ave Summit NJ 07901 Office: Booz Allen & Hamilton 101 Park Ave New York NY 10178

POP, EMIL, research chemist; b. Tirgu Mures, Romania, Aug. 12, 1939; came to U.S., 1983; s. Victor and Rosalia (Graf) P.; m. Elena Petrina Petri, Apr. 28, 1964; 1 child, Andreea Christina. BS, Babes-Bolyai U., Cluj., Romania, 1961; PhD, Inst. Chemistry, Cluj. and Supreme Council of Romanian Acad. Sci., 1973. Chemist Chem. Pharm. Research Inst., Cluj-Napoca, Romania, 1962-65, researcher, 1965-78, sr. researcher, group leader, compartment leader, 1978-83; researcher Rugjer Boskovic Inst., Zagreb, Yugoslavia, 1971-72; postdoctoral research assoc. U. Fla., Gainesville, 1983-86; sr. research scientist Pharmatec, Inc., Alachua, Fla., 1986-87, group leader, 1987-88; assoc. dir. chem. devel., 1988—. Contbr. articles to profl. jours.; inventor in field. Recipient Romanian Acad. award for chemistry. Fellow Am. Inst. Chemists; mem. Am. Chem. Soc., AAAS, Am. Assn. Pharm. Scientists, Internat. Union Pure and Applied Chemistry, N.Y. Acad. Scis. Greek Catholic. Current work: Design and synthesis of pharmaceutical compounds in particular brain chemical drug delivery systems; M.O. calculations. Home: 810 SW 51st Way Gainesville FL 32607

POPE, BARBARA M. HARRAL, editor; b. Lubbock, Tex., Jan. 26, 1937; d. Leonard Paul and Olivette (Stuart) Harral; m. John Rowell Toman (div. 1963); 1 child, Stuart Rowell. BE, Tex. Christian U., 1959; MLS, U. Hawaii, 1968; postgrad., Golden Gate U., 1980-82. Tchr. pub. elem. schs., various cities, Tex. and Hawaii, 1959-66; contracts abstractor, indexer Champlin Oil Co., Ft. Worth, 1963-64; adminstrv. asst. engring. Litton Industries, Lubbock, Tex., 1964-65; mgr. rsch. library Hawaii Employers' Coun., Honolulu, 1968-72; dir. med. library U. S.D.-Sacred Heart Hosp., Yankton, 1977-79; editor, adminstrv. coord. book div. ABC-Clio, Inc., Santa Barbara, Calif., 1981-88; free-lance rsch./editorial cons. Albuquerque, 1988—; rsch. cons. Thailand Hotel, Touche-Ross Assocs., Honolulu, 1974—;

instr. Santa Fe Community Coll., 1989—. Vol., contbr. Boy's Ranch, Amarillo, Tex., 1987—; mem. Lobero Theater Group, Santa Barbara, 1975-76; mem., treas. Yankton Med. Aux., 1977-79. Mem. Spl. Libraries Assn., Med. Libraries Assn., ALA, Am. Soc. Info., Sci., Tex. Christian U. Alumni Assn., Delta Delta Delta. Republican. Episcopalian. Home: 9300 Seabrook NE Albuquerque NM 87111 Office: PO Box 26356 Albuquerque NM 87125

POPE, JOHN CHARLES, airline company executive; b. Newark, Mar. 30, 1949; s. John Aris Coutant and Eleanor Laura (Hillman) P. BA, Yale U., 1971; MBA, Harvard U., 1973. Dir. profit analysis and capital analysis GM, N.Y.C., 1973-77; sr. v.p. fin., treas., chief fin. officer Am. Airlines, Inc., AMR Corp., Dallas-Fort Worth, 1977-88; exec. v.p., chief fin. officer UAL Corp., United Airlines (subs.), Chgo., 1988—; bd. dirs. Fed. Mogul Corp., Detroit; trustee Sta. WTTW, Chgo. Mem. Air Transport Assn. (chmn. fin. com.). Home: 882 S Country Pl Lake Forest IL 60045 Office: United Airlines Inc PO Box 66100 Chicago IL 60666

POPE, KATHY POSTELL, marketing professional; b. Gastonia, N.C., Mar. 7, 1961; d. Donald Anders and Patsy (Wall) Postell; m. George Kenneth Pope Jr., Sept. 22, 1984. Student, Appalachian State U., 1979-83, N.C. Sch. Broadcasting, Charlotte, 1984. Mgr. western regional sales Credit Mgmt., Inc., Capitola, CAlif., 1989—. Mem. NAFE (bd. dirs. 1986—), Women in Cable (publicity com. 1986—), So. Calif. Cable TV Assn., CCTA, NCTA, CTAM. Republican. Baptist. Office: Credit Mgmt Inc 1840 41st Ave Ste 102-277 Capitola CA 95010

POPE, PETER T., forest products company executive; b. 1934; married. B.A., Stanford U., 1957, M.B.A., 1959. With Pope & Talbot Inc., Portland, Oreg., 1960—, asst. sec., 1964-68, v.p., 1968-69, v.p., gen. mgr., 1969-71, chmn. bd., chief exec. officer, 1971—, also dir. Served with USAR, 1957-58. Office: Pope & Talbot Inc 1500 SW 1st Ave Portland OR 97201

POPE, ROBERT GLYNN, telecommunications executive; b. Greenville, Tex., Dec. 5, 1935; s. Edwin R. P.; m. Shirley Hall, Dec. 30, 1958; children: Kenneth, Richard, David. BSME, So. Meth. U., 1958. Registered profl. engr. Chief engr. Southwestern Bell Telephone Co., Houston, 1973-77; v.p. staff Tex. Southwestern Bell Telephone Co., Dallas, 1977-78, v.p. centralized services, 1978-80; v.p. residence and pub. services Southwestern Bell Telephone Co., St. Louis, 1980-81, v.p. transition, 1981-83, v.p. strategic planning, 1983; v.p. corp. devel. Southwestern Bell Corp., St. Louis, 1984-86, vice-chmn. corp. devel., 1986-88, vice chmn. corp. devel., chief fin. officer, 1988—; mem. Adv. Bd. Battery Ventures; bd. dirs. Southwestern Bell Corp., CompuServe. With U.S. Army, 1959. Mem. NSPE, Mo. Soc. Profl. Engrs., Media Club, Arch Soc. St. Louis, Mo. Athletic Club, Univ. Club, Golf Club Okla., Old Warson Country Club, St. Louis Club. Office: Southwestern Bell Corp 1 Bell Ctr Ste 4214 Saint Louis MO 63101

POPEJOY, WILLIAM J., savings and loan association executive; b. 1938; married. B.A., Calif. State U., 1961, M.A., 1962. Pres. Fed. Home Loan Mortgage Corp., 1971-74; pres. Am. Savs. & Loan Assn. subs. Fin. Corp. Am., Los Angeles, 1974-80; chmn., pres., chief exec. officer Am. Savs. & Loan Assn. subs. Fin. Corp. Am., Irving, Calif., 1984-89, also bd. dirs.; pres. Far West Savs. & Loan Assn., 1980-81; pres., chief fin. officer Fin. Fedn. Inc., Culver City, Calif., from 1981; chmn., pres., chief exec. officer Fin. Corp. Am., Irvine, 1984-89, also bd. dirs. Office: Fin Corp Am 18401 Von Karman Ave Irvine CA 92715 *

POPHAM, WM. LEE, investment company executive; b. Washington, July 17, 1950; s. James Edward Popham and Jeanne (Minear) Popham Baker; m. Peggy Crook, Oct. 11, 1968 (div. Apr. 1987); children: William Lee, Erik, Laura. AB, Duke U., 1971; JD, U. Miami, Fla., 1976. Bar: Fla. 1980; CPA, Fla., 1980. Ptnr. Peat Marwick Main & Co., Miami, 1971-83; pres. First Atlantic Capital Corp., Miami, 1983-85; chmn., pres. Caesar Creek Holdings Inc., Miami, 1985—, Adm. Fin. Corp., Miami, 1987—; bd. dirs. Cruise Am. Inc. formerly known as Am. Land Cruisers Inc., Miami, Jeanne Baker Realty Inc., Miami, Haven Fed. Savs. and Loan Assn., Winter Haven, Fla. Editor: Tax Research, 1976. Mem. exec. bd., v.p. S. Fla. Council Boy Scouts Am., 1977—; active U. Miami Citizens Bd., 1985—; bd. dirs. Goodwill Industries of S. Fla. Inc., Miami, 1982—, Vizcayan Found. Bd. Inc., 1985-88. Recipient Silver Beaver award Boy Scouts Am., 1983; named an Outstanding Young Man of Am., U.S. Jaycees, 1983. Mem. ABA, Fla. Bar Assn., Am. Inst. CPA's, Fla. Inst. CPA's, Exec. Assn. Greater Miami, Duke U. Alumni Assn. (nat. bd. dirs. 1981-85), Miami Duke Alumni (pres. 1977-84), Vizcayans. Republican. Presbyterian. Clubs: University (Miami) (social chmn. 1980-83), Coral Reef Yacht (Miami) (fin. com. chmn. 1986-88). Home: 1000 Venetian Way #1204 Miami FL 33139 Office: Caesar Creek Holdings Inc 600 Brickell Ave #600 Miami FL 33131

POPOFF, FRANK PETER, chemical company executive; b. Sofia, Bulgaria, Oct. 27, 1935; came to U.S., 1940; s. Eftim and Stoyanka (Kossoroff) P.; m. Jean Urse; children: John V., Thomas F., Steven M. B.S. in Chemistry, Ind. U., 1957, M.B.A., 1959. With Dow Chem. Co., Midland, Mich., 1959—, exec. v.p., 1985-87, dir., pres., chief executive officer, 1987—, also bd. dirs.; exec. v.p., then pres. Dow Chem. Europe subs., Horgen, Switzerland, 1976-85; bd. dirs. Dow Corning Corp., Chem. Bank & Trust Co., Chem. Fin. Corp., Midland, The Salk Inst. Internat. Com. Dir. Am. Inst. for Contemporary German Studies; bd. dirs. Ind. U. Found.; mem. Dean's Adv. Council, Ind. U.; mem. vis. com. U. Mich. Sch. Bus. Mem. Chem. Mfrs. Assn. (bd. dirs.), U.S. Coun. for Internat. Bus. (sr. vice-chmn.), Bus. Roundtable, Conf. Bd., Am. Chem. Soc. Office: Dow Chem Co 2030 Willard H Dow Ctr Midland MI 48674

POPP, VIRGINIA GAIL, real estate developer; b. Balt., Sept. 10, 1944; d. LaMar John and Virginia Margaret (McComas) Campbell; m. Richard Lyell Guy, 1962 (div. 1964); children: Richard Jr., James (dec.); m. Lawrence Joseph Popp Jr., Feb. 10, 1973 (div. 1988); 1 child, JoElla; 1 stepchild, John. Grad. high sch., Towson, Md. Credit corr. Humble Oil Co., Balt., 1963-68; typist Charles J. Cirelli and Son, Inc., Severna Park, Md., 1969-70, from bookkeeper to adminstrv. asst., 1970-80, v.p., 1980-88; v.p. Tristate Devel. Corp., Severna Park, Md., 1988—, also bd. dirs.; v.p., bd. dirs. Cirelli Co., Severna Park, CJC Devel. Corp. Mem. Chpt. 81 Parents Without Ptnrs., Inc. Mem. Ch. of the Brethren Lodge: Ladies Aux. of the Moose. Avocations: reading, counted cross stitch, needlework, yardwork.

POPPA, RYAL ROBERT, manufacturing company executive; b. Wahpeton, N.D., Nov. 7, 1933; s. Ray Edward and Annabelle (Phillips) P.; m. Ruth Ann Curry, June 21, 1952; children: Sheryl Lynn, Kimberly Marie. BBA, Claremont Men's Coll., 1957. Sales trainee IBM, L.A., 1957-59, sales rep., 1959-62, product mktg. rep., 1963, sales mgr., 1964-66; v.p., gen. mgr. Comml. Computers Inc., L.A., 1966-67; v.p. Greyhound Computer Corp., Chgo., 1967-68, pres., chief exec. officer, bd. dirs., 1969-70; pres., chief exec. officer, bd. dirs., mem. exec. com. Data Processing Fin. & Gen., Hartsdale, N.Y., 1970-72; exec. v.p., chief fin. officer, bd. dirs., mem. exec. com. Mohawk Data Sci. Corp., Utica, N.Y., 1972-73; chmn., pres., chief exec. officer Pertec Computer Corp., L.A., 1973-81, BMC Industries, Inc., St. Paul, 1982-85; pres., chmn., chief exec. officer Storage Tech. Corp., Louisville, Colo., 1985—; bd. dir. Western Digital Corp., Irvine, Calif.; founder Charles Babbage Inst.; past dir. Spacelabs, Inc. Trustee Claremont Men's Coll., Colo. Music Festival; mem. Chmn.'s Circle Colo. Reps.; past mem. Pres. Com. Nat. Medal of Sci. Recipient Exec. of Yr. award U. Colo. MBA Alum Assn., 1986, Community Svc. award Inst. Human Rels. Am. Jewish Com., 1980. Mem. World Bus. Coun., Chief Exec. Orgn., World Bus. Coun., Computer and Communications Industry Assn. (past bd. dirs., chmn., mem. exec. com.), Am. Electronics Assn. (past bd. dirs., mem. exec. com. Colo. chpt.), Electronic Mfrs. Club, Boulder Country Club, The Denver Club. Office: Storage Tech Corp 2270 S 88th St Louisville CO 80028-4315

POPPE, FRANCES WINNIE PEREZ, broadcast executive; b. Agana, Guam, June 3, 1942; d. James Edgar Landis and Remedios (Perez) Roberto; m. Edward H. Poppe Jr., May 15, 1965; children: Edward III, Michelle, Matthew, Cheryl. AA in Bus. Adminstrn., Coll. Guam, Agana, 1963. Sec. Fuchu Air Base, Japan, 1965-66; office mgr. Sta. KSTO-FM, Agana, 1978—; fin. officer Stas. KCNM-AM and KZMI-FM, Saipan, N. Marianas Islands, 1985—, Sta. KSTO-FM, Agana, 1985—; sec., bd. dirs. Inter Island Communications, Inc., Agana, 1978—, Saipan, 1984—. Mem. Territorial Bd. Edn., Agana, 1983-85; pres. St. Francis Sch. PTA, Yona, Guam, 1982-84. Mem. Guam C. of C. (chmn. Christmas parade 1984—, Leadership award 1986). Baptist. Club: Guam Women's (chmn. scholarship fund 1984-85). Home: 25 Kristin Ln Baza Gardens Agana GU 96914 Office: Intern Island Commnunications Inc PO Box 20249 Main Facility Agana GU 96921

PORAT, AVNER MEIR, retail executive; b. Tel Aviv, June 20, 1939; s. Eldad and Meriam (Haiman) P.; m. Joan Gelfond, Aug. 29, 1965; children: Ilana, Gil. BA, Hebrew U., Jerusalem, 1961; MBA, U. Pitts., 1965, PhD, 1967. Textile exec. Israel, 1962-64; cons. Israeli Ministry Fin., 1962-64; asst. prof. U. Rochester, N.Y., 1968-69; cons. D.D. Howard & Assoc., Chgo., 1969-70; cons. Hay Assoc., Chgo., 1970-73, ptnr., 1973-76, gen. and internat. ptnr., 1976-85; sr. v.p. Federated Dept. Stores Inc., Cin., 1985—; bd. dirs. H.G. Pollak Ltd., Tel Aviv. Author: (with J. Vaughan) Banking Computer Style, 1968; contbr. articles to profl. jours. Trustee Sta. WCET-TV, Cin., Kidney Found., Cin. Served with Israeli Army, 1956-58. Fulbright scholar, 1964-67, Ford Found. grantee, 1966-67. Mem. Am. Psychol. Assn. Jewish. Clubs: Losantiville (Cin.); East Bank (Chgo.). Office: Federated Dept Stores Inc 7 W Seventh St Cincinnati OH 45202

PORCELLA, JOHN EDWIN, respiratory therapy equipment executive; b. N.Y.C., July 3, 1950; s. Thomas W. and Mary (Johnson) P.; m. Barbara J. Anderson, Aug. 21, 1971; 1 child, Allison Jeanne. BA, SUNY, New Platz, 1972; MA, St. John's U., 1976, PhD, 1979. Lic. Psychologist, N.Y.; cert. sch. psychologist, N.Y. Staff psychologist II Sagamore Children's Psychiat. Ctr., Melville, N.Y., 1977-78, dir. edn., 1978-79; dir. clin. services Rhinebeck (N.Y.) Country Sch., 1979-85; pres. Transpirator Technologies, Somerset, N.J., 1985—; mem. adj. faculty Marist Coll., Poughkeepsie, N.Y., 1982-86. Mem. Am. Psychol. Assn., Dutchess County Mental Health Assn. (bd. dirs. 1985). Roman Catholic. Home: 8 N Hinterlands Rhinebeck NY 12572 Office: Transpirator Technologies 265 Davidson Ave Somerset NJ 08873

PORGES, WALTER RUDOLF, television news executive; b. Vienna, Nov. 26, 1931; s. Paul and Charlotte (Posamentier) P.; m. Jean Belle Mlotok, Dec. 22, 1953; children: Donald F., Marian E., Lawrence M. B.A., CCNY, 1953. News writer radio sta. WOR, N.Y.C., 1955-56, WCBS Radio and TV, N.Y.C., 1956-57; news writer ABC Radio Network, N.Y.C., 1958-60; news editor ABC Radio Network, 1960-63, asst. dir. radio news, 1963-65; asst. assignment mgr. ABC-TV, 1965-68; asso. producer ABC-TV Evening News, 1968-70, sr. producer, 1973-75; European producer ABC News, London, 1970-73; producer ABC-TV spl. events, N.Y.C., 1975-76; coordinating producer ABC News (Republican Nat. Conv.), 1976; editorial producer, chief writer ABC Evening News, 1976-77, sr. producer, 1977-80; sr. producer ABC World News Tonight, 1978-83; fgn. news dir. ABC News, N.Y.C., 1983—. Served with U.S. Army, 1953-55. Office: ABC News 47 W 66th St New York NY 10023

PORTAL, GILBERT MARCEL ADRIEN, oil company executive; b. Paris, Aug. 2, 1930; came to U.S., 1982; s. Emmanuel Jules and Henriette Josephine (Bonnard) P.; m. Monique Janine Adam, July 12, 1951; children: Dominique, Veronique, Marc-Emmanuel. Baccalaureate, Lycee Charlemagne U., Paris, 1949; Ingenieur Civil des Mines, Sch. of Mines, St. Etienne, 1955; diplome du C.P.A., Ctr. Advanced Bus., Paris, 1969; auditeur 30 eme session IHEDN, Higher Studies Nat. Defense, Paris, 1978. Geophysicist Societe Nationale Elf Aquitaine, Sahara, Algeria, 1957-63; exploration mgr. north sea Societe Nationale Elf Aquitaine, 1963-65, dep. exec. v.p. Europe, 1965-68, dep. exec. v.p. North and South Am., 1968-70; chief exec. officer Societe Nationale Elf Aquitaine, Iraq, 1970-72; dir., chief exec. officer Societe Nationale Elf Aquitaine, Gabon, Africa, 1972-76; dep. exec. v.p. hydrocarbons Societe Nationale Elf Aquitaine, 1976-78, exec. v.p. North Africa, Mid. East, Far East, 1978-82; pres. Elf Aquitaine Petroleum, Houston, 1982—; Bd. dirs. French Am. C. of C., Houston, 1984—; bd. dirs. L'Alliance Francaise, Houston, 1987—; bd. dirs. The Sterling Group, Inc., Houston, 1986—. Trustee The Awty Internat. Sch., Houston, 1983. Served to lt. French Army, 1955-57. Decorated Legion of Honor (France), Nat. Merit Order (France); Equatorial Star (Gabon). Roman Catholic. Clubs: Century, The Petroleum (Houston); Lakeside Country. Office: Elf Aquitaine Petroleum 1000 Louisiana Ste 3800 Houston TX 77002

PORTALE, JOSEPH JOHN, dentist, dental corporation executive; b. N.Y.C., Oct. 20, 1946; s. Joseph Sebastian and Vassie Josephine (Mc Guire) P.; m. Karen Mary Krygowski July 26, 1976 (div. Jan. 1984); children: Michelle, Joseph, Kathryn. BS in Biology, Villanova U., 1968; DMD, UNJ, 1972. Gen. practice dentistry North Bergen, N.J., 1972—; program dir. Gen. Dentistry Residency Program Bergen Pines County Hosp., Paramus, N.J., 1981-82; gen. ptnr. Fine-Dent Data Systems Inc., Phoenix, 1984-85, chmn., 1985-87, ptnr., 1984—, pres., chief exec. officer, 1988—; lectr. Competitive Edge Seminars, North Bergen, 1979-80; cons. Fine-Dent Data Systems Inc., Pvt. Care Inst., Paramus, 1987—, author newsletter, 1988. Author: (newsletter) Competitive Edge, 1982, Napili Internat., 1986-87. Fellow Acad. Gen. Dentistry, Acad. Dentistry Internat. Republican. Roman Catholic. Home: 265 Crescent Ave Wyckoff NJ 07481 Office: Fine Dent Data Systems 8321 Kennedy Blvd North Bergen NJ 07047 also: Bergen Med Ctr 1 W Ridgewood Ave Paramus NJ 07652

PORTER, CARSON PAGE, healthcare company executive, lawyer; b. Bowling Green, Ky., Sept. 22, 1945; s. Carson Omen and Alice Odell (Page) P.; m. Mary Ann Sackfield, Aug. 12, 1967; children: Carson Page Jr., Catherine Clay. BA, U. Ky., 1967, JD, 1970. Bar: Ky. 1971. Assoc. Stites & McElwain, Louisville, 1971-75; ptnr. Reisz, Brown, Rice & Porter, Louisville, 1975-82, Rice, Porter & Seiller, Louisville, 1982-86; pres. Res-Care Devel. Co., Louisville, 1986-88, Pafco Enterpises Inc, Louisville, 1989—; bd. dirs. Dream Factory, Inc., 1985—. Bd. dirs. Preservation Alliance, Louisville, 1976-79, Urban Renewal Commn., Louisville, 1975. Fellow Am. Soc. Healthcare Attys.; mem. ABA, Nat. Health Lawyers Assn., Ky. Bar Assn. Office: Pafco Enterprises Inc 9300 Shelbyville Rd Ste 202 Louisville KY 40222

PORTER, DIXIE LEE, insurance executive, consultant; b. Bountiful, Utah, June 7, 1931; d. John Lloyd and Ida May (Robinson) Mathis. B.S., U. Calif. at Berkeley, 1956, M.B.A., 1957. Personnel aide City of Berkeley (Calif.), 1957-59; employment supr. Kaiser Health Found., Los Angeles, 1959-60; personnel analyst U. Calif. at Los Angeles, 1961-63; personnel mgr. Reuben H. Donnelley, Santa Monica, Calif., 1963-64; personnel officer Good Samaritan Hosp., San Jose, Calif., 1965-67; fgn. service officer AID, Saigon, Vietnam, 1967-71; gen. agt. Charter Life Ins. Co., Los Angeles, 1972-77, Kennesaw Life Ins. Co., Atlanta, from 1978, Phila. Life Ins. Co., San Francisco, from 1978; now pres. Women's Ins. Enterprises, Ltd.; cons. in field. Co-chairperson Comprehensive Health Planning Commn. Santa Clara County, Calif., 1973-76; bd. dirs. Family Care, 1978-80, Aegis Health Corp., 1977—, U. Calif. Sch. Bus. Adminstrn., Berkeley, 1974-76; mem. task force on equal access to econ. power U.S. Nat. Women's Agenda, 1977—. Served with USMC, 1950-52. C.L.U. Mem. C.L.U. Soc., U. Calif. Alumni Assn., U. Calif. Sch. Bus. Adminstrn. Alumni Assn., AAUW, Bus. and Profl. Women, Prytanean Alumni, The Animal Soc. Los Gatos/Saratoga (pres. 1987—), Beta Gamma Sigma, Phi Chi Theta. Republican. Episcopalian. Home and Office: PO Box 64 Los Gatos CA 95031

PORTER, ELSA ALLGOOD, writer, lecturer; b. Amoy, China, Dec. 19, 1928; d. Roy and Petra (Johnsen) Allgood; m. Raeford B. Liles, Mar. 19, 1949 (div. 1959); children: Barbara, Janet; m. G. Hinckley Porter, Nov. 22, 1962; children: David, Brian, Wendy. BA, Birmingham-So. Coll., 1949; MA, U. Ala., 1959; M in Pub. Adminstrn., Harvard U., 1971; LHD (hon.), U. Ala., 1986. With HEW, Washington, 1960-73; dir. clearinghouse on productivity and organizational effectiveness U.S. CSC, Washington, 1973-77; asst. sec. Dept. Commerce, Washington, 1977-81; disting. practitioner in residence Washington Pub. Affairs Ctr., U. So. Calif., Washington, 1982-84; sr. mgmt. assoc. The Prodn. Group, Alexandria, Va., 1985-87; project dir. Cathedral Coll. of the Laity, Washington, 1987—. Author tng. program. Mem. Nat. Acad. Pub. Adminstrs. (trustee 1982-86, treas. 1986-88), Am. Soc. Pub. Adminstrn., Women's Nat. Democratic Club, Human Interaction Research Assn. (bd. dirs. 1984—), Am. Leadership Forum (bd. dirs. 1988—). Home: 1250 S Washington St Alexandria VA 22314

PORTER, HARVEY, bank executive, lawyer; b. Wilmington, Del., Oct. 2, 1931; s. Nathan and Rose May (Rudnick) P.; m. Anna C. Semon, Aug. 17, 1957; children: Lisa, Karen, Robert. AB, U. Del., 1954; student, Boston U., 1956; LLB, U. Pa., 1958. Bar: Del. 1959, Pa. 1961, U.S. Supreme Ct. 1965. Asst. prof. bus. law Oreg. State Coll., 1958-59; v.p. Larami Corp., 1959-61; ptnr. with O. Francis Biondi, Wilmington, Del., 1961-67, Cohen, Verlin, Sherzer and Porter, Phila., 1967-78; vice chmn. First Nat. Bank Wilmington, Del., 1978-87; pres. Regent Bancshares Corp. Regent Nat. Bank, Phila., 1987—; pres. First Nat. Bank Wilmington, 1980-83; mem. Llyod's of London, 1979—. Patent. dir., organizer Wilmington Montessori Assn., 1962-67; mem. annual fund com. Pa. Hosp., Phila., 1979—; chmn. Phila. Cancer Ctr. Pa. Hosp., 1977-79. Mem. ABA, Del. Bar Assn., Pa. Bar Assn., Am. Judicature Assn., Am. Bankers Assn., Am. Trial Lawyers Assn. Clubs: Rodney Square, Bala Golf. Home: 2401 Pennsylvania Ave Ste 15B-24 Philadelphia PA 19130 Office: Regent Nat Bank 1430 Walnut St Philadelphia PA 19102

PORTER, JOHN HILL, public relations executive; b. Kane, Pa., Oct. 22, 1933; s. Hugh Clinton and Louise (Hill) P.; m. Sandra Van Fossen, Aug. 25, 1956 (div. 1981); children—John, Allison, Gardiner; m. Louise Bertels, Aug. 15, 1981; children—Campbell, Colin. B.S. in Econs., U. Pa., 1955; postgrad., U. Minn., 1956-57. Account exec. Benton & Bowles, N.Y.C., 1955, 57-59; sr. v.p. Ogilvy & Mather, N.Y.C. and London, 1959-70; dir. pub. affairs U.S. Peace Corps, Washington, 1970-72; chmn. Porter Novelli, Washington, 1972-86, N.Y.C., 1986—. Bd. overseers Sch. Nursing, U. Pa., Phila., 1982-87; trustee U. Pa., 1980-86, Penn. Med. Ctr., Phila., 1987-89. With U.S. Army, 1955-57. Republican. Office: Porter Novelli 1633 Broadway New York NY 10019

PORTER, JOHN ROBERT, technical executive; b. London, Jan. 5, 1953; came to U.S. 1979; s. Leslie and Shirley P. MA, Oxford U., Eng., 1974; DEA, Paris, 1976; MBA, Stanford U., 1981. Assoc. N.M. Rothschild U.K., 1975; cons. Boston Cons. Group, Paris, 1976-79; with Tesco Stores U.K., 1982-83; chmn. Cast Alloys, Calif., 1984—, VeriFone, Calif., 1985-86, Monogram, 1986—; bd. dirs. PhotoService, France, Lennox Ct., Eng. Office: VeriFone One Lagoon Dr #200 Redwood City CA 94065

PORTER, LANA GARNER, marketing executive; b. Salem, Ill., Dec. 31, 1943; d. Marion E. and Belva M. (Hayden) Garner; B.A., Murray State U., 1965, M.A., 1972; M.B.A., Ohio State U., 1980; m. Michael E. Porter, June 7, 1964; 1 dau., Catherine Diane. Tchr. jr. high sch. French, Hopkinsville, Ky., 1964-66; tchr. high sch. English, French and speech, Benton, Ky., 1966-69; instr. Murray (Ky.) State U., 1969-70; ednl. researcher Battelle Meml. Inst., Columbus, Ohio, 1970-73; coordinator of info., research, and devel. Planned Parenthood of Columbus, 1973-76; account exec. Ohio Bell Telephone Co., Columbus, 1976-78, adminstrv. mgr., Cleve., 1978-79, industry mgr., 1979-82, mgr. strategy planning, 1982-83; dir. advt. and pub. relations Ameritech Communications, Chgo., 1983-85, dir. nat. shared tenant ops., 1985-86; dir. Strategic Vendor Relations and Distbn. Services, 1986-88; Ameritech Info. Systems, dir. mktg. Network Products Ameritech Info. Systems, 1988— . Trustee, sec. United Cerebral Palsy of Columbus, 1977-78; trustee United Cerebral Palsy of Cuyahoga County, 1979-83. Mem. Am. Mgmt. Assn., Am. Soc. Profl. and Exec. Women, NOW, AAUW, Columbus Area Leadership Program Alumna, Jr. League, Alpha Omicron Pi Alumna. Republican. Presbyterian. Home: 546 W Brompton Chicago IL 60657 Office: Ameritech Info Systems 500 W Madioson Ste 1700 Chicago IL 60606

PORTER, MARC A., financial executive; b. Wichita, Kans., July 12, 1954; s. Marvin L. and Mary E.P.; m. Sheryl L. Wolfe, July 24, 1976; children: Jamie, Tracy. BBA in Bus. and Acctg., Wichita State U., 1976, MS in Acctg., 1983. CPA, Kans. Controller Ritchie Enterprises, Wichita, Kans., 1979-85; corp. controller Collins Industries, Hutchinson, Kans., 1985-87; chief fin. officer The Law Co., Inc., Wichita, 1987—. Mem. Am. Inst. CPA's, Fin. Execs. Inst. Office: The Law Co Inc 345 Riverview Wichita KS 67203

PORTER, MILTON, tubular, rail and construction products supplier executive; b. Charleroi, Pa., Mar. 2, 1911; s. Harry S. and Jennie (Mitnick) P.; m. Adrienne Foster, Nov. 11, 1938. B.A. in Bus. Adminstrn., U. Pitts., 1932. With L.B. Foster Co., Pitts., 1945-89, v.p., 1955, dir., 1958, pres., chief exec. officer, 1968, chmn. bd., chief exec. officer, 1981-84, now dir.; pres., chief exec. officer Foster Industries, Inc., Pitts.; chmn. bd. Foster Internat. Devel., Inc., Pitts.; mng. ptnr. various real estate cos. Past pres., life bd. dirs. Montefiore Hosp., Pitts.; bd. dirs. Pitts. Symphony, United Jewish Fedn., United Way Southwestern Pa.; bd. dirs., treas. Univ. Health Ctr., Pitts.; chmn. Health Edn. Ctr., Pitts.; ptnr. Gov.'s Pvt. Sector Initiatives Task Force; bd. trustees The Carnegie; dir. emeritus Carnegie-Mellon Univ. Recipient Benjamin Rush award Pa. Med. Soc., 1984; recognition award N. Am. Soc. for Corp. Planning, Inc. Clubs: Duquesne, Westmoreland Country (life dir.), Concordia, Rivers (dir.) (Pitts.); Longboat Key (Fla.). Home: Gateway Towers 320 Fort Duquesne Blvd Pittsburgh PA 15222 Office: Foster Industries Inc 681 Andersen Rd Pittsburgh PA 15220

PORTER, ROBERT WILLIAM, data processing executive; b. Elyria, Ohio, June 6, 1938; s. E. John and Lucille A. (Penfound) P.; m. L. Sandra Reed, Aug. 15, 1959; children: Matthew, Rebecca, Jonathan. BME, Gen. Motors Inst. Tech., Flint, Mich., 1960. Registered profl. engr., Ohio. Process engr. Fisher Body div. of GMC, Elyria, 1960-66; systems engr. Data Processing div. of IBM, Cleve., 1966-70; industry specialist Data Processing div. of IBM, 1970-78; applications cons. Computer Mgmt. Inc., Cleve., 1978-80; product mgr. Indsl. Systems div. of Anacomp Inc., Cleve., 1980-87; product planning and mktg. support mgr. Electronic Data Systems, Cleve., 1987—; frequent speaker on planning and marketing. Author: The Computerized Purchasing Standard System Description, 1985; co-author: The Computers in Purchasing Handbook, 1984; contbr. numerous articles to profl. jours. Fellow Am. Prodn. and Inventory Control Soc. Mennonite. Office: Electronic Data Systems 20325 Center Ridge Rd Rocky River OH 44116

PORTER, STUART WILLIAMS, investment company executive; b. Detroit, Jan. 11, 1937; s. Stuart Perlee and Alma Bernice (Williams) P.; m. Myrna Marlene Denham, June 27, 1964; children: Stuart, Randall. BS, U. Mich., 1960; MBA, U. Chgo., 1967, postgrad., 1967-68. Investment mgr., ptnr. Weiss Peck & Greer, 1978—. Chmn. Crusade of Mercy, 1973; chmn. investment com. Presbytery of Chgo. Served with USAF, 1961-62. Recipient Excellence in Bus. and Acctg. award Fin. Exec. Inst., 1966; Am. Acctg. Assn. fellow, 1967. Mem. Midwest Pension Conf., Investment Analysts Soc. Chgo., Fin. Analysts Fedn., Investment Tech. Symposium N.Y., Renaissance Club, Turnberry Country Club, Econ. Club, Chgo. Athletic Club, Tower Club, Avondale Club, Wynstone CLub, Beta Gamma Sigma Home: 130 Wyngate Dr Barrington IL 60010 Office: 20 N Wacker Dr Ste 4120 Chicago IL 60606

PORTER, SYLVIA, writer; b. Patchogue, L.I., N.Y., June 18, 1913; d. Louis and Rose (Maisel) Feldman; m. Reed R. Porter, 1931; 1 dau., Cris Sarah; 1 stepson, Sumner Campbell Collins; m. James F. Fox, 1979. B.A. magna cum laude, Hunter Coll., 1932; student, Grad. Sch. Bus. Adminstrn., N.Y. U.; 16 hon. degrees. Founder weekly news letter (Reporting on Governments); assoc. N.Y. Post, 1935-77, N.Y. Daily News, 1978—; syndicated columnist Los Angeles Times Syndicate; chmn. Sylvia Porter Orgn., Inc., 1987—. Editor-in-chief: Sylvia Porter's Personal Finance Mag.; author: How to Live Within Your Income, 1948, Sylvia Porter's Income Tax Guide, pub. annually 1960—, How to Get More for Your Money, 1961, Sylvia Porter's Money Book-How to Earn It, Spend It, Save It, Invest It, Borrow It, and Use It to Better Your Life, 1975, paperback edit., 1976, Sylvia Porter's New Money Book for the 80's, 1979, paperback edit., 1981, Sylvia Porter's Your Own Money, 1983, Love and Money, 1985, Your financial Security, 1988. Named one of Am.'s 25 Most Influential Women World Almanac, 1977-82; Woman of the Decade Ladies Home Jour., 1979. Mem. Phi Beta Kappa. Office: Sylvia Porter Orgn Old Pound Rd RR 5 PO Box 151 Pound Ridge NY 10576

PORTER, WALTER THOMAS, JR., banker; b. Corning, N.Y., Jan. 8, 1934; s. Walter Thomas and Mary Rebecca (Brookes) P.; m. Dixie Jo Thompson, Apr. 3, 1959; children: Kimberlee Paige, Douglas Thompson, Jane-Amy Elizabeth. BS, Rutgers U., 1954; MBA, U. Wash., 1959; PhD, Columbia U., 1964. CPA, Wash., N.Y. Staff cons. Touche Ross & Co., Seattle, 1959-61; NDEA fellow Columbia U., 1961-64; dir. edn. Touche Ross & Co., N.Y.C., 1964-66; assoc. prof. U. Wash., 1966-70, prof., 1970-74; vis. prof. N. European Mgmt. Inst., Oslo, Norway, 1974-75; nat. dir. planning Touche Ross & Co., Seattle, 1975-78, dir. exec. fin. counseling, 1978-84, exec. v.p., mgr. pvt. banking, Rainier Nat. Bank, 1984-87, exec. v.p., mgr. capital mgmt. and pvt. banking, 1987-88, vice chmn. 1988-89; vice chmn. Security Pacific Bank Washington, 1989—; vis. lectr. taxation U. Wash., 1978-85, 1988—. Mem. Seattle adv. bd. Salvation Army, 1975-83; trustee Ryther Child Ctr., 1975-85, pres., 1979-81; trustee Lakeside Sch., 1977-87, treas., 1970-81, 1st v.p. 1982-84, pres. 1984-86; trustee Virginia Mason Rsch. Ctr., 1982-87, Mus. History and Industry, 1982-83, Va. Mason Med. Ctr., 1986—. Served with U.S. Army, 1955-57. Author: Auditing Electronic System, 1966; (with William Perry) EDP: Controls and Auditing, 1970, 5th edit., 1987; (with John Burton) Auditing A Conceptual Approach, 1974; (with D. Alkire) Wealth: How to Achieve It, 1976; Touche Ross Guide to Personal Financial Management, 1984, 3d edit., 1989; (with D. Porter) The Personal Financial Planner's Practice Sourcebook, 1986. Mem. Am. Inst. CPA's. Congregationalist. Club: Wash. Athletic, Sand Point Country. Office: Security Pacific Bank Wash 1301 5th Ave PO Box 3966 Seattle WA 98124

PORTER, WILLIAM HORACE, II, accountant, financial analyst; b. Sheridan, Wyo., May 28, 1952; s. William Horace Sr. and Norma Jeanette (Williams) P. BS in Acctg., U. Wyo., 1974. Acct. Meml. Hosp., Sheridan, 1974—. Mem. Hosp. Fin. Mgmt. Assn. (bd. dirs. 1982-84), Rotary, Masons (membership com.). Home: 950 Clarendon Ave Sheridan WY 82801 Office: Meml Hosp 1401 W 5th St Sheridan WY 82801

PORTER-O'GRADY, TIMOTHY, health science facility adminstrator; b. Edmonton, Alta., Can., Mar. 29, 1947; came to U.S., 1969; s. Thomas Joseph O'Grady and Margaret Porter; m. Josephine Nelson, May 13, 1969 (div.). AA In SCi., Lower Columbia Coll., 1973; BS, Seattle U., 1975; MA, U. Wash., 1977; EdD, Nova U., 1983. Staff nurse Providence Med. Ctr., Seattle, 1973-75, clin. supr., 1975-77; patient care adminstr. Alleghany Regional Hosp., Covington, Va., 1977-79; v.p. patient care services Drs. Meml. Hosp., Richmond, Va., 1979-80; nurse adminstr. St. Joseph's Hosp., Atlanta, 1980-84; pres. Affiliated Dynamics Inc., Atlanta, 1987—, also bd. dirs.; v.p. Mercy Care Corp., Atlanta, 1987—. Author: Shared Governance, 1984, Creative Nursing Administration, 1986, Nursing Finance, 1987; contbr. numerous articles on health adminstrn. to profl. jours. Mem. governing bd. Atlanta Community Health Program, 1987—; trustee Ga. Nurses' Found., Atlanta, 1988—; mem. adv. bd. Ga. State Dept. Human Resources, Atlanta, 1987—. Homeless health care grantee U.S. Dept. HHS, 1987; recipient Ga. Health Care award Ga. League Nursing, 1988, Book Yr. award, Am. Jour. Nursing, 1985, 87. Mem. Nat. League Nursing, Am. Hosp. Assn., Am. Nurses Assn. (nat. cert. advanced adminstrn.), Gerontol. Soc. Am., Health Care Profl. div. Amnesty Internat., Sigma Theta Tau. Democrat. Roman Catholic. Home: 2 Dartmouth Ave Avondale Estates GA 30002-1410 Office: 1100 Johnson Ferry Rd NE Atlanta GA 30342

PORTMAN, GLENN ARTHUR, lawyer; b. Cleve., Dec. 26, 1949; s. Alvin B. and Lenore (Marsh) P.; m. Katherine Seaborn, Aug. 3, 1974 (div. 1984); m. Susan Newell, Jan. 3, 1987. B.A. in History, Case Western Res. U., 1968; J.D., So. Meth. U., 1975. Bar: Tex. 1975, U.S. Dist. Ct. (no. dist.) Tex. 1975, U.S. Dist. Ct. (so. dist.) Tex. 1983, U.S. Dist. Ct. (we. and ea. dists.) Tex. 1988. Assoc. Johnson, Bromberg & Leeds, Dallas, 1975-80, ptnr., 1980—. Asst. editor-in-chief: Southwestern Law Jour., 1974-75; contbr. articles to profl. jours. Mem. ABA, Dallas Bar Assn., So. Meth. U. Law Alumni Assn. (council bd. dirs., v.p. 1980-86, chmn. admissions com., chmn. class agt. program, chmn. fund raising). Republican. Methodist. Clubs: 500 Inc., Assemblage. Home: 9503 Winding Ridge Dr Dallas TX 75238 Office: Johnson Bromberg & Leeds 2600 Lincoln Plaza 500 N Akard St Dallas TX 75201

PORTWAY, PATRICK STEPHEN, telecommunications consulting company executive, telecommunications educator; b. June 18, 1939; s. Christopher Leo and Ceciala (King) P.; children by previous marriage—Shawn, Pam, Vicki. BA, U. Cin., 1963; MA, U. Md., 1973; postgrad., Columbia U. Regional ADP coordinator GSA, Washington, 1963-68; mgr. strategic mkt. planning Xerox Corp., 1969-74; mgr. plans and programs System Devel. Corp., 1974-78; fin. indsl. mktg. exec. Satellite Bus. Systems, 1978-80; western regional mgr. Am. Satellite Co., 1980-81; pres. Applied Bus. Telecommunications, San Ramon, Calif., 1981—; prof., lectr. Golden Gate U. Grad. Sch., San Francisco, 1983—; pub. mag. Teleconference, 1981—. Author: (with others) Teleconferencing. Presdl. elector Electoral Coll., Va., 1976; candidate Va. State Legislature from 19th Dist., 1971. Served to 1st lt. U.S. Army, 1963-65. Mem. Internat. Teleconferencing Assn. (founder, bd. dirs. 1983-88), Nat. Univ. Teleconferencing Networdk (mem. adv. bd., bd. dirs. 1986—), U.S. Distance Learning Assn. (exec. dir. 1987—) Electronic Funds Transfer Assn. (founder, bd. dirs. 1980), Satellite Profls., Jaycees charter pres. Chantilly, VA., Disting. Service award Dale City, VA. Club: Commonwealth. Home: 4024 Greenwich Dr San Ramon CA 94583 Office: Applied Bus Telecommunications 2500 Old Crow Canyon Rd San Ramon CA 94583

POSEIDON, PANTELIS LEE, director strategic planning and business development; b. Athens, Aug. 16, 1955; s. Apostolos A. and Athena (Karageorgi) P.; m. Donna Jean Bertolet, May 27, 1984. BA, Ohio Wesleyan U., Delaware, 1977; MBA, Xavier U., 1979. Mgr. service bus. planning Reynolds & Reynolds, Dayton, Ohio, 1984-85; dir. strategic planning and bus. devel. Computer Systems div. Reynolds & Reynolds, Dayton, Ohio, 1985—; mgr. fin. planning Harris Constrn., Columbus, Ohio, 1979-81; fin. analyst NCR, Dayton, 1981-82, section mgr. fin. and adminstrn., 1982-83, program fin. mgr., 1983-84. Mem. Am. Mktg. Assn., The Planning Forum. Republican. Greek Orthodox. Home: 4720 Witherby Dr Kettering OH 45429 Office: Reynolds & Reynolds PO Box 1005 Dayton OH 45401

POSNER, VICTOR, diversified business executive; b. Balt., 1918. With DWG Corp., Miami, Fla., 1952—, chmn., pres., 1966—, now chmn., chief exec. officer, dir.; chmn., pres., chief exec. officer Southeastern Pub. Service Co. subs. DWG Corp., Miami; with NVF Co., Yorklyn, Del.; chmn. NVF Co., pres., chief exec. officer; chmn. Sharon Steel Corp., Farrell, Pa., pres., chief exec. officer, until 1988; chmn., pres., chief exec. officer Nat. Propane Corp., New Hyde Park, N.Y., Wilson Bros., Miami; chmn., pres., chief exec. officer, dir. Evans Products Co., Miami, Mueller Brass Co., Port Huron, Mich., Birdsboro Corp., Pa., Pa. Engring. Cor., Pitts.; chmn., chief exec. officer, dir. Graniteville Co., S.C. also: Fischbach Corp 485 Lexington Ave New York NY 10017 other: Chesapeake Fin Corp 6917 Collins Ave Miami Beach FL 33141 other: APL Corp 6917 Collins ave Miami FL 33141 *

POSNICK, ADOLPH, chemical company executive; b. Yellow Creek, Sask., Can., May 3, 1926; came to U.S., 1947; s. Frank and Joanne (Shimko) P.; m. Sarah Anne Briggs, May 16, 1947; children—Joann Elizabeth, Barbara Ellen. B.S. in Ceramic Enging, U. Sask., 1947. Research engr. Ferro Corp., Cleve., 1947-50; tech. dir. Ferro Enamel-Brazil, Sao Paulo, 1950-56; mng. dir. Ferro Enamel-Brazil, 1956-65; v.p. internat. ops. Ferro Corp., Cleve., 1965-74; sr. v.p. ops. Ferro Corp., 1974-75, exec. v.p., 1975-76, pres., chief exec. officer, 1976-88, chmn. bd. dirs., chief exec. officer, 1988—; bd. dirs. fgn. subsidiaries; mem. Brazil-Am. Bus. Coun. Mem. Am., Brazilian ceramic socs., Cleve. World Trade. Clubs: Clevelander, Mid Day, Chagrin Valley Country, Union, Pepper Pike Country. Office: Ferro Corp 1 Erieview Pla Cleveland OH 44114

POSPISIL, EVA HOLDRIDGE, systems engineer; b. Hobbs, N. Mex., May 6, 1953; d. Earl Lee and Ruby Pearl (Bryan) Holdridge; m. Charles Henry Beecroft, Oct. 2, 1971 (div.); m. Francis Joseph Pospisil, Oct. 10, 1980. AS, Baylor U., 1977; BS, NYU, 1983; MS in Sci. Counseling Psychology with honors, Am. Technol. U., 1985, MS in Mgmt. Sci. with honors, 1986. Med. technician, instr. Acad. Health Sci., Fort Sam Houston, Tex., 1971-81; med. technician Darnall Army Community Hosp., Fort Hood, Tex., 1982-84; program analyst DOIM, Fort Hood, 1984-88; systems engr. Northern Telecom, Richardson, Tex., 1988-89, network mgr., 1989—; instr. Cen. Tex. Coll., Killeen, 1985-88, research mgr., 1984-85; owner, mgr. SUEDE, Copperas Cove, Tex., 1985—; cons. Mary Kay Cosmetics. Served with U.S. Army, 1971-81. Mem. Am. Med. Technicians, Tex. Assn. Counseling and Devel., Nat. Assn. Underwater Diving Instrs., Nat. Assn. Parachute Clubs, Nat. Assn. Hangliding, Copperas Cove C. of C., Epsilon Delta Phi. Democrat. Roman Catholic. Club: Fort Hood Parachute. Avocations: skydiving, scuba diving, water and snow skiing, racquetball. Home: 1329 Kesser St Plano TX 75023

POSS, JOHN CLAYBRON, construction executive; b. Beaumont, Tex., Mar. 10, 1948; s. Charles Ellis Poss and Ida (Counce) Popham; m. Janice Cimerhanzel, July 15, 1966 (div. Sept. 1969); children: Monica, Jeff; m. Melinda Ann Koester, Feb. 28, 1981; 1 child, Kate. BBA, U. Tex., 1974. CPA, Va. Auditor Arthur Andersen & Co., Washington, 1974-75, cons., 1975-78, mgr. cons., 1978-79; planning mgr. McIntyre Mines, Calgary, Alta., Can., 1980-81, v.p. fin. and planning, 1981-83; planning advisor Superior Oil, Houston, 1983-84; ind. cons., Houston, 1984-86; sr. v.p. corp. devel. Gemcraft Inc., Houston, 1986-87, pres., 1987-89. Sustaining mem. Harris County Dem. Party, Houston, 1987. Mem. Am. Inst. CPA's. Democrat. Office: Gemcraft Inc 1265 San Felipe #1100 Houston TX 77027

POSS, STEPHEN DANIEL, lawyer; b. Buffalo, Jan. 13, 1955; s. Gilbert H. and Bernice L. (Lippman) P. BA magna cum laude, Amherst Coll., 1978; JD, U. Chgo., 1981. Bar: N.Y. 1982, U.S. Tax Ct. 1983, U.S. Dist. Ct. (so. dist.) N.Y. 1984, U.S. Dist. Ct. (ea. dist.) N.Y. 1986, U.S. Supreme Ct. 1986, Mass. 1988, U.S. Dist. Ct. Mass. 1988. Assoc. Cravath, Swaine & Moore, N.Y.C., 1981-87, Goodwin, Procter and Hoar, Boston, 1988—; teaching asst. to Prof. Henry Steele Commager, 1977; lectr. Mass. Continuing Legal Edn., 1987, 88. Advisor campaign Bill Guy for U.S. Senate, N.D., 1974, Quentin Burdick for U.S. Senate, N.D., 1976, Bill Bradley for U.S. Senate, N.J., 1978, Gary Hart for U.S. Senate, Colo., 1980, Jeff Bingaman for U.S. Senate, N.Mex., 1982; pro bono counsel to Dem. Nat. Com., 1986-87; bd. dirs. Internat. Forum, N.Y.C., 1984, council N.Y. Law Assocs., N.Y.C., 1985. John Woodruff Simpson fellow, 1978. Mem. ABA. Club: Circle (dirs.), Sierra (life). Office: Goodwin Procter & Hoar Exchange Pl Boston MA 02109

POSSATI, MARIO, electronic gauge company executive; b. Cordoba, Argentina, Apr. 7, 1922; s. Pompeo and Rosa (Badini) P.; B.S. in Mech. Engring., Bologna U., 1946; m. Manfredi Gabriella, June 4, 1947; children—Stefano, Marco, Edoardo, Alberto. Tech. mgr. Officine Maccaferri, Bologna, Italy, 1946-48; gen. mgr. Baschieri & Pellagri, 1949-52; founder MARPOSS, Bologna, 1952, chmn., chief exec. officer, 1952—. Served with Italian Air Force, 1943. Mem. Profl. Engrs. Assn. Italy, Soc. Mfg. Engrs., Cavaliere del Lavoro. Office: Marposs SpA, Via Saliceto 13 Bentivoglio, 40010 Bologna Italy

POST, DAVID ALAN, broadcast executive; b. N.Y.C., Oct. 20, 1941; s. Emil R. and Ruth (Rosen) P.; m. Arline Goldbrum, June 10, 1962 (div. 1981); children: Randee, Lori, Jill; m. Katlean de Monchy, Dec. 13, 1984. Student, CCNY, 1959-61; grad., Fleigenheimer Ins. Inst., 1961, N.Y. Inst. Fin., 1968. Sales rep. Aetna Life Ins. Casualty, Hartford, Conn., 1961-63; sales mgr. Globe Rubber Products, Phila., 1963-67; ptnr. Zuckerman Smith and Co., N.Y.C., 1968-71; dir. corp. fin. Andersen and Co., N.Y.C., 1971-72; exec. v.p., dir. R.K. Pace Post Investment Bankers, N.Y.C., 1973-76; chmn., chief exec. officer, founder Page Am. Group, Inc., Hackensack, N.J., 1976-86, also bd. dirs.; chmn., chief exec. officer, founder Channel Am. LPTV Holdings, Inc., N.Y.C., 1986—. Contbr. articles to INC. mag. Mem. Nat. Assn. TV Programming Execs., Nat. Greyhound Assn. Republican. Jewish. Home: 400 E 57th St New York NY 10022 Office: Channel Am LPTV Network 24 W 57th St New York NY 10019

POSTAL, EDWARD DAVID, accountant, corporate executive; b. Washington, Sept. 15, 1955; s. Joseph Lewis and Flora Paula (Gottlieb) P.; m. Marjorie Beth Mayer, Mar. 22, 1987; 1 child, Steven William. BS in Acctg. magna cum laude, U. Md., 1977. CPA, D.C., Md. Asst. to sr. acct. Touche Ross & Co., Washington, 1977-81; sr. acct., mgr. fin. reporting and taxes, mgr. acctg. and taxes Satellite Bus. Systems, McLean, Va., 1981-85; controller Wyatt Co., Washington; 1985—. Mem. Am. Inst. CPA's, Md. Assn. CPA's, D.C. Inst. CPA's. Office: Wyatt Co 1850 M St NW Ste 700 Washington DC 20036-5803

POSTE, GEORGE HENRY, pharmaceutical company executive; b. Polegate, Sussex, Eng., Apr. 30, 1944; came to U.S., 1972; s. John H. and Kathleen B. (Brooke) P.; m. Mary E. Mudge, Mar. 9, 1968; 1 child, Eleanor Kathy. DVM, U. Bristol, 1966, PhD, 1969, DSc, 1987. Lectr. Univ. London, 1969-72; assoc. prof. SUNY, Buffalo, 1972-76; prof. pathology Roswell Park Meml. Inst., Buffalo, 1976-80; v.p. rsch. SmithKline Beckman, Phila., 1980-82, v.p. R&D, 1982-86, v.p. worldwide rsch. and pre-clin. devel., 1987-88, pres. R&D, 1988—; mem. pathology B study sect. NIH, Bethesda, Md., 1978-82; chairperson Gordon Conf., N.H., 1985, 86. Editor: Cell Surface Reviews, New Horizons in Therapeutics, Cancer Metastasis Revs., Advanced Drug Delivery Revs., 15 books; contbr. numerous articles to profl. jours. Trustee Gordon Rsch. Confs.; mem. gov. bd. UCLA Symposia; mem. Gov's. adv. com. Sci. and Tech., Pa.; mem. governing bd. Life Sci. Rsch. Found. Mem. F.R.C Pathologists, Royal Coll. Pathologists, AAAS, Am. Soc. Cell Biology, Path. Soc., Nat. Assn. Biomed. Research (bd. govs. 1984), Univ. Assn. Space Rsch. (mem. coun. 1984), Pharm. Mfrs. Assn. (chmn. R&D sect.), U. Pa. Natural Sci. Assn. (mem. bd. govs.), Inst. Sci. Info. (sci. adv. bd.), U. Tex. M.D. Anderson Cancer Ctr. (pres. coun.). Office: Smith Kline Beckman PO Box 1539 King of Prussia PA 19406-0939

POSTLER, ERMIN JOSEPH, audio engineer; b. Prague, Czechoslovakia, Aug. 13, 1942; s. Ladislav and Ermina (Pokorná) P.; m. Blanka P. Postler (div. 1979); 1 child, Richard P.; m. Maria Pavla Zákora. Diploma engring., Czech High Tech. Sch., Prague, 1965. Audio engr. sound dept. Ceskoslovenská Televize (CST), Prague, 1966-78, chief sound dept., 1978-80, researcher tech. devel. dept., 1980-83, audio expert concept and tech. dept., 1983—. Contbr. articles to profl. jours. Mem. Sci. and Tech. Cons. CST. Office: Ceskoslovenska televize, Jindrisska 16, 111 50 Prague Czechoslovakia

POSTLEWAITE, WILLIAM MARC, publishing executive; b. Louisville, Oct. 10, 1944; s. William Cresson and Gretchen (Heingardner) P.; m. Marion Teresa Milton, Dec. 28, 1969; children: Brian, Matthew, Andrew, John. BS, U. Tenn., 1968; degree in profl. mgmt. devel., Harvard U., 1978. Reporter The Knoxville (Tenn.) Jour., 1969-71; editor The Sevier County News Record, Sevierville, Tenn., 1971-73; gen. mgr. The Mountain Press Newspapers subs. Harte-Hawks Communications, Gatlinburg, Tenn., 1973-76, pub., 1976-80; pub. Sunbelt Publs. of Chgo. Tribune Co., New Port Richey, Fla., 1980-82, Life & Home Mag. Visitor Publs. Inc., Tarpon Springs, Fla., 1982-88; co-founder, bus. mgr. Lightning Laser Optical Corp., Tarpon Springs, 1988—; bd. dirs. Tampa Bay Media, Inc. ,1988—. Publisher emeritus Tampa Bay Homes mag.; patentee in field. Pres. Group Positive, Tarpon Springs, 1983. Mem. Tenn. Press Assn. (bd. dirs. 1973-76), Fla. Mag. Assn., Am. Hellenic Ednl. Progam Assn., Harvard Bus. Sch. Club (v.p. S.W. Fla. chpt. 1988), Elks. Home: 262 S Beach Dr Tarpon Springs FL 34689 Office: 131 Hibiscus St Tarpon Springs FL 34689

POTE, HAROLD WILLIAM, banker; b. Phila., Sept. 18, 1946; s. Frank Lafferty and Lucille (Bock) P.; m. Judy Elizabeth Constantine, Oct. 12, 1968. A.B., Princeton U., 1968; M.B.A., Harvard U., 1972. Dir. investor relations Fidelcor/Fidelity Bank, Phila., 1974-76, v.p., head corp. devel. dept., 1976-78, sr. v.p., head corp. devel. dept., 1978-80, exec. v.p., treas. fin. and planning dept., 1980-83, vice chmn., treas. fin. and planning dept., 1983-84; chmn. bd., chief exec. officer Fidelity Bank, Phila., 1984-88; pres., chief exec. officer Fidelcor, Inc., 1986-88; pres. and chief exec. officer First Fidelity Bancorp., Phila., 1988—; adj. asst. prof. LaSalle Coll., Phila., 1972-79; bd. dirs. Smith Kline Beckman Corp. Trustee Pa. Ballet Assn., Phila., 1976—; mem. exec. council Harvard Bus. Sch. Assn., 1980—; bd. dirs., co-chmn. Phila. Urban Coalition. Mem. Am. Inst. C.P.A.s, Res. City Bankers Assn. Clubs: Merion Golf, Locust, Union League. Office: First Fidelity Bancorp Broad & Walnut Sts Philadelphia PA 19109

POTEET, DWAYNE LEE, medical products company executive; b. Waco, Tex., Jan. 15, 1959; s. Aarron Dwayne and Frances Arlene (Freeman) P.; m. Pamela Anne Perry, July 26, 1980; children: Christopher Lee, Perry Stephen. BS in Edn. and Journalism, S.W. Tex. State U., 1980. Sales rep. Dover, Houston, 1980-82, Delmed, Houston, 1982-83; sales rep. Tecnol, Ft. Worth, 1983, western sales mgr., 1983-85, nat. sales mgr., 1985, internat. dir. sales, 1985-87; dir. sales Tecnol, Europe and Middle East, 1987-88, Internat. Midmark Corp., Versailles, Ohio, 1988—. Mem. nat. com. Rep. Party, Dallas, 1981—. Republican. Home and Office: 60 Vista Dr Versailles OH 45380 also: Place de Bastogne 26 BS, 1080 Brussels Belgium

POTENTE, EUGENE, JR., interior designer; b. Kenosha. Wis., July 24, 1921; s. Eugene and Suzanne Marie (Schmit) P.; Ph.B., Marquette U., 1943; postgrad. Stanford U., 1943, N.Y. Sch. Interior Design, 1947; m. Joan Cioffe, Jan. 29, 1946; children—Eugene J., Peter Michael, John Francis, Suzanne Marie. Founder, pres. Studios of Potente, Inc., Kenosha, Wis., 1949—; pres., founder Archtl. Services Assos., Kenosha, 1978—, Bus. Leasing Services of Wis. Inc., 1978—; past nat. pres. Inter-Faith Forum on Religion, Art and Architecture; vice chmn. State Capitol and Exec. Residence Bd., 1981-88. Sec., Kenosha Symphony Assn., 1968-74. Bd. dirs. Ctr. for Religion and the Arts, Wesley Theol. Sem., Washington, 1983-84. Served with AUS, 1943-46. Mem. Am. Soc. Interior Designers (treas., pres. Wis. 1985—, chmn. nat. pub. service 1986), Inst. Bus. Designers, Sigma Delta Chi. Roman Catholic. Lodge: Elks. Home: 8609 2d Ave Kenosha WI 53140 Office: 914 60th St Kenosha WI 53140

POTH, STEFAN MICHAEL, sales financing company executive; b. Detroit, Dec. 9, 1933; s. Stefan and Anna (Mayer) P.; m. Eileen T. McClimon, May 28, 1966; 1 child, Stefan Michael. Cert. in acctg., Walsh Inst., Detroit, 1954. CPA, Mich. Sr. acct. Lybrand, Ross Bros. & Montgomery, Detroit, 1953-56, 58-61; with Ford Motor Credit Co., Dearborn, Mich., 1961—; v.p. leasing truck and recreational products and tractor financing Ford Motor Credit Co., Dearborn, 1973-77; v.p. cen. and western U.S. ops. Ford Motor Credit CO., Dearborn, 1977-79; v.p. mktg. and ops. svcs. Ford Motor Credit Co., Dearborn, 1979-85, v.p. bus. planning, 1985—; bd. dirs. GE Credit Auto Resale Svcs., Inc. Chmn. adv. coun. Credit Rsch. Ctr. Krannert Grad. Sch. Mgmt., Purdue U., 1986—. With AUS, 1956-58. Roman Catholic. Office: Ford Motor Credit Co American Rd Dearborn MI 48121

POTT, JAMES THOMAS, civil engineer, consultant; b. Shanghai, Feb. 28, 1927; (father Am. citizen); s. James Hawks and Nancy (Yang) P.; m. Lois Jane Donaldson, July 16, 1955; children: Nancy, Catherine, Margaret. BSCE, Stanford U., 1949, MSCE, 1950. Registered profl. engr., Calif., Colo. Civil engr. Kennedy/Jenks/Chilton, San Francisco, 1950-60; county engr. County of Santa Clara, San Jose, Calif., 1960-77, dir. pub. works, 1963-73, dir. transp., 1973-77, asst. county exec., 1973-77; city engr., dir. pub. works City of Long Beach, Calif., 1978-84; v.p. O'Brien-Kreitzberg & Assocs., Encino, Calif., 1984-87; propr., engring. cons. James Pott & Co., Long Beach, 1987—. Patentee transit wheelchair lift. Served to 1st lt. U.S. Army, 1944-46, 52-53. Recipient S.I.R. award Assoc. Gen. Contractors Calif., 1976; Disting. Service award Calif. Council Civil Engrs. and Land Surveyors, 1967. Fellow ASCE; mem. Am. Pub. Works Assn. (mem. research found. 1982-84, Top Ten Pub. Works award 1976), County Engrs. Assn. Calif. (pres. 1971-72, life mem.), Nat. Assn. County Engrs. (1st v.p. 1976-77, Urban County Engr. of Yr. 1973), Pub. Works Officers-League Calif. Cities (v.p. 1983-84), Long Beach Area C. of C. (vice chmn. 1986—, chmn. strategic plan task force 1988), Tau Beta Pi. Republican. Episcopalian. Club: Rotary.

POTTER, ANTHONY NICHOLAS, JR., security company executive, consultant; b. N.Y.C., Jan. 6, 1942; s. Anthony Nicholas Sr. and Alta Lorene (Downing) P.; m. Patricia Anne Tlumac, Apr. 4, 1964 (div. Oct. 1981); children: Merika Elizabeth, Victoria Hope Nora; m. Cheryl Kay Dittman, Oct. 15, 1983. AA, Westchester Community Coll., 1970; BS in Criminal Justice, U. Cin., 1975. Cert. protection profl., security trainer. Chief police Tampa Internat. Airport, Fla., 1970-73; prin. cons. Booz, Allen & Hamilton, Cin., 1973-75; chief police City of Danville, Ill., 1976-78; police commr. City of York, Pa., 1978-80; v.p. Omni Internat. Security, Atlanta, 1980-83; exec. dir. Internat. Assn. Shopping Ctr. Security, Atlanta, 1981—; cons. shopping ctr. developers, operators, retailers; faculty mem. Internat. Council Shopping Ctr. Mgmt. Insts., 1970-85; expert witness security matters fed. and state cts. Author: Shopping Center Security, 1976, Recommended Security Practices for Shopping Centers, 1987; contbr. articles to profl. jours. Various positions local, council, regional, nat. Boy Scouts Am., 1950—. Served to sgt. USMC, 1959-65. Recipient Disting. Service award Internat. Security Conf. 1970; Merit award Security World Mag., 1972. Mem. Met. Atlanta Crime Commn., Internat. Assn. Chiefs Police (pvt. security com. 1978-85), Internat. Assn. Profl. Security Cons. (bd. dirs. 1988—), Am. Soc. Indsl. Security (chmn. St. Petersburg chapt. 1970-71, chmn. nat. transp. security com. 1971-74, regional v.p. region VI 1975-76, com. standards and codes 1977-80, chmn. legis. com. 1986-87, pvt. security services council 1988—), ABA (assoc.), Am. Acad. Forensic Scis. (elected mem. 1987), Nat. Acad. Police Specialists (v.p. 1988—). Republican. Lutheran. Avocations: model railroading, gun collecting, scuba diving. Home: 2493 Willow Wood Ct NE Atlanta GA 30345 Office: Internat Assn Shopping Ctr Security 2830 Clearview Pl NE Suite 300 Atlanta GA 30340

POTTER, DONALD ALBERT, manufacturing company executive; b. Indpls., May 9, 1922; s. Donald Holmes and Gertrude Antoinette (Sullivan) P.; m. Marian Helen Loughery, Feb. 6, 1943; children: Donald V., Mary J., Richard J., Ann T., Robert A., William M., James P. BS magna cum laude, Notre Dame U., 1943. Registered profl. engr., Ind. Chief engr. Universal Castings Corp., Chgo., 1946-47; with Stewart-Warner Corp., Chgo., 1947—; gen. mgr. electronics div. Stewart-Warner Corp., 1959—; v.p., dir. subs. Datafax Corp., 1959—, v.p. corp., 1960—; pres., dir. Stewart Warner Microcircuits, Inc., 1963—; v.p., dir. subs. Stewart Warner Display Systems, Inc., 1982—. Patentee heat transfer, elec. controls. Chmn. citizens bd. Loyola U., 1975-77. Served to ensign USNR, 1943-45. Named hon. alumnus, 1978. Mem. ASME, Am. Def. Preparedness (dir. 1977—), Soc. Automotive Engrs., Ill. C. of C., Armed Forces Communications and Electronics Assn. (dir. Chgo. area 1963-67), Chgo. Research and Devel. Council, Loyola U. devel. council. Clubs: Chgo. Athletic, Economics. Home: 250 Franklin Rd Glencoe IL 60022 Office: Stewart-Warner Corp 1826 Diversey Pkwy Chicago IL 60614

POTTER, GEORGE HARRIS, banker; b. Pitts., Dec. 15, 1936; s. William Sommerville and Katharine (Rockwell) P.; A.B., Colgate U., 1959; m. Nicole Enfield Weir, May 1, 1977; children—Clara Potter Mokher, George Harris, Faris Feland, Jonathan Rockwell, Kristin Enfield Weir, David Bruce Weir, Jr., Jennifer Berkey Weir. Life underwriter Equitable Life Assurance Soc. of U.S., Pitts., 1958-59; with Pitts. Nat. Bank, 1959-64; asst. treas. First Nat. Bank of Miami (Fla.), 1964, asst. v.p., 1964, v.p., 1969-79; v.p. Central Nat. Bank of Cleve., 1979-85, Barclays Bank PLC, 1985-87, v.p., dep. mgr. Cleve. office, 1987—; dir. Nik-Pak, Inc., Pitts. Testing Laboratory, Inc., 1973-86; mng. partner PTL Assos., 1978-86. Mem. adv. bd. Vanguard Sch., Coconut Grove, Fla., 1968-79. Mem. Greater Cleve. Growth Assn., Phi Delta Theta. Republican. Congregationalist. Clubs: University (Pitts.); River Oaks Racquet; Hermit, Mid-Day, City of Cleve., Lakewood Country, Colgate (pres. 1982—) (Cleve.). Home: 18151 Clifton Rd Lakewood OH 44107 Office: Barclays Bank PLC 1111 Superior Ave Ste 700 Cleveland OH 44114

POTTER, ROBERT JOSEPH, technical and business executive; b. N.Y.C., Oct. 29, 1932; s. Mack and Ida (Bernstein) P.; m. Natalie Joan Silverstein, Sept. 9, 1956; children: Diane Gail, Suzanne Lee, David Craig. B.S. cum laude (Kroner scholar), Lafayette Coll., 1954; M.A. in Physics, U. Rochester, 1957, Ph.D. in Optics, 1960. Cons. ANPA Research Inst., AEC Brookhaven Nat. Lab., RCA Labs., U.S. Naval Research Labs., 1952-60; mgr. optical physics and optical pattern recognition IBM Thomas J. Watson Research Center, Yorktown Heights, N.Y., 1960-65; assoc. dir. Applied Research Lab., Xerox Corp., Rochester, N.Y., 1965-67; v.p. advanced engring. Xerox Corp., 1967-68, v.p. devel. and engring., 1968-69; v.p., gen. mgr. Spl. Products and Systems div. Xerox Corp., Stamford, Conn. and Pasadena, Calif., 1969-71; v.p. info. tech. group Xerox Corp., Rochester, 1971-73; v.p. info. tech. group Xerox Corp., Dallas, 1973-75, pres. Office Systems div., 1975-78; sr. v.p., chief tech. officer Internat. Harvester Co., Chgo., 1978-82; with R.J. Potter & Co., 1983-84; group v.p. integrated office systems No. Telecom Inc., Richardson, Tex., 1985-87; pres., chief exec. officer Datapoint Corp., San Antonio, 1987—; dir. Molex Inc. Contbr. articles to profl. jours. Bd. dirs. So. Meth. U. Found. Sci. and Tech.; trustee Ill. Inst. Tech.

Recipient IBM Outstanding Tech. Contbn. award, 1964, Disting. Achievement award Soc. Mfg. Engrs., 1981. Fellow Optical Soc. Am., Am. Phys. Soc.; mem. Soc. Automotive Engrs., Phi Beta Kappa, Sigma Xi. Office: Datapoint Corp 9725 Datapoint Dr San Antonio TX 78229-8501

POTTER, WILLIAM BARTLETT, trucking company executive; b. Washington, Jan. 4, 1938; s. George Holland and Virginia (Bartlett) P.; m. Simone Robert, June 6, 1964; children: Eva Simone, William Bartlett. A.B., Princeton U., 1960; M.B.A., Emory U., 1962. With Merc.-Safe Deposit & Trust Co., Balt., 1962—; asst. sec., asst. treas. Merc.-Safe Deposit & Trust Co., 1964-66, asst. v.p., 1966-68, v.p., 1968-69, sr. v.p., 1969-76, exec. v.p., 1976; exec. v.p. Preston Trucking Co., 1976-77, pres., 1977-86; chmn., pres. Preston Corp., 1986—; chmn. Preston Trucking Co., 1986—; bd. dirs. Merc. Bankshares Corp., Md. Econ. Growth Assocs., Md. Bus. for Responsive Govt. Mem. Md. Club, Chesapeake Bay Yacht Club. Home: Rte 4 Peach Blossom Point Easton MD 21601 Office: Preston Corp 151 Easton Blvd Preston MD 21655

POTTER, WILLIAM JAMES, investment banker; b. Toronto, Ont., Can., Aug. 11, 1948; s. William Wakely and Ruby Loretta (Skidmore) P.; m. Linda Lee, Nov. 25, 1972; children: Lisa Michelle, Meredith Lee, Andrew David. AB, Colgate U., 1970; MBA, Harvard U., 1974. With White Weld & Co., Inc., N.Y.C., 1974-75, Toronto Dominion Bank, Toronto (Can.) and N.Y., 1975-78; group mgr. Toronto Dominion Bank, Toronto, 1979-82; 1st v.p. Barclays Bank PLC, N.Y.C., 1982-84; mng. dir. Prudential-Bache Securities, Inc., N.Y.C., 1984—; bd. dirs. Prudential-Bache Securities Can., Toronto, First Australia Fund Inc., Md., First Australia Prime Income Fund Inc., Md., First Australia Prime Income Co. Ltd., New Zealand, Equitilink Internat. Ltd., Jersey, Eng., Impulsora del Fondo Mex., Mexico City. Author: Finance for the Minerals Industry, 1985. Bd. dirs. Glen Ridge (N.J.) Community Fund, 1985—, fin. Glen Ridge Congl. Ch., 1985—. Mem. Nat. Fgn. Trade Council (bd. dirs., chmn. fin. com.). Congregationalist. Clubs: Harvard, Williams (N.Y.C.); National (Toronto); Glen Ridge (N.J.) Country. Office: Prudential-Bache Securities One Seaport Pla New York NY 10292

POTTS, RAMSAY DOUGLAS, JR., lawyer, aviator; b. Memphis, Oct. 24, 1916; s. Ramsay Douglas and Ann Clifton (VanDyke) P.; m. Veronica Hamilton Raynor, Dec. 22, 1945; children: Ramsay Douglas, David Hamilton, Lesley Ann, Lindsay Veronica. B.S., U. N.C., 1941; LL.B., Harvard U., 1948. Bar: Tenn. 1948, D.C. 1954, U.S. Supreme Ct. 1957. Commd. 2d lt. USAAF, 1941, advanced through grades to maj. gen. Res., 1961; various combat and operational assignments (8th Air Force and Air Force Res.), 1942-60; chmn. Air Force Res. Policy Com., 1967-68; practice of law Washington, 1955—; spl. asst. to chmn. Nat. Security Resources Bd., 1951; pres. Ind. Mil. Air Transport Assn., 1952-55; ptnr. Shaw, Pittman, Potts & Trowbridge, 1956—; dir. Emerson Electric Co. Publisher: Air Power History; contbr. articles to profl. jours. Mem. State Council Higher Edn. for Va., 1968-71; Trustee Air Force Hist. Found., pres., 1971-75; pres. Washington Area Tennis Patrons Found. Decorated D.S.C., other combat decorations. Mem. Am., D.C. bar assns., Phi Beta Kappa. Clubs: City Tavern (Washington), Metropolitan (Washington); Harvard (N.Y.C.); Army Navy Country (Arlington, Va.); Internat. Lawn Tennis Clubs of U.S., Gt. Brit., India. Home: 2818 N 27th St Arlington VA 22207 Office: Shaw Pittman Potts & Trowbridge 2300 N St NW Washington DC 20037

POTVIN, ROBERT JOHN, JR., financial planning executive; b. Worcester, Mass., Feb. 20, 1959; s. Robert John and Virginia Marie (Pensky) P.; m. Maureen Vaughn, Sept. 26, 1986. BS in Fin., Acctg. and Entreprenurial Mgmt., Wharton Coll., U. Pa., 1982. V.p., dir. fin. planning ops. Lincoln Fin. Services, Inc., Worcester, Mass. Mem. Internat. Assn. Cert. Fin. Planners. Office: Lincoln Fin Svcs 316 Main St Worcester MA 01608

POULIN, GERALD C., utility company executive; b. Augusta, Maine, Mar. 26, 1942; s. Marcel Gerard and Lucienne (Jean) P.; children: Brian, Melanie. AS, Franklin Inst. Boston, 1966; BS, Tufts U., 1969, MS, 1970. Civil engr. Cen. Maine Power Co., Augusta, 1979-79, supervising design engr., 1979-82, mgr. engring., 1982-84, asst. v.p., mgr. engring., 1984-86, v.p. engring., 1986—; v.p., dir. Maine Electric Power Co., Augusta, 1985—; pres. Kennebec Water Power Co., Waterville, Maine, 1986—; pres., dir. Union Water Power Co., Lewiston, Maine, 1986—. Bd. dirs., vice-chmn. St. Augustine Fed. Credit Union, Augusta; bd. dirs., loans and grants authorization officer Calumet Edn. Found., Augusta. Mem. ASCE, Maine Assn. Engrs. (bd. dirs. 1982). Home: PO Box 972 Augusta ME 04330 Office: Central Maine Power Co Edison Dr Augusta ME 04330

POULOS, MICHAEL JAMES, insurance company executive; b. Glens Falls, N.Y., Feb. 13, 1931; s. James A. and Mary Poulos; m. Mary Kay Leslie; children: Denise, Peter. BA, Colgate U., 1953; MBA, NYU, 1963. With sales dept., mgr. U.S. Life Ins. Co., N.Y.C., 1958-65, asst. v.p., 1965-67, 2d v.p., chief adminstrv. officer sales, 1967-68, sec., treas, dir., v.p adminstrn., mem. exec. com., 1968-70; v.p. adminstrn. Calif.-Western States Life Ins. Co., Sacramento, 1970-71, dir., sr. v.p., exec. v.p., 1971-74, pres., chief exec. officer, dir., 1975-79; sr. v.p., div. head life ins. Am. Gen. Corp., Houston, 1979-81, pres., chief exec. officer, mem. of exec. and fin. coms., dir., 1981—, also bd. dirs. Mem. Sam Houston Area council Boy Scouts Am. Mem. Am. Soc. C.L.U.s, Nat. Assn. Life Underwriters, Houston Assn. Life Underwriters, Life Office Mgmt. Assn., Am. Mgmt. Assn., Beta Gamma Sigma, Delta Sigma Pi. Greek Orthodox. Clubs: Heritage, University. Office: Am Gen Corp 2929 Allen Pkwy Houston TX 77019

POULSON, LAWRENCE VANCE, mining executive; b. Colo. Springs, Colo., July 25, 1940; s. Garrell B. and Esther P. (White) P.; m. Sheryl J. Dotson, June 17, 1967; children: Craig D., Krista N., Kent B. BS, Colo. State U., 1963. Ins. mgr. Colo. Interstate Corp., Colo. Springs, 1966-73, Phillips Industries, Dayton, Ohio, 1973-74; dir. risk mgmt. N.W. Energy, Salt Lake City, 1974-85, Kerr McGee Corp., Oklahoma, 1985-88; v.p. Johnson & Higgins, Dallas, 1988—; bd. dirs. Oil Ins. Ltd., 1987-88, Oil Casualty Ins. Ltd., 1986-88, Bermuda; Am. Casualty Excess, 1987, Cayman Islands. Mem. Risk and Ins. Mgmt. Soc. (pres. Salt Lake City chpt. 1984). Republican. Mormon. Office: Johnson & Higgins One Dallas Ctr Dallas TX 75201

POULTON, CRAIG KIDD, property and casualty insurance broker; b. Salt Lake City, Nov. 22, 1951; s. LaMarr Williams and Marcella (Kidd) P.; m. Diane Adamson, Dec. 28, 1973; children: Brysen, Blake, Marissa, Ashley. BA, U. Utah, 1977. V.p. Poulton Insurance Agy., Inc., Salt Lake City, 1977-84, pres., 1984—; broker Internat. Lines and Comml. Lines, Salt Lake City, 1977—; Pres., chmn. Instar Corp., 1988—. Mem. Rep. Presdl. Task Force, 1983. Paul Harris fellow, 1984. Mem. Profl. Ins. Agts. Am., Ind. Ins. Agts. Assn. (com. chmn), Rotary Internat. Halladay Salt Lake City Club (bd. dirs. 1985, sec. 1986, v.p. 1987, pres. 1988). Republican. Mormon. Office: Poulton Ins Agy 3643 Highland Dr Salt Lake City UT 84106

POUNDS, WILLIAM FRANK, educator, director, advisor; b. Fayette County, Pa., Apr. 9, 1928; s. Joseph Frank and Helen (Fry) P.; m. Helen Ann Means, Mar. 6, 1954; children: Thomas McClure, Julia Elizabeth. B.S. in Chem. Engring., Carnegie Inst. Tech., 1950, M.S. in Math. Econs., 1959, Ph.D. in Indsl. Adminstrn., 1964. Indsl. engr. Eastman Kodak Co., 1950-51, 55-57; cons. Pitts. Plate Glass Co., 1958-59, asst. to gen. mgr. Forbes finishes div., 1960-61; mem. faculty Sloan Sch. Mgmt., MIT, 1961—, prof. mgmt., 1966—, dean, 1966-80; cons. to industry 1958—, sr. adv. Rockefeller Family and Assocs., 1981—; dir. EG&G, Inc., Putnam Funds, Sun Co., Inc., Gen. Mills Inc., M/A COM Inc.,. Served as aviator lt. (j.g.) USNR, 1951-55. Fellow Am. Acad. Arts and Scis.; mem. Inst. Mgmt. Sci. (pres. Boston 1965-66). Home: 33 Prince St West Newton MA 02165 Office: 50 Memorial Dr Cambridge MA 02139 also: 30 Rockefeller Pla Rm 5600 New York NY 10112

POUPORE, NORMA CAREY, former motel executive; b. Burke, N.Y., Sept. 14, 1929; d. Matthew Gabriel and Laura Anna (Moore) Carey; m. Bernard Charles Poupore, Feb. 16, 1952; children—Kevin, Barry, Casey, Michael. Grad. Adirondack Bus. Sch., 1946. With Marine Midland Banks, Malone and Syracuse, N.Y., 1946-53; legal stenographer local attys. and Office Ct. Adminstrn., State of N.Y., 1954-80; owner, operator Gateway Motel, Malone, 1962-86. Extension Service (bd. dirs.), Grange, Malone C. of C., Hotel-Motel Assn., Catholic Daus. Am. Republican. Roman Catholic. Club: Malone Golf and Country (bd. dirs.). Lodge: Elks. Avocations: golf; bowling; reading. Home: 2 Howard Dr Malone NY 12953

POURIAN, HEYDAR, financial economist, consultant; b. Tehran, Apr. 23, 1948; came to U.S., 1972, naturalized, 1978; s. Pasha and Moneer (Hamidi-Khaleghi) P.; student Nat. U. Iran, 1966-70, B.A., 1972; English lang. cert. U. Mich., 1972; M.A. (Internat. Scholar), U. Wis., Oshkosh, 1974; Ph.D., U. Wis., Milw., 1980; public econs. cert. M.I.T., 1979; postgrad. Harvard U., summer 1986. Research asst. dept. econs. and C. of C., U. Wis. Oshkosh, 1974, Fletcher sch. law and diplomacy Tufts U.; teaching asst. dept. econs. U. Wis. Milw., 1975-78, lectr. econs., dept. econs. and Sch. Bus. Adminstrn., 1978-79; asst. prof. econs. U. Mo., St. Louis, 1979-84, asst. prof. fin., 1984-88, assoc. prof., 1988—; research asst. to Council on Fgn. Relations and World Bank; adv. bd. N.Am. Econs. and Fin. Assn.; tax coordinator IRS, U.S. Dept. Treasury; cons. Can. govt., corps. and individual fin. planning. Recipient Grad. Sch. award U. Wis., Milw., 1975. Mem. Am. Econ. Assn., Am. Fin. Assn., Eastern Fin. Assn., UN Assn. of U.S.A., Omicron Delta Epsilon, Phi Kappa Phi (charter mem. U. Mo. at St. Louis chpt.). Contbr. papers to profl. confs.; participant interviews Public Broadcasting Service, Sta. KWMU, St. Louis Globe-Democrat, 1980. Home: PO Box 1960 Cullowhee NC 28723 Office: Western Carolina U Sch Bus Adminstrn Dept Econs & Fin Cullowhee NC 28723

POVEY, THOMAS GEORGE, office systems company executive; b. Norristown, Pa., Dec. 27, 1920; s. Thomas and Blanche (Groff) P.; B.S., Temple U., 1948; m. Bettina O. Houghton, June 2, 1945; children—Bettina C., Denise E. With Sperry Remington div. Sperry Rand Corp., Phila., also Newark, N.Y.C., 1948-76, eastern regional gen. sales mgr., 1960-63, nat. gen. sales mgr., N.Y.C., 1966-67, dir. mktg., Marietta, Ohio, 1968-71, v.p. mktg., 1972-73, v.p. fed. govt. mktg., Washington, 1973-76; pres. Remco Bus. Systems, Inc., Washington, 1976—; lectr. Newark High Sch., 1954-56, Belleville (N.J.) High Sch., 1956-58, Fairleigh Dickinson Coll., Paterson, N.J., 1957-58, Pace Coll., N.Y.C., 1965—, Georgetown U., 1974, ednl. TV, N.Y.C., 1965—. Dir. Community Fund, Essex Fells, N.J., 1967. Served as 1st lt. with USAF, 1942-45. Decorated Air medal; named Remington Dartnell Salesman of Yr., 1950. Mem. Internat. Platform Assn., Smithsonian Assos., Internat. Systems Dealer Assn. (dir. 1977-78), Office Systems Equipment Coop. (pres. 1978-80), Pi Delta Epsilon (pres. 1948). Republican. Methodist. Home: 227 Cape St John Rd Annapolis MD 21401 Office: 8000 Parston Dr Forestville MD 20747

POWELL, DAVID GREATOREX, public affairs executive; b. Princeton, N.J., Apr. 7, 1933; s. Richard Chew P. and Clare Davis Todd; m. Joan Van Nostrand Hitch, Mar. 27, 1956; children: Katherine Dexter Wood, Clare Davis Pitney, Elizabeth Todd. A.B. cum laude, Princeton U., 1954. Asst. mgr. pub. relations Esso Europe Inc., London, 1966-68; asst. to pres. Esso Iberia, Madrid, 1968-70; sr. pub. affairs adv. Exxon Corp., N.Y.C., 1970-74, mgr. pub. info., 1974-76; mgr. pub. affairs Exxon Chem. Co., 1976-79; sr. v.p. pub. affairs Allied-Signal Inc., Morristown, N.J., 1979—; chmn. conf. bd. Pub. Affairs Research Council, 1985-88, mem. exec. com., 1985—. Trustee Ind. Coll. Fund, N.J., 1981-87, Centenary Coll., 1986—, The Seeing Eye Inc., 1988—, Nat. Fgn. Trade Coun., 1988—; bd. dirs. United Way Morris County, 1980-87; dir., vice chmn. Pub. Affairs Coun., 1988—; membership corp. of Morristown Meml. Hosp., 1984, bd. dirs. 1988—. Mem. N.J. C. of C. (bd. dirs. 1985). Clubs: Somerset Hills Country, Somerset Lake & Game (N.J.); Adirondack League (N.Y.). Office: Allied-Signal Inc PO Box 3000 R Morristown NJ 07962-2496

POWELL, ELIZABETH PARKER, manufacturing executive; b. Denver, Dec. 5, 1938; d. Everett Humphreys and Clare Gernon (Davis) Parker; m. David George Powell, Sept. 21, 1963; children: Parker Davis, Clare Madeline, Elizabeth Everett. BA, Smith Coll., Northhampton, Ma., 1960; MA, Tufts U., 1962; MBA, Babson Coll., 1976. Asst. prof. mgmt. Babson Coll., Wellesley, Ma, 1978-80; seminar leader U. Lowell, Babson Coll., Wellesley Coll., Wellesley, 1978-85; co-founder, treas. Diamond Machining Tech., Inc., Marlborough, Ma., 1976—; lectr. U. Lowell, 1976-78, Harvard U. Ctr., Cambridge, Ma., 1980-81; charter trustee Phillips Acad., Andover, Ma., 1980—, trustee Babson Coll., 1984— (chmn. presdl. search com.); bd. dirs., fin. com. Harvard Community Health Plan, bd. overseers, Boston, 1986—; bd. dirs. BayBank Norfolk, Deedham, Ma. Mem. Wellesley Town meeting , 1973—; Rep. Town Com., Wellesley; sec. Wellesley Free Libr. Needs Com., 1974-76; exec. com. Wellesley Free Libr. Centennial Fund, 1983-86. Mem. Jr. League of Boston, Denver and Phila., Inc., Boston Symphony Vol. Assn., Nat. Fedn. of Bus. (Mass. guardian adv. coun. 1987—), Smith Coll. Club (pres. 1975-77, v.p. 1973-75), Vincent Club, Union Club. Home: 109 Edmunds Rd Wellesley Hills MA 02181 Office: Diamond Machining Tech. 85 Hayes Memorial Dr Marlborough MA 01752

POWELL, ERNESTINE BREISCH, retired lawyer; b. Moundsville, W.Va., Feb. 16, 1906; d. Ernest Elmer and Belle (Wallace) Breisch; student Dayton YMCA Law Sch., 1929; m. Roger K. Powell, Nov. 15, 1935; children—R. Keith (dec.), Diane L.D., Bruce W. Admitted to Ohio bar, 1929; tax analyst tax dept. Wall, Cassell & Groneweg, Dayton, Ohio, 1929-31; practiced law, 1931-40; gen. counsel for Dayton Jobbers and Mfrs. Assn., 1931-41; mem. firm Powell, Powell & Powell, Columbus, Ohio, 1944-86, ret. Ohio chmn. Nat. Woman's Party, Washington, 1950-51, nat. chmn., 1953, hon. nat. chmn. Pres. vol. activities com. Columbus State Sch., 1960-61, mem. bd. trustees, 1957-59. Mem. Nat. Assn. Women Lawyers, Am., Ohio, Columbus bar assns., Nat. Soc. Arts and Letters (pres. Columbus chpt. 1963-64), Nat. Lawyers Club (charter mem.), Nat. Mus. Women in Arts (charter mem.). Co-author: Tax Ideas, 1955; Estate Tax Techniques, 1956—. Editor-in-chief: Women Lawyers Jour., 1943-45. Office: 1382 Neil Ave PO Box 8010 Columbus OH 43201

POWELL, GEORGE EVERETT, JR., motor freight company executive; b. Kansas City, Mo., June 12, 1926; s. George Everett and Hilda (Brown) P.; m. Mary Catherine Kuehn, Aug. 26, 1947; children: George Everett III, Nicholas K., Richardson K., Peter E. Student, Northwestern U. With Riss & Co., Inc., Kansas City, Mo., 1947-52, treas., 1950-52; with Yellow Freight System, Inc., Kansas City, Mo., 1952—, pres., 1957-68, chmn. bd., 1968—; pres. Yellow Freight Systems, Inc. of Del., Overland Park, Kans., 1987—; dir. 1st Nat. Charter Corp., Butler Mfg. Co. Trustee, mem. exec. com. Mid-West Research Inst., Kansas City, Mo., from 1961, chmn. bd. trustees, from 1968; bd. govs. Kansas City Art Inst., from 1964, chmn. bd. trustees, 1973-75. Served with USNR, 1944-46. Mem. Kansas City C. of C. (bd. dirs. 1964-68). Office: Yellow Freight System Inc Del PO Box 7563 Overland Park KS 66207 *

POWELL, GEORGE EVERETT, III, trucking company executive; b. Kansas City, Mo., Oct. 18, 1948; s. George Evertt Jr. and Mary Catherine (Kuehn) P.; m. Wendy Jarman, July 29, 1972; children: Jessica Jarman, Ashley Sinclair. BSBA, Ind. U., 1970. From planning analyst trainee to pres. Yellow Freight System Inc., Overland Park, Kans., 1971—, also bd. dirs. Chmn. Kansas City Pub. TV; chmn. Kansas City Target; mem. Young Pres.'s Orgn., Powell Family Found. Mem. Regular Common Carrier Conf. (bd. govs.), Kansas City Country Club. Home: 5801 Ward Pkwy Kansas City MO 64113 Office: Yellow Freight System Inc 10990 Roe Ave Overland Park KS 66207

POWELL, GEORGE GERARD, manufacturing executive; b. Mar. 30, 1920; s. John and Catherine Powell; m. Fay Muriel Richardson, 1944 (dec. 1975); children: Scott Richardson, Pamela Fay, Glen Geoffrey; m. Isabelle Harrison, 1976. Founder East Coast Sales and Svc., Inc., 1952; pres. Lourdes Industries, Inc., 1968—. Recipient Gen. Dynamics Supplier of Month award. Mem. Nat. Assn. Mfrs., Sky Island Club, Sands Point Golf Club, Deepdale Club. Office: Lourdes Industries Inc 65 Hoffman Ave Hauppauge NY 11788

POWELL, JAMES BOBBITT, biomedical laboratories executive, pathologist; b. Burlington, N.C., Aug. 28, 1938; s. Thomas Edward and Sophia (Sharpe) P.; m. Pamela Oughton, Sept. 12, 1969 (div. Sept. 1979); 1 child, Daphne Oughton; m. Anne Ellington, Oct. 20, 1984; children: James Bobbitt (dec.), John Banks. B.A., Va. Mil. Inst., 1960; M.D., Duke U., 1964. Diplomate Am. Bd. Pathology. Intern, Duke U. Med. Ctr., Durham, N.C., 1964-65; resident Cornell Med. Ctr., N.Y.C., 1965-67, Englewood Hosp., N.J., 1967-69; founder Biomed. Labs., Burlington, 1969—, pres., 1969—; dir. Carolina Biol. Supply Co., Burlington, First South Bank, Burlington, First South Bank, N.C. Trust Co., Greensboro. Contbr. articles to sci. publs. Trustee Elon Coll. (N.C.), 1981—; bd. overseers Duke U. Comprehensive Health Ctr. Served as maj. M.C., U.S. Army, 1969-72. Fellow Am. Soc. Clin. Pathologists, Coll. Am. Pathologists; mem. AMA, Young Pres. Orgn. Republican. Club: Alamance Country (Burlington). Home: 2307 York Rd Burlington NC 27215 Office: Roche Biomed Labs 430 Spring St Burlington NC 27215

POWELL, JOE A., law office administrator; b. Palestine, Tex., June 7, 1944; s. Frank K. and Kathleen Ione (Tinsley) P.; m. Judy Carol Crain, May 22, 1964; children: Jody M., Jason A. BBA, Sam Houston State U., 1966, MBA, 1968. Instr. Tyler (Tex.) Jr. Coll., 1968-69; system auditor U. Tex., Austin, 1969-73; asst. v.p. for bus. affairs, assoc. dir. of athletics for fin. U. Tex., San Antonio, 1973-82; office adminstr. Groce Locke & Hebdon P.C., San Antonio, 1982—. Mem. Assn. Legal Adminstrs. (pres. Alamo chpt. 1983). Republican. Mem. Ch. Christ. Club: Monday Morning Quarterback of San Antonio (bd. dirs. 1983—). Office: Groce Locke & Hebdon PC 2000 Frost Bank Tower San Antonio TX 78205

POWELL, JOHN KEY, life insurance underwriter, estate planner; b. Dallas, Dec. 14, 1925; s. Floyd Berkeley and Eloise (Sadler) P.; m. Ann Penniman, July 14, 1950; children: Nena Ann, Scott Key, Elliott Edward. Student, U. Ala., 1946-47, 49-50, So. Meth. U., 1947-48; cert., Inst. Ins. Mktg., So. Meth. U., 1954-55; cert., Am. Coll Life Underwriters, 1972. CLU. Ins. agt. Tuscaloosa, Ala., 1949-56; asst. gen. agt. John Hancock Mut. Life Ins. Co., Lubbock, Tex., 1956-57; asst. supr. of gen. agys. John Hancock Mut. Life Ins. Co., Boston, 1957-59; gen. agt. John Hancock Mut. Life Ins. Co., Columbia, S.C., 1959-85; pres., chief exec. officer First Sun Fin. Services Corp., Columbia, 1987—, also chmn. bd.; mem. adv. bd. NCNB-S.C. Pres. Cen. Carolina Community Found., chmn. Ctr. for Cancer Treatment and Research; bd. dirs. Salvation Army, Columbia. 1985—. Served with AC, U.S. Army, 1943-45. Mem. Am. Soc. CLU's (Golden Key Soc.), Million Dollar Round Table (life), Greater Columbia C. of C. (bd. dirs. 1978-81). Republican. Presbyterian. Lodge: Rotary (local pres. 1985-86). Home: 212 Holliday Rd Columbia SC 29223 Office: First Sun Fin Svcs Corp 1401 Main St Ste 700 Columbia SC 29201

POWELL, JOY LEE (BOK SIN LEE), antique dealer, importer; b. Pyong-Yang, Korea, Jan. 29, 1936; came to U.S., 1956, naturalized, 1962; d. Yong Joon and Chun Jai Lee; m. Jimmy Wayne Powell, Sept. 24, 1960; children—Chn Jai Lee, Miran Victoria. Student Internat. Speech Coll., Pusan, Korea, 1952; Nat. U. Pusan, 1953-55, McMurry Coll., Abilene, Tex., 1956-58; B.A., Wayland Baptist U., Plainview, Tex., 1966; postgrad. Central State Coll., Okla., 1967-68. Cert. antique appraiser and consultant. Nurse, Rok Med. Sch., Pusan, 1950-53; news announcer Pusan Radio Sta., Korea, 1953; sec., choir organizer chaplain's office U.S. Army div. Hqdrs., Pusan, 1954-56, Meth. Mission, Pusan, 1955-56, U.S. A.S.C. Office, Floydada, Tex., 1958, Am. U., Washington, 1958-60; with Washington Post, U.S. Acad. Sci., 1960; survey taker Pub. Schs. Plainview, Tex., 1965-66; tchr. Oklahoma City Sch. Systems, 1968-70; owner Internat. Antiques, Fairfax, Va., 1973—. Contbr. articles to profl. jours., Contbr. (poetry) New Voices in American Poetry, 1978. Contbr. poems and essays to Korean periodicals. Mem. Mang Hiang, Internat. Platform Assn., NOW, Nat. Trust for Hist. Preservation, Smithsonian Assocs. Nat. Hist. Preservation. Mem. Nat. Bus. Assn., Better World Soc., Women's Mus., World Affairs Council Washington, Nat. Assn. Female Execs., Internat. Student House. Avocations: art; painting; music; writing; swimming. Home and Office: PO Box 185 Chantilly VA 22021

POWELL, LARSON MERRILL, investment advisory service executive; b. Pittsfield, Mass., Mar. 8, 1932; s. Harry LeRoy and Elsie Madeline (Larson) P.; m. Anne C. Millett, Dec. 8, 1956; children: Larson Merrill, Anne Coleman, Miles Sloan. AB Harvard U., 1954; student Columbia U. Law Sch., 1957-59. News editor, reporter Boston Daily Globe, 1954, 56-57; security analyst Moody's Investors Service, N.Y.C., 1959-62, regional mgr., 1964-67, v.p., 1967-68; pres. instl. investment mgmt. div. Anchor Corp., Elizabeth, N.J., 1968-70; pres. Res. Research, Ltd., N.Y.C., 1971—, Powell Publs. Corp., N.Y.C., 1980—. Bd. mgrs. W.Side br. YMCA of Greater N.Y., 1970-79, mem.-at-large citywide bd., 1976-79; chmn. men's com. Am. Mus. Natural History, 1970-72; mem. Boro of Manhattan Community Planning Bd. 7, 1966-69; bd. dirs. Children's Home of Portland, 1986—, Sweetser Children's Home, 1988—, Episcopal Camp and Conf. Center, 1978-80. Served with AUS, 1954-56. Fellow Fin. Analysts Fedn.; mem. Internat. Soc. Fin. Analysts, N.Y. Soc. Security Analysts, N.Y. Newsletter Pubs. Assn. Episcopalian. Club: Harvard (N.Y.C.); Cumberland (Portland, Maine). Editor, pub. Powell Monetary Analyst, 1971—, Powell Gold Industry Guide and Internat. Mining Anlayst, 1976—, Powell Alert, 1980-88. Home: 413 Blackstrap Rd Falmouth ME 04105 Office: PO Box 4135 Sta A Portland ME 04101

POWELL, MELINDA SUE, food company executive; b. West Islip, N.Y., Feb. 7, 1963; d. Henry Stuart and Barbara L. (Thompson) P. BBA, U. Vt., 1985. Sales rep. Hershey Chocolate Co., Burlington, Vt., 1985-87, dist. account supr., 1987—. Republican. Home: 851 Coventry Ln #203 Norwood MA 02062

POWELL, MILES, JR., investment and business broker; b. Mt. Holly, N.J., June 27, 1926; s. Miles and Grace (Taylor) P.; m. M. Jeanne Parker, Aug. 28, 1948; children: Phyllis, Kimberlee, Kristin. B Chem. Engring., U. Del., 1950. From salesman to product mgr. E.I. DuPont & Co., Wilmington, Del., 1950-61; from sales mgr. to exec. v.p., bd. dirs. Chemplast, Inc., Wayne, N.J., 1961-82; v.p. Norton Co., Wayne and Worcester, Mass., 1982-84, Chem. Fabrics, Manchester, N.H., 1984-85; pres., owner Powell Assocs., Medford, N.J., 1985—, Siltef, Inc., Medford, 1985—; bd. dirs. Standard Tool, Lyndhurst, N.J. With USAAF, 1944-45. Mem. Soc. Plastics Engrs. (life, pres. R.I.-S.E. Mass. sect. 1955), Soc. Plastic Industries (life, bd. dirs. 1974-78, pres. fluoropolymer div. 1974-76), Plastic Pioneers (life), Plastics Acad. (life), West Hudson Mfrs. Assn. (various offices), Pine Valley Golf Club (N.J.), Jupiter Hills Golf Club (Fla.). Republican. Baptist. Home: 19351 SE Lakeside Dr Tequesta FL 33469 Office: 1-3 N Main St PO Box 68 Medford NJ 08055

POWELL, RAMON JESSE, lawyer, government official; b. Macon, Mo., Mar. 1, 1935; s. Robert Evan and Blanche Odella (Dry) P.; A.B. in Econs. with distinction, U. Mo., 1957; postgrad. (Fulbright scholar) U. Brussels, 1957-58; J.D., Harvard U., 1965. Admitted to D.C. bar, 1966, Va. bar, 1975, U.S. Supreme Ct. bar, 1975; atty., advisor Office Gen. Counsel, Office Chief Engrs., Dept. Army, 1965-70; gen. counsel U.S. Water Resources Council, Washington, 1970-74, 80-82; asst. counsel for interagy. relations Office of Chief Counsel, Office of Chief of Engrs., Dept. Army, Washington, 1982-87, asst. chief counsel for legal services policy and programs, 1987—; sole practice law, Washington, 1975-76; pres., gen. counsel Leman Powell Assos., Inc., Alexandria, Va., 1976-80. Served as officer USAF, 1958-62. Mem. ABA, Fed. Bar Assn., D.C. Unified Bar, Bar Assn. D.C., Va. State Bar, Phi Beta Kappa, Omicron Delta Kappa, Delta Sigma Rho, Beta Theta Pi. Club: Nat. Lawyers. Office: Office Chief Engrs Dept Army 20 Massachusetts Ave NW Washington DC 20314

POWELL, RAYMOND WILLIAM, financial planner; b. Waterbury, Conn., June 17, 1944; s. Don C. and Kathryn (Linhard) P.; B.S., So. Conn. State Coll., New Haven, 1966, M.S., 1969; postgrad. U. Bridgeport (Conn.); m. Janet Yasinski, June 24, 1967; 1 son, Raymond Joseph. Pres., R.W. Powell Enterprises, Inc., fin. and tax cons., Waterbury, Conn., 1972—; dir.-owner Educators Tax Service, Watertown, 1972—, Powell's Acctg. Service, 1975—, Powell's Fin. Planning Service, 1977—. Vice chmn. Watertown Town Council, 1975-76. Cert. fin. planner; enrolled agt. Mem. Nat. Assn. Enrolled Agts., Internat. Assn. Fin. Planners, Am. Soc. Tax Cons., Conn. Assn. Enrolled Agts. Democrat. Author articles in field. Address: 293 Hamilton Ave Waterbury CT 06706

POWELL, ROBERT DOMINICK, lawyer; b. Bklyn., Mar. 30, 1942; s. Ralph and Dorothy Piccola; m. Pamela Van Horn, Aug. 19, 1978; 7 sons. BA, U. Pa., 1963; LLB, St. John's Sch. Law, 1966; LLM, Georgetown

U., 1978. Bar: N.Y. 1967, D.C. 1968, Md. 1974, U.S. Supreme Ct. 1972, U.S. Circuit Ct. Appeals (1st, 2d, 3d, 4th, 5th, 9th and 11th cirs.). Trial atty. FAA, 1966-68; assoc. Welch & Morgan, 1968-69; ptnr. Smith & Pepper, Washington, 1969-72, Powell & Becker, Washington, 1972-73, Sanders, Schnabel, Joseph & Powell, Washington, 1976-82, Joseph, Powell, McDermott & Reiner, Washington, 1982-86; prin. Law Office of Robert D. Powell, P.C., 1986—; pvt. practice law, Washington, 1973-76; gen. counsel Nat. Bus. Aircraft Assn., 1970-87. Author: (poetry) Faint and Low, Soft and Sweet, 1968. Mem. instnl. com. working group Ctr. High Speed Comml. Transp. Mem. ABA (forum com. on air and space law), InterAm. Bar Assn., Fed. Bar Assn., N.Y. State Bar Assn., D.C. Bar Assn., Md. Bar Assn., Montgomery County Bar Assn., Internat. Law Soc., Am. Judicature Soc., Assn. Trial Lawyers Am., Civil Aviation Med. Assn., Internat. Aviation Club, Batelle Inst. High Speed Comml. Flight Working Group. Republican. Episcopalian. Clubs: Aero (Washington), Wings. Lodge: Rotary. Home: 11109 Smokey Quartz Ln Potomac MD 20854 Office: 2033 M St NW Ste 703 Washington DC 20036

POWELL, ROBERT WENDELL, JR., financial executive; b. Potsdam, N.Y., June 1, 1930; m. Betty Ann Greer, Apr. 3, 1954. B.S., Yale U., 1952; M.B.A., Harvard U., 1956. With Martin Marietta Corp., Bethesda, Md., 1956—; treas. Martin Marietta Corp., 1980—, corporate v.p., 1985—. Trustee Severn Sch., Arnold, Md. Served to maj. USAF, 1952-54, ret. Res. Office: Martin Marietta Corp 6801 Rockledge Dr Bethesda MD 20817

POWELL, RODNEY EDSEL, paper company executive; b. Meridian, Miss., Apr. 17, 1953; s. Edsel Herman and Eloise (Lunsford) P.; m. Mary Kathryn Langfitt, Dec. 17, 1974; children: April Brooke, Ashley Nicole. BEE, Miss. State U., 1975. Registered profl. engr. Ala., Fla., N.C., Miss., Tex. Engr. Rust Engring. Co., Birmingham, Ala., 1975-77; design leader Rust Engring. Co., Birmingham, 1977-79; sr. design leader Rust Internat., Birmingham, 1979-82, staff engr., 1982-83, sr. staff engr., 1983-85; regional mfg. mgr. Bailey Controls Co., Atlanta, 1985-86, nat. mfg. mgr., 1986-87, mgr. regional sales, 1987-88; supt. process control Georgia Pacific Co., Atlanta, 1988-89, mgr. engring. and process control, 1989—. Contbr. articles to profl. Mem. fin. com. Dawson Meml. Ch., Birmingham, Ala., 1976-77. Mem. Instrument Soc. Am. (Young Engr. Yr. 1979, 81), Nat. Soc. Profl. Engrs., Ala. Soc. Profl. Engrs. (v.p. 1981-82, Young Engr. 1982), Eta Kappa Nu, Theta Tau. Home: 108 Woodshire Dr Crossett AR 71635 Office: Ga Pacific Co 100 Papermill Rd Crossett AR 71635

POWELL, SHARON LEE, social welfare organization administrator; b. Portland, Oreg., July 25, 1940; d. James Edward Carson and Betty Jane (Singleton) Powell. BS, Oreg. State U., 1962; MEd, Seattle U., 1971. Dir. outdoor edn. Mapleton (Oreg.) Pub. Schs., 1962-63; field dir. Totem Girl Scout Council, Seattle, 1963-68, asst. dir. field services, 1968-70, dir. field services, 1970-72; dir. pub. relations Girl Scout Council of Tropical Fla., Miami, 1972-74; exec. dir. Homestead Girl Scout Council, Lincoln, Nebr., 1974-78, Moingona Girl Scout Coun., Des Moines, 1978—. Pres. agy dirs. assn. United Way of Cen. Iowa, 1987-88; mem. priorities com. United Way of Cen. Iowa, Des Moines, 1986—; mem. priority goals task group United Way Found., Des Moines, 1985—; capt. Drake U. Basketball Ticket Dr., Des Moines, 1983-87. Mem. Assn. Girl Scout Execs. (chair nat. conv. 1985—, nat. bd. dirs. 1985-87, mem. nat. nominating com. 1982-84, nat. treas. 1987—), AAUW, Urbandale C. of C. (bd. dirs., chair edn. com.), Des Moines Obedience Tng. Club (treas. 1987—), Des Moines Golden Retriever Club, Chi Omega Alumni Assn. Democrat. Club: Altrusa (Des Moines) (treas. 1983-85, community service chair 1986-87). Office: Moingona Girl Scout Coun 10715 Hickman Rd Des Moines IA 50322

POWELL, TIMOTHY WOOD, marketing executive, consultant; b. Phila., June 22, 1949; s. James Rennie and Elizabeth Clay (Thurman) P.; children: Michael Ross, David Alexander. BA, Yale U., 1971, M in Pub. and Pvt. Mgmt., 1979. Sr. procedures analyst State of N.J., Trenton, 1975-76; sr. fin. analyst State of N.Y., N.Y.C., 1976-77; sr. cons. Peat, Marwick, Mitchell, N.Y.C., 1979-83; mgr. nat. mktg. Coopers & Lybrand, N.Y.C., 1983—; bd. dirs. WindRose Group Inc. Monsey, N.Y. Mem. Am. Mktg. Assn. (chmn. case devel. com. 1985-87, service mktg. planning council 1987—). Home: 224 First Ave New York NY 10009 Office: Coopers & Lybrand 1700 Broadway New York NY 10019

POWELL, WILLIAM ARNOLD, JR., banker; b. Verbena, Ala., July 7, 1929; s. William Arnold and Sarah Frances (Baxter) P.; m. Barbara Ann O'Donnell, June 16, 1956; children: William Arnold III, Barbara Ann, Susan Frances, Patricia Baxter. BSBA, U. Ala., 1953; grad., La. State U. Sch. Banking of South, 1966. With Am. South Bank, N.A., Birmingham, Ala., 1953—, asst. v.p., 1966, v.p., 1967, v.p., br. supr., 1968-72, sr. v.p., br. supr., 1972-73, exec. v.p., 1973-79, pres., 1979-83, vice chmn. bd., 1983—, also bd. dirs.; pres First Nat. Bank Birmingham, 1983—, also bd. dirs.; pres. AmSouth Bancorp., 1979—; bd. dirs. AmSouth Mortgage Co., Inc., AmSouth Bancorp. Bd. dirs. Am. Cancer Soc., Birmingham Better Bus. Bur.; pres. Sch. Banking of South; trustee, chmn. Ala. Ind. Colls.; bd. visitors, U. Ala.; bd. dirs., sec.-treas. Warrior-Tombigbee Devel. Assn., Met. Arts Council, Sch. Fine Arts Found., Discovery Place, Brookwood Med. Ctr.-AMI, Big Brothers/Big Sisters of Greater Birmingham; campaign chmn. United Way, 1987. Served to lt. AUS, 1954-56. Mem. Birmingham Area C. of C. (pres., bd. dirs.), Birmingham Hist. Soc. (bd. dirs.). Clubs: The Club, Downtown, Mountain Brook, Riverchase Country, Birmingham Country, Green Valley Country (Birmingham). Lodge: Kiwanis (Birmingham) (past pres.). Home: 3309 Thornton Dr Birmingham AL 35226 Office: AmSouth Bancorp PO Box 11007 Birmingham AL 35288

POWER, ELIZABETH HENRY, marketing consultant; b. Hickory, N.C., Sept. 28, 1953; d. William Henry Power and Kathryn Otis (Smith) Nelson. Cert. in creative writing, N.C. Sch. Arts, 1971; BA in Sociology, U. N.C., Greensboro, 1977. With adoption and foster home recruitment Davidson County Dept. Human Svcs., Nashville, 1980-81; behavioral cons. Nutri-System Weight Loss Ctr., Nashville, 1982-84; corp. sec., cons. Quantum Leap Cons., Inc., Nashville, 1984-86; v.p. mktg. Open Communication, Inc., Nashville, 1987-88; pres., owner E. Power & Assocs., Brentwood, Tenn., 1980-84, 86—; seminar presenter, 1977—; cons. GM/Saturn, 1988—. Author: Getting the Fat Out of Your Head So It Stays Off Your Body, 1987, Relocation, survival and the South, 1989, Changimus Maximus Rx: Taking Charge of Change, 1989; co-author, editor: Circle of Love: Child Personal Safety, 1984. Vol. West Chester Women's Resource Ctr., West Chester, Pa., 1977; vol. instr. theology Lay Acad. Episcopal Diocese Western N.C., Asheville, 1976-77; mem. Burke County Coun. on Status of Women, Morganton, N.C., 1977-79, sec., 1978; vol. Western N.C. Flood Com., 1977-78; exec. dir. N.C. Rape Crisis Assn., Raleigh, 1979, Foothills Mental Health Ctr., Morganton, 1978-79; mem. task force, writer, convener, facilitator N.C. Gov.'s Conf. on Mental Health, 1979; trainer, vol. Rape House Crisis Ctr., Nashville, 1979-81; vol., trainer Rape and Sexual Abuse Ctr., Nashville, 1981-82, bd. dirs., 1981-82; mem. quality circles steering com. Tenn Dept. Human Svcs., 1980-81; program cons. Women's Resource and Assistance Program, Jackson, Tenn., 1981-82; vol. devel. cons. AGAPE Christian Counseling Ctr., Nashville, 1988. Recipient numerous awards N.C. Dept. Mental Health/Mental Retardation, 1979, State of N.C., 1979, Central Nashville Optimist Club, 1982, Waco YWCA, Waco, Tex., 1985. Mem. Tenn. Orgn. Profl. Speakers, Nat. Assn. Female Execs. Democrat. Office: 9000 Church St Brentwood TN 37027

POWER, FRANK RAYMOND, transportation company executive; b. N.Y.C., Aug. 12, 1938; s. Frank and Kathleen Bridget (Raymond) P.; m. Marie Frances Lynch, Oct. 27, 1962; children: Kathleen, Elizabeth, Edward. BCE, Manhattan Coll., 1960; MS, Cornell U., 1964; LLB, NYU, 1966, postgrad., 1968-70. Bar: N.Y. 1966; registered profl. engr. Project engr. Foster Wheeler Corp., Livingston, N.J., 1962-65; lawyer Am. Ind. Oil Co., Livingston, 1966-70; gen. mgr. Japan ops. Am. Ind. Oil Co., Tokyo, 1970-73; mgr. mktg. planning Am. Ind. Oil Co., N.Y.C., 1973-75, mgr. bus. planning, 1976-78; dir. devel. R.J. Reynolds Industries, Winston-Salem, N.C., 1976; v.p. bus. planning Aminoil Inc., Houston, 1978-84; v.p. corp. planning Sea-Land Corp., Edison, N.J., 1985—; lectr. Sophia U., Tokyo, 1971-73, U. Houston, 1984-85, MIT, 1987. Contbr. articles to profl. jours. Mem. Houston Planning Forum, Asia Soc., Japan Soc., Petroleum Club, Tau Beta Pi, Chi Epsilon, Phi Kappa Theta. Republican. Home: 23 Olsen Dr Warren NJ 07060 Office: Sea Land Corp 10 Parsonage Rd Edison NJ 08817

POWER, KENNETH D., utilities company executive; b. Weeping Water, Nebr., Dec. 12, 1927; m. Jane Ann Osborne, June 20, 1953; children: Joan, Mary, John. BA in Bus., Cornell Coll., 1952. Installer Northwestern Bell, Davenport, Iowa, 1952-53, traffic chief, 1953-56; dist. supr. Northwestern Bell, Waterlo, Iowa, 1956-58, Mason City, Iowa, 1958-59; dist. mgr. Northwestern Bell, Sioux City, Iowa, 1959-60; bus. office supr. Northwestern Bell, Omaha, 1960-63; staff rep. AT&T, N.Y.C., 1961-63; div. mgr. Northwestern Bell, Mpls., 1963-64; gen. collecting employment coord. Northwestern Bell, Omaha, 1966-67; gen. comml. mgr. Northwestern Bell, Mpls., 1967-68, gen. ops. mgr., 1968-72; sec., treas. Northwestern Bell, Omaha, 1972-78, v.p. support svcs., 1978-81, v.p. residence, 1981, v.p. distbn. svcs., 1981-83, v.p. personnel, 1983-84, v.p. corp. and H.R., 1984-87, v.p., chief exec. officer, 1987—; bd. councillor Al-Sar-Ban; bd. dirs. Belluvue Coll., FirsTier Nat. Bank. Mem. United Way of the Midlands; bd. dirs. Western Heritage Mus. With USN, 1946-48. Mem. NCCJ, Nebraskans for Pub. TV, Nebr. Telophone Assn., Nebr. C. of C. (pres. local chpt.), Nebr. Futures, Omaha Club, Plaza Club, Happy Hollow County Club. Office: Northwestern Bell 100 S 19-1200 Dodge Omaha NE 68102

POWER, RICHARD GEARY, pharmaceuticals executive; b. Darlington, Wis., May 20, 1929; s. Richard James and Prudence Mary (McGuire) P.; m. Barbara Ann Gordon, Nov. 24, 1951; children: Susan Power Miller, Kathleen Power Holmes, Jennifer Jeanne, Richard Theodore. BA cum laude, Loras Coll., 1951; BS, U. Wis., 1955. Mgr. new product mktg. Smith, Kline and French Labs., Phila., 1955-70; dir. internat. mktg. Warner Lambert Co., Ft. Lauderdale, Fla., 1971-72; dir. bus. devel. Rohm and Haas, Phila., 1972-74; dir. corp. devel. G.D. Searle Co., Skokie, Ill., 1974-78; v.p. corp. devel. Ortho Pharm div. Johnson and Johnson Co., Raritan, N.J., 1978-80; pres. R.G. Power Assocs. Inc., Princeton, N.J., 1980—; ptnr. Hayes and Griffith Inc., Chgo., 1988—; pres. Pharmatec Inc., Princeton, 1983-86, HGP Corp., Princeton, 1987—; bd. dirs. HEM Research, Phila. Republican. Roman Catholic. Home and Office: 49 Balcort Dr Princeton NJ 08540

POWERS, CARSON HARDIE, financial services executive, consultant; b. N.Y.C., Nov. 24, 1934; s. Harry Grell and Gladys Lillian (Mars) P.; m. Jon Grenville Dodson, May 4, 1957 (div. May 1978); children—Torii Heath, Elliott Grell; m. Kathleen Ann Osage, July 1, 1978. A.B. in Econs., Princeton U., 1956; postgrad. Harvard U., 1971. Media buyer Cunningham & Walsh, Inc., N.Y.C., 1960-62; account exec. Dancer-Fitzgerald-Sample, Inc., N.Y.C., 1963-68; v.p., dir. mktg. Chem. Bank, N.Y.C., 1968-79; nat. dir. svcs. mktg. Price Waterhouse, N.Y.C., 1979-83, dir. smaller bus. practice dev l., Washington, 1983-85; pres. C.H. Powers & Co., Inc., Upper Montclair, N.J., 1985-87; cons. Downey, Weeks, Toomey, Inc., N.Y.C.; mng. dir. R.S. Carmichael & Co., Inc., White Plains, N.Y., 1986—. Rep., Town Meeting, Greenwich, Conn., 1974-77; trustee Greenwich Library, 1975-77; class fund agt. Harvard Bus. Sch., Boston, 1982-84. Served to lt. USNR, 1956-60. Presbyterian. Clubs: Princeton of N.Y., University, St. Andrews Soc. N.Y. State. Home: 295 N Mountain Ave Upper Montclair NJ 07043

POWERS, ELDON NATHANIEL, data processing executive; b. Wichita, Kans., Feb. 14, 1932; s. Ernie Lee and Bessie Othella (Loomis) P.; m. Betty Jean Zeigler, Sept. 4, 1954; children: Rebekah Jean, Robert John, Samuel Tyler. Student, Friends U., 1950-51; BA in Missions, Central Bible Coll., 1954; BA in Modern Lang. Edn., Evangel Coll., 1963; MS in Math., Tulsa U., 1971. Pastor Assembly of God Ch., Hays, Kans., 1955-60; data processing technician Gospel Pub. House, Springfield, Mo., 1960-63; data processing analyst Amoco Prodn. Co., Oklahoma City, 1963-65; research scientist Amoco Prodn. Co., Tulsa, 1965-67, staff research scientist, 1968-81; sr. system analyst Electro Mech. Research, Bloomington, Minn., 1967-68; mgr. info. service Fox Drilling Co., Tulsa, 1981-82; pres. ENP Software, Inc., Sapulpa, Okla., 1982—; cons. in field. Contbr. articles to profl. jours.; author various computer programs. Adv. bd. Cen. Okla. Vocat. Tech. Sch., Sapulpa, 1986—. Mem. Computer Oriented Geol. Soc., Internat. Assn. Math. Geology. Republican. Methodist. Office: ENP Software Inc 1215 Ridgeoak Cir PO Box 370 Sapulpa OK 74067

POWERS, HENRY MARTIN, JR., oil company executive; b. Bath, Maine, July 18, 1932; s. Henry Martin and Eva (Saunders) P.; m. Hepzibah Hinchey Reed, June 20, 1959; children—Henry Martin III, Carlton Reed. B.S., Maine Maritime Acad., 1954. Marine engr. Am. Export Lines, N.Y.C., 1954-58; staff engr. Bull & Roberts Inc., N.Y.C., 1958-59; gen. sales mgr. Williams Bros., Inc., Portland, Maine, 1959-61; v.p. C.H. Sprague & Son Co., Boston, 1961-72; pres. C.H. Sprague & Son Co., 1972—, chmn. bd., 1987—, also dir.; dir. Portsmouth Trust Co., N.H., Petroleum Heat & Power Co. R.I., Shanley Corp., Strawbery Banke Inc., First N.H. Banks, Seaward Constrn. Co. Vice pres. Seacoast United Fund, 1967-69; chmn. fuels, energy com. New England Council, 1974-75; pres. Portsmouth Council, 1966-67; bd. visitors Maine Maritime Acad. Served to lt. USNR, 1956-58. Mem. Navy League, Mechanic Fire Soc. Clubs: Mason. (Boston), Fort Hill (Boston), Algonquin (Boston); Taratine (Bangor, Maine); Cumberland (Portland). Home: 68 River Rd Box 261 Stratham NH 03885 Office: C H Sprague & Son Co 1 Parade Mall Portsmouth NH 03801

POWERS, HOWARD FRANCIS, pharmaceutical company executive; b. Boston, May 30, 1932; s. Howard and Mary F. (Sullivan) P.; children: Howard Francis, Jennifer, Bradford. B.S., Boston Coll., 1958; M.B.A., Harvard U., 1960. With Merck & Co. Inc., Rahway, N.J.; sr. v.p. Merck & Co. Inc. Served with U.S. Army, 1952-54. Home: 1 B Markham Manor Princeton NJ Office: Merck & Co Inc PO Box 2000 Rahway NJ 07065

POWERS, JAMES FRANCIS, financial executive; b. Worcester, Mass., Aug. 15, 1938; s. Joseph A. and Anita (Gaulin) P.; m. Joanne DeFeudis, June 18, 1961; children: Kim Marie, Lori Jean, James F. Jr. BSBA, Holy Cross Coll., 1961; MBA, Babson Coll., Wellesley, Mass., 1969. C.P.A., Mass. Various fin. positions United Brands, Boston, 1961-74, corp. controller, 1974-77; v.p., controller LTV Corp., Dallas, 1977-83, v.p., treas., 1983-86, sr. v.p., chief fin. officer, 1986—, also bd. dirs. Served with U.S. Army, 1962-63. Mem. Am. Inst. C.P.A.'s, Mass. Soc. C.P.A.'s, Fin. Execs. Inst. Office: LTV Corp 2001 Ross Ave Dallas TX 75201

POWERS, JAMES FRANCIS, financial planner; b. Natick, Mass., Sept. 24, 1931; s. James C. and Ruth C. (McMahon) P.; m. Kathleen M. Crowley, May 20, 1972; children: Rachel M., Janet R. BA, Boston Coll., 1956, MA in Philosophy, 1957. Lic. theologist, Ga.; joined S.J., 1951, ordained priest Roman Cath. Ch., 1963. Priest Boston, 1963-71; with sales and mktg. dept C.H. Dexter Div. Dexter Corp., Windsor Licks, Conn., 1971-82; mfr's rep. WEB Corp., Stone Mountain, Ga., 1982-83; fin. planner Planned Asset Devel., Inc., Norcross, Ga., 1983-84, Conceptual Fin. Adv. Corp., Atlanta, 1984—. Bd. dirs. Seed, Inc., Decatur, Ga., 1988—. Mem. Inst. for Cert. Fin. Planners, Internat. Assn. for Fin. Planning (bd. dirs. 1988—). Democrat. Home: 3693 Marlborough Dr Tucker GA 30084 Office: Conceptual Fin Adv Corp 1100 Johnson Ferry Rd Ste 1080 Atlanta GA 30342

POWERS, JEFFREY KEVIN, risk manager, safety consultant; b. Milw., Oct. 29, 1957; s. Roy R. and Kathleen D. (Dentice) P.; m. Lisa Ann Scheible, June 27, 1987. BBA in Fin., U. Wis., Whitewater, 1979, MS, 1981. Cert. safety exec., hazard control mgr., assoc. safety profl. Comml. underwriter Gen. Casualty Ins. Co., Madison, Wis., 1979-80; safety mgr., cost acct. Motor Castings Co., West Allis, Wis., 1983; mgr. safety engring. and adminstrn. Nat. Tooling and Machining Assn., Ft. Washington, Md., 1983-84; mgr. corp. safety and workers compensation Price Bros. Co., Dayton, Ohio, 1984—; mem. safety adv. bd. Clement Communications, Concordville, Pa., 1984—. Mem. Am. Soc. Safety Engrs. (pres. KittyHawk chpt. 1987-88, del. to All-Ohio Coun. 1987—), Affiliate Socs. Coun., Am. Nat. Standards Inst. (subcom. chmn. 1983-85, mem. Occupational Safety and Health Act coordinating com. 1983—), soc. Ohio Safety Engrs., Hunters Unltd. (treas. 1983—), Dayton C. of C. (labor relations coun.), Lambda Chi Alpha. Home: 4855 Bonnie Rd Kettering OH 45440 Office: Price Bros Co 367 W 2d St Dayton OH 45401

POWERS, JOHN AUSTIN, alcoholic beverage company executive; b. N.Y.C., Oct. 24, 1926; s. Francis A. and Meta Marie (Touwsma) P.; m. Eileen Herlihy, Mar. 23, 1962; children: Maribeth, John Austin, Jennifer, Cecilia. B.A., St. Peters Coll., 1950; A.M.P., Harvard U., 1980. With McCann-Erickson, Inc., 1957-73; chmn. McCann-Erickson, Inc., U.K., 1967-70; pres. McCann-Erickson, Inc., Europe, 1967-71; v.p. internat. McCann-Erickson, Inc., 1968-70; pres. McCann-Erickson, Inc., U.S.A., 1971-73; v.p. Heublein, Inc., Farmington, Conn., 1973-78; group exec. wines group Heublein, Inc., 1975-78, sr. v.p. alcoholic beverages, 1979-81, pres., chief exec. officer, 1982-86, chmn., chief exec. officer, 1986-87, chmn. bd., 1987—; chmn., chief exec. officer United Vintners, Inc., San Francisco, 1973-78; sr. v.p. alcoholic beverages United Vintners, Inc., 1978-81; bd. dirs. Hartford Nat. Corp., Hartford Steam Boiler and Inspection Co., The Pillsbury Co.; dep. chmn. Internat Distillers & Vintners, Ltd. Bd. dirs. Hosp.; regent U. Hartford; trustee Hartford Grad. Ctr., Bus. Advisory Council, Skidmore Coll., Saratoga Springs, N.Y.; dir. San Francisco Ballet, 1975-77. Served to 2d lt. U.S. Army, 1944-46. Mem. Conn. Bus. and Industries Assn. (bd. dirs.). Clubs: Meadow (Southampton, N.Y.); Hartford Golf (West Hartford, Conn.). Office: Heublein Inc Munson Rd Farmington CT 06034-0388

POWERS, MARCUS EUGENE, lawyer; b. Cedarville, Ohio, Apr. 7, 1929; s. Frederick Armajo and Elizabeth Isabel (Rumbaugh) P. B.A., Ohio Wesleyan U., 1951; J.D. (Root-Tilden scholar), NYU, 1954, LL.M., 1958. Bar: Ohio 1954, N.Y. 1959, Calif. 1964. Asst. prof. law NYU Sch. Law, 1956-60; atty. Am. Brake Shoe Co., N.Y.C., 1959-63; asst. gen. counsel Dart Industries, Inc., Los Angeles, 1963-81; sr. v.p., gen. counsel Nat. Med. Enterprises, Inc., Los Angeles, 1981—; exec. v.p., sec. Health Care Property Investors Inc., Los Angeles, 1985-87. Served with U.S. Army, 1954-56. Mem. Los Angeles County Bar Assn. (past chmn. corp. law depts. sect.), Inst. Corp. Counsel (bd. govs., chmn. 1984-86), ABA (mem. Calif. com. on corp. law depts. 1981-86, chmn. com. 1985-86), Assn. of Bar ofCity of N.Y., Calif. State Coastal Conservancy, Phi Beta Kappa (pub.), Omicron Delta Kappa, Phi Delta Theta, Kappa Sigma, Pi Sigma Alpha, Theta Alpha Phi. Office: Nat Med Enterprises Inc 11620 Wilshire Blvd Los Angeles CA 90025

POWERS, MARK JAMES, economist, businessman; b. Mauston, Wis., Sept. 16, 1940; s. James Michael and Emma Agnes (Feldbruegge) P.; m. Josephine Ann Moriarty, June 13, 1964; children: James Michael, Sheila Marie. BS in Agrl. Edn., U. Wis., Platteville, 1963; MS in Agrl. Econs., U. Wis., 1966, PhD in Agrl. Econs., 1966. Asst. prof. econs. S.D. State U., Brookings, 1966-68, assoc. prof. econs., 1968-69; sr. v.p. research edn. Chgo. Merc. Exchange and Internat. Monetary Market, 1969-75; chief economist Commodities Futures Trading Commn., Washington, 1975-77; sr. v.p. dir. commodities Thomson McKinnon Securities, N.Y.C., 1977-80; pres., chief. exec. officer Powers Research Inc., Jersey City, 1980—; bd. dirs. Columbia U. Ctr. Future's Study, N.Y. Author: Inside the Financial Futures Markets, 1981, Getting Started In Commodity Futures Trading, 1983; editor: Jour. of Future Markets, 1982—. Recipient Disting. Alumnus award U. Wis., Platteville, 1979. Mem. Am. Assn. Agrl. Economists; mem. ABA (assoc.). Roman Catholic. Home: 57 Glenmere Dr Chatham NJ 07928 Office: Powers Rsch Inc 30 Montgomery St Jersey City NJ 07302

POWERS, PATRICK JOSEPH, III, corporate executive; b. Den Haag, The Netherlands, Sept. 6, 1957; s. Patrick Joseph Jr. and Maureen (McConeghy) P. BA in History, San Diego State U., 1980; postgrad., Taiwan Normal U., 1981-83. Exec. asst. Bechtel Inc., San Francisco, 1984-86; coordinator tng. Island Creek of China Coal Ltd., Shanxi, People's Republic of China, 1986-87, mgr. tng., 1987, mgr. tng. and safety, 1987—; dir. ATB Support Office, Beijing, 1988—. Office: Island Creek China Ltd, 19 Jianguomenwai #2401, Beijing People's Republic of China

POWERS, PATRICK WILLIAM, defense company owner, retired army officer, author; b. Honolulu, Mar. 21, 1924; s. Patrick Francis and Margaret Mary (Thompson) P.; m. Doris Mildred Hurt, Nov. 12, 1950; children: Robert Warren, Patricia Joanne, Laura Suzanne. BS in Mil. Engring., U.S. Mil. Acad., 1945; MSME, U. So. Calif., 1950. Commd. 2d lt. U.S. Army, 1945, advanced through grades to maj. gen., 1973; comdg. officer 56th arty. group U.S. Army, Schwaebisch Gmuend, Fed. Republic Germany, 1967-68; se. joint staff Hdqrs. Mil. Assistance Command U.S. Army, Vietnam, 1968-69, comdr. 1st inf. div., arty, 1970-72, dep. asst. chief staff ops. Hdqrs., 1970; comdg. gen. readiness region II U.S. Army, Ft. Dix., N.J., 1973-75; comdg. gen. test and evaluation command U.S. Army, Aberdeen Proving Ground, Md., 1975-78; ret. U.S. Army, 1978; pres. Test and Evaluation Internat., Bel Air, Md., 1969—, Test and Evaluation Internat. Svcs., Bel Air, 1984—; mng. dir. Tech. & Engring. Svcs. GmbH, Essen, Fed. Republic Germany, 1986—; exec. v.p. Shielding Technologies, Inc., Bel Air, 1987—. Author: A Guide to National Defense, 1964; developer miniature supersonic wind tunnel, 1952; contbr. to profl. publs. Decorated Disting. Svc. Medal, Legion of Merit with 3 oak leaf clusters, Disting. Flying Cross, Bronze Star medal, Air medal. Mem. Am. Def. Preparedness Assn., Assn. U.S. Army, Md. Golf and Country Club, Army-Navy-Air Force Country Club. Home: 6 McGregor Way Bel Air MD 21014 Office: Test & Evaluation Group 40 Bright Oaks Dr Bel Air MD 21014

POWERS, PETER SHELDON, plastics manufacturing executive; b. Elmira, N.Y., Nov. 20, 1951; s. Whitney Sheldon and Patricia (Lindau) P.; m. Debra Stegenga, Nov. 6, 1982. BSEE, N.C. State U., 1973; MBA, U. So. Miss., 1984. Project engr. Chattanooga (Tenn.) Glass Co., 1975-78; mfg. engr. Chattanooga Glas Co., Gulfport, Miss., 1978-81; sr. project engr. Baby Products div. Johnson & Johnson Corp., Royston, Ga., 1981-84; pres. Clearplass Containers, Lyons, N.Y., 1984-86, chmn. bd., 1986—. Mem. Soc. Plastics Industry (fin. mgmt. com.). Home: 4624 Hogback Hill Rd Palmyra NY 14522 Office: Clearplass Containers Inc 8700 Hills Rd Lyons NY 14489

POWERS, RONALD GEORGE, management consultant; b. N.Y.C., July 9, 1934; s. Lee Whitney and R. Anne Powers; m. Elizabeth Braislin McClellan, July 24, 1980. Pres., Ronald Powers, Inc., Winter Park, Fla. and Westport, Conn., 1971; adviser to chief execs. of banks, corps. and govts. on strategic mgmt. issues, 1971—. Trustee Trinity Sch., Fla. Symphony Orch. Mem. Interlachen C. of C. Republican. Episcopalian. Club: La Coquille (Palm Beach, Fla.), Winter Park Racquet. Home: 561 Virginia Dr Winter Park FL 32789 Office: PO Box 2174 Winter Park FL 32790

POWIS, ALFRED, mining company executive; b. Montreal, Que., Can., Sept. 16, 1930; s. Alfred and Sarah Champe (McCulloch) P.; m. Shirley Haldenby., Aug. 8, 1953; children—Timothy Alfred, Nancy Alison, Charles Robert. B in Commerce, McGill U., 1951. Mem. staff investment dept. Sun Life Assurance Co. Can., 1951-55, now dir.; with Noranda Inc. (formerly Moranda Mines Ltd.), Toronto, 1956—; asst. treas. Noranda Inc. (formerly Noranda Mines Ltd.), Toronto, 1958-62, asst. to pres., 1962-63, exec. asst. to pres., 1963-66, v.p., 1966-67, exec. v.p., 1967-68, pres., 1968-82, chmn., chief exec. officer, 1977—, dir., 1964—; dir. MacMillan Bloedel Ltd., Noranda subsidiaries, Can. Imperial Bank Commerce, Ford Motor Co. Can. Ltd., Gulf Oil Can. Ltd., Placer Devel. Ltd., Kerr Addison Mines Ltd., Simpsons-Sears Ltd., Sun Life Assurance Co. Can. Trustee Toronto Gen. Hosp. Mem. Conf. Bd., Conf. Bd. Can. (chmn.). Anglican. Clubs: York; Mount Royal (Montreal). Office: Noranda Inc PO Box 45, Commerce Ct W Ste 4500, Toronto, ON Canada M5L 1B6 *

POWLUS, LEE CARSON, banker; b. Yardl, Pa., Apr. 8, 1960; s. Robert Addison and Janet Louise (Troy) P.; m. Allyson Jane Fletcher, Aug. 2, 1986. BS, U. Vt., 1982, MBA, 1988. Installment lender Chittenden Bank, Middlebury, Vt., 1982-83; dept. mgr. Chittenden Bank, Burlington, Vt., 1984—; mgr. savs. and time deposit Chittenden Bank, Burlington, 1986-87, asst. v.p., mgr. bookkeeping dept., 1987-88, product mgr., 1988—; loan officer Mountain Trust Co., Stowe, Vt., 1983-84. Asst. scout master Boy Scouts Am., Burlington; advisor Oreder DeMolay, Williston, Vt.; fin. com. Vt. Symphony Orch., 1988-89. Mem. Masons. Home: 69 Hayes Ave South Burlington VT 05403

POYNTER, DANIEL FRANK, publisher; b. N.Y.C., Sept. 17, 1938; s. William Frank and Josephine E. (Thompson) P. BA, Calif. State U., Chico, 1960; postgrad., San Francisco Law Sch., 1961-63. federally lic. master parachute rigger; lic. pilot. Pub., prin. Para Pub., Santa Barbara, Calif., 1969—; listed as expert witness Nat. Forensic Ctr., Tech. Adv. Service for Attys., Consultants and Consulting Organizations Directory, Lawyer's Guide to Legal Consultants, Expert Witnesses, Services, Books and Products. Author: The Parachute Manual, Parachuting, The Skydiver's Handbook, Parachuting Manual with Log, Hang Gliding, Manned Kiting, The Self-Publishing Manual, How to Write, Print & Sell You Own Book, Publishing Short Run Books, Business Letters For Publishers, Computer Selection Guide, Word Processing and Information Processing, Publishing Forms,

Parachuting Manual for Square/Tandem Equipment, Frisbee Players' Handbook, Toobee Players' Handbook, some translated in fgn. languages; past editor news mag. Spotter; monthly columnist Parachute mag., 1963—; contbr. over 400 tech. and popular articles and photographs to mags; patentee parachute pack, POP TOP. Recipient numerous certs. of appreciation for directing parachuting competitions. Mem. U.S. Parachute Assn. (life, chmn. bd., exec. com. 12 yrs., nat. and internat. del., achievement award, 1981, cert. 25 yr. mem., awarded Gold Parachute Wings, 1972), Parachute Industry Assn. (pres. 1985, 86), AIAA, Soc. Automotive Engrs., Nat. Aeronautic Assn., Aviation Space Writers Assn. (internat. conf. mem. 1978,79, 82), Calistoga Skydivers (past sec.), No. Calif. Parachute Council (past sec.), U.S. Hang Gliding Assn. (life, past dir., del.), Internat. Assn. Ind. Pubs. (past bd. dirs., pres. Santa Barbara chpt. 1979-82), Assn. Am. Pubs., Pub. Mktg. Assn. (bd. dirs.), Book Pubs. So. Calif., Am. Booksellers Assn., Commn. Internat de Vol Libre of Fedn. Aero. Internat. in Paris (U.S. del., past pres., lifetime Pres. d'Honneur award 1979, recipient Paul Tissander Diploma, 1984). Home: Rural Rt #1 Box P Goleta CA 93117 Office: Para Publishing PO Box 4232 Santa Barbara CA 93140-4232

POYTHRESS, DAVID BRYAN, lawyer; b. Macon, Ga., Oct. 24, 1943; s. John M. and Dorothy (Bayne) P.; m. Darla Chris Hilton, Aug. 19, 1972. B.A., Emory U., 1964, J.D., 1967. Asst. atty. gen. Dept. Law, State of Ga., Atlanta, 1971-72; dep. commr. Ga. Dept. Revenue, Atlanta, 1972-76; commr. Ga. Dept. Med. Assistance, Atlanta, 1976-79; sec. of state State of Ga., Atlanta, 1979-83; ptnr. Kutak Rock & Huie, Atlanta, 1983-84; sole practice Atlanta, 1984-86; exec. dir. Ga. Health Network, Atlanta, 1986—. Served with USAF, 1967-71. Mem. State Bar Ga. Democrat. Methodist. Office: Ga Health Network 938 Peachtree St Atlanta GA 30309

POZA, ERNESTO J., management consultant; b. Havana, Cuba, Mar. 27, 1950; came to U.S., 1961; s. Hugo Ernesto and Carmen (Valle) P.; m. Karen Elizabeth Saum, Oct. 14, 1978; 1 child, Kali Jennette. BS in Adminstrv. Sci., Yale U., 1972; MS in Mgmt., MIT, 1974. Personnel asst. Digital Equipment, Maynard, Mass., 1973-74; personnel mgr. rsch. Sherwin Williams Co., Chgo., 1974-75; orgn. specialist Sherwin Williams Co., Cleve., 1975-77, dir. orgn. planning, 1977-79; pres., sr. mgmt. cons. E.J. Poza Assoc., Cleve., 1979—; advisor Family Firm Inst., 1986. Author: Smart Growth: Critical Choices for Business Continuity and Prosperity, 1989; contbr. articles to profl. jours. Bd. dirs. Neighborhood Health Care, 1980; mem. program com. United Way, Cleve., 1985, Hispanic Leadership, 1986. Mem. Acad. Mgmt. (entrepreneurship div., 1980—, orgn. devel. network, 1975—). Office: EJ Poza Assocs 37300 Jackson Rd Moreland Hills OH 44022

PRAGER, PAUL, stockbroker; b. Cleve., Sept. 30, 1934; s. Abraham and Rose (Budney) P.; m. Lucille Stein, Jan. 27, 1959; children: Alison, Robert. BA, U. Fla., 1961; MA, Columbia U., 1963. Tchr., adminstr. Mineola (N.Y.) Pub. Schs., 1961-73; v.p. trading and sales Sherman Fitzpatrick and Co., Inc., Mineola, 1973—. Served as sgt. U.S. Army, 1953-56. Mem. Nat. Assn. Securities Dealers (artibrator), Am. Arbitration Assn. (arbitrator), N.Y. State Traders Assn., Jewish War Vets, Pythians, Masons. Jewish. Lodge: Pythians, Masons. Home: 74 Rowe Ave Lynbrook NY 11563 Office: Sherman Fitzpatrick & Co Inc 131 Mineola Blvd Mineola NY 11501

PRANGLEY, LESLIE NATHANIEL, III, accountant; b. Grand Rapids, Mich., Oct. 11, 1943; s. Leslie Nathaniel and Dorothy Phyllis (Sowa) P.; m. Katherine Eileen Tyler, July 25, 1965; children: Michelle Leslie, Michael Todd, Marcus Allen. BSBA, Aquinas Coll., 1968. CPA. Staff acct. James R. Rugg CPA, Grand Rapids, 1969-70, sr. acct., 1970-71, supr., 1971-73; ptnr. Rugg, Merkel & Prangley, Grand Rapids, 1973-76, Prangley & Marks, Grand Rapids, 1976-79; exec. ptnr. Prangley & Marks and Co., Grand Rapids, 1983—. Editor, author: (periodical column) Municipal Forum of the Michigan CPA, 1973-78. Bd. dirs. Am. Cancer Soc.-Kent City, Grand Rapids, 1975-80, chmn. fund drive, 1975-80. Mem. Mich. Assn. CPA's, Am. Inst. CPA's, CPA Assocs. Republican. Roman Catholic. Clubs: Blythefield Country (Belmont, Mich.) (bd. dirs. 1980-82, pres. 1981-82); Grand Rapids Optomists (bd. dirs. 1973-77, pres. 1976-77).

PRAS, ROBERT THOMAS, hotel executive; b. Newark, Dec. 14, 1941; s. Leon Lewis and Helen (McCully) P.; m. Constance Wilson, Nov. 30, 1968; children: Andrew, Douglas, Allison. BS, Delaware Valley Coll., 1965. Sanitarian Phila. Dept. Pub. Health, 1965-66; dir. quality assurance Acme Markets, Phila., 1966-68; merchandiser Alpha Beta Acme Markets, LaHabra, Calif., 1968-72; dir. Wakefern Food Corp., Elizabeth, N.J., 1972-79; exec. v.p. Marriott Corp., Washington, 1979—. Mayor Hillsborough (N.J.) Twp., 1979, mem. twp. council, 1976-77. Mem. Am. Mgmt. Assn., Nat. Restaurant Assn. Office: Marriott Corp 10400 Fernwood Rd Bethesda MD 20058

PRASSEL, FREDERICK FRANZ, construction company executive; b. San Antonio, Nov. 14, 1934; s. Victor, Sr., and Eda Marie (Groos) P.; student U. Tubingen (Germany), Trinity U.; BA, U. Tex., 1959; postgrad. doctoral program Calif. Western U.; m. Barbara Fry, July 2, 1959; children—Charlotte, Victor B., Edie C. Owner, pres. Prassel Constrn. Co., San Antonio, 1959—; sec.-treas., dir. Pras-Mel Corp.; pub. speaker. Bd. dirs. YMCA, 1977-82; mem. allocations com. United Way, 1981-82; deacon First Presbyterian Ch.; pres. Arthur Gray Jones Choir, 1978-80; mem. Leadership San Antonio Program, 1979-80. With U.S. Army, 1957-59. Mem. Am. Mgmt. Assn., Builders Exch. of Tex., Constrn. Specifications Inst., Internat. Platform Assn., San Antonio C. of C., San Antonio Mus. Assn. Presbyterian. Clubs: Downtown (pres. 1980), Toastmasters (pres. 1976, bd. dirs. 1977-78), Oak Hills Country, Beethoven Maennerchor. Lodge: Rotary (sec. 1978-79, svc. chmn. 1979-80, sgt.-at-arms 1980-81, program chmn. 1981-82, v.p. 1982-83, pres. 1984-85, gov.'s rep. 1985-86). Home: Lazy P Ranch Rte 3 Box 37F Floresville TX 78114 Office: Prassel Constrn Co 1000 S Comal St PO Box 830012 San Antonio TX 78283-0062

PRATHER, CHARLES WAYNE, chemist; b. Union, S.C., Feb. 10, 1941; s. Charlie Jentry and Elizabeth (Sprouse) P.; m. Patricia Louise Maynard, Aug. 23, 1969 (div. Jan. 1986); children: Patricia Julianne, Charles Houston. BS, Belmont Abbey Coll., 1963; MS, N.C. State U., 1965, PhD, 1971. Research chemist E.I. DuPont de Nemours & Co., Richmond, Va., 1965-67; sr. research chemist E.I. DuPont de Nemours & Co., Richmond, 1971-73; supr. E.I. DuPont de Nemours & Co., Wilmington, Del., 1973-76, Kinston, N.C., 1976-83; mgr. tech. group E.I. DuPont de Nemours & Co., Richmond, Va., 1983-86, Waynesboro, Va., 1986—. Mem. Am. Soc. Tng. and Devel. Democrat. Episcopalian. Home: 213 Turkey Ridge Rd Charlottesville VA 22901 Office: EI DuPont Co DuPont Rd Waynesboro VA 22980

PRATT, ARTHUR D., printing company executive; b. Indpls., May 7, 1924; s. Arthur D. and Helen L. (Rikhoff) P.; m. Marjorie M. Zwally May 19, 1967 (div. Mar. 1974); m. Amal Marcos, Apr. 11, 1987; children: Margaret, Michael, Sarah. Student, Sorbonne U., Paris, 1947. Pres. Found. Internat. Econ. Devel., 1949-56, Pratt Printing Co., Indpls., 1972-88. Author: The Party's Over, 1976, Christ and America's Survival, 1977, How to Help and Understand the Alcoholic, 1987. Pres. Flynn Christian Fellowship Houses Inc., 1956-88, Community Interfaith Housing Inc., 1966-73. Episcopalian. Club: Athenacum. Home: 2621 Sutherland Indianapolis IN 46205 Office: Pratt Printing Co 4040 W 10th St Indianapolis IN 46222

PRATT, CHARLES DUDLEY, JR., utility company executive; b. Honolulu, Sept. 30, 1927; s. Charles Dudley and Dora (Broadbent) P.; divorced; children by previous marriage: Charles Dudley, Timothy G., Sarah E., Melinda L. BCE with honors, Yale U., 1950, M in Structural Engring., 1951; MBA, U. Hawaii, 1971. Registered profl. engr., Hawaii. With Hawaiian Electric Co., Inc., Honolulu, 1953—, v.p. planning, 1971, exec. v.p., 1980-81, pres., from 1981, now chmn., chief exec. officer; pres., dir. Hawaiian Elec. Industries, Inc. (parent co.), Honolulu, 1983—, now also chief exec. officer; chmn. bd. Hawaii Electric Co. Inc., Hawaiian Electric Renewable Systems Inc., HEI Investment Corp., Malama Pacific Corp., Hawaiian tug & Barge Corp., Young Bros. Ltd., Hawaiian Ins. Group, Am. Savs. Bank. Chmn. bd. Hawaii Bus. Roundtable and Hist. Hawaii Found.; bd. dirs. Econ. Devel. Corp. Honolulu, Friends Iolani Palace, Hawaii Maritime Ctr., Aloha United Way; bd. dirs., v.p. Aloha Council Boy Scouts Am. Served with AUS, 1946-48, 51-53. Mem. ASCE (past pres. Hawaii sect.), Pacific Coast Electrical Assn. (pres. 1988-89), Edison Electric Inst., Hawaii Soc. Corp. Planners, Hawaii C. of C. (bd. dirs.), U. Hawaii MBA Alumni Group, USCG Aux., Beta Gamma Sigma, Tau Beta Pi. Clubs: Pacific, Kaneohe Yacht. Home: 276 N Kalaheo Ave Kailua HI 96734 Office: Hawaiian Elec Co Inc 900 Richards St Honolulu HI 96813

PRATT, DONALD HENRY, manufacturing company executive; b. Hays, Kans., Dec. 2, 1937; s. Donald Edwin and Ida Marjorie (Dreiling) P.; m. George-Ann Hinkle, June 7, 1960; children—Jacqueline, Donald. B.S.I.E., Wichita State U., 1960; M.B.A., Harvard U., 1965. With Butler Mfg. Co., Galesburg, Ill, 1965-67; with Butler Mfg. Co., Kansas City, MO, 1967—; sr. v.p., gen. mgr. bldgs. div. Butler Mfg. Co., 1978-80, exec. v.p., gen. mgr. bldgs. div., 1980-82, exec. v.p., pres. bldgs. div., 1982-86, pres., 1986—; bd. dirs. Union Nat. Bank, Wichita, Kans., Commerce Bank, Kansas City. Trustee Midwest Research Inst.; bd. dirs. Kansas City Art Inst., Mo. Served to capt. USAF, 1960-63. Mem. Metal Bldg. Mfrs. Assn. (chmn. 1983), Am. Royal of Kansas City (bd. dirs.). Republican. Roman Catholic. Home: 433 Ward Pkwy Kansas City MO 64112 Office: Butler Mfg Co PO Box 917 Kansas City MO 64141

PRATT, EDMUND T., JR., pharmaceutical company executive; b. Savannah, Ga., Feb. 22, 1927; s. Edmund T. and Rose (Miller) P.; m. Jeanette Louise Carneale, Feb. 10, 1951; children: Randolf Ryland, Keith Taylor. BS in Elec. Engring. magna cum laude, Duke U., 1947; MBA, U. Pa., 1949; hon. degrees, L.I. U., Marymount Manhattan Coll., Poly. U. of N.Y., St. Francis Coll. With IBM Corp., 1949-51, 54-57, asst. to exec. v.p., 1956-57; with IBM World Trade Corp., 1957-62, controller, 1958-62; asst. sec. financial mgmt. Dept. Army, 1962-64; controller Pfizer Inc., N.Y.C., 1964-67; v.p. operations internat. subsidiaries Pfizer Inc., 1967-69, chmn. bd., pres. internat. subsidiaries, 1969-71, exec. v.p., 1970-71, pres., 1971-72, chmn., chief exec. officer, 1972—, also chmn. exec. com., bd. dirs.; dir. Chase Manhattan Corp., Internat. Paper Co., Gen. Motors Corp.; trustee Com. for Econ. Devel.; trustee Am. Enterprise Inst. Bd. dirs. N.Y.C. Partnership; mem. N.Y. State Bus. Adv. Council; chmn. Emergency Com. for Am. Trade; trustee Duke U.; bd. overseers Wharton Sch. Commerce and Finance.; mem. Adv. Com. on Trade Negotiations; chmn. Nat. Indsl. Adv. Council for Opportunities Industrialization Ctrs. of Am. Served to lt. (j.g.) USNR, 1952-54. Mem. Bus. Roundtable (chmn., mem. policy com.), N.Y. Chamber Commerce and Industry (dir.), Bus. Council (chmn.), Phi Beta Kappa.

PRATT, EUGENE FRANK, financial services executive; b. Wilmington, Del., July 13, 1946; s. Henry Holt and Sarah Sneath (Berlekamp) P.; m. Susan Barron, Jan. 21, 1975 (div. 1983); m. Patricia Burgess, Dec. 17, 1983; children: Keith Losey, Joshua. BS, U. Del., 1968. Cert. fin. planner. Mgr. Pratt's Hatchery, Middletown, Del., 1972-74; account exec. Dean Witter Reynolds Inc., Dover, Del., 1974-80, assoc. v.p. investments, 1980-86, v.p. investments, 1986—; instr. Wesley Coll., 1981—. Bd. dirs. ARC, 1986—, exec. com. Capt. U.S. Army, 1969-72, Vietnam. Decorated Bronze star. Mem. Inst. Cert. Fin. Planners, Dover Racquetball Club. Methodist. Home: 215 Portmarnoch Ct Dover DE 19901 Office: Dean Witter Reynolds 20 E Division St Dover DE 19901

PRATT, HOWARD WILLIAM, insurance executive; b. Bedford, Ind., Apr. 2, 1946; s. Joseph William and Ruth (Baker) P. BS, U. Evansville, 1970. Claim rep. State Farm Ins., Evansville, Ind., 1970-75; sr. claim rep. State Farm Ins., Columbus, Ind., 1975-79; claim specialist State Farm Ins., Indpls., 1979-81; asst. supt. State Farm Ins., Daytona, Ohio, 1981-85; asst. supt. State Farm Ins., Cin., 1985-88, claim specialist, 1988—; seminar trainer State Farm Ins., Cin., 1987-88. Served with Ind. N.G., 1960-75. Home: 3 S Applewood Ct Fairfield OH 45014

PRATT, STANLEY EDWARD, financial company executive; b. Boston, July 21, 1931; s. Waldo Elliott and Virginia (Stanley) P.; m. Maryanne Thomas, Jan. 14, 1956; children: Thomas, Virginia, Cynthia, Johanna. BA, Brown U., 1953. Assoc. W.E. Hutton and Co., Boston, 1955-61; v.p. Diversified Corp. Services, Boston, 1961-68, Creative Resources, Inc., Wellesley, Mass., 1968-77; pres. Venture Econs., Inc., Wellesley, Mass., 1977-84, chmn., 1984-89; chmn., gen. ptnr. Abbott Capital Mgmt. Co., Needham, Mass., 1986—. Editor: Pratt's Guide to Venture Capital Sources, 1977-87; publisher, editor Venture Capital Jour., 1977-88. Served to lt.USNR, 1953-55.

PREDPALL, DANIEL FRANCIS, environmental engineering executive, consultant; b. Rochester, N.Y., May 22, 1946; s. Daniel Francis and Elizabeth K. Predpall; m. Carolyn Jane Kokish, May 29, 1981; 1 child, Robert. BS in Physics, Stevens Inst. Tech., 1968; MS in Marine Sci., L.I. U., 1974; MBA, NYU, 1985. Registered profl. engr., Pa. Mgr. environmental projects Ebasco Services, N.Y.C., 1970-73, 1977-82; v.p., sr. assoc. Woodward-Clyde Cons., Wayne, N.J., 1973-77, 1982—; speaker tech. presentations on risk assessment, site selection and waste mgmt. Contbr. numerous articles to profl. jours. Bd. govs. Packanack Lake Community, 1987—. Mem. Soc. Profl. Engrs., Air and Waste Mgmt. Assn. Republican. Lutheran. Home: 14 Archung Rd Wayne NJ 07470 Office: Woodward-Clyde Cons 201 Willowbrook Blvd Wayne NJ 07470

PREIS, MICHAEL W., investment executive; b. N.Y.C., Oct. 4, 1944; s. William J. and Elinor (Bloomingdale) P. BME, Ohio State U., 1969; MBA, Harvard U., 1972. V.p. Wometco Lathrop Co., Inc., Anchorage, 1975-78; sr. cons. Peat, Marwick, Main & Co., Anchorage, 1978-82; pres. Reynolds Equipment Co., Inc., Anchorage, 1982-87; investment mgr. Alaska Securities Mgmt., Inc., Anchorage, 1987—. Mem. Anchorage Bid Rev. Bd., 1987—; bd. dirs. Anchorage Symphony, 1980—; chmn. Anchorage Telephone Commn., 1982—. Mem. Whittier Boat Owners Assn. (pres. 1987-88), Rotary. Office: Alaska Securities Mgmt Inc PO Box 616 Anchorage AK 99510

PREIS, RICHARD MARK, marketing executive; b. N.Y.C., Feb. 8, 1960; s. John Joseph and Irene Margret (Guilfoyle) P. BBA, Iona Coll., 1982. Sales rep. Canon M.C.S. Inc., N.Y.C., 1982-84; sales mgr. Stratocom, Inc., N.Y.C., 1984-86; equipment sales specialist Ilford Photo Corp, Paramus, N.J., 1986-88, area sales mgr., 1988—. Mem. In-Plant Printing Mgmt. Assn., Nat. Computer Graphics Assn. (sales exec. com.), K.C. Republican. Roman Catholic. Home: 189 Beach 124th St Belle Harbor NY 11694 Office: Ilford Photo Corp W 70 Century Rd Paramus NJ 07653

PREISSER, BERNHARD FRANK, financial executive; b. Bronx, N.Y., Feb. 11, 1947; s. Joseph August and Emilie (Grimm) P.; m. Christina Helen Szolis, Sept. 7, 1974; children: Joseph, Andrew. BS in Acctg., Fordham U., 1968, MBA, 1983. Sr. acct. Price Waterhouse & Co., N.Y.C., 1970-74; asst. controller Am. Export/Farrell Lines, N.Y.C., 1974-82; v.p. fin. Bowe Systems and Machinery, Hicksville, N.Y., 1982—. Treas. Cub Scout Pack 3, Boy Scouts Am., Ardsley, N.Y., 1985—; coach Am. Youth Soccer, Dobbs Ferry, N.Y., 1983—. Served to capt. U.S. Army, 1968-70. Recipient Disting. Service award Kolping Soc. Am., N.Y.C., 1986. Mem. AICPAs, N.Y. State Soc. CPAs. Roman Catholic. Home: 19 Revere Rd Ardsley NY 10502 Office: Bowe Systems and Machinery 200 Frank Rd Hicksville NY 11801

PRENDERGAST, BRIAN, financial planner, investment advisor; b. Denver, July 26, 1948; s. Edmund T. and Yvonne S. (Saliba) P.; B.S., U.S. Air Force Acad., 1970; M.A., Central Mich. U., 1972; m. Alice Sawaya, Dec. 26, 1970; children—Amy L., Christina M., Elizabeth Ann. Ins. agt. United Fidelity Life, 1976-78; partner, registered prin. Colo. Investor Services, Denver, from 1979-83; owner Prendergast & Assocs., Denver, 1979—; founder, sec., treas. Investment Resource and Design, Inc., 1987—; lectr. Sunset Life's Agt. Conf., 1980. Roman Catholic. Club: Cedars of Lebanon (pres. 1979-80). Author: (with Douglas Nutt) Property Profile, 1978. Home and Office: 5665 S Big Canon Dr Englewood CO 80111

PRENDERGAST, JOHN PATRICK, accounting company executive; b. Jersey City, Dec. 13, 1927; s. William James and Hannah (Conmy) P.; m. Peg Prendergast, Dec. 27, 1952; children—Kevin, William, Mary Kay, Brian, Sheila; m. Margaret Teresa McGrath. A.B., Fordham U., 1950; M.B.A., NYU, 1957. Ptnr., cons. Arthur Young & Co., N.Y.C., 1961-63, mng. assoc., 1963-66; prin. Arthur Young, N.Y.C., 1966-68, ptnr., 1968—. Track and field ofcl. Olympic Games, Los Angeles, 1984; mem. adv. council Fordham U., Pace U., N.C. Central U., Durham, 1985. Served to lt. USN, 1950-53, Korea; capt. USNR (ret.). Roman Catholic. Clubs: Fordham (pres. 1970-75) (N.Y.C.); Spiked Shoe. Home: 167 Godwin Ave Wyckoff NJ 07481 Office: Arthur Young 277 Park Ave New York NY 10172

PRENTICE, EUGENE MILES, III, lawyer; b. Glen Ridge, N.J., Aug. 27, 1942; s. Eugene Miles and Anna Margaret (Kiernan) P.; m. Katharine Kirby Culbertson, Sept. 18, 1976; children: Eugene Miles IV, Jessie Kirby, John Francis. BA, Washington and Jefferson Coll., 1964; JD, U. Mich., 1967. Bar: N.Y. 1973, U.S. Dist. Ct. (so. dist.) N.Y. 1973, U.S. Dist. Ct. (ea. dist.) N.Y. 1974, U.S. Ct. Appeals (2d cir.) 1974. Mgmt. trainee Morgan Guaranty Trust, N.Y.C., 1967-68, 71-73; assoc. White & Case, N.Y.C., 1973-78; assoc. Windels, Marx et al, N.Y.C., 1978-80, ptnr., 1980-84; ptnr. Brown & Wood, N.Y.C., 1984—; bd. dirs. various corps. Trustee Vt. Law Sch., South Royalton, 1984—, Washington and Jefferson Coll., Pa., 1985—. Served to capt. U.S. Army, 1968-70. Mem. ABA, Assn. of Bar of City of N.Y. Republican. Clubs: Links, Union League, N.Y. Athletic Club (N.Y.C.), Spring Lake Bath & Tennis. Home: 34 W 95th St New York NY 10025 Office: Brown & Wood One World Trade Ctr New York NY 10048

PRENTICE, JAMES STUART, energy company executive, chemical engineer; b. Louisville, Feb. 4, 1944; s. John Edward and Helen (Staples) P.; m. Mary Joan Kelly, July 24, 1965; children: Holly Michelle, Craig Edward, Brian Andrew. B in Chem. Engring., U. Louisville, 1966; MS, Northwestern U., 1967. Research engr. Esso Research and Engring. Co., Baytown, Tex., 1967-71; engr., supr. ops., mkt. mgr. to plant mgr. No. Petrochem. Co., Morris and Des Plaines, Ill., 1971-82; v.p. mfg. No. Petrochem. Co., Omaha, 1982-85; sr. v.p. corp. planning HNG/Internorth, Omaha, 1985-86; sr. v.p. adminstrn. and human resources Enron Corp., Houston, 1986-87; exec. v.p. Enron Liquid Fuels, Houston, 1987-89; sr. v.p. Enron Gas Pipeline Group, Houston, 1989—; bd. dirs. Chem. Inst. Indsl. Toxicology, Research Triangle, N.C., 1983-85. Patentee in field. Roman Catholic. Clubs: Lakeside Country, Westside Tennis, Petroleum (Houston). Office: Enron Corp PO Box 1188 1400 Smith St Houston TX 77251-1188

PRESCHLACK, JOHN EDWARD, management consultant; b. N.Y.C., May 30, 1933; s. William and Anna M. (Hrubesch) P.; m. Lynn A. Stanley, Dec. 29, 1962; children: John Edward Jr., James S., David C. B.S.E.E., M.I.T., 1954; M.B.A., Harvard U., 1958. Ptnr. McKinsey & Co., Inc., N.Y.C., London, Dusseldorf, W. Ger., 1958-73; pres. ITEK Graphic Products Co., Lexington, Mass., 1973-77; pres., chief exec. officer Gen. Binding Corp., Northbrook, Ill., 1977-83, Roberts & Porter, Inc., Des Plaines, Ill., 1984-86, Spencer Stuart, Chgo., 1987—; bd. dirs. Hycor Corp., Lake Bluff, Ill. Trustee Chgo. Hort. Soc., 1979—; chmn. Lake Forest Planning Commn., 1982-88; mem. MIT Devel. Com. 1986—. With USAF, 1954-56. Decorated Air Force Commendation medal; recipient Corp. Leadership award M.I.T., 1978. Mem. Onwentsia Club, Chgo. Club, Harvard Club of N.Y.C. Republican. Roman Catholic. Office: Spencer Stuart 401 N Michigan Ave Chicago IL 60611

PRESCOTT, DANIEL BERM, accountant; b. Bishopville, S.C., July 10, 1955; s. Daniel and Alice (Scott) P.; m. Felicia Holley, Aug. 11, 1979. BA, Rutgers U., 1976; MA, So. Ill. U., 1979; MBA, Nat. U. San Diego, 1980; PhD, JD, Columbia Pacific U., 1987. CPA, Tex. Asst. regional mgr. Hartford Inc. Co., Dallas, 1982-84; sr. fin. analyst Celenase Chems., Dallas, 1984-85; cost acctg. mgr. Johnson & Johnson, Sherman, Tex., 1985—; bd. dirs. Dallas Occupational Indsl. Council. Treas. Dallas Black Dance Theater, 1986-87, bd. dirs. 1984-85; budget dir. Friendship West Baptist Ch., Dallas, 1988; del. Dem. County Com., 1988. Served to capt. USMC, 1976-82. Mem. Nat. Black MBA's, Cert. Mgmt. Accts., Am. Mgmt. Assn. Home: 707 W Redbird Ln Dallas TX 75232

PRESSLER, PHILIP BERNARD, advertising executive, educator; b. Balt., May 3, 1946; s. James William and Jean Callista (Colgan) P.; m. Catherine Mary Dale, Jan. 11, 1973 (div. Feb. 5, 1987); children: Julie, Brian, Elizabeth. BA, Villanova U., 1969; MA, Washington Theol. Coalition, 1972. Sales rep. 3M Co., Wilmington, Del., 1972-76; systems cons. Tab Products Co., Pennsauken, N.J., 1976-78, Compugraphic Corp., Bala Cynwyd, Pa., 1978-80; advanced to pres., chief exec. officer Pro-file Systems, Inc., Conshohocken, Pa., 1980-88; br. mgr. Document Mgmt. Group, Inc., Malvern, Pa., 1988-89; owner Pressler Assocs., Wayne, Pa., 1988—; prof. Manor Jr. Coll., Jenkintown, Pa., 1985—; bd. dirs. Bus. Systems and Security Mktg. Assn., Kalamazoo, 1986—; chmn. bd. Assn. Records Mgrs. and Adminstrn., Phila. (Pres.'s award, 1986). Author: Equipment Cost Study, 1981; inventor: Acoustical Panel the Baffile, File Directory, Conversion Fileback, 1981-87. V.p. Glenhardie Condominium Assn., Wayne, Pa., 1987-88, pres. 1988—. Named to Inc. 500 Inc. Mag., 1985-86. Mem. Office Automation Soc. Internat., Glenhardie Country Club. Roman Catholic. Home and Office: 322 Drummers Ln Wayne PA 19087

PRESSMAN, THELMA, microwave company executive, consultant; b. N.Y.C., Apr. 10, 1921; d. William and Ida (Neckrich) Rosenson; m. Morris Pressman, May 17, 1942; children: Paul, Richard. Student, UCLA, 1073-77. Cert. coll. instr., Calif. Supr. new product testing Waste King Corp., Los Angeles, 1959-69; cons. Microwave div. Amana Corp., 1969-77; pres., owner Microwave Cooking Ctr., Encino, Calif., 1969—; dir. consumer edn. and services Sanyo Electric, Inc., 1971-87; instr., cookware designer Microwave Cooking Ctr., Encino, 1969—; microwave instr. Calif. State U., Northridge; currently spokesperson for Procter & Gamble Bounty Microwave Paper Towel, The Glass Packaging Inst. Author: The Art of Microwave Cooking, 1983 (selected by Library of Congress to be used as talking book for the blind, 1984), Microwave Cooking/Meals in Minutes, 1982, Microwave Magic, 1985, The Great Microwave Dessert Book, 1985, 365 Ways to Cook in Your Microwave, 1989; also New Product Cookbooks for Sears Roebuck & Co., 1977—; microwave columnist Bon Appetit mag., 1979-82; articles for newspapers and mags. throughout U.S. mem. Mayor's adv. council, Los Angeles, 1979. Recipient trophy Sanyo Electric, Inc., 1985. Mem. Internat. Microwave Power Inst. (editor jour. 1975-77), Elec. Women's Round Table (pres. 1978-79), Am. Women in Radio and TV, Internat. Assn. Cooking Profls., AFTRA. Club: Hadassah (Beverly Hills). Home and Office: 17728 Marcello Pl Encino CA 91316

PRESSON, FRANCIS TENNERY, credit union official; b. Jackson, Tenn., Oct. 31, 1925; s. Norman Z and Mary Isabelle (Tennery) P.; student W. Tenn. Bus. Coll., 1948-49, U. Tenn., 1954; m. Harriet Francis Shires, June 17, 1950; 1 son, Stephen Francis. Car insp. Ill. Central Gulf R.R., Jackson, 1942-86; treas., mgr. ICG Fed. Credit Union, Jackson, 1960—. Mem. Madison County Democratic Exec. com., 1976—; mem. Stadium Com. for City of Jackson, 1970—. Served with USNR, 1942-45. Mem. Am. Mgmt. Assn., Tenn. Credit Union League (dir. 1973-80, treas., vice chmn.), VFW, Brotherhood Ry. Carmen. Baptist. Club: K.P. Home: 407 Lambuth Blvd PO Box 3266 Jackson TN 38303 Office: ICG Fed Credit Union 131 Tucker St PO Box 3334 Jackson TN 38303

PRESTIA, MICHAEL ANTHONY, accounting executive; b. S.I., N.Y., Oct. 6, 1931; s. Anthony and Antoinette (Folino) P.; M.B.A., NYU, 1956; B.A., 1953; m. Nancy Ferrandino, July 4, 1959 (div. May 1970); 1 son, Anthony. Sr. accountant Gluckman & Schacht, C.P.A.'s, N.Y.C., 1953-60; chief financial officer Franklin Broadcasting Co., N.Y.C., 1960-63; chief accountant asst. to bus. officer, sec. Cooper Union for Advancement Sci. and Art, N.Y.C., 1963-66; bus. officer Inst. Pub. Adminstrn., N.Y.C., 1966-71, controller, 1971-78, treas., 1978—. Cons. taxation and tax planning, 1959—. Served with AUS, 1953-55. C.P.A., N.Y. Mem. Am. Inst. C.P.A.'s, N.Y. State Soc. C.P.A.'s. Home: 53-06 Francis Lewis Blvd Bayside NY 11364 Office: Inst Pub Adminstrn 1457 Broadway New York NY 10036

PRESTON, ALAN MICHAEL, data processing executive; b. Newark, July 23, 1948; s. Charles Preston and Lena (Stetner) Paola; m. Evelyn Dorothy Schwartz, Aug. 18, 1974; 1 child, Maxwell Charles. BEE, Rutgers Coll., 1971; MBA, U. Md., 1978. Programmer analyst D.A.T.A. Inc., Orange, N.J., 1972-74; with tech. staff Informatics Inc., Rockville, Md., 1974-76; v.p. Infodata Systems Inc., Falls Church, Va., 1976—. Editor: Electric and Electronics Research in Progress, 1972. Capt. U.S. Army, 1971-78. Mem. IEEE, Data Processing Mgrs. Assn. Jewish. Office: Infodata Systems Inc 5205 Leesburg Pike Falls Church VA 22041

PRESTON, ANDREW JOSEPH, pharmacist, drug company executive; b. Bklyn., Apr. 19, 1922; s. Charles A. and Josephine (Rizzutto) Pumo; B.Sc., St. John U., 1943; m. Martha Jeanne Happ, Oct. 10, 1953; children—Andrew Joseph, Charles Richard, Carolyn Louise, Frank Arthur, Joanne Marie, Barbara Jeanne. Mgr. Press Club, Bklyn. Nat. League Baseball Club, 1941-42; purchasing agt. Drug and Pharm. div. Intrassind, Inc., 1947; chief pharmacist Hendershot Pharmacy, Newton, N.J., 1949; agt. Bur. of Narcotics, U.S. Treasury Dept., 1948-49; with Preston Drug & Surg. Co., Boonton, N.J., 1949-86; chief exec. officer Preston Pharmaceuticals, Inc., Butler, N.J., 1970-80, pres. Preston Cons., Kinnelon, N.J., 1987—; commr. N.J. State Bd. Pharmacy, 1970-72, pres., 1973; organizer State of N.J. Drug Abuse Speakers Program, 1970-76; lectr. drug abuse and narcotic addiction various community orgns., 1968-78; mem. adv. bd. Nat. Community Bank, Boonton, N.J., 1973. Chmn. bldg. fund com. Riverside Hosp., Boonton, 1963; mem. Morris County (N.J.) Republican Fin. Com., 1972—, Pres. Ronald Reagan N.J. Re-Election Adv. Bd., 1984, exec. com. Gov. Tom Kean Annual Ball, 1985—; chmn. Pharmacists of N.J. for election of President Ford, 1976, Pharmacists for Gov. Tom Kean, 1981-84, N.J. Pharmacists for Reagan/Bush '84; mem. exec. com. Morris County Overall Econ. Devel. Com., 1976-82; chmn. Pharmacists for Fenwick, 1982; v.p. Kinnelon Republican Club, 1980. Served to lt. (j.g.), USN, 1943-46; PTO. Recipient Bowl Hygeia award Robbins Co., 1969, E.R. Squibb President's award, 1968, N.J. Pharm. Square Club award, 1969. Mem. Am. Pharm. Assn., N.J. Pharm. Assn. (mem. econs. com. 1960-65, pres. 1967-68, Oscar Singer Meml. award 1987), Nat. Assn. of Retail Druggists, Internat. Narcotic Enforcement Officers Assn., N.J. Narcotic Enforcement Officers Assn., Pharmacists Guild Am. (pres. N.Y. div. 1946-47), Pharmacists Guild of N.J., N.J. Public Health Assn., Morris County Pharm. Assn., Morris-Sussex Pharmacists Soc., Am. Legion, St. John's Alumni Assn. Roman Catholic. Clubs: Elks, K.C., Smoke Rise. Contbr. editorials to profl. jours. Home and Office: 568A Pepperidge Tree Ln Kinnelon NJ 07405

PRESTON, BRUCE MARSHALL, lawyer, educator; b. Trinidad, Colo., Feb. 24, 1949; s. Marshall Caldwell and Juanita (Killgore) P.; m. Mariannina Erra, Aug. 10, 1974; children: Charles Marshall, Robert Arthur. BS summa cum laude, Ariz. State U., 1971; MA, U. Ariz., 1972, JD, 1975. Bar: Ariz. 1975, U.S. Ct. Appeals (9th cir.) 1976, U.S. Ct. Claims 1983, U.S. Tax Ct. 1983, U.S. Supreme Ct. 1983; cert. fin. planner. Atty. Maricopa County Office of Pub. Defender, Phoenix, 1975-84; ptnr. Simonsen & Preston, Phoenix, 1985-86, Simonsen, Preston, Sargeant & Arbetman, Phoenix, 1986; atty. office of atty. gen. State of Ariz., 1987—; judge pro tem Mcpl. Ct., Phoenix, 1984-86; licensee in sales Ariz. Dept. Real Estate, Phoenix, 1981-87; adj. faculty Phoenix Coll. for Fin. Planning, Denver, 1984—, Maricopa County Community Coll. Dist., Phoenix, 1985-87, Ariz. State U. Coll. of Bus., Tempe, 1986-87, Ottawa U., Phoenix, 1986. Chmn. com., treas., pres. bd. dirs Kachina Country Day Sch., 1982—; bd. dirs. Family Svc. Agy., Phoenix, 1988—, Clearwater Hills Homeowners Assn., Paradise Valley, Ariz., 1989—. Named one of Outstanding Young Men in Am., 1984, 85. Mem. ABA, Ariz. Bar Assn. (cert. specialist criminal law 1982-84), Inst. of Cert. Fin. Planning, Internat. Assn. Fin. Planners, Ariz. State U. Coll. of Liberal Arts Alumni Assn. (bd. dirs. 1978-80, 87—). Clubs: Economics (Tempe); Variety (Phoenix). Home: 7247 Black Rock Trail Paradise Valley AZ 85253 Office: Office Atty Gen 1275 W Washington St Phoenix AZ 85007

PRESTON, DONALD, corporate executive; b. Newark, Aug. 26, 1941; s. Edward and Helen (Gould) P.; m. Geraldine Diane Laing, Sept. 4, 1965; children: Tammy, Donald E., Thomas W. BS, Brigham Young U., 1967; postgrad., Fordham U., 1971-73. CPA, N.Y., Vt. Supr. Ernst & Ernst, N.Y.C., 1967-73; group controller U.S. Industries, Inc., Dallas, 1973-80; pres., chief exec. officer Bijur Lubricating Corp., Bennington, Vt., 1980—, also bd. dirs.; bd. dirs. Sterling Gun Drills Ltd., Hemel-Hempstead, Eng.; chmn. bd. Bijur Lubricating Ireland Ltd., Ennis, 1984—. Trustee Bennington Mus., 1985—, Putnam Meml. Health Corp., 1987—, So. Vt. Coll. 1987—; Govs. Commn. on the econ. future Vt. Served with USMC, 1959-63. Recipient Bronze medal for Meritorious Pub. Service, Econ. Devel. Council N.Y.C., 1973. Mem. Am. Inst. CPA's, N.Y. State Soc. CPA's, Nat. Assn. Accts., Am. Mgmt. Assn., Vt. Bus. Roundtable. Home: 22 Monument Ave Old Bennington VT 05201 Office: Bijur Lubricating Corp 50 Kocher Dr Bennington VT 05201

PRESTON, JAMES E., cosmetics company executive; b. 1933. Student, Temple U.; BS, Northwestern U., 1955. With Avon Products, Inc., N.Y.C., 1964—, from mgmt. trainee to dir. sales promotions, 1964-70, dir. personnel, 1970-71, v.p. personnel, 1971-72, from group v.p. mktg. to sr. v.p. field ops., 1972-77, exec. v.p., 1977-81, exec. corp. v.p., pres., 1981-88, pres., chief operating officer, 1988-89, chief exec. officer, 1988—, chmn. bd. dirs., 1989—. Office: Avon Products Inc 9 W 57th St New York NY 10019 *

PRESTON, KENDALL, JR., electro-optical engineer; b. Boston, Oct. 22, 1927; s. Kendall and Dorothy Fletcher (Allen) P.; m. Sarah Malcolm Stewart, Aug. 23, 1952; 1 dau., Louise. Grad., Milton Acad., 1945; B.A. cum laude, Harvard U., 1950, M.S., 1952. Mem. tech. staff Bell Telephone Labs., Murray Hills, N.J., 1952-60; sr. staff scientist Perkin-Elmer Corp., Norwalk, Conn., 1961-74; prof. elec. engring. and bioengring. Carnegie-Mellon U., Pitts., 1974—; prof. radiation engring. Grad. Sch. Public Health, U. Pitts., 1977—; gen. mgr., chief engr. Kensal Cons., 1980—; pres. Pathology Imaging Corp., 1986—; chmn. Internat. Optical Computing Conf., Zurich, Switzerland, 1974, conf. automatic cytology Engring. Found., N.Y.C., 1971-72, conf. Coherent Radiation Systems, 1973, conf. Comparative Productivity of Non-invasive Techniques for Med. Diagnosis, 1976; U.S. chmn. U.S.-Japan Seminar on Digital Processing of Biomed. Images, Pasadena, Calif., 1975; faculty NATO Advanced Study Inst. on Digital Image Processing and Analysis, Bonas, France, 1976; mem. faculty Internat. Sch. Med. Scis., Erice, Italy, 1988; mem. Tech. Audit Bd., Inc., N.Y.C., 1976—. Author: Coherent Optical Computers, 1972, Kogeretnye Optiches; in Russian, 1974; editor: (with Dr. Onoe) Digital Processing of Biomedical Images, 1976, (with Drs. Ayers, Johnson and Taylor) Medical Imaging Techniques: A Comparison, 1979, (with Drs. Onoe and Rosenfeld) Real-Time Medical Image Processing, 1980, Real-Time/Parallel Computing, 1981; (with Dr. Duff) Modern Cellular Automata, 1984; editor: (with Drs. Duff, Levialdi, Uhr) Evaluation of Multicomputers for Image Processing, 1986; assoc. editor: Pattern Recognition; editorial adviser: Biocharacterist, Analytical and Quantitative Cytology; mem. editorial com.: Pattern Analysis and Machine Intelligence; contbr. articles to profl. jours.; patentee blood smear spinning, laser location of chromosomes on microscope slide, acoustic holography, multi-dimensional image processing, others. Chmn. Ecclesia, YMCA, Summit, N.J., 1958-60; chmn. health services industry com. Automation Research Council, Am. Automatic Control Council, N.J., 1973-76; mem. NSF Fact Finding Team on Egyptian Scientific Instrumentation, 1974-75. Served with arty. AUS, 1946-47. Fellow IEEE (chmn. Conn. PTGEC 1966-67); mem. AAAS, Biol. Engring. Soc. Gt. Britain, Biomed. Engring. Soc. (charter), Harvard Engrs. and Scientists (pres. students 1952), N.Y. Acad. Sci., Cum Laude Soc. Clubs: D.U, Hasty Pudding Inst. 1770, Harvard of Western Pa; Country (Brookline, Mass.); Lake (Dublin, N.H.); Hillsboro (Pompano Beach, Fla.); Lawn (New Haven); Capitol Hill (Washington); Athletic (Scottsdale, Ariz.). Office: Carnegie Mellon U Dept Elec & Computer Engring Schenley Park Pittsburgh PA 15213

PRESTON, LEWIS THOMPSON, banker; b. N.Y.C., Aug. 5, 1926; s. Lewis Thompson and Priscilla (Baldwin) P.; m. Gladys Pulitzer, Apr. 17, 1959; children: Linda Pulitzer Bartlett, Victoria Maria Bartlett, Lucile Baldwin, Lewis Thompson, Priscilla Munn, Electra. Grad., Harvard U., 1951. With J.P. Morgan & Co. (merged with Guaranty Trust Co., named Morgan Guaranty Trust Co. 1959), N.Y.C., 1951—; vice chmn. bd., dir. J. P. Morgan & Co. and Morgan Guaranty Trust Co., N.Y.C., 1976-78, mem. corporate office, mem. exec. com., 1976—; pres. J.P. Morgan and Morgan Guaranty Trust Co., N.Y.C., 1978-80; chmn. bd. J. P. Morgan and Morgan Guaranty Trust Co., N.Y.C., 1980—, chmn. exec. com., chief exec. officer; bd. dirs. Fed. Res. Bank of N.Y. Trustee NYU. Served with USMC, 1944-46. Mem. The Pilgrims, Council Fgn. Relations (dir.), Assn. Res. City Bankers. Republican. Episcopalian. Clubs: The Brook (N.Y.C.), The River (N.Y.C.); Bedford Golf and Tennis. Office: J P Morgan & Co Inc 23 Wall St New York NY 10015 *

PRESTON, SEYMOUR STOTLER, III, manufacturing company executive; b. Media, Pa., Sept. 11, 1933; s. Seymour Stotler and Mary Alicia (Harper) P.; m. Jean Ellen Holman, Sept. 8, 1956; children: Courtney J., Katherine E., Alicia D., Shelley S. B.A., Williams Coll., 1956; M.B.A., Harvard U., 1958. With Pennwalt Corp., Phila., 1961—; exec. v.p. in charge of chems. and equipment ops., worldwide Pennwalt Corp., 1975-77, pres., chief operating officer, 1977—, also dir.; bd. dir. Core States Fin. Corp., Phila. Nat. Bank, The Lawrenceville (N.J.) Sch., 1982—. Trustee Shipley Sch., Bryn Mawr, Pa., 1976—, Acad. Natural Scis., 1981—; bd. mgrs. Franklin Inst., Phila., 1980— . Served to 1st lt. USAF, 1958-61. Mem. Soc. for Chem. Industry, Greater Phila. C. of C. (dir. 1979—). Clubs: Union League (Phila.), Urban (Phila.); Radnor Hunt (Malvern, Pa.).

PRETLOW, WILLARD EDWIN, financial services executive; b. Norfolk, Va., May 13, 1947; s. Zenobia (Jeraldine) P.; m. Hellen Mayes, June 17, 1968 (div. 1985); children: D'Allen, Sheree Nicole. AA in Gen. Edn., Fayetteville State U., 1976. ordained 1983. Enlisted U.S. Army, 1967, advanced through ranks to chief warrant officer 3, 1977, resigned, 1984; pres., cons. Titus Fin. Group, Norfolk and Chesapeake, Va., 1986—; with A.L. Williams Co., 1985—, regional mgr. Norfolk, 1985—; pres., cons. Home Credit Assocs., 1986; loan officer Old Dominion Credit Union, 1986-87. Counselor Chesapeake Juvenile Ct., 1986—. Decorated Bronze Star, Vietnam Cross of Gallentry, DFC, Air Medal (25). NTE grantee, 1987-88. Mem. Pacesetters Club (pres. 1987-88), Fin. and Banking Club (pres. 1988-89), Alpha Kappa Mu. Democrat. Baptist. Home: 7224 Chesapeake Blvd 1 Norfolk VA 23513 Office: Titus Fin Group PO Box 2181 Norfolk VA 23501 Other: 3614 Colley Ave Norfolk VA 23504

PRETZINGER, DONALD LEONARD, insurance executive; b. Los Angeles, Sept. 17, 1923; s. Leonard K. and Beatrice K. (Haupt) P.; m. Beverly Helen Winnard, Aug. 30, 1946; children: Christine, Kathryn, Kerry. BS with honors, Oreg. State U., 1948; MS, U. So. Calif., 1949. CLU, chartered fin. cons. Secondary tchr. sci. Fillmore (Calif.) High Sch., 1949-50, Los Angeles City Schs., 1950-51; spl. agt. FBI, Washington, 1951-56; sales supr. Farmers Group Inc., Los Angeles, 1956-60, asst. mgr. sales, 1960-63, mgr. sales, 1963-65, regional mgr., 1966-69, v.p. profl. liability, 1978-84; pres. Farmers Ins. Co. Oreg., 1984-89; v.p., gen. mgr. Farmers New World Life, Mercer Island, Wash., 1969-78. Pres. Northridge (Calif.) Townhome and Homeowners Assn., 1981-82; bd. dirs. St. Martin in the Fields Episc. Ch., Canoga Park, Calif., 1982-84. Lt. (j.g.) USN, 1942-46, PTO. Mem. Oreg. Ins. Mgrs. (bd. dirs. 1984-88), Oreg. Life and Health Guaranty Assn. (chmn., bd. dirs. 1984—), Oreg. Ins. Guaranty Assn. (treas., bd. dirs. 1984—), Oreg. Ins. Council (bd. dirs. 1984—), Masons, Kiwanis. Republican. Home: 18235 Moria Ct Lake Oswego OR 97034 Office: Farmers Group Inc 13333 SW 68th Pkwy Tigard OR 97223

PREUSS, GREGORY EDWARD, insurance association manager; b. West Union, Iowa, Dec. 24, 1946; s. Edward Arthur and Arlene Lucille (Otdoerfer) P.; m. Doreen Kay Williams, Aug. 29, 1969; children: Gretchen, Cara, Bryan, Amy. Student, Casper Coll., 1968; BS in Indsl. Mgmt., U. Wyoming, 1971. CLU; chartered fin. cons. Supr. Western Electric, Phoenix, 1971-75; dist. rep. Aid Assn. Lutherans, Phoenix, 1976-84; gen. agt. Aid Assn. Lutherans, Mission Viejo, Calif., 1984—. Trustee Christ Coll. Irvine (Calif.) Found., 1985. Mem. (life) Million Dollar Round Table (pres. 1984—), Nat. Assn. Life Underwriters, Am. Soc. CLU's, Gen. Agts. & Mgrs. Assn., Nat. Assn. Fraternal Ins. Counselors. Republican. Office: Aid Assn for Luths 25241 Paseo De Alicia Suite 200 Laguna Hills CA 92653

PREVITE, ERNEST LEON, bank executive, consultant; b. Leechburg, Pa., June 22, 1933; s. Angelo G. and Anna (Aleci) P.; m. Mary Taylor, May 21, 1955 (div. 1978); 1 child, Alice; m. 2d, Jessica Carole Pierangei, Dec. 18, 1983; stepchildren—Andrea, William, Maria. Student in pharmacy Ohio No. U., 1951-53; B.A. in Bus., Greenville Coll., 1955. Pres. Atlantic Realtors, Berlin, N.J., 1960-68; pres. Citizens Fed. Savs. and Loan Assn., Berlin, 1968-84; pres. Howard Fed., Berlin, 1984-87; pres. G. Potter King, Inc., Berlin, 1987—; dir. Viking Yacht Co., New Gretna, N.J. Pres. Greater Camden (N.J.) Devel. Corp., 1984; trustee Cooper Hosp., Univ. Med. Coll., Camden, South Jersey Blood Bank; commr. Camden County Mcpl. Utilities Authority. Democrat. Methodist. Club: Rotary. Office: G Potter King Inc 5 W Tauton Ave Berlin NJ 08009

PREVOST, EDWARD JAMES, brewing company executive; b. Baie Comeau, Que., Can., May 26, 1941; s. Omer and Jeanne (Ouellet) P.; m. Anna Marie Murphy, June 20, 1964; children: Marc, Louise, Eric, Luc. BA in History with honors, Loyola Coll., Montreal, Que., 1962; MBA, U. Western Ont., London, 1964. Cert. Advt. Agy. Practitioner. Account exec. J. Walter Thompson Co. Ltd., Montreal, 1964-66; successively account exec., account supr., group mgr. and v.p. Cockfield Brown & Co. Ltd., Montreal, 1966-69; gen. mgr. CJRP Radio, Quebec City, 1969-71; exec. v.p., chief operating officer Mut. Broadcasting Ltd., 1971-72, pres., chief operating officer, 1973; chmn. bd. Stephens and Towndrow Co. Ltd., Toronto, 1973-74; exec. v.p. Civitas Corp. Ltd., Montreal, 1973-74, pres., chief exec. officer, 1974-82, also chmn. bd. operating cos., 1974-82; pres., chief exec. officer La Brasserie O'Keefe Limitée, Montreal, 1983—; sr. v.p. Carling O'Keefe Breweries of Can. Ltd., 1983—; bd. dirs. BBM Bur. Broadcasting Measurement, 1971-78; mem. Montreal Bd. Trade. Gov. Can. Advt. Found., 1982; chmn. Telefilm Can., 1983-86; bd. dirs. U. Western Ont., Nat. Ctr. for Mgmt. R&D, 1986; v.p. bd. dirs. Loyola High Sch. Found. (Concordia), 1987; pres. ann. campaign Provincial March of Dimes, 1978 ; bd. dirs. Que. chpt. Canadian Council Christians and Jews; chmn. Montreal Heart Inst. Research Fund, 1979-81, exec. com. 1981-86; hon. patron Telethon of Stars, 1982; active Que. Diabetes Assn. Mem. Bd. L'Assn. des Brasseurs du Que. (chmn. 1984-86), Montreal C. of C. (dir. 1980, co-pres. cinematographic com. 1980-81), Province Que., Can., chambers commerce, Canadian Assn. Broadcasters (dir. 1975, vice chmn. radio 1976-77, chmn. 1978-79, past chmn., mem. exec. com. 1980-81), Inter-Am. Assn. Broadcasters Uruguay (sec., past treas), Young Pres. Orgn. (chmn. Que. chpt. 1987), Inst. Canadian Advt., Que. Diabetes Assn., Chambre de Commerce Belge et Luxembourgeoise, Am. Mktg. Assn. (pres. Quebec City chpt. 1970), Assn. des MBA du Que. (chmn. 1985-86),. Clubs: St.-Denis (Montreal), Western Bus. Sch. (Montreal) (founding pres. 1972), Royal Montreal Golf. Office: La Brasserie O'Keefe Limitée, 990 Rue Notre Dame W, Montreal, PQ Canada H3C 1K2 also: Carling O'Keefe Breweries Can Ltd, 4100 Yonge St, North York, ON Canada M2P 2C4

PREWITT, WILLIAM CHANDLER, financial executive; b. Phila., Aug. 23, 1946; s. Richard Hickman and Jean Mary (Simpkins) P.; m. Karen Ruth Padgett, May 15, 1971. BA in History, Transylvania coll., 1968; cert., Coll. Fin. Planning, 1987. Dist. exec. Cen. N.C. Council, Albemarle, 1971-74, Transatlantic Council, Heidelburg, Fed. Republic Germany, 1974-78; field dir. Dutchess City Council, Hyde Park, N.Y., 1978-80; prin. Prewitt Properties, Charleston, S.C., 1980—, William C. Prewitt Cert. Fin. Planner, Charleston, S.C., 1986—; regional rep. First Investors Corp., Charleston, S.C., 1982-83; lectr. Charleston Coll., 1987—, Trident Tech. Coll., Charleston, 1987—. Deacon 1st Prebyn. Ch., Rockingham, N.C., 1972-74; 1st Scots Ch., Charleston, 1987—; treas. Historic Ansonborough Neighborhood Assn., Charleston, 1987—. Served to 1st lt. USMCR, 1968-71. Mem. Greater Charleston Inst. Cert. Fin. Planners (pres. 1985-87, chmn. bd. dirs. 1987—), Inst. Cert. Fin. Planners, Internat. Assn. Fin. Planning, Nat. Assn. Personal Fin. Advisors. Republican. Lodge: Rotary. Home: 33 Hasell St Charleston SC 29401 Office: 123 Meeting at Queen Charleston SC 29401

PREYSZ, LOUIS ROBERT FONSS, III, management consultant, educator; b. Quantico, Va., Aug. 1, 1944; s. Louis Robert Fonss, Jr., and Lucille (Parks) P.; BA, U. Wis., Madison, 1968; MBA, U. Utah, Salt Lake City, 1973; grad. Stonier Grad. Sch. Banking, Rutgers U., 1983, The Command and Gen. Staff Coll., Ft. Leavenworth, Kans., 1986; m. Claudia Ann Karpowitz, Sept. 9, 1967; children—Louis Robert Fonss IV, Christine Elizabeth, Michael Anthony, Laura Ann, Daniel Timothy. Teaching and research asst. U. Utah, 1972-73; mktg. and personnel officer Security 1st Nat. Bank of Sheboyan (Wis.), 1973-76; mktg. dir. 1st Nat. Bank Rock Island (Ill.), 1976-77; asst. v.p., mktg. sales mgr. 1st Nat. Bank Birmingham (Ala.), 1977-78; v.p., mktg. mgr. Sun 1st Nat. Bank Orlando (Fla.), 1978-80; pres. Preysz Assocs. (Fla.), 1980—; asst. prof. mgmt. and banking Flagler Coll., St. Augustine, Fla., 1982—; mem. part-time faculty U. Wis., 1973-76, Fla. Inst. Tech., 1976-77, St. Ambrose Coll., Davenport, Iowa, 1976-77, U. Cen. Fla., 1979-81, Columbia Coll. (Mo.), 1981-82; mem. Tng. and Profl. Devel. Council, Bank Mktg. Assn., 1976-78, chmn., 1978; mem. mktg. and pub. relations com. Wis. Bankers Assn., 1975; v.p. Ala. Automated Clearing House Assn., 1978; mem. Wis. Automated Clearing House Assn., 1975-76. Mem. Rep. Presdl. Task Force, Rep. Nat. Com.; bd. dirs. Cath. Charities Bur. Inc., 1988—, v.p., 1989; bd. dirs. United Way St. Johns County, 1989—. Capt. U.S. Army, 1968-72; officer Fla. Army N.G. Mem. Soc. Advancement Mgmt. (internat. v.p., bd. dirs. 1984—), U. Wis. Alumni Assn., U. Utah Alumni Assn., Nat. Geog. Soc., N.G. Officers Assn., Phi Gamma Delta. Republican. Roman Catholic. Clubs: St. Augustine Officers, Anastasia Athletic. Lodge: Rotary. Author: How to Introduce a New Service, 1976; Energy Efficiency Programs and Lending Practices for Florida's Financial Institutions, 1980; Credit Union Marketing, 1981, An Effective Management Structure for Multi-Bank Holding Companies, 1983; contbg. editor: Target Market, an Instructional Approach to Bank Cross Selling of Services, New Accounts Training Manual, 1977; Tested Techniques in Bank Marketing, 1977; contbr. articles to mags. Home: 42 Southwind Circle Saint Augustine FL 32084 Office: PO Box 1027 Saint Augustine FL 32085

PRIBULO, JANET HUDAK, electronics company official; b. St. Petersburg, Fla., Oct. 9, 1955; d. Andrew John and Mary Alice (Stephens) Hudak; m. Kenneth J. Pribulo, July 10, 1976 (div. Aug. 1983). BA, U. South Fla., 1978; MBA, Fla. Inst. Tech., 1985. Fin. adminstr., acct. Sperry Def. Electronics Systems, Inc. (name changed to Hercules Def. Electronics Systems, Inc. 1984), Clearwater, Fla., 1978-84, sr. contract adminstr., 1984—. Mem. Nat. Contract Mgmt. Assn. (treas. Seminole area 1985-87, pres. 1987-88, nat. dir. 1988—). Democrat. Office: Hercules Def Electronics Systems Inc PO Box 4648 Clearwater FL 34618

PRICE, ALAN THOMAS, corporate financial planner; b. Balt., Nov. 11, 1949; s. Alvah Thompson and Doris Elaine (Cole) P.; m. Page Angela Jennings, Sept. 1978 (div. 1980); m. Lauren Ann St. Clare, Aug. 12, 1983. BS, U. N.C., 1972. Cert. estate and bus. analyst, Chartered Fin. Cons. Mgmt. trainee Sears, Atlanta, 1972-73; ins. agt. Aetna Life & Casualty, Atlanta, 1973-76, Pilot Life/New Eng. Life, Virginia Beach, Va., 1976-81; owner, pres. Page II Prodns., Inc., Norfolk, Va., 1981—; veteran judge Miss U.S.A. Pageant System. Fin. columnist News-Herald, 1985-86. Active Mus. Marine Scis., Virginia Beach, 1986—, Hope Found., Windsor, N.C., 1987—, Va. Stage Co., Va. Pops Orch. Named Man of Yr., Pilot Life, Tidewater, Va., 1978, 79, 80. Fellow Life Underwriter Tng. Coun.; mem. Million Dollar Roundtable (life and qualifying), Internat. Assn. Registered Fin. Planners, Am. Coun. Ind. Life Underwriters, Am. Soc. CLU's, Internat. Assn. Fin. Planning (dir. 1987-88), Inst. Cert. Fin. Planners, Nat. Assn. Life Underwriters, Sales and Mktg. Execs., Ct. of the Table, Tidewater Estate Planning Coun., Tidewater Builders Assn., Cen. Bus. Dist. Assn., Hampton Roads C. of C. Methodist. Home: 2645 River Rd Virginia Beach VA 23454 Office: Page II Prodns Inc 2 Koger Exec Ctr Ste 17 Norfolk VA 23502

PRICE, ALFRED LEE, lawyer, mining company executive; b. Little Rock, May 19, 1935; s. Dewey Ernest and Dorothy Ava (Cooper) P.; m. Magdalena Torres, June 20, 1958; children: Gregory L., Ana Maria. BA, Hendrix Coll., 1956; JD, Tulane U., 1967. Bar: La. 1967, Miss. 1974, D.C. Office mgr., dir. personnel Petroleum Helicopters Co., Lafayette, La. and New Orleans, 1956-67; atty., office mgr. Offshore Navigation and Petroleum Helicopters Co., New Orleans, 1967-74; gen. counsel First Miss. Corp., Jackson, 1974—, corp. sec., 1988—. Mem. ABA, La. Bar Assn., Miss. Bar Assn., Fed. Bar Assn., Hinds County Bar Assn., Miss. Mfrs. Assn. (bd. dirs.), Reservoir Exchange Club (bd. dirs.), Miss. Econ. Council (chmn. tort reforms com.), Jackson County Club, University Club. Methodist. Office: First Mississippi Corp 700 North St PO Box 1249 Jackson MS 32915-1249

PRICE, BEN E., electronics executive; b. Caretta, W.Va., May 28, 1938; s. Robert Ralston and Helen (Rogers) P.; m. Barbara Jane Ehyott, Sept. 15, 1962; children: Brett, Bart. Student, Union Coll., 1956-60; grad., G.E. Apprentice Sch. Pres. Brad Cable Electronics, Inc., Schenectady, 1977—. Rep. committeeman Rotterdam, 1961. Mem. Internat. Ins. Agts. Assn., Profl. Ins. Agts. Assn., N.Y. State Cable TV Assn., Jaycees, Friends of Music. Lodge: Kiwanis. Office: Brad Cable Electronics Inc 1023 State St PO Box 739 Schenectady NY 12301

PRICE, DAVID ALAN, business equipment company executive; b. N.Y.C., Oct. 3, 1940; s. Louis and Stella (Friedman) P.; m. Roberta R. Cohen, June 16, 1963; children: Scott, Steven, Lainie. BS, U. Bridgeport, 1963. Sales rep. Proctor & Gamble, Cin., 1964-65, IBM, Armonk, N.Y., 1965-68; sales mgr., dist. mgr., regional mgr., v.p. TAB Products Co., Palo Alto, Calif., 1968—. Author: Attacking the Territory, 1974. Cub master Boy Scouts Am., N.Y.C., 1970-72. Sgt. U.S. Army, 1963-64. Republican. Jewish. Home: 37 Christopher Dr New York NY 10956 Office: TAB Products 280 N Central Ave Hartsdale NY 10530

PRICE, DAVID ROBERT, construction company executive; b. Lafayette, Ind., June 16, 1940; s. James R. and Robert L. (Pierce) P.; m. Jane Hovde, Aug. 19, 1961; children: Rebecca L., James F. BS, Purdue U., 1962. Pres. Price Homes, INc., Kokomo, Ind., 1962-66, Nat. Home Constrn. Corp., Lafayette, 1966-72; exec. v.p. Nat. Homes Corp. (name changed to Nat. Enterprises, Inc. 1987), Lafayette, 1966-72, 1972-77, pres., 1977-87, chmn., 1987—, chief operating officer, 1977-78, chief exec. officer, 1978—, also bd. dirs.; bd. dirs. Bank One (formerly Purdue Nat. Bank), Lafayette. Past mem. bd. dirs. Jr. Achievement, Lafayette, St. Elizabeth Hosp., Lafayette. Mem. Young Pres. Orgn., Nat. Assn. Home Builders (past bd. dirs.), Nat. Housing Ctr. (past trustee), Coun. Housing Producers (past bd. dirs.), Ind. Home Builders Assn. (past bd. dirs., Pres. of Yr. award 1968). Presbyterian. Home: 3500 Cypress Ln Lafayette IN 47905 Office: Nat Enterprises Inc 401 S Earl Ave PO Box 7680 Lafayette IN 47903

PRICE, DENNIS JOSEPH, loss prevention consultant; b. Stamford, Conn., Sept. 22, 1945; s. John Joseph and Mary Ann (Pscheck) P.; m. Bernardene Scott, June 7, 1975 (div. 1979); children: Barbara, Katie; m. Noreen Murphy, Apr. 22, 1989. AA, Dade Jr. Coll., 1966; BS in Criminology, Fla. State U., 1968. Cert. safety profl.; assoc. in loss control mgmt. Property mgr. Key West, Fla., 1971-75; real estate sales Anchor Realty, Tallahassee, Fla., 1975-76; with loss control dept. Mobile Home Industries, Tallahassee, 1977-79; loss prevention cons. Amerisure/Mich. Mut., St. Petersburg, Fla., 1979—. State coord. Operation Lifesaver, 1988. Lt. (j.g.) USNR, 1969-70. Mem. Am. Soc. Safety Engrs. (pres. elect 1989—), Fla. Fedn. for Safety (pres. 1988). Roman Catholic. Home: 12733 83d Ave N Seminole FL 34642 Office: Amerisure Ins Co 6133 Central Ave Saint Petersburg FL 33733

PRICE, EDWARD JOHN, JR., tractor manufacturing company executive; b. Youngstown, Ohio, Sept. 27, 1946; s. Edward John and Margaret (Kaschak) P.; m. Kathleen Mary Elizabeth Eckman, June 2, 1968; children: Amy, Patrick, Karen, Beth. BSBA in Personnel Mgmt., Ohio State U., 1968. Credit supr. Ashland Oil Inc., Dublin, Ohio, 1968-74; credit mgr. White Haines div. Itek Corp., Columbus, Ohio, 1974-76; credit mgr. Dravo Marks div. Dravo Corp., Pitts., 1976-79; fin. mgr. no. div. Kubota Tractor Corp., Columbus, 1979—. Mem. Nat. Assn. Credit Mgrs., Internat. Credit Assn., Consumer Credit Assn., Internat. Diabetic Athletes Assn., Am. Diabetes Assn., Cum Cristo Cursillo. Roman Catholic. Home: 108 Aldrich Rd Columbus OH 43214 Office: Kubota Tractor Corp 438 McCormick Blvd Columbia OH 43213

PRICE, FORD COWAN, JR., real estate officer; b. Lakeland, Fla., Aug. 3, 1958; s. Ford Cowan and Janet (Shields) P.; m. Sheryl Hoover, Apr. 27, 1985; 1 child, Katherine Claire. BBA, Trinity U., 1980. With The Sweetsers Co., Oklahoma City, 1980-88, pres., chief exec. officer, 1985-88; mng. ptnr. Price Edwards, Henderson and Co. (formerly The Sweetsers Co.), Oklahoma City, 1988—. Bd. dirs. Omniplex Mus., 1987. Mem. Nat. Orgn. Indsl. Office Pks. (pres. 1986-87), Young Men's Dinner Club (pres. 1988). Home: 2525 Clermont Oklahoma City OK 73118

PRICE, GARY ANDREW, electrical engineer; b. Cin., June 26, 1960; s. James Orion and Dorothy Jean (McElfresh) P.; m. Karen Marie Steinhoff, May 5, 1984. BSE, Purdue U., 1983. Co-op engr. Cin. Bell, Inc., 1979-82; residence hall counselor Purdue U., West Lafayette, 1982-83; engring. assoc. Cin. Bell Telephone, 1983-84, network supr., 1984-85, network engr., 1985-

86; engr. network communications AT&E Labs., Inc., Portland, Oreg., 1986-87; project mgr. AT&E Labs., Inc., 1987-88; mgr. network svcs. AT&E Corp., 1988—; dir. Engr. & Scientists of Cin., 1982-86; chmn. Engr. for a Day, Cin., 1984-86. Patentee in field. Recipient of Sherwood Engr. Ingenuity award Purdue Engring., 1981, Outstanding Svc. award Purdue Bands, 1981, Outstanding Young Men of Am. Jaycees, 1983. Mem. Cheviot #140 Lodge. Republican. Home: 6915 SW 169th Pl Beaverton OR 97007

PRICE, HARRY STEELE, III, corporate executive; b. Dayton, Ohio, Apr. 19, 1938; s. Harry Steele Jr. and Janet (Smith) P.; m. Valerie Knost, Aug. 29, 1961; children: Harry Steele IV, Paul Tobin. Student, Brown U., 1957-59; BSCE, U. Cin., 1966, MBA, 1967. Div. mgr. Price Bros. Co., Dayton, 1972-79; pres. EWP Corp., Wilmington, Ohio, 1979-81; exec. v.p. ACTS-BSC Inc., Plymouth, Mich., 1985-86; also bd. dirs. ACTS-BSC Inc., Plymouth; pres. Flexiblast Co., Wilmington, 1981—, also bd. dirs. Inventor descaling machine, wire guide aparatus. Grad. Leadership Dayton, 1978; community adv. counsel Sycamore Hosp., Miamisburg, Ohio, former mem. Kettering Med. Assocs. Mem. Wire Assn. Internat. (continuing edn. com. 1986—), Wire Reinforcement Inst. (chmn. 1980-81). Club: Miami Valley Hunt (Spring Valley, Ohio), Camargo Hunt (Cinn.), Dayton Racquet. Lodge: Rotary (bd. dirs. Wilmington club 1981). Office: Flexiblast Co PO Box 291 Bellbrook OH 45305

PRICE, I. EDWARD, financial service company executive; b. N.Y.C., Sept. 14, 1942; s. Harry and Sylvia (Feldberg) P.; m. Diane Gail Miller, June 21, 1964; children: Noah, Stefan. BA, Yale U., 1964. Various positions Prudential Ins. Co. Am., Newark, N.J. and Los Angeles, 1964-81; sr. v.p. Prudential Property and Casualty Ins. Co., Holmdel, N.J., 1981-84; v.p. Prudential Ins. Co. Am., Newark, 1984-86, sr. v.p., corp. actuary, 1986-88; sr. v.p. individual ins. systems and adminstrn. Prudential Ins. Co. Am., Roseland, N.J., 1988—; bd. dirs. Prudential Property and Casualty Ins. Co. Fellow Soc. Actuaries; mem. Am. Acad. Actuaries. Office: Prudential Ins Co Am 55 N Livingston Ave Roseland NJ 07068

PRICE, JAMES NORMAN, sales official; b. Picayune, Miss., Feb. 10, 1959; s. Daniel Jefferson and Helen (Harris) P.; m Lee Ann Miller, Oct.9, 1987. BBA, Miss. Coll., 1981. Sales rep. Am. Greetings Co., Lafayette, La., 1983-84; ter. supr. Am. Greetings Co., Lufkin, Tex., 1984; sales devel. rep. Am. Greetings Co., Houston, 1984-86; field mgr. Am. Greetings Co., Ft. Lauderdale, Fla., 1986-87; dist. mgr. Am. Greetings Co., Memphis, 1987-88, sales rep., 1988—. Sunday sch. worker Bellvue Ch., Memphis, 1988. Republican. Baptist. Home and Office: 4792 Barkshire Dr Memphis TN 38115

PRICE, KEITH MURRAY, engineering construction company executive; b. Los Angeles, Jan. 1, 1937; s. Daniel Duane and Doris Virginia (Disney) P.; children—Paige Nicolle, Piper Danielle, Keitra Suzanne; m. Debra Lynn Deitz, Dec. 22, 1986. Student, Mt. San Antonio Coll., Walnut, Calif., 1955-57; M.B.A., Pepperdine U., 1978. Project engr. Am. Electronics, Los Angeles, 1957-59; test dir. Paul Hardeman, Inc., Stanton, Calif., 1959-64; tech. dir. Morrison-Knudsen Co., Inc., Merritt Island, Fla., 1964-69; project mgr. various locations, 1969-73; v.p. Boise, Idaho, 1973-79, group v.p. power group, 1979-83, exec. v.p., 1983-85; chmn., chief exec. officer MK-Ferguson Co., Cleve., 1985—. Mem. ASME, Am. Soc. Chem. Engrs., Constrn. Industry Inst., Acad. Mgmt., Soc. Mfg. Engrs., Am. Nuclear Soc., Pacific Coast Elec. Assn. Presbyterian. Clubs: Beavers, Masons (32 deg.). Office: MK-Ferguson Co 1 Erieview Pla Cleveland OH 44114

PRICE, MARILYN JEANNE, fund raising and management consultant; b. N.Y.C., Jan. 24, 1948; d. George Franklin and Mary Anastasia (Barnishin) Lawrence; student Temple Bus. Sch., 1964-66; student U. Md., 1973-74; 1 child, Kimberly Jean. Asst. to sr. printing and paper buyer ARC, Washington 1965-67; conf. planner for classified mil. confs. Nat. Security Indsl. Assn., Washington, 1967-69; fund devel. office asst. Nat. Urban Coalition, Washington, 1970; direct mail/membership coordinator Common Cause, Washington, 1970-72; mgr. direct mail fund raising Epilepsy Found. of Am., Washington, 1973-76; exec. v.p. Bruce W. Eberle & Assocs., Vienna, Va., 1977-81; pres. Response Dynamics, Inc., Vienna, Va., 1981-83; v.p. The Best Lists, Inc., Vienna, 1981-83; pres. The Creative Advantage, Inc., Fairfax, Va., 1983—, Creative Mgmt. Services, Inc., Fairfax, 1987—; cons. in field. Asst. to Young Citizens for Johnson, 1964; vol. Hubert Humphrey campaign, 1968, George McGovern campaign, 1972. Recipient Silver Echo award, Direct Mail/Mktg. Assn. Internat. competition for mktg. excellence, 1980. Mem. Nat. Soc. Fund Raisers, Direct Mail Mktg. Assn., Non-Profit Mailers Fedn., Assn. Direct Response Fundraising Council (bd. dirs., treas.), Direct Mktg. Club. Home: 9614 Lindenbrook St Fairfax VA 22031 Office: The Creative Advantage 9401 Lee Hwy Suite 205 Fairfax VA 22031

PRICE, N. LEIGH, bank executive; b. Malin, Oreg., Feb. 6, 1941; d. Clarence Loraine and Nina Ellen (Kamping) P.; children: Brian, Leigh Ann. BA in Psychology, UCLA, 1980, MBA in Mgmt., 1982. Analyst Standard Oil Co., Tulsa, 1967-69; programmer/analyst Honeywell, Inc., Mpls., 1969-73; sr. systems analyst Fabri-Tek, Inc., Mpls., 1974-77; pres. Price & Assocs., Mpls., 1978-79; sr. cons. MRG Assocs., L.A., 1981-83; exec. v.p., chief operating officer Prescription Health Svcs., L.A., 1984-85; v.p., mgr. First Interstate Bank, L.A., 1985-88; v.p. Md. Nat. Bank, Balt., 1988—. Del. Minn. Dem. Conv., 1972; chmn. Parent/Sch. Bd. Coun., Edina, Minn., 1975; pres. Friends L.A. Opera, 1980-81; v.p. Guild Opera Co., L.A., 1983-85; exec. v.p. Opera Guild So. Calif., 1984-85, pres., 1985-87. Unitarian. Office: MNC Info Svcs PO Box 987 Baltimore MD 21203

PRICE, ROBERT, lawyer; b. N.Y.C., Aug. 27, 1932; s. Solomon and Frances (Berger) P.; m. Margery Beth Wiener, Dec. 18, 1955; children: Eileen Marcia, Steven. AB, NYU, 1953; LLD, Columbia U., 1958. Bar: N.Y. 1958, U.S. Dist. Ct. 1958, U.S. Ct. Appeals 1958, U.S. Supreme Ct 1958, ICC 1958, FCC 1958, IRS 1958. With R.H. Macy & Co., Inc., 1955-58; practiced in N.Y.C., 1958—; law clk. to judge U.S. Dist. Ct. (so. dist.) N.Y., 1958-59; asst. U.S. atty. So. Dist. N.Y., 1959-60; ptnr. Kupferman & Price, 1960-65; chmn. bd. pres. Atlantic States Ind. Inc., 1963-66; pres. WNVY, Pensacola, Fla., 1965-66, WLOB, Portland, Me., 1965-66; dep. mayor N.Y.C., 1965-66; exec. v.p., dir. Dreyfus Corp., N.Y.C., 1966-69; v.p., investment officer Dreyfus Fund, until 1969; chmn., pres., dir. Price Capital Corp., N.Y.C., 1969-72; gen. ptnr., spl. counsel Lazard, Freres & Co., 1972-82; pres. N.Y. Law Jour., Nat. Law Jour.; pres., treas., dir. Price Communications Corp., 1979—; chmn., dir. Telemation Inc., 1986—; adv. com. Bankers Trust Co. N.Y.; dir. Holly Sugar Corp., Lane Bryant, Inc.; chmn. N.Y.C. Port Authority Negotiating Com. for World Trade Ctr., 1965-66; mem. N.Y.C. Policy Planning Coun., 1966; spl. counsel N.Y. State Joint Legis. Com. on Ct. Reorgn., 1962-63; asst. counsel N.Y. State Joint Legis. Com. on N.Y. Banking Laws, 1961-62. Author articles. Chmn. govt. and civil svc. div. United Jewish Appeal Greater N.Y., 1966; co-chmn. Met. N.Y. Red Cross Blood Drive, 1966; mem. nat. exec. com. Columbia Law Sch. 16th Ann. Fund Drive, 1966-67; campaign mgr. John V. Lindsay campaigns for congressman, N.Y.C., 1958, 60, 62, 64; del. N.Y. Rep. State Conv., 1962, 66; del. Rep. Nat. Conv., 1988; campaign mgr. Nelson A. Rockefeller, Ore. Rep. presdl. primary campaign, 1964, Lindsay campaign for mayor, N.Y.C., 1965; lectr. Rep. Nat. Com., 1966—; bd. dirs. Am. Friends Hebrew U.; past trustee Columbia U. Sch. Pharm. Scis., Birch Wathen Sch. Served with AUS, 1953-55. Recipient Yeshiva U. Heritage award, 1966, Pub. Svc. award Queens Catholic War Vets., 1966, Pub. Svc. award Phila. 21 Jewel Sq. Club, 1967. Mem. ABA, FCC Bar Assn., Assn. Bar City N.Y., N.Y. State Dist. Attys. Assn., Coun. Fgn. Rels., Columbia Law Sch. Alumni Assn. (dir.), Scribes, Tau Kappa Alpha. Home: 25 E 86th St New York NY 10028 Office: Price Communications Corp 45 Rockefeller Pla New York NY 10020

PRICE, ROBERT MCCOLLUM, computer company executive; b. New Bern, N.C., Sept. 26, 1930. B.S. in Math. magna cum laude, Duke U., 1952; M.S. in Applied Math., Ga. Inst. Tech., 1958. Research engr. Gen. Dynamics div. Convair, San Diego, 1954-56; research mathematician Ga. Inst. Tech., 1956-58; mathematician Standard Oil of Calif., San Francisco, 1958-61; with Control Data Corp., Mpls., 1961—, pres. systems and services, 1973-75, pres. systems, services and mktg., 1975-77; pres. Computer Co., Control Data Corp., Mpls., 1977-80; pres., chief oper. officer Control Data Corp., Mpls., 1980-86, pres., 1986-88, chmn., chief exec. officer, 1986—, also dir. Office: Control Data Corp 8100 34th Ave S Minneapolis MN 55420 *

PRICE, RONALD JAMES, electrical products company executive; b. Wellsville, Ohio, Jan. 26, 1933; s. Thomas Pugh and Dorothy Maud (Saltsman) P.; BA in Math., Wooster Coll., 1953; BS in Mech. Engring., Ohio U., 1955; m. Phyllis Eileen Mangan, Feb. 15, 1958; children—Penny Eileen, Deborah Lynn. Sales engr. Westinghouse Corp., Detroit, 1957-62, dist. mgr., 1962-65, product mgr., standard control div., Beaver, Pa., 1965-68, sales mgr., 1968; v.p., gen. mgr. Fife Fla. Electric Supply, Tampa, Fla., 1968-71; mktg. mgr. Westinghouse Control Products Div., Beaver, 1971-75, engring. mgr., 1975-77, mgr. mktg. and strategic planning Indsl. Control Bus. unit, 1977-78; acting gen. mgr. specialty transformer div., Greenville, Pa., 1976, control equipment group mktg. mgr., 1978-80; gen. mgr. Bryant div. Westinghouse Electric Corp., Bridgeport, Conn., 1980-83, gen. mgr. comml. div., distbn. and protection bus. unit, 1983—; vis. lectr. Mich. State U. M.B.A. program. Trustee Beaver County Recreational Authority, 1972—; mem. Council of 100, Tampa, 1969-71; pres. Beaver Civic Assn.; chmn. Ft. McIntosh dist. Boy Scouts Am., Beaver; bd. assocs. U. Bridgeport, 1982—. Served with U.S. Army, 1958. Recipient Bausch & Lombe Sci. award, 1950. Registered profl. engr., Mich., Ohio, Pa. Mem. Nat. Soc. Profl. Engrs., Nat. Elec. Mfrs. Assn. (indsl. control systems sec., chmn. adv. com. for user needs), Elec. Council of Fla., Nat. Assn. of Elec. Distbrs. (speaker), Nat. Assn. Mfrs. (industry speaker), Am. Mgmt. Assn. (lectr.). Republican. Presbyterian. Home: 840 River Rd Beaver PA 15009 Office: Westinghouse Elec Corp Chatham Ctr Pittsburgh PA 15230

PRICE, STEVEN, lawyer, communications executive; b. N.Y.C., Feb. 14, 1962; s. Robert and Margery (Wiener) P. BA, Brown U., 1984; LLD, Columbia U., 1989. Reporter The Gainesville (Fla.) Sun, 1983—; mergers analyst Goldman Sachs and Co., N.Y.C., 1984-86; v.p. PriCellular, Inc., N.Y.C.; asst. corp. sec. Price Communications Corp., N.Y.C., 1986—, also bd. dirs.; bd. dirs. Telemation Inc., Atlas Broadcast Corp., N.Y. Law Jour. Co. Mem. Phi Beta Kappa. Home: 25 E 86th St New York NY 10028

PRICE, WILLIAM SLOANE, mining equipment company executive; b. Colorado Springs, Aug. 8, 1939; s. Inkerman Sloane and Mary Myrle (Senter) P.; m. Linda Kay Hillegas, Dec. 18, 1960; children: Scott Sloane, Melinda Jane. Engr. of mines, Colo. Sch. Mines, 1961; MBA, Lehigh U., 1970; cert. advanced mgmt. program, Harvard U. Grad. Sch. Bus. Adminstrn., 1985. With Ingersoll-Rand Corp., 1961-73; mktg. mgr. Worthington Compressors, Holyoke, Mass., 1973-76; v.p. Inex Resources, Lakewood, Colo., 1976-77, Reed Mining Equipment, Inc., Sherman, Tex., 1977-78; pres., chmn. bd. Baker-Hughes Mining Tools, Inc., Grand Prairie, Tex., 1978-88; pres. Eimco Jarvis Clark, Burlington, Ont., Can., 1988—; bd. dirs. Eimco Elecon, India, Mitxui Zosen Eimco, Japan, Pakmart, Oakville, Ont., Can. Mem. Young Pres. Orgn, Ft. Worth. Served to 1st lt. U.S. Army, 1962-64. Mem. AIME, Can. Inst. Mining and Metallurgy. Episcopalian. Office: Eimco Jarvis Clark, 4445 Fairview St, Burlington, ON Canada L7R 3Y8

PRICKETT, DAN STEVEN, information services executive; b. Mt. Vernon, Ohio, Sept. 11, 1952; s. Delbert Eugene and Anne H. (Scripter) P.; m. Janice Kathryn Morgan, Apr. 12, 1986; 1 child: Jonathan Lane. AB, Miami U., 1973; postgrad., U. Iowa, 1975-76; MBA, U. Dayton, 1985. Mgr. Nexis operation Mead Data Central, Dayton, Ohio, 1979-81, sr. mktg. rep., 1982, mgr. Nexis strategic planning, 1983-84, product mgr., corp. info. systems, 1984-85, mgr. strategic planning, 1986-87; dir. bus. devel. Bell Atlantic Directory Svcs., Bethesda, Md., 1987—. Mem. Info. Industry Assn. Home: 2595 John Milton Dr Herndon VA 22071 Office: Bell Atlantic Directory Svcs 6701 Democracy Blvd 9th Fl Bethesda MD 20817-1586

PRICKETT, WILL SMITH, JR., textile executive; b. Clanton, Ala., June 27, 1950; s. Will Smith Sr. and Geraldine (Boone) P.; m. Donna Jo Brown, Nov. 27, 1970; children: Lacy Hope, Will Smith III. BS in Maths. and Bus., Jacksonville State U., 1972. CPA, Ala. Indsl. engr. Carisbrook Industries, Blue Mountain, Ala., 1972-73; cost acct. Carisbrook Industries, 1973-74, mgr. cost acctg. dept., 1974-77; gen. mgr. Carisbrook Industries Blue Mountain div., Gardena, Calif., 1977; contr. Carisbrook Industries Blue Mountain div., Luray, Va., 1977-81; plant mgr. Carisbrook Industries Templon div., Wytheville, Va., 1981-82; contr. NFA Corp., Anniston, Ala., 1982-84; v.p., sec., treas. The Tape Craft Corp., Anniston, 1984—. Home: 830 Brookhaven Dr Anniston AL 36201 Office: The Tape Craft Corp 17 S Hunter St PO Box 2027 Anniston AL 36202

PRIEM, THEODORE LUDWIG, fast food company executive; b. Ladysmith, Wis., Oct. 25, 1940; s. Raymond Arthur and Pearl Ann (Pederson) P.; m. Theresa Carolyn Droege, Aug. 16, 1962; 1 child, Troy Raymond. BSBA, BA in Psychology, Eau Claire State U., 1962; MBA, Harvard U., 1982. Vice pres. sales Nat. Cash Register Co., Dayton, Ohio, 1964-69; pres. Comserv Corp., Mpls., 1970-83, bd. dirs., 1980-83; pres. T.L.A.P. Products Inc., Mpls., 1983-85, 1 Potato 2 Inc., Mpls., 1986—; bd. dirs. Communication Scis., Mpls. Pres. Minnetonka Babe Ruth Little League, 1984—, Blake Boosters, Mpls., 1986—. Mem. Am. Data Processing Svc. Orgn. (founding software contracts standards com. 1978-81), Internat. Coun. Shopping Ctr. Developers, Sigma Tau Gamma (pres. alumni Mpls. 1981-85). Office: 1 Potato 2 Inc 5640 International Pkwy New Hope MN 55428

PRIESTLEY, MICHAEL LINN, sales executive; b. Portland, Oreg., Jan. 24, 1953; s. Chester Carroll and Darlene Blanch (Jeske) P.; m. Anna Rebecca Miller, Jan. 1, 1973; children: Benjamin Ivon, Isaac Noel, Abraham Jordan. Grad. high sch., Portland; sales tng., Tom Hopkins and Dale Carnegie; mgmt. tng., Zig Ziglar, Portland. Lic. ins. and real estate agt. Sales mgr. Oreg. Office Systems, Beaverton, Oreg., 1979-80; western region br. mgr. Ontel Corp., Portland, 1980-81; bus. account exec. Rogers Cablesystems, Portland, 1981-84; dist. mgr. A.L. Williams, Portland, 1983-85; corp. and govt. account sales engr. Sentrol, Inc., Portland, 1985—; bus. plan devel. cons. Crawford Svcs., Portland, 1981, 83, L.W. Dennis & Assoc., 1983, 85; mem. rsch. bd. advisors Am. Biographical Inst.; fin. cons. in field. Pres., chmn. Richmond Neighborhood Assn., Portland, 1984-86; founder Clinton St. Coalition, 1983. Recipient Achievement award Dale Carnegie Sales Inst. L.W. Dennis & Assoc., 1981. Mem. Eagles Nest Club. Republican. Evang. Christian. Home: 16991 Maple Circle Lake Oswego OR 97035 Office: Sentrol Inc 10831 SW Cascade Blvd Portland OR 97223

PRIESTNER, EDWARD BERNARD, manufacturing company executive; b. Hamilton, Ont., Can., June 4, 1936; s. William Joseph and Helen Gladys (Osbaldeston) P.; m. Marianne Agnes Baker, May 23, 1959; children: Lorraine, Patricia, Nancy. BA in Econs., U. Western Ont., 1958. Supr., treas. Prudential Ins. Co. Am., Toronto, Ont., 1958-61; treasury asst. Westinghouse Can. Inc., Hamilton, 1961-64, asst. treas., 1964-71, treas., 1971-78, v.p., 1975-78, v.p. fin., 1978-81; v.p. ops. Westinghouse Can. Inc., Toronto, 1981-84, exec. v.p. ops., 1984-85, also bd. dirs.; pres., chief exec. officer Westinghouse Can. Inc., Hamilton, 1985—; v.p. Westinghouse Electric Corp. (parent co. Westinghouse Can. Inc.), Pitts., 1985—; bd. dirs. Allendale Ins. Co., Johnston, R.I., The Hamilton Group, Toronto. Mem. steering com. Hamilton dist. United Way, 1978—; bd. govs. McMaster U., Hamilton, 1985—, Jr. Achievement Hamilton. 1985—. Mem. Hamilton C. of C. (past pres.), Ont. Bus. Adv. Coun. Roman Catholic. Clubs: Hamilton; Hamilton Golf and Country (Ancaster, Ont.). Office: Westinghouse Can Inc, 120 King St W Box 2510, Hamilton, ON Canada L8N 3K2

PRIMACK, LEONARD, mortgage broker; b. Bklyn., Apr. 16, 1936; s. Victor and Jennie (Derechinsky) P.; m. Sandra Lowell, May 19, 1968; children—Jonathan, Adam. B.A., CCNY, 1957; M.B.A., NYU, 1966. Asst. to chmn. T. Rowe Price Assocs., Inc., Balt., 1963-65; fin. analyst SEC, Washington, 1965-67; portfolio mgr. Lazard Freres Co., N.Y.C., 1967-72; v.p. Lionel D. Edie & Co., Inc., N.Y.C., 1972-75; v.p. Steve Grief & Assocs., Inc., Encino, Calif., 1975-77; pres. Leonard Primack Assocs., Ltd., Hauppauge, N.Y., 1977—. Advisor Braintrust pub. Mem. Town of Smithtown Zoning Bd. Appeals. Served with U.S. Army, 1958-60. Recipient Real Estate award Real Estate Newsletter, 1983. Mem. L.I. Assn., Mortgage Bankers Assn. Lodges: Rotary. Home: 133 Parkway Dr N Commack NY 11725 Office: Primack Leonard Assocs 300 Rabro Dr Hauppauge NY 11788

PRIME, STEPHEN RUGGLES, yachting center manager; b. Detroit, Mar. 27, 1948; s. John Prosser and Joan (Mitchell) P.; m. Nancy Kaull, May 19, 1976 (div. Dec. 1982); m. Elizabeth Rooney, Oct. 22, 1983. BA in Polit. Sci., C.W. Post Coll., 1971. Laborer North Sails, Stratford, Conn., 1969-74, sales mgr., 1974-78; nat. sales mgr. AMF Alcort Sailboats, Waterbury, Conn., 1978-80, Pearson Yachts, Portsmouth, R.I., 1980-84; gen. mgr. Newport (R.I.) Yachting Ctr., 1984—; v.p. Sail Newport; lectr. seminars North Sails U., 1975-78. Mem. Mus. Yachting, R.I. Marine Trade Assn., Newport Bus. Alliance, Newport C. of C., Ida Lewis Yacht Club (Newport). Home: 13 South Dr Middletown RI 02840 Office: Newport Yachting Ctr 4 Commercial Wharf Newport RI 02840

PRIMI, DON ALEXIS, advertising and public relations executive, railroad transportation executive; b. N.Y.C., Jan. 14, 1947; s. John Prosper, Sr. and Eileen Mary P.; A. in Advt., State U. N.Y., 1967; B.S. in Mktg. and Advt., Hofstra U., 1971; advanced astron. studies degree, Vanderbilt Mus. and Planetarium, 1967. Gen. mgr., Recreational Pub. Corp.; pres., owner Fantasia Trains/REE R.R. Equipment Exchange, 1980, Don Primi Designs, 1983, First Communications, Inc., 1984, Rail Industries, Rail Fin. Corp., 1987, Gold Coast Ltd./Royal Rail, 1987; cons. to rail industries, 1986, ry. industry, brick and clay products industry; designer corp. identity programs. Recipient awards Printing Industries Met. N.Y., Gold Boli advt. awards, Kimberly-Clark Graphic excellence awards, Astrophotoawards. Mem. Assn. Ry. Progress Inst., R.R. Pub. Relations Assn., Nat. R.R. Assn. Passengers, Sales and Mktg. Execs., Astron Soc. L.I. (pres., pub. rel dir.), Rail Mktg. Club N.Y. Designs published in periodicals. Office: 160 Fifth Ave New York NY 10010 also: PO Box 1199 Port Washington NY 11050

PRIMUTH, ERIC MARK, corporate executive; b. East Cleveland, Ohio, May 25, 1959; s. Elroy Mark and Mary Alice (Klemencic) P. BBA, Cleve. State U., 1982; MBA, Kent State U., 1985, MS in Acctg., 1985. CPA, Ohio; cert. internal auditor. External auditor Deloitte, Haskins & Sells, Cleve., 1983-85; internal auditor Reliance Electric Co., Cleve., 1985-86; controller The Leahey Constrn. Co., Inc., Chagrin Falls, Ohio, 1986-87; asst. controller Matrix Essentials, Inc., Solon, Ohio, 1987-88; pres. Primuth, Hendrickson & Co., CPA's, Independence, Ohio, 1988—; auditing instr. Kent State U., 1985; co-chmn. exam. com. IIA Cleve. chpt. CIA. Mem. research com., spl. events fin. com. Cleve. Waterfront Coalition. Mem. Ohio Soc. CPA's, Inst. Internal Auditors, Assn. MBA Execs., Cleve. State U. Alumni Assn., Kent State U. Alumni Assn., St. Joseph High Sch. Alumni Assn. Home: 1906 Marda Dr Parma OH 44134 Office: 2 Summit Park Dr #300 Independence OH 44131

PRINCE, LARRY L., automotive parts and supplies company executive. With Genuine Parts Co., Atlanta, 1958—, v.p., then group v.p., 1977-83, exec. v.p., 1983-86, pres., chief operating officer, 1986—, also bd. dirs. Office: Genuine Parts Co 2999 Circle 75 Pkwy Atlanta GA 30339 *

PRINCE, ROBB LINCOLN, manufacturing company executive; b. Duluth, Minn., June 30, 1941; s. Milton H. and Katherine (Lincoln) P.; m. Jacqueline H. Marik, June 19, 1965; children: Daniel, Deborah. B.A. in Econs., Carleton Coll., 1963; M.B.A. in Mktg., U. Pa., 1965. With mktg. planning United Airlines, Chgo., 1965-72; dir. planning Jostens Inc., Mpls., 1973-74, treas., 1975-79, v.p., treas., 1979—; dir. AMEV Open End Mut. Funds. Served with USN, 1966-69. Club: Wharton Alumni (dir.). Office: Jostens Inc 5501 Norman Center Dr Minneapolis MN 55437

PRINCE, SIDNEY, financial planning executive, broker; b. N.Y.C., June 15, 1923; s. Marcus and Mollie (Bartel) P.; m. Adele Zweben, June 1, 1946; children: Richard Eric, Jeffrey Mark, Denise Robin. BS, L.I. U., 1943. Life underwriter Penn. Mut. Life Ins., Ridgewood, N.J., 1965-69; staff mgr. Penn. Mut. Life Ins., Orlando, Fla., 1969-70; pres., chief exec. officer Sid Prince & Assoc., Inc., Winter Park, Fla., 1970—; pres. S.P. & Assocs, Inc. Fin. Services, Winter Park. Pres. Life Underwriter Tng. Council, Orlando, Fla., 1978-79. Fellow Nat. Assn. Life Underwriters; mem. Nat. Assn. Security Dealers, Fla. Assn. Life Underwriters, Internat. Assn. Fin. Planners (treas. Orlando chpt. 1985—, designated RFP.). Club: Mercedes Benz (Orlando) (pres. 1985-86). Lodge: Masons (32 degree), Shriners, Kiwanis (pres. Cen. Fla. chpt. 1980-81) (Kiwanian of Yr. 1977). Office: Sid Prince & Assocs Inc 861 W Morse Blvd Ste 200 Winter Park FL 32789

PRINDIVILLE, ROBERT ANDREW, investment executive; b. Chgo., Aug. 18, 1935; s. James A. and Mary (Greening) P.; m. Kathleen Hardie, Aug. 8, 1959; children: Eleanor, Victoria, Christopher, Charles, Anne, Mary Alice, Genevieve. BS, Marquette U., 1958. With Thomson McKinnon Asset Mgmt., N.Y.C., 1958—; bd. dirs. Chgo. Bd. Option Exchange, 1978-82. Mem. City Midday Club, Baltusrol Golf Club. Office: Thomson McKinnon Asset Mgmt Financial Sq New York NY 10005

PRINE, CHARLES W., JR., construction executive; b. Pitts., Apr. 23, 1926; s. Charles W. and Mabel (Kerr) P.; m. Elizabeth Waite, July 23, 1983; children: Linda, Janet, Karen, Roger, Barbara, Alison. A.B., Princeton U., 1948. Journalist Pitts. Sun-Telegraph, 1948-56; pres. P.R. Counselors, Inc., Pitts., 1957-69; sr. v.p. Ryan Homes, Inc., Pitts., 1969—. Chmn. Mt. Lebanon Joint Recreation Commn., 1968-70; bd. dirs. Pitts. Opera, Grantmakers of Western Pa., Three Rivers Shakespear Festival; pres. Action Housing Inc.; bd. dirs. Health and Welfare Planning Assn.; chmn. adv. council YWCA Greater Pitts.; mem. strategic planning and resource mgmt. United Way Allegheny County; elder Bower Hill Community Presbyn. Ch. Served with USNR, 1944-46. Recipient Vol. of Yr. award United Way Allegheny County, 1987. Club: Harvard-Yale-Princeton (Pitts.). Office: Ryan Homes Inc 100 Ryan Ct Pittsburgh PA 15205

PRINGLE, EDWARD GRAVES, management consultant; b. Summit, N.J., Feb. 25, 1941; s. Edward Harvey and Caroline (Mazuco) P.; m. Neta Lindsay, June 14, 1963 (div. 1986); children: Elizabeth, Katherine, Ian; m. Mary S. Coburn, Aug. 23, 1986; children: Robert, Thomas, Susan. BS, Lehigh U., 1963; MBA, U. Pa., 1965. CPA, cert. mgmt. cons. Mem. cons. staff Coopers & Lybrand, N.Y.C., 1964-71, ptnr., 1972-86, vice chmn., 1987—; Area v.p. Acme Assn. Advt. Firms, N.Y.C., 1986—. Recipient Service award Pa. Inst. CPA's, Phila., 1968. Mem. Assn. Service Industries (bd. dirs. 1988—), Am. Inst. CPA's, Inst. Mgmt. Cons. (bd. dirs. 1984-86), Univ. Club, N.Y. Athletic Club. Republican. Presbyterian. Office: Coopers & Lybrand 1251 Ave of the Americas New York NY 10020

PRINGLE, HOMER LYNN, grain company executive; b. Laramie, Wyo., Dec. 26, 1941; s. Homer Lynn, Jr. and Mary Beth (Dumbrill) p.; m. Lorna Ruth Morgan, Mar. 11, 1966; children: Heather, Erin, Cameron. BA, U. Wyo., 1964, postgrad., 1964-66; postgrad., U. Ariz., 1966-67. Mgr. Walgreen Drug Co., Phoenix, 1970-74, Palo Alto, Calif., 1974-76; mgr., v.p. Morgan-Lindsay, Inc., Jerome, Idaho, 1976-79; regional mgr. Wickes Co., Jerome, 1979-80; pres. A&B Bean and Grain, Inc., Burley, Idaho, 1980-85, Haney Seed Co., Twin Falls, Idaho, 1985—. Bd. dirs. Jerome C. of C. 1979-80, N.W. Opera Assn, Twin Falls, 1980-82, Magic Valley Arts Council, Inc., Twin Falls, 1987—. Mem. Western Bean Dealers Assn. (pres. 1979-80), Nat. Dry Bean Council , Inc. (Idaho rep. 1980-84), Elks. Republican. Presbyterian. Home: 601 E Main St Jerome ID 83338 Office: Haney Seed/Bean Growers 347 S Park Ave W Twin Falls ID 83301

PRINGLE, LEWIS GORDON, advertising agency executive; b. Lansing, Mich., Feb. 13, 1941; s. Gordon Henry and Lucile Roxana (Drake) P.; m. Linda Carol Norum; children: Lewis Gordon Jr., William Davis, Thomas Benjamin. B.A., Harvard U., 1963; M.S., M.I.T., 1965, Ph.D., 1969. Vice pres., dir. mktg. sci. BBDO, Inc., N.Y.C., 1968-73, exec. v.p., dir. research services, corp. dir., 1978—; exec. v.p. BBDO Worldwide, 1986—; chmn. BBDO Europe, 1986—; asst. prof. mktg. Carnegie-Mellon U., 1973-74. Author numerous articles in field. Active local Boy Scouts Am. Ford Found. fellow, 1967. Fellow Royal Statis. Soc.; mem. Market Research Council, Inst. Mgmt. Sci., Am. Psychol. Assn., European Soc. Mktg. and Opinion Research, Am. Mktg. Assn. Republican. Congregationalist. Home: Whispers, Riversdale, Bourne End, Buckinghamshire, England SL8 5EB Office: BBDO Worldwide, 1-2 Chester Gate, London NW1 4JB, England

PRINGLE, THOMAS WALKER, stock broker; b. Hartford, Conn., Sept. 19, 1957; s. William George and Polly (Peterson) P. BA in Communications, Boston U., 1981. V.p. Mark Securities, Inc., West Hartford, Conn., 1983—, registered rep., 1983—. Mem. Internat. Assn. Fin. Planning. Club: University (Hartford). Office: Mark Securities Inc 1007 Farmington Ave West Hartford CT 06107

PRINJINSKI, THOMAS JOSEPH, data processing executive; b. Teaneck, N.J., June 1, 1955; s. Joseph Paul and Irene Marie (Hendl) P.; m. Rosanne Jackson, Feb. 15, 1975 (div. Nov. 1986); children: Jennifer Claire, Sarah Grace; m. Cara Krylewitch, Apr1 1, 1989. AAS in Data Processing with distinction, Nat. Coll., 1984, BS in Data Processing summa cum laude, 1985. Computer programmer, analyst U.S. Govt., Kirtland Air Force Base, N.Mex., 1982-85; sr. system analyst Honeywell Fed. Systems Inc., McLean, Va., 1985-88; computer programmer Internat. Union Bricklayers and Allied Crafts, Washington, 1988—. Mem. Beth Messiah Congregation, Rockville, Md. Served with USAF, 1975-78. Home: PO Box 9355 Silver Spring MD 20906-0996 Office: Internat Union Bricklayers & Allied Crafts 815 15th St NW Washington DC 20005

PRITCHARD, LOIS RUTH BREUR, engineer; b. Paterson, N.J., Mar. 26, 1946; d. George L. and Ruth Margaret (Farquhar) Breur; m. Bruce N. Pritchard, Aug. 10, 1968 (div. May 1982); children: John Douglas, Tiffany Anne; m. Robert H. Krause. Student, Keuka Coll., 1964-65; BS in Chemistry cum laude, Fairleigh Dickinson U., 1980; postgrad., Stevens Inst. Tech. With dept. R & D UniRoyal, Wayne, N.J., 1966-68, Jersey State Chem. Co., North Haledon, 1968-69, Inmont, Clifton, N.J., 1969; from chemist to sr. analyst Lever Bros., Edgewater, N.J., 1976-80; process engr. Bell Telephone Labs., Murray Hill, N.J., 1980-84, RCA, Somerville, N.J., 1984-86; sr. engr. electron beam lithography ops. Gain Electronics Corp., Somerville, 1986-88; cons. Pritchard Assocs., Budd Lake, N.J., 1988—; presenter profl. papers for profl. confs. Patentee package design. Troop leader, trainer, cons. Bergen County council Girl Scouts U.S., 1969-80, troop leader Morris Area council, 1980-83, head com. Mt. Olive twp., 1980-81; den leader, den leader coach, trainer Boy Scouts Am., 1973-76. Mem. AAAS, AAUW, NAFE, IEEE, Components, Hybrids, and Mfg. Tech. Soc. (semicondr. tech. subcom. electronic components conf. program com. 1981-86). Soc. Photo-Optical Instrumentation Engrs., Am. Soc. for Quality Control, Soc. Women Engrs., Am. Chem. Soc., Am. Inst. Chemists, Assn. Women in Sci., Internat. Platform Assn., Mensa, Phi Omega Epsilon. Republican. Episcopalian.

PRITCHARD, NILES ARTHUR, mortgage banker; b. Easton, Pa., Aug. 14, 1957; s. Niles Brewer and Shirley Louise (George) P.; m. Carol Diane Bryant, Feb. 14, 1980 (div. Aug. 1984); m. Kimberly Dianne Manworing, Apr. 16, 1988. BBA, U. Houston, 1985, postgrad., 1986. Mortgage loan officer Lumbermens Investment Corp., Houston, 1977-78; sr. comml./residential loan officer Commonwealth Mortgage, Houston, 1978-86; sr. residential loan officer Silver State Mortgage div. Imperial Corp. of Am., Denver, 1986-87; pres., chief exec. officer NAP Holdings, Inc., Denver, 1987—. Bd. dirs. Amateur Bowlers Tour, Denver, 1987. Mem. Mortgage Bankers of Am., Jefferson County Bd. of Realtors (lender relations com. 1987), Am. Bowling Congress. Democrat. Baptist. Office: NAP Holdings Inc 9030 Yukon Suite 3600 Westminster CO 80020

PRITCHARD, RAYMOND JOHN, tobacco company executive; b. Newland, Gloucestershire, Eng., Aug. 2, 1931; came to U.S., 1985; s. David and Hilda (Williams) P.; m. Connie Pritchard, Feb. 25, 1956; children: Julie, Carolyn, Allison. Student, Monmouth Coll., Eng., 1943-50. Dir. Imperial Tobacco Co., India, 1969-70; v.p., dir. CIA de Cigarros, Souza Cruz, Brazil, 1970-77; exec. dir. B.A.T. Co. Ltd., Eng., 1977-79, B.A.T. Services Ltd., Eng., 1979-83; chmn. B.A.T. Ltd., Eng., 1983-85; dep. chmn. B.A.T. Ltd., 1983-85; chmn., chief exec. officer Brown & Williamson Tobacco Co., Louisville, Ky., 1985—; also bd. dirs. Brown & Williamson Tobacco Co., Louisville; Mem. Tobacco Exec. Com., 1981-85. Mem. Nat. Corp. Com. United Negro Coll. Fund, Columbus, Ohio, 1985—; bd. dirs. Nat. Urban League, Opportunities Industrialization Ctrs. of Am., U. Louisville Internat. Ctr. Mem. Jefferson Club, Pendennis Club. Office: Brown & Williamson Tobacco Corp 1500 Brown & Williamson Tower Louisville KY 40202

PRITCHARD, RUTHANN MARY, financial executive; b. Ottawa, Ont., Can., Apr. 14, 1962; came to U.S., 1980; d. Roderick Adrian and Margaret Marie (Schooley) P.; m. Howard A. Silverstein, Feb. 6, 1988. BS in Engring., Yale U., 1984. Analyst Goldman, Sachs & Co., N.Y.C., 1984-86; assoc. fin. insts. First Boston Corp., N.Y.C., 1986-88, assoc. high yield finance, 1988—. Republican. Roman Catholic. Home: 364 North St Greenwich CT 06830 Office: First Boston Corp 55 E 52nd St Park Ave Pla New York NY 10055

PRITCHARD, WILLIAM WINTHER, lawyer, drilling company executive; b. Bartlesville, Okla., Mar. 20, 1951; s. James Edward and Agnes Kathryn (Winther) P.; m. Susan Jane Parsons, Aug. 12, 1972; children—Jane, Kathryn, Robert. BA with honors, U. Kans., 1970; JD, U. Tulsa, 1973. Bar: Okla. 1976. With Parker Drilling Co., Tulsa, 1976—, v.p., gen. counsel, 1984—. Mem. Hillcrest Assocs., Tulsa, 1982—. Mem. ABA, Okla. Bar Assn. Republican. Presbyterian. Club: So. Hills Country (Tulsa). Office: Parker Drilling Co 8 E 3d St Tulsa OK 74103

PRITCHETT, THOMAS CARROLL, accountant; b. Tifton, Ga., Apr. 14, 1952; s. Grafton Lee Pritchett and Geraldine (Sumner) Stephens; m. Linda Faye Oliver, Sept. 15, 1973; children: Thomas C. Jr., Jesse Sumner. BBA, Valdosta (Ga.) State Coll., 1974. CPA, Ga. Staff acct. Herring & Powell CPA's, Tifton, Ga., 1973-75, Allen & Williams CPA's, Tifton, 1975-79; ptnr. Allen, Pritchett & Bassett, CPA's, Tifton, 1980—. Treas. Big Bros.-Big Sisters Tifton; fund raiser Heart Assn., Tifton, 1979-80; active Valdosta State Coll. Blazer 1000 club; Nat. Trust Hist. Preservation, Habitat for Humanity Ptnr. Mem. AICPA (tax div.), Ga. Soc. CPA's, Nat. Soc. Pub. Accts., Springhill Country (Tifton) Club, Pres's. Club. Club: Springhill Country (Tifton). Office: Allen Pritchett & Bassett 405 Tift Ave Tifton GA 31793

PRITZKER, ALAN, controller; b. Pitts., July 22, 1954; s. Marvin and Rose (Kanovsky) P.; m. Brenda Silverman, Aug. 9, 1977; children: Menachem David, Shira Leah. BS in Acctg., Bklyn. Coll., 1979. Mgr. Focus Electronics, Bklyn., 1974-78; mgr. acctg. Holland Am. Line, N.Y.C., 1978-84; controller Vacation Travel Concepts, N.Y.C., 1984-85; sec., controller Regency Cruises Inc., N.Y.C., 1985—. Offices: Regency Cruise Inc 260 Madison Ave New York NY 10016

PRITZKER, JAY ARTHUR, lawyer; b. Chgo., Aug. 26, 1922; s. Abraham Nicholas and Fanny (Doppelt) P.; m. Marian Friend, Aug. 31, 1947; children: Nancy (dec.), Thomas, John, Daniel, Jean. B.Sc., Northwestern U., 1941, J.D., 1947. Bar: Ill. 1947. Asst. custodian Alien Property Adminstrn., 1947; since practiced in Chgo.; partner firm Pritzker & Pritzker, 1948—; chmn. bd. Hyatt Corp., Marmon Group, Inc.; dir. Dalfort Corp.; partner Chgo. Mill & Lumber Co., Mich.-Calif. Lumber Co. Trustee U. Chgo. Served as aviator USNR, World War II. Mem. Am., Chgo. bar assns. Clubs: Standard (Chgo.), Comml. (Chgo.), Lake Shore (Chgo.), Mid-Day (Chgo.), Arts (Chgo.), Vince (Chgo.). Office: Pritzker & Pritzker 200 W Madison Chicago IL 60606

PRITZKER, NICHOLAS J., diversified services corporation executive. Exec. v.p. devel. Hyatt Corp., Chgo.; pres. Hyatt Devel. Corp., Chgo. Office: Hyatt Corp 200 W Madison Chicago IL 60606 *

PRITZKER, ROBERT ALAN, manufacturing company executive; b. Chgo., June 30, 1926; s. Abram Nicholas and Fanny (Doppelt) P.; m. Irene Dryburgh; children: Matthew, Liesel; children by previous marriage: James, Linda, Karen. B.S. in Indsl. Engring., Ill. Inst. Tech., Chgo., 1946; postgrad. in bus. adminstrn., U. Ill. Engaged in mfg. 1946—; pres., dir. Union Tank Car Co., Chgo.; chief exec. officer, pres., dir. The Marmon Group, Inc., Chgo., Marmon Corp., Chgo., Marmon Indsl. Corp., Chgo.; pres., dir. The Colson Group, Inc., Marmon Holdings, Inc., Marmon Industries, Inc., Chgo.; dir. Hyatt Corp., Chgo., Dalfort Corp., Union Tank Car Co., S&W Berisford PLC, TIE Communications. Chmn. bd. Pritzker Found., Chgo.; trustee, vice chmn. Ill. Inst. Tech. Office: The Marmon Group Inc 225 W Washington St Chicago IL 60606

PRITZKER, THOMAS JAY, lawyer, business executive; b. Chgo., June 6, 1950; s. Jay Arthur and Marian (Friend) P.; m. Margot Lyn Barrow-Sicree, Sept. 4, 1977; children—Jason, Benjamin, David. B.A.,, Claremont Men's Coll, 1971; M.B.A., U. Chgo., 1972, J.D., 1976. Assoc. Katten, Muchin, Zavis, Pearl and Galler, Chgo., 1976-77; exec. v.p. Hyatt Corp., Chgo., 1977-80, pres., 1980—; chmn. bd. Hyatt Hotels Corp., Chgo., 1980-86, 1988; chmn. exec. com. Hyatt Hotels Corp., 1986-88; ptnr. Pritzker & Pritzker, Chgo., 1976—; pres. Rosemont Shipping, Chgo., 1980-86; bd. dirs. Dalfort, Chgo., ContinentalBank Corp. Chgo. Trustee Art. Inst. Chgo., 1988—. Mem. ABA, Ill. Bar Assn., Chgo. Bar Assn. Clubs: Standard (Chgo.); Lake Shore Country (Glencoe, Ill.). Office: Hyatt Corp 200 W Madison Ave Chicago IL 60606

PROBERT, JAMES PAUL, insurance company executive; b. Evansville, Ind., Feb. 12, 1951; s. Ralph Engle and Evelyn Louise (Cleavelin) R.; m. Margaret Miles, Oct. 30, 1971; children: Andrew R., Susan E. BS, Ind. State U., 1976; MBA, Webster U., 1988. Multi-line claims adjuster Transam. Ins. Co., Evansville, 1977-79; property claims examiner Transam. Ins. Co., Indpls., 1979-80; asst. zone claims mgr. Transam. Ins. Co., Battle Creek, Mich., 1980-83; claims mgr. CNA Ins. Co., St. Louis, 1983-84, Safety Mut. Casualty Corp., St. Louis, 1984—. Mem. Mo. Bar Assn. (fee disputes com. 1986—), Ins. Arbitration Forums. Republican. Methodist. Home: 113 Hollyleaf Dr Ballwin MO 63021 Office: Safety Mut Casualty Corp 1034 S Brentwood Blvd Ste 1500 Saint Louis MO 63117

PROCHNOW, HERBERT VICTOR, JR., banker; b. Evanston, Ill., May 26, 1931; s. Herbert V. and Laura (Stinson) P.; m. Lucia Boyden, Aug. 6, 1966; children: Thomas Herbert, Laura. A.B., Harvard U., 1953, J.D., 1956; A.M., U. Chgo., 1958. Bar: Ill. 1957. With 1st Nat. Bank Chgo., 1958—, atty., 1961-70, sr. atty., 1971-73, counsel, 1973—, adminstrv. asst. to chmn. bd., 1978-81. Author: (with Herbert V. Prochnow) A Treasury of Humorous Quotations, 1969, The Changing World of Banking, 1974, The Public Speaker's Treasure Chest, 1986, The Toastmaster's Treasure Chest, 1988; also articles in legal publs. Mem. ABA, Ill. Bar Assn., Chgo. Bar Assn. (chmn. com. internat. law 1970-71), Am. Soc. Internat. Law, Phi Beta Kappa. Clubs: Harvard (N.Y.C.); Chicago (Chgo.), Legal (Chgo.), Law (Chgo.), Onwentsia, Economic (Chgo.), Executives (Chgo.), University (Chgo.). Home: 949 Woodbine Pl Lake Forest IL 60045 Office: 1 First Nat Pla Chicago IL 60670

PROCKNOW, EUGENE ALAN, management consultant; b. Oak Park, Ill., Sept. 6, 1954; s. Donald Eugene and Esther (Elhert) P.; m. Mary Ellen Dineen, Oct. 6, 1984. BA with honors, Knox Coll., 1976; MBA, U. Mich., 1978. Assoc. cons. Touche Ross, Detroit, 1978-80, sr. cons., 1980-84, sr. mgr., 1984—. Mem. Assn. for Systems Mgmt. (Speaker's award 1987). home: 3780 Squirrel Rd Bloomfield Hills MI 48013 Office: Touche Ross 200 Renaissance Ctr Detroit MI 48243

PROCTOR, MELODY LOUISE, bank executive; b. Missouri Valley, Iowa, Mar. 29, 1962; d. Herb Martin and Phyllis Louise (Bessire) Brothers; m. William Ross Proctor, Aug. 20, 1983. BBA, Iowa State U., 1984. Personnel asst. Iowa State U., Ames, 1984-85; audit clk. Marine Corps Exchange, Quantico, Va., 1985-86; consumer loan rep. Wells Fargo Bank, Laguna Hills, Calif., 1986-87, personal banking officer, 1987—. Mem. Inst. Cert. Fin. Planners. Republican. Home: 325 Coral Reef Dr Unit 20 Huntington Beach CA 92648 Office: Wells Fargo Bank 2211 Main St Huntington Beach CA 92648

PRODAN, JOHN, aviation executive; b. Orange, N.J., Nov. 17, 1924; s. Vasile and Cleda Blanche (Neville) P.; m. Ruth Jennie Larson, Dec. 29, 1945; children: Susan Ruth, Robert John, John Vernon, Donald Albert, Karen Ruth, Nancy Ann. BS in Aero. Engring., U. Ill., 1948; MS in Aero. Engring., MS in Instrumentation Engring., U. Mich., 1954; MBA, UCLA, 1980. Registered comml. pilot, cert. flight instr. Commd. 2d lt. USAF, 1943, advanced through grades to lt. col., 1966; squadron commdr. and asst. dep. wing commdr. USAF, Vietnam, 1971-72; asst. program dir. and mgr. shuttle program USAF, Los Angeles, 1972-74; ret. USAF, 1974; research pilot and engr. S.D. Sch. Mines and Tech., Rapid City, 1978-80; chief test pilot, sr. engr. Kohlman Systems Research, Lawrence, Kans., 1982-84; pres., chief engr. AV-CON, Rapid City, 1980—; sr. v.p. Highland Mfg. Inc., Rapid City, 1988—; visiting lectr. Workshop on Meteorol. and Environ. Inputs to Aviation Systems, 1978—. Contbr. articles and reports to profl. jours. Treas. First Bapt. Ch. Alamogordo, N.Mex., 1958-61, First So. Bapt. Ch., Canoga Park, Calif., 1974-78. Decorated D.F.C., Legion of Merit with one oak leaf cluster, Meritorious Service medal, Air medal with six oak leaf clusters; named Disting. Alumnus, U. Ill., 1980. Mem. Soc. Exptl. Test Pilots (chmn. weather subcom. 1980-74, sect. sec. 1984-85), AIAA, Soc. Automotive Engrs. (flight test com.), Tau Beta Pi, Sigma Tau. Republican. Baptist. Home and Office: AV-CON 1100 Kings Rd Rt 1 Rapid City SD 57702

PROPP, GAIL DANE GOMBERG, computer consulting company executive; b. N.Y.C., Mar. 22, 1946; d. Oscar and Goody (Rosenburgh) Dane; B.A. in Econs., Barnard Coll., 1965; m. Ephraim Propp; children—Eric Wesley, David Marc, Anna Michelle. Instr., programmer IBM Corp., N.Y.C., 1965-66; systems and programmer analyst R.S. Topas Co., N.Y.C., 1966-67; dir. systems and programming Abercrombie & Fitch Co., N.Y.C., 1967-69; dir. corp. data processing and MIS, 1969-77; founder, 1977, since pres. Met Data Systems, Inc., N.Y.C., 1977—; founder, pres. Datatype International. Inc, 1982—; assoc. dir. Burns Archive of Hist. Med. Photographs, N.Y.C., 1979—. Bd. overseers Bar-Ilan U., Israel; mem. adv. bd. KIRUV. Mem. Internat. Council Computers in Edn., Women in Info. Processing, Assn. Systems Mgmt., Data Processing Mgmt. Assn., Assn. Systems Mgmt., Assn. Inst. Certified Systems Profls., Photog. History Soc. Am., Photog. Historic Soc. N.Y. Author articles in field. Office: 919 3d Ave New York NY 10022

PROROK, CYNTHIA LYNNE, controller, accountant; b. Pitts., Oct. 24, 1959; d. Thomas Martin and Verna Wanda (Wood) P. BS in Econs. and Bus., Slippery Rock (Pa.) U., 1982, M in Adminstrn., 1988. Legis. asst. Nat. Tax Limitation Com., Washington, 1980; acct. Butler (Pa.) Conservation Dist., 1981—; sr. internal auditor County of Butler, 1982-84, asst. fin. dir., 1984-85, dep. controller, 1985—, dep. controller, budget coordinator, 1988—. Mem. Butler County Rep. Women, 1985—, Butler County Rep. Task Force, 1987-88. Washington fellow Nat. Leadership Inst./Heritage Found., 1980. Mem. Nat. Assn. Accts. (bd. dirs. tech. programs and profl. devel. 1987—), Govt. Fin. Officers Assn. (conf. com. 1988—), Assn. of Govt. Accts., Assn. Pub. Adminstrs. Republican. Roman Catholic. Home: 434 W Sunbury Rd #8 Butler PA 16001 Office: County Controller Court House Butler PA 16001

PROSSER, CHARLES LAVERN, metals industry executive; b. Wilkinsburg, Pa., Mar. 18, 1927; s. Edwin Forest-Porter and Ada Mae (Morrow) P.; m. Audrey Mae Doench, Oct. 25, 1952; children: Audrey, Jeffrey, Chris, Jill, Scott, Sean. BS in Indsl. Mgmt., Duquesne U., 1951; postgrad., U. Pitts., 1951-53. Mgmt. trainee U.S. Steel Corp., Pitts., 1951-53; supr. U.S. Steel Corp., Homestead, Pa., 1953-58; mgr. extrusions Curtiss-Wright Corp., Buffalo, 1958-62; v.p. mktg. BLH Corp. Standard Steel div., Burnham, Pa., 1962-65, Firth-Sterling Inc., McKeesport, Pa., 1965-68; prin. Westmoreland Assocs., Murrysville, Pa., 1968-71; pres. Westmoreland Industries Inc., Lewistown, Pa., 1971-77, Westmorelane Steel & Metals Inc., Reedsville, Pa., 1977—. Author: Heavy Press Extrusions, 1961. Served to capt. U.S. Army, 1944-47, 50-51. Mem. Am. Soc. for Metals, Aircraft Owners/Pilots Assn. Lutheran. Club: Pitts. Athletic. Home: Gwydd Aelwyd Back Mountain Rd Reedsville PA 17084 Office: Westmoreland Steel & Metals Inc PO Box 101 Reedsville PA 17084

PROTHERO, CHARLES LESLIE, III, safety and security products executive, lawyer; b. Long Branch, N.J., Dec. 27, 1932; s. Charles Leslie Jr. and Julia W. (Ryan) P.; m. Elizabeth Lloyd Hall, Dec. 30, 1967; children: Charles L. IV, Michael, Kenneth. BS, St. Peter's Coll., 1955; LLB, Georgetown U., 1961. Bar: D.C. 1961. Staff atty. SEC, Washington, 1961-69; v.p. Kidde, Inc., Saddle Brook, N.J., 1969—. Served to 1st lt. U.S. Army, 1955-57. Mem. ABA. Roman Catholic. Office: Kidde Inc 100 Wood Ave S Iselin NJ 08830

PROUD, ROBERT DONALD (ROBERT DONALD PAYTON), radio station executive, broadcaster; b. Cleve., Nov. 1, 1949; s. Lloyd Donald and Eleanore Matilda (Cihon) P.; m. K. Diane Siler, Feb. 17, 1979; 1 child, James Siler. Grad., Cleve. Inst. Broadcasting, 1969. Program dir. Sta. WGCL-FM, Cleve., 1972-74; ops. mgr. Sta. WRBR-FM, South Bend, Ind., 1974-75, Sta. XEROK, Juarez, Mex., 1975-77; program dir. Sta. WZZP-FM, Cleve., 1977-78; gen. mgr. Sta. KELP, El Paso, Tex., 1978-82; sales mgr. Sta. KAMZ-FM, El Paso, 1982-86; gen. mgr. Stas. KAMA/KAMZ-FM, El Paso, 1982-86; dir. nat. sales Thrash Broadcasting, El Paso, Lubbock, Tex., 1987-88; gen. mgr. Sta. KVIV, El Paso, 1987—. Bd. dirs., chmn. communications Am. Heart Assn. Mem. El Paso Assn. Radio Stas. (pres. 1981), Tex. Assn. Broadcasters. Office: Sta KVIV 4180 N Mesa El Paso TX 79902

PROVECT, MARTIN H., financial executive; b. N.Y.C., Oct. 24, 1932; s. Max Provect; children: Christopher, Michele. BA, Columbia U., 1954, JD, 1956. Assoc. Reavis & McGrath, N.Y.C., 1956-59; exec. v.p. Calvin Bullock, Ltd., N.Y.C., 1959-79; pres. Venture Advisers, Inc., Santa Fe, 1979—; dir. various fin. cos.; trustee Venture Trust Money Market Fund, Venture Trust Tax-Free Money Market Fund. Office: Venture Advisers LP 124 E Marcy St PO Box 1688 Santa Fe NM 87504-1688

PROVOST, MARTY WAYNE, retail executive; b. Merced, Calif., Dec. 19, 1957; s. Gilbert Charles and Mary Ellen (Joyner) P.; m. Rebecca Lynn Carter, June 17, 1979; children: Melissa Elizabeth, Laura Lynn, James Carter. AA, El Camino (Calif.) Coll., 1984; BA in Bus. Mgmt., Redlands (Calif.) U., 1986. Sales rep. Royal Crown Cola, L.A., 1981-82; sales rep. Crown Zellerbach Corp., L.A., 1982-83, account mgr., 1983-85, asst. to regional mgr., 1985-86; mgr. merchandising Crown Zellerbach Corp., San Francisco, 1986-87; dist. mgr. Crown Zellerbach Corp., Seattle, 1987—; bd. dirs. Seafair Seattle. Served with U.S. Army, 1976-79. Fellow Mfrs. Reps. Club, Husky Fever, Variety Club of Seattle. Republican. Lutheran. Office: James River/Crown Zellerbach 15400 SE 30th Pl Ste #201 Bellevue WA 98007-6546

PROZAN, LAWRENCE IRA, financial planner; b. Albuquerque, Apr. 8, 1961; s. George and Sylvia (Simmons) P.; m. Charmaine Fiumos, June 25, 1988. AB, U. Calif., Berkeley, 1983. Asst. buyer Macy's, San Francisco, 1984-85; fin. planner Calvert Securities, Oakland, Calif., 1985-87, Intrust, Walnut Creek, Calif., 1987; pres. Wren Pro, Oakland, 1988—. Mem. Bear Backers U. Calif., 1985—. Mem. Internat. Assn. Fin. Planners. Office: Wren Pro 426 17th #319 Oakland CA 94611

PRUD'HOMME, ALBERT FREDRIC, securities compnay executive; b. New Rochelle, N.Y., Sept. 19, 1952; s. Albert O. and Rita R. (Moshier) Prud'h,; m. LuAnn Winfield, June 29, 1985; children: Cherilyn, Alicia. BA, Mercer U., 1975. Cert. fin. planner. Sales rep. Met. Life Ins. co., N.Y.C., 1975-82; sales agt. Ohio Nat. Life, Cin., 1977-82; bd. dirs. DWP, Inc. Pres. Belmont Abbey Coll. Athletic Found., 1985-87. With U.S. Army, 1972-74. Recipient Estate Planning award Winthrop Coll., 1981. Mem. Inst. Cert. Fin. Planners, Internat. Assn. Fin. Planning. Democrat. Presbyterian. Home: 3608 Chevington Rd Charlotte NC 28226 Office: Scepter Securities Inc 112 S Tyron St Ste 1240 Charlotte NC 28284

PRUETT, CLAYTON DUNKLIN, civil engineer; b. Montgomery, Ala., June 16, 1935; s. William Rogers and Myra Eleanor (Ganey) P.; m. Barbara Clapp, Feb. 22, 1974; children: Christopher Blair, Tyler Michael. BSCE, Auburn U., 1956. Cert. profl. engr., Ala. Civil engr. Ala. State Hwy Dept., Montgomery, 1956-57; commd. lt. USAF, 1957; civil engr. USAF, Andrews AFB, 1959-64; resigned USAF, 1964; staff assoc. Gen. Atomic div. Gen. Dynamics, La Jolla, Calif., 1964-68; exec. v.p. Environ Med. Inc., La Jolla, 1968-73; chmn. bd. CDP Inc., Atlanta, 1973—; also bd. dirs. CDP Inc.; bd. dirs. Immunomedics Inc., Warren, N.J., Orion Med. Scis. Inst., Pasadena, Calif., Jack Kelly Yachts Inc., San Diego. Bd. dirs. Am. Cancer Soc., 1986—, U. Calif., San Diego Cancer Ctr. Found., 1989—. Mem. San Diego Yacht Club. Home: PO Box 2304 Rancho Santa Fe CA 92067 Office: CDP Svcs Inc 1050 Crowne Point Pkwy Atlanta GA 30338

PRUETT, SAMUEL H., manufacturing executive; b. Michigan City, Ind., Aug. 19, 1932; s. Samuel K. and Anne S. P.; m. Yvonne C. Jones; children: Carrie, Steven. BS in Bus., Ind. U., 1954. Staff asst. household soap products div. Procter & Gamble Co., 1957-59, with sales tng. household soap products div., 1959, asst. brand mgr. household soap products, 1959-61, brand mgr. household soap products div., 1961-65, assoc. brand promotion mgr. household soap products div., 1965-66, brand promotion mgr. bar soap and household cleaning products div., 1966-75, div. mgr. gen. advt. dept., 1975-81, gen. mgr. citrus products div., 1981-84, v.p. personnel citrus products div., 1984—. Trustee Deaconess Hosp., Cin., 1988—. Capt. USAF, 1954-57. Mem. Bus. Roundtable (employee relations com.), Cowdrick Group, Greater Cin. C. of C. (trustee, 1988), Ind. U. Sch. Bus. Alumni Assn. (bd. dirs.). Office: Procter & Gamble Co 1 Procter & Gamble Pla Cincinnati OH 45202

PRUETT, TIMOTHY IRVING, textile executive; b. Appleton, Wis., Jan. 19, 1954; s. Richard Lawrence and Bernadine Eva (Brockman) P. BA, Lawrence U., 1976. Br. mgr. Means Services, Inc., Portage, Wis., 1978; mgmt. info. system coordinator Means Services, Inc., South Bend, Ind., 1978-79; br. mgr. Means Services, Inc., Terre Haute, Ind., 1979-80; service mgr. Means Services, Inc., Indpls., 1980, ARA Services, Inc. (Aratex), Evansville, Ind., 1980-83; gen. mgr. ARA Services, Inc. (Aratex), East Moline, Ill., 1983-87; N.E. group mgr. ARA Services, Inc., Cherry Hill, N.J., 1987—. Mem. Beta Theta Pi (pres. Gamma Phi chpt. 1974-75). Republican. Lutheran. Clubs: Big Ten Investors (East Moline); Sand Lake Musky Hunters (Big Sand Lake, Wis.). Home: 216 Stratton Ct Mount Laurel NJ 08054 Office: Aratex Svcs Inc 1178 Marlkress Rd Cherry Hill IL 08003

PRUPAS, MELVERN IRVING, video consultant, studio agent; b. Montreal, Que., Can., Dec. 16, 1926; s. Harry and Esther (Braunstein) P.; student Sir George Williams U., 1943-45, Montreal Tech. Inst., 1946, Mt. Allison U., 1967, N.Y. State Coll. Agr., Cornell U., 1971, U. Guelph, 1971-72; m. Sheila Ditkofsky, 1948 (div. 1981); children—Michael, Lorne, Norman, David, Dianne. m. Myrtle Levine, Sept. 17, 1981. Salesman, Crescent Cheese Co., 1947-50, sales mgr., 1951-56, dir., v.p., 1956-72, dir., v.p., sec., 1972-77; v.p., dir. Maycrest Co. Ltd., 1960-77; sec.-treas., dir. Les Produits Laitiers Marieville (Que., Can.) Ltee., 1956-72, v.p., sec., dir., 1972-77; founder En Ville newspaper, 1962; pres., dir. Ambassador Food Sales Ltd., 1981—; sec.-treas., dir. Proops Press Inc., 1967-70 (all Montreal); pres. Dadnaram Ltd. of Montreal, 1972—; pres. MPA Video Distbrs., 1981-85, chmn. 1985-86; chmn. MPA Video Inc., 1985-86; pres. MPA Investment Properties Inc., 1985—; pres. Mel Prupas Cons., 1986—; pres. Prupas Studio Cons., 1987—. Bd. dirs. YM-YWHA of Montreal, 1954-72, gov., 1956-66, gov.-benefactor, 1967—, met. campaign chmn., 1966; cubmaster Boy Scouts of Can., Mount Royal, 1960-71; chmn. food div. Combined Jewish Appeal, Montreal, 1961-63, trade coordinator, 1964-65, vice chmn. trades. 1969-70, vice chmn. spl. names, 1972-73; bd. dirs. Jewish Nat. Fund Montreal, 1970-72; v.p. Algonquin Home and Sch. Assn., 1971-72. Recipient Scouters Warrant, Boy Scouts of Can. 1963; Chevalier Medal, Chaine des Rotisseurs, 1964; Ida Steinberg Meml. trophy Combined Jewish Appeal, 1969; Golden Gloves Heavyweight Boxing Champion, 1941; mem. Can. Olympic Basketball Team, 1948. Mem. Province of Que. Food Brokers Assn. (dir. 1968-70), Food Service Execs., Assn., Can. Restaurant Assn., Chaine de Rotisseurs in Montreal Baillage, Confrerie Des Vignerons De St. Vincents, Guilde des Fromagers Confrerie de Saint-Uguzon, Montreal Bd. of Trade, Can. C. of C., Comml. Travellers Assn. Can., Food Brokers Assn. Can., Can. Importers Assn., Video Distbrs. Assn. Can. (v.p. 1983), Can-Israel C. of C., Am. Mus. Natural History, Playwrights Workshop, Jewish Theol. Sem. Am., Canadian Council Christians and Jews, Mt. Royal Property Owners Assn. (dir. 1968-70). Jewish religion (dir. Congregation Beth El 1960-65, v.p. 1964-65, sec. 1969-70, v.p. 1971-73, pres. 1973-75). Mem. B'nai B'rith. Clubs: Cedarbrooke Golf and Country (St. Sophie); Montreal Anglers and Hunters, Rotary, Canadian, Amici (pres. 1950-51, 65-66). Office: 5350 MacDonald Ave, Ste 1706, Montreal, PQ Canada H3X 3V2

PRUS, FRANCIS VINCENT, tire company executive; b. Sewickley, Pa., 1927; s. Mark Phillip and Mary Agnes Prus; m. Catherine Frances Dumesic, Jan. 30, 1949; children: Cathy, Mark, Linda, David. B.S. in Elec. Engring., Carnegie Mellon U., 1949. Gen. mgr. Goodyear Aerospace Corp., Akron, Ohio, pres., chief exec. officer, until 1981; dir. mfg. services, then v.p. mfg. Goodyear Tire & Rubber Co., from 1981, now exec. v.p. research and devel.; formerly dir. prodn. Kelly Springfield Tire Co.; dir. mfg. services, then v.p.

mfg. Goodyear Tire & Rubber Co., exec. v.p. corp. technology, bd. dirs., 1981—. Mem. Litchfield Park Sch. Bd., 1970-71; bd. dirs. Akron Jr. Achievement, 1974-80, pres., 1977-78. Served with USNR, 1945-46. Mem. Aerospace Industries Assn., Nat. Security Indsl. Assn., Am. Def. Preparedness Assn., Navy League U.S. Club: Portage Country (Akron). Office: Goodyear Tire & Rubber Co 1144 E Market St Akron OH 44316

PRUYN, WILLIAM J., energy industry executive; b. Boston, Aug. 25, 1922; s. William J. and Ida M. (Langan) P.; m. Mary Anton, May 19, 1945; children: William J., Barbara, Ann Marie, Stephen, Christopher. Student, Bentley Coll., 1939-41, Harvard U., 1944-45, 64; BBA, Northeastern U., 1948. Pub. acct. Meahl, McNamara & Co., 1946-51; with Eastern Gas & Fuel Assocs. (name changed to Eastern Enterprises 1989), Boston, 1951—, sr. v.p., 1972-76, trustee, 1973—, pres., chief adminstrv. officer, 1976-77, pres., chief exec. officer, 1977-85, chmn. bd., chief exec. officer, 1986-87, chmn. bd., 1987—; bd. dirs. Shawmut Corp. Bd. dirs. Med. Found., Inc.; trustee Northeastern U.; chmn. New Eng. Aquarium; mem. pres.'s adv. council Bentley Coll. Served with USNR. Clubs: Somerset, Algonquin, Corinthian Yacht. Home: 14 Foster St Marblehead MA 01945 Office: Eastern Enterprises 9 Riverside Rd Weston MA 02193

PRUZAN, PAUL STEPHEN, financial executive; b. N.Y.C., Aug. 29, 1940; s. Michael and Amelia (Fuhrer) P.; BBA, CUNY, 1962, MBA, 1971; m. Linda Feinstein, June 16, 1962; children: Melissa, Lauren. Audit mgr. Arthur Young & Co., N.Y.C., 1965-71; v.p. fin. Rockwood Industries, Inc., Greenwich, Conn., 1971-79, Chessco Industries, Inc., Westport, Conn., 1979—; mng. dir. Southport Capital Group, Ltd., Westport, Conn., 1985—; adj. asst. prof. Pace U., N.Y.C., 1978-81. First v.p. Greenville Community Council, 1980-81. CPA, N.Y. Mem. Am. Inst. CPA's, Assn. Corporate Growth, N.Y. State Soc. CPA's. Club: Scarsdale (N.Y.) Golf. Home: 11 Robin Hill Rd Scarsdale NY 10583 Office: Southport Capital Group Ltd 1300 Post Rd E Westport CT 06880

PRYJMAK, PETER GOTHART, industrial engineer; b. Würzburg, Fed. Republic of Germany, Feb. 25, 1949; came to U.S., 1951; s. Peter and Else Freida (Proske) P.; m. Kathleen Ann Hankla, June 7, 1974; children: Peter Michael, Daniel Gregory, Renae Christine. BA in Physics, U. Nebr., 1974. Enlisted USN, 1968, advanced through grades, commd., 1974; served on USS DEG1 Brooke, Vietnam, 1970, USS AD-19 Yosemite, 1975-77, USS DDG-18 Semmes, 1977-79; staff of comdr. Commandant 6th Naval Dist., Charleston Naval Base, 1979; resigned USN, 1979; lt. comdr. USNR; sr. field service engr. Westinghouse Electric Corp., Pitts., 1981-83, sr. quality assurance engr., 1983—. Served to lt. comdr. USNR. Mem. Am. Welding Soc., Am. Assn. Artificial Intelligence. Republican. Home: PO Box 42 New Stanton PA 15672 Office: Westinghouse Electric Corp PO Box 355 Pittsburgh PA 15230

PRYOR, ALAN MARK, banker; b. Charleston, S.C., Apr. 4, 1949; s. Sidney and Grace (Buchstane) P.; m. Pamela Ray Price, Nov. 22, 1986; 1 child, Johnathan Price. BA in History, U. Mich., 1971, MA in Econs., 1974. Asst. mgr. internat. banking group Citibank, N.A., N.Y.C., 1975-78, mgr., v.p. internat. fin., 1978-82, v.p. internat. capital markets, 1983-85; from v.p. to exec. v.p., head swap dept. Deutsche Bank Capital Corp., N.Y.C., 1985—; guest lectr. bus. sch. Columbia U., N.Y.C., 1987; speaker Inst. for Internat. Rsch., N.Y.C., 1986-87, Euromoney Confs., N.Y.C., 1988. Home: 150 E 77th St Apt 8E/69 New York NY 10021 Office: Deutsche Bank Capital Corp 40 Wall St New York NY 10005

PRYOR, HUBERT, editor, writer; b. Buenos Aires, Argentina, Mar. 18, 1916; (parents Am. citizens); s. John W. and Hilda A. (Cowes) P.; m. Ellen M. Ach, 1940 (div. 1959); children: Alan, Gerald, David. Grad., St. George's Coll., Argentina, 1932; student, U. London, Eng., 1934-36. Corr. in S.Am. for United Press, 1937-39; pub. relations rep. Pan Am. Airways in Buenos Aires, 1939-40; reporter N.Y. Herald Tribune, 1940-41; writer, dir. short-wave newsroom CBS, 1941-46; asst. mng. editor Knickerbocker Weekly, 1946-47; sr. editor Look mag., 1947-62; creative supr. Wilson, Haight & Welch (advt.), 1962-63; editor Science Digest, 1963-67; mng. editor Med. World News, 1967; editor NRTA Jour. Modern Maturity, 1967-82; editorial dir. Dynamic Years, 1977-82; publs. coordinator Modern Maturity, Dynamic Years, 1982-84; editorial cons., writer 1985—. Served to lt. USNR, 1943-46. Mem. Am. Soc. Mag. Editors. Home: 3501 S Ocean Blvd Palm Beach FL 33480

PRYOR, JERRY DENNIS, corporate professional; b. Cin., Apr. 11, 1952; s. Cicero and Pauline (Estill) P. BA in History, Lincoln U., 1978. Collector, mgmt. trainee Gem Savs. & Loan, Dayton, Ohio, 1978-81; loan mgr. Maj. Fed. Savs. & Loan, Cin., 1981; acct. receivable mgr. Sonitrol of Cin., 1983-84; sr. adjuster Cen. Trust Bank, Cin., 1984-86; collector Robert Half/Accountemps, Cin., 1986—; owner J.D. Pryor & Assocs., 1981—. Honoree Am. Chem. Soc., 1969. Mem. Am. Inst. Banking, MBA Execs. Inc., Real Estate Investor Assn., Am. Inst. Constructors Inc. Democrat. Baptist. Club: Dayton. Lodge: Civitan. Home: 3455 Knott St Cincinnati OH 45229 Office: Robert Half/Accountemps 201 E Fifth St Cincinnati OH 45202

PRZYBYLOWICZ, EDWIN PAUL, chemical company executive, research director; b. Detroit, June 29, 1933; s. Ignacy and Antonette Olga (Krezalek) P.; m. Roberta Richardson, June 5, 1954; children: Christine, Margaret, Paul, Sue, Anne, Thomas, Catherine, James, Elizabeth, Sara, Edward. BS in Chemistry, U. Mich., 1953; PhD in Analytical Chemistry, MIT, 1956. Research chemist, lab. head Eastman Kodak Co., Rochester, N.Y., 1956-68, asst. div. head, 1969-74, tech. asst. to dir. of research labs., 1974-75, dir. photographic program devel., 1975-77, asst. dir. research labs., 1977-81, program mgr. copy products, 1981-83, asst. dir. research labs., 1983-85, dir. research, 1985—; acad. assignment Nat. Bur. Standards, Washington, and MIT, Cambridge, 1968-69; bd. dirs. Indsl. Research Inst., N.Y. Co-Author: Activation Analysis with Neutron Generators, 1973, Chem. Analysis, A Series of Monographs on Analytical Chemistry and Its Applications, 1973; patentee in field. Pres. Webster Bd. (N.Y.) Edn., 1965-72; bd. dirs. St. Paul's Ch. Bd., Webster, 1980-85. Eastman Kodak fellow MIT, 1955; recipient Moses Gomberg Prize in Chemistry U. Mich., 1953. Mem. Am. Chem. Soc. Republican. Roman Catholic. Home: 1219 Crown Point Dr Webster NY 14650 Office: Eastman Kodak Co 343 State St Rochester NY 14650

PSAROUTHAKIS, JOHN, manufacturing company executive; b. Canea, Crete, Greece, June 29, 1932; s. Michael and Stamatia (Tsikouldani) P.; m. Inga Lundgren, Aug. 1, 1959; children: Michael, Peter. BS, MIT, 1957, MS, 1962; PhD, U. Md., 1965; student Program for Execs., Carnegie-Mellon U., 1968, DSc. (Hon.) Cleary Coll. Engr. Power Stas., Boston Edison, 1955-58; research and devel. dept. mgr. Martin Marietta/Thermo Electron Corp., Waltham, Mass., 1958-66; dir. tech. and new product planning Allis Chalmers Corp., Milw., 1966-70; corp v.p. planning and engring., Masco Corp., Taylor, Mich., 1970-73, group v.p. internat. ops. and internat. corp. devel., 1973-77; pres., founder, chmn. J.P. Industries, Inc., Ann Arbor, Mich., 1978—; chmn. El Greco chpt. Pan Cretan Assn. Am.; dir. Edwards Bros., Inc. Contbr. articles to profl. jours.; patentee in field. Bd. dirs. Indsl. Tech. Inst; chmn. adv. bd. Coll. of Bus. Eastern Mich. U., adv. bd. Ctr. Enterpreneurship Eastern Mich. U.; mem. adv. com. research and devel. Strategic Fund of Mich., Andrew Carnegie Soc. Carnegie-Mellon U., Pryor Found. award com. Grad. Sch. of Bus. U. Mich.; mem. devel. com. MIT; mem. devel. council grad. sch. indsl. adminstrn. Carnegie Mellon U.; mem. vis. com. grad. sch. of bus. U. Mich.; sustaining fellow Mass. Inst. Tech. Recipient Distinguished Young Scientist award Md. Acad. Sci., 1965, Martin Gold Medal award, 1964, 65, Corp. Leadership award MIT, 1987. Mem. Am. Mgmt. Assn., Am. Metals Soc., Bus. Internat., Conf. Bd., Mich. C. of C., Liberty Lawn Tennis Club (Ann Arbor), Greek Am. Cultural Assn. (founder, chmn.), Pancretan Assn. Am. (pres. El Greco chpt.). Home: 2119 Melrose St Ann Arbor MI 48104 Office: JP Industries Inc 325 Eisenhower Pkwy Ann Arbor MI 48104

PSZCZOLKOWSKI, ROBERT E., oil company executive; b. Natrona Heights, Pa., Mar. 13, 1946; s. Leonard L. and Violet (Lubiniecki) P.; m. Kathleen J. Burin, Apr. 15, 1965; children—Elizabeth M., Susan J. B.A., Columbia U., 1968. Area mgr. Mobil Oil Corp., Fairfax, Va., 1968-74; Middle mgmt. tng. McDonald's Co., Albany, N.Y., 1975; East Coast tng. mgr. Rockwell Internat.-Admiral, Schaumburg, Ill., 1975; pres. Pszczolkowski Service, Inc., Little Falls, N.Y., 1977—, PTS Inc., East Pembroke, N.Y., 1984—, CTS, Inc., Clarence, N.Y., 1984—, MSMM, Inc., Amherst, 1987—, Non-Toxic Housing, Inc., E. Aurora, 1988—, CMSE, Inc., Cooperstown, 1988—. Mem. Human Ecology Action League, Evanston, Ill., 1982—; mem. steering com. H.E.A.L. of West N.Y., 1986—; mem. adv. council Com. for a Republican Assembly, Albany, N.Y., 1984—; mem. Friends of Bassett Hosp., Cooperstown, N.Y., 1984—; chmn. Cooperstown Columbia Coll. Alumni Secondary Schs. Com., N.Y.C., 1985—; dir., Columbia Coll. Alumni Regional Bd., 1988—. Recipient Cert. of Merit, Mobil Oil Corp., Waltham, Mass., 1972. Mem. Gasoline Retailers Assn. (state dir., bd. dirs. 1984—), Nat. Fedn. Ind. Bus., N.Y. State Assn. Service Sta. (steering com. 1984—). Avocations: bicycling, fishing, music, art. Home: 24 Lake St Cooperstown NY 13326 Office: PTS Inc 38 Mahogany Dr Williamsville NY 14221

PTASYNSKI, HARRY, oil producer; b. Milw., May 26, 1926; s. Stanley S. and Frances V. (Stawicki) P.; m. Nola G. Whitestine, Sept. 15, 1951; children: Ross F., Lisa Joy. BS, Stanford U., 1950. Cert. profl. geologist; cert. petroleum geologist. Dist. geologist Pure Oil Co., Amarillo, Tex., 1951-55, Casper, Wyo., 1955-58; ind. geologist, Casper, 1958—. With USN, 1944-46, PTO. Mem. Am. Assn. Petroleum Geologists, Am. Inst. Profl. Geologists, Ind. Petroleum Assn. Am. (v.p., bd. dirs. 1976—), Ind. Petroleum Assn. Mountain States (v.p., bd. dirs. 1976-80). Republican. Episcopalian. Home: 1515 Brookview Dr Casper WY 82604 Office: Pure Oil Co PO Box 43 Casper WY 82601

PUCKETT, JAY MILTON, publishing company executive; b. Hollywood, Calif., Mar. 16, 1946; s. Milton Albert and Margaret Eileen (Bayer) P.; m. Judy Ellen Rau, Aug. 17, 1975; children: Jason, Jennifer. BA in Bus. magna cum laude, So. Oreg. State Coll., 1975. Mktg. lease rep. Western Devel. Svcs., Dublin, Calif., 1982-87; regional pub. Black's Guide McGraw Hill Info. Svcs., Lafayette, Calif., 1987—. Staff sgt. U.S. Army, 1967-69, Vietnam. Mem. Bldg. Owners and Mgrs. Assn., Assn. S. Bay Brokers. Democrat. Office: McGraw Hill Info Svcs 3443 Golden Gate Way Ste G Lafayette CA 94549

PUGH, LAWRENCE R., textile corporation executive; b. 1933; (married). Grad., Colby Coll., 1956. Div. sales mgr. Borden Inc., 1958-66; product mgr., gen. mktg. mgr. Hamilton Beach Co., 1966-70; dir. mktg. Ampex Corp., 1970-72; group pres. Beatrice Foods Co., 1972-80; pres. V.F. Corp., Reading, Pa., 1980-83, chmn., 1983—. Office: VF Corp 1047 N Park Rd Box 1022 (19603) Wyomissing PA 19610 *

PUGLIESE, ROBERT F., lawyer, manufacturing executive; b. W. Pittston, Pa., Jan. 15, 1933. BS, U. Scranton, 1954; LLB, Georgetown U., 1957, LLM, 1959; grad. advanced mgmt. program Harvard U., 1976. Bar: D.C. 1957, U.S. Dist. Ct. 1957, U.S. Ct. Claims 1958, U.S. Tax Ct. 1957, U.S. Ct. Appeals 1957. Assoc. Hedrick & Lane, Washington, 1957-60; tax counsel Westinghouse Electric Corp., Pitts., 1961-70, gen. tax counsel, 1970-75, v.p., gen. tax counsel, 1975-76, v.p., gen. counsel, sec., 1976-86, sr. v.p., 1987, exec. v.p., 1988—; dir. Westinghouse Credit Corp., Westinghouse Broadcasting, Inc., Westinghouse Fin. Svcs., Inc. Trustee U. Scranton; bd. dirs. St. Francis Health System, Pitts., St. Francis Med. Ctr., Pitts.; mem. exec. com. U. Scranton. Mem. ABA, Assn. Gen. Counsel, St. Clair Country Club (bd. govs.). Office: Westinghouse Electric Corp Westinghouse Bldg 6 Gateway Ctr Pittsburgh PA 15222

PUGLISI, ANTHONY JOSEPH, manufacturing company executive; b. N.Y.C., Apr. 7, 1949; s. Nicholas and Gilda (Sorvillo) P.; m. Blanche Lucas, June 4, 1972; 1 child, Eileen Marie. B.B.A., Bernard Baruch Coll., 1972. C.P.A., N.Y. Mgr., Seidman & Seidman, N.Y.C., 1972-79; sr. v.p., chief fin. officer, treas. IMC Magnetics Corp., Jericho, N.Y., 1979—; v.p., chief fin. officer NMB (USA), Inc., 1988—. Home: 15 Carriage Ct Muttontown NY 11791 Office: IMC Magnetics Corp 100 Jericho Quadrangle Jericho NY 11753

PULITZER, MICHAEL EDGAR, newspaper editor; b. St. Louis, Feb. 23, 1930; s. Joseph and Elizabeth (Edgar) P.; m. Cecille Stell Eisenbeis, Apr. 28, 1970; children: Michael Edgar, Elizabeth E., Robert S., Frederick D., Catherine D. Hanson, Christina H. Eisenbeis, Mark C. Eisenbeis, William H. Eisenbeis. Grad., St. Mark's Sch., Southborough, Mass., 1947; AB, Harvard U., 1951, LLB, 1954. Bar: Mass. 1954. Assoc. Warner, Stackpole, Stetson & Bradlee, Boston, 1954-56; reporter Louisville Courier Jour., 1956-60; reporter, news editor, asst. mng. editor St. Louis Post-Dispatch, 1960-71, assoc. editor, 1978-79; editor, pub. Ariz. Daily Star, Tucson, 1971—; pres. chief operating officer Pulitzer Pub. Co. (and subs.), 1979-84, vice chmn., 1984-86, pres., 1986—, also bd. dirs. Clubs: St. Louis Country; Mountain Oyster (Tucson). Office: St Louis Post-Dispatch Pulitzer Pub Co 900 N Tucker Blvd Saint Louis MO 63101 also: Arizona Daily Star PO Box 26807 Tucson AZ 85726 *

PULLEN, RANDALL L., accountant; b. Green Bay, Wis., Nov. 3, 1948; s. Robert R. and Geneva M. (Cole) P.; m. Joyce E. Pullen, Jan. 31, 1970; 1 child, Travis D. BA, Ariz. State U., 1970, MBA, 1983. CPA, Ariz., Oreg. Instr. Yvapai Community Coll., Prescott, Ariz., 1973-74; gen. mgr., ptnr. Charleston (Oreg.) Boat Bldg. Co., 1974-77; programmer, analyst Airesearch Mfg. Co., Phoenix, 1977-79; mgr. Deloitte, Haskins & Sells, Phoenix, 1979-84; v.p. fin. Venture Capital Devel. Co., Scottsdale, Ariz., 1984-86; co-owner Pannell Kerr Forster, Phoenix, 1986—. Editor: Arizona Lodging Forecast, 1987, 2d edit., 1988. Mem. Ariz. Soc. CPAs, Real Estate Securities Syndicate Inst., Nat. Assn. Realtors, Homebuilders Assn. Ariz., Urban Land Inst. Office: Pannell Kerr Forster 2600 N Central #1300 Phoenix AZ 85004

PULLEN, RICHARD OWEN, lawyer, communications company executive; b. New Orleans, Nov. 6, 1944; s. Roscoe LeRoy and Gwendolen Sophia Ellen (Williams) P.; m. Frances G. Eisenstein, Jan. 24, 1976 (div. 1986). B.A. in Econs., Whitman Coll., 1967; J.D., Duke U., 1972. Bar: D.C. 1972. Fin. mgmt. trainee Gen. Electric Co., Lynn, Mass., 1967-69; sr. atty. domestic facilities div. Common Carrier Bur., FCC, Washington, 1972-79, atty. advisor Office of Opinions and Rev., 1979-81; chmn. definitions and terminology of joint industry, govt. com. for preparation of U.S. Proposals 1977 Broadcasting Satellite World Adminstrv. Radio Conf.; v.p. Washington office Contemporary Communications Corp., New Rochelle, N.Y., 1981—. Served with U.S. Coast Guard Res., 1967-75. Mem. ABA, Fed. Communications Bar Assn., Fed. Bar Assn., Internat. Platform Assn. Republican. Unitarian.

PULLEY, CHARLIE HERBERT, medical company executive; b. Kenly, N.C., Aug. 27, 1940; s. Charlie H. and Helen Elizabeth (Jackson) P.; m. Betty Louise Hunt, Dec. 22, 1963; children: Anna, Nathan, Deron. BS, East Carolina U., 1967. Area sales mgr. Am. Hosp. Supply Corp., Evanston, 1967-74; regional sales mgr. Cardiac Pacemakers, Inc., Mpls., 1974-75; v.p. sales, mktg. Medcor, Inc., Hollywood, Fla., 1975-80; dir. dealer sales Squibb Med. Systems, Redmond, Wash., 1980-83; exec. v.p. Am. Med. Electronics, Dallas, 1983—, also bd. dirs. Democrat. Baptist. Office: Am Med Electronics Inc 4125 Keller Springs Rd Dallas TX 75244

PULLEY, GEORGE GRAFTON, data processing executive; b. Amarillo, Texas, Jan. 10, 1947; s. George Henry and Mary Katherine (McInnish) P. AS, Amarillo Coll., 1970; BSBA, Texas Tech U., 1971; postgrad. in bus. adminstrn. West Texas State U., 1972. Systems and program mgr. Sunwest Bank, Albuquerque, 1972-79; pres. G. G. Pulley & Assocs., Inc., Albuquerque, 1979—; computer software provider fin. instns. Mem. Data Processing Mgmt. Assn. (bd. dirs. 1981-82), Spl. Interest Group in Bus. Data Processing (v.p. 1980), Assn. Computing Machinery, Assn. Inst. Cert. Computer Profls. Republican. Methodist. Office: G G Pulley & Assocs Inc 5700 Harper Dr NE Ste 340 Albuquerque NM 87109

PULLIN, JOHN SPENCER, financial executive; b. McAllen, Tex., Apr. 1, 1927; s. John Spencer and Lucille (Dowd) P.; m. Frances Verne Jennings, Feb. 25, 1949; children: John R., Cathy Lynn, Michael S. Student, Schreiner Inst., Kerrville, Tex., 1943; BBA, Tex. A&I U., 1949. With Lone Star Brewing Co., San Antonio, 1949-59; sales mgr. Lone Store Beer Inc., Corpus Christi, Tex., 1959-71; territory mgr. Perry Shankle Wholesale Auto Parts, San Antonio, 1971-85; owner Pullin Enterprises, San Antonio, 1985—; owner, pres. Bi-Weekly Mortgage Systems, San Antonio, 1987—. Served with USN, 1944-46; PTO. Mem. Greater San Antonio C. of C., Am. Legion. Lodges: Elks, Eagles. Home: 6511 Spring Rose San Antonio TX 78249 Office: Bi-Weekly Mortgage Systems and Money Broker 6511 Spring Rose San Antonio TX 78228

PULOS, WILLIAM WHITAKER, lawyer; b. Hornell, N.Y., Aug. 29, 1955; s. William Leroy and Juanita (Whitaker) P. BA magna cum laude Econs., Alfred U., 1977; JD, Union U., 1980. Bar: N.Y. 1982, U.S. Bankruptcy Ct. 1982, U.S. Supreme Ct. 1987. Assoc. Degnan and Hotvet, P.C., Canisteo, N.Y., 1981-82; pvt. practice Alfred, N.Y., 1982—; adj. prof. law Alfred U., 1981—; prof. bus. adminstrn. SUNY-Alfred, 1982-84; tutor Empire State Coll., 1982-85; atty. Town of Alfred, 1982—, Village of Almond (N.Y.), 1983—, Town of West Almond (N.Y.), 1987—; mem. Allegany County and Steuben County Assigned Counsel Program for Indigent Defendants, 1982-85; spl. prosecutor Allegany County, 1984—; asst. counsel N.Y. State Assembly, 1980; hearing officer N.Y. state Small Claims Assessment Rev., 1983-87. Active Alfred Sta. Vol. Fireman's Assn., Inc., 1985—, 2d chief, 1988—; treas. Alfred Community Organizers and Renovators, 1985—. Recipient Outstanding Young Man Am. award U.S. Jaycees, 1982, 86. mem. ABA (profl. standards sect.), Assn. Trial Lawyers Am., N.Y. State Bar Assn. (gen. practice, trial practice, ins. negligence and workers compensation sects.), N.Y. State Trial Lawyers Assn., Steuben County Bar Assn., Steuben County Magistrates Assn., City of Hornell Bar Assn., Canisteo Bar Assn., Allegany County Bar Assn., Am. Abritration Assn., Alfred Bus. Assn., N.Y. State Beef Cattlemen's Assn., N.Y. State Sheriff's Assn. (hon.), U.S. Jaycees, Lions, Elks, Delta Sigma Phi. Office: 44 N Main St PO Box 803 Alfred NY 14802

PULS, DARRELL LEE, labor relations specialist; b. Grand Rapids, Mich., Sept. 6, 1948; s. Leo John and Marjorie Jane (Shoterman) P.; m. Carole Ann DeYoung, May 2, 1969; 1 child, Michelle Suzanne. BA, Western Mich. U., 1971, MA, 1975; postgrad., U. Mich., 1976-79. Tchr. Wyoming (Mich.) Pub. Schs., 1971-79; labor relations specialist Mich. Edn. Assn., East Lansing, 1979-82; uniserv dir. Wash. Edn. Assn., Kennewick, 1982—; organizational cons. West Richland (Wash.) Police Officers Assn., 1983—, NEA, 1979—. Contbr. articles to profl. publs. Mem. exec. bd., labor participation council Monroe County, United Way, Mich., 1980-81; loaned exec. Benton County United Way, Wash., 1982-85; mem. West Richland Planning Commn., 1986, City Council, 1986-87. Mem. Indsl. Relations Rsch. Assn., Am. Arbitration Assn., Columbia Basin Racquet Club. Avocations: weight lifting, photography. Home: 1802 Hummingbird Ct West Richland WA 99352 Office: Wash Edn Assn 8300 Gage Blvd Ste 410 Kennewick WA 99336

PULSIFER, EDGAR DARLING, leasing service and sales executive; b. Natick, Mass., Jan. 11, 1934; s. Howard George and Elvie Marion (Morris) P.; m. Alice Minarik, Feb. 13, 1957 (div. Oct. 1979); children: Mark Edgar, Audrey Carol, Lee Howard; m. Barbara Ann Chuhak, Apr. 19, 1980. BSEE, MIT, 1955. With sales and service dept. Beckman Instruments, Fullerton, Calif., 1956-59; regional sales mgr. Hewlett Packard, Palo Alto, Calif., 1959-72, Gen. Automation, Anaheim, Calif., 1973-74; exec. v.p. Systems Mktg., Elk Grove Vlg., Ill., 1975-79; pres. Consol. Funding, Mt. Prospect, Ill., 1979—. Served as 1st lt. U.S. Army, 1956. Republican. Episcopalian. Clubs: North Shore Country (Glenview, Ill.), Itasca (Ill.) Country. Home: 370 W Dulles Des Plaines IL 60016 Office: Consol Funding Corp 500 W Central Mount Prospect IL 60056

PURCELL, ELAINE IRENE (SCHOCK), banker; b. Pottsville, Pa., Nov. 13, 1946; d. Salem Henry and Ethel Mae (Howells) Schock; m. Jerome James Purcell, June 27, 1969 (div. July 1984). BS in Math., Bloomsburg U., 1968; JD, Duquesne U., 1981; MBA in Fin. and Acctg., Columbia U., 1983. Cert. tchr., Pa. Math. tchr. Pottsville Area High Sch., 1968-69, Keystone Oaks Sch. Dist., Pitts., 1969-81; credit trainee 1st Nat. Bank Chgo., 1983-84; corp. banking officer 1st Nat. Bank Chgo., N.Y.C., 1984-86, asst. v.p., 1987-88; v.p. 1st Nat. Bank Chgo., 1988—. Mem. Women in Cable, Pa. Bar Assn., NAFE, Internat. House, Bklyn. Acad. Music. Office: 1st Nat Bank Chgo 153 W 51st St New York NY 10019

PURCELL, FENTON PETER, engineering consultant; b. Paterson, N.J., Nov. 23, 1942; s. Lee Thomas and Dorothy P.; B.C.E., Rensselaer Poly. Inst., 1965; m. Susan Duggan, Feb. 20, 1971; children—Aimee and Suzie (twins), Jacqueline. Engr., Lee T. Purcell Assocs., cons. engrs., Paterson, 1965-66, partner, 1969—; v.p. Fenton Corp., Paterson, 1970—; partner L.T.P.A. Partnership, Paterson, 1981—. Bd. dirs. Ramapo Valley chpt. ARC, 1978—, 1st v.p., 1980. Served to capt. Med. Service Corps, U.S. Army, 1966-69. Decorated Army Commendation medal; registered profl. engr., N.J., N.Y. State, Pa., Mass.; lic. profl. planner, N.J.; diplomate Am. Acad. Environ. Engrs. Mem. Am. Water Works Assn., Water Pollution Control Fedn., N.J. Cons. Engrs. Council, Am. Cons. Engrs. Council, Rensselaer Soc. Engrs., N.J. Water Pollution Control Assn., Nat. Soc. Profl. Engrs., N.J. Soc. Profl. Engrs. Home: 4 Highview Terr Upper Saddle River NJ 07458 Office: Lee T Purcell Assocs 60 Hamilton St Paterson NJ 07505

PURCELL, MAURICE A., financial executive; b. Frankfort, Ind., Aug. 10, 1946; s. Maurice A. Sr. and Thelma M. (Metzger) P. BS in Econs., Purdue U., 1969; MBA, Ohio State U., 1973. Fin. analyst Formpac div. W.R. Grace and Co., Reading, Pa., 1973-74, mgr. planning, 1974-76; group fin. mgr. corp. office W.R. Grace and Co., N.Y.C., 1976-78, sr. project mgr., 1978-79; v.p., chief fin. officer Grace Distbn. Svcs., Grenville, S.C., 1980—. Mem. Greenville chpt. Habitat for Humanity, 1985—, treas., 1985-87; active Greenville County United Way, 1988—. Mem. Nat. Assn. Accts., Greenville C. of C., Greenville City Club. Republican. Methodist. Office: Grace Distbn Svcs PO Box 24999 Greenville SC 29616

PURCELL, PHILIP JAMES, financial services company executive; b. Salt Lake City, Sept. 5, 1943; s. Philip James and Shirley (Sorenson) P.; m. Anne Marie Mc Namara, Apr. 2, 1964; children: David, Peter, Mark, Michael, Paul, Philip, Thomas. B.B.A., U. Notre Dame, 1964; M.Sc. in Econs., London Sch. Econs. and Polit. Sci., U. London, 1966; M.B.A., U. Chgo., 1967. Mng. dir., cons. McKinsey & Co., Inc., Chgo., 1967-78; v.p. planning and adminstrn. Sears, Roebuck and Co., Chgo., 1978-82; pres., chief operating officer, then chmn., chief exec. officer Dean Witter Fin. Svcs. Inc., N.Y.C., 1982—, also bd. dirs.; bd. dirs. Dean Witter Realty Inc., Dean Witter Reynolds Inc., Dean Witter Reynolds Internat. Inc., Sears, Roebuck and Co., Securities Industry Assn.; mem. council Grad. Sch. Bus., U. Chgo.; mem. adv. council U. Notre Dame Bus. Sch., Ind. Served with USNR. Roman Catholic. Clubs: Economic of Chgo., The Chgo.; Bond of N.Y. (N.Y.C.). Home: 1036 Seneca Rd Wilmette IL 60091 Office: Dean Witter Fin Svcs Inc 2 World Trade Ctr 66th Fl New York NY 10048

PURCELL, RICHARD FICK, lawyer, food company executive; b. Washington, Apr. 19, 1924; s. Richard J. and Clara A. (Fick) P.; m. Judith Wyckoff, Nov. 28, 1964; children: Richard Wycoff, Edward Thomas, Carolyn Elizabeth. B.A., George Washington U., 1948; M.A., Columbia U., 1949; cert., U. Fribourg (Switzerland), 1949; LL.B., Harvard U., 1952; grad., Command and Gen. Staff Coll., Ft. Leavenworth, Kans., 1970. Bar: D.C. 1953, Mass. 1953, Minn. 1953, N.Y. 1954, U.S. Ct. Appeals 1954, U.S. Supreme Ct. 1963. Assoc. Shearman & Sterling, N.Y.C., 1954-74; v.p. office gen. counsel 1st Nat. City Bank (now Citibank N.A.), N.Y.C., 1974-75; sr. v.p., gen. counsel Connell Rice and Sugar Co., Westfield, N.J., 1975—. Author: Government Administration of Wage Incentives in Wartime, 1949, Church and State in Colonial Connecticut, 1953; contbr. to Cath. Ency., legal and banking jours.; law editor (Banking Law Jour.), 1965-67. Served to lt. col. F.A. U.S. Army, 1943-46, 52-53. Mem. ABA, D.C. Bar Assn., Am. Irish Hist. Assn. Republican. Roman Catholic. Clubs: Nat. Lawyers; Army and Navy (Washington); Harvard (N.Y.C.). Office: Connell Rice & Sugar Co Inc 45 Cardinal Dr Westfield NJ 07090-1099

PURCELL, ROBERT HARRY, financial service company executive; b. Beatrice, Nebr., July 21, 1943; s. Harry C. and Anita M. (Finley) P.; B.S., U. Nebr., 1965, J.D., 1968; m. Linda Jo Cook, Sept. 6, 1964; children—Gregory, Jennifer, Christopher. Admitted to Nebr. bar, 1969; tax specialist Arthur Andersen & Co., Omaha and Cin., 1968-73; dir. taxes Ward Foods, Inc., Chgo., 1973-77; tax counsel Walter E. Heller Internat. Corp., Chgo., 1977-80, v.p. corp. planning, 1980-81; sr. v.p. div. hdqrs. accounts Heller Fin., Inc. Chgo., 1981-85, div. pres., project mgmt. orgn.,

1986—. Mem. ABA, Am. Inst. C.P.A.s., Ill. Soc. C.P.A.s., Nebr. Soc. C.P.A.s., Nebr. Bar Assn. Episcopalian. Home: 1020 Mallard Dr Palatine IL 60067 Office: Heller Fin Inc 200 N LaSalle St Chicago IL 60601

PURCELL, STUART MCLEOD, III, financial planner; b. Santa Monica, Calif., Feb. 16, 1944; s. Stuart McLeod Jr. and Carol (Howe) P. AA, Santa Monica City Coll., 1964; BS, Calif. State U., Northridge, 1967; grad., CPA Advanced Personal Fin. Planning Curriculum, San Francisco, 1985. CPA, Calif. Sr. acct. Pannell Kerr Forster, San Francisco, 1970-73; fin. cons. Purcell Fin. Services, San Francisco, 1973-74, San Rafael, Calif., 1980-81; controller Decimus Corp., San Francisco, 1974-76, Grubb & Ellis Co., Oakland, Calif., 1976-78, Marwais Steel Co., Richmond, Calif., 1979-80; owner, fin. counselor Purcell Wealth Mgmt., San Rafael, 1981—; guest lectr. Golden Gate U., San Francisco, 1985—; leader ednl. workshops, Larkspur, Calif., 1984. Contbr. articles to profl. jours. Treas. Salvation Army, San Rafael-San Anselmo-Fairfax, Calif., 1987—; chmn. fin. planners div. United Way Marin County, Calif., 1984; mem. fundraising com. Marin County March of Dimes, 1987—, Marin County Arthritis Found., 1988—; mem. Marin Estate Planning Council. Served to lt. (j.g.) USNR, 1968-76. Named Eagle Scout, 1959, Best Fin. Advisor Marin County Independent-Jour. newspaper, 1987, Top Producer Unimarc, 1986; recipient Outstanding Achievement award United Way, 1984. Mem. Am. Inst. CPAs, Calif. Soc. CPAs, Nat. Speakers Assn., Internat. Assn. for Fin. Planners (exec. dir. North Bay chpt., San Francisco 1984), Internat. Soc. Pre-Retired Planners, Soc. CPA-Fin. Planners (dist. membership chmn. San Francisco 1986), Sigma Alpha Epsilon. Presbyterian. Home: 45 Vineyard Dr San Rafael CA 94901 Office: Purcell Wealth Mgmt 1811 Grand Ave Ste B San Rafael CA 94901

PURDOM, HAROLD E., diversified company executive; b. 1924; married. BS, Abilene Christian Coll., 1947. Drilling engr., Shell Oil Co., 1947-57; gen. mgr. Buck Fishing Tool Co., 1957-61; div. mgr. Nitrogen Oil Well Service Co. subs. Big Three Industries Inc., 1961-63, br. mgr., 1963-70, mgr. mktg., 1970-72; v.p. So. div. Big Three Industries Inc., from 1972, now exec. v.p., also bd. dirs. Served to maj. USAR, 1944-66. Office: Big Three Industries Inc 3535 W 12th St Houston TX 77008

PURDUM, ROBERT L., manufacturing company executive; b. Wilmington, Ohio, 1935; married. BS, Purdue U., 1956. With U.S. Navy and Ind. Toll Road Commn., 1956-62; with Armco Inc., Middletown, Ohio, 1962—, dist. engr. metal product div., 1962-66, sales staff, 1966-72; dist. mgr. Columbus, Ohio, 1972-76; gen. mgr. adminstrn. Armco Inc., Columbus, Ohio, 1976-78; v.p. div. subs., pres. Midwestern Steel, Columbus, Ohio, 1978-80, area v.p., 1980-82; group v.p., chief exec. officer steel svcs. group Middletown, Ohio, 1982-86; exec. v.p., chief operating officer Armco Inc., Middletown, Ohio; pres., chief operating officer Armco Inc., Parsippany, N.J., 1986—; also bd. dirs. Armco Inc., Parsippany. Capt. USNR. Recipient Disting. Engring. Alumnus award Purdue U., 1986. Office: Armco Inc 300 Interpace Pkwy Parsippany NJ 07054

PURDY, FRAZIER RODNEY, advertising executive; b. N.Y.C., Oct. 31, 1929; s. Harris Levitt and Mary Irene (Long) P.; m. Joan Wolverton Smith, Apr. 11, 1953 (div. Aug. 1979); children: Mark C., Kevin B., Christopher P.; m. Susan Soroko, Sept. 23, 1979. Grad. high sch., Westport, Conn. Studio artist Lennen & Mitchell, N.Y.C., 1952-53; asst. art dir. Young & Rubicam, N.Y.C., 1954-57, art dir., 1957-66, art supr., 1966-70, v.p., assoc. creative dir., 1970-73, mgr. copy dept., 1973-75, sr. v.p., creative dir. N.Y. div., 1975-79, exec. v.p., creative dir. USA div., 1979-84; exec. creative dir., exec. v.p. Young & Rubicam Worldwide, N.Y.C., 1984—; speaker in field. Sgt. U.S. Army, 1948-50. Recipient various advt. awards, 1954-84. Mem. Am. Assn. Advt. Agys. (com. 1975-85). Republican. Home: 131 South St PO Box 223 Roxbury CT 06783 Office: Young & Rubicam Inc 285 Madison Ave New York NY 10017

PURPURA, CHARLES GERARD, screenwriter, production company executive; b. N.Y.C., Sept. 14, 1945; s. Charles Carmelo and Jennie (LaMacchia) P.; m. Jennie Simeone, Aug. 22, 1970; children: Simon Henry (dec.), William Charles. Student, N.Y.U. Film Sch., 1975-78. Pres. Bop House Prodns., Los Angeles, 1982—. Screenwriter: (feature films) Heaven Help Us, 1985, Satisfaction, 1988, (TV film) The Day the Senior Class Got Married, 1985 (Emmy award, Humanitas award). Mem. Nat. Acad. TV Arts and Scis., Writers Guild Am. Roman Catholic. Masons. Home: 27 Connecticut Ave Massapequa NY 11758 Office: Bop House Prodns 8955 Norma Pl Los Angeles CA 90069

PURTLE, MARIE JO-ANN See LANKFORD, MARIE JO-ANN

PUTIGNANO, PATRICK ALLEN, aerospace company executive; b. San Angelo, Tex., Aug. 10, 1951; s. Patrick John and Grace Marie (Flanagan) P.; m. Judith Ann Marousek, May 3, 1975. BS, U.S. Mil. Acad., 1973; MPA, Princeton U., 1981. Commd. U.S. Army, 1973, advanced through grades to maj., 1987; mil. legis. asst. Sen. John McCain, Washington, 1988-89; spl. asst. internat. affairs Office Sec. Air Force, Washington, 1989; project devel. mgr. Gen. Dynamics, Arlington, Va., 1989—; staff mem. Nat. Security Coun., Washington, 1980, 83; asst. prof. dept. social scis. U.S. Mil. Acad., West Point, N.Y., 1981-84; student and mem. faculty U.S. Army Command and Gen. Staff Coll., Ft. Leavenworth, Kans., 1985-87; participant Internat. Univ. seminar on Armed Forces and Soc. Contbr. article to profl jours. White House fellow Office Sec. Interior, Washington, 1984-85. Mem. Internat. Inst. Strategic Studies, Army Navy Club (Washington), Phi Kappa Phi. Roman Catholic. Home: 8342 Brockham Dr Alexandria VA 22309 Office: Gen Dynamics Def Initiatives Orgn 1525 Wilson Blvd Arlington VA 22209

PUTNAM, CHARLES DUANE, manufacturing company executive; b. Northport, Mich., Apr. 21, 1928; s. Evits W. and Mabel Ruth (Lanham) P.; Gladys Louise Neiderhiser, July 23, 1955; children: Andrea, Charles Jr., Cynthia, Robert. BEE, Mich. Coll. Mining and Tech., 1950; MD, Cleveland-Marshall Law Sch., 1955. With Clark Controller Co., Cleve., 1950-63; patent atty. Whirlpool Corp., Benton Harbor, Mich., 1963-65, sr. patent atty., 1965-67, dir. corp. labor relations, 1967-77, gen. mgr. personnel, 1977-78, v.p. personnel, 1978-83, sr. v.p. human resources, 1983-84, sr. v.p. adminstrn., 1984-85, exec. v.p. adminstrn., 1985—, also bd. dirs. Mem. ABA, Mich. Bar Assn., Ohio Bar Assn. Home: 1935 Lasein Saint Joseph MI 49085 Office: Whirlpool Corp 2000 M63 N Benton Harbor MI 49022 *

PUTNEY, JOHN ALDEN, JR., insurance company executive; b. Bklyn., Mar. 5, 1939; s. John Alden and Anne Marie (Davenport) P.; m. Theresa Rose Defrisco, Feb. 9, 1964; children—Angela, Alexander. B.S. cum laude in Math, St. John's U., 1960. Systems engr. IBM, N.Y.C., 1961-64; mktg. rep. IBM, 1964-66; cons. Topas Computer Corp., N.Y.C., 1966-67; dir., v.p., sec. Topas Computer Corp., 1967-70; with Tchrs. Ins. and Annuity Assn., N.Y.C., 1971—; v.p. Tchrs. Ins. and Annuity Assn., 1977-79, sr. v.p., 1979-80, exec. v.p., 1980—, office and info. systems area mgr., 1979-87, mgr. ops. support area, 1987—. Served with USMC, 1960. Home: 9 Concord Ave Larchmont NY 10538 Office: Tchrs Ins & Annuity Assn 730 3rd Ave New York NY 10017

PUTNEY, MARK WILLIAM, lawyer, utility executive; b. Marshalltown, Iowa, Jan. 25, 1929; s. Lawrence Charles and Geneva (Eldridge) P.; m. Ray Ann Bartnek, May 25, 1962; children: Andi Bartnek, William Bradford, Blake Reinhart. BA, U. Iowa, 1951, JD, 1957. Bar: Iowa 1957, U.S. Supreme Ct. 1960. Ptnr. Bradshaw, Fowler, Proctor & Fairgrave, Des Moines, 1961-72; pres., dir. Bradford & Blake Ltd., Des Moines; pres., chmn., chief exec. officer Iowa Resources, Inc., 1984—; chmn., chief exec. officer Iowa Power & Light Co., 1984—, Iowa Gas Co.,, 1984-85; dir. Norwest Bank Des Moines N.A., Allied Ins. Group. Civilian aide to Sec. Army for Iowa, 1975-77; bd. dirs. Greater Des Moines YMCA, 1976-86, Boys' Home Iowa, 1982-86, Hoover Presdl. Libr. Assn., 1983—, Living History Farms, 1984—, U. Iowa Found., 1984—; bd. dirs. Greater Des Moines Com., 1984—, pres. 1988, Edison Electric Inst., 1886—, Assoc. Edison Illuminating Cos., 1988—; chmn. Iowa Com. for Employer Support of Guard and Res., 1979-86, Des Moines Devel. Corp., 1984—, pres., 1989. With USAF, 1951-53. Mem. Iowa Utility Assn. (chmn. 1989), Edison Electric Inst., Assn. of Edison Illunminating Cos., Greater Des Moines C. of C., Delta Chi, Phi Delta Phi. Republican. Episcopalian. Clubs: Des Moines (pres. 1977), Wakonda (pres. 1982). Lodges: Rotary, Masons, Shriners. Home: 6675 NW Beaver Dr Johnston IA 50131 Office: Iowa Resources Inc 666 Grand Ave PO Box 657 Des Moines IA 50303

PUTNEY, MARY ENGLER, federal auditor; b. Overland, Mo., May 1, 1933; d. Bernard J. and Marie (Kunkler) Engler; children: Glennon (dec.), Pat Michael, Michelle. Student Fontbonne Coll., 1951-52; AA, Sacramento City Coll., 1975; BS in Bus., Calif. State U., 1981; CPA, Calif. Asst. to acct. Mo. Research Labs., Inc., St. Louis, 1953-55, sec. to controller, 1955-56, adminstrv. asst. to pres., 1958-60; sec. to mgr. Western region fin. Gen. Electric Co., St. Louis, 1960-62; sec. to regional v.p. agrl. loans Crocker Nat. Bank, Sacramento, 1962-67, asst. credit analyst No. region, 1967, sec. to v.p. and mgr. capital office, Sacramento, 1967-72; student tchr. Sacramento County Dept. Edn., 1979-81; acctg. technician East Yolo Community Services Dist., 1983; mgmt. specialist USAF Logistics Command, 1984; staff auditor office Insp. Gen., U.S. Dept. Transp., 1984—. Mem. Sacramento Community Commn. for Women, 1978—, rec. sec., 1980-81, bd. dirs., 1980—; mem. planning bd. Golden Empire Health Systems Agy. Mem. Nat. Assn. Accts. (dir., newsletter editor), Fontbonne Coll. Alumni Assn., AAUW (fin. officer 1983—), Assn. Govt. Accts. (chpt. officer), Am. Soc. Women Accts., Beta Gamma Sigma, Beta Alpha Psi. Roman Catholic. Club: Arden Hills Swim and Tennis. Home: 2616 Point Reyes Way Sacramento CA 95826 Office: US Dept of Transp Office Insp Gen Room 287 PO Box 1915 Sacramento CA 95809

PYKE, JOHN SECREST, JR., polymers company executive; b. Lakewood, Ohio, July 11, 1938; s. John S. and Elma B. P.; student Haverford Coll., 1956-58; B.A., Columbia U., 1960, postgrad. Sch. Grad. Faculties, 1960-61; J.D., Columbia Law Sch., 1964; m. Judith A., Dec. 26, 1970; 1 son, John Secrest, III. Bar: N.Y. 1965. Assoc. firm Townsend & Lewis (now Thacher, Proffit & Wood), N.Y.C., 1964-68; atty. M.A. Hanna Co., Cleve., 1968—, sec., 1973—, v.p., 1979—. Trustee, Western Res. Acad., Cleve., 1976—. Mem. ABA, Am. Soc. Corp. Secs., Assn. Bar N.Y.C. Clubs: Union, Cleveland, Clifton. Author: Landmark Preservation, 1969, 2d edit., 1972. Office: MA Hanna Co 1301 E 9th St Ste 3600 Cleveland OH 44114

PYLE, HOWARD, III, utility executive; b. Richmond, Va., Feb. 1, 1940; s. Wilfrid and Anne Woolston (Roller) P.; m. Caroline Oglesby Smith, June 18, 1965; children: Elizabeth Roller, Howard. AB, Princeton, 1962; JD, U. Va., 1967. Career trainee CIA, Washington, 1967-69; adminstrv. asst. to Congressman Odin Langen, Washington, 1969-70, Congressman Hastings Keith, Washington, 1971; asst. to sec. Dept. Interior, Washington, 1971-73; Washington rep. Standard Oil Co. of Ind., 1973-77; mgr. fed. pub. affairs R.J. Reynolds Industries, Inc., Winston-Salem, N.C., 1977-80; dir. fed. relations Houston Light & Power Co., Washington, 1980—; adv. bd. STRATCO Inc., bd. dirs. Pub. Affairs Coun. Bd. govs., treas. Sevier House Episcopal Ch. Home; bd. dirs., treas. Friendship Terr. Episcopal Ch. Home; treas. St. Alban's Ch. Served to capt. USNR, 1962—. Mem. Am. Bar Assn., Fed. Bar Assn., D.C. Bar, Va. Bar, Fed. Energy Bar Assn., Nat. Rifle Assn., Naval Res. Assn., Res. Officers Assn., SAR, Delta Theta Phi. Republican. Episcopalian. Clubs: Va. Country, Kenwood Golf and Country. Home: 4930 Quebec St NW Washington DC 20016 Office: 1050 17th St NW Suite 550 Washington DC 20036

PYLE, RAYMOND JAMES, JR., advertising executive; b. Oak Park, Ill., Jan. 15, 1932; s. Raymond James and Bessie Inez (Osborn) P.; student U. Wis., 1951-56, U. Notre Dame, 1968; student mgmt. U. South Fla., 1972; m. Mabel Lee Freeman, June 28, 1952; children—Dale, David, Steven, Carol Lynn. Sales rep. London Wholesale Hardware, 1957-58; sales rep. Martin Outdoor Advt., 1958-65, gen. mgr., 1965-66, v.p., 1966-69, pres., 1969-76; Fla. regional mgr., v.p. Foster & Kleiser div. Metromedia, Tampa, Fla., 1976-82, sr. v.p., 1982-86, v p., gen. mgr., Patrick Media Group, 1986—; bd. fellows, counselor U. Tampa, 1970-77. bd. dirs. Town and Country Med. Ctr., Tampa, Hall of Fame Bowl Assn., Gulf Ridge Council Boy Scouts of Am., Tampa. Mem. Outdoor Advt. Assn. Fla. (pres.; Disting. Service award 1981). Inst. Outdoor Advt. S.E. U.S.A. (treas.), Tampa Advt. Fedn. (past pres.; Advt. Man of Year 1969, Silver Medal award 1979-80), Sales and Mktg. Execs. Tampa (past pres. 1970, Sales and Mktg. Exec. Top Mgmt. award 1982, Man of the Year, 1970), Pi Sigma Epsilon. Democrat. Baptist. Clubs: Centre, Rotary (Tampa); Feather Sound Golf and Tennis; Masons. Home: 1206 S Suffolk Dr Tampa FL 33629 Office: Patrick Media Group 5555 Ulmerton Rd Clearwater FL 34620

PYLE, RICHARD ERNEST, securities analyst; b. Fargo, N.D., Feb. 12, 1948; s. Ernest G. and Betty Lou I. (Thompson) P.; m. Nathalie B. Clark, May 16, 1970; children: R. Judson, Rebecca, Nathaniel. BA, Macalester Coll., 1969; postgrad., U. Minn. Analyst lst Trust Co., St. Paul, 1970-73; investment officer lst Northwestern Co., Fargo, 1973-80; investment analyst Investors Diversified Svcs., Mpls., 1980-82; mng. dir. Piper, Jaffray & Hopwood, Mpls., 1982—; bd. dirs. Piper Jaffray Ventures, Mpls. M. Mem. Twin Cities Securities Analysts (treas. 1983-85), Mpls. Athletic Club, Minikahda Club. Republican. Office: Piper Jaffray & Hopwood Box 28 Minneapolis MN 55440

PYLINSKI, ALBERT, JR., insurance company executive; b. New Berlin, N.Y., June 6, 1953; s. Albert and Marian Lucelia (Sprague) P.; m. Danica Camille Adams, June 7, 1980; children: Brenton Thomas. BS, Syracuse U., 1985; diploma specialized tng., Coll. Ins., N.Y.C., 1977, 79, Lloyds of London, 1986. Acct. N.Y. Cen. Mut. Fire Ins. Co., Edmeston, 1973-85, asst. treas., 1985-86, treas., 1986—, v.p., 1987—; also bd. dirs. N.Y. Cen. Mut. Fire Ins. Co. Trustee Edmeston Free Library, 1981-84. Mem. Soc. Ins. Accts., Nat. Assn. Mut. Ins. Cos., Cooperstown (N.Y.) Country Club (bd. dirs., treas. 1980—). Roman Catholic. Office: NY Cen Mut Fire Ins Co Central Pla E Edmeston NY 13335

PYLIPOW, STANLEY ROSS, manufacturing company executive; b. Coudersport, Pa., Apr. 4, 1936; s. Stanley Edward and Helen L. (Haskins) P.; m. Phyllis Beverly Moore, Dec. 1, 1956; children—David, James, Vicky, Kenneth, Sandra. B.B.A. in Acctg. cum laude, St. Bonaventure U., 1957. Various fin. positions Chicopee Mfg., New Brunswick, N.J., 1957-65; various positions to v.p., gen. mgr. Domestic Coatings div. Mobil Chem. Co., N.Y.C., 1965-73; asst. corp. controller Monsanto Co., St. Louis, 1974-76; controller, dir. planning Monsanto Comml. Products, St. Louis, 1976-79; sr. v.p., chief fin. officer Fisher Controls Internat., Inc., St. Louis, 1979—. Treas., City of Town and Country, Mo., 1980-84; bd. dirs. Ecumenical Housing Prodn. Corp., St. Louis, 1980—; sr. warden St. Peter's Episcopal Ch., St. Louis, 1984-87. Served to 1st lt., U.S. Army, 1958. Named Exec. of Yr., Profl. Secs. Internat., 1982. Mem. Nat. Assn. Accts. (chmn. com. chpt. ops. 1984-86, chmn. rsch. com. 1986-87, v.p. 1983-84, exec. com. 1988—), Fin. Execs. Inst., Machinery and Allied Products Inst. (fin. council II 1985—), Clayton Club, Bellerive Country Club. Republican. Home: 244 Carlyle Lake Dr Saint Louis MO 63141 Office: Fisher Controls Internat Inc 8000 Maryland Ave 13th Fl Ste 1300 Clayton MO 63105

PYNE, EBEN WRIGHT, banker; b. N.Y.C., June 14, 1917; s. Grafton H. and Leta Constance (Wright) P.; grad. Groton Sch., 1935; A.B., Princeton, 1939; m. Hilda Holloway, Dec. 16, 1941; children—Constance Howland Pyne Ranges (dec.), Lillian Stokes (Mrs. Lillian Pyne-Corbin), Mary Alison. Clerk 1st Nat. City Trust Co. (formerly City Bank Farmers Trust Co., 1939, v.p., asst. to pres., 1952-56, exec. v.p., 1956, pres., dir., 1957-61; asst. cashier Nat. City Bank of N.Y., 1946-50, asst. v.p., 1950-52, v.p., 1952-53, sr. v.p., 1960-82; vice chmn., bd. dirs. The Home Group Inc.; bd. dirs. U.S. Life Ins. Co. City of N.Y., Home Ins. Co., U.S. Internat. Reins., Inc., Gen. Devel. Corp., Slattery Group, Inc., USLIFE Corp., L.I. Lighting Co., W.R. Grace and Co. Mem. N.Y. State Met. Transp. Authority, 1965-75; commr. N.Y.C. Transit Authority, Triborough Bridge and Tunnel Authority, Manhattan and Bronx Surface Transit Authority, Stewart Airport, S.I. Rapid Transit Operating Authority, all 1965-75; adv. bd. Nassau County council Boy Scouts Am.; bd. dirs. Winthrop U. Hosp.; trustee Juilliard Sch., St. Luke's Hosp., Grace Inst., Grace Found.; mem. exec. com. Pres.'s Pvt. Sector on Cost Control. Served as maj. AUS, 1940-46. Decorated Bronze Star. Mem. Pilgrims of U.S. (exec. com.), Bklyn. Inst. Arts and Scis. (trustee), N.Y. Zool. Soc. (trustee). Clubs: Piping Rock (Locust Valley, L.I.); Bond, Racquet and Tennis, River (N.Y.C.); Ivy (Princeton, N.J.); Links Golf (North Hills, L.I.). Home: 134 Willets Rd Box 195 Old Westbury NY 11568 Office: WR Grace & Co 1114 Ave of the Americas New York NY 10013

PYNE, RUSSELL BRADHURST, venture capitalist; b. Princeton, N.J., Feb. 19, 1955; s. John Insley Blair and Elizabeth Stuyvesant (Fish) P.; m. Helen Darlington Cooke, June 18, 1983; children: Thornton Hamilton, Russell Stuyvesant. AB in Econs. magna cum laude, Princeton U., 1977; JD, MBA, Stanford U., 1981. Bar: N.Y., 1982. Assoc. Davis Polk & Wardwell, N.Y.C., 1981-82; assoc. The Sprout Group, N.Y.C., 1983-86, v.p., 1986-87; gen. ptnr. The Sprout Group, Menlo Park, Calif., 1987—; bd. dirs. AlphaGraphics Inc., Tucson, Compex Services Inc., L.A., PAC Holdings Corp. Trustee Alice & Hamilton Fish Library, Garrison, N.Y., 1981—. Arjay Miller scholar Stanford U., 1981. Mem. Phi Beta Kappa. Republican. Office: The Sprout Group 3000 Sand Hill Rd Bldg 1 Ste 285 Menlo Park CA 94025

PYNN, THOMAS DAMON, consulting firm executive; b. Meredith, N.H., May 26, 1944; s. Leander Giles and Ruth (Bennett) P.; m. Maria Elena Berghmans, Dec. 20, 1966. BA, U. So. Fla., 1971, MA, 1973; postgrad., U. N.Mex., 1972-74. Research asst. U. So. Fla., U. N.Mex., Tampa, Fla. and Albuquerque, 1969-74; lectr. U. N.Mex, Albuquerque, 1974-76, Cath. U., Quito, Ecuador, 1976-77; sr. scientist Creative Socio-Medics Corp., N.Y.C., 1978-82; div. mgr. Lawrence Johnson & Assocs., Inc., Washington, 1982-88; group mgr. Sci. Mgmt. Corp., Landover, Md., 1988-89; sr. cons. Bur. Internat. Narcotics Matters U.S. Dept. State, 1989—; v.p. Eirenicon Corp., Fairfax, Va., 1977-79, MEP Assocs., Falls Ch., Va., 1984—. Editor Nat. Dir. Alcoholism and Drug Treatment, 1979-84; contbr. numerous articles on substance abuse to profl. jours. Served with USMC, 1963-67. Mem. Phi Kappa Phi. Democrat. Roman Catholic. Club: San Martin Soc. Home: 10101 Grosvenor Pl #2014 Rockville MD 20852

QAZI, KHIZIR HAYAT A., civil engineer; b. Ratodero, Larkana, Sindh, Pakistan, Apr. 12, 1945; s. Abdul Hayee A. and Raziya Abdul Hayee Qzai; m. Khursheed Khizir, Aug. 29, 1965; children—Waheeda Khizir, Fahmeeda Khizir, Tahmena Khizir, Sanjeeoa Khizir, Sikandar Aftab Khizir. Debates and fine arts Govt. Coll. Larkana, 1962-64; Sind U. Engring. Coll., Jamshoro, 1964-68. B.E. in Civil Engring., Sind U., Jamshoro, 1968; diploma in fine arts, Bd. Intermidiate Drawing Grade Examinations, Hyderabad, 1958; M.I.E., Inst. of Engrs. Pakistan, Karachi, 1979. Registered profl. engr., Lectr. Sind U. Engring. Coll., Jamshoro, 1969-70, N.E.D. Gov't. Engring. Coll., Karachi, 1970-73; asst. engr. P.I.D.C., Karachi, 1973-75; project engr. N.F.C. (Paksaudi Fertilizer Ltd.), Lahore, 1975-81; exec. engr. Mehran U. of Engring. & Tech., Jamshoro, 1981—; prin. Sikandar Art Gallery, Nawabshah. Author: Engineering Drawing, 1973, (with M.I. Baloch) Engineering Drawing, 1979. Recipient Cash Prize & Certificate, Gov. of Sindh, Karachi, 1984, Gold Medal, Sindh Grad. Assn. Pakistan, Karachi, 1985. Mem. Inst. Engrs. Clubs: Officer's (Mirpur Mathelo, Nawabshah). Home: Al-Manzar Ratodero, Dist Larkana Sindh Pakistan Office: Mehran U of Engring & Tech, Nawabsha Sindh Pakistan Office: Sikandar Art Gallery, PO Box 96, Nawabshah Sindh Pakistan

QAZILBASH, IMTIAZ ALI, engineering company executive, consultant; b. Peshawar, North West Frontier, Pakistan, July 15, 1934; s. Nawazish Ali and Jahan Ara (Samdani Khan) Q.; m. Rubina Satti, Dec. 20, 1964; children—Zulfiqar Ali, Haider Ali, Zainab. Intermediate cert., Islamia Coll., Peshawar, Pakistan, 1951; gen. cert. edn. advanced level Coll. Tech., Northampton, U.K., 1952; diploma in French lang. Geneva U., 1953; B.Sc. in Engring., Imperial Coll. Sci. and Tech., London, 1957; Assoc., City and Guilds of London Inst., 1957. Registered profl. engr., Pakistan. Engr. N.Z. Power Co. Nord Sjaeland Elektricitet og Sporveje Aktieselskab, Copenhagen, 1957; telefoningenior Copenhagen Telephone Co., Kopenhavns Telefon Aktieselskab, Copenhagen, 1957-58; telecomm engr. Pakistan Indsl. Devel. Corp., Karachi, 1958-59; asst. dir. telecommunications Water and Power Devel. Authority, Lahore, Pakistan, 1959-64, dir. telecommunications, 1964-74; mng. dir., pres. Engrs. Internat., Lahore, Peshawar, 1975—; expert to study com. on communications Internat. Conf. on Large High Tension Electric Systems CIGRE, Paris, 1974—; expert roster UN, N.Y.C., 1970—; leader engrs. select com. West Pakistan Gov.'s Panel on Water and Power Devel. Authority Reorgn., Lahore, 1969-70; mem. Pakistan delegation Internat. Conf. on Large High Tension Electric Systems CIGRE, Paris, 1970, 74, 76; chmn. session Conf. on Implementation of Adminstrn. Reforms, Lahore, 1974-75; convenor com. on orgn. and adminstrn. Nat. Conf. on Acceleration of Devel. Process, Lahore, 1974; mem. energy panel Nat. Sci. Policy Group Islamabad, 1974-75; mem., organizer Nat. Seminar on Role of Hydroelectric Resources in Pakistan's Devel., Lahore, 1975; mem. selection com. U. Engring. and Tech., Lahore, 1969—; cons. Pakistan Adminstrv. Staff Coll., Lahore, 1972-74. Contbr. articles to profl. jours. Founder mem., central council mem. Fedn. Engring. Assns. Pakistan, Lahore, 1969—; v.p. Service of Elec. Engrs. Assn., Lahore, 1969-71; convenor ann. conv. Instn. Engrs., Dacca, 1970. Fellow Instn. Engrs. Pakistan (exec. council, vice-chmn. elec. sect. 1986—); mem. Pakistan Engring. Congress (council 1970-72, 76), IEEE, Instn. Elec. Engrs. U.K., Clubs: Lahore Gymkhana; Peshawar; Punjab (Lahore); Golf (Peshawar). Avocations: books; music; ballet; golf; trout fishing; shooting; flying. Home: 9 Mulberry Rd, University Town, Peshawar Pakistan Office: Engrs Internat Pakistan Pltd, 9 Mulberry Rd, University Town, Peshawar Pakistan

QUAAL, WARD LOUIS, broadcasting executive; b. Ishpeming, Mich., Apr. 7, 1919; s. Sigfred Emil and Alma Charlotte (Larson) Q.; m. Dorothy J. Graham, Mar. 9, 1944; children—Graham Ward, Jennifer Anne. A.B., U. Mich., 1941; LL.D. (hon.), Mundelein Coll., 1962, No. Mich. U., 1967; D.Pub. Service, Elmhurst Coll., 1967; D.H.L. (hon.), Lincoln Coll., 1968, DePaul U., 1974. Announcer-writer Sta. WBEO (now sta. WDMJ), Marquette, Mich., 1936-37; announcer, writer, producer Sta. WJR, Detroit, 1937-41; spl. events announcer-producer WGN, Chgo., 1941-42, asst. to gen. mgr., 1945-49; exec. dir. Clear Channel Broadcasting Service, Washington, 1949-52, pres., chief exec. officer, 1964-74; v.p., asst. gen. mgr. Crosley Broadcasting Corp., Cin., 1952-56; v.p., gen. mgr., mem. bd. WGN Inc., Chgo., 1956; exec. v.p., then pres. WGN Continental Broadcasting Co., 1960-74; pres. Ward L. Quaal Co., 1974—; former dir. Tribune Co.; dir., mem. exec. com. U.S. Satellite Broadcasting Corp., 1982—; bd. dirs. Christine Valmy Inc.; chmn. exec. com., dir. WLW Radio Inc., Cin., 1975-81; co-founder, dir. Universal Resources, Inc. 1961-86; mem. FCC Adv. Com. on Advanced TV Systems, 1988—. Author: (with others) Broadcast Management, 1968, rev. edit., 1978, 3d rev. edit., 1989; co-producer (Broadway play) Teddy and Alice, 1988. Mem., Hoover Commn. Exec. Br. Task Force, 1949-59; mem. U.S.-Japan Cultural Exchange Commn., 1960-70; mem. Pres.'s Council Phys. Fitness and Sports, 1983—; bd. dirs. Farm Found., 1963-73; bd. trustees Hollywood (Calif.) Mus., 1964-78, MacCormac Jr. Coll., Chgo., 1974-80; chmn. exec. com. Council for TV Devel., 1969-72; mem. bus. adv. council Chgo. Urban League, 1964-74; bd. dirs. Broadcasters Found., Internat. Radio and TV Found., Sears Roebuck Found., 1970-73; trustee Mundelein Coll., 1962-72, Hillsdale Coll., 1966-72. Served as lt. USNR, 1942-45. Recipient Disting. Bd. Gov.'s award Nat. Acad. TV Arts and Scis., 1966, 87, Freedoms Found. award, Valley Forge, 1966, 68, 70, Disting. Alumnus award U. Mich., 1967, Loyola U. Key, 1970, Advt. Man of Yr. Gold medallion, Chgo. Advt. Club, 1968, Disting. Svc. award Nat. Assn. Broadcasters, 1973, Ill. Broadcaster of Yr. award, 1973, Press Vet. of Yr. award, 1973, Communications award of distinction Brandeis U., 1973; first recipient Sterling Medal, Barren Found., 1985, Lifetime Achievement award in broadcasting Ill. Broadcasters Assn., 1989; 1st person named to Better Bus. Bur. Hall of Fame, Council of Better Bus. Burs. Inc., 1975; named Radio Man of Yr. Am. Coll. Radio, Arts, Crafts & Scis., 1961, Laureate in Order of Lincoln, Lincoln Acad. Ill., 1965, Communicator of Yr., Jewish United Fund, 1969, Advt. Club Man of Yr., 1973, Lifetime Achievement award in Broadcasting Ill. Broadcasters Assn., 1989. Mem. Nat. Assn. Broadcasters (bd. dirs. 1952-56), Broadcast Music Inc. (bd. dirs. 1953-70), Assn. Maximum Service Telecasters Inc. (bd. dirs. 1952-72), Broadcast Pioneers (pres., bd. dirs. 1962-73), Broadcast Pioneers Library (pres. 1981-84), Broadcast Pioneers Ednl. Fund Inc., Am. Advt. Fedn. (ethics com.), Delta Tau Delta (Disting. Service chpt.), Nat. Acad. TV Arts and Scis. (bd. govs. 1966-76). Clubs: Mid-America; Exmoor Country (Chgo.); Marco Polo (N.Y.C.); Kenwood Golf and Country; Internat. (Washington); Lakeside Golf (North Hollywood, Calif.); Boulders Golf (Carefree, Ariz.). Office: Ward L Quaal Co 401 N Michigan Ave Ste 3140 Chicago IL 60611

QUACKENBUSH, DAVID R., manufacturing executive; b. Bedford, Ind., Oct. 22, 1939; s. Russell W. and Eva (Hedge) Q.; m. Carole A. Stanelle, Feb. 10, 1962; children: Sharon Ann, Michael David. Student, Purdue U., 1968, Lake Mich. Coll., 1975-76. Supr. Miami Brass Co., Peru, Ind., 1966-67,

Duramold Castings, Inc., Mishawaka, Ind., 1967-68; quality control mgr. Stedman Foundry & Machine Co., Aurora, Ind., 1968-70; staff engr. Alexander Proudfoot Co., Chgo., 1970-71; gen. foreman Benton Harbor (Mich.) Malleable Industry, 1972-73; gen. supr. Superior Steel Casting Co., Benton Harbor, 1973-78; quality and finishing mgr. Tech-Cast, Inc., Montague, Mich., 1978-80; mfg. analyst Midwest Foundry Co., Coldwater, Mich., 1981—; cons. Miami Brass Co., Peru. Leader 4-H Club, St. Joseph, Mich., 1976-77. Served as radarman 2d class USN, 1957-60. Mem. Am. Foundrymen's Soc., Nat. Rifle Assn. Office: Midwest Foundry Co 77 Hooker St Coldwater MI 49036

QUANDT, RICHARD EMERIC, economics educator; b. Budapest, Hungary, June 1, 1930; came to U.S., 1949, naturalized, 1954; s. Richard F. and Elisabeth (Toth) Q.; m. Jean H. Briggs, Aug. 6, 1955; 1 son, Stephen. BA, Princeton U., 1952; MA, Harvard U., 1955, PhD, 1957. Mem. faculty Princeton U., 1956—, prof. econs., 1964—, Hughes-Rogers prof. econs., 1976—, chmn. dept., 1968-71, 85-88; dir. Fin. Rsch. Ctr., Ford Found., 1983—, rsch. prof., 1967-68; cons. Alderson Assocs., 1959-61; sr. cons. Mathematica, Inc., 1961-67; cons. Internat. Air Transport Assn., 1974-75, N.Y. Stock Exchange, 1976-77, N.Y. State Dept. Edn., 1978; adviser Am.-Hungarian Found., 1977-78; editorial adviser Holt, Rinehart & Winston, 1968-72; fin. adviser Inst. for Rsch. in History, 1981-86; vis. prof. Birkbeck Coll., 1981, Coll. of Leicester, 1989—; mem. Census Adv. Com., 1983-86. Author: (with J. M. Henderson) Microeconomic Theory: A Mathematical Approach, 1958, 2d edit., 1971, 3d edit., 1980, (with W.L. Thorp) The New Inflation, 1959, (with B.G. Malkiel) Strategies and Rational Decisions in the Securities Option Market, 1969; editor: The Demand for Travel: Theory and Measurement, 1970; (with S.M. Goldfeld) Nonlinear Methods in Econometrics, 1972, Studies in Nonlinear Estimation, 1976; (with P. Asch) Racetrack Betting: The Professor's Guide to Strategies, 1986, (with M. Peston) Prices, Competition and Equilibrium, 1986, The Econometrics of Disequilibrium, 1988, (with H.S. Rosen) The Conflict Between Equilibrium and Disequilibrium Theories, 1988; also numerous articles; editorial bd.: Applied Econs.; assoc. editor: Econometrica, 1976-80, Jour. Am. Statis. Assn, 1974-80, Bell Jour. Econs., Jour. of Comparative Econs., 1988—, Empirica, 1988—. Guggenheim fellow, 1958-59; McCosh fellow, 1964; NSF Sr. Postdoctoral fellow, 1971-72. Fellow Am. Statis. Assn., Econometric Soc.; mem. Am. Econ. Assn., Math. Programming Soc., Econometric Soc. (mem. coun. 1985-88). Home: 162 Springdale Rd Princeton NJ 08540 Office: Princeton U Fin Rsch Ctr Dept Econs Princeton NJ 08544

QUANSTROM, WALTER ROY, oil executive, educator; b. Gary, Ind., Nov. 20, 1942; s. Walter Roy and Neita Arlene (Perry) Q.; m. Harriet Fay Sheldon, Aug. 14, 1963; children: Erik Walter, Anna Katherine. BS, So. Nazarene U., 1964; PhD, U. Okla., 1968; cert. Advanced Mgmt., Harvard U., 1986. Asst. prof. Olivet Nazarene U., Kankakee, Ill., 1968-70; assoc. prof., div. chmn. Northwest Nazarene Coll., Nampa, Idaho, 1970-74; staff ecologist Amoco Corp., Chgo., 1974-77, dir. ecology, 1977-78, dir. environ. affairs and energy conservation, 1978-80, dir. indsl. hygiene and toxicology, 1980-82, mgr. indsl. hygiene, toxicology, safety, 1982-84, gen. mgr. environ. affairs and safety, 1984-87, v.p. environ. affairs and safety, 1987—; chmn. membership com. Chem. Industry Inst. of Toxicology., Research Triangle Park., N.C., 1984—; com. chmn. Am. Petroleum Inst., Washington, 1983—; chmn. Internat. Petroleum Industry Environ. Assn., London, 1987—. Mem. Civitan, Nampa, 1971-74; bd. dirs. Keystone (Colo.) Ctr., 1988—. Mem. Ill. Game and Pet Breeders, Am. Soc. Mammalologists, Sigma Xi, Phi Sigma, Phi Delta Lambda. Republican. Mem. Ch. of Nazarene. Office: Amoco Corp 200 E Randolph St Chicago IL 60601

QUARLES, LEO THOMPSON, utilities company executive; b. Raleigh, N.C., July 1, 1944; s. Walter Greyson and Ida Owen (Hayssen) Q.; m. Beverly Kathryn Abernathy, Sept. 16, 1969; children—Kimberly, Blair, Amy. B.S. in Math., Hampden-Sydney Coll., 1966; M.B.A., East Carolina U., 1969. C.P.A. Auditor Peat Marwick Mitchell & Co., Atlanta, 1969-72; supr. balance sheet and income statement Carolina Power & Light Co., Raleigh, 1972-73, tax acct., 1973-74, tax mgr., 1974-77, asst. treas., 1977-79, treas., 1979—. Presbyterian. Lodge: Rotary. Home: 1905 Aurora Dr Raleigh NC 27615 Office: Carolina Power & Light Co 411 Fayetteville St Raleigh NC 27602

QUASHA, WILLIAM HOWARD, lawyer; b. N.Y.C., May 19, 1912; B.S. in Mech. Engring., N.Y. U., 1933, M.A., 1935; LL.B., St. John's U., 1936; m. Phyllis Grant, Apr. 17, 1946; children: Wayne Grant, Alan Grant, Jill. Admitted to N.Y. bar, 1936, Philippine bar, 1945, U.S. Supreme Ct. bar, 1947; practiced in N.Y.C., 1936-42, Manila, Philippines, 1946—; sr. partner Quasha, Asperilla, Ancheta, Peña, and Nolasco; dir. Marcopper Mining Corp., Manila. Faculty, N.Y. U., 1933-35, Santo Tomas U., Manila, 1946-48; vis. asso. prof. L.I. U., summer 1966; lectr. Harvard Law Sch., summer 1976, U. Philippines Coll. Law, 1979. Mem. nat. exec. bd. Boy Scouts Philippines, 1955-74, mem. exec. bd. Manila council, 1949-74, v.p., treas., 1964-74, hon. life pres., 1970; v.p., legal counsel Acacia Mut. Aid Soc., Inc., Manila, 1963—; mem. exec. bd. Far East council Boy Scouts Am., 1973—, mem. nat. exec. bd., 1977—; pres., chmn. bd. trustees St. Luke's Med. Ctr., Manila, 1975—; trustee Jose P. Laurel Meml. Found.; chmn. Republicans Abroad Com., Philippines, 1979-84, chmn. Asia-Pacific region, 1985-86, chmn. adv. com. 1987—. Served with AUS, 1942-46; PTO; lt. col. Res. Decorated Bronze Star with oak leaf cluster, Philippine Legion of Honor (officer rank); recipient Silver Tamaraw, Boy Scouts Philippines, 1959, Silver Fir Tree Br., Boy Scouts Austria, 1960; Distinguished Eagle Scout award Boy Scouts Am., 1970, Silver Buffalo award, 1974. Spl. award and citation City of Manila, 1970; tribute of appreciation U.S. Dept. State, 1983; Conrado Benitez Heritage award Philippine Women's U., 1983. Mem. Am., Fed. bar assns., Integrated Bar of Philippines, Law Asia, Internat. Bar Assn., Am. Soc. Internat. Law, Am. C. of C. of Philippines, Philippine Hist. Soc., Navy League U.S. (judge adv., chartermem.), Am. Assn. Philippines, Propeller Club U.S. (past pres., charter mem. Manila chpt.), Philippine Constn. Assn. (life), Philippine Soc. Internat. Law, Ramon Magsaysay Meml. Soc., Knights of Rizal (knight comdr.), Nat. Sojourners (pres. 1959), Am. Legion (dept. comdr. 1954-55), Manila Jr. C. of C. (asso., v.p. 1949), Internat. C. of C. (gov. Philippine council 1964—). Episcopalian (sr. warden, chancellor). Mason (33 deg., grand master 1962-63, Chevalier of Legion of Honor Supreme Council of Order De Molay 1986), regent, trustee Cathedral St. John the Divine, N.Y., 1988—, Shriner, Elk (bd. dirs. palsy project 1954-69, chmn. 1963-65), Rotarian (past dir. Manila). Clubs: Nat. Lawyers' (Washington); Am. Nat. (Sydney, Australia); Creek (L.I.); University (N.Y.); Army and Navy, Manila Polo, Valle Verde Country; others. Author: (with Rensis Likert) Revised Minnesota Paper Form Board Test. Home: 22 Molave Pl, Makati Metro, Manila Philippines Office: Don Pablo Bldg, 114 Amorsolo St, Legaspi Village, Metro Manila Philippines

QUATTLEBAUM, WALTER EMMETT, JR., telephone company executive; b. Midville, Ga., Dec. 22, 1922; s. Walter Emmett and Eva (Bagley) Q.; student Murvey Vocational Sch., Charleston, S.C., 1941, U. Hawaii, 1943; m. Dorothy Evelyn Clewis, Oct. 19, 1946; children—Walter Emmett III, Amalia Ann. Former owner Fla. Telephone Exchange, Sneads, Cottondale, Grand Ridge, Bonifay, Westville, and Seagrove Beach, Quattlebaum Telephone Supply Co., Quattlebaum Investments, also Spanish Trail Motel, Bonifay, Fla.; v.p., dir. Seminole Telephone Co., Donalsonville, Ga.; now investment analyst Quattlebaum Investments and others. City councilman, Sneads, 1950-52, pres. City Council, 1953. Served with AUS, 1944-46. Mem. Fla. Telephone Assn., Telephone Pioneers Am. Methodist. Office: Bonifay FL 32425

QUELLMALZ, HENRY, printing company executive; b. Balt., May 18, 1915; s. Frederick and Edith Margaret (Shaw) Q.; BA with high honors, Princeton U., 1937; m. Marion Agar Lynch, Aug. 2, 1940; children—Lynn Quellmalz Johnson, Susan Quellmalz Mastan, Jane Quellmalz Carey. Pres. Princeton Advt. Agy., 1936-37; dir. personnel, Macy's Men's Store, 1938-40; asst. mgr. Fowlers Dept. Store, Glens Falls, N.Y., 1940-41; personnel dir. U.S. Army postexchanges, Ft. Meade, Md., 1941-44; with Boyd Printing Co., Albany, N.Y., 1944—, pres., 1952-84, chmn. bd., 1984—; v.p. Q Corp. U.S. agt. for WHO publs., 1965—; adv. bd. First Am. Bank N.Y., 1984-86; dir. Bankers Trust Co. Albany 1965-84. Campaign chmn. ARC, Albany, 1956, 57; bd. govs. Doane Stuart Sch., Albany, 1977-79, treas. bd., 1977-78; vice chmn. Family Service Assn. Am. Salute to Families, 1979—, Nat. UN Day com., 1980-82; mem. adv. bd. Ind. Coll. Fund of N.Y., 1971—; bd. dirs. Am. Assn. World Health, 1977-82, Combined Health Appeal of Capitol Dist., Inc., 1984, Camelot Home for Boys, 1975; mem. adv. bd. Ind. Coll. Fund of N.Y., Inc., 1971; trustee St. Peter's Hosp. Found., Albany, 1982—, asst. sec., 1987—, chmn. bd. dirs., 1989—. Served with AUS, 1943. Recipient Pres.'s award Am. Assn. Mental Deficiency, 1976; 25 Yrs. Service award N.Y. State Bar Assn., 1983, 34 Yrs. Service Award Am. Sociol. Assn., 1985. Mem. Albany Area C. of C., Printing Industry Am. Assn. of East Cen. N.Y., (pres. 1958). Democrat. Episcopalian. Clubs: Princeton (N.Y.C.); Fort Orange, Hudson River. Home: 1 Park Hill Dr Apt 6 Menands NY 12204 Office: 49 Sheridan Ave Albany NY 12210

QUELLO, JAMES HENRY, government official; b. Laurium, Mich., Apr. 21, 1914; s. Bartholomew and Mary Katherine (Cochis) Q.; m. Mary Elizabeth Butler, Sept. 14, 1937; children: James Michael, Richard Butler. B.A., Mich. State U., 1935, D.Humanities (hon.), 1977; D.Pub. Service (hon.), No. Mich. U., 1975. Vice-pres., sta. mgr. Goodwill Stas., Inc., Detroit, 1947-72; v.p. Capital Cities Communications Corp., 1968; communications cons., Detroit, 1972-74; commr. FCC, Washington, 1974—; commr. Detroit Housing and Urban Renewal Commn., 1951-72. Contbr. articles to mags., newspapers. Bd. dirs. Greater Detroit Hosp. Assn.; trustee Mich. Vet. Trust Fund; mem. Gov.'s Spl. Commn. on Urban Problems, Mich., Gov.'s Spl. Study Com. on Legis. Compensation, Mayor's Com. on Human Relations; bd. dirs. Am. Negro Emancipation Centennial; mem. exec. bd. Boy Scouts Am.; TV-radio chmn. United Found. Served to lt. col. AUS, 1940-45. Decorated Bronze Star with oak leaf cluster, Croix de Guerre (France); recipient Internat. Pres.' award Nat. Assn. TV Program Execs., 1985, Silver Satellite award Am. Women in Radio and TV, 1988, Sol Taishoff award Washington Area Broadcasters Assn., 1989; named Outstanding Mich. Citizen Mich. Assn. Broadcasters, 1989. Mem. Nat. Assn. Broadcasters (mem. gov. liaison com. 1964-72), Mich. Assn. Broadcasters (pres. 1958, legis. chmn. 1959-72, dir.), Greater Detroit Bd. Commerce, Sigma Alpha Epsilon. Clubs: Adcraft (Detroit); Detroit Athletic, Army and Navy Country; Nat. Press (Washington). Office: FCC 1919 M St NW Washington DC 20554

QUENON, ROBERT HAGERTY, holding company executive; b. Clarksburg, W.Va., Aug. 2, 1928; s. Ernest Leonard and Josephine (Hagerty) Q.; m. Jean Bowling, Aug. 8, 1953; children: Evan, Ann, Richard. B.S. in Mining Engring., W.Va. U., 1951; LL.B., George Washington U., 1964. Mine supt. Consol. Coal Co., Fairmont, W.Va., 1956-61; mgr. deep mines Pittston Co., Dante, Va., 1964-66; gen. mgr. Riverton Coal Co., Crown Hill, W.Va., 1966-67; mgr. ops. coal and shale oil dept. Exxon Co., Houston, 1967; pres. Monterey Coal Co., Houston, 1969-76; sr. v.p. Carter Oil Co., Houston, 1976-77; exec. v.p. Peabody Coal Co., St. Louis, 1977-78; pres., chief exec. officer Peabody Coal Co., 1978-83, Peabody Holding Co., Inc., St. Louis, 1983—; bd. dirs. Boatmen's Banshares, Inc., St. Louis, Baker Hughes Inc., Houston, Interco Inc., St. Louis, Newmont Gold Co., Denver; chmn. coal industry adv. bd. Internat. Energy Agy. Trustee Blackburn Coll., Carlinville, Ill., 1975-83, St. Louis U., 1981—; pres. St. Louis Art Mus., 1985-88. Served with AUS, 1946-47. Mem. Nat. Coal Assn. (chmn. bd. 1978-80), U.S. C. of C. (dir. 1982-88), Bituminous Coal Operators Assn. (chmn. 1980-83), Am. Mining Congress (vice-chmn.).

QUEST, ARTHUR EUGENE, petroleum company executive; b. Atoka, Okla., Oct. 9; s. Arthur Eugene and Lula (Moore) Q.; m. Audrey Ann Bell, June 30, 1944; children: Jean Ann, Arthur Eugene III. BS, W. Tex. State U., 1939; PhD Bus. Adminstrn., Hamilton State U., 1973. With AT&T 1941-43; engr. Tex. Health Dept., 1943-45; ptnr. A.E. Quest & Sons Mfg. Co., Lubbock, Tex., 1946—; pres. A.E. Quest & Sons, Inc., Lubbock, 1972—; owner cotton farm, Lorenzo, Tex., 1960—; mem. exec. bd. Snake River Ranch Corp., Idaho, Corps Great S.W., Dallas, Twin Lakes Corp., Denver: mem. exec. bd., sr. v.p. Great S.W. Life Co., Houston; ind. oilman. composer: songs. Active Boy Scouts Am.; founder trustee fund A.E. Quest Jr., Student Loan Endowment Fund, W. Tex. State Coll, 1954; ast pres. L.E.A.R.N. student fund; dist. chmn. Masonic Sch. and Old Age Home; bd. dirs. Civic Ctr., 1982—; former bd. regents W. Tex. State U.; bd. dirs. Civic Ctrs., 1982—; bd. mem. Council for Excellence through Continuing Edn., Tex. Tech. U. Recipient Silver Beaver, 1952, Wisdom award Honor. Mem. Canvas Mfrs.Assn. (pres. Tex. and Okla.), W. Tex. Ex-Student Assn. (past pres.), Oil Mill Machinery Mfrs.and Supply Assn. (past pres.). Methodist. Lodge: Shriners (past pres.), Red Raider (Lubbock), Masons, Elks, Lions. Home: 3311 46th St Lubbock TX 79413 Office: AE Quest & Sons Inc 2302 Ave Q Lubbock TX 79405

QUESTROM, ALLEN I., retail executive; b. Newton, Mass., Apr. 13, 1941; s. Irving Allen and Natalie (Chadbourne) Q.; m. Carol Brummer, Sept. 9, 1967. B.S., Boston U., 1964. From exec. trainee to div. mdse. mgr. Abraham & Straus, Bklyn., 1965-73; v.p., gen. mdse. mgr. home store Bullock's, Los Angeles, 1973-74, sr. v.p., gen. mdse. mgr. all stores, 1974-77; exec. v.p. Bullock's div. Federated Dept. Stores, Los Angeles, 1977-78; pres. Rich's div. Federated Dept. Stores, Atlanta, 1978-80, chmn. bd., chief exec. officer, 1980-84; chmn. bd., chief exec. officer Bullock's/Bullocks Wilshire div. Federated Dept. Stores, Los Angeles, 1984-88; corp. exec. v.p. Federated Dept. Stores, Cincinnati, 1987-88, vice-chmn., 1988; pres., chief exec. officer Neiman Marcus Group Inc., Dallas, 1988—. Office: Neiman Marcus Main & Ervay Sts Dallas TX 75201 also: Federated Dept Stores Inc 7 W 7th St Cincinnati OH 45202 *

QUICK, JACK BEAVER, club executive, tax consultant; b. Biloxi, Miss., Oct. 31, 1947; s. Murdoch Alexander and Ethel Christine (Martin) Q. B.S. in Acctg., N.E. La. U., 1971; postgrad. U. So. Calif., 1975-76; AAS in Hotel, Restaurant and Instl. Mgmt., No. Va. Community Coll., 1986. Asst. for systems mgmt. Office of Sec. of Def., Washington, 1977-79; pres. Northeastern Food Corp., Columbia, Md., 1979-80; v.p. Bojangles of Washington, Inc., Washington, 1980-83; adminstrv. asst. The University Club, Washington, 1983-85, gen. mgr., 1985—; tax cons. Profl. Tax Service, Alexandria, Va., 1974—. Served to capt. U.S. Army, 1971-79. Mem. Internat. Food Service Execs. Assn. (1st v.p. 1983, Key award 1983), Club Mgrs. Assn. Am. (chmn. govt. affairs Nat. Capital chpt. 1988—, Wine Soc. Idea Fair award 1988), Nat. Restaurant Assn., Restaurant Assn. Met. Washington (bd. dirs. 1986—, chmn. mem. com., 1987-88, chmn. membership svcs. com. 1989—, sec. 1989—), Am. Soc. Assn. Execs., Knights of the Vine, Delta Sigma Pi (life mem., sr. v.p. 1970-71). Republican. Lutheran. Clubs: Half-Fast Social (Alexandria, Va.) (pres. 1983—), Swan Point Yacht and Country, Mercedes Benz (1st place in class Starfest 88 Concours). Avocations: classic cars; swimming; tennis; jogging. Home: 5902 Mount Eagle Dr Ste 1101 Alexandria VA 22303 Office: The University Club 1135 16th St NW Washington DC 20036

QUICK, SALLY SCHWEPPE, banker; b. Washington, Mar. 14, 1954; d. Homer William and Marian Lucille (Daniel) Schweppe; m. Marlin Jay Quick, Oct. 21, 1978. BA in Bus. Adminstrn., Gettysburg Coll., 1976. Asst. br. mgr. DC Nat. Bank, Washington, 1976-77; bookkeeper Dept. of Justice Fed. Credit Union, Washington, 1977-78; asst. acctg. mgr. Am. Nat. Bank, Morristown, N.J., 1979-83; with cash mgmt. Carteret Savs. Bank, Morristown, N.J., 1983—. Mem. Northern N.J. Assn. Cash Mgmt., Nat. Corp. Cash Mgmt. Assn. Office: Carteret Savs Bank 200 South St Morristown NJ 07960

QUICK, SHARON WELLS, real estate executive, developer; b. Bethesda, Md., Apr. 13, 1945; d. John Ashley and Alicia (Kenyon) Wells; m. Michael K. Mann, Sept. 6, 1966 (div. July 1971); 1 child, Amy C.; m. Winston C. Fulton, Sept. 3, 1984. BA, U. Wis.-Madison, 1965; postgrad. Oxford U., Eng., 1965-67, Purdue U., 1974-77. Cert. real estate broker. Pres. Shaman & Assocs. Ltd., London, 1967-71; vis. lectr. U. Aberystwyth, Wales, 1971-73; sales assoc. Livesay Realty, Lafayette, Ind., 1977-79; owner, pres. The Wells Agy., Lafayette, 1979—; investment cons. Mem. Realtors Polit. Action Com., 1980—, Nat. Trust for Hist. Preservation. Mem. Internat. Council Shopping Ctrs., Women in Bus., Midwest Real Estate Exchangors, Nat. Assn. for Female Execs., Farm and Land Inst., Internat. Exchangors, Nat. Bd. Realtors, Smithsonian Instn., Nat. Fedn. Independent Bus., Nat. Assn. Indsl. and Office Parks, C. of C. Lafayette. Republican. Presbyterian. Office: The Wells Agy 200 Ferry St Suite C Lafayette IN 47901

QUICK, THOMAS CLARKSON, brokerage house executive; b. Westbury, N.Y., Feb. 26, 1955; s. Leslie Charles and Regina (Clarkson) Q. BS in Bus., Fairfield U., 1977. Br. mgr. Quick & Reilly Inc., Palm Beach, Fla., 1977-81; dir., v.p. The Quick & Reilly Group, Palm Beach, 1981—; v.p. Quick & Reilly Inc., Palm Beach, 1981-86, pres., 1986—; mem. Securities Industry Assn. Econ. Edn. Com., N.Y.C., 1986—. Mem. investment adv. bd. St. Jude Children's Research Hosp., Memphis, 1986—; chmn. Wall St. Friends of St. Jude Children's Research Hosp., 1979—. Clubs: University (N.Y.C.), Friendly Sons of St. Patrick (N.Y.C.); Beach (Palm Beach); Apawamis (Rye, N.Y.). Home: 25 East End Ave New York NY 10028 Office: Quick & Reilly Inc 120 Wall St New York NY 10005

QUIGG, DONALD JAMES, lawyer, government official; b. Kansas City, Mo., Apr. 28, 1916; s. James Smith and Lorna (Shields) Q.; m. Louise Marie Heinzelman, Feb. 14, 1942; children: Sandra Louise Quigg Porter, James Michael. Student, Bartlesville Jr. Coll., Okla., 1933-34; B.S. in Bus. Adminstrn., U. Okla., 1937; postgrad., Kansas City Sch. Law, 1937-38; J.D., Kansas City U., 1940. Bar: Mo. 1940, Okla. 1947. Clk. Hovey, Beals & Boley, Kansas City, 1937-42; patent atty. Phillips Petroleum Co., Bartlesville, 1945-81; dep. commr. U.S. Patent and Trademark Office, Arlington, Va., 1981-85, commr., asst. sec., 1985—. Patentee in field. Served to 1st lt. F.A., AUS, 1942-46, PTO. Mem. ABA, Okla. Bar Assn., Mo. Bar Assn., Am. Intellectual Property Law Assn., Assn. Corp. Patent Counsel (emeritus). Republican. Presbyterian. Office: US Patent & Trademark Office Washington DC 20231

QUIGLEY, JEROME HAROLD, management consultant; b. Green Bay, Wis., Apr. 19, 1925; s. Harold D. and Mabel (Hansen) Q.; BS, St. Norbert Coll., 1951; m. Lorraine A. Rocheleau, May 3, 1947; children: Kathy, Ross, Michael, Daniel, Mary Beth, Andrew, Maureen. Personnel adminstr. Gen. Motors Corp., 1959-64; dir. indsl. rels. Raytheon Co., Santa Barbara, Calif., 1964-67; dir. personnel U. Calif., Santa Barbara, 1967-72; corp. dir. indsl. rels. Gen. Rsch. Corp., 1972-73; dir. indsl. rels. ISS Sperry Univac, 1973-75; corp. dir. indsl. rels. Four-Phase Systems, Inc., Cupertino, Calif., 1975; sr. v.p. human resources UNC, Annapolis, Md., 1975-86; pres. Profl. Guidance Assocs. Inc., 1986—. Aviator with U.S. Navy, 1943-47. Mem. Am. Electronics Assn., Assn. Former Intelligence Officers, Machinery and Allied Products Inst., Assn. Naval Aviation, Tailhook Assn., Navy Aviation Mus. Found., Navy League, Am. Soc. Personnel Adminstrs., Scottsdale Racquet Club. Republican. Roman Catholic. Home: 7789 E Joshua Tree Ln Scottsdale AZ 85253 Office: Profl Guidance Assocs Inc 7031 E Camelback Rd Ste 571 Scottsdale AZ 85251

QUIGLEY, JOSEPH JOHN, construction executive; b. Bklyn., Oct. 8, 1947; s. Patrick A. and Rebecca Ann (Conley) Q.; m. Christine Anthony Armstrong, July 12, 1969; children: Ryan, Erin. BBA in Acctg., Notre Dame U., 1969; MBA in Fin., Hartford (Conn.) U., 1979. CPA, Ariz. Auditor Price Waterhouse & Co., Hartford, Conn., 1969-71; controller, mgr. Heublein, Inc., Farmington, Conn., 1971-81; v.p. fin. Kitchell Corp., Phoenix, 1981—, also bd. dirs. Bd. dirs. Met. Youth Symphony, Mesa, Ariz.; asst. scoutmaster Boy Scouts Am., Tempe, Ariz. Mem. Nat. Assn. Accts. (pres. Hartford chpt. 1978-79), Constrn. Fin. Mgr. Assn. (pres. Phoenix chpt. 1988—, nat. exec. bd. 1989—), Assoc. Gen. Contractors (nat. com. 1986—). Home: 1515 E Westchester Dr Tempe AZ 85283 Office: Kitchell Corp 1006 S 24th St Phoenix AZ 85034

QUIGLEY, WILLIAM JOHN, motion picture executive; b. N.Y.C., July 6, 1951; s. Martin S. and Katherine Q.; m. Dorothy (Dee) Carey, Oct. 21, 1978; children: Brian, Michael, Colleen. BA, Wesleyan U., Middletown, Conn., 1973; MS in Bus. Policy, Columbia U., 1983. Tchr. Shanderema Secondary Schl., Kenya, 1974-75; media planner Grey Advt., N.Y.C., 1975; asst. film buyer Walter Reade Orgn., N.Y.C., 1975-77, head film buyer, 1977-82, v.p., 1982-86; sr. v.p. Vestron Pictures Inc., Stamford, Conn., 1986-87, pres., 1987—; dir. Quigley Pub., N.Y.C. Exec. Producer: The Dead, 1987, Steel Dawn, 1987, Salome's Last Dance, 1988, The Unholy, 1988, Lair of the White Women, 1988, Burning Secret, 1988, The Rainbow, 1989, Paint It Black, 1989. Mem. Sundance Instit., ShowEast (hon. com. mem.), Motion Pictures Bookers' Club. Democrat. Roman Catholic. Clubs: Larchmont (N.Y.) Yacht, Variety. Office: Vestron Pictures Inc 1010 Washington Blvd Stamford CT 06907

QUILL, MARTIN WILLIAM, financial services executive; b. Moorhead, Minn., Nov. 1, 1954; s. David Gilmore and Rosemary (Tallis) Q.; m. Karen Sue Betts, June 5, 1982; children: Sarah Elizabeth, Lauren Christine, Graham Tallis. BS in Finance, Towson State U., 1976. CPA, D.C.; lic. gen. securities prin. Asst. treas. Contee Resources, Laurel, Md., 1976-77; chief fin. officer DRG Financial, Washington, DC, 1977-80; sr. v.p., chief fin. officer York Assocs., 1980-82, Fin. Service Group, McLean, Va., 1982-84; pres., chief exec. officer Fin. Service Group, Tysons Corner, Va., 1984-87; pres. FSG Capital Corp., 1987—, Capitol Securities Mgmt., Inc., Vienna, Va., 1986-88; v.p. Driggs Assocs., Capitol Heights, Md., 1988—. Mem. AICPA, IAFP, GAMA, bd. dirs. NAA. Republican. Episcopalian. Clubs: Sporting, Avenel TPC. Lodge: Kiwanis. Home: 10009 Scenic View Terr Vienna VA 22180 Office: Driggs Assocs 8723 Ashwood Rd Rd Capitol Heights MD 20743

QUILLEN, CECIL DYER, JR., corporation lawyer; b. Kingsport, Tenn., Jan. 21, 1937; s. Cecil D. and Mary Louise (Carter) Q.; m. Vicey Ann Childress, Apr. 1, 1961; children: Cecil D., Ann C. BS, Va. Poly. Inst., 1958; LLB, U. Va., 1962. Bar: Va. 1962, N.Y. 1963, Tenn. 1974. Atty., patent dept., Eastman Kodak Co., Rochester, N.Y., 1962-65, atty. patent sect. Tenn. Eastman Co. (div. Eastman Kodak), Kingsport, Tenn., 1965-69, mgr., 1969-72, mgr. licensing, 1972-74, sec. and asst. chief counsel, 1974-76, dir. patent litigation, Eastman Kodak, 1976-82, v.p. and chief counsel, Tenn. Eastman, 1983-85, v.p.,and assoc. gen. counsel, Eastman Kodak, 1986, sr. v.p., gen. counsel, dir., 1986—. Mem. Va. Poly. Inst. Com. of 100, Assn. of Gen. Counsel.

QUILLEN, LLOYD DOUGLAS, oil and gas company executive; b. Red House, Ky., Sept. 9, 1943; s. Carter Livingston and Irene (Bolson) Q.; m. Leslie J. Johnsen (div. Jan. 1980); children: Tracey, David; m. Debra Gale Wagner, Aug. 7, 1982; children: Justin, Meghan. BA, U. Ky., 1965, JD, 1969; student, Emory U., 1966-67. Bar: Ky., 1970, Tex., 1986. Atty. Phillips Petroleum Co., Denver, 1970-76; mgr. real estate and claims Phillips Petroleum Co. Euro. Afr., London, 1976-79; dir. govt. and comml. affairs Phillips Petroleum Co. & Subs., Lagos, Nigeria, 1979-82; mgr. internat. gas devel. Phillips Petroleum Co., Bartlesville, Okla., 1982-84; dir. laws and regulations Phillips 66 Natural Gas Co., Bartlesville, Okla., 1984-88; mgr. bus. devel. and planning Roy M. Huffington, Inc., Jakarth, Indonesia, 1988—; cons. Nigerian Govt., Lagos, 1977-82. Charter mem. Statue of Liberty Ellis Island Found., N.Y.C., 1983; pro bono counsel Landmark Preservation Council, Bartlesville, 1986-87, Washington County Sr. Citizens, Inc., Bartlesville, 1987—. Recipient Speak Out award Am. Petroleum Inst., 1972; named to hon. order Ky. Cols., 1969. Mem. Ky. Bar Assn., Tex. Bar Assn., Fed. Energy Bar Assn. Republican. Unitarian. Home: PO Box 4455 Houston TX 77210

QUINLEY, KEVIN MILTON, insurance company executive; b. Norfolk, Va., Sept. 4, 1954; s. Charles William and Nelleen (Duff) Q.; m. Jane McRee Hodges, Oct. 20, 1979; children: Kevin McRee, Charles Hunter. BA, Wake Forest U., 1976; MA, Coll. William & Mary, 1977. Claims adjuster Crawford & Co., Norfolk, Va., 1977-81; claims supr. Crawford & Co., Fairfax, Va., 1981-86; claims mgr. Hamilton Resources Corp., Fairfax, 1986—. Co-author: Industrial Low Back Pain, 1985, Professional Salesmanship Course, 1983; assoc. editor: Va. Claimsman mag., 1981—; contbr. editor: Claims Mag., 1987—. Mem. Risk and Ins. Mgrs. Soc., Washington Claims Assn., No. Va. Claims Assn., Washington Soc. CPCU, Va. State Claims Assn., Soc. CPCU (dir. 1986-88), Ins. Inst. Am. (assoc., claims and risk mgmt.), Am. Soc. Healthcare Risk Mgmt. Democrat. Episcopalian. Office: Hamilton Resources Corp 3975 University Dr #410 Fairfax VA 22030 Home: 5406 Cabot Ridge Ct Fairfax VA 22032

QUINN, CARL S., oil and gas company executive; b. Moberly, Mo., Mar. 2, 1931; s. Roscoe S. and Mary K. (Woods) Q.; m. Jo Ann Merriott, May 30, 1952; children: Nancy Kathryn, Patricia Ellen. BS, U. Mo., 1953. CPA, La., Mo. Acct. Peat, Marwick, Mitchell, Kansas City, Mo., 1956-59; mgr. Panhandle Ea. Corp., Kansas City, 1960-66; v.p. United Gas Pipe Line Co., Shreveport, La., 1967-70; sr. v.p. Mid. La. Gas Co., New Orleans, 1971-77,

So. Natural Gas Co., Houston, 1978-79; sr. v.p., chief fin. officer Celeron Corp., Lafayette, La., 1980-86, chmn., pres., chief exec. officer, 1986-87; pres., chief operating officer Arkla, Inc., Shreveport, 1988—; bd. dirs. subs. cos. Commr. Water Dist. I, Johnson County, Kans., 1966; bd. dirs. Cen. Mo. State U. Found., 1982-84. Served as lt. USN. Mem. Am. Gas Assn., AICPA, Interstate Natural Gas Assn., So. Gas Assn. Episcopalian. Office: Arkla Inc PO Box 21734 525 Milam St Shreveport LA 71101

QUINN, EDWARD JAMES, banker; b. N.Y.C., Apr. 2, 1911; s. Edward M. and Mary M. (Schneider) Q.; m. Marie A. Stafford, Apr. 22, 1939 (dec. 1972); children—Mary Ann Brown, James E., Patrick M., Sheila G.; m. Margaret B. O'Neill, Nov. 4, 1982. Student, Hofstra Coll., 1946-52; grad., Am. Inst. Banking, 1932-39, Grad. Sch. Banking at Rutgers, 1955-57. Messenger J.S. Bache & Co., N.Y.C., 1926-27; bookkeeper Nassau-Suffolk Bond & Mortgage Guaranty Co., Mineola, N.Y., 1928; sr. v.p. European-Am. Bank & Trust Co., 1928—. Chmn. investment com. United Fund L.I., 1968-71; treas. Nassau County Boy Scouts Am., 1936-39, Nassau County March Dimes, 1947-48, Nassau County Easter Seal Appeal, 1948-55, Suffolk County Cancer Soc., 1955-57, Union Free Sch. Dist. 22, Farmingdale, 1948-57; mem. U.S. Savs. Bond Com., Nassau County, 1952-65; bd. regents Royal Arcanum, 1938-39, grand committeeman, 1940-41; Mem. Bd. Appeals Village Farmingdale, 1941-56. Served with Med. Detachment AUS, 1943-46. 1st Sgt. Army Commendation ribbon, 1986. Mem. Mcpl. Forum N.Y., Mcpl. Finance Officers Assn. U.S., L.I. Bankers Assn. (chmn. check clearing com. 1955, legis. com. 1965-71), Nat. Assn. Accts., Am. Legion. Clubs: St. George's Golf and Country (Stony Brook, N.Y.); Southward Ho Country (Brightwaters, N.Y.); Atlantis (Fla.) Country. Home: 383 West Hills Rd Huntington NY 11743 Home: 130 Driftwood Terr Atlantis FL 33462 Office: European-Am Bank & Trust Co 383 W Hills Rd Huntington NY 11743

QUINN, JANE BRYANT, journalist; b. Niagara Falls, N.Y., Feb. 5, 1939; d. Frank Leonard and Ada (Laurie) Bryant; m. David Conrad Quinn, June 10, 1967; children—Matthew Alexander, Justin Bryant. B.A. magna cum laude, Middlebury Coll., 1960. Assoc. editor Insiders Newsletter, N.Y.C., 1962-65, co-editor, 1966-67; sr. editor Cowles Book Co., N.Y.C., 1968; editor-in-chief Bus. Week Letter, N.Y.C., 1969-73, gen. mgr., 1973-74; syndicated financial columnist Washington Post Writers Group, 1974—; contbr. fin. column to Women's Day mag., 1974—; contbr. NBC News and Info. Service, 1976-77; bus. corr. WCBS-TV, N.Y.C., 1979, CBS-TV News, 1980-87; contbg. editor Newsweek mag., 1978—. Author: Everyone's Money Book, 1979, 2d edit., 1980. Mem. Phi Beta Kappa. Office: Newsweek Inc 444 Madison Ave New York NY 10022

QUINN, JOHN COLLINS, editor; b. Providence, Oct. 24, 1925; s. John A. and Kathryn H. (Collins) Q.; m. Lois R. Richardson, June 20, 1953; children: John Collins, Lo-anne, Richard B., Christopher A. A.B., Providence Coll., 1945; M.S., Columbia U. Sch. Journalism, 1946. Successively copy boy, reporter, asst. city editor, Washington corr., asst. mng. editor, day mng. editor Providence Jour.-Bull., 1943-66; with Gannett Co. Inc., Rochester, N.Y., 1966—; exec. editor Rochester Democrat & Chronicle, Times-Union, 1966-71; gen. mgr. Gannett News Service, 1967-80, pres., 1980-88, v.p. parent co., 1971-75, sr. v.p. news and info., 1975-80, sr. v.p., chief news exec. parent co., 1980-83; exec. v.p. Gannett Co., editor USA TODAY 1983-88, editor in chief, 1988-89, also dir. co. Named to R.I. Hall of Fame, 1975, Editor of Yr. Nat. Press Found., 1986; recipient William Allen White citation, 1987, Women in Communications Headliner award, 1986; Paul Miller/Okla. State U. medallion, 1988. Mem. AP Mng. Editors (past dir., nat. pres. 1973-74), Am. Soc. Newspaper Editors (dir., chmn. editorial bd., chmn. conv. program, nat. pres. 1982-83). Roman Catholic. Home: 365 S Atlantic Ave Cocoa Beach FL 32931 Office: Gannett Co Inc 1100 Wilson Blvd Arlington VA 22209 also: USA Today 1000 Wilson Blvd Arlington VA 22209

QUINN, MICHAEL DESMOND, business executive; b. Balt., Sept. 4, 1936; s. Michael Joseph and Gladys (Baldwin) Q.; m. Mary Annette McHenry, Apr. 11, 1961; children: Cailin A., Maureen K., Patricia B., Marianne P. BA, U. Md., 1970. With Weaver Bros., Inc. of Md., Balt., 1960—, investment v.p., corporate dir. interim loan dept., 1978—; chmn. bd. Wye Mortgage Co., L.P., 1977—, also Christiana Capital Group, Inc., Wye Ins. Agy. Inc., Wye Investment Corp., Wye Securities Inc.; chmn. bd. Wm. R. Alborn & Assocs. Inc., Wye Title Agy., Inc., Wye Leasecorp.; faculty evening coll. Johns Hopkins U., Essex Community Coll., 1967—. Mem. gov.'s task force Md. Housing Ins. Fund; mem. Md. Health Claims Arbitration Panel; bd. visitors U. Md.; dist. adv. council U.S. Small Bus. Adminstrn. Served with USN, 1956-58. Mem. Md. Mortgage Bankers Assn. (pres. bd. govs.), Real Estate Bd. Greater Balt. (bd. dirs.), Home Builders Assn. Md., Md. Bankers Assn., Balt. Econ. Soc., N.Am. Soc. Corp. Planning, Greater Balt. Com., Ancient Order Hibernians, Balt Jr. Assn. Commerce (Richard Troja Meml. award 1967, Outstanding Young Man of Balt. 1969), Balt. County C. of C. (bd. dirs.). Home: 8207 Robin Hood Ct Baltimore MD 21204 Office: 1400 Front Ave Lutherville MD 21093

QUINN, PAUL JOSEPH, JR., food company executive; b. N.Y.C., Mar. 8, 1932; s. Paul Joseph and Alice Elenora (Einzig) Q.; m. Cynthia Edna Faigle, Oct. 15, 1955; children: Kenneth Edward, Bruce Randall, Leslie Ann, Christopher Paul. BA, Williams Coll., 1955. Pres. Vick/Mex. div. Richardson Merrell, Inc., Mexico City, 1968-71; div. v.p. Richardson Merrell, Inc., N.Y.C., 1971-74; v.p. internat. div. Internat. Multifoods, Mpls., 1974-84, group v.p., 1985—. Pres. Edina (Minn.) Soccer Assn., 1977; mem. Minn. State Band Trade Mission, 1985-86. Served to 1st lt. USAF, 1955-57. Mem. Williams Coll. Alumni Assn. (pres. North Cen. chpt. 1975-78). Republican. Episcopalian. Clubs: Edina Country (pres. 1982-83), The Moorings (Vero Beach, Fla.). Home: 5227 Larada Ln Edina MN 55436 Office: Internat Multifoods Corp Box 2942 Minneapolis MN 55402

QUINN, TRUDY LEE, communications executive; b. Rock Hill, S.C., July 28, 1952; d. Joseph Erskine and Amelia Rose (Ford) Q.; m. John Merrill Stoudemayer, Nov. 5, 1978 (div. May 1983). BA in Sociology, Furman U., 1974. Supr. bus. office So. Bell, Columbia, S.C., 1974-75, supr. spl. services, 1975-76, account mgr., 1976-78; mgr. corp. planning Atlanta, 1978-79; mgr. corp. communications Columbia, 1980-84; staff mgr. CCNC Bellsouth Services, Atlanta, 1984-86, staff mgr. network planning, 1986-87, product mgr., 1987—. Bd. dirs. Friendship Ctr., Columbia, 1984. Mem. Phi Beta Kappa. Home: 66 Sycamore St Decatur GA 30030 Office: Bellsouth Svcs 675 W Peachtree St NE Atlanta GA 30375

QUINNAN, EDWARD MICHAEL, aluminum company executive; b. Scranton, Pa., Dec. 11, 1935; s. Francis Patrick and Mary Angela (Mannion) Q.; m. Hilarion Swift, Nov. 22, 1962; children: Edward, Hilarion Doyle, Maryanne. B.S., Georgetown U., 1957; M.B.A., NYU, 1959. With Chase Manhattan Bank, N.Y.C., 1957-65, U.S. Agy. Internat. Devel., Washington, 1965-67; with Kaiser Aluminum & Chem. Corp., Oakland, Calif., 1967—, v.p., chief fin. officer, 1982—; v.p., chief fin. officer Kaiser Tech., Ltd., 1987—. Served to 1st lt. USAR, 1959-64. Republican. Office: Kaiser Aluminum & Chem Corp 300 Lakeside Dr Oakland CA 94642

QUIÑONES, MARTHA IRENE, retail executive; b. Bogotá, Colombia, Sept. 18, 1952; came to U.S. 1967; m. Mark Karavolos. Student, NYU, 1987. Asst. trader Bunge Corp., N.Y.C., 1970-87; export import cons. Export Ease, Park Ridge, N.J., 1987—. Mem. NAFE, Active Core of Exec. (small bus. adminstrn.), World Trade Assn., Internat. Trade Roundtable, Tappan Zee Internat. Trade Assn. Office: Export Ease 58 Ormsay St Park Ridge NJ 07656

QUINTANILLA-VILLANUEVA, ROSALINDA, economist; b. Monterrey, Mex., Feb. 22, 1955; came to U.S., 1978; d. Ernesto Quintanilla and Marina Villanueva. BA in Econs. with high honors, Inst. Tech. Monterrey, 1976; MA in Econs., U. Wis., Milw., 1979; PhD in Econs., U. Minn., 1988. Rsch. assoc. Econometric Unit Inst. Tech. Monterrey, 1976; cons. Grupo Indsl. ALFA, Monterrey, 1977; assoc. prof. econs. U. Autonoma Metropolitana, Mexico City, 1977-78; cons. World Bank, Washington, 1983—. Nat. Coun. Sci. and Technology fellow, 1978-82. Home: 2251 Pimmit Dr Apt 717 Falls Church VA 22043 Office: World Bank 1818 H St NW Washington DC 20433

QUINTON, JOHN EDWARD, real estate developer; b. Oakland, Calif., July 31, 1941; s. John Clarence Quinton and Louella Francis (Puett) Minear; m. Leslie Ann Boke, Mar. 21, 1964; 1 child, Lacey. AA, Graceland Coll., 1961; BS in Engring., San Jose State U., 1965; postgrad., Calif. State U., Fullerton. Application engr. Bourns Electronics, Riverside, Calif., 1965-69; mgr. devel. Diversified Properties, Orange, Calif., 1969-72; v.p., dir. real estate Downey (Calif.) Savs. and Loan, 1972-77; sr. v.p. real estate Far West Savs. and Loan, Newport Beach, Calif., 1977-81; pres. PacDevco Inc., Newport Beach, Calif., 1971—; mng. ptnr. Tri-City Corp. Ctr., San Bernardino, Calif., 1985—; mem. bd. advisors Berkus Group, Newport Beach, 1985—. Bd. dirs. South Coast YMCA, S. Laguna, Calif., 1975-80, mem. chmn. Roundtable, 1988—; bd. dirs. San Bernardino Mus., 1986—, St. John's Acad., Mission Viejo, Calif., 1987—; bd. govs. U. So. Calif. Commerce Assn., Newport Beach, 1975-80. Recipient Excellence in Design award City of San Bernardino, 1986, 87. Mem. Internat. Council of Shopping Ctrs., Nat. Assn. of Indsl. and Office Parks, Urban Land Inst. (mem. Small Scale Devel. Council 1987), Toastmasters (bd. govs. 1965-72), IEEC (bd. dirs. 1985—), Jr. C. of C. Office: PacDevco Inc 303 Vanderbilt Way Ste 275 San Bernardino CA 92408

QUITTMEYER, ROBERT THEODORE, former food and indsl. equipment co. exec.; b. Peekskill, N.Y., Sept. 12, 1920; s. Ernest Martin and Edith Grace (Loreaux) Q.; A.B., Columbia U., 1941, J.D., 1946; postgrad. Exec. Program in Bus. Adminstrn., 1966; m. Marilyn Louise Prehm, Mar. 20, 1948; children—Richard Charles, Susan Louise, James Prehm. Admitted to N.Y. bar, 1946, since practiced in N.Y.C.; asso. firm Sullivan & Cromwell, 1946-56; mem. law dept. Amstar Corp., N.Y.C., 1956-59, asst. sec., 1959-61, asst. gen. counsel, 1961-66, v.p., 1966-71, exec. v.p., 1971, pres., chief exec. officer, 1971-81, chmn. bd., chief exec. officer, 1981-82, chmn. bd., 1982-83; dir. Bank of N.Y., Borden, Inc., Lever Brothers Co.; exec.-in-residence Columbia U. Grad. Sch. Bus., 1983-88 . Chmn., Village of Baxter Estates (N.Y.) Bd. Appeals, 1958—. Served with inf. AUS, 1942-45. Decorated Combat Inf. Badge. Mem Phi Gamma Delta. Episcopalian. Home: 11 Ridgeway Rd Port Washington NY 11050

QUOYESER, CLEMENT LOUIS, corporate executive; b. Norristown, Pa., Mar. 29, 1899; s. Louis Clement and Jane Theresa (Bradley) Q.; m. Rosie Marie Brown, June 6, 1932; children: Patricia Anne, Clement Bradley, Thomas Brown (dec.), Camille James. Grad. high sch., Norristown, Pa. Printer John Hartenstine Printers, Norristown, 1914-19; sales corr. Clarke & Courts, Inc., Galveston, Tex., 1919-22; regional sales mgr. Clarke & Courts, Inc., La., 1922-78; chmn. Quoyeser, Inc., Lafayette, La., 1978—. Home: 1420 St John St Lafayette LA 70506 Office: Quoyeser Inc PO Box 3059 Lafayette LA 70502-3059

RAAB, FREDERICK HERBERT, electronics engineer; b. Ft. Crook, Nebr., Feb. 4, 1946; Herbert Leo and Grace Mable (Johnson) R.; m. Rebecca Ann Staude, June 6, 1970; 1 child, Hans Frederick. BSEE, Iowa State U., 1968, MSEE, 1970, PhD, 1972. Electronics engr. Collins Radio Co., Cedar Rapids, Iowa, 1966-69, NASA Marshall Space Flight, Huntsville, Ala., 1970; staff engr. Cin. Electronics, 1971-75; systems engr. Polhemus Navigation Scis., Burlington, Vt., 1975-80; pres., prin. Green Mountain Radio Research, Winooski, Vt., 1980—. Author: Solid State Radio Engineering, 1980; patentee in field. Sec.-treas. Nat. Railway Hist. Soc., Burlington, 1980-83. Recipient 2nd pl. award FET Design Contest, Signetics, Santa Clara, Calif., 1974, 2nd award FET Design Contest, Siliconix, Santa Clara, 1978. Mem. IEEE (sr., recipient 2nd prize paper, 1980); Can. Aerospace Assn., Internat. Omega Assn., Wild Goose Assn., Omega Assn., Sigma Xi. Office: Green Mountain Radio Research 50 Vermont Ave Winooski VT 05404

RAAB, WALTER FERDINAND, manufacturing company executive; Phila., Nov. 25, 1924; s. BSE, U. Pa., 1945; m. Bernice M. Jacobs, 1952; children: Laurie Ann Kucher, Wendy Louise Robbins, Mandy Margaret. With Coopers Lybrand Co., 1945-53; with AMP Inc., Harrisburg, Pa., 1953—, treas., 1968-71, v.p., treas., 1971-75, v.p., treas., dir., 1975-79, v.p., chief fin. officer, 1979-81, vice chmn., chief fin. officer, 1981, chmn. bd., chief exec. officer, 1982—; dir. The West Co., Harris Corp., Dauphin Deposit Trust Co., Air Products and Chems., Inc. Bd. dirs. Holy Spirit Hosp.; trustee, Harrisburg Area YMCA. Mem. Elec. Mfrs. Club (bd. govs.), Pa. Bus. Roundtable, Machinery and Allied Products Ins. (exec. com.). Office: AMP Inc PO Box 3608 Harrisburg PA 17105

RABB, CARLOS C., JR., petroleum company executive; b. 1924. With Ashland Oil Co., 1958-73; with Scurlock Oil Co. Inc., Houston, 1973—, formerly sr. v.p., now pres., also bd. dirs. Office: Scurlock Oil Co PO Box 4648 Houston TX 77210 *

RABB, IRVING WILLIAM, retired retail chain executive; b. Boston, Feb. 4, 1913; s. Joseph and Lottie (Wolf) Rabinovitz; m. Charlotte Frank, June 23, 1938; children: Betty Ann Rabb Schafer, James Mark. A.B. cum laude, Harvard U., 1934; postgrad., Bus. Sch., 1935. With Stop & Shop, Boston, 1935-83; v.p. retailing, exec. v.p. Stop & Shop, 1957-61, gen. mgr., v.p., 1961-64, pres., 1964-66, vice chmn. bd., dir., 1966-83, also chmn. exec. com. Bd. dirs. Harvard Community Health Plan; trustee Beth Israel Hosp., past pres.; past pres., trustee Combined Jewish Philanthropies Boston; trustee Boston Symphony Orch., kMus. Fine Arts. Fellow Am. Acad. Arts and Scis.; mem. Food Mktg. Inst. (chmn. 1977), Marine Biol. Lab.-Woods Hole (trustee). Office: PO Box 369 Boston MA 02101

RABBE, DAVID ELLSWORTH, oil executive; b. Alexandria, Va., Dec. 17, 1955; s. Raymond Leed and Judith Ann (Ayers) R.; m. Maryann Degroot, Sept. 25, 1982; children: Lisa Ann, Chelsea Nicole. BCE, U. Md., 1979. Terminal trainee Amerada Hess Corp., Balt., 1980-81; terminal supt. Amerada Hess Corp., Syracuse, N.Y., 1981-82, Roseton, N.Y., 1982-83, Pennsauken, N.J., 1983-87; mgr. gas station maintenance Amerada Hess Corp., Woodbridge, N.J., 1987—. Mem. Md. Soc. Surveyors, World Affairs Counci. Republican. Episcopalian. Home: 1408 Weld Ave Cherry Hill NJ 08002

RABE, PAUL ROBERT, marketing executive; b. Napoleon, Ohio, Oct. 3, 1948; s. George Fred and Amanda (Ludemann) R.; m. Karen Sue Behrman, Apr. 25, 1970; children: Kirsten, Brian. BS in Elec. and Computer Engring., Wayne State U., 1976; MS in Elec. and Computer Engring., Mich. State U., 1980. Cert. R.E.T.S., 1968. Research asst. Gen. Motors Research Labs., Detroit, 1968-74, sr. research asst., 1974-77; sr. project engr. diesel equipment Gen. Motors Research Labs., Grand Rapids, Mich., 1977-78; supr. test lab. Gen. Motors Research Labs., Grand Rapids, 1978-80; mgr. staff systems Gen. Motors Research Labs., Detroit, 198-84; dir. product devel. Cummins Electronics Co., Columbus, Ind., 1984-87; v.p. mktg. and sales Cummins Electronics Co., Columbus, 1987—. Contbr. articles to profl. jours.; patentee if field. Mem. IEEE, Soc. Autmotive Engrs. (vice chmn. 1978-80). Home: 428 S Mutz Dr Columbus IN 47201 Office: Cummins Electronics Co 2851 State St Columbus IN 47201

RABENSTINE, JAMES ROBERT, insurance company executive; b. Phila., Nov. 10, 1948; s. James Marcellus and Rita Marie (McGrath) R.; m. Margaret Jean Soltis, June 27, 1970; children: Michael, Matthew, David. BBA, Pa. State U., 1970. CPCU. With Liberty Mut. Ins. Co., 1970—; underwriter bus. risks East Orange, N.J., 1970-73; supervising underwriter bus. risks Lynbrook, N.Y., 1973-76; asst. chief underwriter nat. risks Boston, 1976-78; div. mgr. bus. risks New Castle, Pa., 1978-80; div. underwriter mgr. Chgo., 1980-84; asst. v.p., mgr. mktg. Boston, 1984-85, asst. v.p., mgr. field ops., 1985-86, v.p. interco. and govtl. relations, 1986—; chmn. Mass. Human Service Providers Market Assistance Plan, Boston, 1986—; asst. sec. Liberty Mut. Fire Ins. Co., Boston, 1986—; bd. dirs. Nat. Council on Compensation Inst., N.Y.C., Mut. Atomic Energy Reins. Pool, Chgo. Zone coordinator Worldwide Marriage Encounter, South County, Mass., 1986-87; bd. dirs. Lisle (Ill.) Youth Soccer League, 1983-84. Mem. Soc. CPCU's. Roman Catholic. Home: 46 Idyl Wilde Cir Marshfield MA 02050 Office: Liberty Mut Ins Co 175 Berkeley St Boston MA 02117

RABIDOUX, MARK KENNETH, lawyer; b. Washington, Oct. 14, 1956; s. Kenneth L. and Phyllis M. (Roberts) R.; m. Karen A. Zaleski, May 30, 1981. B in Gen. Studies, U. Mich., 1978; JD, U. Detroit, 1981. Bar: Mich. 1981, U.S. Dist. Ct. (ea. dist.) 1981. Asst. gen. counsel Advance Mortgage Corp., Southfield, Mich., 1981-84; asst. gen. counsel Regency Savs. Bank FSB, Detroit, 1985-86, gen. counsel, 1986-87; v.p., staff atty., corp. sec. Independence One Mortgage Corp., Southfield, 1987—; instr. real estate law Am. Inst. Paralegal Studies, Detroit, 1985-86. Recipient Am. Jurisprudence award Lawyers Co-op Pub. Co., 1980. Mem. ABA, Mich. State Bar Assn. Republican. Roman Catholic. Club: Economic (Detroit). Home: 1866 Lancaster Grosse Pointe Woods MI 48236 Office: Independence One Mortgage Corp PO Box 5076 Southfield MI 48086-5076

RABIN, JOSEPH HARRY, market research company executive; b. Chgo., Dec. 12, 1927; s. Morris and Libby (Broder) Rabinovitz; m. Barbara E. Leader, Oct. 31, 1954; children: Marc Jay, Michelle Ann, Deborah Susan. BSc, Roosevelt U., 1950; MBA, DePaul U., 1951. Account exec. Gould, Gleiss & Benn, 1951-56; asst. dir. mktg. rsch. Paper Mate Co., Chgo., 1953-63; pres. Rabin Rsch. Co., Chgo., 1963—. Pres. Mather High Sch. Council, 1972-74; mem. adv. council U. Toledo, 1976-77, Kellstadt Ctr. DePaul U., 1986-89; mem. adv. com. Bur. of the Census, 1978-83; bd. dirs. Market Rsch. Inst., 1973-75, Ner Tamid Synagogue, 1976-89, Jewish Vocat Svc., 1977-80, With AUS, 1946-47. Mem. Am. Mktg. Assn. (pres. Chgo. chpt. 1961-62, nat. dir. 1973-75, nat. v.p. mktg. rsch. 1978-79, nat. pres. 1981-82), Assn. Consumer Rsch., Am. Statis. Assn. (pres. Chgo. chpt. 1962-63), Am. Assn. Pub. Opinion Rsch. Home: 7061 N Kedzie St Chicago IL 60645 Office: Rabin Rsch Co 520 N Michigan Ave Chicago IL 60611

RABIN, KENNETH HARDY, public relations executive; b. Rochester, N.Y., Apr. 6, 1943; s. Martin and Ruby (Hardy) R.; m. Renee Efland, June 2, 1967; children: Max, Glennie. BA cum laude, Cornell U., 1965; MAT, Yale U., 1966; MA, U. N.C., 1968; PhD, Vanderbilt U., 1974. Accredited pub. relations practitioner. Fgn. svc. info. officer U.S Info. Agy., Uganda, Nigeria, 1967-70; news dir. U. Tenn., Chattanooga, 1970-72; communications specialist Meharry Med. Coll., Nashville, 1972-73; asst. editor Peabody Jour. of Edn. Vanderbilt U., Nashville, 1973-74; assoc. prof. pub. relations Am. Univ., Washington, 1974-80; dir. U.S. pub. affairs Squibb Corp., Princeton, N.J., 1980-83; sr. v.p., dir. health care commn. Hill and Knowlton, Washington, 1984—. Co-editor: Informing the People, 1981; mem. edit. bd. Pub. Relations Rev., 1978—. Bd. dirs. Nat. Alliance Rsch. in Schizophrenia and Depression, Chgo., 1985—, Dystrophic Epidemiologist Bull. Rsch. Assn. Am., N.Y.C., 1984-87; mem. bus. adv. bd. Nat. Down Syndrome Soc., N.Y.C., 1985—. Mem. Am. Med. Writers Assn. (assoc.), Nat. Assn. Sci. Writers (assoc.), Pub. Relations Soc. Am. (Silver Anvil award, 1986). Democrat. Jewish. Home: 3918 Ingomar St NW Washington DC 20015 Office: Hill & Knowlton Inc Washington Harbour Washington DC 20007

RABIN, STANLEY ARTHUR, metal products manufacturer; b. N.Y.C., 1938. B.A., B.S. in Metall. Engring., Columbia U., 1958; M.B.A., U. Santa Clara, 1969. With Comml. Metals Co., Inc., Dallas, 1970—, pres., 1978—, now also chief exec. officer, mem. exec. com., dir. Office: Comml Metals Co Inc 7800 Stemmons Frwy Dallas TX 75247 *

RABINOWITZ, WILBUR M., container company executive, consultant; b. Bklyn., Feb. 18, 1918; s. Harry A. and Caroline (Simmons) R.; m. Audrey H. Perlmutter, Apr. 30, 1944; 1 child, Michael B. PhB, Dickinson Coll., 1940; JD, Harvard U., 1943. Gen. mgr. J. Rabinowitz & Sons, Inc., Bklyn., 1945-67; pres. J. Rabinowitz & Sons, Inc., 1967-81, pres. emeritus cons., 1981—; pres. Met. Glass & Plastic Containers, 1967-81; bd. dirs. Republic N.Y. Corp. Author: Almost Everywhere. Pres. Rabinowitz Found., Bklyn., 1967—; trustee Dickinson Coll. Served with AUS, 1943-45; ETO. Mem. Nat. Assn. Container Distbrs. (past pres.), U.S. Power Squadrons (past comdr.), Explorers Club, Desert Forest Golf Club, Marco Polo Club. Home: 425 E 58th St New York NY 10022 also: PO Box 2121 Carefree AZ 85377 Office: J Rabinowitz & Sons Inc 1300 Metropolitan Ave Brooklyn NY 11237

RABON, WILLIAM JAMES, JR., architect; b. Marion, S.C., Feb. 7, 1931; s. William James and Beatrice (Baker) R.; BS in Arch., Clemson (S.C.) Coll., 1951; BArch, N.C. State Coll., 1955; MArch, MIT, 1956. Registered architect, Calif., Ky., Md., N.Y., N.C., Ohio, Pa., Ga. Designer archtl. firms in N.Y.C. and Birmingham, Mich., 1958-61; designer, asso. John Carl Warnecke and Assos., San Francisco, 1961-63, 64-66, Keyes, Lethbridge and Condon, Washington, 1966-68; prin. archtl. partner A.M. Kinney and William J. Rabon Assocs., Cin., 1968-85; v.p., dir. archtl. design A.M. Kinney, Inc., Cin., 1977-85; v.p., dir. programming services Design Art Corp., 1977-85; assoc. John Portman & Assocs., Atlanta, 1985-88; dir. architectural design and assoc. Robert and Co., Atlanta, 1988—; lectr. U. Calif., Berkeley, 1963-65; asst. prof. archtl. design Cath. U. Am., 1967-68; planning cons. China Nat. Bur. Standards, 1982. Prin. works include Kaiser Tech. Center, Pleasanton, Calif. (Indsl. Research Lab. of Yr. award), 1970; Clermont Nat. Bank, Milford, Ohio, 1971; Pavilion bldg. Children's Hosp. Med. Center, Cin. (AIA design award), 1973; EG&G, Hydrospace, Inc., Rockville, Md. (AIA design award), 1970; Mead Johnson Park, Evansville, Ind. (Indsl. Research Lab. of Yr. hon. mention), 1973; Hamilton County Vocat. Sch., Cin., 1972; hdqrs. lab. EPA, Cin., 1975; Arapahoe Chem. Co. Research Center, Boulder, Colo. (Indsl. Research Lab. of Yr. award 1976; Concrete Reinforced Steel Inst. Nat. Design award), 1976; corporate hdqrs. Ohio River Co., Cin., 1977; Children's Hosp. Therapy Center, Cin. (AIA design award 1978, award of merit Am. Wood Council 1981); VA Hosp. addition, Cin. (ASHRAE award 1980); NALCO Chem. Co. Research Center, Naperville, Ill. (AIA design award 1980, 81), 1980; Proctor & Gamble-Winton Hill Tunnel, Cin. (AIA design award), 1978; Toyota Regional Center, Blue Ash, Ohio (AIA and Ohio Masonry Council combined design award 1981); planning cons. Nat. Bur. Standards, Republic of China, 1982; East-West fleet hdqrs. Complex of Royal Saudi Arabian Navy, 1983, Data Libraries, 1983; corporate hdqrs. The Drackett Co., Cin., 1983; corporate hdqrs. Brown & Williamson, Louisville, 1984, others Served to 1st lt. AUS, 1951-53; Korea. Decorated Silver Star, Bronze Star with V device, Purple Heart with bronze cluster; MIT Grad. Sch. scholar, 1955-56; Fulbright scholar, Italy, 1957-58. Mem. AIA, Nat. Council Archtl. Registration Bds. Office: Robert & Co 96 Poplar St NW Atlanta GA 30335

RABOSKY, JOSEPH GEORGE, engineer, consultant; b. Sewickley, Pa., May 20, 1944; s. Mary Helen (Mayer) Rabosky; m. Suzanne Lazzelle, Aug. 23, 1969. BS, Pa. State U., 1966; MS in Engring., W.Va. U., 1969, MSCE, 1973; PhD, U. Pitts., 1984. Project engr. Chester Engrs., Coraopolis, Pa., 1969-70; project mgr. Calgon Corp., Pitts., 1970-73, sect. leader, 1979-85, mktg. mgr., 1985-86; sr. environ. specialist Mobay Chem. Corp., Pitts., 1975-79; project engr. Morris Knowles, Inc., Pitts., 1973-74; project mgr. Penn Environ. Cons., 1974-75; engring. mgr. Baker/TSA, Inc., Pitts., 1986—; adj. prof. U. Pitts., 1985—, Pa. State U.-Beaver, McKeesport and New Kensington campuses, 1985—. Bd. dirs. Moon Twp. Mcpl. Authority, 1980—. Mem. Nat. Soc. Profl. Engrs., Pa. Soc. Profl. Engrs., Am. Acad. Environ. Engrs. (diplomate), Water Pollution Control Fedn., Water Pollution Control Assn. Pa. (chmn. research com. 1984—, program com. 1984-87), Western Pa. Water Pollution Control Assn. (officer). Home: 104 Wynview Dr Coraopolis PA 15108

RABOY, S. CAESAR, insurance executive; b. N.Y.C., May 20, 1936; s. Murray and Rose (Peckins) R.; m. Deborah Lewis, Dec. 30, 1956; children: Adam, Alyce, James. BA, Brandeis U., 1957; MBA, Pepperdine U., 1975. Agt. Nat. Life of Vt., San Francisco, 1958-62; supr. Conn. Mut., San Francisco, 1963-66; gen. agt. Conn. Mut., Detroit, 1966-70, Los Angeles, 1970-78; sr. v.p. Conn. Mut., Hartford, Conn., 1978-80, exec. v.p., 1980-84, pres., 1985—, chief operating officer, 1988—; bd. dirs. Conn. Nat. Bank, GroupAmerica Ins. Co., 1985; chmn. Life Underwriters Tng. Council; trustee No. Utilities. Chmn. Conn. Law Enforcement Found.; pres. Greater Hartford Arts Council; bd. fellows Brandeis U.; bd. regents U. Hartford. Home: 48 Ledyard Rd West Hartford CT 06117 Office: Conn Mut Life Ins 140 Garden St Hartford CT 06154

RACHMELER, LOUIS, research and development executive; b. N.Y.C., Feb. 16, 1923; s. Jack Nathan and Sophie R.; m. Mary Lou Johnson, June 23, 1950; children: Dale Nelson, Catherine Lynn, Richard Forrest, Kimberley Ann. BS, U.S. Mil. Acad., 1947; MS, Stanford U., 1953. Commd. 2d lt. U.S. Army, 1947, advanced through grades to maj. gen., 1977, ret., 1980; v.p. adminstrn. SCI Systems, Huntsville, Ala., 1980-82; asst. to pres. Nichols Research Corp., Huntsville, 1982-83, dir. AOA project, 1983-85, group v.p., 1985—. V.p. fin. Tennessee Valley Council, Boy Scouts Am., Huntsville, 1978-88; bd. dirs. Salvation Army, Huntsville, 1988; pres.

United Way Am., Huntsville/Madison County, 1984-85; chmn. Vols. Am. North Ala., Inc., Huntsville, 1987-88. Decorated Disting. Service medal, Legion of Merit with three oak leaf clusters. Mem. Am. Def. Preparedness Assn., Assn. U.S. Army, Heritage Club, Huntsville Club, Army Navy Country Club (Arlington, Va.), Rotary (bd. dirs. 1988). Presbyterian. Office: Nichols Rsch Corp 4040 S Meml Pkwy Huntsville AL 35802

RACINE, JEAN CLAUDE B., corporate executive, management consultant; b. Thiviers, France; came to U.S., 1983; s. Charles P. and Juliette (Couvet) R.; m. Martine M. Fangeau, Oct. 25, 1975; children: Isabelle, Xavier. BA, Lycee St. Louis, Paris, 1959; MBA, U. Sorbonne, 1962, PhD, 1965. Personnel mgr. Souriau, Paris, 1967-68; dir. personnel LaFarge Cenent, 1968-72; dir. French Nat. Assn. Mfrs., 1972-76; owner Pragma Internat., Washington, 1976—. Mem. ASPA, N.Y. C. of C., Georgetown Bus. Assn. Home: 11028 Stanmore Dr Potomac MD 20854 Office: Pragma Internat 1050 17th St NW Washington DC 20036

RADEMACHER, HOLLIS WILLIAM, banker; b. Spencer, Iowa, Aug. 19, 1935; s. Bernard William and Helen Dorothy (Hollis) R.; m. Carolyn Alice Frisk, Sept. 21, 1957; children—William, Robert. B.B.A., U. Minn., 1957. With Continental Ill. Nat. Bank & Trust Co. Chgo., 1957—, successively 2d v.p., v.p., sr. v.p., exec. v.p., chief credit officer, now chief fin. officer, 1984—; participant RMA Credit Policy Roundtable, 1983, 84. Mem. Am. Bankers Assn. (div. chmn. 1978-83), Nat. Futures Assn. (bd. dirs. Chgo. sect. 1982-84). Republican. Episcopalian. Clubs: Bankers, Executives, Economic (Chgo.).

RADEN, LOUIS, tape and label corporation executive; b. Detroit, June 17, 1929; s. Harry M. and Joan (Morris) R.; m. Mary K. Knowlton, June 18, 1949; children: Louis III, Pamela (Mrs. T.W. Rea III), Jacqueline. BA, Trinity Coll., 1951; postgrad. NYU, 1952. With Time, Inc., 1951-52; with Quaker Chem. Corp., 1952-63, sales mgr., 1957-63; exec. v.p. Gen. Tape & Supply, Inc., Detroit, 1963-68, pres., chmn. bd., 1969—; pres. Mich. Gun Clubs, 1973-77. Fifth reunion chmn. Trinity Coll., 1956, pres. Mich. alumni, 1965-72, sec. Class of 1951, 81-86, pres. 1986—; trustee, v.p. Mich. Diocese Episcopal Ch., 1980-82, mem. urban evaluation com., 1975-78, chmn. urban evaluation com., 1978, chmn. urban affairs com., 1977-79; vice chmn. bd. dirs. Robert H. Whitaker Sch. Theology, 1983-85; founding sponsor World Golf Hall of Fame; mem. Founders Soc. Detroit Inst. Arts. Mem. Nat Rifle Assn. (life), Nat. Skeet Shooting Assn. (life, nat. dir. 1977-79, 5 Man Team World Champion award 1977), Greater Detroit Bd. Commerce, Automotive Industry Action Group, Mich. C. of C., U.S. C. of C., Greater Hartford Jaycees (exec. v.p. 1955-57, Key Man award 1957), Theta Xi (life; Disting. Service award 1957, alumni pres. 1952-57, regional dir. 1954-57). Republican. Clubs: Detroit Golf, Detroit Gun, Katke-Cousins Golf, Black Hawk Indians, Pinehurst Country; Oakland U. Pres.'s, Round Table. Home: 1133 Ivyglen Cir Bloomfield Hills MI 48013 Office: Gen Tape & Supply Inc 7451 W Eight Mile Rd Detroit MI 48221

RADER, (M.) ELIZABETH, accountant; b. Knoxville, Tenn., May 7, 1951; d. Charles Edward and Eleanor (Wall) R.; m. Donald Floyd McKee. BA summa cum laude, Rice U., 1973; MBA, Tulane U., 1975. CPA, Tex., N.Y. From staff auditor to audit mgr. Arthur Andersen & Co., Houston, 1975-81; securities profl., acctg. fellow U.S. SEC, Washington, 1981-83; audit mgr. nat. office Touche Ross & Co., N.Y.C., 1983-84, audit ptnr. Fin. Services Ctr., 1984—; exchange exec. Pres.'s Commn. on Exec. Exchange, 1983-84. Thomas J. Watson fellow, 1973-74; recipient John Burnis Allred award Tex. Soc. CPA's, 1975. Mem. AICPA, Am. Acctg. Assn. (SEC liaison com. 1985-86), Fin. Women's Assn. of N.Y., Swedish-Am. C. of C., Phi Beta Kappa, Beta Gamma Sigma. Methodist. Club: Roton Point (Rowayton, Conn.). Office: Touche Ross & Co One World Trade Ctr 93d Floor New York NY 10048

RADER, KENNETH CECIL, JR., financial executive, consultant; b. East Chicago, Ind., July 6, 1948; s. Kenneth Cecil and Irma Jeanne (Romer) R.; m. Nora Lee Wolff, Dec. 27, 1969; children—Emilee Jeanne, Bethany Anne. B.S., Ind. U., 1971; M.M., Northwestern U., 1980. C.P.A., Ill., Ind. Branch mgr. Mercantile Nat. Bank, Hammond, Ind., 1971-73; asst. controller Fieldhouse, Inc., Highland, Ind., 1974-75; controller Atlas Steel Fabrication, Inc., East Chicago, 1976-77; div. controller Motorola, Inc., Schaumburg, Ill., 1978-81; v.p., chief fin. officer VCS, Inc., Carol Stream, Ill., 1981-85; v.p. CFO Grayhill, Inc. and Grayhill Taiwan, Inc., 1985—; cons. in bus. planning, St. Charles, Ill., 1976—. Chmn. St. Mark's Lutheran Ch., St. Charles, 1983-84. Mem. Am. Inst. C.P.A.s, Nat. Assn. Accts. Home: 818 Timbers Trail Saint Charles IL 60174-5503 Office: Grayhill Inc 561 Hillgrove Ave La Grange IL 60525

RADER, STEVE ALLEN, accountant; b. El Paso, Tex., July 25, 1954; s. Charles Augusta and Barbara Ann (Cargill) R. BBA, U. Houston, 1976. CPA, Tex.; cert. mgmt. acct. Cons. Seidman and Seidman, Houston, 1976-77; mgr. Deloitte, Haskins and Sells, Houston, 1977-83; mng. ptnr. Rader and Co., Houston, 1983—; adv. dir. Ameriway Bank, Houston, 1984-86. Treas. DeYoung Campaign Com., 1988. Mem. Am. Inst. CPAs, Tex. Soc. CPAs (mem. Houston chpt. com. 1982-83), Inst. Mgmt. Acctg. Club: Dover (Houston). Office: Rader and Co 550 Westcott Ste 500 Houston TX 77007

RADEY, RICHARD GREGER, agricultural cooperative company executive; b. Camden, N.J., Oct. 13, 1933; s. Henry Walter and Vivian Alice (Martin) R.; m. Abigail Elizabeth Irvin, Dec. 29, 1953; children: Donald Neil, Barbara Elizabeth, Dona Lynn. B.S., Syracuse U., 1955. C.P.A., N.Y. Acct. Coopers & Lybrand, N.Y.C., 1955-56; acct. Coopers & Lybrand, 1959-73, audit mgr., 1969; div. controller Cooper Labs., Parsippany, N.J., 1974-75, controller, 1976-79, sr. v.p., treas., 1979; v.p. fin. and control Agway Inc., Syracuse, N.Y., 1980, sr. v.p. fin. and control, 1980—; bd. dirs. Agway Ins. Co., Syracuse, H.P. Hood Co. Inc., Boston, Key Bank of Cen. N.Y., N.A., Syracuse, Agway Gen. Agy., Inc., Syracuse, Agway Data Services, Inc., Syracuse. Bd. dirs. Syracuse Symphony Orch. Served as 1st lt. USAF, 1956-59. Mem. Fin. Exec. Inst. (pres. Syracuse chpt. 1983-84), Am. Inst. CPA's, N.Y. State Soc. CPA's, Nat. Soc. Accts. for Coops. Office: Agway Inc PO Box 4933 Syracuse NY 13221

RADICAN, THERESA FUSCO, controller; b. Providence, Feb. 21, 1937; d. Thomas and Mary Delores (Tundis) Fusco; m. Robert Edward Radican, July 2, 1960; children: Dawn, Stacey, Kelli, Deborah, Robert Jr. BS in Bus. Edn., Bryant Coll., 1958. Cert. tchr., R.I. Tchr. bus. Cranston (R.I.) High Sch., 1958-63; corp. sec., controller R.A.I., Inc., Warwick, R.I., 1966-68; controller Network Solutions, Inc., Warwick, 1968—; corp. sec. Radican Co., Warwick, 1987—. State chmn. sect. of auxs. Hosp. Assn. of R.I., Providence, 1987—; state rep. NE Healthcare Assembly, Durham, N.H., 1988—; trustee Kent County Meml. Hosp., Warwick, 1985-87, incorporator, 1982—, spl. event chmn., 1985-87; pres. Kent County Hosp. Aux., Warwick, 1985-87; mem. R.I. Cancer Soc. Spl. Event, Providence, 1985, Warwick Consortium for Arts and Humanities, Warwick, 1985, Warwick Boys & Girls Club, Trudeau Ctr. for Retarded Children. Mem. Warwick Country Club (chmn. entertainment com.), Warwick Neck Garden Club (pres. 1977-79), St. Thomas Yacht Club, St. Kevin's Women's Club, Surf Club. Home: 99 Briarcliff Ave Warwick RI 02889 Office: Network Solutions Inc 20 Catamore Blvd East Providence RI 02914

RADKE, CARROLL ELDON RAYMOND, oil company executive; b. Beaumont, Tex., Apr. 19, 1937; s. Carroll Vernon and Edith Odessia (Duncan) R.; m. Georgia Mae Barbee, Dec. 6, 1975. Pres. Radke Oil Co. Inc., Jennings, La., 1977—, Carla Oil Co., Inc., Jennings, 1977—; co-owner C.V. Radke Well Service, Jennings, 1977—. With U.S. Army, 1960-62. Democrat. Baptist. Home and Office: 433 Magnolia PO Box 915 Jennings LA 70546

RADLAUER, PATRICIA THOMASINE, designer; b. N.Y.C., Feb. 15, 1940; d. John Joseph and Lucinda Mary (Hinphy) McLoughlin; m. David Max Radlauer, Oct. 6, 1959; children: Mark Alfred, Daniel John. Student Plaza Bus. Sch., 1956-57, New Sch. Social Research, 1957, Palau Studios, 1968-70, Suffolk Community Coll., 1970-72. Legal sec. Giamo & Nicolossi, N.Y.C., 1956; exec. sec. World Wide Auto Corp., N.Y.C., 1956-59; advt. and display Sterns, N.Y.C., 1959-62; pres. Interiors by Patricia, Inc., Centerport, N.Y., 1967-88; designer Designers Showcase, Nassau County, 1981-82. Committeeman Suffolk County Liberal Party, 1975. Mem. Am. Soc. Interior Designers (assoc.), Nat. Assn. Women in Constrn. Office: Interiors by Patricia Inc 8 Fort Salonga Rd Rt 25A Centerport NY 11721

RADLER, F. DAVID, holding company executive. Pres., chief exec. officer, dir. Dominion Stores Ltd., Toronto. Office: Sterling Newspapers, 1827 W 5th Ave, Vancouver, BC Canada V6J 1P5

RADMER, MICHAEL JOHN, lawyer, educator; b. Wisconsin Rapids, Wis., Apr. 28, 1945; s. Donald Richard and Thelma Loretta (Donahue) R.; children from previous marriage: Christina Nicole, Ryan Michael; m. Laurie J. Anshus, Dec. 22, 1983; 1 child, Michael John. B.S., Northwestern U., Evanston, Ill., 1967; J.D., Harvard U., 1970. Bar: Minn. 1970. Assoc. Dorsey & Whitney, Mpls., 1970-75, ptnr., 1976—; lectr. law Hamline U. Law Sch., St. Paul, 1981-84; gen. counsel, rep., sec. 64 federally registered investment cos., Mpls. and St. Paul, 1977—. Contbr. articles to legal jours. Active legal work Hennepin County Legal Advice Clinic, Mpls., 1971—. Mem. ABA, Minn. Bar Assn., Hennepin County Bar Assn. Club: Mpls. Athletic. Home: 4329 E Lake Harriet Pkwy Minneapolis MN 55409 Office: Dorsey & Whitney 2200 First Bank Pl E Minneapolis MN 55402

RADNER, SIDNEY HOLLIS, rug company executive; b. Holyoke, Mass., Dec. 8, 1919; s. William I. Radner; m. Helen Jane Cohen, Dec. 12, 1946; children: William Marc, Richard Scott. Student, Yale U., 1941. Pres. Am. Rug Co., Holyoke, 1946; lectr., cons., investigator crooked gambling, U.S. Armed Forces, FBI, gov. of Canada, various state and mcpl. police vice squads; appearances in BBC film on Houdini as well as various TV shows, including "In Search Of..."; leading collector and expert on Houdini, including nat. pub. TV appearance in "Houdini". Author: Radner on Poker, Radner on Dice, Radner on Roulette and Casino Games, How to Detect Card Sharks; contbr. articles to profl. jours. Past pres. Holyoke C. of C.; co-founder Volleyball Hall of Fame; bd. dirs. Greater Springfield (Mass.) Better Bus. Bur. (past bd. dirs.); hon. curator Radner Houdini Collection Outagamie County Mus., Appleton, Wis. Served with criminal investigation div. U S. Army, 1942-46. Mem. Soc. Am. Magicians (mem. Occult Investigation Com.), Internat. Brotherhood Magicians, Magic Circle (London), Magician's Guild (charter), Magic Collector's Assn., Am. Platform Assn., Houdini Club of Wis. (hon.), Rotary, Masons, Shriners. Jewish. Home: 1050 Northampton St Holyoke MA 01040 Office: Am Rug 1594 Dwight St Holyoke MA 01040

RADON, JENIK RICHARD, lawyer; b. Berlin, Germany, Jan. 14, 1946; came to U.S., 1951, naturalized, 1956; s. Louis and Irmgard (Hinz) R.; m. Heidi B. Duerbeck, June 10, 1971; 1 child, Kaara H.D. BA, Columbia Coll., 1967; MCP, U. Calif., Berkeley, 1971; JD, Stanford U., 1971. Bar: Calif. 1972, N.Y. 1975, U.S. Ct. Appeals (2d cir.) 1975, U.S. Dist. Ct. (so. dist.) N.Y. 1975. Ptnr. Radon & Ishizumi, N.Y.C., Tokyo, Taipei and Munich, 1981—; lectr. Polish Acad. Scis., 1980, Tokyo Arbitration Assn., 1983, Japan External Trade Orgn., 1983, 86, Japan Mgmt. Assn., 1983, Japan Inst. Internat. Bus. Law, 1983-84, Va. Ctr. World Trade, 1985, UN Indsl. Devel. Orgn., Warsaw, 1987-88, Wichita World Trade Council, 1987, Inst. Nat. Economy of Poland, 1987, Hungarian Econ. Roundtable, 1987, USSR. Com. on Sci. and Tech., 1988, USSR Fgn. Trade Ministry, 1988, Taillinn Poly. Inst., 1988, Tartu State U., 1988, U. Ottowa, 1988, Palm Beach World Trade Coun., 1988. Editor The International Acquisitions Handbook, The Toyo-Kaizai Pub. Co., Tokyo, 1987, editor-in-chief Stanford Jour. Internat. Studies, 1970-71; contbr. articles to German and Am. bus. and legal pubs. Active Am. Council on Germany, N.Y.C., 1978—, U.S.-Polish Econ. Council, 1987—; mem. exec. com. Afghanistan Relief Com., N.Y.C., 1980—; mem. bd. dirs. Internat. Video Inst., N.Y.C., 1988—; seminar participant U.S. Polish Trade Commn., Washington, 1981; trustee Direct Relief Internat., Santa Barbara, Calif., 1987; mem. bd. dirs. Freedom Medicine, Honolulu, 1987—; advisor UN Indsl. Devel. Orgn., 1988. NSF grantee, 1966; Slavic and E. European Inst. grantee, 1968; HUD fellow, 1968-70. Mem. German-Am. Law Assn., Asia-Pacific Lawyers Assn., Deutscher Verein, Columbia Coll. Alumni Assn. Roman Catholic. Office: Radon & Ishizumi 269 W 71st St New York NY 10023

RADVANY, CRAIG JOSEPH, pharmaceuticals company executive, accountant; b. Trenton, N.J., Apr. 20, 1949; s. Joseph D. and Marjorie I. (Balla) R.; m. Barbara Ann Prevatil, Aug. 28, 1970; children: Kerry Ann, Kevin Scott. BBA, Rider Coll., 1971, postgrad., 1977. Acct. Princeton (N.J.) Applied Research Corp., 1970-71, Thiokol Chem. Corp., Trenton, 1971-72; acct. Carter-Wallace, Inc., Cranbury, N.J., 1972-74, sr. acct., 1974-77, fin. coordinator, 1977-81, mgr. fin., 1981-88; dir. fin. and adminstrn. research and devel. div. Carter Products, 1988—. Co-rep. Thiokol United Way Campaign, Trenton, 1971; mem. Bd. of Session First Presbyn. Ch. of Hamilton Sq., N.J., 1982-84, utilities adv. com. Hopewell Twp., 1988—; mgr., coach Nottingham Little League, Trenton, 1982-83, Hamilton Twp. Recreation Soccer Assn., Trenton, 1982-83; mgr. Hamilton Lassies Basketball League, Trenton, 1984, Hamilton Police Athletic League Basketball, Trenton, 1985; apptd. to utilities adv. com. Hopewell Twp., 1988. Mem. Nat. Assn. Accts. (Trenton chpt. pres. 1985-86, nat. adv. panel to subcom. of mgmt. acctg. practices com. 1986, nat. com. on pub. relations 1987-88), Am. Mgmt. Assn. Home: PO Box 646 Cranbury NJ 08512 Office: Carter-Wallace Inc PO Box 1 Cranbury NJ 08512

RADVIC, STEPHAN, international management consultant, senior corporate management negotiator, linguist; b. Mar. 5, 1940; s. Melko and Theresa (Cini) R. B.Econs. and Commerce, U. Melbourne (Australia), 1963; M.A. in Internat. Mgmt., U. Tex.-Dallas, 1976. C.P.A., Australia, 1965-69; profl. soccer player, 1963-65; exec. asst. to Lamar Hunt, Hunt Oil Co., Dallas, 1969-73; v.p., controller, chief fin. officer, electronics group Rockwell Internat., London and Paris, 1973-79; v.p.-gen. mgr. Europe, United Technologies, Barcelona and Geneva, 1979-81; pres. Atlantic Group, Inc., Madeira Beach, Fla., 1981—; adj. prof. Internat. Mgmt. U. of Tampa Grad. Sch. of Bus., 1988—; lingust with fluency in 7 languages, good comprehension of 4 others; mem. bd. dirs. 4 European corps.; head coach So. Meth. U. varsity soccer team, 1972; lectr. internat. corp. fin. grad. sch. U. Tex.-Dallas, 1976-77. Mem. Am. Inst. C.P.A.s. Roman Catholic. Home: 845 119th Ave Treasure Island FL 33706 Office: Atlantic Group Inc PO Box 8856 Madeira Beach FL 33738

RAE, MATTHEW SANDERSON, JR., lawyer; b. Pitts., Sept. 12, 1922; s. Matthew Sanderson and Olive (Waite) R.; m. Janet Hettman, May 2, 1953; children: Mary-Anna, Margaret, Janet, Rae-Dupree. AB, Duke, 1946, LLB, 1947; postgrad., Stanford U., 1951. Bar: Md. 1948, Calif. 1951. Asst. to dean Duke Sch. Law, Durham, N.C., 1947-48; assoc. Karl F. Steinmann, Balt., 1948-49, Guthrie, Darling & Shattuck, Los Angeles, 1953-54; nat. field rep. Phi Alpha Delta Frat., Los Angeles, 1949-51; research atty. Calif. Supreme Ct., San Francisco, 1951-52; ptnr. Darling, Hall & Rae and predecessor firms, Los Angeles, 1955—; mem. Calif. Commn. Uniform State Laws, 1985—. V.p. Los Angeles County Rep. Assembly, 1959-64; mem. Los Angeles County Rep. Cen. Com., 1960-64, 77—, exec. com., 1977—; vice chmn. 17th Congl. Dist., 1960-62, 28th Congl. Dist., 1962-64; chmn. 46th Assembly Dist., 1962-64, 27th Senatorial Dist., 1977-85, 29th Senatorial Dist,m 1985—; mem. Calif. Rep. State Cen. Com., 1966—, exec. com., 1966-67; pres. Calif. Rep. League, 1966-67; trustee Rep. Assocs., 1979—, pres., 1983-85, chmn. bd. dirs., 1985-87. Served to 2d lt. USAAF, World War II. Fellow Am. Coll. Probate Counsel; academician Internat. Acad. Estate and Trust Law (exec. council 1974-78); mem. ABA, Los Angeles County Bar Assn. (chmn. probate and trust law com. 1964-66, chmn. legislation com. 1980-86, chmn. program com. 1981-82, chmn. membership retention com. 1982-83, trustee 1983-85, dir. Bar Found. 1987—), South Bay Bar Assn., State Bar Calif. (chmn. state bar jour. com. 1970-71, chmn. probate com. 1974-75, exec. com. estate planning trust and probate law sect. 1977-83, chmn. legislation com. 1977—, probate law cons. group Calif. Bd. Legal Specialization 1977-88, chmn. conf. dels. resolutions com. 1987, exec. com. conf. dels. 1987—), Lawyers Club of Los Angeles (bd. govs. 1981-87, 1st v.p. 1982-83), Am. Legion (comdr. Allied post 1969-70), Legion Lex (dir. 1964—, pres. 1969-71), Air Force Assn., Aircraft Owners and Pilots Assn., Town Hall (gov. 1970-78, pres. 1975), World Affairs Council, Internat. Platform Assn., Los Angeles Com. on Fgn. Relations, Phi Beta Kappa (councilor Alpha Assn. 1983—, v.p. 1984-86), Omicron Delta Kappa, Phi Alpha Delta (supreme justice 1972-74, elected to Disting. Service chpt. 1978), Sigma Nu. Presbyterian. Clubs: Breakfast (law, pres. 1989—), Commonwealth (San Francisco); Chancery, Petroleum (L.A.). Lodge: Rotary. Home: 600 John St Manhattan Beach CA 90266 Office: Darling Hall & Rae 550 S Flower St 6th Floor Los Angeles CA 90071

RAEZER, SALLIE STEWART, software company executive; b. N.Y.C., May 11, 1951; d. John Larry and Margaret Ann (Thompson) Stewart; m. John Raezer, Aug. 18, 1984; children: John Kenneth, Julie Rebecca. BA, Bucknell U., 1973. Programmer to systems analyst Sperry Univac, Blue Bell, Pa., 1973-75; systems analyst Prudential Ins. Co. Am., Dresher, Pa., 1975-76; systems engr. Datapoint Corp., Bala-Cynwyd, Pa., 1976-78; v.p., bus. design architect Finpac Corp., Narberth, Pa., 1978—, bd. dirs., sec.; founder SR Investment Co., Narberth, Pa., 1984—. Mem. Soc. Indsl. and Applied Math., Bucknell U. Alumni Assn. (trustee 1978-83). Club: Island Heights (N.J.) Yacht. Home: 107 Foxhall Ln Narberth PA 19072 Office: Finpac Corp Windsor and Forrest Aves Narberth PA 19072

RAFFAY, STEPHEN JOSEPH, manufacturing company executive; b. McAdoo, Pa., Oct. 25, 1927; s. Stephen John and Stephanie (Severa) R.; m. Audree Eugenia Kuehne, Sept. 12, 1953; children: Andrea, Stephen, Leslie. B.A., Columbia, 1950, M.S., 1951. C.P.A., N.Y. Sr. accountant Arthur Andersen & Co., N.Y.C., 1951-56; asst. controller Emhart Corp., Farmington, Conn., 1956-61, asst. treas., 1961-63, treas., 1963-67, v.p. internat., 1967-72, v.p., group pres., 1972-79, exec. v.p., 1979-84, vice chmn., chief adminstrv. officer, 1984-87, dir., 1980-87; sr. v.p. Dexter Corp., Windsor Locks, Conn., 1987—; bd. dirs. Reflexite Corp., Conn. Bank & Trust Co., Superior Electric Co. Bd. dirs. Hartford Symphony Soc.; chmn. Greater Hartford Arts Coun. Served with AUS, 1946-47. Mem. AICPAs, Conn. Soc. CPAs, Greater Hartford C. of C. (bd. dirs.), World Trade Assn. (bd. dirs.). Office: Dexter Corp One Elm St Windsor Locks CT 06096

RAFFELSON, MICHAEL, financial executive; b. Bklyn., Jan. 2, 1946; s. Leo and Fay Rebecca (Clumpus) R.; B.B.A., Coll. City N.Y., 1967; M.B.A., CUNY, 1969; m. Eileen Judith Tauber, Mar. 23, 1975; 1 dau., Elyse Lauren. Acct., Am. Metal Climax Inc., N.Y.C., 1967-69; fin. analyst Anaconda Co., N.Y.C., 1971-74; sr. fin. analyst corp. staff Internat. Paper Co., N.Y.C., 1975-76, bus. analyst white papers group, 1976-79, applications coordinator paper and packaging mgmt. systems, 1979-81, mgr. mgmt. services info. systems, 1981-85; mgr. ops. analysis and control info. services The First Boston Corp., N.Y.C., 1986-87, mgr. telecommunications analysis and control 1987-88, asst. v.p. 1988; v.p. Chase Manhattan Bank, N.Y.C., 1988—; instr. fin. mgmt. edn. program Internat. Paper, 1977. Served with AUS, 1969-71. Mem. Phi Epsilon Pi (pres. chpt. 1966). Office: Chase Manhattan Bank 1 World Trade Ctr New York NY 10048

RAFFERTY, EDSON HOWARD, lawyer, consultant; b. Newark, N.J., Jan. 7, 1943; s. Martin James and Amber Louise (Leach) R.; m. Sarah Webster, Bartlett, Sept. 18, 1976 (div. 1981); children: Ethan Eric, Heather Knowles. AB in Chemistry, Syracuse U.; BSME; MS in Bio-engring., U. Tex. Grad. Sch. Bio-Med. Scis.; JD, Hamline Law Sch.; MBA, MIT. Bar: Mass., 1982. Chief engr. Artificial Heart Project, VA Hosp., Houston and Syracuse, N.Y., 1966-68; prin. scientist, mgr. Artificial Heart Program Applied Sci. div. Litton Industries, Inc., Mpls., 1968-70; chief operating officer, exec. v.p., chief fin. officer, dir. Bio-Medicus, Inc., Mpls., 1970-78, acting pres., 1970-73; sr. ptnr. Consultus, Inc., Cambridge, Mass., 1978—, sr. ptnr., Attys at Law Rafferty & Polich, Cambridge, 1982—. Contbr. numerous articles to profl. jours. Over 50 patents in field. Legis. dist. Dem. chairperson Mpls., 1970-74; nat. coordinator med. exchange between U.S. and U.S.S.R., Mpls., 1975-79; chmn. corp. fin. Council on U.S./U.S.S.R. Health Care Exchange, Mpls., 1975-79; participant numerous TV spls. on artificial heart, 1968-78. Recipient IR-100 award Indsl. Research Inc., 1972, Bachner award Plastic Industry Trade Org., 1976. Mem. ABA, Mass. Bar Assn., Am. Soc. for Artificial Internal Organs, Assn. Advancement of Med. Instrumentation. Club: Warren Tavern (Charlestown, Mass.) (founder). Office: Rafferty & Polich 1675 Massachusetts Ave Cambridge MA 02138

RAFFERTY, FRANK THOMAS, psychiatrist healthcare executive; b. Greenville, Miss., Jan. 28, 1925; s. Frank Thomas and Mary P. (Jordan) R.; m. Sally Louise App, Feb. 18, 1950 (div. 1976); children: F. Thomas, Margaret, Gerard, Elizabeth, Ann, Christine, Jennifer. BS in Biology and Chemistry, St. Mary's Coll., Winona, Minn., 1944; MD, St. Louis U., 1948; MS in Psychiatry, U. Colo., 1953. Diplomate Am. Bd. Psychiatry and Neurology. Intership St. Louis City Hosp., 1948-49; residency in psychiatry Colorado Psychopathic Hosp., Denver, 1949-52; fellowship in child psychiatry U. Colo. Mental Hygiene Clinic, Denver, 1952-53; dir. child psychiatry U. Utah, Salt Lake City, 1955-61; dir. child psychiatry U. Md., Balt., 1961-71, prof. psychiatry, 1966-71; prof. psychiatry U. Ill., Chgo., 1971-79, dir. Inst. for Juvenile Rsch., 1971-79; dir. child and adolescent Ill. Dept. Mental Health and Devel. Disabilities, Chgo., 1974-79; med. dir. Brown Schs., Austin, Tex., 1979-85; v.p. med. affairs Healthcare Internat., Austin, 1980—; dir. mental health svc. Utah State Prison, Draper, 1955-58; Fogarty scholar Nat. Inst. Mental Health, Bethesda, Md., 1968-69; cons. West Side VA Hosp., Chgo., 1971-79, Cook County Juvenile Detention Ctr., Chgo., 1971-79. Author: Catalog of Psychiatric Procedures, 1988; contbr. articles to profl. jours., chpts to books. Mem. Joint Commn. on Mental Health Children and Adolescents, Washington, 1965-69, Ill. Children's Commn., 1971-79; cons. Presdl. Commn. on Mental Health, 1978-79; adv. com. Mental Health Mental Retardation, Austin, 1988—. Fellow Am. Psychiat. Assn., Am. Acad. Child and Adolescent Psychiatry; mem. AMA, Ill. Child Psychiat. Soc. (pres 1978), Am. Mgmt. Assn., Tex. Soc. Child and Adolescent Psychiatry (pres. 1988). Republican. Office: Healthcare Internat 9737 Great Hills Trail Austin TX 78759

RAGAGLIA, KRISTINE DIANE, lawyer; b. Encino, Calif., Apr. 30, 1962; d. Jack Connor and Beverly Ann (Ladiges) Williams; m. Scott R. Ragaglia, Aug. 23, 1986. BA, U. Conn., 1984; student, U. London, 1982-83; JD, Western New Eng. Coll., Springfield, Mass., 1987. Bar: Conn. 1987, U.S. Dist. Ct. Conn., 1988. Intern to presiding justice U.S. Dist. Ct. Conn., 1987; assoc. Tyler Cooper and Alcorn, Hartford, Conn., 1987—. Vol. atty. Legal Aid, 1988—; legal asst. Corp. Lawyers' Legal Aid to Elderly, Hartford, 1984-86; 2nd vice-chmn. Conn. Fedn. Young Republicans 1984-85, credentials chmn. 1985. Recipient Am. Jurisprudence award Bancroft-Whitney Co., 1987. Mem. ABA, Conn. Bar Assn., Assn. Trial Lawyers Am. Office: Tyler Cooper and Alcorn City Place 35th Floor Hartford CT 06001

RAGALS, WILLIAM CHARLES, JR., lawyer, business executive; b. N.Y.C., Feb. 4, 1939; s. William Charles and Frances (Spiegel) R.; m. Jane Gottlieb, June 26, 1960; children: Jonathan William, David Charles. BA, Colgate U., 1960; LLB, NYU, 1963. Assoc. Wikler Gottlieb Taylor & Howard, N.Y.C., 1963-66, 1970-71; corp. counsel Bermec Corp., N.Y.C., 1966-70; v.p., sec., corp. counsel Creative Capital Corp., N.Y.C., 1971-73; sec., corp. counsel Internat. Controls Corp., Thomaston, Conn., 1973-83, v.p., sec., corp. counsel, 1978-83; v.p., sec. gen. counsel Internat. Controls Corp., Somerset, N.J., 1983—. Mem. planning bd. Town of New Castle, Chappaqua, N.Y., 1980—; adv. bd. local region Am. Youth Soccer Assn. Mem. ABA, N.Y. Bar Assn., N.Y. County Lawyers Assn., Am. Soc. Corp. Secs., Am. Corp. Counsel Assn. Office: Internat Controls Corp 2 Executive Dr Somerset NJ 08873

RAGAN, BARBARA MARY, television and theater producer, financial management and real estate company executive; b. Toledo, Ohio, Feb. 27, 1949; d. Robert Charles and Edith Lucy (Mahoney) R. B.A., Cath. U. Am., 1971; M.B.A., NYU, 1986. Producer, assoc. producer Broadway/Regional Theatre, 1974-77; asst. gen. mgr. Alexander H. Cohen Prodns., N.Y., 1977-79, acct. pub. Livingston Wachtell & Co., C.P.A.'s, N.Y., 1979-82; mgr. theater programming RCTV-Entertainment Channel, N.Y., 1982-83; controller Ornstein Orgn., N.Y., 1983-85; v.p., exec. producer Candico Prodns., Inc. N.Y.C., 19—; cons. to office of chmn. Cen. Fed. Savs. and Loan, N.Y., 1987—; adv. bd. Actors Studio, N.Y.; controller N.Y. Women in Film, N.Y., 1984—; cons. Cable TV Studies, 1976—. Contbr. articles to profl. jours. Intern U.S. House Reps., Washington, 1967-68; conferee White House Conf. on Conservation and Natural Beauty, Washington, 1967; mem. U.S. State Dept. Tour of Europe, 1970-71, Nat. Trust for Hist. Preservation. Recipient Ohio Conservationist award Ohio Forestry Assn., 1967. Nat. Merit Found. scholar 1967-71. Mem. Dramatists Guild, N.Y. Acad. TV Arts and Scis. Avocation: music. Home: 60 E 9th St New York NY 10003

RAGO, NICHOLAS A., transportation company executive; b. 1942. BS, Temple U., 1972. Dist. mgr. Foremost McKesson Corp., Phila., 1960-68, Campbell Soup Co., Camden, N.J., 1968-77; v.p. Armour div. Greyhound Corp., Phoenix, 1977-84; v.p. frozen foods div. ConAgra Corp., 1984-86; pres., dir. Transp. Leasing Co. (formerly Greyhound Lines Inc.), Phoenix, 1987—. Office: Transp Leasing Co Greyhound Tower Phoenix AZ 85077 *

RAGONE, DAVID VINCENT, former university president; b. N.Y.C., May 16, 1930; s. Armando Frederick and Mary (Napier) R.; m. Katherine H. Spaulding, Dec. 18, 1954; children: Christine M., Peter V. S.B., MIT, 1951, S.M., 1952, Sc.D., 1953. Asst. prof. chem. and metall. engring. U. Mich., Ann Arbor, 1953-57; assoc. prof. U. Mich., 1957-61, prof., 1961-62; asst. dir. John J. Hopkins Lab for Pure and Applied Sci., also chmn. metallurgy dept. Gen. Atomic div. Gen Dynamics, La Jolla, 1962-67; Alcoa prof. metallurgy Carnegie-Mellon U., Pitts., 1967-69; assoc. dean Carnegie-Mellon U. (Sch. Urban and Pub. Affairs), 1969-70; dean Thayer Sch. of Engring., Dartmouth Coll., 1970-72, U. Mich. (Coll. Engring.), 1972-80; pres. Case Western Res. U., Cleve., 1980-87; vis. prof., dept. materials sci. and engring. MIT, Cambridge, Mass., 1987—; gen. ptnr. Ampersand Specialty Materials Venture, 1988—; trustee Mitre Corp.; bd. dirs. Cabot Corp., Cleve. Cliffs Iron Co., Augat Inc., Sifco Inc. Mem. Nat. Sci. Bd., 1978-84; mem. tech adv. bd. U.S. Dept. Commerce, 1967-75; chmn. adv. com. advanced auto power systems Council on Environ. Quality, 1971-75; Trustee Henry Luce Found. Named Outstanding Young Engr., Engring. Soc. Detroit, 1957. Mem. Sigma Xi, Tau Beta Pi. Clubs: Cosmos (Washington); Union (Cleve.); University (N.Y.C.). Office: MIT Dept Materials Sci & Engring Rm 8-301 Cambridge MA 02139

RAGSDALE, LINCOLN JOHNSON, insurance company executive; b. Muskogee, Okla., July 27, 1926; m. Eleanor Dickey; children: Elizabeth, Gwendolyn Madrid, Lincoln J. III, Emily. Diploma in instrument and comml. flying, Tuskegee Inst.; diploma in acctg. and mgmt., Lamson Bus. Coll.; diploma magna cum laude, Calif. Coll. Mortuary Sci.; AA with distinction, Phoenix Coll.; BSBA with distinction, Ariz. State U.; LLD (hon.), Shorter Coll.; postgrad., Union Coll., Cin. Lic. real estate broker, Ariz., lic. gen. ins. agt., Ariz., lic. bldg. contractor, Ariz., lic. comml. pilot. Pres. Internat. Investment Co., Phoenix, 1952, also bd. dirs.; pres. Valley Life & Casualty Ins. Group, Phoenix, 1964—, also bd. dirs.; pres. Valley Life Ins. Co. of Ala., 1980—, also bd. dirs.; pres. Valley Life & Casualty Ins. co. of La., 1980—, also bd. dirs.; pres. Valley Life & Casualty Ins. Co. of Tex., 1983—, also bd. dirs.; ptnr. Home Realty and Ins. Agy.; advisor to Pres. Reagan on Small and Minority Bus., 1982—, chmn. sub-com. banking and ins.; bd. dirs. Universal Meml. Ctr., Phoenix, Universal Sunset Chapel, Phoenix, Sun State Savs. and Loan Assn., Phoenix. Mem. Mcpl. Aero. Adv. Bd., Phoenix, 1972-77, chmn. 1976-77; past 2st v.p. NAACP; trustee Rust Coll., Holly Springs, Miss., Nat. Urban League, 1977-82, Meml. Hosp. found., 1978-85; bd. dirs. NCCJ, 1957—, Nat. Bus. League, Washington, Ariz. Civic Unity Council. Served to 2d lt. U.S. Army, 1944-46. Mem. Ariz. State U. Alumni Assn. (pres. 1976-77), Am. Legion, Iota Sigma Alpha, Omega Psi Phi, Sigma Pi Phi (Grand Boule). Club: The Arizona (Phoenix). Lodges: Masons (33 degree), Shriners. Office: Universal Meml Ctr 1100 E Jefferson St Phoenix AZ 85034

RAIFF, FREDERIC KAUFMAN, retail executive; b. N.Y.C., Dec. 18, 1927; s. Isadore Raiff and Maurine Clare (Kaufman) Schreiber; m. Pauline Raiff, June 12, 1975; children: Dorie, Richard, Robert. BBA, Lehigh U., 1949; MS, Columbia U., 1950. Pres., chmn. bd. Raylass Dept. Stores, N.Y.C., 1953—, U.S. Factory Outlets, Inc., N.Y.C., 1983—, Seville, Ltd., N.Y.C., 1985—; bd. dirs. Alleco, Cheverly, Md. Master sgt. U.S. Army, 1946-48. Office: US Factory Outlets Inc 7 Penn Pla New York NY 10001

RAIGO, MARIANO MARCELO, marketing executive, video station partner; b. Buenos Aires, Apr. 20, 1952; came to U.S., 1973; s. Henry and Eva Sara Raigo; divorced; children: Nealy Eve, Cory Brook. Student electronic tech., Buenos Aires; grad., N.C. State U. Sales and service rep. Southeastern Sight & Sound, Raleigh, N.C., 1973-75; ptnr. Le Chocolait, Asheville, 1984-85, Heavenly Hams, Asheville, 1984-85, Video Station, Asheville, N.C., 1976—. Recipient Retailer of Yr. award Videostore Mag., Las Vegas, 1985, NARDA Bell Cow award for Merchandising Innovation. Mem. Nat. Assn. Retailer Dealer Assns., Sales and Mktg., Rotary. Office: Video Sta 513 McDowell St Asheville NC 28803

RAIKES, CHARLES FITZGERALD, lawyer; b. Mpls., Oct. 6, 1930; s. Arthur FitzGerald and Margaret (Hawthorne) R.; m. Antonia Raikes, Dec. 20, 1969; children: Jennifer Catherine, Victoria Samantha. B.A., Washington U., 1952; M.A., Harvard U., 1955, LL.B., 1958. Bar: N.Y. State 1959. Assoc. White & Case, N.Y.C., 1958-69; assoc. gen. counsel Dun & Bradstreet, Inc., N.Y.C., 1969-72; v.p., gen. counsel Dun & Bradstreet, Inc., 1972-73, The Dun & Bradstreet Corp., N.Y.C., 1973-76; sr. v.p., gen. counsel The Dun & Bradstreet Corp., 1976—; cons. Bd. Govs. Fed. Reserve System, 1958—. Served with U.S. Army, 1952-54. Woodrow Wilson fellow, 1952. Mem. Assn. Bar City N.Y., Phi Beta Kappa. Clubs: Board Room, Harvard. Home: 25 Rowayton Woods Dr Norwalk CT 06854 Office: Dun & Bradstreet Corp 299 Park Ave New York NY 10171

RAIMONDI, PETER JOHN III, lawyer, financial consultant; b. Winthrop, Mass., July 28, 1955; s. Peter John Jr. and Erma Dorothy (Oliver) R.; m. Christine Mary Welch, Aug. 29, 1976; children: Elizabeth, Jessica. Student, Mass. Coll. of Art, 1977-80; BLS, Boston U., 1980, JD, 1983. Bar: Mass. 1984. Fin. cons. The AYCO Corp., Inc., Albany, N.Y., 1983-84; portfolio mgr., sr. fin. cons. Weston Fin. Group, Wellesley, Mass., 1984-86; co-founder, mng. dir. The Colony Group, Inc., Boston, 1986—; dir. The Blackstone Bank and Trust, Boston, 1987—. Mng. editor Probate Law Jour., Boston U., 1982-83; contbr. articles to mags. and profl. jours. Mem. ABA, Mass. Bar Assn., Boston Bar Assn., Internat. Assn. of Fin. Planners. Home: 1 Seal Harbor Rd 208 Winthrop MA 02152 Office: The Colony Group Inc 199 State St Boston MA 02109

RAINBOLT, JOHN VERNON, II, lawyer; b. Cordell, Okla., May 24, 1939; s. John Vernon (Mike) and Mary Alice (Power) R.; m. Janice Glaub, Oct. 2, 1976; children—John Vernon, III, Sara McLain, Charles Joseph. B.A., Okla. U., 1961, LL.B., 1964; postgrad. George Washington U. 1971-73. Bar: Okla. 1964, D.C. 1971, U.S. Supreme Ct. 1971. Legis. counsel, adminstrv. asst. U.S. Rep. Graham Purcell, Washington, 1967-72; counsel agr. com. U.S. Ho. of Reps., Washington, 1972-74, chief counsel, 1975; commr. Commodity Futures Trading Commn., Washington, 1975-78; sole practice, Washington, 1978—; ptnr. Miles & Stockbridge, Washington, 1982-86; advisor agr. policy Tokyo Roundtable White House, 1978-81; mem. Adminstrn. Conf., U.S., 1976-79. Author and draftsman Commodity Futures Trading Commn. Act, 1974; contbr. articles to legal jours. Served to 1st lt. Inf., U.S. Army, 1964-67. Vice chmn. Commodity Futures Trading Commn., 1975-78. Mem. ABA (chmn. subcom. on fgn. markets and traders 1982-85), U.S. Futures Industry Assn. (assoc.). Clubs: Commodity of Washington, Pisces. Office: 655 15th St NW Ste 300 Washington DC 20005

RAINES, RONALD BRUCE, accountant; b. Sydney, Australia, Nov. 6, 1929; s. Douglas William and Jean Laurie (Pilcher) R.; m. Helen Janet Cadwallader, Oct. 21, 1977; children: Ronald Douglas, Fenella Jann, Douglas Antony. Diploma Sydney Boys High Sch., 1947. Ptnr. R.A. Irish & Michelmore, Chartered Accts., Sydney, 1955-65; dep. chmn. Alexander Stenhouse Ltd.; chmn. bd. Pastoral & Agrl. Mgmt. Ltd., Australian Elec. Industries Ltd., 1964-68, New South Wales State Dockyard, 1968-77; chmn. Med. Resources Ltd.; dep. chmn. Letona Coop Ltd.; bd. dirs. W.C. Penfold Ltd., Stenhouse Securities Ltd., Found. 41, 600 Machinery Australia Pty. Ltd., Australian Canned Fruits Corp., Case Communication Systems Ltd. Mem. Legis. Council New South Wales, 1977-78, Met. (Sydney) Waste Disposal Authority. Fellow Chartered Inst. Accts. Australia, Australian Inst. Mgmt., Inst. Dirs. Clubs: Australian, Royal Sydney Golf, Australian Jockey, Bowral Golf. Home: Point Piper, New South Wales Australia Office: GPO Box 1742, Sydney, New South Wales, Australia

RAINES, TIM D., real estate corporation executive; b. Everett, Wash., May 8, 1950; s. Richard Thomas and Arvilla Mae (Chick) R.; m. Virginia N. McLaurin, July 21, 1977. BA, U. Ala., Tuscaloosa, 1968-72; MA, U. Alabama, Birmingham, 1977; postgrad., U. Calif., 1976-77. Community planner HUD, Birmingham, 1972-77; dir., program planning and eval. HUD, Atlanta, 1977-83, dir. regional ops. div., 1983-87; exec. v.p. chief operating officer Sanbury Corp., Atlanta, 1987—. Pres. Stonington Homeowners Assn., Atlanta, 1980-83; patron Atlanta Ballet, 1978—; sponsor Pub. TV (WPBA), Atlanta, 1980—. Recipient Cert. of Recognition William A. Jump Found., 1978. Mem. Am. Soc. Pub. Adminstrs., Am. Mgmt. Assn., Atlanta Zool. Soc. Home: 8315 Ison Rd Atlanta GA 30350

RAINEY, JAMES LEE, JR., chemical company executive; b. Nashville, Dec. 4, 1929; s. James Lee and Elsie Mallory R.; m. Edith Esther Normington, Feb. 17, 1952; children—James, Patrick J., Robert L., Sarah Lee, Jason N. B.S., Purdue U., 1952. Gen. mgr. eastern agri-chem. ops. Kerr-McGee Chem. Corp., Balt., 1968-72; v.p., gen. mgr. agri-chem. ops. Kerr-McGee Chem. Corp., Oklahoma City, 1968-72; v.p. chem. mktg. div. Kerr-McGee Chem. Corp., 1972-75, pres., 1975-86; pres., chief exec. officer Farmland Industries, Kansas City, Mo., 1986—; bd. dirs. Commerce Bank Kansas City, NA. Mem. Deer Creek Sch. Bd., 1975-79; dir. Oklahoma County ARC, 1971-73; mem. Deer Creek Sch. Planning Com., Episcopal Diocesan Bishop's Planning Commn. Served with U.S. Army, 1952-54. Mem. Chem. Mfr.'s Assn. Republican. Episcopalian. Home: 4009 Birdneck Route 1 Edmond OK 73034

RAINEY, WILLIAM JOEL, lawyer; b. Flint, Mich., Oct. 11, 1946; s. Ralph Jefferson and Elsie Matilda (Erickson) R.; m. Cynthia Hetsko, June 15, 1968; children—Joel Michael, Allison Elizabeth. A.B., Harvard U., 1968; J.D., U. Mich., 1971. Bar: N.Y. 1973, U.S. Dist. Ct. (so. and ea. dists.) N.Y. 1973, U.S. Ct. Appeals (2nd cir.) 1973, Wash. 1977, U.S. Dist. Ct. (we. dist.) Wash. 1977, U.S. Supreme Ct. 1976, U.S. Ct. Appeals (9th cir.) 1978, Ariz. 1987, U.S. Dist. Ct. Ariz. 1987. Assoc. atty. Curtis, Mallet-Prevost, Colt & Mosle, N.Y.C., 1971-76; atty., asst. corp. sec. Weyerhaeuser Co., Tacoma, Wash., 1976-85; v.p., corp. sec., gen. counsel Southwest Forest Industries Inc., Phoenix, 1985-87; sr. vp., corp. sec., gen. counsel Valley Nat. Corp. and Valley Nat. Bank, Phoenix, 1987—; chmn. taskforce ABA, Chgo., 1984—. Editor U. Mich. Jour. Law Reform, 1970-71. Bd. dirs. Mcpl. League Seattle and King County, 1982-84; bd. dirs. 1st Ave. Svc. Ctr., Seattle, 1977-85 ; chmn. Bellevue Planning Commn., Wash., 1984. Maj. USAR, 1970—. Mem. ABA, Wash. State Bar Assn., Ariz. Bar Assn., Rotary. Presbyterian. Home: 5478 E Cholla St Scottsdale AZ 85254 Office: Valley Nat Corp PO Box 71 Phoenix AZ 85001

RAISANEN, WALFRED RICHARD, electronics company executive; b. Wakefield, Mich., Apr. 3, 1935; s. Isaac Walfred and Edith Matilda (Niemi) R.; m. Jeraldine Dorothy Smith, Dec. 14, 1959; children: Wendy, Carol, Eric. BEE, Mich. Technol. U., 1957; MEE, U. Minn., 1965; MBA, Ariz. State U., 1970. Engr. mech. div. Gen. Mills Co., Mpls., 1957-59; rsch. and devel. dept. mgr. Sperry Rand Univac, Mpls., 1959-65; integrated circuit rsch. and devel. mgr. Motorola Semicondr. Co., Phoenix, 1965-70; product mgr. Motorola Metal Oxide Semicondr. Ops., Mesa, Ariz., 1970-76; chief engr. Motorola Rifle Systems, Scottsdale, Ariz., 1976-78; mgr. Motorola New Venture Lab., Phoenix, 1978-81; chmn. Ariz. Instrument Corp., Tempe, 1981—; adj. prof. Karl Eller Sch., U. Ariz., Tucson, 1986—. Patentee in field. Entrepreneurial fellow U. Ariz. Bus. Sch., 1985. Mem. IEEE (sr., chmn. Phoenix sect. 1981), Enterprise Network (bd. dirs. 1987—, Promethean award 1985), Ariz. Mus. Sci. and Tech. (bd. dirs. 1986—), Ariz. Soaring Assn. (pres. 1980-81). Office: Ariz Instrument Corp PO Box 1930 Tempe AZ 85281

RAKOCHEVICH, WOOLAY, public mediator, behavioral scientist; b. Belgrade, Yugoslavia, Jan. 10, 1939; came to U.S., 1969; s. Milinko and Zivana (Zujovic) R.; married; 1 child, Beck. PhD in Behavioral Sci., Ljubljana U., Yugaslavia, 1964; postgrad., Columbia U., 1976; PhD, NYU, 1980. Pvt. practice psychology Paradise Valley, Ariz., 1977-85; founder Pub. Mediator Office, Inc., Scottsdale, Ariz., 1981—. Author: How to Become a Public Mediator, 1985; contbr. articles on marriage to profl. jours.; inventor method of mind control without drugs, 1987. Republican. Serbian Orthodox.

RAKUNAS, NADINE MARIE, real estate broker, consultant; b. Oak Lawn, Ill., Feb. 15, 1963; d. Jerome Bruno and Carolyn Ann (Contant) R. Student, Moraine Valley Community Coll., Palos Hills, Ill., 1985. Lic. real estate broker. Mgr. svc. and parts dept. Indsl. Forklift, Addison, Ill., 1983-85; mgr. Realty World -Forst, Palos Heights, Ill., 1985-87; broker, mortgage cons. Realty World -Chgo. Diversified Svcs., Oak Lawn, 1987-89, mgr., 1989—. Mem. Nat. Assn. Realtors, Southwest Suburban Bd., Guys n'Dolls Club (pres. 1987—).

RALEIGH, WALTER JAMES, textile company executive; b. Newark, Feb. 28, 1928; s. Walter J. and Eleanor F. (Stevens) R.; widowed; children: Kimberly, Christopher. BS, Seton Hall U., 1950. Gen. sales mgr. Chicopee Mfg. Co., Boston, Evanston, Cornelia, N.Y.C., Ill., Ga., 1964-74; pres. Clinton Mills Sales Co., N.Y.C., 1974—; instr. Northeastern U., 1956-60; sr. v.p. N.Y. Bd. Trade, 1981; chmn. Textile Sect., 1975-77. Past bd. dirs. N.Y. Found. for Sr. Citizens; mem. Mayor's Adv. Coun., N.Y.C., 1981—; exec. v.p. Greater N.Y. Coun. Boy Scouts Am. With USCG, 1945-47. Recipient Svc. to Humanity award March of Dimes, 1984, Man of the Yr. award Textile Salesmen's Assn., Inc., 1986, Silver Beaver award Boy Scouts Am., 1987. Mem. Am. Textile Mfrs. Inst. (chmn. mktg. com. 1980), Amti-Defamation League B'nai B'rith (chmn. 1980, Torch of Liberty award 1982), Univ. Club. Home: 1000 Hudson St Hoboken NJ 07030 Office: Clinton Mills Sales Co 111 W 40th St New York NY 10018

RALES, MITCHELL P., automotive parts company executive; b. 1956; married. Pres. Danaher Corp., Washington, 1984—, also bd. dirs.; with Equity Group Holdings, Washington, 1979—. Office: Danaher Corp 3524 Water St NW Washington DC 20007 *

RALES, STEVEN M., automotive parts company executive; b. Pitts., Mar. 31, 1951; married. BA, DePauw U., 1973; JD, America U., 1978. With Equity Group Holdings, Washington, 1979—; chmn., chief exec. officer Danaher Corp., Washington, 1984—. Office: Danaher Corp 3524 Water St NW Washington DC 20007 *

RALEY, JAMES MORRIS, JR., insurance company executive; b. Leonardtown, Md., Aug. 27, 1950; s. James Morris Sr. and Mary Lou (Johnson) R.; m. Harriet Joanne Condon, July 15, 1972; children: Tracy, Shelley, Richie, Jami. BBA, U. Notre Dame, 1972; MPA, Loyola Coll., Balt., 1983. Staff B. auditor Coopers and Lybrand, Balt., 1972-73, staff A. auditor, 1973-74, audit sr., 1974-75, audit supr., 1975-76; acct. U.S. Fidelity and Guaranty Co., Balt., 1976-77, asst. treas., 1977-78, asst. v.p., 1978-81, v.p., treas., 1981-82, sr. v.p. fin., 1982-88, exec. v.p., 1988—; pres., dir. USF&G Fin. Svcs. Corp. Active Cen. Md. United Way, mem. fin. com., audit com., endowment and investment com., long range planning com. Mem. AICPA, Md. Assn. CPAs, Fin. Execs. Inst., Soc. Ins. Accts. Republican. Roman Catholic. Home: 547 Pointfield Dr Millersville MD 21108 Office: USF&G Corp 100 Light St Baltimore MD 21202

RALLO, JAMES GILBERT, fleet management company executive; b. Balt., Mar. 1, 1942; s. James Vincent and Thelma Mary (Hannahs) R.; m. Frances Elaine Petro, June 13, 1965; children: James Michael, Robert Francis. BS, U. Md., 1965; postgrad., George Washington U., 1967—. Mktg. trainee Chessie System, Balt., 1965-66; market analyst Bendix Corp., Balt., 1966-68, contract adminstr., N.Y.C., 1968-70; account exec. Peterson, Howell & Heather, Inc., Hunt Valley, Md., 1970-75, regional mgr., 1975-80, v.p. sales, 1980-83, v.p. sales and client relations, 1983-87, sr. v.p. sales and client relations, 1987—. Bd. dirs., mem. fin. com. Towson YMCA, Md., 1981—; coach Cockeysville-Springlake Recreation Council, 1973-82. Mem. Nat. Assn. Fleet Adminstrs. (bd. dirs. 1978-81, affiliate chmn. intercounty chpt. 1980). Club: Optimists (chmn. fundraising com., v.p. Springdale-Cockeysville 1982-84). Avocations: sports car racing, skiing, coaching youth sports, antique cars, reading. Office: Fleet Am 307 International Cir Hunt Valley MD 21031

RALSON, LESLEY LLOYD, insurance company executive; b. Rusk, Tex., Oct. 12, 1929; s. James Herbert and Virginia Mae (Sword) R.; m. Dorothy Ralson, Sept. 14, 1984; children: William Garrett, Dana Marie; children by previous marriage—Leslie Ann, Sylvia Simone, Stephanie Jean. B.B.A., U. Houston, 1952; grad., Am. Coll. Life Underwriters, Pa., 1963; postgrad. in bus. adminstrn., Columbia U., 1975. C.L.U. Mgmt. trainee Prudential Ins. Co. Am., Houston, 1957-59, group service rep., 1959-60; group sales rep. Prudential Ins. Co. Am., Tulsa, 1960-61, dist. group mgr., 1961-63, dist. group supr., 1963-64; regional group mgr. Prudential Ins. Co. Am., Milw., 1964-66; assoc. dir. group ins. Prudential Ins. Co. Am., Newark, 1966-67, dir. group sales and service, 1967; dir. group ins. Prudential Ins. Co. Am., Houston, 1967-71, v.p. group ins., 1971-73; v.p. Prudential Ins. Co. Am., Newark, 1973-77; sr. v.p. Prudential Ins. Co. Am., Newark and Roseland, N.J., 1977-87, pres. group ops., 1987—; chmn. PruCare, Houston, PruCare of Okla., PruCo Life of Ill., Tesseract, Inc. Served to 1st lt. USMC, 1952-57. Office: The Prudential Ins Co Am 56 N Livingston Ave Roseland NJ 07068 also: The Prudential Ins Co Am Prudential Pla Newark NJ 07101

RALSTON, GARY MICHAEL, real estate executive; b. Louisville, Nov. 11, 1950; s. Elsworth Emory and Wilma Ruth (Kendall) R.; m. Connie Sue O'Guin, Dec. 19, 1981; children: Lauren, Ruth-Ann. Buyer Maas Bros., Tampa, Fla., 1971-75; v.p. Arthur Richards, Ltd., N.Y.C., 1976-78, Ralston Real Estate, Lakeland, Fla., 1979-82, Exec. Nat. Devel. Corp., Lakeland, 1983—; bd. dirs. Bd. of Realtors, Lakeland, Fla.; nat. instr. Comml. Investment Real Estate Council, Chgo., 1985—; mem. editorial bd. Investment Real Estate Jour., Chgo., 1985—. Mem. Fla. Assn. Realtors, Realtors Nat. Mktg. Inst. (CCIM, CRS), Soc. Indsl. and Office Realtors, Real Estate Securities and Syndication Inst., U.S. C. of C. (bd. dirs. 1985—). Home: One Lake Hollingsworth Pl #10 Lakeland FL 33803 Office: Exec Nat Devel Corp 129 S Kentucky Ste 900 Lakeland FL 33801

RAMADAN, SAR, design automation company executive; b. Ismaila, Egypt, Feb. 8, 1943; came to U.S., 1970; s. Hosny and Saadia (Awad) R.; m. Carol Mulcahy, Aug. 1, 1987; children: Samira, Janine, Celene, Ameer, Ramadan. BS, Ain Shams U., Cairo, 1965; MBA, U. New Haven, 1974; postgrad., Harvard U., 1986. Fin. adminstr. Suez Canal Authority, Ismailia, 1962-70; plant acct. Cities Services Corp., New Haven, 1971-73; corp. controller Home Care Services, New Haven, 1973-74; contract controller GTE Internat., Burlington, Mass., 1974-79; v.p. group controller Computervision Corp., Bedford, Mass., 1979-86; v.p. fin., controller CAD/CAM Resources, Inc., Waltham, Mass., 1986-87; corp. controller Mentor Graphics Corp., Portland, Oreg., 1987—; cons. Supercads Inc., Calif., 1986, TSI Internat., Mass., 1986. Mem. Harvard Alumni Assn. Republican. Home: 2431 Palisades Crest Lake Oswego OR 97034 Office: Mentor Graphics Corp 8500 SW Creekside Beaverton OR 97005

RAMAKRISHNAN, VENKATASWAMY, civil engineer, educator; b. Coimbatore, India, Feb. 27, 1929; came to U.S., 1969, naturalized, 1981; s. Venkataswamy and Kondammal (Krishnaswamy) R.; m. Vijayalakshmi Unnava, Nov. 7, 1962; children: Aravind, Anand. B.Engring., U. Madras, 1952, D.S.S., 1953; D.I.C. in Hydropower and Concrete Tech, Imperial Coll., London, 1957; Ph.D., Univ. Coll., U. London, 1960. From lectr. to prof. civil engring., head dept. P.S.G. Coll. Tech., U. Madras, 1952-69; vis. prof. S.D. Sch. Mines and Tech., Rapid City, 1969-70; prof. civil engring. S.D. Sch. Mines and Tech., 1970—, dir. concrete tech. research, 1970-71, head grad. div. structural mechanic and concrete tech., 1971—, program coordinator materials engring. and sci. Ph.D. program, 1985-86; cons., 1955—; Founding mem. PSGR Children's Sch., 1961; founding dir. World Open U., 1974, v.p., 1980—. Author: Ultimate Strength Design for Structural Concrete, 1969; also over 100 articles. Colombo Plan fellow, 1955-60; recipient Outstanding Prof. award S.D. Sch. Mines and Tech., 1980. Mem. Internat. Assn. Bridge and Structural Engring., ASCE (vice chmn. constrn. div. publs. com. 1974), Am. Concrete Inst. (chmn. subcom. gen. considerations for founds., chmn. com. 214 on evaluation of strength test results, sec.-treas. Dakota chpt. 1974-79, v.p. 1980, pres. 1981), Instn. Hwy. Engrs., Transp. Research Bd. (chmn. com. on mech. properties of concrete), Am. Soc. Engring. Edn., Nat. Soc. Profl. Engrs., Internat. Council Gap-Graded Concrete Research and Application (sec. 1973-78), Sigma Xi (chpt. treas. 1975-78). Address: 1809 Sheridan Lake Rd Rapid City SD 57701

RAMAMURTHY, SABRAMANIAN, management consultant; b. Coimbatore, Madras, India, Nov. 25, 1948. B Tech., Indian Inst. Tech., Madras/Tamilnadu, 1970; MS in Engring., U. Madras, 1972; PhD, Cornell U., 1977. Asst. prof. U. Ill., 1977-79; stress analyst ConRail, Phila., 1979-81; engr. Stone & Webster Engring. Corp., Cherry Hill, N.J., 1981-87; staff engring. group leader Stone & Webster Engring. Corp., 1982, structural engr., 1982; lead engr. Stone & Webster Engring. Corp., Monroe, Mich., 1985; sr. structural engr. Stone & Webster Engring. Corp., 1986; pres. Optimum Mgmt. Inc., Canton, Mich., 1987; bd. dirs. Optimum Mgmt. Inc., 1987—; advisor award-winning projects Lincoln Arc Welding Found., Cleve. Contbr. numerous articles to profl. jours. Mem. Am. Soc. Civil Engring., Am. Soc. Mech. Engrs., Soc. Mnfg. Engrs., Engring. Soc. of Detroit, Am. Concrete Inst., Rotary, Tau Beta Pi, Chi Epsilon, Sigma-Xi. Office: Optimum Mgmt Inc 127 S Main St Plymouth MI 48170

RAMAT, CHARLES SAMUEL, entrepreneur; b. Vienna, Austria, May 25, 1951; came to U.S., 1954; s. Emil and Hana (Landa) R.; m. Ora Maidenbaum, Nov. 22, 1972; children: Hana Leah, Abraham Gabriel. BA, Yeshiva Coll., 1971; JD, Columbia U., 1974. investor, N.Y.C., 1984—. Cochmn. The Mid-Manhattan Polit. Action Com., 1984—. Mem. The Town Club. Jewish. Office: The Marcade Group Inc 805 Third Ave New York NY 10022

RAMBERT, GORDON ARTHUR, management consultant executive, recruitment executive; b. Rochester, N.Y., Mar. 6, 1922; s. Arthur Frederick and Mildred (Baker) R.; B.S., Lehigh U., 1949; m. Jeanne Audrey Bucher, Dec. 27, 1947; children—Paul A., Cynthia L., Gregory N., Michele M. Personnel mgr. Jamestown Malleable Iron Corp. (N.Y.), 1955-58; mgr. compensation Todd div. Burroughs Corp., Rochester, 1958-64; asst. sec., dir. personnel Consol-Vacuum Corp., Rochester, 1964-66; v.p. indsl. relations Joslyn Mfg. & Supply Co., Chgo., 1966-70; pres. Rambert and Co., Inc., mgmt. cons. and exec. recruitment, Gainesville, Fla., 1970—; adv. cons. on exec. compensation Midwest Indsl. Mgmt. Assn. Served with Signal Corps AUS, 1942-46. Mem. Am. Soc. Personnel Adminstrn. (dir. 1968—, treas. 1970, 71). Home: 8419 SW 46th Rd Gainesville FL 32601 Office: 4131 NW 13th St Gainesville FL 32609

RAMER, JAMES LEROY, Civil engineer; b. Marshalltown, Iowa, Dec. 7, 1935; s. LeRoy Frederick and Irene (Wengert) R.; m. Jacqueline L. Orr, Dec. 15, 1957; children: Sarah T., Robert H., Eric A., Susan L. Student U. Iowa, 1953-57; MCE, Washington U., St. Louis, 1976, MA in Polit. Sci., 1978; postgrad. U. Mo., Columbia, 1984—. Registered profl. engr., land surveyor. Civil and constrn. engr. U.S. Army C.E., Tulsa, 1960-63; civil and relocations engr. U.S. State Dept., Del Rio, Tex., 1964; project engr. H. B. Zachry Co., San Antonio, 1965-66; civil and constrn. engr. U.S. Army C.E., St. Louis, 1967-76, tech. advisor for planning and nat. hydropower coordinator, 1976-78, project mgr. for EPA constrn. grants, Milw., 1978-80; chief architecture and engring. HUD, Indpls., 1980-81;civil design and pavements engr. Whiteman AFB, Mo., 1982-86; soil and pavements engr. Hdqtrs. Mil. Airlift Command, Scott AFB, Ill., 1986-88; project manager AF-1 maintenance hangar; cattle and grain farmer, 1982—; pvt. practice civil/mech. engr., constrn. mgmt., expert witness, Sedalia, Mo., 1988—; adj. faculty civil engring. Washington U., 1968-78, U. Wis., Milw., 1978-80. Ga. Mil. Coll., Whiteman AFB.; adj. research engr. U. Mo., Columbia, 1985—. Holder 25 U.S. patents in diverse art, 7 copyrights. Mem. ASCE, Nat. Soc. Profl. Engrs., Soc. Am. Mil. Engrs., AAUP. Lutheran. Club: Optimists Internat. Home: Rte 1 PO Box 50-AA Fortuna MO 65034

RAMIREZ-PORTILLA, CARLOS ALFONSO, architect; b. Guatemala, May 18, 1949; s. Carlos Humberto Ramirez Aldana and Estela Portilla Wright; m. Elisa Sinibaldi Dalton, Nov. 20, 1976; children: Juan Pablo Jose Antonio, Carlos Adolfo. BArch, U. San Carlos, Guatemala City, 1974; postgrad., U. San Carlos; MBA, U. Francisco Mauroquin, Guatemala City, 1985. Exec. architect Comosa, Guatemala City, 1972-78; pres. C.R.P. Assocs., Guatemala City, 1978—, Showbiz Pizza Place, Guatemala City; dir. Jeff Tours Guatemala. Author: Proyeccion Universiaria Dos Parametros,

1974. Recipient hon. mention Guatemalan Archtl. Mag., 1978, Guatemala C. of C. mem. Interam. Assn., AIA Guatemala. Roman Catholic. Lodge: Rotary. Office: 9 Avenida 4-61, Zona 9, Guatemala City Guatemala also: Ave Reforma 7-62, Zona 9, Guatemala City Guatemala

RAMISCAL, ELMER FEBENITO, financial planner; b. Ilocos Norte, Philippines, Sept. 9, 1942; came to U.S., 1961; s. Bernardino Alonzo and Florentina (Febenito) R.; m. Erlinda Oana , Oct. 7, 1968; children: Ermin Ross, Eileen Michelle. Student, Northwestern Coll., Laoag, Ilocos Norte, 1959-61; BS in Mgmt., Golden Gate U., 1982; postgrad., Old Dominion U., Norfolk, Va., 1983-84. Enlisted USN, 1961, advanced through grades to sr. chief petty officer, ret., 1983; ednl. sales rep. LaSalle Extension U., Norfolk, Va., 1972-73; owner, operator Royal Products, Norfolk, 1973-77; real estate agt. St. George Real Estate, Norfolk, 1977-79; rep. Waddell & Reed, Inc., Virginia Beach, Va., 1983-88; fin. planner Waddell & Reed, Inc., 1986—; instr. Coll. Fin. Planning, Virginia Beach, 1987—. Pres. United Ilocano Assn. of Tidewater, Virginia Beach, 1978-79; bd. dirs. Council of United Filipino Orgns., Virginia Beach, 1988; auditor Filipino-Am. Vets, 1988; treas. Filipino Businessmen of Hampton Rds., 1988. Mem. Inst. Cert. Fin. Planners, Internat. Assn. Fin. Planners. Home: 612 Nicklaus Ct Virginia Beach VA 23462 Office: Waddell & Reed Inc 505 S Independence Blvd Ste 110 Virginia Beach VA 23452

RAMO, SIMON, engineering executive; b. Salt Lake City, May 7, 1913; s. Benjamin and Clara (Trestman) R.; m. Virginia Smith, July 25, 1937; children: James Brian, Alan Martin. B.S., U. Utah, 1933, D.Sc. (hon.), 1961; Ph.D., Calif. Inst. Tech., 1936; D.Eng. (hon.), Case Inst. Tech., 1960, U. Mich., 1966, Poly. Inst. N.Y., 1971; D.Sc. (hon.), Union Coll., 1963, Worcester Poly. Inst., 1968, U. Akron, 1969, Cleve. State U., 1976; LL.D. (hon.), Carnegie-Mellon U., 1970, U. So. Calif., 1972, Gonzaga U., 1983, Occidental Coll., 1984, Gonzaga U., 1983, Occidental Coll., 1984. With Gen. Electric Co., 1936-46; v.p. ops. Hughes Aircraft Co., 1946-53; with Ramo-Woolridge Corp., 1953-58; sci. dir. U.S. intercontinental guided missile program 1954-58; dir. TRW Inc., 1954—, vice chmn. bd., 1961-78, chmn. exec. com., 1969-78; chmn. bd. TRW-Fujitsu Co., 1980-83; pres. The Bunker-Ramo Corp., 1964-66; vis. prof. mgmt. sci. Calif. Inst. Tech., 1978—; Regents lectr. UCLA, 1981-82, U. Calif. at Santa Cruz, 1978-79; chmn. Center for Study Am. Experience, U. So. Calif., 1978-80; Faculty fellow John F. Kennedy Sch. Govt., Harvard U., 1980—; dir. Union Bank, 1965—, Atlantic Richfield Co., 1984-86; past dir. Times Mirror Co., 1968-83; Mem. White House Energy Research and Devel. Adv. Council, 1973-75; mem. adv. com. on sci. and fgn. affairs U.S. State Dept., 1973-75; chmn. Pres.'s Com. on Sci. and Tech., 1976-77; mem. adv. council to Sec. Commerce, 1976-77; co-chmn. Transitition Task Force on Sci. and Tech. for Pres.-elect Reagan; mem. roster consultants to adminstr. ERDA, 1976-77; bd. advisors for sci. and tech. Republic of China, 1981—. Author: The Business of Science, 1988, other sci., engring. and mgmt. books. Bd. dirs. Los Angeles World Affairs Council; bd. dirs. Music Center Found., Los Angeles, Los Angeles Philharm. Assn.; trustee Calif. Inst. Tech., Nat. Symphony Orch. Assn., 1973-83; trustee emeritus Calif. State Univs.; bd. visitors UCLA Sch. Medicine, 1980—; bd. dirs. W. M. Keck Found., 1983—; bd. govs. Performing Arts Council of Music Ctr. Los Angeles, pres., 1976-77. Recipient award IAS, 1956; award Am. Inst. Elec. Engrs., 1959; award Arnold Air Soc., 1960; Am. Acad. Achievement award, 1964; award Am. Iron and Steel Inst., 1968; Distinguished Service medal Armed Forces Communication and Electronics Assn., 1970; medal of achievement WEMA, 1970; awards U. So. Calif., 1971, 79; Kayan medal Columbia U., 1972; award Am. Cons. Engrs. Council, 1974; medal Franklin Inst., 1978; award Harvard Bus. Sch. Assn., 1979; award Nat. Medal Sci., 1979; Disting. Alumnus award U. Utah, 1981; UCLA medal, 1982; Presdl. Medal of Freedom, 1983; Jr. Achievement Bus. Hall of Fame award, 1984; others. Fellow IEEE (Electronic Achievement award 1953, Golden Omega award 1975, Founders medal 1980), Am. Acad. Arts and Scis.; mem. Nat. Acad. Engring. (founder, council mem. Bueche award), Nat. Acad. Scis., Am. Phys. Soc., Am. Philos. Soc., Inst. Advancement Engring., Internat. Acad. Astronautics, Eta Kappa Nu (eminent mem. award 1966). Office: TRW 1 Space Pk Redondo Beach CA 90278 *

RAMON, SHARON JOSEPHINE, personnel management executive, real estate salesperson; b. Chgo., Nov. 8, 1947; d. Edward Albert and Helen Josephine (Tomaszewski) Mazur; m. Kevin John Ramon, Aug. 4, 1979. BA, U. Ill.-Chicago, 1969. Caseworker, ct. aide Social Svc. Dept. of Cir. Ct. Cook County, Chgo., 1969-71; investigator aide U.S. Civil Svc. Commn., Chgo., 1971-72, personnel staffing specialist, 1972-74, personnel mgmt. specialist, 1974-80; mgmt. cons. U.S. Office Personnel Mgmt., Chgo., 1980-82, personnel mgmt. specialist, 1982-83, personnel staffing specialist, 1983-86; salesperson First United Realtors, Barrington, Ill., 1987—. Recipient Certs. of Spl. Achievement, U.S. Office Personnel Mgmt., 1980, Cert. of Appreciation, 1981. Mem. Nat. Assn. Female Execs., AAUW, Ill. Assn. Realtors, Nat. Assn. Realtors, Barrington Bd. Realtors, McHenry County Bd. Realtors. Roman Catholic. Office: First United Realtors 115 S Hough St Barrington IL 60010

RAMOS, ANDRES ROACH, railway executive; b. Laredo, Tex., Apr. 8, 1914; s. Baltazar and Pomposa (Roach) R.; m. Chita Novoa, Jan. 1, 1938; 17 children. Student Tex. A&M U., Laredo Jr. Coll., 1947. Auditor, sec. Tex.-Mexican Ry. Co., Laredo, 1970-74, v.p. fin., 1975-77, pres., gen. mgr., 1978-81, chmn., chief exec. officer, 1982—. Roman Catholic. Lodges: Rotary, K.C., Alhambra, Knights of Holy Sepulchre.

RAMSDEN, WILLIAM EARL, religious organization administrator; b. Toronto, Ont., Can., Sept. 6, 1932; came to U.S., 1937; s. William Earl and Eleanor Amelia (Mason) R.; m. Elsa Lucille Boedecker, Mar. 19, 1955; children: Richard C., Ronald W., Karin E. BA magna cum laude, U. Buffalo, 1954; STB summa cum laude, Boston U., 1957, PhD, 1960. Ordained to ministry, 1957. Pastor Stanton Ave. Meth. Ch., Boston, 1959-62, Plymouth Meth. Ch., Buffalo, 1962-66; mem. coordinator Meth. Bd. Missions, Indpls., 1967-69; exec. dir. Opportunity Assocs. (formerly T.E.A.M.), Phila., 1969—; sec., treas. Times Three, Inc., Phila., 1972—; cons. Med. Edn. Systems, Wyndmoor, Pa., 1981—, Ch. Scotland Social Relations Staff, Edinburgh, 1984—, Strategic Mgmt. Assocs., Phila., 1986—, Coun. of Voluntary Socs., Northampton, Eng., 1983; bd. dirs. Theol. Edn. Consortium, Pa. Found. for Pastoral Counseling. Author: Church in Changing Society, 1979, Non-Parish Institutions, 1987, Inward Vigor, Outward Vitality, 1985, Metro: Channel for Urban Mission, 1988. Chmn. bd. Eastern Communities Tng. Inst., Phila., 1985—. Gallahue fellow Boston U., 1958-59, Danielson fellow, 1959-60. Mem. Am. Soc. Tng. Devel., Assn. for Creative Change, Phi Beta Kappa. Democrat. Home: 1045 70th Ave Philadelphia PA 19126 Office: Times Three Inc 8200 Flourtown Ave Ste 2 Philadelphia PA 19118

RAMSEY, DORIS JUNE, corporate professional; b. Milton, Pa., June 7, 1923; d. Earl F. and Kathryn Caroline (Wands) Gordon; m. A. Donald Ramsey, Dec. 22, 1972. Grad. high sch., Milton. With Rohr Industries, Inc., Chula Vista, Calif., 1944—; pres. Transp. Ins. Ltd. (subs. Rohr Industries, Inc.), Chula Vista, 1972-76; v.p., sec. Aircraft Builders Counsel (subs. Rohr Industries, Inc.), Chula Vista, 1976—, also bd. dirs.; bd. dirs. Universal Ins. Co., United Ins. Co., Wrenford Ins. Co. Mem. Women in Bus., Tribute to Women and Industry Forum, Captive Ins. Cos. Assn., Inc. Methodist. Home: 4063 The Hill Rd Bonita CA 92002 Office: Rohr Industries Inc PO Box 878 Chula Vista CA 92012-0878

RAMSEY, THOMAS EDWIN, retired banker, consultant; b. Denver, Mar. 31, 1905; s. William Randall and Edwina Meriwether (Adams) R.; m. Lorraine Lorena Chamberlin, June 1, 1943; 1 child, Robin. B Fgn. Svc., Georgetown U., 1928. Bank supr. Fed. Res. Bd., Washington, 1927-28; market rsch. Colo. Fuel and Iron, Denver, 1928-29; asst. advt. mgr. Mine and Smelter Supply, Denver, 1929-30; economist Fed. Res. Bank, San Francisco, 1930-36; nat. bank examiner U.S. Treasury, San Francisco, 1936-65; cons. and tech. asst. expert Internat. Monetary Fund, Cen. Bank Svc., Uganda, Kenya, Jamaica, Barbados, 1967-76; project dir. Indsl. Devel. Corp., Internat. Exec. Svc. Corp., N.Y.C., 1977; examiner Cen. Bank Botswana, Gabarone, 1979. Maj. U.S. Army, 1943-46. Decorated Knight, Crown of Italy, Italian Govt., 1945; recipient Meritorious Svc. award. Republican. Episcopalian. Home: 11375 SW Walker Rd Portland OR 97225

RAMSEY, WILLIAM DALE, JR., petroleum company executive; b. Indpls., Apr. 14, 1936; s. William Dale and Laura Jane (Stout) R.; m. Mary Alice Ihnet, Aug. 9, 1969; children: Robin, Scott, Kimberly, Jennifer. AB in Econs., Bowdoin Coll., 1958. With Shell Oil Co., 1958—, salesman, Albany, N.Y., 1960, merchandising rep., Milton, N.Y., 1961-63, real estate and mktg. investments rep., Jacksonville, Fla., 1963-65, dist. sales supr., St. Paul, 1965-67, employee relations rep., Chgo., 1967-69, spl. assignment mktg. staff-adminstrn., N.Y.C., recruitment mgr., Chgo., 1970-72, sales mgr., Chgo., 1973-75, sales mgr., Detroit, 1975-79, dist. mgr. N.J. and Pa., Newark, 1979-84, Mid-Atlantic dist. mgr. (Md., D.C., Va.) 1984-87, econ. advisor head office, Houston, 1987-89; mgr. Mktg. Concepts head office, Houston, 1989—; dir. N.Am. Fin. Services, 1971-72; lectr., speaker on energy, radio, TV, appearances, 1972—; guest lectr. on bus. five univs., 1967-72; v.p., dir. Malibu East Corp., 1973-74; mem. Am. Right of Way Assn., 1963-65. James Bowdoin scholar Bowdoin Coll., 1958. Active Chgo. Urban League, 1971-75; mem. program com., bus. adv. council Nat. Republican Congressional Com.; mem. Gov.'s Council on Tourism and Commerce, Minn., 1965-67; mem. Founders Soc., Detroit Inst. Arts, 1978-80; bd. dirs. N.J. Symphony Orch. Corp., 1981-85. Capt. U.S. Army, 1958-60. Mem. Soc. Environ. Econ. Devel., N.J. Petroleum Council (exec. com. 1979-84 vice chmn. 1982-84), Midwest Coll. Placement Assn., Md. Petroleum Council (exec. com. 1984-87). Presbyterian. Clubs: Ponte Vedra (Fla.); Bowdoin Alumni (Houston); Morris County (N.J.) Golf; Kingwood (Tex.) Country; Bethesda (Md.) Country. Author: Corp. Recruitment and Employee Relations Organizational Effectiveness Study, 1969.

RANALLI, MICHAEL PATRICK, utility company executive; b. Syracuse, N.Y., Sept. 23, 1933; s. Patrick and Amelia (Polermo) R.; m. Angela Bigliardi, Apr. 7, 1956; children: David, Mark, Michael. BEE, Syracuse U., 1955. Rsch. scientist NASA, San Jose, Calif., 1957-58; project engr. Niagara Mohawk Power Corp., Syracuse, 1958-65, supr. sta. design, 1965-69, mgr. system engring., 1978-81, asst. project mgr. planning, 1981-82, v.p. engring., 1982-87, sr. v.p., 1987—; mgr. Ea. div. engring. Niagara Mohawk Power Corp., Albany, N.Y., 1969-74; mgr. Western div. engring. Niagara Mohawk Power Corp., Buffalo, 1974-78; pres. N.Mex. Uranium (subs. Niagara Mohawk), 1988—; bd. dirs. INROADS, Syracuse, Empire State Elec. Energy Research Corp. Mem. tech. adv. com. Clarkson U., Potsdam, N.Y., 1983—, Rensselaer Sch. Engring., Troy, N.Y.; bd. dirs. Boy Scouts Am., Syracuse. Served to capt. USNR, 1965-85. Mem. IEEE (various local offices). Republican. Roman Catholic. Office: Niagara Mohawk Power Corp 300 Erie Blvd W Syracuse NY 13202

RANCOURT, JOHN HERBERT, pharmaceutical company executive; b. Troy, N.Y., Aug. 10, 1946; s. Charles Dennis and Helen Mary (Keadin) R.; BS in Mgmt., Rensselaer Poly. Inst., 1968, MS in Mgmt., 1972, MBA, 1981. CPA, Ill.; cert. mgmt. acct.; m. Susan Jane Koneski, Feb. 14, 1970; children—Karen Mary, John Herbert, Alison Jane, Elizabeth Anne, Maureen Ellen. Asst. to dir. rsch. Rensselaer Poly. Inst., 1968-69; mgmt. trainee, buyer/purchasing agt., contr. rsch. div. Huyck Corp., Rensselaer, N.Y., 1969-74, corp. internat. project mgr., Wake Forest, N.C., 1974-76, adminstrv. svc. mgr. Formex div., 1976-77; sr. fin. analyst Abbott Labs., North Chicago, Ill., 1977-79, sect. mgr. sales acctg., 1979-80, mgr. fin. analysis, materials mgmt. div., 1980-82, mgr. fin. planning and analysis, pharm. products div., 1982-84; contr. TAP Pharms subs. Abbott Labs., North Chicago, Ill., 1984—; instr. acctg. Coll. of Lake County, Grayslake, Ill., part-time, 1981—. Indian Guide/Princess Tribal leader YMCA, 1980—; solicitor United Way, 1981, 83, 85, 87, 88-89. Mem. Nat. Assn. Accts., Am. Acctg. Assn., Am. Inst. CPA's, Ill. CPA Soc., Liberty Road and Track Club. Roman Catholic. Home: 826 Furlong Dr Libertyville IL 60048 Office: Abbott Labs 14th and Sheridan Rd North Chicago IL 60064

RAND, JAMES LELAND, plastics company executive; b. Ft. Worth, Tex., Dec. 23, 1935; s. George Leland and Barbara Elizabeth (Meyer) R.; m. Deanne Marie Dyke, Dec. 28, 1956 (div. 1973); children: Patricia, Michael, Theresa, Mary Eileen, Christopher, Elizabeth. BS in Aero. Engring., U. Md., 1961, MS in Areo. Engring., 1963, PhD in Mech. Engring., 1967. Registered profl. engr., Tex., Md. Research engr. U.S. Naval Ordnance Lab., White Oak, Md., 1961-68; profl. aerospace engr. Tex. A&M U., College Station, 1968-78, mem. faculty, 1978-83; mgr. dynamic analysis Southwest Research Inst., San Antonio, 1978-83; pres., chief exec. officer Winzen Internat. Inc., San Antonio, 1983—; adv. and cons. in field. Contbr. articles to profl. jours; inventor in field. Chmn., Brazos Valley Sci. and Engring. Fair, College Station, 1976-78; bd. dirs. Leon Springs Vol. Fire Dept., Tex., 1988—. Served to airman 1st class, USAF, 1954-58, Korea. Recipient Meritorious Civil Service award USN, 1966. Fellow AIAA (assoc.); mem ASME, Soc. Plastics Industry, Am. Soc. Mechanics, NSPE, San Antonio C. of C. Republican. Roman Catholic. Office: Winzen Internat Inc 12001 Network Blvd Ste 200 San Antonio TX 78249

RAND, KATHY SUE, public relations executive; b. Miami Beach, Fla., Feb. 24, 1945; d. William R. and Rose (Lasser) R.; m. Peter C. Ritsos, Feb. 19, 1982. BA, Mich. State U., 1965; M in Mgmt., Northwestern U., 1980. Asst. editor Lyons & Carnahan, Chgo., 1967-68; mng. editor Cahners Pub. Co., Chgo., 1968-71; pub. rels. writer Super Market Inst., Chgo., 1972-73; account supr. Pub. Communications Inc., Chgo., 1973-77; divisional mgr. pub. rels. Quaker Oats Co., Chgo., 1977-82; exec. v.p., dep. gen. mgr. Golin/Harris Communications, Chgo., 1982—. Dir. midwest region NOW, 1972-74. Mem. Pub. Rels. Soc. Am. (Silver Anvil award 1986, 87), Pub. Club Chgo. (Golden Trumpet award 1982, 83, 84, 85, 86, 87), Women in Communications Inc. (Clarion award 1983), Northwestern Club Chgo., Kellogg Alumni Club, Beta Gamma Sigma. Home: 400 Riverwoods Rd Lake Forest IL 60045 Office: Golin/Harris Communications 500 N Michigan Ave Chicago IL 60611

RANDALL, CRAIG, financial management consultant; b. Santa Monica, Calif., Oct. 29, 1957; s. Les Shepard and Marian (Swanson) Hand; m. Jeanne Runsvold, July 14, 1984. Student, Pierce Coll., 1975-76, Calif. State U.-Northridge, 1977-79. Asst. controller Becker CPA Rev., Encino, Calif., 1979-81; sr. staff acct. Kress and Goldstein, CPAs, Sherman Oaks, Calif., 1981-84; owner Ultimate Mktg. Co., Woodland Hills, Calif., 1987—; pres., chief exec. officer Bus. Computers Network, Inc., Woodland Hills, 1984—, Randall Accountancy Corp., Woodland Hills, 1984—; owner Randall & Assocs., Woodland Hills, 1988—. Office: Randall Accountancy Corp 5525 Oakdale Ave Ste 250 Woodland Hills CA 91364

RANDALL, JAMES ALLING, banker, venture consultant; b. New Haven, Sept. 13, 1955. BS in Engring., Mich. State U., 1978; MBA, Harvard U., 1981. Sr. cons. Touche Ross & Co., N.Y.C., 1981-83; exec. v.p. Universal Trading Exch., Inc., N.Y.C., 1983-87; founder, pres. Madison Entrepreneurial Resources, N.Y.C., 1987-88; pres. Bankers Fed. Savs., N.Y.C., 1988—, also bd. dirs.; bd. dirs., pres. BFS Bankorp. Mem. Harvard Club of N.Y.C. Office: Bankers Fed Savs 110 William St New York NY 10038

RANDALL, JAMES R., manufacturing company executive; b. 1924; married. BS in Chem. Engring., U. Wis., 1948. Tech. dir. Cargill Inc., 1948-68; v.p. prodn. and engring. Archer-Daniels-Midland Co., Decatur, Ill., 1968-69, exec. v.p., 1969-75, pres., 1975—, also dir. Served with AUS, 1943-46. Office: Archer-Daniels-Midland Co 4666 Faries Pkwy Decatur IL 62525 *

RANDALL, JOSEPH DUDLEY, JR., advertising executive; b. Phoenix, Oct. 1, 1955; s. Joseph Dudley and Joann Christine (Smith) R. Student, Mesa Coll., Ariz., 1984. Pub. relations dir. Technology Prodns., San Diego, 1984-87; pres., owner Wildcat Prodns., San Diego, 1987—; co-owner ResuME; pres. Calvin Condom Inc.; social dir. Le Tip, San Diego, 1987—. Pub. Neighbors San Diego mag. Mktg. dir. San Diego Walks for Life, 1987—. Served with U.S. Army, 1974-75. Mem. Mid City C. of C. (sec. 1987-88), Log Cabin Club. Republican. Office: Wildcat Prodns 1205 Cleveland Ave San Diego CA 92103

RANDALL, ROBERT L., industrial economist; b. Aberdeen, S.D., Dec. 28, 1936; s. Harry Eugene and Juanita Alice (Barstow) R.; MS in Phys. Chemistry, U. Chgo., 1960, MBA, 1963. Market devel. chemist E.I. du Pont de Nemours & Co., Inc., Wilmington, Del., 1963-65; chem. economist Battelle Meml. Inst., Columbus, Ohio, 1965-68; mgr. market and econ. research Kennecott Copper Corp., N.Y.C., 1968-74, economist, 1974-79, dir. new bus. venture devel., 1979-81; pres., mng. dir. R.L. Randall Assocs., Inc., 1981—; economist U.S. Internat. Trade Commn., Washington, 1983—; exec. dir. Rain Forest ReGeneration, 1986—; indsl. panel policy review of effect of regulation on innovation and U.S.-internat. competition U.S. Dept. Commerce, 1980-81. Mem. AAAS, AIME (council econs.), Am. Econ. Assn., Am. Statis. Assn., Am. Chem. Soc., Soc. Mining Engrs., Chemists Club of N.Y.C., Metall. Soc., N.Y. Acad. Scis. Contbr. articles to profl. jours.; contbg. author: Computer Methods for the '80's. Home: 1727 Massachusetts Ave NW Washington DC 20036 Office: 500 E Street SW Washington DC 20436

RANDALL, WILLIAM B., manufacturing company executive; b. Phila., Jan. 8, 1921; s. Albert and Ann (Fine) R.; m. Geraldine Kempson, Aug. 10, 1943; children: Robert, Erica Lynn, Lisa. Student, Rider Coll., Trenton, N.J., 1940-41. Gen. Sales mgr. Lowres Optical Mfg. Co., Newark, 1946-49; pres., founder Rand Sales Co., N.Y.C., 1949-58; gen. mgr. Sea & Ski Co. div. Botany Industries, Inc., Millbrae, Calif., 1958-61; pres., dir. Botany Industries, Inc., 1961-66, v.p., 1961-65; pres. Renauld of France, Reno, 1967-68; chmn. bd. Renauld Internat., Reading, Pa., 1963-65; pres., chief operating officer Renauld Internat., Ltd., Burlingame and Reno, 1966-67; pres., chmn. bd. Randall Internat., Ltd., 1967-68; sr. exec. v.p. Forty-two Prods. Ltd., 1969-71; pres. Exec. Products Internat. Ltd., 1969-71, New Product Devel. Ctr., Carlsbad, Calif., 1971—; pres. Internat. Concept Ctr. Exec. Products Internat. Ltd., Irvine, 1971—, pres. Sun Research Ctr., 1974—; pres. La Costa Products Internat., 1975-86; mng. dir. merchandising La Costa Hotel and Spa, 1986-88; bd. dirs. Bank of La Costa. Served to 1st lt., navigator USAAF, 1942-45. Mem. Am. Mgmt. Assn., Nat. Wholesale Druggists Assn., Nat. Assn. Chain Drug Stores, Hon. Order Ky. Cols. Home: 7150 Arenal Ln Carlsbad CA 92009

RANDLES, KEVIN LEE, mortgage company executive; b. Sacramento, Oct. 29, 1963; s. Keith Borland and Marlene Ann (Bowman) R. BS in Fin., Calif. State U., Fresno, 1987, Cert. in Mgmt., 1989; Cert. in Mgmt., Am. Mgmt. Assn. Extension Inst., 1989. Lic. real estate salesperson. Loan adminstr. Weyerhaeuser Mortgage Co., Fresno, 1987—. Mem. Fin. Mgmt. Assn., Fresno C. of C., Diplomat Club, Lambda Chi Alpha (chmn. recruitment com. 1986-87). Republican.

RANDMAN, BARRY I., real estate developer; b. Cin., Apr. 1, 1958; s. David I. and Marilyn June (Garfinkel) F. BBA in Fin., U. Denver, 1980. With acctg. dept. Rookwood Pottery & Celestial Restaurants, Cin., 1976-80; asst. to pres., head mktg. and real estate branching Great Am. Banks Inc., Miami, 1980-83; pres. Tower Mgmt. Inc., Cin., 1983-85, also bd. dirs.; pres. Ohio Jet Services Inc., Cin., 1983-85; v.p. Home State Fin. Services Inc., Cin., 1984-85; pres. DNAR Devel. Corp., Cin., 1985—, B.I.R. Properties Inc., Cin., 1985—, Golden Devel. Corp., 1988—. Mem. Jewish Welfare Fund, Cin., 1980. Home: 1034 St Paul Pl Cincinnati OH 45202 Office: BIR Properties Inc 427 Delta Ave Cincinnati OH 45226

RANDOLPH, JACKSON HAROLD, utility company executive; b. Cin., Nov. 17, 1930; s. Dward Bradley and Cora Belle (Puckett) R.; m. Angelina Losito, June 20, 1958; children: Terri, Patti, Todd, Craig. B.B.A., U. Cin., 1958, M.B.A., 1968. C.P.A., Ohio. Acct. Arthur Andersen & Co., Cin., 1958-59; with Cin. Gas & Electric Co., 1959—, v.p. fin. and corp. affairs, 1981-85, exec. v.p., 1985-86, pres., chief exec. officer, 1986—, also dir.; also pres. Union Light Heat and Power Co., Covington, Ky.; bd. dirs. Cen. Trust Bank, N.A., Cin. Fin. Corp., PNC Corp. V.p., bd. dirs. Gen. Protestant Orphan Home, Cin., 1981-86; treas., bd. dirs. Cin. chpt. ARC, 1975—; mem. adv. com. Catherine Booth Home, 1980—, Dan Beard council Boy Scouts Am., 1985. Served with USN, 1951-55. Mem. Cin. Country Club, Queen City Club, Delta Sigma Pi, Phi Eta Sigma, Beta Gamma Sigma. Home: 414 Bishops Bridge Dr Cincinnati OH 45230 Office: The Cin Gas & Electric Co 139 4th St Cincinnati OH 45202 also: Union Light Heat & Power Co 107 Brent Spence Sq Covington KY 41011

RANDOLPH, JAMES GLENN, energy company executive; b. Cleve., Tenn., Jan. 20, 1930; s. James Franklin and Mary (Chambers) R.; m. Nancy Elrod, Aug. 8, 1958 (dec. Jan. 1971); children—James Edward, Charles Franklin, Glenn Thomas, Marilyn Hope; m. Henrietta Kleinpell, May 30, 1973. B.S. in Indsl. Engring., U. Mich., 1962; M.S., U.S. Army Command and Staff Coll., 1964; M.S. in Internat. Relations, George Washington U., 1968. Enlisted U.S. Air Force, 1948, commd. 2d lt., 1951, advanced through grades to maj. gen., 1974, vice comdr. San Antonio Air Logistics Ctr., 1971-73, comdr. Oklahoma City Air Logistics Ctr., 1973-76; ret. 1976; pres. Kerr McGee Coal Corp., 1976—; sr. v.p. Kerr McGee Corp., Oklahoma City, 1984—; pres. Quevira Mining & Sequoyah Fuels, Oklahoma City, 1985—. Mem. exec. com. Okla. Med. Research Found., Oklahoma City, 1978—; trustee Casady Sch., Oklahoma City, 1983—; bd. dirs., treas. Okla. Blood Inst., Oklahoma City, 1977—. Mem. Nat. Coal Council (chmn. 1987-88), Nat. Coal Assn. (bd. dirs. 1977—, vice chmn. 1988), Oklahoma City C. of C. (life mem.; exec. bd. dirs. 1976—). Republican. Home: 2601 Country Club Dr Oklahoma City OK 73116 Office: Kerr McGee Corp PO Box 25861 Oklahoma City OK 73125

RANDOLPH, JAMES HARRISON, SR., realty company executive; b. Springfield, Tenn., Feb. 17, 1917; s. Bayless Jones and Effie Lee (Cummings) R.; BS in Bus. Adminstrn., U. Tenn., 1940; m. Millicent Roma Lincoln, Aug. 14, 1943; 1 child, James Harrison. Spl. agt., adminstrv. asst. to dir. FBI, Washington, 1942-52, also Bur. speaker, insp.; personnel dir. Dallas Housing Authority, 1952-54; real estate broker Bolanz & Bolanz, Dallas, 1954-58; real estate broker, investor Jim Randolph & Co., Realtors, Dallas, 1958—. Bd. govs. U. Tenn. Mem. Soc. Former Spl. Agts. of FBI (chmn. chpt. 1960), Soc. Indsl. Realtors, Dallas C. of C. (hon. life), Scarabbean, Phi Sigma Kappa. Baptist. Club: Brookhaven Country (Dallas). Subject of articles in Nat. Real Estate Investor, July, 1961. Home: Jim Randolph & Co Realtors 5924 Royal Ln Ste 150B Dallas TX 75230 Office: 211 N Ervay Bldg Dallas TX 75201

RANDOUR, PAUL ALFRED, lawyer, holding company executive; b. Bakersfield, Calif., Aug. 15, 1935; s. Alfred Edward and Shirley (Sutherland) R. A.B., Stanford U., 1957, LL.B., 1960; Jur.Drs., Leiden U., The Netherlands, 1961. Bar: Calif. 1962, N.Y. 1963. Assoc. Cahill, Gordon & Reindel, N.Y.C., 1962-65; atty. Gen. Electric Co., N.Y.C., 1965-66; assoc. Chadbourne, Parke, Whiteside & Wolff, N.Y.C., 1966-72, ptnr., 1972-85; sr. v.p., gen. counsel Am. Brands, Inc., N.Y.C., 1986—. Mem. Assn. Bar City N.Y., Internat. Bar Assn. Clubs: University, Explorers. Office: Am Brands Inc 1700 E Putnam Ave Old Greenwich CT 06870-0819

RANELLI, JOHN RAYMOND, steel products company executive; b. New London, Conn., Sept. 25, 1946; s. Frank Robert and Sue Mary (Bongo) R.; m. Paula Jean Contillo, June 8, 1968; children: Carina, Christina, Jennifer. Student, U. Loyola, Rome, 1966-67; A.B. in History, Coll. Holy Cross, 1968; M.B.A., Dartmouth Coll., 1973. Fin. analyst Gen. Motors Corp., N.Y.C., 1973-74; mgr. fin. adminstrn. No. Telecom, Inc., Nashville, 1975-76; asst. treas. No. Telecom. Inc., Nashville, 1976-77; treas. No. Telecom, Inc., Nashville, 1977-78; asst. controller No. Telecom, Ltd., Montreal, Que., Can., 1978-79; treas. ARA Services Inc., Phila., 1980-81, v.p., treas., sec. to fin. com., dir., mem. retirement com., 1981-83, pres. Aero Enterprises div., 1983-85; chief fin. officer, mem. exec. com. Atcor, Inc., Harvey, Ill., 1985-87; v.p., chief fin. officer Cyclops Industries, Mt. Lebanon, Pa., 1987-88; v.p., treas. Ames Dept. Stores, Inc., Rocky Hill, Conn., 1989—. Co-author: Mutual Savings Banking at the Crossroads: Renaissance or Extinction, 1973. Served with submarine force USN, 1968-71. Decorated Nat. Def. medal; Fulbright Scholar, 1968. Mem. Fin. Exec. Inst. Lodges: KC, Folks. Office: Ames Dept Stores Inc 2418 Main St Rocky Hill CT 06067 also: ATCOR Inc 16100 S Lathrop Ave Harvey IL 60426

RANFTL, ROBERT MATTHEW, management consulting company executive; b. Milw., May 31, 1925; s. Joseph Sebastian and Leona Elaine (Goetz) R.; m. Marion Smith Goodman, Oct. 12, 1946. BSEE, U. Mich., 1946; postgrad. UCLA, 1953-55. Product engr. Russell Electric Co., Chgo., 1946-47; head engring. dept. Radio Inst. Chgo., 1947-50; sr. project engr. Webster Chgo. Corp., 1950-51, product design engr., 1951-53, head equipment design group, 1953-54, head electronic equipment sect., 1954-55, mgr. product engring. dept., 1955-58, mgr. reliability and quality control, 1958-59, mgr. adminstrn. 1959-61, mgr. product effectiveness lab., 1961-74; corp. dir. engring./design mgmt., 1974-84, corp. dir. managerial productivity Hughes Aircraft Co., Los Angeles, 1984-86; pres. Ranftl Enterprises Inc., Mgmt. Cons., Los Angeles, 1981—; guest lectr. Calif. Inst. Tech., Cornell U., U. Calif.; mem. White House Conf. on Productivity, 1983; mem. human resources productivity task force Dept. of Def., 1985-86. Author: R&D Productivity, 1974, 78; (with others) Productivity: Prospects for Growth, 1981; contbr. articles to profl. jours. Mem. AAAS, AIAA, Am. Soc. Engring. Edn., Am. Soc. Tng. and Devel., IEEE, Inst. Mgmt. Scis., Acad. Mgmt., N.Y. Acad. Scis., U. Mich. Alumni Assn., UCLA Alumni Assn. Office: Ranftl Enterprises Inc PO Box 49892 Los Angeles CA 90049

RANGOS, JOHN G., waste management company executive; b. Steubenville, Ohio, July 27, 1929; s. Gust and Anna (Svokas) R.; children: John G. Jr., Alexander William, Jenica Anne. Attended, Houston Bus. Coll., 1949-50; grad., U.S. Signal and Communications Sch., Ft. Gordon, Ga. Formerly gen. agt. Rockwell Mfg. Co., Pitts.; also formed several cos. and pioneered technol. advances in waste transp. and disposal resources recovery and recycling during 1960; pres., chief exec. officer Chambers Devel. Co., Inc., Pitts., 1971—; pres., chief exec. officer U.S. Services, U.S. Utilities Corp., William H. Martin, Inc. So. Alleghenies Disposal Service Co. Inc., Assocs. Internat. Inc., Chatham Security Services Inc., Palmetto Security Systems, Sec. Bur. Inc.; del. UN of Am. Innovations include converting powerplant boiler ash into a useful product for cinder block material and anti-skid material for hwys.; contbd. to invention of techniques for recycling bituminous by-products, disposing of sewage sludge; co-developer of techniques for disposing liquid indsl. waste; developer of a resource recovery system which converts waste-generated methane into energy. Fundraising chmn. UNICEF; contbr. Children's Hosp., Pitts., United Cerebral Palsy, Muscular Dystrophy, Leukemia Soc.; nat. del. U.S. Olympic Conf.; mem. Truman Library Found.; bd. dirs. Hellenic Coll., Presentation of Christ Diocese, Clergy Liturgy Council. Served with U.S. Army, 1951-54, Korea. Decorated Nat. Def. medal, U.N. medal, Korean Campaign medal; recipient Presdl. Unit citations; elected Archon of Ecumenical Patriarchate Order St. Andrew the Apostle, Greek Orthodox Ch., 1988. Mem. Nat. Dem. Club, Young Dems., Internat. Platform Assn. Clubs: The Allegheny, The Pitts. Press, U. Pitts. Golden Panther, Churchill Valley Country. Lodges: Masons (32nd degree), Shriners (Syria). Home: 78 Locksley Dr Pittsburgh PA 15235 Office: Chambers Devel Co Inc 10700 Frankstown Rd Pittsburgh PA 15235

RANIERE, MARCIA VICOREK, public relations executive; b. Wilmington, Del., Dec. 4, 1943; d. John A. and Irene J. (Binacewicz) Vicorek; m. Laurence A. Raniere, July 28, 1978; children: Christopher L., Samantha D. Exec. sec. cert., Golden Beacom Coll., 1962. With legal dept. DuPont Co., Wilmington, 1961-72, exec. sec. to chmn. bd., 1972-83, pub. affairs specialist, 1984-88, placement and devel. coord. external affairs dept., 1988—; bd. trustees Golden Brocom Coll., 1983—. Bd. dirs. Am. Ctr. Enterprise Edn., Wilmington, 1987—; bd. trustees Del. Found. Retarded Children, Wilmington, 1975—; dir. emeritus Mary Campbell Ctr., 1988—. Democrat. Roman Catholic. Home: 1004 Thaxten Ln Wilmington DE 19807 Office: DuPont Co 1007 Market St Wilmington DE 19898

RANKIN, ALFRED MARSHALL, JR., manufacturing executive; b. Cleve., Oct. 8, 1941; s. Alfred Marshall and Clara Louise (Taplin) R.; m. Victoire Conley Griffin, June 3, 1967; children: Helen P., Clara T. BA in Econs. magna cum laude, Yale U., 1963, JD, 1966. Mgmt. cons. McKinsey & Co., Inc., Cleve., 1970-73; with Eaton Corp., Cleve., 1974-81, pres. materials handling group, 1981-83, pres. indsl. group, 1984-86, exec. v.p., 1986, vice chmn., chief oper. officer, 1986-89; pres., chief oper. officer NACCO Industries, Inc., Cleve., 1989—, also bd. dirs.; bd. dirs. B.F. Goodrich Co. Former pres., trustee Hathaway Brown Sch.; trustee Holden Arboretum, Oberlin Coll., Univ. Hosps., Musical Arts Assn. Served to 2d lt. USAF, 1966-68. Mem. Ohio Bar Assn. Republican. Clubs: Chagrin Valley Hunt, Union, Tavern, Pepper Pike, Kirtland Country (Cleve.); Rolling Rock (Ligonier, Pa.); Met. (Washington). Home: Old Mill Rd Gates Mills OH 44040 Office: NACCO Indsutries Inc 12800 Shaker Blvd Cleveland OH 44120

RANKIN, BRUCE CHARLES, marketing executive; b. Mpls., May 25, 1954; s. Robert Frank and Barbara Louise (Campbell) R.; m. Janice Marie Congdon, Jan. 11, 1975; children: Jennifer, Jody, Robert. BSBA, U. Minn., 1976. Mgr. Pillsbury Restaurant, Mpls., 1977-78; rep. sales Moore Bus. Forms, Inc., Mpls., 1978-80, mgr. sales, 1981-82, mgr. mktg., 1983-84; dir. mktg. Data Documents div. Pitney Bowes Co., Kansas City, Kans., 1985—. Mem. Am. Mktg. Assn., Direct Mktg. Assn., Kansas City Mktg. Assn., Mail Advt. Service Assn. Office: Data Documents Inc 14601 W 99th St Lenexa KS 66215

RANKIN, CLYDE EVAN, III, lawyer; b. Phila., July 3, 1950; s. Clyde Evan Jr. and Mary E. (Peluso) R. A.B., Princeton U., 1972; J.D., Columbia U., 1975; postgrad. Hague Acad. Internat. Law, 1975. Bar: N.Y., N.J., D.C., U.S. Supreme Ct. Law clk. to judge U.S. Dist. Ct. So. Dist. N.Y., 1975-77; assoc. Debevoise, Plimpton, Lyons & Gates, N.Y.C., 1977-79; assoc. Coudert Bros., N.Y.C., 1979-83, ptnr., 1984—. Stone scholar, 1974. Mem. Assn. Bar City N.Y., ABA, N.Y. State Bar Assn., D.C. Bar Assn., N.J. Bar Assn. Roman Catholic. Club: Amateur Comedy (N.Y.C.). Contbr. article to legal jour. Office: Coudert Bros 200 Park Ave New York NY 10166

RANKIN, JAMES ASBURY, manufacturing executive; b. Covington, Ky., July 25, 1928; s. Grover C. and Alice Mae (Townsend) R.; m. Mary Jane Butsch, July 26, 1952; children—Nancy, Peggy. B.S., Eastern Ky. U., 1951; postgrad., U. Ky., U. Cin., Stanford U. With NuTone div. Scovill, Inc., Cin., 1955—, v.p., gen. mgr., 1970-75; group v.p. NuTone-Yale, Cin., 1975-79; exec. v.p. NuTone-Hamilton Beach, Cin., 1979-85; pres. NuTone Inc.-Scovill, Cin., 1985-86, NuTone Inc., Cin., 1987—. Served with U.S. Army, 1946-48; PTO. Home: 870 Rosewood Villa Hills KY 41017 Office: NuTone Inc Madison & Red Bank Rds Cincinnati OH 45227

RANKIN, WILLIAM EDWARD, banker; b. Balt., May 27, 1952; s. Bernard J. and Nancy Lee (Truxal) R.; m. Marlene Ann Kidda, Aug. 10, 1974; children: Kiara Lynn. BS, Johns Hopkins U., 1973; MBA, U. Pa., 1975. Mgmt. trainee C & P Telephone Co. Md., Balt., 1973-74; mgmt. trainee Mellon Bank, Pitts., 1976-77, cash mgmt. officer, 1978-79; banking officer Mellon Bank, Houston, 1979-82; v.p. Mellon Bank, Dallas, 1982-84; div. head Mellon Bank, Pitts., 1984-87, sr. v.p., 1987—. Mem. Phi Beta Kappa. Club: St. Clair Country (Pitts.). Office: Mellon Bank 1 Mellon Ctr Pittsburgh PA 15258

RANKIN, WILLIAM PARKMAN, educator, former publishing company executive; b. Boston, Feb. 6, 1917; s. George William and Bertha W. (Clowe) R.; m. Ruth E. Gerard, Sept. 12, 1942; children: Douglas W., Joan W. BS, Syracuse U., 1941; MBA, NYU, 1949, PhD, 1979. Sales exec. Redbook mag., N.Y.C., 1945-49; sales exec. This Week mag., N.Y.C., 1949-55, adminstrv. exec., 1955-60, v.p., 1957-60, v.p., dir. advt. sales, sales devel. dir., 1960-63, exec. v.p., 1963-69; gen. exec. newspaper div. Time Inc., N.Y.C., 1969-70; gen. mgr. feature svc. Newsweek, Inc., N.Y.C., 1970-74, fin. and ins. advt. mgr., 1974-81; prof., asst. to the dir. Walter Cronkite Sch. Journalism and Telecommunication, Ariz. State U., Tempe, 1981—; lectr. Syracuse U., NYU, Berkeley Sch.; mem. adv. coun. Sch. Journalism, N.Y. Dutch Treat CLub, Met. Adv. Golf Assn., Mesa Country Club, Syracuse U. Mem. Soc. Profl. Journalists/Sigma Delta Chi, Alpha Delta Sigma. Author: Selling Retail Advertising, 1944; The Technique of Selling Magazine Advertising, 1949; Business Management of Consumer Magazines, 1980, 2 ed. 1984, The Practice of Newspaper Mgmt., 1986. Home: 1220 E Krista Way Tempe AZ 85284 Home: Bridge Rd Bomoseen VT 05732 Office: Ariz State U Walter Cronkite Sch Journalism/ Telecommunication Tempe AZ 85287

RANKINE, ALAN EUGENE, personnel director; b. Oaklyn, N.J., Sept. 18, 1948; s. Mildred (Highsaw) R.; m. Karen Elaine Maskey, Sept. 12, 1969 (dec.); children: Alec Stuart, Ian Trevor; m. Margaret Ann Schlafer, Feb. 23, 1980. BA cum laude, Christian Bros. Coll., 1969; MEd, Memphis State U., 1973; completed sr. exec. program, MIT, 1986. Cert. compensation profl.; accredited personnel mgr., personnel specialist. Tchr. Memphis City Schs., 1970-75; dir. personnel Nat. Trust Life, Memphis, 1976-79; with Fed. Express Corp., Memphis, 1979—, mng. dir. compensation and benefits, 1983-85, mng. dir., mgmt. preceptor, 1985-87, mng. dir. intl. personnel, 1987—; founder, pres. Memphis Bus. Group on Health, 1985—. Sponsor Jr. Achievement, Memphis, 1979-81. Mem. Am. Soc. Personnel Adminstrn., Mid-South Compensation Assn. (pres. 1980-81). Republican. Episcopalian. Office: Fed Express Corp Box 727 Memphis TN 38194-1611

RANSOM, JERRY JR., data processing executive, consultant; b. Hinds County, Miss., Sept. 4, 1950; s. Jerry Sr. and Bernice Marie (Wells) R.; m. Irene Ruth Knoener, Jan. 25, 1973. AA in Bus. Data Processing, Milw. Area Tech. Coll., 1974; BA in Indsl. Mgmt., Milw. Sch. Engring., 1981; MBA, Keller Grad Sch., 1988. Computer system specialist Wis. Electric Power Co., Milw., 1974-80; system analyst Gen. Life Ins. Corp., Milw., 1981-83, mgr. systems and programming, 1983-87; cons. data processing Milw., 1987—. Fellow Life Office Mgmt. Inst.; mem. Upper Ctr. St. Bus. Assn. (treas. 1983-86). Democrat. Home and Office: 4939 N 61st St Milwaukee WI 53218

RANT, WALTER FRANCIS, chemical company executive; b. N.Y.C., Aug. 4, 1925; s. Francis Walter and Anastazia (Kindrick) R.; BS, U. Pitts., 1950, MLitt, 1950; postgrad. Am. Inst. Banking, 1955-57, NYU, 1957-65; m. Evelyn M. Buddy, Oct. 7, 1950; children—Melinda, Nadine, Walter Francis II. Asst. mgr. investment research dept. Walston & Co., N.Y.C., 1951-56, mgr. investment research dept. Cosgrove, Miller & Whitehead, 1956-57, Gregory & Sons, 1957-58; sr. security analyst Lionel D. Edie & Co., 1958-60, Goodbody & Co., 1960-65; v.p. corporate devel. Essex Chem. Corp., Clifton, N.J., 1965-88. 1st lt. USAAF, 1943-47; ret. maj. Res. Recipient Morris award Am. Inst. Banking, 1955. Mem. Am. Econ. Assn., N.Y. Soc. Security Analysts, Inst. Chartered Fin. Analysts. Contbr. articles profl. jours. Home: 19 Beresford Rd Allendale NJ 07401 Office: 1401 Broad St Clifton NJ 07015

RAO, KRISHNA, financial executive, controller; b. Calcutta, India, Dec. 9, 1954; came to U.S., 1979; s. M.N. and Anjani (Katari) R.; m. Roxana Mae Marks, Nov. 21, 1981; children: Sarika Katherine, Nandan Mark. BS, U. Calcutta, 1974; MBA, U. Utah, 1982. Chartered acct., certified mgmt. acct. Mem. audit staff Lovelock and Lewes affiliate of Coopers and Lybrand, Calcutta, 1975-79; teaching fellow U. Utah Coll. Bus., 1979-81; mgmt. cons. SBA Devel. Ctr., Salt Lake City, 1979-81; fin. analyst Hewlett Packard, Corvallis, Oreg., 1982, acctg. supr., 1983-84, acct. mgr., 1985-87, controller, 1988—; lectr. Oreg. State U., Corvallis, 1986—. Advisor Jr. Achievement, Corvallis, 1983-84; treas. United Way Affiliated Agy., Corvallis, 1987. Mem. Inst. Chartered Accts. India (merit rank gold medal 1978), Inst. Cert. Mgmt. Accts., Nat. Assn. Accts., Am. Mgmt. Assn. Office: Hewlett Packard 1020 NE Circle Blvd Corvallis OR 97330

RAPACCIOLI, MICHEL ANTOINE, financial executive; b. Paris, Apr. 1, 1934; came to U.S., 1977; m. Janette Rapaccioli, Sept. 5, 1959; children: François, Philippe. H.E.C., Ecole des Hautes Etudes Commerciales, Paris, 1957; MBA, U. Chgo., 1958; cert. advanced mgmt. program, Harvard U., 1975. Asst. treas. S.N. Elf Aquitaine, Inc., Paris, 1962-66, treas., controller, 1972-74; v.p. Aquitaine Co. Can., Calgary, Alta., Can., 1966-72, Le Nickel, Paris, 1974-77; pres. Elf Petroleum Corp., N.Y.C., 1977-83; sr. v.p., chief fin. officer Elf Aquitaine, Inc., Stamford, Conn., 1983—. Served to lt. French Navy, 1959-62.

RAPOPORT, LAWRENCE SANDY, financial planning company executive; b. Queens, N.Y., May 2, 1951. BS in Applied Math., SUNY, Stony Brook, 1974; MS in Acctg., NYU, 1977. CPA, N.Y., N.J. Mgr. acctg. M. Sternlieb & Co., Hackensack, N.J., 1976-85; v.p. adv. svcs. Ind. Fin. Svcs., White Plains, N.Y., 1985—; instr. fin. planning Iona Coll., New Rochelle, N.Y., 1986—, mem. adv. bd. cert. fin. mgmt. program, 1988—; instr. Conn. Soc. CPAs, 1987—, Mass. Soc. CPAs, 1988—. Mem. editorial adv. bd. S Corp. Planning Alert, Springfield, N.J., 1988—. Mem. AICPA, Internat. Assn. for Fin. Planning (pres. Westchester/Rockland chpt. 1988—), Inst. Cert. Fin. Planners, Am. Assn. Personal Fin. Planners. Office: Ind Fin Svcs 244 Westchester Ave White Plains NY 10604

RAPP, GERALD DUANE, lawyer, manufacturing company executive; b. Berwyn, Nebr., July 19, 1933; s. Kenneth P. and Mildred (Price) R.; m. Jane Carol Thomas, Aug. 14, 1954; children—Gerald Duane Jr., Gregory T., Amy Frances. B.S., U. Mo., 1955; J.D., U. Mich., 1958. Bar: Ohio bar 1959. Practice in Dayton, 1960—; partner Smith & Schnacke, 1963-70; asst. gen. counsel Mead Corp., 1970, v.p. human resources and legal affairs, 1973, v.p., corp. sec., 1975, v.p., gen. counsel, corp. sec., 1976, v.p., gen. counsel, 1979, sr. v.p., gen. counsel, 1981—; chmn. Mead Data Cen., Inc., 1971-73. Sr. editor: U. Mich. Law Review, 1957-58. Past chmn. Oakwood Youth Commn.; past v.p., bd. dirs. Big Bros. Greater Dayton; mem. president's visitors com. U. Mich. Law Sch.; past trustee Urbana Coll., Ctr. Internat. Mgmt. Studies, Internat. YMCA; former pres., past trustee Ohio Ctr. Leadership Studies, Robert K. Greenleaf Ctr., Newton Ctr., Mass.; pres. bd. trustees, Dayton and Montgomery County Pub. Library; mem. bd. visitors Law Sch. U. Dayton. 1st lt. U.S. Army, 1958-60. Mem. ABA, Ohio Bar Assn., Dayton Bar Assn., Phi Kappa Psi, Phi Delta Phi, Beta Gamma Sigma. Presbyterian. Clubs: Rod and Reel, Moraine Country, Dayton Racquet, Dayton Bicycle, Dayton Lawyers, Ye Buz Fuz; Met. (Washington). Office: Mead Corp Courthouse Pla NE Dayton OH 45463

RAPP, JAMES ALLEN, marketing, advertising executive; b. St. Louis, Dec. 30, 1946; s. William Albert and Catherine C. (Book) R.; m. Esther Liselotte Nelson, May 26, 1979. Student, St. John's U., Collegeville, Minn., 1965-66; BA, Benedictine Colls., Atchison, Kans., 1969. Editor Apt. Living mag., St. Louis, 1972-73; mng. editor Daily Record, New Orleans, 1973-74; dir. mktg., devel. WYES-TV, New Orleans, 1974-78; dir. mktg. services Stewart Enterprises Inc., New Orleans, 1978-85; v.p. Perez Corp., New Orleans, 1985-86; principal J.A. Rapp & Assocs., 1987-88; dir. Mktg. Communications ISA and ISA Internat., Raleigh, N.C., 1988—. Editor: Metairie Cemetery, An Historical Memoir, 1983 (Anvil award). Chmn. community bd. Boys Clubs of New Orleans, 1985-86; chmn. programming com., bd. dirs. Cultural Communications, Inc., 1987-88; devel. advisor New Orleans Opera Assn., 1983-85. Mem. Pub. Relations Soc. Am. (Anvil award 1983), World Trade Ctr., Ad Club of New Orleans (Addy award 1984). Clubs: Plimsoll, Internat. House, New Orleans Opera. Home: 509 Mandeville St New Orleans LA 70117 also: 2908 Wycliff Rd Raleigh NC 27607 Office: ISA Corp 67 Alexander Dr Research Triangle Park NC 27709

RAPP, LEA BAYERS, copywriter; b. Bklyn., July 19, 1946; d. Irving and Adele (Emanuel) Bayers; m. Stanley J. Rapp, Sept. 3, 1968; children: Ilana, Justin. BA in Journalism, Thomas A. Edison Coll., 1987. Pres. The Pub. Eye, Sayreville, N.J., 1972—. Author: Put Your Kid in Showbiz, 1981, You Can Overcome Stuttering, Anthology of Diet Plans, How to Operate a Dating Service, Sensuality--It's Primal, How to Meet and Date Women, How to Earn Money in TV Commercials, others; columnist The News Tribune, Woodbridge, N.J., The Japan Times; contbr. articles to mags. and newspapers. Mem. Soc. Profl. Journalist, Authors Guild, Authors League Am., Nat. Fed. of Press Women, N.J. Press Women, N.Y. Bus. Press Editors. Office: The Pub Eye 82 Marsh Ave Sayreville NJ 08872

RAPP, RICHARD TILDEN, economist, consultant; b. Miami, Fla., Nov. 30, 1944; s. Melville Benjamin and Rachel (Marx) R.; m. Wilma J. Levin, Aug. 20, 1967; children: Ethan, Sandra. BA, Bklyn. Coll., 1965; MA, U. Pa., 1966, PhD, 1970. Asst. prof. SUNY, Stony Brook, 1970-75, assoc. prof., 1976-77; pres. Nat. Econ. Research Assocs., Inc., White Plains, N.Y., 1977—. Author: Industry and Economic Decline in Seventeenth-Century Venice, 1976, Trade Warfare and the New Protectionism, 1986; co-author: European Economic History, 1975. Kent fellow Danforth Found., 1968-70. Fulbright fellow, 1968-69. Mem. Am. Econ. Assn., Inst. for Advanced Study. Home: 46 North Pl Chappaqua NY 10514 Office: Nat Econ Rsch Assocs Inc 123 Main St White Plains NY 10601

RAPPAPORT, BARBARA HARRIET, telecommunications systems analyst; b. Newark, July 14, 1948; d. Arthur Oscar and Selma (Sklaw) R. B.A., Douglass Coll., 1970; M.B.A., Fairleigh Dickenson U., 1979; basic data cert. Pace U., 1983. Sr. sales cons. Coradian Corp., N.Y.C., 1980-82; sr. telecommunications analyst Mfrs. Hanover Trust Co., N.Y.C., 1982-83; govt. mktg. specialist Tel Plus Communications/Siemens, Somerset, N.J., 1984-88, Office of Telecommunications and Info. Systems, State of N.J., Trenton, 1988—. Co-chairperson N.J. ERA Campaign, Union, 1974; mem. Union County Democratic Platform Com., N.J., 1973; v.p. Union County Women's Polit. Caucus, 1975; columnist Young Democrats Middlesex County, N.J., 1976. Mem. NAFE (bd. dirs. N.J. chpt. 1988—), AAUW (chpt. publicity chairperson 1985-86). Jewish. Avocations: travel; exercise; theater; concerts; reading.

RAPPAPORT, JAMES WYANT, lawyer, real estate developer; b. Boston, May 9, 1956; s. Jerome Lyle and Nancy (Vahey) R.; divorced; children: James, Jessica. BS in Econs., Wharton Sch., U. Pa., 1977; JD, Boston U., 1980. Assoc. Law Offices of Alan Jacobs, Boston, 1980-81; ptnr. Rappaport and Rakov, Boston, 1981—; co-owner Lylehaven Farms, East Montpelier, Vt., 1980—; gen. ptnr. Charles River Park, Boston, 1981—, Nat. Breeding Co., Wauconda, Ill., 1984—; sr. v.p. Charles River Properties, Ltd., 1986—; pres. Charles River Hawaii Devel. Corp., 1987—. Class chmn. Roxbury Latin Sch., 1978—; vice chmn. Rep. 3d ward, Boston, 1978-82, chmn., 1988—; mem. Young Eagle sect. Rep. Nat. Com., Boston, 1985-88, Rep state fin. com., Boston, 1985—, Concord (Mass.) Rep. Town Com., 1985-87; bd. dirs. Mass. Taxpayers Com., Needham, Mass., 1984—, chmn. 1988—; reunion co-chmn. Boston U. Law Sch., 1985; gen. ptnr. Charles River Hawaii L.P., Kauai, Hawaii. Mem. ABA, Mass. Bar Assn., Vt. Bar Assn., Boston Bar Assn., Greater Boston Real Estate Bd. (bd. dirs. Rental Housing Assn.), Holstein-Friesian Assn. Am., Alpha Chi Rho (fin. chmn. Phi Phi chpt. 1984—). Jewish. Office: Charles River Properties Ltd 1 Longfellow Pl Suite 3612 Boston MA 02114 also: Charles River Hawaii Devel Corp 841 Bishop St Ste 2006 Honolulu HI 96813

RAPPAPORT, STEVEN N., financial information services executive; b. N.Y.C., July 10, 1948; s. Abraham and Frances (Schwartz) R.; m. Judith A. Garson, Dec. 20, 1970; children: Peter Benjamin Garson-Rappaport. BA, Northeastern U., 1971; JD, Washington U., 1974; LLM, NYU, 1980. Ptnr. Hartman & Craven, N.Y.C., 1974-87; exec. v.p. Telerate, Inc., N.Y.C., 1987—, also bd. dirs. Mem. ABA, N.Y. State Bar Assn., Assn. of Bar of City of N.Y. (com. on fgn. and comparative law). Clubs: City Athletic, Downtown Athletic (N.Y.C.); Sedgewood (Carmel, N.Y.). Home: 325 W End Ave New York NY 10023 Office: Telerate Inc 1 World Trade Ctr New York NY 10048

RAPPORT, JACK MICHAEL, financial services company executive; b. Manila, Philippines, Aug. 7, 1952; came to U.S., 1955.; s. Michael and Tatiana (Yastreboff) R.; m. Cecelia Jame Rayhbuck, Aug. 25, 1973; children: Michael, Jason, Victoria, Brianna. BA, Brigham Young U., 1974; MBA, Golden Gate U., 1977. Asst. v.p. Bank Am., L.A., 1974-77; v.p. Mfrs. Hanover Trust, N.Y.C., 1977-81; mgr. dir. JMR Assocs., New Canaan, Conn., 1982-87; treas. Blue Cross and Blue Shield of Md., Balt., 1987-88; pres. Health Line, Inc., Balt., 1988—; bd. dirs. Health Line, Inc. Producer, dir. musical Braithwaithe Castle 1320 A.D., 1985. Scout leader Boy Scouts Am., Calif., N.Y., Md., 1974—; bd. dirs. Liahona Scout Camp, Holmes, N.Y., 1983-87; pres. Arcadia (Calif.), Young Reps., 1980; mem. Leadership Balt. County, 1987. Mem. Dartmouth Coll. Alumni Assn., Brigham Young U. Mgmt. Soc., Hunt Valley Country Club (Md.). Republican. Mormon. Home: 18 Highfield Ct Cockeysville MD 21030 Office: Health Line Inc PO Box 10653 Baltimore MD 21285

RASBERRY, SHAROL BARTA, accountant, management executive; b. Red Cloud, Nebr., Oct. 15, 1947; d. Allen James and Orfa Irene (Copley) Barta; m. Robert E. Rasberry, Dec. 29, 1968; children: Kimberly, Robert E. BBA, U. Nebr., 1969. CPA, Kans. Tax prin. Arthur Young & Co., Wichita, Kans., 1969-79; dir. taxes CWG Enterprises, Wichita, Kans., 1979-80; exec. v.p. fin. Capital Enterprises, Wichita, 1980—. Bd. dirs. YWCA, 1978, Accent on Kids, 1983—, Wichita area council Girl Scouts U.S., 1986—, Leadership 2000, 1986; mem. Wichita Jr. League, 1985—. Mem. AICPA, Kans. Soc. CPAs, Wichita C. of C., Beta Gamma Sigma. Republican. Avocation: skiing. Home: 8501 Tipperary Wichita KS 67206 Office: Capital Enterprises Inc 300 N Main St Ste 200 Wichita KS 67201

RASH, STEVEN BRITTON, health care company executive; b. Dover, Del., Nov. 16, 1947; s. Kensil and Donna Lodema (Britton) R.; m. Joanne Lynn Peterson, Aug. 3, 1969; children: Gregory Steven, Jeffrey Britton. BBS, U. Del., 1969; MBA, So. Ill. U., 1976. Team controller Gen. Foods Corp., Dover, 1973-76; mgr. internal reporting Carborundum Co., Niagara Falls, N.Y., 1976-77, div. mgr., fin. planning and analysis, 1977-79, div. controller, 1979-81; group fin. mgr. BOC Group, Montvale, N.J., 1981-83; v.p. acquisitions BOC Group div. Glasrock, Atlanta, 1983-85, zone v.p., 1985—. Treas. Willow Ridge Civic Assn., Amherst, N.Y., 1978-81; football coach Williamsville/ Sweet Home Jr. Football, Amherst, 1979-80, Ringwood (N.J.) Youth Assn., 1981-83, Atlanta Colts Youth Football Assn., 1984—; bd. dirs. football program Dunwoody High Sch. Served to capt. U.S. Army, 1969-73. Mem. Nat. Assn. Med. Equipment Suppliers, Am. Mgmt. Assn., Omicron Delta Kappa, Beta Gamma Sigma. Republican. Methodist. Club: Georgian, Ravinia, (Atlanta). Home: 5358 Brooke Farm Dr Dunwoody GA 30338 Office: Glasrock Home Health Care 6525 The Corners Pkwy Norcross GA 30092

RASKAUSKAS, FRANCIS XAVIER, construction company executive; b. Washington, Dec. 15, 1954; s. Ernest Constant and Catherine Caroline (Konieczny) R.; m. Nancy Ellen Barrett, Sept. 20, 1980; children: Elizabeth Ann, Mary Catherine, Stephen Michael. BA, U. Md., 1978. Project mgr. East Coast Resorts, Inc., Bethany Beach, Del., 1975-78; exec. v.p. East Coast Resorts, Inc., Bethany Beach, 1978-84; pres. East Coast Constrn. Co., Bethany Beach, 1984—. Mem. rescue squad, ambulance attendant Millville (Del.) Vol. Fire Dept., 1978—; mem. Rep. State Com. Del., Wilmington, 1987-88; chmn. Sussex County Adv. Retirement Bd., Georgetown, Del., 1987—; mem. exec. com. Delmarva Adv. Council, Salisbury, Md., 1988—. Recipient Heroic Fireman of Yr. award Sussex County Fire Chief's Assn., 1983. Mem. Home Builders Assn. Lower Del., Bethany-Fenwick C. of C. (bd. dirs. 1985—, pres. 1988—), Omicron Delta Epsilon, Rep. Club (pres. 1989—). Roman Catholic. Home: 940 Heron Dr Bethany Beach DE 19930 Office: E Coast Constrn Co Drawer S Bethany Beach DE 19930

RASKE, JAMES ROBERT, state agency administrator; b. Pierre, S.D., Jan. 25, 1944; s. Henry E. and Erma B. (Meigs) R.; m. Sharon Ruth Roesler, Jan. 23, 1981; children: David James, Matthew John. BS, U. Oreg, 1966; OPM, Harvard U., 1982. Sales engr. Dow Chem. Co., Bakersfield, Calif., 1966-67; geologist, engr. Union Oil Co., Los Angeles, 1967-71; v.p. mktg. Paine Webber, Portland, Oreg., 1971-76; v.p. mktg. Gerber Legendary Blades, Portland, 1976-79, exec. v.p., 1979-82, pres., 1982-87; dir. internat. trade div. State of Oreg., Portland, 1988—; bd. dirs. Oreg. Dental Svc., Portland, 1st Bank, Portland, Leopold & Stevens, Inc., Portland. Mem. Arlington, Multnomah Athletic, Univ. Club. Republican. Home: 1250 Englewood Dr Lake Oswego OR 97034 Office: State Of Oreg 121 SW Salmon Portland OR 97201

RASMANIS, EGONS, electronics company executive; b. Riga, Latvia, July 12, 1924; came to U.S., 1950, naturalized, 1955; s. Janis Andrejs and Anna (Smemanis) R.; B.Sc., Friedrich Alexander U., Erlangen, Ger., 1949; postgrad. Northeastern U., 1955; m. Vita Anita Skulte, June 30, 1956; children—Anita Ilze, Ingrid Inta, Linda Irene. Mgr. devel. engring. CBS Electronics, Lowell, Mass., 1956-60; project mgr., prin. engr. GT & E Sylvania, Waltham, Mass., 1960-64; mgr. microelectronics Amperex Co., Cranston, R.I., 1964-69, mgr. mfg., 1969-72; co-founder, v.p. sales Micro Components Corp., Cranston, 1972-78; v.p. sales Cherry Semicondr. Co., 1978-86; pres. Ertronics, Inc., 1986—. Pres., Latvian Acad. Soc. Fraternitas Metropolitana, Boston, 1957-59, 62-64, 75-77, 79-81, 86—. Mem. Internat. Soc. Hybrid Microelectronics, Assn. Latvian Acad. Socs., (pres. 1987-88). Lutheran. Patentee in field of semicondrs. and microelectronics. Home: 151 Westwood Dr East Greenwich RI 02818 Office: 5586 Post Rd East Greenwich RI 02818

RASMUSON, ELMER EDWIN, banker, former mayor Anchorage; b. Yakutat, Alaska, Feb. 15, 1909; s. Edward Anton and Jenny (Olson) R.; m. Lile Vivian Bernard, Oct. 27, 1939 (dec. 1960); children: Edward Bernard, Lile Muchmore (Mrs. John Gibbons, Jr.), Judy Ann; m. Col. Mary Louise Milligan, Nov. 4, 1961. B.S. magna cum laude, Harvard U., 1930, A.M., 1935; student, U. Grenoble, 1930; LL.D., U. Alaska, 1970. C.P.A., N.Y., Tex., Alaska. Chief accountant Nat. Investors Corp., N.Y.C., 1933-35; prin. Arthur Andersen & Co., N.Y.C., 1935-43; pres. Nat. Bank of Alaska, 1943-65, chmn. bd., 1966-74, chmn. exec. com., 1975-82, now chmn. emeritus; mayor City of Anchorage, 1964-67, dir., emeritus and cons., 1989; civilian aide from Alaska to sec. army 1959-67; Swedish consul Alaska, 1955-77; Chmn. Rasmuson Found.; Rep. nominee U.S. Senate from Alaska, 1968; U.S. commr. Internat. N. Pacific Fisheries Commn., 1969-84; mem. Nat. Marine Fisheries Adv. Com., 1974-77, North Pacific Fishery Mgmt. Council, 1976-77, U.S. Arctic Research Commn., 1984—. Mem. City Council Anchorage, 1945, chmn. city planning commn., 1950-53; pres. Alaska council Boy Scouts Am., 1953; sec.-treas. Loussac Found.; regent U. Alaska, 1950-69; trustee King's Lake Camp, Inc., 1944—, Alaska Permanent Fund Corp., 1980-82; bd. dirs. Coast Guard Acad. Found. Decorated knight first class Order of Vasa, comdr. Sweden; recipient silver Antelope award Boy Scouts Am., Japanese citation Order of the Sacred Treasure, Gold and Silver Star, 1988; outstanding civilian service medal U.S. Army; Alaskan of Year award, 1976. Mem. Pioneers Alaska, Alaska Bankers Assn. (past pres.), Defense Orientation Conf. Assn., NAACP, Alaska Native Brotherhood, Explorers Club, Phi Beta Kappa. Republican. Presbyn. Clubs: Masons, Elks, Anchorage Rotary (past pres.); Harvard (N.Y.C.; Boston); Wash. Athletic (Seattle), Seattle Yacht (Seattle), Rainier (Seattle); Thunderbird Country (Palm Desert, Calif.); Bohemian (San Francisco); Eldorado Country (Indian Wells, Calif.); Boone & Crockett. Home: PO Box 600 Anchorage AK 99510

RASMUSSEN, EDWARD FREDERICK, airline company official; b. Mpls., June 5, 1940; s. Hans Edward and Lois Ruth (Welch) R.; student public schs., Hopkins, Minn.; m. Lena K. Clement, Feb., 1981; stepchildren: Greg Carvalho, Heather Carvalho; 1 son by previous marriage, John Edward. Served with U.S. Navy, 1959-67; with Western Air Lines, Los Angeles, 1967—, avionics line foreman, Los Angeles, 1975-83, sr. avionics engr., 1983-85, maintenance control tech. coordinator, 1985-86, mgr. aircraft prodn. control, 1986-87; mgr. avionics, Hawaiian Airline, 1987-89; dir. shops Hawaiian Airline, 1989—. Republican. Home: 1579 Molehu Dr Honolulu HI 96818 Home: 94-1103 Kaaholo St Waipahu HI 96797 Office: Honolulu Internat Airport PO Box 30008 Honolulu HI 96820

RASMUSSEN, EVIE WEBB, financial institution executive; b. Wurzburg, Franken, Federal Republic of Germany, June 18, 1952; came to U.S., 1956; d. Robert Daniel and Rosemarie Franziska (Scheidermeier) Webb; m. Terry James Rasmussen, Dec. 29, 1973; 1 child, John Robert. Student, Mt. Hood Community Coll., Portland, Oreg., 1983-84, Claremont Coll., Pamona, Calif., 1984-86. Clk. Unishops Inc., Portland, Oreg., 1969-71; teller Tigard (Oreg.) Community Fed. Credit Union, 1980-81; auditor Nat. Credit Union Adminstrn., Portland, 1981-83; chief exec. officer United Assn. NW Federal Credit Union, Portland, 1983—. Vol. Portland Easter Seals, 1986—, Nat. Fedn. for Blind, 1987. Credit Union Nat. Assns. scholar 1984. Mem. Nat. Assn. Female Execs., Credit Union Womens Assn., Oregon Credit Union League (scholarship com. 1983—, budget com. 1986—, bd. dirs, dir.-at-large, 1987, bd. dirs. Columbia chpt. 1985—), Smithsonian Assocs. Club: Toastmasters (Portland) (treas. 1987—). Office: United Assn NW Fed Credit Union 2111 NE 43d Ave Portland OR 97213

RASMUSSEN, LOUIS CHARLES, electric utility executive; b. N.Y.C., June 28, 1928; s. Lauritz and Anna (Walsh) R.; m. Cecile Doughty, Dec. 28, 1954; children—Louis Charles Jr., Kurt, Jan, Lisa. B.S. in E.E., MIT, 1948; M.B.A., NYU, 1951; J.D., U. Mo., 1968. Registered profl. engr., Mo., Kans.; Bar: Ks. Engr. Pub. Service Electric & Gas, Newark, N.J., 1948-55; mgr. Bangor Gas Co., Maine, 1955; asst. gen. mgr. Citizens Utility Co., Sacramento, Calif., 1956; ops. analyst Citizens Utility Co., Stamford, Conn., 1957; rate cons. Ebasco Internat. Corp., N.Y.C., 1957-60; mgr. rates Kansas City Power & Light, Mo., 1960-65, v.p. corp. planning and fin., 1974-80, sr. v.p. fin. and commerce, 1982-84, exec. v.p., 1984—, also dir.; v.p., treas., officer WYMO Fuels, Inc., Kansas City, Mo. Contbr. articles to law rev. Chmn. Carondelet Health Corp., Kansas City, Mo.; trustee U. Mo., Kansas City. Served to 1st lt. USAF, 1951-53. Mem. Mo. Valley Electric Assn., Kansas City C. of C. Club: Kansas City Club. Office: Kans City Power & Light Co 1330 Baltimore Ave Kansas City MO 64105

RASMUSSEN, RAUN JAY, venture capital company executive; b. Sioux City, Iowa, June 27, 1928; s. Clarence R. and Mamie C. (Johnson) R.; m. Donna Jean Reeves, July 21, 1951; children: Raun J. Jr., Dan C., Terri A., Amy L. BS, U.S. Naval Acad., 1951; MBA, Harvard U., 1959. Commd. 2d lt. USAF, 1951, advanced through grades to capt., 1957, resigned, 1962; ptnr., investment banker G.H. Walker & Co., N.Y.C., 1962-72; pres. InnoVen, Saddle Brook, N.J., 1972—; bd. dirs. Microdynamics, Inc., Dallas, Sigma Design, Inc., Denver, Phoenix Digital Corp. Mem. Glen Rock (N.J.) Bd. Edn., 1966-69. Republican. Lutheran. Club: Ridgewood Country (Paramus, N.J.) (bd. dirs. 1974-77). Home: 60 Midwood Rd Glen Rock NJ 07452 Office: InnoVen Park 80 Pla W-1 Saddle Brook NJ 07662

RASMUSSEN, ROBERT DEE, real estate appraiser; b. Lincoln, Kans., Dec. 24, 1936; s. Sam and Kristena (Andersen) R.; m. Beverly Bert Rowden, Mar. 22, 1959; children: Robert Denis, Kay Lynn. B Gen. Edn., U. Nebr., 1965; MA, Ariz. State U., 1970. Commd. USAF, 1956, advanced through grades to col., 1978, fighter pilot various locations, 1956-75; comdr. 59th Tactical Fighter Squadron Eglin AFB, Fla., 1975-77; chief Europe/Nato Plans USAF, Washington, 1978-80; vice-comdr. 474th Tactical Fighter Wing USAF, Nellis AFB, Nev., 1980-81; chief of plans U.S. European Command USAF, Stuttgart, Fed. Republic of Germany, 1981-84; dir. joint matters Hdqrs. Tactical Air Command USAF, Langley AFB, Va., 1984-86; ret. USAF, 1986; appraiser, cons. Appraisal House Inc., Ft. Walton Beach, Fla., 1987—; dir. U.S. Power Squadrons, Ft. Walton Beach, 1988. Decorated Disting. Flying Cross, Legion of Merit, Def. Superior Svc. Medal. Mem. Air Force Assn., Ret. Officers Assn., Am. Assn. of Individual Investors, Fla. Assn. of Realtors, NAR, Mortgage Lenders Assn., Porsche Club of Am. (v.p. Germany region 1983-84, pres. North Fla. region 1989). Home: 2421 Duncan Dr Niceville FL 32578

RASMUSSEN, WILLIAM OTTO, computer company executive; b. Burley, Idaho, Jan. 29, 1942; s. Otto M. and Eleanor M. (Kinney) R.; m. Bonnie K. Branson, Sept. 5, 1964; children: Robert, Christopher. BS in Physics, U. Idaho, 1964, MS in Physics, 1966; PhD, U. Ariz., 1973. Exploration geophysicist Heinrichs Geoexploration Co., Tucson, Ariz., 1968-70; assoc. prof. agrl. engring U. Ariz., Tucson, 1973—; dir. Western Computer Consortium, Tucson, 1983-87; with Biosystems Engring., Tucson, 1988—; cons. Bell Tech. Ops., Tucson, 1981-87. Author: Computer Applications in Agriculture, 1985. W.K. Kellogg Found. grantee, 1983-87. Mem. AAAS, Am. Water Resources Assn., Assn. Computing Machinery, Assn. of Old Crows, Sigma Pi Sigma. Home: 1325 N Goebel Tucson AZ 85715 Office: Biosystems Engring 507 Shantz UA Tucson AZ 85721

RASMUSSON, CHARLES LEONARD, director of planning analysis; b. Bklyn., Mar. 7, 1954; s. Leonard Beely and Joan Ann (Rees) R.; m. Joanne Louise Stiefel, Aug. 4, 1954; children: Brian, Kristen. BBA in Acctg. magna cum laude, Adelphi U., 1976, MS in Acctg., 1979. CPA, N.Y. Jr. acct. Columbia Ribbon Co., Glen Cove, N.Y., 1976-77, supr. cost acctg., 1977-79, mgr. acctg., 1979-81; plant controller Reliance Plastic, Deer Park, N.Y., 1981; asst. controller Histacount Corp. div. Hanson Industry, Melville, N.Y., 1982, controller, 1982-86, trustee employee salary and hourly pension, 1985—; dir. planning and analysis Histacount Corp. div. Hanson Industry, Melville, 1986—; treas. Legacy Direct div. Histacount, Amityville, N.Y., 1984—. Mem. Nat. Assn. Accts., N.Y. State Soc. CPA's, Long Island Mktg. Assn. Home: 544 Larch Ln East Meadow NY 11554 Office: Histacount Corp 965 Walt Whitman Rd Melville NY 11747

RATCLIFF, GENE AUSTIN, energy company executive; b. Onaga, Kans., Apr. 12, 1930; s. Ralph Stovall and Florence Esther (Perrussel) R.; m. Sharon Lee Burrell, Aug. 23, 1953; children: Brenda Gail, Linda Ann. BS in Geology, Kans. State U., 1956, MS in Geology, 1957. Geologist Sohio Petroleum Co., Amarillo, Tex., 1957-61; chief geologist Ozark Mahoning Co., Amarillo, 1961-69; chief research geologist Kerr McGee Corp., Oklahoma City, 1969-74, dir. exploration, 1974-78, v.p. exploration, 1978-85, sr. v.p. exploration, 1985-87, sr. v.p. adminstrn. and minerals exploration, 1987—. Served as sgt. USAF, 1950-52. Mem. Am. Assn. Petroleum Geologists, Am. Petroleum Inst., Indep. Petroleum Assn. Am. Republican. Methodist. Home: 3841 NW 67th Oklahoma City OK 73116 Office: Kerr-McGee Corp PO Box 25861 Oklahoma City OK 73125

RATCLIFFE, ALLEN THOMPSON, JR., financial and real estate consultant, lawyer; b. Beloit, Wis., Jan. 11, 1947; s. Allen T. Ratcliffe and Phyllis (Woellner) Weigand; m. Leslie Garland, Aug. 23, 1979; children: David A., Anne Meredith. B.A., U. Cin., 1969; J.D., U. Denver, 1972; L.L.M., U. Miami, 1978. Bar: Colo. Assoc. Nicholas & Magill, Steamboat Springs, Colo., 1972-73; ptnr. Ratcliffe & Chamberlin, Steamboat Springs, 1974-83; of counsel, dir. devel. Robert J. Pope & Assocs., Palo Alto, Calif., 1983-84; chief ops. officer Gaither & Fitzgerald, Menlo Park, Calif., 1984-85; investment coord. David White and Assocs., Walnut Creek, Calif., 1986—; town atty. Yampa, Colo., 1972-74; city atty. Steamboat Springs, 1973-77; prof. Colo. Mountain Coll., Steamboat Springs, 1978-83; ptnr. Steamboat Cablevision, 1981-85. Lectr. Steamboat Springs Chamber Resort Assn., 1981, 82; pres. Tree Haus Homeowners Assn., 1981-82; v.p. Tree Haus Water and Sanitation District, 1982. Mem. Colo. Bar Assn., N.W. Colo. Bar Assn., Colo. Criminal Justice Planning Council (chmn. exec. com. 1976-76). Episcopalian. Lodge: Rotary. Home: 1155 Turtle Rock Ln Concord CA 94521 Office: David White & Assocs 309 Lennon Ln Walnut Creek CA 94598

RATCLIFFE, GEORGE JACKSON, JR., lawyer, business executive; b. Charleston, W.Va., Mar. 22, 1936; s. George Jackson and Dorothy (Ward) R.; m. Nancy Lenhardt, Oct. 5, 1963; children: George Jackson III, Dorothy Margaret. AB, Duke U., 1958; JD, U. Va., 1961. Bar: N.Y. 1964, Ohio 1962. Assoc. Taft, Stettinius & Hollister, Cin., 1961-63; lawyer IBM Corp., 1963-65; assoc. Perkins, Daniels & McCormack, N.Y.C., 1965-70, ptnr., 1970; v.p., sec., gen. counsel Helme Products Inc., N.Y.C., 1970, exec. v.p., 1971-74, pres., 1974; v.p., sec., gen. counsel Hubbell Inc., Orange, Conn., 1975-80, sr. v.p. fin. and law, 1980-83, exec. v.p. adminstrn., 1983-87, chmn. bd., 1987—, pres., chief exec. officer, 1987—; bd. dirs. Hydraulic Co., Bridgeport, Conn., Handy & Harman, N.Y.C., People's Bank, Bridgeport. Mem. ABA, Assn. of Bar of City of N.Y., Conn. Bus. and Industry Assn. (bd. dirs.), Nat. Elec. Mfrs. Assn. (bd. govs.), Brooklawn Country Club (Fairfield, Conn.), Aspetuck Fish and Game Club (Bridgeport), Clove Valley Rod and Gun Club (LaGrangeville, N.Y.), Loblolly Pines (Hobe Sound, Fla.), Merion Golf Club (Ardmore, Pa.). Home: 278 Sherwood Dr Southport CT 06490 Office: Hubbell Inc 584 Derby Milford Rd PO Box 549 Orange CT 06477-4024

RATHBLOTT, PAUL LEON, lawyer; b. Phila., May 6, 1940; s. Albert and Ruth (Dorman) R.; m. Katherine M. Mersereau, Sept. 8, 1967; children: Ruth, Aaron. BA, U. Pa., 1962; JD, Temple U., 1966. Assoc. Morgan, Lewis & Backus, Phila., 1966-68; ptnr. Rathblott & Rathblott, Camden, N.J., 1968-70; sr. litigation atty. Xerox Corp., Stamford, Conn., 1970-77; asst. v.p., asst. gen. counsel Avis, Inc., Garden City, N.Y., 1977-80; v.p., sec., gen. counsel Baker Industries, Inc., Parsippany, N.J., 1980—. Served as pvt. U.S. Army, 1962. Mem. ABA, Am. Corp. Counsel Assn., N.J. Gen. Counsel, Westchester-Fairfield Corp. Counsel Assn. Jewish. Home: 1072 Oenoke Rd New Canaan CT 06840 Office: Baker Industries Inc 1633 Littleton Rd Parsippany NJ 07054

RATHER, JEROME WILLIAM, association administrator; b. Fond du Lac, Wis., Mar. 30, 1953; s. Howard Adolph and Dorothy Rose (Diedrich) R.; m. Marsha Lee Hill, Sept. 5, 1981. BBA, U. Wis., 1975. CPA, Wis. Staff acct. Arthur Andersen & Co., Milw., 1975-78; mgr. fin. services Cuna Mut. Ins. Group, Madison, Wis., 1978-82; v.p. fin. Credit Union Nat. Assn., Inc., Madison, 1982—. Mem. Am. Inst. CPA's, Wis. Inst. CPA's, Wis. Com. on Credit Unions. Roman Catholic. Office: Credit Union Nat Assn PO Box 431 Madison WI 53701

RATHER, JONATHAN MASSEY, financial executive; b. Winchester, Eng., May 20, 1960; came to U.S. 1964; s. Hal and Shiela (Balls) R.; m. Mary Frances Caliendo, Apr. 5, 1986. BS, Boston Coll., 1982; MS in Taxation, Pace U. Sr. auditor Arthur Anderson & Co., N.Y.C., 1982-85; asst. treas. Goelet Corp., N.Y.C., 1985—; cons. J & R Assocs., N.Y.C., Atlanta. Mem. World Vision, Pasadena, Calif. Mem. Am. Inst. CPA's, State of N.Y. CPA's, Alpha Sigma Nu, Beta Gamma Sigma. Republican. Office: Goelet Corp 22 E 67th St New York NY 10021

RATI, ROBERT DEAN, data processing executive; b. Pittsburg, Kans., Jan. 8, 1939; s. Steve Julius Rati and Dorothy Bill (Rodebush) McWilliams; m. Margaret Fort Henry, June 7, 1969; children: Susan Margaret, Robert Henry. BA, U. Kans., 1961; MA, Northeastern U., Boston, 1970; MBA, Columbia U., 1973. Systems engr. IBM Corp., Boston, 1965-72; mgr. mgmt. services Arthur Young and Co., N.Y.C., 1973-75; mgr. client systems Touche Ross and Co., N.Y.C., 1975-76; mgr. systems and programs Walker Mfg. div. Tenneco, Racine, Wis., 1976-78; mgr. data processing Schwitzer div. Household Internat., Indpls., 1979-87; mgr. mgmt. info. systems Nat. Machinery Co., Tiffin, Ohio, 1988—. Contbr. articles to fraternal orgs. newsletters. Mem. Rep. Com., Ramsey, N.J., 1972-74; treas. Rep. Club Ramsey, 1972-75; vice chmn. Swimming Pool Commn., Ramsey, 1972-74; bd. dirs., exec. com. Near Eastside Multi-Service Ctr., Indpls., 1984-87; fin. com. Carmel (Ind.) United Meth. Ch., 1984-87, adminstrv. bd., 1987—. Served to lt. (j.g.) USN, 1961-64. Recipient Regional Mgrs. award, IBM Corp., 1967. Mem. Soc. Ind. Pioneers (bd. govs. 1985-89), Huguenot Soc. Ind. (pres. 1985-89), S.R. (Ill. pres. 1980-82, chmn. awards com. 1983—), Pi Mu Epsilon. Republican. Home: 2215 Windsong Dr Findlay OH 45840 Office: Nat Machinery Co 161 Greenfield St Tiffin OH 44883

RATICAN, PETER S., health maintenance organization executive. Now chmn., pres., chief exec. officer Maxicare Health Plans Inc., 1988—, also bd. dirs. Office: Maxicare Health Plans Inc 5200 W Century Blvd Los Angeles CA 90045 *

RATZLAFF, JAMES W., investment banker. BS, U. Kans., 1958; JD, George Washington U., 1968. With Amcap Fund Inc., L.A., 1973—, exec. v.p., 1973-84, chmn., chief exec. officer, 1984—, also pres. bd. dirs. Office: AMCAP Fund Inc 333 S Hope St Los Angeles CA 90071 *

RATZLAFF, STANLEY ABE, diversified holding company executive; b. Bakersfield, Calif., June 22, 1935; s. Abe S. and Verna A. (Heinrichs) R.; m. Bette Anne Riley, July 14, 1957; children: Deborah Ratzlaff Huff, Stephen, Diane. A.A. in Acctg., Bakersfield Coll., 1955; B.A. in Acctg. with distinction, San Jose State U., 1957; grad. advanced mgmt. program, Harvard U., 1978. C.P.A., Calif. Sr. acct. Shell Oil Co., Los Angeles, 1957-61; audit mgr. Ernst & Ernst, Los Angeles, 1961-69; treas., controller Shareholders Capital Programs, Inc., Los Angeles, 1969-72; asst. controller Atlantic Richfield Co., Los Angeles, 1972-79; controller Standard Oil Co., Cleve., 1979-81; v.p., controller Occidental Petroleum Corp., Los Angeles, 1981-84, Pacific Enterprises, Los Angeles, 1984—. Mem. bd. advisors U. So. Calif. Sch. Acctg., 1982—; pres., bd. dirs. Union Rescue Mission, L.A., 1984—. Mem. AICPA, Calif. Soc. CPAs, Fin. Execs. Inst. (pres. L.A. chpt. 1989—, bd. dirs. 1984—), Nat. Assn. Accts. (v.p. local chpt. 1968-69, mgmt. acctg. com. 1987—, named Most Valuable Mem. 1964), Am. Petroleum Inst., Pacific Coast Gas Assn., Am. Gas Assn. Republican. Office: Pacific Enterprises 801 S Grand Ave Los Angeles CA 90017

RAU, ALLEN HOWARD, chemical engineer; b. Pitts., Apr. 6, 1958; s. Eric and Anita Doris (Goldrich) R.; m. Edyce Diane Solomon, Mar. 18, 1989. BS in Chemistry, Rutgers U., 1979; MBA in Mgmt., U. Cin., 1983. Staff engr. Procter & Gamble, Cin., 1979-81, group leader, 1981-85; sr. project mgr. Andrew Jergens Co., Cin., 1985-87, dir. product devel., 1987—. Patentee in field. Mem. leadership council, Jewish Fed. Cin., 1987—. Mem. Am. Inst. Chem. Engrs., Am. Chem. Soc., Am. Oil Chemists Soc, Soc. of Cosmetic Chemists. Home: 1306 Duncan Ave Cincinnati OH 45208 Office: Andrew Jergens Co 2535 Spring Grove Ave Cincinnati OH 45214

RAU, DAVID EDWARD, real estate company executive; b. Lincoln, Nebr., Sept. 27, 1956; s. Leo George and Anne Marie (Pavel) R.; m. Kathy Georgette Wilcox, May 17, 1980; children: Andrew David, Peter Nicholas, Victoria Anne. BBA, U. Ariz., 1978. CPA, Ariz., N.Mex. Sr. Peat Marwick Main, Albuquerque, 1978-82; supervising sr. Peat Marwick Main, Phoenix, 1982-83; asst. treas. Kroy Inc., Scottsdale, Ariz., 1983-85; acct. Zolondek & Blumenthal, Phoenix, 1985; v.p. taxes Del Webb Corp., Phoenix, 1985—. Advisor Phoenix Sky Harbor Ctr. Tech. Adv. panel, 1987. Mem. Assn. for Corp. Growth, Ariz. Soc. CPA's, Greater Phoenix C. of C. (downtown redevel. task force 1986), Albuquerque Jaycees (treas. 1981-82), Beta Alpha Psi. Republican. Roman Catholic. Office: Del E Webb Corp 2231 E Camel Back Rd Phoenix AZ 85038

RAUCH, ARTHUR IRVING, management consultant; b. N.Y.C., Sept. 18, 1933; s. David and Miriam (Frankel) R.; BA magna cum laude (Rufus Choate scholar), Dartmouth Coll., 1954, MS, Amos Tuck Sch. Bus. Adminstrn., 1955; m. Roxane M. Spiller, Aug. 19, 1962 (div. 1977); children—David S., Janine B.; m. Lynn R Saidenberg, Oct. 11, 1987; Security analyst Lionel D. Edie & Co., N.Y.C., 1959-64; group dir. rsch. Eastman Dillon, Union Securities & Co., N.Y.C., 1964-68; v.p., sr. analyst Laird, Inc., N.Y.C., 1968-69, dir. rsch., 1969-71, sr. v.p., 1970-73; ptnr. Oppenheimer & Co., N.Y.C., 1973-77; v.p. corp. devel. Rorer Group Inc., Ft. Washington, Pa., 1977-84; v.p. corp. fin. Arnhold & S. Bleichroeder, Inc., 1984-88; cons. corp. devel. ICN Pharms. Inc., N.Y.C., 1988—; mem. investment com. Becker Fund, 1969-73; bd. dirs. Sonomed Tech., Inc., 1983—, exec. com. Dartmouth Class of 1954, 1968-79. Lt. (j.g.) USNR, 1956-59. Chartered fin. analyst. Mem. N.Y. Soc. Security Analysts, Assn. Corp. Growth, Fin. Analysts Fedn. (corp. info. com.), Phi Beta Kappa. Home: 1185 Park Ave New York NY 10128 Office: ICN Pharms Inc 345 Park Ave 42nd Fl New York NY 10152

RAUNIO, MATTHEW ISAAC, controller; b. Detroit, Aug. 26, 1957; s. Isaac Cedric and Ethel Pearl (Bratt) R.; m. Holly Kristine Beck, June 19, 1982; children: Duncan, Dillon. BBA, Mich. Tech. U., 1979; MBA, U. Wis., Oshkosh, 1982. CPA, Mich., Wis.; chartered fin. analyst. Sr. acct. Jonet & Fountain, CPA's, Green Bay, Wis., 1979-81; controller The Premonstratensian Fathers, De Pere, Wis., 1982—; instr. fin. acctg. St. Norbert Coll., De Pere, 1984; lectr. grad. program U. Notre Dame, South Bend, Ind., 1985-89. Fellow Wis. Inst. CPAs; mem. AICPAs (investments com.), Nat. Assn. Treas. Religious Insts. (discussion leader fin. mgmt. workshop 1984-86), Inst. Chartered Fin. Analysts. Lutheran. Home: 515 Karen Ln Green Bay WI 54301 Office: The Premonstratensian Fathers 1016 N Broadway De Pere WI 54115-2697

RAUSSER, GORDON C(LYDE), agricultural and resource economics educator; b. Lodi, Calif., July 21, 1943; s. Elmer A. and Doyve Ester (Meyers) R.; children: Sloan, Stephanie, Paige. B.S. summa cum laude, Calif. State U., 1965; M.S. with highest honors, U Calif.-Davis, 1968; Ph.D. with highest honors, U. Calif.-Davis, 1971. Prof. econs. and agrl. econs. U. Calif., Davis, 1969-74; vis. prof. U. Chgo., 1972-74; prof. econs. and stats. Iowa State U., 1974-75; prof. bus. adminstrn. Harvard U., 1975-78; prof., chmn. dept. agrl. and resource econs. U. Calif.-Berkeley, 1979-85, Robert Gordon Sproul prof., disting. prof., 1985—; dir. Giannini Found., Berkeley, 1984-86; vis. prof. Hebrew U. and Ben-Gurion U., Israel, 1978; Ford Found. vis. prof., Argentina, 1972; spl. cons. and sr. economist Council Econ. Advisors, 1986-87; chief economist Agy. for Internat. Devel., 1988—; advisor econ. research service U.S. Dept. Agriculture, 1978-80, 86—, Agriculture Can., 1977-79, Bur. Agrl. Econs., Australia, 1987, U.S. Office Mgmt. and Budget, 1986; mem., chmn. planning com. Sch. Bus. Adminstrn. U. Calif., Berkeley, 1986-87, mem. adv. com. Agrl. Issues Ctr., 1984-85, mem. planning com. Agrl. and Natural Resources Program, 1986, mem. econs. programs evaluation com., 1987-88; mem. Citrus Planning Commn., Brazil, 1984. Author numerous books including: Macroeconomic Environment for U.S. Agricultural Policy, Alternative Agricultural and Food Policies and the 1985 Farm Bill, New Directions in Econometric Modeling and Forecasting in U.S. Agriculture, Dynamics of Agricultural Systems: Economic Prediction and Control, Quantitative Methods in Agricultural Economics; editor: Decision-Making in Business and Economics, 1977-79, Am. Jour. Agrl. Econs., 1983-86, Advances in Agricultural. Management and Economics., 1988—; assoc. editor: Jour. Am. Stats. Assn., 1973-77, Jour. Econ. Dynamics and Control, 1978-82; contbr. over 200 articles to profl. jours. Mem. western nutrition ctr. coordinating com. U.S. Dept. Agr., 1980-83; mem. Arab-Am. Council for Cultural and Econ. Exchange, 1979-81; bd. dirs. Giannini Found. Agrl. Econs., 1979—, mem. exec. com., 1979—; mem. planning com. Berkeley Food Coop., 1980-83, planning com. for agrl. and food policy Resources for the Future, 1984-85; mem. adv. com. Calif. State Dept. Agriculture, 1982-84; bd. dirs. Am. Agrl. Econs. Awards. Grantee U.S. Dept. Agr., NSF, World Bank, Chgo. Merc. Exchange, U.S. Bur. Mines; Fulbright scholar, Australia, 1987; sr. fellow Resources for Future, 1984-85; Outstanding Research Discovery award, 1972, 76, 78, 80, 82, 86; outstanding tchr. award Harvard U., 1978. Mem. Am. Econ. Assn., Am. Acad. Polit. and Social Sci., Am. Agrl. Econs. Assn. (agrl. policy planning com. 1984-86, outstanding enduring research contribution com. 1982-84, outstanding PhD dissertation com. 1974-76, chmn. outstanding article com. 1983-86, awards 1976, 80, 82), Am. Statis. Assn., Econometric Soc., Math. Assn. Am., Ops. Research Soc., Western Agrl. Econ. Assn. (award 1978), Alpha Gamma Rho, Alpha Zeta, Phi Beta Kappa. Club: Commonwealth (dir. agriculture study group 1983-84). Home: 649 Creston Rd Berkeley CA 94708 Office: U Calif Dept Agr & Resource Econs Berkeley CA 94720

RAUTH, ROBERT KENNETH, oil company executive; b. Chgo., Jan. 4, 1939; s. Leopold and Helen (Banach) R.; m. Marilyn Sue Boell, June 5, 1959; children: Robert Jr., Susan Lynn, Elizabeth Ann, Jeffrey Scott. BS, Northwestern U., 1960. Sales mgr. D.A. Stuart Oil Co., Chgo., 1961-68; regional mgr. D.A. Stuart Oil Co., Hartford, Conn., 1968-77; pres. Pillsbury Chem. & Oil Co., Detroit, 1977—. Contbr. articles to profl. jours. Chmn. fund raiser com. Boy Scouts Am., Detroit, 1986. Mem. Soc. Mfg. Engrs. (chmn. coolant com. 1982—), ASM, ASLE (sec. 1965). Republican. Roman Catholic. Club: Wabeck (Mich.) Country. Office: Pillsbury Chem & Oil Inc 139 Summit St Detroit MI 48209

RAW, DEBORAH J., bank executive; b. Winchester, Mass., Jan. 10, 1959; d. George William and Vena Geraldine (Hamilton) Hardy; m. David Nathanial Raw, Sept. 12, 1981. BA in Langs., SUNY, Stony Brook, 1981. Office mgr., dir. purchasing World Color Press, Inc., N.Y.C., 1982-85; asst. treas., asst. mgr. N.Y. agy. Bahrain Mid. East Bank, N.Y.C., 1985—. Office: Bahrain Mid East Bank 12 E 49th St New York NY 10017

RAWIE, LATITIA JO (TISH), retail executive; b. Joplin, Mo., Dec. 28, 1954; d. Richard Gail and Betty Joan (Nichols) Auman; m. Mark Edwin Rawie, June 12, 1975; children: John McLane, Ashley Jo, Nicholas Morgan. BSBA, Pitts. (Kans.) State U., 1975. Bookkeeper PITSCO, Inc., Pitts., 1973-75; office mgr. Griner and Schmitz, Inc., Kansas City, Mo., 1975-79; v.p. adminstrn., bd. dirs. Personal COmputer Ctr., Overland Park, Kans., 1981-85; v.p. adminstrn., co-owner Integrated Support, Inc., Lenexa, Kans., 1985—, also bd. dirs. Mem. Nat. Assn. Female Execs., Phi Beta Lambda (pres. 1975), Delta Mu Delta. Republican. Methodist. Home: 8925 Hirning Rd Lenexa KS 66220 Office: Integrated Support Inc 8855 Long St Lenexa KS 66215

RAWITT, PEGGY DEBORAH, lawyer; b. Middletown, N.Y., Dec. 1, 1957; d. Kurt Conrad and Regina (Winter) R.; m. Philip Bernstein, July 1, 1979; 1 child, Jonathan. BA, SUNY, Stony Brook, 1977; JD, N.Y. Law Sch., 1980. Student law clk. to presiding justice U.S. Dist. Ct., So. Dist., N.Y.C., 1979-80; assoc. Kramer, Levin Nessen, Kamin & Frankel, N.Y.C., 1980-84, Baker & McKenzie, N.Y.C., 1984—. Mem. ABA (real estate sect.), Assn. Bar City of N.Y. (real property law com. 1988—), N.Y. State Bar Assn. (real estate sect.), Phi Beta Kappa. Office: Baker & McKenzie 805 3rd Ave New York NY 10022

RAWL, ARTHUR JULIAN, accountant, consultant; b. Boston, July 6, 1942; s. Philip and Evelyn (Rosoff) R.; m. Karen Lee Werby, June 4, 1967; 1 child, Kristen Alexandra. BBA, Boston U., 1967, postgrad, 1972-74. CPA, Mass., N.Y., La. Audit mgr. Touche Ross & Co., Boston, 1967-77; audit mgr. Touche Ross & Co., N.Y.C., 1977-79, ptnr., 1979; ptnr. Touche Ross & Co., Newark, 1980-88, N.Y.C., 1988—; mem. adj. faculty Boston U., 1971-75. Contbr. articles to profl. journals. Mem. Newton Upper Falls Hist. Commn., 1977; dir. Sherburne Scholarship Fund Boston U., 1977-80; mem. Englewood (N.J.) Planning Bd., 1981-83; trustee, Englewood Bd. Edn., 1983-85, 89—; trustee, treas. exec. com. Englewood Econ. Devel. Corp. 1986-89; fin. and compensation com. Dwight Englewood Sch., 1985—. Served to 2d class petty officer USN, 1960-63. Fellow Am. Inst. CPA's, Mass. Soc. CPA's, N.Y. Soc. CPA's; mem. Am. Legion, Navy League U.S., N.J. Hist. Soc. (bd. govs., exec. com., nominating com., treas. 1987—), St. George's Soc. N.Y., Univ. Club (N.Y.C.), Essex Club (Newark), Englewood Field

Club, Englewood Club. Home: 72 Booth Ave Englewood NJ 07631 Office: Touche Ross & Co 1633 Broadway New York NY 10019

RAWL, LAWRENCE G., petroleum company executive; b. 1928. Grad. Okla. U., 1952. With Exxon Corp, 1952—, asst. mgr. East Tex. prodn. div., 1965-66, mgr. ops. 1966-67, exec. asst. to chmn., 1967-69, gen. mgr. supply Exxon Co. USA div. then v.p. mktg., 1969-72, v.p. then sr. v.p., 1972-76, exec. v.p. Exxon Co. USA div., 1976-80, sr. v.p. Exxon Corp., N.Y.C., 1980-86, pres., 1986, chmn., chief exec. officer, 1986—, also dir. Office: Exxon Corp 1251 Ave of the Americas New York NY 10020 *

RAWLES, LEWIS GENE, manufacturing executive; b. Kendallville, Ind., Aug. 26, 1948; s. Lewis G. and Virginia E. (Franks) R.; m. Linda Lou Wright, Sept. 20, 1975; children: Lara Lin, Lesli Ann. Student, Indiana U., 1966-68, 72-73. Gen. mgr. parkway dist. Holiday Rambler Corp., Sweetwater, Tex., 1976-77, v.p. Sweetwater div., 1977-80; pres. formtec plastics and harborcraft marine div.s Holiday Rambler Corp., Wakarusa, Ind., 1980-83; pres. HRO Inc., Wolcottville, Ind., 1983-84; sr. v.p. Coachmen Industries Inc., Elkhart, Ind., 1984, exec. v.p., 1985—, mem. fin. com., 1986—; v.p. bd. dirs. So. Ambulance Builders, La Grange, Ga., 1986—. Served in USAF, 1968-72. Mem. Soc. Plastics Engrs., Elkhart C. of C. Republican. Methodist. Home: 22554 Winchester Dr Elkhart IN 46514 Office: Coachmen Industries Inc 601 E Beardsley Ave PO Box 3300 Elkhart IN 46515

RAWLINGS, BOYNTON MOTT, lawyer; b. El Paso, Tex., Dec. 6, 1935; s. Junius Mott and Laura Bassett (Boynton) R.; m. Nancy Mary Peay, Aug. 24, 1962 (div. 1973); children—Laura Bassett, James Mott; m. Judith Reed, Dec. 10, 1977; 1 child, William Reed. A.B., Princeton U., 1958; LL.B., Stanford U., 1961; Diploma, U. Strasbourg (France), 1963. Bar: Calif., 1962, D.C., 1980, Conseil Juridique Paris, 1973. Assoc. Broad, Busterud & Khorie, San Francisco, 1963-65, Homer G. Angelo, Brussels, 1966; assoc., ptnr. S.G. Archibald, Paris, 1967-74; ptnr. Boynton M. Rawlings, Paris, Los Angeles, 1974-84, Kevorkian & Rawlings, Paris, 1984—; dir. Central Soya France, S.A., Trappes, France. Contbr. articles to profl. jours. Mem. Los Angeles Bar Assn. (bd. dirs. sect. internat. law 1975-82), French Am. C. of C. (bd. dirs., v.p. 1985—). Republican. Episcopalian. Avocations: music; tennis; skiing; hiking. Home: 53 Ave Montaigne, 75008 Paris France Office: Kevorkian & Rawlings, 46 Ave D'Iena, 75116 Paris France

RAWLS, BARBARA WATSON, finance and systems consultant; b. N.Y.C., Mar. 3, 1941; d. Robert W. and Jeanne B. (Rogers) Watson; m. Reuben R. Rawls, May 10, 1969; 1 child, Juliana B. Student, Smith Coll., 1959-62; AB, Stanford U., 1963, MA, 1964; MBA, U. Pa., 1978. Systems engr. in fin. and ins. IBM, Phila., 1964-67; mgmt. cons. in data processing, systems design and fin. planning 1967-77; mgmt. cons. Sun Co. Inc., Radnor, Pa., 1978-80, sr. cons. in external affairs for fin. econ. and bus. issues, 1980-85, corp. fin. planner, 1985-87; instr. in bus. adminstrn., evening div. Temple U., 1968-71. Bd. dirs. Phila. Women's Network, 1979-81; exec. adv. Jr. Achievement, Bryn Mawr, Pa., 1978-79; trustee Ludington Library, Bryn Mawr, Cabrini Coll. Recipient Achievement cert. YWCA. Mem. Nat. Women's Coalition, Phila. Fin. Assn., Nat. Assn. Mfrs., Sun Fin. Forum, Beta Gamma Sigma. Clubs: Wharton of Phila., Acorn.

RAWLS, CATHERINE POTEMPA, commodity trader; b. Chgo., Mar. 19, 1953; d. Stanley Louis and Mary Ann (Kuczmarski) Potempa; m. Stephen Franklin Rawls, July 30, 1983. BA, Marquette U., 1975. Mem. Chgo. Bd. Trade, 1977-79, 83—; fin. futures analyst Geldermann Inc., Chgo., 1979-82, dir. rsch., 1982-86 ; pres. Tiare Trading Co. 1987—; mem. Chgo. Merc. Exchange, 1982. Editor Fax & Figures newsletter, 1983, Geldermann-Peavey newsletter, 1983-86 . Recipient award Marquette U. chpt. Women in Communications, 1975. Mem. Futures Industry Assn. Roman Catholic. Home: 421-C Sandhurst Circle Glen Ellyn IL 60137 Office: O'Connor & Co 141 W Jackson 28th Fl Chicago IL 60604

RAWLS, STEPHEN FRANKLIN, brokerage house executive; b. Tifton, Ga., Sept. 18, 1951; s. Jacob Franklin and Jean Harriet (Gamadanis) R.; m. Catherine Dorothy Potempa, July 30, 1983. BBA, Stetson U., 1973. Mgr. commodity futures Cen. Soya Co., Ft. Wayne, Ind., 1975-79; v.p. Drexel Burnham Lambert, Chgo., 1979-82, Geldermann, Inc., Chgo., 1982-85; pres. Delta Fin. Mgmt. Corp., Chgo., 1986—. Mem. Chgo. Bd. Trade. Episcopalian. Lodges: Masons, Shriners. Home: 27W230 Waterford Dr Winfield IL 60190 Office: Delta Fin Mgmt Corp 1 Energy Ctr 300 E Shuman Blvd Naperville IL 60540

RAY, ARLISS DEAN, environmental consultant; b. Hot Springs, Ark., Apr. 3, 1929; s. Clyde E. and Gladys Lorraine (Wofford) R.; B.Engring., Yale U., 1951; M.S., Oreg. State U., 1957; Ph.D., U. Calif., Berkeley, 1962; m. Ardyth Lee Sharman, Aug. 23, 1952; children—Sandra Lee, Nancy Lynn, Laurie Jean, James Clyde. Asst. prof. environ. engring. Vanderbilt U., 1961-63; assoc. prof., then prof. U. Mo., Columbia, 1963-71; v.p. Woodward-Envicon, also Woodward Clyde Cons., Clifton, N.J. and Houston, 1972-75; pvt. cons., 1975-77; co-founder, 1978, since exec. officer EMANCO Inc., environ. mgmt. and cons., Houston, 1978—; adv. EPA, NSF. Served with USNR, 1951-55. Recipient award merit Mo. Water Pollution Control Assn., 1967. Mem. ASCE, Am. Water Works Assn., Air Pollution Control Assn., Water Pollution Control Fedn., Sigma Xi, Tau Beta Pi, Chi Epsilon, Pi Mu Epsilon. Author papers in field. Home: 1319 W Brooklake St Houston TX 77077

RAY, GEORGE THOMAS, financial executive; b. Kankakee, Ill., Mar. 24, 1958; s. George A. and Adlorene V. (Studer) R.; m. Maria C. Martinez, Oct. 11, 1986. A in Applied Sci., Kankakee Community Coll., 1979. Cert. fin. planner. Registered rep. First Colo. Investments and Securities, Denver, 1979-83, B. J. Leonard & Co., Englewood, Colo., 1983-84; v.p. Genesis Capital Corp., Denver, 1984-85; registered rep. Pittock Fin. Corp., Englewood, 1985-86; fin. planner Woodward Fin. Group Inc., Denver, 1986—. Mem. Internat. Assn. for Fin. Planning, Inst. Cert. Fin. Planners, Colo. Soc. Cert. Fin. Planners (charter). Republican. Roman Catholic. Home: 2370 Cherry St Denver CO 80207 Office: Woodward Fin Group Inc 300 S Jackson St Ste 500 Denver CO 80209

RAY, JACK HARRIS, international business development executive; b. Breckenridge, Tex., Oct. 9, 1924; s. Everson Counts and Bessie Lea (Harris) R.; m. Irma Hernandez; 1 child, Rory. B.S., U.S. Mil. Acad., 1947; B.S. in Petroleum Engring., U. Tex., 1949. Sr. dist. petroleum engr. Magnolia Petroleum Co. now Mobil, 1949-59; dist. prodn. supt. Tenneco Oil Co., Lafayette, La., 1959-62; prodn. supt. Gulf Coast div. Tenneco Oil Co., Houston, 1962, v.p. prodn., 1967-70; v.p. Tenneco Internat. Oil Co., Houston, 1966-67; exec. v.p. Tenn. Gas Transmission, Houston, 1972; pres. TGT, Houston, 1974; sr. v.p. internat. devel. Tenneco Inc., Houston, 1983-88; exec. v.p. Sentry Oilfield Equipment, Houston, 1988—. Contbr. articles to profl. jours. Mem. Am. Gas Assn., Am. Petroleum Inst., Interstate Natural Gas Assn. Am., Ctr. for Internat. Mgmt. Studies, U.S.-USSR Trade and Econ. Council, Am. Com. on East-West Accord. Republican. Home: 41 Legend Ln Houston TX 77024

RAY, JAMES ALLEN, consultant; b. Lexington, Ky., Feb. 21, 1931; s. Allen Brice and Elizabeth Logan (Simpson) R.; m. Mary Ruth Johnston, June 8, 1958; children: James Edward, Allen Bruce, John David. BS in Geology, U. N.C., 1958; MS, N.C. State Coll., 1962. Chief petrographic research Master Builders div. Martin Marietta Corp., Cleve., 1959-73, asst. dir. research, 1973-77, dir. research, 1977-78, v.p. research, 1979-80, v.p. creative research, 1980-82; cons., 1982—; pres. James A. Ray Corp. 1986—. Patentee in field. Served with USAF, 1951-55. Recipient Jefferson cup Martin Marietta Corp., 1977. Fellow Am. Inst. Chemists, Inc.; mem. Mineral. Soc. Am., Mineral. Soc. Can., Am. Concrete Inst., ASTM, Res. Officers Assn. (life), Nat. Rifle Assn. (life), Washington Legal Found. (life), Am. Security Council. Republican. Home: 9891 Stamm Rd PO Box P Mantua OH 44255

RAY, JOHN M., insurance agency executive; b. Gleason, Tenn., Nov. 13, 1938; s. John H. Ray and Elsie Kimbel Innis; m. Phyllis J. Brown, Nov. 8, 1958; children: John F., Joanna P., Jacquelyn J. BS, U. Tenn., Nashville, 1968, Trevecca Coll., 1978. CLU, 1973. Agt. State Farm Ins., Nashville, 1968-82; mgr. State Farm Ins., Columbia, Tenn., 1982-87; agy. dir. State Farm Ins., Memphis, 1987—. Contbr. articles to profl. jours. Mem. adv. bd. Tenn. dist. Ch. of Nazarene 1976-77, bd. dirs. coll. hill dist., 1975-81; pres. Gideons, Nashville camp, 1972-76; mem. adminstrv. bd. Craft United, Columbia, 1985-86. Mem. Nat. Assn. Life Underwriters (v.p., 1982, speaker), Am. Soc. CLUs (pub. relations chmn. 1980-81), Nat. Assn. CLUs (pub. relations chmn., 1974-75), State Farm Ins. Cos. Pres.' Club (life). Home: 2937 Levee Oaks Collierville TN 38017

RAY, JUDY SELF, marketing consultant; b. Neosho, Mo., June 23, 1946; d. Dan J. and Madge Lee (Hager) Self; m. Charles E. Smith, May 8, 1965 (div. 1974); 1 child, Jennifer Charlene; m. John Wallace Ray, June 20, 1974; stepchildren: Donna Sue, Vickie Kay, Wendy Ann. Student, Columbus Coll., 1965, Brunswick Jr. Coll., 1975, Chattahoochee Valley State Coll., 1975-76. Operator So. Bell, Columbus, Ga., 1964-66, service rep., 1966-71, 79-87, service cons., 1987—; service rep. South Cen. Bell, Phenix City, Ala., 1972-74, 75-79; sec. Brunswick (Ga.) Jr. Coll., 1975; trainer/facilitator Communications Workers Am., Columbus, 1984-87, So. Bell, Columbus, 1984-87; tng. course developer So. Bell, 1985-87. Contbr. articles to profl. jours. Vol. campaign com. Sen. Danny Corbett, Phenix City, Ala., 1982, 83, 86; poll worker State of Ala., Russell county, 1982—; legis. sec. Communications Workers Am., 1988—; vol. CWA Charity Golf Tournament, 1986—. Mem. Am. Bus. Women's Assn. (v.p. 1988—, treas. 1987-88), Telephone Pioneers Am. Democrat. Mem. Assembly of God Ch. Home: PO Box 1799 Phenix City AL 36868 Office: So Bell 1251 13th St Columbus GA 31994

RAY, WILLIAM F., banker; b. Cin., Sept. 17, 1915; s. William F. and Adele (Daller) R.; m. Helen Payne, 1939; children: Katharine Ray Sturgis, Barbara Ray Stevens, Mary Ray Struthers, Margaret Ray Gilbert, Whitney Ray Dawson, William F. III, Susan. A.B., U. Cin., 1935; M.B.A., Harvard, 1937. With Brown Bros. Harriman & Co., 1937—, asst. mgr., 1944-49; mgr. Brown Bros. Harriman & Co., Boston, 1950-67; partner Brown Bros. Harriman & Co., N.Y.C., 1968—; trustee emeritus Atlantic Mut. Ins. Co., N.Y.C.; mem. internat. bd. advice Australia and New Zealand Banking Group, Ltd. Bd. dirs., v.p. Robert Brunner Found.; bd. dirs. Downtown-Lower Manhattan Assn., Inc., Am. Australian Bicentennial Found. Mem. Bankers Assn. for Fgn. Trade (pres. 1966-67), Harvard Bus. Sch. Assn. (pres. 1963-64, exec. council), Robert Morris Assocs. (pres. N.E. 1962-63), Pilgrims U.S., Am. Australian Assn. (pres.), Phi Beta Kappa Assocs. (v.p., dir.), Order of Australia (officer, hon.), Sons of the Revolution (life), Order of Malta, Asia Soc. (Am. award 1988), Phi Beta Kappa. Republican. Clubs: Skating (Boston) (pres. 1956-58); Country (Brookline, Mass.); Union, India House (N.Y.C.); Apawamis (Rye, N.Y.); Fishers Island (N.Y.) Country, Ardsley (N.Y.) Curling; Mountain Lake (Lake Wales, Fla.). Home: 1 East End Ave New York NY 10021 Office: Brown Bros Harriman & Co 59 Wall St New York NY 10005

RAYBURN, DOUGLAS DALE, accountant; b. Corpus Christi, Tex., Jan. 17, 1948; s. Clarence Wallace and Dortha Frances (Anthony) R.; m. Colleen Sue McGilvray, Aug. 16, 1985; children: Kristine Noelle, Tara Ann. BS in Acctg., San Diego State U., 1976. CPA, Wash. Auditor Foodmaker, Inc., San Diego, 1976-78; acctg. supr. Paccar, Inc., Seattle, 1979-85; sr. fin. adminstr. John Fluke Mfg., Everett, Wash., 1985—; chmn. supervisory com. Fluke Credit Union, Everett, 1986—; chmn. audit com. Kenworth Credit Union, Seattle, 1984-85. Served with USAF, 1969-72, Vietnam. Mem. Am. Inst. CPA's, Nat. Assn. Accts. Republican. Mem. Christian Ch. Home: 30625 56th Ave S Auburn WA 98001

RAYE, WILLIAM HENRY, retired banker; b. Boston, Sept. 12, 1911; s. William Henry and Clara (Capen) R.; widower; children: Charlotte, Polly. AB, Amherst Coll., 1934; MBA, Harvard U., 1936. With Bank of Boston, from 1934, sr. v.p., from 1945, now ret.

RAYFIELD, ALLAN LAVERNE, electronics company executive; b. Mobile, Ala., May 11, 1935; s. Allan Edger and Clara Louise (Dalee) R.; m. Joan Pilgrim Boucher, July 5, 1958; children: Michael Jon, Mark Allan. BSCE, Pa. State U., 1959; MBA, Rensselaer Poly. Inst., 1965; grad. Advanced Mgmt. Program, Harvard U. Bus. Sch., 1976. Various positons medium A.C. motors GE, Schenectady, 1964-72; gen. mgr. armament systems dept. GE, Burlington, Vt., 1972-77; gen. mgr. transp. equipment dept. GE, Erie, Pa., 1977-80; chmn. bd., chief exec. officer Gen. Electric do Brasil, Sao Paulo, 1980; pres. GTE Communications Products Corp., Stamford, Conn., 1980-83, GTE Diversified Products, Stamford, 1983-87; pres. GTE Products and Systems, Stamford, 1987-89, also bd. dirs., sr. v.p. joint venture ops., 1989—; corporator Burlington Savs. Bank, 1978-79; dir. Parker Hannifin Corp., Cleve. Trustee Com. for Econ. Devel.; mem. bd. overseers Rensselaer Poly. Inst.; pres. Greater Burlington Indsl. Devel. Coun., 1975-77, bd. dirs., YMCA, Burlington, 1976-77, Erie, 1978-79; pres. Family Y, Erie, 1975-77. Recipient Clarence E. Davies award Rensselaer Poly. Inst., 1981, Disting. Alumni award Pa. State U.; named Alumni Fellow Pa. State U., 1985, Disting. Alumnus, 1988. Mem. Nat. Assn. Mfrs. (bd. dirs. 1988), Nat. Action Coun. for Minorities in Engring. (treas., trustee), Brooklawn Club, Tau Beta Pi, Chi Epsilon. Republican. Methodist. Office: GTE Svc Corp 1 Stamford Forum Stamford CT 06904

RAYFIELD, GORDON ELLIOTT, political risk consultant; b. Newark, Sept. 1, 1950; s. Bernard George and Rhoda Gertrude (Glucklisch) R.; m. Jean Metzger, July 12, 1981; children—Michael Evan, Jillian Amy. B.A., The American U., 1972; Ph.D., CUNY, 1980. Adj. lectr. Hunter Coll., CUNY, 1977-79, Bklyn Coll., Bklyn., 1977-79; research assoc. Ralph Bunche Inst., UN, N.Y.C., 1978-79; dir. Assn. Polit. Risk Analysts, N.Y.C., 1980-84; polit. risk analyst Gen. Motors Corp., N.Y.C., 1979-86; prin. Rayfield Assocs., N.Y.C., 1986—. Editor: newsletter Polit. Risk Rev., 1983—; mem. bd. editors: book series Global Risk Assessments, 1983—; columnist World Wide Projects, 1985—. Mem. CUNY Grad. Sch. Corporate Adv. Bd., N.Y.C., 1983-86. Mem. Assn. Polit. Risk Analysts (co-founder 1980, pres. 1981-83, bd. dirs. 1997—). Home: 47 Nance Rd West Orange NJ 07052

RAYMER, DONALD GEORGE, utility company executive; b. Jackson, Mich., July 16, 1924; s. Donald Rector and Vivian Alverda (Wolfinger) R.; m. Joan Elizabeth Steck, Oct. 16, 1948; children: Mary Margaret Dorward, Dorothy Elizabeth, Charles George. B.S.E.E., U. Mich., 1948; M.S. (Sloan fellow), M.I.T., 1960. Relay engr. Central Ill. Public Service Co., Springfield, 1948-56; mgr. system ops. Central Ill. Public Service Co., 1956-65; div. mgr. Central Ill. Public Service Co., Mattoon, Ill., 1965-68; v.p. Central Ill. Public Service Co., Springfield, 1968-78; exec. v.p. Central Ill. Public Service Co., 1978-80, pres., chief exec. officer, 1980—, also dir.; dir. Electric Energy, Inc., Marine Bank of Springfield, Marine Corp. Vice chmn. Springfield United Fund Campaign, 1964, asso. chmn., 1974; vice chmn. Mattoon United Welfare Fund, 1967; bd. dirs. Meml. Med. Center; chmn. Meml. Med. Ctr., 1987—. Served to lt. (j.g.) USNR, 1943-46. Mem. IEEE, Am. Mgmt. Assn., Ill. State C. of C. (dir. 1982-88, vice chmn. 1985-87), Greater Springfield C. of C. (dir. 1968-71, 85-88, vice chmn. 1985-88), Chi Phi. Republican. Episcopalian. Clubs: Illini Country, Sangamo (Springfield); Union League (Chgo.). Office: Cen Ill Pub Svc Co 607 E Adams St Springfield IL 62739

RAYMOND, DOUGLAS STAFFORD, recruitment company executive; b. Worcester, Mass., Dec. 6, 1939; s. Kenneth W. and Catharine C. (Stafford) R.; m. Robin Adelle Miller, Dec. 19, 1964; 1 child, Kendra Ann. AB, Kenyon Coll., 1961; MBA, U. Pitts., 1964. V.p. Equibank Co., Pitts., 1961-74; pres. Cornerstone Corp., Upper St. Clair, Pa., 1974—, also bd. dirs.; cons. Scholarship Search, N.Y.C., 1972—, D.R.K. Assocs., Pitts., 1976—. Mem. adv. bd. Pitts. YMCA, 1974—. Mem. Data Processing Mgmt. Assn. (speaker 1973), Assn. Systems Mgmt. Club: Lucyan Country (Freeport, The Bahamas). Home and Office: 1304 Rolling Meadow Rd Pittsburgh PA 15241

RAYMOND, GEOFFREY PETER, finance company executive; b. New Haven, Oct. 13, 1943. BA in Polit. Sci., Providence Coll., 1965; MBA in Fin., U. Pa., 1967. V.p., sr. investment officer Citibank, N.Y.C., 1967-83; exec. v.p., chief investment officer Tex. Commerce Bank N.A., Houston, 1983-86; pres., chief exec. officer Tex. Commerce Investment Management Co., Houston, 1987—; bd. dirs. The Henry Venture Fund I & II-Isle of Man, Cayman Islands. Mem. finance coun. St. Cecilia Ch. Mem. Wharton Alumni Club Houston (bd. dirs.), Delta Epsilon Sigma. Republican. Roman Catholic. Home: 406 Wolf Ct Houston TX 77024 Office: Tex Commerce Investment Mgmt Co 600 Travis PO Box 2558 Houston TX 77252-8032

RAYMOND, LEE R., oil company executive; b. Watertown, S.D., Aug. 13, 1938; m. Charlene Raymond. BSChemE, U. Wis., 1960; PhDChemE, U. Minn., 1963. Various engring. positions Exxon Corp., Tulsa, Houston, N.Y.C. and Caracas, Venezuela, 1963-72; mgr. planning Internat. Co. div. Exxon Corp., N.Y.C., 1972-75; pres., dir. Nuclear subs. Exxon Corp., Bellevue, Wash., 1979-80; exec. v.p. Enterprises div. Exxon Corp., N.Y.C., 1981-83, sr. v.p., dir., 1984-86, pres., dir., 1987—; v.p., dir. Lago Oil, Netherlands Antilles, 1975-76, pres., dir., 1976-79; pres., dir. Esso Inter-Am. Inc., Coral Gables, Fla., 1983-84, sr. v.p., dir., 1984—; bd. dirs. J.P. Morgan & Co, Inc., N.Y.C., Morgan Guaranty Trust Co. of N.Y., N.Y.C., Bus. Council of N.Y. State Inc., N.Y. Chamber of Commerce and Industry Inc., N.Y.C. Partnership Inc., Am. Petroleum Inst. Bd. dirs. Coun. Aid. to Edn., Inc., N.Y.C., 1987—, Nat. Action Coun. Minorities in Engring. Inc., N.Y.C., 1985—, United Way Tri-State, N.Y.C., 1986—; trustee Wis. Alumni Rsch. Found., 1987—; mem. Am. Coun. on Germany, 1986—, Brit.-N.Am. Com., 1985—, vis. com. U. Wis. Dept. Chem. Engring., 1987—. Mem. Am. Petroleum Inst. (bd. dirs. 1987—), German Am. C. of C. (bd. dirs. 1985—), Coun. Fgn. Rels. Club: Country of Darien (Conn.).

RAYMOND, WILLIAM MARSHALL, real estate and contracting company executive; b. Salt Lake City, Dec. 13, 1934; s. Marshall Wellington and Edna Harriett (Byrne) R.; m. Arnetus Harriett Walton, Feb. 19, 1954; children: Ronna Lee, William Marshall, Cecilia, Ami, Jacob. BBA, Woodbury Coll., L.A., 1956. With Walton Assocs. Cos., Glendora, Calif., 1953—, v.p., 1957-69, pres., 1969-89, chmn. bd., 1969-89; chmn. bd. Ben-Wal Printing, Walton Mgmt. Svcs., Inc. Walton Constrn. Co. Pres. Citrus Coll. Found. Bd.; chmn. bd. dirs. Glendora (Calif.) Hosp., 1985-89. With Air N.G., 1953-59. Mem. Nat. Elec. Contractors Assn. Republican. Mormon. Home: 210 Oak Knoll Dr Glendora CA 91740 Office: Walton Assoc Cos 2011 E Financial Way Glendora CA 91740

RAYMONDA, JAMES EARL, banker; b. Piseco, N.Y., Feb. 20, 1933; s. Floyd E. and Bertha (Kramer) R.; m. Marie A. Countryman, Aug. 18, 1956; children—David J., Diane J., Daniel J. B.S. magna cum laude, Syracuse U., 1955. With Norstar Bank (formerly Oneida Nat. Bank & Trust Co. Central N.Y.), Utica, 1957—; v.p., comptroller Norstar Bank (formerly Oneida Nat. Bank & Trust Co. Central N.Y.), 1968—, adminstrv. v.p., until 1973, exec. v.p., 1973—, regional pres., 1987—. Treas. Oneida County chpt. Nat. Found.; pres. Whitestown Jaycees, 1964; adv. com., sec. Whitestown Sr. Center, 1965-87 ; mem. adv. com. St. Elizabeth Hosp., Utica, N.Y.; gen. chmn. campaign Greater Utica United Way, 1977, pres., 1979-80. Recipient Len Wilbur award Utica Kiwanis, 1980, Indsl. Man Yr., 1981. Mem. Nat. Assn. Accountants, C. of C. Greater Utica Area (v.p. adminstrn.). Clubs: K.C. (Utica), Fort Schuyler (Utica); Yahnundasis Golf (New Hartford, N.Y.). Lodge: Rotary (Utica) (pres. 1985-86). Home: 35 Chateau Dr Whitesboro NY 13492 Office: Norstar Bank Upstate NY 268 Genesee St Utica NY 13502

RAYNER, LORD DEREK GEORGE, business executive; b. Norwich, Norfolk, Eng., Mar. 30, 1926; s. George William and Hilda Jane (Rant) R. Student City Coll., Norwich, Selwyn Coll., Cambridge U. (hon. fellow 1983). Joint mng. dir. Marks and Spencer, London, 1973—, joint vice-chmn., from 1982, chief exec., 1983-88, chmn., 1986— . Spl. adviser to Her Majesty's Govt., 1970; chief exec., procurement exec. MOD, 1971-72; mem. U.K. Permanent Security Commn., 1977-80; dep. chmn. Civil Service Pay Bd., 1978-80; mem. Design Council, 1973-75, Council RCA, 1973-76; adviser to Prime Minister on improving efficiency and eliminating waste in govt., 1979-83. Served with RAF, 1946-48. Fellow Inst. Purchasing and Supply; mem. Coronary Artery Disease Research Assn. Office: Mark & Spencer, Michael Housecer Baker St, London W1A 1DN, England

RAZRAN, GILBERT BRUCE, research company executive, industrial engineer; b. Walsenburg, Colo., Sept. 25, 1926; s. Bernard A. and Carolina I. (De Mallieu) R.; AB, U. Miami (Fla.), 1949, MS, 1950; PhD in Indsl. Bioengring., Purdue U., 1953; m. Charlotte D. Bellant, Nov. 8, 1969; children: Rita Lynn, Steven Barry. Project engr. Gen. Electric Co., Ithaca, N.Y., 1953-55, The George Washington U., research specialization in electrophysiology, 1955-59, systems analyst Burroughs Corp. Research Center, Paoli, Pa., 1959-63; dir. ops. research office Command & Control Systems, Washington, 1963-65; pres. Sci. Operational Systems, San Diego, 1965—; chmn., chief exec. officer Kingrexx, Inc., 1983—; prof. Grad. Sch., U.S. Internat. U., Calif., 1969-73; mem. U.S. Sci. Study Rev. Group, UN, Geneva, 1971. Mem. Library Bd., Upper Merion Twp., Pa., 1960-63. Bd. dirs. SOS-Disc, Inc., Las Vegas, Nev., chmn., 1972-75. Served with USNR, 1944-46; PTO; to capt. USAF, 1950-52. Recipient Inventor of Yr. award Patent Law Assn., 1980; registered profl. engr., N.Y., Pa., Calif. Mem. Nat. Security Indsl. Assn., Assn. for Advancement Med. Instrumentation, Mil. Ops. Research Soc., Am. Psychol. Assn., IEEE, Psi Chi, Sigma Xi. Author: Programmed Instruction Book in Electronics, 1966; CAI in Vocational Training, 1967. Contbr. articles to sci. jours. Inventor of oculometer. Office: ILR Med Clinics Ltd, 9 Tooting High St, London SW17, England

REA-CARTER, SUSAN L., investment executive, consultant; b. Troy, N.Y., Aug. 10, 1966; d. Marshall Lewis and Barbara Eileen (Mack) R.; m. James S. Carter, July 9, 1988. BFA, Russell Sage U., 1984. Mng. ptnr. Imperial Ptnrs. 1, Troy, 1984-87; exec. v.p. Castle Bros., Inc., N.Y.C., 1985-86; pres. Imperial Corp., Troy, 1985—, also chmn. bd. dirs.; cons. Carters Painting and Interiors, Schenectady, N.Y., 1988—; bd. dirs. Accord Mgmt. Co., Miami, Fla., 1987—. Mem. legis. adv. com. N.Y. Senate, Albany, 1986—, Guggenheim Mus., 1985-87. Mem. Turf and Field Club, Turf Club. Republican. Home: 228 Belleview Rd Troy NY 12180 Office: Imperial Corp 100 McChesney Ave Troy NY 12180

REACH, BRIAN LEO, healthcare executive; b. Scranton, Pa., Jan. 18, 1955; s. Donald and Joan (Michcalli) R.; m. Mary M. Brozdowski, Mar. 18, 1977; 1 child, Christopher. BS in Acctg., U. Scranton, 1976. CPA, N.J. Sr. acct. Price Waterhouse, N.Y.C., 1976-80; controller Thomas Tilling, Inc., N.Y.C., 1980-84; v.p. fin. Prime Med. Services, Inc., N.Y.C., 1985-86, sr. v.p., 1985-86; pres. C.P. Rehab Corp., Bedminster, N.J., 1986—. Office: CP Rehab Corp 376 Main St Rt 200 Bedminster NJ 07921

READ, ELEANOR MAY, financial analyst; b. Arcadia, N.Y., July 4, 1942; d. Henry and Lena May (Fagner) Van Koevering; 1 child, Robin Jo. Typist, clk., sec., credit corr. Sarah Coventry, Inc., Newark, N.Y., 1957-61; exec. sec. Mobil Chem. Co., Macedon, N.Y., 1961-68; bus. mgr. Henry's Hardware, Newark, 1968-72; with Xerox Corp., Fremont, Calif., 1973—, internat. clk. analyst, personnel adminstrv. asst., employment coordinator, exec. sec., cycle count analyst, tax preparer H&R Block, 1985—. Mem. Xerox/Diablo Mgmt. Assn., Am. Mgmt. Assn., Profl. Businesswomen's Assn., NAFE. Office: H&R Block 910 Page Ave FM-261 Fremont CA 94538

READ, EMERSON BRACKETT, SR., real estate executive; b. Dobbsferry, S.C., Aug. 9, 1925; s. Thomas Carpenter and Helen (Emerson) R.; m. Marie W. Read, Aug. 19, 1978; children by previous marriage: Anne R. Brandt, Elizabeth E. Sunde, Susan L., Emerson B. BSCE, The Citadel, 1950. Chmn. Read & Read, Inc., Charleston, S.C., 1947-50; exec. v.p., mgr. gen. sales Carlton Dooley Realtors, Miami, Fla., 1950-55; with comml. and investment property sales staff The Keyes Co., Inc., Miami, 1955-60, exec. v.p., chief exec. officer Fla. sales div., 1960-65; chmn. bd. Read & Read, Inc., Charleston, 1960—; lectr. Realtors Ednl. Found. S.C., U. S.C. Extension, Columbia, 1966—. Newspaper columnist, 1970-72, 80. Mem. Nat. Assn. Securities Dealers, Nat. Assn. Realtors, S.C. Assn. Realtors (bd. dirs. 1967-85), Nat. Assn. Ind. Fee Appraisers, Greater Charleston Bd. Realtors (pres. 1971-72, Realtor of Yr. 1979), Carolina Yacht Club, The Long Room Club (Charleston). Episcopalian. Home: 19 King St Charleston SC 29401 Office: Read & Read Inc 37 Broad St Charleston SC 29401

READ, PETER KIP, health care administrator; b. Chgo., Nov. 28, 1941; s. Edwin Lewis and Virginia Beapure (Miller) R.; m. Lucy Pierson Wilson, June 4, 1966; children: Dana Dominick, Peter Kip Jr., Jodi Marie. BS, U. Ariz., 1971; MS, Trinity U., 1973. Conv. coord. Hilton Hotels, Palmer House, Chgo., 1963-67; exec. dir. Dental Found. Colo., Denver, 1967-69;

assoc. dir. St. Luke's Hosp., Cleve., 1973-76, exec. v.p., chief ops. officer, 1976-85; exec. v.p., chief ops. officer Bayfront Med. Ctr., St. Petersburg, Fla., 1985-87; pres. Indsl. Med. Supply Co., Tampa, 1988—; vice-chmn. Cancer Data Systems, Cleve., 1983-85. Served with ANG, 1962-68. Fellow Am. Coll. Health Care Execs.; mem. Health Care Adminstrn. N.E. Ohio (pres. 1983), Am. Hosp. Assn., Bay Area Hosp. Assn., Feather Sound Country Club, Rotary. Republican. Episcopalian. Home: 2964 Sandpiper Pl Clearwater FL 34622 Office: Indsl Med Supply Co 8410 Sunstate St Tampa FL 33634

READ, PHILIP LLOYD, computer design and manufacturing executive; b. Flint, Mich., Jan. 9, 1932; s. Harry Samuel and Maude Elizabeth (Jones) R.; m. Ann Elizabeth Goodall, June 23, 1956; children: Thomas, Elizabeth, Jane. AB, Oberlin Coll., 1953; MS in Physics, U. Mich., 1954, PhD in Physics, 1961. Physicist Gen. Electric Co., Schenectady, N.Y., 1960-67; mgr. Gen. Electric Co., Milw., 1967-70, gen. mgr., 1970-75; corp. v.p., div. gen. mgr. Computervision Corp., Bedford, Mass., 1975-81, sr. v.p., chief operating officer, 1981-83, sr. v.p., 1983-88, also bd. dirs.; cons. Computervision Corp., 1988—. Contbr. articles to profl. jours.; patentee in field. Mem. Am. Phys. Soc. Office: Computervision Corp 80 Whtherell Dr Sudbury MA 01776

READE, CHARLES FALKINER, JR., multinational manufacturing executive; b. Evanston, Ill., June 24, 1941; s. Charles Falkiner and Elizabeth (Boomer) R.; m. Emily Schroeder, Sept. 9, 1978; children: Amanda Browning, Elisabeth Kenyon. BBA in Fin., U. Miami, 1965; PMD, Harvard U., 1971; postgrad. NYU. Salesman, So. Bell Tel. & Tel. Co., 1965-66; instnl. salesman Blyth Eastman Dillon & Co. Inc., 1969-73, also founder R.E.I.T. quar. jour.; regional instl. sales mgr. Reynolds Securities Co., 1973-77; dir. metal powder div., gen. mgr. Reade advt. agy. Reade Mfg. Co., Inc., Lakehurst, N.J., 1977-83; pres., chief exec. officer, Reade Internat. Corp., Rumson, N.J., 1983—; lectr. on world trade and size-reduced advanced materials to colls. and profl. assns. Contbr. articles to internat. bus. and leisure pubs. Chmn. Keep Rumson Safe Com.; active Rumson Vol. Fire Dept.; vol. cons. Harvard Urban Minority Cons.; mem. Rep. Nat. Fin. Com.; nat. chmn. Friends for Reagan Com., 1976, Businessmen for Pres. Ford Com., 1976; mem. fund raising com. United Way; trustee World U., Army of U.S. Spl. Warfare Mus.; mem. council exec. bd. Boy Scouts Am.; mem. fin. com. Vol. Nursing Svc.; mem. County Rep. Com. Capt. U.S. Army, 1966-69, Vietnam. Decorated Air medal, Bronze Star with two oak leaf clusters. Mem. Am. Ceramic Soc., Soc. for Advancement of Material and Process Engring., Internat. Iron and Steel Inst., Am. Foundrymen's Soc., ASTM (com. for internat. standardization), AMVETS (life), AIME, Am. Def. Preparedness Assn., Am. Powder Metallurgy Inst., Air Force Assn., Atlantic Coun. U.S. (internat. trade adv. com.), AAU, Am. Chem. Soc., Am. Pyrotechnics Assn., ASM Internat., Ductile Iron Soc., Internat. Magnesium Assn. (dir.), Internat. Pyrotechnics Soc., Bus./Profl. Advt. Assn., C. of C. of U.S., Royal Soc. Chemistry (U.K.), Monmouth County Hist. Soc. (life), Navy League (life), NAM, Scabbard and Blade. Episcopalian. Clubs: N.Y. Yacht; Harvard (N.Y.C., Boston and Phila.); Associate (life); World Trade; Monmouth Boat, Navesink River Rod and Gun, North Shrewsbury Ice Boat and Yacht, Univ. Barge Club (Phila.). Lodge: Masons. Office: Reade Internat Corp 45 W River Rd Rumson NJ 07760

READE, ROBERT MELLOR, convenience store executive; b. Elmhurst, Ill., Jan. 9, 1940; s. M.G. and Virginia A. (Mellor) R.; m. Carol Jean Coon, May 26, 1962; children—Christopher, Gregory. B.A. in Liberal Arts, U. Ariz., 1962. Charting mgr. Eller Outdoor Advt., Phoenix, 1964-69; sales mgr. Mullins Neon, Denver, 1969-70; pres. Gannett Outdoor Co. Ariz., Phoenix, 1970-84; sr. v.p. Gannett Outdoor Group, N.Y.C., 1984-85; sr. v.p. real estate and devel. Circle K Corp., Phoenix, 1985-86; pres., chief operating officer Circle K Internat., Phoenix, 1986—; bd. dirs. Western Savs. and Loan. Chmn. Phoenix chpt. Am. Humanics, 1983, Valley Youth Coalition, 1981, Phoenix City Bond Election, 1984; active Thunderbirds, 1978-83, Theodore council Boy Scouts Am., Community Council, Phoenix United Way, Camelback Mental Health Found. Served with USAR, 1963-69. Recipient U. Ariz. Alumni Appreciation award, 1975, 77, Slouaker award, 1977; Anti Defamation League Torch of Liberty award, 1981. Mem. Ariz. Safety Assn. (pres. 1981), Young Pres. Orgn., Outdoor Assn. Am., Inst. Outdoor Advt., Phoenix Advt. Club (pres. 1974). Club: Rotary (pres. 1982). Office: The Cir K Corp 1601 N 7th St PO Box 52084 Phoenix AZ 85006

READERMAN, DAVID B., securities analyst; b. Phila., Aug. 21, 1956; s. Irwin H. and Joan A. (Mulvehill) R. BA, Colgate U., 1978; MBA, NYU, 1983; Cert. Fin. Analyst, U. Va., 1986. Staff acct. Price Waterhouse, 1978-80; options strategist Smith, Barney, Harris, Upham & Co., N.Y.C., 1980-82, securities analyst, v.p., 1983-88; 1st v.p. equity rsch. Shearson Lehman Hutton Software and Data Svcs. Analyst, N.Y., 1988—; 1st v.p., security analyst software industry, Sherson Lehman Hutton, 1988—. Mem. N.Y. Soc. Securities Analysts, N.Y. Software Analysts Splinter Group. Home: 11 E 66th St New York NY 10021 Office: Shearson Lehman Hutton Software and Data Svcs Analyst Am Express Tower World Fin Ctr New York NY 10285-1400

READY, BILLY RAY, lawyer; b. Auburndale, Fla., Dec. 4, 1943; s. Earnest Marvin and Ethel (Lashley) R.; B.A., Southeastern Coll., 1968; J.D. with distinction, Miss. Coll., 1980; M. Rachael Elizabeth Ford, Feb. 16, 1973; children—Ray Kelvin, Donald Ashley, Holly Christine and Natalie Nicole (twins). Tchr., Fla., 1968-70; dir. ins. Comml. Carrier Corp., Auburndale, 1971-79; admitted to Miss. bar, 1980, Fla. bar, 1981; staff counsel, dir. ins. Comml. Carrier Corp., 1980-83; pres. Heritage Cons., Inc.; chmn. Fla. Self-Ins. Guaranty Fund, Inc., 1983-84; cons. in field; dir., sec. Fla. Self-Ins. Guaranty Fund, Inc. Pres. North Pointe Homeowners Assn.; chmn. employees Health Care Coalition Polk County, chmn. med. com. Mem. Am. Bar Assn., Fla. Bar Assn., Miss. Bar Assn., Risk and Ins. Mgmt. Soc., Am Jurisprudence Soc., Lakeland Bar Assn., Southeastern Coll. Alumni Assn. (pres. 1984-88), Delta Theta Phi. Democrat. Mem. Assembly of God Ch. Home: 190 Gapway Rd Auburndale FL 33823 Office: Waddell & Ready PA 209 Palmetto St Auburndale FL 33823

REALS, WILLIS BRAITHWAITE, oil company executive; b. Utica, N.Y., Sept. 12, 1925; s. Donald Drawbridge and Jane Owen (Patrick); m. Priscilla Alden Redfield, Nov. 28, 1953; children—Susan B., Jeffrey A. B.S. in Chem. Engring, M.I.T., 1947, M.S., 1949. With Texaco Inc., 1949—; gen. mgr. strategic planning Texaco Inc., White Plains, N.Y., 1972-74, v.p. strategic planning, 1974-79, sr. v.p., 1979—; chmn. Texaco Chem. Co. 1985—; chmn. Whitney Supply Co., Tulsa. Mem. vis. com. for chem. engring. MIT; mem. MIT Energy Lab. Adv. Bd. Mem. Chem. Mfg. Assn. (bd. dirs.). Clubs: Beach (Centerville, Mass.); Ballymeade (Falmouth, Mass.); University (Houston), Pine Forest Country. also: 47 Babbling Brook Centerville MA 02632 Office: Texaco Chem Co 3040 Post Oak Blvd Houston TX 77401

REAMES, TIMOTHY PAUL, lawyer, toy company executive; b. Dallas, Jan. 24, 1935; s. Phillip B. and Grace A. (Plauche) R.; m. Ann Semmes, Nov. 7, 1959; children: Timothy, Peter, Jennifer. B.B.A., So. Methodist U., 1957, LL.B., 1961. Bar: Tex. bar 1961, Calif. bar 1962, N.Y. bar 1971. Atty. Union Oil Co. Calif., 1961-64, Litton Industries, Inc., 1964-68, City Investing Co., 1968-78; v.p., gen. counsel Home Ins. Co., N.Y.C., 1978-81; sr. v.p., gen. counsel Mattel, Inc., Hawthorne, Calif., 1981—. Mem. Am. Bar Assn., N.Y. Bar Assn., Calif. Bar Assn., Tex. Bar Assn. Roman Catholic. Home: 1535 Hillcrest Ave Glendale CA 91202 Office: Mattel Inc 5150 Rosecrans Rd Hawthorne CA 90250

REAMS, BERNARD DINSMORE, JR., lawyer, educator; b. Lynchburg, Va., Aug. 17, 1943; s. Bernard Dinsmore and Martha Eloise (Hickman) R.; m. Rosemarie Bridget Boyle, Oct. 26, 1968; children: Andrew Dennet, Adriane Bevin. B.A., Lynchburg Coll., 1965; M.S., Drexel U., Phila., 1966; J.D., U. Kans., 1972; Ph.D., St. Louis U., 1983. Bar: Kans. 1973, Mo. 1986. Instr., asst. librarian Rutgers U., 1966-69; asst. prof. law, librarian U. Kans., Lawrence, 1969-74; mem. faculty law sch. Washington U., St. Louis, 1974—, prof. law, 1976—, librarian, 1974-76, acting dean univ. libraries, 1987-88. Author: Law For The Businessman, 1974, Reader in Law Librarianship, 1976, Federal Price and Wage Control Programs 1917-1979: Legis. Histories and Laws, 1980, Education of the Handicapped: Laws, Legislative Histories, and Administrative Documents, 1982, Housing and Transportation of the Handicapped: Laws and Legislative Histories, 1983, Internal Revenue Acts of the United States: The Revenue Act of 1954 with Legislative Histories and Congressional Documents, 1983 Congress and the Courts: A Legislative History 1978-1984, 1984, University-Industry Research Partnerships: The Major Issues in Research and Development Agreements, 1986, Deficit Control and the Gramm-Rudman-Hollings Act, 1986, The Semiconductor Chip and the Law: A Legislative History of the Semiconductor Chip Protection Act of 1984, 1986, American International Law Cases, 2d series, 1986, Technology Transfer Law: The Export Administration Acts of the U.S., 1987, Insider Trading and the Law, 1989; co-author: Segregation and the Fourteenth Amendment in the States, 1975, Historic Preservation Law: An Annotated Bibliography, 1976, Congress and the Courts: A Legislative History 1787-1977, 1978, Federal Consumer Protection Laws, Rules and Regulations, 1979, A Guide and Analytical Index to the Internal Revenue Acts of the U.S., 1909-1950, 1979, The Numerical Lists and Schedule of Volumes of the U.S. Congressional Serial Set: 73d Congress through the 96th Congress, 1984, Human Experimentation: Federal Laws, Legislative Histories, Regulations and Related Documents, 1985, American Legal Literature: A Guide to Selected Legal Resources, 1985, The Constitution of the United States: A Guide and Bibliography, 1987, The Congressional Impeachment Process and the Judiciary, 1987, Tax Reform 1986: A Legislative History of the Tax Refrom Act of 1986, 1988, The Constitutions of the States: A State by State Guide and Bibliography, 1988, The Legislative History of the Export Trading Company Act of 1982 Including the Foreign Trade Antitrust Improvements Act, 1989. Thornton award for Excellence Lynchburg Coll., 1986. Mem. ABA, Am. Assn. Higher Edn., ALA, Spl. Libraries Assn., Internat. Assn. Law Libraries, Am. Assn. Law Librarians, Southwestern Assn. Law Librarians (pres. 1977-78), ABA, Nat. Assn. of Coll. and Univ. Attys., Order of Coif, Phi Beta Kappa, Beta Phi Mu, Phi Delta Phi, Phi Delta Epsilon, Kappa Delta Pi., Pi Lambda Theta. Home: 3051 Thornbury Town and Country MO 63131 Office: Washington U Sch of Law 1 Brookings Dr Saint Louis MO 63130-4899

REAP, KATHERINE KISSANE, brokerage executive; b. Chgo., Dec. 27, 1954; d. Elmer Charles and Jeanne (O'Toole) Kissane; m. Thomas Leo Reap, July 19, 1980. BA, John Carroll U., 1976; AM in English, U. Chgo., 1982. Tchr. St. Mary's Sch., Lake Forest, Ill., 1976-77, Willows Acad., Glencoe, Ill., 1978-81; asst. syndicate mgr. Chgo. Corp., 1983—. Mem. Women's Syndicate Assn. (regional rep. 1987—). Office: Chicago Corp 208 S LaSalle St Chicago IL 60604

REARDON, ANDREW FITZPATRICK, lawyer; b. Cin., Nov. 8, 1945; s. William James and Frances Louise (Blasdel) R.; m. Michele Marie Berard, Dec. 27, 1967; children—Andrew F., Elizabeth B., William J., Mark C. BA, U. Notre Dame, 1967; JD, U. Cin., 1974; LLM in Taxation, Washington U., St. Louis, 1975. Bar: Ohio 1974, Mo. 1975, Nebr. 1981, Minn. 1981, Ill. 1985, U.S. Tax Ct. 1981, U.S. Claims Ct. 1981. Assoc. Thompson & Mitchell, St. Louis, 1975-77; gen. tax atty. St. Louis-San Francisco Ry. Co., St. Louis, 1977-79; sr. tax counsel Union Pacific Corp., N.Y.C., 1979-81; asst. gen. counsel Burlington No., St. Paul, 1981-82, asst. v.p. law, 1982-84; gen. counsel, sec. Farm Credit Svcs., St. Paul, 1984-85; sr. v.p. law/adminstrn. Ill. Cen. R.R. Co., Chgo., 1985—; lectr. Practicing Law Inst., 1981. Lt. USN, 1967-71. Mem. ABA (chmn. com. depreciation and credits tax sect. 1982-84), Met. Club, Mid-Am. Club, Knollwood Club. Roman Catholic. Home: 1313 Harlan Ln Lake Forest IL 60045 Office: Ill Cen RR Co 233 N Michigan Ave Chicago IL 60601

REARDON, ROBERT JOSEPH, financial corporation executive; b. Cleve., June 9, 1928; s. Arthur E. and Jane (Clark) R.; m. Josephine Carr, July 25, 1953; children—Jane, John, Patricia, Michael (dec.), Mary, Catherine, Daniel, Sarah, Robert. B.S. in Bus. Adminstrn., U. Mo., 1949. TV salesman Nat. Broadcasting Co., Chgo., 1955-57; mgr. WNBC-TV, Hartford, Conn., 1958-59; sales mgr. WTCN-TV, Mpls., 1959-61; chmn. bd. Bremer Fin. Services, St. Paul, 1973—; chmn. bd. dirs. Bremer Fin. Corp., St. Paul, 1967-89; pres., chief exec. officer Bremer Fin. Corp., 1967-89, chmn. bd. dirs., 1988—; dir. Dakota Bank & Trust, Fargo, N.D., 1st Am. Nat. Bank, St. Cloud, Minn., Drovers 1st Am. Bank, South St. Paul. Trustee Otto Bremer Found., St. Paul, 1967—; bd. dirs. AHW Corp., Mille Lacs Found., United Way, St. Paul, Catholic Charities, Archdiocese of St. Paul-Mpls., Minn. Council on Founds., Mpls.; chmn. bd. Convent of Visitation Sch., St. Paul. Roman Catholic. Office: Bremer Fin Corp 55 E 5th St Suite 700 Saint Paul MN 55101

REATH, GEORGE, JR., lawyer; b. Phila. Mar. 14, 1939; s. George and Isabel Duer (West) R.; children: Eric, Amanda. BA, Williams Coll., 1961; LLB, Harvard U., 1964. Bar: Pa. 1965, U.S. Dist. Ct. (ea. dist.) Pa. 1965. Assoc. Dechert Price & Rhoads, Phila. 1964-70, Brussels 1971-74; atty. Pennwalt Corp., Phila. 1974-78, mgr. legal dept., asst. sec. 1978-87, sr. v.p.-law, sec., 1987—. bd. dirs. Internat. Bus. Forum, Inc. Bd. mgrs. Children's Hosp. Phila. 1974—, sec. 1980-81, vice chmn., 1984—; bd. mgrs. Phila. City Inst. Library 1974—, treas., 1981-89; bd. dirs. Phila. Festival Theatre for New Plays, 1983—, Cen. Phila. Devel. Corp., 1987—, Internat. Bus. Forum Inc., 1978—; trustee Children's Hosp. Found., 1984—. With Pa. Army N.G., 1964-70. Mem. ABA, Pa. Bar Assn., Phila. Bar Assn., Am. Soc. Corp. Secs., Am. Corp. Counsel Assn., Phi Beta Kappa. Clubs: Racquet (Phila.); Penllyn (Pa.); Winter Harbor (Maine) Yacht. Office: Pennwalt Corp 3 Parkway Philadelphia PA 19102

REAVES, DORA ANN WOOLFREY, editor, newspaper; b. Conway, S.C., Sept. 1, 1946; d. Frederick Wilson and Ruth (Paterson) Woolfrey; m. James Joseph Reaves Jr., Jan. 11, 1969; 1 child, James Joseph III. BA in English, Winthrop Coll., 1968. Reporter Evening Post Pub. Co., Charleston, S.C., 1968-81, copy desk chief, 1981, asst. chief copy editor The Evening Post, 1981—. Recipient 2d Place Spot Reporting award S.C. AP, 1972, Sch. Bell award S.C. Ednl. Assn., 1973, Order of the Flying Orchid award Delta Airlines, 1978. Mem. Charleston Press Club (v.p. 1971, pres. 1972), Soc. Profl. Journalists. Lutheran. Home: 9 Dunvegan Dr Charleston SC 29414 Office: Evening Post Pub Co 134 Columbus St Charleston SC 29402

REAVIS, A(RTHUR) DAVID, computer executive; b. Brownsville, Tex., June 21, 1943; s. Walter Terrill Reavis and Molly Cumilla (Ward) Ford; m. Minnie Dolores Napolitano, Jan. 15, 1977 (div. July 1987). BS, Fairleigh Dickinson U., 1969, MBA, 1981. Supr. systems devel. Internat. Paper Co., Denville, N.J., 1969-76; mgr. software Internat. Paper Co., Denville, 1978-81; supr. systems project Societé Normande De Carton Ondule-Barrez, Paris, 1976-77; pres., gen. mgr. MBA-RDDR, Inc., Netcong, N.J., 1981—; v.p. computer tech. Teaching Pathways, Inc., Amarillo, Tex., 1983-85; bd. dirs. adv. com. Altro Health and Rehab. Service, N.Y. Author: (computer software) Property Mgmt. System, 1979, Target Mgmt. System, 1982. Served with USMC, 1964-66. Mem. N.Y. Acad. Scis. Republican. Club: Toastmasters (pres. Denville chpt. 1980-81). Home: 10 E Blackwell St-3D Dover NJ 07801 Office: MBA-RDDR Inc One Maple Ave Netcong NJ 07857

REBANE, JOHN T., lawyer; b. Bamberg, Germany, Oct. 29, 1946; s. Henn and Anna (Inna) R.; m. Linda Kay Morgan, Sept. 22, 1972; children: Alexis Morgan, Morgan James. BA, U. Minn., 1970, JD, 1973. Bar: Minn. 1973. Atty. Land O'Lakes, Inc., Arden Hills, Minn., 1973-80, assoc. gen counsel, 1980-83, v.p., gen. counsel, 1984—. Bd. dirs. Kenwood Isles Area Assn., Mpls., 1982-84, East Calhoun Community Orgn, Mpls., 1976-78. Served with AUS, 1968-70, Vietnam. Mem. Minn. Bar Assn., Hennepin County Bar Assn., Nat. Consel Farm Corp. Office: Land O'Lakes Inc 4001 Lexington Ave N Arden Hills MN 55112

REBECK, DANIEL STANLEY, stationary company executive; b. Kansas City, Kans., May 25, 1938; s. George J. and Helen A. (Loncaric) R.; m. Loretta L. Schuster, Nov. 12, 1966; children: Daniel Jr., Deborah, Robert. BBA, Rockhurst Coll., 1965. Cost acct. Swift & Co., Kansas City, 1961-64; cost acctg. supr. Sealright Co., Inc., Kansas City, 1964-67, plant controller, 1968-69; gen. acct. Sealright Co., Inc., Kansas City, Mo., 1967-68; mgr. ops. acctg. Sealright Co., Inc., Kansas City, 1969-70; div. acctg. mgr. Sealright Co., Inc., Fulton, N.Y., 1970-73; controller Staurt Hall Co., Inc., Kansas City, Mo., 1973-76, v.p. fin., treas., 1976—, also bd. dirs. Mem. Fin. Execs. Inst. Republican. Roman Catholic. Office: Stuart Hall Co Inc PO Box 419381 117 W 20th St Kansas City MO 64141-6381

RECANATI, RAPHAEL, shipping and banking executive; b. Salonique, Greece, Feb. 12, 1924; s. Leon and Mathilde (Saporta) R.; m. Diane Hettena, Oct. 8, 1946; children: Yehuda, Michael. Student Israel and Eng. Chmn. El-Yam Ships Ltd., 1953—; chmn. Discount Bank & Trust Co., Geneva, Switzerland, 1970; chmn., mng. dir. IDB Bankholding Ltd., 1970—. Home: 944 Fifth Ave New York NY 10021 Office: 511 Fifth Ave New York NY 10017

RECHHOLTZ, ROBERT AUGUST, brewing company executive; b. N.Y.C., Mar. 29, 1937; s. Agust Bruno and Frances Maude (Wirth) R.; m. Caroline Morton Osborne, May 2, 1959; children—Laurie Virginia, Jennifer Paige, Kristen Caroline. B.S. in Bus., U. N.C., 1958. Asst. copy supr. Proctor & Gamble, Cin., 1958-60; v.p. mktg. R.J. Reynolds Co., Winston-Salem, N.C., 1961-72, Gallo, Modesto, Calif., 1973; sr. v.p. sales and mktg Liggett Group, Durham, N.C., 1974-77, Joseph Schlitz, Milw., 1977-81; exec. v.p. sales and mktg. Adolph Coors, Golden, Colo., 1981—. Editor: Marketing Management, 1972. Served with USAR, 1958-61. Mem. Assn. Nat. Advertisers (dir. 1983-86), Advt. Council (bd. dirs. 1986-89), Winston-Salem Jr. C. of C. Republican. Episcopalian. Club: Rolling Hills Country. Home: 1375 Southridge Ct Golden CO 80401 Office: Adolph Coors Co Golden CO 80401

RECHNER, JOSEPH, computer company executive; b. Karavucovo, Yugoslavia, Apr. 9, 1940; came to U.S., 1950; s. John I. and Margarete (Berli) R.; m. Lena Greco, Dec. 9, 1985; children: Kathryn, Margaret, Maryanne. BSBA, Monmouth Coll., 1974. Tech. rep. Burroughs Corp., Radnor, Pa., 1961-64; test supr. Electronic Assocs., West Long Branch, N.J., 1964-67; various mgmt. positions Interdata Inc., Oceanport, N.J., 1967-74, gen. mgr. service, 1974-78; gen. mgr. terminals Perkin-Elmer Co., Norwalk, Conn., 1978-81; v.p. customer service Concurrent Computer Corp., Oceanport, 1981-87, v.p. ops., 1987—. Served with U.S. Army, 1958-61. Office: Concurrent Computer Corp 2 Crescent Pl Oceanport NJ 07753

RECHTIN, EBERHARDT, aerospace educator; b. East Orange, N.J., Jan. 16, 1926; s. Eberhardt Carl and Ida H. (Pfarrer) R.; m. Dorothy Diane Denebrink, June 10, 1951; children: Andrea C., Nina, Julie Anne, Erica, Mark. B.S., Calif. Inst. Tech., 1946, Ph.D. cum laude, 1950. Dir. Deep Space Network, Calif. Inst. Tech. Jet Propulsion Lab., 1949-67; dir. Advanced Research Projects Agy., Dept. Def., 1967-70, prin. dep. dir. def. research and engring., 1970-71, asst. sec. def. for telecommunications, 1972-73; chief engr. Hewlett-Packard Co., Palo Alto, Calif., 1973-77; pres., chief exec. officer Aerospace Corp., El Segundo, Calif., 1977-87; prof. U. So. Calif., 1988—. Served to lt. USNR, 1943-56. Recipient major awards NASA, Dept. Def. Fellow AIAA (major awards), IEEE (major awards); mem. Nat. Acad. Engring., Tau Beta Pi. Home: 1665 Cataluna Pl Palos Verdes Estates CA 90274 Office: U So Calif University Pk Los Angeles CA 90089-1454

RECK, DONALD HARRY, public affairs specialist; b. Chgo., Aug. 12, 1936; s. Harry August and Emma Marie (Rauch) R.; m. Joan Ann Lernert, Aug. 11, 1962 (div. Nov. 1975); children: Laurance Russell, Valarie Cheryl, Diana Claire; m. Marie Pearl Nadeau, Nov. 28, 1981. Student, U. Ill., Chgo., 1954-56; BJ, U. Mo., 1958. Reporter Ill. State Jour., Springfield, 1958-60; columnist Chgo. Daily News, 1960-63; info. rep. div. data processing IBM, White Plains, N.Y., 1963-65; mgr. internal communications corp. hdqrs. IBM, Armonk, N.Y., 1965-69; bur. chief div. data processing IBM, Mpls., 1970-73; mgr. area communications IBM, N.Y.C., 1973-77; div. info. mgr. office products IBM, Franklin Lakes, N.J., 1977-80; mgr. communications/community rels. div. gen. products IBM, Tucson, 1980-85, state mgr. external program for Ariz., 1985-88, mgr. policy programs for Ariz., 1988—. Bd. dirs. Arizonans for Cultural Devel., 1988—, Goodwill Industries, 1989; mem. Mayor's Task Force for Econ. Devel., 1988—; bd. dirs. Tuscon Mus. of Art; pres., 1987; Tucson Pima Arts Council; pres., 1986; founder Tucson Bus. Com. for the Arts, 1986—; bd. dirs. Ariz. Coun. on Econ. Edn., 1986—, Ariz. Sonora Desert Mus. Found. Recipient Best Corp. Mag. award Internat. Assn. Bus. Communicators, 1967, Best Corp. Communications award United Way, 1985. Mem. Am. Electronics Assn. (bd. dirs. 1985—), Ariz. C. of C. (vice chmn. 1985—), Tucson C. of C. (bd. dirs. 1981-88), Can. Hills Country Club (Tucson), Ariz. Club (Phoenix), Sigma Delta Chi (bd. dirs. N.Y. Deadline Club 1974-80). Republican. Lutheran. Office: IBM 2850 E Camelback Rd Phoenix AZ 85016

RECTENWALD, GARY MICHAEL, information systems executive; b. Toledo, Dec. 31, 1949; s. Edgar E. and Dorothy C. (Antieau) R. BS (cum laude), Ohio State U., 1971, MS in Computer Sci., 1972, MBA, 1978. Programmer trainee Ohio State U., 1970-71, grad. research assoc., 1971-72; application programmer, 1972-75, system programmer, 1975-77, mgr. application systems programming, 1977-78; mem. Instrn. and Research Computer Ctr.; systems engr. IBM, Columbus, 1978-81, mktg. rep., 1982, large systems mktg. cons., Cin. and Detroit, 1983, mktg. mgr., Lansing, Mich., 1984-86; program mgr. Info. Systems Investmen, Strategies, 1986-88, exec. asst. to group dir., account mktg. dir., customer exec., bus. edn., 1988; br. mgr. San Diego pub. sector and utilities, 1989—. Mem. Ohio State U. Marching Band (Most Inspirational Bandsman 1973). Served with Air N.G., 1970-76. Mem. Phi Beta Kappa, Beta Gamma Sigma, Kappa Gamma Sigma, Pi Mu Epsilon, Kappa Kappa Psi. Roman Catholic. Office: IBM-San Diego Pub Sector and Utilities 8845 University Center Ln San Diego CA 92122

RECUPERO, JOHN, management consultant; b. Schenectedy, N.Y., July 29, 1931; s. Salvatore and Antoinette (Martini) R.; m. Marie J. Lippiello, Aug. 18, 1956; children: Rose-Ann, John J. Cert. in Acctg., Albany Bus. Coll., 1951; BBA, Bryant Coll., 1952. Registered Pub. Acct., N.Y. Acctg. specialist Gen. Electric Co., Schnectady, 1952-65; chief fin. officer Mech. Tech., Inc., Latham, N.Y., 1965-79, corp. treas., 1972—; mgmt. cons. J&M Services Co., Daytona Beach, Fla., 1979—. Mem. Nat. Contract Mgmt. Assn., Soc. Mfg. Engrs. (sr.). Republican. Roman Catholic. Home: 308 American Way Daytona Beach FL 32019 Office: Mech Tech Inc 968 Albany-Shaker Rd Latham NY 12110

REDDAN, E. DOUGLAS, financial consultant, investor; b. East Orange, N.J., Aug. 7, 1916; s. William J. and Catherine E. (Tansey) R.; student Stevens Inst. Tech., 1934-37, Newark Coll. Engring., 1938-40; m. Marian Williams, May 29, 1948; children—Susan (Mrs. Robert Maquire III), Jeffrey, Polly, Lisa Paige. Mech. engr. Aerospace div. Walter Kidde & Co., Inc., Belleville, N.J., 1937-42, sales mgr., 1946-52; v.p. Mil. div. Electronics Corp. Am., Cambridge, Mass., 1952-57; founder, chief exec. officer, dir. Infrared Industries, Inc., Santa Barbara, Calif., 1957-65, chmn. bd., 1965-66; dir. Nash Controls, Inc., Caldwell, N.J., 1961-64, Exotech, Inc., Falls Church, Va., 1961-65; pres., dir. Electro-Nuclear Labs, Inc., Mountain View, Calif., 1961-65, pres., 1961-63; chmn. bd., chief exec. officer Rolair Systems Inc., Santa Barbara, 1970-76; vice chmn., dir. Century Mortgage Co., Fin. Corp. Santa Barbara, Santa Barbara Savs. & Loan. Bd. dirs. Santa Barbara Symphony Orch. Assn., Santa Barbara Mus. Art, Santa Barbara Med. Found., Music Acad. West, Santa Barbara, LaGuna Blanca Sch., Santa Barbara, Am. Nat. Red Cross, Cottage Hosp., Santa Barbara, vice chmn. Arthritis Inst., Arlington, Va. Served to lt. AC, USNR, 1942-46. Mem. Am. Ordnance Assn., Optical Soc. Am., ASME, Am. Mgmt. Assn., I.E.E.E. Clubs: Valley of Montecito (pres., gov.); Santa Barbara (gov.), Birnham Wood Golf. Contbr. articles on flight safety devices, electro-optical techniques to indsl. and aerospace to profl. pubs. Patentee in field. Home: 475 Crocker Sperry Dr Santa Barbara CA 93108 Office: 1129 State St Ste 28 Santa Barbara CA 93101

REDDEN, HARRAL ARTHUR, JR., insurance agency executive; b. Neptune, N.J., Aug. 14, 1936; s. Harral A. and Evelyn Redden; B.A., Ursinus Coll., 1958; m. Bernadine Tenreiro, July 30, 1983; children—Stephen D., Scott H. Owner, mgr. Redden Agy., Fair Haven, N.J., 1958—; instr. Brookdale Community Coll., 1972-80. Pres., Little Silver (N.J.) Community Appeal, 1971—. Served to 1st lt. USAR, 1963-70. Designated CIC. Mem. Monmouth County Ind. Ins. Agts. Assn. (pres. 1966-67), Soc. C.P.C.U.'s (pres. Central Jersey chpt. 1968-69), Ind. Ins. Agts. N.J. (pres. 1982-83). Republican. Methodist. Clubs: Sea Bright Lawn Tennis (Rumson, N.J.); Root Beer & Checker (Red Bank). Office: Redden Agy 718 River Rd PO Box 262 Fair Haven NJ 07704

REDDING, EDWARD JOHN, bank executive; b. Fountain Hill, Pa., Dec. 18, 1941; s. John Patrick and Dorothy Margaret (Beier) R. BS in Econ., Villanova U., 1964. CPA, Pa. Supervisory auditor U.S. Gen. Acctg. Office, Phila., 1964-76; auditor Cement Natl. Bank, Northampton, Pa., 1976-79, controller, 1979-84; v.p. fin. Northeastern Bank of Pa., 1984—. Conv. del. Democratic Party, N.Y.C., 1980; vice chmn. Fountain Hill Planning Commn., Pa., 1982-84. Recipient Letter of Commendation for civilian service in Vietnam Gen. Acctg. Office, 1969. Mem. AICPAs, Pa. Inst. CPAs, Natl. Assn. Accts., Bank Adminstrn. Inst. (pres. 1983-84), Exchange Club (Fountain Hill) (pres-elect, 1983—, Disting. Sec. award), Java Soc. (Northampton) (treas. 1981-85). Roman Catholic. Home: 1124 Wiley St Fountain Hill PA 18015 Office: Northeastern Bank Pa 201 Penn Ave Scranton PA 18503

REDDING, PETER STODDARD, manufacturing company executive; b. Bklyn., June 27, 1938; s. Kenneth Benckert and Frances Elizabeth (Hasselman) R.; B.A., U. Md., 1960; M.Decision Scis., Ga. State U., 1974; m. Mary Lorelei LeBrun, Feb. 4, 1961; children—Shelagh, Mark, Todd, Jill. Dept. mgr. trainee J.C. Penney Co., 1960-62; sales rep. Standard Register Co., Washington, 1962-66, asst. dist. sales mgr., Washington, 1966-68, Atlanta, 1968-69, dist. sales mgr., Atlanta, 1969-76, regional sales mgr. Pacific region, Orinda, Calif., 1976-79, asst. to pres., Dayton, Ohio, 1979-81, v.p. mktg., 1981-87, sr. v.p., 1987—. Bd. dirs. Dayton Contemporary Dance Co.; trustee Dayton Philharm. Orch., The Children's Med. Ctr., Dayton. Republican. Roman Catholic. Clubs: Dayton City, Rotary, Dayton Country, Racquet. Home: 4966 Ashwyck Pl Kettering OH 45429 Office: Standard Register Co 600 Albany St Dayton OH 45408

REDDING, STEVEN WESLEY, financial executive, consultant; b. Asheboro, N.C., Jan. 31, 1947; s. C. Wesley and Ellen Lucille (Jones) R.; m. Miriam Maria Miyares, July 18, 1970; children: Steven, Jason, Bryan. BA in Econs., Guilford Coll., Greensboro, N.C., 1971; MBA Mgmt. and Fin., U. Tenn., 1985. Field cons., auditor N.C. Credit Union League, Greensboro, 1971-75; dir ops. First Carolina Cen. Credit Union, Greensboro, 1975-76; acct. mgr. Y-12 Fed. Credit Union, Oak Ridge, Tenn., 1976-78; ops. mgr., comptroller Y-12 Fed. Credit Union, Oak Ridge, 1978-85, chief investment officer, 1978-87, asst. gen. mgr., asst. treas., 1985-87; pres., chief exec. officer Va. Beach (Va.) Fed. Credit Union, 1987—; treas. Oak Ridge Chpt. Credit Unions, 1976-80, pres. 1980-83; cons. in field. Author numerous research papers in field, 1981-85. Mem. Credit Union Exec. Soc., Tenn. Orgn. MBA's, Assn. MBA Execs., Nat. Assn. Accts., Credit Union Nat. Assns. Founders Club., Guilford Coll. Alumni Assn., U. Tenn. Nat. Alumni Assn., The Bus. Planning Bd., The Controllers Council. Republican. Baptist. Club: Exchange (Oak Ridge).

REDDISH, JOHN JOSEPH, management consulting company executive; b. Albany, N.Y., July 23, 1946; s. Leonard Frank and Marion Elizabeth (McElveney) R.; A.B. in Communication Arts, Fordham U., 1968; M.S.A., West Chester U., 1984; m. Sharon L. Cloud; children—Jorin T., Adam Sledd, Lee Sledd. Pub. relations asst. Civil Service Employees Assn., Albany, 1967-68; assoc. editor Edison Electric Inst., N.Y.C., 1968-69; dir. info. services N.Y. State Nurses Assn., Guilderland, 1969-70; pres. RA Group, Inc., Advt. and Pub. Relations, Albany, 1970-77; v.p. The Presidents Assn. div. Am. Mgmt. Assocs., N.Y.C., 1978—; pres., dir. Advent Mgmt. Assoc., Ltd., West Chester, Pa., 1979—; cons. mktg. and mgmt. Chmn. bd. Kairos Center for Care and Counseling, Albany, 1975-77; trustee N.Y. Theol. Sem.; adv. bd. Hope Med. Emergency Services, Delaware County Community Coll. Bus. Dept.; bd. dirs. Focus Chs. of Albany, 1973-76; bd. deacons Emmanuel Bapt. Ch., 1974-77; hon. trustee Nat. French and Indian Wars Mus., Hudson Falls, N.Y., 1975-77. Mem. Assn. Corp. Growth, Inst. Mgmt. Cons. (cert.), Internat. Platform Assn. Contbr. articles to profl. jours. Office: Advent Mgmt Assoc. Ltd PO Box 3203 W Chester PA 19381

REDDITT, GERALD BRUCE, telecommunications company executive; b. Orlando, Fla., Jan. 18, 1951; s. Richard Cleveland and Grace Joanne R.; m. Sara Patricia Abstein, Apr. 14, 1979; children: Sara Evelyn, David Bruce. AA in Bus. Adminstrn., Valencia Community Coll., 1971; BSBA, Fla. State U., 1975. Pub. info. staff specialist Fla. Pub. Svc. Commn., Tallahassee, 1975-78; coordinator communications Pub. Svc. Colo., Denver, 1979-84; dir. investor relations Key Pharms., Inc., Miami, Fla., 1984-86; dir. investor relations Contel Corp., Atlanta, 1986-87, asst. v.p. investor relations, 1987—. Mem. Nat. Investor Relations Inst. (conf. speaker 1986—), U.S. Telephone Assn., The Peachtree World of Tennis. Republican. Office: Contel Corp 245 Perimeter Ctr Pkwy Atlanta GA 30346

REDDY, VADDI BUTCHI, research chemist; b. Anmangal, India, June 12, 1950; s. V. Veera Reddy and Venkatamma (Chintareddi) Vaddi; m. Premakumari Reddy, Mar. 15, 1979; children: Priyanka, Pranay. BS, Osmania U., Hyderabad, India, 1973; MS, U. Roorkee, India, 1977, PhD, 1981. Pool officer Regional Research Labs., Hyderabad, 1982; postdoctoral appointee Inst. Mining and Minerals Research, Lexington, Ky., 1982-84; research engr. GTE Products Corp., Towanda, Pa., 1984—. Inventor inorganic phosphors for radiography; contbr. articles to profl. jours. Postdoctoral fellow U. Roorkee, 1981-82. Mem. Am. Chem. Soc. (chmn. continuing edn. com. Corning sect. 1988), Soc. Applied Spectroscopy (chmn. elect Pennyork sect. 1988—), Electro Chem. Soc., N.Am. Thermal Analysis Soc. Hindu. Home: 120 Vista Dr Sayre PA 18840

REDDY, YENAMALA RAMACHANDRA, metal processing executive; b. Polavaram, Andhra, India, Feb. 12, 1939; came to U.S., 1974; s. Y. Venkata and Y. Lakshamamma Reddy; m. Y. Uma Reddy, May 30, 1965; children: Y. Sharath, Y. Jay. BME, S.V. U., Andhra, 1961; M in Tech., IIT, Bombay, 1966, PhD, 1970. Lic. profl. engr., Wis. Asst. prof. IIT, Bombay, 1966-69; research and devel. mgr. Jyoti Pumps, Baroda, 1973-74; chief engr. Patterson Pumps, Toccoa, Ga., 1974-80; pres. R.B. Pump Co., Baxley, 1980—, U.B. Cons., Ga., 1980—. Contbr. articles to tech. jours. Postdoctoral fellow U. of Tech., Loughborough, Eng., 1970-73. Mem. Am. Soc. of Mech. Engrs. Office: R B Pump Co #1 Dixie Dr PO Box 557 Baxley GA 31513

REDFERN, JOHN D., manufacturing company executive; b. 1935. Grad. Queen's U., Kingston, Ont., 1958. With Can. Cement Lafarge Ltd. (name changed to Lafarge Can. Inc. 1988), Montreal, 1977—, pres., chief exec. officer, 1977-84, chmn., 1984—; chmn. bd. parent co. Lafarge Corp., Reston, Va., 1985-88, vice-chmn., 1988— Office: Lafarge Can Inc, 606 Cathcart, Montreal, PQ Canada H3B 1L7 *

REDING, NICHOLAS LEE, chemical company executive; b. Algona, Iowa, Nov. 7, 1934; s. Louis Clair and Alice Rosanne (Steil) R.; m. Patricia Jane Finnegan, Aug. 2, 1958; children—Nancy Allison, Scott Nicholas. B.S. in Chem. Engring, Iowa State U., 1956; grad. exec. program, Stanford U., 1975. With Monsanto Co., 1956—; with Monsanto Agrl. Products Co., 1960—; v.p., mng. dir. Monsanto Agrl. Products Co., St. Louis, 1976-78; group v.p., mng. dir. Monsanto Agrl. Products Co., 1978-81, exec. v.p., 1981-86; pres. Monsanto Agrl. Co., St. Louis, 1986—; mem. mgmt. com. parent co., bd. dirs. Internat. Multifoods Corp., 1986—. Trustee Agr. Council Am. Edn. Found., Washington, 1986—; bd. dirs., mem. exec. com. United Way Greater St. Louis, 1982—, St. Louis County Day Sch., 1986—; bd. dirs. St. Louis Children's Hosp., 1986—; mem. chancellor's coun. U. Mo., St. Louis, 1988—. Recipient award for excellence in agrl. mktg. Nat. Agri-Mktg. Assn., 1982. Mem. Nat. Agrl. Chem. Assn. (chmn. exec. com. 1980-81, bd. dirs. 1986—), Alpha Zeta (hon.), St. Louis Club, Bellerive Country Club, Bogey Club. Methodist. Office: Monsanto Co 800 N Lindbergh Blvd Saint Louis MO 63167

REDMAN-JOHNSON, CHLOË LOUISE, controller; b. Amityville, N.Y., Sept. 3, 1942; d. Cecil Bernard and Gladys Lucille (Taylor) R.; m. James W. Barrow, July 31, 1960 (div. Jan. 1966); children: Valerie, Kevin, Joycelyn; m. Joseph Constantine Johnson, July 26, 1970; children: Joanne, Joseph Jr., Jason. BBA in Acctg., Dowling Coll., 1984. Acct. Davis & Raymond Assocs., Uniondale, N.Y., 1982-83, Robbins, Greene et al., N.Y.C., 1983-84; controller Newman, Tannenbaum et al., N.Y.C., 1984-85; controller, U.S.A., Butler, Cox and Ptnrs., Ltd., London, 1985-86; controller, chief acctg. officer British Land of Am., Inc., N.Y.C., 1986-87; dir. of fin. and adminstrn. Johnson, Smith & Knisely, Inc., N.Y.C., 1987—. Democrat. Roman Catholic. Home: 18 South St Old Westfield Selden NY 11784 Office: Johnson Smith & Knisely 475 Fifth Ave New York NY 10017

REDMOND, PAUL ANTHONY, utility executive; b. Lakeview, Oreg., 1937. BSEE, Gonzaga U., 1965. Asst. elec. engr. Wash. Water Power Co., Spokane, 1965-67, maintenance engr., 1967-69, supt. contract constrn., 1969-73, constrn. and maintenance supt., 1973-75, mgr. constrn. and maintenance, 1975-77, asst. to pres., 1977-78, v.p., asst. to pres., 1978-79, sr. v.p. ops., 1979-80, exec. v.p., pres., 1982—, chief operating officer, pres., 1984—, chmn. bd., pres., chief exec. officer, 1985, also bd. dirs.; former pres. Wash. Irrigation & Devel. subs. Wash. Water Power Co., Spokane, now chmn., pres., chief exec. officer, 1985—; bd. dirs. Security Pacific Bank Washington, Spokane Indsl. Park Inc., Limestone Co. Inc., Devel. Assocs. Inc., Pentzer Corp., Water Power Improvement Co., Wash. Irrigation and Devel. Co., Itron Inc. Lt. col. USNG. Office: Wash Water Power Co PO Box 3727 Spokane WA 99220

REDMONT, BERNARD SIDNEY, university dean, journalism educator; b. N.Y.C., Nov. 8, 1918; s. Morris Abraham and Bessie (Kamerman) R.; m. Joan Rothenberg, Mar. 12, 1940; children: Dennis Foster, Jane Carol. B.A., CCNY, 1938; M.J., Columbia U., 1939; D.H.L., Fla. Internat. U., 1980. Reporter, book reviewer Bklyn. Daily Eagle, 1936-38; free lance corr. Europe, 1939, Mexico City, 1939-40; telegraph editor, editorial writer Herkimer (N.Y.) Evening Telegram, 1941-42; newswriter U.S. Office of Inter-Am. Affairs (Washington shortwave radio newscasts to Latin Am.), 1942-43, dir. News div., 1944-46; staff corr., bur. chief U.S. News & World Report, Buenos Aires and Paris, 1946-51; columnist Continental Daily Mail, Paris, 1951-53; chief corr. English Lang. World News Service Agence France-Presse, Paris, 1953-65; European corr. Paris news bur. chief Westinghouse Broadcasting Co., Paris, 1961-76; corr., bur. chief CBS News, Moscow, 1976-79; corr. CBS News, Paris, 1979-81; prof. journalism, dir. broadcast journalism program, dean Boston U. Coll. Communication, 1982-86, dean emeritus, prof. journalism, 1986—. Served with USMCR, 1943-44. Decorated Purple Heart, chevalier Legion of Honor France; Pulitzer Traveling fellow; recipient Columbia Journalism award for advancement of journalism, 1986. Mem. Overseas Press Club (award best radio reporting from abroad 1968, 73), Soc. Profl. Journalists, Nat. Press Club, Anglo-American Press Assn. of Paris (pres. 1961, treas. 1970-73, sec. 1974-76). Unitarian.

REDPATH, RONALD RALPH, manufacturing financial executive; b. Akron, Ohio, Sept. 25, 1946; s. Donald Ralph and Mary Helene (Marzlack) R.; m. Valerie Ann Snyder, Nov. 8, 1975. BS in Econs., Juniata Coll., 1968; MBA in Fin., Oklahoma City U., 1978. Programmer analyst The NCR Corp., Wilmington, Del., 1968-70; systems engr. The NCR Corp., Patchogue, N.Y., 1970-72; systems engr., mgr. The NCR Corp., Oklahoma City, 1972-79; sr. fin. analyst Piper Aircraft Corp., Lock Haven, Pa., 1979-81, adminstr. fin. planning, 1981-82; corp. dir. fin. planning Piper Aircraft Corp., Vero Beach, Fla., 1982-87; chief of fin. Fin. Planning and Controls div. Gen. Dynamics Corp., Ft. Worth, 1987-88; corp. dir. planning analysis and controls Todd Shipyards Corp., Seattle, 1988—. Mem. The Planning Forum, Aircraft Owners and Pilots Assn., Experimental Aircraft Assn. Republican. Presbyterian. Home: 16149 SE 33d Ln Bellevue WA 98008 Office: Todd Shipyards Corp PO Box 84788 Seattle WA 98134

REDRUELLO, ROSA INCHAUSTEGUI, municipal department executive; b. Havana, Cuba, Dec. 6, 1951; came to U.S., 1961, naturalized, 1971; d. Julio Lorenzo and Laudelina (Vazquez) Inchaustegui; m. John Robert Redruello, Dec. 14, 1972; 1 child, Michelle. AA, Miami-Dade Community Coll., 1972; BS, Fla. Internat. U., 1974. Cert. systems profl. With Fla. Power & Light Co., Miami, 1975-81, records analyst, 1981-84, sr. records analyst, 1984-87, office mgr. Miami Beach Sanitation Dept., 1987—; cons. United Bus. Records, Miami, 1985—. Editor South Fla. Record newsletter, 1983-86; editor, producer Files Mgmt. video tape, 1984-85. Rotary Club scholar, 1970. Mem. Assn. Records Mgrs. and Adminstrs. (chpt. chmn. bd. 1985—, chpt. mem. of yr. 1985), Assn. for Info. and Image Mgmt., Exec. Female, Nuclear Info. and Records Mgmt. Assn. (Appreciation award 1985). Republican. Roman Catholic. Avocations: swimming, jazzercise, reading. Office: Miami Beach Sanitation Dept 1100 Washington Ave Miami Beach FL 33139

REDSTONE, SUMNER MURRAY, theatre executive, lawyer; b. Boston, May 27, 1923; s. Michael and Belle (Ostrovsky) R.; m. Phyllis Gloria Raphael, July 6, 1947; children—Brent Dale, Shari Ellin. B.A., Harvard U., 1944, LL.B., 1947. Bar: Mass. 1947, U.S. Ct. Appeals (1st cir.) 1948, U.S. Ct. Appeals (8th cir.) 1950, U.S. Ct. Appeals (9th cir.) 1948, D.C. 1951, U.S. Supreme Ct. 1952. Law sec. U.S. Ct. Appeals for 9th Circuit, San Francisco, 1947-48; instr. law and labor mgmt. U. San Francisco, 1947; spl. asst. to U.S. atty. gen., Washington, 1948-51; partner firm Ford, Bergson, Adams, Borkland & Redstone, Washington, 1951-54; pres., chief exec. officer Natl. Amusements, Inc., Dedham, Mass., 1967—, also chmn. bd., 1986—; chmn. bd. Viacom Internat., Inc.; prof. Boston U. Law Sch., 1982, 85-86. Chmn. met. div. NE Combined Jewish Philanthropies, Boston, 1963; mem. corp. New Eng. Med. Center, 1967—; trustee Children's Cancer Research Found.; chmn. Am. Cancer Crusade, State of Mass., 1984-86; Art Lending Library; sponsor Boston Mus. Sci.; chmn. Jimmy Fund Found., 1960; v.p., mem. exec. com. Will Rogers Meml. Fund; bd. dirs. Boston Arts Festival; bd. overseers Dana Farber Cancer Center, Boston Mus. Fine Arts; mem. presdl. adv. com. on arts John F. Kennedy Center for Performing Arts; bd. dirs. John F. Kennedy Library Found. Served to 1st lt. AUS, 1943-45. Decorated Army Commendation medal; recipient William J. German Human Relations award Am. Jewish Com. Entertainment and Communication Div., 1977, Silver Shingle award Boston U. Law Sch., 1985; named one of ten outstanding young men Greater Boston C. of C., 1958, Communicator of Yr. B'nai B'rith Communications/Cinema Lodge, 1980. Mem. Am. Congress Exhibitors (exec. com. 1961—), Theatre Owners Am. (asst. pres. 1960-63, pres. 1964-65), Nat. Assn. Theatre Owners (chmn. bd. dirs. 1965-66), Motion Picture Pioneers (bd. dirs.), Am., Boston, Mass. bar assns., Harvard Law Sch. Assn., Am. Judicature Soc. Clubs: Mason, University, Variety New Eng., Harvard (Boston). Home: 98 Baldpate Hill Rd Newton Centre MA 02159 Office: Nat Amusements Inc 200 Elm St Dedham MA 02026

REED, DOUGLAS BYRON, chemical company sales executive; b. Colfax, Wash., July 2, 1946; s. Everett B. Reed and Ferne (Stipe) Carlon; m. Patricia L. Bailey, June 28, 1968; children: Chad, Matthew, Michelle, Sarah. BS in Chem. Engring., Wash. State U., 1964-70. Chem. engr. Dow Chem., Midland, Mich., 1970-72; sales rep. Dow Chem., Pitts., 1972-76, Seattle, 1976-82, Houston, 1982-83; sales mgr. Neville Chem. Co., Houston, 1983-84; product mgr. Neville Chem. Co., Pitts., 1984—. Dir. Bilma Mcpl. Utility Dist., Spring, Tex., 1984—. Served to capt. U.S. Army, 1970-72. Mem. Soc. Plastic Engrs., Soc. Cosmetic Chemists, Southwest Chem. Assn., Houston Chem. Club. Republican. Home: 6223 Spring Creek Oaks Dr Spring TX 77379 Office: Neville Chem Co Neville Island Pittsburgh PA 15225

REED, FRANK METCALF, banker; b. Seattle, Dec. 22, 1912; s. Frank Ivan and Pauline B. (Hovey) R.; student U. Alaska, 1931-32; B.A., U. Wash., 1937; m. Maxine Vivian McGary, June 11, 1937; children—Pauline Reed Mackay), Frank Metcalf. Vice pres. Anchorage Light & Power Co., 1937-42; pres. Alaska Electric & Equipment Co., Anchorage, 1946-50; sec., mgr. Turnagain, Inc., Anchorage, 1950-56; mgr. Gen. Credit Corp., Anchorage, 1957; br. mgr. Alaska SBA, Anchorage, 1958-60; sr. v.p. First Interstate Bank of Alaska, Anchorage, 1960-87, also dir., corp. sec.; dir. First Interstate Corp. of Alaska, pres., dir. Anchorage Broadcasters, Inc.; past pres., chmn. Microfast Software Corp.; ptnr. R.M.R. Co.; dir. Anchorage Light & Power Co., Turnagain, Inc., Alaska Fish and Farm, Inc., Life Ins. Co. Alaska, Alaska Hotel Properties, Spa Inc. Pres., Anchorage Federated Charities, Inc., 1953-54; mem. advisory bd. Salvation Army, 1948-58; mem. Alaska adv. bd. Hugh O'Brian Youth Found., 1987—; trustee Anchor Age Sr. Ctr. Endowment Fund, 1988—; mem. City of Anchorage Planning Commn., 1956; mem. City of Anchorage Council, 1956-57; police commr. Ter. of Alaska, 1957-58; chmn. City Charter Commn., 1958; mem. exec. com. Greater Anchorage, Inc., 1955-65; pres. Sch. Bd., 1961-64; mem. Gov.'s Investment adv. com., 1970-72; mem. Alaska State Bd. Edn.; mem. citizens adv. com. Alaska Meth. U.; chmn. Anchorage Charter Commn., 1975; chmn. bldg. fund dr. Community YMCA, 1976—; bd. dirs., mem. exec. com. Arts Alaska, 1976-78; sec.-treas. Breakthrough, 1976-78; bd. dirs. Anchorage Civic Opera, 1978, Rural Venture Alaska, Inc.; bd. dirs Alaska Treatment Ctr., 1980-87, pres. 1985-86; trustee Marston Found., Inc., 1978, exec. dir. 1988. Served as lt. USNR, 1942-46. Elected to Hall of Fame, Alaska Press Club, 1969; named Outstanding Alaskan of Year Alaska C. of C., 1976; recipient Community Service award YMCA, 1975-78. Mem. Am. Inst. Banking, Am. (exec. council 1971-72) Alaska (pres. 1970-71) bankers assns., Nat. Assn. State Bds. Edn. (sec.-treas. 1969-70), C. of C. U.S. (Western region legislative com.), Anchorage C. of C. (pres. 1966-67, dir.), Pioneers of Alaska, Navy League (pres. Anchorage council 1961-62). Clubs: Tower (life), San Francisco Tennis. Lodges: Lions (sec. Anchorage, 1953-54, dir. 1988, pres., 1962-63), Elks. Home: 1361 W 12th Ave Anchorage AK 99501

REED, FREDRIC DAVID, utility company executive; b. Valley View, Pa., Mar. 18, 1937; s. Palmer Harold and Mildred Terell (Reed) R.; m. Barbara Ann Yurick, Aug. 23, 1958; children—Janet Elaine, David Alan. BS, Pa. State U., 1959, MBA in Finance, 1961. Cost analyst, Birmingham (Ala.) So. R.R., 1961-63; sr. cost analyst, Louisville & Nashville R.R., 1963-66; asst. dir. econ. analysis/cost control Chgo., Rock Island & Pacific R.R., Chgo., 1966-69; mgr. budgets and econ. analysis Pacific Power & Light, Portland, Oreg., 1969-74, controller, 1974-79, v.p., 1979-86, sr. v.p., 1986-89; exec. v.p. Utah Power & Light Co., Salt Lake City, 1989—, Northwest Electric Light and Power Assn. Republican. Lutheran. Club: Oswego Lake Country. Avocations: fishing, golf. Home: 560 E South Temple Ste 1001 Salt Lake City UT 84102 Office: Utah Power & Light Co 1407 W North Temple Rm 315 Salt Lake City UT 84110

REED, GEORGE FORD, JR., investment exec.; b. Hollywood, Calif., Dec. 26, 1946; s. George Ford and Mary Anita Reed; B.A. in Econs. with honors, U. So. Calif., 1969, M.A., 1971; m. Kathryn Nixon, 1981. Analyst planning and research Larwin Group, Beverly Hills, Calif., 1971-72; with Automobile Club So. Calif., Los Angeles, 1972—, supr. mgmt. info., research and devel., 1973-74, mgr. fin. and market analysis, 1975-81, group mgr. fin. analysis and forecasting, 1981-86; pres. Reed Asset Mgmt. Co., Inc., Los Angeles, 1986—; instr. bus. and econs. Los Angeles Community Coll. Mem. population task force Los Angeles C. of C., 1974—; mem. Gov. Calif. Statewide Econ. Summit Conf., 1974. Served with U.S. Army, 1969. Mem. Assn. Corp. Real Estate Execs., Nat. Assn. Bus. Economists, Western Regional Sci. Assn., Am. Mgmt. Assn., Am. Fin. Assn., So. Calif. Planners Assn., Rotary Internat., Omicron Delta Epsilon. Home: 1001 S Westgate Ave Los Angeles CA 90049 Office: 10960 Wilshire Blvd Ste 2200 Los Angeles CA 90024

REED, GEORGE FRANKLIN, investment executive, lawyer; b. Beaver, Pa., Jan. 19, 1935; s. Harold Francis and Mary Lou (Eckles) R.; m. Anne Stewart Dixon, May 5, 1962; children—George Franklin, Peter, Carolyn. B.A., Princeton U., 1956; J.D., U. Pa., 1959. Bar: Pa. 1960. Assoc. Morgan Lewis & Bockius, Phila., 1960-67; gen. counsel Pa. Dept. Ins., Harrisburg, 1967-69; ins. commr. Commonwealth of Pa., Harrisburg, 1969-71; sr. v.p., counsel Am. Gen. Corp., Houston, 1971-79, vice-chmn. bd., 1979-83; chmn. bd. Am. Capital Mgmt. & Research Inc., Houston, 1976—, pres., 1976-87; also officer, dir. 38 registered investment cos. managed by Am. Capital Mgmt. & Research, Inc. 1976—. Chmn. state employees div. Tri-County United Fund, Harrisburg, 1969, bd. dirs., 1970-71; mem. Pa. Gov.'s Cabinet, 1969-71; bd. regents Mercersburg Acad., 1971—; trustee Retina Research Found., 1979—, Salvation Army, 1978—, St. Joseph Hosp., 1980-88; bd. dirs. Houston Symphony Soc., 1982-88, Am. Cancer Soc., 1987—. Served with U.S. Army, 1959-60, Pa. N.G., 1960-65. Recipient Disting. Service award Harrisburg Jaycees, 1969. Mem. ABA, Tex. Bar Assn., Pa. Bar Assn. (chmn. young lawyers sect. 1968-69), Phila. Bar Assn. (sec. jr. bar conf. 1962-63), Houston Bar Assn., Houston C. of C. (bd. dirs. 1974-75), Investment Co. Inst. (bd. govs. 1977-88, chmn. 1984-86). Republican. Presbyterian. Clubs: Houston, Lakeside Country, University (Houston); Princeton (N.Y.C.). Home: 514 Clear Spring Dr Houston TX 77079 Office: Am Capital Mgmt & Rsch Inc 2800 Post Oak Blvd Houston TX 77056

REED, JOHN SHEDD, former railway executive; b. Chgo., June 9, 1917; s. Kersey Coates and Helen May (Shedd) R.; m. Marjorie Lindsay, May 4, 1946; children: Ginevra, Keith, Helen, Peter, John Shedd. Student, Chgo. Latin Sch., Hotchkiss Sch.; B.S. in Indsl. Adminstrn, Yale U., 1939; grad., Advanced Mgmt. Program, Harvard U., 1955. With A.T. & S.F. Ry., 1939-83; test dept. asst., successively spl. rep. to gen. supt. transp. Chgo.; transp. insp. Amarillo, Tex.; trainmaster Slaton, Tex., Pueblo, Colo.; supt. Mo. div., Marceline, Mo.; asst. to v.p. Chgo., 1957-59, exec. asst. to pres., 1957-59, v.p. finance, 1959-64, v.p. exec. dept., 1964-67, pres., 1967-78, chief exec. officer, 1968-82, chmn. bd., 1973-83; pres. Santa Fe Industries, Inc., 1968-78, chmn. bd., chief exec. officer, dir., 1973-83; chmn., chief exec. officer Santa Fe So. Pacific Corp., 1987, chmn., 1987-88; bd. dirs. Santa Fe Pacific Corp. (formerly Premark Internat. Inc.). Chmn. Nat. Merit Scholarship Corp.; pres. Shedd Aquarium, Chgo. Served with USNR, 1940-45. Clubs: Chicago; Old Elm, Shoreacres, Onwentsia (Lake Forest). Home: 301 W Laurel Ave Lake Forest IL 60045 Office: Santa Fe So Pacific Corp 224 S Michigan Ave Chicago IL 60604

REED, JOHN SHEPARD, banker; b. Chgo., Feb. 7, 1939; married; 4 children. BA, Washington and Jefferson Coll., 1959; BS, MIT, 1961; MS, Sloan Sch., 1965. Former systems analyst Goodyear Tire & Rubber Co.; with Citibank N.A., 1965—, former vice chmn., now chmn., chief exec. officer, dir.; with Citicorp (parent), N.Y.C., sr. exec. v.p. individual banking, then vice-chmn., 1982-84, chmn., chief exec. officer, 1984—, dir.; dir. Philip Morris, Inc., United Techs. Corp., Rand Corp., Monsanto Co. Mem. Meml. Sloan-Kettering Cancer Ctr, MIT, Ctr. for Advanced Study in Behavioral Scis., Woodrow Wilson Internat. Ctr. for Scholars in Smithsonian Inst.; bd. dirs. Russell Sage Found., Sloan Kettering Inst. for Cancer; bd. dirs., chmn. N.Y. Blood Ctr.; chmn. Russell Sage Found. Served with C.E., U.S. Army, Korea. Office: Citicorp 399 Park Ave New York NY 10043 *

REED, LAURENCE A., chemical company executive; b. 1939. BS, U. Minn., 1961; MS, Northwestern U., 1962; MBA, Cen. Mich. U., 1969. Research asst. U. Minn., 1960-61; with Dow Corning Corp., Midland, Mich., 1964—, chem. engr., 1964-66, staff specialist, 1967-68, econ. evaluation engr., 1968-78, v.p. chief fin. officer, controller, 1978-81, exec. v.p. bus., from 1981, pres., 1984—, chief operating officer, 1984-88, chief exec. officer, 1988—. Served with USN, 1962-64. Office: Dow Corning Corp 220 W Salzburg Rd Midland MI 48686-0994 *

REED, LEON SAMUEL, defense analyst; b. Warren, Ohio, July 6, 1949; s. Walter Charles and Lois Avalene (Botroff) R.; BA in Econs. and Journalism, Antioch Coll., 1971; m. Margaret Smith, Dec. 27, 1975 (separated); children: Samuel Currier, Stephen Walter, Catherine Lois. Project dir. Council on Econ. Priorities, N.Y.C. and Washington, 1970-75; sr. mem. profl. staff Joint Com. on Def. Prodn., U.S. Congress, Washington, 1975-77; mem. profl. staff Com. on Banking, Housing and Urban Affairs, U.S. Senate, Washington, 1977-81; analyst Analytic Scis. Corp., 1981-82, mgr. contingency planning, 1982-85, mgr. indsl. resources dept., 1985—; bd. dirs. Council on Econ. Priorities, 1971-73; del. White House Conf. on Youth, 1971. Mem. exec. com., Randolph Civic Assn., 1977-83, pres., 1978-80; asst. chair Coalition on Sensible Transp.; v.p. North Bethesda Congress of Citizens Assns., 1983-84, pres., 1984-86, sec., 1986-88; mem. Montgomery County Council of Pres., 1982—, chmn. 1986-87. Mem. Disciples of Christ Ch. Co-author: Guide to Corporations, 1973; author: Military Maneuvers, 1975; contbr. Strategic Survey, 1981-82, The American Defense Mobilization Intrastructure, 1983; author numerous congressional reports, mag. and jour. articles.

REED, MARSHA LEE, personnel agency executive, consultant; b. Pitts., Sept. 8, 1953; d. Milton and Ruth (Farber) Denmark; m. David P. Reed, Sept. 4, 1977; children—Diane, Robert. B.Gen. Studies, Ohio U., 1975. Cons. Devonshire Personnel, Garden Grove, Calif., 1977-79, Mgmt. Recruiters, Miami, Fla., 1979-80; unit mgr. Dunhill Personnel, Miami, 1980-82; owner, pres. Markett Personnel, Miami, 1982—. Mem. Nat. Assn. Personnel Cons., Nat. Assn. Female Execs., Nat. Assn. Female Bus. Owners, Fla. Assn. Personnel Cons., Bus. and Profl. Women, Greater Miami Jewish Fedn., Kappa Delta (social chmn. 1973-75), Kappa Delta Alumni Assn. Democrat. Club: Hadassah (Miami). Avocations: reading; piano playing. Home: 11124 SW 132d Ct Miami FL 33186 Office: Markett Personnel 11430 N Kendall Dr Miami FL 33176

REED, PAUL RUTHERFORD, editor; b. Boston, Jan. 20, 1929; s. Paul Rutherford and Elizabeth (Bagley) R.; B.S., Babson Coll., 1955, M.B.A., 1956; m. Barbara Louise Olsen, May 27, 1966. With Spear & Staff, Inc., Wellesley, Mass., 1957-64, in charge generation and editing Spear's Spl.

Situation, 1958-64, editor-in-chief The Spear Market and Group Trend Letter, investment adv. publ., 1964-74; with United Bus. Service Co., Boston, 1974-84, editor United Mut. Fund Selector, investment adv. publ., 1976-84, v.p., 1982-84, ind. fin. cons., 1985—.Served with USAF, 1951-52. Mem. Boston Security Analyst Soc. Office: 210 Newbury St Boston MA 02116

REED, RICHARD WEBSTER, JR., coal company executive; b. Seattle, July 28, 1951; s. Richard Webster Sr. and Garnet Roberta (Gallup) R.; m. Carolyn Prescott Bennett, Apr. 15, 1978; children: John Bennett, Charlotte Vickery, Malcolm DeWitt. BA in Econs., U. Calif., Berkeley, 1974. CPA, Pa., Nev. Treas. Penn Pocahontas Coal Co., Pitts., 1974-78; pres. Penn Enterprises Group, Inc., Pitts., 1978-80; v.p., treas. Shannopin Miing Co., Pitts., 1980—. Republican. Episcopalian. Home: 5310 Wilkins Ave Pittsburgh PA 15217 Office: Shannopin Mining Co 2 Chatham Ctr Ste 1480 Pittsburgh PA 15219

REED, ROBERT GEORGE, III, petroleum company executive; b. Cambridge, Mass., Aug. 9, 1927; s. Robert George and Marjorie B. Reed; m. Maggie L. Fisher, Mar. 22, 1974; children: Sandra McNickle, Valerie Sloan, Jonathan J., John-Paul. BA in Econs., Dartmouth Coll., 1949; AMP, Harvard U., 1970. Mktg. mgr. Tidewater Oil subs. Getty Oil Co., Los Angeles, 1957-64; v.p. mktg. Cities Service Oil Co., Tulsa, 1964-72; exec. v.p. Tesoro Petroleum Corp., San Antonio, 1972-79; chmn. bd., chief exec. officer Clark Oil & Refining Corp., Milw., 1979-81, pres., chief exec. officer div. Apex Oil Co., St. Louis, 1981-85; chmn. bd., chief exec. officer Energy Sources Exchange, Inc., Houston, 1981—; chmn., pres., chief exec. officer Pacific Resources, Inc., Honolulu, 1985—; bd. dirs. Alexander and Baldwin, Inc., Honolulu, First Hawaiian Bank, Hawaiian Telephone Co. Active Aloha United Way. Served with USN, 1945-46. Mem. Am. Petroleum Inst., Nat. Petroleum Refiners Assn., Nat. Petroleum Council, Hawaii C. of C. Clubs: Pacific, Plaza, Waialae Country, Plaza. Office: Pacific Resources Inc 733 Bishop St PO Box 3379 Honolulu HI 96842

REEDE, FRED ALLAN, JR., accountant; b. Ridgewood, N.J., June 13, 1956; s. Fred Allan and Magedela (Deischman) R.; m. Lynn J. Vitartas, Dec. 11, 1976. BBA, Kent State U., 1982. CPA, Ohio. Sales mgr. Park Honda, Canton, Ohio, 1974-80; staff acct. Price Waterhouse, Cleve., 1982-84; budget and personal computer specialist Gen. Electric Corp., Canton, 1984-85; leasing specialist Gen. Electric Credit Auto Lease, Canton, 1985; founding ptnr. Erlitz, Reede, & Nairne, Akron, Ohio, 1985; founding ptnr. Heartland Systems, Akron, 1987, pres., chief exec. officer, 1988—. Mem. acctg. adv. council Kent State U.; vice-pres. Stark County br. Arthritis Found., trustee Northeastern Ohio chpt., bd. dirs. Recipient Honda Council of Sales award Leadership Gold Chpt. Am. Honda Motor Co.Gardena, Calif. 1977-79. Mem. AICPA, Ohio Soc. CPA's, Canton C. of C. (chmn. membership steering com.). Republican. Lutheran. Home: 2411 55th St NE Canton OH 44621 Office: Erlitz Reede & Nairne 3570 Executive Dr Suite 205 Uniontown OH 44685

REEDER, DOUGLAS LEE, corporate executive; b. Kansas City, Mo., Oct. 14, 1937; s. Lee and Madaline Flo (Brown) R.; m. Sheila Ann Foley, June 20, 1959 (div. 1978); children: Douglas L. III (dec.), Kevin Lee, Bradford Scott Lee; m. Anne Marie Murphy, Jan. 27, 1979. BA, U. Mo., 1959; postgrad., Northwestern U., 1963-64. Pres. Wis. Shoe Co., Milw., 1965-77; exec. v.p. Plastic Sales and Mfg. Co., Kansas City, Mo., 1980-82; pres. Tex. Bus. Telephone Service, Dallas, 1982-85, WSC Group, Inc., Dallas, 1983—; chmn. bd. WSC Group, Inc., 1983—; bd. dirs. Reeder Cons., Inc., also cons. Contbr. econ. devel. studies, patentee in field. Officer Young Pres. Orgn., Milw.; bd. dirs. Ctr. for Slower Learners, Dallas, 1986—, 1st Ch. Christ Sci., Richardson, Tex., 1987—. Mem. Leadership Dallas, SAR, Mensa, Rotary (bd. dirs.), Masons. Office: WSC Group Inc 5400 E Mockingbird Ln #122 Dallas TX 75206

REEDER, MICHAEL S., consulting firm executive. BSBA, U. Fla.; MBA, U. Tampa (Fla.). Mgr., employment svcs. Fla. Power Corp.; v.p. (exec. search div.) MSL Internat. Cons., Ltd. Office: Lamalie Assocs Tower Pla 3340 Peachtree Rd NE Atlanta GA 30026

REESE, CAROL ANN YOUNG, insurance company executive; b. Salem, N.J., Oct. 6, 1951; d. Richard Fogg and Alice Elizabeth (Shafer) Young; m. George Russell Reese, Aug. 4, 1973; children: Jonathan Russell, Jason Richard. BS, W.Va. U., 1973. Teller Nat. Bank S.D., Rapid City, 1974-76; secondary tch. math. Douglas Sch. System, Ellsworth AFB, S.D., 1976-78; mgr. agy. Henry D. Young Inc., Salem, 1978-84, owner, mgr., 1984—. Chmn. comml. div. south United Way Salem County, N.J., 1987-88; treas. Cub Scout pack #28 Boy Scouts Am., Salem, 1988; asst. coach Salem Little League, 1987; treas. Elsinboro (N.J.) Sch. Assn., 1986-88; deaconess Meml. Bapt. Ch., Salem, 1987-88. Mem. NAFE, Profl. Ins. Agts., N.J. Assn. Cert. Ins. Counselors (cert.), Cumberland/Salem Ind. Ins. Agts. (treas. 1982-86), N.J. Redshaw Computer Users (dir. edn. 1980-83). Democrat. Baptist. Office: Henry D Young Inc 216 E Broadway Salem NJ 08079

REESE, DANIEL WILLIAM, finance company executive, bank executive; b. Abington, Pa., Apr. 5, 1953; s. Joseph Hammond Reese and Patricia (Welsh) Somers; m. Carol Olwert. Student, Georgetown U. Sch. Fgn. Service, 1974-75; BS in Polit. Sci., Trinity Coll., 1975; MS in Bus., Columbia U., 1985. Researcher Fed. Election Commn., Washington, 1975, spl. asst. to chmn., 1975-77; spl. asst. to gov. State of Conn., 1977-81; mgr. Citibank NA, N.Y.C., 1981-83, ops. mgr., 1983-85; v.p., state mgr. Citicorp, Westport, Conn., 1985-88; sr. v.p. Conn. Nat. Bank, Stamford, Conn., 1988—; bd. dirs. Conn. Pub. TV, Stamford, 1985—, Charles Ives Ctr. Arts, Danbury, Conn., 1986—; alumni dir. Trinity Coll., 1977-79. Chmn. New Fairfield (Conn.) Democrat. Town Com., 1987—. Democrat. Episcopalian. Home: 2 Hudson Dr New Fairfield CT 06812 Office: Conn Nat Bank 1 Landmark Sq Stratford CT 06880

REESE, JOSEPH HAMMOND, JR., insurance company executive, consultant; b. Phila., Aug. 29, 1928; s. Joseph Hammond and Ethel (Allen) R.; m. Joan Barton, Feb. 7, 1975; children: Daniel, Linda Hurd; stepchildren: Anne Kabay, Carol Hancock, Will Harbison. BA in Econs., Washington and Lee U., 1950; postgrad. in bus., U. Pa., 1950; cert. Am. Coll., 1955. Agt. Penn Mut. Life Ins. Co., Phila., 1950-61, asst. gen. agt., 1958-60; chmn., chief exec. officer Reese & Co. Inc., Abington, Pa., 1961-81; chmn., pres. Montgomery Mgmt. Corp., Abington, 1972-82; pres., chief operating officer Provident Indemnity Life Ins. Co., 1982-85; chmn. bd. dirs., chief exec. officer Provident Am. Corp., Provident Indemnity Life Ins. Co., 1983-86; gen. agt. Mass. Mut. Life Ins. Co., Phila., 1961-81. Trustee Franklin and Marshall Coll., 1972-77; bd. dirs. Am. Lung Assn. Phila. and Montgomery County; founder, past chmn. Wellness Council Southeastern Pa. 1st lt. USAF, 1950-53. Mem. Am. Soc. CLU's (pres. Phila. chpt. 1960-61), Nat. Assn. Life Underwriters (life, mem. Million Dollar Round Table 1956—), Young Pres.'s Orgn., Phila. Pres.'s Orgn. (bd. dirs.), Am. Srs. Golf Assn., Internat. Srs. Amateur Golf Soc., So. Srs. Golf Assn. Republican. Episcopalian. Clubs: Huntington Valley Country (Abington, Pa.); Union League (Phila.); Wilderness Country (Naples, Fla.). Home and Office: Hidden Glen Meadowbrook PA 19046

REESE, KENNETH WENDELL, diversified company executive; b. Orange, Tex., Aug. 1, 1930; s. Richard W. and Florence (Mulhollan) R.; m. Mary A. Broom, Aug. 22, 1955; children: Jimmy, Michael, Gary. BBA, U. Houston, 1954. Asst. treas. Firestone Tire & Rubber Co., Akron, Ohio, 1968-70, treas., 1970—, v.p., 1973-75, exec. v.p. finance, 1975; sr. v.p. fin. Tenneco Inc., Houston, 1975-78, exec. v.p., 1978—, also bd. dirs.; bd. dirs. Tex. Commerce Bancshares Inc., Fleming Cos. Inc., Tridon Industries Inc. Bd. dirs. Better Bus. Bur. Met. Houston, Tex. Council on Econ. Edn., Cotton Bowl Athletic Assn.; nat. bd. dirs. Jr. Achievement Inc.; chmn. adv. bd. Coll. Bus. Adminstrn. U. Houston. 1st lt. AUS, 1954-56. Mem. U. Houston Athletic Lettermans Assn. Baptist. Clubs: Heritage, Houston City, Ramada, River Oaks Country. Home: 101 Westcott #1806 Houston TX 77007 Office: Tenneco Inc 1010 Milam Houston TX 77002-2511

REESE, PAUL WESLEY, JR., retail executive; b. Atlanta, Oct. 2, 1949; s. Paul Wesley and Elizabeth Irene (Currington) R.; m. Dianne Hassen Drescher, Sept. 4, 1971; children: Eric Adam, Adrienne Elaine, Lauren Leigh, Meredith Erin. BA, U. Fla., 1971; MBA, Mich. State U., 1984. Mgmt. cons. Behavioral Systems, Inc., Atlanta, 1974-75; indsl. engr. Michelin Tire Corp., Greenville, S.C., 1975-78; cons. engr. Kurt Salmon Assocs., Atlanta, 1978-81; dir. distbn., leased ops. J.L. Hudson Co., Detroit, 1981-86; v.p. distbn. Emporium-Capwell Co., San Francisco, 1986-87; sr. v.p. distbn. and transp. Ames Dept. Stores, Inc., Rocky Hill, Conn., 1987—. Mem. Inst. of Indsl. Engrs., Council of Logistic Mgmt., Beta Gamma Sigma. Republican. Congregationalist. Office: Ames Dept Stores Inc 2418 Main St Rocky Hill CT 06067

REESE, WILLIAM HARRY, psychologist, management development company executive, consultant; b. Stillwater, Okla., Aug. 26, 1947; s. Harry Bryan and Doris Rae (Hays) R.; m. Jill Wayne Astroth, June 19, 1971; children: Bryan, Nathan, Christan, Lizabeth, William. BA, William Jewell Coll., 1969; MA, U. Mo., 1973, 75; PhD, Union, Cin., 1979. Psychologist W.H. Reese & Assocs., Shawnee Mission, Kans., 1973—; cons. W.P. Dolan Inc., Shawnee Mission, 1983—; acting chief exec. officer Generations Techs., Kansas City, Mo., 1987—; chief exec. officer Ctr. for Mgmt. Devel., Kansas City, 1987—; cons. Ctr. Bus. Innovation, Kansas City, 1987; adj. prof. William Jewell Coll., Liberty Mo., 1986; dir. devel. Cen. Solutions Inc. Contbr. articles to profl. jours. Bd. dirs. Nat. Council Alcohol and Drugs, Kansas City, 1981. Mem. Fellowship Christian Athletes (Westwood, Kans.), Pi Kappa Delta. Home: 4931 Mission Rd Westwood KS 66205 Office: 6025 Metcalf Ln Shawnee Mission KS 66202

REESE, WILLIAM WILLIS, banker; b. N.Y.C., July 8, 1940; s. Willis Livingston Meiser and Frances Galletin (Stevens) R.; B.A., Trinity Coll., 1963; M.B.A., J.D., Columbia U., 1970. Admitted to N.Y. bar, 1972; research analyst Morgan Guaranty Trust Co., N.Y.C., 1971-73, investment research officer, 1973-77, asst. v.p., 1977-86, v.p., 1986— . Bd. dirs. N.Y.C. Ballet, 1975-87, Counseling and Human Devel. Center, 1977—, 3d St. Music Sch. Settlement, 1976—; trustee Millbrook Sch., 1972—. Served with USAF, 1963-67. Mem. Am., Inter-Am., N.Y. State (sec. com. on internat. law 1973-76), Dutchess County bar assns., N.Y. Soc. Security Analysts, Certified Fin. Analysts, Assn. Bar City N.Y. Republican. Episcopalian. Clubs: Union, Racquet and Tennis, Rockaway Hunt, Mt. Holyoke Lodge. Home: 345 Meadowview Ave New York NY 11550 Office: Columbia U Law Sch 435 W 116th St New York NY 10020

REEVES, MARK DESMOND, marketing company executive; b. Eden, N.C., Nov. 10, 1958; s. Harry Desmond and Margaret (Rutledge) R.; m. Deaune Wilson, Mar. 26, 1988. BS in Mktg. and Mgmt., N.C. State U., 1981. Dept. mgr. Brendle's, Inc., Greensboro, N.C., 1981-83; regional sales mgr. Rose Enterprises, Atlanta, 1983-85; owner, mgr. Mountain Mktg., Asheville, N.C., 1985—. Mem. Eden Jaycees. Republican. Methodist. Home: 18 Spears Ave Asheville NC 28801 Office: Mountain Mktg Bldg 2 Unit 1 134 Johnston Sch Rd POB1015 Asheville NC 28806

REEVES, RAY LESLIE, marketing professional; b. Denver, Mar. 10, 1959; s. George Raymond and Mary Esther (Willard) R.; m. Bibiana Marie Petras, June 14, 1986. BS, U. Colo., 1982. Gen. mgr. Littso Soccer and Sports, Littleton, Colo., 1977-78, David Clement's Pro Soccer, 1978-81; instl. sales B&H Sports, Denver, 1981-82; account exec. nat. Screenprint, Denver, 1982-84; gen. mgr. nat. Screenprint, Chgo., 1984-88, dir. mktg., 1988—. Mem. Greater O'Hare Assn. (ambassador 1985-87). Office: Nat Screenprint 425 Crossen Ave Elk Grove Village IL 60007

REEVES, WILLIAM HATTON, electronics and chemical company executive; b. Phila., Jan. 18, 1937; s. Jonathan Hatton and Eugene Sue (Headley) R.; m. Carole Lynne Cargal, Aug. 4, 1962; children: Mark Stephen, Jonathan Wyatt, Marion Alicia. Student, U. W.Va., 1955-56; BS in Chemistry and Zoology, Marshall U., 1959; postgrad., Universite Louis Pasteur, Strasbourg, France, 1976-81. Dir. product devel. Internat. Paper Co., N.Y.C., 1967-69; nat. sales mgr. Sherwood Med. Industries, St. Louis, 1969-73; v.p. mktg. Logos Internat., Plainfield, N.J., 1973-76; chmn., founder Vectra Corp., Columbia, Md., 1976-81, Magnum Electronics, Englewood, Ohio, 1981-86; pres., founder Chronodynamics, Ltd., Dayton, Ohio, 1986—; cons. Rhom Pharma NA, Durmstadt, Fed. Republic Germany, 1981—, QMax Tech., Dayton, 1981—; bd. dirs. MedTech Inc., Dayton, Thermology Labs., Centerville, Ohio. Holder 4 patents. Served with U.S. Army, 1959-62. Fellow Am. Acad. Thermology, Internat. Soc. Christian Counselors. Republican. Presbyterian. Home: 10449 Stream Park Ct Spring Valley OH 45370 Office: Chronodynamics Ltd 6012 N Dixie Dr Dayton OH 45404

REGAN, JOHN DENNISS, insurance company executive; b. Bklyn., Oct. 29, 1943; s. Cornelius and Margarite Regan; m. Lynda Louise Hcider, May 5, 1968; children: Alysia, Melissa. CLU, Chartered Fin. Cons. Agt. Washington Nat. Ins. Co., San Francisco, 1968-73; pres. Regan Co., Sausalito, Calif., 1973-84, Regan Group Ins. Mktg., Sausalito, 1979-86; pres. & chief exec. officer Gen. Services Life Holding Co. and Gen. Services Life Ins. Co., Novato, Calif., 1986—; chmn. bd. Regan Reassurance Co., Phoenix, The Regan Group Ins. Mktg., Novato; frequent speaker various groups. Author: Complete Book of Retired Lives Reserves, 1979; contbr. numerous articles to profl. jours. Founder, bd. dirs. Nat. Ins. Polit. Action Com., Washington, 1984—. Mem. Ins. Coalition Am. (founding), Assn. for Advanced Life Underwriting, Nat. Assn. Life Underwriters, Internat. Assn. Fin. Planners, Million Dollar Round Table, Internat. Forum, Top of Table. Republican. Roman Catholic. Office: Gen Svcs Life Holding Co 201 Alameda del Prado Novato CA 94949

REGAN, PAUL E., food company executive; b. Arlington, Mass., Apr. 16, 1939; m. Ellen Seeno, Aug. 19, 1967; children: Courtney, Sarah. AB, Harvard U., 1961. V.p. sales Lever Bros. Co., N.Y.C., 1962-87; v.p. food svc. Chesebrough Ponds, Greenwich, Conn., 1987—. Home: 63 Central Ave Glen Rock NJ 07452 Office: Ragu Foods Inc 75 Merritt Blvd Trumbull CT 06611

REGAN, ROBERT M., small business owner; b. Leominster, Mass., Mar. 28, 1930; s. George Edward and Beatrice Mary (Roberts) R.; m. Carole Marcotte, Feb. 6, 1954; children: Jean Marie, John, Jennifer, Jacqueline, Jessica. BS, Fitchburg State U., 1952. Cert. in real estate appraising. Tchr. elem. sch. Lunenburg (Mass.) Sch., 1954-55; field rep. S.D. Warren Co., Boston, 1955-67, Century Paper, Randolph, Mass., 1967-86; pres. O'Connel-Regan Assocs., Inc., Fitchburg, 1988—; sales rep. Old Colony Real Estate, Leominster, 1966-88. Served to lt. (j.g.) USN. Office: O'Connell-Regan Assoc Inc 280 Main St Suite 315 Fitchburg MA 01420

REGAN, TIMOTHY JAMES, controller; b. Atchison, Kans., July 31, 1956; s. Vincent James and Phyllis (Brull) R.; m. Veronica Sue Kasten, June 25, 1977; children: Katrina Sue, Brian James. BS, Kans. State U., 1978. Corp. acct. Lincoln Grain Co., Atchison, 1978-80; acctg. supr. Pillsbury Co., St. Joseph, Mo., 1980; br. account mgr. Pillsbury Co., St. Joseph, 1980-82, Omaha, 1982; internal auditor Pillsbury Co., Mpls., 1983; regional account mgr. Pillsbury Co., Huron, Ohio, 1983-84; regional account mgr. Scoular Grain Co., Omaha, 1984-87, controller, 1987—. fin. advisor Grace Abbott Sch. PTO, Omaha, 1987. Republican. Roman Catholic. Lodges: KC, Elks. Home: 755 N 153d Ave Omaha NE 68154 Office: Scoular Grain Co 2027 Dodge St Omaha NE 68102

REGAS, WILLIAM GRADY, restaurateur; b. Knoxville, Tenn., Dec. 10, 1958; s. William Frank and Elizabeth (Frost) R. BS in Risk Mgmt., Real Estate, Fla. State U., 1981. Concept developer Grady's Goodtimes, Knoxville, 1981, v.p., mgr., 1981-84; v.p., mgr. Grady's Goodtimes, Charlotte, N.C., 1984-85, v.p., gen. mgr., 1985-88; v.p., gen. mgr., devel. dir. Grady's Goodtimes, Charlotte and Knoxville, 1988—. Mem. Nat. Restaurant Assn., N.C. Restaurant Assn., Tenn. Restaurant Assn., Charlotte C. of C. Republican. Office: Grady's Goodtimes 6739 Kingston Pike at Papermill Dr Knoxville TN 37919

REGAZZI, JOHN HENRY, corporate executive; b. N.Y.C., Jan. 4, 1921; s. Caesar B. and Jennie (Moruzzi) R.; m. Doris Mary Litzau, Feb. 16, 1946; children—Mark, Dale. B.B.A., Pace Coll., 1951. C.P.A., N.Y. Mgr. Price Waterhouse, N.Y.C., 1946-62; comptroller ABC, N.Y.C., 1962-70; sr. v.p., chief fin. officer Avnet, Inc., N.Y.C., 1970—. Contbr. articles to profl. jours. Pres. bd. River Dell Regional High Sch., Oradell, N.J., 1962-65; trustee, treas. Oradell Pub. Library, 1970-79; councilman Borough of Oradell, 1979—. Served as staff sgt. USAF, 1942-45. Mem. Fin. Execs. Inst., Am. Inst. C.P.A.s, Nat. Assn. Accts. Republican. Roman Catholic. Lodge: Lions. Home: 637 Park Ave Oradell NJ 07649 Office: Avnet Inc 767 Fifth Ave New York NY 10153

REGELBRUGGE, ROGER RAFAEL, steel company executive; b. Eeklo, Belgium, May 22, 1930; came to U.S., 1953, naturalized, 1961; s. Victor and Rachel (Roesbeke) R.; m. Dorcas Merchant; children: Anita, Marc, Laurie, Jon, Craig, Kurt, Christiane, Lauren. B.Sc. in Mech. Engring, State Tech. Coll., Ghent, 1951; B.Sc. in Indsl. Engring, Gen. Motors Inst., Flint, Mich., 1955; M.Sc. in Mech. Engring, Mich. State U., 1964. Supr. product engring. dept. Gen. Motors Corp., Antwerp, 1955-58; chief devel. engr., then gen. mgr. Airmaster div. Hayes Industries Inc., Jackson, Mich., 1958-66; with Koehring Co., 1966-74; group v.p. internat. ops. Koehring Co., Milw., 1969-74; exec. v.p. Korf Industries, Inc., Charlotte, N.C., 1974-77; pres., chief exec. officer Georgetown Industries, Inc. (formerly Korf Industries, Inc.), 1977—, also dir.; chmn. bd. dirs., pres. Georgetown Steel Corp.; chmn. bd. Georgetown Investment Corp., Georgetown Fin. Corp., Advanced Wire Tech., Western Lumber Co., Tree Island Industries; bd. dirs. Vesuvious Crucible Co., Waccamaw Corp. Bd. visitors Davidson Coll.; N.C. adv. bd. Fuqua Sch. Bus. Duke U.; bd. dirs. Carolinas Council on World Affairs. Mem. ASME, Am. Soc. Automotive Engrs., Am. Iron and Steel Inst. (dir.). Roman Catholic. Clubs: Charlotte Athletic, Carmel Country, Tower (Charlotte); Georgetown (Washington); Litchfield Country (Pawley Island, S.C.). Office: Georgetown Industries Inc 1901 Roxborough Rd Ste 200 Charlotte NC 28211

REGENSTREIF, HERBERT, lawyer; b. N.Y.C., May 13, 1935; s. Max and Jeannette (Hacker) R.; m. Patricia Friedman, Dec. 20, 1967 (div. July 1968); m. Charlotte Lois Levy, Dec. 10, 1980; 1 child, Cara Rachael. BA, Hobart Coll., 1957; JD, N.Y. Law Sch., 1960; MS, Pratt Inst., 1985. Bar: N.Y. 1961, Ky. 1985, U.S. Dist. Ct. (ea. and so. dists.) N.Y. 1962, U.S. Tax Ct. 1967, U.S. Ct. Appeals (2d cir.) 1962, U.S. Supreme Ct. 1967. Ptnr., Fried & Regenstreif, P.C., Mineola, N.Y., 1963—; cons. in field. Contbr. articles to profl. jours. County committeeman Dem. Com., Queens County, N.Y., 1978-79; arbitrator N.Y. City Civil Ct., 1984-86. Mem. Bar Assn. Nassau County, Phi Delta Phi, Beta Phi Mu. Jewish. Club: Hobart of N.Y. (gov. 1968-69).

REGIER, SUSAN ANNE, trust company executive; b. Clinton, Okla., Dec. 4, 1954; d. John and Shirley Anne (Leonard) R. BS in Acctg., Southwestern Okla. State U., 1977; M in Acctg., U. Okla., 1980. CPA, Okla. Internat. tax acct. Phillips Petroleum Co., Bartlesville, Okla., 1977-78; researcher, teaching asst. U. Okla., Norman, 1979-80; sr. tax acct. Grant Thornton Internat., Oklahoma City, 1981-83; v.p. Trust Co. of Okla., Oklahoma City, 1983—, Kepco Inc., Oklahoma City, 1987—; cons. Robert W. Leonard and Assocs., Houston, 1980—, Continental Ill. Bank, Chgo., 1984—, Kepco Inc., Oklahoma City, 1985-87; bd. dirs. Houston Fitness Ctr. Atlantic Richfield Corp. grantee, 1979. Mem. Am. Inst. CPA's, Okla. Soc. CPA's, Southwestern Okla. State U Alumni Assn., U. Okla. Pres.' Ptnrs., Oklahoma City C. of C., Sigma Kappa Alumni Assn. Republican. Baptist. Club: Desk and Derrick (Oklahoma City). Home: 4400 Hemingway #229 Oklahoma City OK 73118-2244 Office: Trust Co Okla 1001 NW 63d Suite 304 Oklahoma City OK 73116 also: Kepco Inc 3535 NW 58th St Suite 450 Oklahoma City OK 73112

REGUERO, MELODIE HUBER, financial services professional; b. Montebello, Calif., May 10, 1956; d. Adam W. and Helen Carolyn (Antrim) Huber; m. Edward Anthony Reguero, Oct. 3, 1987. BA in Econs. magna cum laude, UCLA, 1978; M in Bus. Taxation, U. So. Calif., 1983. CPA, Calif. Mem. tax audit staff Arthur Young & Co., Los Angeles, 1978-80; sr. mem. Singer, Lewak, Greenbaum & Goldstein, Los Angeles, 1980-82; tax supr. Coldwell Banker & Co., Los Angeles, 1983-84; fin. analyst, acquisitions specialist Coldwell Banker Residential Group, Newport Beach, Calif., 1984-86; fin. services profl. The Acacia Fin. Group, Newport Beach, Calif., 1986-88; chief fin. officer Fin. Engring. Concepts, Inc., Santa Ana, Calif., 1988—; treas. Champions Choice, Inc., 1980—. Active Censer Club, Costa Mesa, 1989—, Ctr. 500 Performing Arts, Costa Meas, 1989—. Mem. Am. Inst. CPA's, Calif. Soc. CPA's (pres. 1980—), Newport Harbor C. of C., Irvine C. of C. Republican. Club: Orange County Triathlon. Office: Fin Engring Concepts Inc 1221 E Dyer Rd Ste 220 Santa Ana CA 92705

REHAGEN, MARK STEVEN, state official; b. Jefferson City, Mo., Jan. 8, 1959; s. Arnold Michael and Juli Ann (Dusheke) R.; m. Susan Kay Sandbothe, Apr. 20, 1985; children: Christopher, Thomas. BA in English, Pontifical Coll. Josephinum, 1981; postgrad., Kenrick Sem., 1981-83. Compliance technician Mo. Div. Ins., Jefferson City, 1985-86, adminstrv. asst., 1986-87, supr. property and casualty, 1988—. Pres. St. Peter's Parish Council, Jefferson City, 1987-88. Named Pinter scholar, 1979. Home: 2020 Meadow Ln Jefferson City MO 65109 Office: Mo Div Insurance 301 W High St Jefferson City MO 65101

REHBEIN, EDWARD ANDREW, exploration geologist; b. Portland, Oreg., Aug. 13, 1947; s. Edward Louis and Marjorie Ann (Simshaw) R.; m. Phyllis Jean Boyer, June 23, 1973; children: Matthew Louis, Angela Mae. BS in Geology, Calif. Inst. Tech., 1969. Geologist U.S. Forest Service, Elkins, W.Va., 1972-74, U.S. Geol. Survey, Billings, Mont., 1974-76; coal geologist W.Va. Geologic Survey, Morgantown, 1977; cons. Morgantown, 1978; geologist Allied Corp., Beckley, W.Va., 1979; sr. exploration geologist Kerr-McGee Corp., Beckley, 1980-82, regional mgr. exploration, Reno, Nev., 1983-85; exploration geologist, Oklahoma City, 1985—. Author: Remembering God's Word, 1989; contbr. articles to profl. jours. Mem. Am. Assn. Petroleum Geologists, Am. Inst. Profl. Geologists. Club: Shotokan Karate Am. Office: Kerr McGee Corp 123 Robert S Kerr Ave MT 2706 Oklahoma City OK 73102

REHER, RAYMOND AGUDO, financial executive, accountant; b. Chgo., Oct. 19, 1948; s. Raymond and Mary Elena (Agudo) R.; m. Margaret Diane Wall, Oct. 28, 1972; children: Brian Anthony, Kevin Raymond. BBA, U. Notre Dame, 1970; MBA, DePaul U., 1972. CPA, Ill. Sr. asst. acct. Deloitte, Haskins and Sells CPA's, Chgo., 1970-73; sr. acct. Allied Van Lines, Inc., Broadview, Ill., 1973-74; project mgr. Baxter Travenol Labs., Inc., Deerfield, Ill., 1974-81; dir. analysis and control UOP, Inc., Des Plaines, Ill., 1981-83; v.p., chief fin. officer CME-SAT, Inc., Longboat Key, Fla., 1983-85; v.p., treas. fin. EyeTech., Inc., St. Paul, 1985—. Capt. USAR, 1970-78. Mem. AICPA, Fla. Inst. CPA's, Beta Alpha Psi. Republican. Roman Catholic. Home: 4172 Centergate Blvd Sarasota FL 34233 Office: Eye Tech Inc 1983 Sloan Pl Saint Paul MN 55117

REHERMAN, RONALD GILBERT, gas company executive; b. Evansville, Ind., Aug. 14, 1935; s. Gilbert and Anna (Lawrence) R.; m. Rosalynn Reherman, Oct. 25, 1959; children: Robin, Chris, David. BS, U. Evansville, 1958; MBA, U. So. Indiana, Evansville, 1971. Registered profl. engr., Ind. With So. Ind. Gas and Electric Co., Evansville, 1960—, v.p., dir. gas ops., 1982-84, exec. v.p., gen. mgr. ops., 1985-88, pres., chief oper. officer, 1988—. Bd. dirs. Evansville Indsl. Found., Evansville Council Boy Scouts Am., Evansville United Way, campaign chmn., 1986-87. With U.S. Army, 1958-60. Mem. Met. Evansville C. of C. (bd. dirs. 1987). Office: So Ind Gas & Electric Co 20 NW 4th St Evansville IN 47741

REHFUSS, WALTER GUY, life insurance company executive; b. Wadena, Minn., Nov. 8, 1936; s. Kenneth Edward and Selma Eldora (Reinsvild) R.; m. Camille Grace Dziedzic, June 20, 1959 (div.); m. Susan Keyser, Dec. 21, 1985; children: Peter, Kenneth, Kay, Sue Ellen. BS in Psychology and Math., Carroll Coll., 1958. Actuary Old Line Ins. Co., Milw., 1958-69; v.p. life systems Network Data Processing, Cedar Rapids, Iowa, 1969-71; v.p. Am. Defender Life, Raleigh, N.C., 1971-74; sr. v.p. adminstrn. Ky. Cen. Life Ins. Co., Lexington, 1974—; adv. bd. Space Design Internat., Cin., 1987—. Vice chmn. United Way, Lexington, 1977; bd. dirs. Lexington Transit Authority, 1977-78, Jr. Achievement, Lexington, 1984-86, Lexington Sister Cities Internat., 1988—. Fellow Life Office Mgmt. Assn.; mem. CLU Assn. (CLU award 1978). Republican. Episcopalian. Office: Ky Cen Life Ins Co Kincaid Towers 300 W Vine Lexington KY 40507

REHM, JACK DANIEL, media executive; b. Yonkers, N.Y., Oct. 10, 1932; s. Jack and Ann (McCarthy) R.; m. Cynthia Fenning, Oct. 18, 1958; children: Lisabeth R., Ann M., Cynthia A., Jack D. Jr. BS in Mktg., Holy Cross Coll., 1954. Advt. sales trainee, asst. account exec. Batten, Barton, Durstine & Osborne, N.Y.C., 1954-59; mgr. Suburbia Today, N.Y.C., 1959-62; with advt. sales dept. Better Homes and Gardens Meredith Corp., N.Y.C., 1962-66; mgr. advt. sales Meredith Corp., Phila., 1966-67; mgr. advt. sales Meredith Corp., N.Y.C., 1967-69, dir. advt. sales, 1969-73, v.p., pub. dir. mag. div., 1973-75, v.p., pub. Better Homes and Gardens, pub. dir. mag. div., 1975-76, v.p. pub. group, gen. mgr. mag. pub., 1976-80; pres. pub. group Meredith Corp., Des Moines, 1980-86, exec. v.p. corp. svcs., 1986-88, pres., chief oper. officer, 1988—, also bd. dirs.; bd. dirs. First Interstate Bank Iowa, Inc., Des Moines, Vernon Co., Newton, Iowa, Equitable of Iowa Cos. Chmn. bd. trustees Des Moines Civic Ctr., 1988—; bd. govs. Drake U., 1988—. With U.S. Army, 1956-57. Mem. Mag. Pubs. Assn. (bd. dirs. 1981—, chmn. 1983-85, Publisher of Yr. 1988), Am. Coun. for Capital Formation (bd. dirs. 1986—), Pine Valley Golf Club, Scarsdale Golf Club, Wakonda Golf Club. Roman Catholic. Home: 2913 Druid Hill Dr Des Moines IA 50315 Office: Meredith Corp 1716 Locust St Des Moines IA 50336

REHMANN, KENNETH ROBERT, accountant, consultant; b. Washington, Feb. 10, 1962; s. Earl John and Felicia Helen (Kwiecinski) R.; m. Kim Elizabeth Doll, Aug. 29, 1987. BS, U. Md., 1984. CPA, Md., 1985. Tax acct. Marriott Corp., Bethesda, Md., 1984-85; sr. cons. Deloitte, Haskins & Sells, Washington, 1985—. Mem. Md. State Bd. Pub. Accts. Republican. Presbyterian. Office: Deloitte Haskins & Sells 1001 Pennsylvania Ave Ste 350 Washington DC 20004

REHNERT, GEOFFREY SCOTT, venture capitalist; b. Jenkintown, Pa., Sept. 23, 1957; s. Francis George and Edythe Elizabeth (Beech) R.; m. Bernadette Theresa Jackman, May 9, 1981. BA, Duke U., 1979; JD, Stanford U., 1984. Bar: Calif. 1984. Account officer Morgan Guaranty Trust Co., N.Y.C., 1979-81; assoc. Kirkland & Ellis, Chgo., 1982, Cooley, Godward, Castro, Huddleson & Tatum, Palo Alto, Calif., 1983; cons. Bain & Co., Palo Alto, 1983-84; sr. assoc. Bain Capital, Boston, 1984-86, prin., 1986-87, gen. ptnr., 1987—; bd. dirs. Calumet Coach Co., Calumet City, Ill., Holson Co., Wilton, Conn., Charles D. Burnes Co., Norwood, Mass., Specialty Retailers Inc., Houston. Contbr. Stanford Law Rev., 1985. Mem. Assn. Corp. Growth, New Eng. Venture Capital Assn., Nat. Venture Capital Assn., U. Club Boston, Bus. Assocs. Club Boston, Phi Beta Kappa, Order of Coif. Office: Bain Capital 2 Copley Pl Boston MA 02116

REHNSTROM, J. BERNARD, utility company executive; b. Linn Grove, Iowa, Jan. 16, 1930; s. Carl Elim and Myrtle Beulah (Halversen) R.; m. Delores Ida Miller, June 19, 1955; children: Alan, Brian, Amy. BS in Commerce, U. Iowa, 1951. Sr. acct. Arthur Andersen & Co., Chgo., 1953-59; sr. v.p. fin., sec., bd. dirs. IE Industries, Inc., Cedar Rapids, 1959—, Iowa Elec. Light and Power Co., 1959—; sec., bd. dirs. Cedar Rapids and Iowa City Ry. Co.; v.p., sec., bd. dirs. Iowa Land and Bldg. Co., Met. Devel. Co.; sec., bd. dirs. Indsl. Energy Applications, Inc.; bd. dirs. Norwest Bank, Cedar Rapids, Telecom USA, Atlanta; v.p., bd. dirs. IEI Container Svcs; sec., treas., bd. dirs. Dubuque Sand & Gravel Co. Bd. dirs. St. Luke's Meth. Hosp., Cedar Rapids, 1984—; bd. trustees Cedar Rapids Pub. Libr., 1984—. Cpl. U.S. Army, 1951-53. Mem. Financial Execs. Inst., Am. Soc. Corp. Secs., Nat. Assn. Accts. (past pres., nat. bd. dirs.), Edison Electric Inst. (mem. fin. com.). Office: IE Industries Inc 200 1st St SE Cedar Rapids IA 54201

REHOR, RAYMOND JAMES, transportation executive; b. Cleve., June 18, 1929; s. Frank V. and Barbara Ann (Stika) R.; B.B.A., Cleve. State U., 1958; J.D., Cleve-Marshall Law Sch., 1972; m. Mary Ann Habdas, May 6, 1961. Cost acct. Willard Storage Battery Corp., 1947-51; tax mgr. Pneumo Corp., Cleve., 1952-65; asst. tax mgr. Harris Corp., Cleve., 1965-69; tax mgr. Leaseway Transp. Corp., Cleve., 1970-73, dir. taxes, 1974-76, v.p. taxes, 1977—. Mem. Acctg. and Fin. Council Tax Exec. Inst., Am. Assn. Equipment Lessors, Am. Mgmt. Assn., Tax Club Cleve. Roman Catholic. Home: 4322 Vezber Dr Seven Hills OH 44131 Office: Leaseway Transp Corp 3700 Park East Dr Beachwood OH 44122

REIBEN, RICHARD HARRY, corporate executive, lawyer; b. N.Y.C., Jan. 2, 1950; s. Bernard and Helene (Berger) R.; m. Karen S. Krouppa, Apr. 28, 1974; children: Joseph Randal, Whitney Claire. BA in Psychology, U. Rochester, 1971; JD, NYU, 1974. Bar: N.Y. 1975, U.S. Dist. Ct. (so. and ea. dist.) N.Y. 1976. Assoc. Wynn & Atlas, N.Y.C., 1972-76, Law Offices Kenneth Carroad, N.Y.C., 1976-78; sole practice Oceanside, N.Y., 1978-80; v.p., gen. counsel Fidelity Mgmt. Corp., Locust Valley, N.Y., 1981-82; pres., chief exec. officer First Stratford Corp., Jericho, N.Y., 1982—; pres. IDT Systems, Inc., 1987—; sole practice law (part-time), Oceanside, 1981-82, Jericho, 1982—; asst. atty. Village of Rockville Centre, N.Y., 1980-82. Speaker to various real estate and industry groups, 1984—. Mem. fin. com. Council for Rural Housing and Devel., Washington, 1985-86. Regents scholar U. Rochester, 1967-71. Jewish. Office: First Stratford Corp 410 Jericho Turnpike Jericho NY 11753

REICE, CHARLES THOMAS, department store, food service and lodging executive; b. Phila., June 3, 1926; s. Charles B. and Frances Elizabeth (Thompson) R.; m. Regina Frances Brown, Aug. 25, 1951; children: Linda Reice Dieter, Regina Reice Rogers, Charlene Reice Piereth, Sharon A., Charles Thomas. B.S., Rider Coll., Trenton, N.J., 1955. Accountant Price Waterhouse & Co. C.P.A.s, Phila., 1955-58; acctg. positions with Campbell Soup Co., 1958-65; v.p., treas. Bunker Ramo Corp., 1965-76; v.p. fin. Chamberlain Mfg. Corp., 1976-80; v.p. fin., treas. Carson, Pirie Scott & Co., Chgo., 1980—. Served with AUS, 1944-46. Mem. Fin. Execs. Inst. (past chmn. membership com.), Econ. Club. Chgo. Club: Chgo. Athletic. Office: Carson Pirie Scott & Co 1 S State St Chicago IL 60603 also: Carson Pirie Scott & Co 36 S Wabash Ave Chicago IL 60603

REICH, JACK EGAN, insurance company executive; b. Chgo., June 17, 1910; s. Henry Carl and Rose (Egan) B.; m. Jean Grady, Apr. 30, 1935; children: Rosemary (Mrs. Jerry Semler), Judith (Mrs. Dan Hoyt). Student, Purdue U., 1928-31; LLD (hon.), Butler U., 1973; PhD (hon.), Marian Coll., 1983; LLD (hon.), Ind. U., 1986. With Inland Steel Co., East Chicago, Ind., 1925-31; field dir. gross income tax and employment security divs. State of Ind., 1933-40; field dir. Ind. C. of C., 1940-52, exec. v.p., 1952-62; chmn. bd., pres. Indpls. Water Co., 1962-67, now mem. exec. com., dir.; chmn. bd. Am. United Life Ins. Co.; bd. dirs., past pres. Assn. Ind. Life Ins. Cos.; bd. dirs. Indpls. Water Resources, Indpls. Health Inst., Inc.; bd. dirs., exec. com. Banc One Ind. Corp., Bank One Indpls., N.A. Bd. dirs., past pres. Greater Indpls. Progress Com.; bd. dirs., pres. Ind. Legal Found.; past chmn. Assoc. Colls. Ind.; bd. govs., past campaign chmn., chmn. bd., pres. United Way Greater Indpls.; bd. dirs. Corp. Community Council, Commn. for Downtown; past mem. bd. lay trustees St. Mary-of-the-Woods Coll.; mem. adv. bd. St. Vincent Hosp.; pres. Ind. Acad.; past local and state pres., nat. v.p. Jr. C. of C. Mem. Ind. C. of C. (dir., past chmn.), Indpls. C. of C. (dir.), Health Ins. Assn. Am. (nominating com., pub. relations policy com.), Pi Kappa Alpha. Clubs: Economic (past pres.), Columbia, Indpls. Athletic, Indpls. Press, Meridian Hills Country, Skyline 100 (chmn.), (Indpls.); Ind. Soc. (Chgo.). Home: 7404 N Pennsylvania St Indianapolis IN 46240 Office: Am United Life Ins Co 1 American Sq PO Box 368 Indianapolis IN 46206

REICHARD, DAVID EDWARD, corporate executive; b. New Martinsville, W.Va., Jan. 1, 1954; s. Edward Leo and Elizabeth Louise (Sankey) R.; m. Denise Ann Popa, June 18, 1977; children: Jamie Ann, Megan Elizabeth. BA, Mount Union Coll., 1975; MBA, Wright State U., 1976. Bus. service analyst Dollar Bank, Pitts., 1977-79; fin. analyst Allegheny Industries, Pitts., 1979-81; fin. analyst Ampco-Pitts. Corp., 1981-84, mgr. corp. fin. planning, 1984-87, asst. treas., 1987—. Mem. Pitts. Cash Mgmt. Assn., Planning Forum. Republican. Methodist. Office: Ampco-Pitts Corp 600 Grant St Ste 4600 Pittsburgh PA 15219

REICHARD, WILLIAM THOMAS, III, insurance company executive; b. Lynchburg, Va., Aug. 31, 1943; s. William Thomas Jr. and Hazel Virginia (Roberts) R.; m. Peggy Ann Crawford, Aug. 2, 1963; children: Jeffrey Thomas, Mark Samuel, Melanie Ann. BA, Lynchburg Coll., 1966. CPCU. Underwriter Nationwide Mut. Ins. Co., Lynchburg, 1961-66, underwriting mgr., 1966-75; supt. pricing Nationwide Mut. Ins. Co., Columbus, Ohio, 1975-77, supt. underwriting, 1977-79; v.p. Heritage Mut. Ins. Co., Sheboygan, Wis., 1979-82, exec. v.p., 1982-84; sr. v.p. Seibels, Bruce & Co., Columbia, S.C., 1984-86; exec. v.p. The Seibels Bruce Group Inc., Columbia, 1986—; bd. dirs. Ky. Ins. Co., Louisville, So. Intermediaries Inc., Columbia, N.C. Reinsurance Facility, Raleigh, Gay & Taylor Inc., Winston-Salem, Catawba Ins. Co., Columbia, Consol. Am. Ins. Co., Columbia; bd. govs. , S.C. Reinsurance Facility, Columbia, 1988—. Adult leader Boy Scouts Am., Columbus, 1977; deacon Northminster Presbyterian Ch., Madison Heights, Va., 1973. Served with USNR, 1966-68. Mem. Soc. CPCU's. Club: Palmetto. Home: 2709 Wales Rd Columbia SC 29223 Office: The Seibels Bruce Group Inc 1501 Lady St PO Box 1 Columbia SC 29202

REICHBART, HOWARD ENOCH, education administrator; b. N.Y.C., May 31, 1943; s. Carl and Judith Lillian (Enoch) R.; m. Susan Hope Shuster, Jan. 28, 1968; children: Joel Ian, Alan Frederick. Student, U. Conn., 1961-63; BS, U. N.H., 1966; MS, Va. Poly. Inst., 1975, postgrad., 1975-77. Asst. dir. mgmt. services Hotel Am., Hartford, Conn., 1966-67; club mgr. Ft. McPherson Officers Club, Atlanta, 1968-70; mgmt. analyst Mayflower Hotel, Washington, 1970; assoc. prof. No. Va. Community Coll., Annandale, 1970—, program head Hotel, Restaurant & Instl. Mgmt. travel & tourism, 1979—; cons. Fairfax, Va., 1970—; evaluator Am. Council on Edn., 1973—. Served to 1st lt. U.S. Army, 1968-70. Mem. Council on Hotel, Restaurant and Instl. Edn., Hotel Sales and Mktg. Assn. Internat. (cert. commr. 1986-88), Va. Hotel and Motel Assn., Nat. Assn. Catering Execs., Hotel Assn. Met. Washington D.C. Jewish. Lodge: B'nai B'rith (pres. 1979-80, Outstanding Lodge Pres. 1980). Office: No Va Community Coll 8333 Little River Turnpike Annandale VA 22003

REICHELT, FERDINAND HERBERT, venture capital company executive; b. Chgo., Jan. 26, 1941; s. Ferdinand W. and Justine E. (Schuetpelz) R.; m. Diane Bethel Peters, Nov. 14, 1964; children: Christine, Brian. BS, U. Ill., 1963; postgrad. Northwestern U., Chgo., 1964. CPA, Ill. Supr., mgr. Peat Marwick & Mitchell, Chgo., 1963-70; actuary, 1966-68, mgr., Omaha, 1970-72; chief fin. officer CMI Investment Corp. and subs., Madison, Wis., 1972-78; exec. v.p. Verex Corp. and subs., Madison, 1978-85, chief operating officer, 1983-86, pres., chief exec. officer, 1986-88, Gemini Corp., 1988—, also bd. dirs. Pres. PDQ Food Stores Inc., 1989—; bd. dirs. Leer Mfg. Corp., Jason Dane Corp. Treas. Madison Civic Ctr. Found., 1981— ; bd. dirs. Festival of Lakes; chmn. Friends of WHA-TV, Inc., 1983; trustee Edgewood Coll.; mem. bd. advisors Clin. Cancer Ctr., U. Wis., Elvehjem Art Ctr., Madison, 1986—. Served with USAF, 1963-69. Mem. Nat. Assn. Accts., Nat. Investor Relations Inst., Wis. Inst. CPAs, Ill. Inst. CPAs, Nebr. Inst. CPAs, Nat. Assn. Ind. Insurers, Fin. Execs. Inst, Madison C. of C. (bd. dirs. 1987—), PGA Nat. Golf (Palm Beach Gardens, Fla.), Nakoma Golf, Madison (Madison). Editor: Secondary Mortgage Market Handbook; guest columnist Barrons; contbr. to profl. publs. Lutheran. Office: Jasen Dane Corp PO Box 5068 Madison WI 53705

REICHERT, JACK FRANK, manufacturing company executive; b. West Allis, Wis., Sept. 27, 1930; s. Arthur Andrew and Emily Bertha (Wallinger) R.; m. Corrine Violet Helf, Apr. 5, 1952; children: Susan Marie, John Arthur. Cert. mktg., U. Wis.-Milw., 1957; AMP, Harvard U., 1970. Various mktg. positions GE, 1948-57; with Brunswick Corp., Skokie, Ill., 1957—; pres. Mercury Marine div. Brunswick Corp., Skokie, 1972-77, corp. v.p., 1974-77, group v.p. Marine Power Group, 1974-77, pres., chief operating officer, 1977—; chief exec. officer Brunswick Corp., 1982—, chmn. bd., 1983—, dir., 1977—; bd. dirs. Greyhound Corp., Phoenix, First Chgo. Corp. Trustee Carroll Coll., Waukesha, Wis., 1972; bd. dirs. INROADS/Chgo., Inc.; indsl. chmn. Fond du Lac United Fund, 1977. Served with C.E. U.S. Army, 1951-53. Named Disting. Alumnus of the Yr., U. Wis., Milw. 1979, Top Chief Exec. Officer in Multi-Industry Group, Fin. World Mag., 1984; recipient Gold award in leisure industry Wall St. Transcript, 1983, 86, Bronze award in multi-industry category Wall St. Transcript, 1985. Mem. Am. Mgmt. Assn. (mem. adv. coun.), U. Wis.-Milw. Alumni Assn., Econ. Club of Chgo., Comml. Club of Chgo., Knollwood Club, Harvard Club, Mid-Am. Club, Met. Club, Beta Gamma Sigma (hon.). Presbyterian. Home: 580 Douglas Dr Lake Forest IL 60045 Office: Brunswick Corp One Brunswick Pla Skokie IL 60077

REICHLE, GEORGE CHRISTOPHER, financial planner; b. Bronx, N.Y., Nov. 14, 1942; m. Dolores Mellon; children: Donna, Christopher. Student, Adelphi U., 1980, The Am. Coll., 1979, 85. CLU, Chartered fin. cons.; cert. fin. planner. Sales mgr. Mutual of N.Y., Westbury, 1968-78; pres. founder Asset Planning Ltd., Huntington, N.Y., 1978—. Conbtr. articles to profl. jours. Mem. planned giving com. Suffolk County Council, Medford, N.Y.; mem. L.I. Assn., Commack, N.Y., Sea Spray Boating Assn., Centerport. Mem. Am. CLU Soc., Nat. Assn. Life Underwriters, Internat. Assn. Registered Fin. Planners (pres. bd. govs., Man of Yr. 1985), Internat. Assn. Fin. Planning (exec. v.p. L.I. chpt. 1981-83), L.I. Assn. Registered Fin. Planners (pres. emeritus), Suffolk County Life Underwriters Assn., N.Y. State Assn. Life Underwriters (downstate v.p. pub. relations), Nat. Assn. Life Underwriters. Office: Asset Planning Ltd 755 New York Ave Ste 230 Huntington NY 11743

REICHMANN, ALBERT, real estate corporation executive. Pres. Olympia and York Devel., Toronto; bd. dirs. Trizec Corp., Calgary, Abitibi-Price Inc., Toronto, Gulf Can. Corp., Toronto, GW Utilities Ltd., Toronto, Campeau Corp., Toronto. Office: Olympia & York Devels, 2 First Can Pl, Toronto, ON Canada M5X 1B4 *

REICHMANN, PAUL, real estate corporation executive. Exec. v.p. Olympia and York Devels., Toronto; bd. dirs. Abitibi-Price Inc., Toronto, Gulf Can. Corp., Toronto, GW Utilities Ltd., Toronto, Trizec Corp., Calgary. Office: Olympia & York Devels, 2 First Can Pl Ste 2700, PO Box 2700, Toronto, ON Canada M5X 1B5 *

REICHMANN, RALPH, real estate corporation executive. Gen. mgr. Olympia and York Devels., Toronto; bd. dirs. Abitibi-Price Inc., Toronto, Gulf Can. Corp, Toronto. Office: Olympia & York Devels, 2 First Can Pl Ste 2800, PO Box 20 130 Kings St W, Toronto, ON Canada M5X 1B5 *

REICHMANN, RENÉE, real estate corporation officer. m. Samuel Reichmann; children: Albert, Ralph, Paul, Eva, Edward, Louis. Chmn. bd. dirs. Olympia and York Devels., Toronto. Office: Olympia & York Devels, 2 First Can Pl Ste 2700, PO Box 20, Toronto, ON Canada M5X 1B5 *

REICKERT, ERICK ARTHUR, automotive executive; b. Newport, Tenn., Aug. 30, 1935; s. Frederick Arthur and Reva M. (Irish) R.; m. Diane Lois Comens, June 10, 1961 (div. Jan. 1979); children: Craig A., Laura L.; m. Heather Kathleen Ross, Sept. 1, 1982. BSEE, Northwestern U., 1958; MBA, Harvard U., 1965. Various positions Ford Motor Co., Dearborn, Mich., 1965-73, exec. dir. small car planning, 1979-84; v.p. export ops. Ford Motor Co., Brentwood, Eng., 1973-79; v.p. advance product devel. Chrysler Motors, Detroit, 1984-86, v.p. program mgmt., 1986-87; v.p., mng. dir. Chrysler Mexico, 1987—. Mem. Soc. Automotive Engrs., Engring. Soc. Detroit, Harvard Bus. Sch., Am. Chamber of Mex., Club of Detroit. Club: Univ. of Mexico City. Office: Chrysler Motors 12000 Chrysler Dr Highland Park MI 48203 also: Chrysler Mex, Lago Alberto 320, 11320 Mexico City Mexico

REID, BELMONT MERVYN, brokerage house executive; b. San Jose, Calif., May 17, 1927; s. C. Belmont and Mary Irene (Kilfoyl) R.; B.S. in Engring., San Jose State U., 1950, postgrad.; m. Evangeline Joan Rogers, June 1, 1952. Pres., Lifetime Realty Corp., San Jose, 1969-77, Lifetime Fin. Planning Corp., San Jose, 1967-77; founder, chmn. bd. Belmont Reid & Co., Inc., San Jose, 1960-77; pres., registered investment adv. JOBEL Fin. Inc., Carson City, Nev., 1980—; pres., chmn. bd. Data-West Systems, Inc., 1984-85 . County chmn. 1982-85, Carson City Rep. Cen. Com., treas., 1979-81; mem. Brewery Arts Ctr., chmn. Carson City Gen. Obligation Bond Commn., 1986—; rural county chmn., 1984-88. Nev. Rep. Cen. Com., 1984—; vice chmn. Carson City Charter Rev. Com., 1986—. Served with USN, 1945-46, 51-55. Decorated Air medals. Mem. Nat. Assn. Securities Dealers, Mcpl. Securities Rulemaking Bd., Nat. Futures Assn., Carson City C. of C. (pres., dir. 1986-87). Clubs: Capital of Carson City. Lodge: Rotary (chpt. sec. 1983-84, 86-87, pres.1988—). Home: 610 Bonanza Dr Carson City NV 89706 Office: 711 E Washington St Carson City NV 89701

REID, EDWARD LOGUE, industrial distribution consulting company owner; b. Newton, Mass., Feb. 21, 1935; s. Edward and Eleanor R.; married, July 16, 1960; 2 children. BSBA, Babson Coll., 1956. Sales mgr. Exxon, 1961-67; from nat. sales mgr., mgr. mktg., v.p. distbn. to v.p., gen. mgr. Loctite Corp., 1967-84; pres. Indsl. Distbn. Cons., College Station, Tex., 1984—; assoc. dir. rsch. Ctr. Distbn. Rsch. and Edn., vis. prof. distbn., instr. for profl. devel. seminars on distbn. Tex. A&M U., College Station, 1986—; cons. B.F. Goodrich, Gerber Sci. Products Inc., Ingersoll-Rand Co., Loctite Corp., Norton Co., Sullair Corp., The Torrington Co., others; guest speaker sales, mktg., mfg., distbg. for various convs. and tng. seminars. Contbr. articles to profl. jours. Jr. warden Episcopal Ch., 1980-86. With supply corps USN, 1956-60. Office: Tex A&M U Dept Engring Tech College Station TX 77843

REID, JACK POWELL, oil company executive; b. Sublette, Kans., Sept. 1, 1936; s. Eldon Gene and Leona M. (Powell) R.; m. Jane B. Logan, June 7, 1958; children: Willie Donald, Tonilou Michelle. BSChemE, U. Kans., 1958. Chief process engr. Refineria Panama, Republic of Panama, 1961-66; process supt. Conoco, Artesia, N.Mex., 1966-67; refinery mgr. Conoco-Navajo, Artesia, 1967-74; gen. mgr. Navajo Refining Co., Artesia, 1974-76, chief operating officer, 1976-82, pres., 1982—; bd.d irs. Holly Corp., Dallas. Office: Navajo Refining Co 501 E Main St PO Box 159 Artesia NM 88210

REID, JAMES SIMS, JR., automobile parts manufacturer; b. Cleve., Jan. 15, 1926; s. James Sims and Felice (Crowl) R.; m. Donna Smith, Sept. 2, 1950; children: Sally, Susan, Anne (dec.), Jeanne. AB cum laude, Harvard U., 1948, JD, 1951. Bar: Mich., Ohio 1951. Pvt. practice law Detroit, 1951-52, Cleve., 1953-56; with Standard Products Co., Cleve., 1956—, pres., 1962—, now also chmn., dir.; bd. dir. Soc. Corp., Cleve. Trustee John Carroll U., 1967—, chmn., 1987—, Musical Arts Assn. of Cleve. Orch., 1973—. Office: The Standard Products Co 2130 W 110th St Cleveland OH 44102

REID, NANCI GLICK, health care professional; b. Brookline, Mass., Sept. 22, 1941; d. Robert Louis and Esther (Shostack) Green; m. Ronald Jay Coleman, July 5, 1962 (div. Sept. 1969); 1 child, Lori Sue; m. Alan Marshall Glick, Jan. 12, 1976 (div. Oct. 1978); 1 child, Staci Alison; m. Raymond Augustus Reid, Feb. 15, 1985. AS, Garland Jr. Coll., Boston, 1960; student, Harvard U. Extension, 1961, 64, 65; BS, Northeastern U., 1983, postgrad. in bus. adminstrn., 1989—. Cert. clin. lab. sci., clin. lab. specialist in cytogenetics. Research technician Children's Hosp., Boston, 1961-63; sr. research technician, med. technician New Eng. Med. Ctr., Boston, 1963-65, 67-69; cytogeneticist supr. Carney Hosp., Boston, 1969-84; instr. medicine Med. Sch. Tufts U., Boston, 1969-86; systems analyst Cognos/Coulter Corp., Waltham, Mass., 1976-77; med. technologist Milton (Mass.) Hosp, 1978-83, Mass. Eye and Ear, Boston, 1983-84; lab. mgr. Harvard Community Health Plan, Braintree, Mass., 1985-88; chairperson com. continuing edn. Harvard Community Health Plan, Boston, 1986-88; quality control mgr. Oncolab Inc., Boston, 1988—; presenter abstracts at 12th and 13th Internat. Hematology Soc. Confs. Contbr. articles to profl. jours. Mem. Assn. Cytogenetic Technologists (pres. 1976-78), Am. Soc. Med. Tech. (lectr.), Sigma Epsilon Rho (v.p. 1987-88, former treas.). Republican. Jewish. Clubs: Plymouth Yacht, Pythian Sisters (sec., editor 1966-67) (Sharon, Mass.). Home: 70 Flintlocke Dr Plymouth MA 02360

REID, RANDALL LEE, controller; b. Midland, Tex., Apr. 2, 1955; s. William T. and Eva L. (Mathews) R.; m. Carole Ann Robertson, June 5, 1976; children: Lauren Rebecca, Matthew Philip. BBA, Baylor U., 1978. CPA, Tex. Sr. acct. Pannell Kerr Forster, Dallas, 1979-84; supr. Tydlaska & Woodard, Dallas, 1984-85; controller Bapt. Gen. Conv. Tex., Dallas, 1985—. Mem. Am. Inst. CPA's, Tex. Soc. CPA's. Republican. Baptist. Office: Bapt Gen Conv 333 N Washington Dallas TX 75245

REID, RUSSELL PETER, fund raising and financial planning company executive; b. Mpls., Oct. 23, 1933; s. Austin and Esther (Munson) R.; m. Carolyn Spurgur, Nov. 5, 1965; children: Conrad, Rachelle. BA in Psychology, San Francisco State U., 1964; cert., Coll. Fin. Planning, Denver, 1987. Glen Eyrie dir. The Navigators, Colorado Springs, Colo., 1965-79, dir. planned giving, 1970-88; dir. resource devel. Compassion Internat., Colorado Springs, 1988—. Bd. dirs. camp bd. YMCA, Colorado Springs, 1981-87, met. bd. YMCA, 1987—. With U.S. Army, 1956-58. Mem. Inst. Cert. Fin. Planners, Internat. Assn. Fin. Planners, Nat. Planned Giving Assn., Nat. Soc. Fund Raising Execs. (cert.). Republican. Presbyterian. Office: Compassion Internat PO Box 7000 Colorado Springs CO 80933

REID, TOY FRANKLIN, chemical company executive; b. York County, S.C., Jan. 13, 1924; s. Toy Fennell and Nellwyn Marteal (Mulliken) R.; m. Martha Josephine Eggerton, May 31, 1947; children: Martha Josephine, Toy Franklin (dec.), Mark Eggerton. BS, U. S.C., 1943; BSChemE, U. Ill., 1947; MS, Ga. Inst. Tech., 1948. Asst. to plant mgr. Holston Def. Corp., 1962, asst. plant mgr., 1963; supt. cellulose esters div. Carolina Eastman Co., 1965-69; asst. research chem. engr. Tenn. Eastman Co., Kingsport, 1948-50, assoc. research chem. engr., 1950-51, research chem. engr., 1951-52, sr. research chem. engr., 1952-54, 55-60, dept. head pilot plant, 1954-55, cellulose esters div. devel., supt. control dept., 1960-62, with, 1963-65, plant mgr., 1969-74, asst. works mgr., 1969-70, asst. to pres., 1970-72; v.p. to sr. v.p. Eastman Kodak Co., Rochester, 1972—; v.p., asst. gen. mgr. Eastman Chems. div., 1974-79, exec. v.p., gen. mgr., 1979—; supt. cellulose esters div. Tenn. Eastman Co., Kingsport, 1963-65, asst. works mgr., 1969-70, asst. to pres., 1970-72, v.p., 1972-73, sr. v.p., 1973-74; plant mgr. Carolina Eastman Co., 1965-69; 1st v.p. Bays Mountain Constrn. Co., 1969-70; asst. gen. mgr. Eastman Chems. Co. div. Eastman Kodak Co., Kingsport, 1974-79, gen. mgr., 1979—; bd. dirs., exec. com. Eastman Kodak Co.; bd. dirs. First Am. Corp., Am. Elect. Power Co., Provident Life and Accident Ins. Co. Bd. dirs. Holston Valley Hosp. and Med. Ctr., Kingsport Area Community Chest, Inc., United Way of Greater Kingsport, Jr. Achievement of Kingsport; trustee Holston Conf. Colls. of United Meth. Ch; bd. govs. Emory and Henry Coll., Tenn. State Bd. Edn. Served to capt. USAF, 1943-46. Mem. Am. Inst. Chem. Engrs., Chem. Mfrs. Assn. (bd. dirs.), Soc. Chem. Industry, Am. Indsl. Health Council (bd. dirs.), NSPE, Ridgefield Country Club (Kingsfield). Home: 2141 Heatherly Rd Kingsport TN 37660 Office: Eastman Chems Div Eastman Kodack Co PO Box 511 Kingsport TN 37662 also: Eastman Kodak Co 343 State St Rochester NY 14650

REID, VIRGINIA (GINNY) A., foundation administrator; b. Niagara Falls, N.Y., Aug. 29, 1936; d. William Russell and Virginia Elizabeth (Hunter) Kennedy; m. James V. Chapman, Mar. 25, 1955 (div. 1964); children: James, Stephen, Scott. BS, U. San Francisco, 1988. Assoc. dir. devel. Easter Seal Soc., Orange, Calif., 1966-76, Oklahoma City, 1979-80; dir. fundraising Am. Heart Assn., Santa Ana, Calif., 1976-79; exec. dir. Leukemia Soc. Am., Oklahoma City, 1980, Tustin, Calif., 1981—. Mem. adv. com. Santa Ana Tournament Roses Com., 1985-87. Mem. Nat. Soc. Fundraising Execs., Pub. Relations Soc. Am. Republican. Presbyterian. Home: 446 S Tustin Ave #34 Orange CA 92666 Office: Leukemia Soc Am 202 Fashion Ln Suite 215 Tustin CA 92680

REIDER, GEORGE MONROE, JR., insurance executive; b. Harrisburg, Pa., Oct. 7, 1940; s. George M. Sr. and Margaret R. (Funk) R.; m. Carol A. Stouffer, June 3, 1961; children: David, Mark, George III, Todd. BS in Bus. Adminstrn. and Econs., Lebanon Valley Coll., 1963. Claim rep. Aetna Life & Casualty Co., Harrisburg, 1963-69; regional claims supt. Aetna Life & Casualty Co., Youngstown, Ohio, 1969-72; claim supr. Aetna Life & Casualty Co., Columbus, Ohio, 1972-73; mgr. claims Aetna Life & Casualty Co., Toronto, Ont., Can., 1973-75; mgr. claims Aetna Life & Casualty Co., Hartford, Conn., 1975-78, dir. regional claims, 1978-80, v.p. underwriting, 1985-88, v.p. claims, 1988—; gen. mgr. Aetna Life & Casualty Co., Wheeling, W.Va., 1980-83, Garden City, N.Y., 1983-85. V.p. Steelton (Pa.) Town Council, 1966-69; mem. Farmington (Conn.) Town Council, 1979-80, 87-89; co-chmn. Ohio Valley United Way, Wheeling, 1982. Named Co. Person of Yr. W.Va. Ind. Agt. Assn., 1982, Outstanding Vol. Ohio Valley United Way, 1982; recipient Chmn.'s Svc. award Wheeling C. of C., 1982. Mem. Nassau Life Underwriters Assn., Hofstra U. Club. Republican.

Lutheran. Home: 9 Glenmore Dr Farmington CT 06032 Office: Aetna Life & Casualty Co 151 Farmington Ave Hartford CT 06156

REIDHAMMER, THOMAS MARTIN, pharmaceutical executive; b. Buffalo, Mar. 18, 1948; s. Harold M. and Marjorie P. (Walsh) R.; m. Evelyn M. Albano, July 25, 1970; children: Michael, Marcus, Tanya. BA, SUNY, Buffalo, 1970; PhD, SUNY, 1975. Dir. rsch. and devel. Bausch and Lamb, Inc., Rochester, N.Y., 1975-84; v.p. Paco Rsch. Corp., Lakewood, N.J., 1984-86; pres. Paco Rsch. Corp., 1986—. Contbr. articles to profl. jours. Home: 1613 Chipmunk Ct Toms River NJ 08753 Office: Paco Rsch Corp 1705 Oak St Lakewood NJ 08701

REIF, LOUIS RAYMOND, lawyer, utilities executive; b. Buffalo, July 4, 1923; s. John Dennis and Sadie (Wilkenson) R.; m. Nancy C. Heuer, Apr. 12, 1958; children: Tracey Lynn, Christopher Louis. Student, Mich. State U., 1941-42, The Citadel, 1943; A.B., U. Buffalo, 1948; J.D., U. Mich., 1951. Bar: N.Y. 1953. Pvt. practice Chgo., 1951-52, Buffalo, 1953—; atty. Continental Ill. Nat. Bank, Chgo., 1951-52, Iroquois Gas Corp., Buffalo, 1952-53; asst. sec. Iroquois Gas Corp., 1953-58, v.p., 1958-63, sr. v.p., 1963-71, pres., 1971—, also bd. dirs.; chmn. N.Y. Gas Group, 1973—; dir. Nat. Fuel Gas Co., N.Y.C., 1966—, v.p., 1960-74, pres., 1974, pres., chief exec. officer, 1975-87, chmn., chief exec. officer, 1988—; chmn. 17th World Gas Conf. Internat. Gas Union, 1986-88; dir. Goldome Bank; asst. to chmn. Delaware North Cos., 1988, chief oper. officer, 1989—. Pres., dir. Buffalo Better Bus. Bur., 1970; trustee SUNY-Buffalo Found. Served with C.E. AUS, 1943-46, ETO. Mem. ABA, N.Y. Bar Assn., Fed. Power Bar Assn., Erie County Bar Assn., Barrister Soc., Am. Gas Assn. (chmn., dir. 1984-85, Disting. Service award 1986), Nat. Alliance Businessmen (dir., chmn. 1967-68), Buffalo C. of C. (dir. 1973—, chmn. nat. affairs com. 1969—), Buffalo Club (bd. dirs. 1988), Phi Alpha Delta. Office: Delaware North Cos 1 Delaware North Pl Buffalo NY 14209

REIFENBERG, JOSEPH OLIVER, financial analyst; b. Evanston, Ill., Aug. 18, 1960; s. John James and Betty J. (Sherman) R.; m. Brenda E. Smith, Nov. 7, 1987; 1 stepchild, Bryauna K. Prassel. Student, Oakton Community Coll., 1978-80; BS in Acctg., No. Ill. U., 1983; postgrad., Loyola U., 1985—. CPA, Ill., cert. mgmt. accountant, Ill. Pvt. practice acctg. 1983—; staff acct. Cook Electric div. No. Telecom, Morton Grove, Ill., 1983-85; cost analyst Cook Electric div. No. Telecom, Morton Grove, 1985-86, sr. fin. analyst, 1986-87, mgr. accts. payable, 1987-88, mgr. gen. acctg., 1988-89; controller Hydraforce, Inc., Wheeling, Ill., 1989—. Mem. Am. Inst. CPA's, Inst. Cert. Mgmt. Accts., Ill. CPA Soc. Roman Catholic.

REILEY, THOMAS NOEL, small business owner; b. Boston, Nov. 28, 1938; s. Francis Xavier and Ann Margaret (Ryan) R.; m. Marcia Canney, Sept. 10, 1961; children: Thomas J., Jennifer Ann, Mary Beth, Matthew Canney. Cert. engring., design, Franklin Tech., Boston, 1959; AS in Bus., Manchester (Conn.) Community Coll., 1972; BA in Art History, Trinity Coll., Hartford, Conn., 1987. With sales and design dept. Grinnel & Automatic, West Hartford, Conn., 1960-65; dist. mgr. Automatic Sprinkler Corp., Manchester, Conn., 1965-69; sales mgr. United Engrs., Springfield, Mass., 1969-70; gen. mgr. Mcpl. Services Inc., East Hartford, Conn., 1971-73; with sales, mgmt. dept. Crown Distbrs., Inc., East Hartford, Conn., 1973-75; pres. Vintage Wine & Liquor, Ltd., Hartford, Conn., 1975-84; owner T.N. Reiley Properties, Vernon, Manchester, Conn., 1985—; chief designer, Grinnell Corp., West Hartford, 1961-62; gen. ptr. Country Club Estates, Manchester, 1984-86; cons. Bassdale (Conn.) Liquors, 1979-80. Commr. Conn. Hist. Commn., Hartford, 1979; mem. Manchester Bldg. Comm., 1970, Com. to Re-Elect Ella Grasso, Hartford, 1978, Dem. Town Com., Manchester, 1985. Mem. Nat. Rifle Assn., Am. Soc. Arms Collectors, Antique Arms Collector's Assn. of Ct. (pres. 1974-76), Conn. Gun Guild. Democrat. Roman Catholic. Lodges: KC, Elks. Office: TN Reiley Properties 312 Hartford Turnpike Vernon CT 06066

REILEY, T(HOMAS) PHILLIP, food company executive; b. Ft. Lewis, Wash., May 5, 1950; s. Thomas Phillip and Anne Marie (Russick) R.; B.Sc. in Biophysics, Pa. State U., 1973; postgrad. in Bus. Adminstrn., Rutgers U. Inventory supr. Leland Tube Co., S. Plainfield, N.J., 1973-76; prodn. inventory control supr. Bomar Crystal Co., Middlesex, N.J., 1976-79; prodn. control mgr. Codi Semicondr. Inc., Linden, N.J., 1979-81; mfg. systems analyst Western Union Info. Systems, Mahwah, N.J., 1981-85; sr. systems analyst Nabisco Brands Biscuit Div., Parsippany, N.J., 1985—. Mem. Am. Prodn. and Inventory Control Soc. (chmn. ednl. com. Raritan Valley chpt.), N.Y. Acad. Scis., Assn. M.B.A. Execs., Mensa. Republican. Home: 56 Carlton Club Dr Piscataway NJ 08854 Office: Nabisco Brands 100 DeForest Ave East Hanover NJ 07936

REILING, HENRY BERNARD, business educator; b. Richmond, Ky., Feb. 5, 1938; s. Henry Bernard and Lucille Frances (Fowler) R.; m. Carol-Lina Maria Schuetz, June 4, 1962; children: Christina Lucille, Maria Hays, Carolina Alexis. B.A., Northwestern U., 1960; M.B.A., Harvard U., 1962; J.D., Columbia U., 1965. Bar: N.Y. 1965. Mem. faculty Columbia U. Bus. Sch., 1965-76, prof., 1974-76; vis. asso. prof. Harvard U. Bus. Sch., 1972-73, prof., 1976—, Eli Goldston prof. bus. adminstrn., 1978—; vis. prof. Stanford U. Bus. Sch., 1974-75. Contbr. bus. and law jours. Trustee Riverside Ch., N.Y.C., 1976-77. Mem. Am., N.Y. bar assns., Bar Assn. City N.Y., Am. Finance Assn., Financial Mgmt. Assn., Nat. Tax Assn., Tax Inst. Am., Beta Gamma Sigma. Club: Union (N.Y.C.). Home: 28 Meriam St Lexington MA 02173 Office: Harvard U Business Sch Boston MA 02163

REILLY, EDWARD JOHN, fire protection consulting company executive; b. Syracuse, N.Y., Apr. 2, 1923; s. John Paul and Margaret (Shamock) R.; m. Marjorie Helen Cook, Jan. 29, 1949; children: Maureen Ann, Patrick Brian, Thomas Kevin, Timothy John, Dennis Edward, Daniel Lawrence. BA, St. Bonaventure U., 1949; postgrad. Fordham U., 1949-51. Dir. info. Nat. Fire Sprinkler Assn., N.Y.C., 1956-70, v.p., Mt. Kisco, N.Y., 1970-77; exec. v.p., Patterson, N.Y., 1976-77, pres., 1977-85, ret., 1985; pres. Ed Reilly Assocs., Kinderhook, N.Y., 1985—. Editor: Sprinkler Quar., 1956-74, Sprinkling of News, 1968-77; contbr. articles to profl. jours. Capt. Rep. Nat. Com., N.Y.C., 1949-52; leader Bronx election campaign, 1950-51; mem. 8th Air Force Hist. Soc. Served with USAAF, 1943-45. Named Fire Protection Engring. Man of Yr., Manhattan Coll., N.Y.C., 1985; recipient Henry Parmalee award for outstanding lifetime achievement to fire protection in Am., 1987. Mem. Full Gospel Businessmen's Fellowship Internat., Am. Legion (chpt. vice comdr. 1950-51). Roman Catholic. Address: 12 Chatham St Kinderhook NY 12106

REILLY, FRANK MICHAEL, publishing executive; b. Atlanta, Mar. 29, 1954; s. Frank Kent Jr. and Blanche (Parks) R.; m. Deborah Stucker, May 29, 1976; children: Brent Michael, Frances Ann., Kathryn Lane. BS, U. Ala., Tuscaloosa, 1976. Sales mgr. Randall Pub. Co., Tuscaloosa, 1978-80, v.p. sales, 1980-82, pres., 1984-87, pres., chief operating officer, 1987—; dist. sales mgr. Gulf Pub. Co., Houston, 1982-84; bd. advisors Cummins Profl. Drivers Assn. Bd. dirs. Boys Club Tuscaloosa County, 1988; vice chmn., bd. dirs. YMCA. Named an Outstanding Bd. Mem. Boys Club Tuscaloosa, 1988. Mem. Am. Mktg. Assn., Internat. Drivers Assn. (bd. advisors), Am. Trucking Assn., Am. Mgmt. Assn., Assn. Bus. Pubs., Indian Hills Country Club (bd. dirs. Tuscaloosa chpt. 1988), Sigma Alpha Epsilon. Roman Catholic. Home: 2409 Trenton Dr Tuscaloosa AL 34506 Office: Randall Pub Co 3200 Rice Mile Rd PO Box 2029 Tuscaloosa AL 35403

REILLY, JOHN LAWRENCE, banker; b. N.Y.C., Jan. 16, 1940; s. John Joseph and Johanna M. (Bernhardt) R.; m. Lois M. Kessel, Aug. 29, 1964; children—John Joseph, Scott Lawrence. Cert., Am. Inst. Banking, 1965; grad., Grad. Sch. Savs. Banking, Brown U., 1972; Grad., Exec. Devel. Sch., U. Mass., 1975. Teller Am. Savs. Bank, N.Y.C., 1958-68, asst. sec. ops., 1968-71, investment officer, 1971-82, 1st sr. v.p., 1982-83, 1st sr. v.p., treas., 1983-87, exec. v.p., chief retail banking officer, 1987—; mem. faculty Nat. Sch. Fin., Fairfield U., 1978—; mem. faculty Am. Inst. Banking, 1974-87, trustee, past pres., Am. Inst. Banking, N.Y.C., 1978—. Pres., bd. dirs. St. Thomas Luth. Ch., Manalapan Twp., N.J., 1981-82; vice chmn. Manalapan Twp. Planning Bd., 1985-87; mem. Lewisboro, N.Y. Planning Bd., 1988— . With M.I., U.S. Army, 1968-71. Mem. Am. Inst. Banking, Nat. Council Savs. Instns. (com. on ops.), N.Y. Investment Officers Assn. (pres. 1980-81), N.Y. Savs. Banks Life Ins. Fund (exec. com.). Republican. Lutheran. Office: Am Savs Bank 99 Church St White Plains NY 10601

REILLY, JOHN PAUL, manufacturing company executive; b. Phila., Aug. 18, 1943; m. Lynda J. Shepley; children: John P., Colleen K., Timothy S. BS, Xavier U., 1965; MBA, U. Detroit, 1967. Mfg. mgr. Chrysler Corp., 1965-79; pres. Mark div. Core Industries, 1979-80; sr. v.p. Internat. Harvester, 1980-83; sr. v.p., gen. mgr. Walker Mfg. Co. div. Tenneco Automotive, Racine, Wis., 1984-87; pres., chief exec. officer Tenneco Automotive, Lincolnshire, Ill., 1987—. Dir. Arden Shore Home for Boys, Lake Forest, Ill.; Racine Area Mfrs. and Commerce, 1984—. Mem. Motor and Equipment Mfrs. Assn. (bd. dirs.). Office: Tenneco Automotive 100 Tri State Internat Ste 300 Lincolnshire IL 60061

REILLY, MICHAEL ATLEE, financial company executive, venture capital investor; b. Ft. Worth, Dec. 10, 1948; s. Thomas William and Alma Margaret (Cox) R.; m. Beverly Ann Yates, Dec. 26, 1974; children—Atlee Michael, Asher Yates, Anson Marcus, Austin Thomas, Axton Carter. B.A., U. Tex., 1971. Ptnr. Michael A. Reilly Co., Dallas, 1971-75, Reilly-Ginsburg, Dallas, 1975-80; pres., chief. exec. officer Ryan Cos., Arlington, Tex., 1980—. Chmn. bd. trustees Charitable and Ednl. Found., Arlington, 1976—, Stars for Children Tex., Arlington, 1983—; trustee Ryan/Reilly Sch. Urban Land Studies, U. Tex.-Arlington, 1982—, Childrens Trust Fund State of Tex. Mem. Urban Land Inst., Mortgage Bankers Assn. Am. Office: Ryan Cos 505 Ryan Plaza Dr Arlington TX 76011

REILLY, PATRICK JOHN, engineering-construction company executive; b. Nutley, N.J., Oct. 10, 1925; s. Philip and Anna (Cox) O'Reilly; m. Marcia Garcia Vazquez, July 27, 1957; children: Anne Maria, Patrick John, Thomas J., Frank P. BSCE, NYU, 1950; cert. practical constrn. law, U. Santa Clara, 1977. Registered gen. engring. contractor, Calif. Shaft engr. Lincoln Tunnel third tube Walsh Constrn. Co., N.Y.C., 1950-54; asst. equipment mgr. Brown-Raymond-Walsh, Madrid, 1954-55, project engr., 1955-57; v.p., project mgr. wastewater treatment plants Shanley Constrn. Co., San Francisco, 1957-65; constrn. mgr. W.W. Kimmins and Sons, Buffalo, 1965-70, gen. supt. hwy., utilities and underground constrn., 1970; dir. mcpl. waste projects, constrn. mgr. Monsanto Environ. Chem. Co., Chgo., 1970-74; v.p., project mgr., dir. constrn. and regional constrn. mgr. solid waste facilities BSP div. Envirotech Corp., Menlo Park, Calif., 1974-84, v.p. project mgmt., 1984-88; ptnr., v.p. Legal/Tech Strategies, Inc., Menlo Park, 1988—; bd. dirs. Bank of Montreal, Laidlaw Transp. Ltd. With USAAF, 1943-45. Decorated D.F.C., Air medal with 5 oak leaf clusters. Mem. ASCE, Am. Arbitration Assn. (panel arbitrators). Roman Catholic. Home: 20719 Woodward Ct Saratoga CA 95070 Office: Legal/Tech Strategies Inc 1720 Amphlett blvd San Mateo CA 94402

REILLY, PETER C., chemical company executive; b. Indpls., Jan. 19, 1907; s. Peter C. and Ineva (Gash) R.; AB, U. Colo., 1929; MBA, Harvard U., 1931; DSc (hon.), Butler U; m. Jeanette Parker, Sept. 15, 1932; children: Marie (Mrs. Jack H. Heed), Sara Jean (Mrs. Clarke Wilhelm), Patricia Ann (Mrs. Michael Davis). With accounting dept. Republic Creosoting Co., Indpls., 1931-32; sales dept. Reilly Tar & Chem. Corp. (became Reilly Industries, Inc. 1989), N.Y.C., 1932-36, v.p., Eastern mgr., 1936-52; v.p. sales, treas. both cos., Indpls., 1952-59, pres., 1959-73, chmn. bd., 1973-75, vice chmn., 1975-82, chmn., 1982—; dir. Environ. Quality Control Inc.; past dir. Ind. Nat. Corp., Ind. Union Ry., Ind. Nat. Bank. Dir. Goodwill Industries Found.; past bd. dirs. United Fund Greater Indpls., Indpls. Symphony Orch.; bd. govs. Jr. Achievement Indpls. Mem. adv. council U. Notre Dame Sch. Bus. Adminstrn., 1947—; mem. adv. council Winona Meml. Hosp. Recipient Sagamore of Wabash award; named Disting. Eagle Scout Boy Scouts Am. Mem. Chem. Spltys. Mfg. Assn. (life; treas. 1950-60, past dir.), Chem. Mfrs. Assn. (past dir.), Am. Chem. Soc., Soc. Chem. Industry (past dir. Am. sect. 1979—). Clubs: Union League, Harvard, Chemist (N.Y.C.); Larchmont (N.Y.) Yacht; Indianapolis Athletic, Pine Valley Golf (N.J.), Meridian Hills Country, Columbia (Indpls.); Rotary (Paul Harris award), One Hundred (past dir.); Crooked Stick Golf. Home: 3777 Bay Rd North Dr Indianapolis IN 46240 Office: Reilly Industries Inc Market Sq Ctr 151 N Delaware St #1510 Indianapolis IN 46204

REILLY, ROBERT FREDERICK, valuation consultant; b. N.Y.C., Oct. 3, 1952; s. James J. and Marie (Griebel) K.; m. Janet H. Steiner, Apr. 16, 1975; children: Ashley Lauren, Brandon Christopher. BA in Econs., Columbia U., 1974, MBA in Fin., 1975. CPA; cert. mgmt. acct.; cert. mfg. engr.; cert. real estate appraiser. Sr. cons. Booz, Allen & Hamilton, Cin., 1975-76; dir. corp. planning Huffy Corp., Dayton, Ohio, 1976-81; v.p. Arthur D. Little Valuation, Inc., Chgo., 1981-85; ptnr., mng. dir. Valuation Engring. Assocs. and ptnr. of Touche Ross & Co., Chgo., 1985—; adj. prof. accounting U. Dayton Grad. Sch. Bus., 1977-81; adj. prof. fin. econs., Elmhurst (Ill.) Coll., 1982-87; adj. prof. fin. Ill. Inst. Tech. Grad. Sch. Bus., Chgo., 1985-87; adj. prof. taxation U. Chgo. Grad. Sch. Bus., 1985-87. Contbr. articles to profl. jours. Mem. AICPA, Nat. Assn. Real Estate Appraisers (cert.), Am. Soc. Appraisers (bd. examiners 1985—, accredited sr. appraiser), Nat. Assn. Accts.(chpt. dir. 1976—), Inst. Property Taxation, Soc. Mfg. Engrs. (cert.), Ill. Soc. CPA's, Ohio Soc. CPA's (chpt. dir. 1978-81). Home: 310 Algonquin Rd Barrington Hills IL 60010 Office: Touche Ross & Co 111 E Wacker Dr Chicago IL 60601

REILLY, WILLIAM FRANCIS, publishing company executive; b. N.Y.C., June 8, 1938; s. William F. and Genevieve Reilly; m. Ellen Chapman, Nov. 19, 1966; children: Anthony Chapman and Jane Wasey (twins). AB cum laude, U. Notre Dame, 1959; MBA, Harvard U., 1964. Mgr. fin. analysis W.R. Grace & Co., N.Y.C., 1964-67, asst. to pres., 1969-71, chief exec. officer Bekaert Textile div., 1971-74; asst. fin. adminstr. City of N.Y., 1967-69; pres. Herman's World of Sporting Goods, Carteret, N.J., 1974-77; v.p. W.R. Grace & Co., N.Y.C., 1977-80, pres. Home Center Div., 1979-80; exec. v.p. Macmillan, Inc., N.Y.C., 1980, pres., chief operating officer, 1981—; pres. Macmillan Pub. Co. div. Macmillan, Inc., N.Y.C., 1987—, Maxwell/Macmillan Pub. & Info. Group, N.Y.C., 1989—. Served to 1st lt. U.S. Army, 1959-61. Home: 8 E 96th St New York NY 10128 Office: Macmillan Pub Co 866 3rd Ave New York NY 10022

REINBOLD, DONNA SPALDING, photographer; b. Burbank, Calif., Aug. 10, 1955; d. William Harrison and Mary Catherine (MacDougall) Spalding; m. Terrence L. Reinbold, May 6, 1984; 1 child, Larissa Marie. Student, San Diego State U., 1973-76. Exec. sec. Sears, Alhambra, Calif., 1976-78; receptionist Gary Studios, Dallas, 1978-79, mgr., photographer, 1979-81; owner, photographer Arsene Studios (named changed to Reinbold GAllery 1984), Anaheim, Calif., 1981—; lectr. in field, 1987—. Trustee West Coast Sch. Profl. Photography, Santa Barbara, Calif., 1986—; bd. dirs. Florence Crittenton Services, Fullerton, Calif., 1987-88. Mem. Profl. Photographers Am. (Print Material award 1983-87), Profl. Photographers Calif., Profl. Photographers Orange County (bd. dirs. 1983-86, pres. award 1984), Rotary Club. Office: Reinbold Gallery 1243 S Euclid St Anaheim CA 92802

REINBOLD, GRACE ANN, artist manager; b. Miles, Tex., June 9, 1941; d. Norbert Joseph and Mary Josephine (Farmer) Renzelman; m. Damon Reinbold (div. 1984); children: Jaqueline, Jeanette, Jay, Jon, Jason. Cert., Harvard U., 1983. Co-founder, pres. Damon and Grace Corp., Lansing, Mich., 1975—; pres. World Wide Mgmt., Los Angeles, 1985—, World Wide Media, Los Angeles and Nashville, 1985—; mgr. The Royal Court of China/A&M Records, The Shakers/Carlyle Records, Mr. Zero/Island Records, Rumble Circus, Rock City Angels/Geffen Records; cons. Saturn Mgmt., Nashville, 1986—. Author: Journey Into 2000, 1981; editor Street Beat mag., 1981-83; creator (videos) Mind Fitness Series, 1983; contbr. ABC's 20/20 show, 1983. Vol., officer Opera Co. of Greater Lansing, 1978-80, Boarshead Theater, Lansing, 1980-81; vol. Am. Lung Assn. of Mich., Lansing, 1982-86; vol., bd. dirs. Kellog Art Mus. at Mich. State Univ., East Lansing, 1984-85. Mem. Nashville Entertainment Assn. (v.p. 1987-88). Clubs: Pres's. (Mich. State Univ.); Harvard Bus. Sch. (Detroit). Home: 1626 Malcolm Ave #204 Los Angeles CA 90024 Office: World Wide Media 9000 Sunset Blvd #601 Los Angeles CA 90069

REINER, BERT LEO, consumer project manufacturing company executive, consultant; b. Dresden, Germany, May 30, 1937; came to U.S., 1949; s. Horace W. and Gertrude (Katz) R.; m. Sandra J. Winkler, June 25, 1960; children: Helaine, Eric, Dana. BME, Resselaer Poly. Inst., 1960. Design engr. Sikorsky Aircraft Div., Stratford, Conn., 1960-62; project engr. Soundscriber Corp., New Haven, Conn., 1962-63; chief engr. A.C. Gilbert Co., New Haven, 1963-66; dir.Far East Mfg. Ideal Toy Co., Jamaica, N.Y., 1967-69; v.p. engring. Coleco IndustriesInc., Hartford, Conn., 1969-85; sr. v.p. Coleco IndustriesInc., West Hartford, Conn., 1985-88; pres. Reiner Assocs. Inc., Wallingford, Conn., 1988—. Patentee in field. Mem. Soc. Plastics Engrs. (sr.), ASME (sr.), IEEE, Am. Mgmt. Assn. Home and Office: Reiner Assocs Inc 21 Blakeslee Rd Wallingford CT 06492

REINERT, PAMELA ANN, social services agency administrator; b. Pipestone, Minn., Dec. 28, 1952; d. Louis Ilse Bickford and Marcella M. (Oye) Hoisington; m. Roger Leo Reinert, Mar. 14, 1970; children: Roger, Aarron, Yolanda, Rosa, Karina, Simone. BA, S.W. Minn. State Coll., 1973; postgrad., Mankato State U., 1974; MA, Coll. St. Thomas, St. Paul, 1982. Lic. social worker. Behavior cons. Robert E. Milton Home, Redwood Falls, Minn., 1972-73; tchr. Renville Co., Olivia, Minn., 1973-74; coord. spl. edn. Region 6E Headstart Program, Cosmos, Minn., 1974-75; therapist WCCSC, Willmar, Minn., 1975; adoption specialist Crossroads, Mpls., 1976-84; founder, exec. dir. Building Families through Adoption, Dawson, Minn., 1984—; co-founder Project Love, Willmar, 1983; cons. Grief Counseling, Mpls., 1987—. Contbr. articles to profl. jours. Treas. Nat. Coalition to End Racism, 1988—; coord. Heal the Children, 1987—. Project Hometown Am. grantee, 1986. Mem. Nat. Assn. Social Workers, N.D. Social Workers Assn. Lutheran. Home: RR 1 PO Box 188 Dawson MN 56232 Office: Building Families through Adoption 7th & Chestnut Sts Dawson MN 56232

REINHARD, CHRISTOPHER JOHN, merchant banking company executive; b. Bridgeport, Conn., Nov. 11, 1953; s. Warren John and Marian Louise (Dutter) R.; m. Maureen Francis, Sept. 24, 1977; 1 child, Griffin John. BS, Babson Coll., 1976, MBA, 1977. Sr. fin. analyst Gen. Motors Corp., Detroit and N.Y.C., 1977-81; asst. sec. Wheelabrator-Frye Inc., N.H., 1981-83; asst. sec., asst. treas. The Signal Cos., Inc., La Jolla, Calif., 1983-86; mng. dir., v.p. The Henley Group, Inc., La Jolla, 1986—; mng. dir. Fisher Sci. Group, Inc., La Jolla, 1986—; mng. dir., v.p. Wheelabrator Tech. Inc., Henley Mfg. Corp., 1987—. Clubs: N.Y. Athletic, Boston Athenaeum, San Diego Polo, Rancho Santa Fe Polo. Office: Henley Group Inc 11255 N Torrey Pines Rd La Jolla CA 92037

REINHARD, ELIZABETH WARING, real estate developer; b. Bryn Mawr, Pa., Dec. 10, 1949; d. John James Jr. and Mary Adelaide (Rozelle) R. BA in History, Smith Coll., 1971; MBA, Harvard U., 1976. Sr. asst. buyer Bonwit Teller, N.Y.C., 1971-72; exec. trainee corp. lending dept. Mfrs. Hanover Trust, N.Y.C., 1972-74, asst. sec., 1976-78, asst. v.p., 1978-80, v.p., 1980-87, v.p. chief of staff N.A. div., 1982-87; fin. analyst treas. officer Gen. Motors Corp., N.Y.C., 1975; sr. v.p. fin. Eisinger Devel. Group, Bethesda, Md., 1987—. Active Jr. League Washington; treas. D.C. chpt. Design Industry Found. for AIDS, Washington, 1989—. Episcopalian. Home: 2301 Connecticut Ave NW Washington DC 20008 Office: Eisinger Devel Group 7315 Wisconsin Ave Bethesda MD 20814

REINS, RALPH ERICH, automotive products company executive; b. Detroit, Sept. 18, 1940; s. Erich John and Florence (Franz) R.; m. Victoria Louise Kolts, Sept. 14, 1963; children—Ann Marie, Christine Louise. B.S.I.E., U. Mich., 1963. Asst. supt. Chevrolet Motor div., Gen. Motors Corp., Detroit, 1963-72; v.p., pres. hwy. product ops. Rockwell Internat., Troy, Mich., 1972-85; sr. v.p. ITT Corp., Bloomfield Hills, Mich., 1985—; pres., chief exec. officer ITT Automotive Inc. Mem. Soc. Automotive Engrs. Republican. Club: Bloomfield Hills Country (Mich.). Home: 4595 Valley View Pointe Rochester MI 48064 Office: ITT Automotive Products 505 N Woodward Bloomfield Hills MI 48013

REINSDORF, JERRY MICHAEL, lawyer, professional athletic franchise executive, real estate executive; b. Bklyn., Feb. 25, 1936; s. Max and Marion (Smith) R.; m. Martyl F. Rifkin, Dec. 29, 1956; children: David Jason, Susan Janeen, Michael Andrew, Jonathan Milton. B.A., George Washington U., 1957; J.D., Northwestern U., 1960. Bar: D.C., Ill. 1960; CPA, Ill.; cert. specialist real estate securities, rev. appraiser; registered mortgage underwriter. Atty. staff regional counsel IRS, Chgo., 1960-64; assoc. law firm Chapman & Cutler, 1964-68; ptnr. Altman, Kurlander & Weiss, 1968-74; of counsel firm Katten, Muchin, Gitles, Zavis, Pearl & Galler, 1974-79; gen. ptnr. Carlyle Real Estate Ltd. Partnerships, 1971, 72; former pres. Balcor Co., Skokie, Ill.; chmn. bd. Balcor Co., 1973-88; mng. ptnr. TBC Films, 1975-83; chmn. Chgo. White Sox, 1981—, Chgo. Bulls Basketball Team, 1985—; lectr. John Marshall Law Sch., 1966-68; former bd. dirs. Shearson Lehman Bros., Inc., Project Academus of DePaul U., Chgo., Sports Immortals Mus., 1987—, Com. Commemorate U.S. Constn., 1987; lectr. in real estate and taxation. Author: (with L. Herbert Schneider) Uses of Life Insurance in Qualified Employee Benefit Plans, 1970. Co-chmn. Ill. Profls. for Sen. Ralph Smith, 1970; mem. Chgo. Region Bd. Anti-Defamation League, 1986—. Mem. ABA, Ill. Bar Assn., Chgo. Bar Assn., Fed. Bar Assn., Nat. Assn. Rev. Appraisers and Mortgage Underwriters, Northwestern U. Law Sch. Alumni Assn. (bd. dirs.), Order of Coif, Omega Tau Rho. Office: Bojer Fin Ltd 980 N Michigan Ave Ste 1011 Chicago IL 60611 also: Chgo Bulls 1 Magnificent Mile 980 N Michigan Ave #1600 Chicago IL 60611

REIPLINGER, JOHN EDWARD, broadcasting executive; b. Ottawa, Ill., Sept. 22, 1942; s. Edward J. and Dorothy (Stephan) R.; m. Barbara Quantock, Oct. 14, 1967 (div. June 1975); m. S. June Lewis, June 15, 1979; children: Richard Wilson, Julie Wilson, Lori. Student bus. adminstrn., St. Mary's Coll., Winona, Minn., 1960-62. News dir. Sta. WCMY, Ottawa, 1963-64; account exec. Sta. WLBK, DeKalb, Ill., 1965-73; account exec. Sta. WLW, Avco Broadcasting Corp., Cin., 1973-75; exec. v.p., gen. mgr. Sta. WGBF, Met. Radio Co., Evansville, Ind., 1975-80; regional sales mgr. South Cen. Communications, Evansville, Ind., 1980-82; gen. sales mgr. Stas. KQKQ and KLNG, Omaha, 1982-83; v.p., gen. mgr. Sta. WYNG, Beasley Broadcasting Group, Evansville, 1983—; guest lectr. broadcasting and mktg. No. Ill. U., U. Nebr., Omaha, So. Ill. U., Carbondale, U. So. Ind., Evansville. mem. aux. U.S. Coast Guard, 1988—, instr. boating safety classes; bd. dirs. Downtown Merchants Assn., Evansville, 1982-85. Mem. Ind. Broadcasters Assn. (bd. dirs. 1983--), S.W. Ind. Broadcasters Assn. (pres. 1983-87), Evansville Area Radio Stas. Assn. (sec.-treas. 1988--), Evansville C. of C. (bd. dirs. 1985), Triad Advt. Club (pres. 1979-80), Civitan Club (bd. dirs. Evansville 1978-80), Kiwanis (bd. dirs. DeKalb 1970-73). Republican. Roman Catholic. Home: 1401 Greenfield Rd Evansville IN 47715 Office: WYNG Radio Beasley Broadcasting PO Box 2777 1133 Lincoln Ave Evansville IN 47714

REIS, EDWARD THOMAS, JR., insurance executive; b. Fresno, Calif., Aug. 27, 1948; s. Edward Thomas and Eleanor Virginia (Read) R.; m. Cheryl Lo Hackett, 1967 (div.); 1 child, Edward Thomas III; m. Patricia Lynn Aiello, Dec. 4, 1981. Cert., Ins. Inst. of Am., 1983; chartered, Am. Inst. for Property and Casualty Underwriters, 1986; chartered life underwriter, Am. Coll., 1988. Agt. Farmers Ins., Simi Valley, Calif., 1975-82; dist. mgr. Farmers Ins., Santa Barbara, Calif., 1982—. Mem. Nat. Assn. Life Underwriters (pres. local chpt.), Profl. Ins. Agts. Assn., Am. Mgmt. Assn., Santa Barbara C. of C., Elks. Republican. Methodist. Office: Farmers Ins 123 W Padre Ste E Santa Barbara CA 93105

REIS, FRANK HENRY, insurance agency executive; b. Kingston, N.Y., Oct. 17, 1936; s. Frank Alfred and Evelyn (O'Brien) R.; m. Kathryn Rose Feeney, Feb. 11, 1961; 1 child, Katherine Feeney Reis. B.S., Rider Coll., 1959. Pres. Frank H. Reis Ins., Inc., Kingston, N.Y., 1966—, Frank H. Reis, Inc., Highland, N.Y., 1966—, Reis Ins. Inc., New Paltz, N.Y., 1966—, Reis Ins. Inc., Saugerties, N.Y., 1983—; regional vice chmn. Continental Nat. Assurance Co., Maine to Va., 1984-85, chmn., 1986; pres., chief exec. officer The Reis Group Ins., 1989—; pres. Rumsey-Reis, Inc. Ins. and Fin. Planning, Newburgh, N.Y.; mem. adv. bd. Am. F.S.A.; nat. chmn. automation com. CNA Ins. Cos.; nat. chmn. CNA Pacer Council, Continental Nat. Assurance Co.; nat. adv. council Crum and Foster; trustee Rondout Savs. Bank, Kingston, N.Y. Pres. Benedictine Hosp. Health Found., Kingston, N.Y., 1984-85, now bd. dirs.; treas. YMCA, Kingston, Ulster County, 1985, bd. trustees. Named Outstanding Agt. N.Y. State, Milton L. Bier award Merchant Mutual Ins. Co., 1974, Outstanding Man of Yr., Ulster County C. of C., 1964. Mem. Profl. Ins. Agts. N.Y. State (pres. 1978-79, Outstanding Profl. Agt. of Yr. 1980), Profl. Ins. Agts. Group of N.Y., N.J. and Conn. (trustee), Service Corp. N.Y. State, N.J. and Conn. (pres. 1979-85), Profl. Ins. Agts. Group (trustee). Republican. Roman Catholic. Clubs: Wiltwyck Country, Callabar Tennis (Kingston) (bd. mem.). Lodge: Kiwanis (past bd.

mem.). Avocations: tennis; golf; skiing; hiking. Home: 1 Lynette Blvd Kingston NY 12401 Office: Reis Ins 79 N Front St Kingston NY 12401

REISER, CHARLES EDWARD, JR., pharmaceutical company executive; b. Louisville, Nov. 2, 1939; s. Charles Edward Sr. and Margaret Christina (Hoffmann) R.; m. Antonia Marie Dominick, Feb. 10, 1944; children: Michelle, Lynette, Jeffery. BA, Ky. Wesleyan Coll., 1963; MBA, U. Mich., 1967. Fin. analyst Ford Motor Co., Dearborn, Mich., 1963-67; v.p. fin. Aluminum div. Atlantic Richfield, Chgo., 1967-85; sr. v.p., chief fin. officer Cardinal Distbn. Inc., Dublin, Ohio, 1985—. Office: Cardinal Distbn Inc 655 Metro Pl S Dublin OH 43017

REISINGER, GEORGE LAMBERT, management consultant; b. Pitts., Aug. 28, 1930; s. Eugene Merle and Pauline Jane (Lambert) R.; m. Judith Ann Brush, Nov. 24, 1967; children—Douglas Lambert, Christine Elizabeth. B.S. in Bus. Adminstrn., Central Coll., 1953; postgrad., Cleveland-Marshall Law Sch., 1962-67. Asst. personnel mgr. Continental Can Co., Houston, 1958-60; mgr. labor relations The Glidden Co., Cleve., 1960-67; dir. employee relations Mobil Oil Corp., N.Y.C., Caracas, Dallas, Denver, 1967-78; sr. v.p. Minton & Assocs., Denver, 1978-82; v.p., ptnr. Korn-Ferry Internat., Denver, 1982-86; pres., mng. ptnr. The Sigma Group, Inc., Denver, 1986—. Bd. dirs. Ponderosa Hills Civic Assn., 1977-80, Arapahoe County Youth League; Republican campaign dir. for county commr., 1978; pres. Douglas County Youth League. Served with USAF, 1953-58. Mem. Am. Soc. Personnel Adminstrs., N.Y. Personnel Mgmt. Soc., Colo. Soc. Personnel Adminstrn., Am. Soc. Profl. Cons., Rocky Mountain Inst. Fgn. Trade and Fin., Employment Mgmt. Assn., Lions Internat. Republican. Methodist. Clubs: Denver Petroleum, Pinery Country, Republican 1200. Lodge: Lions. Home: 7924 Deertrail Dr Parker CO 80134 Office: The Sigma Group Inc 717 17th St Ste 1440 Denver CO 80202-3314

REISLER, HELEN BARBARA, publishing and advertising executive; b. N.Y.C., June 21; d. George and Elizabeth Lois (Schultz) Gottesman; BS, in Edn., N.Y. U., 1954; MS in Edn. and Reading, L.I. U., 1978; m. Melvin Reisler, June 5, 1955; children: Susan O'Brien, Karen Reisler, Keith James. Elem. tchr., N.Y.C., 1954-78; instr. grad. sch., adj. lectr. L.I. U., Bklyn., 1978; account exec. N.Y. Yellow Pages, Inc., N.Y.C., 1979, personnel mgr., 1979, adminstrv. dir., 1980-83, v.p. personnel, 1983-84, v.p. adminstrn./ personnel, 1984-85, also dir.; staff specialist sales and market support Southwestern Bell Publs., 1985-88, NY. mgr. pub. relations and recruitment N.Y. Yellow Pages/Mast Advt. and Publs., Inc. of Southwestern Bell, 1988—; recruiter Northeast Region, N.Y. area community relations rep.; moderator weekly cable TV show New York Business Forum, N.Y.C., 1983-85. Named Ptnr. in Edn., N.Y.C. Bd. Edn., 1984. Mem. Sales Execs. Club N.Y. (bd. dirs., reception, membership and mem. relations coms., chmn. youth edn., v.p. 1987—), Execs. Assn. Greater N.Y. (chmn. com. Sec. Day), NYU Club, Heritage Hills Country Club Westchester, Sales Execs. Club (v.p.), Rotary. Profiled in various bus. publs. Home: 47 Plaza St Park Slope Brooklyn NY 11217 Office: Southwestern Bell Publs 91 Fifth Ave New York NY 10003

REISS, KENNETH MICHAEL, insurance company executive; b. Bklyn., Nov. 9, 1942; s. David A. Reiss and Anne Florence (Finkelstein) Brickman; m. Joan Esther Reisman, July 2, 1967; children: David, Adam, Rachel. BA, Bard Coll., 1966. CLU, chartered fin. cons. Rep. sales Met. Life Ins. Co., N.Y.C., 1969-71, mgr. sales, 1971-76, cons. field tng., 1977-79; mgr. dist. sales Met. Life Ins. Co., S.I., 1979-87; mgr. regional sales Met. Life Ins. Co., Bklyn., 1987—. Contbr. articles to profl. jours. Mem. Nat. Assn. Life Underwriters (local pres. 1983-85), Gen. Agts. & Mgrs. Assn. (local pres. 1984-85, recipient Nat. Mgmt. award 1982-86), Atlantic Agy. Mgr. Assn. (sec. 1986-87, pres. 1988), S.I. Life Underwriters (pres. 1983-85), Bklyn Gen. Agts. & Mgrs. Assn. (pres. 1984), N.Y. Life Underwriters (1st v.p. 1985-87). Office: Met Life Ins Co 9920 4th Ave Brooklyn NY 11209

REISSMAN, MAURICE L., bank executive. Former chief operating officer Crossland Savs., FSB, Bklyn., now pres., chief exec. officer, also chmn. bd. dirs. Office: Crossland Savs FSB 211 Montague St Brooklyn NY 11201 *

REITBERGER, ISAAC, accountant; b. Farenwald, Fed. Republic Germany, Aug. 31, 1950; came to U.S., 1951; s. Jules and Gusta Reitberger; m. Michele Susan Eisenfeld, Aug. 8, 1976; children: Adeena Cheri, Elana Beth. CPA, Md., N.Y., Va., Conn., R.I. Sr. acct. Elmer Fox Westheimer and Co., Washington, 1973-77; controller Spring Mall Dodge, Springfield, Va., 1977-79; mgr. Reznick Fedder and Silverman, Bethesda, Md., 1979-85; pres. Isaac Reitberger, Rockville, Md., 1985—, A&E Computers Inc, Rockville, Md., 1986—. Mem. lawyers and accts. div. State of Israel Bonds, Washington, 1981. Mem. AICPA (ptnrship. subcom. tax div., tax computer applications subcom. tax div., pvt. cos. practice sect.), Md. Soc. CPAs, Am. Friends Ben Gurion U. (bd. dirs. Washington 1988, 89), Md. Soc. Accts. Democrat. Jewish. Office: 6110 Executive Blvd Rockville MD 20852

REITBERGER, LINDA ANN, marketing consultant and director, real estateinvestor; b. Newark, June 13, 1947; d. Herbert J. and June Ellen (Dirgo). Grad., Belleville (N.J.) High Sch. Legal sec. Gaffey & Webb Esq., Newark, 1965-66; legal asst. Leibowitz & Corradino, Newark and East Orange, N.J., 1966-84; adminstrv. asst., dir. investor rels. LCL Equities, Parsippany, N.J., 1976—. Democrat. Roman Catholic. Home: 467 Valley St 3H Maplewood NJ 07040

REITER, RICHARD RONALD, healthcare executive; b. Dubuque, Iowa, Nov. 2, 1938; m. Carol Kueter, Sept. 18, 1964; children: Pamela, Paula, Stephanie. BS, U. Iowa, Iowa City, 1962; MBA, U. Iowa, 1980, MHA, 1984. With Hoelscher's Apothecary, Dubuque, Iowa, 1953-68, Mercy Health Ctr., Dubuque, 1968—; exec. dir. ops. Mercy Health Ctr., 1983-85, v.p. ops., 1985-87, v.p. gen. and profl. svcs., 1987—; pres., chief exec. officer Amicare Home Health Services/Tri-State, Inc., Dubuque, 1986—; bd. dirs. Pharmacy Enterprises, Inc., Des Moines, 1987—, Amicare Home Health Services/Tri-State, Inc., 1986—; dir. United Clin. Labs., Inc., 1987—. Contbr. articles to profl. jours. Mem. MBA adv. council U. Dubuque, 1986—; mem. Planning and Zoning Commn., Dubuque, 1983-87. Iowa Pharmacy Found. scholar, 1958-59. Fellow Am. Acad. Med. Adminstrs.; mem. Am. Coll. Healthcare Execs., Iowa Pharmacists Assn., Iowa Hosp. Assn. (mem. council on patient svcs. 1987—). Home: 1055 Arrowhead Dr Dubuque IA 52001 Office: Mercy Health Ctr Mercy Dr Dubuque IA 52001

REITMEISTER, NOEL WILLIAM, financial planner, insurance broker, author, consultant, educator; b. Bklyn., Aug. 12, 1938; s. Morris G. and Anna (Miller) R.; BA in Econs., Queens Coll., 1960; MBA in Indsl. Psychology and Bus., Baruch Coll., CUNY, 1969; diploma N.Y. Inst. Fin., 1969; CFP, Coll. Fin. Planning, 1974; m. Elaine Schendelman, Sept. 16, 1961; children—Gregg Allen, Stephen Michael. Account exec. duPont Walston, Chgo., Gary and Merrillville, Ind., 1969-71, br. coordinator, 1971-74; sr. investment broker A.G. Edwards & Sons Inc., Merrillville, 1974-79, v.p.-investments, 1979—; ptnr. Ind. Investors, 1980-88, Nat. Property Investors, 1980-84, Petro Lewis, 1979-84. Can. Am. Oil, 1980—, Rollingbrook Properties, 1983—, Nora Assocs., 1981—; vice chmn. bd. Menorah Credit Union, 1979-81, chmn., 1981-82, chmn., chief exec. officer, pres., 1982-83; owner Le Baron TV Prodns.; dir., prin. Arctic Exploration, Inc.; gen. ptnr. Filthy Rich Enterprises; conducted Roundtable at Advanced Conf. on Retirement Planning, Washington, 1986, also attended White House Briefing; lectr. Purdue U. Calumet, Purdue U. North Cen., Roosevelt U., Calumet Coll.; adj. faculty Coll. for Fin. Planning, Denver, 1974—; columnist Star Publs., 1984-86, Am. Med. News Jour., Times. Author: Portfolios, Inc. "Key Objectives in Investments"; co-author text "Retirement Planning" for Coll. Fin. Planning; producer, host cable TV show Money Doctor, 1985—, PBS spl. "Market Crisis of October 1987"; contbr. articles on fin. planning and retirement to profl. jours. including Jour. Inst. Fin. Planning, Fin. Planning and Nursing mags., Post Tribune, Times, Vidette Messenger, The Star, The Economist, Financial Services Weekly, Financial Planning News. Decorated Order William Tell Switzerland, 1986; named col.on staff of Gov. of Ky., 1988, Disting Grad. Coll. for Fin. Planning, 1984, Man of the Yr. B'nai B'rith, 1986; recipient Excellence award Nat. Assn. Accts., 1985. Mem. exec. com., sec., Ill. Theatre Ctr., 1985-88; bd. dirs. South Suburban HELP, 1968-69, N.W. Ind. Pub. Broadcasting, 1986—; trustee Temple Anshe Sholom, 1975-82, chmn. adult edn., 1977-82, chmn. house and grounds, 1977-78, co-chmn. social action com., 1979-82; dir. Drug and Alcohol Edn. Sheriff's Dept. Cook County, Ill., 1989—; v.p., sec. S. Suburban Acad. Jewish Studies, 1979-82; local troop coordinator Boy Scouts Am., 1977-78, vol. Richton Crossing Nursing Home; mem. Anti-Defamation League Cabinet, 1978-82; pres. Young Rep. Club of Queens County, 1958-60; v.p. Chgo. B'nai B'rith Council; co-founder, treas. SESSA. With USAR, 1960-66. fin. planning and retirement cons. Amoco, 1974—, LTV, 1982—, Inland Steel, 1983—, Ford Motor Co., 1987—; cert. fin. planner; examiner in fin. planning, 1974-78; lic. in investments, commodities and ins. sales; registered rep. N.Y. Stock Exchange, Am. Stock Exchange, Midwest Stock Exchange, Pacific Stock Exchange, Boston Stock Exchange, PBW Exchange, Chgo. Bd. Trade, Chgo. Merc. Exchange, Comex, NASD, Chgo. Options Exchange; lic. investment broker, N.Y., N.J., Conn., Mass., Fla., Ariz., Calif., Tex., Pa., Mich., Wis., Okla., Ill., Mich. Ind., Tenn. Mem. Inst. Cert. Fin. Planners (charter mem., pres. Illiana Soc., 1985-86, 87—, Dist. Service award 1987), Internat. Assn. Registered Fin. Planners, Chgo. Assn. Fin. Planners (pres. 1975, charter 1973-78), Michigana Assn. Fin. Planners (charter), Internat. Assn. Fin. Planners (v.p. Chgo. South chpt.), Internat. Soc. Registered Reps. (charter), Registry Fin. Planning Practitioners (charter 1983—), Am. Arbitration Assn. (div. fin. planning, investments and ins.), Am. Psychol. Assn., Midwest Psychol. Assn., Ill. Psychol. Assn., Weisenthal Inst., Chgo. Council on Fgn. Relations, Ind. TV producers Assn. (chmn.'s coun.), Pres.'s Council, Million Dollar Council, Crest Club, Three Million Dollar Council, Queens Coll. Alumni Assn., Baruch Coll. Alumni Assn., Art Inst. Chgo., Goodman Theater Prodn., Tau Delta Phi (chpt. v.p., pres., asst. nat. v.p.), Zetu, Alpha Epsilon Pi (chpt. pres.). Clubs: Crest, Century, Convenent, Idlewild Country, Homewood Flossmoor Racquet and Tennis. Lodges: Masons (32d degree), Lions, Shriners (v.p. south suburban club), B'nai B'rith (pres. lodge), Soc. of Fellows Anti-Defamation League). Home: 2246 Flossmoor Rd Flossmoor IL 60422 Office: 8300 Mississippi Merrillville IN 46410

RELDAN, ROBERT RONALD, legal educator, psychological consultant; b. Bklyn., June 2, 1942; s. William and Marie (Garis) R.; m. Judith Feldman, Nov. 7, 1971 (div. June 1979); 1 child, Edward. BS, Fairleigh Dickinson U., 1965; MS (hon.), Park Coll., 1975; JD, LaSalle U., St. Louis, 1988. Sales mgr. Pistilli Ford, Oradell, N.J., 1967-69; owner Triple "R" Co., Tenafly, N.J., 1969-75; dir. Legal Ltd., Trenton, N.J., 1975—. Served with USN, 1965-67. Mem. Toastmasters Internat., (v.p. Trenton chpt. 1987-88), Am. Entrepreneurs Assn., Aircraft Owners and Pilots Assn. Office: Legal Ltd 3d and Federal Trenton NJ 08625

REMBERT, DONALD MOSBY, financial advisor; b. Washington, Jan. 3, 1939; s. Samuel Harley and Laura Mclellan (Mosby) R.; m. Judith Rae Ellis, June 24, 1961; children: Heather Lynne, Donald Mosby Jr., Charles Ellis. BA in Econs., Western Md. Coll., 1961. Mgr. C&P Telephone Co., Washington, 1964-68; gen. mgr., sec., treas. Charcoal Inn Ltd. and related corps., Bowie, Md., 1968-72; v.p., gen. mgr. Associated Restaurants, Arlington, Va., 1972-74; ptnr. Dilkes, Cooper and Rembert, Falls Church, Va., 1974-78; proprietor, fin. planner Rembert & Assocs., Falls Church, 1978-80; fin. planner Rembert & Hopewell Inc., Falls Church, 1980-83; fin. advisor, dir., v.p. Hopewell Rembert Advisors Inc., Falls Church, 1983—; sec., treas. bd. dirs. Integrated Systems Mgmt. Solutions Inc., Reston, Va. Active in Jaycees, 1964-68. 1st Lt. U.S. Army, 1961-64. Mem. Internat. Assn. Fin. Planning, Inst. Cert. Fin. Planners, Registry Fin. Planners, Nat. Assn. Realtors, No. Va. Bd. Realtors, Ludwig von Mises Inst., So. Econ. Assn., Va. Archery and Rifle Club (Alexandria) (pres. 1980-81). Methodist. Home: 10810 Hunt Club Rd Reston VA 22090 Office: Hopewell Rembert Advisors Inc 7647 Lessburg Pike Falls Church VA 22043

REMMER, JAMES EDWARD, photography equipment company executive; b. Rockport, Calif., Mar. 12, 1927; s. Victor Herbert and Ellen (Stahl) R.; teaching credential San Diego State Coll., 1947; m. Denise O. Sours, Aug. 17, 1947; children: James H., Jan A., Jeffrey B.; m. 2d, Luana Jean Warwick, Mar. 1975. Gen. mgr. San Diego Office Equipment Co., 1956-63; subsidiary v.p. A.B. Dick Co., San Diego, 1959-63; zone mgr. Xerox Corp., Los Angeles, 1963-68; v.p., gen. mgr. Houston Fearless Corp., 1968-70; pres. Cintel Corp., Los Angeles, 1970-72; v.p. Falls Land & Devel. Corp., 1972-74; zone dir. Saxon Bus. Products, 1974-81; nat. dir. ops. Toshiba Corp., 1981-83; dir. Gestetner Corp., 1983-84; pres. Ampco Marine Emergency Network, 1984-87; v.p., gen. mgr. Filmguard Corp., Escondido, Calif., 1987—; dir. Columbis Mgmt. Scis. Corp., Encino, Calif., Gov. Cons., Inc., Washington, CPS Assocs.; cons. Tech., Inc., Dayton, Ohio, 1970—; tchr. sales and mktg. U. Calif., Berkeley, 1951—, Arlington Jr. Coll., 1953-54. Bd. dirs. Calif. Mus. Found., 1967—, So. Calif. Industry and Edn. Council, 1966—, Jr. Achievement, 1960—; mem. Port Commn., San Diego, 1959-62; dir. sales and mktg. execs. Mayor's Speakers Bur., 1959. Served with USMC, 1945, 50-51. Mem. A.I.M., Pres. Council, Research Inst. Am., Soc. Reproduction Engrs., Sigma Alpha Epsilon, Epsilon Eta. Home: 17152 Ruette Campana San Diego CA 92128 Office: 2239 Vineyard Ave Escondido CA 92025

REMMER, RICHARD HENRY, energy company executive; b. Greenport, N.Y., June 28, 1955; s. George Henry and Betty Emora (Bauer) R.; m. Kathleen Hart Geoghan, June 17, 1978; children: Maxwell Henry, Meredith Hart. BA in Biology and Geology, Williams Coll., Williamstown, Mass., 1977; JD, U. Tulsa, 1981. Bar: Okla. 1981; cert. petroleum geologist. Geologist Lenhart & Bennett Inc., Sapulpa, Okla., 1977-78; exploration geologist Buttonwood Petroleum Co., Tulsa, 1978-79; pres. Remmer Oil Co., Tulsa, 1979-88, also bd. dirs.; v.p. Irish Petroleum Corp., Tulsa, 1982-88, also bd. dirs.; v.p. Cayman Resources Corp., Tulsa, 1983-88, also bd. dirs.; exec. dir. Chemtex Petroleum Resources, Tulsa, 1988—. Vol. Tulsa Vol. Lawyers, 1986—, Tulsa Legal Services for Elderly, 1987—, Okla. Nature Conservancy, 1988; bd. dirs. Tulsa Park Friends, 1988. Mem. ABA, Am. Assn. Petroleum Geologists, Okla. Bar Assn., Tulsa Bar Assn., Tulsa, Oklahoma City, N.Y. Geol. Socs. Office: Chemtex Petroleum Resources 560 Lexington Ave New York NY 10022

REMONDINI, WALTER LINO, retail executive; b. Milw., Oct. 4, 1960; s. Arthur S. and Idelma (Formolo) R. AS in Bus. Mgmt., U. Wis.-Parkside, 1981. Sales rep. Northwestern Photo Co., Greenfield, Wis., 1981-83, mgr. retail div., 1983-87; pres. Foto Finish Wis. Inc., W. Allis, 1987—; ind. producer Milw. Access Telecommunications, 1985—. Producer cable TV program Autumnal Impressions, 1986 (award 1987). Mem. Project Literacy, Milw., 1987—. Mem. Nat. Fedn. Ind. Businesses, Photomktg. Assn. Internat., Badgerland Striders. Office: Foto Finish Wis Inc 10534 W Greenfield Ave West Allis WI 53214

REMY, RAY, chamber of commerce executive; b. San Francisco. B in Polit. Sci., Claremont Men's Coll. (now Claremont McKenna Coll.); M in Pub. Adminstrn., U. Calif., Berkeley. Adminstrv. intern City of Berkeley, 1962-63; with So. Office League of Calif. Cities, 1963, then asst. to exec. dir. and mgr., to 1969; exec. dir. So. Calif. Assn. Govt., 1969-76; appointed dep. mayor City of Los Angeles, 1976-84; pres. Los Angeles Area C. of C., 1984—, also prin. spokesman. Mem. exec. com. Mus. Sci. and Industry; past chmn. bd. councilors Sch. Pub. Adminstrn. U. So. Calif., Los Angeles; vice chmn. bd. dirs. Rose Inst. for state and local govt.; mem. state adv. com. Revision of Master Plan for Higher Edn.; trustee, Claremont McKenna Coll., Calif. Trust for the Environ. Recipient numerous awards including Fletcher Bowron award, Donald Stone award, Mus. of Sci. and Industry Fellowship award, others. Mem. Nat. Acad. Pub. Adminstrn., Jr. Statesmen Found. (trustee, vice chmn. So. Calif. region), Am. Soc. Pub. Adminstrn. (past pres.), exec. com. Mus. Sci. and Industry, L.A. County Transp. Com. Office: Los Angeles Area C of C 404 S Bixel St PO Box 3696 Los Angeles CA 90017

RENAUD, PHILIP SYLVESTER, II, retail executive; b. Woonsocket, R.I., Apr. 20, 1951; s. Philip S. Sr. and Jeannette (Fischesser) R.; m. Suzanne Anne Jodoin, May 26, 1973. Claim and loss rep. Royal Globe Ins. Co., Providence, R.I., 1973-77; claim and loss supr. Royal Globe Ins. Co., Newton, Mass., 1977-78; claim and loss mgr. Royal Globe Ins. Co., Hagerstown, Md., 1978-79; risk mgr. JLG Industries, Inc., McConnellsburg, Pa., 1979-83; mgr. corp. risk mgmt. SCOA Industries, Inc., Columbus, Ohio, 1983—; dir. risk mgmt. SCOA Industries?Hills Dept. Stores, Canton, Mass., 1985—. Mem. Risk and Ins. Mgmt. Soc. (sec. 1983, treas. 1984, bd. dirs. 1984-85). Roman Catholic. Home: 67 Countryside Dr Cumberland RI 02864 Office: Hills Dept Stores Inc 15 Dan Rd Canton MA 02021

RENCK, ROBERT LEO, JR., stock brokerage company executive; b. N.Y.C., Apr. 18, 1948; s. Robert Leo and Agnes (Fives) R.; m. Diane Elder, Nov. 22, 1969 (div. May 1978); children: Susan Lynn, Robert Leo III; m. Ellen Sadove, June 30, 1979; children: Andrew, Caroline. BS in Econs., St. John's U., N.Y.C., 1968, MBA in Econs., 1971; postgrad., NYU, 1960-70. Economist, asst. v.p. Bache and Co., Inc., N.Y.C., 1968-70; v.p. Laird, Inc./ G.H. Walker Laird, Inc., N.Y.C., 1972-74, Cyrus J. Lawrence, Inc., N.Y.C., 1974-79, Oppenheimer & Co., Inc., N.Y.C., 1979-82; mng. ptnr. R.L. Renck & Co., N.Y.C., 1983—. Mem. Fin. Analysts Fedn., N.Y. Soc. Security Analysts. Republican. Office: RL Renck& Co 850 3d Ave New York NY 10022

RENDELL, KENNETH W., rare and historical documents dealer, consultant; b. Boston, May 12, 1943; s. Harry H. and Pauline (Walsh) R.; m. Diana J. Angelo, June 3, 1967 (div. 1985); children: Jeffrey H., Jason J.; m. Shirley L. McNerney, July 14, 1985. Student, Boston U., 1961-63. Pres. Kingston Galleries, Inc., Somerville, Mass., 1960-67, Kenneth W. Rendell, Inc., Newton, Mass., 1967—, Kenneth W. Rendell, Ltd., London, 1970—, Kenneth W. Rendell Gallery, Inc., N.Y.C., Tokyo, 1985—; bd. dirs. John Wilson Autographs Ltd., London, 1961-75, Charles Ede Gallery Ltd., London, 1976—; chmn. New England Antiquarian Booksellers Assn., 1975-77; pres. Internat. League Autograph and Manuscript Dealers, 1975-77; cons. to numerous univ. librs., govt. and media orgns. Author: The Fundamentals of Autograph Collecting, 1976, Tax Appraisals of Manuscript Collections, 1983, Changing Concepts of Value and Rarity, 1985, The Hitler Diaries: Bad Forgeries But a Great Hoax, 1986, The Mormon Conman, Forger and Killer, 1987, Other People's Mail: 30 Years As A Dealer In Historical Documents, 1988; co-editor: Autographs and Manuscripts: A Collector's Manual, 1978 (Outstanding Reference Book award ALA); contbr. numerous articles in field to mags. and profl. jours. Fellow Manuscript Soc. (bd. dirs. 1968-74, pres. 1972-74); mem. Assn. Internat. de Bibliophilie Paris. Club: Grolier (N.Y.C.). Office: Kenneth W Rendell Inc 154 Wells Ave Newton MA 02159 also: 125 E 57th St New York NY 10022

RENDINO, ANTHONY, trust company executive; b. Bklyn., June 5, 1926; s. William and Marion (DeMartino) R.; m. Anita F. Prince, Oct. 28, 1950; children: Claire Rendino Ryan, Lynn Rendino Schiro, Luann, Caren, Tracie. B.Elec. Engring., Pratt Inst., 1950; M.B.A., Fairleigh Dickinson U., 1966. With IBM, 1950-70, dir. real estate operations Western area, 1965-68, dir. field real estate, 1968-70; v.p. real estate mgmt. Irving Trust Co., N.Y.C., 1970-72; sr. v.p. adminstrv. services Irving Trust Co., 1972-73, sr. v.p. operational services div., 1973-76, exec. v.p. ops. group, 1976-80, exec. v.p. gen. services group, 1980-87, sr. exec. v.p. gen. services group, 1987—; pres. One Wall Street Corp., Irving Life Ins. Co. Mem. Borough of Manhattan Community Coll. Fund, Inc. Served with USNR, 1944-46. Mem. N.Y. Chamber Commerce and Industry, Downtown Lower Manhattan Assn., Regional Plan Assn. Home: 15 Bramley Ln Dobbs Ferry NY 10522 Office: Irving Trust Co 1 Wall St New York NY 10005

RENDL-MARCUS, MILDRED, artist, economist; b. N.Y.C., May 30, 1928; d. Julius and Agnes (Hokr) Rendl; BS, NYU, 1948, MBA, 1950; PhD (Dean Bernice Brown Cronkhite fellow 1950-51), Radcliffe Coll., 1954; m. Edward Marcus, Aug. 10, 1956. Economist, Gen. Electric Co., 1953-56, Bigelow-Sanford Carpet Co., Inc., 1956-58; lectr. econs. evening sessions CCNY, 1953-58; research investment problems in tropical Africa, 1958-59; instr. econs. Hunter Coll. CUNY, 1959-60; lectr. econs. Columbia U., 1960-61; research econ. devel. Nigeria, W. Africa, 1961-63; sr. economist Internat. div. Nat. Indsl. Conf. Bd., 1963-66; asst. prof. Grad. Sch. Bus. Adminstrn., Pace Coll., 1964-66; asso. prof. Borough of Manhattan Community Coll., City U. N.Y., 1966-71, prof., 1972-85; vis. prof. Fla. Internat. U., 1986; prin. MRM Assos., Rendl Fine Art; corp. art econ. cons.; fine arts appraiser; participant Internat. Economical Meeting, Amsterdam, 1968, Econs. of Fine Arts in Age of Tech., 1984, Internat. Economic Assn. North Am., Laredo, Tex., 1987-88, Soc. Southwestern Economists, San Antonio, 1988, New Orleans, 1989. Exhibited New Canaan Art Show, 1982, 83, 84, 85, New Canaan Soc. for Arts Ann., 1983, 85, New Canaan Arts, 1985, Silvermine Galleries, 1986, Stamford Art Assn., 1987, Women in the Arts at Phoenix Gallery, Group Show, N.Y.C., 1988; symposium participant Sienna, Italy, 1988; contbr. articles to Women in the Arts newsletter, 1986-87, Coalition Womens Art Orgns., 1986-87. Bd. dirs. N.Y.C. Council on Econ. Edn., 1970— ; mem. program planning com. Women's Econ. Roundtable; participant Eastern Econ. Assn., Boston, 1988; Participant Art and Personal Property Appraisal, N.Y.U., 1986-88. Recipient Disting. Service award CUNY, 1985. Fellow Gerontol. Assn.; mem. Internat. Schumpeter Econs. Soc. (founding), Am. (vice chmn. ann. meeting 1973), Met. (sec. 1954-56) econ. assns., Indsl. Relations Research Assn., Audubon Artists and Nat. Soc. Painters in Casein (assoc. 1987-88) Allied Social Sci. Assn. (vice chmn. conv. 1973), AAUW, N.Y.C. Women in Arts, Women's Econ. Roundtable, N.Y. U. Grad. Sch. Bus. Adminstrn. Alumni (sec. 1956-58). Clubs: Radcliffe; Women's City (art and landmarks com.). Author: (with husband) Investment and Development of Tropical Africa, 1959, International Trade and Finance, 1965, Monetary and Banking Theory, 1965; Economics, 1969; (with husband) Principles of Economics, 1969; Economic Progress and the Developing World, 1970; Economics, 1978; also monographs and articles in field. Econ. and internat. research on industrialization less developed areas, internat. debtor nations and workability of buffer stock schemes; columnist economics of art Women in Art. Home: 928 West Rd New Canaan CT 06840 Office: PO Box 814 New Canaan CT 06840 also: 7441 Wayne Ave Miami Beach FL 33141

RENFREW, CHARLES BYRON, oil company executive, lawyer; b. Detroit, Oct. 31, 1928; s. Charles Warren and Louise (McGuire) R.; m. Susan Wheelock, June 28, 1952 (div. June 1984); children: Taylor Allison Ingham, Charles Robin, Todd Wheelock, James Bartlett; m. Barbara Jones Orser, Oct. 6, 1984; 5 stepchildren. AB, Princeton U., 1952; JD, U. Mich., 1956. Bar: Calif. 1956. Assoc. Pillsbury, Madison & Sutro, San Francisco, 1956-65, ptnr., 1965-72, 81-82; U.S. dist. judge No. Dist. Calif., San Francisco, 1972-80; dep. atty. gen. U.S. Washington, 1980-81; instr. U. Calif. Boalt Hall Sch. Law, 1977-80; v.p. law Chevron Corp. (formerly Standard Oil Co. Calif.), San Francisco, 1983—, also bd. dirs.; mem. exec. com. 9th Cir. Jud. Conf., 1976-78, congl. liaison com. 9th Cir. Jud. Council, 1976-79, spl. com. to propose standards for admission to practice in fed. cts. U.S. Jud. Conf., 1976-79; chmn. spl. com. to study problems of discovery Fed. Jud. Ctr., 1978-79; mem. council on role of cts. U.S. Dept. Justice, 1978-83; mem. jud. panel Ctr. for Pub. Resources, 1981—; head U.S. del. to 6th UN Congress on Prevention of Crime and Treatment of Offenders, 1980; co-chmn. San Francisco Lawyers Com. for Urban Affairs, 1971-72, mem., 1983—; bd. dirs. Internat. Hospitality Ctr., 1961-74, pres., 1967-70; mem. adv. bd. Internat. Comparative Law Ctr., Southwestern Legal Found., 1983—; trustee World Affairs Council No. Calif., 1984—, Nat. Jud. Coll., 1985—, Grace Cathedral, 1986—. Contbr. articles to profl. jours. Bd. fellow Claremont U., 1986—; bd. dirs. San Francisco Symphony Found., 1964-80, pres., 1971-72; bd. dirs. Council for Civic Unity, 1968-72, pres., 1971-72; bd. dirs. Opportunity Through Ownership, 1969-72, Marin Country Day Sch., 1972-74, No. Calif. Service League, 1975-76, Am. Petroleum Inst., 1984—, Nat. Crime Prevention Council, 1982—; alumni trustee Princeton U., 1976-80; mem. vis. com. U. Chgo. Law Sch., 1977-79, U. Mich. Law Sch., 1977-81; bd. visitors J. Reuben Clark Law Sch., Brigham Young U., 1981-83, Stanford Law Sch., 1983-86; trustee Town Sch. for Boys, 1972-80, pres., 1975-80; gov. San Francisco Symphony Assn., 1974—; mem. nat. adv. bd. Ctr. for Nat. Policy, 1982—; bd. dirs. Nat. Council on Crime and Delinquency, 1981-82, NAACP Legal Def. and Edn. Fund, 1982—; parish chancellor St. Luke's Episcopal Ch., 1968-71, sr. warden, 1974-76; mem. exec. council San Francisco Deanery, 1969-70; mem. diocesan council Episcopal Diocese of Calif., 1970; mem. adv. council Episcopal Ch. Found., 1974—; chmn. Diocesan Conv., 1977, 78, 79. Served with USN, 1946-48, to 1st lt. U.S. Army, 1952-53. Fellow Am. Bar Found.; mem. ABA (council mem. sect. antitrust law 1978-82, vice chmn. sect. antitrust law 1982-83), San Francisco Bar Assn. (past bd. dirs.), Assn. Gen. Counsel, State Bar Calif., Am. Judicature Soc., Am. Coll. Trial Lawyers, Am. Law Inst., Council on Fgn. Relations, Order of Coif, Phi Beta Kappa, Phi Delta Phi. Office: Chevron Corp 225 Bush St San Francisco CA 94104

RENFRO, CHARLES GILLILAND, economist; b. Paris, Tex., Nov. 23, 1943; s. Charles G. and Virginia Armstrong (Dawsey) R.; m. Patricia Elise Candlin, June 21, 1969; children: Rebecca Elise, James Lawrence. BA, U. of York, Eng., 1966; MSc, London Sch. Econs., U. London, 1968; MA, U. Pa.,

1971, PhD, 1976. Rsch. asst. Indsl. Manpower Project London Sch. Econs., 1967-68; rsch. asst. Brookings Instn., Washington, 1968-70; econ. research fellow U. Pa.-Wharton Econometric Forecasting Assos., Phila., 1970-71; instr. econs. U. Pa., 1971-73; lectr. dept. econs. Swarthmore (Pa.) Coll., 1972-73; rsch. assoc., asst. prof. econs. U. Ky., Lexington, 1973-77, assoc. dir. econ. studies and analysis, 1975-81, dir. ctr. for Applied Econ. Rsch., 1979-81; dir. regional forecasting, chief regional economist Chase Econometrics Assocs., Bala Cynwyd, Pa., 1981-83; pres. C.G. Renfro & Assocs., Bala Cynwyd, 1978—; pres., chief exec. officer, bd. dirs. Alphametrics Corp., Bala Cynwyd, 1984—; bd. dirs. Integrated Modelling Applications Ltd., Cambridge, Alphametrics Ltd., Cambridge, Modler Info. Tech. Ltd., Cambridge; econ. advisor office budget and mgmt. State of Ohio, 1980, 82-83, permanent subcom. investigations, com. govt. ops. U.S. Senate, 1974-75, State Govt. Pa., 1981-83, environ. protection agy. State of N.J., 1982-83, State of Conn., 1982-83, State of Tex., 1982-83, dept. of taxation State of North Dakota, 1981-83, State of Mo., 1982-83; mem. dept. of taxation, mem. Senate budget com. State of Va., 1982-83; econ. info. systems advisor small bus. subcom. U.S. Ho. Reps., 1979-80; cns. Merrill Lynch Econs. Inc., 1986-87, Data Resources Inc., 1985—, Wharton Econometric Forecasting Assocs, Inc., 1984-86, Chase Econometric Assocs, 1983, 85-87, Humana, Inc., 1981, Dames & Moore, 1980-81, Gen. Telephone Co., Ky., 1977-81, 1st Security Nat. Bank and Trust Co., 1979-81, Elsevier Sci. Publ. Co., Inc., 1980-87. Author and developer numerous computer software systems, 1976-86; editor: Review of Public Data Use, 1980-86; Journal of Economic and Social Measurement, 1986—; editorial adv. bd.: Computers and the Social Sciences, 1985-87; contbr. articles to profl. jours. Assoc. dir. Ky. Council Econ. Advisors, 1977-79, exec. dir., 1979-81. Mem. Am. Econ. Assn., Am. Statis. Assn., Southeastern Econ. Analysis Conf. (program chmn. 1977, exec. com. 1977-81), Internat. Assn. for Research in Income and Wealth, Soc. for Econ. Dynamics and Control, Nat. Assn. Bus. Economists, Assn. for Computing Machinery, Royal Econ. Soc.

RENICKER, ROBERT NOLAN, utility executive, controller; b. Urania, La., Feb. 15, 1944; s. Carl A. and Mildred C. (Wooley) R.; m. Barbara L. Gary, Jan. 28, 1966; children: Robert G., Ryan N., Reid C. BSBA, La. Tech. U., 1966, MBA in Econs., 1967; postgrad. in acctg., So. Meth. U., 1972-76; postgrad. pub. utility exec. program, U. Mich., 1985. CPA, Tex., La., Ark. Sr. fin. cons. Middle West Svc. Co., Dallas, 1975-79; asst. treas., coord. fin. planning and analysis Gulf States Utilities, Beaumont, Tex., 1979-81; mgr., prin. Arthur Young & Co., Tulsa, 1981-84; asst. contr. Southwestern Electric Power Co., Shreveport, La., 1984, contr., 1984—, chief acctg. officer, 1987—. Treas. Episcopal Ch., Tulsa, 1982-83; mem. com. troop 14, Boy Scouts Am., Shreveport, 1985—. With USMCR, 1968. Mem. AICPA, La. Soc. CPA's, Nat. Assn. Accts. (v.p. Shreveport chpt. 1988—, Leadership award 1986), Edison Electric Inst., Missouri Valley Electric Assn. (chmn. chief acctg. and fin. officer com. 1987-88), Shreveport C. of C. (long range planning com. 1984—), So. Trace Country Club, Shreveport Athletic Club for La. Tech. U. (pres. 1987-88). Republican. Office: Southwestern Electric Power 428 Travis St Shreveport LA 71156

RENIER, JAMES J., diversified electronic equipment manufacturing company executive; b. 1930. BS in Chemistry, Coll. St. Thomas; PhD in Phys. Chemistry, Iowa State U. With U.S. AEC, to 1956; with Honeywell, Inc., Mpls., 1956—, corp. v.p., gen. mgr. data systems ops., 1970-74, v.p. aerospace and def. group, 1974-76, group v.p., 1976-78, corp. exec. v.p., 1978-79, pres. control systems, 1979-82, vice chmn., 1982-87, also pres. info. systems div., corp. pres., chief operating officer, 1987—, also chief exec. officer. Office: Honeywell Inc Honeywell Plaza Minneapolis MN 55408 *

RENKER, MARSHALL EDISON, SR., cement company executive; b. Cowan, Ind., Dec. 8, 1904; s. Jacob E. and Alberta May (Neff) R.; m. Vera Lea Keesling, Nov. 26, 1925 (dec. Mar. 1985); children: Marshall Edison, David B., John J.; m. Ruby Marian Stewart, Aug. 27, 1987. Student in teaching, Ball State U., 1921-23. With Rinker Materials Corp. (and predecessor); chief exec. officer, chmn. bd. Rinker Materials Corp., West Palm Beach, Fla., Rinker Realty Corp., West Palm Beach. Chmn. West Palm Beach Community Chest, 1954; bd. dirs. West Palm Beach chpt. ARC, 1930-50, Fla. East Coast Industries, 1978—; trustee emeritus Stetson U.; trustee DeLand, Fla.; chmn. bd. deacons 1st Bapt. Ch., West Palm Beach, 1960-62. Recipient Free Enterprise medal Palm Beach Atlantic Coll., 1985; named John D. MacArthur Bus. Leader of Yr., 1985. Mem. Nat. Concrete Masonry Assn. (bd. dirs., pres. 1954), Nat. Ready Mixed Concrete Assn. (pres. 1973), Fla. Concrete and Products Assn. (pres. 1967), West Palm Beach C. of C. (pres. 1954-55). Clubs: Everglades, Old Guard Soc., Govs.' (life) (Palm Beach); Garden of Gods (Colorado Springs, Colo.); Ocean Reef (Key Largo, Fla.); River (Jacksonville, Fla.). Lodge: Rotary. Home: 561 Island Dr Palm Beach FL 33480 Office: Rinker Materials Corp PO Drawer K West Palm Beach FL 33416-4635 also: PO Box 24635 West Palm Beach FL 33416-4635

RENKIS, ALAN ILMARS, plastics formulating company executive; b. Preili, Latvia, Apr. 16, 1938; came to U.S., 1950; naturalized, 1958.; s. Joseph and Malvine (Sturitis) R.; m. Inara Balodis, July 15, 1961; children: Martin Alan, Laura Alise. BSChemE, Pa. State U., 1960. With product devel. and tech. service div. Diamond Alkali Co., Painesville, Ohio, 1960-63; tech. dir. G.S. Plastics Co., Cleve., 1963; founder, pres. Thermoclad Co., Erie, Pa., 1963—, Riverside, Calif., 1972—, Ocala, Fla., 1985—. Developer comml. PVC resins for formulating fluidized bed coating powders; formulations and compounding techniques. Mem. Young Pres. Orgn., Soc. Plastics Engrs., Sigma Pi, Fraternitas Metropolitana (Latvian student frat.). Clubs: University, Erie, Aviation, Kankwa (Erie). Home: 5109 Watson Rd Erie PA 16505 Office: Thermoclad Co 361 W 11th St Erie PA 16501

RENN, PATRICK GEORGE, financial planner; b. Frederick, Md., Mar. 19, 1947; s. Ralph H. and Aurelie (Arcas) R.; m. Suzanne Wiggens McCord, June 26, 1962; children: S. Tyler, Owen McCord. BS, Villanova U., 1969; MBA, Loyola Coll., Balt., 1970. Supr. Phoenix Cos., Hartford, Conn., 1970-72; registered rep. Fin. Svc. Corp. Am., Atlanta, 1972-75; sr. v.p. Consol. Planning Corp., Atlanta, 1975—; mem. Investment Mgmt. and Research Pres. Council, St. Petersburg, 1986—. Pub., author, editor The Renn Fin. Letter, 1984—. Vice chmn. Ga. Spl. Olympics, Atlanta, 1981-88, chmn., 1988-89; mem. Eagle Adv. Council, St. Petersburg, Fla., 1986—; vestry Cathedral St. Philip, Atlanta, 1988—. Mem. Inst. Cert. Fin. Planners, Internat. Assn. Fin. Planning (pres. Ga. chpt. 1984-85), Ga. Soc. Inst. Cert. Fin. Planners (past pres.), Midtown Bus. Assn., So. Pension Conf., Atlanta Estate Planning Council, Am. Soc. CLU's, Registry of Fin. Planners, Sales and Mktg. Execs. of Atlanta, Cherokee Town and Country Club, German Club, Rotary, Toastmasters. Republican. Episcopalian. Office: Consol Planning Corp 400 Colony Sq Ste 325 Atlanta GA 30361

RENSCH, JOSEPH ROMAINE, public utility holding company executive; b. San Bernardino, Calif., Jan. 1, 1923; s. Joseph R. and Lucille (Ham) R.; m. June Elizabeth Burley, Mar. 25, 1946; children: Steven R., Jeffrey P. BS, Stanford U., 1947; JD, Golden Gate U., 1955. Bar: Calif.; registered profl. engr., Calif. Successively sales engr., regional gas engr., asst. regional gas supt., asst. mgr. gas supply and control Coast Counties Gas & Electric Co., San Francisco, 1947-54; sr. pipeline operations engr. Pacific Gas & Electric Co., 1954-56; prodn. control supt. Western div. Dow Chem. Co., Pittsburg, Calif., 1956; asst. counsel So. Counties Gas Co. of Calif., Los Angeles, 1957-58; asst. v.p., spl. counsel Pacific Lighting Gas Supply Co., Los Angeles, 1958- 61, v.p., bd. dirs., 1962-65; sr. v.p. Pacific Lighting Service Co., 1965-67, exec. v.p., 1967-69, pres., 1969-71, chmn. bd., 1971-73; exec. v.p., dir. Pacific Lighting Corp., Los Angeles, 1968-72, pres., 1972-86, vice chmn., 1986-88; bd. dirs. McKesson Corp. Served with USNR, 1942-46. Mem. Pacific Coast Gas Assn. (pres. 1966-67), Am. Gas Assn., Tau Beta Pi, Alpha Tau Omega. Office: Pacific Enterprises 810 S Flower St Los Angeles CA 90017

RENSCHLER, C. ARNOLD, healthcare company executive, pediatrician; b. Sioux Falls, S.D., Jan. 15, 1942; s. Clarence Alvin and Lorraine Ellen (Arnold) R.; m. Barbara Jean Bainum, June 20, 1965 (div. Dec. 1984); children: Scott, Todd; m. D. Sheryl White, Aug. 23, 1986. BA, Walla Walla Coll., 1964; MD, Loma Linda U., 1968. Diplomate Am. Bd. Pediatrics. Resident in medicine Georgetown U., Washington, 1968-69; med. dir. Far Eastern Island Med. Clinic, Agana, Guam, 1969-72; resident in pediatrics Stanford U., Palo Alto, Calif., 1972-74, asst. prof. pediatrics, 1974-75; pres. Child Health Assocs., Warrenton, Va., 1975-79; asst. prof. pediatrics Johns Hopkins U., Balt., 1979-81; v.p. corp. devel. Manor Care, Inc., Silver Spring, Md., 1981-82, pres., chief operating officer, 1985—; pres., chief exec. officer Manor HealthCare Corp., Silver Spring, 1982—. Fellow Am. Acad. Pediatrics; mem. Soc. for Adolescent Medicine, Pres.' Assn. Am. Mgmt. Assn. Democrat. Seventh-Day Adventist. Office: Manor Care Inc 10750 Columbia Pike Silver Spring MD 20901

RENTSCHLER, ALVIN EUGENE, mechanical engineer; b. Havre, Mont., Oct. 24, 1940; s. Alvin Joseph and Pauline Elizabeth (Browning) R.; m. Marilyn Joan Bostrom, Dec. 7, 1974; children—Elizabeth Louise, Richard Eugene, Alison Lynn. BS, Mont. State U., 1964. Sci. and math. instr. Helena (Mont.) Pub. Schs., 1964-66; dist. mgr. Woodmen Accident and Life Co., Helena, 1966-69; profl. med. rep. Abbott Labs., Great Falls, Mont., 1969-72; sales engr. Agribest, Inc., Great Falls, 1973; design engr. Anaconda Co., Mont., 1974-77; ops. and maintenance engr. Rochester Meth. Hosp., Minn., 1977-85; maintenance supervisor, 1985—; mem. engring. coordinating com. Franklin Heating Sta., 1977-85. Bd. dirs. Mont. affiliate Am. Diabetes Assn., 1975-78, pres. Butte-Anaconda chpt., 1974-77; mem. citizens adv. com. Rochester Tech. Inst., 1977— (chmn. 1987—). Recipient Greatest Achievement award Combined Tng., Inc., 1977, Pres.' Club award Woodmen Accident & Life Co., 1968. Mem. ASME, Am. Soc. Hosp. Engring., Internat. Congress Hosp. Engring. Mem. Covenant Ch. Home: 2215 17th Ave NW Rochester MN 55901

REPLOGLE, DAVID ROBERT, publishing company executive; b. Chgo., Feb. 24, 1931; s. Homer Mock and Helen (Fluke) R.; m. Jeanne Lonnquist, Nov. 4, 1954; children: William T., Bruce R., Stewart D., James M., John B. A.B., Dartmouth Coll., 1953; postgrad., Princeton U., 1957-58. V.p., gen. mgr. Doubleday & Co., Inc., N.Y.C., 1958-70; pres., chmn. bd. G. & C. Merriam Co., Springfield, Mass., 1970-75; pres. Praeger Publishers, N.Y.C., 1970-75; exec. v.p. Houghton Mifflin Co., Boston, 1975—. Trustee L.I. Replogle Found., Chgo., 1982—. Served to lt. USNR, 1953-57. Clubs: Cohasset Golf, Cohasset Yacht (Mass.). Home: 84 Gammons Rd Cohasset MA 02025 Office: Houghton Mifflin Co 1 Beacon St Boston MA 02108

RESNICK, ALAN HOWARD, health care and optics executive; b. Boston, Nov. 1, 1943; s. Max Lawrence and Natalie (Levine) R.; m. Barbara Gail Parnes, Jan. 8, 1944; children: Stephen Seth, Helaine Elise, Eilleen Michelle. BS, Tufts U., 1965; MBA, Columbia U., 1967. Fin. analyst E.I. DuPont de Nemours & Co., Wilmington, Del., 1967-73; various positions Bausch & Lomb Inc., Rochester, N.Y., 1973—, treas., 1986—; mem. adv. bd. Allendale Ins. Co., Johnston, R.I., 1987. Bd. dirs. Vis. Nurse Service Rochester and Monroe County, 1977—, Rochester Monroe County chpt. ARC, 1988—. Jewish. Office: Bausch & Lomb Inc 1 Lincoln 1st Sq Rochester NY 14601

RESNICK, MYRON J., insurance company executive, lawyer; b. Louisville, July 13, 1931; s. Harry C. and Sybil G. (Glick) R.; m. Alicia M. Ward, Dec. 16, 1967; children—Hugh, Clay, David. B.S. in Econs., U. Pa., 1953; J.D., U. Mich., 1956. Various positions Allstate Ins. Co., Northbrook, Ill., 1959-88, sr. v.p., treas. bd. dirs., 1989—; chmn. bd. Federated Ins. Co. Ltd. (U.K.), Sale, Cheshire, Eng., 1979-81; dir. Allstate Ins. Co. Ltd. (U.K.), Sale; pres. Allstate Investment Mgmt. Co. Mem. Chgo. exec. com. Anti-Defamation League, 1975—; bd. dirs. Chgo. Urban League, 1987—, St. Scholastica High Sch., Chgo., 1977-79; trustee George Williams Coll., Downers Grove, Ill., 1981—. Served with U.S. Army, 1956-58. Mem. ABA, Chgo. Bar Assn., Ill. Bar Assn., Assn. Life Ins. Counsel, Chgo. Mortgage Attys. Assn. (bd. dirs. 1965-75). Club: Reform (London). Office: Allstate Ins Co Allstate Pla Northbrook IL 60062

RESNIK, DAVID ALAN, manufacturing company executive; b. Providence, R.I., June 9, 1956; s. Sol Leon and Esther (Petersohn) R.; m. Susan Winoker, Aug. 12, 1979; children: Joshua Michael, Alissa Joy. BA, U. Pa., 1978, MS, 1979. Cert. PADL scuba instr. Gen. mgr. Emblem & Badge, Inc., Providence, 1980—; exec. v.p. Emblem & Badge, Inc., 1986-87, pres., 1987-88; pres. North Main Industries, Inc. (formerly Westcalind Corp.), Providence, 1987-88; dir. Emblem & Badge, Inc., Westcalind Corp. Contbr. articles to profl. jours. Mem. Soc. Econ. Paleontologists and Mineralogists, Internat. Orgn. Paleobotany, Paleontol. Soc., Bot. Soc. Am., Boston Computer Soc., Paleontol. Soc. Jewish. Office: Emblem & Badge Inc PO Box 6226 Providence RI 02940

RESNIK, FRANK EDWARD, tobacco company executive; b. Pleasant Unity, Pa., Oct. 14, 1928; s. Vincent and Augusta (Mauser) R.; m. Elizabeth Patterson, June 21, 1952; children—David A., Mary Ann, Anne Margaret. B.S. in Chemistry, St. Vincent Coll., Latrobe, Pa., 1952; M.S., U. Richmond, Va., 1955; D.Sc. (hon.), St. Vincent Coll., 1985. With Philip Morris Inc., 1952—; v.p. ops. adminstrn., then v.p. tobacco ops. Philip Morris Inc., N.Y.C., 1976-80; corp. v.p., exec. v.p. tobacco tech. group Philip Morris Inc., 1980-81, pres. tobacco tech. group, 1981-84; pres., chief exec. officer Philip Morris U.S.A., 1984-89, chmn., 1989—; dir. Philip Morris Inc., Philip Morris Cos.; bd. dirs., chmn. exec. com. Tobacco Inst., 1985—; bd. dirs. Nat. Tobacco Edn. Inst., 1985—. Author numerous papers in field. Bd. dirs. Benedictine High Sch., Richmond, Va., 1965-67; mem. St. Edwards Sch. Bd., Richmond, 1972-75; bd. assocs. U. Richmond, 1986—; bd. dirs. Found. for State Legislatures, 1986—. Served with AUS, 1946-48, 51. Recipient Gold Ring Merit award Philip Morris Inc., 1972, Jewel Ring award Philip Morris Cos., 1986, Horatio Alger Award, 1988; named Letterman of Distinction St. Vincent Coll., 1974. Mem. Am. Chem. Soc., AAAS, N.Y. Acad. Scis., Am. Inst. Chemists. Roman Catholic. Club: Innis Arden Country (Greenwich, Conn.). Home: 341 Riverside Ave Riverside CT 06878 Office: Philip Morris USA 120 Park Ave New York NY 10017

RESO, ANTHONY, geologist; b. London, Eng., Aug. 10, 1934; s. Harry and Marion (Gerth) R.; came to U.S., 1940, naturalized, 1952. A.B., Columbia Coll., N.Y.C., 1954; M.A., Columbia U., 1955; postgrad. U. Cin., 1956-57; Ph.D. (fellow) Rice U., 1960; postgrad. Grad. Sch. Bus. U. Houston, 1964-68. Instr. geology Queens Coll., Flushing, N.Y., 1954; geologist Atlantic Richfield Corp., Midland, Tex., 1955-56; asst. prof. geology and curator invertebrate paleontology Pratt Mus., Amherst (Mass.) Coll., 1959-62; staff research geologist Tenneco Oil Co., Houston, 1962-86; geol. mgr. Peak Prodn. Co., Houston, 1986—, v.p., 1988—. Cons. in geol. research Tenn. Gas and Oil Co., 1960-61; lectr. U. Houston, 1962-65; vis. prof. Rice U., 1980; mem. bd. advisers Gulf Univs. Research Corp., Galveston, Tex., 1967-75, chmn., 1968-69; dir. Stewardship Properties, Houston, 1968—; cons. Gulf Coast Geol. Library, Inc., 1987— . Recipient research grants Am. Assn. Petroleum Geologists, 1958, 59, Geol. Soc. Am., 1958, Eastman Fund, 1962; NSF fellow, 1959. Fellow Geol. Soc. Am. (com. investments 1984—, chmn. 1985—), AAAS; mem. Am. Assn. Petroleum Geologists (life, com. convs. 1977-83, chmn. 1980-83, gen. chmn. nat. conv. 1979, com. on investments 1982-88, chmn. com. group ins. 1986-88, treas. 1986-88; Disting. service award 1985), Paleontol. Soc., Soc. Econ. Paleontologists and Mineralogists, Paleontol. Research Instn., Tex. Acad. Sci., Houston Geol. Soc. (v.p. 1973-75, pres. 1975-76, chmn. constn. revision com. 1981; Disting. service award 1985), English-Speaking Union U.S. (dir. Houston chpt. 1978—, v.p. 1982-88), Sigma Xi, Sigma Gamma Epsilon, Beta Theta Pi. Episcopalian. Contbr. profl. jours. Home: 1801 Huldy Houston TX 77019 Office: care Peak Prodn Co PO Box 130785 Houston TX 77219-0785

RESTER, GEORGE G., architect, painter, sculptor; b. Ponchatoula, La., Oct. 5, 1923; s. Kelly Caldwell Rester and Myra Vira (Adams) Smith; m. Virginia Wilhelmena, June 25, 1955; children: Gina Louise, Taira Elizabeth, Licia Therese. Student, U.S. Army Engring. Sch., Ft. Belvoir, Va., 1943, Soulé Coll., 1945-48, Delgado Tech. Inst., 1949-50, Art Ctr. Coll. Design, 1961-62. Registered architect, La., Calif., Fla., Colo., N.Y., Ariz., Tex., N.J., Mich., Minn., Wash., N.Mex. Architect, designer, draftsman various firms, New Orleans, 1953-60; pvt. practice architecture Culver City, Calif., 1960-61; project architect Welton Beckett Architect, Beverly Hills, Calif., 1961-64; chief architect, dir. archtl. design and prodn. Walt Disney Imagineers, Glendale, Calif., 1965-71, 76-87; sr. prin. engr. Ralph M. Parsons Engring. Co., Pasadena, Calif., 1973-76; prin. George G. Rester Architect & Assocs., Rolling Hills Estates, Calif., 1987—; founder, pres., chief exec. officer New Visions Resorts Inc., Rolling Hills Estates, 1987—. Prin. works include Theme Park, New Orleans Sq., Disneyland, 1965, Destination Resort and Theme Park (internat. accolades 1987), Walt Disney World, Fla., 1967, Resort Community (internat. accolades 1987), E.P.C.O.T. at World Disney World, 1982, Theme Park (Calif. and nat. accolades, 1983), Disneyland, 1983, Theme Park , Tokyo Disneyland, Japan, 1983. Served as pfc. C.E., U.S. Army Engrs., 1943-45, ETO, Africa, Mid. East. Mem. AIA, Internat. Platform Assn., Smithsonian Instn., New Orleans Amateur Artists Soc. (founding pres. 1940-42). Republican. Roman Catholic. Home and Office: 26337 Dunwood Rd Rolling Hills Estates CA 90274

RESTIVO, ALPHONSE CHARLES, educator, consultant; b. N.Y.C., May 2, 1936; s. Arthur and Jeanette (Speciale) R.; m. Diane Cassella, July 7, 1963; children: Kenneth Arthur, Andrew Thomas. BA, Coll. New Rochelle, 1984; MA, Goddard Coll., 1985. Market devel. mgr. Rexham Corp., Charlotte, N.C., 1974-78; nat. accounts mgr. Avery Internat., North Brunswick, N.J., 1978-82, sales devel. mgr., 1982-88; tng. dir. Avery Internat., Pasadena, Calif., 1985—; bd. dirs. Rx Surgical Svcs., N.Y. Trustee Bd. of Edn., Eastchester, N.Y., 1975-78, Eastchester Pub. Library, 1986—; chmn. pub. adminstrn. curriculum adv. bd., Westchester (N.Y.) Community Coll., 1986—; dist. leader Rep. Party 38th Election Dist., Eastchester, 1986—. Served with USAF, 1958-62, Germany. Mem. Packaging Inst., Sales Exec. Club of N.Y. program com. 1984—), Am. Mgmt. Assn. Republican. Roman Catholic. Lodge: Kiwanis (pres. Eastchester club 1981-82, La Canada, Calif. club bd. dirs. 1987—). Home: 4338 Oakwood Ave La Canada CA 91011 Office: Avery Internat Corp 777 E Foothill Blvd Azusa CA 91702

RESTIVO, RAYMOND M., health association executive, public health consultant; b. Chgo., Aug. 19, 1934; s. Frank M. and Angeline (Franzone) R.; children: Laura, Maria, Mark, Susan, Steven, John, Tony, Matthew. BSA, Loyola U., Chgo., 1956; cert. pub. health adminstrn. U. Ill., 1968; CAE, 1978. Adminstrv. asst. to pres. of S.K. Culver Co., Chgo., 1954-59; projects coordinator Chgo. Heart Assn., 1959-66, exec. dir., 1973—; pub. health adminstr. Chgo. Bd. Health, 1966-73, mem. adv. com., 1967-73, mem. editorial rev. com. for newsletter, 1968-73; cons. community health to various pub., vol. and ofcl. health agys., 1962—; del. to Pub. Service Inst. of City of Chgo., 1973; notary pub., Cook County (Ill.), 1971—; mem. oral bd. examiners for cardiovascular technologist, City of Chgo. Civil Service Commn., 1971-73. Sec. Morris Fishbein, Jr. Meml. Fund, 1973—; mem. Zoning Bd. Appeals, Forest Park, Ill., 1964-68; mem. Health Services Task Force, Oak Park, Ill., 1974-75; bd. dirs. Chgo. Health Research Found., 1976—, vice chmn., 1985—; mem. Planning Com. 4th Nat. Congress Quality of Life AMA, 1977-78. Recipient Meritorious Service award Village of Oak Park, 1975, Recognition award Chgo. Pub. Schs., 1982, Founders award Nat. Am. Italian Sports Hall of Fame, 1987. Mem. Am. Pub. Health Assn., Ill. Pub. Health Assn. (mem. policy com. 1971-73, mem. health issues com. 1972-73), Am. Heart Assn. Profl. Staff Soc., Am. Soc. Assn. Execs., Chgo. Soc. Assn. Execs. (Samuel B. Shapiro award 1986), Am. Mgmt. Assn., Nat. Assn. of Emergency Care Technicians, Epidemiology Club of Chgo., City of Chgo. Exec. Devel., Loyola U. Alumni Assns. Clubs: Tower, Univ. Office: 20 N Wacker Dr Chicago IL 60606

RETALLACK, DEBRA LEE, financial executive; b. Aurora, Colo., July 2, 1955; d. Leo George Edmund and Helen Marie (Cathcart) Fromme; m. Jack C. Retallack, May 12, 1974. Acct. Brinkerhof Co., Denver, 1975-78; office mgr. Sherwood Securities, Denver, 1978-80; trader J. Daniel Bell Securities, Denver, 1980-81; office mgr. Hawaiian Plantations, Honolulu, 1981-82, Office Products of Pacific, Honolulu, 1982-85; prin. Boardwalk Capital, Agoura Hills, Calif., 1987—; cons. Hawaii End. Fin. Svcs., Honolulu, 1985—. Mem. Profl. Women Hawaii, Powerful Women of Hawaii, NAFE, Kanehoe C. of C. Demcrat. Roman Catholic. Office: Bruce Wilson & Co Ltd 1750 Kalakaua #3103 Honolulu HI 96826

RETHORE, BERNARD GABRIEL, diversified company executive; b. Bklyn., May 22, 1941; s. Francis Joseph and Katharine Eunice (MacDwyer) R.; BA, Yale U., 1962; MBA, U. Pa., 1967; m. Marilyn Irene Watt, Dec. 1, 1962; children: Bernard Michael, Tara Jean, Kevin Watt, Alexandra Marie, Rebecca Ann, Christopher Philip, Abigail Lyn. Assoc., McKinsey & Co., Inc., Washington, 1967, then sr. assoc., 1973; v.p./gen. mgr. Greer div. Microdot, Inc., Darien, Conn., 1973-77, v.p. ops. connector group, 1977-78, pres. bus. devel. group, 1978-82, pres. fastening systems and sealing devices groups, 1982-84, pres. Microdot Industries, 1984-87, pres., chief exec. officer, 1988—; pres. Microdot Europe Ltd., 1984—; dir. Microdot Aerospace Ltd., 1982—, Ets Proner, S.A. 1984—; cons. U.S. Govt., UN. Mem. dean's adv. bd. Wharton Sch. Bus., U. Pa., 1972-80; chmn. Emmaus adv. bd. Fairfield Prep. Sch.-Lauralton Hall Acad., 1981-85; elected mem. bd. fin. Town of Westport, Conn., 1986—. Served to capt., inf., AUS, 1962-65. Decorated Bronze Star. Mem. Wharton Bus. Sch. Alumni Assn. (dir., pres.), Am. Mgmt. Assn. Clubs: Yale, Wharton Bus. Sch. (N.Y.C.); Union League (Chgo.); Faculty, U Pa. (Phila.); Landmark (Stamford). Home: 18 Crooked Mile Rd Westport CT 06880 Office: Microdot Industries 23 Old Kings Hwy S Darien CT 06820-4518

REUBER, GRANT LOUIS, banker; b. Mildmay, Ont., Can., Nov. 23, 1927; s. Jacob Daniel and Gertrude Catherine (Wahl) R.; m. Margaret Louise Julia Summerhayes, Oct. 21, 1951; children: Rebecca, Barbara, Mary. BA, U. Western Ont., 1950, LLD, 1985; AM, Harvard U., 1954, PhD, 1957; LLD, Wilfred Laurier U., 1983, Simon Fraser U., 1985; postgrad., Cambridge U., 1954-55. Mem. research dept. Bank Can., Ottawa, 1950-52; mem. Can. Dept. Finance, Ottawa, 1955-57; asst. prof. econ. U. Western Ont., London, 1957-59, assoc. prof., 1959-62, prof., 1962—, head dept., 1963-69, dean faculty Social Sci., 1969-74, mem. bd. govs., 1974-78, acad. v.p., provost, 1975-78; sr. v.p., chief economist Bank of Montreal, Que., Can., 1978-79; exec. v.p. Bank of Montreal, 1980-81, dep. chmn., dep. chief exec. officer, 1981-83, dir., mem. exec. com., 1981—, pres., chief operating officer, 1983-87, dep. chmn., 1987—; dep. minister fin. Can. 1979-80; mem. Royal Commn. Banking and Finance, Toronto, 1962-63; chmn. Ont. Econ. Council, 1973-78; cons. Can. Internat. Devel. Agy., 1968-69; hon. research assoc. econs. Harvard U., 1968-69; mem. internat. capital markets advisory com. Fed. Res. Bank N.Y.; cons. devel. centre OECD, 1969-72; bd. dirs. Harris Bancorp Inc., The Inst. Internat. Fin., Genstar Capital Corp.; mem. C.D. Howe Research Inst., also chmn. 1983-88; mem. adv. com. U. Western Ont. Sch. Bus. Author: (with R.J. Wonnacott) The Cost of Capital in Canada, 1961, (with R.E. Caves) Canadian Economic Policy and the Impact of International Capital Flows, 1970, Private Foreign Investment in Development, 1973, Canada's Political Economy, 1980; contbr. articles to profl. jours. Mem. Brit. N.Am. Com.; bd. dirs. Can. Opera Co.; bd. govs. Stratford Shakespearean Festival Found., 1985—. Decorated officer Order of Can. Fellow Royal Soc. Can. (bd. dirs.); mem. Can. Econs. Assn. (chmn. founding com. 1966-67, pres. 1967-68). Office: Bank of Montreal, 1st Bank Tower, 1st Canadian Pl, Toronto, ON Canada M5X 1A1

REULING, MICHAEL FREDERICK, supermarket company and real estate executive; b. Peoria, Ill., May 11, 1946; s. F.H. and Doris (Salzenstein) R.; m. Susan Ruth Morgan, Aug. 10, 1968; children—Jessica Sue, Jeremy Michael. B.A. in Econs., Carleton Coll.; J.D., U. Mich. Bar: Utah, Idaho, Tex., Fla. Assoc. Van Cott, Bagley, Cornwall & McCarthy, Salt Lake City, 1971-73; assoc. real estate Skaggs-Albertson's, Richardson, Tex., 1974-78; assoc. contracts Albertson's, Inc., Boise, Idaho, 1973-74, sr. v.p., gen. counsel, 1978-81, sr. v.p. real estate, 1981-86; exec. v.p. store devel. Albertson's, Inc., Boise, 1986—. Mem. Idaho State Bar Assn., Utah State Bar Assn., Fla. State Bar Assn., Tex. State Bar Assn. Office: Albertson's Inc PO Box 20 Boise ID 83726

REUM, W. ROBERT, financial executive; b. Oak Park, Ill., July 22, 1942; m. Sharon Milliken. BA, Yale U., 1964; JD, U. Mich., 1967; MBA, Harvard U., 1969. Dir. investment analysis City Investing Co., N.Y.C., 1969-72; v.p. corp fin. Mich. Nat. Corp., Bloomfield Hills, Mich., 1972-78; v.p., treas. White Motor Corp., Cleve., 1978-79; v.p. fin., chief fin. officer Lamson & Sessions, Cleve., 1980-82; v.p. fin., chief fin. officer The Interlake Corp., Oak Brook, Ill., 1982-88, exec. v.p., 1988—. Contbr. articles to Harvard Bus. Rev. Mem. Chgo. Golf Club, Chgo. Club. Office: Interlake Corp 701 Harger Rd Oak Brook IL 60521-1488

REUSS, LLOYD EDWIN ARMIN, automobile manufacturing company executive; b. Belleville, Ill., Sept. 22, 1936; s. Lawrence Phillip and Dorthea B. (Juenger) R.; m. Maurcine Kaye Bilderback, Aug. 10, 1957; children: Charlene Faye, Mark Lyle. B.S. in Mech. Engring., U. Mo., Rolla, 1957; grad. sr. exec. course, M.I.T., 1971. With Gen. Motors Corp., 1959—, chief engr., Buick Motor div., 1975-78, dir. engring., Chevrolet div., 1978-80, v.p., gen. mgr., Buick Motor div., 1980-84, v.p., group exec., Chevrolet, Pontiac, GM of Can., 1984-86, exec. v.p. N.Am. passenger cars, 1986—, exec. v.p. N.Am. automotive ops., 1987—; dir. Electronic Data Systems Corp., Tex. Trustee Lawrence Technol. U., Southfield, Mich., 1977—, Louisville Presbyn. Theol. Sem. Ky., 1985—, Vanderbilt U., Nashville, 1987—. Served with C.E. AUS, 1957-59. Mem. Soc. Automotive Engrs., Pi Tau Sigma, Tau Beta Pi. Presbyterian (elder). Office: GM Gen Motors Bldg 3044 W Grand Blvd Detroit MI 48202

REUSS, ROBERT PERSHING, telecommunications executive; b. Aurora, Ill., Mar. 23, 1918; s. George John and Mary Belle (Gorrie) R.; m. Mildred Louise Daly, Dec. 22, 1940 (dec. May 1985); children: Lynn Ann (Mrs. David Bohmer), Robert Cameron; m. Grace K. Brady, Aug. 28, 1986. BS, U. Ill., 1939; postgrad., Harvard U., 1943; MBA, U. Chgo., 1950; D Bus. Adminstrn., Blackburn Coll., 1976. Staff AT&T, 1955-58, asst. compt., 1958-59; v.p. Ill. Bell Tel. Co., 1959-72, dir., 1970-72; pres., chief exec. officer, dir. Centel Corp., Chgo., 1972-76, chmn., 1977-88, corp. dir., cons., 1988—; dir. Tellabs, Inc., Am. Nat. Bank and Trust Co., Chgo., Amsted Industries, Triangle Industries, Inc. Bd. dirs. Jr. Achievement Chgo., 1970-77, pres., 1971-73; bd. govs. Midwest Stock Exch.; trustee Rush-Presbyn.-St. Luke's Med. Ctr., Chgo., Blackburn Coll., 1963-83, Aurora U., 1986—, Lyric Opera, 1987—; bd. dirs. U. Ill. Found. Lt. (s.g.) USNR, 1943-46, PTO. Mem. Chgo. Assn. Commerce and Industry (bd. dirs. 1971-78), Phi Kappa Phi. Presbyterian (deacon, trustee). Clubs: Commercial, Mid-Am., Chicago, Economic (Chgo.); Chicago Golf (Wheaton, Ill.); Old Baldy (Saratoga, Wyo.); Ocean (Ocean Ridge, Fla.); Delray Beach Yacht, Country of Fla. (Delray Beach). Office: Centel Corp 2001 Spring Rd Ste 760 Oak Brook IL 60521

REVEL, GARY NEAL, music publishing executive; b. Florala, Ala., June 29, 1949; s. Leamon Curtise and Martha Marie (Mitchell) R.; m. Linda Marie Willis, Jan. 23, 1973; children: Gary Neal Jr., Curtise Leamon II, Mary Noel, Rebecca Ann, Elisabeth Marie, Sonny Americas. BA in Advanced Theology, Am. Bible Coll., Pineland, Fla., 1983. Pres., chief exec. officer Star City Records, Inc., Nashville, 1979-80; songwriter Milene-Opryland Music, Nashville, 1975—; owner, pub., songwriter Gary Revel Music, Hollywood, Calif., 1980—, Jongleur Music, Hollywood, 1983—; owner, chief exec. officer Top's Records, Hollywood, 1983—; pres., singer, performing artist Revel Mgmt., Canoga Park, Calif., 1987—; owner, chief exec. officer Top's Film Prodn., Canoga Park, Calif., 1988—; cons. Friends Indeed, Hollywood, 1980-84; record producer Top's Records, 1986—, recording artist, 1983—. Author: (novel) Midnight's Calling; (poems) The Poet's Fare, 1986, Wanderings, 1987; (play) And Then I Went Away, 1971; composer (songs) Treat America Like a Lady, 1982, Hollywood Star, 1986, I Know (We're Gonna Make It Love), 1988; (film soundtrack) Last of the American Hoboes, 1971. Founder Ams. for Worldwide Prison Reform, Hollywood Star Project, philanthropic effort to help children on streets of L.A.; bd. dirs. Citizens Com. for Civic Betterment; past scoutmaster Boy Scouts Am. Served with USN, 1967-69. Recipient Humanitarian award So. Calif. Motion Picture Council, Los Angeles Freedoms Day award Citizens Com. for Civic Betterment, Angel Victory cert. award and Angel Victory Patriotic award, Music and Performing Arts Angels. Named one of Outstanding Ams. under the age of 40 Esquire, 1984, 85. Mem. ASCAP, Am. Legion. Home and Office: 9015 Owensmouth Ave #106 Canoga Park CA 91304

REW, WILLIAM EDMUND, civil engineer; b. Corning, N.Y., Nov. 24, 1923; s. Robert James and Clara (Neal) R.; m. Jean Ella Ohls, Aug. 16, 1947 (dec.); children: Virginia Ann, Robert James, John Edward. BE, Yale U., 1954, M in Engring., 1955. Registered profl. engr., N.Y., Fla., Calif., Ill. Project engr. Texaco & Affiliate, USA and Saudi Arabia, 1955-62; sr. engr. Martin-Marietta Corp., Cape Kennedy, Fla., 1962-63, Chrysler Corp, Cape Kennedy, 1963-65, The Boeing Co., Cape Kennedy, 1965-70; project mgr. Brevard Engring. Co., Cape Canaveral, Fla., 1970-74; city engr. City of Vero Beach (Fla.), 1974-77; resident engr. Post, Buckley, Schuh & Jernigan, Miami, Fla., 1977-85; mgr. Keith & Schnars, P.A., West Palm Beach, Fla., 1985—. Active Dem. Party of Brevard County. 1st lt. U.S. Army, 1942-76, ATO. Scholar of 2d rank Yale U., 1953, grad. scholar, 1955. Fellow ASCE (chmn. Fla. ann conv. 1971, Engr. of Yr. 1974); mem. NSPE, Soc. Am. Mil. Engrs. (bd. dirs. 1982-83), Fla. Engring Soc. (chpt. pres. 1976), Yale Club, Browning Assn. Club. Home: 1605 US Hwy 1 Apt V3-204 Jupiter FL 33477 Office: Keith & Schnars PA 1660 Southern Blvd Ste H West Palm Beach FL 33406

REXINGER, DANIEL MICHAEL, retail company executive; b. Buffalo, Apr. 12, 1938; s. John Frank and Mary Cecil (Madigan) R.; m. Joan Elisabeth Fraser, Nov. 26, 1961; children: Robin Ann, Daniel Fraser. AS, U. Buffalo, 1957. V.p. Wards Co., Richmond, Va., 1966-71; sr. v.p. Circuit City, Richmond, 1971-80, exec. v.p., 1980—, also bd. dirs. Bd. dirs. Stony Point Sch., Richmond, 1980, Family & Children's Services. Served with U.S. Army, 1959-61. Republican. Episcopalian. Home: 3365 Cedar Grove Rd Richmond VA 23235 Office: Cir City Stores Inc 2040 Thalbro St Richmond VA 23230

REY, CARLOS RAUL, furniture company execuitve; b. Havana, Cuba, June 12, 1959; came to U.S., 1961; s. Carlos and Berta (Gomez) R.; m. Adelaida Artime, Feb. 2, 1985. Student in bus., Biscayne Coll., 1977-78, 1984. Prodn. cons. Capri Upholstery Corp., Miami, Fla., 1977-79; sec., treas. J.R.C. Mica Corp., Hallandale, Fla., 1979-80, pres., 1981—; pres. J.R.C. Furniture Mfg. Corp., 1987—; adminstrv. cons. Southeast Furniture Corp., Hallandale, 1984—. Counselor Renaissance Outreach Ctr., Miami, 1986. Recipient Young Disting. Leadership award Am. Biog. Inst., 1988. Mem. Fla. Assn. Furniture Mfrs. (youngest ever to be nominated for bd. dirs.). Republican. Home: 4925 Collins Ave # 12A Miami Beach FL 33140 Office: JRC Mfg Corp 11400 NW 36th Ave Miami FL 33167

REYES, RAMON VILLAREAL, venture capitalist; b. Iloilo, Philippines, Aug. 17, 1951; came to U.S., 1951; s. Cesar Potenciano and Elena (Villareal) R.; m. Diane Mary Scully, Dec. 11, 1976; children: Jonathan Alexander and Jaqueline Nicole (twins). BA magna cum laude, De LaSalle Coll., Manila, 1972; MBA, U. Mich., 1975. Project analyst Nat. Electrification Adminstrn., Manila, 1972-73; cons. Interactive Data Corp. (subs. Chase Bank), Boston and N.Y.C., 1976-77; dir. area mgr. Data Resources, Inc. (subs. McGraw Hill), Lexington, Mass., 1977-83; gen. ptnr. Nazem & Co.Pvt. Venture Capital, N.Y.C., 1984—; bd. dirs. Betagen Corp., Boston, Byvideo Inc., Sunnyvale, Calif., Cydrome, Inc., Milpitas, Calif., Spectranetics Corp., Colorado Springs, Colo., Dominion Venture Ptnrs., Inc., San Francisco. Office: Nazem & Co Madison Ave New York NY 10022

REYNAL, THOMAS DOUGLAS, electronics executive; b. Houston, Nov. 19, 1957; s. Thomas Jefferson and Dolores (Wactor) R. Student, Tex. A&M U., 1976-77; BBA in Fin., U. Houston, 1981. Engr. Ross Hills Controls, Houston, 1978-79, acct., 1979-81; chief exec. officer Tex. Security, Inc., Houston, 1981-82; pres. Reynal Controls Corp., Houston, 1982-86; also bd. dirs. Reynal Controls Corp.; v.p. C&K Systems, San Jose, Calif., 1986—. Republican. Methodist. Home: 834 Ivy Wall Dr Houston TX 77079 Office: C & K Systems Inc 580 Westlake Park Houston TX 77079

REYNOLDS, A. WILLIAM, manufacturing company executive; b. Columbus, Ohio, June 21, 1933; s. William Morgan and Helen Hibbard (McCray) R.; m. Joanne D. McCormick, June 12, 1953; children: Timothy M., Morgan Reynolds Brigham, Mary M. AB in Econs., Harvard U., 1955; MBA, Stanford U., 1957. Pres. Crawford Door Co., Detroit, 1959-66; staff asst. to treas TRW Inc., Cleve., 1957-59, asst. to exec. v.p. automotive group, 1966-67, v.p. automotive aftermarket group, 1967-70, exec. v.p. indsl. and replacement sector, 1971-81, exec. v.p. automotive worldwide sector, 1981-84; pres. GenCorp, Akron, Ohio, 1984-85, pres., chief exec. officer, 1985—, chmn., chief exec. officer, 1987—, also bd. dirs.; bd. dirs. Soc. Corp., Cleve., Eaton Corp., Cleve., Boise (Idaho) Cascade Corp.; mem. dean's adv. council Stanford (Calif.) U. Grad. Sch. Bus., 1981-88. Chmn. United Way-Red Cross of Summit County, Ohio, 1987; trustee Univ. Hosps. of Cleve., 1984—, chmn., 1987—. Mem. Soc. Automotive Engrs., Rubber Mfrs. Assn. (bd. dirs., exec. com. 1985—), Bus. Roundtable, Council on Fgn. Relations. Episcopalian. Clubs: Kirtland Country (Willoughby, Ohio); Union (Cleve.); Rolling Rock (Ligonier, Pa.); John's Island (Vero Beach, Fla.); Pepper Pike (Cleve.); Harvard (N.Y.). Office: GenCorp Inc 1 General St Akron OH 44329

REYNOLDS, CARL ROBERT, lawyer; b. Syracuse, N.Y., Feb. 22, 1948; s. Robert Earl and Norma Osborn (Williams) R.; m. Betty Ann Tomchik, Jan. 17, 1970; children: Christopher Robert, Diane Elizabeth. BS in Acctg., U. Rochester, 1969; JD, U. Buffalo, 1974. Bar: N.Y. 1975, Fla. 1977. Acct. Leonard A. Dopkins & Co., Buffalo, 1970-71; ptnr. Kloner, Reynolds, Conover & Mitrano, P.C., Rochester, N.Y., 1976-77, Mitrano & Reynolds, Rochester, N.Y., 1978-80; pvt. practice Rochester, N.Y., 1980—; assoc. producer of motion pictures; pres./treas. New Sky Communications, Inc., 1984—; bd. dirs. First Nat. Bank of Rochester, 1977—. contbr. articles to profl. jours. Mem. N.Y. State Bar Assn., Monroe County Bar Assn., Fla. Bar Assn. Republican. Presbyterian. Office: New Sky Communications Inc One E Main St Suite 910 Rochester NY 14614

REYNOLDS, DAVID PARHAM, metals company executive; b. Bristol, Tenn., June 16, 1915; s. Richard S. and Julia L. (Parham) R.; m. Margaret Harrison, Mar. 25, 1944; children: Margaret A., Julia P., Dorothy H. Student, Princeton U. With Reynolds Metals Co., Louisville, 1937—, salesman, 1937-41, asst. mgr. aircraft parts div., 1941-44, asst. v.p., 1944-46, v.p., 1946-58, exec. v.p., 1958-69, exec. v.p., gen. mgr., 1969-75, vice chmn., chmn. exec. com., 1975-76, chief exec. officer, 1976-86, chmn. bd., 1986-88, chmn. emeritus, 1988—; chmn. bd. dirs. Eskimo Pie Corp. Trustee Lawrenceville Sch. (N.J.), U. Richmond; bd. dirs. United Negro Coll. Fund.; mem. Bus. Com. for the Arts. Mem. AIA (hon.), Primary Aluminum Inst., Aluminum Assn. (past chmn.). Office: Reynolds Metals Co 6601 Broad Street Rd Richmond VA 23261

REYNOLDS, DON WILLIAM, geologist; b. Centerburg, Ohio, Apr. 6, 1926; s. Loren William and Charlotte Lonas (Hunt) R.; m. Betty Jeannette Spears, Sept. 4, 1953; children: Don William, Jr., Richard Allen, Brenda Gay. BS, Ohio State U., 1952. Registered profl. geologist, Calif. Mgr., Geochem. Engring. Inc., Midland, Tex., 1950-52; geologist Union Oil Co. Calif., Midland, 1953-66, dist. exploration geologist, Anchorage, 1966-68, area geologist, Bakersfield, Calif., 1968-76, dist. devel. geologist, Ventura, Calif., 1976-86; dist. devel. geologist mid-continent dist., Oklahoma City, 1986—. Pres. Park Stockdale Civic Assn., Bakersfield, 1970, Clearpoint Home Owners Assn., Ventura, 1980-86; chmn. Kern County Freeway Assn. Bakersfield, 1970-73. Served wtih USAF, 1944-45. Mem. Am. Assn. Petroleum Geologists, West Tex. Geol. Soc. (sec. 1965-66), Kans.-Okla. Oil and Gas Assn. (nomenclature com. 1987—), San Joaquin Geol. Soc. (treas. 1974-75), Am. Assn. Petroleum Geologists (sec. Pacific sect. 1975-76). Republican. Methodist. Home: 4409 St George Dr Oklahoma City OK 73120 Office: UNOCAL 4005 NW Expwy Rm 600 Oklahoma City OK 73116

REYNOLDS, DONNA ALIX, real estate broker; b. Newport, R.I., Jan. 9, 1945; d. Andrew F. and Mildred (Sack) Alix; m. Ernest W. Zirkle, Feb. 25, 1976 (div. 1983); children: Terry Conover, Kelli Webb, Joan L. Webb; m. Samuel M. Reynolds. Cert. in cosmotology, Vineland Sch. of Beauty Coll., 1983. Lic. real estate broker, N.J. Office mgr. Wilwynn Animal Hosp., Bridgeton, N.J., 1970-81; co-owner, cosmotologist Ebony-Ivory Hair Salon, Northfield, N.J., 1982-85; cosmotologist Creativity Salon, Brigantine, N.J., 1984—; real estate broker Century 21 Parade of Homes, Absecon, N.J., 1985-86, chmn. pub. relations, 1987-88. Active South Jersey Cancer Fund, 1988; charity chmn. Easter Seal Soc., 1987-88. Mem. Atlantic Co. Bd. Realtors (chmn. pub. relations 1988), ACCBOR (chairperson pub. rels. 1989—). Democrat. Methodist. Home: 804 Millbridge Ct Smithville NJ 08201

REYNOLDS, GINGER FAY, healthcare company executive; b. Jackson, Miss., July 14, 1950; d. Neville Scott and Mabel Fay (Covington) R. Diploma, Miss. Gulf Coast Jr. Coll. (formerly Perkinston (Miss.) Jr. Coll.), 1969, Bates Bus. Coll., 1970; BSBA in Acctg., U. So. Miss., 1973. With Stallworth Furniture Co., Pascagoula, Miss., 1969-71; asst. sec. U. So. Miss., Hattiesburg, 1972-73; office acct. South Miss. Home Health Found. Inc. (formerly S. Miss. Home Health and Rehab. Agy. Inc.), Hattiesburg, 1973, comptr., 1973—, sec., 1976—, comptr., sec.-treas., 1987—; sec.-treas. Health Care Enterprises Inc., Hattiesburg, 1985—. Vol. Am. Cancer Soc., Hattiesburg, 1984, 85. Mem. U. So. Miss. Alumni Assn., Miss. Gulf Coast Jr. Coll. Alumni Assn. Republican. Baptist. Office: South Miss Home Health Inc PO Box 16929 Hattiesburg MS 39404-6929

REYNOLDS, HELEN ELIZABETH, service executive; b. Minerva, N.Y., Aug. 30, 1925; d. Henry James and Margurite Catherine (Gallagher) McNally; m. Theodore Laurence Reynolds, Feb. 27, 1948; children: Laurence McBride, David Scott, William Herbert. BA, SUNY, Albany, 1967; MA, Union Coll., Schenectady, N.Y., 1971. Owner, mgr. Schafer Studio, Schenectady, 1970-73; co-owner, v.p. Reynolds Chalmers Inc., Schenectady, 1971—; program coordinator Schenectady County, 1980-81; adminstr. Wellspring House of Albany, N.Y., 1981—; cons., examiner N.Y. State Civil Service, Albany, 1971-81; mem. adv. council SBA, Washington, 1978-80. Mem. planning bd. Town of Niskayuna, N.Y., 1977-81, town councilwoman, 1986—; co-chairwoman Great N.E. Festival on the Mohawk River, 1989; bd. dirs. HAVEN, Schenectady, 1978-81; bd. dirs. Schenectady YWCA. Named Woman Vision, 1986, 87, Today's Woman, 1987, Schenectady YWCA. Mem. Antique and Classic Boat Soc. (bd. dirs. 1974—, Disting. Service award 1979), Assn. Adminstrs. Independent Housing (pres. 196-88), Inst. Real Estate Mgmt., Am. Mgmt. Assn., Lake George (N.Y.) Assn. Club: N.Y. State Women's Press. Lodge: Zonta (pres. 1981-82). Home: 2262 Cayuga Rd Schenectady NY 12309 Office: Wellspring House Albany Washington Ave Extension Albany NY 12203

REYNOLDS, JACK MASON, manufacturing company executive; b. East Orange, N.J., Jan. 27, 1927; s. Frederick Lynn and Bernice (Mason) R.; m. Rhea Evans, June 14, 1949; children: Jeff, Jennifer Reynolds Brickley, Mark. B.S., U.S. Mcht. Marine Acad., 1948. With Bendix Corp., Southfield, Mich., 1948-83, exec. v.p. automotive group, 1979-80, pres. automotive group, 1980-83; pres. automotive sector, exec. v.p. Allied-Signal Inc., Morristown, N.J., 1983—; dir. NBD Bancorp Inc. Bd. dirs. Detroit Renaissance, 1983—, Citizens Research Council of Mich., 1983—, Detroit Econ. Growth Corp., 1983—, Detroit Symphony Orch., 1983—. Served with USNR, 1944-48. Mem. Soc. Automotive Engrs. Club: Renaissance (Detroit).

REYNOLDS, JAMES, management consultant; b. Detroit, Mar. 22, 1941; s. Richard James and Esther (Nikander) R.; m. Joanne M.J. B.A. in Econs., NYU, 1965, postgrad., 1965-66. Cons. to pres. Rothrock, Reynolds & Reynolds Inc., N.Y.C., 1966-70; sr. v.p. health, med. div. Booz, Allen & Hamilton, N.Y.C., 1970-80; pres. J.X. Reynolds & Co., Inc. (mgmt. cons.), N.Y.C., 1981—; developer 1978, orgn. concepts for multihosp. systems, 1979, consolidation methods for hosp. industry, 1982, DRG-based planning methods, 1983, product line mgmt. for hosps., managed care contracting strategies, 1988; chmn. bd. J.X. Reynolds Fine Arts, Ltd., 1979—; past dir. Booz, Allen & Hamilton, Inc.; dir. Health Center Mgmt. Inst.; faculty mem. Commn. Profl. and Hosp. Activities; mem. Shared Services Com. of Regional Med. Program, N.Y.C., 1976-78; bd. dirs. Health Center Mgmt. Inst., Richmond, Va., 1977; mem. health adv. bd. Hunter Coll., 1980—, Battelle Inst. Editorial bd. Physicians Fin. News. Recipient NYU Founders award, 1965. Mem. Am. Pub. Health Assn., Am. Mgmt. Assn., Assn. Am. Med. Colls., Am. Hosp. Assn., Hosp. Mgmt. Systems Soc., Hosp. Fin. Mgmt. Assn., Asia Soc., Phi Beta Kappa, Mus. Modern Art, Met. Mus. Art, Met. Opera Guild (N.Y.C.). Episcopalian. Home and Office: 333 E 51st St New York NY 10022 also: 100 Spear St 18th Fl San Francisco CA 94105 also: 1825 I St NW Washington DC 20006

REYNOLDS, KATHRYN ANNE, accountant; b. Kalamazoo, July 31, 1957; d. Ronald Louis and Patricia Anne (Mathers) Blaul; m. Lee Michael Reynolds, Aug. 4, 1979; children: Daniel, Stephani, Joseph. Student, McHenry Community Coll., 1975-76, Knox Coll., 1976-77; BBA in Acctg. magna cum laude, U. Wis.-Whitewater, 1979. CPA, Wis. Intern Arthur Anderson & Co., Milw., 1979; mem. staff Baillies, Denson, Erickson & Smith, CPAs, Lake Geneva, Wis., 1980-82, sr. acct., 1983-84; contr. Rubidell Recreation Inc., Elkhorn, Wis., 1984—. Rotary exchange student, France, 1973-74. Mem. AICPA, NAFE, Wis. Inst. CPAs, Nat. Assn. Accts., Beta Alpha Psi, Phi Gamma Nu. Home: Powers Lake Rd Rte 1 PO Box 585 Genoa City WI 53128 Office: Rubidell Recreation Inc 39 N Washington St Elkhorn WI 53121

REYNOLDS, LEO THOMAS, electronics company executive; b. Mpls., May 24, 1945; s. Donald Charles and Elizabeth (Graham) R.; m. Betty Gail Herrington, Aug. 8, 1966 (div. Apr. 1978); children: William, Nathan; m. Diana Frances Boyd, Feb. 26, 1982; children: Jeffrey, Daniel. BSEE, U. Iowa, 1972; postgrad. in bus., Mankato State U., 1972-74. Registered profl. engr., S.D. Mech. draftsman John Deere Co., Dubuque, Iowa, 1970-71; engring. supr. 3M Co., New Ulm, Minn., 1972-76; supt. Litton Microwave, Sioux Falls, S.D., 1976-80; founder, pres., chief exec. officer Electronic Systems, Inc., Sioux Falls, 1980—. Editor Transit mag., 1972. Mem. Sioux Falls Devel. Found., 1986—. With USAF, 1963-67. Mem. Nat. Soc. Profl. Engrs., Surface Mount Tech. Assn., Inst. Packaging Electronics Cirs., Sioux Falls C. of C. (leadership trainer). Republican. Office: Electronic Systems Inc 600 E 50th St PO Box 5013 Sioux Falls SD 57117

REYNOLDS, PAUL GEORGE, mortgage banking executive; b. Chgo., July 24, 1922; s. Jay Joseph and Mae Ellen (Donohue) R.; m. Sheila Marie Taaffe, Apr. 15, 1944;children: Paul Jr., Shaun D., Christopher J., Tracy M., Damien P., Regina C., Sheila M., Martha V., Molly J., Jill E., Peggy E., Siobhan L. BA, U. Chgo., 1946, MBA in Fin., 1949. Asst. to pres. Chas Ringer Co., Chgo., 1945-52; v.p. Dovenmuehle, Inc., Chgo., 1952-62; chmn., chief exec. officer McElvain-Reynolds Co., Chgo., 1962-86; chmn. Curto Reynold Oelerich Inc., Chgo., 1971-86; chmn., chief exec. officer Mid-Continental Realty Corp., Chgo., 1973-86; instr. mortgage banking schs. Mich. State U., Northwestern U. Bd. dirs. Cath. Charities, Chgo., 1962—, Grant Park Concerts Soc., Chgo., 1983—. Served to 1st lt. USAF, 1942-45. Fellow Nat. Assn. Cert. Mortgage Bankers; mem. Ill. Mortgage Bankers Assn. (pres. 1970—), Mortgage Bankers Assn. Am., Chgo. Mortgage Bankers Assn., Nat. Soc. Real Estate Fin., Mortgage Bankers Legion (hon. life). Republican. Roman Catholic. Clubs: Chgo. Athletic Assn., Beverly Country (Chgo.); Loxahatchee (Jupiter, Fla.). Office: McElvain-Reynolds Co 55 E Monroe St Chicago IL 60603

REYNOLDS, RICHARD ALBEE, JR., marketing professional; b. Reading, Pa., Aug. 11, 1956; s. Richard Albee and Anne (Vernon) R.; m. Katharine Anne McGlinn, July 11, 1981; 1 child, Douglas Richard. BA, Denison U., 1978; MBA, Ga. State U., 1981. Cons. Henry Sherry Assocs., Atlanta, 1981-82; mktg. cons. Warner Annex Satellite Entertainment Co./Showtime, Atlanta, 1982-84, BCI Consulting Group, Atlanta, 1984—. Mem. The Planning Forum, Advanced Tech. Devel. Inst. (co-chair Atlanta conf. 1989). Office: BCI Consulting Group 1430 W Peachtree St Atlanta GA 30309

REYNOLDS, RICHARD BURKE, real estate developer, accountant; b. Mpls., Feb. 5, 1957; s. Thomas Burke and Particia (Pierce) R.; m. Suzanne Odom Reynolds, July 11, 1981; 1 child, Caroline Claire. BS in Acctg., Auburn U., 1979. CPA, Ga. Acct. Cooper & Lybrand, Atlanta, 1979-87, Cushman & Wakefield, Atlanta, 1987—. Mem. Am. Inst. CPA's, Ga. Soc. CPA's. Methodist. Home: 235 Hampstead Ct Duluth GA 30136 Office: Cushman & Wakefield 1201 W Peachtree St Atlanta GA 30303

REYNOLDS, ROBERT HARRISON, export company executive; b. Mpls., Sept. 6, 1913; s. Clarence H. and Helen (Doyle) R.; student pub. schs., Vinton, Iowa; m. Gladys Marie Gaster, Apr. 7, 1934; 1 dau., Shirley Anne (Mrs. Frank S. Potestio); m. 2d, Viola E. Shimel, June 26, 1982. Export sales mgr., rolled products sales mgr. Colo. Fuel & Iron Corp., Denver, 1938-46; pres. Rocky Mountain Export Co., Inc., Denver, 1941—; dir. Electromedics, Inc. Club: Denver. Home: 580 S Clinton St Denver CO 80231 Office: Rocky Mountain Export 11111 Mississippi Ave Aurora CO 80012

REYNOLDS, ROBERT LOUIS, financial services executive; b. San Francisco, Nov. 5, 1939; s. James Clinton and Betty (Harris) R.; m. Sandra Benvenuto, June 14, 1980. B.B.S., U. Calif.-Berkeley, 1961. Sr. v.p. Chrysler Capital Corp., Greenwich, Conn., 1975—; also dir. Mem. Am. Mgmt. Assn., Am. Assn. Equipment Lessors, Southwest Area Conn. Industry Assn. (advisor). Club: Burning Tree Country (Greenwich). Office: Chrysler Capital Corp 51 Weaver St Greenwich CT 06836

REYNOLDS, RUSSELL SEAMAN, JR., recruiting company executive; b. Greenwich, Conn., Dec. 14, 1931; s. Russell Seaman and Virginia Dare (Carter) R.; m. Deborah Ann Toll, July 21, 1956; children: Russell Seaman III, Jeffrey Toll, Deborah Chase. B.A., Yale U., 1954; postgrad., NYU, 1958-61. Asst. v.p. Nat. div. J.P. Morgan & Co., Inc. Morgan Guaranty Trust Co. of N.Y., 1957-66; ptnr. William H. Clark Assocs., Inc., N.Y.C., 1966-69; founder, pres. Russell Reynolds Assocs., Inc., N.Y.C., 1969-71, chmn. bd., 1971—; bd. dirs. Oppenheimer Mgmt. Corp.; past adv. dir. Merrill Lynch Capital Ptnrs. Trustee Westminister Sch., Hotchkiss Schs., Hurricane Island Outward Bound Sch., Internat. House; trustee, life mem. Naval War Coll. Found.; mem. Greater N.Y. adv. bd. Salvation Army; chmn. George Bush for Pres. Fin. Com., Conn., 1987-88. Served to 1st lt., SAC USAF, 1954-57. Mem. Greenwich Hist. Soc. (trustee), Foreign Policy Assn. (bd. dirs.), Pilgrims, Assn. of Exec. Recruiting Cons. (past adv. dir.). Clubs: Round Hill, N.Y. Yacht, Indian Harbor Yacht, Links, Yale, River Club, Mill Reef, Tarrantine, Amateur Ski of N.Y. Office: Russell Reynolds Assocs Inc 200 Park Ave New York NY 10166

REYNOLDS, SCOTT WALTON, banker; b. Summit, N.J., July 15, 1941; s. Clark Leonard and Shirley (Hill) R.; m. Margaret Ann Johnson, July 5, 1969; children: Jane, Amy, David. B.A., Trinity Coll., Hartford, Conn., 1963; M.B.A., Harvard U., 1965. Sr. v.p. fin. control group, mem. asset and liability com. Bankers Trust Co., N.Y.C., 1967—; dir. Bankers Internat. Corp., N.Y.C., 1980-85; pres., bd. dirs. B.T. Securities Co., N.Y.C., 1985-88. Chmn. fund campaign Montclair (N.J.) ARC, 1974; chmn. bus. and fraternal group Montclair Bicentennial Com., 1976; bd. fellow Trinity Coll., 1982-88. 1st lt. U.S. Army, 1965-67. Recipient 150th Anniversary Trinity Coll., 1978, Alumni medal for Excellence, 1988. Mem. Montclair Jaycees (treas. 1973), Trinity Coll. Alumni Assn. N.Y. (pres. 1972-73). Episcopalian. Club: Harvard (N.Y.C.). Office: Bankers Trust Co 280 Park Ave New York NY 10017

REYNOLDS, SIDNEY RAE, editorial director; b. Alliance, Nebr., June 27, 1956; d. Harold Edward and Dolores Jean (Bestol) James; m. Eddie Ellis Reynolds, May 27, 1975; 1 child, Ashley Dawn. BAgr, Kans. State U., 1977. Asst. editor Harvest Pub. Co., Lansing, Mich., 1977-78, assoc. editor, 1978-80; assoc. editor Harvest Pub. Co., Topeka, 1980-82; editor Specialized Agrl. Publs., Raleigh, N.C., 1982-88, editorial dir., 1984-88; rep. NCH Corp., Raleigh, N.C., 1988—. Contbr. articles to profl. jours. Advisor Episcopal Youth Group, Wake Forest, N.C., 1986—, Raleigh, N.C., 1987—. Named Writer of Yr., Harvest Pub. Co., 1978. Mem. Am. Agrl. Editors Assn., Women in Communications (bd. dirs. 1978-79), Soc. Profl. Journalists (reorgnl. chairperson 1985-88), Sigma Delta Chi. Clubs: Spurs (nat. v.p. 1976-78), Agrl. Communicators (pres. Manhatten, Kans. chpt. 1976). Home: 512 Brookfield Rd Raleigh NC 27615 Office: Specialized Agrl Publs 3000 Highwoods Suite 300 Raleigh NC 27625

REYNOLDS, SUSAN ELIZABETH, marketing professional; b. Carlisle, Pa., Dec. 12, 1950; d. Harold Kenneth and Elizabeth (Holman) R. BS, Western Mich. U., 1973, postgrad., 1974-75. Systems engr. IBM, Lansing, Mich., 1977-81; regional mktg. support rep. IBM, Detroit, 1982-83, systems engring. mgr., 1984-85, area systems support mgr., 1985-86, resource programs mgr., 1986-87, area mktg. mgr., 1987; asst. to v.p. and area mgr. IBM, Southfield, Mich., 1987-88; br. mgr. IBM, Youngstown, Ohio, 1988—. Judge retriever field trials Am. Kennel Club. Recipient Grand prize photograph contest Dog's USA, 1985, Nat. Photography awards, 1985-88. Mem. Youngstown C. of C. (bd. dirs.), Rotary, Birmingham Community Women's Club, Wolverine Retriever Club, Buckeye Retriever Club. Republican. Lutheran. Office: IBM 250 Federal Pla E Youngstown OH 44503

REYNOLDS, THOMAS MORGAN, chemical company executive; b. Jackson, Tenn., Nov. 28, 1943; s. Albert Morgan and Tommie Orleigh (Melton) R.; student So. Ill. U., 1962-63; B.S.B.A., Roosevelt U., 1982; 1 son, Brent Morgan. With Wyandotte Chems., St. Louis, 1965-68, Allied-Kelite Div., Witco, Chgo., 1969-82; electronic industry mgr. M & T Chems., Chgo., 1982-84; v.p. NCA Systems, Chgo., 1984-85, pres. Reynolds & Co.,

1985—, v.p. Lamina, Inc., 1985—. Mem. Electronic Connector Study Group (founder Midwest chpt.), Am. Electroplaters Soc., Am. Soc. Metals, Interconnection Packaging Circuitry, Midwest Circuit Assn. (founder). Home: 1605 E Central Rd Arlington Heights IL 60005 Office: 30 N 8th Ave Maywood IL 60153

REYNOLDS, WAYNE MCFALL, restaurant owner; b. Richmond, Va., Nov. 21, 1947; s. Jesse Anthony and Muriel (Clarke) R.; m. Judy Anne Derr, Dec. 22, 1974; children: Stephanie Danielle, Amber Christine, Michael Jesse. Student, Pfeiffer Coll., 1965-67; BA, Humboldt State Coll., 1969; MA, Humboldt State U., 1976. Tech. dir., designer Old Brewery Theatre, Helena, Mont., 1968-69; stage technician Humboldt State U., Arcata, Calif., 1968-69, 75-76; owner Two Traveler's Restaurant, Valier, Mont., 1976—; lectr. drama Coll. Great Falls, Mont., 1984—. Appointed to mont. State Foster Care Review Bd., 1986; sec., chmn. bd. Valier Area Devel. Corp., 1980-82; founder Valier Community Theatre, 1980, artistic dir., 1980—; chmn. bd., 1980-82, pres. Luth. Ch. council, Valier, 1981-85; trainer and speaker for Spl. Needs Adoption Workshops, Mont. State Dept. Social Services, 1983—. Served with USCG, 1969-73. Recipient Five Star Thespian award Nat. Thespian Soc., 1965, Founders award Valier Community Theatre, 1982. Mem. Am. Legion, Alpha Phi Omega. Club; Valier Community (v.p. 1980-81). Home: 307 Teton Ave Valier MT 59486

REZICH, GEORGE F., metal fabrication company executive; b. Lynch, Ky., June 15, 1927. B.S. in Acctg., Western Ky. U., 1951. Sr. v.p. fin. Harsco Corp., Camp Hill, Pa., 1978—; dir. Exel Ltd., X.L. Ins. Co., Ltd., Dartmouth Investments Ltd., Fortuna Ins. Ltd., Harsco Europa. Mem. AICPA, Mo. Soc. CPAs, Machinery and Allied Products Inst. Home: 807 Riverview Rd Lemoyne PA 17043 Office: Harsco Corp 350 Poplar Church Rd PO Box 8888 Camp Hill PA 17011

REZZONICO, RENZO, lawyer; b. Lugano, Switzerland, Nov. 18, 1929; s. Nino and Blanche (Schlaeppi) R. Doctorate summa cum laude, U. Basle, 1955; postgrad. in econs., U. Lausanne, 1956. Sec. Swiss Fed. Tribunal, Lausanne, 1956-58; sole practice, Lugano, Switzerland, 1958-88. Author, editor: Helbing and Lichtenhahn, 1955. Mem. Internat. Bar. Assn., Internat. Tax Planning Assn. Home: Via Orbisana 37, 6932 Biogno di Breganzona Switzerland

RHATIGAN, JOSEPH GERARD, financial executive; b. Boston, Jan. 7, 1956; s. Michael Anthony and Anne Kate (Hennigan) R. BS in Acctg., Bentley coll., Waltham, Mass., 1978; postgrad., Suffolk U., 1987—. Acctg. mgr. Allegheny Internat., Boston, 1982-85; audit mgr. Allegheny Internat., Pitts., 1085-86; controller Pollak Corp., Boston, 1986—. Office: Joseph Pollak Corp 195 Freeport St Boston MA 02122

RHEA, MARTI JEAN, marketing educator; b. Cleve., July 19, 1944; d. W. Howard and Elizabeth (McMillen) R. BBA, Kent State U., 1970; MBA, Ariz. State U., 1980, PhD, 1984. With sales and mktg. div. Cen. Nat. Bank, Cleve., 1970-71, Procter & Gamble, Cleve., 1971-73, Gillette Co., Honolulu, 1974-77, Boise (Idaho) Cascade, 1978; grad. teaching asst. Ariz. State U., Tempe, 1979-82; instr. U. of North Tex., Denton, 1983-84; asst. prof. mktg. North Tex. State U., Denton, 1984—, coord. mktg. MBA program, 1987—. Editorial reviewer Kent Pub., Merrill Pub., McGraw-Hill, Richard D. Irwin, Prentice Hall, Dryden Press, 1985—; contbr. articles to profl. jours. Mem. Acad. Mgmt., Am. Mktg. Assn., Council logistics Mgmt., Sales and Mktg. Execs. Dallas (W.V. Ballew award 1986, Educator Mem. of Yr. 1986), Strategic Mgmt. Soc. Office: U N Tex PO Box 13677 Denton TX 76203-3677

RHEA, MARY ELIZABETH, financial planner; b. Warren, Pa., Nov. 26, 1924; d. Francis Hilding and Wilma (Burkett) Nelson; m. Charles Otis Rhea, June 2, 1984; children by previous marriage; Susan, Judy, Milt, Betsy. Student, Westmar Coll., 1951-52, Coll. of Desert, 1963, Cypress Coll., 1968-69. Cert. fin. planner. Registered rep. Am. Pacific Securities, San Diego, 1972-84, Sequim, Wash., 1984-88; co-owner, mgr., San Diego, 1988—; gen. securities prin., Pasadena, Calif., 1973—. Recipient Big Eagle award Am. Pacific Securities, 1983, 84, 86, 87. Mem. Internat. Assn. Fin. Planning, Inst. Cert. Fin. Planners, C. of C., Soroptimists. Office: Am Pacific Securities Corp 3638 Camino Del Rio N Ste 201 San Diego CA 92108

RHEAD, JAMES ORISON, JR., hotel company executive; b. Salt Lake City, Jan. 14, 1939; s. James Orison Sr. and Verda Elsie (Lillywhite) R.; m. Karin Elizabeth Day, June 30, 1961; children: Elizabeth, Kristen, James, Alisyn, Jill, Amy. BS, U. Utah, 1961, MBA, 1963. Sr. v.p. Western Savs. and Loan, Phoenix, 1963-72, Romney Internat. Hotels, Phoenix, 1972-80; pres.,chmn. bd. Paragon Hotel Corp., Phoenix, 1980—; dir. frachise exec. Embassy Suites Inc., Dallas, 1983-86. Mayor's rep. Phoenix Leap Commn., 1975-76; mem. Phoenix Union High-Segregation Commn., 1978, Phoenix Union High-Budget Com., 1980; dir. Rightway Children Inc., 1984—. Served to lt. U.S. Army, 1961-62. Mem. Am. Hotel/Motel Assn. (pres. adv. com. 1980— Washington). Republican. Mormon. Office: Paragon Hotel Corp 5333 N 7th St Phoenix AZ 85014

RHETT, WILLIAM MEANS SMITH, marketing professional; b. Miami Beach, Fla., Jan. 25, 1930; s. Haskell Smith and Eunice Campbell (Emery) R.; m. Ethelyn Eddy, May 29, 1965 (div. July 1971); children: Ian Christopher, Allison Wingate; m. Mary Frances Amill, Jan. 1, 1980 (dec. Dec. 1988). BA, Hamilton Coll., 1952; MBA, Harvard U., 1957. Account group exec. McCann-Erickson Internat., N.Y.C., 1957-60; dir. client services Colón S.A., Madrid, 1960-61; mgr. mktg. devel. and advt. Motorola Overseas Corp., Chgo., 1962-66; account mgr. Marsteller Internat., N.Y.C., 1966-67; area dir. Latin Am. Wells, Rich, Greene Internat., N.Y.C., 1968-69, account supr., 1969-70; v.p. Mktg. Control Inc., N.Y.C., 1971-73; internat. mktg. mgr. consumer products div. Nat. Semiconductor Corp., Sunnyvale, Calif., 1974-75; mng. dir. Intermarkets Ltd., Orinda, Calif., 1975—. Contbr. articles to profl. jours. Served to commdr. USNR, 1954—. Mem. Internat. Advt. Assn. (dir. at large, 1966-68), Midwest Internat. Mktg. Caucus (founder, chmn. projects com.), Hamilton Alumni (pres. 1964-66, pres. North Calif. Assn. 1983-87, mem. bd. govs. 1988—), Marines Meml. Club., San Francisco Advt. Club, U.S. Naval Inst. Republican. Episcopalian. Club: Am. (Madrid); Hamilton (N.Y.C.); Lawn Tennis de la Exposición (Lima, Peru); Stamford (Conn.) Yacht. Office: Intermarkets Ltd PO Box 141 Moraga CA 94563

RHETTS, PAUL FISHER, public relations executive; b. Washington, Mar. 26, 1946; s. Charles Edward and Ruth (Fisher) R.; m. JoAnn Rhodes, Aug. 26, 1968 (div. Dec. 1979); children: Joanna Katherine, Alexandra Copeland; m. Barbe J. Awalt, Mar. 13, 1982. BA, Bucknell U., 1968; student Pub. Adminstrn. MS program, U. So. Calif., 1975-77. Pub. affairs producer Sta. WMAL-TV, Washington, 1969-70, Md. Pub. TV, Owings Mills, 1970-73; asst. supt. Balt. City Pub. Schs., 1973-74; publs. cons. Community Coll. Balt., 1975-78; pub. info. officer Howard County Schs., Ellicott City, Md., 1976-86; pres. Laser Pub. and Design, 1986—; trainer Pagemaker Desktop Pub. Software, 1986—; mem. adj. faculty Loyola Coll., Balt., 1978-80. Author: Finding Out How People Feel, 1984. Mem. exec. bd. Family Life Ctr., Columbia, Md., 1980-86, Humanities Inst., Columbia, 1978-82, Columbia Archives, 1984-86. Recipient award San Francisco Internat. Film Festival, 1971, Broadcasting award Ohio State U., 1972, Community Service Merit award So. Ednl. Communications Assn., 1973, Nat. Community Service award Corp. for Pub. Broadcasting, 1973, Publ. award of Excellence, 1986. Mem. Nat. Sch. Pub. Relations Assn. (state coordinator 1978-83, pres. Chesapeake chpt. 1981-82, 86-87, mem. exec. bd. 1976—, Gold Medallion award 1985, chmn. nat. conv. planning com., Blue Ribbon award 1982, 87), Ednl. Press Assn., Am. Profl. Graphic Artists Assn., Desktop Pub. Assn., C. of C. (bd. dirs.), Columbia Bus. Exchange. Democrat. Episcopalian. Home: 7481 Broken Staff Columbia MD 21045 Office: Laser Pub & Design 7481 Broken Staff Columbia MD 21045

RHODEN, HUBERT NELSON, JR., credit executive; b. Plant City, Fla., July 13, 1946; s. Hubert Nelson and Lena Udora (Tillman) R.; m. Reta Karole Simons, Dec. 15, 1967 (div. Sept. 1987); children: Lisa Michelle, F. Jason. BA, U. South Fla., 1967. Collection mgr. Cen. Adjustment Bur., Tampa, Fla., 1968-70; pres. Interstate Account Svcs., Tampa, 1970-75, Bus. Edn. Svcs., Tampa, 1975-76; sales mgr. Bert Simons Real Estate, Tampa, 1976-85; pres. Housing Credit Svcs. Inc., Tampa, 1985—, also chmn. bd. Author: Guide to Credit and Collection, 1975. Mem. Nat. Assn. Real Estate Appraisers, Internat. Assn. Real Estate Appriasers, Mortgage Brokers Assn., Tampa Bd. Realtors. Republican. Baptist. Office: Housing Credit Svcs Inc 1306 W Sligh Ave Tampa FL 33604

RHODES, ERIC FOSTER, editor, publisher; b. Luray, Va., Feb. 5, 1927; s. Wallace Keith and Bertha (Foster) R.; A.A., George Washington U., 1949, A.B., 1950, M.A., 1952, Ed.D., 1967; m. Barbara Ellen Henson, Oct. 19, 1946; children—Roxanne Jane, Laurel Lee; m. 2d, Lorraine Endresen, July 29, 1972; m. 3d, Daisy Chun, May 31, 1980. Tchr. high sch., Arlington, Va., 1950-52; counselor Washington Lee High Sch., Arlington, 1952-53, dir. publs., 1953-54, chmn. dept. English, 1954-55; exec. sec. Arlington Edn. Assn., 1952-53, Montgomery County (Md.) Edn. Assn., 1955-57; lectr. edn. George Washington U., 1955-60, 65-70; salary cons. NEA, Washington, 1957-58, asst. dir. membership div., 1958-60, dir. N.Y. regional office, N.Y.C., 1960-64, ednl. cons. Ednl. Research Services, White Plains, N.Y., 1964-65; pres. Ednl. Service Bur., Inc., Arlington, 1965-72, chmn. bd., 1972-80; pres. Negotiations Consultation Services, Inc., 1969-80, Eastern States Advt. Inc., 1970-79, EFR Corp., 1972—; exec. dir. Assn. Negotiators and Contract Adminstrs., 1981—; pres. Employee Futures Research, 1980-87, pres. 1988—; pres. Waterfront Quality Real Estate, 1988—; asst. supt. for adminstrn. Brighton (N.Y.) Schs., 1983-88; owner Frederick Foster Galleries, 1974-80; cons. Va. Dept. Community Colls., 1965-77; employee relations ofcl. City of Orlando, 1980-83; vice chancellor Va. Community Coll. System, 1970-71; lectr. edn. Frostburg (Md.) State Coll., 1967. Mem. Civil Rights Commn., Franklin Twp., N.J., 1962-64; mem. Franklin Twp. Bd. Edn., 1964-65; mem. adv. bd. Keep Am. Beautiful, 1964-75, nat. chmn., 1968. Served with AUS, 1945-47. Mem. Am. Assn. Sch. Adminstrs., Internat. Assn. Sch. Bus. Officials, NEA, Edn. Press Assn., Nat. Assn. Ednl. Negotiators (exec. dir. 1971-81), Phi Delta Kappa (chpt. pres. 1959-60), Fed. Schoolmen's Club, N.Y. Schoolmasters Club. Club: Lions. Author: Negotiating Salaries; 41 Ways to Cut Budget Costs. Editor: Inside Negotiations, Wages and Benefits; Employers' Negotiating Service. Home: 114 N Court St Luray VA 22835

RHODES, JAMES M(ARVIN), lawyer; b. Rosenberg, Tex., June 17, 1940; s. James and Myrtle (McNutt) R.; m. Jane Lewis Janover, June 8, 1969; children—David Gray, Benjamin James. B.A., Rice U., 1962; J.D., U. Tex.-Austin, 1965. Bar: Tex. 1965, N.Y. 1971. Atty., U.S. Justice Dept., Washington, 1967-70; assoc. atty. Simpson Thacher & Bartlett, N.Y.C., 1970-73, Coudert Bros., N.Y.C., 1973-74; ptnr., 1975-81; ptnr. Battle Fowler, N.Y.C., 1981—. Eisenhower Exchange fellow, Am. Council on Germany, 1977. Mem. ABA, Assn. of Bar of City of N.Y., State Bar Tex. Republican. Episcopalian. Clubs: River, Yale. Avocation: skiing. Office: Battle Fowler 280 Park Ave New York NY 10017

RHODES, RICHARD MORSE, university administrator; b. Alamogordo, N.Mex., Jan. 13, 1951; s. James Lewis and Lillian M. (Banks) R.; m. Melinda L. Duncan, May 15, 1971 (div. 1976); 1 child, Carey Ann; m. Katherine P. Linder, Aug. 31, 1978; children: Kristyn Annette, Karyn Alisa, Richard Alexander. BBA, N.Mex. State U., 1974, MA, 1983. CPA, N.Mex., Tex. Auditor Emmons, Adams & Co. CPAs, Albuquerque, 1974-75; acct. N.Mex. State U., Las Cruces, 1975-79, comptroller, 1979-83; v.p. fin. services El Paso (Tex.) Community Coll., 1983—; cons. in field. Bd. dirs. Dona Ana Tchrs. Fed. Credit Union, Las Cruces, 1978-81, Sta. KCOS Pub. TV, El Paso, 1987—, Tax Increment Fin. Bd., El Paso, 1987—, mem. tax. adv. bd. City of El Paso, 1984—. Mem. Am. Inst. CPAs, N.Mex. Soc. CPAs, Tex. Soc. CPAs, Nat. Assn. Coll. and Univ. Bus. Officers, So. Assn. Coll. and Univ. Officers, Delta Sigma Pi. Republican. Mem. Full Gospel Ch. Home: 1553 Avenida Quintas Las Cruces NM 88005 Office: El Paso Community Coll PO Box 20500 El Paso TX 79998

RHODES, STEPHEN MICHAEL, poultry company executive; b. Harrisonburg, Va., Mar. 12, 1949; s. Trovilla Geil and Ogretta (Dove) R.; m. Judy Ann Higgs, June 19, 1971; children: Jeremy, Meridith. AA, Shenandoah Coll., 1969; BA in Biology, Madison Coll., 1971. Mgr. quality control Rocco Farm Foods, Inc., Edinburg, Va., 1971—; wastewater operator Rocco Farm Foods, Inc., Edinbrug, 1973—. Bd. dirs. Broadway Youth Baseball League, Va., 1985—, coach 1985-88; 1st lt., pres. Broadway Emergency Squad, 1971-77; chmn. adminstrv. bd. Sunset Dr. United Meth. Ch., Broadway, 1986-87; coach Timberville Midget League Football, 1985-88; bd. dirs. Community Pk. Bd., Broadway, 1984—. Mem. Va. Poultry Industry Lab. (chmn. bd. dirs. 1983, 87), Southeastern Poultry and Egg Fedn. (sci. adv. com. 1983—). Home: 199 3d St Broadway VA 22815 Office: Rocco Farm Foods Inc Rte 3 Box 370 Edinburg VA 22824

RHODES, WILLIAM REGINALD, banker; b. N.Y.C., Aug. 15, 1935; s. Edward R. and Elsie R.; divorced; 1 child, Elizabeth. B.A. in History, Brown U., 1957. Sr. officer internat. banking group-Latin Am. and Caribbean Citibank, N.A., N.Y.C., 1977-80; sr. corp. officer Latin Am. and Caribbean Citibank, N.A., 1980-84, chmn. restructuring com., 1984—, group exec., 1986—, also chmn. bank adv. coms. for Brazil, Argentina, Peru, and Uruguay, 1982—, co-chmn. bank adv. com. for Mexico, 1982—. Decorated Orden Mérito en el Trabajo, 1st class, Orden Francisco Miranda, 1st and 3d classes (Venezuela). Mem. Americas Soc. (bd. dirs.), Council of Ams. (trustee), Bankers Assn. for Fgn. Trade (past pres.), Council Fgn. Relations, Venezuelan-Am. C. of C. (past pres.). Office: Citicorp 399 Park Ave New York NY 10043

RHYNE, CHARLES SYLVANUS, lawyer; b. Charlotte, N.C., June 23, 1912; s. Sydneyham S. and Mary (Wilson) R.; m. Sue Cotton, Sept. 16, 1932 (dec. Mar. 1974); children: Mary Margaret, William Sylvanus; m. Sarah P. Hendon, Oct. 2, 1976; children: Sarah Wilson, Elizabeth Parkhill. B.A., Duke U., 1934, LL.D., 1958; J.D., George Washington U., 1937, D.C.L., 1958; LL.D., Loyola U. of Calif., 1958, Dickinson Law Sch., 1959, Ohio No. U., 1966, De Paul U., 1968, Centre, 1969, U. Richmond, 1970, Howard U., 1975, Belmont Abbey, 1982. Bar: D.C. 1937. Pvt. practice Washington; sr. partner Rhyne & Rhyne; gen. counsel Nat. Inst. Mcpl. Law Officers; prof. aviation law George Washington U., 1948-53; gen. counsel Fed. Commn. Jud. and Congl. Salaries, 1953-54; spl. cons. Pres. Eisenhower, 1957-60; Dir. Nat. Savs. & Trust Co., ACCIA Life Ins. Co.; Mem. Internat Commn. Rules Judicial Procedures, 1959-61, Pres.'s Commn. on UN, 1969-71; spl. ambassador, personal rep. of Pres. U.S. to UN High Commr. for Refugees, 1971-73. Author: Civil Aeronautics Act, Annotated, 1939, Airports and the Courts, 1944, Aviation Accident Law, 1947, Airport Lease and Concession Agreements, 1948, Cases on Aviation Law, 1950, The Law of Municipal Contracts, 1952, Municipal Law, 1957, International Law, 1971, Renowned Law Givers and Great Law Documents of Humankind, 1975, International Refugee Law, 1976, Law and Judicial Systems of Nations, 1978, Law of Local Government Operations, 1980; editor: Municipal Attorney; Contbr. articles in field. Trustee Geo. Washington U., 1957-67, Duke U., 1951—. Recipient Grotius Peace award, 1958; Freedoms Found. award for creation Law Day-U.S.A., 1959; Alumni Achievement award George Washington U., 1960; Nat. Bar Assn. Stradford award, 1962; 1st Whitney M. Young award, 1972; Harris award Rotary, 1974; U.S. Dept. State appreciation award, 1976; D.C. Bar Assn. Disting. Svc. award, 1976; Nansen Ring for refugee work, 1976, 1st Peacemaker award Rotary Internat., 1988. Mem. ABA (pres. 1957-58, chmn. ho. dels. 1956-58, chmn. commn. world peace through law 1958-66, chmn. com. aero. law 1946-48, 51-54, chmn. internat. and comparative law sect. 1948-49, chmn. UN com., chmn. commn. on nat. inst. justice 1972-76, nat. chmn. Jr. Bar Conf. 1944-45, Gold medal 1966), D.C. Bar Assn. (pres. 1955-56), Inter-Am. Bar Assn. (v.p. 1957-59), Am. Bar Found. (pres. 1957-58, chmn. fellows 1958-59), Internat. Bar (v.p. 1957-58), Am. Judicature Soc. (dir.), Am. Law Inst., Am. Soc. Internat. Law (life), World Peace Through Law Ctr. (pres. 1963—), Nat. Aero. Assn. (dir. 1945-47), Washington Bd. Trade, Duke U. Alumni Assn. (chmn. nat. coun. 1955-56, pres. 1959-60), Barristers, Met. Club, Nat. Press Club, Congl. Club, Nat. Lawyers Club, Univ. Broadcasters, Delta Theta Phi, Order of Coif, Omicron Delta Kappa, Scribes. Clubs: Metropolitan, Nat. Press, Barristers, Congressional, Nat. Lawyers, Easton (Md.) Broadcasters. Home: 1404 Langley Pl McLean VA 22101 Office: Rhyne & Rhyne 1000 Connecticut Ave NW Ste 800 Washington DC 20036

RHYNE, ROBERT GLENN, JR., economist; b. Charlotte, N.C., Mar. 18, 1944; s. Robert Glenn and Louise (Hoover) R.; m. Lelia Lorraine Gunn, Apr. 26, 1968; children: Robert Glenn III, Jacob Daniel, Jesse John. BBA, Western Carolina U., 1966; MBA, Appalachian State U., 1967; D in Bus. Adminstrn., Miss. State U., 1976. Instr. Alexander City (Ala.) Coll., 1967-70; research analyst Miss. Bur. Econs., Starkville, 1970-73; asst. prof. Miss. U. for Women, Columbus, 1973-74, Wake Forest U., Winston-Salem, N.C., 1974-76; sr. economist Duke Power Co., Charlotte, N.C., 1976; dir. research S.C. Pub. Service Commn., Columbia, 1977—; instr. U. S.C., Columbia Coll., 1988—. Contbr. articles on fin. to profl. jours. Mem. So. States Energy Bd., Nat. Assn. Regulatory Utility Commrs. (fin. com. 1984—, computer sci. com. 1985—), S.C. Archeol. Soc. Baptist. Home: 128 Botany Dr Irmo SC 29063 Office: Pub Svc Commn 111 Doctor's Cir Columbia SC 29211

RIBEIRO, FRANK HENRY, bank executive; b. Kowloon, Hong Kong, July 1, 1949; came to U.S., 1955; s. Henry Agusto and Agatha Marie (Rodriguez) R.; m. Margaret Ann Mitchell, July 23, 1988. BA, Calif. State U-Northridge, 1973; M in Pub. and Internat. Affairs, Princeton U., 1976. Cons. Omega Rsch. Assocs., Northridge, 1973; economist Fed. Power Commn., San Francisco, 1974; economist dept. state U.S. Embassy, London, 1975; fin. analyst Exxon Corp., N.Y.C., 1976-81; mgr. swaps Marine Midland Bank, N.Y.C., 1982-83; v.p., dir. Bank of Am., N.Y.C., 1983—; cons. UN, N.Y.C., Malaysia and Thailand, 1984-85. Contbr. articles to profl. publs.; contbr. chpt. to Handbook of Internat. Corp. Fin., 1988. Mem. Internat. Swap Dealers Assn., N.Y.C. Folk Dance Found. (program coordinator 1982-86). Office: Bank of Am 335 Madison Ave New York NY 10017

RIBLE, MORTON, manufacturing executive, lawyer; b. Los Angeles, July 30, 1938; s. Ulysses Floyd and Ruth (Morton) R.; m. Ann Martin, June 22, 1963; children: Kimberly, Kristen. AB cum laude, Princeton U., 1961; JD, Stanford U., 1964; MBA, U. So. Calif., 1973. Bar: Calif. 1964. Ptnr. Darling, Mack, Hall & Call, Los Angeles, 1965-69; v.p., gen. counsel, sec. The Leisure Group Inc., Los Angeles, 1969-76; sr. v.p., gen. counsel Calif. Life Corp., Los Angeles, 1976-78; v.p., gen. counsel, sec. Pacific S.W. Airlines, San Diego, 1978-85, v.p. human resources and adminstrn., 1985-87; v.p., gen. counsel, sec. PS Group Inc., San Diego, 1978-87; sr. v.p. human resources and adminstrn. Am. Internat., Inc., Chgo., 1988—. Bd. dirs. San Diego C. of C., 1983-86, Rancho Santa Fe (Calif.) Community Found., 1981-89; pres. Palos Verdes (Calif.) Community Arts Assn., 1976-77; trustee Rancho Santa Fe Youth Inc., 1980-82. Mem. ABA, Calif. Bar Assn., Am. Soc. Corp. Secs. Club: Executive (Chgo.). Lodge: Rotary (San Diego). Home: 400 E Ohio St Chicago IL 60611

RICCARDO, LEONARD THOMAS, multi-manufacturing company executive; b. White Plains, N.Y., Feb. 18, 1933; s. Vito and Anna (Gigante) R.; m. Jeanette McManus, Sept. 27, 1964; children—Christopher, Robert, Amy. B.B.A., Iona Coll., 1959. Acct. Coopers & Lybrand, N.Y.C., 1959-64, Gen. Foods Corp., White Plains, 1964-66; staff acct. Walter Kidde & Co., Clifton, N.J., 1966-71, v.p. planning, 1971-75, group v.p., 1975-83, sr. v.p., group mgr., Kidde, Inc., Saddle Brook, N.J., 1983, now exec. v.p. Dir. Conn. Pub. Expenditures Council, Hartford, 1975. Served to cpl. U.S. Army, 1953-55, Germany. Recipient Cornelia award Iona Coll., New Rochelle, 1976. Club: Ridgewood Country (N.J.).

RICCI, FRANCO MARIA MARCHESE, publisher, designer; b. Parma, Italy, Dec. 12, 1936; s. A. and Carolina (Vitali) R. Grad. in Geology, U. Parma, 1958. Publs. include: facsimile edit. of Ency. by Diderot et d'Alambert, 1979, various series of art books, FMR (art mags.), 1965—. Recipient Les insignes de Chevalier dans l'ordre des Arts et des Lettres, France, 1980. Club: Grolier (N.Y.C.). Office: Via Durini 19, 20122 Milan Italy

RICCI, ROBERT RONALD, manufacturing company executive; b. N.Y.C., Jan. 11, 1945; s. George and Mary Pauline (Barbieri) R.; m. Sandra Piccione, Jan. 18, 1948; children: Jason, Sean. AAS, S.I. Community Coll., 1972; BBA, Bernard Baruch Coll., 1974, MBA, 1976. Sales mgr. G.A.F. Photo, Elizabeth, N.Y., 1974-76; v.p. Photo Drive Thru, Pennsauken, N.J., 1976-80; head nat. accounts Berkey Photo, Phila., 1980-85; dir. nat. account sales Qualex, Inc., Durham, N.C., 1988—; pres. Sanjasean, Inc., Marlton, N.J., 1978-86. Served with USN, 1966-70. Mem. Photo Mktg. Assn. Republican. Roman Catholic. Home: 11009 Coachmans Way Raleigh NC 27614 Office: Qualex Inc 3000 Croasdaile Rd Durham NC 27705

RICCI, RUSSELL JOSEPH, health care executive; b. Providence, May 6, 1946; s. Joseph and Maria R.; m. Carla Wengren, Feb. 14, 1970; children: Matthew, Catherine. BA, Columbia U., 1968; MD, NYU, 1972. Resident in adult psychiatry McLean Hosp., Belmont, Mass., 1972-74, resident in child psychiatry, 1974-76; dir. child and adolescent services Charles River Counseling, Newton, Mass., 1976-80, Charles River Hosp., Wellesley, Mass., 1979-83; v.p. Community Care System, Boston, 1980-83; v.p., dir. VHA Enterprises, Irving, Tex., 1983-86, exec. v.p., 1986-88, also bd. dirs.; pres., chief exec. officer VHA Physician Svcs., Inc., Irving, 1988—; chmn., med. dir. Behavioral Med. Care, Irvine, Calif., 1983—; Dallas Am. Health Capital, N.Y.C.; chmn. bd. Sutter Ctr. for Psychiatry, Sacramento; chmn., med. dir. Behavioral Med. Care, Irvine. Author: Handbook of Adolescent and Family Therapy, 1985. Mem. AMA, Am. Acad. Child Psychiatry, Mass. Med. Med. Soc., Am. Psychiatric Assn. Office: VHA Enterprises 950 Winter St Suite 4100 Waltham MA 02154

RICCIO, JEROME MICHAEL, medical company marketing executive, consultant; b. Jersey City, June 12, 1983; s. Jerome and Jean (Voza) R.; m. Sonia Kaufman, June 12, 1983; children: Nicole, Jamie, Jerome. AS, Middlesex Coll., 1976. Supr. ultrasound St. Barnabas Med. Ctr., Livingston, N.J., 1976-81; sr. account rep., sales trainer, mktg. cons. Philips Ultrasound, Santa Ana, Calif., 1982-85; dir. mktg. Am. Med. Imaging Corp., Horsham, Pa., 1985—; pres. Sound Advice Cons., Washington Crossing, Pa., 1985—; mktg. and bus. devel. cons. Universal Med. Inc., Yonkers, N.Y., 1984—; mktg. cons. Interspec Inc., Conshohocken, Pa., 1986-88; mktg. and bus. devel. cons. Ultramed Inc., Princeton, N.J., 1986—, Orthosonics Inc., N.Y.C., 1988—, Computer Devel. Lab Inc., Edison, N.J., 1988—; med. leasing cons. Execulease Inc., Elmont, N.Y., 1987—. Mem. Am. Registry Diagnostic Med. Sonographers, Am. Registry Radiologic Technologists, Soc. Noninvasive Technologists, Masons. Home: 7 Bakers Dr Washington Crossing PA 18977 Office: Am Med Imaging Corp 101 Gibraltar Rd Horsham PA 19044

RICCIO, MARGARET MARIE, mortgage corporation executive; b. Boston, July 7, 1942; d. Alfred E. and Loretta (Campbell) Duffy; m. Daniel J. Riccio, Mar. 6, 1961; children: Brian, Daniel Jr., Kristine, Melissa. BS, Boston State Coll., 1977; MBA, Suffolk U., 1987. History tchr. Melrose (Mass.) Sch. System, 1978-80; tax adminstr. Wakefield (Mass.) Savs. Bank, 1980-84; mortgage servicing mgr. 1st Ea. Mortgage Corp., Lowell, Mass., 1984-86, v.p., 1986—; v.p. 2nd Fed. Savs. and Loan, Boston, 1989—. Mem. Mass. Mortgage Bankers Assn., Young Mass. Mortgage Bankers Assn., Suffolk U. Alumni Assn. Roman Catholic. Office: 1st Ea Mortgage Corp One Lowell Research Ctr 847 Rogers St Lowell MA 01852

RICCO, PHILIP A., association administrator; b. N.Y.C., Mar. 25, 1938; s. Angelo A. and Josephine (Vitale) R.; m. Patricia A. Gerzban, July 16, 1966; children: Paul S., Alexis A. BS in Econs. and Acctg., U. Pa., 1960. Assoc. Booz, Allen & Hamilton Inc., N.Y.C., 1962-66; v.p. Dasol Corp., N.Y.C., 1966-72, Prog. Casualty Inc. Co., Mayfield, Ohio, 1973-76; assoc. dir. The Diebold Group Inc., N.Y.C., 1976-79; dir. info. resources mgmt. S.C. Johnson & Son Inc., Racine, Wis., 1979-82, corp. productivity dir., 1982-87, mgr. corp. bus. systems, 1987-88; exec. dir. Am. Productivity Mgmt. Assn., Northfield, Ill., 1988—; U.S. Senate appointee Wis. State Productivity Bd., Milw., 1985. Editor: Automatic Data Procssing Hand Book, 1977. Am. Productivity Mgmt. Assn. (bd. dirs. 1984-87, v.p. 1985-86, pres. 1987-88). Home: 23 Sheffield Dr Racine WI 53402 Office: Am Productivity Mgmt Assn 550 Frontage Rd Ste 395 Northfield IL 60093

RICE, BENJAMIN MANSON, JR., financial analyst; b. Boston, Sept. 1, 1930; s. Benjamin Manson and Roselle (Wall) R.; m. Hannah Coolidge,

Aug. 25, 1954 (div. 1966); children: Benjamin, John, Christopher. BA, Princeton U., 1952; MBA, Harvard U., 1956. In mktg. various cos., U.S., France, Fed. Republic Germany, 1956-69; fin. analyst Old Colony Trust, Boston, 1970-72, Eaton & Howard, Boston, 1973-77, Colonial Mgmt. Co., Boston, 1977-79, Chem. Bank, N.Y.C., 1979-83, Brown Bros., Harriman & Co., N.Y.C., 1983—; bd. dirs. various pvt. cos. 1st lt. arty., U.S. Army, 1952-54, Korea. Mem. Oil Analysts Group N.Y., Am. Assn. Chartered Fin. Analysts, Union Club (N.Y.C.), The Country Club (Brookline, Mass.). Home: 411 West End Ave New York NY 10024 Office: Brown Bros. Harriman & Co 59 Wall St New York NY 10005

RICE, ELIZABETH FISCHER, financial executive; b. Highland Park, Ill., Mar. 25, 1953; d. Thomas Clark and Nancy (Knight) Fischer; m. Larry Alan Rice, Feb. 25, 1984. BA, Coe Coll., 1975; MBA, Northwestern U., 1977. Fin. analyst Xerox Corp., Rochester, N.Y., 1977-81, plant controller, Oak Brook, Ill., 1981-85, program fin. mgr., Rochester, 1985—. Mem. Nat. Assn. Female Execs., Xerox Mgmt. Assn. (pres. 1987-88), Omicron Delta Epsilon, Delta Delta Delta. Republican. Episcopalian. Avocations: racquetball, running, reading. Home: 134 Beckwith Terr Rochester NY 14610 Office: Xerox Corp 1350 Jefferson Rd Henrietta NY 14623

RICE, ERNEST WEBB, JR., rail transportation executive; b. Roanoke, Va., May 15, 1940; s. Ernest Webb Sr. and Martha Louise (Gulker) R.; m. Linda Sue Stennett, June 10, 1976; children: Beverley Tay Warren, Terre Marae Warren. BA, DePauw U., 1963; MBA, U. Utah, 1972; postgrad., U. Tenn., 1973, U. So. Miss., 1974. Pers. asst. Eaton Corp., Galletin, Tenn., 1972-73; mgr. indsl. rels. adminstrn. Eaton Corp., Tifton, Ga., 1973-74; mgr. employee rels. Masonite Corp., Laurel, Mo., 1974-75, asst. pers. dir., 1975-76; asst. pers. mgr. Tenneco Oil (Packaging Corp. Am.), Counce, Tenn., 1976-78; mgr. pers., indsl. rels. Tenneco Oil (Packaging Corp. Am.), Andalusia, Ala., 1978-82; asst. to pres. Corinth and Counce R.R., 1982-83, pres., gen. mgr., 1983—, also bd. dirs.; prof. L.B. Wallace Community Coll., 1981-82. Capt. USAF, 1964-71. Mem. Am. Shortline R.R. Assn. (bd. dirs. 1988—), So. R.R. Conf. (chmn. 1988—), Miss. R.R. Assn., Tenn. Shortline Alliance, Corinth/Alcorn County C. of C. (bd. dirs. 1988), Rotary. Republican. Methodist.

RICE, HERBERT DANIEL, JR., industrial engineer; b. Westfield, Mass., Feb. 1, 1961; s. Herbert Daniel Sr. and Mildred Eva (Frost) R.; m. Laura Jane Zacchigna, Aug. 8, 1987. BS in Indsl. Engring. and Ops. Rsch., Syracuse U., 1983. Cert. in prodn. and inventory control. Supr. Syracuse (N.Y.) U. Food Svc., 1980-82; indsl. engr. Eastman Kodak Co., Rochester, N.Y., 1983—. Mem. Inst. Indsl. Engr. (sr. mem., bd. dirs.), Rochester Indsl. Engring. Soc., Genny Carps Swim. Home: 56 Bly St Rochester NY 14620 Office: Eastman Kodak Co 901 Elm Grove Rd Rochester NY 14653-6105

RICE, HUGH THOMPSON, JR., tax lawyer; b. Charleston, S.C., Aug. 4, 1957; s. Hugh Thompson and Katherine Louise (Miller) R.; m. Wrenzie Lee Calhoun, Aug. 7, 1982; children: Hugh Thompson III, Jacob Calhoun, James Lucas. BS in Acctg., U. S.C., 1979, MS, 1982, JD, 1982. Bar: S.C. 1982; CPA, S.C. Sr. tax cons. Deloitte Haskins & Sells, Charlotte, N.C., 1982-84; tax atty., cons. Van Osdell, Lester, Stewart, Myrtle Beach, S.C., 1984—; adj. prof. acctg. U. S.C., Myrtle Beach, 1985-86. Vol. Brothers and Sisters Community Action, Columbia, S.C., 1978-82. Recipient Outstanding Svc. award Brothers and Sisters Community Action, 1980, 81. Mem. S.C. Bar Assn., S.C. Assn. CPA's, Sertoma (Gem award 1987, Centurion award 1988, sec. 1988-89). Republican. Episcopalian (vestry mem. 1989—, treas. capital bldg. fund 1988—). Home: 5705 Porcher Ave Myrtle Beach SC 29577 Office: Van Osdell et al PA 1301 48th Ave N Myrtle Beach SC 29577

RICE, JOSEPH ALBERT, banker; b. Cranford, N.J., Oct. 11, 1924; s. Louis A. and Elizabeth J. (Michael) R.; m. Katharine Wolfe, Sept. 11, 1948; children: Walter, Carol, Philip, Alan. B.Aero. Engring., Rensselear Poly. Inst., 1948; M.Indsl. Engring., NYU, 1952, MA, 1968. With Grumman Aircraft Engring. Corp., 1948-53; with IBM, N.Y.C., 1953-65, mgr. ops., real estate, constrn. divs., 1963-65; dep. group exec. N.Am. comml. telecommunications group, pres. telecommunications div. ITT, N.Y.C., 1965-67; sr. v.p. Irving Trust Co., N.Y.C., 1967-69, exec. v.p., 1969-72, sr. exec. v.p., 1972-73, vice chmn., 1973-74, pres., from 1974, chmn., 1984-88; exec. v.p. Irving Bank Corp., 1971-74, vice chmn., 1974-75, pres., 1975-83, chmn. bd., chief exec. officer, 1984-88; bd. dirs. N. Am. Phillips Corp., Avon Products, Inc. Trustee John Simon Guggenheim Meml. Found., Hist. Hudson Valley Restorations. 1st lt. C.E. AUS, 1943-46. Mem. Council Fgn. Relations, University Club, Links, Sky Club, Sleepy Hollow County Club. Office: Irving Trust Co 51 W 51st St New York NY 10019

RICE, KENNETH LLOYD, finance company executive; b. St. Paul, June 17, 1937; s. Irving James and Anne Louise (Rogers) R.; m. Elizabeth Lyman Vankat, May , 1963 (div. June 1980); children: Anne Louise, Kenneth L. Jr., Elizabeth Ellen, Stephen James. BBA, U. Wis., 1959; postgrad., N.Y. Inst. Finance, 1960-64; completed Advanced Mgmt. Program, Harvard U., 1975. Trainee corp. finance Irving J. Rice & Co., St. Paul, 1959-64; asst. branch mgr. DB Marron & Co. Inc., St. Paul, 1964-65; mgr. corp. finance JW Sparks & Co. Inc., St. Paul, 1965-69, The Milw. Co., St. Paul, 1969-70; dir. finance Cedar Riverside Assocs. Inc., Mpls., 1970-71; prin. Kenneth L. Rice & Assocs., St. Paul, 1971-88; chmn., chief exec. officer Allegro Tech. Corp., St. Paul, 1988—; Minn. del. World Trade Cens. Assn., 1987, Budapest, Hungary. Founder Chimera Theatre, St. Paul, 1969; vice moderator Presbytery of the Twin Cities, Mpls., 1976; pres. Liberty Plaza Non-Profit Housing Project, St. Paul, 1975-77; judge Leadership Fellows Bush Found., St. Paul, 1985—; co-chmn. Parents Fund, Macalester Coll., St. Paul, 1985-87. Mem. Real Estate Securities Syndication Inst. (chpt. pres. 1977, disting. service award 1978). Presbyterian. Club: Harvard Bus. (local bd. dirs. 1978-83). Lodges: Optimists (local v.p. 1986-88), Masons, KT, Shriners. Office: Allegro Tech Corp 220 S Robert St Ste 208 Saint Paul MN 55107

RICE, LISTON MCLEOD, JR., electronics company executive; b. Dallas, Mar. 12, 1927; s. Liston McLeod and Ruth (Hall) R.; m. Gloria Ross, Sept. 12, 1953; children: Liston McLeod III, Gloria Irene, Patrick Douglas, Kathryn Melinda. BS in Naval Sci. and Tactics, U. Tex., 1948, BS in Elec. Engring., 1949. Engr. GE, Syracuse, N.Y., 1949-53, Collins Radio Co., Dallas, 1953-54; mgr. engring. Tex. Instruments Inc., Dallas, 1956-58, mgr. radar and electro-optic systems, 1958-64; mgr. field mktg. office Washington, 1965-67; mgr. bus. devel. Digital Systems div. Houston, 1970-74; asst. v.p., mgr. corp. rels. Dallas, 1974-80; v.p. Latin Am. div. 1980-84, v.p. corp. communications and mktg., 1985—; cons. Weapon System Evaluation Group. Mem. adv. com. engring. faculty U. Tex., Austin; bd. dirs. N. Tex. Commn., Dallas Coun. World Affairs; pres. Tex. Instruments Found. Lt. USN, 1954-56. Office: Tex Instruments Inc PO Box 655474 MS 5236 Dallas TX 75243

RICE, OTIS LAVERNE, nursing home builder and developer; b. Emerson, Iowa, June 24, 1922; s. William Reuben and Bonnie Elizabeth (Edie) R.; m. Ferill Jeane Dalton, Mar. 7, 1946; children: LeVeria June McMichael, Larry Lee. Student Fox Valley Tech. Sch., 1971-72. Lic. electrician and contractor. With Tumpane Electric, Omaha, 1949-53; ptnr., pres. Rice & Rice, Inc., Kaukauna, Wis., 1953—. Ptnr. Rice Enterprises. Served with U.S. Army, 1942-46. Decorated Bronze Stars. Mem. Associated Builders and Contractors, Fenton Art Glass Collectors of Am. Inc. (founder), Internat. Carnival Glass Collectors, Am. Carnival Glass Collectors. Republican. Clubs: Masons, Shriners, Eastern Star.

RICE, ROBERT AUGUSTUS, public affairs executive; b. Winnipeg, Man., Can., Oct. 11, 1930; children: Katherine, Jennifer, Julie. Diploma in advance mgmt., McGill U., Montreal, Quebec, Can., 1970. News editor CBC, Winnipeg, 1951-52; mng. editor Nassau (The Bahamas) Guardian, 1952-55; staff correspondent The Can. Press, London, Montreal and Ottawa, 1955-64; chief of bur. The Globe and Mail, Montreal, Que., 1964-66; spl. rep. Can. Pacific Ltd., Montreal, 1966-69, mgr. pub. rels., 1969-73, asst. gen. mgr. pub. rels., 1973-81, gen. mgr. pub. rels. and advt., 1981-85; v.p. pub. affairs CP Rail, Montreal, 1985—; journalist Winnipeg Citizen, 1948-50; news editor Prince Albert (Sask.) Herald, 1950-51. V.p. Can. Transport Rsch. Forum, Montreal, 1969-70; sec., bd. dirs. Cath. Community Services, Montreal, 1975-79; pres. English Speaking Cath. Coun., Montreal, 1987—. Mem. Assn. R.R. Advt. and Mktg., R.R. Pub. Relations Assn., Assn. Can. Advertisers, Inc., Can. Advt. Found., The Conf. Bd. (com. pub. affairs execs.), Montreal Press Club, Beaconsfield Yacht Club. Office: CP Rail, PO Box 6042, Sta A, Montreal, PQ Canada H3C 3E4

RICE, THEODORE KARL, lawyer; b. Watertown, N.Y., June 4, 1956; s. Arthur Brownell and Faye (Sweet) R. AA, Jefferson Community Coll., Watertown, 1976; BA, SUNY, Plattsburgh, 1978; postgrad., Union Coll., 1979-80; JD, Hamline U., 1983. Bar: Minn. 1983. Contract analyst No. Telecom, Inc., Minnetonka, Minn., 1983; atty. Universal Pensions, Inc., Brainerd, Minn., 1984-87, First Trust Nat. Assn., St. Paul, 1988—. Contbr. articles to profl. jours., 1986-88. Del. Minn. Dem.-Farmer-Labor State Conv., 1984. Mem. Minn. State Bar Assn. (employee benefits sect.), Minn. Corp. Fiduciaries. Home: 195 E Fifth St #S-1102 Saint Paul MN 55101 Office: First Trust Nat Assn First Trust Ctr SPFT 0307 180 E Fifth St Saint Paul MN 55101

RICE, THOMAS KENNETH, venture capitalist; b. Chgo., Sept. 18, 1941; s. Kenneth Thomas and Alice Betty (Reynolds) R.; m. Judy Anne Balint, Nov. 24, 1967; children: Jennifer Anne, Kenneth Paul. BS, Iona Coll., 1963; M of Natural Sci., U. Okla., 1968, PhD, 1971. Tchr. St. Lawrence High Sch., Stickney, Ill., 1963-66, Marist High Sch., Oak Lawn, Ill., 1966-67; rsch. sci. Purdue U., West Lafayette, Ind., 1971-72; sr. immunologist Riker Labs.-3M Co., St. Paul, 1972-76, rsch. specialist, 1977-82, tech. assessment coordinator, 1983-85; v.p. Minn. Seed Capital Inc., Mpls., 1985—; bd. dirs. Video Care Inc., St. Paul, Seismed Inc., Mpls. Patentee in field. Mem. AAAS, Am. Soc. for Microbiology, Med. Alley Assn., University Club. Office: Minn Seed Capital Inc 1660 S Hwy 100 Minneapolis MN 55416

RICH, ERIC, plastics company executive; b. Znojmo, Czechoslovakia, Oct. 1, 1921; came to U.S., 1955, naturalized, 1962; s. Sandor and Alice (Shifferes) Reich; m. Ilse L.B. Renard, Nov. 14, 1959; children—Susan Frances, Sally Dora, Charles Anthony. Ed., U. Coll., Wales, Bangor, U.K. Export sales mgr. Pilot Radio, Ltd., London, Eng., 1945-49; dir. Derwent Exports, Ltd., London, 1949-55; export sales mgr. Am. Molding Powder & Chem. Corp., N.Y.C., 1956-58; with Gering Plastics Co. div. Monsanto Chem. Co., Kenilworth, N.J., 1958-67; v.p., gen. mgr. Goldmark Plastics Internat., Inc., New Hyde Park, N.Y., 1967—. Served with RAF, 1941-45. Decorated Gallantry medal, 1939-43, Star Atlantic Star. Home: 111 7th St Garden City NY 11530 Office: Nassau Terminal Rd New Hyde Park NY 11040

RICH, HARRY E., footwear and specialty retailing financial executive; b. Wichita, Kans., Mar. 5, 1940; s. Hubert E. and Lorene (Sadler) R.; m. Elfreda Elizabeth Babcock, Aug. 8, 1964; children—Lisa G., Carey E., Ashley H. B.A., Harvard U., 1962, M.B.A., 1968. Pres. instrumentation div. Baxter Travenol, Deerfield, Ill., 1977-78; group v.p. Mallinckrodt, Inc., St. Louis, 1978-83; sr. v.p., chief fin. officer Brown Group, Inc., St. Louis, 1983-88, exec. v.p., chief fin. officer, 1988—, also dir. Pres. bd. dirs. Repertory Theatre, 1988—; treas., v.p. Fair Found., 1985-88; bd. trustees Mary Inst., 1986—. Served to lt. USN, 1962-66. Home: 101 Fair Oaks St Saint Louis MO 63124 Office: Brown Group Inc 8400 Maryland Ave Saint Louis MO 63105

RICH, JAMES ERIC ANTONY, sugar company executive; b. London, Feb. 15, 1929; came to U.S., 1963; naturalized, 1969; s. Eric Ralph and Phyllis (Cook) R.; m. Marjorie Isobel Anderson, July 25, 1953; children—Ian Antony, Alan Stuart. B. Sc., Kings Coll. Durham U. (Eng.), 1950. Chartered Engr. Control engr. British Sugar PLC, Peterborough, Eng., 1950-63; various positions Holly Sugar Corp., Colo. Springs, Colo., Tracy Ca., 1963-81, chief operating officer, Colo. Springs, 1981—; project mgr. Jacobs Engring., Concord, Calif., 1981; vice chmn. Holly Sugar Corp., Colo. Springs, 1981-88. Scout master Pikes Peak Council Boy Scouts Am., 1964-75; adv. Jr. Achievement, Colo. Springs, 1982-84. Served to s/sgt. British Army, 1947-49. Mem. Am. Soc. Sugar Beet Technologists (dir. 1976-78, 87—, Meritorious Service award 1981), Inst. Measurement & Control, Instrument Soc. Am. (sr. mem.), Beet Sugar Devel. Found. (dir. 1981—). Club: Commonwealth Calif. (San Francisco). Office: Holly Sugar Corp Holly Sugar Bldg PO Box 1052 Colorado Springs CO 80901

RICH, ROBERT E., SR., frozen foods company executive. married. Grad., U. Buffalo, 1935. Owner Wilber Farms Dairy, 1935; with Rich Products Corp., Buffalo, chmn. bd., dir., from 1944. Office: Rich Products Corp 1150 Niagara St Buffalo NY 14213

RICHARD, SANDRA CLAYTON, academic administrator; b. Athens, Tex.; d. Chester Armendale and Lola Hybernia (Clayton) R. AA, Trinity Valley Community Coll.; BBA, U. Tex., 1958, MBA, 1959, PhD, 1968. Instr. Am. U. of Beirut, 1959-61, asst. prof., 1968-74, vis. assoc. prof., 1978-81; asst. prof. Haile Selassie I U., Ethiopia, 1965-66, U. Mo., St. Louis, 1966-67; visiting assoc. prof. U. Notre Dame, 1974-77; vis. assoc. prof. Calif. State U., Long Beach, 1977-78; assoc. prof., chair div. bus. adminstrn. Laredo (Tex.) State U., 1981—; prodn. and inventory control cons. Mathes Mfg. Co., Athens, 1958, U.N. Indsl. Devel. Orgn., Vienna, Austria, 1968; mgmt. devel. programs Pakistan Indsl. Devel. Corp., Karachi, 1963, Beirut, Bahrain, Qatar, 1970-74, 78-81. Contbr. articles to profl. jours. Mem. Leadership Laredo, 1985—; founding bd. mem. Laredo Regional Food Bank, 1982—; bd. mem. Animal Protective Soc., Laredo, 1982—; mem. steering com. Am. for Justice in the Middle East, Beirut, 1980-81. Named Outstanding Ex-Student, Trinity Valley Community Coll., Athens, 1983; Fulbright grad. research grantee, Karachi, 1962-63. Mem. Soc. for Internat. Devel., Acad. Internat. Bus., Acad. Mgmt., Tex. Assn. Middle East Scholars, Am. Assn. Univ. Profs., Animal Air Transp. Assn., Phi Kappa Phi. Office: Laredo State U West End Washington St Laredo TX 78040

RICHARDS, BARBARA ANNE, bank executive; b. Scottsville, Ky., Dec. 15, 1955; d. James E. and Mary Ann (Cooksey) Ogles; m. Nathan Edward Richards, Aug. 28, 1973; children: Dustin Erik, Rebekah Christiane. Student, We. Ky. U. V.p. human resources and loans Farmers Nat. Bank, Scottsville, 1973—; sec., treas. Scottsville Allen County Pub. Properties Corp., 1982—, bd. dirs. Mem. Am. Banking Inst. (sec. So. chpt. 1984—), Ky. Banking Assn. (founding bd. young bankers div. 1987—), Profl. Secs. Inst., Nat. Assn. Bank Women (chmn. awards and scholarships com. 1987—). Methodist. Home: 155 Lakeside Dr Scottsville KY 42164

RICHARDS, BERNARD, investment company executive; b. N.Y.C., July 12, 1927; s. Charles and Sadie (Rubin) R.; m. Arlene Kaye, Dec. 23, 1948; children: Carol Leslie, Patricia Ellen, Lori Gale. BBA, Baruch Coll., 1949. CPA, N.Y. Acct. Eisner & Lubin, N.Y.C., 1949-53, S.D. Leidesdorf, N.Y.C., 1953-56; from controller to treas. to v.p. fin. to pres. Slattery Group Inc., N.Y.C., 1956-87; pres. Slattery Investors Corp., N.Y.C., 1988—; chmn. bd. dirs. Slattery Assocs., Inc., N.Y.C., 1968-87. Trustee Temple Sinai, Roslyn, N.Y., 1987—; v.p., bd. dirs. Variety Boys Club, Queens, N.Y., 1972—; bd. dirs. N.Y.C. Indsl. Devel. Bd., 1973-76; pres., bd. dirs. Baruch Coll. Fund, N.Y.C., 1975—, Man Yr., 1972. Named Man of Yr. United Jewish Appeal, 1980, March of Dimes, 1983, Outstanding Alumnus of Yr. Baruch Coll.; recipient Heavy Constrn. award United Jewish Appeal, 1980; Wood fellow Baruch Coll., 1979. Mem. Am. Inst. CPA's, N.Y. State Soc. CPA's, Moles, Beavers (bd. dirs. 1982—). Republican. Jewish. Clubs: Bd. Room (N.Y.C.); Shelter Rock Tennis (North Hills, N.Y.). Home: 18 Applegreen Dr Old Westbury NY 11568 Office: Slattery Investors Corp 1 Hollow Ln Ste 311 Lake Success NY 11042

RICHARDS, DANIEL WELLS, company executive; b. Taylor, Pa., Dec. 16, 1928; s. Daniel Wells and Bernice (Robling) R.; m. Helen Reilly, Feb. 10, 1979; children: Kenneth, Deborah, Thomas. BA, Dickinson Coll., 1950; postgrad., U. Pitts., 1953-54. Mgr. advt. prodn. Miller Machine Co., Pitts., 1954-55; mgr. sales promotion Gen. Paper Co., Pitts., 1955-57; advt. and product mgr. Harris Seybold Co., Cleve., 1957-67; mgr. advt. Colwell Systems Inc., Champaign, Ill., 1967—, also pres., 1986—. Mem. Urbana (Ill.) City Council, 1975-77; budget dir. Ill. Humanities Council, 1980-84; bd. dirs. United Way Champaign County, 1987—, Sinfonia da Camert, 1987—. Served to lt. U.S. Army, 1950-53. Unitarian. Home: 1704 Coventry Dr Champaign IL 61821

RICHARDS, D(ORIS) JEAN, computer equipment sales executive; b. Charleston, Ill., Nov. 2, 1937; d. Albert Leonard and Ruth Erica (Freeland) Anderson; m. Donald Lee Richards, Mar. 21,1956 (div. Mar. 1977); 1 child, Chad Lyn. Student, St. Edwards U., 1981—. Internat. control mgr. KMW Systems Corp., Austin, Tex., 1979-81, controller, 1981-82, corp. sec., treas., 1981—, dir. sales adminstrn., 1982-86, v.p. bus. adminstrn., 1986—. Republican.

RICHARDS, EDWARD COLLYN, JR., engineering company executive; b. Baton Rouge, July 3, 1948; s. Edward Collyn Sr. and Frances Elane (Draughon) R. BS in Elect. Engring., La. State U., 1971. Registered profl. engr. La., Miss., Ala. Sales engr. Bass Electronics, Baton Rouge, 1971-73; sr. design engr. Rust Engring., Baton Rouge, 1973-78; dept. mgr. Process Services, Baton Rouge, 1978-83; pres. Richards-Mead & Assocs., Baton Rouge, 1983—; chmn. bd. dirs. Software Solutions Tech., Baton Rouge; v.p. Flood Control Systems, Inc. Author: (software) Corocomp, 1984, Draw Account Manager, 1984. Served as capt. U.S. Army, 1971-78. Mem. La. Engring. Soc., Nat. Soc. Profl. Engrs., Profl. Engrs. in Pvt. Practice, IEEE, Illuminating Engring. Soc., Baton Rouge Aircraft Pilots Assn. (pres. 1981-83). Republican. Baptist. Home: 3420 San Felipe Rd Baton Rouge LA 70809 Office: Richards Mead & Assocs Inc 11314 Cloverland Ave Baton Rouge LA 70809

RICHARDS, FREDERICK FRANCIS, JR., manufacturing company executive; b. Payette, Idaho, Jan. 28, 1936; s. Frederick Francis and Dorothy Lucille (Taylor) R.; B.S. in Indsl. Engring., So. Meth. U., 1959; M.B.A., Harvard U., 1961; m. DeAnne Aden, Aug. 10, 1958; children—Frederick Francis III, Craig, Jeffrey. Indsl. engr. Collins Radio Inc., 1955-59; research asst. Harvard U., 1961-62; fin. analyst H.F. Linder & William T. Golden, N.Y.C., 1962-65; pres. Adrich Corp. and subs., Dallas, 1965—; v.p. and prin. Capital Alliance Corp., Dallas, 1985—; v.p. GTex., Inc., Dallas, 1986-87; pres. AR Assocs., internat. mgmt. cons., Dallas, 1972—; dir. Dallas Pub. Inc., 1982-84, DPIM, Inc., Alt. Energy Resources, Global Link, Aden-Richards, Inc., Higley Steel Corp. Mem. Am. Inst. Indsl. Engrs. (sr.), ASTM, Airplane Owners and Pilot Assn., Am. Soc. Indsl. Security, Internat. Assn. Chiefs Police, Nat. Pilots Assn., Exptl. Aircraft Assn. Club: Harvard (N.Y.C.). Author papers in field; bus. columnist. Home: 3 Cumberland Pl Richardson TX 75080 Office: 1111 W Mockingbird Ln Suite 737 Dallas TX 75247

RICHARDS, LEONARD MARTIN, investment executive, consultant; b. Phila., June 4, 1935; s. Leonard Martin and Marion Clara (Lang) R.; m. Phyllis Janelle Mowrey, Aug. 26, 1961 (div. Aug. 1978); children: Lisa, David Reed. BS, Pa. State U., 1957; MBA, U. Pa., 1963. Asst. to sr. ptnr. Van Cleef, Jordan & Wood, N.Y.C., 1963-68; v.p., portfolio mgr. Bernstein-Macaulay, Inc., N.Y.C., 1968-72; ptnr. G. H. Walker, Laird Co., N.Y.C., 1972-74; v.p., trust officer Republic Bank N.A., Dallas, 1974-77; v.p., sr. investment officer Variable Annuity Life Ins. Co., Houston, 1977-88; bd. dirs., pres. L.M. Richards & Co., Houston, 1982—. Pres., bd. dirs. Sand Dollar Youth Ctr., Houston, 1985—; bd. dirs. Houston Chorale, 1988—. Served as capt. U.S. Army, 1957-65. Fellow Fin. Analysts Fedn.; mem. Houston Soc. Fin. Analysts. Republican. Avocations: tennis, travel, scuba. Home: 9023 Briar Forest Dr Houston TX 77024 Office: Variable Annuity Life Ins Co 2929 Allen Pkwy Houston TX 77019

RICHARDS, MARTA ALISON, lawyer; b. Memphis, Mar. 15, 1952; d. Howard Jay and Mary Dean (Nix) Richards; m. Jon Michael Hobson, May 5, 1973 (div. Jan. 1976); m. 2d, Richard Peter Massony, June 16, 1979 (div. Apr. 1988); 1 child, Richard Peter Massony, Jr. Student Vassar Coll., 1969-70; AB cum laude, Princeton U., 1973; JD, George Washington U., 1976. Bar: Assoc. Phelps, Dunbar, Marks, Claverie & Sims, New Orleans, 1976-77; assoc. counsel Hibernia Nat. Bank, New Orleans, 1978; assoc. Singer, Hutner, Levine, Seeman & Stuart, New Orleans, 1978-80, Jones, Walker, Waechter, Poitevent, Carrere & Denegre, New Orleans, 1980-84; ptnr. Mmahat Duffy, & Richards, 1984, Montgomery, Barnett, Brown, Read, Hammond & Mintz, 1984-86, Montgomery, Richards & Batlin, 1986-89, Gelpi, Sullivan, Carroll and Laborde, 1989—; lectr. paralegal inst. U. New Orleans, 1984—. Contbr. articles to legal jours. Treas. alumni coun. Princeton U., 1979-81. Mem. ABA, La. State Bar Assn., Fed. Bar Assn., New Orleans Bar Assn., Princeton Alumni Assn. New Orleans (pres. 1982-86). Republican. Episcopalian. Home: 1133 8th St New Orleans LA 70115 Office: Gelpi, Sullivan, Carroll & Laborde 430 Notre Dame St New Orleans LA 70130

RICHARDS, REUBEN FRANCIS, natural resource company executive; b. N.Y.C., Aug. 15, 1929; s. Junius A. and Marie R. (Thayer) R.; m. Elizabeth Brady, Nov. 28, 1953; children—Reuben Francis, Timothy T., Andrew H. A.B., Harvard U., 1952. With Citibank, N.A., N.Y.C., 1953-82, exec. v.p., 1970-82; chmn., pres., chief exec. officer Inspiration Resources Corp., N.Y.C., 1982—; dir. Adobe Resources Corp., N.Y.C., Ecolab, Inc., St. Paul, Engelhard Corp., Menlo Park, N.J., chmn., dir. Minorco, Luxembourg, Potlatch Corp., San Francisco. Served with USNR, 1948-50. Office: Inspiration Resources Corp 250 Park Ave New York NY 10177

RICHARDS, ROBERT CHARLES (BOB), management consultant; b. Portland, Oreg., Jan. 18, 1939; s. Charles Robert and Mildred Marie (Merrill) R.; m. Marilyn Cornelia Poole, Sept. 1, 1961 (div.); children: Kristin Elizabeth, Jeffrey Robert. BA, Lewis and Clark Coll., 1961. Tng. officer, mgr. edn. dept. U.S. Bancorp, Portland, Oreg., 1965-74; mgr. orgn. devel. Coors Container Co., Golden, Colo., 1974-77; mgmt. cons., mgr. western office Cons. Assocs. Internat., Inc., Lakewood, Colo., 1977-84; mgmt cons., pres. Cons. Network, Lakewood, 1985—; pres., chief exec. officer Epoch Prodns., 1986—; instr. Portland State U., 1972-73, U. Oreg., Portland Extension, 1973-74, Portland Community Coll., 1971-74; adj. faculty Bryant Coll. Ctr. for Mgmt. Devel., Smithfield, R.I., 1979—; mgmt. cons.; seminar leader; dir., sec. Sr. Mgmt. Programs, Inc., 1971-73, pres., 1973-74. Author tng. materials; contbr. articles to profl. publs. Mem. adv. com. Community Coll. of Denver, scholarship and employment com. Portland State U. Found.; adj. faculty USMC Service Support Schs., Camp Lejeune, N.C. Served with USMCR, 1961-64; col. Res., 1966—. Mem. Am. Soc. Tng. and Devel. (bd. dirs. chpt. 1976, v.p. 1977, bd. dirs. Oreg. chpt. 1972, pres. 1971, bd. dirs. Western region 1971-72), World Futures Soc., Planning Execs. Inst., Rocky Mountain Orgn. Devel. Network, Marine Corps Res. Officers Assn. (pres. Mile High chpt.), Marine Corps Meml. Assn. (sec.). Home and Office: 13362 W Montana Ave Lakewood CO 80228

RICHARDS, ROBERT JOHN, financial planner; b. Woodbridge, N.J., Dec. 16, 1944; s. Elbur and Eleanore (Larsen) R.; m. Jean T. W., Nov. 6, 1966; children: Robert J. Jr., Heather Beth. BS, Rutgers U., 1966; MBA, Seton Hall U., 1972. Cert. fin. planner, CLU. Asst. dir. market rsch. Squibb Co., New Brunswick, N.J., 1968-70; dir. market rsch. Seatrain Lines., Weehawken, N.J., 1970-72; supr. Aetna Life Ins., Edison, N.J., 1972-74, Mass. Mut. Life Ins., Fairfield, N.J., 1974-76; gen. agt. Am. Gen., Lakewood, N.J., 1976-77; pres., owner Exec. Planning Assocs., Toms River, N.J., 1977—, Resource Mgmt. Co., Toms River, 1980—, EPA Fin. Services, Corp., Toms River, 1982—; faculty Coll for Fin. Planning, 1983—. Coach, mgr. Toms River little, minor, major, sr. leagues, 1974—, bitty basketball league, 1976-85, Carleton high sch. level league baseball, 1987; bd. dirs. N.J. Tournament of Champions for the Learning Disabled and Orthopedically Handicapped, 1979—. Served to 1st lt. with U.S. Army, 1966-68. Office: EPA Fin Svcs Corp 2040 US Hwy 9 Toms River NJ 08753

RICHARDS, STEPHEN IRVING, telephone company executive; b. Cherry Point, N.C., Mar. 2, 1949; s. Irving S. and Marie A. (Andrews) R.; m. Pamela Padrick, Nov. 21, 1972; 1 child, Amelia Marie. BS in Acctg. magna cum laude, U. N.C., Greensboro, 1976; MBA, Duke U., 1981. Staff auditor GTE South, Durham, N.C., 1977-78, sr. auditor, 1978, supr. product line acctg., 1978-79, mgr. product line acctg., 1980-81; mgr. gen. acctg. GTE Calif., Santa Monica, 1982-85; contr. GTE Telemessager, Stamford, Conn., 1985-86, GTE S.W., San Angelo, Tex., 1986—. Mem. Nat. Assn. Accts., Tex. Telephone Assn. (cons. com. acctg.), Aircraft Owners and Pilots Assn. Episcopalian. Home: 5410 Bent Green Ct San Angelo TX 76904 Office: GTE SW Inc 2701 Johnson Ave San Angelo TX 76904

RICHARDS, T. GERALD, banker; b. Llandinham, Wales, Nov. 20, 1913; s. William Nickolas and Margaret Jane (Jones) R.; m. Jean Betty Culliton, Oct. 7, 1947; children: Heidi, Jon J. Student, Wake Forest Coll., 1943, Boston U., 1949-54. Teller Bay Bank Middlesex, Reading, Mass., 1935-49; head teller Malden (Mass.) Trust Co., 1949-56; asst. treas. to v.p. Reading Coop. Bank, 1956—; bd. dirs. Reading Coop. Bank. Bd. dirs. Regional Health Ctr., Wilmington, Mass., 1985—; treas. North Reading Cancer Crusade, 1948-60; trustee North Reading Flint Meml. Library, 1960—; v.p., bd. dirs. Community Regional Health Ctr., Wilmington, Mass., 1989—. Served with U.S. Army, 1942-46. Mem. Young Execs. Club of Mass. Coop. Banks (pres. 1968-69). Republican. Home: Surrey Lane Box 82 North Reading MA 01864 Office: Reading Coop Bank 180 Haven St Reading MA 01867

RICHARDS, TIMOTHY DAVID, lawyer; b. Schenectady, N.Y., Oct. 20, 1952; s. David Emyrs and Helen (Rice) R.; m. Vicki Horner, Aug. 19, 1978; 1 child, Gwendolyn. BA, Brown U., 1974; JD, Suffolk U., 1978. Bar: Fla. 1981. Assoc. Robert Feinschriber & Assocs., N.Y.C., 1978-80, Mann, Dady, Corrigan & Zelman, Miami, Fla., 1981-86, Thomson, Muraro, Bohrer & Razook, Miami, Fla., 1986-89, Katz, Barron, Squitero & Faust, P.A., Miami, 1989—; bd. dirs. Continental Farms Inc., Miami. Author: The Guide To Foreign Investment in U.S. Real Estate, 1985; asst. editor Internat. Tax Jour., N.Y.C., 1978-80; contbr. articles to legal jours. Faculty rsch. fellow Smithsonian Instn.-Am. Inst. Indian Studies, India, 1979. Mem. Inter-Am. Bar Assn., Vol. Lawyers for Arts (svc. awards 1984, 85, 86). Office: Katz Barron Squitero & Faust PA 2699 S Bayshore Dr Miami FL 33133

RICHARDS, WILLIAM GEORGE, b. Lockhart, Tex., Feb. 20, 1920; s. Cyrus F. and Gussie (Baldridge) R.; LL.B., U. Tex., 1948; m. Winnifred Adams, Nov. 23, 1940 (dec. May 1969); children—Bettye Ann (Mrs. Rogers), Mark Andrew; m. 2d, Corrie Marsh, Mar. 29, 1972. Admitted to Tex. bar, 1948; practiced law with father, Lockhart, 1948-55; v.p., atty., dir. Lockhart Savs. & Loan Assn., 1948-55; exec. v.p. Benjamin Franklin Savs. & Loan Assn., 1955-64, pres., 1964-74, vice-chmn. bd., 1974-75; chmn. bd., chief exec. officer Surety Savs. Assn., Houston, 1975-78; trustee Savs. & Loan Found., Inc., 1957-59. Mem. Tex. Ho. of Reps., 1947-50; mayor of Lockhart, 1954-55. Mem. adv. com. Coll. Bus. Adminstrn. U. Houston, 1966-70. Served with USNR, 1942-45. Mem. Nat. League Insured Savs. Assns. (exec. com. 1962-66), Houston C. of C. (dir. 1966, 68-73), Tex. Savs. and Loan League (dir. 1953-63, 63-66; pres. 1967-68), Phi Delta Phi. Democrat. Episcopalian. Clubs: Onion Creek, Austin (Austin). Home: 11007 Pinehurst Dr Austin TX 78747

RICHARDSON, CARL COLLEY, JR., propane gas company executive; b. Inverness, Fla., Sept. 14, 1941; s. Carl Colley and Margaret (Barnes) R.; m. Linda Lou Dale, June 6, 1965; children: Heather Anne, Holly Anne. BA, Cen. Mo. State U., 1965. Spl. agt. U.S. Secret Service, Washington, 1965-66; ins. agt. Coll. Life Ins. Co., Warrensburg, Mo., 1966-67; salesman Skelly Oil Co., Kansas City, Mo., 1967; various positions Mobil Oil Co., nationwide, 1967-76; mgr. co. ops. Amerada Hess Corp., Woodbridge, N.J., 1976-77; v.p., corp. officer Cheker Oil Co., Chgo., 1977-79; dir. mktg. and planning Suburban Propane Gas Corp. (now Suburban Propane div. Quantum Chem. Corp.), Whippany, N.J., 1979-80, area v.p., 1980-86, group v.p. western ops., 1986—, also officer, 1985—. Mem. Am. Gas Assn., Nat. L.P. Gas Assn., Morris County Indsl. Rec. Assn., Suburban Propane Div. Quantum Chem. Corp. Golf Team (capt. 1985-88), Order of Ky. Cols., Theta Chi. Republican. Baptist. Lodge: Order of De Molay. Home: 17 Ironwood Rd Morristown NJ 07960 Office: Quantum Chem Corp Suburban Propane Div PO Box 206 Rt 10 Whippany NJ 07981

RICHARDSON, DAVIS BATES, oil company executive; b. Fayetteville, Ark., Dec. 19, 1929; d. Davis Payne and Frances (Bates) R.; m. Sue Anne Garber, Feb. 11, 1950 (div. 1978); children: Clara Frances, Sue Ellen; m. Norma Jean Eastland, Jan. 20, 1979. BS in Chemistry, U. Ark., 1951, MS, 1955, PhD, 1956. Research chemist Shell Oil Co., Houston, 1958-64; mgr. mfg. ops. Shell Oil Co., Wood River, Ill., 1965-67, mgr. product devel., 1968-70; mgr. mfg. econs. Shell Oil Co., Houston, 1970-73, mgr. chem. research, 1974, gen. mgr. oil prodn. bus. ctrs., 1975-78; co. liaison Shell Group, London, 1978-80; v.p. corp. planning Shell Oil Co., Houston, 1981-83; pres. Shell Refining & Mktg. Co., Houston, 1984-87, Shell Chem. Co., Houston, 1987—. Served to 1st lt. U.S. Army, 1951-53. Mem. AAAS, Nat. Assn. Mfrs. (bd. dirs., exec. com.), Chem. Mfg. Assn. (bd. dirs. exec. com.), Am. Chem. Soc., The Chem. Soc., Soc. Chem. Industry,. Clubs: Petroleum, Houston Racquet. Office: Shell Oil Co 1 Shell Pla Houston TX 77252

RICHARDSON, DEAN EUGENE, banker; b. West Branch, Mich., Dec. 27, 1927; s. Robert F. and Helen (Husted) R.; m. Barbara Trytten, June 14, 1952; children: Ann Elizabeth, John Matthew. A.B., Mich. State U., 1950; LL.B., U. Mich., 1953; postgrad., Stonier Grad. Sch. Banking, 1965. With Indsl. Nat. Bank, Detroit, 1953-55; with Mfrs. Nat. Bank, Detroit, 1955—; v.p. adminstrn. Mfrs. Nat. Bank, 1964-66, sr. v.p., 1966-67, exec. v.p., 1967-69, pres., 1969-73, chmn. bd. dirs., 1973-89, chmn. exec. com., 1989—; chmn. bd. Mfrs.-Detroit Internat. Corp., 1973—; chmn. bd. dirs. Mfrs. Nat. Corp., 1989—; chmn. bd. Mfrs. Nat. Bank, 1973-89, chmn. exec. com., 1989—; bd. dirs. Detroit Edison Co., R.P. Scherer Corp., Fruehauf Corp., Tecumseh Products Co. Served with USNR, 1945-46. Mem. Mich., Detroit bar assns., Assn. Res. City Bankers, Am. Inst. Banking, Mens Forum, Robert Morris Assocs., Econ. Club Detroit (dir.), Newcomen Soc. N.Am. Episcopalian. Clubs: Masons, KT, Detroit Athletic, Detroit, Country of Detroit. Office: Mfrs Nat Bank Mfrs Bank Tower 100 Renaissance Ctr Detroit MI 48243

RICHARDSON, DEBORAH L., manufacturing company executive; b. Hamilton, Tex., Feb. 5, 1952; d. Carl E. and Louella (Ewald) Luker; m. Richard R. Richardson, May 27, 1973 (div. Aug. 1984); 1 child: Dustin Kyle. BS in Acctg., U. Tex., Arlington, 1974. CPA, Tex. Acct. Weaver & Tidwell, Ft. Worth, 1974-77; asst. tax mgr. Bass Enterprises, Ft. Worth, 1977-78; pvt. practice acctg. Ft. Worth, 1978-85, 87—; prin. AVM Products Inc., Ft. Worth, 1985-87. Mem. Am. Inst. CPA's, Tex. Soc. CPA's (state and Ft. Worth chpts.), Jr. Womens Club. Office: 5016 Kemble St Fort Worth TX 76103

RICHARDSON, DONALD CHARLES, engineer, consultant; b. Glendale, Calif., June 6, 1937; s. George Robert and Margaret Josephine (Buchholz) R.; m. Helen Mary Boyd, Aug. 9, 1984. B.A. in Sci., Calif. State U., 1965; M.S. in Engring., Queens U., 1981, M.Ed., 1983; Ph.D., Clarkson U., 1988. Sr. engr. Control Data Corp., Toronto, Ont., Can., 1972-75; tchr. Algonquin Coll., Kingston, Ont., Can., 1975-79; assoc. prof. Royal Mil. Coll. of Can., Kingston, 1982-84; instr. Clarkson U., Potsdam, N.Y., 1988; supercomputer cons., 1989. Author of engring. papers. Served to lt. comdr. USN, 1964-69, Vietnam. Electrochem. Soc. fellow, 1984. Mem. Am. Soc. Engring. Edn., Mensa, Sigma Xi. Lodge: Fraternal Order of Seals.

RICHARDSON, DOUGLAS FIELDING, lawyer; b. Glendale, Calif., Mar. 17, 1929; s. James D. and Dorothy (Huskins) R.; m. Leni Tempelaar-Lietz, June 26, 1959; children—Arthur Wilhelm, John Douglas. A.B., UCLA, 1950; J.D., Harvard U., 1953. Bar: Calif. 1953. Assoc. O'Melveny & Myers, Los Angeles, 1953-68, ptnr., 1968-86, of counsel, 1986—. Author: (with others) Drafting Agreements for the Sale of Businesses, 1971, Term Loan Handbook, 1983. Bd. govs. Town Hall of Calif., Los Angeles, 1974-87, sec., 1977, v.p., 1978-79, pres., 1984, mem. adv. council, 1987—, chmn. sect. on legis. and adminstrn. of justice, 1968-70, pres. Town Hall West, 1975, mem. exec. bd. 1973—; bd. dirs. Hist. Soc. So. Calif., 1976-82, pres., 1980-81. Mem. ABA (com. on devels. in bus. financing, com. state regulation of securities, com. corp. law and acctg., com. employee benefits and exec. compensation of sect corp. banking and bus. law.), Calif. Bar Assn., Los Angeles County Bar Assn. (chmn. com. Law Day 1968, exec. com. comml. law sect. 1974-78, exec. com. corp. law sect. 1975-86), Nat. Assn. Bond Lawyers, Phi Beta Kappa. Republican. Presbyterian (elder). Clubs: California, Harvard So. Calif. Home: 1637 Valley View Rd Glendale CA 91202 Office: O'Melveny & Myers 400 S Hope St Los Angeles CA 90071

RICHARDSON, EMILIE WHITE, manufacturing company executive, investment company executive, lecturer; b. Chattanooga, July 8; d. Emmett and Mildred Evelyn (Harbin) White; B.A., Wheaton Coll., 1951; 1 dau., Julie Richardson Morphis. With Christy Mfg. Co., Inc., Fayetteville, N.C., 1952—, sec. 1956-66, v.p., 1967-74, exec. v.p., 1975-79, pres., chief exec. officer, 1980—; v.p. E. White Investment Co., 1968-83, pres., 1983—; cons. Aerostatic Industries, 1979—; v.p. Gannon Corp., 1981—; cons. govt. contacts and offshore mfg., 1981—; lectr., speaker in field. Vice pres. public relations Ft. Lauderdale Symphony Soc., 1974-76, v.p. membership, 1976-77, adv. bd., 1978—; active Atlantic Found., Ft. Lauderdale Mus. Art, Beaux Arts, Freedoms Found.; mem. East Broward Women's Republican Club, 1968—, Americanism chmn., 1971-72. Mem. Internat. Platform Assn., Nat. Speakers Assn., Fla. Speakers Assn. Presbyterian. Clubs: Toastmasters, Green Valley Country. Home: 1531 NE 51st St Fort Lauderdale FL 33334 Office: 3311 Ft Bragg Rd Fayetteville NC 28303

RICHARDSON, FRANCIS JOSEPH, III, bank consultant, investment counsel, investment analyst, financial analyst; b. New Orleans, Mar. 22, 1943; s. Francis J. and Stella M. (Schulze) R.; BBA, Tulane U., 1965, postgrad. Tax Insts., 1967-74; MBA, Loyola U., New Orleans, 1970; postgrad. Goethe Inst., W. Ger., summer 1966; cert. Am. Inst. Banking, 1972; postgrad. Sch. Banking of South, La. State U., 1975; m. Carolyn Mary Bienvenu, Apr. 17, 1971 (div. Dec. 1978); children: Caroline LeGardeur, Edward Emile. Jr. mech. engr. Michoud plant, Saturn launch systems br. Boeing Aerospace, New Orleans, 1964-66; various positions IBM Computer Systems Engring., New Orleans, 1966-71; investment service rep. First Nat. Bank of Commerce, New Orleans, 1971-75, v.p. and mgr. trust investment dept., 1975-76, investment counsel, fin. analyst, 1978—; account exec., registered rep. William O'Neil & Co. Inc. of Los Angeles, 1978-79; account exec. retail/instl. Bache, Halsey, Stuart, Shields, New Orleans, 1979-80; bond broker Dorsey & Co., New Orleans, 1982-83; bank cons. F.E. DiBacco Inc., 1984-86; chmn., pres., chief exec. officer Richardson Intellectual Property Mgmt., New Orleans, 1986-88; v.p. nat. mktg. Fla. Software Kirchman Corp., 1989—. Mem. Republican State Central Com., 1st Rep. Dist., 1969-70; bd. dirs. Big Bros., 1973-74, Museums Com. Jeuness D'Orleans, 1974-75. Fellow Fin. Analysts Fedn.; mem. Fin. Analysts Soc. New Orleans, Assn. M.B.A. Execs., New Orleans C. of C. (del. 1974-75), AFTRA (New Orleans chpt.), Le Debut de Jeunnes Filles Novelle Orleans, Navy League, Am. Econ. Assn., Am. Mgmt. Assn., La. Soc. SAR (state treas. 1973-74), Mil. Order Fgn. Wars, Mil. and Hospitaller Order St. Lazarus of Jerusalem (So. del. editor), Thackeray Soc. New Orleans (founding dir.), Soc. War of 1812 New Orleans, Tulane Assn. Bus. Alumni, Phi Delta Phi (Cert. of Merit 1970), Young Men's Bus. Club Greater New Orleans (dir. 1965-68), Alpha Tau Omega. Roman Catholic. Clubs: So. Yacht; Calif. Yacht (Marina del Rey); YMCA Health, New Orleans Country, New Orleans Athletic, Roundtable of New Orleans (sec. 1972-74), New Orleans Polo; Wailers Ski (Los Angeles). Lodges: Masons, Rotary.

RICHARDSON, FRANK H., oil industry executive; b. 1933. BS, South Dakota Sch. Mines, 1955. With Shell Oil Co., Houston, 1955—, various engring. and mgmt. positions, 1955-72, prodn. mgr. western exploration/prodn. regions West Coast Div., 1972-74, gen. mgr. prodn., western region, 1975-77, v.p. corp. planning, 1978-80, sr. v.p., 1980-82, exec. v.p., 1982-88, pres., chief exec. officer, 1988—. Office: Shell Oil Co 1 Shell Pla Houston TX 77001 *

RICHARDSON, GARY FRANKLIN, publishing company executive; b. Bloomington, Ind., Sept. 23, 1949; s. Howard Franklin and Dorothy Helen (Norman) R.; m. Janna Sue Fowler, Aug. 19, 1972; children: Christina Suzanne, Nicholas Franklin. BS, Ind. U., 1972; MA in Communications, Wheaton Coll., 1976. Tchr. English/coach Catoctin High Sch., Thurmont, Md., 1972-73; tchr. English/dir. Teen Ctr. Edinburg (Ind.) Community Schs., 1973-75; editorial mgr. Victor Books, Wheaton, Ill., 1976-80; editor 3 mags. Group Pub. Co., Loveland, Colo., 1980-86; editor-in-chief, dir. product acquisition Sch. Book Fairs Inc., Worthington, Ohio, 1986-88; v.p. books and products Youth Specialities, El Cajon, Calif., 1988—. Author: Where's It At?, 1978, The Youth Leader Source Book, 1980; editor fund raising newsletter for street mission, Chgo., 1977-80; contbr. over 100 articles to various publs. Coordinator youth ministry Blanchard Rd. Alliance Ch., Wheaton, 1976-80; youth ministry vol. 1st Bapt. Ch., Loveland, 1981-84, Westerville Community Ch., 1988—; organized 20 ch. consortium, Loveland, 1981. Mem. Phi Delta Kappa. Democrat. Home: 938 W Main St Westerville OH 43081 Offfice: 1224 Greenfield Dr El Cajon CA 92021

RICHARDSON, GERALD CLEMEN, finance company executive; b. Glendale, Calif., Jan. 8, 1937; s. Gerald Q. and Kathleen Richardson; m. JoAnn Cox, Sept. 21, 1963; children: JoAnn H., Gerald D., Charles E., John M. BA, Los Angeles Bapt., 1979; MA, Calif. Grad. Theology, 1981, D in Ministry, 1983; MA, Azusa Pacific U., 1982. Cert. nat. counselor, fin. planner. Account exec. Transport Employer Benefits, Los Angeles, 1967-70; regional dir. agys. Pacific Nat. Capitol Life, Pacific Fidelity NW LIfe, Los Angeles, 1970-75; mgr. employee benefits Speare and Co., Los Angeles, 1975-77; v.p. benefits and fin. services Speare and Co., Santa Monica, Calif., 1988—; assoc. pastor Van Nuys (Calif.) 1st Bapt., 1977-79; sr. pastor Foothill Bapt. Ch., Sylmar, Calif., 1979-86; pres. Growing IED Counseling Ctr., Northridge, Calif., 1983—, Brittain Co., Covina, Calif., 1987—; chmn. North Valley Christian Counseling Ctr., Inc., Northridge, 1982—; trustee SW Bapt. Conf., West Covina, 1984, moderator, 1988. Author: Counseling in Time of Crisis, 1987' contbr. articles to Counseling and Pastoral Ministries, 1983-84. Planning commr. City of Manhattan Beach, Calif., 1967-70, chmn. crime study commn., 1968-69, councilman, 1970-74, mayor, 1972-73; mem. Rep. Cen. Com., Los Angeles, 1958-60. Served with USNG, 2955-63. Recipient commendation County of Los Angeles, 1968, City of Manhattan Beach, 1974, State Senate, 1983. Mem. Am. Assn. Counseling and Devel., Christian Assn. for Counseling and Devel., Internat. Assn. for Fin. Planning, Nat. Assn. Life Underwriters, Inst. Cert. Fin. Planners. Office: Speare & Co 2600 Colorado Ave Ste 100 Santa Monica CA 90404

RICHARDSON, JEROME JOHNSON, food service company executive; b. 1936; married. AB, Wofford Coll., Spartanburg, S.C., 1959. Profl. football player Balt. Colts, 1959-61; with Spartan Food Systems, Inc., Spartanburg, S.C., 1961—, pres., chief exec. officer, 1987—; pres., bd. dirs. TW Services, Inc., N.Y.C. also: Spartan Food Systems Inc Frontage Rd PO Box 3168 Spartanburg SC 29304 *

RICHARDSON, JOHN DAY, banker; b. Memphis, June 3, 1950; s. Harry Morton and Blanche Naomi (Day) R; m. Carol Ann Mocella, Nov. 28, 1975. BS, Ariz. State U., 1972; MBA, Miami U., Oxford, Ohio, 1975. Account exec. Reynolds Securities, Chgo., 1975-76; asst. v.p. 1st Chgo. Corp., 1976-85; v.p. Harris Trust Bank Ariz., Scottsdale, 1985—. Trustee Barrow Neurol. Found., Phoenix, 1987—, Edgar and Ellen Higgins Scholarship Found., Scottsdales, 1987—. Fellow Fin. Analysts Fedn.; mem. Inst. Chartered Fin. Analysts (chartered grader 1986—), Phoenix Soc. Fin. Analysts, Prodesse Soc., Delta Sigma Pi (cons. 1972-74, golden council 1982), John Gardiner's Tennis Ranch Club, Paradise Valley Country Club, Ariz. State U. Pres.'s Club. Republican. Episcopalian. Home: 7251 Clearwater Pkwy Paradise Valley AZ 85253 Office: Harris Trust Bank Ariz 6710 E Camelback Rd Scottsdale AZ 85251

RICHARDSON, JULIEANNA LYNN, cable television executive; b. Pitts., June 10, 1954; d. Julius Laconia and Margaret (Barfield) R. BA, Brandeis U., 1976; JD, Harvard U., 1980. Bar: Ill. 1980. Corp. lawyer Jenner & Block, Chgo., 1980-82; asst. cable adminstr., chmn. Chgo. Cable Commn., 1985; pres. Richardson & Assocs., Chgo., 1985-86; pres., chief exec. officer Shop Chgo., Inc., 1986—. Bd. dirs. Kuumba Theatre, Chgo., 1980-88, Chgo. Reporter, 1986-88. Mem. ABA, Ill. Bar Assn., Nat. Assn. Telecommunications Officers and Adminstrs., Lawyers for Creative Arts (bd. dirs. 1983—). Club: Harvard (Chgo.). Home: 2742 W Logan Blvd Chicago IL 60647

RICHARDSON, KAREN FINNEGAN, lawyer; b. Richmond, Ky., June 24, 1950; d. John Joseph and Juanita (Neal) Finnegan; m. Stephen Cole Richardson, Dec. 26, 1970 (div. Nov. 1987); 1 child, Michael Cole. Student, U. Dayton, 1968-70; BA magna cum laude, Bellarmine Coll., 1974; postgrad., U. Louisville, 1974; JD, Ga. State U., 1987. Bar: Ga. 1987. Tchr. elem. and mid. schs. Cath. Archdiocese Louisville, 1974-78; presch. tchr. Peachtree Rd. United Meth. Ch., Atlanta, 1980-83; assoc. tchr. Westminster Schs., Atlanta, 1983-84; litigation assoc. Smith, Gambrell & Russell, Atlanta, 1987-88; staff atty. Nat. Data Corp., Atlanta, 1988—. Presdl. scholar U. Dayton, 1968-70, Langdale Law scholar Ga. State U., 1984-87. Mem. ABA, Am. Corp. Counsel Assn., State Bar Ga. Assn., Delta Theta Phi (dean 1986-87). Democrat. Roman Catholic. Home: 577 Donna Dr Smyrna GA 30082 Office: Nat Data Corp Nat Data Pla Atlanta GA 30329-2010

RICHARDSON, MARY SAHM, wholesale distribution executive; b. Williamsport, Pa., Jan. 10, 1951; d. Frank Basil Rothrock Sahm and Shirley Winston Slater; m. Michael Ford Richardson, Sept. 4, 1971 (div. 1980). A in Secretarial Sci., Katharine Gibbs Coll., 1971. Pres. Williamsport Beverage Co., Inc., 1975—. Corp. solicitor United Way, Williamsport, 1981—; bd. mem. Lycoming County Water & Sewer Authority, 1989—. Mem. Nat. Beer Wholesalers Assn., Pa. Beer Wholesalers Assn. (treas. 1984—), Malt Beverage Distbrs. Assn., U.S. C. of C., Pa. C. of C., Williamsport-Lycoming C. of C. (bd. dirs., mem. exec. com. 1986—), Clinton County C. of C., Ross Club, Oaks Club. Republican. Office: Williamsport Beverage Co Inc PO Box 3395 Williamsport PA 17701-0395

RICHARDSON, RICHARD THOMAS, banker; b. Hackensack, N.J., Dec. 16, 1933; s. Rolande Herbert and Rose Hortense (Collina) R.; m. Melinda Davis Murphy, children: Lisa Melinda, Heidi Davis, Peter Thomas. B.S., Yale U., New Haven, 1955. With Chem. Bank, N.Y.C., 1960—, v.p., 1969-74; v.p., gen. mgr. Chem. Bank, London, 1974-77; sr. v.p., head audit div. Chem. Bank, N.Y.C., 1977-80, sr. v.p., head Middle East, Africa, 1980-87; mng. dir., head internat. banks & fin. instns. Chem. Bank, 1987—; dir. Wiremold Co., West Hartford, Conn., 1980—. Trustee Internat. Coll., Beirut, Lebanon, 1986—. Clubs: Yale (N.Y.C.); Beacon Hill (Summit, N.J.). Office: Chem Bank 277 Park Ave New York NY 10172

RICHARDSON, ROBERT ALLISON, aviation executive; b. East Corinth, Maine, Apr. 2, 1928; s. Morrall Englas and Rhoda Alice (Palin) R.; m. Betty David, Nov. 2, 1951; children: Mark Jay, Perry Kimball, Lisa Kim. BS, U. Md., 1958. Gen. mgr. Helicopter div. Butler Aviation, Chgo., N.Y.C., 1958-68; pres. Washington Airlines, Balt., 1968-69, Tradewinds and Western Airlines, San Juan, P.R., 1969-71; exec. dir. The Helicopter Assn. Internat., Washington, 1971-82; mktg. dir. Airclaims Info. Services, Inc., Chevy Chase, Md., 1983-88; exec. dir. Seaplane Pilots Assn., Frederick, Md., 1988—. Served to capt. with U.S. Army signal corps., 1951-58. Recipient Winged S award Sikorsky Aircraft, N.Y., N.J., 1954. Mem. Am. Soc. Appraisers, Internat. Soc. Transport Aircraft Traders, Internat. Aviation Club, Aviation/Space Writers Assn., Soc. Sr. Aerospace Execs., Aero Club of Washington, Wings Club. Republican. Episcopalian. Home: 4905 Sangamore Rd Bethesda MD 20816 Office: Seaplane Pilots Assn 421 Aviation Way Frederick MD 21701

RICHARDSON, ROBERT FRANCIS, service company executive; b. Dugger, Ind., Apr. 15, 1929; s. Arlie Franklin and Lillian Edith (Burge) R.; m. Gloria Ann Village, Dec. 31, 1952; children: Michael, Roberta, Peter, Ann, Margaret. Student, Purdue U., 1947-49. Supt. Armco Steel Corp., South Bend, Ind., 1949-52; agt. spl. investigations USAF, Wiesbaden, Fed. Republic Germany, 1953-55; mgr. Am. Service Bur., Inc., Chgo., 1955-65; resident v.p. Am. Service Bur., Inc., N.Y.C., 1965-70; v.p. Am. Service Bur., Inc., Chgo., 1970-77, pres., 1977-79; pres., chief exec. officer Am. Service Bur., Inc., Des Plaines, Ill., 1979—. Staff sgt. USAF, 1951-55. Home: 811 E Valley Ln Arlington Heights IL 60004 Office: Am Svc Bur Inc 1825 Miner St Des Plaines IL 60016

RICHARDSON, ROBERT GEORGE, financial analyst; b. Watertown, N.Y., May 19, 1946; s. Warren Allan and Pauline (Herzig) R.; children: Sarah, Emily. AB, Colgate U., 1968. Registered investment advisor, fin. planner; cert. fin. planner. Owner Sherwood Farms & Co., Aurora, N.Y., 1969-78; pvt. practice investment advisor Syracuse, N.Y., 1978-83; pres. Security Research Co., Inc., Syracuse, 1983—. Contbg. editor, columnist Pension Planning and Financial Product News, 1986—. Mem. Internat. Assn. Fin. Planning, Real Estate Securities and Syndication Inst., Internat. Assn. Registered Fin. Planners, Nat. Assn. Securities Dealers (registered prin. 1984—), N.Y. Soc. Security Analysts, Masons, Shriners, Phi Delta Theta (pres. province 1970-85). Mem. Soc. of Friends. Home: Sherwood Farms Aurora NY 13026 Office: Security Rsch Co Inc The Regency Tower 770 James St Syracuse NY 13203

RICHARDSON, ROBERT WILLIAM, industrial consultant; b. Kirksville, Mo., May 20, 1904; s. William Hart and Grace (Hill) R.; m. Mildred Miller, Dec. 29, 1929 (div. 1971); children: Annette Heynen, Thomas Hill; m. Margaret Upshaw, Aug. 29, 1982. B in Mech. Engring., U. Mich., 1928. With real estate liquidation dept. Union Dime Savs. Bank, N.Y.C., 1933-42; engr. Sanderson & Porter, N.Y.C., 1943-48, Ebasco Svcs., N.Y.C., 1951-65; chief of mission indsl. devel. orgn. UN, N.Y.C. and Bogota, Columbia, 1965-71; indsl. cons. pvt. practice Bogota, 1971—. With U.S. Army, 1942-43.

RICHARDSON, RONALD JAMES, construction consulting company executive; b. Bellows Falls, Vt., Nov. 17, 1948; s. Elwin Andrew and Elizabeth Louise (Barnett) R.; m. Sandra Lee Vastola, Jan. 9, 1970; children: James Anthony, Jared Michael, Jennifer Leigh. Student, Laurel Bus. Coll., 1968. Mgr. constrn. Potomac Country Builders Inc., Washington, 1972-77; supt. Excalibar Inc., Washington, 1977-79; mgr. constrn. Pizza Hut Inc., Atlanta, 1979-81; gen. mgr. Calson Corp., Atlanta, 1981-83; v.p. Bell Constrn. Co. Inc., Atlanta, 1983-85, Foley & Ray Inc., Atlanta, 1985-87; pres. Spectrum Internat., Atlanta, 1987—. Editor (newsletter) Constrn. News, 1987. Served with USMC, Vietnam. Mem. Am. Assn. Cost Engrs., Associated Builders and Contractors (membership com. 1985-86), London Inst. Arbitration, Am. Arbitration Assn., Constrn. Specification Inst., Internat. Ctr. Tech. Expertise, FIDIC Arbitration Experts. Office: Spectrum Internat 2635 Sandy Plains Rd Suite A-12 & A-13 Marietta GA 30066

RICHARDSON, R(OSS) FRED(ERICK), insurance executive; b. Renfrew, Ont., Can., Feb. 4, 1928; came to U.S., 1980; s. Garfield Newton and Grace Mary (MacLean) R.; m. Betty Blanche Betts, Feb. 4, 1972; children by previous marriage—Sheri Joan, Robert John, Paul Frederick. BA in Math. and Physics with honors, Queens U., 1950. Actuarial asst. Empire Life Ins. Co., Kingston, Ont., Can., 1950-55; sec. Maritime Life Ins. Co., Halifax, N.S., Can., 1955-59, dir. sales, 1959-65, chief exec. officer, 1967-72; mng. dir., chief exec. officer Abbey Life Ins. Co., U.K., 1972-80; group gen. mgr. Hartford Europe Group, 1975-80; sr. v.p., dir. worldwide life ins. ops. Hartford Ins. Group, Conn., 1980-83, dir. worldwide life ins. ops., 1983-88; pres., chief operating officer Hartford Life Cos., 1983-88; pvt. ins. cons. Boca Raton, Fla., 1988; pres., chief exec. officer Crown Life Ins. Co., 1988—. Fellow Soc. Actuaries; mem. Inst. Actuaries Gt. Britain, Companion Brit. Inst. Mgmt. CLU. Home: 17038 Royal Cove Way Boca Raton FL 33496

RICHARDSON, ROY, mfg. co. exec.; b. Chgo., Mar. 22, 1931; s. John George and Margaret Beattie (Henderson) R.; B.A. in Psychology, Macalester Coll., 1952; M.A. in Labor and Indsl. Relations, U. Ill., 1953; Ph.D. in Indsl. Relations, U. Minn., 1969; m. Mary C. Westphal, May 16, 1970; children—Beth Allison, Jessica, Adam, Roman, Alexis. With Honeywell, Inc., Mpls., 1956-70, corp. manpower mgr., 1967-70; mgr. manpower devel. and tng. Internat. Harvester, Chgo., 1970-73; dir. personnel U. Minn., 1973-75; v.p. human resources Onan Corp., Mpls., 1975-82; v.p. human resources Graco Corp., Mpls., 1982-84, v.p. human resources and corp. devel., 1985—; pres. Personnel Surveys, Inc., Mpls., 1978-80; dir., chmn. exec. com. Kotz Grad. Sch. Mgmt., St. Paul, 1984—. Vice pres. Mpls. Urban League, 1962-64. Recipient Disting. Citizens award City of Mpls., 1964. Mem. Am. Soc. Personnel Adminstrs., Am. Compensation Assn., U. Minn. Indsl. Relations Alumni Soc. (dir. 1979-85, pres. 1981). Republican. Episcopalian. Club: Edina Country. Author: Fair Pay and Work, 1971. Home: 5509 Goya Ln Edina MN 55436 Office: PO Box 1441 Minneapolis MN 55440

RICHART, DOUGLAS STEPHEN, chemist; b. Harrisburg, Pa., June 6, 1931; s. Howard Winans and Muriel Matilda (Long) R.; B.S. in Chemistry, Franklin and Marshall Coll., Lancaster, Pa., 1954; m. Joan J. Lombardo, Apr. 19, 1986; children—Deborah, Sandra, Stephen, Catherine. Research chemist Union Carbide Corp., Bound Brook, N.J., 1954-60; group leader research and devel. Polymer Corp., Reading, Pa., 1960-65, mgr. research and devel. coatings, 1965-86; mgr. research and devel. Chem. div. Morton Thiokol Inc., Reading, 1986—. Mem. Am. Chem. Soc., Soc. Plastics Engrs., Nat. Assn. Corrosion Engrs., AAAS. Republican. Episcopalian. Author in field; patentee powder coatings. Home: 6 Golfview Ln Reading PA 19606 Office: Morton Chems Flying Hills Corp Ctr 3 Commerce Dr Reading PA 19607

RICHBURG, BILLY KEITH, financial executive; b. Memphis, Dec. 16, 1946; s. Byron C. and Marjorie Mae (Draper) R.; m. Cynthia Marie Fuller, Aug. 23, 1969 (div. 1989); children: Gretchen, Jeremy. BA, U. Alaska-

Anchorage, 1974; MS in Health Care Adminstrn., Trinity U., San Antonio, 1978. Adminstrv. resident Am. Medicorp., Inc., Bluefield, W.Va. and Dallas, 1977-78; asst. exec. dir. San Antonio Community Hosp. (Humana, Inc.), 1978-79; adminstr. Hempstead County Meml. Hosp., Hope, Ark., 1979-83; exec. dir. Med. Park Hosp. (Am. Med. Internat.), Hope, 1983-84; asst. adminstr. Columbia (Mo.) Regional Hosp. (Am. Med. Internat.), 1984-85, v.p., chief fin. officer, 1985—; dir., sec.-treas. Alpha-Omega electronics, Inc., Columbia: preceptor William Woods Coll., Fulton, Mo., 1987—, U. Mo., Columbia, 1988. Active United Way, Hope, 1980-84. Served with USAF, 1969-76. Mem. Am. Coll. Healthcare Execs., Healthcare Fin. Mgmt. Assn., Columbia C. of C. (pub. affairs com. 1985—), Mensa, Rotary. Roman Catholic. Office: Columbia Regional Hosp 404 Keene St Columbia MO 65201

RICHEY, ROBERT WAYNE, real estate executive; b. Bellingham, Wash., Aug. 7, 1929; s. Harry William and Margaret (McDonald) R.; m. Ruth Ann Oetting, Feb. 14, 1953; children: David B., Elise K., Ellen T., Timothy P. BSEE, U. Wash., 1950. Registered profl. engr., Ind., Ill. Apparatus salesman Gen. Electric Co., Chgo., 1951-59; mktg. mgr. Marathon Electric Co., Wausau, Wis., 1959-71; mgr. engring. and mktg. Motors div. Reliance Electric Co., Cleve., 1971-78; gen. mgr. Kato Engring. Co., Mankato, Minn., 1979-81; chief operating officer Fed. Pacific Electric Co., Raleigh, N.C., 1981-83; exec. v.p. gen. mgr. Carolantic Realty Inc., Raleigh, N.C., 1983—. Home: 110 Annandale Dr Cary NC 27511 Office: Carolantic Realty Inc 133 Fayetteville St Mall Raleigh NC 27602

RICHEY, WILLIAM EDWARD, engineering company executive, consultant; b. Lenox, Iowa, Feb. 13, 1931; s. Edwin Lester and Thelma Bell (Cunning) R.; m. Ellen Kay Marcellus, May 25, 1968; children: Craig Eugene, Michael Lynn. A in EE, Wyandotte Tech. Inst., Kansas City, Mo., 1956. Mgr. Integrated Logistics Support Martin Co., Denver, 1958-63; supr. Integrated Logistics Support North American, Tulsa, 1963-65; supr. ILS Gen. Dynamics, Rochester, N.Y., 1965-67; pvt. practice fin. cons. U.S. and Fed. Republic Germany, 1967-76; pres. Logistics Data Services, Hudson, Fla., 1976—; proposal cons. mil. contracts to over 40 cos., including ITT, LTV, Am. Gen., Honeywell, 1967—. Mem. U.S. Def. Com. Served as sgt. USMC, 1948-52, Korea. Mem. Am. Defense Preparedness Assn., Soc. Logistics Engrs. (sr. mem.). Republican. Lutheran. Office: Logistics Data Services Inc 13615 Stacey Dr Hudson FL 34667

RICHEY, WILLIAM WINTHROP, venture capitalist; b. Waco, Tex., Dec. 29, 1951; s. Harvey Mac and Doris (Ray) R; m. Cheryl Diane Ivy, Aug. 15, 1987; 1 child, Alicia Starr. BBA, U. Tex., Arlington, 1975, MBA, 1981; cert., NASBIC Mgmt. Inst., Chgo., 1981. Credit analyst Republic Bank Dallas, 1979-80; investment analyst Republic Venture Group, Inc., Dallas, 1980-81, asst. v.p., 1981-85, treas., asst. sec., 1981—, v.p., 1985—; dir. Martinaire, Inc., Dallas, Pharmacy Practice Group, Inc., Dallas, Care Systems, Inc., Huntsville, Ala. Mem. 500, Inc., Dallas Mus. Art, Omicron Delta Epsilon, Beta Theta Pi, Delta Rho Beta Alumni Assn. Republican. Roman Catholic. Office: Republic Venture Group Inc 325 N Saint Paul St Dallas TX 75201

RICHMAN, ANTHONY E., textile rental company executive; b. Los Angeles, Dec. 13, 1941; s. Irving M. and Helen V. (Muchnic) R.; m. Judy Harriet Richman, Dec. 19, 1964; children: Lisa Michele, Jennifer Beth. BS, U. So. Calif., 1964. With Reliable Textile Rental Services, Los Angeles, 1964—, service mgr., 1969, sales and service mgr., 1970-73, plant mgr., 1973-75, gen. mgr., bd. dirs., 1975-78, chief exec. officer, 1978-82, v.p., sec.-treas., 1975-82, exec. v.p., chief exec. officer, 1982-84, pres., chief exec. officer, 1984—. Bd. dirs. Guild for Children, 1979—, Valley Guild for Cystic Fibrosis, 1974—; Cystic Fibrosis Found., 1985—; founding mem. Patrons for Cystic Fibrosis, 1983—. Recipient cert. of Achievement Linen Supply Assn. Am., 1979. Mem. Textile Rental Services Assn. Am. (past bd. dirs.). Office: Reliable Textile Rental Svcs 3200 N Figueroa St Los Angeles CA 90065

RICHMAN, JOHN MARSHALL, business executive, lawyer; b. N.Y.C., Nov. 9, 1927; s. Arthur and Madeleine (Marshall) R.; m. Priscilla Frary, Sept. 3, 1951; children: Catherine, Diana H. BA, Yale U., 1949; LLB, Harvard U., 1952. Bar: N.Y. 1953, Ill. 1973. Assoc. Leve, Hecht, Hadfield & McAlpin, N.Y.C., 1952-54; mem. law dept. Kraft, Inc., Glenview, Ill., 1954-63; gen. counsel Sealtest Foods div. Kraft, Inc., Glenview, 1963-67, asst. gen. counsel, 1967-70, v.p., gen. counsel, 1970-73, sr. v.p., gen. counsel, 1973-75, sr. v.p. adminstrn., gen. counsel, 1975-79, chmn. bd., chief exec. officer, 1979—; chmn. bd., chief exec. officer Dart & Kraft, Inc. (became Kraft, Inc. 1986), Glenview, 1980; vice chmn. Philip Morris Cos., 1988—; chmn. Kraft Gen. Foods, 1988—. Congregationalist. Clubs: Comml. (Chgo.), Econ. (Chgo.), Mid-Am. (Chgo.); Union League (N.Y.C.); Westmoreland Country (Wilmette, Ill.); Old Elm (Ft. Sheridan, Ill.); Lost Tree (North Palm Beach, Fla.). Office: Kraft Gen Foods Kraft Ct Glenview IL 60025

RICHMAN, MARVIN JORDAN, real estate developer; b. N.Y.C., July 13, 1939; s. Morris and Minnie (Graubart) R.; m. Amy Paula Rubin, July 31, 1966; children—Mark Jason, Keith Hayden, Susanne Elizabeth, Jessica Paige. BArch, MIT, 1962; M Urban Planning, N.Y. U., 1966, postgrad., 1967-69; MBA, U. Chgo., 1977; U.S. Dept. State fellow U. Chile, 1960. Architect, planner Skidmore, Owings & Merrill, N.Y.C., 1964, Conklin & Rossant, N.Y.C., 1965-67; ptnr. Vizbaras & Ptnrs., N.Y.C., 1968-69; v.p. Urban Investment & Devel. Co., Chgo., 1969-79, sr. v.p., 1979; pres. First City Devels. Corp., Beverly Hills, Calif., 1979-80, Olympia & York (U.S.) Devel. (West), 1987—, Olympia & York Calif. Equities Corp., L.A., 1981-87, Olympia & York Calif. Devel. Corp., 1981-87, Olympia & York Hope St. Mgmt. Corp., 1982-87, Olympia & York Homes Corp., 1983—, Olympia & York Calif. Constrn. Corp., 1986—; lectr. NYU, 1967-69, Nat. Humanities Inst., other univs. Adv. Nat. Endowment for Arts. Mem. UCLA Ctr. Fin. and Real Estate Bd. Advisors. With USAF, 1963-64. Registered architect; lic. real estate broker. Mem. AIA, Am Planning Assn.,Internat. Coun. Shopping Ctrs., L.A. World Affairs Coun., Urban Land Inst., Nat. Assn. Office and Indsl. Parks, Chief Exec.'s Round Table, Air Force Assn., Lambda Alpha. Home: 3238 Fond Dr Encino CA 91436 Office: Olympia & York 11601 Wilshire Blvd Los Angeles CA 90025

RICHMAN, STEPHEN I., lawyer; b. Washington, Pa., Mar. 26, 1933; m. Audrey May Gefsky. BS, Northwestern U., 1954; JD, U. Pa., 1957. Bar: Pa. 1958. ptnr. Ceisler, Richman, Smith Law Firm, P.A., Washington. Lectr. W.Va. U. Med. Ctr., Grand Rounds, Am. Coll. Chest Physicians, Pa. Thoracic Soc., Am. Thoracic Soc., The Energy Bur., Coll. of Pathologists, Allegheny County Health Dept., Am. Pub. Health Assn., Indsl. Health Assn., Self-Insurers Assn., Am. Iron and Steel Inst., Can. Thoracic Soc., ABA, Pa. Chamber of Bus. and Industry, Internat. Conf. Pneumoconlosis. Author: Meaning of Impairment and Disability, Chest, 1980, Legal Aspects for the Pathologist, in Pathology of Occupational and Environmental Lung Disease, 1988, Current Medical Methods in Diagnosing Coal Workers Pneumoconiosis, A Review of the Medical and Legal Definitions of Related Impairment and Disability, Labor and the Congress, 1986, Medicolegal Aspects of Asbestos for Pathologists, Arch. Pathology and Laboratory Medicine, 1983, The Franklin Report to The Congress, 1983, Struggle for Reason and Accountability, 1986, Compensation for Occupational Lung Disease, Legal Insight, 1988, other publs. Mem. legal com. Indsl. Health Found., Pitts. Mem. ABA (vice chair workers compensation and employers liability law com.), Pa. Bar Assn. (governing coun. worker's compensation sect.), Assn. Trial Lawyers Am., Pa. Chamber Bus. and Industry (workers' compensation com., chmn. subcom. on legis. drafting). Home: 820 E Beau St Washington PA 15301 Office: Washington Trust Bldg Ste 200 Washington PA 15301

RICHMAN, VICTORIA S., hotel, real estate consultant; b. Boston, June 21, 1959; d. Justin Lewis and Susan (Kadison) R. BA, Brown U., 1981; MBA, U. Pa., 1985. Lic. in real estate sales. Pvt. investigator Pinkerton Security Service, Boston and Providence, R.I., 1980-81; bus. analyst Hibernia Nat. Bank, New Orleans, 1981-83; hotel real estate cons. Stephen W. Brener Assocs., Inc., N.Y.C., 1985—; sponsor's rep. Ann. Hospitality Investment Conf., N.Y.C., 1985—. Interviewer nat. alumni sch. program Brown U., New Orleans and N.Y.C., 1981—. Mem. Nat. Assn. Female Execs., Ednl. Inst. of Am. Hotel and Motel Assn. Clubs: Brown, Wharton (N.Y.C.).

RICHMOND, JOHN MELVYN, jewelry company executive; b. Chgo., Feb. 13, 1939; s. Harry and Clarice (Costulas) R.; student pub. schs., Chgo., Los Angeles; m. Dotty Finberg; children—Kelly, Robyn, Shannan. Salesman Sarong Inc., div. Playtex, Dover, Del., 1964-66; key account coordinator Exquisite Form, Pelham Manor, N.Y., 1964-66; regional mgr., nat. trainer Benrus Corp., Ridgefield, Conn., 1966-70, regional mgr. Wells Inc., div. Benrus Corp., Attleboro, Mass., 1970-74, nat. sales mgr., 1974-75; v.p., nat. sales mgr. Imperial Pearl Syndicate, Chgo., 1975-76; nat. sales mgr., v.p. Gall Fashion Jewelry Co., Dallas, 1977—; pres. JMR Fine Jewelry, 1977—, Classique D'Or Inc., Dallas, Shoe Biz Inc., Avric, Inc.; dir. Town North Nat. Bank, Dallas. Served with U.S. Army, 1958-61. Mem. Retail Jewelers of Am., Jewelers Mfg. Guild. Home: 7309 NW Maple Dr Lawton OK 73505 Office: 3222 SW Airport Indsl Rd Lawton OK 73501

RICHMOND, SAMUEL BERNARD, management educator; b. Boston, Oct. 14, 1919; s. David E. and Freda (Braman) R.; m. Evelyn Ruth Kravitz, Nov. 26, 1944; children: Phyllis Gail, Douglas Emerson, Clifford Owen. AB cum laude, Harvard U., 1940; MBA, Columbia U., 1948, PhD, 1951. Mem. faculty Columbia U., 1946-76, assoc. prof., 1957-60, prof. econ. and statistics, 1960-76; assoc. dean Grad. Sch. Bus. Columbia U., 1971-72, acting dean, 1972-73; dean, prof. mgmt. Owen Grad. Sch. Mgmt., Vanderbilt U., Nashville, 1976-86, Ralph Owen prof. mgmt., 1984-88, Ralph Owen prof. mgmt., dean emeritus, 1988—; vis. prof. U. Sherbrooke, Que., 1967, U. Buenos Aires, Argentina, 1964, 65, Case Inst. Tech., Cleve., 1958-59, Fordham U., N.Y.C., 1952-53; dir. IMS Internat. Inc., N.Y.C., 1978-88, 1st Am. Corp., Nashville, 1981-86, Winners Corp., Nashville, 1983-89, Corbin Ltd., N.Y.C., 1970-85; Ingram Industries Inc., Nashville; cons. to maj. comml., ednl., profl. and govtl. orgns. Author: Operations Research for Management Decisions, 1968, Statistical Analysis, 1957, 2d. edit., 1964, Regulation and Competition in Air Transportation, 1961. Trustee Ramapo Coll. N.J., 1975-76. 1st lt. USAAF, 1943-45. Recipient Honor award CAB, 1971, Alumni award for outstanding svc. Grad. Sch. Bus., Columbia U., 1973. Mem. Am. Statis. Assn. (chmn. adv. com. rsch. to CAB 1966-74, dir. 1965-67), Am. Econ. Assn., Inst. Mgmt. Sci., Ops. Rsch. Soc. Am., Beta Gamma Sigma. Home: 5404 Camelot Rd Brentwood TN 37027 Office: Vanderbilt U Owen Grad Sch Mgmt Nashville TN 37203

RICKARDS, LEONARD MYRON, oil company executive; b. Canton, N.C., Aug. 17, 1927; s. James Cooper and Ethel Naomi (Trull) R.; m. Pauline Hope Murray, Feb. 28, 1953; children—Tim Paul, Lisa Diane. B.S., U. Kans., 1950; advanced mgmt. insead, European Inst. Bus. Adminstrn., Fountainbleau, France, 1974. With Phillips Petroleum Co., Bartlesville, Okla., 1950—; sr. v.p. Europe-Africa Phillips Petroleum Co., London, 1973-76; mgr. N.Am. exploration and prodn. div. Phillips Petroleum Co., Bartlesville, 1976-77, v.p. N.Am., 1977-80, sr. v.p. exploration and production, 1980-85, exec. v.p., 1985—, also bd. dirs. Served with U.S. Coast Guard, 1945-46. Mem. Am. Assn. Petroleum Geologists, Am. Petroleum Inst. (bd. dirs.), Okla. Soc. Profl. Engrs., Sigma Tau, Tau Beta Pi, Theta Tau. Office: Phillips Petroleum Co 4th & Keeler Bartlesville OK 74004

RICKERT, EDWIN WEIMER, investment counsel; b. Connersville, Ind., June 17, 1914; s. Edwin and Grace (Weimer) R.; A.B., Columbia U., 1936; m. Ruth Alma Fulcher, July 9, 1942; children—Jean Adelia, Wendy Grace, Allen Edwin. Security analyst, economist Mackubin, Legg & Co., Balt., 1936-40; indsl. analyst Office of Prodn. Mgmt., Washington, 1940-41; supr. commodity econ. research Standard Brnds, Inc., N.Y.C., 1946-53; with Brundage, Story & Rose, N.Y.C., 1953—, partner, 1966-83, sr. investment cons., 1984—. Trustee, Columbia U. Press, 1977—; bd. visitors Columbia Coll., N.Y., 1986—. Served to capt. U.S. Army, 1941-46; ret. lt. col. Res. Mem. Investment Counsel Assn. Am., N.Y. Soc. Security Analysts. Republican. Presbyterian. Clubs: India House (N.Y.C.); Grachur (Balt.). Home: 56 Dogwood Ln Rockville Centre NY 11570 Office: One Broadway New York NY 10004

RICKMAN, WALLACE RAY, investment broker; b. Washington, Jan. 28, 1926; s. Amos Raymond and Inez (Wade) R.; m. Gladys Rebecca Branch, June 11, 1947; children: David Wallace, Barry Alan. BCS, Benjamin Franklin U., 1951; grad., Am. Inst. Banking, 1957. Cert. fin. planner. Records mgr. John H. Wilkins Co., Washington, 1947-51; credit mgr. Campbell Music Co., Washington, 1951-53; v.p., budget dir. Nat. Bank Washington, 1953-81; broker Wheat First Securities, Inc., Petersburg, Va., 1981—. Treas., bd. dirs. Wakefield (Va.) Found., 1987-88; chmn. planning com. Town of Wakefield, 1985-88; chief election officer Wakefield Precinct, Sussex County, Va., 1988. With USAAF, 1944-46. Mem. Inst. Cert. Fin. Planners, Ruritan Club (treas. 1984-86), Rotary (pres Wakefield chpt. 1984). Republican. Methodist. Home: 108 Wilson Ave PO Box 417 Wakefield VA 23888 Office: Wheat First Securities Inc 129 N Sycamore St PO Box 190 Petersburg VA 23804

RICKS, JACQUELINE POWELL, real estate company official; b. Edenton, N.C., Oct. 11, 1955; d. James Pender and Jacqueline (Burke) R. AA, St. Mary's Jr. Coll., 1975; grad., N.C. Realtors Inst., 1989. Lic. real estate broker, N.C. Sec., rental asst. Kitty Dunes Realty, Kitty Hawk, N.C., 1975-77, rental mgr., 1977-80; rental mgr. Sun Realty, Kill Devil Hills, N.C., 1980-85, assoc. broker, 1985—. Mem. Nat. Mktg. Inst., N.C. Assn. Realtors, Dare County Bd. Realtors (bd. dirs. 1980-81, 85-88, pres. elect 1989, chmn. grievance com. 1987), Dare County C. of C. (chmn. Mariners's Club 1985). Democrat. Episcopalian. Home: Box 1367 Kill Devil Hills NC 27948 Office: Sun Realty 1500 S Croatan Hwy Kill Devil Hills NC 27948

RICKS, THOMAS EDWIN, accounting executive; b. Salt Lake City, May 4, 1946; s. Ben E. and Afton (Bawden) R.; m. Virginia Richey, Aug. 21, 1968; children: Leslie, Thomas Jr., Brian, Brent, Susannah, Stephen. BS in Acctg. cum laude, Weber State Coll., 1972. CPA, Calif., Tex. Audit sr. Arthur Anderson & Co., Los Angeles, 1972-75; internal audit supr. So. Calif. Edison Co., Rosemead, 1975-77; internal audit mgr. El Paso (Tex.) Natural Gas Co., 1977-80, gen. acctg. mgr., 1980-82, fin. forecast dir., 1982-83, v.p., controller, 1985—; asst. v.p. acctg. Burlington No. Co., Seattle, 1983-85. Active Boy Scouts Am., El Paso, 1977; dir. Jr. Achievement, El Paso, 1985—. Mem. Am. Gas Assn. (mem. adv. com.), Interstate Natural Gas Assn., Am. Inst. CPA's, Tex. Soc. CPA's, Phi Kappa Phi. Republican. Mormon. Home: 873 Forest Willow Circle El Paso TX 79922 Office: El Paso Natural Gas Co PO Box 1492 El Paso TX 79978

RICOTTA, ANTHONY VINCENT, publisher; b. N.Y.C., Apr. 26, 1932; s. Vincent James and Jennie (Gianfortuna) R.; m. Mary Ann Theresa Feeley, July 4, 1956; children: Christine, Anthony, Marianne. BS, St. Francis Coll., Bklyn., 1986. Utility analyst Ebasco Services, N.Y.C., 1956-67; editor fin. news Investment Dealer's Digest, N.Y.C., 1967-85; pub. IDD's Security Traders Monthly, N.Y.C., 1985-87, Traders Mag., N.Y.C., 1987—. Pres., chmn. Beachview Mano Civic Assn., Staten Island, N.Y., 1972-76; bd. dirs. Last Chance Pond Found., 1976-79; trustee St. Ann's Ch., 1968-84. Served with cpl. U.S. Army, 1952-54, Korea. Mem. Fin. Writers Assn., Investment Assn. N.Y. Roman Catholic. Club: Comanche Archery Bklyn. Office: Traders Mag 225 Broadway Ste 1607 New York NY 10007

RIDDICK, DOUGLAS SMITH, horticultural industrialist, industrial designer; b. High Point, N.C., Sept. 28, 1942; s. Delmar Smith and Irene Douglas (Sparks) R.; m. Marcia Ann, Feb. 24, 1968; children: Eric Smith, Adrea Anne. Student, Columbus (Ohio) Coll. Art and Design, 1961-65, U. Bridgeport, 1965-66; BFA, U. Del., 1978. Indsl. designer Harper Landell & Assocs., Phila., 1967-70, ILC Industries, Dover, Del., 1970-75, Leeds Travelwear, Clayton, Del., 1975-76, DuPont Co., Glasgow, Del., 1976-79, Consumer Electronics Div. RCA, Indpls., 1979-80; designer Brayton Internat. Coll., High Point, N.C., 1981; owner Riddick Landscape Nursery, High Point, N.C., 1980—; mgr. Riddick Greenhouses & Nursery, High Point, N.C., 1980—. Patentee; designer indsl. instruments in field. Mem. Dover Bicentennial Com., 1975-76, Gov. DuPont's Com. Promotion of Solar Energy and subcom. Consumer Protection, 1978-79. Recipient Best in Packaging award Print Casebooks III, Washington. 1977, Excellence in Advt. award Am. Assn. Nurserymen, 1981. Baptist. Club: Bicycle Club Del. (coordinator 1974-78, pres. 1979). Home and Office: Rte 5 PO Box 490-C High Point NC 27263

RIDDLE, DAVID MICHAEL, banker; b. Pensacola, Fla., Mar. 17, 1945; s. James Alvin and A. Laura (Cone) R.; m. Linda Teague, Dec. 12, 1967 (div.); m. Nancy Beauchamp, Oct. 9, 1975; children: Jeffrey Alan, Kelly Lynn. BS, Fla. State U., 1967, MS, 1971. Ann. fund. coordinator Fla. State U., Tallahassee, 1969-71; v.p. lending Sun Fed. Savs., Tallahassee, 1971-79; sales rep. Republic Mortgage Ins. Corp., Winston-Salem, N.C., 1979-83; exec. v.p. Andrew Jackson Savs. & Loan, Tallahassee, 1983-84; pres., chief exec. officer Citizens & Builders Fed. Savs. Bank, Pensacola, 1984—. Mem. pres.'s club Fla. State U., Tallahassee, 1985-87; treas. Pvt. Industry Coun., Pensacola, 1987-88; chmn. Better Bus. Bur., Pensacola, 1987-88; v.p. Pensacola Area C. of C., 1987-88. Recipient Disting. Leadership award NACLO, 1987; named one of Emerging Leaders, Pensacola Area C. of C., 1988. Democrat. Baptist. Office: Citizens & Builders Fed Savs 33 W Garden St Pensacola FL 32501

RIDDLE, DIXIE LEE, wholesale company executive. Formerly v.p., then sr. v.p. Farmers Union Cen. Exchange, St. Paul, 1st vice chmn. bd., now 2d vice chmn. Office: Farmers Union Cen Exch Inc PO Box 64089 Saint Paul MN 55164-0089 *

RIDDLE, TIMOTHY ALAN, accountant; b. Columbia, Tenn., Mar. 26, 1961; s. Charles Calvin and Frances Sara (Parks) R.; m. Lisa Jean, Aug. 18, 1984. BS cum laude, Tenn. Tech. U., Cookeville, 1983. CPA, Tenn. Staff acct. Arthur Andersen & Co., Chattanooga, 1983-85; chief fin. officer Carter St. Corp., Chattanooga, 1985—. Mem. Citizens Taxpayers Assn. Hamilton County, Chattanooga, 1987. Mem. Tenn. Soc. CPAs. Republican. Mem. Ch. of Christ.

RIDEOUT, EARL HARRISON, manufacturing company executive; b. Lewiston, Maine, Feb. 10, 1946; s. Harrison Earl and Marion Frances (Mitchell) R.; m. Catherine Louise Haubner, Aug. 23, 1969; children: David, Michael, Stacey. BSEE, Northeastern U., 1969, MBA, 1974. Elec. engr. Teledyne TAC, Woburn, Mass., 1969-77; regional sales mgr. MCT, Wakefield, Mass., 1977-79; dir. engring. Handler div. MCT, St. Paul, 1979-81, gen. mgr., 1981-84; pres. Testamatic Corp., Albany, N.Y., 1984-86; exec. v.p. Vitronics Corp., Newmarket, N.H., 1986-88; pres. Vitronics Energy Systems, Newmarket, 1988—. Patentee in field. Mem. Surface Mount Equipment Mfrs. Assn. (co-founder, bd. dirs., pres.). Office: Vitronics Energy Systems 4 Forbes Rd Newmarket NH 03824

RIDER, GREGORY ASHFORD, investment company executive; b. Douglas, Wyo., Nov. 16, 1949; s. Keith Shumway and Margaret Elizabeth (Markle) R.; m. Katherine Elizabeth Winn, June 24, 1979; 1 child, Elizabeth Winn. BS, Georgetown U., 1972; MBA, Harvard U., 1979. Mktg. specialist Marshall Internat., Chgo., 1972-77; asst. to chmn. McLean Securities, N.Y.C., 1978-81; dir. corp. devel. SHV N.Am. Corp., Cin., 1981-83; gen. ptnr. Criterion Investments, Houston, 1983-85; pres. Rider Assocs., Cin., 1986—, Ocean Ventures Mgmt., Inc., N.Y.C., 1987—; bd. dirs. MetaLaser Techs., Ltd., Sydney, San Francisco, (chmn.), Ocean Ventures, Ltd., Sydney. Mem. Soc. Mfg. Engrs. (sr.) Nat. Assn. Small Bus. Investment Cos., Nat. Venture Capital Assn., Circumnavigators Found. (treas. 1980-81, Global Research fellow 1971). Episcopalian. Clubs: Circumnavigators, Harvard (N.Y.C.); Met. Racquet (Houston); Camargo Racquet (Cin.), Kenwood Swim and Tennis (Cin.). Home and Office: 2870 E Galbraith Rd Amberley Village OH 45237

RIDER, LUTHER GLENN, insurance agent; b. Adams County, Pa., Nov. 12, 1936; s. Glenn M. and Virginia O. (Brewer) R.; m. Dorothy L. Stape, Jan. 7, 1956; children: Barbara E., Douglas A., Michael L., Kathy L. Grad. high sch., Biglerville, Pa. Agt. Nationwide Ins. Cos., Columbus, Ohio, 1967—. With USAF, 1955-59. Fellow Life Underwriters Tng. Coun., Hanover-Gettysburg Life Underwriters. Democrat. Office: Luther G Rider Ins Agy PO Box 366 22 N Main St Biglerville PA 17307-0366

RIDLEY, CLARENCE HAVERTY, lawyer; b. Atlanta, June 3, 1942; s. Frank Morris Jr. and Clare (Haverty) R.; m. Eleanor Horsey, Aug. 22, 1969; children: Augusta Morgan, Clare Haverty. BA, Yale U., 1964; MBA, Harvard U., 1966; JD, U. Va., 1971. Bar: Ga. 1971. Assoc. King & Spaulding, Atlanta, 1971-77; ptnr. King & Spaulding, 1977—; adv. bd. Venture 1st Ventrue Capital Fund, 1984—; bd. dirs. Haverty Furniture Cos., Inc. Author: Computer Software Agreements, 1987. Chmn. St. Joseph's Hosp. Found., Atlanta, 1986—; trustee Mercy Health Svcs., 1987—. Lt. U.S. Army, 1966-68, Korea. Roman Catholic. Home: 2982 Habersham Rd Atlanta GA 30305 Office: King & Spaulding 2500 Trust Co Tower Atlanta GA 30303

RIEBESEHL, E. ALLAN, lawyer; b. N.Y.C., July 7, 1938; s. Harold J. and Phyllis Riebesehl; m. Suzanne C. Moore, July 28, 1963; children: Gregory, Christopher. BA, CCNY, 1961; JD, Fordham Law Sch., 1966; LLM, NYU, 1972. Bar: N.Y. 1966, U.S. Tax Ct. 1968, U.S. Supreme Ct. 1970, U.S. Ct. Appeals (2d cir.) 1971, U.S. Dist. Ct. (ea. dist.) N.Y. 1973, U.S. Dist. Ct. (so. dist.) N.Y., 1974. Tax atty. Kennecott Copper Corp., N.Y.C., 1966-69, Celanese Corp., 1969-70, Pan Am. World Airways, N.Y.C., 1970-71; sole practice, Garden City, N.Y., 1971—. adj. prof. Touro Law Sch. Past pres. Woodbury-Syosset Republican Club; past v.p. Syosset Hosp. Community Adv. Bd. Served with USMC, 1961-66. Fellow Am. Acad. Matrimonial Lawyers; mem. ABA, Am. Judicature Soc., C.W. Post Tax Inst., Am. Arbitration Assn., Cath. Lawyers Guild (pres.), N.Y. State Bar Assn., Nassau County Bar Assn. (bd. dirs.), Suffolk County Bar Assn., Nassau Lawyers Assn., Lawyers in Mensa. Club: Kiwanis (past pres.) (Mineola, N.Y.). Co-author: New York Practice Guide: Domestic Relations; contbr. articles to profl. jours. Office: 666 Old Country Rd Garden City NY 11530

RIECHERS, STEPHEN ALLEM, controller; b. Harvey, Ill., Oct. 19, 1948; s. Merith A. and Rose Maria (Brehm) R.; m. Charlotte Jean Bachmann, June 27, 1970; children: Kristin Joy, Marissa Lyn. BS in acctg., No. Ill. U., 1970; Assoc. degree, Nat. Inst. Credit, Park Ridge, Ill., 1984. Staff acct. Interlake, Inc., Riverdale, Ill., 1970-74; acctg. supr. Interlake Inc., Blue Island, Ill., 1974-80; v.p., gen. mgr. Korhumel Steel, 1980-83; controller Korhumel Steel, Bensenville, Ill., 1983-84; asst. controller Allied Structural Steel, Chicago Heights, Ill., 1984; acctg. supr. Hydro Aire Inc., Chgo., 1985; controller Northwest Engring & Constrn., Inc., Gary, Ind., 1985—. Lutheran. Office: Northwest Engring & Constrn Inc 3240 W 5th Ave Gary IN 46406

RIED, ROBERT JEFFREY, automotive executive; b. Rockville Centre, N.Y., Sept. 4, 1946; s. Robert R. and Frances M. (Cherleck) R.; m. Susan Rowland, Aug. 4, 1973; children: Jennifer, Alexander. AB, Villanova U., 1968; JD, Fordham U., 1973. Assoc. Donovan Leisure Newton & Irvine, N.Y.C., 1973-81; sr. counsel Firestone Tire & Rubber Co., Akron, Ohio, 1981-87; chief legal officer Toyota Motor Mfg. U.S.A., Inc., Georgetown, Ky., 1987—. Served with U.S. Army, 1968-70. Home: 2224 Abbeywood Rd Lexington KY 40515 Office: Toyota Motor Mfg USA Inc 1001 Cherry Blossom Way Georgetown KY 40324

RIEDEL, ALAN ELLIS, manufacturing company executive, lawyer; b. Bellaire, Ohio, June 28, 1930; s. Emil George and Alberta (Shafer) R.; m. Ruby P. Tignor, June 21, 1953; children: Ralph A., Amy L., John T. AB magna cum laude, Ohio U., 1952; JD, Case Western Res. U., 1955; grad., Advanced Mgmt. Program, Harvard, 1971. Bar: Ohio 1955, Tex. 1968. Assoc. Squire, Sanders & Dempsey, Cleve., 1955-60; gen. counsel Cooper Industries Inc. (formerly Cooper Bessemer Co.), Mt. Vernon, Ohio, 1960-63, sec., 1963-68, 1963-68, v.p. indsl. relations, 1968-73; sr. v.p. adminstrn. Cooper Industries Inc. (formerly Cooper Bessemer Co.), Houston, 1973—; also dir. Cooper Industries Inc. (formerly Cooper Bessemer Co.); dir. Standard Products Co., Cleve., Arkwright Mut. Ins. Co., Waltham, Mass. Former chmn. bd. dirs. Jr. Achievement of S.E. Tex.; chmn. bd. trustees Ohio U. Endowment Found. Mem. Order of Coif, Phi Beta Kappa, Omicron Delta Kappa, Delta Tau Delta. Home: 803 Creekwood Way Houston TX 77024 Office: Cooper Industries Inc 1001 Fannin 40th Fl PO Box 4446 Houston TX 77210

RIEDEL, PAUL SCHREITER, mobile homes company executive; b. Minden City, Mich., Oct. 8, 1911; s. Louis Herman and Anna (Schreiter) R.; m. Dorothy Artha Slack, Oct. 17, 1932; children: Daniel P., Andrea Lynn. Student Mich. State U., 1928-31, Detroit Bus. U., 1932. Propr. L.H. Riedel Lumber Co., Inc., 1941-46, pres., 1946-53; pres. Marlette (Mich.) Coach Co., 1953-58; pres. Vindale Corp., Dayton, Ohio, 1958-76, hon. chmn. bd. dirs., cons., 1976—. Presbyterian. Clubs: Le Mirador Country (Mont

Pelerin, Switzerland), Moorings Country. Lodges: Shriners, Masons. Office: Vindale Corp 6001 Pelican Bay Blvd Apt 906 Naples FL 33963

RIEDEL, STEVEN DARRELL, data processing company executive; b. Eau Claire, Wis., June 2, 1943; s. Harold W. and Lucy C. (Reiter) R.; m. Fern Margaret Borum, Dec. 19, 1964; children: Phillip B., Mark S. BS in bus. admin., economics, U. Wis., Eau Claire, 1965. Product mgr. Burroughs Corp., Detroit, 1973-75, regional sales mgr., 1975-79; v.p. product mktg. No. Telecom Corp., Mpls., 1979-82, v.p. mktg., 1982-83; pres. Betacom Corp., St. Paul, 1983-85; pres., chief exec. officer Enercon Data Corp., Mpls., 1985—, also bd. dirs.; cons. in field, 1984-85; bd. dirs. Betacom, 1983-84. Pres. St. Clares Parish Council, Detroit, 1979, sec., 1978. Mem. Nat. Tax Limitation Com., Christian Edn. Inst., Mpls. Exec. Group, Pax Christi, Alpha Kappa Lambda. Republican. Roman Catholic. Club: Flagship Athletic (softball mgr., league champions 1986-88). Office: Enercon Data Corp 7464 W 78th St Minneapolis MN 55435

RIEDHAMMER, THOMAS MARTIN, pharmaceutical company executive; b. Buffalo, Mar. 18, 1948; s. Harold M. and Marjorie P. (Walsh) R.; m. Evelyn M. Albano, July 25, 1970; children: Michael, Marcus, Tanya. BA, SUNY, Buffalo, 1970, PhD, 1975. Dir. rsch. and devel. Bausch and Lomb, Inc., Rochester, N.Y., 1975-84; v.p. Paco Rsch. Corp., Lakewood, N.J., 1984-86, pres., 1986—. Contbr. articles to profl. jours.; patentee in field. Office: Paco Rsch Corp 1705 Oak St Lakewood NJ 08701

RIEF, MARVIN L., accounting manager; b. West Point, Nebr., Sept. 4, 1946; s. Leroy John and Madelen (Marksmeier) R.; m. Dorothy R. Krull, Aug. 16, 1969; children: Julie, Angela, Brian, Bradley. BS in Bus. Adminstrn., Creighton U., 1969. Staff acct. Begley, Herbert, Graham, Wering, Omaha, 1968-69; staff auditor Arthur Andersen & Co., Omaha, 1969-71; staff acct. Zeph Telpner, CPA, Council Bluffs, Iowa, 1971-72; acctg. systems supr. Nebr. Pub. Power Dist., Columbus, 1972-76, acctg. mgr., 1976-82, project mgr., 1982-88, acctg. mgr., 1988—. del. Rep. County Conv., Columbus, 1980. Mem. Nat. Assn. Accts. (bd. dirs. 1988—), Am. Pub. Power Assn. (info. com. 1987). Republican. Roman Catholic. Home: 2564 43d Ave Columbus NE 68601 Office: Nebr Pub Power Dist PO Box 499 Columbus NE 68601

RIEFLER, DONALD BROWN, banker; b. Washington, Nov. 10, 1927; s. Winfield W. and Dorothy (Brown) R.; m. Patricia Hawley, Oct. 12, 1957; children—Duncan, Linda, Barbara. B.A., Amherst Coll., 1949. With Morgan Guaranty Trust Co. of N.Y., N.Y.C., 1952—; v.p. Morgan Guaranty Trust Co. of N.Y., 1962-68, sr. v.p., 1968-77, chmn. market risk com., 1977—; dir. Liberty Brokerage Inc., Niagara Mohawk Power Corp., Pvt. Export Funding Corp. Served with U.S. Army, 1950-52. Mem. Am. Bankers Assn., Public Securities Assn. Club: Creek (Locust Valley, N.Y.). Home: 5 Pond View Dr Glen Cove NY 11542 Office: Morgan Guaranty Trust Co 23 Wall St New York NY 10015

RIEGELS, GUY ANTHONY, accounting executive; b. Mombassa, Kenya, Feb. 19, 1945; arrived in Belgium, 1988; s. Ernest Rudolf and Mildred Violet (Hockley) R.; m. Jennifer Vivian Gray, Sept. 9, 1967; children: Lara Jane, Timothy Patrick. Cert., Prince of Wales Sch., Nairobi, Kenya. Chartered acct. Articles clk. Coopers & Lybrand, London, 1961-66, sr. mgr., 1970-74; supr. Coopers & Lybrand, Dar-Es-Salam, Tanzania, 1967-70; ptnr. Michael Angel Paul, Victoria, Seychelles, 1974-81, Binder Hamlyn, Sydney, Australia, 1981-84; mng. ptnr. Parkhills BDO, Sydney, 1984-88; chief operating officer BDO Binder, Brussels, 1988—. Fellow Inst. Chartered Accts in Eng. and Wales, Inst. Chartered Accts. in Australia; mem. Middle Harbour Yacht Club. Office: BDO Binder, 60 Blvd de la Woluwe, 1200 Brussels Belgium

RIEHL, HARRY ERNEST, banker; b. Yonkers, N.Y., Oct. 10, 1943; s. Harry Ernest and Rose (Benza) R.; m. Margaret T. Rossbach, Dec. 28, 1968; children: Kathryn, Monica, Stephen. BE, NYU, 1969; MBA in Fin., Iona Coll., 1974, cert. in mgmt. systems, 1975. Cost analyst Irving Trust Co., N.Y.C., 1968-69; systems analyst Celanese Corp., N.Y.C., 1971-73; sr. analyst Fed. Res. Bank, N.Y.C., 1973-77; asst. v.p. Bradford Nat. Corp., N.Y.C., 1977-82; sr. v.p. Savs. Banks Trust Co., N.Y.C., 1982—; bd. dirs. SBT Investors Brokerage Svcs., N.Y.C. Bd. dirs. Lakeland Sch. Bd., Westchester County, N.Y., 1978. 2d lt. U.S. Army, 1969-71. Mem. Planning Forum. Home: RD 3 229 Lakeview Dr Mahopac NY 10541 Office: Savs Banks Trust Co 330 Madison Ave New York NY 10036

RIEKE, RONALD ALFRED, computer company executive; b. Rugby, N.D., Aug. 16, 1951; s. Lawrence Allen Rieke and Emma Marie (Lord) Cooper; m. Jacquelyn Senger, Dec. 22, 1972 (div. Nov. 1985); m. Madelyn E. Owens, May 2, 1987; 1 child, Ronald Alexander. AS, N.D. State U., 1971; BS, U. N.D., 1973; MA, Webster U., St. Louis, 1976. Operator Lystads, Inc., Kansas City, Kans., 1972-74; sales rep. Parke-Davis Co., St. Louis, 1974-76; with bio-med. engring. and sales Gen. Electric Corp., Tulsa, 1976-78; mgr., sales engr. Digital Equipment Corp., Houston, 1978-85; pres. R.A.R.E. Systems, Inc., Houston, 1985—; bd. dirs. Champions Point Nat. Bank, Houston, Cam-Eng, Inc., Houston, Title Techs., Houston. Mem. Houston Fine Arts Council, 1988. Mem. Am. Mgmt. Assn., Digital Dealer Assn., Digital Equipment Soc. Republican. Mem. Christian Ch. (Ch. of Christ). Office: RARE Systems Inc 10690 Shadowwood #106 Houston TX 77043

RIEPL, FRANCIS JOSEPH, utilities executive; b. Sayreville, N.J., Feb. 7, 1936; s. Frank Joseph and Adeline (Farley) R.; m. Jacqueline Ann York, Dec. 29, 1956; children: Timothy, Frank, Glenn. BS in Econs., U. Pa., 1958. Mgr. adminstrv. systems Pub. Service Electric and Gas, Newark, 1970-72, asst. treas., 1972-80, gen. mgr. systems, 1980-87, v.p., treas., 1987—. Office: Pub Svc Electric & Gas Co 80 Park Pla Newark NJ 07101

RIES, EDWARD RICHARD, petroleum geologist, consultant; b. Freeman, S.D., Sept. 18, 1918; s. August and Mary F. (Graber) R.; student Freeman Jr. Coll., 1937-39; A.B. magna cum laude, U. S.D., 1941; M.S., U. Okla., 1943, Ph.D. (Warden-Humble fellow), 1951; postgrad. Harvard, 1946-47; m. Amelia D. Capshaw, Jan. 24, 1949 (div. Oct. 16, 1956); children—Rosemary Melinda, Victoria Elise; m. 2d, Maria Wipfler, June 12, 1964. Asst. geologist Geol. Survey S.D., Vermillion, 1941; geophys. interpreter Robert Ray Inc., Oklahoma City, 1942; jr. geologist Carter Oil Co., Mont., Wyo., 1943-44, geologist Cutbank, Mont., 1944-49; sr. geologist Standard Vacuum Oil Co., India, 1951-53, sr. regional geologist, Indonesia, 1953-59, geol. adviser for Far East and Africa, White Plains, N.Y., 1959-62; geol. adviser Far East, Africa, Oceania, Mobil Petroleum Co., N.Y.C., N.Y., 1962-65; geol. adviser for Europe, Far East, Mobil Oil Corp., N.Y.C., 1965-71, sr. regional explorationist Far East, Dallas, 1971-73, Asia-Pacific, Dallas, 1973-76, 1976-79, assoc. geol. advisor Regional Geology-Geophysics, Dallas, 1979-82, geol. cons., 1982-83; internat. ind. petroleum geol. cons. Europe, Sino-Soviet and S.E. Asia, 1983—. Grad. asst., teaching fellow U. Okla., 1941-43, Harvard, 1946-47. Served with AUS, 1944-46. Mem. N.Y. Acad. Scis., Am. Assn. Petroleum Geologists (asso. editor 1976-83). Geol. Soc. Am., Am. Hort. Soc., Internat. Platform Assn., Am. Geol. Inst., A.A.A.S., Nat. Audubon Soc., Nat. Wildlife Fedn., Soc. Exploration Geophysicists, Wilderness Soc., Am. Legion, Phi Beta Kappa, Sigma Xi, Phi Sigma, Sigma Gamma Epsilon. Republican. Mennonite. Club: Harvard (Dallas). Contbr. articles to profl. jours. Home: 6009 Royal Crest Dr Dallas TX 75230 Office: 6009A Royal Crest Dr Dallas TX 75230-3434

RIESENBACH, MARVIN S., automotive corporation executive; b. 1929; married. BA, Pa. State U., 1951; MBA, Rutgers U., 1954. Acct. Haskins & Sells, 1957-62; v.p. Inst. for Sci. Info., 1962-68; v.p., treas. 3i Co., 1968-72; mem. staff Subaru of Am., Cherry Hill, N.J., 1972-76, v.p., contr., 1976-77, sr. v.p., 1977-83, exec. v.p., 1983, exec. v.p., chief fin. officer, 1986—. Served with U.S. Army, 1954-56. Office: Subaru of Am Inc PO Box 6000 Cherry Hill NJ 08034-6000

RIFFLE, RICHARD DAVIS, insurance agency administrator; b. Reading, Pa., May 21, 1953; s. F. Richard and Margaret (Eaches) R.; m. Debra Lynn Mathias, June 14, 1975; children: Sarah, Rebecca, Abigail, Amy. BS in Edn., Kutztown U., 1975. Tchr. blind, visually impaired Wellsboro, Pa., 1975-78; coord. health handicapped program Project Head Start, Blossburg, Pa., 1978-79; announcer Sta. WVLJ Radio, Monticello, Ill., 1979-84; sales agt. United Health & Life Svcs. Inc., Taylorville, Ill., 1984; br. mgr. United Health & Life Svcs. Inc., Champaign, Ill., 1984—. Home: 3502 S Vine St Urbana IL 61801 Office: United Health & Life Svcs Inc 1817 S Neil PO Box 6239 Champaign IL 61821

RIGDON, RONALD MILTON, management consultant; b. Balt., Jan. 15, 1937; s. Leland Sanford and Betty Berniece (Roe) R.; student Kansas City (Mo.) Art Inst., 1958-60, William Jewell Coll., Liberty, Mo., 1955-58, 62-63; m. Arlene June Eddington, May 26, 1962; children—Ryan Todd, Rebecca Erin. Field adjuster CNA Ins. Corp., Kansas City, Mo., 1962-63; asst. mgr. Anchor Fin. Corp. Ins. Agy., Overland Park, Kans., 1963-64; mgr. First Mortgage Investment Co. Ins. Agy., Kansas City, Mo., 1964-67; pres. Programming Inst., Mission, Kans., 1967-70, RMR & Assos., Inc., Overland Park, 1970—; dir. Assn. Cons., Inc., Scheduling Systems, Inc. First v.p. Johnson County Mental Health Assn., 1968-70, Kans. Mental Health Assn., 1969-70. Mem. Mgmt. Cons. Inst., Profl. Ins. Mass-Mktg. Assn., Am. Mgmt. Assn., Assn. Chief Exec. Officers, Am. Profl. Assn. Group Ins. Adminstrs., U.S. Dressage Fedn., Kansas City Dressage Soc. Republican. Baptist. Author: Work Flow-Cost Reduction a Management Control System, 1978, Recors, Your Key to Increased Productivity for Paper Flows, 1983 Home: 12200 Big Bone Trail Olathe KS 66061 Office: RMR & Assocs 10875 Benson Dr Ste 103 Overland Park KS 66210

RIGGS, LARRY DEAN, architectural engineer; b. Pittsburg, Kans., Sept. 4, 1951; s. Virgil Maynard and Rosetta Irene (Dockum) R.; m. Dvonna Sue LaRose, Sept. 6, 1975; children: Jeremy Dean, Jason Lee, Jamie Lynn. BS in Arch. Engring., U. Kans., 1974. Registered profl. engr., Kans., Ariz., Calif. Project engr. URS/Hewitt & Royer, Kansas City, 1974-80, HNTB, Kansas City, 1980-82; HVAC engr. Black and Veatch, Overland Park, Kans., 1982-83; engring. mgr. ptnr. The Hollis & Miller Group, Overland Park, 1983-86; mgr. mech. engring., v.p. Gibbens & Swinney Inc., Raytown, Mo., 1986—; design cons. Ch. of God Bible Sch. Kansas City Coll., Overland Park, 1980—; seminar leader Kansas City Power & Light Co., 1987-88. Mem. ASHRAE, U. Kans. Alumni Assn., Kansas City Coll. and Bible Sch. Alumni Assn. Nazarene. Home: 34860 W 95th St De Soto KS 66018 Office: Gibbens & Swinney Inc E 63rd St Ste 200 Raytown MO 64133

RIGSBEE, WILLIAM ALTON, insurance company executive; b. Durham, N.C., July 10, 1926; s. Coley Leonard and Julia Hill (Hackney) R.; m. Shirley Reese Morgan, July 12, 1952. BA, Duke U., 1950. With Home Security Life, Durham, 1950-56, Franklin Life Ins., Springfield, Ill., 1956-61; pres., chmn. Midland Nat. Life Ins. Co., Sioux Falls, S.D., 1961—; pres. and chmn. Investors Life Ins. Co. of Nebr., Sioux Falls, 1968—, N.Am. Mgmt., Inc., Sioux Falls, 1968—; bd. dirs. Sammons Enterprises, Inc., Northwestern Bell Telephone Co, Norwest Bank S.D.. Bd. dirs. Downtown Devel. Corp., Sioux Falls, 1979—. Served with U.S. Army, 1944-46, ETO. Mem. Am. Council Life Ins. Home: 1200 Tomar Rd Sioux Falls SD 57105 Office: Midland Nat Life Ins Co One Midland Pla Sioux Falls SD 57193

RIHERD, THOMAS MALCOLM, II, banker; b. Gainesville, Fla., May 14, 1959; s. Paul Markey and Martha Phillips (Carroll) R.; m. Barbara Ann Bullough, Dec. 27, 1981; children: Paul Markey II, Lynne Shelley. BBA in Fin., Auburn U., 1980; MBA, Jacksonville U., 1987. Cert. internal auditor, Fla. Sr. auditor Barnett Banks Fla. Inc., Jacksonville, 1981-84; v.p. Farmers and Dealers Bank, Lake Butler, Fla., 1984—, also bd. dirs.; owner Riherd Computing, Lake Butler, 1986—; v.p., controller Riherd Bank Holding Co., Lake Butler, 1987—, also bd. dirs.; bd. dirs. Suwannee River Authority, Live Oak, Fla. Fundraiser coordinator Union County (Fla.) Boy Scouts Am., 1988; v.p. 4-H Found., Union County, 1987, pres., 1988—. Mem. Fla. Bankers Assn. (group II vice chmn. 1987, chmn. 1988, coun. 1989&), North Fla. Bankers Assn. (chmn. 1988-89). Democrat. Baptist. Lodge: Rotary. Office: Farmers & Dealers Bank 395 W Main St Lake Butler FL 32054

RIHM, PAUL CHARLES, controller; b. Cin., Dec. 23, 1953; s. Manfred John and Jean Ann (Naber) R. m. Sarah Jane Kolodziej, Sept. 10, 1977. BSBA in Acctg., Xavier U., 1976. CPA, Ohio. Audit mgr. Deloitte Haskins & Sells, Cin., 1977-86; controller Opelika Industries, Inc. (subs. Leshner Corp.), Hamilton, Ohio, 1986—. Mem. Butler County Assn. for Retarded Citizens, Hamilton, Ohio, 1978—. Recipient Five Yr. Participant award Project Bus. (div. of Jr. Achievement) 1988, Letter of Commendation Deloitte Haskins & Sells Working Paper Rev. Project, 1984. Mem. Ohio Soc. CPA's (local v.p. 1985-86), The Planning Forum (local chmn audit com. 1985-87, v.p. fin. 1988—), Adminstrv. Mgmt. Soc. (treas. 1984-87, 1st v.p. 1987-88, pres. 1988—), Am. Inst. CPA's. Roman Catholic. Home: 5450 Joey Terr Cincinnati OH 45248 Office: Opelika Industries Inc 1010 Eaton Ave Hamilton OH 45013

RIKALA, SUSAN CAROL, human resources executive; b. Burlingame, Calif., July 15, 1955; d. Uno William and Ruby Viola (Pomrankee) R. A.A., Coll. San Mateo, 1975; A.B. in Mass Communications magna cum laude, U. Calif.-Davis, 1977; postgrad. Golden Gate U., 1985—. Pub. info. intern Calif. State Dept. Parks and Recreation, Sacramento, 1976; pub. relations intern, Calif. Bur. Land Mgmt., Sacramento, 1976; editorial cons. Central Valley Regional Water Quality Control Bd., Sacramento, 1977-78; pub. relations agt. Aerojet Services Corp., Sacramento, 1978; mgr. TOD Temporary Services, San Mateo, Redwood City, Calif., 1978-82; personnel and tng. mgr. Franklin Resources, San Mateo, 1982-84, dir. human resources, 1985-86, v.p. human resources, 1986—. Mem. Am. Soc. Personnel Adminstrn., Am. Soc. Tng. Devel., Am. Mgmt. Assn., Santa Clara Valley Personnel Adminstrs., San Mateo Employees Adv. Council, Calif. Scholarship Fedn., Alpha Gamma Sigma. Democrat. Methodist. Home: 66 Eddystone Ct Redwood Shores CA 94065 Office: Franklin Resources Inc 777 Mariners Island Blvd San Mateo CA 94404

RIKLIS, MARCIA, retail executive. Formerly vice-chmn. Schenley Industries Inc., Dallas; exec. v.p. EII Holdings, Rapid Am. Corp., N.Y.C. Office: Rapid Am Corp 725 Fifth Ave New York NY 10022 *

RIKLIS, MESHULAM, manufacturing and retail executive; b. Turkey, Dec. 2, 1923; came to U.S., 1947, naturalized, 1955; s. Pinhas and Betty (Guberer) R.; children: Simona Riklis Ackerman, Marcia Riklis Hirschfeld, Ira Doron, Kady Zadora Riklis, Kristofer Riklis. Student, U. Mexico, 1947; BA, Ohio State U., 1950, MBA, 1968. Co-dir. youth activities and mil. tng. Hertzlia High Sch., Tel-Aviv, 1942; tchr. Hebrew Talmud Torah Sch., Mpls., 1951; research dept. Piper, Jaffray & Hopwood, 1951-53, sales rep., 1953-56; vice chmn. McCrory Corp., N.Y.C., 1960-69, vice chmn. exec. com., from 1970, chmn., 1975-85, dir., former pres.; with Rapid-Am. Corp., N.Y.C., 1956—, chmn., 1956—, pres., chief exec. officer, 1957-73, chmn., chief exec. officer, 1973-76, chmn., pres., chief exec. officer, 1976—. Served Brit. 8th Army, 1942-46. Mem. Pi Mu Epsilon. Jewish. Office: Rapid-Am Corp 725 Fifth Ave New York NY 10022 *

RILEY, DEBORAH ANN, marketing executive; b. Pitts., June 30, 1953; d. Lionel Glen and Ethel Louise (Alexander) Davidson; m. Richard Earl Riley, May 27, 1977 (div. Dec. 1983); children: Steven Earl, Michael Glen. BA, W.Va. Wesleyan Coll., 1975. Sec., treas. Anniston Joint Venture, Inc., Dallas, 1982-85; exec. v.p. Insignia Corp., Dallas, 1985—, bd. dirs.; pres. Sports Concepts, Dallas, 1986-88. Mem. Glenshaw (Pa.) Players, 1975-76. Capt. U.S. Army, 1976-77, with Res. 1981—. Mem. Res. Officers Assn., Nat. Assn. Female Execs., Am. Mgmt. Assn. Republican. Presbyterian. Home: 7206 Shawn Rowlett TX 75088

RILEY, DERRELL WAYNE, coal company executive; b. East St. Louis, Ill., Nov. 5, 1951; s. Elmo Martin and Wilma Irene (Hale) R.; m. Barbara Ann Milton, Apr. 15, 1972 (div. May 1985); children: Jonathan, Lauren; m. Dianne Carol Arp Stricker, June 22, 1985; stepchildren: Jeremy Stricker, Nathan Stricker. BBA, So. Ill. U., Edwardsville, 1979. Constrn. clerk Peabody Coal Co., St. Louis, 1979-80, constrn. auditor, 1980-82, office mgr., 1982-83; acctg. mgr. N. Antelope Coal subs. Peabody Holding Co., Gillette, Wyo., 1983-85; materials mgr. Powder River Coal subs. Peabody Holding Co., Gillette, Wyo., 1985—; advisor and instr. materials mgmt. assocs. art program Sheridan Coll., Gillette. Served with U.S. Army, 1970-73. Mem. Purchasing Mgmt. Assn. Wyo. (bd. dirs., dir. at large 1986-87, pres. 1987-88, dir. nat. affairs, 1988—). Office: Powder River Coal PO Box 3034 Gillette WY 82717

RILEY, JOHN BERNARD, chemical company executive; b. Queens, N.Y., Feb. 28, 1930; s. Eugene B. and Margaret (Morrissey) R.; m. Mary Ann Lannig, Sept. 6, 1952 (div. 1980); children: John B. Jr., Peter, Kathy Riley Weaver, Mary; m. Carole Field, Feb. 14, 1981. BS in Chemistry, St. John's U., Jamaica, N.Y., 1950; MS in Organic Chemistry, Stevens Inst. Tech., 1952; M of Chem. Engring., Newark Coll. Engring., 1956. Engr. Tidewater Oil Co., Bayonne, N.J., 1952-53; from engr. to v.p. Exxon Chem. Co., various locations, 1956-84; v.p. Exxon Chem. Co., Houston, 1984—. Served with U.S. Army, 1953-55. Mem. Comml. Devel. Assn. (program com. chmn. 1986). Republican. Roman Catholic. Home: 419 Sandy Bluff Houston TX 77079 Office: Exxon Chem Co 13501 Katy Freeway Houston TX 77079-1398

RILEY, JOHN HALLY, federal railroad administrator, lawyer; b. N.Y.C., Jan. 19, 1947; s. John Joseph and Eileen Johanna (McDermott) R.; m. Karen Jane Youngquist, Mar. 22, 1975. B.A. in Econ., Boston Coll., 1968; J.D., Cornell Law Sch., 1972. Bar: Colo. 1973, Minn. 1975. Trial lawyer Isaacson, Rosenbaum, Spiegleman & Friedman, Denver, 1973-75; trial lawyer Meagher, Geer, Markham & Anderson, Mpls., 1975-79; chief counsel Senator D. Durenberger, Washington, 1979-83; adminstr. Fed. R.R. Adminstrn., Washington, 1983—; exec. dir. U.S. Senate Rail Caucus, Washington, 1981-82, U.S.-Japan-France High Speed Rail Congress, Washington, 1981-83. Contbr. article to profl. jour. Bd. dirs. Amtrak, Washington, 1983—, Union Sta. Redevel., Washington, 1983—; field dir. Mass. Republican State Com., Boston, 1968-69, John Sears for Mayor, Boston, 1967; state chmn. Mass. Young Rep., Boston, 1968. Served with USAR, 1969-75. Roman Catholic. Home: 3411 Cypress Falls Church VA 22042 Office: Fed RR Adminstrn 400 7th St SW Washington DC 20590 *

RILEY, KATHLEEN ANN, pharmaceuticals executive; b. Norfolk, Va., Jan. 30, 1945; d. Edward Miles and Ruth Annette (Powers) R.; m. Wendell Earl Dunn III, Mar. 29, 1981; 1 child, Elissa Brooks Dunn. Student, Tulane U., 1962-64; BS in Chemistry, Coll. William & Mary, 1967; MS, U. Ill., 1970; MBA, Northwestern U., 1977. Pharm. chemist Abbott Labs., North Chicago, Ill., 1970-73; clinical research assoc. Abbott Labs., North Chicago, 1973-75; cons. Mgmt. Analysis Ctr., Northbrook, Ill., 1975-76; mgr. strategic planning agrl. chemicals FMC Corp., Phila., 1977-81, mgr. strategic planning phosphorus chemicals, 1981-82; mgr. new compound opportunities Smith Kline French Internat. Labs., Phila., 1982-86, market planning mgr., 1986-88; assoc. dir. new product evaluation Smith, Kline & French, Phila., 1988—. Patentee in field; contbr. articles to profl. jours. Bd. dirs. Community Arts Alliance, Phila., 1982-87; cons., counselor Girl Scouts Am., Haddonfield, N.J., 1986-87. Mem. Am. Soc. Bone and Mineral Research, Internat. Soc. Chemotherapy, Phila. Womens' Network (bd. dirs. 1980-84, treas. 1983-84, chmn. strategic planning com. 1982-87), Iota Sigma Pi, Sigma Xi. Lutheran. Club: Haddon Fortnightly (Haddonfield) (program speaker 1986-87, bd. dirs. 1987—, chmn. internat. relations com. 1987—, chmn. gardening group, 1987—). Home: 443 Gladstone Ave Haddonfield NJ 08033 Office: Smith Kline & French 1500 Spring Garden St Philadelphia PA 19101

RILEY, LESTER GROVER, federal agency administrator; b. Martin, Kent., June 18, 1947; s. Wallen Everett and Sarah Jane (Keathley) R.; m. Juanita Carmen Harkness, Mar. 28, 1970; children: Maria Lynn, Sheri Ann, Carmen Veronika. BS, S.W. Mo. State U., 1975; MBA, Rockhurst Coll., 1983; grad., U.S. Army Command & Gen. Staff Coll., Ft. Leavenworth, Kans., 1986. Comptroller, treas. Marx Corp., Springfield, Mo., 1975-76; acct. Dept. Agr., Kansas City, Mo., 1976-83, mgmt. analyst, 1983-84, sect. supr., 1984-87, br. mgr., 1987—. Lt. col. U.S. Army, 1966-73, Vietnam. Decorated Bronze Star; recipient Cert. of Merit Dept. Agr., 1986. Mem. Assn. Govtl. Accts. (membership chmn. 1979-81, pres. 1985-86, edn. chairperson 1987—), Reserve Officers Assn. Office: Dept of Agr Kansas City MO 64131

RILEY, ROBERT ANNAN, III, social services administrator, financial consultant; b. Balt., Jan. 2, 1955; s. Robert Jr. and Elfrieda Bertha (Mueller) R.; m. Adama Ly, July 31, 1987. BA in English, Yale U., 1979. Vol. Peace Corps, Gabon, Africa, 1979-83, adminstr. tng., 1983-84; assoc. dir. adminstrn. Peace Corps, Gabon, 1984-86, Mali, 1986-88; mgmt. analyst internat. ops. Peace Corps, Washington, 1988—. Author of several computer fin. software programs, 1985—. Democrat. Episcopalian. Home: 1669 Park Rd NW Apt H Washington DC 20010 Office: Peace Corps 1990 K St Washington DC 20526

RILEY, TIMOTHY MICHAEL, financial planner; b. Norwich, Conn., Nov. 14, 1954; s. Gerard E. and Ruth (Riley) Papineau; m. Linda Ann Gilbert, Sept. 11, 1976; children: Michael, Amy, Sean, Christopher. BS, U. N.H., 1975. CLU; certified fin. cons. Mgr. Met. Co., Manchester, N.H., 1976-80; prin. Harbor Group Inc., Bedford, N.H., 1980—; mem. adj. faculty Coll. Fin. Planning, Denver, 1986—. Mem. Registry Fin. Planning Practitioners, Inst. Cert. Fin. Planners, Internat. Assn. Fin. Planning (v.p. programs 1986-87), Rotary (pres. 1982), Bedford Men's Club. Republican. Roman Catholic. Office: The Harbor Group Inc Bedford Commons Bldg 4 Bedford NH 03102

RILEY, VICTOR J., JR., financial services company executive; b. Buffalo, Aug. 29, 1931; s. Victor J. and Gwenevieve Riley; m. Marilyn A. Felrath, Aug. 8, 1954; children—Victor J. III, Karen, Patricia, Kevin, Shawn, Mary Katherine. B.A. in Econs., U. Notre Dame; LL.D., Coll. St. Rose, 1983. With trust div. 1st Nat. Bank Miami, Fla., 1955-62; mgr. Miami office Bowles, Andrews & Towne, 1962-64; trust officer Nat. Comml. Bank (now Key Bank N.A.), Albany, N.Y., 1964-73; pres., chief exec. officer KeyCorp (formerly Key Banks Inc.), Albany, 1973—, also dir.; chmn. bd. Key Bank N.A., Albany, 1984—, Ctr. Econ. Growth; dir. Albany Med. Ctr.; mem. Interstate Banking Commn. for State of N.Y., 1986—. Hon. chmn. Capital Dist. Cerebral Palsy Telethon, Albany, 1981-87; bd. dirs. Pop Warner Football League; chmn. various fund raising drives. Served with U.S. Army, 1953-55. Apptd. civilian aide to Sec. Army, 1985—. Decorated Knight of Malta. Mem. N.Y. State Bankers Assn. (long-range planning com.), Interstate Banking Com. State N.Y. Republican. Roman Catholic. Home: 166 Van Rensselaer Blvd Mercado NY 12204 Office: KeyCorp 60 State St Albany NY 12207

RIMERMAN, MORTON WALTER, utility executive; b. Wilmington, Del., Aug. 7, 1929; m. Helen Holland, Sept. 1960; 1 dau., Jennifer. B.S., LaSalle Coll., 1958; M.B.A., Drexel U., 1962; postgrad. Exec. Devel. Program, Grad. Sch. Bus. and Pub. Adminstrn., Cornell U., 1973. With Phila. Electric Co., 1948—, asst. treas., 1970-73, treas., 1973-86, v.p. fin. and acctg., 1986—. Served with U.S. Army, 1951-53. Mem. Am. Gas Assn., Fin. Analysts of Phila., Fin. Execs. Inst., Edison Electric Inst. Office: Phila Electric Co 2301 Market St Philadelphia PA 19101

RINEHART, CHARLES R., finance company executive; b. San Francisco, Jan. 31, 1947; s. Robert Eugene and Rita Mary Rinehart; married; children: Joseph B., Kimberly D., Michael P., Scott. BS, U. San Francisco, 1968. Exec. v.p. Fireman's Fund Ins. Cos., Novato, Calif., 1969-83; pres., chief exec. officer Avco Fin. Services, Irvine, Calif., 1983—, also bd. dirs. Served to 2d lt. U.S. Army, 1968-69. Fellow Casualty Actuarial Soc.; mem. Am. Mgmt. Assn., Am. Acad. Actuaries, Young Pres. Orgn. (Calif. Coast chpt.). Repubican. Roman Catholic. Office: Avco Fin Svcs Inc 3349 Michelson Dr Irvine CA 92715-1606

RINEHART, GARY DEAN, data processing executive; b. Santa Barbara, Calif., May 10, 1943; s. Lloyd Stanley and Ruth Burdean (Grim) R.; BS in Math., Calif. State Poly., U. 1969; MS in Mgmt. Sci., U.S. Internat. U., 1974; m. Nancy Tietjen, Dec. 14, 1968; children: Tisha Noelle, Brooke Allison. Systems engr. IBM, San Diego, 1968-69; programmer San Diego Gas & Electric Co., 1969-71, sr. data systems analyst, 1971-76, corp. planning system supr., 1976-81, mgr. decision support services, 1981-85; mgr. Info. Techs., 1985-88; pres. Decision Interface, Inc., 1980—; instr. info. tech. Cert. data processing. Mem. Nat. Assn. Accts. (cert. appreciation 1975), Assn. Internal Mgmt. Cons. (nat. v.p., Man of the Yr. 1985), Data Processing Mgmt. Assn., Planning Forum (pres. S.D. chpt.), Nat. Computer Graphics Assn., MIT Enterprise Forum. Lutheran. Contbr. articles to profl. jours. Internat. lectr. in field. Home: 15043 Paso Del Sol Del Mar CA 92014 Office: Decision Interface Inc 101 Ash St San Diego CA 92101

RINES, JOHN RANDOLPH, automotive company executive; b. Balt., Aug. 3, 1947; s. John William and Betty (Singer) R.; m. Peggy J. Daugaard, Sept. 19, 1969 (dec. 1978); m. Katherine M. Duff, Nov. 29, 1980; children: Jacqueline D., Eleanor W. BS in Econs., Colo. State U., 1970; MBA, U. Va., 1977. With GM, 1970-75, 77—; fin. analyst GM, Detroit, 1977-78, dir. product programs, 1978-80, asst. to pres., 1980-81, gen. dir. fin., 1981-82; exec. dir. GM, Sao Paulo, Brazil, 1982-84; dir. fin. Buick/Oldsmobile/Cadillac group GM, Flint, Mich., 1984-85; gen. mgr. motors holding div. GM, Detroit, 1985—. Trustee Arts Found. Mich., Detroit. Mem. Grosse Pointe (Mich.) Club, Detroit Athletic Club. Office: GM 3044 W Grand Blvd Detroit MI 48202

RING, JAMES EDWARD PATRICK, mortgage insurance company executive; b. Washington, Feb. 12, 1940; s. Edward Patrick and Eleanor (Sollers) R.; m. Kathleen Murphy, Aug. 10, 1979; children: Christopher James, Daniel Edward Patrick. Student, Holy Cross Coll., Worcester, Md., 1958-59; BSEE, U.S. Naval Acad., 1963; MBA in Fin., Wharton Sch. Bus., 1972. Lic. securities broker, comml. pilot. Fin. analyst Exec. Office of the President, Washington, 1972-74; sr. budget analyst Bd. Govs. Fed. Res. System, Washington, 1974-77; dir. fin. planning Fed. Home Loan Mortgage Ins., Washington, 1977-83; dir. mktg. Ticor Mortgage Ins., Falls Church, Va., 1983-84, Gen. Electric Mortgage Ins., McLean, Va., 1985-86; sr. v.p. First Chesapeake Mortgage, Beltsville, Md., 1986-88; v.p. G.E. Mortgage Ins., McLean, Va., 1988—. Vol. Big Bros. of Am., Washington, 1973-81. Lt. USN, 1963-69, Vietnam. Republican. Roman Catholic. Club: Wharton (Washington), Toastmaster (pres. 1977-83, Pres. of Yr. 1981). Home: 1716 Stonebridge Rd Alexandria VA 22304

RINGER, JEROME, public relations executive; b. Los Angeles, Mar. 1, 1935; s. Arthur and Alice (Olds) R.; m. Shirley A. O'Neal, Jan. 5, 1955; children: Julie Ann Allen, Kellie Lynn Burns. BSBA, Calif. State U., Northridge, 1967. Reporter Glendale (Calif.) News, 1956-58; pub. relations Northrop, Van Nuys and Thousand Oaks, Calif., 1956-64; pub. relations and advt. mgr. Walter Kidder Webber A/C Div., Burbank, Calif., 1964-67; account exec. Smith Klitton Advt. Agy., Santa Monica, Calif., 1967-68; asst. to pres. Cubic Corp., San Diego, 1968—; pub. relations trustee U. San Diego, 1985—; teaching assoc. Pub. Relations U. Calif., San Diego, 1984—; bd. dirs. Jr. Achievement, San Diego, 1971—. Pres. Nat. Football Found., San Diego Chpt., 1972—; bd. dirs. U.S. Olympic Tng. Sight Task Force, San Diego, 1986—. Served to Sgt., U.S. Army, 1954-56. Named Profl. of Yr. Pub. Relations Club, 1986. Mem. Press Club of San Diego (Best Com. Relations Program award 1975, 78, 80, Man of Yr. 1986), Fin. Analyst Soc., Aviation Space Writers Assn., Pub. Relations Soc. Am. Club: Trojan (San Diego). Office: Cubic Corp 9333 Balboa Ave San Diego CA 92123

RING-MILLER, BARBARA ANN, management consultant; b. St. Louis, Mar. 7, 1945; d. Oliver C. and Ann (McCarron) Garleb; m. Roland Joseph Tony Miller; 1 son, Michael Francis Ring. AA in Nursing, El Camino Coll., 1964; BA, UCLA, 1967, JD, 1971; BS in Mgmt., Pacific Christian Coll., 1976; BS in Nursing, Am. Nat. U., 1980, MBA, 1982; postgrad. U. So. Calif. With Harbor Gen. Hosp., Torrance, Calif., 1964-66, Gardena Meml. Hosp., 1967-68, UCLA Med. Ctr., 1969-70, Brotman Meml. Hosp., Culver City, 1971-73; cardiac specialist Calif. Hosp. Med. Ctr., Los Angeles, 1974-77; asst. dir. nurses Fountain Valley Community Hosp. (Calif.), 1978-79; cons. Upjohn Health Care Services, 1980-84; mgmt. cons. Ind. Contractor. Dir. Charter Counseling Ctr., De Anza, Riverside; youth camp dir. YMCA, also caravan dir.; bd. dirs. U. Calif.-Riverside Athletic Assn., Urban League; mem. Jurupa 2001 steering com. Bank Am. scholar, 1962; Westmont Coll. scholar, 1962; recipient Woman of Achievement award Riverside YWCA. Mem. Am. Mgmt. Assn., Nat. Assn. Female Execs., Critical Care Nurses Assn. NOW, ACLU, Christian Bus. Women's Fellowship, Riverside C. of C. (ambassador, bd. dirs., steering com.), Jurupa C. of C. (bd. dirs.). Lodge: Soroptimist.

RINGOEN, RICHARD MILLER, manufacturing company executive; b. Ridgeway, Iowa, May 15, 1926; s. Elmer and Evelyn Louise (Miller) R.; m. Joan Marie Brandt, June 7, 1953; children: David, John, Daniel. Student, U. Dubuque, Iowa, 1944-45, Marquette U., Milw., 1945-46; BSEE with highest distinction, U. Iowa, 1947, MS, 1948. Research engr. Collins Radio, Cedar Rapids, Iowa, 1948-55; v.p. engring. Alpha Corp. subs. Collins Radio, Cedar Rapids, 1955-59; dir. spl. projects Martin-Marietta Co., Denver, 1959-70; v.p., gen. mgr. Ball Bros. Research Corp., Boulder, Colo., 1970-74; corp. v.p. ops. Ball Corp., Muncie, Ind., 1974-78, pres., chief operating officer, 1978-80, pres., chief exec. officer, 1981—, chmn. bd., 1986—, also bd. dirs., mem. exec. com.; mem. Conf. Bd.; bd. overseers Exec. Council on Fgn. Diplomats; bd. dirs. Am. Electric Power Co., Inc., Arvin Industries, Inc., CTS Corp., Ralston Purina Co., Am. Nat. Bank, Tokheim Corp.; chief exec. officer Tally Corp., 1973-78. Patentee in communications, navigation and electronics circuitry. Pres. sch. bd. Arapahoe County, Colo., 1963-70, past vice chair sch. planning com.; dir. steering com. Arapahoe Jr. Coll., 1969-70; past pres. United Way of Delaware County, Muncie Symphony Assn., Inc.; trustee Hudson Inst., Purdue U., Muncie YMCA; supt. Christian edn. 1st Congregational Ch. Cedar Rapids; bd. dirs. Ball State U. Found., Ball Bros. Found., Meth. Hosp. Indpls., Nat. Bd. of Joint Council on Econ. Edn., Keep Am. Beautiful Inc., Minnetrista Cultural Found. Served with USN. Recipient Bronze award for top chief exec. officer in container industry Fin. World, 1982, 84, Chief Exec. Officer Silver award Wall St. Transcript, 1982-83, Gold award for best chief exec. officer in container industry Wall St. Transcript, 1984; named Industrialist of Yr. Ind. Bus. Mag., 1988; Ball Corp. named most innovative co. in the packaging industry by Forbes Mag., 1988. Mem. Glass Packaging Inst., Can Mfrs. Inst. (chmn. 1985-86, exec. com. 1986—), Ind. State C. of C. (bd. dirs.), Nat. Assn. Mfs. (bd. dirs.). Lodge: Rotary (bd. dirs. Muncie club). Office: Ball Corp PO Box 2407 Muncie IN 47307-0407

RINKEL, RALPH C., automotive executive; b. Antler, N.D., Nov. 10, 1911; s. Frank A. and Frances (Nelson) R.; m. Ella L. Johnson, Feb. 4, 1936; children: Marlys, Bruce. Student, Jamestown (N.D.) coll. Mgr. No. Chevrolet Co., Thief River Falls, Minn., 1935-49; mgr., owner Merit Chevrolet Co., St. Paul, 1949—. Mem. Minn. Automobile Dealers Assn. (pres. 1948-49), Masons. Home: 2277 S Shore Blvd White Bear Lake MN 55110 Office: Merit Chevrolet 2695 Brookview Dr Saint Paul MN 55119

RINNE, AUSTIN DEAN, insurance company executive; s. Hermann Henry and Marie (Knudsen) R.; m. Martha Jo Runyan, Dec. 29, 1941; children: Erik Knudsen, Barbara Jane Rivera; student Ind. U., 1938-40, grad. Purdue U., 1947. Spl. agt. Northwestern Mut. Life, Indpls., 1946-56, dist. agt., 1956-58, gen. agt., Dallas, 1958-84, gen. agt. emeritus, 1984—; chmn. bd. dirs. Communication and Mgmt. Assocs., Ann Arbor, Mich. Bd. dirs., v.p. English Speaking Union, Dallas, 1972-80; bd. dirs. Dallas Opera, 1984—. Served to capt. USAF, 1941-45, ETO. Decorated Purple Heart. Mem. Dallas Estate Planning Coun. (pres. 1965-66), Dallas Assn. Life Underwriters (bd. dirs. 1960-63), Dallas Knife and Fork (v.p., bd. dirs. 1986—), Mil. Order World Wars, English-Speaking Union (dir., v.p. Dallas chpt. 1972—), Sertoma (pres. Dallas chpt. 1967-68), Phi Kappa Psi Alumni Assn. (pres. 1951-52), Phi Kappa Psi (exec. council 1972-76), City Club, Dallas Country Club, Northshore Club. Republican. Methodist. Home: 4311 Bordeaux St Dallas TX 75205 Office: 3333 Lee Pkwy #900 Dallas TX 75219

RINSKY, JOEL CHARLES, lawyer; b. Bklyn., Jan. 29, 1938; s. Irving C. and Elsie (Millman) R.; m. Judith L. Lynn, Jan. 26, 1963; children: Heidi M., Heather S., Jason W. BS, Rutgers U., 1961, LLB, 1962, JD, 1968. Bar: N.J. 1963, U.S. Dist. Ct. N.J. 1963, U.S. Supreme Ct. 1967, U.S. Ct. Appeals (3d cir.) 1986. Sole practice Livingston, N.J., 1964—. Mem. exec. com. Essex County (N.J.) Dems., 1983—; Dem. com. person Millburn-Short Hills, N.J., 1982—, vice chmn. 1983-87; bd. govs. Lake Naomi Assn. Pocono Pines, Pa., 1983-86; trustee Student Loan Fund, Millburn, 1983—. Fellow Am. Acad. Matrimonial Lawyers; mem. N.J. Bar Assn., Essex County Bar Assn., N.J. Automobile Arbitration Program (arbitrator). Jewish. Home: 23 Winthrop Rd Short Hills NJ 07078 Office: 600 South Livingston Ave Livingston NJ 07039

RINSKY, JUDITH LYNN, foundation administrator; b. Sept. 12, 1941; d. Allen A. Lynn and Sophie (Schwartz); m. Joel C. Rinsky, Esq., Jan. 29, 1963; children: Heidi Mae, Heather Star, Jason Wayne. BA in Home Econs., Montclair State Coll., 1963. Cert. in Home Econs., 1987. Tchr. home econs. Florence Ave. Sch., Irvington, N.J., 1963-66; substitute tchr. Millburn-Short Hills Sch. System, 1978-82, sr. citizen coordinator, 1982-87; respite care coordinator Essex County Respite Care, East Orange, N.J., 1988—; bd. member adv. com. gerontology Seton Hall U., 1984—; coordinator Mayor's Adv. Bd. Sr. Citizens, Millburn-Short Hills, 1982-87. Pres. Deerfield Sch. PTA, 1979-80, Millburn High Sch. PTA, 1983-85; co-chmn. Charles T. King Student Loan Fund dinner dance, 1981; mem. Handicapped Access Study com. 1983-85; bd. dirs. Council on Health and Human Services, 1985—. Mem. Lake Naomi Assn. (chmn. sailing com. 1981), N.J. Home Econs. Assn. Am. Home Econs. Assn., Rotary (chairperson Interact Club 1987—), Notary Pub. N.J. Lodge: Millburn Rotary (bd. dirs. 1987). Home: 23 Winthrop Rd Short Hills NJ 07078

RIORDAN, JAMES FRANCIS, consulting company executive; b. Tampa, Fla., Sept. 4, 1946; s. Howard James and Mary Loretta (McElligot) R.; m. Lynn Louise Gemette, Jan. 25, 1969; children: Jim, Lisa, Brett. Grad. High Sch., San Jose, Calif. Prodn. mgr. Viking Sauna Co., San Jose, 1969-73; owner Almaden Valley Carpet, San Jose, 1973-74; quality assurance engring. FMC, San Jose, 1974-76; mfg. engr. mgr. Atari, Sunnyvale, Calif., 1976-79; pres. Overnight Engring, Inc., San Jose, 1979—; cons. Investors of Calif., Moraga, Calif., 1987-88; seminar speaker Overnight Engring., Inc., San Jose, 1986—; keynote speaker JFK U., Calif., 1988. Inventor in field; author: Converting Potential to Profit, 1988, Path to Profit for New Products, 1988. Chmn. Watsonville Antique Aircraft Fly-in, Watsonville, Calif., 1988. Recipient of Ross Donald Good Citizen award, City of San Jose, 1982. Mem. Inventors of Calif., Nat. Congress of Inventor Orgns., Community Entrepreneurs Assn., Antique Aircraft Assn. (bd. dirs. San Jose chpt. 1987, 88), Aircraft Owners/Pilots Assn. Office: Overnight Engring Inc 1859 Andrews Ave San Jose CA 95124

RIORDAN, JAMES QUENTIN, oil company executive; b. Bklyn., June 17, 1927; s. James A. and Ruth M. (Boomer) R.; m. Gloria H. Carlson, June 23, 1951; children: Nancy, Susan, James, Ruth. B.A., Bklyn. Coll., 1945; LL.B., Columbia U., 1949. Bar: N.Y. 1951, U.S. Supreme Ct 1954. Atty. Winthrop, Stimson, Putnam & Roberts, N.Y.C., 1949-51; mem. staff Ways and Means sub-com., Washington, 1951-52; atty. tax div. Justice Dept., Washington, 1952-55; atty. Chadbourne, Parke, Whiteside & Wolff, N.Y.C., 1955-57; tax counsel Socony Mobil Oil Co., N.Y.C., 1957-59; planning assoc. Socony Mobil Oil Co., 1959-60, mgr. planning, 1961-62; v.p. Mobil Latin Am., 1963-64, pres. internat. div., 1965-69, exec. v.p. fin., 1969—, also dir., mem. exec. com.; sr. v.p. Mobil Corp., 1976-86, vice chmn., chief fin. officer, 1986—; bd. dirs. Dow Jones & Co., Inc., Marcor, Inc.; mem. adv. bd. Chem. Bank. Bd. dirs. Com. Econ. Devel.; trustee Bklyn. Mus., Tax Found., Inc. Mem. N.Y. City Bar Assn. Clubs: Rembrandt (N.Y.C.); Blind Brook, Apawamis. Office: Mobil Oil Corp 150 E 42d St New York NY 10017

RIORDAN, JOHN FRANCIS, oil and gas corporate executive; b. Medina, N.Y., Jan. 12, 1936; s. Francis J. and Harriet (Stork) R.; m. Judith Kathryn Wokna, Feb. 5, 1967; children: Michael, Timothy, Allison. B.A. in Chemisty, Niagara U., 1958; M.B.A., SUNY-Buffalo, 1975. Chemist Durez div. Occidental Chem. Corp., North Tonawanda, N.Y., 1958-61, field sales rep., 1961-67; product mgmr. Durez div. Occidental Chem. Corp., North Tonawanda, N.Y., 1967-75; dir. corp. devel. Occidental Chem. Corp., Grand Island, N.Y., 1965-76; v.p., gen. mgr. internat. Occidental Chem. Corp., Niagara Falls, N.Y., 1976-78, v.p., gen. mgr. ECD, Hooker Chems. Plastic Corp.,, 1978-80, v.p. employee relations Hooker Corp., Houston,, 1980-81, pres. ICG, Hooker Corp.,, 1981-85; exec. v.p. Occidental Chem. Corp., Niagara Falls, 1985-86; exec. v.p. NGL Group Cities Service Oil & Gas Corp., Tulsa, 1986-88; pres. MidCon Oil Corp., Lombard, Ill., 1988—. Roman Catholic. Office: MidCon Corp 701 E 22d St Lombard IL 60148

RIORDAN, MICHAEL LEE, biotechnology company executive; b. Wichita, Kans., Sept. 26, 1957; s. Hugh Desaix and Jan Mary (Brick) R. BS summa cum laude and BA, Washington U., St. Louis, 1979; MD, MA in Internat. Affairs, Johns Hopkins U., 1984; MBA, Harvard U., 1986. Def. analyst Systems Research and Application System, Arlington, Va., 1983-84; biotech. cons. Arthur D. Little, Inc., Cambridge, Mass., 1984-85; mgmt. cons. McKinsey and Co., Los Angeles, 1985; comml. banker Indsl. Bank of Japan, Tokyo, 1986; venture capitalist Menlo Ventures, Menlo Park, Calif., 1986-87; pres. biotech., chief exec. officer Gilead Scis., Inc., Foster City, Calif., 1987—. Contbr. articles to profl. jours.; patentee in field. Langsdorf scholar, 1975-79, Henry Luce Found. scholar, 1979-80. Mem. U.S.-Japan Soc., Am. Chem. Soc., AAAS, Am. Inst. Chem. Engrs., N.Y. Acad. Scis., AOA Med. Soc., Sigma Xi, Phi Beta Kappa. Club: Lincoln of No. Calif. Home: 440 Conil Way Menlo Park CA 94025 Office: Gilead Scis Inc 344 Lakeside Dr Foster City CA 94404

RIOS, EVELYN DEERWESTER, columnist, musician, artist, writer; b. Payne, Ohio, June 25, 1916; d. Jay Russell and Flossie Edith (Fell) Deerwester; m. Edwin Tietjen Rios, Sept. 19, 1942 (dec. Feb. 1987); children: Jane Evelyn Rios Sample, Linda Sue Rios Stahlman. BA with honors, San Jose State U., 1964, MA, 1968. Cert. elem., secondary tchr., Calif. Lectr. in music San Jose State U., 1969-75; bilingual cons., then assoc. editor Ednl. Factors, Inc., San Jose, 1969-76, mgr. field research, 1977-78; writer, editor Calif. MediCorps Program, 1978-85; contbg. editor, illustrator The Community Family Mag., Wimberly, Tex., 1983-85; columnist The Springer, Dripping Springs, Tex., 1985—; author, illustrator, health instr. textbooks elem. schs., 1980-82. Choir dir. Bethel Luth. Ch., Cupertino, Calif., 1965-83; organist Holy Spirit Epis. Ch., Dripping Springs, Tex., 1987—; music dir. Cambrian Park (Calif.) Meth. Ch., 1961-64. Mem. AAUW, Am. Guild Organists (dean 1963-64), Phi Kappa Phi. Republican. Episcopalian. Home and Office: Star Rte 1-B PO Box 427 Dripping Springs TX 78620

RIPP, JOHN PATRICK, accountant; b. Richmond, Va., May 26, 1964; s. Richard Joseph and Mary Francis (Hill) R. B in Fin., Fordham U., 1986; postgrad., U. Richmond, 1986—. Gen. mgr. The Restaurant Co., Richmond, Va., 1986-87; acct. The Restaurant Co., Richmond, 1987—. Republican. Roman Catholic. Home: 304 N Belmont Ave Richmond VA 23221 Office: The Restaurant Co 1132 Hermitage Rd Richmond VA 23220

RIPPEL, ERIC RICHARDS, foundation administrator; b. Morristown, N.J., Jan. 2, 1935; s. Julius Alexander and Carol Winnefred (Richards) R.; m. Caryl Marsh, Aug. 25, 1957 (div. June 1965); 1 child, Schoenly Shearer Alexandra. Student, Choate, Wallingford, Conn., 1951-53, Dartmouth Coll., 1953-54, U. Edinburgh, Scotland, 1954-55; BS, Columbia U., N.Y.C., 1958. Mem. N.Y. Stock Exchange, N.Y.C., 1965-72, Internat. Futures Exchange, Hamilton, Bermuda, 1980—; trustee Fannie E. Rippel Found., Madison, N.J., 1961—, v.p., 1974-86; pres. Fannie E. Ripple Found., Madison, 1987—. Mem. N.Y. State Health Research Council, Albany, N.Y., 1975-80, Royal Naval Assn., N.Y.C.; trustee, chmn. Intersearch Inst., Inc., 1988—. Mem. Met. Club (N.Y.C.), Univ. Club (N.Y.C.), St. Andrews Club (N.Y.C.), Alexandria Hunt and Stirup Cup Assn. Presbyterian. Office: Fannie E Rippel Found 333 Main St PO Box 758 Madison NJ 07940

RIRIE, THOMAS ROBERT, chemical engineer; b. Monogahela, Pa., May 8, 1964; s. Donald Johnston and Mary Rita (Jonas) R. BS in Chem. Engring., Case Western Res. U., 1987; BA in Chemistry, Thiel Coll., 1987. Research engr. Engelhard, Corp., Beachwood, Ohio, 1987; process engr., analytical supr. Engelhard, Corp., Cleve., 1987-88, plant process engr., 1988-89, prodn. supr., 1989—. Mem. Am. Inst. Chem. Engrs. (assoc.), Am. Chem. Soc. Roman Catholic. Office: Engelhard Corp 1000 Harvard Ave Cleveland OH 44109

RISDON, MICHAEL PAUL, manufacturing executive; b. Hamburg, Iowa, Feb. 24, 1946; s. Paul A. and Vesta Mae (Melton) R.; m. Ann Lorraine Grandowski, June 4, 1966; children: Anita Ann, Carter Paul. BS, Iowa State U., 1967, U. Ky., 1968; MBA, U. Pitts., 1971. Budget analyst Cummins Engine Co., Columbus, Ind., 1969-70; sr. acct. Ernst & Ernst, Indpls., 1971-75; audit supr. Ashland (Ky.) Oil, Inc., 1975-77; mgr. corp. audit Cummins Engine Co., Columbus, 1977-78, dir. corp. and EDP audit, 1978-82; v.p. fin. & systems Diesel ReCon Co., Memphis, 1982-86; v.p., dir. fin. and planning power systems group Cummins Engine Co., Columbus, Ind., 1987-88; v.p. Cummins Power Generation, Inc., Columbus, 1989—. V.p. Columbus Child Care Ctr., 1981-82. Mem. AICPA, Ind. CPA Soc., Nat. Assn. Accts. (nat. bd. dirs. 1981-87, v.p. 1984-85). Roman Catholic. Lodge: Kiwanis (Columbus and Broad Ripple, Ind.) (v.p. Columbus chpt. 1981). Office: Cummins Power Generation Inc 8155 Bowline Dr Indianapolis IN 46236

RISHEL, RICHARD CLINTON, banker; b. Oreland, Pa., June 7, 1943; S. Herbert Beale and Evelyn (Lauer) R.; m. Carol Staub, Apr. 3, 1965; children: Christian Daniel, Peter James. B.A., Pa. State U., 1965; postgrad., Drexel Inst. Tech., 1965-66. Credit analyst 1st Pa. Banking & Trust Co., Phila., 1965-69; comml. lending officer Nat. Bank of Chester County, West Chester, Pa., 1969; asst. v.p. Continental Bank of Norristown, Pa., 1969-70; sec. Continental Bank of Norristown, 1970-71, v.p., 1971-73, sr. v.p., chief fin. officer, 1973-75, exec. v.p., chief fin. officer, 1975-81, vice chmn., 1981-83, pres., chief adminstrv. officer, 1984—, also dir.; dir. Continental Bank, 1980—, vice chmn. bd., 1981—; pres. parent co. Continental Bancorp., 1981—; bd. dirs. York Bank & Trust Co., United Penn Bank, World Affairs Council, Urban Affairs Partnership, Midlantic Corp. Mem. Phila. C. of C. (bd. dirs.). also: Midlantic Corp Metro Park Pla PO Box 600 Edison NJ 08818

RISICA, LORETTA CASH, rancher, accountant; b. Marlow, Okla., Jan. 26, 1930; d. Harvey D. and Retie C. (Harris) Cash; m. Sam Risica, Oct. 24, 1948 (dec. Oct. 1984); children: Ronald C., Patrick W., Tony J., Michael D. Cert. in acctg., Draughon's Bus. Coll., 1947. With mgmt. and acctg. Edinburg Glass Co., Tex., 1960-77, M&S Contracting Co., Edinburg, 1977-82, Risica & Sons, Inc., 1977-88; asst. mgr. acctg. Ropatomi Ranch, Inc., 1982—; pres. Risica & Sons, Inc., Edinburg, 1984—; owner Risica & Sons, Inc.; prin., owner, chief exec. officer Risica & Sons Glass Co., Ropatomi Ranch Inc. Sec. Edinburg Gen. Hosp. Aux., 1986; treas. Hidalgo County Hist. Mus. Guild, Edinburg, 1983—; v.p. Edinburg Gen. Hosp. Aux., 1987; bd. dirs., trustee South Tex. Symphony Assn., McAllen, Tex., 1987—; mem. Hidalgo County Hist. Mus. (life). Mem. P.E.O. Democrat. Presbyterian.

RISK, J. FRED, banker, investment banker; b. Ft. Wayne, Ind., Dec. 1, 1928; s. Clifford and Estella (Kline) R.; m. Viola Jean Tompt, July 12, 1953; children: Nancy Jean, John Thomas. B.S. cum laude, Ind. U., 1949, LL.B., J.D., 1951; postgrad., Nortwestern U.; LL.D., Ind. State U. With Harris Trust & Savs. Bank, Chgo., 1951-54, W.T. Grimm & Co., 1954-56; with Ind. Nat. Bank of Indpls., 1956-76, exec. v.p. dir., 1965-68, pres., 1968-76, chmn., 1971-76; chmn. Forum Group, Inc., 1976—, Sargent & Greenleaf Inc., 1980—; dir. Steak n Shake, Inc., Standard Locknut, Inc., Somerset Corp., Nat. Homes Corp., Amli Realty Co., Security Group, Inc., Keystone Distbn., Inc. Lacy Diversified Industries, Inc., Excepticon, Inc., L.R. Nelson Corp., Forum Industries, Breckenridge Corp., Canterbury Corp., Cygnet Enterprises, Inc., Franklin Corp., Forum Fin., Inc.; Dir. Haag Drug Co., Inland Container Corp., Ind. Bell Telephone Co., Ransburg Corp., Hook Drug Co., Northwestern Mut. Life Ins. Co. Bd. dirs. Hanover Coll., 1966-72, Ind. U. Found., 1968—; chmn. Indpls. Center for Advanced Research; bd. dirs. United Student Aid Fund; chmn. Ind. State Scholarship Com., 1968-72. Served as capt. inf. AUS, 1950-51. Mem. Am., Ind., Res. City bankers assns., Ind., Indpls. bar assns. Methodist. Clubs: Meridian Hills Country (Indpls.); Royal Poinciana Golf (Naples, Fla.); Quail Creek Country (Naples). Office: Forum Group Inc 8900 Keystone Crossing Indianapolis IN 46240

RISK, PAMELA JANE, cosmetics company executive; b. South Bend, Ind., June 13, 1962; d. Robert James and Rosemary (DeWood) R. BS, Ind. U., 1984. Asst. buyer Rich's Dept. Store, Atlanta, 1984-85; asst. to owner Bonnie White, Inc., Atlanta, 1985-86; account coord. and mgr. Princess Marcella Borghese, Atlanta and Charlotte, N.C., 1986-87, account exec., 1987—. Mem. NAFE, Am. Home Econs. Assn. (v.p. 1983-84), Charlotte C. of C., Omicron Nu (sec. 1983-84, del. to annual conclave 1983). Republican. Methodist. Home and Office: 1216 Summit N Dr Atlanta GA 30324

RISLEY, DAVID MILO, controller; b. Davenport, Iowa, Dec. 3, 1944; s. Ernest and Emma (Remke) R.; m. Karen Ann McConkey, Aug. 26, 1967; children: Kristen Anne, Matthew Christopher. BBA in Acctg., U. Iowa, 1966; MBA in Fin., Loyola U., Chgo., 1970. CPA, Ill. Staff auditor Authur Young & Co., Chgo., 1970-76; dir. internal audit Trans. Union Corp., Lincolnshire, Ill., 1976-79, group controller, 1979-81; v.p., controller Heizer Corp., Chgo., 1981-84; corp. controller Trinova Corp., Maumee, Ohio, 1984—. Trustee Knox Presbyn. Ch., Naperville, Ill., 1976-84, Toledo Hearing and speech ctr., Ohio, 1988—; bd. dirs. Toledo Opera, 1989—; instr. Jr. Achievement, Toledo, 1985—. Served as 1st lt. U.S. Army, 1966-69, Vietnam. Mem. AICPA, Ohio Soc. of CPAs, Fin. Exec. Inst., Nat. Assn. Accts. Republican. Methodist. Clubs: Inverness Golf (Toledo). Home: 2710 Derby Rd Toledo OH 43615 Office: Trinova Corp 1705 Indian Wood Cir Maumee OH 43537

RISNER, RAY DAVID, foods company executive, finance educator; b. Phila., Feb. 3, 1945; s. Joseph and Frances (Grossman) R.; m. Judy Irene Goodman, Aug. 20, 1972; children: Juliet Danielle, Mariel Francine. BSEE, Brown U., 1967; MBA, Harvard U., 1971. Security analyst Reich and Tang, Inc., N.Y.C., 1971-74; sr. fin. analyst Warner-Lambert Co., Morris Plains, N.J., 1974-75; asst. treas. Standard Brands, Inc., N.Y.C., 1975-82; dir. fin. analysis Nabisco Brands, Inc., Parsippany, N.J., 1982-85, staff v.p. fin. ops., East Hanover, N.J., 1985-86, v.p. fin. adminstrn., Atlanta, Ga., 1987—; treas. Nabisco Brands Program for Active Citizenship, 1983-87; v.p. fin. adminstrn. and ops. RJR Nabisco, Inc., Atlanta, 1987—; adj. prof. fin. Fairleigh Dickinson U., Madison, N.J., 1974-86. Treas., bd. dirs. ARC, Southeast Morris and Madison, N.J., 1984-87, bd. dirs. Atlanta chpt., 1988—. Served to 1st lt. U.S. Army, 1968-70, Vietnam. Mem. Am. Mgmt. Assn., N.Y. Soc. Security Analysts, Fin. Analyst Fedn., Fin. Execs. Inst., IEEE. Jewish. Home: 8175 Grogans Ferry Rd Atlanta GA 30350 Office: RJR Nabisco Inc 300 Galleria Pkwy Atlanta GA 30339

RISS, ROBERT BAILEY, insurance company executive; b. Salida, Colo., May 27, 1927; s. Richard Roland and Louise (Roberts) R.; married; children: Edward Stayton, G. Leslie, Laura Bailey, Juliana Warren. BSBA, U. Kans., 1949. Pres. Riss Internat. Corp., Kansas City, Mo., 1950-80, chmn. bd., 1964-86; founder, chmn. bd., pres. Republic Industries, Inc., Kansas City, Mo., 1969-86; chmn. bd. Grandview Bank and Trust Co., 1969-86, Commonwealth Gen. Ins. Co., 1986—; Chmn. bd. dirs., exec. com. Heart of Am. Fire and Casualty Co.; chmn. bd. dirs. Comml. Equipment Co. Vice chmn. bd. trustees Kansas U. Endowment Assn., 1980—. Recipient Silver Beaver award Kansas City Area coun. Boy Scouts Am., 1972; Disting. Svc. citation U. Kans., 1976; Fred Ellsworth medal U. Kans., 1979; named Most Outstanding Young Man in Mo. U.S. Jr. C. of C., 1956. Mem. Kans. U. Alumni Assn. (nat. pres. 1969-70), Sigma Nu. Episcopalian.

RIST, HAROLD ERNEST, consulting engineer; b. Newcomb, N.Y., Aug. 6, 1919; s. Ernest DeVerne and Iva Cardine (Braley) R.; m. Vera Leona Basuk, July 30, 1942 (div. June 1980); children: Cherry Diana Rist Chapman, Harold Ernest II, Byron Basuk; m. Ruth Ann Mahony, Aug. 16, 1980. BCE, Rensselaer Poly. Inst., 1950, MCE, 1952. Registered profl. engr., N.Y., N.J., N.H., Vt., Mass., Pa., Md., Ky. Project mgr. Seelye, Stevenson, Value & Knecht, N.Y.C., 1952-58; found., prin. Harold E. Rist, Assocs., Glens Falls, N.Y., 1958-60; ptnr., chief exec. officer Rist, Bright & Frost, Glens Falls, 1960-63, Rist, Frost & Assocs., Glens Falls, 1963-79; pres., chief exec. officer Rist, Frost Assocs., P.C., Glens Falls, 1979-84, chmn. bd., 1984—; pres. chief exec. officer 21 Bay Corp., Glens Falls, 1970—, Hudson Heights Moreau, Inc., Glens Falls, 1972—, Mech. Elec. Systems, Inc., Glens Falls, 1983—, Glens Falls Communications Corp., 1985—. Contbr. articles to profl. jours. Bd. dirs. Adirondack (N.Y.) North County Assn., 1960—, v.p., 1986—; commr. Hudson River Valley Commn., Tarrytown, N.Y., 1970-78. Served to staff sgt. U.S. Army, 1942-44. Mem. NSPE, Cons. Engrs. Council N.Y. (pres. 1966-68), Am. Cons. Engrs. Council (v.p. 1970-72), Profl. Services Council (bd. dirs. 1972-85), N.Y. State Assn. of The Professions (charter), Adirondack Regional C. of C. (v.p. 1984—). Republican. Mem. Methodist Episcopal Ch. Clubs: Lake George (Diamond Point, N.Y.); Safari Club Internat.; Surfside Vacation, Kehei, Maui Hawaii (pres.); Lodge: Masons. Home: Lake Shore Dr Box A 1 Diamond Point NY 12824 Office: Rist Frost Assocs P C 21 Bay St Glen Falls NY 12801

RISTAINO, RHONDA SUE, accountant; b. Albuquerque, Sept. 21, 1960; d. Karl Bruno and Margaret Ann (White) Rueb; m. David Connor Ristaino, June 23, 1984; 1 child, Andrea Nicole. BS in Acctg., N.Mex. State U., 1983.

CPA, Tex. Asst. bank examiner Fed. Deposit Ins. Co., Ft. Worth, 1980, Tyler, Tex., 1982, Dallas, 1983-84; bank liquidator Midland, Tex., 1984; auditor, tax cons. Price Waterhouse, Midland and South Bend, Ind., 1984—. Mem. Ind. Soc. CPA's, AICPA. Republican. Presbyterian. Home: 2 Mayfield St Greenville RI 02828

RITCHIE, CEDRIC ELMER, banker; b. Upper Kent, N.B., Can., Aug. 22, 1927; s. E. Thomas and Marion (Henderson) R.; m. Barbara Binnington, Apr. 20, 1956. Student pub. schs., Bath, N.B. With The Bank of N.S., Bath, 1945—; chief gen. mgr. The Bank of N.S., Toronto, Ont., Can., 1970-72, pres., 1972-79, chief exec. officer, 1972—, chmn. bd. dirs., 1974—, also bd. dirs.; chmn. bd., dir. The Bank N.S. Channel Islands Ltd., The Bank N.S. Asia Ltd., The Bank N.S. Trust Co. Channel Islands Ltd., Scotiabank (U.K.) Ltd., Scotia Realty Ltd., The Bank N.S. Trust Co. (Bahamas) Ltd., The Bank N.S. Trust Co. (Caribbean) Ltd., BNS Internat. (U.K.) Ltd., The Bank N.S. Jamaica Ltd., The Bank N.S. Trust Co. Trinidad and Tobago Ltd., 1st So. Bank Ltd., Scotia Leasing Ltd., The West India Co. Mcht. Bankers Ltd., The Bank of N.S. Internat. Ltd., The Bank N.S. Trinidad & Tobago Ltd., The Bank N.S. Trust Co. (Cayman) Ltd.;chmn, chief exec. officer, dir. The Bank of Nova Scotia Properties Inc.; dir. numerous companies; mem. adv. council for Can. Exec. Service Orgn. Mem. sch. bus. adminstrn. adv. com. U. Western Ont., internat. adv. council Ctr. for Inter-Am. Relations; mem. chmn.'s council Ams. Soc.; bd. govs. Jr. Achievement Can., Olympic Trust Can. Decorated Officer Order of Can., 1981. Clubs: Canadian, Donalda, Mt. Royal, Mid Ocean, National, Toronto, York, Lyford Cay. Office: Bank NS Scotia Pla, 44 King St W, Toronto, ON Canada M5H 1H1

RITCHIE, MARK ANDREW, commodities broker; b. Corvallis, Oreg., Apr. 4, 1948; s. Dwight Dameron and Winefred Zoe (Belshee) R.; m. Nancy Lynn Oberg, May 12, 1973; children: Daniel, Joseph, Mark, Jolynn, Marylynn. BA, Trinity Coll., Deerfield, Ill., 1973, MDiv, 1980. Correctional officer Cook County House of Correction, 1970-75; phone clk.-trader A-Mark Trading, Chgo., 1975-76; pvt. practice Chgo., 1977—; founding ptnr. Chgo. Rsch. and Trade, 1977—; founder, owner Ceretech, London, 1984—, Media Conversion, Glen Ellyn, Ill., 1983—. Author: God in the Pits: Confessions of a Commodities Trader, 1989; exec. producer films.

RITCHIE, RICHARD LEE, communications company executive, former railroad and forest products company executive; b. Grand Rapids, Mich., July 20, 1946; s. Robert George and Gertrude (Dryer) R.; m. Marlene Barton, Nov. 16, 1969; children: Gabrielle Gay, Steven Barton. B.A., Mich. State U., 1968, M.B.A., 1972; P.M.D., Harvard U., 1982. C.P.A., Mich. Sr. acct. Peat, Marwick, Mitchell & Co., Detroit, 1968-69, 72-74; mgr. corp. acctg. Grand Trunk Western R.R., Detroit, 1974-76; treas. Grand Trunk Western R.R., 1976-79, asst. v.p., treas., 1980-83; v.p., treas. James River Corp., Richmond, Va., 1984-86; v.p. fin. Harte Hanks Communications, San Antonio, 1987—; prof. Oakland Community Coll., Farmington, Mich. Served with AUS, 1969-71. Mem. Am. Inst. C.P.A.s, Mich. Assn. C.P.A.s, Am. Acctg. Assn., Beta Alpha Psi, Beta Gamma Sigma. Jewish. Office: Harte Hanks Communications PO Box 269 San Antonio TX 78291-0269

RITCHIE, ROBERT JAMIESON, transportation executive; b. Ormstown, Que., Can., Oct. 5, 1944; s. Ian David and Helen Mary (Jamieson) R.; m. Tatiana Miloradovitch, Feb. 2, 1974; children: Nicolai, Ian. BSc, McGill U., Montreal, Can., 1967; MBA, U. Western Ont., London, Can., 1970. Research analyst Can. Pacific Ltd., Montreal, Que., 1970-72; rep. mktg. CP Rail, Vancouver, B.C., Can., 1972-74, dir. mktg., 1974-76, mgr. mktg., 1976-77; mktg. mgr. mktg. CP Rail, Montreal, 1977-79, gen. mgr. mktg. and sales Pacific region, 1979-81, asst. v.p. mktg., 1981-84, v.p. mktg. and sales, 1984-87, exec. v.p., 1987—; bd. dirs. Fording Coal, Toronto Terminal Railway, InCan. Ships. Mem. Nat. Freight Transp. Assn. (regional v.p. 1987—), Ont. Bus. Adv. Council, Toronto C. of C., Toronto Bd. Trade, Tornto & Montreal Ry. Clubs., Au Fond Club. Office: CP Rail, 65 Front St W, Toronto, ON Canada M5J 1E8

RITTENHOUSE, BRUCE DEAN, aerospace engineer; b. Trenton, N.J., May 9, 1951; s. Jean White and Naomi (Emmons) R. BS, Parks Coll. of St. Louis U., Cahokia, Ill., 1974. Aerospace engr. Marine Corps Air Sta. Naval Aviation Depot (formerly Naval Air Rework Facility), Havelock, N.C., 1977—. Republican. Home: PO Box 1960 Atlantic Beach NC 28512 Office: Product Support Directorate Naval Aviation Depot Marine Air Corps Sta Cherry Point Havelock NC 28533-5030

RITTER, ANN L., lawyer; b. N.Y.C., May 20, 1933; d. Joseph and Grace (Goodman) R. B.A., Hunter Coll., 1954; J.D., N.Y. Law Sch., 1970; postgrad. Law Sch., NYU, 1971-72. Bar: N.Y. 1971, U.S. Ct. Appeals (2d cir.) 1975, U.S. Supreme Ct. 1975. Writer, 1954-70; editor, 1955-66; tchr., 1966-70; atty. Am. Soc. Composers, Authors and Pubs., N.Y.C., 1971-72, Greater N.Y. Ins. Co., N.Y.C., 1973-74; sr. ptnr. Brenhouse & Ritter, N.Y.C., 1974-78; sole practice, N.Y.C., 1978—. Editor N.Y. Immigration News, 1975-76. Mem. ABA, Am. Immigration Lawyers Assn. (treas. 1983-84, sec. 1984-85, vice chair 1985-86, chair 1986-87), N.Y. State Bar Assn., N.Y. County Lawyers Assn., Assn. Trial Lawyers Am., N.Y. State Trial Lawyers Assn., N.Y.C. Bar Assn. Democrat. Jewish. Home: 47 E 87th St New York NY 10128 Office: 420 Madison Ave New York NY 10017

RITTER, GUY FRANKLIN, structural engineer; b. Detroit, Feb. 9, 1933; s. Guy Franklin and Ethel (Reed) R.; m. Peggy Anne Maloy, Sept. 20, 1954; children: Constance Elaine, Margaret Anne, Sallie Reed. BS in Architecture, Ga. Inst. Tech., 1954, B Arch. Engring., 1955; MS in Bldg. Engring., MIT, 1956. Registered profl. engr., Ga., Fla., S.C., N.C., Ala., Tenn. Structural detailer I.E. Morris Assocs., Atlanta, 1955-56; structural engr. Morris, Boehmig & Tindel, Atlanta, 1956-58; dist. structural engr. Portland Cement Assn., Atlanta, 1958-61; sr. structural engr. Lindsey Tucker Ritter, Albany, Ga., 1961-74; v.p. Lindsey & Ritter, Inc., Albany, 1974-79; pres., chief exec. officer Lindsey & Ritter, Albany, 1979—. Recipient Value Engr. award GSA, 1974. Mem. ASCE, NSPE, Am. Cons. Engrs. Council, Am. Concrete Inst., Prestressed Concrete Inst. Republican. Presbyterian. Lodges: Elks, Rotary (local pres. 1983-84). Office: Lindsey & Ritter Inc 423 Pine Ave Bldg Albany GA 31702

RITTER, ROBERT JOSEPH, lawyer; b. N.Y.C., Aug. 11, 1925; s. Robert Reinhart and Mary (Mandracchia) R.; m. Barbara Willis Foust, Oct. 1, 1955 (div. May 1977); children: Robert Thornton, Jan Willis, Nancy Carol. Student Bklyn. Poly. Inst., 1943; BA cum laude, Queens Coll., 1949; JD, NYU, 1953, LLM in Internat. Law, 1955. Bar: N.Y. 1953. Acct. UN Secretariat, N.Y.C., 1949-54; asst. counsel RCA Corp., N.Y.C., 1955-58; atty. CIBA-GEIGY Corp., Ardsley, N.Y., 1958-60; atty. AT&T Bell Telephone Labs., Inc., Murray Hill, N.J., 1960-70; tax atty. AT&T Technologies, Inc., N.Y.C., 1970-85; mgr. fin. AT&T Corp. Hdqrs., Parsippany, N.J., 1985-87; asst. sec. 14 AT&T subs. telephone cos.; v.p. CPPS Tax Cons., N.Y.C., 1987—. Contbr. articles to legal jours. Pres. Harry B. Thayer chpt., Telephone Pioneers of Am., N.Y.C., 1983-84; trustee United Way Cen. N.J., Milltown 1989—; corp. program dir. Vol. Action Ctr. of Middlesex County, N.J., 1988—; mem. census com. Middlesex County, 1988—; adv. coun. Project Resources, State N.J., 1987—; bd. dirs. Somerset Hills YMCA, Bernardsville, N.J., 1971-73; candidate (Democratic) N.Y. State Assembly, Westchester County, N.Y., 1965; chmn. Am. Cancer Soc. Fund Drive, Bronxville, N.Y., 1964. Served with USAAF, 1943-46; ATO. Recipient Crusade award Am. Cancer Soc., 1965, Masonic Svc. award, 1947, Am. Legion Citizenship award, 1943, Eagle Scout award Boy Scouts Am., 1941. Mem. Nat. Tax Assn.-Tax Inst. Am. (chmn., advisor state sales and use taxation com. 1984—, chmn. prodn. exemption subcom. 1978-84), Assn. of Bar of City of N.Y., Legal Aid Soc., NYU Law Alumni Assn., Perth Amboy (N.J.) C. of C. (exec. dir. 1988—), Rossmoor Tennis Club (pres. 19876), Church of N.Y. Club, Kiwanis (1st v.p. 1970-71), Sigma Alpha. Democrat. Episcopalian. Home: 3-N Village Mall Jamesburg NJ 08831 Office: CPPS Tax Cons PO Box 7022 Yorkville Station New York NY 10128

RITTMANN, RONALD GEORGE, finance company executive; b. Trenton, N.J., Apr. 7, 1949; s. Charles Harry and Muriel Jean (Manzor) R.; m. Ruth Ethel Nickerson, June 21, 1975; children: Michelle, Melissa. BS in Commerce, Rider Coll., 1971. Sr. mgr. Ernst & Whinney, Trenton, N.J., 1979-81; asst. corp. contr. Imo Delaval, Inc., Lawrenceville, N.J., 1981-84, corp. contr., 1984-86, v.p., treas., 1986—. Bd. dirs. Boy's Club of Am., Trenton, 1979-81. Mem. N.J. Soc. CPAs, Machinery and Allied Products Inst. (fin. coun.). Office: Imo Delaval Inc 3450 Princeton Pike Lawrenceville NJ 08648

RIVA, JOSEPH PETER, JR., geologist; b. Chgo., Oct. 31, 1935; s. Joseph Peter and Anita (Tron) R.; m. A. Susanne Bozenhardt, Dec. 6, 1963; children—Monica, Michaela. B.A., Carleton Coll., 1957; M.S., U. Wyo., 1959. Petroleum geologist Tenneco Oil Co., Casper, Wyo., 1959; geol. cons., Chgo., 1961-66; chief earth sci. br. Smithsonian Sci. Info. Exchange, Washington, 1966-74; specialist in earth scis. Congl. Res. Service, Library of Congress, 1974—; sr. research geologist U.S. Geol. Survey, Reston, Va., 1980—; cons. geologist Great Falls, Va., 1966—; mem. com. offshore Hydrocarbon Resource Estimation Methodology, and com. on undiscovered oil and gas Resources, nat. Research Council of Nat. Acad. Scis. Author: Secondary and Teritary Recovery of Oil, 1974; Energy From Geothermal Resources, 1978; Energy From the Ocean, 1978; World Petroleum Resources and Reserves, 1983; U.S. Conventional Oil and Gas Production Prospects to the Year 2000, 1985; contbr. articles to profl. jours.; contbr. articles to congressional publs.; contbr. articles in field to Encyclopaedia Britannica, 1987 ed. Served with USN, 1959-61. Mem. Am. Assn. Petroleum Geologists, Am. Inst. Profl. Geologists, Sigma Xi. Methodist. Avocations: photography, golf. Home: 9705 Mill Run Dr Great Falls VA 22066 Office: Congl Rsch Svc Libr Congress Washington DC 20540

RIVENBARK, REMBERT REGINALD, shipbuilding executive; b. St. Paul, S.C., Sept. 9, 1912; s. Reginald Vernon and Kathleen Francis (Fussell) R.; m. Marie Barbour, July 20, 1932; children: Patricia Pate, Rembert Reginald, Herbert William Barbour. Grad., Goldsboro (N.C.) High Sch. Foreman bottling dept. Coca Cola Bottling Co., New Bern, N.C., 1927-32; with Barbour Boat Works, New Bern, 1932—, successively bookkeeper, office mgr., gen. mgr., v.p., gen. mgr., 1945-57, pres., 1957-72, bd. chmn., 1957—; bd. chmn., pres. Marine Trading Corp., New Bern, 1948—. Mem. N.C. Med. Assn. (hon.), Am. Mgmt. Assn., U.S. C. of C., Am. Ordnance Assn., Crippled Children's Assn. (life), N.C. Wildlife Assn., N.C. Fisheries Assn. (dir.). Clubs: N.Y. Athletic, East Carolina Yacht (charter), New Bern Golf and Country. Lodges: Mason, Shriners, Elks, Rotary. Home: Trent Shores Dr New Bern NC 28560 Office: 522-525 Tyron Palace Dr New Bern NC 28560

RIVERA, RICHARD E., food products executive; b. Jan. 6, 1947; m. Leslie Suzanne Pliner, Nov. 18, 1984. Student, Washington U., 1963-68; BA, Lee U., 1968. Credit analyst Nat. Bank Commerce, Dallas, 1970-71, 1970-71; from mgmt. trainee to exec. v.p., dir. Steak Ale Restaurants of Am., Dallas, 1971-80; pres. restaurant div. El Chico Corp., 1980-82; v.p., chief oper. officer W.R. Grace & Co. div. T.J. Applebee's and Taco Villa Mexican Restaurant, Dallas, 1982-87; exec. v.p. ops. TGI Friday's Inc., Dallas, 1987-88, pres., chief exec. officer, 1988—. Office: TGI Friday's Inc 14665 Midway Rd PO Box 809062 Dallas TX 75380

RIVERIN, BRUNO, financial center executive; b. Chicoutimi, Que., Can., Mar. 29, 1941. BSEE, Laval U., Que., Quebec, 1966; MBA in Fin., Sherbrooke (Que.), 1970; postgrad., U. Paris, 1971. Sales engr. Esso and Gentec, Toronto and Montreal, Can., 1966-68; analyst Air Can., Montreal, 1968-71; fin. analyst Caisse de dépôt et placement du Québec, Montreal, 1971; account officer Mercantile Bank, Montreal, 1971, asst. to sr. v.p., 1977; v.p. fin., adminstrn. Desjardins Group, Montreal, 1977-80; pres., chief operating officer Caisse Centrale Desjardins (Desjardins Group), Montreal, 1980-87; pres., chief exec. officer The Montreal Exchange, 1987—; dir. Trans-Can. Options Inc., Toronto, 1987—, The Canadian Depository Securities Ltd., Toronto, 1987—, Internat. Options Clearing Corp. B.V., Amsterdam, 1987—; deputy gov. The Nat. Contingency Fund, Toronto, 1987—; chmn. Internat. Fin. Ctrs. Orgn. of Montreal (Ifcom), 1988—. Mem. C.D. Howe Inst. (Que. div.), Que. Engrs. Assn., Montreal C. of C., French C. of C., Laval U. and Sherbrooke U. Alumnae Assn., St. Denis Club, Montreal Amateur Athletic Assn., Richelieu Golf Club. Office: Montreal Exch, 800 Sq Victoria 4th Fl, Montreal, PQ Canada H4Z 1A9

RIVET, DIANA WITTMER, lawyer, developer; b. Auburn, N.Y., Apr. 28, 1931; d. George Wittmer and Anne (Jenkins) Wittmer Hauswirth; m. Paul Henry Rivet, Oct. 24, 1952; children: Gail, Robin, Leslie, Heather, Clayton, Eric. BA, Keuka Coll., 1951; JD, Bklyn. Law Sch., 1956. Bar: N.Y. 1956, U.S. Dist. Ct. (ea. and so. dists.) N.Y. 1975. Sole practice, Orangeburg, N.Y., 1957—; county atty. Rockland County (N.Y.), 1974-77; asst. to legis. chmn. Rockland County, 1978-79; counsel, adminstr. Indsl. Devel. Agy., Rockland County, 1980—, Rockland Econ. Devel. Corp., 1981—; counsel, exec. dir. Pvt. Industry Council Rockland County, 1980—; pres. Environ. Mgmt. Ltd., Orangeburg, 1980—; mem. air mgmt. adv. com. N.Y. State Dept. Environ. Conservation 1984—; pres. Indoor Enviroment Ltd.; v.p. Naturescapes Ltd. Pres. Rockland County council Girl Scouts U.S., 1981-84; chmn. Rockland County United Way campaign, 1983-84, 88-89, bd. dirs. 1988—; bd. dirs. Rockland County Assn., West Nyack, 1981—. Recipient Community Svc. award Keuka Coll., 1965, Disting. Svc. award Town of Orangetown, 1970, Disting. Svc. award Rockland County, 1989; named Businessperson of Yr., Jour. News, Rockland County, 1982. Mem. ABA, N.Y. State Bar Assn. (mcpl. law sect. exec. com. 1976-83, environ. law sect. exec. com. 1974-86). Democrat. Mem. Religious Soc. of Friends. Home: 1 Lester Dr 35 Orangeburg Rd Orangeburg NY 10962

RIVLIN, ALICE MITCHELL, economist; b. Phila., Mar. 4, 1931; d. Allan C. G. and Georgianna (Fales) Mitchell; m. Lewis Allen Rivlin, 1955 (div. 1977); children: Catherine Amy, Allan Mitchell, Douglas Gray. B.A., Bryn Mawr Coll., 1952; Ph.D., Radcliffe Coll., 1958. Mem. staff Brookings Instn., Washington, 1957-66, 69-75, 83—; dir. econ. studies Brookings Inst., 1983-87; dir. Congl. Budget Office, 1975-83; dep. asst. sec. program coordination HEW, Washington, 1966-68, asst. sec. planning and evaluation, 1968-69; Staff Adv. Commn. on Intergovtl. Relations, 1961-62; bd. dirs. UNISYS Corp., Union Carbide Corp. Author: The Role of the Federal Government in Financing Higher Education, 1961, (with others) Microanalysis of Socioeconomic Systems, 1961, The U.S. Balance of Payments in 1968, 1963, Systematic Thinking and Social Action, 1971, Setting National Priorities: The 1974 Budget, 1973, (with others) Economic Choices 1987, 1986; (with others) The Swedish Economy, 1987, (with others) Caring for the Disabled Elderly: Who will Pay?, 1988. Chmn. bd. The Wilderness Soc. MacArthur fellow, 1983. Mem. Am. Econ. Assn. (nat. pres. 1986). Office: Brookings Inst 1775 Massachusetts Ave NW Washington DC 20036

RIZZI, JOSEPH VITO, banker; b. Berwyn, Ill., Dec. 5, 1949; s. Joseph and Mary Catherine (Mancini) R.; m. Candace Kunz, June 24, 1972; children: Jennifer, Joseph. BS in Commerce summa cum laude, DePaul U., 1971; MBA, U. Chgo., 1973; JD magna cum laude, U. Notre Dame, 1976. Bar: Ill. 1976. Law clk. to judge U.S. Dist. Ct. No. Dist. Ill., 1976-77; exec. v.p. T.B.R. Enterprises, Inc., Downers Grove, Ill., 1977-83; v.p. ABN/LaSalle Nat. Bank, Chgo., 1983—; mem. adv. bd. Banking Rsch. Ctr. Northwestern U. Mem. Union League Club, Delta Epsilon Sigma. Roman Catholic. Assoc. editor Notre Dame Lawyer, 1975-76; contbr. articles to profl. publs. Home: 287 Bartram Rd Riverside IL 60546 Office: ABN/LaSalle Nat Bank 135 S LaSalle St Rm 260 Chicago IL 60603

RIZZO, RICHARD DAVID, financial service company executive; b. Boston, May 7, 1944; s. George and Adele Therese (Eonnotti) R.; m. Jacqueline Ann Dugas, Oct. 10, 1971; children: Andrea, Danielle. BA in Math., Boston U., 1966, postgrad., 1967. Analyst to dist. credit mgr. CIT Corp., Boston, 1967-70; nat. credit mgr. to v.p. ops. Ind. Nat. Bank (leasing div.), Providence, 1970-73; v.p. adminstrn. New Eng. Mchts. Bank, Boston, 1973-77; asst. treas., v.p. fin. Wheelabrator Fin. Corp., Hampton, N.H., 1977-81; pres. Signal Capital Corp., Hampton, 1981—; bd. dirs. Northmark Bank, North Andover, Mass. Bd. dirs. New Eng. Council, Boston. With U.S. Army, 1968-74. Mem. Am. Assn. Equipment Lessors, Am. Mgmt. Assn., Prospector's Ski Club (bd. dirs. 1986—, lodge chmn. 1987—). Roman Catholic. Office: Signal Capital Corp Liberty Ln Hampton NH 03842

RIZZO, TERRIE LORRAINE HEINRICH, aerobic fitness executive; b. Oneonta, N.Y., Dec. 15, 1946; d. Steven Joseph Heinrich and Grace Beatrice (Davis) Chamberlin; m. Michael Louis Rizzo, Dec. 28, 1968; 1 child, Matthew Michael. BA, Pa. State U., 1968; MA, Johns Hopkins U., 1971. Tchr. Balt. County Sch. System, 1968-79; asst. dir. univ. relations U. Md., Catonsville, 1980-81; exec. dir. Aerobic Danse de Belgique, Brussels, 1981—; pres. Eurobics Inc., Sunnyvale, Calif., 1984—; aerobics dir. Green Valley Health Clubs, San Jose, Calif., 1985; pres. Personally Fit, 1986; cons. Belgian Ministry Sport, Sabena Airlines, others; lectr., syndicated columnist, 1986—. Author: Sittercise, 1985, How To Keep Fit While You Sit, 1988, Stress Relief Through Exercise, 1988; contbr. articles to profl. jours. Pres. Internat. Study Group, Brussels, 1983-84. Named Marketeer of Yr. Am. C. of C. in Belgium, 1987. Mem. Internat. Dance Exercise Assn., Assn. for Fitness in Bus., Aerobics and Fitness Assn. Am., Pa. State Alumni Assn. (bd. dirs. 1979-88), Brussels and Sunnyvale C. of C., San Francisco VCB, Mensa, Pi Gamma Mu, Phi Alpha Theta. Democrat. Roman Catholic. Clubs: Am. Women's (Brussels) (dir. 1983-84); San Jose Quota (bd. dirs. 1986-87). Avocations: traveling, oenology, gourmet cooking. Home: 19755 Lanark Ln Saratoga CA 95070 Office: 108 E Fremont Ave Sunnyvale CA 94087

RIZZUTO, LEANDRO PETER, corporate executive; b. N.Y.C., Apr. 10, 1938; s. Julian and Josephine (Rizzo) R.; children—Susan, Leandro P. Jr., Denis, Rita. Student, St. Johns U. Pres., chmn. bd. Conair Corp., Edison, N.J., 1959—. Bd. dirs. St. Jude's Children's Hosp., Memphis, 1971—. Recipient Man of Yr. award Boys Town of Italy, 1980, Achievement award Italian Legions of Merit, 1983, Man of Yr. award Am. Beauty Assn., 1987; named Humanitarian of Yr., Cabrini Hosp., 1985; faculty fellow U. Bridgeport, 1984. Roman Catholic. Club: Columbus (N.Y.C.). Office: Conair Corp 1 Cummings Point Rd Stamford CT 06904

ROACH, ANTOINETTE VELORIES, financial brokerage company executive; b. Meridian, Miss., July 8, 1931; d. Otha Lee and Ester (Mayatte) Ethridge; children: Carl Lowell Roach, Nan Roach Kurth, Mike Roach, Jackie Roach Pilkinton. Student public schs., Waco, Tex., Collinsville, Miss. Ins. and real estate investor, 1964-81; pres., owner, operator Lubbock Mortgage Co., Inc. (name now Guaranty Fin. Services, Inc.), Lubbock, Tex., 1976—; pres. Delta Cotton Co., 1977—; pres. Hunter & Roach Advt. Co., Lubbock, 1978—. Mem. Nat. Assn. Fin. Cons., NAFE, Better Bus. Bur., Sheriff Assn., Internat. Bus. Assn., Am. Alliance Small Bus. Club: Presidents of Tex. Home: PO Box 6890 Lubbock TX 79413-6890 Office: 1928 34th St Lubbock TX 79411

ROACH, JOHN D. C., corporate executive; b. West Palm Beach, Fla., Dec. 3, 1943; s. Benjamin Browning and Margaret (York) R.; m. Pam Flebbe, Dec. 29, 1967 (div. Aug. 1981); children: Vanessa, Alexandra; m. Elizabeth Louise Phillips, Aug. 28, 1982; children: Bruce Phillips, Bryce Phillips, Brian Phillips. BS in Indsl. Mgmt., MIT, 1965; MBA, Stanford U., 1967. Cofounder, mgr. Northrop Venture Capital, Century City, Calif., 1970-71; dir. mgmt. acctg. and info. systems Ventura div. Northrop Corp., Thousand Oaks, Calif., 1967-70; v.p., dir. Boston Cons. Group, Boston and Menlo Park, Calif., 1971-80; v.p., strategic mgmt. practice mng. officer Booz, Allen, Hamilton, San Francisco, 1980-82; strategic mgmt. practice mng. officer Houston, 1982-83; mng. dir. Braxton Assocs., Houston, 1983-87; sr. v.p., chief fin. officer Manville Corp., Denver, 1987-88, exec. v.p. ops., 1988—; pres. Manville Sales Corp., Denver, 1989. Author: Strategic Management Handbook, 1983; contbr. articles to profl. jours. Chmn. 65 Rose's Sports Club, Houston, 1986-87; bd. dirs. Am. Leukemia Soc., Houston, 1986, Opera Colo., Denver, 1987—. Mem. N.Am. Soc. Strategy Planners, Colo. Forum, Soc. Corp. Planners (charter), Fin. Execs. Inst. (mem. planning forum), Stanford Grad. Sch. Bus. Club, MIT Alumni Club, Met. Raquet (Houston), Denver Athletic Club, Petroleum Club. Clubs: Met. (Denver), Met. Raquet (Houston), Denver Athletic. Home: 4 Random Rd Englewood CO 80110-6106 Office: Manville Corp 717 17th St Denver CO 80202

ROACH, JOHN H., JR., banker, corporate finance executive; b. N.Y.C., Oct. 24, 1941; s. John Hendee and Julia (Casey) R.; m. Joan Hayden Muchmore, Sept. 23, 1972; children: Hayden, Cameron, John, Lauriston, Schuyler. BA, Washington & Jefferson Coll. Asst. mgr. to asst. v.p. Chem. Bank, N.Y.C., 1968-71, v.p. Wall St. div., 1972-74, v.p. corp. bank, 1974-80; pres. Chem. N.Y. Corp. U.S.A., Chgo., 1983-87; mng. dir. Chem. Bank, N.Y.C., 1987—. Bd. dirs. Banking Rsch. Ctr., J.L. Kellogg Grad. Sch. Mgmt. Northwestern U., Evanston, Ill. Capt. U.S. Army, 1964-66. Republican. Roman Catholic. Clubs: Winter (Lake Forest, Ill.); Field (Greenwich, Conn.); Racquet & Tennis (N.Y.C.); Duquesne (Pitts.); Onwentsia (Lake Forest, Ill.); Chgo. Home: 144 Parsonage Rd Greenwich CT 06830 Office: Chem Bank 277 Park Ave New York NY 10172

ROACH, JOHN VINSON, II, retail company executive; b. Stamford, Tex., Nov. 22, 1938; s. John V. and Agnes M. (Hanson) R.; m. Barbara Jean Wiggin, Mar. 31, 1960; children: Amy, Lori. B.A. in Physics and Math, Tex. Christian U., 1961, M.B.A., 1965. V.p. Radio Shack, 1972-75, Radio Shack Mfg., 1975-78; exec. v.p. Radio Shack, 1978-80; gen. mgr. data processing Tandy Corp., Ft. Worth, 1967-73, pres., 1980—, chief exec. officer, 1981—, chmn., 1982—, also dir.; chmn., chief exec. officer, bd. dirs. Intertan Inc.; bd. dirs. Justin Industries. Bd. dirs. Van Cliburn Found. Arts Coun., Tex. Christian U., Internat. Tex. Dept. of Commerce; chmn. United Way. Mem. Ft. Worth Club, City Club, Rotary. Office: Tandy Corp 1800 Two Tandy Ctr Fort Worth TX 76102

ROACH, RALPH LEE, health science facility administrator; b. Silver Spring, Md., Mar. 27, 1957; s. William A. and Mary B. (Collins) R.; m. Susan Diane Schirmacher, Aug. 17, 1985. BA, Messiah Coll., 1982; MS, Shippensburg U., 1985. Inventory controller Messiah Coll., Grantham, Pa., 1977-85; therapist, crisis interviewer Stevens Mental Health, Carlisle, Pa., 1983-86; psychotherapist Holy Spirit Community Mental Health Inst., Camp Hill, Pa., 1986—; presentor, cons. Lebanon (Pa.) Valley Coll., 1986; vocat. tng. mgr. Ctr. for Indsl. Tng., Mechanicsburg, Pa., 1985-87; program coordinator Hershey Med. Ctr., Elizabethtown, Pa., 1987—; adj. faculty Elizabethtown Coll., 1987—. Edn. dir. Cumberland Valley Ch., Dillsburg, Pa., 1980-83; presentor Gov.'s Com. on Handicapped, Harrisburg, Pa., 1986; presentor Office of Spl. Edn. and Rehab., Harrisburg, 1987. Mem. Pa. Specialists in Group Work, Pa. Crisis Intervention Assn., Nat. Rifle Assn. Presbyterian. Home: PO Box 309 Grantham PA 17027 Office: Hershey Med Hosp Elizabethtown PA 17022

ROACH, WILLIAM RUSSELL, training and education executive; b. Bedford, Ind., Jan. 1940; s. George H. and Beatrice M. (Schoenlaub) R.; m. Margaret R. Balogh, 1961; children: Kathleen L., Keith W. BS, UCLA, 1961. Internal auditor Hughes Aircraft Co., Los Angeles, 1961-62, Lockheed Aircraft Corp., Los Angeles, 1962; sr. acct. Haskins & Sells, Los Angeles, 1962-66; asst. to group v.p. Lear Siegler, Inc., Santa Monica, Calif., 1966-71; v.p. fin., sec. Paul Hardeman Engrs. & Constructors, Inc., Los Angeles, 1971-72; exec. v.p., corp. sec., dir. Optimum Systems Inc., Santa Clara, Calif., 1972-79; pres., dir. Banking Systems Inc., subs. Optimum Systems Inc., Dallas, 1976-79; pres., dir. BancSystems, Inc., Santa Clara, 1976-79, DMA/Optimum, Honolulu, 1978-79; v.p. URS Corp., San Mateo, Calif., 1979-81; pres. URS Internat., Inc., 1980-81; pres., chief exec. officer, dir. Applied Learning Internat., Inc. (formed from merger of Advanced Systems, Inc. and Deltak Training Corp.), Naperville, Ill., 1981-88; sr. v.p., bd. dirs. Nat. Edn. Corp., Irvine, Calif., 1988-89; pres. W.R. Roach & Assocs., Rolling Meadows, Ill., 1989—. Chgo. area vice chmn. Pacific Basin Econ. Coun., 1987-89. Mem. AICPA, Calif. Soc. CPAs, Theta Delta Chi. Clubs: Commonwealth (San Francisco); The Meadow (Chgo.). Home: 45 Hawthorne Ln Barrington Hills IL 60010 Office: WR Roach & Assocs III Crossroads of Commerce Ste 200 Rolling Meadows IL 60008

ROACHE, PATRICK MICHAEL, JR., management consultant; b. Elizabeth, N.J., Oct. 8, 1946; s. Patrick Michael and Rose Marie (Remite) R.; B.S., St. Peter's Coll., 1969. Adminstrv. aide to a state assemblyman, N.J., 1969-71; supr. acctg. Dept. Public Works Newark, 1971-78, asst. to dir. public works, 1978-79, mgr. div. motors, 1979-84; mgmt. specialist Dept. Gen. Services, Newark, 1985-86; pvt. practice as mgmt. and fin. cons., 1986—. Democrat. Roman Catholic. Lodge: Lions (treas. 1983-86, pres. 1988—). Home and Office: 170 Binnacle Rd Brick Town NJ 08723-6704

ROAN, MICHAEL CLARK, bank executive; b. Stillwater, Okla., May 24, 1951; s. Norman C. Jr. and Maudie B. (Cammerer) R.; m. Linda M. Ostler, June 25, 1975 (div. May 1987); children: Dawn Marie, Shiloh M., Spencer C., E. Taylor; m. Amy L. Ferroggiaro, Sept. 1988. AA, Brigham Young U., 1975, BS with high honors, 1975; postgrad., Northwestern U. Kellogg Grad. Sch. Mgmt. Mgr. div. N.A. Mgmt., Orem, Utah, 1975-79; v.p. Foster & Marshall, Richland, Wash., 1979-82, Shearson Lehman Bros., Richland,

1982-85; v.p., mgr. sales Pipper, Jaffray & Hopwood, Richland, 1985-87; v.p., sr. cons. Fin. Cons. Ctr., No. Trust Bank, Chgo., 1987—. Chmn. Rep. Caucus, Richland, 1985—, del., 1986; chmn. long range planning com. Wash. State U. Adv. Council, Tri Cities, 1987—. Mem. Internat. Assn. Fin. Planners, Inst. Cert. Fin. Planners, Estate Planning Council, Richland C. of C. (bd. dirs. 1987), Rotary. Republican. Mormon. Home: 4309 N Kostner Chicago IL 60641 Office: No Trust Bank 50 S La Salle B10 Chicago IL 60675

ROANE, DAVID JAMES, JR., infosystems specialist; b. Petersburg, Va., Nov. 11, 1960; s. David James Roane Sr. and Anne (Vest) Savage; m. Bonnie L. Dear, Dec. 3, 1983, 1 child, Apr. 20, 1987. BS, Va. Commonwealth U., 1984. CPA, Va.; cert. info. systems auditor. Audit intern Continental Fin. Services Co., Richmond, Va., 1983-84, staff auditor, 1984-85; EDP auditor Life Ins. Co. of Va., Richmond, 1985-86, James River Corp., Richmond, Va., 1986-88; technologies group specialist Mgmt. Info. Systems, 1989—. Treas. Civic Assn., Chester, Va., 1985—. Mem. EDP Auditors Assn. Methodist. Home: 2665 Mistwood Forest Dr Chester VA 23831

ROARK, CARL OLIVER, banker; b. Ephrata, Wash., Oct. 8, 1948; s. Carl Oliver Roark and B. Joyce (Hensley) Chrysler; m. Kathryn Anne Swanson, June 7, 1969; children: Emily, Kathryn, Caitlin, Elizabeth. BS, Ind. U., 1970, MBA, 1972. Corp. banking offical Citibank Corp. N.A., N.Y.C., 1972-78; gen. dir. corp. banking Citibank Corp., Mex., 1978-80; sr. v.p. Bankers Trust Co., N.Y.C., 1980-86, mng. dir., 1986. Republican. Presbyterian. Office: Bankers Trust Co 280 Park Ave New York NY 10017

ROATH, ROBERT S., food products executive; b. N.Y.C., Jan. 27, 1943; m. Ann G. Leys; children: David, Jessica. BA, U. Md., 1966; postgrad., Amos Tuck Sch., 1979. CPA, N.Y. Audit mgr. Price Waterhouse, N.Y.C., 1966-73; asst. corp. controller GAF, Wayne, N.J., 1973-75, Gen. Foods Corp., White Plains, N.Y., 1975-81; internat. controller Gen. Foods Internat., Rye, N.Y., 1981-84; v.p. fin., bus. devel. Gen. Foods, Can., Toronto, 1984—. Served to sgt. USAF, 1960-64. Mem. Am. Inst. CPA's, N.Y. Soc. CPA's, Fin. Execs. Inst., Council Fin. Execs. (conf. bd. Can.). Home: 319 Lansdowne Westport CT 06880 Office: Gen Foods Inc, PO Box 1200, Don Mills, ON Canada M3C 3J5

ROBB, ALEXANDER FORBES, aeronautical engineer; b. Bklyn., Nov. 27, 1919; s. Alexander Riddle and Helen (Forbes) R. B in Aero. Engring., Polytech. Inst. of N.Y., 1942; MS, Adelphi U., 1956; postgrad., MIT, 1958-63. Aerodynamicist Grumman Aircraft, Bethpage, N.Y., 1942-47; sr. test engr. Wright Aero., Patterson, N.J., 1947-49; project engr. Curtiss-Wright, Caldwell, N.J., 1948-50; sr. aerodynamicist Republic Aviation, Farmingdale, N.Y., 1950-56; sr. staff scientist AVCO, Wilmington, Mass., 1956-68; design engr. Atkins & Merrill, Maynard, Mass., 1968-70; sr. analyst Kentron Internat., Cambridge, Mass., 1970-79; project engr. H.H. Aerospace, Bedford, Mass., 1980-83; sr. analyst, ADP Support services Unisys, Cambridge, 1983—. Mem. Boston Computer Soc. Democrat. Methodist. Club: Palmer Cove Yacht. Lodge: Masons. Home: 267 Andover St Danvers MA 01923 Office: Unisys 55 Broadway Cambridge MA 02142

ROBB, RAYMOND ROSARIO, manufacturing company executive; b. Latrobe, Pa., Aug. 2, 1942; s. Raymond A. and Mary L. (Ciocco) R.; m. Frances L. Battaglia, Feb. 23, 1968; 1 child, Raymond E. BSME, Cath. U. Am., 1965. Registered profl. engr., Pa. Product engr. Elliott Co., div. Carrier Corp., Jeannette, Pa., 1966-73, project engr., 1973-75, sr. engr., 1975-77, mgr. indsl. products, 1977-79, mgr. spl. projects, 1979-81; dir. engring. Atlas Copco Comptec, Voorheesville, N.Y., 1981-85; v.p. engring. Leybold Vacuum Products, Inc., Export, Pa., 1985—. Patentee in field. Chmn. United Fund Drive, Atlas Copco, 1984-85; religious edn. tchr. St. Thomas Roman Cath. Ch., Delmar, N.Y., 1981-84. Mem. ASME, Semiconductor Equipment and Materials Inst., Penn Ligonier, Model R.R. Club (pres. 1977-80), Elks. Republican. Roman Catholic. Office: Leybold Vacuum Products Inc 5700 Mellon Rd Export PA 15632

ROBB, RICHARD EDWARD, JR., sales executive; b. Honolulu, Jan. 7, 1950; s. Richard Edward Sr. and Margaret Aylett (Poole) R.; m. Patricia Joanne Disciascio, Jan. 31, 1975 (div. Jan. 1983); children: Denise Alexis, David Thomas. BS in Agrl. Econs., Oreg. State U., 1973. Sales rep. Mobay Corp., Anaheim, Calif., 1975-79, Bakersfield, Calif., 1979-81; product mgr. Mobay Corp., Kansas City, Kans., 1981-86; dist. sales mgr. Mobay Corp., Shawnee, Kans., 1986—. With USNR, 1967-74. Mem. Calif. Assn. Pest Control Advisors (bd. dirs. 1978-79, 81), Am. Phytopathilogical Soc. Republican. Home and Office: 17437 W 70th St Shawnee KS 66217

ROBBINS, ARNOLD BRUCE, lawyer; b. Seattle, Mar. 27, 1928; s. Earl and Sara Miriam (Vickerson) R.; m. Esther Haim Zelikovksy, Aug. 23, 1980 (div. Nov. 1986); children: Victoria Lee, Seth Allan; m. Barbara Wessel Hurst, Dec. 2, 1987. BS, U. Wash., 1949, JD, 1950. Bar: Wash., 1951, U.S. Dist. Ct. (we. dist.) Wash. 1956, U.S. Ct. Appeals (9th cir.) 1956, U.S. Supreme Ct. 1980. Ptnr. Breskin & Robbins, Seattle, 1962—; arbitrator Am. Arbitrations Assn., King County Superior Ct., Seattle, 1980—. Pres. Am. Jewish Commn., Seattle, 1978. Sgt. U.S. Army, 1953-60. Mem. Wash. State Bar Assn., Seattle King County Bar Assn. Office: Breskin & Robbins 3401 First Interstate Ctr Seattle WA 98104

ROBBINS, DONALD MICHAEL, lawyer; b. Woonsocket, R.I., Oct. 2, 1935; s. Robert Sidney and Nancy Ruth (Medoff) R.; m. Esther Sharp, Aug. 30, 1959; children: Jeffrey, Benjamin. Student, Brandeis U., 1953-55; A.B., U. Mich., 1957; LL.B., Boston U., 1960. Bar: Mass. 1961, R.I. 1962. Individual practice law 1961-68; v.p., sec., gen. counsel Hasbro, Inc., Pawtucket, R.I., 1968—. Bd. dirs., former chmn. Big Bros. R.I.; bd. dirs. Miriam Hosp.; former pres. Temple Emanu-El; chmn. Israel Bonds State of R.I. Mem. Am. Soc. Corp. Secs., Mass. Bar Assn., R.I. Bar Assn. Home: 93 Pratt St Providence RI 02906 Office: Hasbro Inc 1027 Newport Ave Pawtucket RI 02861

ROBBINS, HARVEY A., textile company executive; b. N.Y.C., Apr. 29, 1922; s. Ira B. and Mildred (Lowy) R.; student U. Mich., 1940-42, Cornell U., 1943, Columbia U., 1945; m. Carolyn Edith Goldsmith, June 8, 1947; children—Margaret Ann (Mrs. Jay Jacobson), James Andrew. Vice pres. Silberstein-Goldsmith, N.Y.C., 1946-50, North Advt., Chgo., 1950-59; v.p. M. Lowenstein & Sons, Inc., N.Y.C., also pres. Wamsutta/Pacific Domestic div., 1959-69; pres. Burlington Domestics div. Burlington Industries, N.Y.C., 1969-73; v.p. United Mchts. & Mfrs., N.Y.C., 1973-78; v.p. PRF Corp., 1978-80; exec. v.p. Whisper Soft Mills, N.Y.C., 1980-84; dir. product devel. Springs Industries, N.Y.C., 1984-85, textile cons., 1985—. Bd. dirs. Fedn. for Handicapped, Ednl. Found. for Fashion Industries; corp. mem. Lesley Coll., Cambridge, Mass. Served with U.S. Army, 1942-45. Decorated Purple Heart, Combat Inf. badge. Mem. Am. Mgmt. Assn., Am. Arbitration Assn., Nat. Bath, Bed and Linen Assn. (dir., treas.), Textile Distbrs. Assn. Clubs: Woodmere Bay Yacht (trustee); U. Mich. Alumni, Hemisphere (N.Y.C.). Home: 35 Brook Rd Valley Stream NY 11581 Office: Arlee Home Fashions 295 Fifth Ave New York NY 10016

ROBBINS, HONEY-MIAM, financial executive; b. Toronto, Ont., Can., Apr. 10, 1930; came to U.S., 1965; d. Daniel David and Fannie (Schidlowski) Serott; m. Julian Pearson, Mar. 25, 1951 (div. 1973)); m. Nat Robbins, Jan. 25, 1976; children: Cheryl Beth Pearson Elbrand, Debra Pearson Abelow, Geoffrey. Student, McGill U., Montreal, Que., Can., 1948-49; AA, U. Miami, 1968; cert., Coll. Fin. Planning, 1985. Pres. Star Investment Group, Montreal, 1964-65; registered rep., dist. mgr. Investors Diversified Services, Miami, Fla., 1974-77; registered rep., fin. planner Nat. Life Vt. and Equity Services, Miami, Fla., 1977-79, Mony Life & Mony Securities, Coral Gables, Fla., 1979-83, 1st Fin. Investment Services, Coral Gables, Fla., 1983-86; pres. Honath Inc. and Fin. Services, Miami, 1981—; cons. World Bus. Brokers, Miami, 1981—, Stetson Co., Miami, 1986—; assoc broker Evensky, Brown Investments, Inc., Coral Gables, 1986—; investment adviser SEC, Washington, 1987. Pres. Temple Beth Am Sisterhood, Miami, 1967; life mem. Sunshine Cancer Group, Miami, 1975. Mem. Internat. Assn. Fin. Planning (bd. dirs. 1976, sec. 1977, Cert Merit 1986), Internat. Assn. Registered Fin. Planners, Inst. Cert. Fin. Planners. Republican. Jewish. Office: Honath Fin Svcs 14720 SW 83d Ave Miami FL 33158

ROBBINS, KATHLEEN GAIL, corporate controller; b. Chgo., Feb. 1, 1953; d. Bertil Reinhold and Lorraine (Czerniak) Edquist. AA in Bus., Thornton Community Coll., 1971-72; postgrad., Valparaiso U., 1976, Purdue U., 1979-80. Cost acctg. clk. Jaymar-Ruby, Inc., Michigan City, Ind., 1972-76; jr. acct. Ind. Gen., Valparaiso, 1976-78, sr. acct., 1978-80, acctg. supr., 1980-81, acctg. mgr., 1981-85; controller The Titan Corp., Valparaiso, 1985—. Mem. Nat. Assn. Female Execs. Republican. Lutheran. Home: 840 S 14th St Chesterton IN 46304 Office: The Titan Corp 5103 Evans Ave Valparaiso IN 46383

ROBBINS, KENNETH L., advertising agency executive. Dep. chmn., chief exec. officer internat. div. Lintas Worldwide, N.Y.C. Office: Lintas Worldwide 1 Dag Hammarskjold Pla New York NY 10017 *

ROBBINS, OREM OLFORD, insurance company executive; b. Mpls., Feb. 5, 1915; s. Douglas Ford and Grace (Rorem) R.; m. Margaret Jane Linderberg, July 4, 1968; children: Ford M., Ross S., Gail R. Tomei, Cynthia R. Rothbard. BBA with distinction, U. Minn., 1936; BS in Law, William Mitchell Coll. Law, 1946, JD, 1948. Comml. rep. NW Bell Telephone Co., Mpls., 1936-48; dep. dir. U.S. Treas. Dept., Mpls., 1948-49; sales rep. Conn. Gen. Life Ins. Co., Mpls., 1949-56; founder, chmn. Security Life Ins. Co. Am., Mpls., 1956—. Bd. dirs., past pres. Family and Children's Service, Mpls., 1968—; bd. govs., past chmn. Meth. Hosp., Mpls., 1960—; past. treas., bd. dirs. Goodwill/Easter Seals, St. Paul, 1958-68, 75—; chmn. bd. trustees Hamline U., St. Paul, 1980—. Served with U.S. Army, 1941-46. Fellow Life Mgmt. Assn.; mem. Am. Soc. CLU (pres. Mpls. chpt. 1953, cert.), Health Underwriters Assn., Charterd Fin. Cons., Am. Legion. Republican. Methodist. Club: Skylight (Mpls.), Mpls., Minikahda Hole in the Wall Golf, Naples Yacht, Naples Sailing and Yacht. Lodge: Masons. Office: Security Life Ins Co Am 6681 Country Club Dr Minneapolis MN 55427-4698

ROBBINS, RAY CHARLES, manufacturing company executive; b. Syracuse, N.Y., Sept. 15, 1920; s. Frederick and Mary Elizabeth (Field) R.; children: Sandra Robbins Jannetta, Ray Charles Jr. With Lennox Industries Inc. (formerly Lennox Furnace Co.), 1940—; with engring. and service depts. Lennox Industries Inc. (formerly Lennox Furnace Co.), Syracuse, 1940-48; asst. sales mgr. Lennox Industries, Inc. (formerly Lennox Furnace Co.), 1948-52; gen. mgr. new factory and sales office, Lennox Industries, Inc. (formerly Lennox Furnace Co.), Toronto, Ont., Can., 1952-67; dir. Lennox Industries, Inc., 1953—; pres. Lennox Can., 1967-76, chmn. bd. dirs., 1976-80; corp. exec. v.p. Lennox Industries Inc., Marshalltown, Iowa, 1969-71; pres., chief exec. officer Lennox world wide Lennox Industries Inc., 1971-77, chmn. bd., chief exec. officer, 1977-80, chmn. bd., 1980—; bd. dirs. Lennox Internat., First Interstate of Iowa, Inc., Hawkeye Security Ins. Co., Des Moines, Fin. Security Group, Inc., Des Moines, Q-Dot, Garland, Tex.; pres., founder, bd. dirs. Exec. Inst., Inc., Dallas, 1983—. Bd. dirs. Metro Toronto Big Bros., 1964-69, Queensway Gen. Hosp., 1957-69; bd. dirs. Texx Found., 1979-81; bd. govs., mem. exec. com. Iowa Coll. Found., 1975-78; v.p., mem. exec. bd. Mid-Iowa County Boy Scouts Am., 1972-78; mem. Pres.' Phys. Fitness Council, from 1979; exec. bd. Circle 10 council Boy Scouts Am., from 1979; mem. Dallas Citizens Council; bd. of govs. Nat. Women's Econ. Alliance Found.; bd. dirs. North Tex. Commn. Served with AUS, 1942-45, PTO. Mem. ASHRAE (life), Am. Refrigeration Inst. (bd. dirs. 1973-74, 78, life from 1979, v.p. 1975-76, chmn. 1977), Nat. Assn. Mfrs. (bd. dirs. 1974-75, dir. at large 1976, dir. State of Iowa 1977-78, dir. State of Tex. 1979—), Nat. Mgmt. Assn. (exec. adv. com.) Gas Appliance Mfrs. Assn. (past bd. dirs.), Can. Gas Assn. (pres.), Can. Mfg. Assn. (chmn. Toronto dist.), U.S. C. of C. (Can.-U.S. sect.). Clubs: Park Cen., Landmark Athletic, Aerobics Activity Ctr. (Dallas); Canyon Creek Country (Richardson, Tex.). Office: Lennox Industries Inc Lennox Ctr Box 809000 Dallas TX 75380-9000

ROBERSON, LAWRENCE R., financial planning executive, investment consultant; b. Birmingham, Ala., Aug. 26, 1946; s. Mack E. and Aressa (Craig) R. BS, Ala. A&M U., 1967; MBA, Ind. U., 1970; cert., Coll. Fin. Planning, 1986. Systems engr. IBM Corp., Huntsville, Ala., 1967-68; fin. analyst IBM Corp., White Plains, N.Y., 1969; fin. analyst Ford Motor Co., Dearborn, Mich., 1970-73, supr., 1973-83; v.p. Asset Mgmt. Internat., Detroit, 1983-85; pres. Wealth Mgmt. Group, Detroit, 1985—; cons. Dearborn Fed. Credit Union, 1979-80; dir. Internat. Exchange Council, Detroit. Fellow Consortium in Grad. Study Mgmt., 1968-70, White House, 1983, 84; recipient Young Men in Am. award Jaycees. Mem. Internat. Assn. Fin. Planning, Inst. Cert. Fin. Planners, Nat. Black MBA Assn. (pres. 1978-79). Office: Wealth Mgmt Group Inc 400 Renaissance Ctr Suite 500 Detroit MI 48243

ROBERTI, MARIO ANDREW, energy company executive; b. Denver, May 12, 1935; s. Emil and Elvira (Ligrano) R.; m. Patricia Ann Ludwig, Apr. 27, 1963; children: Andrea Louise, Paul Richard, Robert Raymond. B.S., Loyola U. (now Loyola Marymount U.), Los Angeles, 1957, J.D., 1960. Bar: Calif. 1961, Hawaii 1977, D.C. 1985. Dep. atty. gen. State of Calif., 1961-69; atty. Pacific Lighting Corp., Los Angeles, 1969-71; asst. gen. counsel, asst. sec. McCulloch Oil Corp., Los Angeles, 1971-76; v.p., gen. counsel Pacific Resources, Inc., Honolulu, 1976-88, sr. v.p., gen. counsel, 1988—. Trustee Hawaii Sch. Girls, 1979-87; regent Loyola Marymount U., Chaminade U. of Honolulu, chmn. bd. regents, 1987—; legal adv. com. Pacific Coast Gas Assn., chmn., 1983-84; adv. bd. Internat. Oil and Gas Ednl. Ctr., Southwestern Legal Found. Mem. Fed. Energy Bar Assn., ABA, D.C. Bar Assn., Hawaii Bar Assn. (chmn. corp. counsel sect. 1979), Calif. Bar Assn., Pacific Club, Outrigger Canoe Club, Oahu Country Club, Phi Alpha Delta, Phi Kappa Theta. Office: Pacific Resources Inc 733 Bishop St Honolulu HI 96813

ROBERTS, BRIAN LEON, communications executive; b. Phila., June 28, 1959; s. Ralph J. and Suzanne F. Roberts; m. Aileen Kennedy, Dec. 28, 1985; 1 child, Sarah Louise. Student, U. Pa., 1981. V.p. ops. Comcast Cable Communications, Inc., Phila., 1985-86; exec. v.p. Comcast Corp., 1986—, also bd. dirs.; bd. dirs. C-Span, Wlater Kaitz Found. Mem. Nat. Cable TV Assn. (rsch. and devel. com., minority affairs com.). Office: Comcast Corp One Belmont Ave Ste 227 Bala-Cynwyd PA 19004

ROBERTS, BURNELL RICHARD, paper company executive; b. Wis., May 6, 1927; s. Roy C. and Ann (Jones) R.; m. Karen H. Ragatz, Aug. 8, 1953; children: Evan, Kari, Paul, Nancy. B.B.A., U. Wis., 1950; M.B.A., Harvard U., 1957. With Bendix Aviation Corp., 1953-58; with Gen. Tire & Rubber Co., 1957-62; treas., controller subsidiary A.M. Byers Co., Pitts., 1962-66; asst. to exec. v.p. Mead Corp., Dayton, Ohio, 1966-68, controller, v.p. finance, 1968-71; group v.p., pres. Mchts. group div. Mead Corp., Dayton, Ohio, 1971-74, Mead Paper div. Mead Corp., Dayton, Ohio, from 1974; sr. v.p. Mead Corp., 1979-81, pres., 1981-83, chmn., chief exec. officer, 1982—, also dir.; bd. dirs. Nat. City Bank, Cleve., Northwood Pulp & Paper, Prince George, B.C., Armco Corp., Perkins-Elmer, Philips Industries, DPL, Inc. Chmn. bd. trustees Kenyon Coll., Sinclair Community Coll., Bus. Roundtable, Aspen Inst. Served with USNR, 1944-46. Mem. Fin. Execs. Inst., Am. Paper Inst. (chmn.). Office: Mead Corp Courthouse Pla NE Dayton OH 45463 *

ROBERTS, DAVID CARON, computer scientist; b. Abilene, Tex., Sept. 13, 1944; s. Robert Henry and Ada Louise (Buckingham) R.; m. Mary Jane Fallis, May 30, 1965; 1 child, Lindsay Ann. BS in Engring. Sci., Johns Hopkins, 1965; MS in Engring., U. Pa., 1968; MS in Computer Sci., U. Md., 1973. Research scientist Pa. Research Assocs., Phila., 1965-69; mgr. image processing systems Informatics Inc., Rockville, Md., 1969-74; tech. dir. Ocean Data Systems, Rockville, 1974-75; project engr. CIA, Washington, 1975-81, info. systems arch., 1985—; v.p. Oracle Systems Corp., Menlo Park, Calif., 1981-85; adj. prof. George Washington U., 1975-87. Contbr. articles to profl. jours. Mem. IEEE, Assn. Computing Machines. Democrat. Club: Potomac Tennis. Home: 8833 Harness Trail Potomac MD 20854 Office: CIA Washington DC 20505

ROBERTS, DAVID EUGENE, financial services executive; b. Mitchell, Ind.; s. Carl William and Helen Rose (Pemberton) R.; m. Margaret JoAnne Keeney, Sept. 26, 1959 (div. 1973); children: Cynthia Ann Bailey, Suzanne D.; m. Carol Beth Feldman (Aug. 7, 1974). BA, U. Md., 1970; MBA, Western New Eng. Coll., 1977. Enlisted USAF, 1959, advanced through grades to staff sgt.; served at various locations USAF, U.S., Fed. Republic of Germany, Turkey, 1959-70; assoc. dir. Mass. Mut. Life Ins. Co., Springfield, 1970-81; v.p. Great So. Life, Houston, 1981-82, Acacia Mut. Life, Washington, 1982-85; sr. v.p. Fannie Mae, Washington, 1985—. Mem. Index Forum. Democrat. Home: 2443 Brussels Ct Reston VA 22091 Office: Fannie Mae 3900 Wisconsin Ave NW Washington DC 20016

ROBERTS, DONALD ALBERT, cable television executive, marketing, media consultant; b. Boston, Dec. 17, 1935; s. Albert Arthur and Linette Violette (Ouelette) R.; m. Gabrielle Dorothy St. Laurent, Apr. 20, 1957; children: Lynne Dianne, Tammy Denise. Student, U. Maine, 1987-88, Liberty U., 1988—. Program mgr., dir. sports Sta. WIMA-TV, Lima, Ohio, 1965-68; v.p., gen. mgr. Sta. WABK/WKME, Gardiner, Maine, 1968-74; pres., owner Sta. WRDO, Augusta, Maine, 1974-77; cons. group gen. mgr. Valley Communications, Bangor, Maine, 1977-78; pres., owner Roberts Advt. Agy., Augusta, 1977-78; v.p., gen. mgr. Sta. WLOB AM/FM, Portland, Maine, 1978-80, Sta. WKCG/WFAU, Augusta, 1980-83; pres., owner Roberts & Co., Augusta, 1983—; exec. v.p. mktg. and programming and sales State Cable TV Corp., Augusta, 1983—; cons. New Eng. Ziebart Dealers Assn., 1982—. Contbr. articles to profl. jours. Pres. Auburn (Maine) City Council, 1957-60; chmn. Jefferson-Jackson Dinner, Rockland, Maine, 1959; del. Dem. State Conv., Bangor, 1980. Named Maine Sportscaster of Yr. Nat. Sportscasters Assn., 1962, 63; recipient Tiger award Maine Broadcasting System, 1965. Mem. So. Kennebec Valley Realtors Assn., Cable Advt. Bur., Cable TV Adminstrs. and Marketers, Ohio Sportscasters Assn. (co-founder 1965), Maine Assn. Broadcasters (bd. dirs.), Kennebec Valley C. of C. (bd. dirs.). Home and Office: 44 Longwood Ave Augusta ME 04330

ROBERTS, DWIGHT LOREN, management executive, novelist; b. San Diego, June 3, 1949; s. James Albert and Cleva Lorraine (Conn) R.; B.A., U. San Diego, 1976, M.A., 1979; m. Phyllis Ann Adair, Mar. 29, 1969; children—Aimee Renee, Michael Loren, Daniel Alexandr. Engring. aide Benton Engring. Inc., San Diego, 1968-73; pres. Robert's Tech. Research Co., also subs. Marine Technique Ltd., San Diego, 1973-76; pres. Research Technique Internat., 1978—; freelance writer, 1979—; owner Agrl. Analysis, 1985-88; constrn. mgr. Homestead Land Devel. Corp., 1988—. Served with U.S. Army, 1969-71. Mem. ASTM, AAAS, Nat. Inst. Sci., N.Y. Acad. Scis., Nat. Inst. Cert. in Engring. Techs., Soil and Found. Engr. Assn., Phi Alpha Theta. Baptist. Author: Geological Exploration of Alaska, 1898-1924, Alfred Hulse Brooks, Alaskan Trailblazer; contbr. articles to profl. jours. Office: 3111 Victoria Dr Alpine CA 92001

ROBERTS, EDWARD BAER, technology management educator; b. Chelsea, Mass., Nov. 18, 1935; s. Nathan and Edna (Podradchik) R.; m. Nancy Helen Rosenthal, June 14, 1959; children: Valerie Jo, Mitchell Jonathan, Andrea Lynne. B.S., MIT, 1958, M.S., 1958, M.S. in Mgmt, 1960, Ph.D., 1962. Founding mem. systems dynamics program MIT, 1958-84, instr., 1959-61, asst. prof., 1961-65, assoc. prof., 1965-70, prof., 1970—, David Sarnoff prof. mgmt. of tech., 1974—, assoc. dir. research program on mgmt. sci. and tech., 1963-73, chmn. tech. and health mgmt. group, 1973—; co-founder, pres. Pugh-Roberts Assocs., Inc., Cambridge, Mass., 1963-89, chmn., 1989—; also dir.; dir. MIT-Boston VA Joint Center on Health Care Mgmt., 1976-80; dir. MIT Joint Program on Mgmt. of Tech., 1980—, Med. Info. Tech. Inc., Advanced Magnetics, Inc., Zero Stage Capital Equity Funds, First Stage Capital Equity Fund; Laser Sci. Inc.; cons. Assn. Am. Med. Colls., also numerous corps.; mem. Task Force on Nuclear Medicine, ERDA, 1975-76, NRC Com. on Ionizing Radiation Effects, NRC Task Force on Mgmt. of Tech., 1986. Author: The Dynamics of Research and Development, 1964, (with others) Systems Simulation for Regional Analysis, 1969, The Persistent Poppy, 1975, The Dynamics of Human Service Delivery, 1976; prin. author, editor: Managerial Applications of System Dynamics, 1978; editor: (with others) Biomedical Innovation, 1981; editor: Generating Technological Innovation, 1987; mem. editorial bd. IEEE Trans. on Engring. Mgmt, 1968—, Indsl. Mktg. Mgmt, 1975—, Health Care Mgmt. Rev, 1976-78, Technol. Forecasting and Social Change, 1980—, Jour. Product Innovation Mgmt., 1983—, Internat. Jour. Tech. Mgmt. 1987—, Jour. Engring. and Tech. Mgmt., 1989—; contbr. articles to profl. jours. Mem. IEEE, Inst. Mgmt. Sci., Sigma Xi, Tau Beta Pi, Eta Kappa Nu, Tau Kappa Alpha. Home: 17 Fellsmere Rd Newton MA 02159 Office: 50 Memorial Dr Cambridge MA 02139

ROBERTS, EDWARD CALHOUN, lawyer; b. Columbia, S.C., Oct. 17, 1937; s. John Cornelius and Cecilia (Allen) R.; m. Margaret C. Roberts, Sept. 1967 (dec. July 1978); children: Kathryn A., John G.; m. Beverley Means, July 10, 1980; 1 child, Beverley M. AB, U. S.C., 1959, JD, 1962; LLM, Georgetown U., 1963. Bar: S.C. 1962, U.S. Ct. Appeals (4th cir.) 1965, U.S. Supreme Ct 1973, U.S. Ct. Appeals (D.C. cir.) 1974. Atty. S.C. Electric and Gas Co., Columbia, 1967-72, sr. atty., 1972-80, gen. counsel, 1980-82, v.p. and gen. counsel, 1982—. Co-author: Freedom from Federal Establishment, 1965; contbr. to profl. jours. Pres. Columbia Urban League, 1977-79, Columbia Lyric Opera Co., 1983-85, Columbia Music Festival Assn., 1986-88. Served to sgt. USMCR, 1963-69. Mem. S.C. Bar Assn. (chmn. com. to revise corp. laws 1976-81), Am. Law Inst., S.C. Law Inst. (treas.), Edison Electric Inst. (legal com.). Home: 8 Woodhill Cir Columbia SC 29209 Office: SC Electric & Gas Co Legal Dept (106) Columbia SC 29218

ROBERTS, FRANCIS STONE, advertising executive; b. Scranton, Pa., Aug. 15, 1944; s. Gordon Link and Eleanor Swartz (Stone) R.; m. Anne Carter Housh, Dec. 21, 1974; children: Francis Stone, Link McGregor. B.A., Grove City (Pa.) Coll., 1966; A.M.P., U. Chgo., 1984. With media dept., then account exec. Compton Advt. Inc., N.Y.C., 1966-69; account exec. Tatham-Laird & Kudner Advt., N.Y.C., 1969-70; account supr., v.p. SSC&B Advt. Inc., N.Y.C., 1970-78, sr. v.p., mgmt. supr., 1978-81; exec. v.p. SSC&B: Lintas Advt. Worldwide, 1981-86, group exec. v.p., 1987—, mem. policy and ops. coms., chmn. strategy rev. bd., also dir. Emergency rm. com. Lenox Hill Hosp. Mem. William Penn Charter Alumni Assn. (pres. N.Y. chpt. 1984—). Republican. Presbyterian. Club: New Canaan Field, New Canaan Winter. Home: 208 Canoe Hill Rd New Canaan CT 06840 Office: Lintas Worldwide Advt Inc 1 Dag Hammarskjold Pla New York NY 10017

ROBERTS, FRANK EMMETT, financial executive; b. Lordsburg, N. Mex., June 1, 1930; s. John J. and Clova (Lovett) R.; m. Gloria Ann Marengo, June 30, 1953; children: Linda, Craig, Laura. BS, U. Calif., 1953, MBA, 1957; postgrad., Harvard U., 1981. Sr. fin. analyst Kaiser Industries, Oakland, Calif., 1957-67; controller Consol. Freightways Inc., San Francisco, 1976-78, controller-treas., 1978-79, v.p., treas., 1979—. Served to lt. comdr. USNR, 1953-57. Mem. Fin. Execs. Inst. (pres., dir.). Republican. Office: Consol Freightways Inc 175 Linfield Dr Menlo Park CA 94025

ROBERTS, GEORGE ADAM, metallurgist; b. Uniontown, Pa., Feb. 18, 1919; s. Jacob Earle and Mary M. (Bower) R.; m. Betty E. Matthewson, May 31, 1941; children: George Thomas, William John, Mary Ellen; m. Jeanne Marie Polk. Student, U.S. Naval Acad., 1935-37; B.Sc., Carnegie Tech., 1939, M.Sc., 1941, D.Sc., 1942. Technician Bell Telephone Labs., N.Y.C., 1938; research dir. Vasco Metals Corp. (formerly Vanadium Alloys Steel Co.), Latrobe, Pa., 1940-45; chief metallurgist Vasco Metals Corp. (formerly Vanadium Alloys Steel Co.), 1945-53, v.p., 1953-61, pres., 1961-66; pres., dir. Teledyne, Inc. (merger with Vasco Metals Corp.), Los Angeles, 1966—, chief exec. officer, 1986—; hon. lectr. Societe Francaise de Metallurgie, 1960. Author: Tool Steels, 1944, 62; contbr. articles to trade jours. Recipient silver medal from Paris, 1955. Fellow Metall. Soc. Am. Inst. Mining, Metall. and Petroleum Engrs., Am. Soc. for Metals (chmn. Pitts. chpt. 1949-50, internat. pres. 1954-55, trustee Found. Edn. and Research 1954-59, 63-64, pres. Found. 1955-56, Gold medal 1977); mem. Nat. Acad. Engring., Metal Powder Industries Fedn. (dir. 1952-55, pres. 1957-61), Am. Soc. Metals, Am. Iron and Steel Inst., Soc. Mfg. Engrs., Tau Beta Pi; hon. life mem. several fgn. socs. Methodist. Office: Teledyne Inc 1901 Ave of the Stars Ste 1800 Los Angeles CA 90067 *

ROBERTS, GEORGE CHRISTOPHER, manufacturing executive; b. Ridley Park, Pa., May 27, 1936; s. George H. and Marion C. (Smullen) R.; m. Adriana Toribio, July 19, 1966; children—Tupac A., Capac Y. Sr. engr. ITT, Paramus, N.J., 1960-65; program mgr. Arde Research, Mawah, N.J., 1965-67; Space-Life Sci. program mgr., research div. GATX, 1967-69; dir.

research and devel. Monogram Industries, Los Angeles, 1969-71; chmn. Inca Mfg. Corp, 1970-72, pres. 1972—; pres. Environ. Protection Center, Inc., L.A.s, 1970-76. Bd. dirs., trustee Fairborn Obs.; founder Culver Nat. Bank, 1983; trustee Calif. Mus. Sci. and Industry, 1988—; trustee Internat. Am. Profl. Photoelectric Photometrists, 1983—, Buckley Sch., 1984—; chmn. solar and stellar physics Mt. Wilson Research Corp., 1984-87; bd. dirs. Peruvian Found. 1981, pres. 1986—, appt. rep. govt. of Peru in L.A., 1988—. Mem. Am. Astron. Soc., Astron. Soc. Pacific. Patentee advanced waste treatment systems, automotive safety systems. Office: 3463 S La Cienega Blvd Los Angeles CA 90016

ROBERTS, GEORGE R., leverage buyout company executive. married; 3 children. JD, U. Calif., San Francisco. With Bears, Stearns, New York, until 1976; now ptnr. Kohlberg, Kravis, Roberts, San Francisco; dir. Beatrice Co., Chgo., Houdaille Industries Inc., Northbrook, Ill., Malone and Hyde, Memphis, Union Tex. Petroleum Holdings Inc., Houston. Office: Kohlberg Kravis Roberts & Co 101 California St San Francisco CA 94111 *

ROBERTS, HARRY MORRIS, JR., lawyer; b. Dallas, June 10, 1938; s. Harry Morris and La Frances (Reilly) R.; m. Nancy Beth Johnson, Mar. 7, 1964; children: Richard Whitfield, Elizabeth Lee. BBA, So. Meth. U., 1960; LLB, Harvard U., 1963. Bar: Tex. 1963, U.S. Dist. Ct. (no. dist.) Tex. 1964, U.S. Ct. Appeals (5th cir.), 1972, U.S. Supreme Ct. 1971. Sr. ptnr. Thompson & Knight, Dallas, 1963—; chmn. real estate, probate and trust law sect. State Bar Tex., 1984-85; vis. scholar U. Tex. Law Sch., 1986. Contbr. articles to legal jours. Trustee, sec. Shelter Ministries of Dallas, 1982—. Mem. ABA, Tex. Bar Found., Dallas Bar Assn. (chmn. real estate sect. 1981), Am. Coll. Real Estate Lawyers. Episcopalian. Clubs: Salesmanship (Dallas), Dallas, Dallas Country. Office: Thompson & Knight 3300 1st City Ctr Dallas TX 75201

ROBERTS, JAMES LAWRENCE (BO), youth camp adminstrator; b. Burlington, N.C., June 3, 1951; s. James Ernest and Lucille (Deneen) R.; m. Helen Powell Graham, Nov. 29, 1975; children: Graham, Hart, Lucy. BS in Biology, U. N.C., 1973. Assoc. dir., dir. personnel Camp Sea Gull, Raleigh, N.C., 1973—; cons. on family programs S.E. regions YMCAs, Atlanta; cons. on camping Nat. YMCA, Chgo., 1977—. Author: Arapahoe Nation-Y Indian Guide Programs, 1987. Elder, White Meml. Presbyn. Ch., Raleigh, 1984-87; mem. PTA Lacy Elem. Sch., Raleigh, 1986—. Mem. Am. Camping Assn., Rotary. Republican. Home: 2201 Saint Mary's St Raleigh NC 27608 Office: Camp Sea Gull 1601 Hillsborough St Raleigh NC 27605

ROBERTS, JAMES OWEN, financial planning executive, consultant; b. Madison, Wis., Aug. 19, 1930; s. John William and Sada (Buckmaster) R.; m. Georgianna Timmons, Jan. 30, 1954; children: Stephen, Susan, Ellen, Timmons. BS, Ohio State U., 1952; MBA, Case Western Res. U., 1970. Sales trainee Owens-Ill., Inc., Toledo, 1952, 54-55, salesman, Atlanta, 1955-58, N.Y.C., 1958-62, food div. mgr., N.Y.C., 1963-66, br. mgr., Cleve., 1966-71; mgr. corp. fin. Stone & Webster Securities Corp., Cleve., 1971-74; regional dir. Mgmt. Planning, Inc., Cleve., 1976-80, v.p., 1980-86, sr. v.p., 1986, pres., 1986—; lectr. in field. Contbr. articles to profl. jours. Chmn. bd. trustees Fairmount Presbyn. Ch., Cleve., 1984; trustee Soc. for the Blind, Cleve., 1983-86, Ohio Motorists Assn., 1985—, vice chmn., 1988—; pres. Children's Svcs., 1986-88; trustee Great Lakes Theater . Named Gem of a Clevelander Cleve. Press, 1981. Mem. Fin. Analysts Fedn., Cleve. Soc. Security Analysts, Cleve. Skating Club, Nassau Club. Republican. Avocations: sailing, skiing, flying, hiking, photography. Home: 2323 Stillman Rd Cleveland Heights OH 44118 Office: Mgmt Planning Inc 545 Hanna Bldg Cleveland OH 44115 also: 101 Poor Farm Rd Princeton NJ 08542

ROBERTS, JOHN JOSEPH, insurance company executive; b. Montreal, Que., Can., June 4, 1922; s. PeterQuila and Irene May (Rich) R.; m. Nancy Lee Rhodes, June 14, 1947; children: John Peter, Christopher Lee. BA, Princeton U., 1945. With Am. Internat. Underwriters Corp., 1947-59, 69—; regional mgr. Europe and Am. Internat. Underwriters Corp., Middle East, to 1959; pres. Am. Internat. Underwriters Corp. (U.S. Overseas ops.), N.Y.C., 1969-75, chmn. bd., 1975—; v.p. for European affairs C.V. Starr & Co., Inc. (subs. Am. Internat. Group, Inc.), N.Y.C., 1960-63; dir. overall worldwide ops. C.V. Starr & Co., Inc. (subs. Am. Internat. Group, Inc.), 1963-68; chmn. bd. Am. Internat. Underwriters Overseas (subs. Am. Internat. Group), N.Y.C., from 1968; exec. v.p. Am. Internat. Group, Inc., N.Y.C., 1976—; bd. dirs. Am. Internat. Group, Inc., Am. Internat. Underwriters Corp., Am. Internat. Underwriters Overseas Am. Internat. Reins. Co., Inc., Am. Life Ins. Co., Am. Internat. Life Assurance Co. N.Y., Am. Internat. Marine Agy. N.Y., Inc., AIG Mktg., Inc., AIG Risk Mgmt., Inc., C. V. Starr & Co., Inc., Starr Internat. Co., Inc., Starr Tech. Risks Agy., Inc., Adams Express Co. Trustee C.V. Starr Found., The Mason Early Edn. Found., Princeton, N.J., Coun. of Ams., Juilliard Sch.; chmn. Internat. Ins. Adv. Coun. to U.S. C. of C., 1977-79, U.S. sect. Polish-U.S. Econ. Coun., 1980-86; 1st v.p. Federaçao Interamericana de Empresas de Seguros; chmn. U.S. sect. Hungarian-U.S. Bus. Coun., 1986—. 1st lt. U.S. Army, 1943-46, Philippines, Japan. Clubs: India House, Knickerbocker, Racquet and Tennis, Brook (N.Y.C.); Nassau (Princeton; George Town (Washington). Office: Am Internat Group Inc 70 Pine St New York NY 10270

ROBERTS, LOUIS WRIGHT, transportation executive; b. Jamestown, N.Y., Sept. 1, 1913; s. Louis Lorenzo and Dora (Wright) R.; m. Mercedes Pearl McGavock, June 8, 1938; children—Louis M., Lawrence E. B.A., Fisk U., 1935, LL.D. (hon.), 1985; M.S., U. Mich., 1937, postgrad., 1941; postgrad., MIT, 1946. Teaching asst. Fisk U., Nashville, 1935-36; instr. St. Augustine's Coll., Raleigh, N.C., 1937-40, assoc. prof., 1941-42; assoc. prof. Howard U., Washington, 1943-44; mgr. tube div. Sylvania Elec. Products Inc., Danvers, Salem and Boston, Mass., 1944-50; tube cons. research lab. for electronics MIT, Cambridge, 1950-51, vis. sr. lectr., 1979-80; founder, pres. Microwave Assocs., Inc., Boston, 1950-55; engring. specialist, cons. Bomac Labs., Inc., Beverly, Mass., 1955-59; founder, v.p., dir. METCOM, Inc., Salem, Mass., 1959-67; pres. Elcon Labs., Peabody, Mass., 1962-66; cons. Addison-Wesley Press, Reading, Mass., 1963-67; chief microwave lab. NASA Electronics Research Ctr., Cambridge, 1967-68, chief optics and microwave lab., 1968-70; dep. dir. Office Tech. Transp. Systems Ctr., Cambridge, 1970-72, dir. Office Tech., 1972-77, dir. Office Energy and Environ., 1977-79, dep. dir., 1979, dir. Office Data Systems and Tech., 1980-82, dir. Office Adminstrn., 1982-83, assoc. dir. Office Ops. Engring., 1983-84, acting dep. dir., 1984, acting dir., 1984-85, dir., 1985—; corporator Wakefield Savs. Bank, Mass., 1975—. Editor: Electronic Tubes, 1964; author, editor: Handbook of Microwave Measurements, 1966; contbr. articles to profl. jours. Mem. Mass. Gov.'s Commn. on Vocat. Rehab., 1966-68, Positive Program for Boston, 1967—; pres. Wakefield Council Chs., 1967-70; mem. adv. bd. U. Mass., Amherst, 1972—, Bentley Coll., Waltham, Mass., 1974—; trustee Univ. Hosp., Boston, 1973—. Recipient Apollo Achievement award NASA, 1969; Meritorious Achievement award Sec. Transp. 1976; Outstanding Achievement award U. Mich., 1978; Meritorious Exec. award Pres. U.S., 1984. Fellow IEEE; mem. AIAA, AAAS, N.Y. Acad. Sci., Phi Beta Kappa Assocs. (life mem.), Sigma Pi Phi (treas. 1980—, pres. 1986—). Episcopalian. Club: Nat. Guardsmen (pres. 1986—). Lodge: Masons. Home: 5 Michael Rd Wakefield MA 01880 Office: Transp Systems Ctr Kendall Sq Cambridge MA 02142

ROBERTS, MARIANNE, realtor; b. Columbus, Ohio, May 27, 1930; d. George W. and Alice L. (Scott) Hunt; m. L.R. Foreman, Sept. 19, 1948 (dec. Aug. 1957); children—Georgia Foreman Masselli, L. Scott, Jeffrey W., Alyce Foreman Heminger; m. Knute Roberts, Apr. 5, 1962; children—Ruthie Roberts McCloud, L. Charlie L. Student Ohio State U., 1980-82; grad. Impact Drug and Alcohol Abuse Tng. Lic. real estate saleswoman, Ohio; Grad. Realtors Inst., Ohio; critique commn. tchr. cert., Ohio. Saleswoman, sec. Hunt Milling Co., Richwood, Ohio, 1947-64; reporter, feature writer Marion Star, Ohio and Marysville Jour., Ohio, 1974-80; saleswoman, appraiser Nelson Blue Agy., Richwood, 1972—. Soloist Ohio OES White Shrine and First Bapt. Ch., supr. Sunday Sch., 1971-74, chmn. fin. com., 1982-85, dir. jr. choir, 1975-80, fin. sec., 1988—; pres. North Union Local Sch. Bd., Richwood, 1984-85, 1988-89, legis. liaison, 1980—; treas. First Baptist Ch., Richwood, 1979—; coordinator Fed./State Relations Network, Washington, 1983—; dir. Richwood Showboat Serenaders, 1980-82; sec. Union County Bd. Mental Retardation, 1971-79; emeritus bd. dirs. Lewis Sch. for Retarded, Marysville, 1983. Recipient numerous civic awards. Mem. Ohio Sch. Bds. Assn. (exec. com. 1983-84, pres. cen. region 1986, com. ploicy and legis. 1985, 86-88), Internat. Platform Assn., Speakers Unltd. Republican. Clubs: Carpe Diem (sec. and v.p. 1982-84, pres. 1988), Mother's Study (Richwood) (pres. 1952-54), Matrons (pres. 1986, Worthy Matron Mt. Carmel chpt. 1962-82); Christian Women (chmn. 1987—). Lodge: Order Ea. Star. Avocations: music, reading, embroidery, writing. Home: 28 George St Richwood OH 43344 Office: Blue Agy E Blagrove St Richwood OH 43344

ROBERTS, PHILIP RICHARD, insurance company executive; b. Bridgeport, Conn., Feb. 18, 1942; s. Frederick William and Dorothy (Allen) R.; m. Lorraine Hazel Lipscomb, June 27, 1964; children: Margaret Cass, Frederick William, Charles Lipscomb. BA in Econs., Harvard U., 1964; MBA, U. Conn., 1971. Various positions Aetna Life & Casualty Ins. Co., Hartford, Conn., 1964-76, asst. v.p., 1976-80, v.p., 1980-85, sr. v.p., 1985—, also bd. dirs.; bd. dirs. Aetna Life Ins. and Annuity Co. Bd. dirs. Hartford YMCA, 1980—, Church Homes of Hartford, 1975—, Local Initiatives Support Corp., 1987—, Conn. Water Service, Inc., 1988—, Inst. of Living, 1988—, Watkinson Sch., 1988—, MBIA, Inc., 1989. Episcopalian. Clubs: Hartford Golf; Pequot Yacht (Southport, Conn.). Office: Aetna Life & Casualty 151 Farmington Ave Hartford CT 06156

ROBERTS, RICHARD HEILBRON, construction company executive; b. Sacramento, Nov. 19, 1925; s. John Montgomery and Mary Lou (Heilbron) R.; m. Jo Anne Sydney Erickson, Feb. 25, 1950; children: Richard, Kurt, Tracy. BSCE, U. Calif., 1949. Registered profl. engr., Calif. Field and resident engr. Calif. Div. Hwys., San Luis Obispo, 1949-51; project and br. mgr. Granite Constrn. Co., Watsonville, Calif., 1951-68, v.p., mgr., 1968-79, pres. engring. constrn. div., 1979-83, exec. v.p., chief operating officer, 1983-89, vice chmn., 1989—, also bd. dirs. Served to corp. U.S. Army, 1944-46. Mem. Soc. Am. Mil. Engrs., Beavers (bd. dirs., pres. 1984, Golden Beaver award 1986, Moles Non-mem. award 1988). Republican. Presbyterian. Clubs: Monterey Peninsula Country (Pebble Beach, Calif.); Silverado Country (Napa, Calif.); Pauma Valley (Calif.) Country. Home: 3481 Taylor Rd Carmel CA 93923 Office: Granite Constrn Co PO Box 900 Watsonville CA 95076

ROBERTS, SANDRA BROWN, realty company executive; b. Boston, May 26, 1939; d. Frederick Thomas and Christine (Peyton) Brown; m. Joseph Peter Roberts, Aug. 26, 1962 (div. May 1984); children: Christine, Joseph, Paul. B.A., Boston Coll., 1981. Lic. real estate broker, Mass. Owner, mgr. real estate, Wellesley, Mass., 1963—; pres. Riverview Realty, Wellesley, 1970—; comml. realtor, Boston, 1974—; cons. Berkshire Hathaway, New Bedford, Mass., 1983—; asst. to pres. BHR, Inc., New Bedford, 1988—. Founder, pres., bd. dirs. Friends of Ft. Washington, Inc.; active Friends of Boston Ballet, 1983—. Mem. DAR (Boston Tea Party chpt. regent 1983-84, 84-85). Navy League of U.S., New Eng. Hist. Geneal. Soc. Republican. Roman Catholic. Club: College (Boston). Lodge: Order of Crown of Charlemagne (life mem.), Order of Lafayette (bd. dirs.). Home: 52 Kenilworth Rd Wellesley MA 02181 Office: BHR Inc 51 River St Wellesley MA 02181

ROBERTS, WILLIAM LAWRENCE, appraiser, broker, real estate executive; b. Boston, Jan. 20, 1924; s. James Joseph and Mary Margaret (Galvin) R.; student Northeastern U., 1949-51, Rutgers U., 1952-54; LL.B., Blackstone Sch. Law, 1959; grad. Realtors Inst., 1975; m. Josephine Mary DeLeo, July 22, 1945; children—James Joseph, Linda Marie (Mrs. John Hamilton Glover), William Lawrence. With RCA, Camden, N.J., 1951-58, Midwest regional rep., 1955, N.E. regional rep., 1956; sr. mem. tech. staff Thompson Ramo Wooldridge Co., Redondo Beach, Calif., 1958-60, N.E. regional mgr., 1960-61; mgr. marketing Sperry Rand Research Center, Sudbury, Mass., 1961-62; research and devel. marketing mgr. Litton Industries, Beverly Hills, Calif., 1962-65, dir. data systems, div. aero Service Corp., 1965-66; with Collins Radio Co., Dallas, 1966-74, venture analyst, mgr. sales service div., 1973-74; with Merrill Lynch-Paula Stringer, Inc., Dallas, 1974-82; v.p. Burchett & Roberts Appraisers, 1975—; chief exec. officer North Tex. Research Inst., St. Paul, Tex., 1982—; instr. real estate appraising Real Estate Career Coll. Chmn. cub scouts Fort Stanwix council Boy Scouts Am., 1956-57, asst. dist. commr., 1965-66; pres. Meadowbrook P.T.A., Pennsauken, N.J., 1953-54; capt. fund drive Plano YMCA, 1975. Campaign mgr. Kennedy/Johnson, Rome, N.Y., 1960. Served with USNR, 1942-45: PTO. Paul Harris fellow Rotary; recipient Citizens award City Utica (N.Y.), 1963. Mem. Nat. Assn. Realtors, Tex. Assn. Realtors (edn. com., inst. instr.), Collin County Cen. Appraisal Dist. Rev. Bd. (chmn. 1986—), Collin County Bd. Realtors (pres. 1981—), Soc. Real Estate Appraisers (edn. com. Dallas chpt. 1981—, designated sr. residential appraiser, bd. dirs. Dallas chpt. 1981-84, chmn. edn. com. 1982-83, instr. 101, 102), Nat. Assn. Rev. Appraisers (cert. rev. appraiser), IEEE (sr. mem., nat. exec. com. 1960-64), Am. Rocket Soc., Am. Inst. Aero. and Astronautics, Armed Forces Communications and Electronics Assn. (nat. dir. 1959-67), Am. Angus Assn., Nat. Mktg. Inst. (cert. residential specialist, cert. residential broker). Author: (with Vernon Poehls) Naval Shipboard Communications Building Block Design Handbook, 1952; Test Agenda and Record of Performance of Shipboard Electronic Systems, 1953. Home: 3021 Princeton Dr Plano TX 75074 Office: Burchett & Roberts Appraisers 1007 20th St Plano TX 75074

ROBERTSON, DOUGLAS GLENN, branch manager; b. Jefferson City, Mo., May 3, 1953; s. Dorsey Franklin and Rosemary Ellen (Glenn) R.; m. Ann Scott Ward, May 26, 1973; children: Joshua Ward, Casey Diane. Student, U. Mo., Columbia, 1972-73, U. N.C., 1974, U. Md., 1975. Sales engr. Motion Industries, Greenville, S.C., 1978-87; br. mgr. Motion Industries, Cin., 1987—. Mem. Rep. Senatorial com., Washington, 1984. Served to staff sgt. U.S. Army, 1972-78. Named one of Outstanding Young Men Am., U.S. Jaycees, 1983. Home: 2440 Orchid Ln Villa Hills KY 41017 Office: Motion Industries PO Box 37405 Cincinnati OH 45222

ROBERTSON, EDWIN DAVID, lawyer; b. Roanoke, Va., July 5, 1946; s. Edwin Traylor and Norma Burns (Bowles) R.; m. Anne Littelle Ferratt, Sept. 7, 1968. BA with honors, U. Va., 1968, LLB, 1971. Bar: N.Y. 1972, U.S. Ct. Appeals (2d cir.) 1972, U.S. Dist. Ct. (ea. and so. dists.) N.Y. 1973, U.S. Supreme Ct. 1975, U.S. Dist. Ct. (ea. dist.) Mich. 1986. Assoc. Cadwalader, Wickersham & Taft, N.Y.C., 1972-80, ptnr., 1980—. Bd. dirs. Early Music Found. N.Y., N.Y.C., 1983—. Served to 1st lt. USAF, 1972. Mem. ABA, Fed. Bar Council, N.Y. County Lawyers Assn. (chmn. bankruptcy com. 1983-87, bd. dirs. 1985-88), Assn. Bar City of N.Y. (mem. com. on state cts. of superior jurisdiction 1987—), Oratorio Soc. N.Y.C., Jefferson Soc., Order of Coif, Phi Beta Kappa, Phi Kappa Psi. Republican. Episcopalian. Club: Down Town (N.Y.C.). Home: 311 E 71st St New York NY 10021 Office: Cadwalader Wickersham & Taft 100 Maiden Ln New York NY 10038

ROBERTSON, GEORGE BERYL, JR., publisher; b. N.Y.C., May 4, 1943; s. George Beryl and Margaret (Gurrie) R.; m. Gratia Bezona, Aug. 28, 1965; 1 child, Karen-Alicia. BA, Calif. State U., Northridge, 1966. Mng. editor News-Chronicle, Thousand Oaks, Calif., 1967-73, Bremerton (Wash.) Sun, 1973-74; editor Lewis River News, Woodland, Wash., 1974-78; pub. The Sun, Sheridan, Oreg., 1978—. Pres. Three Cities Devel. Corp., Sheridan, 1980—. Recipient Best Edn. Reporting award Wash. State Edn. Assn., 1976. Mem. Nat. Newspaper Pubs. Assn., Oreg. Newspaper Pub. Assn. (Best News Reporting award 1981, Best Sports Reporting award 1983, mem. computer/technology ctr. 1987—), Sheridan C. of C. (pres. 1980-81, Citizen of Yr. 1982), Kiwanis Club (pres. 1988), Rotary Club (bd. dirs. 1987-88), K.C. Roman Catholic. Home: PO Box 277 Sheridan OR 97378 Office: The Sun Newspaper 249 S Bridge PO Box 68 Sheridan OR 97378

ROBERTSON, GREGG WESTLAND, diversified company executive; b. Sydney, Australia, Jan. 16, 1934; s. Alexander and Lillian R.; BA in Econs., Fairleigh Dickinson U., 1964; postgrad. Harvard U., 1980; m. Elizabeth Stimper, Apr. 30, 1957; children—Gregg Westland, Lisa. Asst. v.p. Bankers Trust Co., N.Y.C., 1964-69; asst. treas. Dillingham Corp., Honolulu, 1970-73, treas., 1974-77, v.p. fin., treas., chief fin. officer, 1977-82, sr. v.p. strategic devel., 1982-83, pres., chief exec. officer, 1986—; pres., chief exec. officer Calif. Gas Corp. subs., Sacramento, 1983-84, exec. v.p. parent co., San Francisco, 1984—; pres., chief exec. officer Robertson & Co., San Francisco, 1987-88. Bd. dirs. Aloha United Way, 1980-82, Sacramento United Way, 1983-84. Mem. Fin. Execs. Inst. Clubs: Olympic (San Francisco); Outrigger Canoe (Honolulu). Home: 145 Avenida Mira Flores Tiburon CA 94920 Office: 300 Montgomery St San Francisco CA 94104

ROBERTSON, HERBERT CHAPMAN, JR., geoscience consulting company executive; b. Dallas, Nov. 18, 1928; s. Herbert Chapman Sr. and Sarah Grace (Foraker) R. BA, So. Meth. U., 1951, MS, 1959. Geologist Research, Inc., Dallas, 1952-54; seismologist Geophys. Surveys, Inc., Dallas, 1957-59; geologist Exploration Surveys, Dallas, 1959-61; research assoc. Teledyne-Geotech, Dallas, 1961-73; sr. geophysicist PEXCON, Dallas, 1973-75; supr. U.S. Geol. Survey, Washington, 1975-81; sr. geophysicist Mobil Exploration Co., Dallas, 1981-82, Sun Exploration Co., Dallas, 1982-84; pres. The Herbert Robertson Co., Inc., Dallas, 1984—; Dept. of Def. tech. cons. to prin. investigator So. Meth. U., Tex., 1984, mgmt. cons. 1989—. Contbr. articles to profl. jours. Served as cpl. U.S. Army, 1954-56. Mem. Soc. Exploration Geophysicists (Silver cert. 1984), Am. Inst. Profl. Geologists (cert.). Republican. Presbyterian. Home and Office: 8707 Wingate Dallas TX 75209

ROBERTSON, JAMES ALLEN, risk management consultant, author, lecturer; b. Burlington, Iowa, Jan. 24, 1948; s. George Allen and Betty Irene (Beck) R.; student Knox Coll., 1965-66; BA, U. Iowa, 1969; postgrad. San Francisco Theol. Sem./Grad. Theol. Union, 1969-70; MSA, Pepperdine U., 1976; m. Stephanie Peacock. Casualty underwriter Hartford Ins. Group, San Francisco, 1970-72, supervising underwriter, 1972-73, L.A., 1973-74; asst. v.p. Tausch Ins. Brokers, Santa Ana, Calif., 1974-75; cons. Warren, McVeigh, Griffin & Huntington, 1975-76; sr. v.p. Reed Risk Mgmt., San Francisco, 1976-78; pres. James A. Robertson & Assoc., Inc., 1978-87; prin. cons. Warren, McVeigh & Griffin, Newport Beach, Calif., 1979-83; pres. Ins. Litigation Cons., 1984-87; nat. dir. ins. litigation svcs. Coopers & Lybrand, Newport Beach, 1987—; assoc. in risk mgmt. CPCU. Mem. Soc. Chartered Property Casualty Underwriters (pres. Orange Empire chpt. 1985-86, nat. publs. com. 1984-87, chmn. 1987-88, nat. dir. 1988—), Soc. Risk Mgmt. Cons. (chmn. profl. practices com. 1986-87), Omicron Delta Kappa. Republican. Author: The Umbrella Book, 1976, 2d edit., editor, 1979-83, Key Financial Ratios, 1978; ISO Commercial Liability Forms, 1984, 4th edit., 1986, It's Time to Take the Mystery Out of Umbrellas, 1984; editor Risk Mgmt. Letter, 1981-83, Risk Management and Insurance in The Handbook of Cash Flow and Treasury Management, 1988, Going for a Broker in Business Strategy International, 1989; contbr. over 40 articles to profl. jours. Office: Coopers & Lybrand One Newport Pl 1301 Dove St Newport Beach CA 92660

ROBERTSON, JAMES COLVERT, insurance company executive; b. Takoma Park, Md., Feb. 2, 1932; s. Charles Edwin and Mary Louise (Colvert) R.; m. Grace A. Shuler, May 7, 1971. BS in Econs., U. Md., 1957; LLB, George Washington U., 1959. Bar: D.C. 1960, Pa. 1965. Atty/analyst SEC, Washington, 1959-64; atty. McNees, Wallace & Nurick, Harrisburg, Pa., 1964-67; gen. counsel Consumers Life, Camp Hill, Pa., 1967-68; pres., chmn. bd. Consumers Life & Consumers Fin. Corp., Camp Hill, 1968—; dir. Consumers Fin. Bd. dirs. Harrisburg Hosp., 1982-86 , Elizabethtown Coll., 1982—, Keystone Sports Found., 1983-88 . With U.S. Army, 1951-53. Mem. Pa. Bar Assn., Fed. Bar Assn. West Shore Country Club (bd. dirs.). Republican. Home: 86 Greenwood Cir Wormleysburg PA 17043 Office: Consumers Life Ins Co 1110 Fernwood Ave PO Box 26 Camp Hill PA 17011

ROBERTSON, JAMES EARL, real estate executive; b. Kerrville, Tex., 1958; s. George Earl and Betty Lou (Campbell) R.; m. Shari Diane Bush, Oct. 14, 1983. BBA in Real Estate Fin., So. Meth. U., 1981, BA in Econs., 1982. Lic. real estate broker, Tex. Analyst Lomas & Nettleton Fin. Corp., Dallas, 1982; fin. analyst to v.p. First S.W. Equity Corp., Dallas, 1983-85; v.p. to exec. v.p., chief operating officer Bright Capital Corp., Dallas, 1985-88; v.p. comml. leading Guaranty Fed. Savs. Bank, Dallas, 1989—; speaker in field. Mem. Urban Land Inst., So. Meth. U. Alumni Assn., Rutherford Inst. Republican. Home: 5846 Morningside Ave Dallas TX 75206 Office: Guaranty Fed Savs Bank 10440 N Central Expwy Dallas TX 75231

ROBERTSON, JOSEPH EDMOND, grain processing company executive; b. Brownstown, Ind., Feb. 16, 1918; s. Roscoe Melvin and Edith Penina (Shields) R.; m. Virginia Faye Baxter, Nov. 23, 1941; 1 son, Joseph Edmond. BS, Kans. State U., 1940, postgrad., 1940. Cereal chemist Ewing Mill Co., 1940-43, flour milling engr., 1946-50, feed nutritionist, 1951-59; v.p., sec. Robertson Corp., Brownstown, Ind., 1960-80, pres., 1980—. Pres. Jackson County (Ind.) Welfare Bd., 1948-52. mem. Ind. Port Commn., 1986—. Served with USAAF, 1943-45. Mem. Hardwood Plywood Mfrs. Assn. (v.p. affiliate div. 1971-73, 87-88), Am. Assn. Cereal Chemists, Assn. Operative Millers, Am. Legion, Brownstown C. of C. (dir. All Am. city program 1955), Kans. State U. Alumni Assn. (life), Blue Key, Phi Delta Theta, Phi Kappa Phi, Alpha Mu. Presbyterian. Clubs: Country (Seymour, Ind.); Hickory Hills Country (Brownstown, Ind.); Internat. Travelers Century (Los Angeles). Lodge: Elks. Home: Rte 1 Lake and Forest Club PO Box A Brownstown IN 47220 Office: 200 Front St Brownstown IN 47220

ROBERTSON, LINWOOD RIGHTER, electric utility executive; b. Richmond, Va., Feb. 10, 1940; s. Reginald Linwood and Alliene Dewer (Righter) R.; m. Mildred Swift, Apr. 10, 1965; 1 child, William S. B.S., Va. Commonwealth U., 1970. Comml. fisherman Smith Fisheries, Belford, N.Y., 1964; supr. Philip Morris Co., Richmond, Va., 1965-68; various positions to v.p., treas., corp. sec. Va. Power, Richmond, 1969—. Served with USN, 1962-64. Mem. Am. Soc. Corp. Secs. Methodist. Club: Hermitage Country, Richmond. Home: 11 Quail Run Dr Manakin-Sabot VA 23103

ROBERTSON, MONROE WAYNE, JR., oil company executive; b. Oklahoma City, Jan. 8, 1950; s. Monroe Wanye Sr. and Virginia Lee (Barker) R.; m. Marilyn Louise Robertson, June 1, 1973; children: Tiffany Lee, Randall Monroe. BSME in Mech. Engring., MIT, 1973, MS in Mech. Engring., 1973, MS in Nuclear Engring., 1973. Engr. Gen. Atomic, San Diego, 1973-74; sr. engr. Gen. Atomic, 1974-76, sr. bus. analyst, 1976-77; staff bus. analyst 1977-79; sr. assoc. corp. planning Gulf Oil Co., Pitts., 1979-80; mgr. corp. planning Gulf Oil Co., 1980-83; mgr. fin. analyst Gulf Oil Internat., Houston, 1983-85, Gotco, Inc., Houston, 1985-86; dir. planning Terra Resources, Tulsa, 1986-88; dir. corp. planning Apache Corp., Denver, 1988—. Mem. Planning Forum. Mem. Am. Petroleum Inst., Petroleum Club (Tulsa). Republican. Methodist. Home: 7679 S Argonne Aurora CO 80016 Office: Apache Corp 1700 Lincoln St Ste 1900 Denver CO 80203

ROBERTSON, ORAN B., retail company executive; b. Turner, Ore., 1917; married; student, U. Wash. With Boeing Aircraft Co. until 1946, Fred Meyer, Inc., Portland, Oreg., v.p., dir. engring., now chmn., chief exec. officer, also dir. Office: Fred Meyer Inc 3800 SE 22nd St Portland OR 97202 *

ROBERTSON, RICHARD BLAKE, management consultant; b. Ahoskip, N.C., July 28, 1929; s. James Henry and Janie Bell (Baker) R.; m. Elizabeth Parker Gardner, Aug. 19, 1941. BSEE, N.C. State U., 1951; MBA, U. Md., 1956. Design engr. Westinghouse Electric Co., Friendship Airport, Md., 1951-54; product planner Gen. Electric Co., Lynchburg, Pa., 1956-59; dir. mktg. Gen. Motors Corp., Milw., 1959-60; pres. Robertson and Assocs., Pinetops, N.C., 1960—. Mem. Phi Kappa Phi, Tau Beta Pi, Phi Eta Sigma, Theta Tau. Office: Robertson & Assocs Inc PO Drawer B Pinetops NC 27864

ROBERTSON, RICHARD STUART, insurance holding company executive; b. Spokane, Wash., June 14, 1942; s. Stuart A. and Marjory (Moch) R.; m. Trudy Ann Prendergast, July 31, 1976; children: Thomas Stuart, Richard Andrew. B.S., Calif. Inst. Tech., 1963. Chief reinsurance actuary Lincoln Nat. Life Ins. Co., Ft. Wayne, Ind., 1963-74; sr. v.p., chief fin. officer Lincoln Nat. Corp., Ft. Wayne, 1974-86, exec. v.p., chief fin. officer, 1986—; bd. dirs. Ins. Co. Ill., Chgo., Lincoln Nat. Sales Corp., Ft. Wayne, Preferred Fin. Corp., Denver. Fellow Soc. Actuaries (pres. 1985-86); mem. Am. Acad. Actuaries (v.p. 1980-81). Episcopalian. Home: 12618 Aboite Center Rd Fort Wayne IN 46804

ROBERTSON, ROBERT LYNN, JR., controller; b. Leesburg, Va., Jan. 6, 1956; s. Robert Lynn and Mary Helen (Cowger) R.; m. Nancy Albig, Feb. 4,

1978; children: Elizabeth Waters, Bradford Allan. Student, Montgomery Coll., 1974-76, Frederick Community Coll., 1978-79; BS in Acctg., Mt. St. Mary's Coll., 1981. CPA, Md. Staff acct. Stoy, Malone & Co., Frederick, Md., 1981-82; staff acct. Trans-Tech, Inc., Adamstown, Md., 1982-83, asst. contr., 1983-84, contr., 1984—. Mem. AICPA. Home: 5822 Jefferson Blvd Frederick MD 21701 Office: Trans Tech Inc 5520 Adamstown Rd Frederick MD 21710

ROBERTSON, SANDRA DEE (GRAEN), accountant; b. Denver, Nov. 7, 1953; d. Fredrick Philip Arthur Graen and Dorothea Stone (Bell) Kohler; m. Charles E. Robertson Jr., Aug. 4, 1973 (Jan. 1985); 1 child, Daniel Philip. BS in Bus. cum laude, U. Colo., 1980. CPA, Colo. Staff acct. Brock, Cordle & Assocs., CPA's, Boulder, Colo., 1980-82; corp. tax acct. Storage Tech. Corp., Louisville, Colo., 1983-87; state tax supr. RJR Nabisco, Inc., Atlanta, Ga., 1987—. Served with U.S. Army, 1972-75. Mem. Am. Inst. CPA's, Colo. Soc. CPA's, Beta Gamma Sigma. Democrat. Club: Toastmasters. Home: 2074 Arbor Forest Dr Marietta GA 30064

ROBERTSON, WILLIAM ALAN, company financial and administrative executive; b. Long Beach, Calif., Nov. 2, 1938; s. Earl Austin and Alice Isobel (Roberts) R.; m. Lee Ann Rogers, Nov. 1961 (div. 1968); children: Susan Lee, Scott Alan, Bradley Alan; m. Joan Greta Sariego, June 11, 1969; 1 child, Jonathan Alan. Student, Calif. State U., Long Beach, 1956-58, 60-67; MBA, Pepperdine U., 1986. Systems engr. IBM, Long Beach, 1960-64; mgr. data processing Shore Calnevar, Paramount, Calif., 1964-65; mgr. systems and procedures CBS-TV Network, Hollywood, Calif., 1965-68; dir. MIS, Capitol Records EMI, Hollywood, 1968-78; v.p., treas. Thorn EMI-Capitol Industries, Hollywood, 1978-86; v.p. ops., chief fin. officer Signal Tech., Inc., Goleta, Calif., 1986—, also bd. dirs. With USNR, 1958-60. Republican. Office: Signal Tech Inc 5951 Encina Rd Goleta CA 93117

ROBERTSON, WILLIAM RICHARD, banker; b. Schenectady, N.Y., July 26, 1941; s. Bruce Manson and Mary Jo (Gillam) R.; m. Sarah Reed Parker, June 20, 1964; children: Deborah Graham, John William, Julie Elizabeth. AB, Colgate U., 1964; MBA, Case Western Res. U., 1967. With Nat. City Bank, Cleve., 1964-72, v.p., 1972-78; sr. v.p. Nat. City Bank, Cleve., 1978-82; exec. v.p. Nat. City Corp., Cleve., 1982-86, chief fin. officer, 1982-89, vice chmn., 1986-87, dep. chmn., 1987—, also bd. dirs. Trustee Coll. of Wooster, Ohio, 1982—, Fairmount Presbyn. Ch., Cleve., 1983-86, St. Lukes Hosp., Cleve., 1984—; pres., trustee Big Brothers Big Sisters, Cleve., 1973-80, Cleve. Ballet, 1985-89, Salvation Army, 1985—, United Way, 1986—. Mem. Fin. Execs. Inst., Assn. Res. City Bankers, Am. Bank Assn., Cleve. Skating Club (pes. 1980-82), Union Club, Country Club, Tavern Club, Pepper Pike Club. Republican. Home: 2700 Chesterton Rd Shaker Heights OH 44122 Office: Nat City Corp Nat City Ctr 1900 E 9th St Cleveland OH 44114

ROBILLARD, RAYMOND ALFRED, financial official; b. Holyoke, Mass., Jan. 26, 1923; s. Lucien and Nellie (Robillard) R.; B.B.A. in Acctg., Northeastern U., 1952; postgrad. U. Toledo, 1955; M.B.A. in Fin., U. Mass., 1959; Ph.D. in Polit. Sci., Am. Internat. Open U. (now Clayton U.), 1978; m. Jennifer Karzy, July 30, 1960; children—Phillip Raymond, Paul Francis; stepchildren—John Michael Brodowski, Thomas Peter Brodowski. Costs and budget dir. Holyoke Card & Paper Co., Springfield, Mass., 1946-52; supervisory acct. Springfield Armory, 1952-59; mgr. adminstrn. and fin. control surface communications div. RCA, Camden, N.J., 1959-62; fin. mgr. Martin-Marietta Corp., Balt., 1962-65; controller, asst. treas. AAI Corp., Balt., 1965-67; bus. mgr. Eastern Shore campus U. Md., Princess Anne, 1967-83; pres. Lit. Services Inst., Towson, Md., 1979—; lectr. Loyola Coll., Balt., 1963-68, Johns Hopkins U., Balt., 1965-70. Controller, Nat. Chicken Festival, Delmarva Poultry Industry, Georgetown, Del., 1970; mem. arts and crafts com. Wye Inst., Queenstown, Md., 1971-78; mem. adv. council Somerset County (Md.) Bd. Edn.; mem. Md. Ednl. TV Planning Council, 1968-78; founder bd. dirs., pres. Eastern Shore Arts and Crafts Center, Princess Anne, 1971-80; bd. dirs. Olde Princess Anne Days Historic Trust, 1973—; bd. dirs., asst. treas. Samuel Chase House Restoration Council, Princess Anne, 1975—; fin. advisor, bd. dirs. Somerset County Bicentennial Commn., Princess Anne, 1974-80; cons. Inst. Chesapeake Bay Studies, Wye Mills, Md., 1975-82, Inst. Mediterranean Studies, Dubrovnik (Yugoslavia) and Tokyo, 1976-82; project evaluator Md. Com. for Humanities, 1979; mem. acad. council Clayton U., St. Louis, 1979—, mem. internat. adv. bd., 1981—; mem. Baltimore County local bd. SSS, 1981—. Served with M.I., U.S. Army, 1942-46. Decorated Croix de Guerre with bronze star (France); recipient Outstanding Boss award Jaycees, Cambridge, Ohio, 1961; Man of Yr. award Marylander and Herald Newspapers, Princess Anne, 1971; N award Northeastern U., 1951. Mem. Princess Anne Area C. of C. (pres. 1969-83), Fin. Execs. Inst., Nat. Assn. Coll. and Univ. Bus. Officers, Internat. Studies Assn., Overseas Devel. Council, Delmarva Indsl. Devel. Assn., Coll. and Univ. Personnel Assn., Am. Legion, Epsilon Phi Sigma, Phi Kappa Phi (life mem.). Republican. Club: Johns Hopkins. Author: Union Financial Accounting and Reporting Practices, 1959; The Place of Capitalism and Morality in a Free Society, 1959; Free Enterprise as a Factor in National Economies: Problems and Perspectives, 1977; Interdependence of Free Enterprise and Governments in the Global Marketplace, 1979; contbr. articles to profl. jours. Home: Hillcreek 1305 Milldam Rd Towson MD 21204 Office: U Md Ea Shore Princess Anne MD 21853

ROBINETTE, SHEREE, construction executive; b. Tampa, Fla., Mar. 12, 1957; d. William J. and Patricia Ann (Gearhart) R. AA Hillsborough Community Coll., 1977; BA in Acctg. U. South Fla., 1980. Mgr. Fontaine Supply, Tampa, 1977-80; owner,mgr. Tampa Accessory Corp., 1980—. Mem. Constrn. Trade Assn., Nat. Assn. Women in Constrn., Nat. Assn. Profl. Estimators . Republican. Baptist. Avocations: ballet, swimming, cycling. Office: Tampa Accessory Corp 5688B W Crenshaw St Tampa FL 33634

ROBINS, BARRIE JEROME, financial executive; b. Chgo., Aug. 15, 1937; s. Jacob and Ethel (Kaplan) R.; m. Sandra Robert Nierenberg, June 23, 1974; children: Michael, Edward, Steven Solar, Sharon Solar. ScB, De Paul U., 1962. V.p. John M. Shannon and Assocs., Inc., Chgo., 1964-81, Mid-Continent Fin. Group, Chgo., 1982-84, Fin. Planning Group, Ltd., Rosemont, Ill., 1984—; pres. Robins Fin. Corp., Rosemont, 1981—. Mem. Internat. Assn. Fin. Planners, Inst. Cert. Fin. Planners (cert.). Office: Fin Planning Group Ltd 9801 W Higgins Ste 510 Rosemont IL 60018

ROBINS, EDWIN CLAIBORNE, SR., pharmaceutical company executive; b. Richmond, Va., July 8, 1910; s. Claiborne and Martha (Taylor) R.; m. Lora McGlasson, June 24, 1938; children: Lora Elizabeth Robins Porter, E. Claiborne, Ann Carol Robins Marchant. AB, U. Richmond, 1931; BS, Med. Coll. Va. Sch. Pharmacy, 1933, D in Pharm. Sci., 1958, LLD, 1960. Chmn., bd. dirs. A. H. Robins Co., Inc., Richmond. Trustee emeritus Richmond Meml. Hosp., United Givers Fund, Crippled Children's Hosp.; mem. exec. com.; trustee U. Richmond, past pres. alumni council. Recipient Outstanding Alumnus award MCV Alumni Assn., 1986, Disting. Service award U. Richmond, 1960; Dean M. McCann award Pharm. Wholesalers Assn., 1968; Hugo H. Schaefer medal Am. Pharm. Assn., 1969; Liberty Bell award Richmond Bar Assn., 1970; Sertoma Club award, 1970; Thomas Jefferson award Pub. Relations Soc. Am., 1970; named Pharmacist of Year Va. Pharm. Assn., 1967; Bus. Leader of Year Sales and Mktg. Execs. Richmond, 1969; Disting. Service award Va. State Chamber, 1972; Jackson Davis award for disting. service to higher edn. in Va., 1976; Edward A. Wayne medal for Disting. Service Va. Commonwealth U., 1978; Wall of Fame award, Va. Sports Hall of Fame; Wall of Fame award, 1979; award U. Richmond Athletic Hall of Fame, 1980; recipient Gt. Am. Traditions award B'nai B'rith, 1982, Outstanding Alumnus award Med. Coll. Va./Va. Commonwealth U. Sch. Pharmacy, 1983, Richmond Paragon medal, 1986. Mem. Pharm. Mfrs. Assn. (past chmn.), NAM, Va. Mfrs. Assn., Va. Pharm. Assn., Newcomen Soc. N.Am., Richmond C. of C. (past pres.), Med. Coll. Va. Alumni Assn. (past pres., dir.), Phi Beta Kappa, Alpha Kappa Psi, Omicron Delta Kappa, Phi Delta Chi, Kappa Psi, Lambda Chi Alpha, Beta Gamma Sigma (hon.). Baptist (mem. bd. adminstrn.). Clubs: Rotary (past dir.), Commonwealth Forum, Country of Va. Home: Clear View River Rd Richmond VA 23226 Office: A H Robins Co Inc 1407 Cummings Dr Richmond VA 23220 *

ROBINS, EDWIN CLAIBORNE, JR., pharmaceutical company executive; b. Richmond, Va., 1943. BS in Bus. Adminstrn., U. Richmond, 1968. Mgmt. trainee Central Fidelity Banks Inc., 1963-64; with A.H. Robins Co., Inc., Richmond, Va., 1968—, exec. v.p., 1975-78, pres., chief exec. officer, 1978—, also dir.; bd. dirs. Va. Land Trust Inc., Cen. Fidelity Banks Inc. Office: A H Robins Co Inc 1407 Cummings Dr Richmond VA 23220 *

ROBINS, JANIS, chemist; b. Riga, Latvia, Aug. 3, 1925; came to U.S., 1949; s. Janis Eriks and Mirdza (Wagners) R.; m. Brigita Maija Svarcs, Mar. 25, 1951; children: Baiba, Daina, Laila, Zaiga. BS in Chemistry, U. Wash., 1951, PhD in Chemistry, 1957. Sr. chemist 3M Co., St. Paul, 1957-65, sr. research specialist, 1972-82, div. scientist, 1982—; asst. prof. chemistry Macalester Coll., St. Paul, 1960-65; project leader Archer Daniels & Midland, Mpls., 1965-68; research assoc. Ashland Chem. Co., Mpls., 1968-72. Contbr. chpt. to book, articles to sci. jours.; patentee cold bar process. V.p. Latvian Evangl. Luth. Ch. in Am., Chgo., 1980—, Evang. Luth. Ch. Latvia in Exile, Toronto, Ont., Can., 1982—; pres. Latvian Assn. in Minn., Mpls., 1984—; treas. Latvian Sport Council in Free World, N.Y.C., 1983—. Mem. Am. Chem. Soc., Am. Latvian Assn. Republican. Home: 11 Ludlow Ave Saint Paul MN 55108 Office: 3M Co 3M Ctr 209-1C-13 Saint Paul MN 55144

ROBINSON, ADELBERT CARL, lawyer, judge; b. Shawnee, Okla., Dec. 13, 1926; s. William H. and Mayme (Forston) R.; m. Paula Kay Settles, Apr. 16, 1988; children from previous marriage: William, James, Schuyler, Donald, David, Nancy, Lauri. Student Okla. Baptist U., 1944-47; JD, Okla. U., 1950. Bar: Okla. 1950. Practice, Muskogee, Okla., 1956—; with legal dept. Phillips Petroleum Co., 1950-51; adjuster U.S. Fidelity & Guaranty Co., 1951-54, atty., adjuster-in-charge, 1954-56; ptnr. Fite & Robinson, 1956-62, Fite, Robinson & Summers, 1963-70, Robinson & Summers, 1970-72, Robinson, Summers & Locke, 1972-76, Robinson, Locke & Gage, 1976-80, Robinson, Locke, Gage & Fite, 1980-83, Robinson, Locke, Gage, Fite & Williams, Muskogee, 1983—; police judge, 1963-64; mcpl. judge, 1964-70; prin. justice Temp. Div. 36 Okla. Ct. Appeals, 1981—; pres., dir. Wall St. Bldg Corp., 1969-78, Three Forks Devel. Corp., 1968-77, Rolo Leasing, Inc., 1971—, Suroya II, Inc., 1977—; sec. Muskogee Tom's Inc., Blue Ridge Corp., Harborcliff Corp.; bd. dirs. First Bancshares of Muskogee, Inc., First of Muskogee Corp., First City Bank, Tulsa; adv. dir. First Nat. Bank & Trust Co. of Muskogee; mng. ptnr. RLG Ritz, 1980—; ptnr. First City Real Estate Partnership, 1985—. Chmn. Muskogee County (Okla.) Law Day, 1963; chmn. Muskogee Area Redevel. Authority, 1963; chmn. Muskogee County chpt. Am. Cancer Soc., 1956; pres. bd. dirs. Muskogee Community Council; bd. dirs. United Way of Muskogee, Inc., 1980—, v.p., 1982, pres. 1983; bd. dirs. Muskogee Community Concert Assn., Muskogee Tourist Info. Bur., 1964-68; bd. dirs., gen. counsel United Cerebral Palsy Eastern Okla., 1964-68; trustee Connors Devel. Found., Connors Coll., 1981—, chmn., 1987—. Served with if. AUS, 1945-46. Mem. ABA, Okla. Bar Assn. (chmn. uniform laws com. 1970-72, chmn. profl. coop. com. 1965-69, past regional chmn. grievance com.), Muskogee County Bar Assn. (pres. 1971, mem. exec. council 1971-74), Okla. Assn. Def. Counsel (dir.), Okla. Assn. Mcpl. Judges (dir.), Muskogee C. of C., Delta Theta Phi. Methodist. Club: Rotary (pres. 1971-72). Home: 2408 St Andrews Ct Muskogee OK 74403 Office: 530 Court St PO Box 87 Muskogee OK 74401

ROBINSON, BERNARD LEO, lawyer; b. Kalamazoo, Feb. 13, 1924; s. Louis Harvey and Sue Mary (Starr) R.; BS, U. Ill., 1947, MS, 1958, postgrad. in structural dynamics, 1959; JD, U. N.Mex., 1973; m. Betsy Nadell, May 30, 1947; children: Robert Bruce, Patricia Anne, Jean Carol. Rsch. engr. Assn. Am. Railroads, 1947-49; instr. architecture Rensselaer Poly. Inst., 1949-51; commd. 2d lt. Corps Engrs., U.S. Army, 1945, advanced through grades to lt. col., 1965, ret., 1968; engr. Nuclear Def. Rsch. Corp., Albuquerque, 1968-71; admitted to N.Mex. bar, 1973, U.S. Supreme Ct. bar, 1976; practiced in Albuquerque, 1973-85, Silver City, N.Mex., 1985—; sec., treas. Rento Inc., 1987—. Dist. commr. Boy Scouts Am., 1960-62. Vice chmn. Rep. Dist. Com., 1968-70. Decorated Air medal, Combat Infantryman's Badge, Joint Svcs. Commendation medal. Mem. ASCE, ABA, N.Mex. Bar Assn., Grant County Bar Assn., Ret. Officers Assn., DAV, Assn. U.S. Army, Am. Legion, VFW. Home: 3306 Royall Dr Silver City NM 88061 Office: PO Box 4070 Silver City NM 88062

ROBINSON, CHARLES MICHAEL, marketing executive; b. Gadsden, Ala., Aug. 11, 1954; s. Roy Robert and Cleo (Brosmer) R.; m. Pamela Jean Breitenkamp, Aug. 30, 1980. BS in Engring., U.S. Mil. Acad., 1976; MA in Mktg., Webster U., 1988. Cert. fin. mgr. With service dept. Caterpillar Tractor Co., Peoria, Ill., 1982-83; account exec. Merrill Lynch, Kansas City, Mo., 1983-85, E.F. Hutton, Overland Park, Kans., 1985-86; v.p. investments Drexel Burnham Lambert Inc., Kansas City, 1986-89; mktg. exec. Twentieth Century Investors, Kansas City, Mo., 1989—. Served to capt. U.S. Army, 1976-82. Mem. West Point Soc. Kansas City, Assn. Grads. U.S. Mil. Acad. Republican. Lutheran. Club: Ducks Unltd. (Shawnee Mission, Kans.). Home: 11330 King Overland Park KS 66210 Office: Twentieth Century Investors 4500 Main St Kansas City MO 64112

ROBINSON, CHARLES WESLEY, energy company executive; b. Long Beach, Calif., Sept. 7, 1919; s. Franklin Willard and Anna Hope (Gould) R.; m. Tamara Lindovna, Mar. 8, 1957; children: Heather Lynne, Lisa Anne, Wendy Paige. AB cum laude in Econs., U. Calif., Berkeley, 1941; MBA, Stanford U., 1947. Asst. mgr. mfg. Golden State Dairy Products Co., San Francisco, 1947-49; v.p., then pres. Marcona Corp., San Francisco, 1952-74; undersec. of state for econ. affairs Dept. State, Washington, 1974-75, dep. sec. of state, 1976-77; sr. mng. partner Kuhn Loeb & Co., N.Y.C., 1977-78; vice chmn. Blyth Eastman Dillon & Co., N.Y.C., 1978-79; chmn. Energy Transition Corp., Santa Fe and Washington, 1979—; bd. dirs. Arthur D. Little, The Allen Group, Northrop Corp., NIKE, Inc.; internat. adv. bd. Pan Am. World Airways. Patentee slurry transport. Trustee Trilateral Commn., N.Y.C., 1972-74, 77—, Brookings Instn., Washington, 1977—. Served to lt. USN, 1941-46. Recipient Disting. Honor award Dept. State, 1977. Mem. Council on Fgn. Relations N.Y.C. Republican. Methodist. Club: Pacific Union (San Francisco). Office: Energy Transition Corp PO Box 2224 Santa Fe NM 87501

ROBINSON, DANIEL RAYMOND, oil company executive; b. Waynesville, Mo., May 21, 1948; s. Gene Francis and Ruth Beatrice (Rose) R.; m. Theresa Elizabeth Knight, May 28, 1973. BSME, U. Wis., 1971, MBA in Fin., 1973. Credit analyst 1st Nat. Bank of Dallas, 1973-75; project engr. Placid Oil Co., Dallas, 1975-77; mgr. ops., planning Placid Refining Co., Dallas, 1977-83; asst. treas., asst. sec. Placid Oil Co., Dallas, 1983-88, sec., asst. treas., 1988—. Republican. Roman Catholic. Home: Rte 2 PO Box 38 Waxahachie TX 75165 Office: Placid Oil Co 3900 Thanksgiving Tower Dallas TX 75201

ROBINSON, DAVID EARL, pharmaceutical executive; b. Indpls., Nov. 28, 1948; s. Howard Ambler and Irma Katherine (Jones) R.; m. Nancy Margaret Neumann, Feb. 14, 1970; children: David Edward, Robert Steven. BA in Polit. Sci. and Econs., Macquarie U., Australia, 1974; MBA in Fin. and Mktg., U. New South Wales, Australia, 1977. Sales rep. Schering A.G., Australia, 1972-74; various positions Abbott Labs., 1974-84; pres. Adria Labs. div. Erbamont, Columbus, Ohio, 1984-88; chief oper. officer Erbamont N.V., Stamford, Conn., 1988—. Bd. dirs. Columbus Assn. Performing Arts, 1988—. Mem. Pharm. Mfrs. Assn., Am. Social Health Assn. (bd. dirs. 1987—), Young Presidents Orgn., Pvt. Pilots Assn. (Columbus chpt.), Capital Club. Office: Erbamont 1266 Main St Stamford CT 06902

ROBINSON, EARL JAMES, information systems educator, consultant; b. Wilmington, Del., Apr. 15, 1949; s. Harry and Minerva Ruth (James) R.; m. Karen Frances Smith, July 5, 1980; children—Ruth Frances, Sarah Rebecca. A.B., Davidson Coll., 1971; M.S., Bucknell U., 1973; Ph.D., U. Ga., 1977. Asst. prof. U. Ga., Athens, 1977-78, St. Mary's U., Halifax, N.S., 1978-81, assoc. prof., 1981-84, chmn., 1981-84; assoc. prof. St. Joseph's U., Phila., 1984—, chmn., 1984—; cons. Mgmt. Research Assn., Halifax, 1978-84; pres., cons. Earl J. Robinson, Ph.D. & Assocs., Bala Cynwyd, Pa., 1984—. Contbr. numerous articles to profl. jours. Recipient Golden M award St. Mary's U., 1981; grantee St. Joseph's U., 1985, St. Mary's U., 1983, Ashland Oil Corp., 1978, Fed. Aviation Adminstrn., 1978, NSF, 1978. Mem. Decision Scis. Inst., Am. Psychol. Assn., Internat. Bus. Schs. Computer Users' Group, Psychometric Soc., Sigma Phi Epsilon (social chmn. 1969-70), Sigma Xi. Republican. Episcopalian. Avocations: choral music, flying. Home: 150 Union Ave Bala Cynwyd PA 19004 Office: St Josephs U Dept Mgmt and Info Systems 5600 City Ave Philadelphia PA 19131

ROBINSON, EDWARD JOSEPH, food and consumer products company financial executive; b. White Plains, N.Y., May 12, 1940; s. Edward D.J. and Christine (Walsh) R.; m. Gail Lee Robinson, June 15, 1963; 1 son, Michael. B.B.A., Iona Coll., 1962. CPA, N.Y. Supr. Peat, Marwick, Mitchell, N.Y.C., 1963-70; exec. v.p. fin., chief fin. officer RJR Nabisco, Inc., Atlanta, 1987—; mem. So. adv. bd. Allendale Ins.; mem. fin. council AMA. Trustee Iona Coll.; mem. Conf. Bd.'s Council of Fin. Execs. Recipient Loftus award for Disting. Achievement Iona Coll., 1976. Mem. Am. Inst. CPS's, N.Y. Soc. CPA's. Republican. Clubs: Winged Foot Country (Mamaroneck, N.Y.); Metropolitan (N.Y.C.); Country of South, Atlanta Nat. Golf (Alpharetta, Ga.); Georgian, Capital City (Atlanta), Atlanta Nat. Golf. Home: 3642 Castlegate Dr NW Atlanta GA 30327 Office: RJR Nabisco Inc 300 Galleria Pkwy Atlanta GA 30339

ROBINSON, EDWARD TEMPLE, III, seed company executive; b. Omaha, Jan. 25, 1956; s. Edward T. and Donna Mae (Deffenbaugh) R.; m. Cheryl Ann Paustian, Dec. 29, 1979; children: Laurel, Jim, Scott. Student, U. Nebr., 1974-78. With J.C. Robinson Seed Co., Waterloo, Nebr., 1978—; mgr. sunflower product J.C. Robinson Seed Co., Waterloo, 1980-82, mgr. soybean product, 1982-86, v.p. mktg., 1986—, mem. exec. com., bd. dirs., 1983—; chmn. soybean com. Golden Harvest Seeds, Bloomington, Ill., mem. mktg. com., 1986—, mem. biotech. com., 1987—. Pres.'s Adv. Council U. Nebr., Lincoln, 1985—; v.p. Waterloo Jaycees, 1979-80. Mem. Am. Seed Trade Assn., Nat. Agrl. Mktg. Assn., GEMS Investment Club (pres. 1983-84). Republican. Presbyterian. Office: JC Robinson Seed Co N Hwy 64 and 3rd St Waterloo NE 68069

ROBINSON, FLORINE SAMANTHA, marketing professional; b. Massies Mill, Va., Feb. 4, 1935; d. John Daniel and Fannie Belle (Smith) Jackson; m. Frederick Robinson (div. 1973); children: Katherine, Theresa, Freda. BS, Morgan State U., 1976; postgrad., U. Balt., 1977-81, Liberty U., 1987. Writer, reporter Phila. Independent News, 1961-63; free lance writer, editor Balt., 1963-71; asst. mng. editor Williams & Wilkins Pubs. Inc., Balt, 1971-76; mktg. rep., then mktg. mgr. NCR Corp., Balt., 1977—; assoc. minister, trustee Christian Unity Temple, Balt., 1976—; bd. dirs. Armstrong & Bratcher, Inc., Balt. Editor: Stedman's Medical Dictionary, 1972; contbr. articles to profl. jours. Active PTA, Balt., 1963-65; bd. dirs. Howard Park Civic Assn., Balt., 1967—; leader, cons. Girl Scouts USA, 1970-73. Recipient Excellence in Research award Psi Chi, 1976. Mem. Mid-Atlantic Food Dealers Assn., Am. Soc. Notaries, Nat. Assn. Female Execs. Democrat. Club: Edelweiss. Lodge: Order Eastern Star. Home: 3126 Howard Park Ave Baltimore MD 21207

ROBINSON, FRANK WARREN, protective services professional; b. Corpus Christi, Tex., July 20, 1950; s. James William And Shirley (Hayes) R.; m. Shirley Wilson, June 5, 1971 (div. 1988); children: Jerry Don, Carey Leanne. BA in Polit. Sci., North Tex. State U., 1976. Cert. protection profl. Police officer Denton (Tex.) Police Dept., 1971-76; capt. adminstrn. dept. police No. Tex. State U., Denton, 1976-79; chief police City of West University Place, Tex., 1979-80, dir. pub. safety, 1980-82; dir. security Century Devel. Corp., Houston, 1982—; instr. Criminal Justice Ctr. U. Houston, 1981—, mem. adv. bds. criminal justice and loss prevention; chmn. Law Enforcement Minority Coalition U.S. Dept. Justice, Houston, 1980-81; expert witness security-related issues, Houston, 1987—. Mem. Am. Soc. for Indsl. Security (chmn. office and multi-residential bldg. com. 1986-88), Nat. Assn. Bus. and Ednl. Radio., Houston C. of C. (retail crime com. 1988—), Houston City Club. Republican. Office: Century Devel Corp 5 Greenway Pla Ste 1700 Houston TX 77046

ROBINSON, GEORGE RICHARD, construction executive; b. Steubenville, Ohio, Sept. 22, 1935; s. Thomas Arthur and Edna Catherine (Harrell) R.; m. Betty Lou Coleman, May 15, 1954 (dec. June 1962); children: George Thomas, Joyce Ellen; m. Bonita Margaret Kwiecinski, June 12, 1980; 1 child, Christopher John. BS, U. Steubenville, 1962; postgrad., Purdue U., 1965-66, Cleve. State U., 1967-69, U. Md., 1974-78. Registered profl. engr., Va., Md., D.C., Ohio, W.Va. Engr.-in-tng. Ohio Dept. of Hwys., New Philadelphia, 1955-61; project mgr., subcontract mgr. The H.K. Ferguson Co., Cleve., 1961-70; project mgr. Norair Engring. Corp., Washington, 1970-71; v.p. engring. Excavation-Construction Inc., Bladensburg, Md., 1971-78; v.p. MCI Constructors Inc., Springfield, Va., 1978—; pvt. practice civil engring., Woodridge, Va., 1978-88. With U.S. Army, 1953-55, Korea. Mem. NSPE, Am. Assn. Cost Engrs., Am. Concrete Inst., Assn. of Iron and Steel Engrs, Elks, Am. Legion. Republican. Episcopalian. Home: 5009 Bobcat Ct Woodbridge VA 22193 Office: MCI Constructors Inc 7649 Dynatech Ct Springfield VA 22152

ROBINSON, GERALD WILLIAM, II, financial executive; b. Saginaw, Mich., Oct. 22, 1947; s. Gerald William and Donna Elaine (Slinkard) R.; m. Diane Patricia Schmidt Schutt, June 19, 1969 (div. 1983); children: Pat, Jeff; m. Michaelynn Jean Rynd, July 17, 1983. BS in Bus., Cen. Mich. U., 1971, postgrad., 1971-73. CLU, cert. fin. planner. Dist. supr. Mut. Benefit Life Ins. Co., Saginaw, 1971-79; assoc. br. mgr. Mfrs. Fin. Services, Saginaw, 1979-83; pres. Strategic Fin. Systems, Saginaw, 1980-84; sr. v.p. mktg. Pvt. Ledger Fin. Services, San Diego, 1984-87; pres. Anchor Nat. Fin. Services, Phoenix, 1987—. Bd. dirs. Easter Seals, Saginaw, 1980-82. Served with USAR, 1971-77. Mem. Nat. Assn. Life Underwriters, Am. Soc. Chartered Life Underwriters, Internat. Assn. Fin. Planners. Club: Arrowhead Country (Glendale, Ariz.)(mem. adv. bd. 1988—). Office: Anchor Nat Fin Svcs Anchor Ctr 1 2201 E Camelback Rd Phoenix AZ 85016

ROBINSON, GLENN HATCH, gas mining executive; b. Cedar City, Utah, Apr. 2, 1950; s. Leon Durham and Louise (Hatch) R.; m. Bonnie Bradshaw, June 8, 1972; children: Colin, Erin, Quinn, Ryan. BS, Utah State U., 1973; MBA, U. Utah, 1974. Economist Mountain Fuel Supply Co., Salt Lake City, 1974-76, asst. mgr. planning, 1976-78, dir. corp. planning, 1978-80, mgr. corp. devel., 1980-85, v.p. mktg., 1985—. Mem. Am. Gas Assn., Pacific Coast Gas Assn. Republican. Office: Mountain Fuel Supply Co 180 E 100 S Salt Lake City UT 84139

ROBINSON, HAMILTON, JR., investment banker; b. New Haven, May 20, 1934; s. Hamilton and Nancy (Brereton) R.; m. Dorothy Fay (div. 1976); children: Gardner J.H., Victoria Anne; m. Roxana Barry, Feb. 20, 1976. BA, Princeton U., 1955; JD, Harvard U., 1960. Sr. v.p., head corp. fin. So-Gen Swiss Internat., N.Y.C., 1974-76; gen. ptnr. Bradford Assocs., N.Y.C., 1976-85, Hamilton Robinson & Co., N.Y.C., 1985—; bd. dirs. Galveston-Houston Co., DI Industries Inc., Yegen Fin. Group Inc. Mem. bd. Burden Ctr. for Aging, N.Y.C., 1983—; mem. fin. com. Katonah (N.Y.) Gallery, 1984—. Served with USNR, 1955-57. Mem. N.Y. State Bar Assn. Episcopalian. Clubs: Pilgrims, Links, Century Assn., River, N.Y. Yacht (all N.Y.C.). Office: Hamilton Robinson & Co Inc 30 Rockefeller Pla #3320 New York NY 10112

ROBINSON, HARRY NORRIS, finance and insurance company executive; b. Fairmont, W.Va., Mar. 19, 1926; s. Harry N. and Nelle (Rimstidt) R.; m. Janet Noelting, May 1, 1954; 1 child, Melinda. BSEE, Purdue U., 1949. CPCU. Sales rep. Credithrift Fin., Inc., Evansville, Ind., 1953-59, v.p., 1958-61, sr. v.p., 1961-83, pres., 1983—; mem. com. Am. Council Life Ins., Washington, 1986—. Bd. dirs. Evansville Philharm. Orch., 1980-82, Youth Service Bur., Evansville, 1980—, Evansville Mus. Arts and Scis., 1986—. With USN, 1944-46. Mem. Consumer Credit Ins. Assn. (chmn. bd. dirs.), Evansville Country Club, Evansville Petroleum Club. Republican. Presbyterian. Home: 421 Scenic Dr Evansville IN 47715 Office: Credithrift Fin Inc 601 NW 2d St Evansville IN 47708

ROBINSON, IRENE ROSE, financial accounting executive; b. Bklyn., Apr. 18, 1950; d. Wilbur Alfred and Mary Magdalene (Chorik) Wouters; B.A. in Econs., Queens Coll., 1976. Bus. rep. N.Y. Telephone Co., Queens, 1968-71; office mgr. C.S.T. Co., N.Y.C., 1971-72; gen. mgr. Interactive Market Systems, Inc., N.Y.C., 1972-76; v.p. fin. Stewart Capital Corp., N.Y.C., 1976-83; pres. Strategies for Growth Inc., Queens, 1983—; v.p. fin., chief fin. officer Access Capital Inc., N.Y.C., 1986—; asst. sec. Interactive Arbitrage Systems,

Inc., 1974-76; sec., treas. Atlantic Forest Products, Inc., 1980-83. Home: 219-72 64th Ave Bayside NY 11364 Office: 232 Madison Ave New York NY 10016

ROBINSON, IRWIN JAY, lawyer; b. Bay City, Mich., Oct. 8, 1928; s. Robert R. and Anne (Kaplan) R.; m. Janet Binder, July 7, 1957; children: Elizabeth Binder Robinson Schubiner, Jonathan Meyer, Eve Kimberly. AB, U. Mich., 1950; JD, Columbia U., 1953. Bar: N.Y. 1956. Assoc. Breed Abbott & Morgan, N.Y.C., 1955-58; asst. to ptnrs. Dreyfus & Co., N.Y.C., 1958-59; assoc. Greenbaum Wolff & Ernst, N.Y.C., 1959-65; ptnr. Greenbaum Wolff & Ernst, 1966-76; sr. ptnr. Rosenman & Colin, N.Y.C., 1976—; bd. dirs. Bernard Chaus, Inc., N.Y.C.; treas. Saarsteel, Inc., Whitestone, N.Y., 1970—; sec. Takara Toy Corp., N.Y.C., 1983—. Bd. dirs. Henry St. Settlement, N.Y.C., 1960-85, Nat. Jewish Welfare Bd., N.Y.C., 1967—, Philippine-Am. C. of C., 1970—, Am.-Asean Trade Council, Inc., N.Y.C., 1978—, Heart Research Found., 1988—. Served as sgt. U.S. Army, 1953-55. Mem. ABA, N.Y. State Bar Assn., Assn. Bar City N.Y., Internat. Bar Assn. Republican. Jewish. Clubs: Sunningdale Country (Scarsdale, N.Y.); Rockefeller Ctr. (N.Y.C.). Home: 4622 Grosvenor Ave Riverdale NY 10471 Office: Rosenman & Colin 575 Madison Ave New York NY 10022

ROBINSON, JAMES DIXON, III, corporate executive; b. Atlanta, Nov. 19, 1935; s. James Dixon Jr. and Josephine (Crawford) R.; m. Bettye Bradley (div.); children: Emily E. Robinson-Cook, James Dixon IV; m. Linda Gosden, July 27, 1984. BS, Ga. Inst. Tech., 1957; MBA, Harvard U., 1961; LHD (hon.), Spelman Coll., 1982; LLD (hon.), Adelphi U., 1982. Officer various depts. Morgan Guaranty Trust Co. of N.Y., N.Y.C., 1961-66, asst. v.p., staff asst. to chmn. bd. and pres., 1967-68; gen. partner corp. fin. dept. White, Weld & Co., 1968-70; exec. v.p. Am. Express Co., N.Y.C., 1970-75, pres., 1975-77, bd. dirs., 1975—, chmn. bd. dirs., chief exec. officer, 1977—; pres., chief exec. officer Am. Express Internat. Banking Corp., 1971-73; dir. Bristol-Myers Co., Coca Cola Co., Union Pacific Corp.; bd. dirs. Shearson Lehman Hutton Holdings, Inc.; chmn. adv. com. Trade Policy and Negotiations; chmn. N.Y.C. Partnership. Chmn. Meml. Hosp. for Cancer and Allied Diseases; vice chmn. bd. overseers, bd. mgrs. Meml. Sloan Kettering Cancer Ctr.; mem. council Rockefeller U.; vice chmn. bd. govs. United Way Am. Served to lt. USNR, 1957-59. Mem. Bus. Roundtable (co-chmn.), N.Y. C. of C. and Industry (dir., chmn.), Bus. Council (vice chmn.), Council Fgn. Relations. Clubs: Economic (N.Y.C.); Pilgrims of U.S. Office: Am Express Co Am Express Tower 200 Vesey St New York NY 10285-5100

ROBINSON, JAMES MORRIS, financial planner, consultant; b. Savannah, Ga., Oct. 26, 1952; s. James and Gladys (Stone) R.; m. Sandra Michelle Aaron, Aug. 8, 1987. BS in Mktg., DePaul U., 1980; cert., Coll. for Fin. Planning, Denver, 1984. Registered health underwriter, securities dealer. Insp. risk evaluation Hooper Info. Systems, Savannah, Ga., 1971-73; agt. AALIC, Savannah, 1973-76, Mut. of Omaha, Savannah, 1976-77, Mut. of Omaha Cos., 1980-81; sr. cons. Career Sales inst. Mut. of Omaha, 1982-83, sr. assoc. dir. Fund Mgmt. Co., 1983-87, mktg./tng. cons., 1988—; purchasing mgr., supr. Coffield Ungretti Harris and Slavin, Chgo., 1977-80; fin. cons., stockbroker Merrill Lynch, 1987-88. Unit commr. Mid-Am. council Boy Scouts Am., Omaha, 1982; vol. Jr. Achievement, Omaha, 1982-87. Republican. Methodist. Home: 11022 Lafayette Plaza #1722 Omaha NE 68154

ROBINSON, JOSEPH ALBERT, corporate executive; b. Kenton, Ohio, May 10, 1938; s. George Lowell and Georgia Eileen R.; m. Sharon R. Jolliff, May 17, 1964; children—Jeffrey Allen, Mark Joseph. B.B.A., U. Cin., 1961. C.P.A., Ohio. Audit mgr. Arthur Andersen & Co., C.P.A.s, Cleve., 1961-72; controller Standard Products Co., Cleve., 1972-76; v.p. fin. Standard Products Co., 1976—, dir., 1985—. Served with U.S. Army, 1961-62. Mem. Am. Inst. C.P.A.s, Fin. Execs. Inst., Ohio Soc. C.P.A.s. Methodist. Clubs: Union Cleve., Lakewood Country. Home: 575 Marygate St Bay Village OH 44140 Office: Standard Products Co 2130 W 110th St Cleveland OH 44102

ROBINSON, KENNETH, manufacturing executive; b. Steubenville, Ohio, Nov. 11, 1945; s. Hays and Burnetta (White) R.; m. Sara Hukill; children: Steven, Gregory, Lee. BS in Acctg., West Liberty State, 1972. Technician Nat. Steel Corp., Weirton, W.Va., 1966-68; accounts payable clk. Weirton Steel Corp., 1968-75, head clk., 1975-76, supr., 1976-78, property acct., 1978-84, risk mgr., 1984—; instr. community edn. class, W. Va., No. Community Coll., Weirton, 1979-82. Treas. Weirton First Meth. Ch., 1977—, Weirton Internat. Food & Arts Festival, 1985-87; fund raiser, Boy Scouts Am., Weirton, 1985; bd. dirs. fin. Pittsl. Conf. First Meth. Ch., 1987-88. Mem. Risk and Ins. Mgmt. Soc., 1985—. Club: Hall Hunt and Fishing (Weirton) (treas. 1987—). Office: Weirton Steel Corp 400 Three Springs Dr Weirton WV 26062

ROBINSON, KENNETH LEONARD, JR., trade association executive; b. Lynn, Mass., Feb. 14, 1929; s. Kenneth Leonard Sr. and Frances Ruth (Leighton) R.; m. Marie Louise Cormier, Sept. 1, 1951; children: Edward K., Elaine F., Ruth M., Doris A., Gordon M. BA, Boston Coll., 1950; MS, George Washington U., 1969. Commd. 2nd lt. USMC, 1950, commg. officer 3d bn., 1970; commdg. gen. Marine Corp. Base USMC, Camp Butler, Okinawa, 1977-79; commdg. gen. 3d Marine div. USMC, Okinawa, 1980; advanced through grades to maj. gen. USMC, 1979; commdg. gen. Marine Corp. Base USMC, Camp Pendleton, Calif., 1980-83; ret. USMC, 1983; pres., chief exec. officer Nat. Assn. Fed. Credit Unions, Washington, 1984—; bd. dirs. San Diego (Calif.) Navy Fed. Credit Union, San Diego, Calif., 1981-83, Washington, 1975-77. Columnist on fin. topics for trade mags.; contbr. articles to trade publs. Mem. Far East Coun. Boy Scouts Am., Okinawa, 1977-80, San Diego Coun., 1980-83. Recipient Golden Eagle award Far East Coun. Boy Scouts Am., 1980, Silver Beaver award San Diego Coun., 1982. Mem. Am. Soc. Assn. Execs., Greater Washington Soc. Assn. Execs., USMC Hist. Soc. (bd. dirs. 1987—), chmn. audit com. 1987—), Army-Navy, Exchequer (Washington). Republican. Roman Catholic. Home: 2538 N Vermont St Arlington VA 22207 Office: Nat Assn Fed Credit Unions 3138 N 10th St Arlington VA 22201

ROBINSON, LOWELL WARREN, financial services executive; b. White Plains, N.Y., Jan. 20, 1949; s. Joseph S. and Belle V. Robinson; m. Leila Heckman, Sept. 10, 1983; children: Sarah Lisa, Abigail Lindsay. BA in Econs., U. Wis., 1971; MBA in Fin., Harvard U., 1973. Various fin. positions Gen. Foods Corp., White Plains, 1973-79, contr. new product devel., 1979-81, mgr. strategic bus. analysis, 1981-83; dir. fin. and ops. Mars, Inc., Houston, 1983-86; asst. contr. Citibank Consumer Svcs. Group, Internat., N.Y.C., 1986, contr., 1987-88; v.p., chief fin. officer global ins. and capital investments Citibank, N.Y.C., 1988—. Bd. dirs. Houston Grand Opera, 1982-83; fund raiser Harvard Bus. Sch., Cambridge, Mass., 1989; vol. Volunteer Urban Cons. Group. Grantee Rockefeller Found., 1972. Mem. Harvard Bus. Sch. Club, Planning Forum. Home: 470 W End Ave New York NY 10024 Office: Citibank 153 E 53rd St New York NY 10043

ROBINSON, MARK LEIGHTON, oil company executive, petroleum geologist, horse farm owner; b. San Bernardino, Calif., Aug. 4, 1927; s. Ernest Guy and Florence Iola (Lemmon) R.; m. Jean Marie Ries, Feb. 8, 1954; children: Francis Willis, Mark Ries, Paul Leighton. AB cum laude in Geology, Princeton U., 1950; postgrad. Stanford U., 1950-51. Geologist Shell Oil Co., Billings, Mont., Rapid City, S.D., Denver, Midland, Tex., 1951-56, dist. geologist, Roswell, N.Mex., 1957-60, div. mgr., Roswell, N.Mex., 1961-63, Jackson, Miss., 1964-65, Bakersfield, Calif., 1967-68, mgr. exploration econs., N.Y.C., 1969; mgmt. advisor BIPM (Royal Dutch Shell Oil Co.), The Hague, The Netherlands, 1966; pres., chmn. bd. dirs. Robinson Resource Devel. Co., Inc., Roswell, 1970—. Campaign chmn. Chaves County Republican Com., Roswell, 1962; mem. alumni schs. com. Princeton U., 1980—. Served with USNR, 1945-46. Mem. Roswell Geol. Soc. (trustee 1972), Am. Assn. Petroleum Geologists, Stanford U. Earth Scientists Assn., Yellowstone Bighorn Research Assn., Am. Horse Shows Assn., SAR, Sigma Xi. Episcopalian. Discovered Lake Como oil field, Miss., 1971, McNeal oil field, Miss., 1973, North Deer Creek Gas Field, Mont., 1983, Bloomfield East Oil Field, Mont., 1986. Home: Rt 1 Box 31D Roswell NM 88201 Office: Robinson Resource Devel Co Inc PO Box 1227 Roswell NM 88201

ROBINSON, MICHAEL ANDREW, venture capitol company executive; b. Springfield, Ohio, Jan. 4, 1949; s. Andrew Walter and Shirley Ann (Cooper) R.; m. Cheryl Jean Madison, Dec. 6, 1952; 1 child, Ellis Andrew. BS in Indsl. Rels., Cornell U., 1975. Mgmt. trainee Bank One, Dayton, Ohio, 1975-76; asst. mgr. Bank One, Kettering, Ohio, 1976-77, Salem Mall, Ohio, 1977-78; mng. oficer Bank One, Germantown-Gettysburg, Ohio, 1978-80, Dayton Mall, 1980-81; bus. devel. oficer Bank One, Dayton, 1981-84; cons. Ctr. City MESBIC, Inc., Dayton, 1984, pres., bd. dirs., 1984—; bd. dirs. Day-Med. Health Maintenance Plan, Inc., Hooven-Dayton Corp., Dayton Area Health Plan, Inc., Johnsons Communications Inc. Mem. Nat. Assn. Investment Cos. (legis. com. 1986—, membership com. 1986-87). Office: Center City MESBIC Inc 40 S Main St Ste 762 Dayton OH 45402

ROBINSON, MORRIS R., publishing executive, researcher; b. Chgo., Dec. 23, 1928; s. Harry and Frances (Brown) R.; m. Betty Rene Kaiser, Oct. 18, 1953; children: Holly, Peggy. BS, U. Ill., 1951; MBA, DePaul U., 1954. Research mgr. Indsl. Pubs., Chgo., 1955-57, Standard Rate and Data Service, Glenview, Ill., 1957-60; v.p. research Cahners Pub. Co., Des Plaines, Ill., 1960—; adj. prof. bus. Ill. Inst. Tech., 1955-62; cons. in field. Contbr. articles to profl. jours. With U.S. Army, 1946-47, CBI. Mem. Am. Bus. Pubs., Advt. Research Found. Jewish. Office: Cahners Pub 1350 E Touhy Des Plaines IL 60018

ROBINSON, PETER CLARK, general management executive; b. Brighton, Mass., Nov. 16, 1938; s. Richard and Mary Elizabeth (Cooper) R.; m. Sylvia Phyllis Petchek, Aug. 26, 1961 (div. 1973); children: Marc Louis, Nicholas Daniel, Andrea Suzanne.; m. Sarah Lingham, Jan. 1, 1984. B.S. in Fgn. Service, Georgetown U., 1961; M.B.A., Babson Inst., 1963; AMP, Harvard U., 1986. Asst. supt. prodn. Mass. Broken Stone Co., Weston, 1961-62; night shift supt. Mass. Broken Stone Co., 1962-65, v.p. ops., 1968, v.p., 1969-75, 85—, also dir.; gen. supt. Berlin Stone Co., 1965-67, v.p. ops., 1968; v.p. Holden Trap Rock Co., to 1975, also dir.; pres. J.P. Burroughs & Sons, Inc. aggregate div. subs. Blount, Inc., Saginaw, Mich. and Montgomery, Ala., 1975-81; v.p. corp. mktg. Blount, Inc., Montgomery, 1978-79, v.p. corp. planning and mktg., 1979—; group exec., pres. Blount Agri/Indsl. Corp., 1984—; mem. The Planning Forum; bd. dirs. Berlin Stone, 1980—. Mem. Montgomery Civic Ballet. Mem. Nat. Stone Assn. (dir., exec. com., chmn. govt. affairs com., chmn. bd.), Am. Mktg. Assn., Am. Mgmt. Assn., Am. Soc. Agrl. Engrs., Newcomen Soc., Engring. Soc. Detroit, Pres. Assn., SME-AIME. Clubs: Montgomery Country, Capital City (Montgomery), Harvard (Boston). Office: 4520 Executive Park Dr Montgomery AL 36116-1602

ROBINSON, RICHARD GARY, management consultant; b. Oakland, Calif., Aug. 17, 1931; s. William Albert and Inez Wilhelmina (Zetterblad) R.; B.B.A., U. Minn., 1955; grad. Indsl. Coll. Armed Forces, 1972; M. Internat. Mgmt., Am. Grad. Sch. Internat. Mgmt., 1980; m. Lorraine Mary Deshaies, Nov. 13, 1965 (dec.); children—Elisabeth Claudine (dec.), Christopher Paul. CPA, Colo.; cert. mgmt. cons. Commd. 2d lt. U.S. Air Force, 1956, advanced through grades to maj.; dir. radar ops. tactical air warfare, comdr. strategic missile operation and maintenance functions, project mgr., dir. mgmt. info. systems Dept. Def. activities, S.E. Asia; ret., 1976; mgmt. cons., Colorado Springs, Colo., 1976—; pres. Bus. Devel. Specialists; dir., chief fin. officer Unique Equipment Co.; bd. dirs. United Air Freight Ltd.; mem. adj. faculty Embry Riddle Aero. U., Luke AFB, Ariz.; adj. prof. econs. and bus. Colorado Springs br. Regis Coll.; U. So. Colo. Mem. bus. adv. council Colo. Internat. Trade Office. Decorated Meritorious Service medal with oak leaf cluster, AF Commendation medal with 2 oak leaf clusters. Mem. Internat. Trade Assn. Colo. (pres.), Am. Mktg. Assn., Armed Forces Communications and Electronics Assn., Am. Mgmt. Assn., Nat. Assn. Accts., Inst. Mgmt. Cons., Assn. Polit. Risk Analysts, N.Am. Soc. Corp. Planning. Lutheran. Home: 1610 McKay Way Colorado Springs CO 80915 Office: 2340 Robinson St Ste 113 PO Box 2714 Colorado Springs CO 80901

ROBINSON, RICHARD GRIER, JR., retail executive; b. Charleston, S.C., June 11, 1933; s. Richard Grier and Ethel (Shepard) R.; m. alice Stewart, June 12, 1965; children: Alice Stewart, Richard Grier III. BS, Davidson Coll., 1955; MS, NYU, 1958. Mgmt. trainee Belk Buying Office, N.Y.C., 1958; buyer Belk-Beery, Wilmington, N.C., 1959-60; buyer Belk-Simpson, Laurens, Greenville and Easley, S.C., 1961, Greenville, S.C., 1964-73, Easley, S.C., 1964—; bd. dirs. Belk-Robinson, Charleston. Bd. dirs. Belk-Simpson Audit League; deacon First Presbyn. Ch., also pres. men's Bible class; pres. Beaux Arts Greenville. Recipient Service award Nat. Found March of Dimes, Greenville, 1970; named Crafted in Pride in U.S.A. Merchant, S.C. Textile Assn., 1986. Mem. Town & Country Mchts. Assn. (pres.), Easley C. of C. (v.p. bd. dirs. 1983), Davidson Alumni Assn. (pres.), St. Andrews Soc. Charleston, Kiwanis (bd. dirs. 1980-84, 86-87, Outstanding Service award 1987), Greenville Country Club. Republican. Home: 4 Thornwood Ln Greenville SC 29605 Office: Belk Simpson Co PO Box 859 Town & Country Shopping Ctr Easley SC 29640

ROBINSON, ROB, publishing company executive; b. Chgo., June 17, 1955; d. Joseph Ross and Charlotte Evelyn (Harchanko) R. BA, No. Ill. U., 1977. Account exec. Meldrum & Fewsmith, Inc., Chgo., 1978-81; sales rep. Jack O'Grady, Inc., Chgo., 1981-82, Leigh Communications, Inc., Chgo., 1982; sales rep. Midwest region Modern Metals Pub. Co., Chgo., 1982-83; regional sales mgr. Morgan-Grampian Pub. Co., Chgo., 1983-86, Cahners Pub. Co., Des Plaines, Ill., 1986—; bd. dirs. Am. Advt. Fedn. 6th Dist. Mem. Electronic Young Tigers, Women in Electronics (bd. dirs. 1985—), Bus. and Profl. Advt. Assn. (co-chmn., benefit officer, bd. dirs.), Women's Ad Club of Chgo. (co-chmn. ADDY com. 1982—, co-chmn. ednl. benefit 1980—, officer, bd. dirs.), Surface Mount Tech. Assn. (officers, bd. dirs.), Sigma Kappa (1st v.p. 1976-77, chpt. historian 1975-76). Republican. Roman Catholic. Clubs: Chgo. Area Runners Assn.; The Athletic Congress. Home: 200 N Arlington Heights Rd Apt #427 Arlington Heights IL 60004 Office: Cahners Pub Co 1350 E Touhy Ave Des Plaines IL 60018

ROBINSON, ROBERT ARMSTRONG, pension fund executive; b. Waterbury, Conn., Sept. 11, 1925; s. Robert and Ethel (Armstrong) R.; m. D. Ann Harding, June 7, 1947; 1 child, Gayllis Robinson Ward. A.B. magna cum laude, Brown U., 1950, M.A., 1952; postgrad., U. Ill., 1954-55; Litt. D., Episcopal Theol. Sem. Ky., 1971; D.C.L., U. South, 1972; LL.D., Nashotah House, Oconomowoc, Wis. Instr. English Brown U., 1950-53; instr. English, asst. prof. rhetoric U. Ill., 1953-56; trust officer Colonial Bank & Trust Co., Waterbury, 1956-63; v.p., trust officer Colonial Bank & Trust Co., 1963-65, sr. trust officer, 1965-66; v.p., sec. Ch. Pension Fund and Affiliates, Ch. Life Ins. Corp., Ch. Ins. Co., Ch. Agy. Corp., Ch. Hymnal Corp., 1966-67, exec. v.p., 1967-68, pres., dir., 1968—; dir. Seabury Press, Inc., Mariners Instl. Funds, Inc., Mariner Tax Free Instl. Fund, UST Master Funds, Morehouse-Barlow Co., Inc., Mariner Funds Trust, Mariner Equity Trust, Pigmy Corp., U.S.T. Master Money Funds, Rosiclare Lead and Flourspar Mining Co., others; cons. to exec. dir. Pension Benefit Guaranty Corp. Trustee Hillspeak, Eureka Springs, Ark., Canterbury Cathedral Trust in Am., Hoosac Sch., Washington Nat. Cathedral, Nashotah Theol. Sem., Wis., H.B. and F.K. Bugher Found., Living Church Found.; mem. exec. com. N.Y. councils Boy Scouts Am., Ch. Pensions Conf.; mem. econ. adv. bd. Columbia U. Grad. Sch. Bus. Adminstrn. Served with inf. AUS, 1943-46. Decorated Bronze Star, Purple Heart with oak leaf cluster, Knights of Malta, Order St. John. Mem. Conn. Bankers Assn. (v.p., head trust div.), Am. Numis. Assn., Newcomen Soc., Phi Beta Kappa. Republican. Episcopalian (vestryman). Clubs: St. Andrew's Soc. (N.Y.C.), Brown (N.Y.C.), Union League (N.Y.C.), Church (N.Y.C.), Country of New Canaan, Athenaeum (London), Pilgrims, Union, Met. (Washington), Yeaman's Hall (Charleston, S.C.). Home: 251 Laurel Rd New Canaan CT 06840 Office: 800 2d Ave New York NY 10017

ROBINSON, ROBERT BLACQUE, association executive; b. Long Beach, Calif., Apr. 24, 1927; s. Joseph LeRoi and Frances Hansel R.; m. Susan Amelia Thomas, Jan. 21, 1960; children: Victoria, Shelly, Blake, Sarah. Student, Oreg. State Coll., 1946; BA, UCLA, 1950; student, U. Hawaii. Partner, Pritchard Assocs. (Mgmt. Cons.), Honolulu, 1956-58; asst. dir. Econ. Planning and Coordination Authority, Hawaii, 1959; dep. dir. dept. econ. devel. State of Hawaii, 1960-63; asst. mgr. Pacific Concrete and Rock Co., Ltd., Honolulu, 1963-66, exec. v.p. and gen. mgr., 1966-68, pres. and gen. mgr., 1968-75; chmn. Pacific Concrete and Rock Co., Ltd., 1976-77; pres. C. of C. of Hawaii, Honolulu, 1977—. Bd. govs. Hawaii Employers Council, 1969-74, mem. exec. com., 1969-74, vice chmn., 1973-74; bd. dirs. Pacific Aerospace Mus., 1982-86; mem. Hawaii Tourism Conf., 1977—, chmn., 1981-82; bd. dirs. Aloha United Fund, 1970-76, sec., 1972, v.p., 1973-76; bd. dirs. Oahu Devel. Conf., 1970-75; treas., bd. dirs. Crime Stoppers Hawaii, 1981—; mem. Hawaii Joint Council on Econ. Edn., 1985—; bd. dirs. Jr. Achievement Hawaii, 1967-73, pres., 1969; bd. dirs. Hawaii Ednl. Council, 1974-75, Health and Community Services Council Hawaii, 1982-84; mem. exec. com. Hawaii Conv. Ctr. Council, 1984—, Interagency Energy Conservation Council, State of Hawaii, 1978—; trustee Cen. Union Ch., 1983-86; bd. dirs. Waikiki Improvement Assn. Inc., 1986—; mem. Ctr. for Tropical and Subtropical Aquacultute industry Adv. Coun., 1987—; chmn. Mayor's Adv. Com. on Pacific Nations Ctr., 1988—. Lt. comdr. USNR, 1945-46, ret. Mem. Japan-Am. Conf. of Mayors and C. of C. Pres. (mem. Am. exec. com. 1974—ing mem.), Am. Soc. Assn. Execs. (past dir. Hawaii chpt.), Hawaii Execs. Council (found. , Young Pres. Assn. (past mem.), Aloha Soc. Assn. Execs., C. of C. Hawaii (dir. 1972-75, chmn. 1975), Council of Profit Sharing Industries (past dir. Hawaii sect.), Cement and Concrete Products Industry of Hawaii (pres. 1968), Hawaii Mfrs. Assn. (past dir.), Navy League of U.S. (Hawaii council), Engring. Assn. Hawaii, Pacific Club, Rotary, Sigma Chi. Home: 1437 Kalaepohaku St Honolulu HI 96816 Office: C of C Hawaii 735 Bishop St Honolulu HI 96813

ROBINSON, ROBERT JAMES, computer company executive; b. Richland Center, Wis., Jan. 4, 1935; s. Walter D. and Pearl B. (Bresee) R.; m. Faye F. Scherbarth, April 25, 1958; children: Wayne, Warren, Holly. BS, U. Wis., 1957; MS, Marquette U., 1964. Programmer analyst A.C. Sparkplug Co., Milw., 1957-59; computing ctr. dir. Marquette U., Milw., 1959-66; computing ctr. dep. dir. U. Kans., Lawrence, 1966-68; computing ctr. dir. U. Neb., Omaha, 1968-71, SUNY, Albany, 1971-81; sr. v.p. tech. Key Corp., Albany, 1981-85; bd. dirs. Key Services Corp., Albany, 1983-85, Key Mortgage Co., Albany, 1983-85; exec. v.p. Key Services Corp., Albany, 1983-85; pres. Cacheco, Albany, 1985—; cons. Kuwait Inst. Sci. Research, 1979, AT&T Corp., 1981, Renasselaer (N.Y.) Poly. Inst., 1988, SUNY, Albany, 1988; chmn. bd., chief exec. officer Upstate Computing Corp., 1981-84; lectr. various univs. in Kuwait, Peoples Republic China, Europe and U.S. Contbr. numerous articles to profl. jours. Bd. mem. Albany Symphony Orch., 1982-85, EDUCOM, 1974-78, EDUNET, 1976-78. Served to maj., A.N.G., 1953-81. Recipient Author of Yr. award, 1980. Mem. Nat. Assn. Corp. Dirs., Assn. for Computing Machinery. Democrat. Lutheran. Home: 22 Locust Ln Clifton Park NY 12065 Office: Cacheco PO Box 2190 Clifton Park NY 12065

ROBINSON, RONALD JAMES, petroleum engineer; b. Pueblo, Colo., Mar. 10, 1946; s. James Claude and Doris Loraine Robinson; B.S. in Math. and Physics, So. Colo. State Coll., 1968; M.S. in Physics, Baylor U., Waco, Tex., 1971; Ph.D. in Petroleum Engring., Tex. A&M U., 1974; m. Bonnie Lynn Martin, Aug. 31, 1968; children—Kevin James, Kyle Bryant, Kurt David. With Getty Oil Co., 1973-78, dist. reservoir engr., Bakersfield, Calif., 1975-78; mgr. thermal recovery Grace Petroleum Corp., Oklahoma City, 1978-79; sr. cons. INTERCOMP Resource Devel. and Engring., Houston, 1979-80; supr. thermal research Getty Oil Co., Houston, 1980-81; spl. projects coordinator Getty Research Ctr., Houston, 1981-84; mgr. reservoir engring. research Texaco, Inc., 1984—; chmn. RBR Investments, 1988—. NASA fellow, 1968. Mem. Can. Inst. Mining, Soc. Profl. Well Log Analysts, Soc. Petroleum Engrs. (dir.), Scientists Research Soc. North Am., Greater Houston C. of C. (mem. chmn.'s club 1987—), Sigma Xi. Club: Kiwanis. Author papers in field. Office: PO Box 770070 Houston TX 77215

ROBINSON, RONALD JOHN, oil and gas executive; b. Los Angeles, Oct. 31, 1931; s. John Patrick and Florence (Yarrow) R.; m. Dianna Natalie Lebrecht, May 15, 1976; children: Poleete Sue, Colette Elizabeth. Student, Victor Valley Coll., 1958-61, LaSalle U., 1962-67. V.p. Carwood Col., Big Bear Lake, Calif., 1967-70; pres. MarinaVille Corp., Boulder City, Nev., 1970-72, United Gen. Corp., Boulder City, 1972-74, Nev. Exchange Counselors, Las Vegas, 1974-82, Capital Morgage Corp., Las Vegas, 1982-85, NECCO Inc. (formerly Symmar), Las Vegas, 1985—; dir. Cert. Capital Correspondent, Nev., Fin. Holdings Corp., Capital Ins. Co., Necco Investments Hong Kong. Contbr. articles to profl. jours. Served to sgt. U.S.A.F., 1950-54, Korea. Mem. Soc. Exchange Counselors, Nat. Assn. Realtors. Republican. Christian Scientist. Lodge: Mason (master 1967-68). Office: Necco Inc 4220 S Maryland Pkwy #201 Las Vegas NV 89119

ROBINSON, RONALD MICHAEL, healthcare company executive, financial consultant; b. N.Y.C., May 1, 1942; s. Arthur John and Matilda (Siegel) R.; m. Mary Jane Reemelin, Feb. 25, 1972; children—Scott Edward, Elizabeth Drew. B.S., Ohio State U., 1964; M.B.A., Wharton Grad. Sch., U. Pa., 1966. C.P.A., Pa. Fin. mgr. Am. Airlines, Inc., N.Y.C., 1969-72; mgmt. cons. Coopers & Lybrand, Phila., 1973-75; pres. Robinson Assocs., Inc., Paoli, Pa., 1975-81; dir. fin. and adminstr., chief fin. officer Decision Scis. Corp., Jenkintown, Pa., 1981-82; v.p. fin., chief fin. officer Presbyn. Homes, Inc., Camp Hill, Pa., 1982—. Mem. Carlisle (Pa.) Regional Med. Ctr., Maxicare (Pa.) Adv. Bd. Mem. Am. Inst. C.P.A.s, Pa. Inst. C.P.A.s, Health Care Fin. Mgmt. Assn., Fin. Execs. Inst., Pa. Assn. Non-Profit Homes for Aging. Lodges: Masons, Rotary. Home: 243 S Hanover St Carlisle PA 17013 Office: Presbyn Homes Inc 1217 Slate Hill Rd Camp Hill PA 17011

ROBINSON, RUSSELL RAY, medical equipment company executive; b. Calgary, Alta., Can., Oct. 7, 1952; s. Duncan Burdette and Juanita (Williams) R.; m. Barbara Kay Diehl, Dec. 7, 1974; children: Heather Leigh, Dana Michelle, Grant Russell, Quinn Marie. BBA, Metro. Community Coll., Omaha, 1988. Mgr. distbn. ctr. Richmond Gorman, Omaha, 1977-79; mgr. shipping Lozier Corp., Omaha, 1979-80; mgr. warehouse Field Paper Co., 1980-84; supr. customer service Picker Internat., Omaha, 1984-85, mgr. dist. ops., 1985-87; mgr. dist. ops. Picker Internat., Detroit, 1987—. Mem. parent adv. com. Brighton Pub. Sch. Dist. Maj. Army N.G., 1972—. Mem. N.G. Officers Assn., Nebr. Officers Assn. (bd. govs. 1980-84). Republican. Lutheran. Home: 8789 Maltby Brighton MI 48116 Office: Picker Internat 41180 Vincenti Ct Novi MI 48050

ROBINSON, SAMUEL L., wholesale grocery company executive. With Super Food Services, Inc., Dayton, 1972—, merchandising mgr., then div. mgr., sr. v.p. Ohio ops., now pres., chief operating officer. Office: Super Food Svcs Inc 3185 Elbee Rd Dayton OH 45439 *

ROBINSON, STANLEY LAURENCE, health care executive, engineer; b. Saco, Maine, Aug. 24, 1922; s. David Edward and Sara Ruth (Leavitt) R.; m. Lois Sylvia Bobin, June 20, 1948; children: Rebecca, Fredric Leslie. BS, Syracuse U., 1948; MS, Rensselaer Poly. Inst., 1963. Registered profl. engr., N.Y. Automation engr. Beechnut-Lifesavers, Canajoharie, N.Y., 1957-70; mgr. prodn. TEK Hughes, Watervliet, N.Y., 1960-69; v.p. ops. Devro, Inc., Somerville, N.J., 1969-74; v.p. internat. tech. ops. Johnson & Johnson Internat., New Brunswick, N.J., 1974—. Author: Automated Inspection, 1988. With USNR, 1944-46. Mem. NSPE, AAAS, Am. Mgmt. Assn., N.Y. Acad. Sci., Machine Vision Assn. (mem. lit. adv. bd.), Soc. Mfg. Engrs. (mem. lit. adv. bd.), Masons. Office: Johnson & Johnson Internat One Johnson & Johnson Pla New Brunswick NJ 08933-5900

ROBINSON, STEPHEN MICHAEL, applied mathematician, educator; b. Columbus, Ohio, Apr. 12, 1942; s. Arthur Howard and Mary Elizabeth (Coffin) R.; m. Chong-Suk Han, May 10, 1968; children: Diana Marie, James Andrew. B.A., U. Wis., 1962, Ph.D., 1971; M.S., NYU, 1963. Adminstr. U. Wis.-Madison, 1969-72, asst. prof., 1972-75, assoc. prof., 1975-79, prof. indsl. engring. and computer scis., 1979—, chmn. dept. indsl. engring., 1981-84; cons. various agys. Dept. Def., 1971-86; cons. Battelle Meml. Labs., Columbus, 1980-81. Editor: Math. of Ops. Research, 1981-86; assoc. editor: Jour. Ops. Research, 1974-86, Mathematical Programming, 1986—; bd. editors Annals of Ops. Research, 1984—; contbr. numerous articles to profl. jours. Trustee Village of Shorewood Hills, Wis., 1974-76, mem. fin. com. , 1973-87. Served to capt. U.S. Army, 1963-69, Korea, Vietnam. Decorated Legion of Merit; decorated Bronze Star, Air Medal, Army Commendation medal with 2 oak leaf clusters. Mem. Ops. Research Soc. Am., Inst. Mgmt. Scis., Inst. Indsl. Engrs., Soc. for Indsl. and Applied Math. Clubs: Madison. Home: 1014 University Bay Dr Madison WI 53705-2251 Office: Dept Indsl Engring U Wis 1513 University Ave Madison WI 53706

ROBINSON, WARREN LOWE, utilities executive; b. Logan, Utah, Apr. 11, 1950; s. Floyd Comish and Grace (Lowe) R.; m. Ann Decker, May 21, 1977 (div. Dec. 1981); 1 child, Stephanie; m. Joan Cunningham, June 17, 1983; children: Jennifer, John. BBA, Brigham Young U., 1974; MBA, Boise

State U., 1976; cert., Stanford U., 1985. Fin. analyst Intermountain Gas Co., Boise, 1976-77, dir. budgets and fin. planning, 1977-79, mgr. planning services, 1979-80, asst. to pres., 1980-81; v.p., treas., chief fin. officer Great Falls (Mont.) Gas Co., 1981-87, sr. v.p., chief fin. officer, 1987—; pres., co-founder bd. dirs. Mont. Overthrust Energy Found., Great Falls, 1983-87; v.p., treas., co-founder Great Falls Capital Corp., 1984-87; mgr. corp. devel. MDU Resources Group Inc. Commr. Garden City, Idaho, 1981. Served with N.G., 1968-75. Mem. Stanford U. Alumni Assn. Republican. Mormon. Lodge: Rotary (pres. Great Falls chpt. 1985-86, bd. dirs. 1985-87). Home: 1909 N Grandview Ln Bismarck ND 58501 Office: Great Falls Gas Co 2 1st Ave S Great Falls MT 59401

ROBINSON, WILLIAM WALTER, restaurateur; b. Lynn, Mass., July 29, 1919; s. Donald Chase and Elizabeth (Wroughton) R.; married, 1950; children: Christopher, Merriam, Barnaby, Auguste, Peter, Keono, Matthew, Malia. BS, Northeastern U., Boston, 1942; postgrad., Harvard U., 1943. Commd. ensign USN, 1935, advanced through grades to rear adm., 1970, ret., 1970; pres. World Wide Distbrs., Inc., Honolulu, 1974-80, Elima Prodns., Inc., Honolulu, 1983-85, Windows of Hawaii, Inc., Honolulu, 1984—; pres. Waialae Petroleum, Inc., Honolulu, 1986—; pres. bd. dirs. nat. council Northeastern U., 1977—. State rep. U.S. Nat. Olympic Com., Washington, D.C., 1970-74; commr. Hawaii Volleyball Assn., Honolulu, 1970-78; chmn. bd. dirs. Honolulu YMCA, 1977-80; pres. Hawaii Aquarium Soc., 1972. Recipient Nat. Volleyball Leader award U.S. Volleyball Assn., 1972; Hawaii State Father of Yr., Hawaii C. of C., 1971. Mem. Armed Forces Recreation Council (chmn. 1978-84), Hawaii Restaurant Assn. (bd. dirs. 1987—), Hawaii World Trade Assn. (pres. 1979-80), Hawaii Assn. Sales Reps. (pres. 1970-72), Entrepreneurs of Hawaii, Inc. (treas. 1980-84). Club: Variety of Hawaii (treas. 1980-82). Home: 3054 Puiwa Ln Honolulu HI 96817 Office: Windows of Hawaii Inc 1441 Kapiolani Blvd Honolulu HI 96814

ROBINSON, WILLIE EDWARD, law educator, consultant; b. Harrisburg, Pa., Feb. 22, 1952; s. Hazel and Mamie (Mingo) R.; m. Brenda Twyner, Sept. 20, 1980; children—Bryant Francis, Alexandra Rosemary. BA, Yale U., 1974; JD, U. Va., 1977. Bar: Ga. 1977, U.S. Dist. Ct. (no. dist.) Ga. 1978, U.S. Ct. Appeals (5th cir.) 1978, U.S. Ct. Appeals (11th cir.) 1982, U.S. Supreme Ct. 1983. Assoc. Powell, Goldsteinet al, Atlanta, 1977-80, Parks, Jackson, et al, Atlanta, 1980-81; adj. prof. law Woodrow Wilson U., Atlanta, 1980-81; asst. prof. law Emory U., Atlanta, 1981-87; vis. asst. prof. sch. law U. Va., Charlottesville, 1984-85; of counsel Sumner & Hewes, Atlanta, 1983-87, Rogers & Hardin, Atlanta, 1987-88; v.p. CharLee Homes Inc., Atlanta, 1980—; pres. Select Sports Profls., Inc., 1987—; ptnr. Robinson & Gilner, 1989—; spl. advisor Nat. Bar Assn., Washington, 1984—. Contbr. articles to profl. jours. Chmn. Joint Com. to Study Standard of Need AFDC Payments, Atlanta, 1984; v.p. Residential Care Facilities for Elderly of Fulton County, Atlanta, 1983. Mem. Gate City Bar Assn. (sec. 1979, pres.-elect 1988, pres. 1989), Atlanta Bar Assn., Nat. Bar Assn., Order of Coif., Handlers Ltd. Club (Atlanta), Atlanta City Club. Methodist. Home: 228 Peachtree Hollow Ct Box 23 Atlanta GA 30328 Office: 138 Peachtree St NW Atlanta GA 30303

ROBISON, JAMES EVERETT, business consultant; b. Alfred, N.D., Nov. 22, 1915; s. John J. and Myrtle (Klundt) R.; m. Jeanette Hoffman, June 6, 1942 (dec.); 1 child, Martha Ann Davies. A.B., U. Minn., 1938; M.B.A., Harvard U., 1940; Sc. D. (hon.), Suffolk U., 1968. Sales dept. Nashua Mfg. Co., N.Y.C., 1940-46, Textron, Inc., N.Y.C., 1947-53; chief textile br. OPS, Washington, 1951; pres., chief exec. officer, dir. Indian Head, Inc., N.Y.C., 1953-67; chmn. bd., chief exec. officer Indian Head, Inc., 1967-72, chmn. fin. com., 1971-76; pres. Lonsdale Enterprises, Inc., 1976—; bd. dirs. Houbigant, Inc. Mem. com. univ. resources Harvard U., 1966-69; vis. com. Grad. Sch. Bus. Adminstrn., 1966-72, 73-79; chmn. bd. Assos. Harvard Bus. Sch., 1968-70, bd. dirs. 1988—; trustee Air Force Aid Soc., 1968—, fin. com., 1969—; bd. dirs. Bus. Com. for Arts, 1973-80; trustee Com. Econ. Devel., 1965-74, Calif. Inst. Tech., 1970—; vice chmn. Pres.'s Council Sch. of Bus. U. Vt. Served to maj. USAAF, 1942-46. Decorated D.F.C., Air Medal with three oak leaf clusters; recipient Distinguished Service award Harvard Bus. Sch. Assn., 1969; Outstanding Alumni award U. Minn., 1974. Mem. Conf. Bd., Harvard Bus. Sch. Assn. (exec. council 1968-71), Am. Textile Mfrs. Inst. (dir. 1961-64), Soaring Soc. Am., U.S. C.of C., Air Force Res. Assn., Phi Delta Theta. Clubs: Harvard, Racquet and Tennis, Harvard Bus. Sch. Greater N.Y. (past dir., pres. 1967-68) (N.Y.C.); Stanwich (Greenwich, Conn.); Stowe (Vt.) Country; Bedford (N.Y.) Golf and Tennis; Lyford Cay (Bahamas). Home: Windmill Farm 12 Spruce Hill Rd Armonk NY 10504 Office: Lonsdale Enterprises Inc 20 Haarlem Ave White Plains NY 10603

ROBLE, CAROLE MARCIA, accountant; b. Bklyn., Aug. 22, 1938; d. Carl and Edith (Brown) Dusowitz; m. Richard F. Roble, Nov. 30, 1969. MBA with distinction, N.Y. Inst. Tech., 1984. CPA, Calif., N.Y. Comptroller various orgns., 1956-66; staff acct. ZTBG CPA'S, Los Angeles, 1966-67; sr. acct. J.H. Cohn & Co., Newark, 1967-71; lectr. New School, Queens Coll., Empire State Coll., Touro Coll., N.Y. Inst. Tech., N.Y., 1971-82; prin. Carole M. Roble, CPA, South Hempstead, N.Y., 1971—; guest appearances various N.Y. radio and TV stats.; speaker and moderator Found. for Accounting Edn., N.Y., 1971-87. Treas. Builders Devel. Corp. of L.I., Westbury, N.Y., 1985; dir. Women Econ. Devels. of L.I., 1985-87. Recipient Sisterhood citation Nat. Orgn. Women, 1984, 85, cert. of Appreciation Women Life Underwriters, 1988, Women in Sales, 1982, 84; named top Tax Practitioner Money Mag., 1987. Mem. Am. Acct. Assn.(auditing sect.), Am. Inst. CPA's, Am. Soc. Women Accts. (pres. N.Y. chpt. 1980-81), Am. Woman's Soc. CPA's, Nat. Conf. CPA Practitioners (L.I. chpt. trustee 1981-82, sec. 1982-83, treas. 1983-84, v.p. 1984-85, 1st v.p. 1985-86, pres. 1986-87, nat. nomination com. 1983-84, edn. chmn. 88—), Calif. Soc. CPAs, N.Y. State Soc. CPAs (Nassau chpt. bd. dirs. 1981-86, bd. profl. devel. 1982-86, various com. positions 1977-86), Delta Mu Delta. Home and Office: 626 Willis St South Hempstead NY 11550

ROBNETT, MELISSA BETH, adminstrative executive; b. Columbia, Mo., July 14, 1958; d. James Overton Robnett II and Linda Ann (Levy) Bennett. Student, U. Mo., 1979; AS, Columbia Coll., 1984. Sec. to pres. Local 50 AFL-CIO, St. Louis, 1978-79; sec. to dean U. Mo., Columbia, 1979-80, med. sec., 1980-82; sec. to dir. Columbia Coll., 1982-84; administrv. assoc. Christian Ch., Columbia, 1984—; cons. B and R Assocs., Columbia, 1980—, pres. 1982-84, chmn. bd., 1984-86. Contbr. articles to profl. jour. Recording sec. Arts Resources Council, Columbia, 1986—, election judge Boone County Elections Office, Columbia, 1976—. Mem. Profl. Secs. Internat. (pres. 1989—), Diciples Secs. Assn., Am. Mgmt. Assn., Am. Bus. Women's Assn., Women Network, VFW (pres. ladies aux. 1981-83). Democrat. Jewish. Home: 121 Holly Park Village Columbia MO 65202 Office: Christian Ch NE Area 3612 Lenoir St Columbia MO 65201

ROBOHM, PEGGY ADLER, personal manager, writer, illustrator, researcher; b. N.Y.C., Feb. 10, 1942; d. Irving and Ruth (Relis) Adler; m. Jeremy Abbott Walsh, June 1, 1962 (div. Dec. 1968); children: Tenney Whedon, Avery Denison; m. Richard A. Robohm, Dec. 24, 1976; stepchildren: Erick John, Kurt William, Kim Alene (Mrs. John L. Moore). Student, Bennington Coll., 1959-60, Columbia U., 1962. Illustrator, author childrens books 1958—; agt. Jan J. Agy., Inc., N.Y.C., 1981-82; freelance talent scout Cuzzins Mgmt., N.Y.C., 1982-83; ind. personal mgr. Madison, Conn., 1983—; investigative researcher/writer, 1987—. Author, illustrator: The Adler Book of Puzzles and Riddles, 1962, The 2nd Adler Book of Puzzles and Riddles, 1963, Metric Puzzles, 1977, Math Puzzles, 1978, Geography Puzzles, 1979; author: Hakim's Connection, 1988; co-author: Skull and Bones: The Skeleton in Bush's Closet?, 1988; illustrator numerous books including (Humane Soc. of U.S. pubs.) Pet Care, 1974, Caring for Your Cat, 1974, Hot and Cold, 1959, Numbers New and Old, 1960, Do a Zoomdo, 1975, Reading Fundamentals for Teen-Agers, 1973; graphic designer various book covers, posters, co. logos; researcher Passion and Prejudice: A Family Memoir (Sallie Bingham), 1989; cons. Nixon's Private Eye: An Autobiography (Anthony Ulasewicz), 1989. Founder Shoreline, Youth Theater Inc. of Greater New Haven, 1979, mem. adv. bd., 1981—; bd. dirs. The Greens Condominium Assn. of Branford, Conn., 1975-78, Arts Council of Greater New Haven, 1971-73, Planned Parenthood of Greater New Haven, 1972-73; v.p., bd. dirs. Pub. Info. Rsch., Washington, 1989—. Mem. Conf. of Personal Mgrs., Dramatists Guild, Authors League Am. Home and Office: Connections 45 Lawson Dr Madison CT 06443

ROBRIQUEZ, ELADIO, manufacturing executive; b. Havana, Cuba, Apr. 12, 1937; came to U.S., 1960; s. Rafael Rodriguez and Silvia Tejeiro; m. Esther Alonso, June 14, 1958; children: Teresa, Maria Elena, Maytee, Anabel. BA, Inst. Marianao, Havana, 1955; postgrad. in bus. adminstrn., U. Mundial, Rio Piedras, P.R., 1969. Spl. technician Cuban Telephone Co., Havana, 1957-60; supr. COE installation ITT Carribean Mfg., Rio Piedras, 1962-64; project supr. ITT Sales and Services, Saigon, Vietnam, 1964-65; mgr. site project V.I., 1966-68; gen. supr. San Juan, 1968-70, mgr. site project, 1970-71, dir. C.O.E. installation, 1972-75; pres. Teletecnicas de P.R., Inc., San Juan, 1975-77; v.p., gen. mgr. Porta Systems Caribbean Corp., San Juan, 1978—. Mem. Hijas de Maria, Bayamon, P.R., 1986-88, Parents and Daus. Assn., San Jose Acad., Caparra, Guaynabo, 1987, Torrimar (Guaynabo) Cath. Ch., 1987-88. Mem. P.R. Mfg. Assn. (Indsl. del Año award), Assn. Interam. Hombres de Empresa. Roman Catholic. Clubs: Torrimar Tennis (bd. dirs. 1987—), Riomar. Office: Porta Systems Carribbean Corp PO Box 11502 Caparra Heights Puerto Nuevo PR 00922

ROBSHAW, EVERETT LEROY, automotive executive; b. Framingham, Mass., Jan. 27, 1945; s. Leroy Wilfred and Eleanor Louise (Ward) R.; m. Brenda Ann Mochel, July 26, 1974; stepchildren: Michael Tuttle, Traci Tuttle. Student, Bentley Coll., 1963-65. Police officer Holliston (Mass.) Police Dept., 1967-69; dir. purchasing Lee Imported Cars, Wellesley, Mass., 1969-78, Fgn. Autopart Inc., Sharon, Mass., 1979-85; mgr. internat. sourcing Echlin Inc., Branford, Conn., 1985—. Capt. Holliston Fire Dept. Ambulance, 1970-84; scuba diver underwater search and recovery unit Town of Holliston, 1973-85; instr. CPR for ARC and Am. Heart Assn., Holliston, 1968-85, Emergency Med. Technician, Holliston, 1974-85. Mem. Conn. Assn. Purchasing Mgmt., Nat. Assn. Purchasing Mgmt., Charlesgate Yacht Club, Commodores Club Am. Home: 15 Great Oaks Branford CT 06405 Office: Echlin Inc 100 Double Beach Rd Branford CT 06405

ROBY, DONALD FRANKLIN, savings and loan association executive; b. Osceola, Iowa, Jan. 20, 1929; s. William Doyle and Wilma Louise (Hurst) R.; m. Margaret Sarah Watters, July 25, 1953; children: George M., Marcia L. Roby Gilmer, Jeanne Ellen (dec.), Alan R. B.S.C., Drake U., Des Moines, 1950. C.P.A., Iowa. Partner Augustine & Co. (C.P.A.s), Des Moines, 1953-60; controller Dewey Electric, Inc., Ventura, Iowa, 1960-61; sr. accountant Meriwether, Wood & Miller (C.P.A.s), Des Moines, 1961-64; exec. v.p. Fed. Home Loan Bank, Des Moines, 1964-77; pres., dir. First Fed. Savs. and Loan Assn., Mpls., 1977-83; pres. Fed. Home Loan Bank of Des Moines, 1983-86; pres., dir. Farm & Home Savs. Assn., Nevada, Mo., 1986—; pres., dir. FHSA Mortgage Corp., Consol. Agys. of Tex., F&H Mortgage Co., Inc., Caltrop Corp.; bd. dirs. Farm & Home Info. Systems, Century Cos. of Am., Waverly, Iowa. Bd. dirs. Luther Northwestern Theol. Sem., St. Paul, Nat. Fund Med. Edn. Served with USAF, 1950-53, lt. col. Res. ret. Mem. Am. Inst. C.P.A.'s, Scottish Heritage Soc. Iowa. Republican. Clubs: Des Moines Golf and Country; Lakewood Oaks Golf, Ltd. (bd. dirs.). Lodge: Shriners. Office: Farm & Home Savs Assn 221 W Cherry PO Box 1893 Nevada MO 64772

ROBY, JOE LINDELL, investment banker; b. Metropolis, Ill., May 22, 1939; s. Gerald C. and Inez (DeLaine) R.; m. Elizabeth Shute, June 17, 1967 (dec. Oct. 1980); m. Hilppa Pirila, June 15, 1984. BA cum laude, Vanderbilt U., 1961; MBA with distinction, Harvard U., 1967. Asst. v.p. Kidder, Peabody & Co., N.Y.C., 1967-72; v.p. Donaldson, Lufkin & Jenrette, N.Y.C., 1972-75, sr. v.p., 1976-83, mng. dir. investment banking, 1984—, also bd. dirs.; bd. dirs. Sybron, Inc., Muskland Group, Inc. Served to lt. USN, 1961-65. Mem. Down Town Assn., Bond Club of N.Y. Club: Down Town Assn. (N.Y.C.). Office: Donaldson Lufkin & Jenrette Inc 140 Broadway New York NY 10005

ROCCA, MATT JOSEPH, small business owner; b. San Francisco, Sept. 10, 1955; s. Louis J. and Marie Ann (Sole) R. BS and Commerce, U. Santa Clara, 1977. Waiter Original Joe's, San Jose, Calif., 1970-72, mgr., 1973-78, owner, 1978—. Bd. dirs. San Jose Downtown Assn., 1986—. Recipient award Calif. Restaurant Assn. Mem. No. Calif. Restaurant Assn., San Jose C. of C., Beta Gamma Sigma. Republican. Roman Catholic. Home: 6554 Bose Ln San Jose CA 95120 Office: Original Joe's 301 S First St San Jose CA 95113

ROCHA, ARMANDINO CORDEIRO DOS SANTOS, accountant, educator, auditor; b. Porto, Portugal, Oct. 19, 1934; s. Mario dos Santos and Maria dos Conceicão (Cordeiro) R.; m. Maria Laura Oliveira Silva, Sept. 1, 1957 (div. 1976); children: Isabel Maria, Mario Rui; m. Ana Rosalina Sa Ribeiro, July 2, 1977; 1 child, Ana Sofia. B in Acctg., Inst. Comercial, Porto, 1962; B in Social Polit., Inst. Estudos Socials, Lisbon, Portugal, 1969; B in Sociology, Inst. Superior Ciencias, 1982; BBA, Inst. superior C. Trab. Empresas, 1975. Fin. dir. Fabrica Fiacão E Tecidos Da Portela, Delães, Portugal, 1960-72, Tinturaria Vaz Ferreira, S. Mamede De Infesta, Portugal, 1962-73; regional dir. Companhia Seguros Bonanca, Porto, 1973-87; auditor Emaco, Sa, Lisboa, Porto, 1979-85, Imobur S.A. and Riguadiana S.A., Porto, 1979-85, Estaleiros Navais De Viana, Porto, 1979-82; auditor Efi-Ed Ferreirinha and Irmão S.A., Porto, 1984-88, Feruni-Sociedade de Fundicão S.A., Trofa, Portugal, 1984—, Portocork, Internat., S.A., Feira, Portugal, 1987—, Copo Atlantico, Industria De Poliuretano S.A., Santo Tirso, Portugal, 1987—, Vasconcelos Lyncke, LDA, Feira, Portugal, 1989—, CYC, S.A.-Vilamoura, Portugal, 1989—, Ferdeirinmas Maguinas, S.A., Trofa, Portugal, 1989; instr. acctg. U. Do Minho, Braga, Portugal, 1980—. Author: Principios Do Seguro, 1982; contbr. articles to profl. jours. Mem. Assn. Para O Desenvowimento Economico E Social, Portugal Economists Assn., Portugal Mgmt. Assn., Inst. Dos Actuários Portugueses. Clubs: Vigorosa Sport, Fenianos. Home: 357-2 Faria Guimaraes, P-4000 Porto Portugal Office: Universidade Do Minho, Castelo, P-4119 Braga Portugal

ROCHAT, JEAN-PAUL, translator, small business owner; b. Oran, Algeria, North Africa, Feb. 22, 1943; s. Lucien Henri and Manuela (Luis) R.; m. Alice Staeheli, Apr. 26, 1965; children: Janine Alice, Marcel Jean-Paul. Swiss and French nat. Lycée français, Sch. Interpreters, Zurich, 1966; Ph.D., Sussex Coll. Tech., Eng., 1972; D honoris causa, Thomas Jefferson U., 1984, D honoris causa en Ciencias Linguisticas, U. El Salvador, 1985, D honoris causa en Ciencias Sociales U. Politécnica de El Salvador, 1986; Cultural Doctorate of Philosophy in Linguistics, World Univ. Roundtable, Benson, Ariz.; Dr. honoris causa en pilosofia U. Poly. de el Salvador, 1988, U. Prague, 1989. Interpreter, translator Wild Heerbrugg AG, 1961-63; translator Pro Jurentute, Zurich, 1964; translator F. Hoffman-La Roche & Co. S.A., Basle, Switzerland, 1965; translator, asst. mgr. Doetsch, Grether & Co. AG, Basle, 1966; translator, sales mgr. Agence Economique et Financiere, Zurich, 1967; owner Translation Agy., 1969—. Nominated non. consul Burkina Faso, Cameroon in Switzerland. Author: La Traduction en Suisse, 1972. Named a hon. col. a.d.c. Ala. State Militia, 1985. Mem. Swiss Assn. Translator and Interpreter (founder), Swiss Assn. Translation Agys. (pres. 1983). Home: Seestrasse 231, 8700 Kusnacht, Zurich Switzerland Office: Forchstrasse 108, 8032 Zurich Switzerland

ROCHE, BRUCE WARE, advertising educator; b. Ft. Worth, Dec. 25, 1929; s. John Edward and Martha Ione (Hendrick) R.; m. Harriet Sammons Smith, Aug. 21, 1952; children: Dawne, Bernadette, Knight Bruce. BJ, U. Tex., 1951, MJ, 1957; PhD, So. Ill. U., 1975. Mgr. classified advt. Temple (Tex.) Daily Telegram, 1954-56; asst. to commr. Gen. Land Office of Tex., Austin, 1956-58; asst. prof. advt. S.W. Tex. State Coll., San Marcos, 1958-67; lectr. So. Ill. U., Carbondale, 1968-71; asst. prof. West Tex. State U., Canyon, 1971-72; assoc. prof. U. Ala., Tuscaloosa, 1972—. Contbr. articles to profl. jours. Sgt. U.S. Army, 1952-54. Mem. Am. Journalism Historians Assn., Assn. for Edn. in Journalism, Am. Advt. Fedn. (historian. bd. dirs. 7th dist. 1984—, gov. 1980-81, Silver medal 1980, Otis Dodge Meml. award 1982, Hall of Fame 1988, Hileman Advt. Educator of Yr. 1989), Am. Acad. Advt., Greater Tuscaloosa Ad Club (pres. 1966-67, bd. dirs. 1984-88, Ad Man of Yr. 1978). Episcopalian. Office: U Ala PO Box 870172 Tuscaloosa AL 35487

ROCHE, BYRON ATHERTON, retired lawyer; b. East St. Louis, Ill., Aug. 8, 1921; s. Francis D. and Freda L. (Pace) R.; m. Elizabeth Miller, Mar. 5, 1948; children: Byron A. Jr., Linda R., Bradford M., Dorothy L. Roche Auble. JD, Washington U., 1947. Bar: Mo. Assoc. Carter, Bull & Baer, St. Louis; ptnr. Murphy & Roche, St. Louis, 1948-69; v.p., gen. counsel, sec. Hussmann Corp., Bridgeton, Mo., 1969-85, v.p. law, sec., 1985-86, ret., 1987; bd. dirs. Hussmann Corp. and subs. Maj. USAAF, WWII. Republican. Lutheran. Home: 36 Raven's Pointe Dr Lake Saint Louis MO 63367

ROCHE, GEORGE AUGUSTINE, investment management executive; b. Rochester, N.Y., July 6, 1941; s. John David and Elizabeth Ann (Switzer) R.; m. Nancy Keen, July 30, 1966; children: Kathryn Elizabeth, Anne Patricia. Student, U. Fribourg, Switzerland, 1961-62; A.B., Georgetown U., 1963; M.B.A., Harvard U., 1966. Brand asst. Procter & Gamble Co., Cin., 1966-68; with T. Rowe Price, Balt., 1968—; research analyst T. Rowe Price, 1968-72, v.p., 1972—, chief fin. officer, 1984—, also dir.; pres. Rowe Price New Era Fund, Balt., 1979—; dir. B.R.P. Inc. Contbr. articles to profl. jours. Mem. Urban Coalition, Balt., 1976; bd. dirs. Roland Park Country Sch., 1982—, Enoch Pratt Free Library, 1985—. Served with U.S. Army, 1963-64. Mem. AIME, Center Club, L'Hirondelle Club, Harvard Bus. Club, Maryland Club. Republican. Roman Catholic. Office: T Rowe Price Assocs Inc 100 E Pratt St Baltimore MD 21202

ROCHE, KEVIN JOSEPH, finance executive; b. Newburyport, Mass., Mar. 31, 1935; s. Francis A. and Johanna (Murphy) R.; m. Arleen Ann Tangney, Oct. 16, 1965; children: Elizabeth, Edward. BBA, Merrimack Coll., 1962. Various positions Dow Jones & Co., Inc., N.Y.C., 1977-87; comptroller Dow Jones & Co., Inc., Princeton, N.J., 1987—; v.p. fin., chief fin. officer Dow Jones & Co., Inc., 1987—. Contbr. articles to profl. jours. Served to sgt. USAF, 1954-58. Mem. Fin. Exec. Inst., Internat. Newspaper Fin. Execs. Office: Dow Jones & Co Inc 200 Liberty St New York NY 10281

ROCHLIS, JAMES JOSEPH, manufacturing company executive; b. Phila., Apr. 12, 1916; s. Aaron and Gussie (Pearlene) R.; m. Riva Singer, Mar. 21, 1943; children: Jeffrey A., Susan J. Ed. pub. schs. Salesman Mid-City Tire Co., Phila., 1945-46, gen. mgr., 1946-49; pres. Ram Rubber Co., Phila., 1948-49; rep. Blair & Co., Phila., 1949-61, bus. analyst, 1955-61; pres., chief exec. officer Baldwin-Montrose Chem. Co., Inc., N.Y.C., 1961-68; v.p. Chris-Craft Industries, Inc., N.Y.C., 1968-69; pres. Chris-Craft Corp., Pompano Beach, Fla., 1969-71; exec. v.p. Chris-Craft Industries, Inc., N.Y.C., 1969-87, also bd. dirs.; pres. Baldwin-NAFI Industries div. Chris-Craft Industries, 1968-86, Chris-Craft Internat., 1977-87; pres. Chris-Craft Indsl. Products, Inc., Pompano Beach, 1981-86, chmn., bd. dirs., cons., 1986—; bd. dirs. Montrose Chem. Co. Calif., Torrance and Mex., So. Mass. Cablevision Corp., N.Y.C., Piper Aircraft Corp., Lock Haven, Pa., Chris-Craft Pacific, Inc., Calif. Mem. AIAA, Fin. Analysts Soc. Phila., Soc. Naval Architects and Marine Engrs., Antique and Classic Boat Soc. Club: Lotus (N.Y.C.). Home: 150 E 69th St New York NY 10021 also: 10601 Wilshire Blvd Los Angeles CA 90024 Office: Chris-Craft Industries Inc 600 Madison Ave New York NY 10022

ROCHON, JOHN PHILIP, cosmetics company executive; b. Sept. 20, 1951; s. Philip Benjamin and Helena Sylvia (McCullough) R.; m. Donna J. Hewitt, Dec. 15, 1972; children: Heidi C., William J., Lauren. BS, U. Toronto, Ont., 1973, MBA, 1976. Plant mgr. Econs. Lab. Inc., Toronto, 1976-80; dir. mfg. Mary Kay Cosmetics, Inc., Toronto, 1980-82; controller mfg. group Mary Kay Cosmetics, Ltd., Dallas, 1982-84, corp. controller, 1984, v.p. fin., chief fin. officer, 1984-85, exec. v.p., chief fin. officer, 1986-87, vice chmn. bd., 1987-88, also bd. dirs.; bd. dirs. Mary Kay Holding Corp., Dallas; mem. fin. com. U. Tex., Dallas, 1985—. Mem. Fin. Execs. Inst., Cosmetic, Toiletry and Fragrance Assn., Verandah Club. Republican. Home: 4315 Firebrick Ln Dallas TX 75287

ROCK, ARTHUR, venture capitalist; b. Rochester, N.Y., Aug. 19, 1926; s. Hyman A. and Reva (Cohen) R.; m. Toni Rembe, July 19, 1975. B.S., Syracuse U., 1948; M.B.A., Harvard U., 1951. Gen. ptnr. Davis & Rock, San Francisco, 1961-68, Arthur Rock & Assocs., San Francisco, 1969-80; chmn. bd. Sci. Data Systems, Inc. (merged with Xerox Corp.); bd. dirs. Xerox Corp., Echelon, Los Gatos, Calif.; chmn. exec. com., dir. Intel Corp., Santa Clara, Calif.; dir. Diasonics, Inc., South San Francisco, Calif., Apple Computer, Inc., Cupertino, Calif., Argonaut Group, Inc., L.A.; vice chmn., dir. Rational, Santa Clara, Calif.; mem. exec. com., dir. Teledyne, Inc., L.A.; trustee Calif. Inst. Tech. Bd. dirs. San Francisco Opera Assn., San Francisco Mus. Modern Art, Am. Soc. for Technion; mem. vis. com. Harvard U. Bus. Sch., 1982-88; adv. bd. Berkeley Bus. Sch., U. Calif. Recipient Medal of Achievement Am. Electronics Assn.

ROCK, DENNIS KENT, municipal official; b. Rexburg, Idaho, Dec. 9, 1951; s. Dennis Clane and Velma Jean (Tunks) R.; m. Sharon Lee Tracy, Aug. 5, 1977; children: Amanda, Melissa, Megan, Michelle, Merrilee. BA in Bus. Mgmt., Brigham Young U., Hawaii, 1976. Cert. city fin. officer, Idaho. Asst. mgr. Capital Fin. Services, Rexburg, 1976-77; installment loan officer First Security Bank, Rexburg, 1977-80; comptr./planner East Cen. Idaho Planning and Devel., Rexburg, 1980-81; dep. treas. purchasing agt., risk mgr. City of Boise, Idaho, 1981-84, city treas., risk mgr., 1984—; mem. State Treas. Investment Adv. Consortium, Boise, 1987—. Contbr. articles to profl. jours. Leg. dist. vice chmn. Dem. Party, Rexburg and Boise, cand. for state treas., Idaho, 1985-86. Named Boise Mid-Mgr. of Yr., 1983, one of Outstanding Young Men of Am., 1985. Mem. Govt. Fin. Officers Assn. (vice chmn. com. cash. mgmt. 1986-88, chmn. 1988—, U.S. adv. task force on arbitrage 1987, Profl. Achievement Recognition 1983, 84), Idaho City Clks. and Fin. Officers Assn. (bd. dirs. 1985-87, chmn. legis com. 1987—). Mormon. Home: 8209 Crestwood Dr Boise ID 83704

ROCK, MILTON LEE, publisher; b. Phila., Feb. 25, 1921; s. Maurice and Mary (Lee) R.; m. Shirley Cylinder, Aug. 3, 1943; children: Susan Herzog, Robert Henry. BA, Temple U., 1946, MS, 1947; Ph.D., U. Rochester, 1949. Mng. ptnr. Hay Group, Phila., 1949-85; chmn., pub. MLR Pub. Co., Phila., 1985—; pres. Assn. Mgmt. Cons. Firms, Phila., 1972-73. Co-author: The Executive Perceptanalytic Scale, 1963, The Development of Bank Management Personnel, 1969; editor: Handbook of Wage and Salary Administration, 1972, 2d edit., 1983, The Mergers & Acquisitions Handbood, 1987. Chmn. Middle Atlantic Regional Manpower Adv. Com., Labor Dept., 1972-73; mem. Pres.'s Nat. Commn. for Manpower Policy, 1974-77; bd. govs. Temple U. Hosp., 1975—, chmn., 1985—, trustee Univ., 1979—; bd. dirs. Phila. Orch., 1981-87, 89—, Curtis Inst. Music, Phila., 1983—, chmn. 1989—, Pa. Ballet, 1983—, Phila. Mus. Art, 1986—, Fgn. Policy Rsch. Inst. 1987—; mem. adv. coun. J.L. Kellogg Grad. Sch. Mgmt. Northwestern U., 1981—. Fellow Am. Psychol. Assn.; mem. Inst. Mgmt. Cons. (dir., founding). Home: The Barclay Philadelphia PA 19103 Office: MLR Pub Co 229 S 18th St Philadelphia PA 19103

ROCKEFELLER, WILLIAM, lawyer; b. N.Y.C., Dec. 4, 1918; s. William Avery and Florence (Lincoln) R.; m. Mary D. Gillett, July 3, 1947; children: Mary Gillett Fogarty, Edith McKee Laird, Sarah Stillman Bogdanovitch. Grad., St. Paul's Sch., 1936; A.B., Yale U., 1940; student, U. Wis., 1940-41; LL.B., Columbia U., 1947. Bar: N.Y. 1948. Asso. firm Dorr, Hammond, Hand & Dawson, 1947-55, Shearman & Sterling, N.Y.C., 1955-57; partner Shearman & Sterling, 1957—; Dir. Indian Spring Land Co., Conn., Oneida Ltd. Trustee, sec. Meml. Sloan-Kettering Cancer Center; bd. dirs. Am. Soc. Prevention Cruelty to Animals, pres., 1956-64; hon. chmn. Met. Opera Assn.; chmn. Geraldine R. Dodge Found.; trustee Paul Smith's Coll. Served to lt. comdr. USNR, 1941-46. Decorated Bronze Star; recipient gold medal Nat. Inst. Social Sci., 1977, Yale Medal, 1987. Mem. Am., N.Y. bar assns., Assn. Bar City N.Y., Zeta Psi, Phi Delta Phi. Episcopalian. Clubs: N.Y. Yacht, Links, Anglers, Metropolitan Opera, Westminster Kennel (N.Y.C.); American Yacht (Rye), Apawamis (Rye), Racquet and Tennis, Brook, River. Home: 84 Grandview Ave Rye NY 10580 Office: 153 E 53 St New York NY 10022

ROCKELMAN, GEORGIA F(OWLER) BENZ, retail furniture executive; b. Jefferson City, Mo., June 7, 1920; d. Charles Herman and Marinda Julia (Fowler) Benz; m. Elvin John Henry Rockelman, Nov. 9, 1940; 1 child, Barbara Jean. BBA, Lincoln U., 1964, MBA, 1977. Sec./acct. Harry Benz Enterprises, Jefferson City, 1932-52; ptnr. Benz Furniture Co., Jefferson City, 1952-59, Benz-Rockelman Furniture Co., Jefferson City, 1961-82; v.p., sec. Benz-Rockelman Ltd., Jefferson City, 1982—. Pres. Trinity-Luth. PTA, Jefferson City, 1952-54; pres. Jefferson City Council Nat. Congress PTA, 1954-56; mem. City Water Flouridation com., 1956; candidate Jefferson City Council, 1983; bd. dirs. Southside Bus. League, Jefferson City, 1981-82, v.p., 1983-84; Rep. com. women Cole County, 1984, 86. Mem. AAUW, DAR,

Am. Legion, Cole County Hist. Soc., Hist. City of Jefferson City, Cole County Rep. Women's Club. Home: 216 W Ashley St Jefferson City MO 65101 Office: 121 W Dunklin & 129 W Dunklin St Jefferson City MO 65101

ROCKWELL, DORIS ELEANOR, service executive; b. Erie, Pa., Dec. 6, 1932; d. Morris Edward and Audrey Mable (Moore) Vogt; m. Benjamin Clarence Otteni, Oct. 6, 1951 (dec. 1963); children: Ronald Fredrick Otteni, Benjamin Morris Otteni; m. Donald Eugene Netzler, Aug. 24, 1963 (dec. 1981); m. Gerald Edward Rockwell, July 2, 1983. Student, Pa. State U., Erie, 1965-83, Jr. Coll., Ft. Pierce, Fla., 1980-81. Cert. banker Am. Inst. Banking. Banker First Nat. Bank, Erie, 1969-71; owner D&D Restaurant, Ford City, Pa., 1971-77; banker Sun Bank St. Lucie County, Ft. Pierce, 1979-81; chief exec. Qatech Svcs. Fla., Inc., Tequesta, 1986—, pres., 1987, also bd. dirs. Mem. State Rep. Com., St. Lucie County, Fla., 1982-83; pres. St. Lucie County Rep. Club; 2d v.p., bd. dirs. Fla. Fedn. Rep. Women, Palm Beach County, 1987; notary State of Fla., until 1990. Recipient Membership awards State of Pa., 1969, Achievement honor in pub. rels. NORAD, 1971, Rep. Achievement award St. Lucie County, 1983. Mem. Nat. Assn. Women in Constrn., NAFE, Nat. Bus. Womens Network, 500 Club (mem. Rep. Nat. Com. 1982-84), Am. Legion Aux. (officer), Beta Sigma Phi (officer). Lutheran. Home: 6684 Woodlake Rd Jupiter FL 33458 Office: Qatech Svcs Fla Inc 222 Pla US Hwy #1 Ste 202 Tequesta FL 33469-2740

ROCKWELL, ELIZABETH DENNIS, financial planner; b. Houston; d. Robert Richard and Nezzell Alderton (Christie) Dennis. Student Rice U., 1939-40, U. Houston, 1938-39, 40-42. Purchasing agt. Standard Oil Co., Houston, 1942-66; asst. sec. Heights Savs. Assn., Houston, 1967-70, asst. v.p., 1970-75, v.p. mktg., 1975-82; sr. v.p., fin. planner Oppenheimer & Co., Inc., Houston, 1982—; 2d v.p. Desk and Derrick Club Am., 1960-61; instr. Coll. of Mainland, Texas City, Tex.; instr. Downtown Coll. and Continuing Edn. Ctr., U. Houston; mem. Dean's adv. bd. U. Houston, alumni bd. 1987—, treas., 1988. Bd. dirs. ARC, 1985—, Houston Heights Assn., 1973-77, 85—; active Houston Jr. League, 1986-87. Named Outstanding Woman of Yr., YWCA. Mem. Am. Savs. and Loan League (state dir. 1973-76, chpt. pres. 1971-72; pres. S.W. regional conf. 1972-73; Leaders award 1972), Savs. Inst. Mktg. Soc. Am. (Key Person award 1974), Inst. Fin. Edn., Fin. Mgrs., Soc. Savs. Instns., U.S. Savs. and Loan League (com. on deposit acquisitions and adminstrn.), Spring Branch Meml. C. of C., Internat. Platform Assn., Houston Heights Assn. (charter, dir. 1973-77), Houston North Assn., Harris County Heritage Soc., Rice U. Bus. and Profl. Women, River Oaks Bus. Womens Exchange Club, U. Houston Bus. Womens Assn. (pres. 1986). Club: Forum. Author articles on retirement planning and tax options. Home: 3617 Yoakum Blvd Houston TX 77006 Office: Oppenheimer & Co Inc 333 Clay St Ste 4700 Houston TX 77002

ROCKWELL, WILLIAM HEARNE, lawyer; b. Taunton, Mass., Oct. 28, 1919; s. Julius and Alice (Hearne) R.; grad. Philips Acad.; AB, U. Mich., 1941, MA, 1947; LLB, Columbia, 1950; m. Elizabeth Virginia Goode, Feb. 3, 1948; children: Enid Rockwell, Karen Rockwell, William Goode Rockwell (dec.). Bar: N.Y. 1950. Assoc. Donovan, Leisure, Newton & Irvine, 1950-51; asst. sec. The Valve Mfrs. Assn., 1951-55; sec. Am. Carpet Inst., Inc., 1956-66, sec., treas., 1966-68; sec., gen. counsel Am. Nat. Standards Inst., N.Y.C., 1969—, v.p., 1984—; gen. counsel Contemporary Dance, Inc., 1962—, Rondo Dance Theatre, Inc., 1970—, Montserrat Found., 1972—, Turns and Caicos Found., 1985—, Product Liability Prevention Conf., 1974—. Mem. bd. ethics Town of Pound Ridge, N.Y., Heritage Hills Soc., Ltd.; bd. dirs. Heritage Hills Soc., Ltd. Maj. Transp. Corps, AUS, 1941-46. Mem. Assn. Bar City N.Y., ABA. (mem. anti-trust com.), Am. Soc. Assn. Execs. (legal com.), N.Y. Soc. Assn. Execs., Nat. Safety Council, Nat. Panel Arbitrators, Am. Arbitration Assn., Columbia Law Sch. Alumni Assn. (dir.), Pound Ridge Land Conservancy, Heritage Hills Soc., Ltd. (bd. dirs.). Clubs: Belham River Valley Country; Montserrat Yacht; Pound Ridge Tennis; New York Athletic; University (Washington), Heritage Hills Golf. Home: 957 D Heritage Hills Somers NY 10589 Office: 1430 Broadway New York NY 10018

ROCKWOOD, FREDERICK WHITNEY, manufacturing company executive; b. Salt Lake City, Dec. 18, 1947; s. Lewis Frederick and Muriel (Whitney) R.; m. Alyce Jolene Edmunds, Aug. 26, 1970; children—Justin, Melissa, Jennifer, Katherine, Elizabeth. Student, U. Utah, 1966-67, Columbia U., N.Y.C., 1970; AB in Anthropology, Stanford U., 1972; JD, Harvard U., 1975. Bar: Mass. Corp. strategy cons. Boston Cons., 1975-77; corp. strategy cons. Bain & Co., Boston, 1977; dir. corp. strategy Hillenbrand Industries, Inc., Batesville, Ind., 1977-78, sr. v.p., 1978-85; pres. The Forethought Group, Batesville, 1985—; mem. adj. faculty U. Mich. Grad. Sch. Bus., 1980; pres., dir. Rockwood Furniture, Inc., Salt Lake City, 1985—. Rep. Ch. of Jesus Christ of Latter-day Saints, Hong Kong, 1967-69; unit scouting coordinator Dan Beard council Boy Scouts Am., Cin., 1982—. Mem. ABA, Fellow Life Mgmt. Inst., Am. Mgmt. Assn., Phi Beta Kappa. Republican. Office: The Forethought Group Forethought Ctr Batesville IN 47006

RODABAUGH, ROBIN ROY, data processing executive; b. Carbondale, Ill., Feb. 19, 1949; s. Louis Dale and Gulna Louise (Fikes) R.; m. Dianne Michelle Lowe, June 18, 1971. BA, U. Akron, 1971. Cert. data processing. Project mgr. Cooper Energy Services, Mount Vernon, Ohio, 1978-80; mgr. HON Co., Muscatine, Iowa, 1980-82; v.p. Protective Life Corp., Birmingham, Ala., 1982—. Mem. Data Processing Mgmt. Assn. Methodist. Home: 3716 Dover Dr Mountain Brook AL 35223-2862 Office: Protective Life Corp 2801 US Highway 280 South Birmingham AL 35223-2488

RODE, JAMES DEAN, banker; b. Cleve., Feb. 4, 1948; s. Andrew Joseph and Eileen M. (Costello) R.; m. Leslie Ann Biles, June 27, 1970. B.A. in Econs, Ohio U., Athens, 1969; M.B.A. in Fin, Case Western Res. U., 1974. With AmeriTrust Co., Cleve., 1969—; sr. v.p. consumer fin. AmeriTrust Co., 1979-80, exec. v.p. retail banking, 1980-83, sr. exec. v.p. banking services group, 1983, pres., 1984—; dir. AmeriTrust Corp. & Co., Bearings, Inc. Trustee Univ. Hosps. of Cleve., Case Western Res.; dir. United Way Svcs., Cleve. Served with USAFR, 1969. Mem. Assn. Res. City Bankers, Consumers Bankers Assn. (trustee). Roman Catholic. Clubs: Skytop (Pa.); Union (Cleve.); Pepper Pike. Office: AmeriTrust Corp 900 Euclid Ave PO Box 5937 Cleveland OH 44101

RODENBERG, TODD WALTER, marketing professional, educator; b. Davenport, Iowa, Sept. 13, 1949; s. Victor Leroy and Darlene Delores (Dietz) Sharp; m. Jody Bagley Rodenberg, Apr. 20, 1974; children: Gabriel Todd, Mindy Jo. BA, William Penn. Coll., 1971; MA, U. No. Iowa, 1973; cert., U. Mo., 1977. Cert. edn. specialist, mktg. edn. coordinator. With sales dept. Burroughs Corp., Davenport, 1971-72, Chuck Fellmer Imports, Cedar Falls, Iowa, 1972-73; mktg. instr., coordinator Chillicothe (Mo.) R-2 Schs., 1973—; with sales and mktg. depts. Summit Nat. Life, Ohio, 1976-77; instr. Positive Mental Attitude, 1976—. Recipient Outstanding Coll. Athlete of Am. award All Conf. Baseball, Iowa Conf. Coaches, 1968, 71. Mem. Mo. State Tchrs. Assn., Community Tchrs. Assn., Am. Vocat. Assn., Mo. Vocat. Assn., Chillicothe Jaycees, Dist. Edn. Club Am. (chpt. advisor), Optimists, Lions. Office: Chillicothe AVTS 1200 Fair Chillicothe MO 64601

RODENHAUSEN, JOHN, electronics company executive; b. Phila., Mar. 27, 1941; s. John and Audrey (Webster) R.; m. Nancy Lynch, Jan. 27, 1973; children: Kristofer, Kari, John III. Student, U. Md., 1962, Pa. State U., 1965, Ursinus Coll., 1968, U. Pa., 1971. Engr. Burroughs Corp., Paoli, Pa., 1964-69; regional sales mgr. Mohawk Data Scis., Phila., Hartford, Conn. and Chgo., 1969-75; area sales rep. Digital Equipment Corp., Phila., 1975-79; corp. accts. mgr. Digital Equipment Corp., N.Y.C. and Phoenix, 1986—; dist. sales rep. Harris Corp., Phila. and Boston, 1979-83; pres. JN Solar Systems, Phila., 1979-84; dir. nat. sales Motorola, Phila. and Phoenix, 1983-86. Asst. coach Scottsdale Little League, 1987, Scottsdale Soccer League, 1988. With USMC, 1961-66. Mem. Data Processing Mgmt. Assn. (bd. dirs. 1983-86, Achievement award 1984-85). Methodist. Home: 9928 E Cinnabar Ave Scottsdale AZ 85258 Office: Digital Equipment Corp 1901 W 14th St Tempe AZ

RODERICK, DAVID MILTON, oil, gas and steel corporation executive; b. Pitts., May 3, 1924; s. Milton S. and Anna (Baskin) R.; m. Elizabeth J. Costello, Jan. 31, 1948; children: David Milton, Patricia Ann, Thomas Kevin. B.S. in Econs. and Finance, U. Pitts. Asst. to dir. statistics USX Corp. (formerly U.S. Steel Corp.), N.Y.C., 1959-62; acctg. cons.-internat. projects USX Corp. (formerly U.S. Steel Corp.), Paris, 1962-64; v.p. acctg. USX Corp. (formerly U.S. Steel Corp.), 1964-67, v.p. internat., 1967-73, chmn. fin. com., dir., 1973-75, pres., 1975-79, chmn., chief exec. officer, 1979—, also bd. dirs.; dir. Marathon Oil Co., Procter & Gamble Co.; gen. dir. Tex. Instruments, Inc., Aetna Life & Casualty Co., Tex. Oil & Gas Corp., Transtar, Inc.; bd. dirs. Pitts. Pirates; chmn., mem. exec. com. Internat. Iron and Steel Inst.; chmn. U.S.-Korea Bus. Coun. Chmn. Internat. Environ. Bur.; bd. dirs. Allegheny Trails coun. Boy Scouts Am.; bd. dirs. Nat. Action Coun. for Minorities in Engring.; trustee Carnegie-Mellon U.; mem. Allegheny Conf. Community Devel., Bus. Com. Arts Inc., Pres.'s Commn. Exec. Exchange; bd. dirs. Nat. Energy Found.; mem. Bus. Higher Edn. Forum. Mem. Am. Iron and Steel Inst., Nat. Water Alliance, Bus. Roundtable, Conf. Bd. (trustee), Nat. Alliance Bus., Nature Conservancy (corp. relations com.), The Bus. Council. Clubs: Rolling Rock (Ligonier, Pa.), Laurel Valley Golf (Ligonier, Pa.); Fox Chapel Golf (Pitts.), Duquesne (Pitts.); Economic of N.Y. Office: USX Corp 600 Grant St Pittsburgh PA 15219-4776

RODERICK, RICHARD MICHAEL, petroleum and real estate executive; b. Buffalo, Oct. 18, 1948; m. Patricia Suzanne Rosick, Oct. 2, 1971; children: Kristina, Thomas, Carolyn. BBA in Acctg., U. Notre Dame, 1970; MS in Computer Systems Mgmt., U.S. Naval Postgrad. Sch., 1971; MBA, U. Maine, 1985. CPA, Maine. Acct. Arthur Young & Co., Portland, Maine, 1976-79; corp. controller Dead River Group of Cos., Bangor, Maine, 1979-87, v.p., 1987—. Served to lt. USN, 1970-76. Roman Catholic. Office: Dead River Co 55 Broadway Bangor ME 04401

RODGERS, COLLEEN MIRIAM YVONNE, medical publishing company executive; b. Stratford, Taranaki, New Zealand, Jan. 27, 1949; d. Edward John and Jean Clara (Murray) R. came to U.S., 1974;. Advt. sales rep. Ronald Park Davis Inc., Ridgewood, N.J., 1974-79; dir. spl. projects advt., regional sales mgr. Miller Freeman Publs., San Francisco, 1979-83, mktg. mgr., 1984-87, assoc. pub., 1988—; bd. dirs. Calif. Tobacco Corp., San Francisco, Nationwide Marketing. Chmn. North Pacific Council Nat. Peace Inst. Found., 1987—. Office: Miller Freeman Publs 500 Howard St San Francisco CA 94105

RODGERS, HENRY JOHN, JR., information systems specialist; b. Latrobe, Pa., Aug. 25, 1941; s. Henry John Sr. and Mary Elizabeth (Rosko) R.; m. Irene Anna Townsend, Aug. 27, 1966; children: Andrew Thomas, Lisa Erin. BA, Wabash Coll., 1963; MBA, U. Pitts., 1967. Mgr. strategic planning IBM, White Plains, N.Y., 1980-82, mgr. programming process and tools, 1982-85, mgr. info. systems software labs., 1987—; chmn. info. systems coun. IBM, Poughkeepsie, N.Y., 1985-87; chmn. bd. dirs. IBM Poughkeepsie Employees Fed. Credit Union, 1974-79, 87—. Bd. dirs., mgr. Hyde Park (N.Y.) Baseball, 1979-83. Mem. Lions (treas. Hyde Park chpt. 1979, pres. 1981), Beta Gamma Sigma. Home: 32 Putnam Rd Hyde Park NY 12538

RODGERS, JAMES ALDEN, communications executive; b. Johnstown, Pa., Aug. 11, 1941; s. C.H. and Margaret (Wieseman) R.; m. Kate Holway Asquith, Mar. 29, 1969; 1 child, Nathan MacFarland. MEd, Indiana U. of Pa., 1971; AB, Susquehanna U., 1986; postgrad., Temple U. Dir. communications JLG Industries, McConnellsburg, Pa., 1984—; cons. in field. Author: Emerson's Unpublished Discourses, 1971. Scholar Aid Assn. for Luths., 1971, Eliza Catherine Smith Found., 1971. Mem. Chambersburg C. of C., JLG Mgmt. Club. Republican. Lutheran. Home: 1617 Wilson Ave Chambersburg PA 17201 Office: JLG Industries Inc JLG Dr McConnellsburg PA 17233

RODGERS, RICHARD RANDOLPH, association executive; b. Madison, Ind., July 28, 1948; s. Richard Payne and Marjorie Jean (Bishop) R.; BS in Acctg., U. Ky., 1970, postgrad., 1972-73; postgrad. U. Md., 1984-85; m. Sharron Kaye Manley, Aug. 15, 1970; 1 child, Leigh Walker. Acct., Sullivan and Clancy, C.P.A.'s, Lexington, Ky., 1969-72; pvt. practice acctg., Lexington, 1972-73; comptroller Council of State Govts., Lexington, 1973-75; dir. adminstrn. and fin. Nat. Gov.'s Assn., Washington, 1975-86, sec.-treas., 1977-86, treas. Center for Policy Research, 1977-86, treas. Kings Manor Assn., 1988—; chmn. bd. State Services Orgn.; v.p. Adminstrn. Mortgage Bankers Assn. Am., 1986—. Pres., Lansdowne Neighborhood Assn., 1972-73; vice chmn. bd. deacons McLean Baptist Ch., 1979-80. Served with Army. N.G., 1970-76. C.P.A., Va. Mem. Am. Soc. Assn. Execs., Washington Soc. Assn. Execs., Ky. Soc. of Washington, U. Ky. Alumni Assn., Phi Gamma Delta. Baptist. Home: 1119 Brentfield Dr McLean VA 22101 Office: Ste 700 1125 15th St NW Washington DC 20005

RODGERS, ROSEMARY, apartment manager, real estate agent; b. Grafton, N.D., Oct. 14, 1946; d. Edward Max and Ruth Lavonne (Kline) Ebertowski; m. William James Rodgers, Oct. 31, 1964; children: William James II, Brenda Lynn, Rebecca Marie. Grad. high sch., Grafton, 1964. Buyer, mgr. Fashion Shoppe, Grafton, 1970-76, Reylecks, Grafton, 1976-78; apt. mgr. GO Devel., Grafton, 1979—; real estate agt. Country Realty, Inc., Grafton, 1983-88, Town & Country Real Estate, Grand Forks, N.D., 1988—, R&R Properties, 1988—. Chmn. Mchts. Com., Grafton, 1976; advisor Distbn. Edn. Club of Am., Grafton, 1985-89. Roman Catholic. Clubs: Grafton Heathers, Grafton Golf. Home: 167 E 2d St Grafton ND 58237 Office: Town & Country Real Estate 401 Reeves Dr Grand Forks ND 58201

RODHAM, EDWIN SEAVEY, JR., book company executive; b. New Haven, Jan. 7, 1947; s. Edwin S. Sr. Rodham and Adda (Mansfield) Tobin; m. Sandra L. Wight, July, 19 1980. BA, Northeastern U., Boston, 1969; MA, Mich. State U., 1971. Assoc. dir. book store Brown U., Providence, 1971-78; dir. book store Brown U., 1978-80; v.p. Login Bros. Book Co., Fairfield, N.J., 1980—. Home: 11 Leone Terr Kinnelon NJ 07405 Office: Login Bros Book Co 4 Sperry Rd Fairfield NJ 07006

RODIGER, W. GREGORY, III, financial executive; b. N.Y.C., Nov. 23, 1959; s. Walter G. and Elizabeth (King) R.; m. Beverly Bodnar, Aug. 16, 1986. BA, St. Lawrence U., 1984. Cert. fin. planner, registered investment advisor. Investment sales rep. 1st Investors Corp., Norwalk, Conn., 1982-84; fin. planner Money Fin. Svcs., Darien, Conn., 1984—; fin. planning cons. Asset Devel. Group, Stamford, Conn., 1987—. Mem. Inst. Cert. Fin. Planners (bd. dirs. 1986—, Founders award 1986, Pres.'s award 1986), Internat. Assn. Fin. Planning (bd. dirs. 1987—), Nat. Assn. Life Underwriters. Republican. Congregationalist. Office: Mony Fin Svcs 19 Old Kings Hwy S Darien CT 06820

RODINO, VINCENT LOUIS, insurance company executive; b. N.Y.C., June 25, 1929; s. Vincenzo and Sofia (De Toro) R.; m. Marie Green; children: Peter Vincent, Vincent Douglas. BA, NYU, 1957. CLU. With The Equitable Fin. Cos., N.Y.C., 1946—, chief mktg. services sector, 1983-84, chief traditional products sector, 1984-86, chmn., chief exec. officer Traebco subs., 1984-86, chief sales support sector, 1986—; trustee Life Underwriter Tng. Council, Washington, 1987. Served as sgt. U.S. Army, 1951-53. Mem. Assn. Advanced Life Underwriting, Nat. Assn. Life Underwriters, N.Y.C. Chpt. CLU's. Office: The Equitable Fin Cos 135 W 50th St New York NY 10020

RODMAN, ALPINE CLARENCE, arts and crafts wholesaler, entrepreneur; b. Roswell, N.Mex., June 23, 1952; s. Robert Elsworth and Verna Mae (Means) R.; m. Sue Arlene Lawson, Dec. 13, 1970; 1 child, Connie Lynn. Student Colo. State U., 1970-71, U. No. Colo., 1983—. Ptnr. Pinel Silver Shop, Loveland, Colo., 1965-68, salesman, 1968-71; real estate salesman, Loveland, 1971-73; mgr. Traveling Traders, Phoenix, 1974-75; owner Deer Track Traders, Loveland, 1975-85, pres. Deer Track Traders, Ltd., 1985—. Author: The Vanishing Indian: Fact or Fiction?, 1985. Mem. Civil Air Patrol, 1965-72, 87—, dep. comdr. cadets, 1988—; cadet comdr. Ft. Collins, Colo., 1968, 70, Colo. rep. to youth tng. program, 1969, U.S. youth rep. to Japan, 1970. Mem. Bur. Wholesale Sales Reps., Mountain States Men's, Boy's and Western Apparel Club, Eastern States Western Salesman's Assn., Internat. Platform Assn., Indian Arts and Crafts Assn. (bd. dirs. 1988—, exec. com. 1989). Republican. Baptist. Clubs: Crazy Horse Grass Roots. Office: Deer Track Traders Ltd PO Box 448 Loveland CO 80539

RODMAN, RICHARD SEWALL, investment advisor; b. Bklyn., Dec. 6, 1946; s. Frank and Evelyn (Sewall) R.; m. Linda Lewis Rodman, Aug. 29, 1971; children: Alison Faith, Danielle Hope. BS in Commerce, Rider Coll., 1968. Asst. controller N.J. Life INs. Co., Newark, 1968-69; account exec. Harris, Upham and Co., Inc., Elizabeth, N.J., 1969-73; assoc. MJR Assocs., Inc., Summit, N.J., 1973-76, Ford Assocs., Inc., Florham Pk., N.J., 1976-83; pres. Start Now, Inc., Cranford, N.J., 1982—; chmn. bd. Start Now, Inc., Cranford, 1982—; pres. Creative Asset Mgmt, Inc. 1988—, chmn. bd. dirs., Cranford. Author: (booklet) Financial and Investment Consulting, 1988; (manual), 1988; author of numerous articles in field. Bd. trustees Jewish Community Ctr., Scotch Plains, N.J., 1984-86. Recipient of Wall St. Jour. Achievement award, Dow Jones Co., Inc., N.Y.C. (1968). Mem. Am. Assn. Individual Investors, Assn. Investment Mgmt. Sales Execs., N.J. Fin. Soc. (pres. 1968), Temple Emanuel Mens Club, B'nai Brith. Jewish. Office: Start Now Inc 65 Jackson Dr Ste 2000 Cranford NJ 07016

RODMAN, SUE ARLENE, wholesale Indian crafts company executive, artist; b. Fort Collins, Colo., Oct. 1, 1951; d. Marvin F. and Barbara I. (Miller) Lawson; m. Alpine C. Rodman, Dec. 13, 1970; 1 child, Connie Lynn. Student Colo. State U., 1970-73. Silversmith Pinel Silver Shop, Loveland, Colo., 1970-71; asst. mgr. Traveling Traders, Phoenix, 1974-75; co-owner, co-mgr. Deer Track Traders, Ltd., Loveland, 1975-85, exec. v.p., 1985—. Author: The Book of Contemporary Indian Arts and Crafts, 1985. Mem. Rep. Presdl. Task Force, 1982-87; mem. U.S. Senatorial Club, 1982-87, Civil Air Patrol, 1969-73, 87—, personnel officer, 1988—. Mem. Internat. Platform Assn., Nat. Assn. Female Execs., Indian Arts and Crafts Assn., Native Am. Art Studies Assn., Inc. Baptist. Club: Crazy Horse Grass Roots (S.D.). Avocations: museums, recreation research, fashion design, reading, flying. Office: Deer Track Traders Ltd PO Box 448 Loveland CO 80539

RODOLFF, DALE WARD, consultant, sales executive; b. Casa Grande, Ariz., Aug. 5, 1938; s. Norval Ward and Mary Louise (Grasty) Rodolff; m. Kathleen Pennington, Sept. 3, 1960 (div. July 1983); children: David Ward (dec.), Julia Ann. BS in Mining Engring., U. Ariz.; PMD, U. Cape Town. Registered profl. engr., Republic of South Africa. Supt. smelting and fabricating Inspiration Consol. Copper Co., Claypool, Ariz., 1960-72; smelter and refinery supt. Palabora Mining Co, Phalaborwa, Republic of South Africa, 1972-74; asst. mgr. Empress Nickel Mining Co., Gatooma, Zimbabwe, 1974-77; smelter supt. Magma Copper Co., San Manuel, Ariz., 1977-81; v.p., gen. mgr. Sentinel Mgmt. Corp., Tucson, 1981-82; dir., mgr. metallurgy Outokumpu Engring. Inc., Denver, 1982-86, regional (U.S.A.) sales mgr., 1986—, also bd. dirs.; cons. Dale W. Rodolff Cons., 1986—; pres. Bus. Performance Services, Inc., 1986—. Contbr. articles to tech. jours.; inventor scrap rod feed system, 1970. Pres. Y Men's Club, Miami, Ariz., 1969. Kennecott scholar U. Ariz., 1959. Mem. AIME (metall. soc., soc. mining engrs., chmn. smelter div. 1970, 71, pyro metall. com. 1973-77). Lodge: Elks. Home: 6527 Jungfrau Way Evergreen CO 80439 Office: Outokumpu Engring Inc 274 Union Blvd Ste 460 Lakewood CO 80228

RODRIGUEZ, BRIAN JOSEPH, financial executive; b. Glendale, W.Va., Jan. 9, 1956; s. Bienvenido Fernandez and Helen Marie (Reilly) R.; m. Marlene Faye Yoho, Oct. 17, 1981; children: Sarah Ruth, Maria Faye, Jennifer Kay, Jessica Jo. BBA, W. Liberty State Coll., 1978. Sr. acct. clk. Mobay Corp., New Martinsville, W.Va., 1979-81; acct. I Mobay Corp., New Martinsville, 1981-84, acct. II, 1984-85, coordinator fin. systems, 1985-86, supr. mfg. cost and inventory acctg., 1986—. Mem. Am. Mgmt. Assn., Spielers Club (treas.), Moose Lodge, KC. Democrat. Roman Catholic. Home: HCR 26161 Box 60 New Martinsville WV 26155

RODRIGUEZ, JAMES J., real estate tax, lawyer; b. San Francisco, Feb. 3, 1946; s. James J. and Louise Rodriguez; m. Lorraine Alison Myers, Jan. 7, 1978; children: Alison Ruth, James John. BA in Psychology, UCLA, 1969, MBA in Fin., 1971; JD cum laude, Santa Clara (Calif.) U., 1978; M of Tax Law, Golden Gate U., San Francisco, 1984. Bar: Calif., 1978; cert. tax specialist. Fin. analyst, loan officer City of Commerce Investment Co., L.A., 1970-71; mem. planning staff Telecor, Inc., Beverly Hills, Calif., 1971-73; banking officer corp. real estate First Interstate Bank, L.A., 1973-75; pres. Mission Properties, San Jose, Calif., 1975—; ptnr. Talia & Rodriguez, Santa Clara, Calif., 1978—; instr., lectr. San Jose (Calif.) State U., De Anza Coll., Pepperdine (Calif.) U., Mission Coll. Mem. Calif. Bar Assn., San Jose Real Estate Bd. (chmn. investment and exchange com., vice chair edn. com.), Real Estate Cert. Inst. (cert. 1975), Calif. Assn. Real Estate Instrs., Nat. Assn. Realtors, Calif. Assn. Realtors,Santa Clara County Bar Assn. (trustee bd. trustees). Office: Talia & Rodrignez 900 Lafayette St Santa Clara CA 95050

RODRIGUEZ, MAURICIO ARMANDO, financial consultant, securities broker; b. Panama City, Panama, July 3, 1949; came to U.S., 1959; s. Jose A. Rodriquez and Julien (Oliver) Rodriguez-Gray; m. Mary Erlinda Romero Garza, Sept. 3, 1980; children: Lance, Anna-Maria, Cammille. BA, U. N.Mex., 1975, MA in Pub. Administrn., 1980; MBA, Atlanta U., 1983; postgrad., Adelphi U., 1986—. Lic. salesman, ins. agt., N.Y., real estate agt. Grad. asst. U. N.Mex., Albuquerque, 1979; data transcriber HEW, Albuquerque, 1980-81; bus. analyst for econ. devel. Ga. Power Co., Atlanta, 1981-83; account exec. Merrill Lynch, Pierce, Fenner & Smith, Inc., N.Y.C., 1983-85, fin. cons., 1985-88, sr. fin. cons., 1988—. Exec. mgmt. scholar Atlanta U., 1981-83; Exxon fellow, 1982. Home: 2787 Kennedy Blvd Ste 502 Jersey City NJ 07306 Office: Merrill Lynch Pierce Fenner & Smith Inc World Fin Ctr S Tower 4th Fl New York NY 10080-0404

RODZIANKO, PAUL, business executive; b. Washington, Oct. 22, 1945; s. Paul and Aimee Rodzianko; m. Chauncie McKeever, May, 1988. B.A., Princeton U., 1967; M.A., Inst. Critical Langs., 1967. With Gen. Electric Co., 1967-76; pres. U.S. Geothermal Corp., N.Y.C., 1976-77, Geothermal Energy Corp., N.Y.C., 1977-83, Geothermal Food Processors, Inc., Fernley, Nev., 1979-82; exec. v.p. Grace Geothermal Corp., 1981-83; pres. Bay Capital Corp., Oyster Bay, N.Y., 1983-85; pres. Data Port Co., 1985-86; bd. dirs., exec. v.p. Halecrest Co., 1983—; dir. So. Slope Devel., Inc., 1989—; chmn. bd. Mt. Hope Hydro, Inc., Halecon, Inc., Mt. Hope Properties, Inc., Aleph Prodns., Component Bldg. Systems, Inc. Vice chmn. Russian Orthodox Theol. Fund, 1978—. Fellow Royal Geographic Soc., Explorers Club., New Eng. Soc.; mem. Geothermal Resources Council (dir., chmn. audit com. 1980-82), Nat. Inst. Social Scis., New Eng. Soc. Clubs: Explorers, Camp Fire.

ROE, DAVID HUGH, corporate executive; b. Grays, Essex, Eng., Jan. 28, 1946; came to U.S., 1969; s. George William and Elizabeth Evelyn (Jenkins) R.; m. Elsa Joan Kalmus, July 1, 1969; children: Alexander, Eleanor. BA, Pembroke Coll., Cambridge U., 1967; MS, London Grad. Sch. Bus. Studies, 1969. Fin. analyst Gen. Mills Inc., Mpls., 1969-73, asst. product mgr., 1973-75; assoc. cons. McKinsey and Co., Chgo., 1975-77; planning mgr. Batus Inc., Louisville, 1977-81, v.p. planning and analysis, 1981-85, v.p., treas., 1985—. Office: Batus Inc 2000 Citizens Pla Louisville KY 40202

ROE, JOHN H., manufacturing company executive; b. 1939. BA, Williams Coll., 1962; MBA, Harvard U., 1964. With Bemis Co. Inc., Mpls., 1964—, plant supt., 1964-67, sales rep., 1967-68, sales mgr., 1968-70, plant mgr., 1970-73, gen. mgr. film div., 1973-76, exec. v.p. ops., 1976-87, pres., chief operating officer, 1987—, also bd. dirs. Office: Bemis Co Inc 800 Northstar Ctr 625 Marquette Ave Minneapolis MN 55402 *

ROE, THOMAS ANDERSON, building supply company executive; b. Greenville, S.C., May 29, 1927; s. Thomas Anderson and Leila (Cunningham) R.; m. Shirley Marie Waddell, Aug. 2, 1980; children: Elizabeth Overton Roe Mason, Thomas Anderson, Philip Stradley, John Verner. B.S., Furman U., 1948, LL.D., 1980; diploma in bus. mgmt., LaSalle Extension U., 1956. Cancer research asst. Furman U., 1947-48; with Builder Marts of Am., Inc., Greenville, S.C., 1948-87, pres., 1961-69, chmn., 1969-87, chief exec. officer, 1969-78; chmn. First Piedmont Corp., 1967-74, First Piedmont Bank & Trust Co., 1967-74; vice chmn. Gen. Com. Group, Inc.; bd. dirs. Swiss Tex. Mem. Greenville County Redevel. Authority, 1971-75; vice chmn. S.C. Republican Com., 1963-64, fin. chmn. 1986—; mem. Nat. Rep. Fin. Com., 1963-64; hon. asst. sgt.-at-arms Rep. Nat. Conv., Chgo., 1960; past bd. dirs. Greenville chpt. ARC, Nat. Found. Ileitis and Colitis; trustee Christ Ch. Episcopal Sch., 1970-72; past bd. dirs. Greenville United Cerebral Palsy, Greenville chpt. ARC; active Little Theater prodns.; past chmn. adv. council Furman U.; pres. S.C. Policy Council, Greenville, 1986—; bd. govs.

Council for Nat. Policy; trustee Greenville Symphony, Coker Coll., 1975-81, Found. Francisco Marroquin, Guatemala, Intercollegiate Studies Inst., Heritage Found., Free Congress Reserch and Edn. Found., Washington, 1987—; trustee, bd. govs. Internat. Policy Forum, Washington; trustee Free Congress Found., Washington; past trustee Inst. for Rsch. on Economics of Taxation. Named builder of yr. Greenville Home Builders Assn., 1962. Mem. Nat. Assn. Home Builders (internat. housing com.), Greenville Home Builders Assn. (v.p. 1962-63), Nat. Lumber Bldg. Material Dealers Assn., Carolina Bldg. Material Dealers Assn. (pres. 1965-66), Greenville Bldg. Material Dealers Assn. (pres.), Greenville C. of C. (dir. 1967-70, pres. 1970). Clubs: Players (pres. 1951), Sertoma (pres. local club 1960-61, disting service award 1959, superior leadership award 1961), Greenville Country, World Trade Ctr, Poinsett. Home and Office: 712 Crescent Ave Greenville SC 29601

ROEBLING, MARY GINDHART, banker; b. West Collingswood, N.J.; d. I.D., Jr. and Mary W. (Simon) Gindhart; m. Siegfried Roebling (dec.); children: Elizabeth (Mrs. D.J. Hobin), Paul. Student bus adminstrn., econs. and fin., U. Pa., econs. and fin., NYU; LLD (hon.), Ithaca Coll., 1954; DS in Bus. Adminstrn. (hon.), Bryant Coll.; DSc (hon.), Muhlenberg Coll.; HHD (hon.), Wilberforce U.; DFA (hon.), Rider Coll.; DCS (hon.), St. John's U.; LHD (hon.), Marymount Coll., Rutgers U., 1987. Former chmn. bd. Nat. State Bank N.J., Women's Bank, Denver, now chmn. emeritus; chmn. N.Y. World's Fair Corp., 1964-65; dir. Companion Life Ins. Co., N.Y. Mem. adv. com. U.S. commr. gen. for Expo '67; nat. bd. dirs. U.S.O.; pub. gov. Am. Stock Exchange, 1958-62; mem. Regional Adv. Com. on Banking Policies and Practices; econ. ambassador State N.J. Chmn., N.J. Citizens for Clean Water, 1969-70; mem. Ann. Assay Commn., 1971, Nat. Bus. Council on Consumer Affairs; mem. adv. com. N.J. Museum. Life trustee George C. Marshall Research Found., N.J. Dental Service Plan; mem. nat. adv. council Nat. Multiple Sclerosis Soc.; trustee Invest-in-America; adv. bd. Assn. U.S. Army, civilian aide emeritus to Sec. Army, First Army; bd. govs. Del. Valley Council; chmn. N.J. Savs. Bond Com.; mem. 4th dist. Adv. Council Naval Affairs; bd. govs. Swedish Hist. Found.; nat. bd. Jr. Achievement Inc.; emeritus mem. def. adv. com. on women in services Dept. Def.; citizens adv. council Com. on Status of Women; bd. dirs. Am. Mus. Immigration; chmn. N.J. Hospitalized Vets.'s Service; comptroller Trenton Parking Authority; founder Donnelly Meml. Hosp. Women's Com. Decorated Royal Order Vasa (Sweden); commendatore Order Star Solidarity (Italy); recipient Brotherhood award NCCJ; Nat. Assn. Ins. Women award; Distinguished Service award Marine Corps League; Golden Key award N.J. Fedn. Jewish Philanthropies; Spirit of Achievement award women's div. Albert Einstein Coll. Medicine; Holland award N.J. Fedn. Women's Clubs; Outstanding Civilian Service medal Dept. Army, 1969; Humanitarian award N.J. chpt. Nat. Arthritis Found., 1970; Four Chaplains award, 1969; Trenton chpt. Nat. Secs. Boss of Year award, 1969, Internat. Boss of Year award, 1972; Golden Plate award Am. Acad. Achievement; Jerusalem Holy City of Peace award State of Israel; Dept. of Def. medal for Disting. Pub. Service, 1984; others. Mem. Nat. Def. Transp. Assn. (life mem.), U.S. Council of I.C.C. (trustee), N.J. Conf. Christians and Jews, Swedish Colonial Soc., League Women Voters, Am. Inst. Banking, N.J. Investment Council, Am. Bankers Assn., Soc. Mayflower Descs., Colonial Daus. 17th Century, Trenton C. of C., N.J. Firemen's Mut. Benevolent Assn. (hon. life), DAR, Geneal. Soc. Pa., Bus. and Profl. Women's Club, Daus. Colonial Wars, Pilgrim John Howland Soc. Clubs: Zonta, Trenton Country; Colony (N.Y.C.), Sea View Country, Contemporary (Trenton), Greenacres Country (Lawrenceville); Overseas Press (assoc.); Am. Newspaper Women's (asso.), 1925 F Street (Washington); Union League (Phila.). Home: 777 W State St Trenton NJ 08618

ROEBUCK, JOSEPH CHESTER, leasing company executive; b. Detroit, Feb. 6, 1946; s. Joseph Leonard and Stella (Grochocki) R.; m. Susan A. Hatala, Mar. 26, 1977; children—Christopher, Jennifer. A.A., Northwood Inst., 1966; B.S. in Bus., Central Mich. U., 1968. Sales IBM Corp., Southfield, Mich., 1968-70; prin. Roebuck, Schaden & Assoc., Detroit, 1970-73; Salesman U.S. Leasing, Birmingham, Mich., 1973-76; sales mgr. Federated Fin., Southfield, Mich., 1976-77; v.p. Corp. Funding, Inc., Birmingham, 1977-84; pres. Corp. Resources, Inc., Birmingham, 1984—; lease cons., 1984—. Mem. Am. Assn. Individual Investors. Republican. Roman Catholic. Club: Detroit Golf. Avocations: Golf, flying, travel, racquetball.

ROECK, THOMAS J., JR., airline financial executive; b. Berwyn, Ill., June 21, 1944; s. Thomas Joseph and Ruth R. (Lovings) R.; m. Carol A. Hansen, Sept. 29, 1973. B.S. in Acctg., U. So. Calif., 1971. With Global Marine, Inc., Los Angeles, 1966-84, asst. treas., 1973-78, treas., 1978-80, v.p., treas., 1980-84; sr. v.p., chief fin. officer Western Air Lines, Inc., Los Angeles, 1984-87; v.p. fin. adminstrn. Delta Air Lines Inc., Atlanta, 1987-88, sr. v.p. fin., chief fin. officer, 1988—. Served as sgt. U.S. Army, 1968-70, Korea. Republican. Office: Delta Air Lines Inc Hartsfield Atlanta Internat Airport Atlanta GA 30320

ROEDER, MORRIS LEE, manufacturing company executive; b. Louisville, Feb. 28, 1949; s. Lawrence Roeder and Jean (Ferguson) Ponder; m. Barbara Meyer, Feb. 17, 1973; 1 child, Michael. BA, U. Louisville, 1974, MBA, 1977. Sr. application engr. Carborundum Co., Knoxville, Tenn., 1977-80, regional mgr., 1980-81; successively indsl. mktg. mgr., product mgr., dist. mgr. Fuller Co., Bethlehem, Pa., 1981-88, gen. mgr., 1988—. Pres. Lehigh Valley Comets Youth Hockey, Bethlehem, 1985. Mem. TAPPI, Air Pollution Control Assn. Republican. Office: Fuller Co 2040 Ave C Bethlehem PA 18001

ROEGNER, GEORGE PETER, industrial designer; b. Flushing, N.Y., Sept. 3, 1932; s. George Elmer and Margaret (Hanna) R.; B.F.A., Pratt Inst., 1954; m. Jane R. Kramer, Aug. 29, 1959; children—George Curtis, John Hanson, Nicholas Meade. Staff designer Gen. Motors Corp., 1954-55, Raymond Loewy Assocs., N.Y.C., Westinghouse Corp., Metuchen, N.J., 1960-66; product design mgr. RCA, Indpls., 1966-70; dir. design Lenox Inc., Trenton, 1972-74; pres. Curtis Hanson Meade Inc., Far Hills, N.J., 1974—; partner Furniture Concepts Internat. Ltd.; dir. Cove House Corp. Bd. dirs. Clarence Dillon Library; vice chmn. Far Hills Bd. Adjustment; councilman Borough of Far Hills, 1982—, police chmn., 1984—. Served with U.S. Army, 1956-58. Recipient design awards ID Mag., Nat. Paper Box, Consumer Electronics Show, Printing Industries, Print Mag., Wescon. Mem. Indsl. Designers Soc. Am. (past nat. com. chmn.), Somerset Hills Assn., Raritan Valley Watershed Assn. Republican. Clubs: Eastward Ho Country, Stage Harbor Yacht. Designs shown at Mus. Modern Art, Smithsonian Instn., N.Y. World's Fair, Brussels, Zagreb Fairs, Indpls. Art Mus. office: 120 Woodland Way Chathamport MA 02650

ROEHR, WALTER CHARLES, JR., telecommunications engineer; b. N.Y.C., Jan. 5, 1939; s. Walter Charles and Amelia L. (Godlewski) R.; m. M. Eileen Jungherr, Oct. 12, 1963; children: Roger E., Jill M. BEE, CCNY, 1961; MS in Engring., Goerge Washington U., 1969. Mem. tech. staff Def. Communications Agy., Reston, Va., 1970-78; dir. Network Analysis Corp., Vienna, Va., 1978-82, Linkabit, McLean, Va., 1982-84; exec. dir. Telecommunication Networks Cons., Reston, 1984—. Contbr. articles to profl. jours. 2d ltd. U.S. Army, 1961-63. Mem. IEEE, Assn. Computing Machinery. Office: Telecommunication Networks Cons 1511 Farsta Ct Reston VA 22090

ROELL, MRS. C. J. See FLYNN, SHARON ANN

ROELS, OSWALD ALBERT, oceanographer, educator, business executive; b. Temse, Belgium, Sept. 16, 1921; came to U.S., 1958, naturalized, 1965; s. Ghisleen and Elvire (Heirwegh) R.; m. Dorothy Mary Broadhurst, Sept. 16, 1950; 1 dau., Margaret Ann Roels Talarico. B.S., U. Louvain, Belgium, 1940, M.S., 1942; Ph.D., 1944. Prof. Columbia U., N.Y.C., 1960-75, CCNY, 1969-76; prof., dir. dept. marine sci. U. Tex., Austin, 1976-80; pres. Maritek Corp., Corpus Christi, Tex., 1980—; adj. prof. Rockefeller U., N.Y.C., 1969-80; vis. research prof. Laval U., Que., Can., 1972-80; dir. mariculture research Port Aransas (Tex.) Marine Lab., U. Tex. Marine Sci. Inst., 1976-80. Author numerous articles in field.; assoc. editor: Nutrition Revs., 1961-68. Served with Belgian Army, 1940. Recipient Postdoctoral award U. Brussels, 1945, Postdoctoral award U. Liverpool, Eng., 1946, Postdoctoral award Sorbonne, 1957; Research Career Devel. award NIH, 1962-65; WHO fellow, 1957; Hoffman-LaRoche vis. lectr., 1974. Mem. AAAS, Am. Chem. Soc., Am. Inst. Nutrition, Am. Soc. Biol. Chemists, Am. Soc. Limnology and Oceanography, Chemici Lovanienses, Inst. Environ. Scis., Inst. Food Tech., Internat. Conf. Biochem. Lipids, Marine Tech. Soc., N.Y. Acad. Scis., N.Y. Lipid Club, Photoelectric Spectrometry Group Gt. Britain, World Mariculture Soc. Home: 28 Hewit Dr Corpus Christi TX 78404 Office: Maritek Corp PO Box 6755 Corpus Christi TX 78411

ROEMER, ELAINE SLOANE, real estate broker; b. N.Y.C., Apr. 23, 1938; d. David and Marion (Frauenthal) Sloane; m. David Frank Roemer, June 21, 1959; children: Michelle Sloane Wolf, Alan Sloane. BBA, U. Fla., 1959; MEd, U. Miami, 1960. Cert. tchr., Fla.; lic. real estate broker, Fla. Tchr. math. Dade County Pub. Schs., Miami, 1959-80; tchr. math and bus. Miami Dade Community Coll., 1968-80; tchr. edn. Fla. Internat. U., Miami, 1977-80; real estate broker Miami, 1978—; mortgage broker, Miami, 1986—; speaker in field. Contbr. articles to profl. jours. Organizer, officer Colonial Dr. Homeowners Assn., Miami, 1965; mem., officer Dade County Polit. Action League for Unincorporated Areas, Miami, 1965-68; chmn. women's com. state's atty.'s campaign, Miami, 1968. Mem. Kendall-Perrine Bd. Realtors, Fla. Assn. Realtors, Nat. Assn. Realtors, NEA, Fla. Edn. Commn., Classroom Tchrs. Assn., Dade County Edn. Assn., Fla. Coun. Tchrs. of Math., Fla. Bus. Edn. Assn., Assn. Classroom Educators, Dade County Assn. Ednl. Adminstrs., Assn. Supervision and Curriculum Devel., Alpha Delta Kappa, Kappa Delta Pi. Home: 7705 SW 138th Terr Miami FL 33158 Office: 15950 SW 96th Ave Miami FL 33157

ROEMER, JOHN ALAN, financial executive; b. Milw., June 9, 1949; s. John Edward and Jeanette Luella (Fleischmann) R.; m. Janet Francis Maloney, Aug. 8, 1970; children: John Robert, Joseph Michael. BBA in Acctg., Suffolk U., 1977; MBA, Rensselaer Poly. Inst., 1983. Supr. reimbursement Univ. Hosp., Boston, 1977-79; dir. fin. planning Champlain Valley Physician Med. Ctr., Plattsburgh, N.Y., 1979-84; contr. Arnot Ogden Meml. Hosp., Elmira, N.Y., 1984-85; dir. fiscal svcs. Bershire Med. Ctr., Pittsfield, Mass., 1985-87; v.p. fin. Franklin Med. Ctr., Greenfield, Mass., 1987—. Mem. Healthcare Fin. Mgmt. Assn., Am. Mgmt. Assn., Western Mass. Fin. Mgrs. Coun. (sec. 1986-87, v.p. 1987-88), DAV, Ea. English Spring Spaniel Club (v.p. 1987-88), KC (Appreciation award 1983). Roman Catholic. Home: 16 Clydesdale Dr Pittsfield MA 01201

ROEMERMAN, STEVEN DANE, electronics executive; b. Ottumwa, Iowa, Dec. 4, 1951; s. Henry Jr. and Ruth Nadine (Shirley) R.; m. Colleen Kay Goodwin, June 6, 1971; children: Krista Ann, Steven Henry. BS in Applied Math magna cum laude, U. Mo., Rolla, 1974; postgrad., So. Meth. U., 1974-75. Designer software and semiconductors Tex. Instruments, Dallas, 1974, systems engr. missiles div., 1974-78; chief systems engr. missiles div. Tex. Instruments, Ridgecrest, Calif., 1978-80; mgr. bus. devel. program advanced systems div. Tex. Instruments, Lewisville, Tex., 1980-86, mgr. advanced weapons dept., 1986—; cons. electronic warfare USN, 1979-80; gen. dir. Flood Warehouse & Movers, Inc., Carrollton, Tex., 1986—. Contbr. articles to profl. jours. Bd. dirs. Christian Life Cathedral, Dallas, 1984—, treas., 1987—. Mem. IEEE (sr.), Assn. Old Crows, Inst. Navigation, Engring. Mgmt. Soc., Am. Def. Preparedness Assn. (regional dir. 1987—).

ROEMMELE, BRIAN KARL, electronics company executive; b. Newark, Oct. 4, 1961; s. Bernard James and Paula Mary Roemmele. Grad. high sch., Flemington, N.J. Registered profl. engr., N.J. Design engr. BKR Techs., Flemington, N.J., 1980-81; acoustical engr. Open Reel Studios, Flemington, 1980-82; pres. Ariel Corp., Flemington, 1983-84, Ariel Computer Corp., Flemington, 1984—; pres., chief exec. officer Coupon Book Ltrd., 1987—; pres. Ariel Fin. Devel. Corp., Flemington, 1987—; bd. dirs. Waterman Internat., Whitehouse Station, N.J.; electronic design and software cons., Flemington, 1980—. Pub., editor-in-chief: Computer Importer News, 1987—. Organizer Internat. Space Week or Day, 1978-83; lectr. Trenton State Mus., N.J., 1983. Mem. AAAS, AIAA, IEEE, Boston Computer Soc., Ford/Hall Forum, N.J. Amateur Computer Users, Am. Soc. Notaries, Planetary Soc. Office: Ariel Computer Corp PO Box 866 Flemington NJ 08822

ROES, NICHOLAS A., communications executive; b. Jersey City, Dec. 26, 1952; s. Nicholas R. and Mimi (Maresca) R.; m. Nancy Bennett. BS in Edn., U. Bridgeport, 1974, MA in Bus. and Pub. Mgmt., 1983. Registered investment advisor (SEC). Chmn. bd. Tchr. Update, Inc., Saddle River, N.J., 1976—; pres., cons., author Nicholas A. Roes & Assocs., Saddle River, 1979—; ptnr. Barryville (N.Y.) Investors, 1985—; dir. investor relations Gambling Times, Inc., Los Angeles, 1984—, NAR Prodns., 1987. Author: Helping Children Watch TV, 1982, America's Lowest Cost Colleges, 1985, 6th edit., 1989, Gambling for Fun, 1988; editor newsletter Tchr. Update, 1977—; (column) The Investment Column, 1980—. Mem. Internat. Assn. Fin. Planners, Direct Mail Club of N.Y., EDPRESS, C. of C., Mensa, Internat. Platform Assn. Office: Nicholas A Roes & Assocs PO Box 205 Saddle River NJ 07458

ROESELER, WOLFGANG GUENTHER JOACHIM, city planner; b. Berlin, Mar. 30, 1925; s. Karl Ludwig and Therese (Guenther) Ph.D., Philipps State U. of Hesse, Marburg, W.Ger., 1946-49; LL.B., Blackstone Sch. Law, Chgo., 1958; m. Eva Maria Jante, Mar. 12, 1947; children—Marion, Joanie, Karl. Asso. planner Kansas City (Mo.) Planning Commn., 1950-52; city planning dir. City of Palm Springs, Calif., 1952-54; sr. city planner Kansas City, 1954-56; prin. asso. Ladislas Segoe & Assos., Cin., 1956-64; dir. urban and regional planning Howard, Needles, Tammen & Bergendoff, cons. Kansas City, N.Y.C., 1964-68; owner W.G. Roeseler, Cons. City Planner and Transp. Specialist, Bryan, Tex., 1969—; head dept. urban and regional planning Tex. A&M U., 1975-81, 85-88, prof., 1975—, dir. Tex. A&M Ctr. Urban Affairs, 1984-88, exec. officer for edn. College of Architecture, 1988—. Fellow Inst. Transport Engrs.; mem. Am. Inst. Cert. Planners, Am. Planning Assn. Author: Successful American Urban Plans, 1982. Contbr. articles to profl. jours. Home: 2508 Broadmoor PO Box 4007 Bryan TX 77801 Office: Tex A&M U College Station TX 77843

ROESSNER, GILBERT GEORGE, savings and loan executive; b. Irvington, N.J., Apr. 27, 1918; s. John K. and Emma Dora (Kurz) R.; m. Dorothy Anne Hector, Oct. 24, 1942; children: D. Anne Atherton, Martha, Gilbert George, Jane Roessner Ritchie, Barbara Roessner Baggott, Katherine Roessner Thorndike. BS, Rutgers U., 1940; diploma, Am. Savs. and Loan Inst.; grad., Internat. Sch. Bldg. Socs. Inst., Eng., 1964. With City Fed. Savs. Bank, Bedminster, N.J., 1941-86; dir. City Fed. Savs. & Loan Assn., 1955, exec. v.p., 1958-69, pres., 1967-79, chief exec. officer, 1970-85, chmn., chief exec. officer, 1978-86; dir. FHL Bank of N.Y., 1981-85; chmn., chief exec. officer CityFed Fin. Corp., 1984-86; chmn. CityFed Fin. Corp., Palm Beach, Fla., 1984—. Pres. Overlook Hosp. Assn., Summit, N.J., 1963; chmn. N.J. Bd. Higher Edn., 1973-75; mem. Pres.'s Task Force on Housing Policy, 1980. Served with USNR, 1942-45. Mem. Nat. Savs. and Loan League (pres. 1973-74), N.J. Council Fed. Savs. Assns. (pres. 1964-65). Clubs: Baltusrol Golf (Springfield, N.J.); Beacon Hill (Summit); Lost Tree (North Palm Beach, Fla.); N.Y. Yacht. Home: 11768 Lake House Ct North Palm Beach FL 33408 Office: CityFed Fin Corp 293 S County Rd PO Box 2872 Palm Beach FL 33480 *

ROETKEN, THEODORE CHARLES, venture capitalist; b. Muncie, Ind., Apr. 14, 1942; s. Evan Chester and Evelyn Louise (Waite) R.; m. Melanie Ann Turner, Apr. 17, 1945; children: Todd Alan, Clint Andrew. AB in Econs., Wabash Coll., 1965. Cert. fin. planner; registered investment advisor. Rep. K.J. Brown & Co. Inc., Muncie, 1965-67; office mgr. K.J. Brown & Co. Inc., Muncie, Ind., 1968-70; owner, mgr. Traveleez, Inc., Muncie, 1971-73; v.p. Young, Smith & Peacock, Inc., Phoenix, 1974-87; pres., owner Roetken & Co., Inc., Phoenix, 1980—; instr. Phoenix Coll., 1985—, Glendale Community Coll., Ariz., 1985—, Mesa Community Coll., Ariz., 1985—. Bd. dirs. United Way, Marion, 1970-72. Paul Harris fellow Rotary Found., 1977. Mem. Internat. Assn. Fin. Planners (v.p., bd. dirs. 1984-88), Internat. Cert. Fin. Planners (charter pres. Phoenix chpt. 1985-86), Exec. Assn. Greater Phoenix, Scottsdale Tips Club (bd. dirs., v.p. 1979-84), Rotary (charter pres. 1975-76). Office: Roetken & Co Inc 2211 E Highland Ave Ste 210 Phoenix AZ 85016

ROETS, LORI DAWN, systems analyst, consultant; b. Charleston, W.Va., Aug. 12, 1962; d. Paul E. Jr. and Carol A. (Baker) Smith; m. Thomas G. Roets Jr., Sept. 20, 1986; 1 child, Kristopher Ryan. AS, Roane State Community Coll., 1980; BA in Am. History, U. Tenn., 1982, BS in Fin., 1985. Cert. in data processing Inst. Cert. Computer Profls. Programmer analyst U. Tenn., Knoxville, 1982-85; v.p. CompuStock Ltd., Knoxville, 1984-85; programmer analyst Blue Cross/Blue Shield, Jacksonville, Fla., 1985-86; systems analyst Provider Automated Services, Jacksonville, 1986-87; v.p. Concepts: Matrix Inc., Jacksonville, 1987-88; systems analyst Cybernetics and Services Inc., Jacksonville, 1987—. Mem. NAFE, Order Eastern Star (Esther 1988-89, Adah 1989—), Delta Zeta (historian 1981-82). Democrat. Roman Catholic. Lodge: Order Eastern Star (Esther 1988—). Home: 8438 Ivey Rd Jacksonville FL 32216-1525

ROFF, J(OHN) HUGH, JR., energy company executive; b. Wewoka, Okla., Oct. 27, 1931; s. Hugh and Louise Roff; m. Ann Green, Dec. 23, 1956; children—John, Charles, Andrew, Elizabeth, Jennifer. A.B., U. Okla., 1954, LL.B., 1955. Bar: Okla., Mo., N.Y. Law clk. to presiding justice U.S. Ct. Appeals (10th cir.), 1958; atty. Southwestern Bell Telephone Co., St. Louis, 1959-63, AT&T, N.Y.C., 1964-68; v.p., gen. atty. Long Lines, N.Y.C., 1969-73, gen. atty., 1973-74; chmn., pres., chief exec. officer United Energy Resources, Houston, 1974-86; chmn. PetroUnited Terminals Inc. and Ala. Methane Prodn. Co., Houston, 1986—. Past chmn. Central Houston, Inc.; mem. adv. bd. Ctr. for Strategic and Internat. Studies, Washington; mem. council of overseers Rice U. Jones Sch. Bus. Adminstrn.; trustee Baylor Coll. Medicine; pres. Houston Symphony. Served to 1st lt. JAGC, U.S. Army, 1955-58. Mem. Order of Coif, Phi Beta Kappa. Clubs: Houston Country, Houston, Coronado, Houstonian. Office: 333 Clay St Ste 4300 Houston TX 77002

ROGAL, RAYMOND JOSEPH, automotive company executive; b. Detroit, Mar. 6, 1941; s. Chester Steven and Stella (Guzowski) Rogalski; m. Constance Loch, Nov. 29, 1966; children: Carolyn Anne, David Michael. BS, U. Detroit, 1965, MBA, 1966. Prodn. mfg. engring. mgr. Ford Motor Co., Livonia, Mich., 1971-76, mgr. transmission and chassis div., 1977-80; plant mgr. tractor ops. Ford Motor Co., Basildon, Eng., 1980-83; plant mgr. Ford Plastics Products Div., Milan, Mich., 1983-84; mgr. plastic product program Ford Plastics Products Div., Europe, 1984-85; dir. corp. quality office Ford Plastics Products Div., Dearborn, Mich., 1985—. Mem. Engring. Soc. Detroit, Am. Soc. Quality Control (chmn. membership com. Detroit chpt.), Soc. Plastics Engrs., Soc. Mech. and Mfg. Engrs. Office: Ford Motor Co World Hdqrs American Rd Room 575 Dearborn MI 48121

ROGAN, MICHAEL PATRICK, environmental service company executive; b. Toledo, Feb. 23, 1947; s. Martin Phelan and Mary Elizabeth (Hirzel) R.; m. Linda Diane Sales, Aug. 31, 1968; children: William Daniel, Bryan Fitzpatrick. BS, Ind. U., 1969. CPA, Ill. Sr. auditor Main Hurdman, Chgo., 1969-72; controller spl. projects Waste Mgmt., Inc., Oak Brook, Ill., 1972-73; div. controller Waste Mgmt., Inc., Los Angeles, 1973-77; sr. dir. fin. and adminstrn. Waste Mgmt. Saudi Pritchard Joint Venture, Riyadh, Saudi Arabia, 1977-80; v.p. fin. Waste Mgmt. Internat., Inc., London, 1980-83; v.p. fin., treas. Waste Mgmt. Internat., Inc., Oak Brook, 1983-86; v.p. fin. Waste Mgmt. N.Am., Oak Brook, 1987—. Mem. Art Inst. Chgo., 1983—; mem. community adv. bd. LWV; active Oak Brook Community Caucus, Oak Brook Civic Assn. Mem. AICPA, Ill. Soc. CPA's, Fin. Exec. Inst., Ind. U. Alumni Assn., Assn. for Corp. Growth, Ind. U. Deans Assn., Exec. Breakfast Club at Oakbrook, DuPage Club, Butterfield Country Club. Republican. Roman Catholic. Club: Ruth Lake Country (Hinsdale), DuPage (OakBrook), Ind. U. Varsity. Office: Waste Mgmt Inc 3003 Butterfield Rd Oak Brook IL 60521

ROGAN, ROBERT WILLIAM, management educator, osteopath; b. Buffalo; s. Rudolph Roland and Alice May (Saville) R. BA, SUNY, Buffalo, 1965, MBA, 1967; DO, W.Va. Sch. Osteo. Medicine, 1983; postgrad., Virginia Beach, 1986-88. Cert. data processor, data educator; diplomate Nat. Bd. Examiners for Osteo. Medicine and Surgery. Assoc. prof. bus. West Liberty (W.Va.) State Coll., 1976-79; intern Metro Health Ctr., Erie, Pa., 1983-84; asst. prof. computer sci. Gannon U., Erie, Pa., 1984-85; asst. prof. mgmt. Slippery Rock (Pa.) U., 1985-86; practice medicine specializing in osteopathy Harborcreek Family Practice, Erie, Pa., 1985. Couns. Contact Crisis Care, Lewisburg, W.Va., 1980-81; med. vol. in Jamaica, West Indies, 1988, Haiti, 1989—. Named one of Outstanding Young Men Am., 1978; recipient Hon. Sci. award Bausch and Lomb, 1960, scholarship U. Buffalo, 1960, two scholarships N.Y. State Regents, 1960-64; grantee NSF, Cornell U., 1959. Mem. Am. Osteo. Assn., Am. Coll. Gen. Practitioners, Mensa. Home: 3853 N Buffalo Rd Orchard Park NY 14127

ROGÉ, RONALD WILLIAM, financial planning and investment management executive; b. Bklyn., Mar. 7, 1947; s. Frederick William and Nancy (Rinaldo) R.; m. Patricia Mack, March 29, 1970; 1 child, Steven. AAS, N.Y.C. Community Coll., 1968; BS, L.I. U., 1970; MS, Poly. U., Bklyn., 1975. Registered investment advisor. Planning engr. N.Y. Telephone Co., N.Y.C., 1970-78, producr mgr., 1978-83; mgr. fin. planning NYNEX Enterprises, N.Y.C., 1983-85, staff dir. employee benefits, 1985-86; pres. R.W. Rogé & Co., Inc., Centereach, N.Y., 1986—. Served with USN, 1966-72. Mem. Internat. Assn. for Fin. Planning, Nat. Assn. Personal Fin. Advisors (chmn. pub. rels. com.), Am. Mktg. Assn. (exec. mem.), Inst. Cert. Fin. Planners (cert.), Am. Assn. Individual Investors. Republican. Roman Catholic. Home and Office: RW Rogé & Co Inc 86 Woodview Ln Centereach NY 11720-4060

ROGEN, NEIL ELLIOTT, technical group executive; b. N.Y.C., May 1, 1933; s. Harry T. and Sylvia A. (Grayson) R.; BS, Poly. Inst. N.Y., 1954; MS, MIT, 1956, Met. Engr., 1957; m. Elisabeth von Krogh, May 28, 1961; children—Stephanie Elisabeth, John Harald. Prin. metallurgist Battelle Meml. Inst., Columbus, Ohio, 1954-55; research asst. Mass. Inst. Tech., Cambridge, 1955-60; pres. Ilikon Corp./Cambridge Metal Research, Natick, Mass., 1958-62; fellow Royal Sch. Mines, Imperial Coll., London, 1962-65; chief metals and ceramics AVCO Systems Div., Wilmington, Mass., 1965-67; pres. Polyclon, Inc., Woburn, Mass., 1967-71, Neil E. Rogen Assocs., Waltham, Mass., 1971-80; v.p. Nedlog Tech. Group, Arvada, Colo., 1977-79; pres. Elektra Energy Corp., Houston, 1980-83, Hemisphere Licensing Corp., 1981-83, Petroleum Scis., Inc., 1981-84; chmn. Memory Metals, Inc., 1981-86, bd. dirs. 1981—, chmn., 1981-86, chief exec. officer, 1983-86, also bd. dirs. Mem. Am. Inst. Metall. Engrs., Am. Soc. Metals, Licensing Execs. Soc., Royal Norwegian Yacht Club, Sigma Xi. Contbr. articles on materials engring. to profl. jours.; patentee in field. Home and Office: 315 Wellesley St Weston MA 02193

ROGENSKI, THEODORE JOSEPH, financial services executive; b. Moline, Ill., Mar. 20, 1941; s. Felix Joseph and Stella Agnes (Borowski) R.; m. Nancy Elizabeth Moore, July 2, 1966; children: Jeffrey, Mark, Kerry. BBA, U. Wis., 1964; MBA, U. Chgo., 1970. Asst. cashier Am. Nat. Bank, Chgo., 1964-70; dist. mktg. mgr. Greyhound Leasing and Fin., Chgo., 1970-71; v.p. mktg. Am. Fletcher Leasing Corp., Chgo., 1971-74; regional v.p. Wells Fargo Leasing Corp., Phoenix, 1974-75; sr. v.p. Wells Fargo Leasing Corp., San Francisco, 1976-80, pres., chief exec. officer, 1981—, also bd. dirs.; bd. dirs. Wells Fargo Capital Markets, San Francisco, 1983—. Bd. dirs. Oberlin Dance Co., San Francisco, 1987—. Mem. Am. Assn. Equipment Lessors (bd. dirs. 1988—). Republican. Roman Catholic. Office: Wells Fargo Leasing Corp 101 California St San Francisco CA 94111

ROGERS, AMY, management consultant; b. Wilmington, Del.; d. Samuel and Dorothy (Chassen) R. BA in Govt., Am. U., 1969; MSW, Yeshiva U., 1975. Cert. social worker, N.Y. Social worker psychiat. Kings Psychiat. Ctr., N.Y.C., 1975; exec. asst. city council mem. Henry Berger, N.Y.C., 1977; dir. home healthcare services People Care, N.Y.C., 1978-79; exec. asst. Nat. Jewish Archives Broadcasting, N.Y.C., 1982-84, dir. tng. and devel. dept. fin., 1984—; cons. Amy Rogers Assocs., N.Y.C., 1980-83; trainer sales Bloomingdales, N.Y.C., 1983-84. Mem. People for Am. Way, N.Y.C., 1985-87, Nat. Abortion Rights Action League, N.Y.C., 1985-87. Named Hon. Citizen Md., Gov. Tawes, 1964; recipient Americanism medal, Am. Legion, 1964. Mem. Am. Soc. Tng. and Devel. (Chat. award 1987). Democrat. Home: 760 W End Ave New York NY 10025

ROGERS, ARTHUR MERRIAM, JR., banker; b. Rochester, Minn., Apr. 19, 1941; s. Arthur Merriam and Marguerite Wood (MacCoy) R.; m. Barbara Whitney, Nov. 27, 1965; children: Arthur, Alison, Whitney. B.A., Yale U., 1963. Mgr. Banca Morgan Vonwiller, Milan, Italy, 1967-71; dir. Morgan & Cie Internat., Paris, 1972-73; gen. mgr. Bank of Kuwait and the Middle East, Kuwait, 1976-78; asst. gen. mgr. Morgan Guaranty Trust Co.

N.Y., London, 1978-82; sr. v.p. Morgan Guaranty Trust Co. N.Y., N.Y.C., 1982-86; exec. v.p. Morgan Guaranty Trust Co. N.Y., 1986—. Trustee Kips Bay Boys Club, N.Y.C., 1965—. Club: Links (N.Y.C.). Office: Morgan Guaranty Trust Co NY 23 Wall St New York NY 10015

ROGERS, CARLETON CARSON, JR., trade show and convention executive; b. Chgo., Nov. 5, 1935; s. Carleton Carson and Eleanor (Lowell) R.; B.S. in Bus. Adminstrn., Am. U., 1957; postgrad. Northwestern U., 1957, Chgo.-Kent Coll. Law, 1957-58; m. Jo Ann Hurley; children—Kirsten Anne, Mark, Brett, Michelle, Melissa, Douglas. Mgmt. trainee Ill. Bell Telephone Co., Chgo., 1959-61; sales mgr. Programs Internat., Chgo., 1961-64, pres., 1964-71; pres. Internat. Speakers Networks, Elgin, Ill., 1971-75; show mgr. Indsl. & Sci. Conf. Mgmt., Chgo., 1975-78; pres. Expo Mgmt., Inc., Chgo., 1978-82, Trade Expositions & Assoc. Mgmt. Ltd., Chgo., 1982—. Pres. Kane County (Ill.) Young Republican Club, 1962-64; trustee Gail Borden Pub. Library, Elgin; bd. dirs. Area 2 Council on Aging for Ill., Upper Kane County chpt. Am. Heart Assn.; mem. adminstrv. bd., trustee First United Methodist Ch., Elgin. Mem. Nat. Assn. Exhbn. Mgrs. (dir.), Chgo. Assn. Commerce and Industry, Execs. Internat., Conv. and Tourism Bur., Omicron Delta Kappa. Clubs: Masons, Shriners. Home: 11N937 Almora Terr Elgin IL 60123 Office: Trade Expositions and Associated Mgmt Ltd Tyler Creek Pla Box 7338 Elgin IL 60121

ROGERS, DENNIS LEE, architect; b. Athens, Tenn., Jan. 26, 1953; s. Franklin O'Dean and Mary Nell (Benson) R.; m. Hada Luz Chavarria, Dec. 17, 1977; children—O'Dina Maria, Angela Emperatriz. B.Arch., U. Tenn., 1980. Archtl. design draftsman U.S. Air Force, Luke AFB, Ariz., 1980-81; engring. design draftsman Marathon Steel Co., Tempe, Ariz., 1981-82; facilities design engr. Hughes Helicopter, Inc., Mesa, Ariz., 1982-83; facilities engr./planner Four-Phase/ISO, Inc., Tempe, 1983-84; architect Motorola, Inc., Mesa, 1984-85, cons., 1987-88, Ariz. Architects and Planners, Inc., Phoenix, 1985-86; project architect Greyhound Lines, Inc., Phoenix, 1986-87; cons. Motorola, Inc., Mesa, 1987-88, Sun-Mos Tech., Tempe, 1988—. Prin. works include passive solar home, Lake Tahoe, Nev., 1982. Recipient Outstanding Performance award Hughes Helicopter, Inc., 1983. Mem. AIA (assoc.), Toastmasters, Mesa Jaycees (treas. 1984-85). Office: Sun-Mos Tech 1430 W Broadway Tempe AZ 85281

ROGERS, DONALD SHELDON, retired gas corporation executive; b. N.Y.C., July 16, 1921; s. Donald Sheldon and Sally Jean (Pettit) R.; m. Jacqueline Doris Routledge, Aug. 7, 1942; children—Donald Sheldon, Jacqueline Donna. With Hudson Bay Co., Alberta, Man., Can., 1947-69; v.p. Steinbergs Ltd., Montreal, Que., Can., 1969-73; pres. Gambles Can. Ltd., Winnipeg, Man., Can., 1973-78; dep. minister Govt. of Man., Winnipeg, Man., Can., 1978-80; exec. v.p. Inter-City Gas Corp., Winnipeg, Man., Can., 1980-86, bd. dirs., 1986-87; dir. Investor Group, Winnipeg, UMA Group, Vancouver, B.C. With RCAF, 1941-47; ETO. Clubs: Manitoba, St. Charles Country (Winnipeg). Home: 4-102, 65 Swindon Way, Winnipeg, MB Canada R3P 0T8 Office: Inter City Gas Corp, 444 St Mary Ave, Winnipeg, MB Canada R3C 3T7

ROGERS, EDMUND PENDLETON, III, lawyer; b. N.Y.C., May 5, 1941; s. Edmund Pendleton Rogers Jr. and Beatrice (Brown) Guthrie; m. Cynthia Banks Alexandre, June 26, 1965; children: Edmund, James. BA, Yale U., 1965, JD, 1968. Assoc. Davis, Polk & Wardwell, N.Y.C., 1968-76; asst. resident counsel Morgan Guaranty Trust N.Y., N.Y.C., 1976-78, v.p., asst. resident counsel, 1978-86, sr. v.p., resident counsel, 1986—. Bd. health Borough of Fair Hills, N.J., 1988. With USNR, 1960-66. Mem. ABA, N.Y. State Bar Assn., Bar Assn. City of N.Y. (audit com. 1987—), Somerset Hills County Club (gov. 1987—), Anglers Club N.Y. Republican. Episcopalian. Office: Morgan Guaranty Trust Co 23 Wall St New York NY 10015

ROGERS, EDWARD SAMUEL, communications company executive; b. Toronto, Ont., Can., May 27, 1933; s. Edward Samuel and Velma Melissa (Taylor) R.; m. Loretta Anne Robinson, Sept. 25, 1963; children: Lisa Anne, Edward Samuel, Melinda Mary, Martha Loretta. B.A., Trinity Coll., U. Toronto, 1956; LL.B., Osgood Hall Law Sch., 1961. Founder, prin. Rogers Telecommunications Ltd., Toronto, 1960—; pres., chief exec. officer Rogers Communications Inc., 1978—; vice chmn., dir. Rogers Cablesystems Am. Inc., 1983—; chmn. Cantel, Inc., 1986—; bd. dirs. Talcorp Ltd., Can. Pub. Ltd. Mem. Canadian Cable TV Assn. (dir., past chmn.), Canadian Assn. Broadcasters., Progressive Conservative Anglican. Clubs: Toronto, York, Albany, Granite, Royal Can. Yacht; Rideau (Ottawa); Lyford Cay (Nassau). Office: Rogers Communications Inc, PO Box 249, Toronto, ON Canada M5K 1J5 *

ROGERS, GARDNER SPENCER, railroad company executive, retired, consultant; b. Bryn Mawr, Pa., Sept. 16, 1926; s. Gardner Spencer and Frances (Lloyd) R.; m. Margaret Elizabeth Windsor, July 18, 1954; children: Ann Rogers Wilbanks, Barbara Lloyd. Student Episcopal Acad., 1940-44, MIT, 1944-45; BS, U. Colo., 1951. Registered profl. engr., Calif. With Western Pacific R.R. Co., San Francisco, 1947-70, engr. costs, valuation and stats., 1964-69, asst. to gen. mgr. planning and control, 1969, asst. gen. mgr., 1970; gen. mgr. Civil & Mech. Maintenance Pty. Ltd., 1970-77; mgr. Western Australian ops. Fluor Australia Pty. Ltd., 1971-73, gen. mgr. ry. div., 1973-77; gen. mgr. Pilbara Industries, 1971-73; dir. budgets and control Consol. Rail Corp., 1978-79, sr. dir. budgets, planning and control, 1980, dir. corp. planning, 1981-87; cons., 1987—; mem. spl. adv. team R.R. ofcls. to U.S. Govt., 1962; adv. com. on R.R. property ICC, 1966-70. Mng. trustee Daniel B. Gardner Trust, Chgo.; alt. trustee Cathedral Sq. Found., Perth; vestryman Ch. of Eng., 1971-77, mem. synod and provincial synod, 1973-77, mem. diocesan coun., 1974-77, bd. dirs. sch.'s trust, 1975-77. Mem. Instn. Engrs. Australia, Am. C. of C. in Australia (bd. dirs., v.p., chmn. Western Australian exec. com. 1976-77), Swanleigh (chmn. exec. com. 1974-77, coun.), Am. Mgmt. Assn., Am. Ry. Engr. Assn. (sec. com. 11 1983-87), Ry. and Locomotive Hist. Soc., Soc. of Cin., Mil. Order Loyal Legion (vice comdr.), Colo. Alumni Assn. No. Calif. (pres. 1951-52), Alpha Tau Omega (high coun. 1964-68, 82—). Republican. Clubs: Berkeley Tennis, Pacific Railway (San Francisco); Commonwealth (Calif.); Australian-Am. (Perth). Home and Office: 9 Mal Paso Rd Rte 1 Carmel CA 93923

ROGERS, HENRY C., public relations executive; b. Irvington, N.J., Apr. 19, 1914; s. Maurice and Mollie (Harrison) Rogosin; m. Rosalind Jaffe, June 16, 1937; children: Marcia Medavoy Ross, Ronald. Student, U. Pa., 1932-34, NYU, 1934. Founder, chmn. Rogers & Cowan, Inc., Pub. Relations, N.Y.C. and Beverly Hills, Calif. Author: Walking the Tightrope, 1980, Rogers' Rules for Success, 1984, The One-Hat Solution, 1986, Rogers' Rules for Businesswomen, 1988. Trustee Los Angeles County Mus. Art; trustee Am. Film Inst., ACLU Found.; bd. govs. Los Angeles Music Ctr. Mem. Pub. Relations Soc. Am., Acad. Motion Picture Arts and Scis., Filmes Soc. (trustee). Democrat. Jewish. Office: Rogers & Cowan Inc 10000 Santa Monica Blvd Los Angeles CA 90067-7007

ROGERS, HORTON WILLIAM, sales executive; b. Louisville, Aug. 12, 1930; s. August Horton and Mildred (Manning) R.; m. Annabelle June Maier, Feb. 2, 1951; children: Timothy, Gail. BSEE, U. Mo., 1959; MBA, U. of S. Fla., 1967. Engr. McDonnel-Douglas Corp., St. Louis, 1962-63; prin. engr. Honeywell, Inc., St. Petersburg, Fla., 1963-71; v.p. ops. Precise Power Corp., Bradenton, Fla., 1971-72; pres. Lampkin Labs., Bradenton, 1971-78; sales mgr. John Fluke Mfg. Co., Orlando, Fla., 1978—; bd. dirs., automated prodn. cons. R.F. Engring., Inc., Sarasota, Fla. Author: Educating Management, 1965; patentee in field. Bd. dirs. United Residents of Pinellas County, Dunedin, Fla., 1968-70. Served with USN, 1951-55. Republican. Methodist. Lodge: Masons. Office: John Fluke Mfg Co Inc 940 N Ferncreek Ave Orlando FL 32803

ROGERS, HOWARD GARDNER, consultant, photographic company research director emeritus; b. Houghton, Mich., June 21, 1915; s. Gardner and Grace (Phillips) R.; m. Erdna M. Reggio, Jan. 17, 1940; children—Anne Cranford, Peter Nicholas, Mary Phillips Rogers Helmreich, Mark Howard, Lucinda Gardner. Student, Harvard Coll., 1933-35. With Polaroid Corp., Cambridge, Mass., 1936-85; dept. mgr. spl. color photographic research Polaroid Corp., 1954-74, v.p., sr. research fellow, 1976-78, sr. v.p., assoc. dir. research, 1978-80, sr. v.p., dir. research, 1980-85; cons. on photog. systems., light polarizers, 3-D imaging, new polymers. Inventor of instant color photographic systems, dye developers, new light-polarizers and other optical devices. Recipient Wetherill medal Franklin Inst., 1966. Fellow Am. Acad. Arts and Scis., Soc. Photographic Scientists and Engrs. (hon.), Optical Soc. Am., Am. Inst. Chemists; mem. Am. Chem. Soc., Royal Photographic Soc., Indsl. Research Inst. (Achievement award 1987). Home: 20 Newton St Weston MA 02193 Office: Polaroid Corp 549 Technology Sq Cambridge MA 02139

ROGERS, JACK MITCHELL, fire department official; b. Terre Haute, Ind., Jan. 11, 1958; s. Glenn Mitchell and Nellie Lou (Bandy) R. BS, Ind. State U., 1981. Owner Rogers Rentals, Terre Haute, 1980-81, 83; disstbr. Amway Co., Terre Haute, 1978-84; mem. Terre Haute Fire Dept., 1981—; owner, mgr. Capital Group Real Estate Rentals, Terre Haute, 1988. Asst. scoutmaster Boy Scouts Am. Mem. Delta Sigma Pi, Wabash Valley Appliance Ctr. Bowling League (capt. 198s6-88), Coin Club (pres. 1978). Home: 1300 S 29th St Terre Haute IN 47803 Office: Terre Haute Fire Dept 934 S 4th St Terre Haute IN 47807

ROGERS, JAMES BEELAND, JR., investment company executive; b. Balt., Oct. 19, 1942; s. James Beeland and Ernestine Barbara (Brewer) R.; B.A. cum laude, Yale U., 1964; B.A. with honors, M.A. in Politics, Philosophy and Econs., Balliol Coll., Oxford (Eng.) U., 1966. Investment analyst Bache & Co., N.Y.C., 1968-69, R. Gilder & Co., N.Y.C., 1969-70; asst. to chmn. Neuberger & Berman, N.Y.C., 1970-71; with Arnhold and S. Bleichroeder Inc., 1971-73; exec. v.p. Soros Fund Mgmt. N.Y.C., 1973-80; chmn. bd. Rogers Holdings, 1980—; adj. prof. Columbia U. Sch. Bus., 1983-85, prof. fin., 1986—. Served to lt. U.S. Army, 1966-68. Home: 352 Riverside Dr New York NY 10025

ROGERS, JAMES EDWARD, paper company executive; b. Richmond, Va., Aug. 13, 1945; s. Olin Adair and Marjorie (Aiken) R.; m. Susan Young, May 24; children: James Edward Jr., Catherine, Margaret. BS in Physics, Va. Mil. Inst., 1967; MS in Nuclear Engring., U. Va., 1969; postgrad., Harvard U., 1987. Licensing engr. Va. Electric and Power Co., Richmond, 1969-71; sales engr., sales mgr., v.p. sales and mktg. James River Paper Co., Richmond, 1971-77, v.p., gen. mgr. paper making div., 1979-82; v.p., gen. mgr. James River-Rochester (N.Y.), Inc., 1977-79; v.p. corp. planning James River Corp., Richmond, 1982-84, sr. v.p. corp. devel., 1984-87, sr. v.p., group exec., specialty paper bus., 1987—. Bd. dirs. Jr. Achievement Richmond, 1985, Richmond Childrens Mus., 1986, Maymont Found., Richmond, 1987. Republican. Clubs: Commonwealth (Richmond); Fishing Bay Yacht (Deltaville, Va.) (commodore 1980); N.Y. Yacht (N.Y.C.). Office: James River Corp Tredegar St Richmond VA 23217

ROGERS, JOHN S., electronics executive; b. Newton, Mass., May 16, 1929; s. John S. and Emily (Brack) R.; m. Jeanne B. Igoe, Sept. 17, 1955 (dec. Apr. 1985); children: John III, Pamela J., Bryan T., Christopher; m. Joyce Retchin, Dec. 12, 1987. Student, Bryant & Stratton Bus. Sch., 1948-50; Northeastern U., 1955-59. Dept. mgr. Raytheon Co., Boston, 1950-59; v.p. mfg. Silicon Transistor, Long Island, N.Y., 1959-64; v.p., gen. mgr. Slater Electric, Glen Cove, N.Y., 1964-69; pres., chmn. bd. R.S.M. Electron Power, Inc., Deer Park, N.Y., 1969—. Served with USMC, 1946-48, PTO. Republican. Roman Catholic. Office: RSM Electron Power Inc 221 W Industry Ct Deer Park NY 11729

ROGERS, JOHN W., parcel delivery company executive; b. 1933; married. Chmn., chief exec. officer, dir. United Parcel Service Am. Inc., Greenwich, Conn., 1984—; chmn., chief exec. officer United Parcel Service Inc., N.Y.C., 1984—; also dir. parent co. and subs. United Parcel Service of Am. Inc., N.Y.C. Office: United Parcel Svc Am Inc 51 Weaver St Greenwich CT 06836 *

ROGERS, JOHN WILLARD, retired construction company executive; b. Oak Park, Ill., Dec. 20, 1908; s. Walter Alexander and Julia Margaret (Cushing) R.; m. Ruth Woods Stiles, Apr. 16, 1933; 1 child, Diane Rogers Carroll. Student, U. Wis., 1926-29. With Bates & Rogers Constrn. Corp., Chgo., 1929-86; gen. supt. Alcan Hwy. Bates & Rogers Constrn. Corp., Whitehorse, Yukon Ter., Alaska, 1943-45; dir. Bates & Rogers Constrn. Corp., 1944—; sec., treas. Bates & Rogers Constrn. Corp., Chgo., 1946-47, v.p., treas., 1948-61, exec. v.p., treas., 1961-67, pres., treas., 1968-79, chmn. bd., chief exec. officer, 1979—. Pres., trustee Glen Ellyn YMCA, Ill., 1937-58; mem. Glen Ellyn Sch. Bd., 1950-53; trustee, sec. George Williams Coll., 1956-86; vice chmn. Jr. Achievement Chgo., Bates & Rogers Found.; adv. bd. B.R. Ryall YMCA; mem. indsl. liaison council dept. engring. U. Wis. Recipient Spl. Recognition medal George Wiliams Coll., 1984; Disting. Service citation U. Wis., Madison, 1985. Mem. ASCE, Western Soc. Engrs., Am. Inst. Constructors, Cons. Constructors Council (past pres.), Ohio Contractors Assn. (Hall of Fame), Assoc. Gen. Contractors Am. (bd. dirs., exec. com., legis. com., regional coordinator pub. relations com.), Assoc. Gen. Contractors Ill. (chmn. legis. network), Builders Assn. Chgo. (past bd. dirs.), Beavers (founding mem.). Republican. Congregationalist. Clubs: Union League (active Civic and Arts Found.), Executives, Economics (Chgo.); Glen Oak Country (Glen Ellyn); Capitol Hill (Washington); Surf (Surfside, Fla.).

ROGERS, JOHNNIE CALVIN, fraternal organization administrator; b. San Francisco, Aug. 22, 1948; s. Alfred Calvin and Evelyn Blanche (Crouse) R.; m. Gail Ann Rogers, Oct. 23, 1982; children: Dylan, Zachary, Chelsea. BS, Colo. Coll., 1974. CPA, Colo. Auditor May Zima & Co., West Palm Beach, Fla., 1974-76; sr. auditor Grant Thornton, Colorado Springs, 1976-78; city auditor City of Colorado Springs, 1978-86; dep. dir. Fire & Police Pension Assn., Englewood, Colo., 1986-87; exec. dir. Fire & Police Pension Assn., Englewood, 1987—. Served with U.S. Navy, 1967-71. Mem. AICPA, Am. Soc. Pub. Adminstrn., Govt. Fin. Officers, Assn. Institutional Investors. Democrat. Mem. Disciples of Christ. Home: 1306 Whitehouse Dr Colorado Springs CO 80904 Office: Fire & Police Pension Assn 5290 DTC Pkwy Englewood CO 80111

ROGERS, JUDY ANN, accountant; b. Pontiac, Mich., May 25, 1948; d. Charles Michael and Virginia (Perna) Crickon; drug sci. scholar, U. Mich., 1965; B.A. summa cum laude, Oakland U., Rochester, Mich., 1978; postgrad. Wayne State U. Law Sch., 1978-79; m. Ronald Richard Rogers, Aug. 30, 1967; 1 dau., Anne Michelle. Office mgr. Holforty Assos. Inc., Rochester, 1970-76; adminstr. asst. to controller Perry Drug Stores, Inc., Pontiac, 1976-78; office mgr. Artcraft Blueprint Co., Pontiac, 1978-81; plant acct. Gates Rubber Co., Pontiac, 1981-83; mgr. VR Bus. Brokers, Troy, 1983-85; owner, operator Fantastic Sam's (3 locations); instr. Oxford Sch. of Bus.; mem. exec. adv. council Mich. region Fantastic Sams. Mem. Orion Twp. Environ. Task Force; treas. Friends of the Library; active local Republican Party. Walter Reuther Meml. Fund scholar, 1978. Recipient Silver Poet award, 1986. Mem. Nat. Assn. Exec. Females, Women's Comml. Real Estate Assn., Am. Bus. Women, Mich. Profl. Women's Network. Club: Deer Lake Racquet. Contbr. to The Poet, Our Twentieth Century's Greatest Poems, Today's Greatest Poems. Home: 4383 Morgan Rd Pontiac MI 48055 Office: 5034 Dixie Hwy Drayton Plains MI 48020

ROGERS, JUSTIN TOWNER, JR., utility executive; b. Sandusky, Ohio, Aug. 4, 1929; s. Justin Towner and Barbara Eloise (Larkin) R. AB cum laude, Princeton U., 1951; JD, U. Mich., 1954. Bar: Ohio 1954. Assoc. Wright, Harlor, Purpus, Morris & Arnold, Columbus, 1956-58; with Ohio Edison Co., 1958—; v.p., then exec. v.p. Ohio Edison Co., Akron, 1970-79; pres. Ohio Edison Co., 1980—, dir., 1970—; chmn. bd., bd. dir. Pa. Power Co., New Castle; bd. dir. First Nat. Bank Ohio, First Bancorp. of Ohio. Past pres., trustee Akron Community Trusts, Akron Child Guidance Ctr.; past chmn. Akron Associated Health Agys., U. Akron Assocs.; past chmn. bd. trustees Akron Gen. Med. Ctr.; bd. dirs. Akron Devel. Corp.; past bd. dirs. Assn. Edison Illuminating Cos., Edison Electric Inst.; chmn. bd. dirs. Ohio Electric Utility Inst.; bd. dirs. Electric Power Rsch. Inst.; bus. adv. coun. Coll. Bus. Adminstrn. Kent State U. With U.S. Army, 1954-56. Mem. Phi Delta Phi, Beta Gamma Sigma (hon.). Clubs: Akron City, Portage Country, Mayflower (Akron); Rockwell Springs Trout (Castalia, Ohio); Princeton (N.Y.C.); Capitol Hill (Washington); Union (Cleve.). Office: Ohio Edison Co 76 S Main St Akron OH 44308

ROGERS, LEE JASPER, lawyer; b. Fort Monmouth, N.J., May 6, 1955; s. Peter and Ethel Mae (Williams) R.; m. Vanessa Walisha Yarbrough, Apr. 18, 1981; 1 child, Stephanie Alexandria. Student Drew U., 1975, Monmouth Coll., 1975; BA in History, Hampton Inst., 1977; JD, Howard U., 1980. Sole practice law, Red Bank, N.J., 1981—; vol. counsel Pro Bono Legal Services, Red Bank, 1982—; pres., chmn. bd. Jay-Mar Entertainment Enterprises Inc., 1986—. Author numerous poems. Mem. exec. com. NAACP, Red Bank, 1983-86. Mem. Assn. Trial lawyers Am., ABA. Baptist. Lodges: Elks (past acting recording sec.), Bates (sec. house com.). Home: 112 Catherine St Red Bank NJ 07701-1244 Office: 298 Shrewsbury Ave Red Bank NJ 07701-1319

ROGERS, MICHAEL THOMAS, advertising company executive; b. Kansas City, Kans., Apr. 24, 1941; s. Charles Francis and Vada Mae (Presley) R.; m. Catherine Helen Egan, June 9, 1962; children: Mary Ann, Charles William, Michael Joseph, Christina, Benjamin, Sandra. BS in Communications, Xavier U., 1962. Writer Lang, Fisher & Stashower, Cleve., 1963-65, Fuller Smith & Ross, Cleve., 1965-68; sr. v.p., exec. creative dir. Leo Burnett Agys., Chgo., 1969-79, Benton & Bowles, N.Y.C., 1979-81; exec. v.p., exec. creative dir. Foote, Cone & Belding Communications, Chgo., 1981—. Active St. Athanasius Parish, Evanston, Ill., 1976—. Named to Advt. Hall of Fame for Diet Rite Cola campaign, 1983; recipient Advt. awards Sears Fin. Network, 1983, numerous Clio and Addy awards. Roman Catholic. Other: Campbell-Mithun Inc 737 N Michigan Ave Chicago IL 60611

ROGERS, PAUL A'COURT, management consultant; b. Detroit, Oct. 12, 1939; s. Noel and Jessie (Adams) R.; m. Terri M. Rogers; 1 child, Ashley. BSBA, U. Md., 1982. Field engr. Gen. Dynamics, Pomona, Calif., 1962-65, project mgr., 1968-72; field engr. Hughes Aircraft Co., Los Angeles, 1965-68; systems engr. Scientific Mgmt. Assos., Riverdale, Md., 1972-73, program mgr., 1975-72; corp. planner, 1982—; project mgr. Systems Cons., Washington, 1973-75. Bd. dirs. Applied Systems Planning, Mut. Human Concerns. Served with USNR, 1959-62. Mem. Am. Mgmt. Assn., Am. Mktg. Assn., Project Mgmt. Inst., Naval Inst., Am. Soc. Naval Engrs. Democrat. Presbyterian. Home: 8223 Mt Vernon Hwy Alexandria VA 22309

ROGERS, PETER NORMAN, food company executive; b. High Wycombe, Eng., June 23, 1938; came to U.S., 1973; s. Norman John and Constance Jane (Jordan) R.; m. Patricia Mary Short, Nov. 15, 1962; children—Bridget Jane, Simon John. B.Sc., U. Leicester, Eng., 1959, Ph.D., 1963. Pres. Curtiss Candy Co., Chgo., 1973-76, New Eng. Fish Co., Seattle, 1978-80; sr. v.p. Standard Brands, Inc., N.Y.C., 1980-81; pres. Life Savers div. Nabisco Brands, Inc., N.Y.C., 1981-83; pres. biscuit div. Nabisco Brands, Inc., Parsippany, N.J., 1983-85, sr. v.p., 1985-86, pres., 1986-87; pres. Internat. Nabisco Brands, Inc., East Hanover, 1987-88; chmn., chief exec. officer Nabisco Biscuit Co., East Hanover, 1988—. Trustee Lupus Found., Food Industry Crusade Against Hunger. Mem. Biscuit and Cracker Mfrs. Assn. (bd. dirs., vice chmn. 1983-85), Nat. Planning Assn. (trustee), Nat. Confectioners Assn. (dir. 1973-76). Club: Burning Tree Country (Greenwich, Conn.). Home: 44 Dexter Dr N Basking Ridge NJ 07920 Office: Nabisco Biscuit Co River Rd East Hanover NJ 07936-1932

ROGERS, RALPH B., business executive; b. Boston, 1909; married. Ed., Northeastern U. With Cummins Diesel Engine Corp., Edwards Co., Hill Diesel Engine Co., Ideal Power Lawnmower Co., Indian Motocycle Co., Rogers Diesel & Aircraft Corp., Rogers Internat. Corp., Armstrong Rubber Export Corp.; with Tex. Industries Inc., Dallas, 1950—, chmn. bd., pres., chief exec. officer, 1951-75, chmn. bd., 1975—; dir. numerous subsidiaries. Chmn. bd. dirs. Tex. Industries Found.; chmn. emeritus Pub. Communication Found. North Tex., Pub. Broadcasting Service, U. Med. Ctr., Inc.; past bd. dirs. Nat. Captioning Inst.; trustee Northeastern U., St. Mark's Sch. Tex.; former chmn. bd. mgrs. Dallas County Hosp. Dist.; founding chmn., chmn. emeritus Dallas Arboretum and Bot. Soc.; pres. Dallas Found. for Health, Edn. and Research. Lodge: Masons. Office: Tex Industries Inc 8100 Carpenter Frwy Dallas TX 75247

ROGERS, RICHARD HILTON, service executive; b. Florence, S.C., May 26, 1935; s. Leslie Lawton and Bessie (Holloway) R.; children: Richard Shannon, Leslie Anne. Student, U. N.C., 1953-55; BA in Bus. Adminstrn. cum laude, Bryant Coll., 1962. Innkeeper Helmsley Spear, N.Y.C., 1961-62; v.p. Holiday Inns of Am., Memphis, 1962-73; exec. v.p. First Hospitality Corp., Hackensack, N.J., 1974-77; v.p., chief oper. officer Cindy's Inc., Atlanta, 1978-81; v.p. 1982 World's Fair, Knoxville, Tenn.; pres., chief exec. officer Hospitality Internat., Atlanta, 1982—; developer, operator The Warehouse Rest., Oxford, Miss., 1973-75, Beauregard's Rest., Hattiesburg, Miss., 1975-78, Walter Mitty's Rest., Auburn, Ala., 1980-83. Contbr. to profl. jours. Mem. adv. bd. Bethune-Cookman Coll. With USN, 1954-58, Korea. Mem. Am. Hotel/Motel Assn. (mktg. com. 1986—, adv. council 1987—, industry adv. bd.), Economy Lodging Council. Home: 245 Rhine Dr Alpharetta GA 30201 Office: Hospitality Internat Inc 1152 Spring St Ste A Atlanta GA 30309

ROGERS, RICHARD RAYMOND, cosmetics company executive; b. Houston, Apr. 15, 1943; s. J. Ben and Mary Kay (Ash) R.; student North Tex. State U.; children: Terri, Rick, Ryan. Co-founder Mary Kay Cosmetics, Inc., Dallas, 1963, gen. mgr., 1963-65, v.p., 1965-68, pres., 1968-87, chmn. bd., 1987—, also dir. With USMCR. Named Man of Yr., North Tex. Mktg. Assn., 1968. Republican. Baptist. Office: Mary Kay Cosmetics Inc 8787 Stemmons Frwy Dallas TX 75247

ROGERS, ROBERT D., steel company executive; b. 1936. Grad., Yale U., 1958; MBA, Harvard U., 1962. With George A. Fuller Co. div. Okla. Cement Co., 1962-63; with Tex. Industries, Inc., Dallas, 1963—, v.p. ops., 1968-70, pres., chief adminstrv. officer, 1970-74, pres., chief exec. officer, also bd. dirs.; chmn. bd. dirs., chief exec. officer Chaparral Steel Co., Midlothian, Tex., Brookhollow Corp., Dallas. Served with USN, 1958-60. Office: Tex Industries Inc 8100 Carpenter Frwy Dallas TX 75247

ROGERS, THEODORE COURTNEY, investment company executive, consultant; b. Lorain, Ohio, Aug. 25, 1934; s. William Theodore and Leona Ruth (Gerhart) R.; BS in Social Sci., Miami U., Oxford, Ohio, 1956; postgrad. Johns Hopkins U., 1957; MBA summa cum laude, Marquette U., 1968; m. Elizabeth B. Barlow, June 28, 1984; children by previous marriage—Pamela Anne Rogers Harmon, Theodore Courtney Jr. With Armco Inc., 1958-80; pres. Olympic Fastening Systems, 1970-74, with Bathey Mfg. Co. subs., 1970, group v.p. indsl. products, 1971-74, exec. v.p. Nat. Supply Co. subs., Houston, 1974-76, pres., 1976-80, v.p. parent co., 1976-79, group v.p. parent co., 1979-80; pres., chief operating officer NL Industries, Inc., N.Y.C., 1980-82, pres., chief exec. officer, 1982-83, chmn., pres., chief exec. officer, 1983-87; ptnr. Am. Indsl. Ptnrs., N.Y., 1987—; bd. dir. Allied Signal Inc., MCorp. Bd. dirs. United Cerebral Palsy Rsch. and Ednl. Found., Inc.; chmn. N.Y.C. Cerebral Palsy Fund Drive; chmn. nat. com. Houston Ballet; mem. devel. bd. U. Tex. Health Sci Ctr.; mem. campaign com. United Way Tri State; mem. fund leadership com. Lincoln Ctr.; chmn. bd. N.Y.C. Ballet. Lt. USN, 1956-58. Mem. Petroleum Equipment Suppliers Assn. (bd. dirs.), Young Pres. Orgn., Bus. Roundtable, Beta Gamma Sigma (bd. dirs.' table), Kappa Phi Kappa. Clubs: Houstonian, Ramada, Houston Country; Links, Sky, Econ. (N.Y.C.); Met. (Washington). Office: Am Indsl Ptnr 200 Park Ave Ste 3122 New York NY 10166-0114

ROGERS, WILLIAM FENNA, JR., supermarket executive, management consultant; b. Higginsville, Mo., Dec. 25, 1912; s. William Fenna and Emily S. (Moose) R.; m. Thelma Ann Hooper, June 15, 1940 (dec. Mar. 1982); m. Ethel Allene Burgess, Aug. 6, 1983; stepchildren—Dorothy H. Nance, Linda H. Connors. B.A., Ark. Coll., 1933; postgrad. U. Ark., 1933, Tulane U., 1935, U. Fla., 1938-39. Vocat. adv. Nat. Youth Adminstrn., Little Rock, 1936-38; chief field ops. U.S. Employment Service, Little Rock, 1938-43, chief supr. tng., Washington, 1946-47; asst. dir. Civilian Personnel Div., U.S. Dept. Navy, Washington, 1947-55; member productivity team Nat. Mgmt. Council, Paris, 1952;lectr. U.S. Internat. Fair, Amsterdam, 1963; v.p. indsl. relations Giant Food, Inc., Washington, 1955-75; mgmt. cons., Falls Church, Va., 1975—; trustee Teamster Warehouse Fund, 1956—, Carpet Layers Funds, 1968—; lectr. Am. U., 1949-69; pres. Chateau Devel. Corp., Fairfax, Va., 1978-83. Mem. selection bd. U.S. Postal Service, 1969-77; elder New York Ave. Presbyterian Ch., Washington, 1948-72, Falls Church Presbyn. Ch., 1980-83; mem. Falls Church Village Preservation and Improvement Soc., 1967—; cons. Lincoln commn. New York Ave. Presbyn. Ch., 1984—; chmn. bur. edn. and employment Greater Washington Bd. Trade, 1974-76. Served to lt. comdr. USNR, 1943-64. Mem. Am. Soc. Tng. and Devel. (life),

Am. Legion Res. Officers Assn., Naval Res. Assn., Alpha Psi Omega, Kappa Gamma, Pi Kappa Delta, Iota Lambda Sigma. Club: International Town and Country (dir. 1959-61) (Fairfax, Va.). Avocations: golf; fishing. Home: 214 Van Buren St Falls Church VA 22046

ROGULA, JAMES LEROY, consumer products company executive; b. Rock Island, Ill., Nov. 8, 1933; s. Andrew and Nellie Pearl (Cook) R.; m. Adelaide F. Dittbrenner, May 29, 1960; children: James Lyle, Adelaide Ann, John Andrew. B.A., Knox Coll., 1955; M.B.A., NYU, 1964. Group product mgr. Am. Chicle Co., Long Island City, N.Y., 1958-66; v.p. new product devel. Carter Wallace, Inc., N.Y.C., 1966-72; v.p. new products J.B. Williams Co., N.Y.C., 1972-74; sr. v.p. E.J. Brach & Sons, Chgo., 1974-77; v.p., gen. mgr. A.E. Staley Mfg. Co., Oak Brook, Ill., 1977-80; exec. v.p. Booth Fisheries Corp., Chgo., 1980-82; v.p., gen. mgr. Arm & Hammer div. Church & Dwight, Inc., Princeton, NJ, 1982—; chmn. DeWitt Internat. Corp., Greenville, S.C., 1986—; bd. dirs. Church & Dwight Ltd., Toronto, Can., 1983—. Bd. dirs. Jr. Achievement, Mercer County, N.J, 1987—. With U.S. Army, 1956-58. Mem. Grocery Mfrs. Assn., Cosmetic Toiletries and Fragrances Assn., Nat. Detergents Assn., Sunset Ridge Country Club, Hopewell Valley Golf Club, Econ. Club Chgo. Home: 58 W Shore Dr Pennington NJ 08534 Office: Church & Dwight Inc 469 N Harrison St Princeton NJ 08540

ROHDE, JAMES VINCENT, software systems company executive; b. O'Neill, Nebr., Jan. 25, 1939; s. Ambrose Vincent and Loretta Cecilia R.; m. Deborah L. Todd, June 6, 1966; children: Maria, Sonja, Daniele. BCS, Seattle U., 1962. Chmn. bd. dirs., pres., Applied Telephone Tech., Oakland, 1974; v.p. sales and mktg. Automation Electornics Corp., Oakland, 1975-82; pres., chmn. bd. dirs. Am. Telecorp, Inc., 1982—. Pres. Council Regents Heritage Coll., Toppenish, Wash., 1985-88; chmn. emeritus exec. com. Council Regents Heritage Coll. Republican. Roman Catholic. Office: Am Telecorp Inc 10 Twin Dolphin Dr Redwood City CA 94065

ROHDE, JOHN HANS, operations executive; b. Egeln, Germany, July 4, 1929; s. Wilhelm Friedrich and Louise Adele (Buschner) R.; m. Christel Elizabeth Wehrenberg, Apr. 24, 1954; children: Joan Evelyn, Karen Sylvia, Denise Marion. B in Mech Engring., Aachen U., Fed. Republic Germany, 1954; M in Indsl. Engring., Can. Inst. Sci. and Tech., 1959; PhD in Indsl. Mgmt., Aachen U., 1960; postgrad., Inst. Pour l'Etude des Methodes de Direction de l'Enterprise, Switzerland, 1975; D in Sci., London Inst. Applied Research, 1975. Gen. cons. S.A. Birn & Co., Louisville, 1961-70; dir. indsl. engring. Automotive div. ITT, Brussels, 1971-79; dir. ops. Automotive div. ITT, Southfield, Mich., 1979-80; dir. indsl. engring. REVLON, Inc., Edison, N.J., 1981-85; chmn. CSM Mgmt. Cons. Co. Inc., Sea Bright, N.J., 1986—; cons. A.T. Kearney, N.Y.C., 1986-88, Coopers & Lybrand, N.Y.C., 1988—. Author: Indirect Manpower Productivity, 1985; contbr. articles to profl. jours. Mem. Inst. Indsl. Engrs. (sr.), Soc. Automotive Engrs. (sr.), Methods Time Measurement Assn. for Standards and Research, Am. Mgmt. Assn. Republican. Home and Office: 1540 Ocean Ave Ste 5 Sea Bright NJ 07760

ROHN, ELIZABETH G., banker; b. Hartford, Conn., May 25, 1948; d. Charles Alonzo and Julie (Gelston) Harrington; m. Douglas Jerome Gregor (div. 1980); m. William John Rohn, Aug. 29, 1980. AA, Harford Coll. for Women, 1968; BA, U. Ill., Chgo., 1971; MBA, U. Minn., 1975; cert. in exec. program-Sloan Mgmt., MIT, 1988. Coord. svc. TIES-Computer Coop., St. Paul, 1971-73; mgr. svcs. Metro-II Computer Coop, Mpls., 1976-78; sr. cons. Plante & Moran-CPA/Mgmt. Cons., Southfield, Mich., 1979-82; sr. cons. Fed. Nat. Mortgage Assn., Washington, 1982-83, asst. to chief exec. officer and chmn. bd., 1983-84, dir. mortgage acquisition, 1984-86, v.p. mortgage ops., 1987-88; v.p., mgr. consumer lending Mellon Bank (East), Phila., 1988—. Office: Mellon Bank 7th and Market Sts Philadelphia PA 19101-7899

ROHR, DANIEL C., banker; b. Chgo., Apr. 9, 1946; s. Edward C. and Rose V. (Murphy) R.; m. Mildred Molinaro, Oct. 10, 1970; children—Rebecca, David, James, Robert. B.A., St. Ambrose Coll, Iowa, 1968; M.B.A., U. Notre Dame, South Bend, 1970. Group v.p. S.E. Continental Ill. Nat. Bank, Chgo., 1980-83, group v.p. East Coast, 1983-85, departmental credit officer, 1984-86, chmn. loan com., 1985-87, sr. v.p., 1985—, dept. head, energy and minerals, 1986-87, chief credit officer, chmn. credit policy com., 1988; exec. v.p., cheif credit officer Columbia Savs. and Loan Assn., Beverly Hills, Calif., 1988—; chmn. investment com. Columbia Savs. and Loan Assn., Beverly Hills, 1989—; chief Credit Officer and chmn. of credit policy com., Beverly Hills, 1988. Mem. Robert Morris Assocs. Republican. Roman Catholic. Home: 1085 Ashley Rd Lake Forest IL 60045 Office: Columbia Savs & Loan Assn 8840 Wilshire Blvd Beverly Hills CA 90211

ROHRBACH, CLAYTON JOHN, III, investment banker; b. Corning, N.Y., Feb. 17, 1944; s. Clayton John Jr. and Carolee (Anderson) R.; m. Anne O. Wholey, Aug. 3, 1985; 1 child, Jacqueline. BA, St. Lawrence U., 1966; MBA, Columbia U., 1971. Mng. dir. Merrill Lynch and Co., N.Y.C., 1971-81, Morgan Stanley and Co., Inc., N.Y.C., 1981—. Lt. USN, 1966-69, Vietnam. Mem. Internat. Ctr. Photography (trustee), N.Y. Athletic Club, Doubles Club, Links, Stanwich CLub, Rockaway Hunting, Lawrence Beach Club, Landmark Club, Loblolly Pines Club. Home: 136 E 79th St New York NY 10021 Office: Morgan Stanley & Co 1251 Ave of the Americas New York NY 10020

ROHRMAN, DOUGLASS FREDERICK, lawyer; b. Chgo., Aug. 10, 1941; s. Frederick Alvin and Velma Elizabeth (Birdwell) R.; m. Susan Vitullo; children: Kathryn Anne, Elizabeth Clelia, Alessandra Claire. AB, Duke U., 1963; JD, Northwestern U., 1966. Bar: Ill. 1966. Legal coordinator Nat. Communicable Disease Center, Altanta, 1966-68; assoc. Keck, Mahin & Cate, Chgo., 1968-73, ptnr., 1973—; exec. v.p., dir. Kerogen Oil Co., 1967—. Co-author: Commercial Liability Risk Management and Insurance, 2 vols., 1978, 86; contbr. articles on law to profl. jours. Vice chmn., commr. Ill. Food and Drug Commn., 1970-72. Served as lt. USPHS, 1966-68. Mem. Am., Chgo. (chmn. com. on food and drug law 1972-73), 7th Circuit bar assns., Am. Soc. Law and Medicine, Selden Soc. Democrat. Episcopalian. Clubs: Legal, Kenilworth, Metropolitan, River, Wigmore, Washington Duke. Home: 520 Brier St Kenilworth IL 60043 Office: 8300 Sears Tower Chicago IL 60606

ROHSENOW, WARREN MAX, retired mechanical engineer, educator; b. Chgo., Feb. 12, 1921; s. Fred and Selma (Gorss) R.; m. Katharine Towneley Smith, Sept. 20, 1946; children—John, Brian, Damaris, Sandra, Anne. B.S., Northwestern U., 1941; M.Eng., Yale, 1943, D.Eng., 1944. Teaching asst., instr. mech. engring. Yale, 1941-44; mem. faculty Mass. Inst. Tech., 1946-85, prof. mech. engring., 1955-85, dir. heat transfer lab., 1954-85, prof. emeritus, 1985; Chmn. bd. dirs. Dynatech Corp. Author: (with Choi) Heat Mass and Momentum Transfer, 1961; Editor: Developments in Heat Transfer, 1964, (with Hartnett) Handbook of Heat Transfer, 1973, 2d edit., 1985. Served as lt. (j.g.) USNR, 1944-46; mech. engr. gas turbine div. Engring. Expt. Sta. Annapolis, Md. Recipient Pi Tau Sigma gold medal Am. Soc. M.E., 1951; award for advancement sci. Yale Engring. Assn., 1952; merit award Northwestern Alumni, 1955. Fellow Am. Acad. Arts and Scis., Nat. Acad. Engring., Am. Soc. M.E. (hon. mem., Heat Transfer Meml. award 1967, Max Jakob Meml. award 1970); mem. Sigma Xi, Tau Beta Pi, Pi Tau Sigma. Home: 47 Windsor Rd Waban MA 02168 Office: MIT Cambridge MA 02138

ROISLER, GLENN HARVEY, utility official; b. Milw., Apr. 6, 1952; s. George Harvey and Mayme Elvin (Salo) R.; m. Jacqueline Bout, July 27, 1971; 1 child, Renee Jenette. Student electronics tech., DeVry Inst. Tech., Chgo., 1976; student computer engring. tech., Capitol Radio Engring. Inst., Washington, 1980; student, N.C. State U., 1982—. Instr. scuba Pirate's Cove, Inc., Milw., 1969-70; sr. electronics technician Bendix Field Engring. Corp., Columbia, Md., 1977-79; field engr. Technicare, Inc., Solon, Ohio, 1979; supr. electronics Troxler Labs., Inc., Research Triangle Park, N.C., 1979-81; mgr. prodn. Matrix Corp., Raleigh, N.C., 1981; vendor surveillance specialist Carolina Power and Light Co., Raleigh, N.C., 1981-84, sr. quality assurance specialist, 1984—. Contbr. articles to profl. publs. Served with USN, 1971-77. Mem. Am. Soc. for Quality Control (cert. quality engr., reliability engr.), Gamma Beta Phi, Sigma Pi Sigma. Methodist. Home: 208 Mayodan Dr Cary NC 27511 Office: Carolina Power & Light Co PO Box 1551 Raleigh NC 27605

ROLAND, BILLY RAY, electronics company executive; b. Grandview, Tex., June 12, 1926; s. Marvin Wesley and Minnie Mae (Martin) R.; m. Ruth Ranell Sheets, Mar. 9, 1950 (div. 1982); children—Carl Ray and Darla Kay (twins); m. Linda Sue Leslie, Feb. 21, 1986. B.S., Tex. Christian U., 1954. C.P.A., Tex. Ticket and baggage agt. Southwestern Greyhound Co., Ft. Worth, 1943-44, 46-51; supr. acctg. dept. Tandy Leather Co., 1954-60; controller, asst. sec., treas. Tandy Corp., 1960-75, Tandy crafts, Inc., 1975-78; v.p. Tandy Corp., 1978-85. Vice pres., treas. David L. Tandy Found., 1966—; mng. trustee James L. and Eunice West Charitable Trust, 1980—; treas. Benjamin F. Johnston Found., 1984—; retired 1985. Served with inf. U.S. Army, 1944-46. Mem. Am. Inst. C.P.A.s, Tex. Soc. C.P.A.s, Ft. Worth Soc. C.P.A.s, Ft. Worth C. of C. Democrat. Methodist. Clubs: Colonial Country, Petroleum, Lake Country Golf and Country. Home: 8937 Random Rd Fort Worth TX 76179

ROLAND, DAVID LEONARD, broadcast production educator; b. Port Jefferson, N.Y., Oct. 2, 1948; s. Leonard Ernest and Dorothy (Stewart) R.; m. Susan Mary Becht, July 10, 1971 (dec. Nov. 1979); m. Theresa Regina Ryan, Dec. 27, 1980. BS, Empire State Coll., 1976; MA, L.I. U., 1981. Tchr. photography Bd. Coop. Ednl. Svcs., Patchoque, N.Y., 1975-85, tchr. TV prodns., 1985—; mem. pub. relations com. Bd. Coop. Ednl. Services, Patchoque, 1986—. Contbr. photographs to gallery shows, 1981, 84; dir. CBS Television Worth Teaching Video (cert. merit), Camp Pa-gua-tuck Video (Outstanding Service award), Longwood Sch. Dist. Video. Named Disting. Occupational Tchr. of Yr. State of N.Y., 1988. Mem. Vocat. Indsl. Clubs Am. (advisor 1976—, chairperson), Internat. TV Assn., Assn. L.I. Vocat. Educators. Home: 523 Washington Ave Riverhead NY 11901 Office: Bd Coop Ednl Services 2 350 Martha Ave Bellport NY 11713

ROLFE, CYNTHIA ELAINE (JOHNSON), computer information systems educator; b. Arkansas City, Kans., Oct. 20, 1953; d. Frank A. and Carolyn (Ragyne) Crank; m. David W. Johnson, Oct. 22, 1972 (div. 1981); 1 child, Jessica Nicole; m. C. David Rolfe; 1 child (stepdaughter) Audrey Janell. MS, Okla. State U., 1979, EdD, 1983. Tchr. Ripley (Okla.) Pub. Schs., 1976-81; teaching assoc. computer science Okla. State U., Stillwater, 1981-83; assoc. prof. Bryant Coll., Smithfield, R.I., 1983—; cons. computers, applications, tng., Providence. Contbr. articles to profl. jours. Vol. ARC, Stillwater, 1980—; sponsor coll. chpt. Assn. Systems Mgrs., jr. high sch. Bapt. youth group. Mem. Assn. Computer Educators (v.p. 1985-88, pres. 1988-90), Assn. Systems Mgrs., Am. Mgmt. Assn. Republican. Methodist. Office: Bryant Coll 450 Douglas Pike Smithfield RI 02917

ROLFE, GERALD T., financial executive; b. N.Y.C., Mar. 5, 1936; s. Herbert and Barbara Molly (Witas) R.; m. Kathy Ann Lund, Oct. 8, 1961; children: Wendy, David. B Chem. Engring., Poly. Inst. N.Y., 1957. Security analyst Loeb Rhoades & Co., N.Y.C., 1960-79; chief investment strategist Shearson Lehman Hutton, N.Y.C., 1979-83; investment counsel Shearson Asset Mgmt., N.Y.C., 1984—. Mem. N.Y. Soc. Security Analysts, Fin. Analysts Fedn. Office: Shearson Asset Mgmt 31 W 52d St New York NY 10019

ROLFE, MICHAEL N., accounting firm executive; b. Chgo., Sept. 9, 1937; s. Mark Alexander and Antoinette (Wittgenstein) R.; m. Judith Mary Lewis, June 16, 1959; children—Andrew, Lisa, James. A.B. in Econs., U. Mich., 1959; postgrad., Grad. Sch. Bus., U. Chgo., 1963-65. Sales staff Lewis Co., Northbrook, Ill., 1961-62; systems mgmt. staff Brunswick Corp., Chgo., 1962-68; v.p. Kearney Mgmt. Cons., Chgo., 1968-81; ptnr. Peat, Marwick, Main & Co., Chgo., 1981—. Author: AMA Management Handbook, 1969. Bd. dirs. Common, Chgo., 1972-75, U. Chgo. Cancer Research, 1985-88, Am. Cancer Soc., Chgo., 1985—; trustee Michael Reese Med. Ctr., 1986—; pres. Sch. Bd. Dist. 113, Highland Park, Ill., 1977-83. Served to lt. (j.g.) USNR, 1959-61. Clubs: Northmoor Country (Highland Park); Standard, Mid Am. (Chgo.). Home: 1730 Overland Trail Deerfield IL 60015 Office: Peat Marwick Main & Co 303 E Wacker Dr Chicago IL 60601

ROLLAND, IAN MCKENZIE, insurance executive; b. Fort Wayne, Ind., June 3, 1933; s. David and Florence (Hunte) R.; m. Miriam V. Flickinger, July 3, 1955; children: Cheri L., Lawrence D., Robert A., Carol Ann, Sara K. B.A., DePauw U., 1955; M.A. in Actuarial Sci., U. Mich., 1956. With Lincoln Nat. Life Ins. Co., Ft. Wayne, 1956—, sr. v.p., 1973-75, pres., 1977-81, chief exec. officer, 1977—, chmn., pres., 1981—; pres. Lincoln Nat. Corp., 1975—, chief exec. officer, 1977—; bd. dirs. No. Ind. Public Service, Lincoln Nat. Bank and Trust Co., Gen. Telephone Co. Ind., Inc., Tokheim Corp., Lincoln Nat. Sales Corp., Am. States Ins. Cos., Security-Conn. Life Ins. Co., Am. States Ins. Cos., Cannon Assurance Ltd., First Penn-Pacific Ins. Co., The Richard Leahy Corp., Modern Portfolio Theory Assocs., Inc.; past chmn. Am. Council of Life Ins. Agts.; exec. com. Associated Ind. Life Ins. Cos. Chmn. citizens bd. St. Francis Coll., 1978—; S. S. Huebner Found.; exec. com. The American Coll.; mem. adv. bd. Ind. U.-Purdue U., 1977; chmn. Ind. Fiscal Policy Com.; trustee Hudson Inst.; mem. Indiana Acad. Mem. Soc. Actuaries, Acad. Actuaries, Health Ins. Assn. Am., Am. Council Life Ins. (past chmn. bd. dirs.), Assoc. Ind. Life Ins. Cos. (exec. com.), Ind. Ins. Soc. (bd. dirs.), Internat. Ins. Soc. (bd. dirs.), Ind. C. of C. (mem. exec. com.). Office: Lincoln Nat Corp 1300 S Clinton St Fort Wayne IN 46801

ROLLAND, LUCIEN G., paper company executive; b. St. Jerome, Que., Can., Dec. 21, 1916; s. Olivier and Aline (Dorion) R.; m. Marie de Lorimier, May 30, 1942; children: Nicolas, Natalie, Stanislas, Dominique, Christine, Etienne, David. Student, Coll. Jean de Brebeuf, Montreal; Profl. Engr., Loyola Coll., U. Montreal, B.A., B.A.Sc., C.E., also D.C.Sc. (hon.), 1960. Registered profl. engr. With Rolland Paper Co. Ltd. (name changed to Rolland inc. 1979), 1942—, v.p., gen. mgr., 1952, pres., gen. mgr., 1952-78, pres., chief exec. officer, 1978—, chmn. pres., chief exec. officer, 1984, chmn., chief exec. officer, 1985; chmn., bd. dirs. Rolland Paper Corp., Rolland Fitchburg Paper, Inc., Rolland Paper Sales Corp., Select Papers, Inc. (formerly W.H. Smith Paper Corp.); pres. Dessalu Limitée, Tarascon Holdings Inc.; bd. dirs. Bank of Montreal, Mortgage Corp., Canadian Investment Fund Ltd., C.H. Robinson Paper Co. Bd. govs. Notre-Dame Hosp., Montreal Children's Hosp., Montreal Gen. Hosp., Hô pital Marie Enfant. Decorated knight comdr. Order St. Gregory. Mem. Canadian Mfrs. Assn., Can. Pulp and Paper Assn. (exec. bd.), Corp. Profl. Engrs., Montreal Bd. Trade, Province of Que., C of C, Montreal C. of C., Engring. Inst. Can. Home: 1321 Sherbrooke St W, Apt B-60, Montreal, PQ Canada H3G 1J4 Office: Rolland Inc, 2000 McGill College Ave, Montreal, PQ Canada H3A 3H3

ROLLAND, MICHAEL JACKSON, banker; b. St. Andrews, Scotland, July 26, 1943; came to U.S., 1977; s. Jackson and Jean (Simpson) R.; m. Martha Suhr, Mar. 8, 1969; children: Christopher, Mark. MA, St. Andrews U., Scotland, 1965; MBA, Stanford U., Calif., 1967. Mng. dir. A.G. Becker-Paribas, N.Y.C., 1977-84, Merrill Lynch Capital Markets, N.Y.C., 1984—. Office: Merrill Lynch Capital Markets North Tower World Fin Ctr New York NY 10281-1201

ROLLHAUS, PHILIP EDWARD, JR., diversified manufacturing corporation executive; b. Phila., Sept. 29, 1934; s. Philip Edward and Elizabeth Snow (Bedford) R.; m. Jacqueline Merrill, Feb. 13, 1965 (div. 1975); children: Natalie, Philip Edward III; m. Barbara Lynn Walker, Oct. 8, 1983. B.A. in English Lit., Wesleyan U., 1956. Dir. gen. Société Rollhaus, Paris, 1960-64; regional mgr. Bus. Internat., Chgo., 1964-67; mgr. pvt. placements Woolard & Co., Chgo., 1967-69; founder, chmn., pres., chief exec. officer Quixote Corp., Chgo., 1969—; bd. dirs. Chgo. Capital Fund. Bd. dirs. DeVry, Inc., 1987—, Keller Grad. Sch. Mgmt., Chgo., 1974-87; chmn. Starlight Found., Chgo., 1986-88, Gastro-Intestinal Research Found., Chgo., 1984—; trustee Inst. Psychoanalysis, Chgo., 1983—; mem. Am. Bus. Conf., Washington, 1987—. Served to lt. (j.g.) USN, 1956-60. Mem. Newcomen Soc. U.S., Econ. Club of Chgo., Soc. Mayflower Descs. Republican. Presbyterian. Clubs: Chicago, Racquet, Tavern (Chgo.); Bath and Tennis (Palm Beach, Fla.); Michigan City Yacht (Ind.). Home: 1500 N Lake Shore Dr Chicago IL 60610 Office: Quixote Corp One E Wacker Dr Chicago IL 60601

ROLLINO, RICHARD STEVEN, controller; b. Oakland, Calif., July 18, 1958; s. Louis Sam and Dorothy (Duggan) R.; m. Mary Ann Inlow, May 17, 1986; 1 child, James Patrick. BS, U. So. Calif., Los Angeles, 1981. Sr. auditor Arthur Andersen & Co., Los Angeles, 1981-83; mgr. budget Beverly Enterprises, Pasadena, 1983-85; controller TV Fanfare Pubs., Inc., Valencia, Calif., 1985—; dir. debate Calif. Inst. Tech., Pasadena, 1981-82. Republican. Roman Catholic. Home: 5150 Dahlia Dr Los Angeles CA 90041 Office: TV Fanfare Pubs Inc 25300 Rye Canyon Rd Valencia CA 91355

ROLLINS, GARY WAYNE, service company executive; b. Chattanooga, Aug. 30, 1944; s. Orville Wayne and Grace (Crum) R.; m. Ruth Magness; children: Glen William, Ruth Ellen, Nancy Louise, Orville Wayne. BSBA, U. Tenn., 1967. Sales mgmt. Orkin Exterminating Co., Atlanta, 1967-72, v.p. ops., 1975-78, pres., 1978-84; v.p., gen. mgr. Dwoskin, Atlanta, 1972-75; pres., chief operating officer Rollins, Inc., Atlanta, 1984—, also bd. dirs.; bd. dirs. Rollins Leasing Co., Wilmington, Del., Rollins Energy Services, Atlanta. Mem. Atlanta Symphony, 1970—, Atlanta Humane Soc., 1970—, Atlanta High Mus. Art, 1970—, Ga. Structural Pest Control Commn., 1967; founding dir. Tuxedo Park Civic Assn., Atlanta, 1984—. Recipient de Tocqueville Soc. award United Way, 1987. Mem. PADI Open Water Diving, Piedmont Driving Club. Methodist. Club: Cherokee (Atlanta). Office: Rollins Inc 2170 Piedmont Rd NE Atlanta GA 30324

ROLLINS, JOHN WILLIAM, SR., service and transportation company executive; b. Keith, Ga., Aug. 24, 1916; s. William Henry and Claudia Ann (Nance) R.; m. Michele M. Metrinko, June 1977; children: Michele, Monique, Michael, Marc; children by previous marriage: John William, Catharine, Patrick, James (dec.), Theodore, Jeffrey. Student various extension and correspondence courses; Assoc. in Humanities, Reinhardt Coll., 1970. Founder, chmn., chief exec. officer RLC Corp., Wilmington, Del., 1954—; co-founder, dir. Rollins Inc.; founder, chmn. exec. com., dir. Rollins Environ. Services Inc.; bd. dirs. FPA Corp., RPC Energy Services, Inc. Lt. Gov., State of Del., 1953-57. Mem. Horatio Alger Assn. Disting. Ams. (pres.). Republican. Clubs: Metropolitan, Masons. Office: RLC Corp One Rollins Plaza PO Box 1791 Wilmington DE 19899 *

ROLLO, FRANK DAVID, hospital management company executive, radiology educator; b. Endicott, N.Y., Apr. 15, 1939; s. Frank C. and Augustine L. (Dumont) R.; m. Deane M. Walchak, June 8, 1967; children: Mindee, Alex. BA, Harpur Coll., 1959; MS, U. Miami, 1965; PhD, Johns Hopkins U., 1968; MD, Upstate Med. Ctr., Syracuse, N.Y., 1972. Diplomate Am. Bd. Nuclear Medicine. Asst. chief nuclear medicine services VA Hosp., San Francisco, 1974-77; chief nuclear medicine VA Hosp., Nashville, 1977-79; sr. v.p. med. affairs Humana Inc., Louisville, 1980—; dir. nuclear medicine div. Vanderbilt U. Med. Ctr., Nashville, 1977-81; prof. radiology Vanderbilt U., Nashville, 1979—; mem. med. adv. com. IBT, Washington, 1984—; mem. pvt. sector liaison panel Inst. of Medicine, Washington, 1983—. Editor: Nuclear Medicine Physics, Instruments and Agents, 1977; co-editor: Physical Basis of Medical Imaging, 1980, Digital Radiology: Focus on Clinical Utility, 1982, Nuclear Medicine Resonance Imaging, 1983; mem. editorial adv. bd. ECRI, 1981—. Pres. bd. dirs. Youth Performing Arts Council, Louisville, 1984-85; bd. dirs. Louisville-Jefferson County Youth Orch., 1983-85. Named to Hon. Order of Ky. Cols., Gov. State of Ky., 1984. Fellow Am. Coll. Nuclear Physicians (profl. com. 1982-84, chmn. 1984); mem. Soc. Nuclear Medicine (trustee 1979-83, 84—, Cassen Meml. lectr. western region 1980, 84), Radiol. Soc. N.Am. (hon. mention sci. exhibits at ann. meeting 1980), Am. Coll. Radiology, AMA, Assn. Advancement Med. Instrumentation (bd. dirs. 1986—), Louisville C. of C. (chmn. mic com. 1987—). Home: 7012 Butterwood Dr Cincinnati OH 45241 Office: Humana Inc 500 W Main St Box 1438 Louisville KY 40201

ROLLWAGEN, JOHN A., scientific computer company executive; b. 1940; married. BSEE, MIT, 1962; MBA, Harvard U., 1964. Mktg. rep. Control Data Corp., 1964-66; prodn. mgr. Monsanto Corp., 1966-68; v.p. Internat. Timesharing Corp., 1968-75; v.p. fin. Cray Rsch. Inc., 1975-76, v.p. mktg., 1976-77, pres., 1977-80, pres., chief exec. officer, 1980-88, chmn., chief exec. officer, 1981—, also bd. dirs.; bd. dirs. Dayton Hudson Corp., Minn.; chmn. bd. dirs. Fed. Reserve Bank Minn. Office: Cray Rsch Inc 608 2nd Ave S PO Box 154 Minneapolis MN 55402 *

ROLNIK, ZACHARY JACOB, editor, publisher; b. Bayonne, N.J., Oct. 2, 1961; s. Joseph and Katie (Simon) R. BA, U. Rochester, 1982; M. in Pub. Policy, Harvard U., 1984. Ops. analyst, presdl. mgmt. intern U.S. Dept. Treasury, Washington, 1984-85; editor, pub. Kluwer Acad. Pubs., Norwell, Mass., 1985—. Democrat. Jewish. Home: 10 Presidents Ln Apt 9 Quincy MA 02109 Office: Kluwer Acad Pubs 101 Philip Dr Norwell MA 02061

ROM, M. MARTIN, financial and real estate company executive; b. Detroit, Mar. 2, 1946; s. Jack and Thelma (Meyer) R.; m. Barbara Miller, July 12, 1970. B.A. magna cum laude, U. Mich., 1967. Founder MultiVest, Inc., Southfield, Mich., 1969; pres. MultiVest, Inc., 1969-73, chmn. bd., chief exec. officer, 1973-75; Pres. Real Estate Securities and Syndication Inst., Nat. Assn. Realtors, Washington, 1975—; dir., bd. govs. Real Estate Securities and Syndication Inst., Nat. Assn. Realtors, 1972—; pres. Martin Rom Co., Inc., 1976—, Rom Energy Corp., 1980—; vice chmn. Sports Illustrated Ct. Clubs, Inc., 1977-79; dir. The Mocatta Corp., 1979-80, Central Holding Co., 1985-88; mem. joint com. Nat. Assn. Securities Dealers-Nat. Assn. Realtors, 1975-76; mem. adv. com. on market instruments Commodity Futures Trading Commn.; cons., bd. dirs. Guaranty Fed. Savings Bank, 1984-87; bd. dirs. Cen. Holding Corp., 1985-88. Author: Nothing Can Replace the U.S. Dollar . . . and It Almost Has, 1975; Adv. bd.: Housing and Devel. Reporter, Washington. Mem. Nat. Assn. Securities Dealers, Com. on Gold Regulations, Phi Beta Kappa. Home: 60 Quarton Ln Bloomfield Hills MI 48013

ROMAINE, HENRY SIMMONS, insurance executive; b. N.Y.C., May 30, 1933; s. Theodore Cole and Cornelia (Simmons) R.; m. Susan Donaldson; children: Henry, Hilary. B.A., Harvard U., 1954. Asst. security analyst Mutual Life Ins. Co., N.Y.C., 1958-60, investment analyst, 1960-61, investment specialist, 1961-64, asst. dir. investments, 1964, dir. investments, 1964-66, asst. v.p. for securities investment, 1966-68, 2d v.p. for securities investment, 1969-71, v.p. for securities investment, 1971-72, sr. v.p., 1972-78, sr. v.p., chief investment officer, 1976-78, exec. v.p., 1978-81, pres., 1981-86; vice chmn., chief investment officer Am. Gen. Corp., Houston, 1986—; dir. MONY Life Ins. Co. of Can.; chmn. bd. MONY Real Estate Investors, 1978-86; mem. advisory bd. Chem. Bank, 1974—; vice chmn. bd. dirs., chief investment officer Am. Gen. Corp., Houston, Tex. Served with USN, 1954-57. Clubs: The Links, Harvard. Home: 606 W Friar Tuck Houston TX 77024 Office: Am Gen Corp 2929 Allen Pkwy Houston TX 77019

ROMAIRONE, CARLO G., management executive; b. Genoa, Italy, Apr. 26, 1940; came to U.S., 1975; s. Pietro and Rosa (Parodi) R.; m. Margaret Marchisio, Jan. 10, 1980; 1 child, Arianna. Student of Economy and Commerce, U. Genoa, Italy; student of Sociology, U. Trento, Italy. With Cassa Di Risparmio De Genova E Imperia, Genoa, 1960—; U.S. rep. Cassa Di Risparmio De Genova E Imperia, N.Y.C., 1975—. Office: Cassa di Risparmio di Genova e Imperia 375 Park Ave New York NY 10152

ROMAN, KENNETH, JR., advertising executive; b. Boston, Sept. 6, 1930; s. Kenneth J. and Bernice (Freedman) R.; m. Ellen L. Fischer, Mar. 27, 1953. B.A., Dartmouth Coll., 1952. Asst. advt. promotion mgr. Interchem Crp., N.Y.C., 1952-55; mgr. advt. sales promotion Raymond Rosen Co., Phila., 1955-56; advt. mgr. Allied Chem. Corp., 1956-63; account mgr. Ogilvy and Mather, Inc., N.Y.C., 1963-73, v.p., 1968-71, sr. v.p., 1971-79; pres. Ogilvy and Mather Worldwide, 1979-85, chmn., 1987—; vice chmn., dir. The Ogilvy Group, 1985—, chmn., chief exec. officer, 1988—. Bd. overseers Hopkins/Hood Ctr., Dartmouth Coll.; bd. dirs. N.Y. Bot. Garden. Club: Univ. (N.Y.C.). Home: 7 Gracie Sq New York NY 10028 Office: Ogilvy Group Inc 2 E 48th St New York NY 10017

ROMAN-BARBER, HELEN, mining company executive. d. Stephen Roman. Chmn., chief exec. officer Denison mines Ltd., Toronto, Ont., Can. Office: Denison Mines Ltd, S Tower Royal Bank Pla, Toronto, ON Canada M5J 2K2 *

ROMANENKO, LINDA CARMEN, automotive company training specialist; b. Washington, May 8, 1957; d. Ivan and Carmen (Prii) R.; m. K. Craig Fehr, July 6, 1985. BA in English and Philosophy, Allegheny Coll., 1979, MEd, 1980. English tchr. Strongsville (Ohio) High Schs., 1979-82; editor, tng. cons. Fastener Forum, Inc., Cleve., 1982-84; media writer EDR Corp., Shaker Heights, Ohio, 1983-84; tng. coordinator F.X. Coughlin Co., Taylor, Mich., 1984-86; tng. specialist Mazda Motors Mfg., Flat Rock, Mich., 1986—. Mem. Am. Soc. for Tng. and Devel., Northville (Mich.) Hist. Soc., Kappa Delta Epsilon. Home: 1052 Grace Ct Northville MI 48167 Office: Mazda Motor Mfg Inc One Mazda Dr Flat Rock MI 48134

ROMANO, JOHN FRANCIS, medical products company executive; b. Bklyn., Dec. 25, 1947; s. Phillip and Madeline (Spata) R.; m. Cathy Pizzolato, Aug. 15, 1969; children: John Paul, Matthew, Damien. BA, St. Leo Coll., 1970; MBA, Rochester Inst. Tech., 1975. Sales rep. Mead Johnson Co., Evansville, Ind., 1975-79; sales rep. Gambro, Lincolnshire, Ill. and Sweden, 1979-80, product mgr., 1980-82, nat. mktg. mgr., 1982-83, dir. sales, 1983-84, div. mgr., 1985-86; v.p. sales and mktg. Biosearch Med. Products, Inc., Somerville, N.J., 1986-89, Delmed, Inc., New Brunswick, N.J., 1989—. Home: 6 Durham Boat Dr Washington Crossing PA 18977 Office: Delmed Inc 120 Albany St New Brunswick NJ 08879

ROMANOWSKI, KENNETH, savings and loan executive; b. Phila., Mar. 27, 1952; s. Matthew J. and Evalina (Lewandowski) R.; m. Linda M. Romanowski, May 17, 1980. BBA, Temple U., 1974, MBA, 1978. Cert. fin. planner, 1986. Banking asst., ops. and planning specialist First Pa. Bank, N.A., Phila., 1974-77; asst. mgr. Indsl. Valley Bank, Phila., 1978-80; controller, adminstr. Raymond Mungiu & Assocs., Inc., Phila., 1980-82; agt., registered rep. Phoenix Mut. Life Ins. Co., Phila., 1982-84; mgr. main office Polonia Fed. Savs. & Loan Assn., Phila., 1984-88; personal banker Atlantic Fin. Fed., Bala Cynwyd, Pa., 1988—; owner Kenneth Romanowski Fin. Planning and Cons., Phila., 1980—; instr. Inst. Fin. Edn., Phila., 1986—. Composer songs include How Can I Get Through To You, 1976, There's Something About You, 1977. Mem. Inst. Cert. Fin. Planners (dir. 1987, 88, 89). Republican. Roman Catholic. Home: 2908 Disston St Philadelphia PA 19149 Office: Atlantic Fin Fed 50 Monument Rd Bala-Cynwyd PA 19004

ROMBS, VINCENT JOSEPH, retired accountant, lawyer; b. Newport, Ky., Mar. 8, 1918; s. John Thomas and Mathilda (Fromhold) R.; m. Ruth Burns, Aug. 15, 1942; 1 child, Ellen (Mrs. James P. Herman). Student Xavier U., 1936-37; BS with honors, Southeastern U., 1941; JD, Loyola U., Chgo., 1952. Bar: Ill. 1952; CPA, Ill. Tax ptnr. with local and nat. pub. acctg. firms, Chgo., 1952-89; assoc. Laventhol & Horwath, Chgo., 1970-75; of counsel Edelman Chartered, 1975-89; Ostrow Reisin Berk & Abrams, Ltd., 1977-89; pres. Vincent J. Rombs, Ltd., 1982-88. Bd. dirs. Miller Found. Lt. comdr., USNR, 1941-46. Recipient Scholarship Key Lward Delta Theta Phi, 1953. Mem. AICPA., Ill. Soc. CPA's. Home: 915 E Golf Rd Apt 3 Arlington Heights IL 60005

ROME, DONALD LEE, lawyer; b. West Hartford, Conn., May 17, 1929; s. Herman Isaac and Juliette (Stern) R.; m. Sheila Ward, Apr. 20, 1958; children: Adam Ward, Lisa, Ethan Stern. SB, Trinity Coll., 1951; LLB, Harvard U., 1954. Bar: Conn. 1954, U.S. Dist. Ct. 1955, U.S. Cir. Ct. Appeals 1965, U.S. Supreme Ct. 1965. Assoc. Ribicoff and Kotkin, Hartford, Conn., 1954-58, ptnr., 1958-67; ptnr. Rosenberg, Rome, Barnett, Sattin & Santos and predecessor, Hartford, 1967-83; now ptnr. Robinson & Cole, Hartford, 1983—; mem. Conn. Gov.'s Study Commn. on Uniform Consumer Credit Code, 1969-70; chmn. Conn. bar advisory com. of attys. to make recommendations to U.S. dist. ct. for proposed changes of bankruptcy rules in dist. Conn., 1975-77; mem. Bankruptcy Merit Screening Com. for Dist. Ct., 1980-81; mem. adv. com. Conn. Law Revision Commn. on article 2A for Uniform Comml. Code, 1987—; lectr. in law U. Conn., 1965-74, 81-83; mem. faculty Sch. Banking of the South, La. State U., 1982-84; lectr. continuing legal edn. on secured creditors' rights, comml. fin., bankruptcy and uniform comml. code, 1958—; corp. adv. bd. dirs. Conn. Nat. Bank. Co-author: A Comparative Analysis and Study of the Uniform Consumer Credit Code in Relation to the Existing Consumer Credit Law in Connecticut, 1970; author: Business Workouts Manual, 1985; contbg. author: Connecticut Practice Book, 1978, Collier Bankruptcy Practice Guide, 1981, Asset-Based Financing: A Transactional Guide, 1984; contbr. articles to profl. jours. Past mem. bd. dirs. New Eng. region Am. Jewish Com., also Hartford chpt., Hebrew Home for Aged, Hartford; past mem. bd. trustees Temple Beth Israel, West Hartford. Mem. ABA (bus. bankruptcy com. and comml. fin. services com., sect. on corp., banking and bus. law), Fed. Bar Assn. (bankruptcy law com.), Conn. Bar Assn. (chmn. sect. comml. law and bankruptcy 1977-80, chmn. spl. com. scope and correlation 1983-84), Hartford County Bar Assn. (continuing legal edn. com.), Conn. Bar Found., Assn. Comml. Fin. Attys. (pres. 1978-80), Am. Arbitration Assn. (mem. panel comml. arbitrators), Am. Bankruptcy Inst., Comml. Law League Am., Harvard Law Sch. Assn. Conn. (pres. 1970-71). Clubs: Hartford, Harvard of N.Y.C, Trinity. Lodge: Masons (32 deg., trial commn. Conn. grand lodge 1970-82). Home: 46 Belknap Rd West Hartford CT 06117 Office: Robinson & Cole 1 Commercial Pla Hartford CT 06103-3597

ROME, JOHN L., restaurant chain executive; b. Alliance, Ohio, 1954. Pres. internat. div. Wendy's Internat. Inc. Office: Wendy's Internat Inc 4288 W Dublin Granville Rd Dublin OH 43017 *

ROMITI, LORENZO, restaurant executive; b. Balt., Dec. 31, 1951; s. Antonietta (Pastocchi) R.; m. Linda Ann Kellinger, June 2, 1974; children: Tess, Andrew. BA in History, Wheeling Coll., 1973. Sec. Squire's Cafe Inc., Balt., 1973—; cons. in field. Mem. Assn. Italian-Am. Charities, Balt., 1975—. Mem. Nat. Restaurant Assn., Restaurant Assn. Md., BMW Motorcycle Owners Club, Antiquerian Motorcycle Owners. Republican. Office: Squires Cafe 6723 Holibird Ave Baltimore MD 21222

RONALD, PETER, utility executive; b. Duluth, Minn., Aug. 26, 1926; s. George W. and Florence (Jones) R.; m. Mary Locke Boyd, Nov. 25, 1950; children: Peter Webb, Pauline Morton, Samuel Herschel. B.A., U. Va., 1950. With Louisville Gas & Electric Co., 1950-58, treas., 1962—, v.p., 1969-82, sr. v.p., 1982-88, dir., 1979-89. Bd. dirs., mem. exec. com. Bus. Devel. Corp. Ky., 1967-75, pres., 1971-72; bd. dirs. Louisville Community Chest, 1967-72, v.p., 1969-72; bd. dirs., v.p. Louisville Rehab. Center, 1964-82, pres., 1970-71; bd. overseers Louisville Country Day Sch., 1967-70; trustee Children's Hosp. Found., 1978-81, sec.-treas., 1978-81. Served with USNR, 1945-46. Mem. Zeta Psi. Clubs: Louisville Country. Home: Mockingbird Valley Rd Louisville KY 40207 also: 1112 Schefflera Ct PO Box 893 Captiva FL 33924

RONC, MICHAEL JOSEPH, venture capital company executive; b. Chambery, France, June 23, 1944; came to U.S., 1987; s. Albert and Renée (Jeantet) R.; m. Marie Rose E. Lux, Mar. 25, 1967; children: Valerie, Joelle, Cecile. License es Sciences, U. Toulouse, France, 1967; diplome d'ingénieur, Institut Genie Chimique, Toulouse, 1968; PhD in Chem. Engring., McGill U., 1973; grad. advanced mgmt. program, Harvard U., 1987. Head research and devel. project Elf-France, Solaize, 1973-79; head energy mgmt. R & D div. Societe Nationale Elf Aquitaine, Paris, 1979-83; dir. innovation Societe Nationale Elf Aquitaine, 1984-87; dir. research NEU, Lille, France, 1982-84; pres., dir. gen. Inovelf, Paris, 1985—; pres., chief exec. officer Elf Techs., Inc., Stamford, Conn., 1984—; chmn. Societe Elene, Paris, 1983-86, Societe Oric, Paris, 1984-87; bd. dirs. Transgene, Paris, Native Plants Inc., Salt Lake City, Angenics, Cambridge, Mass. Contbr. articles to profl. pubs.; patentee solar roof structure, also others, in France, U.S., Can. Home: 40 Colony Rd Westport CT 06880 Office: Elf Techs Inc High Ridge Park PO Box 10037 Stamford CT 06904

RONCHI, GIORGIO, electronics company executive. Chmn., chief exec. officer Memorex Corp. Office: Memorex Corp 461 S Milpitas Blvd Milpitas CA 95035 *

RONCK, DAVID KENT, real estate executive; b. Enid, Okla., Nov. 25, 1959; s. Leonard Victor and Albina Marie (Ciskowski) R.; married. BS in Acctg. and Econs., Okla. State U., 1982. CPA, Tex. Pub. acct. Arthur Andersen & Co., Dallas, 1982-85; corp. contr. Cambridge Cos., Dallas, 1985-87; sr. v.p. fin. Bright Realty Corp., Dallas, 1987—. Mem. Am. Inst. CPAs, Tex. State Bd. CPAs, Tex. Soc. CPAs, Real Estate Fin. Execs. Assn. Republican. Roman Catholic.

RONDEAU, CLEMENT ROBERT, petroleum geologist; b. Ironwood, Mich., July 6, 1928. BS, Tulane U., 1955. Geol. supr. Texaco, Inc., New Orleans, 1955-63; area mgr. Pubco Petroleum Corp., New Orleans, 1963-69; cons. petroleum geologist Harahan, La., 1969—; owner Natural Gas Exploration Co., Harahan, 1977—. Mem. Am. Assn. Petroleum Geologists, Soc. Exploration Geophysicists, New Orleans Geol. Soc., AAAS, Explorers Club, Ind. Petroleum Assn., N.Y. Acad. Sci., Internat. Platform Assn., Internat. Oil Scouts Assn., Phi Beta Kappa, Sigma Gamma Epsilon. Democrat. Roman Catholic. Clubs: New Orleans Athletic; Bay/Waveland Yacht (Miss.). Home: 632 Stratford Dr Harahan LA 70123 Office: Natural Gas Exploration Co 958 Hickory Ste A Harahan LA 70123

RONDEAU, DORIS JEAN, entrepreneur, consultant; b. Winston-Salem, N.C., Nov. 25, 1941; d. John Delbert and Eldora Virginia (Klutz) Robinson; m. Robert Breen Corrente, Sept. 4, 1965 (div. 1970); m. Wilfrid Dolor Rondeau, June 3, 1972. Student Syracuse U., 1959-62, Fullerton Jr. Coll., 1974-75; BA in Philosophy, Calif. State U.-Fullerton, 1976, postgrad., 1976-80. Ordained to ministry The Spirit of Divine Love, 1974. Trust real estate clk. Security First Nat. Bank, Riverside, Calif., 1965-68; entertainer Talent, Inc., Hollywood, Calif., 1969-72; co-founder, dir. Spirit of Divine Love, Capistrano Beach, Calif., 1974—; pub., co-founder Passing Through, Inc., Capistrano Beach, 1983—; instr. Learning Activity, Anaheim, Calif., 1984—; chmn. bd., prin. D.J. Rondeau, Entrepreneur, Inc., Capistrano Beach, 1984—; co-founder, dir. Spiritual Positive Attitude, Inc., Moon In Pisces, Inc., Vibrations By Rondeau, Inc., Divine Consciousness, Expressed, Inc., Capistrano Beach. Author, editor: A Short Introduction To The Spirit of Divine Love, 1984; writer, producer, dir. performer spiritual vignettes for NBS Radio Network, KWVE-FM, 1982-84; author: Spiritual Meditations to Uplift the Soul, 1988. Served with USAF, 1963-65. Recipient Pop Vocalist First Place award USAF Talent Show, 1964, Sigma chpt. Epsilon Delta Chi, 1985, others. Mem. Hamel Bus. Grads., Smithsonian Assocs., Am. Mgmt. Assn., Nat. Assn. Female Execs. Avocations: long-distance running, body fitness, arts and crafts, snorkeling, musical composition.

RONEL, SAMUEL H., biotechnology company executive; b. Metz. France, Apr. 20, 1936, came to U.S., 1970, naturalized, 1975; m. Hilda Ronel; children: Erella, Daniel. P.C.B., U. Nancy, 1954; student U. Paris, 1956; B.Sc., Technion, Israel Inst. Tech., 1964, M.Sc., 1966, Sc.D., 1969. Asst. prof. analytical and organic chemistry Technion, Israel Inst. Tech., 1966-69; research assoc. Clarkson Coll., Potsdam, N.Y., 1969-70; research chemist Hydron Labs., New Brunswick, N.J., 1970-73, pres., 1976-80; head biomed. research group Hydro Med. Scis., New Brunswick, 1973-75; pres. Interferon Scis., Inc., New Brunswick, also v.p. research and devel. Nat. Patent Devel. Corp., 1980—; pres. Hydro Med. Scis., 1980—. Mem. Am. Chem. Soc., Soc. Biomaterials, N.Y. Acad. Scis., pres. Assn. Biotech. Cos., Am. Soc. Indsl. Microbiology, Assn. Biotech. Cos. Contbr. articles to profl. jours. Patentee in field. Office: Interferon Scis Inc 783 Jersey Ave New Brunswick NJ 08901

RONES, MARIE D., marketing and planning professional; b. Phila., July 6, 1957; d. Sebastian F. and Catherine F. (Helmar) Donnarumma; m. Clifford Todd Rones, Nov. 6, 1983. BS, Drexel U., 1978; MBA, U. Pa., 1980. Pub. info. specialist U.S. EPA, Phila., 1978; mkt. research analyst Honeywel, Inc., Ft. Washington, Pa., 1979-80; asst. to v.p. Western Pub. Co., N.Y.C., 1980-83; mgr. planning info. systems The Lehigh Press, Inc., Pennsauken, N.J., 1983-85, dir. mkt. planning, 1985-87; dir. corp. planning Blue Cross of Greater Phila., 1987—; ind. cons. Voorhees, N.J., 1987—. Sec. Cen. Voorhees Civic Assn., 1987—; campaign mgr. sch. bd. candidate, Voorhees, 1988; mem. Environ. Adv. Bd., Voorhees, 1987—. Mem. The Planning Forum, Am. Mgmt. Assn., Phi Sigma Iota, Phi Kappa Phi. Home: 4 Martindale Dr Voorhees NJ 08043 Office: Blue Cross of Greater Phila 1333 Chestnut St Philadelphia PA 19107

RONEY, ROBERT KENNETH, retired aerospace company executive; b. Newton, Iowa, Aug. 5, 1922; s. Louie Earl and Hazel Iona (Cure) R.; m. Alice Lorraine Mann, Oct. 6, 1951; children: Stephen P., Karen Margaret Dahl. BSEE, U. Mo., 1944; MSEE, Calif. Inst. Tech., 1947, PhD, 1950. Engr. rsch. Jet Propulsion Lab. Calif. Inst. Tech., Pasadena, 1948-50, Hughes Aircraft Co., Culver City, Calif., 1950-54; mgr. system analysis Hughes Aircraft Co., Culver City, 1955-59, dir. tech. R&D, 1960, assoc. mgr. space system div., 1961-68, mgr. space system div., 1968-70, v.p. asst. group exec., 1970-85, sr. v.p. corp. technology, 1986-88, ret., 1988. Mem. adv. bd. Dept. Transpn. Comml. Space, Washington, 1984-87, Engring. Sch. U. Kans., 1988—. Lt. (j.g.) USNR, 1944-46, PTO. Recipient Honor award for Disting. Svc. in Engring. U. Mo.-Columbia, 1979. Fellow IEEE; mem. AIAA, Club de Caza. Home: 1105 Georgina Ave Santa Monica CA 90402

RONNQUIST, JOHN DAVID, financial executive; b. Worcester, Mass., Dec. 1, 1947; s. Nils R.H. and Ellen M. (Davis) R.; m. June E. Baca LeDuc, Oct. 10, 1986; children: Erik J., Mark A., Kristi A. LeDuc. BBA, Nichols Coll., 1970. CPA, Mass. Supervising sr. acct. Peat, Marwick, Mitchell & Co., Worcester, 1970-76; v.p. fin. Curry Copy Ctrs. Am., Worcester, 1976-78; mgr. cost. acctg. ATF Davidson div. White Consol., Whitinsville, Mass., 1978-80; corp. internal auditor, sr. fin. analyst Norton Co., Worcester, 1980-84; treas., chief fin. officer Luxtec Corp., Sturbridge, Mass., 1986—, also bd. dirs. Bd. dirs. Charlton Credit Union. Served with Mass. N.G., 1970-76. Mem. Nat. Assn. Accts. (Worcester chpt.). Republican. Office: Luxtec Corp RT 20/49 Box 225 Sturbridge MA 01566

RONQUILLO, ALLAN LOUIS, automotive financial corporation executive, lawyer; b. New Orleans, July 31, 1941; s. Louis and Rita Henrietta (O'Brien) R.; m. Karen Marie Munster, June 6, 1964; children—Robin, Lesley, Allan Louis. Student La. State U., 1959-62; J.D., Tulane U., 1965. Bar: La. 1965, Mich. 1968. Atty., def. div. Chrysler Corp., New Orleans, 1965-67, staff atty. legal dept., Detroit, 1967-72, sr. atty. internat., legal dept. Chrysler Fin. Corp., Troy, Mich., 1972-78, internat. dir. Europe, Paris, 1978-79, asst. counsel legal dept., Troy, 1979-80, assoc. gen. counsel, 1980-85, v.p. and gen. counsel, 1985—; chmn. law forum Am. Fin. Services Assn., 1987—. Mem. ABA, Mich. State Bar Assn., La. Bar Assn., Am. Fin. Services Assn. (law com.). Office: Chrysler Fin Corp 901 Wilshire Dr Troy MI 48084

RONSON, RAOUL R., music publishing executive; b. Fiume, Italy, Mar. 22, 1931; came to U.S., 1951; s. Mirko and Margaret (Fischer) Ruzicka; m. Susan Kohn, July 22, 1962; 1 child, Paul. DBA, U. Rome, 1950; MA, New Sch Social Research, 1957; postgrad., Inst. for Advanced Internat. Studies, U. Miami, 1967-68, NYU, 1974. Fgn. corr., freelance writer 1953-59; treas. Daron Enterprises, Inc., 1959-63; pres. Seesaw Music Corp., N.Y.C., 1963—, Okra Music Corp., N.Y.C., 1963-77, Ulsyra Prodn. Corp., N.Y.C., 1963—; pres. The Composers Press, 1972-76; acad. lectr. Am., Australian, New Zealand univs. and conservatories; vis. lectr. Youngstown (Ohio) State U., 1985—. Producer documentary films, 1959—, classical music recs., 1963—. Mem. Emergency Control Bd. Office of Mayor, N.Y.C., 1973-82; research analyst Office of the Sec. Defense, Reserve Affairs, Washington, 1984—; liaison officer U.S. Mil. Acad., West Point, 1988—. Served with M.I., AUS, 1952-54, USAR, 1955—. Recipient numerous awards and decorations. Mem. Am. Polit Sci. Assn., Am Acad. Polit. and Social Sci., Internat. Platform Assn., Civil Affairs Assn., Sibelius Soc. (bd. dirs. 1978-85). Club: Masons. Home: 825 West End Ave New York NY 10025 Office: 2067 Broadway New York NY 10023

RONTY, BRUNO GEORGE, phonograph record manufacturing company executive, tenor; b. Lwow, Poland, June 10, 1922; came to U.S., 1946, naturalized, 1955; s. Leon and Hermine (Elsner) R.; student Lwow Lyceum of Humanities, 1938-40; B.A., Conservatory, 1939, M.A., M.F.A., 1941, Ph.D. in History and Polit. Sci., 1945; m. Wanda von Rudolph, Nov. 3, 1943 (div. 1959); 1 dau., Maria; m. 2nd, Michele van Beveren, June 12, 1962 (div. 1972). Tenor, USSR, Poland, Sweden, U.S., 1940-50; pres. Colosseum Records, Inc., N.Y.C., 1950—, Musicart Internat., Ltd., N.Y.C., Wilton, Conn., 1958—; pres. Acropole Corp. Am., N.Y.C., 1972—; producer Bruno Hi-Fi Records; voice instr. N.Y.C.; tenor, gen. dir. cultural exchange program Musica Nostra et Vostra, Nat. Corp. Am., 1973—. Contbr. articles to profl. jours. Bd. dirs. Ministry Culture, Art, Poland, 1945; pres. Narcolepsy and Cataplexy Found. Am., 1975—, Cultural Exchange Soc. Am., 1976—. Served with Polish Army, 1942-45. Decorated Grunwald Cross; Polonia Restituta; recipient 1st prize USSR Internat. Competition, 1940. Roman Catholic. Club: YMCA Greater N.Y. (life mem.). Office: 1410 York Ave PO Box 22 Ste 2D New York NY 10021

ROOD, DON D., insurance executive; b. Flint, Mich., Apr. 3, 1930; s. William and Ruth R.; m. Rose Lorraine Gigure, Apr. 7, 1951; children: Lorraine Cheryl Rood Burris, Don D. B.S., Central Mich. U., 1952; postgrad., U. Mich., 1954-65. Agt. State Farm Ins. Co., Flint, 1955-60; agy. mgr. State Farm Ins. Co., 1960-61; tng. dir. State Farm Ins. Co., Marshall, Mich, 1961-62; agy. dir. State Farm Ins. Co., 1962-71; dep. regional v.p. State Farm Ins. Co., Springfield, Pa., 1971-74; v.p. agy. State Farm Ins. Co., Bloomington, Ill, 1974-76; agy. v.p. State Farm Ins. Co., 1976—, sr. agy. officer, 1980—; dir. State Farm Life & Accident Assurance Co., Bloomington, State Farm Internat. Services Inc., Bloomington; now sr. v.p. State Farm life Ins. Co., Bloomington, Ill.; v.p. sr. agy. State Farm Mut. Auto Ins. Co., Bloomington, Ill. Served with U.S. Army, 1952-54, Korea. Mem. Nat. Assn. Life Underwriters, Agy. Officers Round Table, Life Ins. Mktg. and Research Assn. (dir. 1982—). Office: State Farm Mut Automobile Ins Co 1 State Farm Pla Bloomington IL 61701 *

ROONEY, FRANCIS CHARLES, JR., corporate executive; b. North Brookfield, Mass., Nov. 24, 1921; s. Francis Charles and Evelyn Fullerbrown (Murray) R.; m. Frances Elizabeth Heffernan, June 10, 1950; children—Peter, Michael, Stephen, Jean, William, Carol, Frances, Clare. B.S. in Econs., U. Pa., 1943; D.Comml. Sci. (hon.), Suffolk U., 1968, St. John's U., 1973; PhD (hon.), Boston Coll., 1986. Mem. sales staff John Foote Shoe Co., Brockton, Mass., 1946-48; mem. sales staff Florsheim Shoe Co., Chgo., 1948-53; various positions Melville Shoe Co., N.Y.C., 1953—; pres. Thom McAn div. Melville Shoe Corp., N.Y.C., 1961-64; pres., chief exec. officer Melville Corp., Harrison, N.Y. and N.Y.C., 1964-77; chmn., pres., chief exec. officer Melville Corp., Harrison, 1977-80, chmn., chief exec. officer, 1980-86, chmn. exec. com., 1987—; dir. Bankers Trust Co., N.Y.C., Crystal Brands Inc., Southport, Conn., N.Y.C., The Neiman Marcus Group, Chestnut Hill, Mass. Bd. dirs. United Cerebral Palsy, N.Y.C., 1960, Smithsonian Assocs., 1975; overseers Wharton Sch. U. Pa.; trustee March of Dimes, N.Y. Med. Coll.; bd. dirs. Wilfred Am. Ednl. Corp. Served to lt. (j.g.) USN, 1943-46. Republican. Roman Catholic. Clubs: Round Hill (Greenwich); Links (N.Y.C.); Winged Foot (Mamaroneck, N.Y.). Office: 60 Arch St Greenwich CT 06830

ROONEY, JAMES ALBERT, utilities executive; b. N.Y.C., Sept. 29, 1944; s. James M. Rooney and Monica G. (Kelly) Garrand; m. Dorothy Bartlett, Feb. 11, 1967 (div. 1978); 1 child, James A. III. BA, Georgetown U., 1966. Mgr. Mead Data Cen., Inc., Washington, 1970-73; exec. interchange participant U.S. Dept. Commerce, Washington, 1973-74; sr. staff mem. White House., Washington, 1974-76; mgr. govt. rels. So. Calif. Gas Co., Washington, 1976-79; exec. v.p. J. Makowski Assocs., Boston, 1979—, bd. dirs., 1980—; pres. Boundary Gas, Boston, 1980—, Alta. (Can.) N.W. Gas Ltd., Calgary, 1986—. Vice chmn. Wolf Trap Found., Washington, 1968. Lt USN, 1967-70. Mem. Am. Cas Assn., Can. Gas Assn., New Eng. Gas Assn., Soc. Gas Lighters, Internat. Club (Washington), Met. Club (N.Y.C.), Boca Raton Club (Fla.). Republican. Roman Catholic. Office: J Makowski Assocs Inc 110 Tremont St Boston MA 02108

ROONEY, JOHN EDWARD, rubber company executive; b. Evergreen Park, Ill., Apr. 24, 1942; s. John Edward and Margaret Wilma (Stolte) R.; m. Germaine Rose Dettloff, June 26, 1965; children: Kathleen, John, Colleen. BS, John Carroll U., 1964; MBA, Loyola U., 1969. Credit analyst Fed. Res. Bank, Chgo., 1964-69, adminstrv. asst., 1969-70; asst. treas. Pullman Inc., 1970-73, asst. controller, 1973-78; v.p. fin. Pullman Standard, 1978-79; sr. v.p. fin. Trailmobile, Chgo., 1979-81; treas. Firestone Tire & Rubber Co., Akron, Ohio, 1981-87, v.p. retail fin. services, 1987-88, exec. v.p. MasterCare Automotive Svc., 1988—; instr. fin. Ill. Benedictine Coll., 1975-80. Mem. Ohio Mfrs. Assn. (trustee 1983-87), Ohio Pub. Expenditure Council (trustee 1986-87), Glen Oak Country Club (Chgo.), Portage Country Club (Akron), The Tavern Club (Chgo.). Home: S 311 Davis Ct Wheaton IL 60187 Office: Firestone Tire & Rubber Co 205 N Michigan Ave Chicago IL 60601-5965

ROONEY, PHILLIP BERNARD, waste management company executive; b. Chgo., July 8, 1944; s. Christopher Thomas and Rita Ann (Mitchell) R.; m. Suzanne Victoria Perillo, Jan. 29, 1966; children: Philip B., Trisha A., Michael P., Sean B. BA magna cum laude, St. Bernard Coll., 1966. Asst. to pres. Waste Mgmt., Inc., Oak Brook, Ill., 1969-71, v.p., 1971-74, sr. v.p., 1981-84, pres., chief oper. officer, 1984—, also bd. dirs., mem. exec. com.; bd. dirs. First Nat. Bank La Grange, Ill., Chem. Waste Mgmt., Inc., The Brand Cos., Wheelabrator Techs. Active Robert Crown Ctr., Hinsdale, Ill.; mem. adv. bd. Hinsdale Community House, 1984—; bd. dirs. Lyric Opera Chgo., Keep Am. Beautiful, Nazareth Acad., La Grange, 1981—, Hinsdale Hosp. Found.; trustee Denison U. Capt. USMCR, 1966-69. Decorated Bronze Star, Navy Commendation medal. Mem. Am. Pub. Works Assn., Nat. Solid Wastes Mgmt. Assn. Roman Catholic. Clubs: Butler Nat., Butterfield Country (Oak Brook, Ill.); Jupiter Hills (Fla.) Golf. Office: Waste Mgmt Inc 3003 Butterfield Rd Oak Brook IL 60521 *

ROONEY, SUSAN KAY, financial services manager; b. Fargo, N.D., Aug. 22, 1946; d. Glenn William and Phyllis Elaine (Ellingson) Heaton; m. Carl A. Moreno, May 28, 1976 (div. 1980); m. R. Timothy Rooney. Student, N.D. State U., 1964-68. Acct. asst. Bank of Am., San Francisco, 1969-75; credit analyst Central Bank of Colo., Colorado Springs, 1975-77; ops. mgr. Transamerica Comml. Fin. Corp., Palatine, Ill., 1978—. Republican. Home: 328 Woodbury Ct Schaumburg IL 60193

ROOT, ALAN CHARLES, diversified manufacturing company executive; b. Essex, Eng., Apr. 11, 1925; came to U.S., 1951, naturalized, 1959; s. Charles Stanley and Lillian (Collins) R. B.A., Oxford U., 1943; M.A., Cambridge U., 1951; M.B.A., Stanford U., 1953. Rsch. analyst Dow Chem. Co., Midland, Mich., 1954-55; mgr. mktg. rsch. Gen. Electric Co., 1955-61; v.p. bus. planning Mosler Safe Co., Hamilton, Ohio, 1961-70; v.p. corp. planning Am. Standard Inc., N.Y.C., 1970-76, sr. v.p. ops. svcs., 1976-86, sr. v.p., 1986-88, sr. advisor, 1989—; bd. dirs. Am.-Standard, Inc. Energy, Inc., Amstan Trucking Inc., 1976-86. Bd. dirs. Brit. Schs. and Univs. Found., Inc., admission to Order of St. John of Jerusalem sanctioned by H.M. Elizabeth II, 1986. Served to capt. AUS, 1944-48. Mem. Am. Inst. Chem. Engrs. (assoc. producer TV series Midland sect. 1955), Pilgrims U.S., Newcomen Soc. N. Am. Clubs: West Side Tennis (Forest Hills, N.Y.); Univ. (N.Y.C.); Quogue Field (L.I.); Montclair Golf Club (N.J.). Home: Claridge House II Verona NJ 07044-3027 Office: Am Standard Inc 40 W 40th St New York NY 10018

ROOT, GORDON CURTISS, financial planning executive; b. Farmington, N.Mex., Sept. 5, 1959; s. Jack Bradford and Wilma Louise (Metz) R.; m. Lindalee Marie Darrah, June 26, 1982; children: Cameron Curtiss, Morganne Marie. BS in Polit. Sci., Oreg. State U., 1981. Registered rep. Univ. Securities, Inc., Portland, Oreg., 1982-83, asst. mgr., 1983-84; gen. mgr. Resource Fin. Planning, Portland, 1984-86; v.p. Successful Money Mgmt. Seminars, Inc., Portland, 1985—, Resource Ins. Services, Inc., Portland, 1985-86; pres. Grid Corp., 1986-88. Mem. Internat. Assn. of Fin. Planning, Fin. Profl. Adv. Panel, Am. Assn. for Fin. Planning, Tigard (Oreg.) Jaycees. Republican. . Home: 1804 Hall Ct West Linn OR 97068

ROOT, LARRY DONALD, utilities executive; b. Emmetsburg, Iowa, Dec. 13, 1936; s. Donald Fred and Opal Ruth (Burdick) R.; m. Mary Ann Asby, June 4, 1960; children: Cheryl, Allen, Kara. BME, Iowa State U., 1959; MBA, U. Santa Clara (Calif.), 1967. Lic. nuclear engr., Calif. Engr. Lockheed, Sunnyvale, Calif., 1959-61, Martin Marietta, Balt., 1961-62, United Tech., Sunnyvale, 1962-65; project engr. GE, San Jose, Calif., 1965-70; successively assr. project mgr., mgr., mechanical/nuclear engr., dir. engring., asst. v.p. nuclear, v.p. engring., sr. v.p. ops. and tech. services Iowa Electric Light and Power Co., Cedar Rapids, Iowa, 1970-85, sr. v.p. ops. and prodn., 1985—; bd. dirs. IE Industries, Inc., Cedar Rapids, Teleconnect, Cedar Rapids, Amana (Iowa) Enterprises, Long Lines Ltd., Sergeant Bluff, Iowa. Div. leader United Way, Cedar Rapids, 1985; bd. dirs. Cedar Rapids C. of C. With U.S. Army Res., 1957-63. Mem. Am. Mgmt. Assn., Rotary. Republican. Presbyterian. Office: IE Industries Inc 200 1st St SE Cedar Rapids IA 52401

ROOT, STUART DOWLING, lawyer; b. Chagrin Falls, Ohio, Oct. 14, 1932; s. Elton Albert and Virginia Saxton (Dowling) R.; m. Jean D. Youse, Dec. 28, 1957 (div. Jan. 1972); children: Bryan, Kathleen, Timothy, Todd; m. Patricia Stoneman Graff, Apr. 24, 1976. BA, Ohio Wesleyan U., 1955; JD,

Columbia U., 1960. Bar: N.Y. 1960. Assoc. Cadwalader Wickersham and Taft, N.Y.C., 1960-68, ptnr., 1969-81, 84-87; pres. Bowery Savs. Bank, N.Y.C., 1981-82, vice chmn., 1982-83; exec. dir. Office Fed Savs. and Loan Ins. Corp., Washington, 1988-89; chmn. bd. Fin. Instn. Svcs. Corp., Washington, 1989—; lectr. ABA, Practicing Law Inst., Infocast, Am. Law Inst.; bd. dirs. Fed. Home Loan Bank of N.Y., 1986-87. Bd. dirs. Harlem Sch. Arts, N.Y.C., 1974-83, Open Space Inst., 1976-80, 84-87, Nat. Choral Soc., N.Y.C., 1981-86; trustee emeritus Harlem Sch. Arts, 1984; pub. interest dir. Fed. Home Loan Bank N.Y., N.Y.C., 1985-87. Served with U.S. Army, 1955-57. Mem. ABA, Am. Coll. Mortgage Attys., Down Town Assn. (N.Y.C.), Century Assn. (N.Y.C.). Republican. Episcopalian. Home: 190 Boulevard Pelham NY 10802 Office: Fin Instn Svcs Corp 1667 K St NW Washington DC 20006

ROOTS, PETER CHARLES, data processing company executive; b. Munich, W. Ger., Mar. 19, 1921; came to U.S., 1939, naturalized, 1943; s. Josef and Ruth R.; B.S., Sch. Fgn. Service, Georgetown U., 1948, LL.B., J.D., 1952; m. Sachiko Tamura; children—Stephanie E. Roots-Karsten, Judith A. Roots-Carver, David H., Catherine E. Admitted to Md. bar, U.S. Tax Ct. bar, 1952; atty. Sperry-Rand Corp., N.Y.C., 1952-65; exec. Sperry-Rand Corp. fgn. subs., Germany, Japan, 1965-70; pres. Inverdata GMBH, W. Ger., 1970—. Served with AUS, 1943-46. Mem. ABA. Club: Kronberg Golf & Land (W. Ger.). Author: (with Greene & Thompson) Developing Munitions for War, 1952. Home: Habicht Strasse 1, D6078 Neu Isenburg Federal Republic of Germany Office: Inverdata Electronics, Paul-Ehrlich Strasse 17, D-6074 Roedermark Federal Republic of Germany also: 1666 Newport Blvd Ste E Costa Mesa CA 92627

RORER, JOHN WHITELEY, publisher, consultant; b. Phila., Aug. 4, 1930; s. Ronald Erle and Hazel (Whiteley) R.; m. Beverly Cae, June 6, 1953. BS, U. Pa., 1952; MBA, Drexel U., 1956. Credit analyst Phila. Nat. Bank, 1954-56; with Curtis Pub. Co., Phila., 1956-68; dir. purchasing Chilton Pub. Co., Phila., 1968-70; founding pres. Focus Bus. Weekly, Bus. News, Inc., Phila., 1968—, pres., pub., 1974—; owner Pubs. Systems Assocs., Upper Darby, Pa., 1979—. Mem. Phila. World Affairs Council, 1979—. Served to capt. U.S. Army, 1952-54. Mem. Nat. Assn. Bus. Publs. (co-founder, bd. dirs. 1978-81), Nat. Assn. Indsl. Advt., Mktg. and Communications Execs. Assn. Republican. Episcopalian. Clubs: Union League, Engrs. (Phila.). Avocation: economics research. Home: 7520 Rogers Ave Upper Darby PA 19082 Office: 1015 Chestnut St Philadelphia PA 19107

RORKE, EDWIN GRANT, JR., manufacturing company executive; b. Phila., Mar. 21, 1923; s. Edwin Grant and Florence (Whitman) R.; m. Jean Gailey, June 10, 1950; children: Steven, David. BME, Cornell U., 1948. With Moore Products Co., Spring House, Pa., 1948—, exec. v.p., 1971-72, pres., 1972-87, chief exec. officer, 1972-88, chmn. bd. dirs., 1978—. With AUS, 1944-46. Mem. Instrument Soc. Am., Phila. Cricket Club. Office: Moore Products Co Sumneytown Pike Spring House PA 19477

RORKE, KEVIN HAYDEN, broadcast executive; b. Washington, June 22, 1949; s. James Hayden and Sari (Schwartz) R.; m. Patricia Hardy, July 15, 1972; children: Kelly Ann, Jennifer Hayden, Kathryn Hayden. BS in Bus. Adminstrn., Washington U., St. Louis, 1971; MBA, U. Denver, 1976. System mgr. Albany office Am. TV and Communications Corp., Englewood, Colo., 1977-79, div. mgr., 1979-81, v.p. devel. systems, 1981-83, pres. Orlando div. and sr. v.p., 1983-84, exec. v.p., 1984—; dir. Cabletelevison Advt. Bur., 1986—, Cable Television Adminstrn. and Mktg. Soc., 1987—. Served to 1st lt. U.S. Army, 1971-75.

ROSAR, VIRGINIA WILEY, librarian; b. Cleve., Nov. 22, 1926; d. John Egbert and Kathryn Coe (Snyder) Wiley; m. Michael Thorpe Rosar, April 8, 1950 (div. Feb. 1968); children: Bruce Wiley, Keith Michael, James Wilfred. Attended, Oberlin Coll., 1944-46; BA, U. Puget Sound, 1948; MS, C.W. Post Coll., L.I.U., Greenvale, N.Y., 1971. Cert. elem. music teacher, N.Y.; cert. sch. library media specialist. Music programmer Station WFAS, White Plains, N.Y., 1948; prodn. asst. NBC-TV, N.Y.C., 1948-50; tchr. Portledge Sch., Locust Valley, N.Y., 1967-70; librarian Syosset (N.Y.) Schs., 1970-71, Smithtown (N.Y.) Schs., 1971—; pres. World of Realia, Woodbury, N.Y., 1969-86; founder Cygnus Pub., Woodbury, 1985-87. Active local chpt. ARC, 1960-63, Community Concert Assn., 1960-66, Leukemia Soc. Am., 1978—. Mem. Suffolk Sch. Library Media Assn., AAAS, N.Y. Acad. Scis., Am. Mus. Natural History (assoc.), Am. Library Assn., L.I. Alumnae Club of Pi Beta Phi (pres. 1964-66). Republican. Presbyterian. Home: 10 Warrenton Ct Huntington NY 11743

ROSCHER, WILLIAM GLEN, financial planner; b. Kansas City, Mo., Mar. 18, 1929; s. Richard Lee and Clara Belle (Bryant) R.; m. Jo Ann Ethel Middlesteadt, Apr. 3, 1954; children: Glenn, Karen, Mary Jo. BS, U. Md., 1968; MSA, George Washington U., 1973. Cert. fin. planner. Served as enlisted man, U.S. Army, 1949-52, commd. 2d lt., 1952, advanced through grades to col., 1973, ret., 1974; v.p. Corp. Assistance, Inc., Scottsdale, Ariz., 1970-79, pres., 1979—; mem. faculty Scottsdale Community Coll., 1979-87. Contbr. articles to Nat. Tax Shelter Digest. Decorated Legion of Merit with oak leaf cluster, Bronze Star, Air medal. Mem. Inst. Cert. Fin. Planners. (pres. local soc. 1988—). Democrat. Methodist. Lodge: Rotary (treas. Paradise Valley, Ariz. 1983-87, pres. 1988—). Home: 9836 N 60th Pl Scottsdale AZ 85253 Office: Corp Assistance Inc 8070 E Morgan Trail Scottsdale AZ 85258

ROSCIA, JOHN J., retired multi-industry company executive, lawyer; b. Utica, N.Y., June 25, 1920; s. Angelo and Ida (Salerno) R.; m. Elizabeth Taylor, Jan. 9, 1943; children: Elizabeth, Margaret. A.B., Cornell U., 1942, LL.B., 1947. Bar: N.Y. 1947, Calif. 1951. With firm Chadbourne & Parke and predecessors, N.Y.C., 1947-55; asst. gen. counsel Rockwell Internat. Corp., Los Angeles, 1956-60; v.p., gen. counsel Rockwell Internat. Corp., 1961-82, sr. v.p., gen. counsel, 1982-84, sr. v.p., 1984-88. Bd. dirs. Ind. Colls. So. Calif. Served to capt., F.A. AUS, 1942-46. Mem. ABA, Phi Beta Kappa, Phi Kappa Phi, Delta Sigma Phi. Clubs: California, Riviera (Los Angeles). Home: 1660 N Amalfi Dr Pacific Palisades CA 90272 Office: Rockwell Internat 2230 E Imperial Hwy El Segundo CA 90245

ROSE, ARTHUR MORRIS, wholesale hardware executive; b. Bklyn., Mar. 7, 1943; s. Lawrence and Lillian (Rosen) R.; B.S., N.Y. U., 1964; M.B.A. with distinction, Adelphi U., 1978; m. Nadine Posner; children—Sharon Elisabeth, Kevin Benjamin, Amy Meredith, Erica June, Jonathan Calman. Exec. trainee, mgr. boy's dept. Gertz Dept. Stores, Hicksville, N.Y., 1966; registered rep. Loeb Rhoades & Co., N.Y.C., 1967; pres. L. Rose Hardware Inc., Bklyn., 1968—. Mem. Am. Mgmt. Assn., U.S. Power Squadron, Am. Radio Relay League, Delta Mu Delta. Jewish. Club: Steppingstone Sailing. Home: 33 Georgian Ln Great Neck NY 11024 Office: L Rose Hardware Inc 201 Snediker Ave Brooklyn NY 11207

ROSE, CHRISTOPHER DUNCAN, marketing executive, consultant; b. N.Y.C., Jan. 31, 1944; s. Henry Martin II and Joan (Kastner) R.; m. Susan Jayne Tracy, Mar. 25, 1979 (div. 1985); 1 child, Shannon Whitney; m. Janice Elaine Kreuzburg, Oct. 12, 1985. Student, Norwich U., 1966-68; BS magna cum laude, Rutgers U., 1977; postgrad., Loyola U., Washington, 1981. Mgr. sales Equity Funding Corp., Paramus, N.J., 1968-70; owner, pres. Alexander Duncan Karr, West Yarmouth, Mass., 1971-74; mgr. contract adminstrn. Burns & Roe, Inc., Oradell, N.J., 1974-77, mgr. mktg. adminstrn., instr. contracting basics and claims def., 1980-83; mgr. dep. contracts Stone & Webster Engring. Corp., Boston, 1977-80; mgr. mktg. Centrig Industries, Charlotte, N.C., 1983-85; dir. mktg. Associated Mech. Contractors, Greensboro, N.C., 1985-87; mgr. sales and mktg. Davis Mech. Contractors, Greensboro, 1987-88; owner, pres. The Rose Group, Kernersville, 1988—; cons. in field. Author: (monographs) Piping in Nuclear Plants, 1977, Construction Management, 1983, Selling/Renting Employees, 1985, Approaches to Construction Management for Billion Dollar Projects, 1986, (manuals) Construction Management, 1983, Renting Construction Employees, 1986. V.p. Montclair (N.J.) Jaycees, 1967-68; Rep. campaign mgr. Mayor of Montclair, 1969; sec.-treas. Rep. Com., Montclair, 1969; pres. Abington Village Neighborhood Assn., Kernersville, N.C., 1988. Mason Gross scholar Rutgers U., 1976. Mem. Nat. Contracts Mgmt. Assn., Am. Mktg. Assn., ASHRAE, N.C. Indsl. Developers Assn., Greensboro C. of C., Inland Sea Sailing, U.S. Yacht Racing Union, Alpha Sigma Lambda (life). Episcopalian. Home: 1605 Round Hill Circle Kernersville NC 27284 Office: The Rose Group PO Box 1247 Kernersville NC 27295-1247

ROSE, DAVID ALLAN, trust administrator; b. N.Y.C., Feb. 15, 1937; s. Edward William and Marion (Nadelstein) R.; m. Frances Helaine Dushman, Aug. 16, 1959; children: Evan Denali, Mitchell Franklin. BS in Acctg., Queens Coll., 1958; MBA in Fin., Syracuse U., 1968. Fin. mgr. U.S. Army, Fort Richardson, Alaska, 1961-75; comptroller U.S. Army, Fort Richardson, 1975; exec. dir. Alaska Mcpl. Bond Bank Authority, Anchorage, 1975-82, Alaska Indsl. Devel. Authority, Anchorage, 1980; co-owner Downtown Investment Co., Anchorage, 1980—, Fran's Fashion Juneau (Alaska), Inc., 1985—; pres. Downtown Delicatessen, Inc., Anchorage, 1976—; exec. dir. Alaska Permanent Fund Corp., Juneau, 1982—; fin. advisor Fin. Green Lake Dam, Sitka, Alaska, 1977, Fin. Dutch Harbor Port, Unalaska, Alaska, 1979-80, Fin. Kenai-Anchorage Pipeline, Anchorage, 1979-80, Fin. Pulp Mill Pollution Control, Ketchikan, Alaska, 1979-80. Mem. City Council, Anchorage, 1971-75, Borough Assembly, Anchorage, 1971-75, Mcpl. Assembly, Anchorage, 1975-80; pres. Alaska Mcpl. League, 1975. Served with U.S. Army, 1959-61. Recipient Golden Man award Boys Club Alaska, Anchorage, 1974, Decoration for Meritorious Civilian Service, U.S. Army, 1975, Pub. Service award City and Borough, Juneau, 1986; named Pub. Adminstr. Yr., Am. Soc. Pub. Adminstrn., Alaska chpt., 1986. Mem. Rotary Club (bd. dirs.). Republican. Jewish. Home: 4660 Thane Rd Juneau AK 99801 Office: Alaska Permanent Fund Corp PO Box 4-1000 Juneau AK 99802

ROSE, DAVID CAMERON, discount store executive; b. Vance County, N.C., Nov. 10, 1942; s. Thomas Benton, Jr. and Kathryn (Hunt) R.; m. Margaret Diane Oakley, June 26, 1965; children: David Cameron, Thomas Benjamin. B.B.A., Wake Forest U., Winston-Salem, N.C., 1965; M.B.A., Wharton Sch., U. Pa., 1967. C.P.A., N.C. Staff accountant Haskins & Sells (C.P.A.s), Greensboro, N.C., 1967-69; with Rose's Stores, Inc., Henderson, N.C., 1969—; controller Rose's Stores, Inc., 1971-72, treas., 1972—, v.p. fin., from 1975, also dir.; dir. Central Carolina Bank, Durham, N.C., CCB Fin. Corp., Durham. Chmn. Henderson/Vance County Parks and Recreation Commn., 1979—; pres. Vance Acad., Inc., Henderson, 1982-84; trustee Maria Parham Hosp., 1985. Mem. Am. Inst. C.P.A.s, N.C. Assn. C.P.A.s, Fin. Execs. Inst. Methodist. Club: Henderson Rotary. Home: 3205 Cameron Dr Henderson NC 27536 Office: Rose's Stores Inc PO Drawer 947 Henderson NC 27536 *

ROSE, DEBORAH ELIZABETH, auditor, consultant, accountant; b. Toledo, July 21, 1956; d. James David and Marlene Frances (Roach) R. BBA, U. Mo., 1978, MS, 1979. CPA, Kans., Mo.; cert. internal auditor, fraud examiner. Cost acct. Vendo Co., Overland Park, Kans., 1976-77, tax acct., 1977-78; contr. Vet. Labs., Lenexa, Kans., 1978; staff mgr. Ernst & Whinney, Kansas City, 1979-85; sr. mgr. Price Waterhouse, Oklahoma City, 1985-86; audit mgr. Mut. Benefit Life, Kansas City, 1986—; treas. Sesor, inc., Kansas City, 1986—; bd. dirs. Ins. Internal Auditors Group, Hartford, Conn.; cons. in field. Fellow Life Officer's Mgmt. Inst.; mem. AICPA, Mo. Soc. CPAs, Inst. Internal Auditors, Nat. Assn. Cert. Fraud Examiners, EDP Auditors Assn., Chi Omega (pres. 1977-78, treas. 1980-86). Office: Mut Benefit Life 2323 Grand Ave Kansas City MO 64108

ROSE, EDGAR, mechanical engineer; b. Essen, Fed. Republic Germany, Sept. 17, 1926; came to U.S., 1947; s. Max and Irene Rose; m. Nettie Kardon; children: Linda, Susan. BSME, Robert Coll., Istanbul, Turkey, 1947; MSME, MIT, 1948. Rsch. assoc. MIT, Cambridge, Mass., 1950-52; dir. rsch. Mercury Marine Kiekhaefer Corp., Oshkosh, Wis., 1952-62; project engr. Curtiss Wright, Wood-Ridge, N.J., 1962-67; dir. snowmobile engring. Outboard Marine Corp., Waukegan, Ill., 1968-76, dir. stern drive and accessory engring., 1976-80, dir. marine engring., 1980-83, v.p. marine engring. and rsch., 1983—. Patentee in field. Mem. ASME, Soc. Automotive Engrs., Am. Power Boat Assn. (pres. elect 1988), Sigma Xi. Home: 741 Sycamore Ln Glencoe IL 60022 Office: Outboard Marine Corp 300 Sea Horse Dr Waukegan IL 60085

ROSE, HUGH, management consultant; b. Evanston, Ill., Sept. 10, 1926; s. HOward Gray and Catherine (Wilcox) R.; m. Mary Moore Austin, Oct. 25, 1952; children: Susan, Nancy, Gregory, Matthew, Mary. BS in Physics, U. Mich., 1951, MS in Geophysics, 1952; MBA, Pepperdine U., 1982. With Caterpillar, Inc., Peoria, Ill., 1952-66; v.p., mktg. mgr. Cummins Engine Co., Columbus, Ind., 1966-69; pres., chief exec. officer Cummins Northeastern, Inc., Boston, 1969-77; pres. Power Systems Assocs., L.A., 1980-81, C.D. High Tech., Inc., Austin, Tex., 1984-87; mgmt. cons. Rose and Assocs., Tucson, 1984, 87—. Contbr. paleontol. articles to various publs. Bd. dirs. Raymond Alf Mus., Claremont, Calif., 1979—, Comstock Found., Tucson, 1988. With USAAF, World War II. Fellow AAAS; mem. Soc. Vertebrate Paleontology, Beacon Soc. Boston (pres.), Algonquin Club Boston (v.p., bd. dirs. 1974-80), Duxbury Yacht Club, Longwood Cricket Club, Racquet Club Tucson, Sigma Gamma Epsilon, Beta Beta Beta. Republican. Presbyterian. Office: Rose & Assocs 5320 N Camino Sumo Tucson AZ 85718

ROSE, JUDY SIZEMORE, small business owner; b. Manchester, Ky., Apr. 28, 1939; d. Frank Sizemore and Nancy (Lee) Henson; m. James Lawrence Rose, Apr. 14, 1962; children: Dwayne Scott, Nathan James Franklin, Sonya Lecia. MusB, Cumberland Coll., Williamsburg, Ky., 1958, DHL, 1985; postgrad., Ea. Ky. U., 1966, U. Ky., 1967. Pres. Cumberland Valley Ins. Agy., London, Ky., 1981—; tchr. Clay County High Sch., Manchester, 1965-69; owner Piggy Wiggly Super Market, Manchester, 1964-70, Art Gallery, Knoxville, Tenn., 1980-83, Art Gallery, Atlanta, 1980-83; asst. family owned coal cos., Manchester, 1962-73; mem. jud. nominating commn. Ky. Supreme Ct., Ky. Ct. Appeals. Bd. dirs. Cardinal Hill Hosp., Lexington, Ky., McDowell Cancer Network, Lexington, Scott Rose Found., London, So. Sem. Found., Louisville, Ky. Ctr. Pub. Issues, Forward in the Fifth; mem. adv. bd. Bapt. Regional Med. Ctr.; bd. dirs., sec. Ky. Easter Seal Soc., Louisville; trustee Cumberland Coll., Williamsburg. Named to Hon. Order of Ky. Cols., Commonwealth of Ky.; U. Ky. fellow. Mem. Nat. Fedn. Rep. Women, Manchester Women's Club (v.p., Outstanding Mem. 1975), U. Ky. Women's Club. Baptist. Home: PO Box 756 London KY 40741 Office: United Bancorp Ky 3100 Lexington Financial Ctr Lexington KY 40507

ROSE, JULES FREED, retail food executive; b. N.Y.C., Feb. 4, 1936; s. Myles and Selma (Freed) R.; B.A., Dartmouth Coll., 1957; law and acctg. courses Cornell U.; m. Marilyn Judith Sloan, Apr. 10, 1960; children—Patti Renee, Mitchell Brian, Randi Sloan. With Sloan's Super Markets, N.Y.C., 1960—, exec. v.p., 1969-79, pres., 1979-82, chmn. bd., chief exec. officer, 1982—; dir. Eastern Frosted Foods Assn., 1970—, pres., 1978-80; adv. bd. Eastern Dairy-Deli Assn.; lectr. N.Y. Agrl. Coll., Farmingdale, Fordham U., L.I.U., Cornell U. Nat. trustee NCCJ, 1975-85. Served with AUS, 1958-60. Named Supermarket of Year N.Y. State Food Mchts., 1969, Frozen Food Merchandiser of Year Eastern Frosted Foods Assn., 1979; Man of Yr., Nat. Prepared Frozen Food Assn., 1979; Nat. Frozen Foods Merchandiser of Yr., 1982. Mem. Food Industry Alliance (pres. 1973-74), Greater N.Y. Food Council (1st v.p. 1978-79, pres. 1981—), Soc. Personnel Adminstrn., Nat. Frozen Foods Assn. (dir. 1982—), Pub. Personnel Adminstrn. Lodge: B'nai B'rith (trustee, v.p. 1970-75, pres. 1975-76). Contbr. articles to publs. Office: 2 Bennett Ave New York NY 10033

ROSE, LAWRENCE JOSEPH, retail executive, pharmacist; b. Phila., Aug. 4, 1941; s. Anthony George and Marian (Vitacolonna) R.; m. Elaine Regina Gentile; children: Maria, Anthony. BS in Pharmacy, Temple U., 1963. Registered pharmacist Pilgrim Pharmacy, Phila., 1963-1966; asst. mgr. Thrift Drug, Southampton, Pa., 1966-67, store mgr., 1967; store mgr. Thrift Drug, Doylestown, Pa., 1967-72; asst. dist. mgr. Thrift Drug, Pitts., 1972-73, dist. mgr., 1973-76, dir. store ops., 1976-81, v.p., dir. mktg., 1981-85, sr. v.p., dir. mktg. and mdse., 1985-87, exec. v.p. mktg., mdse., distbn., 1987; pres., chief operating officer Fays Drug Co., Liverpool, N.Y., 1987—. Mem. Nat. Assn. Chain Drug Stores (outstanding service award 1987), Kappa Psi, Beta Omega. Republican. Roman Catholic. Home: 7310 Barberry Ln Manlius NY 13104 Office: Fay's Drug Co 7245 Henry Clay Blvd Liverpool NY 13088 *

ROSE, MICHAEL DAVID, hotel corporation executive; b. Akron, Ohio, Mar. 2, 1942; s. William H. and Annabel L. (Kennedy) R.; children: Matthew Derek Franco, Gabrielle Elaine Franco, Morgan Douglas. B.B.A., U. Cin., 1963; LL.B., Harvard U., 1966. Bar: Ohio 1966. Lectr. U. Cin., 1966-67; atty. firm Strauss, Troy & Ruehlmann, Cin., 1966-72; exec. v.p. Winegardner Internat., Cin., 1972-74; v.p. hotel group Holiday Inns, Inc., Memphis, 1974-76, pres. hotel group, 1976-78, corp. exec. v.p., 1978-79, pres., from 1979, chief exec. officer, 1981—, chmn. bd., dir., 1984—; chmn., chief exec. officer Holiday Corp.; dir. First Tenn. Nat. Corp., Gen. Mills, Inc., Po Folks Inc. Fellow advance mgmt. program Harvard U. Grad. Sch. Bus. Adminstrn.; bd. dirs. Memphis Arts Council, from 1979; mem. Future Memphis, from 1979; mem. bd. advisors U. Cin., from 1979; hon. chmn. bd. trustees Jr. Achievement, Memphis. Mem. Ohio Bar Assn., Young Pres.'s Orgn., Conf. Bd., Service Industry Council of U.S. C. of C., Jobs Skills Task Force, Am. Hotel and Motel Assn. (industry real estate financing adv. council). Club: Econ. Memphis. Office: Holiday Inns Inc 3796 Lamar Ave Memphis TN 38196 *

ROSE, PAUL EDWARD, publishing company executive; b. Spokane, Wash., Apr. 27, 1947; s. Albert Edward and Karen (Murray) R.; m. Karen Pearl Rose, Aug. 23, 1971; children: Marcus, David, Julianne. BS, Brigham Young U., 1970, M in Acctg., 1971. CPA, N.Y., Ill. Auditor Ernst & Whinney, N.Y.C., 1971-75; budget mgr. Dun & Bradstreet, N.Y.C., 1975-77; controller, dir. circulation sales Official Airline Guides, Oak Brook, Ill., 1977-82; fin. controller John Morrell & Co., Northfield, Ill., 1982-83; v.p. fin. Standard Rate and Data Service, Wilmette, Ill., 1983-85; sr. v.p. Macmillan Directory Div., Wilmette, Ill., 1985-87, exec. v.p., 1987—. Recipient Outstanding Pianist award, Wash. State Music Tchrs. Assn., 1968. Mem. IICPA. Office: Macmillan Directory Div 3004 Glenview Rd Wilmette IL 60091

ROSE, ROBERT NEAL, brokerage executive; b. Chgo., Feb. 27, 1951; s. James Allan Rose and Hazel (Gordon) Kaufman; m. Anna Yvette Trujillo, Aug. 23, 1981; 1 child, David James. BS, Georgetown U., 1973; postgrad., U. N.Mex., 1974. Trader Salomon Bros., N.Y.C., 1974-75; regional coordinator Latin Am. Merrill Lynch Govt. Securities, N.Y.C., 1975-76; dir. fed. govt. affairs Pub. Service of N.Mex., Albuquerque, 1977-78; exec. dir. Gov. Jerry Apodaca, Washington, 1979-80; expert cons. U.S. Dept. Commerce, Washington, 1980-81; officer Am. Express Internat. Bank, N.Y.C., 1981-82; sr. v.p. Refco, Inc., N.Y.C., 1982-84; v.p., mgr. Thomson McKinnon Securities, N.Y.C., 1984-88; sr. v.p. futures Shearson Lehman Hutton, N.Y.C., 1988—; cons. BDM Corp., McLean, Va., 1981-88, Seminole Tribe of Hollywood, Fla., 1980-82, GFTA Trendanalysen, Fensisberg, Switzerland, 1988—. Mem. Dem. Nat. Bus. Council, Washington, 1980-85; mem. arrangements com. Dem. Nat. Conv., San Francisco, 1984; founder Dem. State Treas.'s Assn., Washington, 1984, Nat. Dem. Party Hdqrs., Washington, 1984; bd.d irs. Levitt Pavillion for the Performing Arts, Westport, Conn., 1989—. Mem. Delta Sigma Pi, Delta Phi Epsilon. Jewish. Home: One Spring Hill Rd Westport CT 06880 Office: Shearson Lehman Hutton World Fin Ctr New York NY 10285

ROSE, STANLEY JAY, newspaper executive; b. Kansas City, Mo., June 3, 1918; s. Joseph and Mae (Lund) R.; m. Shirley Mallin, Oct. 7, 1942; children: Roberta Susan Rose Small, Stephen F. AA, Los Angeles City Coll., 1939; BJ, U. Mo., 1941. Chmn. bd., pub. Sun Publs., Inc., Overland Park, Kans., 1950—; pub. Kansas City (Mo.) Jewish Chronicle, Inc., 1964—, College Blvd. News, 1984—, Atlanta Jewish Times, 1986—, Olathe (Kans.) Life, 1980. Author: Memo from Russia, 1986. Bd. dirs. Kaw Valley Heart Assn., Heart of Am. council Boy Scouts Am.; past chmn. bd. trustees Humana Med Ctr.; trustee William Allen White Found.; mem. adv. council U. Kans. Med. Center, K.U. Chancellor's Cabinet, 1986—. Served to lt. (j.g.) USNR, World War II; PTO. Recipient Sweepstakes, 1st place awards Kans. Better Newspaper Contest, 1968-70, 72, 73, William Allen White News Enterprise award, 1975, Bea Johnson award Am. Cancer Soc., 1st place winner for gen. excellence Suburban Newspapers Am., 1983-84, Chancellor's award U. Kans., 1988; honoree Matrix Table, 1980, honoree Nat. Conf. Christians and Jews, 1989; Regional Comdr. Kans. Cav. Mem. Kans. State C. of C. and Industry (chmn.), Sigma Delta Chi. Club: Kansas City (Mo.) Press. Lodges: Masons, Shriners, Rotary (Paul Harris fellow 1985). Home: 8600 Mission Rd Leawood KS 66206 Office: Sun Publs Bldg Overland Park KS 66212

ROSE, STEPHEN JAY, advertising company executive; b. N.Y.C., Nov. 24, 1925; s. Herman and Harriet (Greenspan) R.; m. Margitta Braun; children by previous marriage: John Stephen, Daniel Jay. A.B., Univ. Heights Coll., NYU, 1948. Dir. radio-TV-rec. Sol Hurok, N.Y.C., 1948-57; mktg. dir. Revlon, Inc., N.Y.C., 1957-60; account exec. Ogilvie & Mather, N.Y.C., 1960-61; v.p. mktg. Maradel, N.Y.C., 1961-63, J.B. Williams, N.Y.C., 1963-65; with AC&R Advt., Inc., N.Y.C., 1965-87, exec. v.p., sec., 1965-72, chmn. bd., from 1972, chief exec. officer, 1987—, now chmn. exec. com.; chmn. bd., chief exec. officer Saatchi & Saatchi Advt. Affiliates, N.Y.C., 1987; chmn. AC&R Pub. Relations, Inc., AC&R Hellas, Athens, Greece; pres. Ted Bates Internat. Ops., 1977; dir. Ted Bates Advt., Inc. Served with USNR, 1942-46. Club: Orienta Yacht. Office: AC&R/DHB&BESS 16 E 32nd St New York NY 10016 *

ROSE, THEODORE ROBERT (LINDSTROM), manufacturing company executive; b. Rhinelander, Wis., Feb. 13, 1951; s. Theodore Robert Lindstrom and Rosemary Catherine (Slizewski) R. Cert. in hydraulics, Milw. Area Tech. Coll., Milw., 1969, Milw. Sch. Engring., 1970; cert. in computers, Nat. Radio Inst., Washington, 1987; cert. in Computer Numerical Control programming, Waukesha County Tech. Inst., Pewaukee, Wis., 1987. Draftsman Krause Mfg. Co., Milw., 1969-70; v.p., foreman Sanitation Svc., Inc., Menomonee Falls, Wis., 1970-74; foreman Comet, Inc., Menomonee Falls, 1974-75; supr. Rose Industries, Inc., Milw., 1975-87, H&H Tool and Machine Co., Germantown, Wis., 1987—; v.p., cons. R-Svc. Co., Germantown, 1980—; cons. Alrose Realty, Germantown. Mem. Daniel Boone Conservation League. Home: N105 W15750 Hamilton Ct Germantown WI 53022 Office: H&H Tool and Machine Co W151 N11412 Fond du Lac Ave Germantown WI 53022

ROSELLE, ROBERT PAUL, financial executive; b. Detroit, Aug. 19, 1925; s. Clarance Shield and Lydia E. (Dammes) R.; m. Beverly Bushey, Nov. 20, 1945 (dec.); children—Janis, Nancy Lutz, James Roselle, Cindy Capobres; m. J. June Ridgway, Apr. 9, 1983. B.S. in Bus. Adminstrn., Wayne State U., 1955. With City of Detroit, 1947-73, dir. Mayor's Com. for Community Renewal, 1962-64, dir. Mayor's Com. for Total Action Against Poverty, 1964-65, dir. budget bur. Controller's Office, 1965-66, dep. controller, 1966-67, exec. sec. to mayor, 1967-68, commr. Dept. Pub. Works, 1968-70, controller, 1970-72, dir. Community Devel. Commn., 1972-73; chief fin. officer and sr. v.p. Lintas:Campbell-Ewald Co., Warren, Mich., 1973; exec. v.p. Lintas:Campbell-Ewald Co., 1973—, sec.-treas., 1973—, also bd. dirs., 1973—; sec.-treas., dir. Campbell-Ewald N.Y., Inc., 1975—, dir. Ceco Communications. Chmn. bd. dirs. Music Hall, Merrill-Palmer Inst.; treas., bd. dirs. United Community Services; bd. dirs., chmn. Civic Searchlight; bd. dirs. Civic, Inc.; mem. fin. adv. bd. LWV, Detroit Zool. Soc.; chmn. Detroit Zoo; mem. Founders Soc., Detroit Inst. Arts; bd. dirs., treas. Luth. Social Services Mich.; bd. regents Capital U., Columbus, Ohio, 1970-79; mem. Wayne County Stadium Authority, 1971-73; trustee Mich. Mcpl. League, 1968-71; bd. dirs. Mich. dist. Am. Luth. Ch., 1968-70; trustee Friends Sch. in Detroit, 1974-81. Served with U.S. Army, 1944-46; ETO. Mem. Fin. Execs. Inst., Adcraft Club Detroit. Democrat. Clubs: Recess, Detroit, Detroit Golf. Home: 8162 E Jefferson St Apt 11-A Detroit MI 48214 Office: Lintas:-Campbell-Ewald Co 30400 Van Dyke Warren MI 48093

ROSEMAN, JACK, computer services company executive; b. Lynn, Mass., June 13, 1931; s. Abraham and Bessie (Guz) R.; m. Judith Ann Rosenthal, Feb. 21, 1960; children: Laura, Alan, Shari. BA, Boston U., 1954; MS, U. Mass., 1955. Instr. U. Mass., 1958-60; dir. info. processing CEIR, Inc., Washington, 1960-66; v.p. KMS Tech. Ctr., Washington, 1966-70; pres. On-Line Systems, Inc., Pitts., from 1970-79 also bd. dirs.; pres., chmn. United Computing Internat. subs. of United Telecommunications, 1980—; pvt. investor, ptnr. J.R. Assocs., Pitts, 1988—; adj. faculty Carnegie-Mellon U., 1988—; cons. North Side Civic Devel. Coun., Inc., Pitts., 1987—; chmn. bd. Allegheny County Am. Heart Assn.; bd. dirs. Pitts. High Tech. Coun. Mem. Am. Fedn. Info. Processing (program chmn. 1964), Assn. Computing Machinery (program chmn.), Meadowlands Standardbred Horseman's Assn. (bd. dirs.). Home: 117 Doray Dr Pittsburgh PA 15237

ROSEMAN, SCOTT MICHAEL, market official; b. N.Y.C., Feb. 5, 1956; s. Norman B. and Marilyn (Mandel) R. BA, U. Calif., Santa Cruz, 1985. Pub. editor Energy News, Santa Cruz, 1980-83; produce mgr., dir. Neighborhood Food Coop., Santa Cruz, 1983-84; gen. mgr. Westside Community Market, Santa Cruz, 1985—. Mem. Progressive Bus. Network (bd. dirs. 1986—), Santa Cruz C. of C. Democrat. Jewish. Home: 3016 Buckingham Ave Santa Cruz CA 95062 Office: Westside Community Market 328A Ingalls St Santa Cruz CA 95060

ROSEN, BENJAMIN MAURICE, venture capitalist; b. New Orleans, Mar. 11, 1933; s. Isidore J. and Anna Vera (Leibof) R.; m. Alexandra Ebere, Sept. 29, 1967; children—Jeffrey Mark, Eric Andrew. B.S., Calif. Inst. Tech., 1954; M.S., Stanford U., 1955; M.B.A., Columbia U., 1961. Engr. Raytheon Corp., Oxnard, Calif., 1955-56; engr. Sperry Corp., Great Neck, N.Y., 1957-59; v.p. Quantum Sci. Corp., N.Y.C., 1961-65; ptnr. Coleman & Co., N.Y.C., 1965-75; v.p. Morgan Stanley & Co. Inc., N.Y.C., 1975-80; pres. Rosen Research Inc., N.Y.C., 1980-83; ptnr Sevin Rosen Mgmt. Co., N.Y.C., 1981—; chmn. bd. Compaq Computer Corp., Houston, Ansa Corp., Belmont, Calif.; dir. Gen. Parametrics Corp., Berkeley, Calif., Expertel, Inc., Dallas; former founder dir. Lotus Devel. Corp.; mem. adv. bd. Sch. Bus., Tulane U., New Orleans. Bd. dirs. Tech. Ctr. Silicon Valley, San Jose, Calif., mem. pres.'s council Meml. Sloan-Kettering Cancer Ctr., N.Y.C.; trustee Calif. Inst. Tech., Pasadena. Mem. N.Y. Soc. Security Analysts. Office: Sevin Rosen Mgmt Co 200 Park Ave New York NY 10166 also: Compaq Computer Corp 20555 FM 149 Houston TX 77070 *

ROSEN, BERNARD, engineer, engineering company executive; b. Bklyn., Mar. 31, 1927; s. Hyman and F. (Kasofsky) R.; m. Janice Raskin; children: Steven. Stuart, Roberta Sue. BEE, City Coll. N.Y., 1950; MEE, Poly. Tech. U., 1957. Registered profl. engr., N.Y. From mgr. to v.p. Watkins Johnson, Palo Alto, Calif., 1964—. Bd. dirs. Jr. Achievement, Santa Clara, Calif. Mem. Am. Mgmt. Assn., IEEE, AFCEA, Tau Beta Pi, Eta Kappa Nu, Sigma Xi. Office: Watkins Johnson Co 2525 N First St San Jose CA 95131

ROSEN, BERTRAM HARVEY, financial planner; b. Cleve., Mar. 22, 1939; s. Harry and Estina (Weinberger) R.; m. Barbara Sandra Katz, Oct. 13, 1970; children: Dennis, Larry, Elisa, Karen. BS, Ohio State U., 1961. Acctg. and auditing specialist GAO, Washington, 1961-65, asst. dir. for ADP initiatives, 1987; designer income tax course H&R Block Co., Washington, 1965-66; adminstrv. officer Manned Space Program NASA, Washington, 1966-69; exec. sec. Joint Fin. Mgmt. Improvement Program, Washington, 1969-76; pres. B.H. Rosen & Assocs., Silver Spring, Md., 1976—. With USAF, 1961. Mem. Inst. Cert. Fin. Planners, Nat. Soc. Pub. Accts., Assn. Govt. Accts. Democrat. Jewish.

ROSEN, JAY BERNARD, computer company executive; b. Glenridge, N.J., Dec. 4, 1954; m. Nancy Isaacs. BS, U. Mich., 1976; MBA, Harvard U., 1980. Analyst Ford Motor Co., Dearborn, Mich., 1976-78; cons. Touche Ross Co., Detroit, 1980-85; v.p. Lason Systems, Inc., Livonia, Mich., 1985—. Home: 5303 Cedar Grove Ct West Bloomfield MI 48322 Office: Lason Systems Inc Schoolcraft St Livonia MI 48150

ROSEN, J(OSHUA) PHILIP, lawyer; b. N.Y.C., Aug. 24, 1956; s. Irving and Tauba (Krieger) R. BA, Yeshiva U., 1978; JD, Georgetown U., 1981. Bar: N.Y. 1982. Law clk. U.S. Dist. Ct. (so. dist.) N.Y., N.Y.C., 1981-82; ptnr. Weil, Gotshal & Manges, N.Y.C., 1982—; bd. advisers N.Y. Real Estate Law Reporter, N.Y.C., 1987—. Contbr. articles to legal publs. Legal counsel N.Y. Holocaust Meml. Commn., N.Y.C., 1983—. Jewish. Home: 55 E End Ave New York NY 10028 Office: Weil Gotshal & Manges 767 Fifth Ave New York NY 10153

ROSEN, MICHAEL HOWARD, real estate executive; b. N.Y.C., May 22, 1943; s. Irving Edward and Lilyan Ruth (Ruttenberg) R.; A.B., Tufts U., 1965; m. Joni Frances Breckel, Dec. 29, 1978; children by previous marriage—Daniel Matthew, Lenise Gayle; stepchildren—Jeffrey, Kelli, Molli Lynch. Lic. real estate broker, N.Y., Md. Exec. v.p. Rosen Orgn. Inc., N.Y.C., 1971-75, dir., 1971-75; v.p. apt. ops. Monumental Properties, Inc., and Monumental Properties Trust, Balt., 1975-79; exec. v.p. Town and Country Mgmt. Corp., Balt., 1979—, now chief operating officer; Commr. Wellwood Little League Baseball and Pikesville Basketball, 1981-82, Blue Devil Umpire Assn., 1982—, Mason Dixon Umpire Assn., 1989—; div. chmn. maj. firms div. United Way of Central Md., 1983-86; chmn. cen. mid team, 1987—; mem. Kennedy Soc.; bd. dirs. Cystic Fibrosis Found., 1983-88; chmn. Life Line Ministries. Md. Mem. Nat. Realty Com., Apt. Owners and Mgrs. Assn. Am., Home Builders Assn. Md., Apt. Builders and Owners Council Md. (dir. 1976, 77, 83, 84), Packard Soc. Tufts U., Greater Balt. Bd. Realtors, Nat. Apt. Assn. Clubs: Suburban Balt. County, Center. Home: 8003 Melody Ln Baltimore MD 21208 Office: Town & Country Mgmt Corp 100 S Charles St Ste 1700 Baltimore MD 21201

ROSEN, NORMAN EDWARD, lawyer; b. Providence, July 2, 1938; s. Albert and Lillian (Korb) R.; m. Estelle Cutler, Sept. 5, 1966; children: James, Vanessa. AB, Harvard U., 1959; LLB, Columbia U., 1962; MA, George Washington U., 1965. Bar: N.Y. 1962, D.C. 1963, U.S. Supreme Ct. 1966. Trial atty. FTC, Washington, 1962-67; assoc. Paskus, Gordon & Hyman, N.Y.C., 1967-69; ptnr. Levin, Kreis, Ruskin & Gyory, N.Y.C., 1970-72; staff v.p., sr. counsel trade regulation and licensing RCA, N.Y.C., 1972-82, Princeton, N.J., 1982-86; sr. v.p., gen. counsel Gen. Electric and RCA Licensing Mgmt. Operation, Inc., Princeton, 1986—, GE Trading Co., Princeton, 1989—. Contbr. articles to profl. jours. Mem. ABA (chmn. antitrust sect. patent trademark and know-how com. 1983-86, mem. antitrust sect. coun. 1986—, mem. task forces on Dept. of Justice antitrust guidelines and mergers and know-how in European econ. community), Am. Intellectual Property Law Assn., Harvard Club, Surf Club. Office: GE 2 Independence Way PO Box 2023 Princeton NJ 08540

ROSEN, RICHARD ERIC, real estate executive; b. Newark, Mar. 10, 1958; s. Irving and Doris (Frieman) R. BS, Syracuse U., 1980. Mgr. Frieman Realty Co., Union, N.J., 1980-84, v.p., 1984-87; pres. Frieman Realty Co., East Brunswick, N.J., 1987—; pres., founder Rosen Family Partnership, Union, 1987—. Mem. Nat. Assn. Home Builders, Cen. Jersey Bldg. Assn. Home and Office: E-5 Brier Hill Ct East Brunswick NJ 08816

ROSEN, SHERWIN, economist, educator; b. Chgo., Sept. 29, 1938; s. Joe W. and Nell (Rudy) R.; m. Sharon Ginsberg, June 11, 1961; children: Jennifer, Adria. BS, Purdue U., 1960; M.A., U. Chgo., 1962, Ph.D., 1966. Mem. faculty dept. econs. U. Rochester, N.Y., 1964-75; Kenan prof. econs. U. Rochester, 1975-77; prof. econs. U. Chgo., 1977-83, Bergman prof. econs., 1984-88, chmn. econ. dept., 1988—; sr. research fellow Nat. Bur. Econ. Research, Nat. Opinion Research Center, Hoover Instn.; vis. prof. U. Buffalo, 1970, Harvard U., 1971-72, Columbia U., 1973, Stanford U., 1976. Contbr. articles to profl. jours. Fellow Econometric Soc., Am. Acad. Arts and Scis.; mem. Am. Econ. Assn. (exec. com. 1985—). Home: 5714 Kimbark Chicago IL 60637 Office: U Chgo Dept Econs 1126 E 59th St Chicago IL 60637

ROSEN, THEODORE STEVEN, market researcher; b. N.Y.C., July 29, 1946; s. Walter B. and Charlotte (Goldberg) R.; m. Marjorie E. Simon, Sept. 1, 1968; children: Tara Lynn, Joshua Simon. BA, CCNY, 1969; MBA, CUNY, 1974. Market rsch. mgr. Am. Express Internat. Bank, N.Y.C., 1974-76, Internat. Playtex, Inc., Stamford, Conn., 1977-87; sr. assoc. Yankelovich, Shelly & White, Stamford, 1977; dir. market rsch. Sterling Drug, Inc., N.Y.C., 1987-89; v.p. Goldstein/Krall Mktg. Resources Inc., Stamford, Conn., 1989—. Mem. Am. Mktg. Assn., Westport Astron. Soc. (dir. 1987—). Home: 16 Bobwhite Dr Norwalk CT 06851 Office: Goldstein Krall Mktg Resources Inc 25 Third St Stamford CT 06905

ROSENBAUM, PAUL LEONARD, computer company executive; b. N.Y.C., Aug. 25, 1937; s. Nelson and Hattie (Cohen) R.; m. Brenda Zeller, Jan. 26, 1964; children: Glen Edward, Neil Nelson. BEE, Cornell U., 1958; MBA, Harvard U., 1963. Engr. Underwood Corp., Hartford, Conn., 1958-59; project engr. Thompson Ramo Wooldridge, Canoga Park, Calif., 1959-61; asst. to pres. Auerbach Corp., Phila., 1963-65; mktg. mgr. Computer Control Co., Framingham, Mass., 1966-68; v.p. mktg. Memory Tech., Inc., Sudbury, Mass., 1968-73; v.p. internat. Codex Corp., Mansfield, Mass., 1973-81; pres. Scitex Am. Inc., Bedford, Mass., 1981-83, Proteon Inc., Natick, Mass., 1984-85; pres. Xyplex Inc., Concord, Mass., 1986-88, also dir.; co-chmn. nat. fin. com. Dukakis for Pres. Campaign, 1988; gen. ptnr. Am. Rsch. Devel., 1989—; bd. dirs. Proteon Inc. Bd. dirs. Congregation Beth El, Sudbury, 1975-76; founder Tsedaka Hevra; mem. Wayland scholarship com., 1988. Served to 1st lt. U.S. Army, 1959-60. Recipient Fuertes Meml. Pub. Speaking award Cornell Engring. Soc., 1958. Home: 19 Pine Needle Rd Wayland MA 01778 Office: Xyplex Inc 100 Domino Dr Concord MA 01742

ROSENBAUM, RICHARD MERRILL, lawyer; b. Oswego, N.Y., Apr. 8, 1931; s. Jack M. and Shirley (Gover) R.; m. Judith Kanthor, June 1, 1958; children: Amy, Jill, Matthew, Julie Fay. BA, Hobart Coll., 1952; JD, Cornell U., 1955. Bar: N.Y. 1956. Ptnr. Rosenbaum, Agnello, Agnello & Levine, Rochester, N.Y., 1955-70; justice Supreme Ct. N.Y. State, 1970-73; ptnr. Nixon, Hargrave, Devans & Doyle, Rochester, 1977-84, 88—, cons., 1984-88; counsel to chmn. of bd., dir. govt. rels. and pub. affairs. Integated Resources, Inc., 1984-88, cons., 1988—; dir. Integrated Resources, Inc.; past mem. econ. adv. bd. U.S. Dept. Commerce; bd. dirs., sec. Jonathan Inst. Contbr. writings in fields of politics and public affairs, legal opinions to publs. Trustee Hobart Coll., 1971—; nat. committeeman N.Y. State Rep. Nat. Com., 1977—, rules rev. com., subcom. chmn. conv. procedures, 1977—; del.-at-large Rep. Nat. Conv., 1980, 84, 88, congl. dist. del., 1968, chmn. N.Y. State del., 1976; chmn. Monroe County Rep. Com., 1968-70, N.Y. Rep. State Com., 1973-77, Northeastern Rep. State Chairmen's Assn., 1973-76, Nat. Rep. State Chairmen's Assn., 1975-77; justice of peace Town of Penfield (N.Y.), 1962-66; mem. and asst. majority leader Monroe County Legislature, 1966-68; council SUNY, Brockport, 1970-72; appointed by Pres. Ronald Reagan, U.S. Holocaust Meml. Council; bd. dirs. Rockefeller Center, 1977—, Cardozo Sch. Law, Yeshiva U., Rochester Mus. & Sci. Center, 1978—; gen. chmn. devel. fund drive Rochester Mus. & Sci. Center, 1977—; trustee Rochester Area Colls., 1979—; mem. council of governing bds. of Ind. Colls. of State of N.Y., 1979—; apptd. mem. N.Y. Mental Hygiene Council, 1973-77, Nat. Citizens Adv. Com. on Environ. Quality, 1977; past bd. dirs. Jewish Home for Aged, Rochester; exec. com. Cornell Law Sch. Mem. Am. Bar Assn., N.Y. State Bar Assn. Jewish. Clubs: Royal Order of Jesters, Masons, Shriners. Home: 19 Denonville Ridge Rochester NY 14625 Office: Nixon Hargrave Devans & Doyle Lincoln First Tower PO Box 1051 Rochester NY 14506

ROSENBERG, A. RICHARD, supermarket company executive; b. Englewood, N.J., 1938. Grad., Lehigh U., 1959. With Big V Supermarket Inc., Florida, N.Y., 1959—, pres., from 1969, chief exec. officer, dir., from 1981, now chmn. bd. Office: Big V Supermarkets Inc 176 N Main St Florida NY 10921 *

ROSENBERG, HENRY A., JR., petroleum executive; b. Pitts., Nov. 7, 1929; s. Henry A. and Ruth (Blaustein) R.; children: Henry A. III, Edward Lee, Frank Blaustein; m. Dorothy Lucibello, June 30, 1984. B.A. in Econs., Hobart Coll., 1952. With Crown Cen. Petroleum Corp., Balt., 1952—, pres., 1966-75, chmn. exec. com., 1966—, chmn. bd., 1975—, also chief exec. officer; dir. Am. Trading & Prodn. Corp., USF&G Corp., Signet Banking Corp. Bd. dirs. Johns Hopkins Hosp., Am. Petroleum Inst., Goucher Coll., McDonogh Sch., Nat. Flag Day Found., YMCA Greater Balt.; past chmn. Greater Balt. Com.; pres., exec. bd. Balt. Area coun. Boy Scouts Am., mem. N.E. regional bd., nat. exec. bd. With AUS, 1952-54. Mem. Nat. Petroleum Refiners Assn. (chmn., dir., exec. com.), Nat. Petroleum Coun., 25 Yr. Club Petroleum Industry. Office: Crown Cen Petroleum Corp 1 N Charles St PO Box 1168 Baltimore MD 21203

ROSENBERG, JEROME WILLARD, accounting and consulting company executive; b. Scranton, Pa., May 2, 1930; s. Sam and Helen (Jurkowitz) R.; m. Lois Jean Feldstein, Nov. 16, 1952; children: Barbra, J. Richard. BS in Commerce, Pa. State U., 1952. CPA, Pa. Acct. Laventhol Krekstein & Co., Wilkes-Barre, Pa., 1952-60, ptnr., 1960-63, ptnr.-in-charge, 1963-67; nat. tax ptnr. Laventhol, Krekstein, Horwath & Horwath, Wilkes-Barre, 1968-70; ptnr.-in-charge Laventhol & Horwath, Wilkes-Barre, 1970-76; ptnr.-in-charge Laventhol & Horwath, Mpls., 1976-80, regional mng. ptnr., 1980; mng. ptnr. ops. Laventhol & Horwath, Phila., 1980—. Mem. Am. Inst. CPA's, Pa. Soc. CPA's. Republican. Jewish. Office: Laventhol & Horwath PO Box 8509 Philadelphia PA 19101 also: Laventhol & Horwath 1845 Walnut St 19th Fl Philadelphia PA 19103

ROSENBERG, JOEL BARRY, government economist; b. Bronx, N.Y., Aug. 14, 1942; s. Benjamin and Miriam Dorothy (Yellin) R.; B.A., Queens Coll., 1964, M.A., 1966; Ph.D., Brown U., 1972; m. Judith Lynne Jackler, Aug. 26, 1965; children—Jeffrey Alan, Marc David. Cons., Commonwealth Services, Washington, 1970-71; asst. prof. econs. SUNY, Geneseo, 1971-75, Case Western Res. U., Cleve., 1975-76; mgr., industry economist IRS, Washington, 1976—. NDEA fellow, Brown U., 1966-69. Mem. Am. Econ. Assn., Nat. Assn. Bus. Economists, Am. Statis. Assn. Contbr. articles to profl. jours. Home: 13 Glazebrook Ct Gaithersburg MD 20878 Office: IRS 1201 E St NW Washington DC 20226

ROSENBERG, LEE EVAN, financial planner; b. Bklyn., Nov. 6, 1952; s. Daniel and Rita (Blanket) R.; m. Saralee Hymen, Aug. 27, 1977; children: Zachary Martin, Alexandra Lynn. Student, Bklyn. Coll., 1969-74. Cert. fin. planner. Underwriter Fin. Life Ins. Co., N.Y.C., 1974-75, Mony, N.Y.C., 1975-80; pres. Lee Rosenberg Assoc., N.Y.C., 1980-83; co-founder, sr. ptnr. ARS Fin. Services Inc., Valley Stream, N.Y., 1983—. Contbr. book chpt. Building a Successful Financial Planning Practice, 1988. Mem. Internat. Assn. Fin. Planners, Internat. Assn. Registered Fin. Planners, Internat. Soc. Preretirement Planners, L.I. Inst. Cert. Fin. Planners (bd. dirs., pres. 1988—), Nat. Speakers Assn. (bd. dirs. N.Y. chpt.). Home: 984 Iris Ln Baldwin Harbor NY 11510 Office: ARS Fin Svcs Inc 125 Franklin Ave Ste 6 Valley Stream NY 11580

ROSENBERG, MANUEL, retail company executive; b. Boston, Apr. 26, 1930; s. Israel and Lillian (Wirin) R.; m. Audray Merle Gold, Aug. 28, 1955; children: Peter Neal, Beth Susan. A.B., Harvard U., 1951, M.B.A., 1953. V.P. Filene's, Boston, 1967-73; pres., chief exec. officer Gimbel's, Phila., 1973-75, chmn. bd., chief exec. officer, 1975-77; exec. v.p. Garfinckel, Brooks Bros., Miller & Rhoads, Inc., Washington, 1977-79, pres., 1979-82, also dir.; chmn. bd., pres., chief exec. officer Morse Shoe, Inc., Canton, Mass., 1982—. Trustee Beth Israel Hosp., Boston, Mass. Eye and Ear Infirmary, Boston, Judge Baker Guidance Ctr., Boston. Served to lt. USN, 1953-56. Clubs: Univ., Harvard (Boston). Home: 370 Beacon St Boston MA 02116 Office: Morse Shoe Inc 555 Turnpike St Canton MA 02021

ROSENBERG, MARSHAL ERNEST, financial consultant, banker; b. Miami, Dec. 11, 1936; s. Morris Rosenberg; children: Lynne, Daniel H. BBA, U. Miami, 1959, MBA, 1980; PhD, Calif. Western U., 1982. Pres. Marshal E. Rosenberg Orgn., Inc., 1st Investors Corp. of Miami; mem. faculty U. Miami Sch. Bus.; bd. dirs. Intercontinental Bank, Atico Savs. Bank. Life trustee, founder Mt. Sinai Med. Ctr.; trustee, bd. dirs. Miami Heart Inst.; bd. dirs. Dade County unit Am. Cancer Soc.; chmn. coaches com. U. Miami Baseball Program. Mem. Assn. Advanced Life Underwriters, Top of the Table, Million Dollar Round Table. Clubs: Miami, Ocean Reef (Key Largo, Fla.). Home: 10205 SW 68th Ct Miami FL 33156 Office: 1500 Monza Ave Suite 202 Coral Gables FL 33146

ROSENBERG, RONALD ERWIN, insurance company executive; b. N.Y.C., Mar. 23, 1935; s. Daniel and Kathryn Rosenberg; m. Susan Maerz, Dec. 28, 1958; children: Amy Lynn Rosenberg Klein, Robert, Melissa. BS in Pharmacy, Fordham U., 1958; Exec. MBA, Columbia U., 1975. Lic. pharmacist, N.Y. Vice pres. planning and devel. Upjohn Health Care Svcs., Kalamazoo, 1976-82, v.p. mktg. and orgn. devel., 1982-86; sr. v.p. Assoc. Group, Indpls., 1986-87, exec. v.p., 1987—. With U.S. Army, 1958-60. Mem. Am. Assn. Continuity Care, Nat. Assn. for Home Health, Home Health Svcs. and Staffing Assn. (chmn. bd. 1978-83). Office: Assoc Group 8320 Craig St Ste 100 Indianapolis IN 46250

ROSENBERG, SYDNEY J., corporate executive; b. San Francisco, Sept. 3, 1914; s. Morris and Gussie (Kaufman) R.; m. Joyce Wexler, Nov. 15, 1939 (div. Mar. 1968); children: Brad, Jill Rosenberg Hughes, Todd; m. 2d Jaclyn Barde, Mar. 22, 1968; stepchildren: Gregg Cobarr, Glenn Cobarr. B.A., Stanford U., 1936; M.B.A., Harvard U., 1938. Pres., chief exec. officer Am. Bldg. Maintenance Industries, Los Angeles, from 1938; now chmn. bd. Am. Bldg. Maintenance Industries, San Francisco; dir. Craig Corp.; pres. OPTIC Fund. Bd. govs. Performing Arts Council; bd. govs. Los Angeles Music Ctr.; trustee Jewish Big Bros.; mem. dirs. council Children's Orthopaedic Hosp. Mem. Chief Execs. Orgn., Urban Land Inst., World Bus. Council. Republican. Jewish. Clubs: Hillcrest (Los Angeles); Big Canyon (Newport, Calif.). Office: Am Bldg Maintenance Industries 333 Fell St San Francisco CA 94102 *

ROSENBERG, WILLIAM, supermarket company executive; b. 1907; married. With Met. Life Ins. Co., Hackensack, N.J., 1923-33; ins. agt. C. Rosenberg Inc., Teaneck, N.J., 1933-41; pres., chief exec. officer Big V. Supermarkets, Florida, N.Y., 1941-69, chmn. dirs. chief exec. officer, 1969-87, chmn. exec. com. to 1989, chmn. emeritus, 1989—. Office: Big V Supermarkets Ind 176 B Main St Florida NY 10921 *

ROSENBERGER, RONALD ANDREW, research administration executive; b. Sellersville, Pa., Jan. 26, 1936; s. Andrew Bishop and Anna Ruth (Wenger) R.; m. Norma Beaumont Chappell, Oct. 21, 1961; children: Bruce Jeffrey, Brian Kent. BA in Natural Sci., Goshen Coll., 1959; postgrad., Northwestern U., 1960-61. Biologist Merck, Sharp & Dohme Rsch. Labs., West Point, Pa., 1961-63; teratologist Merck, Sharp & Dohme Rsch. Labs., 1963-65, med. data coord., 1965-66, supr. data coordination, 1966-67, mgr. data coordination, 1967-71; asst. to pres. Merck, Sharp & Dohme Rsch. Labs., Rahway, N.J., 1971-74; dir. adminstrv. svcs. Merck, Sharp & Dohme Rsch. Labs., West Point, 1974—. Contbr. articles to profl. jours. Mem. planning commn. Salford Twp., Montgomery County, Pa., 1967-72; mem. steering com. United Way. Mem. Am. Mgmt. Assn., Drug Info. Assn., Soc. Rsch. Adminstrs. (sec.-trea. 1984-86, pres. 1988, bd. dirs. 1987—). Home: 108 S County Line Rd Telford PA 18969 Office: Merck Sharp & Dohme Rsch Labs Sumneytown Pike West Point PA 19486

ROSENBLATT, LEONARD, business executive; b. N.Y.C., Oct. 20, 1929. BBA, CCNY, 1953; grad. Advanced Mgmt. Program, Harvard U., 1973. Gen. mgr. div. Witco Chem., N.Y.C., 1949-63; various positions including exec. v.p. constn. products div. W.R. Grace & Co., Mass., 1963-81; pres., chief exec. officer Ausimont Compo NV, Waltham, Mass., 1981—, also bd. dirs. Bd. dirs. The League Sch. of Boston; trustee Outwardbound; adv. bd. Suffolk U., Fla. Govs. Council of 100. Served to sgt. USAF, 1947-49. Office: Ausimont NV 128 Technology Dr Waltham MA 02254 *

ROSENBLATT, STEVEN, convention center executive; b. Framingham, Mass., Apr. 16, 1947; s. Irving and Alice (Mordis) R.; m. Linda Lipkowitz, Mar. 20, 1977; children: Jaime, Jodi. BSBA, Northeastern U., 1970. Exec. mgr. Kans. Expocentre, Topeka. Bd. dirs. Temple Beth Sholom, Topeka, 1986—. Mem. Internat. Assn. Auditorium Mgrs., Sales and Mktg. Execs., Country Music Buyers Assn., Am. Soc. Assn. Execs. Office: Kans Expocentre One Expocentre Dr Topeka KS 66612

ROSENBLUM, JOHN WILLIAM, business educator, university dean; b. Houston, Jan. 1, 1944; s. H. William and Susan (Ullmann) R.; m. Carolyn Edith Jones, Sept. 12, 1964; children: J. Christopher, Kathryn, Nicholas. A.B., Brown U., 1965; M.B.A., Harvard U., 1967, D.B.A., 1972. Instr. Harvard U. Bus. Sch., Boston, 1969-72, asst. prof., 1972-75, assoc. prof., 1975-79; prof. Darden Grad. Sch. Bus. Adminstrn., U. Va., Charlottesville, 1979-80, assoc. dean, 1980-82, dean, 1982—; bd. dirs. Chesapeake Corp., Cadmus Communications, Inc. Co-author: Strategy and Organization, 1973, (2d edit.), 1977, Cases in Political Economy-Japan, 1980. Mem. Phi Beta Kappa. Home: U Va Pavilion III Charlottesville VA 22903 Office: U Va Grad Sch Bus Adminstrn Box 6550 Charlottesville VA 22903

ROSENBLUM, RICHARD SETH, insurance agent; b. Newark, May 1, 1944; s. Leo and Marjorie (Lewitt) R.; m. Barbara Jean Axelrod (div. Oct. 1982). BA, Upsala Coll., 1966; MAT, William Paterson Coll., 1973; MLS, Pratt Inst., 1974. Cert. fin. planner. Tchr., librarian schs. and libraries in N.J., 1966-81; ins. agt., registered rep. Mut. of Omaha Ins. Cos., Cherry Hill, N.J., 1982—. Mem. West Jersey Chamber Music Soc. Mem. Nat. Assn. Health Underwriters (chmn. health com. Camden County 1987-88), Inst. Cert. Fin. Planners, Princeton Area Soc. Cert. Fin. Planners, Pratt Inst. Alumni Assn., B'nai Brith. Home: 1 Doral Ct Marlton NJ 08053 Office: Mut of Omaha 1930 E Marlton Pike Cherry Hill NJ 08003

ROSENDALE, GEORGE WILLIAM, aircraft company executive; b. Keenan, Okla., Nov. 4, 1933; s. John Webster and Laura Lee (Schawo) R.; m. Penney Sue Tillotson, Dec. 27, 1964; children: James Christopher, Kathleen Marie, John Charles. Student Okla. Baptist U., 1957-58, U. Wichita, 1959-63; BA in English, Wichita State U., 1969, MS in Adminstrn., 1971. Diplomate Personnel Accreditation Inst., 1977-83. Engring. draftsman Skyline Corp., Wichita, Kans., 1952, Boeing Aircraft Co., Wichita, Kans., 1953, O.A. Sutton Corp., Wichita, 1956, enginrg. checker, 1956-57; various positions Cessna Aircraft Co., Wichita, 1958—, personnel rep., 1967-69, tng. supr., 1969-73, mgr. employee tng. and devel., 1973-84, mgr. personnel projects, 1984-85, mgr. mgmt. resource devel., 1985-87, adminstr. Internat. Assembly Programs, 1987-88, mgr. Material Fin. and Adminstrn. 1988—; vocat. instr. Wichita Pub. Schs., 1963; personnel adviser Wichita Police Res., 1969-73; treas. Haysville Police Res., 1975—; chmn. bd. dirs. Corp. Employment Resources, Inc. 1987-88, Area comdr. United Fund, Wichita, 1971; sec. Haysville Jr. Football League, Haysville, Kans., 1973-75; study com. chmn. Wichita Community Planning Council, 1972-73; mem. Haysville Planning Commn., 1976-86, chmn., 1977-79, 80-84; exec. com. Kans. State Employment and Tng. Council, 1979-82, chmn. employment and tng. services com., 1981-82; mem. Kans. 107 Planning Com. for Vocat. Edn., 1981-84, chmn., 1983-84; mem. Kans. High Tech. Task Force for Vocat. Edn., 1983-84; mem. tng. adv. com. div. vocat. and continuing edn. Wichita Pub. Schs., 1974; active various Bapt. Chs., Wichita, Hominy, Okla., Mulvane, Kans., 1951—; bd. dirs. Christian Braille Found., 1971-74; bd. dirs. Amigos de SER, Wichita, 1975-77, 81-88, vice chmn., 1984; bd. dirs. Kans. SER, Inc., 1981-88, treas., 1983-84, vice chmn., 1985-87, chmn., 1987-88; bd. dirs. Am. Cancer Soc., Sedgwick County (Kans.) unit, 1977-88, Ark-Valley Jr. Football League, 1974-75. Served with U.S. Army, 1953-56. Recipient Campaign award United Fund of Wichita, 1969-71, Outstanding Service plaque award Am. Cancer Soc., 1978-79, 81-82; SER Individual Support award, 1979, others., Psi Chi. Republican. Lodge: Optimist (chmn. community service 1985-86, v.p. Haysville club 1986-87, pres. 1987-88, lt. gov. Kans. dist. 1988—). Home: 424 Hollywood Dr Wichita KS 67217 Office: Cessna Aircraft Div PO Box 7704 Wichita KS 67277

ROSENE, LINDA ROBERTS, organizational consultant, researcher; b. Miami, Fla., Nov. 1, 1938; d. Wilbur David and Dorothy Claire (Baker) Roberts; m. Ralph W. Rosene, Aug. 3, 1957; children: Leigh, Russ, Tim. MA, Fielding Inst., 1981, PhD in Clin. Psychology, 1983. Lic. clin. psychologist. Counselor Rapid City (S.D.) Regional Hosp., 1978-81, Luth. Social Services, Rapid City, 1978-83; v.p. Target Systems Inc., Dallas and Irving, Tex., 1983-85, cons., 1985—; cons. S.W. Home Furnishing Assn., Dallas, 1984, Northwestern Bell, Omaha, 1985; presenter, developer seminars gest-Accor Retail Assn. of Can., So. Home Furnishings Conventions, Am. Assn. Med. Assts. Pub. Profl. Furniture Merchants mag., nat. adv. group Nat. Assn. Convenience Stores; developer copyrighted hiring system, 1985, rev., 1987. Bd. dirs. Assn. Children with Learning Disabilities, S.D., 1983-84, West River (S.D.) Alcoholism Services, 1983-84, Health Adv. Com. of Head Start, S.D., 1980-84, St. Martins Acad., S.D., 1971-75; mem. Rapid City Mayor's Commn. on Racial Conciliation, 1971-73, Nat. Trust for Hist. Preservation; charter mem. Nat. Mus. Women in the Arts. Research grantee Nat. Luth. Ch., 1981. Mem. Am. Psychol. Assn., N.C. Psychol. Assn., Aircraft Owners and Pilots Assn., Am. Soc. Tng. and Devel., S.W. Home Furnishing Assn., Internat. Platform Assn. Unitarian. Avocations: aviation, bicycling, racquetball, music, birdwatching. Home: 300 Shinoak Valley Irving TX 75063

ROSENFELD, GERALD, investment banking executive; b. N.Y.C., Dec. 29, 1946; s. Jack and Shirley (Otter) R.; m. Nancy P. Henenfeld, Jan. 18, 1970 (div. Dec. 1984); 1 child, Erica; m. Judith Ellen Zarin, May 26, 1985; 1 child, Jack. BCE, CCNY, 1968; M in Engring. Sci., CUNY, 1970; PhD, NYU, 1973. Instr. NYU, N.Y.C., 1970-73; asst. prof. U. Md., Catonsville, 1973-76; mgr. analytical services McKinsey & Co., N.Y.C., 1976-79; assoc.

Salomon Bros., Inc., N.Y.C., 1979-80, v.p., 1980-85, mng. dir., 1985-87, chief fin. officer, 1987-88; mng. dir. Bankers Trust Co., N.Y.C., 1988—. Home: 580 West End Ave New York NY 10024 Office: Vector Capitol LP 230 Park Ave New York NY 10169

ROSENFELD, MARK KENNETH, retail store executive; b. Jackson, Mich., Mar. 17, 1946; s. Nathan and Marjorie N. (Leopold) R.; children: Edward Robert, Zachary, Alix Caitlin. B.A., Amherst Coll., 1968; S.M., MIT, 1970. With Jacobson's, Jackson, Mich., 1972—; v.p., real estate group mgr. Jacobson's, 1976-78, exec. v.p., 1978-82, pres, 1982—; dir. Jacobson Stores, 275 N Woodward Co., Great Lakes Bancorp. Served with U.S. Army, 1969-70. Jewish. Office: Jacobson Stores Inc 3333 Sargent Rd Jackson MI 49201

ROSENGREN, WILLIAM R., corporation executive; b. 1934; LL.B., U. Minn., 1959. Pvt. practice, 1959-67; instr. bus. law U. Minn., 1963-69; Asst. sec. and sr. atty. Internat. Multifoods Corp., to 1973; with Ecolab Inc., St. Paul, 1973—, v.p., gen. counsel, 1973, v.p., sec., gen. counsel, sec., 1974-83, sr. v.p., gen. counsel, sec., 1983-88, sr. v.p. law and human resources, gen. counsel, sec. Office: Ecolab Inc 370 Wabasha St Osborn Bldg Saint Paul MN 55102

ROSENKRANZ, GEORGE, chemical executive; b. Budapest, Hungary, Aug. 20, 1916; naturalized Mexican citizen, 1949; s. Bertalan and Stella (Weiner) R.; degree as chem. engr., dr. tech. scis. E.T.H. Zurich, Switzerland, 1939, postgrad., 1940-41; D (hon.) U. of las Ams. m. Edith Stein, Sept. 20, 1945; children—Robert Peter, Gerald Michael, Richard Thomas. Tech. dir. Labs. Vieta-Plasencia, Havana, Cuba, 1941-45; with Syntex, S.A. (name later changed to Syntex Corp.), Mexico City, 1945—, tech. dir., 1945-47, research dir., 1947-49, v.p. research, 1949-51, v.p. research and prodn., 1951-53, exec. v.p. 1953-56, pres., chmn. bd., 1956-76, chmn. bd., 1976-81, founding chmn. bd., 1981—, chief exec. officer, 1976-80. Bd. govs. U. Tel Aviv, Israel; bd. govs. mem. sci. commn. Weizmann Inst., Israel; mem. council Rockefeller U., N.Y.C. Created comdr. Order Vasco Nunez de Balboa, Panama. Fellow Internat. Coll. Dentists; mem. Am. Chem. Soc., AAAS, Royal Chem. Soc. Gt. Britain, Nat. Acad. Medicine in Mex. (hon.), Chem. Soc. Switzerland. Author: The Romex System, A Dynamic Approach to Bidding; Win with Romex, Key to Accurate Bidding; Bid Your Way to the Top; Modern Ideas in Bidding, Bridge: The Bidders Game, Everything You Always Wanted to Know About Trump Leads; contbr. articles to profl. publs.; patentee in field. Home: Parque Via Reforma 1730, Delegación Miguel, 11000 Chapultepec, Mexico City Mexico Office: Syntex Corp, Apartado Postal 2679, Mexico City Mexico

ROSENN, HAROLD, lawyer; b. Plains, Pa., Nov. 4, 1917; s. Joseph and Jennie (Wohl) R.; m. Sallyanne Frank, Sept. 19, 1948; 1 child, Frank Scott. BA, U. Mich., 1939, JD, 1941. Bar: Pa. 1942, U.S. Supreme Ct. 1957. Ptnr. Rosenn & Rosenn, Wilkes Barre, Pa., 1948-54; ptnr. Rosenn, Jenkins & Greenwald, Wilkes Barre, 1954-87, of counsel, 1988—; mem. Pa. State Bd. Law Examiners, 1983—; asst. dist. atty Luzerne County, Pa., 1952-54; mem. Gov's. Justice Commn., Pa., 1968-73, Crime Commn., Pa., 1968-73, Fed. Judicial Nominating Com., Pa., 1977-79, Appellate Ct. Nominating Com., Pa., 1979-81; bd. dirs. Franklin 1st Fed. Savs. & Loan Assn., Wilkes-Barre, Am. Homestead, Inc., Mt. Laurel, N.J. Chmn. ARC, Wilkes Barre, 1958-60; pres. Pa. Council on Crime and Delinquency, Harrisburg, 1969-71; bd. dirs. Coll. Misericordia, Dallas, Pa., 1976-86, Hoyt Library, Kingston, Pa., 1971-78, Nat. Council on Crime and Delinquency, N.Y.C., 1969-71; chmn. United Way Campaign of Wyoming Valley, 1975; pres. United Way, Wyoming Valley, 1978-80. Served to capt. USAAF, 1942-45, ETO. Named Honoree, Wyo. Vally Interfaith Council, 1986; recipient Erasmus medal Dutch Govt., 1985. Mem. ABA, Pa. Bar Assn., Am. Judicature Soc. Republican. Jewish. Clubs: U. Mich. (N.E. Pa.) (pres. 1946-76), Westmoreland (Wilkes Barre). Lodge: B'nai Brith (pres. Wilkes Barre 1952-53, Community Service award 1976). Home: 29 Hedge Pl Kingston PA 18704 Office: Rosenn Jenkins & Greenwald 15 S Franklin St Wilkes-Barre PA 18711

ROSENSAFT, LESTER JAY, management consultant, reorganization lawyer, business executive; b. Leominster, Mass., Jan. 11, 1958; s. Melvin and Beatrice (Golombek) R. BS in Econs., Wharton Sch., U. Pa., 1978; JD, Case Western Res. U., 1981, MBA, 1981; LLM in Corporate Law, NYU, 1983. Bar: Ohio 1981, U.S. dist. ct. (no. dist.) Ohio 1982, U.S. dist cts. (ea., we., no., so. dists.) N.Y. 1982. Practice corp. and comml. law, Ohio, 1981—, reorgn. law fed. cts. Ohio, N.Y., 1982—; mem. firm Hall, Rosensaft & Yen, Cleve. and Singapore, 1981—; with Cons. to Mgmt., Inc., Cleve., N.Y.C., Boston, Hong Kong, 1977—, v.p., 1977-80, pres. and chief exec. officer, 1980-83, chmn., 1983—; pres. and chief exec. officer Eljay Devel. Corp., 1985-86; chmn., chief exec. officer Logistix Ltd., 1987—; ptnr. Sanctuary Assocs., Boston, 1988—; exec. v.p., chief fin. officer Omni Teleproductions, Inc. Boston, 1988—, also bd. dirs.; vice chmn. bd. Paramount Systems Design Group, Inc., N.Y.C., 1982—; v.p. corp. devel., mem. bd. dirs. Ameritec Corp., N.Y.C., 1983—; v.p., chief fin. officer, mem. bd. dirs. Chipurnoi Inc., L.I. City, N.Y., 1983—; v.p., chief fin. officer Kinnerton Industries, N.Y.C. and London, 1983—; vice chmn., gen. counsel, mem. bd. dirs. GIOIA Couture, Inc., Akron, Ohio, 1984-86; dir. Honeybee Robotics Ltd., Taiwan and N.Y.C., dir. Pelletier Brothers, Inc., 1986— , Advanced Radiator Techs., Inc., Fitchburg, Mass., 1987—; ednl. cons.; advisor indsl. devel. and strategic urbanism; cons. federally funded biomed. research projects; active Combined Jewish Philanthropies; participant 40th Anniversary II Pres.'s Mission, 1987; chmn. Region V Outreach Mission, 1988; mem. Russian Resettlement Com., 1988; active U. Pa. Secondary Com. of Cen. Mass. Co-author (with Melvin Rosensaft): Industrial Development Survey for City of Leominster, 1978. Contbr. articles to profl. jours. Mem. exec. adv. council Keene State Coll., 1984—. Mem. ABA, Greater Cleve. Bar Assn., Ohio State Bar Assn., Assn. Bar City N.Y., Assn. Trial Lawyers Am., Am. Mgmt. Assn., Am. Mktg. Assn. Wharton Club Cleve. (exec. com.), Wharton Club N.Y., U. Pa. Clubs Cleve., U. Pa. Club N.Y., Bankruptcy Lawyers Bar Assn., N.Y.C. Reorgn. Roundtable, Internat. Soc. Strategic Planning Cons., Soc. Profl. Mgmt. Cons., Inst. of Mgmt. Cons. (cert. mgmt. cons.), North Cen. Mass. C. of C. (indsl. devel. com. 1984—), Phi Alpha Delta (vice justice). Clubs: Boca Beach, Boca Pointe Golf and Racquet, Boca West, Boca Raton Hotel and Club (Boca Raton, Fla.). Home: 59 Crescent Rd Leominster MA 01453

ROSENSHINE, ALLEN GILBERT, advertising agency executive; b. N.Y.C., Mar. 14, 1939; s. Aaron and Anna (Zuckerman) R.; m. Suzan Weston-Webb, Aug. 31, 1979; children: Andrew, Jonathan. A.B., Columbia Coll., 1960. Copywriter J.B. Rundle (advt.), N.Y.C., 1962-65; copywriter Batten, Barton, Durstine & Osborn, N.Y.C., 1965, copy supr., 1967, v.p., 1968, asso. creative dir., 1970, sr. v.p., creative dir., 1975-77, exec. v.p., 1977-80, pres., 1980-82, chief exec. officer, 1981-86, chmn., 1983-86, also dir., mem. exec. com.; pres., chief exec. officer BBDO Internat., N.Y.C., 1984-86, also bd. dirs.; pres., chief exec. officer Omnicom Group, N.Y.C., 1986-88; chmn., chief exec. officer BBDO Worldwide, N.Y.C., 1988—; lectr. gen. studies Bklyn. Coll., 1961-65. Office: BBDO Worldwide 1285 Ave of the Americas New York NY 10019-6095 also: Omnicom Group Inc 437 Madison Ave New York NY 10022 *

ROSENSTEEL, JOHN WILLIAM, insurance company executive; b. Chgo., June 4, 1940; s. Harold Eugene and Alice (Shanahan) R.; divorced; children: Elizabeth, Margaret, Jill. BS in Econs., Holy Cross Coll., 1962. Chartered life underwriter. Home office rep. Aetna Life and Casualty, Chgo., 1967-72, regional dir., 1972-75; dir. Aetna Life and Casualty, Hartford, Conn., 1975-81; nat. dir. Aetna Life and Casualty, Hartford, 1981-83, v.p., 1983-86, service pres., 1986-88; sr. v.p.European region & United Kingdom Aetna Internat., Hartford, London & Madrid, 1988—; bd. dirs. Aetna Internat. U.K., London, 1986, Aetna Chile de Vida, Santiago, Chile, 1986, La Estrella de Seguros, Madrid, 1988. Lt. USN, 1963-66, Vietnam. Mem. Nat. Assn. Life Underwriters. Republican. Roman Catholic. Home: 102 Timberwood Rd West Hartford CT 06117 Office: Aetna Life & Casualty Co 151 Farmington Ave D 143 Hartford CT 06156

ROSENSTEIN, ALLEN BERTRAM, electrical engineering educator; b. Balt., Aug. 25, 1920; s. Morton and Mary (Epstein) R.; m. Betty Lebell; children: Jerry Tyler, Lisa Nan, Adam Mark. B.S. with high distinction, U. Ariz., 1940; M.S., UCLA, 1950, Ph.D., 1958. Elec. engr. Consol. Vultee Aircraft, San Diego, 1940-41; sr. elec. engr. Lockheed Aircraft Corp., Burbank, Calif., 1941-42; chief plant engr. Utility Fan Corp., Los Angeles, 1942-44; prof. engring. UCLA, 1946—; founder, chmn. bd. Inet, Inc., 1947-53, cons. engr., 1954—; founder, chmn. bd. dirs. Pioneer Magnetics, Inc., Pioneer Research Inc., Anadex Instruments Inc.; dir. Internat. Transformer Co., Inc., Fgn. Resource Services; cons. ednl. planning UNESCO, Venezuela, 1974-76. Author: (with others) Engineering Communications, 1965, A Study of a Profession and Professional Education, 1968; contbr. articles to profl. jours.; patentee in field. Bd. dirs. Vista Hill Psychiat. Found. Served with USNR, 1944-46. Fellow IEEE; mem., Am. Soc. Engring. Edn., N.Y. Acad. Scis., AAAS, Sigma Xi, Phi Kappa Phi, Delta Phi Sigma, Tau Beta Pi. Home: 314 S Rockingham St Los Angeles CA 90049

ROSENTHAL, CHARLES MICHAEL, financial executive; b. Bklyn., Nov. 21, 1935; s. David B. and Edna (Lefcourt) R.; m. Eva P. Sonnenberg, July 7, 1963; children: Andrea, Nicole. Research asst., Fed. Res. Bank, N.Y., 1960-62. Research asst. Fed. Res. Bank N.Y., N.Y.C., 1960-62; v.p. L.M. Rosenthal & Co., Inc., 1962-74; ptnr. 1st Manhattan Co., N.Y.C., 1974—. Served to capt. USAF, 1957-60. Mem. Investment Assn. N.Y., Security Traders Assn. N.Y. Jewish. Club: Sunningdale Country. Home: 784 Park Ave New York NY 10021 Office: 1st Manhattan Co 437 Madison Ave New York NY 10022

ROSENTHAL, CLIFFORD NEAL, trade association administrator; b. Newark, Apr. 20, 1945; s. Morris Robert and Edythe (Kurtz) R.; m. Deborah Wright, Jun. 7, 1970 (div. Dec. 1977) m. Elayne Grant Archer, Nov. 26, 1980; 1 child, Dana. BA, Columbia Coll., 1966; MA, Columbia U., 1969. Program dir. Am. Indians for Devel., Meriden, Conn., 1975-77; dir. organizational devel. Nat. Assn. of Farmworker Orgns., Washington, 1977-80; exec. dir. Nat. Fedn. of Community Devel. Credit Unions, N.Y.C., 1980—; Mem. adv. bd. Community Capital Bank, Chem. Community Devel. Inc., Columbia-Barnard Fed. Credit Union; mem. consumer adv. coun. Fed. Res. System, 1989—. Editor, translator: Five Sisters, 1975; contbr. articles. to profl. jours. Bd. dirs. Food and Hunger Hotline, N.Y.C., 1983-86. Fellow Revson Found., 1983-84. Jewish. Office: Nat Fedn Community Devel Credit Unions 29 John St New York NY 10038

ROSENTHAL, MILTON FREDERICK, corporation executive; b. N.Y.C., Nov. 24, 1913; s. Jacob C. and Louise (Berger) R.; m. Frieda Bojar, Feb. 28, 1943; 1 child, Anne Rosenthal Mitro. BA, CCNY, 1932; LLB, Columbia U., 1935. Bar: N.Y. 1935. Research asst. N.Y. State Law Revision Commn., 1935-37; law sec. Fed. Judge William Bondy, 1937-40; asso. atty. Leve, Hecht & Hadfield, 1940-42; sec., treas. Hugo Stinnes Corp., 1946-48, exec. v.p., treas., 1948-49, pres., dir., 1949-64; pres., dir., chief exec. officer Minerals and Chems. Philipp Corp., N.Y.C., 1964-67; pres. Engelhard Minerals & Chems. Corp., N.Y.C., 1967-77, 79-81, chmn., 1977-81, also chief exec. officer and dir. until, 1981; bd. dirs. European-Am. Bank; bd. dirs. emeritus Ferro Corp., Midlantic Corp., Salomon Inc.; ret. dir. Engelehard Corp., Schering-Plough Corp. US/USSR Trade and Econ. Coun., Nat. Coun. for U.S. China Trade, Bus. Coun. for Internat. Understanding. Bd. dirs. Romanian-U.S. Econ. Coun., also chmn. U.S. sect.; trustee Mt. Sinai Med. Ctr. and Mt. Sinai Hosp.; bd. dirs. United Cerebral Palsy Rsch. and Ednl. Found., Inc.; dir., gov. Fgn. Policy Assn.; ret. trustee Am. Fedn. Arts, Manhattanville Coll., Purchase Coll. Found. 1st lt. JAG dept. U.S. Army, 1942-45. Mem. Assn. Bar City N.Y., Chgo. Bar Assn., Columbia Law Sch. Alumni Assn., Judge Adv. Assn., Fgn. Policy Assn. (dir., gov.), Phi Beta Kappa. Home: Woodlands Rd Harrison NY 10528 Office: 1221 Ave of Americas New York NY 10020

ROSENTHAL, PETER, public relations executive; b. N.Y.C., Nov. 1, 1946; s. Walter and Rita (Horn) R.; m. Christine Giglio, Mar. 16, 1978; 1 son, Joel. B.A., Lehman Coll., 1969; M.A., Ball State U., 1972. Tchr., N.Y.C. Bd. Edn., 1969-71; reporter Bklyn. Today, 1972-73; asst. dir. pub. relations St. Vincents Hosp., N.Y.C, 1973-76; account exec. Howard Rubenstein Assocs., N.Y.C., 1976-78, v.p., 1978-81, sr. v.p., 1981-84, exec. v.p., 1984-87, sr. exec. v.p., 1987—. Mem. Internat. Assn. Bus. Communications, Nat. Assn. Real Estate Editors, Urban Land Inst. (assoc.) Jewish. Avocations: reading; theater; travel. Office: Howard J Rubenstein Assocs Inc 1345 Ave of the Americas New York NY 10105

ROSENTHAL, RICHARD LAURENCE, utilities executive, venture capitalist, foundation executive; b. Winnipeg, Man., Can., Aug. 25, 1915; came to U.S., 1921; s. Myer C. and Anne (Frankel) R.; m. Hinda Gould, Dec. 2, 1944; children: Jamie G. Rosenthal Wolf, Richard L. Jr. B.S. summa cum laude, NYU, 1936, postgrad., 1936-37. Chief exec. Citizens Utilities Co. and subs., Stamford, Conn., 1946-81, chmn. bd., exec. com., 1981—; pres., chief exec. Utilities & Industries Corp., 1948-69; chmn. bd., chief exec. Mich. Gas & Electric Co., 1950-67; chief exec. officer Mills Music, Inc. 1964-69; trustee Mills Music Trust, 1964-69; lectr., expert witness; Regents lectr. U. Calif., 1982-83; Disting. Regents prof. GBA UCLA, 1982-83; Disting. adj. prof. BPA NYU, 1983-84; lectr. numerous univs. Contbr. articles to profl. jours. Chmn., trustee Richard and Hinda Rosenthal Found.; past trustee Salk Inst. Biol. Research, La Jolla, Calif., chmn. exec. com.; bd. dirs.Exec. Re Inc., Simsbury, Conn. Nominee Rhodes scholarship, 1936; recipient Madden medal NYU Coll. Bus. and Pub. Adminstrn., 1980; Gordon Grand fellow Yale U., 1982; Olin fellow Fairfield U., 1982. Mem. World Bus. Council. Club: Century Country (Purchase, N.Y.). Office: Citizens Utilities Co High Ridge Pk PO Box 3801 Stamford CT 06905

ROSENTHAL, ROSALIE, sales and marketing professional; b. Bklyn., Apr. 26, 1943; d. Joseph and Esther (Cohen) Strassner; m. Jerrold Rosenthal, Nov. 24, 1962 (div. 1984); children: Shari, Jeffrey, Jay. Student, C.W. Post Coll., 1961; cert. in bus., Berkeley Bus. Sch., Hicksville, N.Y., 1962. Adminstrv. asst. H.J. Heinz Co., Lake Success, N.Y., 1972-78; sales rep. Tura Co., Great Neck, N.Y., 1978-79; sales mgr. U.S. Bus. Corp., Hicksville, 1979-82, Dataline Co., Hicksville, 1982-87; dir. sales and mktg. Sandata Inc., Port Washington, N.Y., 1987-88; dir. sales Softpoint Systems, Carle Place, 1988—. Mem. NAFE, Homecare Assn. N.Y. State, Healthcare Fin. Mgmt. Assn., Nat. Council Jewish Women, N.Y. State Med. Bus. Assn. Democrat. Office: Softpoint Data Systems 200 Stonehinge Ln Carle Place NY 11514

ROSENTHAL, STUART A., retail executive. Formerly sr. v.p. The Vons Cos. Inc., El Monte, Calif., now exec. v.p. mktg. Office: The Vons Cos Inc 10150 Lower Azusa Rd El Monte CA 91731 *

ROSENTHAL, WARREN W., restaurant chain executive; b. Paducah, Ky., 1923; married. Grad., U. Ky., 1947. With Long John Silver's Inc. subs. Ferrico, Inc., Lexington, Ky., 1969—; chmn. bd., dir. Long John Silver's Inc., Lexington, Ky., 1969—; chmn., dir. Jerrico, Inc., Lexington, 1969—. Office: Jerrico Inc 101 Jerrico Dr Box 11988 Lexington KY 40579 other: Long John Silver's Inc 101 Jerrico Dr Lexington KY 40509 *

ROSENWALD, E. JOHN, JR., brokerage house executive, investment banker; b. 1930. AB, Dartmouth Coll., 1952, MBA, 1953. With Bear Stearns Cos. Inc., N.Y.C., 1953—, pres., vice-chmn., sr. mng. dir. Office: Bear Stearns Cos Inc 55 Water St New York NY 10041 *

ROSHON, GEORGE KENNETH, manufacturing company executive, b. Pottstown, Pa., July 30, 1942; s. George Washington 3d and Ellen Eleanor (Knopf) R.; B.S. in Elec. Engring., Pa. State U., 1964; M.S., Drexel U., Phila., 1974, postgrad., 1974-75; m. Ella Maye Brandt, Nov. 21, 1964; 1 dau., Kirsten Renee. Sr. engr. Am. Electronics Labs., Inc., Colmar, Pa., 1966-69; v.p. engring. Acrodyne Industries, Inc., Montgomeryville, Pa., 1969-74; mgr. electric design W-J div. Hayes-Albion Corp., Norristown, Pa., 1974-78; mgr. quality assurance PSMBD, Gen. Electric Co., Phila., after 1978, mem. exec. com. electronics test council after 1980, mgr. advanced systems engring., 1983-84, mgr. communications engring., Malvern, Pa., 1984-86; v.p. quality assurance Hercules Aerospace Display Systems, Inc., Hatfield, Pa., 1986—. Patentee in field. Served to lt. USNR, 1964-66. Registered profl. engr., Pa. Mem. Nat. Soc. Profl. Engrs., Am. Soc. Quality Control (cert. quality engr.), Pa. Soc. Profl. Engrs., Gen. Electric Mgmt. Assn., Elfun Soc., Drexel U. Alumni Assn., Pa. State U. Alumni Assn., Tri-County Arabian Horse Assn. Home: 454 Eagle Ln Lansdale PA 19446 Office: 2321 Topaz Dr Hatfield PA 19440

ROSHON, WILLIAM RAY, management executive; b. Wheeling, W.Va., Apr. 18, 1952; s. Robert Vincent and Rosemary (Rickabaugh) R.; m. Pamela Sue Fjelsted, Sept. 2, 1972; children: Angela Sue, Bradley Michael. BS in Edn., Ohio U., 1974; postgrad., Ohio State U., 1974, U. Ga., 1987-88. Tchr. Reynoldsburg (Ohio) Jr. High Sch., 1974-80, Cape Coral (Fla.) High Sch., 1980-85; with Metro Ft. Myers (Fla.) C. of C., 1981-86; v.p. bus. econ. affairs The Chamber of S.W. Fla., Ft. Myers, 1986—; bd. dirs. S.W. Fla. Bus. Healthcare Coalition, Ft. Myers, Lee County Pvt. Industry Council; mem. adv. bd. S.W. Fla. Consortium Bus./Higher Edn. Author: Newsletter (monthly) Small Business World, 1988. Local dir. Young Life, Lee County, Fla., 1981-85; bd. dirs. S.W. Fla. Regatta, Inc., Ft. Myers, 1985-86; mem. Fla. Gov.'s Challenge Conf., Tallahassee, 1985. Mem. Execs. Assn., Researchers Assn. and Small Bus. Council of U.S. C. of C. Lutheran. Home: 1309 SW 12th Terr Cape Coral FL 33991 Office: The Chamber of SW Fla 1365 Hendry St Fort Myers FL 33901

ROSICA, LUCIA A., accountant; b. Phila., Jan. 24, 1963; d. Joseph Marion and Carmela (D'Amico) R. BS in Accountancy, Villanova U., 1984. CPA, Pa. Sr. acct. Laventhol & Horwath, CPA's, Phila., 1984-87; sr. acct. fin. reporting IU Internat. Corp., Phila., 1987-88; sr. acct. Sun Carriers, Inc., Media, Pa., 1988—; fin. systems analyst Pa. Mfrs. Ins. Co., 1988—. Mem. AICPA, Pa. Inst. CPA's, Am. Women's Soc. CPA's, Nat. Assn. Accts. Roman Catholic.

ROSIER, DAVID LEWIS, investment banker; b. Sioux City, Iowa, Mar. 22, 1937; s. Orel Lewis and Jewell May (Palmer) R.; m. Jackie Dodd, July 1965 (div. 1973); 1 child, Michele, m. Carol Mary Byre, Nov. 25, 1982. BSBA, U. Denver, 1960. V.p., mgr. mktg. Hertz Internat., Ltd., N.Y., 1970-71; regional v.p. Amtrak, N.Y., 1971-73; pres. Rosier & Assocs., Ltd., San Diego, 1973—; sr. v.p. for strategic mktg. Am. Prins. Holdings, Inc., San Diego, 1979-84; v.p., registered prin. Am. Diversified Equity Corp., Costa Mesa, Calif., 1984-85; pres. Glen Eagle, Inc., 1986-87; sr. v.p. Western Region Cozad Investment Svcs. Inc., San Diego, 1987-88; chmn. bd., registered prin. Stringaree Corp. Group, San Diego, 1988—; mng. gen. ptnr. Schooner Bay Ltd., San Diego, 1988—. Appeared as speaker on nat. TV and at various industry conferences. Mem. adv. bd. Nautical Heritage Soc. (Hamburg award 1988). Mem. Rotary, Kona Kai Internat. Yacht Club (commodore 1987), Marina City Club (life).

ROSIN, MORRIS, real estate, land development company executive; b. San Antonio, Feb. 21, 1924; s. Berco and Leia (Dupchansky) R.; student Tex. A&M U., 1942, St. Mary's U., 1941, 45-47; m. Ethel Rosenberg; children—Susan, Charles, Lindsay. Sec.-treas. Bimbi Mfg. Co., 1949-67; pres. Bimbi Shoe Co. div. Athlone Industries, San Antonio, 1970-72; v.p. Athlone Industries, Parsippany, N.J., 1967-72; pres. Ardo Pro, San Antonio, 1966-74, Yoakum Bend Corp., San Antonio, 1968—, Broadway Devel. Corp., 1984—; sec.-treas. R & R Corp., San Antonio, 1970-72. Served with USAAF, 1942-45. Clubs: Masons (32 deg.), Shriners. Home: 4 Parliament Pl Dallas TX 75225 Office: Yoakum Bend Corp 4813 Broadway Dallas TX 75248

ROSMINI, GARY DAVID, financial marketing executive, consultant; b. Sewickley, Pa., Dec. 20, 1952; s. Silvio and Evelyn (Casciola) R.; m. Vivian Hooks, Jan. 7, 1978 (div. July 1984). BA, Pa. State U., 1975. Acct. mgr. Atwood-Vandell Assocs., Inc., N.Y.C., 1976-80, Clayton Brokerage, N.Y.C., 1980-81; assoc. v.p. Whitehall Investors Internat., Inc., N.Y.C., 1981-82; v.p. Monetary Futures Inc., N.Y.C., 1982-84; regional mktg. dir. Barrick Group, New Haven, Conn., 1984-86; pres. Rosmini Assocs., San Raphael, Calif., 1986—; regional mgr. Chilmark Commodities, Emeryville, Calif., 1987-88; mem. bd. advisors Pacific Investment Banking Group, Portland, Oreg., 1986—; bd. dirs. Superior Robotics Am., Petaluma, Calif., 1983-84; cons. in field. Creative dir. corp. brochure, 1986; copy writer bus. publ., 1983-84. Foster parent Save the Children, Ind., 1983-86; counselor Found. for Inner Peace, N.Y.C., 1976-78; choir dir. Saint Frances Cabrini Ch., Monaca, Pa., 1970-72; mem. Sewickley (Pa.) Civic Symphony, 1970-72, N.Y.C. Choral Soc., 1979-81. Recipient Billy Mitchell award CAP, 1970. Mem. Internat. Assn. Fin. Planning. (bd. dirs. 1981-84), Pa. State Alumni Assn. Home: 125 Wild Horse Valley Dr Novato CA 94947

ROSNER, BERNAT, corporate lawyer; b. Budapest, Hungary, Jan. 29, 1932; came to U.S., 1948; s. Alexander and Bertha (Schwartz) R.; m. Natalie Elizabeth Baylies, May 19, 1959 (dec. Jan. 1981); children: Michael, Andrew, Owen.; m. Susan Optner, May 14, 1983. BA, Cornell U., 1954; JD, Harvard U., 1959. Atty. Safeway Stores, Oakland, Calif., 1959-70, sr. atty., 1970-80, v.p., asst. gen. counsel, 1981-83, sr. v.p., gen. counsel, corp. sec., 1984—; guest lectr. law U. Calif., San Francisco, 1979-83, Calif. Inst. Mgmt., Berkeley, 1985-87. Contbr. articles to profl. jours. Served as 1st. lt., U.S. Army, 1954-56. Mem. ABA (com. chair antitrust sect. 1983-87, council mem. 1987—). Club: Round Hills Country. Office: Safeway Stores Inc 201 4th St Oakland CA 94660

ROSNER, T., insurance executive. V.p. Farmers Group Inc., L.A. Office: Farmers Ins Exch PO Box 2478 Terminal Annex Los Angeles CA 90051 *

ROSNESS, BETTY JUNE, advertising and public relations agency executive; b. Oklahoma City, Mar. 4, 1924; d. Thomas Harrison and Clara Marguerite (Stubblefield) Pyeatt; student Oklahoma City U., 1940-41; m. Joseph H. Rosness, Aug. 5, 1960; children—Melody L. Johnson (dec.), Michael C., Randall L., Melinda Rosness Mason, John C. Continuity dir. Sta. KFBI, Wichita, Kans., 1957-58; sales exec. Sta. KFH, Wichita, 1958-60; U.S. senatorial press sec., 1961-66; dir. advt. and public relations Alaska State Bank, Anchorage, 1966-68; prin. Rosness Advt. Assocs., Goleta, Calif., 1968—; bd. dirs. Fin. Corp. Santa Barbara (Calif.), Santa Barbara Savs. & Loan. Pres., Goleta Valley Girls Club, 1972-75, Ret. Officers Womens Assn., 1970; v.p. Santa Barbara Symphony Assn., 1977-80; bd. dirs. Channel City Womens Forum, 1976—, Goleta Valley Community Hosp.; Chmn. U. Calif. at Santa Barbara Affiliates, Pvt. Industry Council Santa Barbara County, 1985-86; bd. dirs. Cancer Found., Santa Barbara, 1978-82, founding mem. Goleta Beautiful, Club West Track and Field; mem. allocations com., bd. dirs. United Way, Santa Barbara; founding mem., bd. dirs. Children's World of Hospice . Named Woman of Year, Santa Barbara County, 1978, Affiliate of Yr., U. Calif.-Santa Barbara, 1983-84. Mem. Greater Santa Barbara Advt. Club. (past v.p.), Goleta Valley C. of C. (past dir.), Santa Barbara C. of C. (bd. dirs. 1982-86), Goleta Valley C. of C. Home: 669 Larchmont Pl Goleta CA 93117

ROSOVSKY, JAY M., computer company executive; b. N.Y.C., Oct. 28, 1945; s. Kermit and Ruth R.; m. Barbara Jane Wolder Rosovsky; children: Lisa, Adam. BS, SUNY, Albany, 1967. Systems engr., mktg. rep. IBM, Albany, N.Y., 1967-71; ops. mgr. Ocean Data Systems, Albany, 1971-74; pres. C.R. Ernst Assocs., Albany, 1974-75; pres. Jay M. Rosovsky Assoc., Albany, 1975-77, MCT/The Computer Room, Albany, 1986—; pres., chief exec. officer Infinite Solutions Inc., Norcross, Ga., 1977-86; pres., chief exec. officer, dir. Computone Systems, Inc., Atlanta, 1983—; dir. Nervene, Inc., Saratoga Springs, N.Y., 1977—. Contbr. articles to profl. jours. Fundraiser Congregation Beth Shalom, Clifton Park, N.Y., 1980; membership com. Schenectady Jewish Community Ctr., 1973; advisor Albany St. Acad., 1972, Jr. Achievement, Albany, 1970. Recipient 100% Club award IBM, 1971. Mem. ABCD-The Microcomputer Industry Assn. (chmn.), Kappa Mu Epsilon, Alpha Pi Omega. Republican. Jewish. Home: 880 Waddington Ct Dunwoody GA 30338 Office: Infinite Solutions Inc 6300 Jimmy Carter Blvd Norcross GA 30338

ROSOWSKI, ROBERT BERNARD, manufacturing company executive; b. Detroit, July 23, 1940; s. Bernard and Anna (Maciag) R.; m. Kathleen Patricia Bates, Aug. 26, 1961; children: John, Paul, Mary, Judith. BS, U. Detroit, 1962; MBA, Mich. State U., 1974. CPA, Mich. Auditor, staff supr. Coopers and Lybrand, Detroit, 1962-71; fin. analyst Masco Corp., Taylor, Mich., 1971-73, controller, 1973-85, v.p., controller, 1985—. Bd. dirs. Econ. Devel. Council City of Taylor, 1983—, Acctg. Aid Soc. Met. Detroit, 1987. Mem. Am. Inst. CPA's, Mich. Assn. CPA's. Office: Masco Corp 21001 Van Born Rd Taylor MI 48180

ROSS, ADRIAN E., diamond drilling company executive; b. Clintonville, N.Y., Mar. 6, 1912; s. James A. and Bertha (Beardsley) R.; B.S. in Elec.

Engring., M.I.T., 1934, M.S. in Elec. Engring., 1935; m. Ruth T. Hill, Mar. 2, 1934; children—James A., Daniel R. Materials engr. USN, 1935-37; devel. engr. Electrolux Corp., 1937-41; chief engr. and asst. to pres. Sprague & Henwood, Inc., Scranton, Pa., 1946-53, dir., 1951—, pres., 1953-74, chmn. bd., 1963—; pres., dir. Sprague & Henwood de Venezuela; dir. Hands Eng. Ltd., Scranton Lackawanna Indsl. Bldg. Co. (emeritus), N.E. Bank of Pa. (emeritus), profl. engrs. Past chmn. bd., dir. emeritus Keystone Jr. Coll.; pres., dir. James A. Ross Found., Sprague & Henwood Found.; former chmn. bd., dir. emeritus Johnson Sch. Tech. Served from lt. to lt. col. Air Communication. USAAF, 1941-46. Registered profl. engr., Pa. Mem. Diamond Core Drill Mfrs. Assn. (past pres.), AIME, ASCE, Soc. Profl Engrs., U.S. Nat. Council Soil Mechanics, Indsl. Diamond Assn. Am. (past pres.), C. of C. Presbyn. Clubs: Mining (N.Y.C.); Scranton, M.I.T. (Scranton, Pa.). Contbr. articles to Mining Congress Jour., Mining Engring., Engring. and Mining Jour., Diamond Drill Handbook. Home: 5 Overlook Rd Clarks Green PA 18411 Office: Sprague & Henwood Inc 221 W Olive St Scranton PA 18501

ROSS, ARTHUR LEONARD, aerospace engineer; b. N.Y.C., Mar. 9, 1924; s. Henry and Anna (Goldhammer) R.; m. Amy Joyce Cohan, July 4, 1948; children: Bradley Alfred, Anne Helen. BS, NYU, 1948, MS, 1950, DSc, 1954. Cons. engr. aircraft nuclear propulsion dept. Gen. Electric Co., Cin., 1954-61; mgr. structural evaluation Knolls Lab. Gen. Electric Co., Schenectady, N.Y., 1961-66; staff engr. Aerospace Group Gen. Electric Co., Phila., 1966—; adj. prof. Drexel U., Phila., 1980-81. Editor: Failure, Prevention and Reliability, 1977; contbr. numerous articles to profl. jours.; patentee in field. With U.S. Army, 1943-45, ETO. Fellow ASME; mem. AIAA, Am. Acad. Mechanics, Sigma Xi. Home: 122 Maple Ave Bala Cynwyd PA 19004 Office: GE 3198 Chestnut St Philadelphia PA 19104

ROSS, BETTY GRACE, medical distributing company executive; b. N.Y.C., July 14, 1931; d. Philip and Nancy Anna (Meredith) Boccella; R.N., Presbyn. Hosp., 1952; student Ariz. State U., 1960-62; m. Robert W. Ross, Mar. 1, 1968 (div. July 1976). Sr. operating rm. nurse Roosevelt Hosp., N.Y.C., 1953-58, pvt. surg. nurse, neurosurgery group, 1958-59, orthopedic surgery group, 1960-64; mem. sales staff Zimmer U.S.A., Phoenix, Ariz., 1964-71, owner, distbr. Zimmer Ross Assocs., Phoenix, 1971—, Zimmer-Ross Ltd., 1978—; instr. operating room nursing Englewood (N.J.) Hosp., 1960. Active on Taskforce for Homeless, Phoenix. Mem. Assn. Operating Room Nurses Phoenix (charter mem.), Maricopa Mental Health Assn., Bloomfield Coll. Alumni Assn. Republican. Club: Century. Home: 5713 Cattletrack Rd N Scottsdale AZ 85253 also: John Gardiner's Enchantment Sedona AZ 86336 Office: 1232 E Missouri St Phoenix AZ 85014

ROSS, BURTON MERRILL, accountant; b. Manchester, N.H., Nov. 21, 1949; s. John Albert and Rose Rachael (Bermont) R.; m. Nancy Jacobson, Aug. 17, 1986; 1 child, Jacob. BS, U. Conn., 1971; MusM, U. Miami, Coral Gables, Fla., 1972. CPA, Washington. Acct. Main Hurdman, Boston, 1981, Rosenfield and Holland, North Dartmouth, Mass., 1982; mem. staff U.S. Postal Service, Brockton, Mass., 1983-84; mem. computer tech. support staff Para Rsch., Gloucester, Mass., 1984-85, Interactive Systmes, Lowell, Mass., 1985-86; tchr. Melrose (Mass.) Pub. Schs., 1986-87; acct. Richard A. Meyers and Co., P.A., Ft. Myers, Fla., 1988—; musician, mgr. Jordan Ross Orch., Bonita Springs, Fla., 1988—. Sgt. USMC, 1976-80. Mem. Fla. Inst. CPAs, Am. Inst. CPAs, Internat. Fedn. Musicians. Home: 3447 Quail Dr SW Bonita Springs FL 33923 Office: Richard A Myers & Co PA 8270 College Pkwy Ste 105 Fort Myers FL 33907-5944

ROSS, COLEMAN DEVANE, accountant; b. Greensboro, N.C., Mar. 18, 1943; s. Guy Matthews and Nancy McConnell (Coleman) R.; B.S. in Bus. Adminstrn., U. N.C., 1965; postgrad. Sch. of Banking of South, 1982-84; m. Carol Louise Morde, Aug. 26, 1965; children—Coleman, Jonathan, Andrew. With Price Waterhouse, Tampa, 1965-76, Toronto, 1970, Hartford, Conn., 1976—, ptnr., 1977—, mng. ptnr. Nat. Ins. Industry Services Group, 1988—. Exec. bd., Long Rivers Council, Boy Scouts Am., 1978—, pres. 1985-88, exec. bd. Northeast Region, Boy Scouts Am., 1988—, pres. New Eng. area, 1988; div. campaign chmn. United Way of Capital Area, 1984; bd. dirs., treas. Family Service Soc. Greater Hartford, 1977-80. C.P.A., C.L.U.; chartered bank auditor. Fellow Life Mgmt. Inst.; mem. Am. Inst. C.P.A.s (ins. cos. com. 1985-88, reins. auditing and acctg. task force 1979-85, relations with actuaries com. 1982-85), N.C. Assn. C.P.A.s, Conn. Soc. C.P.A.s, Soc. Ins. Accts., Am. Soc. CLUs, Nat. Soc. Chartered Bank Auditors, Assn. Mut. Ins. Accts. Clubs: Hartford (bd. govs. 1977-84), Hop Meadow Country. Home: 11 Neal Dr Simsbury CT 06070 Office: 1 Financial Pla Hartford CT 06103

ROSS, DANIEL DELANO, venture capitalist; b. Dodson, La., Sept. 19, 1940; s. Walter James and Phama (Pullen) R.; m. Joan Alden Laborde, Aug. 21, 1965; children: Jeanne, Daniel Jr., Roxanne, Mark, Marguerite, Noelle. BS in Math., La. Tech. U., 1966. With mktg. staff IBM Corp., Shreveport, La., 1966-70; regional mgr. Itel Corp., N.Y.C., 1971-73, v.p., 1973-75; v.p. Itel Corp., Atlanta, 1975-79; exec. v.p. leasing Memorex Corp., Santa Clara, Calif., 1979, exec. v.p. communications, 1979-83; chief operating officer Timex Computer Corp., Middlebury, Conn., 1982-84; gen. ptnr. Advanced Tech. Devel. Fund, Atlanta, 1984—; bd. dirs. Syntellect, Inc., Phoenix, HealthServ, Inc., Atlanta, Integratec, Inc., Atlanta. Bd. dirs. All Saints Cath. Ch., Dunwoody, Ga.; mem. Friendship Force, Atlanta, 1987-88. Sgt. USAFR, 1965-70. Mem. Advanced Tech. Devel. Inst., Venture Forum, Dunwoody Golf Club. Democrat. Home: 1859 Tennille Ct Dunwoody GA 30338 Office: Advanced Tech Devel Fund 1000 Abernathy Rd 400 Northpark Town Ctr Ste 420 Atlanta GA 30328

ROSS, DEBRA BENITA, development executive; b. Carbondale, Ill., May 1, 1956; d. Bernard Harris and Marian (Frager) R. BS, U. Ill., 1978; MA, U. Wis., 1979. Dir. mktg. Ambion Devel., Inc., Northbrook, Ill., 1983—. Mem. Am. Mktg. Assn., Chgo. Advt. Club. Home: 1953 Mission Hills Ln Northbrook IL 60062 Office: Ambion Devel Inc 5 Revere Dr Ste 200 Northbrook IL 60062

ROSS, DONALD EDWARD, engineer; b. N.Y.C., May 2, 1930; m. Jeanne Ellen McKessy, Apr. 4, 1954; children—Susan, Christopher, Carolyn. B.A., Columbia U., 1952, B.S. in Mech. Engring., 1953; M.B.A., NYU, 1960. Registered profl. engr., N.Y., N.J., Calif. Engr. Carrier Corp., N.Y.C., 1955-70; v.p. Dynadata, 1970-71; with. Jaros, Baum & Bolles, 1971—, ptnr. 1977— . Chmn. profl. liability com. Am. Cons. Engrs. Council, Washington, 1984—; mem. engring. council Columbia U. Sch. Engring and Applied Sci. Mem. faculty and alumni adv. council Columbia U. Served to lt. (j.g.) USN, 1953-55. Fellow ASHRAE; mem. ASME, NSPE, N.Y. Assn. Cons. Engrs. (pres. 1984-86, coun. on tall bldgs. and urban habitat), Nat. Bur. Engrs., Univ. Club, Nassau Country Club. Office: Jaros Baum & Bolles 345 Park Ave New York NY 10154

ROSS, DONALD KEITH, insurance company executive; b. Rochester, N.Y., July 1, 1925; s. Alexander L. and Althea G. (Granger) R.; m. Mary F. Fyffe, June 4, 1949; children: Catherine (Mrs. Charles P. Lesher), Susan (Mrs. William Gardner Morris, Jr.), Donald Keith, Deborah Anne (Mrs. Michael Holt). B.E., Yale U., 1946; M.B.A., Harvard U., 1948. With N.Y. Life Ins. Co., N.Y.C., 1948—, exec. v.p., 1974-79, vice chmn., 1979-80, pres., 1980-81, chmn. bd., chief exec. officer, 1981—, also dir.; trustee Consol. Edison of N.Y. Trustee Colonial Williamsburg (Va.) Found.; chmn. N.Y. Life Found.; chmn. bd. dirs. YMCA. Club: Links. Office: NY Life Ins Co 51 Madison Ave New York NY 10010

ROSS, DOUGLAS TAYLOR, software company executive; b. Canton, Republic of China, Dec. 21, 1929; (parents Am. citizens); s. Robert Malcolm and Margaret (Taylor) R.; m. Patricia Mott, Jan. 24, 1951; children—Jane Louise, Kathryn R. Chow, Margaret R. Thrasher. A.B. in Math. cum laude, Oberlin Coll., 1951; S.M., MIT, 1954, postgrad. math., 1958. Head computer applications group elec. systems lab. MIT, Cambridge, 1952-69, lectr. dept. elec. engring. and computer sci., 1960-69, 83—, exec. com. MIT Enterprise Forum, 1984—; pres. SofTech, Inc., Waltham, Mass., 1969-75, chmn. bd., 1975—; bd. dirs. Cognition, Inc., 1985—. Mem. town meeting, Lexington, Mass., 1960-70; trustee, bd. dirs. Charles Babbage Inst., 1984—. Mem. United Ch. of Christ. Home: 33 Dawes Rd Lexington MA 02173 Office: SofTech Inc 460 Totten Pond Rd Waltham MA 02154

ROSS, E. DENNIS, retail executive; b. Springfield, Ohio, Dec. 20, 1941; s. Edward and Thelma (Burkepile) R.; m. Marian Ruth Dreyer; children: Christopher Dennis, Stephanie Dreyer. BCE, Ohio U., 1965, MCE, 1966. Mktg. rep. IBM Corp., Columbus, Ohio, 1966-71; dir. mktg. Applied Mgmt. Systems, Columbus, 1971-74, v.p., 1974-77; sr. cons. assoc. Mgmt. Horizons, Columbus, 1977-78, v.p., 1978-81, exec. v.p., 1981-83; v.p. The Home Depot, Atlanta, 1983-85, sr. v.p., 1985—; bd. dirs. Quality Stores Inc., North Muskegon, Mich.; speaker in field. Methodist. Office: Home Depot 2727 Paces Ferry Rd Atlanta GA 30339

ROSS, ELISE JANE, newspaper executive; b. Manchester, Conn., Aug. 29, 1943; d. Harry and Sophia J. (Osher) R. BA, NYU, 1965. Programmer Met. Life Ins. Co., N.Y.C., 1965-68; systems analyst Bache Co., N.Y.C., 1968-70; mgr. systems and programming Omniswitch, Inc., Lake Success, N.Y., 1970-73; sr. v.p. info. systems N.Y. Times, N.Y.C., 1973—. Jewish. Office: The New York Times 229 W 43rd St New York NY 10036

ROSS, GEORGE C., banker. Sr. v.p. Chem. Bank N.Y. Office: Chem Bank 277 Park Ave New York NY 10172 *

ROSS, GEORGE MARTIN, investment banker; b. Phila., July 24, 1933; s. David L. and Beatrice (Rittenberg) Rosenkoff; m. Lyn Merry Goldberg, Nov. 26, 1959; children: Merry Beth, Michael John. BS, Drexel U., 1955. Mgmt. trainee Sears, Roebuck & Co., Phila., 1955-58; assoc. Goldman, Sachs & Co., Phila., 1959-68, v.p., 1968-70, ptnr., 1971—. Mem. Mayor's Cultural Adv. Council, Phila., 1987—, campaign steering com. Bus. Leadership Organized for Cath. Schs., campaign policy com. United Way Southeastern Pa., We the People 200 com., Gov.'s Pvt. Sector Initiatives Task Force, 1983-84, Gov.'s Commn. on Financing Higher Edn., 1983-84, Wills Eye Hosp. Adv. Council, 1979-81, nat. bd. govs., exec. com., past pres., bd. dirs., past chmn. Phila chpt. Am. Jewish Com.; v.p., exec. com. Fedn. Jewish Agencies Greater Phila.; chmn. emeritus, bd. dirs., exec. com. Phila. Drama Guild; past gov. Phila. Stock Exchange, 1981-84; trustee Episcopal Acad., exec. com. Drexel U., Phila., 1981—; bd. dirs. Phila. Orch. Assn., 1985—, Acad. Music Phila., Urban Affairs Partnership, Cystic Fibrosis Found., 1978-83, Nat. Found. Jewish Culture. Mem. Urban Affairs Partnership (bd. dirs. 1978-83), Fin. Analysts Phila., Phila. Securities Assn., Bond Club Phila., Union League. Clubs: Sunday Breakfast (Phila.), Locust (bd. dirs. 1986—). Home: 1116 Barberry Rd Bryn Mawr PA 19010 Office: Goldman Sachs & Co 3 Mellon Bank Ctr 27th Fl Philadelphia PA 19102

ROSS, HOWARD, financial planner; b. Bklyn., Jan. 4, 1950; s. Harold and Paula (Zeines) R.; m. Marilyn Dennerstein, Jan. 25, 1974; children: Alison, Michael. BBA, Baruch Coll., 1971, MBA, 1982; JD, St. John's U., 1975. Cert. fin. planner. Asst. controller N.Y. Times, N.Y.C., 1970-80; agt. Equitable Life, N.Y.C., 1981-82, fin. planner, 1985—; wholesaler Security First Group, N.Y.C., 1982-85. Contbr. articles to profl. jours. Mem. ABA, Internat. Assn. Fin. Planners, Nassau Life Underwriters. Office: Shulman Group 1983 Marcus Ave Suite 260 Lake Success NY 11042

ROSS, HOWARD PHILIP, lawyer; b. Chgo., May 10, 1939; s. Bernard and Estelle (Maremont) R.; m. Loretta Teresa Benquil, 1962 (div.); children: Glen Joseph, Cynthia Ann; m. Jennifer Kay Shirley, 1984. BS, U. Ill., 1961; JD, Stetson Coll. Law, 1964. Bar: Fla. 1964, U.S. Ct. Appeals (5th cir.) 1965, U.S. Ct. Appeals (11th cir.) 1981, U.S. Supreme Ct. 1969; cert. civil trial lawyer. Assoc. Parker & Battaglia and predecessor firm, St. Petersburg, Fla., 1964-67; ptnr. Battaglia, Ross, Hastings, Dicus & Andrews and predecessor firms, St. Petersburg, 1967-87; ptnr. Battaglia, Ross, Hasings and Dicus, P.A., 1987—; lectr. Stetson Coll. Law, St. Petersburg, 1971-72, adj. prof., 1987—. Author: Florida Corporations; contbr. articles to profl. jours. Recipient Woman's Svc. League Best Groomed award, 1979, Fla. Bar merit citation, 1974. Mem ABA, Fla. Bar Assn., St. Petersburg Bar Assn., Am. Soc. Writers on Legal Subjects, Assn. Trial Lawyers Am., Assn. Fla. Trial Lawyers, Smithsonian Assocs. Republican. Jewish. Office: Battaglia Ross Hastings Dicus PA PO Box 41100 980 Tyrone Blvd Saint Petersburg FL 33743

ROSS, IAN MUNRO, electrical engineer; b. Southport, Eng., Aug. 15, 1927; came to U.S., 1952, naturalized, 1960; m. Christina Leinberg Ross, Aug. 24, 1955; children: Timothy Ian, Nancy Lynn, Stina Marguerite. BA, Gonville and Caius Coll., Cambridge (Eng.) U., 1948; MA in Elec. Engring, Cambridge U., 1952, PhD, 1952; DSc (hon.), N.J. Inst. Tech., 1983; D of Engring. (hon.), Stevens Inst. Tech., 1983. With AT&T Bell Labs. (and affiliates), 1952—, exec. dir. network planning div., 1971-73, v.p. network planning and customer services, 1973-76; exec. v.p. systems engring. and devel. AT&T Bell Labs. (and affiliates), Holmdel, N.J., 1976-79; pres. AT&T Bell Labs. (and affiliates), 1979—; dir. Thomas & Betts Corp., B.F. Goodrich Co. Patentee in field. Recipient Liebmann Meml. prize IEEE, 1963, Pub. Service award NASA, 1969, Founders medal IEEE, 1988. Fellow IEEE (Liebmann Meml. prize 1963, Founders medal 1988), Am. Acad. Arts and Scis.; mem. Nat. Acad. Engring. Home: 5 Blackpoint Horseshoe Rumson NJ 07760 Office: AT&T Bell Labs Inc Crawfords Corner Rd Holmdel NJ 07733 *

ROSS, J(AMES) ROBERT, oil company executive; b. Mexia, Tex., June 9, 1924; s. Dudley Warren and Betty (McGilvary) R.; BBA cum laude, So. Meth. U.; m. Betty Jane Fischer, Sept. 11, 1953. With Magnolia Petroleum Co., Dallas, 1941-59, mgr. controllers dept., 1955-59; mgr. controllers dept. Socony Mobil Oil Co., N.Y.C., 1959-60; asst. controller Mobil Chem. Co., N.Y.C., 1960-68; sr. cons. Mobil Oil Corp., N.Y.C., 1968-72, sr. con. fed. reporting Mobil Corp., N.Y.C., 1972-85, ind. fin. cons., 1985—. CPA, Tex., Conn. Mem. Am. Petroleum Inst., AICPA, Tex. Soc. CPAs, Nat. Accts. Assn., Bus. Adv. Council Fed. Reporting, Am. Mgmt. Assn., Beta Gamma Sigma. Republican. Presbyterian. Clubs: Masons, K.T. Home: Salem Straits Darien CT 06820 Office: Standard Oil Co 200 Public Sq Cleveland OH 44114

ROSS, JUDITH PARIS, life insurance executive; b. Boston, Dec. 23, 1939; d. Max and Ruth Paris; ed. Boston U., 1961, UCLA, 1978; grad. Life Underwriting Tng. Council, 1978; 1 son, Adam Stuart. Producer, co-host Checkpoint TV show, Washington, 1967-71; hostess Judi Says TV show, Washington, 1969; brokerage supr., specialist impaired risk underwriting Beneficial Nat. Life Ins. Co. (now Nat. Benefit Life), Beverly Hills, Calif., 1973-82, dir. Salary Savs. program for West Coast, 1982-87; ins. and benefits specialist, cons. Alliance Assocs., 1987—; mktg. dir. Brougher Ins. Group, 1982-87; ins. and benefits specialist Alliance Assocs., Beverly Hills, 1987—; featured speaker ins. industry seminars. Active local PTA, Boy Scouts Am., Beverly Hills local politics; mem. early childhood edn. adv. com. Beverly Hills Unified Sch. Dist., 1977. Mem. Nat. Assn. Life Underwriters, Calif. Assn. Life Underwriters (dir. W. Los Angeles 1980—, v.p. chpt. 1982—, chmn. pub. relations), West Los Angeles Life Underwriters Assn. (v.p. fin. 1983-84). Office: Alliance Assocs 449 S Beverly Dr #206 Beverly Hills CA 90212

ROSS, MICHAEL FREDERICK, lawyer; b. Coral Gables, Fla., Sept. 20, 1950; s. George Thomas and Frances (Brown) Skaro. BA, Yale U., 1973; JD, U. Conn., 1979; MLS, So. Conn. State U., 1981. Bar: Conn. 1979, U.S. Dist. Ct. Conn. 1979, Fla. 1979, U.S. Ct. Claims 1980, U.S. Tax Ct. 1980, U.S. Ct. Customs and Patent Appeals 1980, U.S. Ct. Mil. Appeals 1980, U.S. Ct. Appeals (1st, 2d and D.C. cirs.) 1980, U.S. Ct. Appeals (5th, 9th and 11th cirs.) 1981, U.S. Ct. Appeals (Fed. cir.) 1982, U.S. Supreme Ct. 1982, N.J. 1983, U.S. Dist. Ct. N.J. 1983, U.S. Ct. Appeals (3d, 4th, 6th, 7th, 8th and 10th cirs.) 1983, Mass. 1984, U.S. Dist. Ct. Vt. 1984, V.I. 1985, U.S. Dist. Ct. V.I. 1985, Temp. Emergency Ct. Appeals 1985. Pvt. practice New Haven, Conn., 1979-82, Madison, Conn., 1985—; chief of adjudications Conn. Motor Vehicle Dept., Wethersfield, 1980-82; adminstrv. law judge State of Conn. Motor Vehicle Dept., Wethersfield, 1985—; asst. atty. gen. State of Conn., Hartford, 1982-84, Dept. of Law, St. Croix, V.I., 1984-85; magistrate Superior Ct. of Middlesex, New Haven and New London Counties, Conn., 1988—; mem. faculty Conn. Bar Assn. Acad. of profl. Devel. of Continuing Legal Edn., 1987. Chmn. selective service system Conn. Local Bd. 11, 1982—. Mem. ABA, Conn. Bar Assn., Mass. Bar Assn., Boston Bar Assn., Mensa. Democrat. Jewish. Club: Fence, Morys Assn. (New Haven). Home: 16 Canborne Way Madison CT 06443-0366 Office: 74 Bradley Rd PO Box 366 Madison CT 06446-0366

ROSS, MYRON DONALD, consultant; b. Chgo., Sept. 30, 1909; s. Michael J. and Bertha (Krutch) R.; m. Marie V. Manning, June 13, 1935; children: Donald R., Darlene M. BS, Northwestern U., 1934. With Jewel Cos., Inc., Melrose Park, Ill., 1932-70, as mgr. inventory control, cost acctg. depts., mgr. cash, payroll dept., store personnel mgr., office mgr., 1932-45, mgr. cash operating div., 1945-54, mgr. systems div., 1954-63, mgr. electronic data processing div., 1963-66, asst. to controller, 1966-68, asst. to exec. v.p., 1968-70; cons. office administrn., 1970—. Vice pres. S.W. Suburban Council on Aging, 1980—. Recipient Merit Award key Office Mgmt. Assn. Chgo., 1950, Leadership plaque Nat. Office Mgmt. Assn., 1951. Mem. Chgo. Office Mgmt. Assn. (pres. 1949-50), Adminstrv. Mgmt. Soc., Bus. Electronics Round Table (pres. 1964-65), Execs. Club (Chgo.). Home: 10543 Dorchester Rd Westchester IL 60154

ROSS, NORMAN ALEXANDER, retired banker; b. Miami, Fla., Jan. 30, 1922; s. Norman DeMille and Beatrice (Dowsett) R.; children—Isabel, Susan Diana. A.B., Stanford U., 1946; postgrad., Trinity Coll., Oxford U., Eng., 1953; D.H.L., Lincoln Coll., Ill., 1959, Fisk U., 1978, Roosevelt U., 1979; Litt.D., Lake Forest Coll., 1967. Airport mgr. Pan Am. Airways, 1943; asst. to producer Metro-Goldwyn-Mayer, 1943-44; ptnr. Norman Ross & Co., 1947-50; owner Norman Ross Record Club, 1951-52; v.p. pub. affairs First Nat. Bank Chgo., 1968-79, sr. v.p. communications dept., 1979-81, sr. v.p. community affairs, 1981-86; pres. Ross-McElroy Prodns., Inc., 1962-68. Radio-TV commentator, NBC, ABC, Chgo., 1953-64, ABC, WGN and WBKB, Chgo., 1964-68, former columnist, Chgo. Daily News. Served with inf. AUS, World War II. Decorated cavaliere Dell Ordine Repubblica Italiana; U.S. Army Outstanding Civilian Service medal; officier and cross of chevalier Legion of Honor France; recipient Peabody award for TV program Off the Cuff 1964. Mem. Phi Gamma Delta. Clubs: Chgo., Racquet, Oxford, Econ. (Chgo.), Wayfarers. Home: PO Box 1280 Pilot Mountain NC 27041

ROSS, PATRICK CONROY, rubber company executive; b. Iron River, Mich., Aug. 27, 1929; s. William D. and Elsie A. (Thompson) R.; m. Ann M. Groves, Feb. 2, 1952; children—Stewart C., Charles E., Nancy J. A.B., U. Mich., 1951, M.A., 1976; grad., advanced mgmt. program Harvard U., 1969. Merchandising mgr. WWJ-Detroit News, 1956-57; sales mgr. Argus Cameras Co., Ann Arbor, Mich., 1957-62; area dir. Europe B.F. Goodrich Co., 1962-68; pres. internat. div. B.F. Goodrich Co., Akron, Ohio, 1969-70; pres. B. F. Goodrich Tire Group, Akron, Ohio, 1972-84; corp. exec. v.p. B.F. Goodrich Co., 1979-84, pres., 1984-86; chmn., chief exec. officer The Uniroyal Goodrich Tire Co., Akron, 1986-88, cons., 1988—. Served with USAF, 1951-55. Club: Portage Country (Akron). Office: Uniroyal Goodrich Tire Co 600 S Main St Akron OH 44397-0001

ROSS, RANDOLPH ERNEST, financial analyst; b. N.Y.C., Mar. 17, 1955; s. David Harvey and Pearl (Frandsen) R.; m. Joan Frances Healey, Apr. 2, 1982. A.B. in History, Brown U., 1977; M.B.A. in Fin., Columbia U., 1981. Chartered fin. analyst. Nat. editor WEAN Radio (CBS affiliate), Providence, 1977-79; research analyst, asst. v.p. Kidder, Peabody & Co., Inc., N.Y.C., 1981-85; research analyst First Manhattan Co., N.Y.C., 1985-86; portfolio mgr. Brundage, Story and Rose, N.Y.C., 1986—. Fundraiser Brown U., Providence, 1981-87, Grad. Sch. of Bus., Columbia U., 1985. Fellow Fin. Analysts Fedn.; mem. Inst. Chartered Fin. Analysts, N.Y. Soc. Security Analysts, N.Y. Hist. Soc., L.I. Hist. Soc., Columbia Club (N.Y.C.), Brown Club, Am. Yacht Club. Republican. Avocations: sailing, archtl. and urban history, fiction, music. Office: Brundage Story & Rose One Broadway New York NY 10004

ROSS, ROBERT GRIERSON, II, publishing executive; b. Bklyn., Jan. 15, 1950; s. Robert Grierson and Margaret Mary (Delaney) R.; m. Cynthia Sampson, Dec. 10, 1983; children: Robert Grierson III, Margaret Jane. BS in Mktg., Bryant Coll., 1973. With advt. sales dept. Cardinal Publishing, San Francisco, 1975-77, Media Networks, Inc., Atlanta, 1977-80; advt. sales Wall St Jour., Dallas, 1980-83; assoc. advt. mgr. Wall St Jour., Houston, 1983-89, Chgo., 1989—. Mem. Houston Advt. Fedn., Bus. Pubs. Assn. Am. Club: Champions Golf (bd. dirs.)(Houston). Office: Wall St Jour One S Wacker Dr Chicago IL 60606

ROSS, ROBERT RESOLVED, JR., data processing executive; b. Bucyrus, Ohio, Sept. 29, 1947; s. Robert Resolved Sr. and Doneta Mae (Young) R.; m. Mary Ann Van Paepeghem, Aug. 10, 1968; children: Christine, Malia, Heather. Systems rep. Shaw Systems Inc., Houston, 1972-74; sr. programmer/analyst M.W. Kellogg, Houston, 1974-75; mgr. data processing Columbia Gas Transmission Co., Houston, 1975-78; mgr. accounts Systems and Programming Resources Co., Houston, 1978-79; project mgr. Brown & Root, Houston, 1979-80; dir. mgmt. info. systems Moron Energy Inc., Houston, 1980-83; v.p. systems Anacomp Inc., Sarasota, Fla., 1983-87; mgr. data communications The Newtrend Group, Orlando, Fla., 1987—. Served with U.S. Army, 1970-71, Vietnam. Republican. Roman Catholic. Lodge: KC. Office: The Newtrend Group 2600 Technology Dr Orlando FL 32804

ROSS, RODERIC HENRY, insurance company executive; b. Jamestown, N.Y., July 14, 1930; s. Edwin A. and Mary (Dornberger) R.; m. Patricia Johnson, Aug. 6, 1955; children: Timothy, Amy, Jane, Christopher. BA, Hobart Coll., 1952, LLD (hon.), 1979. CLU; chartered fin. cons. Gen. agt. Phila. Life Ins. Co., 1957-70, sr. v.p. mktg., 1972-73, pres., 1973-83, vice chmn., 1983-84; chmn., pres. Keystone State Life Ins. Co., Phila., 1985—; bd. dirs. Provident Nat. Bank, Phila., PNC Fin., Pitts., Hunt Mfg. Co., Phila, Pa. Mfrs. Corp., Phila. Sr. warden St. David's Ch., Radnor, Pa., 1988—; chmn. bd. Hobart-William Smith Colls., Geneva, N.Y., 1983-88; bd. dirs. Cen. Phila. Devel. Corp. Sgt. U.S. Army, 1952-54, Korea. Mem. Am. Coll. Life Underwriters, Am. Soc. CLU's, Nat. Assn. Life Underwriters, Million Dollar Round Table (life). Republican. Episcopalian. Clubs: Union League (Phila.), Orpheus; Pine Valley Golf (Clementon, N.J.); St. David's Golf (Wayne, Pa.). Home: 770 Pugh Rd Wayne PA 19087 Office: Keystone State Life Ins Co 1227 Chestnut St Philadelphia PA 19107

ROSS, STEVEN J., communications company executive; b. N.Y.C., 1927; married. Student, Paul Smith's Coll., 1948. Pres., dir. Kinney Services Inc., 1966-72; pres. Warner Communications Inc., N.Y.C., from 1972, now chmn. bd., chief exec. officer, 1972—; Bd. dirs. N.Y. Conv. and Visitors Bur., N.Y. State Alliance to Save Energy; mem. bd. sports medicine Lenox Hill Hosp. Office: Warner Communications Inc 75 Rockefeller Pla New York NY 10019 *

ROSS, STUART B., corporate financial executive; b. N.Y.C., Apr. 16, 1937; s. Bernard Theodore and Ruth R.; m. Stephanie Banks, Dec. 15, 1962; children: Jessica, Benjamin. BS, NYU, 1958; MBA, CCNY, 1966. Pub. acct. Harris, Kerr, Forster, N.Y.C., 1958-63; fin. analyst MacMillan Co., N.Y.C., 1963-66; with Xerox Corp., Stamford, Conn., 1966—, chief fin. officer, 1985—, also mem. pvt. sector coun., conf. bd.; bd. dirs. ECKO Group, Inc. Mem. Am. Inst. CPA's, Fin. Execs. Inst. Office: Xerox Corp Stamford CT 06904

ROSS, SUSAN JULIA, lawyer; b. Phila., July 24, 1943; d. Herbert Joseph and Susan Eshleman (Reese) R.; BA, magna cum laude, U. Pa., 1965, JD magna cum laude, 1969; postgrad. N.Y. U. Law Sch., 1972-75. Bar: N.Y., 1971, N.Mex., 1976, U.S. Dist. Ct. (so. and ea. dists.) N.Y., U.S. Dist. Ct. N.Mex., U.S. Ct. Appeals (2d cir.), U.S. Tax Ct.; assoc. Dewey, Ballantine, Bushby, Palmer & Wood, N.Y.C., 1969-76; ptnr. Natelson & Ross, Taos, N.Mex., 1976—; vis. assoc. prof. law U. Oreg., 1978; dir. Beneficial Corp., Wilmington, Del., 1979—. Trustee Millicent Rogers Mus., Taos, 1979—. Thouron-U. Pa. fellow, Oxford U., 1969-70; Am. Scandinavian Assn. fellow, Stockholm U., 1970. Mem. Phi Beta Kappa, Order Coif. Editor U. Pa. Law Rev., 1967-69; contbr. in field articles to jours. Democrat. Avocations: skiing, tennis, scuba diving, windsurfing, horseback riding.

ROSS, TOM, financial services company. Exec. v.p. client svcs. U.S.A. Leo Burnett Co. Inc., Chgo. Office: Leo Burnett Co Inc One Prudential Plaza Chicago IL 60601 *

ROSS, WILBUR LOUIS, JR., investment banker; b. Weehawken, N.J., Nov. 28, 1937; s. Wilbur Louis and Agnes (O'Neill) R.; m. Judith Nodine, May 26, 1961; children: Jessica, Amanda. AB, Yale U., 1959; MBA with distinction, Harvard U., 1961. Assoc. Wood, Struthers and Winthrop, N.Y.C., 1963-64; pres. Faulkner, Dawkins and Sullivan Securities Corp., N.Y.C., 1964-76; sr. mng. dir. Rothschild, Inc., N.Y.C., 1976—; bd. dirs. Aileen Inc., N.Y.C., Geo Internat. Corp., Stamford, Conn., Biocraft labs Inc., Rutherford, N.J., FurVault Inc., N.Y.C., Investors Ins. Co., Lawrence Harbor, N.J., Revere Copper and Brass Co., Stamford, Syms Corp., Secaucus, N.J., Am. Bankruptcy Inst., Washington, Allis Chalmers Corp., Milw., Mego Corp., Las Vegas, Nev.; fin. advisor equity holders com. Texaco Co., A.H. Robins Co., Pub. Service N.H. Treas. N.Y. State Dem. Com., 1980-83; vice chmn. Bklyn. Mus., 1981—; chmn. council com. on art Yale U., 1983-88; chmn. NAD, N.Y.C., 1985—, Am. Art Forum, Smithsonian Instn., 1987—; trustee, vice chmn. Nat. Mus. Am. Art, Washington, 1986—; trustee Sarah Lawrence Coll., 1986—, chmn. art gallery, 1984—. With U.S. Army, 1961-63. Fellow Jonathan Edward Coll. of Yale U., Met. Mus. Art; mem. Fin. Analysts Fedn. (chartered), Century Assn. Home: The Dakota 1 W 72nd St New York NY 10023 Office: Rothschild Inc 1 Rockefeller Pla New York NY 10020

ROSS, WILLIAM DANIEL, retired chemist; b. Elmira, N.Y., Nov. 22, 1917; s. Walter P. and Mary (Daly) R.; B.A., Columbia, 1938; B.S., Columbia Engring. Sch., 1939; m. Sophie E. Gebert, 1961; 1 dau., Celia Mary. With pigments dept. E. I. du Pont de Nemours & Co., Inc., 1939-82, research assoc., 1962-68, research fellow, 1968-82, ret., 1982. Mem. AAAS, Am. Chem. Soc., Am. Inst. Chem. Engrs., N.Y. Acad. Scis., Phila. Soc. for Coatings Tech., Optical Soc. Am. Patentee in calcination. Home: 36 Ridgewood Circle Wilmington DE 19809

ROSSBACH, PAUL R(OBERT), public relations executive; b. Pitts., Oct. 30, 1946; s. Robert Albert and Margaret Urline (Duffy) R. BA, Duquesne U., 1968. Exec. producer Creative Communications Group, Dallas, 1973-76; dir. pub. relations San Antonio Mus. Assn., 1976-80; with press advance dept. U.S. Dept. State and The White House, Washington, 1978-80; owner Paul Rossbach Pub. Relations, San Antonio, 1980—; assoc. The Konig Ctr., San Antonio, 1980—; affiliate Daniel J. Edelman, Inc., N.Y.C., 1982—. Contbg. editor articles for local bus., mcpl. and lifestyle mags. Mem. Friends of McNay Art Mus., 1981—; chmn. publicity Cattle Barons div. Am. Cancer Soc., San Antonio, 1987-88; chmn. mktg. com. San Antonio Performing Arts Assn., 1988—; commr. Fiesta San Antonio Commn., 1988—. Served to capt. USAF, 1968-72. Recipient Gold Addy award San Antonio Advt. Fedn., 1977, 79, award of excellence Internat. Assn. Bus. Communicators, 1979, also 3 awards of merit. Democrat. Roman Catholic. Office: The Konig Ctr 4001 Broadway Suite 4047 San Antonio TX 78209

ROSSETTI, JOSEPH PAUL, trucking industry executive; b. Weymouth, Mass., Nov. 24, 1938; s. Joseph W. and Louise (Petrucelli) R.; m. Shiela U. Natale, May 8, 1965; children: Brenda, Donna. B.S. in mktg., U. Richmond, 1960. Sales rep. P. Ballantine & Sons., Newark, 1964; with Mack Trucks, Inc., Providence, 1964-72; mgr. Mack Trucks, Inc., Syracuse, N.Y., 1972-74; dist. mgr. Mack Trucks, Inc., Maspeth, N.Y., 1974-75; mgr. western mktg. div. Mack Trucks, Inc., Hayward, Calif., 1975-76; v.p. western product div. Mack Trucks, Inc., 1976-77; v.p. mktg. distbn. Mack Trucks, Inc., Allentown, Pa., 1977-81, sr. v.p. sales, from 1981, now exec. v.p. mktg. Served with U.S. Army, 1962-64. Mem. Allentown-Lehigh County C. of C. (gov. 1981—). Roman Catholic. Office: Mack Trucks Inc 2100 Mack Blvd Allentown PA 18105 *

ROSSI, CARMEN ENRICO, utilities executive; b. Buffalo, Nov. 11, 1939; s. Armando and Mary Dominica (Gismondi) R.; m. Savina jane Lucarelli, Sept. 2, 1957; children: Charles C., Daniel J. Diploma in heating and air conditioning, Erie Community Coll., 1972. With Nat. Fuel Gas Dist. Corp., Buffalo, 1958—, asst. gen. foreman, 1984—; speaker in field. Scanner, observer USAF Civil Air Patrol, 1987—. Sgt. USAR, 1957-64. Mem. Masons. Office: Nat Fuel Gas Dist Corp 2121 Military Rd Tonawanda NY 14150

ROSSI, DOMINICK F., JR., advertising agency executive; b. 1942. BA, Boston U., 1962. Exec. v.p. N.W. Ayer Inc., N.Y.C.; market analyst Beech Nut Inc., 1965-67; with N.W. Ayer Inc., N.Y.C., 1967—, v.p., 1972-73, sr. v.p., 1973-80, exec. v.p., 1980—, also bd. dirs. Lt. USN, 1962-65. Office: NW Ayer Inc 1345 Ave of the Americas New York NY 10105 *

ROSSI, LOUIS GERARD, news service director; b. Providence, May 2, 1948; s. Louis and Palmira (Crenca) R.; m. Cintra Lowell Reeve, July 23, 1983; children: Ariana Lowell, Venetia Lowell. BA, U. Bridgeport, 1970; MFA, Tufts U., 1976. Investment exec. Shearson Am. Express, Inc., Newton, Mass., 1978-80; mktg. dir. Herman Pub. Co., Boston, 1980-81; v.p., mktg. dir. Herman Communications Corp., Boston, 1981-83; pres. News-a-tron Corp., Salem, Mass., 1983—; v.p. Global Venture Network, Lincoln, Mass., 1984—. Mem. Boston Computer Soc., New England Commodity Club, 128 Venture Capital Club. Office: News-a-tron Corp One Peabody St Salem MA 01970

ROSSI, RALPH L., tobacco company executive; b. 1928; married. BBA, Pace Coll., 1952. From salesman to div. mgr. to dir. sales U.S. Tobacco Co., Greenwich, Conn., 1955-73, v.p. sales, 1973-77, exec. v.p. ops., 1977-81, exec. v.p. adminstrn., 1981-85, vice-chmn., 1985—, also bd. dirs., 1985—; vice-chmn. UST Inc., 1987—. Office: US Tobacco Co 100 W Putnam Ave Greenwich CT 06830 *

ROSSI, ROBERT JOHN, newspaper executive; b. Pitts., Jan. 5, 1928; s. John Baptist and Carmella Marie (Pastore) R.; B.A., Denison U., 1950; postgrad. 1963; m. Mary Kathryn Rust, June 30, 1951; children—Shannon Elizabeth, Claudia Irene. Advt. dir., bus. mgr. Willoughby (Ohio) News-Herald, 1953-60; advt. dir. Elgin (Ill.) Courier-News, 1960-64; editor and pub. New Albany (Ind.) Tribune and Sunday Ledger, 1964-71; mgmt. cons. Thomson Newspapers, Inc., Chgo., 1971, gen. mgr. So. div., Tampa, Fla., 1972-73; v.p., chief newspaper ops. officer Park Communications Inc., Ithaca, N.Y., 1974-79, 85—, also dir.; editor, gen. mgr. Courier News, Blytheville, Ark., 1983-85, also Osceola Times, Ark.; Bd. dirs. Ky. Opera Assn., Ky.-Ind. Comprehensive Health Planning Council. Served with U.S. Army, 1946. Mem. Am., So. newspaper pubs. assns., Internat. Execs. Service Corps. Club: Filson. Republican. Presbyterian. Home: 323 Winthrop Dr Ithaca NY 14850 Office: Park Communications Inc PO Box 550 Ithaca NY 14851

ROSSITER, BRYANT WILLIAM, chemist, pharmaceutical company executive; b. Ogden, Utah, Mar. 10, 1931; s. Bryant B. and Christine (Peterson) R.; m. Betty Jean Anderson, Apr. 16, 1951; children: Bryant, Mark, Diane, Steven, Linda, Karen, Matthew, Gregory. BA, U. Utah, 1954, PhD, 1957. Researcher Eastman-Kodak Co., Rochester, N.Y., 1957-63, head color phys. chem. lab., 1963-70, dir. chemistry div., 1970-84, dir. sci., tech. devel., 1984-86; pres. Viratek Inc., Costa Mesa, Calif., 1986-89; sr. v.p. ICN Pharms., Costa Mesa, 1989—; sr. editor John Wiley & Sons, N.Y.C., 1970—; chmn. bd. Nucleic Acid Rsch. Inst., Costa Mesa, 1987—; trustee Eastman Dental Ctr., Rochester, 1974—; bd. dirs. Vera & Corp. Editor: (chem. treatises) Physical Methods of Chemistry (11 vols.), 1970-76, Physical Methods, 2d Edit., 1986, Chemical Experimentation Under Extreme Conditions, 1979. Mem. rsch. adv. com. Agy. for Internat. Devel., Washington; presiding officer Ch. Jesus Christ Latter Day Saints, Ea. U.S. and Can., 1959-86. 1st lt. USAFR, 1951-58. Named Hon. Alumni Brigham Young U., Provo, Utah, 1982. Fellow AAAS, A.I.C. (lect. & fellows award, 1988); mem. Internat. Union Pure and Applied Chemistry (chmn. CHEMRAWN com. 1975-87), Am. Chem. Soc. (chmn. internat. activities). Home: 25662 Dillon Rd Laguna Hills CA 92653 Office: Viratek Inc 3300 Hyland Ave Costa Mesa CA 92626

ROSS-JACOBS, RUTH ANN, retired golf and country club executive; b. Milw., Mar. 10, 1934; d. Arthur Theodore and Mary Marilyn (Digert) Kamman; m. Warren Ross, Aug. 9, 1957 (div. Sept. 1972); 1 child, Michael Edward; m. Albert Jacobs, June 28, 1973 (dec. Apr. 1978). B.S., U. Miami, Coral Gables, Fla., 1958; M.S., Wayne State U., 1961; postgrad. U. Wis., 1967-69. R.N., Fla., Wis., Mich. Staff nurse Lafayette Clinic, Detroit, 1958-59; instr. Milw. Inst. Tech., 1962-67; dir. inservice edn. St. Mary's Hosp., Milw., 1963-69; cons. Hearthside Rehab., Milw., 1968-69; owner Peddler Stores, Milw., 1969-72; pres. Jacobs & Densmore Ltd., Toronto, Ont., Can., 1978-83; v.p. Vaughn Ltd., Toronto, 1978-87; pres. Glen Road Leasing Ltd., Toronto, 1978-79, Evnor Apts. Ltd., Toronto, 1978-79, Norman Lathing Ltd., Toronto, 1978-79; v.p. Elgin Mills Investments Ltd., Toronto, 1978-80. Author: Inservice Education, 1967; Nursing Procedures, 1969. Pres. PTO, Boca Raton, Fla., 1973-76; mem. Republican Nat. Com., Washington, 1984—; mem. Inner Circle, Washington, 1984—, Security and Intelligence Found, 1986—, Second Amendment Found., Washington, 1989—, Presdl. Roundtable, Washington, 1987—, Presdl. Task Force, Washington, 1986—, U.S. Com. for Battle Normandy, Washington, 1987—. Recipient stipend NIH, Bethesda, Md., 1959. Mem. Pres. Club USO, Wayne State Univ. Deans Club, Internat. Platform Assn., NRA, Madisons Eagles, Sigma Theta Tau. Republican. Lutheran. Club: Boca Raton. Avocations: real estate investments; travel; charity. Home: 2000 S Ocean Blvd Penthouse K Boca Raton FL 33432

ROSSKAMM, ALAN, retail company executive; b. 1950. With Fabri-Ctrs. of Am., Inc., 1978—, v.p., from 1980, now pres., chief exec. officer. Office: Fabri-Ctrs Am Inc 23550 Commerce Park Rd Beachwood OH 44122

ROSSKAMM, MARTIN, fabric manufacturing company executive; b. 1915. With Fabri-Ctrs. of Am., Inc., Cleve., 1953—, first pres., chief exec. officer, now chmn. bd. dirs. Served with AUS, 1941-45. Office: Fabri-Ctrs Am Inc 23550 Commerce Park Rd Beachwood OH 44122

ROSSLER, WILLIS KENNETH, JR., executive management consultant; b. Houston, Nov. 17, 1946; s. Willis Kenneth and Fay Lee (Olle) R.; BS in Indsl. Engring., Tex. Tech. U., 1969; m. Melva Sue Booker; children: Nancy Kay, Kristen Sue, Deborah Anne, Ryan Konrad, Eric George. Dist. mgr. Tex.-La. ops. Continental Pipe Line Co., Lake Charles, La., 1974-75, mgr. engring., Houston, 1976-77; asst. mgr. corp. planning and devel. Conoco, Inc., Houston, 1977-78; v.p. project devel. PetroUnited, Inc., Houston, 1978-80, pres., 1981-86, also dir. Pres., Village Pl. Community Assn., Houston, 1978, V.p., gen. mgr., Pilko and Assoc., Inc., Houston, 1986—; Mem. Am. Inst. Indsl. Engrs., Am. Petroleum Inst., Houston Mgmt. Council, Intensive Mgmt. Devel. Inst. (adv. dir. 1983-84), Ind. Liquid Terminals Assn. (vice chmn. 1986, chmn.-elect 1987), Am. Mgmt. Assn., Planning Forum (pres. chpt. 1985), Petroleum Club of Houston. Office: Pilko & Assocs Inc 2707 N Loop W Houston TX 77008

ROSSMAN, WILLIAM J., banker; b. Altoona, Pa., Sept. 29, 1941; s. John McClelland and Kathryn Josephine (Morgan) R.; m. Judith D. Arthur, Oct. 20, 1962; 1 child, William Michael. BA in Bus., Duke U., 1984; grad., Bank Adminstrn. Inst., 1984; postgrad., U. Okla., 1977. With Mid-State Bank & Trust Co., Altoona, 1964—, sr. v.p., 1980-85, exec. v.p., 1985, pres., chief exec. officer, 1985—; dir. Altoona Enterprises; treas. Preferred Provider Orgn., Altoona, 1987—. Chmn. U.S. Savs. Bond, Altoona, 1986—; bd. dirs. Altoona Hosp., 1984—; chmn. bldgs., egupment and fin. com., 1985—, mem. exec. com., 1986—, So. Alleghenies Commn., Pvt. Industry Counc., 1986, 87, 88; co-chmn. R.R. Mus., Altoona, 1987; chmn. region X Campaign for Pa. State U., 1987—. Named U.S. Debate Champion Am. Inst. Banking, 1970, Outstanding Young Altoonan Altoona Jaycees, 1977. Mem. Robert Morris Assocs. (pres. 1981-82, nat. bd. dirs. 1988—), Pa. Bankers Assn. (conv. com. 1987—), Park Hills Country Club, Scotch Valley Country Club. Home: 604 Beaumont Dr Altoona PA 16602

ROSSNICK, RON ELLIOT, computer specialist; b. N.Y.C., Apr. 20, 1965. BA, Queens Coll., N.Y.C., 1987. Sales rep. Turbo Techs., Roslyn, N.Y., 1985-87; mgr.. educator Musication, N.Y.C., 1987; freelance cons. Digital Concepts, N.Y.C., 1987—; part time sales person Gt. Am. Meat & Seafood, N.Y.C., 1986; computer specialist Gips & Balkind MacSolutions, N.Y.C. 1988—; freelance cons. Apple MacIntosh systems; account exec. MacTimes, N.Y.C., 1986. Mem. N.Y. Mug Club, Aftertouch Club. Republican. Jewish.

ROSSO, LOUIS T., scientific instrument manufacturing company executive; b. San Francisco, 1933; married. A.B., San Francisco State Coll., 1955; M.B.A., U. Santa Clara, 1967. Product specialist Spinco div. Beckman Instruments, Inc., Fullerton, Calif., 1959-63; mktg. mgr. Beckman Instruments, Inc., 1963-69, mgr. Spinco div., 1969-70, mgr. clin. instruments div., 1970-74, corp. v.p., mgr. analytical instruments group, 1974-80, corp. sr. v.p., 1980-83, pres., 1983—, also bd. dirs.; v.p. SmithKline Beckman Corp., Phila. Office: Beckman Instruments Inc 2500 Harbor Blvd Fullerton CA 92634 *

ROSSOW, KATHERINE GOETTING, infosystems specialist; b. Mpls., Feb. 28, 1948; d. Trester F. and Helen (Johnson) Goetting; m. Ronald Allan Rossow, July 11, 1970; children: Candace, Justin. BA, Bradley U., 1970; cert. in programming, Brown Inst., 1983. Designer, editor Laidlaw Bros Pub., River Forest, Ill., 1970-74; proofreader Eastwood Pub., LeSeur, Minn., 1976-77; programmer Integral Tech. Corp., Bloomington, Minn., 1983-84; software specialist, trainer Entré Computer Ctr., Green Bay, Wis., 1985-87; cons., Green Bay, Wis., 1987-89; info. cons. Schreiber Foods Inc., Green Bay, 1989—; instr. N.E. Wis. Tech. Coll., 1987—. Home and Office: 2694 Sequoia Ln Green Bay WI 54313

ROSTENBACH, KEVIN VICTOR, infosystems specialist, consultant; b. Davenport, Iowa, Sept. 23, 1959; s. Marvin Henry and Loisfaye (Bahr) R.; m. Jean Lee Sasser, Aug. 16, 1978 (div. June, 1986); m. Karla Lynn Bowden, Nov. 22, 1986. Postgrad., Am. Inst. Commerce, 1982. Data processing coordinator Am. Inst. Commerce, Bettendorf, Iowa, 1982-87; personal computer analyst, programmer First Fed. Savs. and Loan, Davenport, Iowa, 1987—; ptnr. Profl. Assessment Cons., Computer Aided Tools for Psychologists; chief exec. officer KVR Systems; cons. Vera French Mental Health Ctr., Davenport. Mem. Soc. Data Educators, Data Processing Mgmt. Assn. (exec. v.p. Ill. chpt., 1985, local pres. 1986), Internat. Platform Assn. Home: PO Box 2358 Davenport IA 52809 Office: First Fed Savs & Loan 131 W 3d St Davenport IA 52801

ROSTOW, WALT WHITMAN, economist, educator; b. N.Y.C., Oct. 7, 1916; s. Victor Aaron and Lillian (Helman) R.; m. Elspeth Vaughan Davies, June 26, 1947; children: Peter Vaughan, Ann Larner. B.A., Yale U., 1936, Ph.D., 1940; Rhodes scholar, Balliol Coll., 1936-38. Instr. econs. Columbia U., 1940-41; asst. chief German-Austrian econ. div. Dept. State 1945-46; Harmsworth prof. Am. history Oxford (Eng.) U., 1946-47; asst. to exec. sec. Econ. Commn. for Europe, 1947-49; Pitt. prof. Am. history Cambridge (Eng.) U., 1949-50; prof. econ. history MIT, 1950-60; staff mem. Center Internat. Studies, 1951-60; dep. spl. asst. to Pres. for nat. security affairs 1961; counselor, chmn. policy planning council Dept. State, 1961-66; spl. asst. to Pres. 1966-69; U.S. rep., ambassador Inter-Am. com. Alliance for Progress, 1964-66; now Rex G. Baker Jr. prof. polit. economy, depts. econs. and history U. Tex., Austin, prof. emeritus; mem. Bd. Fgn. Scholarships, 1969-72. Author: The American Diplomatic Revolution, 1947, Essays on the British Economy of the Nineteenth Century, 1948, The Process of Economic Growth, 1953, 2d edit., 1960, (with A.D. Gayer, A.J. Schwartz) The Growth and Fluctuation of the British Economy, 1790-1850, 1953, 2d edit., 1975, (with A. Levin, others) The Dynamics of Soviet Society, 1953, (with others) The Prospects for Communist China, 1954, (with R.W. Hatch) An American Policy in Asia, 1955, (with M.F. Millikan) A Proposal: Key to an Effective Foreign Policy, 1957, The United States in the World Arena, 1960, The Stages of Economic Growth, 1960, 2d edit., 1971, View from the Seventh Floor, 1964, A Design for Asian Development, 1965, (with William E. Griffith) East-West Relations: Is Detente Possible?, 1969, Politics and the Stages of Growth, 1971, The Diffusion of Power, 1972, How It All Began, 1975, The World Economy: History and Prospect, 1978, Getting From Here to There, 1978, Why the Poor Get Richer and the Rich Slow Down, 1980, Pre-Invasion Bombing Strategy: General Eisenhower's Decision of March 25, 1944, 1981, British Trade Fluctuations, 1868-1896: A Chronicle and a Commentary, 1981, The Division of Europe After World War II: 1946, 1981, Europe After Stalin: Eisenhower's Three Decisions of March 11, 1953, 1982, Open Skies: Eisenhower's Proposal of July 21, 1955, 1982, The Barbaric Counter-Revolution: Cause and Cure, 1983, Eisenhower, Kennedy, and Foreign Aid, 1985, The United States and the Regional Organization of Asia and the Pacific: 1965-1985, 1986, Rich Countries and Poor Countries, 1987, Essays on a Half Century: Ideas, Policies and Action, 1988, Theorists of Economic Growth From David Hume to the Present with a Perspective on the Next Century, 1989, History, Policy, and Economic Theory, 1989; editor: The Economics of Take-Off Into Sustained Growth, 1963. Served as maj. OSS, AUS, 1942-45. Decorated Legion of Merit, Hon. Order Brit. Empire (mil.); recipient Presdl. Medal of Freedom with distinction. Mem. Am. Acad. Arts and Scis., Am. Philos Soc., Mass. Hist. Soc. Clubs: Cosmos (Washington); Elizabethan (New Haven). Home: 1 Wildwind Point Austin TX 78746

ROSZTOCZY, FERENC ERNO, business exec.; b. Szeged, Hungary, Aug. 16, 1932; came to U.S., 1957, naturalized, 1962; s. Ferenc Lipot and Edith Jolan (Kunzl) R.; M.S., U. Szeged, 1955; Ph.D., U. Calif. at Berkeley, 1961; m. Diane Elder, Dec. 21, 1963; children—Thomas Ferenc, Robert Anthony, Stephanie Elder, Edward Joseph. Phys. chemist Stanford Research Inst., Menlo Park, Calif., 1961-64; mem. tech. staff Bell Labs., Murray Hill, N.J., 1964-68; mgr. semicondr. materials Bell & Howell, Pasadena, Calif., 1968-69; mgr. semicondr. crystal growth and device engring. Varian Assos., Palo Alto, Calif., 1969-75; dir. Ariz. Machinery Co., Avondale, 1974—, pres., 1975—, chmn. bd., 1976—; pres. Stotz Farms, Inc., 1979— ; dir. Ariz. Indsl. Machinery Co., 1975—. Cons. Siltec Corp., Menlo Park, Calif., 1971-72. Bd. trustees Agua Fria High Sch., 1981, pres. 1986—. Roman Catholic. Club: Wigwam Country. Contbr. articles to profl. jours. Patentee in field. Home: 1010 Acacia Cir Litchfield Park AZ 85340 Office: Ariz Machinery Co PO Box 63 Avondale AZ 85323

ROTBERG, EUGENE HARVEY, international investment banker, lawyer; b. Phila., Jan. 19, 1930; s. Irving Bernard and Blanche Grace (Levick) R.; m. Iris Sybil Comens, Aug. 29, 1954; children—Diana Golda, Pamela Lynn. B.S., Temple U., 1951; LL.B., U. Pa., 1954. Bar: Pa., D.C. 1955. Mem. spl. study U.S. Securities Markets, Securities and Exchange Commn., Washington, 1957-63; chief counsel Office Policy Research, Securities and Exchange Commn., Washington, 1963-66; v.p., treas. World Bank Group, Washington, 1969-87; exec. v.p. Merrill Lynch & Co., N.Y.C., 1987—. Served with U.S. Army, 1954-55. Recipient Disting. Service award Securities and Exchange Commn., 1968; named Alumnus of Year Temple U., 1969. Home: 7211 Brickyard Rd Potomac MD 20854 Office: Merrill Lynch & Co Inc Washington Harbour 3000 K St NW Washington DC 20007

ROTCHFORD, PATRICIA KATHLEEN, insurance and finance lawyer; b. Chgo., Nov. 17, 1945; d. Charles E. Sr. and Mary (Rodde) R.; 1 child, John. BA with honors, Rosary Coll., River Forest, Ill., 1966; JD, No. Ill. U., 1979. Bar: Ill. 1979. Tchr. pub. schs. Schiller Park, Ill., 1966-76; sole practice Elmhurst, Ill., 1977-79; assoc. Shand, Morahan, Evanston, Ill., 1979-83; corp. counsel CNA Fin., Chgo., 1983-86; gen. counsel, v.p. and corp. sec. MMI Cos., Bannockburn, Ill., 1986-87; gen. counsel, v.p., corp. sec. Inland Group, Northbrook, Ill., 1987—; legal counsel/fin. and ins. advisor Nat. Med. Assoc., Washington, 1988—; mem. nat. bd. dirs. NAFWIC. Author: (pamphlet) Handle Your Own Claims, 1983, (book) Women's Resource Guide, 1988, Women's Insurance and Financial Resource Guide, 1988. Counselor for battered women. Mem. Womens Bar Assn. Ill. (active coms. and activities), Corp. Councils Am., Womens Exec. Network, Nat. Assn. Women in Careers. Office: PO Box 4422 Northbrook IL 60065

ROTH, DAVID RICHARD, economic analysis manager, accountant; b. Wauseon, Ohio, Dec. 28, 1951; s. Richard Ellis and Imogene R. (Beck) R.; m. Stacia Lynn Taylor, Mar. 30, 1985. BS in Acctg., Bowling Green State U., 1974; MBA, U. Toledo, 1983. CPA, cert. internal auditor, cert. real estate agt. Auditor Ernst & Whinney, Toledo, 1974-75; auditor in charge Ernst & Whinney, 1975-76; auditor Owens Corning Fiberglass, Toledo, 1976-77; sr. auditor Owens Corning Fiberglass, 1977-78, fin. analyst, 1978-81, mgmt. info. systems analyst, 1981-84; planning mgr. Libbey Owens Ford Co., Toledo, 1984-86; econ. analysis mgr. Health Care and Retirement Corp., Toledo, 1986—; pres. programs Planning Forum, Toledo, 1989, bd. dirs., 1986-88; mgmt. instr. u. Toledo, 1984; planning leader Ohio CPA's Health Care Conf., Toledo, 1988. organizer Rep. Com., Toledo, 84-88; exec. advisor Jr. Achievement, 1987-88. Mem. Ohio Soc. CPA's (planning leader 1987-88), Beta Alpha Psi, Beta Gamma Sigma. Republican. Presbyterian. Home: 9613 St Andrews St Perrysburg OH 43551 Office: Health Care & Retirement Corp Summit St Toledo OH 43666

ROTH, DONALD C., banker; b. Washington, May 18, 1943; s. Leo A. and Margaret G. (Gaynor) R.; m. Mary Beth Stanton; children: Stacey, Collins, Matthew, Christopher. BA in Polit. Sci., Princeton U., 1965; MBA in Fin., U. Chgo., 1970; MSc in Econs., London Sch. Econs., 1970. V.p. Merrill Lynch Internat., Tokyo, 1971-73; chmn. Merrill Lynch Internat., London, 1981-83; dir. Merrill Lynch Internat. Bank, London, 1973-77, Chase Manhattan Ltd., Hong Kong, 1977-79; dep. mng. dir. Chase Manhattan Ltd., London, 1979-80; chmn. Merrill Lynch Europe, London, 1983-85, Merrill Lynch Pvt. Capital, N.Y.C., 1985-87; v.p., treas. World Bank, Washington, 1988—. Trustee Gettysburg (Pa.) Coll., 1988—. 1st lt. U.S. Army, 1967-69. Mem. Univ. Coll. Club (trustee Princeton, N.J. chpt. 1986-88), F St. Club (Washington). Roman Catholic. Home: 5020 Millwood Ln Washington DC 20016 Office: World Bank 1818 H St NW Rm E4071 Washington DC 20433

ROTH, HARRY FRANCIS, livestock breeding company executive; b. Nazareth, Pa., Jan. 7, 1931; s. Harry Franklin and Carrie M. (Miller) R.; m. Ruth Young, June 14, 1952; children: Ann, Sarah, Mary. BS, Pa. State U., 1954. Asst. agt. York County Agr. Extension Service, York, Pa., 1954-56; fieldman, sire analyst, mgr. Western Pa. Artificial Insemination Co., Clarion, 1956-64; dir. ops. Western Pa. Artificial Insemination Co. now Atlantic Breeders Coop., Lancaster, Pa., 1964-84, gen. mgr., 1985—; appointed dir. Ptnrship Bd. Econ. Devel., State of Pa., 1987; supt. youth div. All Am. Dairy Show, Harrisburg, 1970-82; chmn. agr. task force Econ. Devel. Pa., 1987. Mem. Nat. Assn. Animal Breeders (pres. 1983—). Home: 1585 Apollo Dr Lancaster PA 17601 Office: Atlantic Breeders Coop 1575 Apollo Dr Lancaster PA 17601

ROTH, JOHN A., communications executive. Exec. v.p. prodn. line mgmt. No. Telecom Ltd., Mississaugai, Ont., Can. Office: No Telecom Ltd, 3 Robert Speck Pkwy, Mississauga, ON Canada L4Z 3C8 *

ROTH, MARTIN G., finance company executive; b. 1937; married. BS, Northwestern U., 1959; JD, DePaul U., 1966. CPA. With Price Waterhouse & Co., Chgo., 1959-63, Fein & Permen, Chgo., 1966-69; asst. sec. Greyhound Fin. Corp., Phoenix, 1969-71, asst. v.p., 1971-72, v.p., asst. sec., 1972-81, sr. v.p. ops., 1981—. Office: Greyhound Fin Corp Greyhound Tower Phoenix AZ 85077 *

ROTH, MERRILL HENRY JACOB, real estate developer; b. Phila., Aug. 8, 1936; m. Helen Margaret Gladman, Apr. 2, 1982; stepchildren: Milena Nicole, Lauren Michele. BA, Pa. State U., 1958; postgrad., Mich. State U., 1970. With Monumental Corp., Balt., 1967-71; ptnr. Deptford Mall Assn., Phila., 1974—, Broadway Sq., Tyler, Tex., 1974-87, Independence Mall Assoc., 1978—, Occasions of Phila., 1971-82, Piedmont Mall Assoc., Danville, Va., 1982—; pres. Occasions of N.C., Wilmington, 1978-82, M.H.J. Roth, Ltd., King of Prussia, Pa., 1986—; exec. dir. TLC Comml. Ventures, Norristown, Pa., 1986—. Mem. com. Panhandle Civic Assn., Tredifryn Twp., Pa., 1986—; mem. exec. com. C.C. Morris Library; donor ARC, Phila., 1983—; cons. City of Savannah, 1986-87. With USAF, 1958-59. Mem. Phila. Bd. Realtors, Internat. Council Shopping Ctrs., Nat. Assn. Office and Industry Parks, Pickwick Club, British Officers Club, Racquet Club, Main Line Ski Club (bd. dirs. 1971—), Merion Cricket Club. Libertarian. Unitarian.

ROTH, MICHAEL I., financial executive; b. Bklyn., Nov. 22, 1945; s. Harry A. and Sally (Kutin) R.; m. Carole A. Snofsky, Aug. 10, 1968; children—Barrie, Marc, Andrew. BS, CCNY, 1967; JD, Boston U., 1971; LL.M., NYU, 1973. Bar: N.Y. 1971. CPA: N.Y. 1973, Conn. 1973. With Coopers & Lybrand, N.Y.C., 1969-76; ptnr. Stamford, Conn., 1976-82; exec. v.p. corp. fin., tax and adminstrn. Primerica Corp. (formerly Am. Can Co.), Greenwich, Conn., 1982-87, exec. v.p., 1987, chief fin. officer, 1987-88; exec. v.p., chief fin. officer MONY Fin. Svcs., N.Y.C., 1989—; bd. dirs. Nat. Benefit Life Ins. Co., N.Y.C., Am. Capital Mgmt. and Research, Inc., Houston. Bd. dirs. Child Guidance Ctr., Stamford, 1984-85; trustee Temple BethEl, Stamford, 1984-85. Mem. Am. Inst. CPA's, Conn. Soc. CPA's, Stamford Tax Assn. (pres. 1981-82). Office: MONY Fin Svcs 1740 Broadway New York NY 10019

ROTH, NORMAN STEWART, accountant, financial planner; b. Passaic, N.J., Oct. 5, 1955; s. Alan and Ellen (Guth) R. BS in Acctg., Rutgers U., 1977; MBA in Taxation, Fairleigh Dickenson U., 1981. CPA, N.J.; cert. fin. planner. Sr. mgr. Ernst & Whinney, Newark, 1977—; adj. prof. St. Peter's Coll., Jersey City, 1985. Mem. N.J. Soc. CPA's (bd.dirs. Passaic County chpt. 1985). Home: 33 Ascension St. Passaic NJ 07055 Office: Ernst & Whinney 550 Broad St Newark NJ 07102

ROTH, RICHARD C., management consultant; b. N.Y.C., July 26, 1937; s. Carl E. and Rose M. Roth; m. Barbara A. Swift, June 13, 1959; children: Steven R., Susan E., Kevin R. BBA, Manhattan Coll., 1959. Account exec. Batten, Barton, Durstine & Osborn, 1959-62; v.p. new products Block Drug Co., Jersey City, 1962-75; sr. v.p. Metaframe Corp., Elmwood Park, N.J., 1975-77; pres. Barich Co., Milltown, N.J., 1977—, Pet Village, Inc., Stroudsburg, Pa., 1980—; exec. v.p. Maspeth (N.Y.) Mills Ltd., 1983-87; pres. County Village Enterprises, Inc., Milltown, 1986—; lectr. NYU, 1974-75; cons. Assn. for Retarded Citizens, Bergen-Passaic, N.J., 1982-83. Patentee medicinal device. Campaign cons. Middlesex County (N.J.) Rep. Com., 1966-71, pres. Milltown Rep. Club, 1969-71; fund drive chmn. Milltown LIbrary Assn., 1973, trustee, 1974-76. Mem. Assn. Nat. Advertisers (founder and chmn. new products mktg. com. 1971-76), Nat. Acad. TV Arts and Scis.

ROTH, RUSSELL ROBERT, holding company executive; b. Chgo., Nov. 18, 1946; s. Robert Bennett and Bernadine J. (Johnson) R.; m. Cheryl Lynne Wait, June 8, 1968 (div.); m. Robbie Robertson, Dec. 15, 1979; children: Danielle, Rebecca. BS in Econs., U. Kans., 1968; MBA in Fin., U. Mich., 1972. Fin. analyst Ford Motor Co., Dearborn, Mich., 1968-72, Rockwell Internat., Troy, Mich., 1972-77; fin. exec. Bendix Co., Southfield, Mich., 1978-82; chief fin. officer Cessna Aircraft Co., Wichita, Kans., 1983-86, Sotheby's Holding Co., N.Y.C., 1986—. Served to 1st lt., U.S. Army, 1969-74. Republican. Avocations: golf, tennis, bridge, flying small planes. Home: 275-B Park St New Canaan CT 06840 Office: Sotheby's Holdings Inc 1334 York Ave New York NY 10021

ROTHBERG, SOL, lawyer, industrialist; b. N.Y.C., July 29, 1910; s. Samuel and Ada (Shayne) R.; m. Dorothy Platka, Jan. 9, 1938; children: David, Richard, Samuel. LL.B., Ind. U., 1933. Bar: Ind. 1933, U.S. Supreme Ct. Since practiced in Ft. Wayne; sr. partner firm Rothberg, Gallmeyer, Fruechtenicht & Logan, from 1951, now of counsel; chmn. bd. Bowser, Inc., 1960—, Wabash Smelting, Inc., 1958—, Gen. Smelting Co.; dir., counsel Ind. Bank & Trust Co., Ft. Wayne, D & N Micro Products, Ft. Wayne, Computer Decision Support, Alexandria, Va., Summit Bank, chmn. fin. compensation com.; former chmn. bd., dir. Summit Labs., Inc. Founder Ft. Wayne Child Guidance Clinic, 1950, pres., 1953; mem. budget and priority coms. Community Chest and United Fund, Ft. Wayne, 1949; pres. Ft. Wayne Jewish Fedn., 1949; mem. Econ. Devel. Authority Ind., 1972; now chmn. bd. Ind. Employment Devel. Commn.; dir. Allen County Dept. Pub. Welfare, 1936; chmn. United Jewish Appeal, Ft. Wayne, 1953; bd. dirs. Parkview Meml. Hosp. Found.; adv. exec. com. Ind. U. Sch. Bus. Appointed to Counsel of Sagamore of the Wabash by Gov. Indiana. Mem. ABA (mem. com. on banking instns. and regulated investment cos., taxation sect.), Ind. Bar Assn. (life, dir. trial sect. 1958), Allen County Bar Assn. (treas. 1943), Am. Judicature Soc., Bar Assn. 7th and 6th Circuit Fed. Ct., Ind. Soc. Chgo., B'nai Brith (pres. Ft. Wayne chpt. 1943), Ind. U. Alumni Assn. (Ft. Wayne pres. 1934), "I" Mens Letter Assn., Ft. Wayne Country Club, Quest Club (Ft. Wayne), Tamarisk Country Club (Palm Springs, Calif.). Jewish (pres. congregation 1951). Home: 4721 Covington Rd Fort Wayne IN 46804 Office: Indiana Bank Bldg Fort Wayne IN 46802

ROTHENBERG, ELLIOT CALVIN, lawyer, writer; b. Mpls., Nov. 12, 1939; s. Sam S. and Claire Sylvia (Feller) R.; m. Sally Smayling; children: Margaret, Katie. B.A. summa cum laude, U. Minn., 1961; J.D., Harvard U. (Fulbright fellow), 1964. Assoc. project dir. Brookings Inst., Washington, 1966-67; fgn. service officer, legal advisor U.S. Dept. State, Washington, 1968-73; Am. Embassy, Saigon; U.S. Mission to the UN; nat. law dir. Anti-Defamation League, N.Y.C., 1973-74; legal dir. Minn. Public Interest Research Group, Mpls., 1974-77; admitted to Minn. bar, 1966, D.C. 1968, N.Y., 1974, U.S. Supreme Ct. 1972, U.S. Ct. Appeals (2nd cir.) 1974, U.S. Ct. Appeals (8th cir.) 1975, U.S. Dist. Ct. Minn. 1966 ; pvt. practice law, Mpls., 1977—; adj. prof. William Mitchell Coll. Law, St. Paul, 1983—. State bd. dirs. YMCA Youth in Govt. Program, 1981-84 ; v.p. Twin Cities chpt. Am. Jewish Com., 1980-84 ; mem. Minn. House of Reps., 1978-82, asst. floor leader (whip), 1981-82; pres., dir. North Star Legal Found., 1983—; Legal affairs editor Public Research Syndicated, 1986—; Mem. citizens adv. com. Voyageurs Nat. Park, 1979-81. Fulbright fellow, 1964-65; recipient Legis. Evaluation Assembly Legis. Excellence award, 1980, Vietnam Civilian Service medal U.S Dept. State, 1970, North Star award, U. Minn., 1961. Mem. Am. Bar Assn., Harvard Law Sch. Assn., Minn. Bar Assn., Am. Legion, Mensa, Phi Beta Kappa. Republican. Jewish. Contbr. articles to profl. and scholarly jours., newspapers, popular magazines; author: (with Zelman Cowen) Sir John Latham and Other Papers, 1965. Avocations: long distance running, classical music, baseball. Home: 3901 W 25th St Saint Louis Park MN 55416 Office: 500 Plymouth Bldg Minneapolis MN 55402

ROTHENBERG, MARK ALAN, architect; b. Jersey City, Feb. 7, 1951; s. Morris and Sylvia (Kurtz) R. BSCE, George Washington U., 1973; BArch, U. So. Calif., 1976. Designer McClellan Cruz Gaylord, Pasadena, Calif., 1976-78; pres. Rothenberg Sawasy Architects, Los Angeles, 1978—. Mem. AIA. Republican. Office: Rothenberg Sawasy Architects 953 E Third St Los Angeles CA 90013

ROTHERMEL, DANIEL KROTT, metals company executive, lawyer; b. West Reading, Pa., Mar. 21, 1938; s. Daniel Grim and Ruth Elizabeth (Krott) R.; m. Sarah Finch, July 9, 1960; children: Anne, Daniel F., K. Melissa. BS, Pa. State U., 1960; JD, Am. U., 1966. Bar: D.C. 1967. Acct. Lukens Steel Co., Coatesville, Pa., 1960-61; sole practice Reading, Pa., 1966-68; atty. Carpenter Tech. Corp., Reading, 1968-70, resident counsel, 1970-78, asst. sec., 1972-73, sec., 1973—, v.p., gen. counsel, 1978—; bd. dirs. Penn Savs. Bank, Sovereign Bancorp, Inc. Mem. Inst. Community Affairs, Pa. State U., 1974-78; bd. dirs. Berks County chpt. ARC, 1983-86; mem., chmn. adv. bd. Pa. State U., Berks campus, 1982—. Served to lt. USNR, 1961-66. Mem. ABA, D.C. Bar Assn., Am. Iron and Steel Inst., Am. Soc. Corp. Secs., U.S. C. of C., Pa. C. of C., Reading C. of C. Republican. Lutheran. Club: Rotary. Home: RD 11 Box 359-C Reading PA 19607 Office: Carpenter Tech Corp 101 W Bern St Reading PA 19603

ROTHFELD, MICHAEL B., investment banker; b. N.Y.C., May 19, 1947; m. Ella Foshay, May 21, 1970; 2 children. BA, Columbia U., 1969, MS, 1971, MBA, 1971. Assoc. editor Fortune Time Inc., N.Y.C., 1971-74, asst. to chmn. bd. dirs., 1974-76; assoc. Salomon Bros., N.Y.C., 1976-79, v.p., 1979-83; v.p. First Boston Corp., N.Y.C., 1983-85, mng. dir., 1985—. Office: 1st Boston Corp Park Avenue Pla New York NY 10055

ROTHMAN, ADAM ALAN, financial consultant; b. Bklyn., Apr. 5, 1960; s. Bernard and Barbara (Schaeffer) R.; m. Suzanne Tiefenbrunn, April 7, 1960; 1 child Seth Daniel. BBA, Am. U., 1982. Acct. exec. Invention Mktg. Co., Washington, 1982-84; sales assoc. Michael Fransblau Assoc., Hartsdale, N.Y., 1984-85, mgr. benefits div., 1985-87; dir. ops. Fransblau Rothman and Assocs., Hartsdale, N.Y., 1987—. Author: Wealth Accumulation Strategy for Educators, 1987. Officer Larchmont Fire Dept. Mem. Interstate Alliance Fin. Planners. Democrat. Jewish. Office: Franzflau Rothman & Assocs 260 E Hartsdale Ave Hartsdale NY 10530

ROTHMAN, BERNARD, lawyer; b. N.Y.C., Aug. 11, 1932; s. Harry and Rebecca (Fritz) R.; m. Barbara Joan Schaeffer, Aug. 1953; children—Brian, Adam, Helene. B.A. cum laude, CCNY, 1953; LL.B., NYU, 1959. Bar: N.Y. 1959, U.S Dist. Ct. (ea. and so. dists.) N.Y. 1962, U.S. Ct. Apls. (2d cir.) 1965, U.S. Supreme Ct. 1966, U.S. Tax Ct. 1971. Assoc. Held, Telchin & Held, 1961-62; asst. U.S. atty. U.S. Dept. Justice, 1962-66; assoc. Edward Gettinger & Peter Gettinger, 1966-68; ptnr. Schwartz, Rothman & Abrams, P.C., 1968-78; ptnr. Finkelstein, Bruckman, Wohl, Most & Rothman, N.Y.C., 1978—; acting judge Village of Larchmont, 1981—, dep. Village atty., 1974-81, former arbitrator Civil Ct. N.Y.C., family disputes panel Am. Arbitration Assn., guest lectr. domestic relations and family law Cardozo Law Sch., Albert Einstein Coll. Med., Hofstra Law Sch.; mem. exec. bd., past v.p. Westchester Putnam council Boy Scouts Am., past mem. nat. council, 1977-81, recipient Silver Beaver award, Wood Badge award; past pres. Congregation B'Nai Israel, 1961-63; pres. B'Nai B'rith, Larchmont chpt., 1981-83. Fellow Am. Acad. Matrimonial Lawyers (co-chmn. interdisciplinary com. on mental health and family law 1986—, bd. govs. N.Y. chpt. 1986-88); mem. ABA (family law sect.), N.Y. State Bar Assn. (exec. com. family law sect. 1982—, co-chmn. com. on mediation and arbitration 1982-88, com. on legis. 1978-88, com. on child custody 1985—, chmn. Commn. on AIDS & matrimonial law, contbr. articles Family Law Review, co-author Leaving Home Family Law Review, 1987—, Aids & Matrimonial law N.Y. State Bar Jour. 1988), Assn. of Bar of City of N.Y., N.Y. State Magistrates Assn., Westchester Magistrates Assn. Democrat. Clubs: N.Y. Road Runners, Limousine 6 Track. Office: Finkelstein Bruckman Wohl Most & Rothman 801 2d Ave New York NY 10017

ROTHMAN, FRANK, lawyer, motion picture company executive; b. Los Angeles, Dec. 24, 1926; s. Leon and Rose (Gendel) R.; m. Mariana Richardson, Aug. 7, 1985; children: Steven, Robin, Susan. B.A., U. So. Calif., 1949, LL.B., 1951. Bar: Calif. 1952, D.C., U.S. Dist. Ct. (cen. dist.) Calif. 1951. Dep. city atty. City of Los Angeles, 1951-55; mem. law firm Wyman, Bautzer, Rothman, Kuchel & Silbert, Los Angeles, 1956-82; chmn. bd., chief exec. officer MGM-UA Entertainment Co., Culver City, Calif., 1982-86; ptnr. Skadden Arps Slate, L.A., 1986—. Bd. editors U. So. Calif. Law Rev., 1948. Served with USAAF, 1945-46. Fellow Am. Coll. Trial Lawyers; mem. L.A. Bar Assn., Calif. Bar Assn., Univ. Club. Democrat. Home: 10555 Rocca Pl Los Angeles CA 90077 Office: Skadden Arps Slate 300 S Grand Ave #3400 Los Angeles CA 90071

ROTHMEIER, STEVEN GEORGE, airline executive; b. Mankato, Minn., Oct. 4, 1946; s. Edwin George and Alice Joan (Johnson) R. BBA, U. Notre Dame, 1968; MBA, U. Chgo., 1972. Corp. fin. analyst Northwest Airlines, Inc., St. Paul, 1973, mgr. econ. analysis, 1973-78, dir. econ. planning, 1978, v.p. fin., treas., 1978-82, exec. v.p., treas., dir., 1982-83, exec. v.p. fin. and adminstrn., treas., dir., 1983, pres., chief operating officer, 1984, pres., chief exec. officer, 1985-86, chmn., chief exec. officer, 1986—, also bd. dirs.; bd. dirs. First Bank System, Honeywell, Inc.; trustee Minn. Mut. Life Ins., U. Chgo. Served to 1st lt. U.S. Army, 1968-71. Decorated Bronze Star. Mem. Air Transport Assn. Am. (chmn. econs. and fin. council 1981). Republican. Roman Catholic. Clubs: Mpls.; Minn. Office: NW Airlines Inc Mpls-St Paul Internat Airport Saint Paul MN 55111 *

ROTHROCK, JAN CAMPBELL, accountant; b. Duncan, Okla., Jan. 24, 1935; d. Robert E. and Mary Louise (Ingram) Campbell; m. Edward Strike Rothrock, Mar. 6, 1972; children: Faun, Ross, Strike III, Robin, Robert, Jon, Jan. Student, U. Houston, 1972, 75, 77, U. St. Thomas, summer 1975, spring 1977, Am. Coll. Advanced Ctr., 1980, Keele U., Eng., summer 1976. CPA, Tex.; cert. real estate broker. Sec.-treas. RES Leasing and Mgmt., Houston, 1967-72; pres. Jan C. Rothrock, Broker, Houston, 1972—; owner Jan Campbell, CPA, Houston, 1979—; bd. dirs. Sandy Reed & Assocs., Inc., Total Life Care Ctr.; lectr. in field. Bd. dirs. Lupus Found. Am., Houston, 1985, 88—, hon. bd. dirs., 1986—, chmn. fund raising, 1986—, mem. chmn., 1986; acctg. advisor S.W. Literary Arts Council, 1986—; trustee Big State Grass Farms, 1979—, AH & LB Wingate Charitable Trust, 1982—; actg. advisor Tex. A&M Marine Mammal Standing Network, Tx. Marine Mammal Stranding Network, 1987, incorporator, bd. dirs., 1988—. Mem. Tex. Assn. Realtors, Nat. Assn. Realtors, Houston Bd. Realtors, Am. Inst. CPA's, Tex. Soc. CPA's, Nat. Conf. CPA Practitioners, Internat. Platform Assn., Phi Eta Sigma, Alpha Lambda Delta. Home: 3257 Ella Lee Ln Houston TX 77019

ROTHSCHILD, DEBORAH EVE, marketing executive; b. N.Y.C., Nov. 22, 1953; d. Siegfried and Mia (Levi) R. BA summa cum laude, CCNY, 1974. Instr. writing Purdue U., West Lafayette, Ind., 1974-75; dir. mktg. communications Price Waterhouse, N.Y.C., 1975—. Mem. Internat. Assn. Bus. Communicators, Phi Beta Kappa. Office: Price Waterhouse 1251 Ave of Americas New York NY 10020

ROTHSCHILD, JAMES ALAN, management consultant; b. N.Y.C., Mar. 23, 1946; s. Lloyd David and Bernice Marjorie (Newmark) R.; B.S. in Chem. Engring., U. Pitts., 1967; M.B.A., Case Western Res. U., 1970; m. Vida Margurette Lauric, June 22 1968; children—Aaron, Haylee. Process engr. Olin Corp., Ashtabula, Ohio, 1968-70, fin. analyst, Stamford, Conn., 1971; mgmt. cons. Touche Ross & Co., N.Y.C., 1972-76; mgmt. cons. J. Rothschild Assoc., Georgetown, Conn., 1976-79; prin. Georgetown Cons. Group, Ridgefield, Conn., 1979-84; prin. Rothschild Fin. Cons., Wilton, Conn., 1985—. Home and Office: 115 Scarlet Oak Dr Wilton CT 06897

ROTHSTEIN, GERALD ALAN, investment company executive; b. Bklyn., Oct. 18, 1941; s. Manuel and Gertrude (Buxbaum) R.; m. Cynthia Bea Pincus, June 11, 1967; children: Michael Neil, Lori Pamela, Meryl Patricia. BBA, City Coll. N.Y., 1962; MBA, U. Pa., 1965. 1st v.p. Shearson Hammill & Co., N.Y.C., 1966-74, Shearson Hayden Store, N.Y.C., 1974-75; v.p. William D. Witter, Inc., N.Y.C., 1975-76; v.p. Oppenheimer & Co. Inc., N.Y.C., 1976-79, sr. v.p., 1979-83, mng. dir., 1983-86, exec. v.p., dir. rsch., 1986—; bd. dirs. The Otto Gerdau & Co., N.Y.C. Mem. N.Y. Soc. Security Analyst, Inst. Chartered Fin. Analyst. Office: Oppenheimer & Co Inc Oppenheimer Tower World Financial Ctr New York NY 10281

ROTHSTEIN, LAWRENCE IRWIN, real estate company executive; b. N.Y.C., Oct. 7, 1952; s. Alex and Audrey (Alexander) R.; m. Nina Gail Mishkin, Dec. 3, 1978; children: Ira, Adam. BSBA in Acctg., U. Denver, 1974; MS in Taxation, Fla. Internat. U., 1982. CPA, N.Y., Fla. Mgr. Touche Ross & Co., N.Y.C. and Miami, Fla., 1974-80; treas. Bayuk Cigars, Ft. Lauderdale, Fla., 1980-82; sr. v.p. Courtland Group, Inc., Miami, 1983; v.p. HMG Capital Corp., Miami, 1983, Transco Realty Trust, Miami, 1983; sr. v.p., chief fin. officer HMG/Courtland Properties, Inc., Miami, 1983—. Charter mem. Beacon Council, Miami, 1985; fundraiser South Broward Fedn., Hollywood, Fla., Israel Bonds, Miami, Rep. Party, Miami. Mem. AICPA, Fla. Inst. CPA's, Grove Isle Club, Emerald Hills Country Club. Republican. Jewish. Home: 3070 N 34th St Hollywood FL 33021 Office: HMG/Courtland Properties Inc 2701 S Bayshore Dr Miami FL 33133

ROTHWEILER, STEPHEN MICHAEL, vocational school administrator; b. St. Louis, Dec. 20, 1951; s. William Judge and Mareta (Christ) R. BA, U. Mo., St. Louis, 1979; MA in Counseling and Mgmt., Webster U., 1981. Facility mgr. Ariz. Bapt. Children's Services, Phoenix, 1973-78; psychiat. specialist Mo. Div. Social Services, St. Louis, 1978-82; dir. Vocat. Tng. Ctr., St. Louis, 1983-86; exec. dir. Profl. Bus. Coll., St. Louis, 1986—. Republican. Roman Catholic. Home: 3923 Dover Pl Saint Louis MO 63116 Office: Profl Bus Sch 9369 Olive Rd Saint Louis MO 63132

ROTHWELL, ALBERT FALCON, retired natural resource company executive, retired lawyer; b. N.Y.C., Sept. 2, 1926; s. Albert Cyril and Finita Maria (Falcon) R.; m. Jane Thomas, June 4, 1949; children—Susan, Peter, Anne, James. AB, Princeton U., 1948; LLB, Columbia U., 1951, postgrad., 1956-58. Bar: N.Y. Assoc. Sullivan & Cromwell, N.Y.C., 1951-56; chief exec. officer Nat. Potash Co., N.Y.C., 1972-75; v.p. Freeport Minerals Co., N.Y.C., 1975-81; sr. v.p., treas. Freeport-McMoRan Inc., N.Y.C., 1981-86, ret., 1986. Pres. Quioque Assn., Westhampton Beach, N.Y., 1982-83, Citizens for Good Schs., Glen Ridge, N.J., 1973-74; vice chmn. civic conf. com., Glen Ridge, 1970-71. Served with USN, 1944-46. Clubs: Quantuck Yacht (commodore 1969-70), Quantuck Beach (Westhampton Beach, N.Y.); Quoque Field (N.Y.), L.I. Wyandanch (Eastport, N.Y.).

ROTHWELL, ROBERT CLARK, agricultural products executive; b. St. Louis, Dec. 7, 1939; s. Fountain and Frances Marie (Bickell) R.; m. Virginia Warren Hubbard, Apr. 18, 1961; children: Sharon Lee, James Clark, Janice Lynn, David Matthews. BSBA, U. Mo., 1967. CPA, Mo. Staff auditor Arthur Andersen & Co., Kansas City, Mo., 1967-71; internal auditor MFA, Inc., Columbia, Mo., 1971-75, mgr. auditing, 1975-79, contr., 1979-81, v.p. fin., 1981-88, treas., 1987—, sr. v.p. fin., 1988—; treas. Agmo Corp., Columbia; mem. investment com. MFA Found., Columbia, MFA Employees Retirement Plan, Columbia; advisor U. Mo. Sch. Accountancy, Columbia, 1987-88. Author various presentations on fin. mgmt. Instr. Mo. Inst. Cooperation, Columbia, 1987-88; bd. dirs. West Broadway Swim Club, Columbia. With U.S. Army, 1959-62. Mem. AICPA, Mo. Soc. CPAs, Fin. Execs. Inst., Nat. Assn. Accts. for Coops., Nat. Coun. Farmer Coops. Republican. Office: MFA Inc 615 Locust St Columbia MO 65201

ROTHWELL, WILLIAM JOSEPH, management consultant, writer; b. Springfield, Ill., Dec. 17, 1951; s. Robert Wood and Delores Jean (Bachstein) R.; m. Marcelina Villaflores, Mar. 22, 1981; children; Froilan Perucho, Candice. BA, Ill. State U., 1973; MA, U. Ill., 1975, PhD, 1985; MABA, *sangamon State U., 1982. Registered orgn. devel. profl., sr. profl. in human resources. Spl. svcs. officer Office Ill. Auditor Gen., Springfield, 1979-87; prin. assoc. R & K Assocs., Springfield, 1987—; mgmt. devel. dir. Franklin Life Ins, Springfield, 1987—. Co-Author: Strategic Human Resources Planning and Management, 1988, Strategic Human Resource Development, 1989; editor: The Critical Resource, 1983. Mem. Am. Soc. for Tng. and Devel. (pres. Cen. Ill. chpt. 1986-87, co-author reference guide 1987), Am. Soc. Personnel Adminstrn. Home: 1317 Lowell Ave Springfield IL 62704

ROTTER, PAUL TALBOTT, retired insurance executive; b. Parsons, Kans., Feb. 21, 1918; s. J. and LaNora (Talbott) R.; m. Virginia Sutherlin Barksdale, July 17, 1943; children—Carolyn Sutherlin, Diane Talbott. B.S. summa cum laude, Harvard U., 1937. Asst. mathematician Prudential Ins. Co. of Am., Newark, 1938-46; with Mut. Benefit Life Ins. Co., Newark, 1946—; successively asst. mathematician, asso. mathematician, mathematician Mut. Benefit Life Ins. Co., 1946-59, v.p., 1959-69, exec. v.p., 1969-80, ret., 1980. Mem. Madison Bd. Edn., 1958-64, pres., 1959-64; Trustee, mem. budget com. United Campaign of Madison, 1951-55; mem. bd., chmn. advancement com. Robert Treat council Boy Scouts Am., 1959-64. Fellow Soc. Actuaries (bd. govs. 1965-68, gen. chmn. edn. and exam. com. 1963-66, chmn. adv. com. edn. and exam. 1969-72); mem. Brit. Inst. Actuaries (asso.), Am. Acad. Actuaries (v.p. 1968-70, bd. dirs., chmn. edn. and exam. com. 1965-66, chmn. rev. and evaluation com. 1968-74), Asso. Harvard Alumni (regional dir. 1965-69), Actuaries Club N.Y. (pres. 1967-68), Harvard Alumni Assn. (v.p. 1964-66),Am. Lawn Bowls Assn. (pres. SW div.), Phi Beta Kappa Assos., Phi Beta Kappa. Clubs: Harvard N.J. (pres. 1956-57); Harvard (N.Y.C.); Morris County Golf (Convent, N.J.). Home: 18278 Canfield Pl San Diego CA 92128

ROTUNDA, DONALD THEODORE, corporate communications official; b. Blue Island, Ill., Feb. 14, 1945; s. Nicholas and Frances (Manna) R.; B.A., Georgetown U., 1967; M.A., London Sch. Econs., 1968, Ph.D., 1972. Analyst, NASA, Washington, 1972; lectr. in econs. U. D.C., 1973; legis. asst. Ho. of Reps., Washington, 1974-76, economist budget com., 1977; mgmt. analyst Office Mgmt. and Budget, Washington, 1977-81; cons., 1981-82; mgr. editorial services United Technologies Corp., Hartford, Conn., 1982-87, mgr. editorial services, Pepsico, Purchase, N.Y., 1987—. Roman Catholic. Contbr. numerous articles to Washington Post, New Republic, Saturday Rev. Home: 20 Church St Apt A-64 Greenwich CT 06830 Office: Pepsico Purchase NY 10577

ROUBOS, GARY LYNN, diversified manufacturing company executive; b. Denver, Nov. 7, 1936; s. Dorr and Lillian Margaret (Coover) R.; m. Terie Joan Anderson, Feb. 20, 1960; children—Lyndel, Leslie. BSChemE with high honors, U. Colo., 1959; MBA with distinction, Harvard U., 1963. With Boise Cascade Corp., 1963-71; with Dieterich Standard Corp., Boulder, Colo., 1971-76; exec. v.p., then pres. Dieterich Standard Corp. (co. acquired by Dover Corp. 1975), 1975-76; exec. v.p. Dover Corp., N.Y.C., 1976, pres., 1977—, chief exec. officer, 1981—; dir. Omnicom Inc., Scott Paper Co., Phila., Gabelli-O'Connor Treas. Fund, Greenwich, Conn.; mem. N.Y. adv. bd. Liberty Mut. Bd. dirs. Colo. U. Found., 1976—. Served to 1st lt. C.E., U.S. Army, 1959-61. Clubs: Tokeneke (Darien, Conn.); Board Room (N.Y.C.); Winged Foot, Econ. Club of N.Y. Office: Dover Corp 277 Park Ave New York NY 10172

ROUDANE, CHARLES, metal and plastics products company executive; b. Los Angeles, July 16, 1927; s. Rudolph and Irene (Warner) R.; BSME, Tulane, 1950; m. Orient Fox, Aug. 20, 1948; children—Mark, Matthew. Gen. mgr. Master div. Koehring Co., Chgo., 1955-67; gen. sales mgr. Wilton Corp., Schiller Park, Ill., 1967-70; dir. mktg. Flexonics div. UOP Inc., Bartlett, Ill., 1970-73, v.p., gen. mgr. div., 1973-83; pres., chief exec. officer Resistoflex Co. div. Crane Co., Marion, N.C., 1983—; dir. Center Indsl. Mktg. Planning, Inc., PowRhouse Products, Inc., Resistoflex, GmbH. Served with AUS, 1945-46. Elected to Inaugural Hall of Fame, Am. Mgmt. Assn., 1978. Mem. Am. Mgmt. Assn. (former trustee, chmn. mktg. council), mem. Internat. Council, Chgo. Pres. Assn., ASME, Newcomen Soc. Gt. Britain. Republican. Presbyterian.

ROUDYBUSH, FRANKLIN, diplomat, educator; b. Washington, Sept. 17, 1906; s. Rumsey Franklin and Frances (Mahon) R.; student U. Vienna, 1925, Ecole National des Langues Orintales Vivantes, Paris, 1926, U. Paris, 1926-28, U. Madrid, 1928, Academie Julian, Paris, 1967; B.Fgn. Service, Georgetown U., 1930; postgrad. Harvard U., 1931; M.A., George Washington U., 1944; Ph.D., U. Strasbourg (France), 1953; m. Alexandra Brown, May 22, 1941. Dean Roudybush Fgn. Service Schs., Washington, Los Angeles, Phila., N.Y.C., 1932—. Prof. internat. econ. relations Southeastern U., Washington, 1938-42; dir. Pan Am. Inst., Washington, 1934; editor Affairs, 1934-45; commodity economist, statistician Dept. State, 1945; with Fgn. Service Inst., Dept. State, 1945-48, Council of Europe, Strasbourg, 1948-54, Am. Embassy, Paris, 1954, Pakistan, 1955, Dublin, 1956. Mem. Am. Soc. Internat. Law, Brit. Inst. Internat. and Comparative Law (London), Delta Phi Epsilon. Clubs: Assns des Amis du Salon d'Automne (Paris); France Amerique; English Speaking Union (London); Nat. Press (Washington); Harvard (Paris), Royal Aberdeen Golf; Miramar Golf (Oporto, Portugal), Yacht (Angiers, France); Pormarnock Golf (Dublin); Les Societe des Artistes Independants Grand Palais (Paris). Author: The Twentieth Century; The Battle of Cultures; Diplomatic Language; Twentieth Century Diplomacy; The Present State of Western Capitalism, 1959; Diplomacy and Art, French Educational System, 1971; The Techniques of International Negotiation, 1979; The Diplomacy of the Cardinal, Duke de Richilieu, 1980. Home: Villa St Honoré, Moledo do Minho, Minho Portugal Office: 15 Ave du President Wilson, Paris 16, France also: Sauveterre de Rouerque, 12800 Aveyron France

ROUGH, DAVID S., marketing professional, consultant; b. Lake Placid, N.Y., Dec. 20, 1933; s. Jack and Veva Lillian (Bickford) R.; m. Patricia Anne Healy, June 10, 1962 (div. Sept. 1974); children: Robert Scott, Patricia Anne, Jonathan Lee; m. Gay Louise Vance, Apr. 9, 1988. BA, U. Conn., 1954; MA, U. Miami, 1963, PhD, 1966. Exec. v.p. Internat. Apparel, Miami, Fla., 1966-69; pres. Outlet Holding Corp., Atlanta, 1969-74; exec. dir. Marco Group, San Bernardino, Calif., 1975-82; exec. v.p., cons. Chroma Concepts, Inc., Irvine, Calif., 1986—; pres. Worldwide Systems, Inc., Laguna, Calif., 1987—; cons. Maxines, Encido, Calif., 1982—, Bobbies, San Diego, 1982—. Served with USAF, 1955-58. Republican. Baptist. Office: Chroma Concepts Inc 18003 Skypark Circle Irvine CA 92651

ROUGHSEDGE, CAROLYN DUNN, advertising agency executive; b. Rocky Ford, Colo., June 9, 1944; d. Joseph Michael and Frances (Barnes) Dunn.; m. Robert Roughsedge, Nov. 29, 1968 (div. Nov. 1978); 1 son, Michael Caine. BA, Manhattanville Coll., 1966. Casting sec. Grey Advt., N.Y.C., 1966-67; TV producer Savage Friedman, N.Y.C., 1967-68; v.p., owner Steppingstone Prodns., N.Y.C., 1968-77; TV producer CBS Records, N.Y.C., 1977-78; v.p., dir. broadcast prodn. Needham, Harper & Steers, L.A., 1978-83; v.p., dir. broadcast prodn. Needham, Harper & Steers, N.Y.C., from 1983, to sr. v.p.; sr. v.p., dir. broadcast prodn. Saatchi & Saatchi Advt. Inc., N.Y.C., exec. v.p., exec. dir. broadcast ops., 1988—. Office: Saatchi & Saatchi Advt Inc 375 Hudson St New York NY 10014

ROULX, RICHARD WILFRED, county official; b. Manchester, N.H., Nov. 25, 1927; s. Wilfred Joseph and Hazel Ellen (Bennett) R.; m. Ruth Ann Noga; children: Mary Ellen, Diane, Gail, Cynthia, Patrice, Lisa, Paula, Christine. BBA, Northeastern U., Boston, 1952. Acct. Booth Meml. Hosp., Boston, 1948-51; dir. ops. J.E. Fattin Met. Transp., Manchester, 1951-66; bus. mgr. County of Hillsborough, Manchester, 1966—. Past pres. Seift Water GS Council, N.E. Roman Cath. Sch. Bd. With USN, 1944-46, PTO. Mem. N.H. Pub. Employment Labor Relations Bd. (mgmt. bd.), N.H. Assn. Counties (treas. 1974—), Exchange Club (past pres. local club). Home: 35

Little Ave Manchester NH 03103 Office: County Hillsborough 300 Chestnut St Manchester NH 03101

ROUMELL, LISA, venture capitalist; b. Grosse Pointe, Mich., Feb. 6, 1959; d. George Theodore and Aphrodite (Doukas) R. BA, Harvard U., 1981, MBA, 1985. Fin. analyst corp. fin. Smith Barney Harris Upham, N.Y.C., 1981-83; assoc. Gen. Electric Venture Co., Fairfield, Conn., 1984; v.p. First Century Ptnrs., N.Y.C., 1985—. Vol., co-chmn. Am. Craft Mus., vol. benefit com. Met. Coun. Student Sponsorship Program. Elizabeth Aguissey scholar Harvard U., 1981. Mem. Nat. Venture Capital Assn., N.Y. Venture Forum, Harvard Bus. Sch. Club. Democrat. Episcopalian.

ROUNICK, JACK A., lawyer; b. Phila., June 5, 1935; s. Philip and Nettie (Brownstein) R.; BBA, U. Mich., 1956; JD, U. Pa., 1959; m. Noreen A. Garrigan, Sept. 4, 1970; children—Ellen, Eric, Amy, Michelle. Bar: Pa. 1960, U.S. Dist. Ct. (ea. dist.) Pa., 1960. Spl. asst. atty. gen., 1963-71; ptnr. Israelit & Rounick, 1960-67, Moss & Rounick, 1968-69, Moss, Rounick & Hurowitz, Norristown, Pa., 1969-72, Moss & Rounick, Norristown, 1972-73; ptnr. Pechner, Dorfman, Wolffe, Rounick and Cabot, Norristown, 1973-87; v.p., gen. counsel Martin Lawrence Ltd. Edits., Inc., 1987—; dir. Martin Lawrence Ltd. Edits., Inc., 1984—, Deb Shops, Inc., 1974—. Fin. chmn. Pa. Young Rep., 1964-66, treas., 1966-68, chmn., 1968-70. Recipient Boss of Yr. award Montgomery County Legal Secs. Assn., 1970, Cert. of appreciation Pa. Bar Inst., 1980. Fellow Am. Acad. Matrimonial Lawyers (pres. Pa. chpt. 1982-84, gov. 1983-85, v.p. 1985-87); mem. ABA, (coun. family law sect. 1982-87), Pa. Bar Assn. (past chmn. family law sect.; Spl. Achievement award 1979-80), Montgomery Bar Assn., Am. Friends of the Hebrew U. (Phila. chpt. pres. 1988, bd. dirs. Nat. Coun. of Trustees 1987—). Republican. Jewish. Author: Pennsylvania Matrimonial Practice, 3 vols., 1982. Editor, Pa. Family Lawyer, 1980-87. Contbr. articles to profl. jours. Office: Martin Lawrence Galleries 151 E 10th Ave Conshohocken PA 19428

ROUNTREE, ROBERT BENJAMIN, utility executive; b. Burnsville, N.C., Oct. 20, 1924; s. Benjamin F. and Carrie R.; m. Martha Jane McBee, Feb. 23, 1946; 1 dau., Janet Fay Rountree Wilson. B.S.E.E., U. N.Mex., 1946. With Pub. Service Co. N.Mex., 1948—; beginning as draftsman successively gen. supt. Pub. Service Co. N.Mex., Belen, N.Mex.; mgr. Pub. Service Co. N.Mex., Deming, N.Mex.; asst. div. mgr. Pub. Service Co. N.Mex., Albuquerque, div. v.p., v.p. div. ops., 1948-72; sr. v.p. Pub. Service Co. N.Mex., 1972-86, ret., 1986, dir.; chmn. bd. Meadows Resources, Inc., 1983—, Sunbelt Minig Co., 1983—. Mem. IEEE, Am. Inst. Mgmt., Nat. Soc. Profl. Engrs.

ROURKE, ARLENE CAROL, publisher; b. N.Y.C., Feb. 1, 1944; d. Ralph and Adele (Rovegno) De Giso; m. Raymond Lawrence Rourke, Oct. 28, 1970; children: Elizabeth, Christopher. BA in English, Pace U., N.Y.C., 1966. Prodn. editor Fawcett Haynes, N.Y.C., 1966-67; prodn. asst., editor McGraw Hill, N.Y.C., 1967-70; owner, pres. Rourke Publs., Inc., Ft. Pierce, Fla., 1980—; v.p. Rourke Enterprises, Inc., Vero Beach, Fla., 1984—. Author: (Looking Good Series) Accesories, Clothing, Skin, Hand and Feet, Diet/Exercise, Hair; (children's book) Things That Move; contbr. various bible stories. Active Ctr. for Arts, Vero Beach, Fla., 1985—, Riverside Theatre, Vero Beach, 1985—; mem. ethics com. Turnabout Modeling Sch. and Agy., 1986. Roman Catholic.

ROUTSON, CLELL DENNIS, manufacturing company executive; b. Elkhart, Ind., Oct. 8, 1946; s. Clell Dean and Olene Maize (Replogle) R.; m. Paula Leone McLallin, Sept. 2, 1967; children: Clell Dustin and Courtney Trevor. BSBA, Ball State U., Muncie, Ind., 1971. With Proctor & Gamble, Cin., 1971-74; nat. sales mgr. Palmer Instruments, Inc., Cin., 1974-76; with Nordson Corp., Amherst, Ohio, 1976-81, MCC Powers, Cleve., Chgo., Singapore, 1981-86; sales mgr., v.p., pres. Burgess, Inc., Freeport, Ill., 1986—; mng. dir. Resource Dynamics, Singapore, Chgo., 1985-86. Contbr. articles to profl. jours. Mem. No. Ill. World Trade Council. Republican. Methodist. Clubs: Beckett Ridge Country (Cin.); Freeport Country. Office: Burgess Inc Foot of Exchange St Freeport IL 61032

ROUTT, KAREN ELIZABETH, management consultant; b. Detroit, May 3, 1955; d. Robert Fletcher and Catherine (Weiss) R. Student, Denison U., 1973-75; BA, U. Mich., 1977; MBA, Stanford U., 1983. Cons. Arthur Andersen & Co., Detroit, 1977-79, sr. cons., 1979-81; project mgr. Bank One Columbus, N.Am., Ohio, 1983-84, project mgr., officer, 1984, mgr. on-line support, 1984-85, mgr. interest rate swap portfolio, 1985-86, mgr. check capture, 1986-87; sr. assoc. Index Group Inc., Cambridge, Mass., 1988—. Active Big Sister, 1986—. Mem. Zonta (bd. dirs. Columbus club 1987-88, chair girls group home 1986-88). Mem. United Ch. Christ. Office: Index Group Inc 5 Cambridge Ctr Cambridge MA 02142

ROVELLO, CAROL LYNN, management consultant; b. Doylestown, Pa., Oct. 9, 1955; d. Michael James and Margaret Jane (Ryan) R. BS, Glassboro State U., 1977; MA, Rider Coll., 1982. Cert. elem. and secondary tchr., N.J. Tchr. Somerdale (N.J.) Bd. Edn., 1977-78; exec. dir. Crossroads, Mt. Holly, N.J., 1978-84; prin. Organizational Mgmt. Cons., Blackwood, N.J., 1984—. Chmn. personnel com. YWCA of Camden County, Stratford, N.J., 1985—. Named one of Outstanding Young Women in Am., 1985. Mem. Inst. Mgmt. Cons. (assoc.), Am. Soc. Tng. and Devel., Am. Soc. personnel Adminstrn., N.J. Assn. Women Bus. Owners, Nat. Assn. Female Execs., Greater Cherry Hill C. of C. Democrat. Methodist. Office: Organizational Mgmt Cons PO Box 345 Blackwood NJ 08012

ROWAN, PATRICK SLOAN, marketing executive; b. LaPorte, Ind.; s. George T. and JoAnne (Sloan) R.; m. Patricia Molinar, Mar. 30, 1985; 1 child, Leslie Anne. BSBA in Mktg., Ohio State U., 1980. Account exec. Communicolor div. Standard Register Co., Chgo., 1980-81; sr. account exec. Communicolor div. Standard Register Co., Dallas, 1981-85; dist. sales mgr. Communicolor div. Standard Register Co., Washington, 1985-86; nat. mktg. mgr. Communicolor div. Standard Register Co., Newark, Ohio, 1986-88; asst. dist. sales mgr. West coast, account dir. Communicolor div. Standard Register Co., Sherman Oaks, Calif., 1988—. Bd. dirs. Leadership Tomorrow, Newark, 1988—. Mem. Direct Mktg. Assn. Republican. Roman Catholic. Home: 28418 N Fig Ct Saugus CA 91350 Office: Communicolor 14101 Valleyheart Dr Ste 102 Sherman Oaks CA 91423-2864

ROWAN, ROBERT DALE, transportation executive; b. Holland, Mich., Mar. 27, 1922; s. Joseph Henry and Mabel Barbara (Streur) R.; m. Ruth Ann Lyons, June 17, 1983; children: Richard Paul, Kristine Louise, Ruthanne Marie. BS, Mich. State U., 1947. CPA, Mich. Audit supr. Touche, Ross and Co., CPA's, Detroit, 1947-55; controller Fruehauf Corp., Detroit, 1955-63, v.p., controller, 1963-65, v.p. fin., 1965-69, exec. v.p. fin., 1969-72, also bd. dirs., pres., chief operating officer, 1972-74, pres., chief exec. officer, 1974-80, chmn., pres., chief exec. officer, 1980-81, chmn. bd., chief exec. officer, 1981-86, chmn., pres., chief exec. officer, 1986-88, chmn., 1988—; bd. dirs. Fruehauf Internat. Ltd., Fruehauf de Mex., Fruehauf France S.A., Decatur Aluminum Co., Jacksonville Shipyards, Inc., also others. Served to capt. U.S. Army, 1942-46, 50-52. Mem. Mich. Assn. CPA's, Detroit C. of C., Nat. Def.-Transp. Assn. Republican. Presbyterian. Clubs: Oakland Hills Country, Detroit, Detroit Athletic, Econ., Renaissance (Detroit); Sky (N.Y.C.); Firestone Country (Akron, Ohio), Hundred. Lodge: Masons. Office: Fruehauf Corp 10900 Harper Ave Detroit MI 48213 •

ROWCLIFFE, GARY DAVID, life insurance company executive; b. Lymn, Cheshire, Eng., Sept. 23, 1959; came to U.S., 1970; s. Arthur F. and Nona (Edwards) R.; m. Lena Lundin, Dec. 26, 1984. BA in Econs., U. South, Sewanee, Tenn., 1981. Coll. unit dir., spl. agt. Northwestern Mut. Life Ins. Co., Knoxville, Tenn., 1981—. Pres. Knoxville Met. Soccer League, 1984-87; capt. Toqua dist. Boy Scouts Am., Knxville, 1987, 88. Mem. AMA (sec. chpt. 1987-88, devel. dir. Knoxville chpt. 1988—), Nat. Assn. Life Underwriters, Million Dollar Round Table, Am. Mktg. Assn. (v.p., sec. interest group Ky. chpt. 1988—). Republican. Episcopalian. Club: Sewanee (Knoxville) (pres. 1985—). Office: Northwestern Mut Life Ins Co 602 S Gay St Knoxville TN 37902

ROWE, ALAN THOMAS, oil company executive; b. Los Angeles, May 6, 1931; s. Charles B. and Mae (Langdon) R.; m. Dona Dee Hadley, Feb. 21, 1952; 1 child, William Thomas. BSME, U. So. Calif., L.A., 1960. Dir. mktg. PCD Ethyl Corp., Houston, 1971-76, Edwin Cooper, St. Louis, 1976-78; dir. mktg. world wide Edwin Cooper, Bracknell, Eng., 1978-81; v.p. sales and supply Tex. City Refining Inc., Texas City, Tex., 1980-83, exec. v.p., 1983-84, pres., chief exec. officer, 1985-87; pres. Allan F. Dow and Assocs., 1988—; bd. dir. Texas City Refining. Del. Rep. State Conv., Tex., 1976. With USAF, 1951-54. Mem. Nat. Petroleum Refiners Assn., Petroleum Club (Houston), Bal Harbour Yacht Club (Nassau Bay). Republican.

ROWE, JACK FIELD, electric utility executive; b. Minn., May 10, 1927; s. William F. and Anna (Stenborg) R.; m. Mary E. Moen, Mar. 26, 1955; 1 dau., Lizette Ann. B.E.E., U. Minn., 1950. Registered profl. engr., Minn., Wis. With Minn. Power and Light Co., Duluth, 1950—; asst. to pres. Minn. Power and Light Co., 1966-67, v.p., 1967-68, exec. v.p., 1969-74, pres., 1974-84, chief exec. officer, 1978—, chmn., 1979—, also mem. exec. com., dir.; chmn. bd., chief exec. officer FiberCore, Inc., Minn. Paper, Inc., So. States Utilities, Universal Telephone, Inc., Topeka Group, Inc., NorLight, Inc.; mem. exec. bd. Nat. Electric Reliability Council, 1970-73; vice chmn. Mid Continent Area Reliability Council, 1970-71, chmn., 1972-73; mem. bus. and econs. adv. bd. U. Minn., Duluth, 1980; bd. dirs. Waldorf Corp., St. Paul, First Bank-Duluth, Edison Electric Inst., Pub. Utilities Reports. Past bd. dirs., v.p. Duluth Jr. C. of C.; mem. exec. bd. Lake Superior council Boy Scouts Am., 1967-75, chmn., Explorers, 1968-72; comml. chmn. Duluth United Fund, 1960-61; vice chmn. Duluth United Way, 1975, chmn., 1976, pres. elect, 1981, U.S. Savs. Bond chmn., St. Louis County, Minn., 1974-77; chmn. St. Louis County Heritage and Arts Center, 1979-81; pres. NE Minn. Devel./Assn., 1981-83; mem. Minn. Bus. Partnership, 1979-88; bd. dirs. Minn. Safety Council, 1979-85, Duluth Downtown Devel. Corp., 1979-81, Duluth Growth Co., 1984-85, Greysolon Mall Corp., 1980-86, Duluth Superior Area Community Found., 1984-86, Duluth Cin. Edn. and Research Found., 1985-86, Benedictine Health System, 1985-88; mem. adv. bd. exec. program U. Minn., 1979; adv. council Inst. Tech., 1979; mem. Minn. High Tech. Council, 1982-87. Served with USNR, 1945-46. Recipient Distinguished Service award Duluth Jr. C. of C., 1960, Outstanding Leadership award in energy conversion scis. N.Y.C. sect. ASME, 1980, Outstanding Achievement award U. Minn. Alumni Assn., 1986, Bronze Chief Exec. Officer of Decade award Fin. World Mag., 1989; named Chief Exec. Officer of Yr., Fin. World mag., 1986, 89; Jack F. Rowe Chair of Engring. named in his honor U. Minn., Duluth, 1986. Mem. NAM (dir. 1975-78), IEEE, Electric Info. Council (pres. 1978-82), North Cen. Electric Assn., Duluth C. of C. (pres. 1972-73, exec. com., bd. dirs.), Kappa Eta Kappa. Lutheran. Clubs: Minneapolis; Engineers (Duluth), Rotary (Duluth) (pres. 1974-75), Kitchi Gammi (Duluth) (dir. 1979—, pres. 1985—), Masons, Shriners. Home: 4735 Villa Mare' Ln Naples FL 33940 Office: Minn Power & Light Co 30 W Superior St Duluth MN 55802

ROWE, JAMES W., food chain executive; b. Chattanooga, Dec. 28, 1923; s. John Howard and Anne Lou (Borders) R.; m. Doris Eileen Carlton, Feb. 19, 1946; children: Carlton, Leigh Anne. Student advanced mgmt, Northeastern U., 1976. Vice pres., sec. Colonial Stores, Atlanta, 1970-77, sr. v.p. adminstrn., 1978, pres., 1979-80; sr. v.p., asst. to chief exec. officer Grand Union Co., Elmwood Park, N.J., 1979; exec. v.p., asst. chief exec. officer Gt. Atlantic and Pacific Tea Co., Inc., Montvale, N.J., 1980-82, vice chmn., chief adminstrn. officer, asst. chief exec. officer, 1982-88, vice chmn. bd. and exec. com., 1988—; bd. dirs. Colonial Stores, Grand Union Co., Gt. Atlantic and Pacific Tea Co. Served with AUS, 1942-45. Republican. Office: Gt Atlantic & Pacific Tea Co 2 Paragon Dr Montvale NJ 07645

ROWE, JOHN WILLIAM, utility executive; b. Dodgeville, Wis., May 18, 1945; s. William J. and Lola (Rule) R.; m. Gail M. Rakitan, Aug. 5, 1977; 1 son, William John. B.S., U. Wis., 1967, J.D., 1970. Bar: Wis. 1970, Ill. 1970, U.S. Supreme Ct. 1979, Pa. 1982. Assoc. Isham, Lincoln & Beale, Chgo., 1970-77, ptnr., 1978-80; counsel to trustee Chgo. Milw. St. Paul & Pacific R.R., Chgo., 1979-80; v.p. law Consol. Rail Corp., Phila., 1980-82, sr. v.p. law, 1982-84; pres., chief exec. officer Central Maine Power Co., Augusta, 1984-89; also dir. Central Maine Power Co., Augusta; pres., chief exec. officer New Eng. Elec. System, Westboro, Mass., 1989—; also bd. dirs. New Eng. Elec. System; bd. dirs. Mid South Corp., UNUM Corp., New England Electric System, Westboro. Trustee Pa. Ballet, 1982-84; chmn. Ft. Western Endowment Fund; mem. Phila. Commn. on Health in '80s, 1983, Maine Econ. Devel. Strategy Task Force; co-chmn. Maine Aspirations Compact, 1988. Mem. Japan Soc., Order of Coif, Chicago Club, Phi Beta Kappa. Home: 6 Sanger Circle Dover MA 02030 Office: New Eng Electric System 25 Research Dr Westborough MA 01582

ROWE, MICHAEL RICHARD, sports arena executive; b. Newark, Oct. 2, 1949; s. Sal Richard and Carol Kay (Moro) R.; m. Constance Mary Wood, May 10, 1975; children: Allyson Rene, Lisa Michelle. BA, Seton Hall U., 1971; MA, Rider Coll., 1978. Sr. career devel. specialist N.J. Civil Svc. Dept., Trenton, 1972-75; manpower employer rels. coord. N.J. Labor Dept., Trenton, 1975-77; exec. asst. to state budget dir. State of N.J., Trenton, 1977-78, dir. adminstrn. to gov., 1978-79; dir. policy and mgmt. Meadowlands Sports Complex, Rutherford, N.J., 1979-83, asst. gen. mgr. Giants Stadium-Meadowlands Arena, 1987, gen. mgr., 1987-89, exec. v.p., gen. mgr., 1989—; bd. dirs. Lakeview Savs. & Loan, Paterson, N.J. Mem. Internat. Assn. Arena Mgrs. (com. chmn. 1987). Roman Catholic. Home: 15 Stockton Dr Cranbury NJ 08512 Office: Meadowlands Sports Compex Rte 3 and Rte 20 Rutherford NJ 07073

ROWE, N. MARK, sales executive; b. Washington, Mar. 25, 1960; s. David Marion and Helen Francis (Miller) R. BBA, Boise (Idaho) State U., 1982; MBA, U. Montana, 1988. Owner, operator The Wood Shop, Boise, 1979-82; sales rep. United Sales, Spokane, Wash., 1982-83; prin. Rowe Furniture, Missoula, Mont., 1984-86; sales rep. The Hoover Co., North Canton, Ohio, 1986—. Mem. Mensa, Garden City Stamp Club (pres. Missoula 1988). Mem. Ch. of Mark. Home: PO Box 630 Bonner MT 59823

ROWE, RICHARD R., online information and management services company executive; b. Burlington, Iowa, Apr. 14, 1933; S. Charles Ronald and Elva Margaret (Gilliland) R.; m. Judy Davis, Jan. 31, 1976; children—Katherine, Susannah, Timothy, Christopher, Jonathan. B.A. in Psychology, UCLA, 1955; S.T.B. in Psychology of Religion, Boston U., 1958; Ph.D. in Psychology, Columbia U., 1963. Cert. and lic. psychologist, Mass. Dir. test devel. and research West African Exams. Council, 1963-67; assoc. dean Grad. Sch. Edn., Harvard U., Cambridge, Mass., 1967-73; dir. program in clin. psychology and pub. practice Harvard U., 1967-73; v.p. Am. Inst. for Research, Cambridge, 1973-79; pres., chief exec. officer The Faxon Co., Westwood, Mass., 1979—; chmn. Serials Industry Systems Adv. Com. Pres. Statewide Adv. Council to Office for Children, Mass., 1980-87, chmn., 1983-87; mem. K-12 computer literacy com. Mass. High Tech Council, 1983-84; spl. adviser Mass. Legis. Com. on Ednl. Excellence, 1983-84; mem. Mass. Legis. Commn. Early Edn., 1988—. Mem. Am. Psychol. Assn., ALA, Library and Info. Tech. Assn. Club: Harvard (N.Y.C.). Home: 37 Goden St Belmont MA 02178 Office: Faxon Co Inc 15 Southwest Pk Westwood MA 02090

ROWE, STANFORD HUNTINGTON, II, data processing executive; b. Boston, Nov. 13, 1942; s. Stanford Huntington Sr. and Katherine Louise (Hampe) R.; children from previous marriage: David, Jeannine, Steven; m. Pamela Jeanne Hendricks, May 26, 1984. AB, U. of Redlands, Calif., 1964; MS, U. So. Calif., Los Angeles, 1966. Software specialist Dow Corning Corp., Midland, Mich., 1966-69, mgr. computer ops., 1972-76, mgr. technical support, 1976-85, mgr. telecommunications, 1985-88; supr. European EDP Dow Corning Corp., Brussels, 1969-72; mgr. Japan Area MIS, 1988—; instr. Delta Coll., Univ. Ctr., Mich., 1973-85. Author: Business Telecommunications, 1988. Bd. dirs. Midland Concert Band, 1979-85. Mem. Data Processing Mgmt. Assn. (past bd. dirs., Saginaw Valley chpt., chmn. 1980, 81-83, Outstanding Performance award 1984), Assn. Computing Machinery, Midland Music Soc. (bd. mgrs. 1988), Am. C. of C. Japan, Tokyo-Am. Club. Republican. Lutheran. Home: Homar Ruby 201, 1-26-6 Minami Aoyama, Minato-Ku, 107 Tokyo Japan Office: Dow Corning Japan, 1-15-1 Nishi Shimbashi, Minato-Ku, 105 Tokyo Japan also: c/o Dow Corning Corp 2200 Salzburg Rd Midland MI 48686-0994

ROWE, WILLIAM JOHN, newspaper executive; b. Detroit, Jan. 11, 1936; s. Howard Tiedeman and Thelma Irene (Fox) R.; m. Ellen McCabe, Nov. 28, 1959; children: Peter William, Susan Victoria. BA in Journalism and Advt., Mich. State U., 1958. With Chgo. Tribune, 1958-79; pres., gen. mgr. Suburban Tribune, 1977-79, Merrill Printing Co., Chgo., 1977-79; pres., chief exec. officer Peninsula Times Tribune, Palo Alto, Calif., 1979-84; exec. v.p., chief operating officer Times Mirror Nat. Mktg., N.Y.C., 1984-85, pres., chief exec. officer, 1985-86; pres. pub., chief exec. officer The Advocate and Greenwich Time, Stamford, Conn., 1986—. Bd. dirs. Boy Scouts Am., Greenwich, Conn., 1987, United Way of Stamford, Nat. Assn. Christians and Jews. Served to 2d lt., inf. U.S. Army Res., 1959. Mem. Am. Newspaper Pubs. Assn, New Eng. Newspaper Assn. Club: Indian Harbor Yacht, Landmark. Home: 9 Hill Rd Greenwich CT 06830 Office: Advocate So Conn Newspapers 75 Tresser Blvd Stamford CT 06904

ROWELL, LESTER JOHN, JR., insurance company executive; b. Cleve., Apr. 2, 1932; s. Lester John and Francis Laureen (Corbett) R.; m. Patricia Ann Loesch, Jan. 16, 1953 (div. Sept. 1970); children: Deborah, Cynthia, Gregory, Maureen, Diane; m. Carol Ann Jankowski, Sept. 26, 1970. B.S., Pa. State U., 1955; grad. Advanced Mgmt. Program, Harvard U. Bus. Sch., 1971. C.L.U. Second v.p., field mgmt. Mut. Life Ins. Co. N.Y., N.Y.C., 1969-70, v.p. agys., 1970-72, v.p. sales, 1972-78, sr. v.p., 1978-80; exec. v.p. Provident Mut. Life Ins. Co., Phila., 1980-84, pres., 1984-86, pres., chief operating officer, 1987; bd. dirs. Provident Mut. Life Ins. Co., Washington Sq. Life Ins. Co., Continental Am. Life Ins. Co., Delfi Am. Corp. Vice chmn. maj. accounts United Way Southeastern Pa., Phila., 1986—; chmn. ad book campaign ARC, 1989; bd. dirs. USO Phila., Paoli Meml. Hosp., World Affairs Council Phila. Capt. USMC, 1953-62. Recipient Alumni award Pa. State U., 1972, Disting. Alumni award Pa. State U., 1988; Alumni Fellow Pa. State U., 1987. Mem. Life Ins. Mktg. and Research Assn. (dir. 1980-83, mem. stategic mktg. issues com. 1987-89), Nat. Assn. Life Underwriters, Agy. Officers Round Table (chmn. 1980-81), Life Underwriters Tng. Council (past trustee). Republican. Office: Provident Mut Life Ins Co 1600 Market St Philadelphia PA 19101

ROWE-MAAS, BETTY LOU, real estate investor; b. San Jose, Calif., Apr. 2, 1925; d. Horace DeWitt and Lucy Belle (Spiker) Rowe; children: Terry Lee, Clifford Lindsay, Craig Harrison, Joan Louise. Real estate investor, Saratoga, Calif., 1968—. Mem. Nat. Trust Hist. Preservation, Smithsonian Instn., San Jose Mus., Saratoga Mus., San Francisco Mus., Los Gatos Mus., San Jose Symphony, Moltalvo; bd. dirs. Valley Inst. Theatre Arts; San Francisco Ballet, City Ctr. Ballet of San Jose and Cleve., Music and Arts Found.; mem. Route 85 Task Force, 1978—, treas., 1984-89; mem. Saratoga Good Govt., 1970—; treas. Traffic Relief for Saratoga. Mem. LWV. Republican. Clubs: Commonwealth of Calif. (life), Saratoga Country. Home: 20360 Saratoga Los Gatos Rd Saratoga CA 95070

ROWLAND, CLIFFORD VANCE, labor relations exec.; b. New Castle, Pa., Apr. 6, 1930; s. Faunt Mitchell and Mary Elizabeth (Lour) R.; B.S., Cornell U., 1953; m. Jeanette Jane Smith, Aug. 29, 1952; children—Theresa Gayle, Mitchell Vance. Vice-pres. indsl. relations Grace Line Inc., N.Y.C., 1969-71; asst. regional postmaster gen. for employee and labor relations N.E., U.S. Postal Service, N.Y.C., Washington, 1971-75, labor relations exec. N. Jersey dist., 1975-86, coordinator of employee involvement northeast region, 1986— . Chmn. bd. dirs. Student Agencies, Inc., Ithaca, N.Y.; pres. Bd. Edn., Berkeley Heights, N.J., 1962-63. Served with USNR, 1948-49. Mem. Indsl. Relations Research Assn., Assn. Quality and Participation, Cornell U. Sch. Indsl. and Labor Relations Alumni Assn. (dir.). Presbyterian. Clubs: Lions Internat., Kiwanis, Columbia Assn. Home: Rowland Farm Rte 1 Box 349 Dallas PA 18612 Office: US Post Office Fed Sq Rm 201 Newark NJ 07102

ROWLAND, HERBERT LESLIE, public relations executive; b. N.Y.C., Dec. 4, 1925; s. I. Martin and Matilda (Appelbaum) R.; m. Joan Feldman, Apr. 9, 1949 (div. 1970); children: Russell Lloyd, Daryl Verne, Julie Anne; m. Patricia Dickson George, Nov. 9, 1985. Grad., CCNY, 1948; M.A., Columbia U., 1951. Corr. N.Y. Times, 1949-50; editor Where mag., also TV Week mag., 1951-53; gen. mgr. Roger Brown, Inc., N.Y.C., 1954-56; ptnr. Brown & Rowland, N.Y.C., 1957-60; pres. Rowland Co., N.Y.C., 1961—. With USAAF, 1944-46. Mem. Pub. Rels. Soc. Am. Home: 1080 Fifth Ave New York NY 10028-0102 Office: Rowland Co Worldwide 415 Madison Ave New York NY 10017

ROWLAND, LANDON HILL, diversified holding company executive; b. Fuquay Springs, N.C., May 20, 1937; s. Walter Elton and Elizabeth Carr (Williams) R.; m. Sarah Fidler, Dec. 29, 1959; children: Sarah Elizabeth, Matthew Hill, Joshua Carr. B.A., Dartmouth Coll., 1959; LL.B., Harvard U., 1962. Bar: Mo. Assoc. Watson, Ess, Marshall & Enggas, Kansas City, Mo., 1962-70; ptnr. Watson, Ess, Marshall & Enggas, 1970-80; v.p. Kansas City So. Industries, Inc., 1980-83, pres., chief operating officer, 1983-86, pres. chief exec. officer, 1987—, also dir.; profl. lectr. antitrust law U. Mo.-Kansas City, 1977-79; chmn. bd., dir. DST Systems, Inc., Kansas City, 1983—, Martec Pharms., Inc., Kansas City, Mo., 1985—; dir. Williams Telecommunications Group, Tulsa, Boatmen's Bank & Trust Co., Kansas City, Kansas City So. Ry. Co., Am. Royal, Kansas City, Mo. Co-author: West's Mo. Practice Series. Trustee Midwest Research Inst., Kansas City, Mo.; bd. dirs. Swope Ridge Health Care Ctr., Kansas City, Lyric Opera of Kansas City; chmn. com. adv. bd. Sta. KCUR-FM, Kansas City; chmn. Met. Performing Arts Fund; bd. govs. Kansas City Art Inst., Mo., 1985—. Mem. ABA, Mo. Bar Assn., Phi Beta Kappa. Clubs: Kansas City Country, Kansas City, River. Home: Ever Glades Farm Rt 29 Kansas City MO 64166 Office: Kans City So Industries Inc 114 W 11th St Kansas City MO 64105

ROWLANDS, T. DEWI, aerospace executive; b. North Wales, U.K., Apr. 11, 1939; came to U.S., 1970; m. Yolande Noella Stevens, Dec. 5, 1961 (dec. 1978); m. Sophia Zezanis, July 29, 1979; children—Francine A., Michael W., Carys M., Kathleen, A.S. ONC, Filton Coll. Tech, Eng., 1961; HNC, Bristol Coll. Tech., Eng., 1963. Apprentice engr. Bristol Aeroplane Co., Eng., 1956; regional sales mgr. Hawker-Siddeley, Eng., 1968-70; sales mgr., dir. com. AC Sales Brit. Aircraft Corp. U.S.A., Inc., 1970-77, v.p. ops., 1977-80, sr. v.p., 1980-81; exec. v.p. Brit. Aerospace Inc., Washington, 1981—. Vol. firefighter Vol. Firedepartment Co. 14, Fairfax County, Va., 1971-73, Co. 11, Loudoun County, Va., 1973-78, also pres., 1975, Vol. Rescue Squad Co. 15, Loudoun County, 1978-81; pres. Sterling Safety Ctr., Loudoun County, 1977-79. Named Outstanding Rescue Person Loudoun Co. WAGE Radio, 1979. Mem. Wings Club, Royal Aero. Soc. AIAA. Methodist. Home: Route 3 Box 137 Leesburg VA 22075 Office: Brit Aerospace Inc PO Box 17414 Washington DC 20041

ROWLANDS, W. JEFF, banker, consultant; b. Utica, N.Y., Jan. 21, 1953; s. William J. and Agnes A. (Griffin) R.; m. Kelly Ann Keim, May 12, 1979. AAS, Hudson Valley Community Coll., 1974. Mgr. sales Comdoc Office Systems, Utica, 1981-87; customer sales rep. Marine Midland Bank, Utica, 1987—; br. mgr. Savs. Bank Utica, Whitesboro, N.Y., 1987—; mem. adv. bd. Utica Devils profl. hockey team. Mem. Oneida County Rep. Exec. Com., 1986—. Roman Catholic. Home: 16 Norris Dr Whitesboro NY 13492 Office: Savs Bank Utica 131 Oriskany Blvd Whitesboro NY 13492

ROWLEY, GEOFFREY HERBERT, management consultant; b. Harrow, Middlesex, Eng., Nov. 10, 1935; s. Herbert and Muriel Jessie (Nicolls) R.; came to U.S., 1962; B.A., Bristol U. (Eng.), 1958; Certificate of Indsl. Adminstrn., Glasgow U., 1962; M.B.A., Harvard U., 1964. Purchasing officer Pirelli Ltd., London, 1958-61; research asso. Assn. for Internat. Research, Inc., Cambridge, Mass., 1964-68, v.p., dir., 1968—, cons. in expatriate compensation, 1964—; lectr. in field. Served with Royal Navy, 1953-55. Mem. Am. Compensation Assn., Am. Soc. Personnel Adminstrn., Brit. Inst. Mgmt. Club: Harvard. Contbr. articles to profl. jours. Home: 11 Berkeley Pl Cambridge MA 02138 Office: care Air Inc 1100 Massachusetts Ave Cambridge MA 02138

ROY, ASIM, business educator; b. Calcutta, India, May 5, 1948; came to U.S., 1975; s. Samarendra Nath and Chhaya (Mukherjee) R.; m. Suchandra Mukherjee, Feb. 10, 1974; 1 child, Sion Roy. B.E., Calcutta U., 1971; M.S. (scholar), Case Western Res. U., 1977; Ph.D., U. Tex.-Austin, 1979. Foreman, Guest, Keen, Williams, Calcutta, 1972-74; mgr. optimization group Execucom Systems Corp., Austin, 1980-82; asst. prof. U. Nebr.-Omaha, 1983, Ariz. State U., Tempe, 1983-89, assoc. prof., 1989—; cons. Mid-Am. Steel Corp., 1976-77, Fabri-Centre, Inc., Cleve., 1976; pres., chief exec. officer Decision Support Software, Inc. Author software: IFPS/Optimum. Contbr. articles to profl. jours. Calcutta U. Merit scholar, 1967; U. Tex. research scholar, 1978-80. Mem. Inst. Mgmt. Sci., Ops. Research Soc. Am. Hindu. Home: 1401 E Brentrup Dr Tempe AZ 85283 Office: Ariz State U Tempe AZ 85287

ROY, BERNARD RUDOLPH, loss prevention executive; b. Frenchville, Maine, Feb. 5, 1933; s. Peter Paul and Catherine Marie (Bouchard) R.; student Assumption Coll., 1951-53; B.A. in Biology and Chemistry, LaSalle Coll., 1955; m. Claire Coffey, Sept. 19, 1970; children—Elaine C., Daniel B. Indsl. hygienist and health physicist Aetna Life and Casualty, 1957-67; dist. environ. health engr. U.S. Steel Corp., Pitts., 1967-72; corp. indsl. hygienist AMAX Inc., Greenwich, Conn., 1972-74, corp. dir. loss prevention, Greenwich, 1974—. Trustee Indsl. Health Found.; bd. dirs. Sera; chmn. bd. NiPERA; chmn. health com. Am. Mining Congress; active People to People Ambassador Program. Served with Signal Corps, U.S. Army, 1955-57. Cert. indsl. hygienist. Mem. Am. Indsl. Hygiene Assn., Am. Acad. Indsl. Hygiene, Am. Soc. Safety Engrs. Roman Catholic. Contbr. articles and papers to profl. publs. and meetings. Home: 162 Putting Green Rd Trumbull CT 06611 Office: AMAX Inc AMAX Center Greenwich CT 06836

ROY, CHARLES ROBERT, machinery manufacturing company executive; b. Duluth, Minn., Oct. 15, 1930; s. John Benjamin and Ruth Laverna (Olsen) R.; m. Patricia Raye Haggins, May 21, 1955; children—Richard, Margaret, John, Joan. B.A., Mich. State U., 1953; A.M.P., Harvard U., 1979. C.P.A., Wis., 1957. Auditor Price Waterhouse & Co., Milw., 1954; auditor, tax accountant, tax mgr. Arthur Andersen & Co., Milw., 1954-62; tax mgr. Rex Chainbelt, Inc. (name now Rexnord Inc.), Brookfield, Wis., 1962-65; asst. sec. Rex Chainbelt, Inc. (name now Rexnord Inc.), 1965-66, asst. sec., chief accounting officer, 1966-68, asst. sec., asst. treas., 1968-69, controller, 1969-81, v.p. fin., treas., 1981-85, v.p. fin., 1985—. Treas., bd. dirs. Wis. Heart Assn.; bus. alumni dir., devel. fund dir. Mich. State U. Served with USAF, 1948-49. Mem. West Milwaukee C. of C. (dir. 1964), Am. Inst. C.P.A.s, Wis. Soc. C.P.A.s (dir. Milw. chpt. 1967), Tax Execs. Inst. (pres. Wis. chpt. 1965), NAM, Fin. Execs. Inst. (pres. Milw. chpt. 1984), Better Bus. Bur. (dir.), Citizens Govtl. Research Bur., Mich. State U. Alumni Assn. of Milw., Delta Sigma Phi. Episcopalian. Home: 14245 Heatherwood Ct Elm Grove WI 53122 Office: Rexnord 350 N Sunny Slope Brookfield WI 53005

ROY, HAROLD EDWARD, research chemist; b. Stratford, Conn., June 2, 1921; s. Ludger Homer and Meta (Jepsen) R.; B.A., Duke U., 1950; m. Joyce E. Enslin, Oct. 9, 1946 (div. 1975); children—Glenn E., Barbara Anne, Suzanne Elizabeth; m. Gail LaVer Jensen, Feb. 11, 1983. Chemist research div. Lockheed Propulsion Co., Redlands, Calif., 1957-61; sec., treas. The Halgene Corp., Riverside, Calif., 1961-63; self-employed chemist, Glendora, Calif., 1963-64; chief engr. propellant devel. Rocket Power, Inc., Mesa, Ariz., 1964-65; cons., Glendora, 1965-66; engring. specialist Northrop Corp., Anaheim, Calif., 1966-69; pres. Argus Tech., Beverly Hills, 1969-70, dir. Harold E. Roy & Assos., Glendora, 1969—. Served to lt. (j.g.) USNR, 1943-46. Mem. Exptl. Aircraft Assn., Am. Ordnance Assn., Am. Inst. Aeros. and Astronautics, Internat. Platform Assn., Acad. Parapsychology and Medicine, Calif. Profl. Hypnotists Assn., World Future Soc. Republican. Home: 143 Warren Rd PO Box 414 Selma OR 97538

ROY, HENRI A., corporate executive; b. Ottawa, Ont., Can., July 29, 1947; m. Diane P. Morin, Aug. 30, 1969; children: Louis Sébastien, Henri Olivier. BMechE, McGill U., 1970; MBA, Harvard U., 1976; grad., Internat. Mgmt. Inst., Geneva, Switzerland, 1982. Chief of staff, exec. asst. to fin. minister and pres. treasury bd. Govt. Que., Can., 1971-74; sr. account mgr. comml. banking Bank of Montreal, Can., 1976-77; with Standard Oil Co., Cleve., 1977-85, dir. fin. and investments, 1983-85, v.p. fin., chief fin. officer processed mineral sector, 1980-83; exec. v.p. Provigo Inc., Montreal, 1985—; chmn., chief exec. officer Consumers Distbg. Co. Ltd., Provigo Corp. (U.S.A), Horne & Pitfield Foods Ltd.; bd. dirs. Provigo Inc., Laurentian Bank, Cambior Inc., SGF, Domtar Inc. Bd. dirs. YMCA Found. Montreal. Mem. Nat.-Am. Wholesale Grocers Assn (gov.), Can.-U.S. Bus. Coun. (chmn.), Fin. Execs. Inst., Order of Engrs. of Que. Clubs: Mt. Royal; Harvard Bus. of Montreal; Le Sanctuaire Sports. Home: 3180 Delavigne, Montreal, PQ Canada H3Y 2C4 Office: Provigo Inc Ste 2600, 800 René-Lévesque W, Montreal, PQ Canada H3B 1Y2 also: Consumers Distbg Co Ltd, 62 Belfield Rd, Rexdale, ON Canada M9W 1G2

ROY, NORMAN E., construction company executive; b. Pawtucket, R.I., Dec. 2, 1926; s. Ernest and Melanie (Morin) R.; m. Jeannette Martel, Oct. 30, 1948; children—Norman E., Jr., Richard R., Jean Roy McGarry, Paul, Deborah Roy Edwards, Ronald, John. B.S. in Acctg., Bryant Coll., 1948; postgrad., Providence Coll., U. R.I. Various positions Gilbane Bldg. Co., Providence, 1949-69; v.p., controller Gilbane Bldg. Co., 1969-79, v.p. fin., 1979-83, sr. v.p. fin., 1983—. Mem. Nat. Assn. Accts., Fin. Execs. Inst., Assoc. Gen. Contractors Am. (mem. ins. info. and surety assn. of Am. coms., 1983—), Adminstrv. Mgmt. Soc., Bryant Coll. Alumni Assn. (mem. exec. bd. 1986-87). Office: Gilbane Bldg Co 7 Jackson Walkway Providence RI 02940

ROYACK, WALTER JOHN, JR., electrical engineer; b. Phila., Feb. 24, 1954; s. Walter Sr. and Julia (Kocur) R.; m. Michelle Anne Quigley, Oct. 23, 1976. BEE, Drexel U., 1986. Instrument calibrator Ametek Instruments & Controls, Feasterville, Pa., 1972-74; instrument mechanic Amstar Corp. subs. Domino Sugar, Phila., 1974-80; instrument engr. Roberts Filter Mfg. co., Darby, Pa., 1980—. Mem. Assn. Computing Machinery, Instrument Soc. Am., Inst. Elec. & Electronics Engrs. Home: 733 Park Ave Collingswood NJ 08108 Office: Roberts Filter Mfg Co 6th & Columbia Ave Darby PA 19023

ROYCHOUDHURI, CHANDRASEKHAR, physicist; b. Barisal, Bengal, India, Apr. 7, 1942; s. Hiralal and Amiyabala (Sengupta) R.; m. Pamela Taren, Aug. 8, 1977; children: Asim, Onnesha. BS in Physics, Jadavpur U., India, 1963; MS in Physics, Jadavpur U., 1965; PhD, U. Rochester, 1973. Asst. prof. U. Kalyani, West Bengal, India, 1965-68; sr. scientist Nat. Inst. Astrophysics, Puebla, Mex., 1974-78; sr. staff scientist TRW Inc., Los Angeles, 1978-86; mgr. laser systems Perkin-Elmer, Danbury, Conn., 1986—. Author: chpt. Optical Shoptesting, 1978; contbr. articles to profl. jours. Mem. IEEE, Optical Soc. Am., Soc. Photo-optical Instrumentation, AAAS, Planetary Soc., Am. Phys. Soc. (life). Office: Perkin-Elmer 100 Wooster Hts Danbury CT 06810

ROYER, DONALD E., corporate lawyer; b. 1949. Grad., Ariz. State U.; JD, Western State U., 1976. V.p. Am. Savs. and Loan Assn., Irvine, Calif., 1983-85, exec. v.p., acting gen. counsel, 1985, sr. exec. v.p., gen. counsel, 1985—; v.p., asst. gen. counsel Fin. Corp. of Am. (parent), Irvine, Calif., 1983-84, sr. v.p., acting gen. counsel, 1984-85; exec. v.p., gen. counsel Fin. Corp. of Am. (parent), Irvine, 1985-88; sr. exec. v.p., gen. counsel Am. Savs. Bank, Irvine, 1988—. Office: Am Savs Bank 18401 Von Karman Ave Irvine CA 92715

ROYER, ROBERT LEWIS, utility company executive; b. Louisville, Jan. 2, 1928; s. Carl Brown and Martha Helen (Garrett) R.; m. Carol Jean Pierce, June 24, 1950; children: Jenifer Lea, Todd Pierce, Robert Douglas. B.S. in Elec. Engring, Rose Hulman Inst. Tech., 1949. Registered profl. engr., Ky. With Louisville Gas and Electric Co., 1949—, asst. v.p. ops., 1962-63, asst. v.p., asst. gen. supt., 1963-64, v.p., gen. supt., 1964-69, v.p. ops., 1969-78, exec. v.p., 1978, pres., chief exec. officer, 1978—, also dir.; mem. exec. bd. East Central Area Reliability Council, 1978—; mem. Ky. Energy Resources Commn., 1975-79; mem. energy task force Gov.'s Econ. Devel. Commn., 1976-79; mem. Ky. Energy Research Bd., 1978—; v.p. Ind.-Ky. Electric Corp., 1979—; dir. Ohio Valley Transmission Corp., Citizens Fidelity Corp., Citizens Fidelity Bank and Trust Co. Mem. exec. bd. Old Ky. Home Council Boy Scouts Am., v.p. dist. ops., 1970-75, 79-80, 1st v.p., 1981-82, pres., 1982-84, commr., 1975-79, rep. to nat. council, 1975—, mem. Southeast Regional Bd., 1985—, S.E. region area pres. 1988—; bd. dirs. East End Boys Club, 1975-78, Louisville Indsl. Found., 1980—, Ky. Council Sci. and Tech.; trustee Spirit of Louisville Found., 1978—, J. Graham Brown Found., 1980—; bd. mgrs. Rose Hulman Inst. Tech., 1979—; mem. Louisville Devel. Com., 1979—. Served with U.S. Army, 1953-55. Recipient Silver Beaver award Boy Scouts Am., 1975. Mem. IEEE, Execs. Club Louisville (dir. 1980-83), Louisville Automobile Club (dir. 1974—, treas. 1977-79, v.p. 1979-81, pres. 1981-83, nat. adv. council 1982—), Louisville Area C. of C. (dir. 1978-80). Methodist. Clubs: Hurstbourne Country, Jefferson, Pendennis, Rotary. Home: 4014 Norbourne Blvd Louisville KY 40207 Office: Louisville Gas & Electric Co 311 W Chestnut St PO Box 32010 Louisville KY 40232

ROYER, THOMAS JERRY, financial planner; b. Coshocton, Ohio, June 17, 1943; s. Walter H. Sr. and Francis (Guerke) R.; m. Felipa T. Pagal, Dec. 24, 1965; children: Matthew Vincent, Brian Eugene, Nicholas Alexander. Student, Xavier U., 1979. Cert. fin. planner. Agt. Met. Life Ins. Co., N.Y.C., 1966-68, mgr., 1968-70; gen. agt. Summit Nat. Life Ins. Co., Akron, Ohio, 1970—; prin. Royer & Co., Fairfield, Ohio, 1985-88; founder, pres. Group-10 Fin., Fairfield, 1988—. Mem. Inst. Cert. Fin. Planners (bd. dirs. Miami Valley chpt.), Internat. Assn. Fin. Planning. Republican. Roman Catholic. Office: Group-10 Fin 5109 Pleasant Ave Ste Q-R-S Fairfield OH 45014

ROY-SANDERS, CATHERINE SUE, accountant; b. Louisville, Oct. 15, 1957; d. Samuel Curtis and Betty Janrose (Phelps) Roy; m. Michael L. Sanders, Nov. 19, 1988. BA in Acctg., Bellarmine Coll., 1979, MBA, 1987. Tax auditor unemployment div. Ky. Dept. Human Resources, Frankfort, 1979-81; acctg. supr. So. Bapt. Theol. Sem., Louisville, 1981-83, purchasing agt., supr., 1983-84; dir. acctg. services dept. Ky. Bapt. Conv., Middletown, 1985—. Flutist River Cities Concert Band, Jeffersonville, Ind., 1980-84; mem. single adult com. Walnut St. Bapt. Ch., Louisville, 1983—, mem. budget planning com., 1985—, deacon, 1987—; vol. Home of the Innocents, Louisville, 1987—. Named Outstanding Young Women in Am., 1987, 88. Office: Ky Bapt Conv 10701 Shelbyville Rd Middletown KY 40243

RUANO, MIGUEL, aeronautical engineer; b. Tangier, Morocco, Spain, July 29, 1928; s. Miguel and M. Dolores (Quero) R.; children: Miguel, Jose C., Fernando, Beatriz, Gonzalo. Degree in Aero. Engring., A.M. Ingenieros Aeronauticos, Madrid, Spain, 1953; D in Aero. Engring., E.S. Ingenieros Aeronauticos, Madrid Spain, 1967. Registered profl. engr. Commd. Spanish Air Force, 1947, advanced through grades to capt.; shop supr. Son Bonet Air Force Depot, Majorca, Spain, 1953-56; maintenance comdr. Spanish Air Force, Son San Juan AFB, Majorca, 1956-59; inspection supr. Spanish Air Force, Barcelona, Spain, 1959-60; head dept. E.N. Motores De Aviacion, Barcelona, Spain, 1960-62; tech. mgr. Fundiciones Industriales, Barcelona, 1962-73; gen. mgr. Sirma, Barcelona, 1973-74, Metron, Barcelona, 1974-82; mng. dir. Corp. Indsl. Catalana, Barcelona, 1982—. Recipient Aero. Merit Cross Ministerio Del Aire, Madrid, 1953. Mem. Assn. Ingenieros España, Assn. Ingenieros Aeronauticos, Colegio Ingenieros Aeronauticos. Office: Corp Industrial Catalana, Pau Claris 165, 08037 Barcelona Spain

RUBACH, JIMMY DALE, vocational services educator; b. Campbell Hill, Ill., Jan. 23, 1946; s. Adolph and Ida (Casten) R.; m. Marlene Susan Bookman, Oct. 25, 1968; children: Jamie Rene, Candace Rose. BS in Occupational Edn., SW Tex. State U., 1977; MS in Adminstrn., Tex. A&I U., 1979, Cert. in Mid-Mgmt., 1986. Tchr. auto mechanics Kingsville (Tex.) Ind. Sch. Dist., 1973-79; instr. curriculum dept. TEX. A&M U., College Station, 1979; tchr. auto mechanics Dickinson (Tex.) Ind. Sch. Dist., 1979-86, asst. prin. vocat. services, 1986—; owner, operator R&B Glass Tinting, Dickinson, 1985. Council mem., fin. sec. Faith Luth. Ch., 1984-85. Mem. Tex. Assn. Secondary Sch. Prins., Tex. Vocat. Adminstrs. and Suprs. Assn., Gulf Coast Vocat. Adminstrs. and Suprs. Assn., Optimists (bd. dirs. Dickinson chpt. 1986-87). Home: 5409 Sycamore Dickinson TX 77539

RUBASH, NORMAN JOSEPH, oil company executive; b. East McKeesport, Pa., Mar. 2, 1932; s. Joseph Robert and Anna (Peckman) R.; m. Alice Elizabeth Chapman, Apr. 20, 1957; children: Karen, Amy, Janet. B.S. in Petroleum Engring., Pa. State U., 1954; J.D., U. Pitts., 1957. Bar: U.S. Ct. Appeals (D.C. cir.), U.S. Dist. Ct. D.C., U.S. Patent Office; registered profl. engr., Okla. Mgr. prodn. Amoco (UK) Exploration Co., London, 1970-71, Amoco Europe, London, 1972-76; pres. Amoco (UK) Exploration Co., London, 1976-77, Amoco Egypt Oil Co., Cairo, 1977-79; v.p. supply Standard Oil Co. (Ind.), Chgo., 1979-81; pres. Amoco Can. Petroleum Co., Ltd., Calgary, Alta., 1981-85; exec. v.p. Amoco Prodn. Co., Chgo., 1985-86, exec. v.p. internat., 1986—; mem. adv. bd. energy tng. program USAID, 1989—. Dep. campaign chmn. Calgary United Way, 1983-85; pres. Jr. Achievement Calgary, 1983-85; U.S. rep. Egyptian Am. Middle Mgmt. Tng. Com., 1978-80; mem. Midwest adv. bd. Inst. Internat. Edn., 1987—; bd. visitors U. Chgo. Oriental Inst., 1987—. Recipient Disting. Alumnus award Pa. State U., 1986. Mem. Am. Petroleum Inst., Soc. Petroleum Engrs., Can. Petroleum Assn. (dir. 1981-85), U.K. Offshore Operators Assn. (bd. dirs. 1976-77), Natural Gas Supply Assn. (exec. com. 1986—), U.S.-Iraq Bus. Forum (bd. dirs. 1986-87), Phi Gamma Delta, Phi Delta Phi. Republican. Presbyterian. Clubs: Petroleum (Calgary); Mid America (Chgo.). Office: Amoco Prodn Co 200 E Randolph Dr Chicago IL 60601

RUBENSTEIN, ALAN, sales executive; b. Memphis, Aug. 2, 1955; s. Samuel and Barbara (Poddel) R. BBA, Memphis State U., 1978. Sales rep. lab. div. Pfizer Inc., Palm Beach Gardens, Fla., 1979-89; dist. hosp. rep. Harvard Med. Sch. system Pfizer Inc., Framingham, Mass., 1989—. Pres. Glenwood Homeowners Assn., 1987, Palm Beach Gardens, 1987—, v.p. 1986-87; mem. com. PGA Srs. Golf Championship, 1984-87, chmn. player relations com., 1987; dist. rep. QTR, 1987. Mem. No. Palm Beach Gardens C. of C. (mem. spl. events com. 1986—), PGA Nat. Men's Golf Assn. (v.p. 1984—), Am. Biographical Inst. (rsch. bd. advisors). Republican. Jewish. Club: PGA Nat. Golf (Palm Beach Gardens). Home and Office: 9 Emily St Framingham MA 01701

RUBENSTEIN, DANIEL ELIAS, business executive; b. N.Y.C., Dec. 18, 1952; s. Bert and Muriel (Krawitz) R.; m. Leah Louise Hirsch, June 22, 1975; children: Harry, Deborah. BS, Cornell U., 1974; MBA, U. Chgo., 1976. Sr. analyst Xerox Corp., Rochester, N.Y., 1976-78; asst. treas. Primerica Corp., Greenwich, Conn., 1978—, also treas. polit. action com., 1986—. Mem. Tau Beta Pi. Office: Primerica Corp PO Box 3610 Greenwich CT 06836

RUBENSTEIN, HOWARD JOSEPH, public relations executive; b. N.Y.C., Feb. 3, 1932; s. Samuel and Ada (Sall) R.; m. Amy Forman, Dec. 17, 1959; children: Roni, Richard, Steven. A.B., U. Pa., 1953; student law, Harvard, 1953; LL.B. (Dean's scholar), St. Johns Sch. Law, 1959. Bar: N.Y. State bar 1960. Pres. Howard J. Rubenstein Assocs., Inc. pub. relations cons., N.Y.C., 1954—; asst. counsel judiciary com. U.S. Ho. of Reps., 1960; cons. U.S. Fgn. Claims Commn., 1961-62; cons. joint legis. com. child care needs N.Y., 1965-66; adviser SBA,, 1965-66. Gov.'s Com. on Sale of World Trade Center, 1981, Mayor's Com. on Holocaust Commemoration, 1981—; mem. N.Y. State Task Force on Energy Conservation, Dept. Housing, 1981—, mem. mayor's council econ. bus. advisors, N.Y.C., 1974-77, mayor's com. pub. interest, 1975-77; past dir. Brownsville Boys Club; bd. dirs. Provide Addict Care Today, Police Athletic League, N.Y. chpt. March of Dimes; mem. U.S. Internat. Council, 1977—; mem. Commn. on Status of Women, 1982—; trustee Cen. Park Conservatory. Mem. Assn. Better N.Y. (mem. exec. com. 1972—), Phi Beta Kappa, Beta Sigma Rho. Jewish (dir. congregation). Home: 141 E 72d St New York NY 10021 Office: Howard J Rubenstein Assocs Inc 1345 Ave of the Americas New York NY 10105

RUBENSTEIN, LAWRENCE ELLIOT, management consultant; b. N.Y.C., Sept. 14, 1948; s. Murray and Lorraine (Sanders) R.; m. Robin Sue Wittlin, Apr. 7, 1970 (div. Feb. 1984); m. Anna Chodos, Sept. 1, 1985; 1 child, Jeremy Ryan. BA in Sociology, Adelphi U., 1970; MBA in Fin., U. Hartford, 1977. Cert. data processing. System mgr. Travelers Ins., Hartford, Conn., 1970-77; cons. Ernst & Whinney, Hartford, 1977-79; audit supr. Timex Corp., Middlebury, Conn., 1979-81; audit mgr. Uniroyal, Middlebury, 1981-84; pres., owner Bus. Mgmt., Avon, Conn., 1984-85; mgr. cons. L&P Friedman & Assoc., Montreal, Que., 1985—; prof. U. New Haven, 1983-84; instr. Women in Data Processing, N.Y.C., 1984. Mem. Inst. Cert. Computer Profls., Can. Info. Processing Soc. Office: L&P Friedman & Assocs, 5075 Rue De Sorel, Montreal, PQ Canada H4P 1G6

RUBIN, CANDACE, brokerage house executive; b. Bakersfield, Calif., Apr. 16, 1952; d. Kal Rubin and Barrie (Barran) Ford. BA, U. Pacific, 1974. Sr. assoc. Henrys Miller Co., Dallas, 1978-82; pres. Andor Investments, Inc., Dallas, 1982—; salesman real estate Darling Delaware, Dallas, 1986—. Campaign mgr. Paul Fielding for City Coun. Rep., Dallas, 1984; vol. Meals on Wheels, 1985-87; with radio show for blind Libr. of Congress, 1987—. Office: 25 Highland Park Village Suite 100 312 Dallas TX 75205

RUBIN, CHARLES ALEXIS, writer; b. Los Angeles, Dec. 4, 1953; s. Herbert Bernard and Jacqueline (Bashor) R.; m. Doris Sara Villalobos, July, 23, 1978; 1 child, Daniel Charles. BA in English magna cum laude, San Francisco State U., 1978, MA in English, 1980. Communications supr. Am. Protective Services, Oakland, Calif., 1982-83; assoc. editor Personal Computing mag., San Jose, 1983-84; free-lance writer Oakland, 1984—; sr. assoc. Waterside Assocs., Fremont, Calif., 1986-87; editorial cons. Televisual Market Strategies, Saratoga, 1985-86. Author: The Endless Apple, 1984, Thinking Small: The Buyer's Guide to Portable Computers, 1984, Appleworks: Boosting Your Business With Integrated Software, 1985, Command Performance: Appleworks, 1986, Microsoft Works, 1986, Macintosh Hard Disk Management, 1988; exec. editor MacIntosh Bus. Rev., San Jose, 1988; contbr. articles to mags. Mem. Media Alliance. Democrat, Jewish. Home: 7036 Exeter Dr Oakland CA 94611

RUBIN, MARTIN A., computer company executive; b. N.Y.C., Feb. 24, 1955. BS, U. Pa., 1976. Co-founder The Mader Group, Narberth, Pa., 1975-76; tech. cons. Radidata, Fairfield, N.J., 1976-77, fin. cons., 1978-79, sales mgr., 1980-81; v.p. Future Techs., Morristown, N.J., 1981-83, Chem. Bank, N.Y.C., 1983-85; pres. Orion Mgmt. Corp. AutoInfo, Inc., Lake Success, N.Y., 1986—; pres. Finnell Corp., Topeka, Kans., 1986—. Office: AutoInfo Inc 5 Dakota Dr Lake Success NY 11042

RUBIN, MARTIN N., meeting planner, consultant; b. N.Y.C., Aug. 9, 1928; s. Max and Esther (Chernow) R.; m. Shirley Anne Rubin, Aug. 22, 1954 (div. Aug. 1964); m. Karen Anne O'Brien, Sept. 21, 1981. AB, U. Mich.; AM, Miami U., Oxford, Ohio; PhD., Sussex U., Eng. Lic. psychologist. With Dayton (Ohio) Sch. System, 1951-60, West Alexandria (Ohio) Sch. System, 1961-63; instr. Wright State U., Dayton, 1961-63; with Devereux Found., Pa., N.Y. Dept. Corrections, Bklyn., 1971-73, Council for Retarded Children, Albany, N.Y., 1973-75; prin. M. Rubin & Co., Inc., Mount Vernon, N.Y., 1975—. Author: Developmentally Disabled, 1965. Candidate Dem. State Legis., 1982; adv. bd. Mt. Vernon Mental Health Bd., 1985. Master's degree scholar Miami U., 1958; Guidance Inst. grantee Miami U., 1959. Fellow Am. Assn. Mental Deficiency (pres. 1967); mem. Soc. Assn. Execs. (bd. dirs. 1985—). Lodge: Masons (sr. warden 1983).

RUBIN, ROBERT EDWARD, investment banking firm executive; b. N.Y.C., Aug. 29, 1938; s. Alexander and Sylvia (Seiderman) R.; m. Judith Leah Oxenberg, Mar. 27, 1963; children: James Samuel, Philip Matthew. A.B. summa cum laude, Harvard U., 1960; postgrad., London Sch. Econs., 1960-61; LL.B., Yale U., 1964. Bar: N.Y. 1965. Assoc. Cleary, Gottlieb, Steen & Hamilton, N.Y.C., 1964-66; assoc. Goldman Sachs & Co., N.Y.C., 1966-70, ptnr., 1971—, mem. mgmt. com., 1980—, vice chmn., co-chief oper. officer, 1987—; bd. dirs. Chgo. Bd. Options Exch., Inc., 1972-76, N.Y. Futures Exch., N.Y.C., 1979-85; mem. Pres.'s Adv. Com. for Trade Negotiations, Washington, 1980-82, mem. adv. com. on tender offers SEC, Washington, 1983, Gov.'s Commn. on Trade Productivity, 1987-88., regulatory adv. com. N.Y. Stock Exch., 1988—, adv. com. internat. capital markets Fed. Res. Bank N.Y., 1989—; Gov.'s Adv. Panel on Fin. Services, 1988—; vice-chmn., trustee Mt. Sinai Hosp., Mt. Sinai Med. Ctr., 1977—; vice-chmn., bd. dirs. Ctr. for Nat. Policy, 1982—; trustee Sta. WNET-TV, 1985—. Trustee Am. Ballet Theatre Found., Inc., N.Y.C., 1969—; trustee Mt. Sinai Med. Ctr., 1977—, Collegiate Sch., 1978-84; mem. bd. overseers' com. to visit econs. dept. Harvard U., 1981-87, com. on univ. resources, 1987—; fin. chmn. N.Y. campaign Mondale for Pres., 1983-84; investment adv. counsel N.Y.C. Pension Fund, 1980—; chmn. Democratic Congressional Dinner, Washington, 1982; bd. dirs. Ctr. for Nat. Policy, 1982—, Democrats For the 80's, 1985-89, Democrats for 90's, 1989—; mem. Commn. Nat. Elections, 1985-86. Recipient award NCCJ, N.Y.C., 1977. Mem. Phi Beta Kappa. Jewish. Clubs: Harvard (N.Y.C.); Century Country (Purchase, N.Y.). Home: 911 Park Ave New York NY 10021 Office: Goldman Sachs & Co 85 Broad St New York NY 10004

RUBINI, EILEEN, fashion designer; b. Union City, N.J., June 2, 1948; d. Julius and Mary (Fitzgerald) R. Student, Iona Coll., Fashion Inst. Tech., N.Y.C.; studied design at Parsons Sch., N.Y.C. With pub. relations and advt. depts. Jaeger Co., N.Y.C., 1972-75; merchandiser Arthur Richards Woman, Inc., N.Y.C., 1975-78; v.p., merchandiser Jerry Silverman Sportswear, N.Y.C., 1978-79, Don Sayres Co., N.Y.C., 1979-81; v.p. design Yukiko Hanai, N.Y.C., 1981-83; v.p., designer Signatures Inc., N.Y.C., 1983-86; designer, owner Eileen Rubini Inc., N.Y.C., 1986—; freelance merchandiser, designer Kellwood Cos., N.Y.C., 1986—. Office: Kellwood Cos 214 W 39th St Ste 902 New York NY 10018

RUBINO, SALVATORE, insurance company executive; b. Bklyn., Feb. 22, 1946; s. Fred and Nettie (Stabile) R.; m. Bernice Robins, June 16, 1968 (div. 1978); children: Christopher Fredrick, Kimberly Elizabeth; m. Nancy Jean Hashagen, Jan. 16, 1982; 1 child, Lisa Marie. BA, Harpur Coll., Binghamton, N.Y., 1968; MBA, Hofstra U., 1983. Cost acct. Empire Blue Cross/Blue Shield Inc., N.Y.C., 1968-69, internal auditor, 1969-73, mgr. internal auditing, 1973-77, dir. internal auditing, 1977—; chmn. Region II auditing com. Blue Cross/Blue Shield Plans. Contbr.: Management Audits, 1986, Case Studies in Internal Auditing, 1986. Mem. Inst. Internal Auditors (cert.), South Shore Power Squadron (Freeport, N.Y.). Democrat. Roman Catholic. Office: Empire Blue Cross & Blue Shield 622 Third Ave New York NY 10017

RUBINOFF, ARNOLD SIDNEY, consultant; b. Toronto, Ont., Can., Feb. 13, 1926; s. Meyer Philip and Sally (Spector) R.; m. Florence Alma Pike, May 19, 1954; children: Carolyn Beth, Philip Andrew, David Matthew. B of Commerce, U. Toronto, 1948, MA, 1949. Statistician Dominion Bur. Statistics, Ottawa, Ont., 1950-56; analyst NATO, Paris, 1956-59; with Can. Dept. Fin., Ottawa, 1959-84, gen. dir. fed.-provincial relations, 1973-76, asst. dep. minister fin., 1976-81, sr. asst. dep. minister, 1981-84; exec. dir. Interam. Devel. Bank, Washington, 1984-88; sr. account exec. pub. policy analysis, econ. and fin. issues Hill and Knowlton, Washington, 1988—. Served to capt. Royal Can. Service Corps (Res.), 1951-56. Jewish. Club: Bretton Woods Recreation Centre (Germantown, Md.). Home: 7811 Whiterim Terr Potomac MD 20854 Office: Govt Rsch Corp 12 S Connecticut Ave NW Washington DC 20036

RUBINOVITZ, SAMUEL, diversified manufacturing company executive; b. Boston, Dec. 26, 1929; s. Benjamin Ephraim and Pauline (Kaufman) R.; m. Phyllis Ann Silverstein; children: David Jay, Robert Neal. BS, MIT, 1951, MS, 1952. Sales engr. Clevite Transistor Products, Waltham, Mass., 1954-63; sales mgr. EG&G Inc., Wellesley, Mass., 1963-72, div. mgr., 1972-79, v.p., 1979-86, sr. v.p., 1986—; bd. dirs. KLA Instruments Inc., Santa Clara, Calif., Richardson Electronics Ltd., Chgo., Kronos Inc., Waltham. Served to 1st lt. USAF, 1952-54. Democrat. Jewish. Office: EG & G Inc 45 William St Wellesley MA 02181

RUBINSTEIN, SHIRLEY JOY, nursing service executive; b. Toronto, Ont., Can., Nov. 19, 1927; came to U.S., 1928, naturalized, 1948; d. Harry Hyman and Ida Ruth (Albert) Adel; m. Philip F. Rubinstein, Aug. 17, 1947; children—David Brian, Wendy Sue, Hope Terri. With Jewish Agy. for Palestine, Washington, 1947-49; coordinator Nursing Staff, Inc., 1975-78; co-founder, pres. Nursing Services, Inc., Silver Spring, Md., 1978—; founder, pres. Fantasy Factory Inc., Pegasus Limosine Services. Democrat. Jewish. Club: B'nai Birth. Office: PO Box 4133 Silver Spring MD 20904

RUBLE, DUANE RUSSELL, retail drug store executive; b. Lewistown, Pa., Apr. 27, 1943; s. Russell Leroy and Jane (Suloff) R.; m. Paula Mae, June 1, 1974; children—Cynthia Jane, Chad Russell, Matthew Ryan. B.S., Juniata Coll., 1965. With Sears Roebuck & Co., Harrisburg, PA., 1965-68; sr. v.p. Rite Aid Corp, Harrisburg, PA., 1968-88; owner Cumberland Truck Equipment Co., 1988—. Served with U.S. Army, 1967-73. Home: 1576 W Lisburn Rd Mechanicsburg PA 17055 Office: Cumberland Truck Equipment Co 25 Roadway Dr Carlisle PA 17013

RUBLE, JAMES KENNETH, insurance company executive; b. Bertram, Tex., Nov. 15, 1923; s. Walter Duey and Sarah Jewel (Reynolds) R.; m. Mary Louise Williams, Jan. 12, 1946; children: Phyllis Ruble McReynolds, Janice Ruble Clements. BBA, U. Tex., 1948. With sales dept. Liberty Mut., Dallas, San Antonio, 1948-54; agt. Ruble & Assocs., San Antonio, 1954-86; bd. dirs. Tex. Ins. Agy. Inc., San Antonio, 1986—; bd. dirs. Alamo Savs. Assn., San Antonio. Fellow Acad. Producer Studies; mem. Soc. Cert. Ins. Counselors (chmn. 1969-75, 86—, chmn. emeritus 1986—), Bus. and Profl. Club. Republican. Baptist. Office: Tex Ins Agy Inc 5368 Fredericksburg Rd San Antonio TX 78229

RUBLOFF, BURTON, real estate broker, appraiser; b. Chisholm, Minn., June 1, 1912; s. Solomon W. and Mary R.; m. Patricia F. Williams, July 17, 1943; 1 dau., Jenifer. Grad, Northwestern U., 1940. With Arthur Rubloff & Co. (now Rubloff Inc.), Chgo., 1930—; v.p. Arthur Rubloff & Co. (now Rubloff Inc.), 1947-76, sr. v.p., 1976—. Bd. dirs. Mcpl. Art League Chgo.; mem. Urbanland Inst. Served with U.S. Army, 1943-46, ETO. Mem. Am. Inst. Real Estate Appraisers (life mem. chpt. 6), Nat. Ill., Chgo. (hon. life mem.) assns. real estate bds., Chgo. Real Estate Bd. (ethics com.), Bldg. Mgrs. Assn. Chgo., Urban Land Inst., Greater State St. Council (real estate com.), John Evans Club, City Club, Northwestern Club of Chgo., Lambda Alpha Internat. (Ely chpt.). Office: Rubloff Inc 111 W Washington St Chicago IL 60602

RUBOTTOM, DONALD J., management consultant; b. Tulsa, Sept. 29, 1926; s. George William and Nellie Dorcas (Core) R.; m. Wanda Mae Stockton, Apr. 29, 1951; children: Rinda Louise, Joy Lynn, Donald Jay, Jill Anna. BS in Fin., Okla. State U.; postgrad., Tulsa U. Chartered fin. analyst; cert. mgmt. cons. V.p., trust officer 1st Nat. Bank & Trust Co., Tulsa, 1955-56; exec. v.p., trust officer, dir. F&M Bank & Trust Co., Tulsa, 1966-68; pres. Rubottom, Dudack & Assocs., Inc., Tulsa, 1986—; tchr. Boston Ave. United Meth. Ch., Tulsa, 1962—. With U.S. Army, 1945-46. Mem. Inst. Mgmt. Cons., Chartered Fin. Analysts Inst., Okla. Soc. Fin. Analysts, Tulsa Knife & Fork Club (pres. 1985-86), Tulsa So. Tennis Club, Tulsa Club, Rotary (pres. 1988—). Office: Rubottom Dudash & AssocsInc 2700 E 51st St Ste 340 Tulsa OK 74105

RUBRECHT, ROBERT LOUIS, sales executive; b. Enid, Okla., Aug. 8, 1944; s. Robert L. and Willie Mae (Sample) R.; m. Margaret Ann, Feb. 13, 1965; children: Robin, Robert. BS in Biology, Cen. State U., Edmond, Okla., 1966. Chemist Wilson & Co., Oklahoma City, 1966-67; with sales dept. Acad. of Reading, Omaha, 1967-69; with pharm. sales dept. Hoechst-Roussel Pharm., Inc., Somerville, N.J., 1969—, with sales mgmt. dept., 1974—. Coach Edmond Soccer Club, 1977-84. Republican. Home: 6129 Stonegate Pl Edmond OK 73034

RUBY, LUCIEN, venture capitalist; b. Knoxville, Tenn., Feb. 9, 1944; s. Clyde and Lorena (Dempster) R.; m. Caryl B. Welborn, Apr. 11, 1987. BS in Civil Engring., Duke U., 1966; MBA, Harvard U., 1977. Founder, chief exec. officer Combined Supply Group, Washington, 1972-74; mgr. Vt. Investment Capital, South Royalton, 1976; cons. The Strategic Planning Inst., Cambridge, Mass., 1977-78; prin. Brentwood Assocs., L.A., 1979-84; cons. Ridgeback Ptnrs., San Francisco, 1984-86; gen. ptnr. Quest Ventures, San Francisco, 1984—; bd. dirs. Chang Labs., San Jose, Calif., Ruby Concrete Co., Madisonville, Ky., Marlstone Corp., San Raphael, Calif., Lokring Corp., Redwood City, Calif., Shirtmakers Ltd., San Francisco. Author: Venture Capital Investing, 1977; contbr.: Corporate Creativity, 1984, Financing and Managing Fast Growth Company, 1987. Mem. Software Entrepreneurs Forum (founder), Harvard Old Boys Club (pres. 1984-88), Boys Rugby Football Club (pres. 1986-88). Office: Quest Ventures 555 California St Ste 5000 San Francisco CA 94104

RUBY, PAUL MICHAEL, investment banker; b. Rome, N.Y., Apr. 22, 1944; s. William Clair and Helen Marion (Dorn) R.; m. Tena Lee Pinuel, Sept. 2, 1972; children: Parker, Taylor, Dylan. BS, MIT, 1966; MBA, Harvard U., 1968. Assoc. Cresap, McCormick & Paget, N.Y.C., 1968-70; dir. fin. Heublein Inc., Hartford, Conn., 1970-75; pres. Massasoit Trading Co., Holyoke, Mass., 1975-77; planning officer Insilco Corp., Meriden, Conn., 1977-79; pres. REN Electronics Corp., South Hadley, Mass., 1979-81; sr. assoc. B.L. McTeague & Co., Hartford, 1981-82; pres. Parker Benjamin Inc., Farmington, Conn., 1982—. Republican. Episcopalian. Clubs: Longmeadow (Mass.) Country; Hartford; Harvard Faculty (Cambridge). Office: Parker Benjamin Inc 160 Farmington Ave Farmington CT 06032

RUCH, RICHARD HURLEY, manufacturing company executive; b. Plymouth, Ind., Apr. 15, 1930; s. Dallas Claude and Mabel (Hurley) R.; m. Patricia Lou Overbeek, June 27, 1931; children: Richard, Michael, Christine, Douglas. BA, Mich. State U., 1952. Stores acctg. supr. Kroger Inc., Grand Rapids, Mich., 1954-55; chief acct. Herman Miller Inc., Zeeland, Mich., 1955-58, controller, 1958-63, dir. mfg., 1963-67, v.p. mfg., 1967-77, v.p. adminstrn., 1978, v.p. corp. resources, 1979-85, chief fin. officer, sr. v.p., 1985-87, chief exec. officer, 1988—; bd. dirs. Milcare, Zeeland, Herman Miller Research Corp., Zeeland, Weldun Internat., Bridgman, Mich. Active Hope Coll., Twentieth Century Club, Holland, Mich.; formerly active Holland C. of C., Zeeland Planning Com. Mem. Scanlon Plan Assocs. (bd. dirs., past pres.). Office: Herman Miller Inc 8500 Byron Rd Zeeland MI 49464

RUCH, WILLIAM VAUGHN, educator, consultant; b. Allentown, Pa., Sept. 29, 1937; s. Weston H. and Dorothy D. (Daubert) R.;. BA, Moravian Coll., 1959; MA in Communications, Syracuse U., 1969; MBA, Fairleigh Dickinson U., 1972; PhD, Rensselaer Poly. Inst., 1980; JD, Western State U. Coll. Law, 1983. Reporter Call-Chronicle Newspapers, Allentown, Pa., 1959-60; tchr. English conversation Jonan Sr. High Sch., Matsuyama, Japan, 1960-62; asst. editor Dixie News, Am. Can Co., Easton, Pa., 1964-65; fin. editor Pa. Power & Light Co., Allentown, 1967-69, sales promotion writer, 1965-66, advt. asst., 1966-67; tech. writer, editor Space Tech. Ctr., Allentown, 1966-67, Gen. Electric Co., King of Prussia, Pa., 1969; prof. mgmt. Monmouth Coll., West Long Branch, N.J., 1985-88; corp. communications cons. Madison, N.J., 1988—; asst. editor Bell System Tech. Jour., Bell Telephone Labs., Murray Hill, N.J., 1969-71; field rep. N.W. Ayer & Son, Inc., N.Y.C., 1972-73; asst. prof. bus. communications Fairleigh Dickinson U., Madison, N.J., 1974-75, Bloomsburg (Pa.) State Coll., 1975-76; lectr. Sch. Bus. and Pub. Adminstrn., Calif. State U., Sacramento, 1977-79; asst. prof. bus. writing Coll. Bus. Adminstrn., San Diego (Calif.) State U., 1979-84; lectr. European div. U. Md., 1984-85; cons. Corporate Communications, 1988—. Author: Corporate Communications: A Comparison of Japanese and American Practices, 1984, Business Reports: Written and Oral, 1988, International Handbook of Corporate Communication, 1989. Mem. Acad. Mgmt., Assn. for Bus. Communication Assn., Internat. Assn. Bus. Communicators, Internat. Platform Assn. Republican. Mem. United Ch. of Christ. Home: 288F Main St Madison NJ 07940

RUCKS, BRIAN LEE, financial services executive; b. Oak Park, Ill., Nov. 2, 1952; s. Bruce ARthur and Beverly (Hedwig Frega) R.; m. Donna Farris, Dec. 21, 1985. BS in Edn., Western Ill. U., 1974. Cert. fin. planner. Fin. planner IDS Fin. Services, Inc., Quincy, Ill., 1974-76; dist. mgr. IDS Fin. Services, Inc., Fort Madison, Iowa, 1976-85; div. mgr. IDS Fin. Services, Inc., Merrillville, Ind., 1985—. Mem. Inst. Cert. Fin. Planners, Airline Owners and Pilots Assn., Internat. Assn. Fin. Planners, Better Bus. Bur. Office: IDS Fin Svcs Inc 80 W 79th Ave Merrillville IN 46410

RUCKSTUHL, KONRAD, waste processing company executive; b. Basel, Switzerland, Aug. 27, 1920; came to U.S., 1977; s. Konrad and Martha (Attinger) R.; m. Judy Sue Adair, June 30, 1968; children: Natasha Lee, Tanya. Student, Basel Bus. Coll., 1938. Founder Waste Processing Corp., Basel, 1940-77; founder, chmn. SPM Group, Inc., Denver, 1977-87, Preston, Minn., 1987—. Patentee in field. With Swiss Army, 1939-45. Lutheran. Office: SPM Group Inc 1601 W 23d Ste 200 Lawrence KS 66046

RUDA, HOWARD, lawyer, finance company executive; b. N.Y.C., Sept. 7, 1932; s. Menahem and Lucy (Gillenson) R.; BA, Coll. City N.Y., 1954; J.D., Columbia, 1959; m. Leah E. Zeliger, Sept. 22, 1963; 1 child, Amy. Bar: N.Y. 1959, U.S. Dist. Ct. (so. and ea. dists.) N.Y. 1959. Assoc., then ptnr. Laporte & Meyers, N.Y.C., 1959-63; staff atty., then gen. counsel Meinhard Comml. Corp., N.Y.C., 1963-68; with C.I.T. Group Holdings, Inc., N.Y.C., 1968-87, asst. gen. counsel, 1968—, gen. counsel, v.p., dir. C.I.T. Corp., C.I.T. Leasing Corp., 1973-84; counsel Hahn & Hessen, N.Y.C., 1987—; lectr. Practicing Law Inst., Banking Law Inst.; dir. Am. Bankruptcy Inst. Editor: Asset Based Financing. Served with U.S. Army, 1954-56. Mem. ABA (chmn. equipment financing com. 1982-85, chmn. ad hoc bulk sales com. 1987—), Am. Law Inst., Phi Beta Kappa. Jewish. Home: 8 Mirrielees Rd Great Neck NY 11021 Office: Hahn & Hessen 350 Fifth Ave New York NY 10118

RUDD, GERALD RAY, retail food and drug company executive; b. Kinsley, Kans., Oct. 6, 1929; s. Linford L. and Bertha Viola (Workman) R.; m. Nicole Cardoso-Ayres, Oct. 4, 1930; children: Christian, Derek. BA, George Washington U., 1958; grad. Program for Mgmt. Devel., Harvard U., 1968. Mgmt. intern AEC, Washington, 1958-59; labor relations mgr. Albertsons, Inc., Boise, Idaho, 1959-62, dir. indsl. relations, 1962-70, v.p. personnel and indsl. relations, 1970-74, sr. v.p. human resources, 1974—. Served to lt. USN, 1951-55. Mem. Am. Soc. Personnel Adminstrn. (Profl. of Yr. awards Boise chpt. 1984, nat. soc. 1986). Republican. Mormon. Club: Hillcrest Country (Boise). Home: 1101 S Owynee Boise ID 83705 Office: Albertson's Inc 250 Parkcenter Blvd Boise ID 83726

RUDD, ORVILLE LEE, II, finance company executive; b. Grove Center, Ky., Dec. 18, 1922; s. Orville Lee and Louie (Collins) R.; m. Margaret Kopsky, Apr. 23, 1944; children: Janice, Keith. AA in Acctg., Brown Bus. Coll., 1952; degree in bus. law, Washington U., 1953. Cert. tax preparer. Dist. mgr. fin. Comml. Credit Corp., Balt., 1953-59; mgr. credit and fin. Iowa Guarantee Corp., Des Moines, 1959-65; fin. mgr. Inland Fin. Co., Clive, Iowa, 1965-77; pers. officer Fawn Engring., Clive, 1977-80, Pella (Iowa) Community Hosp., 1979-80; owner, prin. Rudd Fin. Svcs., Pella, 1980—. Dist. comdr. U.S. Power Squadrons, Des Moines, 1987—. Capt. U.S. Army, 1942-44. Recipient Comdr.'s award U.S. Power Squadrons, 1976, 88, Ky. Col. award Commonwealth of Ky., 1986. Mem. Nat. Assn. Life Underwriters, Kiwanis. Office: Rudd Fin Svcs 739 1/2 Franklin Pella IA 50219

RUDDELL, GARY RONALD, publisher; b. Washington, Feb. 15, 1948; s. Paul Alexander and Jessie Pauline (Barker) R.; m. Mary Lee Receveur, Jan. 25, 1969; children—Mary Elizabeth, Aimee Suzanne, Paul Alexander II. B.S., U. Md., 1973. Pres. Expert Lawn Service, Hyattsville, Md., 1964-68, Manor House Press, Inc., Riverdale, Md., 1969-71, Hobby House Press, Inc., Cumberland, Md., 1971; pub. Doll Reader mag., Teddy Bear and Friends mag. Curator, Western Md. Sta. Ctr. Mus., 1984-87, bd. dirs. Western Md. Hospitality Bur., 1988—; founder, chmn. bd. Internat. Doll Acad., 1985—; pres. Dolls of Yr., 1985—; pres. Crafted Heirlooms, Inc., Cumberland. Mem. bus. adv. curriculum com . Allegany Community Coll., Cumberland, 1987—. Mem. United Fedn. Doll Clubs (treas. 1978-79), Allegany County Hist. Soc. (curator 1983-86, trustee 1983, 87—). Mem. Allegany County C. of C. (bd. dirs. 1988—, chmn. tourism commn. 1987—). Republican. Methodist. Club: Civitan (sec., treas. 1977-79, civitan of yr. 1979) (Hyattsville). Lodge: Rotary (bd. dirs. 1981-83, pres. 1985-86). Office: Hobby House Press Inc 900 Frederick St Cumberland MD 21502

RUDELL, MILTON WESLEY, aerospace engineer; b. Rice Lake, Wis., July 9, 1920; s. George C. and Edna (Bjoraa) R.; m. Doris Lorraine Shella, Nov. 30, 1941; children: Helen, Geoffrey, Lynn, Deborah, Leah, Andrea, Kessea, Eric, Erin. B in Aerospace Engring., U. Minn., 1946. Registered profl. engr. Chief tool engr. Boeing Aircraft Corp., Wichita, Kans. and Seattle, 1941-43, stateside and overseas field engr., 1943-45; chief fueling systems engr. N.W. Airlines, Mpls., 1946-50; pres. Rumoco Co., Frederic, Wis., 1950-68; registrar ECPI-Nat. IBM computer sch., Mpls., 1968-69; pres. Life Engring. Co., Milw. and Frederic, Wis., 1969—. Designer original med. surg. suture tape, 1951; designer 1st match-book cover with strike plate on rear side for safety, 1942; pioneered high-speed underwing fueling systems for comml. aircraft and 1st hydrant ground fueling stems for comml. aircraft; co-author Ops. & Maintenance Manual for B-29 aircraft, 1943. Founder Frederic Found. for Advanced Edn. Recipient WWII Aeronautical Engring. Citation from Pres. Eisenhower, 1944. Mem. Exptl. Aircraft Assn., Northwestern Wis. Mycol. Soc. (charter). Lutheran. Home and Office: 501 N Wisconsin Ave Frederic WI 54837-0400

RUDER, DAVID STURTEVANT, lawyer, educator, government official; b. Wausau, Wis., May 25, 1929; s. George Louis and Josephine (Sturtevant) R.; m. Susan M. Small; children: Victoria Chesley, Julia Larson, David Sturtevant II, John Coulter; stepchildren: Elizabeth Frankel, Rebecca Frankel. B.A. cum laude, Williams Coll., 1951; J.D. with honors, U. Wis., 1957. Bar: Wis. 1957, Ill. 1962. Of counsel Schiff Hardin & Waite, Chgo., 1971-76; assoc. Quarles & Brady, Milw., 1957-61; asst. prof. law Northwestern U., Chgo., 1961-63, assoc. prof., 1963-65, prof., 1965—, assoc. dean Law Sch.,, 1965-66, Dean Law Sch.,, 1977-85; chmn Securities and Exchange Commission, Washington, DC, 1987—; cons. Am. Law Inst. Fed. Securities Code, parts XVI and XVII; planning dir. Corporate Counsel Inst., 1962-66, 76-77 (com. mem. 1962-87); vis. prof. law U. Pa., Phila., 1971; C.R.B. vis. lectr. Universite de Liege, 1967; faculty Salzburg Seminar, 1976; mem. legal adv. com. to bd. dirs. N.Y. Stock Exchange, 1978-82; mem. com. on profl. responsibility Ill. Supreme Ct., 1978-87; mem. adv. bd. Securities Regulation Inst., 1978-87. Editor-in-chief: Williams Coll. Record, 1950-51, U. Wis. Law Rev, 1957; editor: Proc. Corp. Counsel Inst, 1962-66; contbr. articles to legal periodicals. Served to 1st lt. AUS, 1951-54. Fellow Am. Bar Found. (bd. dirs. 1984-86), Ill. Bar Found.; mem. ABA (council sect. on corp., banking and bus. law 1970-74), Chgo. Bar Assn. (com. chmn.), Ill. Bar Assn., Wis. Bar Assn., Am. Law Inst., Order of Coif, Gargoyle Soc., Phi Beta Kappa, Phi Delta Phi, Zeta Psi. Home: 325 Orchard Ln Highland Park IL 60035 Office: SEC 450 5th St NW Washington DC 20549

RUDER, WILLIAM, public relations executive; b. N.Y.C., Oct. 17, 1921; s. Jacob L. and Rose (Rosenberg) R.; m. Betty Cott, May 23, 1980; children—Robin Ann, Abby, Brian, Michal Ellen, Eric. B.S.S., City Coll., N.Y., 1942. With Samuel Goldwyn Prodns., 1946-48; pres. Ruder & Finn, Inc., N.Y.C., 1948-80, William Ruder Inc., 1981—; asst. sec. commerce, 1961-62; Tobe lectr. Harvard Grad. Sch. Bus., 1962; mem. grad. adv. bd. City Coll. N.Y., Baruch Sch. Bus., N.Y.C.; cons. State Dept.; bd. dirs. W.P. Carey & Co., Inc. Author: The Businessman's Guide to Washington. Bd. dirs. Bus. Com. for Arts, Jewish Bd. Guardians, Chamber Music Soc. Lincoln Center, Fund for Peace; exec. com. United Way Am.; former chmn. bd. trustees Manhattanville Coll., Purchase, N.Y., 1974-75; bd. overseers Wharton Sch. U. Pa.; mem. pres.'s council Meml. Sloan-Kettering Cancer Ctr.; chmn. bd. ACCESS. Served to capt. USAAF, 1941-45. Mem. UN Assn. U.S.A. (nat. policy panel dir.). Home: 430 E 86th St New York NY 10028 Office: William Ruder Inc 301 E 57th St New York NY 10022

RUDLOFF, WILLIAM JOSEPH, lawyer; b. Bonne Terre, Mo., Feb. 19, 1941; s. Leslie W. and Alta M. (Hogenmiller) R.; m. Rita Howton, Aug. 5, 1965; children: Daniel, Andrea, Leslie, Susan. AB, Western Ky. U., 1961; JD, Vanderbilt U., 1965. Bar: Ky. 1965, Tenn. 1965, U.S. Supreme Ct. 1975; cert. civil trial specialist Nat. Bd. Trial Advocacy. Mem. Harlin, Parker & Rudloff and predecessors, Bowling Green, Ky., 1965—; U.S. magistrate Western Dist. Ky., 1971-75. NDEA fellow U. Nebr. 1961-62. Fellow Ky. Bar Found. (charter life); mem. Assn. Ins. Attys., Am. Bd. Trial Advocates, Am. Counsel Assn., Def. Research Inst., Ky. Def. Counsel, Nat. Council Self-Insurers, ABA, Bowling Green Bar Assn., Am. Coll. Forensic Psychiatry, Trial Attys. Am., Am. Coll. Legal Medicine, Internat. Assn. Ins. Counsel. Home: 126 Broadway PO Box 146 Smiths Grove KY 42171 Office: Harlin Parker & Rudloff 519 E 10th St Bowling Green KY 42101

RUDOLPH, CARLETON GENE, municipal official, financial services executive; b. Port Angeles, Wash., Oct. 13, 1942; s. Carleton James and Jorgine Evelyn (Boyd) R. AA, Peninsula Coll., 1964; advanced acctg. diploma, LaSalle U., 1974; BS, City Coll. Seattle, 1977; MBA with honors, City U., Bellevue, Wash., 1985. CPA, Wash. Staff Virgil E. Knedlick CPA, Port Angeles, 1977-80; acctg. mgr. City of Port Angeles, 1980-86, fin. services mgr., cons., 1987—; fin. cons. Chmn. Angeles Arts in Action, Port Angeles, 1985. Served to sgt. USNG, 1965-71. Mem. Am. Inst. CPA's, Wash. Soc. CPA's (sec./treas., v.p./pres. elect), Wash. Fin. Officers Assn. Republican. Club: Nor'Wester. Lodge: Rotary. Home: 2714 S Oak St Port Angeles WA 98362 Office: City Port Angeles 321 E 5th St Port Angeles WA 98362

RUDOLPH, JOHN DAVID, optical company executive; b. Camden, N.J., Sept. 26, 1947; s. Garrison E. and Vera (Howe) R.; m. Carolyn Jill Roblou, Aug. 9, 1969; children: Jeffrey D., Jennifer L. B of Chem. Engring., U. Del., 1970; MS in Indsl. Mgmt., MIT, 1973. Mgr. product devel. and applications Corning Glass Co., N.Y., 1980-82, mgr. mfg. planning, 1982-83, dir. tech. planning and mktg., 1983-86, bus. mgr. precision molded optics, 1986-87; v.p. optical components U.S. Precision Lens, Cin., 1987—. Served to capt. U.S. Army, 1970-72. Office: US Precision Lens 4000 McMann Rd Cincinnati OH 45245

RUDOLPH, RICHARD, lawyer; b. Birmingham, Ala., Apr. 28, 1948; s. Carvin and Willie Lee (Harvey) R.; m. Doris Sheppard, Aug. 12, 1978. BA with honors, Ala. A&M U., 1970; JD, So. U., Baton Rouge, 1974. Bar: La. 1975, D.C. 1978, U.S. Dist. Ct. (mid. dist.) La. 1976, U. S. Dist. (we. dist.) La. 1984, U.S. Supreme Ct. 1982. Specialist tax law Regional Counsel's Office, Chgo., 1974-75; asst. atty. gen. La. Dept. Justice, Baton Rouge, 1975-82; pvt. practice law Baton Rouge, 1982—; col., aide de camp staff of Gov. Edwin W. Edwards, 1987; hon. La. state senator, 1987, state rep., 1987, sec. state, 1988. Mem. Community Assn. for the Welfare of Sch. Children, Baton Rouge, 1986—. Rsrch. fellow U. Fla., 1969; named one of Outstanding Young Am. U.S. Jaycees, 1979, hon. La. state senator, 1987, hon. La. state rep., 1987, hon. La. sec. of state, 1988; hon. col. Aide-de-Camp Gov. Office of Gov. State La., 1987-88; recipient cert. of appreciation Moot Ct. Bd. So. Univ. Law Ctr., 1987. Mem. ABA, Nat. Bar Assn., Assn. Trial Lawyers Am., Internat. Platform Assn., Delta Theta Phi (founder, pres. 1978—, western dist. chancellor 1982—), Omega Psi Phi (chmn. community liaison com. 1978—), Beta Kappa Chi (pres. 1969—),. Home: 4123 Raleigh Dr Baton Rouge LA 70814 Office: 200 Government St Ste 150 Baton Rouge LA 70802

RUDOLPH, RICHARD KENNEDY, financial planner, investment advisor; b. Cleve., Dec. 2, 1937; s. Clayton McBride and Mary Grace (Kennedy) R.; student Yale U., 1955-56; B.A., Grove City Coll., 1961; J.D., U. Va., 1964; m. Edith Davis, Sept. 17, 1960; children—Richard, Gretchen, Suzanne, Steven, Kristen. With Esso Standard Eastern (Asian sub.) Exxon Corp., 1964-70; v.p. Investment Data & Research Corp., Boca Raton, Fla., 1970-72; sr. v.p. fin. planning, dir. Raymond James & Assocs., Naples, Fla., 1972—; dir. R.J. Fin. Corp. Served with USAF, 1955-59. Republican. Home: 719 Willowhead Dr Naples FL 33940 Office: Raymond James & Assocs 405 5th Ave S Naples FL 33940

RUDZINSKI, KENNETH WILLIAM, financial planner; b. Phila., Aug. 23, 1947; s. Sigmund Michael and Nina R.; m. Mary Jane Hall Shaup, Aug. 16, 1969; children: Matthew Hylan, Alexander Hall. BA, Villanova U., 1969; MA, U. Del., 1971. CLU, cert. fin. planner, chartered fin. cons. Tchr. French Archmere Acad., Claymont, Del., 1970-73; mgr. sales Lincoln Nat. Sales Corp., Phila. and Bala Cynwyd, Pa., 1973-77, Aetna Life and Casualty, Wayne, Pa., 1977-80; v.p. mktg. Lincoln Nat. Sales Corp., Bala Cynwyd, 1980-85; dir. mktg. The Am. Group Ltd., Radnor, Pa., 1985-88, Wilmington, Del., 1988—; v.p. Fin. Adv. Network Ltd., Radnor, 1987-88; pres. Cardiac Perfusion Inc., Phila., 1986—; advisor Lincoln Nat. Agts. Adv. Bd., Ft. Wayne, 1983-84, SMA Life Agts. Adv. Bd., Worcester, Mass., 1987. Dupont Andelot fellow U. Del., Newark, 1969; recipient Nat. Sales Achievement award Million Dollar Round Table, Des Plaines, Ill., 1987; named One of Top 200 Fin. Planners in U.S. Money mag., 1987. Mem. Internat. Assn. Fin. Planners, Inst. Cert. Fin. Planners, Nat. Assn. Life Underwriters, Pa. Soc. Pub. Accts. (assoc.). Republican. Office: The Am Group 2036 Foulk Rd Ste 204 Wilmington DE 19810

RUF, JOHN FREDERIC, banker; b. Madison, Wis., May 9, 1937. BS, Lawrence U., 1959; JD, U. Wis., 1964. Bar: Wis. 1964. Asst. cashier Continental Ill. Bank, Chgo., 1964-68; v.p. M&I Marshall & Ilsley, Mllw., 1968-81; pres. RBP Chem. Corp., Mllw., 1981-84, First Interstate Bank of Wis., Mllw., 1984—; mem. legis. council Wis. Bankers Assn., Madison, 1974-81; bd. dirs., pres. TYME Corp., Milw., 1974-87. Sec.-treas Inland Lake Yachting Assn., Lake Geneva, Wis.; trustee Lawrence U., Appleton, Wis. Mem. Lawrence U. Alumni Assn. (pres.). Clubs: Kettle Moraine Curling (Hartland, Wis.) (pres.); Pewaukee Yacht (Wis.) (commodore). Home: W277 N2531 Rocky Point Rd Pewaukee WI 53072 Office: First Interstate Bank of Wis 735 W Wisconsin Ave Milwaukee WI 53233

RUFE, REDDING KANE, hotelier; b. Mpls., June 29, 1930; s. Redding Henry and Dorothy (Liese) R.; m. Marta Judith Kern, May 9, 1959; children—Marta Nicole, Michael Kern. B.S. in Hotel Adminstrn., Cornell U., 1952; grad., Program Mgmt. Devel., Harvard U., 1967. With Inter-Continental Hotels Corp., 1957—, sr. v.p. ops. Far East/Pacific, 1970-72; gen. mgr. Inter-Continental Hotels Corp. (Hotel Siam Inter-Continental), 1967-70, pres. Pacific/Asia div., 1973-84, pres. Pacific/Asia/Latin Am. area, 1984-87, pres. Ams. and Pacific/Asia area, 1987—. Served to 1st lt. USAF, 1952-56. Mem. Assn. Internat. Des Skal Clubs Amicale de Tourisme, Am. Soc. Travel Agts., Pacific Area Travel Assn., Hotel Sales Mgmt. Assn. Internat., Cornell Soc. Hotelmen, Theta Delta Chi. Lutheran. Clubs: Harvard Bus. Sch. (N.Y.C.); Waialae Country (Honolulu). Lodge: Rotary. Address: Intercontinental Hotels Corp 100 Paragon Dr Montvale NJ 07645

RUFFLE, JOHN FREDERICK, banker; b. Toledo, Mar. 28, 1937; s. Matthew Frederick and Hazel Ruth (Johnson) R.; m. Eleanor Grace Loock, Nov. 19, 1960; children: Donald Alan, William Charles, John Garrett. B.A., Johns Hopkins, 1958; M.B.A., Rutgers, 1963. C.P.A., N.J. With Price Waterhouse & Co., N.Y.C., 1958-65; sr. accountant Price Waterhouse & Co., 1962-65; asst. treas. Internat. Paper Co., N.Y.C., 1965-70; comptroller Morgan Guaranty Trust Co. N.Y., N.Y.C., 1970-80; exec. v.p. Morgan Guaranty Trust Co. N.Y., 1980-85, vice chmn. bd., 1985—. Served with AUS, 1959-60. Mem. Fin. Execs. Inst. (chmn. bd. 1983-84), Nat. Assn. Accts, AICPA, N.J. Soc. CPAs, Fin. Acctg. Found. (trustee 1984—, pres. 1989—). Home: 34 Wynwood Rd Chatham NJ 07928 Office: Morgan Guaranty Trust Co 23 Wall St New York NY 10015

RUGER, WILLIAM BATTERMAN, firearms manufacturing company executive; b. Bklyn., June 21, 1916; s. Adolph and May R.; m. Mary Thompson, Aug. 26, 1938; children: William Batterman, Carolyn Amalie Ruger Vogel, James Thompson. Student, U. N.C. Firearms design engr. U.S. Armory, Springfield, Mass., 1939-40; machine gun designer Auto Ordnance Corp., Hartford, Conn., World War II; founder, pres. Ruger Corp. (hand tool mfrs.), Southport, Conn., 1946-48; co-founder 1948; since pres., chmn. bd., treas. Sturm, Ruger & Co., Inc., Southport; v.p. Sporting Arms and Ammunition Inst., 1978—; past bd. dirs. Nat. Shooting Sports Found. Author, editor; patentee in field. Trustee Salisbury (Conn.) Sch., 1970-75, Naval War Coll. Found., Buffalo Bill Hist. Ctr. Recipient Nat. Leadership award Hunting Hall of Fame, 1979; named Handgunner of Year Am. Handgunner Found., 1975. Mem. NRA (past dir.), Blue Mountain Forest Assn., Vintage Sports Car Club Am., Auburn-Cord Duesenberg, Rolls Royce Owners Club, Rolls Royce Silver Ghost Assn., Am. Bugatti Club, Bugatti Owners' Club, Bentley Drivers Club, Ea. Packard Auto Club, Vet. Motor Club, Stutz Club, Ferrari Club Am., Campfire Club, Pequot Yacht Club, N.Y. Yacht Club, Boone and Crockett Club, Cat Cay Club, Clambake Club, Delta Kappa Epsilon. Lutheran. Office: Sturm Ruger & Co Lacey Pl Southport CT 06490

RUGG, PETER, banker; b. Glen Cove, N.Y., Apr. 12, 1947; s. Daniel M. and Carol (Van Zandt) R.; m. Meredith Catlin Phelps, Sept. 12, 1969 children—Charlton Alexander, Courtney Caroline. B.A. Columbia U., 1969, BS in Engring, 1970. Asst. treas. Morgan Guaranty Trust Co., N.Y.C., 1972-74, asst. v.p., 1974-76, v.p., London, 1975-79, v.p., head banking, Hong Kong, 1979-82, v.p. mergers and acquisitions, N.Y.C., 1982-85, v.p. corporate fin., 1985—; adj. prof. fin. Fordham U. Grad. Sch. Bus. Adminstrn., 1987—. Clubs: New York Yacht (N.Y.C.); Fishers Island (N.Y.); Fishers Island Yacht (commodore). Avocations: sailing; skiing; arts; reading. Home: 108 E 82d St New York NY 10028 Office: JP Morgan & Co 60 Wall St New York NY 10260

RUGGAARD, RANDALL PAUL, financial consultant; b. Chgo., Oct. 7, 1956; s. Knute and Rita Catherine (Knitter) R.; m. Margaret Mary Bracken, June 20, 1981. BS, Miami U., Oxford, Ohio, 1978; MBA, Case Western Res. U., 1985. Acct. Ernst & Whinney, Cleve., 1978-81; ins. cons. N.Eng. Life, Cleve., 1981-84; fin. planner Am. Fin. Resources Group, Cleve., 1984-86; fin.

cons. New Eng. Fin. Advisors, Cleve., 1986-88, TPF&C, Cleve., 1988—. Contbr. articles to profl jours. Mem. New Eng. Nat. Studies Com., Boston, 1987—. William J. Cook scholar Chgo. Community Trust Found., 1978; Miami U. scholar, 1978. Mem. Registry of Fin. Planning Practitioners, Internat. Assn. Fin. Planning, Internat. Bd. Studies and Practices for Cert. Fin. Planners, Inst. Cert. Fin. Planners, Ohio Soc. CPA's, Am. Coll. CLU's, Hudson Country Club. Home: 7415 Stow Rd Hudson OH 44236 Office: TPF & C 1100 Superior Ave Cleveland OH 44114

RUGGIERI, DAVID THOMAS, marketing executive, consultant; b. Providence, Sept. 3, 1947; s. Rizieri and Dorothy (DiMeo) R., m. Marie Milosovic, Dec. 7, 1975; children: Christopher, Vanessa. BBA, Nat. U., 1975. Dir. Cabrillo Pacific U., San Diego, 1976-78; v.p. sales Nat. Edn. Corp., Newport Beach, Calif., 1978-80; v.p. Mid-Western Edn. Systems, Phoenix, 1983-85; owner, pres. Career Mktg. System, Los Angeles, 1980—; pres. Chgo. Model Mgmt., 1985-87; chmn. Western Edn. and Tng. Systems, Inc., 1987—; bd. dirs., v.p. Chgo. Career Ctrs., 1985—; cons. Drake Coll, Mid-West Ednl. Author: Sales Management, 1978, Telephone Marketing, 1979, Admissions Management, 1980, Sales Strategy for Colleges, 1980-81. Served to lt. USAF, 1968-71. Mem. Am. Mktg. Assn., Sales Execs. Internat. Office: 250 4th St San Francisco CA 94103

RUGGIRELLO, PAT CHARLES, transportation executive; b. Niagara Falls, N.Y., Oct. 3, 1948; s. Charles Ruggirello; m. Mary Margaret O'Hara, Nov. 24, 1972; 1 child, Nicholas Charles. Assoc. in Arts and Scis., Niagara County Comm. Coll., Niagara Falls, 1973; BA in Sociology, BA in Bus., U. Buffalo, 1975. Customer engr. IBM, Buffalo, 1972-76; v.p. Cataract Truck & Rental Corp., Niagara Falls, 1976-79, pres., chief exec. officer, 1985—; exec. v.p. SPC Enterprises, Niagara Falls, 1979-85; pres. Md. Maple Devel. Corp., Niagara Falls, 1988—. Bd. dirs. Niagara Falls Traffic Club, 1986—, Niagara Falls Area C. of C., 1987—; mem. Niagara Falls Econ. Devel. Com., 1987—; committeeman Lewiston (N.Y.) Rep. Party, 1988. Served with USCG, 1967-71. Mem. Ea. Intermodal Draymennt Assn. (bd. dirs. 1985—), Buffalo World Trade Assn., Buffalo Transp. Club., Greater Buffalo C. of C. Roman Catholic. Clubs: Niagara Falls Country, Niagara. Office: Cataract Truck & Car Rental Corp PO Box 2126 Niagara Falls NY 14302

RUGH, WILLIAM BATMAN, manufacturing executive; b. Alton, Ill., Nov. 6, 1947; s. Robert Hanlin and Elizabeth (Batman) R. BS in Engring., Duke U., 1969; MBA, U. N.C., 1972. Indsl. engr. Owens-Ill., Inc., North Bergen, N.J., 1972-74; process control engr. Owens-Ill., Inc., Toledo, 1974-77, handling engr., 1977-79, supr. design group, 1979-83, group supr., 1983—; gen. mgr. engring. and tech. assistance Cisper div. Owens-Ill., Brazil. Bd. dirs. Nat. Flag Found., Pitts.; active Boy Scouts Am., Toledo. Mem. ASME, Toledo Soc. Magicians, Alpha Phi Omega. Republican. Home: 120 Freedom Ln Waterville OH 43566 Office: Owens-Ill Inc One Seagate Toledo OH 43666

RUIZ, SHARON KAY, banker; b. Cleburne, Tex., Jan. 31, 1945; d. Weldon Clyde and Alice Merle (Wallace) Strickland. AS in Mgmt., Richland Coll., Dallas, 1979; postgrad., Am. Inst. Banking, 1987. Adminstrv. officer SBA, Dallas, 1963-78; asst. to pres. Comml. Nat. Bank, Dallas, 1981-83, credit mgr., 1983-85; credit mgr., asst. v.p. BancTexas, Richardson, 1986-87; asst. v.p., credit ops. mgr. BancTexas Group, Inc., Dallas, 1988—. Mem. Nat. Assn. Bank Women (v.p. 1987, pres. 1988), Am. Bus. Women's Assn. (v.p. 1973, pres. 1974, Woman of Yr. 1974). Baptist. Home: 7823 Umphress Rd Dallas TX 75217

RUIZ, WALLACE DAVID, petroleum company executive; b. N.Y.C., May 15, 1951; s. Wallace William and Ruth Diane (Knox) R.; m. Gabriele Lehmann, Aug. 21, 1976; children: Jens Christian, Erik Jeffrey. BA, St. Johns U., 1973; MBA, Columbia U., 1975. Acct. Arthur Young & Co., N.Y.C., 1975-80; dir. fin. planning and analysis Gen. Mills, Inc., N.Y.C., 1980-81; dir. fin. Gen. Mills, Inc., Mexico City, 1981-82; v.p., fin. and adminstrn. Tropigas Internat. Corp., Coral Gables, Fla., 1982—. Mem. Tropical Audubon Soc., Greenpeace, Am. Inst. CPAs (computer edn. subcom., 1980), Fla. Inst. CPAs (legis. action com., 1986), N.Y. State Soc. CPAs, Sierra Club. Home: 9828 SW 108 Terr Miami FL 33176 Office: Tropigas Internat Corp 1701 Ponce de Leon Blvd Coral Gables FL 33134

RUKEYSER, LOUIS RICHARD, economic commentator; b. N.Y.C., Jan. 30, 1933; s. Merryle Stanley and Berenice Helene (Simon) R.; m. Alexandra Gill, Mar. 3, 1962; children: Beverley Jane, Susan Athena, Stacy Alexandra. AB, Princeton U., 1954; LittD (hon.), N.H. Coll., 1975; LLD (hon.), Moravian Coll., 1978, Mercy Coll., 1984; DBA (hon.), Southeastern Mass. U., 1979; LHD (hon.), Loyola Coll., 1982, Johns Hopkins U., 1986. Reporter Balt. Sun newspapers, 1954-65; chief polit. corr. Evening Sun, 1957-59; chief London bur. The Sun, 1959-63, chief Asian corr., 1963-65; sr. corr., commentator ABC News, 1965-73, Paris corr., 1965-66, chief London bur., 1966-68, econ. editor, commentator, 1968-73; host Wall St. Week with Louis Rukeyser PBS-TV, 1970—; nationally syndicated econ. columnist McNaught Syndicate, 1976-86, Tribune Media Services, 1986—; frequent lectr. Author: How to Make Money in Wall Street, 1974, 2d edit., 1976 (Literary Guild selection 1974, 76), What's Ahead for the Economy: The Challenge and the Chance, 1983 (Literary Guild selection 1984), 2d edit., 1985, Louis Rukeyser's Business Almanac, 1988. Served with AUS, 1954-56. Recipient Overseas Press Club award, 1963, Overseas Press Club citation, 1964, G.M. Loeb award U. Conn., 1972, Janus award for excellence in fin. news programming, 1975, George Washington Honor medal Freedoms Found., 1972, 78, N.Y. Fin. Writers Assn. award, 1980, Free Enterprise Man of the Yr. award Tex. A&M U. Ctr. for Edn. and Research in Free Enterprise, 1987. Office: 586 Round Hill Rd Greenwich CT 06831

RUKEYSER, M. S., JR., television executive; b. N.Y.C., Apr. 15, 1931; s. Merryle Stanley and Berenice (Simon) R.; m. Phyllis L. Kasha, May 16, 1975; children: Jill Victoria, Patricia Bern. Student, U. Va., 1948-52. Reporter Albany (N.Y.) Times-Union, 1949, Internat. News Service, N.Y.C., 1951; TV publicist Young & Rubicam, Inc., N.Y.C., 1952-57; with NBC, 1958-80, 81-88; dir. news info. NBC, Washington, 1962; v.p. press and publicity NBC, N.Y.C., 1963-72; v.p. corp. info. NBC, 1972-74, v.p. pub. info., 1974-77, exec. v.p. pub. info., 1977-80, 81-84, exec. v.p. corp. communications, 1984-88; sr. v.p. GTG Entertainment, N.Y.C., 1988—; v.p. communications Newsweek Inc., 1980-81. Served with U.S. Army, 1953-54. Mem. Acad. TV Arts and Scis., Internat. Radio and TV Soc. Home: 275 Central Park W New York NY 10024 Office: GTG Entertainment 150 E 52d St New York NY 10022

RUKEYSER, ROBERT JAMES, manufacturing executive; b. New Rochelle, N.Y., June 26, 1942; s. Merryle Stanley and Berenice Helene (Simon) R.; m. Leah A. Spiro, July 26, 1964; children: David Bern, Peter Lloyd. BA, Cornell U., 1964; MBA with distinction, N.Y.U., 1969. Mun. services analyst Dun & Bradstreet, N.Y.C., 1964-65; bond analyst Standard & Poors, N.Y.C., 1965-66; mktg. rep. data processing div. IBM, N.Y.C., 1967-72, regional mktg. staff, 1973-74, mktg. mgr., 1974-76; corp. mgr. internal communications IBM, Armonk, N.Y., 1976-79; mgr. communication ops. IBM, Franklin Lakes, N.J., 1979-81; pub. affairs dir., asst. to chmn. Am. Brands, Inc., N.Y.C., 1981-83, v.p. pub. affairs, asst. to chmn., 1983-85; v.p. office products Am. Brands, Inc., Old Greenwich, Conn., 1986-87, v.p. ops., 1987—, also bd. dirs.; bd. dirs. Am. Brands, Inc. subs. ACCO World Corp., Am. Brands Internat. Co., Jim Beam Brands Co., Am. Franklin Co., Acushnet Co., MasterBrand Industries. Communications com. Boy Scouts Am., 1982-86; personal solicitation chair Cornell U., 1985-87; bd. dirs. The Hole in the Wall Gang Camp. Mem. Nat. Office Products Assn., Wholesale Stationer's Assn. Office: Am Brands Inc 1700 E Putnam Ave PO Box 819 Old Greenwich CT 06870

RUMSFELD, DONALD H., former government official, corporate executive; b. Chgo., July 9, 1932; s. George Donald and Jeannette (Husted) R.; m. Joyce Pierson, Dec. 27, 1954; 3 children. A.B., Princeton U., 1954; hon. degree, Ill. Coll., Lake Forest Coll., Park Coll., Tuskegee Inst., Nat. Coll. Edn., Bryant Coll., Claremont (Calif.) Grad. Sch. Adminstrv. asst. U.S. Ho. of Reps., 1958-59; with A.G. Becker & Co., Chgo., 1960-62; mem. 88th-91st congresses from 13th Dist. Ill., Pres's Cabinet, 1969-73; dir. OEO, asst. to pres., 1969-70; counselor to Pres. Richard Nixon, dir. econ. stabilization program 1971-72; U.S. ambassador and permanent rep. to NATO, 1973-74; Chief of Staff, mem. Pres.'s cabinet Washington, 1974-75; sec. Dept. Def., 1975-77; pres., chief exec. officer G.D. Searle & Co., Skokie, Ill., 1977-85; sr. adviser William Blair & Co., Chgo., 1985—; Pres. Reagan's spl. envoy to Middle East, 1983-84; bd. dirs. Rand Corp., Kellogg Co., Vulcan Materials Co., Union Camp Corp., Sears, Roebuck & Co., Gilead Scis., Inc. Chmn. Eisenhower Exchange Fellowships, 1986—; chmn. bd. trustees Inst. Contemporary Studies. Served as naval aviator USN, 1954-57. Recipient Presdl. medal of Freedom. Office: care William Blair & Co 135 S LaSalle St Ste 1740 Chicago IL 60603

RUNGE, DONALD EDWARD, food wholesale company executive; b. Milw., Mar. 20, 1938; s. Adam and Helen Teresa (Voss) R.; divorced; children: Roland, Richard, Lori. Grad., Spencerian Coll., Milw., 1960. Fin. v.p. Milw. Cheese Co., Waukesha, Wis., 1962-69; dir. Farm House Foods Corp., Milw., 1966—, pres., 1966-84, chief exec. officer, 1984—, treas., 1984-85, chmn., pres., 1985-87; chmn., chief exec. officer Retailing Corp. Am., Milw., 1982-84; chief exec. officer Drug Systems Inc., Milw., 1984-85, treas., 1984—; chmn. Drug Systems Inc. (now Retailing Corp. of Am.), Milw., 1985—; chmn., pres., chief exec. officer Farm House Foods Corp., Milw.; bd. dirs. Convenient Food Mart, CasaBlanca Industries, Inc., City of Industry, Calif.; sec. The Diana Corp., Milw., 1985-86, treas. 1986—, pres. 1987—; chmn. Economy Dry Goods Co. Inc.; treas. Fairbanks Farms Inc. Adventist. Home: 2204 W Kenboern Dr Glendale WI 53209 Office: Farm House Foods Corp 111 E Wisconsin Ave #190 Milwaukee WI 53202 *

RUNION, EMILY OLIVA, accountant, financial planner; b. Newark, Apr. 30, 1952; d. Charles and Maria Irene (Raffetto) Oliva; m. Robert Lee Runion, Oct. 3, 1976; children: Christopher, Kelly. BS in Biology, Fairleigh Dickinson U., 1974, BS in Med. TEch., 1975, MBA in Acctg., 1980. CPA, N.J., cert. fin. planner, N.J. Asst. supr. biochemistry dept. St. Peters Hosp., New Brunswick, N.J., 1978; supr. tax dept. Amper, Politziner & Mattia, Flemington, N.J., 1981—. Fellow N.J. Soc. CPA's (fed. and state taxation com. Hunterdon/Warren chpt. 1987—); mem. Am. Inst. CPA's, Am. Inst. Cert. Fin. Planners, Princeton Soc. Cert. Fin. Planners. Home: PO Box 591 Flemington NJ 08822 Office: Amper Politzner & Mattia CPA PA 3Minneakoning Rd PO Box 415 Flemington NJ 08822

RUNKE, JAMES FREDERICK, stamp and engraving company executive; b. Algoma, Wis., July 23, 1946; s. LaFollette John and Barbara (Wehausen) R.; m. Susan J. Kloppmann, Oct. 11, 1969; 1 child, Shannon R. BS, U. Wis., Stevens Point, 1971; MA, Ind. U., 1974. Dir. transp. rsch. Coun. State Govts., Lexington, Ky., 1974-79; dir. rail transport Ky. Transp. Cabinet, Frankfort, 1979-80, sec., 1982-83; commr. Ky. Dept. Vehicle Registration, Frankfort, 1980-82; asst. to pres. Telemktg. Communications Mgmt. Co., Louisville, 1985-86; pres. Koehler Stamp & Engraving Co., Louisville, 1986—, also bd. dirs.; chmn., chief exec. officer Valley Engraving Co., Green Bay, Wis., 1987—, also bd. dirs.; cons. U. Wis., Milw., 1978-79, Assn. Am. R.R.'s, Washington, 1984. Co-author:. Bd. dirs. Cedar Lake Lodge, LaGrange, Ky., 1987. Sgt. USAF, 1966-69. Mem. Louisville Forum, Downtown Athletic Club, Jefferson Club. Democrat. Lutheran. Office: Koehler Stamp & Engraving 1600-B Main St Louisville KY 40203

RUNNELLS, CLIVE, entrepreneur; b. Chgo., Jan. 16, 1926; s. Clive and Mary (Withers) R.; children from previous marriage: Helen Rutherford, Clive III; m. Nancy Morgan, June 14, 1967; children: Amy Firestone del Valle, David Firestone, Jeff Firestone, Calvin Garwood, John Garwood, Thomas Pierce. BA, Yale U., 1948. Pres. Mid-Coast Cable Tv, Inc., El Campo, Tex., 1972—, Runnells Cattle Co., Bay City, Tex., 1980—; bd. dirs. Criterion Group, Houston, Western Gulf Savs., Bay City, Tex. and S.W. Cattle Raisers, Ft. Worth, Fed. Reserve Bank Houston, Gulf Coast Med. Found., Wharton, Tex. Bd. dirs. Dallas Boys Clubs, Houston Symphony Soc.; bd. dirs., chmn. Tex. Turnpike Authority, 1987—; chmn. Mental Health and Mental Retardation Authority Harris County, 1988—; mem. Rep. Senatorial Trust, 1978. Recipient John Mankin award Tex. Cable TV Assn., Cable TV Pioneer award. Mem. Assn. Community TV (bd. dirs. Houston 1984-85), Nat. Cable TV Assn. (nat. bd. dirs. 1979—), Houston C. of C. (chmn. arterial subcom. 1987, regional mobility com. 1986—). Republican. Episcopalian. Clubs: Bayou, River Oaks Country, Houston Country, Houston City, Ramada; Anglers (Key Largo, Fla.); Jupiter Island (Hobe Sound, Fla.); Iron City Fishing (Parry Sound, Ont., Can.); The Brook (N.Y.C.). Office: Criterion Group PO Box 22738 Houston TX 77227

RUNNION, HOWARD J., JR., banker; b. Hot Spring, N.C., May 23, 1930; s. Howard Jackson and Blanche Mae (Elam) R.; m. Betty Ann Bishop, June 30, 1951; children—Debra Joy Sizemore, Jill Marie Glenn. B.S., U. N.C., 1952. Various postions Wachovia Bank and Trust Co.-Wachovia Corp., Winston-Salem, N.C., 1952—, now sr. exec. v.p.; dir. Recognition Equipment Inc., Dallas, Depository Trust Co., N.Y.C.; chmn. bd. PSA Treasury Com, 1984-85; also exec. v.p. First Wachovia Corp. Vice chmn. bd. trustees Coll. Found. Raleigh, 1978—. Mem. Res. City Bankers Assn., Pub. Securities Assn. (dir. 1976-79, 84-85). Republican. Presbyterian. Clubs: Forsyth Country, Roaring Gap. Lodge: Elk. Home: 3521 York Rd Winston-Salem NC 27104 Office: 1st Wachovia Corp PO Box 3099 Winston-Salem NC 27150

RUNYON, RITA JULIET, marketing executive; b. Ranchi, Bihar, India, Nov. 6, 1954; came to U.S., 1970; d. Bernard Mohan and Geeta Rani (Sinha) L. BS in Psychology and Communications, U. Sask., Regina, Can., 1975. Dist. agt. Prudential Ins., Irvine, Calif., 1975-77; mgr. dept. cosmetics Bullocks div. Federated Dept. Stores, Costa Mesa, Calif., 1977-79, Saks Fifth Ave., Costa Mesa, 1979-80; cons. Mary Kay Cosmetics, Dallas, 1980-81; makeup artist Burbank (Calif.) Studios, 1975-80; owner Enchanté Cosmetics, South Bend, Ind., 1980-87, Image Cons., South Bend, 1985—; pres. Dennis Rsch. & Data Collection, Inc., South Bend, 1983—; exec. cons. SBA, South Bend, 1981—. Author: Beauty Secrets, 1980; exec. producer About Face, 1984. Mem. Aestheticians Internat. Assn. (Aesthetician of Yr. 1981), Am. Mktg. Assn., Market Rsch. Assn. (Appreciation award 1987, 88). Democrat. Office: Dennis Rsch & Data Collection 115 W Colfax Ave South Bend IN 46601

RUPER, JERAY MARIAN, accountant; b. Painesville, Ohio, May 10, 1952; d. Richard Lewis and Nancy Jean (Few) Bunnell; children—Heather Lynn, Heidi Marie; m. Ronald Thomas Ruper, June 6, 1981. B.A. in Acctg., Thiel Coll., 1974; postgrad. W.Va. U., 1985—. C.P.A., Pa., Ohio, W.Va. Acct., Rex Walker & Assocs., Grove City, Pa., 1976-78; mgr. fin. acctg. Harris Wholesale Co., Solon, Ohio, 1978-83; spl. asst. to chief fin. officer W.Va. U., Morgantown, 1983-84, mgr. mgmt. analysis, 1984-86; coordinator fin. ops. and analysis Dept. Publs., Printing & News Service, Office of Instl. Advancement, W.Va. U., 1986—; cons. fin. systems Human Interface, Morgantown, 1983—. Mem. Am. Inst. C.P.A.s, Am. Women's Soc. CPA's, W.Va. Soc. C.P.A.s, Ohio Soc. C.P.A.s. Republican. Roman Catholic. Avocation: travel. Office: West Va U #117 Communications Bldg Morgantown WV 26505

RUPP, GLENN N., sporting goods executive; b. Washington, Sept. 27, 1944; s. Glenn N. and Verda Mae (McCullough) R.; m. Judith Carpenter, Dec. 28, 1968; children: Kerry, Edward. BS, Duke U., 1966; MBA, Harvard U., 1968. Pres. N.Am. Van Lines Can., Toronto, Ont., 1971-75; v.p., gen. mgr. N.Am. Van Lines, Ft. Wayne, Ind., 1975-79; v.p. internat. PepsiCo Inc., Purchase, N.Y., 1979, 82, Frankfurt, Fed. Republic Germany, 1980-82; v.p., gen. mgr. internat. Wilson Sporting Goods Co., River Grove, Ill., 1983-85, pres., chief ops. officer, 1985-87, pres., chief exec. officer, 1987—; also bd. dirs.; bd. dirs. Nat. Golf Found., Jupiter, Fla., 1986—. Mem. Sporting Goods Mfgs. Assn., Caribbean, Cen. Am. Action Com., Lake Forest Club, Knollwood Club, Harvard Club (N.Y.C.). Office: Wilson Sporting Goods Co 2233 West St River Grove IL 60171

RUPP, JAMES M., communications executive; b. Pocatello, Idaho, Nov. 7, 1935; s. Mahlon and Ila Grace (Burnham) R.; m. Sharon Elaine, Aug. 28, 1955; children: Julie Rupp Dasher, Sandra, Steven. BA, Idaho State U., 1957; MA, Ohio State U., 1959. Mktg. dir., product mgr. Am. Research Bur., 1959-64; v.p. Media Stat, 1965; group v.p., gen. mgr. Cox Broadcasting, Atlanta, 1965-76; exec. v.p. Midwest Communications, Inc., Mpls., 1976-81, pres. and chief operating officer, then chief exec. officer, 1981—, also bd. dirs.; bd. dirs. United Video, Inc., Tulsa, United Video Cablevision of Hawaii, Inc., First Trust Co., Mpls. and St. Paul, Satellite Music Network, Inc., Dallas, Satellite Radio Network, Charlotte, King World Prodns., Inc. Mem. TV cooperation subcom. US Japan Conf. on Cultural and Ednl. Interchange; trustee Sci. Mus. Minn. Recipient Abe Lincoln award, So. Bapt. Radio and TV Commn., 1985. Mem. Minn. C. of C. (bd. dirs.), Greater Mpls. C. of C. Office: Midwest Communications Inc 90 S 11th St Minneapolis MN 55403

RUPPRECHT, SCOTT BRIAN, controller, accountant; b. Milw., June 11, 1959; s. Herbert Frank and LaVerne Amalia (Krueger) R.; m. Olivia Ann McInnis, Nov. 29, 1986; children: Nora Corrine, Dylan Paul, Laura Leigh, Stephanie Hope, Molly Ruth. BS, U. Wis., LaCrosse, 1981; MBA, Tex. Tech. U., 1988. CPA, Tex. Staff acct. Price Waterhouse, Milw., 1981-83; mgr. acctg. indsl. constrn. equipment div. Eagle-Picher, Lubbock, Tex., 1983-84; div. controller Eagle-Picher, Lubbock, 1984—. Mem. Nat. Assn. Accts., Tex. Soc. CPAs, Blue Key. Republican. Lutheran. Home: 2301 58th St Lubbock TX 79412

RUSH, EUNICE MARIE, computer training manager; b. Logansport, Ind., Mar. 18, 1951; d. Charles Lavaughn and Janet Louis (Ervin) Grant; m. Randy Lynn Rush, Aug. 26, 1978; 1 child, Brandon Michael. Student, Patricia Stevens Modeling Coll., 1968-69; BS, Ind. U., Indpls., 1977; MS, Ball State U., 1982. Freelance model 1970-78; programmer Miller Steel Kokomo, 1973-75; engring. technician Delco Electronics, Kokomo, Ind., 1973-74, systems engr., 1974-79, systems security officer, 1979-80, office automation specialist, 1980-83, supr. data processing tng., 1983-85; mgr. end user computing tng. Electronic Data Systems, Kokomo, 1985-87, Ind. regional tng. mgr., 1987—; part-time instr. Purdue U., Kokomo, 1982-84, Ind. U., Kokomo, 1982—; cons. data processing Sturm Ins. Co., Walton, Ind., 1982-83. Author: High Chair to High School Math, 1983, Adventures in Cooking. Fundraiser Howard County chpt. Am. Cancer Assn., 1975, Am. Heart Assn., 1977; loaned exec. Howard County United Way, 1976; mem. sch. bd., Kokomo, 1988—; scoutmaster Kokomo Explorer Post Boy Scouts Am., 1982-83. Named Miss Miami County, 1968. Fellow Cen. Ind. Educators Data Processing Assn.; mem. Nat. Businessmen's Assn. (program dir.). Home: Rte 1 PO Box 235 Bunker Hill IN 46914 Office: Electronic Data Systems 1815 S Plate St Kokomo IN 46902

RUSH, HENRY LESTER, data processing executive; b. Shreveport, La., May 22, 1951; s. Katherine (Wilkins) R. BS, La. Tech. U., 1973. Cert. systems profl. Systems mgr. Tex. Ea. Corp., Houston, 1975-80, dir. corp. planning, 1980-83, dir. info. services, 1983-86; pres. Summit Computing, Inc., Houston, 1987—; dir. Info. & Human Resources Svcs., Tex. Eastern Corp., 1988—. Bd. dirs. Houston Symphony Orch., 1988; gen. chmn. Handicapped Computer Tng., Houston, 1987-88. Mem. Am. Mgmt. Assn., Houston C. of C. Democrat. Baptist. Club: Houston Ctr. Office: Summit Computing Inc 1221 McKinney Houston TX 77252

RUSHING, KATHIE CANTRELL, financial executive; b. Shamrock, Tex., Oct. 5, 1947; d. Royce and Violette (Parrish) Cantrell; m. Charles Wayne Rushing, Jan. 27, 1967; 1 child, Darren Wade. Student, Tex. Tech U., 1966-72. V.p. fin. Royal Cantrell Corp., Shamrock, 1980—; prin. R & R Rental Properties. Mem. Panhandle Apt. Assn. Office: Royce Cantrell Corp 1400 N Main St Shamrock TX 79079

RUSK, DAVID WILLIAM, investment broker; b. Dubuque, Iowa, Sept. 9, 1954; s. Ross Phillip and Marguerite Elizabeth (Brodbelt) R.; m. Jane Ann Schmit; children: David William Jr., Benjamin Dominic. B in Gen. Studies, U. Iowa, 1976. Mktg. rep. IBM Corp., Cedar Rapids, 1978-83; advt., mktg. programs adminstr. IBM Corp., Chgo., 1983-85; mktg. mgr. IBM Corp., Terre Haute, Ind., 1985-88; investment broker A.G. Edwards and Sons, Dubuque, 1989—. Bd. dirs. Wabash Valley Vol. Action Ctr., Terre Haute, 1987, Arts Illiana, 1988—; bd. assocs. Rose-Hulman Inst. Tech., Terre Haute, 1988—; grad. Leadership Terre Haute; mem. Pres.' Soc. Ind. State U., Terre Haute, 1987—. Mem. Terre Haute Area C. of C. (bd. dirs.), Country Club of Terre Haute, Harbour Club of Bloomington. Home: 2340 Coates St Dubuque IA 52001 Office: AG Edwards & Sons 190 Cycare Pla Dubuque IA 52001

RUSKIN, ARNOLD MILTON, engineer, educator; b. Bay City, Mich., Jan. 4, 1937; s. Dave Burnard and Florence Shirley (Ruttenberg) R.; m. Dorothy Lee Hadley; 1 child, Sandra. BSChemE, BS in Materials Engring., U. Mich., 1958, MS in Engring. Materials, 1959, PhD, 1962; M of Bus. Econs., Claremont Grad. Sch., 1970. Registered profl. engr., Calif., Colo.; chartered engr., Eng. Lectr. Rugby (Eng.) Coll. Engring. Tech., 1962-63, asst. prof. engring., 1963-66, assoc. prof., 1966-72; assoc. prof. bus. and econs. Claremont (Calif.) Grad. Sch., 1970-72—, prof., 1972-73; assoc. prof. bus. and econs. Harvey Mudd Coll., 1970-72; prof. engring. Harvey Mudd Coll., Claremont, 1972-73; engr. mgr. Everett/Charles, Inc., Pomona, Calif., 1973-74; v.p., program mgr. Claremont Engring. Co., 1974-78; system engr. Jet Propulsion Lab., Pasadena, Calif., 1978-80, mgr. network strategy devel., 1980-86, dep. mgr. system engring. resource ctr., 1986—; founder, ptnr. Claremont Cons. Group, 1979—; lectr. UCLA, 1974-77, adj. prof engring., 1977-84, coordinator engring. exec. program, 1978-84; lectr. Indsl. Relations Ctr., Calif. Inst. Tech., Pasadena, 1985—. Author: Materials Considerations in Design, 1967, What Every Engineer Should Know About Project Management, 1982; patent thermally metamorphosing oil shale to inhibit leaching, 1980; book rev. editor Engring. Mgmt. Internat., 1981-84, mem. editorial bd. 1984-87, mem. editorial rev. bd. Project Mgmt. Jour., 1988—; mem. editorial bd. Engring. Mgmt. Jour., 1989—; contbr. papers to profl. publs. Mem. Archtl. Commn., Claremont, 1974-76, chmn. 1976; mem. Profl. Adv. Group, Claremont, 1968; bd. dirs. ARC, Claremont, 1970-72. Fellow AIAA (assoc. tech. com. mgmt. 1986—); mem. Am. Soc. Engring. Edn. (founding chmn., engring. mgmt. com. 1972-73, vice chmn. materials div. 1972-73, sec. materials div. 1963-67, editor Pacific Southwest sect. 1965-66, editorial com. Engring. Edn. 1970-71), Project Mgmt. Inst. (cert.), Am. Inst. Chem. Engrs., Assn. Mgmt. Cons. (cert.), Am. Soc. Engring. Mgmt., Sigma Xi, Tau Beta Pi, Phi Lambda Upsilon, Omicron Delta Epsilon, Phi Kappa Phi. Office: Claremont Cons Group 545 W 12th St Claremont CA 91711

RUSKIN, UZI, diversified manufacturing company executive; b. 1945; married. Pvt. investor to 1981; pres., chief operating officer United Mchts. and Mfrs. Inc., N.Y.C., 1981—; also chief exec. officer, dir. United Mchts. and Mfrs. Inc., N.Y.C. Office: United Mchts & Mfrs Inc 1407 Broadway New York NY 10018 *

RUSS, ARTHUR ALBERT, JR., lawyer; b. Buffalo, Nov. 26, 1942; s. Arthur Albert and Mary P. (Meyers) R.; m. Audrey Galinski, Nov. 12, 1975; children: Laura, Kevin, Allison. BA, Northwestern U., 1964; LLB, SUNY, Buffalo, 1967. Bar: N.Y. 1967, U.S. Dist. Ct. (no. dist.) N.Y. 1970, U.S. Tax Ct. 1969, U.S. Ct. Appeals (2d cir.) 1970, U.S. Supreme Ct. 1974. Ptnr. Albrecht Maguire Heffern & Gregg, P.C., Buffalo, 1969—; bd. dirs. various local pvt. corps., N.Y. Contbr. articles to profl. jours. Bd. dirs. Mercy Hosp., Buffalo, 1984—. Mem. ABA, N.Y. State Bar Assn., Erie County Bar Assn., Country Club Buffalo (chmn. legal com. 1983), Buffalo Club. Republican. Episcopalian. Office: Albrecht Maguire et al 2100 Empire Tower Buffalo NY 14202

RUSSELL, CHARLES ANDREW, investment company executive; b. Detroit, Oct. 29, 1941; s. William M. and Esther R.; m. Nancy Tussey; children: Andrew Keith, Amy Esther. BS, U. Mo., 1963, MBA, 1967. Profl. linebacker Pitts. Steelers, 1963-76; salesman Oliver Tyrone Corp., Pitts., 1967-68; regional rep. Simpson Emery & Co., Pitts., 1978-80; oil and gas operator Three Rivers Energy, Pitts., 1981—; ptnr. Russell, Rea & Zappala, Pitts., 1980—; broker, dealer Russell Investments, Pitts., 1974—; bd. dirs. Equimark, Pitts. Dinner chmn. Rep. Fundraiser, 1987—; bd. dirs. United Way, Pitts., 1984—. Served to lt. U.S. Army, 1964-65. Recipient Byron Whizzer award NFL Players Assn., 1975; named Most Valuable Player Pitts. Steelers, 1970, Man of Yr. Pitts. YMCA, 1987. Mem. NFL Alumni Assn., Parents Anonymous. Clubs: Duquesne, Rolling Rock, Fox Chapel Golf. Office: Russell Rea & Zappala Inc 2 North Shore Ctr Pittsburgh PA 15212

RUSSELL, CHUCK, marketing and management professional; b. Rome, Ga., May 6, 1949; s. James Leo and Virginia (Johnson) R.; m. Lauretta LaBarbera, Dec. 3, 1987. Buyer, dir. merchandising Rhodes, Inc., Pensacola, Fla., 1972-75; design and merchandising cons. Pensacola, 1975-77, profl. tennis coach, 1977-82; sr. exec. Macy's, Atlanta, 1982-85; v.p., ptnr.

Creative Mgmt. Group, Atlanta, 1985—; cons. numerous cos., Atlanta, 1985—; pub. speaker various organs. and cos.; pres. Attitude Accessories, Inc., Atlanta, 1987—. Mem. Nat. Speakers Assn. Office: Creative Mgmt Group 9755 Dogwood Rd Ste 350 Roswell GA 30075

RUSSELL, CLOVIA E., communications company executive; b. Sarasota, Fla., Apr. 18, 1953; d. Harold E. and Ruby Byrd. BS, U. No. Fla., 1980. Asst. mgr. customer svcs. So. Bell, Jacksonville, Fla., 1980-87; mgr. corp. affairs So. Bell, Jacksonville, 1987—. Chmn. Visions Taskforce 2005 Crime Prevention, Jacksonville, 1988; bd. dirs. Ritz Theatre Dist., 1988, Pace Ctr. for Girls, 1989, N.W. Area Coun., 1989, Mental Health, 1989; mem. mktg. com. Arts Assembly, 1989, adv. coun. Nassau County Vol. Ctr., Fernandina Beach, Fla., 1989. Served with U.S. Army, 1972-75. Mem. ASPA, NAFE, Fla. Pub. Relations Assn., Nat. Assn. Negro Bus. and Profl. Women, Nat. Coun. Negro Women, NAACP, Jacksonville Urban League, Civitan, Jacksonville C. of C. (bd. dirs.). Democrat. Baptist. Office: So Bell 301 W Bay St Ste 2600 Jacksonville FL 32202

RUSSELL, DAVID C., JR., brokerage firm executive; b. N.Y.C., Nov. 5, 1951; s. David C. and Catherine (Crawford) R.; m. Grace Ester Ben-Ezra, Sept. 28, 1985. Student, NYU, 1969-71. Sr. reporter N.Y. Coffee Sugar and Cocoa Exchange, N.Y.C., 1971-75; trader B.W. Dyer and Co., N.Y.C., 1975-77; supr., ops. and sales W.C.L., N.Y.C., 1977-79; v.p. ops., account exec. A.C.L.I. Internat./DLJ Futures, N.Y.C., 1979-84; sr. v.p. ops. DM Brokers, N.Y.C., 1984-85; v.p. ops., mgr. sales Mocatta Futures Corp., N.Y.C., 1985-87; dir. Hornblower Fischer and Co., N.Y.C., 1987—. Founding mem. Joyce Dance Co., N.Y.C., 1984; supporter Boy Scouts Am., N.Y.C., 1970—. Mem. Futures Industry Assn., Commodities Exchange Inc., N.Y. Mercantile Exchange. Democrat. Office: Hornblower Fischer & Co 20 Broad St 25th Fl New York NY 10005

RUSSELL, DAVID WILLIAMS, lawyer; b. Lockport, N.Y., Apr. 5, 1945; s. David Lawson and Jean Graves (Williams) R.; A.B. (Army ROTC scholar, Daniel Webster scholar), Dartmouth Coll., 1967, M.B.A., 1969; J.D. cum laude, Northwestern U., 1976; m. Frances Yung Chung Chen, May 23, 1970; children—Bayard Chen, Ming Rennick. English tchr. Talledega (Ala.) Coll., summer 1967; math. tchr. Lyndon Inst., Lyndonville, Vt., 1967-68; instr. econs. Royalton Coll., South Royalton, Vt., part-time 1968-69; asst. to pres. for planning Tougaloo (Miss.) Coll., 1969-71, bus. mgr., 1971-73; mgr. will and trust rev. project Continental Ill. Nat. Bank & Trust Co. Chgo., summer 1974; law clk. Montgomery, McCracken, Walker & Rhoads, Phila., summer 1975; admitted to Ill. bar, 1976, Ind. bar, 1983; Winston & Strawn, Chgo., 1976-83; ptnr. Klineman, Rose, Wolf & Wallack, Indpls., 1983-87, Johnson, Smith, Densborn, Wright & Heath, 1987—; cons. Alfred P. Sloan Found., 1972-73; dir., sec. Forum for Internat. Profl. Svcs., 1985-88, pres. 1988—; U.S. Dept. Justice del. to U.S. China Joint Session on Trade, Investment & Econ. Law, Beijing, 1987; lectr. Ind. Law, Gov's Ind. Trade Mission to Japan, 1986, internat. law Ind. Continuing Legal Edn. Forum, 1986-88, chmn., 1987-88. Mem. Ind. ASEAN Coun., Inc. (dir. 1988—), nat. selection com. Woodrow Wilson Found. Adminstrv. Fellowship Program, 1973-76 ; vol. Lawyers for Creative Arts, Chgo., 1977-83; dir. World Trade Club of Ind., 1987—; v.p., dir., Sister Cities of Ind., 1988—; v.p., dir. Internat. Ctr. Indpls., 1988—. Woodrow Wilson Found. Adminstrv. fellow, 1969-72. Mem. ABA, Ill. Bar Assn., Ind. Bar Assn. (vice chmn. internat. law section, 1988—), Indpls. Bar Assns., Dartmouth Lawyers Assn., Indpls. Assn. Chinese Ams., ACLU, Chinese Music Soc., Zeta Psi. Presbyterian. Club: Dartmouth of Ind. (sec. 1986-87, pres. 1987-88). Home: 10926 Lakeview Dr Carmel IN 46032 Office: Johnson Smith Densborn & Heath Indiana Nat Bank Tower 1800 One Indiana Sq Indianapolis IN 46204

RUSSELL, EDWARD THOMAS, banker; b. Stamford, Conn., June 15, 1941; s. Thomas B. and Margaret L. (Mead) R.; AS, Quinnipiac Coll., 1962, BS in Acctg. 1964; student Stonier Grad. Sch. Banking, 1977; MBA U. New Haven; m. Beverly J. Richards, June 17, 1967; children: David R. and Deborah L. (twins), Kevin C. With Fidelity Trust Co., Stamford, 1964-88, asst. v.p. treas.'s dept., 1972-74, v.p., 1974-81, v.p., treas., 1981-82, sr. v.p., treas. 1982-88; sr. v.p., chief fin. officer Stamford Savs. Bank, 1988—. Cubmaster, Cub Scout Pack 46, Stamford, 1976-78; bd. dirs. Stamford Youth Soccer League, 1977—, pres., 1979-86, coach, 1976—; coach Stamford Basketball for Youth, 1977—, v.p. 1988—, Northrop Little League, 1978-84; treas. Northrop Little League, 1985—; treas. Emmanuel CH., 1980-81. 1972-76, jr. warden, 1978-79, vestryman, 1980—. Recipient chpt. leadership award Bank Adminstrn. Inst., 1979, nat. award, 1979; award for Service and Achievement Stamford Bd. of Recreation, 1979, 80, 81, 82; Proclamation for Service to Youth City of Stamford, 1986; chartered bank auditor; cert. office automation profl., cert. payroll profl. Mem. Am. Payroll Assn., Am. Inst. Banking (dir. Stamford chpt. 1977-79, pres. Western Conn. chpt. 1978-79, dir. 1979-80, instr. banking), Fin. Execs. Inst., Nat. Assn. Bank Cost and Mgmt. Accts., Inst. Mgmt. Accts., Nat. Corp. Cash Mgmt. Assn., Nat. Soc. Chartered Bank Auditors, Nat. Assn. Accts., Office Automation Soc. Internat. Club: Hubbard Heights Men's (gov., pres. 1976-81). Lodge: Lions (v.p. Stamford club 1985—). Home: 31 Sussex Pl Stamford CT 06905 Office: Stamford Savs Bank 117 Prospect St Stamford CT 06904

RUSSELL, EDWIN LARSON, manufacturing company executive; b. N.Y.C., Feb. 15, 1945; s. Edwin Fortune and Betty Louise (Larson) R.; m. Alicia Zintl, May 30, 1972; 1 child, Robert Larson. BA, Bowdoin Coll., 1967; MBA, Harvard U., 1971. Exec. trainee Chase Manhattan Bank, N.Y.C., 1967; mgmt. cons. McKinsey & Co., N.Y.C., 1971-74; mgr. mach. group planning dept. FMC Corp., Chgo., 1974-77, dir. bus. planning, 1977-78; pres., mng. dir. FMC Food Machinery Europe, St. Niklaas, Belgium, 1978-81; v.p. devel. corp. Stanadyne Inc., Windsor, Conn., 1981—; bd. dirs. New Med. Techniques, Bystol, Conn. Mem. Zoning Commn., Essex, Conn., 1988; mem. vestry St. John's Epis. Ch., Essex, 1988; chmn. class com. capital campaign Bowdoin Coll., Brunswick, Maine, 1988. Lt. U.S. Army, 1967-69. Mem. Saddle & Cycle Club (bd. dirs. 1977-78), Micguamicut Club, Hartford Club. Republican. Office: Stanadyne Inc 100 Deerfield Rd Windsor CT 06095

RUSSELL, HAROLD JOHN, civic worker for handicapped, management consultant; b. North Sydney, N.S., Can., Jan. 14, 1914; came to U.S., 1921, naturalized, 1936; m. Elizabeth Marshallsea; children by previous marriage: Gerald J., Adele Rita. B.A., Boston U., 1949; L.D.H. hon., LaSalle Coll.; L.D.H., U. Mass. Pres. Harold Russell Assocs., Winchester, Mass. Appeared in supporting role in movie: Inside Moves, 1980; author: Victory in My Hands, 1949. Vice chmn. President's Com. on Employment of People with Disabilities, 1962-64, chmn., 1964—; mem. Nat. Council on Vocat. Rehab., 1966-68, Mass. Indsl. Accident Rehab. Commn., Nat. Orgn. on Disability, Nat. Challenge Com. on Disability; active ARC, NCCJ; mem. adv. council Nat. Easter Seal Soc., Goodwill Industries Am., People to People com. for Handicapped Bd. Served with U.S. Army, 1941-45. Named One of 10 Outstanding Young Men U.S. C. of C., 1950. Mem. AMVETS (nat. comdr. 1950-51, 1960), World Vets. Fedn. (v.p. 1960-67). Office: Pres's Com Employment People Disabilities 1111 20th St NW Washington DC 20210

RUSSELL, JAY D., marketing executive; b. Milw., Dec. 20, 1950; s. John Frank and Veronica Cecilia (Jones) R.; m. Carol Jean Croft, Feb. 14, 1976 (div. 1980); 1 stepchild, Kirsten Jean. BS, Ariz. State U., 1984, MBA, 1987. Prin. Southwest Casting Corp., Albuquerque, 1973-77; exec. v.p. Creative Constrn. Inc., Albuquerque, 1977-78; ops. supt. Demas Constrn. Inc., Alameda, N.M., 1978-81; adminstrv. mgr. Investment and Retirement Systems Inc., Phoenix, 1984-85; research asst. dept. communications Ariz. State U., Tempe, Ariz., 1985-86; grad. asst. Ariz. State U., 1986-87; project coordinator CHR Interiors, Scottsdale, Ariz., 1987-88; assoc. CHR Equipment and Space Planning, Scottsdale, 1988-89; prin. AJR Enterprises/Equipment Co., Tempe, 1985—; research intern Gov's Office State of Ariz., Phoenix, 1986; mktg. intern Chase Bank Ariz., cons. 1988—, Fin. Ctr., Scottsdale, 1987; grad. liaison Econ. Club of Phoenix, Tempe, 1986-87. Named Outstanding Grad. Student Fin., Wall St. Jour., 1987; Exxon Ednl. Found. scholar, 1986. Mem. Ariz. State U. Alumni Assn., Sigma Iota Epsilon, Phi Kappa Phi, Beta Gamma Sigma. Roman Catholic. Club: Econ. (Phoenix). Office: AJR Enterprises PO Box 24429 Tempe AZ 85282

RUSSELL, KEITH PALMER, JR., financial services executive; b. Los Angeles, Oct. 23, 1945; s. Keith Palmer and Betty Jane (Stratton) R.; m. Margaret Ann Richards, Mar. 18, 1967; 1 child, Hope Ann. BA, U. Washington, 1967; MA, Northwestern U., 1970. V.p. Security Pacific Corp., London and Hong Kong, 1979-81; sr. v.p. Security Pacific Corp., Los Angeles, 1981-83; exec. v.p. Glendale (Calif.) Fed. Savs. & Loan Assn., 1983-84, sr. exec. v.p., 1984-85, chief operating officer, 1985-88; dir., chief oper. officer Glenfed, 1988-89, pres., 1989—, also bd. dirs. Republican. Episcopalian. Club: Jonathan (Los Angeles). Office: GLENFED Inc 700 N Brand Blvd Glendale CA 91209

RUSSELL, NORMAN THOMAS, marketing executive; b. Phila., May 26, 1952; s. John W. and Florence Marie (Collins) R.; m. Maryann Rogers, Oct. 6, 1973; children: Benjamin, Meredith, Bradley, Amanda, Andrew. BS, La. Tech., 1977; MBA, Southern Ill. U., 1982. Office mgr. Okonite Co., Phila., 1978-79; sales rep. Okonite Co., Vienna, Va., 1979-81; area mgr. Pirelli Cable Corp., Manassas, Va., 1981-83; regional mgr. Pirelli Cable Corp., Greenwood, S.C., 1983-86; mktg. mgr. Pirelli Cable Corp., Greenwood, 1986—. With USAF, 1973-77. Mem. IEEE, Greenwood C. of C., K.C. Republican. Roman Catholic. Office: Pirelli Cable Corp PO Box 1097 Greenwood SC 29646

RUSSELL, RANDALL L. C., chemical company executive; b. Pitts., Jan. 13, 1945; s. Homer and Agnes (McBride) R.; m. Barbara Wright, June 11, 1966; 1 child, Randall Lee. BA magna cum laude, Slippery Rock U., 1966; MBA, U. Pitts., 1970, PhD in Chemistry, 1970. V.p., gen. mgr. Koppers Co., Inc., Pitts., 1970-84; pres. Ranbar Tech., Inc., Pitts., 1984—, Ball Chem. Co., Pitts., 1984—; bd. dirs. Union Nat. Bank, Pitts., Union Nat. Corp., Pitts. Mem. Duquesne Club, Oakmont Country Club. Republican. Episcopalian. Office: Ball Chem Co 1114 William Flinn Hwy Glenshaw PA 15116

RUSSELL, RICHARD BRUCE, capital management executive; b. Seattle, Nov. 14, 1949; s. William Ellis and Miriam Jeanette (Savage) R.; m. Eleonore Klara Crane, Dec. 27, 1985. BBA, U. Wash., 1972. Registered investment advisor. Pvt. portfolio mgr. Russell Investments, Issaquah, Wash., 1972-77; pres. Ariston Capital Mgmt. Corp., Issaquah, 1977-85, Bellevue, Wash., 1985-88; portfolio mgr. Concord income trust Ariston Capital Mgmt. Corp., Florham Park, Wash., 1988—; portfolio mgr., trustee bd. dirs. Concord Income Trust Convertible Portfolio Mut. Fund, 1988—. Author several research studies on econ. forecasting, asset allocation and security investments, 1981, 84-88; contbr. articles to profl. jours. Mem. Am. Assn. Individual Investors, Found. for Study of Cycles, Market Technicians Assn. Home: 9705 NE 13th Bellevue WA 98004 Office: Ariston Capital Mgmt Corp 12301 NE 10th Pl Ste 250 Bellevue WA 98005

RUSSELL, ROBERT EMMET, defense contractor executive; b. Buffalo, Apr. 28, 1947; s. Edward E. and Carol (Person) R.; B.S. in Metall. Engring., U. Ill., 1970, M.S., 1971; M.B.A., Ill. Inst. Tech., 1975; m. Nancy J. Doody, June 17, 1972; children—William E., Catherine E., David C. Welding engr. Ill. Inst. Tech. Research Inst., Chgo., 1971-72; materials engr. quality assurance group Northrop Corp., Rolling Meadows, Ill., 1972-74, chief of materials 1975-78, project mgr., 1977-78; sr. analyst Northwest Industries, Chgo., 1978-79, mgr. capital expenditures, 1979-86; sec. mgr. Engring. Northrop Corp., Arlington, Heights, Ill., 1986—. Registered profl. engr., Ill. Mem. Am. Mgmt. Assn., Nat. Soc. Profl. Engrs., Am. Soc. Metals, Sigma Iota Epsilon. Home: 1502 S Fernandez Arlington Heights IL 60005 Office: Engring Northrop Corp 600 University Arlington Heights IL 60004

RUSSELL, ROBERT LEONARD, association executive; b. Mt. Vernon, Ill., July 18, 1916; s. Charles Arthur and Edna Mabel (Yearwood) R.; m. Jeanne Lucille Tackenberg, May 21, 1942. Student, St. Petersburg Jr. Coll., 1971-72; BS, U. Mid. Fla., 1973, MS, 1974. Reporter Peoria (Ill.) Jour., 1939-42, 46-47, Chgo. Daily News, 1947-57; asst. exec. dir. Profl. Golfers Assn., Dunedin, Fla., 1957-65; exec. dir. United Vol. Services, San Mateo, Calif., 1965-66; reporter St. Petersburg (Fla.) Evening Ind., 1967-70; pres. Aldrich & Assocs., 1967-70; exec. v.p. Fla. Health Care Assn. (formerly Fla. Nursing Home Assn.), Orlando, 1970-77; exec. v.p. Mortgage Bankers Assn. Fla., Orlando, 1977—, Mortgage Bankers Assn. Cen. Fla., Orlando, 1978—; exec. v.p. Mortgage Bankers Ednl. Found. Fla., Orlando, 1986—; adminstr. Fla. Health Care Self Insurers Fund, 1972-78; sec.-treas. Mortgage Bankers Fla. Polit. Action Com., 1977-85, treas., 1987—; pres. Profl. Assn. Services, Inc., 1977-81, chmn. bd., 1981—. Editor: Profl. Golfer mag., 1957-65, Nat. Golfer mag., 1965-66, Communicator, 1977-80, Bull., 1980-81, The Messenger, 1986—; exec. editor Rx Sports and Travel mag., 1966-67. Elder Park Lake Presbyn. Ch., Orlando, 1979-83, St. Paul's Presbyn. Ch., Orlando, 1983-87, Presbyn. Ch. of Lakes, 1987—; mem. coord. coun. Presbytery of Cen. Fla., 1989—. Served with USAAF, 1942-46. Mem. Am. Soc. Assn. Execs. (cert.), Fla. Soc. Assn. Execs., Cen. Fla. Soc. Assn. Exec., Am. Coll. Health Care Adminstrs. (hon.), Fla. Sheriffs Assn. (hon.), U.S. Basketball Writers Assn. (pres. 1956-57), Football Writers Assn. Am. (bd. dirs. 1955-57), Nat. Rifle Assn. (life), Am. Legion. Republican. Home: 7316 Lismore Ct Pembrooke Orlando FL 32811 Office: 4401 Vineland Rd Ste A-11 Orlando FL 32811

RUSSELL, SUZANNE DAVIS SHEPARD, mortgage company executive; b. Kirkland, Wash., Apr. 28, 1956; d. Dodd Vincent and Mary Wharton (Jennings) Shepard; m. James Brant Russell, Aug. 7, 1976 (div. Feb. 1985); children: James Dodd, Chase Brant. Student, Wash. State U., 1974-75, Spokane (Wash.) Community Coll., 1976-83. Loan processor Bancshare Mortgage Co., Spokane, 1975-78; loan processor/closer Rainier Mortgage Co., Spokane, 1978-79; asst. v.p. Hoover 1st Mortgage Corp., Spokane, 1979-83; exec. sec. Carnation Dairies, Spokane, 1983-85; corp. real estate specialist ISC Systems Corp., Spokane, 1985-88; mgr. of leasing CityFed. Mortgage Co., Bellevue, Wash., 1988—. Mem. United Way Spokane County, 1987-88; mem. Employee Relocation Council. Republican. Episcopalian. Office: CityFed Mortgage Co 10900 NE 4th ST Bellevue WA 98004

RUSSELL, THOMAS FRANK, manufacturing company executive; b. Detroit, Apr. 7, 1924; s. Frank W. and Agnes V. (Kuhn) R.; m. Ruth Helen Costello, June 25, 1949; children: R. Brandon, Scott K. B.S. in Acctg., U. Detroit, 1948. Cost acct. Fed.-Mogul Corp., Southfield, Mich., 1946-47, internal auditor, 1948-49, asst. controller, 1950-58, controller, 1959-64, v.p. fin., 1964-68, group mgr. adminstrn., 1968, v.p., group mgr. service group, 1968-69, exec. v.p., 1969-72, pres., 1972-76, chief exec. officer, 1975—, chmn. bd., 1976—; dir. Comerica Inc., Detroit, Comerica Bank-Detroit, Consumers Power Co., Cross & Trecker Corp., Bloomfield Hills, Mich., A.O. Smith Corp., Milw. Mem. exec. bd. Detroit Area council Boy Scouts Am., 1972—, treas., 1976-77, 1st v.p., 1978-79, pres., 1979-80; bd. dirs. United Found., 1975—, exec. com., 1977—, v.p., 1978—; trustee Detroit Symphony Orch., Bus./Edn. Alliance, Com. for Econ. Devel., St. John Hosp. Served to sgt. U.S. Army, 1943-45. Mem. Machinery and Allied Products Inst. (fin. council 1967-71, exec. com. 1973—, v.p., treas. 1978—, treas. Council for Technol. Advancement 1976—), Greater Detroit C. of C. (bd. dirs. 1978-80, asst. treas. 1978-79), Automotive Info. Council (bd. dirs. 1973—, 1st vice chmn. 1976-77, vice chmn. 1977-78), Citizens Research Council (trustee), Hwy. Users Fedn. (bd. dirs. 1975—), Assn. Ind. Colls. and Univs. (trustee 1976-81). Republican. Roman Catholic. Clubs: Bloomfield Hills Country; Country of Detroit (Grosse Pointe Farms, Mich.); Detroit Athletic, Renaissance (chmn. bd. govs.); Country of Fla. (Golf). Office: Fed-Mogul Corp PO Box 1966 Detroit MI 48235 also: Fed-Mogul World Trade 26555 Northwestern Hwy Southfield MI 48076 *

RUSSELL, WILLIAM THOMAS, III, banker; b. Balt., Dec. 29, 1958; s. William Thomas and Rose Marie (Stanek) R. BBA, James Madison U., 1980. Sr. acct. Peat Marwick Mitchell & Co., Balt., 1980-83; sr. v.p. Second Nat. Fed. Savs. Bank, Salisbury, Md., 1983—; dir. Panda Foods Corp., Salisbury, Md. Mem. Republican Cen. Com., Md., 1986—; bd. dirs. YMCA, Salisbury, 1984—. Roman Catholic. Lodge: Kiwanis (pres. 1987-88). Office: Second Nat Bank Rt 50 and Phillip Morris Dr Salisbury MD 21801

RUSSO, PETER FRANCIS, manufacturing company executive, financial executive; b. Bklyn., Oct. 7, 1942; s. Frank Joseph and Elvira Ann (Gallo) R.; m. Catherine Joan Dillon; children: Peter M., Michele J., Michael J. BBA, St. Francis Coll., 1967. Controller with aerospace and marine group Singer Co., Bridgeport, Conn., 1969-70; mgr. fin. analysis indsl. sewing Singer Co., Piscataway, N.J., 1971-73; dir. ops. Far East mktg. Singer Co., Osaka, Japan, 1974-75; dir. product and mktg. plan indsl. ops. Singer Co., N.Y.C., 1976-79; v.p. fin. Am. Meter Co., Singer Co., Phila., 1979-82, v.p. internat. ops., 1982—; rep., shareholder Sejong/AMC, Seoul, Republic of Korea, 1986—; bd. dirs. Internat. Gas Apparatur, A/S, Hjorring, Denmark, Internat. Gas Apparaten, B.V., Waalwijk, The Netherlands, Internat. Gas Apparatus Ltd., Camberley, Eng. Chmn. com. Cub Scouts Am., Clinton, N.J., 1973-76, cubmaster, 1976-79; co. advisor Pa. Free Enterprise Week, Erie, 1986, 87. Named one of Outstanding Young Men in Am., 1978. Mem. Inst. Gas Engrs. New Zealand (assoc.), Australian Gas Assn., Am. Mgmt. Assn., Internat. Bus. Forum (speaker, various coms.). Republican. Roman Catholic. Home: 73 Water Crest Dr Doylestown PA 18901 Office: Am Meter Co 13500 Philmont Ave Philadelphia PA 19116

RUSSO, PETER JOHN, corporate controller; b. Jersey City, June 20, 1946; s. Patrick John and Josephine Rose (Papalia) R.; B.B.A., Niagara U., 1968; m. Susan M. Poharski; children—Peter, Michele, Elizabeth; step children: Nicole, Amy Hallwood. Audit mgr. Price Waterhouse Co., Rochester, N.Y., 1968-76, sr. audit mgr., Hartford, Conn., 1976-80; corp. contr. Gerber Sci. Inc., South Windsor, Conn., 1980—, treas., 1989—. With Army NG, 1969-75. CPA, N.Y. Mem. AICPA, Nat. Assn. Accts. (co-chmn. profl. devel. com. Rochester 1973), Fin. Execs. Inst., Nat. Corp. Cash Mgmt. Assn., Newcomen Soc., Somers Town Planning Com., N.Y. Soc. CPA's, Conn. Soc. CPA's. Democrat. Roman Catholic. Club: Court House One Tennis. Lodge: Rotary. Contbr. articles to profl. jours. Office: Gerber Sci Inc 83 Gerber Rd W South Windsor CT 06074

RUSSO, SAMUEL LOUIS, JR., planner; b. Utica, N.Y., Jan. 2, 1950; s. Samuel Louis and Eleanor (Santina) R.; B.A., Syracuse U., 1972; cert. in Public Adminstrn., MA in Govt. and Politics, St. John's U., 1981, postgrad., 1988—; m. Janice Furtek, Aug. 21, 1971. With Oneida County Legal Aid Soc., Rome, N.Y., 1970-71, urban planner J.G.K. Assos., Utica, 1971; with U.S. Postal Service, 1970-72; community supr. Urban Renewal Agy. and Mcpl. Housing Authority, Rome, 1970-71; planning analyst City of Utica, 1972; exec. dir. Nat. Found. March of Dimes, Oneida-Herkimer-Madison-Otsego counties, 1972-74; housing, community, econ. devel. planning dir. City of Utica, 1974-78; cons./asst. exec. dir. Oneida County Assn. Retarded Children and Progress Industries, Inc., Utica, 1977; communications and fin. devel. cons./dir. Am. Lung Assn., N.Y. counties, 1978-79; cons. Bur. Census, U.S. Dept. Commerce, Utica, 1980; devel. specialist/exec. dir. Chemung, Schuyler and Steuben counties So. Finger Lakes Devel., Inc., Corning, N.Y., 1980, So. Tier Regional Planning, Corning, 1980; profl. planner Russo Asso., Utica, 1977-81; pub., owner The Voice of the People newspaper, Utica, 1978-80; planning cons. N.Y.C. Community Bd. #4, Elmhurst, Queens, 1980-81; profl. planner/community devel. specialist/ research analyst City of Utica, 1982-85; dir. instl. research SUNY-Herkimer County Community Coll., 1985—; owner S. Russo Assocs., Inc., Utica, N.Y., 1986—; adj. prof. SUNY-Mohawk Valley Community Coll.; discussant N.Y. State Polit. Sci. Assn., Northeastern Polit. Sci. Assn.; adv. com. N.Y. State Sch. Indsl. and Labor Relations, Utica and Rome. Editor Mohawk Valley Times. Mem. exec. com. Utica Coll. Council, 1966-68; chmn., mem. Utica Charter Rev. Commn., 1972, 74, 75; bd. dirs. Upward Housing and Industry Corp., 1967-68; mem. devel. council St. Elizabeth Hosp.; former mem. legis. research com. N.Y.S.H.R.O., 1968-71. Recipient award Community Chest and United Fund. Mem. Am. Planning Assn., Am. Acad. Polit. Social Sci., Am. Soc. Public Adminstrn., Ctr. for Study of the Presidency, Acad. Polit. Scis., Manhattan Inst., Internat. Platform Assn., Sons of Am. Legion, Sons of Italy, Herkimer County C. of C., Utica Area C. of C., Alpha Phi Delta. Lodge: KC (4 deg.). Home: PO Box 411 Utica NY 13503

RUST, EDWARD BARRY, JR., insurance company executive, lawyer; b. Chgo., Aug. 3, 1950; s. Edward Barry Sr. and Harriett B. (Fuller) R.; m. Sally Buckler, Feb. 28, 1976; 1 child, Edward Barry III. Student, Lawrence U., Appleton, Wis., 1968-69; BS, Ill. Wesleyan U., Bloomington, 1972; JD and MBA, So. Meth. U., Dallas, 1975. Bar: Tex. 1975, Ill. 1976. Mgmt. trainee State Farm Ins. Cos., Dallas, 1975-76; atty. State Farm Ins. Cos., Bloomington, 1976, sr. atty., 1976-78, asst. v.p., 1978-81, v.p., 1981-83, exec. v.p., 1983-85, pres. and chief exec. officer, 1985—, chmn., 1987—; pres. and bd. dirs. State Farm Investment Mgmt. Corp., State Farm Internat. Services, Inc., State Farm Cos. Found.; chmn. State Farm Mut. Automobile Ins. Co., 1987; bd. dirs. exec. and investment coms. State Farm Annuity and Life Ins. Co., State Farm Mut. Automobile Ins. Co., State Farm Life Ins. Co., State Farm Fire and Casualty, State Farm Gen. Trustee Ill. Wesleyan U., 1985—. Mem. ABA, Tex. State Bar Assn., Ill. Bar Assn., Am. Inst. Property and Liability Underwriters (trustee 1986—), Ins. Inst. Am. (trustee 1986—), Inst. for Civil Justice (bd. overseers). Office: State Farm Ins Cos One State Farm Pla Bloomington IL 61710

RUST, S. MURRAY, III, building contractor; b. Pitts., Oct. 31, 1939; s. S. Murray and Gladys (Over) R.; m. Shirley Irene Bone, Dec. 22, 1964; children: Robert Bruce, Richard Mark. BA in Applied Sci., Lehigh U., 1961, BS in Mech. Engring., 1962. With Rust Engring. Co., Pitts., 1962-72; pres. Montgomery and Rust, Pitts., 1972—; Bd. dirs. Nursing Home Loan Agy., Harrisburg, Pa.; com. chmn. Housing Opportunities, Inc., McKeesport, Pa. (pres. 1979-81); trustee Shadyside Hosp., Pitts., Chatham Coll. Mem. Builders Assn. Met. Pitts. (pres. 1980, Builder of the Yr. 1977), Pa. Builders Assn. (bd. dirs., v.p., treas.), Harrisburg, Nat. Assn. Home Builders, Washington (bd. dirs.). Episcopalian. Club: Pitts. Golf. Office: Montgomery & Rust Inc Castle Town Sq S 4284 Rte 8 Allison Park PA 15101

RUSTAM, MARDI AHMED, film and television producer, publisher; b. Kirkuk, Iraq, Nov. 25, 1932; came to U.S., 1954; s. Ahmed Baker and Fatima (Behram) R.; m. Sarah Alice Shoup, Apr. 15, 1960; children: Sandra Nesreen, Karima Marguerite. BFA, Art Inst. Chgo., 1960; MFA, U. So. Calif., 1973. Free-lance film editor L.A., 1962-69, free-lance motion picture technician, 1962-72; film producer Mars Prodns. Corp., L.A., 1972—; pub. The Tolucan, Toluca Lake, Calif., 1984—. Cons. Nat. Assn. Arab Ams., Washington, 1980—, Am. Arab Anti-Discrimination Com., Washington, 1984—. Recipient Golden Scroll Merit award Acad. Sci. Fiction, Fantasy and Horror, 1984, Best Horror Film award, 1977, Outstanding Film of Yr. award London Film Festival, 1977. Mem. L.A. Press Club., Calif. Publishers Assn., Lions, Elks. Home: 7 Toluca Estates Dr Toluca Lake CA 91602 Office: Mars Prodns Corp 4405 Riverside Dr Ste 106 Burbank CA 91505

RUSTERHOLZ, KENNETH GEORGE, credit company executive; b. Bklyn., July 21, 1928; s. George and Adeline (Weitz) R.; m. Joan Martha Sinnott, June 12, 1955; children: Ellen Margaret, Kenneth Paul, Mary Catherine. BBA, Pace Coll., 1956. With Gen. Electric Credit Corp., N.Y.C., 1956—, mgr. corp. placements, 1971-75; v.p., mgr. leasing and indsl. loans Gen. Electric Credit Corp., Stamford, Conn., 1975-79, v.p., mgr. transp. and maj. project financing, 1979-81, v.p., gen. mgr. transp. fin. dept., 1981-84, v.p., mgr. internat. fin. ops., 1984—. Served with AUS, 1966-68. Mem. Assn. Equipment Lessors, Sigma Lambda Iota. Republican. Congregationalist. Home: 14 Scatter Good Circle Trumbull CT 06611 Office: GE Credit Corp 260 Long Ride Rd Stamford CT 06904

RUTH, FRANKLIN WILLIAM, JR., metals manufacturing company executive; b. Dayton, Ohio, Oct. 14, 1917; s. Frank William and Florence U. (Iobst) R.; m. Pearl Showers, Mar. 23, 1940; children: Betsy Ann (Mrs. Derle M. Snyder), Pamela Jane, Franklin William III. BA, Pa. State Coll., 1939. Supr. bookkeeper Pa. Treasury dept., 1939-42; sr. accountant Main & Co. C.P.A.s, Harrisburg, Pa., 1942-44; chief accounting officer Reiff & Nestor, Co., Lykens, Pa., 1944-46; sec., dir. Reiff & Nestor Co., 1946-83, gen. mgr., 1951-83, treas., 1965-83; sec. dir., gen. mgr. Medco Developing Co. Inc., Lykens, 1955-83; treas. Medco Developing Co. Inc., 1965-83; sec., gen. mgr. Medco Process Inc., Lykens, 1957-83, treas., 1965-83, dir., 1957—; bd. dirs. Miners Bank Lykens, sec. 1962-87, pres. 1987—; treas. New Eng. Tap Co. Inc., 1967-83; also dir.; dir., mem. exec. com. Capital Blue Cross, Harrisburg, vice chmn. bd., 1980-82, chmn. bd., 1984—; dir. Camp Hill Ins. Co. Trustee Pa. State U., 1956-63; sec., dir. Nestor Charitable Found., 1953-83, treas., 1965-83; sec., dir. Mary Margaret Nestor Found., 1953-83, treas., 1965-83; chmn. Upper Dauphin Area Sch. Authority, 1972-80. Mem. N.A.M., Nat. Soc. Pub. Accountants, Am. Soc. Tool and Mfg. Engrs. Methodist. Club: Mason (Shriner). Home: 422 S 2d St Lykens PA 17048

RUTHERFORD, CLYDE E., dairy products company executive; b. 1939; married. Vice president, mem. exec. com. Dairylea Coop., Syracuse, N.Y., 1976-77, 2d v.p., 1977-78, pres., dir., 1978—. Office: Dairylea Coop Inc 831 James St Syracuse NY 13203

RUTHERFORD, REID, finance company executive; b. Morristown, N.J., Dec. 30, 1952; s. Clinton Homer and Bonnie Beth (Bergner) R.; m. Beth Ann Husak, Apr. 3, 1977; children: Ian Michael, Laurel Bryce, Corinne Leigh, Alyse Allyne. BA, Pepperdine U., 1975; MBA, Stanford U., 1981. Exec. v.p. Analytics, Inc., N.Y.C., 1976-79; pres. Softlink Corp., Santa Clara, Calif., 1981-83, Research Applications for Mgmt., Menlo Park, Calif., 1984-85, Concord Growth Corp., Palo Alto, Calif., 1985—. Contbr. articles to profl. jours. Office: Concord Growth Corp 1086 E Meadow Cir Palo Alto CA 94303

RUTKOWSKI, JANET EUNICE, marketing professional; b. Albany, N.Y., Mar. 31, 1965; d. Nicholas and Doris Shirley (Colbert) R. B SUNY, Plattsburgh, N.Y., 1986; postgrad., Université de Quebec à Chicoutimi, 1986. Trade show coord. Econ, Tech. Assistance Ctr., SUNY, Plattsburgh, 1986-87; crafts devel. program ctr. dir. Adirondack North Country Assn., Lake Placid, N.Y., 1987—. Home: The Lodge Lake Clear NY 12945 Office: ANCA 93 Saranac Ave Lake Placid NY 12946

RUTLAND, GEORGE PATRICK, banker; b. Tifton, Ga., Sept. 4, 1932; s. George Patrick Sr. and Peggy (Roberts) R.; m. Dawn Mary O'Neill, Jan. 2, 1954; children: Michael, Kathleen, Dawn Kelly, Mary Linderman. BBA, Pace Coll. N.Y., 1961; postgrad., Rutgers U., 1962-64. With Citicorp, N.Y.C., 1954-75; sr. v.p. corp. svcs. Citicorp, 1970-73; exec. v.p. Citicorp (Advance Mortgage subs), 1973-75; exec. v.p., cashier Crocker Nat. Bank, San Francisco, 1975-81, sr. exec. v.p. ops, 1981-82; exec. v.p. Calif. Fed. Savs. and Loan Assn., L.A., 1982-83, pres., chief exec. officer, 1983-84, vice chmn., 1984-88; pres., chief exec. officer CalFed Inc., L.A., 1985-88, also bd. dirs.; chmn., pres., chief exec. officer N.E. Savs., Hartford, 1988—, also bd. dirs. Trustee Pace U. With USN, 1950-53. Mem. Town Hall of Calif., The Newcomen Soc., L.A. World Affairs Coun. Republican. Roman Catholic. Clubs: Wilshire Country (L.A.), The Hartford, Golf Club of Avon (Conn.), St. James's (London). Home: 83 Stagecoach Rd Avon CT 06001

RUTLEDGE, EUNICE FREESE, financial planner; b. Dallas, Nov. 22, 1928; d. Simon W. and Eunice E. (Brooks) Freese; m. Robb H. Rutledge, Aug. 4, 1950; children: David, Peter, Susan, John. BA, Wellesley Coll., 1949. Cert. fin. planner. Tchr. Fessenden Sch., West Newton, Mass., 1950, Rivers Country Day Sch., Brookline, Mass., 1951-54; ptnr. Neil & Rutledge, Ft. Worth, 1982—; bd. dirs. Summit Nat. Bank, Ft. Worth. Pres. Jr. League, Ft. Worth, 1967; bd. dirs. City Park and Recreation, Ft. Worth, 1968-71; mem. exec. com. Streams and Valleys Com., Ft. Worth, Ft. Worth Nature Ctr. and Refuge, Trinity Terr. Retirement Ct., Ft. Worth. Mem. Inst. Cert. Fin. Planners. Episcopalian. Office: Neil & Rutledge Ridglea Bank Bldg Ste 904 Fort Worth TX 76116

RUTLEDGE, GLORIA JUDITH, engineering company executive; b. Jackson, Tenn., Nov. 22, 1961; d. Rustico Dizon and Kathryn Lillian (Crump) Garcia; m. Corey Neal Rutledge, Oct. 28, 1983. Student, Okla. A&M Coll., 1979-80; AAS, San Jacinto Coll., 1986. Asst. mgr. Southland Corp., Norman, Okla., 1980-81; hydrologic rsch. asst. U.S. Geol. Survey, Oklahoma City, 1982-83; service adminstr. Berkey Mktg. Co., N.Y.C., 1983; exec. adminstr. First Computer Corp., Houston, 1984; mktg. support asst. IBM/NYNEX, Houston, 1984-86; exec. adminstr. Coulson and Assocs. Engrs., Houston, 1987—; pres. Quality, Time & Money, Inc., Houston, 1988—. Author: (short story) Inverted Origins, 1980. Asst., Rep. Campaign, Houston, 1984; vol. fundraiser, Muscular Dystrophy Assn., Am. Cancer Soc., United Jewish Appeal, 1979—; pres. Camp Fire, 1976-80, Horizon Rep., 1977, congress rep. 1979-80. Mem. Am. Council Cons. Engrs., B'nai Brith, Alpha Sigma Epsilon (named Outstanding Pledge 1982). Home: 19334 Lazy Valley Dr Katy TX 77449 Office: Quality Time & Money PO Box 218586 Houston TX 77218

RUTLEDGE, KENNETH DEAN, food company executive; b. Fayette, Ala., Nov. 29, 1946; s. Murray Frederick and Lula Vaudine (Sawyer) R.; m. Brenda Catherine Lanman, July 19, 1969; children: Scott Christopher, John Andrew. BS, Ind. State U., 1969. Elem. tchr. Franklin (Ind.) Sch. Corp., 1969-70; middle sch. tchr. No. Harrison Schs., Ramsey, Ind., 1970-73; procurement mgr. Swift and Co., Jasper, Ind., 1973-76; adminstrv. asst. Swift and Co., Chgo., 1976-77; asst. mgr. Swift and Co., Jasper, Ind., 1977-78; comlpex mgr. Swift and Co., Jasper, 1978-80; prodn., procurement mgr. Swift and Co., Chgo., 1980-82; complex mgr. Marshall, Minn., 1982-83; dir. proc. and processing Chgo., 1983; dir. ops. Norbest, Inc., Salt Lake City, 1983-86, exec. v.p., 1986-87, pres., gen. mgr., 1988—; mem. sec. of agriculture's USDA Com. on Meat and Poultry Inspection; bd. dirs., exec. com. Nat. Turkey Fedn., Reston, Va., 1984-88; bd. dirs. Pacific Egg and Poultry Assn., Modesto, Calif., 1985-88. Republican. Methodist. Office: Norbest Inc 6925 Union Park Ctr Midvale UT 84047

RUTSTEIN, DAVID W., lawyer, food company executive; b. N.Y.C., July 7, 1944; s. David and Mazie (Weissman) R.; m. Rena E. Rutstein, July 19, 1967; children: Sara E., Charles B. B.A., U. Pa., 1966; J.D. with honors, George Washington U., 1969. Bar: Pa. 1969, D.C. 1969. Dep. atty. gen. Pa., 1969-70; partner firm Danzansky, Dickey, Tydings, Quint & Gordon, Washington, 1970-78; sr. v.p., gen. counsel Giant Food, Inc., Washington, 1978—; bd. dirs. Washington Met. Bd. Trade, Fed. City Council. Bd. dirs., pres. Washington Hebrew Home for Aged; mem. exec. com. Fed. City Council; trustee Agnes and Eugene Meyer Found., Wash Met. Bd. Trade. Mem. ABA, D.C. Bar Assn., Washington Met. Area Corp. Counsel Assn. (pres. 1986). Jewish. Home: 9 Greentree Ct Bethesda MD 20817 Office: Giant Food Inc PO Box 1804 Washington DC 20013

RUTSTEIN, SHELDON, electronics executive; b. Boston, Oct. 25, 1934; s. Herman and Betty (Altman) R.; m. Susan Rutstein, June 4, 1961; children: Michael, Robin. BBA, U. Mass., 1956. With Raytheon, Lexington, Mass., 1958—, v.p., contr., 1987—. Mem. Fin. Exec. Inst. Jewish. Home: 60 Thunder Rd Sudbury MA 01776 Office: Raytheon Co Spring St Lexington MA 01776

RUTTENBERG, ERIC MAXIMILIAN, private investor; b. Chgo., Feb. 21, 1956; s. Derald Herbert and Janet (Kadesky) R. BA, Hampshire Coll., 1979. Pres. Computer Data Access, Inc., Clifton, N.J., 1978-83; exec. v.p. Tinicum Inc., N.Y.C., 1983-87; gen. ptnr. Tinicum Investors, L.P., N.Y.C., 1988—; gen. ptnr. Tinicum Ptnrs., N.Y.C., 1984—; bd. dirs. Rexa Corp., Medfield, Mass., Environ. Strategies Corp., Vienna, Va. Conservative. Jewish. Office: Tinicum Investors LP 885 2d Ave New York NY 10017

RUTTENCUTTER, BRIAN BOYLE, construction company executive; b. Long Beach, Calif., June 15, 1953; s. Wayne Andrew and Florence Mae (Heckman) R.; m. Marilyn Ruth Grubb, Sept. 9, 1978; 1 child, Christi Anne. BS in Bus. Adminstrn. and Acctg., Biola U., 1976; MBA, Calif. State U., Long Beach, 1983. Cert. mgmt. acct. Controller Fuller Theol. Sem., Pasadena, Calif., 1976-80; dir. gen. acctg. Air Calif., Newport Beach, 1980-84; corp. controller PBS Bldg. Systems, Inc., Anaheim, Calif., 1984-88, v.p. fin. and adminstrn., 1988—. Mem. Drivers for Hwy. Safety, Irvine, Calif., 1986; bd. dirs. Grace Brethren Ch., Long Beach, 1978-80; vice chmn. bd. dirs. Woodbridge Community Ch, Irvine, 1986-88. Mem. Inst. Cert. Mgmt. Accts., Nat. Assn. Accts., Christian Ministries Mgmt. Assn., Fin. Execs. Inst. Republican. Baptist. Home: 14262 Wyeth Ave Irvine CA 92714 Office: PBS Bldg Systems Inc 155 N Riverview Dr Anaheim CA 92808

RUTTER, LINDA CHARLOTTE, realtor; b. Mt. Pleasant, Pa., Sept. 28, 1949; d. Thomas Leland and Charlotte (Fisher) R.; m. Roy Lawrence Murphy, July 7, 1970 (div. July 1977); children: Sean Patrick, Scott Christopher; m. William Arthur Layton, Oct. 7, 1987. Realtor Charlotte F. Rutter Real Estate, Greensburg, Pa., 1972—; pres. Countywide Funding and Fin. Svcs., Greensburg, 1985—. Sec. Women's Svcs. of Westmoreland County, Greensburg, 1981-84. Fellow Bus. and Profl. Women's Club. Republican. Office: Charlotte F Rutter Real Estate 438 S Maple Ave Greensburg PA 15601

RUTTER, RALPH FREDERICK, architect, consultant; b. Corvalis, Oreg., Mar. 6, 1944; s. Milton Frederick and Gloria Jean (Berry) R.; m. Julie Margaret Kniffen, Oct. 1968 (div. 1976); m. Julie Margaret Meisinger, Jan 17, 1976; children: Bryan Wells, Chelsea Jean. BArch, U. Notre Dame, 1967; postgrad., U. Pa., 1969-70. Registered architect Idaho 1973, Calif. 1987; registered contractor Calif. 1986. Architect Neil M. Wright, Architect, Sun Valley, Idaho, 1969-73; pvt. practice architecture, contracting Ketchum, Idaho, 1973-85; ptnr. Space Planning and Architecture Co., Ketchum, 1978-82; pvt. practice architecture, contracting Newport Beach, Calif., 1986—; architect Eckland Cons. Inc., Irvine, Calif., 1987—. Organizer, designer, builder Harriman Sq., Ketchum, 1984. Served with U.S. Army, 1967-69. Republican. Home: 2452 Vista Hogar Newport Beach CA 92660 Office: Eckland Cons Inc 3333 Michelson Suite 580 Irvine CA 92715

RUTZEN, ARTHUR COOPER, JR., investment company executive; b. Chgo., Nov. 18, 1947; s. Arthur Cooper and Helen Doyle Rutzen; B.S. in Bus. & Econs., Lehigh U., 1970, M.B.A., 1972; postgrad. in advanced mgmt. Stanford U., 1982; m. Dolores Cornachia, May 26, 1973; children—Sandy, Arthur C., Judy. Account exec. Merrill Lynch Pierce Fenner & Smith, N.Y.C., 1971-75; mgr. bus. analysis and mktg. positions Union Carbide Corp., N.Y.C., 1975-77, San Francisco and Los Angeles, 1977-83; dir. nat. accounts Liquid Air Corp., San Francisco, 1979-83; v.p., dir. investment mktg. Security Pacific Nat. Bank, Pacific Century Advisors, San Francisco, 1983-85, sr. v.p., 1985-86, exec. v.p., 1986-88; mng. dir. sales and mktg. Asset Mgmt. div. Wells Fargo Bank, 1988—; participant nat. accounts mgmt. study Mktg. Sci. Inst., Harvard U. Sch. Bus., 1980—. Head wrestling coach PAL, Nassau County, L.I., N.Y., 1974. Recipient Spl. Service award Union Carbide, 1976, Meritorious Achievement award, Union Carbide, 1977. Mem. Nat. Accounts Mktg. Assn. (dir., v.p.), Merrill Lynch Exec. Club, Bay Area Sales and Mktg. Execs. Assn. (div. 1981—, v.p. 1982—). Clubs: Golden Gateway Tennis, Family, Lehigh U. Alumni, The Family. Home: 245 Estates Dr Piedmont CA 94611

RUVKUN, FREDERICK JON, securities analyst; b. Berkeley, Calif., Apr. 26, 1957. BSME, Stanford U., 1979; MS in Mgmt., MIT, 1983. Cost engr. IBM Corp., San Jose, Calif., 1979-81; assoc. Merrill Lynch Venture Capital, N.Y.C., 1983-86; securities analyst Morgan Stanley, N.Y.C., 1986—. Office: Morgan Stanley 1251 Ave of the Americas New York NY 10020

RUWITCH, ROBERT SIMON, banker; b. Chgo., Mar. 19, 1914; s. Simon and Selma (Froehlich) R.; m. Shirley Mayer, Aug. 2, 1947; children: Susan Elliott, Robert S., Elizabeth. BA, U. Mich., 1935; postgrad., Northwestern U., 1960-65. Exec. v.p. Buhay Pub. Co., Chgo., 1956-60; 2d v.p. City Nat. Bank & Trust Co., Chgo., 1960-61; v.p. Continental Nat. Bank, Chgo., 1961-76, gen. mgr. gen. merchandising div., 1976-80; self employed fin. cons. Chgo., 1981—; bd. dirs. Salant Corp., N.Y.C., Carson Pirie Scott Found. Contbr. articles to profl. jours. Chmn. archtl. control commn. Village Northbrook, Ill., 1964-70, mem. fire and police commn., 1982-87; trustee U. Chgo. Cancer Research Found., Chgo., 1971—; trustee Ravinia Festival Assn., Chgo., 1968-76, Highland Park (Ill.) Hosp., 1965-74. Served to maj. USAAF, 1942-45, ETO. Decorated Air medal with oak leaf cluster. Mem. Am. Bankers Assn., Robert Morris Assocs., Nat. Assn. Corp. Dirs. Clubs: The Attic, U. Chgo.; Lake Shore Country (Glencoe). Home: 3 Eastwood Dr Northbrook IL 60062 Office: 105 W Adams St Ste 3850 Chicago IL 60603

RUYAN, JERRY LEE, diagnostics company executive; b. Columbus, Ohio, June 17, 1946; s. John and Rosemary Helen (McGee) R.; 1 child, Alexander Christian Willner. BS, Ashland Coll., 1968; MS, Ohio State U., 1972. Microbiologist Henry Ford Hosp., Detroit, 1972-75; sales exec. Analytab Products, Detroit, 1975-77; pres., chief exec. officer Meridian Diagnostics, Cin., 1977—; also bd. dirs. With U.S. Army, 1967-72. Republican. Methodist. Office: Meridian Diagnostics 3471 River Hills Dr Cincinnati OH 45244

RUZZO, GERARD DONALD, small business investor, educator; b. Boston, Sept. 6, 1936; s. Pasquale and Alvina (Moccia) R.; children: Priscilla, Pamela, Elizabeth, Gerard, William. BS, Boston Coll., 1958; MEd, Boston State Coll., 1963. Computer programmer John Hancock Ins. Co., Boston, 1960-61; ind. real estate broker Boston, 1962-65; tchr. pub. schs., Marshfield, Mass., 1965—; owner dry cleaning plant, laundries, investment properties, Mass. and Vt., 1974—. Home: 718 Metropolitan Ave Hyde Park MA 02136 Office: 60 Regis Rd Marshfield MA 02136

RYALS, STANLEY DEE, investment counsel; b. Boise Valley, Idaho, Nov. 23, 1925; s. Oren Franklin and Etta Grace (Gibby) R.; B.A. in Econs., Willamette U., 1949; grad. (fellow) Am. Inst. Econ. Research, 1953, Pacific Coast Banking Sch., U. Wash., 1962; m. Barbara Louise Robinson, May 27, 1949; children—Steven D., Stuart D., Stanton D., Scott D., Spencer D. Trust officer Nat. Bank of Commerce, Seattle, 1955-64; v.p./investment officer Bank of Calif., Los Angeles, 1964-70; vice-chmn., dir. portfolio mgmt. Transam. Investment Mgmt. Co., Los Angeles, 1970-72; v.p./mgr. Western region Standard & Poor's/Intercapital, Los Angeles, 1972-73; exec. v.p., dir. Everett Harris & Co., Los Angeles, 1973-75; pres., dir. Beneficial Standard Investment Mgmt. Corp., Los Angeles, 1975-78, investment counsel, 1978—; instr. U. Wash., Seattle, 1955-60. Trustee, Myrtle L. Atkinson Found., 1973—. Served with U.S. Army, 1943-46. Chartered fin. analyst. Mem. Nat. Assn. Bus. Econs., Los Angeles Soc. Fin. Analysts (past pres.), Inst. Chartered Fin. Analysts, Beta Theta Pi, Blue Key; fellow Fin. Analysts Fedn. Republican. Unitarian. Club: Lions (past pres.) (Seattle). Author: How to Invest Wisely, 1954; Investment Trusts and Funds, 1954; The Ryals Investment Report, 1978—. Asso. editor C.F.A. Digest, 1973—. Home: 26103 N Rainbow Glen Dr Newhall CA 91321 Office: 2930 Honolulu Ave Suite 202 La Crescenta CA 91214

RYAN, ALICE JOY, chemical company executive; b. Staten Island, N.Y., Aug. 13, 1959; d. Carl and Irene (Mandel) Horowitz; m. John Ryan, Aug. 17, 1985. BA, Bklyn. Coll., 1980. Sec. Polymer Research Corp., Bklyn., 1980-82, mgr., 1982-83, dir., 1983-84, v.p. research mktg., 1984—. Contbr. articles to profl. jours. Home: 3035 Lonni Ln Merrick NY 11566 Office: Polymer Rsch Corp 2186 Mill Ave Brooklyn NY 11234

RYAN, CHARLES KENNETH, financial executive; b. Mineola, N.Y., May 23, 1930; s. Charles Clinton and Kathryn (Meyer) R.; m. Catherine Frances O'Brien, June 25, 1955; children: Carol, Pamela. BS in Econs., Fordham U., 1952; MBA, NYU, 1957. Trainee Merrill Lynch, N.Y.C., 1954-56, portfolio unit supr., 1957-61, stock analyst, 1961-62, industry specialist, 1962—; all Am. team mem. Elec. Consumer Products and Photography, 1977—. Served with U.S. Army, 1952-54. Mem. N.Y. Soc. Security Analysts, N.Y. Stock Exchange. Avocations: photography, travel, orchid growing. Office: Merrill Lynch World Fin Ctr New York NY 10281

RYAN, DENNIS JAMES, accounting executive; b. N.Y.C., Sept. 6, 1949; s. Martin J. and Margaret (Egan) R.; m. Carmella Mary Patti, Sept. 2, 1972; children: Danielle Marie, Christina Elizabeth. BBA, Pace U., 1977; grad., Coll. Fin. Planning, 1987. Cert. fin. planner. Securities clk. Chem. Bank, N.Y.C., 1966-69, supr. securities, 1969-71, adminstr. investments, 1971-75, trust fund reviewer, 1975-76; staff acct. St. Clares Hosp., N.Y.C., 1976-78; sr. tax acct. Rockefeller Family & Assocs., N.Y.C., 1978-84, mgr. acctg., 1984—. Treas. Wendell Gilley Mus., Southwest Harbor, Maine, 1987—. Mem. Inst. Cert. Fin. Planners. Home: 186 Cedar Ave Rockville Centre NY 11570 Office: Rockefeller Family & Assocs 30 Rockefeller Pla New York NY 10112

RYAN, EDWIN JOSEPH, JR., auditor; b. Detroit, Oct. 18, 1961; s. Edwin Joseph Sr. and Helen (Kennedy) R. BS magna cum laude in Acctg., Providence Coll., 1983; MBA, Bentley Coll., 1987. Cert. Info. Systems Auditor, Mass. Mgr. Friars Desires, Providence, 1980-83; examiner Bank of New Eng. NA, Boston, 1983-85, audit micro specialist, 1986, EDP examiner, 1986-87, audit systems analyst, 1987-88; sr. systems analyst, corp. audit services Bank of New Eng. div. New Eng. Corp., Boston, 1988—; ptnr. Montagna Spaccada, Inc.; pub. and editor newsletter New England Systems Auditor, 1986—. Publicity chmn. Xaverian Alumni Assn., Westwood, Mass., 1982-83, activities co-chmn., 1983; rep., town meeting mem. Town of Walpole, Mass., 1984-87. Standex Internat. Corp. scholar, 1979; Corp.'s Spotlight award Bank New Eng., 1988. Mem. Auditec Users Group of New Eng., Friar Front Ct. Democrat. Home: 5 Juniper Circle Walpole MA 02081 Office: Bank of New England 1 Washington Mall Boston MA 02109

RYAN, ERIK O., accountant; b. Seattle, Aug. 3, 1962; s. Halvor O. and Myrtle I. (Monson) R. BBA, Pacific Luth. U., 1984. CPA, Wash. Account closure coord. Sea 1st Nat. Bank, Seattle, 1981-85; trade show coord. Wash. Council Internat. Trade, Seattle, 1984; acct. Mahrt & Assocs., Seattle, 1984-86; pension plan adminstr. Benefit Svc. Corp., Seattle, 1986-87; account support rep. WM Fin., Seattle, 1987-88; corp. trust adminstr. 1st Interstate Bank Wash., Seattle, 1988—. Mem. games com. Wash. State Spl. Olympics, 1985-88. Mem. Western Pension Conf., Norwegion Coml. (v.p. 1988, pres. 1989), Toastmasters (treas. 1985). Lutheran. Home: 3264 41st St SW Seattle WA 98116 Office: 1st Internat Bank Wash Trust Div PO Box 21927 Seattle WA 98111

RYAN, FRANK J., chemical company executive; b. Phila., Sept. 15, 1931; s. Frank J. and Mildred (Schowers) R.; m. Jane E. Loughran, July 16, 1955; children: Laurene, Christopher, Carolyn, William. B.S. in Chem. Engring., Villanova U., 1953; M.B.A., Lehigh U., 1961; A.M.P., Harvard U., 1976. With Air Products and Chems., Inc., 1957—; Allegheny Regional mgr. indsl. gas div. Air Products and Chems., Inc., Pitts., 1964-65; asst. gen. mgr. indsl. indsl. gas div. Air Products and Chems., Inc., Allentown, Pa., 1965-68, gen. mgr. agrl. chems., 1968-71; pres. indsl. chems. Air Products and Chems., Inc., Valley Forge, Pa., 1971-77; group v.p. chems. Air Products and Chems., Inc., Allentown, 1978-88, pres., chief oper. officer, 1988—. Fin. chmn. exploring com. Minsi Grails council Boy Scouts Am., 1983; treas. bd. assos. Muhlenberg Coll., Allentown, 1983. Served to lt. USN, 1953-57. Mem. Am. Inst. Chem. Engrs., Soc. Chem. Industry, Allentown-Lehigh County C. of C. Republican. Roman Catholic. Home: 2898 Fairfield Dr Allentown PA 18103 Office: Air Products & Chems Inc 7201 Hamilton Blvd Allentown PA 18195-1501

RYAN, JAMES HERBERT, security and retail services company executive; b. Petersburg, Va., Feb. 1, 1931; s. Richard Hillsdon and Mary Orgain (Mann) R.; BS, U.S. Mil. Acad., 1955; M.A., U. Pa., 1962; MS, George Washington U., 1972; grad. Program for Mgmt. Devel. Harvard U., 1972; Ph.D., Walden U., 1984; m. Patricia Louise Abbott, June 7, 1955; 1 child, Pamela Louise. Commd. 2nd lt. U.S. Army, 1955, advanced through grades to lt. col., 1968, ret., 1972; gen. mgr. U.S. ops. Ryan Enterprises, Washington, 1970-73; pres. Ford Enterprises, Ltd., Mt. Rainier, Md., 1973-87; pres. James H. Ryan Assocs., Inc., Petersburg, Va.,1987—. Advisor to Sec. of Army, 1975, chief of naval material, 1980-82; mem. Pres.'s Pvt. Sector Survey on Cost Control, 1982; bd. govs. USO, 1977-86. Decorated Legion of Merit, Soldiers medal, Bronze Star, Air medal, Vietnamese Gallantry Cross. Mem. Chief Execs. Orgn., Am. Mgmt. Assn., Am. Soc. Indsl. Security, Nat. Retail Mchts. Assn., Internat. Assn. Profl. Security Cons., Ret. Officers Assn., West Point Soc. D.C., Chief Execs. Orgn. Episcopalian. Home: 1666 Westover Ave Petersburg VA 23805 Office: James H Ryan Assocs Inc 522 Grove Ave PO Box 2126 Petersburg VA 23804

RYAN, JERRY GLENN, company executive; b. Muscatine, Iowa, Jan. 23, 1941; s. Glenroy and Violet Marie (Heerd) R.; m. Gerda Ryan, June 1, 1961; children: Jerry, William, Karen. AA, SUNY, Albany, 1974; BS in Mgmt., Shenendoah Coll., 1978. Commd. U.S. Army, 1958-79, advanced through grades to chief warrant officer, 1979; mgr. govt. accounts Xonics Med. Systems, Chgo., 1979-84; dir. govt. and nat. accounts Liebel-Flarsheim Co., Cin., 1984—; cons. in field. Author: Long Term Storage of Medical Equipment, 1977, Preventive Maintenance of Medical Equipment, 1978. Republican. Methodist. Home: 7902 Runnymeade Dr Frederick MD 21701 Office: Liebel-Flarsheim Co 2111 E Galbraith Rd Cincinnati OH 45215-6305

RYAN, JOHN THOMAS, JR., business executive; b. Pitts., Mar. 1, 1912; s. John Thomas and Julia (Brown) R.; m. Irene O'Brien, Aug. 1, 1939; children: John, III, Irene (Mrs. L. Edward Shaw, Jr.), Michael, Daniel, Julia (Mrs. Robert F. Parker), William. B.S., Pa. State Coll., 1934; M.B.A., Harvard U., 1936; D.Sc. (hon.), Duquesne U.; LL.D., U. Notre Dame, 1973. Engr. with Mine Safety Appliances Co., 1936-38, asst. gen. mgr., 1938-40, gen. mgr., 1940-48, exec. v.p. and dir., 1948-53, pres., dir., 1953-63, chmn., 1963—. Mem. exec. com. Allegheny Conf. Community Devel.; trustee emeritus U. Notre Dame; bd. dirs. Children's Hosp. Pitts.; trustee Thomas A. Edison Found. Mem. Am. Mining Congress (dir. mfg. div.), Council on Fgn. Relations, Am. Inst. Mining and Metall. Engrs., ASME, Phi Delta Theta, Tau Beta Pi, Pitts. Athletic Assn. Roman Catholic. Clubs: Pitts. Golf, University, Duquesne; N.Y. Yacht, Union League (N.Y.C.); Chicago; Metropolitan (Washington); Fox Chapel (Pa.); Rolling Rock (Ligonier, Pa.), Allegheny (Laurel Valley). Lodge: Knights of Malta. Home: W Woodland Rd Pittsburgh PA 15232 Office: Mine Safety Appliances Co PO Box 426 Pittsburgh PA 15230

RYAN, JOHN THOMAS, III, safety equipment company executive; b. Pitts., Aug. 6, 1943; s. John Thomas and Mary Irene (O'Brien) R.; m. Catharine Marie Murray, Nov. 18, 1946; children: Mary Catharine, Maureen Emily, John Thomas IV. AB, U. Notre Dame, 1965; MBA, Harvard U., 1969. Mgmt. trainee Mine Safety Appliances Co., Pitts., 1969-70, asst. to dir. of product planning, 1970-74, mgr. S.Am., 1974-78, v.p. internat., 1978-82, v.p., 1982-86, exec. v.p., 1986—, also dir.; dir. Auergesellschaft, Berlin. Bd. dirs. Catholic Youth Assn. of Pitts., 1972—, Mercy Hosp. Found., 1985—; mem. adv. council Coll. Bus. Adminstrn., U. Notre Dame, Ind., 1978—. Served to lt. U.S. Army, 1967-69. Mem. N.Y.C. Council on Fgn. Relations, Am. Mining Congress (chmn. mfrs. div. 1988—, chmn. export com). Republican. Roman Catholic. Home: 5708 Lynne Haven Rd Pittsburgh PA 15217 Office: Mine Safety Appliances Co PO Box 426 Pittsburgh PA 15230

RYAN, KATHLEEN MARY, business executive; b. Chgo., Sept. 11, 1948; d. Albert P. and Betty J. (Kroll) Cavicchioni; divorced; children: Clifford Allen, Jefferey Thomas. BS, Ea. Ill. U., 1970. Jr. account exec. E.H. Brown Advt. Inc., Chgo., 1968-73; sec. Scott Foresman & Co., Glenview, Ill., 1973; sec., treas. Circulation Promotions Inc., Chgo., 1973-88; owner, pres. RYMER Internat., Arlington Heights, Ill., 1988—. Bd. dirs. Spectrum Edn. Ctr., 1985-87; mem. Ill. Council for Gifted, 1986-87. Mem. Nat. Assn. Women in Careers (bd. dirs. Northbrook chpt. 1988—). Lutheran. Home and Office: 616 E Redwood Ln Arlington Heights IL 60004

RYAN, KENNETH ANDREW, finance executive; b. Washington, Sept. 23, 1958; s. Edward Frances and La Nelva T. (Creel) R.; m. Elizabeth Ford, Nov. 27, 1982; children: Elise DuVal, Ann Marie Ryan. BBA in Acctg., James Madison U., 1980. CPA. Va. Asst. acct. Peat, Marwick, Mitchell & Co., Washington, 1980-81, staff acct., 1981082, sr. acct., 1982-84; controller Van Metre Cos., Alexandria, Va., 1984-87; v.p. fin. Van Metre Cos., Burke, Va., 1988—. Mem. Franklin Farm Jaycees (treas.), Phi Beta Lambda (pres. 1980). RRoman Catholic. Home: 12769 Flat Meadow Ln Hernon VA 22071 Office: Van Metre Cos 5252 Lyngate Ct Burke VA 22015

RYAN, KENNETH NEAL, bank executive; b. Boston, Jan. 6, 1938; s. Cornelius James and Dorothy Elizabeth (Wells) R.; m. Carolyn Margaret Hurlebaus, Apr. 28, 1962; children: Theresa Marie, Diana Elizabeth. Student, Boston Coll., 1959-62; cert. in banking, Williams Coll., 1973-74; postgrad., Rutgers U., 1982-84. Credit card rep. State St. Bank & Trust, Boston, 1966-70, budget officer, 1970-74, ops. officer, 1974-78, lending officer, mgr., 1978-86, v.p. lending, 1986—; mem., chmn. bd. dirs. Bay Cove Human Svcs. Inc., Dorchester, Mass., 1974-86; trustee Laboure Ctr. Inc., Boston, 1985—, vice-chmn., 1989—. Mem. adv. bd. Por Cristo, Inc., Brockton, Mass., 1987—; chmn. Civic Reception for Laboure Ctr., Boston, 1987; dir. Assocs. Cath. Hosps., Inc., Boston, 1988; chmn. Bay Cove Capital Campaign, 1988; trust fund commr. Town of Braintree, Mass., 1989—. Recipient Helping Hand award Mass. Bankers Assn., 1987. Mem. KC (state treas. 1988—, state auditor 1982-84, state warden 1984-86, state advocate 1986-88). Republican. Roman Catholic.

RYAN, LEO VINCENT, business educator; b. Waukon, Iowa, Apr. 6, 1927; s. John Joseph and Mary Irene (O'Brien) R. BS, Marquette U., 1949; MBA, DePaul U., 1954; PhD, St. Louis U., 1958; postgrad., Catholic U. Am., 1951-52, Bradley U., 1952-54, Northwestern U., 1950; LLD, Seton Hall U., 1988. Joined Order Clerics of St. Viator, 1950; mem. faculty Marquette U., Milw., 1957-65; dir. continuing edn. summer sessions, coordinator evening divs. Marquette U., 1959-65, prof. indsl. mgmt., 1964; prof. and chmn. dept. mgmt. Loyola U., Chgo., 1965-66; adj. prof. mgmt. Loyola U., 1967-69; dep. dir. Peace Corps, Lagos, Nigeria, 1966-67; dir. Western Nigeria Peace Corps, Ibadan, 1967-68; asst. superior gen. and treas. gen. Clerics of St. Viator, Rome, 1968-69; dir. edn. Am. province Clerics of St. Viator, Arlington Heights, Ill., 1969-74; pres. St. Viator High Sch., 1972-74; dean, prof. mgmt. Coll. Bus. Adminstrn. U. Notre Dame, Ind., 1975-80; dean Coll. Commerce, DePaul U., 1980-88, prof. mgmt., 1980—; prof. mgmt. DePaul U., Chgo., 1988—; dir. Peace Corps. tng. programs Marquette U., 1962-65; adj. prof. human devel. St. Mary's Coll., Winona, Minn., 1972-74; mem. sch. bd. Archdiocese Chgo., 1972-75, vice chmn., 1973-75; mem. nat. edn. com. U.S. Cath. Conf., 1971-75, mem. exec. com., 1973-75; mem. nat. adv. bd. Benedictine Sisters of Nauvoo, 1973— ; mem. nat. adv. council SBA, 1982-85, vice chmn. minority bus., 1982-85, exec. com. Chgo. chpt., 1982-84; vis. prof. U. Ife, Ibadan, 1967-68; bd. dirs. 1st Bank-Milw., chmn. trust audit com., 1980-85, chmn. audit and trust com., 1985—; bd. dirs. 1st Bank-LaCrosse, Vilter Mfg. Co., McHugh-Freeman Assos., Filbert Corp., Vilter Sales & Service, Vilter Internat., Henricksen & Co., Inc., Gebhardt Refrigeration Co.; mem. fin. commn. Clerics of St. Viator, 1978—, mem. provincial chpt., 1985—; cons. Pontifical Commn. on Justice and Peace, 1968-70. Mem. editorial adv. bd. The Internat. Trade Jour. Mem. Pres.'s Com. on Employment Handicapped, 1959-65, Wis. Gov.'s Com. on Employment Handicapped, 1959-65, Wis. Gov.'s Com. on UN, 1961-64, Burnham Park Planning Commn., 1982-88; bd. dirs. Ctr. Pastoral Liturgy U. Notre Dame, 1976-79; trustee St. Mary of Woods Coll., 1978-81; regent Seton Hall U., 1981-87, mem. acad. affairs com., 1981-87, chmn., 1983-87. Recipient Freedom award Berlin Commn., 1961; chieftaincy title Asoju Atoaja of Oshogbo Oba Adenle I, Yorubaland, Nigeria, 1967; Brother Leo V. Ryan award created in his honor Cath. Bus. Edn. Assn., 1962, Ryan Scholars in Mgmt. established in his honor St. Louis U., 1989 and DePaul U., 1989; recipient Kapp Meml. Disting. Alumni award St. Louis U., 1989; named Man of Year Jr. C. of C. Milw., 1959, Marquette U. Bus. Adminstrn. Alumni Man of Year, 1974, Tchr. of Yr. U. Notre Dame, 1980; recipient B'nai B'rith Interfaith award Milw., 1963, Disting. Alumnus award DePaul U., 1976, Tchr. of Yr. award Beta Alpha Psi, Notre Dame U., 1980, Centennial Alumni Achievement award Marquette U., 1981, Boland Meml Disting. Alumni award St. Louis U., 1989; Milw. Bd. Realtors travelling fellow, 1964; Nat. Assn. Purchasing Agts. faculty fellow, 1958; German Am. Acad. Exchange Council fellow, summer 1983; Scholar-in-Residience The Mgmt. Sch., Imperial Coll. of Sci. and Tech., U. of London, 1988; Presidl. fellow Am. Grad. Sch. of Internat. Mgmt; vis. scholar U. Calif., Berkeley, Spring, 1989. Mem. Cath. Bus. Edn. Assn. (nat. pres. 1960-62, nat. exec. bd. 1960-64), Assn. Sch. Bus. Ofcls. (nat. com. chmn. 1965-67), Am. Assembly Collegiate Schs. Bus. (com. internat. affairs 1977-84, chmn. 1981-84, bd. dirs. 1981-87, program chmn. 1979-80, exec. com., chmn. projects/svc. mgmt. com. 1984-86), Am. Fgn. Svc. Assn., Acad. Internat. Bus., Acad. Mgmt., August Derleth Soc., Econ. Club Chgo., Chgo. Counvil Fgn. Relations, Council Fgn. Relations (Chgo. com.), European Found. Mgmt. Edn., European Bus. Ethics Network, Internat. Trade and Fin. Assn. (founder), Milw. Press Club (hon.), Alpha Sigma Nu, Alpha KappaBronze Disting. Service award 1949, silver Disting. Service award 1958), Beta Alpha Psi, Beta Gamma Sigma (co-chair 75th Anniversary committee), Delta Mu Delta, Pi Gamma Mu, Tau Kappa Epsilon. Office: De Paul U Coll Commerce Mgmt Dept 25 E Jackson Blvd Chicago IL 60604-2287

RYAN, LEONARD EAMES, lawyer, public affairs consultant; b. Albion, N.Y., July 8, 1930; s. Bernard and Harriet Earle (Fitts) R.; m. Ann Allen, June 18, 1973; 1 child, Thomas Eames Allen-Ryan. Grad., Kent Sch., 1948; A.B., U. Pa., 1954; J.D., N.Y. U., 1962. Bar: D.C., N.Y. bars 1963, U.S. Ct. of Appeals, D.C 1963, U.S. Dist. Ct. for So. and Eastern Dists. of N.Y 1965, U.S. Ct. of Appeals for the Second Circuit 1966, U.S. Supreme Ct. bar 1967. Reporter Upper Darby (Pa.) News, 1954; newsman AP, Pitts., Phila., Harrisburg, N.Y.C., 1955-62; reporter, spl. writer on law N.Y. Times, 1962-63; info. adviser corp. hdqrs. IBM, N.Y.C., 1963; atty. firm Perrell, Nielsen & Stephens, N.Y.C., 1964-66; trial atty. Civil Rights Div. Dept. Justice, Washington, 1966-68; asst. to dir. bus. affairs CBS News, N.Y.C., 1968; program officer Office Govt. and Law, Ford Found., N.Y.C., 1968-74; pvt. practice, cons. pub. affairs N.Y.C., 1974—; v.p., sec. W.P. Carey & Co., Inc., N.Y.C., 1976-81; adminstrv. law judge N.Y. State Div. Human Rights, 1976—, N.Y. State Dept. Health, 1982—, N.Y. State Dept. Agr. and Mkts., 1987—; impartial hearing officer Edn. for All Handicapped Children Act of 1975, 1976—; hearing examiner Family Ct. of State of N.Y., N.Y. County, 1981-82; arbitrator Small Claims Ct., N.Y.C., 1974-84; bd. dirs. Community Action for Legal Services Inc., N.Y.C., 1971-77, vice-chmn., 1975-77; co-chmn. Citizens Com. to Save Legal Services, N.Y.C., 1975-76; bd. dirs. Lower East Side Service Center, N.Y.C., 1977-89. Author: (with Bernard Ryan Jr.) So You Want to Go Into Journalism, 1963; contbr. articles to profl. jours. Served with USAR, 1950-57. Mem. Am. Judicature Soc., Assn. of Bar of City of N.Y., N.Y. State Bar Assn. Democrat. Clubs: St. Elmo, Phila. Office: 32 Orange St Brooklyn NY 11201

RYAN, LYNN BANKER, professional speaker; b. Holtville, Calif., Oct. 8, 1935; d. Fredrick William and Mary (Setz) Waterman; m. Edward Everett Banker, Sept. 18, 1954 (div. Sept. 1987); children: Bret Howard, Bruce Edward, Bradley Allen; m. Vernon Joseph Ryan, Sept. 19, 1987. Office mgr. Design Scis., Inc., El Centro, Calif., 1967-74; office mgr. U. Calif., Irvine, 1979-81, fin. bus. mgr., 1981-85; pres. Lynn Banker & Assoc., Costa Mesa, Calif., 1984—; mem. classification com. U. Calif., 1980-84; pres., v.p. Internat. Tng. in Communications, Huntington Beach, Calif., 1982-84. Author audio tape album and single tapes; contbr. articles to profl. jours. Mem. by laws task force, 1st v.p., bd. dirs. congregation St. Matthews Old Cath. Mission, Huntington Beach, 1988. Mem. Nat. Speakers Assn. (bd. dirs. 1986-87, membership chair 1985-87, 2d v.p. 1987-88, 1st. v.p., program chmn. 1988-89, pres. 1989—, Bronze Mike 1986, Silver Mike 1987, Gold Mike 1988), Women's Bus. Assn. Republican. Clubs: Connections (Cerritos) (ethics com. 1986-88), Ind. Cons. (Los Angeles). Home: 1953 Flamingo Dr Costa Mesa CA 92626 Office: Lynn Baker & Assoc PO Box 2397 Costa Mesa CA 92628

RYAN, MICHAEL EDMOND, communications company executive, lawyer; b. N.Y.C., May 30, 1938; s. John J. and Mary K. (Mulligan) R.; m. Ellen Todaro, Feb. 10, 1962; children: Michael, Patrick, MaryEllen. B.B.A., St. John's U., Jamaica, N.Y., 1963; J.D., Fordham U., 1967; grad. Advanced Mgmt. Program., Harvard U., 1983. Bar: N.Y. 1967, U.S. Supreme Ct. 1972. With N.Y. Times Co., 1956—, prodn. mgr., 1960-63, asst. controller, 1963-67, corp. atty., 1967-70, asst. sec., 1970-74, sec., corp. counsel, 1974-79, v.p. law, fin., adminstrn., 1979-80, sr. v.p. corp. devel., broadcasting, cable-TV and forest products, 1980-89, sr. v.p. corp. devel., corp. staff, 1989—. Bd. dirs. Fordham U. Law Sch. Served with U.S. Army, 1961-62. Recipient Am. Jurisprudence Corps. award Lawyers Coop. Pub. Co., 1967. Mem. ABA, Fed. Bar Assn., Assn. Bar City N.Y. Clubs: Sands Point Golf, Forest Hills, West Side Tennis. Office: NY Times Co 229 W 43rd St New York NY 10036

RYAN, MICHAEL LOUIS, controller; b. Corning, Iowa, Feb. 22, 1945; s. Leo Vincent and Elda May (Lawrence) R. AAS in Constrn. Tech., Iowa State U., 1965; BS in Acctg., Drake U., 1972. CPA, Iowa, Wyo. Acct. Ernst & Ernst, Des Moines, 1972-75, Becker, Herrick & Co., Pueblo, Colo., 1975-78; pvt. practice acctg. Gillette, Wyo., 1978-81; acct. Karen M. Moody, CPA's, Sheridan, Wyo., 1981-85; controller T-C Investments, Inc., Sheridan, 1985—. With U.S. Army, 1966-68, Vietnam. Mem. Am. Inst. CPA's (tax div.), Wyo. Soc. CPA's, Am. Legion (fin. officer 1977-81), Lodge (sec. Sheridan club 1982—), Phi Kappa Phi, Beta Alphs Psi, Beta Gamma Sigma. Democrat. Roman Catholic. Home: 735 Canby St Sheridan WY 82801 Office: T-C Investments Inc 856 Coffeen Ave Sheridan WY 82801

RYAN, MICHAEL THOMAS, financial planner; b. Providence, July 9, 1952; s. Thomas Michael and Dorothy Mary (Houlihan) R.; m. Leslie Michele Fonsh, June 21, 1980. BA, U. R.I., 1974; MA, U. Conn., 1972, PhD, 1987. Cert. fin. planner. Lectr. U. Conn., Storrs, 1976-78, research asst., 1978-79; psychologist East Lyme (Conn.) Pub. Schs., 1981-87; fin. planner Profl. Planning Group, Westerly, R.I., 1985—. Mem. Spl. Edn. Adv. Com., Westerly, 1988. Mem. Inst. Cert. Fin. Planners, Internat. Assn. Fin. Planners. Lodge: Lions. Home: 37 Woodlund Ave Westerly RI 02891 Office: Profl Planning Group 7 Grove Ave Westerly RI 02891

RYAN, MIKE, II, financial planning company executive; b. Evansville, Ind., Oct. 5, 1951; s. Mike and Mabel (Mason) R.; m. Pamela Marie Bogdalik, Aug. 19, 1973; children: Dylan Michael, Devin Michael. BA, Ind. U., 1974, MA, 1978. Cert. fin. planner, 1983. Filmmaker Image Makers, Bloomington, Ind., 1978-79; travel cons. Am. Express Co., Chgo., 1979; pvt. investor Wilmette, Ill., 1979-82; pres. Ryan Fin. Advisors, Ltd., Wilmette, 1983—; mem. adj. faculty Coll. for Fin. Planning, Denver, 1984—. Named One of Am's. Best Fin. Planners Money Mag., 1987. Mem. Inst. Cert. Fin. Planners (v.p. Greater Chgo. Soc. 1985-86, pres. 1986-87, chmn. 1987-88, nat. bd. dirs. 1989, Svc. award 1988), Internat. Assn. Fin. Planners (bd. dirs. Greater O'Hare chpt. 1984-86, North Shore chpt. 1987-88, Svc. award 1986), Registry Fin. Planning Practioners, Nat. Assn. Pers. Fin. Advisors, Am. Assn. Ind. Investors (life), Michigan Shores Club. Republican. Office: Ryan Fin Advisors 1000 Skokie Blvd Ste 570 Wilmette IL 60091

RYAN, PATRICK J., electric utility company executive; b. Chgo., July 31, 1938; s. Phillip W. and Estelle F. Ryan; m. Grace M. Marko, Sept. 5, 1959; children: Rachel, Nicole. BS in Elect. Engring., U. Okla. 1961; hon. degree in mgmt. Edison Electric Inst., 1976. Registered profl. engr., Okla Western div. service mgr. Okla. Gas and Electric, Oklahoma City, 1971-73, chief environ. affairs, 1973-76, asst. treas., 1976-78, treas., 1978-80, v.p. and treas., 1980-81, sr. v.p. and treas., 1981-84, exec. v.p. fin. and adminstrn., 1984-86, exec. v.p. and chief operating officer, 1986—; bd. dirs. St. Anthony Hosp. Found., Inc., ARC, Oklahoma City, 1981—, Last Frontier council Boy Scouts Am., 1985—, Okla. Philharm. Soc., United Way Cen. Okla.; bd. visitors Coll. Engring. U. Okla. Served with U.S. Army, 1962. Mem. U. Okla. Assocs., Okla. Soc. Profl. Engrs., NSPE, Okla. City C. of C. (bd. dirs.). Republican. Episcopalian. Clubs: Oklahoma City Golf and Country, Petroleum. Office: Okla Gas & Electric Co 321 N Harvey PO Box 321 Oklahoma City OK 73101

RYAN, PATRICK JOHN, mining company executive; b. Krugersdorp, Transvaal, Republic of South Africa, Feb. 11, 1937; came to U.S., 1984; s. Maurice and Nora (Knapp) R.; m. Dorothy Barclay, Mar. 30, 1963; children: Jennifer, Jacqueline, Richard, Rosemary, Catherine. BSc in Mining/Geology, U. Witwatersrand, Johannesburg, South Africa, 1960, MSc in Geology, 1963, PhD in Geology, 1967. Registered profl. engr., Ariz. Sr. v.p. Phelps Dodge Corp., Phoenix, 1984—. Capt. South African Army, 1956-72. Fellow AIME, South Africa Inst. Mining and Metallurgy, South Africa Geol. Soc. Home: 5481 E Lupine Scottsdale AZ 85254 Office: Phelps Dodge Corp 2600 N Central Ave Phoenix AZ 85004

RYAN, PATRICK MICHAEL, food products company executive, corporate lawyer; b. S.I., N.Y., Feb. 16, 1937; s. Thomas Francis and Helen Anne (Kelly) R.; m. Judith Maurine Steelman, July 16, 1977; 1 child, Courtney. BA, St. Francis Coll., 1957; JD, Villanova U., 1960. Bar: N.Y. 1961, Calif. 1965. Atty. U.S. Dept. Justice, Washington, 1960-64; antitrust counsel Hunt Foods and Industries, Fullerton, Calif., 1964-68; asst. gen. counsel Hunt-Wesson Foods, Inc., Fullerton, 1968-70, v.p., gen. counsel, 1970-83; v.p., gen. counsel Swift/Hunt-Wesson Foods, Inc., Fullerton, 1983-84, Beatrice/Hunt-Wesson, Inc., Fullerton, 1984—. Served to capt. USAR, 1960-66. Mem. ABA, Calif. Bar Assn., Am. Corp. Counsel Assn. Home: 22565 Skyline Dr Yorba Linda CA 92632 Office: Beatrice/Hunt-Wesson Foods 1645 W Valencia Dr Fullerton CA 92634

RYAN, PATRICK ORIE, software consultant; b. Nevada, Iowa, July 5, 1955; s. Archie Earl and Madonna Kay (Wright) R.; m. Debra Jane Tharp, May 24, 1986. BS in Computer Sci. and Math., Iowa State U., 1977, postgrad., 1983-86. Devel. engr. Hewlett-Packard Co., Palo Alto, Calif., 1977-83; pres. Starbyte Co., Washington, Iowa, 1986-88, Des Moines, 1988—; cons. Fisher Controls, Marshalltown, Iowa, 1987—. Contbr. articles to profl. jours. Mem. IEEE.

RYAN, RICHARD JAMES, retail company executive; b. Buffalo, June 24, 1937; s. James Joseph Ryan and Mary Lenore (Driscoll) Schryver; m. Suzanne Guarnieri, May 16, 1939; children: Colleen P., Dennis C., Richard T., Christopher, Kathleen M. BSME, U. Notre Dame, 1959; MBA, Harvard U., 1964. Sr. systems analyst Cleve. Pneumatic Tool Co., 1964-66; v.p. mfg. Cole Nat. Corp., Cleve., 1967-78; pres. ophthalmic labs. Bausch & Lomb Inc., 1978-79; pres. Jim Watler Doors div. Jim Walter Corp., 1979-83; exec. v.p. fin. and adminstrn., chief fin. officer Child World Inc., Avon, Mass., 1984—. Co-author: The Management of Racial Integration in Business, 1964. Pres. Carriage Park Homeowners Assn., Solon, Ohio, 1976, Carrollwood Village Jr. Tennis Assn., Tampa, Fla., 1983. Served to lt. USN, 1959-62. Roman Catholic. Office: Child World Inc 25 Littlefield St Avon MA 02322

RYAN, RICHARD KEENAN, scientific instruments manufacturing executive; b. Springfield, Ill., Sept. 23, 1937; s. Richard Francis and Anne Marie (Keenan) R.; children: Richard W., Scott K. Student, Loyola U., Chgo., 1955-57, Ill. Inst. Tech., 1957-59; MBA, Lake Forest Sch. Mgmt., 1984. Lab. technician Buehler Ltd., Evanston, Ill., 1957, inside sales specialist, 1957-58, sales mgr., 1972-73, gen. sales mgr., 1973-76, v.p. sales and mktg., 1976—, exec. v.p., 1984—, also bd. dirs.; bd. dirs. Buehler UK Ltd., Coventry, Eng., Buehler Internat., Lake Bluff. Patentee mold closure system, 1976. Mem. Am. Soc. Metallographic Internat. (publs. council), Internat. Metallographic Soc. (bd. dirs. 1981-85), Am. Ceramic Soc. Office: Buehler Ltd 41 Waukegan Rd Lake Bluff IL 60044

RYAN, ROBERT JOHN, JR., agricultural cooperative executive; b. Boston, July 31, 1944; s. Robert John and Marjorie MacFarland (Collins) R.; m. Linda Marie Villa, Dec. 28, 1968; children—Robert, Melissa. B.S. in Mech. Engring., U. Vt., 1966; M.B.A., Cornell U., 1971. Asst. treas. Agway, Inc., Syracuse, N.Y., 1971-79, treas., 1979-82, v.p., treas., 1982—; dir. Curtice Burns, Inc., Rochester, N.Y., Blue Cross, Syracuse; adv. bd. Marine Midland Bank, Syracuse, 1980—. Pres. Syracuse Boys Club, 1983—. Served to lt. USN, 1967-70, Vietnam. Mem. Fin. Mgmt. Assn. Democrat. Roman Catholic.

RYAN, ROBERT LESLIE, oil company executive; b. Detroit, Apr. 15, 1943; s. Henry and Venicee (Beavers) R.; m. Sharon Goode, July 3, 1971; children: Lesley M., Eric A. BSEE, Wayne State U., 1966; MSEE, Cornell U., 1968; MBA, Harvard U., 1970. Mgmt. cons. McKinsey and Co., N.Y.C., 1970-75; v.p. Citibank N.A., N.Y.C., 1975-82; v.p., treas. Union Tex. Petroleum Corp., Houston, 1982-83, v.p., controller, 1983-84, v.p. fin., 1984—; bd. dirs. Syndicated Communications Corp., Washington, Syncom Capital Corp., Washington. Dir. Tex. Opera Theatre, Houston, 1988—. Office: Union Tex Petroleum Corp 1330 Post Oak Blvd Houston TX 77252

RYAN, ROBERT SEIBERT, consulting company executive; b. Columbus, Ohio, July 25, 1922; s. Howard L. and Jannie Gertrude (McComis) R.; m. Esther Lee Moore, Mar. 15, 1947; children: Phillip Craig, Lynda Joyce, Lois Jean. BS in Indsl. Engring, Ohio State U., 1947. Registered profl. engr., Ohio, Ind. Maintenance foreman Internat. Harvester Co., Richmond, Ind., 1947-52; prin. welding engr. Battelle Meml. Inst., Columbus, 1952-55; dir. engring. Columbia Gas System, Columbus, 1955-67; sr. v.p. Columbia Gas System, Pitts., 1967-73; sr. v.p., dir. Columbia Gas Distbn. Cos. in, Ohio, Pa., Ky., W.Va., Md., Va., N.Y., 1973-75; dir. Columbia Gas, Inc. of, N.Y., Md., Ky., Ohio, W.Va., Va., Ohio Energy and Resource Devel. Agy., 1975-76, Ohio Dept. Energy, 1977-80; mem. Gov.'s Cabinet; pres. Robert S. Ryan & Assocs., 1981—. Contbr. articles profl. jours. Served to capt. U.S. Army, 1943-46, Japan. Recipient Disting. Alumnus award Ohio State U. Coll. Engring., 1970. Mem. NSPE, Am. Gas Assn., Pa. Gas Assn. (pres. 1974). Republican. Methodist. Clubs: Duquesne (Pitts.), Capital (Columbus), Press. Home: 6566 Plesenton Dr S Worthington OH 43085-2931 Office: Robert S Ryan & Assocs 90 E Wilson Bridge Rd Columbus OH 43085-2325

RYAN, SHEENA ROSS, financial planner; b. Perth, Scotland, Aug. 1, 1944; came to U.S., 1972; d. Douglas George Haig and Johanna Adams (Brown) Ross; m. Raymond John Ryan, Dec. 17, 1978 (div. Feb. 1985); 1 child, Ross McCarthy. Assoc., Inst. Bankers, Glasgow, Scotland, 1964; B. Profl. Studies, Pace U., 1985. Banker, Clydesdale Bank, Glasgow, 1962-65; acct. Newmont Pty. Ltd., Melbourne, Australia, 1965-72; acctg. mgr. Hertz Internat., N.Y.C., 1972-73; asst. controller Marsh & McLennan Internat., N.Y.C., 1974-76; v.p. human resource planning Marsh & McLennan, N.Y.C., 1976-80; dir. data processing, Town of Ridgefield, Conn., 1986-87, Rotondo Real Estate, Katonah, N.Y., 1981-87; dir. corp. svc. info. systems, asst. to v.p. fin. Children's TV Workshop, N.Y.C., 1988—; v.p., trustee Hammond Mus., 1987—, N. Salem, N.Y., 1988—. founder, dir. New Eng. Sch. of Needle Art, Wilton, Conn., 1985-86; dir. Rotondo Real Estate, Katonah, N.Y., 1983-87; treas. Playwrights Preview Prodns., N.Y.C., 1988—. Editor: Human Resource Planning newsletter, 1979. Mem. Embroiderers Guild Am., Mensa. Avocation: reading.

RYAN, THOMAS W., financial executive; b. Detroit, Jan. 28, 1947; m. Barbara L. Schembri, Sept. 6, 1968; children: Thomas III, Kristie, Kelly, Stephanie, Michael. BSBA, Wayne State U., 1969. Controller Leasing Internat. Industries, 1973; controller Kenosha mfg. complex Am. Motors Corp., Ill., 1974-78; controller mktg. Am. Motors Corp., 1978-80, dir. fin. planning, 1981-82; dir. internat. operations Am. Motors Corp., Southfield, Mich., 1982-85; v.p. A.O. Smith Corp., Milw., 1985—, treas., 1987—. Trustee Wis. Nat. Multiple Sclerosis Soc., Milw., 1986; bd. dirs. Greater Milw. Healthcare Network, 1987—; mem. Zoning Bd. of Appeals, Whitefish Bay, Wis., 1987; bd. dir., treas. A.O. Smith Found., 1987. Mem. Fin. Exec. Inst., Nat. Assn. Accts. Office: A O Smith Corp 11270 W Park Pl 1 Park Pla Milwaukee WI 53224

RYAN, TODD MICHAEL, mergers and acquitions consultant; b. Milw., Oct. 8, 1947; s. William George and Virginia Mary (Jurcek) R.; m. Margaret Ellen Schantz, Oct. 7, 1967; 1 child: Jennifer Ann. BA, U. Wis., Milw., 1970, BS, 1971, MSc, 1974. Fin. analyst The Falk Corp., Milw., 1969-74; mgr. sales, services and devel. Miller Brewing Co. div. Philip Morris, Milw., 1974-79; dir. planning Seven-Up div. Philip Morris, St. Louis, 1979-85; merger cons. Arthur Andersen, Chgo., 1985—. Mem. Assn. Corp. Growth, Council on Fgn. Relations, Chgo. United, Ducks Unltd., Inc. Club: University (Chgo.). Office: care Arthur Andersen & Co 10 S LaSalle St Chicago IL 60603

RYAN, WILLIAM FRANK, management consultant, insurance and risk consultant; b. Inkster, Mich., May 6, 1924; s. William Henry and Gertrude Mary (Kling) R.; m. Loke Waiau Akoni, Oct. 5, 1963; children—Ilima, Lokelani, Eugene. Student Georgetown U., 1948-49, Columbia U., 1951-52, U. Padua (Italy), 1950-51; B.A., U. Mich., 1948. Diplomatic assignments in Russia, Italy and Japan, 1949-53; investment broker N.Y.C., Detroit and Honolulu, 1953-63; mgmt. cons. Bus. Mgmt. Internat., Honolulu, 1963-68; officer, dir. numerous corps.; ins. and risk mgr. U. Mich., Ann Arbor, 1969-88; mem. Nat. Univ. Property Pool Ins. Study Group, 1969-70; chmn. ins. com. Mich. Council State Coll. Pres., 1971-73; mem. Nat. Task Force on Instl. Liability, 1974-76; exec. cons. William Ryan Risk Mgmt. Assocs., 1984—; v.p. Higher Edn. Liability Mut. Ins. Co., 1988; chmn. adv. com. Assoc. Degree program in health care risk mgmt. Oakland Community Coll., 1984-88; pres. Veritas Ins. Corp, 1986-88; pres. Risk Mgmt. Internat. Ltd., 1986—. Trustee Assn. Ind. Colls. and Univs. Mich. Workers Compensation Self-Ins. Fund; mem. Bishop Mus., Honolulu, Friends of Iolani Palace, Honolulu. Served to lt. (j.g.) USN, 1943-46. Recipient Instl. Risk Mgr. of Yr. award Bus. Ins. mag., 1981, Disting. Service award Assn. Ind. Colls. and Univs. of Mich., 1986. Mem. Am. Soc. Hosp. Risk Mgmt. (bd. dirs. 1981-84, pres. 1983), Univ. Risk Mgmt. and Ins. Assn. (dir.), Mich. Coll. and Univ. Risk Mgmt. Officers Assn. (chmn. 1973-75), Midwest Univ. Risk and Ins. Mgmt. Assn. (chmn. 1977-78), Hist. Soc. Mich., Nat. Trust for Hist. Preservation, Irish Georgian Soc., Am. Conf. for Irish Studies, Royal O'Connor Clan Assn. Democrat. Roman Catholic. Home: 801 Center Dr Ann Arbor MI 48103

RYAN, WILLIAM JOSEPH, communications company executive; b. Nyack, N.Y., Apr. 14, 1932; s. william Joseph and Elizabeth (Langley) R.; m. Jane Householder, June 27, 1970; children: Ashley Allison, William Joseph, III. BA, U. Notre Dame, 1954. TV producer Jules Power Prodn., Chgo., 1954-56; pres., gen. mgr. Radio Naples, Naples, Fla., 1956-70; gen. mgr. Radio Naples (Fla.) div. Palmer Broadcasting, 1970-73; v.p., cable-radio Palmer Broadcasting, Fla. and Calif., 1973-80; v.p. cable Palmer Communications, Naples, 1980-82; pres. Palmer Communications, Inc., Des Moines, 1982-84, pres., chief exec. officer, 1984—; bd. dirs. Norwest Bank, Des Moines. State committeeman Rep. Com., Collier County, Fla., 1970-72; pres. Navy League, Naples, local chpt. Am. Cancer Soc.; bd. govs. Drake U., Des Moines; chmn. Collier County Econ. Devel. Coun. Recipient Walter Kaitz award Nat. Cable TV Assn. Mem. Cable Advt. Bur. (founding chmn., bd. dirs.), So. Cable Assn. (pres.), Fla. Cable Assn. (pres.), Fla. Assn. Broadcasters (pres.), Cable TV Pioneers, Broadcast Pioneers, Cable TV Adminstrn. and Mktg. Soc. (Grand Tammy award 1981), Naples C. of C. (pres.), Wakonda Club, Royal Poinciana Club, Rotary, KC (Grand Knigh6). Office: Palmer Communications Inc 1801 Grand Ave Des Moines IA 50308

RYBACK, WILLIAM ALLAN, bank executive; b. Massilon, Ohio, Feb. 7, 1946; s. William Allan and Helen Marie (Bredhold) R.; m. Nancy Jane Bernard, Aug. 24, 1968; children: Steven, Dana. BS, Seton Hall U., 1968. Nat. bank examiner Comptroller Currency, N.Y.C., 1968-79; dir. internat. banking Comptroller Currency, Washington, 1979-82, dir. multinat. bank policy, 1982-86; dep. assoc. dir. Bd. Govs. Fed. Res. System, Washington, 1986—. Served with U.S. Army, 1969-71. Home: 9300 Wynyard Pl Burke VA 22015 Office: Bd Govs Fed Res System 20th and C Sts Washington DC 20551

RYDER, PAUL RODNEY, manufacturing executive; b. New Haven, Conn., Apr. 8, 1950; s. Harold W. and Elizabeth (Kinney) R.; m. Maureen Callahan, July 1, 1972; children: Victoria B., Matthew J. BS in Mgmt.Sci., Rensselaer Poly Inst., 1972, MS %, 1973. Analyst mgmt. info. Echlin Inc., Branford, Conn., 1973-78; dir. bus. info.analysis Echlin Inc., Branford, 1978-84, dir. investor relations, 1984—. V.p., pres. North Branford (Conn.) Scholarship Assn., 1973-78; bd. dirs. East Shore Regional Adult Daycare, 1985-89. Recipient Annual Report awards Fin. World, 1984, 87, 88; ARC award for Annual Report, 1988. Mem. Automotive Market Rsch. Coun. (treas., sec., v.p., pres. 1973—, Outstanding Service award 1984), Nat. Investor Relations Inst., Rotary (treas., pres. North Branford chpt. 1977—). Office: Echlin Inc 100 Double Beach Rd Branford CT 06405

RYDER, SANDRA SMITH, communications specialist, publicist; b. Great Lakes, Ill., July 6, 1949; d. Dennis Murrey and Olga (Grosheff) Smith. BS, Northwestern U., 1971; MA, Annenberg Sch. Communications at U. So. Calif., 1986. Columnist Camarillo Daily News (Calif.), 1971-76; editor Fillmore Herald (Calif.), 1976-78; pub. info. officer Oxnard Union High Sch. Dist. (Calif.), 1980-82; pub. info. officer Ventura County Community Coll. Dist., 1982-83; pub. relations dir. Murphy Orgn., Oxnard, Calif., 1983-84; pub. affairs rep. Gen. Telephone Calif., Thousand Oaks, 1984-88; adminstr. internat. communications, Gen. Telephone Ops., Irving, Tex., 1988—. Co-chmn. Ventura County Commn. for Women, 1981—. Mem. Women in Communications, Soc. Profl. Journalists, Pub. Info. and Communications Assn. (life). Office: GTE Telephone Ops Wlliams Sq W Tower 5205 N O'Connor Rd Irving TX 75039

RYE, KARL ERIK, telecommunications engineer; b. Decorah, Iowa, Nov. 7, 1952; s. Gordon Dean Rye and Miriam Ester (Hofstad) Hartwick; m. Barbara Callesen, Sept. 9, 1974; children: Christian Björn, Finn-Olaf, Nils-Erik. AA, Everett (Wash.) Community Coll., 1976; BS in Technology, Western Wash. U., 1978. Cert. secondary tchr., Wash. Prodn. mgr. Pacifica Crafts, Inc., Ferndale, Wash., 1978-79; outside plant engr. GTE Northwest, Everett, 1979-81; planning engr. GTE Calif., Pomona, 1981-83; sr. project engr. for Pacific Northwest area Tesinc Inc., Phoenix, 1983-84, Denali Communications, Inc., Palmer, Alaska, 1984; network planning engr. Matanuska Telephone Assn., Inc., Palmer, 1984—; pres. Ursa Major Internat., Ltd., Palmer, 1987—; bd. dirs. Regional Econ. Devel. Corp., Wasilla, Alaska, 1988—. Commr. Matanuska-Susitna Borough Planning Commn., Palmer, 1986—; project leader Mat-Su Bus. Devel. Ctr., 1988—; chmn. Palmer Planning and Zoning Commn., 1985—; vice chmn. Alaska Dems. Dist. 16, 1988. Served with USCG, 1972-75. Recipient Cheechako award Mat-Su Dems., 1987-88. Mem. Nat. Assn. Radio and Telecommunications Engrs. (cert. Class 1), Am. Planning Assn., Amnesty Internat. Democrat. Lutheran. Lodge: Moose. Home: 445 N Alaska St Palmer AK 99645 Office: Matanuska Telephone Assn Inc Pouch 5050 Palmer AK 99645

RYE, MORRIS LYNN, real estate corporation officer; b. New Albany, Miss., Oct. 30, 1948; s. Jesse H. and Ophie (Ruthledge) R.; m. Lynn Marie Valley, Dec. 22, 1973; children: Anthony Michael, Daniel Morris. BBA, U. Miss., 1972. Acct. Walker Mfg., Racine, Wis., 1973-75; auditor Walker Mfg., Racine, 1975-76, First Wis., Milw., 1977-79; auditor sr. Tenneco, Inc., Houston, 1979-81; audit dir. Tenneco Realty, Inc., Houston, 1981-84, cons. dir., 1984—. Served to sgt. U.S. Army, 1970-71, Vietnam. Republican. Baptist. Home: 9903 Green Creek Dr Houston TX 77070 Office: Tenneco Realty 1100 Milan #4400 Houston TX 77001

RYERSON, W. NEWTON, association executive; b. N.Y.C., Sept. 29, 1902; s. William Newton and Martha (Taft) R.; m. Jean Hamilton, May 15, 1936 (dec. Sept. 1973); children: Timothy (dec.), Amy Ryerson Borer, Marjorie, William N.; m. Henriette Keil, July 13, 1974. BS in Engring., Yale U., 1925. Cadet engr. to personnel supr. Phila. Gas Works Co., 1927-44; various positions with Sun Oil Co., Phila., 1944-67; dir. placement Vt. Tech. Coll., Randolph Center, Vt., 1967-82; exec. dir. Randolph C. of C., 1983—; bd. mem. Green Mountain Econ. Devel. Corp., Am. Heart Assn. White River Valley unit; vis. instr. Pa. State U., University Park, 1962-68. Vice pres. Swarthmore Sch. Bd. (Pa.), 1956-62; chmn. troop Boy Scouts Am., Swarthmore, 1952-55; mem. Republican Com., Swarthmore, 1951-55; jr. warden Trinity Ch. Vestry, Swarthmore, 1953-56. Recipient Disting. Service award Vt. Tech. Coll., 1982; named Randolph Bus. Exec. of Yr., 1988. Mem. Vt. Assn. Chamber Execs., Vt. Soc. Career Counselors, Vt. Soc. Assn. Execs., Tau Alpha Pi. Episcopalian. Club: Phila. Foremen's, Appalachian Mountain. Home: Randolph Center VT 05061 Office: Randolph C of C PO Box 9 Randolph VT 05060

RYKER, NORMAN J., JR., manufacturing company executive; b. Tacoma, Dec. 25, 1926; s. Norman Jenkins and Adelia Gustine (Macomber) R.; m. Kathleen Marie Crawford, June 20, 1947 (div. 1983); children: Jeanne Ryker Flores, Christina, Vickie Ryker Risley, Norman Jenkins, Kathy; m. Judith Kay Schneider, Dec. 18, 1983. B.S., U. Calif.-Berkeley, 1949, M.S., 1951; postgrad. Advanced Mgmt. Program, Harvard U., 1973. Asst. chief engr. space div. Rockwell Internat., Downey, Calif., 1962-68, v.p. research engring. and testing, 1968-70, v.p. research and engring. graphic systems group, 1970-74, v.p., gen. mgr. Webb div., 1974, v.p., gen mgr. transp. and equipment div., 1974-76; pres. Rocketdyne div. Rockwell Internat., Canoga Park, Calif., 1976-83; sr. v.p. aerospace and indsl. group Pneumo Corp., Boston, 1983-84, exec. v.p., chief operating officer, 1984-85; pres., chief exec. officer Pneumo Corp. subs. IC Industries, 1985-86, Pneumo Abex Corp., 1986-88; vice chmn., chief exec. officer Cross & Trecker Corp., 1989—; lectr. in field. Contbr. articles to profl. jours. Served with U.S. Army, 1944-46. Recipient cert. of appreciation NASA, 1969, merit award, 1979, Silver Knight award Nat. Mgmt. Assn., 1979, Tech. Mgmt. award Calif. Soc. Profl. Engrs., 1979. Fellow Inst. Advancement Engring., AIAA; mem. ASCE, Am. Astronautical Soc., Nat. Mgmt. Assn., Instn. Prodn. Engrs. (elected companion). Republican.

RYLAND, GLEN LEROY, airline executive; b. Stockton, Calif., Aug. 10, 1924; s. Hawkesbury Ridgway and Lola Myrle (Stevens) R.; m. Corinne Vere Zurick, June 29, 1947; children: Sally, Gail, Stephen. B.S., U. Calif.—Berkeley, 1949. Purchasing agt. Calif. & Hawaiian Sugar Corp., San Francisco, 1949-51; ins. mgr. Calif. & Hawaiian Sugar Corp., 1954-57; mgr. contract, program adminstr. Aerojet-Gen. Corp., Sacramento and Azusa, Calif., 1957-68; controller, chief fin. officer Aerojet Nuclear Systems Co., 1968-71; v.p. fin., chief fin. officer Frontier Airlines, Inc., Denver, 1971-73; exec. v.p., chief operating officer Frontier Airlines, Inc., 1973-80, pres., chief exec. officer, 1980-85, chmn. bd., 1981-85; pres., chief exec. officer RYCO, Inc., 1985—, Ryland Equipment Services Corp., 1988—; dir. Homestake Mining Co., US West, Cen. Bancorp., Cen. Bank of Denver. Vice chmn. Rancho Cordova Park and Recreation Dist., Calif., 1959-61; mem. Parents of Hearing Handicapped, 1964-71, Alexander Graham Bell Assn., 1962-79; trustee Colo. Outward Bound Sch., 1982—; chmn. LifeWorkshop, Covina, Calif., 1962-64; dir. LifeWorkshop Found., Los Angeles, 1962-64; bd. dirs. Sacramento Hearing Soc., 1964-71, Sacramento Hearing and Speech Center, 1964-71; mem. exec. bd. Denver Area council Boy Scouts Am., 1975—, pres., 1978-81, chmn. bd., 1981-84, bd. dirs. N. Central region, 1982—, v.p., 1983—, mem. nat. council 1978—; campaign chmn. Listen Found., 1978-79; mem. Colo. Gov.'s Blue Ribbon Panel, 1979-81, Pres.'s Council for Youth Exchange, 1983-85; adv. bd. Bus. Sch. U. Calif., Berkeley, 1983—. Served to lt. col. USAF, 1942-45; served to capt. USAAF, 1951-54. Recipient Boffey award Nat. Assn. Purchasing Agts., 1949, Airline Fin. Mgmt. award Air Transport World Mag., 1977, 81, Disting. Alumni award Calif. Assn. Community Colls., 1983; named The Outstanding Chief Exec. Officer Regional Airlines, Wall St. Transcript., 1981. Mem. Am. Mgmt. Assn., Air Transport Assn. (dir., exec. com. 1971-84), Econ. and Fin. Council (chmn. 1977-78), Assn. Local Transport Airlines (vice chmn. 1980-84, chmn. 1981), Soaring Soc. Am., Alumni Assn. U. Calif. at Berkeley, Aircraft Owners and Pilots Assn., Silver Wings Frat., Phi Kappa Sigma. Republican. Episcopalian. Clubs: Wings, Columbine Country. Home: PO Box 37068c St Denver CO 80237

RYLAND, MERLE EDWARD, JR., consultant; b. Key West, Fla., Oct. 11, 1944; s. Merle Edward and Maria R. (Rodrigues) R.; m. Michele Gordon Eddy, Mar. 21, 1978; children: Tahereh Marisa, Tatiana Jordan, Tabitha Ryland. BBA, Nat. U., 1982; postgrad. in bus. adminstrn., U. Colo. Pres. Surfer Pub. Group-Products, Capistrano Beach, Calif., 1977-79; gen. mgr. Baha'i Pub. Trust, Wilmette, Ill., 1979-80; prof. bus. dept. Palomar Coll., San Marcos, Calif., 1981-83; pres. Ryland Fin., San Marcos, 1981-83; v.p. fin. Sullins Electronics, San Marcos, 1981-83, also bd. dirs.; gen. counsel Anisa, Inc., 1981-83; bd. dirs. Crutchfield Concessions; adj. lectr. Coll. Aurora (Colo.) Bus. Dept., 1983—. Pub.: Anisa Process Curriculum, 1981. Served with USN, 1962-64. Mem. Nat. Assn. Accts. (past founding bd. dirs.), Nat. Mgmt. Assn., Am. Arbitration Assn. (panel of arbitrators). Baha'i. Office: 1300 30th D7/12 Boulder CO 80303

RYLE, WILLIAM EDWARD, JR., data processing executive; b. Covington, Ky., Jan. 10, 1956; s. William Edward and Martha (Jones) R.; m. Shelia Lynn Felty, Feb. 5, 1977; 1 child, Ashley Danielle. BSBA, Ky. Wesleyan Coll., 1978. Cert. data processor. With Tex. Gas Transmission Corp., Owensboro, Ky., 1978—, supr. bus. systems, 1984—, mgr. data base adminstrn., 1988—. Coach Owensboro Babe Ruth Baseball, 1986, 87. Recipient 1987 award of Excellence CSX Corp., 1988. Mem. Data Processing Mgmt. Assn. (chmn. program 1988, bd. dirs.). Democrat. Baptist. Home: 3801 Springtree Dr Owensboro KY 42301 Office: Tex Gas Transmission Corp 3800 Frederica St Owensboro KY 42301

RYLEE, R(OBERT) TILMAN, III, real estate consultant; b. Corpus Christi, Tex., Dec. 23, 1958; s. Robert T. II and Sarah Jane (English) R. BA, U. Tex., 1980; postgrad., Columbia U., 1981; JD, NYU, 1983. Cons. Channing Weinberg & Co., N.Y.C., 1983-85; ptnr. Alster Internat., N.Y.C., 1985-88; cons. Weatherall Green & Smith, N.Y.C., 1988—; bd. dirs. USA Real Estate Acquisition Corp. Author: (screenplay) Deep Dark River, 1988. Asst. sgt.-at-arms State of Tex. Senate, Austin, 1979. National Merit Scholar, 1976.

RYMAR, JULIAN W., manufacturing company executive; b. Grand Rapids, Mich., June 29, 1919; student Grand Rapids Jr. Coll., 1937-39, U. Mich., 1939-41, Am. Sch. Dramatic Arts, 1946-47, Wayne U., 1948-52, Rockhurst Coll., 1952-53; Naval War Coll., 1954-58; m. Margaret Macon Van Brunt, Dec. 11, 1954; children—Margaret Gibson, Gracen Macon, Ann Mackall. Entered USN as aviation cadet, 1942, advanced through grades to capt., 1964; chmn. bd., chief exec. officer, dir. Grace Co., Belton, Mo., 1955—; chmn. bd. dirs. Shock & Vibration Research, Inc., 1956-66; chmn. bd., chief exec. officer Bedtime Story Fashions; dir. Am. Bank & Trust; comdg. officer Naval Air Res. Squadron, 1957-60, staff air bn. comdr., 1960-64. Mem. Kansas City Hist. Soc.; bd. dirs. Bros. of Mercy, St. Lukes Hosp.; adv. bd. dirs. St. Joseph Hosp.; trustee Missouri Valley Coll., 1969-74; pres. Rymar Found. Mem. Mil. Order World Wars, Navy League U.S. (pres. 1959-60, dir. 1960-70), Rockhill Homes Assn. (v.p.) Friends of Art (pres., chmn. bd. govs. 1969-70, exec. bd. 1971-74), Soc. of Fellows of Nelson Gallery Found. (exec. bd. 1972-77), Soc. Profl. Journalists, Press Club, Univ. of Mich. Club, Arts Club, Quiet Birdman Club, Sigma Delta Chi. Episcopalian (dir., lay reader, lay chalice, vestryman, sr. warden, diocesan fin. bd., parish investment bd.). Home: 815 Camino Del Poniente Santa Fe NM 87501 Office: Grace Co 614 W Mill St Belton MO 64012

RYND, DAVID PAUL, environmental services company executive; b. Pitts., Oct. 12, 1952; s. Christopher and Ruth (Lockhart) R.; m. Lisa Ann Clements, Dec. 23, 1978; children: Allison, Drew. BS, U.S. Mil. Acad., 1974; MBA, Pepperdine U., 1978. Dist. rep. Nalco Chem. Co., Birmingham, Ala., 1979-84; exec. asst. to chief ops. officer Riedel Environ. Svcs., Portland, Oreg., 1984-85; v.p., regional mgr. Riedel Environ. Svcs., St. Louis, 1985-87; v.p. ops. Peterson-Riedel Svcs. div. Riedel Environ. Svcs., New Orleans, 1987-88; v.p., exec. asst. to chmn. parent co. Riedel Environ. Techs. Inc., Portland, 1988—. Capt. U.S. Army, 1974-79. Mem. Nat. Assn. Corrosion Engrs., New Orleans C. of C. Republican. Roman Catholic. Home: 3781 Tempest Dr Lake Oswego OR 97035 Office: Riedel Environ Techs Inc 4611 N Channel Ave Portland OR 97208

RYPCZYK, CANDICE LEIGH, employee relations manager; b. Norman, Okla., Apr. 24, 1949; d. John Anthony and Lee (Brunswick) Wirth; m. Peter Charles Rypczyk, Nov. 27, 1976. BA, Kalamazoo Coll., 1971; cert. labor studies extension program, Cornell U., N.Y. Sch. Indsl., Labor Relations, Middletown, 1985. Personnel asst. PFW div. Hercules Inc., Middletown, N.Y., 1973-77, asst. personnel mgr., 1977-79, mgr. employee relations, 1979—. Mem. Am. Soc. for Personnel Adminstrn. (v.p. Mid-Hudson Valley chpt. 1985, pres. 1986, treas. N.Y. State council 1986, dist. dir. 1988—, cert.), Orange County (N.Y.) Pvt. Industry Council, Orange County C. of C. (Vol. of Yr. 1986, program com., treas., mem. exec. com.). Office: PFW Div Hercules Inc 33 Sprague Ave Middletown NY 10940

RYSKA, EDWARD MICHAEL, insurance executive; b. Chgo., July 23, 1950; s. Edward Anothany and Mary K. (Mangan) R.; m. Edwina M. Mazur, Aug. 11, 1973; 1 child, Stephanie Noel. BS in Mgmt., Northern Ill. U., 1972, MS in Safety, 1975. Loss control cons. Fireman's Fund Ins. Co., Chgo., 1972-75; comml. group sr. cons. Fireman's Fund Ins. Co., San Francisco, 1975-78; mgr. comml. group loss control Fireman's Fund Ins. Co., San Rafael, Calif., 1978-80; mgr. loss control Pacific Compensation Ins. Co., 1980-81, asst. v.p. loss control, 1981-82, v.p. loss control, 1982-85; v.p., div. mgr. Pacific Compensation Ins. Co., San Bruno, Calif., 1983-85; v.p. loss control Pacific Compensation Ins. Co., 1985; v.p. Beaver Ins. Co., San Francisco, 1985—. Mem. Am. Soc. Safety Engrs., Nat. Safety Mgmt. Soc., Nat. Safety Council (consumer product adv. com., pub. safety exec. com., chmn. risk mgmt. com., vice chmn. pub. safety div.). Office: Beaver Ins Co 100 California St San Francisco CA 94111

RYSKAMP, CARROLL JOSEPH, chemical engineer; b. Grand Rapids, Mich., Dec. 25, 1930; s. Henry C. and Edna E. (Robinson) R.; m. Joanne Ruth Winter, Nov. 17, 1951; children: Jan C., John M., Julie K., Jay A. BS in Chem. Engring., Wayne State U., 1953. Registered profl. control systems engr. Chem. engr. Reichhold Chem. Co., Ferndale, Mich., 1953-55; process supv. and specialist Marathon Oil Co., Detroit, 1955-65; process control coordinator Marathon Oil Co., Findlay, Ohio, 1965-70; control cons. Foxboro (Mass.) Co., 1970-85; owner Process Performance Co., Foxboro, 1986. Contbr. articles to profl. jours.; patentee in field. Bristol fellow, The Foxboro Co., 1985. Sr. mem. Instrument Soc. Am. (Philip T. Sprague award, 1981). Republican. Home and Office: 48 Prospect St Foxboro MA 02035

RZEMINSKI, PETER JOSEPH, hospital administrator; b. Chgo., Apr. 19, 1947; s. Casmir Stanley and Bertha Emma (Rudisill) R.; m. Dorothy Morowczynski, Jan. 10, 1970; children: Peter Joseph II, Stacey Bobbe. BS in Mgmt., U. Ill., Chgo., 1973; MBA, DePaul U., 1976; grad., U.S. Army Command and Gen. Staff Coll., 1981; MS in Indsl. Relations, Loyola U., Chgo., 1985. Asst. dir. personnel St. Francis Hosp., Blue Island, Ill., 1974-79; assoc. dir. personnel St. Francis Hosp., Blue Island, 1979-80, dir. personnel, 1980-82, v.p. human resources, 1982-88; corp. dir. compensation and benefits Chgo. Osteopathic Health Systems Inc., 1988-89; v.p. human resources Little Company of Mary Hosp., Evergreen Park, Ill., 1989—; mem. ex officio St. Francis adv. bd., 1982. Mem. subcom. Tinley Park (Ill.) Econ. Devel. Commn., 1984—; chmn. med. office program Sauk Area Adv. Com., Crestwood, Ill., 1974-77, 80-86; bd. dirs. United Way of Blue Island/Calumet Park, Ill., 1985-89. Capt. U.S. Army, 1967-72, Vietnam; col. with res., 1972—. Decorated Bronze Star, D.F.C., Purple Heart, Meritorious Service medal with one oak leaf cluster, Air medal with twenty-two oak leaf clusters, Nat. Defense Service medal, Vietnam Campaign medal with five campaign stars, Vietnam Cross of Gallantry with palm, Army Res. Achievement medal with one oak leaf leaf cluster, Vietnam Civil Actions medal 1st class. Mem. Am. Coll. Healthcare Execs., Am. Soc. for Personnel Adminstrn., Am. Soc. for Hosp. Personnel Adminstrn., Chgo. Healthcare Human Resources Assn.(chmn. survey com. 1980-85, sec. 1975-76, 86-87, sr. mem. at large 1985-87, treas. 1987-88); Southwest Area Hosp. Personnel Dirs. Assn. (sec. 1975-76, treas. 1979-80), Compensation Assn. of Chgo. Area Hosps., Young Adminstrs. of Chgo. (mem. program com. 1979), Chgo. Health Exec. Forum, Hosp. Mgmt. Systems Soc., Sisters of St. Mary's Personnel Dirs. Assn., Res. Officer's Assn. (sec., treas. 1977-79), Interallied Confederation of Res. Officers, Ill. Soc. Human Resource Adminstrn., U. Ill. Alumni Assn., 101st Airborn Assn., Tippers Internat. Republican. Roman Catholic. Home: 13417 Medina Dr Orland Park IL 60462 Office: Little Co of Mary Hosp 2800 W 95th St Evergreen Park IL 60642

RZOMP, KIMBERLY MCCARTHY, controller; b. Gettysburg, Pa., July 11, 1956; d. Thomas Humphrey and Patricia Anne (Shealer) McC.; m. Thomas Gerard Drake, Aug. 19, 1978 (div. Mar. 1980); m. Casimir Leonard Rzomp Jr., Dec. 27, 1986. BA in Econs. and Bus. Adminstrn., Lycoming Coll., 1978; MBA, Shippensburg U., 1987. Mgr. office Aratex Services div. ARA Services, Scranton, Pa., Cherry Hill, N.J., 1978-80; dist. controller trainee Ryder Truck Rental, Inc., Cherry Hill, 1981-83; mgr. bus. office The Chambersburg (Pa.) Hosp., 1983, staff acct., 1983-84, asst. controller, 1984-87, controller, 1987—; mem. continuing edn. adv. com. Wilson Coll., Chambersburg, 1987. Mem. Health Care Fin. Mgmt. Assn., Chambersburg C. of C. (mem. small bus. com. 1987). Republican. Mem. Ch. of Christ. Club: Soroptimist Internat. (Chambersburg) (treas. 1987—). Office: The Chambersburg Hosp 112 N 7th St Chambersburg PA 17201

SAAD, THEODORE SHAFICK, microwave company executive; b. Boston, Sept. 13, 1920; s. Wadie Assad and Mary (Shalhoub) S.; m. Afeefi Abdelnour, May 5, 1943; children: Karen Jeanne, Janet Elaine. BSEE, MIT, 1941. Engr. Sylvania Electric Products, Danvers, Mass., 1941-42; engring. specialist Sylvania Electric Products, Woburn, Mass., 1953-55; rsch. assoc. radiation Lab. MIT, Cambridge, 1942-45; sr. engr. Submarine Signal Co., Boston, 1945-49; v.p., chief engr. Microwave Devel. Labs., Waltham, Mass., 1949-53; pres., chmn. Sage Labs. Inc., Natick, Mass., 1955—; cons. Horizon House Microwave, Norwood, Mass., 1958—. Editor: Microwave Engineers Handbook, 1971, Historical Perspectives of Microwave Technology, 1984; patentee in microwavetech. and passive components fields. Fellow IEEE; mem. Microwave Soc. of IEEE (hon. life, nat. lectr. 1972, Disting. Service award 1983, Centennial medal 1984). Home: 52 Doublet Hill Rd Weston MA 02193 Office: Sage Labs Inc 11 Huron Dr Natick MA 01763

SAADIAN, JAVID, accountant, consultant; b. Tehran, Iran, Dec. 25, 1953; came to U.S., 1971; s. Avshalom and Akhtar (Barookhian) S.; m. Janet Elissa Salins, Dec. 30, 1978; children: Jason, Sarah, Susan. Student, Montgomery Coll., spring 1972; BS in Acctg., U. Md., 1976. CPA, Md., Va. Acct. Lewis Kest and Co., Washington, 1977-78; auditor, sr. acct. Aronson, Greene, Fisher & Co., Bethesda, Md., 1978-80; auditor Price Waterhouse, Washington, 1980-81; controller Mt. Vernon Inn Inc. subs. Mt. Vernon Ladies Assn. of the Union, 1981-83; dir. fin. Mt. Vernon Ladies Assn. of the Union and subs., 1983—; cons. various orgns. Washington Met. area, 1979—. Fin. advisor Ft. Hunt Coop. Presch., Alexandria, 1986-89; treas. Collingwood on the Potomac Homeowners Assn., Alexandria, 1987-89; mem. budget and fin. com. Mt. Vernon Council of Citizens Assns., 1988, treas., 1988—. Recipient cert. of Merit SBA, Washington, 1976. Mem. Am. Inst. CPA's, Va. Soc. CPA's, Am. Soc. Assn. Execs., Am. Assn. Mus., Am. Mgmt. Assn., Fairfax C. of C., Mt. Vernon-Lee C. of C., Beta Alpha Psi (chmn. tutoring com. 1976). Jewish. Home: 910 Neal Dr Alexandria VA 22308 Office: Mt Vernon Ladies Assn of the Union George Washington Meml Pkwy Mount Vernon VA 22121

SAALFIELD, JAMES ALBERT, venture capitalist; b. Akron, Ohio; s. Henry Robinson and Mary (Albercht) S.; m. Roseanne Brady, Mar. 20, 1982; children: Sarah, Peter, Jonathan. BA, Oberlin Coll., 1969; MBA, Harvard U., 1971. Assoc. dir. Harvard U., Boston and Cambridge (Mass.), 1973-76, asst. dean sch. bus., 1976-80; trainee Citibank, N.Y.C., 1976-77; pvt. practice venture capitalist Boston, 1980-85; gen. ptnr. Fleet Venture Ptnrs., Boxborough, Mass., 1985—; bd. dirs. Advanced Materials Technology, Oriskany, N.Y., KVH Industries, Middletown, R.I., Kronos, Waltham, Mass., Logicraft, Nashua, N.H., Tracer Tech., Somerville, Mass., Amherst Process Inst., Stellar Scientific, Cardinal Instruments, Suffield, Systems Engring. & Mfg. Co., Stoughton, Mass., Wainroy, Hubbardston, Mass. Trustee Harvard Conservation Trust, 1986—. Club: Harvard Bus. Sch. Home: PO Box 638 120 Bolton Rd Harvard MA 01451 Office: Fleet Venture Ptnrs 1740 Massachusetts Ave Boxborough MA 01719

SAAREL, DOUGLAS A., soft drink, foods and entertainment company executive; b. 1939; m. Brenda Elizabeth Arlett; children—Douglas A., Edward Ernest. B.A., Rutgers U., 1961; grad., Loyola U. Law Sch., 1974. Dir. personnel Johnson & Johnson, 1965-74; dir. human resources Cleve. Clinic Found., 1974-77; v.p. employee relations Pepsi Co. Inc, 1977-78; v.p. adminstrn. E.R. Squibb & Sons Inc., 1978-81; v.p. human resources The Coca-Cola Company, 1981-82, sr. v.p. human resources, 1982—. Office: The Coca-Cola Co One Coca-Cola Pla NW Atlanta GA 30313

SAASK, AAPO, research company executive; b. Tartu Estonia, Mar. 22, 1943; came to Sweden, 1944; s. Alexander and Asta (Kallas) S.; m. Helny Cecilia Sundin, July 15, 1966; children: Fredrik, Markus. BA, Brown U., 1964; postgrad. Rutgers U., 1964-65; M in Polit. Sci. and Philosophy, U. Stockholm, 1968; MSc.in Edn., U. Linkoping (Sweden), 1970; MBA, U. Stockholm, 1973. Ptnr., Scarab Devel. Group, Stockholm, 1973-77; mng. dir. AB Scarab Devel., Stockholm, 1977-83, 83—; chmn. Scarab Energy AB, Taby, Sweden, 1983—; pres. Internat. Coconut Devel. Assn., Stockholm, 1979-86. Author: Integrated Processing of Coconuts, 1981; pub. Coconut Industries Quarterly, 1978-82; contbr. articles on coconuts, desalination to profl. jours. Mem. Internat. Desalination Assn. (Topsfield, Mass.), Coconut Industries Consultancy Service (London), Mem. European Desalination Assn. (Glasgow). Office: Scarab, Gardesvagen 11, 18330 Taby Sweden

SAATCHI, CHARLES, communications and marketing company executive; b. June 9, 1943; m. Doris Lockart, 1973. Student, Christ's Coll., Finchley. Assoc. dir. Collett Dickenson Pearce, 1966-68; dir. Cramer Saatchi, 1968-70; owner, dir. Saatchi & Saatchi, 1970—. Office: 80 Charlotte St, London England W1A 1AQ also: Saatchi & Saatchi Co, 15 Lower Regent St, London SW1Y 4LR, England •

SAATCHI, MAURICE, communications and marketing company executive; b. June 21, 1946; s. Nathan and Daisy Saatchi; m. Josephine Hart, 1984; 1 son, 1 stepson. BS in Econs., London Sch. Econs. and Polit. Sci., 1967. Co-founder Saatchi & Saatchi Co, 1970, chmn., 1984—. Office: 80 Charlotte St, London W1A 1AQ, England also: Saatchi & Saatchi Co, 15 Lower Regent St, London SW1Y 4LR, England

SAAVEDRA, CHARLES JAMES, banker; b. Denver, Nov. 2, 1941; s. Charles James and Evangeline Cecilia (Aragon) S.; m. Ann Helen Taylor, 1967; children: Michael, Kevin, Sarah. BSBA, Regis Coll., Denver, 1963; postgrad. U. Calif., San Francisco, 1964-66. Vice-pres., Western States Bankcard Assn., San Francisco, 1969-77; dir. info. systems World Airways, Inc., Oakland, Calif., 1977-79; v.p. computer services First Nationwide Bank, San Francisco, 1979-83; sr. v.p. Wells Fargo Bank, San Francisco, 1983—; instr. Programming & Systems Inst., San Francisco, 1968-69; lectr. Am. Mgmt. Assn., 1984—. With USNR, 1963-64. Mem. Data Processing Mgrs. Assn. (bd. dirs., chmn. program com. 1981), Am. Nat. Standards Inst., Am. Bankers Assn., San Francisco Jaycees. Clubs: Commonwealth of Calif.; Lake Lakewood Assn. Home: 210 Lakewood Rd Walnut Creek CA 94598 Office: Wells Fargo Bank 464 California St San Francisco CA 94163

SABALA, JAMES ANTHONY, mining company executive; b. Aug. 5, 1954; s. Tony Joe and Dorthy Molly (Kirkpatrick) S.; m. Janice Rae Oman, Aug. 14, 1976; children: Dominick James, Toni Marie. BS in Bus., U. Idaho, 1978. Acct. Price Waterhouse and Co., Seattle, 1978-81; asst. treas. Coeur d'Alene Mines Corp., Coeur d'Alene, Idaho, 1981, controller, 1981-82, treas., 1982-86, sec., treas., 1986-87, v.p. fin., 1987—. Bd. dirs. Excell Edn. Found., Coeur d'Alene, 1986—, North Idaho Coll. Pvt. Founs.; treas. Statler for Sheriff, 1987—. Recipient Elijah Watt Sells award AICPA, 1978. Mem. Hayden Lake Country Club. Republican. Roman Catholic. Office: Coeur d'Alene Mines Corp 505 Front Ste 400 Coeur d'Alene ID 83814

SABBAGH, ANN MARIA, cost control professional; b. Waterbury, Conn., Sept. 3, 1959; d. Joseph John and Rose Frances (Ranando) Ciaccio; m. Kenneth John Sabbagh, Sept. 20, 1986. BS in Fin., Bryant Coll., 1980; MBA, Suffolk U., 1984. Fin. assoc. GTE Hdqrs., Stamford, Conn., 1981-82; fin. analyst GTE Govt. Systems Corp, Needham, Ma., 1982-83, sr. fin. analyst, 1983-85, supr. cost performance, 1985-86, mgr. cost control, 1986—. Mem. St. John The Evangelist Choir, Attleboro, Ma, 1986—, St Basils Ch., Central Falls, R.I. 1988—. Delta Omega. Roman Catholic. Office: GTE Govt Systems Corp 400 John Quincy Adams Rd Taunton MA 02780

SABBETH, STEPHEN J., diversified company executive, entrepeneur; b. Bronx, N.Y., July 31, 1947; s. Herbert H. and Belle (Bartfield) S.; m. Carole Fiore; children: Brian Jay, Lisa Joy, Michael Jonathan. Student, Hofstra U., 1965. Chmn. bd. Sabbeth Industries, Deer Park, N.Y., 1972—, Triple S Lumber Co., Waverly, N.Y., 1980—, Atlantic Lumber Co., Norwood, Mass., 1981—; chmn. bd. dirs. Sabbeth Internat. Ltd., Deer Park, N.Y., Sabbeth Worldwide Wood Corp., Crystal Springs, Pa., Sabbeth-York, Haverhill, Mass., Sabbeth Millwork, Ltd., Deer Park, N.Y., Internat. Lumber Processing, Crystal Springs. Pres. Long Beach (N.Y.) City Council, 1976-78; chmn. Long Beach Urban Renewal Commn., 1976-78; mem. N.Y. State Econ. Devel. Commn.; bd. dirs. L.I. Philharm., 1984—; apptd. by N.Y. Gov. Mario Cuomo to L.I. Econ. Devel. Bd., mem. Council for the Maritime Coll., mem. Forest Industry Task Force. Recipient Award of Honor, United Jewish Appeal, 1982. Mem. N.Am. Wholesale Lumber Assn., Northeast Lumber Mfrs. Assn., Nat. Hardwood Lumber Assn., L.I. Lumbermen's Assn., N.Y. and Suburban Lumbermen's Assn. (v.p. 1968-86), Freight Users Assn. (chmn. bd.). Home: 7 Pound Hollow Rd Old Brookville NY 11545 Office: Sabbeth Industries 55 N Industry Ct Deer Park NY 11729

SABIN, JACK CHARLES, engineering and construction firm executive; b. Phoenix, June 29, 1921; s. Jack Byron and Rena (Lewis) S.; B.S., U. Ariz., 1943; B.Chem.Engring., U. Minn., 1947; m. Frances Jane McIntyre, Mar. 27, 1950; children—Karen Lee, Robert William, Dorothy Ann, Tracy Ellen. With Standard Oil Co. of Calif., 1947-66, sr. engr., 1966—; pres., dir. Indsl. Control & Engring., Inc., Redondo Beach, Calif., 1966—; owner/mgr. Jack C. Sabin, Engr.-Contractor, Redondo Beach, 1968—; staff engr. Pacific Molasses Co., San Francisco, 1975-77; project mgr. E & L Assos., Long Beach, Calif., 1977-79; dir. Alaska Pacific Petroleum, Inc., 1968—, Marlex Petroleum, Inc., 1970, 71—. Served with U.S. Army, 1942-46; capt. Chem. Corps, Res., 1949-56. Registered profl. engr., Calif., Alaska; lic. gen. engring. contractor, Ariz., Calif. Mem. Nat. Soc. Profl. Engrs., Ind. Liquid Terminals Assn., Conservative Caucus, Calif. Tax Reduction Com., Tau Beta Pi, Phi Lambda Upsilon, Phi Sigma Kappa. Republican. Clubs: Elks; Town Hall of Calif. Address: 151 Camino de las Colinas Redondo Beach CA 90277

SABUCO, LYNNE ADELE, publishing company executive, consultant; b. Chgo., Apr. 29, 1950; d. Vincent Arthur and Irene Carolyn Pecelunas; m. John Joseph Sabuco; 1 child, Bryan James. AA, Chgo. City Jr. Coll., 1970; BA, DePaul U., 1972. Sec. Playboy Enterprises, Chgo., 1972-73; exec. sec. Smith Barney, Harris Upham, Chgo., 1973-76; office mgr. Tom McCall Exec. Search, Matteson, Ill., 1976-81; office mgr. Allstate Appraisal, Inc., Chicago Heights, Ill., 1981-87, corp. v.p., 1987-88; cons., computer programmer Good Earth Pub., Ltd., Glenwood, Ill., 1983-88, v.p., 1988—. Editor: The Best of the Hardiest, 1987. Pres. South Suburban Food Coop., Park Forest, Ill., 1979. Mem. Burroughs Distributed Intelligence Group (sec. 1986—), Folks on Spokes. Office: Good Earth Pub Ltd PO Box 104 Flossmoor IL 60422

SACCHETTA, PASQUALE JOSEPH, financial services executive; b. Bristol, Conn., July 11, 1964; s. Gaetano and Angela (DiMatteo) S. BBA, Cen. Conn. State U., New Britain, 1984. Svc. mgr. First Nat. Supermarkets, Bristol, Conn., 1980-84; account exec. First Investors Corp., Glastonbury, Conn., 1984-86; chmn., pres. Cambridge-Newport Co., Wethersfield, 1986—. Chmn. St. Anthony's Ch. Altar Soc., Bristol, 1978. Mem. Internat. Assn. Fin. Planning, Nat. Assn. Securities Dealers, Inc., Pres's. Assn., First Investors Stratosphere Club, Hundred Club of Conn., Wethersfield C. of C. (nominating com.). Democrat. Roman Catholic. Home: 308 Divinity St PO Box 1835 Bristol CT 06010-1835 Office: Cambridge-Newport Co 530 Silas Deane Hwy Wethersfield CT 06109-2297

SACCHITELLA, LAURIE ANN, brokerage claims supervisor; b. Oak Park, Ill., Jan. 14, 1955; d. Douglas Farrington Smith and Barbara Ann (McLaughlin) Smith Wilson; m. Michael Anthony Sacchitella, Nov. 1, 1986. BS in Criminal Justice, Ill. State U., Normal, 1977; assoc. realtor, Century 21 Acad., 1979; student real estate law, Fla. Atlantic U., 1983. Realtor assoc. All-Rite Real Estate, Inc., Hollywood, Fla., 1979-80; personal injury claims rep. Indsl. Fire & Casualty Ins., Hollywood, 1980-81; claims adjuster, investigator Riley Adjustment Bur., Ft. Lauderdale, Fla., 1981-82; claims rep. Dixie Ins. Co., Lauderhill, Fla., 1982-84; brokerage claims supr. Am. Internat. Adjustment Co., Ft. Lauderdale, 1984—. Republican. Episcopalian. Home: 861 NW 85 Terr #1813 Plantation FL 33324 Office: Am Internat Adjustment Co 10400 Griffin Rd Ste 206 Fort Lauderdale FL 33328

SACCO, ROBERT ROSARIO, health science association administrator; b. Bklyn., Aug. 14, 1951; s. Gasper and Josephine (Allocca) S.; m. Roberta Mustico, Aug. 4, 1985; children: Eileen, Robert, Maureen. BS, N.Y. Inst. Tech., 1979; MBA, Marymount Coll., 1985. Asst. corp. controller M.S. Ginn Co., Hyattsville, Md., 1980-85; dir. fin. N.Y. Nurses Assn., Guilderland, N.Y., 1985—. 2nd v.p. Tri-County Council Vietnam Era Vets., Albany, N.Y., 1985—. With USMC, 1969-75, Vietnam; capt. inf., 1975—. Mem. Am. Soc. Assn. Execs., Internat. Found. Employee Benefits Plans. Office: NY Nurses Assn 2113 Western Ave Guilderland NY 12084

SACERDOTE, PETER M., investment banker; b. Turin, Italy, Oct. 15, 1937; came to U.S., 1940; s. Giorgio S. and Luciana (Levi) S.; m. Bonnie Lee Johnson, June 18, 1967; children: Alisa, Alexander, Laurence. B.E.E., Cornell U., 1960; M.B.A., Harvard U., 1964. Assoc. investment banking div. Goldman, Sachs & Co., N.Y.C., 1964-69, v.p. investment banking div., 1969-73, gen. ptnr., 1973—; dir. Weis Markets, Inc., Sunbury, Pa., Maxwell Labs., Inc., San Diego. Trustee Day Sch., N.Y.C., 1980—. Served to lt. (j.g.) USNR, 1960-62. Clubs: Union League (N.Y.C.), Harvard (N.Y.C.), Downtown Assn. (N.Y.C.); Yacht (Nantucket, Mass.); Stanwich Golf (Greenwich, Conn.). Office: Goldman Sachs & Co 85 Broad St New York NY 10004 *

SACHS, ROBERT JAY, cable television company executive; b. New Rochelle, N.Y., Dec. 16, 1948; s. Monroe and Norma (Gantz) S.; m. Caroline A. Taggart, Feb. 20, 1982. BA, U. Rochester, 1970; MS in Journalism, Columbia U., 1974; JD, Georgetown U., 1978. Bar: D.C. 1978. Adminstrv. asst. Sen. Chas E. Goodell, N.Y., 1971-73; legis. asst. U.S. Rep. Tim Wirth, Colo., 1975-77; cons. White House Office of Telecommunications Policy, Washington, 1977-78; legis. counsel Na.t Telecommunications and Info. Adminstrn., Washington, 1978-79; dir. corp. devel. Continental Cablevision Inc., Boston, 1979-83, v.p. corp. devel., 1983-88, sr. v.p. corp. and legal affairs, 1988—. Bd. dirs. Community Antenna TV Assn., Washington, 1987—. Democrat. Office: Continental Cablevision Inc Pilot House Lewis Wharf Boston MA 02110

SACKETT, HUGH F., financial services executive; b. Tulsa, Sept. 6, 1930; s. Hubert F. and Frances (Cozier) S.; B.S. in Bus. Adminstrn., Ind. U., 1955; m. Claudette Despres, Aug. 31, 1968; children—Michael Stanton, Deborah Faye, Stephanie Frances. Vice pres., gen. mgr. vender products group Cornelius Co., Anoka, Minn., 1969-72; group v.p. automotive Stellar Industries, Inc., Los Angeles, also pres. lawn care group, 1972-74; exec. v.p. Jefferson Mint, San Diego, 1974-79; pres. Graver Energy Systems, Inc., East Chicago, Ind., 1976-80, HFS, Inc., Guilford, Conn., 1976—, New H.S. Industries, Inc., 1980-82, Calif. Design Group, 1980-83, Am. Prins. Holdings, Inc. and Pvt. Ledger Fin. Svcs. Group, 1982-84, also dir.; chmn. Pacific Capital Ltd., 1984—. Mem. chancellors council Purdue U., Calumet, Ind., 1977. Served with USNR, 1951-52. Mem. Soc. Mayflower Desc., Alden Kindred Am., SAR, Ind. U. Alumni Assn. (life), Nat. Assn. Life Underwriters, Guilford Keeping Soc., Goodspeed Opera Assn., Rotary, Delta Tau Delta. Republican. Presbyterian, Congregational. Home: 13 Orcutt Dr Guilford CT 06437-2221 Office: PO Box 365 Guilford CT 06437-0365 Office: 2323 N Broadway #200 Santa Ana CA 92706

SACKETT, ROBERT ENNIS, small business owner; b. Scotch Grove, Iowa, Oct. 11, 1912; s. Clarence Alden and Mary Louise (Tritten) S.; m. Florence Evelyn Nelson, Mar. 14, 1936; children: Marie, Nancy, Morris, Robert, Stephen, Jane. Student, Waterloo Bible Coll., 1940-42. Owner Morris Printing Co., Waterloo, Iowa, 1930—. Mem. Christian Bus. Men's Com., 1953—, chmn., 1950-54. Served as cpl. inf. U.S. Army, 1944-45, ETO, prisoner of war, Germany. Mem. Waterloo C. of C. Republican. Mem. Brethren Ch. Office: Morris Printing Co 326 W Park Ave Waterloo IA 50701

SACKIN, STANLEY OWEN, broadcasting and restaurant executive; b. Los Angeles, May 16, 1936; s. Ernest and Fanny (Shatkin) S.; m. Stephanie Cook, June 30, 1968; children: Samantha, Courtney, Marvin, Alexandra. BA, UCLA, 1959. Ptnr. SOS Telephone Exchange, Hollywood, Calif., 1959-82; gen. mgr. Answer Page, Inc., Los Angeles, 1982-83; regional mgr. Graphic Scanning Corp., Los Angeles, 1983-84; sr. v.p., chief operating officer A Beeper Co., Atlanta, 1984-86; bd. dirs. Faver Broadcasting Income Fund, Atlanta; cons. Telephone Answering Services, Balt., 1986—; pres. Sacro Corp. doing bus. as Johnny Rockets, Atlanta, Chgo., Beverly Hills, Calif., 1986—. Dir. agy. relations Los Angeles United Way, 1979. Mem. Telephone Answering Services (pres. Calif. chpt. 1968, pres. Internat. Assn. 1966-68), Associated Telephone Answering Services (pres. Washington chpt. 1966-68), C. of C. Democrat. Jewish. Club: Friars (Beverly Hills), Los Angeles. Home: 8 Heards Overlook Ct Atlanta GA 30328 Office: Sacro Corp 6065 Roswell Rd Ste 2233 Atlanta GA 30328

SACKS, DAVID G., distilling company executive, lawyer; b. N.Y.C., Jan. 6, 1924; s. Irving and Jeannette (Greenhoot) S.; m. Naomi Gostin, Oct. 12, 1947; children: Jonathan E., Deborah A., Judith A., Joshua M. A.B., Columbia U., 1944, LL.B., 1948. Ptnr. Simpson Thacher & Bartlett, N.Y.C., 1961-67, sr. ptnr., 1967-76, counsel, 1981-83; chief adminstrv. officer Lehman Bros., Inc., N.Y.C., 1976-81; exec. v.p. fin. adminstrn. The Seagram Co. Ltd., Montreal, Que., Can., 1983-86, pres., chief operating officer, 1986-89, also bd. dirs.; exec. v.p. fin. adminstrn. Joseph E. Seagram & Sons, N.Y.C., 1983-86, pres., chief operating officer, 1986-89; vice chmn. The Seagram Co. Ltd. and Joseph E. Seagram & Sons, Inc., Montreal and N.Y.C., 1989—. Pres. United Jewish Appeal, Fedn. Jewish Philanthropies, N.Y.C., 1989—. Cpl. USAAF, 1943-46. Club: Beach Point (Mamaroneck, N.Y.). Office: Joseph E Seagram & Sons 375 Park Ave New York NY 10152

SADDOCK, HARRY G., utilities executive; b. 1929; married. BS, Rensselaer Poly. Inst., 1950. With Rochester (N.Y.) Gas & Electric Corp., 1950—, asst. div. supt. electric dept., 1968-71, div. supt. electricity and steam, 1971-74, v.p., 1974-80, sr. v.p., 1980-84, exec. v.p., 1984-88, also bd. dirs., pres., chief operating officer, 1988-89, chmn., chief exec. officer. Office: Rochester Gas & Electric Corp 89 East Ave Rochester NY 14649

SADEL, HARRIET RUTH, marketing professional; b. Washington, Dec. 22, 1949; d. Jacob and Jean (Bloom) S. BEd, U. Miami, Coral Gables, Fla., 1971. With sales and risk mgmt. Mass. Indemnity & Life Ins. Co., Silver Spring, Md., 1974-82; with fin. planning dept. T. Levin & Assocs., Vienna, Va., 1982-85; mgr. sales and mktg., v.p. Sovran Ins. Inc., Gaithersburg, Md., 1985—. Mem. Friends of the Kennedy Ctr. Mem. U.S. Tennis Players Assn., D.C. Med. Soc. (corp. contbn. com. 1988—), Variety Club, Washington Area Tennis Patrons Assn. Democrat. Jewish. Home: 5225 Pooks Hill Rd #1109N Bethesda MD 20814

SADIK-KHAN, ORHAN IDRIS, financial executive; b. Laghman, Afghanistan, July 3, 1929; came to U.S., 1951; s. Alim Jan and Shemsulbenat (Ashrat) Idris; m. Karen Lamond, May 3, 1969; children: Janette, Alim Jan, Karim, Kadria, Altan. BA, Am. U. at Cairo, 1951; MBA, Stanford (Calif.) U., 1953; PhD, Ricker Coll., 1970. Dir. tech. research and services Dean Witter & Co., N.Y.C., 1954-61; instl. research Schirmer Atherton & Co., 1961-62, F. Eberstadt, 1962-63; ptnr. charge research Ira Haupt Co., 1963; dir. research N.Y. Securities Co., N.Y.C., 1964-65; v.p. planning bus. equipment group Litton Industries, Inc., Beverly Hills, Calif., 1965-67; sr. v.p. Norton Simon Inc., N.Y.C., 1967-81; pres. Millicom, Inc., N.Y.C., 1982-84; mng. dir. Paine Webber, Inc., N.Y.C., 1986-88—; bd. dirs. Firecom, Inc.; pres. ADI Corp., Old Greenwich, Conn., 1975—. Mem. N.Y. Soc. Security Analysts, Boston Soc. Security Analysts. Republican. Clubs: The Board Room, Economics, Chemists (N.Y.C.). Office: Paine Webber Inc 1285 Ave New York NY 10019

SADILEK, VLADIMIR, architect; b. Czechoslovakia, June 27, 1933; came to U.S., 1967, naturalized, 1973; s. Oldrich and Antoine (Zlamal) S.; Ph.D. summa cum laude in City Planning and Architecture, Tech. U. Prague, 1957; m. Jana Kadlec, Mar. 25, 1960; 1 son, Vladimir, Jr. Chief architect State Office for City Planning, Prague, 1958-67; architect, designer Bank Bldg. Corp., St. Louis, 1967-70, asso. architect, San Francisco, 1970-74; owner, chief exec. officer Bank Design Cons., San Mateo, Calif., 1974-81, West Coast Development Co., San Mateo, 1975—; pres., chief exec. officer Orbis Devel. Corp., San Mateo, 1981—. Served with Inf. of Czechoslovakia, 1958. Recipient awards of excellence from Bank Building Corp. and AIA for planning and design of fin. instns. in Hawaii, Calif. (1971), Ariz., N.Mex., Tex. (1972), Colo., Wyo. (1973), Idaho, Oreg., Washington (1974); lic. architect, 28 states. Republican. Roman Catholic. Home: 80 Orange Ct Hillsborough CA 94010 Office: 1777 Borel Pl San Mateo CA 94402

SADLER, DAVID GARY, office copier company executive; b. Iowa City, Mar. 14, 1939; s. Edward Anthony and Elsie June (Sherman) S.; children: Angela, Laura, David Cary. Student, St. Ambrose Coll., 1957-59; BS in Indsl. Adminstrn. and Prodn., Kent State U., 1961. Various mgmt. positions Ford Motor Co., Lorain, Ohio, 1962-67, Sperry-New Holland, Lebanon, Ohio, 1967-71; mgr. mfg. Allis Chalmer, Springfield, Ill., 1971-72; dir. mfg. Purolator, Inc., Fayetteville, N.C., 1972-73; v.p. mfg. farm equipment and ops. truck div. White Motor Co., Eastlake, Ohio and Chgo., 1973-78; corp. v.p. mfg. Massey Ferguson Ltd., Toronto, Ont., Can., 1978-80; corp. v.p. mfg. Internat. Harvester, Chgo., 1980-81, sr. v.p. ops. staff, 1981-82, v.p. bus. devel., 1982, pres. diversified group, 1982-83, pres. internat. group, 1983-85; pres. AMI, Inc., Chgo., 1985-86; vice chmn., chief exec. officer Savin Corp., Stamford, Conn., 1986, chmn., chief exec. officer, 1986—, also bd. dirs.; bd. dirs. Greater Chgo. Safety Council, 1981-84. Roman Catholic. Home: 296 Pine Creek Ave Fairfield CT 06430 Office: Savin Corp 9 W Broad St Stamford CT 06904

SADOWSKI, ANDREW GREGORY, insurance broker; b. Stockholm, Apr. 16, 1941; s. Kazimierz and Angeline (Domachowski) S.; m. Kathleen Mary Jagelski, June 20, 1964; children: Angela K., Derek A., Lisa M., Sean M. Student, Portland State U., 1963-68. Investment analyst U.S. Nat. Bank of Oreg., Portland, 1962-67; surety underwriter Gen. Ins. Co., Portland, 1967-69; fin. mgr. various constrn. cos., Portland, 1969-74; ins. broker Salem, Oreg., 1974-76; pres. A.G. Sadowski Co., Salem, 1976-82, 88—; sr. v.p. Fred S. James & Co., Portland, 1982-88; underwriting mem. Lloyd's of London, 1985. Served to corp. USMC, 1958-62. Mem. Assn. Gen. Contractors of Am., Nat. Assn. of Surety Bond Producers, Ind. Ins. Agts. of Oreg. Republican. Roman Catholic. Club: Les Ambassadeurs, London. Home: 385 Snead Dr N Salem OR 97303

SADOWSKI, CHESTER PHILIP, JR., real estate executive; b. Pensacola, Fla., May 28, 1946; s. Chester P. and Florence Edna (Perry)S.; m. Jerriann Gibson Steller, Oct. 4, 1975; children: Julie K., Charles P., Robert T., David A. BSBA, U. Fla., 1968. CPA, Fla. Sr. auditor Arthur Andersen & Co., Tampa, Fla., 1969-74; sr. auditor U.S. Home Corp., Clearwater, Fla. and Houston, 1974-77, audit mgr., 1977-81, sr. audit mgr., 1981-82, audit dir., 1982-85, controller, 1985-87, v.p., controller, chief acctg. officer, 1987—. Mem. AICPA (real estate com. N.Y.C., 1986-88), Fla. Inst. CPA's, Nat. Assn. Accts. Office: US Home Corp 1800 W Loop South Ste 2100 Houston TX 77027

SADRUDDIN, MOE, oil company executive, consultant; b. Hyderabad, India, Mar. 3, 1943; came to U.S., 1964; m. Azmath Oureshi, 1964; 3 children. BSME, Osmania U., Hyderabad, 1964; MS in Indsl. Engring., NYU, 1966; MBA, Columbia U., 1970. Cons. project engr. Ford, Bacon & Davis, N.Y.C., 1966; staff indsl. engr. J.C. Penney, N.Y.C., 1966-68; sr. cons. Drake, Sheahan, Stewart & Dougall, N.Y.C., 1966-70, Beech-Nut Inc. subs. Squibb Corp., N.Y.C., 1970-72; founder, pres. Azmath Constrn. Co., Englewood, N.J., 1972-77; crude oil cons., fgn. govt. rep. 1977—; pres. A-One Petroleum Co., Fullerton, Calif., 1985—; govt. advisor Puerto Rico, 1980-82, Dominica, 1983-84, St. Vincent, 1981-82, Kenya, 1983-84, Belize 1984-85, Costa Rica 1983-86, Paraguay 1984-87. Mem. Los Angeles World Affairs Council. Mem. Internat. Platform Assn. Address: A-One Petroleum Co 2656 Camino Del Sol Fullerton CA 92633

SAENGER, BRUCE WALTER, consulting firm executive; b. Hanover, N.H., July 16, 1943; s. Werner Hugo and Natalie Bertha (Brown) S.; m. Cheryl Jeanne Bouchard, Nov. 6, 1976. B.A., Pa. State U., 1969; postgrad. Am. Coll., Bryn Mawr, Pa., 1979, Coll. Fin. Planning, Denver, 1980; C.P.C.U., Am. Inst., Malvern, Pa., 1981. Chartered fin. cons; C.L.U. Agt., Nationwide Ins., Lansdale, Pa., 1969-73, dist. sales mgr., Springfield, Ma., 1973-75; dist. sales mgr. Am. Mut., Braintree, Ma., 1975-77; dir. mktg. Bankers Life & Casualty, Chgo., 1977-78; pres., founder Sales Tng. Techs., Southboro, Mass., 1979-81, The Saenger Orgn., Medway, Mass., 1981—; faculty Notre Dame U., South Bend, Ind., 1977-78, Northeastern U., Boston, 1984—; commr. RHU Commn., Washington, 1979-81; dir. Northeastern U. Ins. Inst., Boston, 1985—; cons. in field. Author: Series 6 Study Book, 1983, Series 22 Study Book, 1984, Tax Shelter Market Guide, 1985, Marketing Mutual Funds, 1985; also articles. Bd. dirs. Lansdale Gen. Hosp., Pa., 1971-73. Served with U.S. Army, 1960-66. Recipient Ednl. Achievement award Profl. Ins. Agts. Assn., 1983. Fellow Soc. C.L.U.s (ednl. adv., bd. dirs. 1987—), Soc. CPCU's (ednl. adv.), Life Mgmt. Inst. (Outstanding Lectr. award 1984); mem. Internat. Assn. Fin. Planners (ednl. adv., bd. dirs. 1986—, pres.), Soc. Cert. Ins. Counselors (ednl. adv.), Life Underwriters Assn. (ednl. adv.). Republican. Roman Catholic. Avocations: golf, fishing. Home: 1 Stephanie Dr Medway MA 02053 Office: The Saenger Orgn 77 Main St Medway MA 02053

SAENZ, GREGORIO, JR., utilities administrator; b. Arroyo, Tex., May 22, 1933; s. Gregorio Saenz and Trinidad (Rodriguez) S.; m. Ofelia Ponce, June 29, 1956; children: Luis Alberto, Leonel, Rene. Grad. high sch., Edcouch, Tex. Various positions Tex., 1953-64; machine operator Virtue Bros. Mfg., Inc., Compton, Calif., 1964-66; router operator McDonnell Douglas Corp., Santa Monica, Calif., 1966-67, leadman, 1967-68; with Mission Screwworm Eradication USDA, Mission, Tex., 1969-70; from operator to systems supt. City of Edinburg, Tex., 1970—. Served as sgt. U.S. Army N.G., 1951-64. Mem. Citrus Water and Wastewater Assn. (awards com. 1984—), Tex. Water Utilities Assn., Am. Water Works Assn., Water Pollution Control Fedn., County Mcpl. Credit Union (bd. dirs. 1987—). Democrat. Roman Catholic. Home: 917 S 15th St Edinburg TX 78539 Office: City of Edinburg PO Box 1079 Edinburg TX 78540

SAEWERT, SCOTT GEORGE, automotive executive; b. Chgo., Nov. 12, 1953; s. George Charles and Lillian Marie (Curtain) S.; m. Janet Ann Kertz, Dec. 24, 1978. BS, U. Colo., 1984. Tech. mgr. Nugent, Glenview, Ill., 1973-78; dist. mgr. Nissan Motor Corp./USA, Chgo., 1978-82; owner World Automotive, Golden, Colo., 1982-84; mgr. Audi of Americas Inc., Lincolnshire, Ill., 1984-86; dist. mgr. Audi of Americas Inc., Lincolnshire, 1986—. Dir. Astor House Hist. Soc., Golden, 1983-84. Mem. Soc. Automotive Engrs., Automotive Svc. Excellence, U. Colo. Alumni Assn., Park Ridge Sports Car. Home: 207 Elm St Prospect Heights IL 60070 Office: Volkswagen Am Audi Div 420 Barclay Ltd Lincolnshire IL 60069

SAFANE, CLIFFORD JAY, wholesale executive; b. N.Y.C., Feb. 13, 1947; s. Milton David and Lydia (Cantor) S.; m. Penny Linet, Apr. 8, 1978; children: Aaron Michael, Nina Vivian. BFA, Union Coll., 1970; MusB, Syracuse U., 1972; MusM, Boston U., 1975. Mgr. sales and mktg. Savage Universal Corp., N.Y.C., 1980-84; sales mgr. Quadriga Art, N.Y.C., 1984-85, Frame Co., Jersey City, 1985-86; pres. Saflin, Inc., Bergenfield, N.J., 1986—. Author: Bud Powell, 1978; contbr. numerous articles to profl. jours. Coach Washington Twp. Little League, 1988—. Mem. Sales Execs. Club N.Y., Photog. Mktg. Assn., Photog. Adminstrs., Assn. Profl. Color Labs. Jewish. Office: Saflin Inc 93B S Railroad Ave Bergenfield NJ 07621

SAFE, KENNETH SHAW, JR., professional trustee; b. Providence, Oct. 13, 1929; s. Kenneth Shaw and Louise (King) S.; m. Elizabeth Kelley, Dec. 20, 1952; children: Hope, Elizabeth, Kenneth, Thorn and Edith (triplets). AB, Harvard U., 1951. Intelligence officer CIA, Washington, 1954-56; with trust dept. Old Colony Trust Co., Bank of Boston, 1956-59; registered rep. Tucker, Anthony & R.L. Day, Boston, 1959-68; ptnr. Welch & Forbes, Boston, 1968—, mng. ptnr., 1983—. Pres. Travelers Aid Soc. Boston, 1956-82, Community Workshops, Inc., Boston, 1968—; asst. treas. Wellesley (Mass.) Coll., 1970-80; trustee Georgiana Goddard Eaton Meml. Trust, Boston, 1975—, G. Howland Shaw Found., Boston, 1977—, Manomet Bird Observatory, Plymouth, Mass., 1984—; treas. Woods Hole (Mass.) Oceanographic Inst., 1981—; bd. dirs. Beverly Land Co., Providence, 1982—; corporator New Eng. Deaconess Hosp., Boston, R.I. Hosp., Providence; bd. dirs., treas. Boys and Girls Camps, Inc., Boston; bd. dirs., asst. treas. Boston Port and Seaman's Aid Soc. With CIC, U.S. Army, 1952-54. Mem. Boston Security Analysts Soc., Somerset Club, Duxbury Yacht Club, Marshall St. Hist. Soc., Country Club. Republican. Episcopalian. Home: 207 King Caesar Rd Duxbury MA 02332 Office: Welch & Forbes 45 School St Boston MA 02108

SAFENOWITZ, MILTON, petroleum company executive; b. Bklyn., 1927. Exec. v.p. Getty Petroleum Corp., Jericho, N.Y., also bd. dirs.; bd. dirs. Slattery Group Inc., Roslyn, N.Y. Office: Getty Petroleum Corp 125 Jericho Turnpike Jericho NY 11753

SAFFEIR, HARVEY JOSEPH, insurance company executive; b. N.Y.C., Nov. 17, 1929; s. Harry and Pauline (Fleischman) S.; m. Lois Marshall Allen, Sept. 17, 1959; children: Robin, Jo Daviess. AB, Cornell U., 1951. Sr. v.p. Travelers Corp., Hartford, Conn., 1974—; sr. v.p. numerous subs. Travelers Corp., Hartford. Fellow Soc. Actuaries, Am. Acad. Actuaries; mem. Inst. Internal Auditors. Republican. Clubs: Hartford (dir. 1979-82), Hartford Golf. Home: 61 Glenwood Rd West Hartford CT 06107 Office: The Travelers Corp 1 Tower Sq Hartford CT 06183

SAFFELL, TED ALLAN, administrative manager; b. Lubbock, Tex., Dec. 16, 1943; s. Edwin Leon and Ruby (Tribble) S.; m. Julia Marie Flournoy, Aug. 25, 1966; children: Cameron Lee, Justin Allan. BA, Tex. Tech. U., 1972. Mgr. 7-11 Stores Southland Corp., Lubbock, 1971-72; audio-visual sales mgr. Baker Graphic Methods, Lubbock, 1972-73, svc. mgr., 1973-79, micrographics sales mgr., 1979-88; adminstrv. mgr. Module Truck Svc. Inc., Lubbock, 1988—. Coach Lubbock Soccer Assn., 1982—, v.p., 1984-87; referee South Plains Soccer Referees Assn., 1987—. With U.S. Army, 1967-70. Mem. Assn. Record Mgrs. and Adminstrs. Baptist. Office: Module Truck Svc Inc 6801 66th St Lubbock TX 79424

SAFFER, BRIAN HARVEY, banker; b. N.Y.C., June 16, 1942; s. George and Mildred (Stein) S.; m. Judith Mack, June 13, 1965; children: Amy L., Ian L. AB, Columbia Coll., 1964; LLB, St. John's U., N.Y.C., 1967. Bar: N.Y.; registered securities dealer. V.p. Irving Trust Co., N.Y.C., 1967-77; v.p. Financo, Inc. Shearson Lehman Hutton Co., Phila., 1978-80; 1st v.p. Prudential-Bache Securities, N.Y.C., 1980-83; sr. v.p. Hay Group div. Saatchi & Saatchi, PLC, N.Y.C., 1984-86; v.p. Swergold, Chefitz & Sinsabaugh, N.Y.C., 1986—; guest lectr. Wharton Sch., U. Pa., Phila., 1979-80, SUNY, New Paltz, 1980-83. Mem. Mergers and Acquisitions Mag. Round Table, Phila., 1980-84; contbr. articles to profl. jours. and chpts. to books. Pres. Countryside Assn., Summit, N.J., 1975-76. Mem. N.Y. State Bar Assn., Assn. Bar of City of N.Y. Clubs: Princeton U. (N.Y.C.); Morris Aero. (Morristown, N.J.). Home: 77 Winchip Rd Summit NJ 07901 Office: Swergold Chefitz & Sinsabaugh 110 Wall St New York NY 10005

SAFFT, STUART J., manufacturing company executive; b. Bklyn., May 21, 1941; s. Abe and Florence Dorothy (Greenberg) S.; children: Andrea, Kenneth. BS in Mech. Engring., Swarthmore (Pa.) Coll., 1962; MBA with distinction, Harvard U., 1964. Analyst, mktg. devel. specialist Corning (N.Y.) Glass Works, 1964-66, supr. mktg., devel. and sales, 1967-69; gen. mgr. hosp. planning Sandoz, Inc., East Hanover, N.J., 1970-74, dir. corp. data services, 1974-78, dir. corp. planning, devel., data services, 1975-77, v.p., treas., 1978-80; v.p. fin. Sandvik, Inc., Fairlawn, N.J., 1980-83, Dianon Systems, Stamford, Conn., 1984-86, Rogers (Conn.) Corp., 1986—. Mem. Ambulance Assn., Old Saybrook, Conn., 1988. Mem. Am. Mgmt. Assn., Fin. Execs. Inst. Jewish. Office: Rogers Corp 1 Tech Dr Rogers CT 06263

SAFIOL, GEORGE E., electronics company executive; b. Bklyn., Apr. 23, 1932; s. Charles and Effie (Patika) S.; m. Demetra Karambelas, July 12, 1958; children: Olympia Safiol Twomey, Peter, Christina. BS in Engring., NYU, 1954; postgrad. Sch. Engring., Columbia U., 1954-55. V.p., gen. mgr. No. Am. Telecom, ITT, Memphis, 1960-69; exec. v.p., chief operating officer Sycor, Inc., Ann Arbor, Mich., 1969-70; v.p. investments Heizer Co., Chgo., 1970-71; sr. v.p. Gen. Instrument Corp., Chicopee, Mass., 1971-77; pres., chief exec. officer Am. Biltrite, Framingham, Mass., 1977-83; various sr. exec. positions Gen. Instrument Corp., N.Y.C., 1984-87, chief operating offficer, pres., 1987—, also dir.; pvt. practice mgmt. cons., 1983-84. Served to 1st lt. U.S. Army, 1955-57. Mem. Alpha Omega. Republican. Greek Orthodox. Club: Metropolitan (N.Y.C.). Home: 64 Juniper Rd Weston MA 02193 Office: Gen Instrument Corp 767 Fifth Ave New York NY 10153

SAFKO, DEBORAH LEE, health care administrator; b. Alliance, Ohio, Sept. 19, 1951; d. Joseph Paul Safko and Doris Marie (Wolf) Sniegocki; m. Samuel John Costa, Jr., Sept. 2, 1972 (div. April 1984); children: Mario Benjamin, Jeremy Michael. BS magna cum laude in Human and Social Scis., Drexel U., 1974; MBA in Health Adminstrn., Temple U., 1982. Bus. mgr., mktg. dir. Occupational Health Services, Pennsauken, N.J., 1983-86; patient service mgr. Children's Hosp., Phila., 1986-87; dir. Resources Human Devel., Phila., 1988—. Active mem. Phila. Com. on City Policy, 1972—. Recipient Am. Coll. Hosp. Adminstrs. award, 1981; grantee Pub. Health Services Traineeship, 1980, 81. Mem. NAFE, Phi Mu. Democrat. Roman Catholic. Home: 4809 Beaumont Ave Apt #3-F Philadelphia PA 19143

SAHLEIN, DON H(OWE), manufacturing executive; b. Jackson, Mich., Mar. 7, 1924; s. David A. and Paula (Byoir) S.; m. Lee Winifred Silver, Mar. 28, 1952; children: Gail Laurie, Stacey Anne. BS, UCLA, 1948. V.p. Leoff & Rose Publicist, L.A., 1948-52; sales mgr. L.A. Wholesale Electric Co., 1952-56; pres. Hollywood (Calif.) Camera Co., 1956-71; corp. exec. Alan Gordon Enterprises, Inc., North Hollywood, Calif., 1971—. Mem. World Affairs Council, Los Angeles, Los Angeles Internat. Visitors Com., Los Angeles Bordeaux Sister City Affiliation, H.O.M.E. (Charitable Aid to the Homeless). With USAAF, 1942-45, U.S. and Europe. Decorated D.F.C., Air medal with three clusters. Mem. Am. Soc. Photogrammetry, Soc. Photo Instrumentation Engrs., Soc. Motion Picture and TV Engrs., Profl. Photographers Assn., Soc. Photo Techs., Internat. Micrographic Congress, Assn. Records Mgrs. and Adminstrn., Inc. Republican. Jewish. Clubs: Founders Guild, Vikings, Wine and Food Soc. Hollywood, Les Gastronomes, Red Barons. Lodge: Masons. Office: Alan Gordon Enterprises Inc 5362 Cahuenga Blvd North Hollywood CA 91601

SAHOTA, GURCHARN SINGH, mechanical engineer; b. Talwandi Jattan, Punjab, India, Jan. 4, 1940; came to U.S., 1971; naturalized, 1980; s. Karam Singh and Amar Kaur (Nijjar) S.; m. Gurvindar Kaur Johal, May 4, 1966 (dec. Mar. 1978); 1 child, Saryadvinder Singh; m. Kamaljit Kaur Grewal, Jan. 10, 1979; 1 child, Parmeet Kaur. BS in Mech. Engring., Punjab U., 1957-61; MS in Mech. Engrin., N.J. Inst. Tech., 1975-77. Engr. Heavy Elecs., Bhopal, India, 1962-70; mnfg. engr. Engelhard Industries, Union, N.J., 1974-76; from sr. plant engr. to supr. plant engring. group Am. Cyanamid Co., Stamford, Conn., 1976—. Home: 34 Duke Dr Stamford CT 06905 Office: Am Cyanamid Co 1937 W Main St Stamford CT 06904

SAID, MOHSIN M., insurance company executive, consultant; b. Cairo, Egypt, Nov. 7, 1954; came to U.S., 1978, naturalized 1981; s. M. Said and Hanem (Hagag) Mohamoud; m. Therese Hanson, Nov. 7, 1977; children: Sharif, Summer, Jihan. BA in Phys. Edn., Cairo U., 1976. Fin. planner Aetna Ins., Milw., 1978-79; ins. exec. Lincoln Fin. Resources, Milw., 1979—; dir. Lincoln Fin. Resources Fin. & Investment Corp., Milw., 1979—. Chmn. Milw. chpt. Am. Arab Anti-Discrimination Com.; active Republican Party, Washington, 1983—; soccer coach Elm Grove (Wis.) Warriors soccer team, Milw. Kicker Club. Mem. Internt. Assn. Fin. Planners (accredited), Nat. Assn. Life Underwriters (life, Nat. Sales Achievement award, 1981-88), Nat. Assn. Health Underwriters (life, leading producer roundtable, Nat. Quality award 1981-88), Athletic Club. Avocations: soccer, bicycling, traveling, tennis, stamp collecting. Home: 14505 Watertown Plank Rd Elm Grove WI 53122 Office: Lincoln Fin Resources Bishops Woods West I 150 S Sunnyslope Rd Ste 101 Brookfield WI 53005

SAINANI, RAM HARIRAM, civil engineer; b. Ratodero, Sind, India, Feb. 22, 1925; came to U.S., 1981; s. Hariram Gurdasmal and Radha Hariram (Ahuja) S.; m. Usha Ram Devkaran-Nanjee, Jan. 16, 1956; 1 child, Devkumar Ram. BA in Math. with honors, U. Bombay, 1943, BA in Physics and Chemistry with honors, 1944, BS in Math. and Physics, 1945, BCE, 1948; MCE, U. Colo., 1958. Registered profl. engr., Ont., Can., Mass., Maine, N.H. Dep. dir. designs Cen. Water & Power Commn. Govt. India, New Delhi, 1951-59; sr. hydraulic engr. SNC Group, Montreal, Que., Can., 1959-65; asst. chief hydraulic engr. Tecult Internat., Montreal, 1965-79; staff engr. Acres Internat., Niagara Falls, Ont., Can., 1979-81; prin. engr. Internat. Engring. Co. Inc., Norwalk, Conn., 1981-85; v.p. engring. Consol. Hydro Inc., Greenwich, Conn., 1985—. Pres. India Can. Assn., Montreal, 1974-77. Mem. ASCE, Rotary. Democrat. Hindu. Office: Consol Hydro Inc 2 Greenwich Pla Greenwich CT 06830

SAINI, GULSHAN RAI, soil physicist; b. Hoshiarpur, India, Oct. 1, 1924; s. Ram Saran and Parmeshri Devi (Bhondi) S.; B.Sc., U. Panjab, 1945, M.Sc., 1956; Ph.D., Ohio State U., 1960; postgrad. Bus. Adminstrn. and Computers, U. N.B., 1983, Harvard, 1986. m. Veena Chaudhri, Jan. 14, 1950; 1 son, Vikas. Research asst. Govt. Agrl. Coll., Ludhiana, India, 1945-57; research assoc. Ohio State U., Columbus, 1957-60; asst. prof. Punjab Agrl. U., Ludhiana, India, 1960-61; research scientist Can. Dept. Agr., Fredericton, N.B., 1962-84; adj. prof. Faculty of Forestry, U. N.B., Fredericton, 1968-76; vis. prof. Rutgers U., 1984-85; dir. fin./adminstrn. Lawyers Alliance for Nuclear Arms Control, Inc., 1985—. Mem. Canadian Inst. of Internat. Affairs, 1974-82, treas. fredericton br. 1979-81; mayor's com. on Languge and Culture, 1970-71. Mem. Indian Sci. Congress Assn. (life), Multicultural Assn. Fredericton (life, pres. 1980-81), Profl. Inst. Pub. Service Can. (nat. v.p. 1980, 81, chmn. Atlantic regional council 1978, 79), Rotary Club (dir. internat. svc. 1967-68), Sigma Xi, Phi Lambda Upsilon. Contbr. articles to profl. jours. Home: 24 Brook St Brookline MA 02146

ST. CLAIR, THOMAS MCBRYAR, manufacturing company executive; b. Wilkinsburg, Pa., Sept. 26, 1935; s. Fred C. and Dorothy (Renner) St. C.; m. Sarah K. Stewart, Aug. 1, 1959; children—Janet, Susan, Carol. AB, Allegheny Coll., 1957; MS, MIT, 1958; grad. advanced mgmt. program, Harvard U. With Koppers Co., Inc., Pitts., 1958—; asst. to gen. mgr. engring. and constrn. div. Koppers Co., Inc., 1966-69, comptroller, asst. treas., 1969-78, pres. Engineered Metal Products Group, 1978-83, v.p., asst. to chmn., 1983-84, v.p., treas., chief fin. officer, 1984—. Trustee Allegheny Coll.; trustee, treas. North Hills Passavant Hosp. Mem. Fin. Execs. Inst., Allegheny Coll. Alumni Assn. Presbyterian. Clubs: Duquesne, Univ. (Pa.). Office: Koppers Co Inc 601 Koppers Bldg Pittsburgh PA 15219

ST. CLEMENT, COURTNEY TOLSON, advertising executive; b. Fort Worth, Nov. 8, 1951; d. J.B. and Dorothy Allison (Marshall) Tolson; m. Reginald St. Clement, Sept. 13, 1981. Art dir. Bloom Advt., Dallas, 1973-77, Cunningham & Walsh, N.Y.C., 1977-82; pres., creative dir. St. Clement Group, N.Y.C., 1982—. Bd. dirs. East Meets West. Recipient Mead award Mead Paper, 1976; Silver Microphone award All Star Radio, 1985. Mem. Dutch Reform Ch. Clubs: Snarks (N.Y.C.); Bklyn. Avocation: equestrian activities. Office: St Clement Group 106 E 19th St New York NY 10003

SAINT-DONAT, BERNARD JACQUES, finance company executive; b. Avignon, France, May 22, 1946; came to U.S., 1971; s. Jean Eugene and Paule Louise (Chastan) S.; m. Ingrid Claire Armstrong, June 6, 1986. PhD in Sci., U. Paris, 1973. Research fellow Harvard U., 1971-74; asst. prof. Columbia U., N.Y.C., 1974-76; assoc. prof. Yale U., New Haven, Conn., 1976-81; assoc. Lehman Bros. KuhnLoeb, N.Y.C., 1981-84; v.p. Shearson Lehman Bros., N.Y.C., 1984-86, sr. v.p., 1986-89; mng. gen. ptnr. Knox Parthers, N.Y.C., 1989—; bd. dirs. New Haven Sister Cities, Inc. Author: Toroidal Embeddings, 1975; contbr. articles to profl. jours. Fellow Berkeley Coll., Yale U. Roman Catholic. Clubs: Elizabethan (New Haven), Yale (N.Y.C.). Home: 315 E 72d St New York NY 10021

ST. ETIENNE, GREGORY MICHAEL, bank executive; b. New Orleans, Dec. 24, 1957; s. Emanuel Anthony and Geraldine Barbara (Dionne) St. E.; m. Valencia Ann Tanner, June 30, 1984. BBA, Loyola U., New Orleans, 1979, MBA, 1981. Sr. account auditor Laporte, Sehrt, Romig & Hand CPA, New Orleans, 1981-85; v.p., auditor Liberty Bank and Trust Co., New Orleans, 1985-87, v.p., controller, 1987-88, sr. v.p., 1988—; dir. Kingsley House, New Orleans, 1987—. Active Young Leadership Council, New Orleans, 1987—, Met. Area Com., New Orleans, 1987—, Urban League Greater new Orleans, 1985—. Mem. Nat. Black MBA Assn. Roman Catholic. Office: Liberty Bank and Trust Co 4101 Pauger St New Orleans LA 70122

ST. GEORGE, NICHOLAS JAMES, lawyer, manufactured housing company executive; b. Waltham, Mass., Feb. 11, 1939; s. Louis and Rose (Argonti) St. G.; B.A. in Econs., Coll. William and Mary, 1960, J.D., 1965; children—Blane Stephen, Nicholas John; m. Eugenia Metzger, July 25, 1987. Trainee, Gen. Electric Co., Schenectady, 1960; admitted to Va. bar, 1965; trust rep. Va. Nat. Bank, Norfolk, 1965-66; group v.p.-in-charge investment banking dept., dir. Legg Mason-Wood Walker, Washington, 1966-76; v.p. Ferguson Enterprises, Newport News, Va., 1977-78; pres., chief exec. officer Oakwood Homes Corp., Greensboro, N.C., 1979—, also dir.; dir. Am. Bankers Ins. Group, First Union Nat. Bank Greensboro, Legg Mason, Inc., vice chmn. Coordinating Council on Manufactured Housing Fin. Served to 1st lt. U.S. Army, 1960-62. Mem. Manufactured Housing Inst. (dir., fin. chmn.), Am. Mgmt. Assn., Am. Bar Assn., Va. State Bar Assn. Republican. Roman Catholic. Office: Oakwood Homes Corp 2225 S Holden Rd Greensboro NC 27407

ST. JAMES, LYN, business owner, professional race car driver; b. Cleve., Mar. 13, 1947; d. Alfred W. and Maxine W. (Rawson) Cornwall; m. John Raymond Carusso, Dec. 7, 1970 (div. 1979). Cert. in piano, St. Louis Inst. Music, 1967. Sec. Cleve. dist. sales office U.S. Steel Corp., 1967-69, Mike Roth Sales Corp., Euclid, Ohio, 1969-70; co-owner, v.p. Dynasales Fla., Hollywood, 1970-79; owner, pres. Autodyne, Dania, Fla., 1974—, Creative Images, Inc., 1979—; race car driver Ford Motor Co., Dearborn, Mich., 1981—, spokesperson, cons., 1981—; media spokesperson 3M Co., Mpls., 1987. Author: LSJ Car Owners Manual for Women, 1985; contbg. editor automotive articles Seventeen mag, 1987—, Cosmopolitan mag., 1988. Bd. trustees Women's Sports Found., N.Y.C., 1988—. Recipient Woman of Yr. award McCalls mag., 1986, Leadership award Girl Scouts U.S., 1988. Mem. Internat. Motorsports Assn., Sports Car Club of Am. Republican. Office: Creative Images Inc 175 SW 20th Way N6 Dania FL 33004

ST. JOHN, ANTHONY PAUL, automotive executive; b. Washington, Jan. 13, 1937; s. Sterling and Beulah (Marston) St. J.; m. Myra Grace Cornfeld, Oct. 30, 1959; children: James Sterling, Ivy Kemp, Mary Marston. LLB, U. Va., 1960; cert. Advanced Mgmt., Harvard U., 1979. Bar: Md. 1961. Various positions Bethlehem (Pa.) Steel Corp., 1960-78, asst. v.p. indsl. relations, 1978-83, asst. v.p., asst. gen. counsel, 1983, v.p. union relations, 1984-86; v.p. human resources Chrysler Motors Corp., Detroit, 1986—; chmn. litigation com. Bus. Roundtable, Washington, N.Y.C., 1974-77; bd. dirs. Labor Policy Assn., Washington, 1988—. Vice-chmn. Moravian Acad. Bd. Trustees, Bethlehem, 1982-85, Greater Detroit Alliance of Bus., 1987—; bd. dirs. ARC Southeastern Mich., Detroit, 1986—. 1st lt. U.S. Army, 1960-61. Mem. ABA, Orchard Lake Country Club, Suncon Valley country Club (Bethlehem), Lehigh Country Club (Allentown, Pa.). Republican. Home: 3701 Lake Crest Dr Bloomfield Hills MI 48013 Office: Chrysler Motors Corp 12000 Chrysler Dr Highland Park MI 48288

ST. JOHN, HENRY SEWELL, JR., utility company executive; b. Birmingham, Ala., Aug. 18, 1938; s. H. Sewell and Carrie M. (Bond) St. J.; student David Lipscomb Coll., 1956-58, U. Tenn., 1958-59, U. Ala., 1962-64; m. J. Ann Morris, Mar. 7, 1959; children—Sherri Ann, Brian Lee, Teresa Lynn, Cynthia Faye. Engring. aide Ala. Power Co., Enterprise, 1960-62, Birmingham, 1962-66; asst. chief engr. Riviera Utilities, Foley, 1966-71, sec.-treas., gen. mgr., 1971—. Deacon, Foley Ch. of Christ, 1975-82, elder, 1983—; active Am. Cancer Soc., chmn. bd. Baldwin County unit, 1977; bd. dirs. AGAPE of Mobile, 1977-80; treas. Christian Care Center, Inc., 1981—; bd. dirs. South Baldwin Civic Chorus, pres., 1979—. Mem. IEEE., South Ala. Power Distbrs. Assn. (chmn. 1973-74), Ala. Consumer-Owned Power Distbrs. Assn. (chmn. 1974-75, 82-83, vice-chmn. 1981, sec.-treas. 1980), S.E. Electric Reliability Council (assoc.), Mcpl. Electric Utility Assn. Ala. (exec. com., dir. 1971—), Ala. Mcpl. Electric Authority (bd. dir. 1981—, vice chmn. 1981-82, chmn. 1983—), United Mcpl. Distbrs. Group (bd. dirs. 1972—), Am. Pub. Power Assn. (cable communications com.), Pub. Gas. Assn. Ala. (bd. dirs. 1987-88), South Baldwin C. of C. (pres. 1974, dir. 1972-75, 81—). Clubs: Foley Quarterback (sec.-treas. 1984-85); Gulf Shores Golf (dir. 1974-75), Classic Chevy, Internat. (life mem.), Azalea City Classic Chevy. Rotarian. Home: PO Box 818 Foley AL 36536 Office: PO Box 550 Foley AL 36536

ST. JOHN, HOWARD C., banker. m. Phyllis Ertrel; 3 children. LL.B, Albany Law Sch., 1948. Sr. ptnr. Howard C. St. John and Assocs., 1948—; former dist. attorney Ulster County, N.Y.; with Ulster Savs. Bank, Kingston, N.Y., 1965—, chmn. bd. dirs., chief exec. officer, 1988—; bd. dirs. Mid-Hudson Pattern Inc.; bd. dirs. Cen. Hudson Corp., vice-chmn., 1987—; chmn. com. on fin. Cen. Hudson Corp., 1986—; chmn. Stavo Industries, Kingston; former assoc. gen. counsel N.Y. Joint Legis. Com. on Reapportionment. U.S. del. to Switzerland, Spain, China, 1978; appointed by Gov. Cuomo to N.Y. State Banking Bd., 1986; former mem. Ulster County Community Coll. Adv. Coun. New Devel. Ctr. for Bus.; trustee Kingston YMCA, Albany Law Sch. With USAF, 1943-45. Mem. Savs. Bank Assn. N.Y. State, Nat. Coun. Savs. Insts., N.Y. State Bar Assn., ABA, Justinian Soc., Kiwanis. Home: Glenford NY 12433 Office: Cen Hudson Gas & Electric Corp 284 South Ave Poughkeepsie NY 12601

SAINT-PIERRE, GUY, agri-business executive; b. Windsor Mills, Que., Can., Aug. 3, 1934; s. Arm and Alice (Perra) Saint-P.; m. Francine Garneau, May 4, 1957; children—Marc, Guylaine, Nathalie. B.Applied Sci. in Civil Engring, Laval U., 1957; diploma, Imperial Coll., London, 1958; M.Sc., U. London, 1959. Registrar, Corp. Engrs. Que., 1964-66. Dir. Irnes Inc., 1966-67; v.p. Acres Que., 1967-70; minister of edn. Govt. Que., 1970-72, of industry and commerce, 1972-76; asst. to pres. John Labatt Ltd., Montreal, 1977-80; sr. v.p. John Labatt Ltd., 1980—; pres., chief operating officer Ogilvie Mills Ltd., Montreal, 1977-80; pres., chief exec. officer Ogilvie Mills Ltd., 1980—; dir. McGavin Foods, Popular Industries Ltd., Miron Inc., Suncor Inc., Commerce Group Ins. Co., SNC, Inc. Bd. dirs. Clin. Research Inst., Montreal, U. Montreal. Served as officer C.E. Can. Army, 1959-64. Mem. Montreal Bd. Trade, Engring. Inst. Can., Can. Mfrs. Assn. (chmn. bd.), Order Engrs. Que., Council Can. Unity (v.p.), Mil. and Hospitalier Order St. Lazarus Jerusalem. Liberal. Roman Catholic. Clubs: Mt. Royal, St. Denis, Mt. Bruno, Forest and Streams. Office: 1 Pl Ville Marie Ste 2100, Montreal, PQ Canada H3B 2X2 also: John Labatt Ltd, 451 Ridout St N, London, ON Canada N6A 5L3

SAINT-PIERRE, MICHAEL ROBERT, funeral director, consultant; b. Indpls., July 12, 1947; s. Robert Ross and Gaile Russell (Cousins) S.; m. Betty Carolyn Wilhoit, Jan. 14, 1967; children: Michelle René, Paul Christopher. Student Milligan Coll., 1965-67, Butler U., 1966; B.S., East Tenn. State U., 1969; diploma Ind. Coll. Mortuary Sci., 1970; postgrad. Nat. Found. Funeral Service, 1970, 71, 73, 74, 76, Ind. U., Indpls., 1977. Intern, Hamlett-Dobson, Kingsport, Tenn., 1967-69; pres. J.C. Wilson & Co., Inc., Indpls., 1969—, St. Pierre Funeral Mgmt. Corp., 1984—; evaluator/practitioner rep. Am. Bd. Funeral Service Edn., 1980—; prof., trustee Ind. Coll. Mortuary Sci., 1971-76; prof. Nat. Found. Funeral Service, 1987—; bd. advisors Nat. Bank Greenwood (Ind.), 1978-80; bd. dirs. Premier Mgmt. Corp., Metro Media Inc. Contbr. articles to profl. jours. Mem. Johnson County (Ind.) Sheriff's Merit Bd., 1989—; bd. dirs. Cen. Ind. Better Bus. Bur., Indpls., 1982-86, Adult/Child Mental Health Ctr., Indpls., 1982-85, Allied Meml. Council, Indpls., 1979—; elder Greenwood (Ind.) United Presbyn. Ch., 1976; past mem., treas. bd. dirs. Consumer Info. Bur., Inc.; past mem. bd. dirs. Cen. for Life/Death Edn., Indpls. Recipient Nat. Bd. Cert., Conf. Funeral Service Exam. Bd., 1970; Disting. Service awards Ind. Coll. Mortuary Sci., Indpls., 1978, Mid Am. Coll. Funeral Service, Jeffersonville, Ind., 1982. Fellow Nat. Found. Funeral Service (pres. alumni assn. 1978); mem. Associated Funeral Dirs. Service Internat. (pres. 1981), Nat. Selected Morticians (bd. dirs. 1988—), Nat. Funeral Dirs. Assn. (practitioner, resource and ourtreach, edn., supplementary speakers bur. and arbitration coms., chmn. employee/employer task force, chmn. mgmt. practice com.), Acad. Profl. Funeral Service Practice, Ind. Funeral Dirs. Assn. (bd. dirs., pres. 1982-83), Funeral Dirs. Forum, Prearrangement Assn. Am., Marion County Funeral Dirs. Assn. (pres. 1974), Nat. Eagle Scout Assn. Republican. Presbyterian. Clubs: Valle Vista Country, Skyline. Lodges: Rotary (past pres., Paul Harris fellow), Masons (past master), Scottish Rite, Shriners; Order Eastern Star. Office: Wilson St Pierre Funeral Svc PO 147 481 W Main St Greenwood IN 46142

SAINT-REMY, PIERRE LEON, import-export executive; b. Gonaïves, Artibonite, Haiti, Mar. 8, 1934; s. Leon and Yvonne (Forbin) Saint-R.; m. Michaelle Marie Delaquis, July 29, 1961; children: Pierre Leon Jr., Nathalie. BA, Coll. St. Martial, Port-au-Prince, Haiti, 1954; BS in acctg. and fin., NYU, 1958. With Madame Leon Saint-Remy Import-Export, Gonaïves, 1958-60, dir. export dept., 1961-69, under-dir. gen., 1969-73, dir. gen., 1973-76, pres., dir. gen., 1976—; pres., dir. gen. Les Allumettes Haïtiennes, S.A., Gonaïves, 1976—. Mem. Constitutional Assembly, Haiti, 1987; bd. dirs. Assn. for the Def. of the Constitution, 1987. Mem. Assn. des Industries d'Haiti (exec. bd. 1984), Soc. Financiere Haitienne de Devel. (exec. bd. 1986). Roman Catholic. Club: Cercle Bellevue (Port-au-Prince). Home: Ave des Dattes, Gonaives Haiti also: Rue Ludovie, Chante Brise, Delmas 83, Port-Au-Prince Haiti Office: Les Allumettes Haitiennes SA, Detour Laborde, Gonaives Haiti

ST. THOMAS, LLOYD LEROY, entrepreneur; b. Salt Lake City, Oct. 26, 1934; s. Evan Leon Thomas and Vivian Ruth (Hurt) Royce; m. Wilma Gean Kirkland, Mar. 2, 1961 (div. Oct. 1972); children: Lance Gregory Thomas, Craig Lloyd Thomas; m. Karen Diane Madsen, Dec. 23, 1973. BS, Westminster Coll., 1975, U. Utah, 1979; MPA, Brigham Young U., 1983; PhD, Am. Inst. Hypnotherapy, Santa Ana, Calif., 1988. Salesman Arden Dairy, Salt Lake City, 1956-57, Holsum Baking Co., Salt Lake City, 1957-60; salesman, supr. Arthur Murray Studio, Salt Lake City, 1960-65; ptnr., mgr. Arthur Murray Studio, Salt Lake City and Denver, 1969-71; account rep. Helena Rubinstein Inc., San Diego, 1965-67; med. salesman William H. Rorer, San Diego, 1967-69; sales cons. Sales Tng. Inc., Salt Lake City, 1972-73; clin. hypnotherapist Bionomics Cons., Anaheim, Calif., 1985-87; ptnr. The Plush Touch, Orange, Calif., 1987—; mem. faculty Am. Inst. Hypnotherapy, 1985-86. With USN, 1951-55, Korea. Recipient Dorothy Carnegie award Dale Carnegie, Salt Lake City, 1971, Best Speaker award Sales Tng. Inst., Salt Lake City, 1972. Mem. N.Am. Soc. Hypnotherapists, Am. Hypnotherapy Assn. Roman Catholic. Office: The Plush Touch 1485 N Tustin Ste 215 Orange CA 92667

SAKAI, KATSUO, electrophotographic engineer; b. Matsumoto, Nagano, Japan, Apr. 9, 1942; s. Mototeru and Fumi (Iida) S.; m. Toshiko Hagiwara, Feb. 7, 1976; children: Asako, Akiharu, Hirohiko. B in Applied Physics, Waseda U., Tokyo, 1967. Engr. Ricoh Co. Ltd., Tokyo, 1967—; lectr. in field. Contbr. articles to profl. jours.; inventor, patentee two-color electrophotography, 1980. Mem. Soc. Electrophotography of Japan, Soc. for Imaging Sci. and Tech. Club: Minami Fuji Country. Home: 25-64 Moegino Midori-ku, Yokohama 227, Japan Office: Ricoh Co Ltd, 1-3-6 Nakamagome, Ohta-ku, Tokyo 143, Japan

SAKANASHI, MARK TAKESHI, financial consultant; b. Oakland, Calif., Oct. 13, 1952; s. Takeshi Henry and Kay Keiko (Yokoyama) S.; m. Akiko Fukami, June 26, 1977; children: Philip Takeshi, Stephen Hiroshi. BA, Seattle Pacific U., 1974; postgrad., Fuller Sem., 1976-78. CLU, cert. fin. planner. Agt. Penn Mut. Life Ins. Co., Los Angeles, 1978-80; dist. mgr. Penn Mut. Life Ins. Co., Anaheim, Calif., 1980-81; prin., owner Mark Sakanashi & Assocs., Los Angeles, 1978-82; pres. Matrix Fin. Ins. Services, Inc., Pasadena, Calif., 1982—, Matrix Fin. Cons., Inc., Pasadena, 1982—, Matrix Fin. Corp., Pasadena, 1988—. Bd. dirs. Los Angeles Nagoya Sister City Affiliation, Los Angeles, 1988, Pasadena Christian Sch., 1989—. Named Outstanding Young Am. Jaycees, 1981; Seattle Pacific U. fellow, 1986. Mem. Inst. Cert. Fin. Planners, Internat. Assn. Fin. Planning, Nat. Assn. Securities Dealers (registered prin. 1983—), Nat. Assn. Realtors. Republican. Methodist. Office: Matrix Fin Corp 140 S Lake Ave Ste 304 Pasadena CA 91101

SAKOWITZ, SIDNEY NATHAN, food products executive; b. Indpls., July 8, 1925; s. Louis and Nesha (Marks) S.; married, 1947; children: Marcia Sakowitz Sklare, Anita Sakowitz Kramer, Jeffrey. Student, Purdue U., 1943. Ptnr., chief fin. officer Grocers Supply Co., Inc., Indps., 1946—. Bd. dirs. Gleaners Food Bank, Indpls., Jewish Fedn. Indpls., 1988—; pres. Hooverwood Home for Aged, Indpls., 1988—. Mem. Fin. Execs. Inst., Risk Mgmt. Ins. Assn., Nat. Am. Wholesale Grocers Assn. (bd. govs. 1980-83, 1988—), Shriners, B'Nai Torah (pres. 1975-77). Office: Grocers Supply Co Inc PO Box 1846 Indianapolis IN 46206

SALAMON, RENAY, real estate broker; b. N.Y.C., May 13, 1948; d. Solomon and Mollie (Friedman) Langman; m. Maier Salamon, Aug. 10, 1968; children: Mollie, Jean, Leah, Sharon, Eugene. BA, Hunter Coll., 1969. Licensed real estate borker, N.J. Mgr. office Customode Designs Inc., N.Y.C., 1966-68; co-owner Salamon Dairy Farms, Three Bridges, N.J., 1968-86; assoc. realtor Max. D. Shuman Realty Inc., Flemington, N.J., 1983-85; pres., chief exec. officer Liberty Hill Realty Inc., Flemington, N.J., 1985—; cons. Illva Saronna Inc. (Illva Group), Edison, N.J. 1985—; real estate devel. joint venture with M.R.F.S. Realty Inc. (Illva Group), 1986—. Environ. Commr. Readington Twp. Environ. Commn., Whitehouse Sta., N.J. 1978-87; fund-raiser Rutgers Prep. Sch., Somerset, N.J. 1984-87; mem. N.J. Assn. Environ. Commrs., Trenton, N.J. 1978-87. Named N.J. Broker Record, Forbes Inc., N.Y.C. 1987. Mem. Nat. Assn. Realtors, N.J. Assn. Realtors, Hunterdon County Bd. Realtors (mem. chair 1986), Realtor's Land Inst. Republican. Jewish. Office: Liberty Hill Realty Inc 415 Hwy 202 Flemington NJ 08822

SALANDRA, JOHN A., accountant, financial operations director; b. N.Y.C., June 3, 1952; s. Michael R. and Ida C. (Cannata) S.; m. Kathryn A. Tota, Oct. 12, 1975; children: Justin, Erika, Lindsay. BBA in Acctg., Iona Coll., 1974. Sr. mgr. Peat Marwick Co., N.Y.C., 1974-84; v.p. fin. Nyack (N.Y.) Hosp., 1984-85; dir. fin. ops. Cath. Med. Ctr. of Bklyn. and Queens, Inc., Queens, N.Y., 1985—; bd. trustees, chmn. fin. com. Dominican Sisters Family Health Services, Ossining, N.Y., 1986—; bd. trustees St. Jerome's Health Svcs., Inc., bd. dirs., chmn., treas. 1989—; vice-chmn. fin. program com. Fin. Mgmt. Assn., N.Y.C., 1987—. Treas. Hawthorne (N.Y.) Fire Co. no. 1, 1985—. Mem. Am. Inst. CPA's, N.Y. State Soc. CPA's, Am. Mgmt. Assn., Nat. Assn. Accts., Am. Hosp. Assn. Republican. Roman Catholic. Office: Catholic Med Ctr 88 25 153rd St Jamaica NY 11432

SALAZAR-CARRILLO, JORGE, economics educator; b. Havana, Cuba, Jan. 17, 1938; came to U.S., 1960; s. Jose Salazar and Ana Maria Carrillo; m. Maria Eugenia Winthrop, Aug. 30, 1959; children: Jorge, Manning, Mario, Maria Eugenia. BBA, U. Miami, 1958; MA in Econs., U. Calif., Berkeley, 1964, cert. in econ. planning, 1964, PhD in Econs., 1967. Sr. fellow, non-resident staff mem. Brookings Instn., Washington, 1965—; dir., mission chief UN, Rio de Janeiro, Brazil, 1974-80; prof. econs. Fla. Internat. U., Miami, 1980—, chmn. dept. econs., 1980—; advisor U.S. Info. Agy., advisor, contbg. editor Library of Congress, Washington, 1972—; editorial bd. Jour. of Banking and Fin.; chmn. program com. Hispanic Profs. of Econs. and Bus.; cons. econs. Agy. for Internat. Devel., Washington, 1979—; council mem. Internat. Assn. Housing, Vienna, 1981—; exec. bd. Cuban Am. Nat. Council, Miami, 1982—; bd. dirs. Insts. of Econ. and Social Research of Caribbean Basin, Dominican Republic, 1983—, U.S.-Chile Council, Miami, 1984—. Co-author: Trade, Debt and Growth in Latin America, 1984; Prices for Estimation in Cuba, 1985; The Foreign Debt and Latin America, 1983; External Debt and Strategy of Development in Latin America, 1985; The Brazilian Economy in the Eighties, 1987, Foreign Investment, Debt and Growth in Latin America, 1988; World Comparisons of Incomes, Prices, and Product, 1988; author: Wage Structure in Latin America, 1982. Fellow Brit. Council, London, 1960, Georgetown U., Washington, 1961-62, OAS, Washington, 1962-64, Brookings Instn., Washington, 1964-65. Mem. Am. Econ. Assn., Internat. Assn. Research in Income and Wealth, Econometric Soc. Latin Am., N.Am. Econs. and Fin. Assn., Internat. Assn. Energy Economists (pres. Fla. chpt.), Nat. Assn. Forensic Economists, Latin Am. Studies Assn., Knights of Malta. Roman Catholic. Home: 1105 Almeria Ave Coral Gables FL 33134 Office: Fla Internat U Tamiami Campus DM 347 Miami FL 33199

SALBERG, JOEL LEWIS, graphics company executive; b. N.Y.C., Feb. 3, 1936; s. Arthur Isaac and Pearl (Polansky) S.; m. Linda Heller, June 24, 1962 (div. June 1981); children: Seth Harris, David Ian; m. Elisabeth Phillips, Oct. 6, 1985. Ba, U. Conn., 1957. Claims examiner State of Conn., Hartford, 1958-59; radio announcer Sta. WTOR, Torrington, Conn., 1959-60; news dir. Sta. WSOR, Windsor, Conn., 1961-62; typographer, v.p. New Eng. Typographic Service, Bloomfield, Conn., 1962-79; sales exec. York (Pa.) Graphic Service, 1980-83; regional sales mgr. Univ. Graphics, Inc., Atlantic Highlands, N.J., 1983-86, v.p., 1986—; bd. dirs., speaker Harris Industries, Winchester, Va., 1971; cons. Pub.s Phototype, Inc., Carlstadt, N.J., 1980, CBS Ednl. Pubs., Mexico City, Mex., 1983. Bd. dirs. Aguda Achim Synagogue, West Hartford, Conn., 1978-79. Capt. USAR, 1957-66. Mem. Nat. Composition Assn. (chmn. 1977-79, bd. dirs. 1970—, Service award 1984, 85, 86, 87), Typographers Internat. Assn. (bd. dirs. 1973-79), Printing Industries Am. (bd. dirs. 1976-79, Service award 1978, 79). Jewish. Home: 64 Skylark Ct Matawan NJ 07747 Office: Univ Graphics Inc 21 W Lincoln Ave Atlantic Highlands NJ 07716

SALDIN, THOMAS R., corporate lawyer; b. 1946. BA, Carleton Coll., 1968; JD, Cin. Coll. Law, 1974. Law clk. to presiding justice U.S. Dist. Ct. (so. dist.) Ohio, 1974-76; assoc. Benjamin, Faulkner & Tepe & Sach, Cin., 1976-78; asst. gen. counsel Albertson's Inc., Boise, Idaho, 1978-81, v.p., gen. counsel, 1981-83, sr. v.p. gen. counsel, 1983—. Office: Albertson's Inc 250 Parkcenter Blvd Boise ID 83706

SALE, TOM S., economist, educator; b. Haynesville, La., July 27, 1942; s. Thomas and Mary Belle (Fagg) S.; BA, Tulane U., 1964; MA, Duke U., 1965; PhD, La. State U., 1972; m. Liza Spivey, July 13, 1966 (div. June 1988); children: Thomas Sanderson IV, Jennifer Elizabeth, Sarah Elaine. Mem. faculty La. Tech. U., Ruston, 1965—, prof. econs., 1975—, head dept. econs. and fin., 1974-86, dir. grad. studies Coll. Adminstrn and Bus., 1988—. Bd. dirs. La. Council for Econ. Edn., 1974—. Chartered fin. analyst. Mem. Am. Econs. Assn., So. Econs. Assns., Southwestern Fin. Assn. (pres. 1985-86), Am. Fin. Assn., Inst. Chartered Fin. Analysts (exam. com.), SW Fedn. Adminstrv. Disciplines (v.p. 1988-89), Dallas Assn. Fin. Analysts, Omicron Delta Kappa, Omicron Delta Epsilon. Episcopalian. Contbr. articles to profl. jours. Home: PO Box 1365 Ruston LA 71273-1365 Office: La Tech U Ruston LA 71272

SALEM, GEORGE RICHARD, lawyer; b. Jacksonville, Fla., Dec. 24, 1953; s. Kamel Abraham and Margaret Virginia (Bateh) S.; m. Rhonda M. Ziadeh, June 28, 1980; children: James George, Jihan Camille, Laila Suad. BA, Emory U., 1975, JD, 1977; LLM, Georgetown U., 1984. Bar: Ga. 1978, Fla. 1979, D.C. 1981. Ptnr. Thompson, Mann & Hutson, Washington, 1977-85, 89—; dep. solicitor of labor U.S. Dept. Labor, Washington, 1985-86, solicitor of labor, 1986-89; bd. dirs. Overseas Pvt. Investment Corp. Contbr. articles to profl. jours. Nat. exec. dir. ethnic voters div. Reagan-Bush '84; bd. dirs. United Palestinian Appeal, Inc., 1981-85, 86—, Arab Am. Inst., Jan.-Mar., 1985, Dec. 1986—; mem. Am. Arab Anti-Discrimination Com., Interagy. Coordinating Coun.; chmn. Arab-Ams. for Bush-Quayle '88. Mem. ABA (labor and employment law sect.), Ga. Bar Assn. (labor relations div.), Fla. Bar Assn. (labor relations div.), D.C. Bar Assn. (labor relations div.), Nat. Assn. Arab Ams. (bd. dirs. 1987—), Am. Ramallah Club (pres. D.C. chpt. 1984, Wash. rep. 1982-84), Am. Ramallah Fedn. (chmn. human rights com., Washington rep. 1982-84), Arab Am. Rep. Fedn. (chmn. 1985), Assn. Am. Arab Univ. Grads., Century Club Nat. Rep. Heritage Groups Council, Delta Theta Phi, Omicron Delta Kappa. Mem. Eastern Orthodox Christian Ch. Office: Thompson Mann and Hutson 3000 K St NW Ste 600 Washington DC 20007

SALIBA, RICHARD JAMEEL, construction company executive; b. Dothan, Ala., May 29, 1957; s. Richard and Karen (Hightower) S.; m. Robbie Jane Royal, Jan. 23, 1982; children: Lauren Elizabeth, Richard Michael. BS in Chemistry, Auburn U., 1979, BS in Bldg. Sci. with honors, 1981. Field engr. McDevitt and Street Co., Atlanta, 1982-83, supt., 1983-84; supt. Patterson-West Constrn. Co., Atlanta, 1984-86; owner, exec. officer Saliba Constrn. Co., Inc., Dothan, 1986—. Mem. Associated Gen. Contractors Am. (sec.-treas. Dothan chpt. 1987—), Houston County C. of C. (legis. affairs com. 1987—, edn. com. 1988—), Internat. Platform Assn., Bus. Coun. Ala., Alpha Epsilon Delta, Sigma Alpha Epsilon, Phi Kappa Phi, Sigma Lambda Chi, Sigma Tau Delta. Republican. Episcopalian. Club: Dothan Country. Home: 6 Holly Hill Rd Dothan AL 36301 Office: Saliba Constrn Co 1103 N Park Ave Dothan AL 36303

SALIG, RONALD JAMES, land developer, engineer, consultant; b. N.Y.C., Mar. 22, 1950; s. Henry Charles and Gladys Dorothy (Brier) S.; m. Marie Ann Baxter, Dec. 29, 1977; children: Jeremy Ronald, Eric Henry. BSCE, Polytech. Inst. N.Y., 1975; MS in Mech. Engring, MIT, 1982, MS in Fire Protection Engring., 1984. Registered profl. engr., N.Y., Mass. Prin., dir. MBS Fire Tech., Inc., Grafton, Mass., 1982—; engring. specialist elec. boat div. Gen. Dynamics, Groton, Conn., 1985-86; pres. Premier Design, Inc., South Grafton, Mass., 1986—. Contbr. articles to profl. jours. Mem. Soc. Fire Protection Engrs. (pres. New Eng. chpt. 1989—, past chmn. scholarship com., chmn. membership com., chmn. publ. com., chmn. program com.), Salamander Hon. Fire Protection Engring. Soc. (nat. bd. dirs. alumni sec.), Nat. Fire Protection Assns., ASCE, Internat. Union Operating Engrs. Home: 23 Barbara Jean St Grafton MA 01519 Office: Premier Design Inc 153 Main St PO Box 2 South Grafton MA 01560

SALIGMAN, HARVEY, consumer products and services company executive; b. Phila., July 18, 1938; s. Martin and Lillian (Zitin) S.; m. Linda Powell, Nov. 25, 1979; children: Martin, Lilli Ann, Todd Michael, Adam Andrew, Brian Matthew. B.S., Phila. Coll. Textiles and Sci., 1960. With Queen Casuals, Inc., Phila., 1960—; v.p. Queen Casuals, Inc., 1966-68, pres., chief exec. officer, 1968-81, chmn., 1981—; pres., chief operating officer Interco Inc., St. Louis, 1981-83, chief exec. officer, 1983-85; chmn., chief exec. officer Interco Inc., 1985—, also bd. dir.; dir. Merc. Bank. Trustee Jewish Hosp. St. Louis, Washington U., St. Louis; bd. dirs. St. Louis Symphony Soc.; dir. Union Electric.; commr. St. Louis Art Mus. Mem. Young Pres. Orgn. Club: St. Louis. Lodge: Masons. Office: Interco Inc 101 S Hanley Rd Saint Louis MO 63105

SALIMBENI, LAURIE ANNE, accountant; b. Lancaster, Pa., Jan. 14, 1964; d. Thomas and Regina Bertha (Ziemba) Posipanko; m. Eugene Vincent Salimbeni, June 29, 1985; children: Amanda, Matthew. BSBA, Millersville U., 1985. Asst. accounting Maj. Smith, New Holland, Pa., 1985; gen. acct. Playskool Inc. (formerly CBS Toys), Lancaster, 1985-86, cost acct., 1986—. Mem. Nat. Assn. Accts. Roman Catholic. Office: Playskool Inc 110 Pitney Rd Lancaster PA 17602

SALINAS, LARRY, marketing executive; b. N.Y.C., May 13, 1947; s. Harry and Victoria (Sasson) S.; m. Rosalind Roth, June 22, 1968; children: Kimberly, Danny. BS, N.Y. Inst. Tech., 1970; MBA, St. John's U., S.I., 1978. Sr. auditor Peat, Marwick, Mitchell and Co., N.Y.C., 1970-73; mgr. personnel Supermarkets Gen. Corp., Woodbridge, N.J., 1975-76, mgr. tng., devel., 1976-77, mgr. benefit planning, 1977-79, dir. mkt. research, 1980-87, v.p. mkt. research, 1987—; mem. rsch. com. Food Mktg. Inst., 1988—. Coach Little League, W. Windsor, 1987. With USAR, 1969-75. Mem. Am. Mgmt. Assn., Am. Numismatic Assn. Republican. Jewish.

SALISBURY, ROBERT CAMERON, finance executive; b. N.Y.C., NY, Nov. 7, 1943; s. Robert Elmore and Grace Louise (Rowe) S.; m. Linda C. Lindefield, Jan. 4, 1965; children: Dianne, Brenda. BS in Fin., Fla. State U., 1965, MBA, 1972. Asst. v.p. First Union Nat. Bank, Charlotte, NC, 1972-74; cash adminstr.; mgr. cash mgmt.; group mgr. cash and planning. The Upjohn Co., Kalamazoo, MI, 1974; dir. internat. fin. Upjohn Internat., Inc., Kalamazoo, 1981-82, dir. corp. fin., 1982-87, v.p. fin., 1988—; bd. dirs. NBD Portage (Mich.) Bank, ACE Ltd., Bermuda, CODA Lmtd. Bermuda. Capt. USAF, 1965-71. Mem. Fin. Execs. Inst. Republican. Office: Upjohn Co 7000 Portage Rd Kalamazoo MI 49001

SALITERMAN, RICHARD ARLEN, lawyer, educator; b. Mpls., Aug. 3, 1946; s. Leonard Slitz and Dorothy (Sloan) S.; m. Laura Shrager, June 15, 1975; 1 child, Robert Warren. BA summa cum laude, U. Minn., 1968; JD, Columbia U., 1971; LLM, NYU, 1974. Bar: Minn. 1972, D.C. 1974. Mem. legal staff U.S. Senate Subcom. on Antitrust and Monopoly, 1971-72; acting dir., dep. dir. Compliance and Enforcement div. Fed. Energy Office, N.Y.C., 1974; mil. atty. Presdl. Clemency Bd., White House, Washington, 1975; sr. ptnr. Saliterman & Siefferman, Mpls., 1975—; adj. prof. law Hamline U., 1976-81. Chmn. Hennepin County Bar Jour., 1985-87. Bd. dirs. Mpls. Urban League, 1987—, pres. Am. Jewish Com., Mpls. St. Paul chpt., 1988—. With USN, 1972-75. Mem. ABA, Minn. State Bar Assn., Hennepin County Bar Assn. (governing council 1985-87), Oakridge Country Club (Hopkins, Minn.), Mpls. Club, Wayzata Yacht Club.

SALIZZONI, FRANK LOUIS, financial executive; b. Bridgeville, Pa., July 21, 1938; s. Augustine and Alice (Berteotti) S.; m. Sarah B. Russel, June 27, 1964; children—Susan, Laura, John. B.S.I.E., Pa. State U., 1960; M.E.A., George Washington U., 1964. Vice-pres., treas. Trans World Airlines, N.Y.C., 1971-76, sr. v.p. fin., treas., 1976-78, also dir.; sr. v.p. fin. Transworld Corp. (name changed to TW Services, Inc. 1987), N.Y.C., 1979-81, sr. v.p. fin. and real estate, 1981-82, sr. v.p. fin. and adminstrn., 1982-84, vice-chmn., chief fin. officer, from 1984, now chmn., chief exec. officer, also dir.; instr. Fairleigh Dickinson U., Rutherford, N.J., 1966-68. Home: 707 Somerset St Franklin Lakes NJ 07417 Office: TW Svcs Inc 605 3d Ave New York NY 10158 *

SALK, PETER L., research company executive; b. Ann Arbor, Mich., Jan. 21, 1944; s. Jonas and Donna (Lindsay) S.; m. Ellen Schreibman, Oct. 1971; 1 child, Michael. AB, Harvard U., 1965; MD, Johns Hopkins U., 1969. Exec. v.p. Westbridge Rsch. Group, San Diego, 1984—; bd. dirs. Westbridge Research Group. Co-author articles for profl. publs. Chmn. San Diego Capital of Age of Enlightenment, 1984-86. Mem. Phi Beta Kappa, Alpha Omega Alpha. Office: Westbridge Rsch Group 9920 Scripps Lake Dr Ste 103 San Diego CA 92131

SALKO, HENRY S., textile company executive; b. N.Y.C., Feb. 24, 1925; s. Max and Louise M. (Ginsberg) S.; BS in Econs., U. Pa., 1949; children: Richard Michael, Karen Leslie, Amy Lynn. With Max Salko Corp., N.Y.C., 1949—, v.p., 1958—; bd. dirs. Ritz Tower Hotel. Chmn. Citizens for Eisenhower; mem. Rep. Town Com., Mamaroneck, 1953-56; trustee Harrison (N.Y.) Jewish Community Ctr., 1970-73; mem. Pub. Employees Rels. Bd. Harrison, 1970-73. With 75th Inf. Div., U.S. Army, 1943-45. Decorated Bronze Star, Purple Heart. Mem. N.Y. Acad. Sci., Retail Assocs. Group, Textile Sq. Club, Wharton Club, City Athletic Club, B'nai B'rith (N.Y. state regional bd. Anti-Defamation League 1979-83, nat. commr. 1989—, chmn. various coms., pres. Westchester Putman coun. 1984-85, v.p. dist. 1 N.E. U.S., pres. 1989-90, internat. bd. govs.), Delta Sigma Rho, Alpha Epsilon Pi. Home: Palmer Landing 123 Harbor Dr #209 Stamford CT 06902 Office: Max Salko Corp 17 W 31st St New York NY 10001

SALLAH, MAJEED JIM, real estate developer; b. Boston, Aug. 5, 1920; s. Herbert K. and Rose (Karem) S.; student Gloucester (Mass.) Pub. Schs.; m. Aline C. Powers, Apr. 10, 1970; children: Christopher M., Melissa Rose. Pres., dir. Glo-Bit Fish Co., Gloucester, 1947-48, Live-Pak of Ohio, Inc., 1947-51, Cape Ann Glass Co., Inc., Gloucester, 1950-72, Cape Ann Realty Corp., Gloucester, 1961—, Marias Restaurant, Gloucester, 1960—; pres., treas., dir. Gloucester Hot-Top Constrn. Co., Gloucester, 1967-75; pres., bd. dirs. SGF Corp., Gloucester, 1983-85, DALFAD, Inc. Rossford, Ohio; pres., treas. Points East, Inc.; trustee Christopher Investment Trust; dir. Lutsal, Inc. Pres. Lebanese-Am. Bus. Men's Club; treas. Lebanese-Maronite Soc. Served with U.S. Army, 1942-45. Decorated Bronze Star. Mem. Gloucester Assocs., Cape Ann Investment Corp., Am. Legion, Amvets, Hon. Order Ky. Cols. Roman Catholic. Lodges: Lions, Elks, Moose. Home and Office: 56 Hilltop Rd Gloucester MA 01930

SALLEN, IRA BRUCE, human resources executive, psychologist; b. Boston, Apr. 14, 1954; s. Melvin Julius and Lois Sheila (Margil) S.; m. Susan Laurie Lubarsky, Dec. 26, 1976; children: Marisa Beth, Amanda Joy. BS in Edn. and Psychology, Bridgewater State U., 1976; MA in Clin. Psychology, New Sch. Social Research, 1978; MBA, Boston U., 1982. Research fellow Rockefeller U., N.Y.C., 1977-78; psychologist Counseling and Family Services, Inc., Brockton, Mass., 1978-81; staff cons. Arthur Young & Co., N.Y.C., 1981-82, sr. supr., 1982-83; mgr. human resource planning Computervision Corp., Bedford, Mass., 1983-85; mgr. human resources Ciba Corning Diagnostics, Medfield, Mass., 1985-88; v.p. human resources Clean Harbors, Inc., Braintree, Mass., 1988—; vis. lectr. Boston U., 1983—, Providence Coll., 1985; bd. dirs. Boston U. Grad. Sch. Mgmt.; faculty U. Conn., Storrs, 1981-83. Mem. Organizational Resources Internat. Roundtable, Human Resources Policy Inst., Human Resources Planning Soc. Office: Clean Harbors Inc 325 Wood Rd Braintree MA 02184

SALMANS, CHARLES GARDINER, banker; b. Washington, Apr. 23, 1945; s. Marion K. and Agnes A. (Gardiner) S.; m. Robin Elizabeth Wakeman, June 8, 1986. BS, Northwestern U., 1967; MBA in Fin., Columbia U., 1970. Account supr. Burson-Marsteller, N.Y.C., 1970-74; v.p. Bankers Trust Co., N.Y.C., 1974-84; sr. v.p. Chem. Bank, N.Y.C., 1984—; mem. editorial adv. bd. Grad. Sch. of Bus. Columbia U., N.Y.C., 1984—. Home: 103 E 75th St New York NY 10021 Office: Chem Banking Corp 277 Park Ave New York NY 10172

SALMON, EUGENE RICHARD, food industry executive; b. Bronx, N.Y., Dec. 13, 1931; s. Reginald Jesse and Regina (Shatzman) S.; m. Jacqueline Yola Gertsman, June 5, 1954; children: Robin, Karen, Michael. Student, Bklyn. Coll., 1954-58; LLD, London Inst. Applied Research, 1973. Store mgr. Fairmart Food Stores, Inc., Bklyn., 1954-61; store mgr. Big Apple Supermarkets, Inc., N.Y. and N.J., 1961-65, store planning and resets mgr., 1966-67, dist. sales mgr., 1967-69, div. mgr., 1969-70, v.p. store ops., 1970-72; v.p. store ops. Foodtown/Melmarkets, Inc., Nassau County, N.Y., 1972—, exec. v.p., 1972—. Campaign worker Rep. Nat. Task Force, Washington, 1982-88; vol. Nat. Com. Furtherance Jewish Edn., Hicksville, N.Y., 1984—; hon. Lubavitch Youth Orgn., 1983, Harvest Lodge B'nai B'rith, Queens, N.Y., 1986. Served as cpl. U.S. Army, 1952-54. Named Man of Yr. N.Y. Foundling Hosp., 1988. Mem. N.Y. Food Mchts. Assn. (bd. dirs. 1982—), Food Industry Exec. Council (mem. trade relations com. 1982—). Lodges: Masons, B'nai Brith. Home: 2625 Karen St Bellmore NY 11710 Office: Melmarkets Inc 33-50 Hempstead Turnpike Levittown NY 11756

SALMON, LEE WILLIAM, psychologist, financial planner; b. Howell, Mich., May 6, 1938; s. William Lee Salmon and Mildred Sue (Seyfried) Thompson; m. Betty Lynn Weeks, Aug. 23, 1958; children: James, Jill, Jon, Jeni. BS, Mich. State U., East Lansing, 1969; MA, Mich. State U., 1972, EdS, 1975; Cert., Coll. Fin. Planning, 1986. Pers. technician dept. civil svc. State of Mich., Lansing, 1970-73; sch. psychologist Livingston Intermediate Sch. Dist., Howell, 1973—; prin. Lee W. Salmon & Co., East Lansing, Mich., 1986—; Mich. rep. Active Parenting Pub. Co., 1989—; registered rep. Mariner Fin. Svcs., Livonia, Mich., 1986—. With USMC, 1956-58. Mem. Inst. Cert. Fin. Planners. Republican. Presbyterian. Home: 831 King Ct East Lansing MI 48823 Office: Livingston Intermediate Sch Dist 1425 W Grand River Howell MI 48843

SALMON, THOMAS MARTIN BRANDEN, banker, lawyer; b. Elizabeth, N.J., Feb. 17, 1945; s. Edward Francis John and Florence Jean (Martin) S. BA, Colgate U., 1967; JD, U. Va., 1975. Bar: Va. 1975. Corp. counsel Citicorp, N.Y.C., 1975-80; pvt. practice internat. law Charlottesville, Va., 1980-81; pvt. practice banking cons. Switzerland, 1982-86; sr. v.p. Am. Security Bank, Washington, 1986—. Lt. USNR, 1962-72, Vietnam. Decorated Bronze Star, air medal (5); decorated Honour Medal (1st class) Republic Viet Nam. Fellow Morgan Library; mem. ABA, Va. State Bar Assn., Army and Navy Club (Washington), University Club (N.Y.C.), Keswick (Va.) Hunt Club, Am. Alpine Club. Office: Am Security Bank 730 15th St NW Washington DC 20013

SALO, DENNIS LLOYD, corporate systems director; b. Detroit, Mar. 12, 1944; s. Matt E. and Wilma S. (Heikkela) S.; m. Trudy L. Baker, Aug. 20, 1966; children—Scott, Carrie. B.B.A., Western Mich. U., 1966; M.B.A., U. N.Mex., 1968. Mktg. rep. IBM, New Haven, 1973-76; sr. systems analyst Yale-New Haven Hosp., 1976-77; project leader NCR Corp., Dayton, Ohio, 1977-78; sr. sci. systems analyst Eli Lilly & Co., Indpls., 1978-80; mgr. info. systems devel. Teledyne CAE, Toledo, 1980-84; corp. dir. systems and data processing Tecumseh (Mich.) Products Co., 1984—. Coach Bedford Women's Softball Assn., Temperance, Mich., 1981-84; mem. adv. com. Vo-Tech Occupational Sch., Adrian, Mich., 1984—. Served to lt. USN, 1968-71. Mem. Am. Prodn. and Inventory Contol Soc., Assn. Systems Mgmt., Delta Sigma Pi. Methodist. Home: 8005 Kingsboro Ct Temperance MI 48182 Office: Tecumseh Products Co 100 E Patterson St Tecumseh MI 49286

SALOM, ROBERTO, financial executive; b. Bogota, Columbia, July 12, 1944; came to U.S., 1966; m. Estell Kathleen Millard; children: David Andres, Robert W.A. Student, U. Andes, Bogota, 1965; BS, San Francisco State U., 1969, MBA, 1972; postgrad., U. Calif., Berkeley, 1973; PhD in Econs., NYU, 1977. Rsch. assoc. Fed. Res. Bank San Francisco, 1968-70, fin. analyst, 1970-73; mem. staff UN Devel. Program/Fund for Population Activities, N.Y.C., 1973-82, dep. chief program planning, 1982-83, dep. chief fin. br., 1983-87, chief fin. br., 1987—; presenter seminars in field. Home: 5 Elmwood Ave Rye NY 10580 Office: UN Fund Population Activities 220 E 42d St New York NY 10017

SALTARELLI, EUGENE A., retired engineering and construction company executive, consultant; b. Buffalo, Feb. 22, 1923; s. Joseph A. and Mary (Cataldo) S.; m. Jean Marie Cray, Nov. 25, 1950; children—Margaret, Joseph, Thomas, Paul, Mary, John. B.Mech. Engring., U. Detroit, 1949; M.S. in Mech. Engring., Northwestern U., 1951. Registered profl. engr., Calif., Md., Mich., N.Y., Pa., Tex., W.Va., Ariz., Ala., Ga. Design engr. Bell Aircraft Corp., Buffalo, 1950-56; sr. mgr. Bettis Atomic Power Lab., Pitts., 1956-67; group v.p. NUS Corp., Gaithersburg, Md., 1967-80; sr. v.p., chief engr. power Brown & Root, U.S.A., Inc., Houston, 1980-88; now pvt. cons. Contbr. articles to profl. jours.; patentee in field. Served to 1st lt. USAAF, 1942-46. Mem. ASME (George Westinghouse Gold medal 1985), Atomic Indsl. Forum, Am. Nuclear Soc. (exec. com. power div. 1975), Nat. Soc. Profl. Engrs. Roman Catholic. Club: Champions Golf (Houston).

SALTER, DOUGLAS NEEL, real estate developer; b. Merced, Calif., Feb. 23, 1940; s. Woodrow Wilson and Catherine (Neel) S.; m. Charlotte Ann Sheldon, Feb. 9, 1963 (div. Dec. 1979); children: Shelley, Rex-Richard; m. 2d Sharanne Braine, June 11, 1983. BS Mech. Engring., U. Nev., 1962. Registered engr.-in-tng., Calif. Constrn. mgr. Bailey Assocs., Mpls., 1968-69; pres. Grubb & Ellis Devel. Co., Oakland, Calif., 1969-81; exec. v.p. Bramalea Colo., Denver, 1981-82; sr. v.p. Bramalea Ltd., Dallas, 1983-85, pres. Urban Properties Group div., 1985—, exec. v.p.; mem. urban devel.-mixed use council Urban Land Inst., Washington. Served to capt. C.E. U.S. Army, 1962-67, Germany, Vietnam. Decorated Bronze Star U.S.; decorated Order of Merit Republic South Vietnam. Republican. also: Bramalea Ltd, 1867 Yonge St, Toronto, ON Canada M4S 1Y5 *

SALTMAN, WILLIAM M., chemist; b. Perth Amboy, N.J., Nov. 19, 1917; m. Juliet Zion, Feb. 14, 1943; children: David, Nina, Daniel. BS in Math., U. Mich., 1938, BS in Chem. Engring., 1938, MS in Chem. Engring., 1939; PhD in Chemistry, U. Chgo., 1949. Research engr. Calif. Inst. Tech., Pasadena, 1945; research chemist Shell Chem. Co., Denver, 1951-54; sr. scientist Goodyear Tire & Rubber Co., Akron, Ohio, 1955-82; cons. Akron, 1982—. Author, editor: Stereo Rubbers, 1977; contbr. articles to profl. jours.; patentee in field. Served with USN, 1942, U.S. Army, 1942-45. Mem. Am. Chem. Soc. Home and Office: 844 Frederick Blvd Akron OH 44320

SALTZ, RALPH, corporate lawyer; b. May 31, 1948; s. Peter and Eve (Bass) S.; m. Linda Bergman, Mar. 15, 1970; children: Erica, Alan. BA, Queens Coll., 1969; JD, St. John's U., 1972. Bar: N.Y. 1973, N.J. 1975. Atty. The Port Authority of N.Y. and N.J., N.Y.C., 1972-76, The Great Atlantic and Pacific Tea Co., Montvale, N.J., 1976-77; asst. real estate counsel Supermarkets Gen. Corp., Woodbridge, N.J., 1977-82, Toys 'R' Us, Inc., Rochelle Park, N.J., 1982-84; v.p., house counsel, asst. sec. Jamesway Corp., Secaucus, N.J., 1984—. Mem. ABA. Democrat. Office: Jamesway Corp 40 Hartz Way Secaucus NJ 07096-1526

SALTZMAN, IRENE CAMERON, perfume manufacturer, art gallery owner; b. Cocoa, Fla., Mar. 23, 1927; d. Argyle Bruce and Marie T. (Neel) Cameron; m. Herman Saltzman, Mar. 23, 1946 (dec. May 1986); children: Martin Howard (dec.), Arlene Norma Hanly. Owner Irene Perfume and Cosmetics Lab., Jacksonville, Fla., 1972—, Irene Gallery of Art, Jacksonville, 1973—. Mem. Cummer Gallery of Art, Jacksonville, 1972—; mem. Jacksonville Gallery of Art, 1972—; mem. The Nat. Mus. of Women in the Arts, Washington, 1972—. Mem. Internat. Soc. Fine Arts Appraisers, Nat. Assn. for the Self Employed, NAFE, Internat. Platform Assn., Women Bus. Owner Jacksonville, Am. Soc. Profl. and Exec. Women. Democrat. Episcopalian. Club: Ponte Vedra. Home: 2701 Ocean Dr S Jacksonville Beach FL 32250

SALUTI, DEAN JULIUS, management consultant, educator; b. Quincy, Mass., Dec. 23, 1948; s. Frank John and Louise Theresa (Frattasio) S. BSBA, Boston U., 1970; MEd, U. Mass., 1971; MBA, Boston Coll., 1973; EdD, Boston U., 1976. Cert. systems profl. Asst. prof. S.E. Mass. U., N Dartsmouth, 1974-78, U. Mass., 1978-84; assoc. prof. Simmons Coll., Boston, 1984-86; dir. Saluti Assocs., Boston, 1978—; cons. Putnam Investor Services, Boston, 1987, Bank Of Boston, 1987—, Shawmut Bank, 1986-87, State St. Bank, Boston, 1987. Contbr. numerous articles to profl. jours. Dir. Boy Scouts of Am./Blue Granite, Boston, 1988, Sons of Italy/Rennaissance Lodge, Boston, 1988; mem. Gov.'s Small Bus. Adv. Com., Boston, 1987, Greater Boston Childcare Study Com., 1988. Served as major U.S. Army, 1970—. Recipient of Official Citation award Mass. House Reps., 1983, Official Citation award Mass. Gov. Dukakis, 1985, Most Valuable Prof. award Student Govt. Assn. U. Mass., 1979, Chapter Pres.'s award AFSM Minuteman chpt., 1987. Mem. Am. Prodn. and Inventory Control Soc. (dir. 1986—), Assn. Systems Mgmt. (dir. 1986—), Assn. Field Service Mgrs. (dir. 1986—), Data Processing Mgmt. Assn., Am. Arbitration Assn., Ancient and Honorables Arty., 1st Corps of Cadets. Roman Catholic. Clubs: Sky (Boston), Army Officers. Lodges: Renaissance, Sons of Italy (dir. 1988). Office: Saluti Assocs 15 Court Sq Ste 340 Boston MA 02108

SALVANESCHI, LUIGI, real estate and construction executive; b. Casale, Italy, 1929; arrived in U.S., 1959; s. Ernesto and Carolina (Bassignana) S.; m. Lenore M. Rickels, Aug. 20, 1958; 1 child, Margherita Lina. Classical Maturity, Valsalice, Torino, Italy, 1950; PhD, Vatican U., Rome, 1958; cert. in real estate, UCLA, 1965. Restaurant mgr. McDonalds Co., Chgo., 1959-61; restaurant mgr. McDonalds Co., Los Angeles, 1961-63, real estate mgr., 1964-68; v.p. real estate McDonalds Co., Oakbrook, Ill., 1969-83; sr. v.p. real estate and constrn. Kentucky Fried Chicken, Louisville, 1983-88; exec. v.p. Blockbuster Entertainment, Ft. Lauderdale, Fla., 1988—; adj. prof. U. Louisville. Served as 2d lt. in Italian Infantry, 1945-46, ETO. Named Colonel of the Commonwealth of Ky., 1984. Mem. Nat. Assn. Real Estate Execs. (co-founder, bd. dirs.). Roman Catholic. Home: 6803 Shadwell Pl Prospect KY 40059 Office: Ky Fried Chicken Corp PO Box 32070 Bishops Ln Louisville KY 40232

SALVATORE, RICHARD JOHN, cinematographer, company executive; b. Bklyn., May 25, 1950; s. Peter Louis and Julia (Stampano) S. AA, Los Angeles Valley Coll., 1972. Artist George Whiteman & Assocs., Hollywood, Calif., 1968-72; ind. cinematographer Hollywood, 1976—; tchr. Am. Film Inst., Beverly Hills, Calif., 1984—, Producers Assn., Hollywood, 1975—; chief exec. officer Omnicom Systems, Canoga Park, Calif., 1981—; bd. dirs. and cinematographer Davidson Design Prodns., San Diego, 1986—. Photographer: Solace, 1968 (Memorable mention Los Angeles County Fair 1968), Night Wind Dragon, 1972. Pres. Robert F. Kennedy campaign com., Los Angeles, 1967, Gun Control Act of 1968, Los Angeles; dist. leader/area leader Muscular Dystrophy Assn., Los Angeles County, 1966-70. Recipient fin. grant U. Calif., 1972. Mem. Soc. Operating Cameramen (assoc.), Acad. TV Arts and Scis. (assoc.).

SALVATORI, VINCENT LOUIS, corporate executive; b. Phila., Apr. 22, 1932; s. Louis and Lydia (Tofani) S.; children: Leslie Ann, Robert Louis, Sandra Ann. BA, Temple U., 1954; BSEE, Pa. State U., 1958. Registered profl. engr., Pa., Va. Dept. head Radiation Systems, Inc., McLean, Va., 1966-68; founder, v.p. Quest Rsch. Corp., McLean, Va., 1968-80; exec. v.p. QuesTech, Inc., McLean, Va., 1980-88; pres., chief exec. officer QuesTech, Inc., Falls Church, Va., 1988—, also bd. dirs.; bd. dirs. Engring. Resources Inc., QuesTech Ventures, Inc., QuesTech N.Am. Ltd., Dynamic Engring. Inc., Profl. Svcs. Coun.; mem. adv. bd. THe Entrepreneurship Inst. Author: Investigations into Microwave Multipath Interferometer, 1959,Investigation of Luxembourg Effect Utilizing Cubic Function Solid State Devices, 1960, Factors Influencing Communications with Satellites, 1959. Pres. PTA, Springhill Sch., Fairfax County, Va., 1973. Sgt. USAF, 1948-52. Mem. IEEE, Assn. of Old Crows, AIAA, Am. Def. Preparedness Assn., Armed Forces Communications & Electronics Assn., Profl. Svcs. Coun., Am. Mgmt. Assn., Security Affairs Support Assn., AAAS, Annaplois Yacht Club, Chesapeake Bay Racing Assn. (chmn. bd. dirs. 1984-85). Office: QuesTech Inc 7600-A Leesburg Pike Falls Church VA 22043

SALVATTI, WAYNE A., public relations and marketing executive; b. Los Angeles, Dec. 8, 1956; s. Keith Wayne and Eleanor Mary Salvatti. AA in Bus. Adminstrn., Rio Hondo Coll., 1986; BA in Pub. Rels., UCLA, 1986. Gen. mgr. Gen. Dynamics Co., Pomona, Calif., 1980-81; v.p. Enhance Pub. Relations and Mktg., Monterey Park, Calif., 1981—; cons. U.S. Olympics, Los Angeles, 1984, World Entertainment Network, Los Angeles Gear Athletic, 1986, Los Angeles Marathon, 1987. Author: Sexual Harassment in Business, 1984, The Max Marketing Approach, 1986. Spokesperson Just Say No for Am. Campaign, Los Angeles, 1986, Rep. com. Los Angeles, 1987; bd. dirs. San Marino Hist. Soc. Mem. Pub. Relations Soc. Am., Am. Soc. Advt. & Promoting, Am. Mktg. Assn., Hollywood Radio and TV Soc., L.A. Publicity Club, L.A. Press Club. Office: Enhance Pub Rels and Mktg 600 Villa Monte Monterey Park CA 91754

SALVESON, MELVIN ERWIN, business executive, educator; b. Brea, Calif., Jan. 16, 1919; s. John T. and Elizabeth (Green) S.; m. Joan Y. Stipek, Aug. 22, 1944; children: Eric C., Kent Erwin. B.S., U. Calif. at Berkeley, 1941; M.S., Mass. Inst. Tech., 1947; Ph.D., U. Chgo., 1952. Cons. McKinsey & Co., N.Y.C., 1948-49; asst. prof., dir. mgmt. sci. research U. Calif. at Los Angeles, 1949-54; mgr. advanced data systems Gen. Electric Co., Louisville and N.Y.C., 1954-57; pres. Mgmt. Scis. Corp., Los Angeles, 1957-67; group v.p. Control Data/CEIR, Inc., 1967-68; pres. Electronic Currency Corp., 1968—; chmn. OneCard Internat., Inc., 1983—; bd. dirs. OneCard Internat. Inc., Diversified Earth Scis., Inc., Algeran, Inc., Electronic Currency Corp.; founder Master Card System, Los Angeles, 1966; chmn. Corporate Strategies Internat.; prof. bus. Pepperdine U. 1972-85; adj. prof. U. So. Calif.; adviser data processing City of Los Angeles, 1962-64; futures forecasting IBM, 1957-61; adviser strategic systems planning USAF, 1961-67; info. systems Calif. Dept. Human Resources, 1972-73, City Los Angeles Automated Urban Data Base, 1962-67; tech. transfer NASA, 1965-70, others; mem. bd. trustees, Long Beach City Coll. Contbr. articles to profl. jours. Served to lt. comdr. USNR, 1941-46. Named to Long Beach City Coll. Hall of Fame. Fellow AAAS; mem. Inst. Mgmt. Sci. (founder, past pres.). Republican. Club: Founders (Los Angeles Philharmonic Orch.), Calif. Yacht. Home: 1577 N Bundy Dr Los Angeles CA 90049

SALYER, MARCY T. ROGERS, foundation administrator, marketing consultant; b. Passaic, N.J., Aug. 15, 1951; d. Bart Michael and Phyllis Marie (White) Rogers; m. Kenneth Everett Salyer, May. 1, 1983. BA, Mary

Washington Coll., 1973; postgrad., U. Va., 1975-76. Coord., counselor U. Va. Dept. Plastic Surgery, Charlottesville, Va., 1974-78; coord., counselor div. plastic surgery City of Dallas, 1976-78; adminstrv. asst. K.E. Salyer, M.D. & Assocs., Dallas, 1978-88, Tex. Craniofacial Ctr., Dallas, 1984-88; pres. Nat. Craniofacial Found., Dallas, 1984-88; mem. founder Craniofacial Deformities Guild, Dallas, 1985—; ex officio bd. dirs. Humana Advanced Surg. Insts. Active March of Dimes Aux., 1985—. Mem. Am. Cleft Palate Assn., Plastic Surgery Adminstrn. Assn., Internat. Craniomaxillofacial Soc., Nat. Soc. Fund Raising Execs.

SALZANO, EDWARD P., food company executive; b. Bklyn., Apr. 9, 1947; s. Edward F. and Carmela Salzano; m. Evelyn Mulinaro; children: Danielle, Noelle, Jocelyn. BS in Indsl. Engring., NYU, 1973. Salesman Bulkley Dunton Linde Lathrop, Inc., N.Y.C., 1966, asst. dir. splty. products, 1969-70, dir. disposable products, 1970-72; pres., chief exec. officer Bell Beer & Ice Distbrs., Inc., Little Neck, N.Y., 1976-79, Auburndale Beer & Ice Distbrs., Inc., Flushing, N.Y., 1972-79; pres., chief operating officer Francesco Rinaldi Food Co., Bklyn., 1979-82; exec. v.p. Omni Continental, Inc., Ft. Lee, N.J., 1979-82; v.p. Cantisano Foods, Inc., Rochester, N.Y., 1982—; pres. Francesco Rinaldi div., Fort Lee, N.J., 1985—. Mem. Italian-Am. C. of C. (dir.), Pres. Assn., Am. Mgmt. Assn.. Roman Catholic. Clubs: NYU, Westwood Racquet. Home: 197 Graney Dr River Vale NJ 07675 Office: 1605 John St Fort Lee NJ 07024

SALZMAN, DAVID ELLIOT, entertainment industry executive; b. Bklyn., Dec. 1, 1943; s. Benjamin and Rose Harriet (Touby) S.; m. Sonia Camelia Gonsalves, Oct. 19, 1968; children: Daniel Mark, Andrea Jessica, Adam Gabriel. B.A., Bklyn. Coll., 1965; M.A., Wayne State U., 1967. Dir. TV ops. Wayne State U., 1966-67; producer Lou Gordon Program, 1967-70; program mgr. Sta. WKBD-TV, Detroit, 1970-71, Sta. KDKA-TV, Pitts., 1971-72; gen. mgr. Sta. KDKA-TV, 1973-75; program mgr. Sta. KYW-TV, Phila., 1972-73; chmn. bd. Group W Prodns., N.Y.C and Los Angeles, 1975—; founder, pres. United Software Assocs., 1980-81; creator News Info. Weekly Service, 1981; exec. v.p. Telepictures Corp., from 1980; now pres. Lorimar Telepictures Corp.; pres. Lorimar TV, 1985—; creator Newscope: Nat. TV News Cooperative, 1983; guest lectr. at schs.; bd. govs. Films of Coll. and Univ. Students. Contbr.: articles to Variety and; numerous communications trade publs. Bd. dirs. Pitts. Civic Light Opera, Am. Blood Bank, Pitts., Hebrew Inst., Jewish Community Center, Harrison, N.Y., Temple Etz Chaim. Recipient award Detroit chpt. Am. Women in Radio and TV, 1969, award Golden Quill, 1971, award Golden Gavel, 1971, local Emmy award, 1972, award AP, 1974, Gold medal Broadcast Promotion Assn., 1983; BPME Gold medal San Francisco Film Festival, 1984, N.Y., 1985, Chgo., 1986, Tree of Life award Jewish Nat. Fund., 1988. Mem. Acad. TV Arts and Scis., Nat. Assn. TV Program Execs., Radio-TV News Dirs. Assn., Am. Mgmt. Assn., Am. Film Inst. Office: Lorimar Telepictures Corp 10202 W Washington Blvd Culver City CA 90232 *

SALZMAN, MARILYN B. WOLFSON, service company executive; b. Chgo., Dec. 25, 1943; d. Joseph and Sera (Krol) Wolfson; 1 son, Lawrence Todd. Student, U. Ill., Barat Coll., Lake Forest, Ill., 1961-64. Adminstrv. project asst. Sci. Research Assocs., Chgo., 1964-70; reporter Suburban Trib of Chgo. Tribune, 1979-80; pres. MWS Assocs., Los Angeles and Fullerton, Calif., 1980—; exec. adminstrv. dir. Crystal Tips of No. Ill., Inc., 1980-83; dir. adminstrn. Ice Dispensers, Inc., 1981-83, Sani-Serv of Ill., Inc., 1981-83; adminstrv. and organizational cons. 1140 Corp., 1980-83; adminstrv. dir. Iceman's Ico Co., Inc., 1980-83; founder, moderator DWC Workshops, 1984; mgr. support svcs., data processing Florence Crittenton Svcs. Orange County 1984—; panelist computers in residential treatment Child Welfare League Am. Biennial Conf. Workshop, 1986. Active Friends of Fullerton Library, Boy Scouts Am.; panelist Child Welfare League Am., Bienniel Conf. Workshop. Mem. Mgmt. Forum, Women's Am. ORT. Contbr. articles to newspapers and indsl. jours. Home: 1112 N Ferndale Dr Fullerton CA 92631

SAMARTINI, JAMES ROGERS, appliance company executive; b. Cleve., Apr. 13, 1935; s. Leonard Henry and Grace Rogers (Tully) S.; m. Irene Ann Kurnava, Sept. 16, 1961; children: David L., James F., Patrick R. A.B., Dartmouth Coll., 1957; M.B.A., Harvard U., 1961. Fin. supr. Ford Motor Co., Dearborn, Mich., 1966-72; v.p. fin. and adminstrn. Thonet Industries Inc., York, Pa., 1972-74; asst. controller Mead Corp., Dayton, 1974-78, assoc. treas., 1974-78, 1978-79, v.p. fin. resources, 1982-84, v.p., chief fin. officer, 1985-86; exec. v.p., chief fin. officer Whirlpool Corp., Benton Harbor, Mich., 1986—, also bd. dirs.; bd. dirs. Peoples State Bank, St. Joseph, Mich. Trustee Dayton Opera Assn., 1977-86, pres., 1985-86; adv. bd. Salvation Army; bd. dirs. Epilepsy Assn. Western Ohio, 1986. Mem. Fin. Execs. Inst. (dir. 1983-86). Home: 1315 Lake Blvd Saint Joseph MI 49085 Office: Whirlpool Corp 2000 M-63 Benton Harbor MI 49022

SAMEK, EDWARD LASKER, service company executive; b. N.Y.C., Oct. 26, 1936; s. Richard E. and Jane L. Samek; B.S. in Commerce and Fin., Bucknell U., 1958; M.B.A., Columbia U., 1960; m. Marthann Lauver, June 26, 1960; children—Anne, Margaret, Elizabeth. Brand mgr. Procter & Gamble Co., Cin., 1960-62; dir. New products Johnson & Johnson, New Brunswick, N.J., 1962-67; v.p., gen. mgr. Avon Products Inc., N.Y.C., 1967-75; pres., chief exec. officer Childcraft Edn. Corp., Edison, N.J., 1975-78, also dir.; pres. Hudson Pharm. Corp., W. Caldwell, N.J., 1978-82; chmn. bd., pres. Secrephone Ltd., Jenkintown, Pa., various locations, 1982—; bd. dirs. A. Gary Shilling & Co., Inc. Pres. bd. trustees Hartridge Sch., Plainfield, N.J., 1969-76; v.p. bd. trustees Wardlaw-Hartridge Sch., Plainfield and Edison, 1975—; trustee, v.p. bd. Plainfield Symphony, 1976—. Served with Ordnance Corps, U.S. Army, 1958-59. Mem. Young Pres.'s Orgn. Clubs: Williams, Metuchen (N.J.) Golf and Country, World Bus. Council. Home: 1717 Woodland Ave Edison NJ 08820

SAMETZ, DR. ARNOLD WILLIAM, financial educator; b. Bklyn., Dec. 4, 1919; s. Milton William and Natalie (Holland) S.; B.A., Bklyn. Coll., 1940; M.A., Princeton U., 1942, Ph.D., 1951; m. Agnes Baroth, Nov. 23, 1956; children—Margaret Rutherford, Laura. Instr., Princeton U., 1948-51, asst. prof. econs., 1951-57; assoc. prof. banking and finance NYU, N.Y.C., 1957-62, prof. finance Grad. Sch. Bus. Adminstrn. and dir. Salomon Bros. Center for Study Fin. Instns., 1975—, Charles Simon and Sidney Homer dir., 1981—; trustee Am. Savs. Bank; econ. cons.; editor Studies in Banking and Fin. Served to lt. USN, 1942-46. Mem. Am. Econ. Assn., Am. Fin. Assn., Royal Econ. Soc. Author: Prospects for Capital Formation and Capital Markets, 1978; Securities Activities of Commercial Banks, 1981; The Emerging Financial Industry, 1984; The New Financial Environment of the U.S., 1986. Office: NYU Salomon Bros Ctr for Study of Fin Inst 90 Trinity Pl New York NY 10006

SAMORS, NEAL S., marketing executive; b. Chgo., July 10, 1943; s. Joseph and Bernette (Schulman) S.; m. Frieda Anschel, May 25, 1969; 1 child, Jennifer Laura. BS, U. Wis., 1965; MA, No. Ill. U., 1967; PhD, Northwestern U., 1979. Lectr. polit. sci. Loyola U., Chgo., 1967-69; instr. polit. sci. Barat Coll., Lake Forest, Ill., 1969-74; profl. assoc. Ednl. Testing Service, Evanston, Ill., 1974-80, asst. dir., 1980-84, sr. field mktg. rep., 1984-88, asst. dir. field mktg., 1989—; cons. and evaluator Alverno Coll., Milw., 1978-81, Madonna Coll., Livonia, Mich., 1978-81, Coll. St. Scholastica, Duluth, Minn., 1980-81. Researcher Stevenson for Sen., Chgo., 1970. Ford Found. fellow, 1967. Mem. Phi Delta Kappa (research v.p. Northwestern chpt. 1980). Home: 282 Stanton Dr Buffalo Grove IL 60089 Office: Ednl Testing Svc One Rotary Ctr St 300 1560 Sherman Ave Evanston IL 60201

SAMPER, JOSEPH PHILLIP, photographic products company executive; b. Salt Lake City, Aug. 13, 1934; s. Juan M. and Harriet (Howell) S.; m. Barbara Fleming, June 15, 1957; children—Joaquin P., Christopher F. With Eastman Kodak Co., Rochester, N.Y., 1961—; asst. to gen. mgr. mktg. div. Eastman Kodak Co. (U.S. and Can. photog. div.), 1976-77, asst. v.p., asst. gen. mgr. mktg. div., 1977-79; v.p., gen. mgr. mktg. div. Eastman Kodak Co., 1979—, exec. v.p., gen. mgr. photgraphic div., 1983-86, vice chmn., exec. officer, 1986—; bd. dirs. Armstrong World Industries, Inc., Lancaster, Pa., Marine Midland Bank, N.A., Rochester region. Trustee St. John Fisher Coll., Rochester. Served with USNR, 1952-56. Recipient Alfred Knight award Am. Grad. Sch. Internat. Mgmt., 1961, Barton Kyle Young award, 1961; Sloan fellow, 1972-73. Mem. Photo Mktg. Assn., Rochester C. of C. Roman Catholic. Club: Oak Hill Country (Rochester). Office: Eastman Kodak Co 343 State St Rochester NY 14650 *

SAMPSELL, ROBERT BRUCE, toy company executive; b. Evanston, Ill., July 22, 1941; s. David Sylvester and Harriet Corson (Fenner) S.; m. Bonnie Louise McClelland, June 26, 1965. B.S., Yale U., 1963; M.B.A., Harvard U., 1965. Plant mgmt. Procter & Gamble Co., Chgo., 1965-69; with Quaker Oats Co., Chgo., 1969—; pres. chems. div. Quaker Oats Co., 1978-81; v.p. U.S. Grocery Products Research and Devel., Barrington, Ill., 1980-83; pres. Fisher-Price div., East Aurora, N.Y., 1983—; dir. M&T Bank, Buffalo, 1984—; bd. dirs. First Empire State Corp., First Ops. Resource, Inc. Bd. dirs. Indian Creek Nature Center, Cedar Rapids, Iowa, 1973-76, pres., 1975-76; trustee Mercy Hosp., Cedar Rapids, 1973-76, Mt. Mercy Coll., 1975-83; bd. dirs. Cedar Rapids Symphony, 1973-76, Greater Buffalo Devel. Found., 1983—, Buffalo State Coll. Found., 1985; bd. dirs. Planned Parenthood Chgo. Area, 1980-83, Buffalo and Erie County, 1984—. Mem. Toy Mfrs. Am. (bd. dirs. 1984—), Buffalo C. of C. (1984—). Home: 324 Rivermist Dr Buffalo NY 14202 Office: Fisher-Price 636 Girard Ave East Aurora NY 14052 *

SAMSELL, LEWIS PATRICK, municipal finance executive; b. Morgantown, Va., Feb. 20, 1943; s. Lewis Hildreth and Harriet Elizabeth (Gidley) S.; m. Linda Joyce Hewitt, July19, 1967. BSBA in Acctg., W.Va. U., 1970; MBA in Acctg., George Washington U., 1975. CPA, V.I.; cert. mgmt. acct. Auditor GAO, Washington, 1971-79, Office of the U.S. Govt. Controller, St. Thomas, V.I., 1979-82; fin. officer City of Merced, Calif., 1982-86; dir. fin. City of Stockton, Calif., 1986—; mem. state controllers task force on single audit, Calif. CAP Composite Squadron 147 Sr. Programs Oficer, Merced, 1985. Served with USN, 1964-67. Recipient Cert. of Achievement Service Corps of Retired Execs., St. Thomas, 1982. Mem. Calif. Soc. Mcpl. Fin. Officers (profl. and tech. standards com. 1983—), Govt. Fin. Officers Assn., Nat. Assn. Accts. (pres. MPG chpt., 1979), Calif. Mcpl. Treas. Assn., Am. Mgmt. Assn. Lodges: Kiwanis, Elks. Office: City of Stockton 425 N El Dorado St Stockton CA 95202

SAMUEL, ROBERT ALLEN, banker; b. Alexandria, Va., Oct. 15, 1949; s. Allen T. and Mildred (Fare) S.; m. Betty Tiffany, May 24, 1975; children: Justin Ryan, Taylor Allen. BS, High Point Coll., 1971; MBA, George Mason U., 1978. Cert. fin. planner. With Am. Security Bank NA, Washington, 1971-78, 81—, asst. v.p., complaince officer, 1981-86, v.p. consumer credit, 1986—; asst. v.p. open end credit 1st Am. Bank NA, Washington, 1978-81. Treas. Mt. Vernon Youth Athletic Assn., 1988. Mem. Internat. Credit Assn. (bd. dir. Washington chpt. 1988), Inst. Cert. Fin. Planners. Republican. Methodist. Office: Am Security Bank NA 1501 Pennsylvania Ave NW Washington DC 20013

SAMUELIAN, MARK GEORGE, marketing professional; b. Boston, Dec. 28, 1963; s. Samuel and Florence (Derderian) S. BS in Indsl. Engring., Ga. Inst. Tech., 1985; postgrad., U. Pa., 1988—. Field sales rep. Morse Indsl. Corp. subs. Emerson Electric Co., Detroit, 1985-88. Mem. media rels. staff gubernatorial campaign, Detroit, 1986. Recipient Master title U.S. Chess Fedn., 1981. Mem. Am. Mktg. Assn. (assoc.); Assn. MBA Execs. Republican. Home: PO Box 0145 3650 Chestnut St Philadelphia PA 19104-6107

SAMUELS, JAMES P., manufacturing executive; b. Lowell, Mass., Mar. 5, 1947; s. Walter F. and Marion F. (Gilligan) S.; m. Cheryl L. Harper; 1 child: Jonathan E. BSBA, Lowell Tech. Inst., 1970; cert. lang., Goethe Inst., Munich, 1971; MBA, Suffolk U., 1972; cert. mktg., Harvard U., Vevey, Switzerland, 1984. Mgr., also bd. dirs. Bowmar Co., Wiesbaden, Fed. Republic of Germany, 1974; plant controller, asst. div. controller Fram Corp., Providence, 1975-79, dir. market research and planning, 1979-81; dir. mgmt. cons. Worldwide Automotive div. Bendix Corp., 1981-83; dir. strategic planning and mktg. Purolator Products, Inc., Rahway, N.J., 1983-85; pres. Purolator Products, Ltd., Mississauga, Ont., Can., 1985—, Facet of Canada Inc. holding co. Facet Enterprises Inc. div. Penzoil Corp., Mississauga, Houston and Tulsa, 1988. Office: Facet of Canada Inc, 1180 Lakeshore Rd E, Mississauga, ON Canada L5E 3B7

SAMUELS, LESLIE EUGENE, marketing and management consultant; b. St. Croix, V.I., Nov. 12, 1929; s. Henry Francis and Annamartha Venetia (Ford) S.; m. Reather James, Oct. 24, 1959; children: Leslie Jr., Venetia, Yvette, Philip. MusB, NYU, 1956; JD, Blackstone Sch. Law, 1975; MBA, Columbia Pacific U., 1984, PhD, 1985. Concert soloist Van Dyke Studios, N.Y.C., 1956-65; dir. Housing, Preservation and Devel., N.Y.C., 1966—; bandmaster N.Y. State Dept. Rehab. and Recreation, N.Y.C., 1967-76; pres., chief exec. officer Samuels and Co., Inc., N.Y.C., 1986—; cons. in field, 1984—; mem. N.Y., N.J. Minority Purchasing Coun., Inc., Nat. Minority Bus. Coun., Inc., Internat. Trade div. Mem. Bronx County Com., N.Y., 1969; dist. leader Bronx 86th Assembly Dist., 1969; advisor Astor Home for Children, Bronx, 1973, Bronxville C. of C., Bklyn., 1975; mem. Smithsonian Assocs. Served with U.S. Army, 1951-53. Mem. Nat. Black MBA Assn., Am. Mgmt. Assn., Harvard Bus. Review, Sloan Mgmt. Review, Calif. Mgmt. Rev., Columbia Pacific U. Alumni Assn. Democrat. Club: Ind. Citizen's (Bronx) (pres. 1967-77). Home: 2814 Bruner Ave Bronx NY 10469

SAMUELS, ROBERT T., supermarket chain executive; b. 1934. Student, Case Western Res. U. Pres. M.H. Hausman Co., 1978; sr. v.p. corp. mgmt. First Nat. Supermarkets Inc., Cleve., 1978-79, sr. v.p. adminstrn., 1979-81; sr. v.p., pres. Eastern div. First Nat. Supermarkets Inc., 1981; then exec. v.p., pres. Eastern div. First Nat. Supermarkets Inc., Cleve.; now corp. pres., chief operating officer Maple Heights, Ohio; also dir. Office: First Nat Supermarkets Inc 17000 Rockside Rd Cleveland OH 44137 *

SAMUELS, ROBERT WALTER, chemical corporation executive; b. Bklyn., Dec. 21, 1929; s. Alexander and Henrietta (Dietzel) S.; m. Audrey Jane Fitzgerald, July 3, 1954; children: Barbara, Carol, Joanne. B.A., St. Lawrence U., 1951; M.B.A., NYU, 1959. Fin. analyst W.R. Grace & Co., N.Y.C., 1951-60; mgr. fin. analysis Dewey & Almy div. Grace, Cambridge, Mass., 1960-63, treas., 1963-65, v.p. fin., 1965-69; pres. Polyfibron div. Grace, Lexington, Mass., 1969-82; sr. v.p. W.R. Grace & Co., N.Y.C., 1982-84, exec. v.p., 1984-87, also bd. dirs.; pres. Grace Specialty Chem. Co., N.Y.C., 1987—. Trustee St. Lawrence U., Canton, N.Y., 1982—; bd. dirs. Nat. Spinal Cord Injury Assn., Newton Lower Falls, Mass., 1978—. Congregationalist. Club: Princeton (N.Y.C.) (assoc.); Woods Hole Golf; Morrings of Vero Beach (Fla.). Home: 144 Birch Ln PO Box 826 North Falmouth MA 02556 Office: W R Grace & Co 1114 Ave of the Americas New York NY 10036 *

SAMUELS, SUSAN JILL, lawyer; b. Madison, Wis., July 2, 1957; d. Warren Joseph and Sylvia Joan (Strake) S. BA, U. Mich., 1982; JD magna cum laude, Yeshiva U., 1986. Bar: N.Y. 1987. Atty. Skadden, Arps, Slate, Meagher & Flom, N.Y.C., 1986—. Mem. ABA. Home: 162-01 Powells Cove Blvd Beechhurst NY 11357 Office: Skadden Arps Slate Meagher & Flom 919 3d Ave New York NY 10022

SAMUELSON, BARBARA SHALITA, securities company manager; b. N.Y.C., Apr. 8, 1943; d. Harry and Celia Shalita; m. John Samuelson, Feb. 27, 1966; children: Charles Aaron, Richard Adam. AB, Wheaton Coll., 1964; MBA, NYU, 1967. Feature editor Investment Dealers' Digest, N.Y.C., 1965-67; fin. writer Barron's, 1967-77; sr. editor Merrill Lynch, Pierce, Fenner & Smith, Inc., N.Y.C., 1977-79, dir. investor relations Merrill Lynch & Co., Inc., 1979-87, dir. corp. and fin. services, 1987—. Mem. N.Y. Soc. Security Analysts, Fin. Women's Assn., Nat. Investor Relations Inst. Office: 165 Broadway New York NY 10080

SAMUELSON, ERIC CARL, financial planner, investment adviser; b. Saffle, Sweden, May 18, 1958; came to U.S., 1958; s. Armin O. and A. Ellen (Banman) S.; m. Julie Kaye Nicholson, Sept. 27, 1986; 1 child, Erin N. BBA in Acctg. and Fin., Kans. State U., 1982, BS in Econs., 1988. CPA, Kans., Mo. Sr. auditor Price Waterhouse, Kansas City, Mo., 1982-85; assoc. planner Fin. Designs, Inc., Overland Park, Kans., 1985-86; v.p. Neill and Assocs., Kansas City, 1986—. Bd. dirs. Nall Ave. Ch. of Nazarene, Prairie Village, Kans., 1987—. Mem. Am. Inst. CPA's, Inst. Cert. Fin. Planners. Home: 5721 Walmer St Mission KS 66202 Office: Neill and Assocs PO Box 13423 Kansas City MO 64199

SAMUELSON, KENNETH LEE, lawyer; b. Natrona Heights, Pa., Aug. 22, 1946; s. Sam Abraham and Frances Bernice (Robbins) S.; m. Marlene Ina Rabinowitz, Jan. 1, 1980; children: Heather, Cheryl. BA magna cum laude, U. Pitts., 1968; JD, U. Mich., 1971. Bar: Md. 1972, D.C. 1980, U.S. Dist. Ct. Md. Trial Bar 1984. Assoc. Weinberg & Green, Balt., 1971-73; assoc. Dickerson, Nice, Sokol & Horn, Balt., 1973; asst. atty. gen. State of Md., 1973-77; pvt. practice, Balt., 1978; ptnr. Linowes and Blocher, Silver Spring, Md. and Washington, 1979—. Author in field. Second v.p., bd. dirs. D.C. Assn. for Retarded Citizens, Inc., 1981—. Capt. U.S. Army, to 1976. Mem. ABA (vice-chmn. comml. leasing com., sect. real property, probate and trust law 1988—), D.C. Bar (comml. real estate com., chmn. subcom.legal opinions 1987—), Md. State Bar Assn. (real property, planning and zoning sect., chmn. environ. subcom. legal opinions project, 1987—, litigation sect. 1982-84, chmn. comml. trans. com., speaker Md. Inst. Continuing Profl. Edn. Lawyers, 1989; speaker environ. considerations in real estate transactions, 1988, speaker on retail leasing, 1989, moderator programs before ABA on comml. leases, 1987, 88, Internat. Council Shopping Ctrs. U., 1988; speaker before D.C. Bar program on lawyer's opinion letters in real estate transactions, 1987), Montgomery County Bar Assn. (judicial selections com. 1988—), Phi Beta Kappa. Office: Linowes and Blocher PO Box 8728 Silver Spring MD 20907

SAMUELSON, PAUL ANTHONY, economics educator; b. Gary, Ind., May 15, 1915; s. Frank and Ella (Lipton) S.; m. Marion E. Crawford, July 2, 1938 (dec.); children: Jane Kendall, Margaret Wray, William Frank, Robert James, John Crawford, Paul Reid.; m. Risha Eckaus, 1981. B.S., U. Chgo., 1935; M.A., Harvard U., 1936, Ph.D. (David A. Wells prize 1941), 1941; LL.D., U. Chgo., Oberlin Coll., 1961, Boston Coll., 1964, Ind. U., 1966, U. Mich., 1967, Claremont Grad. Sch., 1970, U. N.H., 1971, Keio U., 1971, Widener Coll., 1982, Cath. U. at Riva Aguero U., Lima, Peru, 1980; D.Sc., East Anglia U., Norwich, Eng., 1966; D.Litt. (hon.), Ripon Coll., 1962, No. Mich. U., 1973; L.H.D., Seton Hall Coll., 1971, Williams Coll., 1971; D.Sc., U. Mass., 1972, U. R.I., 1972; LL.D., Harvard, 1972, Gustavus Adolphus Coll., 1974, U. So. Calif., 1975, U. Pa., 1976, U. Rochester, 1976, Emmanuel Coll., 1977, Stonehill Coll., 1978, Widener Coll., 1982; Doctorate Honoris Causa, U. Catholique de Louvain, Belgium, 1976, City U., London, 1980, New U. Lisbon, 1985; DLitt., Valparaiso U., 1987; DLitt, Columbia U, 1988; DSc, Tufts U., 1988; Doctor Honoris Causa, Univ. Nat. de Educacion a Distancia, Madrid, 1989. Prof. econs. MIT, 1940—, inst. prof., 1966, prof. emeritus, Gordon Y. Billard fellow, 1986—; mem. staff Radiation Lab., 1944-45; prof. internat. econ. relations Fletcher Sch. Law and Diplomacy, 1945; cons. Nat. Resources Planning Bd., 1941-43, WPB, 1945, U.S. Treasury, 1945-52, 61—, Bur. Budget, 1952, RAND Corp., 1948-75, Fed. Res. Bd., 1965—; council Econ. Advisers, 1960—; econ. adviser to Pres. Kennedy; sr. adviser Brookings Panel on Econ. Activity; mem. spl. commn. on social scis. NSF, 1967—; cons. int Econ. Council, Congl. Budget Office; Inst. prof., Inst. prof. emeritus, Gordon Y Billard Fellow MIT, Boston, 1986—; vis. prof of polit. econ. Ctr. Japan-U.S. Bus. and Econ. Studies, NYU, 1987—; Stamp Meml. lectr., London, 1961, Wicksell lectr., Stockholm, 1962, Franklin lectr., Detroit, 1962; Hoyt vis. fellow Calhoun Coll., Yale, 1962; Carnegie Found. reflective year, 1965-66; John von Neumann lectr. U. Wis., 1971; Gerhard Colm Meml. lectr. New Sch. for Social Research, N.Y.C., 1971; Davidson lectr. U. N.H., 1971; Sulzbacher Meml. lectr. Columbia Law Sch., N.Y.C., 1974; J. Willard Gibbs lectr. Am. Math. Soc., San Francisco, 1974; John Diebold lectr. Harvard, 1976; Horowitz lectr. Jerusalem and Tel Aviv, 1984; lectr. Harvard 350 Symposium, Harvard U., 1986; Vernon F. Taylor vis. disting. prof. Trinity U., San Antonio, Tex., 1989; Olin lectr. U. Va. Law Sch., 1989, many other lectureships; acad. cons. Fed. Reserve Bd. Author: Foundations of Economic Analysis, 1947, enlarged edit., 1983, Economics, 1948-85, Readings in Economics, 1955, 13th edit., 1989 (with R. Dorfman and R.M. Solow) Linear Programming and Economic Analysis, 1958, Collected Scientific Papers, 5 vols., 1966, 72, 78, 86; co-author numerous other books.; Contbr. numerous articles to profl. jours.; Columnist for, Newsweek, 1966-81; assoc. editor: Jour. Pub. Econs., Jour. Internat. Econs., Jour. Fin. Econs., Jour. Nonlinear Analysis; adv. bd. Challenge Mag.; editorial bd. Proceedings Nat. Acad. Scis. Chmn. Pres.'s Task Force Maintaining Am. Prosperity, 1964; mem. Nat. Task Force on Econ. Edn., 1960-61; econ. adviser to Pres. John F. Kennedy, 1959-63; mem. adv. bd. Nat. Commn. Money and Credit, 1958-60. Hon. fellow London Sch. Econs. and Polit. Sci. Guggenheim fellow, 1948-49; Ford Found. research fellow, 1958-59; recipient John Bates Clark medal Am. Econ. Assn., 1947, Alfred Nobel Meml. prize in econ. sci., 1970, Medal of Honor U. Evansville, Ill., 1970, Albert Einstein Commemorative award, 1971, Alumni medal U. Chgo., 1983, Britannica award, 1989. Fellow Brit. Acad. (corr.), Am. Philos. Soc., Econometric Soc. (v.p. 1950, pres. 1951), Am. Econ. Assn. (hon.; pres. 1961); mem. Com. Econ. Devel. (commn. on nat. goals, research adv. bd. 1959-60), Am. Acad. Arts and Scis., Internat. Econ. Assn. (pres. 1966-68, hon. pres.), Nat. Acad. Scis., Leibniz-Akademie der Wissenschaften und der Literatur (corr. mem. 1987—) Nat. Assn. of Investment Clubs (disting. Svc. award in Investment Edn. 1974), Phi Beta Kappa, Omicron Delta Kappa (trustee), Omicron Delta Epsilon (trustee). Home: 75 Clairemont Rd Belmont MA 02178 Office: MIT Dept Econs Cambridge MA 02139

SAMUELSON, RANDALL ALBERT, mortgage company executive; b. Eau Claire, Wis., June 28, 1957; s. Robert Lee and Tina (Fedele) S. Student, St. Louis Community Coll., 1975-78, U. Mo., 1986. Collection clk. Gen. Bancshares Corp., St. Louis, 1975-80; asst. mgr. Beneficial Fin. Corp., St. Louis, 1980-82, Security Pacific Fin. Co., St. Louis, 1982-83; account exec. Mass. Indemnity and Life Ins. Co., St. Louis, 1983-84; exec. recruiter, sr. account rep. J.E. Wottowa and Assocs., St. Louis, 1984—. Recipient Dale Carnegie Inst. award, 1983. Mem. Rotary. Home: 12277 Corrida Ct Maryland Heights MO 63043

SANADA, RANDALL PAUL, financial executive; b. Los Angeles, Sept. 7, 1951; s. Vincent Michael and Fran Marie (Ferrara) S.; m. Kaylene Luetta Green, June 24, 1972; children: Randall P. Jr., Jerry V., Chad M., Joseph D. BS in Bus. Mgmt. and Data Processing, Calif. Poly. U., 1972; MS in Fin. Services, Am. Coll., 1982, MS in Mgmt., 1987. CLU, chartered fin. cons. Fin. planner IDS Fin. Services, Am. Express, Pasadena, Calif., 1972-74, dist. mgr., 1974-76; div. mgr. IDS Fin. Services, Am. Express, Northridge, Calif., 1976-83, fin. planner, gold team founder, 1983-87; pres. Alliance Adv. Group Inc., Chatsworth, Calif., 1987—; tchr. U. So. Calif. Fin. Planning, Los Angeles, 1983-85; lectr. IDS Fin. Services, 1984; media spokesman Am. Express, 1984-87. Mem. Internat. Assn. Fin. Planning, Inst. Cert. Fin. Planners (bd. dirs. 1987—, pres. elect 1989—), Chatsworth C. of C. (bd. dirs. 1987—). Republican. Office: Alliance Adv Group Inc 21053 Devonshire Ste 103 Chatsworth CA 91311

SANBORN, ALLEN WEBBER, commercial banker; b. Balt., Mar. 12, 1942; s. Fred M. Sanborn and Sally (Webber) Sanborn Nevin; m. Mary Anne Hawley, June 19, 1965; children—Wendy Anne, Jenny. B.A. in Econs., Gettysburg Coll., 1964; M.B.A. in Fin., U. Pitts., 1968. Loan officer Citibank, N.Y.C., 1968-71; various positions Bank of Am., San Francisco and Chgo., 1971-79, head cash mgmt., San Francisco, 1979-81, head credit and mktg., London, 1981-82, sr. v.p., head Calif. corp. banking, San Francisco, 1982-84, head retail asset mgmt., 1984—, head comml. real estate industries div., 1987—; adv. dir. Bank Am. Capitol Corp., San Francisco, 1983—. Club: Bankers. Home: 556 Silverado Dr Lafayette CA 94549 Office: Bank Am Nat Trust & Savs Assn 555 California St San Francisco CA 94104 *

SANCHEZ, CLAUDIO R., electronics company executive; b. San Cristobal, Venezuela, Aug. 30, 1943. BS in Bus. Adminstrn., Emporia State U., 1970; MS in Computer Scis., MBA in Bus. Mgmt., Am. Technol. U., 1980. Sr. budget analyst IV Menegrande Oil Co., San Tomé, Venezuela, 1974-78; v.p. human resources Bus. Machines Inc., Houston, 1980-83; pres. Total Software Systems Inc., Austin, Tex., 1984-85, D. Kosh & Assoc., Austin, 1983-85, Abacus Tech., Austin, 1986-88, Tex. State Bd. Ins., Austin, 1988—; bd. dirs. O.S. Tile and Brick, Inc., Austin, Citizens Ins. Co. Am., Austin; cons. bd. dirs. Remington Group, Inc., Austin. Mem. Am. Security Council, Rep. Presdl. Task Force, Tex. Computer Ind. Council. Home: 917 Peggotty Place Austin TX 78753 Office: Abacus Techs PO Box 15776 Austin TX 78761-5776

SANDALLS, WILLIAM THOMAS, JR., bank company executive; b. Newport, R.I., Jan. 7, 1944; s. William Thomas Sr. and Marion Harriett (Hellman) S.; m. Katharine Anne Flood, June 22, 1968; children: William Thomas III, Benjamin Flood (dec. 1987), Katharine Anne. BS cum laude in

Indsl. Adminstrn., Yale U., 1966; MBA, Harvard Grad. Sch. Bus. Adminstrn., 1972; MS in Taxation, Bentley Coll., 1979. CPA, Mass. With Arthur Andersen & Co., Boston, 1972-74; with BayBanks, Inc., Boston, 1974—, chief fin. officer, 1977—, vice chmn., 1983—, also bd. dirs.; chmn. CIRRUS System, Inc.; bd. dirs. MasterCard Internat. Inc.; dir.-at-large Bank Adminstrn. Inst. Corporator Boston's Mus. Sci.; chmn. fin. com. Town of Weston, Mass.; trustee Mass. Taxpayers Found., Inc. Served to lt. USN, 1966-70, Vietnam. Mem. Am. Inst. CPAs, Mass. Soc. CPAs, Tax Execs. Inst., Fin. Execs. Inst. Clubs: Union, Harvard; Yale (N.Y.C.); Boston Econ. Office: BayBanks Inc 175 Federal St Boston MA 02110

SANDBULTE, AREND JOHN, utility executive; b. Sioux Center, Iowa, Dec. 9, 1933; s. Ben and Rena (Rensink) S.; m. Verna VanDeBerg, June 30, 1953; children: Ruth Marie, Gregory Bern, Kristin Ann, Rachel Lynn. B.S. in Elec. Engring., Iowa State U., 1959; M.B.A., U. Minn., 1966. Registered profl. engr., Minn., N.D., Wis. Rate engr. No. States Power Co., Mpls., 1959-64; with Minn. Power, Duluth, 1964—, asst. v.p. budgets and corp. planning, 1972-74, v.p. corp. planning, 1974-76, v.p., fin., chief fin. officer, 1976-78, sr. v.p. fin. and adminstrn., chief fin. officer, 1978-80, exec. v.p., chief fin. officer, 1980-83, exec. v.p., chief operating officer, chief fin. officer, dir., 1983-84, dir., 1983—, pres., chief oper. officer, 1984-88, pres., chief exec. officer, 1988-89, chmn., pres., chief exec. officer, 1989—, also bd. dirs.; bd. dirs. Norwest Bank Duluth Community Bd., Royal D. Alworth Jr. Inst. Internat. Studies, Assn. Edison Illuminating Cos., Iowa State U. Elec. Engring. Adv. Bd., Lake Superior Cen. Bd., Minn. Bus. Ptnrship., St. Mary Parish Land Co., Utech Venture Capital Corp. Bd. dirs. Northeastern Minn. Devel. Assn., 1987-88, Minn. C. of C. and Industry, 1984—, St. Luke's Found., 1985—; trustee Coll. St. Scholastica, Duluth, 1979—, vice chmn. bd., 1983, chmn. bd., 1984-87; dir. St. Luke's Hosp., Duluth, 1977-88, chmn. bd., 1982-84; trustee Duluth YMCA, 1977—; bd. dirs. Ordean Found., 1983—, Minn. Safety Council, 1986-88, bd. dirs. United Way, 1984—, campaign chmn., 1986, chmn. bd. 1989—. Served with U.S. Army, 1954-55. Recipient Nikola Tesla award Midwest Area Power Utilities, 1975; named Boss of Year, Duluth Jaycees, 1974. Mem. Engrs. Club of No. Minn., IEEE, Duluth Area C. of C. (pres. 1982), North Cen. Electric Assn. (pres. 1987-88), Edison Elect. Inst. Policy on Strategic Planning. Republican. Presbyterian. Clubs: Mpls. Athletic (Mpls.); Kitchi Gammi (Duluth); Northland Country. Home: 2930 London Rd Duluth MN 55804 Office: Minn Power 30 W Superior St Duluth MN 55802

SANDE, BARBARA, interior decorating consultant; b. Twin Falls, Idaho, May 5, 1939; d. Einar and Pearl M. (Olson) Sande; m. Ernest Reinhardt Hohener, Sept. 3, 1961 (div. Sept. 1971); children: Heidi Catherine, Eric Christian. BA, U. Idaho, 1961. Asst. mgr., buyer Home Yardage Inc., Oakland, Calif., 1972-76; cons. in antiques and antique valuation, Lafayette, Calif., 1977-78; interior designer Neighborhood Antiques and Interiors, Oakland, Calif., 1978-86; owner, Claremont Antiques and Interiors, Berkeley, Calif., 1987—; cons., participant antique and art fair exhibits, Orinda and Piedmont, Calif., 1977—. Decorator Piedmont Christmas House Tour, 1983, 88, Oakland Mus. Table Setting, 1984, 85, 86, Piedmont Showcase Family Room, 1986, Piedmont Showcase Music Room, 1986, Piedmont Kitchen House Tour, 1985, Santa Rosa Symphony Holiday Walk Benefit, 1986, Piedmont Benefit Guild Showcase Young Persons Room, 1987, Piedmont Showcase Library, 1988, Peidmont Showcase Solarium, 1989, Jr. League Table Setting, Oakland-East Bay, 1989. Bd. dirs. San Leandro Coop. Nursery Sch., 1967; health coord. parent-faculty bd., Miramonte High Sch., Orinda, 1978, Acalanes Sch. Dist., Lafayette, Calif., 1978; bd. dirs. Orinda Community Ctr. Vols., 1979; originator Concerts in the Park, Orinda, 1979. Assoc. Am. Soc. Interior Design, Am. Soc. Appraisers; mem. Am. Decorative Arts Forum, De Young Mus., Nat. Trust Historic Preservation, San Francisco Opera Guild, San Francisco Symphony Guild. Democrat. Avocations: travel; hiking.

SANDE, THOMAS PAUL, toy manufacturing company executive; b. Grand Forks, N.D., Dec. 6, 1935; s. Gerald Elliot and Colleta Barbara (Backes) S.; m. Audrey Joan Hoffer, June 29, 1963; children: Theodore, Matthew. BBA, U. N.D., 1957. CPA. Audit mgr. Price Waterhouse and Co., 1957-72; v.p., treas., controller Monroe Auto Equipment Co., 1972-78; corp. controller Dayton-Walther Corp., 1978-84; sr v.p. fin., chief fin. officer Coleco Industries Inc., Avon, Conn., 1984—. Office: Coleco Industries Inc 80 Darling Dr Avon CT 06001

SANDEFUR, THOMAS EDWIN, JR., tobacco company executive; b. Cochran, Ga., Dec. 4, 1939; s. Thomas Edwin and Elsie (Camp) S.; m. Annette Crawford Meginniss, May 8, 1965. B.S. in Bus. Acctg., Ga. So. U., 1963. Sales and mktg. positions R.J. Reynolds Tobacco Co., Winston-Salem, N.C., 1964-76, sr. v.p. advt. and brand mgmt., 1976-79; sr. v.p. R.J. Reynolds Internat., Winston-Salem, N.C., 1979-81; exec. v.p. Europe, Geneva, 1981-82; sr. v.p. internat. mktg. Brown & Williamson Tobacco Corp., Louisville, 1982-84, exec. v.p., 1984-85, pres., chief operating officer, 1985—. Office: Brown & Williamson Tobacco Corp 1500 Brown & Williamson Tower Louisville KY 40202

SANDELL, RICHARD ARNOLD, international trade executive, economist; b. Buenos Aires, Argentina, Oct. 22, 1937; s. Kurd Wolfcang and Isolde Mary (Josevich) S.; m. Phyllis H. Levinson, July 6, 1968; children: Laurie Alyssa, Karyn Joy, Sylvie Jennine. B.A. in Social Sci., U. Buenos Aires, 1957, JD in Internat. Law, 1959; M.S. in Econs., U. San Marcos, 1960; LL.M., NYU, 1962; Ph.D., Columbia U., 1972, M.B.A., 1977. Dir. bus. planning Guerrero Merc. Internat. Ltd., Buenos Aires, 1954-62; gen. mgr. Acquatronic Universal, Inc., 1965-68; corp. v.p. indsl. econs. Mgmt. Analyst Group, Ins., Van Nuys, Calif., 1968-70; pres., chief exec. officer A.I.M. Internat. Corp., Alameda, Calif., 1970-76; pres., chief exec. officer, dir. Aurag Internat. Corp. and Aura Tech. Corp., Larchmont, N.Y., 1979—; dir. FerroCement Internat. Ltd. of Panama, Consorcio Pesquero Marmesa of Guayaquil, Ecuador, INTEX S.A., Buenos Aires, Export Marketeers Ltd., Auckland, N.Z., Aledo Transnat. Trading Corp., Panama, Geneva, Oakland, Calif.; dir. Nexus Corp., Santa Rosa, Calif., Guanabara Mining Co., Rio De Janeiro, Brazil, Primax Electronics Ltd., Aimore Internat. Corp., Stockton, Calif., Premisa, S.A., Venezuela; former cons. U.S. Dept. State, govts. Ecuador, Nicaragua, Guyana, Zaire, Fiji, El Salvador, currently cons. to Taiwan, Chile, former cons. to Venezuela, Brazil, 1972-88, N.Z., Ghana, 1968-82; adj. prof. bus. adminstrn. Elbert Covell Coll. and Coll. Pacific at U. Pacific, 1972-77; adj. prof. internat. bus., mgmt. U. Am. States, Miami, Fla., 1977-79, prof. internat. trade and tech., chair bus. enterprise , 1987—; adj. prof. internat. bus., mgmt. U. Francisco Marroquin, Guatemala City, 1977-79; dir. Grad. Inst. Free Enterprise Studies, prof. internat. bus., govt. Mercy Coll. and L.I.U., Dobbs Ferry, N.Y., 1980-83; prof. internat. fin. and bus., chair bus. enterprise Ramapo Coll. of N.J., Mahwah, 1983-87. Author: The Politics of Marketing in Latin America, 1970, Private Investment in the Andean Block - A Study in Conflicts, 1970, Santa Cruz - Crosswords of Heaven and Hell, 1971, U.S.-Latin America - a Time for Reciprocity, 1972, Use of Consultants - How Valuable an Investment, 1972, The Role of U.S. Multinational Corporation, 1972, Summary of Controls on the International Movement of Capital, 1973, The Effects of Rising Energy Costs on LDC Development, 1974, Trade in the Andean Common Market, 1975, U.S. Private Investment - Its Future Role in Interamerican Development, 1976, Tourism in Latin America - Cornerstone of Development, 1976, Administration of Human Resources - Its Effectiveness in the Modern Organization, 1977, A System Called Capitalism, 1977, Marketing Plague - The Regulators, 1978; Prescription for Survival - Can Free Enterprise Make It?, 1979, The Intellectual Defense of Free Enterprise, 1980, Freedom at Bay - Government Controls in the Economy, 1982, American Values: the Economy, the Polity, the Society, 1986, The Debt Bomb: In the Shadow of Depression, 1987, Finance and Stress: The Market Crash of '87, 1988; editor Interam. Econ. Journal, Univ. Am. States. Advisor Explorer post Alameda council Boy Scouts Am., 1969-71, post. com. chmn., 1971-75; bd. dirs. San Francisco-Bay Area council Girl Scouts U.S.A., 1975-80, v.p., 1978-80; trustee Sagitario Fund, Buenos Aires, 1960-62, Amigos de las Americas, Houston, 1975-80, U. Am. States, Santiago, Chile, 1976-80, Am. Research Inst. for Social Environments, Alameda, 1975-82, Princeton Fund, 1976-82, Found. for Free Enterprise, 1983-87, Aura Tech. Found., 1987—, Coll. Electro Bio-Scis., 1987-89. With AUS, 1962-65. Decorated Bronze Star; decorated Purple Heart; recipient medal Sagitario Found., 1962, Silver Condor award U. Andina, 1969, Kenneth Chilton Meml. award, 1972. Fellow AAAS (life); mem. Nat. Rifle Assn. (life benefactor), N.Y. Acad. Scis. (life), Am. Numis. Assn. (life), Inst. Mgmt. Cons. (dir., v.p. Latin Am. 1975-80), Am. Econ. Assn., Internat. Inst. Economists (dir. 1968-70), Interam. Soc. Polit. Economists (rustee 1971-81), Inst. Mgmt. Sci., Internat. Execs. assn. (dir. 1971-80), Fgn. Policy Assn., 2d Amendment Found., Am. Security Council, Am. Soc. Internat. Execs., N.Am. Corp. Planning Assn. (pres. 1972-73), Soc. Internat. Trade Planning, Am. Sociol. Assn., Am. Psychol. Assn., Latin Am. Studies Assn., Pacific Coast Council Latin Am. Studies (gov. 1972-75, treas. 1975-79, exec. com. 1972-79), The Atlantic Council (bd. govs. 1986—, pres. 1988), Oakland C. of C., Mensa. Clubs: Commonwealth (San Francisco) (chmn. sect. Latin Am. 1969-75); Oakland World Trade. Lodge: Rotary. Home: 2250 Boston Post Rd Larchmont NY 10538 Office: 1 Chatsworth Ave Ste 508 Larchmont NY 10538

SANDER, SUSAN BERRY, environmental planning engineering corporation executive; b. Walla Walla, Wash., Aug. 26, 1953; d. Alan Robert and Elizabeth Ann (Davenport) Berry; m. Dean Edward Sander, June 3, 1978. BS in Biology with honors, Western Wash. U., 1975; MBA with honors, U. Puget Sound, 1984. Biologist, graphic artist Shapiro & Assocs., Inc., Seattle, 1975-77, office mgr., 1977-79, v.p., 1979-84, pres., owner 1984—, also bd. dirs. Merit scholar Overlake Service League, Bellevue, Wash., 1971, Western Wash. U. scholar, Bellingham, 1974-75, U. Puget Sound scholar, 1984. Mem. Soc. Mktg. Profl. Services (treas., bd. dirs., Employer of Yr. 1987, Small bus. of Yr.), Seattle C. of C. Club: Wash. Athletic (Seattle). Avocations: swimming, hiking, traveling, painting. Office: Shapiro & Assocs Inc 1400 Smith Tower Seattle WA 98104

SANDERS, ARTHUR JAY, lawyer; b. N.Y.C., Apr. 24, 1957; s. Samuel and Thea (Weiss) S.; m. Sharon Rose Post, Aug. 29, 1981. BA, CUNY, 1978; JD, Bklyn. Law Sch., 1981. Bar: N.Y. 1982. Assoc. Mitchell M. Kay, N.Y.C., 1982-85, Finkelstein, Kaplan, Levine, Gittlsohn, Tetenbaum, Newburgh, N.Y.C., 1985; pvt. practice New City, N.Y., 1985—. Assoc. dir. Rockland County Ctr. Physically Handicapped Children, New City, 1987—. Mem. ABA, Comml. Law Assn. Am., N.Y. State Bar Assn., Rockland County Bar Assn., Soc. Profl. Investigators (co-counsel 1988—). Democrat. Jewish. Office: 14 S Main St New City NY 10956

SANDERS, CHARLES ADDISON, pharmaceutical company executive, physician; b. Dallas, Feb. 10, 1932; s. Harold Barefoot and May Elizabeth (Forrester) S.; m. Elizabeth Ann Chipman, Mar. 6, 1956; children: Elizabeth, Charles Addison, Carlyn, Christopher. M.D., U. Tex., 1955. Intern, asst. resident Boston City Hosp., 1955-57, chief resident, 1957-58; clin. and research fellow in medicine Mass. Gen. Hosp., Boston, 1958-60; chief cardiac catheterization lab. Mass. Gen. Hosp., 1962-72, gen. dir., 1972-81, physician, 1973-81, program dir. myocardial infarction research unit, 1967-72, program dir. MEDLAB systems, 1969-72; exec. v.p. E.R. Squibb and Sons, 1981-84; exec. v.p. Squibb Corp., 1984-88, vice chmn., 1988—; assoc. prof. medicine Harvard U. Med. Sch., 1969-80, prof., 1980-83; lectr. MIT, 1973-81; bd. dirs. Merrill Lynch and Co. Inc., N.Y.C., Commonwealth Fund N.Y.C., Mt. Sinai Med. Ctr., N.Y.C., Princeton (N.J.) Med. Ctr.; mem. Inst. Medicine, Nat. Acad. Scis., Charles Stark Draper Lab.; chmn. Nat. Council Health Care Tech., 1980-81. Mem. editorial bd. New Eng. Jour. Medicine, 1969-72. Past trustee Mass. Hosp. Assn. Served to capt. M.C. USAF, 1960-62. Mem. Am. Fedn. for Clin. Research, Am., Mass. heart assns., Mass. Med. Soc., A.C.P., Am. Physiol. Soc., Am. Clin. and Climatol. Soc., Am. Coll. Cardiology, Am. Soc. for Clin. Investigation, Soc. Hosp. Adminstrs., Greater Boston C. of C. (dir. 1977-81). Unitarian. Club: Harvard. Home: 70 Independence Dr Princeton NJ 08540 Office: Squibb Corp PO Box 4000 Princeton NJ 08540 *

SANDERS, CURTIS REMMELL, management and investment consultant; b. Jonesboro, Ark., Mar. 12, 1929; s. Macon Remmell and Dorothea Auttie Irene (McAuliffe) M.; m. Dorothy Elizabeth Dalton, Sept. 6, 1950; children: Elizabeth, Linda, Eric. BS in Chemistry, San Diego State U., 1958; student, U. So. Calif. and UCLA, 1962-66. Dir. product forecasting IBM Product Group div. IBM Corp., U.S.A., 1972-74; group dir. bus. vols. IBM Europe div. IBM Corp., 1974-79; dir. bus. plans IBM Office Products div. IBM Corp., U.S.A., 1979-82; dir. market research IBM Corp., White Plains, N.Y., 1982-87; pres., chief exec. officer Haigh Assoc., Inc., Stamford, Conn., 1983—. Served with USN, 1946-49, PTO. Mem. Mktg. Sci. Inst., Conf. Bd. Council on Mktg. Research.

SANDERS, DAVID CLIFTON, electrical engineer; b. Sanford, N.C., Dec. 29, 1940; s. David C. II and Katherine (Aldridge) S.; m. Diane Hamilton, June 22, 1963; children: Susan A., Elizabeth W. BSEE, U. Ky., 1962. With dept. polymer products E.I. Dupont, Wilmington, Del., 1962—, dir. dept. fluropolymers, 1987—. Mem. Soc. of Plastics Inst., Rotary. Republican. Home: 2314 Ridgeway Rd Wilmington DE 19805 Office: EI Dupont Dept Polymer Products Wilmington DE 19898

SANDERS, EUGENE THOMAS, electrical engineer; b. San Mateo, Calif., Nov. 18, 1950; s. John Andrew and Betty Mary Elizabeth S.; m. Marlene Mae Louie, Jan. 16, 1984; 1 child, Aaron Matthew. BSEE, U. Calif., Berkeley, 1973, MSEE, 1974. Sr. staff engr. Datapoint Corp., San Antonio, 1977-82; v.p. Gen. Parametrics Corp., Berkeley, 1982—. Mem. IEEE.

SANDERS, GARY GLENN, electronics engineer, consultant; b. Gettysburg, Pa., Dec. 21, 1944; s. James Glenn Sanders and Martha Maybelle (Fleming) Ehlert; m. Elizabeth Marie Rega, Sept. 9, 1977 (div. Sept. 1981). Cert. med. technologist, Chgo. Inst. Tech., 1970; AA, Mayfair Coll., 1972; BS in Electronic Engring., Cooks Inst., Jackson, Miss., 1982. Registered Internat. Med. Techs. Cons. engr. Electronics Design Services, Chgo., 1977-79; applications engr. Nationwide Electronics Systems, Streamwood, Ill., 1979-80; mng. engr. Electronics Design Ctr. Case Western Res. U., Cleve., 1980-82; sr. project mgr. Scott Fetzer Co., Cleve., 1982—; Comml. piloting. Contbr. articles on medicine and biology to profl. confs. and publs.; patentee in biomed. electronics and indsl. instrumentation; inventor, 1985-88. Alumni mem. Boy Scouts Am. Served with U.S. Army, 1962-68, Vietnam. Decorated DFC, Bronze Star, Air medal. Fellow Internat. Coll. Med. Technologists; mem. IEEE, AAAS, Instrument Soc. of Am. (sr. mem.), Internat. Soc. Hybrid Microelectronics, N.Y. Acad. Scis., DAV, Am. Legion, Ohio Acad. Sci., Nat. Eagle Scout Assn., Legion Disabled Am. Vets., Boys Scouts Am. (alumni mem.), Internat. Soc. Hybrid Microelectronics, NRA. Republican. Home: 1360 Brockley Ave Lakewood OH 44107-2415 Office: Scott Fetzer Co Meriam Div 10920 Madison Ave Cleveland OH 44102

SANDERS, GREGORY LAWRENCE, data processing executive; b. Glendale, Calif., Jan. 27, 1948; s. Luther Ansel and Patricia (Begley) S.; m. Barbara Kay Long, Aug. 20, 1982; 1 child, Corrie Ann. BA in Acctg., U. Queensland, Australia, 1971. Adminstrn. mgr. Computer Technology, Adelaide, Australia, 1972-80; support mgr. Telecredit, Inc., Tampa, Fla., 1981-83; dir. prodn. Automated Data Processing, Tampa, 1983-86; v.p. S.E. region Com-Pro (subs.of Continental Info. Systems Corp.), Orlando, Fla., 1986—. Active Leadership Orlando. Cpl. Australian Army, 1966-68. Republican. Roman Catholic. Office: COM PRO 1209 Edgewater Dr Ste 202 Orlando FL 23804

SANDERS, HASSEL MARTEEN, gas company executive; b. Altus, Okla., Apr. 26, 1930; s. William Andrew and Gertrude Eloise (Kingston) S.; m. Thelma Jacqueline Barr, Feb. 18, 1950; children: Robert, David, John, Melanie, Jacqueline. BBA in Acctg., Baylor U., 1955. CPA, Colo., Tex. Sr. acct. Arthur Andersen & Co., Houston, 1955-60; sec.-treas. Plateau Natural Gas Co., Colorado Springs, Colo., 1960-70; v.p. rates and consol. acctg. KN Energy, Inc., Lakewood, Colo., 1970-1988; sr. v.p. KN Energy, Inc., Lakewood, 1988—. With USN, 1949-52. Fellow Am. Inst. CPAs, Colo. Soc. CPAs, Tex. Soc. CPAs. Republican. Baptist. Home: 2439 S Medinah Dr Evergreen CO 80439

SANDERS, JOHN DAVID, investor, management consultant; b. Louisville, Aug. 2, 1938; s. Wallace W. Sr. and Mary Jane (Brownfield) S.; m. Carole C. Ewing, Aug. 19, 1967; children: Elaine R., Paul D. BEE, U. Louisville, 1961; MS, Carnegie-Mellon U., 1962, PhD, 1965. Registered profl. engr., Va., Ky. Devel. engr. GE, Schenectady, N.Y., 1961; mem. tech. staff RCA Labs, Princeton, N.J., 1962; resch. scientist U.S. CIA, Washington, 1964-68; investment banker Wachtel and Co. Inc., 1968-88; chmn., chief exec. officer Washington Tech. Newspaper, Vienna, Va., 1988—; bd. dirs. Radiation Systems Inc., Sterling, Va., Daedalus Enterprises Inc., Ann Arbor, Mich., Data Measurement Corp., Gaithersburg, Md., Indsl. Tng. Corp., Gaithersburg. Author: Parables for Entrepeneurs, 1985. Mem. IEEE, Nat. Assn. Corp. Dirs. (pres. Wash. chpt. 1988—), Wash. Soc. Investment Analysts (bd. dirs. 1980-82). Republican. Baptist. Home: 4600 N 26th St Arlington VA 22207 Office: Washington Tech 1953 Gallows Rd #130 Vienna VA 22180

SANDERS, ROBERT MAYER, investment company executive; b. N.Y.C., Nov. 10, 1923; s. Albert and Beulah (Mayer) S.; m. Evelyn Frenkel, Apr. 14, 1955; 1 child, Patricia Ann. D (hon.), Coll. Oral Surgery, 1950. Ptnr. Josios Comercio, Rio de Janeiro, 1947-55; pres. Herodent, Inc., N.Y.C., 1948-55; pres., chmn. R.M. Sanders & Co., Inc., N.Y.C., 1955-59; mng. ptnr. Frenkel Group, San Salvador, El Salvador, 1958-82; chmn. Monel Inc., Miami, Fla., 1982—; pres., chmn. bd. Auto Palace S.A. and related cos., San Salvador, Merident S.A. and related cos., San Salvador; bd. dirs. exec. com. Am. Capital Corp., Miami, Transcaptial Fin. Corp., Cleve. Mem. citizens bd. U. Miami, 1987. Named to French Legion of Honor, 1979. Mem. Am. Soc. French Legion of Honor (patron). Republican. Home: 2333 Brickell Ave Terr F Miami FL 33129 Office: Monel Inc 4238 NW 37th Ave Miami FL 33142

SANDERS, TERESSA IRENE, health care marketing consultant; b. Atlanta, May 29, 1951; d. Floyd Roscoe Jr. and Marian Teressa (Rutland) S.; m. John Christian Yoder, Apr. 23, 1983. BS in Nursing, Duke U., 1973; MS in Nursing, Med. Coll. Ga., 1975. Psychiatric staff nurse Grady Meml. Hosp., Atlanta, 1973-74, adult health practitioner, 1975-77; cons., fed. liaison Ga. Dept. Human Resources, Atlanta, 1978-81; legis. asst. U.S. Sen. Sam Nunn, Washington, 1981-83; dir. mktg. and pub. affairs Nat. Rehab. Hosp., Washington, 1983-86; pres. Sanders & Co., Washington, 1986—, Pizzagram Inc., Washington, 1987—. Originator, assoc. producer, host TV series Lifelines, 1980-81. Founding dir., treas., chairperson legis. task force Ga. Assn. for Primary Health Care, Atlanta, 1978-81; co-chairperson Sesquicentennial Commn., Decatur, Ga., 1973-74; vice chairperson Bicentennial Commn., Decatur, 1976; bd. dirs. Samuel L. Jones Boys Club, Decatur, 1976-77; mem Ga. Drug Abuse Adv. Council, Atlanta, 1976-77; mem. adv. bd. Nat. Assn. for Craniofacially Handicapped, Chattanooga, 1986—. Orgn. 2d Community systems fellow Johns Hopkins U., 1987-88. Mem. Women in Govt. Relations, U.S. C. of C. (pvt. sector task force on Social Security, 1985-86, health care cost mgmt. task force, 1985—). Democrat. Home: 4435 Garrison St NW Washington DC 20016 Office: Sanders & Co 1667 K St NW Ste 801 Washington DC 20006

SANDERS, WALTER JEREMIAH, III, electronics company executive; b. Chgo., Sept. 12, 1936; s. Walter J. and Kathleen (Finn) S.; m. Linda Lee Drobman, Nov. 13, 1965 (div. 1982); children: Tracy Ellen, Lara Whitney, Alison Ashley. BEE, U. Ill., 1958. Design engr. Douglas Aircraft Co., Santa Monica, Calif., 1958-59; applications engr. Motorola, Inc., Phoenix, 1959-60; sales engr. Motorola, Inc., 1960-61; with Fairchild Camera & Instrument Co., 1961-69; dir. mktg. Fairchild Camera & Instrument Co., Mountain View, Calif., 1961-68, group dir. mktg. worldwide, 1968-69; pres. Advanced Micro Devices Inc., Sunnyvale, Calif., until 1987, chmn. bd., chief exec. officer, 1969—; dir. Donaldson, Lufkin & Jenrette. Mem. Semicondr. Industry Assn. (co-founder, dir.), Santa Clara County Mfg. Group (co-founder, dir.). Office: Advanced Micro Devices Inc 901 Thompson Pl Sunnyvale CA 94086 *

SANDERSON, WILLIAM H., investment real estate broker; b. Phillipsburg, N.J., Oct. 6, 1917; s. William H. and Florence (Garis) S.; m. Helen Mahoney, Feb. 20, 1966. BS cum laude, Fairleigh Dickinson U., 1959. Sec., treas. Acacia Realty, Inc., Port Charlotte, Fla., 1976—. Mem. Cert. Residential Specialists (pres. Fla. chpt. 1984), Realtors Nat. Mktg. Inst. (designated cert. comml. investment mem., cert. real estate brokerage mgr.). Republican. Presbyterian. Office: Acacia Realty Inc 2195 Tamiami Trail Port Charlotte FL 33948

SANDFORD, BRUCE THOMAS, film and pharmaceutical company executive; b. Paterson, N.J., Oct. 20, 1947; s. Raymond C. and Elizabeth (Talerico) S.; m. Elizabeth DeVita, June 21, 1969 (div. 1975); children: David, Jason; m. Lorraine M. Gettings, May 19, 1979; children: Ashley, Erica. BA in Philosophy, Bloomfield Coll., 1968. Asst. ins. mgr. Instrument Systems Corp., Huntington, N.Y., 1973-75; mgr. ins. and employment benefits Henkel Inc., Teaneck, N.J., 1975-78; dir. risk mgmt. Sterling Drug Inc., N.Y.C., 1978-80, asst. treas., 1980-88; asst. mgr. corp. ins. Eastman-Kodak Co., Rochester, N.Y., 1988—; v.p., bd. dirs. Wheeling Ins. Ltd., Hamilton, Bermuda, 1980—. Staff sgt. USAF, 1969-73. Mem. Risk and Ins. Mgmt. Soc. Democrat. Club: Glen Ridge (N.J.) Country. Home: 6 Summerfield Circle Pittsford NY 14534

SANDIDGE, KANITA DURICE, communications company executive; b. Cleve., Dec. 2, 1947; d. John Robert Jr. and Virginia Louise (Caldwell) S. AB, Cornell U., 1970; MBA, Case Western Res. U., 1979. Supr. assignments service ctrs. and installation AT&T, Cleve., 1970-78, chief dept. data processing and acctg., 1979-80; adminstrn. mgr. exec. v.p. staff AT&T, N.Y.C., 1980-83; sales forecasting and analysis mgr. resources planning AT&T, Newark, 1983-86; planning and devel. mgr. material planning and mgmt. AT&T Network Systems, Morristown, N.J., 1986-87; dir. adminstrv. services AT&T Network Systems, Lisle, Ill., 1987—. Mem black exchange program Nat. Urban League, N.Y.C., 1986—. Named Black Achiever in Industry, Harlem YMCA, 1981; recipient Tribute to Women and Industry Achievement award YWCA, 1985. Mem. Nat. Black MBA's, Alliance Black AT&T Mgrs., Am. Mgmt. Assn., Nat. Assn. for Female Execs., NAACP, Beta Alpha Psi. Mem. African Meth. Episcopal Ch. Home: 820 Cardiff Rd Naperville IL 60565 Office: AT&T Network Systems 2600 Warrenville Rd Lisle IL 60532

SANDLER, HERBERT M., savings and loan association executive; b. N.Y.C., Nov. 16, 1931; s. William B. and Hilda (Schattan) S.; m. Marion Osher, Mar. 26, 1961. B.S.S., CCNY, 1951; J.S.D., Columbia U., 1954. Bar: N.Y. 1956. Asst. counsel Waterfront Commn. N.Y. Harbor, 1956-59; partner firm Sandler & Sandler, N.Y.C., 1960-62; pres., dir., mem. exec. com. Golden West Savs. & Loan Assn. and Golden West Fin. Corp., Oakland, Calif., 1963-75; chmn. bd., chief exec. officer, dir., mem. exec. com. World Savs. & Loan Assn. and Golden West Fin. Corp., Oakland, 1975—; charter mem. Thrift Instns. Adv. Council to Fed. Res. Bd., Oakland, 1963-75; mem. com. on industry restructuring U.S. League of Savs. Instns.; bd. dirs. Fed. Home Loan Bank, San Francisco; bd. dirs. adv. com. Fed. Home Loan Mortgage Corp.; m. task force U.S. League of Savs. Inst.; former chmn. legis. and regulation com. Calif. Savs. Loan League. Pres., trustee Calif. Neighborhood Services Found.; chmn. Urban Housing Inst.; mem. policy adv. bd. Ctr. for Real Estate and Urban Econs. U. Calif., Berkeley. Served with U.S. Army, 1954-56. Office: Golden W Fin Corp 1901 Harrison St Oakland CA 94612 *

SANDLER, MARION OSHER, savings and loan association executive; b. Biddeford, Maine, Oct. 17, 1930; d. Samuel and Leah (Lowe) Osher; m. Herbert M. Sandler, Mar. 26, 1961. BA, Wellesley Coll., 1952; postgrad., Harvard U.-Radcliffe Coll., 1953; MBA, NYU, 1958; LLD (hon.), Golden Gate U., 1987. Asst. buyer Bloomingdale's (dept. store), N.Y.C., 1953-55; security analyst Dominick & Dominick, N.Y.C., 1955-61; sr. fin. analyst Oppenheimer & Co., N.Y.C., 1961-63; sr. v.p., dir. Golden West Fin. Corp. and World Savs. & Loan Assn., Oakland, Calif., 1963-75, vice chmn. bd., co-mng. officer, dir., mem. exec. com., 1975-80, pres., co- chief exec. officer, dir., mem. exec. com., 1980—. Vice-chmn. industry adv. com. Fed. Savs. and Loan Ins. Corp., 1987-88; controller's office idea audit task force State of Calif., 1987; bd. overseers NYU Schs. Bus., 1987-89; mem. capital formation task force White House Conf. on Small Bus., 1979; mem. Pres. Carter's Housing Task Force, 1980, Pres.'s Mgmt. Improvement Council, 1980; mem. exec. com., policy adv. bd. Ctr. for Real Estate and Urban Econs. U. Calif., Berkeley, 1981—; mem. ad hoc com. to rev. Schs. Bus. Adminstrn. U. Calif., Berkeley, 1984-85; past mem. adv. council Fed. Nat. Mortgage Assn.; mem. Thrift Insts. Adv. Coun. to Fed. Res. Bd., 1989—. Mem. Phi Beta Kappa, Beta Gamma Sigma. Office: Golden W Fin Corp 1901 Harrison St Oakland CA 94612

SANDLER, ROBERT MICHAEL, insurance company executive, actuary; b. N.Y.C., Apr. 20, 1942; s. Albert and Ruth (Marcus) S.; m. Annette L. Marchese, Aug. 18, 1963; children—David, Glenn. B.A. in Math., Hofstra U., 1963. Various actuarial positions Met. Life, N.Y.C., 1963-68; various actuarial positions Am. Internat., N.Y.C., 1968-80; v.p., casualty actuary American Internat. Group, Inc., N.Y.C., 1980-84, sr. v.p., sr. actuary, sr. claims officer, 1984—, dir. various subs. Mem. Casualty Actuarial Soc. (assoc.), Am. Acad. Actuaries, Internat. Actuarial Assn. Republican. Home: 3 Crestwood Dr Bridgewater NJ 08807 Office: Am Internat Group 70 Pine St New York NY 10270

SANDLIN, GEORGE WILSON, real estate broker, mortgage banker; b. Glen Rose, Tex., May 13, 1912; s. Walter Algie and Margaret (Parks) S.; student pub. schs., also Schreiner Inst.; m. Ruth Ina Zollinger, Sept. 21, 1941 (dec. 1975); children—George Walter Raoul, Carole Ruth, Sarah Louise, Margaret Ina; m. Ann Marie Anderson, Nov. 11, 1984. Field rep. HOLC, San Antonio, 1934-36; pres. Sandlin Mortgage Corp., Austin, Tex.; owner Sandlin & Co., 1936—; pres., dir. Trans-Pacific Resorts, Inc.; pres. Profl. Arts, Inc.; ind. fee appraiser. Chmn., Tex. Real Estate Commn., 1949-55. Mem. Austin City Planning Commn., 1947-52, chmn., 1951-52. Chmn., Tex. Dem. Exec. Com., 1954-56. Pres. chmn. bd. Tex. Found., 1955—. Served as lt. comdr. USNR, World War II; PTO. Recipient Silver Citizenship medal VFW, 1957. Mem. Tex. Assn. Realtors (dir., pres. 1979, Realtor of Yr. 1981), Austin Real Estate Bd. (past pres.), Inst. Real Estate Mgmt., Inst. Real Estate Brokers, Mortgage Bankers Assn., Nat. Assn. Realtors (dir., chmn. polit. action com. 1982), Am. Legion, V.F.W. Episcopalian. Clubs: Austin Country, Headliners. Home: 11301 Spicewood Pkwy Austin TX 78750 Office: 6010 Balcones Dr Austin TX 78731

SANDNER, JOHN FRANCIS, lawyer, commodity futures broker; b. Chgo., Nov. 3, 1941; s. James and Margaret (Elmore) S.; m. Carole Ruth Erhardt, Feb. 14, 1970; children: Kathleen Dyan, Christopher John, Angela Marie, Michael John, Nicholas James, Allysann Elizabeth. B.A., So. Ill. U., 1965; J.D., U. Notre Dame, 1968. Bar: Ill. 1968, U.S. Dist. Ct. 1969, U.S. Supreme Ct. 1975. Pvt. practice Chgo., 1968-88; mem. Chgo. Merc. Exch., 1971-89, chmn. bd. govs., sr. policy advisor, 1980-82, 86-89; mem. Internat. Monetary Market, 1973—; pres. John F. Sandner & Assocs. (commodity futures brokers), Chgo., 1973—, Rufenacht, Bromagen, & Hertz, Inc. (commodity futures clearing firm), Chgo., 1978—. Mem. Commodity Adv. Com., State of Ill., 1980—; bd. dirs. Fund for Integrative Bio-med. and Ednl. Research, 1981, Jones Inst. for Reproductive Medicine, Eastern Va. Med. Sch., 1984—; mem. Ill. Vol. Parole Officer Program, 1976-78; commr. Prospect Heights (Ill.) Park Dist., 1977-78; trustee Found. for Brain Life Research, 1983—. Mem. Am. Bar Assn., Am. Arbitration Assn., Ill. Bar Assn., Chgo. Bar Assn. (arbitration com. 1976-77, mental health com. 1976-77), Nat. Futures Assn. (bd. dirs. 1982, chmn. central region bus. conduct com. 1982—), Notre Dame Law Assn. (bd. dirs. 1984—). Clubs: Notre Dame of Chgo. (gov.), Mid-America, Metropolitan. Office: 30 S Wacker Dr Chicago IL 60606

SANDS, DANIEL LEE, accountant, consultant; b. Copenhagen, July 18, 1947; came to U.S., 1948, naturalized, 1965; s. Robert Lee and Grete Anne (Birkhøj) S.; B.A., U. South Fla., 1972; M.S., Fla. Internat. U., 1974; m. Elizabeth Jean, July 31, 1976; children—Christopher Lee, Brian Stephen. Asst. controller North Dade Med. Complex, Miami, Fla., 1972-74; staff auditor Touche Ross & Co., Miami, 1974-76; div. controller Burger King Corp., Miami, 1976-79; dist. sales mgr. Automatic Data Processing, Inc., Miami, 1979-82; ptnr. Holyfield & Co., P.A., CPA's, West Palm Beach, Fla., 1982-87, pvt. practice, 1987—. Served with USAR, 1972. C.P.A., Fla. Mem. Fla. Inst. C.P.A.s (mgmt. services com. 1982-83, pub. relations com. 1987), U.S. Jaycees (chpt. v.p. 1981), Palms West C. of C., Rotary, Toastmasters, Alpha Tau Omega. Republican. Roman Catholic. Home: 13651 Ishnala Circle West Palm Beach FL 33414 Office: 2326 S Congress Ave West Palm Beach FL 33406

SANDS, DON WILLIAM, agricultural products company executive; b. Durant, Okla., Aug. 30, 1926; s. William Henry and Mary (Crutchfield) S.; m. Joan Cantrell, Mar. 28, 1947; children: Susan Sands Stone, Stan W., Steve J. B.S., Southeastern Okla. State U., 1949. Office mgr. Durant Cotton Oil & Peanut Corp., Okla., 1949-53; asst. mgr. Greenwood Products Co., Graceville, Fla., 1953-57; with Cotton Producers Assn. (changed name to Gold Kist Inc., 1970); exec. v.p. Gold Kist Inc., Atlanta, 1978-84, pres., 1984—, mem. mgmt. exec. com., 1986-89, chief oper. officer, chief exec. officer, 1989—; chmn. Golden Poultry Co., Inc. subs. Gold Kist Inc., Atlanta, 1987—; pres., chmn. exec. com., chief exec. officer Gold Kist Inc., Atlanta, 1989—; bd. dirs. C & S Agribusiness Adv. Bd., Atlanta, C & S Trust Co., Atlanta, Ill. Coop. Futures Co., Chgo., InTrade, Inc., Curacao, Netherlands Antilles, Ga. World Congress Ctr., Atlanta. Adv. bd. mem. Inst. Internat. Edn., Atlanta, 1980; adv. bd. mem. Japan-U.S. Southeast Assn., 1975; bd. dirs. Ga. Bd. Industry and Trade, 1979. Served with USN, 1944-46. Mem. Ga. C. of C. (dir.). Democrat. Presbyterian (elder). Club: Atlanta Athletic (pres.). Office: Gold Kist Inc 244 Perimeter Ctr Pkwy NE Atlanta GA 30346

SANDS, ERIC ALAN, financial consultant, bank officer; b. N.Y.C., Nov. 10, 1959. BBA in Fin., U. Fla., 1981; MBA in Fin., Loyola U., New Orleans, 1982; BBA in Acctg., Fla. Atlantic U., 1984. Pres. Sands Cons. Group, Ft. Lauderdale, Fla., 1985—; mgmt. trainee Barnett Bank So. Fla., Pompano Beach, 1988—. Active Ft. Lauderdale Multiple Sclerosis Soc., 1985—, Ft. Lauderdale United Way, 1988. Recipient Key to City of New Orleans, Cert. of Merit for Outstanding Service. Mem. Gold Coast Venture Capital Club, Mus. Art Contemporaries. Office: Sands Cons Group PO Box 26036 Tamarac FL 33320

SANDS, I. JAY, corporate, business, marketing and real estate consultant, lecturer, realtor; b. N.Y.C.; m. Kiti Reiner; children: Nelson, Tiffany, Summer Paige. B.A., NYU; J.D., Columbia U. Bar: N.Y., U.S. Supreme Ct. Mng. partner Korvette Bldg. Assocs., N.Y.C.; mng. dir., founder, chmn. bd. dirs., sec. First Republic Corp. Am.; chief exec. officer, sec. First Republic Corp., N.Y.; gen. partner Velvex Mid-City Parking Center, N.Y.C., Manhattan Parking Assocs.; dir., chmn. First Republic Underwriters, Inc.; pres., dir. Waltham Mgmt. Inc., Mass.; partner Cypress Parking Assocs., Cypress Plaza Shopping, Pompano Beach, Fla., Randolph House Co., Syracuse, N.Y., Beau Rivage Hotel Co., Bal Harbour, Fla., Gulf Assocs., Fla., Sahara Motel Assocs., Miami Beach, Fla.; chmn. Waltham (Mass.) Engring. & Research Co.; gen. partner Allstate Ins. Bldg. Co., N.Y.C., Fairfax Bldg. Assos., Kansas City, Mo., Engring. Bldg. Assos., Chgo., Manhattan Parking Co., Williamsbridge Assocs., N.Y.C., First Republic Funding Agy., N.Y.C., Atlantic Co., Miami, Syracuse-Randolph House Hotel, N.Y.C., Marchwood Realty Co., Phila., Video Film Center Assocs., N.Y.C., Hempstead Real Estate Enterprises, N.Y.C., Imperial Sq. Assocs., N.Y.C., DeMille Theatre Co., N.Y.C., Ohio Indsl. Assocs., Cleve., Pelham Park Assocs., Pa., Peoria (Ill.) Parking Assocs.; chmn., dir. Triple P Parking Corp., Peoria, Ill., Square Mgmt. Corp., N.Y.C., Park Circle Apts., Inc., N.Y.C., Holme Circle Apts., Inc., Phila.; sec. F.S. Mgmt. Corp., N.Y.C.; founder, chmn. exec. com., sec., dir. Imperial Sq. Mgmt. Corp., Hempstead, N.Y.; chmn. bd., chmn. exec. com., sec., dir. Nat. Med. Industries, Inc., Health Insts. Leasing Corp., Am. Med. Computer Corp.; pres. Med. Contract Supply Corp., City Capital Corp., N.J., Claredon Co.; vis. lectr., instr. mktg., real estate, comml. mktg. NYU, New Sch. for Social Research, U. Fla.; gen. agt. Northeastern Life Ins. Co., Patriot Life Ins. Co., Citizens Life Ins. Co. Past trustee Baldwin Sch., N.Y.C.; hon. trustee Pres. Harry S Truman Library. Served with AUS, 1942. Harlan Fiske Stone fellow, 1975; named Man of Year, Real Estate Weekly. Mem. Nat. Real Estate Club, ABA, N.Y. Real Estate Bd., Columbia U. Law Sch. Alumni Assn. (class chmn. 1978). Clubs: Shriners, Masons (32 deg.), Merchants.

SANDS, M(AYNARD) DALE, environmental science executive; b. Highland Park, Mich., Feb. 13, 1951; s. Maynard Duffy and Claire (Martin) S.; m. Debra Heath, Aug. 25, 1973; children: Hilaria, Trenton, Kendrick. BS in Chemistry and Biology, Cen. Mich. U., 1973; MS in Environ. Health Sci., U. Mich., 1974; MBA, Calif. State U., Hayward, 1984. Instrumentation chemist Raytheon Oceanography and Environ. Service, Portsmouth, R.I., 1974-77; ocean scis. dir. Interstate Electronics, Anaheim, Calif., 1977-81; v.p. Marine Ecol., Encinitas, Calif., 1981; v.p., gen. mgr. McKesson Environ. Svcs., Inc., Pleasanton, Calif., 1981-87; gen. mgr. Clayton Environ. Cons., Pleasanton, 1987-88; v.p. analytical svcs. CH2M Hill, Montgomery, Ala., 1988—. Contbr. articles to profl. jours. Schlar faculty Cen. Mich. U., 1969-73, U. Mich., 1973-74. Mem. Air Pollution Control Assn., Water Pollution Control Assn., Hazardous Materials Control Rsch. Inst., Am. Chem. Soc., U. Mich. Alumni Assn. Republican. Episcopalian. Home: 8137 Wynlakes Blvd Montgomery AL 36117 Office: CH2M Hill Inc 2567 Fairlane Dr Montgomery AL 36116

SANDS, THOMAS E., heavy machinery company executive; b. 1931. BS, Coffeyville Coll., 1951. With Parkersburg Rig & Reel Co., 1954-63; with Big Three Industries Inc., Houston, 1963—, treas., asst. sec., 1967-74, now pres., chief fin. officer. Served with AUS, 1951-54. Office: Big Three Industries Inc 3535 W 12th St Houston TX 77008 *

SANDSTROM, ALICE WILHELMINA, accountant; b. Seattle, Jan. 6, 1914; d. Andrew William and Agatha Mathilda (Sundius) S. BA, U. Wash., 1934. CPA, Wash. Mgr. office Star Machinery Co., Seattle, 1935-43, Howe & Co., Seattle, 1943-46; pvt. practice acctg., Seattle, 1945—; controller Children's Orthopedic Hosp. and Med. Ctr., Seattle, 1948-75, assoc. adminstr. fin., 1975-81; lectr. U. Wash., Seattle, 1957-72. Mem. Wash. State Title XIX Adv. Com., 1975-82, Wash. State Vendors Rate Adv. Com., 1980-87, Mayor's Task Force for Small Bus., 1981-83; bd. dirs. Seattle YWCA, 1981—, pres., 1986-88; bd. dirs. Sr. Services Seattle/King County, 1985, treas., 1986, pres. 1988—; bd. dirs. Children's Orthopedic Hosp. Found., 1982—. Fellow Hosp. Fin. Mgmt. Assn. (charter, state pres. 1956-57, nat. treas. 1963-65, Robert H. Reeves Merit award 1970, Frederick T. Muncie award 1985), Wash. State Hosp. Assn. (treas. 1956-70), Am. Soc. Women Accts. (pres. Seattle chpt. 1946-48), Am. Soc. Women CPA's. Club: Women's Univ. (Seattle); City (Seattle). Home and Office: 5725 NE 77th St Seattle WA 98115

SANDY, WILLIAM HASKELL, training and communications systems executive; b. N.Y.C., Apr. 28, 1929; s. Fred and Rose S.; A.B., U. Md., 1950, J.D., 1953; postgrad. Advanced Mgmt. Program, Harvard Bus. Sch., 1970-71; m. Marjorie Mazor, June 15, 1952; children—Alan, Lewis, Barbara. Admitted to Md. bar, 1953; planner-writer, account exec., account supr. Jam Handy Orgn., Detroit, 1953-64, v.p., 1964-69, sr. v.p., 1969-71; pres. Sandy Corp., Troy, Mich., 1971-88; chmn., 1988—. Bd. govs. Northwood Inst., 1976-80; bd. dirs. Cranbrook Sci. Inst.; v.p. nat. exec. coun. Harvard Bus. Sch., 1985—. Mem. Am. Mktg. Assn. (pres. Detroit chpt. 1975), Am. Soc. Tng. and Devel., Southeastern Mich. Better Bus. Bur. (bd. dirs.), Adcraft Club, Nat. Assn. Ednl. Broadcasters. Clubs: Harvard Bus. Sch. (pres. Detroit club 1983-85), The Hundred. Home: 596 Rudgate Bloomfield Hills MI 48013 Office: Sandy Corp 1500 W Big Beaver Rd Troy MI 48084

SANFORD, CHARLES STEADMAN, JR., banker; b. Savannah, Ga., Oct. 8, 1936; s. Charles Steadman and Ann (Lawrence) S.; m. Mary McRitchie, June 19, 1959; children: Ann Whitney, Charles Steadman III. AB, U. Ga., 1958; MBA, U. Pa., 1960. Vice pres. nat. div., account officer Bankers Trust Co., N.Y.C., 1961-68, 1st v.p., asst. to head resources mgmt., 1969-71, sr. v.p., 1973, exec. v.p., head resources mgmt., from 1972, pres., 1983-86, dep. chmn., from 1986, chmn., chief exec. officer, 1987—, mem. mgmt. com., 1979—; chmn. N.Y. Clearing House Com., 1987-88; dir. Gen Re Corp., Council for Aid to Edn., Inc., Internat. Monetary Conf., Wharton Bus. Sch. Club N.Y. Mem. bd. overseers Wharton Sch. of the U. Pa.; trustee U. Ga. Found., Com. for Econ. Devel. Served with arty. U.S. Army, 1958-59. Mem. Public Securities Assn. (dir. 1977-78), Securities Industry Assn. (exec. com. gov., dir., mem., 1976), Assn. Res. City Bankers (dir.), Council Fgn. Relations Inc., The Conf. Bd., Econ. Club of N.Y., Bond Club of N.Y., Inc. Office: Bankers Trust NY Corp Church St Sta PO Box 318 New York NY 10015

SANGER, SCOTT HOWARD, b. Chgo., Nov. 8, 1948; s. Alvin Beryl and Elaine June (Elman) S.; m. Betty Jane Gordon, June 27, 1971; children: Aaron Lee, Abby Gordon. BA, Tulane, U., 1970; JD, Northwestern U., 1973. Bar: Ill. 1973, N.Mex. 1980, U.S. Dist. Ct. (no. dist.) Ill. 1973. Assoc. Altman, Kurlander & Weiss, Chgo., 1973-74; Newman, Hess & Stahl, 1974, assoc. Newman, Stahl & Shadur, Chgo., 1975-79; pvt. practice law, Taos, N.Mex., 1981—; gen. ptnr. Taos Inn Assocs., Taos, 1982—. Mem. Taos Hist. Commn., 1983-88. Mem. ABA, Chgo. Bar Assn., Ill. Bar Assn., N.Mex. Bar Assn, Taos County Bar Assn.

SANGUINETTI, JACK ANTHONY, contracting executive; b. San Jose, Calif., Aug. 15, 1953; s. Benjamin and Grace Catherine (Navarra) S.; m. Diane Marie Taormino, Oct. 14, 1973; children: Jaclyn Christine, Anthony Paul, Benjamin Ross. Sales mgr. H.V. Welker Co., Inc., San Jose, 1974-78, v.p., 1978-88, exec. v.p., 1988—; founder, mng. owner Paragon Industries, San Jose, 1981—. Mem. Downtown Am. Cancer Soc. League, San Jose, 1986—. Served to staff sgt. USNG, 1971-77. Mem. Archbishop Mitty High Sch. Alumni Assn. (founding exec. com. mem., pres. 1989), Rotary. Republican. Office: H V Welker Co Inc 1390 Piper Dr Milpitas CA 95035

SANS, STEPHEN MICHAEL, retail executive; b. Harrison, N.J., Dec. 29, 1960; s. Edmond Walter and Mary Anne (Kapec) Smolski; m. Maria E. DeBarros, June 3, 1984 (div. April 1988); 1 child, Phillip Leland. BFA, Fairleigh Dickinson U., 1989. Pres. The Shop, Clifton, N.J., 1985-87; store mgr. Sharper Image, N.Y.C., 1987—; v.p. Three Star Sports, Rutherford, N.J., 1988—. Office: Sharper Image 4 W 57th St New York NY 10019

SANT, JOHN TALBOT, lawyer; b. Ann Arbor, Mich., Oct. 7, 1932; s. John Francis and Josephine (Williams) S.; m. Almira Steedman Baldwin, Jan. 31, 1959; children: John Talbot Jr., Richard Baldwin, Frank Williams. AB, Princeton U., 1954; LLB, Harvard U., 1957. Bar: Mo. 1957. Assoc. Thompson, Mitchell, Douglas & Neill, St. Louis, 1958-60; atty. McDonnell Aircraft Co., St. Louis, 1960-61, asst. sec., 1961-62, sec., 1962-67; sec. McDonnel Douglas Corp., St. Louis, 1967-76, asst. gen. counsel, 1969-74, corp. v.p. legal, 1974-75, corp. v.p., gen. counsel, 1975-88, sr. v.p., gen. counsel, 1988—. Vestry Ch. of St. Michael and St. George, St. Louis, 1979-82, 87—; bd. dirs. St. Luke's Hosp., St. Louis, 1986, Consolidated Neighborhood Services, Inc., St. Louis, 1987. Mem. ABA (pub. contracts sec., mem. council), Mo. Bar. Assn., St. Louis Bar Assn. Home: 9 Ridgewood Rd Saint Louis MO 63124 Office: McDonnell Douglas Corp PO Box 516 Saint Louis MO 63166

SANTANGELO, DANIEL LOUIS, food products executive; b. Norwalk, Conn., June 21, 1945; s. Daniel and Vivian (D'Alessio) S.; m. Janice Diane Smith, May 4, 1968; children: Kimberly, Heather, Daniel. BS magna cum laude, U. New Haven, 1968; MBA, CUNY, 1971. Mgr. mktg. research Campbell Soup Co., Camden, N.J., 1977-78, group mgr. mktg. research, 1978-79, dir. strategy planning, 1979-80, mktg. dir. soup, 1980-82, gen. mgr. main meals bus. unit, 1982-83, gen. mgr. refrigerated foods bus. unit, 1983-84, group gen. mgr. fresh foods div., 1984-85, v.p., group gen. mgr. Soup/Dry Foods bus. units, 1985—; trustee U. Medicine and Dentistry, Newark; mem. bus. adv. bd. Rider Coll., Lawrenceville, N.J. Pres. Moorestown (N.J.), 1984; mem. Rep. Town Com., Norwalk. Served with Conn. N.G., 1968-74. Recipient Diamond award Dupont Co., 1987. Mem. Planning Exec. Inst., Am. Mktg. Assn., Assn. Nat. Advt., Am. Mgmt. Assn. Roman Catholic. Home: 209 Demarest Rd Moorestown NJ 08057 Office: Campbell Soup Co Campbell Pl Camden NJ 08101

SANTANGELO, JOSEPH ANTHONY, corporation executive; b. Norristown, Pa., Apr. 13, 1954; s. Anthony Charles and Grace (Bonfiglio) S.; m. Susan Eldred, Sept. 16, 1978; children: Jenifer, Mark. BS in Acctg., Drexel U., 1977. CPA, Pa. Staff acct. to sr. mgr. Price Waterhouse, Phila., 1977-87; treas. FPA Corp., Huntingdon Valley, Pa., 1987—. Mem. Mt. Laurel, N.J. Newcomers Orgn. Mem. Am. Inst. CPA's, Pa. Inst. CPA's, Pi Kappa Phi (bd. dirs. 1978-81). Republican. Roman Catholic. Home: 59 Horseshoe Dr Mount Laurel NJ 08054 Office: FPA Corp 2507 Philmont Ave Huntingdon Valley PA 19006

SANTARELLA, ROY THEODORE, health care executive; b. Bklyn., Apr. 24, 1953; s. Benidetto and Mary (Giangrasso) S.; m. Joan P. Lacker, Sept. 11, 1977; children: Ryan, Devin. AS, Nassau Community Coll., 1973; BBA, Hofstra U., 1975; MBA, Adelphi U., 1977. Fin. analyst Unisys Corp., Detroit, 1976-79, St. Joseph Mercy Hosp., Pontiac, Mich., 1979-80; mgr. fin. planning The Toledo Hosp., 1980-83; cons. Touche Ross and Co., Detroit, 1983-84; sr. v.p., treas. Mercy Med. Ctr., Springfield, Ohio, 1984—. Planning com. Roman Cath. Conf. Ohio, Columbus, 1985—; bd. dirs. Dayton Area Health Plan, 1985-87, McKinley Hall, Springfield, 1985—, High St. United Meth. Ch., 1987-90. Mem. Ohio Hosp. Assn. (fin. com.), Physician Hosp. Orgn. (treas.), Greater Dayton Hosp. Assn. (fon., planning com.), Fin. Execs. Inst., Health Care Fin. Mgmt. Assn., Am. Coll. Health Care Execs., Springfield Country Club, Kiwanis. Methodist. Home: 519 Sparta Dr Springfield OH 45503 Office: Mercy Med Ctr 1343 N Fountain Blvd Springfield OH 45501

SANTAVICCA, ADAM, computer company executive; b. Turtle Creek, Pa., July 18, 1943; s. Flavian and Josephine (Zablocki) S.; m. Catherine A. Sekerchak, Nov. 26, 1965; children: Ann Marie, Daniel J. BBA, Robert Morris Coll., 1974. Mgr. corp. sales Equibank, Pitts., 1966-74; br. mgr. Computer Scis., Pitts., 1974-81; regional v.p. Anacomp, Pitts., 1981—. Served with U.S. ARmy, 1962-65. Mem. Data Processing Mgmt. Assn., Am. Records Mgmt. Assn. (advisor, cons., Pitts. 1981-85), Assn. Image Mgmt. Republican. Roman Catholic. Home: 1710 Craig Dr North Huntingdon PA 15642 Office: Anacomp 2020 Ardmore Blvd Pittsburgh PA 15642

SANTIAGO, CARLOS MANUEL, bank executive; b. Ponce, P.R., Dec. 1, 1961; s. Carlos M. Sr. and Marian Teresa (Irrizarry) S.; m. Sandra L. Hammond, Apr. 6, 1985; children: Christopher M., Sandra Marie. AA, Seminole Community Coll., 1980; BA, U. C.F., 1983. Adjuster Barnett Banks, Winter Park, Fla., 1984-85; br. mgr. C&S Family Credit, Tallahassee, 1985-87, Security First Fed. Savs. and Loan, Tallahassee, 1987-89; v.p. The Kirchman Corp., Altamonte Springs, Fla., 1989—; dir., instr. Inst. Fin., Tallahassee, 1987. Mem. Nat. Rifle Assn., Armed Forces Communications, Res. Officers Assn., Assn. MBA Execs., U.S. Jaycees. Republican. Presbyterian. Home: 1016 Danson Dr Deltona FL 32725 Office: 711 E436 Altamonte Springs FL 32725

SANTILLAN, ANTONIO, banker, motion picture finance executive; b. Buenos Aires, May 8, 1936; naturalized, 1966; s. Guillermo Spika and Raphaella C. (Abaladejo) S.; children: Andrea, Miguel, Marcos. Grad., Morgan Park Mil. Acad., Chgo., 1954; student, Coll. of William and Mary, 1958. Cert. real estate broker. Asst. in charge of prodn. Wilding Studios, Chgo., 1964; pres. Adams Fin. Services, Los Angeles, 1965-88. Writer, producer, dir. (motion pictures) The Glass Cage, co-writer Dirty Mary/Crazy Harry, Viva Knievel; contbg. writer Once Upon a Time in America; TV panelist Window on Wall Street; contbr. articles to profl. fin. and real estate jours. Served with USNR, 1959. Recipient Am. Rep. award San Francisco Film Festival, Cork Ireland Film Fest, 1961. Mem. Writer's Guild Am., Los Angeles Bd. Realtors, Beverly Hills Bd. Realtors (income/investment div. steering com.), Westside Realty Bd. (bd. dirs.), Los Angeles Ventures Assn. (bd. dirs.). Lodge: Rotary. Office: Adams Fin Svcs Inc 425 N Alfred St Los Angeles CA 90048

SANTONOCITO, PAULA JOAN, bank executive, writer; b. Riverhead, N.Y., Apr. 1, 1957; d. Anthony Philip and Clara Joan (Doman) S.; m. Francis Thaddeus Kennedy, Feb. 4, 1983. Student, L.I. U., 1975-78. Asst. mgr. legal advt. dept. San Diego Daily Transcript, 1979; methods analyst Saks Fifth Ave., N.Y., 1979-80, forms analyst, 1980-81, corp. purchasing exec., 1981-84; asst. cashier, mgr. materials mgmt. Midlantic Nat. Bank, Edison, N.J., 1984-85; asst. v.p., dir. materials mgmt. Midlantic Nat. Bank, Edison, 1985-87, v.p. materials mgmt., 1987—. Author poetry (3 poems) pub. in Street Mag., 1980; contbr. articles to newspapers, mags. Vol. tutor Literacy Vols. Am., Woodbridge, N.J., 1983-84. Mem. Nat. Assn. Purchasing Mgmt, Purchasing Mgmt. Assn. N.J., Internat. Platform Assn., LWV. Club: Barefoot Bay Golf and Country (Sebastian, Fla.). Office: Midlantic Nat Bank 10 Jersey Ave Metuchen NJ 08840

SANTOPIETRO, ALBERT ROBERT, lawyer; b. Providence, R.I., Oct. 18, 1948; s. Alfred and Marie (Epifanio) S.; m. Linda Williams Standridge, Nov. 22, 1974; children: Hope, Spencer, Anna. BA, Brown U., 1969; JD, U. Va., 1972. Bar: R.I. 1973, U.S. Dist. Ct. R.I. 1973, Ill. 1974, Conn. 1983. Atty. Met. Life Ins. Co., Oak Brook, Ill., 1974-75, Seligman Group, N.Y.C., 1975-76; atty. Mut. Benefit Life Ins. Co., Newark, 1976-78, asst. counsel, 1978-81; atty. Aetna Life and Casualty, Hartford, Conn., 1981-82, counsel, 1982—. Mem. ABA, Am. Corp. Counsel Assn. Office: Aetna Life and Casualty City Pl Hartford CT 06156

SANTOS, DAVID EARL, public relations executive; b. Fresno, Calif., Oct. 31, 1947; s. Earl E. and Hazel M. (Sanders) S. BA, Fresno State Coll., 1969; MA, Calif. State U., Fresno, 1972. Pub. relations officer Wells Fargo Bank, San Francisco, 1972-77, Marine Midland Bank, N.Y.C., 1977-78; v.p. Irving Trust Co., N.Y.C., 1978-88; sr. mgr. pub. rels. Equitable Life Assurance Soc., N.Y.C., 1988—. Mem. Pub. Relations Soc. Am. Home: 155 E 29th St Apt 8G New York NY 10016 Office: Equitable Life 787 7th Ave New York NY 10019

SANTOS, ISABELLE MARIA, retail company executive; b. Newark, N.J., May 11, 1964; d. Raymond and Maria (Rodrigues) De Almeida. BA, Rutgers U., 1986. Jr. exec. Macy's N.E., Newark, N.J., 1986—. Participant Hands Across Am., 1986. Mem. NAFE, Rutgers U. ALumni Assn. (v.p.), Pi Sigma Alpha. Home: 222 Chestnut St Kearny NJ 07032

SANTOSUOSSO, VINCENT, JR., personnel executive; b. Needham, Mass., Feb. 28, 1942; s. Vincent and Lenore (Elwyn) S.; m. Paula A. Tuzzo, Mar. 31, 1979. Student, Northeastern U., 1966-69, Boston State Coll., 1969; cert. in banking, Williams Coll., 1977. Vocat. counselor Action for Boston Com. Devel., 1965-69; skills tng. instr. Bank of New Eng., Boston, 1969-70, job analyst, 1970-71, personnel counselor, 1971-73, staff recruitment officer, 1973-79; dir. personnel Spaulding and Slye Corp., Burlington, Mass., 1979-80, New Eng. Rare Coin Galleries, Boston, 1981-82; corp. dir. personnel, voting trustee Tech. Aid Corp., Newton, Mass., 1982—; cons. V.S. Assocs., Boston, 1980-81. Hon. trustee S.W. Boston Community Services, 1982—; mem. Balsamo Meml. Charitable Found., Dover, Mass., 1985—, Cath. Charitable Bur. Boston, 1985—; clk. Tri-Lateral Council for Quality Edn., Inc., 1975; monitor sch. desegregation U.S. Dist. Ct. Appointee, 1975; mem. Mayors Manpower Adv. Planning Council, 1974; vol. interviewer/screener Commonwealth of Mass. Exec. Dept., 1973. Named Outstanding Vol., Nat. Ctr. for Vol. Action, 1978. Mem. Nat. Assn. Temp. Services, Am. Soc. Personnel Adminstrn., Mass. Assn. Temp. Services, New Eng. Soc. Personnel Mgmt., Am. Compensation Assn. Roman Catholic. Club: Italian Am. Citizens. Lodge: Sons of Italy. Office: Tech Aid Corp 109 Oak St Newton MA 02164

SANTRY, ARTHUR JOSEPH, JR., retired engineering company executive; b. Brookline, Mass., Aug. 1, 1918; s. Arthur Joseph and Suzanne (Cawley) S.; m. Julia Timmins, June 4, 1955; children—Arthur Joseph III, Suzanne (Mrs. Claude Robert Cochin), Peter, Charles, Robert. B.A., Williams Coll., 1941; LL.B., Harvard, 1948. Bar: Mass. bar 1948. Ptnr. Putnam, Bell, Santry & Ray, Boston, 1948-56; ret. chmn. Combustion Engring., Inc., Stamford, Conn.; also bd. dirs.; bd. dirs. AMAX, Inc., Greenwich, Conn., N.Am. Reins. Corp., N.Y., N.Am. Reassurance Co., N.Y. Served to lt. (s.g.) USNR, 1942-46. Mem. Navy League U.S. Clubs: New York Yacht (N.Y.C.); Seawanhaka Corinthian Yacht (Oyster Bay, N.Y.); Storm Trysail (Larchmont, N.Y.); Country (Brookline, Mass.); Eastern Yacht (Marblehead, Mass.); Indian Harbor Yacht (Greenwich, Conn.), Round Hill (Greenwich, Conn.); Lyford Cay (Nassau, Bahamas); Royal Bermuda Yacht (Hamilton); Royal Ocean Racing (London, Eng.). Office: Combustion Engring Inc 900 Long Ridge Rd PO Box 9308 Stamford CT 06904

SANTRY, BARBARA LEA, securities analyst and investment banker; b. Key West, Fla., Jan. 20, 1948; d. Jere Joseph and Frances Victoria (Appel) S. BS in Nursing, Georgetown U., 1969; MBA, Stanford U., 1978. Enlisted USN, 1969, advanced through grades to lt., 1971, resigned, 1972; program analyst, br. chief U.S. Dept. HEW, Washington, 1973-76; mgr. cons. div. Arthur Andersen and Co., San Francisco, 1978-80; asst. v.p. Am. Med. Internat., Washington, 1980-83; v.p. Alex Brown and Sons, Inc., Balt., 1983-86; ptnr. Wessels, Arnold and Henderson, Mpls., 1986-88; v.p. Dain Bosworth Inc., Mpls., 1988—. Home: 2521 Princeton Ct Saint Louis Park MN 55416

SANTUCCI, J. DENNIS, electronics executive; b. N.Y.C., Jan. 31, 1948; s. John J. and Eileen C. S.; m. Karen A. McNally, June 14, 1969; children: J.

Brian, David C. BEE, Manhattan Coll., 1969; MBA, Northeastern U., 1973. Electronics engr. Raytheon Co., Wayland, Mass., 1969-74; internat. sales mgr. Teledyne Philbrick, Dedham, Mass., 1974-79; sales mgr. Analogic Corp., Wakefield, Mass., 1979-85; v.p. Dymec, Inc., Winchester, Mass., 1985—. Chmn. Christian Svc. Com., St. Brigid's Ch., Lexington, Mass., 1987, pres. parish counc., 1988. Mem. Northeastern MBA Assn., Mass. Mktg. Assn., Instrument Soc. Am., IEEE. Home: 20 Birch Hill Ln Lexington MA 02173 Office: Dymec Inc 8 Lowell Ave Winchester MA 01890

SAPERSTEIN, JEFFREY STANLEY, marketing executive; b. N.Y.C., Dec. 4, 1949; s. Harry and Ruth (Dworsky) S.; m. Chantal Marie El-Bez, Apr. 24, 1974; children: David, Michael. BA in Communications cum laude, Queens Coll., 1971; MA in Communications, U. Denver, 1972. Media planner Rosenfield, Sirowitz & Lawson, N.Y.C., 1973-75; account exec. Marschalk, N.Y.C., 1975-76, Ted Bates, N.Y.C., 1976-77; account supr. Foote, Cone & Belding, San Francisco, 1978-83; dir. mktg. Jewish Community Fed., San Francisco, 1983-85; prin. Jeff Saperstein & Ascs., Mill Valley, Calif., 1985—; instr. U. Calif. Berkeley Ext., San Francisco, 1983-88; cons. Sosnick Cos., Santa Clara, Calif., 1985-88. Author: Practical Applications of Impromptu Speaking, 1988; contbr. articles to profl. jours. Fund raiser Jewish Community Fed., San Francisco, 1981-88; bd. dirs. Mgmt. Ctr., San Francisco, 1988. Democrat. Home and Office: 18 Azalea Dr Mill Valley CA 94941

SAPERSTEIN, ROSE, learning consultant; b. Seattle, Dec. 28, 1956; d. Harold and Sylvia (Kettleman) S. Student, Western Wash. State U., 1975-76, Brandeis U., 1976-77; BA, U. Wash., 1981; MA, Antioch U., Seattle, 1987. Mgr., instr. Inst. Reading Edn. and Devel., Seattle, 1979-84; tng. cons. Learning Internat., Bellevue, Wash., 1985-88; owner, learning cons. Rose Saperstein and Assocs., Seattle, 1985-88; organizational devel. specialist Amdahl Corp., Sunnyvale, Calif., 1988—; adv. bd. New Horizons for Learning, Seattle, 1987—; mem. steering com. The Edn. Summit Conf., Fairfax, Va., 1988. Co-author Read Your Way to the Top, 1987. Mem. Pacific Northwest Orgn. Devel. Network, Nat. Coun. Jewish Women (bd. dirs. 1984-87), Phi Beta Kappa. Home: 292 E Iowa Sunnyvale CA 94086 Office: Amdahl Corp 1250 E Arques Ave Sunnyvale CA 94088-3470

SAPIDIS, NICKOLAS, engineer; b. Edessa, Greece, Sept. 16, 1961; came to U.S., 1985; s. Savas and Aliki (Iosiphidis) S. Diploma in Naval Architecture and Marine Engring., Nat. Tech. U., Athens, 1985; MA in Applied Math., U. Utah, 1987; MSME, U. Rochester, 1988. Research asst. Nat. Tech. U., Athens, 1985; research fellow mech. engring. dept. U. Rochester, 1987—; vis. lectr. in ocean engring. Computer-Aided Design Lab. MIT, Cambridge, Mass., 1986. Contbr. articles to profl. jours. Greek Govt. scholar, 1983. Mem. Am. Math. Soc. Greek Orthodox. Office: U Rochester Dept Mech Engring Rochester NY 14627

SAPP, KENNETH JOHN, marketing analyst; b. Gt. Lakes, Ill., Feb. 11, 1961; s. Carl Edward and Genevieve Marie (Litka) S.; m. Kathi Suzanne Myers, Apr. 11, 1987. AS in Computer Sci., Cypress Coll., 1981; BS in Fin., Calif. State U., Long Beach, 1988. Computer operator Carter, Hawley, Hale Stores, Anaheim, Calif., 1980-81; computer operator, ops. analyst then supr. computer ops. Ralph's Grocery Store, L.A., 1981-86; mktg. analyst NCR Comten, L.A., 1986-89; ter. sales mgr. NCR Comten, San Diego, 1989—. Mem. Long Beach Yacht Club, Balboa Sailing Club. Republican. Roman Catholic. Home: 804 Spindrift Ln Carlsbad CA 92009 Office: NCR Comten 8304 Clairemont Mesa Blvd Ste 110 San Diego CA 92111

SAPP, WALTER WILLIAM, lawyer, energy company executive; b. Linton, Ind., Apr. 21, 1930; s. Walter J. and Nona (Stalcup) S.; m. Eva Kaschner, July 10, 1957; children: Karen Elisabeth, Christoph Walter. A.B. magna cum laude, Harvard, 1951; J.D. summa cum laude, Ind. U., 1957. Bar: Ind. 1957, N.Y. 1959, Colo. 1966, U.S. Supreme Ct. 1972, Tex. 1977. Pvt. practice N.Y.C., 1957-60; practice in Paris, France, 1960-63, Colorado Springs, 1966-76; assoc. atty. Cahill, Gordon, Reindel & Ohl, N.Y.C., 1957-60, Paris, 1960-63, N.Y.C., 1963-65; partner Cahill, Gordon, Reindel & Ohl, 1966; gen. counsel Colo. Interstate Corp., 1966-76, v.p., 1968-76, sec., 1971-76, sr. v.p., dir., exec. com., 1973-75, exec. v.p., 1975-76; v.p. Coastal States Gas Corp., 1973-76; sr. v.p., gen. counsel Tenneco, Inc., Houston, 1976—, sec., 1984-86; Editor-in-chief Ind. U. Law Jour., 1956-57. Trustee Houston Ballet, 1982-85; bd. dirs. Harris County Met. Transit Authority, 1982-84; mem. adv. bd. Inst. for Internat. Edn. S.W. region, 1987—, Internat. and Comparative Law Ctr. Southwestern Legal Found., 1976—. Served to lt. USNR, 1951-54. Mem. ABA, N.Y. State Bar Assn., Tex. Bar Assn., Assn. of Bar of City of N.Y., Houston Bar Assn., Order of Coif, French-Am. C. of C. (bd. dirs. 1987—), Alliance Française Houston (bd. dirs. 1989—). Mem. United Ch. of Christ. Clubs: Coronado, Houston Racquet. Office: Tenneco Inc Tenneco Bldg PO Box 2511 Houston TX 77001

SAPPENFIELD, DIANE HASTINGS, real estate executive, civic worker; b. Marion, Ohio, Apr. 22, 1940; d. Edgar Dean and Marguerite Elizabeth (Alexander) Hastings; B.A. in Sociology and Econs., Mills Coll., 1962; tchr.'s cert. Calif. State U., Los Angeles, 1963; M.S. in Fin. and Real Estate, Am. U., 1986; m. Ronald Eugene Sappenfield, July 6, 1962; children—Derek Ronald, Ann Elizabeth. Tchr. elem. sch., El Segundo, Calif., 1963-66; asst. dir. admissions Mills Coll., 1972-74; v.p., dir. DDA Assocs., Inc., McLean, Va., 1978—; real estate investment cons., Shannon and Luchs, Washington, 1987—; asst. to chmn. bd. Watergate Complex, Washington, 1979-81; dir. corp. mktg. Watergate Devel. Inc., McLean, 1981-82; pres. Am. U. Real Estate Alumni Chpt.; Vol. tchr. Saugatuck Elem. Sch., Westport, Conn., 1976-79; active benefits for Corcoran Sch. Art, Nat. Symphony Orch., Women's Bd. Am. Heart Assn., Hope Ball, Meridian House, Washington; bd. dirs. Westport-Weston Arts Council, 1973-79, Young Concert Artists, 1984—; mem. Levitt Pavilion Governing Com., 1974-79; pres. Friends of Levitt Pavilion, 1977; trustee Stauffer-Westport Fund, 1976-79; mem. Westport Young Woman's League, 1969-79, pres., 1975-76, Jr. League of Washington D.C., 1980—; bd. dirs. Stamford-Norwalk br. Jr. League, 1977-78. Mem. Washington D.C. Bd. Realtors, Mills Coll. Club N.Y., Washington Jr. League. Home: 7612 Georgetown Pike McLean VA 22102

SAPSOWITZ, SIDNEY H., entertainment and media company executive; b. N.Y.C., June 29, 1936; s. Max and Annette (Rothstein) Sapsowitz; m. Phyllis Skopp, Nov. 27, 1957; children—Donna Dawn Chazen, Gloria Lynn Aaron, Marsha Helene Gleit. BBA summa cum laude, Paterson (N.J.) State Coll., 1980. Various fin. and systems positions Metro Goldwyn Mayer, N.Y.C., 1957-68; exec. v.p., chief fin. officer Metro Goldwyn Mayer, Los Angeles, 1980-86, also bd. dirs.; exec. v.p. Penta Computer Assoc. Inc., N.Y.C., 1968-70, Cons. Actuaries Inc., Clifton, N.J., 1970-73, Am. Film Theatre, N.Y.C., 1974-76; exec. v.p., chief fin. officer Cinema Shares Internat. Distributors, N.Y.C., 1976-79; sr. cons. Solomon, Finger & Newman, N.Y.C., 1979-80; various positions leading to exec. v.p.fin. and adminstrn., chief fin. officer MGM/UA Entertainment Co., Culver City, Calif., 1985-86; sr. exec. v.p., bd. dirs. exec. com. Beverly Hills, Calif., 1986—; chmn. bd., chief exec. officer MGA/UA Telecommunications Corp., Beverly Hills, 1986—; dir. Penta Computer Assoc., N.Y.C., 1968-70, Metro Goldwyn Mayer, N.Y.C., 1985-86; MGM/UA Communications Co., Beverly Hills, 1986—. Pres., Wayne Conservative Congregation, N.J., 1970-77. Mem. Am. Mgmt. Assn. (cons., lectr. 1967), Am. Film Inst., Acad. Motion Picture Arts & Scis., Fin. Exec. Inst. Lodge: Knights of Pythias (chancellor 1970).

SARETSKY, PETER STEVEN, financial services executive; b. Bronx, N.Y., Feb. 23, 1951; s. Eli and Helen (Lesikin) S.; m. Nancy Evans, May 25, 1974; children: Jason S., Heather R. BS, Carnegie-Mellon U., 1974, MS, 1974; Cert. in Profl. Accountancy, Northwestern U., 1975. CPA, N.Y. Auditor, then sr. auditor Arthur Young and Co., N.Y.C., 1974-77; with Am. Express Co., N.Y.C., 1977—, with travel related svcs. div., 1981—, dir. fin. acctg., 1983, v.p. fin. and planning, 1987—; dir. fin. and planning Am. Express Co., Singapore, 1983-87. Mem. AICPA, N.Y. State Soc. CPAs. Democrat. Jewish. Home: 111 Ridge Rd Ardsley NY 10502 Office: Am Express Co Am Express Tower World Fin Ctr New York NY 10285-3600

SARGENT, CHARLES LEE, recreation vehicle and pollution control systems manufacturing company executive; b. Flint, Mich., Mar. 22, 1937; s. Frank T. and Evelyn M. (Martinson) S.; m. Nancy Cook, June 9, 1962; children: Wendy L., Joy A., Candace L. B ME, GM Inst., 1960; MBA, Harvard U., 1962. Reliability engr. AC Spark Plug div. GM, Flint, 1962-63; with Thetford Corp., Ann Arbor, Mich., 1962—, pres., chmn. bd. dirs., 1974—; pres., chmn. bd. dirs. Thermassan Corp., 1969-72; bd. dirs. Ann Arbor Bank & Trust Co., First of Am. Bank Ann Arbor; bd. dirs., pres.' coun. GM Engring. and Mgmt. Inst., Flint, 1987—. Patentee in field. Elder Presbyn. Ch.; trustee Lincoln Consolidated Sch. Bd., 1973-77; bd. dirs. Stirling Power Systems, 1977-86, Harvard Bus. Sch. Club of Detroit, 1983—. Named Entrepreneur of the Yr. Harvard Bus. Sch. Club of Detroit, 1981; recipient Entrepreneurial Achievement award, 1987. Mem. Recreational Vehicle Industry Assn. (bd. dirs. 1979-80), Barton Hills Country Club (bd. dirs. 1985-87, pres. 1987). Home: 3000 Glazieiz Way #160 Ann Arbor MI 48105 Office: Thetford Corp PO Box 1285 Ann Arbor MI 48106

SARGENT, HENRY BARRY, JR., holding company executive; b. Jackson, Miss., June 19, 1934; s. Henry Barry and Grace Richmond (Ellis) S.; m. Caroline Huey, Aug. 8, 1964 (div. 1978); children: Catherine Sargent Warshawsky, Carolyn, Henry B. III; m. Claire King, Dec. 23, 1978. BA, Ariz. U., 1956; MS, Columbia U., 1957. Various positions Ariz. Pub. Service Co., Phoenix, 1957-67, controller, 1967-69, v.p. mktg. then customer service, 1969-75, v.p. fin., 1975-81, also bd. dirs., exec. v.p., 1981-86; exec. v.p., chief fin. officer Pinnacle West Capital Corp., Phoenix, 1985—, also bd. dirs.; bd. dirs. MeraBank, Phoenix, Magma Copper Co., San Manuel, Ariz. Pres., dir. Phoenix Symphony Assn., 1969-79; chmn. Nat. Alliance Businessmen, Phoenix, 1970-71; chmn. Ariz. Theatre Co., Phoenix and Tucson, 1985—; chmn. Cen. Phoenix Com., 1987—. Mem. Phi Beta Kappa. Republican. Episcopalian. Clubs: Phoenix Country; Univ. (N.Y.C.). Home: 2201 N Central Ave Phoenix AZ 85004 Office: Pinnacle W Capital Corp 411 N Central Ave Phoenix AZ 85004 *

SARGENT, JOHN C., oil company executive. V.p., treas. Conoco Inc., Wilmington, Del. Office: Conoco Inc 1007 Market St Wilmington DE 19898 *

SARGENT, WILLIAM LEROY, life insurance company executive; b. Coalville, Utah, May 10, 1947; s. William Copley and Evelyn Shirley (Kincade) S.; B.A., U. Utah, 1972; m. Margaret P. Patterson, June 27, 1979; children—Catherine, William Patterson, Jonathan Browning, Sara Jane. Acct. to sec.-treas. SNL Fin. Corp., Salt Lake City, 1969—. bd. dirs. Hansen Planetarium Found. Served to capt. USAR, 1972-80. Mem. Internat. Acctg. and Statis. Assn. (pres. chpt., nat. com. co-chmn. program 1987, 88, 89), Utah Life Conv. (pres.). Republican. Address: 6822 Pineview Circle Salt Lake City UT 84121

SARICH, JOHN THOMAS, insurance company executive, consultant; b. DeKalb, Ill., Oct. 22, 1948; s. Victor F. and Laura (Allen) S.; m. Virginia Rae Swearingen, Aug. 10, 1974; children: Jonathan, Jeremy, Lora. BA, U. Nebr., 1974; MBA, Creighton U., 1978. Analyst, corp. planner Mut. of Omaha, 1974-78; dir. mktg. Nebr. AAA, Omaha, 1978-80, v.p. ins., 1983—; v.p. ops. Redland Group, Council Bluffs, Iowa, 1980-83. Bd. dirs. Fontenelle Forest Assn., Bellevue, Nebr., 1988—; mem. alumni bd. Creighton U., 1985-88; mem. athletic bd., 1988—; fin. chmn. Kountze Meml. Luth. Ch., Omaha, 1988—. With USAF, 1969-72. Republican. Office: AAA Nebr 910 N 96th St Omaha NE 68114

SARKIS, BARBARA LOUISE, commercial credit manager, educator; b. Detroit, Jan. 9, 1941; d. Charles Robert and Fern C. (Harris) Hankins; m. Daniel Roy Nelson, Dec. 19, 1959 (div. Oct. 1977); children: Tamara Ann Oquist, Angela Marie Moyes; m. S. Walter Sarkis, July 9, 1982. Student, U. Nebr., 1958-59; degree in bus. machines, Davis Bus. Sch., Omaha, 1959. Cert. bus. credit exec. Credit mgr. and mktg. Western Farmers Assn., Seattle, 1970-78; mgr. credit, asst. sec. Associated Sand and Gravel Co., Inc., Everett, Wash., 1978—; adj. prof. Seattle Pacific U., 1984—; bd. dirs., founder Lien Research Corp. Contbr. articles to profl. jours. Mem. Mountain Rescue Council, Seattle, 1973—, South Snohomish County Econ. Devel. Council, Lynnwood, Wash., 1979-83; instr. mountaineering first aid Seattle chpt. ARC, 1973-80; mem., bd. dirs. Driftwood Theatre, Edmonds, Wash., 1973-80. Nat. Inst. Credit fellow, 1981. Mem. Nat. Assn. Credit Mgmt. (bd. dirs. Western Wash. and Alaska chpts. 1982-86, mem. adv. council Task Force on Edn. 1987-88, Nat. Credit Exec. of Yr. 1984), Pacific N.W. Credit Council (pres. 1986-88), Credit Edn. Orgn. (bd. dirs. 1978-88, pres. 1987-88), Soroptimist Internat. Republican. Office: Associated Sand and Gravel Co Inc PO Box 2037 Everett WA 98203

SARNI, VINCENT ANTHONY, manufacturing company executive; b. Bayonne, N.J., July 11, 1928; s. Alfred M. and Louise M. (Zoratti) S.; m. Dorothy Bellavance, Nov. 4, 1950; children: Louise Marie, Karen Lee, Vincent Anthony. B.S., U. R.I., 1949; postgrad., N.Y. U., 1950-52, Harvard U., 1973; LL.D. (hon.), Juniata Coll., 1979, U. R.I., 1985. Plant acct. Rheem Mfg. Co., Linden, N.J., 1950-53; dir. mfg. services Crown Can Co., Balt., 1953-57; dir. mktg. services Olin Corp., Stamford, Conn., 1957-68; with PPG Industries Inc., Pitts., 1968—, v.p. mktg. indsl. chem. dept., 1968-69, v.p., gen. mgr. indsl. chem. dept., 1969-75, v.p., gen. mgr. chem div., 1975-77, group v.p. chems. group, 1977-80; sr. v.p. PPG Industries Inc. (parent co.), Pitts., 1980-83, vice chmn., 1984, chmn., chief exec. officer, 1984—; bd. dirs. Brockway, Inc., Honeywell, Inc., Pitts. Baseball Assocs.; chmn. bus. adv. com. Inst. for Tng. of Handicapped in Advanced Tech. Exec. com. Allegheny Conf. on Community Devel.; trustee U. R.I. Found., Juniata Coll.; bd. dirs. Pitts. Guild for Blind, 1980; bd. dirs., vice chmn. Allegheny Gen. Hosp.; mem. bus. adv. council U. R.I., 1975—. Mem. Chem. Mfrs. Assn. (bd. dirs.), Soc. Chem. Industry, Bus. Higher Edn. Forum, Bus. Roundtable. Clubs: Duquesne, Rolling Rock, Laurel Valley Country, Chartiers Country, Allegheny, Point Judith Country. Office: PPG Industries Inc 1 PPG Pl Pittsburgh PA 15272 *

SARNOFF, ALBERT, communications executive; b. N.Y.C., July 19, 1925; s. Morris and Clara (Oppenheimer) S.; m. Nancy Hanak, July 25, 1968; children: Gary, Ken, Doug. B.A., Yale U., 1947. Buyer R.H. Macy & Co., N.Y.C., 1950-52; v.p. Pease & Elliman, N.Y.C., 1952-58; pres. Club Razor Blade Mfg. Co., N.J., 1958-62; sr. v.p., treas. Warner Communications Inc., N.Y.C., 1962—. Clubs: Metropolis Country, City Athletic. Office: Warner Communications Inc 75 Rockefeller Pla New York NY 10019

SARTOR, ANTHONY J., environmental engineer; b. Englewood, N.J., Mar. 28, 1943; s. John and Catherine (Dottino) S. Sr.; m. Maria C. Crisonio, Dec. 26, 1964; children: Lisanne, Colette (twins), John. BS in Engring., Manhattan Coll., 1964; MS in Engring., Mich. U., 1965, PhD, 1968. Devel. engr. Celanese Co., 1968-70; sr. water quality engr. Con Edison, N.Y.C., 1970-72; mgr. environ. affairs N.Y. Power Pool, 1972-74; pres. Sartor Associates, Warren, N.J., 1974-77; exec. v.p., treas., sec. Paulus, Sokolowski, Sartor, Inc., Warren, 1977—. Mem. Environ. Commn., Fanwood, N.J., gov.'s transition team N.J. Dept. Environ. Projection. Recipient Disting. Service award Fanwood-Scotch Plains Jaycees, 1974. Mem. Am. Chem. Soc., Am. Inst. Chem. Engrs., Nat. Soc. Environ. Engrs., Jaycees (bd. dirs. 1971-72, pres. 1973-74), Sigma Xi, Phi Lambda Upsilon. Club: Italian-Am. (Fairview, N.J.). Home: 19 Kevin Rd Scotch Plains NJ 07076 Office: 67A Mountain Blvd Extension Warren NJ 07060

SARTORE, DONALD GINO, financial executive; b. Pitts., Sept. 17, 1949; s. Gino and Mary K. (Ricci) S.; m. Deborah Ann Gegick, July 11, 1975; children: Adele Marie, Megan Elizabeth. BBA, Robert Morris Coll., 1971; grad., Bucknell U. Pa. Sch. Banking, 1981; postgrad., Rutgers U. Stonier Grad. Sch., 1985. Asst. controller JetNet Corp., Carnegie, Pa., 1971-73; v.p. fin. JetNet Corp., Carnegie, 1986—, also bd. dirs.; sr. fin. analyst Equibank, Pitts., 1973-75, mgr. performance reporting, 1975-79, mgr. fin. analysis, 1979-81, v.p., mgr. market research, 1981-86. Mem. Nat. Assn. Bus. Econs. (forecast panel 1983—), Bank Mktg. Assn., Nat. Assn. Bank Cost Analysts. Home: 2131 Coventry Dr Allison Park PA 15101 Office: JetNet Corp Keystone Dr Carnegie PA 15106

SARVER, LARRY DAVID, chemical engineer; b. Feb. 17, 1947; s. Glen Edward and Claretta (Fulmer) S.; m. Judith Annette Moran, Aug. 31, 1968; children: Jon David, Benjamin Glen, Janet Michal. BS in Chemistry, David Lipscomb Coll., 1970; BS in Chem. Engring., Tenn Tech. U., 1970. Engr. prodn. devel. Borg Warner Plastics, Parkersburg, W.Va., 1970-77; engr. prodn. Mobay Corp., New Martinsville, W.Va., 1977-79, prodn. supt., 1979-82; extrusion specialist Mobay Corp., Pitts., 1984—; prodn. supt. Bayer Corp., Uerdingen, Fed. Republic Germany, 1982-84; Patentee in field. Mem. Soc. Plastics Industries. Home: 130 McCandless Pl Wexford PA 15090 Office: Mobay Corp Mobay Rd Pittsburgh PA 15205

SASAKI, Y. TITO, business services company executive; b. Tokyo, Feb. 6, 1938; came to U.S., 1967, naturalized, 1983; s. Yoshinaga and Chiyoko (Imada) S.; m. Janet Louise Cline, June 27, 1963; 1 child, Heather N. BS, Chiba U., 1959; postgrad. Royal Coll. Art, London, 1961, U. Oslo, 1962; MS, Athens Tech. Inst., Greece, 1964; postgrad. U. Calif., Berkeley, 1969. Chief designer Aires Camera Industries Co., Tokyo, 1958-59; tech. officer London County Council, 1961-62; researcher Athens Ctr. Ekistics, 1964-66; sr. researcher Battelle Inst., Geneva, 1966-68; project engr. Marin County Transit Dist., San Rafael, Calif., 1968-69; chief planning, research Golden Gate Bridge Dist., San Francisco, 1969-74; pres. Visio Internat. Inc., Somona, Calif., 1973—; chmn. steering com. Kawada Industries Inc., Tokyo, 1974-82; chief exec. officer Quantum Mechanics Corp., Somona, 1981—; bd. dirs., v.p. Sonoma Skypark, Inc., 1986—. Mem. Rep. Nat. Com. Mem. ASME, Am. Welding Soc., Helicopter Assn. Internat., AIAA, Am. Inst. Cert. Planners, World Soc. Ekistics, Brit. Soc. Long-Range Planning, Am. Vacuum Soc., Aircraft Owners and Pilots Assn. Roman Catholic. Office: Visio Internat Inc PO Box 1888 Sonoma CA 95476

SASDI, GEORGE P., utilities company executive; b. Budapest, Hungary, Mar. 4, 1934; came to U.S., 1963; s. Miksa and Margaret (Krausz) S.; m. Susan T. Feldman, July 17, 1964; children: Richard, David. Diploma in Elec. Engring., Tech. U. Budapest, 1956; BS in Elec. Engring., U. Toronto, 1959. Registered profl. engr., Mass. Engr. Gatineau Power Co., Hull, Que., Can., 1959-63; with New England Electric System, Westborough, Mass., 1963—; planning mgr. New England Power Service Co., Boston, 1963-69; project mgr. mgmt. info. systems New England Power Service Co., 1969-70; head engring. computer applications dept., New England Power Service Co., Westboro, Mass., 1970-73, project mgr. power plant projects, 1973-75, dir. power plant engring., 1975-77, v.p., chief engr., 1977—; v.p., chief engr. New England Power Co., Westboro, Mass., 1984—; also bd. dirs. New England Power Service Co., Westboro, Mass.; v.p., chief engr. New England Electric System, Westboro, Mass., 1985-87, sr. v.p., chief engr., 1987—; mem. Electric Power Research Inst. Coal Combustion Systems Div., 1988—, Energy Mgmt. and Utilization Div. Com., 1985-87 Utility Air Regulatory Group Steering-Audit Com., 1985—. Mem. Internat. Energy Adv. Council Fletcher Sch. Law and Diplomacy Tufts U., 1984—. Named Young Engr. of Yr. Engring. Soc. Mass., 1969. Mem. IEEE (sr. mem., past chmn. power engring. Boston chpt. 1972), Am. Soc. Macro Engring., EEI Engring. and Ops. Exec. Adv. Com. Office: New Eng Electric System 25 Research Dr Westborough MA 01582

SASS, DANIEL RAYMOND, energy company executive; b. St. Paul, Nov. 16, 1957; s. Thomas and Margaret (Traxler) S. BS in Fin. cum laude, St. Cloud State U., 1980; MBA in Fin., U. Minn., 1984. Cert. mgmt. acct. Supr. Northwest Airlines, St. Paul, 1981-83; program acct. Apache Corp., Mpls., 1984; sr. fin. analyst Diversified Energies Inc., Mpls., 1984-86, sr. treasury analyst, 1986—. Active Am. Lung Assn., Mpls., 1987-88. Office: Diversified Energies Inc 201 S 7th St Minneapolis MN 55402

SATRE, PHILIP GLEN, business executive, lawyer; b. Palo Alto, Calif., Apr. 30, 1949; s. Selmer Kenneth and Georgia June (Sterling) S.; m. Jennifer Patricia Arnold, June 30, 1973; children—Malena Anne, Allison Neal, Jessica Lilly, Peter Sterling. B.A., Stanford U., 1971; J.D., U. Calif.-Davis, 1975; postgrad sr. exec. program MIT, 1982. Bar: Nev., Calif. Assoc. Vargas & Bartlett, Reno, 1975-79; v.p., gen. counsel, sec. Harrah's, Reno, 1980-83, sr. v.p., 1983-84, pres. Harrah's East, Atlantic City, 1984; pres., chief exec. officer Harrah's Hotels and Casinos, Reno, 1984—. Mem. ABA, Nev. Bar Assn., Calif. Bar Assn., Order of Coif, Phi Kappa Phi, Stanford Alumni Assn. (pres. Reno chpt. 1976-77), Young Pres. Orgn. Office: Harrah's 300 E 2d St PO Box 10 Reno NV 89504 *

SATULOFF, BARTH, accounting executive; b. Buffalo, Dec. 13, 1945; s. Bernard and Annette (Lurie) S.; m. Marsha Steiner, May 25, 1974. BBA in Acctg., U. Miami, 1967, MBA, 1969. CPA, Fla., N.Y., Ill., La. Staff acct. Price Waterhouse, Miami, Fla., 1969-71; tax specialist Laventhol & Horwath, Miami, 1973-74; mng. dir. Barth Satuloff, CPA, Miami, 1974—; pres., bd. dirs. Satuloff Bros., Inc., Buffalo, 1974—; sec., treas. Chartered Investment Research Corp., Miami, 1980—, also bd. dirs. Mem. endowment fund com. U. Miami, 1979, Estate Planning Council Greater Miami, 1974; bd. dirs. Fellowship House Found., Miami, 1980; mem. Fla. Inst. CPA's Ednl. Found., 1975, Polit. Action Com., 1983. Served with Fla. N.G., 1970-76. Mem. Am. Inst. CPA's, Fla. Inst. CPA's, N.Y. State Soc. CPA's, Ill. Soc. CPA's, Soc. La. CPA's. Home: 9614 SW 134th CT Miami FL 33186 Office: 8090 SW 81 Dr Miami FL 33143

SAUDER, JOHN WAGGONER, oil company executive, communications executive; b. Wichita Falls, Tex., June 10, 1955; s. Aaron L. and Johnnie M. (Waggoner) S.; m. Cheryl L. Bryant, Aug. 16, 1980; children: John Jr., Grace. BBA, U. Tex., 1977; student, Harvard U., 1986-88. Exec. asst. A.L. Sauder, Oil Operator, Wichita Falls, 1973-79; pres. Sauder Mgmt. co., Wichita Falls, 1978—; v.p. Leland Corp., Wichita Falls, 1978—; pres. Cerebrus Corp., Wichita Falls, 1980—; chmn. Tex. Caribe Holdings, British West Indies, 1986—; pres., chief exec. officer Micro Com Internat., Dallas, 1988—; bd. dirs. MBank Wichita Falls, Austin (Tex.) Movie and Sports Cable. Chmn. county campaign Slover for Congress, Wichita Falls, 1982; bd. dirs. Wichita Falls Mus. Art, 1986, Wichita Falls Faith Mission, 1986-87. Mem. Ind. Petroleum Assn. Am., North Tex. Oil and Gas Assn. (bd. dirs. 1984-86), Phi Kappa Psi. Republican. Methodist. Club: Harvard (Dallas). Office: Sauder Mgmt Co 5949 Sherry Ln #1255 Dallas TX 75225

SAUER, MARVIN BRIAN, financial executive, small business owner; b. L.A., Oct. 25, 1959; s. Samuel and Phyllis (Levine) S. BS, UCLA, 1981; MBA, U. Mich., 1986. Cons. Katke Co., Ann Arbor, Mich., 1981-83, sr. cons., 1983-85, v.p., 1985-87, treas., 1986—, chief fin. officer, 1987—; fin. advisor DataServ, Farmington Hills, Mich., 1987—; v.p., treas. Direct Dial Advt. Network, L.A., 1988—; bd. dirs. Mediquest, Canton, Mich. Chmn. Walk for Life, Ypsilanti, Mich., 1982. Mem. Am. Mgmt. Assn., Assn. Individual Investors. Republican. Roman Catholic. Home: 266 Village Green Blvd #208 Ann Arbor MI 48105 Office: Katke Co 2750 S State St Ann Arbor MI 49104

SAUERS, CLAYTON HENRY, financial executive; b. Mont., Apr. 7, 1926; m. Patricia Davis; children: Gale Elizabeth, Peter D. BS, U. Wash., 1948; MBA, Harvard U., 1951. Credit analyst The Northern Trust Co., Chgo., 1951-54; exec. v.p. A.B. Dick Co., Chgo., 1954-79; v.p. fin., chief fin. officer West Point (Ga.) Pepperell Inc., 1979—. With USN, 1944-46, PTO. Mem. Fin. Execs. Inst. (pres. Chgo. chpt. 1974-75). Republican. Mem. Christian Science Ch. Office: West Point-Pepperell Inc PO Box 71 West Point GA 31833

SAUERWEIN, JAMES CHARLES, management consultant; b. Belleville, Ill., July 31, 1937; s. Lee Roy Albert and Carmela (Houser) S.; (div.); children: Thomas, David, Theresa, Anne, Laura, Mark, Mary Anne. AA, Boise Coll., 1957; BA, Idaho State Coll., 1959; MBA, U. Nev., 1969; postgrad., U. Calif., 1974. Cert. purchasing mgr. Various positions Boeing Co., Seattle, 1959-64; mgr. purchasing EG&G Inc., Las Vegas, Nev., 1964-71; mgr. mktg. and purchasing Beckman Instruments, Fullerton, Calif., 1971-78; ptnr. Karrass Seminars Internat., Santa Monica, Calif., 1978—. Home: 20872 Serrano Creek El Toro CA 92630 Office: Karrass Seminar Internat 1633 Stanford St Santa Monica CA 90404

SAUFFERER, WARREN BENJAMIN, manufacturing executive; b. Faribault, Minn., Sept. 3, 1928; s. Walter and Emily (Lipps) S.; m. Audrey Mae Barrett, Nov. 8, 1955; children: Mark, Mary Beth, Sara Mae, Peter. BS in Agrl. Engring., U. Minn., 1959. Cert. profl. engr., Minn., Ind., Ariz., Calif. Dir. mktg. Farmhand Inc., Hopkins, Minn., 1964-71, Nat. Car Rental, Mpls., 1971-74; pres. Agrifim Irrigation, Phoenix, 1974-78; dir. mktg. DMI, Goodfield, Ill., 1978-82; exec. v.p. Farm Bus. Software Systems, Aledo, Ill., 1982—; pvt. practice cons., Morton, Ill., 1980—. Author: (manual) Farming in the Profit Zone, 1983. Vice-chmn. Minnetonka Sch. Bd., Hopkins, Minn., 1978. Served in U.S. Army, 1953-55. Republican.

Mem. Mennonite Ch. Home: 300 W Birchwood Morton IL 61550 Office: Farm Bus Software Systems PO Box 248 Aledo IL 61231

SAUFLEY, WILLIAM EDWARD, lawyer, savings banker; b. Washington, Mar. 7, 1956; s. Franklin Dewit and Ruth Constance (Wright) S.; m. Leigh Ingalls, Jan. 3, 1981. BA, Dartmouth Coll., 1977; JD, U. Maine, 1980. Bar: Maine 1980, U.S. Dist. Ct. Maine 1980. Of counsel Maine Legislature, Augusta, 1981-84; v.p. counsel Maine Savs. Bank, Portland, 1984-88, gen. counsel, sec., 1988—; corp. sec. The One Bancorp, Portland, 1984—, gen. counsel, 1989—. Trustee 75 State St Home for Elderly, Portland, 1986—. Mem. ABA (banking, corp. law sect.), Maine Bar Assn. (consumer law sect.). Democrat. Roman Catholic. Home: 10 Newell Rd Yarmouth ME 04096 Office: Maine Savs Bank One Maine Savs Plaza Portland ME 04101

SAUL, B. FRANCIS, II, bank executive; b. Washington, Apr. 15, 1932; s. Andrew Maguire and Ruth Clark (Sheehan) S.; m. Elizabeth Patricia English, Apr. 30, 1960; children: Sharon Elizabeth, B. Francis III, Elizabeth Willoughby, Andrew Maguire II, Patricia English. Grad. Georgetown Prep. Sch., 1950; BS, Villanova U., 1954, DCS (hon.), 1989; LLB, U. Va., 1957. Bar: D.C. 1959. With B.F. Saul Co., Chevy Chase, Md., 1957—, asst. v.p., 1959-62, v.p., 1962-65, sr. v.p., 1965-69, pres., 1969—, pres., chmn., 1985—; chmn., trustee B.F. Saul Real Estate Investment Trust Co., Chevy Chase, 1969—; pres. Chevy Chase Savs. Bank, 1969-88, pres., chmn., 1985-88, chief exec. officer, chmn., 1988—; chmn. Fin. Gen. Bankshares, Inc., 1978-82; chmn. bd. dirs. 1st Am. Bankshares, Inc., Washington, 1978-85, Colonial Williamsburg Hotel Properties, Inc., 1983—. Trustee Fed. City Council, Nat. Geographic Soc., 1985—, Suburban Hosp., 1972-76, Wadsworth Preservation Trust, 1983—, Brookings Inst., 1987—; life trustee Corcoran Gallery Art, Washington; mem. vis. com. Sch. Architecture U. Va., 1985—; bd. dirs. Garfinckel, Brooks Bros., Miller & Rhoads, 1970-81, Madeira Sch., Greenway, Va., 1978-88, Portsmouth Abbey Sch., R.I., 1979-84, United World Coll. of Am. West, Montezuma, N.Mex., 1982-85, D.C. Found. for Creative Space, 1980-82, D.C. chpt. ARC, 1964-86; chmn. Folger Shakespeare Library Com., 1985—; pres. D.C. Soc. for Crippled Children, 1972-76; trustee Brookings Inst., 1987—. Mem. Mortgage Bankers Assn. Met. Washington (pres. 1968), Nat. Assn. Real Estate Investment Trusts (pres. 1973-74), Alfalfa Club, Chevy Chase Club, Burning Tree Golf Club (Bethesda, Md.), Met. Club (Washington), Wianno Club (Cape Cod, Mass.), The Brook Club (N.Y.C.), Farmington Country Club. Home: 1 Quincy St Chevy Chase MD 20815 Office: BF Saul Co 8401 Connecticut Ave Chevy Chase MD 20815

SAUL, BRADLEY SCOTT, communications, advertising and entertainment executive; b. Chgo., June 29, 1960; s. Richard Cushman and Yolanda (Merdinger) S. BS, Northwestern U., 1981, MA, 1982; postgrad., Loyola U., 1983-84. With info. services dept. Sta. CBS/WBBM Radio, Chgo., 1978-80; gen. mgr. Sta. WEEF Radio, Highland Park, Ill., 1979-81, Sta. WONX, Evanston, Ill., 1981-83; faculty advisor Sta. WNUR Radio, Evanston, 1981-83; pres., ptnr., co-founder Pub. Interest Affiliates, Chgo., N.Y., 1981—; pres. Chgo. Antique Radio Corp., 1986—; prof. Columbia Coll., Chgo., 1985-87; bd. dirs. Lake View Mental Health Ctr., Chgo. Contbr. articles to prof. jours. Named Outstanding Investigative Journalist, Warner Books, 1977. Mem. Nat. Assn. Broadcasters, Ill. Assn. Broadcasters. Jewish. Club: East Bank (Chgo.). Office: Pub Interest Affiliates 680 N Lake Shore Dr Ste 800 Chicago IL 60611 also: 12 W 31st St New York NY 10001

SAUL, KENNETH LOUIS, utility company executive; b. Columbus, Ohio, Aug. 29, 1923; s. Aloysius Louis and Ruth Geneva (Duke) S.; m. Shirley Ann Todd, Feb. 14, 1953; children: Carl, Deborah, Kenneth, Mark, Lori, Richard. BBA, Ohio State U., 1949. Various mgmt. positions Columbus & So. Ohio Elec. Co., 1955-70, asst. controller, 1970-74; v.p., controller Tucson Elec. Power, 1974-84, sr. v.p., chief fin. officer, 1984-88, also bd. dirs.; bd. dirs. Ohio Steel Products, Columbus, Engring. Rsch. Assocs., Ariz. Commerce Bank, Tucson. Chmn. bd. Bishop Hartley High Sch., Columbus, 1967-73; treas., bd. dirs. United Way, Tucson, 1975-81, Carondelet Health Care, Tucson, 1982-85, St. Joseph's Hosp., Tucson, 1976-82. Served to sgt. USAF, 1943-45, PTO. Mem. Nat. Assn. Accts., Edison Electric Inst., Pacific Coast Electric Assn., Skyline Country Club (pres. 1979-80), SMOO Investment Club (pres. 1970-73). Republican. Roman Catholic. Home: 4830 Camino La Brinca Tucson AZ 85718 Office: Tucson Electric Power Co 220 W 6th St Tucson AZ 85702

SAUL, RALPH SOUTHEY, financial executive; b. Bklyn., May 21, 1922; s. Walter Emerson and Helen Douglas (Coutts) S.; m. Bette Jane Bertschinger, June 16, 1956; children: Robert Southey, Jane Adams. B.A., U. Chgo., 1947; LL.B., Yale U., 1951. Bar: D.C. 1951, N.Y. 1952. With Am. Embassy, Prague, Czechoslovakia, 1947-48; assoc. firm Lyeth & Voorhees, N.Y.C., 1951-52; asst. counsel to Gov. N.Y. State, 1952-54; staff atty. RCA, 1954-58; with SEC, 1958-65, dir. div. trading and markets, 1963-65; v.p. corporate devel. Investors Diversified Services, Inc., Mpls., 1965-66; pres. Am. Stock Exchange, N.Y.C., 1966-71; chmn. mgmt. com. First Boston Corp., 1971-74; chmn., chief exec. officer INA Corp., Phila., 1975-82; chmn. bd. CIGNA Corp., Phila., 1982-84; bd. dirs. Sun Co., Peers & Co., Pennwalt Corp., CertainTeed Corp., Drexel Burnham Group, Fidelity Group, Alco Health Services. Trustee Com. for Econ. Devel.; vice chmn. bd. trustees Brookings Instn.; chmn. Com. to Support Phila. Pub. Schs. Served with USNR, 1943-46, PTO. Mem. ABA, AICPA. Clubs: Union League (Phila.); Merion Golf; Links (N.Y.C.), Board Room (N.Y.C.). Home: 549 Avonwood Rd Haverford PA 19041 Office: CIGNA Corp 1600 Arch St Philadelphia PA 19103

SAUNDERS, ALEXANDER HALL, real estate executive; b. Tallahassee, Oct. 5, 1941; s. Irvin Jasper and Perry Francis (Watson) S.; m. Pamela Wightman, July 24, 1970; 1 child, Anne Marguerite. AA, Norman Coll., 1961; BA, Mercer U., 1966. Planning adminstr. Ga. Dept. Corrections, Atlanta, 1969-70; mgmt. analyst Ga. Dept. Transp., Atlanta, 1970-71, tng. adminstr., 1971-72, asst. to research and devel., 1972-73, adminstr., asst. to dir., 1974-82; pres. ERA Towne Square Realty, Inc., Stone Mountain, Ga., 1982—. Named one of Top Real Estate Execs. in Am., ERA, 1987. Mem. Nat. Assn. Realtors, Ga. Assn. Realtors, DeKalb Bd. Realtors, ERA North Ga. Brokers Council (trustee 1983-86, pres. 1988—), Metro Listing Service, U.S. C. of C., DeKalb C. of C., Better Bus. Bur., Alpha Tau Omega, Delta Theta Phi. Club: Metro Golf and Tennis. Lodge: Elks. Home: 4845 Banner Elk Dr Stone Mountain GA 30083

SAUNDERS, DONALD HERBERT, utility company executive; b. Gallipolis, Ohio, Dec. 1, 1935; s. Clyde Edwin and Daisy Mae (Betz) S.; m. Dolores Marie Martin, Jan. 4, 1958; children: Scott, Glenn, Laura, Ellen. BBA, U. Toledo, 1957, MBA, 1964. Budget and statis. analyst Toledo Edison Co., 1957-60, supr. customer records and acctg., 1960-63, supr. property acctg., 1963-66, mgr. gen. acctg., 1966-68, asst. controller, dir. acctg. records, 1968-71, controller, dir. acctg., 1971-79, treas., 1979-86, v.p. fin. and adminstrn., 1986—. Treas. City Oregon, Ohio, 1972—; mem. adv. bd. St. Charles Hosp., Oregon, 1981—; mem. acctg. mgmt. com. Edison Elec. Inst., 1977—; trustee Metro Toledo YMCA, 1980—, St. Charles and Mercy Hosp., 1989—; bd. dirs. Toledo Area Govtl. Research Assn., 1987—. Served to col. USAFR, 1957—. Named Outstanding Citizen of Oregon, Oregon C. of C., 1983. Mem. Fin. Analysts Soc. Toledo, Fin. Execs. Inst. (sec. Toledo chpt. 1986-87, treas. Toledo chpt. 1987-88, 2d v.p. 1988-89, 1st v.p. 1989—), Toledo C. of C. (named one of Outstanding Young Men of Toledo 1970), Air Force Assn., N.G. Assn., N.G. Assn. U.S., The Oregonian Club, U. Toledo Alumni Assn., Blue Key. Republican. Club: Toledo Automobile (corp. bd. 1984—). Lodge: Masons, Yondota F. & Am, Scottish Rite (Toledo). Home: 239 Ponderosa Dr Oregon OH 43616 Office: Toledo Edison Co 300 Madison Ave Toledo OH 43652

SAUNDERS, DORIS SYLVIA, financial planner, columnist; b. Cornwall-on the-Hudson, N.Y., Dec. 16, 1935; d. George H. and Bessie H. (Marshall) St. Mary; m. James Mack Saunders, Dec. 17, 1951; children: Alexcia Synder, Allan James, Neal George, Maurice Mark. Degree, Coll. for Fin. Planning, Denver. Lic. ins. dealer, Vt., N.Y. Ptnr. Jador Jersey Farms, Greenwich, 1954-81; registered rep. First Investors Corp., N.Y.C., 1981-84, Waddell & Reed, Inc., Kansas City, Mo., 1984—; ptnr. Fin. Planning Assocs., Saratoga Springs, N.Y., 1987—; instr. Knowledge Network, Albany. Columnist Resources Northeast Sell, 1988—. Bd. dirs., mem. women's com., dir. polit. action com. Washington County Farm Bur., 1969-82; chmn. PTA, Greenwich, 1961-68; trustee Sunday Sch. South Argyle United Presbyn. Ch., youth leader; chmn. Greenwich Town Election Inspector, 1965-82; clk. Greenwich Town Zoning Commn., 1972-81, Greenwich Town Planning Bd.; founding dir. Citizen Environmentalists Against Sludge Encapsulation, 1977-82. Mem. Internat. Assn. Fin. Planners, Am. Bus. Women's Assn., Saratoga C. of C. Home: RD #2 Box 2222A Argyle NY 12809 also: 268 Washington Ave Extension Corp Plaza West Albany NY 12203

SAUNDERS, DOROTHY ANN, insurance company executive, sales management; b. Roxbury, N.C., Nov. 29, 1932; d. James William and Anna Bell (Wesley) Rice; m. Bernard L. Lewis, June 10, 1950 (dec. Jan. 1957); m. J.R. Saunders, Nov. 26, 1976 (dec. May 1981). Student, Md. U., 1950-53. Bookeeper, office mgr. ANT Cosmetics, Bethesda, Md., 1958; owner, mgr. Donnel's Hall of Gifts, Washington, 1959-63, Gifts, Inc., Washington, 1959-63; with U.S. Govt. Health, Edn., Welfare, Bethesda, 1965-73; owner, mgmt. in sales Dorothy Saunders Ins. Agy., Forest, Va., 1973—; vis. spkr. Bus. & Profl. Woman's Assn., Brookneal, Va., 1986-87. Mem. Nat. Trust for Historic Preservation. Democrat. Baptist. Home: Rt 1 Huddleston VA 24104 Office: Dorothy Saunders Ins Agy 100 Old Forge Rd Forest VA 24551

SAUNDERS, GEORGE LAWTON, JR., lawyer; b. Mulga, Ala., Nov. 8, 1931; s. George Lawton and Ethel Estell (York) S.; children: Kenneth, Ralph, Victoria; m. Terry M. Rose. B.A., U. Ala., 1956; J.D., U. Chgo., 1959. Bar: Ill. 1960. Law clk. to chief judge U.S. Ct. Appeals (5th cir.), Montgomery, Ala., 1959-60; law clk Justice Hugo L. Black, U.S. Supreme Ct., Washington, 1960-62; assoc. Sidley & Austin, Chgo., 1962-67, ptnr., 1967—. Served with USAF, 1951-54. Mem. ABA, Ill. State Bar Assn., Chgo. Bar Assn., Am. Coll. Trial Lawyers, Order of Coif, Phi Beta Kappa. Democrat. Baptist. Clubs: Chicago, Saddle and Cycle, Mid-Am., Quadrangle, Law, Legal (Chgo.). Home: 179 E Lake Shore Dr Chicago IL 60611 Office: Sidley & Austin 1 First Nat Pla Chicago IL 60603

SAUNDERS, JOSEPH ARTHUR, office products manufacturing company executive; b. Creston, Mont., July 9, 1926; s. Albert Henry and Edith Margaret (Rhodes) S.; m. Lois Evelyn White, June 19, 1948 (dec. Oct. 1986); children: Albert Henry II, Margaret Jean; m. Eva Homor, July 18, 1987; stepchildren: Rodney, Charmaine. Ed. pub. schs., Youngstown, Ohio and Winthrop, Maine. With Saunders Mfg. Co. Inc., Winthrop, 1947—, exec. v.p., 1967-77, pres., 1977-88 , chief exec. officer, 1967—, chmn. bd., 1988—; chmn. Saunders Internat. B.V., Netherlands; co-founder, sec., bd. dirs. Dirigo Bank and Trust Co., Augusta, Maine, 1969-86; co-founder, dir. Cushnoc Bank and Trust Co., Augusta, Maine. Served with U.S. Army, 1945-47. Patentee in field. Mem. Maine C. of C. and Industry (bd. dirs. 1976-81, chmn. mfg. council 1978-82), Maine Metal Products Assn. (bd. dirs. 1983-84), Soc. Mfg. Engrs. (cert. new product engr.), Internat. Bus. Forms Industries (chmn. assocs. 1976-77, co-chmn. exhbts. com. 1978-82), Nat. Bus. Forms Assn., Nat. Office Products Assn., Maine Metal Products Assn., Printing Industries New Eng. Am. Soc. Metals, Printing Industries Am., Am. Legion, others. Lodges: Masons, Shriners. Home: Touisett Point Readfield ME 04355 Office: Saunders Mfg Co Box 243 Winthrop ME 04364

SAUNDERS, PETER PAUL, finance executive; b. Budapest, Hungary, July 21, 1928; emigrated to Can., 1941, naturalized, 1946; s. Peter Paul and Elizabeth (Halom) Szende; m. Nancy Louise McDonald, Feb. 11, 1956; children: Christine Elizabeth, Paula Marie. Student, Vancouver Coll., 1941-44; B.Com., U. B.C., 1948. Acct. Canadian Pacific Ry. Co., 1948-50; founder, pres. Laurentide Fin. Corp., Ltd., 1950-66, vice chmn., 1966-67; pres. Coronation Credit Corp. Ltd., Vancouver, B.C., Can., 1968-78; chmn., pres. Cornat Industries Ltd., Vancouver, B.C., Can., 1969-78, Versatile Corp. (formerly Coronation Credit Corp. and Cornat Industries Ltd.), Vancouver, B.C., Can., 1978-87; prin. Saunders Investment Ltd., Vancouver, 1987—; bd. dirs. China Bus. Machines, Inc., B.C. Broadcasting Co. Ltd., Wajax Ltd., N.W. Sports Enterprises Ltd., WIC Western Internat. Communications Ltd., Laurentian Pacific Ins. Co., Jannock Ltd.; mem. Vancouver adv. bd. Nat. Trust Co. Ltd. Adv. com. inmate employment Correctional Svc. Can.; gov. Vancouver Opera Assn.; pres. Vancouver Symphony Soc., 1968-70, Can. Cancer Soc., B.C. and Yukon region, 1975-77, Vancouver Art Gallery Assn., 1981-83; pres., chmn. Vancouver Soc. for Bus. and Arts; bd. dirs. Coun. for Bus. and the Arts in Can., Coun. for Can. Unity. Clubs: Vancouver Lawn Tennis and Badminton, Shaughnessy Golf and Country, Royal Vancouver Yacht, Vancouver; Thunderbird Country (Rancho Mirage, Calif.). Home: 2186 SW Marine Dr, Vancouver, BC Canada V6P 6B5 Office: Saunders Investment Ltd, PO Box 49352 Bentall Centre, Vancouver, BC Canada V7X 1K4

SAUNDERS, PHYLLIS S., financial and business consultant; b. N.Y.C., May 2, 1932; d. Jack and Bella (Bader) Bloom; widowed; children: Todd B., Dean B. Grad. U. Miami. Pres. P.S. Export Co., buying service, bus. cons., fin. cons., money mgmt. for Cen. and S.Am., Bahamas, Caribbean; cons., investor since 1961. Mem. Am. Bus. Women's Assn., Nat. Assn. Women Bus. Owners, Am. Liver Found., Am. Jewish Com., Nat. Home Asthmatic Children, Hope Ctr. Mentally Retarded, U. Miami Booster Club, U. Miami Ctr. for Liver Diseases, U. Miami AIDS Research Ctr., Fla. Feminist Bank. Republican. Avocations: golf, tennis, aerobics, fishing, boating. Home: 2 Grove Isle Apt #205 Coconut Grove FL 33133

SAUNDERS, R. REED, financial services company executive; b. Manchester, N.H., Feb. 27, 1948; children: Hunter, Ramsey. BA in English, Dartmouth Coll., 1970, MBA, 1972. Dir. mktg. Tonka Corp., Hopkins, Minn., 1972-78; v.p. advt. HBM, Boston, 1978-81; v.p. mktg. IDS Fin. Corp., Mpls., 1981-86, sr. v.p. mktg., 1986-88, sr. v.p. field resource mgmt., 1988—, also bd. dirs.; sr. v.p. mktg. IDS Fin. Services Inc., Mpls., 1987—, also bd. dirs. Clubs: Wayzata Country; Voyageur Outward Bound. Home: 19110 Ramsey Rd Wayzata MN 55391 also: 11 Cleveland Rd Marblehead NH 03455 Office: IDS Fin Svcs Inc IDS Tower 10-T29 Unit 75 Minneapolis MN 55440

SAUNDERS, RICHARD J., financial services company executive; b. San Francisco, July 3, 1947; s. Robert Scott and Virginia Dorothy (Lawless) S.; m. Memri Hearn (div. 1987); children: Jason, Andrew, Patrick. BA, Duke U., 1969; grad. Securities Industry Inst., U. Pa., 1985. Cert. fin. planner. Trust officer Merc.-Safe Deposit & Trust Co., Balt., 1969-73, 1st Nat. Bank Atlanta, 1973-77; mgr., fin. planning cons. Personal Capital Planning Group subs. Merrill Lynch & Co., Atlanta, 1977-78; fin. planning cons. Robinson-Humphrey Co., Atlanta, 1978-80, dir. investments, 1980-83, dir. personal fin. planning, 1983-85, mng. dir. fin. svcs. group, 1985-88. Elder Peachtree Presbyn. Ch., Atlanta, 1983—; trustee Rabun Gap (Ga.) Nacoochee Sch., 1988. Mem. Internat. Assn. for Fin. Planning, Inst. Cert. Fin. Planners.

SAUNDERS, ROBERT SAMUEL, investment company executive; b. Akron, Ohio, Dec. 3, 1951; s. Samuel Robert and Rose Annette (Shulman) S.; m. Heidi Ruth Fulkerson, Mar. 18, 1978. AB with distinction, Stanford U., 1973; MSc with distinction, London Sch. Econs., 1974; diploma, U. Stockholm, 1976; MA, Harvard U., 1978. Cons. World Bank, Washington, 1975-79; sr. cons. Boston Cons. Group, 1978-82; dir. competitive strategy analysis Bain and Co., Boston, 1982-86; sr. v.p., chief planning officer Krupp Cos., Boston, 1986-88; mng. dir. Abbey Holdings, Boston, 1988—; mem. investment com. Briercroft Savs. and Loan, Austin, Tex., 1986-88; vice-chmn. Kinmont Industries, Kings Mountain, N.C., 1988—; bd. dirs. Simon Boyle Group, Inc., Boston, Scand-Tech, Inc., Lincoln, Mass. Editor Stanford Quar. Rev., 1973. Del. Mass. Dem. Nat. Conv., San Francisco, 1984; co-founder Lexington Group Mass., Boston, 1985. Marshall scholar, 1973-75; NEH fellow, 1978; Swedish Govt. Fulbright grantee, 1975, U.S. Congress Profl. Devel. grantee, 1976. Mem. Am. Econ. Assn., Internat. Union for Sci. Study of Population, Nat. Assn. Sr. Living Industries. Unitarian.

SAUNDERS, WILLIAM ARTHUR, management consultant; b. Ottawa, Ont., Can., Oct. 13, 1930. BS with honors, McGill U., 1954; MBA in Econs. and Fin., U. Western Ont., 1956, M of Commerce in Econs. and Mktg., 1960. Econ. analyst Imperial Oil Ltd., Toronto, Ont., 1956-63; supr. distbrn. Polysar Ltd., Sarnia, Ont., 1963-69; venture mgr. Polysar Plastics, Inc., Westport, Conn., 1969-77; adv. strategy devel. Gulf Oil Chems. Co., Houston, 1977-82; mgmt. cons. Houston, 1982—; pres. William A. Saunders Co., 1987—. Mem. Soc. Plastics Engrs., Assn. Corp. Growth, The Planning Forum. Methodist. Home and Office: 7490 Brompton Rd Apt #351 Houston TX 77025

SAUNDERS, WILLIAM RALPH, magazine publisher; b. Rosedale, L.I., N.Y., Apr. 6, 1930; s. Mitchell E. and Dorothy A. (Munzer) S.; Asso. B.S., Leicester Jr. Coll., 1954; B.S., U. Bridgeport, 1956; postgrad. N.Y. U., 1957-58; m. Dorothy A. Braun, Aug. 29, 1954; children—Stephen Scott, Scott Stuart, Robert Mitchell; m. 2d, Marie E. Nellis, July 16, 1977. With Mut. Benefit Life Ins. Co., 1956-57; estate planner Mitchell E. Saunders Co., 1956-58; account exec. Diamond Internat. Corp., 1958-60; account mgr. Nations Bus. mag., N.Y.C., 1960-65, Eastern advt. mgr., 1965-68; advt. dir. IEEE Spectrum mag., N.Y.C., 1968-77, asso. pub., 1978—, assoc. staff dir., 1980—; cons. The William Co., 1974—. Served with USMC, 1948-52; Korea. Decorated Purple Heart. Mem. IEEE, AAAS, Bus./Profl. Advt. Assn. (cert. bus. communicator), Am. Soc. Assn. Execs., Soc. Nat. Assn. Publs. (bd. dirs.), Mag. Pubs. Assn., Eastern Mktg., Golf Assn. (past pres., exec. dir.), N.Y. State Consumer Mag. Club (past pres.), First Marine Div. Assn. (life), DAV (life), Met. Advt. Golf Assn., Theta Sigma, Advt. Club N.Y., Wyantenuck (Mass.) Country Club, Cornell Club. Republican. Roman Catholic. Home: 145 E 27th St New York NY 10016 Home: PO Box 254 71 Mount Washington Rd South Egremont MA 01258 Office: 345 E 47th St New York NY 10017

SAUTER, CHARLES HERMAN, personnel director. s. Alex and Florence (Schultz) S.; m., Sept. 1964; children: Stephen, David, Jennifer. BBA, St. Norbert Coll., 1964; MBA, U. Wis., Oshkosh, 1971. Trainee mgmt. N.Y. Life Ins. Co., Appleton, Wis., 1966-67; mgr. personnel Wis. Tissue Mills, Menasha, 1966-67; v.p. human resources Bancorp., Appleton, 1967—. Active Am. Cancer Soc., Boy Scouts Am, Fox Cities Scouting Fund Dr.; chmn. adv. bd. Salvation Army; mem. Edison Sch. PTA; bd. dirs. Fox Cities United Way. Served to 1st lt. U.S. Army, 1964-66. Mem. Fox Valley Personnal Assn., St. Norbert Coll. (nat. alumni bd.), Am. Soc. Personnel, Wis. Bank Holding Co. Personnel Group. Roman Catholic. Club: Ephraim Yacht (commodore). Office: Valley Bancorp 100 W Lawrence Appleton WI 54912

SAVAGE, WILTON ALBERT, financial executive; b. N.Y.C., Dec. 16, 1942; s. Wiley Wilton and Jewel Alberta (Johnson) S.; m. Helen Marie Marshall, June 17, 1965; children: Monyka, Andreama. BBA, Cleve. State U., 1971; MBA, Harvard U., 1973. Purchasing agt. Warner & Swasey Co., Cleve., 1964-71, v.p. fin., 1984—; controller small signal prodn. Fairchild Camera, Mountain View, Calif., 1973-75; fin. analyst Bendix Corp., Southfield, Mich., 1975-77; controller Tex. Pipe Bending Co. div. Bendix Corp., Houston, 1977-82; dir. fin. analysis Bendix Indsl. Corp., Cleve., 1982-84; bd. dirs. Kirloswkar Warner & Swasey, Hubli, India, 1985—. Trustee United Way Services, Cleve., 1985, Phyllis Wheatley, Cleve., 1984; bd. dirs. Mid Town Corridor, Cleve., 1988. Served with U.S. Army, 1965-67. Fellow George Gund Found., Cleve., 1971. Methodist. Club: Harvard Bus. Sch. (Cleve.). Office: Warner & Swasey Corp 11000 Cedar Ave Cleveland OH 44106

SAVASTANO, JOHN HENRY, accounting company executive; b. Paterson, N.J., Sept. 27, 1949; s. John Frank and Anne Pesacreta Savastano; m. Linda Lou Perrone, Oct. 14, 1972. B.S., Fairleigh Dickinson U., 1971. CPA, N.J., N.Y., Fla. Staff acct. Yardley of London, Inc., Totowa, N.J., 1971-72, Malesardi, Quackenbush, Swift & Co., Englewood, N.J., 1972-75; sr. acct. Arlook, Shinder & Co., P.A., Paramus, N.J., 1975-79, ptnr., prin., 1979-86, Savastano, Kaufman & Co., PC, Paramus, 1986—; dir., treas. Graphic Media, Inc., Fairfield, N.J., 1981—. Tax tips columnist for Hudson Forum and Commerce mags., 1980-86. Fellow N.J. State Soc. CPAs; mem. AICPA, Nat. Assn. Accts. (Meadowlands chpt. treas. 1974-76, dir. 1974-80, v.p. 1977-79). Roman Catholic. Office: Savastano Kaufman & Co PC 625 From Rd Paramus NJ 07652 also: Graphic Media Inc 373 Rte 46 W Bldg E Fairfield NJ 07006

SAVIDGE, JACK W., international consulting executive; b. Bklyn., June 14, 1932; married; 5 children. Student, St. Lawrence U., Lehigh U. Dir. mktg. 3M Co., St. Paul, 1957-69, cons.; pres. Venture Strategies Inc., LaJolla, Calif., 1969-81; v.p. corp. devel. Spin Physics Inc. sub. Eastman Kodak, San Diego, 1975-80; sr. v.p. Continuous Curve Contact Lenses Inc., San Diego, 1978; pres. Savidge & Savidge Inc., LaJolla, 1981—; lectr. in field; cons. Warner Bros., 3M Co., Bank of Am., Memorex, Motorla, bd. dirs., Brooktree Corp., San Diego, Western Health Plans Inc., San Diego, Computer Accessories Inc., San Diego. Chmn. investment com. City of San Diego Employees Retirement Bd., 1981-88. Served with U.S. Army, 1954-56. Home: 7946 Ivanhoe Ave La Jolla CA 92037

SAVIN, ROBERT SHEVRYN, health care products company executive; b. Bridgeport, Conn., Mar. 17, 1925; s. Harry and Agnes (Jacobs) S.; m. Barbara Low, July 15, 1951; children: Deborah Joyce, Scott Martin. Student U. Bridgeport. Pres. Savin Jewelers, 1948-55, also dir.; salesman IPCO Corp., White Plains, N.Y., 1955-61, v.p., dir., 1962-66, pres., chief exec. officer, 1966-73, chmn., 1973-77, chmn., pres., 1977-84, chmn. chief exec. officer, 1984—. Chmn. United Home for Aged Hebrews; co-pres. Am. Friends of Hebrew U., N.Y.; bd. dirs. Nat. Sports. Served with U.S. Army, 1943-46. Mem. Hosp. Industry Assn., Old Oaks Country Club. Home: 1045 Nautilus Ln Mamaroneck NY 10543 Office: IPCO Corp 1025 Westchester Ave White Plains NY 10604

SAVIN, RONALD RICHARD, chemical company executive, inventor; b. Cleve., Oct. 16, 1926; s. Samuel and Ada (Silver) S.; m. Gloria Ann Hopkins, Apr. 21, 1962; children: Danielle Elizabeth, Andrea Lianne. Student, U. Cin., 1944-46; BA in Chemistry and Literature, U. Mich., 1948; postgrad., Columbia U., 1948-49, Sorbonne, Paris, 1949-50; grad., Air War Coll., 1975, Indsl. Coll. Armed Forces, 1976. V.p. Premium Finishes, Inc., Cin., 1957-58, pres., owner, 1958—. Contbr. articles on aerospace, marine industry and transp. to profl. jours.; adv. coun. Chem. Week mag; patentee corrosive prevention coatings for aerospace use. With USAF, 1950-55, Korea, col. Res., ret. Mem. Nat. Assn. Corrosion Engrs., Air Force Assn., Am. Internat. Club, Res. Officers Assn., Mission Hills Country Club. Office: Premium Finishes Inc 10448 Chester Rd Cincinnati OH 45215 also: LOBO, St Symphorien, Lyon France

SAVITZ, SAMUEL J., actuarial consulting firm executive; b. Phila., Dec. 23, 1936; s. Paul and Ann (Gechman) S.; B.S. in Bus. Adminstrn., Temple U., 1958; postgrad. U. Pa., 1960-62, Temple U., 1965; m. Selma Goldberg, June 15, 1958; children—Jacqueline Beverly, Steven Leslie, Michelle Lynn. Pension analyst Provident Mut. Life Ins. Co., Phila., 1958-61; v.p. The Wirkman Co., Phila., 1961-64; pres. Samuel J. Savitz & Assoc., Inc., Phila., 1964-86; chmn. bd., cons. Exec. Compensation Plans, Inc., Phila., 1984—; sr. prin. Laventhol & Horwath, Phila., 1986—; mng. ptnr. Samuel J. Savitz & Assocs. div. Laventhol & Horwath, 1986—; vis. lectr. U. Pa., Phila., 1960, La. State U., 1972-74; faculty Villanova U., 1971-75; cons. in field. Mem. pension com. Fedn. Jewish Agencies, Phila., 1960; bd. dirs. Am. com. Weizmann Inst. Sci., 1984-85, Phila. All-Star Forum, 1987—. Served with USAR, 1954-62. Mem. Am. Soc. Pension Actuaries (dir. 1969-75), Am. Soc. C.L.U.'s, Assn. Advanced Life Underwriting. Jewish. Club: Locust. Contbr. articles in field to profl. jours. Home: 470 Conshohocken State Rd Bala Cynwyd PA 19004 Office: REBC Assocs 1845 Walnut St Philadelphia PA 19103

SAVOLT, LOUANN SUE, retailer; b. Ft. Wayne, Ind., Sept. 28, 1942; d. Harold Edwin and Norma Esther (Mertz) Hartman; m. Larry Gene Savolt, Sept. 6, 1980; children: Neil Reith, Sheila Reith. AD in Nursing, Garden City Community Coll., 1977. RN, Kans. Health nurse Garden City Community Coll., Kans., 1977-80; staff nurse St. Catherine Hosp., Garden City, 1983; owner, mgr. Personally Yours Lingerie, Garden City, 1984—. Hot line vol. Family Crisis Services, Finney County, Kans., 1982-84; pub. edn. chmn. Am. Cancer Soc., Finney County, 1978-84; co-chmn. Coalition for Prevention of Child Abuse and Neglect, Finney County, 1978-79, chmn., 1979-80. Recipient Service award Finney County Am. Cancer Soc., 1981, Family Crisis Services, 1984. Mem. Women's C. of C., Nat. Retail Mchts. Assn., Nat. Assn. Female Execs. Lutheran. Avocations: reading, snowmobiling, traveling. Home: Rte 2 Box 51 Holcomb KS 67851 Office: Personally Yours Lingerie 503 N Main Garden City KS 67846

SAVORY, MARK, management consultant, insurance company executive; b. Englewood, N.J., Oct. 5, 1943; s. William A. and Marion J. (Garland) S.; m. Rose Marie Proietti, Feb. 5, 1988. BA with honors, Rutgers U., Newark, 1965; MA, Columbia U., 1966; MBA, U. Conn., 1973. Sec.-dir. Hartford (Conn.) Ins. Group, 1971-81; ptnr. Coopers & Lybrand, N.Y.C., 1981—. Contbr. articles to profl. jours. V.p. Tallott Glen Assn., 1985. Capt. USAF, 1966-71. Mem. Internat. Ins. Soc., Planning Forum, Ins. Acctg. and Systems, Beta Gamma Sigma, Pi Sigma Alpha. Home: 26 Vom Eigen Dr Convent Station NJ 07961 Office: Coopers & Lybrand 1251 Ave of the Americas New York NY 10020

SAVRANN, RICHARD ALLEN, lawyer; b. Boston, July 29, 1935; s. Abraham B. and Doris (Curhan) S.; m. Diane Barbara Kleven, Dec. 22, 1957; children: Stephen Keith, Russell Carl. BA, Harvard U., 1956, JD, 1959. Bar: Mass. 1959, U.S. Dist. Ct. Mass. 1963, U.S. Ct. Appeals (1st cir.) 1965. Exec. Klev Bro. Mfg., Derry, N.H., 1959-63; assoc. Law Office of Jerome Rappaport, Boston, 1963-68; asst. atty. gen. Commonwealth of Mass., Boston, 1968-70; ptnr. Newell, Savrann & Miller, Boston, 1970-75; sr. ptnr. Kunian, Savrann & Miller, Boston, 1976-81, Singer, Stoneman, Kunian & Kurland, P.C., Boston, 1981—. Chmn. Andover (Mass.) Housing Authority, 1972—; pres. Hospice of Greater Lawrence, North Andover, Mass., 1984; bd. dirs. Boston Latin Sch. Found., 1986—. Mem. ABA, Mass. Bar Assn., Boston Bar Assn., Ferncroft Country Club, Golf and Racquet (Palm Beach Gardens, Fla.), Harvard (Andover) (pres. 1984—), Harvard (Boston). Home: 11 Sheridan Rd Andover MA 01810 Office: Singer Stoneman Kunian & Kurland PC 100 Charles River Pla Boston MA 02114

SAWABINI, NABIL GEORGE, banker; b. Beirut, Sept. 11, 1951; came to U.S., 1980; s. George Issa and Yvonne (Slim) S.; m. Nadia Abdelnour, Dec. 15, 1973; children: Karim, Zina. BBA, Am. U. Beirut, 1973. Mgmt. trainee Bank Almashrek (affiliate Morgan GTY), Beirut, 1973-74, head corp. lending, 1977, head corp. lending, fgn. dept., 1978, head corp. lending, fgn. dept., treasury fgn. exch., 1979-80; with mgmt. tng. program Morgan Guaranty Trust Co., N.Y.C., 1974-75; with shipping and commodities dept. Morgan Guaranty Trust Co., London, 1975-76; petroleum banker Morgan Guaranty Trust Co., N.Y.C., 1980-81, unit head petroleum dept., 1981-84, govt. bond sales rep., 1984; head internat. sales and trading J.P. Morgan Securities, N.Y.C., 1984-86, mng. dir., head domestic and internat. taxable sales, 1987-89, mgr. securities group, 1989—. Greek Orthodox. Home: 88 Secor Rd Scarsdale NY 10583 Office: JP Morgan Securities 23 Wall St New York NY 10015

SAWICKI, EDWARD JAMES, corporate consulting service executive; b. Phila., Aug. 24, 1946; s. Edward Joseph and Catherine (Rita) S.; m. Anita Gale Sottler, July 15, 1972. AS in Sci. and Math., West Valley Coll., 1972; student, San Jose State U., 1973-76, U. San Francisco, 1977-78. Watch comdr. Ampex Corp., Redwood City, Calif., 1973-74; watch comdr., safety engr. Signetics, Sunnyvale, Calif., 1974-76; corp. safety dir. Intel Corp., Santa Clara, Calif., 1976-82; pres. Microsafe, Inc., Santa Clara, 1982—. Served as staff sgt. U.S. Army, 1966-70, Vietnam. Decorated Bronze Star with V device; recipient Plaque City of Santa Clara, 1980, Award of Merit City of Sunnyvale, 1981. Mem. World Safety Orgn. (cert.), Am. Soc. Safety Engrs. (pres. San Jose chpt. 1985-86), Am. Indsl. Hygiene Assn., Health Physics Assn., Nat. Safety Council (research and devel. com.), Nat. Fire Protection Assn., Semiconductor Safety Assn. (bd. dirs. Cen. Counties Nat. Safety Council), Bay Area Electronics Safety Group (founder 1978). Home: 854 Hilmar St Santa Clara CA 95050 Office: Microsafe Inc 1500 Wyatt Dr Ste #5 Santa Clara CA 95051

SAWYER, JOHN GILMAN, management/data processing consultant; b. Syracuse, N.Y., Aug. 20, 1942; s. Arthur Gilman and Muriel Ruth (Smith) S.; m. Sydney Gayle O'Brien, July 29, 1967 (div. 1977); children: Jason Gilman, David James. BSBA, Boston U., 1965. Store mgr. Sears, Roebuck & Co., Warwick, R.I., 1966; inside sales rep. Rollway Bearing Co., Syracuse, 1966-67, sr. prodn. scheduler, 1968-69; sr. systems analyst Morse Borg-Warner, Ithaca, N.Y., 1970-73; sr. programmer/analyst Fairchild Semiconductor, South Portland, Maine, 1973-76; mgr. mfg. systems Winchester Group Olin Corp, New Haven, 1976-81; dir. MIS U.S. Repeating Arms Co., New Haven, 1981-84; pres. The Sawyer Group, Inc., New Haven, 1985—. Mem. Am. Prodn. and Inventory Control Soc., Ind. Computer Cons. Assn. Office: The Sawyer Group Inc PO Box 3381 New Haven CT 06515-0164

SAWYER, KRISTIN LEE, executive search consultant; b. Salem, Mass., July 12, 1951; d. Jack Nichols and Carol Margary (Forsyth) Arnold; m. Alan Irwin Sawyer, Nov. 12, 1972 (div. Nov. 1985); children—Carrie Lee, Jeremy Scott. Student Harbor Jr. Coll., San Pedro, Calif., 1969, El Camino Coll., Redondo Beach, Calif., 1970, Monserrat Sch. Visual Art, Beverly, Mass., 1975. Vice pres., sales Custom Clean, Topsfield, Mass., 1975-77; mfrs. rep. Sawyer Assocs., Topsfield, 1977-79; account exec. Exxon Office Systems, Waltham, Mass., 1979-80; facility cons. M. Brown, Inc., Boston, 1980-83; pres. The Sawyer Co., Topsfield, 1984—; cons. in field. Speaker, Mass. Com. to Ratify E.R.A., 1975. Mem. Nat. Assn. Personnel Cons., North Shore Women in Bus. (bd. dirs. 1988—), Nat. Assn. Female Execs., Ms. Found. for Women, NOW. Club: Ipswich Bay Yacht. Avocations: sailing; skiing; horseback riding.

SAWYER, RAYMOND LEE, JR., motel chain executive; b. New Orleans, Oct. 7, 1935; s. Raymond Lee Sawyer and Eloise Falvy (Searcy) Easley; m. Dolores Jean Young, June 11, 1960; children: Lisa Kay, Linda Fay. BA, Northwestern State U., 1959. Art dir., advt. mgr. Natural Food and Farming Mag., Atlanta, Tex., 1959-66, editor, 1963-66; asst. editor, editor Tourist Court Jour./Southwest Water Works Jour., Temple, Tex., 1966-73; editor Tourist Court Jour./Southwest Water Works Jour., Temple, 1973-75; founding ptnr., sr. v.p. Budget Host Inns, Ft. Worth, 1975-83, pres., chief exec. officer, 1983—. Named Man of Yr. Motel Brokers Assn. Am., 1974; recipient Bob Gresham Meml. award Nat. Innkeeping Assn., 1975. Methodist. Office: Budget Host Inns 2601 Jacksboro Hwy Ste 202 Box 10656 Fort Worth TX 76114

SAWYER, THOMAS EDGAR, management consultant; b. Homer, La., July 7, 1932; s. Sidney Edgar and Ruth (Bickham) S.; B.S., UCLA, 1959; M.A., Occidental Coll., 1969; m. Joyce Mezzanatto, Aug. 22, 1954; children—Jeffrey T., Scott A., Robert J., Julie Anne. Project engr. Garrett Corp., Los Angeles, 1954-60; mgr. devel. ops. TRW Systems, Redondo Beach, Calif., 1960-66; spl. asst. to gov. State of Calif., Sacramento, 1967-69; prin., gen. mgr. Planning Research Corp., McLean, Va., 1969-72; dep. dir. OEO, Washington, 1972-74; asso. prof. bus. mgmt. Brigham Young U., 1974-78; pres. Mesa Corp., Provo, 1978-82, chmn. bd., 1978-82; pres. and dir. Sage Inst. Internat., Inc., Provo, Utah, 1982-88; pres., chmn. bd. Pvt. Telecom Networks, Inc., Orem, Utah, 1988—; dir. Intechna Corp., HighTech Corp., Nat. Applied Computer Tech. Inc. (chmn.), Indian Affiliates, Inc. Chmn. Nat. Adv. Council Indian Affairs; chmn. Utah State Bd. Indian Affairs; mem. Utah Dist. Export Council; mem. Utah dist. SBA Council; chmn. So. Paiute Restoration Com.; mem. adv. council Nat. Bus. Assn.; mem. Utah Job Tng. Coordinating Council. Served with USMC, 1950-53. Mem. Am. Mgmt. Assn., Am. Soc. Public Adminstrn., Utah Council Small Bus. (dir.). Republican. Mormon. Club: Masons. Author: Assimilation Versus Self-Indentity: A Modern Native American Perspective, 1976; Computer Assisted Instruction: An Inevitable Breakthrough. Home: 548 W 630 S Orem UT 84058 Office: Pvt Telecom Networks Inc 744 South 400 E Orem UT 84058

SAWYER, W(ALDRON) TOM, waste management company executive; b. Bangor, Me., Mar. 17, 1949; s. Waldron E. and Winona (Cole) S.; m. Bonnie Prince, May 28, 1970; children: Shannon, Patricia. BA in Edn. cum laude, Denver U., 1972. Gen. mgr. Truck-a-Way Systems, Inc., Bangor, 1972-80, pres., 1980—; pres. Tom Sawyer, Inc., Hampden, Me., 1980—, Sawyer Environ., Hampden, Me., 1980—, Mid Coast Disposal Union, Union, Me., 1985—, Eagle Equipment Co., Bangor, 1982—, WES, Inc., Portland, Me., 1986—, Sawyer Mgmt. Svcs., Bangor, 1987—, Sawyer Consol., Beddington, Me., 1987—; dir. Merrill Bankshares, Bangor, Ea. Me. Devel. Dist.; dir. Blue Cross/Blue Shield of Me., Portland audit chmn., 1987—. Bd. dirs. Sch. Bd., Hampden, 1980-82, Me. Motor Transp. Assn., 1984-87, Bangor Ednl. Found., 1987—; trustee Husson Coll., Bangor, 1987—; elected to Bangor City Coun., 1987-89; chmn. United Way Penobscot Valley, 1988; 2d v.p. Bangor YWCA, 1988; mem. consumer adv. coun. Blue Cross and Blue Shielf Maine, 1974-79, chmn., 1977-79. Mem. Nat. Solid Waste Mgmt. Assn., Detachable Container Assn. (treas. 1988—), Bangor C. of C., Newcomen Soc., Am. Mgmt. Assn., Bangor Jaycees (pres. 1980), Kappa Delta Phi, Gyro Club of Bangor (pres. 1985), Rotary, Masons, Shriners. Republican. Methodist. Office: Sawyer Mgmt Svcs PO Box 1388 Bangor ME 04401

SAWYER, WILLIAM CURTIS, pest control company executive; b. Lockport, N.Y., Jan. 25, 1933; s. Fletcher D. and Mildred R. (Schnurstein) S.; m. Noreen T. Doran, Aug. 8, 1959 (div. 1987); children: Curtis P., Todd T.; m. Gail P. Mangan, 1988. Student, Cornell U., 1950-52. Technician McCleod Indsl. Fumigators, Buffalo, 1949-50; v.p. Sawyer's Exterminating, Rochester, N.Y., 1958-76, pres., 1976—. Sgt. USMC, 1952-56. Mem. Nat. Pest Control Assn. (bd. dirs. 1981—), Empire State Pest Control Assn. (treas. 1981-85, bd. dirs. 1978-85), N.Y. State Pest Control Assn. (bd. dirs. 1981-85), Small Bus. Assn. Rochester (bd. dirs. 1981-85), Meml. Art Gallery, Rochester Area C. of C., Rochester Club, Masons, Shriners. Republican. Home: 3126 Brockport Rd Spencerport NY 14556 Office: Sawyers Exterminating 201 Monroe Ave Rochester NY 14607

SAXBY, LEWIS WEYBURN, JR., glass fiber manufacturing company executive; b. Oak Park, Ill., Dec. 17, 1924; s. Lewis Weyburn Saxby and Dorothy (Porter) Willey; m. Kathryn Hutchinson, Sept. 7, 1947; children: Steven Lewis, Ann, Jane Porter. BS, U. Calif., Berkeley, 1945; MBA, Stanford U., 1948. Prodn. trainee Owens-Corning Fiberglas Corp., Newark, Ohio, 1948-49; prodn. scheduler Santa Clara, Calif., 1949-51; estimator salesman San Francisco, 1951-52, dept. supr., 1952-56; br. mgr. Sacramento, Calif., 1956-58; br. mgr. Detroit, 1958-60, mgr. supply and contracting East, 1960-61; mgr. supply and contracting Toledo, 1961-66, v.p., mgr. supply and contracting, 1966-70, v.p. mech. products and constrn. services, 1971-74, v.p. mech. ops. div., 1974-78, sr. v.p., 1978—; bd. dirs. OC-Birdair, Inc., Buffalo. Nat. bd. dirs. Jr. Achievement, Inc., Colorado Springs, 1979—, chmn. com., 1980—; bd. dirs., chmn. com. Toledo Conv. and Visitors Bur., 1986-87. Served to ensign USNR, 1942-46, PTO. Recipient Gold Leadership award Jr. Achievemnt, Inc., 1981. Mem. Nat. Insulation Contractors (chmn. com. 1984—, Man of Yr. 1985). Republican. Presbyterian. Club: Inverness (Toledo) (bd. govs. 1976-80). Office: Owens-Corning Fiberglas Corp Fiberglas Tower Toledo OH 43659

SAXBY, SARA BETH, financial planner; b. N.Y.C., July 9, 1944; d. Russell George and Mary Elizabaeth (Altsman) S.; m. Charles Ford Sydnor, Aug. 27, 1966 (div. Sept. 1978); 1 child, Russell. BA, Hollins Coll., 1966; BS, N.C. State U., 1975. Cert. fin. planner. Adminstrv. asst. HEW Region III, Charlottesville, Va., 1966-69; admissions advisor Grad. Inst. Edn. Washington U., St. Louis, 1969-70; owner, mgr. Braeburn Farm, Snow Camp, N.C., 1975-78; bookkeeper, office mgr. Fed. Homes Inc., Auburn, Ala., 1982-83; fin. planner Machen, McChesney & Chastain, Auburn, 1983-88, Lincoln Investment Planning, Phila., 1988—. Sec. Alamance County Extension Svc., Burlington, N.C., 1976; vol. tchr. Cin. Nature Ctr., Long Branch Farm, 1980-82; vestry mem. Chapel of St. Dunstan, Auburn, 1983-85; chmn. football program. Lee-Scott Acad., Auburn, 1986; speaker on conflict resolution Beyond War, 1988—. Mem. Inst. Cert. Fin. Planners (sec. Ala. 1987-88), Delaware Valley Inst. Cert. Fin. Planners, Bucks County Estate Planning Council. Republican. Episcopalian. Home: 2004 Makefield Rd Yardley PA 19067 Office: Lincoln Investment Planning Inc Benson E Ste 1000 Jenkintown PA 19046

SAYLE, EDWARD FRANCIS, management consultant; b. Waukegan, Ill., Sept. 26, 1928; s. Edward Arthur and Grace Adeline (Burke) S.; m. Mae Helena Mitchell, Nov. 14, 1953. Student, Mich. State U., 1950-51. Intelligence officer CIA, Washington and Overseas, 1951-84, curator hist. intelligence, 1974-84; pres. Foxhall Communications, Arlington, Va., 1984—; hon. rep. in U.S. Isle of Man Govt., Douglas, 1978—; vis. prof. Def. Intelligence Coll., Washington, 1983—. Editor (jour.) Periscope, 1984—; contbr. articles on intelligence and diplomatic history to profl. jours. Pres. Arlington Hist. Soc., 1973; chmn. Arlington County Hist. Commn., 1974-75, Bicentennial Commn., 1975-76. Served with U.S. Army, 1946-49. Mem. SAR (pres. George Mason chpt. 1976, nat. pub. relations chmn. 1977), Internat. Assn. Computer Crime Investigators, Assn. Former Intelligence Officers, Computer Security Inst., Soc. Colonial Wars of Washington. Republican. Roman Catholic.

SAYRE, WILLIAM HEYSHAM, banker; b. Montclair, N.J., Apr. 1, 1933; s. William Heysham and Lee (Stuart) S.; m. Eleanor deVore, June 18, 1955; children: Carolyn Beldon, Catherine Brooks, Robert deVore, William H. BBA, Lehigh U., 1958; postgrad., Harvard Bus. Sch., 1976. Asst. treas. Fidelity Bank, Phila., 1962-66, asst. v.p., 1966-70, v.p., 1970-73, sr. v.p., 1973-75; exec. v.p. Fidelcor and Fidelity Bank N.A., Phila., 1975—, chief credit officer, 1982—; dir. Am. Abrasive Metals Co., Irvington, N.J. Contbg. author: The Banker's Handbook, 1978. Past chmn. bd. dirs., chief exec. officer Cathedral Village, Phila.; treas. Cathedral chpt. Episcopal Diocese of Pa. Mem. Am. Bankers Assn. (cert. comml. lender 1976), Robert Morris Assocs. (nat. pres. 1987-88, pres. Phila. chpt. 1979-80, chmn. policy div. 1980-81, bd. dirs., chmn. chpts. council div. 1982-84). Home: 850 Mt Pleasant Rd Bryn Mawr PA 19010 Office: Fidelity Bank Broad & Walnut Sts Philadelphia PA 19109

SBARBARO, RICHARD DONALD, executive search consulting firm executive; b. Chgo., Dec. 16, 1946. BSC, DePaul U., 1967, MBA, 1971. Mktg. mgr. Ill. Bell Telephone, 1967-69; sr. cons. Fry Cons., Chgo., 1969-71; sr. v.p. Midwest Stock Exchange, Chgo., 1971-78; prin. Booz, Allen, & Hamilton Assocs., Chgo., 1978—; pres. Lauer, Sbarbaro Assocs., Chgo. Bd. dirs. DePaul U. Pres's Club, 1982—, DePaul U. Athletic Bd., 1984—. Recipient Disting. Alumni award DePaul U., 1983. Mem. Assn. Exec. Search Cons. (v.p., sec. 1982—), Nat. Assn. Corp. and Profl. Recruiters, Pres. Assn., Am. Mgmt. Assn., Attic Club, Chgo. Athletic Club, St. Charles Country Club, Beta Gamma Sigma. Office: Lauer Sbarbaro Assocs Inc Three 1st Nat Pla Ste 650 Chicago IL 60602-4205

SBRAGIA, GARY W., communications company executive; b. Chgo., Aug. 25, 1941; s. Gertrude Harriet (Legge) S.; m. Sharyn Lee Simpson, Aug. 26, 1961; children: Marci Lee, Melissa Ann. Student, Waldorf Jr. Coll., 1959-60, 61-62, Colo. State U., 1962-65. V.p. Lift Trucks, Inc., Denver, 1972-74; mgr. Levenworth (Kans.) Cable TV, 1974-75; gen. mgr., then div. mgr. Athena Cablevision of Corpus Christi (Tex.), Inc., 1976-81; regional mgr., then asst. dir. ops. Telecommunications, Inc., Corpus Christi and Denver, 1981-84; v.p. Telecrafter Corp., Denver, 1984—; pres. Telecrafter Services Corp., Denver, 1987—. Home: 11425 Last Dollar Pass Littleton CO 80127 Office: Telecrafter Svcs Corp 12596 W Bayaud St Ste 300 Denver CO 80228

SCAGGS, ROGER THOMAS, information service executive; b. Tulsa, June 17, 1939; s. Wilburt Thomas and Dorothy (Townsend) S.; m. Penny Ehrle, Apr. 4, 1961; 1 child, Sarah Kay. BS, U. Tulsa, 1961. Br. mgr. URS Data Sci. Corp., San Mateo, Calif., 1965-71; systems engring. mgr. Electronic Data Systems, Dallas, 1971-80; v.p. Am. Physician Service Group, Dallas, 1980-83; sr. v.p. Am. Physician Service Group, Austin, Tex., 1984-87, pres., 1988—, also bd. dirs.; bd. dirs. Capitol View Ctr., Austin. Deacon Riverbend Bapt. Ch., Austin, 1986. Served to 1st lt. USAF, 1961-64. Home: 1908 Winter Park Austin TX 78746 Office: Am Physician Svc Group 1301 Capitol of Tex Hwy B220 Austin TX 78746

SCAGLIONE, CECIL FRANK, marketing executive; b. North Bay, Ont., Can., Dec. 2, 1934; came to U.S., 1967, naturalized, 1982; s. Frank and Rose (Aubin) S.; m. Mary Margaret Stewart, Nov. 11, 1954 (div. 1982); children: Cris Ann, Michael Andrew, Patrick Andrew; m. Beverly Louise Rahn, Mar. 25, 1983; student North Bay Coll., 1947-52, Ryerson Tech. Inst., Toronto, Ont., 1955-56, San Diego State U. Inst. World Affairs, 1979. Fin. writer Toronto Telegram, 1955; reporter Sarnia (Ont.) Observer, 1956-57; reporter, editor Kitchener-Waterloo (Ont.) Record, 1957-61; reporter, editor, analyst Windsor (Ont.) Star, 1961-67; writer, editor, photo editor Detroit News, 1967-71; reporter, assoc. bus. editor San Diego Union, 1971-80; mgr. corp. communications Pacific Southwest Airlines, San Diego, 1981-83; sr. v.p. media rels. Berkman & Daniels, Inc., San Diego, 1984-87, prin. Scaglione Mktg. Communications, 1987—; chmn., chief exec. officer Spl. Info. Svcs., Inc. Mem. adv. coun. SBA, Accredited Pub. Rels. Soc. Am. Recipient award B.F. Goodrich Can., Ltd., 1962, 66, Spl. Achievement award Nat. Assn. Recycling Industries, 1978, award SBA, 1980; Herbert J. Davenport fellow, 1977; Can. Centennial grantee, 1966. Mem. San Diego Press Club (hon. life, past pres., awards 1978, 80, 84), Airline Editors Forum awards 1982, 83), Pub. Rels. Soc. Am., Sigma Delta Chi. Roman Catholic. Founding editor-in-chief Aeromexico mag., 1973; contbr. articles, columns and photographs to various publs. Home and Office: 3911 Kendall St San Diego CA 92109

SCALLEY, JOHN J., automotive parts company executive; b. 1930. BS, Ga. Inst. Tech., 1951. With Genuine Parts Co., Atlanta, 1951—, various mgmt. positions, 1951-74, v.p. S.E. div., 1974-77, now exec. v.p. Office: Genuine Parts Co 2999 Circle 75 Pkwy Atlanta GA 30339 *

SCALLY, SEAN PATRICK, lawyer, communications executive, consultant; b. Columbia, Mo., May 26, 1960; s. William Patrick and Margaret Ann (Schaeffer) S. BS, U. Tenn., 1984; JD, Washburn U., 1987; MA, St. John's Coll., 1989. Legal cons., communications analyst Scally Communications, Washington, 1985—. Arbitrator Better Bus. Bur., Topeka, 1987. Home and Office: 1044-C Spa Rd Annapolis MD 21403

SCANLAN, JEAN M., infosystems specialist; b. Portland, Maine, Apr. 6, 1945; d. John Joseph and Patricia Ruth (Fox) S. BA, U. Maine, 1967; MS, Simmons Coll., 1969. Head reader svc. Babson Coll., Wellesley, Mass., 1969-73; bus. reference librarian U. Mass., Amherst, 1973-76; dir. info. ctr. Price Waterhouse, Boston, 1976—. Mem. Spl. Librs. Assn. (chmn. bus. and fin. div. 1986—). Roman Catholic. Home: 126 Walnut St Natick MA 01760 Office: Price Waterhouse 160 Federal St Boston MA 02110

SCANLAN, ROBERT MICHAEL, financial management company executive; b. Boston, May 2, 1936; s. Michael Henry and Grace Agnes (Thorne) S.; BS magna cum laude in Econs., Boston Coll., 1959, postgrad., 1963-66; cert. Stonier Grad. Sch. Banking, Rutgers U., 1968, Greater Boston Exec. Program, MIT, 1969; m. Joanne J. Radosta, Aug. 12, 1961; children—Robert M., Timothy J., Daniel F., Grace M. Asst. bank examiner, 1959-62; with Fed. Res. Bank Boston, 1959-69, asst. v.p., 1968-69; pres., chief exec. officer Investment Cos. Services Corp., computer services to investment cos., Boston, 1969-79; pres., chief exec. officer Eagle Income Mgmt. Co., Inc., Boston, 1980-84; chmn., The Harborview Group Inc., Boston, 1985—; pres., trustee Am. Liquid Trust, 1978-79; pres. ALT Mgmt. Corp., 1978-79; dir., prin. Cornerstone Fin. Services, 1976-79; trustee Keystone Employees Benefit Fund, 1974-79; mem. pension com. Keystone Retirement Equity Trust, 1974-79; mem. ops. com. Investment Co. Inst., 1970-79, chmn., 1973-75, chmn. broker/dealer subcom., 1971-72, chmn. electronic funds transfer adv. com., 1978—. Mem. alumni fund-raising com. Boston Coll., 1976—, alumni admissions counselor, 1977—. Roman Catholic. Home: 96 Hinckley Rd Milton MA 02186 Office: One Post Office Sq Boston MA 02109

SCANLON, PETER REDMOND, accountant; b. N.Y.C., Feb. 18, 1931; s. John Thomas and Loretta Dolores (Ryan) S.; m. Mary Jane E. Condon, Mar. 7, 1953; children: Peter, Barbara, Mark, Brian, Janet. B.B.A. in Accounting, Iona Coll., 1952. C.P.A., N.Y. Mem. profl. staff Coopers & Lybrand, N.Y.C., 1956-66; partner Coopers & Lybrand, 1966, chief exec. officer, chmn. exec. com. Pres. Coopers & Lybrand Found.; trustee Iona Coll.; vis. com. Sloan Sch. MIT. Served to lt. USN, 1952-56. Decorated Knight of Malta, Knight Holy Sepulchre; recipient Arthur A. Loftus award Iona Coll., 1974. Mem. AICPA, N.Y. State Soc. CPA's. Roman Catholic. Clubs: N.Y. Athletic, Marco Polo. Office: Coopers & Lybrand 1251 Ave of the Americas New York NY 10020

SCANLON, TERENCE JOHN, publisher; b. St. Joseph, Mo., July 26, 1931; s. Byron Bernard and Margaret Susan (Zirkle) S.; m. Doris Jean Blasdel, Mar. 8, 1969; children: Kerry, Brooke, Erin, Thomas, Duffy, Tanner. BA, Wichita (Kans.) State U., 1956. Mem. mgmt. dept. City of Wichita, 1956-66; dir. adminstrn. State of Kans., Topeka, 1966-70, dir. econ. devel., 1972-73; pres. Cen. Devel., Inc., Topeka, 1970-71, Coors of Kans., Inc., Wichita, 1973-79, Scanlon Enterprises, Wichita, 1980-85; pres. and publisher Wichita Bus. Jour., 1986—; bd. dirs. Kans. Gas and Electric Co.; chmn. bd. trustees St. Joseph Med. Ctr. Vice chmn. bd. trustees Wichita State U., 1981-88; chmn. Dem. State Com., Topeka, 1977-79. Roman Catholic. Home: 132 N Fountain Wichita KS 67208 Office: Wichita Bus Jour 138 Ida Wichita KS 67211

SCANLON, TERRENCE MAURICE, foundation administrator; b. Milw., May 1, 1939; s. Maurice John and Anne (Hayes) S.; m. Judy Ball, June 14, 1969; children: Michael Mansfield, Justin Ball, Brendan Hayes. BS, Villanova U., 1961. Staff asst. The White House, Washington, 1963-67; with SBA, Washington, 1967-69; with Dept. of Commerce, Washington, 1969-83, mem. office Minority Bus. Enterprise, 1969-80, with Internat. Trade Adminstrn., 1980-81, with Minority Bus. Devel. Agy., 1981-83; mem. Consumer Product Safety Commn., Washington, 1983—, vice chmn., 1983-84, chmn., 1985, 86-89; v.p., treas. Heritage Found., Washington, 1989—. Am. Polit. Sci. Assn. Congl. fellow, 1967-68. Mem. University Club. Home: 4510 Dexter St Washington DC 20007 Office: Heritage Found 214 Massachusetts Ave NE Washington DC 20002

SCANNELL, PHILIP LAWRENCE, treasurer, consultant; b. Lowell, Mass., Apr. 19, 1919; s. Philip and Mary (Cooney) S.; m. Ellen H. Slattery, June 23, 1948; children: Jo Ellen, Philip III, Dennis, Maureen, Susan, Priscilla, Kathleen, George, Maryann. Cert. in Mech. Tech., Poly. Tech., Troy, N.Y. Registered profl. engr., N.H., Mass. Treas. Lowell (Mass.) Iron, Steel Co., 1956—, Scannell Boiler Works, Lowell, 1956—; trustee Menans Investment Trust, Lowell. Served as tech. sgt. U.S. Army, 1942-46, PTO. Mem. Com. of Mass. (constrn. supr.). Roman Catholic. Club: Vesper Country, Tynsboro, Mass. (pres. 1982-83). Lodge: Elks. Office: Scannell Boiler Works PO Box 1313 Lowell MA 01853

SCARBOROUGH, MARION KENNETH, real estate company executive; b. Celeste, Tex., Apr. 18, 1941; s. Marion H. and Knovis Elizabeth (Arnold) S.; m. Lynn Wilford Scarborough (div.); children: Valerie, Adam, Chris. BS, North Tex. State U., 1971, postgrad., 1976; postgrad., Inst. Orgn. Mgmt., 1981. Chmn., chief exec. officer Scarborough and Cotton Polit. & Pub. Affairs Consulting, Dallas, 1945-86; pres. Scarborough Rose Tekemktg. Co., Scarborough Prodns.; co-gen. ptnr. TV Album Ltd.; legis. aide Congressman Dale Milford, 1971-74; dist. aide Congressman Graham Purcell, 1968-71; dir. Learning Tree Mgmt. Systems Inc., LWS Communication, Wilford Scarborough Prodns. Contbr. articles to profl. jours. Mem. adv. bd. dirs. Yale Literary Mag.; mem. adv. bd. Heartwise Found.; bd. dirs. Swiss Ave. Counseling Ctr., Maverick Cinema Group; bd. advs. New Am. Patriots; bd. advs. Inst. Pub. Policy Research; mem. sustentation council Episcopal Found. for Drama; active Boy Scouts Am.; bd. regents Walden Prep. Sch.; chmn. bd. regents Scarborough Acad. Performing Arts. Served with U.S. Army, M.I., 1962-65. Mem. U.S. C. of C. (pub. affairs mgr. S.W. region 1974-83), Tex. C. of C. Execs. Assn. (Meritorious Service awards), N.Mex. C. of C. Execs. Assn. (Disting. Service award), Okla. C. of C. Execs. Assn., Mo. C. of C. Execs. Assn., Ark. C. of C. Execs. Assn., La. C. of C. Execs. Assn., Dallas Friday Group, Dallas Study Group, Dallas Bd. Realtors, Dallas 40, Dallas Rep. Mens, North Dallas C. of C., Waxahachie C. of C. Lodge: Rotary. Home: 2611 Fairmount St #A Dallas TX 75201 Office: 6311 N O'Connor Ste 216 LB110 Irving TX 75039-3510

SCARBOROUGH, YANCEY WILCOX, JR., insurance company executive; b. Charleston, S.C., July 31, 1922; s. Yancey Wilcox Scarborough; m. Helen Cox, July 3, 1945; children: LouAnn Scarborough Pratt-Thomas, Frances Cameron Scarborough Gunter, Yancey Wilcox III, George C., John C. BA, The Citadel, 1943, LLD (hon.), 1987. CLU. With Atlantic Coast Life Ins. Co., Charleston, 1946—, asst. to pres., 1951-52, exec. v.p., 1952-56, pres., 1956-88, chmn., chief exec. officer, 1988—; bd. dirs. Citizens & So. Trust Co. S.C.; mem. Charleston adv. bd. C&S Corp. Trustee Episcopal Diocese S.C.; past chmn. Charleston Devel. Bd., Charleston Trident United Way Campaign, S.C. Bd. for Tech. and Comprehensive Edn.; past mem. Trident Tech. Coll. Found., S.C. Council on Vocat. and Tech. Edn., S.C. Commn. Higher Edn.; scoutmaster Boy Scouts Am., Charleston, 1950-52; past sr. warden Cathedral St. Luke and St. Paul; former mem. bd. dirs. Charleston YMCA, Nat. YMCA; past mem. fin. com. S.C. Dem. Com; past trustee Health Sci. Found. Med. U. S.C.; bd. dirs. S.C. Research Authority. Served with USMCR, 1943-46. Mem. S.C. Life and Health Guarantee Assn. (bd. dirs.), Life Insurers Conf. (past chmn.), Assn. S.C. Life Ins. Cos. (past pres.), Charleston Indsl. Assn. (past pres.), Charleston Trident C. of C. (past pres.). Lodge: Sertoma (charter pres. Charleston, past gov. S.C.). Office: Atlantic Coast Life Ins Co PO Box 20010 Charleston SC 29413-0010

SCARBROUGH, ERNEST EARL, stockbroker, fin. planner; b. Memphis, Jan. 7, 1947; s. Earl Carson and Mary Lillian (Keileber) S.; m. Cindy Cowley, Sept. 22, 1973; children: Michael E., William E. AA, Phoenix Coll., 1974. Cert. fin. planner. Profl. pilot, airline transport rating, flight instr. various gen. aviation cos., Memphis and Phoenix, 1968-72; transp. analyst leasing and sales Rollins Leasing Co., Phoenix, 1971-73; cost analyst Ariz. Pub. Service Co., Phoenix, 1973-75; air traffic contr. FAA, Ariz. and Calif., 1977-81; account exec. E.F. Hutton & Co., Phoenix, 1982-83, asst. v.p., 1984-86, v.p., 1987; v.p., portfolio mgr. Prudential-Bache Securities, Inc., Phoenix, 1988—. Chmn. stewartship, vice chmn. fin. Cross in Desert United Meth. Ch., Phoenix, 1987-88; exec. bd. dirs. Sojourner Ctr., 1987—. With USAF, 1966-70. Mem. Internat. Assn. for Fin. Planning, Internat Assn. Cert. Fin. Planners, Profl. Air Traffic Controllers Orgn. (local pres. 1975-81), Rotary (v.p. Phoenix chpt. 1987, pres.-elect 1988). Democrat. Home: 2419 E Synnyside Dr Phoenix AZ 85028 Office: Prudential-Bache Securities Inc 4340 E Camelback Rd Phoenix AZ 85018

SCARFF, EDWARD L., diversified company executive; b. 1930. BS, Mich. Tech. U., 1954. With Ansul Chem. Co., 1953-56, Stanford Research Inst., 1956-60; dir. investment research Investors Diversified Services, Inc., 1960-63; pres., chief exec. officer N. Am. Securities Co., 1963-65; v.p., then pres. Transam. Corp., 1965-71; pres. Edward L. Scarff and Assocs., San Francisco, 1971—; with Arcata Corp., San Francisco, 1971—, now chmn. bd. dirs., also bd. dirs. Office: Arcata Corp 601 California St San Francisco CA 94108 *

SCARLETT, JOHN ARCHIBALD, III, physician, pharmaceutical executive; b. Evansville, Ind., Mar. 5, 1951; s. John Archibald, Jr. and Albion Adele (Ritte) S.; m. Susan Ellenstein, June 17, 1972; children: Jessica Lee, Lauren Elizabeth. BA, Earlham Coll., 1973; MD, U. Chgo., 1977. Diplomate Am. Bd. Internal Medicine. Intern, then resident Internal Medicine Hosp. U. Pa., Phila., 1977-80; asst. dir. med. rsch. and svcs. McNeil Pharm., Spring House, Pa., 1982; fellow in endocrinology and metabolism Sch. Medicine U. Colo., 1980-82; dir. med. rsch. and svcs. McNeil Pharm., Spring House, Pa., 1982-85; v.p. sci. affairs Greenwich Pharms., Ft. Washington, Pa., 1985—. Edward K. Cox scholar Earlham Coll., 1972. Fellow ACP; mem. Drug Info. Assn., Am. Fedn. for Clin. Rsch. Republican. Mem. Soc. of Friends. Home: 570 Penllyn Blue Bell Pike Blue Bell PA 19422 Office: Greenwich Pharms Inc 501 Office Center Dr Fort Washington PA 19034

SCARRY, MARY, financial executive; b. Pitts., Apr. 1, 1934. BS in Edn., Slippery Rock U., 1956, MEd, 1970; cert., Coll. Fin. Planning, 1982. Tchr. McGuffy Sch., Claysville, Pa., 1956-58; tchr., chmn. dept. Elizabeth (Pa.) Forward Sch., 1958-62; dir. student activities Allegheny Gen. Hosp., 1962-66; tchr. econs. Ringgold Sch. Dist., Monongahela, Pa., 1966-67; registrar, counselor U. Pitts., 1967-77; registered rep., fin. planner Shoal P. Berer Assocs., Pa., 1977-87; fin. services mgr. United Resources, Inc., Pitts., 1987-88; with Hackett Assocs. Inc., Pitts., 1988—. Mem. Inst. Cert. Fin. Planning (chief exec. officer Pitts. chpt., pres. 1984-87, founder), Internat. Assn. Fin. Planning (Pitts. chpt., v.p. programs 1980-84, v.p. ethics com. 1984-86). Home: 218 Rock Run Rd Elizabeth PA 15037 Office: Hackett Assocs Inc PO Box 10911 Pittsburgh PA 15236

SCARTH, JOHN CAMPBELL, paper company executive; b. Sherbrooke, Que., Can., July 5, 1924; s. Hubert Ashley and Christine (McIntosh) S.; m. Ellen Marion Frazar, June 3, 1948; children—Ian, Jane. B.Sc., U. Bishops Coll., Lennoxville, Que., 1945. With KVP Co. Ltd., Can., 1948-61, v.p. sales, 1958-61; asst. to pres. KVP Sutherland Paper Co. subs. Brown Co., Kalamazoo, 1961-63; v.p. KVP Sutherland Paper Co. subs. Brown Co., 1963-68; pres. Deerfield Glassine Co., Monroe Bridge, Mass., 1968; exec. v.p. E.B. Eddy Paper Co. (name now E.B. Eddy Forest Products, Ltd.), Hull, Que., Can., 1968-72; pres. E.B. Eddy Paper Co. (name now E.B. Eddy Forest Products, Ltd.), 1972-88, chief exec. officer; chief exec. officer Eddy Paper Co. Ltd., Ottawa, Ont., Can., 1988—. Office: Eddy Paper Co Ltd, 1335 Carling Ave, Ottawa, ON Canada K1Z 8N8 *

SCHACHAR, HENRY, materials marketing executive. Pres. Philipp Bros., Inc., N.Y.C. Office: Philipp Bros Inc 1221 Ave of the Americas New York NY 10020 *

SCHACHMAN, STEPHEN, lawyer; b. Phila., Nov. 12, 1944; s. Bernard Kapnik and Hannah (Levi) S.; m. Sharyn Negus (div. Nov. 1979); m. Toby Schmidt. BS, U. Pa., 1966; JD, Georgetown U., 1969. Bar: Pa. 1969, Washington 1969, U.S. Supreme Ct. 1975. Atty. various govt. agys., Washington and Phila., 1973-77; pvt. practice Washington and Phila., 1973-77; pres., chief exec. officer Phila. Gas Works, 1977-83; v.p. externatl affairs Bell Atlantic Mobile System, Basking Ridge, N.J., 1983-85; exec. v.p. Bell Atlantic Mobile System, Basking Ridge, 1985; exec. dir. external affairs Bell Atlantic NSI, Arlington, Va., 1986; v.p., dir. Internat. Cogeneration Corp., Phila., 1987—; of counsel Dilworth, Paxson, Kalish & Kauffman, Phila., 1988—; bd. dirs. Elizabethtown (N.J.) Gas Co., Internat. Cogeneration Corp.; exec. dir. Middle States Ind. Power Producer, Phila., 1987—. Bd. dirs. Urban League, Phila., 1981—; exec. com. to Re-elect U.S. Senator Arlen Spector, Phila., 1986. Served to capt., USMC, 1970-73. Recipient Pres.'s Award for Excellence in Energy U.S. Govt., 1982, cert. merit Am. Gas Assn., 1982. Mem. Locust Club, Zebra Group (bd. dirs. 1981—). Republican. Jewish. Home: 713 Lombard St Philadelphia PA 19107 Office: Dilworth Paxson Kalish & Kauffman 2600 The Fidelity Bldg Philadelphia PA 19109

SCHACHT, HENRY BREWER, diesel engine manufacturing company executive; b. Erie, Pa., Oct. 16, 1934; s. Henry Blass and Virginia (Brewer) S.; m. Nancy Godfrey, Aug. 27, 1960; children: James, Laura, Jane, Mary. B.S., Yale U., 1956; M.B.A., Harvard U., 1962. Sales trainee Am. Brake Shoe Co., N.Y.C., 1956-57; investment mgr. Irwin Mgmt. Co., Columbus, Ind., 1962-64; v.p. finance Cummins Engine Co., Inc., Columbus, 1964-66; v.p., central area mgr. internat. Cummins Engine Co., Inc., London, Eng., 1966-67; group v.p. internat. and subsidiaries Cummins Engine Co., Inc., 1967-69; pres. Cummins Engine Co., Inc., Columbus, 1969-77; chmn., chief exec. officer Cummins Engine Co., Inc., 1977—; bd. dirs. AT&T, CBS., Chase Manhattan Corp., Chase Manhattan Bank N.A. Mem. Bus. Council, Council Fgn. Relations; mem. The Assocs., Harvard Bus. Sch.; trustee Brookings Instn., Com. Econ. Devel., Conf. Bd., The Ford Found., Yale Corp. Served with USNR, 1957-60. Mem. Assocs. Harvard Bus. Sch. (bd. dirs.), Tau Beta Pi. Republican. Office: Cummins Engine Co Inc MC-60910 Box 3005 Columbus IN 47202

SCHACHTER, ESTHER RODITTI, lawyer, author, publisher; b. Los Angeles, Feb. 7, 1933; d. David and Lucy Roditti; m. Oscar H. Schachter, Aug. 8, 1957; children—Charles David, Susan Dayana. B.A., UCLA, 1954; J.D., Harvard U., 1957. Bar: N.Y. 1959. Assoc. Stickles, Hayden and Kennedy, N.Y.C., 1957-62; asst. dir. Legis. Drafting Fund Columbia U., N.Y.C., 1962-65, cons., 1965-67; cons. N.Y.C. Air Pollution Control Dept., 1965-67; instr. and cons. New Sch. for Social Research, N.Y.C., 1968-70; cons. Internat. League for Rights of Man, N.Y.C., 1969, Rand Inst., N.Y.C., 1969, U.S.-Soviet Environ. Studies Program, UN Assn., N.Y.C., 1969; sr. research assoc. Ctr. for Policy Research Columbia U., 1970-73; sr. program officer Ford Found., N.Y.C., 1972-78; pres. Esther Roditti Schachter, P.C., N.Y.C., 1978-83; ptnr. Schachter & Froling, N.Y.C., 1983-85, Schachter, Courter, Purcell & Kobert, N.Y.C., 1985—; speaker, lectr., panelist profl. assn. confs., forums, workshops, U.S., Can., Tokyo, London. Author: N.Y.C. Air Pollution Control Code Annotated, 1965; Enforcing Air Pollution Controls, 1979; Financial Support of Women's Programs in the 1970's, 1979; Computer Contracts Reference Directory, 1979-83; co-author: Charities and Charitable Foundations, 1974; author, co-author articles in field; legal editor: Computer Economics, 1983—; editor Computer Law & Tax Report, 1984-86, pub., editor, 1986—. Nat. governing bd. Common Cause, 1979-82, mem. state governing bd., N.Y., 1982-84; mem. com. on urban environ. Citizens Union, N.Y.C., 1969-73; mem. West Side Democratic Club, 1958-63. Ford Found. grantee, 1970; NSF grantee, 1971; recipient Award for Outstanding Service Brandeis U., Nat. Women's Com., 1973. Mem. ABA (lectr. 1987), Assn. Bar City N.Y. (founder, chmn. com. on computer law 1980—), N.Y. State Bar Assn., Computer Law Assn. (lectr. 1985), Am. Arbitration Assn. (chair com. for computer disputes 1985—), Phi Beta Kappa. Club: Panther (Alamuchy, N.J.).

SCHAD, THEODORE GEORGE, JR., food company executive; b. N.Y.C., Mar. 4, 1927; s. Theodore George and Helen (Tennyson) S.; m. Karma Rose Cundell, Mar. 21, 1957 (dec. June 1978); children: Roberta Gay Hill, Theodore George III, Olive Schad Smith, Peter Tennyson.; m. Mary Nell Jennings, June 20, 1981. Student, Va. Mil. Inst., 1944-45; B.S. in Bus. and Econs, Ill. Inst. Tech., 1950, M.S. in Bus. and Econs, 1951. V.p. mktg. Great Western Savs. Co., Los Angeles, 1961-63; prin., nat. dir. mktg. and econs. cons. Peat, Marwick, Mitchell, N.Y.C., 1964-71; chmn. bd., pres., chief exec. officer Lou Ana Foods, Inc., Schad Industries, Inc. (formerly Lou Ana Industries, Inc.), 1971—, Lou Ana Industries Internat., 1971-84, Schad Industries Internat., Opelousas, La., 1985—, Lou Ana Foods of Tex., Inc., Kingwood, 1986—, Lou Ana Gardens Inc., Kingwood, 1989—; instr. mktg. and econs. U. Calif., Riverside, U. So. Calif., Los Angeles State Coll., U. Calif., Los Angeles, 1956-63. Pres. Assn. Parents Retarded Children, Mamaroneck, N.Y., 1970-71; pres. Greater Opelousas C. of C., 1972-73, bd. dirs. 1973-74, 88—; bd. dirs. Council for Better La., Baton Rouge, 1975-80, La. Assn. Bus. and Industry, 1980-85; chmn. U.S. Bus. and Indsl. Council, 1987—, bd. dirs., 1979-84, mem. exec. com., 1984-87, bd. dirs. U.S. Indsl. Council Ednl. Found., 1987—; trustee Va. Mil. Inst. Found., 1978-88; v.p., mem. exec. bd. Evangeline Area council Boy Scouts Am., 1984-85. Recipient Disting. Eagle Scout award Boy Scouts Am., 1985; named Citizen of Yr. Opelousas, La., 1979, Man of Yr. Sertoma of Opelousas, 1978, Paul Harris fellow Rotary, 1987. Mem. Am. Mktg. Assn. (pres. So. Calif. chpt. 1961-62, dir. 1962-63), Greater Opelousas C. of C. (pres. 1972-73, bd. dirs. 1973-74, 88—), Greater Opelousas Econ. and Industrial Coun. (bd. dirs. 1988—). Republican. Methodist. Lodge: Sertoma (founding pres. local chpt. 1963). Office: Lou Ana Foods PO Box 591 Opelousas LA 70570

SCHADER, HARRY W., III, real estate developer, financial consultant; b. Alameda, Calif., Oct. 21, 1956; s. Harry W. Jr. and Evelyn A. (Smith) S.; m. Lynnette Hazelrigg, Jan. 9, 1975 (div. Feb. 1986); children: Harry W. IV, Shari V. Owner Beverly Hills (Calif.) Devel. Co., 1980—, Beverly Hills Constrn. Services, 1980—; chief fin. officer Beverly Hills 1st Capital Corp., 1983-85; bd. dirs. Market Street, Newport Beach, Calif. Office: Beverly Hills Devel Co PO Box 1833 Beverly Hills CA 90213

SCHAEFER, C. BARRY, railroad executive, lawyer; b. Elizabeth, N.J., Feb. 23, 1939; s. Carl H. and Evelyn G. (Conk) S.; m. Carol Ann Craft, July 11, 1970; children: Sara Elizabeth, Susan Craft. B.S. in Engring., Princeton U., 1961; M.S. in Engring., U. Pa., 1962; LL.B., Columbia U., 1965; M.B.A., NYU, 1970. Bar: N.Y. 1966, Nebr. 1972. With Kelley, Drye, Warren, N.Y.C., 1966-69; asst. gen. counsel Union Pacific Corp., N.Y.C., 1969-72; western gen. counsel Union Pacific R.R. Co., Omaha, 1972-74, v.p., western gen. counsel, 1974-77, v.p. law, 1977-82; sr. v.p. planning and corp. devel. Union Pacific Corp., N.Y.C., 1984-88; exec. v.p. Union Pacific Corp., Bethlehem, Pa., 1988. Contbr. articles to law revs. Nat. bd. dirs. Jr. Achievement, Colorado Springs, Colo., 1986—. Mem. ABA, Nebr. Bar Assn. Clubs: Rockaway Hunting (N.Y.), Racquet and Tennis (N.Y.C.), Round Hill (Greenwich, Conn.), Princeton of N.Y., Board Room. Office: 2 Greenwich Pla Ste 6830 Bethlehem PA 18018

SCHAEFER, GEORGE ANTHONY, manufacturing company executive; b. Covington, Ky., June 13, 1928; s. George Joseph and Marie Cecelia (Sandheger) S.; m. Barbara Ann Quick, Aug. 11, 1951; children: Mark Christopher, Sharon Marie. BS in Commerce, St. Louis U., 1951. With Caterpillar Inc., Peoria, Ill., 1951—, div. mgr., 1968-73; plant mgr. Caterpillar Inc., Decatur, Ill., 1973-76, v.p., 1976-81, dir., 1981-84; vice chmn., exec. v.p. Caterpillar Inc., Peoria, 1984-85, chmn., chief exec. officer, 1985—; fin. and acctg. mgr. Caterpillar France S.A., Grenoble, 1962-68; db. dirs. San Diego, 1st Chgo. Corp.; mem. bus. council Emergency Com. for Am. Trade Negotiations. Mem. adv. council Coll. Commerce and Bus. Adminstrn. U. Ill, Champaign, 1979; trustee Bradley U.; econ. devel. com. Proctor Community Hosp. Served with USMC, 1946-48. Mem. Bus. Council. Republican. Roman Catholic. Club: Peoria Country. Office: Caterpillar Inc 100 NE Adams St Peoria IL 61629 *

SCHAEFER, JEFFREY A., financial planner; b. Denver, Aug. 14, 1964; s. Kenneth R. and Marilyn (Ulrich) S. BS in Fin., U. Colo., 1986, postgrad., 1987—. Cert. fin. planner. Registered rep. B.J. Leonard & Co., Inc., Englewood, Colo., 1984-85; assoc. Fin. Svcs. Group, Denver, 1985-86, Fin. Architects, Inc., Denver, 1986-87; owner, mgr. Capital Fin. Mgmt. Inc., Englewood, 1987—. Mem. Inst. Cert. Fiin. Planners. Republican. Office: Capital Fin Mgmt Inc 5299 DTC Blvd Ste 500 Englewood CO 80111

SCHAEFER, LOUIS BERNHARDT, IV, manufacturing executive; b. Cleve., Feb. 19, 1941; s. Louis B. III and Betty (Iles) S.; m. Jane Nash, Dec. 26, 1964; children: Julie, Lou, Jayne, Beth. BS, Ohio State U., 1963. Salesman Schaefer Bros. Inc., Akron, Ohio, 1963-71; v.p. sales Schaefer Bros. Inc., Cleve., 1972-73, pres., 1974—; pres. Indsl. Furnace Services Inc., Cleve., 1976-83, Steel Ceramics Inc., Cleve., 1979-83, HiTemp Inc., Cleve., 1985—; cons. Ceramic Fiber Anchor, 1988. Patentee in field. Served with U.S. Army, 1963-69. Mem. Air Pollution Control Assn. Republican. Home: 810 Beechwood Dr Medina OH 44256 Office: Schaefer Bros Inc 12500 Berea Rd Cleveland OH 44111

SCHAEFER, PATRICK MICHAEL, real estate development consultant; b. Kansas City, Mo., Mar. 31, 1955; s. James Michael and Elizabeth (Oieckich) S.; m. Carolyn Edney, Dec. 17, 1983. BS, U. Kans., 1977. Dist. mgr. Hydro-Air Engring., St. Louis, 1977-8l, dir. mktg., 198l-84; assoc. Vandermeer & Co., Dallas, 1985; mgr. real estate feasibility Arthur Young & Co., Dallas, 1986—; bd. dirs. Systems Machinery Engring., Kansas City. Contbr. articles to profl. jours. Mem. stewardship coun. Highland Park Presbyn. Ch., Dallas, 1985-86. Republican. Home: 2937 Fondren St Dallas TX 75205

SCHAEFFER, BARBARA HAMILTON, transportation company executive; travel consultant; b. Newton, Mass., Apr. 26, 1926; d. Peter Davidson Gunn and Harriet Bennett (Thompson) Hamilton; m. John Schaeffer, Sept. 7, 1946; children—Laurie, John, Peter. Student, Skidmore Coll., 1943-46; AB in English, Bucknell U., 1948; postgrad. Montclair State U., 1950-51, Bank St. Coll. Edn., 1959-61, Yeshiva U., 1961-62; student Daytona Beach Coll., 1984. Cert. primary, secondary tchr., N.J. Dir. Pompton Plains Sch., N.J., 1959-62; adviser Episcopal Sch., Towaco, N.J., 1968-70; v.p. Deltona-DeLand Trolley, Orange City, Fla., 1980-81; pres. Monroe Heavy Equipment Rentals, Inc., Orange City, 1981—, also Magic Carpet Travel, 1986-88 cons. TLC Travel Club, Orange City, 1981-88; lectr. on children's art, 1959-70. Contbr. articles to profl. publs. Mem. Internat. Platform Assn., Am. Soc. Travel Agts., Deltona C. of C., Orange City C. of C., Small Bus. Devel. Regional Ctr. (Stetson U. chpt.), DeLand Area C. of C. (transp. com. 1981-85). Episcopalian. Avocations: restoring old homes, oil painting, piano. Home: 400 Foothill Farms Rd Orange City FL 32763 Office: Magic Carpet Travel 2425 Enterprise Rd Orange City FL 32763

SCHAEFFER, FREDERICK ROBERT, small business owner; b. Chgo., May 9, 1941; s. Bertram Frederick and Evelyn Pearl (Benson) S.; m. Carol Eleanor Witte, Feb. 8, 1964; children: Frederick Henry, Kysa Lynn. BS with honors, U. Ill., 1964; MBA with distinction, Northeastern U., 1965. Asst. brand mgr. Procter & Gamble, Inc., Cin., 1965-68; v.p. subs. Polaroid, Inc., Cambridge, Mass., 1968-71; treas., chief exec. officer Salomon/N.Am., Inc., Peabody, Mass., 1971-77; owner, pres., chief exec. officer Sailboard, Inc., Danvers, Mass., 1980-87; pres., chief exec. officer Schaeffer & Co., Inc., Danvers, 1977—; owner, founder Wadsworth Village, Danvers, 1982—. Alderman City of Beverly, Mass., 1980-82; gov.'s transition sec. State House, Boston, 1978-79; co-founder, pres., bd. dirs. Beverly Coalition for Youth, 1979—; mem. ch. vestry, Beverly, 1985. Recipient Ruth Hahn Achievement in Mktg. award U. Ill., 1979-89, Outstanding Svc. award Men's Assn. Mem. 49'ers (forum moderator 1984—), Young Pres. Orgn. (forum moderator 1975-78), Rotary, Gideons Internat. (v.p. Boston North 1987-88, camp v.p.), Danvers Hist. Soc. (Hist. award 1987, v.p. 1988—). Democrat. Episcopalian. Home: 3 Wilson Ave Beverly MA 01915 Office: Wadsworth Village 130 Centre St Danvers MA 01923

SCHAFER, CARL WALTER, investment executive; b. Chgo., Jan. 16, 1936; s. MacHenry George and Gertrude (Herrick) S.; m. June Elizabeth Perry, Feb. 2, 1963; 1 child, MacHenry George II. BA with distinction, U. Rochester, 1958. Budget examiner Budget Bur., Exec. Office Pres., Washington, 1961-64, legis. analyst, 1964-66, dep. dir. budget preparation, 1966-68, dir. budget preparation, 1968-69; staff asst. U.S. Ho. of Reps. Appropriations Com., 1969; dir. budget Princeton (N.J.) U., 1969-72, treas., 1972-76, fin. v.p., treas., 1976-87, lectr. indsl. adminstrn., 1975; prin. Rockefeller & Co., Inc., 1987—, also bd. dirs.; pres., chief exec. officer Palmer Square Inc., 1979-81; trustee, treas. McCarter Theatre Co. Inc., 1974-76; co-chmn. N.J. Gov.'s Task Force on Improving N.J. Econ. and Regulatory Climate, 1982-83; trustee, dir. Wainoco Oil Corp., Bio Techniques Labs. Inc., Ecova Corp., Electronic Clearing House Inc., the Kidder, Peabody Group of Mutual Funds, Harbor Br. Inst. Inc., Am. Bible Soc., The Jewish Guild For the Blind, Atlantic Found, The Johnson Atelier and Sch. Sculpture; adv. dir. Hamilton and Co.; chmn. investment adv. com. Howard Hughes Med. Inst.; mem. adv. council Domain Ptnrs. Mem. Phi Beta Kappa. Republican. Episcopalian. Clubs: Princeton (N.Y.C.); Nassau (Princeton). Home: PO Box 1164 Princeton NJ 08542 Office: Rockefeller and Co Inc Rm 5425 30 Rockefeller Pla New York NY 10112

SCHAFER, JERRY SANFORD, film company executive, producer, writer, director; b. Los Angeles, July 4, 1934; s. Sidney Sanford and Belle (Bass) S.; children : Mark, Morgan, Martin, Aaron, Erik; m. Marianne Marks, Oct. 1, 1979. Masters, UCLA, 1956. Writer, producer, dir. The Legend of Billy the Kid Repuplic Studios, 1958; writer, producer, dir. worlds fair presentation The Quick Draw Theatre, Seattle, N.Y.C., 1962, 66; writer, producer, dir. mus. shows Speaking of Girls, Las Vegas, Nev., 1963, That Certain Girl, Las Vegas, 1967, Belle Starr, London, 1968, The Piece-Full Palace, Las Vegas, 1969; writer, producer, dir. western stunt show Cowboys, Cowgirls & Kata, Osaka, Japan, 1970; pres. Sanford Internat. Entertainment, Inc., Las Vegas, 1978—; freelance writer, producer, dir. 1981—; entertainment dir. Del E. Webb Corp., Las Vegas, 1961-69; lectr., vis. prof. U. Nev., Las Vegas, 1985—. Writer, producer, dir.: (feature films) Tonight For Sure, 1959, The Little People, 1960, Along Came Jasper, 1961, The Blackhawk Gunfighters, 1963, Like it Is, 1972, Not My Daughter, 1972, The Low Price of Fame, 1973, Shortcut to Terror, 1975, Horace & Fred, 1976, Go for Your Gun, Fists of Steel, 1988, (mus. prodns.) On Stage with Judy Garland, An Evening with Pat Boone, Presenting Mr. Jack Benny!, Betty Grable/A Musical Musical!, Robert Goulet The Camelot Prince, The Polly Bergen Show, Brenda Lee on Stage!, Girls a la Carte, C'est la Femme; producer, dir., 1962-69, Soul Follies, Flower Drum Song, Under the Yum Yum Tree, The Ziegfeld Follies, numerous TV spls., 1983-87. Named Producer of Yr. Am. Guild Variety Artists, 1964, 66; recipient PAVCA award Profl. Audio-Visual Communications Assn., 1985; holder world record for fastest draw. Mem. Nat. Constables Assn. (comd. 1985—), Nat. Counter Intelligence Assn. (invited), Ky. Cols. Assn. (invited), Nat. Orch. Leaders Assn., ASCAP, Nev. Motion Picture and TV Bd. (appointed to adv. com. by Gov. Richard Bryan 1987), Dirs. Guild Am. Office: Sanford Entertainment PO Box 15101 Las Vegas NV 89114-5101

SCHAFER, SANDRA LEE, healthcare executive; b. Sioux City, Iowa, Apr. 2, 1951; d. Wallace Lafe and Marydona (Blades) Hansen; children from previous marriage: Leah, Tavis. BSBA, U. Iowa, 1981, MA in Hosp. Adminstrn., 1983. Svc. assoc. Amherst Assocs., Chgo., 1983-84, market analyst, 1984-85; sr. specialist fin. and decision support HBO & Co., Atlanta, 1985-86, mgr. nat. sales ops., 1986-88, dir. bus. devel., 1988—. Mem. Healthcare Fin. Mgmt. Assn., Electronix Computing Health Oriented, U. Iowa Alumni Assn. Office: HBO & Co 301 Perimeter Ctr N Atlanta GA 30346

SCHAFF, PAULA KAY, industrial company executive; b. Cape Girardeau, Mo., Oct. 10, 1945; d. Charles Henry Sr. and Elnora Pauline (Ridge) Canine; m. Fred Jon Schaff; 1 child, Kevin Jon. Student, Washtenaw Community Coll., U. Ill., Dana U. Successively records clk. PTO div., accounts payable clk., sec., sales specialist, exec. sec., plant mgr., customer svc. specialist Dana Corp., Chelsea, Mich., 1967-78, supr. customer svc., 1978-79, supr. customer svc., shipping and assembly PTO div., 1979-81; distbn. mgr. Dana Corp., Athens, Ga., 1981-85, Maumee, Ohio, 1985-88; gen. mgr. warehouse ops. div. Dana Corp., 1989—. Mem. NAFE, Toledo Women in Industry. Republican. Methodist. Office: Dana Corp Warehouse Ops Div PO Box 455 Toledo OH 43692

SCHAFFER, DAVID EDWIN, management systems executive; b. N.Y.C., Nov. 3, 1929; s. Karl and Jeanette (Gotthelf) S.; student Wharton Sch. of U. Pa., 1948-49; B.A., New Sch. for Social Research, 1959; m. Ariel Williams Sullivan, May 3, 1951; stepchildren—Adrienne Sullivan Smith, James W. Sullivan. Spl. edn. tchr. of emotionally disturbed children, various schs. and hosps., 1954-65; br. mgr. First Westchester Nat. Bank, New Rochelle, N.Y., 1965-66; v.p. Longines-Symphonette Inc., spl. asst. to chmn. bd. Longines Wittnauer Inc., Larchmont, N.Y., 1966-72; pvt. practice mgmt. cons., Franconia, N.H., 1973-77; v.p., dir. ops. Carroll Reed Ski Shops, Inc., 1978-80; co-pres.-owner Bus. Mgmt. Systems, Inc., Franconia, N.H. instr. econs. Am. Inst. Banking, 1965-66. Moderator, Town of Franconia, 1973—, co-chmn. Frost Pl. com.; bd. dirs. White Mountain Community Services, 1973-77; bd. dirs., pres. No. N.H. Mental Health Services, 1975-77. Served with Signal Corps, AUS, 1951-53. Mem. Direct Mail Credit Assn. Am. (founding mem.), Asso. Retail Credit Men of N.Y.C., Direct Mail Assn. Am. (past chmn. subcom. on consumer affairs and regulator agys.). Republican. Episcopalian. Club: Profile (pres., dir.). (Franconia). Producer numerous record albums. Home: River Rd Franconia NH 03580 Office: Dow Acad Bldg Franconia NH 03580

SCHAFFER, DONALD L., retired insurance company executive, lawyer; b. Charleston, W.Va., July 1, 1923; s. Philip F. and Irma (Williams) S.; m. Phyllis J. Holmes, Aug. 22, 1944; children—Steven G., Jeffrey H., Susan B. B.A., W.Va. U., 1947; LL.B., 1949. Bar: W.Va. 1949, Ill. 1958. Atty. Litton, Fisher & Schaffer, Charleston, 1949-57; asst. gen. counsel Allstate Ins. Cos., Skokie, Ill., 1957-61; v.p., gen. atty. Allstate Ins. Cos., Northbrook, Ill., 1961-72, v.p., sec., gen. counsel, 1972-77, sr. v.p., sec., gen. counsel, 1977-85, exec. v.p., sec., gen. counsel, 1986-88, also dir.; dir. Northbrook Ins. Co. Mem. Jud. Council W.Va., 1956-60; Ill. Crusade chmn. Am. Cancer Soc., 1963-64; bd. govs. Ins. Inst. Hwy. Safety, 1961—, chmn., 1968-69; bd. govs. Ill. Ins. Info. Service, 1963—, pres., 1965, 73, 83; v.p. Allstate Found., 1962—. Served with inf. U.S. Army, 1942-46. Mem. ABA, W.Va. Bar Assn. (certificate of merit 1960), Chgo. Bar Assn., Internat. Assn. Ins. Law, Nat. Assn. Ind. Insurers (gov. 1972-85, chmn. 1986), Fedn. Ins. and Corp. Counsel. Methodist. Clubs: Nat. Lawyers (Washington); Mid-Am. (Chgo.), Metropolitan (Chgo.); Westmoreland Country (Wilmette, Ill.), The Executives (Chgo.); Ironwood Country (Palm Desert, Calif.). Home: 2658 Sheridan Rd Evanston IL 60201

SCHAFFNER, PHILIP MACKENZIE, human resources executive, consultant; b. New Orleans, July 3, 1934; s. Philippe Val Louis Schaffner and Ethelyn (Mackenzie) Connor; m. Rebecca Lee, June 17, 1961; children: John Philip, Suzanne Lee. AS in Pre-engring., Perkinston Coll., 1956; BS, Miss. State U., 1964; MA, Webster U., 1989. Lic. comml. aviator. Employee relations rep. Pan Am. Airways, Cocoa Beach, Fla., 1964-65; employee relations specialist Gen. Electric Co., Bay St. Louis, Miss., 1965-66, Cin., 1966-67; mgr. employee and community relations Gen. Electric Co., Arkansas City, Kans., 1967-68, Charleston, S.C., 1968-71, Selmer, Tenn., 1971-73; mgr. industrial and community relations Bosch Corp., Charleston, 1973—; exec. bd. mem. Trident Tech. Found., Charleston, 1986—; bus. mgmt. advisor Trident Tech. Coll., Charleston, 1979—; task force advisor S.C. C. of C., Columbia, S.C., 1982-84, Gov.'s Office, 1984-86. Exec. bd. mem. Boy Scouts Am. Coastal Carolina Council, Charleston, 1981-86, S.C. Council on Econ. Edn., 1986—; pres. Rep. Party Precinct Club, Summerville, S.C., 1985—; chmn. Dorchester County S.C. Devel. Bd., Summerville, 1984-86; exec. bd. mem. Farmer Asst. Relief Mission, Summerville, 1986-87. Served to lt. USNR, 1956-62. Recipient Silver Beaver award Boy Scouts Am., 1986, Congratulatory Cert. S.C. Legislature, 1986, S.C. Amb. for Econ. Devel. award from Gov. Mem. Am. Soc. Personnel Assn., Tri County Personnel Assn., Charleston Devel. Bd. and Indsl. Relations Com., S.C. C. of C., Summerville C. of C. (c.p. 1978). Methodist. Club: Sertoma. Lodge: Rotary. Home: 114 Willow Oaks Ln Summerville SC 29483 Office: Bosch Corp PO Box 10347 Charleston SC 29411

SCHALCOSKY, S. RICHARD, insurance and investment company executive; b. Latrobe, Pa., Oct. 3, 1947; s. Stanley P. and Helen (Bush) S.; m. Sherry A. Donato, Apr. 9, 1979; 1 child, John David. Student, Point Park Coll., 1966-71. Adminstrv. mgr. H&R Block, Greensburg, Pa., 1973-75; controller, treas. Luttner Assocs., Inc, Pitts., 1975-78; v.p. Luttner Assocs., Inc, 1978-81; gen. agt. Gen. Am. Life Ins. Co., Pitts., 1981—; pres. chief exec. officer Ins. Benefit Coordinators Inc., Pitts., 1981—; sec. Gen. Agts. Adv. Council, St. Louis, 1987—; chmn. adminstrn. and commn. task force coms. Gen. Am. Life Ins. Co. Corp. sponsor Pitts. Symphony Soc., 1986—. Mem. Nat. Assn. Life Underwriters (Nat. Quality award), Nat. Assn. Securities Dealers, Walnut St. Securities, Ct. of Table, Pitts. Life Underwriters Assn., Million Dollar Round Table, Lambda Chi Alpha. Democrat. Roman Catholic. Club: The Rivers (Pitts.). Home: 103 Elrose Dr Pittsburgh PA 15237 Office: Ins Benefit Coords Inc 4 Gateway Ctr Ste 1800 Pittsburgh PA 15222

SCHALLER, MICHAEL DAVID, accountant; b. Chgo., Oct. 3, 1953; s. Dayle A. and Catherine (Doherty) S.; m. Denise Waterstraat, Mar. 18, 1978; children: Michael D., Jennifer. BBA, Loyola U., 1975; MBA, Ill Inst. Tech., 1987. Controller, treas. Indsl. Erectors Inc., Chgo., 1975-84; mgr. fin. services Ill. Auto Electric Co., Elmhurst, 1985; controller T. Nagai Assocs. Ltd., Elmhurst, 1886-87; mgr. acctg. N.Am. Paper Co., Berkeley, Ill., 1987—. Home: 129 Caroline Ave Elmhurst IL 60126

SCHALLER, VERN GEORGE, real estate corporation officer; b. St. Louis, Sept. 10, 1959; s. Vern lewis and Georgia (Seil) S.; m. Ramela Elizabeth Rai, Dec. 18, 1986; 1 child, Devanna. BS in Bus., U. Mo., 1982. Resident mgr. Gordon Properties, Columbia, Mo., 1981-82; area mgr. Midwest Diversified Properties, St. Louis, 1982-83, regional mgr., 1983-85, v.p. ops., 1985—. Mem. Mo. Assn. Realtors, St. Louis Inst. Real Estate Mgmt., St. Louis Home Builders Assn., St. Louis Apt. Owners Assn. Republican. Home: 4610 Avalon Boca Raton FL 33428

SCHANTZ, HERBERT FELIX, computer executive; b. Trenton, N.J., Aug. 7, 1930; s. Herbert Frank and Anna Marie Schantz; m. Letty Louise Moxley, June 9, 1954; children: Louise Anne, Felice Marie. BSME, Drexel U., 1954, MS in Mgmt. Sci., 1968. Registered profl. engr. Md., Tex. Sr. engr. RCA Corp., Moorestown, 1957-67; chief scientist Black & Decker, Towson, Md., 1962-65; dept. mgr. Computest Inc., Moorestown, 1965-68; product line gen. mgr. Recognition Equipment, Dallas, 1968-80; v.p. Graham Carlisle, Ft. Worth, 1980-87; pres. HLS Assocs., Southlake, Tex., 1987-88; pres., gen. ptnr. HLS Assocs., Sterling, Va., 1988—; dir. tech. ops. Fed. Nat. Computer Systems, Washington, 1988-89; assoc. Strategic Mktg. and Communications Inc., Boston, 1988—; v.p., bd. dirs. Edn. Assn, Inc., Southlake, Tex.; bd. dirs. Graham Magnetics Ltd., Graham Japan. Author: History of OCR, 1980; tech. editor OCR Today; editorial adv. bd. ID Systems mag., 1988—; contbr. articles to mags. including ID Systems and RTLA-Today; inventor several high-speed mechanisms. Pres. Towson Civic Assn. D.W. Hills, Towson, 1964, elected charter commn. City of Southlake, 1986, mem. Southlake Noise Awareness Commn., Zoning Bd. Adjustments. 1st It. C.E., U.S. Army, 1955-57. Mem. IEEE (sr.), NSPE, Data Processing Mgmt. Assn., Assn for Computing Machinery, Dallas Engrs. Club, Am. Standards Com. for Info. Processing, Internat. Tape Assn., Computer and Communication Industry Assn., Recognition Technologies Users Assn. (v.p., bd. dirs. Tex. chpt. 1979-82), Drexel Alumni (chmn. Southwest Chpt.), Mensa, KC, Optimists (dir. Sterling chpt.), Kiwanis, Lions (pres. Southlake club 1985-88, charter, bd. dirs.). Home: 19 Halifax Ct Sterling VA 22170

SCHANZ, MARTIN WILLIAM, beverage distributing company executive; b. Troy, N.Y., Apr. 16, 1927; s. Martin Michael and Evelyn Ruth (Langford) S.; m. Pearl Emily Humphrey, June 17, 1950; 1 child, Jo-Ann Ruth. Student, Siena Coll.; diploma in real estate, Hudson Valley Community Coll. Ptnr. Schanz Realty Partnership, Schenectady, N.Y., 1946—; sec., treas. Albany Beverage Corp., Schenectady, 1963—, G.B. Lee, Inc., Schenectady, 1967—, Schanz Bros. Realty Corp., Schenectady, 1969—; bd. dirs. Empire Beer Distbg. Assn., N.Y. Former sec. Albany Exec. Assn.; vol. Heart Assn., Albany, N.Y., 1986. Served as staff sgt. U.S. Army, 1944-46, 50-51, Korea. Mem. VFW, Am. Legion, Albany Execs. Assn. Roman Catholic. Lodge: Elks (Organist 1960-63). Home and Office: 103 Southbury Rd Clifton Park NY 12065

SCHAPIRO, GEORGE A., electronics company executive; b. Richmond, Va., Mar. 21, 1946; s. Irwin Abraham and Jeanne (Goldman) S.; B.A., U. Va., 1967; M.S. Indsl. Adminstrn., Carnegie-Mellon U., 1969; m. Jo Ann Katzman, Aug. 6, 1978; children—Rebecca Jeanne, Amy Elizabeth. Fin. analyst data processing group IBM, Harrison, N.Y., 1968; product mktg. mgr. data systems div. Hewlett-Packard Co., Cupertino, Calif., 1969-74, med. electronics div., Waltham, Mass., 1974-76; pres., chief exec. officer Andros Inc., Berkeley, Calif., 1976-80, Andros Analyzers Inc., Berkeley, 1979—; guest lectr. Stanford U. Sch. Bus., U. Calif. at Berkeley Coll. Engring. and Extension Sch., Am. Mgmt. Assn. Seminar Series. Bd. dirs. Anesthesia Patient Safety Found. Mem. Assn. Computing Machinery, Assn. Advancement Med. Instrumentation, Soc. Computer Medicine, Young Pres.'s Orgn. Democrat. Jewish. Home: 3880 Ralston Ave Hillsborough CA 94010 Office: 2332 4th St Berkeley CA 94710

SCHAPIRO, JEROME BENTLEY, chemical company executive; b. N.Y.C., Feb. 7, 1930; s. Sol and Claire (Rose) S.; B.Chem. Engring., Syracuse U., 1951; postgrad. Columbia U., 1951-52; m. Edith Irene Kravet, Dec. 27, 1953; children—Lois, Robert, Kenneth. Project engr. propellents br. U.S. Naval Air Rocket Test Sta., Lake Denmark, N.J., 1951-52; with Dixo Co., Inc., Rochelle Park, N.J., 1954—, pres., 1966—; lectr. detergent standards, drycleaning, care labeling, consumers standards, orgns., U.S., 1968—; U.S. del. spokesman on drycleaning Internat. Standards Orgn., Newton, Mass., 1971, Brussels, 1972, U.S. del. spokesman on dimensional stability of textiles, Paris, 1974, Ottawa, 1977, Copenhagen, 1981; chmn. U.S. del. com. on consumer affairs, Geneva, 1974, 75, 76, spokesman U.S. del. on textiles, Paris, 1974, mem. U.S. del. on care labeling of textiles, The Hague, Holland, 1974, U.S. del., chmn. del. council com. on consumer policy, Geneva, 1978, 79, 82, Israel, 1980, Paris, 1981; leader U.S. del. com. on dimensional stability of textiles, Manchester, Eng., 1984; fed. govtl. appointee to Industry Functional Adv. Com. on Standards, 1980-81. Mem. Montclair (N.J.) Sch. Study Com., 1968-69. Served as 2d lt. USAF, 1952-53. Mem. Am. Inst. Chem. Engrs., Am. Nat. Standards Inst. (vice chmn. bd. dirs., 1983-85 , exec. com. 1979-81, 83-85 , dir. 1979-85, fin. com. 1982-85 , chmn. consumer council 1976, 79, 80, 81, mem. steering com. to advise Dept. Commerce on implementation GATT agreements 1976-77, mem. exec. standards council, 1977-79), internat. standards council, chmn. internat. consumer policy adv. com. 1978-86), Am. Assn. Textile Chemists and Colorists (mem. exec. com. on research 1974-77, chmn. com. on dry cleaning 1976-88, vice chmn. internat. test methods com.) Am. Chem. Soc., Standards Engring. Soc. (cert.), ASTM (award 1970, chmn. com. D-12 Soaps and Detergents, 1974-79, mem. standing com. on internat. standards 1980-84, hon. mem. award com. D-13, textiles), Internat. Standards Orgn. (mem. internat. standards steering com. for consumer affairs 1978-81), Nat. Small Bus. Assn. (assoc. trustee 1983-85). Jewish (v.p., treas. temple). Mason. Home: 197 N Mountain Ave Montclair NJ 07042 Office: 158 Central Ave Rochelle Park NJ 07662

SCHAPIRO, MARY, federal agency administrator. Commr. Securities and Exchange Commn., Washington, D.C. Office: SEC 450 5th St NW Stop 6093 6 7 Washington DC 20549 *

SCHAPIRO, MORRIS A., investment banker; b. Lithuania, Apr. 9, 1903; came to U.S., 1907, naturalized, 1914; s. Nathan M. and Fanny (Adelman) S.; m. Alma Binion Cahn, Mar. 28, 1929; children: Linda S. Collins, Daniel E. BA, Columbia U., 1923, Engr. Mines, 1925, LLD (hon.), 1987. Engr. geologist Am. Metal Co., 1925-27; bank analyst Hoit, Rose & Troster, 1928-31; ptnr. Monahan, Schapiro & Co., 1931-39; pres. M.A. Schapiro & Co., Inc., N.Y.C., 1939—; chmn. adv. com. N.Y. State Joint Legis. Com. to Revise Banking Law, 1957-60. Contbr. articles on banking to profl. jours. Mem. Am. Inst. Mining and Metall. Engrs. (hon.), N.Y. Soc. Security Analysts, Securities Industry Assn. Club: Columbia U. (N.Y.C.). Home: 910 Fifth Ave New York NY 10021 Office: 1 Chase Manhattan Plaza New York NY 10005

SCHAPIRO, RUTH GOLDMAN, lawyer; b. N.Y.C., Oct. 31, 1926; d. Louis Albert and Sarah (Shapiro) Goldman; m. Donald Schapiro, June 29, 1952; children: Jane Goldman, Robert Andrew. A.B., Wellesley Coll., 1947; LL.B., Columbia U., 1950. Bar: N.Y. 1950, D.C. 1978. Asst. to reporters Am. Law Inst. Fed. Income Tax Statute, N.Y.C., 1950-51; assoc., then ptnr. Proskauer Rose Goetz & Mendelsohn, N.Y.C., 1955—; mem. nominating commn. U.S. Tax Ct., 1978-81. Notes editor: Columbia Law Rev., 1949-50; editor: Tax Shelters, Practising Law Inst., 1983; contbr. articles to legal jours. Vice-chmn. adv. com. NYU Inst. Fed. Taxation, 1979-85; mem. adv. com. NYU-IRS Continuing Legal Edn. Project. Fellow Am. Bar Found., N.Y. Bar Found.; mem. ABA, N.Y. State Bar Assn. (chmn. tax sect. 1981-82, exec. com. 1982-84, ho. of dels. 1981-84, chmn. fin. com. 1984-87, chmn. spl. com. on Women in the Cts. 1986—), Assn. Bar City N.Y. (taxation com. 1972-75, 78-79), N.Y. County Lawyers Assn., Am. Judicature Soc. Jewish. Club: N.Y. Wellesley (N.Y.C.). Home: 1035 Fifth Ave New York NY 10028 Office: Proskauer Rose Goetz & Mendelsohn 300 Park Ave New York NY 10022

SCHAPS, ALLEN JAY, investment properties rentals and corporate relocation company executive; b. Milw., Jan. 29, 1932; s. Sidney and Betty (Golin) S.; children: Marci, Scott and Steven (twins), Susan. BSC, Roosevelt U., 1954. Buyer Spiegel, Inc., Chgo., 1955-70; new products mgr. Venetianaire Corp., Yonkers, N.Y., 1970-73; v.p. E. Coast sales Unitron, Inc., Los Angeles, 1973-74; dir. mktg. Nat. Curtain Corp., N.Y.C., 1974-79; v.p., ptnr. Bigelow & Schaps, Inc., Stamford, Conn., 1980—. Co-chmn. real estate div. United Way Greater Stamford, 1983-84, co-chmn. small bus. div., 1986; bd. dirs., co-chmn. Small Bus. div., 700 Summer Assn. Mem. Nat. Bd. Realtors, Conn. Bd. Realtors, Stamford Bd. Realtors (pres.-elect 1989—), Area Commerce and Industry Assn. Home: Barnes Rd Stamford CT 06902 Office: William Raveis Real Estate 945 Summer St Stamford CT 06905

SCHARF, MICHAEL, metal processing company executive; b. 1942. Chmn. Edgcomb Metals Corp., Nashua, N.H., 1983-86; chmn., sec. Edgcomb Metals Co., Tulsa, 1984—; also bd. dirs. Edgcomb Metals Corp., Tulsa. Office: Edgcomb Metals Co 2 W 2nd St Tulsa OK 74136 *

SCHARFFENBERGER, GEORGE THOMAS, diversified industry executive; b. Hollis, N.Y., May 22, 1919; s. George L. and Martha L. (Watson) S.; m. Marion Agnes Nelson, July 17, 1948; children: Ann Marie, George Thomas, John Edward, Thomas James, James Nelson, Joan Ellen. BS, Columbia U., 1940; DHL (hon.), U. So. Calif., 1984, Georgetown U., 1987. C.P.A., N.Y. With Arthur Andersen & Co., 1940-43; with ITT (subs.'s and divs.), 1943-59; v.p. Litton Industries, Inc., 1959-66; chmn., chief exec. officer, dir. City Investing Co., N.Y.C., 1966-85; chmn. The Home Group, Inc., 1984—, also dir.; bd. dirs. Whitman Corp., Chgo., Earle M. Jorgensen Co., Los Angeles, Northrop Corp., Los Angeles, Interim Systems Corp., N.Y.C., Rockefeller Group, Inc., Gen. Devel. Corp., Miami. Chmn. bd. trustees U. So. Calif.; bd. dirs. Georgetown U., U.S. Equestrian Team, N.J.; chmn. Acad. Polit. Sci. With AUS, World War II. Clubs: California, Regency (Los Angeles); Brook, River, Down Town Assn. (bd. dirs.), Rockefeller Ctr. (N.Y.C.). Home: 40 E 94th St New York NY 10128 also: 4 Appaloosa Ln Rolling Hills CA 90274 also: Snowmass Village CO 81654 Office: Home Group Inc 59 Maiden Ln New York NY 10038

SCHARFFENBERGER, WILLIAM J., steel company executive; b. N.Y.C., 1921. Degree, Columbia U., 1942. With Wheeling-Pittsburgh Steel Corp., pres., chief exec. officer, 1987—; bd. dirs. Alco Standard Corp., Allegheny Internat. Corp., Health Mgmt. Assocs.; trustee Magnavox Govt. and Electronics Co. Bd. dirs. Pub. Svc. Co. N.H. Office: Wheeling-Pitts Steel Corp 1134 Market St Wheeling WV 26003 *

SCHARFY, G. CHARLES, lawyer, bank executive; b. Cleve., Nov. 26, 1916; s. Gottlieb Charles and Teresa (Klemm) S.; m. April Mildred Stemple, Sept. 27, 1942; children: Philip, Madelon, Ralph. PhB magna cum laude, U. Toledo, 1938, LLB cum laude, 1940, JD, 1968. Bar: Ohio 1940. Acct. The Barrett Co., Toledo, 1936-40; assoc. Shumaker, Loop & Kendrick, Toledo, 1940-51, ptnr., 1951-82, of counsel, 1982—; bd. dirs. Bank of Fountain Hills, Ariz. Trustee Fountain Hills Spl. Rd. Dists., 1984-88, joint powers chmn., 1986-87; mem. Com. for Incorporation Fountain Hills; former trustee Toledo Area C. fo C. Served to lt. col. USMCR. Mem. ABA, Ohio State Bar Assn., Toledo Bar Assn. (past exec. com.). Republican. Episcopalian. Club: Kiwanis (Scottsdale, Ariz.). Home: 15232 E Palomino Blvd Fountain Hills AZ 85268

SCHARLATT, HAROLD, management company executive; b. N.Y.C., Dec. 9, 1947; s. Bertram and Miriam Louise (Stone) S.; BEd, SUNY, 1969, MA in Liberal Studies, 1973; advanced cert. adminstrn. and supervision, Oxford U., 1975; m. Mary Moore, June 10, 1978. Tchr., in-service instr. N.Y., 1970-77; mgmt. devel. specialist Union Carbide Corp., N.Y.C., 1977, mgmt. devel. cons., 1978-80; regional dir. Vector Mgmt. Systems, Inc., Lexington, Ky., 1980-83; pres. Tng. and Devel. Assocs., Inc., Lexington, 1983—. Mem. Am. Soc. Tng. and Devel., Assn. For Psychol. Type, Oxford Soc. for Applied Studies in Edn., Assn. for Continuing Edn. Office: 3608 Bircham Way Lexington KY 40515

SCHATZ, EDWARD GARY, personnel consultant; b. Williston, N.D., May 31, 1929; s. Chester Edward and Betty Louise (Warner) S.; m. Rita Marie Hirsch, June 11, 1940; children: Philip, Karen, Curtis, Kristina, Deborah, Lisa. BA in Psychology, U. Minn., 1953; MS in Tech. Mgmt., Rensselaer Poly. Inst., 1958; postgrad., Harvard U., 1975; PhD in Indsl. Orgnl. Psychology, LaSalle U., 1986. Employee relation exec. Gen. Electric Co., N.Y.C., 1953-69; v.p. ops. Internat. Dairy Queen, Bloomington, Minn., 1969-73; chief exec. officer Minnetonka (Minn.) Mills Inc., 1973-79, also chmn. bd. dirs.; chief exec. officer Chanute (Kans.) Mfg., 1979-83; prin. Your Human Investments, Hopkins, Minn., 1983—; chief operating officer, mfg. Westfield (Ind.) Decorator, 1988—; bd. dirs. Gear Raceway Calif., Banning Compete Inc., Minnetonka, Rose E. Dee Can. Ltd.; mem. Inst. Reality Therapy, Canoga Park, Calif., 1985—. Bd. dirs. Nightime Outreach , Mpls., 1986—, Joint Labor Council, Mpls., 1986—; arbitrator Am. Arbitration Assn., Mpls., 1987—. Served with USAF, 1951-52. Fellow IIE; mem. ASME, Am. Psychol. Assn. (affiliate), Am. Soc. Performance Improvement, Ind. Soaring Soc. Republican. Roman Catholic. Clubs: Harbour Trees Country, Ind. Athletic (Noblesville); Mpls. Athletic, Indpls. Aero, Golf Club Ind. Lodges: Shriners, KC, Elks. Home: 516 Currant Dr Noblesville IN 46060 Office: Your Human Investments 810 1st St S Hopkins MN 55343

SCHATZ, MARTIN, college dean, business educator; b. N.Y.C., Aug. 1, 1936; s. Murray and Florence (Hollander) S.; m. Harriet M. Cohen, June 26, 1970; children—Karen, Lauren. B.S., U. Ala.-Tuscaloosa, 1959; M.B.A., U. Fla., 1965; Ph.D., NYU, 1972. Asst. to dean N.Y.U., N.Y.C., 1966-69; project mgr. Office of Mayor, N.Y.C., 1970-71; asst. prof. Worcester Poly. Inst., Mass., 1972-74; assoc. dean Adelphi U., Garden City, N.Y., 1974-76; dean sch. bus. SUNY-Utica, 1976-78; dean grad. sch. bus. Rollins Coll., Winter Park, Fla., 1979—. Contbr. articles to profl. jours. Mem. Acad. Mgmt., Am. Inst. for Decision Scis., Inst. Mgmt. Scis., Fin. Mgmt. Assn. Home: 102 Coveridge Ln Longwood FL 32779 Office: Roy E Crummer Grad Sch Bus Rollins Coll Winter Park FL 32779

SCHAUB, SHERWOOD ANHDER, JR., management consultant; b. Rahway, N.J., Jan. 8, 1942; s. Sherwood Anhder Sr. and Doris (Beecher) S.; m. Diane Katherine Wells, July 29, 1967; children: Whitney, Kristen. BBA with honors, Nichols Coll., 1964; postgrad. in bus. adminstrn., Fairleigh Dickinson U., 1965-69. Dir. Gilbert Lane, N.Y.C., 1965-67; exec. v.p. Ward Clancy, N.Y.C., 1967-71; founder, chmn., chief exec. officer, sr. mng. ptnr. Goodrich & Sherwood Co., N.Y.C. 1971—; pres., chmn., chief exec. officer Reed, Cuff & Assocs., 1980—; pres., chief exec. officer Exec. Change, Inc. Author: Breakpoints, 1986, Doubleday; contbr. articles on mgmt. to mags. and profl. jours. Rep. Congl. advisor Pres. Ronald Reagan, 1986; head Bus. Task Force N.Y. for Reagan Adminstrn., 1987-89; bd. dirs. Conn. Pub. Broadcasting. Mem. Nat. Human Resources Planners Assn., Nat. Assn. Corp. and Profl. Recruiters, Young Pres. Orgn. (chpt. chmn. elect, 1988, bd. dirs. 1986-88, vice chmn. met. chpt. sounding bd. com, hospitality com., edn. chmn., chpt. chmn. elect 1989), Internat. Platform Assn., Pvt. Pilots Assn. (sr.), Nat. Ski Patrol, Safari Club Internat. (bd. dirs., 1987-89), U.S. Equestrian Team. Congregationalist. Clubs: University, Westfield Tennis, New Canaan Racquet, New Cannan Field, Rolling Rock, Porcupine Rod and Gun, Mashomak Field and Game, Econ. of N.Y., Explorers (fellow), Madison Ave Sports Car Driving, Chowder Society, Greenwich Polo, Ducks Unlimited. Avocations: scuba diving, equestrian riding, collecting and restoring vintage race cars, big and small game hunting. Office: Goodrich and Sherwood Co 521 Fifth Ave New York NY 10175 also: #4 Greenwich Office Park Greenwich CT 06831 also: The Office Ctr Plainsboro Rd Plainsboro NJ 08536 also: 6 Century Dr Parsippany NJ 07054

SCHAUER, THOMAS ALFRED, insurance company executive; b. Canton, Ohio, Dec. 24, 1927; s. Alfred T. and Marie A. (Luthi) S.; BSc, Ohio State U., 1950; m. Joanne Alice Fay, Oct. 30, 1954; children: Alan, David, Susan, William. Ins. agt., Canton, 1951—; with Schauer & Reed Agy., 1951—, Kitzmiller, Tudor & Schauer, 1957—, Webb-Broda & Co., 1971—, Foglesong Agy., 1972—; pres. Ind. Ins. Service Corp. Akron, Dover and Canton, Canton, 1964—, Laurenson Agy., 1978—, Wells-Williams, 1978—, JD Craig Agy., 1981—; dir. Central Trust Co. NE Ohio (N.A.). Chmn., Joint Hosp. Blood Com., 1974; bd. dirs. Better Bus. Bur., Canton, 1970-81, chmn., 1979-80; bd. dirs. area YMCA, 1974, v.p., 1975-82, pres., 1982-84; trustee Canton Cemetery Assn., 1988—, Stark County Blue Coats, 1987—; bd. dirs. Hosp. Bur. Central Stark City, 1972-78; vice chmn. bd. Aultman Hosp., 1981-84, chmn., 1984-87; pres. Aultman Hosp. Found., 1987—; chmn. bd. JMS Found., 1968—; bd. dirs. United Way, 1974-84, pres., 1976-78; mem. distbn. com. Stark County Found., 1977-87, chmn. distbn. com.; 1984-87; adv. bd. Malone Coll., 1979—; trustee Kent State U., 1980-88, trustee emeritus, 1988—, N.E. Ohio Univs. Coll. Medicine, 1983-88; past trustee Canton Urban League, Boys Village (Smithville, Ohio), Canton Art Inst., Buckeye Council Boy Scouts Am. Served with USNR, 1946-48. Recipient Gold Key award United Way of Cen. Stark County, 1981, Award of Merit Canton C. of C., 1984, Red. Triangle award Canton Area YMCA, 1985. Mem. Chartered Ins. Inst. London, Nat. Assn. Mfg., Am. Soc. CPCUs, Am. Soc. CLUs, Am. Mgmt. Assn., Assn. Advanced Life Underwriters, Am. Risk and Ins. Assn., Am. Soc. Pension Actuaries, Stark County Accident and Health Underwriters (past pres.), Canton Club, Brookside Country Club, Atwood Yacht Club. Home: 1756 Dunbarton Dr NW Canton OH 44708 Office: Carnegie Library Bldg 236 3d St SW Canton OH 44702

SCHAUMBERG, WILLIAM LLOYD, retired banker; b. Lincoln, Nebr., May 4, 1923; s. Edward George and Claire Elizabeth (Barentsen) S.; m. Patricia Louise Ward, Sept. 4, 1948; children: DeeAnn, William Ward, Denise Lynn, Kirstin. B.S., U. Nebr., 1947, LL.B., 1949. Bar: Nebr. 1949, Oreg. 1953. Dep. county atty. Lancaster County, Nebr., 1949-51; v.p. 1st Nat. Bank of Oreg., 1952-69, Columbia Mgmt. Co., Portland, Oreg., 1970-73; exec. v.p., mgr. capital mgmt. div. Rainier Nat. Bank, Seattle, 1973-87. Bd. dirs. Willamette Valley Camp Fire Girls, 1955-62, pres., 1960-61; bd. dirs. Ind. Colls. Wash.; bd. dirs. Multnomah County chpt. Nat. Found. March of Dimes, 1963-70, pres. Multnomah County chpt., 1968; bd. visitors Puget Sound U.; mem. Trustees Assn. Wash., pres., 1975, 84; mem. adv. com. Fred Hutchinson Cancer Research Ctr., 1983-87. Served with U.S. Army, 1943-46, 51-52. Mem. Seattle Estate Planning Council, Assn. Corp. Trustees Wash., Beta Theta Pi. Republican. Episcopalian. Clubs: Broadmoor Golf, D'Anza Country. Home: 8520 SE 80th St Mercer Island WA 98040

SCHAUWECKER, MARGARET LIDDIE, construction executive; b. Louisa, Ky., July 28, 1934; d. Mitchell and Mary Lou (Thompson) McKinster; m. Norman Walter Schauwecker, Aug. 30, 1953 (div. Oct. 1968); children: Johanna L., Mitchell Walter, Shawna Ann. Student, Bliss Coll., 1952-54, El Segundo Coll., 1957-59. Sec. N. Am. Aviation, Columbus, Ohio, 1952-1955, Gilfillan Electronics, Los Angeles, 1956-62; adminstrv. asst. Columbus Wood Preserving Co., 1970-78; pres. Ohio State Tie and Timber Inc., Louisa, Ky., 1978—. Named to Honorable Order Ky. Cols. Commonwealth Ky., 1984; recipient Outstanding Achievement in Sales Vol. award Ohio Dept. Econ. Devel., 1980, 81, 82; recipient Top 100 Small Bus's. in Ohio award Ohio House Reps., 1983. Mem. Am. Wood Preservers Assn., Railway Tie Assn., Bus. and Profl. Women in Constrn. Baptist. Club: Louisa Woman's. Lodges: Order Eastern Star, Rebekah. Home: Rte 1 Box 2360 Louisa KY 41230 Office: Ohio State Tie and Timber Rte 1 Box 2360 Louisa KY 41230

SCHECHTER, ARTHUR LOUIS, lawyer; b. Rosenberg, Tex., Dec. 6, 1939; s. Morris and Helen (Brilling) S.; m. Joyce Proler, Aug. 28, 1964; children—Leslie, Jennifer. B.A., U. Tex., 1962, J.D. 1964; postgrad. U. Houston, 1964-65. Bar: Tex. 1964, U.S. Dist. Ct. (ea. and so. dists.) Tex. 1966, U.S. Ct. Appeals (5th cir.), U.S. Supreme Ct. 1976, cert. Tex. Bd. Legal Specialization to Personal Injury Trial Law. Pres. firm Dowman, Jones & Schechter, Houston, 1964-76, Schechter and Eisenman, Houston, 1976—; speaker Marine Law Seminar, 1983. Contbr. to Law Rev., 1984. Bd. dirs. Theatre Under the Stars, Houston, 1972-78, Congregation Beth Israel, Houston, 1972-84, Am. Jewish Com., Houston, 1982-84; mem. fin. council Nat. Dem. Orgn., 1979; mem. Deans Council, U. Tex. Law Sch. Found., Austin, 1981-84; pres. Beth Israel Congregation; chmn. fgn. relations commn. Am. Jewish Com. Recipient Service award Congregation Beth Israel, 1976. Mem. Tex. Trial Lawyers Assn. (chmn. admiralty sect.), Am. Jewish Com. (exec. com.), Houston Trial Lawyers Assn., Houston Bar Assn., Am. Trial Lawyers Assn. Democrat. Jewish. Clubs: Westwood Country (bd. dirs., sec.), Houston Racquet (Houston). Home: 19A Westlane Houston TX 77019

SCHECHTMAN, IRVING SEYMOUR, data processing executive; b. Phila., Sept. 27, 1933; m. Beverly Bell, Aug. 4, 1963; children: Stephanie, Jeffrey, Michelle. BA in English, U. Pa., 1955, MA in Math., 1957. Programmer Remington Rand Univac, Phila., 1955-57; EDP specialist RCA, Camden, N.J., 1957-59; sr. staff member Nat. Computer Analysts, Princeton, N.J., 1960-72, sec., treas., 1972-82, v.p., treas., 1982-86; v.p. M Tech. Northeast, Princeton, 1986—; trustee NCA 401k Savs. Plan, Princeton, 1984—; mng. ptnr. Farber Rd. Assocs., Princeton, 1981—. Chmn. fin. com. MARC, Norristown, Pa., 1978-82. Mem. AAAS, Data Processing Assn., Assn. for Computing Machinery, ACLU (Phila. chpt. 1968-80), Tourette's Syndrome Assn. Democrat. Home: 3604 Walsh Ln Huntingdon Valley PA 19006 Office: M Tech NE 99 Farber Rd Princeton NJ 08540

SCHECTMAN, HERBERT A., corporate executive, lawyer; b. N.Y.C., Aug. 8, 1930; s. Leon and Ethel (Brown) S.; m. Evelyn P. DePalma, Apr. 15, 1956 (div. 1974); children: Bart T., Robert; m. Lois Regent Driscoll, Apr. 11, 1974. A.B., Syracuse U., 1952; M.A., Columbia U., 1958, JD. Bar: N.Y. 1959. Atty. U.S. Govt., Bklyn., 1958-60; atty. The Lummus Co., N.Y.C., 1960-62; assoc. gen. counsel Gen. Electric Credit Corp., N.Y.C. and Chgo., 1962-67; div. counsel General Electric Co., N.Y.C., 1967-69; atty.-ptnr. Belfer, Bogart & Schectman, N.Y.C., 1969-74; sr. v.p. ops. and adminstrn., gen. counsel Chrysler Capital Corp. (formerly E.F. Hutton Credit Corp.), Greenwich, Conn., 1974-87, sr. v.p./group exec. mergers, acquisitions and corp. fin. group, 1988—; also dir. Chrysler Capital Corp. (formerly E.F. Hutton Credit Corp.); arbitrator N.Y.C. Civil Ct. Small Claims, N.Y.C., 1974—. Served with USAF, 1951-54; ETO. Mem. Am. Judges Assn., N.Y. State Bar Assn. Office: Chrysler Capital Corp 51 Weaver St Greenwich CT 06836

SCHECTMAN, STEPHEN BARRY, corporate executive; b. Washington, Oct. 20, 1947; s. Samuel and Rae (Tarnef) S.; m. Barbara Lea Butcher, Sept. 10, 1969; children: Christopher, Matthew. BS, Randolph-Macon Coll., 1969; postgrad., U. Tenn., 1969-74, Georgetown U., 1974-75. Staff scientist Enviro Control Inc., Rockville, Md., 1975-76; sr. cons. JRB Assocs. Inc., McLean, Va., 1976-78; dir. IMS Am. Ltd., Washington, 1979-81; pres., founder Alpha 1 Biomeds. Inc., Washington, 1981-84; pres. Research Data Corp., Haddenfield, N.J., 1984-85; pres., chief exec. officer Large Scale Biology Corp., Rockville, 1985—; pres. CM Group Internat., Rockville, 1985—; prin. Med. Tech. Ventures, Ft. Lauderdale, Fla., 1985—. Author: (with others) Biomedical Innovation, 1981. NIMH fellow U. Tenn., 1969-73. Mem. AAAS, Am. Mgmt. Assn., Beta Beta Beta. Jewish. Office: Large Scale Biology Corp 7503 Standish Pl Rockville MD 20855

SCHEDLER, SPENCER JAIME, consultant; b. Manila, Philippines, Oct. 23, 1933; s. Edmund W. and Ruth (Spencer) S.; m. Judy Hamilton, Aug. 30, 1969; children: Ryan Edmund, Spencer Hamilton, Peter Joseph. BS, U. Tulsa, 1955; MBA, Harvard U., 1962. Petroleum engr., Humble Oil & Refining Co., 1957-60; fin. analyst Sinclair Oil Corp., Tulsa, 1963-65, asst. dir. budgets, N.Y.C., 1965-66, mgr. budgets and fin. analysis for mfg. and mktg., 1966-67, corp. mgr. budget and analysis, 1968-69; asst. Sec. of Air Force, 1969-73; exec. v.p. Hycel Inc., Houston, 1973-74; gen. mgr., asst. to vice chmn. fin. and adminstrn. Continental Can Co., Inc., N.Y.C., 1974-76; gen. mgr. corp. bus. devel. Continental Group, Inc., 1977-81, chief resources staff, 1981-82; v.p. Continental Resources Co., 1982-83; pres. Maxam Corp. (cons. in U.S. acquisitions to maj. fgn. cos.), 1984—; bd. dirs. Myers Group Inc., Nova Fund. Served as pilot USAF, 1955-58. Club: Innis Arden Golf. Office: PO Box 542 Old Greenwich CT 06870

SCHEEL, PAUL JOSEPH, insurance company executive; b. Balt., Nov. 15, 1933; s. Joseph A. and Julia S.; m. Beverly Ann Mitchell, June 1, 1957; children: Mary Claire, Paul Joseph. B.S. in Math., Loyola Coll.-Balt., 1959. With U.S. Fidelity & Guaranty Co., Balt., 1959—, assoc. actuary, 1971, v.p., sr. actuary, 1971-78, exec. v.p., 1978-82, pres., chief operating officer, 1982—; bd. dirs. Fidelity and Guaranty Ins. Co., Thomas Jefferson Life Ins. Co., Fidelity Ins. Co. Can., First Md. Bancorp. Served with U.S. Army, 1953-55. Fellow Casualty Actuarial Soc.; mem. Am. Acad. Actuaries. Roman Catholic. Home: 32 Oak Ridge Ct Lutherville MD 21093 Office: US Fidelity & Guaranty Corp 100 Light St PO Box 1138 Baltimore MD 21202

SCHEFFY, HUBERT, JR., real estate company executive; b. Rochester, N.Y., Aug. 13, 1940; s. Hubert and June Clark (Brackett) S.; m. Elgonde Marleen Van Assen, Sept. 9, 1967; children: Clark Willem, Marieke Sarah. AB in Econs., Harvard U., 1962, MBA, 1965. Audit mgr. Arthur Andersen & Co., Boston, 1965-70; mgr. mgmt. info. USM Corp., Boston, 1970-72; controller Midland-Ross Corp., Somerset, N.J., 1972-74; asst. v.p. City Investing Co., N.Y.C., 1974-76; sr. v.p. fin. Wood Bros. Homes, Inc., Denver, 1976-81; v.p. fin. Miller-Klutznick-Davis-Gray Co., Denver, 1982-83; gen. ptnr. Crestone Investment Co., Denver, 1983-85; sr. v.p., chief fin. officer Pacific Scene Inc., San Diego, 1985; v.p., controller Lewis Homes Co., Upland, Calif., 1985—. Mem. Am. Inst. CPA's, Mass. Soc. CPA's. Episcopalian.

SCHEIBLE, WAYNE G., printing company executive; b. Rochester, N.Y., July 21, 1938; s. George H. and Elinor M. Scheible; m. Patricia J. Alexander, Nov. 26, 1960; children: Karl F., Bryan W., Susan P. Prepress supr. Scheible Press, Inc., Rochester, 1960-68, gen. mgr., 1968-70; co-founder, pres. Flower City Printing, Inc., Rochester, 1970—; chmn. bd. Award Image, Barbados, West Indies, 1987—. Patentee in printing field. Exec. bd. dirs. Ptnrs. of Ams., Rochester, 1984—; mem. Nathaniel Soc. of Rocheater Inst. Tech., Rochester, 1983—. Named Small Bus. Person of Yr., Rochester Small Bus. Assn., 1987, Connunicator of Yr., 1988. Mem. Small Bus. Council Rochester (bd. dirs.), Rochester Ad Council, Nat. Assn. Printers/ Lithographers, Rochester Printing House Craftsmen Club, Rochester C. of C., Nat. Rifle Assn., Sports Car Club Am. Republican. Roman Catholic. Home: 3800 Dewey Ave Ste 5300 Rochester NY 14616 Office: Flower City Printing 4800 Dewey Ave Rochester NY 14612

SCHEIDE, RICHARD GILSON, bank executive; b. Hartford, Conn., May 14, 1929; s. Philip W. and Virginia R. (Gilson) S.; B.A., U. Va., 1952; m. Geraldine A. Pierre, June 14, 1952; children—William C., Robert G., Susan R. Vice pres. trust Conn. Bank and Trust Co., Hartford, 1956-72, 1st Interstate Bank, Los Angeles, 1972-76; exec. v.p., mgr. trust and pvt. banking div. Bank of New Eng., N.A., Boston, 1976—; dir. New Eng. Capital Corp. and BNE Life Ins. Co., Boston; Bank New Engl. Trust Co., Fla.; dir. Constn. Capital Mgmt. Co. Bd. dirs., treas. Mass. Taxpayers Found., Inc., Boston, Friends of the Pub. Garden Inc.; trustee Wheaton Coll., Norton, Mass. Served with USMC, 1952-54. Mem. Am. Bankers Assn. (past chmn. Trust and Investment Div., investment adv. com.), Mass. Bankers Assn. (past chmn. exec. com. trust div.). Republican. Congregationalist. Club: Dedham Country and Polo. Office: Bank New Eng 28 State St Boston MA 02109

SCHEIFELE, RICHARD PAUL, cosmetics and chemical manufacturing company executive; b. Phila., Mar. 6, 1934; s. E. Paul and Kathryn Edith (Weidner) S.; m. Wanda Louise Bruch, June 15, 1957; 1 child, Kristina Louisa. BCE, Cornell U., 1957. Area mfg. dir. Colgate Palmolive Ltd. S.A., Guatemala City, Guatemala, 1965-68; tech. dir. Toddy Venezolana S.A., Caracas, Venezuela, 1968-69; mfg. dir. Chesebrough-Pond's Inc., Clinton, Conn., 1969-72, dir. internat. mfg., Geneva, 1972-76, corp. v.p. mfg., Greenwich, 1976-82, group v.p., 1982-85, vice chmn., Westport, Conn., 1985—; also bd. dirs. Mem. AAAS, Indsl. Research Inst., Dirs. Indsl. Research. Club: Bailiwick. Avocations: archeology, art, real estate, biking, tennis. Home: 35 Birchwood Dr Greenwich CT 06831

SCHEINESON, IRWIN B., insurance and investment company executive; b. Cin., Aug. 8, 1955; s. Julian and Joan (Klein) S.; m. Judith Office, Apr. 27, 1985; children: Kate Marie, John Philip. BBA, U. Cin., 1978. Exec. v.p., prin. Lang-Kruke Fin. Group, Cin., 1978—; agt. adv. liaison Community Mut. Ins. Co. (Blue Cross), Cin., 1987—, Cen. Benefits Mut., Columbus, Ohio, 1986—; lectr. in field. Contbr. articles to profl. jours. Fund raiser Guilford Sch., Cin., 1985—; chmn. Life Underwriters Polit. Action Com., Cin., 1987. Mem. Internat. Assn. Fin. Planning, Nat. Assn. Health Underwriters, Nat. Assn. Life Underwriters (Nat. Sales Achievement award 1979), Cin. Assn. Health Underwriters (bd. dirs. 1986—), Cin. Assn. Life Underwriters (bd. dirs. 1984-87), Nat. Soc. CLU's and Chartered Fin. Cons., Crest Hills Country Club (bd. dirs. 1988—). Republican. Jewish. Home: 9480 Bluewing Ter Cincinnati OH 45241 Office: Lang Kruke Fin Group Inc 9549 Montgomery Rd Ste 300 Cincinnati OH 04524-0002

SCHEINMAN, DAVID CLARK, consultant; b. N.Y.C., Aug. 24, 1948; s. Sidney Charles and Diana Helen (Friedenberg) S.; 1 child, Nina. BA, Am. U., 1970; MS, Cornell U., 1979. Community devel. worker Peace Corps, Kathmandu, Nepal, 1973-76; rural devel. specialist, project mgr. U.S.A.I.D., Mlingano, Tanzania, 1980-83; cons. Netherlands Fgn. Ministry, Tanga, Tanzania, 1984—, German Agy. Tech. Assistance, Tanga, 1985—. Author: Inservice Training For Extension Workers, 1984, Village Farm and Livestock Study, 1984, Caring for the Land of the Usambaras, 1985, Animal Draft Use in Tanga Region, 1986. Democrat. Jewish. Club: Tanga Yacht. Home: 973 Southern Rd York PA 17403 Office: Box 859, Tanga Tanzania

SCHEITZACH, EVELYN B., manufacturing company executive; b. Seminole, Okla., June 14, 1941; d. Roy A. and Ida (Kirkpatrick) Boggs; m. James R. Mestepey (div. 1973); 1 child, Philip Todd; m. Duane R. Scheitzach; children: Michael Dean, Clay Bradley. BS in Indsl. Enging., La. State U., 1960; MBA, Ball State U., 1969; PhD, Walden U., 1983. Indsl. engr. E.I. DuPont de Nemours & Co., Inc., Orange, Tex., 1960-62, Chrysler Air Temp, Bowling Green, KY., 1967-73; ops. mgr. Popped Right, Marion, Ohio, 1978-83; cons. Dresser Ind., Marion, 1973-78, Mgmt. Co., Columbus, Ohio, 1983-84; owner S & A Enterprises, Inc., Clinton, Mich., 1984—; bd. dirs. Wyandotte Popcorn. Contbr. articles to profl. jours. Bd. dirs. Big Bros. Am., Marion, 1980-84; trustee First Presbyn. Ch., Marion, 1982-84; campaign organizer Reagan for Pres., Marion, 1983. Named Woman of Yr. Bus. and Profl. Women of Marion, 1982; Dept. Edn. grantee, 1968-69. Mem. Soc. Mfg. Engrs., Indsl. Enging. Soc. (pres. 1982-84), Am. Prodn. and Inventory Control Soc. (v.p. 1981-85). Republican. Home: 4004 Blakemore Ct Midland TX 79707 Office: S&A Enterprises Inc 301 W Franklin Clinton MI 49236

SCHELL, W. H., oil company executive. Exec. v.p. PEPCO div. Pennzoil Co., Houston. Office: Pennzoil Co PO Box 2967 Houston TX 77252-2967 *

SCHELLER, SANFORD GREGORY, printing company executive; b. Newark, July 7, 1931; s. John Arthur Scheller and Harriet (Gregory) Tate; m. Marjory Meyer, Dec. 31, 1950; children: Sanford Gregory Jr., Douglas Meyer, Bradford John, Frances Scheller Lavin, Eric Bruce. BBA, Westminster Coll., New Wilmington, Pa., 1953. V.p., gen. mgr. St. Regis Corp., N.Y.C., 1978-84, Champion Internat., Stamford, Conn., 1984-85; pres., chief exec. officer Treasure Chest Advt., Glendora, Calif., 1986—. Republican. Office: Treasure Chest Advt Co Inc 511 W Citrus Edge Glendora CA 91740

SCHELLHOUS, NANCY SHICK, outplacement executive; b. Youngstown, Ohio, Feb. 15, 1940; d. Robert C. and Nell Louise (Redman) Shick; m. James H. Reed. Apr. 21, 1960 (div. May. 1972); children: Bradley, Tobin, Steven; m. Edward A. Schellhous, Oct. 4, 1974. AA, U. Cin., 1975, BS, 1979, postgrad., 1979-84. Mgr. office H. Derringer Co., Cin., 1970-72; researcher Promark Co., Cin., 1972-73; asst. to treas. Frederick Rauh & Co., Cin., 1973-75; v.p. adminstrn. Promark Co., Cin., 1975-78, pres., 1978—; bd. dirs. Outplacement Internat., Phoenix. Pres. to vice chmn. Pvt. Ind. Council, Cin., 1985—, ARC, 1985; mem. adv. bd. Great Oaks Career Resource Ctr., 1985—. Recipient annual achiever award, Greater Cin. C. of C., 1980-85. Mem. Cin. Affiliate Internat. Assn. Personnel Women (pres. 1985-86), Employment Mgmt. Assn., Am. Soc. Personnel Adminstrs., Leadership Cin. Alumni Assn. Republican. Club: Milford Amateur Radio. Home: 6296 Glade Ave Cincinnati OH 45230 Office: Promark Co 3814 West St Cincinnati OH 45227

SCHELLING, THOMAS CROMBIE, educator, economist; b. Oakland, Calif., Apr. 14, 1921; s. John M. and Zelda M. (Ayres) S.; m. Corinne T. Saposs, Sept. 13, 1947; children: Andrew, Thomas, Daniel, Robert. AB, U. Calif., Berkeley, 1943; PhD, Harvard U., 1951. U.S. govt. economist Copenhagen, Paris, Washington, 1948-53; prof. econs. Yale U., 1953-58, Harvard U., Cambridge, Mass., 1958—; Lucius N. Littauer prof. polit. economy John F. Kennedy Sch. Govt.; sr. staff mem. RAND Corp., 1958-59; chmn. research adv. bd. Com. Econ. Devel., 1978-81, 84-85; mem. sci. adv. bd. USAF, 1960-64, def. sci. bd., 1966-70; mem. mil. econ. adv. panel CIA, 1980-85; trustee Aerospace Corp. Author: National Income Behavior, 1951, International Economics, 1958, The Strategy of Conflict, 1960, Arms and Influence, 1966, Micromotives and Macrobehavior, 1978, Choice and Consequence, 1984; co-author: Strategy and Arms Control, 1961. Recipient Frank E. Seidman Disting. award in polit. economy, 1977. Fellow Am. Acad. Arts and Scis., AAAS, Assn. for Pub. Policy Analysis and Mgmt., Am. Econ. Assn. (disting.); mem. Nat. Acad. Scis., Inst. Medicine. Office: Harvard U John F Kennedy Sch of Govt Cambridge MA 02138

SCHEMBRI, DAVID CHARLES, automotive executive; b. Detroit, June 9, 1953; s. Anthony Joseph and Mary (Barbara) S.; m. Michele Ann Dunn, May 10, 1974; children: Anthony Joseph, Dana Marie. BSBA, U. Detroit, 1974, MBA, 1977. Accounts payable auditor, acct. Am. Motors Corp., Southfield, Mich., 1975-77, sr. analyst fgn. investments, 1977-78, sr. analyst profit planning, 1978-79; supr. investment analysis Volkswagen U.S., Troy, Mich., 1979-80, mgr. adminstrv. budgets, 1980-81, mgr. capital investments, 1981-84, mgr. nat. bus. mgmt., 1984-85, mgr. field sales, 1985-86; mgr. region sales Volkswagen U.S., Culver City, Calif., 1987-88; mgr. field ops. Volkswagen U.S., Troy, Mich., 1988—. Ambassador United Found. United Way, Detroit, 1983. Roman Catholic. Home: PO Box 3951 Troy MI 48007

SCHENCK, FREDERICK A., business executive; b. Trenton, May 12, 1928; s. Frederick A. and Alwilda M. (McLain) S.; m. Quinta Chapman, Jan. 25, 1974. Student, Howard U., 1948-50; B.S., Rider Coll., 1958, M.A., 1976. With N.J. Dept. Community Affairs, 1967-72; dir. youth and family services div. N.J. Dept. Instns. and Agys., 1972-74; dep. dir. adminstrn. purchase and property div. N.J. Treasury Dept., 1974-77; secretarial rep. Fed. Region II, Dept. Commerce, 1977-78; dep. under sec. Dept. Commerce, 1978-79; sr. v.p. adminstrn. Resorts Internat. Hotel Casino, Atlantic City, 1979-88; v.p. personnel Cunard Lines Ltd., N.Y.C., 1988—. Mem. N.J. Gov.'s Commn. on Disabled. Served with USNR, 1946-48. Mem. Am. Soc. Public Adminstrn., N.J. C. of C. Presbyterian. Club: Sundowners, Nat. Guardsmen, Inc. Home: 569 Sanderling Ct Secaucus NJ 07094 Office: Cunard Lines Ltd 555 Fifth Ave New York NY 10017

SCHENCK, JACK LEE, electric utility executive; b. Morgantown, W.Va., Aug. 2, 1938; s. Ernest Jacob and Virginia Belle (Kelley) S.; m. Rita Elizabeth Pietschmann, June 7, 1979; 1 son, Erik. B.S.E.E., B.A. in Social Sci., Mich. State U., 1961; M.B.A., NYU, 1975. Engr. AID, Tunis, Tunisia, 1961, Detroit Edison Co., 1962-63; engr./economist OECD, Paris, 1963-70; v.p. econ. policy analysis Edison Electric Inst., N.Y.C. and Washington, 1970-81; v.p., treas. Gulf States Utilities Co., Beaumont, Tex., 1981—. Mem. Internat. Assn. Energy Economists, Eta Kappa Nu, Triangle Frat. Republican. Office: Gulf States Utilities Co 285 Liberty Ave Beaumont TX 77701

SCHENCK, PHILIP KNIGHT, city manager; b. Norwalk, Conn., Aug. 4, 1944; s. Philip Knight and Kathryn Minnie (Thompson) S.; m. Pauline Ann DiMuzio, July 28, 1968; children: Lynn Ann, Michael. AB, Hiram Coll., 1966; MA, Northeastern U., 1968. Asst. to town mgr. Town of Brattleboro, Vt., 1972-74; town mgr. Town of Farmington, Maine, 1974-78, Town of Avon, Conn., 1978—; bd. dirs. Conn. Conf. Municipalities, New Haven, Conn. Interlocal Risk Mgmt. Assn., New Haven; chmn. North Cen. Conn. Emergency Med. Services Com., Newington, 1983-88. Contbr. articles to profl. jours. Bd. dirs. Farmington Valley YMCA, Simsbury, Conn., 1980-86. Served to lt. col. U.S. Army, 1968-72. Recipient Cert. Achievement Govt. Fin. Officers Assn. U.S. and Can., 1983-88; named Businessman of Yr. Avon C. of C., 1987. Mem. Conn. Town and City Mgrs. Assn. (pres. 1986-87), Internat. City Mgmt. Assn. (mem. nominating com. 1988). Episcopalian. Lodge: Rotary (v.p. 1988, pres. 1989). Home: 126 New Rd Avon CT 06001 Office: Town of Avon 60 W Main St Avon CT 06001

SCHENK, RAY M(ERLIN), electronics company executive; b. Logan, Utah, Dec. 18, 1946; s. Merlin F. and Thelma E. (Birch) S.; B.S. in Acctg. magna cum laude, Utah State U., 1969. C.P.A., Utah. Staff acct. Haskins and Sells, Phoenix, 1969, Salt Lake City, 1969-71; controller Kimball Electronics, Salt Lake City, 1971—. Recipient Scholastic Achievement cert. Phi Kappa Phi, 1967, 68; 1st Security Found. scholar, 1968; Alpha Kappa Psi scholarship award, 1969; C.P.A. medallion, 1970. Mem. Nat. Assn. Accts., Am. Acctg. Assn., Utah Assn. C.P.A.s, Am. Inst. C.P.A.s. Home: 5044 S Boabab Dr Salt Lake City UT 84117 Office: Kimball Electronics 350 Pierpont Ave Salt Lake City UT 84101

SCHERBA, ELAINE LOUISE, investment banker, financial analyst; b. Milw., Mar. 24, 1949; d. Raymond Arthur and Isabelle (Benson) Podolske; m. Stephen Scherba Jr., June 19, 1971. BA, Carroll Coll., 1971; MBA, U. Wash., 1977. Fin. analyst Rainier Nat. Bank, Seattle, 1977-78; officer fin. analysis Seattle-1st Nat. Bank, 1978-79, asst. v.p., mgr. capital investment analysis, 1979-80, v.p., mgr. fin. analysis and cons., 1980-81, v.p., mgr. asset-liability div., 1982-83, sr. v.p., mgr. fin. planning and reporting div., 1983-84, sr. v.p., mgr. retail delivery systems div., 1985-86, sr. v.p., mgr. fin. adv. services, 1986-89; treas. Egghead Discount Software, Issaquah, Wash., 1989—. Pres., bd. trustees Univ. Prep. Acad., Seattle, 1987-89; bd. dirs. Friends of Youth, Seattle, 1987-89. Republican. Episcopalian. Clubs: Rainier, Wash. Athletic (Seattle). Home: 509 Crockett St Seattle WA 98109 Office: Egghead Discount Software 22011 SE 51st St Fl PO Box 7004 Issaquah WA 98027

SCHERER, HAROLD NICHOLAS, JR., electric utility company executive, engineer; b. Plainfield, N.J., Apr. 5, 1929; s. Harold Nicholas and Nora (McDonough) S.; m. Jane Neely, Sept. 6, 1952 (div.); children—Anne Scherer McConnell, Peter; m. Patricia Condon, May 4, 1974; stepchildren: James, John, Joseph, Jeffery Ludwig, Jean Ludwig Ransdell. B.E., Yale U., 1951; M.B.A., Rutgers U., 1955. Registered profl. engr., N.J., Va., Tenn., W.Va., Ky., Ohio, Ind., Mich. Various engring. positions Pub. Service Electric and Gas Co., Newark, 1951-63; various engring. positions Am. Electric Power Service Corp., N.Y.C., 1963-68, asst. chief. elec. engr., 1968-69, chief elec. engr., 1969-73, v.p. elec. engr., 1973-82; sr. v.p. elec. engring. Am. Electric Power Service Corp., Columbus, Ohio, 1982—; also dir. Am. Electric Power Service Corp.; bd. dirs. Ohio Power Co., Canton; mem. joint U.S.-USSR working group on power transmission, 1975-81, joint U.S.-Italy working group on power transmission, 1979—; vice chmn. Am. Nat. Standards, N.Y.C., 1985-87; v.p. U.S. nat. com., chmn. U.S. tech. com. CIGRE, 1985—; mem. rev. bd. Bonneville Power Adminstrn. Enging., 1984—. Contbr. articles to profl. jours. Councilman, City of Plainfield, 1963-65; mem. Watchung (N.J.) Hills Regional High Sch. Bd. Edn., 1970-72; pres. Woods at Josephinum Civic Assn., Worthington, Ohio, 1983-84. Recipient Clayton Frost award U.S. Jaycees, 1961; recipient Young Man of Yr. award Plainfield Jaycees, 1963. Fellow IEEE (v.p. power engring. soc. 1988-89, pres. 1990—, William Habirshaw award for transmission and distbn. engring. 1986); mem. Conf. Internat. des Grands Reseaux (v.p. U.S. com. 1985—, internat. adminstrv. coun. 1988—), Nat. Acad. Enging., Worthington Hills Country Club, Columbus Athletic Club, Tau Beta Pi, Beta Gamma Sigma. Republican. Home: 7703 Cloister Dr Worthington OH 43235 Office: Am Electric Power Svc Corp 1 Riverside Pla Columbus OH 43215

SCHERF, PAUL HENRY, JR., electronics company executive; b. Lancaster, Ohio, Sept. 2, 1947; s. Paul Henry and Patricia (Pease) S.; m. Victoria H. King, Dec. 20, 1970 (div. 1984); children: Kathryn, Kelly. BS in Aero. Enging., U.S. Naval Acad., 1969; MSME, N.C. State U., 1970; MBA, Stanford U., 1981. Mktg. mgr. Itek Corp., Mountain View, Calif., 1981-82, Zehntel Inc., Walnut Creek, Calif., 1983-85; spl. bids mgr. Rolm Systems, Santa Clara, Calif., 1985-88; nat. dir. sales Domestic Automation Co., Foster City, Calif., 1988—. Co-author: Principles of Naval Weapons Systems, 1977. Bd. dirs. Big Brothers/Big Sisters of Cen. Md., Balt., 1976-78, Big Brothers/ Big Sisters of Anne Arundel County, Annapolis, Md., 1976-78. Lt. comdr. USN, 1969-79, comdr. res. Republican. Lutheran. Home: 3820 Park Blvd Apt 15 Palo Alto CA 94306

SCHERFF, RICHARD LEE, financial planner, employee benefit consultant; b. Canton, Ohio, Jan. 5, 1937; s. Lester Maynard and Evelyn Jeannette (Heacock) S.; m. Helen Sue Ritchie; children: Susan Lee, Richard Heacock. AB, Dartmouth Coll., 1959; MA, Columbia U., 1961, EdD, 1974. Tchr. history Jonathan Dayton High Sch., Springfield, N.J., 1960-62, Lompoc (Calif.) High Sch., 1962-63; instr. history Hancock Jr. Coll., Santa Maria, Calif., 1963; dir. admissions Columbia U., N.Y.C., 1964-66, asst. to dean, dean student activities Grad. Sch. Bus., 1966-69, asst. to v.p., acting dean students Coll. Physicians and Surgeons, 1970-77; v.p. corp. and fin. planning Compensation Planning Corp., N.Y.C. and Sparta, N.J., 1978-87; v.p. ECIS, Kansas City, Los Angeles, N.J., 1988—; mem. Canton (Ohio) Symphony, 1951-55. Author: Faculty Attitudes Toward Decision Making in Colleges and Universities, 1974. Pres. bd. trustees Riverside Ch., N.Y.C., 1976-80, chmn. bd. ushers, 1975-77; chmn. fin. com. Bd. Edn., Sparta, 1988-89; bd. dirs. Infant Day Care Ctr. Riverside, N.Y.C., 1976-80, Sta. WRVR-FM Radio, N.Y.C., 1975-77; cons. Teaneck N.J. Scholarship Fund, 1964—, Peace Corps, Washington, 1964. Internat. Paper Co. grantee, 1963-64; finished in 1st Place State of Ohio String Bass Competition, 1955. Mem. Internat. Assn. Fin. Planning, N.J. Underwriters Assn., Am. Philatelic Soc., N.J. Sch. Bds. Assn., Am. Fedn. Musicians, N.J. State Golf Assn., Alpha Theta, Phi Delta Kappa. Presbyterian. Clubs: Dartmouth (N.Y.C.); Lake Mohawk Golf (Sparta, N.J.). Lodge: Order of Demolay (Chevelier 1956). Home and Office: 19 Fairway Trail Sparta NJ 07871

SCHERICH, ERWIN THOMAS, civil engineer, consultant; b. Inland, Nebr., Dec. 6, 1918; s. Harry Erwin and Ella (Peterson) S.; student Hastings Coll., 1937-39, N.C. State Coll., 1943-44; B.S., U. Nebr., 1946-48; M.S., U. Colo., 1948-51; m. Jessie Mae Funk, Jan. 1, 1947; children—Janna Rae Scherich Thornton, Jerilyn Mae Scherich Dobson, Mark Thomas. Civil and design engr. U.S. Bur. Reclamation, Denver, 1948-84, chief spillways and outlets sect., 1974-75, chief dams br., div. design, 1975-78, chief tech. rev. staff, 1978-79, chief div. tech. rev. Office of Asst. Commr. Enging. and Research Ctr., 1980-84; cons. civil engr., 1984—. Mem. U.S. Com. Internat. Commn. on Large Dams. Served with AUS, 1941-45. Registered profl. engr., Colo. Fellow ASCE; mem. Nat. Soc. Profl. Engrs. (nat. dir. 1981-87), Profl. Engrs. Colo. (pres. 1977-78), Wheat Ridge C. of C. Republican. Methodist. Home and office: 3915 Balsam St Wheat Ridge CO 80033

SCHERMER, HARRY ANGUS, insurance company executive; b. Dubois, Pa., Apr. 13, 1942; s. Herman Victor and Dorothy Evelyn (Postlethwait) S.; m. Marsha Ann Rockey, Jan. 3, 1970 (div. 1982); m. Linda Lou Smith, Feb. 5, 1983. B.S., Ohio State U., 1964. Chartered fin. analyst, 1971. Various postions Nationwide Ins. Co., Columbus, Ohio, 1965-79, v.p. equity securities, 1979—; v.p. Nationwide Fin. Svcs. Inc., Nationwide Gen. Ins. Co., Nationwide Life Ins. Co., Nationwide Mut. Fire Ins. Co. Mem. Fin. Analysts Fedn., Inst. Chartered Fin. Analysts. Office: Nationwide Mut Ins Co One Nationwide Plaza Columbus OH 43216 *

SCHERSCHEL, MARK ERIC, controller, city councilman; b. Bedford, Ind., Dec. 10, 1949; s. John Peter and Tressie Louise (Steele) S.; m. Susan June Larkin, May 10, 1980; children: Mark Eric II, Christopher Kent, John Scott. AB, Ind. U., 1972, MBA, 1975, postgrad., 1972-73; postgrad., Ind. U., Indpls., 1979-80. Staff acct. T. F. Simma Accountancy Corp., Terre Haute, Ind., 1975-78, office mgr., 1978-82; prin. Mark E. Scherschel CPA, Bedford, Ind., 1982-86; contr. South Cen. CMHC, Inc., Bloomington, Ind., 1984—; adj. faculty Bedford Coll. Ctr., 1982-84. Bd. dirs. Dist. Camping Com. Boy Scouts of Am., Bedford, 1984—; city councilman, City of Bedford, 1987—. Mem. Ind. CPA Soc., Am. Inst. CPAs, Bedford C. of C. Republican. Roman Catholic. Lodge: Elks. Home: 1405 M Bedford IN 47421 Office: South Cen CMHC Inc 645 S Rogers Bloomington IN 47401

SCHEUERMANN, MONICA, construction manager; b. Newark, N.J., Oct. 20, 1951; d. Joseph Peter and Dorothy May (Ade) S. BA, Rutgers U., 1973. Various retailing positions N.J., N.C., 1973-79; project mgr. Carl E. Widell & Son, Haddonfield, N.J., 1979-84, Larwin Constrn. Co., Cherry Hill, N.J., 1984—. Mem. Phila. Zoo, Phila. Mus. Art. Mem. NAFE. Home: 303 Nature Dr Cherry Hill NJ 08003

SCHEURING, HELEN, real estate company executive, developer, consultant; b. Greene, Ohio, Apr. 12, 1940; d. Donald and Wilma (Harvey) Gibbs; m. Bob Gunther, 1960 (dec. 1967); children: Arthur, Alvin; m. Tim Scheuring, Apr. 8, 1969. Student real estate devel., Lakeland Coll., 1982, Ohio U., 1984. Salesperson Old Reserve Realty, Jeferson, Ohio, 1982-84, Lin-Con Inc., Columbus, Ohio, 1984-86; saleswoman, comml. and indsl. specialist Delores Knowlton Realtors, Chardon, Ohio; pres. Global Mktg., Exporting and Importing Co., New Bloomington, Ohio, 1984. Mem. Ohio Council Vocat. Edn., Westerville, Chardon Realty Bd. Mem. Ohio Planning Dirs. (treas.), Ohio Devel. Assn., Future Farmers Am. Republican. Office: Knowlton Realtors 145 Main St Chardon OH 44024

SCHEWE, CHARLES DANIEL, marketing educator, author, consultant; b. Detroit, Aug. 10, 1942; s. Ralph E. and Marion R. (Dietz) S.; m. Anne Robin Montgelas, Sept. 9, 1967; children: Charles Daniel Jr., Sara Christie. AB, U. Mich., 1964, MBA, 1965; PhD, Northwestern U., 1972. Instr. mktg. Lansing (Mich.) Community Coll., 1966-67; asst. prof. mktg. Roosevelt U., Chgo., 1970-72; prof. mktg. U. Mass., Amherst, 1972—; cons. IBM, White Plains, N.Y., 1984—; cons., bd. dirs. Stephen Winchell & Assocs., Washington, 1977—; bd. dirs. Atlantic List Co., Washington, Woodbridge Assocs., Holyoke, Mass. Author: Marketing: Principles and Strategies, 1987, Marketing: Concepts and Applications, 1980, 2d edit. 1983; editor: The Elderly Market: Selected Reading, 1985, Marketing Information Systems: Selected Readings, 1976. Recipient Fulbright Hays award, 1979. Mem. Am. Mktg. Assn., Am. Assn. for Advances in Health Care Rsch. (sec. 1983-90, v.p. 1990—), Assn. Consumer Rsch. Home: 23 Ash Ln Amherst MA 01002 Office: U Mass Sch of Mgmt Amherst MA 01003

SCHICK, THOMAS EDWARD, airline executive; b. N.Y.C., July 1, 1941; s. Frederick and Nora (Ahearn) S.; m. Collete Olga Salvator; children: Margaret Escobar, Carole, Suzanne. AAS in Mgmt., Farmingdale Coll.; BSBA, SUNY, Albany. Various mgmt. positions to dir. material mgmt. Pan Am Airlines, N.Y.C., 1961-78; sr. cons. Coopers and Lybrand, N.Y.C., 1978-79; dir. purchase services USAir Inc., Pitts., 1979-81, asst. v.p. material services, 1980-81, asst. v.p. maintenence services, 1981-82, v.p. maintenence ops., 1982-86; v.p. maintenence and engring. Piedmont Airlines, Winston-Salem, N.C., 1986-87, sr. v.p. ops., 1987—; elected pres., chief operating officer Piedmont Aviation, Inc., 1988—, also bd. dirs.; chmn. bd. Air Service, Inc., Aviation Supply Corp., Piedmont Aviation Services, Inc., all subs. Piedmont Aviation, Inc., 1988—. Mem. aeronautic edn. adv. commn. Bd. Edn. N.Y.C., 1984—. Mem. Air Transport Assn. (various coms. 1984—), Soc. Aero. Engrs. Club: Wings. (N.Y.C.). Office: Piedmont Airlines Inc 1 Piedmont Pla Winston-Salem NC 27156-1000

SCHIERL, PAUL JULIUS, paper company executive, lawyer; b. Neenah, Wis., Mar. 28, 1935; s. Julius Michael and Erna (Landig) S.; m. Carol Schierl; children: Michael, Kathryn, Susan, David, Daniel. B.S. in Polit. Sci, U. Notre Dame, 1957, LL.B., 1961. Mem. Wickham, Borgelt, Skogstad & Powell (attys.), Milw., 1961-64; with Fort Howard Corp., Green Bay, Wis., 1964—; sec., gen. counsel Fort Howard Corp., 1967-74; pres. Fort Howard Paper Co., 1974-84, chief exec. officer, 1974—, chmn. bd., 1984—; pres., bd. dirs. Fort Howard Paper Found. Inc.; bd. dirs. Fed. Res. Bank Chgo., Green Bay Packers, Wis. Trustee St. Norbert Coll.; mem. adv. council Sch. Law U. Notre Dame; bd. regents Milw. Sch. Enging.; bd. dirs. Green Bay Area Cath. High Sch. Found., Ltd. Served with AUS. Mem. ABA, State Bar Wis,

Nat. Assn. Mfrs. (bd. dirs.). Clubs: Union League, University (Chgo.). Office: Ft Howard Corp 1919 S Broadway PO Box 19130 Green Bay WI 54307 *

SCHIESSWOHL, CYNTHIA RAE SCHLEGEL, lawyer; b. Colorado Springs, July 7, 1955; d. Leslie H. and Maime (Kascak) Schlegel; m. Scott Jay Schiesswohl, Aug. 6, 1977; children: Leslie Michelle, Kristen Elizabeth. BA cum laude, So. Meth. U., 1976; JD, U. Colo., 1978; postgrad. U. Denver, 1984. Bar: Colo. 1979, U.S. Dist. Ct. (Colo.) 1979, U.S. Ct. Appeals (10th cir.) 1984, Wyo. 1986, Ind. 1988. Research clk. City Atty.'s Office, Colorado Springs, 1976; investigator Pub. Defender's Office, Colorado Springs, 1976; dep. dist. atty., 4th Jud. Dist. Colo., 1979-81; pvt. practice law, Grand Junction, Colo., 1981-82, Denver, 1983-84; assoc. Law Offices of John G. Salmon P.C., 1984-85; pvt. practice, Laramie, Wyo., 1985-88, Indpls., 1988—; guest lectr. Pikes Peak Community Coll., 1980. Staff U. Colo. Law Rev., 1977. Advisor, Explorer Law Post, Boy Scouts Am., 1980-81; ex officio mem. ch. devel. com. Cen. Rocky Mt. region Christian Ch. (Disciples of Christ), 1986-88; active evangelism commn. United Meth Ch., 1987-88, fin. com. youth and music depts., 1979-81, lay del. Rocky Mountain Ann. Conf., 1986-87; mem. Meridian St. United Meth. Ch., 1988—; hearing officer Wyo. Dept. Edn., 1987-88; vol. Project Motivation, Dallas, 1974; chairperson Wyo. Med. Rev. Panel, 1987. Named U. Scholar So. Meth. U., 1973. Mem. ABA, Wyo. State Bar, Colo. Bar Assn. (ethics com. 1984-85, long range planning com. 1985-88, chairperson 1986-87), Denver Bar Assn., Ind. State Bar Assn., Pi Sigma Alpha, Alpha Lambda Delta, Alpha Delta Pi. Republican.

SCHIFF, ALBERT JOHN, insurance company executive; b. N.Y.C., June 4, 1942; s. Charles Schiff and Katherine (Thompson) Weinstein; m. Jayne Nenerow, Mar. 7, 1971; children: Matthew Even, Kara Anne. BBA, U. N.C., 1965. Pres., chief exec. officer Schiff, Goldstein & Weiner, Greenwich, Conn., 1968-85; pension specialist Mut. Life Ins. Co. of N.Y., N.Y.C., 1966-68, exec. v.p., 1986-88; sr. exec. v.p. MONY Fin. Svcs., 1988—. Served to capt. USNR, 1964—. Mem. Am. Soc. CLU's (chmn, continuing edn. 1983-84), Assn. Advanced Life Underwriting (1s v.p. 1985-86), Million Dollar Round Table (Top of the Table, chmn. 1984-85). Republican. Jewish. Clubs: Ocean Reef, Y.C. (Key Largo, Fla.). Home: 30 Stanwich Rd Greenwich CT 06830 Office: Mut Life Ins Co of NY Glenpointe Ctr West Teaneck NJ 07666

SCHIFF, JAYNE NEMEROW, insurance underwriter; b. N.Y.C., Aug. 8, 1945; d. Milton E. Nemerow and Shirley (Kaplan) Wachtel; m. Albert John Schiff, Mar. 7, 1971; children: Matthew Evan, Kara Anne. Student, Fashion Inst. Tech., 1962-63, Am. Coll., 1977, NYU, 1976-77; BS in Bus., Marymount Coll., 1981. Corporate sec., treas. Albert J. Schiff Assocs., Inc., N.Y.C., 1970-78; field underwriter MONY Fin. Services, Greenwich, Conn., 1973—; freelance employee benefit cons. Greenwich, 1979—; regional dir. mktg., MONY Fin. Services, N.Y.C., 1978-79. Bd. dirs. N.Y. League Bus. and Profl. Women, 1976-78, Temple Sinai, Stamford, Conn., 1979-84, N.Y. Ctr. Fin. Studies; leader Webelos Cub Scouts, 1977-78; treas. Annual Mother's Bd. Benefit Greenwich Acad., 1988, upper sch. acquisitions chmn., 1989. Named Ct.'s Outstanding Young Woman, 1979. Mem. Am. Soc. Chartered Life Underwriters, N.Y. Ctr. Fin. Studies, N.Y.C. Life Underwriters Assn. (bd. dirs. 1977-78), League Women Voters. Jewish. Office: 30 Stanwich Rd Greenwich CT 06830

SCHIFF, RON, drug store company executive; b. 1938; married. BS, N.D. State U., 1960. With PayLess Drug Stores Northwest, Wilsonville, Oreg., 1960—, sr. v.p. ops., 1980-86, pres., chief operating officer, 1986—. Office: Pay Less Drug Stores NW Inc 9275 SW Peyton Ln Wilsonville OR 97070

SCHIFFMAN, LOUIS F., management consultant; b. Poland, July 15, 1927; s. Harry and Bertha (Fleder) S.;m. Mina R. Hankin, Dec. 28, 1963; children: Howard Laurence, Laura Lea. B.Chem. Engring., NYU, 1948, M.S., 1952, Ph.D., 1955. Research engr. Pa. Grade Crude Oil Assn., Bradford, 1948-50; teaching fellow in chemistry NYU, 1950-54; research chemist E.I. duPont de Nemours & Co., Wilmington, Del., 1954-56, Atlantic Refining Co., Phila., 1956-69; project leader, group leader, head corrosion sect. Amchem Products Inc., Ambler, Pa., 1959-70; pres. Techni Research Assocs. Inc., Willow Grove, Pa., 1970—, real estate developer: ptnr. Bay Properties Co., Bay Club Marina, Margate, N.J., Willow Grove (Pa.) Assocs.; pub., editor Patent Licensing Gazette, 1968—, World Tech., 1975—; mem. adv. oversight com. NSF, 1975, moderator energy conf. ERDA, Washington, 1976, Las Vegas, 1977. Editor: (with others) Guide to Available Technologies, 1985; contbr. to Encyclopedia of Chemical Technology, 1967; contbr. articles to profl. jours. Patentee in field. Recipient Founders Day award NYU, 1956. Fellow Am. Inst. Chemists; mem. Am. Chem. Soc., N.Y. Acad. Scis., Lic. Execs. Soc., Am. Assn. Small Research Cos. (editorial contbr. newsletter), Sigma Xi, Phi Lambda Upsilon. Home: 1837 Merritt Rd Abington PA 19001 Office: Techni Rsch Assocs In Willow Grove Pla Willow Grove PA 19090

SCHILLER, JERRY A., manufacturing company executive; b. Moline, Ill., Sept. 2, 1932; s. Walter A. and Mae (Sears) S.; m. Betty Fuller; children: Michele Schiller Smead, Susan Schiller Fortune, Richard, Lisa Schiller Swank, Sandra Schiller Rogers, Sara. BA in Bus. Adminstrn. and Acctg., Augustana Coll., 1954. CPA, Iowa. Mgr. internal auditing Maytag Co., Newton, Iowa, 1962-75, asst. controller, 1975-84, asst. v.p., controller, 1984-85; v.p., chief fin. officer Maytag Corp., Newton, 1985-86, sr. v.p., chief fin. officer, 1986—, trustee; mem. various coms. Maytag Mgmt. Club, Newton. Chmn. Newton Community Childrens Day Care Ctr., 1967; pres. Newton YMCA, 1970; auditor Newton Community Ctr. Fund Dr., 1973; various offices Our Savior Luth. Ch., Citizens Com. for Schs.; bd. dirs. Des Moines Ballet, 1986. Recipient Outstanding Religious Leader award Newton Jaycees, 1968. Mem. Fin. Execs. Inst., Iowa Soc. CPAs, Am. Inst. CPAs. Home: Box 515 Newton IA 50208 Office: Maytag Corp 403 W 4th St N Newton IA 50208

SCHILLER, MARGERY KABOT, financial planner; b. Hartford, Conn., Nov. 26, 1947; d. Ben William and Anne Lillian (Smulovitz) Kabot; m. Eugene Allan Schiller, Nov. 21, 1973; children: Jonathan Michael, Jeremy Andrew. BS, U. Conn., 1969, MA, 1975. Cert. fin planner, registered investment advisor. County agt. N.Y. State Coop. Extension, Liberty, 1969-70, Conn. Coop. Extension, Hartford, 1970-73; lectr. U. Vt., Burlington, 1975-77; extension specialist U. Conn., Storrs, 1977; cons. East Hampton, Conn., 1978-81; fin. planner East Hampton, 1981-86, St. Paul, 1986—; guest lectr. So. N.E. Telephone Co., New Haven, 1981-86; lectr. St. Joseph Coll., West Hartford, 1981-86. Author: (with E. Carr and V. Jodoin) Consumer Education: A Green Thumb Guide, 1975: (with E. Fetterman) Let the Buyer Be Aware, 1976; Personal and Family Finance: Principles and Applications, 1981; Connecticut Guide to Curriculum Development in Comsumer Education K Through Adult, 1981; Money Management: A Packet for Teaching Adults, 1984; Guidebook for Teaching Consumer Credit, 1984; contbr. articles in to profl. jours. Recipient award Registry Fin. Planning Practitioners, 1987. Mem. Inst. Cert. Fin. Planners, Internat. Assn. Fin. Planning, Nat. Assn. Personal Fin. Advisors.

SCHILLER, PIETER JON, venture capital executive; b. Orange, N.J., Jan. 14, 1938; s. John Fasel and Helen Roff (Roberts) S.; m. Elizabeth Ann Williams, Nov. 20, 1965; children—Cathryn Ann, Suzanne Elizabeth. B.A. in Econs. with honors, Middlebury (Vt.) Coll., 1960; M.B.A., N.Y. U., 1966. Fin. analyst Merck & Co., Inc., N.Y.C., 1960-61; fin. analyst, asst. div. controller, dir. auditing, then asst. controller Allied Chem. Corp., N.Y.C. and Morristown, N.J., 1961-75; treas. Allied Chem. Corp., 1975-79, v.p. planning and devel., 1979-83; exec. v.p. diagnostic ops. Allied Health & Sci. Products Co., 1983-86; pres. subs. Instrumentation Lab., Lexington, Mass., 1983-86; exec. v.p. The Winbridge Group Inc., Cambridge, Mass., 1986-87; gen. ptnr. Advanced Tech. Ventures, Boston, 1986—; bd. dirs. The Chatham Trust Co., N.J., 1982-83, The Winbridge Group, Inc., Cambridge, Data Acquisition Systems, Inc., Boston, SpectroVision, Inc., Chelmsford, Mass., Quidel, Inc., La Jolla, Calif., Vestar, Inc., San Dimas, Calif., Cytyc Corp., Marlborogh, Mass. Chmn. bd. trustees Newark Boys Chorus Sch., 1976-78, pres. bd., 1974-76; trustee Colonial Symphony Soc., 1978-85, v.p., 1980-82, pres., 1982-83, Morris Mus., Morristown; bd. dirs. New Eng. Coun., Boston, 1983-86, Middlebury Coll. Alumni Assn., 1989—; chmn. allocations com. United Way of Morris County, 1974-79, v.p., bd. dirs., mem. exec. com., 1979-80; trustee Morris Mus. Arts and Scis., 1980-83; co-chmn. devel. com. Lawrence Acad., Groton, Mass., 1988—. Mem. Fin. Execs. Inst. Republican. Episcopalian.

SCHILLING, CLAIRE ELIZABETH, financial executive; b. Balt., July 24, 1959; d. Edward M. and Anne F. (Zimmermann) Schilling. BA magna cum laude, James Madison U., 1981. Lic. security dealer. Sales rep. Tenneco Corp., Balt., 1981-82, Chesapeake Corp., Winston-Salem, N.C., 1982-86; account exec. Prudential-Bache Securities, McLean, Va., 1986-87; dir. fin. inst. services Packard Press, Washington, 1987—. Campaign coordinator Com.. to Reelect Del Cox, Bel Air, Md., 1978, 82, 86. Mem. Nat. Assn. Female Execs., McLean Bus. and Profl. Women's Assn., AAUW. Democrats. Presbyterian. Office: Packard Press 1025 Connecticut Ave NW Ste 905 Washington DC 20036

SCHILT, ANDREW A., data processing executive; b. Ypsilanti, Mich., Aug. 8, 1962; s. Alfred Ayars and Mary Ann (Squire) S. BS in Computer Sci., Purdue U., 1986. Programmer, analyst NCR, Cambridge, Ohio, 1986-89. Advisor Jr. Achievement, Cambridge, 1986—. Mem. Assn. for Computing Machinery. Republican. Episcopalian. Home: 7704 NW 44th Pl Gainesville FL 32606

SCHILT, CHRISTIAN RUSSELL, newspaper publisher; b. Denver, Mar. 21, 1951; s. Bernerd Earl and Valerie Gale (Shaver) S.; m. Annette Grete-Marie Bjerke, June 6, 1981; children: Russell Samson, Emily Ayavs. BA in History, U. Colo., 1973. Circulation mgr. Boulder (Colo.) Daily Camera, 1971-78, Nev. State Jour. Gannett Co., Reno, 1979-81; circulation dir. Bradenton (Fla.) Herald, Knight-Ridder, Inc., 1978; circulation dir. Bryan (Tex.)-College Station Eagle, HHC, Inc., 1981-85, advt. dir., 1985; pub. Lewisville (Tex.) Daily Leader, Colony Leader, 1986—, Farmers Br. Times, Carrollton (Tex.) chronicle, coppell (Tex.) Gazette, 1988—. Pres. Bryan-College Station Jaycees, 1982-83; pub. rels. chmn. Keep Lewisville Beautiful, 1988—; pres. Christian Community Action, Lewisville, 1988—; campaign chmn. United Way Lewisville, 1987, chmn., 1988. Mem. Am. Newspaper Pubs. Assn., Tex. Newspaper Pubs. Assn., Tex. Daily Newspaper Assn., Lewisville C. of C. (vice chmn. 1988), The Colony C. of C. (bd. dirs. 1988—, pres. 1989—), Rotary (treas. The Colony 1988—, pres. 1989—). Office: Lewisville Daily Leader 591 W Main St Profl Bldg Ste 100 Lewisville TX 75067

SCHINASI, DEBRA LYN, securities company executive; b. N.Y.C., July 22, 1954; d. Hyman and Jean (Urshansky) S. BA in Psychology, Vassar Coll., 1976; MSc in Econs., London Bus. Sch., 1984. Banking assoc. mktg. and new bus. devel. Interfirst Intrenat. Corp., N.Y.C., 1980-82; account exec. internat. instl. sales Merrill Lynch, N.Y.C., 1984-87; v.p. dept. head far eastern instl. sales Baring Securities, Inc., N.Y.C., 1987—. Mem. Asia Soc., London Bus. Sch. Alumni Assn., Vassar Club (N.Y.C.). Home: 220 Central Park S New York NY 10019

SCHINDELIN, JUERGEN WOLFGANG, engineer, scientist; b. Bad Friedrichshall, Germany, Aug. 8, 1928; s. August Friedrich and Emma Maria (Mueller) S.; M.S. in Elec. Engring., U. Karlsruhe, 1953; M.S., UCLA, 1959; Dr.Ing., U. Brunswick, 1967; m. Karin Anna Schlieper, May 5, 1967; 1 child, Tanya. Research engr. Convair, San Diego, 1957-59; design specialist Martin Marietta Corp., Orlando, Fla., 1959-61; sr. staff scientist Friedrich Krupp, Essen, Fed. Republic Germany, 1961-67; tech. staff Bellcomm, Inc., and Bell Tel. Lab., Washington and Whippany, N.J., 1967-73; chief scientist Def. Systems Center, Computer Scis. Corp., Moorestown, N.J., 1973-74; tech. staff, sci. advisor Messerschmitt-Boelkow-Blohm, Munich, Fed. Republic Germany, 1974—. Served with German Army, 1944-45. Recipient NASA Apollo Achievement award, 1970; AT&T Manned Space Flight award, 1971; Convair grantee, 1958-59. Mem. IEEE, N.Y. Acad. Scis., Deutsche Gesellschaft für Luft-und Raumfahrt, Sigma Xi. Contbr. articles to sci. jours. Patentee in field. Home: 28 Winzerstrasse, D-7100 Heilbronn Federal Republic of Germany Office: PO Box 801160, D-8000 Munich Federal Republic of Germany

SCHINDLER, ROBERT DAVID, sales executive; b. N.Y.C., Sept. 12, 1952. BA, CUNY, 1973. Dir. sales Studio 8 Inc., Bellerose, N.Y., 1975-81; regional sales mgr. Ikegami Electronic Inc., Maywood, N.Y., 1981-86; nat. sales mgr. Sony Corp. of Am., Paramus, N.Y., 1986-88; nat. sales, mktg. mgr. Toshiba Am. Inc. (name to Toshiba Am. Comsumer Products Inc.), Wayne, N.J., 1988—. Home: PO Box 603 Pomona NY 10970 Office: Toshiba Am Consumer Products Inc 82 Totowa Rd Wayne NJ 07470

SCHIPPER, LARRY ARTHUR, trade association executive; b. Newark, Mar. 10, 1953; s. Norman and Elana (Golden) S.; m. Marcia Mollenkopf, Aug. 24, 1975; children: Michael, Daniel, Kevin, Lauren. BA, U. Toledo, 1975; MBA, Fairleigh-Dickinson U., 1985. V.p. sales Maxnor Metals Co., Newark, 1975-77; pres., chief exec. officer Internat. Alloys Inc., Florham Park, N.J., 1977—. Office: Internat Alloys Inc PO Box 509 Florham Park NJ 07932

SCHIRMER, ROBERT HAMILTON, advertising executive; b. Detroit, Mich., July 19, 1940; s. Edward Adolph and Frances (Hamilton) S.; m. Alice Louise Mayes, Feb. 12, 1940; children: Allison, Mark, Cathrine. BA, Denison U., 1962. Account exec. MacManes, John & Adams, Detroit, 1965-68; account supr. Grey Advt., Detroit, 1968-72; Dodge advt. mgr. Chrysler Corp., Detroit, 1972-75, dir. merchandising, 1977-79; sr. v.p. McCann-Erickson, Detroit, 1975-77; exec. v.p. Campbell-Ewald, Detroit, 1979—. Trustee Mercy Coll. of Detroit, 1985—. Served to lt. (j.g.) USN, 1962-65. Mem. Detroit Adcraft Club (bd. dirs. 1984—), Mich. Council Am. Assn. Ad. Agys. (bd. dirs. 1984—). Republican. Episcopalian. Clubs: Orchard Lake (Mich.) Country; Recess (Detroit). Office: Campbell-Ewald 30400 Van Dyke Warren MI 48093 *

SCHIRR, GARY RICHARD, securities firm executive; b. Toledo, July 26, 1954; s. Richard William and Jean (Howard) S.; m. Laurel Elizabeth Dunkle, June 25, 1977; children: Christine Marie, Stephen Richard. BS in Math., Miami U., Oxford, Ohio, 1976; MS in Fin., Carnegie Mellon U., 1978. Strategic analyst Continental Bank, Chgo., 1978-80; investment analyst Met. Life Ins. Co., Chgo., 1980-82; fin. futures cons. Chgo. Merc. Exchange, Chgo., 1982-84; v.p. bank hedging Prudential Bank Securities, Chgo., 1984—; lectr. on bank risk mgmt. to various fin. assns., 1982—; mem. Chgo. council on fgn. relations,. Contbr. articles to fin. jours. Mem. Japan-Am. Soc. Home: 94 E Stone Ave Lake Forest IL 60045 Office: Prudential-Bache Securities 141 W Jackson St Ste 1930A Chicago IL 60604

SCHISSLER, LEE L., advertising professional; b. Colby, Kans., Jan. 22, 1955; s. C.L. and Blanche (Simpson) S.; m. Dawn Peterson, June 28, 1980; children: Megan, John. BS in Edn., Asbury Coll., 1977; MA in Socio-cultural Anthropology, U. Ky., 1983; MA in Advt., Northwestern U., 1985. Assoc. dean students Asbury Coll., Wilmore, Ky., 1979-84; asst. account exec. Ted Bates Advt.-Worldwide, N.Y.C., 1985-86; exec. dir. Hot Springs (Ark.) Advt. Commn., 1986—; pres. LSA Cons.-Tourism Mktg., Hot Springs, 1986—. Author: TETRA-Team Training, 1984. Mem. Internat. Assn. Conv. and Visitor Burs., Am. Soc. Assn. Execs., Tourism Travel Rsch. Assn. (bd. dirs.). Republican. Methodist. Office: Hot Springs Advt Commn Box K Hot Springs AR 71902

SCHKEEPER, PETER ALBERT, II, manufacturing company executive; b. Plainfield, N.J., Nov. 21, 1944; s. Peter Alexander and Marguerite Elizabeth (Leibner) S.; m. Carolyn Ann Gayer, June 11, 1966; children: Theresa, Daniel, Amy. BS in Indsl. Engring., N.J. Inst. Tech., 1966; postgrad., SUNY, Buffalo, 1970, U. Calif., Berkeley, 1968. Registered profl. engr., N.J. Engring. aide Port N.Y. Authority, N.Y.C., 1965-66; sr. mgmt. cons. Marpet Cons., Inc., Somerville, N.J., 1970-72; mgr. systems devel. Valcor Engring. Corp., Kenilworth, N.J., 1972-73, plant mgr., 1973-84; gen. mgr. Valcor Indsl. Products Div., Kenilworth, 1977-84; chief operating officer Valcor Sci. Div., Springfield, N.J., 1984—; v.p. mfg. Valcor Engring. Corp., Springfield, 1984—. Contbr. articles to profl. jours. Counselor N.J. Boys State, New Brunswick, 1962-67; chmn. Kenilworth Mfrs. Bicentennial, 1976; coordinator Tall Ship Denmark visit to Perty Amboy, N.J., 1982; host., chmn. Tall Ship Gloria Op-Sail Statue of Liberty Centennial, 1986. Lt. USCG, 1966-70. Recipient Dir. of Yr. award South Plainfield Jaycees, 1975, Disting. Pres. award Kenilworth Mfrs. Assn., 1980. Mem. Nat. Soc. Profl. Engrs., Am. Soc. Mech. Engrs. (com. chmn.), Employers Assn. N.J. (dir. 1988—), Raritan Yacht Club (fleet capt. 1983-85). Republican. Roman Catholic. Home: 228 Longwood Ave Chatham Township NJ 07928 Office: Valcor Engring Corp 2 Lawrence Rd Springfield NJ 07081

SCHLACK, CARL WILLIAM, general manager company executive; b. Buffalo, N.Y., Oct. 29, 1946; s. Carl Eaml and Mildred (Waltz) S.; Brenda Fay Knowlton, Aug. 25, 1987. AAS, Rochester Inst. Tech., 1967, BS, 1970, MBA, 1976. Fin. analyst Mfg. Xerox Corp., Rochester, N.Y., 1969-71; foreman Mfg. Xerox Corp., 1971-73, bus. analyst U.S. Ops., 1973-74, product mgr., 1974-80, mgr. high vol. strategy, 1980-82; market analyst Eastman Kodak, Rochester, N.Y., 1982-83; asst. dir. bus. devel. Eastman Kodak, 1984-85, gen. mgr., 1986—; cons. Med. Markets, Rochester, N.Y., 1980-82; bd. dirs. Erros Corp., Buffalo, 1978—. Active The Planning Forum. Mem. Soc. for Imaging Sci. and Tech. Republican. Episcopalian. Home: 80 Hollyvale Dr Rochester NY 14618 Office: Eastman Kodak Co 343 State St Rochester NY 14650

SCHLAIFER, CHARLES, advertising executive; b. Omaha, July 1, 1909; s. Abraham Schlaifer; m. Evelyn Chaikin, June 10, 1934 (dec. Oct. 1978); children: Arlene Lois Silk, Roberta Semer; m. Ann Mesavage, July 31, 1980. Privately ed.; Litt.D. (hon.), John F. Kennedy Coll., 1969. Newspaper reporter Omaha, 1926-29; advt. dir. Publix Tri-States Theatres, Nebr., Iowa, 1929-37; mng. dir. United Artists Theatres, San Francisco, 1937-42; nat. advt. cons. United Artists Producers, 1937-42; nat. advt. mgr. 20th Century-Fox Film Corp., N.Y.C., 1942-45; v.p. charge advt. and pub. relations 20th Century-Fox Film Corp., 1945-49; pres. Charles Schlaifer & Co., Inc., N.Y.C., 1949—; vis. prof. New Sch. Social Research; expert witness U.S. Congl. and Senatorial coms. on mental health, 1949—. Co-author: Action for Mental Health, 1961; contbr. articles to psychiat. jours. Mem. Pres.'s Com. Employment Handicapped, 1960—; founder, co-chmn. Nat. Mental Health Com., 1949-57; mem. nat. mental health adv. council Surgeon Gen. U.S., 1950-54; sec.-treas. Joint Commn. Mental Illness and Health, 1955-61; vice chmn. Found. Child Mental Welfare, 1963; mem. Gov.'s Youth Council State N.Y.; chmn. N.Y. State Mental Hygiene Facilities Improvement Corp., 1963—, White House Conf. Children, 1970; sec.-treas., bd. dirs. Joint Commn. Mental Health Children; chmn. N.Y. State Facilities Devel. Corp., 1963-78; mem. adv. council NIMH, 1976—; bd. dirs. Hillside Hosp., League Sch. For Seriously Disturbed Children, Menninger Found., Nat. Mental Hygiene Com. Recipient Social Conscience award Karen Horney Clinic, 1972; Hon. fellow Postgrad. Center Mental Health. Fellow Am. Psychiat. Assn. (hon.), Brit. Royal Soc. Health (hon.), Am. Orthopsychiat. Assn. (hon.); Mem. Nat. Assn. Mental Health (founder), Acad. for Motion Picture Arts and Scis., Harmonie Club. Home and Office: 150 E 69th St New York NY 10021

SCHLANG, DAVID, real estate executive, lawyer; b. N.Y.C., May 2, 1912; s. Alexander and Blanche (Cohen) S.; m. Arlene Roth, May 9, 1948. LLB, NYU, 1933. Bar: N.Y., 1935, U.S. Dist. Ct. (so. dist.) N.Y. 1940. Individual practice law, 1935-42; sec. Schlang Bros. & Co., Inc., N.Y.C., 1945—, pres., 1978—; gen. ptnr. 67 Wall St. Co., Maidgold Assocs.; pres. Corner Gold Realty Corp. Bd. trustees Brookdale Hosp., Bklyn., 1980—, v.p., 1983—; bd. dirs. Samuel Schulman Inst. Nursing and Rehab. of Brookdale Hosp., 1973—, sec. bd. dirs., 1976—; dir. Legion Meml. Sq., Inc., 1983—; sec. Schlang Found., 1953—; founding mem. U.S. Congl. Adv. Bd.; mem. U.S. Def. Com. Served with AUS, 1942-45. Decorated Croix de Guerre with palm (France); recipient Conspicuous Service award State of N.Y., 1965. Mem. Criminal Investigation Div. Agts. Assn., ABA, N.Y. State Bar Assn., N.Y. County Lawyers Assn., Real Estate Bd. N.Y., N.Y. State Assn. Realtors and Appraisers, Internat. Orgn. Real Estate Appraisers, Nat. Assn. Real Estate Appraisers. Clubs: New Nautilus Beach and Country (Atlantic Beach, N.Y.); NYU (N.Y.C.), U.S. Senatorial, Town (N.Y.C.) Home: 737 Park Ave New York NY 10021 Office: 67 Wall St New York NY 10005

SCHLEEDE, GLENN ROY, energy company executive, public policy researcher; b. Lyons, N.Y., June 12, 1933; m. Sandra Christine Klafehn, Dec. 27, 1958; children: Kristen M., Kimberly J., Kendall E. BA, Gustavus Adolphus Coll., 1960; MA, U. Minn., 1968; advanced mgmt. program, Harvard U., 1987. Research asst. Indsl. Relations Ctr., U. Minn., Mpls., 1960-61; mgmt. intern, then contractor personnel specialist AEC, Argonne, Ill. and Germantown, Md., 1961-65; asst. chief div. natural resources U.S. Office Mgmt. and Budget, Exec. Office of Pres., Washington, 1965-72, exec. assoc. dir., 1981; dep. assoc. dir. Office of Policy Analysis, AEC, Germantown, 1972-73; assoc. dir. energy and sci. Domestic Council, The White House, Washington, 1973-77; sr. v.p. Nat. Coal Assn., Washington, 1977-81; pres. New Eng. Energy Inc., Westborough, Mass., 1982—, also bd. dirs.; v.p. New Eng. Power Service Co., Westborough, 1982—, also bd. dirs.; v.p. New Eng. Electric System, Westborough, 1986—. Author numerous speeches, papers and congl. testimony on various nat. energy policy issues. Recipient Disting. Alumni in Bus. award Gustavus Adolphus Coll. Alumni Assn., St. Peter, Minn., 1987. Republican. Lutheran. Home: 2 Thornton Ln Concord MA 01742 Office: New Eng Electric System 25 Research Dr Westborough MA 01582

SCHLEICHER, JOEL ARTHUR, manufacturing executive; b. Mpls., Mar. 9, 1952; s. Gordon C. and Shirley J. (Palmer) S.; m. Diane Marie Devine, June 30, 1979; 1 child, Kelli Lyn. BSB in Acctg., U. Minn., 1974. CPA. Sr. acct. Peat Marwick Mitchell, Mpls., 1974-78; v.p., treas. Murray Resources Inc., Pikeville, Ky., 1978-80; controller Seis Pros Inc., Houston, 1980-81; asst. to chief fin. officer Phoenix Mgmt. Corp., Houston, 1981-82; chief exec. officer Murray Chris-Craft Boat Co., Brandenton, Fla., 1982—; also bd. dirs.; bd. dirs. Gulf Coast Marine Inst., Sarasota, Fla., 1986—, Am. Community Devel. Corp., St. Petersburg, Fla., 1986-87. Recipient Beta Alpha Psi award U. Minn., Mpls., 1974, Beta Gamma Signa award U. Minn., 1974. Mem. Nat. Marine Manufacturers Assn. (govt. relations com. 1988—), Young Pres.'s Orgn., Tampa, Fla., 1988. Mem. Econ. Devel. Com. Manatee County, Fla., Bradenton, 1988. Office: Murray Chris-Craft Boat Co 101 Riverfront Blvd Bradenton FL 34205

SCHLEICHER, NORA ELIZABETH, bank executive, treasurer, accountant; b. Balt., Aug. 10, 1952; d. Irvin William and Eleanor Edna Schleicher; m. Ray Leonard Settle Jr., July 27, 1985. AA cum laude, Anne Arundel Community Coll., 1972; BS summa cum laude, U. Balt., 1975. CPA, Md. Staff auditor Md. Nat. Bank, Balt., 1975-76, sr. staff auditor, 1976-77, supr. auditing dept., 1977-78; full charge acct. Wooden & Benson, CPA's, Balt., 1978-81; asst. to treas. First Fed. Savs. & Loan Assn., Annapolis, Md., 1981, asst. treas., 1982-83, v.p., 1984, v.p., treas., 1984—. Mem. Am. Inst. CPA's, Md. Assn. CPA's, Fin. Mgrs. Soc., Inc. Methodist. Office: First Fed Savs & Loan Assn Annapolis MD 21401

SCHLEIN, DOV C., banker. Vice chmn. Republic N.Y. Corp. Office: Republic NY Corp 452 Fifth Ave New York NY 10018 *

SCHLEIN, MARLIN WILLIAM, manufacturing executive; b. Lancaster, Pa., Apr. 15, 1941; s. Marlin Elwood and Mae H. (McCready) S.; m. Diane Lynne Anderson, June 25, 1966; 1 child, Marlin W. Jr. AA, Catonsville Coll., Balt., 1964; BA, Towson State U., 1966; MA, U. N.C., Greensboro, 1972. V.p. Advanced EQ Co., Inc., Charlotte, N.C., 1967-73, Gregory Poole Equipment Co., Raleigh, N.C., 1973-74; pres. Falcon Equipment Co., Greensboro, 1975—, Marlin Equipment Co., Asheboro, N.C., 1980—; chmn. bd. Marlin Equipment Co., Inc., Asheboro, 1981—; pres. Marlin Fabricating, Inc., Randleman, N.C., 1984—, also chmn. bd. dirs. Scout asst. Cub Scouts Boy Scouts Am., 1985. Democrat. Presbyterian. Office: Marlin Equipment Inc PO Box 2326 Asheboro NC 27204

SCHLESINGER, ALBERT R., diversified products company executive, controller; b. Pitts., Oct. 25, 1941; s. Harry and Anne (Dugan) S.; m. Joan Saul, Aug. 8, 1964; children: Marc D., Todd E. AS in Acctg. and Taxation, Robert Morris Coll., 1964; BS in Acctg. and Econs., Gannon U., 1966. CPA, Ohio, Ind. Mgr. Schlesingers Food Store, Pitts., 1960-66; mgr. acctg. and auditing Price Waterhouse & Co., Cleve., 1966-76; asst. controller Ball Corp., Muncie, Ind., 1976-87, v.p., controller, 1987—; treas., bd. dirs. Ball Packaging Products, Inc. Bd. dirs. Boy's Club, Muncie, 1986—; co-chmn. hospitality Sta. WIPB-Telesale 49,Muncie, 1986; v.p. Beth El Temple,

Muncie, 1987—. Mem. Tax Execs. Inst., Fin. Execs. Inst., Am. Inst. CPA's, Ohio Soc CPA's. Office: Ball Corp 345 So High St Muncie IN 47305

SCHLESS, PHYLLIS ROSS, investment banker; b. N.Y.C., Apr. 16, 1943; d. Lewis H. and Doris G. Ross; m. Aaron Backer Schless, July 7, 1970; 1 son, Daniel Lewis Ross. Cert., N.Y. Playhouse Sch. of Theatre, 1962, N.Y. Sch. Interior Design, 1964; B.A. in Econs., Wellesley Coll., 1964; M.B.A., Stanford U., 1966. Assoc. in internat. fin. Kuhn Loeb & Co., N.Y.C., 1966-70; fin. cons. 1971-73; sr. analyst fin. Trans World Airlines, N.Y.C., 1974-75; assoc. corp. fin., mergers and acquisitions Lazard Freres & Co., 1976-79; dir. mergers and acquisitions Am. Can Co., Greenwich, Conn., 1979-82; v.p. mergers and acquisitions Bear, Stearns & Co., N.Y.C., 1982-84; sr. v.p. corp. acquisitions Integrated Resources, 1984-85; chmn. Ross Fin. Services Group Ltd., 1985—; fin. adv. Children's Theatre, N.Y.C. Parks Dept., 1969. Pres. Greater Bridgeport Nat. Council Jewish Women, 1972-73, bd. dirs., 1974-75;on Cause, 1973-75; treas. Wellesley Class 1964, 1984-89; bd. dirs. Girls Clubs Am., 1979-89, mem. exec. com., 1982-89, pres., 1984-86; bd. dirs. Pauline Koner Dance Co., 1979-81, Child Guidance Clinic Greater Stanford, 1981-83, New Canaan United Way, 1981-83; trustee Nat. Child Labor Bur., 1981—, mem. exec. com., 1983—; trustee, New World Found., 1986—, treas., 1988—, chair fin. com., 1988—. Recipient Bravo award Greenwich YMCA, 1980. Mem. Assn. Corp. Growth. Clubs: Grolier, Atrium. Home: 214 Sunset Hill Rd New Canaan CT 06840 Office: Ross Fin Svc Group Inc 122 E 42d St Ste 5300 New York NY 10168

SCHLIEFER, MARC SCOTT, financial planning company executive; b. Phila., July 3, 1957; s. Edward I. and Arlene (Solovitz) S.; m. Christine Marie Sokol, Oct. 4, 1981; 1 child, Trevor Scot. Student, Montgomery Coll., 1975-77, U. Md., 1977-78; cert., Coll. for Fin. Planning, 1984. Ins. salesman J.E. Walter Assocs., Silver Spring, Md., 1978-79; v.p., fin. planner, bd. dirs. Equity Planning Inst., Inc., 1979—; bd. dirs. E.A. Merrifield, P.A., Gaithersburg, Md., Sandy Botkin Show, Silver Spring; fin. planning hotline vol. USA Today, Arlington, Va., 1986-87; speaker to ins. groups, 1986; instr. fin. Ben Franklin U., Washington, 1980; condr. fin. planning seminars Southeastern U., Washington, 1988. Mem. budget com. Rockshire Home Owners Assn., Rockville, Md., 1986. Mem. Inst. for Cert. Fin. Planners, Nat. Assn. Life Underwriters, Internat. Assn. Fin. Planners, Suburban Md. Life Underwriters Assn., Rotary (speaker). Home: 15504 Summer Grove Ct Gaithersburg MD 20878 Office: 7910 Woodmont Ave Ste 222 Bethesda MD 20814

SCHLOEMER, PAUL GEORGE, diversified manufacturing company executive; b. Cin., July 29, 1928; s. Leo Bernard and Mary Loretta (Butler) S.; m. Virginia Katherine Grona, Aug. 28, 1954; children: Michael, Elizabeth, Stephen, Jane, Daniel, Thomas. BS in Mech. Engring., U. Cin., 1951; MBA, Ohio State U., 1955. Rsch. and devel. engr. Wright Patterson AFB, Dayton, Ohio, 1951-52; R&D officer Wright Patterson AFB, Dayton, 1952; resident engr. Parker Hannifin Corp., Dayton, 1957; also Ea. area mgr. Parker Hannifin Corp., Huntsville, Ala., 1957-65; v.p. aerospace group Parker Hannifin Corp., Irvine, Calif., 1965-77; pres. aerospace group Parker Hannifin Corp., Irvine, 1977, corp. v.p., 1978-81, exec. v.p., 1981; pres. Parker Hannifin Corp., Cleve., 1982-84, chief exec. officer, 1984—; bd. dirs. Ameritrust Corp., Cleve., Ohio Bell Tel. Co. Capt. USAF, 1952-53. Mem. Machinery and Allied Products Inst. (exec. com.), Conf. Bd., Inc. Republican. Roman Catholic. Club: The Country, Big Canyon Country, The Pepper Pike. Office: Parker Hannifin Corp 17325 Euclid Ave Cleveland OH 44112

SCHLOSS, EUGENE MATHIAS, JR., healthcare services company executive, lawyer; b. Philadelphia, Pa., Apr. 19, 1932; s. Eugene Mathias and Jeanette (Kenin) S.; m. Sherna L. Goldberg, Apr. 3, 1955; children—Karen L., David M. B.S., Trinity Coll., Hartford, Conn., 1953; J.D., Temple Univ., Philadelphia, Pa., 1957. Bar: Pa. 1958. Assoc., Brumbelow & Comisky, Phila., 1957-59; ptnr. Rappeport, Magil, Schulman & Schloss, Phila., 1959-73; corp. counsel, sec., dir. R.H. Med. Services, Elkins Park, Pa., 1974-80; gen. counsel, sec., dir. MEDIQ Inc., Pennsauken, N.J., 1981—; mem. Regional Comprehensive Health Planning, Montgomery City, Pa., 1974-77; mem. Inst. Rev. Bd., Rolling Hill Hosp., Elkins Park, Pa., 1979—. Mem. exec. bd. Old York Rd. Temple Beth Am, Abington, Pa., 1976-84, pres., 1977-79; chmn. Democratic Party Congl. Dist., Abington, 1965-69. Mem. Am. Corp. Counsel Assn. (bd. dirs., 2d v.p. Del. Valley chpt.), Am. Acad. Hosp. Attys., Phila. Bar Assn. Democrat. Jewish. Home: 1700 Cary Rd Huntingdon Valley PA 19006 Office: MEDIQ Inc One Mediq Pla Pennsauken NJ 08110

SCHLOSS, LAWRENCE MICHAEL VAN DAELEN, investment banker; b. N.Y.C., Sept. 28, 1954; s. Alfred Simon and Elizabeth (Van Daelen) S.; m. Laurie Sue Klayman, June 25, 1978; 1 child. BA in Econs. cum laude, Tulane U., 1976; MBA, U. Pa., 1978. Assoc. investment banker Donaldson, Lufkin & Jenrette Securities Corp., N.Y.C., 1978-81, v.p., 1981-84, sr. v.p. mergers and acquisitions, 1984—; vice chmn., dir. DLJ Bridge Fund.; dir. Krueger Internat., Inc., Green Bay, Wis., MPB Corp., Keene, N.H. Office: Donaldson Lufkin & Jenrette 140 Broadway New York NY 10005

SCHLOSSER, FRANKLIN ROGER, retail executive; b. Peoria, Ill., July 3, 1941; s. Ernest Carl and Julia Margaret (Shields) Higgins; m. Carol Sue Holt, June 2, 1962; children—Patrick, Timothy, Andrew. Student St. Louis Coll Pharmacy, 1959-62. Store mgr. Abbey Sales Co., St. Louis, 1965-71, regional supr., 1971-74; buyer Wetterau Co., 1975-77, sr. buyer hardlines, 1976-77; with Pamida Inc., Omaha, Nebr., 1977—, sr. v.p., 1981-83, exec. v.p., 1983-88, pres., 1989—. Bd. dirs. Goodwill Industries, Omaha, 1983—. Named Store Mgr. of Yr., Diversified Industry Abbey Sales, 1970, Buyer of Yr., Wetterau Inc., 1976. Mem. Fontenelle Forest Com., Nat. Mass Retailing Inst., Macomb C. of C., Chapel Hill Recreation Assn. (v.p. 1981—), St. Louis Housewares Assn; Republican. Roman Catholic. Office: Pamida Inc 8800 F St Omaha NE 68127 *

SCHLOTTERBACK, EDWARD EARL, manufacturing engineer; b. Garrett, Ind., Feb. 11, 1952; s. Earl Malcolm and Elsie Emma (Kleiber) S.; m. Darlene Louise Conner, Sept. 26, 1982; children: Kim Miceli, Brett, Bethany, Emily. AS, Los Angeles Community Coll., 1979, State Tech. Inst., Memphis, 1979; BS in Industrial Tech., So. Ill. U., 1984. Enlisted USMC, 1970, resigned, 1979; assoc. elec. engr. King Seeley Thermos Co., Kendallville, Ind., 1980-82; sr. instrument lab. technician Magnavox Co., Garrett, 1982-87; tech. foreman Magnavox Co., Auburn, Ind., 1987-88, mfg. engr., 1988—. Republican. Lutheran. Home: RR 1 Box 306-AA Kendallville IN 46755

SCHLOTTERBECK, WALTER ALBERT, manufacturing company lawyer; b. N.Y.C., Dec. 22, 1926; s. Albert Gottlob and Maria Louise (Fritz) S.; m. Pauline Elizabeth Hoerz, Sept. 2, 1951; children—Susan, Thomas, Paul. A.B., Columbia U., 1949, LL.B., 1952. Bar: N.Y. bar 1953. Counsel Gen. Electric Co. (various locations), 1952-87; v.p., corp. counsel Gen. Electric Co. (various locations), N.Y.C., 1970-77; sec. Gen. Electric Co. (various locations), 1975-76, gen. counsel, 1976-87, sr. v.p., 1977-87. Served with USNR, 1944-46. Home: 752 Town House Rd Fairfield CT 06430

SCHLOTZHAUER, DAVID EUGENE, certified public accountant; b. Boonville, Mo., Mar. 10, 1954; s. John Eugene and Elizabeth Lorraine (Day) S.; m. Sallie Suzanne Bornhauser, Aug. 23, 1975; children: Susanne, Anna, Patrick. BS in Bus. Adminstr. cum laude, Cen. Mo. State U., 1976. Staff acct. Jackson and Co., CPA's, Kansas City, Mo., 1976-80, mgr., 1981-83, ptnr., 1984-88; ptnr. Mills and Schlotzhauer, Overland Park, Kans., 1988—; bd. dirs. Community Group Health Plan, Kansas City, treas. 1984—, chmn. fin. com. 1986—; speaker group trg. seminars. Named one of Outstanding Young Men of Am., U.S. Jaycees, 1979. Mem. Am. Inst. CPA's (mem. com., computer applications subcom.), Mo. Soc. CPA's (fellow 1978—, chmn. continuing profl. edn. com. 1983-85, mgmt. acctg. practice com. 1985—, sec. Kansas City chpt.), Accts. Computer Users Tech. Exchange (conf. del. 1983—, author trg. manual 1985). Republican. Office: Mills & Schlotzhauer 5330 College Blvd Ste B Overland Park KS 66210

SCHLUTER, PETER MUELLER, electronics company executive; b. Greenwich, Conn., May 24, 1933; s. Fredric Edward and Charlotte (Mueller) S.; m. Jaquelin Ambler Lamond, Apr. 18, 1970; children: Jane Randolph, Charlotte Mueller, Anne Ambler. BME, Cornell U., 1956; postgrad. Harvard U. Grad. Sch. Bus. Adminstrn., 1982. Sr. engr. Thiokol Chem. Corp., Brigham City, Utah, 1958-59; asso. Porter Internat. Co., Washington, 1960-65, v.p., 1965-66, pres., treas., dir., 1966-70; pres., treas. dir. Zito Co., Derry, N.H., 1970-72; internat. bus. cons., Washington, 1972-74; v.p., dir. Buck Engring. Co. Inc., Farmingdale, N.J., 1975, pres., chief exec. officer, dir., 1975—; dir. Keystone Forging Co., Northumberland, Pa.; trustee Monmouth Med. Ctr. Mem. Republican Inaugural Book and Program Com., 1969; mem. community adv. bd. Monmouth council Girl Scouts U.S.; mem. adv. council Monmouth (N.J.) Coll. Sch. Bus. Admin.; bd. dirs. United Way of Monmouth County., trustee Monmouth Med. Ctr. Mem. Pi Tau Sigma. Clubs: Metropolitan (Washington), Rumson Country. Home: 1607 Channel Club Towers Monmouth Beach NJ 07750 Office: PO Box 686 Farmingdale NJ 07727

SCHMALZ, J. P., oil company executive; b. 1916. BS, Tex. A&M U., 1942; MS, Okla. U., 1950. With Shell Oil Co., Houston, 1945-47, Magnolia Oil, Houston, 1947-52, Tenneco Oil, Houston, 1952-69; with Tesoro Petroleum Corp., San Antonio, 1969—, exec. v.p., 1980—. Office: Tesoro Petroleum Corp 8700 Tesoro Dr San Antonio TX 78286 *

SCHMECHEL, WARREN P., utilities executive; b. 1927; married. BS, Mont. State U., 1953; student, Harvard U., 1965. With Mont. Power Co., Butte, 1953—, various mgmt. positions, 1953-73, v.p., 1973-79, from pres. to pres., chief exec. officer, 1979-84, chmn. bd., chief exec. officer, 1984—. Office: Mont Power Co 40 E Broadway Butte MT 59701 *

SCHMEISER, RONALD CHARLES, finance executive; b. Pitts., June 6, 1930; s. Philip and Esther (Fineman) S.; m. Ethel Fine, Nov. 23, 1952; children: Jane Marian Power, Diane Ellen, Susan Rebecca. BBA, U. Pitts., 1952, ML, 1953. CPA, Pa. Prof. Duquesne U., Pitts., 1956-67; ptnr. Touche Ross & Co., Pitts., 1967-80; dir. fin. City of Pitts., 1980-87; v.p. Butcher & Singer, Inc., Pitts., 1987-89; sr. v.p. W.R. Lazard & Co., Pitts., 1989—. Author articles Statement of Funds, 1964, Accounting for Mergers & Acquisitions, 1966. Chmn. City of Pitts. Sinking Fund Commn., 1978-80, Pub. Parking Authority of Pitts., 1979—; treas. City of Pitts. Equipment Leasing Authority, 1981-87; vice chmn. The Pitts. Water & Sewer Authority, 1984-87. Served with U.S. Army, 1953-55. Named Man of Yr. in Fin. Vectors Pitts., 1982. Mem. AICPA, Pa. Inst. CPA's (coun., pres. 1976), Govt. Fin. Officers Assn., U. Pitts. Sch. Bus. Alumni (pres. 1986—), U. Alumni Coun., Concordia Club, Rivers Club, Duquesne Club. Democrat. Jewish. Office: WR Lazard & Co 2460 City Centre Tower Pittsburgh PA 15222

SCHMELZER, PATRICIA ANNE, health physicist; b. West Union, Iowa, June 7, 1951; d. William John and Shirley Anne (Coglan) S. BS, U. Iowa, 1976. Lab. asst. U. Iowa, Iowa City, 1974-78, lab. technician, 1978-82, chemist, 1982-84; health physicist Iowa Elec. Light & Power, Cedar Rapids, 1984-87, ALARA coordinator, 1987-88; radiol. engr. Detroit Edison, 1988—. Foster parent Dept. Human Services, Iowa City, 1987-88; vol. Dept. Corrections, Cedar Rapids, 1982, 83. Mem. Health Physics Soc. Democrat. Roman Catholic. Office: Fermi II Nuclear Power Plant Detroit Edison 6400 N Dixie Hwy Newport MI 48166

SCHMERTZ, HERBERT, advertising executive; b. Yonkers, N.Y., Mar. 22, 1930; s. Max and Hetty (Frank) S.; children: Anthony, Lexy, Nicole, Thomas. AB, Union Coll., 1952, LLD (hon.), 1977; LLB, Columbia U., 1955. Bar: N.Y. State 1958. With Am. Arbitration Assn., N.Y.C., 1955-61; gen. counsel, asst. to dir. Fedn. Mediation and Conciliation Svc., N.Y.C., 1961-66; with Mobil Oil Corp., N.Y.C., 1966—; pres. Mobil Shipping and Transp. Co., 1973-74; v.p. pub. affairs Mobil Oil Corp., 1974-88; pres. The Schmertz Co., Inc., N.Y.C., 1988—, Schmertz/Hilton Advt., 1989—; also dir. Mobil Oil Corp., Mobil Corp. Author: Good-bye to the Low Profile, 1986; co-author Takeover, 1980. Appointee Pres.'s Commn. on Broadcasting to Cuba, U.S. Adv. Commn. on Pub. Diplomacy; dir. internat. coun. Nat. Acad. TV Arts and Scis.; mem. adv. coun. NYU Sch. Arts; bd. dirs. USO Met. N.Y.C., Bedford Stuyvesant Devel. and Svcs. Corp., The Vista Orgn., Ltd.; trustee Media Inst., Silver Shield Found.; bd. govs. Media and Society Seminars Columbia U. Grad. Sch. Journalism. Served with CIC U.S. Army, 1955-57. Mem. Coun. Fgn. Rels., Fed. City Club, Internat. Club, N.Y. Athletic Club. Democrat. Jewish. Office: Schmertz/Hilton Advt 230 Park Avee Ste 805 New York NY 10169 also: Schmertz Co 285 Central Pk W 11th Fl New York NY 10024

SCHMID, JOHN GEORGE, JR., auditor; b. Rochester, N.Y., Feb. 22, 1942; s. John G. Sr. and Bertha D. (Hept) S.; m. Luba P. Stobierski, Apr. 10, 1981; children: Thomas, Laura B. Mebert. BA, Boston Coll., 1964; MBA, Rochester Inst. Tech., 1973. CPA, Conn., N.Y. Mgr. market research Bausch & Lomb Inc., Rochester, 1967-73; tax specialist Peat, Marwick & Mitchell, N.Y.C., 1973-77; mgr. internat. div. Chesebrough Pond's Inc., Greenwich, Conn., 1977-84; co-owner Schmid Assocs., Branford, Conn., 1984-88; audit mgr. Insilco Corp., Meriden, Conn., 1988—. Asst. majority leader Branford Rep. Town Meeting, 1985-87, majority leader, 1987—, dist. chmn., 1985—; chmn. fin. com. St. Elizabeth Ch., Branford, 1987—. Capt. U.S. Army, 1965-67, Vietnam. Mem. Nat. Assn. Accts. (pres. Bridsgeport, Conn. chpt. 1982-83, Outstanding Achievement award 1980), Am. Inst. CPA's, N.Y. State Soc. CPA's, Conn. Assn. CPA's. Home: 5 Mirage Dr Branford CT 06405 Office: Insilco Corp 1000 Research Pkwy Meriden CT 06450

SCHMIDT, CHARLES WILSON, electronics products company executive; b. N.Y.C., Mar. 18, 1928; s. William Charles and Anita (Wilson) S.; m. Martha Moore, Dec. 29, 1951; children: Anne, Martha, William, Heidi. Grad., Deerfield Acad., 1945; A.B., Williams Coll., 1948; postgrad., Carnegie Inst. Tech., 1950; grad., Advanced Mgmt. Program, Harvard U., 1973. With S.D. Warren Co. div. Scott Paper Corp., 1948-83; apprentice Westbrook, Maine, 1948; salesman N.Y.C., 1950-52; dist. sales mgr. Rochester, N.Y., 1952-56, West Coast, 1956-59, Phila., 1963-67, N.Y.C., 1967-69; asst. sales mgr. Boston, 1969; v.p. mktg. and sales 1969-72; pres. S.D. Warren Co. div. Scott Paper Corp., from 1972, also sr. v.p. parent co., 1975-83; pres., chief exec. officer S.C.A. Services, 1984; exec. in residence, prof. Babson Coll., Wellesley, Mass., 1985-86; sr. v.p., group exec. Raytheon Co., Lexington, Mass., 1987—; dir. Boston Co., Boston Safe Deposit and Trust Co., Dennison Mfg. Co., Environ. Treatment and Technol. Corp., Mass. Investors Trust, The Stop & Shop Cos., Inc., pres. 66th Advanced Mgmt. Program, Harvard U. Mem. Recreation Commn., Irvington, N.Y., 1964-67; trustee chmn. U. Maine Pulp and Paper Found.; bd. dirs. New Eng. Colls. Fund; mem. corp. Mass. Gen. Hosp.; bd. dirs. Smithsonian Instn.; trustee Deaconess Hosp. Mem. Am. Paper Inst. (exec. com. printing-writing div., chmn. 1977-78, 82-83), Sales Assn. of Paper Industry (pres. 1973-74), New Eng. Paper Trade Assn. (past pres.), Gargoyle Alumni Assn. (past pres.), Deerfield Acad. Alumni Assn. (pres., trustee 1974-75, 81—), Alpha Delta Phi. Clubs: Ardsley Country (Irvington, N.Y.) (past gov.); Williams of N.Y. (N.Y.C.) (past gov.); Weston (Mass.) Golf; Royal Cork Yacht (Ireland); Vineyard Haven Yacht, Pine Valley Golf. Home: 63 Claypit Hill Rd Wayland MA 01778 Office: Raytheon Co 141 Spring St Lexington MA 02173 other: Amana Refrigeration Inc Amana IA 52204

SCHMIDT, HERMAN J., former oil company executive; b. Davenport, Iowa, Feb. 26, 1917; s. Herman and Lillian (Beard) S.; m. Eileen Carpenter, Dec. 20, 1967; children: Paul David, Sarah Louise. AB, U. Iowa, 1938; JD, Harvard U., 1941. Bar: N.Y. 1943. With Cravath, Swaine & Moore, 1941-44, 47-51; tax counsel Socony Mobil Oil Co. Inc. (now Mobil Corp.), N.Y.C., 1951-55, adminstrv. asst. to gen. counsel, 1955, assoc. gen. counsel, 1955-56, gen. counsel, 1956-59, exec. v.p., 1959-74, vice chmn., 1974-78, dir., 1957-78; pres. Mobil Internat. Oil Co., 1959-63; bd. dirs. H.J. Heinz Co., MAPCO Inc., Ryder System Inc., HON Industries Inc., Tri-Continental Corp. Former chmn. bd. trustees Am. Enterprise Inst.; hon. life trustee U. Iowa Found. Served to 1st lt. M.I. Corps, AUS, 1944-47. Mem. Harvard Law Rev. Assn., Phi Beta Kappa, Phi Gamma Delta. Club: Blind Brook (Ryebrook, N.Y.). Home: 15 Oakley Ln Greenwich CT 06830

SCHMIDT, JAMES CRAIG, savings bank executive; b. Peoria, Ill., Sept. 27, 1927; s. Walter Henry and Clara (Wolfenbarger) S.; m. Jerrie Louise Bond, Dec. 6, 1958; children: Julie, Sandra, Suzanne. Student, Ill. Wesleyan U., 1945, 48-50, Ph.B. in Bus. Adminstrn, 1952; postgrad., U. Ill. Coll. Law, 1950-52; J.D., DePaul U., 1953. Spl. agt. Fidelity & Deposit Co., Chgo., 1956-58; with Home Fed. Savs. & Loan Assn., San Diego, 1958-67; asst. sec. bus. and transp. State of Calif., 1967-69; vice-chmn. Gt. Am. 1st Savs. Bank, San Diego, 1969—; pres. Conf. Fed. Savs. and Loans of Calif., 1974-75; Mem. Calif. Toll Bridge Authority, 1969-74; mem. Calif. State Transp. Bd., 1972-78; past chmn. San Diego Bal. Commn. Task Force; bd. dirs. Fed. Home Loan Bank of San Francisco. Pres. San Diego Holiday Bowl Football Game, 1986; bd. dirs. Greater San Diego Sports Assn., Californians for Better Transp. Served with USN, 1945-48. Mem. Calif. Bar Assn., Ill. Bar Assn., Calif. League Savs. Insts. (chmn. 1986-87), Calif. Savs. and Loan League (chmn. 1986-87, bd. dirs.), Calif. C. of C. (bd. dirs. 1987), U.S. Savs. Instn. League (exec. com. 1983-86), Sigma Chi, Phi Delta Phi. Clubs: Rancho Las Palmas Country, San Diego Country, Univ. Office: Gt Am First Savs Bank 600 B St San Diego Fed Bldg San Diego CA 92183

SCHMIDT, JOHN LOUIS, architect, trade association executive; b. Kansas City, Mo., Oct. 31, 1931; s. John Louis and Helen Edna (Stuntz) S.; m. Sally Louise Schmidt, Aug. 15, 1953; children: John Eric, Peggy Lynn, Kathy Louise, Jo Ann. BArch, U. Ill., 1955. Registered profl. architect, Ill. Sr. architect Clark, Dailey & Dietz, Urbana, Ill., 1959-61; dir. archtl. research U.S. League Savs. Instns., Chgo., 1961-72; v.p. Environ. Systems Internat., Los Angeles, 1972-74; pres. Berkus Group, Los Angeles, 1974-76; v.p. Inst. Fin. Edn., Chgo., 1976—; lectr. various indsl. and ednl. orgns., 1970—. Co-author: Construction Principles Materials and Methods, 1966, 6th rev. edit., 1983, Construction Lending Guide, 1964; author (monthly column) Housing Report, 1964-72. Mem. Riverwoods (Ill.) Planning Commn., 1967; pres. Riverwoods Residents Assn., 1968; mem., vice chmn. Lake County (Ill.) Regional Planning Commn., 1977—. 1st lt. USAF, 1956-59. Named Top Performer House and Home mag., N.Y.C., 1964. Mem. AIA, Urban Land Inst., Sigma Pi (bd. dirs. 1977-81). Republican. Club: Tennaqua (Deerfield, Ill.) (bd. dirs. 1984-87, pres. 1988). Home: 2627 Gemini Ln Riverwoods IL 60015 Office: Inst Fin Edn 111 E Wacker Dr Chicago IL 60601

SCHMIDT, JOSEPH W., lawyer; b. Jeffersontown, Ky., July 6, 1946; s. A.W. and Olivia Anne (Hohl) S.; m. Angela Petchara Apiradee, Dec. 20, 1969; children: Narissa Ann, Suriya Christine. BA in Psychology, Bellarmine Coll., 1969; AB in Commerce, U. Md., Bangkok, 1972; JD, Columbia U., 1975. Bar: N.Y. 1976. Law clk. to presiding judge U.S. Dist. Ct. (so. dist.), N.Y., 1975-76; assoc. Breed, Abbott & Morgan, N.Y.C., 1976-83, ptnr., 1983—. Adminstrv. editor Columbia Jour. of Law and Social Problems, 1974-75. Woodrow Wilson fellow, 1968; Harlan Fiske Stone scholar, 1975. Mem. ABA, Assn. of Bar of the City of N.Y., N.Y. Bar Assn., Am. Coll. Investment Counsel. Office: Breed Abbott & Morgan Citicorp Ctr 153 E 53d St New York NY 10022

SCHMIDT, KARL FRANK, JR., engineering services company executive; b. Newark, June 5, 1947; s. Karl Frank and Ruth Elaine (Rose) S.; m. Candace McCann, Feb. 3, 1971 (div. June 1981); 1 child, Karl Frank III; m. Priscilla Woodehouse, Aug. 29, 1987; 1 stepchild, J.O. Spencer Sullivan. BA in Physics, U. Calif., Berkeley, 1969; postgrad. in bus., Lynchburg Coll., 1974-75. Project mgr. Babcock & Wilcox Co., Lynchburg, Va., 1972-75; v.p. Nuclear Energy Services, Inc., Danbury, Conn., 1975—; mem. task force on reactor pressure vessel integrity Atomic Indsl. Forum, 1982-86; mem. ad hoc com. for recommended changes to regulatory guide on ultrasonic testing of reactor vessels welds Electric Utility Industry, 1982. Pres., Newbury Crossing Condo Assn., Brookfield Ctr., Conn., 1984-88. Served with USN, 1969-72. Mem. Am. Nuclear Soc., Am. Soc. for Nondestructive Testing, Am. Inst. Plant Engrs. Republican. Lutheran. Home: 339 Florida Hill Rd Ridgefield CT 06877 Office: Nuclear Energy Svcs Inc Shelter Rock Rd Danbury CT 06810

SCHMIDT, MARTIN H., cosmetic company exective; b. 1927; married. A.B., Manhattan Coll., 1951; postgrad., Columbia U., NYU. Mgr. adminstrv. services Arthur Andersen & Co., 1965; with Squibb Corp., 1965-85, corp. v.p. mgmt. services, 1974-79, group v.p., 1979-85, sr. cons., 1989—; exec. v.p. Charles of the Ritz Group Ltd., 1975-76, pres., chief exec. officer, 1976-89, also dir.; now sr. cons. Squibb Corp. Office: Squibb Corp PO Box 4000 Princeton NJ 08543-4000 *

SCHMIDT, PETER GUSTAV, shipbuilding industry executive; b. Tumwater, Wash., Dec. 3, 1921; s. Peter G. and Clara Louise (Muench) S.; m. Elva Mary Ingalls, Dec. 3, 1945; children: Mimi Schmidt Fielding, Jill Schmidt Crowson, Janet Schmidt Mano, Hans. BSME, U. Wash., 1948; MS in Naval Architecture and Marine Engring., U. Mich., 1950. Naval architect Nat. Steel Shipbldg. Corp., San Diego, 1950-52, Carl J. Nordstrom/P. Spaulding, Seattle, 1952-53; pres. Marine Constrn. & Design Co., Seattle, 1953—, Astilleros Marco Chilena Ltd., Santiago, Chile, 1960—, Marco Peruana S.A., Lima, Peru, 1965—, Marco España, Bilbao and Canary Islands, Spain, 1970—, Marco Panama, Panama City, 1976—, Campbell Industries, San Diego, 1979—. Author papers on fishing gear and vessels. Served to lt (j.g.) USN, 1942-45, PTO. Recipient Puget Sound's Maritime Man of Yr. award Puget Sound Press Assn., 1975. Mem. Soc. Naval Architects and Marine Engrs., Wash. State Boatbuilders Assn. (pres. 1956-58), Alpha Delta Phi. Office: Marine Constrn & Design 2300 W Commodore Way Seattle WA 98199

SCHMIDT, RICHARD FREDERICK, business executive; b. N.Y.C., Mar. 11, 1930; s. George and Hermine (Hanatschek) S.; m. Faith Segui, Sept. 12, 1958; children: Julia, Carl. B.A., Princeton U., 1953; M.B.A., U. Pa., 1960. Fin. analyst Gen. Motors Corp., Detroit, 1960-61, Ford Motor Co., 1961-63; asso., mgmt. cons. McKinsey & Co., N.Y.C., 1963-69; dir. fin. planning Reuben H. Donnelly Corp., N.Y.C., 1969, v.p. fin., 1969-72, v.p. fin. and adminstrn., 1972-74; pres. Mgmt. Cons. div. Dun & Bradstreet Corp., N.Y.C., 1974-79, sr. v.p. planning and devel., 1976-81, exec. v.p. fin. and planning, 1982—, also dir. Served with AUS, 1953-54. Mem. Fin. Execs. Inst. Republican. Clubs: Sky, Bronxville Field. Home: 5 Fordal Rd Bronxville NY 10708 Office: The Dun & Bradstreet Corp 299 Park Ave New York NY 10171

SCHMIDT, RICHARD KENNETH, marketing executive; b. Milw., May 3, 1951; s. Richard H. Schmidt and Arletta L. (Oravez) Peters; m. Karen Ann Scherer, Aug. 28, 1976. BSEE with Honors, Milw. Sch. Engring., 1974; MBA, Xavier U., 1986. Trainee sales div. Allen-Bradley Co., Milw., 1974-76; sales engr. Allen-Bradley Co., Stratford, Conn., 1976-78; br. mgr. Allen-Bradley Co., Scottsdale, Ariz., 1978-83; area mgr. Allen-Bradley Co., Cin., 1983-86; mgr. comml. mktg. Allen-Bradley Co., Ann Arbor, Mich., 1986-88; nat. sales mgr. Allen-Bradley Co., Milw., 1989—; pres. Milw. Air, Inc., 1973-76. Mem. MBA exec. mktg. com. Xavier U., 1986-87. Mem. Soc. Mfg. Engrs. (speaker 1987), Local Area Network Dealers Assn. (corp. com.), Milw. Sch. Engring. Alumni Assn. (treas. Phoenix 1980-83). Republican. Office: Allen-Bradley Co 1201 S 2d St Milwaukee WI 53204

SCHMIDT, ROBERT ADOLPH, accountant; b. Chgo., Dec. 26, 1947; s. Edward Fred and Josephine (Roggen) S.; m. Margaret Ann Sheridan, July 27, 1968; children: Catherine Anne, Deborah Lynn. BA in Econs., DePauw U., 1969; MBA in Acctg., Northwestern U., 1972. Mem. audit staff Arthur Young & Co., Chgo., 1972-76; controller FAI, Inc., Northfield, Ill., 1976-78; fin. v.p. C&L, Inc., Bensenville, Ill., 1978—. With USAR, 1969-75. Presbyterian. Home: 4139 Yorkshire Ln Northbrook IL 60062 Office: C&L Inc 703 Foster Bensenville IL 60106

SCHMIDT, WENDY SUE, financial executive; b. Neenah, Wis., May 6, 1959; d. Allan Gilbert and Marlene Jean (Beimborn) Wohlers; m. Charles Donald Schmidt, Oct. 17, 1981. Grad., pvt. schs. Cert. profl. sec. Cert. clk. AAL/Life Issue Services, Appleton, Wis., 1977-79; cert. verifier AAL/Life Issure Services, Appleton, Wis., 1979; cor. AAL/Premium Services, Appleton, 1979-81; investment analysis clk./mortgages and real estate AAL/Investment Div., Appleton, 1981-87; exec. asst. to pres. AAL Distbrs. Inc., AAL Advisors Inc., Appleton, 1987—. Vol. ICT (vol. orgn.) of AAL, Appleton, 1980—. Mem. Profl. Secs. Internat. (pres. 1988—), Internat. Assn., Fin. Planning. Office: AAL Mut Fund Cos 222 W College Ave Appleton WI 54919-0007

SCHMIED, WILLIAM F., aerospace electronics company executive; b. 1928; married. BSEE, Purdue U., 1951, DEng (hon.), 1987. Project dir. N.Am. Rockwell, 1953-56; v.p., dir. engring. Litton Industries, Inc., 1959-69;

with The Singer Co., Stamford, Conn., 1969—, pres. Kearfott div., 1969-71, group v.p. aerospace and marine systems, 1971-74, exec. v.p., 1974-78, exec. v.p. products and service govt. group, 1978-80, pres., 1980-88, chief operating officer, mem. fin. com., 1980-88, co-chmn., co-chief exec. officer, 1988, also bd. dirs. Served with USAF, 1952-53. Office: Singer Co 110 Summit Ave PO Box 426 Montvale NJ 07645 *

SCHMIEDER, CARL, jeweler; b. Phoenix, Apr. 27, 1938; s. Otto and Ruby Mable (Harkey) S.; m. Carole Ann Roberts, June 13, 1959; children: Gail, Susan, Nancy, Amy. Student Bradley Horological Sch., Peoria, Ill., 1959-61; B.A., Pomona Coll., 1961; Owner timepiece repair service, Peoria, 1959-61; clock repairman Otto Schmieder & Son, Phoenix, 1961-65, v.p., 1965-70, pres., 1970—, chief exec. officer, 1970—. Mem. subcom. Leap Commn., 1966; area rep. Pomona Coll., 1972-76. Cert. jeweler; cert. gemologist, gemologist appraiser; recipient Design award Diamonds Internat., 1965, Cultured Pearl Design award, 1967, 68, Diamonds for Christmas award, 1970; winner Am. Diamond Jewelry Competition, 1973; bd. dirs. Lincoln Hosp., 1983—, Ariz. Mus., 1984-88; delegate White House Conf. on Small Bus., 1986; chmn. Gov.'s Conf. on Small Bus., 1988—; col. Confederate Air Force. Mem. Am. Gem. Soc. (dir. 1973-86, nat. chmn. nomenclature com. 1975-77, chmn. membership com. 1977-81, officer 1981-86), Ariz. Jewelers Assn. (Man of Yr. 1974), Jewelers Security Alliance (dir. 1974-78), Jewelers Vigilance Com. (dir. 1981-87), Jewelry Industry Council (dir. 1982-88), 24 Karat Club So. Calif., Exptl. Aircraft Assn., Deer Valley (Ariz.) Airport Tenants Assn. (dir. 1980—, pres. 1983—), Ariz. C. of C. (bd. dirs. 1985—), Small Bus. Council (bd. dirs. 1985—, chmn. 1988, del. to White House Conf., 1986). Republican. Methodist. Lodges: Kiwanis (pres. Valley of the Sun chpt. 1975-76), Friends of Iberia. Home: 537 W Kaler St Phoenix AZ 85021 Office: Park Central Phoenix AZ 85013

SCHMIEDER, FRANK JOSEPH, banker, business executive; b. Granite City, Ill., June 26, 1941; s. Frank John and Ione Mina (Scheller) S.; m. Anne Loraine Murray, Aug. 26, 1961; children—Kevin Frank, Craig Michael. BS (Nat. Merit scholar, State Assembly scholar), U. Ill., 1963, MA, 1964; postgrad. (U. Ill. grad. research fellow), Mass. Inst. Tech., 1966, Stanford U., 1977. Asst. to v.p. indsl. relations Cummins Engine Co., Columbus, Ind., 1964-66, mgr. corp. devel. systems, 1966-68; dir. corp. planning Samsonite Co., Denver, 1969-71, v.p. finance, 1971-73; v.p., treas. Fairchild Camera & Instrument Corp., Mountain View, Calif., 1973-76; v.p. adminstrn. Peterson, Howell & Heather Inc., Hunt Valley, Md., 1976-79, sr. v.p., chief fin. officer, 1979-81, exec. v.p., chief fin. officer, 1981-87; chief operating officer Mason Best Mcht. Bank, Dallas, 1987—; pres., dir. Vail Restaurant & Food Services, 1973—; Spl. cons. on econs. and efficiency to Gov. Colo., 1968; bd. dirs. EIL Instruments, 1984—, Aviation Office of Am., Plexus Fin. Services, Aviation Internat. Airline. Author: Application of Game Theory to Collective Bargaining, 1965. Bd. dirs. Retarded Children Unltd., 1969-71; dir. Council Econ. Edn. in Md., 1983—. Mem. Nat. Assn. Accountants (award of merit 1971), Am. Econ. Assn., Inst. Mgmt. Sci. Republican. Roman Catholic. Home: 3702 Harvard Ave Dallas TX 75205 Office: PHH Group Inc 11333 McCormick Rd Hunt Valley MD 21031

SCHMIEGE, ROBERT W., railroad executive; b. Madison, Wis., May 24, 1941; married. AB, U. Notre Dame, 1963, JD, 1966. Atty. Nat. Ry. Labor Conf., Chgo., 1966-68, Chgo. & N. Western Transp. Co., Chgo., 1968-74, So. Pacific Transp. Co., L.A., 1974-75; ptnr. Albert & Schmiege, L.A., 1975-76; asst. v.p. labor rels. Chgo. & N. Western Transp. Co., Chgo., 1976-79, v.p. labor rels., 1979-84, sr. v.p. adminstrn., 1984-88, chmn., pres., chief exec. officer, 1988—; chmn., pres., chief exec. officer CNW Corp. and Chgo. & N. Western Transp. Co., Chgo., 1988—, also bd. dirs. Office: CNW Corp 1 Northwestern Ctr Chicago IL 60606 *

SCHMITT, CARVETH JOSEPH RODNEY, office supplies manufacturing official; b. Manitowoc, Wis., Sept. 10, 1934; s. Clarence C. and Thelma J. (White) S.; m. Carolyn Sue Jarrett, May 14, 1965. diploma in bus. adminstrn. and acctg. Skadron Coll. Bus., 1959; A.A. in Bus. Mgmt., San Bernardino Valley Coll., 1962; B.S. in Bus. Adminstrn., U. Riverside-Calif., 1970; M.A. in Edn.-Manpower Adminstrn., U. Redlands, 1975; B.S. in Liberal Studies, SUNY-Albany, 1977; B.A. in Social Sci., Edison State Coll., Trenton, 1978; cert. in Human Services, U. Calif. Extension, Riverside, 1977, postgrad., 1977-80. Registered rep. Ernest F. Boruski, Jr., N.Y.C., 1956-61; acct. Barnum & Flagg Co., San Bernardino, Calif., 1959-70; registered rep., ins. agt. (part-time) Inland Am. Securities, Inc., San Bernardino, 1966-70; registered rep. (part-time) Parker-Jackson & Co., San Bernardino, 1970-73, LeBarron Securities, Inc., 1973-74. credit mgr. Stationers Corp., San Bernardino, 1970-77, office mgr., credit mgr., 1977-83; internal auditor Stockwell & Binney Office Products Ctrs., San Bernardino, 1983-85, corp. credit mgr., 1985—. Served with USAF, 1954-58. cert. tchr., community coll. counselor and personnel worker, Calif. Mem. Nat. Geog. Soc., Nat. Rifle Assn. (life), Nevada Mining Assn., Colo. Mining Assn., N.W. Mining Assn., Modern Woodmen Am., Am. Philatelic Soc., Nat. Travel Club, Edison State Coll. Alumni Assn., U. Redlands Fellows, Friends of Library Assn. U. Redlands, Valley Prospectors (life), SUNY Regents Alumni Assn., U. Redlands Alumni Assn., Am. Legion, Am. Assn. Ret. Persons, Gold Prospectors Assn. Am. (life mem.). Republican. Rosicrucian. Clubs: Fontana Tour, Hiking, Badminton, Bowling, Arrowhead Stamp, M & M Tour, Rosicrucian (San Jose). Lodge: Masons. Home: 538 N Pampas Ave Rialto CA 92376 Office: 420 South E St PO Box 5129 San Bernardino CA 92412

SCHMITT, JOHN PATRICK, consulting company executive; b. Spartanburg, S.C., July 11, 1944; s. Herbert S. and Regina T. (King) S.; m. Lois Merkel, Aug. 5, 1967; children: Stacey Regina, John Garrett. BS in Psychology, St. Louis U., 1966; MBA in Mgmt., Fla. State U., 1971; PhD in Bus., U. Fla., 1978. Chief fin. officer Wuesthoff Meml. Hosp., Rockledge, Fla., 1970-74; dir. research and devel. Physicians Trust Fund, Miami, Fla., 1976-78; asst. prof. U. Fla., Gainesville, 1979-82; pres. J.P. Schmitt & Assocs., Gainesville, Fla., 1977-83, MEDIRISK, Inc., Atlanta, 1983—; developer, mng. agt. ALPHA Health Network, Pitts., 1983-86. Contbr. articles to health care jours. Tech. advisor Fla. Dept. Ins., Tallahassee, Fla., 1981-84. Capt. USAF, 1966-70. Fellow Am. Soc. Hosp. Risk Mgmt.; mem. Nat. Assn. Health Underwriters (registerd mem.), Healthcare Fin. Mgmt. Assn. (bd. dirs. 1974-76, Follmer award 1982, jour. award for Article of Yr. 1984). Republican. Lodge: Kiwanis (bd. dirs. Rockledge. Fla. club 1972-74). Home: 1240 Dunwoody Knoll Atlanta GA 30338 Office: MEDIRISK Inc 5655 Spalding Dr Norcross GA 30092

SCHMITT, LOUIS CHARLES, insurance company executive; b. Lafayette, Ind., Jan. 12, 1946; s. Stanley Joseph and Dolores Rose (Moser) S.; m. Virginia Louise Weger, Feb. 2, 1969; children: Kimberly Ann, Tamara Lynn, Angela Marie. BBA, U. Notre Dame, 1968. CPA, Ind. Acct., audit mgr. Ernst & Whinney, Indpls., 1968-82; sr. v.p., chief fin. officer United Presdl. Life Ins. Co., Kokomo, Ind., 1982—. Treas. Woodlands Homeowners Assn., Carmel, Ind., 1974-80; chmn. finance com. St. Elizabeth Seton Ch., Carmel, 1981—. With USAR, 1968-74. Mem. Am. Inst. CPAs, Ind. CPA Soc., Nat. Assn. Corp. Treasurers, Ins. Accts. and Systems Assocs. Republican. Roman Catholic. Home: 10919 Braewick Dr Carmel IN 46032 Office: United Presdl Life Ins Co 217 Southway Blvd E Kokomo IN 46902

SCHMITT, PAUL STEVEN, business developer; b. New Haven, Apr. 7, 1956; s. William Joseph Schmitt and Alyce Jean (Schultz) Gendall. BA in Biol. Sci., Cornell U., 1978. Commd. ensign USN, 1978, advanced through grades to lt., 1982, resigned, 1986; dir. bus. devel. northeast region Am. Systems Corp., Middletown, R.I., 1987—. Active R.I. Spl. Olympics, 1987, Newport County Cath. Youth Orgn., 1988. Lt. comdr. USNR, 1987—. Mem. Am. Mgmt. Assn., U.S. Naval Inst., Armed Forces Communication & Electronics Assn. (R.I. chpt. bd. dirs., facilities chmn.), Common Fence Paint Improvement Assn. (com. mem.), R.I. Marksmen, Gov.'s Footguard, Cornell U. Alumni Assn. (R.I. chpt. pres.), Naval Reserve Assn. (life mem.), Nat. Rifle Assn. (life mem.). Democrat. Roman Catholic. Office: Am Systems Corp 1274 W Main Rd Middletown RI 02840

SCHMITT, PETER ALLAN, physical therapist, corporate consultant; b. Buffalo, July 29, 1947; s. Norman Peter and Elsie (Iverson) S.; m. Rosalind Giulietti, Oct. 7, 1978; children: Sllegra, Logan. BA in English, U. Rochester, 1970; BS in Phys. Therapy, SUNY, Buffalo, 1974; MS in Rehab. Systems Mgmt., DePaul U., 1987. Lic. phys. therapist. Clin. intern Morristown (N.J.) Meml. Hosp., 1973, Detroit Rehab. Inst., 1974; staff phys. therapist Schwab Rehab. Ctr., Chgo., 1974-75, asst. dir. phys. therapy, 1976-78; dir. phys. therapy Oak Forest (Ill.) Hosp. of Cook County, 1979-85; dir. rehab. services West Suburban Hosp. Med. Ctr., Oak Park, Ill., 1985-88; corp. cons. on health and injury risk mgmt. Preventive Therapeutics, Inc., Oak Park, Ill., 1986—; lectr. seminars on stress mgmt., indsl. injury prevention, 1985—. Inventor ambulation analysis grid. Mem. curriculum com., program n phys. therapy Northwestern U. Med. Sch. Chgo., 1985—; supporter Greenpeace, 1983—; sponsor, supporter Found. for Phys. Therapy Research, 1986—; mem. Citizens Utility Bd., Chgo., 1985—. Recipient Speaker's award Kiwanis of Tinley Park, Ill., 1983, Chgo. Lung Assn., 1984-85. Mem. Am. Phys. Therapy Assn. (nat. del. 1981), Ill. Phys. Therapy Assn. (chmn. nominations com. 1981-82, 85, treas. East dist. 1981-83, state del. 1988), Chicagoland Phys. Therapy Dirs. Forum (treas. 1981-85), Peoples Med. Soc. Democrat. Office: Preventive Therapeutics Inc 610 Clinton Ave Oak Park IL 60304

SCHMITT, PETER JOSEPH, insurance company executive; b. Medina, N.Y., Feb. 13, 1949; s. William Thomas Sr. and Genevieve Margaret (Gaughan) S.; m. Soon Wha Lee, May 25, 1974; children: Claire, Thomas. BA magna cum laude in Asian Studies, SUNY Coll. at Brockport, 1975; MBA in Fin., SUNY, Albany, 1977. Asst. v.p. mcpl. research dept. First Boston Corp., N.Y.C., 1977-80, asst. v.p. pub. fin. research dept., 1980-81; instl. salesman Prescott, Ball & Turben, Inc., N.Y.C., 1981-82, sr. v.p., dir. fixed income research, 1982-85; exec. v.p., dir. risk mgmt. Fin. Guaranty Ins. Co., N.Y.C., 1985-89, chief oper. officer, 1989—; bd. trustees St. Andrew Kim Fed. Credit Union, Orange, N.Y., 1984-87. Treas. St. Cassian Sch. Found., Upper Montclair, N.J., 1987—. 2d-class petty officer USN, 1967-71. Recipient Korean-Lang. Book award Def. Lang. Inst., 1968. Mem. Mcpl. Bond Club N.Y. Office: Fin Guaranty Ins Co 175 Water St New York NY 10038-4972

SCHMITT, RALPH GEORGE, manufacturing company executive; b. Tarrytown, N.Y., Aug. 8, 1944; s. Alfons George and Otillie Lucie (Mehler) S.; B.S., Mass. Inst. Tech., 1966, M.S., 1967; M.S., U. Calif., 1970; m. Sandra Lee Watt, Feb. 5, 1965; children—Ralph Scott, Carrie Lee, Kurt Ryan. Engr., McDonnell Douglas, Huntington Beach, Calif., 1967-70, Rockwell Internat., Downey, Calif., 1970-72; pres., chmn. bd. TBG Industries, Los Angeles, 1972-74; gen. mgr. Columbia Yacht div. Whittaker Corp., Chesapeake, Va., 1975-76; v.p. ops., dir. R & G Sloane Mfg. Co., Los Angeles, 1976-83; dir. mfg.-plastics Sweetheart Products Group, Ft. Howard Paper Co., Wilmington, Mass., 1983-86; gen. mgr. PHI, City of Industry, Calif., 1986—; v.p. Tulip Corp., City of Industry, 1986—. Mem. MIT Ednl. Council., Am. Mgmt. Assn., Tau Beta Pi, Sigma Xi, Sigma Gamma Tau, Sigma Alpha Epsilon. Republican. Clubs: MIT of So. Calif. (pres.). Home: 1709 Calle Catalina San Dimas CA 91773 Office: PHI 14955 E Salt Lake Ave Industry CA 91746

SCHMITT, ROLAND WALTER, university president; b. Seguin, Tex., July 24, 1923; s. Walter L. and Myrtle F. (Caldwell) S.; m. Claire Freeman Kunz, Sept. 19, 1957; children: Lorenz Allen, Brian Walter, Alice Elizabeth, Henry Caldwell. B.A. in Math, U. Tex., 1947, B.S. in Physics, 1947, M.A. in Physics, 1948; Ph.D., Rice U., 1951; D.Sc. (hon.), Worcester Poly. Inst., 1985, U. Pa., 1985; D.C.L. (hon.), Union Coll., 1985; DL (hon.), Lehigh U., 1986; D.Sc. (hon.), U. S.C., 1988. With Gen. Electric Co., 1951-88; research and devel. mgr. phys. sci. and engring. Gen. Electric Corp. Research and Devel. Gen. Electric Co., Schenectady, 1967-74; research and devel. mgr. energy sci. and engring. Gen. Electric Corp. Research and Devel. Gen. Electric Co., 1974-78, v.p. corp. research and devel. Gen. Electric Corp. Research and Devel., 1978-82, sr. v.p. corp. research and devel. Gen. Electric Corp. Research and Devel., 1982-86, sr. v.p. sci. and tech., 1986-88, ret., 1988; pres. Rensselaer Poly. Inst., Troy, N.Y., 1988—; past pres. Indsl. Research Inst.; mem. energy research adv. bd. Dept. Energy, 1977-83; chmn. CORETECH; mem. Nat. Research Council's. Com. on Japan, NASA's Comml. Devel. Ind. Adv. Group; exec. com. Council on Competitiveness. Trustee Northeast Savs. Bank., 1978-84, bd. advisors Union Coll.; vice chmn. bd. dirs., chmn. investment rev. com. N.Y. State Sci. and Tech. Found., 1978-84; bd. govs. Albany Med. Center Hosp., 1979-82, 1988—; trustee Union Coll., Schenectady, 1981-84, Argonne Univs. Assn., 1979-82; bd. trustees RPI, 1982-88; bd. dirs. Sunnyview Hosp. and Rehab. Center, 1978-86; dir. Gen. Signal Corp., 1987—; mem., bd. dirs. Council on Superconductivity for Am. Competitiveness, 1987—; mem. exec. com. N.Y. State Ctr. for Hazardous Waste Mgmt., 1988-89. Served with USAAF, 1943-46. Recipient award for disting. contbns. Stony Brook Found., 1985, Disting. Alumnus award Rice U., 1985. Fellow Am. Phys. Soc., Am. Acad. Arts and Scis., IEEE, AAAS; mem. Am. Inst. Physics (chmn. com. on corp. assocs., mem. governing bd. 1979-83), Nat. Acad. Engring. (council), Nat. Sci. Bd. (past chmn.), Dirs. Indsl. Rsch. Club: Cosmos. Office: Rensselaer Poly Inst Office of Pres Troy NY 12180-3590

SCHMITT, WOLFGANG RUDOLPH, consumer products executive; b. Koblenz, Fed. Republic Germany, Mar. 12, 1944; s. Josef H. and M.H. (Baldus) S.; m. Toni A. Yoder, June 30, 1974; children: Christopher, Corey, Clayton. BA, Otterbein Coll., 1966; AMP, Harvard U. Bus. Sch., 1986. With Rubbermaid Inc., Wooster, Ohio, 1966—, pres., gen. mgr., 1984—; exec. v.p., bd. dirs. Rubbermaid Inc., 1987—. Pres. bd. dirs. Wooster United Way, 1987; Trustee Ch. of the Saviour. Mem. Nat. Housewares Mfrs. Assn. (bd. dirs. 1986—). Republican. Office: Rubbermaid Inc Home Products Div 1147 Akron Rd Wooster OH 44691

SCHMITZ, EDWARD HENRY, electrical equipment manufacturing executive; b. Glenbeulah, Wis., June 21, 1929; s. John Charles and Angeline Ann (Gundrum) S.; m. Janyth Lanier, Dec. 26, 1959; stepchildren: Janyth Lynn, Leslee; children: Robert, Ellen. BS in Bus. Adminstrn., Bryant Coll., 1955. Cert. purchasing mgr. Mgr. purchasing and traffic Hooker Glass Co., Chgo., 1961-65; materials mgr. API Industries, Chgo., 1965-71; purchasing mgr. G&W Electric Co., Blue Island, Ill., 1971—; cons. engr. A. Proudfoot, Chgo., 1957-60. Served with U.S. Army, 1951-53. Mem. Purchasing Mgmt. Assn. (bd. dirs. Chgo. chpt. 1971-73, 83-85), Nat. Assn. Purchasing Mgmt. (dist. chmn. 1980—), Am. Prodn. and Inventory Control Soc. Home: 112 Elizabeth Ln Downers Grove IL 60516 Office: G&W Electric Co 3500 W 127th St Blue Island IL 60406

SCHMITZ, EUGENE GERARD, engineer; b. Brackenridge, Pa., Sept. 17, 1929; s. Wienand Gerard and Florence Marie (Grimm) S.; student Phoenix Coll., 1946-47, Ariz. State U., 1959-61; m. Anna May Lee, May 3, 1952; children—Joyce Marie, Michael Paul, Carol Ann, John David, Eugene Jr. Dist. mgr. Field Enterprise Ednl. Corp., Phoenix, 1955-59; designer, engr. Motorola Inc., Scottsdale, Ariz., 1961-67; project engr. space and reentry systems div. Philco-Ford Co., Palo Alto, Calif., 1967-70; engring. program adminstr. Memorex Equipment Co., Santa Clara, Calif., 1970-71; plant mgr. Tijuana (Mex.) ops. Philco-Ford, 1971-72; engring. cons. FMC Corp., San Jose, Calif., 1972-75; staff cons. engr. Stetter Assos., Inc., Palo Alto, 1975-80, Schmitz Engring. Assocs., 1980-82, 1986—; project engr. Ordnance div. FMC Corp., 1982-86; instr. electronic design Middlton Inst., Phoenix, 1965-66. Served with U.S. Army, 1948-55. Registered profl. engr., Calif. Mem. Soc. Mfg. Engrs. (cert.), Nat. Soc. Profl. Engrs., Profl. Engrs. in Pvt. Practice, Am. Inst. Indsl. Engrs. Republican. Home and Office: 302 Shuksan Way PO Box 401 Everson WA 92247 Office: 3061 Vesuvius Ln San Jose CA 95132

SCHMITZ, RALPH KARL, life insurance company executive; b. Frankfurt am Main, Germany, Jan. 29, 1932; came to U.S., 1954; s. Peter A. and Edith (Widder) S.; m. Marianne A. Panzer, Nov. 29, 1953; children: Wilfried, Keith, Edith, Peter. Student, Tex. Christian U., 1964-66. V.p. mktg. World Service Life Ins. Co., Ft. Worth, 1954-74; pres. Schmitz and Co., Ft. Worth, 1974-77, IMC, Inc., Ft. Worth, 1977-84; v.p. fed. mktg. Nat. Western Life Ins. Co., Austin, Tex., 1984—. Author software. Roman Catholic. Lodge: Rotary. Office: Nat Western Life Ins Co 850 E Anderson Ln Austin TX 78752-1602

SCHMOE, WILFRED PICKERING, chemical, oil and gas company executive; b. Seattle, June 18, 1927; s. Floyd Wilfred and Ruth (Pickering) S.; m. Lillian Agnes Standing, Aug. 26, 1947; children: Lee Alan, Lynne Marie Higerd, Lori Ann Schmoe Field. Student, Pasadena City Coll., 1947-48, U. Wash., 1948-50; BS in Mech. Engring., Okla. State U., 1953. With Conoco, Wyo., Colo., 1953-66; mgr. personnel Conoco, Houston, 1966-70, v.p. internat. prodn., 1980-81; mgr. internat. prodn. Stamford, Conn., 1970-75; vice-chmn. Conoco, Stamford, Conn., 1981-84; exec. v.p. Conoco North Sea, London, 1975-80, E.I. DuPont, Wilmington, Del., 1984—; chmn., mng. dir. Conoco U.K. Ltd., London, 1980-81; bd. dirs. E.I. DuPont de Nemours & Co., Bank of Del.; pres. U.K. Offshore Operators Assn., London, 1977-78. Trustee Med. Ctr. Del., 1986—. Mem. AIME, Am. Petroleum Inst. Republican. Clubs: Wilmington Country, Wilmington; Teton Pines (Jackson, Wyo.). Home: PO Box 906 Mendenhall PA 19357 Office: E I Du Pont de Nemours & Co 1007 Market St Wilmington DE 19898

SCHMOKE, L(EROY) JOSEPH, III, financial consulting company executive; b. Detroit, July 15, 1944; s. LeRoy Joseph and Leona Rita (Barkhaus) S.; m. Diana Lynn Dragon, July 12, 1969. BA in Fin., U. Detroit, 1966; postgrad., Wayne State U., 1971-73. Account exec. First Am. Corp., Southfield, Mich., 1967-69; mgr. corp. svcs. Merrill Lynch Pierce Fenner & Smith, Southfield, 1969-74; pres. Versatile Van Works of Detroit, Inc., Livonia, Mich., 1974-77, Am. Radio Distbrs., Dearborn Heights, Mich., 1976-80, Univ. Cons., Inc., Boca Raton, Fla., 1980—; pres. Fla. Restaurant Investment Corp., Boca Raton, 1983—, also bd. dirs.; pres. Mariner Capital, 1984; chmn., treas. Schmoke & McBath Enterprises, Garden City, Mich., 1973-76; exec. v.p. Servico Bus. Systems, Ft. Lauderdale, Fla., 1983; bd. dirs. Univ. Cons., Inc., Secom Gen. Corp., Cherry Hill, N.C. Author: Vital Business Secrets for New and Growing Companies, 1988. With USMCR, 1965-71. Mem. Assn. Corp. Growth, Seagate Club (Delray Beach). Republican. Home: 1005 Russell Dr #1 Highland Beach FL 33487 Office: Univ Cons Inc 621 NW 53d St Ste 325 Boca Raton FL 33487

SCHMULTS, EDWARD CHARLES, lawyer, corporate executive; b. Paterson, N.J., Feb. 6, 1931; s. Edward M. and Mildred (Moore) S.; m. Diane E. Beers, Apr. 23, 1960; children: Alison C., Edward M., Robert C. B.S., Yale U., 1953; J.D., Harvard U., 1958. Bar: N.Y. State 1959, D.C. 1974. Assoc. White & Case, N.Y.C., 1958-65; ptnr. White & Case, 1965-73, 77-81; gen. counsel Treasury Dept., Washington, 1973-74; undersec. Treasury Dept., 1974-75; dep. counsel to Pres. U.S., 1975-76; dep. atty. gen. of U.S., Dept. Justice, Washington, 1981-84; sr. v.p. external rels., gen. counsel GTE Corp., Stamford, Conn., 1984—, also bd. dirs.; lectr. securities laws. Bd. dirs. Germany Fund, USA-Republic of China Econ. Council; trustee Refugee Policy Group, Trinity Sch., N.Y.C., 1977-81. Served with USMCR, 1953-55. Mem. Am., N.Y. State, Fed. bar assns., Assn. Bar City N.Y., Adminstrv. Conf. U.S. (council 1977-84). Clubs: Sakonnet Golf (Little Compton, R.I.); Metropolitan (Washington). Office: GTE Corp One Stamford Forum Stamford CT 06904

SCHMUTZ, JOHN FRANCIS, lawyer; b. Oneida, N.Y., July 24, 1947; s. William L. and Rosemary S.; m. H. Marie Roney, June 7, 1969; children—Gretchen, Jonathan, Nathan. B.A. cum laude, Canisius Coll., 1969; J.D. cum laude, Notre Dame U., 1972; LL.M., George Washington U., 1975. Bar: Ind. 1972, U.S. Ct. Mil. Appeals 1972, U.S. Tax Ct. 1973, D.C. 1975, U.S. Supreme Ct. 1975. Legislation and major projects officer Office Judge Adv. Gen., 1972-74; appellate atty. U.S. Army Legal Services Agy., 1974-75; assoc. Ice, Miller, Donadio & Ryan, Indpls., 1976-77; staff atty. Burger Chef Systems, Inc., Indpls., 1977-78, sr. atty., 1979, asst. chief legal counsel, 1978-70, chief legal counsel, 1980, v.p., gen. counsel, sec., 1981—; v.p. legal Hardee's Food Systems, Inc., 1983—; dir., v.p. Bursan Credit Union; dir. Food Service and Lodging Inst.; dir., v.p. Blahs, Inc., RIX Systems, Inc., Burger Chef Distributive Corp.; v.p. Hardee's Food Systems, Inc. Mem. ABA, Fed. Bar Assn., Ind. Bar Assn., D.C. Bar Assn., Indpls. Bar Assn., Am. Assn. Corp. Counsel, Nat. Restaurant Assn. Republican. Roman Catholic. Lodge: K.C. Exec. editor Notre Dame Law Rev., 1971-72. Home: 305 Old Coach Rd Rocky Mount NC 27801 Office: 1233 N Church St Rocky Mount NC 27801

SCHNAPP, ROGER HERBERT, lawyer; b. N.Y.C., Mar. 17, 1946; s. Michael Jay and Beatrice Joan (Becker) S.; m. Candice Jacqueline Larson, Sept. 15, 1979. BS, Cornell U., 1966; JD, Harvard U., 1969; grad. Pub. Utility Mgmt. Program, U. Mich., 1978. Bar: N.Y. 1970, Calif. 1982, U.S. Dist. Ct. (so. dist.) N.Y. 1975, U.S. Dist. Ct. (no. dist.) Calif. 1980, U.S. Dist. Ct. (cen. dist.) Calif. 1982, U.S. Dist. Ct. (ea. dist.) Calif. 1984), U.S. Ct. Appeals (2d cir.) 1970, U.S. Ct. Appeals (4th and 6th cirs.) 1976, U.S. Ct. Appeals (7th cir.) 1977, U.S. Ct. Appeals (8th cir.) 1980, U.S. Supreme Ct. 1974. Atty. CAB, Washington, 1969-70; labor atty. Western Electric Co., N.Y.C., 1970-71; mgr. employee relations Am. Airlines, N.Y.C., 1971-74; labor counsel Am. Electric Power Service Corp., N.Y.C., 1974-78, sr. labor counsel, 1978-80; indsl. relations counsel Trans World Airlines, N.Y.C., 1980-81; sr. assoc. Parker, Milliken, Clark & O'Hara, Los Angeles, 1981-82; ptnr. Rutan & Tucker, Costa Mesa, Calif., 1983-84; ptnr. Memel, Jacobs, Pierno, Gersh & Ellsworth, Newport Beach, Calif., 1985-86; ptnr. Memel, Jacobs & Ellsworth, Newport Beach, 1986-87; sole practice, Newport Beach, 1987—; commentator labor rels. Fin. News Network; lectr. Calif. Western Law Sch., Calif. State U.-Fullerton, Calif. State Conf. Small Bus.; lectr. collective bargaining Pace U., N.Y.C. N.E. regional coordinator Pressler for Pres., 1979-80. Mem. ABA (R.R. and airline labor law com., internat. labor law com.), Calif. Bar Assn., Am. Arbitration Assn. (adv. com. Orange County area, cons. collective bargaining com.), Conf. R.R. and Airline Labor Lawyers, Newport Harbor Area C. of C. Republican. Jewish. Clubs: Balboa Bay, Lincoln of Orange County, Center. Lodge: Masons. Author: Arbitration Issues for the 1980s, 1981; A Look at Three Companies, 1982; editor-in-chief Industrial and Labor Relations Forum, 1964-66; contbr. articles to profl. publs. Office: PO Box 9049 Newport Beach CA 92658

SCHNECKENBURGER, KAREN LYNNE, finance executive; b. Peoria, Ill., Sept. 12, 1949; d. Walter Carl and Judith Jane (Grimshaw) S. BS in Acctg., Bradley U., 1971. CPA, Ill. Auditor Ernst & Whinney, Chgo., 1971-76; controller C.A. Roberts Co., Franklin Park, Ill., 1976-78; mgr. fin. and investments Gould Inc., Rolling Meadows, Ill., 1978-86; dir. fin. Fairchild Industries, Inc., Chantilly, Va., 1986—. adviser Jr. Achievement, Chgo., 1979-83. Mem. Am. Inst. CPA's, Ill. CPA Soc., Chgo. Fin. Exchange. Home: 2249 Cedar Cove Ct Reston VA 22091-4108 Office: Fairchild Industries Inc 300 Service Rd Chantilly VA 22021-9998

SCHNEIDER, ARNOLD, accounting educator; b. N.Y.C., June 30, 1953; s. Henry and Irene (Bleier) S.; m. Marcy Lynn Newman, May 18, 1980; children: Julie, Evan. BS, Case Western Res. U., 1975; MA, Ohio State U., 1980, PhD, 1982. CPA, Md. Auditor GAO, Washington, 1975-76; grad. teaching assoc. Ohio State U., Columbus, 1976-81; asst. prof. Ga. Inst. Tech., Atlanta, 1982-87, assoc. prof., 1987—; cons. spl. instr. in field. Mem. editorial bd. Issues in Acctg. Edn., 1988—; contbr. articles to profl. jours. Rec. sec. Congregation Beth Jacob, Atlanta, 1988—, treas., 1986-87; mem. Worldwide Jewish Affairs Com. Atlanta Jewish Fedn., 1984-88; advisor Bnai Brith Youth Orgn., Atlanta, 1983-84. Recipient Young Investigator Ga. Inst. Tech., 1986, Mem. of Yr. Congregation Beth Jacob, 1987. Mem. Am. Acctg. Assn., Atlanta Jewish Community Ctr. Home: 851 Vistavia Circle Decatur GA 30033 Office: Ga Inst Tech Coll Mgmt Atlanta GA 30332

SCHNEIDER, CHARLES I., newspaper executive; b. Chgo., Apr. 6, 1923; s. Samuel Hiram and Eva (Smith) S.; m. Barbara Anne Krause, Oct. 27, 1963; children: Susan, Charles I. Jr., Kim, Karen, Traci. BS, Northwestern U., 1944. Indsl. engr., sales mgr., v.p. mktg. Curtis-Electro Lighting Corp., Chgo., 1945-54, pres., 1954-62; pres. Jefferson Electronics, Inc., Santa Barbara, Calif., 1962-64; pres. 3 sub., v.p., asst. to pres. Am. Bldg. Maintenance Industries, Los Angeles, 1964-66; group v.p. Times Mirror Co., Los Angeles, 1966-88; bd. dirs. Jeppesen Sanderson, Inc., Denver, Graphic Controls Corp., Buffalo, Regional Airports Improvement Corp., CPG Internat., Irvine, Calif. Bd. regents Northwestern U., Evanston, Ill.; trustee, past pres. Reiss-Davis Child Study Center, Los Angeles; bd. dirs. Music Center Operating Co. of Los Angeles County, chmn.; Constl. Rights Found.; bd. govs., past pres. Performing Arts Council; bd. visitors UCLA Grad. Sch. Edn.; trustee the Menninger Found. Served with AUS, 1942-44. Mem. Chief Execs. Orgn. (past pres., bd. dirs.). Clubs: Standard (Chgo.); Beverly Hills Tennis (Calif.); Big. Ten of So. Calif. Home: 522 N Beverly Dr Beverly Hills CA 90210 Office: Times Mirror Times Mirror Sq Los Angeles CA 90053

SCHNEIDER, DENNIS EUGENE, purchasing executive; b. Bellevue, Ohio, Dec. 27, 1957; s. Vernon Edwin and Marquerite Mary (Best) S.; m. Sandra Lynn Seavolt, June 26, 1982. BS, Bowling Green State U., 1981. Buyer Teledyne Continental Aviation and Engring. Co., Toledo, 1981-84; div.

purchasing mgr. Tappan Appliances, Mansfield, Ohio, 1984-85; corp. purchasing mgr. Marathon Electric Mfg. Corp., Wausau, Wis., 1985-88; materials mgr. Pacific Scientific Corp., Rockford, Ill., 1988—. Vol. Toledo Bid Bros./Big Sisters, 1982-85. Mem. Am. Prodn. Inventory Control Soc., Nat. Assn. Purchasing Mgmt., Ducks Unltd, Am. Chesapeake Club, KC. Republican. Roman Catholic. Home: 914 W River Rd Mosinee WI 54455 Office: Pacific Scientific Corp 4301 Kishwaukee St Rockford IL 61105-0106

SCHNEIDER, DONALD ALFRED, sales executive; b. Chgo., Dec. 19, 1951; s. Albert and Julia Bernice (Smith) S.; m. Rosemary Veronica Wayand, Sept. 29, 1973; 1 child, Jaymes Albert. AS, Wright Jr. Coll., Chgo., 1983; BA, Roosevelt U., 1986. Graphic arts asst. Lawson Products, Inc., Des Plaines, Ill., 1970-73, product mgr. rsch. and devel., 1973-81, mgr. indsl. rsch. and devel. dept., 1981-83, dir. merchandising, 1983-84, v.p. merchandising, 1984—. Teaching cons. project bus. Jr. Achievement, Chgo., 1986—. Republican. Roman Catholic. Home: 1145 Estes Ave Lake Forest IL 60045 Office: Lawson Products Inc 1666 E Touhy Ave Des Plaines IL 60015

SCHNEIDER, FREDERICK P., food products company executive; b. Kitchener, Ont., Can., Mar. 14, 1926; s. Frederick Henry and Ella E. (Daniels) S.; m. Frances Jane, July 11, 1953; children: Peter Frederick, Daniel John, Thomas Ervin, Anne Cecile, Margaret Ella. BA, McMaster U., 1947; M in Commerce, U. Toronto, 1949. With Schneider Corp., 1949-89, mgr. by-products, 1961-62, v.p., 1963-66, exec. v.p., 1967, pres., 1968-88, chief exec. officer, 1969-87, chmn. bd., 1970—, also bd. dirs. Past pres. K-W Symphony Orch. Assn., Inc., and Can. Meat Council. Office: Schneider Corp, 321 Courtland Ave E, PO Box 130, Kitchener, ON Canada N2G 3X8

SCHNEIDER, FREDERICK WILLIAM, JR., utility company executive, retired; b. Jersey City, Dec. 20, 1923; s. Frederick William and Violet Ruth (Hunt) S.; m. Margaret M. Davis, Jan. 21, 1945; children—Frederick William III, David P., Mark S. B.S.M.E., N.J. Inst. Tech., 1949, M.S.M.E., 1959. Registered profl. engr., N.J. Mgr. engring. Pub. Service Electric and Gas Co., Newark, 1971-74, v.p. prodn., 1974-82, sr. v.p. corp. planning, 1982-84, exec. v.p. ops., 1984-88, ret., Dec. 1988. Served to lt. j.g. Air Force USN, 1943-45. Recipient Edward F. Weston award for Disting. Profl. Achievement N.J. Inst. Tech., 1987. Mem. ASME (Outstanding Leadership award 1985). Roman Catholic. Clubs: Essex (Newark); Essex Fells Country (N.J.).

SCHNEIDER, HAROLD NORMAN, actuary; b. L.A., Nov. 17, 1950; s. George Herman and Rosa (Fuller) S. AB in Math. summa cum laude, UCLA, 1972; MA in Math., SUNY, Stony Brook, 1973. Actuarial analyst Farmers Group Inc., L.A., 1973-76, asst. actuary, 1976-78, actuary, 1978-84, v.p., 1985—. Fellow Casualty Actuarial Soc.; mem. Am. Acad. Actuaries, So. Calif. Casualty Actuarial Club (pres. 1988-89), Phi Beta Kappa. Office: Farmers Group Inc 4680 Wilshire Blvd Los Angeles CA 90010

SCHNEIDER, HAROLD WILLIAM, insurance executive; b. Rochester, N.Y., Oct. 8, 1943; s. Fred George and Ida (Shulman) S.; m. Ellyn Joyce Silverstein, Oct. 26, 1969; children: Melissa, Rachelle, Amy. AB, U. Rochester, 1965; MS, U. Chgo., 1966, PhD, 1972. From lectr. to prof. math. Roosevelt U., Chgo., 1969-86; actuarial cons. CNA Ins. Co., Chgo., 1981-86; assoc. dir. fin. planning and analysis Lincoln Nat. Ins. Corp., Ft. Wayne, Ind., 1986—. Mem. Soc. Actuaries, Maths. Assn. Am., Phi Beta Kappa. Democrat. Jewish. Home: 3927 Ravenscliff Pl Fort Wayne IN 46804 Office: Lincoln Nat Ins Corp 1300 S Clinton St Fort Wayne IN 46801

SCHNEIDER, HERBERT C(ARPENTER), oil products distribution company executive; b. Newburgh, N.Y., Nov. 20, 1945; s. Floyd R. and Katharyn (Carpenter) S.; m. Judith S. Seidowitz, Feb. 14, 1976; 1 child, Victoria. BA, Dartmouth Coll., 1967; MBA, Columbia U., 1969. Researcher Iran Nat. Tourist Orgn. Peace Corps., Tehran, 1969-71; trainee Carpenter & Smith, Inc., Monroe, N.Y., 1972-75, treas., 1975-82, pres., 1982—; bd. dirs. Met. Energy Council, N.Y.C., 1986—, Hudson Valley Oil Heat Council, Middletown, N.Y., 1985—. Sec., Hudson Valley Oil Heat Council, 1987—; bd. dirs. Orange County Community Coll. Ednl. Found., 1988—. Republican. Lodge: Rotary (pres. Monroe-Woodbury 1987-88, Paul Harris fellow 1986). Home: 51 Laurel Hill Rd Croton-on-Hudson NY 10520 Office: Carpenter & Smith Inc 100 Spring St PO Box 686 Monroe NY 10950

SCHNEIDER, HOWARD JAY, accountant; b. Miami Beach, Fla., Oct. 20, 1951; s. Bernard and Henrietta (Gerson) S.; m. Gail Rockoff, Dec. 18, 1981; children: Briana, Danielle. BBA, CUNY (Baruch Coll.), 1974. CPA. Staff acct. David Berson & Co., N.Y.C., 1971-76; acct. Shapiro Fleischman & Co., Miami, Fla., 1979; pvt. practice Miami, Fla., 1979—. Mem. Am. Inst. CPA's, Fla. Inst. CPA's (outstanding com. mem. 1983, contact person polit. action com., 1987—), U. Miami Acctg. Conf. Com. Lodges: Kiwanis (v.p. Miami club, 1987-88), Elks. Office: Howard J Schneider CPA 5975 Sunset Dr #807 South Miami FL 33143

SCHNEIDER, JOSEPH RAYMOND, JR., merger and acquisition intermediary executive; b. St. Paul, Jan. 10, 1929; s. Joseph Raymond Sr. and Adella (Hoffmann) S.; m. Kathryn Ione Kjellsen, June 22, 1985; children: Joseph, William, Richard, Robert. BS, Coll. St. Thomas, 1952; car. Pres. Schneider Lincoln Mercury Co., St. Paul, 1967-76, Joseph R. Schneider & Assocs., Inc., St. Paul, 1979—. 1st lt. USAF, 1951-52. Mem. Internat. Assn. Merger and Acquisition Cons. (v.p., bd. dirs. 1984—), Assn. for Corp. Growth., North Oaks Golf Club (St. Paul, pres. 1975). Home: 4453 Ellsworth Dr Edina MN 55435 Office: 1983 Sloan Pl Ste 14 Saint Paul MN 55117

SCHNEIDER, MICHAEL IRA, data processing executive; b. N.Y.C., June 26, 1936; s. Charles and Gussie (Josephson) S.; m. Jane Madeline Silverstein, July 28, 1943; children: Jeffrey, Valerie. BSEE, MIT, 1957, MSEE, 1958; PhD, Harvard U., 1962. V.p. Data Gen. Corp., Westboro, Mass., 1971—; bd. dirs. Microcom Corp., Norwood, Mass. Home: 13 Crestwood Dr Framingham MA 01701 Office: Data Gen Corp 4400 Computer Dr Westborough MA 01580

SCHNEIDER, MICHAEL JOSEPH, financial executive; b. Salt Lake City, Oct. 14, 1960; s. John Joseph and Liesel Ann (Riechmann) S.; m. Christina Elizabeth Tewes, June 28, 1985. BBA in Acctg., Tex. Tech U., 1985. Staff acct. Ervin, Prater, Pickens, Snodgrass & Koch, CPAs, Arlington, Tex., 1985-86; controller, bus. mgr. Bill Miller Cos., Arlington, 1986—; cons. S.P.E. Svcs., Arlington, 1986—. Mem. Tex. Tech Acctg. Soc., U. Tex. Acctg. Alumni Assn., Tex. Tech Ex-Student Assn., IBM PC Users Club (Ft. Worth). Republican. Roman Catholic. Home: 6218 Paradise Dr Arlington TX 76017

SCHNEIDER, SANDRA PHYLLIS, financial advisor; b. Washington, Apr. 8, 1949; d. Morris and Faye (Sudack) Schwartz; m. Lewis C. Schneider, June 19, 1971. BA, U. Md., 1972. Cert. fin. planner; registered rep., investment advisor; CPA, Md. Contr. Donatelli, Rudolph & Schoen, Washington, 1971-75, Dental Corp. Am., Rockville, Md., 1974-76; ptnr. Understein & Assocs., Bethesda, Md., 1976-82; pres. Schneider Fin. Svcs., Washington, 1983—. Mem. Inst. Cert. Fin. Planners, Internat. Assn. Fin. Planning, AICPA, Washington Bd. Trade. Democrat. Jewish. Home: 5805 Tudor Ln Rockville MD 20852 Office: Schneider Fin Svcs 1155 21st St NW Ste 400 Washington DC 20036

SCHNEIDER, WILLIAM GEORGE, JR., savings and loan executive; b. N.Y.C., Jan. 22, 1941; s. William George and Erna (Doscher) S.; m. Barbara E. Gattiker, May 9, 1964; children: Jill, Jennifer. B.S. in Econs., Wagner Coll., 1962, M.B.A. in Fin., 1968. V.p. fin. Anchor Savs. Bank, Northport, N.Y., 1970-72, sr. v.p. fin., 1972-75, exec. v.p., 1975-77, pres., 1977-82, pres., chief operating officer, 1982—; dep. chmn., treas. Anchor Mortgage Services, N.J., 1983; treas. Mortgage Resources, Atlanta, 1980—. Trustee Indsl. Home for Blind, N.Y.C., 1972; trustee Lutheran Med. Center, Bklyn., 1981, Wagner Coll., S.I.,N.Y., 1979. Served with Air N.G., 1962-68. Republican. Lutheran.

SCHNOLL, HOWARD MANUEL, accounting firm executive; b. Milw., June 6, 1935; s. Nathan P. and Della (Fisher) S.; married; children: Jordan, Terry, Jeffrey, Robert, Tammy, Daniel. BBA, U. Wis., 1958. CPA, Wis. Mng. ptnr. Nankin, Schnoll & Co., S.C., Milw., 1966-86, Seidman & Seidman, Milw., 1986—. Bd. dirs. Milw. World Festival, Inc., 1968—, City of Festivals Parade, Milw., 1983—, Milw. Coun. on Alcoholism, Aurora Health Care Ventures; treas. Am. Heart Assn., Milw., 1978-82; capt. United Way, Milw., 1985; mem. greater Milw. com. Nat. Found. Ileitis and Colitis, Milw. chpt. Served to sgt. U.S. Army, 1956-63. Mem. Am. Inst. CPA's, Wis. Inst. CPA's, Acct. Computer Users' Tech. Exchange. Jewish. Club: Brynwood Country (Milw.). Lodge: B'nai B'rith (pres. 1960-62). Office: BDO Seidman 330 E Kilbourn Ave Milwaukee WI 53092

SCHNUR, ROBERT ARNOLD, lawyer; b. White Plains, N.Y., Oct. 25, 1938; s. Conrad Edward and Ruth (Mehr) S.; children: Daniel, Jonathan. BA, Cornell U., 1960; JD, Harvard U., 1963. Bar: Wis. 1965, Ill. 1966. Assoc. Michael, Best & Friedrich, Milw., 1966-73, ptnr., 1973—; chmn. Wisconsin Tax News, 1983—. Author: Organizing a Wisconsin Business, 1979, (with others) Taxation of Partnerships, 1970. Capt. U.S. Army, 1963-65. Mem. ABA, Wis. Bar Assn. (chmn. tax sect. 1986-88), Milw. Bar Assn. Home: 929 N Astor St Milwaukee WI 53202 Office: Michael Best Friedrich 250 E Wisconsin Ave Milwaukee WI 53202

SCHOCH, DAVID HENRY, real estate executive; b. N.Y.C., May 21, 1947; s. Theodore W. and Carol (Malmquist) S. AB, Syracuse U., 1968; MBA, UCLA, 1971. Cost analyst So. Pacific, San Francisco, 1971-72; acct. Peat Marwick Mitchell & Co., San Francisco, 1972-76; fin. analyst Rocor Internat., Palo Alto, Calif., 1976-77; v.p. property sales McNeil Corp., San Mateo, Calif., 1977-84; v.p. real estate fin. The Fox Group, Foster City, Calif., 1984—. Mem. Am. Fin. Assn., Nat. Assn. Bus. Economists, Bay Area Mortgage Assn. Republican. Lutheran. Office: The Fox Group 950 Tower Ln Foster City CA 94404

SCHOCK, THOMAS CRAIG, real estate developer; b. Grand Forks, N.D., Apr. 14, 1952; s. Gottlieb and Lorraine (Hollan) S.; m. Debra Sue Haakenson, July 17, 1982 (div. 1986). BE, Valley City (N.D.) State U., 1974, BBA, 1988. Mgr. sales Dynamic Homes, Inc., Detroit Lakes, Minn., 1977-82; asst. v.p. Met. Svc. Corp., Fargo, N.D., 1982-84; real estate syndicator First Investments of Fargo, 1984-86; investment real estate analyst Regan Weiland Investment Co., Fargo, 1986—. Mem. Econ. Devel. Commn., 1988—. Mem. Nat. Assn. of Realtors, Fargo C. of C., Elks. Republican. Lutheran. Office: Regan Weiland Investment Co 112 University Dr N Fargo ND 58102

SCHOECK, STEPHEN RICHARD, dining services executive; b. Glen Ridge, N.J., Nov. 10, 1952; s. Edward Meredith and Marion Amelia (Hertzel) S.; m. Patricia Louise Hughes, Aug. 17, 1974; children: William Meredith, Robert Hughes, John Edward Alexander. BS in Chemistry, Ga. Inst. Tech., 1975. Mgr. Arthur Treacher's, Atlanta, 1975-77; asst. kitchen mgr. T.G.I. Friday's Restaurant, Atlanta, 1977-81; sous chef Boardwalk at Park Place Restaurant, Dunwoody, Ga., 1981-82, 57th Fighter Group Restaurant, Chamblee, Ga., 1982; chef Joe Dale's Cajun House, Atlanta, 1981-83, Shutter's Restaurant, Atlanta, 1983; exec. chef Thursday's Restaurant, Atlanta, 1983-84; dining svcs. mgr. Canteen Corp., Waltham, Mass., 1984—. Lutheran. Home: 28 Indian Rd Waltham MA 02154 Office: Canteen Corp 71 First Ave Waltham MA 02154

SCHOEGGL, GERALD RAY, hospital financial executive; b. Seattle, May 5, 1945; s. Martin and Margery (Johnson) S.; m. Teresa Anderson, Dec. 26, 1987; 1 child, Scott. BA in Acctg., U. Wash., 1968. Acct. Deloitte Haskins & Sells Corp., Los Angeles, 1968-70; controller Scripps Clinic & Resh Found., La Jolla, Calif., 1970-80; chief fin. officer Rogue Valley Med. Ctr., Medford, Oreg., 1980-87, Rogue Valley Health Services, Medford, 1987—; chief fin. officer Rogue Valley Health Found., Medford, 1980—, Rogue Valley Nursing Services, Medford, 1983—; bd. dirs. So. Oreg. Imagining, Medford, Rogue Valley Serenity Ln., Central Point, Oreg. Treas. Siskiyou Wheelman, Medford, 1988. Mem. Healthcare Fin. Mgrs. Assn., Rogue Valley Country Club, La Jolla Country Club. Republican. Home: 1861 Wagontrail Dr Jacksonville OR 97530 Office: Rogue Valley Health Svc 2650 Siskiyou Blvd Medford OR 97502

SCHOELD, CONSTANCE JERRINE, financial planner; b. Wichita, Kans., July 20, 1935; d. Joe Delos and Volna May (Liston) Lumbert; m. Edmund Allan Schoeld, Oct. 4, 1953 (div. Dec. 1974); children: Nancy Ann., Elsa Charlene, Jennie Marie, Brian Shelton, Richard Zweibruck. Student, St. Olaf Coll., 1953-54, Lindenwood Coll., 1960-62, U. Mich., 1967-68, Harper Jr. Coll., 1970. Cert. fin. planner. Mgr. Walden Books, Schaumburg, Ill., 1972-74; owner Books, Etc., Mt. Prospect, Ill., 1974-77; sales rep. Fawcett Books/CBS, N.Y.C., 1977-78, Lawyers Cooperative Pub., Rochester, N.Y., 1978-83; owner Associated Lawyers Svc., Palatine, Ill., 1982-86; broker investments A.G. Edwards & Sons, Aurora and Roselle, Ill., 1983—. Sec. Northwest Mental Health/Retardation Ctr., Arlington Hts., Ill., 1971, Mental Health Ctr. Elk Grove/Schaumburg Twp., Ill., 1970-72, vice chmn., bd. dirs.; v.p. PTA, St. Charles, Mo., 1964; pres. St. Charles Girl Scouts Am., 1965-66; mem. com. Dist. 54 Bd. Edn., Schaumburg, 1969-72; bd. dirs. Mental Health Ctr. St. Charles, 1963-66, Mental Health Ctr. Schaumburg Twp., chmn. 1969-72. Named one of Outstanding Young Women Am., 1964. Mem. Internat. Bd. Cert. Fin. Planners, LWV (bd. dirs. St. Charles 1964-66, Hoffman Estates/Schaumburg 1969-71), DAR (outstanding mem. award 1964), Greater O'Hare Assn. (ambassador, co-chmn. 1989), Nat. Assn. Women in Careers, NAFE, Northwest Bus. and Profl. Women (rec. sec. 1988-89, asst. treas. 1989—), Epsilon Sigma Alpha (outstanding mem. award 1970). Republican. Episcopalian. Office: AG Edwards & Sons 1350 W Lake St Roselle IL 60172

SCHOELLHORN, ROBERT A., pharmaceutical company executive; b. Phila., Aug. 29, 1928. Grad., Phila. Coll. Textiles and Sci., 1957. With Am. Cyanamid Co., 1947-73; pres. Lederle Labs., 1971-73; with Abbott Labs., North Chicago, Ill., 1973—; exec. v.p. hosp. group Abbott Labs., 1973-76, pres., 1976-81, chief operating officer, 1976-79, 85—, chief exec. officer, 1979—, chmn. bd., 1981—, also dir. Office: Abbott Labs Abbott Pk Rte 137 & Waukegan Rd North Chicago IL 60064

SCHOEN, CHARLES JUDD, service executive; b. Owatonna, Minn., Sept. 6, 1943; s. John Nicholas and Dorothy Georgine (Jacobson) S.; m. Birgitta Marianne Haggren, Dec. 15, 1972; 1 child, Vanja Karina. BA, U. Minn., 1965. Stockbroker Harris, Upham and Co., Mpls., 1967-70; with Litton Industries, Sydney, Australia, 1970-71; gen. mgr. Westinghouse Electric, Mpls., 1971-77; pres. Westec Security, Mpls., 1977—. Served with USN, 1966-67. Mem. Alarm Dealers Assn. (pres.), Nat. Trade Group. Office: Westec Security 3280 Gorham Ave S Minneapolis MN 55426

SCHOEN, MARC ALAN, pension and employee benefits executive; b. Worcester, Mass., May 30, 1938; s. A. Robert and Ruth D. (Kulin) S.; m. Joanne S. Schultz, June 24, 1962; children: Elliott, Aaron, Jennifer, Matthew. BBA, BS, U. Miami, 1965. Asst. buyer Allied Stores, Miami, Fla., 1965-66; agt. Fidelity Mut. Ins., Miami, 1966-67, Prudential Ins. Co., Miami, 1967-68; pvt. practice registered rep., agt. Miami, 1973-81; pres. Pencoa, Miami, 1981—; cons. Criterion Funds, Inc., Houston, 1983—, Hibbard Brown & Co., Inc., Greenbelt, Mo., 1987—, Wood Logan Assocs., Inc., Old Greenwich, Conn.; bd. dirs. Beagle Group-Miramar, Fla., 1987—, Integrated Capital Planning Corp., Miami, Fla. Columnist for newspapers, 1969-76, 84. Mem. So. Fla. Employee Benefits Council, N. Dade Estate Planning Council; Scoutmaster Boy Scouts Am., Miami, 1966—; exec. bd. dirs. Crouse Found. to Pub. Arts, N.Y.C., 1983—. Served with USN, 1957-62. Recipient Community Service award Prudential Ins., 1968; named Outstanding Young Man Yr., Optimists, 1967; named to Rollins Coll. Sports Hall of Fame, 1987. Mem. assoc. mem. Am. Soc. Pension Actuaries, Internat. Assn. Fin. Planners, Million Dollar Round Table (qualifying life). Lodges: Optimists, Rotary, Masons. Home: 6725 SW 90 Court Miami FL 33173

SCHOEN, REM, investment executive; b. N.Y.C.; d. Harry L. and Rita (Connors) S.; B.S., Trinity Coll. Burlington, Vt., 1951. Registered rep. Bache & Co., N.Y.C., 1956-61; instl. sales Gruntal & Co., 1961-65; v.p., partner, dir. instl. sales Pressman, Frohlich & Frost, Inc., N.Y.C., 1965-74; allied mem. N.Y. Stock Exchange; with Bernard Herold & Co., Inc., N.Y.C., 1974-77, Hamershlag, Kempner & Marks, N.Y.C., 1978-80; v.p. North East Securities, N.Y.C., 1980-82; sr. account exec. Smith Barney Harris Upham, N.Y.C., 1982-84, Gruntal & Co., N.Y.C. (formerly Herzfeld & Stern), 1984—; fin. adviser to banks in Paris, Milan, Geneva. Vol., Lighthouse, N.Y. Assn. for Blind; fund chmn. ex-officio Trinity Coll., also trustee. Author: Childhood Poems, 1972. Home: 225 E 70th St New York NY 10021 Office: Gruntal and Co 635 Madison Ave New York NY 10022

SCHOENBERG, LAWRENCE JOSEPH, computer services company executive; b. N.Y.C., July 4, 1932; s. Samuel and Selma (Shapiro) S.; m. Barbara Ann Zuckerman, June 24, 1956; children—Douglas, Eric, Julie. A.B., U. Pa., 1953, M.B.A., 1956. Sr. systems analyst IBM, N.Y.C., 1956-59; asst. mgr. systems Litton, Orange, N.J., 1959-61; sr. cons. Computer Scis., N.Y.C., 1961-63; exec. v.p. Automation Scis., N.Y.C., 1963-65; chmn., chief exec. officer AGS Computers, Mountainside, N.J., 1966—; chmn. ADAPSO, Arlington, Va., 1983; bd. dirs. VM Software, Essex Life, Microam. Contbr. articles to profl. jours. Trustee St. Barnabas Hosp., Charles Babbage Inst. Served to cpl. U.S. Army, 1953-55. Mem. Software Industry Assn. (dir. 1976—). Club: East Orange Tennis (N.J.) (pres. 1984-86). Home: 276 Westgate Sq Edison NJ 08820 Office: AGS Computers Inc 1139 Spruce Dr Mountainside NJ 07092

SCHOENDORF, WALTER JOHN, supermarket bakery executive; b. Jersey City, Mar. 16, 1927; s. John Peter and Elizabeth S.; m. Dorothy Mary Myers, Jan. 22, 1949; children: Mary Beth, Patrice, Walter John. Student, Princeton U., 1944-48; B.S. in Chemistry, St. Peter's Coll., Jersey City, 1949. Quality control mgr. Safeway Stores, Inc., Oakland, Calif., 1952-54; plant mgr. Safeway Stores, Inc., 1954-57, prodn. mgr. bakery div., 1957-66, v.p., mgr. bakery div., 1966-86, sr. v.p., exec. officer supply ops., 1986—; lectr. San Jose State U. Foreman Santa Clara Grand Jury, 1967; chmn. bd. St. Francisco Archdiocese Sch. Bd., 1966, Santa Clara County Cath. Charities.; trustee Bakery and Industry Internat. Health and Benefits Pension Fund. Served with AUS, 1944-46. Mem. Am. Chem. Soc., Am. Mgmt. Assn., Am. Baker's Assn. (gov. 1983-87), Am. Soc. Bakery Engrs. Republican. Home: 16508 Far Vue Ln Los Gatos CA 95030 Office: Safeway Stores Inc 201 4th St Oakland CA 94660

SCHOENENGERGER, TOM A., publishing company executive; b. Canton, Ill., Dec. 19, 1940; s. John Harold and Mary Grace (Morgan) S.; m. Virginia Caroline Schoenberger, Sept. 29, 1962; children: Scott, Heidi, Denise, Paula. Grad. high sch. Owner, operator Westgate (Iowa) DX, 1961-62; ter. mgr. Rockford (Ill.) Life Ins. Co., 1962-64; area mgr. Old N.W. Agy., Mpls., 1964-76; state mgr. Directory Svc. Co., Boulder, Colo., 1976-77, Rockford Map Pubs., 1977-78; owner, pub. Maps Midwestern, Oelwein, Iowa, 1978—, Upper Midwest Pubs., Oelwein, 1987—; owner The Touurister, 1988—. Dir. Peace Luth. Ch., Iowa, 1962—, sec. sunday sch. tchr., sunday sch. supt., elder, 1962—; precinct del. Westgate Democratic Com., 1988, mem. platform com., 1988; regional chaplin Iowa Jaycees, chpt. sec., v.p., local dir.,sec. Mem. Ea. Iowa Tourism Assn., Fayette County Tourism Coun. (mktg. chmn. 1987—), Oelwein Hist. Soc. (bd. dirs. 1987—), Iowa Small Bus. Assn. (bd. dirs. 1983—). Home: PO Box ll4 Westgate IA 50681 Office: Maps Midwestern City Park Rd Oelwein IA 50662

SCHOENFEIN, ROBERT A., advertising executive; b. N.Y.C., Feb. 19, 1937; s. Benjamin P. and Elizabeth (Weiss) S.; m. Sandra Feldman, June 10, 1959; children—Liza, Karen. B.A., Union Coll., 1958; M.S., Columbia U., 1959. Staff asst. Grey Advt., Inc., N.Y.C., 1965-66; v.p., account supr. Grey Advt., Inc., 1969-73, sr. v.p., mgmt. supr., 1973-78, exec. v.p., mgmt. rep., 1978—. Bd. dirs. Big Bros./Big Sisters Am. Club: City Athletic (N.Y.C.). Home: 142 E 71st St New York NY 10021 Office: Grey Advt Inc 777 3d Ave New York NY 10017

SCHOENFELD, RICHARD HOLLEMAN, financial counselor; b. Washington, Feb. 19, 1958; s. John Short and Florence Sillers (Holleman) S.; m. Anne Hunter Joyner, May 24, 1986. BA in History, Washington and Lee U., 1980; MBA, Coll. of William and Mary, 1985. Dep. press sec. Rep. Nat. Com., Washington, 1980-81; spl. asst. to dir. pub. affairs U.S. Dept. Transp., Washington, 1981-83; v.p. InterVest, Ltd., Bethesda, Md., 1985—. Home: 5308 Yorktown Rd Bethesda MD 20816 Office: InterVest Ltd 4405 East-West Hwy Ste #406 Bethesda MD 20814

SCHOENKE, RICHARD WARREN, banker; b. Milw., Dec. 13, 1943; s. Robert W. and Bernice A. (Heiser) S.; m. Sandra Jean Tornquist, June 13, 1964; children—Peter, Michael, Andrew. B.B.A., U. Wis., 1965, M.B.A., 1966. Banker Continental Ill. Nat. Bank, Chgo., 1970-79; sr. v.p. Tex. Commerce Bank, Houston, 1979; exec. v.p. First Bank Mpls., 1980-82, pres., from 1982, also dir.; vice chmn. First Bank Systems Inc., Minneapolis, until 1988, chief adminstrv. officer, 1988—; dir. First Bank Internat., Mpls. Served with USAR, 1966-72. Mem. Am. Bankers Assn. Office: 1st Bank System Inc 1200 1st Bank Pl E Minneapolis MN 55480 also: 1st Bank Mpls 120 S 6th St Minneapolis MN 55402 *

SCHOENSTADT, STEVEN E., marketing executive; b. Phila., Dec. 16, 1939; s. Gerald H. and Anna (Opshelor) S.; m. Barbara Laison, June 18, 1961; children: Scott Carl, Bruce Alan, Cori Maxine. BS in Bus. Adminstrn., Temple U., 1961. Prodn. coordinator Johnson and Johnson, New Brunswick, N.J., 1966-69; nat. sales mgr. Tesa Corp. div. Beiersdorf, Inc., Denville, N.J., 1970-83; gen. mgr. Nitto Denko Am., Inc., Port Washington, N.Y., 1983-87; v.p. sales and mktg. American Biltrite, Inc., Mt. Laurel, N.J., 1987—. Chmn. bd. Neshaminy Sch., Langhorne, Pa., 1973-79. Served to capt. U.S. Army, 1961-66, Germany. Mem. Am. Mgmt. Assn., Nat. Rifle Assn. Democrat. Jewish. Home: 736 Hunter Dr Langhorne PA 19047 Office: Am Biltrite Inc 106 Gaither Dr Mount Laurel NJ 08054

SCHOENWALD, ARTHUR ALLEN, financial advisor; b. Bklyn., Mar. 3, 1940; s. Saul Morris and Charlotte (Lipschitz) S.; B.B.A., Baruch Sch. Bus., CCNY, 1961; M.B.A. (Baruch Sch. honor scholar), U. Chgo., 1962; D.B.A. (Arthur Andersen & Co. fellow), Harvard U., 1968; m. Maxine Rapchik, Nov. 4, 1961; children—Scott M., Ellen Beth. Asst. prof. bus. adminstrn. Rutgers U., Newark, 1967-68, asso. prof., 1968-72; exec. dir. N.J. Public Utilities Commn., Newark, 1972-74; mgr. electric utilities group Salomon Bros., N.Y.C., 1974-75; pres. A.A. Schoenwald Assos., Inc., Colonia, N.J., 1975—; lectr. in field. Fin. cons. N.J. Gov.'s Commn. to Evaluate Capital Needs of N.J., 1968; mem. N.J. Gov.'s Commn. on Public Electric Power Authority, 1975, N.J. Gov.'s Econ. Recovery Commn., 1975; treas. Middlesex County (N.J.) Republican Orgn. Recipient Chgo. Control award Controllers Inst. Am., 1962; named Tchr. of Yr., Rutgers U. Grad. Sch. Bus., 1971. Mem. Fin. Mgmt. Assn., Beta Gamma Sigma, Beta Alpha Psi. Jewish. Clubs: Colonia Country, Channel, K.P., Harvard Bus. Sch. of Greater N.Y., U. Chgo. Bus. of N.Y. Home and Office: 26 Cambridge Dr Colonia NJ 07067

SCHOFIELD, DOUGLAS FRANKLIN, financial advisor; b. New Castle, Pa., Aug. 9, 1945; s. Douglas Franklin and Mary Bell (Duncan) S.; m. Janet Ward, Sept. 1, 1968; children: Alanya, Heather, Emily. BA cum laude, Yale U., 1967; MBA, Harvard U., 1969, DBA, 1972. Asst. to exec. sec. Atlanta U. Ctr. Corp., 1969-70; policy analyst U.S. Dept. Transp., Washington, 1972-74; asst. v.p., mgr. fgn. exchange Mellon Bank, Pitts., 1974-83; v.p., mgr. strategic planning Equimark Corp., Pitts., 1983-84; pres. FSA Fin. Counselors, Inc., Pitts., 1985-88, Schofield Fin. Counseling, Inc., Pitts., 1988—. Chmn. fin. com., bd. dirs. La Roche Coll., Pitts., 1976-87. Mem. Internat. Assn. Fin. Planners, Harvard U. Bus. Sch. Assn. Office: Schofield Fin Counseling Inc Box 369 Indianola PA 15051

SCHOFIELD, GEORGE H., corporate executive; b. Newark, Nov. 18, 1929; s. George H. and Louise (Minder) S.; m. Barbara Shimmin; children—George, Linda, Lauren, Robert. B.S., U. Vt., 1951. Various fin. positions Gen. Electric Co., 1951-72; gen. mgr. medium steam turbine generator prodn. dept. Gen. Electric Co., Lynn, Mass., 1972-75; gen. mgr. mech. drives turbine dept. Gen. Electric Co., Fitchburg, Mass., 1975-78; v.p., gen. mgr. indsl. and marine turbine div. Gen. Electric Co., Lynn, 1978-85; pres., chief exec. officer Zurn Industries Inc., Erie, Pa., 1985-86, chmn., chief exec. officer, 1986—. Mem. bd. corporators St. Vincent Found. for

Health & Human Svcs., adv. com. ACES; trustee Gannon U.; bd. dirs. Erie Conf. Community Devel., United Way Erie County, 1988—. Mem. Pa. Bus. Roundtable, Nat. Assn. Mfrs. (bd. dirs.), Pa. Chamber Bus. and Industry, Key Contbr. Club (co-chmn.). Office: Zurn Industries Inc 1 Zurn Pl Erie PA 16505

SCHOFIELD, PAUL MICHAEL, finance company executive; b. Wilmington, Del., Mar. 30, 1937; s. John Edward and Sabina A. (Clarke) S.; m. Carol Ann Hane, July 11, 1964; children—Paul Michael, Andrew Clarke, Dennis Charles. B.A., LaSalle U., Phila., 1960; postgrad., U. Del., 1963. Asst. treas. Sears Roebuck Acceptance Corp., Wilmington, Del., 1971-73, asst. v.p., 1973-74, treas., 1974-83, v.p., treas., 1983-87; pres., treas. Discover Credit Corp., Wilmington, 1987—. Campaign capt. United Way of Del., 1978; campaign capt. Boys Club Del., 1979. Mem. Del. Fin. Assn. (treas.), Phila. Treas. Club. Democrat. Roman Catholic. Club: Irish Culture of Del. (treas. 1980). Home: 2014 Delaware Ave Wilmington DE 19806 Office: Discover Credit Corp PO Box 15185 Wilmington DE 19850

SCHOLES, CLIFFORD ROWLAND, accountant, publishing company executive; b. Dayton, Ohio, Sept. 17, 1927; s. Clifford William and Sarah Mildred (Butts) S.; m. Arlene Mabel Hanson, Aug. 25, 1956; children: Peter R., Andrew H., Sheila G. BS in Acctg., U. Dayton, 1951. Acct. Deloitte, Haskins and Sells, Cin., 1951-57; treas. Anderson Pub. Co., Cin., 1957-88, v.p. fin., 1988—; cons. Coll. Bus. U. Cin., 1985—. Served to sgt. USAF, 1946-47. Mem. Adminstrv. Mgmt. Soc. Baptist. Office: Anderson Pub Co 2035 Reading Rd Cincinnati OH 45202

SCHOLL, DANIEL JOHN, real estate appraiser; b. N.Y.C., Jan. 10, 1949; s. Morton John and Lena (Ghio) S. Assoc. diploma, Bryant and Stratton Sch. Bus., 1969; comml. diving cert., Coastal Sch. Deep Sea Diving, 1971. Cert. non-destructive testing technician. Owner, diver Underwater Technicians Inc., Orleans, Mass., 1971-76; owner D.J. Scholl Real Estate Appraiser & Broker, Orleans, Mass., 1984—; owner, mgr. D.J. Scholl, The Investment Co., Orleans, 1988—. Developer shellfish processing equipment. Home: Alston Ave Eastham MA 02642 Office: DJ Scholl Real Estate Appraiser 95 Rayber Rd Orleans MA 02653

SCHOLL, GLENN LEWIS, international real estate and finance company executive, marketing consultant; b. Wilkes-Barre, Pa., Oct. 6, 1947; s. John Harold and Beverly Jean (Lewis) S.; m. Jane Frances Smith, May 28, 1973; children: Alexy Anna, Amanda Rita. BA, Bates Coll., 1969; JD, U. Conn., 1973. Bar: Conn. 1974, U.S. Dist. Ct. (Conn. dist.) 1974. Pvt. practice New Britain, Conn., 1974-82; account rep. Cert. Lab. div. NCH Corp., Paramus, N.J., 1982-84; fin. cons. Merrill Lynch Pierce Fenner & Smith, Hartford, Conn., 1984-85; pres. Transatlantic Investment Svcs., Inc., Farmington, Conn., 1985-86, Horizon Capital Corp., Farmington, 1986—; bd. dirs. Capitol Partnerships, Inc., Hartford. Mem. Conn. World Trade Assn., Farmington C. of C., Greater Hartford C. of C., Civitan (pres. New Britain chpt. 1983-85), Rotary. Democrat. Episcopalian. Office: Horizon Capital Corp 270 Farmington Ave Farmington CT 06032

SCHOLTEN, KIM DIANE STANDRIDGE, accountant; b. Santa Ana, Calif., Apr. 26, 1957; d. Howard Vernon and Mary Louise (Countryman) Horner; m. Roger Odell Standridge, Jan. 7, 1978 (div. Aug. 1983). BSBA, Okla. State U., 1984. CPA, Okla. Acct., Kerr-McGee Corp., Oklahoma City, 1980-82, Warren Petroleum Co., Tulsa, 1983, Oxy USA Inc., Tulsa, 1985—; owner Multinet Internat., 1988—; auditor Arthur Young & Co., Tulsa, 1984-85. Mem. AICPA, Okla. Soc. CPA's, Nat. Assn. Accts., NAFE, Toastmasters, Phi Kappa Phi, Beta Gamma Sigma, Beta Alpha Psi. Republican. Mem. Assembly God Ch. Avocations: singing and performing in musicals, snow and water skiing, sailing, softball. Home: 1430B E 38th Pl Tulsa OK 74105 Office: Oxy USA Inc PO Box 300 Tulsa OK 74102

SCHONHOFF, ROBERT LEE, marketing and advertising executive; b. Detroit, May 24, 1919; s. John Clement and Olympia Regina (Diebold) S.; m. Kathleen O'Hara, Dec. 24, 1971; children: Rita, Elise, Robert. Student, Wayne State U., 1940-41. Artist, J.L. Hudson, 1939-42; v.p. advt. and mktg. Dillard Dept. Stores, Little Rock and San Antonio, 1963-77; owner R.L. Schonhoff Advt. and Mktg., San Antonio, 1977-83; owner Ad Graphics, AMC Printers Inc.; co-owner New Orleans Saints football team; mem. faculty Bus. Sch., St. Mary's U., 1975-81; bd. dirs. Comml. Nat. Bank, San Antonio. Permanent deacon Roman Catholic Ch., San Antonio Diocese. Served to 1st lt. USAF, 1942-46. Mem. Am. Mktg. Assn. (founding dir. San Antonio chpt.). Clubs: Tapatio Springs Country; Josef (San Antonio). Home: 501 Hillside Dr San Antonio TX 78212 Office: 1528 Contour St Ste 101 San Antonio TX 78212

SCHOOLEY, KENNETH RALPH, manufacturing company executive; b. Anamosa, Iowa, Jan. 22, 1943; s. Ralph Kenneth and Kathleen Ann (Eilers) S.; m. Sharon Faye Foster, July 11, 1964; children by previous marriage: Blaine Evan, Lynette Kay. Student, Kirkwood Community Coll., Cedar Rapids, Iowa, 1971-75. Asst. warehouse mgr. Trico Auto Parts, Bakersfield, Calif., 1964-65; mail carrier U.S. Post Office, Bakersfield, 1965, Marion, Iowa, 1965-66; asst. traffic mgr. Cargill Corn Starch & Syrup, Cedar Rapids, 1966-68; traffic mgr. LeFebure Corp., Cedar Rapids, 1968-71; traffic mgr. to mgr. traffic and warehouse Amana Refrigerator, 1971-80; traffic mgr. Service Merchandise Co., Nashville, 1980-84; mgr. reg. warehouses Heil Quaker Corp., La Vergne, Tenn., 1984—. Mem. Iowa Indsl. Traffic League (sec.-treas. 1973-74). Republican. Lutheran. Club: Nashville Traffic. Home: 517 Idlewood Dr Mount Juliet TN 37122 Office: Heil Quaker Corp 1136 Heil Quaker Blvd La Vergne TN 37086

SCHOOLS, CHARLES HUGHLETTE, banker, lawyer; b. Lansing, Mich., May 24, 1929; s. Robert Thomas and Lillian Pearl (Lawson) S.; B.S., Am. U., 1952, M.A., 1958; J.D., Washington Coll. of Law, 1963; LL.D., Bethune-Cookman U., 1973; m. Rosemarie Sanchez, Nov. 22, 1952; children—Charles, Michael. Dir. phys. plant Am. U., 1952-66; owner, 1957—, Gen. Security Co., Washington, 1969—; chmn., pres. Consol. Ventures Ltd.; pres., chmn. bd. McLean Bank (Va.), 1974—, Instl. Environ. Mgmt. Services; chmn. bd. Harper & Co.; chmn., pres. Community Assos. of Va., Associated Real Estate Mgmt. Services; dir. Computer Data Systems Inc., DAC Devel. Ltd., Am. Indsl. Devel. Corp., Intercoastal of Iran; mem. Met. Bd. Trades. Pres., McLean Boys' Club; bd. dirs. D.C. Spl. Olympics, Nat. Kidney Found.; trustee Bethune Cookman Coll., Western Md. Coll., Randolph Macon Acad. Served with USAAF, 1946-47, USAF, 1947-48. Mem. Va. C. of C., Profl. Businessman's Orgn., Alpha Tau Omega. Democrat. Clubs: Georgetown of Washington, Touchdown of Washington, Univ. of Washington, Washington Golf and Country, Pisces (Washington); Halifax (Daytona Beach, Fla.); Masons. Home: 1320 Darnall Rd McLean VA 22101 Office: 1340 Old Chain Bridge Rd Ste 301 McLean VA 22101

SCHOON, WARREN EUGENE, automotive executive; b. Ash Creek, Minn., Oct. 3, 1921; s. Jacob and Viola (Hansen) S.; m. Elizabeth Johnson, Dec. 25, 1943 (div. 1969); children: Steven, Susan, Peter, Christian, Robert; m. Marjorie Costello, Oct. 10, 1969. BA, U. Minn., 1943. Various jr. exec. positions GM, Mpls. and St. Louis, 1947-50; nat. advt. and N.Y. zone mgr., Pontiac div. GM, N.Y.C., 1957-60; ptnr. McKean and Schoon Ford, Sioux Falls, S.D., 1951-54; pres. and owner Schoon Motors, Luverne, Minn., 1960—; pres. New Chrysler Inc., Luverne, 1977—, Luverne Oil Co., 1971—; master adv. bd. dirs. Met. Fin. Corp., Fargo, N.D.; chmn. bd. dirs. Dakota Savs. and Loan, Sioux Falls (merger Met. Fed. Bank, Fargo), 1982-86. Mayor City of Luverne, 1955-57; small bus. adv. com. U.S. Sen. R. Boschwitz, Minn., 1982—, U.S. Sen. Pressler, S.D., 1985—; adv. bd. McKennan Hosp., Sioux Falls, 1985—, pres. 1988—; bd. dirs. S. Dakota Crippled Children's Sch., 1986—; chmn. Rock County (Minn.) Reps., 1954-57, 60-70; mem. Nat. Bd. Ctr. Western Studies Augustana Coll., Sioux Falls. Served to lt. (j.g.) USN, 1943-47, PTO. Mem. Oldsmobile Zone Deal Coun. (chmn. 1984-85), U. Minn. Alumni Assn. (pres. Rochester chpt. 1974-75), Minn./S.D. Cadillac Dealer's Mktg. Assn. (pres. 1986-88), Am. Legion, VFW, Phi Beta Kappa. Republican. Presbyterian. Club: Minnehaha Country (Sioux Falls). Lodges: Rotary (bd. dirs. Sioux Falls Downtown Club 1984-85), Masons, Shriners, Elks. Home: 1942 S First Ave Sioux Falls SD 57105 Office: Schoon Motors Cedar & Maple Luverne MN 56156

SCHOPPA, ELROY, accountant, financial planner; b. Vernon, Tex., Aug. 25, 1922; s. Eddie A. and Ida (Foerster) S.; m. Juanita C. Young, Aug. 11, 1956 (div.); children: Karen Marie, Vickie Sue; m. Gail O. Martin, May 12, 1984; stepchildren: Veronica, Vanessa. BBA, Tex. Tech U., 1943; postgrad. Law Sch., U. Tex., 1946-47; MA, Mich. State U., 1950. CPA, Tex., Calif.; cert. real estate broker; cert. ins. agt. Mem. faculty Tex. Tech U., Lubbock, 1943, U. Tex., Austin, 1946-47, Mich. State U., East Lansing, 1947-50; auditor Gen. Motors Corp., 1950-56; dir. systems and procedures Fansteel Metall. Corp., 1956-59; gen. auditor Consol. Electro Dynamics Corp., 1959-60; auditor, sr. tax acct. Beckman Inst. Inc., Fullerton, Calif., 1960-70; pres. Elroy Schoppa Acctg. Corp., La Habra, Calif., 1960—; cons. to bus. Treas. La Habra Devel. Corp.; organizer, pres. 4-H Club, Vernon; adviser Jr. Achievement, Waukegan, Ill.; bd. dirs. Klein Ctr. for Prevention of Domestic Violence; asst. football and basketball coach, Manzanola, Colo.; coach Am. Girls Sport Assn., La Habra. Served with USN, 1942-46. Mem. Calif. Soc. CPA's, Alpha Phi Omega, Theta Xi. Republican. Lutheran. Club: Phoenix (Anaheim, Calif.). Avocations: hunting, fishing, camping. Office: 801 E La Habra Blvd La Habra CA 90631

SCHORB, EUGENE JOHN, accountant; b. Columbia, Ill., Jan. 2, 1931; s. Elton John and Ottilda (Beckerle) S.; m. Elaine C. Frye, Aug. 17, 1963; children: Lisa, Laura, Christine. BS in commerce, St. Louis U., 1954. CPA, Mo., Ill. Staff acct. Arthur Anderson & Co., Chgo., 1957-58; sr. cons. Touche Ross & Co., St. Louis, 1958-68; sole practice acctg. Eugene J. Schorb, CPA, P.C., Columbia, 1968—. Mem. Am. Inst. Cert. Pub. Accts., Am. Legion (jr. vice comdr. Columbia post 1968), Rotary (past. dist. gov. 1967-68, dist. treas. 1988—). Home: 503 N Metter St Columbia IL 62236 Office: 518 N Main St Columbia IL 62236

SCHORSTEN, BRUCE MICHAEL, realtor; b. Canton, Ohio, Oct. 28, 1948; s. Walter M. and Sara (Shilvely) S.; m. Elizabeth Loichot, June 19, 1971; children: Amanda, Erica. BS in Edn., Kent State U., 1970. Agt. Nationwide Ins. Co., Canton, 1969-71; tchr. Canton City Schs., 1972-73; realtor DeHoff Realtors, North Canton, Ohio, 1971-76; realtor/sales mgr. T.K. Harris Realtors, Canton, 1976-79; realtor/broker United Realty & Investment Co., North Canton, 1979-88; broker Putman Properties, Inc., Canton, 1988—; prin. Stark Cellular, North Canton, 1986—. Mem. Sales and Mktg. Execs., Realtors Nat. Mktg. Inst., Nat. Assn. Realtors, Ohio Assn. Realtors (pres.'s sales award 1983-88), Canton-Massillon Bd. Realtors (named Profl. of the Year 1983-88), Congress Lake Club, Canton Rotary. Office: Putnam Properties Inc 220 Market Ave S Canton OH 44720

SCHOTANUS, EUGENE LEROY, agricultural and industrial equipment manufacturing company executive; b. Eldora, Iowa, Apr. 19, 1937; s. Robert and Caroline (Jutting) S.; m. Ruth Anderson, Sept. 14, 1957. Student, Drake U., 1955-56; B.S., Iowa State U., 1959. Auditor Deere & Co., Moline, Ill., 1959-66, asst. treas., 1968-71, treas., 1971-74, v.p., treas., 1974-81, sr. v.p., 1981—, also bd. dirs.; chief fin. officer John Deere Iberica, subs. Deere & Co., Spain, 1966-68. Office: Deere & Co John Deere Rd Moline IL 61265

SCHOTZ, GARY STEPHEN, general contracting company executive, civil engineer; b. Syracuse, N.Y., Dec. 10, 1953; s. William Julius Schotz and Lucille Fern (Schwartz) Ferguson; m. Leslie Ellen Boris, Sept. 20, 1977. BS in Forestry, SUNY, Syracuse, 1976; BS in Civil Engring., Syracuse U., 1976; MS in Civil Engring., Stanford U., 1977. Project engr. Charles Pankow Inc., San Francisco, 1977-78; project mgr., mktg. dir. Olson Constrn. Co., San Diego, 1978-85; pres. Westwinds Engring. Co., Oceanside, Calif., 1982—, Quest Constrn. Engring. and Mgmt. Inc., San Diego, 1985—. N.Y. Regents Scholar, 1972-76; engring. scholar Stanford U., 1977. Mem. ASCE (assoc.), Am. Concrete Inst., San Diego C. of C. Office: Quest Constrn Engring & Mgmt Inc 8380 Miramar Mall Ste 125 San Diego CA 92121

SCHRADER, LYNWOOD, utility company executive; b. Detroit, Aug. 15, 1930; s. Henry Atwood and Viola (Hall) S.; m. Patricia Page, May 31, 1952; children: John, Joel, James. B.S., U. Ky., 1952. Dir. residential sales Ky. Utilities Co., Lexington, 1973, asst. v.p., 1973-75, v.p., 1975-78, sr. v.p., 1978—; dir. Old Dominion Power Co., Lexington. Served with U.S. Army, 1952-54. Recipient Service award Optimist, 1982; recipient Thomas Poe Cooper award U. Ky., 1983. Mem. Ky. C. of C. (chmn. 1979-80). Democrat. Baptist. Home: 616 Tally Rd Lexington KY 40502 Office: Ky Utilities Co One Quality St Lexington KY 40507

SCHRADER, THOMAS F., utilities executive; b. Indpls., 1950. Grad., Princeton U., 1972, 78. Pres., chief oper. officer Wis. Gas Co., Milw. Office: Wis Gas Co 626 E Wisconsin Ave Milwaukee WI 53202

SCHRADER, WILLIAM CUTLER, banker; b. St. Paul, Apr. 15, 1933; s. Ernst-Joseph and Lydia (Cutler) S.; m. Carolyn Miller, Aug. 4, 1956; children—Elizabeth, William. B.S., Yale U., 1955; M.B.A., Rutgers U., 1966; A.M.P., Harvard U., 1980. Ops. mgr. Procter & Gamble Co., 1958-68; v.p. prodn. William Underwood Co., Watertown, Mass., 1968-74; sr. v.p. Chem. Bank, N.Y.C., 1974-82; exec. v.p. Shawmut Corp., Boston, 1982—; dir., mem. exec. com./Bank Administn. Inst., Rolling Meadows, Ill., 1980-85; chmn. Exec. Svc. Corps of New Eng.; bd. dirs. New Eng. Banking Inst. Bd. dirs. Boston council Boy Scouts Am., Boston, 1983—, Brighter Day, Boston, 1973-74. Served to capt. USMC, 1955-58. Mem. Tau Beta Pi, Beta Gamma Sigma. Clubs: Short Hills, Cohasset Golf, Hingham Yacht, Harvard of Boston. Office: Shawmut Corp 1 Federal St Boston MA 02211

SCHRAGE, PAUL DANIEL, fast food executive; b. Chgo., Feb. 25, 1935; s. William and Rose Marie (Bruell) S.; m. Janet Carolyn Sievers, June 15, 1957; children: Paul Daniel, Gordon Clark. B.A., Valparaiso U., 1957; M.S. in Advt., U. Ill., 1959. Media buyer Young & Rubicam Advt., Chgo., 1959-61; brand mgr. Quaker Oats Co., Chgo., 1961-65; salesman This Week mag., Chgo., 1965-66; asso. media dir. D'Arcy Advt., Chgo., 1966-67; sr. exec. v.p., chief mktg. officer McDonald's Corp., Oak Brook, Ill., 1967—; dir. Century Co. Am., Safety-Kleen Corp. Office: McDonald's Corp 1 McDonald's Pla Oak Brook IL 60521 *

SCHRAGER, MINDY RAE, corporate executive; b. Paterson, N.J., Jan. 18, 1958; d. Julius Maxwell and Miriam (Max) S. Student Middlebury Coll., 1977, Inst. European Studies, Nantes, France, 1977-78; BA, Dickinson Coll., 1979; MBA, Babson Coll., 1981. Cons., Nolan Norton & Co., Lexington, Mass., 1981-86; mgr. sales support Logos Corp., Dedham, Mass., 1986-87; resource ctr. supr. Codex Corp., Canton, Mass., 1987—. Mem. NAFE, ACLU, Internat. Customer Svc. Assn., Am. Mgmt. Assn., Women in Mgmt., Boston Computer Soc. Avocations: reading, travel, music, dance. Home: 80 Walnut St Canton MA 02021

SCHRAMM, EUGENE JOSEPH, manufacturing company executive; b. Grassflat, Pa., July 12, 1925; s. Eugene George and Helen Ann (Jackson) S.; m. Virginia Mary Wyckoff, Aug. 16,1946; children: Karen L., Stephen R. BA, Lycoming Coll., 1950. Cert. tchr., Md. Tchr. Balt. County Pub. Schs., Towson, Md., 1951-56; group engr. I Martin Marietta Corp., Middle River, Md., 1956-66; test mgr. Martin Marietta Corp., Denver, 1966-67; product mgr. Gen. Electric Corp., Phila., 1967-73; v.p. engring. Somat Corp., Pomeroy, Pa., 1973-77; pres. VSC Inc. subs. Vibration Splty. Inc., Phila., 1977-88. Patentee in field. Served with Seabees USN, 1943-46, PTO. Mem. Vibrations Inst., Am. Soc. Inventors. Democrat. Roman Catholic. Home: Box 242G Rd 3 Cogan Station PA 17728 Office: VSC Inc 100 Geiger Rd Philadelphia PA 19115

SCHRECK, ALBERT FRANKLIN, III, financial executive; b. Hackensack, N.J., Aug. 8, 1953; s. Albert F. Jr. and Rhoda (Fahnestock) S.; m. Patricia Ann Reiser, July 4, 1975; children: David, Amber, Arielle. AA, St. Petersburg Jr. Coll., 1973; BS cum laude, Fla. State Coll., 1975; cert., Coll. Fin. Planning, 1986. Sales rep. Shell Oil Co., Tampa, Fla., 1975-79; sales devel. rep. Shell Oil Co., Cleve., 1979-80; fin. cons. Merrill Lynch Pierce Fenner & Smith Inc., New Port Richey, Fla., 1981-86, sr. fin. cons., 1986-87, asst. v.p., 1987—. Recipient Speakers award Fla. Petroleum Coun., 1972, 78, 79. Mem. Inst. Cert. Fin. Planners, Phi Theta Kappa, Sigma Iota Epsilon, Beta Gamma Sigma. Republican. Roman Catholic. Home: 1482 Treetop Dr Palm Harbor FL 34683 Office: Merrill Lynch Pierce Fenner & Smith 4821 US Hwy 19 New Port Richey FL 34652

SCHREIBER, ALLAN CHARLES, banker; b. Mineola, N.Y., Jan. 23, 1941; s. Charles A. and Alvena M. (Heurmann) S.; m. Patricia Biggard, Mar. 7, 1971; children: David, Stephanie. B.S., The Citadel, 1962. Vice pres. Chase Manhattan Bank, N.Y.C., 1964-79; sr. v.p. Nat. Westminster Bank U.S.A., N.Y.C., 1979-82, exec. v.p., 1982—. Mem. Harrington Park Planning Bd., 1981—; mem. Harrington Park Environ. Com., 1982—, Lower Manhattan Cultural Coun. Robert Morris Assocs.ž Served to 1st lt. U.S. Army, 1962-64. Mem. Real Estate Bd. N.Y., Mortgage Bankers Assn.; mem Urban Land Inst. Republican. Home: 5 Pine Pl Harrington Park NJ 07640 Office: Nat Westminster Bank USA 175 Water St New York NY 10038

SCHREIBER, HARRY, JR., management consultant; b. Columbus, Ohio, Apr. 1, 1934; s. C. Harry and Audrey (Sard) S.; B.S., Mass. Inst. Tech., 1955; M.B.A., Boston U., 1958; m. Margaret Ruth Heinzman, June 12, 1955; children—Margaret Elizabeth, Thomas Edward, Amy Katherine Schreiber Garcia. Accountant truck and coach div. Gen. Motors Corp., Pontiac, Mich., 1955; instr. Mass. Inst. Tech., 1958-62; pres. Data-Service, Inc., Boston, 1961-65; pres. Harry Schreiber Assos., Wellesley, Mass., 1965; mgr., nat. dir. merchandising Peat, Marwick, Mitchell & Co., N.Y.C., 1966-70, partner, Chgo., 1970-75; chmn. bd. Close, Martin, Schreiber & Co., 1975-82; partner Deloitte Haskins & Sells, 1983-85; chmn. bd. Harry Schreiber & Assocs., Ltd., 1985—. Staff, Work Simplification Conf. Lake Placid, N.Y., 1960-61. Served to 1st lt. AUS, 1956-58. Mem. Am. Inst. Indsl. Engrs. (chmn. data-processing div. 1964-66, chpt. v.p. 1961, 65, chmn. retail industries div. 1976-78), Com. Internat. Congress Transp. Confs., Assn. for Computing Machinery, Assn. for Systems Mgmt., Inst. Mgmt. Scis., Retail Research Soc., Retail Fin. Execs., Nat. Retail Mchts. Assn. (retail systems specifications com.), Food Distbn. Research Soc. (dir. 1972—, pres. 1974), Japan-Am. Soc. Chgo. Republican. Methodist. Clubs: MIT Faculty; Hidden Creek Country (Reston, Va.); Army and Navy (Washington); Plaza (Chgo.). Home and Office: 12137 Stirrup Rd Reston VA 22091

SCHREIBER, KURT GILBERT, lawyer; b. Milw., Aug. 22, 1946; s. Raymond R. and Mildred L. (Kleist) S.; m. Nelda Beth Van Buren, May 3, 1974; children—Katharine Anne, Matthew Edward. A.B. in Econs., Cornell U., 1968; J.D., U. Mich., 1971. Bar: Wis. 1971, Tex. 1979. Internat. atty. Tenneco Internat. Holdings Co., London, 1974-78; atty. Tenneco Inc., Houston, 1978-80; 2d v.p., asst. gen. counsel Am. Gen. Corp., Houston, 1980-83, v.p., gen. counsel, 1983-84, sr. v.p., gen. counsel, 1984-85, exec. v.p., gen. counsel, 1985—. Mem. ABA, Wis. Bar Assn., Tex. Bar Assn., Houston Bar Assn. Clubs: Heritage, Forum (Houston). Home: 306 Fall River Ct Houston TX 77024 Office: Am Gen Corp 2929 Allen Pkwy Houston TX 77019

SCHREIBER, OTTO WILLIAM, manufacturing company executive; b. Greenwood, Wis., July 4, 1922; s. Otto Waldemar and Meta Wilhelmina (Suemnicht) S. BSEE, U. Wis., Madison, 1944. Electroacoustic scientist Navy Electronics Lab., San Diego, 1946-56; electronics engr. then mgr. electronic engring. dept., ordnance div. Librascope, Sunnyvale, Calif., 1956-65; chief engr. Teledyne Indsl. Electronics Co., San Jose, Calif., 1965-68; exec. v.p. Marcom Corp., San Francisco, 1969; test mgr. MB Assocs., San Ramon, Calif., 1970-71; ops. mgr. Am. Service Products, Inc., Newhall, Calif., 1972-75; mfg. mgr. UTI, Inc., Sunnyvale, Calif., 1975-80; dir. mfg. Hi-Shear Ordnance/Electronics, Torrance, Calif., 1980-82; tech. writing supr. Marine div. Westinghouse, Sunnyvale, 1980—. Mem. IEEE (life), Soc. Tech. Communication, Eta Kappa Nu, Kappa Eta Kappa. Republican. Lutheran. Home: 1623 New Brunswick Ave Sunnyvale CA 94087 Office: Westinghouse Marine Div 1623 New Brunswick Ave Sunnyvale CA 94087

SCHREIBER, RICHARD ALAN, foundation administrator; b. N.Y.C., May 4, 1941; s. Lester H. and Celia F. Schreiber; m. Marilynn K. Smith, Feb. 1, 1963; children: J. Scott, Leslie A. BA in History, U. Va., 1963, MBA, 1965. With Lever Bros. Co., N.Y.C., 1965-80, mktg. mgr., 1972-74, dir. mktg., 1975-78, dir. strategic planning, 1979-80; v.p., gen. mgr. products and mktg. Colonial Williamsburg (Va.) Found., 1981-86, v.p., gen. mgr. bus. ops., 1987-88, v.p., chief bus. officer, 1988—; lectr. bus. Coll. of William and Mary, Williamsburg, 1988—; bd. dirs. Mystic (Conn.) Seaport Mus. Stores Corp. Chmn. exec. com. Williamsburg Conv. and Visitors Bur., 1987—; trustee fund for Am. Studies, 1989—. Mem. Va. State C. of C. (bd. dirs. 1986—). Home: PO Box 353 Williamsburg VA 23187 Office: Colonial Williamsburg Found Goodwin Bldg Williamsburg VA 23185

SCHREINER, JOAN MAU, accountant; b. Appleton, Wis., July 12, 1944; d. John F. and Agnes M. (Hartzheim) Mau; m. Edwin A. Schreiner, June 17, 1967; children: Teri Lee, Douglas Edwin, Catherine Anne. BBA, U. Wis., Madison, 1966, MS, 1968. CPA, N.Y. Staff acct. Price Waterhouse & Co., Milw., 1968-69; sr. tax acct. Price Waterhouse & Co., Seattle, 1969-72; pvt. practice acct. Rochester, N.Y., 1973-80; tax analyst GTE Corp., Stamford, Conn., 1981-83; tax mgr. U.S. Tobacco Co., Greenwich, Conn., 1983-84; dir. tax acctg. UST Inc., Greenwich, 1984—. Mem. AICPA, Tax Execs. Inst. Home: 529 Nod Hill Rd Wilton CT 06897 Office: UST Inc 100 W Putnam Ave Greenwich CT 06830

SCHREYER, MANFRED RICHARD, marketing professional, consultant; b. Clausthal, Zellerfeld, Germany, May 23, 1957; came to U.S., 1984; s. Richard Ewald and Elsbeth (Kottke) S.; m. Marilyn Louise Varvel, Mar. 2, 1979; 1 child, Manfred Richard II. Tech. degree, Fachhochschule Nord Ost Niedersachsen, Buxtehude, Germany, 1979. Pres. Auktionshaus Manfred Schreyer, Buxtehude, 1977-84, Mktg. and Promotion, Richmond, Ind., 1984—; cons. Graphic Press, Richmond, 1988—, Furniture Showcase, Richmond, 1988—, Koon's Appliances, Richmond, 1988—; dir. of ops. Farm Bur., Inc., P.S., Indpls., 1988—. Author: Reference Book for Critical Sales, 1987. Chmn. Rose Festival Richmond, 1986, Rose Garden Com., Richmond, 1987—. Mem. Richmond C. of C., Kiwanis (chmn. local chpt. 1986-88), Masons. Home and Office: Mktg and Promotion 101 S 13th St Richmond IN 47374

SCHREYER, WILLIAM ALLEN, investment firm executive; b. Williamsport, Pa., Jan. 13, 1928; s. William L. and Elizabeth (Engel) S.; m. Joan Legg, Oct. 17, 1953; 1 dau., Drue Ann. B.A., Pa. State U., 1948. With Merrill Lynch, Inc. and predecessors, N.Y.C., 1948—; v.p. Merrill Lynch, Pierce, Fenner & Smith, Inc., N.Y.C., 1965-78, sales dir., 1969-72, met. regional dir., 1972-73; chmn. Merrill Lynch Govt. Securities, Inc., N.Y.C., 1973-76, exec. v.p. capital markets activities, 1976-78, pres., 1978-85, chmn., 1981-85, pres., chief operating officer, 1982-85; chief exec. officer Merrill Lynch & Co., N.Y.C., 1984—, chmn., 1985—, also bd dirs. various subs.; bd. dirs. N.Y. Stock Exchange, Inc., Schering-Plough Corp. Trustee Med. Center at Princeton, 1974-80, Am. Mgmt. Assns., 1979—; chmn. Sigma Phi Epsilon Ednl. Found., 1979—. Served with USAF, 1955-56. Mem. Securities Industry Assn. (gov. 1979—, vice chmn. 1978-83), Bus. Roundtable (budget task force com.), Com. of Econ. Devel. (trustee), Fgn. Policy Assn. (gov.), Ctr. for Strategic and Internat. Studies (internat. councillor). Roman Catholic. Clubs: Bond (N.Y.C.), River, Links; Saturn (Buffalo); Springdale Golf (Princeton), Nassau; Knights of Malta. Office: Merrill Lynch & Co Inc 165 Broadway New York NY 10080 *

SCHRIER, STUART TED, lawyer, real estate company executive; b. Bklyn., Feb. 15, 1956; s. Melvin Henry and Anita Ruth (Finkelstein) S.; m. Alicia Joan Protas, Dec. 22, 1979; children: Danielle, Jaclyn Rose, Sarah Beth. BA in Philosophy with honors, SUNY, Stony Brook, 1978; JD, Boston U., 1981. Bar: Mass. 1981, U.S. Dist. Ct. Mass. 1983, U.S. Supreme Ct. 1987. Pvt. practice Boston, 1981-87; ptnr. Schrier & Balin, Boston, 1987—; pres., bd. dirs. Real Estate Co., Inc., Boston, 1983—. Mem. ABA, Mass. Bar Assn. Jewish. Office: Schrier & Balin 1011 Dorchester Ave Boston MA 02125

SCHRIEVER, BERNARD ADOLPH, management consultant; b. Bremen, Germany, Sept. 14, 1910; came to U.S., 1917, naturalized, 1923; s. Adolph Niholaus and Elizabeth (Milch) S.; m. Dora Brett, Jan. 3, 1938; children: Brett Arnold, Dodie Elizabeth Schriever Moeller, Barbara Alice Schriever Allan. B.S., Tex. A&M U., 1931; M.S.M.E., Stanford U., 1942; D.Sc. (hon.), Creighton U., 1958, Rider Coll., 1958, Adelphia Coll., 1959, Rollins Coll., 1959; D.Aero. Sci. (hon.), U. Mich., 1961; D.Eng. (hon.), Bklyn. Poly. Inst., 1961; LL.D. (hon.), Loyola U., Los Angeles, 1960. Commd. 2d lt. U.S. Army Air Force, 1938; advanced through grades to gen. U.S. Air Force, 1961; comdr. ICBM Program, 1954-59, AFSC, 1959-66; ret. 1966; chmn. bd.

Schriever & McKee, Washington, 1971-87; cons. B.A. Schriever, 1987—; dir. Am. Med. Internat., Emerson Electric Co., Wackenhut Corp. Decorated D.S.M., D.S.M. with oak leaf cluster, Legion of Merit, Air medal, Purple Heart; named to Aviation Hall of Fame, 1980; recipient Forrestal award, 1987. Fellow AIAA; mem. Nat. Acad. Engring., Am. Astron. Soc., Air Force Assn. Clubs: Burning Tree, Los Angeles Country. Home: 4501 Dexter St NW Washington DC 20007 Office: 2000 N 15th St Ste 707 Arlington VA 22201

SCHRIEVER, FRED MARTIN, consulting company executive; b. N.Y.C., June 5, 1930; s. Samuel and Sara S.; m. Cheri G. Spatt, Aug. 2, 1953; children: Melissa Ann, Elizabeth Ellen. B.M.E., Poly. U. N.Y., 1952, M.M.E., 1958. Registered profl. engr., N.Y., Wash. cert. mgmt. cons. Chief engr. div. Sperry Corp., N.Y.C., 1956-64; v.p. Booz, Allen and Hamilton, N.Y.C. and Washington, 1964-71; sr. v.p. Reliance Group Holdings, Inc., N.Y.C., 1971—; chmn., pres. RCG Internat. Inc., N.Y.C., 1971—; chmn. Werner Mgmt. Consultants Inc.; pres. RCG Personnel Scis., Inc.; bd. dirs. Moody Tottrup Inc., P-E Internat. PLC, RCG Vectron Systems Inc., RCG Hagler Bailly Inc. Served to 1st lt. U.S. Army, 1952-54. Fellow Inst. of Dirs., Inst. Mgmt. Consultants U.K.; mem. ASME, Inst. Mgmt. Consultants. Club: Metropolitan. Home: PO Box 32 Westport CT 06881 Office: RCG Internat Inc 111 W 40th St New York NY 10018

SCHROEDEL, HUBERTA GOWEN WOLF, non-profit foundation administrator; b. Phila., Oct. 8, 1943; d. Richard O'Shea and Huberta Horan (Gowen) Wolf; m. Serafettin Vgur; 1 child, Kemal. BS in Sociology, Daemen Coll., 1967; MS in Counseling, U. Ariz., 1969. Lic. notary pub.; cert. infant massage educator. Rehab. counselor Fountain House, Inc., Rockland State Hosp., N.Y.C., 1969-72; tchr. of the deaf N.Y.C. BD. of Edn., Hearing Edn. Services, 1974—; exec. dir. N.Y. Ctr. for Law and the Deaf, N.Y.C., 1980—; cons. St. Joseph Sch. for the Deaf, Bronx, N.Y., 1978-82; mem. nat. adv. com. The Captions Ctr., 1987—. Exec. producer TV video series, New York Connection, 1987—. Chairperson N.Y. Deaf Women, 1981; adv. bd. N.Y.C. Mayor's Office for Handicapped, 1984—. Recipient Durfee award for enhancing human dignity Durfee Found., 1987. Mem. Nat. Assn. Female Execs., Lexington Mental Health Ctr. for the Deaf (adv. bd.). Democrat. Roman Catholic. Office: NY Ctr for Law and the Deaf 275 Seventh Ave New York NY 10001

SCHROEDER, CHARLES EDGAR, bank executive, investment management executive; b. Chgo., Nov. 17, 1935; s. William Edward and Lelia Lorraine (Anderson) S.; m. Martha Elizabeth Runnette, Dec. 30, 1958; children: Charles Edgar, Timothy Creighton, Elizabeth Linton. BA in Econs., Dartmouth Coll., 1957; MBA, Amos Tuck Sch., 1958. Security analyst Miami Corp., Chgo., 1960-69, treas., 1969-78, pres., 1978—, dir., 1969—; security analyst Cutler Oil & Gas Corp., Chgo., 1960-69; treas. Cutler Oil & Gas Corp., Chgo., 1969-78, pres., 1978—, dir., 1969—; chmn. bd., dir. Blvd. Bank of Chgo., 1981-86; dir. Nat. Blvd. Bank of Chgo.; bd. dirs. Blvd. Bank, N.A., Blvd. Bancorp, Inc., Nat.-Standard Co., Niles, Mich. Assoc. Northwestern U., 1975—; trustee First Presbyterian Ch. of Evanston, Ill., 1968—; bd. dirs. Presbyn. Home, Evanston, 1979-83; trustee Wayland Acad., Beaver Dam, Wis., 1982-88, Northwestern Meml. Hosp., 1985—. Lt. (j.g.) USN, 1958-60. Mem. Fin. Analysts Soc. of Chgo., Beta Theta Pi. Clubs: Chicago, Glen View (v.p.), Mid-America, Michigan Shores, Casque and Gauntlet, Comml. Office: Miami Corp 410 N Michigan Ave Chicago IL 60611

SCHROEDER, DAVID HAROLD, healthcare facility executive; b. Chgo., Oct. 22, 1940; s. Harry T. and Clara D. (Dexter) S.; m. Clara Doorn, Dec. 27, 1964; children: Gregory D., Elizabeth M. BBA, Kans. State Coll., 1965; MBA, Wichita State U., 1968; postgrad., U. Ill., 1968-69. CPA, Ill. Supt. cost acctg. Boeing Co., Wichita, Kans., 1965-68; sr. v.p., treas. Riverside Med. Ctr., Kankakee, Ill., 1971—; treas. Kankakee Area Care Corp., 1982—, Kankakee Valley Health Inc., 1985—, Riverside Medi-Ctr., Kankakee, 1983—; v.p., treas. Oakside Corp., Kankakee, 1982—; bd. dirs. Harmony Home Health Svc. Inc., Naperville, Ill.; mem. faculty various profl. orgns. Contbg. author: Cost Containment in Hospitals, 1980; contbr. articles to profl. jours. Pres. Riverside Employees Credit Union, 1976-79; founder Kankakee Trinity Acad., 1980, Riverview Hist. Dist., Kankakee, 1982; pres. Kankakee County Mental Health Ctr., 1982-84, United Way Kankakee County, 1984-85; chmn. Ill. Provider Trust, Naperville, 1983-85; trustee, treas. Am. Luth. Ch.; preceptor Gov.'s State U., University Park, Ill, 19876. Capt. U.S. Army, 1969-71. Fellow Am. Coll. Healthcare Execs., Healthcare Fin. Mgmt. Assn. (pres. 1975-76, cert. mgr. patient accounts 1981); mem. Ill. Hosp. Assn. (chmn. council health fin. 1982-85), Inst. Chartered Fin. Analysts, Am. Inst. CPAs, Ill. CPA Soc., Nat. Assn. Accts., Healthcare Fin. Mgmt. Assn. (William G. Follimer award 1977, Robert H. Reeves Award 1981, Muncie Gold award 1987), Classic Car Club Am., Packard Club, Kiwanis (pres.-elect), Masons. Home: 901 S Chicago Ave Kankakee IL 60901 Office: Riverside Med Ctr 350 N Wall St Kankakee IL 60901

SCHROEDER, ERVIN EDWARD, petrochemical executive; b. Evansville, Ind., Sept. 24, 1934; s. George Frederick and Martha L. (Boeke) S.; m. Marcia Lee Metzger, Jan. 11, 1958; children: Timothy, Cynthia. BS, Purdue U., 1956. Process devel. Firestone Tire & Rubber Co., Akron, Ohio, 1958-68; research group leader Firestone Tire & Rubber Co., 1968-70, mgr. customer service, 1970-72, tech. dir., 1972-79; plant mgr. Shintech, Inc., Freeport, Tex., 1980-84; dir. mfg. Shintech, Inc., 1984-88. Author: Reigels Handbook Industrial Chemistry-Rubber, 1983; contbr. articles to profl. jours.; numerous patents in field. Paul Harris fellow, Rotary Internat., Chgo. 1987. Mem. Akron Section Am. Inst. Chem. Engrs. (chmn. elect, sec., treas. 1966-68), Freeport C. of C. (bd. dirs., v.p.). Republican. Episcopalian. Lodge: Rotary (chmn. projects local chpt.). Home: 106 Fawn Trail Lake Jackson TX 77566 Office: Shintech Inc 5618 Hwy 332 E Freeport TX 77541

SCHROEDER, FREDERICK JOHN, JR., investment banker; b. Detroit, July 13, 1934; s. Frederick John and Evelyn (Calalan) S.; m. Janet Bachrach, Dec. 29, 1977; children: Yvelyn, Frederique Lory. BA in English, Georgetown U., 1956; MBA, Harvard U., 1962. Intern, lending officer Nat. Bank Detroit, 1962-68; v.p. corp. fin. 1st of Mich. Corp., Detroit, 1968-78, sr. v.p., mgr. corp. fin., 1978-83, exec. v.p., 1983—, also officer, bd. dirs. 7 corp. subs.; pres., chief exec. officer Omni Petroleum, Detroit. Bd. dirs. Goodsports Found., Detroit, 1988. Lt (j.g.) USNR, 1956-60. Mem. Securities Industry Assn. (com. 1985—), Bayview Yacht Club, Grosse Pointe Club. Home: 115 Lewiston Rd Grosse Pointe Farms MI 48236 Office: 1st of Mich Corp 100 Renaissance Ctr Detroit MI 48243

SCHROEDER, HORST WILHELM, food products executive; b. Schwerin, Fed. Republic Germany, May 5, 1941; m. Gisela I. Kammin; 1 child, Bernd; stepchildren: Ralph, Isabel Lange. BBA, U. Gottingen, Hamburg, Fed. Republic of West Germany, 1965. Sr. auditor Price Waterhouse, Hamburg, 1966-70; fin. contr. Kellogg Co. of West Germany, Bremen, 1970-71, dir. fin., 1971-76, mng. dir., 1976-81; pres., chief exec. officer Kellogg Salada Can., Toronto, 1981-83; pres. Kellogg Internat., Battle Creek, Mich., 1983-86, Kellogg N.A., Battle Creek, 1986-88; exec. v.p. Kellogg Co., Battle Creek, 1988, pres., chief oper. officer, 1988—. Bd. of govs. St. Joseph Acad. of Food Mktg., Phila., 1986-88; mem. com. external affairs U. Ill., Chgo., 1987-88. Mem. Am. Health Found. (bd. dirs. 1987—), KC (pres. 1988—, bd. dirs. 1989—). Office: Kellogg Co 1 Kellogg Sq Box 3599 Battle Creek MI 49016-3599 *

SCHROEDER, MARY ESTHER, wood products executive; b. Dayton, Ohio, July 29, 1947; d. James Walter and Mary Agnes (Danzig) McIver; m. Reinhard Schroeder, Sept. 10, 1966 (div. Mar. 1989). BS in Forest Industries Mgmt., Ohio State U., 1978. Fiber supply supr. Crown Zellerbach, Inc., Port Townsend, Wash., 1978-83; fiber supply and transp. mgr. Port Townsend Paper Corp., Bainbridge Island, Wash., 1983-87; dir. Pacific Wood Fuels, Redding, Calif., 1987—; bd. dirs. Peninsula Devel. Assn., Port Angeles, Wash., 1985—. Screenwriter: As the Chips Fall, 1988. Precinct committeeman Kitsap County Reps., Poulsbo, Wash., 1984-86; active Rep. Presdl. Task Force. Mem. Soc. Am. Foresters, Shasta Alliance for Resources and Environment, Am. Pulpwood Assn., Western Timber Assn., Timber Assn. Calif., Writers' Forum, Am. Film Inst. Home: 320 Hilltop Dr #216 Redding CA 96003 Office: Pacific Wood Fuel 2659 Balls Ferry Rd Anderson CA 96007

SCHROEDER, ROBERT ANTHONY, lawyer; b. Bendena, Kans., May 19, 1912; s. Anthony and Nanon (Bagby) S.; m. Janet Manning, Nov. 21, 1936; 1 child, Robert Breathitt. LLB cum laude, U. Kans., 1937. Bar: Mo. 1937. Atty. Allstate Ins. Co., Chgo., 1937-38; assoc. Madden, Freeman, Madden & Burke, Kansas City, Mo., 1938-48; ptnr. Swofford, Schroeder & Shankland, Kansas City, 1948-59; pvt. practice law 1959-67; ptnr. Schroeder & Schroeder, 1967-84; commr. 16th Jud. Circuit, 1974-80, Appellate Jud. Commn. of Mo., 1980-86; pres., bd. dirs. Roxbury State Bank, Kans., 1954-77, chmn. bd. dirs., 1977—; chmn. bd. dirs. Roxbury Bancshares Inc., 1984—; pres. Douglas County Investment Co., 1967-88; chmn. bd. dirs. Hub State Bank, 1974-82; hon. chmn. Mark Twain Bank Noland, 1982—; regional dir. Mark Twain Bancshares; sr. counsellor Mo. Bar, 1987. Author: Twenty-Five Years Under The Missouri Plan, Twenty-Five Years Experience with Merit Judicial Selection in Missouri; editorial bd.: Kan. Bar Jour, 1935-36. Hon. trustee Kansas City Art Inst.; bd. dirs. Mo. Inst. for Justice; mem. dirs. club U. Kans. Williams Ednl. Fund, 1978-81, execs. club, 1981-85, All Am. club, 1986—. Recipient Disting. Alumnus award U. Kans. Sch. Law; hon. fellow Harry S. Truman Library Inst., disting. charter fellow Kansas City Bar Found.; donor Robert A. Schroeder endowed chair for disting. prof., 1981; established Robert A. Schroeder scholarships and fellowship at U. Kans. Sch. Law.; donor Roberta Schroeder Scholarship at Midway High Sch., Kans., 1985. Fellow Am. Coll. Probate Counsel, Am. Bar Found., Kans. U. Law Soc. (trustee 1970-74); mem. ABA (Mo. chmn. membership com. 1961-65, del. 1966-70, lawyer referral com.), Mo. Bar Found. (v.p. 1965-69, pres. 1969-73), Mo. Bar Assn. (bd. govs. 1959-67), Mo. Bar (exec. com. 1963-67, pres. 1965-66, v.p., pres. found., chmn. legal edn. com. 1964-65, chmn. cts. and judiciary com. 1971-72, mem. bench and bar com. 1970-80, vice chmn. 1970-71; Pres.'s award 1972), Bar Assn. State Kans. (hon. life), Kansas City Bar Assn. (pres. 1957-58, chmn. exec. com., chmn. law day com., chmn. program com. 1968-70, chmn. prepaid legal services com. 1975-76; Achievement award 1976), Am. Judicature Soc. (bd. dirs. 1967-69), Nat. Legal Aid and Defender Assn., U. Kans. Law Alumni Assn. Greater Kansas City (past pres.), Order of Coif, Delta Tau Delta, Phi Delta Phi. Club: Mason. Office: 11324 Madison St Kansas City MO 64114

SCHROEDER, WALTER ALLEN, lawyer, director; b. San Francisco, July 29, 1954; s. Carl Walter and Mary (Lee) S.; m. Lee Walthall, Jan. 1, 1982; BS in Bus. Adminstrn., Georgetown U., 1976; JD, U. Houston, 1979. Bar: Tex. 1979, D.C. 1984, U.S. Dist. Ct. (we., no. and so. dists.) Tex., U.S. Ct. Appeals (5th, 11th and D.C. cirs.), U.S. Supreme Ct. Asst. treas. G.U. Fed. Credit Union, Washington, 1976-77; asst. to pres. U.S.E. Credit Union, Houston, 1977-79; analyst Banc Systems, Inc., Houston, 1979; briefing atty. Tex. Ct. Civil Appeals, Ft. Worth, 1979-80; asst. counsel Am. Ins. Assn., Houston, 1980-81; atty. Rolston & Hausler, Houston, 1981-85, Chamberlain, Hrdlicka, White, Johnson & Williams, 1985-86, Hollrah, Lange & Thoma, 1986-87, Eikenburg & Stiles, 1987—; dir. Fayetteville Bank, 1988—, Fayetteville Bancshares Inc., 1988—; pres. 1985-86, dir. 1985-86, 87—, Park Regency Coun. Co-owners. Trustee Found. Amateur Radio, Inc. Washington, 1972-76, chmn. audit com., 1975-76; treas. Houston Echo Soc., 1979. Mem. ABA, D.C. Bar Assn., Houston Bar Assn., Houston Young Lawyers Assn., State Bar Tex., Tex. Assn. Bank Counsel. Republican. Lutheran. Clubs: Univ. (Houston). Author articles in field. Home: 6201 Olympia Houston TX 77057 Office: Eikenburg & Stiles 1100 First City Nat Bank 1021 Main St Houston TX 77002

SCHROER, EDMUND ARMIN, utility company executive; b. Hammond, Ind., Feb. 14, 1928; s. Edmund Henry and Florence Evelyn (Schmidt) S.; children: James, Fredrik, Amy, Lisa, Timothy, Suzanne. BA, Valparaiso U., 1949; JD, Northwestern U., 1952. Bar: Ind. 1952. Sole practice Hammond, 1952—; assoc. Crumpacker & Friedrich, 1952; ptnr. Crumpacker & Schroer, 1954-56; assoc., then ptnr. Lawyer, Friedrich, Petrie & Tweedle, 1957-62; ptnr. Lawyer, Schroer & Eichhorn, 1963-66; sr. ptnr. Schroer, Eichhorn & Morrow, Hammond, 1967-77; pres., chief exec. officer No. Ind. Pub. Service Co., Hammond, 1977—, chmn., 1978—, also bd. dirs.; asst. dist. atty., No. Ind., 1954-56; bd. dirs., mem. exec. com. Ind. Electric Assn.; bd. dirs. Harris Bank Corp., Assoc. Electric and Gas Ins. Services, Ltd., Bankmont Fin. Corp. Trustee Sch. Bd., Munster, Ind., 1969-71, pres., 1971; fin. chmn. Rep. Party, Hammond, 1958-62; del. Ind. Rep. Conv., 1958, 60, 64, 66, 68. Mem. ABA, Fed. Bar Assn., Ind. Bar Assn. (bd. mgrs. 1969-71), Hammond Bar Assn. (pres. 1966-67), Am. Gas Assn. (mem. exec. com., chmn. 1986), Gas Research Inst. (mem. exec. com., chmn. budget com., bd. dirs.), Edison Electric Inst. (bd. dirs.). Lutheran. Lodge: Rotary (pres. Hammond club 1968). Office: No Ind Pub Svc Co 5265 Hohman Ave Hammond IN 46320

SCHROETER, LOUIS C., pharmaceutical company executive; b. St. Louis, Dec. 13, 1929; s. Clarence Edward and Eleanor (Schindler) S.; m. Julann Griffin, June 7, 1952; children: John Louis, Lois Celeste, Julie Ann, Robert Louis. BS, St. Louis Coll. Pharmacy, 1952, MS, 1956, DSci. (hon.), 1982; PhD, U. Wis., 1959. Lic. pharmacist, Mo. Rsch. assoc. Upjohn Co., Kalamazoo, 1959-63, head rsch., 1963-66, asst. rsch. mgr., 1966-69, rsch. mgr., 1969-70, v.p. pharm. mfg., 1973-77, v.p., gen. mgr., 1977-85, v.p. worldwide mfg., Eng., 1985-88, corp. sr. v.p., 1988—; exec. dir. Merck, Sharpe & Dohme, West Point, Pa., 1969-70; chmn. U.S. Pharmacopeia Adv. Panel, 1975; bd. dirs. Nat. Pharm. Coun., Washington, 1979-85, Mich. Pharm. Coun., Lansing, 1981-83; bd. advisers Rsch. Inst. Pharm. Edn., Oxford, Miss., 1985-87. Author: Sulfur Dioxide, 1966, Ingredient X, 1969, Organizational Elan, 1970, Self-Discipline, 1978. Trustee St. Louis Coll. Pharmacy, 1986—; chmn. Kalamazoo Symphony Soc., 1980-83, trustee, 1982-87; bd. dirs. Am. Found. Pharm. Edn., N.Y.C., 1985— With U.S. Army, 1953-55. Recipient Disting. Svc. to Pharmacy award Alumni St. Louis Coll. Pharmacy, 1968, Citation for Profl. and Literary Accomplishments, U. Wis., 1980. Fellow Acad. Pharm. Scis. (v.p. 1968-69); mem. Am. Pharm. Assn. (mem. exec. com. 1968—). Republican. Roman Catholic. Office: Upjohn Co 7000 Portage Rd Kalamazoo MI 49001

SCHROPFER, DAVID WALDRON, advertising executive, educator, consultant; b. Plainfield, N.J., Oct. 27, 1939; s. Frank Jeremiah and Edna Mae (Mueller) S.; m. Gloria Weaver, Aug. 10, 1963; children: Suzanne, David Jr., Kathleen. BS, NYU, 1961; postgrad., Hunter Coll., 1972-74. Asst. product mgr. Procter and Gamble, Cin., 1961-63; account exec. Ted Bates, N.Y.C., 1963-65; sr. account exec. Ogilvy and Mather, N.Y.C., 1965-68; v.p., mgmt. supr. SSC&B, N.Y.C., 1969-72, D'Arcy McManus and Masius Inc., N.Y.C., 1973-75; exec. v.p. James Neal Harvey, Inc., N.Y.C., 1976-79; exec. v.p., ptnr. Mike Sloan, Inc., Miami, Fla., 1980-82; pres., chief exec. officer Knudsen Moore Schropfer Advt., Inc., Stamford, Conn., 1983-88; pres. DWS Advt Inc., Stamford, 1988—; adj. prof. Fla. Internat. U., Miami, 1982; lectr. U. Mass., Amherst, 1985-86, U. New Haven, 1985, Providence Coll., 1987. Author: What Every Account Executive Should Know About Marketing Plans, 1989. Chmn. Charter Revision Commn., Stamford, 1986-87; mem. Stamford Bd. Fin., 1987—; chmn. ARC, Stamford, 1987—, bd. dirs. 1984—, Jr. Achievement, Miami, 1982-83. Mem. Am. Assn. Advt. Agys. (lectr. 1982-85), Am. Mktg. Assn., Am. Mgmt. Assn. (lectr. 1984—). Democrat. Roman Catholic. Club: Landmark (Stamford).

SCHROTH, PETER W(ILLIAM), lawyer, educator; b. Camden, N.J., July 24, 1946; s. Walter and Patricia Anne (Page) S.; m. Keven Anne Murphy, Jan. 2, 1986; children: Laura Salome Erickson-Schroth, Julia James. AB, Shimer Coll., 1966; JD, U.Chgo., 1969, M in Comparative Law, 1971; SJD, U. Mich., 1979; postgrad. U. Freiburg (W.Ger.), Faculté Internationale pour l'Enseignement de Droit Comparé; MBA, Rensselaer Poly. Inst., 1988. Bar: Ill. 1969, N.Y. 1979, Conn. 1985. Asst. prof. So. Meth. U., 1973-77; fellow in law and humanities Harvard U., 1976-77, vis. scholar, 1980-81; assoc. prof. N.Y. Law Sch., 1977-81; prof. law Hamline U., St. Paul, 1981-83; dep. gen. counsel Equator Bank Ltd., 1984-87, v.p., dep. gen. counsel, Equator Holdings Ltd. 1987—; adj. prof. law U. Conn., 1985-86, Western New Eng. Coll., 1988—, of mgmt. Rensselaer Poly. Inst., 1988—. Mem. ABA, Am. Fgn. Law Assn., Internat. Bar Assn., Internat. Law Assn. (coms. multinat. banking and internationalization securities markets), Assn. Trial Lawyers Am., Conn. Civil Liberties Union (bd. dirs.), Environ. Law Inst. (assoc.), Columbia U. Peace Seminar (assoc.). Author: Foreign Investment in the United States, 2d edit., 1977; (with Stiefel) Products Liability: European Proposals and American Experience, 1981; bd. editors Am. Jour. Comparative Law, 1981-84, Conn. Bar Jour.; editor in chief ABA Environ. Law Symposium, 1980-83; contbr. articles to profl. jours. Office: Equator House 111 Charter Oak Ave Hartford CT 06106

SCHUBERT, BLAKE H., corporate executive, lawyer; b. Wheeling, W.Va., Apr. 21, 1939; s. John Arnold and Esther Elizabeth (Masters) S.; m. Carol Jean Cramp, Jan. 13, 1962; children—Cheryl Lynn, Charles Bradley, Elisabeth Anne. BA, Ohio Wesleyan U., 1961; JD, U. Chgo., 1964. Bar: Ill. 1964, U.S. Dist. Ct. (no. dist.) Ill. 1968. Atty., Brunswick Corp., Chgo., 1964-68; asst. group counsel FMC Corp., Chgo., 1968-73; gen. counsel Dresser Tool Group, Chgo., 1973-79; chmn. Schubert Securities Corp., Oak Park, Ill., 1979-84, Inter-Am. Investments, Inc., Oak Park, 1980—; gen. ptnr. Investment Trust Ltd., St. Petersburg, Fla., 1981—, Inter-Am. Fund, Oak Park, 1982—, Inter-Am. Fund I, Oak Park, 1982-87, Inter-Am. Fund II, Oak Park, 1984—; chmn. Compath Video Corp., Oak Park, 1984-85; lectr. Am. Inst. Banking, 1965, Chgo. Inst. Fin. Studies, 1984-85. Chmn. 1st United Ch. Endowment Fund, Oak Park, 1975-80, Park Forest Co-op. (Ill.), 1966-70. Recipient Bancroft-Whitney Prize U. Chgo., 1964. Mem. Ill. State Bar Assn., Chgo. Bd. Options Exch. Author: THe Well-Kept Secrets of Investing, 1982. Home and Office: 522 Linden Ave Oak Park IL 60302

SCHUBERT, MARTIN WILLIAM, investment bank executive; b. N.Y.C., Oct. 27, 1935; s. Charles and Ann (Kaplan) S.; m. Irene Ginsberg, Jan. 17, 1960 (div. July 1974); children: Lisa, Douglas, Jeffrey; m. Carol Sue Howard, Dec. 28, 1986.. BA, Bklyn. Coll., 1957; MBA, CCNY, 1962; postgrad., NYU, 1962-65. Trader Phillip Bros. (PHIBRO), N.Y.C., 1959-64; sr. v.p. Rosenthal & Rosenthal Inc., N.Y.C., 1964-82; pres. Rosenthal Internat. Ltd., N.Y.C., 1976-82; chmn., chief exec. officer European Interam. Fin. Co., N.Y.C., 1982—; bd. dirs. Singer & Friedlander Ltd., London; chmn., bd. dirs. Finex Corp., N.Y.C., 1985-87; vice chmn., bd. dirs. Trade Credit Underwriters Agy., N.Y.C., 1985-86; mng. ptnr., bd. dirs. Eurinam Capital Ptnrs., N.Y.C., 1985-86. Co-author: Pick's Currency Annual, 1963, Challenge of International Finance, 1966; contbr. numerous articles on internat. fin. to profl. jours. Mem. U.S. Council of Mex.-U.S. Bus. Com. Council of Americas, 1987—. Mem. Brazilian-Am. C. of C., Venezuelan-Am. C. of C. Republican. Home: 245 E 40th St Apt 25C New York NY 10016 Office: European Interamerican Fin Corp 400 Madison Ave Ste 401 New York NY 10017

SCHUBERT, NANCY ELLEN, beauty industry executive, management consultant, franchise director; b. Chgo., June 25, 1945; d. Raymond James and Kathleen Mary (Gibbons) Nugent; m. Emil Joseph Schubert, Jan. 14, 1967; children—James Bryant, Erin Heather, Shannon Kathleen. B.F.A., Mundelein Coll., 1968. Freelance artist, Chgo., 1968; tchr. St. Pius X Sch., Lombard, Ill., 1975-76; pres., treas., dir. Super Style Inc., Hoffman Estates, Ill., 1981—, Super Six, Inc., Glendale Heights, Ill., 1983—, N.E.S. Mgmt. Inc., Schaumburg, Ill., 1985—, Super Style III, Inc., Berwyn, Ill., 1985—; created and developed Super Style concept and system of operation; created SuperStyle logo and design trademarked in 1983. Mem. Cermak Plaza Mcht. Assn. (bd. dirs.). Republican. Roman Catholic. Avocations: licensed pilot, downhill skiing, horseback riding. Office: Super Style Inc 707 W Golf Rd Hoffman Estates IL 60194

SCHUCHARD, JAMES ANTHONY, information systems specialist; b. Abilene, Tex., Feb. 27, 1953; s. James Harold Schuchard and Rose Mary (Tunnell) Burch; m. Melissa Joan Reiter, June 14, 1975; children: Jason Ryan, Patrick Aaron. BBA in Fin., Tex. Tech U., 1975, MS in Fin., 1976. Cons. mgr. Arthur Andersen & Co., Dallas, 1976-85; v.p. mgmt. info. systems Am. Heart Assn., Dallas, 1985—. Bd. dirs. Plano (Tex.) YMCA, 1987—. Mem. Soc. Info. Mgmt. Republican. Methodist. Office: Am Heart Assn 7320 Greenville Ave Dallas TX 75231

SCHUCHART, JOHN ALBERT, JR., utility executive; b. Omaha, Nov. 13, 1929; s. John A. and Mildred Vera (Kessler) S.; m. Ruth Joyce Schock, Dec. 2, 1950; children: Deborah J. Kelley, Susan K. Felton. B.S. in Bus, U. Nebr., 1950; grad., Stanford U. Exec. Program, 1968. With No. Natural Gas Co., Omaha, 1950-71, asst. sec., 1958-60, mgr. acctg., 1960-66, adminstrv. mgr., 1966-71; v.p., treas. Intermountain Gas Co., Boise, Idaho, 1972-75, chief fin. officer, 1973-75; fin. v.p. and treas., chief fin. officer Mont.-Dakota Utilities Co. (now MDU Resources Group, Inc.), Bismarck, N.D., 1976-77, pres., chief operating officer, 1978—, pres., chief exec. officer, 1980—, chmn. bd., 1983—, also dir.; bd. dirs. First Bank Bismarck, Fidelity Oil Holdings Inc., Bismarck, Knife River Coal Mining Co., Bismarck, Williston Basin Interstate Pipeline Co., Bismarck; mem. Midwest adv. bd. Arkwright Mut. Ins. Co., Waltham, Mass.; mem. Midwest adv. com. Mountain States Legal Found., Denver. Contbr. articles to profl. jours. Mem. budget com. United Way, Omaha, 1969-70; mem. Council U.S. Savs. Bonds Vols.; bd. dirs. Girl Scouts U.S.A., Boise, 1975, Greater N.D. Assn., Fargo; chmn. bd. trustees Bismarck YMCA; trustee, treas. N.D. chpt. Nature Conservancy; mem. lay adv. bd. St. Alexius Med. Ctr., Bismarck; bd. regents U. Mary, Bismarck. Served with AUS, 1951-53. Recipient Scroll and Merit award Adminstrv. Mgmt. Soc., 1972, U. Nebr. at Omaha citation for Alumnus Achievement, 1987. Mem. Am. Gas Assn. (past bd. dirs., Merit award 1968, 78), Midwest Gas Assn., Edison Electric Inst., North Central Elec. Assn., Fin. Execs. Inst., Delta Sigma Pi. Republican. Methodist. Clubs: Elks, Apple Creek Country. Home: 1014 Cottage Dr Bismarck ND 58501 Office: MDU Resouces Group Inc 400 N 4th St Bismarck ND 58501

SCHUCK, MARJORIE MASSEY, publisher, editor, authors' consultant; b. Winchester, Va., Oct. 9, 1921; d. Carl Frederick and Margaret Harriet (Parmele) Massey; student U. Minn., 1941-43, New Sch., N.Y.C., 1948, N.Y. U., 1952, 54-55; m. Ernest George Metcalfe, Dec. 2, 1943 (div. Oct. 1949); m. 2d, Franz Schuck, Nov. 11, 1953 (dec. Jan. 1958). Mem. editorial bd. St. Petersburg Poetry Assn., 1967-68; co-editor, pub. poetry Venture Mag., St. Petersburg, Fla., 1968-69, editor, pub., 1969-79; co-editor, pub. Poetry Venture Quar. Essays, Vol. I, 1968-69, Vol. 2, 1970-71; pub., editor poetry anthologies, 1972—; founder, owner, pres. Valkyrie Press, Inc. (name changed to Valkyrie Pub. House 1980), 1972—; cons. designs and formats, trade publs. and ann. reports, lit. books and pamphlets, 1973—; founder Valkyrie Press Roundtable Workshop and Forum for Writers, 1975-79; established Valkyrie Press Reference Library, 1976-80; pub., editor The Valkyrie Internat. Newsletter, 1986—; exec. dir. Inter-Cultural Forum Villanor Ctr., Tampa, Fla., 1987—; pres. Found. for Human Potentials, Inc., Tampa, 1988—; lectr. in field. Judge poetry and speech contests Gulf Beach Women's Club, 1970, Fine Arts Festival dist. 14. Am. Fedn. Women's Clubs, 1970, South and West, Inc., 1972, The Sunstone Rev., 1973, Internat. Toastmistress Clubs, 1974, 78, Beaux Arts Poetry Festival, 1983; judge Fla. Gov.'s Screenwriters Competition, 1984—. Corr.-rec. sec. Women's Aux. Hosp. for Spl. Surgery, N.Y.C., 1947-59; active St. Petersburg Mus. Fine Arts (charter), St. Petersburg Sister City Com., St. Petersburg Arts Center Assn.; mem. Orange Belt express com. 1988 Centennial Celebration for St. Petersburg, mem. Com. of 100 of Pinellas County, Inc., exec. bd., 1975-77, membership chmn., 1975-77; pub. relations chmn. Soc. for prevention Cruelty to Animals, 1968-71, bd. dirs., 1968-71, 75-77; mem. Pinellas County Arts Council, 1977-79, chmn., 1977-78; mem. grant rev. panel for lit. Fine Arts Council of Fla., 1979. Named One of 76 Fla. Patriots, Fla. Bicentennial Commn., 1976; a recipient 1st ann. People of Dedication award Salvation Army, Tampa, 1984. Mem. Acad. Am. Poets, Fla. Suncoast Writers' Confs. (founder, co-dir., lectr. 1973-83, adv. bd. 1984—), Fla. Poets Assn., Com. Small Mag. Editors and Pubs., Coordinating Council Lit. Mags., Friends of Library of St. Petersburg, Suncoast Mgmt. Inst. (exec. bd.; chmn. Women in Mgmt. 1977-78), Pi Beta Phi. Republican. Episcopalian. Author: Speeches and Writings for Cause of Freedom, 1973. Contbr. poetry to profl. jours. Home: 8245 26th Ave N Saint Petersburg FL 33710 Office: 8245 26th Ave N Saint Petersburg FL 33710

SCHUELE, ALBAN WILHELM, chemical company executive; b. Stuehlingen, Baden-Wuerttemberg, W. Ger., Apr. 28, 1944; came to U.S., 1963; s. Wilhelm and Emma (Utz) S.; m. Grayce Winifred LaGrotta, Jan. 25, 1969; children: Jason Alban, Kathleen Marie. B.S. in Econs., Ariz. State U., 1969; B. Internat. Mgmt., Am. Grad. Sch. Internat. Mgmt. Thunderbird, Glendale, Ariz., 1970. V.p. Chase Manhattan Bank, N.Y.C., 1970-80; treas. Am. Hoechst Corp. (now Hoechst Celanese Corp.), Somerville, N.J., 1980—, v.p., treas., 1985-88; treas. Hoechst-Roussel Pharms., Inc., 1985—, Hoechst-Roussel Agri-Vet Co., 1985—; v.p. quality and communications Hoechst Celanese Corp., 1988—, corp. v.p. and pres. splty. products group, 1989—; treas. P.B. Diagnostics, Inc., 1985—. Mem. Nat. Assn. Corp. Treas., Fin.

Exec. Inst. Roman Catholic. Office: Hoechst Celanese Corp Splty Products Group 1 Main St Chatham NJ 07928

SCHUENKE, DONALD JOHN, insurance company executive; b. Milw., Jan. 12, 1929; s. Ray H. and Josephine P. (Maciolek) S.; m. Joyce A. Wetzel, July 19, 1952; children: Ann, Mary. Ph.B., Marquette U., 1950, LL.B., 1958. Bar: Wis. 1958. Spl. agt. Nat. Life of Vt., 1958-59; real estate rep. Standard Oil Co. of Ind., Milw., 1959-63; atty. Northwestern Mut. Life Ins. Co., Milw., 1963-65; asst. counsel Northwestern Mut. Life Ins. Co., 1965-67, asst. gen. counsel, 1967-74, v.p., gen. counsel, sec., 1974-76, sr. v.p. investments, 1976-80, pres., 1980—, chief operating officer, 1981-83, pres., chief exec. officer, 1983—; bd. dirs. Mortgage Guaranty Ins. Corp., No. Telecom Ltd., Regis Group. Bd. dirs. Milw. Symphony Orch., Com. Econ. Devel., Marquette U., United Way of Greater Milw., Med. Research Fund, Milw. Redevel. Fund, Badger Meter, Milw. Regional Med. Ctr., Milw. Art Mus., Milw. Boys and Girls Club, Grand Ave Corp., Greater Milw. Com., Wis. Taxpayers Alliance, Med. Coll. Wis.; mem. adv. council Am. Heart Assn.; mem. Competitive Wis. Milw. Redevel. Corp. Mem. Wis. Bar Assn., Am. Council Life Ins. (bd. dirs.), Met. Milw. Assn. Commerce (bd. dirs.). Club: University (local bd. dirs.). Home: 3704 N Lake Shore Dr Shorewood WI 53211 Office: Northwestern Mut Life Ins Co 720 E Wisconsin Ave Milwaukee WI 53202 *

SCHUETTINGER, ROBERT LINDSAY, international studies center executive; b. N.Y.C., Sept. 12, 1936; s. Edward Andrew and Mildred (McKenna) S. MA, U. Chgo., 1968; BPhil, St. Andrews U., 1975; postgrad., Columbia U., 1959-60, Oxford U., Eng., 1962-64. Asst. prof. polit. sci. Cath. U. Am., Washington, 1965-68; sr. research assoc. U.S. Ho. Reps., Washington, 1973-77; dir. studies Heritage Found., Washington, 1977-79; asst. dir. nat. security affairs Reagan Transition Office, Washington, 1980-81; dep. to undersec. of state U.S. State Dept., Washington, 1981; sr. policy analyst The White House, Washington, 1981-83; dir. long range policy planning Office Sec. Def., Washington, 1984; pres. Washington Internat. Studies Ctr., 1985—; vis. lectr. polit. sci. Yale U., New Haven, 1974, 75; assoc. fellow Davenport Coll. Yale U., 1974—; assoc. mem. Mansfield Coll., Oxford U., 1988—. Author: Lord Acton: Historian, 1977; co-author: Forty Centuries of Wage-Price Controls, 1978; editor: (anthology) Conservative Tradition, 1970, Policy Rev., 1977-79; co-author or editor 16 other books. N.Y. State Regents scholar, Grad. fellow, 1954-60. Mem. Phila. Soc. (trustee 1988—), Cosmos Club (Washington), Beefsteak Club, Reform Club, Oxford Univ. Club, Cambridge Univ. Club (London). Home: 901 6th St SW Apt 713A Washington DC 20024 Office: Washington Internat Studies Ctr 214 Massachusetts Ave Washington DC 20002

SCHULER, JACK WILLIAM, healthcare company executive; b. N.Y.C., Sept. 17, 1940; m. Renate Rosita Schuler; children—Tino, Tanya, Tessi. B.S. in Mech. Engring., Tufts U., 1962; M.B.A., Stanford U., 1964. Various positions Tex. Instruments, France, W.Ger. and Japan,, 1964-72; dir. sales and market diagnostics Abbott Labs., North Chicago, Ill., 1972-74, div. v.p. sales and mktg., 1974-76, v.p. diagnostic ops., 1976-83, group v.p., 1983-85, exec. v.p., 1985-86, pres. Abbott Labs., North Chicago, 1987—, also bd. dirs.; bd. dirs. Cooper Industries, 1988. Bd. dirs. Lake Forest Hosp., Ill., 1983—; mem. vis. com. Harvard Sch. Pub. Health. Office: Abbott Labs Abbott Park IL 60064

SCHULER, JOHN HAMILTON, holding company executive; b. Birmingham, Ala., Oct. 15, 1926; s. Robert Eustace and Doris (Moughon) S.; m. Elizabeth Locke, Dec. 14, 1954; children—George Augustus Mattison IV, Elizabeth Schuler Ogburn, John Hamilton Jr., Robert Eustace II. B.S. in Indsl. Mgmt., Auburn U., 1952. Vice pres. ops. Anderson Electric Corp., Leeds, Ala., 1957-59, exec. v.p., 1959-66, pres., 1966-69, chmn., chief exec. officer, 1969-72; pres. Schuler Investment Co., Birmingham, Ala., 1972-80; exec. v.p. Steego Corp., West Palm Beach, Fla., 1980—; dir. So. Research Inst., Birmingham, Palm Beach Ventures, Fla., WSEF Corp., Palm Beach. Pres., chmn. Associated Industries of Ala., Birmingham, 1962-64, Birmingham Symphony, 1967-69; pres. Ala. Opera Assn., Birmingham, 1970; mem. exec. com. Republican Party of Ala., Birmingham, 1964-68, Soc. Four Arts, Palm Beach Preservation Found. Exec. Com.; mem. nat. fin. com. Nat. Rep. Party, 1968-72. Recipient Erskine Ramsay award Citizenship Group, Birmingham, 1969. Mem. Newcomen Soc. Am., AmSouth Bank, NA (dir. 1973-81), Sq. D Corp. (dir. 1972-78), First Nat. Bank (dir. 1970-81). Episcopalian. Clubs: Mountain Brook, Birmingham Country (Birmingham); Everglades Bath and Tennis (Palm Beach); Duquesne (Pitts.). Home: 624 N Lake Way Palm Beach FL 33480 Office: Steego Corp 319 Clematis St Ste 900 West Palm Beach FL 33402

SCHULMAN, BRUCE DAVID, investment banker; b. Chgo., Aug. 16, 1950; s. Leonard and Berneice (Weiner) S.; m. Sandra Jo Evans, July 16, 1983; 1 child, Barri Skyler, July 11, 1985. B.A., U. Colo., 1972; M.B.A., So. Meth. U., 1975. Chief exec. officer Chesters, Salt Lake City, 1975-77; v.p. A. David Silver & Co., N.Y.C., 1972-73, 77-78; pres. B.D. Schulman Inc., N.Y.C., 1978-81; pres. Niederhoffer, Cross & Zeckhauser, Inc., N.Y.C., 1981—; dir. Ludwig Industries, Inc., Bklyn.; bd. dirs., pres. R.B. Studio, N.Y.C.; cons. small businesses. Jewish. Avocations: skiing, aikido. Home: 170 E 88th St Apt 4C New York NY 10128 Office: Niederhoffer Cross & Zeckhauser Inc 49 W 57th St New York NY 10019

SCHULMAN, STUART M., real estate executive; b. Bklyn., Sept. 29, 1953; s. Nathan David and Gloria (Steiner) S.; m. Lillian Susan Lubin, Sept. 9, 1979; children: Jaclyn. BA in History cum laude, Adelphi U., 1975, MBA, 1977. Bank loan officer NatWest USA, N.Y.C., 1977-80, Aetna Bus. Credit (Barclays Am.), Hartford, Conn., 1980-81; dir. fin. Nat. Property Analysts, Inc., Phila., 1981-82; sr. v.p. fin. The Patrician Group, Inc., N.Y.C., 1982-86, Concord Assets Group, Inc., N.Y.C., 1986-89; 1st v.p., mgr. real estate lending div. DnC Am. Banking Corp., N.Y.C., 1989—. Office: DnC Am Banking Corp 600 Fifth Ave New York NY 10020

SCHULMERICH, STEPHEN CRAIG, financial planner; b. Portland, Oreg., Jan. 9, 1949; s. Norman R. and Ruth (Beach) S.; m. Sharon Ruth McGehee, Feb. 26, 1971; children: Stephanie, Heather, Stephen Craig Jr. BBA, Oreg. State U., 1977; cert. in fin. planning, Coll. Fin. Planning, 1988. Owner Schulmerich Assocs. Investment Advisors, Portland, 1970—; instr. life underwriter tng. course in estate and bus. planning, Portland. Grantor Oreg. Art Inst., Portland, 1988—. Mem. Internat. Bd. Standards and Practices for Cert. Fin. Planners, Tualatin (Oreg.) Country Club. Home: 10585 NW Reeves Port OR 97229 Office: 10220 SW Greenburg Rd #215 Portland OR 97223

SCHULTE, MARY ANN, finance executive; b. Phoenix, Feb. 6, 1953; d. Walter Barry and Norma Gladys (Caffey) S. BSBA, U. So. Calif., 1975, MBA, 1989. Mgr. acctg. Coldwell Banker, Los Angeles, 1975-78; controller Adams, Ray and Rosenberg, Inc. (now Triad Artists), Century City, Calif., 1978-81; co-owner Marwal, Inc., Los Angeles, 1976-82; controller, chief fin. officer DNA Group, Inc., Pasadena, Calif., 1982-86; chief fin. officer Sukut Constrn., Inc., Santa Ana, Calif., 1986—; cons. Mikeselle DeKorff, Los Angeles, 1981-82, Hollywood (Calif.) High Sch., 1986-87; cons., bd. dirs. Inner Ear Prodns., Los Angeles, 1983-85. Staff leader drop out prevention program Hollywood High Sch., 1986. Mem. Nat. Assn. Accts. (past bd. dirs.), U. So. Calif. Commerce Assocs., Alpha Chi Omega. Republican. Roman Catholic. Office: Sukut Constrn Inc 4010 W Chandler Santa Ana CA 92704

SCHULTZ, FREDERICK CARL, die casting company executive; b. Toledo, Sept. 23, 1929; s. Oswald Charles and Margarete Joanne (Schoeneberg) S.; m. Anita Margarete Lueller, Sept. 10, 1955; children: David, Elisabeth, Mary, Martha. BSChemE, U. Mich., 1951, MS in Indsl. Engring., 1952. Research engr. LECO Corp., St. Joseph, Mich., 1956-61, dir. research, 1961-67, market research mgr., 1967-71; exec. v.p. Benton Harbor (Mich.) Malleable, 1971-75; pres. Cast-Matic Corp., Stevensville, Mich., 1975—. Patentee in field. Bd. dirs. Community Concerts Assn., St. Joseph, 1960-69, S.W. Mich. Symphony, St. Joseph, 1965—, Blossomland Area Safety Council, St. Joseph, 1972-79, Krasl Art Ctr., St. Joseph, 1985—. Served to cpl., U.S. Army, 1951-54. Republican. Lutheran. Home: 2816 Evergreen Dr Saint Joseph MI 49085 Office: Cast-Matic Corp 2800 Yasdick Dr Stevensville MI 49127

SCHULTZ, GERALD ERNEST, manufacturing company executive; b. Princeton, Ill., July 17, 1941; s. Charles C. and Margaret L. Schultz; m. Barbara E. Potocny, May 18, 1978; children: Barry, Jennifer, Gregory, Julee, Christopher. B.S. in Fin., U. Ill., 1963. With Ford Motor Co., 1963-65; div. controller TRW, Inc., Mex., 1967-69; from div. controller to v.p. controller Gould, Inc., 1969-80; v.p., chief fin. officer and adminstrv. officer Hoover Universal, Inc., Ann Arbor, Mich., 1980-82; exec. v.p. Bell & Howell Co., Skokie, Ill., 1982-86, chief fin. officer, 1982-86, pres., chief operating officer, 1986—, now pres., chief exec. officer. Office: Bell & Howell Co 5215 Old Orchard Rd Skokie IL 60077 *

SCHULTZ, JAMES CLEMENT, railroad executive, lawyer; b. Council Bluffs, Iowa, Nov. 24, 1934; s. John William and Lillian Ruth (Clement) S.; m. Nancy Jean Dixon, May 29, 1969; children: James Vincent, Erica Ruth. B.S., U. Nebr., 1956; J.D. with honors, George Washington U., 1961. Minority counsel Senate Anti-trust Subcom. of Judiciary Com., 1965-68; trial atty. antitrust div. U.S. Dept. Justice, 1969-70; asst. gen. counsel U.S. Dept. Transp., 1971-74; chief counsel Nat. Hwy. Traffic Safety Adminstrn., 1975; gen. counsel CAB, Washington, 1976-77; sr. v.p., gen. counsel Trailways, Inc., Dallas, 1978-79; partner firm Baker & Hostetler, Washington, 1979-83; Sr. v.p. law and risk mgmt. Seaboard System R.R., Jacksonville, Fla., 1983-85; v.p. law and gen. counsel CSX Transp. Inc., distbn. svcs. grp., Balt., 1986—. Served with AUS, 1957-58. Office: CSX Transp Inc Distbn Svcs Grp 100 N Charles St Baltimore MD 21201

SCHULTZ, JANET DARLENE, credit union executive; b. Oakland, Calif., July 22, 1942; d. Charles Emile and Viola Iva (Ogden) Ranvier; m. Orville Carl Schultz Sr., Apr. 7, 1971; children: Carol Marie, Donald Courtland. BSBA, U. Wis., 1978. Cert. credit union mgmt. Loan officer Sierra Schs. Fed. Credit Union, Reno, 1974-79; mgr. Nev. Realtors Credit Union, Reno, 1979-81; pres., chief exec. officer Reno Fed. Credit Union, 1979-85; cons. Union Credit Union, Sparks, Nev., 1986; mgr., chief exec. officer Union Credit Union, Sparks, 1986—; vice chmn. Nev. Cen. Credit Union, Las Vegas, 1980-83; treas. Western Nev. Chpt. Nev. CLU, Reno, 1980-84. Tng. chmn. Boy Scouts Am., 1980, Pow Wow chmn., 1978; treas. Pop Warner Football League, Sparks, 1981, pres. 1987. Recipient Dist. Award of Merit, Boy Scouts Am., 1978. Mem. Nat. Assn. Female Execs., Reno Women Bus. Network, Nat. Notary Assn., Cuna Mktg. Inst., Cuna Fin. Inst., Cuna Alumni Assn., Inc. Democrat. Roman Catholic. Home: 914 Glen Martin Dr Sparks NV 89431 Office: Union Credit Union 1110 Greg St Sparks NV 89431

SCHULTZ, LOUIS EDWIN, management executive; b. Foster, Nebr., Aug. 8, 1931; s. Louis Albert and Lula Pusey (Cox) S.; m. Mary Kathleen Peck, Mar. 3, 1962; children: Kurt Michael, Kristen Leigh. BSEE, U. Nebr., 1959; MBA, Pepperdine U., 1974. Mktg. mgr. Bell & Howell, Pasadena, Calif., 1962-70; dir. mktg. Cogar Corp., Utica, N.Y., 1970-71; product mgr. Pertec Corp., L.A., 1971-73; gen. mgr. Control Data Corp., Mpls., 1973-84; pres., chief exec. officer Process Mgmt. Inst. Inc., Bloomington, Minn., 1984—; adv. bd. Inst. for Productivity Through Quality, U. Tenn., Knoxville, 1983-85. Mem. Gov.'s Commn. on Productivity, St. Paul, 1986; chmn. Wirth Park Tree Restoration Com., Mpls., 1983; mem. Productivity Planning Com., St. Paul, 1985—. Staff sgt. USMC, 1952-54. Mem. Am. Soc. for Performance Improvement (bd. dirs. 1984—), Minn. High Tech. Coun., Minn. Assn. Commerce and Industry, Asia-Pacific Orgn. for Quality Control. Republican. Methodist. Club: Garden (Mpls.). Lodge: Masons. Home: 6901 Gleason Circle Edina MN 55435 Office: Process Mgmt Inst 7801 E Bush Lake Rd Ste 360 Bloomington MN 55435

SCHULTZ, LOUIS MICHAEL, advertising agency executive; b. Detroit, Aug. 24, 1944; s. Henry Richard and Genevieve (Jankowski) S.; m. Susan Kay Hammel, Sept. 10, 1966; children—Christian David, Kimberly Ann. B.A., Mich. State U., 1967; M.B.A., Wayne State U., 1970. Staff Campbell-Ewald, Warren, Mich., 1967-74; v.p. group dir. Campbell-Ewald, 1975-77, sr. v.p., assoc. dir., 1977-82, group sr. v.p., 1982-83, exec. v.p., 1984-87; exec. v.p. Lintas: USA, 1987—; mem. devel. council IPG, N.Y.C., 1984—; guest lectr. Mich. State U., East Lansing, Mich., 1983-85, U. Mich., Ann Arbor, 1983-84; bd. dirs. Lintas USA, Lintas N.Y., Lintas Campbell-Ewald. Advisor, Detroit Renaissance Com., 1981—. Served with USAR, 1967-73. Mem. Nat. Acad. TV Arts and Scis., Am. Women in Radio and TV, Am. Mktg. Assn., Detroit Advt. Assn., Ad Club N.Y. Democrat. Roman Catholic. Clubs: Great Oaks Country, Adcraft. Home: 472 Streamview Ct Rochester MI 48063 Office: Lintas USA 30400 Van Dyke Warren MI 48093

SCHULTZ, RICHARD JOHN, architect; b. St. Louis, July 1, 1949; s. Donald Emmett and Jean Lee (Auld) S.; m. Joan Cathy Holubeck, Aug. 30, 1969; children: Jennifer Lynn, Laura Marie, Patricia Lee. BS in Computer Sci., U. Mo., Rolla, 1973. Registered profl. architect, Mo., Ill. Cons. Tex. Instruments, Dallas, 1973-74; pres. Schultz Group, Inc., Saint Charles, Mo., 1974—; pres. Schultz Partnership, Saint Charles, 1987—. Vice-chmn. Planning and Zoning Commn., Saint Charles, 1979; chmn. Bd. Adjustment, Saint Charles, 1979—. Mem. AIA, Yeo-Mark Twain Club. Republican. Roman Catholic. Home: 28 Green Five Dr Saint Charles MO 63303 Office: Schultz Group Inc 220 Compass Point Saint Charles MO 63301

SCHULTZ, T. PAUL, economics educator; b. Ames, Iowa, May 24, 1940; s. Theodore W. and Esther (Werth) S.; m. Judith Hoenack, Sept. 16, 1967; children: Lara, Joel, Rebecca. BA, Swarthmore Coll., 1961; PhD, MIT, 1966; MA (hon.), Yale U., 1974. Cons. Joint Econ. Com., Washington, 1964; researcher econs. dept. Rand Corp., Santa Monica, Calif., 1965-72, dir. population research, 1968-72; prof. econs. U. Minn., Mpls., 1972-75; prof. econs. Yale U., New Haven, 1974—, dir. Econ. Growth Ctr., 1983—; cons. World Bank, Rockefeller Found.; mem. com. on population Nat. Acad. Scis., Washington, 1987—. Author: Structural Change in a Developing Country, 1971, Economics of Population, 1981; editor: (book) The State of Develoment Economics, 1988, (periodical) Research in Population Econs., 1985, 88. Fellow AAAS (population resources environ. com. 1985—, nomination com. 1987—); mem. Am. Econ. Assn., Population Assn. Am. (bd. dirs. 1979-81), Internat. Union for Scientific Study Population, Soc. for Study Social Biology (bd. dirs. 1986—). Office: Yale U Econ Growth Ctr Box 1987 Yale Sta 27 Hillhouse Ave New Haven CT 06520

SCHULTZ, TERRY ALLEN, architect; b. Elmhurst, Ill., May 18, 1946; s. Clarence Frederick Theodore and Elvera Stella (Landmeier) S. BArch, U. Ill., 1970, MS, 1971; MBA, Keller Grad. Sch. Mgmt., 1980. Registered architect, Wis. Sr. project structural engr. Skidmore Owings & Merrill, Chgo., 1971-75; gen. mgr. Archtl. Engring. Cons., Arlington Heights, Ill., 1975-77; project engr. Gillum-Colaco, Chgo., 1977-79; prin. A/E Consulting, Arlington Heights, 1979—; Bd. dirs. Evang. Health Systems Corp., Oak Brook, Ill., 1978-88, Audit Fin. Med. Affairs and Facilities Com.; chmn. bd. dirs. Evang. Care Corp., Oak Brook, 1985-88. Mem. bd. govs. fin. and strategic planning coms. Good Sheperd Hosp., Barrington, Ill., 1978-83; trustee, fin. and strategic planning quality assurance, facilities coms. Bethany Hosp., Chgo., 1980—; v.p. Good Sheperd Manor, Barrington, 1985—; pres., treas. St. John United Ch. of Christ, Arlington Heights, 1976-80. Mem. AIA, Nat. Assn. Corp. Dirs. Republican. Club: American (Hong Kong). Lodge: Lions. Home and Office: 316 E Euclid St Arlington Heights IL 60004

SCHULTZ, THEODORE WILLIAM, retired educator, economist; b. Arlington, S.D., Apr. 30, 1902; s. Henry Edward and Anna Elizabeth (Weiss) S.; m. Esther Florence Werth; children: Elaine, Margaret, T. Paul. Grad., Sch. Agr., Brookings, S.D., 1924; B.S., S.D. State Coll., 1927, D.Sc. (hon.), 1959; M.S., U. Wis., 1928, Ph.D., 1930; LL.D. (hon.), Grinnell Coll., 1949, Mich. State U., in 1962, U. Ill., 1968, U. Wis., 1968, Cath. U. Chile, 1979, U. Dijon, France, 1981; LL.D., N.C. State U., 1984. Mem. faculty Iowa State Coll., Ames, 1930-43; prof., head dept. econs. and sociology Iowa State Coll., 1934-43; prof. econs. U. Chgo., 1943-72, chmn. dept. econs., 1946-61, Charles L. Hutchinson Disting. Service prof., 1952-72, now emeritus; econ. adviser, occasional cons. Com. Econ. Devel., U.S. Dept. Agr., Dept. State, Fed. Res. Bd., various congl. coms., U.S. Dept. Commerce, FAO, U.S. Dept. Def., Germany, 1948, Fgn. Econ. Adminstrn., U.K. and Germany, 1945, IBRD, Resources for the Future, Twentieth Century Fund, Nat. Farm Inst., others.; dir. Nat. Bur. Econ. Research, 1949-67; research dir. Studies of Tech. Assistance in Latin Am.; bd. mem. Nat. Planning Assn.; chmn. Am. Famine Mission to India, 1946; studies of agrl. developments, central Europe and Russia, 1929, Scandinavian countries and Scotland, 1936, Brazil, Uruguay and Argentina, 1941, Western Europe, 1955. Author: Redirecting Farm Policy, 1943, Food for the World, 1945, Agriculture in an Unstable Economy, 1945, Production and Welfare in Agriculture, 1950, The Economic Organization of Agriculture, 1953, Economic Test in Latin America, 1956, Transforming Traditional Agriculture, 1964, The Economic Value of Education, 1963, Economic Crises in World Agriculture, 1965, Economic Growth and Agriculture, 1968, Investment in Human Capital: The Role of Education And of Research, 1971, Human Resources, 1972, Economics of the Family: Marriage, Children, and Human Capital, 1974, Distortions of Agricultural Incentives, 1978, Investing in People: The Economics of Population Quality, 1981; co-author: Measures for Economic Development of Under-Developed Countries, 1951; editor: Jour. Farm Econs., 1939-42; contbr. articles to profl. jours. research fellow Center Advanced Study in Behavioral Sci., 1956-57; recipient Nobel prize in Econs., 1979. Fellow Am. Acad. Arts and Scis., Am. Farm Econs. Assn., Nat. Acad. Scis.; mem. Am. Farm Assn., Am. Econ. Assn. (pres. 1960, Walker medal 1972), Royal Econ. Soc., Am. Philos. Soc., others. Home: 5620 Kimbark Ave Chicago IL 60637 Office: U Chgo Dept Econs 1126 E 59th St Chicago IL 60637

SCHULTZ, THOMAS ARNOLD, manufacturing company executive; b. Oakland, Calif., Aug. 7, 1950; s. Arnold Max and Barbara (Pratt) S.; m. Jenny Gispen, June 15, 1972 (div. Oct. 1979); children: Matthew, Cathryn; m. Diana Lee Lovato, Jan. 3, 1982; children: Elizabeth, Nicholas. Student, U. Calif.-Santa Barbara, 1968-70; BS, Johns Hopkins U., 1972; MBA, Harvard U., 1975. Cons. Boston Cons. Group, Menlo Park, Calif., 1975-79; ptnr. Booz, Allen and Hamilton, San Francisco, 1979-83; v.p. Castle and Cooke Corp./, San Francisco, 1983-86; pres. Crystallume, Menlo Park, 1986—; bd. dirs. U.S. Comml. Telephone, Redwood City, Calif. Mem. Phi Beta Kappa, Tau Beta Pi. Home: 833 Orchid Pl Los Altos CA 94022 Office: Crystallume 125 Constitution Dr Menlo Park CA 94025

SCHULZ, RAINER WALTER, computer company executive; b. Berlin, Jan. 29, 1942; s. Horst and Marta S.; came to U.S., 1959, naturalized, 1964; B.A. summa cum laude in Math., San Jose State U., 1964; children—Heidi, Kenneth, Kirsten. System devel. asso. IBM, San Jose, Calif., 1964-65, SDS, Santa Monica, Calif., 1965-67, U. Calif., Berkeley, 1967-70; system mgmt. asso. Stanford (Calif.) U., 1970-77; v.p. Computer Curriculum Corp., Palo Alto, Calif., 1973-81, dir., sec., 1978-81; mgr. Tandem Computers Inc., Cupertino, Calif., 1981-83; v.p. computing and info. systems Teknowledge, Palo Alto, 1983-88; pres. Modernsoft, Palo Alto, Calif., 1989—; cons. NSF., 1974-77. Mem. Am. Electronics Assn., Conf. Bd. Republican. Lutheran. Home: PO Box 50243 Palo Alto CA 94303 Office: Modernsoft 260 Sheridan #210 Palo Alto CA 94306

SCHULZ, RODNEY RAY, petroleum engineer; b. Ellinwood, Kans., Sept. 24, 1958; s. Harold Dee and Lora Louise (Swicegood) S. BS in Petroleum Engring., U. Kans., 1982; postgrad., Duke U., 1987—. Engr. Conoco, Inc., Corpus Christi, Tex., 1982-85; reservoir engr. Conoco, Inc., Anchorage, 1985-86, Midland, Tex., 1986-87, New Oreleans, 1988—. Contbr. articles to profl. jours. Co-sponsor high sch. youth group 1st Christian Ch., Corpus Christi, 1982-85, Meml. Christian Ch., Midland, 1987. Mem. Gas Processors Assn. (vice chmn. 1983-84, cert. Appreciation 1985), Soc. Profl. Well Log Analysts (sec. treas. Anchorage 1985-86), Soc. Petroleum Engrs., Pi Kappa Alpha. Republican. Mem. Disciples of Christ Ch. Club: Operations (com. chmn.)(Duke U.). Home: 1315 Morreene Re Apt 9Y Durham NC 27705

SCHULZ, WALTER KURT, accountant; b. Hamburg, Fed. Republic Germany, Apr. 9, 1940; came to U.S., 1970; s. Richard and Karla (Halm) S.; m. Beth Ann Edwards, June 21, 1972; children: Alec, Elli, Peter, Andrew, Heidi. MBA, U. Münster, Fed. Republic Germany, 1969; MBA in Acctg., Ohio State U., 1972. Auditor Dr. Kaase, CPA, Bad Oeynhausen, Fed. Republic Germany, 1966-71; systems analyst United Airlines, Chgo., 1973-77; v.p. fin. Eickhoff-Nat. Corp., Pitts., 1977-79; div. controller Mobay Corp., Pitts., 1979-86; pres. Computer Renaissance, Charlotte, N.C., 1986—; cons. Westinghouse Corp., Mercy Hosp., Pitts. Served to lt. Fed. Republic Germany Air Force, 1960-63. Mem. Am. Mgmt. Assn., Assn. MBA Execs. Republican. Home: 301 Sardis Rd N Charlotte NC 28226

SCHULZE, ERWIN EMIL, manufacturing company executive, lawyer; b. Davenport, Iowa, May 4, 1925; s. Erwin F. and Hazel (Sorensen) S.; m. Jean E. Steele, June 21, 1952; children: Suzanne Schulze Walker, William Steele, Donna Schulze Ballard, Stephen Johnson. B.A., De Pauw U., 1947; LL.B., Yale, 1950. Bar: Ill. 1950. Practiced in Chgo.; partner firm Rooks, Pitts, Fullagar & Poust (and predecessor firms), 1950-67, counsel, 1967-80; pres., dir. Standard Alliance Industries, Inc., 1967-79; pres., chief operating officer, dir. Ceco Industries, 1980-85; pres., chief exec. officer The Ceco Corp., 1985-86; pres., chief exec. officer, chmn., dir. Ceco Industries, Inc., 1986—; chief counsel Standard Forgings Corp., Chgo., 1963-65; exec. v.p. Standard Forgings Corp., 1965-67; treas., dir. Transue & Williams Steel Forging Corp., Alliance, Ohio, 1965-66; dir. AAR Corp., Interlake, Inc.; mem. com. on specialist assignment and evaluation and space planning com. Midwest Stock Exchange, bd. govs., 1979—; Mem. Adv. Council Zoning, Chgo., 1955-57. Bd. visitors De Pauw U., 1979-81, trustee, 1981—; co-chmn. Joint Com. Codify Ill. Family Law, 1958-61; mem. Mayor Chgo. Adv. Council Juvenile Delinquency, 1958-62; v.p., dir. Midwestern Air Pollution Prevention Assn., 1958-72, chmn. legal com., 1960-63; Vice pres., dir. Chgo. Tennis Assn., 1964-71; sec., dir. Chgo. Tennis Patrons, 1960-74; chmn. men's ranking com. U.S. Lawn and Tennis Assn., 1961-71. Served as lt. (j.g.) USNR, 1943-46, PTO. Mem. ABA, Ill. Mfrs. Assn. (bd. dirs. 1983—, vice chmn. 1986—, chmn. 1987—), Phi Beta Kappa. Presbyterian (deacon, elder trustee). Clubs: Chicago, Economics, Chicago Golf, Legal; Shoreacres. Office: The Ceco Corp 1 Tower Ln Oakbrook Terrace IL 60181

SCHULZE, JOHN B., manufacturing executive. BBA, So. Meth. U., 1959; postgrad., Harvard U., 1984. From group v.p., sr. group v.p., sr. exec. v.p. to pres. and chief exec. officer White Consol. Industries, 1962-87; pres., chief oper. officer Lamson & Sessions Co., Cleve., 1987—, also bd. dirs. Capt. USMC, 1959-62. *

SCHULZE, RICHARD WILFRED, machinery company executive; b. St. Paul, May 27, 1937; s. Wilfred Karl Schulze and Norene Margaret (Sturgeon) Schulze Newton; m. Kay Ann Dumdey, Aug. 29, 1959 (div. Nov. 1977); children—Elizabeth, Amy; m. Charlene Elfrieda Ryder, July 5, 1978; children—Nicole, Kathryn. B.A., Ripon Coll., 1959. Mgr. pub. relations Speed Queen, Ripon, Wis., 1959-62; pub. Regional Reporter, Markesan, Wis., 1962-64; employee communications specialist Gen. Electric Co., Milw., 1964-65; dir. pub. relations Harnischfeger Corp., Milw., 1965-82, sr. v.p. human resources and pub. relations, 1982—; bd. dirs. Century II Inc. Mem. Pub. Relations Soc. Am., Nat. Investor Relations Inst., Am. Soc. Personnel Adminstrs., Indsl. Relations and Research Assn. Republican. Methodist. Clubs: Press (Milw.); Westmoor Country (Brookfield, Wis.). Office: Harnischfeger Corp 13400 Bishops Ln Brookfield WI 53025

SCHULZETENBERG, JOHN MARTIN, finance company executive, accountant; b. Greenwald, Minn., Apr. 5, 1946; s. Al and Del Schulzetenberg; m. Jane Planer, June 10, 1968; children: J. Peter, Jay P. BA, St. Cloud (Minn.) U., 1968. CPA, Colo., Minn. With professional staff Touche Ross and Co., Mpls., 1967-77, audit ptnr., 1977-84; mng. ptnr. Touche Ross and Co., Bloomington, Minn., 1985-86, Denver, 1986—; dir. recruiting and tng. Touche Ross and Co., Mpls., 1976-84, Denver, 1986—; mem. mgmt. adv. council Touche Ross and Co., 1979-82; asst. prof. acctg. St. Cloud U. Sch. of Bus., 1973. Bd. dirs., treas. Denver Civic Ventures, 1988; v.p., treas., bd. dirs., Denver Children's Mus., 1988; bd. advisors U. Denver Sch. Accountancy, 1988; found. bd. dirs. and dir. fin. St. Cloud U., 1988. Mem. AICPA (mem. personal fin. statements com. 1987—), Colo. Soc. CPAs (bd. dirs., com. chmn. 1987—), Nat. Assn. Accts. (bd. dirs.). Republican. Office: Touche Ross & Co 370 17th St Ste 2600 Denver CO 80202-5626

SCHUMACHER, ALAN THOMAS, financial planner, insurance company official; b. Wichita, Kans., Mar. 29, 1956; s. Robert Eugene and Rosemary Barbara (Staab) S.; m. Gloria Jean Linenberger, Jan. 31, 1975 (div. June 1980); m. M. Kathleen Nichols, Feb. 27, 1982; children: Angela Lynn, Alan Robert,

Amber Rose. Student parochial schs., Hays, Kans. Supr. Silicon Systems, Inc., Tustin, Calif., 1977-80; v.p. Ins. Planning, Inc., Hays, 1980-87; account exec. Dorth Coombs Ins., Inc., Wichita, 1987—; mem. Internat. Bd. Cert. Fin. Planners. With USMC, 1974-77. Mem. Nat. Assn. Life Underwriters, Soc. Cert. Ins. Counselors, Hays C. of C. Ambassadors, Smoky Hill Country Club (Hays, v.p. 1987, pres. 1989), K.C., Kiwanis. Republican. Roman Catholic. Home: 3719 Fairway Dr Hays KS 67601 Office: Dorth Coombs Ins Inc 111 W 10th St Hays KS 67601

SCHUMACHER, FREDERICK RICHMOND, lawyer; b. N.Y.C., Sept. 4, 1930; s. Frederick William and Anna De Rose Elizabeth (Richmond) S.; A.B., Princeton U., 1952; J.D., Cornell U., 1957; postgrad. in law, cert. in taxation, U. So. Calif., 1959-61; m. Birte Vestel, Dec. 1, 1973; children: Anna Lisa, Ian, Eric. Admitted to N.Y. bar, 1957, Calif. bar, 1960; assoc. firm Clark, Carr & Ellis, N.Y.C., 1957-59, firm Thelen, Marrin, Johnson & Bridges, Los Angeles, 1960-62; individual practice law, 1963—, pres. Frederick R. Schumacher, Ltd., Carlsbad, Calif. 1988 ; dir. Phrobis III Ltd.; cons. fed. and internat. taxes. Active Republican Nat. Com., 1981—. Served with USMC, 1952-54. Mem. N.Y. State Bar Assn., Calif. Bar Assn., Hunting Hall of Fame Found. (charter mem.), So. Calif. Safari Club. Author: International Letters of Credit, 1960. Office: 2310 Faraday Ave Carlsbad CA 92008

SCHUMAKER, DALE H., paper manufacturing company executive; b. 1933. BS, U. Wis., 1955. Engr. Am. Can Co., Neenah, Wis., 1955-65; with Appleton (Wis.) Papers, Inc., 1965—, v.p. mfg., 1965-79, 1979-84, sr. v.p. mfg., 1984-85, exec. v.p., 1985-86, pres., chief operating officer, 1986—, also bd. dirs. Office: Appleton Papers Inc 825 E Wisconsin Ave Appleton WI 54912

SCHUMAN, ALLAN L., chemical company executive; b. 1937. BS, NYU, 1955. With Ecolab Inc., St. Paul, 1957—, v.p. mitg. and nat. acctg., 1974-78, v.p. mktg. devel., 1978—, now exec. v.p. instl. group. Office: Ecolab Inc Ecolab Ctr Saint Paul MN 55102 *

SCHUMANN, WILLIAM HENRY, III, financial executive; b. Iowa City, Aug. 28, 1950; s. William Henry Jr. and Eunice Vere (Doak) S.; m. Denise Suzane Hargrove, Sept. 29, 1979; children: Stefanie Lynn, John William, Kimberly Ann. BS, UCLA, 1972; MS, U. So. Calif., 1973. Program mgmt. analyst Hughes Helicopters, Culver City, Calif., 1973-75; mgr. fin. planning Sunkist Growers, Sherman Oaks, Calif., 1975-81; treas. FMC Corp., Chgo., 1981—; trustee Ill. State Bd. Investment, Chgo., 1986—. Republican. Office: FMC Corp 200 E Randolph Dr Chicago IL 60601

SCHUMITZ, ELIZABETH DOROTHY, mathematics educator, tutor; b. Newark, N.J., Dec. 29, 1935; d. Lester Herbert Sr. and Elizabeth (Snowden) Erickson; m. Rudolph William Schumitz Jr., Aug. 31, 1957 (dec. Sept. 1971); children: Robert Wayne, William Richard. BA, Montclair State Coll., 1957; postgrad., Rutgers U., 1959, N.J. Inst. Tech., 1959-60; MA, Fairleigh Dickinson U., 1977; postgrad., Kean Coll., Jersey City State Coll. Tchr., N.J.; prin./supr. cert., N.J. Tchr. math. various high schs., N.J., 1957-86; coordinator math. dept. Thompson Jr. High, Middletown, N.J., 1979—; tchr. math. Red Bank Regional Bd. Edn., Little Silver, N.J., 1985—; tchr. math. and computers Thompson Jr. High, Middletown, 1986—; mem. curriculum devel. com. Middletown Twp. Bd. Edn., 1969—; external tchr. Marlboro (N.J.) State Hosp., 1966-67. Author: Eric and the Red Beard, 1977. Election challenger, Middletown Rep. Com., 1976, 80; com. chmn., treas., merit badge counselor, Boy Scouts. Am., Middletown, 1971—; elder, choir, bell choir Westminster Presbyn Ch., Middletown, 1963—. Recipient schlarship Horace A. Moses Found., 1953, Newark Tchrs. Assn., 1953, N.J. State, 1954-57, and others; grantee Rutgers U., 1959. Mem. NEA, Middletown Twp. Edn. Assn., Monmouth County Edn. Assn., N.J. Edn. Assn., Nat. Council Tchrs. of Math. (ref. to editorial panel 1988-89), Nat. Middle Schs. Assn., Assn. of Math. Tchrs. of N.J., Newark Tchrs. Assn., Order Rainbow (advisor 1950-55), Math. Assn. Am., Kappa Mu Epsilon, Kappa Delta Pi. Home: 1 Lakewood Pl Port Monmouth NJ 07758 Office: Thompson Middle Sch Middletown Lincroft Rd Middletown NJ 07748

SCHUMSKY, STANLEY, marketing executive; b. N.Y.C., Sept. 3, 1932; s. Benjamin and Betsy (Yudin) S.; m. Felice Roberta Trayman, Aug. 27, 1961 (div. Sept. 1978). BA, NYU, 1955, MA, 1978, PhD, 1982. V.p. Alfred Politz, Inc., N.Y.C., 1956-62, Bennett Chalken, Inc., N.Y.C., 1962-65; sr. v.p. Daniel Yankelovich, Inc., N.Y.C., 1965-74; exec. v.p. Felicie, Inc., N.Y.C., 1965-78; sr. v.p. Doyle Dane Bernbach, N.Y.C., 1978-86; sr. mng. dir. N.Y. Strategy Group Internat., 1986—. Author: Jan Steen, 1980. Bd. dirs. Reach-Out, N.Y.C., 1981-85. Served with U.S. Army, 1953-55, PTO. Fellow Met. Mus. Art, N.Y.C., 1976-78; mem. Am. Mktg. Assn., Am. Soc. Consultants. Democrat. Home: 320 E 58th St New York NY 10022 Office: 50 E 78th St New York NY 10021

SCHUPAK, DONALD, merchant banker, stategic planner, lawyer; b. N.Y.C., Apr. 2, 1943; s. Sidney and Helen (Smith) S.; m. Leslie Silverman, June 21, 1964 (div. 1981); children: Andrew, Jessica; m. Cynthia Saul, Nov. 19, 1981; children: Amanda, Philip Nicholas. BA, Syracuse U., 1964, JD, 1966; LLM in Taxation, NYU, 1970. Bar: N.Y. Assoc. various law firms, N.Y.C., 1966-70; ptnr. Schupak, Rosenfeld, Fishbein, et al, N.Y.C., 1970-82; chmn. bd., chief exec. officer Donald Schupak and Co., Inc., N.Y.C., 1982—, Bright Star Holding Inc., N.Y.C., 1985—, Safety Harbor Corp., N.Y.C., 1985—, Rudy's Restaurant Group Corp., Miami, Fla., 1985—; vice chmn. Horn and Hardart Co., N.Y.C., 1977-88, chmn. bd., chief exec. officer, pres., 1988—. Mem. Assn. Bar City N.Y., N.Y. Bar Assn., Phi Kappa Phi, Order of Coif. Club: Rombout Hunt (Hyde Park, N.Y.). Office: Horn & Hardart Co 730 Fifth Ave New York NY 10019 also: 101 Convention Ctr Dr Las Vegas NV 89109

SCHURMAN, DONALD GLENN, aluminum company executive; b. Pitts., June 13, 1933; s. Andrew Matthew and Mary Ann (Plavan) S.; m. Barbara Jean Burby, Oct. 20, 1962; children—Lonnette, Kathleen, William, Marianne. B.B.A., M. Litt., U. Pitts., 1950-54. C.P.A., Pa., Ohio. With Lybrand, Ross Bros. & Montgomery, Pitts., 1954-59, U.S. Steel Corp., Pitts., 1959-62, The Chesapeake & Ohio Ry., Cleve., 1962-65; asst. to v.p. and controller Liquid Carbonic div. Gen. Dynamics Corp., Chgo., 1965-66; treas. Alcan Aluminum Corp., Cleve., 1966—; v.p. Alcan Aluminum Corp., 1975-81, v.p. fin., chief fin. officer, 1981-85, v.p. fin. and adminstrn., chief fin. officer, 1985—. Served with AUS, 1956-58. Home: 8 Cortland Ln Lynnfield MA 01940 Office: Alcan Aluminum Ltd 124 Mount Auburn St Cambridge MA 02138

SCHURMANN, WILLIAM JOSEPH, investment counselor; b. N.Y.C., Feb. 12, 1946; s. William Joseph and Martha Elizabeth (Ruelens) S.; m. Anna Mae Griesgraber, Sept. 17, 1977; 1 child, Robert Andrew. BA, Iona Coll., 1968; JD, Western State U., San Diego, 1978; MBA, Nat. U., San Diego, 1980. Mcpl. trader, underwriter Eldredge & Co., San Diego, 1973, J.C. Bradford & Co., San Diego, 1973-77; v.p. Frank Henjes & Co., San Diego, 1977-79, First Affiliated Securities, San Diego, 1979-81; chmn. Fin. Designs Ltd., San Diego, 1981-87; exec. v.p. Briarwood Fin. Group, Escondido, Calif., 1987—; instr. Coll. Fin. Planning, Denver, 1981-86; prof. U. Calif. San Diego extension, 1982—; instr. Am. Coll., 1980-81, bd. dirs., v.p. The Guyer Group, San Diego, 1985—; bd. dirs. Valve Equities Corp. Mem. bus. adv. bd., U Calif., San Diego, 1983—, Calif. Commerce Bank, 1986—. Capt. USMC, 1968-72. Mem. Internat. Assn. for Fin. Planning, Inst. Cert. Fin. Planners, Registry Fin. Planning Practitioners. Mem. Internat. Assn. Fin. Planning, Inst. Cert. Fin. Planners, Registry Fin. Planning Practitioners, Kiwanis (bd. dirs. 1982-87, pres. 1987-88). Home: 1509 Tutela Heights Escondido CA 92026 Office: Briarwood Fin Group 613 W Valley Pkwy Ste 210 Escondido CA 92025

SCHUSTER, PHILIP FREDERICK, II, lawyer; b. Denver, Aug. 26, 1945; s. Philip Frederick and Ruth Elizabeth (Robar) S.; m. Barbara Lynn Nordquist, June 7, 1975; children: Philip Christian, Matthew Dale. BA, U. Wash., 1967; JD, Willamette U., 1972. Bar: Oreg. 1972, U.S. Dist. Ct. Oreg. 1974, U.S. Ct. Appeals (9th cir.) 1986, U.S. Supreme Ct. 1986. Dep. dist. atty. Multnomah County, Portland, Oreg., 1972; title examiner Pioneer Nat. Title Co., Portland, 1973-74; assoc. Buss, Leichner et al, Portland, 1975-76; from assoc. to ptnr. Kitson & Bond, Portland, 1976-77; sole practice Portland, 1977—; arbitrator Multnomah County Arbitration Program, 1985—. Contbr. articles to profl. jours. Organizer Legal Aid Services for Community Clinics, Salem, Oreg. and Seattle, 1969-73; dem. committeeman, Seattle, 1965-70. Mem. ABA, NAACP (exec. bd. 1979—). Lodge: Sertoma. Office: 1500 NE Irving Ste 540 Portland OR 97232

SCHUTTE, GILES W., mail order company executive; b. Erie, Pa., Dec. 5, 1931; m. Joan G. Todaro, June 12, 1954; children: Sharon, Anna. B.A. in Bus. Adminstrn, Pa. State U., 1954. C.P.A., Pa. V.P., treas. New Process Co., Warren, Pa., 1974—; also dir. New Process Co.; dir. Pa. Bank and Trust Co. Bd. dirs. Warren Gen. Hosp. Served to lt. (j.g.) USCG, 1955-58. Mem. Am. Inst. C.P.A.s, Pa. Inst. C.P.A.s. Home: 7 Quaker Ct Warren PA 16365 Office: New Process Co 220 Hickory St Warren PA 16366

SCHUTTE, PAULA MARION, information systems strategist, consultant; b. St. Paul, Oct. 29, 1941; d. Paul Maurice and Marion (McAllister) S. BA in Chemistry, Rosary Coll., River Forest, Ill., 1963; MBA, NYU, 1985. Med. research chemist Geigy Chem. Corp., Ardsley, N.Y., 1964-70; group leader, sci. systems CIBA-Geigy Corp., Ardsley, N.Y., 1970-77, mgr. sci. info., 1980-83, sr. research fellow, 1985-86, dir. end user services, 1986-87; dir. info. techs. CIBA-Geigy Corp., Ardsley, 1987—; dir. med. systems pharm. div. CIBA-Geigy Corp., Summit, N.J., 1977-80; dir. sci. info. systems pharm. div. CIBA-Geigy Corp., Summit, 1983-85; research coordinator Prism, Cambridge, Mass., 1985—; info. systems cons. St. Jude's, Thornwood, N.Y., 1985-86; adv. Pace U. Computer Sci. and Info. Systems Bd. Patentee in field. Mem. Am. Mgmt. Assn., Assn. Computing Machinery, Chem. Notation Assn. Office: CIBA-Geigy Corp 444 Saw Mill River Rd Ardsley NY 10502

SCHUTTLER, ROBERT JAMES, environmental risk management consultant; b. Sioux Falls, S.D., Sept. 23, 1947; s. Reynold Charles Schuttler and Louila Elizabeth (Scott) Wasserburger. BS in Chem. Engring., S.D. Sch. Mines Tech., 1970. Numerous engring. and environ. positions 1970-79; mgr. environ. protection Occidental Chem. Corp., Niagara Falls, N.Y., 1979-80, project mgr., 1980-81, dir. environ. health and safety, 1981-84; sr. assoc. Pilko & Assocs., Inc., Houston, 1984—. Mem. AAAS, Am. Chem. Soc., Am. Inst. Chem. Engrs., U.S. Figure Skating Assn., Ice Skating Inst. Am., Alpha Chi Sigma. Republican. Home: 2323 Mid Ln #23 Houston TX 77027 Office: Pilko & Assocs Inc 2707 N Loop W Ste 960 Houston TX 77008

SCHUTTS, PHILIP LOWDON, printing company executive; b. Ft. Worth, Oct. 6, 1947; s. Robert and Kathryn (Lowdon) S.; m. Heidi Lynne Shearer, Sept. 20, 1986; B.B.A., Tex. A&M U., 1970; m. Carolyn Elizabeth Reeves, July 12, 1969 (div.); children—William Lowdon, Emily Elizabeth. With Stafford-Lowdon, Inc., Ft. Worth, 1970—, pres. Stafford-Lowdon Bank Stationery Co., 1979—; sr. v.p., gen. mgr. Am. Bank Stationery Co., 1980—; pres., chief exec. officer Stafford-Lowdon Printing Printing and Lithography, 1984—, Royer & Schutts Comml. Printing div., 1987—; pres., bd. dirs. Ft. Worth Sister Cities Inc.; bd. dirs. YMCA of Ft. Worth; bd. dirs., Tex. Heritage, Inc.; chmn., dir. Cutting Horse Heritage Found.; pres., bd. dirs. Chisholm Trail, Inc.; bd. dirs. N. Fort Worth Bus. Assn. Served with USMCR, 1970-76. Republican. Presbyterian. Mem. Ft. Worth C. of C. (bd. dirs.). Clubs: Rotary, Rivercrest Country, Ft. Worth Boat, Ft. Worth Petroleum, Ft. Worth, Steeplechase, Julian Field Lodge. Home: 6325 Genoa Rd Fort Worth TX 76116 Office: Royer & Schutts Comml Printing Div 1114 W Dagget Fort Worth TX 76102

SCHUTZ, JOHN THOMAS, real estate developer; b. Jasper, Ind., Jan. 3, 1932; s. William Ludwig and Marcella Elizabeth (Schneider) S.; m. Mary Alice Gramelspacher, Sept. 5, 1953; children: Sandra, Stephen, Scott, Stanley, Stuart, Sarah. BSEE, Purdue U., 1955. Engr. H.D. Tousley, Indpls., 1955; purchsing agt. DeCamp Reality, Indpls., 1959-60; gen. mgr. R.V. Welch, Indpls., 1960-64; construction supr. Brendon Park, Indpls., 1964-68; pres., owner Quadrant Devel. Co., Carmel, Ind., 1968—; part owner Chandelle Enterprises, Carmel, 1983—, Eden Devel., Carmel, 1985—, Peak Group, Carmel, 1986—. Mem. pres. council, Purdue U., West Lafayette, Ind., 1980. Served to capt. USAF, 1956-59. Mem. Gold Coats (dir.). Republican. Roman Catholic. Clubs: Gold Coats, John Purdue (West Lafayette). Lodge: KC. Home: 3234 McLaughlin St Indianapolis IN 46227 Office: PO Box 864 445 Gradle Dr Carmel IN 46032

SCHUTZMAN, LEONARD, beverage company executive; b. N.Y.C., Aug. 5, 1946; s. Samuel and Lillian (Bader) S.; m. Dale Ann Wenglowski, June 14, 1970; children: Joel, Rachel, Adam. BA, Queens Coll., 1967; MBA, U. Rochester, 1969. CPA, N.Y. Audit mgr. Arthur Young & Co., N.Y.C., 1969-76; asst. controller PepsiCo Inc., Purchase, N.Y., 1976-78; v.p. fin. Taco Bell, Irvine, Calif., 1978-79; v.p, controller PepsiCo Inc., Purchase, 1979-82; v.p. fin. PepsiCo Bottling Internat., Purchase, 1982-84, Pepsi-Cola Internat., Purchase, 1984-86; sr. v.p. fin. Frito-Lay, Plano, Tex., 1986-87; sr. v.p., treas. PepsiCo Inc., Purchase, 1987—; chmn. bd. Bus. Consortium Fund, N.Y.C. Recipient Disting. Alumnus award William E. Simon Grad. Sch., U. Rochester, 1987. Mem. Am. Mgmt. Assn. (fin. adv. council), Fin. Execs. Inst., Fairchester Treas.'s Group. Office: Pepsico Inc 700 Anderson Hill Rd Purchase NY 10577

SCHUYLER, ROBERT LEN, forest products company executive; b. Burwell, Nebr., Mar. 4, 1936; s. Norman S. and Ilva M. (Hoppes) S.; m. Mary Carol Huston, June 13, 1958; children: Kylie Anne, Nina Leigh, Melynn Kae, Gwyer Lenn. BS, U. Nebr., 1958; MBA, Harvard U., 1960. Asst. to treas. Potlatch Forests, Inc., Lewiston, Idaho, 1962-64; dir. corp. planning Potlatch Forests, Inc., San Francisco, 1964-66; mgr. fin. analysis Weyerhaeuser Co., Tacoma, 1966-68; mgr. investment evaluation dept. Weyerhaeuser Co., 1968-70, v.p. fin. and planning, 1970-72, sr. v.p. fin. and planning, 1972-85, exec. v.p., chief fin. officer, 1985—; mem. nat. adv. bd. Chem. Bank. Mem. adv. bd. Univ. Wash., council of fin. exec. of the Conf. Bd., MBA program adv., pvt. sector council. Mem. Fin. Exec. Inst., Am. Paper Inst. (bd. dirs., fin. mgmt. com.), U.S. C. of C. (econ. policy com.). Club: Anglers (N.Y.C.). Home: 12101 Gravelly Lake Dr SW Tacoma WA 98499 Office: Weyerhaeuser Co Tacoma WA 98477

SCHWAB, MARTIN JAY, textile company executive; b. N.Y.C., Nov. 26, 1922; s. Jacob Walter and Dora (Kaiser) S.; m. Betty Brand, June 5, 1949; children: Jeffrey, Sally, Steven. B.S., U. N.C., 1946. With United Mchts. & Mfrs., Inc., N.Y.C., 1946—, trainee, 1946-49, asst. to treas., 1949-55, treas., 1955-59, bd. dirs., 1955—, exec. v.p., mem. exec. com., 1959-67, chief fin. officer, chmn. fin. com., 1967-68, pres., 1968-75, chief exec. officer, from 1975, chmn., 1975—; dir. Am. Broadcasting Cos.; mem. adv. bd. Mfrs. Hanover, Arkwright-Boston Ins. Co. Trustee Inst. on Man and Sci., Montefiore Hosp., Hudson Guild. Served to 1st lt. USAF, 1942-45. Mem. Am. Textile Mfrs. Inst. (dir.). Club: Quaker Ridge Golf (Scarsdale, N.Y.) (treas.). Home: 71 Sheldrake Rd Scarsdale NY 10583 Office: United Mchts & Mfrs Inc 1407 Broadway New York NY 10018 *

SCHWAGER, JOHN LOUIS, oil company executive; b. East St. Louis, July 21, 1948; s. George Nicholas and Elizabeth Jane (Hanley) S.; m. Sharon Margaret Martin, Nov. 5, 1969 (div.); 1 child, Melanie Marie; m. Anna Carol Adams, Jan. 3, 1976; children: John Jr. (Jack), Casey Peyton. BS in Petroleum Engring, U. Mo., 1970. Engr. Shell Oil Co., New Orleans, 1970-76; div. engr. Shell Oil Co., 1976-79, supt. drilling, 1979-80; v.p., prodn. Callon Petroleum co., Natchez, Miss., 1980-84; sr. v.p. Alamco Inc. Clarksburg, W.Va., 1984-87; exec. v.p. Clarksburg, 1987, pres., chief exec. officer, 1987—; Bd. dirs. Alamco Inc., Clarksburg, W.Va., 1986-88. Mem. Soc. of Petroleum Engrs. Home: 49 Carriage Ln Bridgeport WV 26330 Office: Alamco Inc 200 W Main St PO Box 1740 Clarksburg WV 26301

SCHWAMB, DONALD FREDERICK, financial consultant; b. West Bend, Wis., July 21, 1952; s. Franklin Harvey and Maxine Ida (Oechsner) S.; A.S., U. Wis., 1972, B.S., 1975. With West Bend Co. (Wis.), 1969-73, indsl. and mfg. engr., 1973-76; mem. appraisal and project staff Valuation Research Corp., Milw., 1976—, dir. research, 1977—, asst. v.p. corp. adminstrn., 1980-87, asst. v.p. data processing, 1987—, mgr. price indexes and trends, fin. statistics, 1980—; cons. as archtl. historian. Chmn. Preservation Coordinating Council Milw., 1987—. Mem. Milw. County Hist. Soc., Wis. Heritages, Wis. State Hist. Soc., Nat. Trust for Hist. Preservation, Am. Inst. Indsl. Engrs., Am. Assn. Cost Engrs., Am. Mgmt. Assn., Nat. Assn. Rev. Appraisers (CRA designation). Home: 2233 N Summit Pl Milwaukee WI 53202 Office: 411 E Wisconsin Ave Milwaukee WI 53202

SCHWANDER, GARY L., toy manufacturing executive; b. 1933. BS, U. Wis., 1955. Engr. Chrysler Corp., Highland Park, Mich., 1959-61; internat. dir. Mattel Toys, Inc., Hawthorne, Calif., 1961-69; v.p. ops. Aurora Products Corp., Hawthorne, 1969-72; with Mattel, Inc., Hawthorne, 1972—, v.p. domestic ops., 1972-78, v.p. ops., 1972-78, sr. v.p. ops., 1980-86, exec. v.p., 1986—. Office: Mattel Inc 5150 Rosecrans Ave Hawthorne CA 90250 *

SCHWANHAUSSER, ROBERT ROWLAND, aerospace engineer; b. Buffalo, Sept. 15, 1930; s. Edwin Julius and Helen (Putnam) S.; m. Mary Lea Hunter, Oct. 17, 1953 (div. 1978); children—Robert Hunter, Mark Putnam; m. Beverly Bohn Allemann, Dec. 31, 1979. S.B. in Aero. Engring., MIT, 1952. V.p. aerospace systems, then exec. v.p. programs Teledyne Ryan Aero., San Diego, 1954-74, v.p. internat. requirements, 1977-79, v.p. Remotely Piloted Vehicles programs, 1979-81; pres. Condur, La Mesa, Calif., 1973-74; v.p. bus. devel. All Am. Engring., 1976-77; v.p. advanced programs Teledyne Brown Engring., Huntsville, Ala., 1981-83; pres. Teledyne CAE, Toledo, Ohio, 1983—; bd. dirs. Ohio Citizen's Bank, Toledo, 1987. Bd. dirs. Riverside Hosp., Toledo, 1985. Lt. USAF, 1952-54. Fellow AIAA (assoc., Outstanding Contbn. to Aerospace award 1971); mem. Assn. Unmanned Vehicle Systems (Pioneer award 1984), Nat. Mgmt. Assn. (Silver Knight of Mgmt. award 1972, Gold Knight of Mgmt. award 1987), Air Force Assn., Am. Def. Preparedness Assn., Nat. Rifle Assn., Navy League, Theta Delta Chi. Republican. Presbyterian. Clubs: Greenhead Hunting (Pine Valley, Calif.), Inverness (Toledo), Maumee River Yacht (Ohio), Gulf Shores Country (Ala.), The Crew's Nest (Ohio). Avocations: boating; hunting, skiing, golf. Home: 7928 Hidden Harbour Dr E Holland OH 43528 Office: Teledyne CAE 1330 Laskey Rd Toledo OH 43612

SCHWARK, AUGUST CARL, banker; b. Cape Girardeau, Mo., Jan. 10, 1948; s. August C. and Mabel A. (Roth) S.; m. Mary Ruth Brauer, July 5, 1975 (div. Jan. 1983); m. Janette Wiley Field, Sept. 21, 1985; 1 child, Ashley Catherine. BA, Valparaiso (Ind.) U., 1970; MBA, Washington U., 1972; diploma, Stonier Grad. Sch. Banking. Comml. banking officer Continental Ill. Nat. Bank, Chgo., 1972-76; asst. v.p. Bank One, Milford, Ohio, 1976-79, v.p., 1979-84, sr. v.p., 1984—, sec. bd. dirs.; instr. Am. Inst. Banking, Cin., 1986—. Mem. adv. com. Cancer Family Care, 1980-83; treas. Clermont County YMCA, Batavia, Ohio, 1983-85; chmn. Clermont Mercy Hosp. Devel. Council, 1984-85; chmn. United Way Campaign, Clermont and Brown Counties, 1989, asst. chmn., 1982, asst. v.p. 1987, vice chmn. 1988. Recipient Community Service award Greater Cin. Community Chest, 1982. Mem. Clermont County C. of C. (bd. dirs. 1981—, chmn. 1986, Pacesetter of Yr. award 1988). Club: Terrace Park Country. Home: 6385 Turpin Hills Dr Cincinnati OH 45244 Office: Bank One I-275 and State Rte 28 Milford OH 45150

SCHWARTZ, ALAN PAUL, consulting company executive; b. N.Y.C., Nov. 5, 1949; s. William and Dorothy Schwartz; m. Lori Jill Kleinman, Aug. 5, 1979. BS in Biology, CCNY, 1972. Investigator law and procedures N.Y. dist. FDA, 1972-77, supervisory investigator, 1977-78; cons., pres. Med. Device Inspection Co., Inc., Great Neck, N.Y., 1978—; cons., v.p. Foodworks Inc., Flushing, N.Y., 1978-85; pres. Foodworks Quality Assurance Cons., Great Neck, 1985—; exec. v.p. Creative Sci. Tech., Inc., Great Neck, 1987—; sec.-treas. Gum Tech. Inc., Flushing, 1983-85; bd. advisers Gen. Med. Corp., Cohasset, Mass.; regulatory affairs advisor MEIPEC Cons. Group, Cohasset, 1983-84; lectr. Ctr. for Profl. Advancement, 1981—; mem. adv. bd. BCR Ltd. 1986—, Preventa-Pak USA, 1986-87, Crystal Biotech Corp., 1987—. Mem. Regulatory Affairs Profl. Soc., Inst. Food Technologists, Environ. Mgmt. Assn., Small Mfrs. Med. Devices Assn., Assoc. Health Found. Club: Toastmasters (sec./treas. 1985-86). Lodge: KP (Man of Yr. 1985). Home: 80-45 Surrey Pl Jamaica Estates NY 11432 Office: 55 Northern Blvd Great Neck NY 11021

SCHWARTZ, BERNARD L., electronics company executive; b. 1925. BBA, CCNY, 1948. Ptnr. Schnee, Hover & Schwartz, 1948-62; sr. v.p. APL Corp., Miami Beach, Fla., 1962-68; with Leasco Corp., Miami Beach, 1969-72, chmn. bd., chief exec. officer, 1969-72; with Loral Corp., N.Y.C., 1972—, former pres., from 1973, now chmn., chief exec. officer. Served with U.S. Army, 1943-45. Office: Loral Corp 600 3d Ave New York NY 10016 *

SCHWARTZ, CAROLYN RAND, financial executive; b. Bedford, Ky., Dec. 12, 1938; d. John William and Sarah (Bray) Rand; m. Leonard Paul Schwartz, May 1, 1970; children: Sarah Roselyn, Daniel. Student, Hanover Coll., 1957-59; BS, U. Ky., 1961; cert. in merchandising, Tobe Coburn Sch., 1962. Cert. fin. planner. Exec. trainee, assoc. buyer Shillito's Dept. Stores, Cin., 1962-65; buyer, merchandiser Jacobson's Stores, Jackson, Mich., 1965-70; mgr. pro shop Colonial Racquet Club, Cin., 1976-82; rep. Chubb Securities, Cin., 1982-86; v.p. Spectrum Fin. Services, Cin., 1986—. Chmn. N.W. fundraising WCET pub. TV sta., Cin., 1980; chmn. fundraising Finneytown schs. PTA, Cin., 1980-82; pres., chmn. fundraising Kindervelt #37, Cin., 1981-82. Mem. Inst. Cert. Planners, Miami Valley Soc. Inst. Cert. Fin. Planners (pres. 1987—), Internat. Assn. Fin. Planners (bd. dirs. Cin. chpt., ethics chmn. 1988). Democrat. Presbyterian. Club: Newcomers (Wyoming, Ohio) (program chmn. 1986). Office: Spectrum Fin Svcs 10260 Alliance Rd Cincinnati OH 45242

SCHWARTZ, CHARLES EUGENE, manufacturing executive; b. Abington, Pa., May 22, 1933; s. Charles Schwartz and Mae (Swartz) Buzard; m. Margaret C. Hammer, Mar. 29, 1958; children: Cynthia L. Cunningham, Eric C. BSChemE, U. Pa., 1959. Engr. Lansdale Tube, Spring City, Pa., 1959-61; plant chemist, process engr. Scott Paper Co., Chester, Pa., 1961-65; chief process engr. Scott Paper Co., Marinette, Wis., 1965-71, div. mgr., 1971-75; plant mgr. to mgr. mfg. Scott Paper Co., Landisville, N.J., 1975-80, dir. mfg., 1980-84; v.p. ops. Scott Paper Co., Phila., 1984—. Bd. dirs. YMCA, Vineland, 1980-82. Mem. Rotary Club (bd. dirs. Vineland chpt. 1980-82). Republican. Lutheran. Home: 1070 Country Club Rd West Chester PA 19382 Office: Scott Paper Co Plaza II Indsl Hwy Philadelphia PA 19113

SCHWARTZ, CHARLES PHINEAS, JR., replacement auto parts company executive, lawyer; b. Chgo., Apr. 23, 1927; s. Charles Phineas and Lavinia Duffy (Schulman) S.; m. Joan Straus, Aug. 12, 1954 (div. 1971); children: Alex, Ned, Debra, Emily; m. Susan Lamm Hirsch, Dec. 18, 1976. A.B., U. Chgo., 1945; LL.B., Harvard U., 1976. Bar: Ill. 1950, N.Y. 1951, U.S. Supreme Ct. 1955. Assoc. Szold & Brandwen, N.Y.C., 1950-52; research assoc., teaching fellow Harvard U. Law Sch., Cambridge, Mass., 1952-56; sole practice law Chgo., 1956-61; ptnr. Straus, Blosser & McDowell, Chgo., 1961-67; fin. and bus. cons. Chgo., 1967-75; pres., chief exec. officer Champion Parts Rebuilders, Inc., Oak Brook, Ill., 1975-86, chmn. bd., chief exec. officer, 1986—; dir. Supercrete Ltd., Winnipeg, Man., Can., 1964-80, Athey Products Corp., Raleigh, N.C., 1967-86. Trustee, officer Hull House Assn., Chgo., 1958-70; dir., officer Chgo. Fedn. Settlements, 1972-79; dir. Friends of the Parks, Chgo., 1982—; dir., pres. Hyde Park Coop. Soc., 1962-68; trustee KAM Isaiah Israel Congregation, 1975-85. Served with USNR, 1945-46. Recipient Boulton Meml. award for disting. bus. statesmanship and dedicated service rendered to the entire industry Automotive Parts Rebuilders Assn., 1987. Mem. Motor Equipment and Mfrs. Assn. (dir. 1977-81), Automotive Pres. Council, Heavy Duty Bus. Forum, Automotive Sales Council, Soc. Automotive Engrs., Am. Bar Assn., Chgo. Council Lawyers. Jewish. Clubs: Quadrangle (Chgo.); Harvard (N.Y.C.). Office: Champion Parts Rebuilders Inc 2525 22d St Oak Brook IL 60521

SCHWARTZ, DARRELL MICHAEL, banker, economist; b. Chgo., July 17, 1958; s. Fred and Irene (Kahn) S.; m. Mary Irene Strok, June 28, 1982. A.A. in Econs., Miami Dade Community Coll., 1980; B.A. in Econs., Fla. Atlantic U., 1982; MBA in Banking, Nova U., 1988; student Leadership Sch. U. S. Fla., 1985, cert. Inst. Fin. Edn., 1986. Mgr. trainee Eckerd Drugs, Miami, 1974-77; sales mgr. Jefferson/Ward, Miami, 1981-82; br. mgr., asst. v.p. Coral Gables Fed. Savings and Loan, Fla., 1982-86; relationship mgr., asst. treas. Chase Manhattan of Fla., 1986-87; lending agy. mgr. Coral Gables Fed. Savs. and Loan, 1987; asst. v.p. consumer real estate lending, First Union Nat. Bank Fla., 1987—; dir. Inst. Fin. Edn., 1984-86. Mem.

Broward County Dem. Exec. Com., 1986. Recipient Outstanding Young Men of Am. award U.S. Jaycees, Montgomery, Ala., 1981. Mem. Am. Econ. Assn., Econ. Soc. South Fla., Fla. Acad. Scis., Fla. Atlantic U. Alumni Assn. (life, bd. dirs. 1985—), Mirimar-Pembroke Pines C. of C., DECA Club (North Miami Beach) (pres. 1975-77), Fla. Atlantic U. Sailing Club (pres. 1981-82), Rotary (charter mem. Weston, 1986-87, Boca Raton West 1987—), Fla. Atlantic Builders Assn. Jewish. Home: 16806 Royal Poinciana Dr Fort Lauderdale FL 33326 Office: First Union Nat Bank Fla 77 East Camino Real Boca Raton FL 33432

SCHWARTZ, EDWARD ARTHUR, digital equipment manufacturer; b. Boston, Sept. 27, 1937; s. Abe and Sophie (Gottheim) S.; m. Linda Washburn; children: Eric Allen, Jeffrey Michael. AB, Oberlin Coll., 1959; LLB, Boston Coll., 1962; postgrad., Am. U., 1958-59, Northeastern U., 1970; student exec. program, Stanford U., 1979. Bar: Conn. 1962, Mass. 1965. Legal intern Office Atty. Gen., Commonwealth of Mass., 1961; assoc. Schatz & Schatz, Hartford, Conn., 1962-65, Cohn, Reimer & Pollack, Boston, 1965-67; v.p., sec. Digital Equipment Corp., Maynard, Mass., 1967-88, gen. counsel, 1988—; vis. prof. law Boston Coll., 1986, adj. prof., 1987—; bd. dir. Stanmar, Inc., N.E. Legal Found., Am. Corp. Counsel Assn. Editor Boston Coll. Indsl. and Comml. Law Rev, 1960-62, Ann. Survey Mass. Law, 1960-62. Bd. dirs. Mass. chpt. Nat. Kidney Found., The Computer Mus. Mem. ABA, Mass. Bar Assn., Boston Bar Assn., Am. Corp. Counsel Assn. (bd. dirs.). Home: 62 Todd Pond Rd Lincoln MA 01773 Office: Digital Equipment Corp 146 Main St Maynard MA 01754

SCHWARTZ, FRANCES BETH (FRAN), public relations executive; b. N.Y.C., Apr. 20, 1950; d. Paul and Rhoda (Browner (Duchon) S. Student Ohio U., 1968-70, N.Y. Inst. Tech., 1971. Reporter Dun's Rev., N.Y.C., 1971-72; asst. to designer Catalina Sportswear, N.Y.C., 1972-74; advt. account asst. Wunderman Ricotta & Kline, Inc., N.Y.C., 1974-76; adminstrv. asst. CBS Mags., N.Y.C., 1976-79, communications coordinator communications dept., 1979-80, mgr. public relations, 1980-83, mgr. pub. relations and publicity, 1983-85; dir. public relations and assoc. editor J.R. O'Dwyer Co., N.Y.C., 1986-87; pub. relations mgr. mags. div. Globe Communications Corp., N.Y.C., 1987-88; pub. relations counselor, N.Y.C., 1988—; guest speaker Ohio U., 1982, CCNY, 1988. Mem. Internat. Assn. Bus. Communicators (bd. govs. chpt. 1982-88, v.p. spl. programs 1983-85, pub. relations chair 1985-86, chair, moderator breakfast club 1986-88, award of Merit 1980), Women in Communications.

SCHWARTZ, GEORGE EDWIN, paper company executive; b. Nampa, Idaho, May 28, 1924; s. Arthur Earl and Alpha Mable (White) S.; m. Marjorie May Allen, Apr. 1, 1944; children—Kathryn Dee Schwartz Schroeder, Thomas George, Steven George. BA in Econs. and Bus., U. Wash., 1948. Sr. acct. Price Waterhouse & Co., Portland, Oreg., 1948-53; instr. acctg. Multnomah Coll., Portland, 1952-53; successively asst. treas., sec., treas., v.p. fin., v.p. adminstrn. Longview (Wash.) Fibre Co., 1953-75, v.p. prodn., asst. sec., 1975-86, exec. v.p., asst. sec., 1986—; also bd. dirs. Trustee through pres. Monticello Med. Ctr., Longview, 1959-84, The Health Care Found., Longview; mem. hosp. and med. facilities adv. council Dept. Soc. and Health Services, State of Wash., Tacoma, 1968-74. Served to cpl. AUS, 1943-46, ETO. Mem. Northwest Pulp and Paper Assn. (trustee, pres. 1979-80), Wash. Pulp and Paper Found. (trustee, pres. 1985-87), Paper Industry Mgmt. Assn., TAPPI, Oreg. Soc. CPA's. Methodist. Lodges: Lions (Longview), Masons. Office: Longview Fibre Co PO Box 639 Longview WA 98632

SCHWARTZ, HENRY GERARD, JR., consulting engineering company executive; b. St. Louis, Aug. 3, 1938; s. Henry Gerard and Edith Childs (Robinson) S.; m. Sally Arlene Dunbar, July 2, 1960; children: Thomas D., Jeffrey R. BS, Washington U., St. Louis, 1961, MS, 1962; PhD, Calif. Inst. Tech., 1966. Registered profl. engr. Mo. project mgr., head environ. div. Sverdrup & Parcel and Assocs., Inc., St. Louis, 1966-72, asst. v.p., 1972-74, v.p. chief engr., 1974-75; v.p. environ. div. Sverdrup Corp., St. Louis, 1975-80, v.p., corp. prin., 1978—, bd. dirs., 1978—; pres. Sverdrup Environ., Inc., St. Louis, 1988—. Contbr. articles to profl. jours. Bd. dirs. St. Louis Psychoanalytic Inst., 1984—, United Way, St. Louis, 1985—; trustee Sverdrup Charitable Trust, 1987—; chmn. troop com. Boy Scouts Am., St. Louis; deacon, elder Ladue Chapel, St. Louis. Mem. Water Pollution Control Fedn. (Arthur Sidney Bedell award 1975, pres. 1986-87), ASCE, Nat. Soc. Profl. Engrs., Am. Acad. Environ. Engrs. (diplomate, lectr. 1989), Mo. Athletic Club, Media Club, Algonquin Golf Club. Presbyterian. Home: 10 Deerfield Rd Saint Louis MO 63124 Office: Sverdrup Corp 801 N 11th St Saint Louis MO 63101

SCHWARTZ, HOWARD MYRON, sales and marketing company executive; b. Phila., Aug. 27, 1935; s. Morton J. and Dorothy (Molden) S.; m. Jerrie Turick, Apr. 8, 1958; children: Robert Jon, Andrea Beth. BS in Mktg., Temple U., 1958. V.p. Phila. Coll. Art., 1958-66, Burns Internat. Security Inc., Phila., 1980-83, Fortress Sci., Inc., Toronto, Ont., Can., 1984-86, Ortho-Kinetics, Inc., Waukesha, Wis., 1986-87; pres. Howard M. Schwartz, Inc., Phila., 1966-76, Creative Communications, Inc., Phila., 1976-80, Rainbow Rock Advt., Inc., Sewell, N.J., 1983-84; prin. Howard M. Schwartz, Inc., Waukesha, 1987—; cons. to med. equipment mfrs. throughout U.S. and Can. Author: The Psychology of Effective Fund Raising, 1979, Computer-Assisted Fund Raising, 1980, Direct Mail for Business and Industry, 1981. Pres. Germantown Community Coun., Phila., 1979. Named hon. citizen City of Houston, 1979. Mem. Pub. Relations Soc. Am. (accredited, pres. 1979, citation 1978), Am. Alumni Coun. (citation 1976), coun. for Advancement and Support Edn. (citation 1975), Nat. Soc. Fund Raising Execs. (chmn. 1976-80), Nat. Direct Mail Coun. (founder, chmn. 1976-86), Phila. Art Alliance, Peale Club (Phila.).

SCHWARTZ, JAMES PETER, real estate broker; b. Bridgeport, Conn., Oct. 30, 1919; s. Joseph and Fannie (Tischler) S.; m. Natalie Postol, Mar. 12, 1941; 1 child, Joseph William. Student Coll. Commerce New Haven, 1939-41. Reporter Bridgeport Times-Star, 1940-41; reporter, photographer Bridgeport Post, 1942-43, 45-49; pres. Jay James Inc., Fairfield, Conn., 1949-70; owner James P. Schwartz & Assocs., Fairfield, 1970—; dir. Lafayette Bank & Trust Co., 1965—, Lafayette Bancorp, 1985-88. Treas. Greater Bridgeport Bd. Realtors, 1974-77, sr. v.p., 1978, pres., 1979. Contbg. editor Photog. Trade News, 1960-70. Pres. Barnum Festival Soc., 1975-76; ringmaster Barnum Festival, 1979; justice of peace, 1970—; mem. Easton (Conn.) Zoning Bd. Appeals, 1971-76; police commr., Easton, 1976—, chmn. bd. police commrs., 1986-88; bd. dirs. Bridgeport div. Am. Cancer Soc., 1977—; bd. assocs. U. Bridgeport, 1962—. Served with AUS, 1943-45. Named Man of Yr. dept. sociology U. Bridgeport, 1962, Realtor of Yr. award Greater Bridgeport Bd. Realtors, 1979. Mem. Fairfield Bd. Realtors, Nat. Assn. Realtors (bd. dirs.), Conn. Assn. Realtors (treas. 1981-82, pres. 1984-85). Lodge: Masons. Home: 78 Blanchard Rd Easton CT 06612

SCHWARTZ, JOSEPH, container company executive; b. N.Y.C., Apr. 22, 1911; s. Nathan and Ida (Estrich) S.; m. Hazel Shapiro, Dec. 25, 1932; children—Arlene Schwartz Bornstein, Linda Schwartz Rosenbaum. Grad., high sch. Ptnr. Mut. Paper Co., Lynn, Mass., 1928-38; treas. Allied Container Corp., Hyde Park, Mass., 1938-56; pres., treas. Allied Container Corp., Dedham, Hyde Park, 1956-84; chmn. bd. Cargal, Ltd., Lod Israel; dir. Macmillan Inc.; ret. v.p. Union Camp Corp., Wayne, N.J. Fellow Brandeis U. Home: 3960 Oaks Clubhouse Dr #307 Pompano Beach FL 33069

SCHWARTZ, KENNETH ERNST, communications executive; b. Detroit, July 12, 1922; s. Bernath and Sadie (Weiss) S.; m. June Henry; m. 2d, Eileen Frances Lamb, Dec.13, 1969; children: Joshua, Sarah. BS, U.S. Merchant Marine Acad., 1944; student, Am. Acad. Dramatic Arts, 1944-46. Producer/dir. Great Lakes Drama Festival, Saginaw, Mich., 1951-53; gen. mgr. Weil & Co., Detroit, 1953-55; producer/director Northland Playhouse, Southfield, Mich., 1955-69; deck officer U.S. Merchant Marine, 1969-71; freelance film producer/writer 1971-73; pres. Cutting Edge Enterprises, Inc., Easy Edit, V & W Sound Rec., Inc., N.Y.C., 1973—; pres. U.S. Editing Systems, N.Y.C.; dir. Midwest Alliance Summer Theatres, Detroit. Asst. producer (Broadway prodn.) Raisin in the Sun, 1959; co-producer (Broadway prodn.) Once There Was a Russian, 1961; co-author (film) Snapshots, 1973. Served to lt. USNR, 1944-47. Mem. B'nai B'rith Cinema, Radio, TV. Jewish. Office: Cutting Edge Enterprises Inc 630 9th Ave New York NY 10036

SCHWARTZ, LEONARD PAUL, management consultant; b. N.Y.C., Feb. 16, 1934; s. Theodore M. and Rose (Diamond) S.; m. Harriet Gale Meltz, Sept. 7, 1958 (div. Feb. 1966); children: Andrea Pearl, Gary Martin; m. 2d, Carolyn Rand, May 1, 1970; children: Sarah Roselyn, Daniel Lee. AB, U. Miami, 1956, student law, 1958-59; student Inst. Fin., N.Y.C., 1959-60. Cert. Inst. Cert. Profl. Bus. Cons. Registered rep., Walston & Co., Miami, Fla., 1959-62; owner, operator shoe store, Margate, N.J., 1962-65; regional mgr. Gulf Am. Land Corp., Miami, 1965-70; pres. MedGroup Mgmt., Inc., Cin., 1970—; mem. accts. and cons. adv. bd. Safeguard Industries Inc., 1988—; condr. seminars; vis. faculty lectr. Health Learning Systems Corp., 1989; tchr. residency programs. Pres. North Miami Beach Jaycees, 1961. Served to 2d lt. USAF, 1956-58. Recipient 2d place Spoke award Fla. Jaycees, 1961, Achievement in Editorial Excellence award Physician's Mgmt. Mag., 1978. Mem. Nat. Assn. Bus. Economist, Soc. Med.-Dental Mgmt. Cons. (dir. 1976-78, pres. 1980-81, Pres.' award 1983 Outstanding Mgmt. Cons of Yr. 1983), Inst. Cert. Profl. Bus. Cons. (trustee 1983-84, v.p. 1985). Democrat. Jewish. Clubs: Mercedes Benz (Cin.); K.P. (Atlantic City). Contbg. editor Physician's Mgmt., Dental Mgmt., Physicians Fin. News mags.; monthly byline question and answer column; contbr. articles to profl. jours. Office: MedGroup Mgmt Inc 10361 Spartan Dr Cincinnati OH 45215

SCHWARTZ, LOU, newspaper executive; b. N.Y.C., Jan. 14, 1932; s. Harry Milton and Beatrice (Skelton) S.; children—David, Jill. B.A., Syracuse U., 1953. Various position Newsday, Inc., N.Y.C., 1957-70, mng. editor, 1970-81, exec. editor, 1981-85; pres. Los Angeles Times Syndicate, 1985—; pres. Qwert Stables, 1977-78; juror investigative reporting panel Pulitzer Prize Jury, N.Y.C., 1985. Served to lt. j.g. USN, 1953-57. Recipient 1st place Lifestyle Journalism award J.C. Penney-U. Mo., 1966. Mem. Am. Assn. Sunday and Mag. Editors (pres. 1978), AP Mng. Editors Assn. (dir.), Am. Soc. Newspaper Editors, Newspaper Features Council (dir.), Horseman's Benevolent Protective Assn. Home: 11365 Canton Dr Studio City CA 91604 Office: LA Times Syndicate Times Mirror Sq Los Angeles CA 90053

SCHWARTZ, M. DAVID, retail executive. Pres., chief oper. officer Perry Drug Stores Inc., Pontiac, Mich. Office: Perry Drug Stores Inc 5400 Perry Dr PO Box 1957 Pontiac MI 48056 *

SCHWARTZ, NEIL DAVID, financial planner; b. Bklyn., Jan. 21, 1942; s. Louis and Rose (Kaplan) S.; m. Gloria Blatt, Jan. 24, 1965; children: Lisa I., Karen J. BS in Acctg., Bklyn. Coll., 1963; MBA in Taxation, CUNY, 1965. CPA, N.Y.; CLU, CFP, ChFC. Auditor, Coopers & Lybrand, N.Y.C., 1965-66; tchr. N.Y.C. Bd. Edn., 1966-67; sr. auditor Price Waterhouse & Co., N.Y.C., 1967-70; divisional controller, sr. fin. analyst ITT World Hdqrs., N.Y.C., 1970-72; sr. v.p. fin. Sun Life Ins. Co. Am., Balt., 1972-77; pres. FPC, Inc., Plantation, Fla., 1977—, Fin. Planning Services, Inc., Plantation, 1977—, NDS Fin. Group, Inc. Author: Corporate Financial Planning: Profit and Prophet, 1975, Current GAAP Accounting and Actuarial Practices for Life Insurance Companies, 1976, Good Acquisition Accounting Principles for Life Insurance Companies, 1976, Tax Sheltered Investments, 1981, Tax Deferred and Tax Sheltered Investments, 1982, How to Develop Financial Planning Practice, 1986. Treas. Jacaranda Lakes Homeowners Assn. Mem. Am. Inst. CPA's, N.Y. State Soc. CPA's, Fla. State Soc. CPA's, Inst. Cert. Fin. Planners (chpt. v.p.), Registry Fin. Planners, Nat. Assn. Life Underwriters, Assn. for Fin. Planning (pres. South Fla. chpt.), Plantation C. of C. (treas.), Million Dollar Round Table, Beta Gamma Sigma, Beta Alpha Psi. Jewish. Lodge: B'nai B'rith. Home: 5744 Waterford Boca Raton FL 33496 Office: Fin Planning Svcs Inc 150 S University Dr Plantation FL 33324 also: 980 N Federal Hwy Boca Raton FL 33432

SCHWARTZ, PERRY LESTER, infosystems engineer, consultant; b. Bklyn., July 29, 1939; s. Max David and Sylvia (Weinberger) S.; m. Arlene Metz, Jan. 24, 1960; 3 children. BEE, CUNY, 1957-62; MS in Indsl. Engring. and Computer Sci., NYU, 1967. Registered profl. engr., N.J.; registered profl. planner, N.J.; cert. mediator and arbitrator. Microwave engr. Airbourne Inst. Lab., Deer Park, N.Y., 1962-63, ITT Fed. Labs., Nutley, N.J., 1963-64; program mgr. Western Electric Co., N.Y.C., 1964-69; dept. head RCA, Princeton, N.J., 1970-71; dir. engring. Warner Communications Inc., N.Y.C., 1972-74; cons. engr. Intertech Assocs., Englishtown, N.J., 1974—; adj. faculty CCNY, 1962-71, Ocean County Coll., Toms River, N.J., 1981-83, Rutgers U., New Brunswick, N.J., 1984-87. Mem. Am. Cons. Engrs. Council, Nat. Assn. Radio and Telecommunications Engrs. (sr. mem., charter mem.), IEEE (sr.), Intelligent Bldgs. Inst. Found. (steering com., trustee 1982—), Nat. Soc. Profl. Engrs., Cons. Engrs. Council N.J., Am. Arbitration Assn., Zeta Beta Tau (chpt. founder 1958). Lodge: K.P. Office: Intertech Assoc 7 Plaza Nine Englishtown NJ 07726

SCHWARTZ, RICHARD THEOPHILE, retired actuary, consultant; b. Columbus, Ohio, Aug. 10, 1904; s. John Joseph and Clara (Vogelgesang) S.; m. Ann Novak Shuliga, Sept. 2, 1944; children—June Elaine Schwartz Tupper, Martha Lynn, Richard Alan. B.A., Princeton U., 1926; postgrad. Columbia U., 1933-34, Pace U., 1955-56, New Sch. Social Research, 1961-62. Assoc. actuary N.Y. Life Ins. Co., N.Y.C., 1926-68; actuarial cons. N.Y. State Employees Retirement System, Albany, 1968; v.p., actuary First Colony Life Ins. Co., Lynchburg, Va., 1969-73; cons. in field. Author: How They Prayed, 1979; (play) Coming of Jesus, 1980. Translator: Gospel of Mark, 1984, Mortality at Ages 65 and Over in 19th and 20th Centuries, 1984; Sermon on the Mount, 1985, Moments with Jesus, 1988, Gospel of John, 1989. Recipient 4th place ribbon U.S. Nat. Sr. Olympics Swimming, St. Louis, 1987. Bd. dirs. Bd. Pensions Lutheran Ch. in Am., Mpls., 1965-73; pres. Track and Field Club, Lynchburg, 1975-77; mem. track and field div. Nat. Ofcls. Com. Served to lt. comdr. USNR, 1942-46. Fellow Soc. Actuaries; mem. Am. Acad. Actuaries, Vickroy Soc. (Lebanon Valley Coll.), Gideons Internat. Republican. Club: Princeton (N.Y.C.); Appalachian Trail. Lodge: Lions. Avocations: swimming; walking; Latin and Greek translation; gardening. Home: 41 Clark Rd Hershey PA 17033 Office: Cons Actuary Ins Counselor 41 Clark Rd Hershey PA 17033

SCHWARTZ, ROBERT GEORGE, insurance company executive; b. Czechoslovakia, Mar. 27, 1928; came to U.S., 1929, naturalized, 1935; s. George and Frances (Antoni) S.; m. Caroline Bachurski, Oct. 12, 1952; children: Joanne, Tracy, Robert G. BA, Pa. State U., 1949; MBA, NYU, 1956. With Met. Life Ins. Co., N.Y.C., 1949—, v.p. securities, 1962-70, v.p., 1970-75, sr. v.p., 1975-78, exec. v.p., 1979-80, vice chmn. bd., chmn. investments com., 1980-83; chmn. Met. Asset Mgmt. Corp., 1983—, also dir., chmn. bd. parent co. State St. Rsch. Mgmt. Corp. and various subs.; bd. dir. Potlatch Corp., San Francisco, Lowe's Cos., Inc., North Wilkesboro, N.C., Communications Satellite Corp., Washington, Mobil Corp., N.Y.C. Trustee Com. for Econ. Devel.; mem. Greater N.Y. coun. Boy Scouts Am., NYU Schs. Bus. Bd. Overseers; trustee Nat. Urban League. With AUS, 1950-52. Mem. Alpha Chi Rho. Clubs: Seaview Country (Absecon, N.J.); Springdale Country (Princeton, N.J.); Sky (N.Y.C.). Office: Met Life Ins Co 1 Madison Ave New York NY 10010 also: Mobil Oil Corp 150 E 42d St New York NY 10017

SCHWARTZ, ROBERT NASH, public relations executive; b. Chgo., Mar. 6, 1917; s. Jacob and Sarah (Nerush) S.; m. Judith Goldman, June 3, 1940; children: Frances, James. B.A. magna cum laude, U. Ill., 1940. Reporter, Champaign (Ill.) News-Gazette, 1941-42; reporter, editor St. Louis Post-Dispatch, 1942-43; writer, editor N.Y. Times Sunday dept., 1943-46; editorial writer Chgo. Sun, 1946; bur. mgr., sci. editor Internat. News Service, Chgo., 1947-51; with Manning, Selvage & Lee, N.Y.C., 1957—; sr. v.p. Manning, Selvage & Lee, 1967-71, vice chmn. bd., 1971-73, pres., 1973-78, pres., chief exec. officer, 1978-83, chmn., chief exec. officer, 1983-85, chmn., 1985—; bd. dirs. Nat. Found. Infectious Disease, Deafness Research Found. Mem. Nat. Assn. Sci. Writers, Pub. Relations Soc. Am., Phi Beta Kappa. Clubs: Univ. (N.Y.C.). Home: 33 W 93d St New York NY 10025 Office: Manning Selvage & Lee Inc 79 Madison Ave New York NY 10016

SCHWARTZ, ROBERT WILLIAM, consultant; b. N.Y.C., Oct. 23, 1944; s. Edward and Bertha R. Schwartz; B.S., Cornell U., 1967; postgrad. in bus. adminstrn. SUNY, Albany, 1970; m. Gail Beth Greenbaum, Mar. 18, 1967; children—Jill, Evan. Asso., IBM, 1967-68; cons. Peat, Marwick, Mitchell & Co., Albany, 1970-71; v.p. Security Gen. Services, Inc., Rochester, N.Y., 1971-73; v.p. fin. and adminstrn. Gardenway Mfg. Co., Troy, N.Y., 1973-77; exec. v.p. United Telecommunications Corp., Latham, N.Y., 1977-79, pres., 1980-82, also dir.; pres., chief exec. officer Winsource, Inc., Albany, N.Y., 1982-85; pres., chief exec. officer Robert W. Schwartz, Inc., 1985—; dir. Caddim Corp., Union Nat. Bank, Albany; dir. Esarci Internat., Inc., Sprinfield, Mo.; assoc. Video hut, Inc., Albany, N.Y.; adj. prof. Rochester Inst. Tech., 1971-73. Bd. dirs. United Cerebral Palsy of Capital Dist., 1973—; trustee Newman Found., Rensselaer Poly. Inst., 1974-78, Gov. Clinton council Boy Scouts Am. Mem. Am. Mgmt. Assn., N.Am. Telephone Assn., Assn. for Systems Mgmt. Republican. Clubs: Ft. Orange; Economic, Cornell (N.Y.C.). Home and Office: 2 Myton Ln Menands NY 12204

SCHWARTZ, SAMUEL, chemical company executive; b. Moose Jaw, Sask., Can., Nov. 12, 1927; came to U.S., 1951, naturalized, 1965; s. Benjamin and Rose (Becker) S.; m. Margaret Patterson, Feb. 20, 1956; children: Michael R., Thomas R., David C., Janet C. B.A., U. Sask., 1948, B.Comm., 1950; M.B.A., Harvard U., 1953. Research assoc. Harvard Bus. Sch., Boston, 1953-57; with Conoco Inc., 1957-83; sr. v.p. coordinating and planning Conoco Inc., Stamford, Conn., 1974-75; sr. v.p. corp. planning Conoco Inc., 1975-78, sr. v.p. adminstrv., 1978-80, group sr. v.p. adminstrv., 1980-83; sr. v.p. adminstrv. E.I. duPont de Nemours & Co., Wilmington, Del., 1983-87, sr. v.p., corp. plans dept., 1987-88; dir. Conoco Inc., Consol. Coal Co.; mem. coordinating subcom. Nat. Petroleum Council's Study of U.S. Energy Outlook, 1970-72. Bd. dirs. Grand Opera House, Wilmington, 1981—; trustee Inst. for the Future, Menlo Park, Calif., 1975—, Henry Francis du Pont Winterthur Mus., Winterthur, Del., 1981—. Mem. Am. Petroleum Assn. Office: E I DuPont de Nemours & Co 2038 DuPont Bldg Wilmington DE 19898

SCHWARTZ, (ELLEN) SHIRLEY ECKWALL, chemist; b. Detroit, Aug. 26, 1935; d. Emil Victor and Jessie Grace (Galbraith) Eckwall; m. Ronald Elmer Schwartz, Aug. 25, 1957; children: Steven Dennis, Bradley Allen, George Byron. B.S., U. Mich., 1957; M.S., Wayne State U., 1962, Ph.D., 1970; B.S., Detroit Inst. Tech., 1978. Asst. prof. Detroit Inst. Tech., 1973-78, head div. math. sci., 1976-78; research staff mem. BASF Wyandotte Corp., Wyandotte, Mich., 1978-81, head sect. functional fluids, 1981; staff research scientist Gen. Motors Corp., Warren, Mich., 1981—. Contbr. articles to profl. jours.; patentee in field. Corr. sec. Childbirth Without Pain Edn. Assn., 1962; corr. sec. Warren-Centerline Human Relations Council, 1968. Recipient McCuen award Gen. Motors Rsch., 1988, Kettering award Gen. Motors Corp., 1989, Gold award Engring Soc. Detroit, 1989. Mem. Soc. Tribologists and Lubrication Engrs. (treas. Detroit sect. 1981, vice chmn. 1982, chmn. 1982-83, chmn. Wear Tech. com. 1987-88, dir. 1985—, assoc. editor 1988—, Wilbur Deutsch award 1987), Am. Chem. Soc., Tissue Culture Assn., Soc. Automotive Engrs. (Excellence in Oral Presentation award 1988), Mensa, Sigma Xi. Lutheran. Club: Classic Guitar Soc. Mich., U.S. Power Squadrons, Detroit Navigators. Office: Gen Motors Rsch Labs Warren MI 48090

SCHWARTZ, STEPHEN ALFRED, historian, consultant; b. Columbus, Ohio, Sept. 9, 1948; s. Horace Osman and Mayme Eileene (McKinney) S.; m. Mary Uhren, July 7, 1969 (div. 1974); 1 child, Matthew; m. Rebecca Rae Long, Mar. 22, 1984. AA, City Coll., San Francisco, 1972; student, U. Calif., Berkeley, 1972-76, 89—, U. London, 1985—. Freelance writer San Francisco, 1966-81; sr. editor Internat. Thomson Bus. Press, San Francisco, 1981-84; historian Sailors Union Pacific, AFL-CIO, San Francisco, 1983-86; fellow Inst. for Contemporary Studies, San Francisco, 1984—; cons. U.S. Info. Agy., Washington, 1988—, U.S. Inst. for Peace, Washington, 1988—; steward, publicist Brotherhood Ry. Clks., San Francisco, 1973-81; publicist Fomento Obrero, San Francisco, 1977-83; guest speaker Mont Pelerin Soc., Indpls., 1987; publicist ARDE/Nicaraguense, San Francisco, 1983-85; cons. author Hoover Inst., 1989—. Author: Brotherhood of the Sea, 1986; co-author: Spanish Marxism vs. Soviet Communism, 1988; editor: The Transition, 1987; contbg. editor Reason mag., 1987—; translator: What is Surrealism?, 1978. Recipient Editorial Excellence award, Communications Arts Mag., 1975; fellow Earhart Found., N.Y.C., 1987, 89; research fellow Olin Found., N.Y.C., 1988-89. Democrat. Jewish. Office: Inst Cont Studies 243 Kearny San Francisco CA 94133

SCHWARTZ, STEPHEN ALLAN, toy company executive; b. Bronx, N.Y., Apr. 18, 1949; s. Edward and Shirley (Silver) S.; m. Hana Solomon, July 4, 1971; children: Joshua, Daniel, Kathryn. BA, NYU, 1971. Mgr. mktg. Ideal Toy Co., Queens, N.Y., 1972-76, Child Guidance, Bronx, 1976-78; dir. mktg. Hasbro, Inc., Pawtucket, R.I., 1978-80, v.p. mktg., 1980-82, sr. v.p. mktg., 1982-87, exec. v.p. mktg., product devel., 1987-89, pres. Playskool div., 1989—. Office: Hasbro Inc 1027 Newport Ave Pawtucket RI 02862

SCHWARTZ, STEPHEN BLAIR, data processing executive; b. Chgo., Oct. 19, 1934; s. Herbert S. and Gertrude (Weinstein) S.; m. Nancy Jean Astrof, Dec. 18, 1955; children: Debra Lee Schwartz Zaret, Susan Beth Schwartz Derene. B.S. in Indsl. Engring., Northwestern U., 1957. With IBM Corp., 1957—; various mgmt. positions, dir. product programs IBM Corp., Harrison, N.Y., to 1977, v.p. Systems Communications div., 1977-81; v.p. IBM Corp., Armonk, N.Y., 1982—, Am. Far East Corp. subs. IBM Corp., Tokyo, 1981-84; pres., chief exec. officer Satellite Bus. Systems IBM Corp., McLean, Va., 1984; v.p., asst. group exec. Telecommunications IBM Corp., 1985-86, v.p., pres. Systems Products Div, 1986-88, v.p., gen. mgr. Application Bus. Systems, 1988—. Mem. adv. bd. Jr. Achievement, United Way. Mem. Am. C. of C. in Japan (com. chmn. 1981-84). Republican. Jewish. Clubs: Rolling Hills Country (Wilton, Conn.); PGA National (Palm Beach Gardens, Fla.). Office: IBM Corp 44 S Broadway White Plains NY 10601

SCHWARTZ, STEVEN GARY, lawyer, insurance executive; b. Newark, Feb. 18, 1954; s. Bert and Maidie (Heimberg) S.; m. Debra Faye Ryals, Apr. 26, 1986. BA in Govt. with honors, Franklin and Marshall Coll., 1975; JD, Washington and Lee U., 1978. Bar: Va. 1978, U.S. Ct. Appeals (4th cir.) 1978, Md. 1986. Assoc. Seawell, Dalton, Norfolk, Va., 1977-83, Scanelli, Shapiro, Norfolk, 1984-85; gen. counsel, mgr. claims Boat Owners Assn. U.S., Alexandria, Va., 1986—; gen. counsel Boat Am. Corp., Alexandria, 1986—. Author: Supreme Court in the Eyes of Presidents, 1975. Chmn. water events Norfolk Harborfest, 1982-84, fireworks 1983-84; chmn. water events Hampton Bay Days Fireworks, 1986, 87, 88, 89, bd. dirs. Mem. ABA, Va. Bar Assn., Md. Bar Assn., Maritime Law Assn., Young Lawyers Bar Assn. (exec. com. 1979-85, pres. 1985), Phi Beta Kappa, Pi Gamma Mu. Democrat. Jewish. Home: PO Box 22171 Alexandria VA 22304 Office: Boat Owners Assn US 880 S Pickett St Alexandria VA 22304

SCHWARTZ, STEVEN MARK, marketing executive; b. Phila., Feb. 26, 1948; s. Edward and Erika (Schneier) S.; m. Paula Mae Levine, May 15, 1979; 1 child, Roger. AB magna cum laude, Bowdoin Coll., 1970; MFA in Writing, Columbia U., 1973. Writer, account exec. Schneider & Rich Assocs., N.Y.C., 1973-76; sr. account exec. Richard Weiner Inc., N.Y.C., 1976-78; account supr., v.p. The Rowland Co., N.Y.C., 1978-79; project mgr. exec. communications GE, Fairfield, Conn., 1979-83; mgr. exec. communications GE, Fairfield, 1983-84; v.p. corp. communications Interleaf Inc., Cambridge, Mass., 1984-86, v.p. mktg. programs and communications, 1986-88, v.p. mktg., 1989—. Recipient Silver medal for documentary script 8th Internat. Film Festival of Ams., 1975. Mem. Phi Beta Kappa, Theta Delta Chi. Republican. Jewish. Home: 85 Old Colony Rd Wellesley Hills MA 02181 Office: Interleaf Inc 10 Canal Pk Cambridge MA 02141

SCHWARTZ, VALERIE BREUER, interior designer; b. Senica, Czechoslovakia, May 13, 1912; came to U.S., 1928, naturalized, 1928; d. Jacob and Ethel (Weiss) Breuer; m. Leo Schwartz, Feb. 5, 1939; children—Catherine, Robert, William. Student States Real Gymnazium, Prague, 1925-28; Parsons N.Y. Sch. of Fine and Applied Arts, 1930-32. Cert. Am. Soc. Interior Designers. Self-employed interior designer, N.J., 1932—. Contbr. to various mags. including N.Y. Times, House & Garden, Cue Mag., Confort, Argentina; guest radio talk shows. Mem. Hadassah (life). Designed Holocaust Room, Kean Coll., N.J.

SCHWARTZBERG, HARVEY JAY, technical sales representative; b. Sheveport, La., Aug. 27, 1928; s. Meyer and Ida (Goldberg) S.; m. Betty Adele Jacobs, Mar. 28, 1951; children: Alan Landau, Glen Jay, Michael Henry. BSEE, La. State U., 1949; MSEE, U. Ill., 1950. Registered profl. engr. La., Tex. Test engr. Gen. Electric Co., Schenectady, N.Y., 1950-51;

v.p. Gremco, Inc., Ft. Worth, 1953-57; design specialist Gen. Dynamics, Ft. Worth, 1957-63; regional mgr. Trans-sonics, Inc., Burlington, Mass., 1963-70; spl. sales rep. Westinghouse Electric Corp., Baton Rouge, La., 1971—; ind. market cons. flame safety, Dallas, 1970-76; bd. dirs. Power div. ISA, Research Triangle, N.C., 1986. Bd. dirs. Temple Sinai Brotherhood, New Orleans, La., 1970, Temple Rodef Sholem Brotherhood, Pitts., 1979; treas. Found. for Hist. La., 1987-88. Served as 1st lt. USAF, 1951-53. Recipient numerous sales proficiency awards Westinghouse Corp., 1971—. Mem. Instrument Soc. Am. (power symposium com. 1975, 78, 85), IEEE, Press Club, Camelot Club, Kiwanis. Jewish. Clubs: Press (Pitts.); Camelot (Baton Rouge). Home: 6135 Riverbend Blvd Baton Rouge LA 70820 Office: Westinghouse Electric Corp 2762 Continental Baton Rouge LA 70808

SCHWARTZBERG, HUGH JOEL, lawyer, corporate executive, educator; b. Chgo., Feb. 17, 1933; s. Ralph M. and Celia (Kaplan) S.; m. Joanne Gilbert, July 7, 1956; children: Steven J., Susan Jennifer. BA cum laude, Harvard Coll., 1953; JD, Yale U., 1956. Bar: Ill. 1957, Conn. 1956. Assoc. Ribicoff & Kotkin, Hartford, Conn., 1956-57, Lederer, Livingston, Kahn & Adsit, Chgo., 1957-62; assoc. Marks, Marks & Kaplan, Chgo., 1962-67, ptnr., 1967-70; ptnr. Schwartzberg, Barnett & Schwartzberg, Chgo., 1970-75, Schwartzberg, Barnett & Cohen, Chgo., 1975—; pres. Arizi Corp., Green Valley, Ariz., 1972-73, BMDC Warehouse Inc. Buffalo, 1975—; adj. prof. Medill Grad. Sch. Journalism Northwestern U., 1976, 78; ptnr. Ledgecrest Village, New Britain, Conn., 1975-86, SFS Lambert, Hyde Park Apts., Bath, Maine, 1975-88, Delaware Park Apts., Buffalo, 1972-86, High Wall, Highland Park, Ill., 1975—; chmn. bd. Zytek Mfg. Inc., Manila, 1987—. Chmn. Ill. State Adv. Com. to U.S. Civil Rights Commn., 1985—; bd. dirs. Fund for an Open Soc., Phila., chmn. exec. com.; bd. dirs. Home Health Svc. of Chgo. North, 1974-88; mem. Cook County (Ill.) Sheriff's Adv. Com., 1972-86; trustee Modern Poetry Assn., pub. Poetry Mag., Chgo., 1980—; chmn. com. in internat. affairs, pub. affairs com. Jewish United Fund, Chgo., 1980-83; bd. govs. Nat. Conf. Soviet Jewry, 1978-83; co-chmn. Emergency Task Force on Indo-Chinese Refugees, 1978-80; bd. dirs. Jewish Edn., 1973-76, 87—. Recipient testimonial Joint Youth Devel. Com., 1957, citation of Merit WAIT Radio, Chgo., 1974. Fellow Ill. Bar Found. (charter); mem. ABA (regional atty. sect. on individual rights and responsibilities 1985-86),Chgo. Bar Assn. (chmn. com. civil rights 1979-80), Tau Epsilon Rho (nat. historian 1988). Clubs: Harvard, Yale, Chgo. Lit., Soc. of Clubs, Union League, Chaine des Rotisseurs. Lodge: B'nai B'rith (pres. dist. 6 1986-88, internat. bd. 1982—, Appreciation award Anti-Defamation League 1975, Torch of Freedom award 1988). Avocations: poetry, photography. Home: 853 W Fullerton Ave Chicago IL 60614 Office: Schwartzberg Barnett & Cohen 55 W Monroe Ste 2400 Chicago IL 60603

SCHWARTZBERG, MARTIN M., chemical company executive; b. N.Y.C., Dec. 10, 1935; s. Morris H. and Anne C. (Steskanin) S.; m. Florence M. Bloom, Sept. 22, 1957; children: Steven E., Michael C., Scott A. B ChemE, NYU, 1956; MBA, Wayne State U., 1965. Asst. to div. mgr. Pennwalt Corp., Phila., 1969-72, mgr. mktg. service, 1972-74, asst. to chief exec. officer, 1974-76, mng. dir. chems. Europe, 1976-78, mng. dir. splt. chems., 1978-80, pres. agrichems. div., 1980-85, pres. inorganic chems. div., 1985, v.p. chems., 1985-87, sr. v.p. chems., 1987—; bd. dirs. Three Rivers Ventures, Pitts., The Chlorine Inst., Inc., Washington. Served with U.S. Army, 1959. Mem. Sigma Iota Epsilon. Avocations: volleyball, golf. Office: Pennwalt Corp 3 Parkway Philadelphia PA 19102

SCHWARTZENTRUBER, DANIEL CHARLES, marketing professional, educator; b. Dayton, Ohio, Dec. 2, 1956; s. Charles Alphonse and Elizabeth (Bogner) S.; m. Karla Ann Kozlowski, May 5, 1984. AS in Bus. Adminstrn., Sinclair Community Coll., 1977; BS in Bus., Wright State U., 1980. Mgr. stock systems Rike's Kumler, Dayton, 1973-76; inventory specialist Levi Strauss Co., Dayton, 1973-76, Farah Sales Corp., Dayton, 1976-77; registered interviewer Shiloh Mktg. Rsch. Co., Dayton, 1977-82; telephone sales rep. L.M. Berry & Co., Dayton, 1982-84, premise sales rep., 1984-86, with sales tng. assn., 1986-88; dist. sales mgr. L.M. Berry & Co., Madison, Wis., 1988—; cons. real estate mktg., advt. mgr. Century 21 Goldgate, Inc., Dayton, 1977-82; adj. prof. Sinclair Community Coll., Dayton 1988. Mem. Fair River Oaks Priority Bd., Dayton, 1980-82. Recipient Outstanding Achievemment award Ohio div. United Telephone Systems, 1984; Wright State U. scholar, 1978-80. Mem. Am. Soc. Tng. and Devel., Greater Dayton Jaycees (chmn., Outstanding Svc. award 1984), Sinclair Community Coll. Alumni Assn. Home: 2571 Petersburg Circle Madison WI 53719 Office: LM Berry & Co 6417 Odana Rd Madison WI 53719

SCHWARTZMAN, JACK, lawyer, educator, writer; b. Vinnitsa, USSR, Mar. 22, 1912; came to U.S., 1925; s. Solomon and Anna (Toporoff) S.; m. Vivian Reicher; children: Steven, Marcia, Robert. BS, CCNY, 1936; LLB, Bklyn. Law Sch., 1936, JSD, 1953; PhD, NYU, 1970. Bar: N.Y. 1938. Instr., Henry George Sch., N.Y.C., 1938-40, 46-49, 68-72, Rhodes Sch., N.Y.C., 1956-60; editor, writer Fragments Quar., Floral Park, N.Y., 1963—; prof. Nassau Community Coll., SUNY, Garden City, 1964—; sole practice, N.Y.C., L.I., 1938—; lectr. in field. Author: Rebels of Individualism, 1949; Alleged Rights to Organize Under the Soviet Constitution, 1953, The Philosophy and Politics of Paul N. Miliukov, 1970; contbr. chpts. to books and over 400 articles to profl. jours. Served to capt. AUS, 1942-46. Decorated Citation for the Army Commendation; recipient Founders Day award NYU, 1971; N.Y. State Chancellor's award for excellence in teaching SUNY, 1974. Mem. N.Y. State Bar Assn., Disting. Teaching Professorship (rev. com.), MLA, Thoreau Soc., Albert Jay Nock Soc., Council of Georgist Orgns., Univ. Profs. Acad. Order, Acad. of Polit. Sci., Found. for Econ. Edn., Albert Keith Chesterton Soc., Christopher Morley Knothole Assn., Internat. Platform Assn., N.Y. Acad. of Sci., Walt Whitman Birthplace Assn., Henry George Inst. (bd. dirs.), Walden Forever Free (bd. sponsors), Townsend Harris Assn., Pi Sigma Alpha, Phi Theta Kappa. Office: 87-16 Winchester Blvd Ste 3E Bellerose NY 11427

SCHWARTZMAN, MICHAEL ISAAC, investment management firm executive; b. Kutais, Krasnodar, USSR, Oct. 23, 1945; came to U.S., 1974; s. Isaac and Esther Schwartzman; m. Natalie Vera Belikhova, 1967; children: Elya, Anthony. MS in Computer Sci., Novosibirsk U., USSR, 1970. Researcher Acad. Scis., USSR, 1970-73, Columbia U., N.Y.C., 1974-75; cons. Chase Manhattan Bank, N.Y.C., 1975-76; mgr. Digital Equipment Corp., Maynard, Mass., 1976-78, Prime Computer, Inc., Natick, Mass., 1978-79; pres., founder Lang. Processors, Inc., Framingham, Mass., 1979-87; also bd. dirs. Lang. Processors, Inc., Waltham, Mass.; mng. ptnr. ENT Capital Mgmt., Acton, Mass., 1987—. Office: ENT Capital Mgmt 53 Newtown Rd Acton MA 01720

SCHWARZ, FREDERIC GEORGE, investment banker; b. N.Y.C., Feb. 22, 1926; s. Gottlob David and Luise (Nagel) S.; m. Ingeborg Wieland, Sept. 19, 1953; children: Tracey Ingrid, Leslie Ann. B.B.A., Manhattan Coll., 1951; M.B.A., N.Y. U., 1955. Credit analyst Chase Manhattan Bank N.A., N.Y.C., 1951-56; adminstrv. asst. Chase Manhattan Bank N.A., 1956-57, asst. treas., 1958-62, asst. v.p., 1962, v.p., 1967-71; v.p. Salomon Inc. (formerly Englehard Minerals & Chems. Corp. and Phibro Corp.), N.Y.C., 1971—; treas. Salomon Inc. (formerly Englehard Minerals & Chems. Corp. and Phibro Corp.), 1973-87; chief fin. officer Ecoban Assocs., Ltd., N.Y.C., 1988—. Served with U.S. Army, 1944-46. Home: 11 Seneca Rd Scarsdale NY 10583 Office: Ecoban Assocs Ltd 825 3d Ave New York NY 10022

SCHWARZ, LOUIS JAY, financial planning business executive; b. Chgo., May 15, 1946; s. Milton J. and Anita (Holtschutz) S.; m. Doris E. Fowler, May 31, 1969; children: Jovialis O., Iris N., Janis A. BA, Gallaudet U., 1968; postgrad, Ill. Inst. Tech., 1968-69. Cert. fin. planner; registered fin. planner. Tchr. Ill. Sch. for Deaf, Jacksonville, 1969-70; tax preparer Silver Spring, Md., 1971—; chemist U.S. Geol. Survey, Reston, Va., 1971-85; agt. Nat. Fraternal Soc. of Deaf, Mt. Prospect, Ill., 1975—; owner, mgr., fin. planner Schwarz Fin. Concepts, Silver Spring, 1983—; stockbroker Integrated Resources Equity Corp., N.Y.C., 1984—; cons., instr., ednl. speaker Nat. Ctr. for Fin. Edn., San Francisco, 1986—. Active Nat. Assn. of Deaf, 1972—, Md. Assn. of Deaf, 1972—; consumer adv. C&P Tel. Co., 1981-84; bd. dirs. Telecommunications for Deaf Inc., 1976-82, consumer adv., mem. adv. coun., 1981-87; cons. Montgomery County Commn. for Handicapped Individuals, 1979-83; adv. coun. Telecommunications Exch. of the Deaf, Inc., 1981-87. Named Outstanding Handicapped Fed. Employee U.S. Dept. Interior, 1974, 77; recipient Internat. Yr. of Disabled Persons' Honor award U.S. Dept. Interior, 1981, award Montgomery County Coun. Bus. Svc., 1988. Mem. Internat. Assn. for Fin. Planning, Inst. Cert. Fin. Planners, Internat. Assn. Registered Fin. Planners. Office: Schwarz Fin Concepts 814 Thayer Ave Ste 301 Silver Spring MD 20910

SCHWASS, GARY L., utilities executive; b. Ludington, Mich., Sept. 30, 1945; s. Philip V. and Greta (Beebe) S.; m. Peggy Ann McElroy, Nov. 29, 1968; children: John P., Jeree A. BS, Western Mich. U., 1968; MBA, Eastern Mich. U., 1971. Tchr. maths. Annapolis High Sch., Dearborn Heights, Mich., 1968-71; corp. systems analyst Consumers Power Co., Jackson, Mich., 1971-73; prin. planning analyst Consumers Power Co., Jackson, 1974-78, dir. fin. planning, 1979-80, dir. fin. planning and projects, 1981-83, exec. dir. fin. planning and projects, 1984-85; treas. Duquesne Light Co., Pitts., 1985—, v.p., 1987—, v.p. finance group, chief fin. officer, 1988—; bd. dirs. Western Pa. Devel. Credit Corp., Pitts.; v.p., treas., bd. dirs. Monongahela Light and Power Co., Pitts., Allegheny Devel. Corp., Pitts. Treas., bd. dirs. Cath. Social Services, Jackson, 1984-85; bd. dirs. Holy Family Inst., Pitts., 1988—. Methodist. Office: Duquesne Light Co One Oxford Centre 301 Grant St Pittsburgh PA 15279

SCHWEIG, MARGARET BERRIS, meeting and special events company executive; b. Detroit, Mar. 23, 1928; d. Jacob Meyer and Anne Lucille (Schiller) Berris; m. Eugene Schweig Jr., Nov. 24, 1951 (dec.); children: Eugene III, John A., Suzanne. Student, U. Mich., 1945-47. Pres., owner St. Louis Scene, Inc., 1975—. Mem. St. Louis Conv. and Visitors Commn., St. Louis Forum. Mem. Meeting Planners Internat., Am. Soc. Assn. Execs., Profl. Conv. Mgmt. Assn., Meeting Cons. Network, Nat. Assn. Exposition Mgrs., Internat. Spl. Events Soc., Hotel Sales Mgmt. Assn. (bd. dirs. 1977-80), Regional Commerce and Growth Assn., The Network (pres. 1980-81). Office: St Louis Inc 711 N 11th St Saint Louis MO 63101

SCHWEITZER, CONRAD, timber company executive; b. 1928. BS, U. So. Calif., 1954. With Ga.-Pacific Corp., Atlanta, 1961—, various mgmt. positions, v.p. ops., 1961-82, sr. v.p., 1982-83, group sr. v.p., 1983-85, exec. v.p., 1985—. Served with USMC, 1946-48, 50-52. Office: Ga-Pacific Corp 133 Peachtree St NE Atlanta GA 30303 *

SCHWEMM, JOHN BUTLER, printing company executive, lawyer; b. Barrington, Ill., May 18, 1934; s. Earl M. and Eunice (Butler) S.; m. Nancy Lea Prickett, Sept. 7, 1956; children: Catherine Ann, Karen Elizabeth. AB, Amherst Coll., 1956; JD, U. Mich., 1959. Bar: Ill. 1959. With Sidley & Austin, Chgo., 1959-65; with legal dept. R.R. Donnelley & Sons Co., Chgo., 1965-69; gen. counsel R.R. Donnelley & Sons Co., 1969-75, v.p., 1971-75, dir. Mattoon Mfg. div., 1975-76, group v.p., 1976-79, sr. group v.p., 1980-81, pres., 1981-87, chmn., 1983—, dir., 1980—; bd. dirs. Growth Industry Shares, Inc., Square D Co., Walgreen Co., USG Corp., Switzer Inc. Adv. bd. O.I.C. Am., Inc.; bd. dirs. Am. Productivity Ctr., The Conf. Bd., United Fund/Crusade of Mercy, Chgo., Evangel. Health Systems, Northwestern U. Mem. Law Club Chgo., Order of Coif, Phi Beta Kappa. Clubs: Chgo., Univ., Mid-Am., Comml., Commonwealth (Chgo.); Hinsdale (Ill.) Golf, Old Elm, Blind Brook. Home: 2 Turvey Ln Downers Grove IL 60515 Office: R R Donnelley & Sons Co 2223 Martin Luther King Dr Chicago IL 60616

SCHWERT, G(EORGE) WILLIAM, III, finance educator; b. Durham, N.C., Jan. 26, 1950; s. George William Jr. and Margaret (Houlton) S.; m. Camille Matthews, Dec. 19, 1970 (div. 1983); 1 child, Lisa Margaret; m. Patricia Michel, Dec. 23, 1983; children: Michael William, Andrew Patrick. AB in Econs. with honors, Trinity Coll., 1971; MBA, U. Chgo., 1973, PhD in Fin., 1975. Asst. prof. Grad. Sch. Bus. U. Chgo., 1975-76; from asst. prof. to prof. Grad. Sch. Mgmt. U. Rochester, N.Y., 1976-86; chmn. Knollwood Cons. Group, Inc., Rochester, 1987—. Co-editor Jour. Fin. Econs., 1979-86, adv. editor, 1986—; assoc. editor Jour. Fin., 1983—, Jour. Monetary Econs., 1984—; contbr. articles to econs. jour. NSF grantee, 1978-82; fellow Batterymarch Fin. Mgmt., Boston, 1982-83; rsrch. assoc. Nat. Bur. Econ. Rsrch., 1988—. Mem. Am. Fin. Assn. (bd. dirs. 1987—), Am. Econs. Assn., Econometrics Soc., Am. Statis. Assn. (chair-elect bus. econs. sect. 1989—). Home: 71 Knollwood Dr Rochester NY 14618 Office: U Rochester W E Simon Grad Sch Bus Adminstrn Rochester NY 14627

SCHWESINGER, EDMUND A., JR., consulting executive; b. Manila, June 22, 1939; s. Edmund A. and Dora (Axthelm) S. BA, St. Lawrence U., 1961; MBA, Columbia U., 1963. Fin. analyst GM, N.Y.C., 1961-69; mgr. Peat Marwick, N.Y.C., 1970-79; prin. A.S. Hansen, N.Y.C., 1980-81; ptnr. Coopers & Lybrand, N.Y.C., 1982-88; pres. Greenwich (Conn.) Cons. Group, 1989—. 1st lt. U.S. Army, 1964-66, Vietnam. Mem. Am. Compensation Assn., Indian Harbor Yacht Club. Home: 94 Cutler Rd Greenwich CT 06831 Office: Greenwich Cons Group 94 Cutler Rd Greenwich CT 06831

SCHWIER, PRISCILLA LAMB GUYTON, television broadcasting company executive; b. Toledo, Ohio, May 8, 1939; d. Edward Oliver and Prudence (Hutchinson) L.; m. Robert T. Guyton, June 21, 1963 (dec. Sept. 1976); children—Melissa, Margaret, Robert; m. Frederick W. Schwier, May 11, 1984. B.A., Smith Coll., 1961; M.A., U. Toledo, 1972. Pres. Gt. Lakes Communications, Inc., 1982—; vice chmn. Seilon, Inc., Toledo, 1981-83, also dir.; pres. Lamb Enterprises, Inc., Toledo, 1983—; dir. Lamb Enterprises, Inc., Toledo, 1976—. Contbr. articles to profl. jours. Trustee Wilberforce U., Ohio, 1983—, Planned Parenthood, Toledo, 1979-83; trustee Maumee Valley Country Day Sch., Toledo. Episcopal Ch., Maumee, Ohio, 1983—; bd. trustees Toledo Hosp. Democrat. Episcopalian. Home: 345 E Front St Perrysburg OH 43551 Office: 1630 Ohio Citizens Bank Toledo OH 43604

SCHWITALLA, STEPHEN EDWARD, food service executive; b. Tacoma, Nov. 16, 1953; s. Alfred M. and Joan E. (Howard) S.; m. Susan Eileen Schwitalla, Mar. 10, 1973; children: Michael Howard, Diane Kelly. Region mgr. Servomation, Fremont, Calif., 1971-73; distbn. supr. Fleming Foods Co., Fremont, 1973-77; warehouse and transp. mgr. Fleming Foods Co., Oakland, Calif., 1977-79; warehouse and purchasing mgr. Distron/Burger King, San Jose, Calif., 1979-80; div. mgr. Nat. Convenience Stores, Los Angeles, 1980-82; v.p. distbn. and foodservice Circle K Corp., Phoenix, 1982-85, corp. sr. v.p. foodservice, 1985—, pres. Deli Pride Foods Inc. div.; bd. dirs. IICA Corp., Phoenix. Recipient Clio award for Advt. Excellence, 1985. Mem. Am. Mgmt. Assn., Nat. Assn. Convenience Stores, Ariz. Retail Grocers Assn., Internat. Food Mfg. Assn., Internat. Deli/Bakery Assn. Republican.

SCHYMAN, ALBERT WILLIAM, marketing executive; b. Chgo., Apr. 26, 1961; s. William Robert and Helen Mary (Daniels) S. Student, Montgomery Coll., Rockville, Md., 1980-82; BA, Hampden Sydney Coll., Va., 1985. Mgmt. trainee U.S. Lines, N.Y.C., 1985; acct. mgr. U.S. Lines, Detroit, 1985-86, Atlanta, 1986-88; mkt. research exec. R.A.S., Inc., Atlanta, 1988—. Author: The Auto Embargo, 1986. Mem. Atlantic Task Force on Homeless, 1987, Marietta Community Devel., 1988, Detroit Improvement Commn., 1986, Let's Speak Japanese, Atlanta, 1988—. Mem. Atlanta Intermaritime Assn., World Trade Club, Japan-Am. Soc. Republican. Roman Catholic. Club: Japan. Home: 2055 B Powers Ferry Rd Marietta GA 30067

SCIABICA, VINCENT SAMUEL, chemist, researcher; b. Greensburg, Pa., July 4, 1959; s. Samuel Vincent and Sallie (Scichilone) S. BS in Chemistry, St. Vincent Coll., 1981; MBA, W.Va. U., 1984. Project chemist Kennametal Inc., Latrobe, Pa., 1980-81; research chemist U. Pitts., 1981; environ. chemist Wheeling (W.Va.)-Pitts. Steel Corp., 1982-85; environ. gas chromatography/mass spectrometry chemist Internat. Tech., Pitts., 1985-89; mgr. Radian Corp., Raleigh, N.C., 1989—; lighting cons. Perfect Image Lighting, 1986—; audio cons. Ears Ahead Audio/Ear Force Sound, Greensburg, 1979—; v.p. S.S.V. Inc., Greensburg, 1981—; pres. Ear Force Sound, Inc., Greensburg, Pa., 1988—. Mem. Soc. Audio Cons. (cert.), Nat. Assn. MBA's, SEC (registered rep.), Am. Chem. Soc. Republican. Roman Catholic. Office: Radian Corp Research Triangle Park Raleigh NC 27560

SCIBILIA, PHILIP CHESTER, publishing company executive; b. Irvington, N.J., Oct. 17, 1940; s. Joseph P. and Delores J. (Padovano); m. Donna Leigh Mills, Mar. 26, 1977; 1 child, Andrew Philip. BCE, N.J. Inst. Tech., 1963; BBA, Rutgers U., 1968; postgrad., Rochester Inst. Tech., 1973-74. Plant engr. Tenco div. Coca Cola Co., Linden, N.J., 1964-65; product mgr. CIBA/Geigy Corp., Summit, N.J., 1968-74; advt. mgr. Cliggot Pub., Greenwich, Conn., 1974-76; assoc. pub. PW Communications, N.Y.C., 1976-80; v.p., pub. Sieber & McIntyre, Morristown, N.J., 1980-84; pres. Macmillan Healthcare, Florham Park, N.J., 1984—; bd. dirs. Individual Asset Planning Corp., Morristown, N.J. Served with USCG. Mem. Pharm. Advt. Council, Mid-West Pharm. Advt. Club, West Coast Med. Mktg. Assn. Republican. Methodist. Home: 47 Round Hill Rd Kinnelon NJ 07405 Office: Macmillan Healthcare Info 25 Hanover Rd Florham Park NJ 07932

SCICCHITANO, CARMINE DAVID, broadcast executive; b. Danville, Pa., June 26, 1962; s. David C. and Peggy (Corcoran) S.; m. Maria Henninger, July 9, 1988; 1 child, Don Filippo David. Lic. FCC 1st class radiotelephone operator. Maintenance engr. Sta. WBRE-TV, Wilkes-Barre, Pa., 1978-79; transmission and quality control engr. Group W Satellite Communications, Stamford, Conn., 1979-81; sr. engr. TeleLink Communications, Hollywood, Fla., 1981-83; chief engr. TeleCom Broadcasting, Inc., Oceanside, Calif., 1983-85, v.p. ops. and engring., 1985-88; v.p. ops. and engring. Wash. Internat. Teleport, Alexandria, Wash., 1988—; designer and builder of transportable Earthstations; supr. 2 satellite Earthstations and Teleports, 1981-88. Mem. Soc. Broadcast Engrs. (broadcast technologist), Nat. Assn. Radio and Telecommunications Engrs. (cert. 1st class), Soc. Satellite Profls. Roman Catholic. Home: 48 N Market St Mount Carmel PA 17851 Office: Wash Internat Teleport 6461 Stephenson Way Alexandria VA 22312

SCIPIONE, RICHARD STEPHEN, insurance company executive, lawyer; b. Newton, Mass., Aug. 27, 1937; s. Charles John and Alice (Scotto) S.; m. Lois Mugford, Aug. 29, 1964; children: Jeffrey Charles, Douglas Loring. B.A., Harvard U., 1959; LL.B., Boston U., 1962. Bar: Mass. 1962. Atty. John Hancock Mut. Life Ins. Co., Boston, 1965-69, asst. counsel, 1969-74, assoc. counsel, 1975-79, sr. assoc. counsel, 1980-82, 2d v.p., counsel, 1982-84, v.p., gen. solicitor, 1984-85, sr. v.p. and gen. solicitor, 1986-87, gen. counsel, 1987—. Served to capt. U.S. Army, 1962-65. Mem. Assn. Life Ins. Counsel, ABA, Am. Corp. Counsel Assn, N.E. Legal Found. (adv. bd.). Club: Chatham Yacht. Office: John Hancock Mut Life Ins Co Po Box 111 Boston MA 02117

SCOATES, WESLEY MARVIN, mining company executive; b. Jacksonville, Fla., Apr. 21, 1938; s. Harry William and Orlene (Buffkin) S.; m. Patty Ann Flora, 1958 (div. 1969); children: Teresa, Lesa, Leslie, Randall; m. Anneliese Marie Knorlein, May 11, 1970; children: Stephen, Cherry. B in Mech. Engring., U. Dayton, 1962; MBA, Fla. Internat. U., 1983. Commd. 2d lt. U.S. Army, 1962, advanced through grades to lt. col., 1982; artillery officer U.S. Army, Ft. Sill, Okla., 1962-65; mech. engr. U.S. Army Corps of Engrs., Jacksonville, 1965-66; artillery officer U.S. Army, Republic of Vietnam, Republic of Korea, Federal Republic of Germany, 1968-76, resigned, 1975; project engr. U.S. Gypsum Co., Jacksonville, 1966-67; div. chief City of Jacksonville, 1976-78; asst. equipment supt. Metro Dade County, Miami, Fla., 1978-79; asst. service mgr. Kelly Tractor Co., Miami, 1979-81; maintenance supt. Vulcan Materials Co., Miami, 1981-87, area mgr., 1987—; CGSOC instr. USAR Sch., 1979-88. Contbr. articles to army logistican mag. Mem. Darmstadt (Fed. Republic of Germany) Sch. Bd., 1974; bd. dirs. Via de Cristo, Miami, 1986. Decorated Bronze Star with oak leaf cluster, Air medal. Mem. Acad. Polit. Sci., Council on Fgn. Relations, Am. Def. Preparedness Assn., Am. Assn. Individual Investors. Republican. Methodist. Office: Vulcan Materials Co PO Box 660097 Miami FL 33166

SCOCOZZA, MATTHEW VINCENT, lawyer; b. Bklyn., Oct. 13, 1948; s. Frank and Stella (Bartone) S. B.S., Murray State U., Ky., 1970; J.D., U. Tenn.-Knoxville, 1973. Bar: Tenn. 1973, D.C. 1974. Law clk. Tenn. Supreme Ct., 1973-74; minority counsel U.S. Ho. of Reps. com. on Appropriations, subcom. on transp., 1975-76; trial atty. Bur. Investigations and Enforcement, ICC, 1974-75, 76; sr. counsel U.S. Senate Com. on Commerce, Sci. and Transp., 1977-82; dept. asst. sec. U.S. Dept. State, 1977-82; asst. sec. for policy and internat. affairs U.S. Dept. Transp., Washington, 1983-88; ptnr. McNair Law Firm, P.A., Washington, 1988—. Contbg. author: Mandate for Leadership, 1980, The First Year, 1982. Recipient Ann. Cooperstown conf. award Cooperstown Rail conf., 1981, Delta Nu Alpha Presdl. award, 1984-85, Delta Nu Alpha Nat. Transp. Man of Yr., 1987. Mem. ABA, Tenn. Bar Assn., D.C. Bar Assn., Omicron Delta Kappa, Phi Alpha Delta, Delta Nu Alpha, Sigma Phi Epsilon. Roman Catholic. Office: McNair Law Firm 1155 15th St NW Ste 400 Washington DC 20005

SCOFIELD, SCOTT JON, financial services company executive; b. Bemidji, Minn., Jan. 25, 1955; s. Levi Russell and Eva (Belle) S.; m. Lancey Leone Cheesebrough, Aug. 28, 1976 (div. Mar. 198l); m. Cheryl Pauline Bath, Mar. l2, 1988. BA, Augsburg Coll., 1979. Produce mgr. Country Club Markets, Mpls., 1974-84; ins. salesman Bankers Life & Casualty, Minnetonka, Minn., 1985; fin. svcs. rep. Century Co. Am., Minnetonka, 1985—. Mem. St. Paul Life Underwriters. Office: Century Co Am Minnetonka MN 55313

SCOFIELD, TODD CARVER, marketing professional; b. Bridgeport, Conn., Dec. 26, 1956; s. Richard Anthony and Gertrude (Johnson) S. Student, U. Conn., 1974-75, 77-80. Sales rep. Digital Equipment Corp., Piscataway, N.J., 1980-83; sales exec. Victor Tech., Union, N.J., 1983; regional sales mgr. Sharp Electronic Corp., Paramus, N.J., 1983-84; dir. mktg. Entre Computer Ctr., Allamuchy, N.J., 1984-85; exec. v.p. sales and mktg. Hugh Carver Group, Inc., Monmouth Junction, N.Y., 1985-89, pres., 1989—; bd. dirs. Hugh Carver Group, Inc., Monmouth Junction. Mem. Sigma Chi (pres. 1978-80). Office: Hugh Carver Group Inc 7 Deer Park Dr Monmouth Junction NJ 08852

SCOLLARD, PATRICK JOHN, banker; b. Chgo., Apr. 20, 1937; s. Patrick J. and Kathleen (Cooney) S.; m. Gloria Ann Carroll, July 1, 1961; children: Kevin, Maureen, Daniel, Thomas, Brian. B.S. in Econs., Marquette U., 1959; grad. sr. exec. devel. program, MIT, 1976. With Equitable Life Assurance Soc. U.S., N.Y.C., 1962-79, advanced systems analyst, 1964-65, mgr. profl. placement, 1965-67, mgr. salary adminstrn., 1967-68, dir. compensation, 1968-69, asst. v.p., 1969-71, v.p., personnel dir., 1971-75, v.p. adminstrv. services, 1975-79, v.p. corp. adminstrv. and employee services, 1978-79; sr. v.p. Chem. Bank, N.Y.C., 1979-80, exec. v.p., 1980-87, chief adminstrv. officer, 1987—; bd. dirs. Nat. Inst. Work and Learning. Mem. adv. bd. Marquette U.; chmn. Woodstock Theol. Ctr.; bd. dirs. St. Francis Hosp.; mgmt. and orgn. adv. bd. Columbia U., N.Y.C. Served with USN, 1959-62. Mem. Nat. Assn. Securities Dealers, Am. Mgmt. Assn., Am. Soc. Personnel Adminstrn., N.Y. Personnel Mgmt. Assn., Personnel Round Table. Office: Chem Bank 277 Park Ave New York NY 10172

SCONCE, MARK CURTIS, modeling school and talent agency executive; b. Dodge City, Kans., Jan. 5, 1944. Student, Trinity Coll., Dublin, 1965-66; BA in Polit. Sci., Antioch Coll., 1967; postgrad., U. Calif., Berkeley, 1971. Mgr. Oharco, Omaha, 1971-73; co-owner, mgr. Nancy Bounds Internat., Omaha, 1972—; v.p. Internat. Talent and Model Assn., N.Y.C., 1979-81. Vol. U.S. Peace Corps, Nepal, South Asia, 1967-69; polit. aide Unruh for gov. campaign, San Francisco, 1970. Democrat. Unitarian. Home and Office: 4803 Davenport St Omaha NE 68132

SCONYERS, JEFF, federal banking executive; b. Cottondale, Fla., Feb. 4, 1935; s. John Grady Sconyers and Ida Mae (Roberts) Buchanan; 1 foster child. B.A. in English Lit., George Mason U., 1974; postgrad. St. Mark's Sem., U. Va. Office mgr. Congresswoman Gracie Pfost, U.S. Ho. of Reps., Washington, 1958-60; asst. to Senator John J. Sparkman, U.S. Senate, Washington, 1961-72, 74-76; dir. subcom. on fin. and investment of Senate Select Com. on Small Bus., Washington, 1972-73; asst., office mgr. Congressman J. Herbert Burke, U.S. Ho. of Reps., Washington, 1977-78; editor Fed. Home Loan Bank Bd. Jour., 1981-84; spl. asst. to exec. staff dir. office of chmn. Fed. Home Loan Bank Bd., Washington, 1984-85; sec. Fed. Home Loan Bank Bd., 1985—; corp. sec. Fed. Savs. and Loan Ins. Corp., 1985-87; EEO counselor Fed. Home Loan Bank Bd. Contbr. articles to profl. jours. Instr. Sacred Heart Acad., Washington. Mem. Jaycees, Birmingham, Ala., 1965-66. Served with USAF, 1954-57. Recipient Superior Performance awards Fed. Home Loan Bank Bd. Republican. Roman Catholic.

SCOPAZ, JOHN MATTHEW, banker; b. N.Y.C., June 24, 1948; s. John J. and Alice L. (Zustovich) S.; m. Linda N. Nelson, Mar. 17, 1973; children: Jennifer, Lauren, Kristen. BSChemE, Manhattan Coll., 1970; MBA, NYU, 1973. Plant engr. Colgate Palmolive, Jersey City, 1970-72; systems analyst

Colgate Palmolive, N.Y.C., 1973-74; mng. dir., v.p. Citicorp (BHC Resources), N.Y.C., 1975-81; exec. v.p. Republic Nat. Bank, N.Y.C., 1981—; pres., bd. dirs. Republic Info. & Communications Svcs., N.Y.C. Coach Pelham (N.Y.) Little League; bd. dirs. N.Y. League Hard of Hearing. Mem. Am. Mgmt. Assn. Republican. Roman Catholic. Office: Republic Nat Bank 452 Fifth Ave New York NY 10018

SCOPINICH, JILL LORIE, editor, writer; b. Seattle, Dec. 7, 1945; d. Oscar John and Marcella Jane (Hearing) Younce; 1 child, Lori Jill. AA in Gen. Edn., Am. River Coll., 1969; BA in Journalism with honors, Sacramento State U., 1973. Reporter Carmichael (Calif.) Courier, 1968-70; mng. editor Quarter Horse of the Pacific Coast, Sacramento, 1970-75, editor, 1975-84; editor Golden State Program Jour., 1978, Nat. Reined Cow Horse Assn. News, Sacramento, 1983-88, Pacific Coast Jour., Sacramento, 1984-88, Nat. Snaffle Bit Assn. News, Sacramento, 1988; pres., chief exec. officer Communications Plus, Bellevue, Wash., 1988—; mag. cons., 1975—. Interviewer Pres. Ronald Reagan, Washington, 1983; assoc. editor Wash. Thoroughbred, 1989—. Mem. 1st profl. communicators mission to the U.S.S.R., 1988; bd. dirs. Carmichael, Winding Way, Pasadena Homeowners Assn., Carmichael, 1985-87. Recipient 1st pl. feature award, 1970, 1st pl. editorial award Jour. Assn. Jr. Colls., 1971, 1st pl. design award WCHB Yuba-Sutter Counties, Marysville, Calif., 1985. Mem. Am. River Jaycees (recipient speaking award 1982), Am. Horse Publs. (recipient 1st pl. editorial award 1983, 88), Mensa (bd. dirs., asst. local sec., activities dir. 1987-88, membership chair 1988—). Republican. Roman Catholic. Club: 5th Wheel Touring Soc. (Sacramento) (v.p. 1970). Home: 440 Adelma Beach Rd Port Townsend WA 98368

SCOTT, ANDREW, corporate executive; b. St. Paul, Apr. 5, 1928; s. Ulric and Annamay (Gorry) S.; m. Kathleen Kennedy, May 7, 1960; children: Andrea Kennedy Scott, Lucia Scott Lambert. BS, U. Minn., 1950, LLB, 1952. Bar: Minn. 1952. Ptnr. Doherty, Rumble & Butler, Mpls. and St. Paul, 1952-77; chmn. Andrew Scott Ltd., Mpls., 1978-81; vice chmn. Cray Research Inc., Mpls., 1981—, also bd. dirs.; bd. dirs. First Trust Co. Inc., St. Paul. Bd. dirs. Minn. Orchestral Assn., Mpls., 1961-78; trustee Mpls. Soc. Fine Arts, 1966-78, Twin City Area Pub. TV Corp., St. Paul, 1967-74, St. Paul Acad./Summit Sch., 1972-75. Mem. ABA, Computer Law Assn. Roman Catholic. Clubs: Mpls.; Somerset (St. Paul). Home: 1941 Penn Ave S Minneapolis MN 55405 Office: Cray Rsch Inc 608 2d Ave S Minneapolis MN 55402

SCOTT, BLAINE WAHAB, III, insurance executive; b. Phila., Apr. 22, 1927; s. Blaine W., Jr., and Dorothy (Fox) S.; ed. Friends' Central Sch.; m. Mary L. Howe, Nov. 14, 1964; 1 son, Robert P.; children by previous marriage—M. Kathleen, Bruce K., Sharon L., Linda, Blaine Wahab, Carol. Registered Health Underwriter. Pres., dir. World Life & Health Ins. Co. of Pa.; pres., dir. Worlco Inc., also pres., dir. all affiliates and subsidiaries; pres. Upper Merion Investment Corp.; sec., dir., Royal Bank Pa., 1963-88; dir. Gen. Devices, Inc., Agy. Rent-A-Car, Worlco Data Systems, Madison Bank. Mem. Upper Merion Bd. Suprs., 1960-66, chmn., 1961-66; trustee Temple U., 1969-73, Valley Forge Mil. Acad. and Jr. Coll., 1978-84, 86—; dir. Valley Forge Country Convention Vis. Bur., dir. emeritus King of Prussia C. of C., mem. Pa. Rep. State Com. Served in U.S. Army, World War II, Korea. Named one of 5 outstanding young men of commonwealth, Pa. Jr. C. of C., 1962, Republican of Yr. Upper Merion Rep. Com., 1984. Mem. VFW, Nat. Assn. Health Underwriters, Greater Delaware Valley Assn. Health Underwriters (dir.), Ins. Fedn. of Pa., Inc. (chmn. 1985-86, bd. dirs. 1964—), Greater Valley Forge Hotel Assn. (Man of the Yr. 1987). Clubs: Union League (Phila.). Home: 480 General Washington Rd Wayne PA 19087 Office: 215 W Church Rd King of Prussia PA 19406

SCOTT, BRADLEY STERLING, automotive executive; b. Santa Monica, Calif., Apr. 20, 1948; s. Milton and Jeanne Scott; m. Jillian A. Miller, May 12, 1979; children: Jilina, Sterling. BA, U. So. Calif., 1970. V.p. sales United Visuals Corp., Los Angeles, 1972-76; mgr. nat. sales Technicolor Corp., Costa Mesa, Calif., 1976-80; dir. sales Microsonics Corp., Los Angeles, 1980-81; pres., founder Los Angeles Auto Salvage, Inc., Van Nuys, Calif., 1982—; v.p., dir. Valley Auto Dismantlers Assn., Sun Valley, Calif., 1984—; adv. council dirs. U. So. Calif. Sch. of Bus. Entrepreneur Program, 1984—; owner Golden State Equipment Leasing Co., Woodland Hills, Calif., 1982—. Patentee sound motion picture projection and viewing device, 1976. Mem. Young Pres. Orgn. Republican. Clubs: Los Angeles Country, Balboa Bay (Newport Beach, Calif). Office: LA Auto Salvage 7245 Laurel Canyon North Hollywood CA 91605

SCOTT, BRIAN E., insurance company executive; b. Akron, Ohio, Oct. 2, 1936; s. Parker and Theresa Scott; m. Carole Leiser, Aug. 27, 1960; children—David, Kelly. B.S. in Math., Kent State U., 1962. Actuarial student Aetna Life & Casualty, Hartford, Conn., 1962-67, asst. sec., 1969-73, dir., 1973-76, asst. v.p., 1976-82, v.p., 1982-87, sr. v.p., 1987—. With U.S. Army, 1956-57. Fellow Casualty Actuarial Soc., Am. Acad. Actuaries; mem. Ga. Underwriters Assn. (bd. dirs. 1984—). Republican. Roman Catholic. Club: Avon Golf (pres. 1984—). Home: 78 Brookmoor Rd Avon CT 06001 Office: Aetna Life & Casualty Co 151 Farmington Ave Hartford CT 06156

SCOTT, CHARLES R., diversified company executive; b. 1928. With Dallas Morning News, 1949-51, Branham Co., 1951-55, Southwestern Investment, Inc., 1955-56, Parker Ford and Co., 1957-62; with Intermark, Inc., 1970—, now pres., also bd. dirs.; chmn. Pier One Imports Inc., Fort Worth, until 1988, vice chmn., 1988—; also chmn., pres., chief exec. officer Triton Grp. Ltd., La Jolla, Calif., 1987—. Office: Intermark Inc 1020 Prospect St La Jolla CA 92037 *

SCOTT, DAVID WILLIAM, automotive company executive; b. Shillong, Assam, India, July 24, 1940; came to U.S., 1962; s. Ronald Bayne and Patricia (Cooper) S.; m. Virginia Del Crowley, Jan. 12, 1962; children: Virginia, Kelley, Tara, Meredith. BA in Polit. Sci., Southeast Mo. State U., 1967. Trainee Ford Motor Co., Dearborn, Mich., 1967-68, pub. affairs mgr. truck div., 1969-73, exec. asst., 1973-75; regional pub. affairs mgr. Ford Motor Co., Los Angeles, 1975-76; internat. pub. affairs mgr. Ford Motor Co., Dearborn, 1976-77; v.p. pub. affairs Ford of Can., Oakville, Ont., 1971-78; dir. internat. pub. affairs Ford Motor Co., Dearborn, 1978-81, dir. N. Am. pub. affairs, 1981-85, v.p. pub. affairs, 1986-88, v.p. external affairs, 1988—. bd. visitors Medill Sch. Journalism Northwestern U. Mem. Pub. Relations Soc. Am., Arthur Page Soc., Detroit Press Club, Bloomfield Hills Country Club. Office: Ford Motor Co The American Rd Dearborn MI 48121

SCOTT, GEORGE HAHN, metals company executive; b. Toronto, Ont, Can, Oct. 23, 1941; came to U.S., 1965, naturalized, 1971; s. George H. and Grace (Hahn) S.; m. Sally Sepic, June 22, 1968; children—David P., Douglas C., Heather L. B.S. in Metall. Engring., Lafayette Coll., 1965; M.B.A., Fairleigh Dickinson U., 1972. Gen. mgr. Engelhard Corp. Specialty Metals Div., Plainville, Mass., 1976-78; v.p. Engelhard Corp. Specialty Metals Div., 1978-81; group v.p. Engelhard Corp. Specialty Metals Div., Iselin, N.J., 1981; sr. v.p. Engelhard Corp. Specialty Metals Div., 1981-86; pres. Art Wire/Doduco Corp., Cedar Knolls, N.J., 1986—. Mem. Gold Filled Assn. (bd. dirs. 1981—), Am. Soc. Metals, Jewelers Vigilance Com. (dir. 1981—), N.J. Employers Assn. (bd. dirs. 1987). Republican. Office: Art Wire/Dudoco Corp 9 Wing Dr Cedar Knolls NJ 07927

SCOTT, GERALD FRANCIS, management consultant; b. Melrose, Mass., July 14, 1958; s. James Milton and Alfreda Yvonne (Grady) S. BA, Westfield State Coll., 1980; MA in Pub. Adminstrn., Northeastern U., 1982. Grad. research fellow Northeastern U., Boston, 1981-82; fin. cons., dir. tng. E.F. Hutton & Co., Boston, 1983-87; v.p. mktg. Saluti Assocs. Mgmt. Cons., Boston, 1987—; adj. prof. Anna Maria Coll., Paxton, Mass., 1987—; adj. prof. fin. Boston U., 1989—. Campaign coordinator Gov. Dukakis Election Campaign, Boston, 1982; bd. dirs. Big Brother Assn. Boston, 1983—; state coordinator 50th Presdl. Inaugural Parade, Washington, 1985; mem. Gov.'s Bus. Adv. Council, 1986—. Served to capt. Army N.G., 1975—. Recipient Israeli Paratrooper Wings, 1987. Mem. Boston C. of C. (small bus. affairs com. 1986—), U.S. Parachute Assn. Roman Catholic. Club: First Corp of Cadets. Home: 38 Kimball Ave #4 Ipswich MA 01938

SCOTT, HOWARD WINFIELD, JR., temporary help service company executive; b. Greenwich, Conn., Feb. 24, 1935; s. Howard Winfield and Janet (Lewis) S.; B.S., Northwestern U., 1957; m. Joan Ann MacDonald, Aug. 12, 1961; children—Howard Winfield III, Thomas MacDonald, Ann Elizabeth. With R.H. Donnelly Corp., Chgo., 1958-59; sales rep. Masonite Corp., Chgo. also Madison, Wis., 1959-61; sales rep. Manpower Inc., Chgo., 1961-63, br. mgr., Kansas City, Mo., 1963-65, area mgr., Mo. and Kans., 1964-65, regional mgr. Salespower div., Phila., 1965-66; asst. advt. mgr. soups Campbell Soup Co., Camden, N.J., 1966-68; pres. PARTIME, Inc., Paoli, Pa., 1968-74; dir. marketing Kelly Services Inc., Southfield, Mich., 1974-78; pres. CDI Temporary Services, Inc., 1978—. Trustee Internat. House Phila. Served with AUS, 1957-58. Mem. Nat. Assn. Temporary Services (sec. 1970-71, pres. 1971-73, bd. dirs. 1982—), Kappa Sigma. Republican. Episcopalian. Home: PO Box 237 Paoli PA 19301-0237 also: 1204 Annapolis Sea Colony E Bethany Beach DE 19930 Office: CDI Temp Svcs Inc 10 Penn Ctr Philadelphia PA 19103-1670

SCOTT, I. B., railroad executive; b. Feb. 2, 1930. Student, McGill U., Montreal, Que., Can. Joined Can. Pacific Ltd., Montreal, 1949, gen. mgr. pub. relations and advt., 1973-81, v.p. adminstrn. and pub. affairs, 1981-85; chmn., chief exec. officer CP Rail div. Can. Pacific Ltd., Montreal, 1985—; exec. v.p. Can. Pacific Ltd., Montreal, 1988—; dir. Montreal Trust, Royal Victoria Hosp. Found., Can. Pacific Ltd., AMCA Internat. Ltd. Mem. Conf. Bd. Can. (past chmn. pub. affairs council), Am. R.R. Pub. Relations Assn., Nat. Freight Transp. Assn. Office: CP Rail Windsor Sta, Box 6042 Sta A, Montreal, PQ Canada H3C 3E4

SCOTT, J. D., oil company executive; b. 1931. BS, Tex. A&M U., 1954. With Oneok, Inc., Tulsa, 1954—, various mgmt. positions, 1954-70, v.p. ops., 1970-76, exec. v.p., 1976-80, pres. Okla. natural gas div., 1980-85, exec. v.p., 1985-86, pres., chief exec. officer, 1986—, now chmn., pres., chief exec officer; now chmn., pres., chief exec. officer Oneok Exploration Co., Tulsa. Office: Oneok Inc 100 W 5th St Tulsa OK 74103 *

SCOTT, JACK HOWITT, food company executive; b. Windsor, Ont., Can., Feb. 24, 1941; s. John I. and Esther A.; m. Fleurette Morrison, July 10, 1969; children: Jason, Andrea. B in Commerce, U. Detroit. With Gen. Foods, Inc., Don Mills, Ont., 1966—, salesman, 1966-77; pres. Hostess Food Products, Ltd. div. Gen. Foods, Inc., 1978-84, gen. mgr. grocery div., 1983-84; pres., chief exec. officer Gen. Foods, Inc., 1984—. Clubs: Granite; Bd. of Trade. Office: Gen Foods Inc, PO Box 1200, Don Mills, ON Canada M3C 3J5 *

SCOTT, JOHN ROLAND, oil company executive, lawyer; b. Wichita Falls, Tex., May 13, 1937; s. John Robert and Margaret Willena (Rouse) S.; m. Joan Carol Redding, Sept. 5, 1959; 1 child, John Howard. LLB, Baylor Sch. Law, Waco, Tex., 1962. Bar: Tex. 1962, Alaska 1970, U.S. Dist. Ct. (we. dist.) Tex. 1965, U.S. Dist. Ct. Alaska 1975. Assoc. litigation sect Lynch & Chappell, Midland, Tex., 1962-65; regional atty. Atlantic Richfield Co., Midland, 1965-79; sr. atty., Anchorage, 1969-77, sr. atty., Dallas, 1977-80; v.p., assoc. gen. counsel Mitchell Energy & Devel. Corp., Houston, 1980-82; asst. gen. counsel Hunt Oil Co., Dallas., 1982-84, v.p., chief counsel, 1984—; bar examiner in Alaska, 1974-77. Mem. State Bar Tex. (lectr.), Dallas Bar Assn., ABA, Phi Alpha Delta. Republican. Clubs: Petroleum, University (Dallas). Office: Hunt Oil Co 2900 1401 Elm St Ste 2900 Dallas TX 75202-2970

SCOTT, KERRIGAN DAVIS, investor; b. Magdalene, Fla., Sept. 26, 1941; s. Thurman Thomas and Jacqueline (Glenister) S.; children: Katherine, Stephanie, Jennifer. degree U. Va., 1964. Investor Mcht. Marine and Plantation Properties, Hilton Head Island, S.C., 1965—. Author: Aristocracy and Royalty of the World, 1983. Capt. U.S. Mcht. Marines. Mem. Million Dollar Round Table, RMS Queen Mary Hist. Soc. (founder). Episcopalian. Club: Shipyard Plantation Racquet (Hilton Head Island). Avocations: maritime subjects, Southern history, art. Home: Hilton Head Plantation 10 Windflower Ct Hilton Head Island SC 29928

SCOTT, LARY R., freight transportation company executive; b. 1936; married. BS, Bowling Green U., 1961. With Roadway Express, 1961-67; with Consolidated Freightways Motor Freight, 1967—, staff asst., 1967-68, asst. to pres., 1968-69, div. mgr., 1969-70, area v.p., 1970-76, exec. v.p. ops., 1976-80, pres., chief exec. officer, 1980—; with Consolidated Freightways, Inc., Palo Alto, Calif., 1967—, exec. v.p., from 1983, pres., chief operating officer, 1986—, chief exec. officer, 1988—, dir.; v.p. Am. Trucking Assn. Served with USMC, 1954-57. Office: Consol Freightways Inc 3240 Hillview Ave Palo Alto CA 94303 *

SCOTT, LEE ALLEN, securities company executive; b. Daniels, W.Va., Oct. 28, 1940; s. Minor Lee and Margaret Allen (Kay) S.; BS in Bus. Adminstrn., W.Va. U., 1962; MBA, U. Ky., 1967; CLU; cert. fin. planner, chartered fin. cons.; m. Myrah Lou Erickson, July 15, 1962; children—Elizabeth Ashley, Stephanie Erickson, Lee Allen. Mgmt. trainee Gen. Tel. & Electronics Co., 1965-66; regional group mgr. Prudential Ins. Co., 1967-76; pres. Scott & Assocs., Inc., employee benefit cons., Parkersburg, W.Va., from 1976; pres., chmn. bd., chief exec. officer Union Trust Nat. Bank, 1980-82; v.p. investments Prudential-Bache Securities, 1983—. Bd. dirs. Parkersburg YMCA, W.Va. Found. Ind. Colls., chmn.; pres. Mid Ohio Valley United Fund, Wood County Devel. Authority; bd. dirs. Parkersburg United Fund. With USAR, 1963-65. Decorated Army Commendation medal. Mem. Am. Soc. CLU's, Inst. Cert. Fin. Planners, Nat. Assn. Life Underwriters, Am. Mgmt. Assn., Health Ins. Assn. Am. (chmn. health care com. W.Va.), Estate Planning Coun., Registry Fin. Planners. Methodist. Club: Parkersburg Country. Lodge: Elks. Home: 141 N Hills Dr Parkersburg WV 26101 Office: 2108 Dudley Ave Parkersburg WV 26101

SCOTT, LEE HANSEN, holding company executive; b. Atlanta, Sept. 25, 1926; s. Elbert Lee and Auguste Lillian (Hansen) S.; m. Margaret Lee Smith, July 20, 1951; children: Bradley Hansen, Randall Lee. B.E.E., U. Fla., 1949. With Fla. Power Corp., St. Petersburg, 1949—; dir. constrn., maintenance and operating Fla. Power Corp., 1968-71, v.p. customer ops., 1971-77, sr. v.p. ops., 1977-83, pres., 1983-88, chmn. bd., 1988—, also bd. dirs.; vice chmn. Fla. Progress Corp., 1988—, also bd. dirs.; bd. dirs. Edison Electric Inst.; v.p. Southeastern Electric Exchange, Southeastern Electric Reliability Council. Pres. St. Petersburg chpt. ARC, 1977, Pinellas Com. of 100, 1980, Community Services Council, 1970, St. Petersburg Progress, 1983, Bus. and Industry Employment Devel. Council, 1983; chmn. bd. United Way. Served with USAF, 1944-46. Mem. Am. Mgmt. Assn., Fla. Engring. Soc., IEEE, Elec. Council Fla. (pres. 1979), St. Petersburg C. of C. (v.p. 1980), Fla. C. of C. (pres. 1987-88), Pinellas Suncoast C. of C. (past chmn., chmn. bd. trustees). Presbyterian. Office: Fla Progress Corp 240 First Ave S Saint Petersburg FL 33701

SCOTT, PETER BRYAN, lawyer; b. St. Louis, Nov. 11, 1947; s. Gilbert Franklin and Besse Jean (Fudge) S.; m. Suzanne Rosalee Wallace, Oct. 19, 1974; children: Lindsay W., Sarah W., Peter B. Jr. A.B., Drury Coll., 1969; J.D., Washington U., St. Louis, 1972, LL.M., 1980. Bar: Mo. 1972, Colo. 1980; diplomate Ct. Practice Inst. Sole practice, St. Louis, 1972-80; assoc. firm McKie and Assocs., Denver, 1980-81; ptnr. firm Scott and Chesteen, P.C., Denver, 1981-84, Veto & Scott, Denver, 1984—; tchr. Denver Paralegal Inst. Served to capt. USAR, 1971-79. Mem. ABA, Mo. Bar Assn., Colo. Bar Assn., Denver Bar Assn. Republican. Mem. United Church of Christ. Home: 26262 Wolverine Trail Evergreen CO 80439 Office: Veto & Scott 6595 W 14th Ave Ste 200 Lakewood CO 80214

SCOTT, PETER FRANCIS, food products company executive; b. Honolulu, 1927; married. B.S., U. Calif., 1952. Staff acct. Touche Ross Bailey & Smart, 1952-58; with Tay-Holbrook, Inc., 1958-63; asst. treas. Di Giorgio Corp., San Francisco, 1963-64, treas., 1964-69, v.p., treas., 1969-74, v.p., chief fin. officer, mem. exec. com., 1974-80, pres., chief operating officer, dir., 1980-84, pres., chief exec. officer Di Giorgio Corp., 1984—; dir. Hale Tech. Corp./Scott Corp. Calif. Served to capt. U.S. Army, 1946-49. Office: Di Giorgio Corp 1 Maritime Pla San Francisco CA 94111 *

SCOTT, RAY VERNON, JR., chemical executive; b. Lexington, Ky., Jan. 30, 1950; s. Ray Vernon Sr. and Eloise (Young) S.; m. Michelle Aller, June 30, 1973 (div. 1974); m. Diane Marie Fenner, June 21, 1976; children: Jason Michael, Amanda Marie. BS in Chem. Engring., N.C. State U., 1972; MBA, Keller Sch. Mgmt., 1984. Sales rep. Goodyear Tire & Rubber Co., Akron, Ohio, 1972-77; regional sales mgr. Air Products & Chems., Chgo., 1977-80; products sales mgr. UOP, Inc., Des Plaines, Ill., 1980—; sales trainer UOP, Inc., 1980—. Mem. Chgo. Comml. Devel. Assn. (pres. 1985-87), Comml. Devel. Assn. (bd. dirs. 1986-89, treas. 1989—), Chem. Mktg. Rsch. Assn., Chgo. Sales Trainer Assn., Polyurethane Mfrs. Assn. Home: 825 Kingspoint Dr W Addison IL 60101 Office: UOP Inc 25 E Algonquin Rd Des Plaines IL 60017

SCOTT, RICHARD ALAN, retail drug chain executive; b. Berkeley, Calif., May 2, 1935; s. Alan R. and Jessie (W.) S.; m. Alice L. McCrudden, Aug. 13, 1966; children: Kelly, Kristin. B.S., U. Calif.-Berkeley, 1961. With Longs Drug Stores, Inc., Walnut Creek, Calif., 1971—, sr. v.p., 1976-77; exec. v.p. Longs Drugs Stores, Inc., Walnut Creek, Calif., 1977—; dir. Longs Drug Stores, Inc., Walnut Creek, Calif.; chmn. Good Govt. Council-Longs Drugs. Bd. dirs. Diabetes Soc.; bd. dir.s Contra Costa. Served with USAF, 1953-57. Mem. Calif. Retailers Assn. (dir., chmn. chain drug com.). Republican. Home: 917 Kirkcrest Rd Alamo CA 94507 Office: Longs Drug Stores Inc 141 N Civic Dr Walnut Creek CA 94596 *

SCOTT, ROBERT KENT, lawyer; b. New Eagle, Pa., July 25, 1936; s. James Philip Scott and D. Mildred (Jeannot) Scott Crisp; m. Patricia Ann Gamble, Aug. 23, 1958 (div.); children—Elizabeth, Philip, Noelle, David; m. Anne Rodgers, May 29, 1982. B.A., Kenyon Coll., 1958; LL.B., Columbia U., 1961. Bar: Ohio 1962, Ill. 1969, Mich. 1977, Wis. 1979, Fla. 1982. Gen. counsel Cutler-Hammer, Milw., 1978-79; v.p., gen. counsel CF Industries, Long Grove, Ill., 1979-81, A.E. Staley Mfg. Co., Decatur, Ill., 1982-85; v.p., sec., gen. counsel Staley Continental, Inc., Rolling Meadows, Ill., 1985-87, sr. v.p. law, sec., 1987-88; v.p. law, sec. The Singer Co., Tampa, Fla., 1988—. Reporter Illinois Criminal Code, 1970. Mem. Ill. Bar Assn., Ohio Bar Assn., Mich. Bar Assn., Wis. Bar Assn., Fla. Bar Assn., Chgo. Crime Commn.

SCOTT, RODGER GENE, personnel executive; b. Antigo, Wis., July 4, 1931; s. Wyman and Faye (Marshall) S.; m. Norma A. Schoenborn, June 6, 1953; children—Bruce Franklin, Lynnette Gay. Grad., Antigo High Sch., Wis., 1949. Store mgr. Krambo Food Store, Merrill, Wis., 1951-65; store mgr. Sentry Foods, Waukesha, Wis., 1965-66, tng. dir., 1966-67, retail supr., 1967-72, sr. v.p. personnel, 1972—. Mem. ch. council Reformation Luth. Ch., pres., 1982-84. Republican. Home: 19945 Bittersweet New Berlin WI Office: Godfrey Co 1200 W Sunset Dr Waukesha WI 53187

SCOTT, ROGER STEPHEN, financial planner; b. Spokane, Wash., Mar. 29, 1943; s. Paul W. and Virginia Ellen (Haggerty) S.; m. Phyliss Tibbetts, Apr. 26, 1987. BA, U. Wash., 1966. Asst. dir. Beaton-Franklin Community Action Com., Pesco, Wash., 1970; planner Seattle Model City Porgram, 1971-73, elderly program dir., 1974, evaluation cons., 1974; planner and policy analyst Wash. State Employment Soc., Olympia, 1974-79; investment advisor Life Planning Co., Seattle, 1981-84; cert. fin. planner Scott Fin. Advisor Inc., Seattle, 1984-88. Bd. dirs. Puget Sound SANE, Seattle, 1983-85; asst. treas. Erxlebenpur for Atty. Gen., Seattle, 1988. Mem. Internat. Assn. Fin. Planners, Inst. Cert. Fin. Planners, Soc. Investment Forum, World Affairs Council, City Club. Democrat. Home: 6285 20 Ave NE Seattle WA 98115 Office: Resource Planning Svcs 2615 4th Ave 2d Fl Seattle WA 98121

SCOTT, STANLEY DEFOREST, lithography company executive; b. Hudson County, N.J., Nov. 2, 1926; s. Stanley DeForest and Anne Marie (Volk) S.; B.A., U. So. Calif., 1950; m. Mary Elizabeth Hazard, Dec. 30, 1953. Gen. mgr. Alfred Scott Publishers, N.Y.C., 1951-56; chmn., pres. S.D. Scott Printing Co., Inc., N.Y.C., 1956—; gen. ptnr. 145 Hudson St. Assocs. Mem. Mayor's Industry Adv. Council; bd. dirs. Bus. Relocation Commn. Served with USNR, 1944-46. Mem. Printing Industries N.Y. (past dir.), Am. Inst. Graphic Arts, Young Printing Execs., Printers League (past v.p.), Soc. Mayflower Descs., Soc. Colonial Wars, Sons of Revolution (treas. 1972-73, 3d v.p. 1975-77, 2d v.p. 1977-79, past co-chmn. Fraunces Tavern Mus. devel. com. 1973-87, chmn. mus. and art com. 1987, N.Y. Hist. Soc. (Frick Collection fellow), Met. Mus. Art, Mus. Modern Art, Morgan Library, rare book libraries. Am. Mus. Natural History, Am. Mus. in Britain (council 1986—); mem. adv. com. Mt. Vernon (Va.) Ladies Assn., Knickerbocker, Union, Downtown Athletic, Merchants (v.p.1985—). Republican. Episcopalian. Home: 1 Sutton Pl S New York NY 10022 Office: 145 Hudson St New York NY 10013

SCOTT, STANLEY SOUTHALL, public relations executive; b. Bolivar, Tenn., July 2, 1933; s. Lewis Augustus and Clinora Neely (Hamer) S.; m. Bettye L. Lovejoy, Dec. 23, 1962; children: Kenneth Earl, Susan Lovejoy, Stanley Southall II. Student, U. Kans., Lawrence, 1951-53; B.S. in Journalism, Lincoln U., Jefferson City, Mo., 1959. Editor, gen. mgr. Memphis World, 1960-61; gen. assignment news reporter, copy editor, editorial writer Atlanta Daily World, 1961-64; gen. assignment news reporter UPI, N.Y.C., 1964-66; asst. dir. public relations NAACP, N.Y.C., 1966-67; radio newsman Westinghouse Broadcasting Corp., N.Y.C., 1967-71; asst. to dir. communications exec. br. White House, Washington, 1971-73; spl. asst. to pres. White House, 1973-75; asst. adminstr. AID, 1975-77; asst. dir. corp. relations Philip Morris, Inc., N.Y.C., 1977; dir. corp. public affairs Philip Morris, Inc., 1978-79, v.p. public affairs, 1979-84, dir. corp. affairs, 1984—; pres., sole owner Crescent Distbg. Co., New Orleans, 1988—; v.p. Philip Morris Cos., Inc., 1984—; lectr. journalism Columbia, New Sch., N.Y.C. Bd. dirs. Jacob K. Javits Conv. Ctr. N.Y., St. Lukes/Roosevelt Hosp. Ctr., Citizen's Research Found., Keep America Beautiful, Inc.; bd. visitors N.C. Central U. Sch. Law; vice chmn. N.Y. Fire Safety Found.; mem. Pres.' Commn. on White House fellowships; mem. N.Y. State Martin Luther King, Jr. Commn; nat. com. mem. Nat. Mus. African Art, Smithsonian Inst.; adv. bd. John Jay Coll. Criminal Justice. Served with U.S. Army, 1954-56. Recipient Russwurm award for excellence in radio news reporting, 1967, Silurians award, 1965, Pulitzer nomination for Malcolm X coverage, 1965, Wisemens award for series on police-minority community confrontation in Atlanta, 1961. Mem. AFTRA, New York Reporters Assn., NAACP, Huntington Civic Assn. Republican. Presbyterian. Home: 4564 Bancroft Dr New Orleans LA 70122 Office: Crescent Distbg Co 5733 Citrus Blvd Harahan LA 70123

SCOTT, THOMAS ROBIE, JR., forestry consultant; b. Monticello, Ark., Mar. 4, 1924; s. Thomas Robie and Bessie (Adcock) S.; m. Verby Opal Belt, Jan. 7, 1951; children: Thomas Robie III, Michael Robert, Phillip Roland. BS in Forestry, La. State U., 1948. Forester Pomeroy and McGowin Forest Mgrs., Monticello, 1948-52, jr. ptnr., 1952-70, sr. ptnr., 1970—. Served as staff sgt. USAR, 1942-46, ETO. Mem. Soc. Am. Forester, Ark. Forestry Assn., La. Forestry Assn., Tex. Forestry Assn. Methodist. Lodge: Rotary (Monticello) (pres. 1984-85). Office: Pomeroy and McGowin Forest Mgrs Hwy 81 N PO Box 29 Monticello AK 71655

SCOTT, WALTER COKE, sugar company executive, lawyer; b. Norfolk, Va., July 20, 1919; s. Walter Coke and Rosemary (White) S.; m. Virginia Kemper Millard, May 14, 1949; children: Mary Lyman Jackson, Roberta Gatewood, Alexander McRae, Buford Coke. B.S., Hampden-Sydney Coll., 1939; J.D., U. Va., 1948. Bar: Va. 1947, Ga. 1954. Atty. U.S. Dept. Justice, Jacksonville, Fla., 1948; commerce atty. S.A.L. Ry., Norfolk, 1948-54; commerce counsel, gen. solicitor Central of Ga. Ry., Savannah, 1954-60; v.p. Central of Ga. Ry., 1960-62, dir., 1960—; partner law firm Hitch, Miller & Beckmann, Savannah, 1956-60; sr. v.p., sec. Savannah Foods & Industries, Inc. (formerly Savannah Sugar Refining Corp.), 1962-72, exec. v.p., mem. exec. com., 1972-87, also dir.; exec. v.p., sec., mem. exec. com. dir. Everglades Sugar Refinery, Inc., Clewiston, Fla., 1964-87; sec., mem. exec. com., dir. The Jim Dandy Co., Birmingham, Ala., 1968-81; bd. dirs. 1st Union Nat. Bank Savannah, First Union Ga. Corp, Atlanta. Pres., chmn. exec. com. Historic Savannah Found., 1963-64; bd. dirs. United Community Services, 1965-68, pres., 1967; gen. chmn. United Community Appeal, 1966; mem. Chatham-Savannah Met. Planning Commn., 1963-68; trustee, chmn. finance com. Telfair Acad. Arts and Scis., 1964-67; trustee, vice chmn. Savannah Country Day Sch., 1967-69, chmn., 1970-72; Bd. dirs., chmn. finance com. Savannah Speech and Hearing Center, 1967-70; bd. dirs. Savannah Symphony Soc., Inc. Mem. U.S. C. of C., Va. State Bar, Ga. State

Bar, St. Andrews Soc., Savannah Benevolent Assn., Kappa Sigma, Omicron Delta Kappa, Phi Alpha Delta, Chi Beta Phi, Pi Delta Epsilon. Episcopalian. Clubs: Chatham, Oglethorpe, Savannah Golf; Farmington Country (Charlottesville, Va.). Home: 56 E 54th St Savannah GA 31405 Office: Savannah Foods & Industries Inc 1st Union Bank Bldg Savannah GA 31401

SCOTT, WILLIAM LAWRENCE, chemical engineer; b. Holden, W. Va., Dec. 26, 1935; s. William Ward and Janyce (Bragg) S.; B.S., Northwestern U., 1961; m. Anita Broad; children—Lawrence Michael, Julia Ann, Jennifer Jo, James David. Draftsman, Internat. Harvester Co., Chgo., 1955; paint formulator U.S. Gypsum, Chgo., 1956; successively chemist, foreman, asst. plant mgr., plant mgr. Witco. Chem. Corp., Chgo. and Burlingame, Calif., 1957-76, plant mgr., Houston, 1976-79, div. mgr. engring., 1979—; condr. seminars on disposal wells, sulfonation, and processes. Cub and scout master Boy Scouts Am. Mem. Am. Chem. Soc., Tex. Chem. Council, U.S. Auto Club, Nat. Model R.R. Assn., Instrument Soc. Am. Republican. Methodist. Home: 5540 Furnace Rd Manvel TX 77578

SCOTT, WILLIAM PICKETT, data processing executive; b. Nashville, Sept. 28, 1950; s. Henry Pickett and Lolitta (Bassham) S. Grad. high sch., Nashville. Programmer Baltz Bros., Nashville, 1968-73; systems analyst, programmer Chattem Drug and Chem., Chattanooga, 1973-74; data processing mgr., programmer Universal Tire and Rubber, Nashville, 1974-78; cons., programmer Creasy Systems, Nashville, 1978-79; pres. Bus. Computer Systems, Nashville, 1979—. Author: (computer program) System 3 to 3740 Printer Transmition, 1975. Office: Bus Computer Systems Inc 1101 Kermit Dr Ste 625 Nashville TN 37217

SCOTT, WINFIELD JAMES, marketing executive; b. Worcester, Mass., Jan. 4, 1933; s. Gherald Dean and Helen L. S.; B.A., Norwich U., 1955; postgrad. Marquette U., 1961-62; m. Betty Joan Price, June 29, 1957; children—Mary Jo, Susan Elizabeth. With sales dept. Norton Co., Worcester, 1956, sales rep. Chgo. dist., 1957, sales supr. Wis. dist., 1960-71; founder, pres. The Abrasive Group, Wauwatosa, Wis., 1971—; ad hoc prof. mktg. U. Wis. Extension. Mem. Abrasive Engring. Soc. (co-gen. chmn. internat. conf.), Nat. Small Bus. Assn., Wis. Mfrs. and Commerce, Ind. Bus. Assn. Wis., Met. Milw. Assn. Commerce, Nat. Fedn. Ind. Bus. Republican. Episcopalian. Author: Modern Machine Shop, 1967. Home: 11037 W Derby Ave Wauwatosa WI 53225 Office: PO Box 13244 Wauwatosa WI 53213

SCOTT-ENSLEY, DEBORAH ANN, bank executive; b. Tenn., Apr. 18, 1954; d. Newty L. Jr. and Elaine Jones; married; 1 child, Keenyattrice LaDelmarquice. BS with honors, Tenn. State U.; cert. banking, La. State U. Audit and tax acct. Peat, Marwick, Mitchell & Co., Nashville, 1974-79; auditor Citizens Bank, Nashville, 1979, controller, 1980-81, asst. v.p., cashier, 1981-86, exec. v.p., 1986—. Bd. advisors Tenn. State U., Nashville; active Nashville Opportunities Industrialization Ctr.; bd. dirs. Inroads, Nashville; bd. dirs Nashville Urban League; vol. Outlook Nashville; mem. Jr. Achievement, 1985. Recipient Kizzy award as one of Outstanding Young Women Am. Mem. Tenn. Banking Assn. (credit conf. 1986), Am. Inst. Banking (bd. dirs.), Nat. Assn. Bank Women, Am. Soc. Women Accts., Nat. Assn. Accts., Young Leaders Council, Nat. Assn. Bus. Profl. Womens' Clubs. Baptist. Office: Citizens Savs Bank and Trust Co Box 2624 Nashville TN 37219-0624

SCOTTI, BRUCE FREDERICK, financial executive; b. Bronxville, N.Y., Aug. 7, 1950; s. Vincent John Thomas and Marilyn (Dieke) S.; m. Maria Angela Benedetti, Nov. 7, 1987. BA, U. Conn., 1972, MA, 1973. Pres. Scotti Corp., Westport, Conn., 1975-85; v.p. Marsh Ruscoe Scotti Assocs., Norwalk, Conn., 1985-86; pres. Scotti Assocs., Cheshire, Conn., 1987—; cons. Mansfield State Tng. Sch., 1971-72, Arch Tech, Inc., Lewiston, Mass., 1987-88. Supr. State Conn. Juvenile Ct. System Vols., Norwalk, Conn., 1974-76; vol. HUD Affordable Housing Program, 1988—. Mem. Internat. Assn. Fin. Planners, Am. Mgmt. Assn. Roman Catholic. Office: Scotti Assocs Fin Resources Inc 100 Hinman St Ste 4 Cheshire CT 06410

SCOTT MORTON, MICHAEL STEWART, educator; b. Mukden, Manchuria, Peoples Republic of China, Aug. 25, 1937; came to U.S., 1958; s. William and Alice (Gleysteen) S.M.; m. Mary Louise Mansell, June 20, 1964; children: Fiona Margaret, Lesley Elizabeth. Student, Glascow U., Scotland, 1957-58; BS, Carnegie Mellon, 1961; DBA, Harvard U., 1967. Asst. prof. Sloan Sch. MIT, Cambridge, 1966-69, assoc. prof., 1969-75, prof., 1975—; bd. dirs. Index Corp., Cambridge, 1970—, Emhart Corp. Farmington, Conn., 1976—; trustee, chancellor, corp. dir. Met. Life State St. Author: Decision Support System, 1978, Strategic Control, 1986; contbr. articles to profl. jours. Mem. Assn. for Computing Machinery, Am. Acctg. Assn., Inst. Mgmt. Sci. Presbyterian. Club: Somerset, Harvard (Boston). Home: 31 Somerset Rd Lexington MA 02173 Office: Sloan Sch Mgmt MIT 50 Memorial Dr Cambridge MA 02139

SCOVILLE, JAMES GRIFFIN, economist; b. Amarillo, Tex., Mar. 19, 1940; s. Orlin James and Carol Howe (Griffin) S.; m. Judith Ann Nelson, June 11, 1962; 1 child, Nathan James. B.A., Oberlin Coll., 1961; M.A., Harvard U., 1963, Ph.D., 1965. Economist ILO, Geneva, 1965-66; instr. econs. Harvard U., Cambridge, Mass., 1964-65; asst. prof. Harvard U., 1966-69; assoc. prof. econs. and labor and indsl. relations U. Ill.-Urbana, 1969-75, prof., 1975-80; prof. indsl. relations Indsl. Relations Center, U. Minn., Mpls., 1979—, dir., 1979-82; cons. ILO, World Bank, U.S. Dept. Labor, Orgn. for Econ. Cooperation and Devel., labor, mgmt. arbitrator. Author: The Job Content of the US Economy, 1940-70, 1969, Perspectives on Poverty and Income Distribution, 1971, Manpower and Occupational Analysis: Concepts and Measurements, 1972, (with A. Sturmthal) The International Labor Movement in Transition, 1973. Mem. Am. Econ. Assn., Indsl. Relations Research Assn. Home: 4849 Girard Ave S Minneapolis MN 55409 Office: U Minn Ind Rels Ctr 271 19th Ave S Minneapolis MN 55455

SCRANTON, WILLIAM WARREN, banker; b. Madison, Conn., July 19, 1917; s. Worthington and Marion Scranton; m. Mary Lowe Chamberlin, July 6, 1942; children—William W., Joseph C., Peter K., Susan. B.A., Yale U., 1939, LL.B., 1946; recipient numerous hon. degrees. With Northeastern Bank of Pa., Scranton; dir. Cummins Engine Co., IBM, N.Y. Times Co., Mobil Corp. Mem. 83d Congress from 10th Pa. dist.; gov. State of Pa., 1963-67; ambassador U.S. Mission to the UN, 1976-77. Chmn. Nat. Policy Panel on U.S./Soviet Relations; mem. exec. com. Trilateral Commn.; U.S. chmn. Soviet/Am. Parallel Studies, chmn. nat. adv. com. Yale U. Sch. Orgn. and Mgmt.; chmn. Major Powers in Asia Project; numerous apptd. positions under Pres. Johnson, Nixon, Ford and Carter. Republican. Presbyterian. Office: Northeastern Bank Pa Pennsylvania Ave Scranton PA 18503 other: Mobil Corp 150 E 42nd St New York NY 10017 *

SCREPETIS, DENNIS, consulting engineer; b. Hoboken, N.J., Feb. 12, 1930; s. George and Athanasia (Stasinos) S.; student Stevens Inst. Tech., Bklyn. Poly. Inst., Cooper Union, Rutgers U.; m. Betty Pravasilis, Sept. 17, 1960. Registered profl. engr., N.J., N.Y. Nuclear engr. Vitro Corp. Am., N.Y.C., 1957-60; project engr. Gen. Cable Corp., Bayonne, N.J., 1960-63; project mgr. AMF Atomics, York, Pa., 1963-65; sr. staff engr. nuclear div. Combustion Engring. Corp., Windsor, Conn., 1965-66; corp. engr. Standard Packaging Corp., N.Y.C., 1966-68; v.p. engring. Eastern Schokbeton, Bound Brook, N.J., 1968-74; cons. engr., Ft. Lee, N.J., 1974—; Patentee in nuclear sci. Mem. Am. Concrete Inst., Pre-Stressed Concrete Inst., Concrete Reinforcing Inst., Nat. Safety Council, Am. Nat. Standards Inst., Internat. Platform Assn., Am. Inst. Steel Constrn., ASTM, Am. Welding Soc., Concrete Industry Bd., Bldg. Ofcls. and Code Adminstrs. Soc. of Am. Mil. Engrs., Nat. Forensic Ctr., Am. Biog. Inst. Research Assn. (bd. dirs.), Internat. Biog. Ctr. (dir.). Greek Orthodox. Home and Office: 2200 N Central Rd Fort Lee NJ 07024

SCRIBANTE, ADRIAN JAMES, entrepreneur; b. Osage City, Kans., Jan. 7, 1930; s. Otto Joseph and Mary Amelia (Vieta) S.; m. Marguerite Anne Hallas, Apr. 30, 1960; children: Kristen Bayer, Lynn, John. BSChemE, Kans. State U., 1956; MBA, Alexander Hamilton Inst., 1968. Tech. sales rep. Union Carbide Corp., Omaha, 1956-60; pres. Nat. Allied Products, Omaha, 1960-63; founder, chief exec. officer Majers Corp., Omaha, 1963-87; chmn. bd. dirs. ViTal Resources Inc., Omaha, 1988—; bd. dirs. FirsTier Bank, Omaha, Guarantee Mut. Life Ins. Co.; lectr. Creighton U., 1985—. Bd. dirs. consultation com. SAC, 1983—; gov. AK-SAR-BEN, Omaha, 1985—; chmn. community rels. Nat. Boy Scouts Am., Washington, 1986—. With USN, 1947-51, Korea. Named Free Enterprise Man of Yr. Omaha Rotary, 1986. Mem. Omaha Country Club, Castle Pines Golf Club. Republican. Roman Catholic. Home: 6634 Burt St Omaha NE 68132 Office: ViTal Resources Inc 444 Regency Pkwy Dr Omaha NE 68114

SCRIPTER, FRANK C., mfg. co. exec.; b. Dansville, Mich., June 21, 1918; s. Edgar and Maggie Alice (Havens) S.; student Warren's Sch. of Cam Design, 1946. Lic. firmarms mfg.; m. Dora Maebelle Smalley, Nov. 2, 1940 (dec. Sept. 1945); 1 child, Karen Scripter Allen; m. Elvira Elaine Taylor, Aug. 6, 1951; children—James Michael, Mark Lee, Anita Elaine, Warren Arthur, Charles Edward. Apprentice, Lundberg Screw Products Co., 1940-41; set-up man Reo Motors, Inc., 1942-43; night supt. Manning Bros. Metal Products Co., 1943; with McClaren Screw Products Co., 1946-47; ptnr. Dansville Screw Products Co., 1946-54, pres., dir. Scripco Mfg. Co., Laingsburg, Mich., 1954-88, ret. 1988; mfg. of ASP Pistol, 1980-81. Chmn., Citizens Com. Laingsburg, 1956-58; mem. Laingsburg Community Schs. Bd. Edn., 1971-75, sec., 1973-74, pres., 1974-75. With USNR, 1944-45. Mem. Nat. Rifle Assn. (life), The Am. Leopard Horse Assn. (founder 1967). Republican. Methodist. Patentee in field. Home: 9701 E Round Lake Rd Laingsburg MI 48848

SCRITSMIER, JEROME LORENZO, lighting fixture manufacturing company executive; b. Eau Claire, Wis., July 1, 1925; s. Fredrick Lorenzo and Alvera Mary (Schwab) S.; B.S., Northwestern U., 1950; m. Mildred Joan Lloyd, June 27, 1947; children—Dawn, Lloyd, Janet. Salesman, Sylvania Elec. Products, Los Angeles, 1951-69; chmn. Cameron Properties Inc.; chief fin. officer Environ. Lighting for Architecture Co., Los Angeles, 1973—. Served with USAAF, 1943-46. Mem. Apt. Assn. (pres., dir. Los Angeles County). Republican. Club: Jonathan (Los Angeles). Home: 2454 N Cameron Ave Covina CA 91724 Office: 17891 Arenth St City of Industry CA 91748

SCROGGINS, RICHARD MUIR, real estate executive; b. Detroit, Dec. 11, 1932; s. Olin and Florence Marie (Muir) S.; m. Jeanne Addison Joslyn, June 30, 1956; children: Laura Scroggins Wolf, Lisa Scroggins Keith, Sarah. BBA, U. Mich., 1955. Salesman , real estate rep. Shell Oil Co., Lansing, Mich., 1958-62; real estate negotiator Burroughs Corp., Detroit, 1962-64; supr. dealership facilities Ford Motor Co., Dearborn, Mich., 1964-68; mgr. dealership facilities and real estate Ford of Europe, London, 1969-74; dir. property mgmt. Ford Motor Land Devel. Corp., Dearborn, 1974-75; v.p. real estate Am. Express Co., N.Y.C., 1975-85, v.p. real estate and gen. services, 1984—. v.p. Myasthenia Gravis Found., Chgo., 1987—; pres. Rockview Dr. Assn., Greenwich, Conn., 1987—. 1st lt. USMC, 1955-58. Mem. Internat. Orgn. Corp. Real Estate Execs. (chpt. adv. com. 1986—), Nat. Assn. Corp. Real Estate Execs. (Master of Corp. Real Estate award 1982, dir.), Urban Land Inst. Republican. Home: 15 Rockview Dr Greenwich CT 06830 Office: Am Express Co Am Express Tower World Fin Ctr New York NY 10285

SCULLEY, DAVID W., food company executive; b. N.Y.C., July 17, 1946; s. John and Margaret Blackburn (Smith) S.; m. Paula Cook; children—Heather Kahrl, David. B.A. in Econs. cum laude, Harvard U., 1968. Group product mgr. Lever Bros. Co., N.Y.C., 1971-73; gen. mgr. mktg. H.J. Heinz-U.S.A., Pitts., 1974-77, v.p. mktg., 1978-81; dep. mng. dir. H.J. Heinz-U.K., Middlesex, Eng., 1982-85; pres., chief exec. officer Heinz U.S.A., Pitts., 1985—. Trustee Sewickley Valley Hosp., Pa., 1981, Allegheny Gen. Hosp, Pitts., 1986—; chmn. D.T. Watson Home Charity Golf Tournament, Sewickley, 1986. Republican. Episcopalian. Clubs: Allegheny Country (Sewickley); Duquesne (Pitts.); Laurel Valley Golf (Ligonier, Pa.). Office: Heinz USA Divs PO Box 57 Pittsburgh PA 15230

SCULLEY, JOHN, computer company executive; b. N.Y.C., Apr. 6, 1939; s. John and Margaret (Blackburn) S.; m. Carol Lee Adams, Mar. 7, 1978; children: Margaret Ann, John Balckburn, Laura Lee. Student, R.I. Sch. Design, 1960; BArch, Brown U., 1961; MBA, U. Pa., 1963. Asst. account exec. Marschalk Co., N.Y.C., 1963-64, account exec., 1964-65, account supr., 1965-67; dir. mktg. Pepsi-Cola Co., Purchase, N.Y., 1967-69, v.p. mktg., 1970-71, sr. v.p. mktg., 1971-74, pres., chief exec. officer, 1977-83; pres. PepsiCo Foods, Purchase, 1974-77; pres., chief exec. officer Apple Computer Inc., Cupertino, Calif., 1983—; also chmn. Apple Computer Inc., Cupertino, Calif, 1986—; bd. dirs. Comsat Corp. Chmn. Wharton Grad. Exec. Bd., 1980; mem. art adv. com. Brown U., 1980; bd. dirs. Keep Am. Beautiful.; mem. bd. overseers Wharton Sch., U. Pa. Mem. U.S. C. of C. Clubs: Indian Harbor, N.Y. Athletic; Coral Beach (Bermuda); Wharton Bus. Sch. of N.Y. (bd. dirs.); Camden (Maine) Yacht. Office: Apple Computer Inc 20525 Mariana Ave Cupertino CA 95014 *

SCULLY, ERIK VINCENT, tax attorney; b. Pitts., Mar. 24, 1957; s. Vincent C. A. and Gloria Dolores (Peterson) S; m. Margaret Mary Scully, Sept. 10, 1982. BA, Syracuse U., 1979; JD, St. Louis U., 1982; postgrad., Duquesne U., Pitts., 1986. Bar: Pa. 1982, U.S. Tax Ct. 1983. Asst. bank officer Mark Twain Bankshares, Inc., St. Louis, 1980; law clk. Thomas, Mottaz & Eastman, Alton, Ill., 1981-82; ptnr. Mercer, Mercer, Carlin and Scully, Pitts., 1982—. Mem. Pitts. Ctr. for the Arts, Soc. Sculptors of Pitts. Mem. Pa. Bar Assn., Allegheny County Bar Assn. Home: 719 Washington Dr Pittsburgh PA 15229 Office: 1218 Frick Bldg Pittsburgh PA 15219

SCULLY, JOHN CARROLL, life insurance company executive; b. Springfield, Mass., Mar. 16, 1932; s. James and Frances (Carroll) S.; m. Barbara A. Fougere, Sept. 7, 1953; children: Kathleen, Margaret, John, James, Patricia, Mary Ellen, Susan. B.A., Holy Cross Coll., 1953; C.L.U., Boston U., 1963; postgrad., Dartmouth Inst., 1977. With John Hancock Mut. Life Ins. Co., 1953—; gen. agent John Hancock Mut. Life Ins. Co., Indpls., 1966-75; sr. v.p. agency dept. John Hancock Mut. Life Ins. Co., Boston, 1975-80; pres. retail sector John Hancock Mut. Life Ins. Co., 1980—; bd. dirs. John Hancock Subs. Inc., John Hancock Distbrs., Inc., Tucker Anthony Holding Corp.; chmn. bd. John Hancock Advisors, Inc., John Hancock Variable Life Ins. Co. Bd. dirs. Greater Boston YMCA, 1975—, chmn., 1978—; trustee, overseer New Eng. Med. Ctr., 1981—; bd. overseers Dartmouth Inst., 1984—; mem. Mass. campaign steering com. Holocaust Meml. Mus., 1985—; div. chmn. United Way, 1985—; bd. dirs. Cath. Charities, 1986—; trustee Springfield Coll., 1986, Suffolk U., 1986, Babson Coll., 1988. Served with U.S. Army, 1954-56. Mem. Am. Coll. Life Underwriters, Nat. Assn. Life Underwriters (v.p. Ind. 1973-75), Life Ins. Mktg. and Research Assn. (past chmn.), Gen. Agts. and Mgrs. Assn. (past pres. Indpls., Nat. Mgmt. award 1973-75), Life Underwriter Tng. Council (past chmn.), Greater Boston C. of C. (bd. dirs. 1985—). Roman Catholic. Clubs: Wellesley, Executives (past pres.), Algonquin (dir.). Lodge: K.C. Home: 67 Maugus Ave Wellesley Hills MA 02181 Office: John Hancock Mut Life Ins PO Box 111 Boston MA 02117

SCULLY, JUDITH RUDOLPH, financial services company executive; b. Scottsbluff, Nebr., Aug. 8, 1948; d. Ralph Gordon and Sally Ruth (Hochstatter) Rudolph; m. Gus Scully, Dec. 19, 1970; children: David, Mark, Daniel. Student, U. Salzburg, Austria, 1966-67, 69-70; BA, BEd, Bowling Green State U., 1970, MA, 1971; cert. in fin. planning, Coll. Fin. Planning, Denver, 1987. Rep. A.L. Williams Co., Edgemont, S.D., 1984-85, dist. mgr., 1985, div. mgr., 1985; regional mgr. A.L. Williams Co., Edgemont, 1985-86; regional v.p. A.L. Williams Co., Rapid City, S.D., 1986—. Office: AL Williams Co 405 E Omaha St Ste 8 Rapid City SD 57701

SCULLY, ROGER TEHAN, lawyer; b. Washington, Jan. 10, 1948; s. James Henry and Marietta (Maguire) S.; m. Martha Anne Seebach, Dec. 29, 1979. BS, U. Md., 1977; JD, Cath. U., 1980. Bar: Md. 1980, D.C. 1981, U.S. Tax Ct. 1982, U.S. Supreme Ct. 1988. V.p. Bogley Related Cos., Rockville, Md., 1971-75; law clk. to presiding justice Superior Ct. of D.C., Washington, 1979-81; assoc. Lerch, Early & Roseman, Bethesda, Md., 1981-82; gen. counsel Westwood Corps., Bethesda, 1982—, Jefferson Meml. Hosp., Alexandria, Va., 1988—, Laszlo N. Tauber & Assocs., Bethesda, 1988—; cons. in real estate Order of Friar Minor, N.Y.C. 1977—; lectr. Mortgage Bankers Assn., Washington, 1984—. Mem. Pres.'s Council St. Bonaventure U., Olean, N.Y., 1986—; trustee Edmund Burke Sch., Washington, 1984—; bd. dirs. Nat. Children's Choir, Washington, 1980—, Manor Montessori Sch., Potomac, Md., 1981-84; bd. of govs. Goodwill Industries, Washington, 1987—. Recipient First Order Affiliation Order of Friars Minor, 1985; named one of Outstanding Young Men in Am., 1982. Mem. ABA, Fed. Bar Assn., Md. Bar Assn., D.C. Bar Assn. (fellow), Assn. Trial Lawyers Am., Am. Judicature Soc., Selden Soc., U.S. Judicial Conf. of the Fourth Cir., World Karate Boxing Assn. (bd. dirs. 1988), Phi Delta Phi. Republican. Roman Catholic. Clubs: Nat. Press (Washington); Nat. Aviation (Arlington, Va.). Home: 10923 Wickshire Way Rockville MD 20852 Office: Westwood Ctr II 5110 Ridgefield Rd Ste 408 Bethesda MD 20816

SCURRY, RICHARDSON GANO, JR., financial executive; b. Dallas, June 7, 1938; s. Richardson Gano and Josephine (DuVall) S.; m. Pamela Ruth Edith McGinley, Oct. 11, 1975; children: Richardson, Kristina. BA, U. Tex., 1961; MBA, Stanford U., 1963. Mktg. rep. DP div. IBM, Dallas, 1963-68; mgr. fin. planning, DP group IBM, Harrison, N.Y., 1968-72; exec. asst., group exec. IBM, Armonk, N.Y., 1973; mgr. fin. planning office products div. IBM, Franklin Lakes, N.Y., 1974; mgr. fin. analysis, antitrust litigation IBM, N.Y.C., 1975; controller system communication div. IBM, White Plains, 1976-80; dir. plans, controls internal info. systems & communications IBM Corp., Purchase, N.Y., 1981-84; sr. v.p. fin. Chem. Bank, N.Y.C., 1985-89; pres., chief exec. officer Pearce, Mayer & Greer Realty Co., N.Y.C., 1989—; v.p. fin., ptnr. Wicker Garden's Children, N.Y.C., 1984—; dir. Info Mart, Dallas, 1987—; treas., bd. dirs. 1158 Fifth Ave Corp., N.Y.C., 1985—. Mem. bus. com. Met. Mus. Art, N.Y.C., 1986—. Mem. Fin. Exec. Inst. (com. info. mgmt. 1979—, dir. N.Y.C. chpt. 1988—), Salesmanship Club, Phi Delta Theta. Republican. Presbyterian. Home: 1158 Fifth Ave New York NY 10029 Office: Pearce Mayer & Greer Realty Co 90 Park Ave New York NY 10016

SCZUDLO, RAYMOND STANLEY, lawyer; b. Olean, N.Y., July 5, 1948; s. Raymond Stanley and Ann Marie (Frisina) S.; m. Jane Marie Ehrensberger, May 9, 1970; children: Gregory Martin, Edward James. BChemE, U. Detroit, 1971; JD, Georgetown U., 1974. Bar: D.C., 1975., U.S. Dist. Ct. (fed. dist.) D.C. 1975, U.S. Ct. Appeals (D.C. cir.) 1975, U.S. Ct. Appeals (5th cir.) 1980, U.S. Supreme Ct. 1981. Assoc. Martin, Whitfield, Thaler & Bebchick, Washington, 1974-78, Verner, Liipfert, Bernhard & McPherson, Washington, 1978-80; ptnr. Verner, Liipfert, Bernhard, McPherson & Hand, Washington, 1981-87, Weil, Gotshal & Manges, Washington, 1987—; bd. dirs. Benlink, Inc., Washington, 1984—. Contbr. articles on banking to profl. jours. Mem. corporate bd. Children's Hosp. Nat. Med. Ctr., Washington, 1983-89, bd. dirs. 1985—, chmn. fin. com., 1988—. Mem. ABA, Fed. Bar Assn., D.C. Bar Assn., Am. Coll. Investment Counsel. Club: University (Washington). Office: Weil Gotshal & Manges 1615 L St NW Washington DC 20036

SEAGRAM, NORMAN MEREDITH, beverage company executive; b. Toronto, Ont., Can., July 10, 1934; s. Norman Oliver and Constance Beatrice (Mills) S.; m. Joyce Elizabeth Seagram, Aug. 21, 1958; children: Susan Dlizabeth , Norman Philip, Joseph Frederick, Samanatha. Student, Trinity Coll., Port Hope, Ont.; BA in Sci., U. Toronto, 1958; MS, U. Birmingham, Eng., 1964. Engr. dept. prodn. systems Rootes Ltd., Coventry, Eng., 1958; cons. Associated Indsl. Cons. Ltd., London, 1960, Nairobi, Kenya and Salisbury, Rhodesia, 1961-63; cons. Mgmt. Scis. Ltd., London, 1964; prin. Inbucon Svcs. Ltd., Halifax, N.S. and Toronto, 1965; exec. asst. to v.p. Can. Indsl. Group Molson Industries Ltd., Toronto, 1968; mgr. mktg. Anthes Equipment Ltd., Port Credit, 1969; dir. planning Molson Breweries Can. Ltd., Montreal, 1970, v.p. planning, pers. and industry affairs, 1972-77, sr. v.p. adminstrn., 1982-83, chmn.; pres. Seaway/Midwest Ltd., Toronto, 1978-82, Molson Western Breweries Ltd., Calgary, 1983-85, Molson Ont. Breweries Ltd., 1985-86; exec. v.p. brewing group The Molson Cos. Ltd., 1986—; chmn. Club de Hockey Can. Inc., Vancouver Can. Baseball Ltd., Santa Fe Beverage Co. Mem. Assn. Profl. Engrs. Ont., Alpha Delta Phi, Toronto Golf Club, Toronto Badminton and Racquet Club, Montreal Badminton and Squash Club, Hillside Tennis Club, Empire Club. Conservative. Anglican. Office: The Molson Cos Ltd, 2 International Blvd, Rexdale, ON Canada M9W 1A2 *

SEAL, JOHN S., JR., construction company executive; b. Phila., May 20, 1944; s. John S. Sr. and Gertrude Eva (Abbott) S.; m. Anna M. Salcedo; children: Kathryn, Ashley and Kristen (twins), Heather. BBA in Econs., Drexel U., 1967; MBA, Dartmouth Coll., 1971. CPA, N.Y. Asst. to exec. v.p. fin. Gould Inc., Chgo., 1971; dir. electronics group fin. planning Gould Inc., Newton Upper Falls, Mass., 1972-73; pres., treas., chief exec. officer Nat. Communications Industries Co., Greenwich, Conn., 1973-76, chmn., 1973-79; exec. v.p. Boyerton (Pa.) Burial Casket Co., 1976-77; v.p., gen. mgr. communications products div. FSC Corp., Pitts., 1977-79; sr. v.p. Butcher and Singer Inc. subs. Butcher and Co. Inc., Phila., 1979-85; pres. Sovereign Group Inc. subs. Butcher and Co. Inc., Phila., 1983-85, Seal Devel. Co., Phila., 1985-88; mng. dir. Essex Fin. Group, Phila., 1988—; pres. Seal Devel. Co., Phila., 1988—; bd. dirs. Essex Fin. Group, Atlanta, Rittenhouse Sq. Fitness Club, Phila. Trustee Please Touch Mus., Phila., 1987—; bd. dirs. alumni bd. Drexel U., Phila., 1983—. Served as sgt. U.S. Army, 1967-68. Mem. Am. Inst. CPAs, N.Y. Soc. CPAs, Conn. Soc. CPAs. Republican. Mem. Ch. of Christ. Club: Union League (Phila.). Home: 208 Llanfair Rd Ardmore PA 19003 Office: Seal Devel Co 714 Market St Philadelphia PA 19106

SEAL, MICHAEL, physicist; b. Weston Super Mare, Eng., Apr. 15, 1930; s. Carl Cyril and Ina May (Hurford) S.; m. Cynthia Ida Austin Leach, Aug. 7, 1954; children: David, Anne, Rosemary, Susan, Christopher. BA, Cambridge U., 1952, MA, 1956, PhD, 1957. Head diamond research Engelhard Industries Inc., Newark, 1959-67, tech. coordinator research and devel. div., 1965-67; dir. research Amsterdam Diamond Test and Devel. Ctr., D. Drukker & Zn. N.V., Amsterdam, 1967—; adj. dir. 1970—; bd. dirs. Dubbeldee Diamond Corp., Mt. Arlington, N.J. Contbr. articles to profl. jours. Served with RAF, 1948-49. Postdoctoral research fellow Cavendish Lab., Cambridge, 1957-59. Fellow Explorers Club, Inst. Physics of London, Mineral Soc. Am.; mem. IEEE, N.Y. Acad. Scis. (life), Am. Chem. Soc., Dutch Phys. Soc., Indsl. Diamond Assn. Am. (assoc.), Dutch Abrasives Soc. (chmn. 1977—), European Fedn. Abrasives Mfrs. (premier del. for Netherlands, chmn. diamond grains subcom. 1976—). Club: United Oxford and Cambridge Univs. Home: 5 Guido Gezelle St, 1077 WN Amsterdam The Netherlands Office: 12 Sarphatikade, 1017 WV Amsterdam The Netherlands

SEALS, HENRY CHAIM, industrial company executive; b. B. Lodz, Poland, Jan. 3, 1924; came to U.S., 1949, naturalized, 1955; s. Josef and Leah (Zimmerkorn) Sliski; B.A., U. Munich, 1949; M.B.A., So. Meth. U., 1958; Ph.D., Am. Internat. U., St. Louis, 1976; m. Elayne Smith, Oct. 27, 1967; 1 son, Jason T.; children by previous marriage—Richard J., Laura S. Comptroller, WJB Corp., Dallas, 1951-56; comptroller Linda-Jo Shoe Co., Dallas, Denton, Gainesville, Tex., 1956-59; v.p. fin. N.Am. Mdse. Corp., N.Y.C., Dallas, 1959-63; v.p. fin. adminstrn. Bogart Industries, Inc., Ft. Worth, 1963-80; pres. Basic Co., Ft. Worth, Seals Realty Co., Ft. Worth, 1980—, fin. cons., trustee in bankruptcy; chmn. bd. Brighton Investment Corp.; dir., pres. Seals & Assocs., Inc., Ft. Worth; dir. Bank of Commerce; trustee Trinity Valley Sch., Ft. Worth. Mem. Am. Bankruptcy Inst., Nat. Assn., Bankruptcy Trustees, Am. Inst. Mgmt., Tex. Assn. of Realtors, Ft. Worth Bd. Realtors, Am. Soc. Profl. Cons., Gainesville Jr. C. of C. (pres., 1957-59). Jewish religion. Clubs: Ft. Worth, Colonial Country (Ft. Worth). Home: 4600 Briarhaven Rd Fort Worth TX 76109 Office: 3417 Hullen St Fort Worth TX 76107

SEAMAN, BYRON JAMES, oil company executive; b. Rouleau, Sask., Can., Sept. 7, 1923; s. Byron L. and Mae (Patton) S.; m. Evelyn Virginia Shirkey, Sept. 4, 1948; children: Karen Gayle, Ronald James, Deborah Joan, Allan Byron. BS in Mech. Engring., U. Sask., 1945. Registered profl. engr. Geophysicist Carter Oil, Saskatoon, Sask., 1945-49; liaison engr. Gulf Oil, Saskatoon, 1945-49; seismograph operator Western Geophysical, Saskatoon, 1945-49; with Bow Valley Industries, Ltd. (formerly Seaman Engring. & Drilling Co.), Saskatoon, 1949-60; v.p., dir. Bow Valley Industries, Ltd. (formerly Seaman Engring. & Drilling Co.), Calgary, Alta., Can., 1960-68, sr. v.p., 1968-75, exec. v.p., 1975-76; chief exec. officer Bow Valley Resource Svcs. Ltd. (subs. Bow Valley Industries, Ltd.), Calgary, Alta., 1977-87, chmn. bd. dirs., 1987—; instr. U. Sask., Saskatoon, 1945-49; bd. dirs. Bow Valley Industries, Ltd., Calgary, Bow Valley Resource Svcs. Ltd., Calgary, Western Rock Bit Co., Calgary, Encal Energy Ltd., Calgary, Champion Bear Resources Ltd., Calgary; chmn. Can. Com. Det norske Veritas, Calgary.

Mem. Can. Soc. for Mech. Engrs., Assn. Profl. Engrs., Geologists and Geophysicists Alta. (spl. award 1987), Can. Soc. Petroleum Geologists, Earl Grey Golf and Country Club, Calgary Golf and Country Club, Calgary Petroleum Club, Calgary Ranchmen's Club, Glencoe Club. Home: 11 Bel Aire Pl SW, Calgary, AB Canada T2V 2C3 Office: Bow Valley Resource Ltd, PO Box 6620 Postal Sta D, Calgary, AB Canada T2P 3R3

SEAMAN, DARYL KENNETH, oil company executive; b. Rouleau, Sask., Can., Apr. 28, 1922; s. Byron Luther and Letha Mae (Patton) S.; m. Lois Maureen deLong (dec.); children: Diane Maureen Lefroy, Robert Byron, Kenneth Alan, Gary Ross Seaman. B.S. in Mech. Engring., U. Sask., 1948, LLD (hon.), 1982. Cert. mech. engr. Chmn., chief exec. officer Bow Valley Industries Ltd., Calgary, Alta., Can., 1962-70, 1970-82, chmn., pres., chief exec. officer, 1985-87, chmn., chief exec. officer, 1988—; bd. dirs. Pan-Alta. Gas Ltd., Calgary, NOVA, Calgary, Vencap Equities Alta. Ltd., Edmonton, BioTechnica Internat. of Can., Calgary, Bow Valley Resource Services Ltd.; co-owner, dir. Calgary Flames Hockey Club. Mem. Royal Commn. Econ. Union and Devel. Prospects for Can., 1982-85; active numerous coms. for fundraising U. Sask. Served with RCAF, 1941-45, Eng., North Africa, Italy. Mem. Assn. Profl. Engrs., Geologists and Geophysicists (hon. life) (Frank Spragins award, 1985, McGill Mgmt. Achievement award, 1979), Ranchmen's Club, RAF Club, Earl Grey Golf Club, Calgary Petroleum Club, Calgary Golf and Country Club, U. Calgary Chancellor's Club. Progressive Conservative. Mem. United Ch. Can. Home: Rural Rt #8, Calgary, AB Canada T2J 2T9 Office: Bow Valley Industries Ltd, 321 6th Ave SW Ste 1800, Calgary, AB Canada T2P 3R2

SEAMAN, RICHARD HARPER, service executive; b. Phila., Nov. 2, 1916; s. Samuel Arthur and Isabel Curry (Gibson) S.; m. Jane Drenning, Nov. 22, 1941; children: Richard D., Cynthia Jane, Mark Cameron. Student, Wyomissing Poly. Inst., 1933-35, Pa. State U., 1936-37. Pres., chief exec. officer Berkleigh Equipment Co., Reading, Pa., 1946-54, Seaman Mill Supplies, Inc., Reading, Pa., 1954-88, 200 Pa. Ave. Realty Corp., W. Reading, Pa., 1960—, S&B Leasing Co., Inc., W. Reading, Pa., 1970-88; chmn. bd. ABE Berkleigh Corp., W. Reading, Pa., 1984—; pres. U.S. Mobile Energy Co., Inc., Reading, 1985—. Served as capt. Ordnance Dept., U.S. Army, 1941-46, PTO. Decorated Bronze Star, Bronze Arrowhead. Mem. Phi Kappa Sigma. Club: Young Rep. (Wyomissing, Pa.) (bd. dirs. 1948-60, pres. 1954-60). Office: Berkleigh Power Equip Co Inc 10 S 2d Ave West Reading PA 19611

SEARBY, DANIEL MACLEOD, venture capitalist; b. Milw., June 24, 1934; s. Edmund Wilson and Muriel Marjorie (MacLeod) S.; m. Joan Innes Hinsch, June 16, 1960 (div. 1974); children: Daniel MacLeod, David Porter, Bruce Hamilton; m. Catharine Ann Rollins, Jan. 31, 1976; 1 child, Katharine MacLeod. AB, Dartmouth Coll., 1957; MA, Columbia U., 1958. Product mgr. Procter & Gamble, Co., Cin., 1958-69; fin. dir. OPIC, Washington, 1970-72; dep. asst. sec. Dept. State, Washington, 1973-74; sr. v.p. Triad, Los Altos, Calif., 1974-76; pres. Kearns Internat., San Francisco, 1976-83, MacLeod Investment, Palo Alto, Calif., 1984—; bd. dirs. PCC Systems, Palo Alto. Contbr. articles to profl. jours. Active Town of Portola Valley Traffic Com., 1987—. Cpl. USMC, 1959-64. Republican. Episcopalian. Home: 190 Golden Hills Portola Valley CA 94025 Office: MacLeod Investments 22300 Foothill Ste 509 Hayward CA 94541

SEARCH, ROGER MACK, employee relations executive; b. Crooksville, Ohio, Apr. 16, 1931; s. Kenneth M. and Alice Louise (Colburn) S.; B.S., Ohio State U., 1958; M.B.A., New Haven U., 1981; m. Betty J. McPeek, Oct. 28, 1950; 1 dau., Lisa A. With The Mead Corp., Dayton, Ohio, 1958-69, Harris Corp., Melbourne, Fla., 1969-74; v.p. personnel, Hubbell, Inc., Orange, Conn., 1974—. Served with USAF, 1951-55. Mem. Nat. Elec. Mfrs. Assn. (mem. indsl. relations com.), Am. Mgmt. Assn., Human Resources Council, Conn. Personnel Assn. Methodist. Office: 584 Derby-Milford Rd Orange CT 06477

SEARCY, JOEL BRADFORD, data processing executive; b. Crestview, Fla., Dec. 17, 1935; s. William Edward Searcy and Virginia (Campbell) Barr; m. Elaine Cram, Jan. 20, 1957 (div. 1968); children: Jennifer Doyle, Lauren Linder; m. Elizabeth Norris, Sept. 6, 1969; 1 child, Samantha. BS, MIT, 1957, MS, 1960, ScD, 1967. Research assoc. MIT, Cambridge, Mass., 1967-68; v.p. Harbridge House, Inc., Boston, 1968-75; gen. mgr. Constrn. Data Systems, Inc., Kansas City, Mo., 1975-81; pres. Compudyne, Inc., Acton, Mass., 1981-87; pres. Pamet Systems, Inc., Acton, Mass., 1987—, also bd. dirs.; bd. dirs. Compudyne Inc. Bd. dirs. Acton Community Chest, 1987, Acton Arts Council, 1984—, A-B Jamboree, 1986—. Recipient A/C Fellowship for Doctoral Study in Astronautics, Gen. Motors, Inc., 1966. Republican. Episcopalian. Home: 15 Balsam Dr Acton MA 01720 Office: Pamet Systems Inc 989 Main St Acton MA 01720

SEARCY, MICHAEL JOHN, financial consultant; b. San Diego, Oct. 18, 1954; s. John H. Jr. and Rosemary A. (Richards) S.; m. Teresa Ann Andrews, Dec. 28, 1978; children: Jessica Ann, Sarah Suzanne. BBA, U. Mo., 1976. Chartered fin. cons., cert. fin. planner. Auditor Probate Court, Kansas City, Mo., 1974-75; prin. Searcy Fin. Services, Kansas City, Mo., 1976—. Mem. Western Assn. Fin. Planning (exec. v.p. western region 1985—), Internat. Assn. Fin. Planning (v.p. edn. 1983-84, pres. 1984-85, bd. chmn. 1985—, adv. com. 1985), Inst. Cert. Fin. Planners, Registry Fin. Planning Practitioners. Republican. Home: 5841 Wornall Kansas City MO 64113 Office: 1 Ward Pkwy #333 Kansas City MO 64112

SEARLE, STEWART A., transportation equipment holding company executive; b. Winnipeg, Man., Can., 1923; s. Stewart Augustus and Sally Elizabeth (Appleyard) S.; m. Maudie Jessiman, Nov. 9, 1949; children: Stewart A., David J. Student, Trinity Coll., Port Hope, Ont., Queen's U., Kingston, Ont. Chmn. bd. dirs. Fed. Industries, Ltd., Winnipeg. Served to lt. RCAF. Office: Fed Industries Ltd, 1 Lombard Pl, Winnipeg, MB Canada R3B 0X3 *

SEARS, PETER A., finance company executive; b. Cleve., Oct. 28, 1938; s. John Andrew and Mildred (Peterson) S.; m. Cary Webb Hank, June 16, 1962; children: William Peterson, Kevin Alden. AB, Colgate U., 1960; JD, Harvard U., 1963. Atty. Smith Kline Beckman Corp., Phila., 1963-71, asst. gen. counsel, 1971-73; gen. mgr. Smith Kline Beckman Corp., Tokyo, 1973-76; v.p. Asia, Pacific and Can. Smith Kline Beckman Corp., Phila., 1976-77, dir. corp. devel., 1977-80, v.p. corp. devel., 1980-85, v.p. bus. investments, 1985—; pres. S.R. One, Ltd. Venture Investments, Phila., 1985—; bd. dirs. KVM Biotech., Inc., Houston, Internat. Canine Genetics, Inc., Malvern, Pa., Cruachem Holdings, Ltd., Glasgow, Scotland; chmn. bd. Delaware Valley Venture Venture Group, Phila., 1985-88; lectr. in field. Chmn. Dem. Com. Radnor Twp., Pa., 1968-69; bd. dirs. Univ. City Sci. Ctr., Phila., 1986—, Sci. Ctr. Internat., Kyoto, Japan, 1988—. Mem. ABA, Am. Arbitration Assn., Assn. for Corp. Growth (bd. dirs., v.p. 1984-86, bd. dirs., pres. Phila. chpt. 1982-86), Greater Phila. C. of C. (bd. dirs. 1987-88), Union League Phila., Japan Soc., Tokyo Am. Club. Office: Star Rte 1 One Franklin Pla Philadelphia PA 19101

SEARS, ROBERT REED, manufacturing company executive; b. Miami, Fla., Aug. 7, 1951; s. Audley Pearson and Elma (Hamilton) S.; m. Natalia Toyos, Nov. 1, 1986. BBA, U. Miami, 1976, MBA, 1977. With Fla. Power and Light Co., Miami, 1971—, assoc. bus. analyst, 1977-78, investment analyst, 1978-79, sr. investment analyst, 1979-80, mgr. investment funds, 1980-81, mgr. corp. fin., 1982-83, asst. treas., mgr. corp. fin., 1983-84, asst. treas., dir. fin., 1984-85, treas., 1985-86; asst. treas. FPL Group, Inc., North Palm Beach, Fla., 1984-86, treas., 1986—; treas., chief fin. officer FPL Group Capital, Inc., 1985—; treas. Palm Ins. Co. Ltd., 1988—, also bd. dirs.; pres., bd. dirs. FPL Employees Fed. Credit Union, 1979-81; mem. Pres.'s Commn. on Exec. Exchange, The White House, Washington, 1981-82; treas. Telesat Cablevision, Inc., 1985—, Group Cable, Inc., 1987—; v.p. FPL Investments, Inc., 1986—. Active Leadership Miami, 1984. Recipient Disting. Service cert. U.S. EEOC, 1982. Mem. Nat. Assn. Corp. Treas., Beta Gamma Sigma, Phi Kappa Phi. Office: FPL Group Inc PO Box 08801 North Palm Beach FL 33408-8801

SEATON, JOHN RICHARD, distribution company executive; b. Boone, Iowa, Nov. 30, 1934; s. Donald F. and Florence (Park) S.; m. Elizabeth Kirch, Sept. 20, 1961; children: Catherine, Elizabeth, Anne. BS in Indsl. Adminstrn., Gen. Sci., Iowa State U., 1958; MBA, U. Pa., 1961. CPA, N.Y., Mo. Group ins. salesman Conn. Gen., Des Moines, 1958-60; with Arthur Young, N.Y.C., 1961-82, gen. ptnr., 1970-82; v.p. Graybar Electric Co., St. Louis, 1982—, also bd. dirs. trustee, v.p. Lawrence Hosp. Bronxville, N.Y., 1977-82. Served to 2nd lt. U.S. Army, 1958-59. Mem. Am. Inst. CPA's, N.Y. Soc. CPA's, Mo. Soc. CPA's, Fin. Execs. Inst. Clubs: Old Warson Country, St. Louis. Office: Graybar Electric Co Inc 34 N Meramec Saint Louis MO 63105

SEATON, W. B. (BRUCE), container transport and distribution executive; b. Phila., Apr. 1, 1925; married. B.S., UCLA, 1949. With J.F. Forbes & Co., 1950-53; treas., controller Douglas Oil Co., 1953-66; asst. treas. Occidental Petroleum Co., 1966-70; v.p., sec., treas. Natomas Co., 1970-72, v.p. fin., treas., 1972-74, sr. v.p., 1974-78, exec. v.p. mktg. and transp., 1978-79, exec. v.p., dir., 1979-83, pres., 1983; pres., chief operating officer Am. Pres. Lines Ltd., Oakland, Calif., 1977-87, chief exec. officer, 1983—; chmn., pres., chief exec. officer, bd. dirs. Am. Pres. Cos., Oakland, 1983—. Bd. trustees UCLA Found. Recipient Excellence in Tech. award Gartner Group, 1988, Internat. Achievement award World Trade Club of San Francisco, 1988; named Maritime Man of Yr. U.S. Propeller Club, 1987. Office: Am Pres Cos Ltd 1800 Harrison St Oakland CA 94612

SEAWELL, WILLIAM LACY, II, insurance company executive; b. Greensboro, N.C., Nov. 29, 1949; s. William Lawrence Jr. and Mary Heilig (McDow) S. ; m. Debra Mae Mundy, Nov. 24, 1973; children: Lacy Allison, Meredith Heilig, Diana Leigh. BS, Appalachian State U., 1972. CLU, cert. fin. planner; chartered fin. cons. Tchr., coach Greensboro City Schs., 1975; regional mgr. Pilot Life Ins. Co., Greensboro, 1976-79; regional agy. mgr. Jefferson-Pilot Life, Greensboro, 1979—; chmn. mgrs. field adv. com. Jefferson-Pilot Life, 1985-86; instr. Agy. Mgmt. Tng. Course, Greensboro, 1985-85. Mem. Greensboro Assn. Life Underwriters (pres. 1985-87, Man of Yr. 1987), Am. soc. CLU's, Gen. Agts. & Mgrs. Conf. (pres. 1983-84, speaker nat. meeting 1988), Internat. Assn. Fin. Planners, Nat. Assn. Life Underwriter Pol. Action Com. (grandee 1986), Nat. Assn. Secutities Dealers (registered rep.), Greensboro City, Starmount Forest Country, Rotary. Republican. Presbyterian. Home: 511 Hobbs Rd Greensboro NC 27403 Office: Jefferson Pilot Life 3101 N Elm St Ste 400 Greensboro NC 27408

SEAY, SUZANNE, financial planner, educator; b. Tulsa, May 3, 1942; d. James Paul and Ann (Maxey) S. BS, Hardin-Simmons U., 1964; MA, Ariz. State U., 1966. Tchr. Baker (Oreg.) Pub. Schs., 1964-65, Govt. of Guam, Agana, 1968-74, Tehran (Iran) Am. Sch., 1974-75, Am. Sch. Isfahan, Iran, 1975-78; internat. pubs. rep. World Editions, Hollister, 1978-87; fin. planner Christopher Weil & Co. (name now Integrated Resources), Monterey, Calif., 1984—; tchr. fin. planning Gavilan Coll., Gilroy, Calif., 1988—, Monterey Peninsula Coll., 1988—, Hartnell Coll., Salinas, Calif., 1989—; speaker Monterey County Women's Fair, Salinas, Calif., 1988—. Mem. Am. Field Svc., Hollister, 1987—; treas. San Benito Hospice, Hollister, 1987-89; speaker in field. Mem. Internat. Assn. for Fin. Planning, S.E. Asia Tchrs. and Counselors Conf. (speaker 1987), Inst. Cert. Fin. Planners, Registry Fin. Planning Practitioners. Republican. Home: 130 George's Dr Hollister CA 95023 Office: Integrated Resources 1139 Victoria St Hollister CA 95023

SEAY, THOMAS PATRICK, retail company real estate executive; b. Hot Springs, Ark., Oct. 21, 1941; s. Paul H. and Fayetta M. (Seversen) S.; children: Christopher, Michael, Eric; m. Brenda Barbee; step-children: Lauren, Lane. BSBA, U. Ark., 1963, MBA, 1975. Dir. market research Cooper Communities, Bella Vista, Ark., 1971-73; with Wal-Mart Stores, Inc., 1973—; store assoc. Wal-Mart Stores, Inc., Rogers, Ark., 1973-74; real estate mgr. Wal-Mart Stores, Inc., Bentonville, Ark., 1974-77; dir. real estate Wal-Mart Stores, Inc., Bentonville, 1977-78, v.p., 1978-83, sr. v.p., 1983—. Served to capt. U.S. Army, 1963-70, Korea, Vietnam. Decorated Bronze Star. Mem. Internat. Council Shopping Ctrs. (trustee 1987-90). Presbyterian. Office: Wal-Mart Stores Inc 701 S Walton Blvd Bentonville AR 72716

SEBALD, CHARLES WILLIAM, JR., electrical company executive; b. Danville, Ill., Feb. 3, 1947; s. Charles William and Harriet (Hecker) S.; m. Jane Marie Mitchell, Feb. 25, 1967; children: Charles Dale, Delora Marie. BA in Bus., Ball State U., 1969, MA in Mgmt., 1970. Mgmt. trainee Ind. Nat. Bank, Indpls., 1970-71; sr. materials planner Western Electric div. AT&T, Westminster, Colo., 1971-74; sr. buyer Storage Tech., Louisville, Colo., 1974-78, mgr. procurement, 1978-80; gen. mgr. Ren Electronics Corp., Canon City, Colo., 1980—; chmn. Mfg. Round Table, Fremont County, Colo., 1983—; lectr. bus. colls., Colo., 1976—. Chmn. bd. dirs. Jr. Achievement, Fremont County, Colo., 1984—, United Way, 1987—. Mem. Colorado Springs Exec. Assn. Lodges: Rotary, Elks. Home: 1006 Beech Canon City CO 81212 Office: Ren Electronics Corp PO Box 1410 Canon City CO 81212

SEBASTIAN, MICHAEL JAMES, manufacturing company executive; b. Chgo., July 8, 1930; s. Michael and Larraine (DeAmicis) S.; m. Sally Ervin, Nov. 29, 1953; children: Michael, Mark, Lisa. B.S. in M.E., Santa Clara U., 1952; A.M.P., Harvard U., 1972. Div. mgr. FMC Corp, Indpls., 1953-77; pres. Rotek, Aurora, Ohio, 1977-78; v.p. Gardner-Denver, Dallas, 1978-79; group pres. Cooper Industries, Dallas, 1979-81; v.p. Cooper Industries, Houston, 1981—. Republican. Roman Catholic. Clubs: Petroleum, Lakeside Country (Houston). Home: 11511 Shadow Way Houston TX 77024 Office: Cooper Industries Inc 1001 Fannin 40th Fl PO Box 4446 Houston TX 77210

SEBESTYÉN, ISTVÁN, computer scientist, educator, consultant; b. Budapest, Hungary, Aug. 14, 1947; arrived in Austria, 1977; s. János and Hedvig (Vadnai) S.; m. Eszter Molnár, Oct. 25, 1975; children: Adam, David Richard, Sylvia Anna. MS in Elec. Engring., Tech. U. Budapest, 1970, PhD in Elec. Engring., 1974. Diplomate in elec. engring. Research asst. dept. high voltage techniques Tech. U. Budapest, 1968-70; sci. collaborator Inst. for Coordination Computer Techniques, Budapest, 1970-77; mgmt. cons. UN Indsl. Devel. Orgn., Vienna, Austria, 1977-78; scientist, research scholar Internat. Inst. Applied Systems Analysis, Laxenburg, Austria, 1978-84; systems planner, telecommunications adviser, standardization expert Siemens AG, Munich, 1985—; vis. prof. Tech. U. Graz, Austria, 1983-85; lectr., tchr. U. Klagenfurt, Austria, 1985—; cons. to internat. orgns. Author: Experimental and Operational East-West Computer Networks, 1983, Transborder Data Flows and Austria, 1986; mem. adv. bd. Jour. Transnat. Data Report, Washington, 1983—; contbr. over 80 articles to sci. jours. Mem. Austrian Computer Soc., Hungarian Computer Soc. Avocations: travel, sports. Home: Sollnerstrasse 10, 8000 Munich 71, Federal Republic of Germany Office: Siemens AG, Hofmannstrasse 51, 8000 Munich 70, Federal Republic of Germany

SEBODA, EARL FRANK, state government administrator; b. Balt., Aug. 10, 1938; s. Max Frank and Mary Margaret (Black) S.; m. Carol Ann Okonski, Nov. 24, 1962; children: Debra, Jacqueline, Earl Frank Jr. BSME, U. Md., 1961; postgrad., Rutgers U., 1965, Stevens Inst. Tech., 1966-67, Johns Hopkins U., 1967-69. Registered profl. engr., Md., N.J. Project engr. E.I. DuPont Co., Linden, N.J., 1965-67; plant engr. Nat. Brewing Co., Balt., 1967-68; bldg. engr. Md. Dept. Budget and Fiscal Planning, Balt., 1968-71; chief capital budget engring. and maintenance Md. State Dept. Health and Mental Hygiene, Balt., 1971-77; asst. sec. Md. Dept. Gen. Svcs., Balt., 1977-83, sec., 1983—; tchr. Catonsville Community Coll., Balt., 1969, Community Coll. Balt., 1973-77. Editor: Comprehensive Maintenance and Repair Program, 1978. Chmn. Westchester Improvement Assn., Catonsville. Lt. (j.g.) USN, 1961-65. Mem. Md. Soc. Profl. Engrs. (officer, Profl. Engr. of Yr. award 1986), Nat. Conf. State Gen. Svcs. Officers, Nat. Assn. State Facilities Adminstrs., Bldg. Offls. and Code Adminstrs. Internat., U.S. Naval Inst., Balt. Yacht Club. Democrat. Roman Catholic. Home: 2412 Harbor Wood Rd Baltimore MD 21228 Office: Md Dept Gen Svcs 301 W Preston St Baltimore MD 21201

SECREST, LARRY, company chief executive officer; b. Ft. Smith, Ark., Aug. 19, 1941; s. Cyrus Grady and Sallie Larue (Mosley) S.; m. Julia Marie Kilkelly, July 12, 1980; children: Olivia Paula, Erik Stephen, Elise Nicole. BA, Tulane U., 1963; MBA, U. Pa., 1965; PhD, U. Tex., 1971. Fin. analyst Ford Motor Co., Dearborn, 1965-68; group planner Lear Siegler, Inc., Santa Monica, Calif., 1968-69; vis. prof. Keio U., Tokyo, 1971-72; dir. internat. planning Cooper Industries, Houston, 1973-74; asst. prof. U. Tex., Arlington, 1974-77; exec. v.p. Standard Meat Co., Ft. Worth, 1978-82; pres. Secrest & Assocs., Dallas, 1983-85; pres., chief exec. officer Sci. Measurement Systems, Austin, Tex., 1986—. Author: Texas Entrepreneurship, 1971; editor: The Prado Oil Company, 1971; contbr. articles on entrepreneurship and mgmt. to profl. jours. Dir. Pastoral Counseling and Edn. Ctr., Dallas, 1983—. Capt. USAF Res., 1967-72. Presbyterian. Home: Rte 1 Box 274A Mountainburg AR 72946 Office: Sci Measurement Systems 2201 Donley Dr Austin TX 78758

SEDACCA, ROSALIND PEARL, marketing professional, copywriter, consultant; b. Bklyn., Mar. 7, 1947; d. Sidney J. and Dorothy (Stein) Lipson; m. Michael L. Sedacca, July 4, 1966; 1 child, Cassidy Daniel. BFA, Pratt Inst., 1967; postgrad., NYU, 1967-68. Creative dir. circulation promotion dept. The Condé Nast Pub., N.Y.C., 1967-70; direct response copywriter Altman, Vos & Reichberg, N.Y.C., 1970-72; advt., freelance copywriter The Parker Group, Nashville, 1973-78; pres. Creative Copywriting Services, St. Louis, 1978-80; copy dir. MBI Advt., Palm Beach Gardens, Fla., 1981-84; pres. Rosalind Sedacca & Assocs., Lake Worth, Fla., 1984—; cons. small bus. devel. ctr. Fla. Atlantic U., 1986—. speaker in field. bd. dirs. The Sunshine Network, West Palm Beach, Fla., 1986-87. Recipient numerous awards Advt. Fedn. Am. Mem. Fla. Freelance Writer Assn., Am. Mktg. Assn., Fla. Pub. Relations Assn. (directoral com. 1983, communications workshop). Office: Rosalind Sedacca & Assocs 4594 Centurian Circle Lake Worth FL 33463

SEDWAY, LYNN MASSEL, real estate economist; b. Washington, Nov. 26, 1941; d. Mark S. and Jean M. (Magnus) Massel; m. Paul H. Sedway, June 12, 1966; children: Mark, Carolyn, Jan. BA in Econs., U. Mich., 1963; MBA, U. Calif., Berkeley, 1976. Economist San Rafael (Calif.) Redevel. Agy., 1976-78; prin. Sedway & Assocs., San Francisco, 1978—; instr. Appraisal Bus. Sch. U. Calif., Berkeley; bd. dirs. San Francisco Devel. Fund. Mem. Berkeley Bus. Sch. Fund Council, 1984-86; chmn San Rafael Downtown Retail Com., 1985; bd. dirs. San Francisco Devel. Fund, 1985—; CAC mem. Dominican Coll., San Rafael, 1983-87. Mem. Urban Land Inst. (vice-chair Devel. Regulations Council), Internat. Council of Shopping Ctrs., Housing Devel. Fin. Corp. (bd. dirs. Marin, Calif. chpt. 1984—), Marin C. of C. (bd. dirs. 1984-87), San Rafael C. of C., Lambda Alpha (past pres., bd. dirs.), Internat. Land Econs. Soc. Home: 2449 Pacific Ave San Francisco CA 94115 Office: Sedway & Assocs Four Embarcadero Ctr Ste 720 San Francisco CA 94111

SEE, HENRY WESSELMAN, retired oil company executive; b. Mar. 8, 1923; s. Alva Benjamin and Helena (Wesselman) S.; m. Gail Sullivan, June 24, 1950; children: Henry W. Jr., Virginia Stanley, Helena Williams. Student, Yale U., 1942-43. Salesman Celco Corp., N.Y.C., 1947-48; asst. account exec. Batten Barton Durstine & Osborn, N.Y.C., 1949-52, account exec., 1952-56, v.p., mgmt. supr., 1956-61; v.p., regional mgr. Batten Barton Durstine & Osborn, Mpls., 1962-66, v.p., bd. dirs., 1966-67; asst. pub. and promotions dir. Life mag., N.Y.C., 1967-69; exec. v.p. Tarkenton Ventures, Atlanta, 1969-72; v.p mktg. and communications Apache Corp., Mpls., 1972-83, sr. v.p. mktg., 1983-88; Pres., bd. dirs. Pine Valley Farm Inc., Shell Lake, Wis.; chmn. bd. Bookcase Inc., Wayzata, Minn. Dist. leader Greenwich (Conn.) Community Chest, 1950-53; promotion dir. United Fund, Mpls., 1965-67; trustee Internat. Coll., Beirut, 1964-89. Served with USCG Res. Mem. Ind. Petroleum Assn. Am. (bd. dirs. 1978-86), Woodhill Country Club (trustee 1983—), Pine Valley Golf Club, Mpls. Club. Home: 1389 Orono Ln Wayzata MN 55391 Office: 435 Peavey Bldg 730 2d Ave S Minneapolis MN 55402

SEEBART, GEORGE E., insurance executive; b. Niles, Calif., 1928. Grad., Whitman Coll., 1952. V.p. field ops. Farmers Ins. Group Cos. Office: Farmers Ins Exch PO Box 2478 Terminal Annex Los Angeles CA 90051 *

SEEBERT, KATHLEEN ANNE, international trade consultant; b. Chgo.; d. Harold Earl and Marie Anne (Lowery) S.; BS U. Dayton, 1971, M.A., U. Notre Dame, 1976; M.M., Northwestern U., 1983. Publs. editor ContiCommodity Services, Inc., Chgo., 1977-79, supr. mktg., 1979-82; dir. mktg. MidAm. Commodity Exchange, 1982-85; internat. trade cons. to Govt. of Ont., Can., 1985—; guest lectr. U. Notre Dame. Registered commodity rep. Mem. Futures Industry Assn. Am. (treas.). Republican. Roman Catholic. Clubs: Notre Dame of Chgo., Northwestern Mgmt. of Chgo. Office: 208 S LaSalle St Ste 1806 Chicago IL 60604

SEELBACH, CHARLES WILLIAM, chemist; b. Buffalo, Dec. 13, 1923; s. Charles George and Marcia (Grimes) S.; AB, Cornell U., 1948; MS, Western Res. U., 1952; PhD, Purdue U., 1955; m. Patricia O'Reilly, July 7, 1946; children: Janet, Jeanne, Paul. Group leader Ohio Rsch., Cleve., 1948-52; asst. sect. head Esso Standard Oil, Baton Rouge, 1956-57; sect. head Esso Rsch. and Engring., Linden, N.J., 1955-56, 58-63; bus. mgr. Esso Chem. Inc., N.Y.C., 1963-67; mgr. devel. USS Chems., Pitts., 1968-83; cons., 1983-89 . Elder Presbyn. Ch., Cranford, N.J., also trustee. Served with USMC, 1942-46. Purdue U rsch. fellow, 1953-55. Mem. Am. Chem. Soc., Comml. Devel. Assn., Am. Mgmt. Assn., AAAS, Catalysis Soc., N.Y. Acad. Scis., Am. Oil Chemists Soc., Psi Lambda Upsilon. Patentee in field. Office: 100 Norman Dr #167 Mars PA 16046

SEELENFREUND, ALAN, distribution company executive; b. N.Y.C., Oct. 22, 1936; s. Max and Gertrude (Roth) S.; m. Ellyn Bolt; 1 child, Eric. BME, Cornell U., 1959, M. in Indsl. Engring., 1960; PhD in Mgmt. Sci., Stanford U., 1967. Asst. prof. bus. adminstrn. Grad. Sch. Bus. Stanford U., Palo Alto, Calif., 1966-71; mgmt. cons. Strong, Wishart and Assocs., San Francisco, 1971-75; various mgmt. positions McKesson Corp., San Francisco, 1975-84, v.p., chief fin. officer, 1984-86, exec. v.p., chief fin. officer, 1986—, also bd. dirs.; bd. dirs. Armor All Products Corp., PCS, Inc. Mem. Fin. Execs. Inst., Fin. Officers No. Calif., Washington Pvt. Sector Coun., World Affairs Coun. No. Calif., San Francisco C. of C. (bd. dirs.), Bankers CLub, St. Francis Yacht Club, San Francisco Yacht Club, Villa Taverna Club. Office: McKesson Corp One Post St San Francisco CA 94104

SEELEY, FRED COOLEY, retail executive; b. Ann Arbor, Mich., Mar. 23, 1942; s. Ralph Kinnie and Charlotte Ruth (Striffler) S.; m. Marlyn Kay Deyo, Nov. 22, 1969; children: Matthew, Marnie. BS, Mich. State U., 1965, MBA, 1972. With Mich. Nat. Bank, Lansing, 1962-65; asst. cashier Bank of Commonwealth, Detroit, 1966-72; mgr. Multivest, Southfield, Mich., 1972-73; sr. v.p. real estate Perry Drug Stores Inc., Pontiac, Mich., 1973—. Dir. Oakland County Econ. Devel. Corp., Pontiac, 1980—, Oakland County Local Devel., Pontiac, 1980—, Pontiac Econ. Devel. Co., 1980—. With USNG, 1966-72. Mem. Nat. Assn. Corp. Real Estate, Internat. Council Shopping Ctrs., Oakland County C. of C. (chmn. bd. dirs. 1982). Office: Perry Drug Stores Inc 5400 Perry Dr PO Box 1957 Pontiac MI 48056

SEELIG, GERARD LEO, diversified company executive; b. Schluchtern, Germany, June 15, 1926; came to U.S., 1934, naturalized, 1943; s. Herman and Bella (Bach) S.; m. Lorraine Peters, June 28, 1953; children: Tina Lynn, Robert Mark and Carol Ann (twins). B.E.E., Ohio State U., 1948; M.S. in Indsl. Mgmt, N.Y. U., 1954. Registered profl. engr., Ohio. Electronics engr. Martin Corp., Balt., 1948-50; sr. engr. Fairchild Aircraft Co., Farmingdale, N.Y., 1950-54; program mgr. RCA, Moorestown, N.J., 1954-59, Van Nuys, Calif., 1959-61; div. mgr. Missile & Space Co. div. Lockheed Aircraft Corp., Van Nuys, 1961-63; v.p., gen. mgr. Lockheed Electronics Co. (Lockheed Electronics div.), Los Angeles, 1963-68; exec. v.p. Lockheed Electronics Co., Inc., Plainfield, N.J., 1968-69; pres. Lockheed Electronics Co., Inc., 1969-71; group exec., exec. asst. to office of pres. ITT, N.Y.C., 1971-72; corp. v.p. ITT, 1972-79, sr. v.p., 1979-81, exec. v.p., 1981-83; pres. Electronic and Instrumentation Sector; exec. v.p. Allied Corp., Morristown, N.J., 1983-87; cons. Lazard Freres and Ctr. Ptnrs., 1987—; disting. exec. lectr. Rutgers Grad. Sch. Mgmt.; exec.-in-residence, vis. prof. Columbia U. Grad. Sch. Bus. Served with AUS, 1944-46. Recipient Disting. Alumnus award Ohio State U., 1987. Fellow AIAA (assoc.); mem. IEEE (sr.). Office: Columbia U Grad Sch Bus Uris Hall New York NY 10027

SEELIG, MAURICE DONALD, planning, design and construction company executive; b. Ballston Spa, N.Y., Sept. 22, 1930; s. Russell L. and Emily (Davidson) S.; m. Joyce Boudreau, Aug. 30, 1958; children: Kimberley, Avis. BE in Indsl. Engring., Johns Hopkins U., 1954; MBA, Northeastern U., 1960. Engr. Standard Oil Co., Cleve., 1954-56; sr. indsl. engr., plant layout supr. Raytheon Co., Lowell, Mass., 1956-60; mgr. facilities programs Gen. Electric Co., Valley Forge, Pa., 1961-65; purchasing agt. J.I. Case Co., Racine, Wis., 1965-67; sr. cons. R. Muther & Assocs., Kansas City, Mo., 1967-71; corp. dir. facilities G.D. Searle Co., Skokie, Ill., 1972-76; mgr. facilities Massey-Ferguson Inc., Racine, 1976-79; chief indsl. engring. H.K. Ferguson Co., San Francisco, 1980-84; project dir. Morrison Knudson Internat., Hong Kong and China, 1984-85; dir. indsl. planning M.K. Ferguson Co., Cleve., 1986—. Lectr. adult edn. programs. Mem. Am. Inst. Indsl. Engrs. (sr. mem.), Internat. Materials Mgmt. Soc., Johns Hopkins Alumni Assn., Council of Logistics Mgmt. Episcopalian. Republican. Home: 21302 Meadows Edge Ln Strongsville OH 44136 Office: MK Ferguson Co 1 Erieview Pla Cleveland OH 44114

SEELY, ROBERT EUGENE, financial and management consultant; b. Bangor, Mich., Oct. 23, 1941; s. Leroy W. and Ruth A. (Hosier) S. Cert., A&M U., 1961; BBA, West Mich. U., 1969. Officer AM. Nat. Bank, Kalamazoo, 1969-74; v.p. fin. and mktg. Rapid Cut, Inc., Vicksburg, Mich., 1974-78; chief exec. officer Suthiff & Case, Inc., Peoria, Ill., 1978-81; chief oper. officer Allied Material Handing Co., Peoria, 1981-83; pres. S.E.R., Inc., Kalamazoo, 1983-86; pvt. practice fin. and mgmt. cons. Portage, Mich., 1986—; mem. adv. com. C & S Plastics, Climax, Mich., 1986-88; bd. dirs. Ventureprise, Inc., Kalamazoo. Served with U.S. Army, 1966-68, Vietnam. Recipient Cert. South Mich. Water Quality Commn., 1978, Cert. of Achievement Entrepreneurship Inst., 1983. Mem. Soc. Plastics Engrs., Nat. Assn. Corp. Dirs., Court Players Club, Masons, Elks. Home and Office: 9930 E Shore Dr Kalamazoo MI 49002

SEEMAN, BERNARD, author, editor; b. N.Y.C., Oct. 19, 1911; s. William J. and Lena (Kerner) S.; student pub. schs.; m. Geraldine Adele Micallef, Jan. 19, 1933. Freelance writer Ken mag., 1938-39; mil. writer, Far East specialist Friday mag., 1939-40; Latin Am. corr. Click mag., 1940-41; war corr. Far East Theatre, 1945 for Readers Scope, Internat. Digest; asso. editor Mag. Digest, also med. and sci. editor, Hillman Publs., 1946-54; exec. editor Internist Observer, Inc., 1958-76; exec. v.p. Sci. & Medicine Pub. Co., 1976-78; editor, spl. editorial cons. Science & Medicine Pub. Co., 1978-81. Spl. cons. on Japan OWI, 1944. Mem. Nat. Assn. Sci. Writers, Acad. Polit. Sci., Fedn. Am. Scientists, Nat. Acad. Rec. Arts and Scis., Authors League Am., Authors Guild, AAAS, Mus. Modern Art, Astron. Soc. Pacific, Leakey Found. Author: Enemy Japan, 1945; The River of Life, 1961 (winner Howard W. Blakeslee award Am. Heart Assn.); Man Against Pain, 1962; The Story of Electricity and Magnetism, 1962; (with Lawrence Salisbury) Cross-Currents in the Philippines, Inst. of Pacific Relations, 1946; (with Dr. Henry Dolger) How to Live with Diabetes, 1958, 5th edit., 1985; Your Sight, 1968. Office: 372 Central Park W New York NY 10025 Office: One Obtuse Rocks Rd Brookfield Center CT 06805

SEENEY, RUSSELL PAUL, computer company executive; b. Pitts., Sept. 27, 1948; s. Dalton Emory and Alice (Angelopolous) S.; m. Pamela Aiko Murashige, Sept. 25, 1976; 1 child, Nicole Naoye. BBA in Mgmt., U. Hawaii, 1973. Cert. data processor. Programmer U. Hawaii, Honolulu, 1971-73, NCR Corp., Honolulu, 1976-78; v.p. ops. Sequel Corp., Honolulu, 1973-76; v.p., software mgr. Century Computer Svcs., Honolulu, 1978-82; project mgr. Unitek Computer Svcs., Honolulu, 1982-84; pres. Pacific Bus. Svcs. Inc., Honolulu, 1984—; cons., lectr. in field. Contbr. articles to profl. jours. With U.S. Army, 1967-70. Recipient Appreciation award Waikiki Jaycees, 1980. Mem. Data Processing Mgmt. Assn. Democrat. Presbyterian. Office: Pacific Bus Svcs Inc 1100 Ward Ave Ste 1050 Honolulu HI 96814

SEETHALER, WILLIAM CHARLES, international business executive, consultant; b. N.Y.C., Dec. 4, 1937; s. William Charles and Catherine Frances (Flaherty) S.; student Quinnipiac Coll., Conn., 1955-56, Ohio State U., 1956-58; BS in Bus. Adminstrn., U. San Francisco, 1977; MBA, Pepperdine U., 1982. Asst. to v.p. sales T. Sendzimir, Inc., Waterbury, Conn. and Paris, 1960-66; mgr. internat. ops. Dempsey Indsl. Furnace Co., E. Longmeadow, Mass., 1966-67; mgr. internat. sales Yoder Co., Cleve., 1967-74; mng. dir., owner Seethaler & Assocs.; owner, chief exec. officer Seethaler Internat. Ltd., Palo Alto, Calif., 1974—; ptnr. DFS Computer Assocs., San Jose, Calif., 1976-87. Bd. dirs. Palo Alto Fund, 1979—, chmn., 1986—; mem. community adv. panel Stanford U., 1986—. Mem. Menlo Park C. of C., Palo Alto C. of C. (v.p. orgn. affairs 1976-77, pres. 1977-78, dir. 1975-79), Assn. Iron and Steel Engrs., Am. Inst. Indsl. Engrs. (sr. mem., v.p. profl. relations Peninsula chpt. 1988—), U. San Francisco Alumni Assn., Stanford U. Alumni Assn., Pepperdine U. Alumni Assn., Assn. MBA Execs., Am. Mgmt. Assn. Clubs: Stanford Buck, Stanford Cardinal Cage, Stanford Diamond. Office: 701 Welch Rd Ste 1119 Palo Alto CA 94304

SEFKO, JOHN ANTHONY, pharmaceutical company executive; b. Windber, Pa., May 7, 1948; s. John and Jennie (Semich) S.; m. Roseanne Rovansek, Apr. 28, 1973; children: Jonathan, Ryan, Julianne. BA in Edn., U. Pitts., 1970. Cert. med. rep. Sales rep. W.T. Grant Co., Johnstown, Pa., 1970-73, dept. mgr., 1973-74; dept. mgr. W.T. Grant Co., Cressona, Pa., 1974-75; sales rep. Del Boring Tire Service, Johnstown, 1975-76; ter. rep. Merrell Dow, Johnstown, 1976-84; div. mgr. Lakeside Pharmaceuticals, Allentown, Pa., 1984—. With U.S. Army, 1970-76. Roman Catholic. Office: Lakeside Pharmaceuticals 227 Burrell Blvd Allentown PA 18104

SEGAL, DAVID A., manufacturing company executive; b. N.Y.C., Aug. 21, 1939. BBA, CCNY, 1960; LLB, Columbia U., 1963. Bar: N.Y. State 1963. Pvt. practice N.Y.C., 1964-67; pres. Bryant Am. Corp., N.Y.C., 1967-84; chmn., chief exec. officer SFM Corp., N.Y.C., 1984—. Office: SFM Corp 870 Seventh Ave 27th Fl New York NY 10019

SEGAL, PHILIP RICHARD, finance company executive; b. Bklyn., June 9, 1949; s. Jacob L. and Vivian (Fain) S.; m. Carolyn Foster, June 3, 1972; children: Jessica, Edward. BA, SUNY, Buffalo, 1971; MLS, SUNY, 1974. CLU. Sales rep. Met. Life Ins. Co., Easton, Pa., 1977-82; fin. cons. Merrill Lynch, Allentown, Pa., 1982-87; regional v.p. Capstone Fin. Svcs., Houston, 1987—. Mem. Selective Svc. Bd., Bethlehem, Pa., 1986—. Mem. Nat. Assn. Life Underwriters and Chartered Fin. Cons. Home: 394 Yorkshire Dr Bethlehem PA 18017 Office: Capstone Fin Svcs 1100 Milam St Ste 3500 Houston TX 77002

SEGAL, STEPHEN MARTIN, advertising executive; b. N.Y.C., Mar. 22, 1938; s. Abraham and Elsie (Dinberg) S. AB, Cornell U., 1959; postgrad., Columbia U. Grad. Sch. Bus., 1959-60. Media research supr. Grey Advt., N.Y.C., 1962-65; v.p. bus. and media research Marschalk Co., N.Y.C., 1965-70; v.p. mktg. intelligence services McCann-Erickson, Inc., N.Y.C., 1970-74; mgr. mktg. services Lever Bros., N.Y.C., 1976-78; v.p. Tinker Campbell & Ewald, N.Y.C., 1978-80; v.p., dir. media planning Lowe-Marschalk, Inc., N.Y.C., 1980-84, sr. v.p., media dir., 1984, exec. v.p., media dir., 1985—, also bd. dirs., 1984—. Jewish. Office: Lowe-Marschalk Inc 1345 Ave of the Americas New York NY 10105

SEGALAS, HERCULES ANTHONY, investment banker; b. N.Y.C., Mar. 21, 1935; s. Anthony Spiros and Katherine A. (Michas) S.; m. Margaret Wharton, Sept. 18, 1956; children—Donnell Anthony, Stephen Wharton, Katherine Lacy. BS, Yale U., 1956. Various engring. and mfg. positions Procter & Gamble Co., Cin., 1956-65; pres. for Latin Am., mgr. Internat. Flavors and Fragrances, N.Y.C., 1965-68; exec. v.p., mem. bd. dirs. William D. Witter Inc., N.Y.C., 1969-76; sr. v.p. Drexel Burnham Lambert Inc., N.Y.C., 1976-87, mng. dir., 1987-88, also bd. dirs., 1976-88; mng. dir. head consumer products investment banking group Paine Webber Inc. Investment Banking Group, N.Y.C., 1988—. Bd. dirs. Nantucket Land Coun., Mass., 1982-85; mem. corp. Nantucket Cottage Hosp., 1984-85. Republican. Clubs: Morristown Field (N.J.); Nantucket Yacht (bd. govs. 1987—, mem. exec. com. 1988—). Home: 17 Hilltop Circle Morristown NJ 07960 Office: Paine Webber Inc 1285 Ave of the Americas New York NY 10019

SEGALL, MAURICE, retail company executive; b. Joliette, Que., Can., May 16, 1929; came to U.S., 1962; s. Jack and Adela (Segall) S.; m. Sarah Ostrovsky, Nov. 25, 1951; children: Elizabeth, Eric, Peter. B.Econs., McGill U., Montreal, Que., 1950; M.Econs., Columbia U., 1952; Hudson Bay Co. fellow, London Sch. Econs., 1953-54. Economist Canadian Fed. Govt., 1951-55; chief economist, dir. research planning and orgn. Steinbergs Ltd. of Montreal, 1955-62; dir. ops. treasury stores J.C. Penney Co., N.Y.C., 1962-70, dir. treasury stores, 1970-71; sr. v.p. Am. Express Co., N.Y.C., 1971, gen. mgr. credit card div., 1971-74; pres. Am. Express Co./Credit Card Div., N.Y.C., 1974-78; chmn., pres., chief exec. officer Zayre Corp., Framingham, Mass., 1978-89; chmn. TJX Cos., Inc., Natick, Mass., 1987-89; sr. lectr. MIT Sloan Sch., Cambridge, 1989—; chmn. TJX Cos., Inc.; bd. dirs. Shawmut Nat. Corp., AMR Corp., Gen. Cinema Corp.; Ames Dept. Stores, Inc. Trustee Mus. of Fine Arts, Boston, Mass. Gen. Hosp., Boston, Beth Israel Hosp., Boston. Mem. Mass. Bus. Roundtable (bd. dirs.). Office: TJX Cos Inc 1 Mercer Rd Natick MA 01760 also: Zayre Corp 770 Cochituate Rd Framingham MA 01701

SEGE, THOMAS DAVIS, electronics company executive; b. Novi Sad, Yugoslavia, May 17, 1926; came to U.S., 1941; m. Dorothea Zimmer; children—Kathy, Ron. B.S. in Elec. Engring., Columbia U., 1946, M.S. in Elec. Engring., 1948. With Sperry Gyroscope Co., N.Y.C., 1948-63, chief engr. Electron Tube div., until 1963; mgr. Power Grid Tube div. EIMAC, San Carlos, Calif., 1963-65, v.p. ops., 1965; v.p., gen. mgr. EIMAC div. Varian Assocs., Palo Alto, Calif., 1965-68, v.p. equipment group, 1968-71, pres. electron device group, 1971-81, pres., chief exec. officer, 1981-84, chmn. bd. dirs., chief exec. officer, 1984—; mem. adv. council SRI Internat., Menlo Park, Calif.; dir. Calif. Microwave. Patentee microwave output window, 1957, electron beam forming device, 1959. Campaign chmn. United Way Santa Clara County, 1983, chmn. policy com., 1984. Mem. IEEE (sr.), Santa Clara County Mfg. Group (bd. dirs. 1981-86). Home: Woodside CA Office: Varian Assocs Inc 611 Hansen Way Palo Alto CA 94303

SEGEL, J. NORMAN, garment manufacturing company executive; b. Toledo, Aug. 1, 1939; s. Sam S. and Dorothy (Gross) S.; B.B.A., Western Res. U., 1961; M.B.A., Adelphi U., 1980; m. Sheila Benkovitz, Jan. 14, 1961; children—Scott Jonathan, David Seth, and Hope Deborah. Accountant, Bobbie Brooks, Cleve., 1961-62; controller Stacy Ames, Long Island City, N.Y., 1962-65, dir. finance, 1965-66, sec.-treas., 1966-70, exec. asst. to pres., 1968-70; v.p. Fairfield-Noble, Inc., N.Y.C., 1970-77; treas. Levin & Hecht Inc., N.Y.C., 1977-79; v.p. fin. Parsons Place Apparel Co. Ltd., N.Y.C., 1979-89, dir., 1982-86; v.p. fin., sec.-treas. DLH Apparel Co. dba Diana Hartman; treas. Stephanie Queller Ltd., 1982-86. Mem. alumni admission bd. Case Western Res. U.; v.p., bd. dirs. Hewlett East Rockaway Jewish Center. Mem. Adminstrn. Mgmt. Soc., Nat. Assn. Accts., Am. Apparel Mfrs. Assn., Am. Arbitration Assn., Am. Assn. Corp. Controllers, Delta Sigma Pi, Sigma Alpha Mu, Alpha Phi Gamma. Home: 3447 5th St Oceanside NY 11572 Office: 500 Seventh Ave #3B New York NY 10018

SEGEL, JOSEPH M., broadcasting executive; b. Phila., Jan. 9, 1931; s. Albert M. and Fannie B. (Scribner) S.; m. Renee A., June 1, 1951 (div. 1960); children: Sandy, Marvin; m. Doris G. Greenstein Usem, Dec. 20, 1963; 1 child, Alan. BS in Econs., U. Pa., 1951. Chmn. Nat. Bus. Services, Inc., Phila., 1950-63; chmn., cons. Franklin Mint Corp., Franklin Center, Pa., 1963-85; chmn. Presdl. Airways Corp., Phila., 1975-79; chmn. Software Digest, Inc., Wynnewood, Pa., 1983-86, Nat. Software Testing Labs., Inc., Phila., 1984-86. Editor The Counselor mag., 1951-61. Chmn. UN Assn. U.S. Am., N.Y.C., 1973-75; mem. U.S. delegation UN Gen. Assembly, , 1974; chmn. QVC Network Inc., 1986—. Republican. Jewish. Club: LeMirador Country (Switzerland) (chmn. 1974—). Home: 1038 Raffles Ln Bryn Mawr PA 19010 Office: QVC Network Inc Goshen Park Westchester PA 19380

SEGELEON, RICHARD ROCKIE, manufacturing executive; b. Sewickley, Pa., Mar. 19, 1951; s. Vincent B. and Eleanor R. (Zappie) S.; m. Mary C. Segeleon, Jan. 23, 1971; children: Jason Richard, Patrick Kent, Catherine Ann. BS in Indsl. Systems, Ohio U., 1974; MBA, Rochester (N.Y.) Inst. Tech., 1978. Registered profl. engr., N.Y., Ohio, Ky. Indsl. engr. Eastman Kodak Co., Rochester, 1974-76, advanced indsl. engr., 1976-79; strategic tech. planning analyst Owens Corning Fiberglass Corp., Toledo, 1979-81, successively sr. sales rep., div. engr., mgr. competitive intelligence, mgr. mktg., 1981-86; v.p. sales and mktg. J.T. Nelson Co. Inc., Louisville, 1986—. Soccer coach Newark YMCA, Ohio, 1979-83; pres. North Elem. PTA, Newark, 1982-83. Republican. Roman Catholic. Office: JT Nelson Co 7647 National Turnpike Louisville KY 40214

SEGER, MARTHA ROMAYNE, government official, economist; b. Adrian, Mich., 1932. B.B.A., U. Mich., 1954, M.B.A., 1955, Ph.D., 1971. Began career in econs. dept. Gen. Motors Corp.; later with Fed. Res. Bank Chgo., 3 yrs.; economist Detroit Bank & Trust Co., from 1967; v.p. Bank of Commonwealth, Detroit, from 1974; adj. assoc. prof. bus. econs. U. Mich., 1978-79; commr. fin. instns. State of Mich., from 1980; mem. bd. govs. FRS, Washington. Office: FRS 20th & C Sts NW Washington DC 20551 *

SEGER, RONALD EARL, management consultant; b. Auburn, Maine, July 29, 1928; s. Guy Lee and Gladys Leona (Wile) S.; B.A., U. Maine, 1954; m. Eileen Sullivan, Sept. 2, 1950; children—Ronald Sullivan, Kathleen Marie. With Libby, McNeill & Libby, Chgo., 1954-69, asst. gen. sales mgr., 1965-67, dir. distbn., 1967-69; dir. distbn. Philip Morris, Inc., N.Y.C., 1969-70; dir. distbn. Chesebrough-Pond's, Inc., Greenwich, Conn., 1970-74, dir. corp. distbn., 1974-82; v.p., mgmt. cons. A. T. Kearney, Inc., Chgo., 1983—; past mem. bus. adv. council New Sch. Social Research; past mem. faculty U. Tenn. Exec. Devel. Program for Distbn. Mgrs.; mem. freight adv. bd. Am. Airlines; frequent lectr. assn. and univ. seminars on distbn. and bus. logistics. Mem. Republican Town Com., Wilton, Conn., 1981-83. Served with U.S. Army, 1947-49. Recipient Traffic Mgmt. Achievement award Traffic Mgmt. Mag., 1979. Mem. Nat. Council Phys. Distbn. Mgmt. (pres. 1981-82, chmn. 1982-83), Conn. Westchester Roundtable (founder, past pres.), Grocery Mfrs. Am. (mem. distbn. exec. com. 1980-82, chmn. customer service panel 1981—), Council Safe Transp. of Hazardous Materials. Roman Catholic. Contbr. articles to profl. jours.; editorial rev. bd. Internat. Jour. Phys. Distbn. and Materials Mgmt., 1982—, Jour. Bus. Logistics, 1982—. Recipient Coun. Logistics Mgmt. award for disting. contbns. Office: 875 3d Ave New York NY 10022

SEGIL, LARRAINE DIANE, materials company executive; b. Johannesburg, South Africa, July 15, 1948; came to U.S., 1974; d. Jack and Norma Estelle (Cohen) Wolfowitz; m. Clive Melwyn Segil, Mar. 9, 1969; 1 child, James Harris. BA, U. Witwatersrand, South Africa, 1967, BA with honours, 1969; JD, Southwestern U., Los Angeles, 1979; MBA, Pepperdine U., 1985. Bar: Calif. 1979, U.S. Supreme Ct. 1982. Cons. in internat. transactions, Los Angeles, 1976-79; atty. Long & Levit, Los Angeles, 1979-81; chmn., pres. Marina Credit Corp., Los Angeles, 1981-85; pres., chief exec. officer Electronic Space Products Internat., Los Angeles, 1985-87; mng. ptnr. The Lared Group, Los Angeles, 1987—. Bd. govs. Cedars Sinai Med. Ctr., Los Angeles, 1984—; bd. dirs. So. Calif. Tech. Execs. Network. Mem. ABA (chmn. internat. law com. young lawyers div. 1980-84), Internat. Assn. Young Lawyers (exec. council 1979—, council internat. law and practice 1983-84), Word Tech. Execs. Network (chmn.). Club: Regency (Los Angeles) (house com.). Avocations: piano, horseriding. Office: 1901 Avenue of the Stars Ste 280 Los Angeles CA 90067

SEGINSKI, WILLIAM ENOCH, sales company executive; b. Englewood, Colo., July 9, 1933; s. Ignatius Albert and Helen Veronica (Mescier) S.; BS in Metall. Engring., U. Ariz., 1960; m. Cora Creswell, July 12, 1957; children: Cynthia, Catherine, Joseph. Mechanic, Am. Airlines, 1956-57; nuclear design engr. GE, Richland, Wash., 1960-61; sales engr. Worthington Air Conditioning Corp., L.A., 1962; pres., owner J & B Sales Co., Phoenix, 1963—; vice chmn. Ariz. State Boiler Adv. Bd., 1977-82; lectr. solar energy. Mem. adv. bd. T-Roosevelt Coun. Boy Scout of Am., 1987-89. With USN, 1950-55. Mem. U. Ariz. Alumni Assn. (bd. dirs. 1972-73, pres. Phoenix chpt. 1971-72), Ariz. Elec. League (pres. solar div.), Ariz. Solar Energy Industries Assn. (bd. dirs., founding officer), NSPE (sr.), ASHRAE (bd. dirs. 1985-86), Am. Soc. Plumbing Engrs. (affiliate), Ariz. Plumbing Mfrs. Rep. Assn. (pres. 1982), Internat. Solar Energy Soc., U. Ariz. Alumni Assn. (pres. Dean's Assocs. 1981), Roosevelt Rough Riders (bd. dirs. 1986, pres.-elect 1986, pres. 1987), Sigma Gamma Epsilon (pres., founding mem.), Sigma Alpha Epsilon. Episcopalian. Clubs: Moon Valley Country, Arizona, Masons. Home: 7050 N 11th Ave Phoenix AZ 85021 Office: J & B Sales 3441 N 29th Ave Phoenix AZ 85017

SEGNAR, SAM F., banking company executive; b. Lonsdale, Ark., Sept. 16, 1927; s. Harry R. and Verda (Honeycutt) S.; m. Dixie Davidson (div. 1982); children: Sam F. Jr., Kathryn E.; m. Linda Foster, March 7, 1984. Student, Tex. A&M U., 1944-46; BSME, U. Okla., 1950; postgrad., U. Miss., 1954; AMP, Harvard U., 1967; LLD (hon.) U. Neb. With InterNorth, Inc., Omaha, 1961-76; pres., chief exec. officer, chmn. bd. InterNorth, Inc. (now Enron Corp.), Omaha and Houston, 1976-85; chmn. bd., Vista Chem. Co., Houston, 1986-88, chmn. bd., Collecting Bank, N.A., Houston, 1988—; adj. prof. Fordham U.; dir. Textron, Inc., Providence, R.I., Seagull Energy Corp., Houston, Hartmarx Corp., Houston, Gulf States Utilities Co., Chgo., Petrolane, Inc., Houston. Dir. exec. com. Boy Scouts Am.; dir. Carribean/Cen. Am. ACtion Com., Washington, Am. Air Power Heritage Found., Bishop Clarkson Meml. Hosp., Omaha, Booker T. Washington Found., Washington, Bus.-Higher Edn. Forum, Washington, Creighton U., Pres.'s Council for Internat. Youth Exchange, Washington; mem. Strategic Air Command Cons. Com., Washington, Am. Council for the Arts, Houston Econ. Devel. Council; pres. bd. John Cooper Sch., Woodlands Tex.; bd. trustees Tex. A&M U. Coll. Bus. Adminstrn. Mem. Inst. Biosci. and Tech., Corp. Council for Internat. Policy, Com. for Econ. Devel., Houston Area Rsch. Soc., The Ams. Soc., Nat. Alliance for Bus. (dir.), River Oaks Country Club, Ramada Club, Alexis Tocqueville Soc., KC (gov.). Home and Office: 9 Deerberry Ct The Woodlands TX 77380

SEHORN, MARSHALL ESTUS, music industry executive; songwriter; b. Concord, N.C., June 25, 1934; s. William Thomas and Bertha (Mesmer) S.; m. Barbara Ann Darcy, May 11, 1974. BS in Agr., N.C. State Coll., 1957; BA in Music, Belmont Coll., 1981, Coun. Devel. of French in La., 1983. Owner, operator comml. farm, Concord, 1957-58; producer, co-owner Fury/Fire Records, N.Y.C., 1958-63; producer EMI, London, 1963-64; pres., co-owner Marsaint/Sansu Enterprises, New Orleans, 1965—; sec., co-owner Sea-Saint Studio, New Orleans, 1972—; pres. Jefferson Jazz, New Orleans, 1980—; pres., owner Red Dog Express, Inc., 1985—. Producer: (recording) Kansas City (gold record 1959), 1959; co-producer: (recording) Lady Marmalade (gold record 1974), 1974; pub.: (song) Southern Nights (Broadcast Music, Inc. award 1977), 1977; exec. producer: (album) Elvis Live at La. Hayride, 1983. Presdl. appointee Civil Rights Com., Washington, 1961; mem. NAACP, New Orleans, 1965—; gov.'s appointee La. Music Commn., Baton Rouge, 1981—; presdl. appointee Anti-Piracy Commn., Washington, 1981-85. Named Record Man of Yr. Am. Record Mfg. and Distbrs. Assn., 1961, Producer of Yr., 1961; recipient Outstanding Svc. award Gov. of La., 1979, 82; Outstanding Music Contbn. award Mayor of New Orleans, 1982. Mem. Broadcast Music Inc., Am. Songwriters Assn. (cons., Merit award), Am. Fedn. Musicians, Recording Engrs. Assn., New Orleans C. of C., Ducks Unltd. (Slidell, La.). Republican. Methodist. Clubs: Bass Anglers Am. (New Orleans) (life). Avocations: boating, fishing, songwriting, hunting, art collecting. Home: 10136 Idlewood Pl River Ridge LA 70123 Office: Sea-Saint Recording Studio 3809 Clematis Ave New Orleans LA 70122

SEIBERT, DONALD CHARLES, venture capital investor; b. Montclair, N.J., Nov. 9, 1926; s. Walter Emil and Johanna Elsa (Franz) S.; children—Donald Charles Jr., Mary Johanna, Edward John. B.S. in E.E., MIT, 1948; M.B.A. in Indsl. Mgmt., U. Pa., 1951. Asst. head research and devel. Brown Div. M-H, Phila., 1951-53; govt. control coordinator RCA, Camden, N.J., 1953-54; import rep. AEG, Wilmington, Del., 1954-55; cons. Booz Allen & Hamilton, N.Y.C., 1955-56, Stevenson Jordan & Harrison, N.Y.C., 1956-59; v.p. eastern region Electronics Capital Corp., N.Y.C., 1960-63; mgr. venture capital investment Bessemer Securities Corp., N.Y.C., 1963-67; pres., chmn. Silicon Transistor Corp., Garden City, N.Y., 1967-68; owner, mgr. DCS Growth Fund, Old Greenwich, Conn., 1968—; mng. dir. Marine Mining Cornwall Ltd., Eng., 1965—; dir. Straight Line Filters Inc., Wilmington, Cleveland-St. Lawrence Fluorspar, Inc., Seibert Assocs., Wilmington, South County Vineyard S. Served with USAAF, 1946-47. Republican. Lutheran. Clubs: Mining, University, Racquet and Tennis, Innis Arden Golf (N.Y.C.). Home: 52 Arcadia Rd Old Greenwich CT 06870 Office: DCS Growth Fund PO Box 740 Old Greenwich CT 06870

SEIDEL, SELVYN, lawyer, legal educator; b. Longbranch, N.J., Nov. 6, 1942; s. Abraham and Anita (Stoller) S.; m. Deborah Lew, June 21, 1970; 1 child, Emily. B.A., U. Chgo., 1964; J.D., U. Calif.-Berkeley, 1967; Diploma in Law, Oxford U., 1968. Bar: N.Y. 1970, U.S. Dist. Ct. (so. and ea. dists.) N.Y. 1970, D.C. Ct. Appeals, 1982. Ptnr. Latham & Watkins, N.Y.C., 1984—; adj. prof. Sch. Law, NYU, 1974-85; instr. Practicing Law Inst., 1980-81, 84. Mem. ABA, New York County Bar Assn., N.Y.C. Bar Assn. (mem. fed. cts. com. 1982-85, internat. law com. 1989—), Boalt Hall Alumni Assn. (bd. dirs. 1980-82), Contbr. articles to profl. jurs. Club: Union League. Home: 110 Riverside Dr New York NY 10024 also: North St Lichfield CT 06759 Office: 885 3d Ave New York NY 10022

SEIDEN, HENRY (HANK SEIDEN), advertising executive; b. Bklyn., Sept. 6, 1928; s. Jack S. and Shirley (Berkowitz) S.; m. Helena Ruth Zaldin, Sept. 10, 1949; children: Laurie Ann, Matthew Ian. B.A., Bklyn. Coll., 1949; M.B.A., CCNY, 1954. Trainee Ben Sackheim Advt. Agy., 1949-51; nat. promotion mgr. N.Y. Post Corp., 1951-53; promotion mgr. Crowell-Collier Pub. Co., Inc., 1953-54; copy group head Batten, Barton, Durstine & Osborn, Inc., 1954-60; v.p., creative dir. Keyes, Madden & Jones, 1960-61; sr. v.p., assoc. creative dir. McCann-Marschalk, Inc., 1961-65, chmn. plans bd., 1964-65; creative dir., dir., prin. Hicks & Greist, Inc., N.Y.C., 1965—, sr. v.p., 1965-74, exec. v.p., 1974-83, chief operating officer, 1983—, pres., 1986—; chief exec. officer Ketchum/Hicks & Greist Inc., 1987-89; chmn., chief exec. officer Ketchum Advt., 1989—; Guest lectr. Bernard M. Baruch Sch. Bus. and Pub. Adminstrn., Coll. City N.Y., 1962—, Baruch Coll., CCNY, 1969—, New Sch. Social Scis., 1968, 72, 73, Sch. Visual Arts, 1979, 80—, Lehman Coll., CCNY, 1980—, Ohio U., 1981, Newhouse Grad. Sch., Syracuse U., 1981, NYU, 1983; cons. pub. relations and communication to mayor of New Rochelle, N.Y., 1959—, also; marketing dept. Ohio State U.; Cons. to pres. N.Y.C. City Council, 1972-73, to Postmaster Gen. U.S., 1972-74; communications adviser to Police Commr. N.Y.C., 1973—; bd. dirs. Transmedia Network Inc., 1988—, Cancer Research and Treatment Fund Inc., 1988—. Author: Advertising Pure and Simple, 1976; Contbg. editor: Madison Ave. mag, 1966—, Advt. Age, Mag. Age; guest columnist: N.Y. Times, 1972. Vice commr. Little League of New Rochelle.; Bd. dirs. Police Res. Assn. N.Y.C., 1973—, Cancer Research and Treatment Fund, Inc., Transmedia Network, Inc.; bd. dirs., exec. v.p. N.Y.'s Finest Found., 1975—. Recipient award Four Freedoms Found., 1959, award Printers Ink, 1960, promotion award Editor and Publisher, 1955, Am. TV Commls. Festival award, 1963-69, Effie award Am. Marketing Assn., 1969, 70, award Art Directors Club N.Y., 1963-70, award Am. Inst. Graphic Arts, 1963, Starch award, 1969; spl. award graphic art lodge B'nai B'rith Greater N.Y., 1971, 87. Mem. A.I.M. (asso.), Nat. Acad. TV Arts and Scis., Advt. Club N.Y. (exec. judge Andy awards, award 1963-65), Advt. Writers Assn. N.Y. (Gold Key award for best newspaper and mag. advts. 1962-64), Copy Club (co-chmn. awards com., Gold Key award for best TV comml. 1969), Alpha Phi Omega. Home: 1056 Fifth Ave New York NY 10028 Office: 220 E 42d St New York NY 10017

SEIDENFELD, GLENN KENNETH, JR., real estate developer, lawyer; b. Oceanport, N.J., Feb. 13, 1944; s. Glenn Kenneth and Mary Louise (Lawton) S.; m. Patricia O'Donnell, Sept. 1, 1974; 1 child, Glenn Kenneth III. B.S., Northwestern U., 1966; J.D., U. Ill., 1969. Atty.-advisor SEC, Washington, 1970-72; atty. McDermott, Will & Emery, Chgo., 1972-76; sec., gen. counsel Bally Mfg. Corp., Chgo., 1977—, v.p., sec., gen. counsel, 1981-85; cons., pres. Catalina West Corp., Tucson, 1985—; prin. The SWS Group. Contbr. articles to profl. jours. Mem. Am. Soc. Corp. Secs. (mem. securities law com. 1984-87), ABA, Chgo. Bar Assn. Home: 5010 Valley View Rd Tucson AZ 85719

SEIDL, JOHN MICHAEL, oil company executive; b. Milw., Mar. 24, 1939; s. Lawrence E. and Dorothy (Gilbert) S.; m. Madelyn S., July 7, 1962; children: Michele A., John D., Sarah C. BS, U.S. Mil. Acad., 1961; MBA, Harvard U., 1966, Ph.D., 1969. Commd. capt. U.S. Air Force, 1961-71; pres. Natomas N. Am., Houston, 1981-83; sr. v.p. Houston Natural Gas, 1984-85; exec. v.p. Enron Corp. (formerly HNG Internorth PL Co), Houston, 1985-86; pres., chief operating officer Enron Corp., Houston, 1986—; chmn. HNG Interstate P L Co, Houston, from 1985. Author: Politics American Style, 1972. Contbr. articles to profl. jours. Bd. dirs., trustee Houston Ballet Found., Alley Theatre, Soc. Performing Arts,

Houston Grand Opera, Houston YMCA, Tex. Nature Conservancy. Served to capt. USAF, 1961-71. Mem. Young Pres.' Orgn., Ind. Petroleum Assn. Am. Clubs: Ramada (Houston), Petroleum. Office: Kaisertech Ltd 300 Lakeside Dr Oakland CA 94643 *

SEIDMAN, L(EWIS) WILLIAM, federal agency administrator; b. Grand Rapids, Mich., Apr. 29, 1921; s. Frank E. and Esther (Lubetsky) S.; m. Sarah Berry, Mar. 3, 1944; children: Thomas, Tracy, Sarah, Carrie, Meg, Robin. A.B., Dartmouth Coll., 1943; LL.B., Harvard U., 1948; M.B.A., U. Mich., 1949. Bar: Mich. 1949, D.C. 1977. Spl. asst. fin. affairs to gov. of Mich. 1963-66; nat. mng. partner Seidman & Seidman C.P.A.s, N.Y.C., 1969-74; asst. for econ. affairs to Pres. Gerald R. Ford, 1974-77; dir. Phelps Dodge Corp., N.Y.C., 1977-82; vice chmn. Phelps Dodge Corp., 1980-82; dean Coll. Bus. Adminstrn. Ariz. State U., Tempe, 1982-85; chmn. FDIC, Washington, 1985—; chmn. Detroit Fed. Res. Bank Chgo., 1970; co-chmn. White House Conf. on Productivity, 1983—. Served to lt. USNR, 1942-46. Decorated Bronze Star. Mem. Am. Instn. C.P.A.s, Mich. Bar Assn., D.C. Bar Assn. Clubs: Chevy Chase (Md.); Univ. (N.Y.C. and Washington); Crystal Downs (Mich.). Home: 1694 31st St NW Washington DC 20007 Office: FDIC 550 17th St NW Washington DC 20429

SEIKEL, LEWIS ANDREW, III, tax accountant; b. Akron, Ohio, Oct. 2, 1958; s. Lewis Andrew Jr. and Kathleen Marie (McDonald) S.; m. Carolyn Rose Aylward, June 14, 1986. BS in Acctg., U. Akron, 1982, postgrad., 1989—. CPA. Fin. analyst MBank, The Woodlands, Tex., 1982-83; acct. Seikel, Koly & Co., Akron, 1984—. Trustee Cath. Youth Orgn. of Summit County, Akron, 1987-88, coach, 1982—. Mem. Am. Inst. CPA's, Ohio Soc. CPA's. Democrat. Roman Catholic. Home: 48 Mull Ave Akron OH 44313 Office: Seikel Koly & Co 1655 W Market St Ste 520 Akron OH 44313

SEIM, WILLIAM BURKE, retail photographic supply executive; b. Balt., Sept. 12, 1963; s. William Albert and Patricia Ann (Eldridge) S. BBA in Fin., Villanova (Pa.) U., 1985. Stockbroker First Jersey Securities, Falls Church, Va., 1985-86; salesperson Svc. Photo Supply Co., Balt., 1986—, v.p., 1988—; v.p. Towson Photo Supply Co., Balt., 1988—, Rotunda Photo Supply, Balt., 1988—. Mem. Am. Soc. Profl. Photographers. Republican. Roman Catholic. Office: Svc Photo Supply Co 3016 Greenmount Ave Baltimore MD 21218

SEIP, CHARLES FORD, financial planner; b. Jersey City, Sept. 19, 1938; s. Norman Winfield and Katherine (Ford) S.; m. Evelyn Watson, June 28, 1959; children: Cynthia, Charlotte, Charles, Edmund. Student, Broward Community Coll., 1976-82. CLU; chartered fin. cons.; cert. fin. planner. Life ins. salesman Franklin Life Ins. Co., Ft. Pierce, Fla., 1967-69; assoc. regional sales mgr. Franklin Life Ins. Co., Ft. Lauderdale, Fla., 1969-80; regional sales mgr. Beneficial Standard Life, Ft. Lauderdale, 1980-82; pres. Fin. Planning Cons., Inc., Plantation, Fla., 1982—. Contbr. articles to profl. jours. Mem. Inst. Cert. Fin. Planners, Nat. Assn. Enrolled Agts., Nat. Assn. Securities Dealers, Internat. Assn. Fin. Planners, Am. Soc. CLU's. Office: Fin Planning Cons Inc 7301 NW 4th St Ste 101 Plantation FL 33317

SEIPPEL, THOMAS J., insurance executive. Pres. Am. Internat. Group Data Ctr. Inc., N.Y.C., also bd. dirs.; v.p. Am. Internat. Group Inc., N.Y.C.; sr. v.p. Commerce and Industry Ins. Co., N.Y.C. Office: Am Internat Group Inc 70 Pine St New York NY 10270 *

SEITER, CARL WILLIAM, financial planner, investment counselor; b. Provo, Utah, Jan. 4, 1939; s. Walter Harry and Alice June (Facer) S.; m. Honalee Green, July 26, 1961; children: Christine, Shawn, David, Annalisa, Marcus. BA, U. Utah, 1966; PhD, Ohio State U., 1970. Cert. fin. planner. NSF trainee Columbus, Ohio, 1966-70; rsch. assoc. Dept. Biochemistry U. N.C., Chapel Hill, 1970-72; rsch. dir. Armour Pharm. Co., Phoenix, 1972-81; agt. Bankers Life and Casualty Co., Phoenix, 1981-82; owner, ptnr. Fin. Security Advisors, Phoenix, 1982-85; rep. Inland Securities Corp., Phoenix, 1985-87; account mgr. Acacia Group, Phoenix, 1987—. Recipient citation Money mag., 1987. Mem. Internat. Assn. for Fin. Planning (v.p. ethics Phoenix 1987—), Inst. Cert. Fin. Planners (pres. Greater Phoenix chpt. 1987-88), Kiwanis. Republican. Mormon. Home: 6601 E Pershing Rd Scottsdale AZ 85254 Office: Acacia Group 7310 N 16th St Ste 285 Phoenix AZ 85026

SEITZ, LAURA RUTH, graphic design company executive; b. Detroit, Nov. 29, 1951; d. John Calvin and Charlotte Mary (Collins) S. Student Western Mich. U., 1969-73, Los Angeles Mcpl. Art Galleries, 1975-78, UCLA, 1978. Sales coordinator Edward Bros., Ann Arbor, 1973-74; clothing designer, dressmaker, owner Moonshadow Designs, Ann Arbor and Los Angeles, 1974-77; sales coordinator Edwards Bros. Inc., Ann Arbor, 1973-74; sec. Maher Elen Advt., Los Angeles, 1976-79; account exec., 1979-80, account supr., 1980-81; sales mgr. Sojourn Design Group, Pico Rivera, Calif., 1981-82; dir. sales and mktg. John Anselmo Design Assocs., Santa Monica, Calif., 1982-83, owner O'Mara-Seitz Design Group, Santa Monica, 1983-87; mktg. cons., 1987-88; dir. account svcs. Scott Mednick and Assocs., L.A., 1988; freelance copywriting, lectr. Mem. task force NOW, 1977; mem. Olympics Steering Com., Muscular Dystrophy Assn., 1979; mem. Superwalk Steering Com., March of Dimes, 1981. Mem. NAFE, Los Angeles Ad Club, Internat. Assn. Bus. Communicators, Visual Artists Assn. (v.p. 1989—), Mktg. Assn. Calif. Office: 7412 Beverly Blvd Los Angeles CA 90036

SEITZ, THOMAS BING, communications company executive, aerospace engineer; b. Starkville, Miss., Apr. 5, 1941; s. Henry Morris and Mary Bernice (Kennedy) S.; m. Joyce Ann Gastineau, June 5, 1965; children—Bret, Melissa. B.S. in Aerospace Engring., Miss. State U., 1963; M.S. in Aerospace and Mech. Engring., Air Force Inst. Tech., Wright-Patterson AFB, Ohio, 1965; M. in Aerospace Ops. Mgmt., U. So. Calif., 1969. Project mgr. AT&T Long Lines, San Francisco, 1972-73, product mgr., N.Y.C., 1973-75, dist. engr. staff, San Francisco, 1975-77, dist. mktg. mgr., Los Angeles, 1977-79, div. sales mgr., 1982-84; div. mktg. mgr. Pacific Telephone Co., Los Angeles, 1979-82; sr. mgr. nat. accounts sales MCI Telecommunications, Los Angeles, 1985-87, dir. sales nat. accounts sales, 1987—. Chmn. fin. Eastern service area Los Angeles council Boy Scouts Am., 1983-84. Served to capt. USAF, 1963-69. Decorated Air Force Commendation medal. Mem. AIAA, Am. Legion, Amvets, Tau Beta Pi, Sigma Alpha Epsilon. Republican. Home: 131 Terraza Santa Elena La Habra CA 90631 Office: MCI Telecommunications 333 S Grand Ave Ste 440 Los Angeles CA 90071

SEITZINGER, HARRY OTIS, manufacturing company executive; b. Lawrenceville, Ill., May 13, 1928; s. Fay L. and Beulah E. (Bass) S.; m. Phyllis J. Daily, Feb. 12, 1950 (dec. Mar. 1981); 1 child, David; m. Josephine M. Post Gutscher, Dec. 19, 1981; children: Lorraine, Charles, Curtis, Christopher. BS in Acctg., U. Ill., 1951. Sr. acct. Servel, Inc., Evansville, Ind., 1951-54; mgr. mgmt. info. systems Ball Corp., Muncie, Ind., 1954-57; mgr. fin. analysis automotive assembly group Chrysler Corp., Detroit, 1957-66; v.p., controller, asst. treas. Diebold, Inc., Canton, Ohio, 1966—. Bd. dirs. United Way, Birmingham, Mich., 1964-65, Consumer Credit Assn. Stark County, Canton, 1977-81, Jr. Achievement Stark County, 1977-87. Served to sgt. U.S. Army, 1946-47, Korea. Mem. Fin. Execs. Inst. (com. on investment of employee benefit assets), Nat. Assn. of Accts., Planning Forum. Republican. Presbyterian. Club: Lake Cable Recreation Assn. (Canton). Lodge: Masons. Office: Diebold Inc PO Box 8230 Canton OH 44711

SEIVER, BENJAMIN CALEB, financial executive; b. Phila., Oct. 18, 1955; s. Lawrence M. and Alice M. Seiver. BA, Yale U., 1977; postgrad., U. Stockholm, 1977-79; MBA, U. Chgo., 1981. Assoc. McKinsey & Co., N.Y.C., 1981-84, Morgan Stanley, N.Y.C., 1984-85; asst. v.p. Am. Internat. Group Overseas Fin. (Europe), Inc., N.Y.C., 1985—. Fellow Union Oil Co., 1979, Am. Scandanavian Found. Mem. Fgn. Policy Assn. (speakers com.), The Down Town Assn., N.Y. Road Runners Club. Home: 40 W 87th Apt 2-A New York NY 10024 Office: Am Internat Group 70 Pine St New York NY 10270

SEKELY, GEORGE FRANK, computer and communications executive; b. Budapest, Hungary, Mar. 22, 1931; came to Can., 1956; s. Alfred and Vilma (Polak) Szekely; m. Veronique M. Dezseny, Apr. 23, 1955; children—Robert F., Sandra M. Diploma civil engring., Tech. U. of Budapest, 1953. Registered profl. engr., Ont., Can. Design engr. Dept. Constrn., Budapest, 1953-56; chief engr. A.M. Lount and Assocs., Toronto, Ont., Can., 1957-59; various mgmt. positions IBM Can., Toronto, 1959-64; mgr. systems engring. tech. programs IBM World Trade, N.Y.C., 1964-69; br. mgr. IBM Can., Montreal, Que., 1969-71; gen. mgr. C&S, Montreal, 1971-72; v.p. computers and communications Can. Pacific Limited, Toronto, 1972—; program chmn., sec. Can. Info. Processing Soc., Montreal, 1973-75. Contbr. articles to profl. jours. Home and sch. exec. PTA, Montreal, 1969-71; cub scout exec. Boy Scouts Can., Montreal, 1971-72. Mem. Assn. Profl. Engrs. of Ont., Assn. of Am. Railroads (exec. com., chmn. gen. com. data systems div. 1976-81). Club: Senneville Yacht (commodore 1978-80)(Montreal). Office: Can Pacific Ltd, 40 University Ave Ste 1200, Toronto, ON Canada M5J 1T1

SEKICH, KAREN S., collection agent; b. Longmont, Colo., June 12, 1944; d. Clarence Herbert and Pauline (Leinweber) Newman; m. Nicholas John Sekich Jr., July 7, 1962; children: Nicholas John III, Dominick Donald, Veronica June Herren. AA in Liberal Arts, Aims Jr. Coll., 1986; BBA, Regis Coll., 1988. Writer Phillips Mktg., Longmont, 1974-77; ptnr. Sekich Bus. Park, Longmont, 1974—; accounts receivable specialist Sekich Equipment Co., Longmont, 1977-82; mgr. Furrow Restaurant, Longmont, 1980-86; pres. mgr. Quest R&I Ltd., Longmont, 1981—; seminar leader, regional mgr. Sklar Fin. Control Corp., San Mateo, Calif., 1987-88; chmn. S.W. Weld Devel. Group, Longmont, 1988. Campaign coordinator Weld County Reps., Greeley, Colo., 1982; bd. dirs. St. Vrain Valley Sch. Dist., Boulder and Weld Counties, Colo., 1977-80, Olde Columbine Sch., Longmont, 1985—; candidate House Seat 49, Longmont, 1980. Mem. NFIB, Associated Collection Agys., Inc. (bd. dirs. Colo. and Wyo. chpts.), Platteville C. of C., Longmont C. of C. (bd. dirs.), Greeley C. of C., Carbon Valley C. of C., Ft. Lupton C. of C., Phi Beta Lamda (named bus. person of yr. 1984). Roman Catholic. Office: Quest R&I Ltd 4311 Hwy 66 Longmont CO 80501

SEKIGUCHI, TAIJI, engineer; b. Tokyo, Apr. 13, 1931; s. Toyozo and Hideko (Ichiba) S.; m. Midori Okura, Mar. 30, 1958; children: Atsuko, Seiichiro. B in Engring., Tokyo U., 1954. Chief platemaking Tosho Printing Co., Ltd., Numazu, Japan, 1959-64; chief of tech. devel. Tosho Printing Co., Ltd., Tokyo, 1964-70; mgr. system engring Sha-ken Co., Ltd., Tokyo, 1970-75, chief tech. coordinator, 1975—. Author (with others): The Japanese Character, 1985. Mem. Japanese Soc. Printing Sci. and Tech., Info. Processing Soc. Japan. Home: 7-33-2, Negishidai, Asaka, Saitama 351, Japan Office: Sha-ken Co Ltd, 2-26-13, Minamiotsuka, Toshima-ku, Tokyo 170, Japan

SELBERHERR, SIEGFRIED, microelectronics educator, researcher, consultant; b. Klosterneuburg, Austria; Aug. 3, 1955; s. Johannes and Josefine (Henninger) S.; m. Margit Leonhard, Oct. 12, 1979; children—Andreas, Julia. Dipl. Ing. Tech. U., Vienna, Austria, 1978, Dr. techn., 1981, venia docendi, 1984. Research assoc. Tech. U. Vienna, 1978-79, asst. prof. microelectronics, 1979-84, prof. computer-aided design, 1984-88, dean microelectronics, 1988—; cons. to bus. and industry. Author: Analysis and simulation of Semicondr. Devices, 1984. Editor: Jour. Transactions of the Soc. for Computer Simulation, 1983—, Jour. Electrosoft, 1986—, Jour. Mikroelektonik, 1988; book series Computational Microelectronics, 1985—. Contbr. articles to profl. jours. Recipient Dr. Ernst Fehrer award Tech. U. Vienna, 1983, Heinz Zemanek award, 1988, Dr. Herta Firnberg Fed. award. Mem. IEEE (sr.), Assn. Computing Machinery, Soc. Indsl. and Applied Math., Nachrichtentechnische Gesellschaft (award 1985). Home: Fasanstrasse 1, A 3430 Tulln Austria Office: Tech U Vienna, Gusshausstrasse 27-29, A 1040 Vienna Austria

SELBY, CECILY CANNAN, educator, scientist; b. London, Feb. 4, 1927; d. Keith and Catherine Anne Cannan; m. Henry M. Selby, Aug. 11, 1951 (div. 1979); children: Norman, William, Russell; m. James Stacy Coles, Feb. 21, 1981. A.B. cum laude, Radcliffe Coll., 1946; Ph.D. in Phys. Biology, MIT, 1950. Teaching asst. in biology MIT, 1948-49; adminstrv. head virus study sect. Sloan-Kettering Inst., N.Y.C., 1949-50; asst. mem. inst. Sloan-Kettering Inst., 1950-55; research assoc. Sloan-Kettering div. Cornell U. Med. Coll., N.Y.C., 1953-55; instr. microscopic anatomy Cornell U. Med. Coll., 1955-57; tchr. sci. Lenox Sch., N.Y.C., 1957-58; headmistress Lenox Sch., 1959-72; nat. exec. dir. Girl Scouts U.S.A., N.Y.C., 1972-75; mem. speakers program Edison Electric Inst., 1976-78; adv. com. Simmons Coll. Grad. Mgmt. Program, 1977-78; mem. Com. Corp. Support of Pvt. Univs., 1977-83; spl. asst. acad. planning N.C. Sch. Sci. and Math., 1979-80, dean acad. affairs, 1980-81, chmn. bd. advisors, 1981-84; cons. U.S. Dept. Commerce, 1976-77; dir. Avon Products Inc., RCA, NBC, Loehmanns Inc., Nat. Edn. Corp. pres. Am. Energy Ind., 1976; mem. nominating com. N.Y. Stock Exchange, 1988-90; co-chmn. commn. pre-coll. math. and sci. Nat. Sci. Bd., 1982-83; adj. prof. NYU, 1984-86, prof. sci. edn., 1986—. Contbr. articles to profl. jours., chpt. to book. Founder, chmn. N.Y. Ind. Schs. Opportunity Project, 1968-72; mem. invitational workshops Aspen Inst., 1973, 75, 77, 79; Trustee Mass. Inst. Tech., Bklyn. Law Sch., Radcliffe Coll., Woods Hole Oceanographic Instn., Women's Forum N.Y., N.Y. Hall of Sci., 1982—, vice chmn., 1989—; mem. Yale U. Peabody Mus. Adv. Council, 1981—. Mem. Headmistresses of East (hon. mem.; pres. 1970-72), Cutaneous Rsch. Soc., Nominating Com. N.Y. Stock Exchange, Cum Laude Soc. (past chpt. pres., dist. regent), Sigma Xi. Clubs: Cosmopolitan (N.Y.C.). Home: 45 Sutton Pl S New York NY 10022 Office: 933 Shimkin Hall 50 W 4th St New York NY 10003

SELBY, JUDY SANDERS, marketing professional; b. Butler, Pa., Jan. 26, 1938; d. Gerald Beckwith and Pauline (Sloan) Sanders; m. Elliott Hoelz Bechtel, Oct. 10, 1960 (div. 1977); children: Robin Sloan, Amy Susan; m. Frederic Litten Selby, Nov. 6, 1982. BA, Ohio Wesleyan U., 1959; MBA, U. Dayton, 1984. Dist. rep. Girl Scouts USA, Findlay, Ohio, 1959-60; real estate broker Easton, Conn., 1967-69; tennis instr. Little Rock, 1975-77; account exec. Sta. KARN Radio, Little Rock, 1977-79; dir. mktg. Human Performance Ctr., Little Rock, 1979-81; asst. dir. mktg. Grandview Hosp., Dayton, Ohio, 1981-84; dir. planning and mktg. Trident Regional Med. Ctr., Charleston, S.C., 1984—; substitute tchr. Easton Pub. Schs., 1963-69. Bd. dirs. Jr. League, 1965-80; cert. chair umpire U.S. Tennis Assn., 1980-85. Recipient Silver Addy, 1986. Mem. Soc. for Hosp. Planning and Mktg., Carolina Soc. for Hosp. Planning and Mktg. (bd. dirs. 1987—), Am. Hosp. Assn., Charleston C. of C. (mktg. com. 1986-88), Charleston Women's Network, Charleston Tennis Club. Episcopalian. Home: 977 Equestrian Dr Mount Pleasant SC 29464 Office: Trident Regional Med Ctr 9330 Medical Plaza Dr Charleston SC 29418

SELBY, MICHAEL DAVID, financial and business consultant; b. Rochester, N.Y., May 11, 1954; s. Bernard and Norine (Chatman) S.; m. Windrati Pramono, Nov. 15, 1977 (div. 1988); children: Jaclyn, Elizabeth. BA in Polit. Sci., George Washington U., 1973, MA in Internat. Relations, 1974. Mgr. internat. projects group Sci. Radio Systems, Rochester, 1974-76; fin. advisor ANTARA (Indonesian Nat. Press Agy.), Jakarta, Indonesia, 1977-82; mng. ptnr. Bus. Adv. Group, Jakarta, Singapore, Hongkong, Bangkok, Manila, Kuala Lumpur and L.A., 1983—; fin., project adv. to minister, Ministry Def., Jakarta, 1976-78; fin. advisor to v.p. of Indonesia, 1976-79, Directorate Gen. Tourism, Jakarta, 1976-80; advisor Directorate Gen. Domestic Monetary Affairs, Indonesia, 1980-85, Bangkok Bank, Ltd., 1987—, Ongco Singapore, 1987—; bd dirs. Airfast Indonesian Airlines, Internat. Capital Corp. Bank Ltd., Siam Citizens Leasing Ltd., Bangkok, Siam Motors Corp., Bangkok, Siam United Fund, Bangkok, Siam Elec. Parts, Bangkok. Author: Financial Development of the Indonesian Tobacco Industry, 1981; contbr. articles on credit analysis and debt. restructuring to profl. publs. Nat. Merit scholar, 1970. Mem. Am. C. of C., Young Pres. Orgn. Clubs: American (Jakarta); Royal Bangkok Sport. Office: Bus Adv Group, Kuningan Pla Ste 34, North Tower J1 HR Rasuna, Said C11-14, Jakarta Indonesia

SELIG, MARVIN, metal products company executive; b. 1923; married. Student, CCNY; B.S.M.E., U. Tex., 1946, Met.E., 1947. With Wiener Machinery Co., 1936-41, Arma Corp., 1941-43; with Structural Metals Inc. subs. Comml. Metals Co., Dallas, 1947—, founder, pres., chief exec. officer; exec. v.p., gen. mgr., now pres. steel group, mem. exec. com., dir. Comml. Metals Co., 1947—. Served with U.S. Maritime Service, 1943-46. Office: Comml Metals Co 7800 Stemmons Freeway Dallas TX 75247 *

SELIG, OURY LEVY, port financial consultant; b. Galveston, Tex., Sept. 24, 1924; s. Andrew Lionel and Freda (Schreiber) S.; m. Miriam Claire Pozmantier, Aug. 22, 1948; children: Michael, Debra, Madeline, James. BBA, U. Tex., 1949, postgrad., 1950; postgrad., U. Houston, 1953-56. Asst. bus. adminstr. of hosp. U. Tex. Med. Br., Galveston, 1952-54; acct. Port of Galveston, 1954-57, asst. auditor, 1957-64, asst. to gen. mgr., 1964-69, dir. fin. and adminstrn., 1966-74, dep. exec. dir., 1974-88. Life mem. Bay Area council Boy Scouts Am., Galveston, 1963—; bd. dirs. Galveston County Jewish Welfare Assn., 1982-84. Served as sgt. USAF, 1943-46. Recipient Nehemiah Gitelson award, Alpha Epsilon Pi, 1948, Silver Beaver award Boy Scouts Am., 1968, Shofar award, Boy Scouts Am., 1968, Disting. Service award, Galveston Jaycees, 1968. Mem. Am. Assn. Port Authorities (chmn. fin. com. 1972-76, chmn. risk mgmt. com. 1981-85, vice chmn. task force on tax reform 1985-86, Import Service award 1987) Tex. Water Conservation Assn. (pres. 1979-80), Galveston Hist. Found., Friars Club, Sierra Club. Democrat. Lodge: B'nai B'rith (pres. Tex. State Assn. 1960-61, local club 1958-59). Home and Office: 11 Colony Park Circle Galveston TX 77551

SELISTE, MARIE HELEN, financial executive; b. Bklyn., Oct. 27, 1946; d. Bruno Voldemar and Frances Ann (Castagna) S.; m. Frank Codispoti, Oct. 26, 1968 (div. 1982); m. Ralph J. Pisacrita, Nov. 26, 1988. Student DataPoint, N.Y.C., 1983. Auditing clk. Edward Thompson Co., St. Paul, 1964-68; full charge bookkeeper Arnessen Marine System, Bklyn., 1968-74; gen. mgr. Composite Films, N.Y.C., 1974-83; fin. comptroller Zaro Bake Shop, Bronx, N.Y., 1983-84; gen. mgr. A Cut Above Editorial, N.Y.C., 1984—. Bd. dirs. Marriage Encounter, Bklyn., 1974-77. Mem. Nat. Assn. Female Execs. Republican. Roman Catholic. Office: A Cut Above Editorial 17 E 45th St New York NY 10017

SELKIRK, RODERICK ALISTAIR, finance executive; b. Bristol, Eng., Feb. 13, 1957; came to U.S., 1986; s. Angus Sutherland and Rosina (Holmes) S.; m. Sarah Jane Bryant, Sept 19, 1986. BPharm, Nottingham (Eng.) U., 1978; MBA, London Bus. Sch., 1981. Pre-registration pharmacist Upjohn Ltd., Crawley, Eng., 1978-79; investment controller Investors in Industry plc dba 3i, Bristol, 1981-85, London, 1985-86; v.p. Investors in Industry plc dba 3i, Boston, 1986—. Office: 3i Capital 99 High St Ste 1530 Boston MA 02110

SELL, WILLIAM EDWARD, legal educator; b. Hanover, Pa., Jan. 1, 1923; s. Henry A. and Blanche M. (Newman) S.; m. Cordelia I. Fulton, Aug. 20, 1949; 1 son, Jeffrey Edward. AB, Washington and Jefferson Coll., 1944, LHD, 1973; JD, Yale U., 1947; LLD, Dickinson Sch. Law, 1968. Bar: D.C. 1951, Pa. 1952. Instr. law U. Pitts., 1947-49, asst. prof. law, 1949-51, assoc. prof. law, 1953-54, prof. law, 1954-77, assoc. dean, 1957-63, dean, 1966-77, disting. service prof. law, 1977—; sr. counsel firm Meyer, Unkovic & Scott, Pitts.; atty. U.S. Steel Corp., 1951-53; vis. prof. U. Mich. Law Sch., 1957; past pres. Pa. Bar Inst.; bd. dirs. Landmark Savs. Assn. Author: Fundamentals of Accounting Lawyers, 1960, Pennsylvania Business Corporations, 3 vols, 1969, Sell on Agency, 1975, also articles; editor: Pennsylvania Keystone Lawyers Desk Library. Past pres., bd. dirs. St. Clair Meml. Hosp. Served with USAAF, World War II. Mem. Am., Pa., Allegheny County bar assns., Assn. Am. Law Schs., Am. Law Inst., Univ. Club, Phi Beta Kappa, Order of Coif, Pi Delta Epsilon, Phi Gamma Delta, Phi Delta Phi, Omicron Delta Kappa. Presbyterian (elder, deacon). Home: 106 Seneca Dr Pittsburgh PA 15228 Office: U Pitts Sch Law 531 Law Bldg Pittsburgh PA 15260

SELLA, GEORGE JOHN, JR., chemical company executive; b. West New York, N.J., Sept. 29, 1928; s. George John and Angelina (Dominoni) S.; m. Janet May Auf-der Heide, May 14, 1955; children: George Caldwell, Jaime Ann, Lorie Jean, Michael Joseph, Carlie. B.S., Princeton U., 1950; M.B.A., Harvard U., 1952. With Am. Cyanamid Co., Wayne, N.J., 1954—; corp. v.p. Am. Cyanamid Co., 1977, sr. v.p., 1977-78, vice chmn., 1978-79, pres., 1979—, chief exec. officer, 1983—, chmn. bd., 1984—; bd. dirs. Pillsbury Co., Union Camp Corp., Equitable Life Assurance Soc. U.S. Bd. dirs. Multiple Sclerosis Soc.; mem. bus. adv. council Carnegie-Mellon U. Grad. Sch. Indsl. Adminstrn.; trustee Princeton U. Served with USAF, 1952-54. Mem. NAM (bd. dirs.), Soc. Chem. Industry (exec. com., chmn.), Pharm. Mfrs. Assn. (bd. dirs.), N.J. State C. of C. (bd. dirs.).

SELLERS, EMORY ROBINSON, banker; b. Pinehurst, N.C., Feb. 29, 1948; s. Emory Robinson Jr. and Minnebelle (Fry) S.; m. Janice Ruth Tudor, Aug. 12, 1972; children: Travis, John. BS, Va. Poly Inst. and State U., 1971; postgrad., Oklahoma City U., 1977. Mgmt. trainee Universal Tire Corp., Rockville, 1971; owner, mgr. Advanced Tire Corp., St. Louis, 1972; sales rep. Dun & Bradstreet, St. Louis, Oklahoma City, 1973-75; comml. lender 1st Nat. Bank Okalhoma City, 1976-78; asst. v.p., comml. lender S.E. Bank, N.A., Orlando, Fla., 1978-80, v.p., mgr. Hub Banking Ctr., 1980-83; sr. v.p., area mgr. S.E. Bank, N.A., Melbourne, Fla., 1983-85; sr. v.p., regional area mgr., regional loan adminstr. S.E. Bank, N.A., Orlando, 1985-89; regional area mgr. S.E. Bank, N.A., Tallahassee, 1989—. Bd. dirs. Jr. Achievement, Orlando, 1982-83, Crime, Inc., Orlando, 1985—; bd. dirs., treas. Community CoordinatedChild Care, Orlando, 1981-83; mem. found bd. Holmes Regional Hosp., Melbourne, 1984—, Fla. Hosp., Orlando, 1986—; exec. bd. Orlando Sci. Ctr. Mus., 1986—. Mem. Indsl. Devel. Commn., Fla. Bankers Assn., Orlando C. of C. (mem. Project 2000, 1985, chmn. Cen. Fla. Small. Bus. Conf. 1981). Republican. Episcopalian. Clubs: Interlachen (Winter Park, Fla.), Univ. (Orlando). Home: 1920 Chatsworth Way Tallahassee FL 32308

SELLERS, FRED STANTON, personnel consultant; b. Moline, Ill., July 10, 1950; s. Earl S. and Beverly J. (Schneider) S.; m. Peggy D. Murphy; children: Rochelle, Craig. BS in Sociology and Phys. Edn., Upper Iowa U., 1973. Lic. ins. agt., Nebr., Iowa. Salesman Earl's Water Conditioning, Davenport, Iowa, 1968-74; br. mgr. ITT Fin. Services, Mpls., 1974-80, regional dir., br. mgr., 1981-85; regional dir. Money Shop Fin., Rock Island, Ill., 1980; loan officer, asst. v.p. Bank Nebr., Omaha, 1985-86; personnel cons., v.p. Quest Personnel, Omaha, 1986—; pres. Cedar Rapids Lenders Exchange, Iowa, 1977-78. Trustee Valley View Bapt. Ch., Council Bluffs, Iowa, 1987-88. Named to Leaders Council, ITT Fin. Services, 1979, 80; named Profl. of Yr., Quest Personnel, Omaha, 1987, 88. Republican. Baptist. Home: 210 Brentwood Heights Council Bluffs IA 51503 Office: Quest Personnel 3020 N 102d St Omaha NE 68134

SELLERS, GREGORY JUDE, physicist; b. Far Rockaway, N.Y., June 20, 1947; s. Douglas L. and Rita R. (Dieringer) S.; m. Lucia S. Kim, Nov. 26, 1983; 1 child, Kristin Kim. A.B. in Physics, Cornell U., 1968, M.S., U. Ill., 1970, Ph.D., 1975. Sr. scientist B-K Dynamics, Inc., Rockville, Md., 1974-76; with Allied-Signal Corp., Morristown, N.J., 1976-88, applications physicist, 1977—, product supr. amphenol fiber optic product, 1985-88; mgr. Cinch Connectors, 1988—; bd. dirs. Thermo-Tek, Inc., Madison, N.J. Mem. AAAS, Am. Phys. Soc., IEEE. ESubspecialties: Fiber Optics; Polymers; Materials. Current work: Development and commercialization of electronic connectors and fiber optic products; development of applications for polymeric materials and glassy metals in the electrical and electronics arena. Co-inventor adhesive bonding metallic glass, electromagnetic shielding, testing of thermal insulation, amorphous antipilferage marker, amorphous spring-shield. Home: 7S 515 Oak Trails Dr Naperville IL 60540 Office: Amphenol Fiber Optic Products 1925 Ohio St Lisle IL 60532

SELLERS, HAYWOOD CONRAD, banker; b. Greenville, N.C., Sept. 29, 1927; s. Robert Earl and Annie (Andrews) S.; m. Anne Clarke, June 23, 1962; children: Mark Conrad, Joanne. BA, Wake Forest U., 1956; postgrad., Duke U., 1956-57. Mgr. Esso Standard Oil Co., Raleigh, N.C., 1957-58; account rep., agt. various cos., Raleigh, Charlotte, N.C., 1959-66; mgr. Advance Indsl. Security, Charlotte, 1966-67; v.p., trust officer First Union Nat. Bank, Charlotte, 1967-76, So. Nat. Bank, Charlotte, 1976-80, Piedmont Bank, Charlotte, 1980-84, 86; v.p. Hosp. Trust Co. Fla., Naples, 1985-86, Comerica Trust Co. Fla., Naples, 1987—; instr. Am. Inst. Banking, 1969-86. Adv. bd. Wake Forest U., East Carolina U., 1970-83. Served with USN, 1945, 1st lt. U.S. Army, 1949-53, Korea. Mem. Estate Planning Council, Naples C. of C., Mason, Oasis Shrine (dir. Charlotte staff 1976-82). Republican. Presbyterian. Home: 1907 Princess Ct Naples FL 33942 Office: Comerica Trust Co Fla 4501 Tamiami Trail N Naples FL 33940

SELLERS, MARK ALLEN, engineering geologist, hydrogeologist; b. Honolulu, Aug. 11, 1958; s. Walter R. and Jaynie L. (Mosley) S.; m. Kenna E. Marchbank, Aug. 23, 1980; children: Justin, Christopher. BS, Old Dominion U., 1980. Registered profl. geologist, Ga., S.C., N.C., Va. Engring. technician Law Engring. Inc., Virginia Beach, Va., 1980, staff geologist, engr., 1980-81; project geologist, engr. Law Engring. Inc., Chesapeake, Va., 1984, dept. mgr., hydrogeologist, 1984-86; project hydrogeologist Law Environ. Inc., Marietta, Ga., 1986; dept. mgr., hydrogeologist Law Environ. Inc., Kennesaw, Ga., 1986—; sr. engring. geologist Law Environ. Inc., 1987, prin. engring. geologist, 1987-88, program mgr., 1988. Author: (computer programs) OGWBAS, 1983, GEOSTAT, 1985; co-author: RCRATABS, 1987. Asst. scoutmaster Boy Scouts Am., Virginia Beach, 1975-78. Mem. Am. Soc. Testing and Materials (voting), Soc. Am. Mil. Engrs., Hazardous Materials Control Research Inst., Assn. Ground Water Scientists and Engrs. Republican. Methodist. Home: 4213 Machupe Dr Louisville KY 40241 Office: Law Environ Inc 9420 Bunsen Pkwy #106 Louisville KY 40220

SELLO, ALLEN RALPH, oil company executive; b. Winnipeg, Man., Can., June 22, 1939; m. Mary Lou Sello, June 3, 1972; children: Clint, Monique, Daren. B of Commerce (hon)., U. Man., 1963; MBA, U. Toronto, Ont., Can., 1964. Mgr. mktg. analysis Ford Motor Co. of Can., Oakville, Ont., Can., 1972-75, mgr. product plans, 1975-78, asst. treas., 1978-79; dir. acctg. Gulf Can. Ltd., Toronto, 1979-81, dir. fin. planning, 1981-82, contr., 1982-85; v.p., contr. Gulf Can. Corp., Calgary, Alta., Can., 1985-86; v.p. fin. Gulf Can. Resources, Ltd., Calgary, 1986-88, v.p. fin., chief fin. officer, 1988—; bd. dirs. Peace Pipeline Ltd., Calgary, Asamera Minerals, Inc., Whenantchee, Wash. Mem. Fin. Execs. Inst., Glencoe Club, Bow Valley Club. Office: Gulf Can Resources Ltd, 401 9th Ave SW, Calgary, AB Canada T2P 2H7

SELLS, BOAKE ANTHONY, retail company executive; b. Ft. Dodge, Iowa, June 24, 1937; s. Lyle M. and Louise (Gadd) S.; m. Marian S. Stephenson, June 20, 1959; children: Damian, Brian, Jean Ann. BSC, U. Iowa, 1959; MBA, Harvard U., 1969. Bus. office mgr. Northwestern Bell Telephone, Des Moines, 1959-63; salesman Hydraulic Cos., Ft. Dodge, Iowa, 1964-67; pres. Cole Nat. Corp., Cleve., 1969-83; vice chmn. Dayton Hudson Corp., Mpls., 1983-84, pres., 1984-87; chmn., pres., chief exec. officer Revco D.S., Inc., Twinsburg, Ohio, 1987—; bd. dirs. Holiday Corp., Ecolab Inc. Pub.-sector rep. to adv. bd. U.S. Olympic Com., 1989—. Mem. Am. Retail Fedn. (bd. dirs.), Nat. Assn. Chain Drug Stores, Inc. (bd. dirs.), Nat. Retail Mchts. Assn. (bd. dirs.). Home: 3105 Topping Ln Hunting Valley OH 44022 Office: Revco DS Inc 1925 Enterprise Pkwy Twinsburg OH 44087

SELLS, HAROLD ROBERT, petroleum and geothermal engineer; b. Effingham, Kans., June 26, 1917; s. William H. and Bertha E. (McPhilimy) S.; m. Alice Plunkett Starbuck, June 25, 1978; 1 child, Jo Jo Starbuck. B.S. in Petroleum Engring., Kans. U., 1940; M.B.A., Columbia U., 1953. Registered profl. engr., Tex. Petroleum engr. Kerr-McGee Corp., Oklahoma City, 1940-42, Sohio Petroleum Corp., Oklahoma City, 1947-50; instr. Kans. U., Lawrence, 1946-47; cons. engr. Amstutz & Yates, Wichita, Kans., 1950-51; petroleum engr. Rockefeller Bros., N.Y.C., 1953-59; pres. Sells Cons. Services, N.Y.C., 1959-79; geothermal engr. San Diego Gas & Electric, 1979-87; pres. Sells Cons. Service, Las Vegas, 1987—. Served to lt. comdr. USN, 1942-46. Bronfman fellow, 1952, 53. Mem. NSPE, Soc. Petroleum Engrs. (tech. editor; legion of honor), Am. Assn. Petroleum Geologists, Geothermal Resources Council, Tau Beta Pi, Sigma Tau, Beta Gamma Sigma, Kappa Sigma. Republican. Presbyterian. Lodges: Masons (32 deg.), Shriners, Elks. Home and Office: 5025 Pacific Grove Dr Las Vegas NV 89130

SELM, ROBERT PRICKETT, architectural engineer; b. Cin., Aug. 9, 1923; s. Frederick Oscar and Margery Marie (Prickett) S.; m. Rowena Imogene Brown, Nov. 25, 1945 (div. Jan. 1975); children: Rosalie C. Selm Pace, Linda R. Selm Partridge, Robert F., Michael E.; m. Janis Claire Broman, June 24, 1977. BSChemE, U. Cin., 1949. Enlisted U.S. Army, 1943; advanced through grades to sgt. U.S. Army, CBI Marianas, 1943-46; commd. capt. U.S. Army, 1949, resigned, 1954; design engr. Wilson & Co., Salina, Kans., 1954-67, gen. ptnr., 1967-81, sr. ptnr., 1981-89; ptnr. in charge Wilson Labs., Salina, Kans., 1956-88, chmn. bd. dirs.; ind. investor Salina, Kans., 1989—. Contbr. articles to profl. jours.; patentee in field. Mem. Gov.'s Adv. Commn. on Health and Environ. Named Engr. of Yr. Kans. Engring. Soc., Topeka, 1986. Fellow Am. Inst. Chem. Engrs.; mem. Am. Chem. Soc., NSPE (state chmn. environ. resource com., nat. legis. and govt. affairs com. 1988—), Am. Water Works Assn., Water Pollution Control Fedn., Am. Acad. Environ. Engrs. (diplomate), Petroleum Club, Salina Country Club (pres. 1986), Elks, Shriners. Republican. Episcopalian. Home: 135 Mt Barbara Rd Salina KS 67401 Office: Wilson & Co 631 E Crawford Salina KS 67402-1640

SELONICK, JAMES BENNETT, department store executive; b. N.Y.C., July 6, 1925; s. Stanley E. and Cecile R. (Rosenblum) S.; m. Peggy Frieder, Nov. 19, 1949; children: Ellen, James, William. AB, U. Cin., 1948, LLB, 1949. Bar: Ohio bar 1949, U.S. Dist. Ct. bar 1949. Asso. firm Harmon Colston, Goldsmith & Hoadley, 1949-52; asso. co. counsel, asst. mgr. real estate Federated Dept. Stores, Cin., 1952-61; exec. v.p. Simon Enterprises, Inc., Reston, Va., 1961-64; v.p. Simon Enterprises, Inc., 1964-65, exec. v.p., 1965-68; v.p. Mugar Group, Boston, 1968-70; v.p. property devel. Federated Dept. Stores, 1970-73, sr. v.p., 1973-87; pres. Federated Stores Realty, Inc., 1973-78, chmn. bd., chief exec. officer, 1978-83. Treas. Rockdale Temple, Cin., 1975-79, 1st v.p., 1981, pres., 1985-87; chmn. Cin. Historic Conservation Bd., 1980—. With USNR, 1943-46. Mem. Internat. Coun. Shopping Ctrs. (trustee), Urban Land Inst. (trustee 1983—), Losantiville Country Club. Home: 11 Corbin Dr Cincinnati OH 45208 Office: Federated Dept Stores Inc 7 W 7th St Cincinnati OH 45202

SELTZER, JEFFREY LLOYD, lawyer, investment banker; b. Bklyn., July 27, 1956; s. Bernard and Sue (Harris) S.; m. Ana Isabel Sifre, Aug. 24, 1985; 1 child, Ian Alexander. BS in Econs. cum laude, U. Pa., 1978; JD, Georgetown U., 1981. Bar: N.Y. 1982. Assoc. Austrian, Lance & Stewart, N.Y.C., 1981-85; assoc. gen. counsel, asst. v.p. Shearson Lehman Bros. Inc. (now Shearson Lehman Hutton Inc.), N.Y.C., 1986; sr. v.p. Shearson Lehman Hutton Inc., N.Y.C., 1986—. Author: The U.S. Greeting Card Market, 1977, Starting and Organizing a Business, 1984, Swap Risk Management: A Primer, 1988. Mem. nat. adv. council SBA, Washington, 1982-87; mem. small bus. adv. council Rep. Nat. Com., Washington, 1984—; advisor New Yorkers for Lew Lehrman, N.Y.C., 1981-82; policy analyst Reagan-Bush com., Arlington, Va., 1980. Named one of Outstanding Young Men Am., 1981, 87. Mem. ABA, Republican Nat. Lawyers Assn., Federalist Soc. Home: 45 W 60th St #21J New York NY 10023 Office: Shearson Lehman Hutton Inc Am Express Tower World Fin Ctr New York NY 10285-1200

SELVAGE, WILLIAM CARL, architect, real estate developer, consultant; b. East Orange, N.J., May 27, 1947; s. John Coe and Barbara (Stobeaus) S.; m. Margaret Ann Tsumagari, June 24, 1971; children: Christiana Ann, Patrick Coe. BArch, U. Utah, 1971. Registered architect. Prin., founder Wm. C. Selvage Architects, Salt Lake City, 1975-84; chief exec. officer, chmn. WCSA Architects, 1984-86; chmn., founder Salt Lake Land Acquisition, 1983-87; pres. Wm. C. Selvage, Inc., 1986—; mem. coun. Urban Land Inst., Washington, 1986—. Mem. Bus. Incentive Com., Salt Lake City, 1984—; chmn. Equip Sch. Community Coun., Salt Lake City, 1985—. Mem. AIA, Mortgage Banker Assn. (speaker), C. of C. (econ. devel. com. 1983—). Republican. Presbyterian. Office: Wm C Selvage Inc PO Box 6218 Salt Lake City UT 84106

SELZ, BERNARD, brokerage company executive; b. Paris, Feb. 7, 1940; s. Georges and Germaine Seiz; m. Barbara Reithoffer. BA, Columbia U., 1960. Security analyst Furman Seiz Siden & de Cuevas, N.Y.C., 1967-73, chmn., 1973—; chmn. Lazard Freres, 1960-67. Treas. Bklyn. Mus. Mem. N.Y. Soc. Security Analysts. Clubs: University (N.Y.C.); Tuxedo Park (N.Y.). Home: 1035 Fifth Ave New York NY 10028 Office: Furman Selz Mager Dietz & Birney Inc 230 Park Ave New York NY 10169

SELZNICK, STEPHEN ANDREW, computer software executive; b. N.Y.C.; s. Murray and Gertrude S.; m. Cynthia A.; children—Jonathan, Marc, Kimberly. BSEE, U. Miami (Fla.), 1963. Programmer, Boeing Corp., Huntsville, Ala., 1963-64; systems analyst Gen. Dynamics, Pomona, Calif., 1964-66, Walter V. Sterling, Inc., Claremont, Calif., 1966-69; dir. data processing Genge, Inc. (Systems Planning Corp.), Los Angeles, 1970-77; pres. Professional Software Applications, Inc., Los Angeles, 1977-86; v.p. PPS, Inc., 1986—, Los Angeles; instr. Calif. Poly. U., 1974-77.

SEMANS, TRUMAN THOMAS, investment company executive; b. Oct. 27, 1926; s. William Ritchie and Ann (Thomas) S.; A.B., Princeton U., 1949; postgrad. U. Va. Law Sch., 1950; m. Nellie Merrick, Dec. 14, 1961; children—Truman Thomas, William Merrick. Chmn. bd., pres. Robert Garrett & Sons, Balt., 1951-74; ptnr. Alex Brown & Sons, Balt., 1974—, mem. exec. com., 1979—, vice chmn. bd., 1987—; Trustee Md. Mus. and Hist. Soc., Balt., 1982—, v.p. bd., 1982—; trustee Chesapeake Bay Found., Annapolis, Md., Lawrenceville, (N.J.) Sch., Eaton Found.; mem. fin. com. Roman Catholic Archdiocese Md. Served with USN, 1944-46; PTO. Democrat. The Brook, Green Spring Valley Hunt, Hamilton St., Govs., Knights St. Gregory; Va. Hot Springs Golf and Tennis; Ivy (Princeton, N.J.). Office: Alex Brown & Sons 135 E Baltimore St Baltimore MD 21202

SEMEL, TERRY, motion picture company executive; b. N.Y.C., Feb. 24, 1943; s. Ben and Mildred (Wenig) S.; m. Jane Bovingdon, Aug. 24, 1977; 1 child, Eric Scott. BS in Acctg., L.I.U., 1964; postgrad. in market research, CCNY, 1966-67. Domestic sales mgr. C.B.S. Cinema Center Films, Studio City, Calif., 1970-72; v.p., gen. mgr. Walt Disney's Buena Vista, Burbank, Calif., 1972-75; pres. W.B. Distbn. Corp., Burbank, 1975-78; exec. v.p., chief operating officer Warner Bros., Inc., Burbank, 1979-80, now pres., chief operating officer, 1980—; bd. dirs. Revlon. Office: Warner Bros Inc 4000 Warner Blvd Burbank CA 91522

SEMELSBERGER, KENNETH J., household products company executive; b. 1936. BBA, Ohio State U., 1970; MBA, Cleve. State U., 1972. Product mgr. Holan Corp., 1954-66; mgr. sales and contracts Barts Corp., 1966-73; with Scott Fetzer Corp., Cleve., 1973—, v.p. mfg., 1974-75, div. pres., 1975-78, group v.p., 1978-83, sr. v.p. fin. adminstrn., 1983-86, pres., chief operating officer, 1986—. Served with AUS, 1959-62. Office: Scott Fetzer Co 28800 Clemens Rd Westlake OH 44145 •

SEMORE, MARY MARGIE, abstractor; b. Cowlington, Okla., Feb. 11, 1920; d. William Leonard and Bessie Mae (Bellah) Barnett; m. Jack Sanford Semore, Mar. 3, 1940 (dec. Jan. 1985). Grad. high sch., Wagoner, Okla., 1938. Legal sec. W.O. Rittenhouse, Wagoner, Okla., 1938-40; abstractor Wagoner County Abstract Co., 1941—. Mem. Title Industry Polit. Action Com., Washington, 1986; Wagoner Hist. Soc. Mem. Okla. Land Title Assn., Am. Land Title Assn., Wagoner C. of C., Daus. Am. Colonists, Am. Legion Women's Aux. Democrat. Methodist. Home: 902 S White Ave Wagoner OK 74467 Office: Wagoner County Abstract Co 219 E Cherokee PO Box 188 Wagoner OK 74477

SEMPLE, CECIL SNOWDON, retired manufacturing company executive; b. Assam, India, Aug. 12, 1917; came to U.S., 1927, naturalized, 1948; s. Fordyce B. and Anne (Munro) S. B.A., Colgate U., 1939. Buyer R.H. Macy & Co., 1939-42, 46-48; buyer, div. supt. Montgomery Ward, 1948-50; v.p. Nachman Corp., Chgo., 1950-55; sales mgr. radio receiver dept. Gen. Elec. Co., Bridgeport, Conn., 1955-60; mktg. cons. merchandising Gen. Elec. Co., N.Y.C., 1966-67, gen. mgr. audio products dept., 1967-68, dep. div. gen. mgr. housewares div., 1968-69, gen. mgr. housewares div., 1969, v.p., 1969-71, v.p. corp. customer relations, 1971-85; v.p. Rich's Inc., Atlanta, 1960-62, sr. v.p., dir., 1962-66; trustee Peoples Savs. Bank., Bridgeport. Bd. dirs. Nat. Jr. Achievement Inc., 1974-86, Bridgeport Area Found.; chmn. bd. dirs. Bridgeport Hosp.; vice chmn. bd. trustees Colgate U., 1978-84; trustee emeritus, past pres., bd. dirs. Alumni Corp. Served to maj. USAAF, 1942-46. Mem. St. Andrews Soc. State N.Y. (chmn. bd. mgrs. 1968-70), Delta Kappa Epsilon. Clubs: Brooklawn Country (Fairfield, Conn.), Fairfield Country. Home: 25 Cartright St Bridgeport CT 06604

SEMRAD, ROBERT, oil and gas company executive; b. 1926. BS, Tex. Tech U., 1950. Exec. v.p., tech. dir. Pan Am. Sulphur, 1965-72; with Duval Corp., 1972-84, gen. supt. Culberson Mine, 1972-74, resident mgr., 1974; with Pennzoil Co., Houston, 1984—, group v.p. sulphur, 1984—; pres., chief exec. officer Pennzoil Sulphur Co., Houston, 1985—. Office: Pennzoil Sulphur Co PO Box 2967 Houston TX 77252 •

SEMROD, T. JOSEPH, banker; b. Oklahoma City, Dec. 13, 1936; s. L.J. and Theda Jo (Hummel) S.; m. Janice Lee Wood, June 1, 1968 (div. 1988); children: Ronald, Catherine, Christopher, Elizabeth. B.A. in Polit. Sci., U. Okla., 1958, LL.B., 1963. Bar: Okla. 1963. With Liberty Nat. Bank, Oklahoma City, 1963-81; v.p. Liberty Nat. Bank, 1967-69, sr. v.p., 1969-71, exec. v.p., 1971-73, pres., 1973-81; pres. Liberty Nat. Corp., Oklahoma City, 1976-81; chmn. bd., pres., chief exec. officer United Jersey Banks, Princeton, N.J., 1981—; chmn. bd. dirs. United Jersey Bank, Hackensack, N.J., 1981—. Trustee, mem. exec. com. Nat. Urban League; bd. advs. Outward Bound Inc., 1984—, Ind. Coll. Fund of N.J., 1986—; bd. dirs. The Nature Conservancy, New Brunswick Cultural Ctr.; treas. Coalition in Support Edn.; commr. Citizens Commn. on AIDS, bd. dirs. internat. fin. conf.; chmn. bd. regents Stonier Grad. Sch. Banking, Rutgers U., 1983; mem. N.J. Transp. Trust Fund Authority, 1985-87; mem. The Partnership for N.J., chmn. edn. task force com., 1985—. 1st lt. U.S. Army, 1958-60. Mem. Am. Bankers Assn., N.J. Bankers Assn. (exec. com.), N.J. Bar Assn., Okla. Bar Assn., Assn. Res. City Bankers, (bd. dirs.), Regional Plan Assn. (bd. dirs.), Young Pres. Orgn., Am. Running and Fitness Assn. (dir. 1983-85), N.J. State C. of C. (bd. dirs.). Democrat. Roman Catholic. Clubs: Bedens Brook (Skillman, N.J.); River (N.Y.C.); Metedeconk (Jackson, N.J.). Office: United Jersey Bank 210 Main St Hackensack NJ 07602

SENECAL, EUGENE GERALD, retail executive; b. Holyoke, Mass., Aug. 19, 1943; s. Raymond Jean and Lottie Barbara (Nowalk) S.; m. Carol Ann Basile, May 3, 1969 (div. 1976); 1 child, Lisa Marie; m. Marie Theresa Doyle, Aug. 15, 1981. Programmer Aetna Ins. Co., Hartford, Conn., 1964; programmer, analyst Conn. Gen., Bloomfield, 1964-66; system-program mgr. Advo System, Hartford, 1966-70; cons. Keane Assocs., East Hartford, Conn., 1970-73; dir. mgmt. info. systems Ames Dept. Stores, Rocky Hill, Conn., 1973-78, asst. v.p., 1978-81, v.p., 1981-85, sr. v.p. MIS, 1985-88; pres. Nat. Store Systems, Dallas, 1988—. USAF, 1961-63. Mem. Assn. Systems Mgmt., Data Processing Mgmt. Assn., Internat. Mass. Retailing Assn. (mgmt. info. systems steering com. 1986-88), Am. Inst. Cert. Computer Profls. Republican. Roman Catholic. Home: 4632 De Grey Ln Plano TX 75093 Office: Nat Store Systems 3418 Midcourt Rd Ste 119 Carrollton TX 75006

SENEKER, STANLEY A., automobile manufacturing company executive; BS Santa Clara U., 1953, MBA, U. Pa., 1957. With Ford Motor Co., 1957—, mgr. investment & system analysis, 1963-65, regional fin. mgr. fin. staff, 1965-66, mgr. facilities & property dept., fin. staff, 1966-69, exec. v.p. Ford Land Devel., 1969-77, asst. treas., 1977-84, pres. fin. & ins. subs. Ford Motor Credit Co., 1984-86, corp. v.p. and treas., 1986-87, corp. exec. v.p. and chief fin. officer, 1987—. Served to 1st lt. U.S. Army, 1953-55. Office: Ford Motor Co The American Rd Dearborn MI 48121

SENGSTACK, DAVID KELLS, publisher; b. Bklyn., June 22, 1922; s. John Fred and Edna Josephine (Maloney) S.; m. Anita Elizabeth Browne, Aug. 12, 1944 (div. 1975); children: Jeffrey Scott, Lynn Ann, Gregg Clift; m. Alice H. Stolzberg, Sept. 30, 1988. BSME, Rutgers U., 1944. Mktg. dir. Birch Tree Group Ltd., Princeton, N.J., 1947-57, pres., 1957—. Trustee Bucknell U., Lewisburg, Pa., 1980-84, McCarter Ctr. for Performing Arts, Princeton, 1983-89; mem. vis. com. Eastman Sch. Music, Rochester, N.Y., 1984—. Served with U.S. Army Corps of Engrs., 1942-47, 50-52, Korea. Mem. Union League Club, Cliff Dwellers Club, Nassau Club, N.Y. Athletic Club. Office: Birch Tree Group Ltd 180 Alexander St Princeton NJ 08540

SENIOR, ENRIQUE FRANCISCO, investment banker; b. Havana, Cuba, Aug. 3, 1943; came to U.S., 1960; s. Frank and Dolores (Hernandez) Senior; m. Robin Suffern Gimbel, Sept. 7, 1977; children: Tailer, Heather, Fern, Seanna. B.A. in Architecture, Yale U., 1964, B.S. in Elec. Engring., 1967; M.B.A., Harvard U., 1969. Corp. fin. exec. White, Weld & Co., N.Y.C., 1969-73; v.p. Allen & Co., Inc., N.Y.C., 1973-80, mng. dir., 1980—; bd. dirs. Environ. Testing and Certification, Edison, N.J., PSO Delphi Corp., L.A., R-C Holding, Inc., Branchburg, N.J., Metcalf & Eddy Cos., Inc., Wakefield, Mass., Dick Clark Prodns, Inc., Burbank, Calif. Mem. Phi Beta Kappa, Tau Beta Pi. Clubs: The Brook (N.Y.C.); Piping Rock (Locust Valley, N.Y.). Office: Allen & Co Inc 711 Fifth Ave New York NY 10022

SENNETT, JOHN F., investment banker; b. Sheboygan, Wis., Dec. 6, 1949; s. Francis J. and Shirley E. Sennett; m. Nancy J. Sennett; children: Amy, Laura. B in Bus. Sci., U. Wis., 1972; MBA, De Paul U., 1979. Investment banker corp. fin. dept. Robert W. Baird & Co. Inc., Milw., 1979—. Pres. Milw. Mgmt. Support Orgn., 1988-90. Mem. U. Wis. Alumni Assn. (bd. dirs. 1984—). Home: 1206 E Fox Ln Fox Point WI 53217 Office: Robert W Baird Co Inc 777 E Wisconsin Ave Milwaukee WI 53202

SENSABAUGH, MARY ELIZABETH, financial consultant; b. Eastland, Tex., Aug. 15, 1939; d. Johnnie and L.G. (Tucker) Roberts; m. Dwight Lee Sensabaugh, Dec. 22, 1956; children: Robert Lee, Mark Jay. Student, Odessa Jr. Coll., 1959-63, North Tex. State U., 1963-67. Sr. acct. Braniff Internat. Airlines, Dallas, 1967-68; acct. Computer Bus. Services, Dallas, 1968-76; sec.-treas. Robert D. Carpenter, Inc., Dallas, 1972-76; controller Broadway Warehouses, Dallas, 1976-78; asst. controller S.W. Offset, Dallas, 1978-79; sec.-treas., cons. Carpenter, Carruth & Hover, Inc., Dallas, 1979—. Mem. Nat. Assn. Women in Constrn. (bd. dirs. Dallas chpt. 1983-84), Internat. Platform Assn., Beta Sigma (pres. Irving, Tex. chpt. 1973-74). Home: 702 Hughes Irving TX 75062 Office: Carpenter Carruth & Hover Inc 1210 River Bend Dr Ste 200 Dallas TX 75247

SENSEBE, RODNEY KARL, retail executive; b. New Orleans, July 23, 1960; s. Phillip Malcolm and Salvadora Mary (Sciortino) S.; m. Lauren Denise Smith, June 14, 1986. BSBA, U. New Orleans, 1985. Lic. real estate, La. Various positions Nat. Tea Co., Metairie, La., 1976-87, category mgr., buyer, 1987—; computer operator Imperial Trading Co., Metairie, La., 1980-81. Mem. Am. Mgmt. Assn. Home: 3743 Whitehall Dr Destrehan LA 70047 Office: Nat Tea Co 5110 Jefferson Hwy Harahan LA 70183

SENTER, ROGER CAMPBELL, hotel company executive; b. Manchester, N.H., Apr. 21, 1932; s. Kenneth Lee and Beatrice (Campbell) S. B.A., Boston U., 1954, LL.B., 1956. Mem. grad. student tng. program Westinghouse Co., Pitts., 1956-59; asst. mgr. recruiting Semi-Condr. div. Raytheon Co., Boston, 1959-61; founder McGovern, Senter & Assocs., Inc., Boston, 1961; v.p. McGovern, Senter & Assocs., Inc., 1961-65; dir. recruiting ITT World Hdqrs., N.Y.C., 1965-70; sr. v.p., dir. adminstrn. Sheraton Corp., Boston, 1970—; also dir. Sheraton Corp.; bd. dirs. Am. Hotel Found., Bay Tower Restaurants Inc. Bd. dirs. Mass. Mental Health Assn. Mem. Am. Hotel and Motel Assn., Hotel Sales Mgmt. Assn. (pres.), Nat. Assn. for Corp. and Profl. Recruiters (pres., dir.). Clubs: Algonquin, Corinthian Yacht (Marblehead, Mass.); Quechee (Vt.). Office: Sheraton Corp 60 State St Boston MA 02109

SENTER, WILLIAM JOSEPH, publishing company executive; b. N.Y.C., Dec. 4, 1921; s. Joseph and Sarah (Greenglass) S.; m. Irene Phoebe Marcus, Aug. 3, 1952; children: Adam Douglas, Caren Amy. B.B.A., CCNY, 1947. Chmn. bd., mng. editor Deadline Data, Inc., N.Y.C., 1962-66; pres. Unipub, Inc. (merged with Xerox Corp. 1971), N.Y.C., 1966-72; v.p. planning and devel. Xerox Info. Resources Group (includes AutEx Systems, R.R. Bowker Co., Ginn & Co., Univ. Microfilms Internat., Unipub Inc., Xerox Edn. Publs., Xerox Learning Systems, Xerox Computer Services), Greenwich, Conn., 1973-74; v.p. info. pub. Xerox Info. Resources Group, Greenwich, 1974-75; pres. Xerox Info. Resources Group, 1976-80, chmn., 1980-86; v.p. Xerox Corp., Stamford, Conn., 1978-86; pres. R.R. Bowker Co., N.Y.C., 1974-75. Served with U.S. Army, 1942-46. Mem. Assn. Am. Pubs. (dir. 1978-81), Info. Industry Assn. (dir. 1980-83). Office: Box 364 Cos Cob CT 06807

SENTURIA, TODD ALEXANDER, treasurer; b. Boston, Jan. 28, 1965; s. Stephen David and Alice Jean (Werlin) S.; m. Chindaree Prou, Sept. 28, 1985. AB magna cum laude, Harvard U., 1985. Mktg. analyst Micromet Instruments Inc., Cambridge, Mass., 1985-86, bus. mgr., 1986-88, v.p. ops., treas., 1988—; treas., bd. dirs. Alice Senturia Assocs., Boston. advisor, cons. Metro. Indochinese Children and Adolescent Services, Boston, 1982—. Mem. Smaller Bus. Assn. New Eng. Club: Harvard. Office: Micromet Instruments Inc 26 Landsdowne St Ste 150 Cambridge MA 02139

SEPLAKI, LES, economics educator, consultant; b. Budapest, Hungary, Aug. 14, 1947; came to U.S., 1956; s. Joseph and Elisabeth (Kun) S.; m. Barbara Jean Sproull, Dec. 20, 1968; children: Lesley, Julie, Christopher, Timothy. BA in Acctg. and Econs., Concordia U., 1962; MA in Econs. and Fin., McGill U., 1966; PhD in Econs., U. Calif., 1970; postdoctoral, U. Chgo., 1972-73, Harvard U., 1976-77. Prof. econs. Rutgers U., New Brunswick, N.J., 1973—; sr. cons. Econ. Cons. and Rsch. Systems Inc., N.Y.C., 1976—; vis. scholar antitrust Harvard U., 1985-86, health care and econs. Columbia U., 1988—; mem. adv. bd. nat. Ctr. for Air Traffic Safety; del. People's Republic of China. Mem. ABA (assoc.), Am. Fin. Assn., Regional Econ. Assn., Acad. Social and Polit. Scis., Am. Econ. Assn. GE Found. fellow U. Chgo., 1984, Harvard U. fellow, 1976-77. Home: 2505 Chestnut Ln Riverton NJ 08077 Office: 303 East Pan Am Bldg 200 Park Ave New York NY 10166

SERCHUK, IVAN, lawyer; b. N.Y.C., Oct. 13, 1935; s. Israel and Freda (Davis) S.; children: Camille, Bruce Mead, Vance Foster. BA, Columbia U., 1957, LLB, 1960. Bar: N.Y. 1961, U.S. Dist. Ct. (so. dist.) N.Y. 1963, U.S. Ct. Appeals (2d cir.) 1964, U.S. Tax Ct. 1966. Law clk. to judge U.S. Dist. Ct. (so. dist.) N.Y., 1961-63; assoc. Kaye, Scholer, Fierman, Hays & Handler, 1963-68; dep. supt., counsel N.Y. State Banking Dept., N.Y.C. and Albany, 1968-71; mem. Berle & Berle, 1972-73; spl. counsel N.Y. State Senate Banks Com., 1972; mem. Serchuk & Siwek, White Plains, N.Y., 1974; sr. ptnr. Serchuk & Zelermyer, White Plains, 1976—; lectr. Practising Law Inst., 1968-71; bd. dirs. United Orient Bank, N.Y.C. Mem. Assn. Bar City of N.Y., N.Y. State Bar Assn. Home: Mead St Waccabuc NY 10597 Office: 81 Main St White Plains NY 10601

SERNETT, RICHARD PATRICK, lawyer; b. Mason City, Iowa, Sept. 8, 1938; s. Edward Frank and Loretta M. (Cavanaugh) S.; m. Janet Ellen Ward, Apr. 20, 1963; children: Susan Ellen, Thomas Ward, Stephen Edward, Katherine Anne. BBA, U. Iowa, 1960, JD, 1963. Bar: Iowa 1963, Ill. 1965, U.S. Dist. Ct. (no. dist.) Ill. 1965, U.S. Supreme Ct. 1971. House counsel, asst. sec. Scott, Foresman & Co., Glenview, Ill., 1963-70; sec., legal officer Scott, Foresman & Co., Glenview, 1970-80; v.p., law sec. SFN Cos., Inc., Glenview, 1980-83, sr. v.p., sec., gen. counsel, 1983-85, exec. v.p., gen. counsel, 1985-87; pvt. practice Northbrook, Ill., 1988—; mem. U.S. Dept. State Adv. Panel on Internat. Copyright, 1972-75. Mem. ABA (chmn. copyright div. 1972-73, com. on copyright legislation 1967-68, 69-70, com. on copyright office affairs 1966-67, 79-81, com. on program for the revision of copyright law sect.; corp., banking and bus. law sect.), Ill. Bar Assn. (chmn. copyright com. 1971-72), Chgo. Bar Assn., Patent Law Assn. Chgo. (bd. mgrs. 1979-82, chmn. copyright law com. 1972-73, 77-78), Am. Patent Law Assn., Am. Judicature Soc., Copyright Soc. USA, Am. Soc. Corp. Secs., North Shore Country Club, Eagle Ridge Country Club. Democrat. Home: 2071 Glendale Ave Northbrook IL 60062 Office: 3420 W Dundee Rd Northbrook IL 60062-2257

SERRANO, RONALD MICHAEL, management consultant; b. Syracuse, N.Y., June 21, 1955; s. Arthur V. and Frances R. (Settineri) S.; m. Heather E. Parus, Sept. 19, 1981. BSE, U. Pa., 1977; MBA, Harvard U., 1981. Supr. constrn. Newport News (Va.) Shipbuilding, 1977-79; assoc. Strategic Planning Assocs., Washington, 1981-83, mgr., 1984, v.p., ptnr., 1985—. Mem. Harvard Bus. Sch. Club. Republican. Roman Catholic. Home: 3702 Huntington St NW Washington DC 20015 Office: Strategic Planning Assocs 2300 N St NW Washington DC 20037

SERSEN, HOWARD HARRY, interior design with cabinetry consultant; b. Chgo., Apr. 20, 1929; s. Harry S. and Bertha A. S.; B.F.A., Sch. Art Inst. Chgo., 1956; m. Judith Ann Nelson, Sept. 22, 1956; children—Mark Howard, Diane Lynn, Karen Judith, Amy Louise. Engaged in store planning, merchandising display and furniture design concepts Paul MacAlister and Assos., Lake Bluff, Ill., 1952-55, Silvestri Art, Chgo., 1955-56, Montgomery Ward & Co., Chgo., 1956-60, Riebold Co., Chgo., 1960-61, Sears, Roebuck & Co., Chgo., 1961-68; custom cabinet and kitchen design Reynolds Enterprises, Inc., River Grove, Ill., 1967-76; prin. Howard Sersen-Design, Park Ridge, Ill., 1976—; design and planning cons. for kitchens and related storage cabinetry for homes, offices; mfr., distbr. showrooms; visual merchandising display cons. to small retail stores. Art dir. Park Ridge Party, 1964. Served with U.S. Army, 1952-54. Recipient 1st place award Bicentennial Kitchen Design Contest, Wood-Mode Cabinets, 1975; Design award Wood Office Furniture Inst. Design Competition, 1952; award Design in Hardwoods Competition, 1958; cert. kitchen designer Council Cert. Kitchen Designers. Mem. Soc. Cert. Kitchen Designers (sec. Chgo.-Midwest chpt. 1974-75, bd. councillors 1977-81, gov. 1978-82, recipient Kitchen Design award 1972), Park Ridge Jaycees, Park Ridge C. of C. Clubs: Park Ridge Univ., Park Ridge Rotary, Masons, Order De Molay. Kitchen editor Qualified Remodeler mag.; contbr. articles to display, home improvement and kitchen mags.; custom cabinets and kitchen designs featured in several books, also Chgo. Tribune. Home and Office: 1608 S Courtland Ave Park Ridge IL 60068

SERVENTI, MICHAEL JAMES, food product executive; b. Butler, Pa., Nov. 4, 1950; s. Mark Lewis and Olive Charlotte (Hartman) S.; m. Gail Brennan Weir, Feb. 10, 1950; children: Jesse Devin, Michaela Brennan. BS, Ithaca Coll., 1972; MBA, Suffolk U., 1973. Ter. rep. Johnson & Johnson, Atlanta, 1973-74; sales rep., mktg. and sales dir., pres., chief exec. officer Lew-Mark Baking Co., Inc., Perry, N.Y., 1974—; chmn. State Gas & Oil Co., Inc., State Coll., Pa., 1986; bd. dirs. Wyo. County Bank, Warsaw, N.Y., Uni-Marts Inc. Rep. pvt. Industry Coun., Batavia, N.Y., 1986—; trustee United Ch. Warsaw, 1988; mem. exec. bd. Boy Scouts Am. Mem. Food Industry Execs. Coun., Biscuit & Cracker Mfrs. Assn., N.Y. State Food Mchts. Assn., Rotary. Presbyterian. Home: 158 W Buffalo St Warsaw NY 14569 Office: Lew-Mark Baking Co Inc 1 Lincoln Ave Perry NY 14530

SERVISON, ROGER THEODORE, investment executive; b. Columbus, Ohio, June 6, 1945; s. Theodore Calvin and Hilda Augusta (Longmack) S.; m. Kristin Landsteiner, Jan. 8, 1972. BA, U. Iowa, 1967; MBA, Harvard U., 1972. Chmn. Tax Man, Inc., Cambridge, Mass., 1970-72; v.p. Continental Investment Corp., Boston, 1972-75, Phoenix Investment Counsel, Boston, 1975-76; mng. dir. Fidelity Investments, Boston, 1976—; bd. dirs. Tax Man, Cambridge, Digital Techniques, Inc., Burlington, Mass., No-load Mutual Fund Assn., N.Y.C. Dir. First Night, Inc., Boston, 1985, Lena Park Community Devel. Corp., Boston, 1985. Mem. Longwood Cricket Club, Bay Club.

SERVODIDIO, PAT ANTHONY, broadcast executive; b. Yonkers, N.Y., Nov. 9, 1937; s. Pasquale and Catherine (Verdisco) S.; m. Ulla I. Schalien, May 4, 1968; children: Christian, Alexa. BS, Fordham U., 1959; postgrad., St. John's U., N.Y.C., 1960-63. Asst. to bus. mgr. Sta. WCBS-TV, N.Y.C., 1960-64; account exec. Sta. WTNH-TV, New Haven, 1964-66; account exec., N.Y. sales mgr. RKO TV Reps., N.Y.C., 1967-74; v.p., N.Y. sales mgr. Sta. WOR-TV, N.Y.C., 1974-79, v.p., gen. sales mgr., 1979-81; v.p., gen. mgr. Sta. WNAC-TV, Boston, 1981-82; pres. RKO TV, N.Y.C., 1982-87, RKO Gen., Inc., N.Y.C., 1987—. Mem. adv. council United Cerebral Palsy, N.Y.C., 1982—; bd. regents St. Peter's Coll., 1983—; mem. com. future financing Rutgers U., New Brunswick, N.Y., 1983-85. With U.S. Army, 1959-62. Mem. Internat. Radio and TV Found. (bd. dirs. 1983—). Office: RKO Gen Inc 1440 Broadway New York NY 10018

SERWATKA, WALTER DENNIS, publishing executive; b. Irvington, N.J., July 19, 1937; s. Walter F. and Grace R. (Sheehan) S.; m. Beverly M. Farrell, Aug. 10, 1963 (div. Feb. 1988); children—David, Nora, Nancy. B.B.A. in Acctg., Upsala U., 1959; M.B.A. in Fin., Fairleigh Dickinson U., 1966; postgrad. in bus., Harvard U., 1978, Columbia U., 1979, Stanford U., 1985. With treas.'s dept. WESTVACO, N.Y.C., 1964-68; dir. fin. analysis Random House Co., N.Y.C., 1968-72; with McGraw-Hill Info. Systems Co., 1972-83; controller Sweet's div. McGraw-Hill, Inc., N.Y.C., 1972-73, dir. profit planning, 1973-75, asst. controller, 1975-76, sr. v.p.-controller, 1976-79, group v.p. real estate info. services, 1979-83; exec. v.p. fin. and services McGraw-Hill Publs. Co., N.Y.C., 1983-84; sr. v.p. group mfg. and circulation services McGraw-Hill, Inc., N.Y.C., 1985, exec. v.p., chief fin. officer, 1985-88; pres. McGraw-Hill Info Svcs., N.Y.C., 1988—. Trustee Upsala Coll., East Orange, N.J. Served with U.S. Army, 1959-62. Mem. Fin. Exec. Inst., Mag. Pubs. Assn., Am. Inst. Accts., Planning Execs. Inst., Pvt. Sector Council. Office: McGraw-Hill Inc 1221 Ave of the Americas New York NY 10020 *

SESHADRI, RAJEEV, retail executive; b. Bombay, Apr. 3, 1951; s. Coimbatore Krishna Rao and Shakuntala (Badami) S.; m. Vindhya Rao, May 22, 1981. B in Tech., Indian Inst. Tech., Kanpur, India, 1972; MBA with distinction, U. Mich., 1983. Head engring. dept. Metal Box India, Ltd., Delhi, 1972-76; mech. engr. Pars Group, Teheran, Iran, 1976-80; prodn. engr. Monotype India, Ltd., Bangalore, India, 1980-81; research analyst K.A. Knapp & Co., Inc., Grand Rapids, Mich., 1983-86, pres., 1986, also bd. dirs., sr. v.p. corp. fin. and investment research, 1986; pres. Race Systems, Inc., Englewood, Colo., 1987-88, Topco Office Supply, Inc., Redwood City, Calif., 1988—. Mem. Fin. Mgmt. Assn., Beta Gamma Sigma. Hindu. Home: 8000 S Jasmine Circle Englewood CO 80112

SESLOWSKY, HARVEY MICHAEL, publishing company executive; b. N.Y.C., Apr. 25, 1942; s. Alan Seslowsky and Geraldine (Dworkin) Brescia; divorced; children: Edward, Wendy, Cheryl, Alan; m. Helen Walker, Aug. 2, 1986; 1 child, Amy Jane. Cert. TV prodn., NYU, 1960; BA in Radio-TV, CUNY, 1964. Acct. exec. ABC-TV, N.Y.C., 1964-66; program buyer, cons. TV Stations Inc., N.Y.C., 1966-70; v.p. Film Service Corp., N.Y.C., 1970-88; pres. Nat. Video Clearinghouse, Inc., Syosset, N.Y., 1972-88, Media Merchandising Corp., Syosset, N.Y., 1988—; chmn., pres. Media Assets Inc., 1988—; bd. dirs. Family Home Shopping Corp., N.Y.C., 1987—, Techknits, N.Y.C., 1987—. v.p. Tranquillity Alumni Inc., N.Y.C., 1987. Mem. Nat. Assn. TV Program Execs. Jewish. Home: 253 Berry Hill Rd Syosset NY 11791 Office: Media Merchandising Corp 100 Lafayette Dr Syosset NY 11791

SESSAMEN, DONALD WILLIAM, communications company executive; b. Whitpain Twp., Pa., Sept. 3, 1932; s. Guy Raymond and Sylvia Marion (Harlan) S.; m. Sandra Roberta MacFarland, Apr. 2, 1954 (div. Aug. 1972); children: Victoria Leigh, Deborah Reneé, Pamela Suzanne, Guy Raymond II; m. Alice Catherine Cusumano, Nov. 10, 1974. Student, Glassboro State U., 1964-65. Various positions-plant, engring., mktg. N.J. Bell Telephone Co., 1954-69; v.p., gen. mgr. Princeton (N.J.) Timesharing Services Inc., 1970-72; western region v.p. Telecommunications Systems of Am., Oklahoma City, 1973-75; cen. region ops. mgr. So. Pacific Communications Co., McLean, Va., 1975-79; nat. ops. mgr. So. Pacific Communications Co., Burlingame, Calif., 1979-80; v.p. ops. Sprint Communications, Burlingame, 1980-82, sr. v.p. planning and bus. devel., 1982-83; sr. v.p. ops. Allnet Communication Services Inc., Birmingham, Mich., 1983-88, exec. v.p., 1988-89; pres., chief operating officer FiberTel, Inc., Columbus, Ohio, 1989—; mem. telecommunications adv. bd. U. Colo., Boulder, 1981—. Chmn. Cape May (N.J.) County Young Republicans, 1965; pres. Stone Harbor (N.J.) Lions Club, 1966; bd. dirs. Am. Speech-Lang.-Hearing Assn., Palo Alto, Calif., 1982-84, Am. Social Health Assn. Served to sgt. major USNG. Republican. Methodist. Home: 5600 Knobby Hill Dr Highland MI 48031 Office: ALC Communications Corp 30300 Telegraph Rd Birmingham MI 48010

SESSLER, JERI DECARLO, technical and corporate researcher, consultant; b. Oak Park, Ill., Oct. 6, 1953; d. Michael A. and Esther (Galucci) DeCarlo; m. Nicholas Eugene Sessler, Dec. 3, 1977; children: Michael Joseph, Nicole Christina. Student Loyola U., 1972-75; BA in Anthropology, No. Ill. U., 1976; cert. emergency med. technician, Kishwaukee Coll., 1976; MBA Lake Forest Sch. Mgmt., 1989. Instr., fellow in anthropology No. Ill. U., 1973-76; emergency med. technician, paramedic Berz Ambulance Svc., Chgo., 1976-77; trade fair coordinator Schenkers Internat., Schiller Park, Ill., 1977-79; rsch. assoc. Staub Warmbold Co, Chgo., 1979-81; dir. rsch. A.T. Kearney Inc. Chgo., 1981-85, dir. rsch. svcs. div., 1985-88, mng. dir. rsch. svcs. group, 1988—; adult edn. instr. Moraine Valley Community Coll., Orland Park, Ill., 1982. Mem. Am. Network of Exec. Women (pres. 1980-83), Am. Chem. Soc., Planning Forum, Am. Soc. Tng. and Devel. Democrat. Roman Catholic. Home: 5167 Winona Ln Gurnee IL 60031 Office: A T Kearney Inc 222 S Riverside Pla Chicago IL 60606

SESTAK, JOE JOHN, gas company administrator; b. Prague, Okla., Apr. 4, 1942; s. Joe J. Sr. and Blanche (Fisher) S.; m. Mikeal Sue McGough, Aug. 21, 1965; children: Andrea Lynn, Michael John. BS in Engring., U. Okla., 1966, MS in Structural Engring., 1967. Design engr. Fluor Corp., Houston, 1967, M.W. Kellogg Co., Dallas, 1967-68; v.p. Trend Constrn. Corp., Oklahoma City, 1968-81, Beard Oil Co., Oklahoma City, 1981-88; mgr. engring. Sid Richardson Carbon & Gasoline Co., Ft. Worth, 1988—. Mem. ASCE, Gas Processors Assn., Natural Gas Men Okla. Republican. Mem. Christian Ch. (Disciples of Christ). Home: 3024 Bedford Rd #1120 Bedford TX 76021 Office: Sid Richardson Carbon & Gas Co 201 Main St Ste 3000 Fort Worth TX 76102

SESTINA, JOHN E., financial planner; b. Cleve., Mar. 17, 1942; s. John J. and Regina Sestina; B.S., U. Dayton, 1965; M.S. in Fin. Service, Am. Coll, 1982; m. Mary Barbara Jezek, Dec. 20, 1970; 1 dau., Alison. Cert. fin. planner, chartered fin. cons. With Sestina, Budros and Ruhlin, Inc., Columbus, Ohio, 1967—. Mem. Soc. Ind. Fin. Advisers (past pres., Fin. Planner of Yr. award 1982), Internat. Assn. Fin. Planners, Nat. Assn. Personal Fin. Advisors (pres.), Inst. Cert. Fin. Planners. Author: Complete Guide to Professional Incorporation, 1970; contbr. articles to profl. jours.; contbr. weekly fin. planning segment AM Columbus, WOSU-AM, 1979—. Office: 3726 Olentangy River Rd Columbus OH 43214

SETHNESS, CHARLES HENRY, JR., food company executive; b. Chgo., July 30, 1910; s. Charles Henry and Mabel Anna (Pehlke) S.; student U. Ill., 1928-31; m. Mary G. Buckley, Feb. 12, 1938; children—Mary B. Arnold, Charles B., Daniel B., Henry B. With Sethness Products Co., Chgo., 1931—, shipping clk., 1931-33, salesman, 1933-36, pres., 1936—; dir., sec.-treas. Sethness Products, Inc. (formerly Food Concentrates, Inc.), Woodbridge, N.J., 1965—; past dir. Chgo. Bank Commerce. Past trustee Latin Sch. Chgo.; past dir. Chgo. Maternity Center, 1500 Lake Shore Dr. Bldg. Corp. Mem. Phi Delta Theta. Clubs: Casino, Saddle and Cycle, Tavern; Capitol City, Piedmont Driving (Atlanta). Home: 1500 Lake Shore Dr Chicago IL 60610 Office: 2367 Logan Blvd Chicago IL 60647

SETHNESS, CHARLES OLIN, international finance executive; b. Evanston, Ill., Feb. 24, 1941; s. Charles Olin and Alison Louise (Burge) S.; 1 son, Peter Worcester; m. Geraldine Greene, June 25, 1977; stepchildren: John, Carla, Sarah Houseman. A.B., Princeton U., 1963; M.B.A. with high distinction (Baker scholar), Harvard U., 1966. Sr. credit analyst Am. Nat. Bank & Trust Co., Chgo., 1963-64; research asst. Harvard Bus. Sch., 1966-67; asso. Morgan Stanley & Co., N.Y.C., 1967-71; v.p. Morgan Stanley & Co., 1972, mng. dir., 1975-81; mgr. Morgan & Cie Internat., S.A., Paris, 1971-73; U.S. exec. dir. World Bank; spl. asst. to sec. treasury Washington, 1973-75; assoc. dean for external relations Harvard U. Bus. Sch., Boston, 1981-85; asst. sec. treasury for domestic fin. Dept. Treasury, Washington, 1985-88; dir. capital markets dept. Internat. Fin. Corp., 1988—. Home: 6219 Garnett Dr Chevy Chase MD 20815 Office: Internat Fin Corp 1818 H St NW Washington DC 20433

SETO, WILLIAM RODERICK, public accounting company executive; b. N.Y.C., July 2, 1954; s. James and Dorothy (Tsang) S. BS, U. Pa., 1976; JD, Cornell Law Sch., 1979. CPA. Bar: N.Y. 1980. Ptnr. Ernst & Whinney, N.Y.C.; lectr. in field. Mem. ABA, N.Y. Bar Assn., Am. Inst. CPA's, Internat. Fiscal Assn. Office: Ernst & Whinney 1800 Peachtree CtrS Tower 225 Peachtree St NE Atlanta GA 30303

SETSER, MARIE ELOISE, credit manager, financial programmer; b. Richmond, Calif., Sept. 25, 1943; d. Denver D. and Frances Marie (Daughtry) Newsom; m. Raymond H. Setser Jr., June 10, 1965; children: Raymond H. III, Kenneth Franklin. BS, U. Ky., 1965; Masters, Citadel Coll., 1978. Technician U. Ky. Sch. Medicine, Lexington, 1965; research asst. Med. U. S.C., Charleston, 1973-80, instr., 1980-82; registered rep. USPA/IRA, Charleston, 1982-84, Gales Ferry, Conn., 1984-86; dist. agt. USPA/IRA, Charleston, 1986—. Pres. Democratic Precinct, Charleston, 1976-77; active City of Charleston Commn. for Women, 1983-84. Mem. AAUW (state pres. 1978-80). Home: 5 Trail Hollow Dr Charleston SC 29414 Office: USPA/IRA 4280 Executive Pl Ste 206 Charleston SC 29405

SETZLER, ROBERT GASTON, oil company executive; b. Shiprock, N.Mex., Dec. 21, 1939; s. Robert Kenneth and Myrtle Lisle (Taylor) S.; m. Susan Darling Johnson, Jan 29, 1960; children: Robert Eric, Michael Kean. BS in Petroleum Engring., N.Mex. Inst. Mining & Tech., 1961. Div. engr. Texaco, Inc., West Tex., 1961-77; dist. mgr. J.M. Huber Corp., Midland, Tex., 1977-83; cons., chief exec. officer Robert Setzler & Assocs., Midland, 1983—; cons. in field. Mem. Midland Art Assembly, Midland Diabetes Assn., Casa de Amigos. Mem. ASPE, Am. Petroleun Inst. Republican. Episcopalian. Home: 4101 Dawn Cir Midland TX 79707 Office: Robert Setzler & Assocs PO Box 8771 Midland TX 79708-8771

SETZLER, WILLIAM EDWARD, chemical company executive; b. Bklyn., Dec. 20, 1926; s. William Edward and Gertrude A. (Seyer) S.; m. Dorothy C. Kress, Dec. 2, 1950; children: William John, Heather A. B of Chem. Engring., Cooper Union, 1950. V.p. ops. Argus Chem. Corp., N.Y.C., 1950-66; v.p. engring., then group v.p. Witco Chem. Corp., N.Y.C., 1966-75, exec. v.p., 1975—; also bd. dirs. Witco Chem. Corp. (now Witco Corp.), N.Y.C. Author and patentee in field. Served with USAAF, 1945-46. Mem. Am. Inst. Chem. Engrs., Soap and Detergent Assn. (bd. dirs.). Home: 3921 Lincoln St Seaford NY 11783 Office: Witco Corp 520 Madison Ave New York NY 10022 *

SEVERANCE, MICHAEL RADFORD, financial consultant; b. Seattle, Oct. 24, 1953; s. Radford Henry and Helen Ann (Gross) S.; married, Apr. 1, 1978; children: Jacob D., Adam T., Luke R. BS in Bus. Adminstrn., Ohio State U., 1976. CLU. Dealer, sales rep. UNOCAL, Mpls., 1976-79; equipment sales mgr. Convex Mktg. Corp., Mpls., 1979-81; pres. Severance and Assocs., Mpls., 1981—; instr. Am. Coll., Mpls., 1986. Mem. Am. Soc. CLU's and Chartered Fin. Cons., Inst. Cert. Fin. Planners, Nat. Assn. Life Underwriters, Minn. Assn. Life Underwriters, Twin Cities Soc. Inst. Cert. Fin. Planners (chartered). Office: Severance and Assocs 6800 France Ave S Ste 735 Edina MN 55435

SEVERINO, ELIZABETH FORREST, consulting company executive; b. Bryn Mawr, Pa., Dec. 29, 1945; d. John Joseph and Elizabeth (Patton) Girard-diCarlo; m. Joseph Domenic Severino, Oct. 20, 1973 (div. Oct. 1983); 1 child, Nicole Marie. AB, Vassar Coll., 1967; MS in Computer Sci., Syracuse U., 1969. Systems programmer IBM Corp., Poughkeepsie, N.Y., 1967-71; competitive analyst IBM Corp., Phila., 1977-79; systems analyst Fidelity Bank, Phila., 1971-72; mng. editor Auerbach Pubs., Phila., 1972-77; v.p. editorial and technology McGraw-Hill Pubs., Delran, N.J., 1979-81; v.p. Symcro Systems, Pennsauken, N.J., 1981-82; pres. The PC Group, Inc., Cherry Hill, N.J., 1982—, also bd. dirs.; bd. dirs. CompCar Leasing, Cherry Hill. Author over 125 articles on computers. Mem. Assn. of Personal Computers Cons. (bd. dirs. Phila. chpt., pres. 1987-88), Nat. Assn. Female Execs., Phila. Area Computer Soc. Republican. Episcopalian. Office: The PC Group Inc 1020 N Kings Hwy Ste 114 Cherry Hill NJ 08034

SEVERINSON, KENNETH J., athletic and electronic equipment manufacturing company executive. Chmn., chief exec. officer AMF Inc., White Plains, N.Y., 1985—, also dir.; pres. Minstar Inc., Mpls., also bd. dirs. Office: Minstar Inc 100 S 5th St Ste 2400 Minneapolis MN 55402

SEVERSON, ROGER ALLAN, bank executive; b. Thief River Falls, Minn., Sept. 2, 1932; s. Alfred Gerhard and Esther Olga (Landro) S.; m. Beverly Diane Hays, Aug. 30, 1953; children: Eric Hays, Holle Diane. BS, U. Minn., 1954. Group v.p. First Nat. Bank, Mpls., 1952-73; pres. FBS Fin., Inc., Mpls., 1974-77; exec. v.p. F&M Savs. Bank, Mpls., 1977-82; sr. v.p. First Nat. Bank, St. Paul, 1983-85; exec. v.p. Shelard Nat. Bank, Mpls., 1985-86, TCF Banking and Savs. FA, Mpls., 1986—; mem. Robert Morris Assocs., 1980—; trustee Heitman Mortgage Investors, Chgo., 1970-71, Mass. Mut. Mortgage Realty Investors, Springfield, 1972-85. Vice chmn. bd. of trustees The Am. Luth. Ch., Mpls., 1976-81; trustee Children's Health Ctr., Mpls., 1971-72; bd. dirs. Goodwill Industries, Mpls., 1967-70. Fellow Vesterheim Mus.; mem. Sons of Norway. Home: 11232 Mt Curve Rd Eden Prairie MN 55344 Office: TCF Fin Inc 801 Marquette Ave Minneapolis MN 55402

SEWARD, GEORGE CHESTER, lawyer; b. Omaha, Aug. 4, 1910; s. George Francis and Ada Leona (Rugh) S.; m. Carroll Frances McKay, Dec. 12, 1936; children: Gordon Day, Patricia McKay (Mrs. Dryden G. Liddle), James Pickett, Deborah Carroll (Mrs. R. Thomas Coleman). Grad., Louisville Male High Sch., 1929; BA, U. Va., 1933, LLB, 1936. Bar: Va. 1935, N.Y., Ky., D.C., U.S. Supreme Ct. With Shearman & Sterling, N.Y.C., 1936-53, Seward & Kissel, N.Y.C., 1953—; Mem. legal adv. com. N.Y. Stock Exchange, 1984-87; chmn. group on internat. capital markets Fedn. Internat. des Bourses de Veleurs-Internat. Fedn. Accts.-Internat. Bar Assn. Author: Basic Corporate Practice; Seward and Related Families; co-author: Model Business Corporation Act Annotated. Trustee Edwin Gould Found. for Children; mem. U. Va. Arts and Scis. Council. Fellow Am. Bar Found. (chmn. model corp. acts com. 1956-65); mem. Internat. Bar Assn. (founder, chmn. bus. law sect. 1969-74, hon. life pres. assn., also hon. life pres. sect.), ABA (chmn. sect. corp. banking bus. law 1958-59, chmn. sect. com. corp. laws 1952-58, chmn. sect. banking com. 1960-61, mem. ho. of dels. 1959-60, 63-74), Am. Law Inst. (mem. joint com. with Am. Bar Assn. on continuing legal edn. 1965-74), Knickerbocker Club, N.Y. Yacht Club, University Club, Met. Club, Bohemian CLub, Scarsdale Golf Club, Shelter Island Yacht CLub, Gardiner's Bay Country Club, Down Town Assn., Cum Laude Soc., Raven Soc., Order of Coif, Phi Beta Kappa Assos. (pres. 1969-75), Phi Beta Kappa, Theta Chi, Delta Sigma Rho. Home: 48 Greenacres Ave Scarsdale NY 10583 also: Ram Head Shelter Island NY 11964 Office: Seward & Kissel Wall St Pla New York NY 10005 also: 818 Connecticut Ave Washington DC 20006

SEWARD, JOHN EDWARD, JR., insurance company executive; b. Kirksville, Mo., June 12, 1943; s. John Edward and Ruth Carol (Connell) S.; B.S. in Fin., St. Joseph's Coll., 1968; children—Mitch, Justina. Mgr. acctg. services Guarantee Res. Life Ins. Co., Hammond, Ind., 1964-69; asst. controller Gambles Ins. Group, Mpls., 1969-71, N.Am. Cos., Chgo., 1971-73; pres., dir. mem. exec. com. Home & Auto. Ins. Co., Chgo., 1975-83; pres. and chief exec. officer, dir., mem. exec. com., chmn. of bd. Universal Fire & Casualty Ins. Co., 1983—; Park Lane Ins. Agy., Bd. dirs. Calumet Council Boy Scouts Am., 1979-85, Teddy Bear Club for Shriners Hosp., 1979-81, Chgo. Baseball Cancer Charities, 1981—. Mem. Munster C. of C., F.L.M.I., C.L.U., C.P.C.U. Home: 1124 Lisa Ln Schererville IN 46375 Office: 730 W 45th St Munster IN 46321

SEWARD, JOHN WESLEY, JR., management consultant; b. Port Chester, N.Y., Sept. 30, 1948; s. J. Wesley and Grace N. (Normand) S.; m. Mary Ann Grimes, Sept. 24, 1977; children: John Wesley III, Thomas Christopher, Madison Bridges. BS, U.S. Naval Acad., 1970; MBA, Emory U., 1983. Commd. ensign USN, 1970, advanced through grades to lt., 1973, resigned, 1978; engr. Systems Control, Inc., Palo Alto, Calif., 1977-79, Lockheed-Calif. Co., Burbank, 1979-81; mgmt. cons. Cresap, McCormick & Paget (now Cresap, a Towers Perrin Co.), Atlanta, 1983—. Mem. Am. Mgmt. Assn., Assn. MBA Execs.

SEWELL, BEVERLY JEAN, finanacial executive; b. Oklahoma City, July 10, 1942; d. Benjamin B. Bainbridge and Faith Marie (Mosier) Allision; m. Ralph Byron Sewell, Jan. 23, 1962; children: M. Timothy, Pamela J. Student, U. Okla., 1960-61, Jackson Community Coll., 1973-77; BA in Bus., Mesa Coll., 1982; cert., Coll. Fin. Planning, 1984. Sole practice fin. planning Grand Junction, Colo., 1985-87; fin. planner, broker Interpacific Investors Services, Grand Junction, 1987-88; investment broker A.G. Edwards & Sons, Inc., Grand Junction, 1988—. Alt. del. Rep. Party, Grand Junction, 1986, del., 1988, precinct capt., Grand Junction, 1988; commr. Grand Junction Planning Commn., 1987—. Mem. Inst. Cert. Fin. Planners, Internat. Assn. Fin. Planning. Home: 717 Wedge Dr Grand Junction CO 81506 Office: A G Edwards & Sons Inc 501 Main St Grand Junction CO 81501

SEWELL, GRAHAME TERENCE, financial executive; b. Sydney, N.S.W., Australia, Mar. 29, 1950; s. Horan Clifton and Joan (Eileen) S.; m. Jennifer Elizabeth Hall, Sept. 6, 1980; children: Anthony, Nicholas. Grad. pub. schs., Wimborne, Eng. Chartered acct. Acct. trainee Thornton Baker & Co., Bournemouth, Eng., 1968-72; audit sr. Arthur Young & Co., London, 1973-74; audit mgr. Ernst Whinney & Co., Brussels, 1975-77; controller AM Internat., The Netherlands, U.K., 1977-83; dir. fin. internat. Lotus Devel. Corp., Windsor, Eng., 1984—. Fellow Inst. Chartered Accts. in Eng. and Wales. Home: Little Felbrigg Farm Ln, East Horsley Surrey England Office: Lotus Devel Corp Consort House, Victoria St, Windsor Berkshire England

SEWELL, MICHAEL JAMES, accountant; b. Cin., Mar. 10, 1963; s. Robert E. and Ellen C. (Caldwell) S.; m. Monique Ann Napoli, June 11, 1988. BSBA, U. Dayton, 1985. CPA, Ohio. Asst. broker E.F. Hutton and Co., Dayton, Ohio, 1984; sr. acct. Deloitte, Haskins and Sells, Cin., 1985—. Advisor Jr. Achievement, Cin., 1986-87. Mem. Am. Inst. CPAs, Ohio Soc. CPAs, Delta Sigma Pi (dist. dir. 1986-88). Home: 5259 Londonderry Dr Cincinnati OH 45241 Office: Deloitte Haskins and Sells 250 E 5th St Cincinnati OH 45201

SEWELL, PHYLLIS SHAPIRO, retail chain executive; b. Cin., Dec. 26, 1930; d. Louis and Mollye (Mark) Shapiro; m. Martin Sewell, Apr. 5, 1959; 1 child, Charles Steven. B.S. in Econs. with honors, Wellesley Coll., 1952. With Federated Dept. Stores, Inc., Cin., 1952-88, research dir. store ops., 1961-65, sr. research dir., 1965-70, operating v.p., research, 1970-75, corp. v.p., 1975-79, sr. v.p., research and planning, 1979-88; dir., mem. exec. compensation com. and audit com. Lee Enterprises, Inc., Davenport, Iowa; dir., mem. nominating and exec. compensation coms. Huffy, Inc., Dayton, Ohio; bd. dirs. Pitney Bowes Inc. Bd. dirs. Nat. Cystic Fibrosis Found., Cin., 1963—; chmn. div. United Appeal, Cin., 1982; mem. bus. adv. council Sch. Bus. Adminstrn., Miami U., Oxford, Ohio, 1982-84; bd. trustees Cin. Community Chest, 1984—. Named One of 100 Top Corp. Women Bus. Week mag., 1976; named Career Woman of Achievement YWCA, 1983; recipient Alumnae Achievement award Wellesley Coll., 1979, Disting. Cin. Bus. and Profl. Woman award, 1981; named to Ohio Women's Hall of Fame, 1982. Office: Federated Dept Stores Inc 7 W 7th St Cincinnati OH 45202

SEWRIGHT, CHARLES WILLIAM, JR., banker; b. Great Lakes, Ill., Feb. 22, 1946; s. Charles William Sewright Sr. and Selma Joy (Nickerson) Kester; m. Bonnie Joyce Knight, July 2, 1967; children: Kimberly Ann, Traci Lynn, Megan Paige. BBA in Acctg., Calif. State U., Long Beach, 1969, MBA, 1974. Fin. analyst aeronautic div. Philco-Ford Corp., Newport Beach, Calif., 1969-73; sr. acctg. analyst Calif. Computer Products, Anaheim, 1973-74; product line controller McGaw Labs. div. Am. Hosp. Supply Corp., Irvine, Calif., 1974-75, div. acctg. mgr., 1975-76, fin. planning dir., 1976-80; v.p., controller critical care div. McGaw Park, Ill., 1980-85; v.p., controller EZ Painter Corp., Milw., 1985-86; v.p. dept. mgr. automotive fin. services secondary mkts. Marine Midland Bank, Buffalo, N.Y., 1986-87; pres., chief exec. officer Marine Midland Mortgage Corp., Buffalo, 1987—; Chair credit com. Am. Employees Fed. Credit Union, McGaw Park, Ill., 1980-85; vice chmn. Bd. Am. Employees Fed. Credit Union, 1981-85; speaker in field. Bd. dirs. Brotherhood North Shore Congregation Israel, Glencoe, Ill., 1980-81. Mem. Nat. Assn. Accts., Inst. of Cert. Mgmt. Accts. (cert.), Beta Gamma Sigma, Phi Kappa Phi. Office: Marine Midland Mortgage Corp One Marine Midland Ctr Buffalo NY 14203

SEXTON, DAVID FARRINGTON, lawyer, investment banking executive; b. Montclair, N.J., Aug. 20, 1943; s. Dorrance and Marjorie (McComb) S.; m. Ann Hemelright, Feb. 27, 1971; children: James, Ashley, Christopher. A.B. cum laude, Princeton U., 1966; J.D. cum laude, U. Pa., 1972. Bar: N.Y. 1972. Assoc. Sullivan & Cromwell, N.Y.C., 1972-77; with First Boston Corp., N.Y.C., 1977—; v.p., gen. counsel First Boston Corp., 1980-83, mng. dir., gen. counsel, 1983-86; mng. dir., pres. First Boston Internat. Ltd., 1986—; adj. prof. law Fordham U., 1985-86. Served to lt. USNR, 1966-69. Mem. ABA, Assn. Bar City N.Y. Republican. Presbyterian. Clubs: Links, Racquet and Tennis (N.Y.C.); Apawamis (Rye, N.Y.); Ivy (Princeton); Bucks Harbor Yacht (South Brooksville, Maine).

SEXTON, DONALD LEE, business administration educator; b. New Boston, Ohio, June 14, 1932; s. Benjamin Franklin and Virgie Marie (Jordan) S.; m. Levonne Bradley, June, 1954 (div. June 1964); 1 child, Rhonda Jane; m. Carol Ann Schwaller, Dec. 18, 1965; children: David Lee, Douglas Edward. BS in Math. and Physics, Wilmington Coll., 1959; MBA, Ohio State U., 1966, PhD in Mgmt., 1972. Indsl. engr. Detroit Steel Corp., Portsmouth, Ohio, 1959-61; sr. research engr. Rockwell Internat., Columbus,

Ohio, 1961-68; v.p. merchandising R.G. Barry Corp., Columbus, 1968-74; v.p., gen. mgr. Henri Fayette, Inc., Chgo., 1976; gen. mgr. M.H. Mfg. Co., Jackson, Miss., 1976-77; assoc. prof. Sangamon State U., Springfield, Ill., 1977-79; Caruth prof. entrepreneurship Baylor U., Waco, Tex., 1979-86; Davis prof. free enterprise Ohio State U., Columbus, 1986—; mem. adv. bd. SBA, Columbus, 1986—; research adv. bd. U. So. Calif., Los Angeles, 1986—; bd. dirs. Bus. Horizons, Inc., Columbus. Co-author: Entrepreneurship Education, 1981, Experiences in Small Business, 1982, Starting A Business in Texas, 1983; co-editor: Encylopedia of Entrepreneurship, 1981, Art and Science of Entrepreneurship, 1986. Served to staff sgt. USAF, 1951-55. Recipient Leavy Free Enterprise award, Freedom Found., Valley Forge, Pa., 1985, Cert. Appreciation SBA, Washington, 1984, 85; named Advocate of Yr.-Innovation SBA, Dallas, 1982, 83, 84. Mem. Internat. Council for Small Bus. (sr. v.p. 1986), U.S. Assn. for Small Bus. (v.p. pub. relations 1987), Acad. Mgmt. (chmn. entrepreneurship com. 1981, adv. bd. 1984-85), Alpha Tau Omega. Republican. Baptist. Lodges: Masons, Shriners. Home: 5466 Eaglesnest Dr Westerville OH 43081 Office: Ohio State U 1775 College Rd Columbus OH 43210

SEXTON, RICHARD, lawyer, diversified manufacturing company executive; b. Madison, Wis., 1929; s. Joseph Cantwell and Eleanor Carr (Kenny) S.; m. Joan Fleming, 1957; children: Molly, Joseph, Lucy, Michael, Ann, Katherine. Student, Amherst Coll., 1947-49; B.S., U. Wis., 1951; LL.B., Yale U., 1958. Bar: N.Y. 1959, U.S. Supreme Ct. 1968. Assoc. firm Sullivan & Cromwell, N.Y.C., 1958-64; with SCM Corp., N.Y.C., 1964-86; asst. counsel SCM Corp., 1964-67, div. gen. counsel Smith-Corona Marchant div., 1967-72, v.p., gen. counsel parent co., 1972-86, sec., 1977-86. Served to lt. (j.g.) USNR, 1951-55. Mem. Assn. Bar City N.Y., ABA, BNA Antitrust Adv. Bd. Club: Yale. Home: 532 3d St Brooklyn NY 11215 Office: 230 Park Ave Ste 1635 New York NY 10169

SEYMOUR, DALE JOSEPH, insurance company executive; b. Toledo, Mar. 2, 1947; s. Robert A. Sr. and Jane E. (Root) S.; m. Phyllis Jean Brimmer, Nov. 29, 1949; children: Michelle Lynn, Brett Joseph, Marc Allan. CLU; chartered fin. cons. Agt. Columbus Mutual Ins. Co., Toledo, 1968-80; gen. agt. Mass. Mutual Life Ins. Co., Toledo, 1980—; pres. SeaGate Benefit Adminstrs., Inc., Toledo, 1982—, Seymour & Assocs. The Fin. Designs Group, Toledo, 1983—; v.p. SeaGate Ins. Agy., Toledo, 1983—. Mem. Toledo Cen. Bd. Edn., 1986—. Mem. Million Dollar Round Table, Toledo Club, Toastmasters. Home: 2401 Wealdstone Toledo OH 43617 Office: 3930 Sunforest Ct Ste 200 Toledo OH 43623

SEYMOUR, HARLAN FRANCIS, computer services company executive; b. East St. Louis, Jan. 25, 1950; s. Harlan Edward and Agnes Wilhelmina (Noakes) S.; m. Ellen Katheleen Schmitt, Aug. 17, 1973; children: Melissa Ann, Harlan Francis Jr. BA in Math., U. Mo., 1973; MBA, Keller Grad. Sch. Mgmt., 1980. Corp. v.p. Statis. Tabulating Corp., Chgo., 1973-80; dist. mgr. Datacorp, Chgo., 1980-83; sr. v.p. First Fin. Mgmt. Corp., Atlanta, 1983—; Mem. mgmt. info. systems adv. bd. U. Ga., Athens, 1986, 87. V.p. St. Joseph's Home and Sch., Marietta, Ga., 1987—. Mem. Nat. Assn. Bank Servicers, Bank Mktg. Assn., Fin. Mgrs. Soc. Roman Catholic. Home: 1662 Barnswallow Pl Marietta GA 30062 Office: First Fin Mgmt Corp 3 Corporate Sq Atlanta GA 30324

SEYMOUR, HORACE WALTON, III, manufacturing engineer; b. Atlanta, Mar. 16, 1958; s. Horace Walton Jr. and Marjorie Elizabeth (Self) S.; m. Sookkai Smith, June 15, 1985; children: Horace Walton IV, David Andrew. BS in Pnysics, Ga. Inst. Tech., 1980, MS in Physics, 1982. Sr. engr. Sanders Assocs., Inc., Manchester, N.H., 1982-85; mfg. engr., mgr. M/A-Com, Inc., Chelmsford, Mass., 1987—. Author: Manufacturing Methods for Microwave Circuits, 1985; patentee in field. Mem. Am. Vacuum Soc., Am. Optical Soc., Assn. Old Crows. Republican. Methodist. Home: 13 Mike Ln Litchfield NH 03103 Office: M/S Com Inc 6 Omni Way Chelmsford MA 01824

SEYMOUR, JEFFREY ALAN, governmental relations consultant; b. Los Angeles, Aug. 31, 1950; s. Daniel and Evelyn (Schwartz) S.; m. Valerie Joan Parker, Dec. 2, 1973; 1 child, Jessica Lynne. AA in Social Sci., Santa Monica Coll., 1971; BA in Polit. Sci., UCLA, 1973, M Pub Adminstrn., 1977. Councilmanic aide Los Angeles City Council, 1972-74; county supervisor's sr. dep. Los Angeles Bd. Suprs., 1974-82; v.p. Bank of Los Angeles, 1982-83; prin. Jeffrey Seymour & Assocs., Los Angeles, 1983-84; mem. comml. panel Am. Arbitration Assn., 1984—; Chmn. West Hollywood Parking Adv. Com., Los Angeles, 1983-84, chmn. social action com. Temple Emanuel of Beverly Hills., 1986, bd. dirs. 1988—; mem. Pan Pacific Park Citizens Adv. Com., Los Angeles, 1982—; bd. dirs. William O'Douglas Outdoor Classroom, Los Angeles, 1981—; exec. sec. Calif. Fedn. Young Democrats, 1971; mem. Calif. Dem. Cen. Com., 1979-82; pres. Beverlywood-Cheviot Hills Dem. Club, Los Angeles, 1978-81; co-chmn. Westside Chancellor's Assocs. UCLA, 1986-88; mem. Los Angeles Olympic Citizens Adv. Com.; mem. liaison adv. commn. with city and county govt. for 1984 Olympics, 1984; v.p. community relations metro region, Jewish Fedn. Council of Los Angeles, 1985-87, co-chmn. urban affairs commn., 1987—; mem. platform on world peace and internat. relations Calif. Dem. Party, 1983; pres. 43d Assembly Dist. Dem. Council, 1975-79; arbitrator Better Bus. Bur., 1984—. Recipient Plaques for services rendered Beverlywood Cheviot Hills Dem. Club, Los Angeles, 1981, Jewish Fedn. Council Greater Los Angeles, 1983; Certs. of Appreciation, Los Angeles Olympic Organizing Com., 1984, County of Los Angeles, 1984, City of Los Angeles, 1987; commendatory resolutions, rules com. Calif. State Senate, 1987, Calif. State Assembly, 1987, County of Los Angeles, 1987, City of Los Angeles, 1987. Mem. Am. Soc. Pub. Adminstrn., Am. Acad. Polit. and Social Scis., Town Hall of Calif., So. Calif. Planning Congress, Bldg. Industry Assn. So. Calif., Greater Los Angeles C. of C., UCLA Alumni Assn. (govtl. affairs steering com. 1983—). Office: Morey/Seymour and Assocs 12424 Wilshire Blvd Ste 1050 Los Angeles CA 90025-1044

SFORZO, ROBERT J., publishing company executive. Contr. Macmillan Inc., N.Y.C. Office: Macmillan Inc 866 3rd Ave New York NY 10022 *

SGARLATA, JULIE MARIE, business administration educator; b. Chgo., May 24, 1941; d. Robert Eugene and Anna Louise (Catalona) Merlotti; m. Louis Mark Sgarlata, July 7, 1965; children: Robert, Anthony, Linda. BS, Notre Dame U., 1963. Cert. secondary tchr., Ill. Tchr. bus. adminstrn. South Shore High Sch., Chgo., 1963-66, Mather High Sch., Chgo., 1966-70, Schaumburg (Ill.) Sr. High Sch., 1970-76; assoc. prof. bus. adminstrn. U. Ill., Chgo., 1976—. Contbr. to profl. jours. Mem. NEA, Soc. Secondary Tchrs. Bus. Adminstrn., North Shore Country Club. Home: Werik Towers 25 E Washington Ste 939 Chicago IL 60602

SGARLATO, RICHARD CHARLES, small business owner; b. Jackson Heights, N.Y., June 16, 1943; s. Charles Fortunato and Helen (Wildish) S.; m. Marilyn Ann tucker, Dec. 12, 1971; children: Dru-Ann, Paul Andrew. BBA, Adelphi U., 1966, MBA, 1971. Assoc. prof. Germanna Community Coll., Locust Grove, Va., 1971-83; agt. ins. Southwestern Life, Fredericksburg, Va., 1973—; owner Sgarlato Ins. Services, Fredericksburg, 1983—. Vol. tchr. Council for Literacy, Fredericksburg, 1987—; Foster parent Va. Emergency Foster Care Program, 1987—. Named Life Underwriter Yr., 1987. Mem. Fredericksburg Life Underwriters. Club: Kiwanis. Office: 408 Westwood Office Pk Fredericksburg VA 22401

SHACKELFORD, JOHN HILARY, JR., diamond company executive; b. Murray, Ky., Aug. 4, 1939; s. John Hilary and Alice (Bell) S.; BS, Murray State U., 1961; MBA, U. Md., 1968; m. June Pierce, Sept. 26, 1964; children—Millicent, Hillary, Alison. Asst. prof. mgmt. and mktg. U. Balt., 1968-71; founder, pres., owner DMA Diamond Importers, Inc., Union, N.J., 1968—, Diamond & Jewelry World, 1968—, Synergetic Mktg. Assocs., 1968—; mktg. rsch. and mgmt. cons. for bus. and govt. Mem. Am. Mktg. Assn. Office: 1523 Morris Ave Union NJ 07083

SHACKLEY, DOUGLAS JOHN, fire alarm company executive; b. Oakland, Calif., Sept. 21, 1938; s. Floyd H. and Margaret I. Shackley; student San Jose State U., 1957, Chabot Coll., 1962-63; diploma in bus. mgmt. LaSalle Extension U., 1972; m. Chloe Jeanne Olson, Sept. 11, 1965; children—Derek Todd, Darren James, Daniel John, Christina Louise. Office mgr. service dept. Am. Dist. Telegraph Co., Oakland, 1961-67; office mgr. Pacific Aux. Fire Alarm Co., San Francisco, 1967-69, mgr., 1969-73, pres., gen. mgr., 1973—, also dir.; contbg. mem. Alarm Industry Telecommunications Com. Pres., Chabot Sch. Dad's Club, 1969-70, Chabot Sch. Parent's Club, 1971-72; moderator Eden United Ch. of Christ, 1980-81, vice moderator 1987-88; mem. Eden Area YMCA, San Francisco YMCA, Boy Scouts Am.; sustaining mem. Calif. Republican Com.; mem. Rep. Presdl. Task Force. Served with USMC, 1957-61. Mem. Nat. Fire Prevention Assn., Calif. Automatic Fire Alarm Assn. (bd. dirs. 1986-87, pres. 1988—, v.p. for No. Calif. 1987-88), Lake Mont Pine Home Owner Assn. (bd. dirs. 1988—), San Francisco C. of C. (code com.). Lodge: San Francisco Rotary. Home: 18716 Dubin Ct Castro Valley CA 94546 Office: Pacific Aux Fire Alarm Co 95 Bontwell St San Francisco CA 94124

SHAD, JOHN, diplomat, investment banker; b. Brigham City, Utah, June 27, 1923; s. John Sigsbee and Lillian (Rees) S.; m. Patricia Pratt, July 27, 1952 (dec.); children: Leslie Anne, Rees Edward. BS cum laude, U. So. Cal., 1947; MBA, Harvard U., 1949; LLB, NYU, 1959; LD (hon.), Rochester U., 1987. Security analyst, account exec., investment banker 1949-62; with E.F. Hutton Group, Inc., 1963-81, v.p. to vice chmn. bd.; chmn. SEC, Washington, 1981-87; ambassador to The Netherlands 1987-89; chmn. Drexel Burnham Lambert Group, N.Y.C., 1989—; faculty N.Y. U. Grad. Sch. Bus. Adminstrn., 1961-62; mem. fin. adv. panel Nat. R.R. Passenger Corp. (Amtrack), 1970-75; speaker, writer on fin. markets, corp. fin. and mergers. Author: How Investment Bankers Appraise Corporations, Financial Realities of Mergers and others. Chmn. Reagan-Bush N.Y. Fin. Com., 1980. Served to lt. (j.g.) USNR, 1943-46. Recipient Investment Banker of Year award Fin. mag., 1972, Brotherhood award NCCJ, 1981, Bus. Statesman of Yr. award Harvard Bus. Sch. Club N.Y., 1988, others. Mem. Met. Mus. Art, Navy League, Beta Gamma Sigma, Phi Kappa Phi, Alpha Kappa Psi. Clubs: University (N.Y.C.), Century (N.Y.C.), Harvard Business Sch. ,India House (N.Y.C.); Metropoliton (Washington); Greenwich Country; Chevy Chase Country. Office: 60 Broad St New York NY 10000-0004 Other: Am Embassy, Lange Voorhout 102, Hague Netherlands

SHAERF, PETER SIMON, shipping company executive; b. London, June 19, 1954; came to U.S., 1977; s. David and Valerie Estelle (Cope) S.; m. Jill Carrie Kornberg, Sept. 1, 1977; children: David, James. BA in Bus. Law, City of London Poly., 1975. Shipbroker Eggar Forrester Ltd., London, 1975-77; gen. mgr. Common Bros. USA, N.Y.C., 1977-80; pres. Commonwealth Shipping Ltd., N.Y.C., 1980—; bd. dirs. Specialized Travel Ltd., N.Y.C., Queen Ann Corp., N.Y.C. Trustee Horace Mann Sch., N.Y.C., 1983—. Mem. Baltic Freight Futures Exch., Brit. Am. C. of C. (trade com.), Town Club. Home: 155 E 76th St New York NY 10021 Office: Commonwealth Shipping Ltd 12 E 86th St New York NY 10028

SHAFER, ROBERT LEROY, drug company executive; b. Amery, Wis., May 10, 1932; s. William Charles Enoch and Margaret Gertrude (Porter) S.; m. Ellen Schlafly, Mar. 18, 1972; children: Adelaide, Katherine, Daniel, Margaret. BS, St. John's U., Collegeville, Minn., 1954; JD, Georgetown U., 1960. Bar: Wis. 1961, D.C. 1978. Adminstrv. and legis. asst. Dean-Wis. Congl. Del., Washington, 1960-66; asst. to dir. govt. relations Pfizer Inc., Washington, 1966-67, assoc. dir. govt. relations, 1967, dir. govt. relations, 1968-73; v.p. pub. affairs Pfizer Inc., N.Y.C., 1973-82, v.p. pub. affairs and govt. relations, 1982—; bd. dirs., mem. audit com. USLIFE Corp., N.Y.C.; bd. dirs., mem. bd. ops. and audit coms., Seligman Funds, N.Y.C. Mem. Cardinal's Com. on the Laity, N.Y.C.; past regent St. John's U.; trustee Citizens Budget Commn., N.Y.C. Served with U.S. Army, 1955-56. Mem. UN Assn. U.S.A. (bd. dirs.), Nat. Assn. Mfrs. (pub. affairs steering com.), Bus. Roundtable (chmn. pub. info. com.), Conf. Bd., U.S. C. of C. (health care council), Pub. Affairs Council. Roman Catholic. Clubs: Economic (N.Y.C.); Harbor (Seal Harbor, Maine), N.E. Harbor (N.W. Harbor, Maine), Apawamis (Rye, N.Y.). Lodge: Knights of Malta. Office: Pfizer Inc 235 E 42d St New York NY 10017

SHAFER, ROBERTA W. CROW, human resources administrator, consultant; b. Long View, Tex., Oct. 31, 1950; d. George Clifford and Marie (Mitchell) C.; m. Gary Stuart Shafer, July 23, 1988. Student U. Ala., 1968-70; A.A.S. in Fine Arts-Drama, Music, Am. Musical & Dramatic Acad., N.Y.C., 1972. Cert. personnel cons., Nat. Assn. Personnel Cons. Exec. trainee/retail merchandising and mgmt. Bergdorf-Goodman, N.Y.C.; account exec., cons. Lawrence Agy., N.Y.C., 1974-77; store mgr., dist. sales mgr. Career House, Bensalem, Pa. and N.Y.C., 1977-82; dir. research and recruting Retail Recruiters, Internat., N.Y.C., 1982-83; dir. exec. search/retail and mfg. Lloyd Cons., Inc., N.Y.C. and Chgo., 1983-85; dir. human resources R.P. McCoy Apparel, Ltd. dba Labels for Less, N.Y.C., 1985-87 ; pvt. practice venture capital and human resources consulting, N.Y.C., 1985—; ind. cons. Donaldson, Lufkin & Jenrette, N.Y.C., 1985; guest lectr. Lab. Inst. Tech., N.Y.C., 1985—. Mem. Nat. Assn. Female Execs., Nat. Assn. Personnel Cons., Am. Mgmt. Assn. Democrat. Episcopalian. Avocations: attending theatre and concerts, internat. traveling, study of foreign cultures and languages, collecting antiques, vintage collectibles. Home: 1365 York Ave Apt 26G New York NY 10021 Office: Ann H Tanners Inc 30 E 42d St New York NY 10017

SHAFFER, DAVE H., publishing company executive; b. Ottawa, Ohio, 1942. MBA, Northwestern U., 1983. With Northwest Airlines, govt. Bahama Islands, Eastern Airlines, to 1974; with Official Airlines Guides Inc., Oak Brook, Ill., 1974—, account mgr. airline mktg., 1974-79, gen. mktg. mgr., 1979-80, v.p., 1980-83, sr. v.p. electronic pub., 1983-85, exec. v.p., 1985-86, pres., 1986—, exec. vice chmn.; vice chmn. Thomas Cook Travel USA; bd. dirs. Northwestern Transp. Ctr.; pres., bd. dirs. Travel Easy Publs. Mem. Travel Industry Assn. (bd. dirs.). Office: Official Airlines Guides 2000 Clearwater Dr Oak Brook IL 60521 *

SHAFFER, OREN GEORGE, manufacturing company executive; b. Sharpsville, Pa., Aug. 13, 1942; s. Oren G. and Alice Marie (Miller) S.; m. Evelyne Soussan, Oct. 2, 1965; children: Kathleen R., Oren O. BSBA, U. Calif., Berkeley, 1968; MS, MIT, 1985. Mem. internal tng. squad Goodyear Tire and Rubber Co., Akron, Ohio, 1968-69, asst. comptroller, 1983-84, v.p., treas., 1985-87, exec. v.p., chief fin. officer, 1987—; mem. fin. staff Goodyear SA, Diegem, Belgium, 1969-70, fin. mgr. Benelux, 1970-75; chief fin. officer Goodyear France, Paris, 1975-80, pres., 1981-83; chief fin. officer Goodyear Tyre and Rubber Co., Wolverhampton, Eng., 1980-81. bd. dirs. Akron Priority Corp., pres. 1987. Mem. Nat. Assn. Accts., Fin. Execs. Inst., Officer's Conf. Group. Clubs: Firestone Country, Portage Country (Akron). Home: 2229 Stockbridge Rd Akron OH 44313 Office: Goodyear Tire & Rubber Co 1144 E Market St Akron OH 44316

SHAFFER, RICHARD JAMES, lawyer, manufacturing company executive; b. Pe Ell, Wash., Jan. 26, 1931; s. Richard Humphrys and Laura Rose (Faas) S.; m. Donna M. Smith, May 13, 1956; children: Leslie Lauren Shaffer and Stephanie Jane Athenton. B.A., U. Wash.; LL.B., Southwestern U. Bar: Calif. Vice pres., gen. counsel, sec. NI, Inc., Long Beach, Calif., 1974—; gen. counsel Masco Bldg. Products Corp., Long Beach, 1985—. Trustee Ocean View Sch. Dist., 1965-73, pres., 1966, 73; mem. fin. adv. com. Orange Coast Coll., 1966; mem. Long Beach Local Devel. Corp., 1978—, Calif. Senate Commission on Corp. Governance, Shareholder Rights and Securities Transactions. Served in USN, 1954-57. Mem. Am. Bar Assn., Calif. Bar Assn. (exec. com. corp. law dept. com. bus. sect. 1981-88), Los Angeles County Bar Assn. Clubs: Huntington Harbour Yacht, Wanderlust Skiers of Huntington Harbour. Office: Masco Bldg Products Corp 1 Golden Shore Long Beach CA 90802

SHAFFNER, GEORGE VAN CLEVE, computer manufacturing executive; b. Joliet, Ill., Dec. 27, 1947; s. George Elden and Annie Jo (Moore) S.; m. Grace Virginia MacIntosh, June 7, 1970; children: Mary, Carl, Tyrrell. BA in Math., U. Nebr., 1970, MBA, 1974. With IBM, Lincoln, Nebr., 1974-80; v.p. Applied Communications Co., Omaha, 1982; mng. dir. Applied Communications Co., Europe; dir. Masstor Systems, Sunnyvale, Calif., 1982-83; sr. v.p. Britton Lee Inc., Los Gatos, Calif., 1984—; mng. dir., sr. v.p. Britton Lee (Europe) Ltd., Eng., 1988—. Producer (video) There Has to be a Better Way, 1983 (distinction award for creativity, Art Direction Mag., 1984). Served to 1st lt. USAF, 1970-72. Office: 71-73 Victoria St, Windsor SL4 1EY, England

SHAFTO, ROBERT AUSTIN, insurance company executive; b. Council Bluffs, Iowa, Sept. 15, 1935; s. Glen Granville and Blanche (Radigan) S.; m. Jeanette DeFino, Dec. 17, 1954; children: Robert, Dennis, Teri, Shari, Michael. BS in Actuarial Sci., Drake U., Des Moines, 1959. Mgr. computer services Guarantee Mut. Life Ins. Co., Omaha, 1959-65; v.p. Beta div. Electronic Data Systems, Dallas, 1965-71; from 2d v.p. to v.p. for computer systems devel. and info. svcs. The New Eng., Boston, 1972-75, sr. v.p. policy holder and computer svcs., 1975-81, adminstrv. v.p., 1981-82, exec. v.p. individual ins. ops., 1982-88, pres. ins. and personal fin. svcs., 1988—, also bd. dirs., and chmn. bd. fin. advisors; bd. dirs., pres. New Eng. Variable Life; bd. dirs. Conn. Nat. Life; chmn. bd. dirs. New Eng. Securities; mem. ChFC's vis. com. Am. Coll. Bd. dirs. Greater Boston YMCA, 1989—; bd. of overseers Children's Hosp., Boston, 1989—. Mem. Life Ins. Mktg. and Research Assn. (mem. sr. mktg. officers rsch. group, strategic mktg. issues com.), IBM Ins. Industries Customer Adv. Coun. Roman Catholic. Office: The New Eng 501 Boylston St Boston MA 02117

SHAGOURY, JOHN DEEB, retail sales executive, software company executive; b. Cambridge, Mass., Mar. 12, 1958; s. John and Priscilla Ann (Derany) S.; m. Yvonne Maria Ciardiello, May 30, 1982; children: Danielle, Lyndsey. BS in Mktg., Babson Coll., 1980, MBAin Mgmt., 1981. Account exec. Mitch Hall Assocs., Dedham, Mass., 1981; v.p. sales, mktg. Software Wholesalers, Inc., Randolf, Mass., 1982; mgr. sales ops. Lotus Devel. Corp., Cambridge, 1983-85, dir. sales ops., 1985-87, dir. sales and distbn. planning, 1987-88; v.p. mktg., corp. software Westwood, Mass., 1988—. Mem. Assn. Better Computer Dealers. Home: 131 Buckskin Dr Weston MA 02193 Office: Corp Software 410 University Ave Westwood MA 02090

SHAH, AMRITLAL JIVRAJ, textile and clothing industry executive; b. Mombasa, Kenya, Nov. 6, 1941; s. Jivraj Devraj and Vejiben Shah; m. Manjula Amritlal, Oct. 23, 1967; children—Reshma, Amar. B.Com., Sydenham Coll. Commerce and Econs., Bombay U., 1963. Trustee, Nat. Provident Fund, Dar Es Salaam, Tanzania, 1975-79; vice chmn. Tanzania Soc. for the Deaf, Dar Es Salaam, 1974-84; vice chmn. Assn. Tanzania Employer, Dar Es Salaam, 1969—, chmn., 1987—; mng. dir. Garments Mfrs. Ltd., Dar Es Salaam, 1966—, Polyknit Textile Industries Ltd., Dar Es Salaam, 1977—; trustee Nat. Provident Fund, 1975-79, 88—. Fellow Inst. Dirs.; mem. Brit. Inst. Mgmt., Assn. Tanzania Employers (chmn. 1987-89), The Textile Mfrs. Assn. of Tanzania (chmn. 1986—). Lodges: Guiding Star; Rotary (dist. gov.). Home: 15 Ocean Rd, PO Box 2358, Dar Es Salaam Tanzania Office: Garments Mfrs Ltd, 62 Migeyo Rd, Dar Es Salaam Tanzania

SHAH, BIPIN, banker; b. Bombay, July 23, 1938; s. Manilal and Keshar Shah; m. Fay Shah, 1962 (div. 1985); m. Ellen T. Dever, Sept. 20, 1985; 1 child, Nelie. BA, Baldwin-Wallace Coll., 1962; MA, U. Pa., 1965. Pres. Vertex Systems, Inc., King of Prussia, Pa., 1970-74; sr. v.p. Fed. Res. Bank, Phila., Pa., 1974-78, Am. Express, N.Y.C., 1979-80; exec. v.p. Phila. Nat. Bank, 1980-84; exec. v.p. CoreStates Fin. Corp., Phila., 1984-86, vice chmn., 1986—; bd. dirs. VISA, USA, San Matteo, Calif., Franklin Inst., Phila., Phila. Internat. Bank, N.Y.C., U.S. Pro Indoor Tennis, Phila.; chmn. bd. dirs. CoreStates Bank Del., Wilmington. Fund raiser Phila. Indoor Tennis, 1985-88. Mem. Union League. Republican. Office: CoreStates Fin Corp PO Box 7618 FC 2-4-21 Philadelphia PA 19101-7618 *

SHAH, CHANDRA SUMANLAL, data processing executive; b. Sonipur, Kaira, Inda, Aug. 23, 1948; came to U.S., 1969; s. Sumanlal H. and Savitaban C. (Mazmudar) S.; m. Usha J. Parilch, Jan. 19, 1975; children: Poorvi, Neervi. BSEE, Pacific States U., 1970. Digital test engr. Hughes Aircraft Co., L.A., 1970-73; ptnr. D. Shah & Co., Bombay, 1973-83; pres. Advanced Bus. Computers, Nashua, N.H., 1983—. Mem. Boston Computer Soc. Hindu. Office: Advanced Bus Computers 49A Caldwell Rd Nashua NH 03060-4207

SHAH, HEMANT KAUJIBHAI, securities analyst; b. Bombay, Dec. 7, 1952; came to U.S., 1976; s. Kamjibhai and Kevaliben K. (Bagadia) S.; m. Varsha H. Shah, Nov. 28, 1980; children: Sachin, Symeet. BS in Pharmacy, U. Bombay, 1974, MS in Pharmacy, 1975; MBA, NYU, 1982. Sr. scientist J.B. Williams Co. (div. of Nabisco Co.), Cranford, N.J., 1978-80; mktg. mgr. Merck and Co., Rahway, N.J., 1980-83; v.p. Mabon Nugent, N.Y.C., 1983-85, Nomura Securities, N.Y.C., 1985—. Mem. N.Y. Soc. Securities Analysts, Inst. Chartered Fin. Analysts. Club: Cardio-Fitness, Centurion (N.Y.C.). Office: Nomura Securities 180 Maiden Ln New York NY 10038

SHAH, JAYANT BHIMSHI, financial analyst; b. Kutch, India, Feb. 18, 1939; came to U.S., 1962; s. Bhimshi Vijpar and Hansa B. S. BS, U. Bombay, 1961; MS, Tex. A&M U., 1969. Process engr. Delta Engring. Corp., Houston, 1967-68; sales rep. Computer Complex, Inc., Houston, 1968-73, Sperry-Univac, Houston, 1973-74; pvt. practice loan broker and fin. cons. Houston, 1974—. Mem. Internat. Soc. Fin. Home and Office: 9647 Judalon Ln Houston TX 77063

SHAH, KETAN DEVENDRA KUMAR, retail executive; b. Bombay, July 18, 1955; came to U.S., 1980; s. Devendra Kumar and Sarala (Kapadia) S.; m. Minaxi Mehta, July 15, 1980 (dec. 1985); children: Miten, Manan; m. Asha Shah, Jan. 25, 1986; 1 child, Ami. Ptnr. Ketan Gems, Bombay, 1972-77; pres. Sparkling Gems, Antwerp, Belgium, 1977-80, Subha Diamond, Inc., N.Y.C., 1980—. Office: Subha Diamond Inc 62 W 47th St Ste 1406 New York NY 10036

SHAH, MIRZA MOHAMMAD, mechanical engineer; b. Delhi, India, Aug. 11, 1941; came to U.S., 1971; s. Mirza Iqbal and Kishwar Jehan (Begum) S.; m. Gulrukh Rehman, Oct. 28, 1977; children: Alvira Sultana, Mirza Akbar. BSc in Physics, Math., Aligarh Muslim U., India, 1959; B in ME, Aligarh Muslim U., 1963; M in ME, Calif. State U., 1973. Registered profl. engr., Calif. Scientist in charge air conditioning, refrigeration div. Central Mech. Engring. Research Inst., Durgapur, West Bengal, India, 1964-68; researcher Tech. U. Norway, Trondheim, 1968-69; mech. engr. Bechtel Power Corp., Norwalk, Calif., 1973, United Engrs. & Constructors, Phila., 1974-76; sr. engr. Gilbert-Commonwealth, Jackson, Mich., 1976-78; prin. engr. Ebasco Services, Inc., N.Y.C., 1978—; cons. in field. Contbg. editor Genium Pub. Co., Schenectady, N.Y., 1984-86; contbr. articles to profl. jours.; patentee in field. NSF grantee, 1986. Mem. ASHRAE (tech. com. 1979-83), ASME (chmn. heat transfer com. 1981-82, L.I. chpt.). Muslim. Home: 15 Rush St Port Jefferson Station NY 11776 Office: Ebasco Svcs Inc Two World Trade Ctr New York NY 10048

SHAH, PULIN RAJENDRA, financial analyst; b. Ahmedabad, India, Jan. 14, 1955; came to U.S., 1977; s. Rajendra Bhagubhai and Premila Rajendra (Jhaveri) S.; m. Aarti Pulin Jhaveri, Dec. 14, 1980; 1 child, Raj Pulin. B Tech., Indian Inst. Tech., Bombay, 1977; MS in Engring., U. Calif., Berkeley, 1978; MS in Mgmt., Stanford U., 1984. Registered profl. engr., Calif. Sr. engr. EDS Nuclear, San Francisco, 1978-80; assoc. engr. URS/Blume Assocs., San Francisco, 1980-81; cons. Nutech Engrs., San Jose, Calif., 1981-83, San Francisco, 1983; staff fin. analyst IBM Corp., Owego, N.Y., 1984—. Mem. Am. Civic Orgn., Binghamton, N.Y., 1984-85. Home: 1609 Parkwood Rd Vestal NY 13850 Office: IBM Corp Rte 17C Owego NY 13827

SHAHEEN, HENRY JOHN, real estate developer; b. Cranford, N.J., Aug. 23, 1912; s. Shaheen A. and Riija (Asmer) S.; widowed; children: S. Henry, Raja E. Student, Lehigh U. Real estate developer various communities in N.J., 1945—; apptd. to state commn. to build housing for returning WWII vets. N.J. Dept. Econ. Devel., 1947—. chmn. West Long Branch Planning Borough, N.J.; mem. N.J. Housing and Fin. Commn. for Sr. Citizen Housing, 1970—; past trustee Cerebral Palsy Monmouth County; past city councilman, then mayor, City of West Long Branch; trustee Monmouth Med. Hosp.; appt. by Gov Cahil sr. citizens com., 1970; mem. pres.'s coun. Monmouth Coll., 1971—. Mem. N.J. Homebuilders Assn. (past pres., cofounder 1945), Home Builders Council Met. N.Y., N.J. and Conn. (pres. 1947-48), Long Branch C. of C. (past pres.). Republican. Roman Catholic. Club: Deal Golf and Country (N.J.). Home and Office: Shaheen Agy 344 Norwood Ave W Long Branch NJ 07764

SHAHEEN, SHAHEEN AZEEZ, textile executive; b. Chgo., Jan. 23, 1928; s. Azeez and Saleemeh (Balluteen) S.; m. Pierina Barbaglia, June 30, 1951; children: John A., David M. BS, Ill. Inst. Tech., 1949. Regional sales Katherine Rug, Dalton, Ga., 1949-53; chmn., pres., founder World Carpets, Inc., Dalton, Ga., 1954—; established modern carpet prodn., pioneering methods and techniques resulting in world-wide common usage of carpets. Author: World Carpets-The First Thirty Years, 1984. Minister Jehovah's Witnesses, 1946—; helped establish Fed. Housing Authority carpet standards, Washington, 1970-75; mem. stay-in-sch. task force Dalwhichcom Found., Dalton, 1984—. Office: World Carpets Inc One World Pla PO Box 1448 Dalton GA 30722

SHAIN, IRVING, chemical company executive; b. Seattle, Jan. 2, 1926; s. Samuel and Selma (Blockoff) S.; m. Mildred Ruth Udell, Aug. 31, 1947; children—Kathryn A., Steven T., John R., Paul S. B.S. in Chemistry, U. Wash., 1949, Ph.D. in Chemistry, 1952. From instr. to prof. U. Wis., Madison, 1952-75, vice chancellor, 1970-75, chancellor, 1977-86; provost, v.p. acad. affairs U. Wash., Seattle, 1975-77; v.p., chief scientist Olin Corp., Stamford, Conn., 1987—, also bd. dirs.; mem. tech. adv. group Johnson Controls, Inc., Milw., 1980—; mem. Nat. Commn. on Superconductivity, 1989—; bd. dirs. Olin Corp., Stamford, Conn.; mem. Univ. Rsch. Park Inc., Madison, chmn. 1984-86. Contbr. articles on electroanalytical chemistry to profl. jours. Bd. dirs. Madison Gen. Hosp., 1972-75; mem. Wis. for Research Inc., Madison, 1983-86; v.p. Madison Community Found., 1984-86. Served with U.S. Army, 1943-46, PTO. Fellow AAAS; mem. Am. Chem. Soc., Electrochem. Soc., Internat. Soc. Electrochemistry, N.Y. Acad. Sci., Conn. Acad. Sci. and Engring., Phi Beta Kappa, Sigma Xi, Phi Kappa Phi. Home: 224 Blackberry Dr Stamford CT 06903 Office: Olin Corp 120 Long Ridge Rd Stamford CT 06903

SHAIN, KENNETH STEPHEN, industrialist; b. Bridgeport, Conn., Sept. 24, 1952; s. Albert Benjamin and Gladys Ann (Lustig) S.; m. Nancie Ann Taylor, Apr. 23, 1983; children: Ian Alexander, Kevin Mitchell. BA, U. Mass., 1978. Prin. Shain Assocs., Atlanta, 1982—; chmn., pres. Geovision, Inc., Norcross, Ga., 1985—. Pub. Geodisc U.S. Atlas. Chmn. mech. engring. curriculum com. Gov.'s High-Tech Adv. Council, State of Ga., 1984. Recipient Cert. Appreciation Gov.'s Office of Ga., 1985. Mem. Soc. Mfg. Engrs. (sr.) (chmn. 1983-84), Nat. Computer Graphics Assn., Computer and Automated Systems Assn. (sr.), Assn. Am. Geographers, Nat. Info. Standards Orgn., Southeastern Software Assn., CD-Map Forum (co-chmn. 1986—). Office: Geovision Inc 270 Scientific Dr Norcross GA 30092

SHAINIS, MURRAY JOSEPH, management consultant; b. N.Y.C., June 9, 1926; s. Henry and Lena (Edelman) S.; m. Hilda Gertler, June 28, 1953; children: Daniel, Julie, Janet. BEE, CCNY, 1949; MME, Poly. Inst. N.Y., 1957, MS in Mgmt., 1970. Registered profl. engr., N.Y. Mgr. quality control, production control mgr., production engr. Presto Recording Corp., Paramus, N.J., 1949-55; staff mgmt. engr. Mergenthaler Linotype, Bklyn., 1955-57; asst. dir. electronics Fairchild Electronics, Syosset, N.Y., 1957-59; mgr. ops. Advanced Devel. Lab., Westbury, N.Y., 1959-62; mgr. engring. Gen. Instrument, Hicksville, N.Y., 1962-69; pres. Murray J. Shainis, Inc., Beechhurst, N.Y., 1969—. Author: Engineer as Manager, 1972, Office Furniture Industry, 1974, Engineering Management, 1976, Operations Managers Desk Book, 1982. Served with USN, 1943-46, ETO, PTO. Mem. Engring. Mgmt. Soc., Soc. Profl. Mgmt. Cons., Inst. Mgmt. Cons. (cert.), IEEE (sr.). Home: PO Box 730 Sheffield MA 01257 Office: 157-11 9th Ave Beechhurst NY 11357

SHAIR, DAVID IRA, publishing executive; b. N.Y.C., May 1, 1921; s. Henry and Jessie (Brinn) S.; m. Hortense Spitz, Oct. 18, 1947. BA, CUNY, 1940; MBA, NYU, 1950. Assoc. Benj. Werne Assocs., N.Y.C., 1952-70; dir. labor relations London Records, Inc., N.Y.C., 1970-80; v.p. personnel Carl Fischer, Inc., N.Y.C., 1980—. Author various articles on personnel and labor relations. Served with inf. U.S. Army, 1942-45, ETO. Decorated Purple Heart. Mem. Adminstrv. Mgmt. Soc. (v.p. 1986-87, exec. v.p. 1987—), Indsl. Relations Research Assn., Am. Soc. Personnel Adminstrn., N.Y. Personnel Mgmt. Assn. Jewish. Home: 6 Peter Cooper Rd New York NY 10010 Office: Carl Fischer Inc 62 Cooper Sq New York NY 10003

SHALHOUP, JUDY LYNN, marketing communications executive; b. Charleston, W.Va., Oct. 25, 1940; s. George Ferris and Mary Margaret (Moses) S.; BA, Morris Harvey Coll., Charleston, 1967; MS, W.Va. U., 1970. With Union Carbide Corp., 1960—, publicity mgr. plastics, N.Y.C., 1971-73, coatings materials div. advt. mgr., 1973-82, mgr. mktg. communications splty. chems. div., 1982-85; mgr. mktg. communications, solvents and coatings materials div., 1982—. v.p., gen. mgr. Fruit Bowl, Charleston, 1975-78. Recipient Best Teller award Bus. Profl. Advt. Assn., 1978-84, 86-87; Objectives and Results Advt. award Am. Bus. Press, 1978; Clio Advt. Recognition award, 1978-86; Clio award, 1984; Andy award, 1983, 84, Nutmegger award, 1985. Mem. Telefood Assn., Internat. Platform Assn., Assn. Nat. Advt., Inc., SSPC, AAAS, Nat. Paint and Coatings Assn. (communications com.), Fedn. Socs. Coatings Tech. Office: 39 Old Ridgebury Rd Danbury CT 06817

SHANAHAN, WILLIAM STEPHEN, consumer products company executive; b. Cin., Apr. 15, 1940; s. William Stephen and Dorothea (Murken) S.; children: Kimberly, Michael Erika, Alejandra. B.A., Dartmouth Coll., 1962; postgrad., U. Calif.-Berkeley, 1962-63, Internat. Christian U., Tokyo, 1963-64, U. Philippines-Manila, 1964-65. Pres., gen. mgr. Colgate-Palmolive Co., Sao Paulo, Brazil, 1972-76; v.p. mktg. services div. Colgate U.S.A. Colgate-Palmolive Co., N.Y.C., 1976-78, v.p. western hemisphere, group v.p., sr. exec. v.p. ops., until 1989, now chief oper. officer, 1989—; pres., chief exec. officer Helena Rubinstein, N.Y.C., 1978-80. Office: Colgate-Palmolive Co 300 Park Ave New York NY 10022 *

SHANDS, WILLIAM EDWARD, city official; b. Dinwiddie, Va., May 16, 1941; s. James Alfred and Littie Elizabeth (Chatman) S.; m. Annette Rosylin Oliver, June 19, 1971; 1 child, Jamille Rosylin. AA, Va. State Coll., 1959; BS, Del. State Coll., 1965; MBA, CUNY, 1976. Cert. pub. housing mgr. Mgmt. trainee Western Electric Co., N.Y.C., 1970-72; cost acct. Cities Service Oil Co., N.Y.C., 1972-74; fin. analyst Gen. Foods Corp., White Plains, N.Y., 1974-82; job developer, counselor Westchester Coalition, Inc., White Plains, 1982-84; exec. dir. Peekskill (N.Y.) Housing Authority, 1984—; mem. adv. bd. Peekskill Dept. Social Services, 1985—. Pres. United Bapt. Deacons Union, 1984—; chmn. bd. deacons Mt. Olivet Bept. Ch., Peekskill, 1985—; bd. dirs. Family Resource Ctr., Peekskill, 1986—; mem. exec. com. Substance Abuse Council, Peekskill, 1987—. Served with USAF, 1966-70. Recipient Outstanding Leadership award Mt. Olivet Bapt. Ch., 1985. Mem. Nat. Assn. Housing and Redevel. Ofcls. (bd. dirs.), N.Y. State Assn. Renewal and Housing Ofcls., Empire State Assn. (sec. Westchester, Rockland and Dutchess counties, 1986—), Hudson Valley Assn. Housing Authorities (pres. 1988—). Democrat. Home: 27 Winthrop Dr Peekskill NY 10566 Office: Peekskill Housing Authority 807 Main St Peekskill NY 10566

SHANE, JOSEPH LAWRENCE, paper company executive; b. Trenton, N.J., Jan. 27, 1935; s. Joseph Brooks and Theresa (Cooper) S.; m. Mary Martha Porter, July 12, 1957; children—Susan Brooks, Carol Ruth, Martha Ann, Sara Lynn. BSME, Swarthmore Coll., 1956; MBA, U. Pa., 1960. Project engr. Scott Paper Co., Phila., 1956-64, asst. treas., 1964-67, treas., 1967-71, v.p. fin., 1971-75, v.p., group exec fin., 1975-80, exec. v.p., chief fin. officer, 1980-85, exec. v.p. staff services, 1985-86, vice chmn. bd., 1986—, also bd. dirs.; dir. Phila. Nat. Bank and Corp., Drexel Bond-Debenture Trading Fund. Chmn. fin. com. Swarthmore Coll., 1986. Office: Scott Paper Co Scott Plaza Philadelphia PA 19113 *

SHANE, LEONARD, savings and loan executive; b. Chgo., May 28, 1922; s. Jacob and Selma (Shayne) S.; m. Marjorie Cynthia Konecky, Jan. 14, 1941; children: Judith Shane Shenkman, Marsha Kay Shane Palmer, William Alan, Shelley Rose Shane Asidon. Student, U. Chgo., 1939-41, Ill. Inst. Tech., 1941-42. Writer-editor UPI, 1942-44; cons. indsl. areas 1944-46; writer-rancher Tucson, 1946-48; writer-producer ABC, Los Angeles, 1948-49; owner cons. agency Los Angeles, 1949-64; chmn. bd., dir., chief exec. officer Mercury Savs. and Loan Assn., Huntington Beach, Calif., 1964—. Chmn. United Jewish Welfare Fund of Orange County, 1972-73; pres. Western region, mem. internat. bd. govs. Am. Assos. Ben Gurion U., Israel; pres. Los Angeles Recreation and Park Commn., 1960-63, Jewish Fedn. Council of Orange County, 1973-74; trustee Ocean View Sch. Dist., 1970-72, City of Hope, 1968—. Mem. U.S. League Savs. Instns. (vice chmn. 1981-82, chmn. 1982-83, legis. chmn. 1987-89—), Calif. Savs. and Loan League (dir. 1969-73, v.p. 1979-80, pres. 1980-81), Phi Sigma Delta. Clubs: Big Canyon Country, Masons, Shriners. Office: Mercury Savs & Loan Assn 7812 Edinger Ave Huntington Beach CA 92647

SHANK, KENNETH EARL, manufacturing company executive; b. Priest River, Idaho, Feb. 24, 1929; s. Robert Phillip and Audra Ester (Eckley) S.; LL.B., LaSalle Coll., 1959; B.S. in Bus. Adminstrn., Northeastern U., 1969; certificate in Indsl. Relations, U. Calif., 1969; m. Bonnie Lee Snapp, Feb. 19, 1954. Supervisory engr., tech. advisor U.S. Air Force, Colorado Springs, Colo., 1958-64; mgr. ops. research Raytheon Co., Sudbury, Mass., 1965-71; pres. NHA and Applied Electronics Co., Andover, Mass., 1972-76; pres. Internat. Pammcorp., East Boston, Mass., 1977-78; dir. Nat. Radio Co., Inc., Melrose, Mass., 1979—; pres. Orion Assos., Inc., 1979—, Valtron Div. Kel Corp., Melrose, Mass., 1981—. Served with U.S. Army, 1949-52. Mem. IEEE. Home: 3 Briarwood Rd Framingham MA 01701 Office: 37 Washington St Melrose MA 02176

SHANKS, EUGENE B., JR., banker. BA, Vanderbilt U., 1969; MA, PhD, Stanford U., 1972. V.p. Bankers Trust Co., 1981-82, sr. v.p., 1982-84, exec. v.p., 1984-86, mng. dir., 1986; exec. v.p. Bankers Trust N.Y. Corp., N.Y.C., 1987—. Office: Bankers Trust NY Corp 280 Park Ave New York NY 10017 *

SHANLEY, WILLIAM C., III, sugar company executive; b. N.Y.C., Aug. 22, 1925; s. William Carlton and Molly (Kelly) S.; m. Grace Ross, May 1, 1954; children: Sharon, William, Thomas, Lynn, Timothy, Patrick. BSEE, Cornell U., 1946; MSChemE, Columbia U., 1949. Chem. engr., asst. supt. Amstar Sugar Corp., Bklyn., 1949-53; asst. to refinery mgr. Amstar Sugar Corp., Bklyn. and Phila., 1954-57; mgr. ind. sales and sales mgr. Amstar Sugar Corp., N.Y.C. and Balt., 1957-61; dir. sales Amstar Sugar Corp., Balt. and N.Y.C., 1961-68; gen. sales mgr. Amstar Sugar Corp., N.Y.C., 1968-69, asst. v.p., v.p. Am. sugar sales div., 1969-76, exec. v.p., 1976-79, pres., 1979-88, pres., chief exec. officer, 1989—; Chmn. bd. dirs. Mineral Mining Corp., Kershaw, S.C., The Sugar Assn.; bd. dirs. East NY Savs. Bank, N.Y.C., First Empire State Corp., Buffalo. Lt. (j.g.) USNR, 1943-46. Mem. Sales Exec. Club N.Y., Sugar Club N.Y., Blooming Grove Hunting and Fishing Club, Woodway Country Club. Office: Amstar Sugar Corp 1251 Ave of the Americas New York NY 10020

SHANNON, ANTHONY DARNELL, health care official; b. Pontiac, Mich., Oct. 4, 1963; s. James Prince and Sharon (Lowe) S. AS with honors, Ea. Ky. U., 1985, student, 1986—; cert. foodservice mgrs.'s sanitation, No. Va. Community Coll., 1988. Restaurant health cert., 1988. Food svc. coord. State Dept of Richmond (Ky.), 1984-85; svc. mgr. Chi-Chi's, Louisville, 1986-87; kitchen mgr. Chi-Chi's, Clinton, Md., 1987-88; health care mgr. Marriott-Nat. Orthopedic Hosp, Arlington, Va., 1988—. Track and football scholar Ea. Ky. U., 1982-85; named one of Outstanding Young Men. of Am., 1988; recipient Healthcare Cert. Marriott Symposium, 1988. Mem. NAACP, Newington Jaycees, Smithsonian, Alpha Kappa Alpha (little bro.). Home: 8350 Moline Pl Springfield VA 22153 Office: Marriott-Nat Orthopedic Hosp 2455 Army Navy Dr Arlington VA 22006

SHANNON, JOHN SANFORD, railway executive, lawyer; b. Tampa, Fla., Feb. 8, 1931; s. George Thomas and Ruth Evangeline (Garrett) S.; m. Elizabeth Howe, Sept. 22, 1962; children: Scott Howe, Elizabeth Garrett, Sandra Denison. AB, Roanoke Coll., 1952; JD, U. Va., 1955. Bar: Va. 1955. Assoc. Hunton Williams Gay Powell & Gibson, Richmond, Va., 1955-56; solicitor Norfolk & Western Ry., Roanoke, Va., 1956-60, asst. gen. solicitor, 1960-64, gen. atty., 1964-65, gen. solicitor, 1965-68, gen. counsel, 1968-69, v.p. law, 1969-80, sr. v.p. law, 1980-82; exec. v.p. law Norfolk So. Corp., Roanoke, Va., 1982—; bd. dirs. Wabash R.R. Co., So. Ry. Co., Pocahontas Land Corp., Va. Holding Corp., Norfolk and Western Ry. Co. Editor-in-chief: Va. Law Rev, 1954-55. Chancellor Episcopal Diocese Southwestern Va., 1974-82; pres. bd. trustees North Cross Sch., Roanoke, 1973-82; trustee, past chmn. exec. com. Roanoke Coll., Salem, Va.; bd. dirs. Legal Aid Soc., Roanoke Valley, 1969-80, pres., 1970-79; trustee Chrysler Mus., Norfolk, Norfolk Acad., 1987—. Mem. ABA, Va. Bar Assn., Norfolk and Portsmouth Bar Assn., Order of Coif, Omicron Delta Kappa, Phi Delta Phi, Sigma Chi. Clubs: Shenandoah, Roanoke Country (Roanoke); Norfolk Yacht and Country, Harbor; Met. (Washington). Home: 7633 Argyle Ave Norfolk VA 23505 Office: Norfolk So Corp Three Commercial Pl Norfolk VA 23510

SHANNON, LORIS KAY, association executive; b. Butte, Mont., Sept. 27, 1941; d. George Robert and Loris Marguerite (Brown) Powe; m. James Norman Bertelson, Aug. 8, 1964 (div. 1973); children—Christopher James, Bonnie Kay; m. Donald Sutherlin Shannon, Dec. 30, 1977; stepchildren—Stacey Eileen, Gail Alison, Michael Corbett. B.A. in English, Carleton Coll., 1963; M.A. in Teaching., Coll. St. Thomas, St. Paul, 1964; M.B.A., U. Ky., 1982. Tchr., Central Jr. High Sch., St. Louis Park, Minn., 1964-67; lab. technician U. Ky., Lexington, 1973-80, grad. research asst., 1980-81; assoc. editor Am. Assn. Individual Investors, Chgo., 1982-84, dir. communications, 1984—. Mem. Pub. Relations Soc. Am. Office: Am Assn Individual Investors 625 N Michigan Ave Chicago IL 60611

SHANNON, MARTHA ALBERTER, portfolio manager; b. Johnstown, Pa., Oct. 9, 1958; d. Rodman Russell and Eleanor Ruth (Christner) S. BA in Econs., U. Pitts., Johnstown, Pa., 1980; MBA magna cum laude, U. Alaska, 1987. Area mgr. Fed. Gold Exchange, Inc., Denver, 1980-81; dept. mgr. Time Service, Inc., Aurora, Colo., 1981-82; exec. dir. John E. Randall II, Investments, Anchorage, 1982-85; portfolio mgr. M.B.A. Co., Anchorage, 1986-87; v.p. portfolio mgmt., corp. sec./treas. Security Portfolio Mgrs., Inc., Anchorage, 1987-88, also bd. dirs.; agt. N.Y. Life Ins. Co., Anchorage, 1988—; field underwriter Mony Fin. Svcs., Anchorage, 1989—; agt. Retirement Planning Assocs., Anchorage, 1989—; adj. prof. fin. U. Alaska., 1988—; bd. dirs. Matrax, Inc. Mem. Am. Mktg. Assn., Fin. Analysts Fedn., Internat. Chartered Fin. Analysts Fedn., Women Life Underwriters Confederation, Nat. Assn. Life Underwriters. Office: NY Life Ins Co 1400 W Benson Blvd Suite 200 Anchorage AK 99503

SHANNON, MICHAEL EDWARD, specialty chemical company executive; b. Evanston, Ill., Nov. 21, 1936; s. Edward Francis and Mildred Veronica (Oliver) S.; m. A. Laura McGrath, July 4, 1964; children: Claire Oliver Mary, Kathryn Ann Elizabeth. BA, U. Notre Dame, 1958; MBA, Stanford U., 1960. bd. dirs. Am. Nat. Bank, St. Paul. With Continental Oil Co., Houston, 1960-62; with Gulf Oil Corp., 1962-75, asst. treas., 1970-75; treas. Gulf Oil Co. U.S., Houston, 1970-72, Gulf Oil Co.-Ea. Hemisphere, London, 1972-75; treas. Republic Steel Corp., Cleve., 1975-84, v.p., 1978-82, exec. v.p., 1982-84; exec. v.p., chief fin. officer Ecolab Inc., St. Paul, 1984, chief fin. and adminstrv. officer, 1984—; pres. ChemLawn Svcs. Corp., Columbus, Ohio, 1988—. Mem. Fin. Execs. Inst., Univ. Club, Rolling Rock Club, St. Paul Athletic Club, Mpls. Club, Minikahada Club. Roman Catholic. Office: Ecolab Inc Ecolab Ctr Saint Paul MN 55102 also: Chemlawn Corp 8275 N High St Columbus OH 43085

SHANNON, SHERRI GALE, auditor; b. Charleston, W.Va., Feb. 3, 1957; d. Clyde Roy and Ida May (Cyrus) Bird; m. Robert William Shannon, June 2, 1984. BA in Acctg. and Fin. summa cum laude, W.Va. State Coll., 1978. CPA, W.Va. Chmn. supr. com., acct. Charleston (W.Va.) Area Med. Ctr., 1979-84, ops. auditor, 1983-88, auditor, 1988, dir. internal audit, 1988—. Mem. Am. Inst. CPA's, W.Va. Soc. CPA's, Inst. Internal Auditors (W.Va. chpt., mem. Directory 1984-85), Health Care Internal Audit Group, Hosp. Fin. Mgmt. Assn., Alpha Kappa Mu. Democrat. Baptist. Office: Charleston Area Med Ctr Brooks and Washington Charleston WV 25326

SHANNON, WILLIAM NORMAN, III, food service executive, marketing educator; b. Chgo., Nov. 20, 1937; s. William Norman Jr. and Lee (Lewis) S.; m. Bernice Urbanowicz, July 14, 1962; children: Kathleen Kelly, Colleen Patricia, Kerrie Ann. BS in Indsl. Mgmt., Carnegie Inst. Tech., 1959; MBA in Mktg. Mgmt., U. Toledo, 1963. Sales engr. Westinghouse Electric Co., 1959-64; regional mgr. Toledo Scale, Chgo., 1964-70; v.p. J. Lloyd Johnson Assoc., Northbrook, Ill., 1970-72; mgr. spl. projects Hobart Mfg., Troy, Ohio, 1972-74; corp. v.p. mktg. Berkel, Inc., La Porte, Ind., 1974-79; gen. mgr. Berkel Products, Ltd., Toronto, Can., 1975-78; chmn. Avant Industries, Inc., Wheeling, Ill., 1979-81; chmn., pres. Hacienda Mexican Restaurants, Mishawaka, Ind., 1978—; chmn. Ziker Shannon Corp., South Bend, Ind., 1982-88, Hacienda Franchising Group, Inc., South Bend, Ind., 1987—; assoc. prof. mktg. Saint. Mary's Coll., Notre Dame, Ind., 1982—, London Program Faculty, 1986, 89. Co-author: Laboratory Computers, 1971; columnist small bus. Bus. Digest mag., 1988—; contbr. articles to profl. jours. V.p. mktg. Jr. Achievement, South Bend, Ind., 1987—; pres. Small Bus. Devel. Council, South Bend., 1987—; bd. dirs. Ind. Small Bus. Council, Indpls., Mental Health Assn., South Bend, 1987—, Entrepreneurs Alliance Ind., 1988—, Women's Bus. Initiative, 1986—, dir. edml. confs., 1986—; chmn. bd. trustees, Holy Cross Jr. Coll., Notre Dame, Ind., 1987—; chmn. St. Joseph County Higher Edn. Council, 1988—, Nat. Council Small Bus. Com. on Bus. and Econ. Devel., Washington, 1988—. Midwest region adv. council U.S. SBA, 1988—; at-large mem. U.S. Govt. Adv. Council on Small Bus., Washington, 1988—; elected del. White House Conf. Small Bus., 1986, Washington, 1986; bd. dirs. Ind. Small Bus. Devel. Ctrs. Adv. Bd. Named Small Bus. Person of Yr., City of South Bend, 1987, Small Bus. Advocate of Yr., State of Ind., 1987. Mem. Am. Mktg. Assn. (chmn. Mich./Ind. chpt., pres. 1985-86), Ind. Inst. New Bus. Ventures (mktg. faculty 1987—), Michiana Investment Network (vice chmn. 1988—), SBA (adminstrn. adv. council 1988—, contbg. editor Our Town Michiana mag. 1988—), South Bend C. of C. (bd. dirs. 1987—), Assn. for Bus. Communication (nat.conf. program chmn. 1988—), Assn. for Bus. Communications (co-chmn. internat. conf. program 1988, undergrad. studies nat. com.), Ind. Small Bus. Edn. Network (co-chmn. Indpls. chpt. 1986—). Roman Catholic. Club: University of Notre Dame (vice chmn.). Lodge: Rotary. Home: 2920 S Twyckenham South Bend IN 46614 Office: Hacienda Franchising Group Inc 3302 Mishawaka Ave South Bend IN 46615

SHANSBY, JOHN GARY, investment banker; b. Seattle, Aug. 25, 1937; s. John Jay and Jule E. (Boyer) S.; m. Joyce Ann Dunsmore, June 21, 1959 (div.); children: Sheri Lee, Kimberly Ann, Jay Thomas.; m. Barbara Anderson De Meo, Jan. 1, 1983 (div.). B.A., U. Wash., 1959. Sales exec. Colgate-Palmolive Co., N.Y.C., 1959-67; subs. pres. Am. Home Products Corp., N.Y.C., 1968-71; v.p. Clorox Co., Oakland, Calif., 1972-73; ptnr. Booz, Allen & Hamilton, San Francisco, 1974-75; chmn. bd., chief exec. officer, dir. Shaklee Corp., San Francisco, 1975-86; mng. gen. ptnr. The Shansby Group, San Francisco, 1986—. Bd. dirs. San Francisco Symphony, Calif. Econ. Devel. Corp.; chmn. Calif. State Commn. for Rev. of Master Plan Higher Edn.; founded J. Gary Shansby chair Mktg. Strategy, U. Calif., Berkeley; trustee Calif. State U. Mem. San Francisco C. of C. (past pres.), Sigma Nu. Republican. Clubs: Villa Traverna, Olympic (San Francisco); Silverado (Calif.) Country; Lincoln of No. Calif; Pennask Lake Fishing (B.C.); St. Francis Yacht; Sky Club (N.Y.). Office: The Shansby Group 250 Montgomery St San Francisco CA 94104

SHANTI, WAEL MOHAMED, engineer; b. Qalgilia, Jordan, Feb. 12, 1946; s. Mohamed Darwish Shanti and Amina Musa Tayeh; m. Amira Ramzia Vezovic, Nov. 28, 1969; children—Raji, Ruba. BSc in Mech. Engring., Univ. Sarajevo (Yugoslavia), 1970. Mech. engr. S.A.C.C. Co., Das-Island, United Arab Emirites, 1972-74, project mgr., 1974-79; constrn. mgr. E.M. In. Co., Amman, Jordan, 1980-83; gen. mgr., pres. Electro Mech. Engring. Group, Amman, 1983—; del. to 3d World Advt. Congress, Beijing, 1987. Recipient 3d Arab Trophy, Geneva, 1986, Internat. award for Technol. Innovation, London, 1986. Mem. Jordan Engrs. Assn., Jordan Contractors Assn., Jordan Industries Assn., Jordan Traders Assn., Internat. Traders Leader Club. Avocations: books, sports. Home: PO Box 926510, 7th Circle, Amman Jordan Office: Electro-Mech Engring Group Co, PO Box 926510, Amman Jordan

SHAPER, CHRISTOPHER THORNE, sales executive; b. Columbus, Ohio, Sept. 6, 1955; s. Charles R. and M. Caroline (Garringer) S.; m. Teresa Marie King, Oct. 29, 1983. BA, Wake Forest U., 1977. Sales rep. Intex Products Inc., Winston-Salem, N.C., 1978; tech. sales rep. Am. Can Co., Oak Brook, Ill., 1979-81, J.T. Baker Chem. Co., Atlanta, 1981-83; corp. accts. rep. Chemetals, Inc., Glen Burnie, Md., 1983-84, industry sales mgr., 1984—. Mem. Am. Chem. Soc., Balt. Chem. Assn., Nat. Feed Ingredient Assn. (chair scholarship com. 1988—, mineral div. 1988—), Am. Feed Industries Assn. Republican. Roman Catholic. Home: 354 Butternut Ct Millersville MD 21108 Office: Chemetals Inc 711 Pittman Rd Baltimore MD 21226

SHAPIRA, DAVID, food chain executive; b. 1942; married. B.A., Oberlin Coll., 1964; M.A., Stanford U., 1966. V.p. Giant Eagle, Inc. (formerly Giant Eagle Markets, Inc.), Pitts., 1974-81, pres., from 1981, chief exec. officer, also bd. dirs. Office: Giant Eagle Inc 101 Kappa Dr Pittsburgh PA 15238 *

SHAPIRO, BARRY, toy company executive; b. Bklyn., Apr. 18, 1942; s. Sidney and Anne (Sokol) S.; m. Frances Rosenfeld, Apr. 5, 1970; children: David Scott, Sean Jonathan. BA in English, Rutgers U., 1963. Asst. buyer J.C. Penney Co., N.Y.C., 1966-69; dir. product planning and internat. ops. Gabriel Industries, Inc., N.Y.C., 1969-78; exec. v.p. Lakeside Games div. Leisure Dynamics, Inc., Mpls., 1978-79, pres., 1979-80; exec. v.p. Toy Game & Hobby Group div. Leisure Dynamics, Inc., Mpls., 1980-81; exec. v.p., gen. mgr., chief exec. officer Wham-O, San Gabriel, Calif., 1981-83; exec. v.p., gen. mgr. Imagineering, Inc., Phoenix, 1984—; cons. to various toy cos. Vol. mem. Jewish Big Brothers, 1964-78, vice chmn. Big Brothers of N.Y., 1976-78; coach Little League, Mpls., Arcadia, Calif., 1979—; v.p. Temple Shaarei Tikvah, Arcadia, 1982-84; bd. dirs. Har Zion Synagogue, 1988—, v.p. 1989—. 1st lt. U.S. Army, 1963-66. Recipient Army Commendation medal. Mem. Assn. Toy Mfg. Am. Jewish. Home: 5421 E Via Buena Vista Paradise Valley AZ 85253

SHAPIRO, GARY MERRILL, statistician; b. Detroit, July 22, 1943; s. Hymin and Bernice (Bassichis) S.; m. Jean Elizabeth Kay, June 14, 1969; children: Rachel, Kim, Justin. BA, U. Mich., 1965; M Exptl. Statistics, N.C. State U., 1968. Math. statistician U.S. Census Bur., Suitland, Md., 1965-70, chief recurring surveys br., 1970-74, asst. chief statis. methods div., 1974—; cons. CBS News, N.Y.C., 1974—. Mem. Prince George's County Adoption Adv. Com., Hyattsville, Md., 1979-81; bd. dirs. Children's Adoption Resource Exchange, Washington, 1982-84; pres. Council on Adoptable Children, Washington, 1983. Recipient Silver medal U.S. Dept. Commerce, 1985. Mem. Am. Statis. Assn., Internat. Assn. Survey Statisticians. Home: 1813 Glendora Dr District Heights MD 20747

SHAPIRO, GEORGE M., lawyer; b. N.Y.C., Dec. 7, 1919; s. Samuel N. and Sarah (Milstein) S.; m. Rita V. Lubin, Mar. 29, 1942; children: Karen Shapiro Spector, Sanford. BS, LIU, 1939; LL.B. (Kent scholar), Columbia U., 1942; LL.D. (hon.), L.I. U., 1986. Bar: N.Y. 1942. Mem. staff gov. N.Y. 1945-51, counsel to gov., 1951-54; partner firm Proskauer, Rose, Goetz & Mendelsohn, N.Y.C., 1955—, mem. exec. com., mng. ptnr., 1974-84; pres. Edmond de Rothschild Found., 1964—; dir. Bank of Calif., 1973-84; counsel, majority leader N.Y. Senate, 1955-59; counsel N.Y. Constl. Revision Commn., 1960-61. Chmn. council State U. Coll. Medicine, N.Y., 1955-71; mem. Gov.'s Com. Reapportionment, 1964, Mayor's Com. Jud. Selection, 1966-69; chmn. Park Ave. Synagogue, 1973-81. Served with USAAF, 1943-45. Mem. Council on Fgn. Relations. Club: Harmonie. Home: 1160 Park Ave New York NY 10128 Office: 300 Park Ave New York NY 10022

SHAPIRO, GERRI ELLEN, insurance agent; b. Bklyn., Dec. 19, 1961; d. Milton and Harriet (Zamkoff) S. BA, SUNY, Binghamton, 1983. Asst. mgr. Waldenbooks, Garden City, N.Y., 1983-84; ins. agt. Phoenix Mut. Life Ins. Co., Uniondale, N.Y., 1984—. Named New Orgn. Leader, Phoenix Mut., 1985, 86, Rookie of Yr., Phoenix Mut., 1984; recipient Sales Achievement award Pres.' Club Assoc.-Phoenix Mut., 1986. Mem. Womens' Life Underwriters, Nat. Assn. Life Underwriters (Nat. Quality award 1987, Nat. Sales Achievement award 1987), Pres.'s Club Assocs., Million Dollar Round Table. Home: 270 Jericho Turnpike Floral Park NY 11001 Office: Phoenix Mut Life 50 Charles Lindbergh Blvd Ste 600 Uniondale NY 11553

SHAPIRO, HENRY L., electronics company executive; b. Bklyn., Apr. 14, 1926; s. Morris Abraham and Sylvia (Golding) S.; m. Fay Rees Shapiro, March 19, 1950; children: Kenneth, Stephen, Lynne. BSME, Duke U., 1948; MS in Aeronautics, U. Va., 1957; MBA, Sacred Heart U., 1988. Aero. rsch.

engr. NASA, Langley Field, Va., 1948-50; aero. engr. Republic Aviation Corp., Farmingdale, N.Y., 1950-52; engring. sect. head Sperry Gyroscope Co., Gt. Neck, N.Y., 1952-62; mgr. electronic systems Boeing Co., Morton, Pa., 1962-72; pres. Computrol, Bala Cynwyd, Pa., 1972-75; mgr. mktg. Burroughs Corp., Paoli, Pa., 1975-78; program, mgr. bus. devel. Norden Systems/UTC, 1978—. Inventions in field. Fireman USN, 1945-48, PTO. Mem. Am. Soc. Mech. Engrs., Boston Computer Soc., Navy League. Republican. Jewish. Office: Norden Systems/UTC PO Box 5300 Norwalk CT 06856

SHAPIRO, ISADORE, material scientist, consultant; b. Mpls., Apr. 25, 1916; s. Jacob and Bessie (Goldman) S.; B. in Chem. Engring. summa cum laude, U. Minn., 1938, PhD, 1944; m. Mae Hirsch. Sept. 4, 1938; children: Stanley Harris, Jerald Steven. Asst. instr. chemistry U. Minn., 1938-41, rsch. fellow, 1944-45; rsch. chemist E. I. duPont de Nemours and Co., Phila., 1946; head chem. lab. U.S. Naval Ordnance Test Sta., Pasadena, Calif., 1947-52; dir. rsch. lab. Olin-Mathieson Chem. Corp., 1952-59; head chemistry Hughes Tool Co., Aircraft div., Culver City, Calif., 1959-62; pres. Universal Chem. Systems Inc. 1962—, Aerospace Chem. Systems, Inc., 1964-66; dir. contract rsch. HITCO, Gardena, Calif., 1966-67; prin. scientist Douglas Aircraft Co. of McDonnell Douglas Corp., Santa Monica, Calif., 1967; prin. scientist McDonnell Douglas Astronautics Co., 1967-70; head materials and processes AiResearch Mfg. Co., Torrance, Calif., 1971-82, cons., 1982—. Rater U.S. Civil Svc. Bd. Exam., 1948-52. Served 1st lt. AUS, 1941-44. Registered profl. engr., Calif. Fellow Am. Inst. Chemists, Am. Inst. Aeros and Astronautics (assoc.); mem. AAAS, Am. Ordnance Assn., Am. Chem. Soc., Soc. Rheology, Soc. Advancement Materials and Process Engring., Am. Inst. Physics, AIM, Am. Phys. Soc., N.Y. Acad. Sci., Am. Assn. Contamination Control, Am. Ceramic Soc., Nat. Inst. Ceramic Engrs., Internat. Plansee Soc. for Powder Metallurgy, Sigma Xi, Tau Beta Pi, Phi Lambda Upsilon. Author articles in tech. publs. Patentee, discoverer series of carborane compounds; creater term carborane. Home: 5624 W 62d St Los Angeles CA 90056

SHAPIRO, JAMES ELMER, imaging company executive; b. Chgo., Feb. 3, 1931; s. Elmer Irving and Marion Alice (Hurley) S.; m. Nancy Ann Hoehl, Aug. 1, 1964; children: Susan, James, Jeffrey, Michael, Megan. BS in Mktg., U. Notre Dame, 1952. Sales rep. IBM, Chgo., 1956-60; various mktg. positions IBM, N.Y.C., 1961-69; dist. mgr. IBM, Chgo., 1970-71; with Xerox Corp., Rochester, N.Y., 1971-83, sr. staff officer, sr. v.p., 1979-80, v.p. product programming office, 1981, gen. mgr. comml. printing div., 1982-83; pres., corp. v.p. So. Pacific and China ops. Xerox, 1984-86; pres., chief exec. officer Du Pont-Xerox Imaging, Lionville, Pa., 1987—; dir. Xerox Shanghai (Republic of China) Ltd., 1987—. Bd. dirs. Ctr. for Govt. Rsch., Rochester, 1976—; trustee Rochester Inst. Tech. Lt. USN, 1952-56. Roman Catholic. Home: 1004 Roundhouse Ct West Chester PA 19380 Office: Du Pont-Xerox 101 Gordon Dr Lionville PA 19353

SHAPIRO, JEFFREY DAVID, broadcast executive; b. Trenton, N.J., Nov. 6, 1961; s. Robert Sander and Lois (Kunzman) S. AB, Dartmouth Coll., 1983. Internal cons. Morgan Guaranty Trust Co., N.Y.C., 1983-84; pres., gen. mgr. Stas. WHDQ and WTSV DynaCom Corp., Claremont, N.H., 1984-88; chmn. Stas. WCIZ and WNCQ Northstar Broadcasting Corp., Watertown, N.Y., 1988—; bd. advisers City Bank & Trust Co., Claremont, 1987—. Bd. dirs. United Way Sullivan County, Claremont, 1985—. Mem. N.H. Assn. Broadcasters (bd. dirs., sec. 1987—), Claremont C. of C. (bd. dirs. 1987—), Rotary. Office: Sta WHDQ/WTSV PO Box 1230 Claremont NH 03743

SHAPIRO, LEO J., social researcher; b. N.Y.C., July 8, 1921; m. Virginia L. Johnson, Feb. 9, 1952; children: David, Erik, Owen, Amy. BA, U. Chgo., 1942, PhD, 1952. Survey specialist Fed. Govt. Youth Agy., Washington, 1941-45, Sci. Research Assn., Chgo., 1948-52; prin., chmn. Leo J. Shapiro and Assocs., Chgo., 1952—; bd. dirs. Circle Fine Art, Chgo., Frank Purcell Lumber, Kansas City. Mem. vis. com. bd. trustees U. Chgo. Fellow U. Chgo., 1949. Fellow Social Sci. Research Council; mem. Am. Mktg. Assn., Am. Assn. Pub. Opinion Research, Am. Sociol. Assn., AAAA, Phi Beta Kappa. Office: Leo J Shapiro Assocs 505 N Lake Shore Dr Chicago IL 60611

SHAPIRO, MARVIN LINCOLN, communications company executive; b. Erie, Pa., Feb. 12, 1923; s. Hyman and Flora (Burstein) S.; m. B. Gertrude Berkman, Oct. 25, 1946; children: Susan Jo, Barbara Ann, Jonathan David. BS, Syracuse U., 1948; postgrad., Williams Coll., 1966, Columbia U., 1975. Account exec. radio sta. WSYR, Syracuse, 1948-50; account exec. sta. WCAU-TV, Phila., 1950-55; nat. sales mgr. sta. WCAU-TV, 1956-58; account exec. CBS TV spot sales, Chgo., 1955-56, N.Y.C., 1958-60; with TV Advt. Reps., Inc., N.Y.C., 1961-66; exec. v.p. TV Advt. Reps., Inc., 1965-66, pres., 1968-69, dir., vice chmn., 1969-77, chmn., 1978; pres. Radio Advt. Reps., Inc., N.Y.C., 1966-68; dir., vice chmn. Radio Advt. Reps., Inc., 1969-77; exec. v.p., chief operating officer, pres. sta. group Westinghouse Broadcasting Co., Inc., N.Y.C., 1969-77; sr. v.p. Westinghouse Broadcasting Co., Inc., 1978-83, also dir., 1969-83; pres. Foxwood Communications Inc., N.Y.C., 1983—; exec. v.p. Veronis, Suhler & Assocs., N.Y.C., 1983—; dir. Queen City Broadcasting, Inc., N.Y.C., 1986—; chmn. bd. Micro-Relay, Inc., 1974-83; chmn. bd., pres. CATV Enterprises, Inc., 1970-83. Boxing official Pa. Athletic Commn., 1952-55; Bd. dirs. TV Bur. Advt., 1974-81, chmn., 1977-79; bd. dirs. Radio Advt. Bur., 1970-77; With USAAF, 1942-45. Decorated Air medal with 9 oak leaf clusters.; recipient Communications Alumni award Syracuse U., 1960. Mem. Internat. Radio and TV Soc., DAV, Alpha Epsilon Rho (hon.). Clubs: Long Ridge (Stamford). Home: 26 Foxwood Rd Stamford CT 06903 Office: Foxwood Communications Inc 866 United Nations Pla New York NY 10017

SHAPIRO, MICHAEL, supermarket chain executive; b. N.Y.C., Mar. 3, 1942; s. Jack and Celia (Schwartzbaum) S.; m. Sara Louise Ress, Mar. 22, 1964; children: Jeffrey, Lisa, Kenneth. B.S., CCNY, 1962. C.P.A., N.Y. Acct. Sidney Kaminsky & Co., N.Y.C., 1964-68; supr. Hurdman Cranston, Penney & Co. (C.P.A.s), N.Y.C., 1968-71; with Mayfair Super Markets Inc., Elizabeth, N.J., 1971-87; v.p. fin. and adminstrn. Mayfair Super Markets Inc., 1978-80, sr. v.p. fin. and adminstrn., 1980-86, exec. v.p. fin. and corp. devel., 1986-87, also dir.; self employed ins. cons. 1988—. Mem. Am. Inst. C.P.A.s, N.Y. State Soc. C.P.A.s. Office: Ins Cons Assocs PO Box 369 Hasbrouck Heights NJ 07604

SHAPIRO, MICHAEL J., real estate developer, lawyer; b. Bklyn., Feb. 1, 1951; s. Sam and Jean (Moak) S.; m. Theresa Vorgia, Aug. 14, 1975; children: Benjamin, Gregory. BA, Columbia Coll., 1973; MMus, Julliard Sch. Music, 1975; JD, NYU, 1978. Assoc. Kurzman Karelsen & Frank, N.Y.C., 1979-83, Finley Kumble Wagner et al, N.Y.C., 1983-87; ptnr. Serchuk Wolfe & Zelermyer, White Plains, N.Y., 1987—. Composer symphonies, chamber music, vocal works. Henry Evans Traveling fellow, 1973; Martha Baird Rockefeller grantee, 1976, 86; recipient ASCAP award, 1987. Mem. N.Y. State Bar Assn. (subcom. on coops. and condominiums 1979—), Assn. of Bar of City of N.Y. Club: Chappaqua (N.Y.) Swim and Tennis. Office: Serchuk Wolfe & Zelermyer 81 Main St White Plains NY 10601

SHAPIRO, NINA BETH, financial analyst; b. N.Y.C., June 29, 1948; d. Arthur Leon and Helen (Wiener) S. BA, Smith Coll., 1970; MBA, MRP, Harvard U., 1976. Sr. fin. officer Internat. Fin. Corp. (World Bank Group), Washington, 1978—; bd. dirs. Source For Automation, Mass., Madwill Food Co., Calif., Richard Wolffers Auctions Inc., Calif. Vol. Dem. Party, Washington, 1978—. Home: 1747 Church St NW Washington DC 20036 Office: World Bank 1818 H St NW Washington DC 20433

SHAPIRO, RALPH J., retail lumber and homebuilding products company executive. Chmn., pres., chief exec. officer Michigan Gen. corp., Beverly Hills, Calif., 1987—. Office: Michigan Gen Corp 1200 Ford Rd Pkwy Ste 300 Dallas TX 75234 also: Michigan Gen Corp 1555 Walwood Pkwy Carrollton TX 75011 *

SHAPIRO, ROBERT ALAN, retail executive; b. Denver, Dec. 24, 1946; s. George and Ruth Bearnice (Horn) S.; m. Jan Laurelle Tilker, Nov. 8, 1980; children: Aaron Phillip, Michael Samuel. BA, U. Denver, 1968; student, Northwestern U. Law Sch, 1968-70. V.p. Draper and Kramer, Inc., Chgo., 1970-73; asst. v.p. Urban Investment & Devel. Co., Chgo., 1973-75; dir. real estate The Limited, Columbus, Ohio, 1975-78; pres. Robert A. Shapiro & Assocs., Chgo., 1978-85; sr. v.p., asst. sec. County Seat Stores, Inc., Dallas, 1985—; lectr. Northwestern U., Evanston, Ill., Ohio State U., Columbus, 1976-78. Mem. Internat. Coun. Shopping Ctrs. (tenant com. 1975-78). Jewish. Office: County Seat Stores 17950 Preston Rd Dallas TX 75252

SHAPIRO, ROBERT M., electronics company executive; b. San Diego, June 13, 1945; s. Oscar J. and Mary (Schneider) S.; m. Nancy J. Sattinger, July 1, 1966 (div.); children: Scott H., Todd M.; m. Judith Ann Gable, Aug. 22, 1975. BA, U. San Diego, 1967. Mktg. rep. Proctor and Gamble, Riverside, Calif., 1967-68; adminstrv. ops. mgr. IBM, Riverside, 1968-71; adminstrn. mgr. Prodigy Svc. Co., Oakland, Calif., 1971-73; regional mgr. Prodigy Svc. Co., Detroit, 1973-75; fin. mgr. Prodigy Svc. Co., Franklin Lakes, N.J., 1975-81; mgr. resource Prodigy Svc. Co., Rye Brook, N.Y., 1981-84; dir. human resources Prodigy Services Co. (partnership IBM and Sears), White Plains, N.Y., 1984-87, v.p. market relations and mgmt. services, 1987—; Mem. The Conf. Bd., N.Y.C. Mem. Am. Mgmt. Assn. Office: Prodigy Svcs Co (IBM/Sears Ptnrs) 445 Hamilton Ave White Plains NY 10601

SHAPIRO, STANLEY, research executive; b. Bklyn., Jan. 3, 1937; s. George Israel and Dora (Richman) S.; m. Janet Skolnick, Aug. 24, 1958; children: Shari Lynne, David Elliot, Jill Diane. B in Chem Engring., CCNY, 1960; MS, Rensselaer Poly. Inst., Troy, N.Y., 1964; PhD in Metallurgy and Materials Sci., Lehigh U., 1966. Research engr. Pratt & Whitney Aircraft Co., 1960-61, United Aircraft Corp., 1961-64; instr., research asst. Lehigh U., 1964-66; research scientist, supr. metals research lab. Olin Corp., New Haven, 1966-79; dir. research, pres., dir. Revere Research Inc. subs. Revere Copper & Brass, Inc., Edison, N.J., 1979-84; v.p. research and devel. Nat. Can Corp. Research Ctr., Des Plaines, Ill., 1984-87; v.p. research and devel. ops. Am. Nat. Can Co., Barrington, Ill., 1987—. Patentee in field. Mem. AAAS, ASTM, Metall. Soc., Am. Soc. Metals, Am. Mgmt. Assn., Electron Microscopy Soc., Inst. Metals, Sci. Research Soc., N.Y. Acad. Scis., Packaging Inst., Inst. Food Technologists, Research Dirs. Chgo., Indsl. Research Inst., Sigma Xi.

SHAPIRO, TODD MARTIN, food products company executive; b. Kankakee, Ill., Apr. 13, 1957; s. Milton S. and Dorothy E. (Hefter) S.; m. Leslie Genel Callihan, May 27, 1979; 1 child, Elizabeth Diane. BS in Fin., U. Ill., 1979; MBA, DePaul U., 1982. Auditor Continental Bank, Chgo., 1979-80; fin. analyst Zenith Electronics, Glenview, Ill., 1981-82; fin. analyst Quaker Oats, Chgo., 1982-84, sr. fin. analyst, 1984-85, supr. fin., 1985-86, mgr. fin., 1986-87, planning controller, 1987—. Trustee LaGrange Park (Ill.) Library Dist., 1987—; mem. task force Cook County Pollution Control Bd., Chgo., 1985—. Mem. LaGrange Area Jaycees (pres. 1986-87). Office: Quaker Oats 321 N Clark Chicago IL 60604

SHAPOFF, STEPHEN H., financial executive; b. N.Y.C., Nov. 1, 1944; s. Barney and Freda Shapoff; m. Andrea Dorin, May 30, 1967; 1 child, Matthew F. BBA, Pace U., 1967. CPA, N.Y. With audit dept. Ernst & Whinney, N.Y.C., 1967-72; asst. controller Seeburg Industries, Inc., 1972-74, 1967-72; with Estee Lauder, Inc., N.Y.C., 1974-78; controller Coleco Industries, Inc., Hartford, Conn., 1978-79; sr. v.p. fin. Ivy Hill Corp. subs. Warner Communications Inc., N.Y.C., Conn., 1979-85, exec. v.p., 1985—; adj. asst. prof. Pace U., N.Y.C., 1971—. Mem. Fin. Exec. Inst. (pres. L.I. Chpt.), Am. Inst. CPAs, N.Y. State Soc. CPAs, Nat. Assn. Accts. Office: Ivy Hill Corp 170 Varick St New York NY 10013

SHARETT, ALAN RICHARD, lawyer; b. Hammond, Ind., Apr. 15, 1943; s. Henry S. and Frances (Givel) Smulevitz; children—Lauren Ruth, Charles Daniel; m. Sarah Rebecca Gaber, June 6, 1987; 1 stepchild, Gary Robert Twist. Student Ind. U., 1962-65; J.D., DePaul U., 1968. Bar: N.Y. 1975, Ind. 1969, U.S. Ct. Appeals (2d cir.) 1975, U.S. Ct. Appeals (7th cir.) 1974, U.S. Supreme Ct. 1973. Assoc. Call, Call, Borns & Theodoros, Gary, Ind., 1969-71; judge protem Gary City Ct., 1970-71; environ. dep. prosecutor 31st Jud. Circuit, Lake County, Ind., 1971-75; mem. Cohan, Cohan & Smulevitz, 1971-75; judge pro tem Superior Ct., Lake County, Ind., 1971-75; professorial dir. NYU Pub. Liability Inst., N.Y.C., 1975-76; asst. atty. gen. N.Y. State, N.Y.C., 1976-78; sole practice, Flushing, N.Y., 1980-82, Miami Beach, Fla., 1982—; chmn. lawyers panel for No. Ind., ACLU, 1969-71; mem. Nat. Dist. Attys. Assn., 1972-75, mem. environ. protection com. Recipient Honors award in medicolegal litigation Law-Sci. Acad. Am., 1967. Mem. ABA, Assn. Bar City N.Y., N.Y. County Lawyers Assn. (com. on fed. cts. 1977-82), Am. Judicature Soc., Assn. Trial Lawyers Am., N.Y. State Trial Lawyers Assn., N.Y. State Bar Assn., Ind. State Bar Assn., Queens County Bar Assn., Am. Acad. Poets. Democrat. Contbr. articles to profl. jours. Address: 3100 Collins Ave Miami Beach FL 33140

SHARF, STEPHAN, automotive company executive; b. Berlin, Federal Republic Germany, Dec. 30, 1920; came to U.S., 1947; s. Wilhelm and Martha (Schwartz) S.; m. Rita Schantzer, June 17, 1951. Degree in Mech. Engring., Tech. U., Berlin, Fed. Republic Germany, 1947. Tool and die maker Buerk Tool & Die Co., Buffalo, 1947-50; foreman Ford Motor Co., 1950-53; gen. foreman Ford Motor Co., Chgo., 1953-58; with Chrysler Corp., Detroit, 1958-86, master mechanic Twinsburg stamping plant, 1958-63, mfg. engring. mgr., 1963-66, mrg. prodn. Twinsburg stamping plant, 1966-68, plant mgr. Warren stamping plant, 1968-70, plant mgr. Sterling stamping plant, 1970-72, gen. plants mgr. stamping, 1972-78, v.p. Engine and Casting div., 1978-80, v.p. Power Train div., 1980-81, exec. v.p., mfg., dir., 1981-85; exec. v.p. internat. Chrysler Corp., 1985-86; bd. dirs. Chrysler Corp, 1981-86; pres. SICA Corp., 1986—; dir., bd. dirs. Medar, Inc., 1986—; bd. dirs. Republic Telecom Systems, Inc., 1986—, PBM Industries, 1988—; bd. dirs. Republic Telcom Systems, Inc., Channel 56 Pub. TV; pres. SICA;. Bd. dirs. Jr. Achievement, Troy Council Boy Scouts Am.; trustee, v.p. Oakland U. Mem. Soc. Auto Engr.s, Detroit Engring. Soc. Club: Wabeek Country. Home: 966 Adams Castle Dr Bloomfield Hills MI 48013 Office: SICA Corp PO Box 623 Troy MI 48099

SHARKO, THOMAS JOSEPH, manufacturing executive, consultant; b. N.Y.C., July 10, 1945; s. Sam and Olga (Taraykovich) S.; m. Frances M. Higgins, Feb. 24, 1968; children: Marianne, John E. BA, Columbia U., 1966, BS, 1967; MS, U. Pa., 1970; MBA, Lehigh U., 1980. Research engr. Boeing Co., Phila., 1967-70; project supr. Ingersoll-Rand Co., Phillipsburg, N.J., 1970-79; dir. ops. Kollsman Instrument Co., Englewood, N.J., 1980-87; cons. Consultec, New Rochelle, N.Y., 1988—.

SHARMA, SUSHIL, hospital administrator; b. Feb. 2, 1956; s. Chandra Dhar and Sushila Sharma; m. Heena Sharma, Feb. 19, 1988. MBA in Fin., Gannon U., 1978, MS in Health Adminstrn., 1981. Internal auditor Hamot Med. Ctr., Erie, Pa., 1977-80; controller and dir. fin. Community Health Services Crawford County, Meadville, Pa., 1980-82; dir. fin. Jamestown (N.Y.) Gen. Hosp., 1982-83; dir. fin. and ops. Buffalo Columbus Hosp., 1983-85, pres., chief exec. officer, 1985—; bd. dirs. Victory Garden Nursing Home, Duncannon, Pa.; mem. corp. Blue Cross Western N.Y., Buffalo, 1984—; developer Preventive Health Services Wellness Wagon, 1985—. Mem. Congress U.S., 1987, N.Y. State senator, 1987. Recipient resolution Erie County, 1987, City of Buffalo, 1987. Mem. Western N.Y. Hosp. Assn. (govt. relations com. 1986—), Am. Hosp. Assn. Ambulatory Soc., Am. Coll. Health Execs., Statue of Liberty Found., Pres. Assn. Clubs: Village Glen (Williamsville, N.Y.); Waterfront (Buffalo). Lodge: Rotary (civic affairs com. Buffalo 1987—). Office: Buffalo Columbus Hosp 300 Niagara St Buffalo NY 14201

SHARP, ESTHER BYNUM, venture capitalist; b. Sumter, S.C., Nov. 6, 1951; d. Robert Glenmore and May Clark (Bynum) S.; m. John Michael Haggerty, June 3, 1978; 1 child, Galen Michael Haggerty. Student, Converse Coll., 1969-72; BA, U. S.C., 1973; MBA, Simmons Coll., 1983. Reporter Sumter (S.C.) Daily Item, 1974-76; account analyst Browning-Ferris Industries, Brighton, Mass., 1977-78; asst. to pres. Harvard Real Estate Inc., Cambridge, Mass., 1979-80; v.p. Burr, Egan, Deleage & Co., Boston, 1983—; dir. Intelco Corp., Concord, Mass., Hologic Inc., Waltham, Mass., Med. Energy Generation Assocs., Boston. Mem. Nat. Venture Capital Assn., New England Entrepreneurship Council (exec. com. 1987—), Simmons Grad. Sch. Mgmt. Alumnae Assn. (v.p. bd. dirs. 1986-87, chair person conf. com. 1986-87). Methodist. Home: 44 Stearns St Cambridge MA 02139 Office: Burr Egan Deleage & Co 1 Post Office Sq Ste 3800 Boston MA 02109

SHARP, J(AMES) FRANKLIN, investments manager and educator; b. Johnson County, Ill., Sept. 29, 1938; s. James Albert and Edna Mae (Slack) S. B.S. in Indsl. Engring., U. Ill., 1960; M.S., Purdue U., 1962, Ph.D., 1966, cert. mgmt. acctg., 1979. Chartered fin. analyst, 1980. Asst. chmn. fin. dept. Pace U. Grad. Sch. Bus., N.Y.C., 1987—; asst. prof. engring., econs. Rutgers U., New Brunswick, N.J., 1966-70; assoc. prof. NYU Grad. Sch. Bus., N.Y.C., 1970-74; supr. bus. research AT&T, N.Y.C., 1974-77, dist. mgr. corp. planning, 1977-81, dist. mgr. fin. mgmt. and planning, 1981-85; prof. fin. Grad. Sch. Bus., Pace U., N.Y.C., 1975—; asst. chmn. dept. fin. Pace U. Grad. Sch. Bus., N.Y.C., 1987—; speaker, moderator meetings, 1965—, cons. sharp investment mgmt., 1967—. Contbr. numerous articles to profl. publs.; corr.: Interface, 1975-78; fin. editor: Planning Rev., 1975-78. Mem. N.Am. Soc. Corp. Planning (treas. 1976-77, bd. dirs. at large 1977-78), Inst. Mgmt. Sci. (chpt. v.p. acad. 1973-74, chpt. v.p. program 1974-75, chpt. v.p. membership 1975-76, chpt. pres. 1976-77), Internat. Affiliation Planning Socs. (council 1978-84), N.Y. Soc. Security Analysts (CFA Rev. 1985-87), Ops. Rsch.Soc. Am. (pres. corp. planning group 1976-82), Am. Assn. U. Profs. (v.p. Pace U. chpt. 1988—), Theta Xi. Republican. Home: 315 E 86th St New York NY 10028 Office: Pace U W 440 Pace Pla New York NY 10038

SHARP, JANE ELLYN, human resources director; b. Chgo., Jan. 5, 1934; d. Truman V. and Mildred L. (Sweitzer) Lasswell; m. David H. Sharp, July 24, 1965 (div. Aug. 1979); children: Michelle Lynn, Lisa Elizabeth. BBA, Coll. Santa Fe, 1985, MBA, 1988. Adminstrv. asst. San Diego State U., 1956-58; dir. classified personnel Grossmont (Calif.) Union High Sch. and Jr. Coll. Dist., 1959-62; legal asst. Stockly & Boone, Attys., Los Alamos, N.Mex., 1974-75; with adminstrn. Los Alamos (N.Mex.) Nat. Lab., 1976-78, pub. rels. specialist, 1978-81, asst. group leader, 1981-82, dep. group leader, 1982-83, asst. div. leader, 1983-84, office dir. protocol, 1984—. Mem. adv. bd. Youth Working for Youth, Los Alamos, 1985—; mem. Adults Working for Youth, Los Alamos, Bingaman Circle, Santa Fe Rail Link Task Force, 1987—, Los Alamos Community Devel. Com., 1989—. Recipient Woman at Work award Coun. on Working Women, 1984. Mem. Tri Area Assn. for Econ. Devel., Los Alamos Nat. Lab. Community Coun. (rep. exec. bd. 1986—). Democrat. Office: Los Alamos Nat Lab PO Box 1663 MS P368 Los Alamos NM 87544

SHARP, RICHARD L., retail company executive; b. Washington, Apr. 12, 1947. Student, U. Va., Coll. of William and Mary, 1965-66. Programmer 1970-75; founder, pres. Applied Systems Corp., Washington, 1975-81; with Circuit City Stores Inc., Richmond, Va., 1982, exec. v.p., 1982-84, pres., chief exec. officer, 1984-86, chief exec. officer, 1986—; also bd. dirs. Circuit City Stores Inc.; bd. dirs. S&K Famous Brands, Inc., Am. Filtrona Corp. With USAF, 1967-70. Office: Circuit City Stores Inc 2040 Thalbro St Richmond VA 23230

SHARP, ROBERT CHARLES, corporate executive; b. Clyde, N.Y., July 5, 1936; s. Robert Napier and Bernice Cyrene (Bower) S.; m. Nancy Dickinson, Sept. 3, 1955; 1 child, Penelope Sharp Bedford. BA, BS, U. Rochester, 1960; MS in Mgmt., MIT, 1981. Sales rep. Recordak Eastman Kodak Co., Rochester, N.Y., 1960-63, product specialist mktg. bus. systems, 1963-68; dist. mgr. bus. systems Eastman Kodak Co., Houston and N.Y.C., 1968-75; regional mgr. bus. systems Eastman Kodak Co., Atlanta, 1975-79; mgr. distbn. Eastman Kodak Co., Rochester, 1979-80, mgr. profl. and finishing markets, 1981-83, v.p. gen. mgr. consumer/profl. and finishing markets, 1983-85, v.p., gen. mgr. photofinishing systems div., 1985-86, v.p., gen. mgr. U.S. sales div., 1986—. Served with U.S. Army, 1954-56. Mem. Photographic Mktg. Assn., Sales Execs. Club, Am. Records Mgmt. Assn. Republican. Office: Eastman Kodak Co 343 State St Rochester NY 14650

SHARP, WILEY HOWARD, III, investment banker; b. Jefferson Parish, La., Jan. 14, 1957; s. Wiley H. Jr. and Maude (Saunders) S.; m. Julia Scott O'Brien, June 14, 1980 (div. Jan. 1986); m. Debra Ann Hoffmann, July 3, 1986; children: Katharine M. Sharpe Thorbeck, Kennedy O'Brien, Stein P. Thorbeck, Wiley H. IV. BS in Mgmt., Tulane U., 1979. Asst. to pres. Alstead, Strangis & Dempsey, Inc., Mpls., 1979-80; with instnl. fixed income sales dept. Dain Bosworth, Inc., Mpls., 1980-83, with corp. fin. dept., 1983—, mgr. pvt. capital group, 1987—. Author: The Private Placement of Debt Securities, 1987. Mem. Boston Club (New Orleans), Lafayette (Mpls.). Republican. Episcopalian. Office: Dain Bosworth Inc 100 Dain Tower Minneapolis MN 55402

SHARP, WILLIAM WHEELER, geologist; b. Shreveport, La., Oct. 9, 1923; s. William Wheeler and Jennie V. (Benson) S.; m. Marsha Simpson, 1948 (div.); 1 child, John E.; m. Rubylin Slaughter, Aug. 15, 1958; children: Staci Lynn, Kimberly Cecile. BS in Geology, U. Tex., Austin, 1950, MA, 1951. Geol. Socony-Vacuum, Caracas, Venezuela, 1951-53; surface geol. chief Creole, 1953-57; dist. devel. geologist, expert geol. witness, coll. recruiter, research assoc. ARCO, 1957-85; discovered oil and gas at Bayou Boullion, Bayou Sale, Jeanerette, La.; Petroleum exploration in Alaska, Aus., Can., U.S. and S.A. Author/co-author geol. and geophys. publs. Past dir., past chmn. U.S. Tennis Assn. Tournaments, Lafayette; pres. Lafayette Tennis Adv. Com., 1972. Served as sgt. USAF, 1943-46, PTO. Winner and finalist more than 75 amateur tennis tournaments including Confederate Oil Invitational, Gulf Coast Oilmen's Tournament, So. Oilmen's Tournament, Tex.-Ark.-La. Oilmen's Tournament; named Hon. Citizen of New Orleans, 1971. Mem. Dallas Geol. Soc., Lafayette Geol. Soc. (bd. dirs. 1973-74), Am. Assn. Petroleum Geologists, Am. Legion, Appaloosa Horse Club, Palomino Horse Breeders Am. Republican. Methodist. Avocations: sports, music, breeding and training Appaloosa and Palomino horses.

SHARPE, JOHN INNES, mining exploration executive; b. Montreal, Que., Can., Feb. 24, 1934; s. Festus Saunders and Lucille (Waterworth) S.; m. Henrietta Morrow, Mar. 29, 1958; children: John Craig, Cameron Saunders, Colin James, Catherine Lucille. BS with honors, U. N.B., 1956, MS, 1958; PhD, McGill U., 1964. Field geologist Govt. Que., Quebec City, 1958-66; dist. officer Ministere des Richesses Naturelle, Noranda, Que., 1967-68; dist. geologist Duval Corp., Toronto, Ont., Can., 1969-70; mng. dir. Pennzoil Australia, Sydney, 1971-73; gen. mgr., v.p. Duval Corp., Tucson, 1978-84; v.p. exploration Battle Mountain Gold Co., Houston, 1985—; bd. dirs. Battle Mountain (Can. Inc.), Battle Mountain (Australia Inc.). Contbr. articles to profl. jours. Fellow Soc. Econ. Geologists, Geol. Soc. Can.; mem. Australian Inst. Mining, Can. Inst. Mining Metallurgy (councillor 1970, Barlow gold medal 1965), Am. Inst. Mining Metallurgy. Clubs: Tex., Engrs. Office: Battle Mountain Gold Co PO Box 1383 Houston TX 77007

SHARPE, WILLIAM PERCY, electronics company executive; b. St. Louis, July 4, 1929; s. William Percy and Elisabeth (Hart) S.; m. Lynne Rogers, May 13, 1955 (div. 1981); m. Patricia Ann Kappel, Dec. 24, 1981; children: Terry, Peter, Gayle. AB, Williams Coll., 1952; MS, Dartmouth Coll., 1954; MBA, Boston U., 1961. V.p. Potter Instrument Co., Plainview, N.Y., 1964-74; pres. Omni Spectra, Inc., Nashua, N.H., 1974-77, PCK Tech. Div., Melville, N.Y., 1977-83, Questec Enterprises, Inc., Huntington, N.Y., 1983-87; chmn. PCK Elastomeric Technologies, Inc., Hatboro, Pa., 1987—; dir. Vicor Corp., Andover, Mass., Procomics, Internat., Woburn, Mass., Innovus, Inc., San Jose, Calif. Mem. IEEE. Republican. Episcopalian. Clubs: Dartmouth (N.Y.C.), Ida Lewis Yacht (Newport, R.I.). Office: Elastomeric Technologies Inc 2940 Turnpike Dr Hatboro PA 19040

SHARRAH, MARION LESTER, oil company executive; b. Hamilton, Mo., Oct. 23, 1922; s. Thomas Lester and Eunice Catherine (Bear) S.; m. Mary Emma Norris, Aug. 16, 1957; children: John T., Karl L., Cynthia K. B.A. in Chemistry, U. Colo., 1943, M.A., 1946, Ph.D. in Organic Chemistry, 1948. With Conoco Inc., 1948—, mgr., then gen. mgr. research and engring., 1958-66, v.p., gen. mgr. research and engring., 1966-74; sr. v.p. research and engring. Conoco Inc., Stamford, Conn., 1974-82; sr. v.p. tech. Conoco Inc., Wilmington, Del., 1983—; dir. Conoco Splty. Products, Conoco Methanation Co.; chmn. U.S. Nat. Com. for World Petroleum Congress. Served to lt. (j.g.) USNR, 1944-46. Mem. Am. Chem. Soc., Phi Beta Kappa, Sigma Xi, Phi Delta Chi. Methodist. Clubs: Darien (Conn.) Country, Wilmington Country, Quail Creek Country. Home: 12856 Coco Plum Ln Quail Creek Estates Naples FL 33999

SHARRON, AVERY B., management executive; b. Tel Aviv, Mar. 27, 1950; s. Bernard D. and Miriam G. (Singer) S.; m. Ruth S. Noy, Feb. 19, 1986. LLB, Hebrew U., Jerusalem, 1974; MA, Tel Aviv U., 1977; PhD, U. Ill., 1981. Assoc. prof. U. Ky., Lexington, 1981-84; dir. rsch. Ernst, Brand, West & Greene, Great Neck, N.Y., 1984-85, v.p. rsch., 1985-87, exec. v.p., 1987—; cons. West Side Assocs., N.Y.C., 1984—. Contbr. articles to profl. jours. Office: Ernst Brand West & Greene 98 Cuttermill Rd #262 S Great Neck NY 11021

SHARRON, BETH ANN, computer executive; b. Birmingham, Ala., July 6, 1958; d. Durward Justice and Peggy Jo (Bailey) Sharron. BS in Computer and Info. Scis., U. Ala., Birmingham, 1982. Programmer Anderson Computers, Birmingham, 1982-85; owner, pres. So. Data Svcs., Birmingham, 1985-86; systems analyst Tel-Data Systems, Birmingham, 1986-87; account rep. Okidata, Inc., Orlando, Fla., 1987-88; br. sales mgr. Okidata, Inc., Dallas, 1988-89, Orlando, 1989—; cons. Jr. League Birmingham, 1982-87. Republican. Baptist. Home: 5601 Rosebriar Way #101 Orlando FL 32822 Office: 532 Fellowship Rd Mount Laurel NJ 08054

SHARTLE, STANLEY MUSGRAVE, civil engineer, land surveyor; b. Brazil, Ind., Sept. 27, 1922; s. Arthur Tinder and Mildred C. (Musgrave) S.; m. Anna Lee Mantle, Apr. 7, 1948 (div. 1980); 1 child, Randy. Student Purdue U., 1947-50. Registered profl. engr., land surveyor, Ind. Chief dep. surveyor Hendricks County, Ind., 1941-42; asst. to hydrographer Fourteenth Naval Dist., Pearl Harbor, Hawaii, 1942-44; dep. county surveyor Hendricks County (Ind.), Danville, 1944-50, county engr., surveyor, 1950-54, county hwy. engr., 1975-77; staff engr. Ind. Toll Rd. Commn., Indpls., 1954-61; chief right of way engring. Ind. State Hwy. Commn., Indpls., 1961-75; owner, civil engr. Shartle Engring., Stilesville, Ind., 1977—; right of way engring. cons. Gannett Fleming Transp. Engrs., Inc., Indpls., 1983—; part-time lectr. Purdue U. for Ind. State Hwy. Commn., 1965-67; adv. com. Hendricks County (Ind.) Subdiv. Control Ordinance, 1988—. Author: Right of Way Engineering Manual, 1975, Musgrave Family History, 1961, Shartle Genealogy, 1955; contbr. tech. articles in sci. jours. Ex-officio mem., charter mem. exec. sec. Hendricks County (Ind.) Plan Commn., 1951-54; mem. citizen adv. com. Hendricks County Subdivision Control Ordinance, 1988—. Recipient Outstanding Contbn. award Hendricks County Soil and Water Conservation Dist., 1976. Mem. Am. Congress Surveying and Mapping (life), Nat. Soc. Profl. Surveyors, Ind. Soc. Profl. Land Surveyors (charter, bd. dirs. 1979), Nat. Geneal. Soc. (Quarter Century club), Ind. Toll Road Employees Assn. (pres. 1959-60), The Pa. German Soc. Republican. Avocations: astronomy, genealogy, geodesy. Home and Office: Shartle Engring RR 1 Box 33 Stilesville IN 46180

SHASTEEN, DONALD EUGENE, government official; b. Englewood, Colo., Dec. 3, 1928; s. George Donald and Frances True (Meyers) S.; m. Shirley Mae Johnson, Aug. 8, 1954; children: Jon Randolph, Ron Winston, Sherilyn Sue. B.A. in Journalism, U. Colo., 1950. Reporter Omaha World-Herald, Des Moines, 1954-58, Lincoln, Nebr., 1958-66; exec. asst. to Senator Carl T. Curtis of Nebr., Washington, 1966-73, adminstrv. asst., 1973-78; adminstrv. asst. to Sen. Gordon J. Humphrey, 1979-80; with transition group Senate Republican Conf., 1980; dep. under sec. for legislation and intergovtl. affairs Dept. Labor, 1981-83, dep. asst. sec. for vets. employment, 1983-85, asst. sec. for vets. employment and tng., 1985—. Rep. nominee for U.S. Senate Nebr., 1978. Served with U.S. Army, 1951-52. Mem. Am. Legion, VFW, Am. Vets., Phi Delta Theta. Republican. Lutheran. Office: Vets Employment and Tng 200 Constitution Ave NW Washington DC 20210

SHATZ, ARTHUR MARK, financial executive; b. N.Y.C., May 12, 1948; s. Alexander and Blanche (Sohn) S.; m. Marsha Joyce Whitman, May 27, 1972; children: Alexander, Steven, Lauren. BS in Acctg., NYU, 1971; MBA in Fin., Adelphi U., 1975. Sr. staff acct. Cerro Metals Corp., N.Y.C., 1971-74; sr. fin. analyst Internat. Playtex, N.Y.C., 1975-76; div. controller Kaiser Roth div. Gulf Western, N.Y.C., 1976-78; asst. chief fin. officer Phillips Van Heusen Corp., N.Y.C., 1978-85; chief fin. officer (formerly MSC Indsl. Supply) Sid Tool Co., Inc., Plainview, N.Y., 1985—. Office: Sid Tool Co Inc 151 Sunnyside Blvd Plainview NY 11803

SHAUGHNESSY, AMY ELISABETH, association administrator; b. N.Y.C., Dec. 6, 1942; d. John Arthur and Alice (Miller) S.; m. David T. Humes, June, 14, 1984; 1 stepchild, Amy Elizabeth Humes. BS in Linguistics, Georgetown U., 1964, MS in Linguistics, 1970. Editorial assoc. Ctr. Applied Linguistics, Washington, 1964-70; asst. mng. editor Am. Jour. Psychiatry, Am. Psychiat. Assn., Washington, 1970-74; mng. editor, bus. mgr. Ctr. Personalized Instrn. Georgetown U., Washington, 1974-76; sr. editor Transp. Research Bd. Nat. Acad. Scis., Washington, 1976-81; freelance editor, writer Washington, 1982-83; dir. publs. Am. Ednl. Research Assn., Washington, 1983-88; Judge typographic excellence competition Nat. Composition Assn., Washington, 1972-75. Mem. Washington Edpress, NAFE, AAUW, MENSA (officer Washington chpt. 1978-79, pres. Washington chpt. 1979-81, nat. gov. com. 1981—, 1st vice chmn. 1983-85, chief exec. officer nat. chpt. 1985-89, internat. bd. dirs. 1985—, bd. trustees Edn. and Rsch. Found. 1985—). Home: 369 0 Street SW Washington DC 20024

SHAUGHNESSY, MARIE KANEKO, broker-distributor warehouse company executive, artist; b. Detroit, Sept. 14, 1924; d. Eishiro and Kiyo (Y-oshida) Kaneko; m. John Thomas Shaughnessy, Sept. 23, 1959. Assocs. in Liberal Arts, Keisen Women's Coll., Tokyo, 1944. Ops. mgr. Webco Alaska, Inc., Anchorage, 1970-88; ptnr. Webco Partnership, Anchorage, 1983—, also bd. dirs. Paintings include Lilacs, 1984, Blooms, 1985, The Fence, 1986 (Purchase award 1986). Bd. dirs. Alaska Artists Guild, 1971-87; commr. Mcpl. Anchorage Fine Arts Commn., 1983-87; organizing com. Japanese Soc. Alaska, 1987. Recipient Arts Affiliates award, Anchorage Community Coll., 1975, 1978, 1984; named Univ. Artist, Alaska Pacific U., 1986. Mem. Potomac Valley Watercolorists (bd. dirs.), Va. Watercolor Soc., Art League, Sumi-e Soc. Am. (Washington chpt.), San Diego Watercolor Soc., Alaska Watercolor Soc. (life). Republican. Episcopalian. Home: 1200 Allendale Rd McLean VA 22101

SHAUGHNESSY, STANLEY H., utility contracting company executive; b. 1938. BSEE, Princeton U. With Doris Carrero and Tristoni, San Juan, P.R., 1968-71; pres. Delta Electric Co., San Juan, 1972-77; with Fischback and Moore Inc., Dallas, 1977—, exec. v.p. opss., from 1982, now pres., chief operating officer, dir. Office: Fischbach & Moore Inc 11050 Ables Ln Dallas TX 75229

SHAVER, CARL HUTCHENS, retail company executive; b. Richland, Oreg., June 10, 1913; s. Charles Jacob and Minne (Mary) S.; m. Georgia Bruce, Oct. 17, 1934 (dec. Apr. 1980); children—Carl B., Dennis G.; m. Laura Frazier, Aug. 12, 1983. Student N.W. Nazarene Coll., Nampa, Idaho, 1931-32. Clk., Stockwells, Nampa, 1935-36, mgr., Donnelly, Idaho, 1936-41; mgr. Shavers, Donnelly and New Meadows, Idaho, 1941-53; pres. Shaver's Inc., Boise, Idaho, 1953-80, chmn. bd., 1980—; pres. Boise Wholesale Drygoods Co., Inc., 1953-77; chmn. bd. Citizens Nat. Bank, Boise, 1981—; vice-chmn. Associated Food Stores, also bd. dirs.; bd. dirs., v.p. Shore Club Lodge Inc., McCall, Idaho. Bd. dirs. United First Meth. Ch., Boise, 1968-74. Named Small Businessman of Yr., State of Idaho, 1973; recipient Disting. Citizen award Idaho Daily Statesman, 1984. Mem. Nat. Assn. Textile and Apparel Wholesalers (bd. dirs. 1962-74, pres. 1974-76), Idaho Retailers (pres. 1951), Greater Boise C. of C. (bd. dirs. 1965-71). Republican. Clubs: Hillcrest Country, Arld (bd. dirs.) (Boise). Lodges: Masons, Shriners. Home: 3100 Crescent Rim Apt 401 Boise ID 83706 Office: Shavers Inc 705 S 8th PO Box 7278 Boise ID 83706 other: Associated Food Stores Inc 3100 Cresent Rim Dr Boise ID 83706 *

SHAVER, ROBERT BRADY, real estate executive; b. Rochester, N.Y., July 23, 1949; s. Samuel Lelus and Dorothy (Brady) S.; children: Robert, William Alexander, Benjamin Daniel. BS in Math. and Bus., Western Carolina U., 1971. Cert. shopping ctr. mgr. Mgr. sales Sperry Rand Corp., Charlotte, N.C., 1971-74; sr. credit officer Barclay's Am. Factors, Charlotte, 1975-78; gen. mgr. Hawaii Mgmt. Corp., Honolulu, 1978-80, The Beall Cos., Honolulu, 1980-83; prin. broker REDEVCO Properties, Inc., Honolulu, 1983-85; pres. Comml. Mgmt. Corp., Honolulu, 1985—; cons. R.B. Shaver & Assocs., Honolulu, 1983—. Mem. Small Bus. Hawaii, 1985—; bd. dirs. Cen. YMCA, 1989. Mem. Internat. Council of Shopping Ctrs., Honolulu Bd. Realtors, C. of C. of Hawaii, Honolulu Club, Rotary. Democrat. Roman Catholic. Home: 3015 Hibiscus Dr Honolulu HI 96815 Office: Comml Mgmt Corp 500 Ala Moana Blvd 7 Waterfront Pla Ste 425 Honolulu HI 96813

SHAW, FRANK, manufacturing company executive; b. Toronto, Ont., Canada, 1926. B.B.A., U. Toronto, 1948; B.S.M.E., Ryerson Poly. Inst., 1952; postgrad., MIT, 1968. With Coleman Co., Inc., 1940—; asst. dir. mfg. and engring. Can. Coleman Co., Ltd., Toronto, 1953-64, v.p., dir. mfg. and engring., 1964-68, corp. coordinator, 1968-71, exec. v.p., gen. mgr. Outing Products Group, 1971-84; mem. office of chief exec. Coleman Co., 1985—; dir. Coleman Co., Inc. Office: Coleman Co Inc 250 N St Francis Ave PO Box 1762 Wichita KS 67201

SHAW, HARRY ALEXANDER, III, manufacturing company executive; b. Tacoma, Sept. 27, 1937; s. Harry Alexander and Gladys (Reynolds) S.; m. Phoebe Jo Crouch, Nov. 27, 1966; children: Harry Alexander IV, Austin R., Christine N. A.B., Dartmouth Coll., 1959. Various sales positions U.S. Steel Corp., 1962-69; div. mktg. v.p. Huffy Corp., 1969-73, corp. mktg. v.p., 1973-75, Calif. div. pres., 1975-77; group v.p. Huffy Corp., Dayton, Ohio, 1977-78; pres. and chief exec. officer, chief operating officer Huffy Corp., 1979-82, pres., chief exec. officer, 1982-85, chmn. bd., chief exec. officer, 1986—; bd. dirs. Duriron Co., Society Corp., Huffy Corp. Trustee Miami Valley Hosp., Wilberforce U.; trustee, past pres. bd. trustees Dayton Art Inst.; sr. warden St. Paul's Ch.; past chmn. Dayton area U.S. Olympic Com., United Negro Coll. Fund; mem. exec. com., past chmn. Dayton area Boy Scouts Am.; past chmn. Dayton Area Progress Coun., Young Pres. Orgn., Bicycle Mfrs. Assn.; mem. cabinet United Way. With USN, 1959-62. Mem. Rotary. Home: 1135 Ridgeway Rd Dayton OH 45419 Office: Huffy Corp 7701 Byers Rd Miamisburg OH 45342

SHAW, HENRY D., insurance company executive; b. Presque Isle, Maine, Nov. 20, 1933; s. Otis Edwin and Hanna Bera (Tweedie) S.; m. Mary A. Shaw, Nov. 24, 1965; children—Edward, Leslie. B.A., Bowdoin Coll., 1956. With John Hancock Mut. Life Ins. Co., Boston, 1966—, asst. actuary, 1966-70, assoc. actuary, 1970-76, 2d v.p. actuarial, 1976-81, v.p. actuarial, 1981-82, v.p. underwriting, 1972-73, sr. v.p. underwriting, 1983—. Fellow Soc. Actuaries; mem. Am. Acad. Actuaries, Home Office Life Underwriters Assn., Inst. Home Office Underwriters. Home: 42 Woodridge Rd Wayland MA 01778 Office: John Hancock Mut Life Ins Co PO Box 111 Boston MA 02117 *

SHAW, JEROME, computer executive; b. 1926. BSEE, N.Mex. State U., 1950. V.p., sec. Volt Info. Scis. Inc., N.Y.C., until 1982, exec. v.p., 1982—, also bd. dirs. Office: Volt Info Scis Inc 101 Park Ave New York NY 10178 *

SHAW, JULIUS C., carpet manufacturing company executive; b. 1929. Student, Ga. Inst. Tech. Supt. Crown Cotton Mills Inc., 1950-57; with Rocky Creek Mills, 1957-63; v.p., gen. mgr. Dan River Carpets, Danville, Va., 1965-67; with Sabre Carpets Inc. (merged into Shaw Industries), Dalton, Ga., 1967—, now chmn., dir. Office: Shaw Industries Inc 616 E Walnut Ave Dalton GA 30720 *

SHAW, MAURICE KENNETH, utility company executive; b. N.Y.C., Apr. 16, 1939; s. Philip Edward and Virginia (Hiney) S.; m. Mary Elizabeth Humphreys, Aug. 26, 1961; children—Elizabeth, Victoria, Anne. B.S. in Indsl. Mgmt., Lehigh U., 1960; M.B.A. in Fin., Wagner Coll., Staten Island, N.Y., 1969; grad. advanced mgmt. program, Harvard U., 1978. With Bklyn. Union Gas Co., 1968—, v.p., 1975-81, sr. v.p., 1981-87, sr. v.p., chief mktg. officer, 1987—; pres. Gas Energy Inc., 1979-84; bd. dirs. Richmond County Savs. Bank, Staten Island; chmn., pres. Cogeneration & Ind. Power Coalition Am. Inc. Mem. adv. bd. St. Vincent's Med. Ctr., Staten Island, 1983—; bd. dirs. USO of Met. N.Y., 1985—, Boys Hope, 1987. Mem. Staten Island C. of C. (bd. dirs. 1983—, vice chmn. 1986), Natural Gas Vehicle Coalition. Roman Catholic. Clubs: Keyport Yacht (N.J.); Monmouth Boat (Redbank, N.J.); Brooklyn, Harvard. Home: 49 Fish Hawk Dr Middletown NJ 07748 Office: Bklyn Union Gas Co 195 Montague St Brooklyn NY 11201

SHAW, RAY, financial publishing company executive; b. 1934; married. Ed., Tex. Western U., U. Okla. With Dow Jones & Co. Inc., N.Y.C., 1960—; mng. editor AP-Dow Jones, Dow Jones & Co., 1966-71, asst. gen. mgr., 1971-72, dir. devel., 1972-73, v.p. devel., 1973-75, v.p. gen. mgr., 1975-77, exec. v.p., 1977-79, pres., chief operating officer, 1979—; dir. Dow Jones & Co.; dir. O'Haway Newpapers Inc., Extel Corp., Far Eastern Econ. Rev., Hong Kong. Office: Dow Jones & Co Inc 200 Liberty St New York NY 10281 also: Dow Jones & Co Inc 200 Liberty St New York NY 10281 *

SHAW, RICHARD DAVID, SR., marketing and management educator; b. Pitts., Kans., Aug. 25, 1938; s. Richard Malburn and Jessie Ruth (Murray) S.; m. Adolphine Catherine Brungardt , Aug. 21, 1965; children: Richard David Jr., John Michael, Shannon Kathleen. BSBA, Rockhurst Coll., 1960; MS in Commerce, St. Louis U., 1964. Claims adjuster Kemper Ins. Group, Kansas City, Mo., 1961; tchr. acctg. Corpus Christi High Sch., Jennings, Mo., 1961-63; assoc. prof. econs. Fontbonne Coll., St. Louis, 1963-70; chmn. social behavioral sci. dept. Fontbonne Coll., 1968-70; mem. faculty, chmn. bus. div. Longview Community Coll., Lee's Summit, Mo., 1970-81, coord. mktg., 1979-81; assoc. prof. mktg. Rockhurst Coll., Kansas City, 1981—, chmn. mgmt. and mktg., 1983-85; workshop leader Rockhurst Coll., 1975—; pvt. cons., 1981—. Author: Personal Finance, 1983. Mem. alumni bd. Rockhurst Coll., 1971-73, 78-80; chmn. Eastwood Hills Coun., Kansas City, 1974-76, bd. dirs., 1988—; co-chmn. Kansas City Vols. Against Hunger, 1975-80; campaign mgr. for Larry Ferns for City Coun., Kansas City, 1975; bd. govs. Citizens Assn., 1976—. Hallmark fellow Rockhurst Coll.; faculty devel. grantee Rockhurst Coll., 1984. Mem. Hallmark fellow Sales and Mktg. Execs. Internat., Sales and Mktg. Execs. Kansas City (chmn. coll. rels. 1982-84), Raytown C. of C., Alpha Sigma Nu. Democrat. Roman Catholic. Home: 4917 Wallace St Kansas City MO 64129 Office: Rockhurst Coll 1100 Rockhurst Rd Kansas City MO 64110-2599

SHAW, RICHARD MELVIN, gemologist, gold company executive; b. Los Angeles, Jan. 14, 1947; s. Melvin and Harriet Louise (Hammond) S.; m. Deanna Lee Revel, Mar. 9, 1968 (div. 1973); 1 child, Katharine Lillian; m. Janet Lynne Gribble, Dec. 31, 1981; 1 child, Jacquelyn Louise. Student Los Angeles Valley Coll.-Van Nuys, 1965-67; grad. Gemological Inst. Am., 1976. Design coordinator Foxy Jon's Smokehouse Cabins, Inc., Los Angeles, 1968-71; Pantera specialist, used car mgr. Bricker Lincoln-Mercury, Los Angeles, 1971-74; designer Melvin Shaw & Assos., Santa Monica, Calif., 1974-76; instr. Gemological Inst. Am., Santa Monica, 1976-79, dir. research and devel., 1979-82; ptnr., dir. sales and mktg. N.W. Gold Mktg., Woodland Hills, Calif., 1982-83; exec. v.p. Nat. Gold Distbr., Ltd., Canoga Park, Calif., 1983-86; pres., chief exec. officer Campbell Shaw, Inc., Woodland Hills, 1986—; founder, ptnr. Rick Shaw & Co., 1982—. Developer, designer Diamond Pen instrument; gemelogical cons., 1988. Mem. Los Angeles County Mus. Alliance, Mineral. Soc. So. Calif., Nat. Assn. Underwater Instrs., Instrument Soc. Am.

SHAW, ROBERT E., carpeting company executive; b. 1931. Pres., chief exec. officer Star Finishing Co. Inc. (merged into Shaw Industries Inc.), Dalton, Ga., until 1969; now pres., chief exec. officer Shaw Industries Inc., Dalton, Ga., also bd. dirs. Office: Shaw Industries Inc 616 E Walnut Ave Dalton GA 30720 *

SHAW, SAMUEL ERVINE, II, retired insurance company executive, consultant; b. Independence, Kans., Apr. 10, 1933; s. Samuel Ervine and Jessie Elizabeth (Guernsey) S.; m. Dale Foster Dorman, June 19, 1954; children—Samuel Ervine III, Christopher Atwood, Elizabeth Foster. B.A., Harvard U., 1954; J.D., Boston Coll., 1965. Bar: Mass. 1965, U.S. Supreme Ct. 1971; enrolled actuary 1976; cons. actuary, 1987. With John Hancock Mut. Life Ins. Co., Boston, 1957-87, group pension and ins. actuary, 2d v.p., 1979-85, v.p., group ins. actuary, 1985-87; dir. Health Reins. Assn. Conn., Hartford, 1980-87; cons. Internat. Exec. Service Corps, Guayaquil, Ecuador, 1973, Jakarta, Indonesia, 1988, Pension Benefit Guaranty Corp., Washington, 1974-75. Contbr. articles to actuarial jours. Mem. Brookline Hist. Commn. (Mass.), 1981, Brookline Retirement Bd., 1985; chmn. Brookline Com. on Town Orgn. and Structure, 1975-79. Served to maj. USAF, 1954-57. Fellow Soc. Actuaries; mem. Am. Acad. Actuaries, Internat. Actuarial Assn., ABA, Mass. Bar Assn., Boston Bar Assn. Episcopalian. Home and Office: 131 Sewall Ave Brookline MA 02146

SHAW, VERONICA, government employee, business executive; b. Milw., Jan. 29, 1953; d. Robert Lee and Mattie Mary (Taylor) S. Student in polit. sci., Marquette U., 1973-77. Cert. dental asst. Govt. clk. County of Milw., 1982—; chief exec. officer Shaw's Inc., Milw., 1988—. Vol. Career Youth Devel., Milw., 1987, foster care project, 1989. Mem. Nat. Assn. Female Electives. Democrat. Lutheran.

SHAW, WILLIAM, diversified telecommunications company executive; b. 1924; married. BS, Bklyn. Coll. Mgr. Remington Rand Co., Inc., 1945-48; with Nat. Lead Industries, 1948-50; now chmn. bd., pres., chief exec. officer Volt Info. Scis., Inc., N.Y.C. Office: Volt Info Scis Inc 101 Park Ave New York NY 10178 *

SHAWHAN, SAMUEL F., JR., telecommunications executive; b. Lexington, Ky., Sept. 19, 1932; s. Samuel F. and Lucille (Holman) S.; m. Ruth Edwards, December 15, 1962; 1 child, Kevin F. BS, Syracuse U., 1955. Various mgmt. positions Gen. Tel of Upstate N.Y., Johnstown, 1958-62, gen. sales adminstr., 1962-64; dist. mgr. Gen. Tel of Upstate N.Y., Pulaski, 1964-66; nat. accounts adminstr. GTE Service Corp., N.Y.C., 1966-68; market devel. adminstr. GTE Communications, Inc., N.Y.C., 1968-71; div. mgr. Gen. Tel of the S.E., Dalton, Ga., 1971-75; dir. regulatory affairs GTE Service Corp., Washington, 1975-80, asst. v.p. regulatory affairs, 1980-84; v.p. govt. affairs GTE Corp., Washington, 1984—. Mem. George Town Club, Internat. Club. Presbyterian. Office: GTE Corp 1850 M St #1200 Washington DC 20036

SHAW-JACKSON, HAROLD NICHOLAS, coal company executive; b. Springs, South Africa, Jan. 13, 1942; came to Belgium, 1978; s. Harold Shaw and Doreen Edna (Woolley) J.; m. Beatrice Valerie Marie Dondelinger, May 6, 1965; children—Flavia, Chloe, Catherine, Philippe. Founder, mng. dir. Fibreglass Devel. Co., Johannesberg, South Africa, 1963—, Jackson's Fibreglass Pty. Ltd., Johannesburg, 1964—; mng. dir. H.N.S. Jackson Athracite Pty. Ltd., Johannesburg, 1974—; dir. Rauli Kohlen Ag, Zug, Jackson Shipping and Coal SA, Brussels. Clubs: Chevaliers du Tastevin, Rand (Johannesburg). Home: 11 Chemin de la Brire, 1328 Ohain, Brussels Belgium

SHAWSTAD, RAYMOND VERNON, computer specialist; b. Brainerd, Minn., Mar. 17, 1931; stepson Klaas Ostendorf, s. Ruth Catherine Hammond; student West Coast U., 1960-62, UCLA Extension, 1966-81, Liberal Inst. Natural Sci. and Tech., 1973-83, Free Enterprise Inst., 1973-83. Salesman, Marshalltown, Iowa, 1952-53; asst. retail mgr. Gamble-Skogmo, Inc., Waverly, Iowa, 1953-54, retail mgr., Iowa Falls, 1954-57; sr. programmer County of San Bernardino (Calif.), 1958-64; info. systems cons. Sunkist Growers, Inc., Van Nuys, Calif., 1965-75, sr. systems programmer, 1975—; univ. extension instr. UCLA, 1980-81; propr., artificial intelligence researcher Lang. Products Co., Reseda, Calif., 1980—; propr., fin. educator Pennyseed Mgmt. Co., Reseda, 1987—; cons., tchr. in field, 1961-63. Vol. VA Hosp., 1984—; bedside music therapist Vets, Adminstrn., 1984—; musician Project Caring, 1984-87; rep. U.S. Senatorial Bus. Adv. Bd., Calif., 1988—. Mem. L.A. VM User Group, Am. Def. Preparedness Assn., Res. Officers Assn., Jewish Vegetarian Soc., U.S. Naval Inst., Am. Math. Soc., Aircraft Owners and Pilots Assn., Math. Assn. Am. Author numerous software programs; editor VM Notebook of GUIDE Internat. Corp., 1982—. Mem. B'nai B'rith. Home: PO Box 551 Van Nuys CA 91408 Office: PO Box 1667 Reseda CA 91335

SHAY, FRANCIS JOSEPH, business executive; b. N.Y.C., July 26, 1942; s. Francis Augustine and Margarite Muriel (Boles) S.; m. Sandra Harman, Aug. 17, 1968; children: Brian Francis, Michael Patrick. BS in Biology, Morehead State U., 1965, MS in Biology, 1968; MBA, Shippensburg State U., 1979; PhD in Science, Va. Poly. Inst., 1971. Dean instrn. Madisonville (Ky.) Community Coll., 1971-72; post-doctoral fellow NASA, Ft. Collins, Colo., 1972-74; asst. prof biology Dickinson Coll., Carlisle, Pa., 1974-78; staff analyst AMP Inc., Harrisburg, Pa., 1978-79, mgr. new products research, 1979-83, mgr. new techs., 1983—. Contbr. numerous articles to profl. journals. Asst. scoutmaster Boy Scouts Am., Harrisburg, 1982-84; bd. dirs. Bishop McDevitt High Sch. Mem. Internat. Soc. Hybrid Microelectronics, Internat. Electronics Packaging Soc., Joint Electronic Device Engring. Council, Am. Soc. Plant Physiologists, Sigma Xi. Republican. Roman Catholic. Home: RD 1 Box 430 E Palmyra PA 17078 Office: AMP Inc PO Box 3608 Harrisburg PA 17105

SHAY, PHILIPP WENDELL, management consultant, professional writer, professor; b. Elberta, Utah, Apr. 17, 1914; s. Robert Martin and Ida Beth (Kelly) S.; m. Agnes Cecilia Schaefer, July 22, 1940; children: Katherine Ann, Philip Brian, Mary Eleanor, Robert Joseph, Peter Fabian, Brooke Elizabeth, Philip W. Jr. BA, Seattle U., 1935; MA, Cath. U., 1937; PhD, U. Toronto, 1941. Prof. Stanford U., Calif., 1941-42, NYU and Columbia U., 1962-66; nat. program asst. dir. USO, N.Y.C., 1942-46; mgmt. cons. Harry Hopf & Co., Ossining, N.Y., 1946-49; ednl. cons. U.S. Army of Occupation, Tokyo, 1949-50; research dir. Am. Mgmt. Assns., N.Y.C., 1950-54; exec. dir. Inst. Mgmt. Cons. of U.S., 1969-75, Assn. Cons. Mgmt. Engrs., N.Y.C., 1954-77; pres. Shay Assocs., Inc., Yonkers, N.Y., 1977—; cons. part-time Assn. Exec. Recruiting Cons., Inst. Mgmt. Cons. of Ont., Can., Mgmt. Cons. Assn. of Australia, Japan, N.Z., India and S.Africa. Editor of 14 publs. on mgmt. cons. published by Assn. Cons. Engrs.; also articles. Recipient Outstanding award 6th Annual N.Am. Conf. Mgmt. Cons., 1977. Democrat. Roman Catholic. Home and Office: 119 Hawthorne Ave Yonkers NY 10701

SHAY, ROBERT MICHAEL, manufacturing company executive, consultant; b. Phila., Sept. 14, 1936; s. Harry and Bertha (Shaivitz) S.; m. Elaine Lee Rosenthol-Kushner, June 8, 1956; children: Susan, Lauri, Robert Michael Jr., Heather. BS in Econs., U. Pa., 1958, JD, 1961. Bar: Pa. 1962, U.S. Supreme Ct. 1962. Pres. Nat. Crematory Corp., 1987—; chief operating officer, sec., treas. Montefiore Cemetery Co., Phila., 1952-88, pres. 1988—; dir., sec., treas. Metachron Research Corp., Phila., 1955-59; assoc. Fox, Rothschild, O'Brien & Frankel, Phila., 1961-74, ptnr., 1973; treas., dir. Forest Hills Cemetery Corp., Phila., 1964-83; chmn. bd., chief exec. officer, officer, dir. various operating subs. Morlan Internat., Inc. and its domestic and fgn. subs., Phila., 1969-83; chmn. bd. Superior Holding Corp., Cleve., Bike-O-Matic, Ltd., Internat. and Commerce Bank, Phoenix; chmn. bd., chief exec. officer Terraplex Corp. and subs., Phila., 1983—; chmn. bd., chief exec. officer Regal Corrugated Box Co., Inc., 1986—; chmn. Bd. Internat. and Commerce Bank, Phoenix, 1988—; pres., chief exec. officer Nat. Crematory Corp., Luna, N.Mex., 1988—; also bd. dirs.; chmn. ALS, Inc., Phila., 1988—; dir. Am. Cemetery Services, Inc., 4-U Corp., also various fin. corps.; lectr. Am. Coll. Life Underwriters, Bryn Mawr, Pa.; cons. in health care field. Contbr. articles to profl. publs. Shelter mgr., mem. Abington CD and Race Network, Pa., 1960-61; co-leader Sawmill Hill council Boy Scouts Am., 1974; co-pres. Huntingdon Jr. High Sch. PTO, Abington, 1973-74; fin. chmn. Coyle for State Rep. Com., Abington, 1978, Swan for State Rep. Com., Abington, 1980, Greenleaf for State Senate Com., Abington, 1982, 86; co-fin. chmn. Fox for State Rep. Com., Abington, 1984, 86; alt. del. Rep. Nat. Conv., 1988; chmn. Century Club, Abington Twp. Rep. Orgn., 1983-86; chmn. bd. dirs. Contemporary Opera Co. Am., Phila., 1983-84; bd. dirs. Mann Music Ctr., Phila., 1975—, Nat. Mus. Am. Jewish History, Phila., 1982-84, Am. com. Phila. br. Shaare Zedek Hosp., 1982—; bd. dirs., sec. Phila. br. Am. Friends of Haifa U., 1982-86, pres., 1986—, also bd. dirs.; treas., trustee Abington Free Library, 1981-88 . Mem. ABA, World Bus. Council, Phila. Pres. Orgn., Am. Cemetery Assn. (bd. dirs. 1979-81, chmn. spring conf. 1982), Cemetery Consumer Service Council (pres. 1982-83), Keystone State Assn. Cemeteries, Cemetery Assn. Greater Phila. and Vicinity, Md. Cemetery Assn., Nat. Assn. Cemeteries, Casket Mfrs. Assn., Jewish Cemeteries Assn. Greater Phila. and Vicinity (pres. 1967), Cremation Assn. N.Am., Tech. Assn. Pulp and Paper Industry, Aircraft Owners and Pilots Assn., Beta Gamma Sigma, Beta Alpha Psi. Avocations: travel, swimming, reading. Home: 1326 Panther Rd Rydal PA 19046 Office: Terraplex Corp Church Rd and Borbeck St Philadelphia PA 19111

SHAYKIN, LEONARD P., investor; b. Chgo., Nov. 17, 1943; s. Lawrence L. and Rose (Yaker) S.; m. Norah Josephine Kan, June 26, 1966; children:

Benjamin, Gabriel, Rebecca. BA, U. Chgo., 1965, MA, 1966, MBA, 1973; postgrad., U. Sussex, Brighton, Eng., 1970. Investment officer First Capital Corp., Chgo., 1970-74; asst. to chmn. Apeco Corp., Chgo., 1975-76; div. pres. Brown Mfg. Co., Woodstock, Ill., 1976-78; v.p. Citicorp Venture Capital, N.Y.C., 1978-79; v.p., dir. Citicorp Capital Investors, N.Y.C., 1979-82; mng. ptnr. Adler & Shaykin, N.Y.C., 1983—; owner Chicago Sun Times, from 1986; bd. dirs. Addiction Recovery Corp. Waltham, Mass., GP Tech. Inc., Somerville, N.J., Joy Techs., Inc., Pitts., Best Products, Inc., Richmond, Folger-Adam Inc., Ill., Athena Ptnrs., Israel; chmn., pres. N.Y. Venture Capital Forum, N.Y.C., 1983; chmn. USIL Investments, Israel. Chmn. Hebrew Arts Sch. and Merkin Concert Hall, N.Y.C., 1983-86. Home: 101 Central Pk W Apt 2F New York NY 10023 Office: Adler & Shaykin 375 Park Ave New York NY 10152

SHEA, BERNARD CHARLES, pharmaceutical company executive; b. Bradford, Pa., Aug. 7, 1929; s. Bernard and Edna Catherine (Green) S.; m. Marilyn Rishell, Apr. 12, 1952; children—David Charles, Melissa Leone. B.S. in Biology, Holy Cross Coll., Worcester, Mass. Dir. mktg. Upjohn Co., Kalamazoo, Mich., 1954-80; pres. Pharm. div. Pennwalt Corp., Rochester, N.Y., 1980-86; v.p. Health div. Pennwalt Corp., Phila., 1986, sr. v.p. health, 1987-88, sr. v.p. chemicals, 1988—. Served to lt. (j.g.) USN, 1951-54, Korea. Office: Pennwalt Corp Corp Hdqrs 3 Parkway Philadelphia PA 19102

SHEA, DEBORAH ANNE, banker; b. Des Moines, Sept. 1, 1964; d. Donald M. and Diane (Wiegerhof) S. Student, Universidad Complutense, Madrid, 1985-86; BA cum laude, U. Calif., Santa Barbara, 1987. Gen. office clk. M. Barry Semler Enterprises, Santa Barbara, Calif., 1984, Office of the Provost U. Calif., Santa Barbara, 1984-85; clk. acctg. Harada Industry Am., Gardena, Calif., 1986; sec./bookkeeper Deinhard Electric Co., Santa Barbara, 1986-87; exec. asst. Banco di Napoli, Los Angeles, 1988—. Home: 3838 W 234th St Torrance CA 90505 Office: Banco di Napoli 333 S Grand Ave Ste 3220 Los Angeles CA 90071

SHEA, FRANCIS XAVIER, banker; b. N.Y.C., Feb. 8, 1941; s. Francis Xavier and Virginia S.; m. Joy Allison, May 24, 1980; children—Francis Xavier, Caitlin Allison; children by previous marriage—Deirdre Ellen, Maura Elizabeth. BS cum laude, Lehigh U. Trainee Chase Manhattan Bank, N.Y.C., 1962-64, asst. treas., 1964-68, bank forward planning group mgr., 1968-70, staff group mgr. internat. dept., 1970-75, service products group mgr. domestic instnl. banking, 1975-80; Asia instnl. mgr. Chase Manhattan Bank, Hong Kong, 1980-83; country mgr. Chase Manhattan Bank, Jakarta Selatan, Indonesia, 1983-88; Asia trade fin. exec. Chase Manhattan Bank, Jakarta Selatan, 1989—. Contbr. articles to profl. jours. Home: #4 Red Hill Park, #12 Pak Pat, Shan Rd, Tai Tam Hong Kong Office: Chase Manhattan Bank, World Trade Ctr-12, Causeway Bay Hong Kong

SHEA, JOHN FRANCIS, JR., insurance executive; b. Manchester, Conn., Sept. 11, 1928; s. John Francis and Irene Ann (Moriarty) S.; m. Grayce Elinore Kummel, Apr. 28, 1956; children—Martin, Kevin, Christine, Daniel. B.A., Providence Coll., 1950; J.D., U. Conn., 1953. Bar: Conn. 1954, U.S. Dist. Ct. Conn. 1964, U.S. Supreme Ct. 1967. Atty., Aetna Life & Casulty Co., Hartford, 1953-55, v.p., claim counsel, 1980—; ptnr. Marte, Shea & Keith, Attys., Manchester, Conn., 1955-73; judge Superior Ct., State of Conn., 1973-80; dir. Soc. for Savs., Hartford. Mem. Conn. Ho. of Reps., 1960-62; chmn. Republican Town Com., Manchester, Conn., 1959-64; Mem. Conn. Rep. Central Com., 1965-73. Mem. ABA, Conn. Bar Assn., Internat. Assn. Ins. Counsel, Conn. Criminal Justice Commn. Roman Catholic. Club: Manchester Country. Lodge: K.C. Home: 57 Boulder Rd Manchester CT 06040 Office: Aetna Life & Casualty Co 151 Farmington Ave Hartford CT 06156

SHEA, JOHN J., catalogue and retail company executive; b. 1938. BS, La Salle Coll.; MBA, U. Pitts. With John Wanamaker, Phila., 1953-80; pres., chief exec. officer Spiegel, Inc., Hinsdale, Ill., 1981—. Office: Spiegel Inc 1515 W 22nd St Oak Brook IL 60522 *

SHEA, WILLIAM ALFRED, lawyer; b. N.Y.C., June 21, 1907; s. Ashley P. and Olive L. (Martin) S.; m. May Nora Shaw, Sept. 16, 1937; children: William A. Jr., Kathy Ann Anfuso, Patricia A. Ryan. LLB, Georgetown U., 1931, LHD (hon.), 1971; LHD (hon.), St. Johns U., 1973, St. Francis Coll., 1974; LLD (hon.), L.I. U., 1986. Bar: D.C. 1931, N.Y. 1932. Now partner firm Shea & Gould, N.Y.C.; counsel liquidation bur. N.Y. State Banking Dept., 1934-36; asst. gen. counsel to supt. ins. N.Y. State, 1936-41; mem. N.Y. State Ins. Bd., 1956; trustee emeritus, sec., gen. counsel Cross Land Savs., FSB; dir., gen. counsel Interboro Mut. Indemnity Ins. Co., N.Y.C.; bd. dirs. Nat. Benefit Life Ins. Co., N.Y.C., Companion Life Ins. Co. Vice chmn. bd. Benjamin N. Cardozo Sch. Law, N.Y.C., North Shore Univ. Hosp., Manhasset, N.Y., Taft Inst. Two-Party Govt. Mem. ABA, Fed. Bar Assn., N.Y. State Bar Assn., Assn. of Bar City of N.Y., N.Y. County Lawyer's Assn., Bklyn. Bar Assn., Lawyer's Club of Bklyn., Sands Point Golf Club, Sky Club, University Club. Office: 1251 Ave of Americas New York NY 10020

SHEAFFER, JAY MICHAEL, electronics executive; b. Harrisburg, Pa., Oct. 12, 1950; s. Jason P. and Vivian (Nell) S.; 1 child, Jack Brett. BBA, Tex. Tech. U., Lubbock, 1975. Adminstrv. Hi-Line Electric Co., Dallas, 1975-76; salesman Hi-Line Electric Co., 1976-78, regional sales mgr., 1978-79, purchasing dir., 1979-81, nat. sales dir., 1981-86, pres., chief exec. officer, 1986—; cons. Jr. Achievement, Dallas, 1985—; corp. dir. Hi-Line Electric Co., 1987—, Roxor, Inc., Dallas, 1987—; dir. Brookhaven Men's Tennis League, Dallas, 1987—. Fellow mem. Dallas Young Republicans, 1986—. Mem. Nat. Assn. Wholesalers. Republican. Clubs: Chief Exec. Officers, The Exec. Com., Jr. Achievement, CEO. Home: 150 Maywood Coppell TX 75019

SHEALY, WALTER DIXON, III, banker; b. Charleston, S.C., Apr. 14, 1949; s. Walter Dixon Jr. and Celia Louise (Snipes) S.; m. Dottie Jean Cummings. BS, Presbyn. Coll., Clinton, S.C., 1971. V.p. Citizens and So. Nat. Bank, Atlanta, 1971-78; sr. v.p. Mortgage Guaranty Ins. Corp., Milw., 1978-84; sr. exec. v.p., chief mktg. officer CenTrust Mortgage Corp. subs. CenTrust Savs. Bank, Deerfield, Fla., 1984, now dir. mgmt., also bd. dirs.; sr. exec. v.p., dir. Capital Markets Group CenTrust Savs. Bank, Miami, Fla., 1984—, chmn. asset and liability mgmt. com., pres., 1988—; bd. dirs. Old Am. Ins. Co., Kansas City, Mo., Securnet Securities Corp., Phoenix. Author (with others): The MGIC Secondary Market Guide; contbr. articles to profl. jours. Mem. Fla. League Fin. Instns. (dist. dir.), Greater Miami C. of C. (bd. govs.), Blue Key Soc., Brickell Club. Presbyterian. Office: CenTrust Savs Bank 101 E Flagler St Miami FL 33131

SHEASBY, EDWARD GORDON, pipeline company executive, lawyer; b. Redcliff, Alta., Can., Mar. 5, 1925; s. Henry Gordon and Mary Jane (Webb) S.; children: Patricia Jane, Henry Gordon, Charlotte Maria, Bruce R. LL.B., U. B.C., 1952. Bar: B.C. 1953, Ont. 1969. Assoc. Campbell, Brazier & Co., Vancouver, B.C., 1953-55; sr. solicitor, asst. sec. Trans Mountain Oil Pipe Line Co., Vancouver, 1955-66; asst. gen. counsel Interprovincial Pipe Line Ltd., Toronto, Ont., 1966-72; gen. counsel Interprovincial Pipe Line Ltd., Toronto, 1972-87, asst. sec., 1967-73, sec., 1973-77, v.p., 1977-87; v.p. law Interhome Energy Inc., Calgary, Alta., Can., 1987—; sec. Lakehead Pipe Line Co., Superior, Wis., 1973-82. Served with Canadian Navy, 1942-47. Mem. Law Socs. B.C. and Ont. Clubs: Masons (Redcliff), Univ. (Toronto), Petroleum (Calgary). Home: 303 Lake Mead Crescent SE, Calgary, AB Canada T2J 4A2 Office: Interhome Energy Inc, 3200 Home Oil Tower 324-8 Ave SW, Calgary, AB Canada T2P 2Z5

SHEEHAN, CHARLES VINCENT, investment banker; b. London, Dec. 19, 1930; came to U.S., 1931; s. Charles Vincent and Mary Margaret (Stokes) S.; m. Susan Ellen Rosar, May 5, 1962. BS, Georgetown U., 1952. Chief fin. officer Gen. Electric Co., Tokyo, Sydney, Australia and Sao Paulo, Brazil, 1962-64, 64-66, 67-71; staff exec. Gen. Electric Co., Fairfield, Conn., 1972-83, v.p. corp. exec. office, 1983-87; sr. v.p., chief fin. and adminstrn. officer Kidder, Peabody Group, Inc., N.Y.C., 1987—; bd. dirs. Anderson Oil Co., Portland, Conn. Chmn. Non-partisan Polit. Action Com. for Gen. Electric Co. employees, Fairfield, 1982-83. Served to lt. USN, 1952-54. Republican. Roman Catholic. Clubs: Westchester County (Harrison, N.J.); Johns Island (Vero Beach, N.J.); Wildcat Cliffs Country (Highlands, N.C.). Home: 186 Lake Ave Greenwich CT 06830 Office: Kidder Peabody Group Inc 10 Hanover Sq New York NY 10005

SHEEHAN, DENNIS WILLIAM, lawyer, business executive; b. Springfield, Mass., Jan. 2, 1934; s. Timothy A. and H. Marjorie (Kelsey) S.; m. Elizabeth M. Hellyer, July 27, 1957; children: Dennis William, Catherine Elizabeth, John Edward. BS, U. Md., 1957; JD, Georgetown U., 1960, LLM, 1962. Bar: D.C., Md. 1960, Mo. 1976, Ohio 1977. Legal asst. to chmn. NLRB, Washington, 1960-61; trial atty. U.S. SEC, Washington, 1962-63; corp. atty. Martin Marietta, Balt., N.Y.C., 1963-64; v.p., gen. counsel, sec. Bunker Ramo Corp., Oak Brook, Ill., 1964-73; exec. v.p., gen. counsel, dir. Diversified Industries, Inc., St. Louis, 1973-75; v.p., gen. counsel, dir. N-ReN Corp., Cin., 1975-77; v.p., gen. counsel, sec., dir. AXIA Inc., Oak Brook, Ill., 1977-84, chmn., pres., chief exec. officer, 1984—; bd. dirs. Ames Taping Tools of Can. Ltd., Ont., Andamios Atlas, Mexico City, Jensen Tools & Alloys Inc., Phoenix, Compagnie Fischbein (S.A.), Brussels, Bliss & Laughlin Steel Co., Chgo., Ednl. Mgmt. Corp., Pitts. Bd. dirs. St. Margarets Sch. Found., Evang. Hosp. Found., Mid-Am. Inst. for Pub. Policy Rsch., Nat. Coun. on Crime and Delinquency. With AUS, 1954-56. Mem. ABA, St. Louis Club, Econ. Club, Carlton Club (Chgo.), Metropolitan Club (Washington), Bankers Club (Cin.), Nat. Lawyers Club, Downtown Club (Richmond, Va.), Metropolitan Club, Phi Delta Phi, Pi Sigma Alpha, Delta Sigma Phi. Republican. Home: 450 Lexington Dr Lake Forest IL 60045 Office: Axia Corp 122 W 22d St Oak Brook IL 60521

SHEEHAN, JAMES PATRICK, media company executive; b. Jersey City, June 6, 1942; s. John Patrick and Helen Teresa (Woods) S.; m. Mary Ellen Finnell, July 1, 1967; children—James, Elisabeth, Christopher. B.S., Seton Hall U., 1965; M.B.A., Wayne State U., 1973. Controller Otis Elevator Co. N.Am., Farmington, Conn., 1976-78; dir. mfg. Otis Elevator Co. N.Am., Yonkers, N.Y., 1978-80; v.p., controller Pratt & Whitney Aircraft, East Hartford, Conn., 1980-82; sr. v.p. A. H. Belo Corp., Dallas, 1982-84, chief fin. officer, 1984-86, pres., chief operating officer, 1987—; also dir. A. H. Belo Corp. Mem. devel. bd. U. Tex.-Dallas, 1985—; trustee Goals For Dallas, 1985; bd. dirs. United Way, Dallas Partnership, Ctr. for Non-profit Mgmt., Dallas Morning News Charities; adv. bd. Ursuline Acad. of Dallas; trustee St. Paul Med. Ctr. Found. Lt. (j.g.) USN, 1967-69, Vietnam. Mem. Am. Newspaper Pubs. Assn., So. Newspaper Pubs. Assn. Roman Catholic. Office: A H Belo Corp Communications Ctr Young & Houston Sts Dallas TX 75265

SHEEHAN, JOHN JOSEPH, data processing executive; b. Phila., Sept. 25, 1930; s. James Patrick and Irene Julia (Talbot) S.; m. Michele Bencivengo, July 13, 1975; 1 child, John II. BS, LaSalle U., 1953; MBA, NYU, 1954. Auditor Union Bank and Trust Co., Bethlehem, Pa., 1956-60, v.p., 1960-62; gen. mgr. Nat. Computer Analysts, Princeton, N.J., 1962-64, v.p., treas., 1964-67, exec. v.p., 1967-70, pres., 1970-86; pres., chief exec. officer MTech Northeast Corp. (formerly Nat. Computer Analysts), Princeton, 1986—; bd. dirs. Neuwirth Fund, Inc., N.Y.C., 1973—; United Scis., Princeton, 1972—. Republican. Roman Catholic. Home: 4 Bennington Pl Newtown PA 18940 Office: MTech NE Corp 99 Farber Rd Princeton NJ 08940

SHEEHAN, KEVIN EDWARD, engine company executive; b. Deerfield, Mass., June 17, 1945; s. Walter Francis and Lillian (Fontaine) S.; m. Barbara Ann Frank, July 6, 1974; children: Timothy John, James Frank. BA, Williams Coll., 1966; MBA, Harvard U., 1971. Traffic mgr. New England Tel., Boston, 1966-69; foreman H Block Line Cummins Engine Co., Columbus, Ind., 1971, employee rels. mgr., 1972-75, dir. employee rels., 1975-77, mgr. engine plant, 1977-80, v.p. mgmt. systems, 1980-83, v.p. parts, 1984, v.p. parts and distbn., 1984-86, v.p. components group, 1986—; bd. dirs. Haynes Internat., Kokomo, Ind. Pres., bd. dirs. Quinco Mental Health Ctr., Columbus, 1976-80, St. Agnes Parish, nashville, Ind., 1980-84. Mem. Country of Brown County Club (Nashville, Ind., pres., bd. dirs. 1984-88). Home: RR 5 Box 550 Nashville IN 47448 Office: Cummins Engine Co PO Box 3005 Columbus IN 47202

SHEEHAN, MONICA MARY, banker; b. New Milford, Conn., Apr. 27, 1955; d. Walter F. and Lillian (Fontaine) S. BA cum laude, Williams Coll., 1977; MBA, NYU, 1984. Cable franchise adminstr. Viacom Internat. Inc., N.Y.C., 1978-81, corp. fin. analyst, 1981-82, mgr. fin. planning, 1982-83, mgr. corp. fin. planning, 1983-84; asst. to chief fin. officer Viacom Internat Inc., N.Y.C., 1984-85; fin. analyst, chmn. bd. Citibank/Citicorp., N.Y.C., 1985-86; project dir. World Corp. Group/Citibank, N.Y.C., 1986-87; relationship banker NCD-East/Citibank, N.Y.C., 1987-88; area mgr. N.E. region The Mitsubishi Bank Ltd., N.Y.C., 1988—. Mem. pres.'s council St. Vincent's Hosp., N.Y.C., 1986—. Democrat. Roman Catholic. Club: Williams (N.Y.C.) (bd. govs. 1979-84). Home: 310 E 44th Apt 507 New York NY 10017 Office: The Mitsubishi Bank Ltd One World Trade Ctr Ste 8527 New York NY 10048

SHEEHAN, THOMAS HENRY, JR., management consultant; b. Detroit, Dec. 28, 1935; s. Thomas H. Sheehan and Ethel Knechtel. B.S. in Mech. Engring., U. Mich., 1959; M.B.A. in Prodn. and Mktg., U. Chgo., 1963; Ph.D. in Mineral Econ., Colo. Sch. Mines, 1976. Engr. Reliable Electric Co., Chgo., 1959-60; mgmt. systems specialist Lockheed Aircraft Corp., Marietta, Ga., 1960-64; mgmt. cons. Touche Ross & Co., N.Y.C., 1965-69, ptnr., Madrid and N.Y.C., 1969-72; mgmt. cons. Spencer Stuart, Chgo., 1972-74; exec. dir. Colo. Dept. Adminstrn., Denver, 1976-78; pres. Sheehan Internat., Golden, Colo., 1979-85, prin. mgmt. cons. SRI Internat., Menlo Park, Calif., 1985—. Served with USMC, 1960, with Res., 1961-66. Mem. N.Am. Soc. for Corp. Planning (exec. v.p. 1984—), U. Chgo. Alumni Assn. San Francisco Area (pres. 1986—). Office: SRI International 333 Ravenswood Ave Menlo Park CA 94025

SHEEHAN, WILLIAM JOSEPH, hotel company executive; b. Plattsburgh, N.Y., July 2, 1944; s. William J. and Anna (McKeefe) S.; m. Ann Lakschewitz, July 3, 1971; children: Emily, William J. IV. BS, Boston U., 1967. Acct. Arthur Andersen & Co., Boston, 1967-79, ptnr., 1979-82; exec. v.p., chief fin. officer Omni Hotels, N.Y.C., 1982-88, pres., chief exec. officer, 1988—. Contbr. articles to profl. jours. Chmn. adv. and fin. com. Town of Nahant, Mass., 1981-83; pres. Tower Sch., Marblehead, Mass., 1987—. Fellow AICPA; mem. Fin. Execs. Inst., Urban Land Inst. Office: Omni Hotels 515 Madison Ave New York NY 10022

SHEEHY, PATRICK, manufacturing company executive; b. Sept. 2, 1930; s. Sir John Francis Sheehy and Jean Newton Simpson; m. Jill Patricia Tindall, 1964; 2 children. Grad., Ampleforth Coll., Yorkshire, Eng.; LHD (hon.), Va. Union U., 1985. Joined Brit.-Am. Tobacco Co., 1950, sales mgr., Nigeria, 1953-54, mktg. dir., Jamaica, 1957-61, gen. mgr., Barbados, 1961-67, Holland, 1967-70, bd. dirs., 1970-82, chmn. bd. dirs., 1976-81; vice chmn. B-A-T Industries, London, 1976-82, chmn. bd. dirs., 1982—; now also chmn., bd. dir. Batus, Inc., Louisville, 1986—; chmn. B-A-T Fin. Services, London, 1985—; bd. dirs. Brit. Petroleum, London . Served to 2d lt. Irish Guards, 1948-50. Mem. Confedn. Brit. Industry (task force on urban regeneration), Trade Policy Research Ctr., Action Com. for Europe. Avocations: golf, reading. Office: Batus Inc 2000 Citizens Pla Louisville KY 40202

SHEEHY, THOMAS DANIEL, apparel and textile manufacturing company executive; b. Lawrence, Mass., Dec. 9, 1946; s. Bernard Agustine and Frances Patricia (Noone) S.; m. Lisa Mary Hartmann; children: Christine Judith, Matthew Thomas. BBA, Suffolk U., 1969, MBA, 1974. Research and devel. engr. Malden Mills, Inc., 1970-71, prodn. control mgr., 1972-77; corp. mgr. Champion Products, Inc., Rochester, N.Y., 1977-80, mgr. mfg. resource planning, 1980-81, dir. mfg. resource planning, 1981-83, dir. mfg., 1984-85, v.p. mfg., 1985-86, v.p. ops., 1986—. Area chmn. Suffolk U. Alumni Fund, 1975-77. Served with U.S. Army, 1970-71. Mem. Am. Prodn. and Inventory Control Soc. (cert. practitioner inventory mgmt.). Home: 91 Great Wood Circle Fairport NY 14450 Office: Champion Products Inc 3141 Monroe Ave Rochester NY 14618

SHEELINE, PAUL CUSHING, hotel executive; b. Boston, June 6, 1921; s. Paul Daniel and Mary Cushing (Child) S.; m. Harriet White Moffat, May 23, 1948 (dec. 1962); children: Christopher White, William Emerson, Mary Child, Leonora Moffat; m. Sandra Dudley Wahl, July 24, 1965; 1 dau., Abby Tucker. B.S., Harvard U., 1943, J.D., 1948. Bar: N.Y. 1949, D.C. 1986. Assoc. Sullivan & Cromwell, N.Y.C., 1948-54; with Lambert & Co., N.Y.C., 1954-65, gen. ptnr., 1958-65; chief fin. officer Intercontinental Hotels Corp., N.Y.C., 1966-71, pres., 1971-74, chief exec. officer, 1971-85, chmn. bd., 1972-87, cons., 1987—; of counsel Verner, Liipfert, Bernhard, McPherson & Hand, Washington; chmn. bd. Valex Energy Corp.; bd. dirs. Nat. Westminster Bancorp, Inc., Nat. Westminster Bank U.S.A., Pan Am Corp., Pan Am. World Airways; mem. Presdl. Bd. Advisors on Pvt. Sector Initiatives, Washington, 1987-89. Vice chmn. Community Service Soc. of N.Y., 1962-63; dir. Am. Assn. for UN, 1951-58; former mem. Harvard Overseers Com. to visit Center for Internat. Affairs and Dept. Romance Langs.; trustee East Woods Sch., Oyster Bay Cove, N.Y., 1959-68, Camargo Found., St. Luke's/Roosevelt Hosp. Ctr.; bd. dirs. Bus. Council for Internat. Understanding., Fgn. Policy Assn., Scientists' Inst. Pub. Info., U.S. Com. for Battle of Normandy Mus. Served to capt. USAAF, 1942-46. Decorated Silver Star medal, French Legion of Honor, Croix de Guerre with palm, Moroccan Ouissam Alaouite. Mem. Council Fgn. Relations, Am.-Arab Assn. Commerce and Industry (chmn. bd. 1984-86), Phi Beta Kappa. Clubs: Cold Spring Harbor Beach; Anglers (N.Y.); Harvard (N.Y.C. and L.I.); Sky (N.Y.C.). Office: care Vale & Co 6 E 43d St New York NY 10017

SHEEN, BRIAN JEFFREY, financial planner; b. Bklyn., Oct. 17, 1952; s. Mickey and Marilyn (Connor) S.; children: Springsong Tawna, Ariel Voyager. Student, Bklyn. Coll., 1971, Hubbard Coll., Sussex, Eng., 1974. Cert. fin. planner, 1984. Mgmt. cons. Voight Ind., Lubec, Maine, 1974-75, Mgmt. Expansion Unltd., Palm Beach, Fla., 1975-77, Bache & Co., Palm Beach, 1977; account exec. Dean, Witter, Reynolds, Palm Beach, 1977-79; investment planner Merrill, Lynch, Pierce et al, North Palm Beach, Fla., 1979-81, E. F. Hutton & Co., North Palm Beach, 1981-82; pres. ins. sales investment Planning Cons., West Palm Beach, Fla., 1982-84; rep. BNL Securities, Parsipanny, N.Y., 1983, Pvt. Ledger Fin. Svcs., San Diego, 1983-84; mng. exec. Integrated Resources Equity Corp., N.Y.C., 1984-88; pres., owner Sheen Fin. Resources, Boca Raton, Fla., 1988; chief exec. officer Sheen Investment Mgmt. Group, Boca Raton, 1986—, Sheen Investment Adv. Svcs., Boca Raton, 1986—, Sheen Fin. Network, Boca Raton, 1986—. Author: Your Money or Your Life, 1982, Preserving Wealth, 1985, Nest Egg Investing, 1987; co-author: Financial Planning Encyclopedia, 1984, Financial Planning Can Make You Rich, 1987, About Your Future, 1988; columnist various S.E. newspapers; composer, musician Colouring Dreams, New Morning, Tenderly, Simple Song, 1973. Mem. Internat. Assn. Fin. Planning, Nat. Speakers Assn., Inst. Cert. Fin. Planners, Nat. Ctr. for Fin. Edn., Nat. Assn. Life Underwriters, U.S. Jaycees (past pres., Seiji Horiuchi award 1984-85, Tommy Thompson award, others). Office: The Sheen Group 1515 N Federal Hwy Ste 406 Boca Raton FL 33432

SHEERAN-EMORY, KATHLEEN MARY, executive consultant; b. Wilmington, Del., Feb. 27, 1948; d. Stanley Robert and Eileen Ann (Walsh) Sheeran. BA, St. Mary's Coll., Notre Dame, Ind., 1970. Asst. editor Conde Nast Publs., N.Y.C., 1970-76; account exec. Working Woman mag., N.Y.C., 1976-77; account exec. Foote Cone & Belding Communications, Inc., N.Y.C., 1977-78; v.p. John P. Holmes & Co., Inc., N.Y.C., 1978-83, Korn Ferry Internat., N.Y.C., 1983-84, Sheeran-Emory Assocs., N.Y.C., 1984—; mem. faculty YWCA, 53d St. chpt., N.Y.C., 1980—. Mem. nominating com. Girl Scouts Greater N.Y. Fellow Internat. Biog. Assn.; mem. MIT Enterprise Forum, Nat. Assn. for Female Execs., Women's Nat. Rep. Club, Am. Soc. Profl. and Exec. Women. Roman Catholic. Home and Office: PO Box 1754 Church St Sta New York NY 10008

SHEETS, KIM RAY, financial consultant, financial planner; b. Waco, Tex., Sept. 29, 1855; s. Whilman George and Molly Mae (Melder) S.; m. Beth Ellen Hartline, Feb. 16, 1961. Student, La. State U., 1973-77. Chief fin. officer SCC Corp., Baton Rouge, 1981-84; futures specialist Merrill Lynch, New Orleans, 1984; fin. cons. Pierce Fenner & Smith Merrill Lynch, Baton Rouge, 1984-89; v.p., fin. cons. Shearson Lehman Hutton, Baton Rouge, 1989—; mem. fin. com., bd. dirs. Young Life, Baton Rouge, 1987—; v.p., fin. cons. Shearson Lehman Hutton, 1989—. Mem. Bd. Trade City of Chgo., Chgo. Merc. Exch., Nat. Assn. Security Dealers, N.Y. Stock Exch., Baton Rouge C. of C., Gonzales C. of C. Republican. Mem. Christian Ch. Home: 10219 Veranda Ct Baton Rouge LA 70810 Office: Shearson Lehman Hutton 8550 United Pla Blvd Ste 901 Baton Rouge LA 70809

SHEETZ, DAVID PATRICK, chemical company executive; b. Colebrook, Pa., Dec. 4, 1926; s. David S. and Ella (Youtz) S.; m. Mary Blumer, Feb. 24, 1946; children: Michael, Matthew, Martha. B.S. in Chemistry, Lebanon Valley Coll., 1948; M.S. in Phys. Chemistry, U. Nebr., 1951, Ph.D. in Phys. Chemistry, 1952. In various research and devel. mgmt. positions Dow Chem. Co., Midland, Mich., 1952-67, asst. dir. research and devel. Mich. div., 1967-71, dir. research and devel. Mich. div., 1971-78, v.p., dir. R & D, 1980-85, sr. v.p., chief scientist, 1985—, also bd. dirs.; tech. dir. Dow Chem. U.S.A., Midland, 1978, v.p., dir. R & D, 1978-80; mem. Chem. Scis. and Tech. Bd. NRC; mem. Matrix Midland Sci. Com., 1978—; adv. bd. Nat. Sci. Resources Ctr., Soc. Chem. Industry; mem. Merrell Dow Bd. Patentee in field. Served with USN, 1945-46. Fellow Am. Inst. Chemists; mem. Am. Chem. Soc., Indsl. Rsch. Inst. (alt. rep.), Coun. for Chem. Rsch. (alt. rep.), Sigma Xi.

SHEETZ, RALPH ALBERT, lawyer; b. Dauphin County, Pa., June 13, 1908; s. Harry Wesley and MaNora (Enders) S.; m. Ruth Lorraine Bender, May 19, 1938; 1 son, Ralph Bert. Ph.B., Dickinson Coll., 1930; J.D., U. Ala., 1933. Bar: Pa. 1934, U.S. Dist. Ct. (mid. dist.) Pa. 1944. Solicitor, East Pennsboro Twp., Pa., 1937-53, Peoples Bank of Enola (Pa.), 1935-75; atty. Lawyers Title Ins. Corp., Richmond, Va., 1956—, Commonwealth Land Title Ins. Co., Phila., 1957—; atty. Employees Loan Soc., 1966-76. Ofcl. Appeal Area no. 4, SSS, Pa., assoc. legal adviser to Draft Bd. No. 2, adviser to registrants to Local Bd. No. 55, Harrisburg, Pa., 1974—; counselor Camp Kanestake, Huntingdon County, Pa., Methodist Ch.; treas., atty. Enola Boys Club, from 1950; pres. East Pennsboro Twp. PTA, 1951-52; atty. hon. mem. Citizens Fire Co. No. 1, Enola, 1951; apptd. bd. gov's. Am. Biog. Inst. Rsch. Assn.; del. arts and communications 15th Internat. Congress, Singapore; sec., treas. West Shore Regional Coordinating Com., Cumberland County, 1956-66; mem. bd. adjustments East Pennsboro Twp., 1959, chmn., 1959, mem. planning commn, 1956-59, vice-chmn., mem. zoning commn., 1958, chmn., 1959; mem. East Pennsboro Twp. Republican Club, from 1936. Recipient numerous awards and honors from Pres. of U.S. for service to SSS; Order of the Silver Trowel, Council of Anointed Kings Commonwealth of Pa., Altoona, 1948. Mem. Dauphin Bar Assn. (social com. 1934—), Cumberland County Bar Assn., Pa. Bar Assn., ABA. Clubs: Tall Cedars of Lebanon (historian Harrisburg Forest No. 43 1980—, exec. com.), Shriners, Masons (York cross of honor), K.T. (comdr. 1946).

SHEFFIELD, DON B., wholesale distribution company executive; b. 1935. BS, U. Tex., 1958. With Geosource Inc., Houston, 1958—, various mgmt. positions, 1958-73, sr. v.p., 1973-76, exec. v.p. geophys. ops. western hemisphere, 1976-78, exec. v.p. geophys. ops. worldwide, 1978-79, pres. mgr. exploration services, 1979-80, pres. petroleum exploration group, 1980-81, v.p. service ops., 1981-82, pres., chief exec. officer, 1984—. Office: Geosource Inc 6909 SW Freeway Houston TX 77074 *

SHEFFIELD, TYLER W., broadcast financial executive; b. Salt Lake City, Dec. 8, 1956; s. Loftis Jolley and Blanche (Whiteley) S.; m. Christine Harmon, June 11, 1987. BS in Acctg., Brigham Young U., 1980; MBA in Fin., Northwestern U., 1982. CPA. Auditor Peat Marwick Mitchell, Oakland, Calif., 1981; bus. analyst Deloitte Haskins & Sells, Chgo., 1982-84; fin. analyst Northwest Ind., Chgo., 1984-85; chief fin. officer Burnham Broadcasting, Chgo., 1985—. Republican. Mormon. Home: 5640 W Kolmar Chicago IL 60646 Office: Burnham Broadcasting 980 N Michigan Ste 1200 Chicago IL 60611

SHEFFIELD, VERNON GERALD, financial planner; b. Houston, Oct. 7, 1913; s. Norris and Mary Benjamin (Rowe) S.; m. Frances Jane Burton, Oct. 30, 1932 (div.); children: Walter, Robert, Carol; m. Marjorie Evaughn Carlock, July 24, 1965; stepchildren: John, William. BBA, South Tex. Coll., 1937. Cert. fin. planner; CPA Tex. Acct. Texaco Inc., Houston, 1930-37; acct. auditor Ernst & Whinney CPA, Houston, 1937-47, mgr. tax. dept., 1949-51; ptnr. Aubrey Fariss & Co., Houston, 1948-49, Alwin Adam & Co.,

Houston, 1951-53; mng. ptnr. Sheffield, Pridgen & Iverson, Houston, 1953-72; sr. ptnr. Grant Thornton CPA, Houston, 1972-77; asst. controller Gauranty Fed. Savs. & Loan Assn., Galveston, Tex., 1977-79; tax acct. R. Wayne Swift, Galveston, 1979-82; v.p. U.S. Nat. Bank, Galveston, 1982-84; sec., treas. Sheffield Fin. Mgmt. Inc., Houston, 1984-85; pres. Galveston Fin. Planning Inc., 1985—. Treas. United Ministry for Port of Galveston, 1985—, also dir.; trustee Galveston Pks. Bd., 1987—. Mem. Calveston County Fair and Rodeo Assn., Tex. Navy Assn. (adml.), Greater Houston C. of C., Houston Livestock Show and Rodeo Assn., Inst. Cert. Fin. Planners, Internat. Assn. Fin. Planners, Am. Inst. CPA's, Nat. Assn. Accts. (pres. Houston chpt. 1955-56), Galveston Estate Planning Council, Tex. State Bd. Realtors, Galveston Country Club, Galveston Pelican, Rotary (past pres.). Home: 4806 Woodrow Ave Galveston TX 77551 Office: Galveston Fin Planning 2201 Market St Ste 907 Galveston TX 77550

SHEFFLER, GEORGE JUSTUS, real estate developer and broker; b. L.A., Dec. 10, 1944; s. Russell Noble and Dorothy Katherine (Sutherland) S. AA, Golden West Coll., Huntington Beach, Calif., 1967; BS, East Tex. State U., 1970; postgrad., So. Meth. U., 1972-73, U. So. Calif., 1977. Cert. real estate brokerage mgr., Ariz. Prin. Sheffler Properties, Phoenix, 1973—; v.p. Vans Improvement Co., Salome, Ariz., 1978-80, pres., chief exec. officer, 1980—, also bd. dirs. Chmn. Hunt County Rep. Com., Greenville, Tex., 1974-80; del. Young Rep. Nat. Conv., 1975; alt. del. Rep. Nat. Conv., 1976. Mem. Realtors Nat. Mktg. Assn., Am. Resort and Residential Assn., Nat. Assn. Home Builders (land devel. com. 1977-79), Real Estate Securities and Syndication Inst. (publs. com. 1977-78), Nat. Assn. Realtors, Ariz. Assn. Realtors, Carlsbad Bd. Realtors (com. chmn. 1982), Ariz. C. of C., McMullen Valley C. of C. (pres.-elect), Parker Area C. of C., UCLA Alumni Assn. (life), SCV, Ariz. Club (Phoenix), Optimists (life), Rho Epsilon. Republican. Episcopalian. Home: Hwy 60 Harcuvar Twp Salome AZ 85348 Office: Vans Improvement Co 3855 N 29th Ave St F Phoenix AZ 85017

SHEFRIN, HAROLD (HERSH) MARVIN, economist, educator, consultant; b. Winnipeg, Man., Can., July 27, 1948; came to U.S., 1974, s. Samuel and Clara Ida (Danzker) S.; m. Arna Patricia Saper, June 28, 1970. B.Sc. with honors, U. Man., Winnipeg, 1970; M.Math., U. Waterloo, Can., 1971; Ph.D., London Sch. Econs., 1974. Asst. prof. econs. U. Rochester, N.Y., 1974-79; asst. prof. U. Santa Clara, Calif., 1979-80, assoc. prof., 1981, chmn. econs., 1983-88, full prof., 1986—; cons. Nuclear Regulatory Commn., U.S. Dept. Energy, Livermore, Calif., 1979-82, Syntex Corp., Palo Alto, Calif., 1983—. Contbr. articles to profl. jours. Mem. Am. Econ. Assn., Econometric Soc., Western Econ. Assn., Western Fin. Assn., Fin. Mgmt. Assn., Am. Profs. for Peace in the Mid. East., European Fin. Assn., Internat. Assn. Math. Modeling. Jewish. Co-developed econ. theory of self control, behavioral finance; contbr. econ. theory of uncertainty, and consumer aggregation. Office: Santa Clara U Dept Econs Santa Clara CA 95053

SHEFTEL, ROGER TERRY, merchant banking executive; b. Denver, Sept. 10, 1941; s. Edward and Dorothy (Barnett) S.; m. Phoebe A. Sherman, Sept. 7, 1968; children: Tisha B., Ryan B. BS in Econs., U. Pa., 1963. Comml. lending officer Provident Nat. Bank, Phila., 1963-65; asst. to pres. Continental Finance Corp., Denver, 1965-68; v.p. Eastern Indsl. Leasing Corp., Phila., 1968-71, exec. v.p., dir., 1971-73; exec. v.p., dir. HBE Leasing Corp., Phila., 1971-73; pres., dir. Zebley & Strouse, Inc., Phila., 1973-75; dir. Kooly Kupp, Inc., Boyertown, Pa., 1974-77, pres., dir., 1977; prin. Trivest, Phila., 1973-77; pres. Trivest, Inc., Phila., 1977-78, 1670 Corp., mgmt. cons.'s, 1978-82; pres. Am. Cons. Group, Inc., 1982-83; exec. v.p., dir. Argus Research Labs., Inc., 1982-83; pres. Leasing Concepts, Inc., 1983—, Barclay Assocs., 1988—. Mem. bd. organized classes, exec. com. U. Pa. Mem. Am. Assn. Equipment Lessors, Eastern Assn. Equipment Lessors (bd. dirs.), Western Assn. Equipment Lessors, Kite and Key Soc. Clubs: Nantucket Yacht; Friars. Lodge: Rotary. Home: 414 Barclay Rd Rosemont PA 19010

SHEH, ROBERT BARDHYL, engineering and construction company executive; b. N.Y.C., July 29, 1939; s. Talat and Nedime (Karali) S.; m. Mary Cheney Fleming, Dec. 29, 1961; children—Andrea K., Jonathan C., Robert R., Elisabeth F., Theresa N. BS in Civil Engring, Rensselaer Poly. Inst., 1960; grad. PMD, Harvard U., 1974. With Ralph M. Parsons Co., 1971—; sr. v.p., mgr. petroleum and chem. div. Ralph M. Parsons Co., Pasadena, Calif., 1981—; also bd. dir. Ralph M. Parsons Co.; bd. dir. Saudi Arabian Parsons; mem. adv. bd. Sch. Chem. Engr. U. Calif., Berkeley, 1986—. Bd. regents Marymount Internat. Sch., London, 1979. With USNR, 1960-64. Mem. Annandale Golf Club (Pasadena), Am. Club (London). Office: Ralph M Parsons Co 100 W Walnut St Pasadena CA 91124

SHEI, VICKI IRENE, accountant; b. Highland, Ill., Nov. 15, 1949; d. Gerard Conrad and Alice Irene (Lee) Mueller; m. Edwin Arthur Shei, July 5, 1969. BS in Math., Loyola U., Chgo., 1971. Officer mgr., acct. Clawson Mfg. Co., Missoula, Mont., 1979, Roemer's Tire Ctr. Inc., Missoula, Mont., 1979-83, Agy. Tile Co., Spring Valley, N.Y., 1983-84; sr. acct. Ford Products Corp., Valley Cottage, N.Y., 1984-88. Republican.

SHEINBERG, ERIC P., investment banker. Ptnr. div. trading and arbitrage Goldman Sachs and Co., N.Y.C. Office: Goldman Sachs & Co 85 Broad St New York NY 10004 *

SHEINBERG, ISRAEL, computer company executive; b. Fort Worth, Apr. 15, 1932; s. Samuel I. and Pauline C. (Fram) S.; m. Betty S. Topletz, Aug. 19, 1962; children—Amy, Karen, David, Paula. B.S. in Physics, U. Tex., 1953; student, UCLA, 1957-58, Arlington (Tex.) State Coll., 1960, Southwestern Med. Sch., 1961. Electronic engr. Hughes Aircraft Co., 1956-60, Nat. Data Processing Corp., 1961; exec. v.p., chief operating officer Recognition Equipment Inc., 1961—; now exec. v.p. responsible for corp. devel., also dir. numerous wholly owned subs.; dir. Tex. Commerce Bank, Cygnet Systems Inc. speaker on image technology, optical character recognition and related subjects. Contbr. articles to profl. jours. Served with AUS, 1954-56. Mem. Optical Soc. Am., Am. Mgmt. Assn. Jewish (bd. dirs. synagogue). Home: 5706 Watson Circle Dallas TX 75225 Office: Recognition Equipment Inc PO Box 660204 Dallas TX 75266

SHEINBERG, SIDNEY JAY, recreation and entertainment company executive; b. Corpus Christi, Tex., Jan. 14, 1935; s. Harry and Tillie (Grossman) S.; m. Lorraine Gottfried, Aug. 19, 1956; children: Jonathan J., William David. A.B., Columbia Coll., 1955; LL.B., Columbia U., 1958. Bar: Calif. 1958. Assoc. in law UCLA Sch. Law, 1958-59; with MCA, Inc., Universal City, Calif., 1959—, pres. TV div., 1971-74, corp. exec. v.p., 1969-73, corp. pres., chief operating officer, 1973—. Mem. Assn. Motion Picture and Television Producers (chmn. bd.). Office: MCA Inc 100 Universal City Pla Universal City CA 91608 *

SHEINKMAN, JACK, union official, lawyer; b. N.Y.C., Dec. 6, 1926; s. Shaia and Bertha (Rosenkrantz) S.; m. Betty Francis Johnson, May 31, 1954; children: Michael, Joshua, Mark. B.S., Cornell U., 1948, LL.B., 1952; cert. in econs., Oxford U., 1949. Bar: N.Y. 1952. Atty. NLRB, Washington, 1952-53; atty. Amalgamated Clothing Workers Am., N.Y.C., 1953-58, gen. counsel, 1958-72, v.p., 1968-72, sec.-treas., 1972-76; sec.-treas. Amalgamated Clothing and Textile Workers Union, N.Y.C., 1976-87, pres., 1987—; chmn. bd. Amalgamated Bank of N.Y.; v.p. indsl. union dept. AFL-CIO, Internat. Textile, Garment and Leather Workers Fedn., Brussels. Contbr.: Labor and the New South, 1977. Trustee Cornell U.; dir. internat. rescue com. Phelp Stokes Fund, N.Y.C.; exec. com. Citizen's Labor-Energy Coalition; trustee Postgrad. Ctr. Mental Health; co-chmn. Econ. Policy Council, United Housing Found. Served to lt. (j.g.) USNR, 1944-46, PTO. Mem. Workers Def. League (dir.), Am. Arbitration Assn. (dir.), Afro-Asian Inst. (chmn.), Council Fgn. Relations, UN Assn. U.S.A. (bd. govs.), Brit.-N.Am. Com. (exec. com.), Can.-Am. Com. (exec. com.). Democrat. Jewish. Home: 52 W 76th St New York NY 10023 Office: Amalgamated Clothing & Textile Workers Union 11-15 Union Sq New York NY 10003 *

SHEKAILO, LORETTA ANNE, accountant; b. Rockville Ctr., N.Y., July 27, 1957; d. Arthur Joseph and Anne Elizabeth (McGunnigle) McCormick; m. Victor Francis Shekailo, Oct. 11, 1985. BS, SUNY, Oswego, 1979. CPA, N.Y. Jr. acct. Harry R. Lipps, CPA, Deer Park, N.Y., 1979-80; controller Evangelista Enterprises, L.I., N.Y., 1980-84, EIL Petroleum Inc., Jericho, N.Y., 1984-86, The Redco Orgn., Oceanside, N.Y., 1986-87; staff acct. Reffsin Delle Fave & Co., Jericho, N.Y., 1987—; pvt. practice tax cons. Dix Hills, N.Y., 1980—. Republican. Roman Catholic. Home: 465 Wolf Hill Rd Dix Hills NY 11746 Office: Reffsin Delle Fave & Co 99 Jericho Turnpike Jericho NY 11753

SHELBY, JAMES STANFORD, cardiovascular surgeon; b. Ringgold, La., June 15, 1934; s. Jesse Audrey and Mable (Martin) S.; BS in Liberal Arts La. Tech. U., 1956; M.D., La. State U., 1958; m. Susan Rainey, July 15, 1967; children—Bryan Christian, Christopher Linden. Intern, Charity Hosp. La., New Orleans, 1958-59, resident surgery and thoracic surgery, 1959-65; fellow cardiovascular surgery Baylor U. Coll. Medicine, Houston, 1965-66; practice medicine specializing in cardiovascular surgery, Shreveport, La., 1967—; mem. staff Schumpert Med. Center, Highland Hosp., Willis-Knighton Med. Ctr.; assoc. prof. surgery La. State U. Sch. Medicine, Shreveport, 1967—. Served with M.C., AUS, 1961-62. Diplomate Am. Bd. Surgery, Am. Bd. Thoracic Surgery. Recipient Tower of Medallion award La. Tech. U., 1982. Mem. Am. Coll. Cardiology, AMA, Soc. Thoracic Surgeons, Am. Heart Assn., Southeastern Surg. Congress, So. Thoracic Surg. Assn. Home: 6003 East Ridge Dr Shreveport LA 71106 Office: 2751 Virginia Ave Shreveport LA 71103

SHELDON, ELEANOR HARRIET BERNERT, sociologist; b. Hartford, Conn., Mar. 19, 1920; d. M.G. and Fannie (Myers) Bernert; m. James Sheldon, Mar. 19, 1950 (div. 1960); children: James, John Anthony. A.A., Colby Jr. Coll., 1940; A.B., U. N.C., 1942; Ph.D., U. Chgo., 1949. Asst. demographer Office Population Research, Washington, 1942-43; social scientist U.S. Dept Agr., Washington, 1943-45; asso. dir. Chgo. Community Inventory, U. Chgo., 1947-50; social scientist Social Sci. Research Council, N.Y.C., 1950-51; research grantee Social Sci. Research Council, 1953-55, pres., 1972-79; research asso. Bur. Applied Social Research, Columbia, 1950-51; social scientist UN, N.Y.C., 1951-52; lectr. sociology Columbia U., 1951-52, vis. prof., 1969-71; research assoc., lectr. sociology UCLA, 1955-61; assoc. research sociologist, lectr. Sch. Nursing U. Calif., 1957-61; sociologist, exec. assoc. Russell Sage Found., N.Y.C., 1961-72; vis. prof. U. Calif. at Santa Barbara, 1971; dir. Equitable Life Assurance Soc., Mobil Corp., H.J. Heinz Co. Author: (with L. Wirth) Chicago Community Fact Book, 1949, America's Children, 1958, (with R.A. Glazier) Pupils and Schools in N.Y.C, 1965; Editor: (with W.E. Moore) Indicators of Social Change; Concepts and Measurements, 1968, Family Economic Behavior, 1973; Contbr. (with W.E. Moore) articles to profl. jours. Bd. dirs. Colby-Sawyer Coll., 1979-85, UN Research Inst. for Social Devel., 1973-79; trustee Rockefeller Found., 1978-85, Nat. Opinion Research Ctr., 1980-87, Inst. East-West Security Studies, 1984-88. William Rainey Harper fellow U. Chgo., 1945-47. Fellow Am. Acad. Arts and Scis., Am. Sociol. Assn., Am. Statis. Assn.; mem. U. Chgo. Alumni Assn. (Profl. Achievement award), Sociol. Research Assn. (pres. 1971-72), Council on Fgn. Relations, AAAS, Am. Assn. Pub. Opinion Research, Eastern Sociol. Soc., Internat. Sociol. Assn., Internat. Union Sci. Study of Population, Population Assn. Am. (2d v.p. 1970-71), Inst. of Medicine (chmn. program com. 1976-77). Club: Cosmopolitan. Home: 630 Park Ave New York NY 10021 Office: Mobil Corp 150 E 42nd St New York NY 10017

SHELDON, FRANCES DOROTHY GIGANTE, retail executive; b. Bronx, Mar. 9, 1949; d. John C. and Frances T. Gigante; m. Thomas Hewey Sheldon, Aug. 22, 1970 (div. Mar. 1978); children: Thomas Hewey Jr., John Edward. Student, Brevard Community Coll., 1967, Cornell U., 1969. Various positions Publix Supermarkets, Inc., Jacksonville, Fla., 1967-81; asst. store mgr. Publix Supermarkets, Inc., Lakeland, Fla., 1981-85, store mgr., 1985—. cons. adv. bd. for coop. edn. students Titusville High Sch., 1986—; mem. St. Theresa's PTA, Titusville, Fla., 1978—; active St. Teresa's Catholic Womens Club, Titusville, 1980—. Mem. Am. Bus. Women's Assn., Nat. Assn. Female Execs., Nat. Police Res. Officers, Am. Nat. Red. Cross. Home: PO Box 1035 Titusville FL 32780 Office: Publix Supermarkets Inc PO Box 407 Lakeland FL 33802

SHELDON, KIRK ROY, financial company executive; b. San Diego, Aug. 17, 1958; s. Gale W. and Ruth Charlotte (Krueger) S. AS, Grossmont Coll., 1983; BSBA in Fin., San Diego State U., 1989; cert., Coll. Fin. Planning, 1983. Registered gen. securities rep.; lic. real estate broker, life and disability ins. agt. V.p. Guardian Broker, San Diego, 1977-87; pres. The Capital Group, San Diego, 1987—. Mem. Inst. Cert. Fin. Planners (cert.), Internat. Assn. Fin. Planning, Nat. Assn. Realtors, Calif. Assn. Realtors, San Diego Bd. Realtors. Methodist. Office: The Capital Group 2535 Camino del Rio S Ste 130 San Diego CA 92108

SHELDON, NANCY WAY, management consultant; b. Bryn Mawr, Pa., Nov. 10, 1944; d. John Harold and Elizabeth Semple (Hoff) W.; m. Robert Charles Sheldon, June 15, 1968. BA, Wellesley Coll., 1966; MA, Columbia U., 1968, M in Philosphy, 1972. Registered pvt. investigator, Calif. Mgmt. cons. ABT Assocs., Cambridge, Mass., 1969-70; mgmt. cons. Harbridge House, Inc., 1970-79, Los Angeles, 1977-79, v.p., 1977-79; mgmt. cons., pres. Resource Assessment, Inc., 1979—; ptnr., real estate developer Resource Devel. Assocs., 1980—; ptnr. Anubis Group, Ltd., 1980—. Author: Social and Economic Benefits of Public Transit, 1973. Contbr. articles to profl. jours. Columbia U. fellow, 1966-68; recipient Nat. Achievement award Nat. Assn. Women Geographers, 1966. Mem. Am. Mining Congress, Am. Inst. Mining, Metall. and Petroleum Engrs., Nat. Wildlife Fedn., Nat. Audubon Soc., Nature Conservancy, World Wildlife Fund (charter mem.), Nat. Assn. of Chiefs of Police, Grad. Faculties Alumni Assn. Columbia U., DAR, Am. Wildlife Soc., Air Pollution Control Assn., East African Wildlife Soc. Club: Wellesley (Los Angeles). Office: Resource Assessment Inc 1431 Washington Blvd Ste 2811 Detroit MI 48226

SHELDON, WILLIAM CHARLES, marketing professional; b. Muskegon, Mich., Apr. 20, 1943; s. John Pitt and Doris Augustus (Spafford) S.; m. Judith Ann Roughton; children: Elizabeth Ann, William Charles Jr. BA, Lakeland Coll., 1966. Sales rep. Ciba-Geigy Pharms., Summit, N.J., 1966-69, hosp. sales rep., 1970-73, dist. mgr., 1974-78, mgr. hosp. sales, 1979, dir. instl., 1980-81, product dir., 1982, exec. dir., portfolio mgmt., 1983, v.p. sales, 1984-85, sr. v.p. mktg., 1986—; bd. dirs. Biocine Co., Emeryville, Calif. Bd. dirs. Epilepsy Found. N.J.; trustee Overlook Hosp., Summit, N.J.. Mem. Nat. Pharm. Council (bd. dirs. 1986). Office: Ciba-Geigy Corp 556 Morris Ave Summit NJ 07901

SHELESKI, STANLEY JOHN, accountant, comptroller, consultant; b. Harleigh, Pa., Feb. 20, 1931; s. Stanley Joseph and Agnes Rose (Yeshmond) S.; m. Sandra Lee Atkins. BS in Fin. Acctg., Rider Coll., 1958. Treas., mgr. United Savs. and Loan, Trenton, N.J., 1958-62; mgr. acctg. dept. Allstates Engring. Co., Trenton, 1962-85, asst. treas., asst. sec., comptroller, 1985—; v.p. fin. Allstates Design and Devel. Co., Trenton, 1988—; bd. dirs. Allstates Credit Union, Trenton, 1966—, treas. and gen. mgr. Allstates Credit Union, 1968—. Planner Jr. C. of C., Trenton, 1959. Served to sgt. USMC, 1952-54, Korea. Mem. Nat. Assn. Accts., Ewing Bus. Assn. (treas. 1959-62). Republican. Roman Catholic. Lodge: North Star Club (v.p. 1953-58).

SHELEY, DONALD RAY, JR., manufacturing company executive; b. Vincennes, Ind., May 20, 1942; s. Donald R. and Norma M. (Cardinel) S.; m. Pamela J. Petho, Jan. 6, 1968; children: Stephanie L., Anne E. AS in Bus. Adminstrn., Vincennes U., 1962; BS in Bus. and Fin., Ind. U., 1964; MBA, U. Chgo., 1971. Acct. Inland Steel Co., East Chicago, Ind., 1964-66, asst. supr. billing and services, 1966-68, supr. ops. acctg., 1968-71; fin. analyst FMC Corp., Chgo., 1971-74; controller petroleum equipment group, wellhead ops. FMC Corp., Houston, 1974-77; controller petroleum group Joy Mfg., Houston, 1977-80; asst. controller Cooper Industries Inc., Houston, 1980-81, dir. bus. analysis, 1981-86, controller, 1986-88, v.p., controller, 1988—. Pres. Greenwood Residence Club Inc., Houston, 1979-80; treas. Greenwood Forest Fund Inc., Houston, 1983-87. Mem. Nat. Assn. Accts. Republican. Home: 5414 Havenwoods Dr Houston TX 77066 Office: Cooper Industries Inc 1001 Fannin Ste 4000 Houston TX 77002

SHELL, OWEN G., JR., banker; b. Greenville, S.C., June 19, 1936; s. Owen and Katherine S.; m. Mary Ruth Trammell, Aug. 9, 1980; children: Katherine Sloan, Mary Carroll, Robert Owen, James Walker. B.S., U. S.C., 1960; post grad., Stonier Grad. Sch. Banking, 1971; grad., Advanced Mgmt. Program, Harvard U., 1979. Tech. supt. Deering-Milliken, Inc., 1962-63; v.p. Citizens & So. Nat. Bank S.C., Columbia, 1968-71; sr. v.p. Citizens & So. Nat. Bank S.C., 1971-74, exec. v.p., 1974-79; pres., dir., chief exec. officer First Am. Nat. Bank, Nashville, 1979-86; vice chmn. bd., dir. First Am. Corp., 1979-86; pres., chief exec. officer Sovran Fin. Corp./Cen. South, Nashville, 1986—, Sovran Bank/Cen. South, Nashville, 1986—; dir. Nashville br. Fed. Res. Bank of Atlanta, 1986—; dir. Engineered Custom Plastics Corp., 1972-80, Sloan Constrn. Co., 1972-81; dir. Nashville br. Fed. Res. Bank of Atlanta. Active Tenn. Performing Arts Found., Middle Tenn. council Boy Scouts Am., Girl Scouts U.S., Cumberland Valley Girl Scout Council, Owen Grad. Sch. Mgmt. Served to maj. USAF, 1960-64. Mem. Assn. Res. City Bankers, Nashville Area C. of C., Kappa Alpha, Omicron Delta Kappa. Presbyterian. Clubs: Rotary, Cumberland, Belle Meade Country. Home: 4412 Chickering Ln Nashville TN 37215

SHELLER, GARY STEVEN, financial analyst; b. St. Louis, Feb. 18, 1955; s. Arthur Lawrence and Elinor Louise (Jenner) S.; m. Rebecca Ann Stark, Mar. 12, 1977; children: Emily Suzanne, Ashley Elizabeth, Amanda Christine. Student, Coll. Fin. Planning, Denver, 1987—. Agt. Met. Life Ins. Co., St. Charles, Mo., 1975-77, Farm Bur. Ins. Co., Troy, Mo., 1977-78; owner, prin. Sheller Ins. Agy., Troy, 1978-87, Sheller Fin. Services, Troy, 1987-88. Contbr. articles to popular mags. Named Citizen of Yr. Game Trails, 1987. Republican. Club: Woods Fort Sportsmans (Troy) (bd. dirs. 1987—). Lodge: Rotary (Troy chpt.). Home: Rte 2 Box 39 Troy MO 63379 Office: Sheller Fin Svcs 481 Main St Troy MO 63379

SHELLEY, EDWIN FREEMAN, engineer, university official; b. N.Y.C., Feb. 19, 1921; s. Robert and Jessie (Sinick) S.; A.B., Columbia Univ., 1940, BSEE, 1941; postgrad. Harvard U., 1957; ScD (hon.) Nova U., 1984; m. Florence Dubroff, Aug. 29, 1941; children—William, Carolyn. Exptl. flight test engr. Curtiss-Wright Corp., Propeller div., Caldwell, N.J., 1941-47; cons. electronics Wilson Mech. Instrument Co., N.Y.C., 1945-47, Bridgeport, Conn., 1945-47; pres., chief engr. Am. Chronoscope Corp., Mt. Vernon, N.Y., 1948-50; spl. cons. Mercury Totalizator Co., Inc., N.Y.C., 1949-50; co-founder, v.p., gen. mgr. Bulova Research & Devel. Labs., Inc., Flushing, N.Y., 1950-57; dir. advanced programs U.S. Industries, Inc., N.Y.C., 1957-60, v.p., 1960-64; pres. U.S. Industries Robodyne Div., 1958-60; pres. E.F. Shelley & Co., Inc., 1965-71, chmn. bd., 1971-75; dir. Center for Energy Policy and Research, N.Y. Inst. Tech., Old Westbury, 1975—. Past pres. Nat. Council on Aging. Trustee N.Y. Inst. Tech.; trustee Nova U., Ft. Lauderdale, Fla., 1970-85; bd. dirs. Center for Community Change, Inst. Responsive Edn.; adv. bd. N.Y. State Legis. Commn. Sci. and Tech. Mem. IEEE (sr.), Am. Phys. Soc., Am. Inst. Aeros. and Astronautics, AAAS, N.Y. Acad. Scis., Newcomen Soc. in N.Am. Patentee in field. Home: 339 Oxford Rd New Rochelle NY 10804 Office: NY Inst Tech Old Westbury NY 11568

SHELLEY, PAMELA DENISE, mortgage banker; b. Greenville, S.C., Oct. 12, 1956; d. Dennis Lee and Eula Mae (Bryson) S. BSBA, Regis Coll., 1986. Adminstrv. asst. Wells Fargo Mortgage Co., Santa Rosa, Calif., 1978-82; customer support mgr. Chase Home Mortgage Co., Montvale, N.J., 1982-84; tng. ops. mgr. Colo. Nat. Mortgage Co., Denver, 1985-86; v.p., servicing mgr. Security Pacific Mortgage, Denver, 1986-87, NCNB Nat. Bank of N.C., Charlotte, 1987—. Mem. Colo. Mortgage Bankers Assn. (mem. edn. com. 1986-87), Mortgage Bankers Assn. Office: NCNB Nat Bank of NC Charlotte NC 28233

SHELLEY, RULON GENE, manufacturing company executive; b. 1924; s. John Franklin and Linda Marie (Gutke) S.; m. Theora Whiting, June 21, 1946; children: Dennis, Kenneth, Ronald, Patricia. BSEE, U. Ariz., 1948; MS, MIT, 1949. Chief engr. aerospace div. N.Am. Aviation, 1949-61; v.p. Tamar Electronics Inc., 1961-64; with Raytheon Co., Lexington, Mass., 1964—, from mgr. Santa Barbara Ops. to v.p. gen. mgr. equipment div., 1964-78, v.p. gen. mgr. group exec. equipment div., 1978-79, sr. v.p. group exec., 1979-86, pres., 1986—, also bd. dirs.; also chmn. bd. dirs. Raytheon Svc. Co.; bd. govs. AIA, Washington, 1986—; bd. trustees Nat. Security and Internat. Affairs, Washington, 1986—. Served to 2d lt. A.C., U.S. Army, 1943-46. Mem. Assn. Old Crows, Air Force Assn., Am. Defense Preparedness Assn., Assn. U.S. Army, Nat. Space Club, Navy League U.S., Tau Beth Pi. Office: Raytheon Co 141 Spring St Lexington MA 02173 *

SHELLY, FRANKLIN JEFF, investor; b. Bay City, Tex., Mar. 13, 1942; s. Franklin E. and Josephine (Anderson) S.; m. Lynne C. Cruickshank, Nov. 20, 1965; children: Jennifer Lynn, Heather Leigh. AA, Harbor Coll., 1963; BS in Mktg., Loyola U., Los Angeles, 1965. Owner, pres. Almar Corp., Palos Verdes, Calif., 1963-65; sales dir. I.B.M. Corp., Glendale, Calif., 1965-70; dir. nat. accounts W.T.C. Air Freight, Los Angeles, 1970-78; v.p. sales Travel Guard Inc., San Juan Capastrano, Calif., 1978-81; gen. mgr., lic. capt. Cormorant Cruises, New Port Beach, Calif., 1981-85; pres. Shelly Enterprises, Channel Islands, Calif., 1985—. Inventor wheeled suitcase and shrinkwrap damage frame. Dir. Project Mex.-Orphanage, Rolling Hills, Calif., 1984-86; mem. Palos Verdes City Council, 1976-77. Recipient Angel of Mercy award Girl Scouts, 1979. Fellow Sales Mktg. Execs. (dir. 1972-73, Top Sales award 1973); mem. Navy League (sr., v.p. 1976-77). Republican. Congregationalist. Clubs: King Harbor Yacht (Redondo Beach, Calif.) (social chmn. and bd. dirs. 1983—); Palos Verdes Breakfast (bd. dirs. 1979-82). Home: 3251 Harbor Blvd Channel Islands CA 93035 Office: Shelly Enterprises 1209 Via Coronel Palos Verdes CA 90274

SHELLY, LISA MAUREEN, communication executive, marketing professional; b. Akron, Ohio, June 1, 1955; d. Melvin Joseph and Mary Jayne (Nerone) Cruder; m. Robert Patrick Shelly, Apr. 30, 1983; 1 child, Victoria. BSBA, U. Akron, 1977. Order adminstr. portable div. Motorola Inc., Plantation, Fla., 1977-78, bid analyst portable div. MT500 products, 1978-81, product planner portable div. MT500 products, 1981-84, sr. product planner expo products communications sector, 1984-88; mgr. product planning Marketized Products Local Area Communications Products, Plantation, Fla., 1988—. Advisor Jr. Achievement, Ft. Lauderdale, Fla., 1978-83. Mem. Am. Mktg. Assn. (exec., sr. v.p. meeting planning 1987—, v.p. chpt. devel. 1985-86). Republican. Roman Catholic. Home: 9011 NW 23d St Coral Springs FL 33065 Office: Motorola Inc 8000 W Sunrise Blvd Plantation FL 33322

SHELNUTT, ROBERT CURTIS, manufacturing company administrator; b. Shawmut, Ala., Sept. 2, 1928; s. Curtis Lee and Odell (Campbell) S.; B.S. in Chemistry, U. Ga., 1954; M.B.A., Pepperdine U., 1981; m. Faye Mahan; children—Robert Curtis, Susan Elaine. With Am. Enka Co., Lowland, Tenn., 1954-79, gen. tech. supr. chem., spinning and finishing depts., 1969-71, tech. mgr. rayon filament plant, 1971-75, tech. mgr. rayon staple plant, 1975-76, energy and devel. mgr. rayon staple plant, 1976-77, energy and devel., mgr. Tenn. ops., 1977-79; gen. mgr. chem. ops. Chatsworth div. Organon Teknika Corp., Chatsworth, Calif., 1979-81, dir. mfg. and chem. engring. research and devel., Oklahoma City, 1981-82, dir. quality assurance and chem. activities, 1982—. Served with USAF, 1946-49. Mem. Am. Chem. Soc., Am. Mgmt. Assn. Republican. Baptist. Clubs: Masons, Shriners. Home: 9105 Pebble Ln Oklahoma City OK 73132 Office: Organon Teknika Corp 5300 S Portland Oklahoma City OK 73119

SHELTON, CHARLES BASCOM, III, investment banker; b. Atlanta, Oct. 14, 1941; s. Charles Bascom Jr. and Elizabeth (Colley) S.; m. Deborah Jackson, July 3, 1965; children—Lara Elizabeth, Ashley Howell. B.S., U. N.C., 1963; M.B.A., U. Pa., 1970. Assoc. McKinsey & Co., Cleve., 1970-74; asst. to treas. Aladdin Industries, Nashville, 1974-75, London, 1975-76, Nashville, 1976-77; mng. dir. Robinson-Humphrey/Am. Express, Atlanta, 1977—. Bd. dirs. Fine Arts Guild Lovett Sch., Atlanta, 1987-88. Served to lt. comdr. USN, 1963-70. Mem. Beta Gamma Sigma. Republican. Episcopalian. Club: Piedmont Driving (Atlanta). Avocations: tennis, golf, travel. Home: 1766 West Paces Ferry Rd Atlanta GA 30327 Office: The Robinson-Humphrey Co Inc 3333 Peachtree St Atlanta GA 30326

SHELTON, GEORGE PERRY, manufacturing company executive; b. St. Louis, Aug. 9, 1952; s. George Perry and Janet Francis (Lutkehaus) S.; m. Breda Louise Bey, Nov. 21, 1981; children: Candace Louise, John Louis. BBA, U. Notre Dame, 1974. CPA, Tex. Mgr. ops. and fin. Zale Corp., Washington, 1974-82; controller Animated Playhouses Corp., Los Angeles, 1982084, White Cube, Buena Park, Calif., 1984-86; v.p. fin. and adminstrn. Premier Products, El Cajon, Calif., 1986-87; div. mgr. Premier Products, Corona, Calif., 1987—; income tax preparer, 1981—. Mem. Rep. Victory Fund, Washington, 1981; chmn. fin. com. Guardian Angels Ch.,

Santee, Calif., 1987; mem. Citizens Against Santee Jail, 1987; fundraiser San Diego Ctr. for Abused Children, Santee, 1987. Republican. Roman Catholic. Club: Notre Dame (San Diego). Home: 10844 Mercer Ave Riverside CA 92505 Office: Premier Products 1436 E 6th St Corona CA 91719

SHELTON, JAMES TED, lawyer; b. Childress, Tex., Sept. 21, 1957; s. Ted. L. and Wilma L. (Helmstetler) S.; m. Cindy G. Trollinger, Aug. 2, 1980; children: Lindsey Gayle, Taylor James. BBA in Acctg., Tex. Tech U., 1980, JD, 1983. Bar: Tex. 1983, U.S. Dist. Ct. (no. dist.) 1985. Assoc. Shannon, Porter, Johnson & Sutton, San Angelo, Tex., 1983-85; ptnr. Lowe, Courtney & Shelton, Clarendon, Tex., 1985—; county atty. Donley County, Clarendon, 1987—; instr. Clarendon Jr. Coll., 1986-87. Bd. dirs. Burton Meml. Libr., Clarendon, 1986-87. Mem. State Bar Tex., Tex. Trial Lawyers Assn., Tex. Dist. and County Attys. Assn., Donley County C. of C. (bd. dirs. 1987—), Lions (pres. 1987-88). Home: PO Box 855 Clarendon TX 79226 Office: Lowe Courtney & Shelton PO Box 550 Clarendon TX 79226

SHELTON, JERRELL WILSON, communications company executive; b. Dickson, Tenn., Aug. 12, 1945; s. James Ellison and Helen Elizabeth (Spann) S.; m. Virginia Zubl, Dec. 28, 1968 (div. 1987); 1 child, Julianne; m. Linda Kay Elliott, Mar. 12, 1988; 1 child, Philip. B in Fin. and Bus. Adminstrn. cum laude, U. Tenn., 1970; MBA, Harvard U., 1973. Tooling inspector AVCO Aerostructures, Nashville, 1965-1968, v.p., asst. gen. mgr., 1979-80; asst. to v.p. Aladdin Electronics, Nashville, 1970-71; mgr. prodn. ops. Berkline Corp., Morristown, Tenn., 1973-74; mgr. gen. mdse. Reed Wallcovering Div., Toronto, Ont., Can., 1974-76; gen. mgr. Wholesale Bldg. Products, Nashville, 1976-78, 1976-79; pres., chief exec. officer Tridon, Inc., Nashville, 1980-83, Cherokee Forest Products, Paris, Tenn., 1983-84; pres., chief exec. officer Advantage Cos. Inc., Nashville, 1984—, also bd. dirs.; bd. dirs. Tulnoy Lumber. Co., Inc., New Rochelle, N.Y. Mem. Pres.'s (Reagan) Council, Nashville, 1984-85, Ambassador for Tenn., Nashville, 1982-84, Jr. Achievement, Vanderbilt Grad. Sch. Bus. Adminstrn. Mem. Nat. Assn. Securities Dealers, Nat. Over-the-Counter Stock Cos., Nat. Assn. Corp. Dirs., Am. Assn. Bus. Publs., Am. Mgmt. Assn., Pres.'s Assn., Competitive Telecommunications Assn., U. Tenn. Alumni Assn., Harvard Alumni Assn., Nashville C. of C. Republican. Episcopalian. Lodge: Rotary, Masons. Home: 980 Overton Lea Rd Nashville TN 37220 Office: Advantage Cos Inc 1801 W End Ave Nashville TN 37203

SHELTON, ROBERT WARREN, marketing executive; b. Albuquerque, Apr. 26, 1943; s. Eugene and Rusty M. (Jentsch) S.; divorced; children: Elise, Samantha; m. Ginger Lee Rapp, Feb. 14, 1984. BBA in Mktg., St. Mary's U., San Antonio, 1969; postgrad., Ga. State U., 1972-73, MBA in Mktg., 1973. Dist. mgr. Ford Motor Co., Atlanta, 1969-78; dir. fleet ops. Rollins, Inc., Atlanta, 1978-81; v.p. sales and ops. Lease Plan U.S.A., Atlanta, 1981-85; v.p. mktg. Spencer Services, Inc., Roswell, Ga., 1985-87; v.p. FX-10 Corp., 1987-88; pres. Motors Distbn. Corp., 1988—. Mem. Lost Forest Civic Assn. (pres. 1980-81). Mem. Nat. Assn. Fleet Adminstrs., Am. Fleet and Leasing Assn. Republican.

SHELTON, WAYNE VERNON, professional services and systems integration company executive; b. Mpls., Nov. 27, 1932; s. Olen George and Evelyn Ruth (Karpen) S.; m. Mary Kay Schwappach, Dec. 29, 1956; children: William David, Susan Evelyn. BS, U. Minn., 1954. Instr. U. Minn., Mpls., 1954-56; tchr. Mpls. Pub. Schs., 1956-57; mathematician Rand Corp., Santa Clara, Calif., 1957-62; sr. assoc. Planning Research Corp., Los Angeles, 1963-72; v.p. Planning Research Corp., McLean, Va., 1972-83, sr. v.p., 1983-85, pres., chief operating officer, 1985-87, pres., chief exec. officer, 1987—; v.p. Emhart Corp., Farmington, Conn., 1987-88; exec. v.p., pres. Emhart Info. and Engring. Systems, Farmington, 1988—; instr. data processing Santa Monica (Calif.) Coll., 1960-62; pres. Assn. Ind. Software Cos., McLean, 1970-71; v.p. Profl. Services Council, Washington, 1972-73; chmn. bd. dirs. Security Affairs Support Assn., Annapolis, Md., 1983-85. Mem. Armed Forces Communications and Electronics Assn. (assoc. dir. 1987—), Navy League (life), Assn. U.S. Army, Air Force Assn., Nat. Security Indsl. Assn., Am. Def. Preparedness Assn. Republican. Mem. Unitarian Universalist Ch. Home: 8521 Brickyard Rd Potomac MD 20854

SHELTON, WILLIAM CHASTAIN, retired government statistician, investor; b. Athens, Ga., May 5, 1916; s. William Arthur and Effie Clyde (Landrum) S.; m. Helen Higgins, Dec. 17, 1938; children: Stuart H., Terry Ann Shelton Coble, Jean R. Shelton Jaffray, Alvic C. AB, Princeton U., 1936; postgrad. U. Chgo., 1937-38. Economist, statistician Fed. Govt., Washington, 1936-48; chief stats. sect. USRO-Marshall Plan, Paris, France, 1948-55; mgr. bus. research Fla. Devel. Com., Tallahassee, 1956-60; asst. com. foreign labor Bur. Labor Stats., Washington, 1960-75; spl. asst. statis. policy div. Office Mgmt. and Budget, 1975-77. Author: (with Joseph W. Duncan) Revolution in U.S. Government Statistics, 1926-76, 1978; contbr. articles to profl. jours. Mem. Am. Statis. Assn., Washington Soc. Investment Analysts, Nat. Economists Club, Sigma Xi, Phi Beta Kappa. Republican. Presbyterian. Home: 8401 Piney Branch Rd Silver Spring MD 20901

SHEMELY, CHARLES LOUIS, food company executive; b. Galien, Mich., Mar. 4, 1938; s. Ward Clifford S. and Mildred Ruth (Renbarger) Shepardson; m. Yolanda Zupko, Mar. 26, 1960; 1 dau., Elizabeth. B.A., Mich. State U., 1961. Assoc. dir. product mgmt. Keebler Co., Elmhurst, Ill., 1965-71, v.p. mktg., 1975-80, sr. v.p. retail mktg. and sales, 1980—, sr. v.p. direct to warehouse bus. and new product devel., 1985-88, sr. v.p. food service and internat. divs., 1988—; v.p. mktg. Planters Curtiss div. Standard Brands, Chgo., 1972-74; dir. L. Karp & Sons, Elk Grove Village, Ill., 1980-85. Mem. Downers Grove Planning Commn., Ill., 1972-78, chmn., 1979-83. Served with U.S. Army, 1961-63. Recipient Outstanding Alumni award Coll. of Communication Arts and Scis., Mich. State U., 1988. Mem. Assn. Nat. Advertisers (bd. dirs. 1984-87, exec. com. 1985-87, chmn. agy. relations com., 1980-81, chmn. advt. mgmt. policy com. 1981-83, chmn. membership com. 1986, chmn. supervising and editing com. for publs. 1979, 81). Clubs: River Forest Golf (Elmhurst, Ill.); Executives (Chgo.). Office: Keebler Co One Hollow Tree Ln Elmhurst IL 60126

SHEMIN, BARRY L., insurance company executive; b. Bklyn., Dec. 17, 1942. A.B. magna cum laude, Brown U., 1963; M.A., U. Mich., 1964. With John Hancock Mut. Life Ins. Co., Boston, 1968—, sr. v.p., 1980—; pres. John Hancock Variable Life Ins. Co., 1987—; bd. dirs. Unigard Ins. Group, Seattle. Fellow Soc. Actuaries; mem. Am. Acad. Actuaries, Internat. Actuarial Assn., Phi Beta Kappa, Sigma Xi. Club: Brown Univ. (Boston). Office: John Hancock Mut Life Ins Co PO Box 111 Boston MA 02117

SHEN, THEODORE PING, investment banker; b. N.Y.C., Feb. 18, 1945; s. Shih-Chang and Clara Grace (Low) S.; m. Carol Lee Wing, June 13, 1968; 1 child, Carla Patricia. B.A. in Econs., Yale U., 1966; M.B.A. in Fin., Harvard U., 1968. Securities analyst Donaldson, Lufkin & Jenrette, N.Y.C., 1968-71, v.p., securities analyst, 1971-78, mng. dir. research, 1978-81, mng. dir. equities div., 1981-84, pres. DLJ Capital Markets Group, 1984-86, chmn. DLJ Capital Markets Group, 1986—; dir. Donaldson, Lufkin & Jenrette, Inc., N.Y.C., 1984—; bd. dirs. Donaldson, Lufkin & Jenrette Securities Corp., N.Y.C., 1979—, N.Y. Urban Coalition; trustee The Packer Collegiate Inst. (Bklyn.). Named to All-Am. Research Team, Instl. Investor mag., 1972-80. Mem. N.Y. Soc. Securities Analysts. Clubs: The Bond Club of N.Y., Heights Casino (Brooklyn Heights, N.Y.); City Midday (N.Y.C.). Office: Donaldson Lufkin & Jenrette Inc 140 Broadway New York NY 10005

SHENDURE, ASHOK SHANTAPPA, financial planner; b. Mangur, Karnataka, India, Aug. 6, 1944; came to U.S., 1967; s. Shantappa Jinnappa and Chandrabai S. (Chougule) S.; m. Rajanee Ashok Datar, Aug. 28, 1969; children: Rahul, Jay. BME, U. Pune, Maharashtra, India, 1966; MSME, U. Wis., 1968; MBA, Case Western Res. U., 1976. Cert. fin. planner. Design engr. Crawford Fitting Co., Solon, Ohio, 1968-72, chief engr., 1972-87; v.p. BDS Fin. Services Corp., Chagrin Falls, Ohio, 1986-87; pres. BDS Fin. Services Corp., Solon, 1988—. Mem. Inst. Cert. Fin. Planners, Internat. Assn. for Fin. Planning, Rotary. Republican. Home: 32200 Haverhill Dr Solon OH 44139 Office: BDS Fin Svc Corp 33595 Bainbridge Rd Solon OH 44139

SHENK, HOWARD FRED, association executive; b. Greenville, S.C., Feb. 14, 1939; s. Donald Hugh and Ruth Aletha (Swartz) S. BSBA, U. Ala., 1961. Gen. mgr. H & R Block Co., Honolulu, 1967-71; v.p. ops. E. K. Fernandez Shows, Honolulu, 1971-75; pres. Micrographics Ltd., Honolulu, 1975-78; pres. Colo. Indsl. Communications, Denver, 1978-83; exec. dir. Arabian Horse Owners Found., 1983—; v.p. So. Ariz. Internat. Livestock Assn., The World Crabbet Trust; devel. and spl. events cons. Nat. Western Stock Show and Rodeo, So. Ariz. Internat. Livestock Assn., 1984—; dir. Fred Graham Communications Ltd., Frank C. Howard Holdings Ltd., Micrographics Ltd. Chmn. Hawaii State Fair, 1970. Served with USAF, 1962-67. Mem. Kings Alley Mchts. Assn. (pres. 1976-78), SAR, Internat. Assn. Amusement Parks and Attractions, Outdoor Amusement Bus. Assn., Internat. Arabian Horse Assn., Am. Horse Shows Assn., Royal Hawaiian Showmen. Republican. Presbyterian. Home: 1200 River Rd #G-84 Tucson AZ 85718 Office: PO Box 30125 Tucson AZ 85751

SHENK, JOHN HENRY, engineering company executive; b. Junction City, Kans., Dec. 19, 1939; s. Henry Arthur and Katherine Phobe (Frick) S.; B.S.B.A., U. Kans., 1963, B.S.C.E., 1963. Constrn. engr. Dupont Corp., Seaford, Del., 1963; engring. supt. Tumpane Co., Sinop, Turkey, 1965-67; with Pacific Architects and Engrs., Inc. and subs., 1967—, v.p. PAE, Bangkok, Thailand, 1971-72, v.p. S.E. Asia, Pacific Architects and Engrs., Inc., Bangkok, 1972-80, sr. v.p. Pacific Architects and Engrs., Inc., 1980-87; dir. PAE Internat., PAE (Thailand) Co. Ltd., pres. 1987—, Pacific Architects and Engrs. Co., Ltd., Pacific Services Co. Ltd., PAE (Singapore) Pte. Ltd., Maenning Corp., Syalin PAE Sdn. Bhd., Service Systems PTE Ltd., Heavylift Internat. B.V., Active Corp., Rand B Corp.; mng. dir. Nus Antara Pacific Ltd., Soon Pacific Ltd., Facilities Engring. Cons. Ltd., PAE (Thailand) Co., Ltd. (pres. 1987) Hong Kong, PAE Constrn. Co., Ltd. (pres. 1987). Served to 1st lt. C.E., U.S. Army, 1963-65. Decorated Army Commendation medal, Army Commendation medal with oak leaf cluster (U.S.); for pub. service (Thailand). Mem. ASCE, Soc. Am. Mil. Engrs., Delta Upsilon (Man of Yr. 1961). Home: 39 Pongsrichan Sapenkwai, Suthisarn, Bangkok Thailand Office: Sinkahakarn Bldg, 55 Rachadapisek Rd 6th Fl, Bangkok Thailand

SHENKMAN, MARK RONALD, portfolio manager; b. Providence, Aug. 17, 1943; s. George and Florence (Littman) S.; m. Gloria Abrams, May 26, 1974; children: Andrew Harris, Gregory Alexander. BA, U. Conn., 1965; MBA, George Washington U., 1967. Security analyst New Eng. Mchts. Bank, Boston, 1969-71; fin. analyst Stone & Webster Securities Corp., Boston, 1971-73; portfolio mgr. Fidelity Mgmt. & Research Co., Boston, 1973-79; v.p. Lehman Bros. Kuhn Loeb, N.Y.C., 1979-83; pres. First Investors Asset Mgmt. Co., N.Y.C., 1983-85; pres., chief exec. officer Shenkman Capital Mgmt. Inc., N.Y.C., 1985—; vice chmn., bd. dirs. Wilshire Restaurant Group, Inc. Served to 1st lt. U.S. Army, 1967-69. Mem. N.Y. Soc. Security Analysts, Boston Security Analysts Soc., Fin. Analyst Fedn., Am. Stats. Assn., Internat. Power Machines (bd. dirs.). Home: Gaston Farm Rd Greenwich CT 06831 Office: 575 Fifth Ave New York NY 10017

SHENSON, HOWARD L., management consultant; b. Seattle, Sept. 16, 1944; m. Sidney and Hermine (Levitt) S.; m. Joan Seligmann, June 11, 1967; children: David, Jonathan, Brian. BCS, Seattle U., 1966; MBA, U. Wash., 1968; postgrad., U. So. Calif., 1968-70. Cert. mgmt. cons., Inst. Mgmt. Cons.; life cert. jr. coll. instr., Calif., Wash. Asst. dir. Research Inst. for Bus. and Econs. U. So. Calif., Los Angeles, 1968-69, instr., 1968-70; chair dept. mgmt., asst. prof. Calif. State U., Northridge, 1969-71, instr., 1969-77; v.p., tech. dir. The Eckman Ctr., Woodland Hills, Calif., 1971-76; pvt. practice cons. Woodland Hills, 1976—; instr. Shoreline Community Coll., Wash., 1967-68, Los Angeles City Coll., 1968-69; lectr. in field. Author: How To Strategically Negotiate the Consulting Contract, rev. edit. 1986, How To Build and Maintain Your Own Consulting Practice, rev. edit. 1985, The Consulting Handbook, rev. edit. 1982, Economics of Consulting: 1980-1990, 1980, The Consultant and Productization, 1980, How To Develop and Promote Profitable Seminars and Workshops, rev. edit. 1985, Successful Consultant's Guide to Fee Setting, rev. edit. 1986, How To Start and Promote Your Own Newsletter, rev. edit. 1984, How To Buy a Business With No Money Down, 1981, How To Create and Market a Successful Seminar or Workshop, 1981, The Consultant's Guide to Proposal Writing, 1982, How To Select, Manage and Compensate Consultants, 1984, Marketing Your Professional Services, 1985, Strategic Seminar and Workshop Marketing, 1985, Complete Guide to Consulting Success, rev. edit. 1989, Beyond Consulting: How to Develop, Package and Market Information Products and Services, 1987, How To Build a Profitable Consulting Practice, Vols. 1 and 2, 1987, 101 Proven Strategies For Building A Successful Practice, 1988, Entrepreneurial Style and Success Indicator (ESSI), 1988; co-author: The Marketing of Consulting Services, 1980, How To Build a Lucrative Paid Speaking Business, 1982, Profitably Managing Your Consulting Business, Vols. 1 and 2, 1987, Publishing Is Your Second Business, 1987; author The Profl. Cons. and Seminar Bus. Report, 1977—; contbr. articles to profl. jours. Bd. dirs. Las Virgenes Edn. Found., Calabasas, Calif., Woodland Hills Little League. Mem. Am. Assn. Profl. Cons. (cert., gov. 1986), Beta Gamma Sigma. Republican. Jewish. Office: 20750 Ventura Blvd Ste 206 Woodland Hills CA 91364

SHEPARD, A. COURTENAY, consumer products company executive; b. N.Y.C., Apr. 19, 1939; s. Donald and Suzanne (Mercadier) S.; m. Faith Eland (div. 1980); children: David C., Scott B., Andrew M.; m. Belinda Kirby, Sept. 17, 1982. B.A., Brown U., 1961. With Procter & Gamble Co., Cin., 1961-68, Philip Morris Inc., N.Y.C., 1968-71; gen. mgr. R.J. Reynolds Foods, N.Y.C., 1971-73; mktg. and gen. mgmt. Colgate Palmolive Co., Brazil, Venezuela, Fed. Republic Germany, Can. and U.S.A., 1973-81; corp. v.p., pres. Colgate U.S.A., N.Y.C., 1981—. Mem. Soap and Detergent Assn. (chmn. dir.), Grocery Products Mfrs. Can. (dir. 1980-81). Home: 24 Harbor Rd Westport CT 06880 Office: Colgate-Palmolive Co 300 Park Ave New York NY 10022

SHEPARD, CHARLES VIRGIL, human resource executive; b. Springfield, Ill., Nov. 14, 1940; s. Charles Woodrow and Catherine Elizabeth (Vlakovich) S.; B.A. in Bus. Adminstrn. and Econs., 1962; postgrad. U. Ill., Urbana, 1966-72; M.B.A., Sangamon State U., 1972; m. Judy A. Wells; children—Cynthia Lynn, Kimberly Lynn. With Allis-Chalmers Corp., Springfield, 1962-73, supr. employee benefits, 1962-67, adminstrv. asst., 1967-68, mgr. personnel services, 1968-70, mgr. orgn. planning and devel., 1970-72, mgr. indsl. relations, 1972-73; mem. corp. indsl. relations staff Rockwell Internat. Corp., Dallas, 1973, dir. indsl. relations, 1973-74, group dir. personnel, 1974-76, v.p. personnel, 1976-77, staff v.p. electronics personnel, 1977-78, corp. staff v.p. employee relations, 1978-80, v.p. electronic operations and human resources Gen. Industries, 1980-81, v.p. human resources, 1981—. Mem. Adv. Council Amigos de Ser, 1976—; mem. adv. bd. Richland Coll., 1975-76; bd. dirs. Jr. Achievement, 1981—, Dallas Theater Center, Pitts. Public Theatre, 1979—, Dallas Opera, 1982—, TACA, 1982, Boy Scouts Am., 1982—. Mem. Electronic Industries Assn. (indsl. relations council), Am. Soc. Personnel Adminstrn., Dallas C. of C. (bd. dirs. 1974-76, mem. Leadership Council 1988—). Republican. Methodist. Club: Masons. Home: 5404 Vista Meadow Dallas TX 75248 Office: Rockwell Internat Dallas TX 75207

SHEPARD, EARL ALDEN, government official; b. Aurora, Ill., Sept. 30, 1932; s. Ralph George and Marcia Louise (Phelps) S.; AS magna cum laude in Bus. Adminstrn. (fed. and local govt. employee scholar), Southeastern U., 1967, BS magna cum laude in Bus. Adminstrn., 1969; MBA (Ammunition Procurement Supply Agy. fellow), U. Chgo., 1974; m. Carolyn Mae Borman, Sept. 1, 1959; 1 son, Ralph Lyle. Chief program budget div. U.S. Army Munitions Command, Joliet, Ill., 1971-73; comptroller, dir. adminstrn. U.S. Navy Pub. Works Center, Gt. Lakes, Ill., 1973-77; dep. comptroller U.S. Army Electronics Command/U.S. Army Communications Electronics Materiel Readiness Command, Ft. Monmouth, N.J., 1977-79; dir. resource mgmt., comptroller, dir. programs U.S. Army White Sands Missile Range, N.Mex., 1979—; bd. dirs. 1st Nat. Bank Dona Ana County, 1987—; adv. com. Rio Grande Bancshares/First Nat. Bank of Dona Ana County, 1983-84. Bd. govs., Southeastern Univ. Ednl. Found., 1969-71; chmn. fin. com. No. Va. Assn. for Children with Learning Disabilities, 1966-67, treas., 1968-70; pres. West Long Branch (N.J.) Sports Assn., 1979. Mem. Assn. U.S. Army, Am. Soc. Mil. Comptrollers. Assn. Govt. Accts., Fed. Mgrs. Assn. Republican. Home: 2712 Topley Ave Las Cruces NM 88005 Office: Attention: STEWS-RM White Sands Missile Range NM 88002

SHEPARD, GEOFFREY CARROLL, lawyer, corporation executive; b. Santa Barbara, Calif., Nov. 7, 1944; s. James J. and Barbara (Hoose) S.; m. Saundra Gayle Carlton, Jan. 10, 1973; children: Jonathan Pettus, William Dabney. B.A., Whittier Coll., 1966; J.D., Harvard U., 1969. Bar: Wash. 1970, D.C. 1972, U.S. Supreme Ct. 1973, Pa. 1977. White House fellow 1969-70; staff asst. to Pres. White House, 1970-72, assoc. dir. domestic coun., 1972-75; sr. assoc. Steptoe & Johnson, Washington, 1975-77; dir. govt. and industry affairs INA Corp., Phila., 1977-80, v.p., sec., 1980-84; v.p., corp. sec. CIGNA Corp., Phila., 1982-84, v.p. govt. and industry rels., 1984-87, sr. v.p., chief counsel property/casualty group, 1988—; mem. pvt. security adv. coun. Dept. Justice, 1975-77; bd. dirs. Ins. Co. N.Am. Mem. adv. coun. on gen. govt. Rep. Nat. Com., 1977-78; mem. Phila. Community Leadership Seminar, 1978-79; mem. exec. com. Boy Scouts Am., Phila., 1981-82; bd. dirs. Sacred Heart Med. Ctr., 1983-85, Swarthmore Presbyn. Ch., 1984-86, Wallingford Hills Civic Assn., 1983-85, Com. of Seventy, 1985-87, Acad. Natural Scis., Phila., 1987—, Pub. Affairs Coun., Washington, 1986—, Episcopal Acad., 1987—. Mem. ABA, Pa. Bar Assn., D.C. Bar Assn., White House Fellows Alumni Assn., Met. Club (Washington), Union League Club (Phila.), Harvard Club (N.Y.C.). Office: Cigna Property & Casualty Group 1600 Arch St 12th Fl Philadelphia PA 19103

SHEPARD, GREGORY MARK, insurance company executive; b. Bloomington, Ill., Oct. 15, 1955; s. Trent Allen and Myra Jane (Rodgers) S. BS in Fin., U. Ill., 1977; JD, Northern Ill. U., 1980. Bar: Ill. 1980. Adminstrv. analyst Union Ins. Co., Bloomington, 1981, v.p., 1981-85, pres., 1985—. Mem. ABA, Ill. Bar Assn., McLean County Bar Assn., Phi Gamma Delta. Home: 15 Country Club Pl Bloomington IL 61701 Office: Union Ins Group 303 E Washington St Bloomington IL 61701

SHEPARD, MARGO ANN, financial consultant; b. Starke, Fla., Dec. 6, 1957; d. Michael Joseph and Carroll May (Emerson) Warhola; m. Michael Eugene Shepard, Sept. 4, 1982; children: Andrew Eugene, Ann Emerson. BSBA, U. N.C., 1978; MBA, U. Kans., 1981. Cert. fin. planner. Product planner Hallmark Cards, Kansas City, Mo., 1979-81; grad. teaching asst. Sch. Bus. U. Kans., Lawrence, 1981; account exec. Kidder, Peabody Co., Kansas City, 1981-83; fin. cons. Shearson, Lehman, Hutton Co., Kansas City, 1983—; vis. lectr. Math. Assn. Am., 1986—; mem. faculty Webster U., Kansas City, 1987—. Bd. dirs. Mid-Continent Coun. Girl Scouts U.S., 1987—. Named One of Am.'s Best Stockbrokers Money Mag., 1987. Mem. Am. Inst. Cert. Fin. Planners, Greater Kansas City C. of C., Kansas City Club, Zonta (pres. found. devel. com. Kansas City chpt. 1983-84), Phi Beta Kappa, Beta Gamma Sigma. Republican. Roman Catholic. Home: 3706 Locust St Kansas City MO 64109 Office: Shearson Lehman Hutton Co 401 Ward Pkwy Ste C Kansas City MO 64112

SHEPARD, ROBERT M., lawyer, investment banker, engineer; b. Amityville, N.Y., Feb. 15, 1932; s. Sidney M. and Undine L. (Lehmann) Shapiro; m. Barbara S. Stannard, June 25, 1955 (div. 1980); children: Karen Michele Shepard Sweer, Daniel Robert; m. 2d Joanne E. Devlin, May 16, 1981. B.C.E., Cornell U., 1954; M.B.A., Hofstra Coll., 1960; LL.B., Yale U., 1963; LLM, NYU, 1988. Bar: N.Y. 1964; registered profl. engr., N.Y., Conn. Project engr. Lockwood Kessler & Bartlett, Syosset, N.Y., 1956-60; assoc. atty. Cravath, Swaine & Moore, N.Y.C. and Paris, 1963-70; gen. ptnr. Kuhn, Loeb & Co., N.Y.C., 1970-77; sr. v.p. Donaldson, Lufkin & Jenrette, N.Y.C., 1977-83; gen. ptnr. Donovan Leisure Newton & Irvine, N.Y.C., 1983—. Note and comment editor: Yale Law Jour., 1962-63. Bd. dirs. N.Y. Grand Opera, 1987—. Recipient Fuertes Medal Cornell U., 1953. Mem. ABA, Am. N.Y. State Bar Assn., Pub. Power Assn., Nat. Assn. Bond Lawyers, Order of Coif, Tau Beta Pi, Chi Epsilon. Club: Union League. Home: 650 Park Ave Apt 11/12B New York NY 10021 Office: Donovan Leisure Newton & Irvine 30 Rockefeller Pla New York NY 10112

SHEPARD-TAGGART, GLORIA HARVEY, communications company executive; b. Ridgeland, S.C., June 20, 1932; d. Leroy Everett and Addie Gertrude (Gray) Harvey; m. Ray Lester Shepard (dec.); children: Michael Ray, Glenn Eric; m. Eugene Sheppard Taggart, June 1, 1986. Student Armstrong Coll., 1950-52. Head bookkeeper Liberty Nat. Bank, Savannah, Ga., 1952-55; v.p. Hargray Telephone Co., Inc., Hilton Head Island, S.C., 1953-82, pres., 1982—; bd. dirs. Citizen & So. Nat. Bank of S.C. Bd. dirs. Better Bus. Bur., Hilton Head Heart Assn., Cultural Council Hilton Head Island. Mem. U.S. Telephone Assn., S.C. C. of C., S.C. Indsl. Developers Assn., Nat. Assn. Female Execs., Am. Mgmt. Assn., Ind. Telephone Pioneers, Profl. Women's Club, Beta Kappa. Baptist. Club: Christian Women's. Avocations: biking, cards. Office: Hargray Telephone Co Inc PO Box 5519 Hilton Head Island SC 29938

SHEPHERD, CHARLES CLINTON, real estate executive; b. Westport, Conn., May 25, 1929; s. J. Clinton and Gail Fleming (English) S.; m. June Stalls, June 19, 1956; children: Gail Paige, Susan Arlen, Richard Clinton. B in Landscape Arch., U. Fla., 1951, M in City Planning, 1956. Lic. real estate broker, mortgage broker; registered landscape architect. Pres. Kendree and Shepherd, Phila., 1958-72; regional pres. Robino-Ladd Co., Palm Beach, Fla., 1972-75; v.p. Hovnanian Co., Lake Worth, Fla., 1975-78; pres. Gamina Co., Lake Worth, 1978—; chmn. Whitpain Planning Commn., Blue Bell, Pa., 1967-72; mem. land use adv. bd. Palm Beach County, 1989—. Contbr. articles to profl. jours. Mem. Palm Beach County Task Force, 1984, Downtown Devel. Authority, Lake Worth, 1985-88, chmn., 1988—. Served to 1st lt. arty. U.S. Army, 1952-54. Mem. Am. Soc. Planners, Home Builders Assn. Clubs: Gov.'s, Forum (Palm Beach). Home: 216 Monterey Rd Palm Beach FL 33480

SHEPHERD, JAMES MANNY, financial planner; b. Richmond, Va., June 11, 1954; s. Francis DuVal and Kathleen (Boyle) S.; m. Theresa Taylor, Oct. 23, 1982; children: Stephanie Lynn, Jamie Aaron. BS, Va. Poly. Inst. and State U., 1977; postgrad., Coll. for Fin. Planning, 1986-88. Cert. fin. planner. Lab. technician Phillip Morris Inc., Richmond, 1977-78; prin. Shepherd Logging, Dillon, Colo., 1978-82; v.p. Va. Planning Corp., Richmond, 1982-87, pres., 1987—; adj. prof. Coll. Fin. Planning, Richmond, 1987; tchr. fin. planning Richmond Area High Sch., 1988. Pres. Civitan Club, Southside Richmond, 1987; bd. dirs. Va. chpt. Am. Cancer Soc., Richmond, 1987. Mem. Internat. Assn. Fin. Planners (bd. dirs. Richmond chpt. 1987), Inst. Cert. Fin. Planners (bd. dirs. Richmond chpt. 1987). Republican. Roman Catholic. Club: Briarwood Swim (Richmond). Home: 510 Overcliff Ct Midlothian VA 23113 Office: Va Planning Corp 601 Twin Ridge Ln Richmond VA 23235

SHEPHERD, MARK, JR., retired electronics company executive; b. Dallas, Jan. 18, 1923; s. Mark and Louisa Florence (Daniell) S.; m. Mary Alice Murchland, Dec. 21, 1945; children: Debra Aline Shepherd Robinson, MaryKay Theresa Shepherd Welker, Marc Blaine. BSEE, So. Meth. U., 1942; MSEE, U. Ill., at Urbana, 1947. Registered profl. engr., Tex. With GE, 1942-43, Farnsworth TV and Radio Corp., 1947-48; with Tex. Instruments, Dallas, 1948-88, v.p., gen. mgr. semicondr.-components div., 1955-61, exec. v.p., chief operating officer, 1961-66, pres., chief operating officer, 1967-69, pres., chief exec. officer, 1969-76, chmn. bd. dirs., chief exec. officer, 1976-84, chmn. bd. dirs., chief corp. officer, 1984-85, chmn., also bd. dirs.; mem. internat. coun. Morgan Guaranty Trust Co.; mem. adv. com. for trade policy and negotiations Office U.S. Trade Reps. Mem. U.S.-Japan Bus. Coun.; U.S. Korea Bus. Coun.; hon. trustee Com. for Econ. Devel.; trustee Am. Enterprise Inst. Pub. Policy Rsch.; councillor Conf. Bd.; mem. Bus. Coun., Dallas Citizens Coun. Lt. (j.g.) USNR, 1943-46. Fellow IEEE; mem. Soc. Exploration Geophysicists, Coun. on Fgn. Rels., Nat. Acad. Engring., Sigma Xi, Eta Kappa Nu. Office: Tex Instruments PO Box 655474 MS 407 Dallas TX 75265

SHEPHERD, RONALD WILLIAM, management consultant; b. Dallas, July 14, 1947; s. James Clarence and Betty Joyce (Stockard) S.; m. Kathryn Kramer, July 28, 1967; children: Patricia Lyn, Kathryn Kristine. BA, So. Meth. U., 1969; MSIA, U. Dallas, 1971. With Weber Mgmt. Cons., Huntington, N.Y., 1988—. Mem. Young Pres.'s Orgn. Home: 3741 Cortez Dallas TX 75220 Office: Weber Mgmt Cons 46 Green St Huntington NY 11743

SHEPLEY, ETHAN ALLEN HITCHCOCK, JR., banker; b. St. Louis, Mar. 5, 1923; s. Ethan Allen Hitchcock and Sophie (Baker) S.; m. Margaret B. Meyer, June 18, 1970; children by previous marriage: Michael Ethan, Lela Lockwood, Virginia Cochran. B.A., Yale U., 1945; J.D., Washington U., St. Louis, 1949-53. Bar: Mo. 1949. With Shepley, Kroeger, Fisse & Shepley, St. Louis, 1949-53; with Boatman's Nat. Bank, St. Louis, 1953-88, vice chmn., 1977-88, also bd. dirs., now ret.; counsel Bryan, Cave, McPheeters & McRoberts, St. Louis, 1988—; pres., dir. Boatman's Bancshares, Inc., St. Louis, 1969-88. Home: 215 Graybridge Rd Saint Louis MO 63124 Office: Bryan Cave McPheeters & McRoberts 500 N Broadway Ste 2000 Saint Louis MO 63102

SHEPPARD, JAMES C., banker; b. Pierre, S.D., Jan. 7, 1936; s. Don A. and Ethel M. (Bowles) S.; m. Loretta A. Scarry, Mar. 2, 1963; children: Kelly L., J. Andrew. Student, U. S.D., 1954-56, 58. Asst. cashier Cherry Creek Nat. Bank, Denver, 1964-69; sr. v.p., cashier First Nat. Bank, Durango, Colo., 1969-82; pres., chief exec. officer First Nat. Bank, Cortez, Colo., 1982-83, Centennial Savs. Bank, Durango, Colo., 1983—. Pres. Durango Indsl. Devel., Colo., 1987—. Mem. Durango C. of C. (pres. 1981). Republican. Episcopalian. Office: Centennial Savs Bank PO Box 1590 1101 E 2d Ave Durango CO 81302

SHEPPARD, STEVEN BRADLEY, computer software executive, lawyer; b. Manhattan, N.Y., July 6, 1949; s. Harvey Phillip and Marcia (Lipson) S.; m. Paula Annette Licastro, Aug. 31, 1968; children: Michael, Nicole. BA, SUNY, Buffalo, 1974; JD, Hofstra U., 1977, MBA, 1977. Bar: N.Y. 1979. Tax cons. Touche Ross & Co., N.Y.C., 1977-81; atty. Reiter & Sabellico, N.Y.C., 1981-83; exec. v.p., chief ops. officer, chief fin. officer Advanced Instl. Mgmt. Software Inc., Syosset, N.Y., 1983—. Mem. ABA, Nassau County Bar Assn., Hofstra Sch. of Law Alumni Assn. (treas. 1984-87, fund raising com. 1982-84), N.Y. State Bar Assn., Phi Beta Kappa. Jewish. Office: Advanced Instl Mgmt Software Inc 485 Underhill Blvd Syosset NY 11791-3413

SHEPPARD, WILLIAM STEVENS, investment banker; b. Grand Rapids, Mich., Apr. 29, 1930; s. James Herbert and Emily Gilmore (Stevens) S.; m. Jane Steketee, 1956 (dec. 1975); children: Stevens C., Elizabeth W., Emily R.; m. Patricia Gillis Bloom, Dec. 2, 1978. B.A. in Econs, U. Va., 1953. Trainee J.P. Morgan & Co., Inc., N.Y.C., 1955-58; investment adv. Delafield & Delafield, N.Y.C., 1958-71; from salesman to sr. v.p. and dir. F.S. Smithers & Co., N.Y.C., 1971-76; sr. v.p., dir. successor Paine, Webber, Jackson & Curtis, Inc., 1976-81; pres., chief exec. officer, dir. Paine Webber Real Estate Securities Inc., 1980-85; mng. dir. Paine Webber Capital Markets, N.Y.C., 1985-88, Berkshire Capital Corp., N.Y.C., 1988—; bd. dirs. Public Securities Assn. Inc., Ea. Bancorp. An editor: Ginny Mae Manual, 1979; contbr. to handbooks. Bd. mgrs. Seamens Ch. Inst., N.Y.C., 1965—; trustee, treas. Riot Relief Fund City N.Y., 1970—. Served to lt. (j.g.) USNR, 1953-55. Republican. Clubs: N.Y. Yacht; Country of Fairfield (Conn.); Pequot Yacht; Mashomack Fish and Game. Home: 405 Sasco Hill Rd Southport CT 06490 Office: Berkshire Capital Corp 405 Lexington Ave The Chrysler Bldg New York NY 10174

SHEPPARD, WILLIAM VERNON, transportation engineer; b. Harlan, Ky., Apr. 18, 1941; s. Vernon L. and Margaret M. (Montgomery) S.; B.S.E., The Citadel, 1964; m. Charlotte A. McGehee, Nov. 6, 1981; children—W. Kevin, Candice Gaye. Registered profl. engr., Pa., Calif. and 10 other states. Hwy. engr. Howard Needles, Tammen & Bergendoff, Kansas City, Mo., 1964-65; with Wilbur Smith & Assos., Columbia, S.C., 1967-80, various positions to western regional v.p., so. regional v.p.; v.p., dir. transp. Post Buckley, Schuh & Jernigan, Inc., Columbia, 1980-85; v.p., dep. corp. prin. for transp. Sverdrup Corp., 1985—; guest lectr. U. So. Calif. Sch. Architecture and Urban Planning. Mem. engring. adv. bd. Clemson U., 1977-80. Served to capt. U.S. Army, 1965-67. Decorated AEM medal. Fellow ASCE, Inst. Transp. Engrs. (pres. S.C. div. 1979); mem. Nat. Soc. Profl. Engrs., S.C. Council Engring. Socs. (pres. 1978). Republican. Roman Catholic.

SHEPPS, REGINALD RONALD, industrial psychologist, consultant; b. Bklyn., Jan. 11, 1939; s. I. Robert and Lillian (Eisenberg) S.; m. Florence Pearl Zahn, June 4, 1966; children: David, Sari. BA, Queens Coll., 1960; MA in Clin. Psychology, Case Western Res. U., 1967; PhD in Indsl. Psychology, Am. Coll., 1979. Lic. psychologist, N.J., N.Y. Dir. personnel rsch. and planning Metro. Ins. Cos., N.Y.C., 1967-82; dir. edn. design and evaluation Coopers & Lybrand, Newark, 1982-83; pres. Productivity Strategies, Jamaica Estates, N.Y., 1983-84; dir. mgmt. devel. Sandy Corp, Troy, Mich., 1984-86; v.p. Drake Beam Morin, Birmingham, Mich., 1986-88; mgr. tng. Harley Davidson, Inc., Milw., 1988—. Contbr. articles to profl. jours. Chmn. rsch. planning com. for Life Ins. Industry, Hartford, Conn., 1980-81; founding sec. Holliswood (N.Y.) Civic Assn., 1972-74; bd. dirs. Temple Israel Jamaica, Jamaica Estates, 1980-83. USPHS fellow Yale U., 1960-62. Mem. Am. Psychol. Assn., Mich. Assn. Indsl. Organizationl Psychology, Met. N.Y. Assn. Applied Psychology (bd. dirs. 1979-85, pres. 1982-83), Soc. Indsl./Organizational Psychology, Life Ins. Mgmt. and Research Assn. (chmn. bd. 1979, ins. ind. research planning com.), Psi Chi. Democrat. Home: 4390 Ramsgate Ln Bloomfield Hills MI 48013 Office: Drake Beam Morin 5505 Corporate Dr Troy MI 48098

SHER, ALLAN L., brokerage company executive; b. Superior, Wis., Oct. 19, 1931; s. Robert Edward and Pearl (Wolpert) S.; m. Judy Biegel, June 17, 1962; children: Allison, Victoria, Robert. BA, Princeton U., 1953; grad. Advanced Mgmt. Program, Harvard U., 1975. With Merrill Lynch, Pierce, Fenner & Smith Inc., N.Y.C., 1956—; exec. v.p. services Merrill Lynch, Pierce, Fenner & Smith Inc., 1976-79, exec. v.p. fin./adminstrn., 1979—, also bd. dirs.; sr. v.p. Merrill Lynch & Co. Inc., 1980—; sr. v.p. Merrill Lynch Realty Assos., Inc., regional pres., 1981—; ptnr. Wertheim and Co.; pres. Wertheim Asset Mgmt. Services, Inc., 1983—; sr. exec. v.p., bd. dirs. Drexel Burnham Lambert Inc.; bd. dirs. Depository Trust Co.; ofcl. Am. Stock Exchange. Trustee Congregation Emanu-El, Scarsdale, N.Y. Served with U.S. Army, 1954-56. Democrat. Club: Century Country. Home: 51 Paddington Rd Scarsdale NY 10583 Office: Drexel Burnham Lambert Inc 60 Broad St New York NY 10004

SHERBLOM, JAMES PETER, biopharmaceutical executive; b. Fall River, Mass., Oct. 6, 1955; s. Edward R. and Ruth P. (Howard) S.; m. Loretta Ho Sherblom, Mar. 11, 1979; children: Sarah, Robert. MBA, Harvard U., 1980. Cons. Bain & Co., Boston, 1980-81, London, 1981-82; sr. cons. Bain & Co., Munich, 1982-83; dir. fin. Genzyme Corp., Boston, 1984-85; chief fin. officer Genzyme Corp., 1985-89; chmn., chief exec. officer Transgenic Scis. Inc., 1989—. Mem. Fin. Execs. Inst., Mass. Biotech. Coun. (pres. 1987-88), Boston Treas.'s Club. Home: 199 Park Ln Concord MA 01742 Office: Genzyme Corp 75 Kneeland St Boston MA 02111

SHERIDAN, JOAN MARIE, automotive engineering executive; b. Charlevoix, Mich., Nov. 26, 1957; d. Thomas Leslie and Ruthann (Kratochvil) S.; 1 child, Peter Thomas. BA in English, Wayne State U., 1985. Admistrv. mgr. Pioneer Engring., Madison Heights, Mich., 1985—. Mem. Mich. Corp. Vol. Coun., Detroit. Capt. USNG 1980—. Mem. NAFE, Nat. Guard Assn. Mich., Nat. Guard Assn. U.S., Am. Mgmt. Assn., Mensa. Republican. Roman Catholic. Home: 77 Highland Lake Orion MI 48035 Office: Pioneer Engring 32384 Edwards St Madison Heights MI 48071

SHERIDAN, PATRICK MICHAEL, finance company executive; b. Grosse Pointe, Mich., Apr. 13, 1940; s. Paul Phillip and Frances Mary (Rohan) S.; m. Diane Lorraine Tressler, Nov. 14, 1986; children: Mary, Patrick, Kelly, Kevin, James. BBA, U. Notre Dame, 1962; MBA, U. Detroit, 1975. Acct. Peat, Marwick, Mitchell & Co., Detroit, 1962-72, audit mgr., 1969-72; exec. v.p. fin. Alexander Hamilton Life Ins. Co., Farmington, Mich., 1973-76; sr. v.p. ops. Sun Life Ins. Co. Am., Balt., 1976-78, exec. v.p., 1978-79; pres. Sun Ins. Services, Inc., 1979-81; pres., chief exec. officer Am. Health & Life Ins. Co., Balt., 1981-85; chief exec. officer Gulf Ins. Co., 1985-86; sr. v.p., chief fin. officer Comml. Credit Co., 1985-86, sr. v.p. audit, 1987; exec. v.p., chief fin. officer The Associated Group, Indpls., 1987—. Republican candidate for U.S. Congress, 1972; past pres. Charlesbrooke Community Assn.; past v.p. Jr. Achievement of Met. Balt., 1984-85; bd. dirs. Goodwill Industries of Balt., 1986; bd. govs. Served to capt. AUS, 1963-65. Recipient various Jaycee awards. Fellow Life Mgmt. Inst.; mem. Am. Mgmt. Assn. (pres.'s assn.), Am. Inst. C.P.A.s, Mich. Assn. C.P.A.s, Md. Assn. C.P.A.s, Am. Soc. C.L.U.s, U.S. Jaycees (treas. 1973-74), Mich. Jaycees (pres. 1971-72), Detroit Jaycees (pres. 1968-69), Balt. C. of C. (bd. dirs.), Mensa. Clubs: Notre Dame (Balt., Indpls.); Indpls. Athletic.

SHERK, WARREN ARTHUR, counselor, educator; b. Buffalo, July 12, 1916; s. Warren E. and Jennie (Taylor) S.; m. Martha Jean Kritzer, June 11, 1954; children: Elena E., Adra K., Lydian M., Warren M., Wilson E. Student Hiram Coll., 1934-35, U. Rangoon, Burma, 1938-39, Duke U., 1939-40; AB, Allegheny Coll., 1938; BD, Berkeley Bapt. Div. Sch., 1945, ThM, 1952; STD, Burton Sem., 1958. Minister, Meth. chs. in western N.Y., 1941-43; Protestant chaplain Ariz. State Prison, 1971-72; vis. prof. Iliff Sch. Theology, U. Denver, 1945-47; field sec. to Pearl S. Buck, 1948-49; minister edn., Indiana, Pa., 1949-51; minister Waitsburg Meth. Ch., Washington, 1951-52, Community Ch., Watertown, Mass., 1955-58, Savanna, Ill., 1958-59, Nogales (Ariz.) United Ch., 1960-61; exec. Dynamics Found., Tucson, 1962—; personal counselor, 1962—; faculty Phoenix Coll., 1963-66, Mesa Community Coll., Eastern Ariz. Coll., Pima Coll., 1963-78, Western Internat. U., 1984—; cons. spl. seminars Pepsi Cola Mgmt. Inst., 1967-68; dir. bus. and profl. seminars for execs., 1968—; lectr. U. Durham (Eng.), summer 1981, Iliff Sch. Theology, summer 1982, Elder Hostels, N.Y., summer 1983, St. Deinels Library, Wales, summer 1985, S.S. Rotterdam N.Y.C. to South Africa, 1984; founder, exec. sec. Valley of Sun Forum, Phoenix, 1963-67; coordinator Assoc. Bus. Execs. Phoenix, 1963-67. Author: Wider Horizons, 1941, Agnes Moorehead: A Biography, 1976, Pearl Buck, 1987; contbr. numerous articles to mags. Chmn. spl. gifts div. Maricopa County Heart Fund. Corporate mem. Perkins Sch. for the Blind; bd. dirs. Boston World Affairs Council, N.E. Assn. UN; hon. bd. govs., bd. dirs. Pearl S. Buck Found. Fellow Am. Acad. Polit. Sci., Am. Geog. Soc.; mem. Thoreau Soc., Emerson Soc., Watertown Hist. Soc., Pimeria Alta Hist. Soc., Maricopa Mental Health Assn., Internat. Winston Churchill Soc., Theodore Roosevelt Assn., Execs. Internat. (founder, exec. dir. 1967—), Nat. Assn. Approved Morticians (exec. sec. 1967-69), Internat. Platform Assn., Tucson Com. Fgn. Relations, Phoenix Com. Fgn. Relations, NCCJ, AAUP, Theta Chi. Republican. Clubs: Ariz., Univ., Kiva. Address: 10032 N 8th St Phoenix AZ 85020

SHERMAN, BEATRICE ETTINGER, business executive; b. N.Y.C., May 29, 1919; d. Max and Stella (Schrager) Ettinger; m. Herbert Jacob Howard, Feb. 15, 1942 (dec. 1971); children—Robert David Howard, Carolyn Howard Smith; m. Ernest John Sherman, Dec. 29, 1974. Student, Shimer Jr. Coll., Mt. Carroll, Ill., 1936-38; B.A., U. Miami, Fla., 1940; postgrad. Harvard U., 1940, Paris-Am. Acad., Paris, 1972, Alliance Française, Paris, 1973. Corp. sec., dir. Save Electric Corp., Toledo, 1940-67, Verd-A-Ray Corp., Toledo, 1944-67, Penetray Corp., Toledo, 1962-67; ptnr. Stella Assocs., Newark, 1960-80; pres. Besman Inc., Coral Gables, Fla., 1975—, All Am. Mobile Telephone Co., Coral Gables, 1986—; with BHS Ptnrs., Miami, 1983—. Vol. worker Jewish Welfare Fedn., Toledo, 1942-69; nat. speaker United Jewish Appeal; mem. womens div. Greater Miami Jewish Fedn., 1969—, trustee, 1986; active Miami advertiser adv. bd. Bell South Advt. and Pub. Co. Recipient Lion of Judah award. Mem. Assn. Telemessaging Services Internat., Telocator Network Am. Home: 5108 SW 72d Ave Miami FL 33155 Office: Besman Inc 141 Aragon Ave Coral Gables FL 33134

SHERMAN, EUGENE JAY, marketing executive, economist; b. N.Y.C., Jan. 10, 1935; s. Samuel and Sarah (Lavinsky) S.; m. Mary Eileen Van, Apr. 22, 1966; 1 child, Rebecca. BA, CCNY, 1956; MBA, NYU, 1959, postgrad., 1959-63. Economist Fed. Res. Bank N.Y., 1959-62, Chase Manhattan Bank, N.Y.C., 1962-65; v.p. Bank of N.Y., N.Y.C., 1965-72; sr. v.p., exec. dir., dir. research Merrill Lynch and Co., N.Y.C., 1972-78; v.p., chief economist, internat. mgr. Internat. Gold Corp., N.Y.C., 1980-86; sr. v.p., chief economist Fed. Home Loan Bank N.Y., 1986—; gold cons., N.Y.C., 1986—. Author: Gold Investment: Theory and Application, 1986; contbr. articles to profl. jours. Clubs: Money Marketeers (pres. 1971-72, honored fellow 1987), Downtown Economist (program chmn. 1985-86, vice chmn. 1987-88, chmn. 1988-89), Forecasters (winner 1986), Treasury Securities Luncheon, Money Mkt. Luncheon. Home: 115 E 9th St New York NY 10003

SHERMAN, FREDERICK WISE, JR., civil engineer; b. Charlottesville, Va., June 26, 1956; s. Frederick Wise and Lula Mae (Herndon) S.; m. Sherry Ann Wiggins, Aug. 16, 1980; children: Taylor Ashton, Amy Rose. BSCE, Va. Mil. Inst., 1978. Registered profl. engr., Va. Owner W. A. Sherman Co., Orange, Va., 1981—. Bd. dirs. zoning com. Town of Orange, 1986—; pres. Orange Presbyn. Mem, 1983-84. Capt. U.S. Army, 1978-81, USAR, 1981—. Decorated Army Commendation medal. Mem. Optimist (v.p. 1985-86). Home: 272 Mimosa Ln Orange VA 22960

SHERMAN, GEORGE M., manufacturing company executive; b. N.Y.C., Aug. 6, 1941; s. Joseph B. and Fredericka (Hand) S.; m. Betsy Rae Bicknell, Nov. 26, 1966; children: Jonathan, David, Michael, Matthew. B.S., L.I. U., 1963; M.B.A., U. Louisville, 1971. Product gen. mgr. Gen. Electric Co., Bridgeport, Conn., 1966-79; pres. Weed Eater div. Emersen Electric Co., Houston, 1979-80; pres. Skil Corp. div. Emerson Electric Co., Chgo., 1980-82; group v.p. U.S. power tools group Black & Decker Corp., Balt., 1985, sr. v.p., pres. power tools group, 1986—; mem. adv. bd. Nat. Home Ctr. Show, Chgo., 1987; bd. dirs. D.I.Y. Research Inst., Lincolnshire, Ill., 1988. Bd. dirs. Ctr. Stage, Balt., 1988. Served with U.S. Army, 1964-66. Mem. Am. Mgmt. Assn. (mem. gen. mgmt. council 1988). Clubs: Center (Balt.); Hillendale Country (Phoenix, Md.). Office: Black & Decker Corp 10 N Park Dr Hunt Valley MD 21030

SHERMAN, JEFFREY BARRY, retail executive; b. Passaic, N.J., June 25, 1948; s. Maxwell and Elinor (Richman) S.; m. Karin Lynn Swann, May 1, 1971; children—Erik, Brett, Peter, Kristin. B.S. in Econs., CCNY, 1971; M.B.A., NYU, 1975. With Bloomingdale's, N.Y.C., 1971—; v.p. merchandising Bloomingdale's, 1982-83, sr. v.p., 1983-85, exec. v.p., 1985—. Office: Bloomingdale's 59th St & Lexington New York NY 10022 *

SHERMAN, MALCOLM LEE, retail company executive; b. Boston, Aug. 3, 1931; s. Samuel Richard and Celia (Marcus) S.; m. Barbara Cantor, Jan. 28, 1959; 1 dau., Robin. B.A., Cornell U., 1953. Distbr. Morse Shoe, Boston, 1957-60; Men's shoe buyer Morton shoe, Boston, 1960-63; exec. v.p., gen. mdse. mgr. Ideal Shoe Co., Phila., 1963-68; with Zayre Corp., Framingham, Mass., 1968—, asst. v.p., footwear gen. mgr., 1968-73; sr. v.p., gen. mdse. mgr. Zayre Corp., 1973-76, exec. v.p., gen. mdse. mgr., 1976-80, exec. v.p., gen. mgr. Zayre Stores, 1980-83; exec. v.p. Zayre Corp., pres. Zayre Stores 1983—; exec. v.p. Zayre Corp., 1983—; past pres., dir. Two/Ten Nat. Found., Boston, 1970—; dir. CompuChem Labs., Inc., U.S. Trust Co., Reging Electronics, Mass. Eye and Ear Infirmary. Bd. dirs. Horizons for Youth, Sharon, Mass., 1978—; trustee Brandeis U., Waltham, Mass., 1980—, chmn. bd. fellows, 1980-83; trustee Civic Edn. Found., Tufts U., 1982—; overseer Boston Symphony Orch., 1983—. Served with U.S. Army, 1953-56. Recipient Jack Martin Man of Yr., Mt. Sinai Med. Ctr., 1981; T. Kenyon Holly award, 1982; Discounter of Yr., Discount Store News, 1983; named Israel Bonds Man of Yr., B'nai B'rith Youth Services, 1983;. Mem. Footwear Retailers Assn. (dir.), Nat. Mass Retailing Inst. (dir.), Confrerie de la Chaine des Rotisseurs (chevalier 1968—). Home: 10 Albion Rd Wellesley MA 02181 Office: Zayre Corp 235 Old Connecticut Path Framingham MA 01701 *

SHERMAN, MARY KENNEDY, business executive; b. Chgo., June 17, 1919; d. Robert Thomas and Mary Cecelia (Hammond) Kennedy; A.A., Los Angeles Valley Coll., 1966; B.S., Pepperdine U., 1973; M.B.A., 1974; Accredited Personnel Accreditation Inst. m. Lloyd McBean Sherman, Dec. 1, 1967; children—Tom D. Akins, Mary Patricia Kraakevik. Indsl. relations supr. Douglas Aircraft Co., Inc., Santa Monica, Calif., 1942-61; dir. personnel Helene Curtis Industries, Studio Girl, Glendale, Calif., 1961-65; dir. personnel Semtech Corp., Newbury Park, Calif., 1965-73, v.p., 1973—; lectr., cons. in field. Mem. Am. Mgmt. Assn., Internat. Assn. for Personnel Women (Mem. of Yr. 1982-83), Am. Soc. for Personnel Adminstrn., Personnel and Indsl. Relations Assn., Am. Bus. Women's Assn., Personnel Women of Los Angeles. Republican. Roman Catholic. Club: Zonta Internat. (dist. gov. 1984-86). Office: Semtech Corp 652 Mitchell Rd Newbury Park CA 91320

SHERMAN, SAUL S., manufacturing company executive; b. 1917. BA, U. Chgo., 1939. Profl. football player Chgo. Bears, 1939-40; pres., treas. Emerson Machinery Corp., 1937-66; with Davis & Thompson Corp., 1948—; pres. Am. Eagle Corp. merged Allied Products Corp., 1962-65; with Allied Products Corp., 1963—, chmn. bd. dirs., 1973—. Office: Allied Products Corp 208 S LaSalle St Chicago IL 60603 *

SHERMAN, SCOTT BRADLEY, business executive; b. N.Y.C., Nov. 4, 1954; s. Allen Maurice and Phyliss (Soloff) S.; m. Sherry Jane Salzmann, May 6, 1979; children: Jennifer Leigh, Zachary Samuel. BS, U. Fla., 1976. V.p. Jay Scott Furniture, Inc., Ft. Lauderdale, 1977-83; pres., founder J. Robin Scott Creative Cons., Ft. Lauderdale, 1983-86; pres. Integrated Bus. Corp., Boca Raton, Fla., 1985—, chmn. bd., bd. dirs., 1986—; pres. Integrated Fin. Group, Boca Raton, 1986—; bd. dirs. Medi-Quip, Inc., Davie, Fla., Sherman, Goelz & Assoc., Kansas City, Metro Systems, Inc., Boca Raton, Design Gifts Internat., Inc., Corona, Calif. Advance team H. Hmphrey for pres., Fla., 1972; pres. Arrowhead Homeowners. Assn., Davie, 1983-84. Ellen Fishback scholar, 1972. Home: 22467 Ensenada Way Boca Raton FL 33433 Office: Integrated Bus Corp 7100 W Camino Real Ste 402 Boca Raton FL 33433

SHERMAN, STEVEN RYAN, software duplicating company executive; b. Palo Alto, Calif., Jan. 7, 1950; s. Gordon Henry and Helen (McAlister) S.; m. Linda Kay Ligon, May 22, 1971; children: Michael Ryan, Daniel James, Amanda Michele. Grad. pub. schs., Cupertino, Calif. Automobile mechanic Sherman's Auto Service, Palo Alto, 1965-74, gen. mgr., 1974-78; realtor assoc. O'Tiffany Properties, Sunnyvale, Calif., 1978-81; pres. L & S Computerware, Sunnyvale, 1981-83, HLS Duplication, Inc., Sunnyvale, 1983—. Home: 1589 Fraser Dr Sunnyvale CA 94087 Office: HLS Duplication Inc 520 Almanor Ave Sunnyvale CA 94086

SHERRELL, LARRY CLINTON, personnel executive; b. Dallas, Dec. 25, 1950; s. Bonnie Maurice and Dorothy Eloise (Connor) S.; m. Gloria Joy Butler, Feb. 26, 1972; children: Jeremy Brandon, Timothy Michael, Melanie Joy Colleen. B in Indsl. Engring., Gen. Motors Inst., Flint, Mich., 1973; MBA, U. Mich., 1975. Employee relations rep. Gen. Motors Corp., Arlington, Tex., 1975-78; personnel analyst Gen. Motors Corp., Warren, Mich., 1978-79; sr. personnel analyst Gen. Motors Corp., Detroit, 1979-80; employment mgr. Gen. Motors Corp., Lake Orion, Mich., 1981-84, employee relations mgr., 1984-85; div. personnel mgr. Abbott Labs., North Chicago, Ill., 1985—. Republican. Baptist. Home: 520 Hemlock Ln Libertyville IL 60048

SHERRILL, HUGH VIRGIL, investment banker; b. Long Beach, Calif., 1920. Ed., Yale. Sr. dir. Prudential-Bache Securities, Inc., 1977—. Trustee Meml. Hosp., N.Y.C., Boys' Club. Office: Prudential-Bache Securities Inc 1 Sea Port Pla 34th Fl New York NY 10292

SHERROD, SUSAN, banker; b. N.Y.C., Apr. 29, 1941; d. Nomer and Emelia (Freberg) Gray; m. John Hudson Sherrod, June 17, 1961 (div. 1977); children: Amy Elizabeth, William Gray. BS in Chemistry, U. Pa., 1963; MBA, U. Pitts., 1977, postgrad., 1980—. Comml. lending officer Equibank, Pitts., 1977-82; comml. lending officer Pitts. Nat. Bank, 1982-86, mgr. cash mgmt. mktg., 1986—. Bd. dirs. Pitts. Dance Council, 1982—, Housing Opportunities, Inc., Pitts., 1982—, Katz Sch. Bus., U. Pitts., 1985—, Pitts. YWCA, 1986—; trustee Sewickley Acad., Pitts., 1971-80. Republican. Episcopalian. Home: 25 Briar Cliff Rd Pittsburgh PA 15202 Office: Pitts Nat Bank Fifth Ave at Wood St Pittsburgh PA 15265

SHERRY, JOHN ERNEST HORWATH, lawyer, educator; b. N.Y.C., Mar. 17, 1932; s. John Harold and Marguerite (Horwath) S.; m. Margaret Louise Singer, Sept. 16, 1961; children: John, Suzanne Cover, Douglas Marshall. BA, Yale U., 1954; JD, Columbia U., 1959; LLM, NYU, 1968. Bar: N.Y., 1961, Ohio, 1967, U.S. Supreme Ct., 1967. Law clk. to pres. justice U.S. Dist. Ct. So. Dist. N.Y., 1959-60; assoc. Baker, Nelson and Mitchell, N.Y.C., 1960-61, John H. Sherry, N.Y.C., 1961-63; law asst. N.Y. State Ct. Claims, N.Y.C., 1963-65; assoc. John H. Sherry and John F. Gilligan, N.Y.C., 1965-67; asst. prof., dir. clin. programs U. Akron, Ohio, 1967-70; assoc. prof., dir. clin. programs U. San Diego Sch. Law, 1970-72; assoc. prof. law Sch. Hotel Adminstrn. Cornell U., Ithaca, N.Y., 1972-85, prof., 1985—, grad. fac. rep., 1988—; ptnr. Sherry & O'Neill, N.Y.C., 1985—; cons. World Tourism Orgn., Madrid, Spain, 1985; mem. U.S. State Dept. Adv. Com. Hotelkeepers Contract, 1974-78. Author: The Laws of Innkeepers, 1981; Business Law, 1984; Legal Aspects of Foodservice Management, 1984. Contbr. articles to profl. jours. 1st lt. U.S. Army, 1955-57, 61-62, Korea. Recipient Merit award Greater Akron Community Action Coun., 1968; Cert. Merit award Fedn. Comml. Counsellors Brazil, 1979. Mem. Internat. Forum Travel and Tourism (pres. 1983—), Advocates Jerusalem, Internat. Bar Assn. (various coms.), Univ. Club. Avocations: photography, stamp collecting. Home: 1026 Hanshaw Rd Ithaca NY 14850 Office: Cornell U Sch Hotel Adminstrn Ithaca NY 14853

SHERWAN, ROY GLENN, travel agency executive; b. St. Louis, Aug. 19, 1930; s. August Carl and Florence (Worth) S.; student Spencerian Coll., Milw., 1949; m. Carol Lee Sorenson, Nov. 10, 1951; children—Scott, Kimberly. Adminstrv. asst. Wis. N.G., Whitefish Bay, 1949-50; teller Home Savs. Bank, Milw., 1951-52; sales corr. Centralab div. Globe Union Co., Milw., 1952-54; sales rep. Am. Airlines, Milw. and Chgo., 1954-70; pres. 1st Maine Travel Agy., Des Plaines, Ill., 1970-85, also chmn. bd. Mem. United Air Lines Travel Agts. Council, Eastern Air Lines Travel Agts. Adv. bd., Norwegian Caribbean Lines Agts. Council. Bd. dirs. United Way of Des Plaines, 1982-85, gen. chmn., 1983-84, 84-85, v.p., 1985-86, pres. 1986-87. Served to capt. U.S. Army, 1951-52, 61-62. Mem. Am. Soc. Travel Agts.(bd. dirs. Midwest chpt. 1986—, v.p. Midwest chpt. 1988—), Assn. Bank Travel Burs., Chgo. Bon Vivants, Pacific Area Travel Assn., Chinese Passenger Club Chgo., Des Plaines C. of C. (dir. tourism 1984-85, bd. dirs. 1986—, v.p. 1989—). Presbyterian. Clubs: Elks, Bus. Breakfast (pres. 1976), Rotary (dir. Des Plaines 1978, 79-81). Home: 700 Graceland Ave Des Plaines IL 60016 Office: 728 Lee St Des Plaines IL 60016

SHERWIN, JAMES TERRY, lawyer, chemical company executive; b. N.Y.C., Oct. 25, 1933; s. Oscar and Stella (Zins) S.; m. Judith Emlyn Johnson, June 21, 1955 (div. Apr. 1984); children—Miranda, Alison Dale, Galen Leigh; m. Hiroko Inouye, June 15, 1985. BA, Columbia U., 1953, LLB (Stone scholar), 1956. Bar: N.Y. 1956, U.S. Supreme Ct. 1963. Assoc. Kaye, Scholer, Fierman, Hays & Handler, N.Y.C., 1957-60; with GAF Corp., N.Y.C., 1960-83, 84—, asso. counsel, gen. mgr. European ops., 1969-71, group v.p. photography, 1971-74, exec. v.p. fin. and adminstrn., 1974-78, exec. v.p. legal and investment services, 1978-83; vice chmn., chief adminstrv. officer GAF Corp., Wayne, N.J., 1984—; exec. v.p., chief fin. officer Triangle Industries, Inc., 1983-84; vice chmn., chief adminstrv. officer GAF Corp., Wayne, N.J., 1984—. Bd. dirs., chmn. exec. com., v.p. Internat. Rescue Com. Served to lt. comdr. USCGR, 1956-57. Named U.S. intercollegiate chess champion, 1951-53, N.Y. State champion, 1951, U.S. speed champion, 1956-57, 59-60, internat. master. Mem. ABA, Assn. Bar City N.Y., Am. Chess Found. (pres., dir.), Marshall (N.Y.) Chess Club (pres. 1967-69, gov.), Econ. Club N.Y., Phi Beta Kappa. Home: 15 Poor Farm Rd Princeton NJ 08540 Office: GAF Corp 1361 Alps Rd Wayne NJ 07470

SHERWOOD, JEFFRY RAND, utility executive; b. Calgary, Alta., Can., Aug. 28, 1950; came to U.S., 1955; s. L. Keith and LaVeda (Jensen) S.; m. Debra Gourdin Sherwood, Dec. 29, 1973; children: Jason, Jeremy, Aimie. BS, Brigham Young U., 1974, MA, 1975. Dept. mgr. Procter & Gamble Co., Grande Prairie, Alta., 1975-79; group mgr. Americus, Ga., 1979-81; mgr. human resource devel. Portland (Oreg.) Gen. Electric Co., 1981-83, dir. mgmt. services, 1983-87, mgr. compensation benefits and human resource info. ctr., 1987—; guest speaker Am. Mgmt. Assn., 1982—; mem. adv. com. pub. utility exec. course U. Idaho. Contbr. articles to profl. jours. Mem. Bus. Group on Health, Am. Compensation Assn., Edison Elecric Inst. (cons. 1982-87, chmn. human resources com. 1987), Mormon. Office: Portland Gen Electric Co 121 SW Salmon St Portland OR 97204

SHERWOOD, NED LEWIS, investment company executive; b. Bklyn., Oct. 13, 1949; s. Irving and Helen Sherwood Burka; m. Emily Layzer, Oct. 10, 1976; children: Matthew, Richard, Mark. BS in Econs., U. Pa., 1971. Asst. to pres. Hazeltine Corp., Greenlawn, N.Y., 1971-76; v.p. W.R. Grace & Co., N.Y.C., 1976-81, AEA Investors, Inc., N.Y.C., 1981-85; pres. Zaleski,

Sherwood & Co., Inc., N.Y.C., 1985—; bd. dirs. Consol. Stores Corp., Columbus, Ohio, Colo. Prime, Inc., Farmingdale, N.Y., Ford Meter Box Co., Inc., Wabash, Ind., So. Electric Corp., Atlanta. Mem. Beta Gamma Sigma. Office: Zaleski Sherwood & Co Inc 1270 6th Ave Ste 2414 New York NY 10020

SHESLOW, EVERETT A., stockbroker; b. N.Y.C., June 3, 1930; s. Julius and Nettie (Nadel) S.; m. Marion Engelman, Aug. 21, 1960 (div. Apr. 1987); children: Faith Ellen, Stephen James. BA, Drake U., 1951; MS, Columbia U., 1952. Trainee Newborg & Co., N.Y.C., 1955-58; v.p., floor broker Ernest Smith & Co., N.Y.C., 1958-59; pvt. practice securities trading N.Y.C., 1959-69; prin., pres. E.A. Sheslow, Inc., N.Y.C., 1969—; founding chmn. Am. Stock Exchange Floor Brokers Assn., N.Y.C., 1969; dir. Oxford First Corp., 1987. Mem. alumni bd. Columbia U. Grad. Sch. Bus., N.Y.C., 1983-86; trustee Drake U., Des Moines, 1986. Served as sgt. U.S. Army, 1952-54. Office: 2 Rector St New York NY 10006

SHETH, DIPAK RAMANLAL, financial advisor, investment analyst; b. Bahadarpur, Gujarat, India, Feb. 26, 1955; came to U.S., 1978; s. Ramanlal C. and Manjulaben R. (Desai) S.; m. Rachana D. Sheth, May 13, 1984; children: Komal, Hetal. BS, Gujarat U., 1975; grad., Coll. for Fin. Planning, Denver, 1983. Owner miscellaneous retail cos., Gujarat and N.Y.C., 1976-78; with Assoc. Fin. Planners, Metairie, La., 1979-82; v.p. Houston Investment Group, 1983-87, cons., 1988—; sr. ptnr. Krystyniak, Sheth & Assocs., Houston, 1986—; cons. Diagnostic Systems Labs., Webster, Tex., 1986—, Pinky Baby Products, Houston, 1987—. Mem. Internat. Assn. Fin. Planners, Inst. Cert. Fin. Planners. Hindu. Office: 1003 Wirt Rd Ste 302 Houston TX 77055

SHICK, BRADLEY ULLIN, construction company executive; b. Upper Darby, Pa., Dec. 26, 1956; s. Charles David and Jeanette Vivian (Reuter) S.; m. Lucille Marie DeSanto, Oct. 31, 1981. BSCE, U. Pitts., Johnstown, Pa., 1978; MBA, U. Scranton, 1981. Project mgr. Sordoni Constrn. Co., Forty Fort, Pa., 1978-83; project mgr. PepsiCo site Sordoni Constrn. Co., Somers, N.Y., 1983-86; mgr. procedures and controls Sordoni Constrn. Co., Parsippany, N.J., 1986—. Mem. ASCE, Delta Chi. Republican. Presbyterian. Home: RD 5 Box 5580 Spring Lake Estates East Stroudsburg PA 18301 Office: Sordoni Constrn Co 119 Cherry Hill Rd Parsippany NJ 07054

SHIELDS, FRANK COX, merchant banker, stockbroker, economist; b. Dublin, Ireland, Sept. 10, 1944; s. Joseph Francis and Alice (Cox) S.; m. Elizabeth Kinross, Oct. 9, 1971; children—Henrietta Olivia, Oliver Elliot Maxwell, Alexander Sheridan Grant. AB with honors, Harvard Coll., 1966; MBA, U. Pa., 1969. Mem. rsch. staff London Sch. Econs., 1969-71; stockbroker Cazenove & Co., London, 1971-73, Grieveson, Grant & Co., London, 1973-78; mcht. banker European Banking Co. Ltd., London, 1978-85, EBC Amro Bank Ltd., 1985-86; sr. rep. Maruman Securities Co., Ltd., London, 1987, bd. dir., gen. mgr., 1987—; econ. cons. Oesterreichische Kontrollbank Aktiengescellschaft, Vienna, Austria, 1979-83. Club: Buck's (London). Home: 24 Church Row, Hampstead, London NW3, England also: Piso Atico, Edificios Altamar Cap de Ras, Llansa, Gerona Spain Office: Maruman Securities Ltd(Europe), 1 Liverpool St, London EC2M 7NH, England

SHIELDS, ROBERT FRANCIS, stockbroker; b. Chgo., Oct. 22, 1923; s. Francis Hugh and Adele Marie (Melcher) S.; B.S. in Econs., St. Joseph's Coll., 1944; M.B.A. in Fin., Governors' State U., 1970; children: Debra, Cynthia, Judith. With instl. bonds dept Bear Stearns & Co., Chgo., 1946-49; resident mgr. Reynolds & Co., Chgo., 1949-62; v.p., resident mgr. Dempsey Tegeler & Co., Chicago Heights, Ill., 1962-70; sr. v.p., resident mgr. Stifel Nicolaus & Co., Chicago Heights, 1970—. Served to maj. USMC, 1943-46, 1950-52. Decorated Purple Heart. Registered fin. planner. Roman Catholic. Club: Olympia Fields Country. Home: 1402 Woodhollow Ln Unit D Flossmoor IL 60422 Office: Stifel Nicolaus & Co 233 W Joe Orr Rd Chicago Heights IL 60411

SHIELDS, TAMARA WEST-O'KELLEY, accountant; b. Lewiston, Idaho, Oct. 23, 1948; d. Brooks E. and Dona J. (Rogers) O'Kelley; 1 son Stewart Alan. BBA cum laude, North Tex. State U., 1976; Staff acct. James C. Beach CPA, Carrollton, Tex., 1972-76, Deloitte, Haskins & Sells, CPA, 1976-77; chief fin. officer Communications Systems, Inc. (name changed to Scott Cable Communications 1983), Irving, Tex., 1977-84; pvt. practice acctg., Dallas, 1984—. lectr. in field. Pres. local sch. charity; active St. Andrews United Meth. Ch. Mem. AICPA, Tex. Soc. CPAs (Dallas chpt. vice chmn. ethics com.), Beta Alpha Psi.

SHIELDS, WILLIAM MAURICE, wood products company executive; b. Vancouver, Wash., Feb. 24, 1937; s. Marshall Joseph and Pearl Elizabeth (Wardle) S.; m. Catherine Diane D'Orsa, June 16, 1962; children—Debi, Janelle, Jackie. B.S. in Bus. Administrn., U. Oreg., 1959. Prodn. supt. Willamette Industries, Inc., Lebanon, Oreg., 1970-71, prodn. mgr., 1971-73; gen. prodn. mgr. Willamette Industries, Inc., Albany, Oreg., 1973-76; sr. v.p. Willamette Industries, Inc., Ruston, La., 1976-80; exec. v.p. Willamette Industries, Inc., Portland, Oreg., 1980—. Served to 1st lt. U.S. Army, 1960-62. Mem. Nat. Forest Products Assn. (bd. govs., chmn. bd. dirs.), Western Wood Products Assn. (bd. dirs. 1982—). Republican. Office: Willamette Industries Inc 1300 SW Fifth Ave Portland OR 97201

SHIELY, JOSEPH LEO, III, construction materials company executive; b. Burlington, Iowa, Apr. 18, 1941; s. Joseph L. Jr. and Rosemary (Clark) S.; m. Georgann C. McIntyre, Nov. 26, 1965; children: Bridget, Matthew. BS in Civil Engring., U. Notre Dame, 1963; MBA, U. Minn., 1971. Registered profl. engr., Minn., Colo. Asst. prodn. mgr. J.L. Shiely Co., St. Paul, 1965-69, chief engr., 1969-75, v.p. ops., 1975-79, v.p., gen. mgr., 1979-82, exec. v.p., 1982-86, pres., chief operating officer, 1986—, pres., chief exec. officer, 1988—. Bd. dirs., v.p. Indianhead coun. Boy Scouts Am., St. Paul, 1980—. 1st lt. U.S. Army, 1963-65. Mem. St. Paul C. of C. (bd. dirs. 1985—), Athletic Club (bd. dirs. 1982-85). Office: JL Shiely Co 1101 N Snelling Ave Saint Paul MN 55108

SHIERY, JULIE ANN, engine parts and machine shop owner, trainer and owner thoroughbreds; b. Scottdale, Pa., July 31, 1963; d. George Edward and Toni Lee (Helmick) S.; 1 child, Clarissa Renee. Grad. with honors, Bus. Career Inst., Greensburg, Pa., 1982. Mgr. HY SY Stable, Connellsville, Pa., 1976-78, mgr., trainer Black Creek Stable, Connellsville, 1978-80; sec., machinist Bill's Performance Shop, New Alexandria, Pa., 1982-83, owner, 1983—; owner J.A.S. Stables, New Alexandria, 1984—; cons. to several auto racing orgns., 1983—. Teen leader Ripple Ridge 4-H Club, Scottdale, 1978-81. Named Grand Nat. Champion, Madison Sq. Gardens, N.Y.C., 1978, Grand Nat. Champion, All Am. Quarter Horse Congress, Ohio, 1979, Grand Champion, Ky. Horse Trails, 1979, Grand Champion, Pa. State 4-H Show, 1977. Democrat. Avocations: stock car racing, drag racing, tractor/truck pulling, equestrian events. Home: RD 1 New Alexandria PA 15670 Office: Bill's Performance Shop RD 1 Box 12 New Alexandria PA 15670

SHIFF, J. RICHARD, real estate corporation executive. Chmn. Brumalea Ltd., Toronto, Ont., until 1987, bd. dirs. Office: Bramalea Ltd, 1867 Yonge St, Toronto, ON Canada M4S 1Y5 *

SHIFF, RICHARD ALAN, film distribution executive; b. N.Y.C., Mar. 3, 1942; s. Morris and Louise (Vogel) S.; children from previous marriage: Jaqui, Jason; m. Carol Ann Freed, Dec. 29, 1985; stepchildren: Nicole Golob, Shana Golob. BA, Queens Coll., 1965, MA, 1969; profl. diploma, Bklyn. Coll., 1974. Cert. secondary sch. tchr., sch. dist. adminstr., prin., N.Y. Tchr., administrator Jr. High Sch. 142 Q, Queens, N.Y., 1965-77; sales analyst Warner Bros., Burbank, Calif., 1977-79, asst. dir. sales adminstrn., 1979-81, dir. sales adminstrn., 1981-87, v.p. sales ops., 1987—. Office: Warner Bros 4000 Warner Blvd Burbank CA 91522

SHIFFER, JAMES DAVID, utility executive; b. San Diego, Mar. 24, 1938; s. Kenneth Frederick and Thelma Lucille (Good) S.; m. Margaret Edith Rightmyer, Sept. 5, 1959 (div. July 1986); children: James II, Elizabeth Warren, Russell; m. Esther Zamora, Sept. 13, 1986. BS ChemE, Stanford U., 1960, MS ChemE, 1961. Registered profl. engr., Calif. Nuclear engr. Pacific Gas & Electric Co., Humboldt Bay Power Plant, Eureka, Calif., 1961-71; tech. mgr. Pacific Gas & Electric. Co., Diablo Canyon Power Plant, Avila Beach, Calif., 1971-80; mgr. nuclear ops. Pacific Gas & Electric Co., San Francisco, 1980-85, v.p. nuclear power generation, 1985—. Mem. Am. Nuclear Soc., Am. Inst. Chem. Engring. Republican. Episcopalian. Home: 1860 Washington St Apt 304 San Francisco CA 94109 Office: Pacific Gas & Electric Co 77 Beale St Rm 1451 San Francisco CA 94106

SHIFRIN, KENNETH STEVEN, financial service executive; b. N.Y.C., Apr. 16, 1949; s. Bernard and Frieda (Morgenstern) S.; m. Yvonne Barber, Mar. 4, 1959; children: Zachary, Joshua, Jacob. BS, Ohio State U., 1971, MBA, 1973. CPA, D.C., Tex. Mgmt. cons. Arthur Andersen & Co., Washington, 1973-76; mgr. forecasting Fairchild Industries, Inc., Germantown, Md., 1976-78; v.p. fin. and contracts Fairchild Aircraft Corp., San Antonio, 1978-85; chief fin. officer Am. Physicians Service Group, Austin, Tex., 1985-87; pres. Am. Physicians Service Group, Austin, 1987—, also bd. dirs. Mem. Young Pres. Organ. With USAR, 1969-75. Mem. AICPA. Jewish. Home: 220 Hurst Creek Austin TX 78734 Office: Am Physicians Svc Group Inc 1301 Capital Tex Hwy #B220 Austin TX 78746

SHIGLEY, ORVILLE LEROY, insurance brokerage executive; b. Nebraska City, Nebr., Apr. 26, 1942; s. Orville LeRoy and Mildred (Dierking) S.; m. Sharla DeAnn McCallum, June 10, 1962; children: Veronica Lyn, Christopher Todd. BSBA, U. Nebr., 1964. Underwriter Hartford Ins. Group, Chgo., 1965-71; mktg. mgr. Ruhl & Ruhl, Bettendorf, Iowa, 1971-73; salesman Becher Curry Co., Columbus, Nebr., 1973-76; v.p. First State Ins. Co., Council Bluffs, Iowa, 1976-78; salesman Anderson Divan & Cottrell, Kearney, Nebr., 1978-80; pres. Rollins Burdick Hunter of Nebr., Omaha, 1980—. Mem. Am. Inst. for Property and Liability Underwriters (chartered property and casualty underwriter), Ind. Agts. Assn., Nebr. Found. for Ins. Edn. (bd. dirs. 1981—, instr. 1976—), Omaha C. of C. Republican. Methodist. Office: Rollins Burdick Hunter 11414 W Center Rd Omaha NE 68144

SHIM, SANG KOO, state mental health official; b. Tokyo, Japan, Oct. 1, 1942; came to U.S., 1968; s. Sang Taek and Kum Ryon (Bae) S.; m. Jae Hee Lee, July 12, 1972; children: Tammy, David. BS, Seoul Nat. U., Korea, 1967; MBA, No. Ill. U., 1970; MS, U. Wis., 1975. CPA, Ill. Acct. Vaughn Mfg. Co., Chgo., 1970-72, Stewart-Warner Corp., Chgo., 1972-73; fin. cons. Cen. Acctg. Assn., New Baden, Ill., 1977-79; auditor Ill. Dept. Mental Health, Springfield, 1980-82, chief fiscal officer, 1983—. Treas. Korean Assn. Greater St. Louis, 1982. Mem. Ill. CPA Soc., Assn. Govt. Accts. Home: 5 Settlers Ln Springfield IL 62707 Office: Ill Dept Mental Health Bur Fin Svcs 401 S Spring St Springfield IL 62706

SHIMA, RICHARD JOHN, insurance company executive; b. Mpls., Aug. 11, 1939; s. Stanley John and Isabel Kathryn (Coyle) S.; m. Denise Marie Buckley, June 26, 1965; children: Kathleen Ann, Patrick John, Mary Elisabeth. B.A. cum laude, Harvard U., 1961. With The Travelers Ins. Co., Hartford, Conn., 1961—, 2d v.p., 1971-73, v.p., 1973-76, sr. v.p., 1976-80, exec. v.p., 1980—; bd. dirs. The Travelers Corp., Conn. Natural Gas Corp. Bd. dirs. Hartford Hosp.; trustee The Hartford Grad. Ctr., Kingswood-Oxford Sch.; corporator Inst. of Living. Served with USNR, 1961-63. Mem. Soc. Actuaries, Am. Acad. Actuaries. Roman Catholic. Club: The Hartford. Office: The Travelers Corp 1 Tower Sq Hartford CT 06183

SHIMEALL, WARREN GLEN, lawyer; b. Topeka, Nov. 13, 1925; s. Glen Woodard and Pearl Agnes (Thoroughman) S. Student, U. Tulsa, 1943, George Washington U., 1947; JD, U. Okla., 1950; grad., USMSRTA Acad., Boston, 1944; postgrad., Harvard U., 1979. Bar: Okla. 1950, Korea 1952, Japan 1954, U.S. Ct. Internat. Trade 1971, U.S. Ct. Mil. Appeals 1980. Assoc. Leon I. Greenberg, Tokyo, 1954-59; ptnr. Bushell & Shimeall, Tokyo, 1959-74, Welty & Shimeall, Tokyo, 1974-79; sr. ptnr. Welty, Shimeall & Kasari Internat. Law and Patents, Tokyo, 1979—; pres. Fast Food Y.K., Tokyo, 1982—; pres. Japan Pizza Co., Roman Meal Co., Japan, Suntown Co. Ltd., Hong Kong; pres., pub. Japan TV Guide; realtor Calif. Pres. Tokyo Union Ch. Shuyko Hojin, TUC Found., Dela; co-founder, dir. Clark Hatch Athletic Ctr., Seoul, Republic of Korea, 1971—. Served to col. U.S. Army, 1951-82. Mem. Am. C. of C.-Japan, Am.-Japan Soc., Asiatic Soc. Japan, Japan-Am. Soc. Legal Studies, Internat. House Japan, Tokyo Dai-Ni Bar Assn., ABA, Okla. Bar Assn., Japan Bar Assn., Assn. U.S. Army, Navy League, U.S. Naval Inst., VFW, Mil. Order World Wars, Res. Officers Assn., LABR, CAR, NAR, Phi Delta Phi. Clubs: Tokyo, Fgn. Corrs., American; Commodore (Washington). Lodges: Masons (master Tokyo club 1985-88), Order Rose Croix (past wise master), Grand Lodge Japan (grand orator 1987). Office: Welty Shimeall & Kasari, New Otemachi Bldg 450 1-2-1, Otemachi, Tokyo 100, Japan

SHIMER, DANIEL LEWIS, corporate executive; b. San Angelo, Tex., July 30, 1944; s. Lewis V. and Mary A. (Slick) S.; divorced. BS in Acctg. and Mktg., Ind. U., 1972; postgrad., Loyola U., New Orleans, 1977. CPA. Sr. acct. Peat, Marwick, Mitchell & Co., Indpls., 1973-75; corp. audit mgr. Lykes-Youngstown Corp., New Orleans, 1975-76, asst. treas., 1976-78; asst. treas. LTV Corp., Dallas, 1978-79; v.p. fin. Stoller Chem. Co., Houston, 1979-81, Petro-Silver, Inc., Denver, 1981-83; v.p., treas. FoxMeyer Corp., Denver, 1983-86; v.p., treas., sec. CoastAmerica Corp., Denver, 1986-88; exec. v.p. Bard & Co., Denver, 1989—; bd. dirs. TechNat. Bank, Denver, IMS Corp., Denver. Mem. Am. Inst. CPA's, Nat. Assn. of Corp. Treas., Colo. Cash Mgmt. Assn., Multiple Sclerosis Soc. Colo. (dir.), Cherry Creek Commerce Assn. (bd. dirs.). Roman Catholic. Home: 445 N Clarkson Denver CO 80218 Office: Bard & Co 3200 Cherry Creek S Dr #600 Denver CO 80209

SHIMIZU, NORIHIKO, consulting company executive; b. Kamiosaki, Japan, Apr. 1, 1940; s. Shirokichi and Itsuko (Gohko) S.; m. Hinako Miyazaki, Dec. 18, 1970; children—Daijo, Hironobu. B.A., Keio U., Tokyo, 1963; M.B.A., Stanford U., 1967. Mem. staff Tokio Marine & Fire Ins. Co., Tokyo, 1963-67; cons. Boston Cons. Group, Inc., 1967-69, mng. dir., Tokyo, 1970-74, v.p., dir., 1970-87; pres. Shimizu & Co., Inc., 1987— ; adviser Japan Devel. Bank, 1969-73; lectr. Sophia U., Tokyo, 1969-73; vis. lectr. UCLA, 1974. Author: (with others) Japanese Management, 1970; editor: (with others) Business Strategy, 1970. Recipient award Sophia U., 1956. Mem. New Mgmt. Club (v.p.), Bus. Research Inst., Stanford Alumni Assn. Japan (trustee), Stanford Bus. Sch. Alumni Assn. Japan (pres.). Office: 39 Mori Bldg 2-4-5 Azabudai, 601C 6th Fl, Minato-ku Tokyo 106, Japan

SHIMP, RICHARD LEE, telecommunications company executive; b. Denver, Pa., Feb. 24, 1942; s. Lee Strickler and Faye (Wallace) S.; m. Shirley May Ruegg; 1 child, Denise Nadine Sowder. Diploma, Cleve. Inst. Electronics, 1970; student, U. Va., 1970-75. Dir. rsch. and devel. Warren L. Braun Cons. Engrs., Harrisonburg, Va., 1969-72; Dir. rsch. and devel. Comsonics, Inc., Harrisonburg, 1972-80, v.p. rsch. and devel., 1980-84, v.p. advanced concepts and system svcs., 1984—. Patentee in field; contbr. articles to various publs. Mem. curriculum adv. com. Blue Ridge Community Coll., 1978—. With USAF, 1960-64. Mem. IEEE, Soc. Cable TV Engrs., Nat. Cable TV Assn. Office: ComSonics Inc 1350 Port Republic Rd Harrisonburg VA 22801

SHIN, BONG GONPHILLIP, economist, educator; b. Inchon, Korea, Apr. 13, 1942; came to U.S., 1964; s. Kyung Hee and Booza (Cho) S.; m. Sharon Ann Sandilla, Jan. 13, 1968; children: Sarah, Cris, Jeff. BS, U. Wis., Superior, 1967; MBA, No. Ill. U., 1969; PhD, U. Ga., 1974. Postdoctoral fellow U. So. Calif., 1980-81; instr. U. Wis., Superior, 1969-71, asst. prof., 1974-76; instr. U. Ga., Athens, 1973-74; asst. prof. Western Ill. U., Macomb, 1979-80, assoc. prof., 1981-83; prof., chmn. Boise (Idaho) State U., 1983—. Editor Jour. Behavioral Econs., 1983—, Idaho's Economy, 1984—; contbr. articles to profl. jours. Bd. dirs. Nat. Bus. Hall of Fame. Mem. Acad. Mgmt., Boise Racquet and Swim Club, Beta Gamma Sigma, Sigma Iota Epsilon. Roman Catholic. Home: 207 N Atlantic St Boise ID 83706 Office: Boise State U Boise ID 83725

SHINABERRY, HENRY RICHARD, real estate broker, developer; b. Marlinton, W.Va., Mar. 29, 1950; s. Wilbur T. and Iva P. (Heimes) S.; m. Victoria Y. Barlow, Aug. 21, 1976; children: Cameron, Brooke. BA, United Electronic Inst., 1970; BS, W.Va. U., 1976. Cert. residential broker. Agt. Village Realty Inc., Odenton, Md., 1976-83; broker, pres. ERA Village Realty, Inc., Odenton, 1983—. Coach YMCA, 1987-88. Served with U.S. Army, 1972-74. Mem. DSAC Anne Arundel Bd. Realtors, Nat. Mktg. Realtors Inst., Realtors Land Inst., Nat. Assn. Real Estate Appraisers. Office: ERA Village Realty Inc 1416 Annapolis Rd Odenton MD 21113

SHINDELL, HOWARD STEVEN, chemical and oil distributing company executive; b. Savannah, Ga., Oct. 26, 1953; s. David Israel and Ruth (Kaplan) S. BS cum laude, Northeastern U., 1976; MBA, Ga. State U., 1979. Lending officer Chem. Bank, N.Y.C., 1979-82, First Nat. Bank Chgo., N.Y.C., 1982, Chase Manhattan Bank, N.Y.C., 1982-83; chief fin. officer Hexagon Enterprises, Inc., Mountain Lakes, N.J., 1983-84, pres., chief exec. officer, 1984-85; pres., chief exec. officer Dynamic Chem. Products, Clark, N.J., 1985-87; gen. mgr. dynamic div. Novick Chem. Co., Inc., Clark, 1987—. Democrat. Jewish. Office: Novick Chem Products 35 Walnut Ave Clark NJ 07066

SHINE, WILLIAM WALTER, management executive; b. Boston, Apr. 22, 1925; s. Bernard Joseph and Eleanor Fay (Lannon) S.; m. Joan M. Kearns, Nov. 24, 1951; children—Kevin J., Eleanor F. B.S. in Math, Boston Coll., 1951. With mktg. dept. Eastern Gas & Fuel, Boston, 1952-54; mathematician Avco Research Lab., Everett, Mass., 1954-58; cons. Arthur D. Little, Inc., Cambridge, Mass., 1958-61; sr. v.p. Chase Manhattan Bank (N.A.), N.Y.C., 1961-87; pres. Shine Assocs., Inc., N.Y.C., 1987—; instr. N.Y. U., 1962-65. Pres. 52 Assn., N.Y.C., 1967—; bd. dirs. Sch. Banking and Money Mgmt., Adelphi U. Served with USMC, 1942-46, 51-52. Mem. Boston Coll. Alumni Assn. (dir.). Office: Shine Assocs 2329 Lancaster Ave New York NY 11510

SHINEHOUSE, JAMES PERRETEN, accountant; b. Bryn Mawr, Pa., Mar. 16, 1958; s. Robert Russel and Efreda Jane (Perreten) S.; m. Patricia Dawn Minard, Mar. 26, 1983. BS magna cum laude, West Chester U., 1980. CPA, Pa. Mgr. to sr. mgr. Peat, Marwick, Mitchell & Co., Phila., 1980-86; dir. internal audit Internat. Signal and Control Group, 1986—. Mem. World Affairs Council Phila.; vol., Delaware Valley Community Accts., Phila., 1981—, coach debate team West Chester U., 1981—, Intercollegiate Speech and Debate Tournament judge; tchr. Project Bus. Program; mem., past chmn. adv. com. YWCA, West Chester, 1985—; bd. dirs. Lancaster County Jr. Achievement. Named one of Outstanding Young Men Am., 1985, Pa. State Intercollegiate Varsity debate Champion, 1979-80; recipient Chester County Marshall award, 1980. Mem. AICPA, Pa. Inst. CPA's, Omicron Delta Epsilon (pres. 1978-80), Pi Kappa Delta (v.p. 1978-79, pres. alumni assn. West Chester chpt.), Pi Gamma Mu, Alpha Lambda Delta. Republican. Lutheran. Avocations: tennis, political debates, trombone.

SHINN, GEORGE LATIMER, investment banker; b. Newark, Ohio, Mar. 12, 1923; s. Leon Powell and Bertha Florence (Latimer) S.; m. Clara LeBaron Sampson, May 21, 1949; children: Deborah, Amy, Martha, Sarah, Andrew. A.B., Amherst Coll., 1948, LL.D. (hon.), 1982; LL.D. (hon.), Denison U., 1975. Trainee Merrill Lynch, Pierce, Fenner & Beane (now Merrill Lynch, Pierce, Fenner & Smith Inc.), 1948-49, various exec. positions, 1949-73, pres., 1973-75; also pres. Goodbody & Co., Inc., Merrill Lynch & Co., Inc., 1974-75; chmn. bd., chief exec. officer 1st Boston Corp., 1975-83; chmn. bd., chief exec. officer First Boston Inc., 1976-83, chmn. exec. com., 1983—; mem. exec. com. Pres.' Pvt. Sector Survey on Cost Control, 1982-84; exec.-in-residence Columbia U. Grad. Sch. Bus., 1983-85; bd. dirs. N.Y. Times Co., Phelps Dodge Co., N.Y.C., N.Y. Life Ins. Co., First Boston, Inc., Financiere Credit Suisse; gov. Am. Stock Exchange, 1970-74; bd. dirs. N.Y. Stock Exchange, 1977-83, vice chmn., 1981-83; bd. dirs., trustee Colonial Group Mutual Funds. Gen. chmn. United Hosp. Fund, N.Y.C., 1973-74; trustee Kent Pl. Sch., Summit, N.J., 1966-73, Carnegie Found. for Advancement Teaching, 1976-85, Pingry Sch., 1977-79, Lucille P. Markey Chantall Trust, 1985—, Amherst Coll., 1968-82, chmn. bd. trustees, 1973-80; bd. dirs. Rsch. Corp., 1975-86; trustee Arts Council Morris Area, 1978—; bd. dirs., trustee Philharm. Symphony Soc. N.Y., 1983—, Nat. Humanities Ctr., 1988—. Capt. USMCR, 1943-46. Clubs: River, Links, Century Assn., Morris County Golf. Office: First Boston Inc care The First Boston Corp Park Ave Pla New York NY 10055

SHINNERS, STANLEY MARVIN, electrical engineer; b. N.Y.C., May 9, 1933; d. Earl and Molly (Planter) S.; m. Doris Pinsker, Aug. 4, 1956; children: Sharon Rose Cooper, Walter Jay, Daniel Lawrence. BEE, CCNY, 1954; MS in Elect. Engring., Columbia U., 1959. Equipment engr. Western Electric Co., N.Y.C., 1953-54; staff engr. electronics div. Otis Elevator Co., Bklyn., 1954-56; project engr. Consol. Avianoics Corp., Westbury, N.Y., 1956-58; sr. rsch. sect. head Unisys Corp. (name formerly Sperry Corp.), Great Neck, N.Y., 1958—; adj. prof. engring. The Cooper Union, N.Y.C., 1966—, N.Y. Inst. Tech., Old Westbury, N.Y., 1972—, Poly. Inst. Bklyn., 1959-72. Author: Control System Design, 1964, Techniques of Systems Engineering, 1967, A Guide to Systems Engineering, 1976, Modern Control System Theory and Application, 1978. Recipient Career Achievement medal CCNY Alumni Assn., 1980. Fellow IEEE; mem. Am. Soc. for Engring. Edn., Eta Kappa Nu, Tau Beta Pi. Home: 28 Sagamore Way N Jericho NY 11753

SHINSATO, FRANCIS GENE, electronics executive; b. Hawiawa, Hawaii, Jan. 22, 1951; s. Yoshtioshi S.; m. Julienne K. Mikasa, Aug. 9, 1973. BEE, Calif. State Poly. U., 1972; MEE, U. So. Calif., 1974; MBA, Harvard U., 1976. CPA, Calif.; registered profl. engr., Calif. Engr. Rockwell Internat., Downey, Calif., 1972-74; fin. adminstr. Rockwell Internat., Downey, 1976-79; mgr., cons. Price Waterhouse & Co., L.A., 1979-83; v.p. fin. Bell Helmets Co., Norwalk, Calif., 1983-85; v.p. fin., chief fin. officer Newport Electronics Inc., Santa Ana, Calif., 1985—. Mem. Am. Electronics Assn., Harvard Bus. Sch. Alumni Assn. Democrat. Methodist. Office: Newport Electronics Inc 630 Young St Santa Ana CA 92705

SHIOKARI, DAVID, trust officer; b. Santa Barbara, Calif., Aug. 11, 1957; s. Tom and Nobuko (Sakioka) S.; m. Ellen A. Rostvold, May 15, 1987. BS, UCLA, 1980; MBA, Pepperdine U., 1983. Cert. fin. planner. Mgr. Nautilus II, Fullerton, Calif., 1980; real estate agt., asst. mgr. ERA Now! Real Estate, Westminster, Calif., 1981-83; fin. planner Fin. Services Unlimited, Newport Beach, Calif., 1982-84; asst. v.p. trust dept. Bank Am., Newport Beach, Calif., 1984-87, Wells Fargo Bank, Newport Beach, Calif., 1987-88; v.p. First Interstate Bank Calif., Newport Beach, Calif., 1988—. Contbr. articles to profl. jours. Com. mem. Plan Giving Council Goodwill Orange County, Santa Ana, Calif., 1986—, Orange County, Newport-Irvine Estate Planning Councils, 1984, South East Repertory Plan Giving Council, 1986—, Am. Heart Assn. Plan Giving Council, 1987—; mem. Charitable Giving Soc. of Orange County. Mem. Inst. Cert. Fin. Planners, Orange County Soc. of Inst. Cert. Fin. Planners, Orange County Estate Planning Council, Newport Beach/Irvine Estate Planning Council, Orange County Soc. Investment Mgrs., Orange County Trust Officers Assn., Sigma Pi. Republican. Methodist. Office: 1st Interstate Bank Calif 5000 Birch Rd Ste 10200 Newport Beach CA 92660

SHIPLEY, L. PARKS, JR., banker; b. Orange, N.J., Aug. 2, 1931; s. L. Parks and Emily Catherine (Herzog) S.; m. Micheline Genevieve Oltramare, Apr. 2, 1966; children—Christiane, Daniel, Alix. B.A., Yale U., 1953. From internat. banking officer to v.p. Marine Midland Bank, N.Y.C., 1969-76; v.p. Irving Trust Co., N.Y.C., 1976-84, exec. v.p., 1984-89; exec. v.p. Bank of N.Y., N.Y.C., 1989—; bd. dirs. Banco Irving Austral, Young Life Found, Irving Trust Internat. Bank. Vol. Moral ReArmament, Europe, Africa, S.Am., 1954-64; participant in founding Up With People Inc. Home: 77 Bellevue Ave Summit NJ 07901 Office: Bank of NY One Wall St New York NY 10015

SHIPLEY, NORMAN DAVID, marketing and sales executive; b. Houston, Aug. 13, 1945; s. Norman Stewart amd Mary (Abbott) S.; m. Ursula Christine Hiebutzki, Dec. 20, 1970; children: Christopher, Ryan. BBA in Acctg., North Tex. State U., Denton, 1968. With Southland Corp., Dallas, 1966-70; salesman Uarco, Dallas, 1970-73; dist. mgr. Uarco, Lubbock, Tex., 1973-82; region mgr. Uarco, St. Louis, 1982-85; gen. ptnr. Data Flow Media Systems, Dallas, 1985—; pres. Dealer News Promotional Products, Inc., Dallas, 1988—. Pres. St. John Neuman PTA, Lubbock. Mem. Nat. Bus. Forms Assn., Assn. Splty. Advt. Republican. Methodist. Lodge: Lions. Home: 3117 Sandy Trail Plano TX 75023 Office: Data Flow Media Systems 1721 W Plano Pkwy Plano TX 75075

SHIPLEY, WALTER VINCENT, banker; b. Newark, Nov. 2, 1935; s. L. Parks and Emily (Herzog) S.; m. Judith Ann Lyman, Sept. 14, 1957; children: Barbara, Allison, Pamela, Dorothy, John. Student, Williams Coll., 1954-56; BS, NYU, 1960. With Chem. Bank, N.Y.C., 1956—, exec. v.p. in charge internat. div., 1978-79, sr. exec. v.p., until 1981, pres., 1982-83; chmn. bd. Chem. Banking Corp., N.Y.C., 1983—; Dir. Champion Internat. Corp., NYNEX Corp. Bd. dirs. Japan Soc., Lincoln Ctr. for Performing Arts Inc., N.Y. City Partnership Inc., N.Y. Chamber Commerce and Industry, Goodwill Industries Greater N.Y. Inc., United Way Tri-State. Mem. The Bus. Council, Bus. Roundtable, Council Fgn. Relations, English Speaking Union, Pilgrims of U.S., Links, Augusta Nat. Golf Club, Baltusrol Golf Club (Springfield, N.J.), Blind Brook Golf Club. Office: Chem Banking Corp 277 Park Ave New York NY 10172

SHIPMAN, MARK JAMES, insurance executive; b. Tampa, Fla., Aug. 28, 1955; s. Robert Allen and Pauline (Ulm) S. BA, U. South Fla., 1976. Career trainee Marine Office Am. Corp., Tampa, 1978-79, asst. underwriter, 1979-81, underwriter, 1981-82; mgr. service office Marine Office Am. Corp., Miami, Fla., 1982-83, Richmond, Va., 1983-86; asst. mgr. Marine Office Am. Corp., Balt., 1986—. Mem. Chesapeake Skyhawks Club of Balt. (sec. 1987—). Home: 16 Millbridge Ct Baltimore MD 21236 Office: Marine Office Am Corp 110 West Rd Towson MD 21204

SHIPPER, FRANK MARTIN, management educator, consultant, author; b. Martinsburg, W.Va., June 27, 1945; s. Paul Bishop and Lillian Foreman (Flagg) S.; m. Frances Irene Clarke, Dec. 19, 1981; children: Christopher Clarke, James Ford, Jay Martin. BSME, W. Va. Univ., 1968; MBA, U. Utah, 1973, PhD, 1978. Asst. prof. Ariz. State U., Tempe, 1977-81, assoc. prof., 1982—; human productivity cons., U.S. Navy, Washington, 1980-81; cons. Dushoff & Sacks, Phoenix, 1979-80, 1984-86, Streich, Lang, Weeks & Cardon, Phoenix, 1981-85, De Concini, McDonald, Brammer, Yetwin & Lacy, Tucson, 1982—, Penton Learning Systems, N.Y.C., 1986-87, Booth-Wright Mgmt. Systems, Boulder, Colo., 1986-87, City of Phoenix, 1987, Phoenix VA, 1987, Holsum Bakeries, 1987, prin. investigator VA, Phoenix, 1986—. Author: Business Strategy for the Political Arena, 1984, Avoiding and Surviving Lawsuits: The Executive Guide to Strategic Legal Planning, 1988; contbr. numerous articles to profl. jours. Co-founder, pres. Data Based Organizational Research Group, Tempe, 1979-80; bd. dirs. East Valley Big Bros., 1983; mem. exec. com. Ariz. State U., 1984-85. Served to capt. USAF, 1968-72. Faculty grantee Ariz. State U., 1979, 82; Fed. Faculty fellow Am. Assembly of Collegiate Schs. of Bus., 1980-81. Mem. Am. Psychol. Assn., Decision Scis. Inst., Acad. Mgmt., Assn. for Quality and Participation, Morrison Inst. Pub. Policy, Internat. Assn. Quality Circles (bd. dirs. chpt. 1983-85, pres. 1984-85). Republican. Presbyterian. Avocations: skiing, cycling, swimming. Office: Ariz State U Coll Bus Dept Mgmt Tempe AZ 85287

SHIRCLIFF, JAMES VANDERBURGH, restaurant executive; b. Vincennes, Ind., Dec. 11, 1938; s. Thomas Maxwell and Martha Bayard (Somes) S.; A.B., Brown U., 1961; postgrad. U. Va., 1963-64; m. Sally Anne Hoing, June 20, 1964; children—Thomas, Susan, Anne, Catherine, Caroline. Asst. gen. mgr. Pepsi Cola Allied Bottlers, Inc., Lynchburg, Va., 1964-65; gen. mgr. First Colony Canners, Inc., Lynchburg, 1965-66; v.p., divisional coordinator Pepsi Cola Allied Bottlers, Inc., Lynchburg, 1966-68, v.p., dir. personnel, 1968-70; v.p., gen. mgr. GCC Beverages, Inc., Lynchburg, 1970-74, group v.p. Va., 1974-75; corp. v.p. Gen. Cinema Corp., Beverage Div., Lynchburg, 1976-77; owner/mgr. WLLL-AM, WGOL-FM, Lynchburg, 1977-86; pres. Jamarbo Corp., 1977-88; chmn. bd. Signwaves, Inc., presdl. interchange exec., 1975-76; exec. dir. Nat. Indsl. Energy Council, Dept. Commerce, Washington, 1975-76. Vice pres. JOBS, Lynchburg, 1970; dir. Central Va. Health Planning Council, 1974-75; mem. Govs. Indsl. Energy Adv. Council, 1976—; dir. Piedmont council, Boy Scouts Am., 1972-73; mem. City of Lynchburg Keep Lynchburg Beautiful Commn., 1974-75, chmn. emergency planning bd., 1974-75, chmn. overall econ. planning council, 1977-88; bd. dirs. Lynchburg Broadway Theatre, 1973-75, Acad. Music, 1973-74, United Fund, Lynchburg, 1966-67, Central Va. Industries, 1971-72, Va. Public Telecommunications Council; chmn. campaign United Way, 1982, pres., 1983; chmn. Citizens for a Clean Lynchburg; campaign chmn. United Way of Central Va.; trustee Va. Episc. Sch.; mem. pres.' council Randolph-Macon Women's Coll., Cen. Va. Community Coll. Found. Bd.; mem. Va-Israel Commn. Served to lt. (j.g.), USN, 1961-63. Recipient Cloyd Meml. award for outstanding service, Greater Lynchburg C. of C., 1975; Va. Soft Drink Assn. citation, 1970, 73, 74; NCCJ Brotherhood Citation; Public Service award Radio-TV Commn. of So. Bapt. Conv., NCCJ State Adv. Bd., Exec. Com. Swensen's Owners Council, 1988. Va. C. of C. (dir. 1976-79), Greater Lynchburg C. of C. (dir., v.p. 1973-74, chmn. community appearance task force 1977-79), Va. Soft Drink Assn. (pres. 1973-74), Va. Pepsi Cola Bottlers Assn. (pres. 1970-73), Nat., Va. (dir. 1974, pres. 1985-86) assns. broadcasters, Lynchburg Advt. Club (v.p.), Va. AP Broadcasters Assn. (pres.), Lynchburg Fine Arts Center (pres.). Roman Catholic. Clubs: Mensa (N.Y.); Commonwealth (Richmond, Va.); Farmington Country (Charlottesville, Va.); Army-Navy (Washington); Oakwood Country (Lynchburg); Piedmont (Lynchburg); Navy League, Galliard, Visa Yacht, Pelican Point Yacht, Lynchburg Sports (bd. dirs.). Lodge: Rotary (pres., Paul Harris fellow 1982, dist. gov. 1986-87). Home: 3525 Otterview Pl Lynchburg VA 24503

SHIRE, DONALD THOMAS, air products executive, lawyer; b. Boston, Jan. 13, 1930; s. Thomas J. and Nellie M. S.; m. Anne Court Bither, Nov 21, 1953; children: Jennifer Anne, Andrew Carter, Daniel Orchard. B.S. in Bus. Adminstrn, Boston U., 1951, LL.B., 1953. Atty. Air Products and Chems., Inc., 1957-64, sec., atty., 1964-75, sec., asst. gen. counsel, 1975-78, v.p. energy and materials, 1978-85, v.p. human resources, 1986—. Trustee Muhlenberg Coll.; bd. dirs. Allentown Hosp.-Lehigh Valley Hosp. Ctr. Served to lt. USNR, 1954-57. Mem. Boston Bar Assns. Episcopalian. Home: 1133 N Main St Allentown PA 18104 Office: Air Products and Chems Inc 7201 Hamilton Blvd Allentown PA 18195-1501

SHIREK, JOHN RICHARD, savings and loan executive; b. Bismarck, N.D., Feb. 5, 1926; s. James Max and Anna Agatha (Lala) S.; student U. Minn., 1944-46; B.S. with honors, Rollins Coll., 1978; m. Ruth Martha Lietz, Sept. 22, 1950; children: Barbara Jo (Mrs. James A. Fowler), Jon Richard, Kenneth Edward. Sports editor Bismarck (N.D.) Tribune, 1943-44; with Gate City Savs. and Loan Assn., Fargo, N.D., 1947-65, v.p., dir., 1960-65; exec. v.p., dir. 1st Fed. Savs. and Loan Assn., Melbourne, Fla., 1966-70; pres., dir. 1st Fed. Savs. and Loan Assn., Cocoa, Fla., 1970-82; exec. v.p., dir. The First, F.A. (formerly 1st Fed. Savs. and Loan Assn. of Orlando), 1982—; interim pres. Freedom Savs. and Loan Assn., Tampa, Fla., 1987-88; trustee Savs. & Loan Found., Inc., 1980-84; dir. Fin. Trans. Systems, Inc., Magnolia Savs. Corp., 1st Cocoa Corp., Magnolia Realty Co., 1982. Chmn., dir. United Fund, Fargo, N.D., 1962-65; dir., exec. bd. mem. Boy Scouts Am., 1960-70, mem. adv. bd. Central Fla. council, 1983-85, exec. bd., 1985—; bd. assos. Fla. Inst. Tech., founding pres., 1968; moderator St. Johns Presbytery, 1979, chmn. coordinating council, 1980-81; moderator Synod of Fla., 1983;mem. adv. bd. Brevard Art Center and Mus., 1980-82; bd. dirs., founding chmn. devel. council Holmes Regional Med. Center, Melbourne, 1981-84; bd. dirs. Orlando Regional Med. Ctr. Found., 1982-85; mem. fin. com. Mayor's Task Force on Housing, 1983-84; chmn. spl. com. on Nat. Council Chs./World Council Chs. relations Presbyn. Ch. in U.S.A., 1983-86; pres. Ecumenical Ctr. Inc., Orlando, 1985—. Served to lt. (j.g.) USN, World War II. Mem. Fla. Savs. and Loan League (past dir.), Fla. Savs. and Loan Services (past dir.), Savs. and Loan Found. (state membership chmn. 1976), Fla. Savs. and Loan Polit. Action Com. (dir. 1976-82), U.S. Savs. and Loan League (chmn. advt. and pub. relations com. 1969-70), Downtown Melbourne Assn. (past pres.), Beta Theta Pi, Omicron Delta Epsilon. Republican. Clubs: Cocoa Country, Cocoa Rotary (pres. 1979); Sapphire Lake Country (N.C.); Orlando Rotary, Rio Pinar Country, University, Citrus (Orlando), Masons, Shriners, Elks. Office: PO Box 2073 Orlando FL 32802

SHIREY, BRUCE REYNOLDS, marketing professional; b. Detroit, Oct. 13, 1952; s. Wallace Franklin and June Ann (Reynolds) S.; m. Teresa Marie Amoroso, May 1, 1982, 1 child, Erik Bruce. Student of mktg. and econs., Calif. State U., Fullerton, 1981. ATE programmer, technican Pertec Computer Corp., Irvine, Calif., 1977-78, mgr., nat. repair depot, 1978-80, adminstr. spl. projects, 1980-81; western region sales mgr. MMI Computer Services, San Clemente, Calif., 1981-82; v.p. mktg., sales MMI Computer Services, Dallas, 1982, v.p. and gen. mgr., 1982-84; founder, v.p. mktg., sales FRS Inc., Sacramento, 1984—; cons. The B. Reynolds Shirey Assoc., Sacramento, 1986—. Served with USN, 1971-76. Mem. Assn. Field Service Mgrs. Internat., Sacramento Valley Venture Capital Forum, C. of C. Republican. Roman Catholic. Office: FRS Inc 1101 National Dr Sacramento CA 95834

SHIREY, DAVID THOMAS, clothing executive; b. Greenville, Tex., Aug. 4, 1932; s. Ferrell E. and Mary (Breedlove) S.; m. Johanna Griffin, Nov. 29, 1952; children: Sheila Patterson, David T., Stewart C. BBA, Baylor U., 1953; MBA, Pepperdine U., 1980. Dir. mfg. Shirey Co., Greenville, Tex., 1953-68, pres., chief exec. officer, 1968—; bd. dirs. Century Factors, Dallas. Deacon Ridgecrest Bapt. Ch., Greenville; adv. bd. Consumer Product Safety Commn., Washington, 1978-80; chmn. bd. Dallas Bapt. Coll., 1958-72, Greenville Ind. Sch. Dist., 1960-71. Served to capt. USAF, 1953-56. Mem. Am. Apparel Assn. (chmn. bd.), Internat. Apparel Fedn. (pres.), Tex. Mfrs. Assn. (chmn. bd. 1976). Republican. Office: Shirey Co Inc 1917 Stanford Greenville TX 75401

SHIRILAU, MARK STEVEN (SHIREY), utilities executive; b. Long Beach, Calif., Dec. 13, 1955; s. Kenneth Eugene and Marjorie Irene (Thorvick) Shirey; m. Jeffery Michael Lau, Nov. 25, 1984. BSEE, U. Calif., Irvine, 1977, MS Bus. Adminstrn., 1980; M in Engring., Calif. Poly. State U., 1978; Diploma in Theology, Episc. Theol. Sch., Claremont, Calif., 1984; MA in Religion, Sch. Theology at Claremont, 1985; PhD, U. Calif., Irvine, 1988. Ordained priest Ecumenical Cath. Ch., 1987. Grad. asst. Electric Power Inst., 1977-78; pres., chief exec. officer M.S.E., Santa Ana, Calif., 1977—; adminstrv. mgr. EECO Inc., Santa Ana, Calif., 1979-83; fin. engr. So. Calif. Edison Co., Rosemead, 1983-84, conservation engr., 1984-85, conservation supr., 1985—; part-time instr. Santa Ana Coll., 1982-84; lectr. engring. West Coast U., Orange, Calif., 1984—; bd. dirs. Aloha Systems, Inc., Heat Pump Coun. So. Calif. Pastor St.John's Ecumenical Cath. Ch., Santa Ana. Mem. IEEE (sr. mem.), Assn. Energy Engrs. (sr. mem.), Eta Kappa Nu. Democrat. Author: Triune Love: An Insight into God, Creation, and Humanity, 1983. Home: 2302 W Adams St Santa Ana CA 92704 Office: 2244 Walnut Grove Ave Rosemead CA 91770

SHIRKEY, WILLIAM DAN, manufacturing executive; b. Roswell, N.Mex., Nov. 6, 1951; s. Robert Johnson and Joan (Savage) S.; m. Karel Kay Czanderna, May 4, 1985. BS in Physics, SUNY, Brockport, 1973; MS in Physics, Clarkson Coll., 1979; MBA, Cornell U., 1984; postgrad. sr. exec. program, MIT. Quality control engr. Corning Glass Works, Canton, N.Y., 1974-77, sr. process engr., 1979-80, devel. engr., 1980-81, sr. process/prodn. devel. engr., 1981-82; mktg. mgr. Corning Glass Works, Corning, N.Y., 1983; project mgr. Eastman Kodak Co., Rochester, N.Y., 1984-87, tech. asst. to v.p. and gen. mgr. fed. systems div., 1987-88, strategic planning bus. imaging systems div., 1988; strategic planning bus. info. system div. Eastman Kodak Co., Rochester, 1988, mgr. bus. devel. advanced technology products Fed. Systems Div., 1988—. Mem. Optical Soc. Am., Tech. Mktg. Soc. Am., Sigma Pi Sigma. Home: 515 Bay Rd Webster NY 14580 Office: Eastman Kodak Co 121 Lincoln Ave Rochester NY 14650

SHIRLEY, MICHAEL JAMES, construction company executive; b. Flagstaff, Ariz., Oct. 25, 1941; s. James Watson and Lorraine Elizabeth (Thomson) S.; m. Gloria Marie Bruni, Aug. 20, 1966; children: Brian Michael, Cynthia Marie. BS, No. Ariz. U., Flagstaff, 1969; MBA, U. Ariz., 1970. Sr. acct. Morrison-Knudsen Co., Inc., Boise, Idaho, 1970-72; asst. treas. Morrison-Knudsen Co., Inc., 1972-74, corp. treas., 1974-75, v.p. adminstrn., 1975-85; v.p. adminstrn. Morrison Knudsen Corp., 1985—. Bd. dirs. United Way Ada County, 1975-81; bd. dirs. Jr. Achievement of S.W. Idaho, 1978-86, pres., 1983-86; mem. Idaho Coun. Econ. Edn., 1978—; bd. dirs. Boise Philharm. Assn., 1982-85, Bogus Basin Recreation Assn., 1984—. Staff sgt. USAF, 1963-67. Recipient Wall St. Jour. award No. Ariz. U., 1969, Alumni Achievement award, 1978. Mem. Boise Area C. of C. (bd. dirs. 1985—). Republican. Office: Morrison Knudsen Corp PO Box 73 Boise ID 83707

SHIVELY, GLEN M., marketing professional; b. Noble County, Ind., Mar. 27, 1936; s. Murry and Eva Joan (Strouse) S.; m. Norma Jean Vought, Aug. 24, 1958; children: Renee, Kim, Karen, Brian. BS, Manchester Coll., 1959; MDiv, Bethany Theol. Sem., 1962. Ordained to ministry Ch. of the Brethren, 1962. Pastor Milledgeville Ch., Brethren, Ill., 1962-70, Ft. McKinley Brethren Ch., Dayton, Ohio, 1970-77, Happy Corner Brethren Ch., Clayton, Ohio, 1977-86; dir. mktg. and planned giving The Brethren's Home, Greenville, Ohio, 1986—. Adv. com. Montgomery County Joint Vocat. Sch., 1986—. Mem. Mins. Assn. (nat. com.), Nat. Soc. Fund Raising Execs., Kiwanis. Home: 5538 Olive Tree Dr Dayton OH 45426 Office: The Brethren's Home 750 Chestnut St Greenville OH 45331

SHIVERS, GARY MELVILLE, broadcasting executive; b. Salina, Kans., Nov. 17, 1945; s. Raymond M. and Blanche Viola (Pyle) S. BA, U. Kans., 1967, MA, 1972. News dir. Sta. KANU/U. Kans., Lawrence, 1968-70, program dir., 1971-75; reporter Sta. WDAF-AM-FM-TV, Kansas City, Mo., 1970-71; program dir. Sta. WUNC/U. N.C., Chapel Hill, 1975-78, gen. mgr., dir., 1978—; cons. Corp. for Pub. Broadcasting, Washington, 1978-86; chmn. Radio Research Consortium, Silver Spring, Md., 1981—. Corr. Downbeat mag., 1974-75; columnist Am. Arts mag., 1980-83; contbr. articles, revs. to profl. jours., 1972—. Bd. dirs. Nat. Pub. Radio, Washington, 1983-85. Recipient Outstanding News Coverage award AP, 1968, 70 (2), Local Radio Program award Corp. for Pub. Broadcasting, 1977. Mem. Assn. for Recorded Sound Collections (chmn. broadcast collections com. 1983—), Music Critics Assn., Nat. Assn. Jazz Educators, So. Ednl. Communications Assn. (bd. dirs. 1981—). Home: PO Box 1346 Chapel Hill NC 27514 Office: Sta WUNC Univ NC Chapel Hill NC 27599-6230

SHOCKEY, THOMAS EDWARD, retired real estate executive, engineer; b. San Antonio, Aug. 17, 1926; s. Verlie Draper and Margaret Ruth (Shuford) S.; BS (Davidson fellow Tau Beta Pi), Tex. A&M U., 1950; postgrad. St. Mary's U., 1964, San Antonio Coll., 1972, Pacific Western U., 1981; m. Jacqueline McPherson. June 4, 1949; children—Cheryl Ann, Jocelyn Marie, Valerie Jean. With Petty Geophys. Survey, summers 1947-49, J.E. Ingram Equipment Co., 1950-51; co-owner, archtl. engr., realtor Moffett Lumber Co., Inc., San Antonio, 1952-76; cons. gen. contracting, gen. real estate, 1944—, retailer wholesale bldg. material, 1951—, v.p., 1959—; real estate counselor, appraiser, 1972—; real estate appraiser Gill Appraisal Service, San Antonio, 1977—; comml. loan appraiser, underwriter, analyst Gill Savs. Assn., Gill Cos., San Antonio, 1979; chief appraiser, underwriter, architect, engr., insp. Gill Cos., 1981, v.p., 1981-87, ret., 1987. Served with inf. Signal Corps, U.S. Army, 1944-46; ETO. Mem. San Antonio C. of C., Nat. Lumber Dealers, Nat. Home Builders, Nat. Real Estate Bd.. Nat. Inst. Real Estate Brokers, Internat. Soc. Real Estate Appraisers, Tex. Assn. Real Estate Insps., Real Estate Appraisers Tex., Nat. Assn. Rev. Appraisers and Mortgage Underwriters, Internat. Inst. Valuers, Internat. Platform Assn. Home: Star Rte Box 87 Mico TX 78056

SHOCKLEY, WILLIAM EARL, communications company executive; b. Jefferson City, Mo., Oct. 20, 1945; s. William Robert and Nancy (Ott) S.; m. Gloria Kay Brown, June 16, 1967; children: Matthew Scott, Christy Charm. BSBA in Acctg., U. S.C., 1968. Pres. Comml. Communications, Inc., Spartanburg, S.C., 1979-87, Cable of Carolinas, Inc., Spartanburg, 1987—. Republican. Presbyterian. Home: 121 Lake Land Dr Moore SC 29369 Office: Cable of Carolinas Inc 157 E St John St PO Box 6324 Spartanburg SC 29304

SHOEMAKER, ALVIN VARNER, investment banker; b. Somerset, Pa., Oct. 4, 1938; s. Alvin Moore and Sarah Rosemary (Varner) S.; m. Sally Prevost, June 30, 1962; children: Peter, John, Christopher, Julie. B.S. in Econs, U. Pa., 1960; J.D., U. Mich., 1963. Bar: Pa. bar, D.C. bar. Atty. Office Controller of Currency, Dept. Treasury, Washington, 1963-65, Investment Bankers Assn., Washington, 1965-69; sr. v.p., dir., mem. mgmt. com. First Boston Corp., 1969-78, chmn. bd., 1981—; pres., chief exec. officer Blyth Eastman Dillon & Co., Inc., N.Y.C., 1978-80, Blyth Eastman Paine Webber Inc., N.Y.C., 1980—. Clubs: Links, Canoe Brook Country, Seaview Country; University (Washington). Office: First Boston Corp Park Ave Pla New York NY 10055

SHOEMAKER, ELEANOR BOGGS, small business owner, beef producer; b. Gulfport, Miss., Jan. 20, 1935; d. William Robertson and Bessie Eleanor (Ware) Boggs; m. D. Shoemaker, April 9, 1955 (div. 1987); children: Daniel W., William Boggs. Student in protocol, Southeastern U., 1952-53; student, George Washington U., Washington, 1953-56; BA in Communications and Polit. Sci. with honrs, Goucher Coll., 1981; MS in Human Organ. Sci., Villanova U., 1989. Feature writer Washington Times Herald, 1951-54; dir. Patricia Stevens Modeling Agy., Washington, 1955-56; free-lance model Julius Garfinkel, Woodward & Lothrop, Washington, 1951-56; research analyst Balt. County Council, Towson, Md., 1980-81; feature news reporter WGCB-TV, Red Lion, Pa., 1980—; pub. speaker, protocol The Reliable Corp., Columbia, Md., 1982-86; media cons. The Enterprise Found., Columbia, Md., 1985-86; faculty, TV prodn. and communication St. Francis Prep Sch., Spring Grove, Pa., 1985—; owner Windswept Productions Co., Spring Grove, Pa., 1989—; mem. conservation bd. Pa. Parks and Recreation Soc., 1984—. Producer: The Pa. County TV prodn., 1981. Bd. dirs. York (Pa.) County Parks and Recreation, 1972-87; exec. com. York County Republicans, 1972-82; bd. dirs. YWCA, York, 1957-82; accreditation adv. com. York Coll. of Pa., instr. YWCA Women in politics; founder, mem. Child Abuse Taskforce, York, 1983—; founder Women in Politics, York, 1985—; mem. select com. Pa. Agrl. Zoning, 1988. Recipient pro bono child legal representation grant Pa. Bar Assn., 1983. Pa. Tree Farmer of Yr., 1987; named Pa. Lay Person of Yr. Pa. Recreation and Parks Soc. and Gov. Thornburg, 1982. Mem. York Area C. of C., Masters of Foxhounds Assn., The Weybright Hounds. Episcopalian. Home and Office: PO Box 167 Felton PA 17322

SHOEMAKER, ROGER LANE, corporate professional; b. Detroit, Apr. 30, 1947; s. Robert Harold and Lois Adele (Lane) S.; m. Kathleen Martha McGinnis, June 4, 1976; children: Peter, Melissa, Timothy. BEd, Ohio U., 1970. Tech. service rep. Kolene Corp., Detroit, 1970-74, customer service mgr., 1974-76, chemicals mgr., 1977-84, corp. sec., 1985—, v.p., 1988—; pres. Custom Elec. Mfg. subs. Kolene Corp., Livonia, Mich., 1986—. Asst. dir. Nat. Ski Patrol, Gaylord, Mich., 1985—. Mem. Indsl. Heating Equipment Assn. (treas. 1983—), Soc. Automotive Engrs., Am. Soc. Materials. Clubs: Plum Hollow Country, Great Oaks Country. Office: Kolene Corp 12890 Westwood Rd Detroit MI 48223

SHOENFELT, CATHERINE RUTH, marketing executive; b. Dallas, Dec. 9, 1954; d. Marion Justus and Nell (Harden) S. B of Music Edn., U. Tex., San Antonio, 1980. Tchr. music Viva Musica, San Antonio, 1980-81, Northside Ind. Sch. Dist., San Antonio, 1981-84; mktg. mgr. Austin Pathology Assocs., Tex., 1984-86; dir. mktg. Nat. Lab. Services, Inc., Austin, 1987; clin. sales rep. Roche Biomed. Labs., Inc., 1987—. Singer Chamber Choralet Symphony, San Antonio, 1982; vol. Symphony Designer Showplace, Austin, 1986-87, Healthfest-Pathology Booth, Austin, 1986. Mem. Nat. Assn. Female Execs. Republican. Lutheran. Club: Blair County Genealogy Soc. (Altoona, Pa.). Avocations: music, tennis, reading, needlework, swimming. Home: 18307 Elmdon Dr Houston TX 77084 Office: Roche Biomed Labs Inc 1 Roche Dr Raritan NJ 08869

SHOFNER, CYNDI MARIE, investment executive; b. Iowa City, Oct. 29, 1950; d. Paul Eugene and Shirley Mary (Motty) Southern; m. Ben Quinn Ward Shofner, Aug. 28, 1970. BBA in Econs., Rollins Coll., 1976. Asst. to pres. Anderson, Clayton and Co., Houston, 1976-78; exec. asst. Fayez Sarofim and Co., Houston, 1978-83; v.p., sec., treas. Daniel Breen and Co., Houston, 1983—, Breen Trust Co., Houston, 1987—. Pres. Bellfort Pl. Homeowners Assn., Houston, 1985—; mem. NOW. Mem. Select Houston Execs. Roman Catholic. Office: Daniel Breen and Co 700 Louisiana Ste 3400 Houston TX 77002

SHOHET, ALBERT JACOB, manufacturing company executive; b. Baghdad, Iraq, Feb. 15, 1938; s. Jacob M. and Sally A. (Nissan) S.; m. Ivy N. Mussaffi, Nov. 21, 1963; children: Jack, Michael, Tanya. BS in Engring. Physics, Alhikma U., Baghdad, 1960; MS in Mech. Engring., U. Cin., 1962. Registered profl. engr., Ont. Design engr. Buffalo Springfield div. Koehring, Ohio, 1962-64; chief research and devel. engr. Littleford Bros., Inc., Cin., 1964-68; v.p. engring. Buck div. Royal Industries, Inc., Cin., 1968-73, Littleford Bros., Florence, Ky., 1973-83; pres., chief exec. officer Processall, Inc., Cin., 1983—. Patentee multipurpose mixer, high intensity mixer, rack and pinion hoist. Com. chmn. Boy Scouts Am., Cin., 1976-81; mem. Syrian Shrine Temple, 1970—. Mem. AIME, Internat. Food Techs., Soc. Automotive Engrs. Republican. Home: 11168 Embassy Dr Cincinnati OH 45240

SHOLTZ, JERROLD, financial executive; b. Bklyn., Nov. 28, 1943; s. Irving and Helen (Madison) S.; B.B.A., Pace U., 1965; m. Debra Mirman, May 7, 1967; children—Elyssa, Michelle. Mgr., Clarence Raines & Co., C.P.A.s, N.Y.C., 1963-76; controller Gelmart Industries, College Point, N.Y., 1977-78; mgr. Goldstein Golub Kessler & Co., N.Y.C., 1979-80; v.p. fin. Bidermann Industries U.S.A., Inc., Secaucus, N.J., 1980—. Served with N.Y. State N.G., 1965-69. C.P.A., N.Y. Mem. Credit Orgn., Am. Inst. C.P.A.s, Am. Apparel Mfg. Assn. (fin. mgmt. com.), N.Y. Soc. C.P.A.s. Club: Bus. Credit. Home: 17 Pecan Valley Dr New City NY 10956 Office: 77 Metro Way Secaucus NJ 07094

SHONK, ALBERT DAVENPORT, JR., b. Los Angeles, May 23, 1932; s. Albert Davenport and Jean Spence (Stannard) S.; BS in Bus. Adminstrn., U. So. Calif., 1954. Field rep. mktg. div. Los Angeles Examiner, 1954-55, asst. mgr. mktg. and field supr. mktg. div. 1955-56, mgr. mktg. div., 1956-57; account exec. Hearst Advt. Svc., Los Angeles, 1957-59; account exec., mgr. Keith H. Evans & Assos., San Francisco, 1959-65; owner, pres. Albert D. Shonk Co., L.A., 1965—; pres., Signet Circle Corp., Inc., 1977-81, dir., 1962-81, hon. life dir., 1977-86. Bd. dirs., sec., 1st v.p. Florence Crittenton Svcs. of Los Angeles, exec. v.p., 1979-81, pres., 1981-83, chmn. bd., 1983-85, hon. life dir., 1986—; founding chmn. Crittenton Assos. Recipient Medallion of Merit Phi Sigma Kappa, 1976, Founders award, 1961. Mem. Advt. Club Los Angeles, Bus. and Profl. Advt. Assn., Pubs. Rep. Assn. of So. Calif., Nat. Assn. Pubs. Reps. (past v.p. West Coast 1981-83), Jr. Advt. Club Los Angeles (hon. life; dir., treas., 1st v.p.), Trojan Club, Skull and Dagger, U. So. Calif., USC Assocs., Inter-Greek Soc. (co-founder, hon. life mem. and dir., v.p. 1976-79, pres. 1984-86), Phi Sigma Kappa (dir. grand council 1962-70, 77-79, grand pres. 1979-83, chancellor 1983-87, court of honor , life, trustee, v.p. meml. found. 1979-84, pres. 1984, trustee pres. Phi Sigma Kappa found. 1984—), Alpha Kappa Psi, Los Angeles Club. Home: 3460 W 7th St Los Angeles CA 90005 Office: Albert Shonk Co 3156 Wilshire Blvd Ste 7 Los Angeles CA 90010

SHOOP, GLENN POWELL, investment consultant; b. Gracemont, Okla., Sept. 1, 1920; s. Roy Alonzo and Myrtle Nancy (Goodfellow) S.; m. Louise Wilhelmina Vollmer, Mar. 19, 1943; children: Merilou Love, Paul, Nancy Caver. Student, U. Okla., 1938-42. Pilot Braniff Internat. Airways, Dallas, 1946-80; ptnr. Shoop, Rogers, Morton, Dallas, 1960—; cons., bd. dirs. Braniff Inc., Justin State Bank, Tex. Bd. dirs. First Bapt. Ch., Dallas, 1950-88; mem. devel. bd. Golden Gate Bapt. Sem., San Francisco. Served to maj. USAF, 1942-46. Republican.

SHORB, EUGENE MURRAY, utility executive; b. Cleve., Mar. 6, 1920; s. Charles F. and Beth L. (Murray) S.; m. Harriet Elizabeth Colman, July 14, 1951; children: Janet E., William M., Thomas C. BS in Mech. Engring., Purdue U., 1949. Gas engr. No. Ind. Pub. Service Co., Hammond, 1949-52, various managerial positions, 1952-73, v.p. gas ops., 1973-74, v.p. gas ops. and fuel procurement, 1974-77, sr. v.p. ops., 1977-79, 1st v.p., 1979-81, exec. v.p., chief operating officer, 1981-85, cons. mgmt., 1985—, also bd. dirs.; bd. dirs. NIPSCO Industries, Inc., Hammond, Mercantile Bankorp, Hammond, Mercantile Bank Ind., Hammond. Past officer or bd. dirs. various civic orgns. Served with USNR, 1942-45. Mem. Am. Gas Assn., Ind. Gas Assn. (life, past pres. and bd. dirs.). Republican. Methodist. Home: 1401 Fran-Lin Pkwy Munster IN 46321 Office: No Ind Pub Svc Co 5265 Hohman Ave Hammond IN 46320

SHOREY, GREGORY DAY, JR., advertising/public relations company executive; b. Arlington, Mass., June 27, 1924; s. Gregory Day and Lucille (McNara) S.; m. Betty Young, Mar. 14, 1943; children: Pam, Day, Cindy, Amy. B.S., Boston U., 1948. Founding pres. Style-Crafters Inc., Greenville, S.C., 1950-71; exec. v.p. Gladding Corp., Syracuse, N.Y., 1971-72; pres. apparel div. Reigel Textile Corp., Greenville, 1972-74; co-founder, chmn. bd., chief exec. officer Shorey & Assocs. Inc., Greenville, 1974—. State chmn. S.C. Republican party, 1956-61, life mem. exec. com., 1956—, life mem. exec. com. Greenville Rep. party, 1954—; bd. dirs. YMCA, Greenville, 1962-72; bd. dirs., v.p. Goodwill Industries, Greenville, 1970-72; vice chmn. S.C. Dairy Commn., 1972-78; mem. Fed. Jury Commn., 1958-60. Served with USN, 1943-45. Decorated Order of Palmetto, S.C. Gov., 1978. Mem. Nat. Advt. Agy. Network, Greenville C. of C., Am. Legion. Episcopalian. Office: Shorey & Assocs Inc 450 E Park Ave Greenville SC 29601

SHORNEY, GEORGE HERBERT, publishing executive; b. Oak Park, Ill., Dec. 16, 1931; s. George Herbert and Mary (Wallace) S.; m. Nancy Leith, Aug. 27, 1955; children: Cindy, Herb, John, Scott. BA, Denison U., 1954. Office mgr. Hope Pub. Co., Carol Stream, Ill., 1958-61, v.p., 1961-70, pres., 1970—; bd. dirs. Gary-Wheaton (Ill.) Bank, 1986—. Contbr. New Grove Handbook of Music, 1989. Pres. West Suburban Choral Union, Wheaton, 1984—, Cen. DuPage Hosp. bd. govs., Winfield, Ill., 1985—; governing mem. Chgo. Symphony Orch., 1986—; chmn. Wheaton Fire and Police Commrs., 1974-81; bd. dirs. Healthcorp Affiliates, Naperville, Ill., 1982—; bd. trustees Westminster Choir Coll., Princeton, N.J. Served with USN, 1954-56. Mem. Ch. Music Pubs. Assn. (pres. 1986-87), Denison Univ. Alumni Soc. (pres. 1976-78). Democrat. Presbyterian. Club: Univ. (Chgo.). Home: 160 W Elm Wheaton IL 60187 Office: Hope Pub Co 380 S Main Pl Carol Stream IL 60188

SHORT, BRANT ALISON, manufacturing executive, engineer; b. Bay City, Mich., Sept. 5, 1933; s. Hugh Alison and Thelma Bernice (Sundquist) S.; m. Barbara Marie Peterson, Aug. 18, 1956; children: Eric, Susan, Kathryn. BSME, Mich. State U., 1955, MS in Mech. Engring., 1957, MBA, 1967. Registered profl. engr., Mich. Resch. engr. Whirlpool Corp., St. Joseph, Mich., 1957-65, mgr. mech. engring., 1965-68, dir. engring. resch., 1968-70; mgr. devel. engring. Whirlpool Corp., St. Paul, 1970-72, mgr. refrigeration engring., 1972-77, dir. quality control, 1977-78; mgr. corp. engring. Graco Inc., Mpls., 1978-82; v.p. engring. Century Mfg. Co., Bloomington, Minn., 1982-85, Doboy Packaging Machinery Inc., New Richmond, Wis., 1985—; dir. mech. engring. adv. coun. U. Minn., Mpls., 1980—. Author: (with others) Role of Mechanical Action in Soil Removal, 1974; Automatic Icemakers, 1979; contbr. articles to profl. jours. Mem. ASME, Am. Soc. Quality Control, Am. Mgmt. Assn., Nat. Soc. Profl. Engrs., Sigma Xi. Episcopalian. Home: 2080 Cameron Dr Woodbury MN 55125 Office: Doboy Packaging Machinery 869 S Knowles Ave New Richmond WI 54017

SHORT, DONALD JAMES, food processing executive; b. Weymouth, Mass., Apr. 5, 1942; s. Charles D. and Elizabeth V. (Noone) S.; m. Lynn Winchester Smith, June 19, 1965; children—Kristin Lynn, Ashley Elizabeth. B.A., Colby Coll., 1964; M.B.A., Wharton Sch. U.Pa., 1970. Asst. product mgr. Gillette Co., Boston, 1970-72, product mgr., 1972-73; mktg. mgr. Braun N.Am., Cambridge, Mass., 1973-78; mktg. mgr. Pillsbury Co., Mpls., 1978-80; v.p. mktg. and sales Fishery Products Inc., Danvers, Mass., 1980-83, pres., 1983—, dir., 1985—. Bd. dirs. Nat. Fisheries Edn. and Research Found. Served to capt. USAF, 1964-68. Mem. Nat. Fisheries Inst. (sec., chmn. promotions com., exec. com., dir. region 1, bd. dirs. Washington, 1985—), New Eng. Fisheries Inst., Gloucester Fisheries Assn. (exec. bd.), Fishery Council Can., Am. Seafood Distbrs. Assn. (bd. dirs. 1985—, pres. 1987-88), North Atlantic Seafood Assn. (chmn. mktg. com.), N. Eng. Fisheries Devel. Assn., Colby Coll. Athletic Com. Alumni Council (exec. bd., chmn. athletic com.), Suffolk U. Sch. Mgmt. Adj. Faculty. Clubs: Manchester Bath and Tennis, Manchester Yacht, Bay, Manchester, Downtown, Manchester Tennis, N. Shore Colby (pres.), Crow's Nest. Home: 102 School St Manchester MA 01944 Office: Fishery Products Inc 18 Electronics Ave Danvers MA 01923

SHORT, HAROLD WAYNE, small business owner; b. Williamsport, Ind., Mar. 24, 1949; s. Jesse Harold and Oma Dell (Cook) S.; m. Martha Ann Goodrich, Mar. 27, 1970; children: John, Kirk. Student, Ind. State U., 1967-69; BBA, Cen. State U., 1974; MBA, Corpus Christi State U., 1982. Cert. residential specialist. Sheet metal journeyman Dept. Def., Oklahoma City, 1973-75; air traffic controller FAA, various locations, 1975-81; sales assoc. Colonial Realtors, Wichita, Kans., 1981-83; co-owner Creative Assocs. Real Estate, Wichita, 1983-84; mgr. ReMax Realty Profls., Inc., Wichita, 1984-87, broker, owner, 1987—; pres. ReMax Realty Profls. P.F.S. Group, Ltd., Wichita, 1987-88. Sgt. USAF, 1969-73. Mem. Nat. Assn. Realtors, Wichita Assn. Realtors (Master Circle award 1986-87), Kans. Assn. Realtors. Democrat. Methodist. Lodge: Optomist. Office: ReMax Realty Profls 10100 W Maple Wichita KS 67209

SHORT, LAUREL JOSEPH, financial executive; b. Archbold, Ohio, Nov. 16, 1930; s. Laurel Albert and Marjorie Mural (Beck) S.; m. Wyona Imogene Meyer, Mar. 17, 1951; children: Denise, Kerrwin, Doreen, Sandra. Student, Internat. Coll., Ft. Wayne, Ind., 1951. V.p., dir. Town and Country Food Co., Ft. Wayne, 1953-69; co-founder, v.p., treas., dir. Town and Country Food Co., Kingsford Ind. and Ft. Wayne, 1955-86, pres., treas., chief exec. officer, 1986; treas., chief fin. officer Harding Dahm and Co., Inc., Ft. Wayne, 1986—. Del. White House Conf. on Small Bus., 1980, 86. Mem. Ind. State C. of C. (mem. sml. bus. coun. 1980). Republican. Ch. of God. Home: 3219 Inwood Dr Fort Wayne IN 46815 Office: Harding Dahm and Co Inc 1910 Fort Wayne National Bank Building Fort Wayne IN 46815

SHORT, ROBERT HENRY, retired utility executive; b. Klamath Falls, Oreg., Oct. 15, 1924; s. Judge Haywood and Henrietta Luella (Lyon) S.; m. Ruby Madalyn Rice, Aug. 1, 1946; children—Robert L., Victoria (Mrs. Gregory Baum), Casey. BS in Journalism, U. Oreg., 1950; PhD in Humane Letters (hon.), Linfield Coll., 1984. City editor Klamath Falls Herald and News, 1950-52; dir. pub. rels. Water and Elec. Bd., Eugene, Oreg., 1952-55; mgr. pub. info. Portland Gen. Electric Co., Oreg., 1955-57, asst. to chmn., 1957-62, v.p., 1962-71, sr. v.p., 1971-73, exec. v.p., 1973-77, pres., 1977-80, chmn. bd., chief exec. officer, 1980-88, ret., 1989; bd. dir. First Interstate Bank of Oreg. Bd. dirs. Oreg. Ind. Colls. Found., Oreg. United Way; trustee Oreg. Grad. Ctr., Willamette U., St. Vincent Hosp. and Med. Ctr. With USNR, 1942-45. Mem. Astoria Country Club, Portland Golf Club, Arlington Club. Home: 1210 SW 61st Ct Portland OR 97221

SHORT, ROGER JOHN, manufacturing company executive; b. Birmingham, Eng., Sept. 17, 1939; came to Can., 1964; s. Bertram C.; m. Susan Short, Dec. 15, 1962; children: Timothy, Helen. B in Chemistry with 1st class honors, Oxford U., Eng., 1961, MS in Theoretical Physics, 1962; MBA, U. Toronto, Can., 1979. With Courtalds Ltd., Eng., 1962-64; mgr. dissolving pulp sales then tech. mgr. Columbia Cellulose Ltd., Prince Rupert, B.C., Can., 1964-68; project dir. MacMillan Bloedel Ltd., Vancouver, B.C., Can., 1968-69; asst. mgr. mill MacMillan Bloedel Ltd., Harmac Nanaimo, B.C., Can., 1969-71; mng. dir. Europe MacMillan Bloedel Ltd., 1973-75; v.p., gen. mgr. Parsons and Whittemore Inc., 1971-73, sr. v.p. ops., 1976-80; group v.p. Reed Paper Ltd., 1975-76; exec. v.p. ops. Celanese Can. Inc., 1980-81; v.p. copr. planning and devel. Canron Inc., 1981-85, exec. v.p., fin. and planning, 1985-88; pres. Canron Industries Inc., 1987-88, also bd. dirs.; v.p., pres. packaging group Domtar Inc, Mississauga, Ont., Can., 1989—. Mem. Can. Assn. Corp. Growth, Confreie des Chevaliers du Tastevin (souscommanderie de Toronto), Royal Soc. Chemistry, Oxford Soc., Cambridge Club, Bd. Trade. Home: 616 Avenue Rd, Toronto, ON Canada M4V 2K8 Office: Domtar Packaging Group Inc, Malton Postal Sta Box 1010, Mississauga, ON Canada L4T 3E9

SHORT, STEVE EUGENE, engineer; b. Crockett, Calif., Oct. 17, 1938; s. Roger Milton and Ida Mae (Mills) S.; B.S. in Gen. Engring. with honors, U. Hawaii, 1972, M.B.A., 1973; M.S. in Meteorology, U. Md., 1980; m. Yumie Sedaka, Feb. 2, 1962; children—Anne Yumie, Justine Yumie, Katherine Yumie. With Nat. Weather Service, NOAA, 1964—, govt. exec. Silver Spring, Md., 1974-81, program mgr. ASOS, 1980—; cons. engring. and mgmt.; cons. SBA. Contbr. articles to sci. jours. Served with USMC, 1956-60. Registered profl. engr., Hawaii. Mem. Am. Meteorol. Soc., Japan-Am. Soc., Am. Soc. Public Adminstrn. Home: 3307 Rolling Rd Chevy Chase MD 20815 Office: Nat Weather Svc 8060 13th St Silver Spring MD 20910

SHORT, WALTER JOSEPH, airline executive; b. Blairsville, Pa., Jan. 10, 1918; s. Charles J. and Margaret E. (Caulfield) S.; m. Martha J. Hammill, June 13, 1942; children: Charles W., Robert A., Debra Ann. BS cum laude, U. Notre Dame, 1939. Acctg. supr. Capital Airlines, Washington, 1941-46; treas. Luke Harris Industries, Inc., Willow Run, Mich., 1946-47; office mgr. Giant Food Co., Washington, 1948-49; chief acct. U.S. Air Inc. (formerly All Am. Airways, Inc.), Washington, 1949; asst. treas. U.S. Air Inc. (formerly Allegheny Airlines), Washington, 1949-53, treas., 1953-59, v.p., treas., 1955-59, v.p. fin., 1959-61, sr. v.p. fin. and adminstr., 1961-69, exec. v.p. fin., 1969-79, vice chmn., 1979—; first v.p. Airline Finance and Acctg. Conf., 1955, pres., 1956, 2d v.p., 1968. Mem. Air Transp. Assn. (chmn. econs. and fin. coun. 1974), Fin. Execs. Inst. (past nat. dir., chpt. pres., bd. dirs., area v.p.). Club: Notre Dame (Fla. West Coast). Home: 3222 Citrus Ct Largo FL 34640 Office: USAIR Inc Crystal Park Four 2345 Crystal Dr Arlington VA 22227

SHOTT, GERALD LEE, human resources executive; b. Elgin, Ill., Jan. 7, 1934; s. Lester A. and Lillian M. (Gould) S.; m. Janet Strang, Aug. 20, 1955; children: Nancy Lynn, Robert Gerald. B.A., Coe Coll., Cedar Rapids, Iowa, 1955; M.B.A., U. Chgo., 1964. Employee rels. rep. Standard Oil Co., Ind., 1959-65; mgr. personnel rels. Johnson & Johnson, 1965-69; v.p. First Nat. Bank Chgo., 1969-76; exec. v.p. First Interstate Bancorp, Los Angeles, 1976—; bd. dirs. First Interstate Bank Okla. Bd. dirs. Los Angeles chpt. Am. Heart Assn.; bd. dirs. Blue Cross of Calif. Served with USAF, 1956-59. Mem. Am. Bankers Assn., Am. Mgmt. Assn., Am. Soc. Personnel Adminstrn., Am. Compensation Assn., Human Resource Planning Soc. Republican. Office: First Interstate Bancorp PO Box 54068 Los Angeles CA 90054

SHOUB, EARLE PHELPS, chemical engineer; b. Washington, July 19, 1915; B.S. in Chemistry, Poly. Inst. Bklyn., 1938, postgrad., 1938-39; m. Elda Robinson; children—Casey Louis, Heather Margaret Shoub Dills. Chemist, Hygrade Food Products Corp., N.Y.C., 1940-41; regional dir. Nat. Bur. Standards, 1943-70; with U.S. Bur. Mines, 1962-70, chief div. accident prevention and health, Washington, 1963-70; dep. dir. Appalachian Lab. Occupational Respiratory Diseases, Nat. Inst. Occupational Safety and Health, Morgantown, W.Va., 1970-77, dep. dir. div. safety research, 1977-79; mgr. occupational safety, indsl. environ. cons., safety products div. Am. Optical Corp., Southbridge, Mass., 1979, cons., 1979—; asso. prof. dept. anesthesiology W.Va. U. Med. Center, Morgantown, 1977-82, prof. Coll. Mineral and Energy Resources, 1970-79. Recipient Disting. Service award Dept. Interior and Gold medal, 1959. Registered profl. engr.; cert. safety profl. Fellow Am. Inst. Chemists; mem. Am. Indsl. Hygiene Assn., Vets. of Safety, AIME, Am. Soc. Safety Engrs., Nat. Fire Protection Assn., Nat. Soc. Profl. Engrs., Am. Conf. Govtl. Indsl. Hygienists, Internat. Soc. Respiratory Protection (pres.), ASTM, Am. Nat. Standards Inst., Sigma Xi. Methodist. Contbr. articles to profl. jours. and texts. Home: Apt 202C 5850 Meridian Rd Gibsonia PA 15044-9605

SHOULDERS, ALLEN MITCHELL, accountant; b. Denton, Tex., June 20, 1957; s. Donald Ray and Joetta Janet (McDonald) S.; m. Laura Lee Boston; children: Anna Lee, Erin. BBA, Abilene Christian U., 1979. CPA, Tex. Mgr. entrepreneurial svc. group Arthur Young & Co., Ft. Worth, 1979-83, 1988—; v.p., controller Pulte Home Corp./ICM Mortgage, Ft. Worth, 1983-87; dir. fin. Shopper's Guide, Harte-Hanks Communications, Arlington, Tex., 1987-88. Mem. Am. Inst. CPAs, Tex. Soc. CPAs. Republican. Mem. Ch. of Christ. Home: 7325 Vanessa Dr Fort Worth TX 76112 Office: Arthur Young & Co 2200 Tex Am Bank Bldg Fort Worth TX 76102

SHOUMATE, BELFORD WASHINGTON, architect; b. Aberdeen, Ohio, June 5, 1903; s. William Francis and Lora Dean (Insko) S.; m. Beatrice Stanford Owens, Aug. 18, 1937; children: William Stanford, Thomas Stanford. BArch, U. Pa., 1929. Registered architect, Fla. Owner, prin. Belford Shoumate Architect and Assocs., Palm Beach, Fla., 1937—; AIA appointee Nat. Preservation Hist. Bldgs. Mem. Palm Beach Civic Assn.; participant landmark and preservation activities. Recipient Efficiency award Army Civilian Dept. Engring., 1941-43. Mem. Beta Theta Pi Alumni Club. Republican. Episcopalian. Avocations: antique cars, sailing, photography, old houses. Home and Office: 222 Phipps Pla Palm Beach FL 33480

SHOUP, JAMES RAYMOND, computer systems consultant; b. McKees Rocks, Pa., Apr. 9, 1932; s. Jacob Daniel and Violet May Shoup; student U. Md., 1953-54, U. Miami, 1957-58, Palm Beach Jr. Coll., 1964-68; AA, Fla. Jr. Coll., 1978, AS, 1980; m. Caren Michelle Gagner, Nov. 20, 1988; children—Emily Ruth, Rhonda Lou, Richard Eugene, Sean Jason, Amy Marisa, Rodney Warren. With Fla. Power and Light Co., Delray Beach 1954-68; pres. JSE Corp., 1954-68; fin. cons. area bus., 1954-68; with FAA, 1968-72; with sales and mgmt. depts. Montgomery Ward Co., 1972-75; project mgr. JR Shoup & Assocs., Jacksonville, Fla., 1975—; v.p. rsch. and devel. JP Computing Co., Jacksonville Beach, 1981—, Alken Computer Systems Co., Flower Mound, Tex., 1979-82; with U.S. Postal Svc., Jacksonville, 1975—; systems instr. microcomputer sci. Duval County Community Schs., Jacksonville, 1980-84; cons. on EDP acctg. applications analysis and EDP systems engring., 1976—; fin. cons., 1967—. Author manuals on computer applications in indsl. and transp. mgmt., 1975-84. Asst. chief, pres., dir. Tri-Community Fire Dept., 1955-57; Sunday sch. tchr., deacon, treas., elder, local Presbyn. chs., 1955—; pub. rels. officer N.B. Forrest High Sch. Band Parents Assn., 1973-79; mem. Rep. Presdl. Task Force. With USAF, 1950-54. Mem. EDP Auditors Assn., Jacksonville C. of C. (com. of 100), Mensa, Internat. Platform Assn. Lodge: Masons. Designer Alken computers, disk patch for tiny Pascal, system 800 computers, IMAS acctg. system for microcomputers; oil painter represented in pvt. collections, Fla. Home and Office: 1832 N Lane Ave Jacksonville FL 32205-1526

SHOURD, ROY R., manufacturing company executive; b. 1927. BA, U. Mo., 1950. With Schlumberger Ltd., N.Y.C., 1950—, from v.p. to exec. v.p., 1977—. Served with USN, 1945-46. Office: Schlumberger Ltd 277 Park Ave New York NY 10017 *

SHOWELL, JOHN DALE, III, investment company executive, banker; b. Washington, Mar. 2, 1923; s. John Dale Jr. and Sarah Elizabeth (Hickling) S.; m. Ann Lockhart, Mar. 22, 1947; children—John Dale, Ann, Sarah Elizabeth, Adam. B.S., Duke U., 1946-49. With Bank of Ocean City, 1945—, now v.p.; pres. Showell Investments, Ocean City, 1956—. Mem. Ocean City Council, 1960-72. Served with USMC, 1943-45; PTO. Democrat. Clubs: Governors, Old Guard (Palm Beach, Fla.); Annapolis Yacht (Md.). Home: 3700 Ocean Front PO Box 190 Ocean City MD 21842

SHPILBERG, DAVID, management consultant, artificial intelligence researcher; b. Lima, Peru, Sept. 28, 1950; came to U.S., 1970; s. Salik and Rosa (Colcher) S.; m. Anita Vaidergorn, June 28, 1970; children: Patricia Elizabeth, Samuel Alexander, Tamara Selma. BS, M.I.T., 1972, MS, 1973, PhD, 1975. Prof. Sch. Mgmt. IESA, Caracas, Venezuela, 1975-79; pres. Sinergica, Caracas, 1979-83; ptnr. Coopers and Lybrand, N.Y.C., 1983—; vis. prof. Wharton Sch. Bus. U. Pa., Phila., 1979; adj. prof. Ga. State U., Atlanta, 1977-84; advisor UNESCO, Paris, 1985—. Atuhor: Statistical Decomposition Analysis, 1980, Seismic Risk, 1980; contbr. to profl. publs. Mem., bd. dirs. Bi-Cultural Day Sch., Stamford, Conn., 1986—. Grantee Factory Mutual Rsch. Corp., 1973, U.S. Geological Survey, 1982; recipient ANCLA award Venezuealan Ins. Assn., Caracas, 1979, rsch. honorarium Am. Risk and Ins. Assn., 1985, Literary Excellence award Assn. Cons. Mgmt. Engrs., 1987. Mem. Am. Assn. Artificial Intelligence, Inst. Mgmt. Sci., Ops. Rsch. Soc. Am., Assn. Computing Machinery, Internat. Ins. Soc. (chmn. program com. 1981), Sigma Xi. Jewish. Home: 16 Hedge Brook Ln Stamford CT 06903 Office: Coopers & Lybrand 1251 Ave of the Americas New York NY 10020

SHRADER, CARL MICHAEL, publishing executive; b. Lafayette, Ky., Sept. 21, 1928; s. Raymond Hill and Larue (Clardy) S.; m. Mary Lunsford, Apr. 4, 1951; children: James Michael, Kenneth Raymond. Cert. in aerial and mapping photography, USAF Sch. of Photography, 1948, Nat. Art Sch., 1954. Circulation mgr. Clarksville (Tenn.) Leaf Chronicle, 1945-47; asst. dir. photogrammetry lab., multiplex map compiler USN Hydrographic Office, Suitland, Md., 1952-55; with Nat. Geog. Soc., Washington, 1955—; establisher Photomech. Reprodn. Lab., 1958, mgr. 1959-69; chief Photog. Labs. (Color, B&W, Photomech.), 1969-71, dir. photog. svcs. div., 1971-84, asst. v.p. prodn. svcs., 1985—. Contbr. articles to profl. jours.; internat. speaker in field; inventor numerous map reproducing techniques. Bd. govs. Washington Litho Club, 1964-65; chmn. adminstrn. bd., council ministries Lanham United Meth. Ch., 1958-61; chmn. Cliff Parks com. city council, New Carrollton, Md., 1966; mem. adminstrn. bd. Severna Park United Meth. Ch., 1986-88; bd. dirs. Chartwell Community Assn., 1988; testified on Olympic Coinage legis. banking subcom. consumer affairs U.S. Ho. Reps., Washington, 1984. Staff sgt. USAF, 1948-52. Named Hon. Ky. Col. Univ. Photographers Assn., 1986. Mem. Graphic communications Assn. (program advisor 1974-75) Tech. Assn. Graphic Arts (ednl. coun. 1977), Gravure Assn. Am., Am. Numis. Assn. (Spl. Commendation cert. 1982, Silver medal with Regalia 1985, gen. chmn. ann. conv. 1985), Mid. Atlantic Numis. Assn. (Numismatist of Yr. 1986, Alex Kapik award 1986), Md. State Numis. Assn. (pres. 1985), Prince Geroges County Coin Club (pres. 1980-81, Numismatist of Yr. 1979, gen. chmn. Tri-Club coin conv. 1980-81), Chartwell Golf and Country Club. Republican. Office: Nat Geographic Soc 1145 17th St NW Washington DC 20036

SHRADER, CHRISTINE NYBURG, insurance agent, financial planner; b. Pensacola, Fla., Aug. 29, 1945; d. Willard Lloyd and Olga (Hendrickson) Nyburg; m. Stephen C. Shrader, June 21, 1981; children: Sarah, Cory. Student, James Madison Coll., Harrisonburg, Va., 1963-64; BA, San Jose State U., 1969; postgrad., U. Wash., 1978-79. CLU, cert. fin. planner. Social worker Dept. Pub. Soc. Svcs.-Exposition Park, Los Angeles, 1969-71; rehab. social worker Los Angeles County Parks and Recreation, 1971-73; freelance illustrator Los Angeles and San Francisco, 1973-76; personnel researcher City of Seattle, 1977-78; social worker, adminstr. Homesharing for Seniors Inc., Seattle, 1978-80; fin. planner Shrader Fin. Services, Seattle, 1980—; ins. agt. Richards Agy.-Mass. Mut. Life Ins., Seattle, 1982—. Del. Kitsap County Rep. Conv., 1988; active St. Barnabas Ch., Bainbridge Island, Wash., 1987—, mem. edn. com., choir, chair outreach commn. Mem. Am. Soc. CLU's, Am. Soc. Chartered Fin. Cons., Inst. Cert. Fin. Planners, Internat. Assn. Fin. Planners, Nat. Assn. Life Underwriters (Nat. Quality award 1983, 84, 85), Million Dollar Round Table, Mass. Mut. Agents' Assn. (Seattle del. 1985-88). Republican. Episcopalian. Lodge: Kiwanis. Office: Richards Ins Agy 2300 The Financial Ctr Seattle WA 98161

SHREVE, THEODORE NORRIS, construction company executive; b. St. Louis, Feb. 14, 1919; s. Truxtun Benbridge and Beulah (Dyer) S.; B.S., U. Colo., 1942; m. Caroline Prouty, Jan. 7, 1943; children—Sara Ann Caile Shreve, Suzanne Godfrey Shreve, Theo Carol. Sec., treas. Trautman & Shreve, Inc., Denver, 1946-68, pres., 1965-86, chmn. bd., 1984—; pres. 4030 Corp., 1984—. Mem. Colo. U. Found. Bd., 1988—; Rep. County Assembly, 1962. Served with USNR, 1942-45. Registered profl. engr., Colo. Mem. Mech. Contractors Assn., Colo. Soc. Profl. Engrs., Rotary, Gyro Club, Denver Country Club, Sigma Phi Epsilon. Republican. Episcopalian. Home: 1510 E 10th Ave #13W Denver CO 80218 Office: Trautman & Shreve 4406 Race St Denver CO 80216

SHRIER, ADAM LOUIS, investment firm executive; b. Warsaw, Poland, Mar. 26, 1938; came to U.S., 1943, naturalized, 1949; s. Henry Leon and Mathilda June (Czamanska) S.; m. Diane Kesler, June 10, 1961; children: Jonathan, Lydia, Catherine, David. B.S., Columbia U., 1959; M.S. (Whitney fellow), M.I.T., 1960; D.Engr. and Applied Sci. (NSF fellow), Yale U., 1965; postdoctoral visitor, U. Cambridge, Eng., 1965-66; J.D., Fordham U., 1976. With Esso Research & Engring. Co., Florham Park and Linden, N.J., 1963-65, 66-72; head. environ. scis. research area Esso Research & Engring. Co., 1969-72; coordinator pollution abatement activities, tanker dept. Exxon Internat. Co., N.Y.C., 1972-74; project mgr., energy systems Exxon Enterprises Inc., N.Y.C., 1974-75; mgr. solar energy projects Exxon Enterprises Inc., 1975-77, pres. solar thermal systems div., 1977-81; corp. planning cons., sec. new bus. investments Exxon Corp., N.Y.C., 1981-82; mgr. industry analysis Exxon Internat. Co., N.Y.C., 1983-86, mgr. policy and planning, 1986-88; dir. Solar Power Corp., North Billerica, Mass., Solar Power, Ltd., London, Daystar Corp., Burlington, Mass.; adj. lectr. chem. engring. Columbia U., N.Y.C., 1967-69; industry adv. bd. Internat. Energy Agy., 1984-88, Energy and Environ. Policy Ctr., Harvard U., 1986-88, Internat. Energy Program, Johns Hopkins U., 1987-88; sr. assoc. Global Bus. Forum, 1988—, Cambridge Energy Rsch. Assocs., 1988—. Patentee in field; contbr. articles to profl. jours. Mem. Am. Inst. Chem. Engrs., Am. Chem. Soc., AAAS, N.Y. Acad. Scis., Am. Inst. Energy Economists, Am. Bar Assn., Sigma Xi, Tau Beta Pi, Phi Lambda Upsilon. Club: United Oxford and Cambridge (London). Home: 543 Park St Upper Montclair NJ 07043 Office: Splty Tech Assocs 100 Park Ave 17th fl New York NY 10017

SHRIEVES, GEORGE MATTHEWS, civil engineer; b. Hopkins, Va., Nov. 27, 1935; s. Tully F. and Mary (Matthews) S.; m. Harriet Janet Stockley, June 4, 1960; children: William, Robert Matthews, Anne Elizabeth. BS, Va. Mil. Inst., 1958; cert. of mgmt., U. Miss., 1975. With Fed. Hwy. Adminstrn., Washington, 1958—, asst. state programs officer, 1979, dir. Nat. Hwy. Inst., 1979—, chmn. tech. transfer com., 1982. Served with U.S. Army, 1959-60. Recipient Fed. Hwy. Adminstrn. Adminstrs. Bronze medal, 1975, Sec. Transp. Silver medal, 1981. Mem. Am. Assn. State Hwy. and Transp. Ofcls., Am. Rd. and Transp. Builders Assn., Am. Pub. Works. Assn. Episcopalian. Office: Dept of Transp Nat Hwy Inst 6300 Georgetown Pike McLean VA 22102

SHRINER, ROBERT DALE, economist, management consultant; b. Hobart, Okla., Nov. 28, 1937; s. William Dale and Mildred Ellen (Goodson) S.; m. Nancy Lee Thompson, June 6, 1961; 1 child, Leslie Annette. BA, U. Okla., 1965, MA, 1967; PhD, Ind. U., 1974. Asst. to chief ops. Gen. Dynamics Astronautics, Altus, Okla., 1961-63; dir. Wyo. tech. asst. program U. Wyoming, 1966-69; research assoc. Ind. U. Bur. Bus. Research, 1969-71; asst. prof. Ind. U. Sch. Pub. and Environ. Affairs, 1972-77; assoc. dir. resource devel. internship program Council of State Govt., 1970-72; dir. aerospace research application ctr. Ind. U., 1972-76; mng. assoc., sr. economist Booz Allen & Hamilton, Washington, 1977-79; dir. Washington ops. Chase Econometrics, Washington, 1979-82; mng. ptnr. Shriner-Midland Co., Washington, 1982—; cons. U.S. Cath. Conf., Aerospace Industries Assocs., Nat. Endowment for Arts., Nat. Restaurant Assn., Presl. Commn. on Social Security; also cons. to various major corps. and nat. assns. Editor, Pub.: Managing Technology and Change, 1972-75, 1986—; creator computer program, 1982; contbr. articles to profl. jours. Pres. grad. students assn. U. Okla., Norman, 1965-66; chmn. Rocky Mountain Tech. Services Council, Wyo., 1967-69; sci. advisor, Wyo. Gov., 1968-69; vice chmn. YMCA Fairfax County, Va., 1978-82; bd. dirs. YMCA of Metro Washington, 1982—, fin. com. 1983—, treas. 1986—; exec. com. Gettysburg Coll. Parents Council, 1985—. Served with USAF, 1957-61. Recipient Disting. Service award YMCA Metro Washington, 1985. Mem. AAAS, Nat. Assn. Bus. Economists, Am. Mgmt. Assn., Am. Econs. Assn., Bus. Planning Forum, Northern Va. Advanced Tech. Assn. (v.p. programs, 1986—). Club: Nat. Economists. Lodge: Rotary (pres. 1976-77). Home: 6432 Quincy Pl Falls Church VA 22042 Office: Shriner-Midland Co 1825 Eye St NW Washington DC 20006

SHROFF, FIROZ SARDAR, merger and acquisition professional; b. Karachi, Pakistan, Feb. 27, 1950; s. Sardar Mohammad Shroff and Kulsum (Bano) Dhanji; m. Munira Firoz, Oct. 27, 1977; children: Khurram, Sara, Ally. Grad. high sch., Nairobi, Kenya. Apprentice, duty incharge Empire Investment Ltd., Nairobi, 1966-67; asst. mgr. to mgr. Trade Aids Inc., Karachi, 1967-69, asst. gen. mgr., 1969-72; gen. mgr. Canorient Overseas Distbrs. Ltd., London, 1972-74; dir., gen. mgr. Westland Securities Ltd., Nairobi, 1974-75; dep. mng. dir. Sasi Ltd., Karachi, 1975-78; dir. internat. expansion Sasi Group Cos., Karachi, 1978-80, mng. dir., 1984—; dir. operation Key Internat. S.A., London, 1980-84; participant Nat. Book Devel. Council, Singapore, 1980, Arthur D. Little Mgmt. Edn. Inst. and Pakistan Inst. Mgmt., 1986; trustee Sasi Found., Karachi, 1985; developer bus. info. and rsch. ctr.; advisor/cons. various corp. bodies on takeover acquisition of bus. in U.S., U.K. and the Pacific; involved in group discussions on internat. bus. opportunities, contacts in fin. circles. Recipient Cert. Recognition Asia-Pacific Real Estate Congress, 1987. Mem. Pakistan Pubs. and Booksellers Assn. (copyright com. 1975-80), Internat. Real Estate Fedn., Assn. Builders and Developers (convenor 1985), Internat. Real Estate Inst. (chpt. head 1986), Inst. Dirs., Pakistan C. of C. and Industry, United Coop. Credit Soc. (bd. dirs. 1977-79), Property Cons. Soc., Internat. Airline Passengers Assn. Muslim. Clubs: Karachi Golf; Def. Lodge: Rotary. Office: Sasi Group Cos, Sasi House, F-95, Khayaban-e-Roomi, Block-7, Clifton, Karachi 6, Pakistan

SHRONTZ, FRANK ANDERSON, airplane manufacturing executive; b. Boise, Idaho, Dec. 14, 1931; s. Thurlyn Howard and Florence Elizabeth

(Anderson) S.; m. Harriet Ann Houghton, June 12, 1954; children: Craig Howard, Richard Whitaker, David Anderson. Student, George Washington U., 1953; LLB, U. Idaho, 1954; MBA, Harvard U., 1958; postgrad., Stanford U., 1969-70. Asst. contracts coordinator Boeing Co., Seattle, 1958-65, asst. dir. contract adminstrn., 1965-67, asst. to v.p. comml. airplane group, 1967-69, asst. dir. new airplane program, 1969-70, dir. comml. sales operations, 1970-73, v.p. planning and contracts, 1977-78; asst. sec. Dept. Air Force, Washington, 1973-76, Dept. Def., Washington, 1976-77; v.p., gen. mgr. 707/727/737 div. Boeing Comml. Airplane Co., Seattle, 1978-82, v.p. sales and mktg., 1982-84; pres. Comml. Airplane Co. Boeing Div., Seattle, 1986—; pres., chief exec. officer The Boeing Co., Seattle, 1986—, chmn., chief exec. officer, 1988—; bd. dirs. Ctr. for Strategic and Internat. Studies, 1986; mem. adv. bd. Stanford Bus. Sch., 1986; mem. The Bus. Council, 1987. Mem. Bus. Roundtable (policy com.). 1st lt. AUS, 1954-56. Mem. Phi Alpha Delta, Beta Theta Pi. Clubs: Rainier, Overlake Golf and Country, Columbia Tower. Home: 8434 W Mercer Way Mercer Island WA 98040 Office: Boeing Co 7755 E Marginal Way S Seattle WA 98108

SHUEY, JOHN HENRY, graphics products company executive; b. Monroe, Mich., Mar. 14, 1946; s. John Henry and Bertha (Thomas) S.; children: Katherine, John Henry. B.S. in Indsl. Engring., U. Mich., 1968, M.B.A., 1970. With Tex. Instruments Co., Dallas, 1970-74; asst. treas. The Trane Co., La Crosse, Wis., 1974-78, treas., 1978-81, v.p., treas., 1981-83, v.p. fin., chief fin. officer, 1983-86; also v.p., group exec. Am. Standard; sr. v.p. and chief fin. officer AM Internat. Inc., Chgo., 1986—; dir., chmn. audit com. State Bank of La Crosse, 1981-87. Bd. dirs. Pub. Expenditure Survey of Wis., La Crosse, 1980-83; bd. dirs., pres. Luth. Hosp. Found., 1983-87. Mem. Fin. Execs. Inst., Machinery and Allied Products Inst. Congregationalist. Office: AM Internat Inc 333 W Wacker Dr Chicago IL 60606

SHUGART, ALAN F., electronic computing equipment company executive; b. L.A., Sept. 27, 1930. BS in Engring. and Physics, U. Redlands, 1951. Dir. engring. IBM, San Jose, Calif., 1952-69; v.p. Memorex Corp., Sunnyvale, Calif., 1969-73; pres. Shugart Assocs., 1973-78; chmn., chief exec. officer Seagate Tech., Scotts Valley, Calif., 1978—, also bd. dirs. Office: Seagate Tech 920 Disc Dr Scotts Valley CA 95066 *

SHUGRUE, MARTIN ROGER, JR., airline executive; b. Providence, Aug. 31, 1940; s. Martin Roger and Dorothy Elizabeth (Campbell) S.; BA in Econs., Providence Coll., 1962; PhD in Bus. Adminstrn. (hon.), 1987; m. Marianne Zaalberg van Zelst, Mar. 9, 1979; children: Catherine, Michael, Marijke, Martijn. Pilot, flight engr. Pan Am. World Airways, N.Y.C., 1968-70, dir. performance measurements, 1970-72, dir. orgn. planning, 1972-74, staff v.p. corp. personnel, 1974-77, mng. dir. Eastern Central U.S., Washington, 1977-78, mng. dir. U.K. and Western Europe, London, 1978-80, v.p. indsl. relations, N.Y.C., 1980, v.p. personnel, 1980-81, sr. v.p. adminstrn., 1981-82, sr. v.p. mktg., 1982-84, chief operating officer, 1984-88; vice chmn. Pan-Am. Corp., 1984-88; also dir.; pres. Continental Airlines Inc., 1988; bd. dirs. Continental Airlines; bd. dirs. Bus. Council for Internat. Understanding; chmn., bd. dirs. Am./Arab Council for Commerce and Industry; chmn. Govt. Affairs Council of Travel and Tourism Industry; mem. U.S. Senate Adv. Com. for Travel and Tourism; dir. adv. bd. U.S. Travel and Tourism Adminstrn., Dept. Commerce, Pres.'s Commn. on Pvt. Sector Initiatives. Mem. pres.'s council Providence Coll. Served with USN, 1962-68; capt. USNR, 1968—. Mem. Travel Industry Assn. Am. (bd. dirs.), Airline Orgn. Planning and Adminstrn. Assn. (founding), Res. Officers Assn., Assn. for Naval Aviation, Navy League, U.S. C. of C., Westminster C. of C. Clubs: Wings, Sky, Union League. (N.Y.C.); American (London). Home: 3260 Del Monte Houston TX 77019 Office: Continental Airlines Inc 2929 Allen Pkwy Houston TX 77019 *

SHULAR, CRAIG STEVEN, financial executive; b. San Antonio, Nov. 13, 1952; s. Herbert Elton Shular and Susan Ruth (Harris) Davis. BS, SUNY, Buffalo, 1974; MBA, SUNY, 1976. CPA, N.Y. Mgmt. acct. Union Carbide Corp., Niagara Falls, N.Y., 1976-78; prodn. mgr. Union Carbide Corp., Niagara Falls, 1978-79; corp. internal auditor Union Carbide Corp., N.Y.C., 1979-81; country controller Union Carbide Corp., Jakarta, Indonesia, 1981-83; area fin. mgr. ea. div. Union Carbide Corp., Hong Kong, 1983-86; fgn. exchange risk mgr. Union Carbide Corp., Danbury, Conn., 1987—; pvt. practice as tax cons., 1987—. Named Fgn. Exchange Risk Mgr. of Yr. Intermarket Mag., 1987. Mem. Nat. Assn. Accts. (bd. dirs.), Omicron Delta Epsilon, Beta Phi Sigma. Office: Union Carbide Corp 39 Old Ridgebury Rd Sec C-4214 Danbury CT 06817

SHULL, WILLARD CHARLES, III, retailing financial executive; b. St. Paul, Dec. 6, 1940; s. Willard Charles II and Rosanna (Robbins) S.; m. Laurie Jane Syverton, Dec. 17, 1977; children by previous marriage: Martha Williams, Willard Charles IV. B.A., Yale U., 1963; M.B.A., Harvard U., 1965. Budget dir. Archer Daniels Midland Co., Mpls., 1965-69; v.p., treas. Northland Equity Corp., Mpls., 1969-71; mgr. fin. services Dayton Hudson Corp., Mpls., 1971-72, asst. treas., 1972-74, treas., 1974-79, v.p., 1975-76, v.p. fin., 1976-79, sr. v.p. fin., 1979—; bd. dirs. First Trust Co. Hon. bd. mem. Sci. Mus. Minn. Clubs: Minneapolis, Woodhill Country; Yale (N.Y.C.). Office: Dayton-Hudson Corp 777 Nicollet Mall Minneapolis MN 55402

SHULTS, ROBERT LEE, real estate executive, airline executive; b. Helena, Ark., Feb. 23, 1936; s. Albert and Mary Shults; m. Belinda Housley, Aug. 21, 1965; children: Catherine Ann, Robert L. BS in Acctg. magna cum laude, U. Ark.-Fayetteville, 1961. CPA, Ark. Mgr., Arthur Andersen & Co., Memphis, 1961-70; exec. v.p. Allied Telephone Co., Little Rock, 1970-80; chmn. bd. Scheduled Skyways, Inc., Little Rock, 1980-85, chmn. bd., chief exec. officer, Fin. Ctr. Corp., Little Rock, 1980—, cons. Alltel Corp., Little Rock, 1980—; dir. Fin. Ctr. Corp., Air Midwest Inc.; past chmn. bd. Regional Airline Assn., Washington, 1984. Bd. dirs. Ark. Children's Hosp., 1985—, Am. Cancer Soc., Little Rock, 1976—, Inst. Pub. Utilities, Mich. State U., 1976-80; mem. Ark. Arts Ctr.; chmn. bd. trustees Trinity Cathedral, 1982—. Served with USMC, 1956-58. Recipient Pres.'s citation, U.S. Ind. Telephone Assn., 1978, 80. Mem. Am. Inst. CPA's, Fin. Execs. Inst., Nat. Assn. Accts., Mo. Bd. Accts., Tenn. Bd. Accts., Met. Little Rock C. of C., Little Rock Club, The Capital Club, Summit Club, Little Rock Country Club, Rotary (bd. dirs. 1988-89). Episcopalian. Office: Fin Ctr Corp PO Box 56350 Little Rock AR 72215

SHULTZ, LEBERT DEAN, lawyer, industrial company executive; b. Cobleskill, N.Y., Mar. 17, 1942; s. Lebert R. and Ruth (Urquhart) S.; m. Merrily Price Tribble, Jan. 30, 1965; children: David, Pamela. BS, U. Kans., 1964, JD, 1967. Bar: Mo. 1967, Kans. 1981. Assoc. Knipmeyer, McCann & Millett, Kansas City, Mo., 1967-70; gen. counsel Data-Sys-Tance, Inc., Kansas City, 1970-71, Maurice L. Brown Co., Kansas City, 1976-77; atty. Commerce Bancshares, Inc., Kansas City, 1971-74, assoc. gen. counsel, 1974-75; atty. Koch Industries, Inc., Wichita, Kans., 1978-81; assoc. gen. counsel Koch Industries, Inc., Wichita, 1982-87, asst. gen. counsel, 1988—. Mem. ABA, Kans. Bar Assn., Mo. Bar Assn., Internat. Bar Assn., Maritime Law Assn. (proctor), Wichita Bar Assn., St. Louis Bar Assn., Am. Corp. Counsel Soc., Wichita Club, Crestview Country Club. Episcopalian. Home: 8220 Tamarac Ln Wichita KS 67206 Office: Koch Industries Inc 4111 E 37th St N Wichita KS 67220

SHULTZ, ROBERT E., pension asset executive; b. Boston, Mar. 21, 1940; s. Earle Lawrence and Cora (Falconer) S.; m. Nancy Allayne Lee; children: Gary, James, Tracy, Tanya. BSBA, Norwich U., 1961. Mgr. accting. N.Y. Telephone Co., L.I., 1963-70; mgr. fin. ops. N.Y. Telephone Co., Bklyn., 1970-73; gen. fin. supr. N.Y. Telephone Co., N.Y.C., 1973-79; mgr. pension fund adminstrn. Western Electric Co., N.Y.C., 1979-80; dir. U.S. retirement fund IBM Corp., Stamford, Conn., 1980-87; v.p. pension asset mgmt. RJR Nabisco Inc., Atlanta, 1987—; mem. adv. com. N.Y. Stock Exchange, 1988—, client adv. bd. Chase Manhattan Bank, N.Y.C., 1984-87. Trustee 1st Presbyn. Ch., Smithtown, N.Y., 1978-83; scout master Boy Scouts Am., Huntington, N.Y., 1967-73. Capt. U.S. Army, 1961-63. Mem. Nat. Investment Sponsors Fedn. (pres. 1987—), Investment Tech. Assn. (adv. council 1988—), Inst. Quantitative Research Fin. (bd. dirs. 1985—), Employee Retirement Income Security Act Industry Com. (bd. dirs. 1988—), Pension Group East (pres. 1984). Republican. Office: RJR Nabisco Inc 300 Galleria Pkwy Atlanta GA 30339

SHUMAN, JOYCE COLLEEN, savings and loan executive; b. West Union, Ill., Sept. 26, 1928; d. John and Helen (Baber) Coryell; m. Raymond Hiner, Oct. 11, 1947 (div. Feb. 1957); m. Robert E. Shuman, June 14, 1970. Grad. high sch., Indpls. Teller, sec. Shelby Street. Fed. Savs. and Loan, Indpls., 1946-57; office mgr. Gersten Constrn. Co., Ft. Belvoir, Va., 1958-60; sec. Dreyfus Bros. Realty, Washington, 1960-62; office mgr., appraiser trainee Carl G. Harding, MAI, Ft. Lauderdale, Fla., 1963-71; comml. appraiser 1st Fed. of Broward, Ft. Lauderdale, 1975-80; appraisal mgr. 1st Nationwide Savs. and Loan Assn., Deerfield Beach, Fla., 1981; v.p., chief apraiser Hollywood (Fla.) Fed. Savs. and Loan Assn., 1981—. Mem. Am. Soc. Appraisers (pres. 1975-76), Soc. Real Estate Appraisers (sec. 1986-87, 2d v.p. 1987-88, 1st v.p. 1988—). Republican. Home: 2701 NE 58th St Fort Lauderdale FL 33308 Office: Hollywood Fed Savs & Loan Assn 1909 Tyler St Hollywood FL 33020

SHUMAN, STANLEY S., investment banker; b. Cambridge, Mass., June 22, 1935; s. Saul A. and Sarah L. (Saxe) S.; m. Ruth H. Lande, 1967 (div. 1979); children—David Lande, Michael Adam. B.A., Harvard U., Boston, 1956, J.D., 1959, M.B.A., 1961. Bar: Mass. 1959. Exec. v.p., mng. dir. Allen & Co., Inc., N.Y.C., 1961—; bd. dirs. Hudson Gen. Corp., News Corp. Ltd., News Am. Holdings Inc. Mem. Fin. Control Bd., N.Y.C., 1977—; trustee, The Dalton Sch., 1977-1984; hon. trustee The Dalton Sch., 1984—; class agt. Phillips Acad., Andover, Mass., 1972—; pres. Wiltwyck Sch., 1971-78; v.p. exec. com. Jewish Guild for the Blind, 1973-80; trustee Jewish Publication Soc., 1986—; chmn. Nat. Econ. Devel. and Law Ctr., 1978-83. Mem. ABA (comml. arbitration com., sect. corp. banking and bus. law 1974—). Clubs: Harvard (Boston); City Athletic, Quaker Ridge Golf, Harvard (N.Y.C.); East Hampton Tennis. Home: 17 E 73rd St New York NY 10021 Office: Allen & Co Inc 711 Fifth Ave New York NY 10022

SHUMWAY, MICHAEL BRIAN, sales executive; b. Des Moines, Feb. 10, 1961; s. Jerry Lee and Phyllis Jean (Thomas) S.; m. Lee Ann Eisenreich, Oct. 11, 1986. BA, Creighton U., 1983. Sales rep., br. mgr. CFC Polymers Co., North Kansas City, Mo., 1983-89; gen. mgr. CFC Polymers Co., Des Moines, 1989—. Mem. Soc. Plastics Engrs. (bd. dirs. 1987—). Home: 3424 SW 31st St Des Moines IA 50321 Office: 512 Tuttle Des Moines IA 50309

SHUPPERT, SCOTT ANTHONY, sales executive; b. Hastings, Minn., Nov. 3, 1958; s. Paul Ray and Mary Jo (Steekler) S.; m. Patty Parsons, July 31, 1988. BEE, U. Minn., 1981. Asst. sales mgr. Audio King, Mpls., 1982-85; with outside sales staff Valcom Computer Ctr., Springfield, Mo., 1985-86; dir. computer aided design sales Entre Computer Ctr., Dallas, 1985-86; dir. sales The Gt. Softwestern Co., Denton, Tex., 1986—; ind. cons., Dallas, 1985—. Contbr. articles to profl. jours. Mem. IEEE. Republican. Home: 4436 Denver St Plano TX 75075 Office: Gt Softwestern Co 207 W Hickory St Ste 202 Denton TX 76201

SHUR, WALTER, insurance company executive; b. N.Y.C., Feb. 1, 1929; m. Ruth Schram, Aug. 28, 1949; children: Robert, Richard, James. B.S., U. Tex., 1949, M.A., 1951; grad., Advanced Mgmt. Program, Harvard U., 1975. With N.Y. Life Ins. Co., N.Y.C., 1952—, asst. actuary, 1956-59, asso. actuary, 1959-62, actuary, 1962-64, group actuary, 1964-65, 2d v.p., group actuary, 1965-69, v.p. in charge group ins., 1969-71, sr. v.p. in charge individual ins. ops., 1971-74, exec. v.p., 1974-81, exec. v.p., chief actuary, 1981—. Fellow Soc. Actuaries; mem. Am. Acad. Actuaries. Office: NY Life Ins Co 51 Madison Ave New York NY 10010

SHUSTER, JOHN A., civil engineer; b. Santa Fe, Jan. 18, 1939; S. William H. and Selma (Dingee) S.; m. Carol Habberiey, July 1958 (div. Feb. 1960); m. Susan Handy Shuster, Aug. 20, 1962; children: David Brian, Karen. Student, U. N.Mex., 1961-63; BCE, U. Alaska, 1965; MCE, Stanford U., 1966. Registered profl. civil engr., Alaska, Calif., R.I., Mass., Va., Washington, Wis. Project engr. Woodward Clyde Assocs., Oakland, Calif., 1966-67, sr. project engr., 1969-72; resident project engr. Soil Cons. of S.E. Asia, Bangkok, Thailand, 1967-69; v.p. engring. Am. Drilling Co., Providence, 1972-74, also bd. dirs.; exec. v.p. Terrafreeze Corp., Lorton, Va., 1974-79, also bd. dirs.; pres. Geocentric Engring. Corp., Newington, Va., 1979—; vis. lectr. on constrn. ground freezing and related techs., numerous univs. and profl. assns., 1975-88; bd. dirs. Geofreeze Corp., Lorton. Contbr. numerous tech. papers to internat. confs. Bd. dirs. Harbor View Civic Assn., Lorton, 1974-79; sect. dir. Operation Zap The Blackstone, Providence, 1972. Served with U.S. Army, 1957-61. Mem. ASCE, Internat. Soc. Soil Mechanics and Founds., Engring. Inst. Can., Am. Underground Space Assn. (charter), Deep Founds. Inst., Nat. Rsch. Coun. Transp. Rsch. Bd., Internat. Organizing Com. for Ground Freezing (internat. contractors rep.), Harbor View Recreation Club (bd. dirs. 1977-80). Democrat. Unitarian.

SHUSTERMAN, NATHAN, underwriter, financial consultant; b. Montreal, Que., Can., Aug. 27, 1927; came to U.S., 1950; s. Aaron and Annie (Nulman) S.; m. Norma Thalblum, Jan. 1950; children: Mark D., Claudia S. Student, Sir George Williams Coll., Montreal, 1944-47; grad. N.Y. Inst. Fin. CLU, chartered fin. cons. Retailing mgr. Jefferson Stores, Miami, Fla., 1950-65; gen. agt. Protective Life Ins. Co., Miami, 1965—, also chmn. agts. adv. com.; fin. and estate planning cons.; pres. Am. Fin. Counseling Corp., Miami; instr. in estate and tax planning Am. Coll., Bryn Mawr, Pa., 1972—, U. Miami, Coral Gables, Fla., 1972—; registered rep. Protective Equity Services Inc. Mem. North Dade- South Broward Estate Planning Council. Named Man of Yr., Gen. Agts. and Mgrs. Assn., Miami, 1965-67. Mem. Million Dollar Round Table (life), Top of Table, Assn. Advanced Life Underwriting, Am. Soc. CLU's and Chartered Fin. Cons. (past pres. Miami chpt.), Nat. Assn. Life Underwriters (Nat. Sales Achievement award, Nat. Quality award), Fla. Assn. Life Underwriters, Miami Assn. Life Underwriters, Internat. Assn. Fin. Planners, Am. Soc. Pension Actuaries (assoc.), Internat. Platform Assn. Club: Optimists (pres. 1971) (North Miami Beach, Fla.). Lodges: Masons, Shriners, B'nai B'rith (pres. 1950) (Miami). Home: 2320 NE 196th St North Miami Beach FL 33180 Office: Am Fin Counseling Corp 16121 NE 18th Ave North Miami Beach FL 33162

SHUTE, DAVID, retail executive, lawyer; b. Crystal, Mich., Feb. 6, 1931; s. Bert M. and Bessie M. (Gleason) S.; m. Lorna Mae Lesnick (div. Apr. 1976); children: David K., Douglas R.; m. Roxanne J. Decyk (div. June 1987). BA, Princeton U., 1953; JD, U. Mich., 1959. Assoc., then ptnr. Foley & Lardner, Milw., 1959-81; sr. v.p., gen. counsel Seraco Enterprise Inc., Chgo., 1981, Coldwell Banker Real Estate Group, Chgo., 1982-84, Sears Consumer Fin. Corp., Lincolnshire, Ill., 1984-86; corp. gen. counsel Sears Roebuck and Co., Chgo., 1987—, v.p., 1987-88, sr. v.p., sec., 1988—. Mem. adv. com. Corp. Counsel Ctr., Northwestern U. Sch. Law, Chgo., 1987—, chmn. planning com. Corp. Counsel Inst., 1987—; mem. adv. bd. Nat. Ctr. Fin. Svcs., U. Calif., Berkeley, 1988—, Chgo. Vol. Legal Svcs. Found., 1988; vice chmn. New City YMCA, Chgo.; mem. lawyers com. Nat. Ctr. for State Cts., Washington, 1987. Lt. (j.g.) USNR, 1953-56. Mem. ABA (com. on corp. law depts.), Ill. Bar Assn., Chgo. Bar Assn., Assn. Gen. Counsel, Am. Enterprise Inst. (mem. fin. svcs. adv. com.), The Law Club, Economic Club of Chgo., Saddle and Cycle Club, Metropolitan Club. Home: 1448 N Lake Shore Dr #10C Chicago IL 60610 Office: Sears Roebuck & Co Sears Tower 68th fl Chicago IL 60684 *

SHUTT, EDWIN HOLMES, JR., consumer products executive; b. St. Louis, July 28, 1927; s. Edwin Holmes and Louise Davenport (Tebbetts) S.; m. Mary Truesdale, Oct. 12, 1953; children: Mary Anne, Edward Truesdale, Amy Louise. BS in Engring., Princeton U., 1950. Mgr. internat. div. for Asia and Latin Am., then v.p. internat. Procter & Gamble Co., Cin., 1968-77; exec. v.p., then pres., chief exec. officer Clorox Co., Oakland, Calif., 1977-81; pres. Tambrands, Inc., Lake Success, N.Y., 1981-89; chief exec. officer Tambrands, Inc., Lake Success, 1982-87, chmn., chief exec. officer, 1987-89; mem. adv. bd. Bus. Sch., U. Calif.-Berkeley, 1980-81; bd. dirs. BTC Diagnostics Inc., 1984-85. Pres. Cin. Coun. World Affairs, 1975-77, Princeton Club So. Ohio, 1976-77; mem. exec. coun. San Francisco Bay Area council Boy Scouts Am., 1980-81, exec. bd. Nassau County coun., 1981—, pres., 1985—; bd. dirs. Oakland Mus. Assn., 1981, Friends of the Arts, 1983-87, Nassau County Mus. Fine Arts, 1986-88, L.I. Assn., 1987—; L.I. Philharm., 1982—. With USNR, 1945-46; with AUS, 1950-52. Mem. L.I. Assn. (bd. dirs. 1987-89), Grocery Mfrs. of Am. (bd. dirs. 1980, 1986—), Phi Beta Kappa. Republican. Clubs: Pacific Union (San Francisco); Creek; Univ. Cottage (Princeton). Office: Tambrands Inc 1 Marcus Ave Lake Success NY 11042

SHYMKUS, JAMES LOWERY, advertising agency executive; b. Chgo., Apr. 5, 1939; s. Frank W. and Margaret (Lowery) S.; m. Karen Siebert, Jan. 24, 1962; children: Tracy, Marni, Timothy. B.S., Miami U., 1961; postgrad., Harvard U., 1974. With Leo Burnett Co., Chgo., 1961—, exec. v.p., 1981—, also bd. dirs. Served with USMCR, 1962-68. Mem. Alpha Epsilon Pi, Phi Gamma Delta. Republican. Methodist. Clubs: Chgo. Athletic Assn, Lincolnshire Country. Home: 387 Aberdeen Dr Lincolnshire Crete IL 60417 Office: Leo Burnett Co One Prudential Plaza Chicago IL 60601 *

SIALOM, SEDAT SAMI, advertising executive; b. Istanbul, Turkey, Dec. 14, 1940; s. Elie Guy and Sarah (Barzilay) S.; M in Econs., Istanbul U., 1961; Technicien en Publicite, Ecole Superieure Technique de Puplicite, Brussels, 1963; 1 child from previous marriage, Sandy; m. Cana Lakse, Mar. 3, 1985; 1 child, Selin. Account exec. Bodden Et Dechy S.A., Brussels, Belgium, 1962-63, D.T.V., London, 1963-64; account dir., group dir. Client Contract dir. Grafika-Maya A.S., Istanbul, Turkey, 1964-70, vice chmn., 1970-73, chmn., 1973; chmn. Grafika-Lintas A.S., 1987—; cons. in field. Served with Turkish Navy, 1960-61. Recipient Rizzoli award, 1972. Mem. Internat. Advt. Assn., Turkish Advt. Assn., Turkish Mgmt. Assn., Internat. C. of C. Office: Maslak Meydani #41, 80620 Levent Istanbul Turkey

SIANO, JERRY J., advertising agency executive. Vice chmn. NW Ayer, Inc., 1987-89, pres., chief exec. officer, 1989— Office: NW Ayer Inc 1345 Ave of the Americas New York NY 10105

SIART, WILLIAM ERIC BAXTER, banker; b. Los Angeles, Dec. 25, 1946; s. William Ernest and Barbara Vesta (McPherson) Baxter; m. Noelle Ellen Reid, Sept. 17, 1966; children—Shayne Allison, Tiffany Ann. B.A. in Econs., U. Santa Clara, 1968; M.B.A., U. Calif., Berkeley, 1969. With Bank of Am., 1969-78; v.p. corp. banking Bank of Am., Brussels, 1977-78; sr. v.p. charge mktg. Western Bancorp, Los Angeles, 1978-81; pres., chief operating officer First Interstate Bank of Nev. N.A., Reno, 1981-82; formerly pres., chief exec. officer First Interstate Bank of Nev. N.A., 1982—; now chmn., pres., chief exec. officer First Interstate Bank Calif., L.A., also bd. dirs. Trustee U. Nev.-Reno Found.; bd. dirs. Sierra Arts Found. Mem. Am. Bankers Assn. (mem. govt. relations council), Reno-Sparks C. of C. (dir.). Republican. Roman Catholic. Office: First Interstate Bank Calif 707 Wilshire Blvd Los Angeles CA 90017 *

SIBBALD, JOHN RISTOW, management consultant; b. Lincoln, Nebr., June 20, 1936; s. Garth E.W. and Rachel (Wright) S.; B.A., U. Nev., 1958; M.A., U. Ill., 1964; divorced; children—Allison, John. Office mgr. Hewitt Assos., Libertyville, Ill., 1964-66; coll. relations mgr. Pfizer Inc., N.Y.C., 1966-69; pres., chief exec. officer Re-Con Systems, N.Y.C., 1969-70; v.p. Booz, Allen & Hamilton, N.Y.C., 1970-73, Chgo., 1973-75; pres., founder John Sibbald Assos., Inc., Chgo., 1975—. Served to capt. AUS, 1958-64. Mem. Met. Club Chgo., St. Louis Club. Episcopalian. Office: 8725 Higgins Rd Chicago IL 60631

SIBLANO, LINDA MARIE, banker; b. N.Y.C., Feb. 21, 1953; d. Joseph Michael and Angela Gloria (Deluca) S. BS, Marymount Coll., 1987. With Dime Savs. Bank, 1974—; supr. Dime Savs. Bank, Bklyn., 1981-82; ops. officer and liaison Dime Savs. Bank, N.Y.C., 1982-83, ops. adminstr., 1983-84, asst. v.p., br. mgr., 1984-85, v.p., br. mgr., 1985-86; 1st v.p., mortgage sales mgr. Dime Savs. Bank, Port Washington, N.Y., 1986—. Mem. L.I. Bd. Realtors, L.I. Assn. Profl. Mortgage Women, Nat. Assn. Female Execs., Am. Mgmt. Assn., Bklyn. Hist. Soc. (bd. dirs., trustee 1984-86). Democrat. Roman Catholic.

SIBOLSKI, JOHN ALFRED, JR., educational association executive; b. Pittsfield, Mass., Nov. 4, 1946; s. John A. and Isabelle Barcaster S.; A.A. in Data Processing, Andover Inst. of Bus., 1966; B.S. in Tech. of Mgmt., Am. U., 1967, cert. in data processing, 1974, grad. cert. in data processing, 1978; m. Elizabeth Gallup, Aug. 15, 1970. With Automated Systems Corp., Washington, 1969-71, KMS Tech. Center, Arlington, Va., 1971-72; ind. cons., 1972-73, 74-76; with Law Enforcement Assistance Adminstrn., Dept. Justice, Washington, 1973-74, D.A. Lewis, Assos., Clinton, Md., 1974; with Bur. of Nat. Affairs, Inc., Washington, 1976-80; mgr. systems devel. NEA, Washington, 1980—. Recipient spl. achievement award Dept. Justice, 1974. Mem. Data Processing Mgmt. Assn., Am. Soc. for Info. Sci. Home: 565 Wayward Dr Annapolis MD 21401 Office: NEA 1201 16th St NW Washington DC 20036

SICHENZE, CELESTE MARIE, business educator; b. Bklyn., Aug. 28, 1937; d. Louis R. and Carmela M. (Esposito) Costagliola; m. John Anthony Sichenze, July 4, 1959; children: John A. II, Louis D., Andrea C. BS in Gen. Bus. cum laude, L.I. U., 1959, MS in Bus. Adminstrn. cum laude, 1965; PhD, George Washington U., 1988. Adminstrv. asst. to v.p., provost L.I. U., 1959-61; tchr. adult edn. Manchester (Mass.) Schs., 1965-68; tchr. Pingree Sch., Hamilton, Mass., 1968-71; substitute tchr. Fairfax City (Va.) Pub. Schs., 1972-74; from lectr. to prof. bus. mgmt. No. Va. Community Coll., Annandale, 1974—. Contbr. articles to profl. jours. Mem. Fairfax County Fedn. Citizens Assn., bus. mgmt. curriculum adv. com. No. Va. Community Coll.; pres. Carriage Hill Civic Assn., Vienna, Va., 1975-76, 88—, v.p. 1985-86, Oakton High Sch. PTA, Vienna, 1977-79; chmn. ways and means com. Oakton High Sch. Band Boosters, Vienna, 1980-83. Named an Outstanding Young Woman of Am., Chgo., 1969. Mem. Am. Mgmt. Assn., Indsl. Relations Research Assn., Va. Community Coll. Assn. (chmn. research and publs. commn. 1984-86). Roman Catholic. Home: 2020 Post Rd Vienna VA 22180 Office: No Va Community Coll 8333 Little River Turnpike Annandale VA 22003

SICILIANO, A. VINCENT, banker; b. Washington, July 19, 1950; s. Rocco Carmine and Marion Stiebel; m. Susan Campbell; 1 child, Michael Carmine. BA, Stanford U., 1972, BS, 1972; MLA, U. Calif., Berkeley, 1976. Spl. asst. Dept. Commerce, U.S. Govt., Washington, 1972-73; energy planner, spl. cons. Calif. Coastal Commn., San Francisco, 1974; various positions with Bank Am., Manila, Singapore, 1976-84; v.p., mgr. corp. banking office Bank Am., San Diego, 1984-86; pres., chief exec. officer Internat. Savs. Bank, San Diego, 1986—. Contbr. articles to profl. jours. Bd. dirs. World Affairs Coun., San Diego, 1985—, San Diego-Yentai Sister City, 1987—; chmn. Internat. Trade Commn., San Diego, 1988—; vice-chmn. Mus. Photographic Arts, San Diego, 1984—. Honoree Anglo-Am. Successor Generation Program, John Hopkins Sch. Advanced Internat. Studies and Royal Inst. Internat. Affairs, 1987. Republican. Office: Internat Savs 1455 Frazee Rd San Diego CA 92122

SICILIANO, ROCCO CARMINE, business executive, lawyer; b. Salt Lake City, Mar. 4, 1922; s. Joseph Vincent and Mary (Arnone) S.; m. Marion Stiebel, Nov. 8, 1947; children: Loretta, A. Vincent, Fred R., John, Maria. B.A. with honors, U. Utah, 1944; LL.B., Georgetown U., 1948; LHD, Hebrew Union Coll. Bar: D.C. bar 1949. Legal asst. to bd. mem. NLRB, Washington, 1948-50; asst. sec.-treas. Procon Inc., Des Plaines, Ill., 1950-53; asst. sec. labor charge employment and manpower Dept. Labor, Washington, 1953-57; spl. asst. to Eisenhower for personnel mgmt., 1957-59; ptnr. Wilkinson, Cragun & Barker, 1959-69; pres. Pacific Maritime Assn., San Francisco, 1965-69; undersec. of commerce Washington, 1969-71; pres., chmn. bd., chief exec. officer Ticor, Los Angeles, 1971-84; chmn., exec. com. Ticor, 1984-85; of counsel Jones, Day, Reavis & Pogue, 1984-87; chmn. bd., chief exec. officer Am. Health Properties, Inc., 1987-88; bd. dirs. Pacific Enterprises, Am. Med. Internat., United TV, Inc.; mem. Fed. Pay Bd., 1971-73; trustee J. Paul Getty Trust. Vice chmn., bd. dirs. Los Angeles Philharm. Assn.; past chmn. Calif. Bus. Roundtable; trustee Com. for Econ. Devel.; Co. chmn. Calif. Commn. on Campaign Financing. bd. dirs. Mus. Contemporary Art; mem. adv. council Johns Hopkins Sch. Advanced Internat. Studies. Served with AUS, 1943-46; 1st lt., 10th Mountain Div. Italy; personnel officer G-1, Hdqrs., U.S. Forces Austria. Decorated Combat Infantryman Badge, Bronze Star, Army Commendation Ribbon U.S.; Order Merit Italian Republic. Mem. Nat. Acad. Pub. Adminstrn., Nat. Commn. on Pub. Service. Clubs: Met. (Washington); California (Los Angeles). Home: 612 N Rodeo Dr Beverly Hills CA 90210 Office: PO Box 2249 Beverly Hills CA 90213

SIDES, JAMES RALPH, aerospace executive; b. Carbon Hill, Ala., Apr. 17, 1936; s. James Beatty and Ruby (Kilpatrick) S.; m. Martha Sue Ryland,

Nov. 1, 1955; children: James R. Jr., Christopher Kent, Patrick Ryland. BS in Chemistry, U. Ala., 1958. Chemist Thiokol Chem. Corp., Huntsville, Ala., 1958-60; chemist, group leader Amcel Propulsion Co. (subs. Celanese), Asheville, N.C., 1960-65; head process engring., chief mfg. and engring., project office mgr. Atlantic Research Corp., Gainesville, Va., 1965-69, dir. engring., 1969, asst. dir. propulsion div., mgr. engring dept., 1970-78, asst. gen. mgr. propulsion div., dir. engring. dept., 1978-80, v.p., gen. mgr. propulsion div., 1980-85, sr. v.p., gen. mgr. propulsion div., 1985-87, group pres., 1987—. Contbr. articles to profl. jours.; patentee in field. Mem. Dulles Airport Task Force, Va., 1987. Recipinet Cert. of Commendation USAF, 1964. Fellow Am. Inst. Astronautics and Aeronautics; mem. Am. Defense Preparedness Assn. (chmn. missiles and astronautics), Air Force Assn., Assn. U.S. Army, Field Artillery Assn., Navy League, Alpha Chi Sigma. Home: 11133 Tattersall Tr Oakton VA 22124 Office: Atlantic Rsch Corp Propulsion Div 5390 Cherokee Ave Alexandria VA 22312

SIDES, PAUL BLOWERS, retail executive; b. Lubbock, Tex., Dec. 11, 1948; s. Teddy Paul and Betty Louise (Blowers) S.; m. Linda Gayle Weaver, Jan. 13, 1968; 1 child, Teri Lyn Sides Sullivan. Student, U. Houston, 1967-69. Owner, chief exec. officer Sides Supply Inc., San Antonio, 1970—; prin. Wood Products Am., San Antonio, 1983-85, Colortyme Rental, 1981-84; cons. R.L. Schonhoff Mktg., San Antonio, 1983-88; speaker in field. Served with U.S. Army, 1969-70. Mem. San Antonio Builders Assn., NARDA, Nat. Speakers Assn., South Tex. Speakers Assn. Republican. Baptist. Club: Toastmasters (pres. San Antonio chpt. 1982-83, area gov. 1985-86). Home: 6 Royal Crest New Braunfels TX 78130 Office: Sides Supply Inc 611 NWW White Rd San Antonio TX 78219

SIDEWATER, ARTHUR, retail executive; b. Phila., June 15, 1914; s. Iaasic and Fanny S.; m. Estelle Czarzasty; children—June, Jacalyn. Founder, sr. exec. v.p. Charming Shoppes, 1940—. Home: 44 Parkview Rd Cheltenham PA 19012 Office: Charming Shoppes Inc 450 Winks Ln Bensalem PA 19020

SIDNEY, WILLIAM WRIGHT, aerospace company executive; b. Anaconda, Mont., Dec. 31, 1929; s. Paul and Lily Maud (Wright) S.; divorced; children: Kay Elise, Paul Daniel. Student U. Calif., Berkeley, 1953-56. Supr. prodn. Kaiser Aerospace, San Leandro, Calif., 1953-57, project engr., 1957-67, chief engr., 1967-69, gen. mgr., 1969-77; pres. Kaiser Aerotech, San Leandro, Calif., 1977—, Kaiser Space Products, Pueblo, Colo., 1988—. With USN, 1948-52. Recipient NASA Pub. Svc. medal 1981. Mem. U. Calif. Alumni Assn., Smithsonian Assocs., Nat. Audubon Soc., Am. Mus. Natural History. Home: 6025 Ridgemont Dr Oakland Hills CA 94619 Office: 880 Doolittle Dr San Leandro CA 94577

SIEBENEICHER, PAUL ROBERT, 2ND, engineer; b. Houston, Sept. 29, 1943; s. Karl Stephen and Rosa Lee (Jones) S.; m. Catherine Veronica Varallo, Jan. 8, 1966; children: Paul Robert III, Kristen Beth. AS in Engring. Tech., U. Houston, 1968, BS in Tech., 1969. Cert. mfg. engr. Project engr. Am. Can. Co., Morrisville, Pa., 1969-70; asst. plant mgr., indsl. engr. Flexitallic Gasket Co., Camden, N.J., 1971-72; plant engr., plant mgr. Frances Denney Co., Phila., Pa., 1972-73; mgr. ops., plant engr. Camden (N.J.) Iron & Metal, Inc., 1974-77; mgr. maintenance engring. NL Industries, Inc., Pedricktown, N.J., 1977-79; mgr. indsl. engring. Congoleum Corp., Kearny, N.J., 1979-80; engr. in-charge Mech. Bur. of Inspection State of N.J., Burlington County, 1980—; dir. corp. engring., facilities, indsl. and mfg. engring. Infotron Systems Corp., Cherry Hill, N.J.; adj. faculty instr. Glassboro State Coll.; chmn. bd., pres. Southern N.J. Tech. Consortium, Pleasantville, 1986—; lectr. in field. Contbr. articles to profl. jours. Dir., Goodwill Industries of Southern N.J., Camden, 1973-76, v.p. ops., 1974-76; mem. Vols. for Internat. Assistance, Washington, 1967—, Camden County YMCA; mem. indsl. adv. tech. com. Glassboro State Coll., 1979—, indsl. tech. adv. com., 1988—, adv. com. Liberal Arts Dept., 1988—; mem. CIM indsl. adv. com., Camden County Coll., 1988—; vol. N.J. Sheltered Workshop for the Handicapped. With USN, 1963-65; also USAF. Recipient Garden State Commerce and Industry award N.J. Gov.'s Office, 1988. Vol. Orgn. of the Year award Goodwill Indsutries. Fellow Inst. Indsl. Engrs. (dir. profl. devel. 1972—, dir. area 1, dist. 2 1982—, sr. mem., chmn. bd., pres. South Jersey Chpt. 1988—, past v.p., trustee bd. dirs. 1980-82, recipient Excellence award 1977, 84, 85, 87, 88); mem. Soc. Mfg. Engrs. (sr. mem., cert.), Bldg. Officials Code Adminstrsn. Internat., Assn. Records Mgrs. and Adminstrs., Explorers Club, Hutton Hill Club, NRA (life). Roman Catholic. Home: 143 Canterbury Rd Mount Laurel NJ 08054-1414 Office: Infotron Systems Corp Cherry Hill Indsl Ctr-9 Cherry Hill NJ 08003-1688

SIEBERN, ROBERT ANTHONY, financial planning consultant; b. N.Y.C., July 31, 1931; s. Clarence F. and Mary D. (Quinn) S.; m. Roberta Gold, Sept. 1, 1955 (div. Sept. 1960); children: Leslie, Janet; m. Marlene F. Lasby, Sept. 19, 1966. LLB, U. Chgo., 1969. Cert. fin. planner; registered fin. planner. Montgomery Ward ops. mgr. E.B.S. Tax Svcs. Inc., St. Petersburg, Fla., 1970-73; nat. ops. mgr. Montgomery Ward Tax Svcs., St. Petersburg, 1973-76; gen. ptnr. Ober & Siebern, St. Petersburg, 1976-81; pres. R.A. Siebern & Assocs. Inc., St. Petersburg, 1981-85; pvt. fin. planning cons. Tampa Bay, Fla., 1985—; bd. dirs. C.A. Turner Svcs., Clearwater, Fla. With U.S. Army, 1953-55. Mem. Inst. Cert. Fin. Planners (pres. 1988), Internat. Assn. Registered Fin. Planners, Tampa Bay Soc., Rotary.

SIEBERT, MURIEL, business executive, former state official; b. Cleve.; d. Irwin J. and Margaret Eunice (Roseman) Siebert; student Western Res. U., 1949-52; D.C.S. (hon.), St. John's U., St. Bonaventure U., Molloy Coll., Adelphi St. Francis Coll., Mercy Coll. Security analyst Bache & Co., 1954-57; analyst Utilities & Industries Mgmt. Corp., 1958, Shields & Co., 1959-60; partner Stearns & Co., 1961, Finkle & Co., 1962-65, Brimberg & Co., N.Y.C., 1965-67; individual mem. (first woman mem.) N.Y. Stock Exchange, 1967; chmn., pres. Muriel Siebert & Co., Inc., 1969-77; trustee Manhattan Savs. Bank, 1975-77; supt. banks, dept. banking State of N.Y., 1977-82; dir. Urban Devel. Corp., N.Y.C., 1977-82, Job Devel. Authority, N.Y.C., 1977-82, State of N.Y. Mortgage Agy., 1977-82; chmn., pres. Muriel Siebert & Co., Inc., 1983—; assoc. in mgmt. Simmons Coll.; mem. adv. com. Fin. Acctg. Standards Bd., 1981; guest lectr. numerous colls. Mem. women's adv. com. Econ. Devel. Adminstrn., N.Y.C.; trustee Manhattan Coll.; v.p., mem. exec. com. Greater N.Y. Area council Boy Scouts Am.; mem. N.Y. State Econ. Devel. Bd., N.Y. Council Economy; bd. overseers NYU Sch. Bus., 1984-88; bd. dirs. United Way of N.Y.C.; trustee Citizens Budget Commn.; mem. bus. com. Met. Mus. Recipient Spirit of Achievement award Albert Einstein Coll. Medicine, 1977; Women's Equity Action League award, 1978; Outstanding Contbns. to Equal Opportunity for Women award Bus. Council of UN Decade for Women, 1979; Silver Beaver award Boy Scouts Am., 1981; Elizabeth Cutter Morrow award YWCA, 1983; Emily Roebling award Nat. Women's Hall of Fame, 1984; NOW Legal Def. and Edn. Fund award, 1981, Brotherhood award Nat. Conf. of Christians and Jews, 1989. Mem. River Club, Doubles Club, Nat. Arts Club, Econ. Club. Home: 435 E 52nd St New York NY 10022 Office: Muriel Siebert & Co Inc 444 Madison Ave New York NY 10022

SIEBRASSE, RICHARD W., food products executive; b. Quincy, Ill., 1926. Grad., Augustana Coll., Rock Island, Ill., 1951. Pres. Best Foods N.Am.; formerly exec. v.p. CPC Internat. Inc., Englewood Cliffs, N.J.; now vice-chmn. CPC Internat. Inc., Englewood Cliffs, also bd. dirs. Office: CPC Internat Inc International Plaza Englewood Cliffs NJ 07632 *

SIECKMANN, WALTER, industrial manufacturing and engineering company executive; b. Duesseldorf, Germany, June 7, 1931; came to U.S., 1958; s. Heinrich and Erni (Neschen) S.; M.S. in Metallurgy, Tech. Hochschule Aachen, 1958; m. Edith Erdelyi, July 28, 1956; children—Michael, Martin. Metallurgist, Crucible Steel Co., 1958-59; project engr., dir. vacuum process dept. Lectromelt Corp., 1959-65, pres., 1967-69; exec. v.p. Heraeus-Engelhard Co., 1965-67; sr. v.p. Pa. Engring. Corp., 1967-69, exec. v.p., chief operating officer, 1969—; group exec. v.p. NVF Co., Sharon Steel Corp., Pa. Engring. Corp., 1983—; chief operating officer, exec. v.p., dir. Birdsboro Corp.; v.p., dir. Alaska Gold Co.; dir. Chesapeake Ins. Co., Ltd.; sr. v.p. DWG Corp.; sr. v.p., dir. Evans Products Co., Mueller Brass Co.; dir. Salem Corp., Sharon Steel Corp. Birdsboro Corp. Mem. Am. Iron and Steel Inst. (dir.), Am. Iron and Steel Engrs., AIME. Clubs: Duquesne, Univ. (Pitts.); St. Clair Country (Upper St. Clair, Pa.); Edeworth (Sewickley, Pa.). Home: Treetops RD 5 Sewickley PA 15143 Office: NVF Co PO Box 4055 Pittsburgh PA 15201 also: NVF Co Yorklyn Rd Yorklyn DE 19736

SIEFERT, DIANE LYNN, accountant; b. S.I., N.Y., Nov. 8, 1948; d. George Vincent and Dorothy (Bauer) Stergious; m. Edward George Siefert, Nov. 9, 1968; children: Jennifer Lynn, Edward Charles. BS in Acctg. and Sociology, La. State U., 1983. Credit analyst Hallgarten and Co., N.Y.C., 1967-69; acctg. supt. comml. air conditioning div. Singer Co., Carteret, N.J., 1969-74; owner, pres. D.L. Siefert Acctg., Carteret, N.J., 1971-80, Baton Rouge, 1980—; acctg. mgr. Kean Miller Hawthorne D'Armond, McCowan & Jarman, Baton Rouge, 1983-85; v.p. fin. KJM Inc. doing bus. as Baton Rouge Mag., 1986-88; owner, pres. DLS Mktg. Co., Baton Rouge, 1987—; part-time owner, pres. D.L. Siefert Acctg. Svcs., Carteret, 1971-80. Mem. VIP Vols. in Pub. Schs., East Baton Rouge Parish, 1987-88; bd. dirs. Camelot Civic Assn., Baton Rouge, 1983-85; tutor Southeast Middle Sch., Baton Rouge, 1987-88. Mem. NAFE, Nat. Assn. Acct., Am. Soc. Women Accts., Women's Info. and Networking Groups (co-founder/pres. 1987—), Am. Bus. Women's Assn. (past treas., v.p., pres., del. nat. conv. 1985-86, 87-88, Woman of Yr. award Baton Rouge 1987), La. State U. Alumni Found., Camelot Garden Club (pres. Baton Rouge 1983). Home and Office: 2746 Lancelot Dr Baton Rouge LA 70816

SIEFERT-KAZANJIAN, DONNA, corporate librarian; b. N.Y.C.; d. Merrill Emil and Esther (Levins) S.; m. George John Kazanjian, June 15, 1974; 1 child, Merrill George. BA, NYU, 1969; MSLS, Columbia U., 1973; MBA, Fordham U., 1977. Asst. librarian Dun & Bradstreet, N.Y.C., 1969-73; research assoc. William E. Hill & Co., N.Y.C., 1973-76; sr. info. analyst Info. for Bus., N.Y.C., 1976-77; librarian Handy Assocs., N.Y.C., 1979—. Chmn. Cub Scout pack 49 Boy Scouts Am., Bayside, N.Y., 1987—. Mem. Bus. & Fin Group Spl. Librs. Assn. (chmn. pub. rels. com.), Rsch.Roundtable, Am. Mensa Ltd. Roman Catholic. Office: Handy Assocs 250 Park Ave New York NY 10177

SIEFKIN, WILLIAM CHARLES, oil and chemical company executive, author, marketing consultant; b. Glendale, Calif., Jan. 15, 1946; s. Ernest Roosevelt and Violet May (Richardson) S.; m. Deborah Sue Olinger, Dec. 21, 1971; children: Barbra Anne, Katherine Marie, William Andrew. BBA, Calif. Polytech. U., San Luis Obispo, 1968; postgrad., U. Del., 1985. Tech. rep. photo products dept. Du Pont, Houston and San Antonio, 1968-71; sr. tech. rep. photo products dept. Du Pont, Louisville, 1971-73; sr. export sales rep. photo products dept. internat. ops. div. Du Pont, Wilmington, Del., 1973-74; tech. sales mgr. internat. dept. Du Pont, Tokyo, 1974-79; internat. planning mgr. photo systems and electronics dept. Du Pont, Wilmington, 1979-85, mktg. mgr. imaging systems dept., 1985-87, mgr. sales devel. corp. plans dept., 1987—; pres., bd. dirs., chief cons. Montchanin Corp., Wilmington, 1981—; mem. adv. bd. Calif. Poly. State U. sch. graphic communications. Life mem., dir. Rep. Nat. Com., Washington, 1985; v.p. Jr. Achievement Del. (Bronze Nat. Leadership award 1985), Wilmington, 1986. Named Honored Alumni of the Year Calif. Polytech. U. Sch. Bus., 1984. Mem. Antique Automobile Club of Am. (life), Mensa, Brandywine Pops Orchestra. Republican. Methodist. Club: Mercedes-Benz Club of Am. Home: 717 Foxdale Rd Edenridge III Wilmington DE 19803-1603 Office: EI DuPont de Nemours & Co Inc Corp Plans Dept DuPont Bldg 2165 Wilmington DE 19898-0001

SIEGEL, ABRAHAM J., economics educator, academic administrator; b. N.Y.C., Nov. 6, 1922; s. Samuel J. and Dora (Drach) S.; m. Lillian Wakshull, Dec. 22, 1946; children: Emily Jean Siegel Stangle, Paul Howard, Barbara Ann Pugliese. B.A. summa cum laude, CCNY, 1943; M.A., Columbia U., 1949; Ph.D., U. Calif., Berkeley, 1961. Instr. dept. econs. CCNY, 1947-49; research economist Inst. Indsl. Relations, U. Calif., Berkeley, 1952-54; instr. dept. econs. M.I.T., Cambridge, 1954-56, asst. prof., 1956-59, assoc. prof., 1959-64, prof. dept. econs. Sloan Sch. Mgmt., 1964—, assoc. dean Sloan Sch. Mgmt., 1967-80, acting dean, 1980-81, dean, 1981-87; spl. lectr. Trade Union Program, Harvard U., 1961-64; vis. prof. Brandeis U., 1956-60; vis. prin. mem. dir. Internat. Inst. Labour Studies, Internat. Labor Office, Geneva, 1964-65; asso. staff dir. Com. Econ. Devel., Study Group on Nat. Labor Policy, 1960-61; trustee, chmn. adminstrv. com. M.I.T. Retirement Plan for Staff Mems., 1970—. Co-author: Industrial Relations in the Pacific Coast Longshore Industry, 1956, The Public Interest in National Labor Policy, 1961, The Impact of Computers on Collective Bargaining, 1969, Unfinished Business: An Agenda for Labor, Management and the Public, 1978. Bd. dirs. Whitehead Inst. Biomed. Rsch.; Analysis Group, Inc.; Adams Russell Electronics; Internat. Data Group; Syska & Hennessy, Inc.; mem. adv. internat. adv. group Inst. for Applied Systems Analysis, Laxenburg, Austria; mem. Framingham Sch. Com., South Middlesex Regional Dist. Vocat. Sch. Com., 1968-71. Served with USAF, 1943-46. Mem. Am. Econ. Assn., Indsl. Relations Research Assn., Nat. Acad. Arbitrators, Am. Arbitration Assn. (mem. various panels), Inst. Mgmt. Scis. Bus. Roundtable (exec. com.), Phi Beta Kappa. Clubs: Comml, St. Botolph's. Home: 112 Gardner Rd Brookline MA 02146 Office: MIT Sloan Sch Mgmt 50 Memorial Dr Cambridge MA 02139

SIEGEL, ARTHUR HERBERT, accounting company executive; b. N.Y.C., Jan. 5, 1938; s. Joseph Kenneth and Gertrude Sylvia (Hecker) S.; m. Eleanor Novick, June 5, 1960; children: Joan Aileen, Linda Beth, Mark Eric. AB, Columbia, 1958, MBA, 1960. With Price Waterhouse, N.Y.C., 1960-61, mgr., L.I., 1961-72, ptnr., Boston, 1972-83, nat. dir. acctg. services, N.Y.C., 1984-88, vice-chmn. acctg. and auditing services, 1988—; mem. Fin. Acctg. Standards Bd. Emerging Issues Task Force, 1985-88, Fin. Acctg. Standards Adv. Council; mem. adv. council Sch. Acctg. U. So. Calif. Past trustee, treas., 1st v.p. Temple Beth Avodah, Newton Centre, Mass. Mem. AICPA (chmn. task force on risks and uncertainties, mem. SEC practice exec. com.), N.Y. Soc. CPA's (Silver Medal award), Mass. Soc. CPA's (pres.-elect 1983), Beta Gamma Sigma. Home: 179 E 70th St New York NY 10021 Office: Price Waterhouse 1251 Ave of the Americas New York NY 10020

SIEGEL, CHARLES HOLLADAY, wholesale company executive; b. Balt., Dec. 13, 1941; s. Rudolph Augustus and Elsie Marion (Kasten) S.; m. Mary Ann Garvin, Sept. 2, 1967; children: Emily Hughes, Charles H. Jr., Margaret Shafer. BA, Yale U., 1963, LLB, 1966. Bar: Ga., 1966. Carpet mgr. The R.A. Siegel Co., Atlanta, 1969-73, chmn., exec. v.p., 1973-80, chmn., pres., and chief exec. officer, 1980—. Bd. dirs. Atlanta Symphony Orch., 1978-84, 87—, mem. exec. com. 1978-84; bd. dirs. Atlanta Hosp. Hospitality House; vice chmn. bd. Galloway Sch., Atlanta, 1985—; mem. Cathedral of St. Philip. Served as 1st lt. with USAF, 1966-69. Mem. Young Pres. Orgn., Piedmont Driving Club, Yale Club of Ga., Yale Club of N.Y.C., Rotary (local pres. 1985-86). Republican. Episcopalian. Office: 1175 Chattahoochee Ave NW PO Box 19753 Sta N Atlanta GA 30325

SIEGEL, EDWARD MALCOLM, lawyer; b. N.Y.C., Apr. 14, 1934; s. Charles and Rose (Fritzhand) S.; m. Elyse R. Roth, Mar. 9, 1969; children: Eric, Eve-Lynn. BA, Columbia Coll., 1955; MA, Columbia U., 1957, JD, 1960. Bar: N.Y. 1961. Legal asst. to dean Columbia U. Law Sch., N.Y.C., 1960-65; gen. counsel Transp. Displays, Inc., N.Y.C., 1965-75, corp. sec., 1968-75, v.p., 1972-73, sr. v.p., 1973-75; pub. affairs mgr. J.C. Penney Co., N.Y.C., 1975-77; gen. counsel, corp. sec. Electro Audio Dynamics, Inc., Great Neck, N.Y., 1977-85, v.p., 1981-85; v.p. legal affairs East View Co., N.Y.C., 1985-87; ptnr. Bangser & Weiss (formerly Danziger, Bangser & Weiss), N.Y.C., 1988—. Mem. N.Y. State Bar Assn., Columbia Law Sch. Alumni Assn. (dir. 1966-70). Home: 1036 Park Ave Apt 6D New York NY 10028 Office: Bangser & Weiss 230 Park Ave Ste 2600 New York NY 10169

SIEGEL, JOEL ROBERT, marketing executive; b. Bklyn., June 6, 1942; s. William and Lillian (Kochmalnick) S.; m. Pearl Rosenkranz, Aug. 19, 1967; children: Lynn, Susan. BS in Physics and Elec. Engring., CUNY, 1970. Application engr. Holophane Co., Inc., N.Y.C., 1962-65, asst. to v.p. research, 1965-68, asst. mktg. mgr., 1968-72; dist. sales mgr. Manville Corp., Inc., N.Y.C., 1972-78; archtl. sales mgr. Lightolier Co., Inc., N.Y.C., 1978-83; v.p. mktg. and sales Edison Price Inc., N.Y.C., 1983—; also bd. dirs. Inventor low brightness lighting, 1968. Mem. Illuminating Engring. Soc. (chmn. emergency lighting com. 1975-76). Jewish. Club: Men's (Rumson, N.J.) (pres. 1986-88). Office: Edison Price Inc 409 E 60th St New York NY 10022

SIEGEL, JOHN EDWARD, computer information company executive, consultant; b. Buffalo, Mar. 5, 1957; s. Vernon Harold and Lattie Lulu (Kenworthy) S.; m. Sarah Ann Sly, July 3, 1982. BS in Mech. Engring., SUNY, Buffalo, 1979; MBA in Fin. and Ops. Mgmt., U. Rochester, 1982. Ops. engr. Calspan Corp., Buffalo, 1979-80; fin. analyst Xerox Corp., Webster, N.Y., 1981; quality engr. Wang Labs., Lowell, Mass., 1982-83; mgr. prodn. Wang Labs., Holyoke, Mass., 1983-85; quality assurance mgr. software Wang Labs., Lowell, 1985-87; treas., chief ops. officer SR Instruments, Tonawanda, N.Y., 1987—; staff cons. Hadco Corp., Salem, N.H., 1986-87; cons. microcomputers Renaissance Systems, Hudson, N.H., 1986—. bd. dirs. Eleanor and Wilson Greatbatch Found., Clarence, N.Y., 1988—. Mem. ASME. Republican. Presbyterian. Home: 224 Paramount Pkwy Kenmore NY 14223 Office: SR Instruments 600 Young St Tonawanda NY 14150

SIEGEL, LAWRENCE IVER, real estate development company executive; b. Cleve., Aug. 19, 1925; s. Edward I. and Mary (Mentz) S.; B.B.A., Western Res. U., 1949, LL.B., 1952; m. Joyce Reske, Nov. 4, 1950; children—Leslie, Diane, Frederic, Edward. Pres., Lawrence I. Siegel Co., Baton Rouge, 1980—; chmn. bd. Lisscorp. Inc. Bd. dirs. Tara High Sch. Backers, Baton Rouge, Community Concerts Assn., New Orleans; Cub Scout master, 1967-68. Served with inf. U.S. Army, 1943-46; ETO, PTO. Col. on Staff of gov. La. Mem Internat. Council Shopping Centers, Mortgage Bankers Assn. Am., Am. Bankers Assn., U.S. C. of C., Baton Rouge C. of C. Club: Kiwanis. Home: 10039 Jefferson Baton Rouge LA 70809 Office: 10455 Jefferson Baton Rouge LA 70809

SIEGEL, MELVYN HARRY, financial consultant, securities company executive; b. Bronx, N.Y., Oct. 19, 1944; s. Herbert and Minnie Siegel; m. Nancy S. Levine (div.); stepchildren: Laurie Levine, Amy Levine, Elise Levine. BBA, CCNY, 1965; MBA, U. Chgo., 1974. CPA, Ill., Md. Asst. prof. bus. and econs. Calumet Coll., East Chicago, Ind., 1967-71; mgmt. cons., 1971-75, 77-79; mgr. mgmt. adv. service Naron, Wagner, Voslow, CPA's, Balt., 1975-77; pres. Stone Mill Assocs., Ltd., Balt., 1980—, Stone Mill Co., Inc., Balt., 1982—; Stone Mill Securities Corp., 1983—, Stone Mill Group, Balt., 1986—. Bd. dirs. Pro Musica Rara, Balt., 1978—, Sinai Hosp., Balt., 1986—, Beth Am Synagogue, 1985-87; chmn. Friends of Symphony, Balt., 1984-86. Mem. Am. Econ. Assn., AICPA, Md. Assn. CPAs. Jewish. Office: The Stone Mill Group 821 N Charles St Ste 1810 Baltimore MD 21201

SIEGEL, MILTON P., international executive, educator, health foundation executive, management consultant; b. Des Moines, July 23, 1911; s. Barney and Sylvy (Levinson) S.; m. Rosalie Rosenberg, May 25, 1934; children: Betsy Lee, Larry (dec.), Sally (dec.). Ed., Drake U., Des Moines. Dir. finance, statistics Iowa Emergency Relief Adminstrn., also treas.; Iowa Rural Rehab. Adminstrn., 1933-35; regional finance and bus. mgr. Farm Security Adminstrn., U.S. Dept. Agr., 1935-41, chief fiscal officer, 1942-44; asst. treas., dir. Office for Far East, UNRRA, 1944-45; asst. dir. fiscal br. prodn. and marketing adminstrn. U.S. Dept. Agr., 1945-47; asst. dir.-gen. WHO, 1947-71; prof. internat. health Sch. Pub. Health, U. Tex. Health Scis. Center, Houston, 1971-75, 87—; health mgmt. cons. Imperial Govt. of Iran, Nat. Health Ins. Orgn., 1975-76; sr. cons. to adminstr. UN Devel. Program, 1976-77; chmn. bd. trustees Mgmt. Planning Systems Internat., Inc., 1977—; pres., chief exec. officer Fedn. World Health Founds, 1978—; prof. internat. health, mgmt. and policy scis. Sch. Pub. Health, U. Tex. Health Scis. Ctr., 1988-89, emeritus, 1989—; mem. permanent scale contbns. commn. League Red Cross Socs., 1967-81; sr. mgmt. scientist Children's Nutrition Research Center, Baylor Coll. Medicine, Houston, 1979-80; cons. Sch. Pub. Health, U. N.C., Chapel Hill, 1970, Carolina Population Center, 1970; vis. prof. Sch. Pub. Health, U. Mich., 1967; awarded acad. chair U. Tex. Health Sci. Ctr., Houston, 1984. Chmn. bd. trustees World Health Found. U.S.A., 1976—. Recipient Sam Beber award, 1960. Mem. Am. Public Health Assn. Home: 2833 Sackett Houston TX 77098-1125 also: 1 Rue Viollier, CH-1207 Geneva Switzerland

SIEGEL, RICHARD ALLEN, economist; b. Chgo., Mar. 11, 1927; s. Mandel Irving and Mary Marsha (Shulman) S.; m. Shirley Platin, Dec. 17, 1950 (dec. June 1980); children: Joel, Barry, Robert, Peter; m. Rosalyn Sandra Miller, June 28, 1981. AB, UCLA, 1953, MBA, 1959, PhD, 1961. Asst. prof. econs. SUNY, Buffalo, 1962-64; economist Bank of Am., San Francisco, 1964-66, Calif. Dept. Fin., 1967-68, Arthur D. Little, Inc., Cambridge, Mass., 1968-70; economist, pres. Richard Siegel Assocs., Boston, 1970-79; economist, prin. Econ. Research Assocs., Boston, 1979-83; economist, pres. Applied Econs., Inc., Boston, 1983—. Contbr. articles to profl. jours. Served with USN, 1945-46, PTO. Jewish. Club: Appalachian Mountain (chmn. Boston chpt. 1983-84). Office: Applied Econs Inc 126 State St Boston MA 02109

SIEGEL, SAMUEL, metals company executive; b. Elizabeth, N.J., Oct. 30, 1930; s. Morris and Anna (Fader) S.; m. Raenea Kershenbaum, Mar. 29, 1953; children—Daryl Lynn, Annie Roslyn. B.B.A., CUNY, 1952. C.P.A., N.Y., Ariz. Cost accountant Seaporcel Metals, Inc., Long Island City, N.Y., 1955-56; asst. to controller Deltown Foods, Inc., Yonkers, N.Y., 1956-57; sr. accountant Touche Ross & Co., N.Y.C., 1957-61; exec. v.p. chief fin. officer, treas., sec., dir. Nucor Corp., Charlotte, N.C., 1961—. Mem. Am. Soc. Corp. Secs., Fin. Execs. Inst., Am. Inst. C.P.A.s. Home: 3421 Windbluff Dr Charlotte NC 28226 Office: Nucor Corp 4425 Randolph Rd Charlotte NC 28211

SIEGEL, STANLEY, import company executive; b. N.Y.C., Nov. 22, 1935; s. Samuel and Betty (Krinsky) S.; m. Joan G. Lerner, Jan. 26, 1958 (div. Dec. 1988); children: Gregg Mitchell, Holli Beth. BBA, Bernard M. Baruch Coll., 1957. CPA, N.Y. Jr. acct. Henry Rosenberg, N.Y., 1957-59; sr. acct., mng. acct. Zvi Levavy & Co. CPA's, N.Y., 1959-68; treas. Uniweave Corp., Paterson, N.J., 1968-79; exec. v.p., treas. Chromatex, Inc., Paramus, N.J., 1972-87; also bd. dirs; v.p., chief fin. officer EPI Internat. Inc., Port Newark, N.J., 1987—; bd. dirs. EPI Internat. Inc.; bd. dirs. Tenney Engring, Union, N.J. Chmn. George Mantore Fund, Livingston, N.J., 1975. With USNG, 1959-64. Recipient Heritage award. Mem. N.Y. State Soc. CPA's. Democrat. Jewish. Club: Cedar Hill Country (v.p. 1981-85, pres. 1985-87). Lodge: KP.

SIEGER, JOHN ANTHONY, lawyer; b. Chgo., Sept. 1, 1942; s. Joseph F. and Alice J. (Hayes) S.; m. Mary K. Heffernan, Feb. 19, 1966; children—Maggie, Kerry, Matt, Bill, Mike. B.A., U. Notre Dame, 1964; J.D., Georgetown U., 1967. Bar: Ill. 1967, U.S. Dist. Ct. (no. dist.) Ill. 1967, U.S. Ct. Appeals (5th cir.) 1973, Tex. 1974, U.S. Dist. Ct. (so. dist.) Tex. 1984. Atty., U.S. Dept. Labor, Chgo., 1967-70, Texaco Inc., Chgo., 1970-71, Houston, 1971-78; atty., sr. atty., assoc. gen. atty. Panhandle Eastern Corp., Houston, 1978-82, gen. atty., 1982-86, v.p., gen. counsel, 1986—. Mem. exec. com. Harris County Democratic party, Houston, 1982-85; election judge City of Hunters Creek Village, Tex., 1982-83. Research fellow Southwestern Legal Found., 1986—. Mem. Chgo. Bar Assn., State Bar Tex. (committeeman 1982—). Roman Catholic. Office: Panhandle Ea Corp 5400 Westheimer Ct Box 1642 Houston TX 77251-1642

SIEGERT, BARBARA MARIE, health care administrator; b. Boston, May 22, 1935; d. Salvatore Mario and Mary Kathleen (Wagner) Tartaglia; m. Herbert C. Siegert (dec. Apr. 1974); children: Carolyn Marie, Herbert Christian Jr. Diploma, Newton-Wellesley (Mass.) Hosp. Sch. Nursing, 1956; MEd, Antioch U., 1980. RN, Diplomate Am. Bd. Med. Psychotherapists. Supr. nursing Hogan Regional Ctr., Hathorne, Mass., 1974-78; community mental health nursing advisor Cape Ann area office Dept. Mental Health, Beverly, Mass., 1978-79, dir. case mgmt., 1979-87, dir. case mgmt. north shore area office, 1988—; nursing edn. adv. com. North Shore Community Coll., Beverly, Mass., 1983—; tng. staff Balter Inst., Ipswich, Mass., 1987-88. Mem. Internat. Cultural Diploma Honor, 1989—. Recipient Spl. Recognition award Lexington (Mass.) Pub. Schs., 1973, Peter Torci award Lexington Friends of Children in Spl. Edn., 1974. Mem. Mass. Nurses Assn., World Inst. Achievement, Am. Biographical Inst. (rsch. bd. advisors 1989—), Internat. Platform Assn. Home: 63 B Willow Rd Boxford MA 01921 Office: Dept Mental Health Greater North Shore Area Office 180 Cabot St 2nd Fl Beverly MA 01915

SIEGFRIED, ROBERT EDWIN, engineering company executive; b. Allentown, Pa., Jan. 16, 1922; s. Harold Edwin and Bessie (Davies) S.; m. Blanche Worth, Aug. 17, 1945; children: Martha Siegfried Fritz, Jay Worth. BS in Chem. Engring., Lehigh U., 1943; MS, MIT, 1947; postgrad., Center Mgmt. Devel., Northeastern U., 1960. Registered profl. engr., Mass.,

Ky., La. Process engrng. supr. Stone & Webster Engrng. Co., London, 1951-52; process engr. E.B. Badger & Sons Co., Boston, 1947-51; process engrng. supr. Badger Co., Cambridge, Mass., 1952-54, project mgr., 1954-56, project and engrng. coord., 1956-59, asst. engrng. mgr., 1959-60, engrng. mgr., 1960-65, dir., 1963-84, v.p., engrng. mgr., 1965-68, pres., 1968-77, chief exec. officer, 1971-84, chmn. bd., 1977—; bd. dir. State St. Bank & Trust Co., State St. Boston Corp., 1975-85. Patentee desalination of sea water. Mem. corp. Boston Mus. Sci.; mem. corp. Northeastern U.; trustee, chmn. bd. Commonwealth Energy System, Belmont Hill Sch. With AUS, 1943-46. Mem. Am. Inst. Chem. Engrs., Fla. Engrng. Soc., Nat. Soc. Profl. Engrs., Sigma Xi, Tau Beta Pi. Office: Commonwealth Energy System 1 Main St Cambridge MA 02142

SIEGFRIED, S(AMUEL) CEDRIC, lawyer; b. Independence, Mo., July 31, 1914; s. Mark Harrison and Madge May (Craig) S.; AB, Mo. U., 1938, JD, 1939; student Kirksville State U., 1932, Cen.Mo. State Coll., 1934; children—Mary Elizabeth, Martha Jane, Cedric Mark. Admitted to Mo. bar, 1939, Fed. bar, 1939, Fed. Communications bar, 1949; asst. pros. atty. Jackson County (Mo.), 1948-50; gen. counsel Jackson County Zoning and Planning Commn., 1950-52; city counselor City of Independence (Mo.), 1966-67; individual practice law Cedric Siegfried, Atty. At Law and Assocs., Inc., P.C., Independence, 1939—; incorporator, gen. legal counsel, dir. Noland Rd. Merc.Bank, Independence, 1964—, White Tractor Parts, 1954—, L.S.B. Corp., 1974—, Turner Contracting Co., 1955—, M.H. Siegfried & Co., 1932—, Sterling Corp., 1962—, Isokinetic Corp., 1976—; incorporator, counsel 1st State Bank, Olathe, Kans.; founder 1st Citibank, Olathe, 1977-78, now gen. counsel, treas.; trial examiner Midwest region CAB, 1950-55. Founder, Independence Area Devel. Corp., 1952, Midcontinent Devel. Council, 1960; mem. U. Mo. Law Sch. Found.; bd. dirs. Kansas City Heart Assn., 1955-69, Mo. Heart Assn., 1960-65, Am. Heart Assn., 1965. Served as flight instr. USAF, 1942-45. Hon. fellow Harry S Truman Library, U. Mo. Mem. C. of C., Independence Bar Assn., Mo. Bar Assn., ABA, Jackson County Bar Assn. (pres. 1958-60), SAR, Phi Delta Phi. Democrat. Mem. Reorganized Ch. of Jesus Christ of Latter Day Saints. Clubs: Rotary, Jefferson (U. Mo.). Office: 308 W Maple Bldg Ste 200 Independence MO 64050

SIEMER, PAUL JENNINGS, public relations executive; b. St. Louis, Jan. 24, 1946; s. Robert Vincent and Pauline Mary (Nece) S.; m. Susan MacDonald Arnott, Aug. 26, 1967. Student, U. Notre Dame, 1964-67. Reporter South Bend Tribune, Ind., 1967-69; reporter St. Louis Globe-Democrat, 1969-76; account exec. Fleishman-Hillard Inc., St. Louis, 1976-79, v.p., sr. ptnr., 1979-84, exec. v.p., sr. ptnr., 1984—. Mem. Pub. Relations Soc. Am. Roman Catholic. Club: St. Louis Press. Home: 2961 Hatherly Dr Bel-Nor MO 63121

SIEMIATKOWSKI, RICHARD THADDEUS, electronics system manufacturing executive; b. Amsterdam, N.Y., Dec. 19, 1938; s. Thaddeus Mathew and Isabell Bernice (Bara) S.; m. Barbara Rae Burkhart, Aug. 19, 1962; children: Samantha, Stephen, Sharon. BSME, Tri-State Coll., 1959; cert. real estate, Golden West Coll., Huntington Beac, Calif. Cert. real estate broker. Sales mgr. Siliconix Inc., Santa Clara, Calif., 1968-72; western area mgr. ITT Semicondrs., Inglewood, Calif., 1972-74, Xciton Corp., Huntington Beach, 1974-76, Monolithic Memories Inc., Santa Clara, 1976-82; v.p. AMCC, San Diego, 1982-84; pres. Silicon Devel. Corp., Huntington Beach, 1984—; cons. Dataquest, San Jose, Calif., 1984; speaker in field. Office: Silicon Devel Corp 16162 Beach Blvd Ste 210 Huntington Beach CA 92647

SIESS, ALFRED ALBERT, JR., engineering executive, management consultant; b. Bklyn., Aug. 16, 1935; s. Alfred Albert and Matilda Helen (Suttmeier) S.; m. Gale Murray Scholes, Dec. 17, 1966; children: Matthew Alan, Daniel Adam. BCE, Ga. Inst. Tech., 1956; postgrad. in bus. Boston Coll., 1968; MBA, Lehigh U., 1972. With fabricated steel constrn. div. Bethlehem Steel Corp. (Pa.), 1958-76, project mgr., 1969-76, engr., projects and mining div., 1976-86; sr. cons. T.J. Trauner Assocs., Phila., 1986-87; assoc. S.T. Hudson Internat., Phila., 1987—; mem. adj. faculty Drexel U., 1976—. Weekly columnist Economic and Environmental Issues, East Pa. edit. The Free Press, 1981-86; co-patentee suspension bridge erection equipment. Founder S.A.V.E. Inc., Coopersburg, Pa., 1969, pres., 1970, 75, 81, bd. dirs., 1970—. Served with C.E., USN, 1956-58. Recipient Environ. Action award S.A.V.E. Inc., 1975. Mem. ASCE (chmn. environ. tech. com. Lehigh Valley sect. 1971-83), Chi Epsilon. Republican. Mem. United Church of Christ. Lodge: Lions. Home: Rte 3 PO Box 145 Coopersburg PA 18036 Office: ST Hudson Internat 1339 Chestnut St 6th Fl Philadelphia PA 19107

SIESS, ECKART CLAUS, retail food company executive; b. Hamburg, Ger., Oct. 23, 1936; came to U.S., 1955, naturalized, 1960; m. Gustav Karl and Gertrud (Ecker) S.; m. Leonore Helbing, Sept. 1, 1959; children: Theresa, Romy. BA in Econs, Ohio Wesleyan U., 1957. Distbn. and purchasing exec. Procter & Gamble Co., Cin., 1957-66, 68-77; logistics dir. Procter & Gamble Co. Ger., Frankfurt, 1966-68; dir. distbn. and buying Procter & Gamble Co. Mex., Mexico City, 1977-79; vice chmn. strategic planing, also bd. dirs. Gt. Atlantic & Pacific Tea Co., Inc., Montvale, N.J., 1980—. Served with USAF, 1962. Mem. German-Am. C. of C. (bd. dirs.). Home: PO Box 63 Lahaska PA 18931 Office: Great Atlantic & Pacific Tea Co Inc 2 Paragon Dr Montvale NJ 07645

SIEVERS, JUDY LOUISE, lumber company executive, controller, treasurer; b. Everett, Wash., May 27, 1942; d. Ralph Clarence and Peggy Joyce (Martin) Hershaw; m. John Henry Sievers, Aug. 31, 1972; children: Larry W. Jr., Lon Gregory, Lena Marie, Lee Edgar. Grad. high sch., Arlington, Wash. Harvest truck driver Twin City Foods, Stanwood, Wash., 1957-60; pvt. practice in comml. art Arlington and Everett, Wash., 1960-69; mem. floral staff Peg's Floral Shop, Arlington, 1961-68; receptionist Reinell Boat Co., Marysville, Wash., 1969; log inventory, asst. to controller Buse Timber & Sales, Inc., Marysville, 1969-84; store owner Clearwood Community Assn., Yelm, Wash., 1984-86; controller Brazier Forest Products, Inc., Tacoma, 1984-86, 89; controller, corp. treas. Arlington Forest Products, Inc., Arlington and Tacoma, 1986-89, controller, 1989—. Tchr. Trinity Episcopal Ch., Everett, 1978; mem. Bald Hills Fire Dept., Yelm, 1984-86. Office: Arlington Forest Products Inc PO Box 3189 Arlington WA 98223

SIEWERT, ROBIN NOELLE, chemical engineer; b. Heidelberg, Fed. Republic Germany, Dec. 14, 1956; (parents Am. citizens); d. Orville Ray and Norma Idella (Sprink) S. BS in Chem. Engrng., U. Tex., 1979. Registered profl. engr. Start-up engr. Cen. Power and Light Co., Fannin, Tex., 1979-81; chem. engr. Cen. Power and Light Co., Corpus Christi, Tex., 1981-85, performance analysis engr., 1985-87, performance analysis supr., 1987—. Mem. NSPE, Am. Inst. Chem. Engrs., Soc. Women Engrs., Alpha Chi Sigma (pres. 1975), ASME. Republican. Baptist. Home: 4005 C Acushnet Corpus Christi TX 78413 Office: Cen Power & Light Co PO Box 2121 Corpus Christi TX 78403

SIGEL, MARSHALL ELLIOT, financial consultant; b. Hartford, Conn., Nov. 25, 1941; s. Paul and Bessie (Somer) S. BS in Econs., U. Pa., 1963; JD, U. Miami, 1982, LLM in Taxation, 1983. Exec. v.p. Advo-System div. KMS Industries, Inc., Hartford, 1963-69, pres., 1969-72; pres. Ad-Type Corp., Hartford, 1963-69, Ad-Lists, Inc., Hartford, 1963-69; fin. cons. Hartford, 1972-83, Boca Raton, Fla., 87—; atty., 1983-87; bd. dirs. Boca Raton First Nat. Bank. Bd. dirs. Hebrew Acad. of Hartford; trustee South County Jewish Community Found. Mem. World Bus. Coun., 100 of Conn., 200 Club of Miami, Wharton Sch. Club of South Fla., Tower Club, Boca West Club, Home and Office: PO Box 273408 Boca Raton FL 33427

SIGETY, CHARLES EDWARD, lawyer, health care executive; b. N.Y.C., Oct. 10, 1922; s. Charles and Anna (Toth) S.; m. Katharine K. Snell, July 17, 1948; children: Charles, Katharine, Robert, Cornelius, Elizabeth. B.S., Columbia U., 1944; M.B.A., Harvard U., 1947; LL.B., Yale U., 1951. Bar: N.Y. 1952, D.C. 1958. With Bankers Trust Co., 1939-42; instr. adminstrv. engrng. Pratt Inst., 1948; instr. econs. Yale U., 1948-50; vis. lectr. acctg. Sch. Gen. Studies Columbia U., N.Y.C., 1948-50, 52; rapporteur com. fed. taxation for U.S. council Internat. C. of C., 1952-53; asst. to com. fed. taxation Am. Inst. Accts., 1950-53; vis. lectr. law Yale U., 1952; pvt. practice law N.Y.C., 1952-67; pres., dir. Video Vittles, Inc., N.Y.C., 1953-67; dep. commr. FHA, 1955-57; of counsel Javits and Javits, 1959-60; 1st asst. atty. gen. N.Y., 1958-59; dir., mem. exec. com. Gotham Bank, N.Y.C., 1961-63; dir. N.Y. State Housing Finance Agy., 1962-63; pres., exec. adminstr. Florence Nightingale Health Ctr., N.Y.C., 1965-85; chmn. bd. Profl. Med. Products, Inc., Greenwood, S.C., 1982—; professorial lectr. Sch. Architecture, Pratt Inst., N.Y.C., 1962-66; mem. Sigety Assocs. (cons. in housing mortgage financing and urban renewal), 1957-67; Housing cons. Govt. Peru, S.Am., 1956. Bd. dirs., sec., v.p., treas. Nat. Council Health Centers, 1969-85; bd. dirs. Am.-Hungarian Found., 1974-76; trustee Cazenovia (N.Y.) Coll., 1981-87; bd. visitors Lander Coll., U. S.C., Greenwood, 1982-84; mem. fin. com. World Games, 1989, Karlsruhe, Fed. Republic of Germany, Confrerie des Chevaliers du Tastevin, Confrerie de la Chaine des Rotisseurs, Wine and Food Soc., Wednesday 10. Served to lt. (j.g.) USNR, 1943-47. Baker scholar Harvard U., 1947. Mem. ABA, N.Y. County Lawyers Assn., Harvard Bus. Sch. Assn. (exec. council 1966-69, area chmn. 1967-69), Alpha Kappa Psi, Phi Delta Phi. Presbyterian. Clubs: Yale (N.Y.C.), Harvard Bus. Sch. (N.Y.C.) (pres. 1964-65, chmn. 1965-66, dir. 1964-70), Harvard (N.Y.C.); Metropolitan (Washington). Home: 2600 S Ocean Blvd Boca Raton FL 33432 Office: Profl Med Products PO Box 3288 Greenwood SC 29648

SIGLER, ANDREW CLARK, forest products company executive; b. Bklyn., Sept. 25, 1931; s. Andrew J. and Eleanor (Nicholas) S.; m. Margaret Romefelt, June 16, 1956; children: Andrew Clark, Patricia, Elizabeth. A.B., Dartmouth, 1953; M.B.A., Amos Tuck Sch., 1956. With Champion Papers Co., Hamilton, Ohio, 1957—; pres. Champion Papers div. Champion Internat. Corp., 1972, exec. v.p., dir. parent co., 1972-74, pres., chief exec. officer, Stamford, Conn., 1974-79, chmn. bd., chief exec. officer, 1979—; dir. Bristol-Myers, Chem. Bank, Gen. Electric Co. Served from 2d lt. to 1st lt. USMCR, 1953-55. Office: Champion Internat Corp 1 Champion Pla Stamford CT 06921

SIGMAN, BOBBY, real estate broker, builder; b. Monroe, Ga., Jan. 19, 1941; s. Grady E. and Alma Irene (Womack) S.; m. Sandra M. Sigman (div. Nov. 1987); m. Alice Faye Atha. Student data processing, Fla. Tech. Coll., 1963. Data processing specialist Lockheed Ga., 1963-70; real estate broker Colony Realty Co., Covington, Ga., 1970—; owner, mgr. Sigman Constrn. Co., Covington, 1984—. Mem. Ga. Ho. of Reps., 1974-75; chmn. Newton County Democratic Com., 1976. With USN, 1959-63. Mem. Newton County Bd. Realtors (pres. 1979-80, bd. dirs. 1980/6), Piedmont Bd. Realtors, Am. Legion, VFW, Masons, Elks, Moose (charter). Office: PO Box 2085 Covington GA 30209

SIGMON, ANNE ELIZABETH, marketing professional; b. Roanoke, Va., May 12, 1953; d. William E. and Betty (Hale) S.; m. John David Sutton, Feb. 14, 1987. ABJ magna cum laude, U. Ga., 1974; MBA, Golden Gate U., 1984. Writer Publs. South, Atlanta, 1973-74, Univ. System Ga., Atlanta, 1974-75; with pub. relations dept. Bechtel Group, Inc., San Francisco, 1975-79, editor, 1979-81, mgr. employee communications, 1981-84, mgr. communications, 1985-87; mgr. pub. relations Bechtel Petroleum, Inc., Houston, 1984-85; mgr. mktg. Bechtel Nat., Inc., San Francisco, 1987—; instr. profl. seminars, 1980—. Recipient profl. achievement awards Internat. Assn. Bus. Communicators, profl. achievement awards Film and TV Festival N.Y.C. Mem. Am. Mktg. Assn., Pub. Relations Soc. Am. (accredited), The Planning Forum, Phi Beta Kappa, Kappa Tau Alpha. Office: Bechtel Nat Inc PO Box 3965 San Francisco CA 94119

SIGNORE, JOSEPH A., baking company executive; b. New Haven, May 25, 1934; s. Daniel D. and Lucy (Porto) S.; m. Jacqueline A. Beckwith, Dec. 28, 1953; children: Beth, Kim, Sue. B.A., Yale U., 1956. With Continental Baking Co., Rye, N.Y., 1963—, successively regional sales mgr., regional v.p., v.p. and dir. sales, exec. v.p. Eastern div., pres., chief operating officer, 1983; dir. Ralston Purina Co., 1985—; dir. Paniplus Co., Olathe, Kans., Nat. Continental Corp., Ltd., Kingston, Jamaica. Mem. Wheat Industry Council, Am. Bakers Assn. (dir.). Club: Yale (Darien, Conn.).

SIGNOROVITCH, DENNIS JAMES, director corporate communications, public affairs executive; b. Norristown, Pa., July 23, 1945; s. James and Regina (Ziemak) S.; m. Susan E. McLaughlin, Aug. 24, 1968; children: James Edward, Sarah Elizabeth. BS in Fgn. Svc., Georgetown U., 1967; MA, Old Dominion U., 1972; postgrad. U. Toledo. Instr., U. Toledo, 1972-77; writer/editor Doehler Jarvis div. NL Industries, Toledo, 1977-78; mgr. pub. rels. Eltra Corp., N.Y.C., 1979, mgr. planning, 1980; spl. assignment staff Allied Corp., Morristown, N.J., 1981; dir. pub. affairs Eltra Corp., Morristown, 1981-82; dir. pub. affairs Allied Info. Systems, Trumbull, Conn., 1982-83, dir. pub. affairs indsl. and tech. sector, 1983-86, dir. corp. communications, 1986—. Bd. dirs. N.W. Ohio Lung Assn., 1980-81; mem. pub. rels. adv. com. Morris Mus. With U.S. Army, 1967-70. Decorated Bronze Star with oak leaf cluster. Mem. Toledo Area C. of C. (com. chmn.), Morris County C. of C. (editorial bd.), Pub. Rels. Soc. Am., Internat. Assn. Bus. Communication (chpt. pres. 1978-79). Home: 5 Williams Rd Chatham NJ 07928 Office: PO Box 2245R Morristown NJ 07962

SIGUION-REYNA, LEONARDO, lawyer, business executive; b. Dagupan City, Philipines, Apr. 18, 1921; s. Lamberto and Felisa (Tiongson) S.; m. Armido Ponce-Enrile, Nov. 24, 1951; children: Monica, Leonardo, Carlos. Student, Ateneo de Manila, 1937-41; LLB, U. Santo Tomas, Manila, 1946-48. Bar: Philippines, 1948. Assoc. firm Perkins and Ponce Enrile, Manila, 1953-56; ptnr. Ponce Enrile, Siguion Reyna, Montecillo & Belo, Manila, 1956-67; sr. ptnr. Siguion Reyna, Montecillo and Ongsiako, Makati Metro Manila, 1967—; chmn. bd. Phimco Industries, Inc., Manila, Sandvick Philippines, Inc., Communication Found. for Asia, Electrolux Mktg. Corp.; pres. Electronic Tele. Systems Industries, Inc., Foremost Wood Products, MLC Agro-Indsl. Corp., Data scope Philippines, Inc., Manila Meml. Park Cemetary, Inc., Zamboanga Rubber Corp., Philippine Global Communications, Inc., Valmora Investment & Mgmt. Corp.; dir. Asian Savs. Bank, BA Fin. Corp., Complex Electronics Corp., Consultasia Mgmt. Services, Inc., Crismida Realty Corp., Dole Philippines, Inc., Electrolux Philippines, Inc., Filflex Indsl. & Mfg. Corp., First Pacific Capital Corp., Goodyear Philippines, Inc., Indsl. Realties, Inc., Investment & Capital Corp. of the Philippines, Perafilms, Inc., Philippine Refining Co., Inc., Rizal Comml. Banking Corp., Rubicon, Inc., Stal-Astra Refrigeration, Inc. Decorated Order of White Elephant (Thailand). Mem. Philippine Bar Assn., Philippine Brit. Soc., Casino Español de Manila. Roman Catholic. Clubs: Manila Yacht, Manila Polo. Lodge: Rotary. Home: No 7 Tangile Rd/ North Forbes, Makati Metro Manila Philippines Office: 5th Floor Soriano Bldg, Ayala Ave, Makito Metro Manila Philippines

SIGURDSON, EDWIN D., small business owner; b. Port Townsend, Wash., May 3, 1942; s. Clarence E. and Beverly Mabel S. BA in Bus. Adminstrn., Oreg. State U., 1970. CPA, Oreg. Regional controller Arcata Communications Co., Portland, Oreg., 1971-73; acct. Ed Luoma CPA, Astoria, Oreg., 1973-75; sr. utility auditor Oreg. Pub. Utility Commn., Salem, Oreg., 1975-84; owner Formula 1 Computers, Salem, 1981—; cons. Oreg. Computer Resource, Salem, 1985—; instr. Chemeketa Community Coll., 1986—. Served with U.S. Army, 1964-66. Mem. Oreg. Soc. CPAs, PHi Theta Kappa, Beta Alpha Psi. Office: Formula 1 Computers Co 1115 Madison St NE #601 Salem OR 97303

SIGURDSSON, THORDUR BALDUR, data processing executive; b. Reykjavik, Iceland, July 9, 1929; s. Sigurdur and Olafia (Hjaltested) Thordarson; m. Anna Hjaltested, Nov. 30, 1951; children—Magnus, Bjoern, Sigurdur, Anna, Ingveldur, Olafur, Katrin. Grad., Comml. Coll. Iceland, 1949; postgrad. U. Iceland, 1949-52. Chief acct. Icelandic State Land Reclamation, Reykjavik, 1947-72; mng. dir. Raftaekjaverzlunin Ltd., 1959-65; EDP mgr. Agrl. Bank of Iceland, Reykjavik, 1972-77, br. mgr., Stykkisholmur, 1974-75; tchr. math. Vogaskoli, Reykjavik, 1966-71; mng. dir. Icelandic Banks Data Ctr., Reykjavik, 1977—, dir. adv. bd., 1973-77. Editor Verzlunarskolabladid, 1947, Studentabladid, 1949, Ithrottabladid, 1967-68. Vestryman, Langholt Parish, Reykjavik, 1969-76. Recipient Gold Emblem, Athletic Union Iceland, 1968, Iceland Sports Fedn., 1972; Ace-Emblem, Athletic Union Iceland, 1967. Club: Reykjavik Football (Emblem Gold/Laures 1974). Home: Langholtsvegur 179, 104 Reykjavik Iceland Office: Icelandic Banks Data Ctr, Kalkofnsvegur 1, 150 Reykjavik Iceland

SIKES, ALFRED C., communications company executive; b. Cape Girardeau, Mo., Dec. 16, 1939; s. William Kendall and Marcia (Weber) S.; m. Martha Pagenkopf, Aug. 19, 1961; chldren: Deborah Sue, Christine Louise, Marcia Cay. AB, Westminster Coll., 1961; student, U. Wis., 1960; LLB, U. Mo., 1964. From asst. atty. gen. to atty. gen. Mo. Atty. Gen.'s Office, Jefferson City, 1970-72; campaign mgr. Bond. for Gov. Com., Jefferson City, 1972; dir. govt. elect. bond transition staff Mo. Transition Inc., Jefferson City, 1972; dir. dept. community affairs, dir. consumer affairs Mo. State Govt., Jefferson City, 1973-76; exec. v.p. Mahaffey Enterprises, Springfield, Mo., 1977-78; pres., chief exec. officer Sikes & Assocs., Springfield, Mo., 1978-86; asst. sec. Commerce for Info. and Communications, 1986—. contbr. articles to profl. jours. Pres. Springfield Council of Chs., 1984. Recipient Alumni Achievement award Westminster Coll., 1987. Mem. Mo. Bar Assn., Orgn. Mo. Jaycees (pres. 1968-69), U.S. Jaycees (v.p. 1969-70), Orgn. Internat. Jaycees (legal counsel 1971-72). Republican. Methodist. Home: 5907 Aberdeen Rd Bethesda MD 20817 Office: Nat Telecommunications & Info Adminstrn 14th & Constitution Ave NW Washington DC 20230

SIKORA, EUGENE STANLEY, engineer; b. Duquesne, Pa., July 21, 1924; s. Adam Joseph and Helen (Pietrowska) S.; student Okla. Bapt. U., 1943-44; B.S. in Indsl. Engrng., U. Pitts., 1949; C.E., Carnegie Inst. Tech., 1951; m. Corinne Mary Coliane, Sept. 7, 1946; children—Karyn Ann, Leslie Ann. Bridge design engr. Gannett, Fleming, Corddry & Carpenter, Pitts., 1949-50; structural designer Rust Engrng. Co., Pitts., 1950-51, chief field engr., 1951-52, asst. project engr.; project engr. Frank E. Murphy & Assos., Bartow, Fla., 1952-55; v.p. Wellman-Lord Engrng. Co., Lakeland, Fla., 1955-61; pres. Gulf Design Co., Lakeland, 1961-74, chmn. Lakeland Constrn., 1974-85; pres. Witcher Creek Coal Co., Belle, W.Va., 1979-84; ptnr. Gulf Atlantic Mgmt. Assocs., Lakeland; chmn. Horizon Constrn. & Devel. Inc., 1974—. Bd. dirs. Polk County Mus. Art. Served with USAAF, 1943-45. Mem. Nat. Soc. Profl. Engrs., Am. Inst. Mining, Metall. and Petroleum Engrs., Am. Mgmt. Assn., Am. Inst. Chem. Engrs., Am. Inst. Indsl. Engrs., Fla. Engrng. Soc., Lakeland C. of C. (dir.). Democrat. Episcopalian. Home: 1400 Seville Pl Lakeland FL 33803 Office: One Lone Palm Pl Lakeland FL 33801

SIKORA, MARTIN JOSEPH, magazine editor, columnist; b. N.Y.C., Dec. 16, 1934; s. Louis and Anna (Bergman) S.; m. Vivian Harris, Sept. 20, 1959; 1 child, Clifford S. BS in Journalism, NYU, 1956. Reporter UPI, Harrisburg, Pa., 1958-66; bur. mgr. UPI, Trenton, N.J., 1966-67; fin. reporter Phila. Inquirer, 1967-82; v.p. Sindlinger & Co., Media, Pa., 1982-83; editor Mergers and Acquisitions mag., Phila., 1983—, Corp. Restructuring Newsletter, Phila., 1988—; instr. in mergers, acquisitions Wharton Sch. U. Pa., Phila., 1986—. Served with U.S. Army, 1957, with Res. 1957-63. Office: Mergers & Acquisitions Mag 229 S 18th St Philadelphia PA 19103

SIKOROVSKY, EUGENE FRANK, lawyer; b. Jackson, Mich., Nov. 27, 1927; s. Frank Joseph and Betty Dorothy (Malik) S.; m. Patricia O'Byrne, July 11, 1953; children: Paul, Charles, Catherine, Elizabeth, Emily. B.S. in Elec. Engring, U. Mich., 1948; LL.B., Harvard U., 1951. Bar: N.Y. 1952, Va. 1970, Ill. 1978. Assoc. predecessor firms Cahill, Gordon & Reindel, 1954-63, ptnr., 1964-68; v.p., gen. counsel, dir. Reynolds Metals Co., Richmond, Va., 1969-76; gen. counsel Gould Inc., Rolling Meadows, Ill., 1977-79; v.p. Gould Inc., 1977-81; dep. gen. counsel Bell & Howell Co., Chgo., 1981-83, v.p., 1983-88, gen. counsel, 1983—, sec., 1984—, sr. v.p., dir., 1988—. Served to lt. USNR, 1951-54. Mem. ABA, Va. Bar Assn., Ill. State Bar Assn., Assn. of Bar of City of N.Y., Tau Beta Pi, Eta Kappa Nu, Phi Eta Sigma, Phi Delta Theta. Episcopalian. Home: 31 E Pembroke Dr Lake Forest IL 60045

SILAS, CECIL JESSE, petroleum company executive; b. Miami, Fla., Apr. 15, 1932; s. David Edward and Hilda Videll (Carver) S.; m. Theodosea Hejda, Nov. 27, 1965; children—Karla, Peter, Michael, James. BSChemE, Ga. Inst. Tech., Atlanta, 1953. With Phillips Petroleum Co., Bartlesville, Okla., 1953—; pres. Europe-Africa, Brussels and London Phillips Petroleum Co., 1968-74; mng. dir. natural resource group Europe/Africa London, 1974-76; v.p. gas and gas liquids div. natural resources group Bartlesville, 1976-78, sr. v.p. natural resources group, 1978-80, exec. v.p. natural resources group, 1980-82, pres., chief operating officer, 1982-85, chmn., chief exec. officer, 1985—; also bd. dirs., mem. exec. com.; dir. First Nat. Bank, Tulsa. Bd. dirs. Jr. Achievement, Stamford, Conn., Regional Med. Devel. Found., Bartlesville, Business-Industry Polit. Action Com., Washington, Okla Research Found., Oklahoma City, TARGET-Drug Prevention div. Nat. Fedn. High Schs., Boys Clubs Am., N.Y.C.; trustee U. Tulsa, Ga. Tech. Found. Inc., Atlanta; trustee Frank Phillips Found., Bartlesville, Okla. Served to 1st lt. Chem. Corps AUS, 1954-56. Decorated comdr. Order St. Olav (Norway). Mem. Conf. Bd., Am. Petroleum Inst. (bd. dirs.). Office: Phillips Petroleum Co 4th & Keeler Bartlesville OK 74004

SILBAUGH, PRESTON NORWOOD, savings and loan consultant, lawyer; b. Stockton, Calif., Jan. 15, 1918; s. Herbert A. and Della Mae (Masten) S.; m. Maria Sarah Arriola; children—Judith Ann Freed, Gloria Stypinski, Ximena Carey Braun, Carol Lee Morgan. A.B. in Philosophy, U. Wash., 1940; J.D., Stanford U., 1953. Bar: Calif. With Lockheed Aircraft Corp., 1941-44, Pan Am. World Airways, 1944, Office Civilian Personnel, War Dept., 1944-45; engaged in ins. and real estate in Calif., 1945-54; mem. faculty Stanford Law Sch., 1954-59, asso. prof. law, 1956-59, asso. dean, 1956-59; chief dep. savs. and loan commnr. for Calif., 1959-61, bus. and commerce adminstr., dir. investment, savs. and loan commr., mem. gov.'s cabinet, 1961-63; dir. Chile-Calif. Aid Program, Sacramento and Santiago, 1963-65; chmn. bd. Beverly Hills Savs. & Loan Assn., Calif., 1965-84; dir. Wickes Cos., Inc.; chmn. bd., pres. Simon Bolivar Fund, Del Mar, Calif.; of counsel firm Miller, Boyko & Bell, San Diego. Author: The Economics of Personal Insurance, 1958; also articles. Mem. pres.'s real estate adv. com. U. Calif., 1966—; mem. Beverly Hills Pub. Bldg. Adv. Com., 1970—. Served with USMCR, 1942-43. Mem. ABA, San Diego County Bar Assn., Soc. Internat. Devel., U.S., Nat., Calif. Savs. and Loan Leagues, Inter-Am. Savs. and Loan Union, Internat. Union Building Socs., U. Wash., Stanford Alumni Assns., Calif. Aggie Alumni Assn., Order of Coif, Phi Alpha Delta. Clubs: Commonwealth (San Francisco), Town Hall (Los Angeles). Home: Costenera del Sur, Zapallar Chile

SILBERMAN, H. LEE, public relations executive; b. Newark, Apr. 26, 1919; s. Louis and Anna (Horel) S.; m. Ruth Irene Rapp, June 5, 1948; children: Richard Lyle, Gregory Alan, Todd Walter. B.A., U. Wis., 1940. Radio continuity writer Radio Sta. WTAQ, Green Bay, Wis., 1940-41; reporter Bayonne (N.J.) Times, 1941-42; sales exec. War Assets Adminstrn., Chgo., 1946-47; copy editor Acme Newspictures, Chgo., 1947; reporter, editorial writer Wichita (Kans.) Eagle, 1948-55; reporter Wall St. Jour., N.Y.C., 1955-57; banking editor Wall St. Jour., 1957-68; 1st v.p., dir. corporate relations Shearson-Hamill & Co., N.Y.C., 1968-74; N.Y. corr. Economist of London, 1966-72; contbg. editor Finance mag., 1970-74, editor in chief, 1974-76; v.p., dir. Fin. Services Group, Carl Boyir & Assos., Inc., N.Y.C., 1976-78, sr. v.p., 1978-80, exec. v.p., 1981-86; sr. counselor Hill & Knowlton, Inc., N.Y.C., 1986—. Contbr. articles to profl. jours. Served to capt. C.E. AUS, 1942-46. Recipient Loeb Mag. award U. Conn., 1965; Loeb Achievement award for distinguished writing on fin. Gerald M. Loeb Found., 1968. Mem. N.Y. Fin. Writers Assn., Deadline Club N.Y., Overseas Press Club, Soc. Profl. Journalists, Sigma Delta Chi, Phi Kappa Phi, Pub. Relations Soc. Am., Zeta Beta Tau, Phi Sigma Delta. Republican. Home: 80 Miller Rd Morristown NJ 07960 Office: 420 Lexington Ave New York NY 10017

SILBERSTEIN, ALAN MARK, banker; b. Munich, Fed. Republic Germany, Dec. 22, 1947; came to U.S., 1949; s. Leon and Rose (Rosenblatt) S.; m. Carol Krongold, Aug. 30, 1970; children: Eric Michael, Adam Eli, Meredith Natania. BS in Engrng., Columbia U., 1969; MBA, Harvard U., 1972. Design engr. Ford Motor Co., Dearborn, Mich., 1969-70; budget analyst N.Y.C. Bur. of Budget, 1972-74; various fin. positions Chem. Bank, N.Y.C., 1974-78, v.p., dir. profit planning, 1978-82, sr. v.p., head retail ops., 1982-86, sr. v.p., head consumer fin. group, 1986-87, head consumer banking suburban N.Y., 1987-89, head consumer banking N.Y., 1989—; chmn. Chem. Fin. Svcs. Corp., Cleve., 1986-87, Chem. Card Svcs. Corp., Chgo., 1986-87;. Trustee Tenafly Bd. Edn., N.J., 1983-86. Mem. Harvard Bus. Sch. Club N.Y. (sec. 1981-85, dir. 1982-83, 85-88), Chem. Bank Nat. Assn. (chmn. Jericho, N.Y. 1986-87), Fed. Res. Bd. (consumer adv. coun. 1989—). Office: Chem Bank 277 Park Ave New York NY 10172

SILBERSTEIN, N. RONALD, lawyer; b. Boston, Feb. 23, 1927; s. Moses and Rose (Silverman) S.; m. Ruth Gerst, Dec. 26, 1954; children: Peter, Margery, Amy. A.B., Yale U., 1949; LL.B., Harvard U., 1952. Bar: Mass. 1952, N.Y. 1955. Clk. Judge John C. Knox, Chief Judge U.S. Dist. Ct., N.Y.C., 1955; v.p., gen. counsel Sheraton Corp. Am., Boston, 1956-73; sec. Sheraton Corp. Am., 1969-73, sr. v.p., gen. counsel, 1973—, also dir. Served with AUS, 1944-46. Office: Sheraton Corp 60 State St Boston MA 02109

SILCOX, GORDON BRUCE, career consulting executive; b. Takoma Park, Md., May 11, 1938; s. Walter Bruce and Ruth May (Davis) S.; A.B., Princeton U., 1960; M.B.A., U. Pa., 1965; m. Judith Andrea Smith, Mar. 7, 1970; children—Andrea Davis, Jessica Lyn. Trust investment officer Am. Security Bank, Washington, 1965-69; v.p., trust investment officer, head trust investment div. First Am. Bank of Washington, 1969-77; v.p., prin. Paul Stafford Assocs., Ltd., Washington, 1977-83; v.p., mgr. MSL Internat. Ltd., Washington, 1983-86; v.p. Manchester Inc., Washington, 1987—. Treas., Princeton U. Class of 1960, v.p., 1980-85. Served to lt. (j.g.) USN, 1960-63. Methodist. Clubs: Wharton Sch. (sec. 1980-81, treas. 1981-82) University (Washington); Princeton (treas. Washington 1972-74) (Washington and N.Y.C.); Montclair (Va.) Country.

SILER, JOYCE REYNOLDS, office supply manufacturing company executive; b. Durham, N.C., Oct. 23, 1949; d. Marion H. Reynolds and Rosa R. (Leslie) Scarborough; m. Carl E. Siler (div. june 1979); 1 child, Tammi L. BBA, N.C. Cen. U., 1984. Project coord. Employment and Tng. Administrn., Graham, N.C., 1976-80; adminstrv. asst. to dir. fin. aid. N.C. Cen. U., Durham, 1980-82; mktg. and tng. rep. Systems Rsch. and Devel. Corp., Research Triangle Park, N.C., 1984-86; pres. Office Plus, Durham, 1987—. Pres. Riverwalk Homeowners Assn., Durham, 1986-88; mem. adv. bd. Triangle March of Dimes, Durham, 1987—; mem. Coal. Battered Women, Durham, 1984—, co-facilator, 1988. Mem. NAFE, Durham C. of C., N.C. Cen. U. Alumni Assn. (chairperson fundraising com. 1986—), Delta Sigma Theta, Alpha Kappa Mu. Home: 16 Riverwalk Terr Durham NC 27704

SILER, OWEN WESLEY, retired military officer, consultant; b. Seattle, Jan. 10, 1922; s. Walter Orlando and Hylda Ruth (Jackson) S.; m. Betty Lilian Walford, Oct. 27, 1945 children: Gregory John, Marsha Joan S. Antista. BS, USCG Acad., 1943; MS, George Washington U., 1968. 2d dist. comdr. USCG, St. Louis, 1971-74; adm. USCG, Washington, 1974-78; ret. USCG, 1978; mem. bd. dirs. Panama Canal Co., Washington and Panama, 1977-81; v.p. mgmt. Forensic Tech. Internat. Corp., Annapolis, Md., 1980-81; pres. Ann-Bay Trans. Co., Annapolis, 1980-81; chmn. adv. bd. Med. Adv. Systems, Owings, Md., 1981-87; assoc. Burdeshaw Assocs. Ltd., Bethesda, Md., 1985—. Recipient Gold Medal award Dept. of Transp., 1976, Minute Man of Yr. Res. Officers Assn., 1978. Mem. Propeller of U.S., Navy League of U.S. (bd. dirs., chmn. resolutions com. 1985-87)The Retired Officers Assn. (1st v.p. 1982-84). Republican. Club: Edgemoor Tennis (Bethesda). Lodges: Rotary (bd. dirs. Washington club 1985-87), Masons.

SILER, WALTER ORLANDO, JR., retired business executive; b. Atascadero, Calif., May 21, 1920; s. Walter Orlando and Hylda Ruth Martyn (Jackson) S.; m. Carolyn Louise Townsend, 1978; children by previous marriage: Robert Eugene, Barbara Ellen, Susan Jane,Donald Walter, David Brian. B.S., U. So. Calif., 1941. C.P.A., Calif. Partner Arthur Andersen & Co. (C.P.A.'s), Phoenix, 1958-61; pres., treas., dir. Bargain City, U.S.A., Inc., Phila., 1962; treas., dir. Getty Oil Co., Los Angeles, 1963-67; v.p. Getty Oil Co., 1966-67, asst. controller, 1968-70; controller Fluor Corp., Los Angeles, 1970-72; gen. mgr. Saudi Arabian ops. Whittaker Corp., 1972-73; bus. mgr. Northrop Aircraft Div., Taif, Saudi Arabia, 1973-74; v.p. fin. Fluor Arabia Ltd., Dhahran, Saudi Arabia, 1974-77; mgr. accounting The Ralph M. Parsons Co., Pasadena, Calif., 1977-78; v.p., treas., sec. Parsons Constructors Inc., Pasadena, 1978-85; treas., dir. Mission Corp., 1963-68; treas. Mission Devel. Co., 1963-67; dir. Skelly Oil Co., 1963-68. Served to maj. USAAF, 1941-46. Mem. Fin. Execs. Inst., Am. Inst. C.P.A.s, Calif. Soc. C.P.A.s, Sigma Nu, Phi Kappa Phi, Beta Gamma Sigma, Beta Alpha Psi. Republican. Club: University (Pasadena). Home: 703 N Stoneman Ave Apt G Alhambra CA 91801

SILK, BERTRAM EDWARD, winery executive; b. Boston, Dec. 27, 1931; s. Abraham Jacob and Deborah Naomi (Gordon) S.; m. Barbara Nancy Ostroff; children: Marilyn Elaine Silk Copeland, David Michael. Student, MIT, 1950-51, U. Mass., 1953-58. Wine chemist Yosemite Wine Co., N.Y., 1958-60; v.p., dir. Delano Growers Winery, N.Y., 1960; enologist, quality control dir. United Vinters, San Francisco, 1961-65; v.p. ops.. Canadaigua (N.Y.) Wine Co., Inc., 1965—; chmn. N.Y. Wine and Grape Found., 1986—. Bd. dir. Wood Library, Canandaigua, 1976-80; chmn. Finger Lakes adv. bd. Rochester Philharm. Orch., Ont. County Libr. Bd.; chmn. N.Y. Wine and Grape Found. With U.S. Army, 1951-53, Japan. Mem. Am. Soc. Viticulture and Enology (chmn. ea. sect. 1978), N.Y. State Assn. Wine Producers (pres. 1981-84), Am. Soc. Enologists, Kiwanis (pres. 1973-74). Jewish. Office: Canandaigua Wine Co Inc 116 Buffalo St Canandaigua NY 14424

SILK, FREDERICK C. Z., treasurer, corporate executive; b. Pretoria, Transvaal, South Africa, July 29, 1934; arrived in Canada, 1964; s. Frederick Charles and Edythe D'Olier (Ziervogel) S.; m. Margaret Colbourne, May 12, 1962; children: Michael, Alison, Jennifer. BS, Rhodes U., Grahamstown, Republic South Africa, 1954; cert. acctg. theory, U. Witwatersrand, Johannesburg, Republic South Africa, 1957. Acct., cons. Deloitte, Plender, Haskins & Sells, Johannesburg, London and N.Y.C., 1954-64; mgmt. cons. P.S. Ross & Ptnrs., Montreal, Que, Can., 1964-68; v.p. fin. and adminstrn. J&P Coats (Can.) Ltd., Montreal, 1968-74; treas. Standard Brands, Ltd., Montreal, 1974-75; asst. treas. Standard Brands, Inc., Montreal, 1975-78; treas. Harlequin Enterprises, Ltd., Toronto, Ont., Can., 1978-82; v.p., treas. Nabisco Brands, Ltd., Toronto, 1982—. Fellow Inst. Chartered Accts., Soc. Chartered Accts., Fin. Execs. Inst., Soc. Internat. Treas., Granite Club. Office: RJR Nabisco Securities Ltd, Royal Bank Pla, PO Box 188 Ste 2700, Toronto, ON Canada M5J 2J4 also: Nabisco Brands Ltd, Ste 2700 S Tower, PO Box Royal Bank Pla, Toronto, ON Canada M5J 2J4

SILKETT, ROBERT TILLSON, food manufacturing company executive; b. Columbia, Mo., Nov. 12, 1929; s. Ross Jacob and Marion Dorchester (Tillson) S.; m. Sally Forrest Lash, Dec. 23, 1954; children—Robert Tillson, Elizabeth L. B.A., Duke U., 1951; M.B.A. with distinction, Wharton Grad. Sch., U. Pa., 1956. With mktg. dept. Anderson Clayton Co., 1956-58; with Gen. Foods Corp., 1958-78, group exec. corp. mktg. and sales, 1976-78; chmn. bd., chief exec. officer Reckitt & Colman N.A., Rochester, N.Y., also R.T. French Co., 1978-86; exec. v.p., dir. Curtice-Burns Foods, Rochester, 1986—. Past bd. dirs. Rochester United Way, Rochester Mus.; mem. exec. bd. Wharton Grad. Sch., Rochester council Boy Scouts Am. Served to lt. USNR, 1951-54. Mem. Wharton Grad. Sch. Alumni Assn. (past chmn.), Beta Gamma Sigma. Republican. Episcopalian. Clubs: Rochester Country, Wilton Riding (past pres.); Wharton M.B.A. (N.Y.C.) (past dir.). Office: Curtice-Burns Foods Inc 1 Lincoln First Sq PO Box 681 Rochester NY 14603-0681

SILL, GERALD DE SCHRENCK, hotel executive; b. Czechoslovakia, Dec. 11, 1917; s. Edward and Margaret (Baroness von Schrenck-Notzing) S.; B.S., Budapest Tech. U., 1942; m. Maria Countess Draskovich, May 11, 1946; children—Susan, Gabrielle. Came to U.S., 1948, naturalized, 1953. With econs. div. U.S. Hdqrs., Vienna, Austria, 1945-48; exec. hotel positions N.Y.C., 1948-52; managerial positions with Hilton Hotel Corp., 1953-61; exec. v.p. Houston Internat. Hotels, Inc., 1961-72, pres., chief exec. officer, 1972-84, chmn. bd., 1984-86; v.p., bd. dirs. 1986-88; sr. chmn. bd. Preferred Hotels Worldwide; dir. Tex. Commerce Med. Bank, Houston, regional bd. dirs., mem. Silver Fox Advisors, Inc.; pres. GdSS Mgmt. and Cons. Inc., The Warwick Hotel, Houston. Clubs: Warwick (pres.), River Oaks Country (Houston). Home: 2227 Pelham Dr Houston TX 77019 Office: 1669 South Voss Ste W Houston TX 77057

SILLIMAN, MICHAEL BARNWELL, real estate developer; b. Louisville, May 5, 1944; s. Clarence August and Margaret Elizabeth (Barnwell) S.; m. Margaret Louise Morris, July 20, 1974; children: M. Scott, M. Elizabeth. BS, U.S. Mil. Acad., 1966. Commd. 2d lt. U.S. Army, 1966, stationed in Korea, advanced through grades to capt., resigned, 1970; basketball player Buffalo, 1970-71; salesman Paul Semonin Co., Louisville, 1971-72; mortgage banker Pence Co., Louisville, 1972-76; owner Semco, Louisville, 1976-77; v.p. mortgage loans Langan Corp., Louisville, 1977-80; pres. Capital Mortgage Investors, Louisville, 1980-85, Silliman Devel. Co., Louisville, 1985—; bd. dirs. U. Louisville Bd. Overseers, U. Louisville Athletic Assn. Co-chmn. Paul Patton for Lt. Gov., Ky., 1987; bd. dirs. Boy Scouts Am., Old Ky. Home, Louisville, 1986-88, St. Xavier High Sch., Louisville, 1987—. Mem. River Rd. Country Club (bd. dirs. 1986-88), Valhalla Golf Club (Louisville). Democrat. Roman Catholic. Home: 645 Upland Rd Louisville KY 40206 Office: Silliman Devel Co PO Box 7216 Louisville KY 40207

SILLS, ROBERT DALE, insurance company agent; b. Evansville, Ind., May 31, 1944; s. Dale Arbury and Norma Vera (Leaf) S.; m. Barbara Ann Bininger, Oct. 9, 1971; children: Brooke Ellen, Bergen Lynn. BS, Purdue U., 1966. Asst. mgr. Baldwin Wallace Coll., Berea, Ohio, 1966-68; mgr. Saga Foods, Balt., Chgo. and Columbus, Ohio, 1968-71; asst. mgr. trainee Lazarus Dept. Store, Columbus, 1971-72; agt. N.Y. Life Ins. Co., Columbus, 1972—. 2d v.p. devel. bd. Children's Hosp., Columbus, 1984—; pres. Our Lady of Peace Parish Council, Columbus, 1985—, mem. Charity Newsies, Columbus, 1987. Mem. Ohio Life Underwriters, Columbus Life Underwriters, Nat. Assn. Life Underwriters, Am. Soc. of Cert. Life Underwriters and Chartered Fin. Cons., Million Dollar Round Table (life). Clubs: Capital (Columbus), Hide Away Hills (Sugar Grove, Ohio). Office: NY Life Ins Co 140 E Town Suite 1500 Columbus OH 43215

SILLS, WILLIAM HENRY, III, investment banker; b. Chgo., Jan. 2, 1936; s. William Henry II and Mary Dorothy (Trude) S.; m. Ellen Henriette Gervais, Apr. 24, 1971; children: William Henry IV, David Andrew Henry. AB, Dartmouth Coll., 1958; MA, Northwestern U., 1961. Stockbroker Bache & Co., Chgo., 1961-64; investment banker Chgo. Corp., 1964-84, First of Mich. Corp., Chgo., 1984-86, Sills & Co., Inc., Zenda, Wis.; bd. dirs. Pacific Enterprises, Inc., San Francisco, 1979—, GSW, Inc., Chgo., 1983—; with Chgo., Harvard and Geneva Lake R.R. Co., 1965—, Rail Funds Corp., 1973—, S & S Steamship Lines Inc., 1978—, Chgo., Elkhorn and Milw. R.R. Co., 1988—; cons. in field. Author papers in field. Chmn. Geneva Lake (Wis.) Area Joint Transp. Commn., 1978-86, Coalition for Balanced Transp., Madison, Wis., 1981-85, 88. With USMCR, 1955-61. Recipient Wood Badge award Boy Scouts Am., 1987, Sea Badge award Boy Scouts Am., 1988. Mem. Am. Soc. Traffic and Transp., Am. Short Line R.R. Assn., United States Yacht Racing Union (judge), Inland Lake Yachting Assn. (sr. judge), Lake Geneva Yacht Club (commodore), Lake Geneva Country Club, Skeeter Ice Boat Club. Republican. Anglican Catholic. Avocations: sailing, ice boating, chess, hunting, rugby. Home: 506 Lake Shore Dr Fontana WI 53125-9615 Office: Sills & Co Inc PO Box 40 Zenda WI 53195-0040

SILTON, MICHAEL, computer marketer; b. Los Angeles. BA, Swarthmore Coll. Mktg. mgr. MAI Basic Four, Inc., Tustin, Calif.; dir. mktg. Siton AMS, Inc., Los Angeles; gen. mgr. Focus Software, Los Angeles. Home: 902 Teakwood Rd Los Angeles CA 90049

SILVATI, JOHN DONALD, financial consultant and executive; b. Cin., July 29, 1937; s. Joseph and Ida Margaret (Muzzo) S.; m. Mary Ann Rawe, June 13, 1959 (div. Aug. 1978); children: Robert, Laura, Lauren, David, Brian, John; m. Linda Lee Snyder, July 4, 1981. BSBA, Xavier U., Cin., 1959. Account exec. Merrill Lynch Pierce Fenner & Smith, Cin., 1959-72, v.p., fin. cons., 1974—; br. mgr. Prescott Ball Turben, Cin., 1972-74; guest speaker on TV and radio, Cin. area. Contbr. articles to profl. publs. Chmn. Interparish Ministry, Cin., 1982-83; bus. chmn. United Way, Cin., 1987; v.p. Dater Found., Cin., 1987—. 1st lt. U.S. Army, 1960-62. Athletic scholar Xavier U. Mem. Internat. Assn. Fin. Planners (charter, v.p. Cin. chpt. 1980-81), Inst. Cert. Fin. Planners (cert), Kenwood Country Club. Home: 5740 Windridge View Cincinnati OH 45243 Office: Merrill Lynch 2600 1st National Ctr Cincinnati OH 45202

SILVER, GEORGE, metal trading and processing company executive; b. Warren, Ohio, Dec. 17, 1918; s. Jacob and Sophie (Bradlyn) S.; m. Irene Miller, Aug. 5, 1945. Student U. Ala., 1938; BA, Ohio U., 1940, postgrad. law sch., 1940-41; grad. Adj. Gen. Sch., 1944. Pres., Riverside Indsl. Materials, Bettendorf, Iowa, 1947-70, Metalpel subs. Continental Telephone Co., Bettendorf, 1970-71, Riverside Industries Inc., Bettendorf, 1971—; pres. Scott Resources Inc., Davenport, Iowa; v.p. Durbin Midwest, Davenport, Iowa, 1987—; founder Iowa Steel Mills (name changed to North Star Steel), Cargill and Wilton. Contbr. articles to profl. jours. Mem. Nat. UN Day Com., 1975-83. Served to capt. AC, U.S. Army, 1941-46, 50-51; Korea. Mem. Nat. Assn. Recycling Industries (co-chmn. nat. planning com., bd. dirs.), Copper Club, Paper Stock Inst. Am. (mem. exec. com.), Bur. Internat. de la Recuperation (chmn. adv. com.), Mining Club N.Y.C., Phi Sigma Delta. Republican. Jewish. Clubs: Outing, Hatchet Men's Chowder and Protective Assn.; Jockey (N. Miami, Fla.), Williams Island (N. Miami); Island Arsenal Officer's, Chemist (N.Y.C.), Crow Valley Country. Lodge: Elks (Davenport). Office: Durbin Paper Stock Co 2303 NW 70th Ave Miami FL 33122

SILVER, JACK MICHAEL, computer industry executive, consultant; b. Providence, Jan. 24, 1945; s. Ben and Mollie Zelda (Berman) S.; m. Marsha Diane Huttler, June 29, 1969; children: David Lee, Lauren Beth. BSBA, U. R.I., 1966, MBA in Fin., 1969. Underwriter Liberty Mut., Boston, 1966-67; data processing mgr. City and Sch. Sytem of Warwick, R.I., 1969-70; prof. mgmt. scis. U. R.I., Kingston, 1970-71; programming mgr. Am. Insulated Wire, Pawtucket, R.I., 1971-75; fin. systems supr. Raytheon Corp., Portsmouth, R.I., 1975-79; prin. Arthur Young and Co., Boston, 1979-83; v.p., gen. mgr. bd. dirs. ASA Internat. Ltd., Westboro, Mass., 1983—. Contbr. articles to profl. jours. Cons. R.I. Spl. Olympics, Warwick, 1986—. Jewish. Home: 10 Sycamore Dr E Greenwich RI 02818 Office: ASA Internat Ltd 1700 W Park Dr Westborough MA 01581

SILVER, JULIUS, lawyer; b. Phila., Dec. 17, 1900; s. Louis and Esther (Miller) S.; m. Roslyn Schiff, July 3, 1929; 1 dau., Enid (Mrs. Winslow). B.A., NYU, 1922, D.C.L. (hon.); J.D., Columbia U., 1924; D.Sc. in Tech. (hon.), Israel Inst. Tech.; D.H.L. (hon.), Jewish Theol. Sem. Am. Bar: N.Y. 1925. Since practiced in N.Y.C.; sr. ptnr. firm Silver & Solomon and predecessor, 1944—; dir. Polaroid Corp., Cambridge, Mass., v.p., chmn. exec. com., 1937—; assoc. counsel com. on banking and currency U.S. Senate, 1932-34. Donor Julius Silver Residence Center, NYU, 1963; founder Julius Silver Inst. Biomed. Engring., Technion U., Israel, 1968; trustee NYU, mem. exec. and finance coms., 1963-75, emeritus, 1975—; trustee Middlesex Coll. (now Brandeis U.), 1946, Jewish Theol. Sem.; pres. Library Corp., 1965-80. Recipient Achievement award NYU Alumni Assn., 1961; Silver Towers named in his honor NYU, 1974; Columbia U. Sch. of Law Julius Silver professorship named in his honor, 1984. Mem. Bar Assn. N.Y.C., N.Y. County Lawyers Assn., Gallatin Soc. (v.p. 1964-68), Phi Beta Kappa, Phi Epsilon Pi (Achievement award 1963), Zeta Beta Tau. Clubs: Old Oaks Country (Purchase, N.Y.); Harmonie. Home: Byram Shore Rd Greenwich CT 06830 Office: Polaroid Corp 549 Technology Sq Cambridge MA 02139 *

SILVER, MARC LAURENCE, sales executive; b. Detroit, Oct. 10, 1953; s. Jerome Sidney and Muriel (Shamovsky) S.; m. Rhonda Dorothy Isner, Aug. 4, 1974; children: Bryan Michael, Daniel Adam. Student, Berklee Coll. Music, 1971-72, Wayne State U., 1973-75. With retail sales dept. Alexander Stationers, Los Angeles, 1976-80; factory rep. Ultra Systems, Detroit, 1980-81; with internal sales dept. David's Office Supply, Southfield, Mich., 1981-82; co-owner, exec. v.p. The Office Connection, Farmington Hills, Mich., 1982-84; account exec. United Stationers, Forest Park, Ill., 1984-85, vendor rels. mgr., 1985-86, internal sales mgr., 1986; midwest regional sales mgr., nat. accounts mgr. office products div. Rubbermaid Comml. Products, Winchester, Va., 1986-88; dir. sales devel. Micro United Computer Products div. United Stationers Inc., Des Plaines, Ill., 1988—. Author: Contemporary Guitar Improvisation, 1977, G.U.T.S. (Guide to Utilizing Telemarketing Skills), 1988, M.U.S.T. (Micro United Specialist Training), 1989; co-patentee cutting system for document shredder, 1989. Mem. Nat. Office Products Assn., ABCD Microcomputer Assn., Gt. Lakes Travelers Club. Office: United Stationers Inc Exec Offices 2200 E Golf Rd Des Plaines IL 60016-1267

SILVER, RALPH DAVID, distilling company executive; b. Chgo., Apr. 19, 1924; s. Morris J. and Amelia (Abrams) S.; m. Lois Reich, Feb. 4, 1951; children: Jay, Cappy. B.S., U. Chgo., 1943; postgrad., Northwestern U., 1946-48; J.D., DePaul U., 1952. Bar: Ill. bar 1952. Staff accountant David Himmelblau & Co. (C.P.A.'s), 1946-48; internal revenue agt. U.S. Dept. Treasury, 1948-51; practice in Chgo., 1952-55; atty. Lawrence J. West, 1952-55; exec. v.p. fin., dir. Barton Brands, Ltd., Chgo., 1955—. Bd. dirs., pres. Silver Found. Served to lt. (j.g.) USNR, 1943-46. Mem. Am., Chgo. bar assns., Am. Inst. C.P.A.s. Clubs: Green Acres Country; University (Chgo.). Home: 1124 Old Elm Ln Glencoe IL 60022 Office: Barton Brands Ltd 55 E Monroe St Chicago IL 60603

SILVER, STERLING PATRICK, manufacturing executive; b. Massena, N.Y., Dec. 20, 1952; s. Leo James and Edrie Doris (Oney) S.; m. Jill Esther Compo, Aug. 12, 1972; children: Dacia, Tammy, Sterling II, Michelle. Diploma in gen. mgmt., Rochester Inst. Tech., 1973, A in Bus. Mgmt., 1974. With Dollinger Corp., Rochester, N.Y., 1972—, gen. foreman, 1980-84, plant supt., 1984-87; plant mgr. Dollinger Corp., Rich Creek, Va., 1987—; mem. welding adv. com. New River Community Coll., Dublin, Va., 1988—. Pres. Palymra/Macedon (N.Y.) Youth Baseball, 1983-87. Mem. Soc. Mfg. Engrs. (sr.). Democrat. Roman Catholic. Home: 109 Caudill St Pearisburg VA 24134 Office: Dollinger Corp 101 Spruce St Rich Creek VA 24147

SILVERMAN, ALAN, accounting firm partner; b. London, May 10, 1938; s. Michael and Hannah (Israel) S.; m. Helene Shaw, Nov. 22, 1959 (dec. Mar. 1984); 1 child, Simon Joel. BSc, U. London, 1959. Mathematician Nuclear Power Group, Knutsford, Eng., 1959-60; tchr. London County Council, 1960-61; salesman Diehl Machine Co., London, 1961-63; with mktg. support IBM, London, 1963-66, San Francisco, 1966-68; tng. instr. IBM, L.A., 1968-69; mktg. mgr. IBM, San Francisco, 1970-73, dir. litigation analysis, 1973-80; ptnr. Coopers & Lybrand, San Francisco, 1980—; vis. lctr. U. London, 1960-65, Hastings Coll. Law U. Calif., San Francisco, 1986—. Author: Attorney Client Privilege and the Work Product Doctrine, 1983; editor: Construction Litigation, 1986. Dir. San Francisco Hearing and Speech Ctr., 1984-87. Mem. ABA (assoc.), Am. Arbitration Assn. (panel of arbitrators 1986—), Inst. Mgmt. Cons., Calif. CPA Soc. (hon., com. on litigation services). Office: Coopers & Lybrand 333 Market St San Francisco CA 94105

SILVERMAN, ALBERT A., lawyer, manufacturing company executive; b. Copenhagen, Oct. 14, 1908; came to U.S., 1909, naturalized, 1921; s. Louis and Anna (Mendelsohn) S.; m. Gertrude Adelman, 1929 (div. 1934); 1 child, Violet (Mrs. Robert Blumenthal); m. Florence Cohen, Aug. 5, 1939 (dec. 1966); m. Francie Seifert, Oct. 1, 1975. Student, Northwestern U., 1929-34; AA, Cen. YMCA Coll., Chgo., 1936; JD, Loyola U., Chgo., 1940. Bar: Ill. 1940, Wis. 1959, U.S. Supreme Ct. 1960. With Cen. Republic Bank & Trust Co., Chgo., 1926-32; sec.-treas. Cen.-Ill. Co., 1932-42; sec. Republic Drill & Tool Co., 1942-44; asst. to treas. Hansen Glove Corp., Milw., 1944-45; v.p. Vilter Mfg. Corp., Milw., 1945-49, pres., 1949-88, chmn., chief exec. officer, 1970—, also bd. dirs., chief legal counsel; bd. dirs., pres. Vilter Found., Inc.; mem. council Marquette U. Engring. Sch., 1974—. bd. dirs. Albert J. and Flora H. Ellinger Found., 1974—. Named Man of Year Milw. chpt. Unico Nat., 1967; recipient Francis J. Rooney-St. Thomas More award Loyola U. Law Sch., Chgo., 1974, Community Relations award Milw. police chief, 1974, Antonio R. Rizzuto Gold Medal award Unico Nat., Community Svc. award VFW, 1989, award Wis. Regional Bd. NCCJ, 1989; honored by VFW for continuing svc., 1988. Mem. ABA, Wis. Bar Assn., Milw. Bar Assn., Chgo. Bar Assn., ASHRAE, Master Brewers Assn. Am., Zool. Soc. Milw. County, Loyola U. Alumni Assn., (hon.) Beta Gamma Sigma. Jewish. Clubs: Tripoli Country, Milw. Athletic, Milw. Press (Knight of Bohemia award 1979, Headliner award 1981), Wis. Lodges: Masons (32 deg.), Shriners. Office: 2217 S 1st St Milwaukee WI 53207

SILVERMAN, ARNOLD BARRY, lawyer; b. Sept. 1, 1937; s. Frank and Lillian Lena (Linder) S.; m. Susan L. Levin, Aug. 7, 1960; children: Michael Eric, Lee Oren. B Engring. Sci., Johns Hopkins U., 1959; LLB cum laude, U. Pitts., 1962. Bar: U.S. Dist. Ct. (we. dist.) Pa. 1963, Pa. 1964, U.S. Patent and Trademark Office 1965, U.S. Supreme Ct. 1967, Can. Patent Office 1968, U.S. Ct. Claims 1975, U.S. Ct. Appeals (3d cir.) 1982, U.S. Ct. Appeals (fed. cir.) 1985. Patent atty. Alcoa, New Kensington, Pa., 1962-67, 68-72, sr. patent atty., 1972-76; ptnr. Price and Silverman, Pitts., 1967-68; v.p., gen. patent counsel Joy Mfg. Co., Pitts., 1976-80; ptnr. Murray Silverman & Keck, Pitts., 1980-81, Buell, Blenko, Ziesenheim & Beck, Pitts., 1984, Eckert, Seamans, Cherin & Mellott, Pitts., 1984—; spl. asst. atty. gen. State of W.Va., 1985—; spl. counsel patents U. Pitts., 1975—; speaker on patents, trademarks, copyright, computer law. Contbr. articles to profl. jours. on intellectual property law and computer law. Mem. Churchill CSC (Pa.), 1967—, chmn., 1975—; mem. Pitts. law com. Anti-Defamation League, 1981—, regional adv. bd., 1982—, co-chmn. Pitts. region ann. dinner, 1983, mem., chmn. by-laws com., 1983; bd. govs. Slippery Rock U. Found., 1985—; Pitts. steering com. MIT Enterprise Forum, 1986-87. With U.S. Army, 1963-64. Recipient Cert. of Recognition Project on Pub. Policy and Tech. Transfer of Coun. of Ams. and Internat. C. of C. Joint Com. on Tech. Transfer, 1978, Am. Spirit Honor medal Ft. Knox, 1963-64; Univ scholar U. Pitts., 1960-62. Mem. ABA, ASME, Allegheny County Bar Assn. (chmn. pub. rels. com. 1978-80, vice-chmn. intellectual property sect. 1981-83 chmn.), Pitts. Patent Law Assn. (chmn. pub. rels. com., 1968-69, chmn. patent laws com., 1970-72, chmn. nominating com., 1973, chmn. legis. action com., 1972-75, bd. mgrs. 1974-88, newsletter editor 1974-88, sec.-treas. 1976-84, v.p. 1984-85, pres. 1985-86), Am. Intellectual Property Law Assn. (membership com. 1985-88), U.S. Trademark Assn. (chmn. task force on advt. agys. 1981, membership com. 19876—), D.C. Bar Assn., Pa. Bar Assn., Nat. Assn. Coll. and Univ. Attys., Am. Chem. Soc. (membership com. 1989), Licensing Execs. Soc., Brit. Inst. Chartered Patent Agts. (fgn. mem.), Johns Hopkins U. Alumni Assn. (chmn. publicity com. 1963-66, exec. com. 1966-87, v.p. 1969-70, pres. 1971-72), U. Pitts. Gen. Alumni Assn., U. Pitts. Law Alumni Assn., Robert Bruce Assn. Law Fellows (life), Golden Panthers, Stratford Community Assn. (v.p. 1966-67, gov. 1966-70, pres. 1967-68), Mensa (charter fellow lawyers in Mensa 1978—, nat. assoc. counsel patents and trademarks copyrights 1980-82, inventors' spl. interest group 1980-86), Intertel (treas. Pitts. Forum 1983—), Order of Coif, Tau Epsilon Rho, Psi Chi. Republican. Jewish. Clubs: Churchill Valley Country, Duquesne, Downtown of Pitts. (sec. and bd. dirs. 1985-87). Home: 221 Thornberry Dr Pittsburgh PA 15235 Office: 600 Grant St 42nd Fl Pittsburgh PA 15219

SILVERMAN, HENRY RICHARD, diversified business executive, lawyer; b. N.Y.C., Aug. 2, 1940; s. Herbert Robert and Roslyn (Moskowitz) S.; m. Susan H. Herson, June 13, 1965 (div. Jan. 1977); children: Robin Lynn, Deborah Leigh; m. Nancy Ann Kraner, Jan. 22, 1978; 1 child, Catherine Anne. Grad. cum laude, Hackley Sch., Tarrytown, N.Y., 1957; B.A. with honors, Williams Coll., 1961; LL.B., U. Pa., 1964; postgrad. in corp. fin. and taxation, NYU, 1965. Bar: N.Y. 1965, U.S. Tax Ct. 1965, U.S. Ct. Appeals (2d cir.) 1965. Practice law 1965-66; with White, Weld & Co., beginning 1966; then gen. ptnr. Oppenheimer & Co., until 1970; pres., chief exec. officer ITI Corp., 1970-72; founder, pres. Trans-York Securities Corp., 1972; exec. v.p., chmn. exec. com. Ladenburg, Thalmann & Co., 1973; pres., chief exec. officer Vavasseur Am. Ltd., subs. U.K. mcht. bank, 1974-75; gen. ptnr. Brisbane Ptnrs., 1976-77; prin. various investment groups, 1977—, Silverman Energy Co., N.Y.C., 1977—, NBC Channel 20, Springfield, Ill., 1977-83, ABC Channel 9, Syracuse, N.Y., 1977-81; prin., dir. Delta Queen Steamboat Co., New Orleans, 1977-86; also prin. outdoor advt., music pub., motion picture prodn., radio broadcasting & hardware mfg. cos; pres., chief exec. officer Reliance Capital Corp., subs. Reliance Group Holdings, Inc., N.Y.C., 1982—; sr. v.p. bus. devel. Reliance Group Holdings, Inc., N.Y.C., 1982—; chmn., chief exec. officer Days Inns Am., Inc., Atlanta, 1984—; also dir; pres., chief executive officer Telemundo Group, Inc., N.Y.C., 1986—. Trustee Dance Theatre Harlem, N.Y.C., 1984-87; bd. dirs. N.Y. Univ. Hosp., N.Y.C., 1987—. Served to lt. USNR, 1965-73. Republican. Jewish. Club: Harmonie (N.Y.C.). Office: Days Inns Am Inc 2751 Buford Hwy NE Atlanta GA 30324

SILVERMAN, MICHAEL DAVID, beverage company executive; b. Newark, Mar. 1, 1946; s. Norman Richard and Florence (Cantor) S.; m. Barbara Lerner, Sept. 23, 1970; 1 child, Aaron Daniel. BA, Yale U., 1968; postgrad., Berklee Coll. Music, 1972-73. Ops. mgr. The Jaydor Corp., Millburn, N.J., 1978-79, v.p., 1979-80, exec. v.p., chief operating officer,

1980-88, pres., 1988—; mem. Heublein Distbr. Adv. Council. Composer, arranger, performer numerous songs; winner Am. Music Festival awards 1975, 76, 77. Mem. Schieffelin & Somerset Distbn. adv. council. Mem. Wine and Spirit Wholesalers of Am. (bd. dirs. 1986—), Wine and Spirit Wholesalers Assn. N.J., Seagram Family Assn. Home: 8 S Beechcroft Rd Short Hills NJ 07078 Office: The Jaydor Corp 16 Bleeker St Millburn NJ 07041

SILVERMAN, STEPHEN MAYER, retail executive; b. Pitts., Jan. 8, 1960; s. Jerry T. and Marjorie Helen (Katz) S. BA, Mich. State U., 1981. Sr. branch coordinator R.H. Macy, Inc., N.Y.C., 1981-85; part owner, mdse. mgr. Retail Ventures, Inc., Pitts., 1986—; owner, pres. Help Ur Self Inc., Pitts. Artist paintings on wood and canvas; designer modern furniture. Active United Jewish Fedn., Pitts.; bd. dirs. Rodef Shalom Synagogue Jr. congregation; founder QA-Bluna Social Orgn., Pitts.; vol. Pitts. Rehab. Inst. Jewish.

SILVERSMITH, DAVID LAWRENCE, charitable organization executive; b. Bklyn., Aug. 27, 1962; s. Jordan B. and Annette L. (Klimer) S. BA in Polit. Sci. and Econs., Union Coll., 1984; MPA, Syracuse U., 1985. Resch. asst. Met. Studies Ctr. Syracuse (N.Y.) U., 1984-85; systems analyst Booz Allen and Hamilton Co., Bethesda, Md., 1985-86, United Way Am., Alexandria, Va., 1986-87; mgr. Project Flagship, Alexandria, Va., 1987—; cons. Ctr. Devel. and Population Activities, Washington, 1987. Vol. Smithsonian Mus., Washington, 1987—. Mem. Am. Soc. Pub. Adminstrn., Maxwell Sch. Alumni Assn. (bd. dirs. D.C. chpt., editor 1987—). Jewish. Home: 712 N Howard St Apt 204 Alexandria VA 22304 Office: United Way Am 701 N Fairfax St Alexandria VA 22314

SILVERSMITH, DEBRA BURSTEIN, investment banking executive; b. Eau Claire, Wis., Dec. 17, 1953; d. Allen David and Florence (Golper) Burstein; m. Donald Alan Silversmith, July 16, 1983; children: Ashley Renee, Lara Emily. BA in Econs., Cornell U., 1976; MBA, U. Pa., 1978. Portfolio mgr. employee benefit trust Bank of N.Y., N.Y.C., 1978-80; v.p. risk arbitrage Salomon Bros. Co., N.Y.C., 1980-83; dir. rsch. Hanifen, Imhoff, Inc., Denver, 1983-88; sr. v.p., dir. rsch. Boeettcher & Co., Denver, 1988—. Active Allied Jewish Fedn., Denver, 1980—, Children's Diabetes Found., Denver, 1983—, Denver Art Mus., 1984—, Nat. Jewish Hosp., Denver, 1986—. Mem. Inst. Chartered Fin. Analysts, Denver Soc. Security Analysts, Fin. Analysts Fedn. Office: Boettcher & Co 828 17th St Denver CO 80201

SILVERWATER, BETH, marketing professional; b. Manhasset, N.Y., May 10, 1962; d. Bernard Fred and Gladys (Koleditsky) S. BS, Cornell U., 1983. Instr. Coop. Extension, Ithaca, N.Y., 1980; legis. aide N.Y. State Asssembly, Albany, 1982; rsch. chemist Pall Corp., Glen Cove, N.Y., 1983-84; account exec. Ingredient Tech. Corp., Pelham Manor, N.Y., 1984-85; tech. mktg. specialist Food Splty. Ingredients, 1984—, Centerchem, Inc., Tarrytown, N.Y., 1986—. Div. leader N.Y. Am. Youth Hostel. Mem. Am. Assn. Candy Technologists (treas. N.Y. chpt. 1985-88), Inst. Food Technologists, Women in Flavor and Fragrances, League Am. Wheelmen (area rep. 1988—), Cornell U. Alumni Assn. Democrat. Jewish. Home: 14 Gould Pl Caldwell NJ 07006 Office: Centerchem Inc 660 White Plains Rd Tarrytown NY 10591

SILVESTRIS, ELAINE JOY, employee relations administrator, notary public; b. Worcester, Mass., Jan. 8, 1943; d. Roland Joseph and Margaret Ann (Arnieri) Gustafson; m. Maurice Richard Silvestris, Nov. 6, 1965. Cert. in Human Resources, Moravian Coll., Bethlehem, Pa., 1985; student, Allentown Coll. of St. Francis de Sales, Center Valley, Pa., 1988—. Legal sec. Mirick, O'Connell, DeMallie and Lougee, Worcester, 1961-65, Edward J. Brady, Camden, N.J., 1966-69; legal sec. to ptnr. Sigmon, Briody, Littner and Ross, Bethlehem, 1969-70; legal sec. to sr. ptnr. Weaver, Weaver and Weaver, Catasauqua, Pa., 1970-76; adminstrv. sec. to pres. and v.p. sales Lehigh Sales and Products, Allentown, Pa., 1976-78; sr. stenographer U.S. Postal Service, Lehigh Valley, Pa., 1978-82, injury compensation supr., 1982-85, employee relations mgr., 1985—; account rep. DialAmerica Mktg., Inc., 1988; notary pub., Lehigh County, Pa., 1974—. Recipient Cert. Appreciation for Outstanding Efforts in Hiring Visually Disabled People, Commonwealth Pa., 1987. Mem. Nat. Assn. Profl. Saleswomen (Lehigh Valley chpt.), Pa. Assn. Notaries, Pa. Soc. Profl. Engrs. (aux. group chmn. 1983-84, sec. 1978-80, v.p. 1978-79, 2nd v.p. and Pa. del. 1976-77), Nat. Assn. for Female Execs. Inc. Republican. Methodist. Office: US Postal Svce 1000 Postal Rd Lehigh Valley PA 18001-4024

SILVEY, DANIEL JOSEPH, controller, accountant; b. Amityville, N.Y., May 7, 1956; s. Daniel Henry and Joan (Keating) S. AS, Adirondack Community Coll., Glens Falls, N.Y., 1981; BS, L.I. U., 1983. Preprofl. Peat, Marwick, Mitchell & Co., Jericho, N.Y., 1981-82, auditor, 1982-83; auditor Peat, Marwick, Mitchell & Co., Albany, N.Y., 1983-84; sr. corp. auditor Cluett, Peabody, Troy, N.Y., 1984-85; controller Transglobal Industries Inc., Whitehall, N.Y., 1985-87; corp. controller J.E. Sawyer & Co. Inc., Glens Falls, 1987-88; sr. plant acct. Allied Signal, Hoosick Falls, N.Y., 1989—; pvt. practice tax acct., Glens Falls, 1984—; part-time instr. Adirondack Community Coll., Glens Falls, 1986. Treas. Town of Moreau Rep. Com., South Glens Falls, N.Y., 1983—. Served as sgt. U.S. Army, 1975-78. Mem. Town of Moreau/ South Glens Falls C. of C. (bd. dirs. 1988—). Roman Catholic. Lodge: Rotary (pres. elect 1988). Home: 143 Main St South Glens Falls NY 12803 Office: Oak-Mitsui Inc First St Hoosick Falls NY 12090

SILVIA, JOHN EDWIN, economist; b. Providence, Sept. 22, 1948. BA in Econs. magna cum laude, Northeastern U., 1971, PhD in Econs., 1980. MA in Econs., Brown U., 1973. Research asst. Boston Mcpl. Research Bur., 1969-70; cons. Mass. Pub. Finance Project, 1973; assoc. tech. staff Mitre Corp., Bedford, Mass., 1974-75; instr. econ. St. Anselm's Coll., Manchester, N.H., 1977-79; asst. prof. Ind. U., Indpls., 1979-82; econ. research officer Harris Bank, Chgo., 1982-83; v.p., fin. economist Kemper Fin. Services, Chgo., 1983—. Contbr. articles to mags., newspapers including Wall Street Jour. Mem. Am. Econ. Assn., Am. Fin. Assn., Nat. Assn. Bus. Economists, Chgo. Assn. Bus. Economists (past sec./treas., now pres.), Blue Chip Survey. Home: 913 Turnbridge Circle Naperville IL 60540 Office: Kemper Fin Svcs 120 S LaSalle St Chicago IL 60603

SIMAPICHAICHETH, PRATAK, real estate developer, researcher; b. Bangkok, Thailand, June 6, 1941; s. Hui and Lang Simpichaicheth; married; 1 child, Weeratos. B.Econ., Thammasat U., Bangkok, 1961; MBA, Victoria U., Wellington, New Zealand, 1964. Dir. DTEC Lang. Inst., Ministry of Nat. Devel., Bangkok, 1966-72; mgr. Trok Chan br. Thai Mil. Bank, Bangkok, 1972-77; mng. dir. Bangkok Friendship Credit Foncier, 1977-81; pres. Krung Thai Health Ins. Co., Bangkok, 1981; former chmn., chief exec. officer Thai Engring. & Mgmt., Bangkok, Thai Real Estate Co., Bangkok; chmn., chief exec. officer Town Home Co., Bangkok, 1981—; bd. dirs. Thai Exim Co. Ltd., Bangkok, Group of Thai Cons. Co., Bangkok; cons. Padco Bangkok Land Study; chmn. Suan-Bangkhen Community Co-op. Bangkok; mem. study team Applied Rsch. for Thai Govt., 1981; trustee Land Inst. Found., Thailand. Bd. dirs. Indsl. Authority of Thailand, Bangkok, Econ. sect. Nat. Research Council, Bangkok; mem. Nat. Housing Policy Com., Bangkok; adv. Green E-Sarn Found. Mem. Credit Foncier Trade Assn. (charter pres. 1975-77), Asean Assn. Planning and Housing (council mem. 1982—), AAPH (hon. treas.), Asean Valuers Assn. (hon. sec.-gen.), Thai Real Estate Assn. (v.p.). Lodge: Rotary (pres. Bangkok chpt. 1986-87). Home: 1236 Soi 43 Klongchan, Bangkok Thailand 10240 Office: Thai Real Estate Co Ltd, 32/13-15 Asoke Rd, Bangkok 10110, Thailand

SIMARD, HOUSTON HERBERT, manufacturing company executive; b. Fort Smith, Ark., Aug. 27, 1930; s. Joseph George and Vera Beatrice (Jackson) S.; student Ark. Poly. Inst., Russellville, 1948; m. Cogene Diffee Simard, Sept. 1, 1984; children—Rodney Joe, Timothy Vick. Vice-pres. Jackson's Furniture, Inc., Fort Smith, 1947-65; salesman Pratt & Lambert, Inc., Kansas City, Mo., 1965-69; sales mgr. Belwood, Inc. (formerly Belwood div. U.S. Industries), Ackerman, Miss., 1969-70, v.p. mktg., 1970-72, exec. v.p., 1972-74, pres., 1974-86, chmn., pres., 1986—. Served with AUS, 1947-48, 50-51. Mem. Nat. Kitchen Cabinet Assn. (chmn. standards com. 1981-83, dir. 1981-87). Republican. Lutheran. Home: 1591 Peabody Memphis TN 38104 Office: Belwood Inc PO Drawer A Hwy 15 S Ackerman MS 39735

SIMBORG, PHILIP JAY, real estate associate, consultant; b. Lincoln, Nebr., July 7, 1944; s. Hugh Meyer and Rose (Fair) S.; m. Nancy Jan Simborg, Aug. 11, 1967 (div. Feb. 1983); m. Nancy Elaine, Mar. 9, 1988; children from previous marriage: Michael, Daniel. BBA, U. Tex., 1967. Sales engr. Triple-S Dynamics, Dallas, 1967-69; salesperson HTO & Co., Chgo., 1969-74; prin. Simborg Real Estate, Chgo., 1974-83; sr. assoc. Bennett & Kahnweiler, Inc., Chgo., 1983—. Contbr. articles to profl. jours. Mem. Assn. Indsl. Real Estate Brokers (pres. 1978), Real Estate Consortium (pres. 1988—), Nat. Council Jewish Women. Lodge: Civitan (membership com. 1985—). Home: 8208 Dolphin Lake Dr Homewood IL 60430 Office: Bennett & Kahnweiler Inc 9700 Bryn Mawr Rosemont IL 60018

SIMEONE, ALLEN THOMAS, sales executive; b. Bklyn., Apr. 17, 1945; s. Anthony Thomas and Margaret (Carrino) S.; m. Carol Ann Greco, Mar. 23, 1968; children: Michael, Thomas, Carolyn. BS, NYU, 1966; MBA, Fairleigh Dickinson U., 1979. Circulation sales dir. Dow Jones and Co., The Wall St. Jour., Princeton, N.J., 1964—. Home: 24 Princeton Dr Manalapan NJ 07726 Office: Dow Jones & Co PO Box 300 Princeton NJ 08540

SIMERAL, WILLIAM GOODRICH, retired chemical company executive; b. Portland, Oreg., May 22, 1926; s. Claire Cornelius and Geneva B. (Goodrich) S.; m. Elizabeth Louise Ross, June 25, 1949; children: Linda Simeral McGregor, Karen Simeral Schousen, William Goodrich Jr., John David. B.S. in Physics, Franklin and Marshall Coll., Lancaster, Pa., 1948; Ph.D. in Physics, U. Mich., 1953. With E.I. duPont de Nemours and Co., Inc., 1953-87; v.p., gen. mgr. plastics dept. E.I. duPont de Nemours and Co., Inc., Wilmington, Del., 1974-76; v.p., gen. mgr. plastic products and resins dept. E.I. duPont de Nemours and Co., Inc., 1976-77, sr. v.p., dir., mem. exec. com., 1977-81, exec. v.p., dir., mem. exec. com., 1981-87; vice chmn. bd., chief operating officer Conoco Inc., 1984-85. Trustee Franklin and Marshall Coll., 1977—; trustee, bd. dirs. Wilmington Med. Center, 1978—, chmn. bd., 1982-86; bd. dir. YMCA Wilmington and New Castle County, 1978-81. Served with USNR, 1944-46. Mem. Chem. Mfrs. Assn. (vice chmn. bd. 1980-81, chmn. exec. com. 1981-82, chmn. bd. 1982-83), Am. Phys. Soc., Phi Beta Kappa, Sigma Xi. Clubs: Wilmington Country, Quail Creek Country, The Club at Pelican Bay.

SIMMONS, BRADLEY WILLIAMS, pharmaceutical company executive; b. Paterson, N.J., Apr. 16, 1941; s. John Williams and Grace Law (Van Hassel) S.; m. Diane Louise Simmons, June 6, 1964 (div. May 1986); children: Susan, Elizabeth, Jonathan; m. Cheryl Lynne Westrum, Aug. 16, 1987. AB, Columbia U., 1963, BSChemE, 1964; MBA, NYU, 1974. Chem. engr. Pfizer, Inc., N.Y.C., 1969-73, analyst, 1973-76, dir. planning, 1976-79; dir., bus. analysis Bristol-Myers, N.Y.C., 1979-82, v.p., 1982-85; pres. Oncogen subs. Bristol-Myers, Seattle, 1985-87, sr. v.p. adminstrn., 1987—; adj. prof. Farleigh Dickinson U., Teaneck, N.J., 1974-84. Council mem. borough of Allendale, N.J., 1977-82; mem. Bergen County (N.J.) com., 1974-82. Served to lt. USN, 1964-69, Vietnam. Republican. Mem. Unity Ch. Office: Oncogen 3005 1st Ave Seattle WA 98121

SIMMONS, CARL KENNETH, cooperative executive; b. Kingman, Ind., Dec. 5, 1914; s. Claud Elmer and Sylvia Ethyl (Myers) S.; grad. exec. devel. program Ind. U., 1959; m. Allice Lucille Weaver, Dec. 16, 1939; 1 child, Erma Jane (Mrs. Thomas Stephen Barlow). Petroleum dept. mgr. Fountain County Coop., Veedersburg, Ind., 1936-40; dist. mgr. Ind. Farm Bur. Coop., Indpls., 1946-47; treas., mgr. Delaware County Coop., Muncie, 1940-46, 48-86; emeritus gen. mgr., treas. 1986—. Mem. Mayor's Citizens Com. Muncie, 1962; bd. dirs. Delaware County Airport Authority, 1972—, pres., 1983—. Mem. Ind. Flying Farmers. Lodge: Masons (32 degree). Club: Muncie Rifle. Home: 225 E Centennial St Muncie IN 47303 Office: 2101 N Granville Ave Muncie IN 47305

SIMMONS, CLINTON CRAIG, human resources executive; b. Cleve., Nov. 25, 1947; s. Benjamin F. and Catharin (Thornton) R.; m. Cheryl LeRoy, June 16, 1973; 1 child, Eric. BBA, Miami U., Oxford, Ohio, 1969; grad. quality mgmt. course Winter Park, Fla., 1986. Cert. quality edn. system instr. Specialist employee and community relations Euclid Lamp Plant, GE, Cleve., 1970-75; employee and indsl. rels. rep. Bailey Controls Co., Wickliffe, Ohio, 1975-78; mgr., coll. recruiting Gen. Tire and Rubber, Akron, Ohio, 1978-81, profl. staffing coord., 1981-82; regional human resource mgr. Gilbane Bldg. Co., Cleve. 1982-86, human resource mgr. Western regions, 1987-88; asst. v.p., dir. human resources western regions, St. Alexis Hosp. Med. Ctr., 1988—. Author: (with W.J. McBurnry Jr.) Course Procurement: Effective Program and Practice. Past chmn. orgn. and extension com. Newton D. Baker Dist., Greater Cleve. coun. Boy Scouts Am., 1970-71; mem. Human Resource Com. for Greater Cleve. United Way, NAACP, Urban League of Cleve.; mem. pension and benefit coms. Greater Cleve. Hosp. Assn. Bd. Edn. commr. Villa Angela Acad., Cleve., 1983—, pres., 1986-88 (U.S. Edn. Dept. award 1987); founder, advisor Explorer Post, Gilbane Bldg. Co., Cleve., 1984-88; Cleve., 1988—; v.p. adv. bd. Cath. Social Svcs. Cuyahoga County; mem. urban regional bd. Cath. Edn. Cleve., 1986; trustee Marotta Montessori Sch. of Cleve., Harambee Svcs. Orgn. Cleve., 1987—. Recipient commendation Nat. Alliance of Bus., Akron, 1979, Community Svc. award WJW-Northwest Orient Airlines, 1975. Mem. Cleve. EEO Assn., Am. Soc. Personnel Adminstrn., Mid-West Coll. Placement Assn. (chmn. rubber industry com. 1979-81), Ctr. for Human Svcs. (v.p., trustee), Indsl. Rels. Rsch. Assn., , Alpha Phi Alpha. Democrat. Roman Catholic. Home: 24400 Emery Rd Warrensville Heights OH 44128 Office: St Alexis Hosp Med Ctr 5163 Broadway Cleveland OH 44127

SIMMONS, CORINNE, hotel executive; b. Washington, Sept. 19, 1940; d. John Malloy Shaw and Ruby Louise (Jordan) Mau; m. James E. Hammock, Apr. 30, 1962 (div. 1981); children: Michele Marie, James E. Jr.; m. Michael Simmons, Nov. 21, 1981. BS, SW Tex. State U., 1971. Supr. purchasing N.E. Sch. Dist., San Antonio, 1976-78; dir. purchasing LaQuinta Motor Inns, San Antonio, 1978-82; v.p. Econo Lodges Am., Inc., Norfolk, Va., 1982-84; sr. v.p. Econo Lodges Am., Inc., Charlotte, N.C., 1986—; v.p. Mariner Corp., Houston, 1984-85; pres. Hotal Furnishings, Santa Ana, Calif., 1985-86; cons. Va. Beach Sales Assn., 1986. Mem. Ad Hoc Mayoral Com., San Antonio; instr. Women's Self Help Group, San Antonio, 1980. Recipient Citizen Achiever award Jefferson Circle, 1987. Mem. Bus. and Profl. Women's Club, Sales and Mktg. Execs., Nat. Purchasing Execs., NAFE, Motel and Hotel Assn., NRA. Republican. Baptist. Home: 3730 Winding Creek Rd Charlotte NC 28226 Office: Econo Lodges Am Inc 6135 Park Rd Ste 200 Charlotte NC 28210

SIMMONS, EDGAR HAMLETT, management consultant; b. Emory, Ga., Oct. 31, 1929; s. Thomas Heyward and Beatrice (Hamlett) S.; m. Ramie Lee Bedwell, Apr. 2, 1955; children: Mark Justin, Brenda, Bridget. BSME, Auburn U., 1951. Mktg. mgr. distbn. assemblies dept. Gen. Electric Co., Plainville, Conn., 1972-76; mgr. Plainville plant Gen. Electric Co., 1976-78; v.p. planning, power systems group Dresser Industries Inc., Houston, 1978-83, gen. mgr. N.Am. industrial ops., 1981-83; pres. Strategic Mgmt. Assocs., Kingwood, Tex., 1984—. Served to lt. USN, 1951-54, Korea. Mem. Assn. Corp. Growth, Internat. Soc. for Pln. and Strat. Mgmt. Republican. Presbyterian. Club: Kingwood Country (Tex). Home and Office: 2003 Spruce Grove Dr Kingwood TX 77339

SIMMONS, EDWARD LEE, turbodrilling engineer; b. Kobe, Japan, Apr. 22, 1953; came to U.S., 1956; s. Reddick Fulton and Margaret Elizabeth (Smith) S.; m. Nancy Yvonne Bell, Aug. 9, 1979 (div. 1982). Student, N.C. State U., 1972, Fayeteville State U., 1972, Pearl River Coll., 1973-75, U. Southwestern La., 1986. Oilwell logger Location Sample Service, Jackson, Miss., 1975-76; oilwell logging mgr. The Analysts, Laurel, Miss., 1976-78; wellsite geologist Hydrocarb Logging Co., Florence, Miss., 1978-81; turbodrilling specialist Neyrfor Turbodrilling Co., Lafayette, La., 1981-86; turbodrilling engr. Neyrfor Turbodrilling Co., Valencia, Calif., 1986-88, Lafayette, 1988—. Served with U.S. Army, 1970-73. Decorated Army Commendation medal. Mem. Soc. Petroleum Engrs., Am. Legion. Republican. Home: 221 Verat School Rd #187 Lafayette LA 70508 Office: Neyrfor Turbodrilling Co 104 Row 3 Canebrake Lafayette LA 70508

SIMMONS, ESTHER GRACE, paralegal; b. Savannah, Ga., May 13, 1961; d. Jephthah and Della L. (Goshea) S. BA, Howard U., 1984, postgrad., 1988—. Office asst. St. Paul Jr. High Sch., Washington, 1981-82; office clk. Dept. Housing and Comml. Devel., Washington, 1982-83; paralegal EGS & Assocs., Savannah, 1986—; substitute tchr. Bd. Edn., Savannah, 1984-86; parliamentarian Charles H. Houston Pre-Law Soc. Bd. trustees scholarship Howard U., Washington, 1981-82; organizer Chancellor Williams Hist. Soc., Washington, 1980-81; sec. Martin Luther King Forencics team, Washington, 1980-81; v.p. Frederick Douglass Honor Soc., Washington, 1982-83. Mem. NAFE. Republican. Pentecostal. Home: 623 M St NW #7 Washington DC 20001

SIMMONS, HARDWICK, investment banker; b. Balt., June 8, 1940; s. Edward Ball and Margaret (Hardwick) S.; m. Sarah Bradlee Dolan, Sept. 9, 1962; children—Elizabeth, Huntington, Benjamin. B.A., Harvard U., 1962, M.B.A., 1966. With Shearson Lehman Bros. Inc., 1966—; regional officer Shearson Lehman Bros. Inc., New Eng., 1972-75; vice chmn. Shearson Lehman Hutton Inc. (formerly Shearson Lehman Bros. Inc.), N.Y.C., 1975—, also bd. dirs.; dir. Chgo. Bd. Options Exchange. Served with USMCR, 1959-60. Mem. Bond Club N.Y.C. Republican. Office: Shearson Lehman Hutton Inc Am Express Tower World Fin Ctr New York NY 10285 *

SIMMONS, HAROLD C., sugar company executive; b. 1931. BA, MA, U. Tex., 1952. Investigator U.S. Civil Service, Dallas, 1952-55; book examiner Fed. Deposit Ins. Corp., Dallas, 1955-56; loan officer Republican Nat. Bank, Dallas, 1956-61; with Amalgamated Sugar Corp., Dallas, 1961—, chmn., chief exec. officer, also bd. dirs.; also pres., chief exec. officer, dir. Contran Corp., Dallas; chmn., dir. NL Industries Inc., Houston. Office: Valhi Inc Three Lincoln Centre 5430 LBJ Frwy Ste 1700 Dallas TX 75240-2697 Office: Amalgamated Sugar Co PO Box 1520 Ogden UT 84402 alsor: NL Industries Inc 3000 N Belt E Houston TX 77032 *

SIMMONS, HARRIS H., banker; b. Salt Lake City, June 25, 1954; s. Roy William and Elizabeth (Ellison) S. B.A. in Econs., U. Utah, 1977; M.B.A., Harvard U., 1980. Comml. loan officer Allied Bancshares, Houston, 1980-81; asst. v.p. Zions Bancorp, Salt Lake City, 1981; fin. v.p., Zions Utah Bancorp, Salt Lake City, 1981-82, sr. v.p. fin., 1982-83, exec. v.p., sec., treas., 1984-86, pres., 1986—; pres. Zions Mortgage Co., 1987—; adj. instr. U. Utah, Salt Lake City, 1981-86; bd. dirs. S.F.I., Inc., Salt Lake City, Zions 1st Nat. Bank, Salt Lake City, Nevada State Bank, Las Vegas. Bd. dirs. United Way, Salt Lake City, 1983—, Utah Symphony, 1986—; trustee L.D.S. Hosp., Salt Lake City, 1987—; co-chair Greater Salt Lake Shelter-the-Homeless Com., 1986—. Mem. Utah Bankers Assn. (bd. dirs. 1987—), Am. Inst. Banking (bd. dirs. Salt Lake City chpt.), Phi Beta Kappa. Mormon. Office: Zions Bancorp 1380 Kennecott Bldg Salt Lake City UT 84133

SIMMONS, HARVEY OWEN, III, lawyer; b. Schenectady, N.Y., Nov. 20, 1948; s. Harvey Owen and Mary Elizabeth (Wall) S.; m. Doreen Anne Buranich, Oct. 12, 1974; children—Olivia Mary, Grace Catherine, Harvey O. Simmour IV. B.S. in Fgn. Service, Georgetown U., 1970; J.D., Union U., 1973; LL.M., NYU, 1984. Bar: N.Y. 1974. System atty. Niagara Mohawk Power, Syracuse, N.Y., 1977-80; asst. gen. counsel, asst. sec. Goulds Pumps, Inc., Seneca Falls, N.Y., 1980-86, dir. govt. affairs, gen. counsel, sec. Crucible Materials Corp., Syracuse, N.Y., 1986—. With USAR, 1970-77. Decorated Army Commendation medal; Georgetown U. scholar, 1966-70, scholar, Union U., 1970-73. Mem. N.Y. State Bar Assn. (Co-chmn. corp. counsel environ. com. 1984—, chmn. govt. affairs com. water systems council 1984-86), Onondaga County Bar Assn., Mfrs. Assn. central N.Y. (chmn. govt. affairs 1982-84). Republican. Roman Catholic. Club: Syracuse Men's Athletic. Home: 38 W Lake St Skaneateles NY 13152 Office: Crucible Materials Inc PO Box 977 Syracuse NY 13201

SIMMONS, HOWARD ENSIGN, JR., research administrator, chemist; b. Norfolk, Va., June 17, 1929; s. Howard Ensign and Marie Magdalene (Weidenhammer) S.; m. Elizabeth Anne Warren, Sept. 1, 1951; children: Howard Ensign III, John W. B.S. in Chemistry, MIT, 1951, Ph.D. in Organic Chemistry, 1954; D Sci. (hon.), RPI, 1987. Mem. research staff central research and devel. dept. E.I. du Pont de Nemours & Co., Wilmington, Del., 1954-59, research supr., 1959-70, asso. dir., 1970-74, dir. research, 1974-79, dir., 1979-83, v.p., 1983—; adj. prof. chemistry U. Del., 1974—; Sloan vis. prof. Harvard U., 1968; Kharasch vis. prof. U. Chgo., 1978. Author: (with A.G. Anastassiou) Theoretical Aspects of the Cyclobutadiene Problem in Cyclobutadiene, 1967; Editorial bd.: (with A.G. Anastassiou) Jour. Organic Chemistry, 1969-74, Synthesis, 1969—, Chem. Revs, 1972-74. Trustee Gordon Research Confs., 1974—. Fellow N.Y. Acad. Scis., Am. Acad. Arts and Scis.; mem. Nat. Acad. Scis., Soc. Chem. Industry, Am. Chem. Soc., Indsl. Research Inst., AAAS, Delta Kappa Epsilon. Home: PO Box 3874 Wilmington DE 19807 Office: E I du Pont de Nemours & Co 1007 Market St Wilmington DE 19898

SIMMONS, J. GERALD, management consultant; b. Atlanta, Sept. 17, 1929; s. Joseph D. and Nell (Ray) S.; m. Barbara McNeeley, Apr. 24, 1955. BBA, U. Miami, 1956; student advanced mgmt. program, Harvard U., 1969. With IMB Corp., 1956-71; dir. mktg. Data Processing div. IMB Corp., White Plains, N.Y., 1969-71; v.p., gen. mgr. dept. and specialty store div. Revlon Inc., N.Y.C., 1971-73; v.p. mktg. Wiltek Inc., Norwalk, Conn., 1973-76; pres. Handy Assocs., N.Y.C., 1976—. With U.S. Army, 1951-54. Mem. University Club, Greenwich (Conn.) Country Club. Office: Handy Assocs 250 Park Ave New York NY 10177

SIMMONS, JAMES BOYD, commodity broker-trader; b. Leavenworth, Kans., Oct. 2, 1944; s. James Louis and Louise (Boyd) S.; B.A. in Bus. and Polit. Sci., William Jewell Coll., 1966; m. Mary Susan Bauman, Oct. 4, 1969; children—Erin Michelle, James Bauman. Vice pres. Andco, Inc., Chgo., 1969-71 (merged with Heinold Commodities 1971); commodity broker and trader, mem. Chgo. Mercantile Exchange, 1971-79, 85—; exec. v.p. First Fidelity Investments, Phoenix; cons. Heinold Commodities; pres. Simmons-Rufenacht Securities Corp., Southwest Cattle Co., Simmons Trading Co.; ptnr. Rufenacht, Engler & Simmons; chmn. instl. rev. bd. ND: YAG Laser; mem. faculty Ariz. State U., Tempe; Pres. agrl. adv. council Ariz. State U. Republican. Mem. United Chs. of Christ. Club: Masons. Home: 800 S Wells St #1116 Chicago IL 60607 Office: 6045 N Scottsdale Rd Scottsdale AZ 85254

SIMMONS, JAMES PAT, JR., electronics company executive; b. Houston, Oct. 15, 1949; s. James Pat and Betty Lou (Baird) S.; m. Barbara Louise Furne, Nov. 29, 1975 (div. 1984); children: James P., Bradley M.; m. Silvia S. Colombetti, Oct. 1, 1988. BS in Applied Physics, Calif. Inst. Tech., 1972; MBA, Harvard U., 1974. From sect. mgr. to mgr. engring. to product mgr. Hewlett Packard Co., Palo Alto, Calif., 1974-83; mgr. product mktg. KLA Instruments Corp., Santa Clara, Calif., 1983-85; v.p. mktg. Applied Scanning Tech., Mt. View, Calif., 1985-87, Electronic Scanning Systems, Mt. View, Calif., 1987-88; v.p. mktg. and sales Nanometrics, Inc., Sunnyvale, Calif., 1988—. Contbr. articles to profl. jours; presenter Vision 86 Conf; presenter, program chmn. Vision West Conf., 1986. Mem. Harvard Bus. Sch. Assn. No. Calif. Republican. Lodge: Kiwanis (v.p. 1979-82). Home: 19863 Lindenbrook Ln Cupertino CA 95014 Office: Nanometrics Inc 690 E Arques Ave Sunnyvale CA 94085

SIMMONS, JOHN DEREK, securities analyst; b. Essex, Eng., July 17, 1931; s. Simon Leonard and Eve (Smart) S.; BS, Columbia, 1956; MBA, Rutgers U., 1959; postgrad. NYU, 1959-62; m. Rosalind Wellish, Mar. 5, 1961; children: Peter Lawrence, Sharon Leslie. Came to U.S., 1952. Chief cost accountant Airborne Accessories, Hillside, N.J., 1952-57; sr. cost analyst Curtiss-Wright Corp., Wood Ridge, N.J., 1957; sr. financial analyst internat. group Ford Motor Co., Jersey City, N.J., 1958-60; research asso. Nat. Assn. Accountants, N.Y.C., 1960-64; asst. to v.p. finance Air Reduction Co., Inc., 1965-67; mgr. corporate planning Anaconda Wire & Cable Co., N.Y.C., 1968; ind. financial cons., 1968-71; asso. cons. Rogers, Slade and Hill, Inc., N.Y.C., 1969-71; v.p., security analyst, economist Moore & Schley, Cameron & Co. (name now changed to Fourteen Research Corp.), 1972-81; v.p., security analyst Merrill Lynch Capital Markets, N.Y.C., 1981-88; security analyst Arnhold and S. Bleichroeder, Inc., N.Y.C., 1988—; lectr. profl. socs. and confs.; lectr. econs., mgmt., polit. sci. Rutgers U., 1957-64. Served to 1st lt. Brit. Army, 1950-52; granted personal coat of Arms By Queen Elizabeth II: manorial Lord of Ash., Suffolk, Eng. Mem. Am. Econ. Assn., Assn. Managerial Economists, Royal Econ. Soc., N.Y. Soc. Security Analysts. Contbr. articles on econs. of underdeveloped nations, polit. sci., mgmt., finance to U.S. and fgn. profl. and sci. jours. Home: 360 E 72d St New York NY 10021 Office: 45 Broadway New York NY 10006

SIMMONS, JOSEPH JACOB, III, federal commissioner; b. Muskogee, Okla., Mar. 26, 1925; s. Jacob, Jr. and Eva (Flowers) S.; m. Bernice Elizabeth Miller, Jan. 30, 1947; children: Jacob IV, Mary Agnes, Bernice, Jacolyn, Eva Frances. Student, U. Detroit, 1942-44, 46-47; B.S. in Geol. Engring., St. Louis U., 1949. Registered profl. engr., Okla. V.p., sec.-treas., geologist Simmons Royalty Co., Muskogee, 1949-61; regional oil and gas mobilization specialist U.S. Dept. of the Interior, Battle Creek, Mich., 1961-62; domestic petroleum production specialist Office of Oil and Gas U.S. Dept. of the Interior, Washington, 1962-66, asst. dir. Office of Oil and Gas, 1966-68, dep. adminstr. Oil Import Adminstrn., 1968-69, adminstr. Oil Import Adminstrn., 1969-70, Under Sec., 1983-84; v.p. govt. relations Amerada Hess Corp., N.Y.C., 1970-82; commr. ICC, Washington, 1982-83, 84—; vice chmn. ICC, 1986, 89; mem. fuel oil mktg. adv. com. Dept. Energy, 1978-82; commr. Pres.'s Commn. on Exec. Exchange, 1970-81; commr. Statue of Liberty Ellis Island Commn., 1983-88, bd. dirs. Found., 1984-86 ; mem. NAS Bd. of Earth Scis. and Resources, 1984—; mem. adv. bd. Dept. of Interior Outer Continental Shelf, 1984—. Youth dir. NAACP, 1950-55; candidate Okla. Ho. of Reps., 1956, City Council, 1956; trustee Madonna Coll., Livonia, Mich., 1969-76. Served with USAAF, 1944-46. Recipient Alumni Merit award St. Louis U., 1968, Spl. Act of Service award Dept. Interior, 1963, Outstanding Performance award, 1968, Disting. Service award, 1970. Mem. Am. Assn. Petroleum Geologists (Pub. Service award 1984), Soc. Petroleum Engrs., AIME.

SIMMONS, JOSEPH THOMAS, accountant, educator; b. Forest Lake, Minn., Jan. 23, 1936; s. Roland Thomas and Erma (Rabe) S.; m. Winola Ann Zwald, Aug. 18, 1962 (div.); children: Thomas E, Kevin M. BS in Bus. and Econs., Morningside Coll., 1964; MBA, U. S.D., 1965; PhD in Bus., U. Nebr., 1974. CPA, S.D. Prof. acctg. and fin. U. S.D., Vermillion, 1966-69, 75—, dir. sch. bus., 1975—; prof. U. Nebr., Lincoln, 1969-71, U. Man., Winnipeg, Can., 1971-75; prin. Simmons and Assocs. Mgmt. Cons., Rapid City, S.D., 1981—; pvt. practice acctg. Rapid City, 1982—; pres. Simmons Profl. Fin. Planning, Rapid City, 1983—; bd. dirs. MDU Resources Inc., Bismarck, N.D., Vermillion, Black Belt Inc., Rapid City, Spearfish, S.D., RE/Spec, Rapid City, Gro/Tech, Rapid City. Served with U.S. Army, 1958-60. Mem. Am. Acctg. Assn., AICPA, Fin. Mgmt. Assn., Investment Co. Inst., S.D. Soc. CPA's. Republican. Methodist. Home: 1407 E Main Vermillion SD 57069 Office: 1407 E Main Vermillion SD 57069

SIMMONS, KEITH ERNEST, consulting company executive; b. Seattle, Oct. 2, 1942; s. Harold E. and Lois Elaine (Hand) S.; m. Susan I. Balko, Dec. 26, 1980; children: Kristin, Matthew, Courtney. BA, Calif. State U., Sacramento, 1965; MSW, Wayne State U., 1969; MBA, Nat. U., 1989. Vol. Peace Corps, Columbia, 1965-67; social worker Sacramento County Dept. Social Welfare, 1969-71; chief community services, asst. dir. housing Sacramento Housing and Redevel. Agy., 1971-76; county dir. Peace Corps, Bahrain and North Yemen, 1976-80; project mgr. U.S. Aid, The Gambia, 1980-83; project devel. officer U.S. Aid, Sahel, Western Africa, 1983-85; dir. ops., then v.p. ops. RDA Internat., Inc., Placerville, Calif., 1985-87, exec. v.p., 1987—; chmn. U.S. Mission/Coop. Assn., The Gambia, 1981-82. V.p. United Cerebral Palsy Assn., Sacramento, 1972-73. State of Calif. grad. scholar Wayne State U., 1967-69; recipient Superior Performance award U.S. Aid The Gambia, 1981; commd U.S. Fgn. Service Officer, 1985. Mem. Soc. for Internat. Devel., Am. Fgn. Service Assn. Democrat. Presbyterian. Office: RDA Internat Inc 801 Morey Dr Placerville CA 95667

SIMMONS, RICHARD DE LACEY, mass media executive; b. Cambridge, Mass., Dec. 30, 1934; s. Ernest J. and Winifred (McNamara) S.; m. Mary DeWitt Bleecker, May 20, 1961; children: Christopher DeWitt, Robin Bleecker. Grad. Phillips Exeter Acad., 1951; AB, Harvard Coll., 1955; LLB, Columbia U., 1958. Bar: N.Y. 1959. V.p., gen. counsel Dun & Bradstreet Corp., N.Y.C., 1969-73, exec. v.p., 1976-79, vice chmn., 1979-81; pres. Moody's Investors Service, N.Y.C., 1973-75; pres. Dun & Bradstreet, Inc., N.Y.C., 1975; pres., chief operating officer Washington Post Co., Washington, 1981—; bd. dirs. Union Pacific Corp. Bd. dirs. Children's Aid Soc., Internat. House, Phillips Collection, Rockefeller U. Council. Office: The Washington Post Co 1150 15th St NW Washington DC 20071 *

SIMMONS, RICHARD P., steel company executive. Chief exec. officer Allegheny Ludlum Steel Corp., Pitts.; also dir. Allegheny Ludlum Corp. (formerly Allegheny Ludlum Steel Corp.), Pitts., formerly also pres. Office: Allegheny Ludlum Steel Corp 1000 6th PPG Pl Pittsburgh PA 15222 *

SIMMONS, RICHARD SHERIDAN, lawyer, banker; b. N.Y.C., Sept. 28, 1928; s. William and Mary E. (Sheridan) S.; m. Margaret Patricia Casey, June 30, 1955; 1 son, William. B.A. summa cum laude, Princeton U., 1951; LL.B., Yale U., 1954. Bar: N.Y. 1956. Mem. firm Cravath, Swaine and Moore, N.Y.C., 1956—; partner firm Cravath, Swaine and Moore, 1963-85; vice chmn. Chem. Banking Corp. and Chem. Bank, 1985—; Dep. supt. Banks of State of N.Y., 1959-60. Editor: Yale Law Jour, 1954. Served with U.S. Army, 1954-56. Mem. Internat. Bar Assn., ABA (chmn. banking com. 1970-75), N.Y. State Bar Assn., Assn. Bar City of N.Y., Council on Fgn. Relations, Soc. Colonial Wars, St. Nicholas Soc., SAR. Mem. Dutch Reformed Ch. Clubs: University, Links, North Hempstead Country, Sailfish Point Golf. Office: Chem Banking Corp 277 Park Ave New York NY 10172

SIMMONS, ROBERT J., medical products company executive; b. 1943. BS, U. Ill., 1965; student, Northwestern U., 1980. With Am. Hosp. Supply Corp., Evanston, Ill., 1965-85, various sales positions, 1965-74, from v.p. corp. sales to exec. v.p. mktg., 1974-85; formerly group v.p. Baxter Travenol Labs., Deerfield, Ill., 1985; now exec. v.p. Baxter Internat. Inc., Deerfield, Ill. Office: Baxter Internat Inc 1 Baxter Pkway Deerfield IL 60015 *

SIMMONS, ROSS ROBERT, small business executive; b. Bend, Oreg., Aug. 28, 1955; s. Robert Edward and Shirley Francis (Braker) S.; m. Wendy Jane Melander, July 8, 1978; 1 child, Gregory Russell. Student, Cen. Oreg. Community Coll., 1973-74, Lewis and Clark Coll., 1974-77. Reporter Sta. KGRL, Bend, 1970-74; sports writer The Bull, Bend, 1971-74; news writer Lewis and Clark Coll., Portland, 1974-77; reporter, editor Valley Times, Beaverton, Oreg., 1977-78; buyer Meier & Frank Co., Portland, 1978-81; asst. mgr. Total Office Products Co., Portland, 1984-85; tech. writer Century Environ. Scis., Portland, 1985-86; prin. SRH Assocs., Inc., Portland, 1986—; freelance tech. writer, Portland, 1984-85. Mem. Bend Sch. Budget Adv. Com., 1974, Metro Diesel Study Task Force, Portland, 1985; chmn. Portland Parking Adv. Com., 1984-86. Mem. City Club. Democrat. Home: 3776 NW 163d Terr Beaverton OR 97006 Office: SRH Assocs 123 NE 3d Ave Ste 230 Portland OR 97232

SIMMONS, ROY WILLIAM, banker; b. Portland, Oreg., Jan. 24, 1916; s. Henry Clay and Ida (Mudd) S.; m. Elizabeth Ellison, Oct. 28, 1938; children—Julia Simmons Watkins, Matthew R., Laurence E., Elizabeth Jane Simmons Hoke, Harris H., David E. Asst. cashier First Nat. Bank Layton, Utah, 1944-49; Utah bank commr. 1949-51; exec. v.p. Bank of Utah, Ogden, 1951-53; pres. Lockhart Co., Salt Lake City, 1953-64, Zion's First Nat. Bank, Salt Lake City, 1964-81; chief exec. officer Zion's First Nat. Bank, 1965—; chmn., chief exec. officer Zion's Utah Bancorp., 1965—; chmn. bd. Zion's Savs. & Loan Assn., 1961-69; pres. Lockhart Co., 1964—; bd. dirs. Salt Lake City br. Fed. Res. Bank San Francisco, 1971-77, Kennecott Copper Corp., 1964-81, Beneficial Life Ins. Co., 1964—, Hotel Utah, 1964-85, Utah Portland Cement Co., Mountain Fuel Supply Co., 1964-83, Denver & Rio Grande R.R., 1964-83, Rio Grande Industries, 1964-85, Ellison Ranching Co., 1969—. Chmn. Utah Bus. Devel. Corp., 1969-80; Mem. Utah State Bd. Regents, 1969-81. Mem. Salt Lake City C. of C. (treas. 1964-65), Sigma Pi. Republican. Mem. Ch. of Jesus Christ of Latter Day Saints. Home: Crestwood Rd Kaysville UT 84037 Office: Zions Utah Bancorp 1380 Kennecott Bldg Salt Lake City UT 84133

SIMMONS, SAMUEL LEE, lawyer; b. St. Louis, Dec. 27, 1929; s. David Mayo and Mayme Pearle (Looney) S.; m. Joan Miller, Oct. 8, 1959; children—Lesley, Samuel Lee. B.A. with honors, Principia Coll., 1951; J.D. cum laude, Harvard U., 1957. Bar: N.Y. 1958. Atty. Standard Oil Co. N.J., N.Y.C., 1957-59; firm Arthur, Dry & Dole, N.Y.C., 1959-63; with ITT, 1963-75; staff counsel, gen. counsel ITT Credit Corp., 1963-67; v.p. parent co., gen. counsel European hdqrs. Europe Inc., Brussels, Belgium, 1967-75; v.p., gen. counsel Revlon Inc., N.Y.C., 1975-76; sr. v.p., gen. counsel Revlon Inc., 1976-86, dir., 1976-85, corp. sec., 1979-81; sr. v.p. dir. corp. devel. ITT Corp., 1987—. Served with U.S. Army, 1952-54. Home: ITT Corp 320 Park Ave New York NY 10022

SIMMONS, SUZANNE, financial executive; b. Vicksburg, Miss., July 1, 1955; d. Henry and Mary Lee (Washington) S. AS in Secretarial Sci., Utica Jr. Coll., 1975; BSBA, Jackson State U., 1980. Procurement clk. U.S. Dept. Agr., Jackson, Miss., 1977; pub. info. officer U.S. Dept. Agr., Jackson, 1977-83; computer operator VA, Jackson, 1987-88; adjudication clk. Dept. Vets. Affairs (formerly 1989), Jackson, 1988—. Active Big Bros./Bis Sisters Orgn., Jackson, 1977-83. With USAF, 1983-87. Mem. Nat. Alliance Postal and Fed. Employees (editor newsletter 1978-83, hospitality com. 1978-83, registration com. 1988—), Fed. Employees Assn., Operation PUSH, Jr. Matrone (v.p. 1988—), Govt. Employees Assn., Heroines of Jericho (mem. courtesy and project com.). Democrat. Methodist. Home: 2950 Oakmont Dr Jackson MS 39209 Office: VA 100 W Capitol St Jackson MS 39269

SIMMONS, VICTOR J., mortgage and insurance broker; b. Vallejo, Calif., June 17, 1945; s. Victor J. Simmons; 1 child from previous marriage: Miriam Victoria. BA, U. Nev., 1968. Bid coordinator Dietary Products div. Am. Hosp. Supply Corp., Irvine, Calif., 1972-73; loan officer, appraiser Brentwood Savs., Los Angeles, 1973-77; loan cons. Union Fed. Savs., Los Angeles, 1978-79; mortgage banker Far West Mortgage, Los Angeles, 1980-81; ins. agt. Met. Life Ins., Los Angeles, 1981-84; mortgage, ins. broker Far West Mortgage, Los Angeles, 1984-85; loan cons. Coast Savs., Beverly Hills, Calif., 1985—. Contbr. articles to profl. jours., 1967-71. Served to 1st lt. USMCR, 1968-71. Democrat. Baptist. Home: PO Box 78281 Los Angeles CA 90016-0281 Office: Coast Savs 9090 Wilshire Blvd #200 Beverly Hills CA 90211

SIMMS, ROBERTA CLARK, accountant; b. LaCrosse, Wis., Dec. 20, 1945; d. Lawrence Andrew and Margaret Louise (Knight) Clark; m. Thomas Earl Simms, June 19, 1965; 1 child, Davine. Student, U. Colo., 1986—. Lic. real estate broker, Colo. Operator supr. Mountain Bell., Boulder, Colo., 1964-68; title clk. Crouch Motors, Boulder, 1968-69; office mgr. Foothill Lincoln Mercury, Boulder, 1970-75; bookkeeper Donald C. Davies, Boulder, 1975-76, acct., 1985-86; owner Boulder Music Centre, Inc., 1976-83; owner, acct. Office Assocs., Ltd., Boulder, 1983-85, acct., 1987—; acct. Jack Kopp & Assocs., Boulder, 1986-87. Treas. Boulder Sci. of Mind Ctr., 1983-85; chmn. fund raising Mapletree Sch., Boulder, 1986; troop leader Girl Scouts U.S.A., Boulder, 1981-83; area rep. Am. Intercultural Student Exchange, 1985—. Mem. Colo. Soc. Pub. Accts., Beta Sigma Phi. Republican. Mem. Religious Sci. Ch. Club: Boulder Country. Home: 4543 Starboard Dr Boulder CO 80301 Office: Office Assocs Ltd 4543 Starboard Dr Boulder CO 80301

SIMON, ALEXANDER A., real estate developer; b. Delray Beach, Fla., Nov. 23, 1937; s. Alexander Abraham and Linda (Zaine) Simon-Eassa; m. Dona W. Simon, May 29, 1976. BS, Ga. Inst. Tech., 1960; MBA, U. Pa., 1965. Salesman Ga. Pacific Corp., Atlanta, 1961-63; v.p. Scott Hudgens Properties, Inc., Atlanta, 1965-68; pres. Oglethorpe Properties, Savannah, Ga., 1968-73, Shenandoah Devel., Inc., Atlanta, 1973-77; v.p. Ackerman & Co., Atlanta, 1977-78; pres. Simon Enterprises, Inc., Delray Beach, 1978—; bd. dirs. Midatlantic Bank and Trust Co., Ft. Lauderdale, Fla.; chmn. bd. dirs. Morikami Mus., Delray Beach, 1986—. Chmn. planning and zoning bd., Delray Beach, 1983-86; chmn. Visions 2000, 1987—; mem. vestry Episc. Ch., 1988—. Recipient Law Day award Savannah Bar Assn, 1972. Mem. Delray Beach Bd. Realtors. Republican. Club: Loggerhead (v.p. Boca Raton, Fla. chpt. 1987—). Lodge: Kiwanis (bd. dirs. Delray Beach club 1986—). Office: Simon Enterprises Inc 777 E Atlantic Ave Suite 310 Delray Beach FL 33483

SIMON, ANDREA JUDITH, bank executive, anthropologist; b. N.Y.C., Dec. 1, 1946; d. Bernard T. and Helen (Handelsman) Wollman; m. Andrew L. Simon, June 30, 1968; children: Alexandra Beth, Rachel Heather. BA, Pa. State U., 1968; PhD, CUNY, 1977. Asst. prof. anthropology Ramapo Coll., Mawah, N.J., 1973-80; consultant Citibank, White Plains, N.Y., 1981; distbn. mgr. Citibank, White Plains, 1981-82; branch mgr. Citibank, Mohegan Lake, N.Y., 1982-84; regional sales mgr. Citibank, N.Y.C., 1984-85; sr. v.p. consumer banking Poughkeepsie (N.Y.) Savings Bank, 1985-88, sr. v.p. mktg. and corp. devel., 1988—; ind. cons. Producer, dir.: CBS Sunrise Semesters series, 1980-81; contbr. articles to profl. jours. Dir. mktg. Main Mall Commn. for City of Poughkeepsie, 1986—. Recipient Nat. Endowment for Humanities grant, 1979. Mem. Assn. of Savings Banks of N.Y. State (operations com. 1986—), Hudson Valley Mktg. Assn. Home: RD 1 Box 346 Hunterbrook Rd Yorktown Heights NY 10598 Office: Poughkeepsie Svs Bank PO Box 31 2 Garden St Poughkeepsie NY 12602

SIMON, DAVID HAROLD, public relations executive; b. Washington, Dec. 3, 1930; s. Isaac B. and Marjorie S. (Felstiner) S.; m. Ruth Lurie, Mar. 2, 1962; children: Rachel, Jessie. B.E.E., Cornell U., 1954. Mktg. engr. Sylvania Elec. Products, Inc., Boston, 1957-58; advt. mgr. Sylvania Elec. Products, Inc., Mountain View, Calif., 1958-60; regional sales engr. Sylvania Elec. Products, Inc., Los Angeles, 1960-63; mgr. advt. and public relations Electronic Splty. Co., Los Angeles, 1963-66; corp. dir. advt. and public relations Teledyne, Inc., Los Angeles, 1966-67; pres. Simon/Public Relations, Inc., Los Angeles, 1967—. Contbr. articles on public relations to various publs. Res. dep. sheriff Los Angeles Sheriff's Dept., 1973—; mem. Los Angeles Olympic Citizen's Adv. Commn., 1980-84; commr. City of Los Angeles Cultural Affairs Commn., 1987—; trustee Calif. Chamber Symphony, 1981-84. Served with USN, 1954-57. Mem. Public Relations Soc. Am., Nat. Assn. Sci. Writers, Nat. Assn. Corp. Dirs. (founding pres. Los Angeles chpt.), Opera Buffs Inc. (bd. dirs. 1986-87), Mensa. Home: 13025 Weddington St Van Nuys CA 91401 Office: Simon McGarry Pub Rels Inc 11661 San Vicente Blvd Ste 903 Los Angeles CA 90049

SIMON, DAVID SIDNEY, consumer goods manufacturing executive; b. Cleve., Feb. 5, 1941; s. Edwin and Dena (Katz) S.; m. Evelyn Wendy Kulber, Jan. 27, 1963; children: Eric Marc, Todd Alan. BS in Mgmt. Sci., Case Inst. Tech., 1963; MBA, Wharton Sch. U. Pa., 1965. Sr. fin. advisor Mobil Oil Corp., N.Y.C., 1965-69; asst. treas. Dart Industries, Los Angeles, 1969-81, Dart and Kraft Inc., Northbrook, Ill., 1981-82; exec. v.p. fin. and adminstrn. Dart and Kraft Fin. Corp., Northbrook, 1982-86; v.p., treas. and info. systems Premark Internat. Inc., Deerfield, Ill., 1986—; instr. Lake Forest Grad. Sch. Mgmt. Mem. Village Ctr. Devel. Com., Deefield, 1987—. Mem. Fin. Exec. Inst. (chmn. North Shore Luncheon group 1985-86), Econ. Club Chgo., Nat. Vehicle Leasing Assn. (dir. at large 1985-86). Republican. Club: Ravinia Green Country (Deerfield). Office: Premark Internat Inc 1717 Deerfield Rd Deerfield IL 60015

SIMON, DEBRA WAGNER, accountant; b. Phila., July 24, 1959; d. Joseph and Annette (Schmerling) Wagner; m. Paul Stephen Simon, Sept. 5, 1982; 1 child, Jessica M. BSBA, Drexel U., 1982. CPA, Pa. Jr. acct. Mann Judd Landau, Phila., 1983-84, staff acct., 1984, sr. acct., 1985—. Mem. Surrey Pl. Civic Assn., Cherry Hill, N.J., 1985-86. Mem. AICPA, Pa.Inst. CPA's, Am. Women's Soc. CPA's, Am. Soc. Women Accts., Beta Alpha Psi. Avocations: tennis, computers. Office: Mann Judd Landau 1401 Walnut St Philadelphia PA 19102

SIMON, EDWARD R., JR., furniture manufacturing company executive; b. 1940; married. Formerly with Ford Motor Co., GM; with Herman Miller Inc., Zeeland, Mich., 1970—, pres., chief operating officer, 1985—. Office: Herman Miller Inc 8500 Byron Rd Zeeland MI 49464 *

SIMON, HERBERT A(LEXANDER), social scientist; b. Milw., June 15, 1916; s. Arthur and Edna (Merkel) S.; m. Dorothea Pye, Dec. 25, 1937; children: Katherine S. Frank, Peter Arthur, Barbara. A.B., U. Chgo., 1936, Ph.D., 1943, LL.D., 1964; D.Sc., Case Inst. Tech., 1963, Yale U., 1963, Marquette U., 1981, Columbia U., 1983, Gustavus Adolphus U., 1984, Mich. Tech. U., 1988; Fil. Dr., Lund U., Sweden, 1968; LL.D., McGill U., Montreal, Que., Can., 1970, U. Mich., 1978, U. Pitts., 1979; LLD., U. Paul Valery, France, 1984; Dr. Econ. Sci., Erasmus U. Rotterdam, Netherlands, 1973, Duquesne U., 1988; D.SC., LHD, Ill. Inst. Tech., 1988; D. Polit. Sci., U. Pavia, Italy, 1988. Research asst. U. Chgo., 1936-38; staff mem. Internat. City Mgrs.' Assn.; also asst. editor Pub. Mgmt. and Municipal Year Book, 1938-39; dir. adminstrv. measurement studies Bur. Pub. Adminstrn., U. Calif., 1939-42; asst. prof. polit. sci. Ill. Inst. Tech., 1942-45, asso. prof., 1945-47, prof., 1947-49; also chmn. dept. polit. and social sci. 1946-49; prof. adminstrn. and psychology Carnegie-Mellon U., Pitts., 1949-65, Richard King Mellon univ. prof. computer scis. and psychology, 1965—, head dept. indsl. mgmt., 1949-60; asso. dean Grad. Sch. Indsl. Adminstrn., 1957-73, trustee, 1972—; cons. to Internat. City Mgrs. Assn., 1942-49, U.S. Bur. Budget, 1946-49, U.S. Census Bur., 1947, Cowles Found. for Research in Econs., 1947-60; cons. and acting dir. Mgmt. Engring. br. Econ. Cooperation Adminstrn., 1948; Ford Distinguished lectr. N.Y. U., 1959; Vanuxem lectr. Princeton, 1961; William James lectr. Harvard, 1963, Sigma Xi lectr., 1964, 76-78, 86; Harris lectr. Northwestern U., 1967; Karl Taylor Compton lectr. MIT, 1968; Wolfgang Koehler lectr. Dartmouth, 1975; Katz-Newcomb lectr. U. Mich., 1976; Carl Hovland lectr. Yale, 1976; Ueno lectr., Tokyo, 1977; Gaither lectr. U. Calif., Berkeley, 1980; Camp lectr. Stanford U., 1982; Gannon lectr. Fordham U., 1982, ; Oates vis. fellow Princeton U., 1982; Marschak lectr. UCLA, 1983; Auguste Comte lectr. London Sch. Econs., 1987; Lee Kuan Yew lectr. U. Singapore, 1989; hon. prof. Tianjin (China) U., 1980, Beijing (China) U., 1986; hon. research scientist Inst. Psychology, Chinese Acad. Scis., 1985; chmn. bd. dirs. Social Sci. Research Council, 1961-65; chmn. div. behavioral scis. NRC, 1968-70; mem. President's Sci. Adv. Com., 1968-72; trustee Carnegie Inst., Pitts., 1987—; cons. bus. and govtl. orgns. Author or co-author: books relating to field, including Administrative Behavior, 1947, 3d edit., 1976, Public Administration, 1950; Models of Man, 1956, Organizations, 1958, New Science of Management Decision, 1960, rev. edit., 1977, The Shape of Automation, 1965, The Sciences of the Artificial, 1968, 2d edit., 1981, Human Problem Solving, 1972, Skew Distributions and Business Firm Sizes, 1976, Models of Discovery, 1977, Models of Thought, vol. I 1979, vol. II 1989, Models of Bounded Rationality, 1982, Reason in Human Affairs, 1983, Protocol Analysis, 1984, Scientific Discovery, 1987. Chmn. Pa. Gov.'s Milk Inquiry Com., 1964-65. Recipient adminstrs. award Am. Coll. Hosp. Adminstrs., 1957; Frederick Mosher award Am. Soc. Pub. Adminstrn., 1974; Alfred Nobel Meml. prize in econ. scis., 1978; Dow-Jones award, 1983; scholarly contbns. award Acad. Mgmt., 1983; Nat. Medal of Sci., 1986, Pender award U. Pa., 1987; Fiorino d'Oro City of Florence, Italy, 1988, Am. Psychol. Found. Gold Medal, 1988. Distinguished fellow Am. Econ. Assn. (Ely lectr. 1977); fellow Econometric Soc., AAAS, Am. Acad. Arts and Scis., Am. Psychol. Assn. (Disting. Sci. Contbn. award 1969), Am. Sociol. Soc., Inst. Mgmt. Scis. (life, v.p. 1954), Brit. Psychol. Assn. (hon.); mem. N.Y. Acad. Scis. (hon.), Jewish Acad. Arts Scis., Am. Polit. Sci. Assn. (James Madison award 1984), Assn. for Computing Machinery (A.M. Turing award 1975), Nat. Acad. Scis. (mem. com. sci. and pub. policy 1967-69, 82—, chmn. com. air quality control 1974, chmn. com. behavioral scis. NSF 1975-76, mem. council 1978-81, 83-8 chmn. com. scholarly communication with PRC, 1983-87 co-chmn. com. behavioral sci. in prevention of nuclear war, 1986—), Soc. Exptl. Psychologists, Am. Philos. Soc., IEEE (hon.), Royal Soc. Letters (Lund) (fgn. mem.), Orgnl. Sci. Soc. (Japan) (hon.), Yugoslav Acad. Scis. (fgn.), Indonesian Economists Assn. (hon.), Phi Beta Kappa, Sigma Xi (Procter prize 1980). Democrat. Unitarian. Clubs: Cosmos (Washington); University (Pitts.). Office: Carnegie-Mellon U Dept Psychology Schenley Pk Pittsburgh PA 15213

SIMON, H(UEY) PAUL, lawyer; b. Lafayette, La., Oct. 19, 1923; s. Jules and Ida (Rogere) S.; m. Carolyn Perkins, Aug. 6, 1949; 1 child, John Clark. B.S., U. Southwestern La., 1943; J.D., Tulane U., 1947. Bar: La. 1947; CPA, La., 1947. Pvt. practice New Orleans, 1947—; asst. prof. advanced acctg. U. Southwestern La., 1944-45; staff acct. Haskins & Sells, New Orleans, 1945-53, prin., 1953-57; ptnr. law firm Deutsch, Kerrigan & Stiles, 1957-79; founding sr. ptnr. law firm Simon, Peragine, Smith & Redfearn, 1979—. Author: Community Property and Liability for Funeral Expenses of Deceased Spouse, 1946, Income Tax Deductibility of Attorney's Fees in Action in Boundary, 1946, Fair Labor Standards Act and Employee's Waiver of Liquidated Damages, 1946, Louisiana Income Tax Law, 1956, Changes Effected by the Louisiana Trust Code, 1965, Gifts to Minors and the Parent's Obligation of Support, 1968; co-author: Deductions—Business or Hobby, 1975, Role of Attorney in IRS Tax Return Examination, 1978; assoc. editor: The Louisiana CPA, 1956-60; bd. editors Tulane Law Rev., 1945-46; estates, gifts and trusts editor The Tax Times, 1986-87. Mem. ABA (mem. tax sect. com. ct. procedure 1958—), La. Bar Assn. (com. on legislation and adminstrv. practice 1966-70), New Orleans Bar Assn., Inter-Am. Bar Assn., Internat. Bar Assn. (com. on securities issues and trading 1970-88), Am. Judicature Soc., Am. Inst. CPA's, Am. Assn. Atty.-CPA's, Soc. La. CPA's, New Orleans Assn. Notaries, Tulane Alumni Assn., New Orleans C. of C. (council 1952-66), New Orleans Met. Area Com., Council for Better La., NYU Tax Conf.-New Orleans (co-chmn. 1976), Tulane Tax Inst. (program com. 1960—), La. Tax Conf. (program com. 1968-72), Tulane Law Sch. Dean's Coun., Bur. Govtl. Research, New Orleans Bd. Trade, Pub. Affairs Research Council, Internat. Platform Assn., Met. Crime Commn., Phi Delta Phi (past pres. New Orleans chpt.), Sigma Pi Alpha. Roman Catholic. Clubs: Young Men's Bus., Petroleum, City, Press, Toastmasters Internat., New Orleans Country, International House (dir. 1976-79, 82-85), World Trade Ctr. (dir. fin. com. 1985-86) (New Orleans), various others. Office: Energy Centre 30th Fl New Orleans LA 70163

SIMON, JAMES MICHAEL, natural resources company executive; b. Montgomery, Ala., Sept. 17, 1951; s. Alfred Philip and Ellen Rae (Shattuck) S.; m. Erica J.B. Burnett, Aug. 9, 1972 (div. Sept. 1976); 1 child, Tristan Michael; m. Karen Ann Kendig, Sept. 29, 1984; 1 child, Lauren Elliott. Student, U. London, 1971-72; BA, Denison U., 1973; postgrad., Cin. U., 1976-78. Examiner, pub. info. officer State of Ohio, Columbus and Cin., 1973-78; account exec. Paul Werth Assocs., Inc., Columbus, 1978-79; dir. devel. Cleve. Ballet, 1979-80; mgr. communications services TRW, Inc., Cleve., 1980-81; mgr. pub. affairs Allied Corp., Morristown, N.J., 1981-85; dir. corp. affairs Inspiration Resources Corp., N.Y.C., 1985—; tchr., trustee Montclair (N.J.) Adult Sch. 1987—; cons. various firms, N.Y. and N.J., 1986—. Contbr. articles to newspapers, mags. Bd. dirs. Voluntary Action Ctr., Morristown, 1982-85. Named one of Outstanding Young Men Am., 1986. Mem. Nat. Investor Relations Inst., Am. Mining Congress Communications Com., The Bd. Room Club. Presbyterian. Home: 14 Fairmount Ave Upper Montclair NJ 07043 Office: Inspiration Resources Corp 250 Park Ave New York NY 10177

SIMON, JOSEPH PATRICK, food services executive; b. Phila., Nov. 9, 1932; s. Joseph Patrick and Elizabeth Gertrude (McLaughlin) S.; m. Vera Cornelia Steiner, Sept. 15, 1956; children: Joseph Walter, Walter Joseph, Leslie Vera, Ernest William. B.S., Cornell U., 1955. With Slater Systems, 1955-59; with ARA Services, Inc., Phila., 1959-72; regional v.p. ARA Services, Inc., 1964-66, area v.p., 1966-68, group v.p. and sr. v.p., 1968-70, pres. community and school food service div., 1970-71, gen. mgr. internat. ops., 1971-72; v.p., gen. mgr. airline services div. Dobbs Houses Inc., Memphis, 1972-73; group v.p. Service Systems Corp., Buffalo, 1973-79; pres. Service Systems Corp., 1980-85, also nat. dir.; group v.p. P.J. Schmitt subs. Loblaw Ltd., 1984, sr. v.p., 1985-88. Dist. chmn. Detroit United Fund, 1966-67, Nat. Alliance of Businessmen, 1969; mem. adv. bd. McComb Jr. Coll.; mem. council Cornell U., 1980-83; chmn. bd. Sheehan Emergency Hosp., Buffalo, 1984-85; trustee D'Youville Coll. Served as 1st lt. U.S. Army, 1955-56. Mem. Assn. Food Service Mgmt. (dir.), Nat. Automatic Merchandising Assn. (dir.), Buffalo C. of C. (dir.), Cornell Hotel Soc. Mich. (pres.), Zeta Psi. Episcopalian. Clubs: Memphis Athletic, Detroit Athletic; Buffalo (Buffalo), Park Country (Buffalo). Home: 4422 Whisperwood Sarasota FL 34235

SIMON, LEONARD SAMUEL, banker; b. N.Y.C., Oct. 28, 1936; s. Nathaniel and Lena (Pasternack) S.; m. Marion Appel, Sept. 1, 1957; children: Andrew, Jonathan. B.S., MIT, 1958; M.S., Columbia U., 1959, Ph.D., 1963. Mem. faculty Grad. Sch. Mgmt., U. Rochester, 1962-79, prof., 1974-79; v.p. Community Savs. Bank, Rochester, N.Y., 1969-74; sr. v.p. Community Savs. Bank, 1974-77, exec. v.p., 1977-83; exec. v.p. Rochester Community Sav. Bank, 1983-84, chmn., chief exec. officer, 1984—; chmn. Telephone Computing Service Corp., 1974-79; trustee Tchrs. Ins. Annuity Assn. Editor-in-chief, founding editor: Interfaces, 1970-76; Author books and articles in field. Past chmn. Rochester-Monroe County chpt. ARC, Rochester Area Ednl. TV Assn.; chmn. Women's Career Ctr.; treas. Ctr. for

Govt. Research; mem. Urban Policy Conf., Brookings Instn., 1972-73, 64th Am. Assembly. Ford Found. grantee, 1964; recipient MIT Corp. Leadership award, 1987. Mem. Savs. Bank Assn. N.Y. State, Nat. Council Savs. Instns., Beta Gamma Sigma. Clubs: Ski Valley, Genesee Valley. Office: Rochester Community Savs Bank 235 Main St E Rochester NY 14618

SIMON, MARTIN STANLEY, commodity marketing company executive, economist; b. St. Louis, Sept. 6, 1926; s. Elmer Ellis and Bessye Marion (Werner) S.; m. Rita Edith Scheinhorn, June 18, 1950; children: Deborah, Richard. B.B.A., CCNY, 1949; M.A., NYU, 1953. Econ. statistician Indsl. Commodity Corp, N.Y.C., 1949-52; agrl. econ. statistician Dept. Agr., Washington, 1952-58; commodity analyst Connell Rice & Sugar Co., Inc., Westfield, N.J., 1958-62; asst. to pres. Connell Rice & Sugar Co., Inc., 1962-67, v.p., 1967-74, sr. v.p., 1974—; cons. AID, Jamaica, 1963; mem. Rice Insp. Industry Adv. Com., Washington, 1971-72. Served with U.S. Army, 1944-46, ETO. Recipient Class of 1920 award for merit in econ. stats. CCNY, 1949. Mem. Am. Econ. Assn., Rice Millers Assn. (chmn. legis. options working group 1984-86, govt. programs com. 1986-87, chmn. PL480 subcom. 1988-89), Nat. Economists Club, Beta Gamma Sigma. Office: Connell Rice & Sugar Co Inc 45 Cardinal Dr Westfield NJ 07092

SIMON, MICHAEL RICHARD, invesent banker; b. Phila., June 26, 1959; s. Sanford R. and Arlene May (Krasnor) S.; m. Karen O. Kesserl, Oct. 16, 1987. BA, U. Pa., 1981; MBA, NYU, 1987. Engr. Mgmt. Systems and Controls, Orange, Calif., 1981-82; assoc. Am. Corp. Svcs., N.Y.C., 1983-85, v.p., 1985—; bd. dirs., v.p. Ferranti High Tech., Inc., N.Y.C., D.A. Electronics Cons., Holbrook, N.Y. Mem. Am. Mgmt. Assn., Am. Electronic Assn., Friends of Wine Club. Office: Am Corp Svcs 515 Madison Ave Ste 1225 New York NY 10022

SIMON, RONALD ISAAC, corporate financial executive; b. Cairo, Nov. 4, 1938; came to U.S., 1942, naturalized, 1949; s. David and Helene (Zilkha) S.; BA, Harvard U., 1960; MA, Columbia U., 1962, PhD (Ford Found. fellow), 1968; m. Anne Faith Hartman, June 19, 1960; children: Cheryl Lynne, Eric Lewis, Daniel Jay. Vice pres. Harpers Internat. Inc., N.Y.C., 1959-62; fin. analyst Amerace Corp., N.Y.C., 1965-66; v.p. Am. Foresight Inc., Phila., 1966-67; asst. to pres. Avco Corp., N.Y.C., 1967-70, exec. v.p., treas., Avco Community Developers Inc., 1970-73, dir. Avco Community Developers Inc., 1969-73; pres. Ronald I. Simon Inc., La Jolla, Calif., 1973—; pres., chief exec. officer Delta Data Systems Corp., 1980-81; exec. v.p., sec., dir. Towner Petroleum Co., Houston, 1983-85, mng. dir., chief fin. officer The Henley Group, Inc., La Jolla, Calif., 1986—; dir. Craig Corp., Reading Corp. Club: University (N.Y.C.). Office: Henley Group Inc 11255 N Torrey Pines La Jolla CA 92037

SIMON, WALTER L., brokerage executive; b. Stuttgart, Germany, Oct. 28, 1936; came to U.S., 1939; s. Sali and Bianka (Ottenheimer) S.; m. Marla H. Amato, Dec. 31, 1976; 1 child, David Andrew. BBA, Baruch Coll., 1957. Mcpl. bonds trader E.F. Hutton & Co., N.Y.C., 1959-63; mcpl. bonds broker N.Y. Hanseatic, N.Y.C., 1963-65; sr. v.p. bond dept. Swiss Am. Securities, Inc., N.Y.C., 1965—. With U.S. Army, 1957. Mem. Wall St. Club, Bond Club N.Y., Mcpl. Bond Club N.Y. Office: Swiss Am Securities Inc 100 Wall St New York NY 10005

SIMONDS, G. NICHOLS, automotive company executive; b. Kansas City, Mo., Aug. 18, 1939; s. L. Goodman and Margaret A. (Nichols) S.; m. Nanne W. Barth, Nov. 28, 1964; children: Stephanie N., Timothy W. BS in Indsl. Engring., Northwestern U., 1962, MBA, 1964. Mgr. systems devel. Inland Steel Co., Chgo., 1969-77, mgr. mfg. systems, 1976-79, dir. systems, 1979-81; dir. mgmt. svcs. Nat. Steel Co., Pitts., 1981-84, Nat. Intergroup, Pitts., 1984; mgr. info. systems Chrysler Motors, Highland Park, Mich., 1984-85; dir. mgmt. info. systems Chrysler Motors, Highland Park, 1985-87, exec. dir. mgmt. info. systems, 1987—. Pres. Elmhurst (Ill.) Pk. Dist., 1979; mem. adv. bd. United Found. Systems, Detroit, 1987—. Mem. U. Mich. Systems Exec. Forum (rsch. bd. 1981—), Northwestern Alumni Assn. (treas. 1980-81), Northwestern Club Chgo. (pres. 1980-81). Office: Chrysler Corp 1200 Chrysler Dr Highland Park MI 48288

SIMONI, JOSEPH PILIE, banking association official; b. San Francisco, Feb. 26, 1945; s. Joseph Mario and Vittoria (Baldassari) S.; B.A. in Bus., Calif. State U., San Francisco, 1977; M.B.A., Coll. Notre Dame, 1979; m. Patricia Sue Mazza, Mar. 23, 1969. With Wells Fargo Bank, 1970-84, asst. v.p., San Lorenzo, Calif., 1982-84; mgr. program devel. and instrn. Am. Inst. Banking, San Francisco, 1984-86; asst. v.p., mgr. First Comml. Bank, San Francisco, 1986—; mgr. program devel./instrn. Am. Inst. Banking, San Francisco, 1984-86; asst. v.p., mgr. 1st Comml. Bank, San Francisco, 1986—; past gen. partner, prin. cons. ASC Assos.; mem. banking and adv. bd. Foothill Coll.; leader Joe Simoni Orch.; dir. Ohio Valley Gen. Hosp., McKees Rocks, Penn.; instr. music Burlingame Recreation Center. Served with U.S. Army, 1967-70; Vietnam. Decorated Army Commendation medal; recipient various certs. merit. Mem. Am. Inst. Banking (instr. mgmt. skills), Am. Mgmt. Assn., Am. Fedn. Musicians, Native Sons Golden West, Coll. Notre Dame Alumni Assn. (bd. dirs.), Italian-Am. Fedn. San Mateo County, Sons of Italy, Italian-Catholic Fedn. Democrat. Roman Catholic. Home: 9 12th Ave San Mateo CA 94402 Office: 550 Kearny St Ste 310 San Francisco CA 94108

SIMONS, ELLEN ANN, advertising executive; b. N.Y.C., Dec. 26, 1941. Cert. of completion, Sch. Visual Arts, N.Y., 1961-63; student, Adelphi Coll., 1959-61. Sr. copy writer Della Femina Travisano, N.Y., 1968-70; copy supr. DKG, Inc., N.Y., 1970-73; pres., creative dir. Simons, Madden & Ptnrs., Honolulu, 1975-79; v.p., assoc. creative dir. Foote Cone Belding/L.A., Los Angeles, 1980-81; assoc. creative dir. Saatchi & Saatchi Compton, N.Y., 1982-85; pres., creative dir. Manhattan Advt., Inc., Sugar Loaf, N.Y., 1985-88, Drackett & Lavidge, Phoenix, 1988; v.p., assoc. creative dir. Patchen Brownfeld/RSHS, Phoenix, 1988—. Recipient The Merit award The Copy Club, 1968, Distinctive Merit award Art Dirs. Club of N.Y., 1970, Award of Excellence, Ad Infinitum 1, 1972, Cert. of Merit award, Ad Infinitum 4, 1974.

SIMONS, ERIC WARD, financial executive; b. N.Y.C., Sept. 21, 1958; s. Theodor Leonard and Jean Lenore (Farbman) S.; m. Dorothy Ann Shiloff, Apr. 30, 1989. BS in Mgmt. and Internat. Bus., NYU, 1980. Sales cons. Paris Health Club, N.Y.C., 1979-81; registered rep. First Investors Corp., N.Y.C., 1981-82; fin. courses instr. Network for Learning, N.Y.C., 1981-83; cert. aquatics dir. West Side YMCA, N.Y.C., 1973—; founder, dir. Simons Fin. Network, N.Y.C., 1982—; chmn. bd. dirs. Found. in Motion, N.Y.C., 1983-85; dir., treas. Rockville Dance Co., N.Y.C., 1984-86. Mem., spl. activities coord. West 83d St. Block Assn., N.Y.C., 1970-76. Named to Million Dollar Round Table, First Investors Corp., N.Y.C., 1982; recipient Highest Sales award Paris Health Club, N.Y.C., 1981. Mem. Internat. Assn. Fin. Planning, Am. Coll. Sports Medicine, Psi Upsilon (chmn. traditions and edn. com., Resolution of Appreciation exec. council 1987). Democrat. Jewish. Home and Office: 110 Riverside Dr New York NY 10024

SIMONS, RAY D., consumer products company manager; b. Cin., July 5, 1946; s. C. S. and V. H. Simons; m. Christa Hermann, May 1978; children: Suzanne, Jonathan. BSBA, U. Cin., 1969. Nat. sales mgr. Keene Corp., Pennsauken, N.J., 1975-81; with Sarama Industries, Bala Cynwyd, Pa., 1981-82; dir. mktg. and sales consumer products div. McCloskey Varnish Co., Phila., 1982-83; v.p. Nat. Home Products Inc., Daily Dryer Corp., Inc., Telford, Pa., All Dry Corp., Inc., Emmaus, Pa., 1983—; bd. dirs. R & C Industries, Mt. Laurel, N.J., "By Design," Laurel, Aegis Products, Inc.; cons. in field. Contbr. articles to profl. jours. Mem. Sales and Mktg. Execs. Internat. Home: 87 Bunning Dr Voorhees NJ 08043 Office: Nat Home Products 535 Schoolhouse Rd Telford PA 18969

SIMONSON, MICHAEL, lawyer, judge; b. Franklin, N.J., Feb. 5, 1950; s. Robert and Eleanor (Weiss) S. BA, U. Ariz., 1973; JD, Southwestern U., Los Angeles, 1976; LLM in Taxation, Washington U., St. Louis, 1978. Bar: Ariz. 1977, U.S. Dist. Ct. Ariz. 1979, U.S. Tax Ct. 1978. Bailiff, law clk. Superior Ct. Maricopa County Div. 2, Phoenix, 1976-77; sole practice, Scottsdale, Ariz., 1978-79; ptnr. Simonson, Groh, & Lindteigen, Scottsdale, 1979-81, Simonson & Preston, Phoenix, 1984-86, Simonson, Preston & Arbetman, 1986-87, Simonson & Arbetman, 1987—; judge pro tempore Mcpl. Ct., City of Phoenix, 1984—; adj. prof. Ariz. State U Coll. Bus., Tempe, 1984—, Coll. for Fin. Planning, Denver, 1984—, Maricopa County Community Colls., 1984—, Western Internat. U., Phoenix, 1984—, Ottawa U., 1987—; prof. law Univ. Phoenix, 1985—, area chmn. legal studies, 1986—. Mem. Maricopa County Foster Child Care Rev. Bd. No. 17, 1978-81; pres. Camelback Mountainview Estates Homeowners Assn., 1980-81, Congregation Tiphereth Israel, 1979-81. Co-author: Buying and Selling Closely Held Businesses in Arizona, 1986, Commercial Real Estate Transactions, 1986. Mem. ABA (taxation sect., various coms.), State Bar Ariz. (cert. specialist in tax law), Maricopa County Bar Assn., Cen. Ariz. Estate Planning Council, Mensa. Democrat. Jewish. Club: Nucleus. Lodge: Masons. Office: Simonson & Arbetman 4645 N 32d St Ste 200 Phoenix AZ 85018

SIMPICH, GEORGE CARY, investment banker; b. Washington, June 25, 1923; s. Frederick and Margaret (Edwards) S.; 1 dau., Juliet Elizabeth. Mem. advt. staff Washington Post, 1945-47, Nat. Geog. Mag., 1947-49; with Young & Rubicam Advt. Agy., 1949-51; with Davidson & Co., 1951-56; div. mgr. Fin. Programs, Inc., Washington, 1956-61; investment cons. O'Boyle, Hearne & Fowler, Ltd., Washington, 1961-66; with various investment banking firms, 1966—; now 1st v.p. Janney Montgomery Scott, mem. N.Y. Stock Exchange, Washington. Served as fighter pilot USAAC, 1943-45. Mem. N.Y. Economists Club, Mcpl. Fin. Forum, Bond Club. Clubs: Del Ray, Nat. Press. Republican. Episcopalian (investment com. D.C. diocese, vestryman). Home: 3210 Wisconsin Ave NW Apt 110 Washington DC 20016 Office: 1225 23d St NW Washington DC 20037

SIMPLOT, SCOTT R., diversified food products company executive; b. 1946. BA, U. Idaho; MBA, U. Pa. Exec. v.p. J.R. Simplot Co., Boise. Office: J R Simplot Co PO Box 27 Boise ID 83707 *

SIMPSON, ALAN CARTER, portfolio manager; b. Stafford Springs, Conn., June 23, 1951; s. Deane Carter and Mary Esther (Clasby) S.; m. Janet Lee Brandon, July 5, 1980; children: Brandon Carter, Tyler Deane. BS, U. N.H., 1973; PhD, Clark U., 1981. Chartered fin. analyst, cert. fin. planner. Trust investment officer State St. Bank and Trust, Boston, 1977-80; asst. prof. fin. Clark U., Worcester, Mass., 1980-85; v.p., dir. internat. investments R.I. Hosp. Trust Nat. Bank, Providence, 1986-87; v.p., portfolio mgr. Boston Safe Deposit and Trust, 1987—; cons. in field. Mem. Inst. Chartered Fin. Analysts, Fin. Analysts Fedn., Internat. Soc. Fin. Analysts, Inst. Cert. Fin. Planners, Boston Security Analysts Soc. Republican. Roman Catholic. Office: Boston Safe Deposit & Trust 1 Boston Pl Boston MA 02106

SIMPSON, ALLAN BOYD, real estate company executive; b. Lakeland, Fla., Nov. 24, 1948; s. Alfred Forsythe and Ruth Jeanette (Coker) S.; 1 child, Lauren Leigh. B in Indsl. Ingring., Ga. Inst. Tech., 1970; MBA, U. Pa., 1972. Cert. rev. appraiser; lic. realtor, Ga. Dir. mortgage banking Ackerman & Co., Atlanta, 1972-73; v.p. B.F. Saul & Co., Atlanta, 1973-79; pres. L.J. Hooker, Atlanta, 1979-88; also bd. dirs. Hooker/Barnes, Atlanta; bd. dirs. Hooker Holdings (USA), Inc., Century Ins. Co., Hooker Internat. Devels. Ltd., Hooker Internat. Fin. BV, Charter Credit Corp. Ltd.; bd. dirs., treas. Midtown Bus. Assn., 1979-88; chmn., chief exec. officer The Simpson Orgn., Inc., Coker Capital Corp., 1989—. Mem. Am. Inst. Indsl. Engrs., MBA Execs. Assn., Bldg. Owners and Mgrs. Assn., Nat. Assn. Realtors., U.S. C. of C., Atlanta C. of C., Internat. Coun. of Shopping Ctrs., Urban Land Inst., Nat. Assn. of Office and Indsl. Pks. Democrat. Methodist. Clubs: Cherokee Town and Country, Atlanta City, Big Cande, The Crescent. Home: 1847 Homestead Ave Atlanta GA 30306 Office: 600 W Peachtree St Atlanta GA 30308

SIMPSON, ANDREA LYNN, energy communication executive; b. Altadena, Calif., Feb. 10, 1948; d. Kenneth James and Barbara Faries Simpson; m. John R. Myrdal, Dec. 13, 1986. BA, U. So. Calif., 1969, MS, 1983; postgrad. U. Colo., Boulder, 1977. Asst. cashier United Calif. Bank, L.A., 1969-73; asst. v.p. mktg. 1st Hawaiian Bank, Honolulu, 1973-78; v.p. corp. communications Pacific Resources, Inc., Honolulu, 1978—. Bd. dirs. Kapiolani Women's and Children's Hosp., 1988—, Hawaii Heart Assn., 1978-83, Child and Family Svcs., 1984-86, Coun. of Pacific, Girl Scouts U.S., 1982-85, Arts Coun. Hawaii, 1977-81; trustee Hawaii Loa Coll., 1984-86; commr Hawaii State Commn. on Status of Women, 1985-87. Trustee Hawaii sch. for girls at LaPietra, 1989—; Bd. dirs. Honolulu Symphony Soc., 1985-87. Named Panhellenic Woman of Yr. Hawaii, 1979, Outstanding Woman in Bus. Hawaii YWCA, 1980, Outstanding Young Woman of Hawaii Girl Scouts Coun. of the Pacific, 1985, 86, Hawaii Legis., 1980. Mem. Am. Mktg. Assn., Pub. Rels. Soc. Am. (bd. dirs. Honolulu chpt. 1984-865, Silver Anvil award 1984), Pub. Utilities Communicators Assn. (Communicator of Yr. 1984), Honolulu Advt. Fedn. (Advt. Woman of Yr. 1984), U. So. Calif. Alumni Assn. (bd. dirs. Hawaii 1981-83), Outrigger Canoe Club, Pacific Club, Kaneohe Yacht Club, Rotary (state pub. rels. chmn. 1988—, Hawaii chpt.), Alpha Phi (dir. Hawaii), Hawaii Jaycees (Outstanding Young Person of Hawaii 1978). Office: Pacific Resources Inc 733 Bishop St Ste 3100 Honolulu HI 96813

SIMPSON, CAROL LOUISE, corporate investment specialist; b. Phila., Jan. 30, 1937; d. William Huffington and Hilda Agnes (Johnston) S. Student, Community Coll., 1985, 86, 87, U. Minn., 1986, 87, 88. Cert. Nat. Assn. Securities Dealers, Inc., Washington; registered options, mcpl. securities, gen. securities, fin. and ops. prin.; lic. life, accident, health ins. Exec. asst. Germantown Fed. Savs., Phila., 1954-67; asst. sec. Am. Med. Investment Co., Inc. (formerly Cannon and Co., Inc.), Blue Bell, Pa., 1967—; v.p., sec. AMA Advisers, Inc. (formerly PRO Services, Inc.), Blue Bell, Pa., 1967—; bd. dirs. Cannon and Co., Inc., Pro Svcs., Inc. Mem. World Affairs Council, Investment Co. Inst. (Fed. Legis. com. 1984—, investment advisers com. 1988—), Internat. Assn. Fin. Planners, Investment Women's Club, Nat. Notary Assn., Pa. Assn. Notaries. Republican. Clubs: Whitemarsh, Valley Country. Home: 7701 Lawnton St Philadelphia PA 19128 Office: AMA Advisers Inc 5 Sentry Pkwy W Ste 120 PO Box 1111 Blue Bell PA 19422

SIMPSON, CATHY ANN, land title company executive, real estate broker; b. Ripley, Miss., Aug. 6, 1953; d. Booth Obed and Annette Grace (Tapp) Simpson. m. Thomas Earl Jones, July 21, 1973 (div. Dec. 1981). B.A. with honors, Harding U., 1975. Real estate broker Houston Bd. Realtors, 1976—; mktg. broker cons. Capital Title Co., Houston, 1979-81; founder, owner The Settlers, 1979—, asst. v.p. Commerce Title Co., Houston, 1981-85; mktg. broker Capital Title Co., 1985—; faculty The Real Estate Sch. Mem. Tex. Real Estate Polit. Action Com. Mem. Nat. Assn. Realtors, Houston Bd. Realtors. Republican. Mem. Ch. of Christ. Home: 11710 Bowlan Ln Houston TX 77035 Office: Capital Title Co 2929 Allen Pkwy Ste 200 Houston TX 77019

SIMPSON, GRACE WILLIS, management professional; b. Shelby, N.C., Apr. 26, 1947; d. Flay Alexander and Florance Edna (Wright) Willis; m. V. David Simpson, Aug. 2, 1964 (div. Feb. 1981); 1 child, Darin Charles. Student, Catawba Valley Tech. Coll., Hickory, N.C., 1966, 82-83, 86, Western Piedmont Community Coll., Morganton, N.C., 1974, U. N.C., 1983. Lic. ins. agt., N.C. Asst. cashier, loan officer 1st Citizens Bank & Trust Co., Hickory, 1965-84; asst. v.p., city exec. Preferred Savs. & Loan, Hickory, 1984-85; asst. v.p., contr. Copi Corp., Hickory, 1985-86; bus. mgr. Dale Earnhardt Chevrolet Inc., Newton, N.C., 1987—. Vice-chmn. Catawba County United Way, Hickory, 1978-81, bd. dirs. 1982-84; chmn. fund drive Catawba Valley Arts Coun., 1986; active Hickory Mus. Art, 1983-88; mem. Catawba Valley steering com. for re-election Jim Broyhill, 1986; treas. Bd. Adminstrn., Fin. and Budget St. Luke's United Meth. Ch., Hickory, 1980-84; bd. dirs. Catawba County Assn. for Spl. Edn., Conover, 1982-88, treas. 1985-86; bd. dirs. Catawba County Area Rehab. Employment Svcs., Conover, 1984-88. Mem. NAFE (dir. networking 1988—), Am. Bus. Womens Assn., Nat. Assn. Notaries (life), Am. Inst. Banking (pres. Hickory chpt. 1982-83, bd. dirs. emeritus 1983-84), Nat. Assn. Bank Women (chmn. edn. and tng. Winston-Salem chpt. 1982-83, instr. 1983-84), N.C. Bankers Assn. (sec. women's div. Raleigh chpt. 1981-82, v.p. 1982-83), Catawba Valley Exec. Club, Hickory C. of C., Altrusa (v.p. Hickory club 1978-79), Beta Sigma Phi. Home: Rte 9 Box 34 Hickory NC 28601 Office: Dale Earnhardt Chevrolet Inc Hwy 16 S Newton NC 28658

SIMPSON, JACK BENJAMIN, medical technologist, business executive; b. Tompkinsville, Ky., Oct. 30, 1937; s. Benjamin Harrison and Verda Mae (Woods) S.; student Western Ky. U., 1954-57; grad. Norton Infirmary Sch. Med. Tech., 1958; m. Winona Clara Walden, Mar. 21, 1957; children—Janet Lazann, Richard Benjamin, Randall Walden, Angela Elizabeth. Asst. chief med. technologist Jackson County Hosp., Seymour, Ind., 1958-61; chief med. technologist, bus. mgr. Mershon Med. Labs., Indpls., 1962-66; founder, dir., officer Am. Monitor Corp., Indpls., 1966-77; founder, pres., dir. Global Data, Inc., Ft. Lauderdale, Fla., 1986—; mng. partner Astroland Enterprises, Indpls., 1968—, 106th St. Assocs., Indpls., 1969-72, Keystones Ltd., Indpls., 1970-82 Delray Rd. Assoc., Ltd., Indpls., 1970-71, Allisonville Assocs. Ltd., Indpls., 1970-82, Grandview Assocs. Ltd., 1977—, Rucker Assocs., Ltd., Indpls., 1974—; mng. ptnr. Raintree Assocs., Ltd., Indpls., 1978—, Westgate Assocs., Ltd., Indpls., 1978—; pres., dir. Topps Constrn. Co., Inc., Bradenton, Fla., 1973—, Acrouest Corp., Asheville, N.C., 1980—; dir. Indpls. Broadcasting, Inc.; founder, bd. dirs. Bank of Bradenton, 1986—. Mem. Am. Soc. Med. Technologists (cert.), Indpls. Soc. Med. Technologists, Ind. Soc. Med. Technologists, Am. Soc. Clin. Pathologists, Royal Soc. Health (London), Internat. Platform Assn., Am. Mus. Natural History. Republican. Baptist. Clubs: Columbia of Indpls.; Harbor Beach Surf, Fishing of Am., Marina Bay (Fort Lauderdale, Fla.). Lodge: Elks.

SIMPSON, MICHAEL, metals service center executive; b. Albany, N.Y., Dec. 10, 1938; s. John McLaren Simpson and Constance (Hasler) Ames; B.A., U. Mich., 1965, M.B.A., 1966; m. Barbara Ann Bodtke, Jan. 5, 1963; children—Leslie Ann, Elizabeth McLaren. Product mgr. Armour & Co., Chgo., 1966-68; with A. M. Castle & Co., Franklin Park, Ill., 1968—, pres. Hy-Alloy Steels Co. div., 1974-79, v.p. Midwestern region, 1977-79, chmn. bd., 1979—, dir., 1972—. Trustee, Rush-Presbyterian St. Luke's Med. Center, Chgo., 1978—, exec. com., 1980—; trustee Oldfields Sch., Glencoe, Md., 1982-87. Served in USMC, 1957-58. Mem. Steel Service Center Inst. (chmn. exec. com. 1982-84, exec. com. 1981—). Republican. Episcopalian. Clubs: Shore Acres; Onwentsia; Racquet of Chicago. Office: A M Castle & Co 3400 N Wolf Rd Franklin Park IL 60131

SIMPSON, PAULA GAIL, hotel executive; b. Lone Oak, Tex., July 24, 1938; d. J.P. Jr. and Cloyce (Bellamy) Bowen; m. Darrel Craig Simpson, June 24, 1982; children: Steven Dale, Nancy Gail McCormack Breeden. B.S. in Bus. Adminstrn., So. Meth. U., 1972; grad. Holiday Inn U., 1980, Dale Carnegie, 1983; Cert. in Hotel Adminstrn., Ednl. Inst., East Lansing, Mich., 1984. Formerly sec. with various orgns.; front desk mgr. Holiday Inn, Greenville, Tex., 1979; gen. mgr. Holiday Inn, Ada, Okla., 1979-85, 87-88; owner Trails Motel, 1986-87; pvt. practice bus. cons., Ada, 1987—; grad. asst. Dale Carnegie Courses, Ada, 1984. Dir. Little Theatre prodns. Mem. Ada Arts and Humanities Com., 1982-84, pres., 1984, del. 1987—; mem. Ada Rodeo Com., 1984-85, sec., 1984-85; bd. dirs. Ada Community Theatre, 1982. Recipient cert. appreciation Boy Scouts Am., 1981; spl. citation State of Okla., 1982; cert. mgmt. excellence Holiday Inn, 1983, Holiday Inn Staff, 1984; named Employee of Yr. 1988 Job Fair. Mem. Ada C. of C. (chmn. recreation and tourism com. 1983-84). Republican. Episcopalian. Lodge: Soroptimists. Avocations: stained glass; sailing. Home: 801 W 23d Ada OK 74820 Office: 400 NE Richardson Bypass Ada OK 74820

SIMPSON, PHIL, gypsum and paperboard company executive; b. Dallas, Feb. 15, 1935; s. Rhyne and Avis (Miller) S.; m. Lorraine Hammerich, Dec. 27, 1957; children: Catherine Simpson Askew, David P., Marimon. BA, Rice U., 1956; MBA, U. Pa., 1958; postgrad., U. Tex. V.p., treas. Republic Gypsum Co., Dallas, 1961-64, pres., 1964-67, 73-75, 86-87, chief exec. officer, 1964-69, 73-82, 86—, chmn. bd. dirs., 1967—. Office: Republic Gypsum Co PO Box 750 Dallas TX 75221

SIMPSON, SAMUEL RANDOLPH, III, materials company executive; b. Annapolis, Md., July 10, 1953; s. Samuel Randolph Jr. and Lucy (Bardwell) S.; m. Cynthia Detweiler, Apr. 8, 1978; 1 child, Clark Randolph. BA, Vanderbilt U., 1975; MBA, U. Va., 1983. Asst. v.p., comml. loan officer Hamilton Bank, Harrisburg, Pa., 1975-81; asst. to pres. Southwire Co., Carrollton, Ga., 1983-85, v.p. fin., 1985-88; v.p., chief fin. officer Fla. Crushed Stone Co., Leesburg, Fla., 1988—. V.p. Am. Heart Assn., Carrollton, 1987-88. Mem. Fin. Execs. Inst. Office: Fla Crushed Stone Co 1616 S 14th St Leesburg FL 32748

SIMPSON, VINSON RALEIGH, manufacturing company executive; b. Chgo., Aug. 9, 1928; s. Vinson Raleigh and Elsie (Passeger) S.; m. Elizabeth Caroline Matte, Sept. 9, 1950; children: Kathleen Simpson Jackson, Nancy Simpson Ignacio, James Morgan. S.B. in Chem. Engring, Mass. Inst. Tech., 1950; M.B.A., Ind. U., 1955. With Trane Co., LaCrosse, Wis., 1950-75, mgr. mktg. services, 1957-64, mgr. dealer devel., 1964-66; mng. dir. Trane Ltd., Edinburgh, Scotland, 1966; v.p. internat. Trane Co., LaCrosse, Wis., 1967, exec. v.p., 1968-70; exec. v.p., gen. mgr. comml. air conditioning div. 1970-73, pres., 1973-75; pres. Simpson and Co., La Crosse, 1975-76; pres., chief operating officer Marathon Electric Mfg. Corp., Wausau, Wis., 1976-80; chmn., pres., chief exec. officer Marion Body Works, Inc., Wis., 1980—; bd. dirs. NTEA. Regional chmn. edn. council MIT; trustee Northland Coll.; past pres., bd. dirs. Wausau Area Jr. Achievement; mem. Marion Minutemen, Adv. Team, U. Wis., Clintonville Community Hosp. Assn. Served with USAF, 1951-53. Decorated Korean War Commendation ribbon. Mem. Fire Apparatus Mfrs., Nat. Truck Equipment Assn. (dir.), Am. Prodn. and Inventory Control Soc., Kappa Kappa Sigma, Alpha Tau Omega, Beta Gamma Sigma (mem. dirs. table), Am. Legion. Methodist. Clubs: Clintonville Riverside Golf, U. Chgo. Lodges: Masons, Shriners, Jesters, Rotary (past pres. Marion club). Home: 419 W Ramsdell St Marion WI 54950 Office: Marion Body Works Inc 211 W Ramsdell PO Box 500 Marion WI 54950-0500

SIMPSON, WILLIAM ARTHUR, insurance company executive; b. Oakland, Calif., Feb. 2, 1939; s. Arthur Earl and Pauline (Mikalasic) S.; m. Nancy Ellen Simpson, Mar. 31, 1962; children—Sharon Elizabeth, Shelley Pauline. B.S., U. Calif.-Berkeley, 1961; postgrad. Exec. Mgmt. Program, Columbia U. C.L.U. Br. mgr. Occidental Life of Calif., Los Angeles, 1965-73, v.p. agys., 1976-79; v.p. mktg. Countrywide Life, Los Angeles, 1973-76; pres., chief exec. officer Vol. State Life, Chattanooga, Tenn., 1979-83; exec. v.p. Transam. Occidental Life Ins. Co., Los Angeles, 1983-86, pres., 1986-88, pres., chief oper. officer, 1988—, also bd. dirs. Pres. Chattanooga coun. Boy Scouts Am., 1982, bd. dirs., L.A., 1983, v.p., 1983-85, vice-chmn, chmn. L.A. Area, 1988; pres. bd. councillors L.A. County Am. Cancer Soc.; trustee Calif. Med. Ctr. 1st lt. U.S. Army, 1961-64. Mem. Am. Soc. CLUs, Life Ins. Mktg. and Rsch. Assn. (bd. dirs. 1986—). Republican. Presbyterian. Lodge: Rotary. Office: Transam Occidental Life Ins Co 2101 Terminal Annex Los Angeles CA 90051

SIMPSON, WILLIAM LOUIS, II, management consultant; b. Miami Beach, Fla., Mar. 14, 1952; s. William Louis and Frieda (Mengani) S.; m. Ellen Kirby, Aug. 31, 1974 (div. May 1979); m. Valerie Dawn Rhoads, Aug. 1, 1981. BS, Stetson U., 1974, MBA, 1975. Cert. systems profl. Programmer analyst Fla. Software Services, Altamonte Springs, 1976-77; budget dir. Lykes Bros., Inc., Tampa, Fla., 1977-80; cons. John E. Kearney, CPA, St. Petersburg, Fla., 1980-82; dir. mgmt. info. services Fed. Constrn./Mills & Jones, St. Petersburg, 1982-84; sr. cons. Touche Ross & Co., Washington, 1984—; lectr. Coll. Engring., U. Fla., Gainesville, 1983; instr. St. Petersburg Jr. Coll., 1984; speaker Nat. Inst. Mgmt. Research, Washington, 1985, Fed. Computer Conf., Washington, 1986, Office Automation Soc. Internat. 4th Ann. Conf., Chgo., 1986. Mem. Assn. Systems Mgmt. Avocations: piano, scuba diving, breeding Arabian horses. Office: 7200 Wisconsin Ave Suite 1100 Bethesda MD 20814

SIMS, CHARLES, JR., financial analyst; b. Memphis, Jan. 25, 1952; s. Charles Sr. and Florence Elizabeth (Boykins) S.; m. Yvonne Irene Frank, June 26, 1984; children: Reginald, Treina, Derron, Anthony, Kyra. Student, Memphis State U., 1972. Cert. fin. planner. Agt. Universal Life Ins. Co., Memphis, 1972-76; registered rep. John Hancock Fin. Svcs., 1976—. Mem. Fellow Life Underwriter Tng. Coun.; mem. Nat. Assn. Life Underwriters (chmn. pub. rels. com. 1987), Inst. Cert. Fin. Planners, Million Dollar Roundtable. Democrat. Baptist. Home: 3030 Oakleigh Ln Germantown TN 38138 Office: John Hancock Fin Svcs 1255 Lynnfield Rd Ste 249 Memphis TN 38119

SIMS, EUGENE RALPH, JR., industrial engineer; b. N.Y.C., Oct. 12, 1920; s. Eugene Ralph and Rose (Simmons) S.; B. Adminstrv. Engring., N.Y. U., 1947; MBA, Ohio U.; m. Ethel Jane Smith, June 8, 1945; children—Pamela Jeanne, Gary Wardner, Phyllis Anne. Tool and instrument maker Sperry Gyroscope Co., N.Y.C., 1939-43; rsch. test engr. N.Y. U., 1947; cons. indsl. engr. Drake, Startzman, Sheahan, Barclay, Inc., N.Y.C., 1947-49; plant mgr. Lit Bros. Warehouse & Furniture Plant, Phila., 1949-50; project indsl. engr. Jeffrey Mfg. Co., Columbus, Ohio, 1950-51; prin. indsl. engr., mgmt. ops. rsch. Battelle Meml. Inst., Columbus, 1951-54; corp. materials handling engr. Anchor Hocking Glass Corp., Lancaster, Ohio, 1954-56; chief indsl. engr., asso. Alden E. Stilson & Assocs. Ltd., Columbus, 1956-58; pres. E. Ralph Sims, Jr. & Assocs., Inc. (name changed to The Sims Cons. Group, Inc.), Lancaster, 1958-86, chmn., 1986—; pres. Fairhill Devel. Co., Lancaster, 1959—; assoc. prof. Ohio U., Athens, 1985—; Dist. commr. Cen. Ohio coun. Boy Scouts Am., 1954-56; past mem. adv. coun. Ohio Tech. Svcs. Program; past mem. Bd. Zoning Appeals Lancaster; command pilot/maj. CAP. 1st lt. USAAF, 1943-46. Registered profl. engr., Ohio, Wis., N.Y., Pa., Calif., Mass., Ind.; chartered engr., U.K. Fellow Inst. Indsl. Engrs., Brit. Inst. M.E., ASME (life fellow), Inst. Mgmt. Cons. (founding mem., past dir.), Assn. Mgmt. Cons. (pres. 1975-76), Nat. Soc. Profl. Engrs. (life), Air Force Assn. (charter life mem.), Psi Upsilon. Clubs: N.Y. U., Minn. Press, Masons, Shriners. Author: Euphonious Coding, 1967, Planning and Management of Material Flow, 1968, Contemporary Comment in Retrospect, 1973; contbg. editor: Production Handbook, 1958, Materials Handling Handbook, 1958, 84, Handbook of Business Adminstrn., 1967, Ency. Profl. Mgmt., 1978, Handbook of Industrial Engineering, 1982, The Distribution Handbook, 1984, The Warehouse Management Handbook, 1988; contbr. articles to trade jours. Home: 114 Luther Ln Lancaster OH 43130 Office: Ohio U 282 Stocker Ctr Athens OH 45701

SIMS, GEORGE OREN, III, financial advisor, contractor, real estate broker; b. Geneva, Ala., Aug. 29, 1955; s. George Oren Jr. and Annie Clyde (Smith) S.; m. Ann Virginia McClow, May 23, 1981; children: Melissa Ann, Andrew George. BBA, Auburn U., 1977. Cert. gen. contractor, Fla.; lic. real estate broker, Fla. V.p., mgr., broker and contractor Gate Land Co., Jacksonville, Fla., 1984-86; fin. advisor, citrus grower, broker and contractor Hugh F. Culverhouse, Tampa, Fla., 1986—; pres. Mode Realty, Inc., Tampa; also citrus grower, jet pilot. Served to lt. USN, 1977-84. Mem. Fla. Waterworks Assn., Assn. Gen. Contractors, Fla. Realtors Assn. Republican. Baptist. Clubs: Big Cypress (Lakeland); Prestancia (Sarasota). Home: 1004 W Imogene St Arcadia FL 33821 Office: Hugh Culverhouse 1408 N Westshore Blvd #908 Tampa FL 33623

SIMS, JEFFREY LLOYD, accounting executive; b. Austin, Tex., Nov. 16, 1958; s. O.T. Sims Jr. and Carol Marie Rose; m. Brenda Kay Strueber, June 22, 1977; 1 child, Hunter Ryan. BBA, U. Tex., 1982. CPA, Tex. Mng. ptnr. Tex. Sign Co., Austin, 1979-82; sr. auditor Ernst & Whinney, Austin, 1982-86; chief fin. analyst Am. Founders Life Ins. Co., Phoenix, 1986-87, v.p., controller, 1988—. Advisor Jr. Achievement, Austin, 1982-83; rep. Austin in Action, 1985-87; past mem. U. Tex. Young Reps. Sgt. USMC, 1975-79. Mem. AICPA, Tex. Soc. CPA's, Nat. Assn. Accts., Austin Jaycees. Republican. Baptist. Home: 10421 N 75th Pl Scottsdale AZ 85258 Office: Am Founders Life Ins Co 2720 E Camelback Phoenix AZ 85258

SIMS, ROBERT BARRY, lawyer; b. N.Y.C., Aug. 20, 1942; s. Irving Zach and Laura (Levine) S.; m. Roberta Jane Donner, Nov. 17, 1973; children: Alexandra Lauren, Andrew Michael. A.B., Franklin and Marshall Coll., 1964; J.D., George Washington U., 1967; M.B.A., N.Y. U., 1969. Bar: N.Y. 1968, D.C. 1969, U.S. Dist. Ct. D.C. 1969, U.S. Dist. Ct. (so. and ea. dists.) N.Y. 1970, U.S. Dist. Ct. Conn 1978, U.S. Ct. Appeals (2d and D.C. cir.) 1969, U.S. Ct. Claims 1977, U.S. Ct. Customs and Patent Appeals 1978, U.S. Supreme Ct. 1979, Conn. 1980, U.S. Ct. Internat. Trade 1981. Assoc. firm Cahill, Gordon & Reindel, N.Y.C., 1967-69, Whitman & Ransom, N.Y.C., 1969-72; asst. counsel Gen. Signal Corp., N.Y.C., Stamford, Conn., 1972-76; v.p., sec., gen. counsel Raymark Corp. (formerly Raybestos-Manhattan, Inc.), Trumbull, Conn., 1976-82; assoc. gen. counsel Lever Bros. Co., N.Y.C., 1983; asst. to pres., corp. counsel Math. Applications Group, Inc., Elmsford, N.Y., 1984; v.p., sec., gen. counsel Summagraphics Corp., Fairfield, Conn., 1984—. Mem. ABA, N.Y. State Bar Assn., Assn. Bar City N.Y., D.C. Bar Assn., Conn. Bar Assn., Westchester-Fairfield Corp. Counsel Assn. Office: Summagraphics Corp 60 Silvermine Rd Seymour CT 06483

SIMS, WALLACE, JR., consultant; b. Greenwood, Miss., Aug. 30, 1936; s. Wallace Sr. and Priscilla (Marshall) S.; m. Beatrice Hinton, Sept. 28, 1958; children: Sharon, Michael, Tasha. Student, Wilson Jr. Coll., 1954-56, Am. Inst. Banking, 1961-63, Northwestern U., 1963-65, Alexander Hamilton Inst., 1965-66. Asst. cashier Drexel Nat. Bank, Chgo., 1961-68; acct. dept. fin. City of Chgo., 1968-70; fin. specialist Chgo. Econ. Devel. Corp., 1970-75; pres. Deluxe Printing Corp., Chgo., 1981-84; owner Wallace Simms & Assocs., Chgo., 1974—. Mem. NCCJ. Mem. Inst. Mgmt. Cons., East Bank Club. Republican. Baptist. Office: Wallace Simms & Assocs 200 W Madison St Ste 630 Chicago IL 60606

SIMUNEK, FRANK GERALD, investment executive; b. N.Y.C., Oct. 2, 1941; s. Frank Charles and Louise (Reininghaus) S. BA, Williams Coll., 1963; LLB, Harvard U., 1966. Vol. U.S. Peace Corps, Kenya, 1967-68; with MONY Capital Mgmt. Corp., N.Y.C., 1969—, v.p. fixed income securities, 1984-88, mng. dir., 1988—; bd. dirs. Long Mfg. Co., Tarboro, N.C. Office: MONY Capital Mgmt Corp 1740 Broadway New York NY 10019

SIMUNEK, NICHOLAS, investment banker; b. London, Jan. 30, 1939; came to U.S., 1963; s. George and Alison (Cook) S. Student Sorbonne U., Paris, 1956, McGill U., Montreal, Que., Can., 1961. Pres. SEI, Inc., N.Y.C., 1970—; ptnr. Cobb Capital Corp.; bd. dirs. Cavendish Capital Corp., N.Y.C., Fersdon Ltd, L.I., N.Y., Lansdowne Investment Trust Inc., Cigar Sales Ltd., Nassau, Forsyth Holdings (U.K.) Ltd., London & Dunedin (N.Z.) Ltd. Author: International Merger Strategy, 1972. Served with Brit. Coldstream Guards, 1956-59. Clubs: N.Y. Athletic; Turf (London). Office: 180 Central Park S Box 932 New York NY 10019

SINAI, ALLEN, economist, educator; b. Detroit, Apr. 4, 1939; s. Joseph and Betty Paula (Feinberg) S.; m. Lee Davis Etsten, June 23, 1963; children—Lauren Beth, Todd Michael. A.B., U. Mich., 1961; M.A., Northwestern U., 1966, Ph.D., 1969. Asst. prof. to assoc. prof. econs. U. Ill.-Chgo., 1966-75; chmn. fin. info. group, chief fin. economist Data Resources, Lexington, Mass., 1971-83; chief economist, mng. dir. Lehman Bros. and Shearson Lehman Bros. Inc., N.Y.C., 1983-87; chief economist, exec. v.p. The Boston Co. Inc., 1988—; pres., chief exec. officer The Boston Co. Econ. Advisors Inc., Boston and N.Y.C., 1988—; cons. Laural Cons., Lexington and Evanston, Ill., 1966—; vis. assoc. prof. econs. and fin. MIT, Cambridge, 1975-77; adj. prof. econs. Boston U., 1977-78, 81-83, NYU, 1984-88, Lemberg Disting. Visitor's Program Brandeis U., 1988—, vis. prof. Sloan Sch. MIT, 1989. Contbr. articles to profl. jours. and books. Mem. reducing the fed. budget deficit task force Roosevelt Ctr., Washington, 1984; bd. govs. Com. on Developing Am. Capitalism, 1984—. Recipient Alumnus Merit award Northwestern U., 1985. Mem. Am. Econ. Assn., Ea. Econs. Assn. (v.p. 1988-89, pres.-elect 1989—, Otto Eckstein prize 1988), Western Econ. Assn. Jewish. Club: Nat. Economists (bd. govs. 1984-88). Home: 16 Holmes Rd Lexington MA 02173 Office: The Boston Co 1st Boston Pla Boston MA 02208

SINCLAIR, JOHN EDWARD, management holding company executive; b. Hamilton, Ont., Can., Dec. 9, 1936. B.A. in Bus., McMaster U., 1958. With Bell Can., 1958-85; v.p. systems Bell Can., Toronto, Ont., 1977-80, v.p. regulatory matters, 1980-83, exec. v.p. corporate, 1983-85, now exec. v.p.; exec. corp. v.p. Bell Can. Enterprises, Inc., Toronto, 1985—; chmn. Tel-Direct (Can.) Inc.; dir. Ronalds-Federated Ltd., Nat. Telephone Directory Corp, Telemap Ltd., New Brunswick Telephone Co. Ltd. Bd. govs. U. Waterloo; v.p. nat. council Boy Scouts Can.; mem. met. Toronto adv. bd., ter. adv. bd. Exec. of Salvation Army. Mem. Canadian C. of C. (chmn. exec. com.). Club: Ontario (dir.) (Toronto). Home: 33 Courtsfield Crescent, Islington, ON Canada M9A 4T1 Office: Bell Can, South Tower 10th Fl, 483 Bay St, Toronto, ON Canada M5G 2E1 *

SINCLAIR, JUDSON WILLIAM, business executive; b. Feb. 3, 1920; s. Warren Fife and Marjorie (Calhoun) S.; m. Velma Irene Hogarth; children: Mark, Paul, Marie, Susanne, Trisha. Chartered accts. auditor Robertson, Robinson, McConnell & Dick, 1941-47; with internal audit dept. Moore Corp., Ltd., Toronto, 1947-51; asst. comptroller So. div. Moore Bus. Forms, Inc., 1951-60, comptroller So. div., 1960-71; treas., comptroller Moore Corp. Ltd., 1971-74, v.p., treas., 1974-76, sr. v.p. fin., 1976-83, pres., chief exec. officer, 1983-86, chmn. bd., 1987—; also chmn., dir. Moore Bus. Forms, Inc.; dir. The Bank of Novia Scotia, Can. Life Assurance Co.; chmn., Moore Corp. Ltd. Avocation: golf. Clubs: Nat. (dir.), Granite, York Downs Golf and Country, Toronto. Office: Moore Corp Ltd, 1 First Can Pla 72F, Toronto, ON Canada M5X 1G5

SINCLAIR, KENNETH ROGER, entrepreneur; b. Williamsport, Pa., Nov. 10, 1927; s. Peter James and Florence (Marquardt) S.; m. Anne Schuman, Aug. 1950 (div. 1974); children: Peter, Suzanne; m. Charlene Happ, Dec. 28, 1974. BS, Washington & Jefferson U., 1947; BS in Edn., MIT, 1949; MBA, Harvard U., 1951. V.p. Westinghouse Air Brake, Geneva, Switzerland, 1960-68; pres. TRW Internat., Cleve., 1969-71; v.p. Questor Corp., Toledo, 1972-74; pres. Agrico Internat., Tulsa, 1974-75; chmn. Sinclair Corp., Tulsa, 1976—; pres. Diamond Head Enterprises, Sand Springs, Okla., 1985—; ptnr. Villa Jerene, Elmira, N.Y., 1972; exec. dir. Keystone Assocs., Mannford, Okla., 1980—; cons. Internat., Geneva, 1975—. Pres., bd. dirs. Mid-Continent Harvard Bus. Sch. Assn., Tulsa, 1980—; bd. dirs. Keystone Lake Area Assn., Cleve., 1981—. Capt. USAF, 1951-53, Tex., Korea. Mem. Phi Gamma Delta (sec. treas. 1946-48). Republican. Presbyterian. Home: Rte 3 S Ridge Estate Cleveland OK 74020

SINDEROFF, RITA JOYCE, property management company executive, real estate broker, mortgage broker; b. Bklyn., June 22, 1932; d. Joseph George and Mary (Cohen) Rothkopf; m. Arthur B. Schneider, Oct. 18, 1953 (div. Sept. 1973); children: Linda Ellen, Debra Carol. Degree in comml. art Pratt Inst., 1953; BA in Acctg., Bklyn. Coll., 1954. Controller Central Funding Co., Bklyn., 1973-80; owner, controller, realtor Riteway Mgmt. Inc., Coral Springs, Fla., 1980-86, Riteway Internat. Realty Corp., Coral Springs, 1986-87, realtor Regal Internat. Realty Inc., Regal Fin. Services and Regal Assn. Services, Coral Springs, Fla., 1987—; cons. in field. Active Cancer Soc., Bklyn., 1954-73, March of Dimes, Bklyn., 1960-70. Recipient 1st art award City of N.Y., 1950. Mem. Nat. Bd. Realtors, Pompany Beach-North Broward Bd. Realtors, Fla. Assn. Mortgage Brokers, Nat. Real Estate Assn. Democrat. Jewish. Avocations: reading, dancing, swimming. Office: Riteway Fin 2930 University Dr #33 Coral Springs FL 33065-2035

SINGER, DAVID MICHAEL, marketing and public relations company executive; b. Bklyn., N.Y., Feb. 11, 1957; s. Seymour Allen and Ellen Sybil (Pavnick) S.; m. Pamela Rae Silton, July 20, 1986. BA in History, NYU, 1978; MA in Communications, Syracuse U., 1979; MA in Media, New Sch. Social Research, 1983; JD, Yeshiva U., 1981. Cons. pub. relations Burson-Marsteller, N.Y.C., 1979-80, Singer & Co., N.Y.C., 1980-81, The Haas Group, N.Y.C., 1981-84; pub., editor-in-chief Lodestone Pub., N.Y.C., 1984-87; cons. pub. relations Braff & Co., N.Y.C., 1987-89; chief operating officer Pentagon Ltd., N.Y.C., 1989—; lectr. evening div. NYU, 1982-83. Contbr. articles and poems to profl. and consumer jours. and mags. Pres. Jewish Cultural Found., N.Y.C., 1976. Named Mem. of Yr., N.Y. State Kiwanis, 1976, Outstanding Young Man of Am., Jaycees, 1977; recipient Cert. Recognition Am. Film Inst., 1982, ANDY Design award Advt. Club N.Y., 1983, Proclamation Bklyn. Borough Pres., 1987. Mem. Alpha Epsilon Pi (Bro. of Yr. 1976).

SINGER, DIANA ROSE, jewelry industry executive; b. N.Y.C., Aug. 25, 1953; d. Leonard Rothblum and Tina Singer; m. Robert Kushner, Apr. 12, 1981. B in French magna cum laude, NYU, 1975, B in Polit. Sci. magna cum laude, 1975; cert., Gemological Inst. Am., 1982. Salesperson, mgr.-in-tng. Halston dept. Bloomingdales, N.Y.C., 1969-71; asst. mgr. Women's Haberdasher's, N.Y.C., 1973; mgr., buyer Antoinette's Heirloom Jewelry, San Francisco, 1975-80; salesperson, buyer, dir. estate jewelry promotions, advt. M & L Singer, Inc., N.Y.C., 1980-89; pres., chief exec. officer D & E Singer, Inc., N.Y.C., 1989—; asst. sec. M & L Singer, Inc., N.Y.C., 1984—; sec.-treas. Antoinette's Heirloom Jewelry of Washington, 1986—; treas. Matthews Jewelry, N.Y.C., 1985—; pastry chef restaurant, N.Y.C., 1981-82. Contbr. articles, recipies to various mags. Vol. Project Dorot, N.Y.C., 1988, Friday Breakfast for Homeless Program Cen. Synagogue, 1987-88; mem. Varsity Fencing Team N.Y.C. Recipient silver medal Maccabian Games, 1974. Mem. Women's Jewelry Assn. (bd. dirs. 1987—, dir. ann. awards dinner 1983-86, Excellency in Retailing award 1987), Circolo Italiano (v.p. 1975). Democrat. Jewish. Office: D & E Singer Inc 580 Fifth Ave New York NY 10036

SINGER, KURT DEUTSCH, news commentator, author; b. Vienna, Austria, Aug. 10, 1911; came to U.S., 1940, naturalized, 1951; s. Ignaz Deutsch and Irene (Singer) S.; m. Hilda Tradelius, Dec. 23, 1932; children—Marian Alice Birgit, Kenneth Walt; m. Katherine Haw, Apr. 8, 1989. Student, U. Zurich, Switzerland, 1930, Labor Coll., Stockholm, Sweden, 1936; Ph.D., Div. Coll. Metaphysics, Indpls., 1951. Escaped to Sweden, 1934; founder Ossietzky Com. (successful in release Ossietzky from concentration camp); corr. Swedish mag. Folket i Bild, 1935-40; founder Niemoller Com.; pub. biography Göring in Eng. (confiscated in Sweden), 1940; co-founder pro-Allied newspaper Trots Allt, 1939; corr. Swedish newspapers in, U.S., 1940; editor News Background, 1942; lectr. U. Minn., U. Kans., U. Wis., 1945-49; radio commentator WKAT, 1950; corr. N.Am. Newspaper Alliance, N.Y.C., 1953—; pres. Singer Media Corp., 1987—; dir. Oceanic Press Service, Buena Park, Calif. Author, editor: underground weekly Mitteilungsblätter, Berlin, Germany, 1933; Author: The Coming War, 1934, (biog.) Carl von Ossietzky, 1936 , Germany's Secret Service in Central America, 1943, Spies and Saboteurs in Argentina, 1943, Duel for the Northland, 1943, White Book of the Church of Norway, 1944, Spies and Traitors of World War II, 1945, Who are the Communists in America, 1948, 3000 Years of Espionage, 1951, World's Greatest Women Spies, 1952, Kippie the Cow; juvenile, 1952, Gentlemen Spies, 1953, The Man in the Trojan Horse, 1954, World's Best Spy Stories, 1954, Charles Laughton Story; adapted TV, motion pictures, 1954, Spy Stories and Asia, 1955, More Spy Stories, 1955, My Greatest Crime Story, 1956, My Most Famous Case, 1957, The Danny Kaye Saga; My Strangest Case, 1958, Spy Omnibus, 1959, Spies for Democracy, 1960, Crime Omnibus Spies Who Changed History, 1961, Hemmingway-Life and Death of a Giant, 1961, True Adventures in Crime, Dr. Albert Schweitzer, Medical Missionary, 1962, Lyndon Baines Johnson-Man of Reason, 1964, Ho-i-man; juveniles, 1965; Kurt Singer's Ghost Omnibus, 1965; juvenile Kurt Singer's Horror Omnibus; The World's Greatest Stories of the Occult, The Unearthly, 1965, Mata Hari-Goddess of Sin, 1965, Lyndon Johnson-From Kennedy to Vietnam, 1966, Weird Tales Anthology, 1966, I Can't Sleep at Night, 1966, Weird Tales of Supernatural, 1967, Tales of Terror, 1967, Famous Short Stories, 1967, Folktales of the South Pacific, 1967, Tales of The Uncanny, 1968, Gothic Reader, 1968, Bloch and Bradbury, 1969, Folktales of Mexico, 1969, Tales of the Unknown, 1970, Tales of the Macabre, 1971, Ghouls and Ghosts, 1972, Satanic Omnibus, 1973, Gothic Horror Omnibus, 1974, Dictionary of Household Hints and Help, 1974, They are Possessed, 1976, True Adventures into the Unknown, 1980, I Spied—And Survived, 1980, First Target Book of Horror, 1984, 2d, 1984, 3d, 1985, 4th, 1985; editor: UN Calendar, 1959-58; contbr. articles to newspapers, popular mags., U.S., fgn. countries, all his books and papers in Boston U. Library-Spl. Collections. Mem. UN Speakers Research Com., UN Children's Emergency Fund, Menninger Found. Mem. Nat. Geog. Soc., Smithsonian Assos., Internat. Platform Assn. (v.p.), United Sch. Assemblies (pres.). Address: 3164 Tyler Ave Anaheim CA 92801

SINGER, MICHAEL HOWARD, lawyer; b. N.Y.C., Nov. 22, 1941; s. Jack and Etta (Appelbaum) S.; m. Saundra Jean Kupperman, June 1, 1962; children: Allison Jill, Pamela Faith. BS in Econs., U. Pa., 1962; JD, NYU, 1965, LLM in Taxation, 1968. Bar: N.Y. 1965, U.S. Ct. Claims 1968, U.S. Supreme Ct. 1969, U.S. Ct. Appeals (6th cir.) 1970, D.C. 1972, U.S. Tax Ct. 1972, Nev. 1973, U.S. Ct. Appeals (9th cir.) 1973. Law asst. Appellate Term Supreme Ct., N.Y.C., 1965-68; trial lawyer Ct. Claims Tax Div., Washington, 1968-72; tax lawyer Beckley, DeLanoy & Jemison, Las Vegas, 1972-74; ptnr. Oshins, Singer, Segal & Morris, Las Vegas, 1974-87; sole practice law Las Vegas, 1987; ptnr. Michael H. Singer Ltd., Las Vegas, 1987—. Pres. Las Vegas chpt. NCCJ, 1980-82. Mem. ABA, Nev. Bar Assn., Las Vegas Country Club, Ctr. Ct. Racquet Club. Democrat. Jewish. Home: 3730 Pama Ln Las Vegas NV 89121 Office: 520 S 4th St 2d Floor Las Vegas NV 89101

SINGER, SANFORD ROBERT, diversified energy company executive; b. Murfreesboro, Tenn., Aug. 25, 1930; m. Ella Rita Raab; children: Halley, Michael. BA, U. Tenn., 1952, MS, 1955; PhD in Econs, Ohio State U., 1960. With Fed. Res. Bank Dallas, 1960-63; economist R & D ENSERCH Corp. (formerly Lone Star Gas Co.), Dallas, 1963-67, v.p. planning and info. data systems, 1967-68, sr. v.p., chief fin. officer, 1968—. 1st lt. U.S. Army, 1952-54, Korea. Mem. Am. Gas Assn., Nat. Assn. Bus. Economists, Fin. Execs. Inst., Dallas Club (bd. dirs. 1983-86), City Midday Club (N.Y.C.), Reform Club (London). Republican. Office: ENSERCH Corp ENSERCH Ctr 300 S St Paul St Dallas TX 75201

SINGER, S(IEGFRIED) FRED, geophysicist, educator; b. Vienna, Austria, Sept. 27, 1924; came to U.S., 1940, naturalized, 1944; s. Joseph B. and Anne (Kelman) S. B.E.E., Ohio State U., 1943, D.Sc. (hon.), 1970; A.M., Princeton, 1944, Ph.D. in Physics, 1948. Instr. physics Princeton, 1943-44; physicist, applied physics lab. Johns Hopkins, 1946-50; sci. liaison officer Office Naval Research, Am. embassy, London, 1950-53; asso. prof. physics U. Md., College Park, 1953-59; prof. U. Md., 1959-62; dir. Nat. Weather Satellite Center, Dept. Commerce, 1962-64; dean Sch. Environ. and Planetary Scis., U. Miami, 1964-67; dep. asst. sec. for water quality and research Dept. Interior, Washington, 1967-70; dep. asst. adminstr. EPA, Washington, 1970-71; prof. environ. scis. U. Va., Charlottesville, 1971-87; chief scientist U.S. Dept. Transp., Washington, 1987—; vis. research prof. Jet Propulsion Lab., Calif. Inst. Tech., 1961-62; Fed. Exec. fellow Brookings Instn., 1971; vis. Sid Richardson prof. LBJ Sch., U. Tex., 1978; sr. fellow Heritage Found., 1982-83; vis. eminent scholar George Mason U., 1984-86; head sci. eval. group, astronautics and space exploration com. Ho. of Reps., 1958; mem. research adv. bd. Center for Strategic and Internat. Studies, Georgetown U.; cons. U.S. Treasury, GAO, Office Tech. Assessment, U.S. Congress.; Mem. bd. Nat. Com. on Am. Fgn. Policy; mem. White House Panel on U.S.-Brazil Sci. and Tech. Exchange, 1987—. Author: Geophysical Research with Artificial Earth Satellites, 1956, Manned Laboratories in Space, 1970, Global Effects of Environmental Pollution, 1970, Is There an Optimum Level of Population, 1971, The Changing Global Environment, 1975, Arid Zone Development: Potentialities and Problems, 1977, The Economic Effects of Demographic Changes, 1977, Energy, 1979, Price of World Oil, 1983, Free Market Energy, 1984; sci. adv. com. Dept State 1981; vice chmn. Nat. Adv. Com. Oceans and Atmosphere, 1981-86; Contbr. articles on space, energy, environment and population problems to profl. pubs. Served with USNR, 1944-46. Recipient Presdl. commendation, 1958, gold medal for exceptional service Dept. Commerce, 1965; named Outstanding Young Man U.S. Jr. C. of C., 1959. Fellow Am. Geophys. Union, Am. Phys. Soc.; mem. Internat. Acad. Astronautics, AAAS (com. council affairs 1970), Pan Am. Med. Assn. (pres. sect. on environ. health scis. 1973—), AIAA. Club: Cosmos (Washington). Office: U S Dept of Transp Rsch & Spl Programs Adminstrn 400 7th St SW Washington DC 20590

SINGER, SUSAN ANN, advertising executive; b. Ashton, Idaho, Oct. 30, 1946; d. Orville Arnold and Irma Hazel (Kortesja) Jensen; m. Paul Singer, Oct. 1, 1983. BA, U. Oreg., 1971; MBA, U. Wash., 1974. Dir. research Cole Weber, Seattle, 1972-75, v.p., 1975-79; v.p. Ogilvy Mather, N.Y.C., 1979-84; sr. v.p. Rapp Collins, N.Y.C., 1984-87, Wells, Rich, Greene, N.Y.C., 1987—. Mem. Direct Mktg. Assn. Home: 170 E 88th St New York NY 10128

SINGER, THOMAS DAVID, corporate lawyer; b. Waynesboro, Pa., Sept. 5, 1952; s. David Luther and Eva Helen (Snowberger) S.; m. Deborah Jean McCracken, Aug. 18, 1974; children: Allison Katherine, Thomas David. BA, Grove City Coll., 1974; JD, Temple U., 1978. Bar: Pa. 1978. Assoc. Keler & Reichard, Waynesboro, 1978-79; mgr. legal svcs. Grove Mfg. Co., Shady Grove, Pa., 1979-84; v.p., gen. counsel JLG Industries, Inc., McConnellsburg, Pa., 1984—; instr. Pa. State U. Bd. dirs. Waynesboro Area Sch. Dist., 1979-86; chmn. Waynesboro chpt. Am. Cancer Soc., 1980. Mem. ABA, Pa. Bar Assn., Franklin County Bar Assn., Am. Corp. Counsel Assn. Republican. Presbyterian. Home: 9477 Hesshire Hill Ct Waynesboro PA 17268 Office: JLG Industries Inc JLG Dr McConnellsburg PA 17233

SINGH, JAGDIP, business educator; b. Chandigarh, India, June 3, 1954; came to U.S., 1982; s. Surjit and Kamla S.; m. Neena Singh, May 7, 1982; children: Abhijit, Tanya. BTech, Indian Inst. Tech., 1975; PhD, Tex. Tech. U., 1985. Jr. engr. Nat. Radio and Electronics Co., Bombay, 1975-76; ops. officer Indian Oil Corp., Bombay, 1976-77; contracts engr. Raunaq Internat., Ltd., New Delhi, 1978-82; asst. prof. mktg. Case Western Reserve U., Cleve., 1985—. Ad hoc reviewer Jour. Mktg. mag., 1987—, Jour. Bus. Rsch. mag., 1988—; contbr. articles to mktg. jours. Recipient 2d prize Acad. Mktg. Sci., 1986, Doctoral Proposal award Acad. Mktg. Sci., 1985. Mem. Am. Mktg. Assn., Am. Psychol. Assn., Assn. Consumer Rsch. Office: Case Western Res U University Circle Cleveland OH 44106

SINGHVI, SURENDRA SINGH, specialty retail company executive; b. Jodhpur, Rajasthan, India, Jan. 16, 1942; came to U.S., 1962, naturalized 1986; s. Rang Raj and Ugam Kanwar (Surana) S.; m. Sushila Bhandari, July 7, 1965; children: Seema, Sandeep. B. Commerce, Rajasthan U., 1961; MBA, Atlanta U., 1963; PhD, Columbia U., 1967. Cert. mgmt. acct., CPA. Asst. prof. fin. Miami U., Oxford, Ohio, 1967-69, assoc. prof., 1969-70; fin. mgr. ARMCO Inc., Middletown, Ohio, 1970-79, asst. treas., 1979-83, gen. fin. mgr., 1983-86; v.p. and treas. Edison Bros. Stores, Inc., St. Louis, 1986—; adj. prof. Miami U., 1970—. Author: Planning for Capital Investment, 1980; co-editor: Frontiers of Financial Management, 4th ed., 1984; contbr. articles to profl. jours. Treas. local PTO, 1981; treas. local Boy Scouts Am., 1982; treas. N. Am. Fedn. Indian Orgns., 1984-86; pres. Jain Ctr. of Greater St. Louis, 1986—; dir., treas. Fedn. Jain Assn. of N.Am., 1986—; v.p. fin. Middletown Symphony, Inc., 1984-86. Fellow Planning Forum; mem. Inst. Mgmt. Accts. (Bayer Silver medal 1978), Fin. Mgmt. Assn., Nat. Assn. Corp. Treas., Fin. Execs. Inst., Assn. Indians in Am. (life). Clubs: Mo. Athletic, India (Dayton, Ohio, pres. 1980). Lodge: Rotary. Home: 13263 Laurel Lake Ct Saint Louis MO 63131 Office: Edison Bros Stores Inc 501 N Broadway Saint Louis MO 63102

SINGLE, RICHARD WAYNE, SR., lawyer; b. Balt., June 17, 1938; s. William and Lillian (Griffin) Single; m. Emily K. Kaffl, Nov. 4, 1962; children: Richard W. Jr., Stacey Lyn. AB, U. Md., 1959, JD, 1961. Bar: Md. 1961, U.S. Dist. Ct. Md. 1961, U.S. Supreme Ct. 1978. Staff atty. Legal Aid Bur. Balt., 1962-64; house counsel Gen. Automatic Prodns. Corp., Balt., 1964-67; resident counsel Nat. Industries, Inc., Odenton, Md., 1967-69; asst. counsel McCormick & Co., Inc., Hunt Valley, Md., 1969-72, asst. sec., asst. counsel, 1972-75, asst. sec., assoc. gen. counsel, 1975-82, div. gen. counsel, v.p., 1983-86, gen counsel, v.p., sec., 1986—, also bd. dirs.; bd. dirs. Club House Foods, Inc., London, Ont., Can., McCormick de Mexico, Mexico City. Trustee Franklin Sq. Hosp., Balt., 1986—. Mem. ABA, Md. Bar Assn. Republican. Office: McCormick & Co Inc 11350 McCormick Rd Hunt Valley MD 21031

SINGLETARY, ALVIN D., lawyer; b. New Orleans, Sept. 27, 1942; s. Alvin E. and Alice (Pastoret) S.; m. Judy Louise Singletary, Dec. 3, 1983; children: Kimberly Dawn, Shane David, Kelly Diane. B.A., La. State U., 1964; J.D., Loyola U., New Orleans, 1969. Bar: La. 1969, U.S. Dist. Ct. (ea. dist.) La. 1972, U.S. Ct. Appeals (5th cir.) 1972, U.S. Supreme Ct. 1978, U.S. Ct. Appeals (11th cir.) 1981, U.S. Ct. Internat. Trade 1981, U.S. Ct. Customs and Patent Appeals 1982. Instr. Delgado Coll., New Orleans, 1976-77; sole practice, Slidell, La., 1970—; sec.-treas. St. Tammany Pub. Trust Fin. Authority, Slidell, 1978—; Councilman-at-large City of Slidell, 1978—, interim mayor, 1985; mem. Democratic State Central Com., 1978-82; del. La. Constl. Conv., 1972-73; chmn. sustaining membership enrollment Cypress dist. Boy Scouts Am., 1989—; chmn. Together We Build Program First Baptist Ch. of Slidell, La.; treas. Slidell Centennial Commn. Mem. Delta Theta Phi. Baptist. Lodge: Lions. Office: PO Box 1158 Slidell LA 70459

SINGLETON, CHARLES EDWARD, public relations executive, pastor; b. Tallulah, La., Jan. 26, 1950; s. Isaac Sr. and Pearl Beatrice (Dexter) S.; m. Charlyn Michelle Palmer, Jan. 27, 1973; children: Charles Mark, Christopher Courtland, Cory Christian, Carey Palmer. BS, So. Ill. U., 1971; MA, Cin. Grad. Sem., 1972. Recruiter Expo '72, Dallas, 1971-72; dir. Campus Crusade, San Bernardino, Calif., 1971-74; pastor Loveland Ch., Fontana, Calif., 1974—; pres. Harambee, Ontario, Calif., 1974—; ltd. ptnr. So. Garvey Med. Bldg., Pomona, Calif, 1986—; chapel speaker Los Angeles Rams,

1973—; adj. prof. Internat. Grad. Sch., San Bernardino, 1984—; cons. Fontana Unit Schs., 1986—; speaker, lectr. Author articles and books. Founder, chmn. BARAC (African relief orgn.), Pasadena,, 1983; pres. Agape Acad., Ontario, 1985. Democrat. Baptist. Clubs: Holiday (Montclair, Calif.); Men's (Fontana). Home: 19689 Kauri Ave Rialto CA 92376 Office: Harambee 16888 Baseline Ave Fontana CA 92335

SINGLETON, EUSTACE BYRON, lawyer; b. Lufkin, Tex., Oct. 3, 1909; s. James Madison and Carolyn Elizabeth (Haygood) S.; m. Elsie Adeline Bell, May 15, 1935; children: Eustace Byron, Savannah Adeline. AB, U. Tex., 1933, JD, 1933. Bar: Tex. 1933, U.S. Supreme Ct. 1941, U.S. Ct. Claims 1952, U.S. Ct. Customs and Patent Appeals 1956, U.S. Ct. Appeals (5th cir.) La., U.S. Ct. Appeals (10th cir.) Colo., U.S. Ct. Appeals (11th cir.) Ga., U.S. Ct. Appeals (D.C. cir.). Assoc. Underwood, Strickland & Singleton, Amarillo, Tex., 1933-38; ptnr. Monning & Singleton, Amarillo, 1939-49, Singleton & Trulove, Amarillo, 1950-60; sole practice Amarillo, 1961—; corp. counsel City of Amarillo, 1941-48; at various times gen. counsel, dir., exec. mgr. BC & M Drilling, Inc., Mesa, Draughon's Bus. Colls., Amarillo and Lubbock, Inc., Beef Industries, Inc., Amarillo Industries, Inc., Ark. Valley Feed Yard, Lamar, TransEra Research of Dallas, Inc., Am. Grain & Cattle Mgmt., San Antonio, Soweco, Inc., Continental Dynamics Ltd of Las Vegas, Venture Assocs Mgmt. Corp., Gems Internat., Santa Barbara; former spl. referee in bankruptcy and U.S. Concilliation Commn., Spl. Bankruptcy Master, Amarillo div. and Lubbock div., 1933-39; gen. counsel TLC Veternarians Assn., Am. Gen. Homewatch, Golden Springs Community Homewatch, 1984-87. Exec. committeeman Young Dems. of Tex., 1935-46; fin. committeeman Amarillo Dem. Com., 1936-40; chmn. Amarillo chpt. ARC, 1938-46; dep. dir. War Savs. Staff, AUstin, Tex., 1939-43; nat. committeeman War Fin. Com., Dallas, 1943-46; bd. dirs. Edna Gladney Home; bd. govs. Nat. Arthiritis Found. Mem. ABA, Amarillo Bar Assn., State Bar Tex., Am. Judicature Soc. Home and Office: 2405 Lipscomb St Amarillo TX 79109 Office: 1409 Atrium Pla 619 S Tyler Amarillo TX 79101-2345

SINGLETON, HENRY EARL, industrialist; b. Haslet, Tex., Nov. 27, 1916; s. John Bartholomew and Victoria (Flores) S.; m. Caroline A. Wood, Nov. 30, 1942; children: Christina, John, William, James, Diana. S.B., S.M., Mass. Inst. Tech., 1940, Sc.D., 1950. Vice pres. Litton Industries, Inc., Beverly Hills, Calif., 1954-60; chief exec. officer Teledyne Inc., Los Angeles, 1960-86; chmn. Teledyne Inc., 1960—. Home: 384 Delfern Dr Los Angeles CA 90024 Office: Teledyne Inc 1901 Ave of the Stars Los Angeles CA 90067 *

SINGLETON, LARRY WILLIAM, financial officer; b. Miami, Fla., Aug. 7, 1950; s. Ollice Monroe and Shirley (Surles) S.; m. Gloria Leonard, Aug. 19, 1972; children: Adam B., Tyler M. BS, Fla. State U., 1972; MBA, U. North Fla., 1982. CPA. Tax mgr. Peat, Marwick & Mitchell, Jacksonville, Fla., 1972-79; with The Charter Co., Jacksonville, 1979—, exec. v.p., chief fin. officer, 1987—. Mem. Fla. Inst. CPA's, Am. Inst. CPA's. Democrat. Methodist. Club: Seminole. Home: 9085 Bay Cove Ln Jacksonville FL 32217 Office: The Charter Co 1 Charter Pla Jacksonville FL 32202

SINGLETON, RAYMOND LEVON, investment broker; b. Rosedale, Okla., Oct. 26, 1927; s. James William and Ruby Mae (Robison) S.; student Okla. State U., 1946; m. Anna Lou Bates, Apr. 2, 1946; children—Sherrie Lurea, Gayla Jean. Dist. mgr. sales Okla. Office & Bank Supply Co., Shawnee, 1948-51; partner Nat. Office & Bank Supply Co., Enid, Okla., 1951-53; v.p., sales mgr. Southwestern Stationery & Bank Supply Co., Lawton, Okla., 1954-83, also dir.; investment broker Stifel, Nicolaus & Co., Inc., Lawton, 1983—. Served with USN, 1946-47. Mem. C. of C., VFW, Am. Legion. Democrat. Mem. Ch. of Christ. Club: Lawton Country (pres.). Lodge: Rotary. Home: 2115 Atlanta St Lawton OK 73505 Office: Stifel Nicolaus & Co Inc 601 C Ave Ste 100 Lawton OK 73501

SINHA, ASHOK KUMAR, electronics company executive; b. Patna, India, Feb. 23, 1944; s. Kedar Nath and Shanti (Prasad) S.; m. Rekha Verma, Feb. 19, 1969; children: Gita Anjali, Anoop Kumar. BE, Indian Inst. Scis., 1964; PhD, Oxford U., 1966. With tech. staff AT&T Bell Labs, Murray Hill, N.J., 1970-76; group supr. AT&T Bell Labs., Murray Hill, N.J., 1976-82, dept. head, 1982-84; dept. head AT&T Bell Labs., Allentown, Pa., 1984-88; v.p., mfg. technology devel. Sematech Consortium, Austin, Tex., 1988—; com. mem. Nat. Materials Adv. Bd., Washington, 1983-84. Contbr. over 80 articles to profl. jours.; holder over 18 patents. Mem. IEEE (sr., assoc. editor IEEE Jour. Semiconductor Mfg.), Electrochem. Soc. (div. editor 1979-80, Callinan award for Outstanding Contbrn. to Dielectrics and Insulation Sci., 1985). Home: 1305 Possum Trot Austin TX 78703 Office: SEMATECH 2706 Montopolis Dr Austin TX 78741

SINN, ROBERT SAMUEL, securities company executive, pharmaceutical company executive, systems management executive; b. Phila., Mar. 9, 1930; s. Charles M. and Dorothea (Koenig) S.; A.B., U. Pa., 1952, M.S., 1957; m. Pamela Gaye; children—Nina A., Robert M., Charles Gordon. Engr., RCA, Camden, N.J., 1952-60; chmn. bd. Elkins-Sinn Corp., 1967-76; chmn. bd. Microwave Semiconductor Corp., 1968-79; pres. Ultronic Systems Corp., 1960-70, dir., 1960-73; chmn. Wall Street Venture Capital Corp., 1969-73; chmn. Robert S. Sinn Securities, Inc., 1976—; chmn. Tel Systems Mgmt. Corp., 1983-84; pres., chmn. Angio Med. Corp., 1984—; pres., chmn. Bion Corp., 1985—. Mem. IEEE, Young Pres.'s Orgn., Engrs. Club Phila., N.Y. Acad. Sci., Ops. Research Soc. Am. Clubs: Wall Street, Metropolitan. Patentee in field. Home: 248 W 88th St Penthouse B New York NY 10024

SINNINGER, DWIGHT VIRGIL, research engineer; b. Bourbon, Ind., Dec. 29, 1901; s. Norman E. and Myra (Huff) S.; student Armour Inst., 1928, U. Chgo., 1942, Northwestern U., 1943; m. Coyla Annetta Annis, Mar. 1, 1929; m. 2d, Charlotte M. Lenz, Jan. 21, 1983. Electronics research engr. Johnson Labs., Chgo., 1935-42; chief engr. Pathfinder Radio Corp., 1943-44, Rowe Engring. Corp., 1945-48, Hupp Electronics Co. div. Hupp Corp., 1948-61; dir. research Pioneer Electric & Research Corp., Forest Park, Ill., 1961-65, Senn Custom, Inc., Forest Park and San Antonio, 1967—. Registered profl. engr., Ill. Mem. IEEE, Instrument Soc. Am., Armed Forces Communications Assn. Holder several U.S. patents. Address: PO Box 982 Kerrville TX 78028

SINOPOLI, PAUL LOUIS, treasurer; b. Pittsfield, Mass., July 17, 1951; s. Vito J. and Rose E. (Tamburello) S.; m. Linda Marie Macone, Sept. 22, 1979; children: Alison, Mark. AS in bus. Adminstrn., Berkshire Community Coll., 1972; BS in Bus. Adminstrn., Salem State Coll., 1975. With Kay Bee Toy and Hobby Shops, Inc., Pittsfield, Mass., 1976—, treas., 1986—. Roman Catholic. Home: 43 Kimberly Dr Dalton MA 01226 Office: Kay Bee Toy & Hobby Shops Inc 100 West St Pittsfield MA 01201

SINSHEIMER, WARREN JACK, lawyer, electronic equipment company executive; b. N.Y.C., May 22, 1927; s. Jerome William and Elizabeth (Berch) S.; m. Florence Dubin, Mar. 30, 1950; children: Linda Ruth, Ralph David, Alan Jay, Michael Neal. Student, Ind. U., 1943-47; J.D. cum laude, N.Y. Law Sch., 1950; LL.M., NYU, 1957; M.Phil., Columbia U., 1977. Bar: N.Y. bar 1950. Ptnr. Sinsheimer, Sinsheimer & Dubin, N.Y.C., 1950-78, Satterlee & Stephens, N.Y.C., 1978-86, Patterson, Belknap, Webb & Tyler, N.Y.C., 1986—; pres. Plessey, Inc., N.Y.C., 1956-70, chmn., chief exec. officer, 1970—; dir. overseas ops. and devel. The Plessey Co., Ltd., Ilford, Essex, Eng., 1969-70, now dep. chief exec., dir.; dir. Plessey, Inc.; dir. Exide Electronics Group, Inc. Chmn. Com. of 68, 1964-67; Mem Westchester County Republican Com., 1956-73; chmn. Nat. Scranton for Pres. Com., 1964; mem. N.Y. State Assembly, 1965-66; Bd. visitors Wassaic State Sch., 1962-64. Served with USNR, 1944-45; with USAF, 1950-52. Mem. Am. Bar Assn., Assn. Bar City N.Y., Torch and Scroll, Zeta Beta Tau. Jewish. Clubs: Beach Point (Mamaroneck, N.Y.); Harmonie (N.Y.C.); Century (Purchase, N.Y.). Home: 22 Murray Hill Rd Scarsdale NY 10583 Office: Patterson Belknap Webb & Tyler 30 Rockefeller Pla New York NY 10112

SIOUKAS, JACK, dentist, business and investments executive; b. Kastoria, Greece, Apr. 21, 1936; came to U.S., 1955; s. Anastasios Kyriakos and Nerantzia (Kopatsis) S.; m. Lillian Sutter, Apr. 28, 1968; children: Chris, Dean, Alex. BS, U. Ill., Chgo., 1960, DDS, 1962. Pvt. practice Sacramento, 1964; investor Jack Sioukas Investments, Sacramento, 1964—; pres. Lexington Homes Inc., Sacramento, 1986—, JAS Devel. Corp., Sacramento, 1986—. Founding mem. Dynamis, San Francisco, 1979; mem. Parish Council-Greek Orthodox Ch. Capt. USAF, 1962-64. Mem. ADA, Acad. Gen. Denstistry, Sacramento Dist. Dental Assn., Am. Hellenic Profl. Soc. No. Calif., Del Paso Country Club, NorthRidge Country Club. Republican. Home: 3331 American River Dr Sacramento CA 95864 Office: Sioukas Investments 7700 College Town Dr Suite 109 Sacramento CA 95826

SIPPL, JAMES GEORGE, JR., manufacturing and wholesaling executive; b. Wassau, Wis., July 28, 1947; s. James G. and Etta (Lenzner) S.; m. Deborah P. Pollreis, Nov. 14, 1975; children: Zachary, Samuel, Rachel. BS, U. Wis., 1970. Ptnr. Coopers & Lybrand, Mpls., 1970-86; chief fin. officer Chgo. Cutlery, Inc., Mpls., 1986—; pres., chief operating officer Chgo. Cutlery, Inc., New Hope, Minn., 1988—; bd. dirs. Mailhouse, Mpls., Beef Specialists Iowa, SPencer. Founder, bd. dirs. World Legends of Golf, Horseshoe Bay, Tex.; bd. dirs. Freeport Group Homes, Mpls., 1978-88, Cath. Charities, St. Paul, Internat. Entrepreneurship Acad., Mpls., Highland Park Hockey Assn., St. Paul. Mem. Fin. Execs. Inst., AICPA, Town and Country Club, Rotary Club. Home: 271 Mt Curve Blvd Saint Paul MN 55105 Office: Chgo Cutlery 5420 N County Rd New Hope MN 55428

SIROTEK, NORMAN ALAN, controller; b. Ottawa, Ont., Can., Aug. 9, 1958; s. Nadia Maria (Bostandjian) S.; m. Lori Beatrice Sears, Aug. 17, 1985. Student, Clarkson Coll. Tech., 1978-80, Algonquin Coll., 1982. Controller Sir-Tech Software, Inc., Ogdensburg, N.Y., 1980—. Mem. Software Pubs. Assn., Rotary. Home: 323 Washington St Ogdensburg NY 13669 Office: Sir Tech Software Inc PO Box 245 Ogdensburg NY 13669

SISITZKY, LEONARD HAROLD, food company executive; b. Springfield, Mass., Aug. 25, 1924; s. Max and Nellie (Tober) S.; m. Dorothy Ertman, Nov. 16, 1952; children: Nancy Alderman, Brian R. BBA, U. Conn., 1950. Sales rep. Beech-Nut Packing Co., Canjoharie, N.Y., 1950-56; div. mgr. James O. Welch/Nabisco Co., Cambridge, Mass., 1956-65; nat. sales mgr. Schrafft Candy Co., Charlestown, Mass., 1965-76; pres. L.H. Sisitzky Sales Inc., Woburn, Mass., 1976—. Pres. Windsor (Conn.) Vol. Fire Dept., 1950-62. Served with U.S. Navy, 1942-46. Mem. Nat. Candy Brokers Assn. (pres. 1986-87), Nat. Candy Wholesalers (candy ambassador 1981), Nat. Candy Salesmen's Club, Boston Confectioner's Club (bd. dirs. 1987—), Knights Grip Conn. (pres. 1962-63), Elks (chaplain 1961-63, Elk Yr. 1963). Office: LH Sisitzky Sales Inc 244 W Cummings Pk Woburn MA 01801

SISK, ALBERT FLETCHER, JR., insurance agent; b. Easton, Md., Nov. 25, 1928; s. Albert Fletcher and Helen (Marvel) S.; m. Mary Douglass Tweedy, Jan. 8, 1955; children: Douglass Fletcher, Geoffrey Price. Student, Washington and Lee U., 1946-49. CLU. With Albert W. Sisk & Son, Preston, Md., 1950-66; ins. agt. Conn. Gen. Life Ins. Co., 1968—; pres. Farrell & Sisk, Inc.; v.p. Atlantic Pension Planners, Inc.; dir. Preston Trucking Co., Inc., Preston Corp., Provident State Bank, Preston. Trustee Meml. Hosp., Easton, Md., 1965-71, mem. Sch. Nursing Com.; mem. Delmarva Estate Planning Council, bd. visitors Horn Point Labs. U. Md., Served with USN, 1952-54. Mem. Nat. Assn. Life Underwriters, Nat. Rifle Assn., Am. Soc. CLU's, Balt. Life Underwriters Assn., Meml. Hosp. Assn. Clubs: Lions (past pres.) (Preston); Chesapeake Bay Yacht. Home: Gilpin's Point Rte I Box 209A Preston MD 21655 Office: 1 Mill Pl Ste 100 Box 179 Easton MD 21601

SISSEL, GEORGE ALLEN, lawyer, manufacturing executive; b. Chgo., July 30, 1936; s. William Worth and Hannah Ruth (Harlan) S.; m. Mary Ruth Runsvold, Oct. 5, 1968; children: Jenifer Ruth, Gregory Allen. B.S. in Elec. Engring., U. Colo., 1958; J.D. cum laude, U. Minn., 1966. Bar: Colo. 1966, Ind. 1973, U.S. Supreme Ct. 1981. Assoc. Sherman & Howard, Denver, 1966-70; with Ball Corp., Muncie, Ind., 1970—; asso. gen. counsel Ball Corp., 1974-78, gen. counsel, 1978—, corp. sec., 1980—, v.p., 1981-87, sr. v.p., 1987—. Asso. editor: U. Minn. Law Rev., 1965-66. Served with USN, 1958-63. Mem. MIT Soc. Sr. Execs. (bd. govs. 1987—), Am. Soc. Corp. Secs., ABA, Colo. Bar Assn., Ind. Bar Assn., Order of Coif, Sigma Chi, Sigma Tau, Eta Kappa Nu. Methodist. Lodge: Rotary. Home: 2600 W Berwyn Rd Muncie IN 47304 Office: Ball Corp 345 S High St Muncie IN 47305

SISSON, EVERETT ARNOLD, industrial developer, executive; b. Chgo., Oct. 24, 1920; s. Emmett B. and Norma (Merbitz) S.; m. Betty L. DeGrado, Apr. 7, 1984; children: Nancy Lee Sisson Rassbach, Elizabeth Anne Sisson Levy. AB, Valparaiso U., 1942. Sales mgr. Ferrotherm Corp., Cleve., 1946-51, Osborn Mfg. Co., Cleve., 1951-56; dir. sales Patterson Foundry & Machine Co., East Liverpool, Ohio, 1956-58; mgr. sonic energy products Bendix Corp., Davenport, Iowa, 1958-60; pres., chief exec. officer, dir. Lamb Industries, Inc., Toledo, 1960-65, Lehigh Valley Industries, Inc., N.Y.C., 1965-66, Am. Growth Industries, Inc., Chgo., 1966—, Workman Mfg. Co., Chgo., 1966-69, Am. Growth Devel. Corp., Chgo., 1968—; chmn. bd., chief exec. officer G.F.I. Inc., 1976-87; pres. Peru Properties, Inc., Oak Brook, 1976-87; chmn. AMBRIANCE! Inc., Burr Ridge, Ill., 1988—; bd. dirs. Century Life of Am., Waverly, Iowa, Telco Capital Corp., Hickory Furniture Co., N.C., Sunstates Corp., Raleigh, N.C., Century Life Ins. Co., Waverly, Iowa, Indiana Fin. Investors Inc., Indpls., Acton Corp., Raleigh, N.C.; trustee Wis. Real Estate Investment Trust, 1980—. Pres. coun., Mayfield Heights, Ohio, 1952-57; adviser to bd. trustees Valparaiso (Ind.) U., 1960-69; bd. regents Calif. Luth. Coll., 1968—, fellow, 1969. Capt. USAAF, 1943-46. Mem. Am. Mgmt. Assn., Cleve. Engring. Soc., Pres.'s Assn., Tau Kappa Epsilon. Clubs: Burr Ridge, Gt. Lakes Yachting, Ocean Reef. Home: 15 Ambriance! Burr Ridge IL 60521 Office: Am Growth Group Inc 745 McClintock Dr Burr Ridge IL 60521

SISTO, FERNANDO, mechanical engineering educator; b. La Coruña, Spain, Aug. 2, 1924; s. Fernando Cartelle and Clara (Reiss) S.; m. Grace Jeanette Wexler, June 27, 1946; children: Jane Caroll, Ellen Gail, Todd Frederic. Student, NYU, 1940-43; BS, U.S. Naval Acad., 1946; ScD, MIT, 1952; M Engring. (hon.), Stevens Inst. Tech., 1962. Registered profl. engr., N.J. Commd. ensign USN, 1946, service in the Pacific, ret., 1949; propulsion div. chief Curtiss-Wright Research, Clifton, N.J., 1952-58; prof. mech. engring. Stevens Inst. Tech., Hoboken, N.J., 1959—, chmn. dept., 1966-79, George M. Bond prof., 1978—; bd. dirs., trustee Am. Capital Mut. Funds, Houston, 1960—; bd. dirs. Dynalysis of Princeton, 1971—; cons. UN Devel. Program, India, 1978. Co-author textbook: A Modern Course in Aeroelasticity, 1978, 2d edit. 1989. Lt. USN, 1943-49. R.C. DuPont fellow MIT, 1951-52. Fellow ASME; mem. Adirondack Mountain Club. Office: Stevens Inst of Tech Dept of Mech Engring Hoboken NJ 07030-5991

SIT, EUGENE C., investment executive; b. Canton, China, Aug. 8, 1938; s. Hom Yuen and Sue (Eng) S.; B.S.C., DePaul U., 1960, postgrad. Grad. Sch. Bus., 1962-65; m. Gail V. Chin, Sept. 14, 1958; children—Ronald, Debra, Roger, Raymond, Robert, Richard. Fin. analyst Commonwealth Edison, Chgo., 1960-66, fin. asst. to chmn. finance com., 1966-68; asso. portfolio mgr. Investors Stock Fund, Investors Diversified Services, Mpls., 1968-69; portfolio mgr. IDS New Dimensions Fund, Mpls., 1969, v.p., portfolio mgr., 1970-72; v.p., sr. portfolio mgr. IDS New Dimensions, IDS Growth Fund, Mpls., 1972-76; pres. IDS Adv., 1976-77, pres., chief exec. officer, 1977-81; chief exec. officer IDS Trust Co., 1979-81; chmn., chief exec. officer IDS Adv./Gartmore Internat. Ltd., 1979-81; pres., chief exec. officer Sit Investment Assocs., Inc., Mpls., 1981—; chmn., pres., dir. Sit New Beginning Growth Fund, Sit New Beginning Income and Growth Fund, Sit New Beginning Investment Res. Fund, Sit New Beginning Tax Free Income Fund, Sit New Beginning U.S. Govt. Securities Fund. CPA, Ill. Bd. pensions Presbyterian Ch. Mem. AICPA, Inst. Chartered Fin. Analysts (trustee), Fin. Analysts Fedn., Twin Cities Soc. Security Analysts, Investment Analysts Soc. Chgo., University Club, Chicago Club, Minneapolis Club, Edina Country Club, World Trade Club. Home: 6216 Braeburn Circle Edina MN 55435 Office: 4600 Norwest Ctr 90 S 7th St Minneapolis MN 55402

SITKO, JERE CONRAD, corporate psychologist; b. Akron, Ohio, Dec. 14, 1950; s. Michael and Joyce Rosalie (Geisinger) S.; m. Donna Jean Gareiro, June 19, 1976 (div. June 1978); children: Maria, Bela-Guido; m. Sheila Sara Gannon, Oct. 31, 1979; children: Jon, Carrie, Melissa, Sara, Gustav, Frederic. BA, Kent State U., 1973, MEd, 1975; PhD, Wright Inst., 1988. Urinologist Townhall II Med. Ctr., Kent, Ohio, 1971-74; adminstr. mental health Western Res. Psychol. Habilitation Ctr., Cleve., 1976-82; asst. dir. San Mateo (Calif.) County Mental Health, 1982-84; cons., researcher Xerox Corp., San Francisco, 1982-85; cons. Chevron USA, San Francisco, 1985—. Author: the Corporate Mind, 1981, Caught in the Corporate Tornado, 1985. Pamphleteer Jews for Jesus, Oaklnd Calif., 1984-86; U.S. Ambassador to Liege U., Belgian Govt., 1972. Recipient Best Score award home documentary ASCAP, 1987. Mem. Psychologists for Ethical Lawyers (dir., founder 1986-87), Psychologists for Ethical Taxi Drivers (asst. dir. 1986-87), Internat. Transaction Analysis Assn., Calif. Psychol. Assn., San Francisco C. of C. (sec. 1986-88), Bohemian Club (treas. 1986-87), Odd Fellows, Phi Beta Bida (v.p. 1985-88). Democrat. Mem. Ch. of Scientology. Home: 2425 Market St #3 San Francisco CA 94114 Office: Psychologist Ethical Lawyers 2728 Durant St Berkeley CA 94704

SITOMER, KENNETH MARK, apparel company executive; b. N.Y.C., Sept. 12, 1946; s. Harry and Beatrice (Katz) S.; BA, CCNY, 1968, MBA, 1974. Pres. Ernst and Whinney, CPA's, N.Y.C., 1969-70, Mann Judd Landau, CPA's, N.Y.C., 1970-74; pres. Bidermann Industries (parent Co. Calvin Klein Menswear, Ralph Lauren Womenswear, Yves St. Laurent, Daniel Hechter and Jean Paul Germain, Karl Lagerfeld), N.Y.C., 1974—, pres., 1977—. Served with U.S. Army, 1969. CPA, N.Y. Mem. Am. Inst. CPA's, N.Y. State Soc. CPA's, Young Pres. Orgn. Home: 303 E 57th St New York NY 10022

SITRICK, MICHAEL STEVEN, communications executive; b. Davenport, Iowa, June 8, 1947; s. J. Herman and Marcia B. (Bofman) S.; m. Nancy Elaine Eiseman, July 1, 1969; children: Julie, Sheri, Alison. BS in Bus. Adminstrn. and Journalism, U. Md., 1969. Coordinator press services Western Electric, Chgo., 1969-70; asst. dir. program services City of Chgo., 1970-72; asst. v.p. Selz, Seabolt & Assocs., Chgo., 1972-74; dir. communications and pub. affairs Nat. Can Corp., Chgo., 1974-81; dir. communications Wickes Cos., Inc., San Diego, 1981-82; v.p. communications Wickes Cos., Inc., Santa Monica, Calif., 1982-84, sr. v.p. communications, 1984-89; chmn., chief exec. officer Sitrick and Co., L.A., 1989—. Mem. Pub. Relations Soc. Am., Nat. Investor Relations Inst. Club: Ad of Los Angeles. Office: Sitrick & Co 10920 Wilshire Blvd Ste 910 Los Angeles CA 90024

SITTERLY, CONNIE SUE, management training specialist; b. Fairfax, Okla., Oct. 9, 1953; d. Claude O. and Virda (Smith) S. AA, Frank Phillips Coll., 1973; BS, West Tex. State U., 1975, MA, 1978; postgrad., Tex. Woman's U., 1985-89. Instr. Frank Phillips Coll., Borger, Tex., 1978-80; asst. prof. Amarillo (Tex.) Coll., 1980-85; owner, operator, pres. Mgmt. Tng. Specialists, Ft. Worth, 1983—; adj. assoc. prof. Tex.'s Women's U., Denton, 1986—. Author: A Woman's Place: Management, 1988; contbr. articles to profl. jours. Mem. Am. Soc. Tng. and Devel., Nat. Mgmt. Educators Assn., Am. Soc. Quality Control. Republican. Lodge: Eastern Star. Home: 2808 5th Ave Fort Worth TX 76110 Office: 1201 W Presidio Ste 204 Fort Worth TX 76102

SIVINSKI, JAMES ANTHONY, automobile dealer; b. Grand Island, Nebr., June 4, 1938; s. Ignatius Paul and Anna (Smedra) S.; m. Suzanne Bee, May 1, 1959 (div. June 1964); children: Anita Cecille Sivinski Kangas, Shaun Lynn; m. Janet Elaine Larson, Nov. 5, 1966; 1 child, Paris Lynn. Grad. banking sch., St. Olaf Coll., 1973; grad. sch. bank adminstrn. with honors, U. Wis., 1978. Credit and collections clerk Comml. Credit Co., Mankato, Minn., 1967-68; mgr. Community Credit Co., Richfield, Minn., 1968-70; exec. v.p. Bank of Mpls. & Trust Co., 1970-78; pres., owner Gemini Auto Sales & Acceptance Co., Mpls., 1979—. Recipient advanced ednl. achievement award Am. Inst. Banking, Mpls., 1976. Mem. Entrepreneurs Resource Group of Mpls. Republican. Roman Catholic. Home: 14116 Whiterock Rd Burnsville MN 55337 Office: Gemini Auto Sales & Acceptance Cos 501 W Lake St Minneapolis MN 55408

SIVRIGHT, JOHN AVERY, banker; b. Mpls., Jan. 26, 1929; s. Harry H. and Mary (Avery) S.; m. Marion Louise Smith, June 6, 1950; children: John Avery Jr., Scott David, Barbara Sivright Costin. BS, U.S. Naval Acad., 1950; MBA, U. Chgo., 1958. Commd. 2d lt. USMC, 1950, advanced through grades to capt., resigned, 1954; with Harris Trust and Savs. Bank, Chgo., 1954—, sr. v.p., 1975-80, exec. v.p., 1980—; bd. dirs. Maytag Corp., Newton Iowa, Harris Bank Winnetka, Ill. Bd. dirs. Chgo. Youth Ctrs., 1962—, pres., 1974-76; trustee Shedd Aquarium, Chgo., 1982—. Mem. Assn. Res. City Bankers, Chgo. Club, Mid-Am. Club, Commonwealth Club, Glen View Club, Riomar Country Club. Republican. Home: 640 Winnetka Mews Apt 408 Winnetka IL 60093 Office: Harris Trust & Savs Bank PO Box 755 Chicago IL 60690

SJOLANDER, LINDA ARLENE, marketing executive; b. Portland, Oreg., Aug. 7, 1943; d. Nathaniel David and Ardis Margaret (Gisselberg) S.; m. James Earl Pennington, Aug. 7, 1965 (div. Sept. 1974); m. John Derek Lyons, Feb. 14, 1986. BA in English, U. Oreg., 1965; MEd in English, Boston U., 1970. Tchr., David Douglas Schs., Beaverton, Oreg., 1965-69; clin. supr., Portland State U., 1965-69; tchr., Winchester Schs., Mass., 1970-73; co-dir., counselor John F. Kennedy Sch., Queretaro, Mex., 1973-74; asst. v.p. pub. relations Newspaper Advt. Bur., N.Y.C., 1975-76; self-employed, Boston, 1977; editor, writer Intermetrics, Inc., Cambridge, Mass., 1978-85; cons., propr., by Sjolander, Belmont, Mass., 1983-85, Sjolander Lyons Communications, Concord, Mass., 1986-88, mktg. cons. Parks and Recreation Dept. Town of Mashpee, Mass., 1988—; guest lectr. U. Lowell, Mass., 1985, Northeastern U., Mass., 1987. Contbr. articles to profl. jours. Mem. Belmont Citizens Com., Mass., 1983-85; chmn. adv. com. Town of Mashpee. Recipient Outstanding Performance award NASA, 1983. Mem. Am. Mktg. Assn., Alpha Omicron Pi. Republican. Episcopalian. Avocations: art, music, dance, literature. Home and Office: 159 Thoreau St #7 Concord MA 01742

SKAGGS, L. SAM, retail company executive; b. 1922; married. With Am. Stores Co., Salt Lake City, 1945—, chmn. bd., chief exec. officer, from 1966, pres., chief exec. officer, until 1988, also bd. dirs.; chmn. Sav-On Drugs, Anaheim, Calif., bd. dirs. Served with USAAF, 1942-45. Office: Am Stores Co PO Box 9649 Newport Beach CA 92658 also: Am Stores Co 19100 Von Karman Ave Irvine CA 92715 *

SKAGGS, SANFORD MERLE, lawyer; b. Berkeley, Calif., Oct. 24, 1939; s. Sherman G. and Barbara Jewel (Stinson) S.; m. Sharon Ann Barnes, Sept. 3, 1976; children—Stephen, Paula, Barbara, Darren Peterson. B.A., U. Calif.-Berkeley, 1961, J.D., 1964. Bar: Calif. 1965. Atty. Pacific Gas and Electric Co., San Francisco, 1964-73; gen. counsel Pacific Gas Transmission Co., San Francisco, 1973-75; ptnr. firm Van Voorhis & Skaggs, Walnut Creek, Calif., 1975-85, McCutchen, Doyle, Brown & Enersen, San Francisco and Walnut Creek, 1985—; bd. dirs. Civic Bank Commerce, Oakland, Calif.; adv. council Lawrence Hall of Sci. U. Calif.-Berkeley, 1988—. Councilman City of Walnut Creek, 1972-78, mayor, 1974-75, 76-77; bd. dirs. East Bay Mcpl. Utility Dist., 1978—, pres., 1982—; trustee Regional Arts Ctr., Inc., 1980-88, Contra Costa County Law Library, 1978—. Mem. Calif. State Bar Assn., Contra Costa County Bar Assn., Alpha Delta Phi, Phi Delta Phi. Republican. Club: World Trade. Office: McCutchen Doyle Brown & Enersen 1855 Olympic Blvd PO Box V 3rd Fl Flagg Pla Walnut Creek CA 94596

SKARSAUNE, RAGNAR MARTIN, purchasing executive; b. Leksvik, Norway, May 18, 1945; came to U.S., 1961; s. Anders Olsen and Karen Gurine (Solem) S.; m. Sandra Kaye Young, July 2, 1966; 1 child, Charles Anders. BS in Geology, N.D. State U., 1971; MBA in Mgmt., Western Mich. U., 1982. With Minnkota Mfg. Co., Moorhead, Minn., 1966-68; officer vets. svc. N.D. State U., Fargo, 1972-73; chief of ops. Cotevensa Agricola, San Felipe, Venezuela, 1974-76; mfg. engr., buyer Rockwell Internat., Battle Creek, Mich., 1977-82; purchasing agt. Buckley Air N.G., Aurora, Colo., 1982-83; contract adminstr. Stearns-Catalytic, Denver, 1984; sr. buyer engine component div. Eaton Corp., Marshall, Mich., 1985, mgr. purchasing div., 1986—. With U.S. Army, 1963-66, USAFR, 1980—. Mem. Cen. Mich. Assn. Purchasing Mgrs., Am. Legion, Sons of Norway, N.D. State U. Vets. Club. Episcopalian. Home: 8190 Pennfield Rd Battle Creek MI 49017 Office: Eaton Corp Engine Component Div Homer Rd & B Dr S Marshall MI 49068

SKATES, RONALD LOUIS, computer manufacturing executive; b. Kansas City, Mo., Sept. 25, 1941; s. Raymond and Suzanne (Lispi) S.; m. Mary Austin; children: Melissa, Elizabeth. AB cum laude, Harvard U., 1963,

MBA, 1965. Acct. Price Waterhouse, Boston, 1965-76, audit ptnr., 1976-86; sr. v.p. fin. and adminstrn. Data Gen. Corp., Westboro, Mass., 1986-88, exec. v.p., chief oper. officer, 1988—. Trustee Brigham and Women's Hosp, Boston, Winsor Sch., Boston. Mem. AICPA, Mass. Soc. CPAs, Boston C. of C. (pres. Execs. Club). Office: Data Gen Corp 4400 Computer Dr Westborough MA 01580

SKEEN, DAVID RAY, computer systems administrator; b. Bucklin, Kans., July 12, 1942; s. Claude E. and Velma A. (Birney) S.; B.A. in Math., Emporia State U., 1964; M.S., Am. U., 1972, cert. in Computer Systems, 1973; grad. Fed. Exec. Inst., 1983, Naval War Coll., 1984; m. Carol J. Stimpert, Aug. 23, 1964; children—Jeffrey Kent, Timothy Sean, Kimberly Dawn. Cert. office automation profl. Computer systems analyst to comdr.-in-chief U.S. Naval Forces-Europe, London, 1967-70; computer systems analyst Naval Command Systems Support Activity, Washington, 1970-73; dir. data processing Office Naval Research, U.S. Navy Dept., Arlington, Va., 1973-78, dir. mgmt. info. systems Naval Civilian Personnel Command, Washington, 1978-80; dep. dir. total force automated systems Dept. Naval Mil. Personnel Command, Washington, 1980-85; dir. total force info. resource and systems mgmt. div. Chief Naval Ops., 1985—; lectr. Inst. Sci. and Public Affairs, 1973-76; cons. Electronic Data Processing Career Devel. Programs, 1975—; detailed to Pres.'s Reorgn. Project for Automated Data Processing, 1978, Pres.'s Fed. Automated Data Processing Users Group, Washington, 1978-80; assoc. prof. Sch. Engring. and Applied Sci., George Washington U. Served with USN, 1964-67, with Res., 1967—. Recipient Outstanding Performance award Interagy. Com. Data Processing, 1976. Mem. Sr. Exec. Assn., Am. Mgmt. Assn., Assn. Computing Machinery, Data Processing Mgmt. Assn., Naval Res. Assn. Contbr. articles to profl. jours. Home: 707 Forest Park Rd Great Falls VA 22066 Office: Dept Navy Washington DC 20370

SKELLY, THOMAS FRANCIS, manufacturing company executive; b. Boston, Jan. 19, 1934; s. Michael Gerard and Katherine Agnes (Kelly) S.; m. Patricia A. Limerick, Sept. 6, 1958; children—Thomas Francis, John M., Peter G., Matthew M. B.S., Northeastern U., 1956; M.B.A., Babson Coll., 1966. Mgr. Peat, Marwick, Mitchell & Co. (C.P.A.'s), Boston, 1957-67; with Gillette Co., Boston, 1967—; controller Gillette Co., 1973—, v.p., 1979-80, sr. v.p. fin., 1980—; mng. dir. Gillette Overseas Fin. Corp. N.V., Netherlands Antilles; dir. Neworld Bank, Boston. Bd. dirs. nat. council Northeastern U., Nat. Fgn. Trade Council. Served to capt. AUS, 1957-59. Home: 54 Magnolia Dr Westwood MA 02090 Office: Gillette Co Prudential Tower Bldg Boston MA 02199

SKELTON, HOWARD CLIFTON, advertising and public relations executive; b. Birmingham, Ala., Mar. 6, 1932; s. Howard C. and Sarah Ethel (Holmes) S., Sr.; B.S., Auburn U., 1955; m. Winifred Harriet Karger, May 19, 1962; 1 dau., Susan Lynn. Copywriter, Rich's, Inc., Atlanta, 1955-59, Ga. Power Co., Atlanta, 1959-61; dir. advt. and sales promotion Callaway Mills, Inc. LaGrange, Ga., 1961-65; dir. advt. and sales promotion Thomasville (N.C.) Furniture Industries, 1965-66; v.p. in charge of fashion and textiles Gaynor & Ducas, N.Y.C., 1966-70; dir. communications Collins & Aikman, N.Y.C., 1970-73; v.p. Marketplace, Inc., Atlanta, 1973-74; v.p. communications and mktg. Internat. City Corp., Atlanta, 1974-75; pres. Howard Skelton Assocs., Sarasota, 1976—. Served with Signal Corps, AUS, 1956-58. Recipient Danforth Found. award, 1950. Mem. Omicron Delta Kappa, Lambda Chi Alpha, Sigma Delta Chi. Home: 770 S Palm Ave #501 Sarasota FL 34236 Office: 950 S Tamiami Trail Ste 207 Sarasota FL 33577

SKEWES, WILLIAM FREDERICK, lawyer; b. Luverne, Minn., Feb. 13, 1945; s. Mortier B. and Mildred Gladys (Pettes) S; m. Kathleen Audrey Hogan, June 24, 1978; children: Elizabeth Brittany, Wiley Boulden. BA, U. Minn., 1967, JD, 1970. Bar: Minn. 1970, Colo. 1971, U.S. Tax Ct. 1981, U.S. Supreme Ct. 1981. Asst. atty. gen. taxation State of Minn., St. Paul, 1970-72; assoc. Kelly, Stansfield & O'Donnell, Denver, 1972-76, ptnr., 1977-88; pvt. practice, Denver, 1988—; bd. dirs. Colo. Pub. Expenditures Council, Credo Petroleum Corp., SECO Energy Corp., Denver, United Oil Corp., Denver. Bd. dirs. Evergreen (Colo.) Ctr. for the Arts, 1975-79, Colo. State Ballet, Denver, 1979-81; personal advisor U.S. Senator Rudy Boschwitz, 1978—. Mem. ABA, Colo. Bar Assn., Minn. Bar Assn., Colo. Bar Assn. (corp. code revision). Republican. Episcopalian. Club: Denver Athletic. Lodge: Masons. Office: 555 17th St Ste 870 Denver CO 80202

SKIDMORE, DONALD EARL, JR., government official; b. Tacoma, Apr. 27, 1944; s. Donald E. and Ingeborg (Johnsrud) S.; BSc, Evangel Coll., 1968. With Dept. Social and Health Svcs., State of Wash., Yakima, 1967-74; quality rev. specialist Social Security Adminstrn., Seattle, 1974-76, program analyst, Balt., 1976-79, Seattle, 1979-81, quality assurance officer, mgr. Satellite office, Spokane, Wash., 1981-84, program analyst, Seattle, 1984—. Pres., bd. dirs. Compton Court Condo Assn., 1980-81; bd. trustees, v.p. Norwood Village, 1987—; vice chair ops. subcom., mem. citizen's adv. com. METRO, 1987-89; mem. citizen's adv. com. land use planning, Bellevue, Wash., 1988—. Office: 2201 6th Ave M/S RX-56 Seattle WA 98121

SKIDMORE, FRANCIS JOSEPH, JR., securities company executive; b. Newark, June 4, 1943; s. Francis Joseph and Gertrude Elizabeth (Auth) S.; stepson Patricia Ann (Jaekel) Skidmore; student U. Md., 1961-63; B.S. in Econs., Duquesne U., 1968; m. Catherine Ann Stepanek, Mar. 27, 1971; children—Francis Joseph, Patrick Edward, Melissa Catherine. Trust adminstr. Chase Manhattan Bank N.A., N.Y.C., 1968-71, asst. v.p. corp. adv., 1971-74; asst. v.p. sales Lombard Wall Co., N.Y.C., 1974-75; v.p., sales mgr. Foxton Securities Co., N.Y.C., 1975-77; v.p., salesman Cantor Fitzgerald Securities Corp., N.Y.C., 1977-87; sales mgr. money market instruments, 1983-87; v.p. sales, mgr. money market dept. Yamaichi Internat. (Am.), Inc., N.Y.C., 1987—; instr. N.Y. Inst. Fin., 1981-82 . Mem. Berkeley Heights (N.J.) Drainage Com., 1976-79; various offices Young Republicans of Essex County, 1963-70; pres. Rep. Club of Berkeley Heights, 1977-79; chmn. Berkeley Heights Corp. Devel. Com., 1977-79; active United Fund, 1975-77; pres. Chester Ridge Property Owners Assn., 1981-82; head coach Mendham Soccer Club; Longhouse chief YMCA Indians Guide Program, 1982-84, Longhouse chief Indian Princess program 1984-87, fedn. chief YMCA Indian Guide, Indian Princess programs, 1988—; co-chmn. Home-Sch. Assn. of St. Joseph Sch., Mendham, N.J., 1983-84; mem. fin. and long-range planning coms. St. Joseph Parish. Mem. Jaycees, N.Y.C. Am. Legion, Essex Troop, Kappa Sigma Phi. Roman Catholic. Club: K.C. Home: 3 Cromwell Dr RD 2 Mendham NJ 07945 Office: Yamaichi Internat (Am) Inc 2 World Trade Ctr 95th Fl New York NY 10048

SKIFF, RUSSELL ALTON, plastic company executive; b. Waterford, Pa., Feb. 26, 1927; s. Albert Alton and Leah Gladys (Allen) S.; B.S., U. Pitts., 1950; m. Dolores Theresa Molnar, June 25, 1950; children—Russell James, Sandra Lee, Eric Alan, Rebecca Lynn. Metall. chemist Jones & Laughlin Steel Co., Alliquippa, Pa., 1950-51; research and devel. chemist Gen. Electric Co., Erie, Pa., 1951-57; mgr. tech. sales and plant operation Hysol Corp. of Calif., El Monte, 1957-60; sr. research engr. autonetics div. N.Am. Aviation, Downey, Calif., 1960-62; pres. Delta Plastics Co., Inc. (now Delta D.P.C., Inc.), Tulare, Calif., 1962—. Served with USAAF, 1944-46. Mem. Constrn. Specifications Inst. Republican. Presbyterian. Club: Exchange (past pres. Calif.-Nev. dist.). Lodge: Lions (dir.). Contbr. articles to profl. jours. Home: 15170 Avenue 260 Visalia CA 93277 Office: Delta DPC Inc 983 E Levin Tulare CA 93274

SKILLIN, EDWARD SIMEON, magazine publisher; b. N.Y.C., Jan. 23, 1904; s. Edward Simeon and Geraldine Madeleine (Fearons) S.; m. Jane Anne Edwards, Jan. 27, 1945; children: Edward John, Elizabeth Ann Skillin Flanagan, Arthur Paul, Susan Geraldine Skillin Thuvanuti, Mary Jane Skillin Davis. Grad., Phillips Acad., Andover, Mass., 1921; AB, Williams Coll., 1925; MA, Columbia U., 1933; LHD (hon.), St. Benedict's Coll., Atchison, Kans., 1954, Fordham U., 1974; LLD, St. Vincent's Coll., Latrobe, Pa., 1959, St. Francis Xavier U., Antigonish, N.S., Can., 1966, Stonehill Coll., 1979. With ednl. dept. Henry Holt & Co., N.Y.C., 1925-32; mem. staff Commonweal Found., N.Y.C., 1933-38, editor, 1938-67, pub., 1967—. Editor: The Commonweal Reader, 1949. Recipient Centennial citation St. John's U., Collegeville, Minn., 1957, St. Francis de Sales award Cath. Press Assn., 1987. Mem. Cath. Commn. on Intellectual and Cultural Affairs, Phi Beta Kappa, Phi Gamma Delta. Office: Commonweal Found 15 Dutch St New York NY 10038

SKILLINGSTAD, CONSTANCE YVONNE, social services administrator, educator; b. Portland, Oreg., Nov. 18, 1944; d. Irving Elmer and Beulah Ruby (Aleckson) Erickson; m. David W. Skillingstad, Jan. 12, 1968 (div. Mar. 1981); children: Michael, Brian. BA in Sociology, U. Minn., 1966; MBA, Coll. St. Thomas, St. Paul, 1982. Cert. vol. adminstr. Social worker Rock County Welfare Dept., Luverne, Minn., 1966-68; social worker Hennepin County Social Services, Mpls., 1968-70, vol. coordinator, 1970-78; vol. coordinator St. Joseph's Home for Children, Mpls., 1978-89, mgr. community resources, 1989—; mem. community faculty Met. State U., St. Paul and Mpls., 1982—; trainer, mem. adv. commn. Mpls. Vol. Ctr., 1978—, cons., 1980—. Contbr. articles to Jour. Vol. Adminstrn. Mem. adv. bd. Mothers Against Drunk Driving, Mpls., 1986-88. Named one of Oustanding Young Women Am., 1974. Mem. Minn. Assn. Vol. Dirs. (pres. 1979-80, sec., ethics chmn. 1987—), Assn. for Vol. Adminstrn. (v.p. regional affairs 1985-87, mem. assessment panel 1986—, coordn. nat. tng. team, cert. process for vol. administs. 1988—), Minn. Social Service Assn. (pres. 1981, Disting. Service award 1987). Mem. Dem.-Farmer-Labor Party. Methodist. Office: St Joseph's Home for Children 1121 E 46th St Minneapolis MN 55407

SKILTON, HARRY, diversified manufacturing company executive; b. 1938. B in Mech. Engring., Cornell U., 1961; MBA, Harvard U., 1965. From v.p. treas. to exec. v.p. ops. Celanese Corp., N.Y.C., 1965-80; v.p., gen. mgr. Gen. Instrument Corp., N.Y.C., 1980-83; v.p. gen. mgr. Ill. Tool Works Inc., Chgo., 1983-85; exec. v.p. ops. Philips Industries Inc., Dayton, Ohio, 1985—. Lt. USNR, 1961-63. Office: Philips Industries Inc 4801 Springfield Inc Dayton OH 45401

SKILTON, PETER THOMAS, software company executive; b. Norristown, Pa., Jan. 13, 1948; s. Thomas Malcolm and Amorette Pearce (Lacher) S.; m. Ann Marie Gately, Aug. 14, 1971; children: Michael, David, Zachary. BS, Pa. State U., 1970. Mgr. Flinchbaugh Products, Inc., Red Lion, Pa., 1975-78, Kaufman Mfg., Red Lion, 1978-82; master scheduler AAI Corp., Cockeysville, Md., 1982-84; dir. customer support Oriole Software, Inc., Towson, Md., 1984-88; logistics cons. STSC, Inc., Rockville, 1988—. Mem. Am. Prodn. and Inventory Control Soc., Coun. of Logistics Mgmt. Home: 10601 Lancewood Rd Cockeysville MD 21031 Office: STSC Inc 2115 East Jefferson St Rockville MD 20852

SKINNER, B. FRANKLIN, telecommunications executive; b. Covington, Va., Nov. 4, 1931; s. B. Franklin and Charlotte Frances (Walton) S.; m. Ruth Ann Gee, Nov. 25, 1955; children: Ruth Anne, Christian Franklin, Lisa Page. B.A., U. Richmond, 1952, D.C.S. (hon.), 1985; L.L.D. (hon.), Jacksonville U., 1986; DHL (hon.), Interdenominational Theological Ctr., Atlanta, 1987. Div. traffic mgr. Chesapeake & Potomac Telephone Cos., Richmond, Va., 1964-66, gen. comml. mgr., 1966-70; v.p. ops. Chesapeake & Potomac Telephone Cos., Washington, 1970-73; v.p., gen. mgr. So. Bell Tel. & Tel., Charlotte, N.C., 1973-79; v.p. Fla. So. Bell Tel. & Tel., Miami, 1979-82; exec. v.p. mktg. and external affairs. co. hdqrs. So. Bell Tel. & Tel., Atlanta, 1982, pres., chief exec. officer, 1982—; bd. dirs. So. Bell, Atlanta, Bell South Svcs., Birmingham, Citizens & So. Corp., Atlanta; chmn. Cen. Atlanta Progress. Please spell out first name. Trustee U. Richmond, Agnes Scott Coll., Atlanta; dir. High Mus. Art, Atlanta ; bd. visitors Emory U., Atlanta; chmn. adv. bd. Met. Atlanta United Negro Coll. Fund.; chmn. nat. adv. bd. Salvation Army, 1988-89; campaign chmn. United Way Met. Atlanta. With U.S. Army, 1952-54. Recipient Top Mgmt. award Sales and Mktg. Execs., 1978, Reubin Askew Awareness award Greater Miami Urban League, 1980. Mem. Telephone Pioneers Am. (assn. pres. 1986-87), Atlanta C. of C. (bd. dirs.), Capital City Club, Commerce Club, Rotary, Omicron Delta Kappa, Sigma Phi Epsilon, Pi Delta Epsilon. Presbyterian. Home: 675 Tuxedo Pl NW Atlanta GA 30342 Office: So Bell Tel & Tel Co 675 Peachtree St NW Rm 4500 Atlanta GA 30375

SKINNER, GARY GERALD, sales executive; b. Montclair, N.J., Feb. 28, 1955; s. Arthur Harvey and Janet Joan S.; m. Caryn Newell; 1 child, Travis Restyn. BA, Rutgers U., 1977; MBA, Oral Roberts U., 1981. Sr. mktg. rep. Xerox Corp., N.Y.C., 1981-83; dist. mktg. mgr. Wang Labs, Inc., Rutherford, N.J., 1983-87; account exec. Gen. Electric Info. Svcs., Lyndhurst, N.J., 1987; sales mgr. Atlantic Computer Systems, N.Y.C., 1987—. Republican. Baptist. Home: 28 Byrd Ave Bloomfield NJ 07003 Office: Atlantic Computer Systems 400 Madison Ave New York NY 10017

SKINNER, JOHN VERNON, retail executive; b. Merryville, La., Aug. 21, 1938; s. Vernon and Margaret (Kleinpeter) S.; m. Gail Grinnell, Sept. 1, 1960 (div. Sept. 1981); children: Sondra Skinner Keefer, Sherrin Skinner Mitzner, Stacy, Jonathan; m. B. Jean Kevane, Nov. 1, 1983. Student, U. Houston, 1957-60. Cert. consumer credit exec. Mgr. collections, asst. mgr. Sears Roebuck & Co., Fitchburg, Mass., 1963-64; mgr. credit Torrington, Conn., 1964-65; mgr. collection/authorization Hartford, Conn., 1965-67; mgr. group collection Albany, N.Y., 1967-68; supr. credit field Boston, 1968; mgr. credit ctr. Balt., 1968-73, Washington, 1973-84; pres. Jewelers Fin. Service subs. Zale Corp., Irving, Tex., 1984—; v.p., mgr. gen. credit Zale Corp., Irving, 1987—; officer, bd. dirs. Consumer Credit Counseling and Edn. Service, Washington and Balt., 1968-84, pres., 1978-84; mem. governing bd. dirs. Credit Research Ctr., Purdue U., 1985—. Contbr. numerous articles to profl. jours. Recipient Disting. Service award Internat. Consumer Credit Assn., 1982. Mem. Consumer Credit Assn. (pres. Greater Washington chpt. 1963-84, bd. dirs.), Internat. Credit Assn. (officer, bd. dirs. dist. XII chpt. 1975-84, bd. dirs., mem. exec. com. St. Louis chpt. 1980—, pres. dist. XII chpt. 1981, v.p. St. Louis chpt. 1985—, Outstanding Mem. award dist. XII 1979, Outstanding Mem. award Greater Washington chpt. 1979, Service award 1985, Merit award 1988), Nat. Found. for Consumer Credit (trustee and officer 1980—, mem. exec. com. 1980—, v.p. 1985—, Chmn.'s award 1982, Harry E. Fuller award for outstanding leadership in establishment of consumer credit counseling services 1985, Linkwilder award 1987), Nat. Retail Mchts. Assn. (bd. dirs. 1985—). Republican. Methodist. Home: 1912 Crockett Circle Irving TX 75038 Office: Zale Corp 901 W Walnut Hill Ln M/S 6A-6 Irving TX 75038-1003

SKIPPER, HENRY T., JR., manufacturing company executive; b. 1924. Sales mgr. Great Dane Trailers Inc., Savannah, Ga., 1949-64, from v.p. to exec. v.p., 1964—. Office: Great Dane Trailers Inc PO Box 67 Savannah GA 31402 *

SKJEI, KEVIN RUSSELL, financial advisor; b. Grand Forks, N.D., June 26, 1955; s. Mark David and Jane (Dushinske) S.; m. Mary Suzanne Armstrong, June 30, 1982. BA in Fgn. Policy, U.S. Naval Acad., 1977; MBA, So. Ill. U., 1985. Commd. ensign USN, 1977, advanced through grades to lt. comdr., 1986, served as aviator, resigned, 1986; bus. fin. cons. Merrill, Lynch, Pierce, Fenner & Smith, San Diego, 1987—; mem. Western Pension Conf., San Diego, 1987, Connect Program U. Calif., San Diego, 1988. Mem. steering com. Butterfield for Congress, San Diego, 1988. Mem. Cash Mgmt. Assn., San Diego C. of C., San Diego Athletic Club, Toastmasters, Order Ancient Mariners. Republican. Office: Merrill Lynch Pierce Fenner & Smith 701 B St Ste 2400 San Diego CA 92101

SKLAR, ALEXANDER, electric company executive, educator; b. N.Y.C., May 18, 1915; s. David and Bessie (Wolf) S.; student Cooper Union, N.Y.C., 1932-35; M.B.A., Fla. Atlantic U., 1976; m. Hilda Rae Gevarter, Oct. 27, 1940; 1 dau., Carolyn Mae (Mrs. Louis M. Taff). Chief engr. Aerovox Corp., New Bedford, Mass., 1933-39; mgr. mfg., engring. Indsl. Condenser Corp., Chgo., 1939-44; owner Capacitron, Inc., 1944-48; exec. v.p. Jefferson Electric Co., Bellwood, Ill., 1948-65; v.p., gen. mgr. electro-mech. div. Essex International, Detroit, 1965-67; adviser, dir. various corp., 1968—; vis. prof. mgmt. Fla. Atlantic U., Boca Raton, 1971—; lectr. profl. mgmt. U. Calif. at Los Angeles, Harvard Grad. Sch. Bus. Adminstrn., U. Ill. Mem. Acad. Internat. Bus., Soc. Automotive Engrs. Address: 4100 Galt Ocean Dr Fort Lauderdale FL 33308

SKLAR, LARRY, investor, real estate developer; b. N.Y.C., Apr. 21, 1946; s. Jacob and Sophia (Epstein) S.; m. Brenda Ann Katz, Oct. 10, 1958; children: Jeffrey, Jamie, Steven. Student, U. Cin., 1964-66. Chief exec. officer Acme Barrel Drum Co., Cin., 1964-71, Bali Realty FKA Acme Realty, Cin., 1971-88, 4th Elm Asst.'s, Inc., Cin., 1979—, Advanced Data Computing, Cin., 1980-81, Fin. Computing/Bali Computing, Henderson, Nev., 1981—; bd. dirs. My-Neil Import, Cin. Bd. dirs. Hillel Found., Cin., 1979-82; mem. allocation com. United Jewish Appeal, Cin., 1980. Mem. B'nai B'rith (cabinet mem. 1980-82, dist. gov. 1979-81). Home: PO Box 50083 Henderson NV 89016 Office: 32 Stone Cress Henderson NV 89014

SKLENAR, HERBERT ANTHONY, industrial products manufacturing company executive; b. Omaha, June 7, 1931; s. Michael Joseph and Alice Madeline (Spicka) S.; m. Eleanor Lydia Vincenz, Sept. 15, 1956; children—Susan A., Patricia I. B.S. in Bus. Adminstrn. summa cum laude, U. Omaha, 1952; M.B.A., Harvard U., 1954. C.P.A., W.Va. Vice pres., comptroller Parkersburg-Aetna Corp., W.Va., 1956-63; v.p., dir. Marmac Corp, Parkersburg, 1963-66; mgr. fin. control Boise-Cascade Corp., Idaho, 1966-67; exec. v.p. fin. and adminstrn., sec. Cudahy Co., Phoenix, 1967-72; pres., chief exec. officer Vulcan Materials Co., Birmingham, Ala., 1972—, also dir.; bd. dirs. AmSouth Bancorp., Birmingham. Author: (with others) The Automatic Factory: A Critical Examination, 1955. Bd. dirs. YMCA, Birmingham; trustee So. Research Inst., Ala. Symphony Assn. Recipient Alumni Achievement award U. Nebr.-Omaha, 1977, cert. merit W.Va. Soc. C.P.A.s. Mem. Chem. Mfrs. Assn. (bd. dirs.), Am. Inst. C.P.A.s (Elizah Watts Sells award 1965), Delta Sigma Pi (leadership award 1952), Omicron Delta Kappa, Phi Kappa Phi, Phi Eta Sigma. Republican. Presbyterian. Clubs: Shoal Creek (Ala.); Birmingham Country, The Club (Birmingham); Wall Street, University (N.Y.C.); Chgo. Home: 3908 Knollwood Dr Birmingham AL 35243 Office: Vulcan Materials Co 1 Metroplex Dr Birmingham AL 35209

SKOLROOD, ROBERT KENNETH, lawyer; b. Stockton, Ill., May 17, 1928; s. Myron Clifford and Lola Mae (Lincicum) S.; m. Marilyn Jean Riegel, June 18, 1955; children: Cynthia, Mark, Kent, Richard. BA, Ohio Wesleyan U., 1952; JD, U. Chgo., 1957. Bar: Ill. 1957, Va. 1985, U.S. Dist. Ct. (no. dist.) Ill. 1959, Okla. 1981, U.S. Ct. Appeals (7th cir.) 1970, U.S. Dist. Ct. (no. dist.) Okla. 1982, U.S. Supreme Ct. 1982, U.S. Ct. Appeals (10th cir.) 1983, Va. 1985, U.S. Dist. Ct. Nebr. 1985, U.S. Dist. Ct. (so. dist.) Ala. 1986, U.S. Dist. Ct. (so. dist.) N.Y. 1986, U.S. Dist. Ct. (ea. and we. dists.) Va. 1986, U.S. Ct. Appeals (4th and 8th cirs.) 1986, D.C. 1987, U.S. Dist. Ct. D.C. 1987, U.S. Ct. Appeals (11th cir.) 1987, U.S. Ct. Appeals (2d cir.) 1988. Ptnr. Reno, Zahm, Folgate, Skolrood, Lindberg & Powell, Rockford, Ill., 1957-80; prof. Ohio Wesleyan U. Coburn Sch. Law; prof. Oral Roberts U., Tulsa, 1980-81, exec. dir., gen. counsel Nat. Legal Found., Virginia Beach, Va., 1984—. Contbr. articles to legal jours. Pres., John Ericsson Rep. Club, 1964; trustee No. Ill. conf. United Meth. Ch., 1957-74, chmn., 1972-74; pres. Ill. Home and Aid Soc. Served with U.S. Army, 1952-54, Korea. Fellow Am. Coll. Trial Lawyers; mem. ABA, Ill. Bar Assn., Okla. Bar Assn., Winnebago County Bar Assn., Assn. Trial Lawyers Am., Va. Trial Lawyers Assn., Tex. Trial Lawyers Assn., Ill. Trial Lawyers Assn., Okla. Trial Lawyers Assn., Nat. Assn. Coll. and Univ. Attys., Christian Legal Soc., Kappa Delta Pi, Pi Sigma Kappa. Mem. Evangelical Free Ch. Home: 808 Donnington Dr Chesapeake VA 23320 Office: Nat Legal Found 6477 College Park Sq Ste 306 Virginia Beach VA 23464

SKOMOROWSKY, PETER P., accounting company executive; b. Leipzig, Germany, Nov. 14, 1932. Home: 25 E 86th St New York NY 10028 Office: care Grant Thornton 605 3rd Ave New York NY 10158

SKRAINKA, ALAN FREDERICK, securities analyst; b. St. Louis, May 8, 1961; s. Frederick Ralph and Yvonne M. (Oelawder) S.; m. Julie Lynn Wussler, Jan. 24, 1987. BBA in Acctg. and Fin., U. Mo., 1983; postgrad., Washington U. Chartered fin. analyst. Utility analyst Edward D. Jones & Co., St. Louis, 1983—; ltd. ptnr. Edward D. Jones & Co., Maryland Heights, Mo., 1986-88, gen. ptnr., 1988—. Mem. Fin. Analysts Fedn. Home: 13047 Vinson Ct Maryland Heights MO 63043 Office: Edward D Jones & Co 201 Progress Pkwy Maryland Heights MO 63043

SKULAN, THOMAS DAVID, publisher; b. Milw., Jan. 17, 1954; s. Thomas William Skulan and Ruth Mary (Loris) Welch. BS in Art Edn., SUNY, New Paltz, 1977. Cert. art tchr., N.Y. Tchr. Carmel (N.Y.) Cen. Sch., 1977; pres., founder FantaCo Enterprises, Inc., Albany, N.Y., 1978—. Author (with other) mag. Smilin' Ed, 1980; exec. editor jour. Chronicles Series, 1981; editor mag. Gore Shriek, 1986; publisher jour. Deep Red, 1987. Mem. Am. Numismatic Soc. (assoc.), Am. Numismatic Assn., Can. Numismatic Assn. Office: FantaCo Enterprises Inc 21 Central Ave Albany NY 12210-1391

SKULINA, THOMAS RAYMOND, lawyer; b. Cleve., Sept. 14, 1933; s. John J. and Mary B. (Vesely) S. A.B., John Carroll U., 1955; J.D., Case Western Res. U., 1959, LL.M., 1962. Bar: Ohio 1959, U.S. Supreme Ct. 1964, ICC 1965. Ptnr. Skulina & Stringer, Cleve., 1967-72, Riemer Oberdank & Skulina, Cleve., 1978-81, Skulina, Fillo, Walters & Negrelli, 1981-86, Skulina & McKeon, Cleve., 1986—; atty. Penn Cen. Transp. Co., Cleve., 1960-65, asst. gen. atty., 1965-78, trial counsel, 1965-76; with Consol. Rail Corp., 1976-78; dir. High Temperature Systems, Inc., Active Chem. Systems, Inc.; tchr. comml. law Practicing Law Inst., N.Y.C., 1970. Contbr. articles to legal jours. Income tax and fed. fund coordinator Warrensville Heights, Ohio, 1970-77; spl. counsel City of N. Olmstead, Ohio, 1971-75; pres. Civil Service Commn., Cleve., 1977-86, referee, 1986—, fact-finder SERB, Ohio, 1986—; spl. counsel Ohio Atty. Gen., 1983—, Cleve. Charter Rev. Commn., 1988. With U.S. Army, 1959. Mem. Am. Arbitration Assn. (labor panel 1988—), Nat. Assn. R.R. Trial Counsel, Internat. Assn. Law and Sci., ABA (R.R. and motor carrier com. 1988—, jr. chmn. 1989—), Cleve. Bar Assn. (grievance com. 1987—, vice chmn. 1989—), Ohio Bar Assn. (bd. govs. litigation sect. 1986—), Fed. Bar Assn., Ohio Trial Lawyers Assn., Pub. Sector Labor Relations Assn. Democrat. Roman Catholic. Clubs: River Run Racquet, Lakewood Country. Home: 3162 W 165th St Cleveland OH 44111 Office: Skulina & McKeon 709 Ohio Savings Pla 1801 E 9th St Cleveland OH 44113

SKURDAHL, DALE MAYNARD, bank holding company executive; b. Warren, Minn., July 5, 1927; s. Norman Arthur and Helen Irma (Kays) S.; m. Hilda G. Jones, June 1, 1948; children: Gail Constance, Dale Norman. B.B.A., U. Minn., 1960, postgrad., 1960-63. C.P.A., Minn., Calif. Audit mgr. Ernst & Ernst, Mpls., 1961-74; sr. v.p., treas. First Interstate Bancorp., Los Angeles, 1974—; instr. U. Minn., 1969-71. Served with USAAF, 1945-46; Served with USN, 1948-56. Mem. Am. Inst. C.P.A.s, Minn., Calif. socs. C.P.A.s, Nat. Assn. Accountants. Republican. Methodist. Club: Jonathan (Los Angeles). Office: First Interstate Bancorp PO Box 54068 Los Angeles CA 90054

SKUTT, THOMAS JAMES, insurance company executive; b. Omaha, Nov. 1, 1930; s. Vestor Joseph and Angela (Anderson) S.; m. Jeanne Cecille Plunkett, Sept. 3, 1955; children: Mary Elizabeth Skutt Sutton, Kimberly Ann, Thomas V. J. BA, Yale U., 1952; LLB, Creighton U., 1957; postgrad., Harvard U., 1979. Ptnr. Spire, Morrow & Skutt, Omaha, 1961-69; with Mut. of Omaha, 1969—, exec. v.p., sec., 1980-81, vice chmn. bd. dirs., 1981-84, 1st vice chmn. bd. dirs., chief exec. officer, 1984-86, chmn. bd. dirs., chief exec. officer, 1986—, chmn. bd. dirs., chief exec. officer United of Omaha subs., 1986—; bd. dirs. United of Omaha, Norwest Bank Omaha. Pres. Mid-Am. Council Boy Scouts Am., 1987, 89, mem. exec. bd. 1980—; mem. consultation com. SAC, Omaha, 1984; bd. dirs. Omaha Zool. Soc., 1978—, pres., 1987-88, past bd. dirs.; gen. chmn. campaign United Way of Midlands, 1979-80, bd. dirs., 1981—; bd. dirs. Creighton U., Omaha, 1983—. Served to 1st lt. U.S. Army, 1952-54, Korea. Mem. Greater Omaha C. of C. (bd. dirs. 1979—, chmn. 1983, past chmn.). Republican. Roman Catholic. Clubs: Mpls.; Yale of N.Y. (N.Y.C.). Lodge: Knights of Ak-Sar-Ben (bd. govs. 1985). Home: 656 N 57th St Omaha NE 68132 Office: Mut Omaha Ins Co Mutual Omaha Pla Omaha NE 68175

SLABE, JAMES F., financial executive; b. Johnstown, Pa., Nov. 29, 1940; s. Frank and Antoinette Marie (Draksler) S.; m. Elaine Werner, July 14, 1973. BA, Washington and Jefferson Coll., 1962; postgrad., U. Md., 1962-64. Div. controller Pfizer, Inc., N.Y.C., 1967-72; treas., controller Pharmacaps, Inc., Elizabeth, N.J., 1972-73; dir. profit planning McGraw-Hill, Inc., N.Y.C., 1973-78; v.p. fin. Parade Publs., Inc., N.Y.C., 1978-79; exec. v.p. fin., pub. and adminstrn. Exec. Enterprises, Inc., N.Y.C., 1979—, also bd. dirs.; bd. dirs. The 21 Bldg. Corp., N.Y.C., Jersey Shore Properties, Lair Realty Co. Inc. Pub. Nat. Productivity Rev., Banks in Insurance Report, S Corporation Strategies and Benefits Law Journal. Capt. U.S. Army, 1964-66. Mem. Fin. Execs. Inst., Assn. Am. Planners, Assn. Am. Controllers, Phi Beta Kappa. Roman Catholic. Home: 17 Mountainview Dr Mountainside NJ 07092 Office: Exec Enterprises Inc 22 W 21st St New York NY 10010

SLABY, FRANK, business educator; b. South Bend, Ind., Aug. 3, 1936; s. Frank A. and Alice E. (Michalec) S.; m. Carolyn Kay Carr, Jan. 20, 1960 (div. Sept. 1977); children: Cami Lynn, Keriann; m. Kristi Lynn Courtright, May 18, 1978, 1 child, Joy Marie. BS, Ind. U., 1961, MBA, 1963; ABD, U. Cin., 1970. CLU. Prof. bus. adminstrn. Ill. Inst Tech., Chgo., 1970-72; spl. asst. to pres. St. Mary's Coll., Notre Dame, Ind., 1972-74; dean, grad. studies coll bus. adminstrn. Ind. U. Northwest, Gary, 1974-78; prof. bus. adminstrn. Valparaiso (Ind.) U., 1978-81; prof. bus. adminstrn. network, coord. div. commerce St. Joseph's Coll., Rensselaer, Ind., 1981—; sr. assoc. Mark-Killian Assocs., Collegeville, Ind., 1978—. Contbr. articles to profl. jours. Del. Rep. State Conv., Indpls., 1972-86; mem. Rep. Cen. Com., Jasper County, Ind., 1982—, adv. coun. Union Twp., Jasper County, 1982—, chmn. 1986—; life mem. Rep. Presdl. Task Force. Capt. USNR, 1963—. Named Ky. Col. by Gov. State of Ky., 1968, Ky. Admiral, 1969; Sagamore of the Wabash by Gov. State Ind., 1981. Mem. Ind. U. Alumni Assn. (life), Midwest Bus. Adminstrn. Assn., Midwest Bus. Econ. Assn. (adv. com., v.p., mem. exec. com.), Masons, Alpha Kappa Psi (life), Beta Gamma (life, chpt. pres. Bronze Medallion award), Kappa Delta Rho (life, alumni pres.). Home: Stonehedge Glen Rt 6 Box 54 Rensselaer IN 47978 Office: St Joseph's Coll Collegeville IN 47978

SLACHTA, GREGORY ANDREW, urologist; b. Paterson, N.J., Mar. 17, 1946; s. Andrew Gregory and Mary Catherine (Shimko) S.; children: Gregory Andrew, Lara Ann, Andrea; m. Patricia A. Albano, Nov. 7, 1981. BS, Pa. State U., 1966; MD, Jefferson Med. Coll., 1968. Diplomate Am. Bd. Urology. Intern Lankenan Hosp., Phila., 1968-69; resident in urology Temple U. Hosp., Phila., 1969-70, 1973-75; ptnr. Urology Group of Western New Eng., Springfield, Mass., 1975—; owner Puppy Ctr. & Aquarium, Springfield, 1982—; cons. Protocare, Inc., Waltham, MAss., 1985—. Author (with others): Inflammatory Diseases of the Male Genital Tract, 1982. Mem. City Council Com. for Health Ins., Springfield, 1984. Maj. U.S. Army, 1971-73. Fellow Am. Coll. Surgeons; mem. AMA (alt. del. Mass. Med. Soc. 1986-89), Am. Urol. Assn. (vice-chmn. socioeconomic com. 1986-89, chmn. New Eng. sect. 1989—, chmn. New Eng. chpt. 1986-89), MAss. Med. Soc. (vice-chmn. legis. and nat. legis. affairs com. 1987—), Hampden Dist. MEd. Soc. (pres. 1986-88), Mass. Assn. Practicing Urologists (pres. 1986-88). Democrat. Roman Catholic. Office: Urology Group of Western New Eng 222 Carew St Springfield MA 01104

SLACK, JOHN LOUIS, aerospace engineering executive; b. Sandsprings, Okla., Feb. 6, 1938; s. John G. and Bertha F. (Husted) S. BSME, Okla. State U., 1960; BS in Aerospace Engring., U. Colo., 1962, MS in Aerospace Engring., 1962; postgrad., Cath. U. Am., 1968. Div. chief Nat. Security Agy., Ft. Meade, Md., 1965-72; dept. mgr. Martin Marietta Corp., Denver, 1972-73, v.p., 1976-79; dep. asst. sec. of def. intelligence Dept. Def., Washington, 1973-76; pres. ZETEC Corp., Arlington, Va., 1979-85; pres. ARDAK Corp., McLean, Va., 1985—, also bd. dirs.; bd. dirs. ZETEC Corp., Arlington, Fingermatrix, Inc., North White Plains, N.Y. Capt. USAF, 1960-65. Mem. Sigma Tau, Pi Tau Sigma, Tau Beta Pi. Republican. Office: ARDAK Corp 1493 Chain Bridge Rd McLean VA 22101

SLACK, ROBERT JOHN, courier services company executive, management consultant; b. Glens Falls, N.Y., Nov. 28, 1958; s. Patrick Gregory and Jean (Holleran) S.; m. Kelley Marie Carlton, June 21, 1986; 1 child, Zachary John. Student, Siena Coll., 1976-79. Asst. mktg. mgr. 1980 Winter Olympic Com., Lake Placid, N.Y., 1979-80; clk. U.S. Post Office, Glens Falls, 1980-81; pres. L.E.D.F.O.O.T. Express Inc., Glens Falls, 1980—; ptnr. Landscapes Photography, Glens Falls, 1985—; v.p. Adirondack Presort Enterprises, Glens Falls, 1986—. Treas. Tri-County Transp., 1986—. Republican. Roman Catholic. Home: 326 Saratoga Rd South Glens Falls NY 12803 Office: LEDFOOT Express 17 Luzerine Rd Glens Falls NY 12801

SLADE, HARRY WARREN, neurological surgeon; b. Highland Park, Mich., Nov. 29, 1922; s. Leon Harrison and Clara A. (Nestrom) S.; m. Betty Arlene Hummer, Jan. 28, 1950; children: Theodore Leigh, Cynthia Ann Slade Bennetzen; Steven Lawrence, Christina Louise. BS, Wayne U., 1944; MD, Baylor U., 1946. Diplomate Am. Bd. Neurol. Surgeons. Intern Grace Hosp., Detroit, 1946-47; resident in gen. surgery Meth. Hosp., Houston, 1949; resident in neurosurgery Hosp. U. Pa., Phila., 1949-52; resident in neurology Grad. Hosp. U. Pa., Phila., 1950-51; resident in pediatric neurosurgery Childrens' Hosp. Phila., 1951; pvt. practice neurosurgery Cleve., 1953-57, Waco, Tex., 1957—; instr. neurosurgery, U. Pa. Sch. Medicine, Phila., 1949-53; sr. instr. neurosurgery, Western Res. U., Cleve., 1953-57; med. adviser Waco March of Dimes, 1959-87. Co-editor audio cassettes on neurology, neurosurgery. Fellow ACS; mem. AMA, Tex. Med. Assn., McLennan County Med. Soc., Am. Assn. Neurol. Surgeons, Congl. Neurol. Surgeons, Tex. Assn. Neurol. Surgeons, Rocky Mountain Neurosurg. Soc., So. Clin.-Neurol. Assn., Pan Pacific Surg. Soc. Baptist. Lodges: Lions, Shriners. Office: Waco Neurol Assn 3500 Hillcrest Dr Waco TX 76708-3195

SLADE, JARVIS JAMES, banker; b. Paris, Feb. 12, 1926; s. Henry Lewis and Elena (de Arostegui) S.; m. Alice Patterson, June 25, 1954 (div. Jan. 1976); children: Shelley, Georgiana, Jarvis Jr.; m. Mary Carlyle Lind, June 2, 1977. BA, Yale U., 1947; MBA, Stanford U., 1950. Assoc. N.Y. Trust, N.Y.C., 1947-50; assoc. F. Eberstadt, N.Y.C., 1950-56, ptnr., 1956-62; founder, co-chmn. N.Y. Securities Inc., N.Y.C., 1962-75; pres. Computer Investments, N.Y.C., 1975-76; gen. ptnr. Hampton Capital Co., N.Y.C., 1976—; chmn. bd. dirs. MCRB Service Bur., North Hollywood, Calif.; bd. dirs. Church & Dwight, Princeton, N.J., Cosmo Communications, Miami, Fla.; cons., bd. dirs. Hanley Co., N.Y.C. With CIC, U.S. Army, 1945-46. Office: Hampton Capital Co 420 Lexington Ave Ste 2018 New York NY 10170

SLADOWSKI, ROBERT THADDEUS, packaging company executive; b. Bayonne, N.J., Sept. 5, 1949; s. Stephen Francis and Estelle (Bober) S.; m. Jennifer Gilarmo, Apr. 7, 1973 (div. Feb. 1985); children: Robert Jr., Jennifer; m. Jean Lou Schmidlein, Dec. 28, 1985; 1 child, Lindsay Helen. BS in Acctg., St. Peter's Coll., 1973; MBA in Fin., Fairleigh Dickinson U., 1975. Chief acct. Metaframe Corp., Elmwood Park, N.J., 1973-74; acctg. mgr. Sealed Air Corp., Fairlawn, N.J., 1974-76; controller U.S. ops. Sealed Air Corp., Danbury, Conn., 1977-81; mktg. rep. Sealed Air Corp., Saddle Brook, N.J., 1981-82; pres. Designs in Cushion Packaging, Inc., Irvington, N.J., 1983—. Republican. Roman Catholic. Office: Designs in Cushion Packaging Inc 390 Nye Ave Irvington NJ 07111

SLAGO, DOUGLAS F., support engineer; b. Chgo., Nov. 12, 1951; s. Frank John and Irene (Sojka) S.; m. Barbara Jane Cox, Mar. 13, 1971; children: Christopher, Michael, Danielle. AS, Coll. Lake County, Grayslake, Ill., 1976; BS, Nat. Coll. Chiropractic, Lombard, Ill., 1978; D of Chiropractic, Nat. Coll. Chiropractic, 1980. Supr. U.S. Navy Drug Screening Lab., Great Lakes, Ill., 1983-87; product mgr. Cole Parmer Instruments, Chgo., 1987; tech. engr. Nelson Analytical, Oakbrook, Ill., 1987—; pvt. practice chiropractic, Libertyville, Ill., 1980—. Contbg. editor The Family Forum, 1981-83. Active Lake County Adv. Council Mental Health, Substance Abuse and Devel. Disabilities, 1981, vice-chmn., 1982-83. Recipient Human Service award Lake County Bd. Health, 1983. Mem. Am. Chem. Soc. Home: 336 Kenloch Libertyville IL 60048

SLAIGHT, BRIAN WRIGHT, newspaper executive; b. Galt, Ont., Can., Mar. 30, 1934; s. John Edgar and Florence Eileen (Wright) S.; m. Carol Annabel Slaight, Aug. 31, 1967. Student in journalism, Ryerson Inst. Tech., Toronto, 1951-54. With Thomson Newspapers Ltd., Toronto, Ont., 1953—; asst. gen. mgr. Can. Thomson Newspapers Ltd., 1963-68; gen. mgr. Thomson Newspapers Ltd., Can., 1968-75; gen. mgr. Thomson Newspapers Ltd., 1975-78, sr. v.p., 1979-81, exec. v.p., 1982-89, dir., 1975-89; exec. v.p., dir. Thomson Newspapers Inc., Des Plaines, Ill., 1981-89; dir. Newspaper Mktg. Bur. Mem. Can. Press, AP, Commonwealth Press Union, Am. Newspaper Pubs. Assn., Internat. Press Inst. Office: Thomson Newspapers Ltd, 65 Queen St W, Toronto, ON Canada M5H 2M8

SLAIN, GEORGE CEDRIC, finance executive; b. Chgo., Oct. 3, 1950; s. Cedric Cletis and Violet (decker) S.; m Susan Diane Childers, Sept. 25, 1976 (div. Dec. 1987). BA in Fin., MBA in Fin., Ind. U., 1973. Asst. v.p. Security Pacific Nat. Bank., Los Angeles, 1973-78; v.p., mng. dir. Security Pacific SW, Inc., Houston, 1978-81; v.p., treas. Pacific Resources, Inc., Honolulu, 1981—. Mem. Fin. Execs. Inst., Nat. Assn. Corp. Treas.'s, Beta Gamma Sigma. Office: Pacific Resources Inc 733 Bishop St Honolulu HI 96813

SLAKIS, ALBERT GEORGE, insurance company executive, consultant; b. Chgo., Feb. 19, 1929; s. Paul P. and Cicilia (Mack) S.; m. Mary M. Pierzynski, Nov. 15, 1958; children: Steven, Paula. BS, De Paul U., 1950, MS, 1952; MBA, U. Chgo., 1961. CPCU. Various positions with ins. cos. 1952-72; v.p., gen. mgr. Reliable Ins. Co., Columbus, Ohio, 1972-74; dir. Gt. Am. Ins. Co., Cin., 1974-79; exec. v.p., sec. Ohio Bar Liability Ins. Co., Columbus, 1979—, bd. dirs., 1988—. Author: Rules, Rates and Forms, 1980; editor Profl. Liability Ins. Policy, 1988—. U. Chgo. scholar, 1960. Mem. Nat. Bar Related Ins. Cos. (chmn. 1984-86), Soc. CPCU, Assn. MBA Execs., U. Chgo. Alumni Assn., De Paul U. Alumni Assn. Roman Catholic. Office: Ohio Bar Liability Ins Co 1550 Old W Henderson Rd Columbus OH 43220

SLANSKY, RICHARD BRUCE, finance company executive; b. N.Y.C., Mar. 28, 1957; s. Paul Herbert and Diane Ruth (Levin) S. BS in Econs., U. Pa., 1979; MBA, U. Ariz., 1982. Exec. v.p. Cottonwood Corp., Millbrook, N.Y., 1979-81; tax researcher JNC Tax Planning Corp., Tucson, 1981-82; devel. coord. JNC Devel. Corp., Tucson, 1982; contr., v.p. DePaul Properties Inc., Sedona, Ariz., 1983-85; fin. analyst Vega Biotechnologies Inc., Tucson, 1985-86, chief fin. officer, v.p., adminstrn. sec., 1986-88, also bd. dirs., pres., chief oper. officer, 1988—; bbd. dirs. Matterhorn Shoppes Inc., Sedona. Active Chazon div. Jr. Achievement, Tucson, 1987—; mem. Rep. Nat. Com., 1984. Mem. Nat. Assn. Accts. Jewish. Home: 4826 N Territory Loop Tucson AZ 85715 Office: Vega Biotechs Inc 1250 E Aero Park Blvd Tucson AZ 85706

SLANSKY, WILLIAM RUDOLPH, manufacturing corporate executive; b. Riverside, Ill., July 21, 1952; s. William Joseph and Sylvia S.; B.B.A., U. Miami, 1973, M.B.A., 1974; m. Elaine Bautista, Jan. 18, 1986. CPA, Ill. Group ins./pension rep. Met. Life Ins. Co., Chgo., 1975-76; auditor Coopers & Lybrand, CPAs, Chgo., 1976-79; corp. controller Johann Haviland China Corp., Des Plaines, Ill., 1979-81, corp. treas., 1982-84, v.p. fin., 1985-87; v.p. fin. and adminstrn. Benetech, Inc., Aurora, Ill., 1987-88, CPS/FlorStar Sales, Inc., Elk Grove Village, Ill., 1988—. Mem. AICPA, Ill. Soc. CPAs, Nat. Assn. Corp. Treas. Home: 1450 N Astor St #7B Chicago IL 60610 Office: CPS/FlorStar Sales Inc 2400 Arthur Ave Elk Grove Village IL 60007

SLATER, CHRISTINE ANNE, marketing executive; b. Syracuse, N.Y., Feb. 17, 1956; d. Albert Charles and Myrtle Anita (Armstrong) S.; m. Gary Lynn Sturtevant, Aug. 30, 1980 (div. 1984); 1 child, Sarah K. Slater-Sturtevant. BS, Ind. U., 1978; postgrad., U. Ill., 1979-80. Cert. elem. and secondary tchr., Ill. Statistician Lawless Commodity Futures Analyst, Champaign, Ill., 1980-82; corres. sec. Tower Hobbies, Inc., Champaign, Ill., 1983-84, spl. project coordinator, 1984-85; exec. mktg. asst. Hobbico, Inc., Champaign, Ill., 1985, mktg. prodn. supr., 1985-86, mktg. prodn. mgr., 1986-88, dir. merchandising, 1988—. Episcopalian. Home: 1828 Tahoe Ct Champaign IL 61821 Office: Hobbico Inc 1608 Interstate Dr Champaign IL 61821

SLATER, DORIS ERNESTINE WILKE, business executive; b. Oakes, N.D.; d. Arthur Waldemar and Anna Mary (Dill) Wilke; grad. high sch.; m. Lawrence Bert Slater, June 4, 1930 (dec., 1960). Sec. to circulation mgr. Mpls. Daily Star, 1928-30; promotion activities Lions Internat. in U.S., Can., Cuba, 1930-48; exec. sec. parade and spl. events com. Inaugural Com., 1948-49; exec. sec. Nat. Capital Sesquicentennial Commn., 1949-50, Capitol Hill Assos., Inc., 1951, Pres.'s Cup Regatta, 1951; adminstrv. asst. Nat. Assn. Food Chains, 1951-60; v.p., sec.-treas. John A. Logan Assos., Inc., Washington, 1960—; v.p., sec.-treas. Logan, Seaman, Slater, Inc., 1962—; mng. dir. Western Hemisphere, Internat. Assn. Chain Stores, 1964—. With pub. relations div. Boston Met. chpt. ARC, 1941-42; mem. Nat. Cherry Blossom Festival Com., 1949—; mem. Inaugural Ball Com., 1953, 57, 65. Methodist. Lion. Home and Office: 2500 Wisconsin Ave Washington DC 20007

SLATER, JOHN WILEY, JR., investment banker, lawyer, financial consultant; b. Memphis, May 10, 1948; s. John Wiley and Dorothy (Ferguson) S.; m. Louise Archer, June 13, 1970; children: Alexandra, Bennet. BA, Princeton U., 1970; JD, U. Va., 1973. Bar: Tenn. 1973; chartered fin. analyst. Assoc. Martin, Tate, Morrow & Marston, P.C., Memphis, 1973-79; ptnr. Winchester, Huggins, Charleton, Leake, Brown & Slater, Memphis, 1979-82; 1st v.p. Morgan Keegan & Co., Memphis, 1982-85; mng. ptnr. Asset Services, L.P., Memphis, 1985—; bd. dirs. Alco Properties, Inc., Memphis; chmn. Staff Line, Inc., Memphis, 1987—; sec. WJG Maritel Corp., Memphis, 1988—. Contbr. articles to profl. jours. Bd. dirs. Memphis Mus., Inc., 1984-87. Mem. ABA, Fin. Analyst Fedn., Memphis Area C. of C. (sec. 1977-82), Memphis Country Club, Econ. Club. Presbyterian. Office: Asset Svcs LP 22 N Front St Ste 1020 Memphis TN 38103

SLATER, S. DONALD, brokerage executive; b. N.Y.C., Apr 8, 1927; s. Moss and Rose (Warshaw) S.; B.A. cum laude, Syracuse U., 1949; M.A., Columbia, 1951, postgrad., 1955; children—Donald, Julia. Investment cons. Standard & Poor's Corp., N.Y.C., 1951-53; lectr. econs. U. Conn., lectr. accounting and fin. Upsala Coll., 1954-55; investment banking and dir. research Shields & Co., N.Y.C., 1955-58; investment banking and research Blyth Eastman Dillon & Co., N.Y.C., 1958-61, E.F. Hutton & Co., N.Y.C., 1962-64; pres. Good Rds. Machinery Corp., pres. MainTek, Inc., Canton, Ohio, 1965-67; pres. Amadon Corp., Boston, 1964—; chmn. bd. Richardson Polymer Corp., Madison, Conn.; asst. prof. fin. Bentley Coll. Grad. Sch., Waltham, Mass. Bd. dirs. World Affairs Council, Boston. Served with US Navy; 1945-46. Mem. Tabard, Pi Sigma Rho, Pi Gamma Mu, Theta Beta Phi. Clubs: Columbia U. Alumni New Eng. (dir.); Badminton and Tennis (Boston). Author: The Strategy of Cash: A liquidity approach to maximizing the company's profits, 1974.

SLAVICH, DENIS MICHAEL, engineering and construction company executive, economist; b. San Francisco, June 1, 1940; s. Francis Luke and Betsy Florence (Carpenter) S.; m. Michele Christine Meyer, June 15, 1963 (div. July 1, 1979) 1 child: Samantha Nicole; m. Debbie Teh-Yan, Nov. 22, 1980; children: David Francis, Destinie Florence. BSEE, U. Calif., Berkeley, 1964; MBA, U. Pitts., 1967; PhD, MIT, 1971. Elec. engr. Douglas Aircraft, Santa Monica, Calif., 1964-65, Hughes Aircraft, Culver City, Calif., 1965-66; prof. Boston U., 1969-71, Stanford U., Palo Alto, Calif., 1984; v.p., chief fin. officer Bechtel Group, Inc., San Francisco, 1971—. Contbr. articles to profl. jours. Mem. Am. Finance Assn., Atomic Indsl. Forum Inc., Nat. Assn. Bus. Econs., U. Calif. Engring. Alumni Soc., San Francisco C. of C. (bd. dirs. 1987—), Bankers Club (San Francisco), Beta Gamma Sigma. Office: Bechtel Group Inc 50 Beale St PO Box 3965 San Francisco CA 94119

SLAVIN, JOHN JEREMIAH, lawyer, corporation director; b. Yonkers, N.Y., Apr. 5, 1921; s. John Lawrence and Carolyn (Lyons) S.; m. Jean Celeste Murphy, Aug. 23, 1943; children: Jean, Susan, Paul, Thomas, Margaret. BA, Manhattan Coll., 1943; JD, Harvard U., 1949. Bar: Mich. 1949. Atty. Detroit Edison Co., Detroit, 1949-51; ptnr. Freud, Markus, Slavin & Galgan and predecessor firms, Troy, Mich., 1951—; bd. dirs. Fed. Screw Works, Detroit, Mac Valves, Inc., Wixom, Mich., various other corps. Served to 1st lt. USAAC, 1942-46, ETO. Mem. ABA, Mich. Bar Assn., Detroit Bar Assn., Oakland County Bar Assn., Am. Judicature Soc. Clubs: Birmingham (Mich.) Athletic (pres. 1967-68), Hillsboro (Fla.). Home: 4688 Haddington Ln Bloomfield Hills MI 48013 Office: Freud Markus Slavin & Galgan PC 100 E Big Beaver Rd Suite 900 Ameritech Bldg Troy MI 48083

SLAWIAK, SHEILA IAQUINTO, data processing executive; b. Erie, Pa., Nov. 1, 1956; d. Salvatore and Carrie (Veneziano) Iaquinto; m. Thomas Arthur Slawiak, Oct. 23, 1976. Cert. lab. asst., Hamot Med. Ctr., 1975; B.S. in Chemistry, Gannon U., 1981, M.B.A., 1981. M.S. in Communications, Rensselaer Poly. Inst., 1983. Tech. rep. Hughson Chems. Co., Erie, 1976-81; sales assoc. J.C. Penney Co., Erie, 1981-82; tech. writer Allen-Bradley Corp., Highland Heights, Ohio, 1983-84, product engr., 1984-87; office automation cons. First Nat. Bank, Erie, 1985—; demand mgr. Digital Equipment Corp., Westfield, Mass., 1987-88, info. systems cons., 1988—. Contbr. articles to tech. jours. Mem. Soc. Tech. Communications (research grant com.), Nat. Assn. Female Execs., Am. Soc. for Profl. and Exec. Women, Phi Sigma Sigma. Republican. Roman Catholic.

SLAYEN, HOWARD THEO, accounting company executive; b. San Diego, May 6, 1947; s. Elijah Al and Pearl Minnette (Lehrer) S.; m. Susan Marie Drake, Aug. 23, 1970; children: Matthew Drake, Samuel William. BA in Econ., Claremont McKenna U., 1968; JD, U. Calif. at Berkeley, 1971. Bar: Calif., 1972; CPA, Calif., 1972. Tax specialist Coopers & Lybrand, Palo Alto, Calif., 1971-76; ptnr. in charge tax svcs. Coopers & Lybrand, Houston, 1976-82, San Jose/Menlo Pk., Calif., 1982—; lectr. taxation Golden Gate U., San Francisco, 1973, San Jose State U., 1987-88. Commr. Am. Youth Soccer Orgn., Menlo Pk., 1987—. Mem. Calif. Soc. CPA's, Calif. State Bar Assn., Tex. Soc. CPA's (chmn. tax curriculum com. 1980-82). Office: Coopers & Lybrand Ten Almaden Blvd #1600 San Jose CA 95113

SLAYTON, JOHN HOWARD, business lawyer, financial consultant; b. Sparta, Wis., July 6, 1955; s. Rex Gordon and Elizabeth (Ward) S.; m. Judith Hughes. BA in Polit. Sci. with honors, Marquette U., 1977; JD with honors, George Washington U., 1980, MBA in Fin., 1982; LLM in Taxation, Georgetown U., 1986. Bar: D.C. 1981, U.S. Ct. Appeals (D.C. cir.) 1981, U.S. Dist. Ct. (D.C. dist.).1981. Assoc. Metzger, Shadyac & Schwarz, Washington, 1980-83, Pillsbury, Madison & Sutro, Washington, 1983-87, Vallejo Co., Washington, 1987—; instr. real estate syndication, Arlington (Va.) County Continuing Edn./Realty Bd., 1982. Contbr. articles to profl. jours. Mem. ABA (mem. com. fed. regulation of securities), D.C. Bar Assn. Roman Catholic. Home: 6802 McLean Province Circle Falls Church VA 22043 Office: Vallejo Co 600 New Hampshire Ave NW Ste 953 Washington DC 20037

SLAYTON, RICHARD COURTNEY, executive recruiting consultant; b. Toledo, Apr. 3, 1937; s. Walter Lee and Virginia Adair (Wuerfel) S.; m. Donna Lynn Stage, July 26, 1962; children: Richard Stage, Robert Courtney. BS Indsl. Engring., U. Mich., 1960, MBA, 1965. With mfg. mgmt. program, tech. sales specialist Gen. Electric Co., 1960-64, subsect. mgr., 1965-67; assoc. dir., cons. R.W. Tunnell Co., Phila., 1967-70; pres. Bus. Tech. Assocs., Inc., Phila., 1970-76; assoc. Boyden Assocs., Inc., Toledo, 1976-78, v.p., mgr., 1981-82, sr. v.p., mgr. Midwest ops., 1982-85; founder, pres. Kreutz Internat., Inc., Chgo., 1985—; Bd. dirs. Alloy Engring. and Casting Co., 1988—. Bd. dirs. Lake Forest Symphony Orch., 1984—. Served with USNR, 1954-62. Mem. Am. Inst. Indsl. Engrs., Alpha Pi Mu, Phi Kappa Phi, Beta Gamma Sigma. Republican. Presbyterian. Clubs: Met., Toledo. Home: 2069 Knollwood Rd Lake Forest IL 60045 Office: Kreutz Internat Inc 10 S Riverside Pla Ste 312 Chicago IL 60606

SLEDGE, DONALD RAY, banker, financial planner, stockbroker, money manager; b. San Antonio, Apr. 3, 1953; s. Marvin Ray and Vivian Louise (Porter) S.; m. Maryann Hope Shimkus, Feb. 14, 1982; children: April Dawn, Chelsea Lynn. Grad. pub. schs., Oxon Hill, Md. Cert. fin. planner; registered rep. Supt. telecommunications Navy Fed. Credit Union, Washington, 1971-73; mgr. various depts. Pentagon Fed. Credit Union, Vienna, Va., 1973-83; mgr. investments ISFA Corp., Tampa, Fla., 1984-88; v.p. United Savs. Bank, Vienna, 1984-88; pres. United Securities Corp., Vienna, 1987-88, Gt. Falls, Va., 1989—. Mem. Internat. Assn. Fin. Planning, Inst. Cert. Fin. Planners, Mensa. Republican. Office: United Savs Bank 10144 Yorktown Dr Great Falls VA 22066

SLEDGE, REGINALD LEON, financial analyst; b. Balt., July 8, 1954; s. Herbert Clifton and Juanita (Brantley) S. Grad., Lawrence Acad., 1972; BS, Boston U., 1976; MBA, Columbia U., 1984. Fin. analyst West Point-Pepperell, Inc., N.Y.C., 1976-77; fin. futures trader European Am. Bank, N.Y.C., 1978-82; portfolio mgr. Fuji Bank, N.Y.C., 1984-85; fin. cons. Control Assocs., N.Y.C., 1986-87; acct., fin. analyst Spicer & Oppenheim, N.Y.C., 1987-88; fin. analyst Security Pacific Bus. Credit, Inc., N.Y.C., 1988—; v.p., dir. Columbia Bus. Sch., N.Y.C., 1986—. Mem. Rep. Nat. Com. Republican. Roman Catholic. Club: Columbia Bus. Sch. N.Y. (v.p. 1986—). Home: 282 E 35th St Apt 6W Brooklyn NY 11203 Office: Security Pacific Bus Credit Inc 228 E 45th St New York NY 10017

SLEEMAN, THOMAS BARRETT, oil company executive; b. Chgo., May 3, 1932; s. Barrett Ayers and Marie J. (Henning) S.; m. Martha June Netzel, Aug. 29, 1953; children: Kevin, Daniel, Gary, Michael. BS in Acctg., U. Ill., 1954. CPA, Ill. Various positions Unocal Corp., Chgo., 1954-67; supr. corp. accts. Unocal Corp., Los Angeles, 1967-69, mgr. budgets, 1970-73, v.p. corp. planning, 1974-79; pres. Molycorp., Inc. subs. Unocal Corp., Los Angeles, 1979-85, Unocal Chems. div. Unocal Corp., Los Angeles, 1986—; sr. v.p. and dir. Unocal Corp., Los Angeles, 1988—; dir. Unocal Corp., 1988—. Office: Unocal Corp 1201 W 5th St PO Box 60455 Los Angeles CA 90060

SLEMMONS, ROBERT SHELDON, architect; b. Mitchell, Nebr., Mar. 12, 1922; s. M. Garvin and K. Fern (Borland) S.; AB, U. Nebr., 1947, BArch, 1948; m. Dorothy Virginia Herrick, Dec. 16, 1945; children: David (dec.), Claire, Jennifer, Robert, Timothy. Draftsman, Davis & Wilson, architects, Lincoln, Nebr., 1947-48; chief designer, project architect Office of Kans. State Architect, Topeka, 1948-54; asso. John A. Brown, architect, Topeka, 1954-56; partner Brown & Slemmons, architect, Topeka, 1956-69; v.p. Brown-Slemmons-Kreuger, architects, Topeka, 1969-73; owner Robert S. Slemmons, A.I.A. & Assos., architects, Topeka, 1973—. Cons. Kans. State Office Bldg. Commn., 1956-57; lectr. in design U. Kans., 1961; bd. dirs. Kaw Valley State Bank & Trust Co., Topeka, 1978—. Bd. dirs. Topeka Civic Symphony Soc., 1950-60, Midstates Retirement Communities, Inc., 1986—, Topeka Festival Singers; v.p. Ministries for Aging, Inc., Topeka, 1984—; mem. Topeka Bd. Bldg. and Fire Appeals. With USNR, 1942-48. Mem. AIA (Topeka pres. 1955-56, Kans. dir. 1957-58, mem. com. on architecture for justice, com. for hist. resources), Internat. Conf. Bldg. Ofcls., Topeka Art Guild (pres. 1950), Am. Corrections Assn., Kans. Council Chs. (dir. 1961-62), Shawnee County Hist. Soc., Greater Topeka C. of C., Downtown Topeka, Inc., St. Andrews Soc., SAR, U. Nebr. Alumni Assn. (life), Band Alumni Assn., Kiwanis (pres. 1966-67). Presbyterian (elder, chmn. trustees). Prin. archtl. works include: Kans. State Office Bldg., 1954, Topeka Presbyn. Manor, 1960-74, Meadowlark Hills Retirement Community, 1979, Shawnee County Adult Detention Facility, 1985. Office: Slemmons Assocs Architects Townsite Pla Ste 1515 Topeka KS 66603

SLEVIN, JOSEPH RAYMOND, editor, publisher; b. N.Y.C., Nov. 27, 1918; s. Theodore and Katherine (Bluh) S.; m. Zillah Katherine Day, Dec. 8, 1943; children: Ann Day, Michael Scott, Jonathan Day, Peter Day. BA, Yale U., 1939; student, Yale U. Law Sch., 1939-40, U. Ill., 1941-42; MA, U. Nebr., 1942. Staff editor Changing Times mag., Washington, 1946-47; econ. corr. Jour. of Commerce, Washington, 1947-55; Washington corr. Fin. Times, London, England, 1952-57; nat. econs. editor N.Y. Herald Tribune, Washington, 1955-66; syndicated econs. columnist Newsday, Times Mirror and Phila. Inquirer, 1966-85; econs. commentator Westinghouse Broadcasting, Washington, 1974-77; editor, publisher Washington Bond Report, 1962—; fin. sec. Nat. Press Club, Washinton, 1979, v.p. 1980, pres. 1981; pres. Nat. Press Bldg. Corp., 1981-82; bd. dirs. Nat. Press Found., Inc., pres. 1983-87. Lt. USNR, 1942-45, PTO. Mem. Am. Polit. Sci Assn., White House Corr Assn., Overseas Writers, Periodical Press Gallery, Nat. Press Club, Yale Club, Fed. City Club. Home: 16 E Melrose St Chevy Chase MD 20815 Office: Washington Bond Report Nat Press Bldg Washington DC 20045

SLEVIN, PATRICK JOSEPH, engineer; b. Orange, N.J., Nov. 28, 1951; s. John Francis and Bridie (Devaney) S.; m. Jacqueline Eileen Cavalero, July, 29, 1978; children: Patrick Joseph, John. BS in Indsl. Engring., N.J. Inst. Tech., 1976; MME, L.I. U., 1980. Engr. Fairchild Rep. Corp., Farmingdale, N.Y., 1977-79; engr. Kearfott (formerly Singer Kearfott), Little Falls, N.J., 1979-84, mem. engring. mgmt. staff, 1984-89, mgr. telecommunications, 1989—. Mem. Soc. Mfg. Engrs. (chpt. chmn. 1985-86), Am. Prodn. and Inventory Control Soc., Am. Assn. Individual Investors, Glen Ridge Country Club (N.J.). Roman Catholic. Home: 10 Sutherland Rd Montclair NJ 07042-2443 Office: Kearfott 1150 McBride Ave Little Falls NJ 07424

SLIGH, ROBERT LEWIS, furniture manufacturing company executive; b. Grand Rapids, Mich., Mar. 27, 1928; s. Charles Robert Jr. and Charlotte Pelton (Klumph) S.; m. Lois Hadley Patterson, Oct. 26, 1951; children:

Robert Lewis, Barbara, John. BS, U. Mich., 1950. Asst. sales mgr. Sligh-Lowry Furniture Co., Holland, Mich., 1954-57; exec. v.p. Sligh-Lowry Furniture Co., Holland, 1963-68; pres. Sligh Furniture Co., Holland, 1968—; bd. dirs. NBD-Grand Rapids N.A. Campaign chmn. United Way, Holland, 1958; pres. Harrington Bd. Edn., Holland, 1958-65; vice chmn. bd. dirs. Kendall Coll. Art and Design, Grand Rapids, 1987—. With USAF, 1952-54. Mem. Rotary (pres. Holland chpt. 1971-72, fellow Rotary found. 1985), Macatawa Bay Yacht Club (commodore 1967-68). Office: Sligh Furniture Co 1201 Industrial Ave Holland MI 49423

SLIJK, RICHARD PHILIP, financial executive; b. Akron, Ohio, May 17, 1955; s. K. Niek and Pat (Larson) S.; m. Noriko Togashi, Nov. 23, 1982. BA, UCLA, 1979; MBA, Am. Grad. Sch. Internat. Mgmt., 1985. Product mgmt. analyst Time-Life Inc., Tokyo, 1980-84; market mgmt., internat. fin. cons. Mitsui Internat., Los Angeles, 1985-86; mktg. analyst, portfolio mgmt. Daiwa Bank and Trust, Los Angeles, 1986-87; internat. mktg. mgr. Sheldahl Rd, Northfield, Minn., 1987—. Home: 4450 Vista Nacion Chula Vista CA 92010 Office: Sheldahl Inc PO Box 170 Northfield MN 55057

SLOAN, DAVID EDWARD, corporate director, consultant; b. Winnipeg, Man., Can., Mar. 29, 1922; s. David and Annie Maud (Gorvin) S.; m. Kathleen Lowry Craig, Dec. 26, 1947; children: Pamela Jane, John David, Kathleen Anne. B.Commerce, U. Man., 1942. With Monarch Life Assurance Co., Winnipeg, 1946-47; with Can. Pacific Ltd., 1947-88, treas., 1969-88; pres. and chief exec. officer Can. Pacific Securities Ltd., 1985-88; bd. dirs. Citadel Gen. Assurance Co., Citadel Life Assurance Co., Citadel Capital Corp., Winterthur Can. Fin. Corp., Norma Products of Can. Ltd.; mem. adv. com. Can. Pension Plan, Can. Govt., 1967-74, chmn., 1974-76. Served to lt. Royal Can. Army Service Corps, 1942-45. Mem. Fin. Execs. Inst. Can. (Toronto chpt., past pres. Montreal chpt.), Toronto Soc. Fin. Analysts, Soc. Investment Analysts (U.K.), Soc. Internat. Treas. (chmn. 1985-86, mem. council advs. 1978-87), Nat. Assn. Bus. Economists, U. Man. Alumni Assn. Mem. United Ch. Can. Clubs: Toronto Hunt (Scarborough, Ont.); Royal Montreal Golf (Ile Bizard, Que.). Home: 316 Rosemary Rd, Toronto, ON Canada M5P 3E3

SLOAN, LANE EVERETT, oil company executive; b. Houston, June 1, 1947; s. James Everett and Margaret A. (Weiss) S.; m. Diane C. Smith, June 1, 1980; children: Jonathan L., Natalie E. BS in Bus., U. Colo., 1969, MS in Mgmt. Sci., 1970; MS in Accountancy, U. Houston, 1979, MBA in Fin., 1984. CPA. Analyst Shell Oil Co., Houston, 1970-72, corp. auditor, 1972-74, supr., 1975-76, staff economist, 1976-79, asst. to treas., 1980-81, adminstrv. mgr., 1981-83, mgr. services, 1983-84, gen. mgr., 1985-86, liaison, 1987, v.p., 1987—. Flatirons Found. scholar U. Colo., 1970. Mem. Fin. Execs. Inst., Tex. Soc. CPA's, Sigma Iota Epsilon, Gov.'s Club. Republican. Baptist. Office: Shell Oil Co PO Box 2463 Houston TX 77252

SLOAN, MACEO KENNEDY, lawyer, investment executive; b. Phila., Oct. 18, 1949; s. Maceo Archibald and Charlotte (Kennedy) S.; m. Melva Iona Wilder, July 3, 1971; children: Maceo S., Malia K. BA, Morehouse Coll., 1971; MBA with honors, Ga. State U., 1973; JD with honors, N.C. Cen. U., 1979. Investment analyst N.C. Mut. Life Ins. Co., Durham, 1973-77, asst. to treas., 1977-78, asst. v.p., 1978-83, treas., 1983-85, v.p., treas., 1985-86; pres. NCM Devel. Group subs. N.C. Mut. Life Ins. Co., Durham, 1985-86; of counsel Moore & Van Allen, Durham, 1985-86; pres., chief exec. officer NCM Capital Mgmt. Group, Inc., Durham, 1986—; adj. vis. profl. N.C. Cen. U. Sch. Law, Durham, 1979-86; workshop rev. leader Study Seminar for Fin. Analysts, Windsor, ONt., Can., 1980—; bd. dirs., chmn. trust com. Mechanics & Farmers Bank, Durham; bd. dirs. Nat. Ins. Assn., Chgo.; networking leader Black Enterprise Mag., 1987—. Bd. dirs. United Way Durham, 1980-87, Urban Ministries Durham, 1983-88; bd. visitors N.C. U. Sch. Law, Durham, 1979-86. Recipient Outstanding Service award Better Bus. Bur., 1980, Freedom Guard award Durham Jaycees, 1982, Outstanding Leadership award United Way Durham, 1984, Resolution in Appreciation Durham City Council, 1983. Mem. Fin. Analysts Fedn., N.C. Soc. Fin. Analysts (v.p. 1977-78), N.C. State Bar, Durham C. of C., Nat. Investment Mgrs. Assn. (founder, pres. 1988—). Democrat. Baptist. Clubs: Univ. (Durham), The George Town (Washington D.C.). Home: 24000 S Lowell Rd Bahama NC 27503 Office: NCM Capital Mgmt Group Inc Two Mutual Pla 501 Willard St Durham NC 27701-3642

SLOAN, ROBERT FRANCIS, management consultant; b. Los Angeles, June 19, 1935; s. Lafayette F. and Frances (Walsh) S.; B.A. in Zoology, UCLA, 1957; Ph.D. in Oral Radiology, Osaka Dental U., 1977; m. Paula Sy, Apr. 22, 1987; children—Patrick, Cristina, Brett. Research asso. U. Calif. Med.-Dental Sch., Los Angeles, 1957-67; founding pres. Rocky Mountain Data Systems, 1967-70; founding exec. dir. Found. Orthodontic Research, 1968-70; exec. dir. InterAm. Orthodontic Seminar, 1964-70; mgmt. cons., Calif., 1978; chmn. bd. Radiol. Mgmt. Communications, Ltd., ITA Ltd., prof. Grad. Sch. of Business, U.S. Internat. U., San Diego, 1977-79; producer documentary and tech. films. Served to capt. M.S.C., U.S. Army, 1957-69. Recipient Bronze N.Y. Film Festival award, 1973, 79, Chris award, 1965, 73, Cine awards, 1964, 65, 74. Mem. ADA, Brit. Inst. Radiology, AMA, Found. Orthodontic Research (hon.), Socieda de Brasileira de Foniatria (hon. mem.). Editor: (book) Craniofacial Radiological Diagnosis and Management, 1988; developer Dental Telesis, 1988. Home: 10342 Wilkins Ave Los Angeles CA 90024

SLOCUM, DONALD HILLMAN, product development executive; b. Flushing, N.Y., Jan. 6, 1930; s. John G. and Frances H. S.; m. June Manning, Sept. 22, 1952 (dec. 1976); children: Richard, Mark, Carol; m. Barbara M. Ruane, Nov. 29, 1986. BS, Davis and Elkins Coll., 1951; MS, U. Vt., 1956; PhD, Ohio State U., 1958; LLD, Fla. Tech. Inst., 1968; MBA, Rider Coll., 1971; ScD, Morton U., 1972; Dr. Profl. Studies, Pace U., 1974. Rsch. Charles Pfizer, Inc., Bklyn., 1954; rsch. scientist Procter & Gamble, Cin., 1958-68; mgr. product devel. E.I. DuPont de Nemours & Co., Wilmington, Del., 1960-68; dir. new ventures N.L. Industries, N.Y.C., 1968-71; dir. fin. planning Hoffmann LaRoche, Nutley, N.J., 1971-74; v.p. Curtiss-Wright Corp., Woodridge, N.J., 1974-78; sr. v.p. Masonite-USA, Chgo., 1978-85; pres. Doner-Viking Corp., Madison, N.J., 1985-87, Woodtec, Inc subs. Masco, Detroit, 1987—. Author: New Venture Methodology, 1974; contbr. articles to tech. and bus. publs.; patentee in field. Lt. U.S. Army, 1951-54, Korea. Home: 61 Chimney Ridge Dr Convent NJ 07961 Office: 505 Newfield Rd Raritan Ctr Edison NJ 08818

SLOCUM, GEORGE SIGMAN, energy company executive; b. East Orange, N.J., Sept. 9, 1940. B.A., Cornell U., 1962, M.B.A., 1967. Mgmt. trainee Richardson-Merrell, Inc., 1962; v.p. Citibank N.A., 1967-78; v.p. fin. Transco Energy Co., Houston, 1978-80, sr. v.p., 1980-81, exec. v.p., chief fin. officer, dir., 1981-84, pres., chief operating officer, dir., 1984-87, pres., chief exec. officer, dir., 1987—; bd. dirs. Tex. Commerce Bank, Houston, Am. Petroleum Inst. Bd. dirs. Tex. Research League, Soc. for the Performing Arts, Houston; trustee Boy Scouts Am., Cornell U., U. Houston Found.; mem. alumni exec. council Cornell U. Grad. Sch. Mgmt. Served with U.S. Army, 1963-65. Mem. Am. Gas Assn. (exec. com., gas demand com., bd. fin. com., bd. dirs.), Southeastern Gas Assn. (fin. com.). Home: 10776 Bridlewood Houston TX 77024 Office: Transco Energy Co 2800 Post Oak Blvd PO Box 1396 Houston TX 77251

SLOCUM, JOHN WESLEY, JR., business educator; b. N.Y.C., Sept. 3, 1940; s. John Wesley Sr. and Florence (Brenner) S.; m. Gail Gustin, June 20, 1964; children: Christopher, Bradley, Jonathan. BBA, Westminster Coll., New Wilmington, Pa., 1962; MBA, Kent State U., 1964; PhD, U. Wash., 1967. With indsl. relations dept. B.F. Goodrich, Akron, Ohio, 1963-64; asst. prof. bus. Pa. State U., University Park, 1967-69, assoc. prof., 1969-73, prof., 1973-79; O. Paul Copley prof. orgnl. behavior So. Meth. U., Dallas, 1979—; vis. prof. Ohio State U., Columbus, 1975-76; cons. Bklyn. Union Gas Co., 1980—, NASA, Huntsville, Ala., 1979—, Transnat. Trucking, Addison, Tex., 1981-85; pres. Mgmt. Cons. Service, Dallas, 1981—; bd. dirs. Optigraphics Corp., Grand Prarie, Tex. Author: Management, 1972, 6th rev. edit. 1989, Organizational Behavior, 1974, 5th rev. edit., 1989, Management in the World Today, 1975, Readings in Organizational Behavior, 1977; contbr. numerous articles to profl. jours. Pres. Bent Tree West Homowners Assn., Dallas, 1983-84. Named Nicolas Salgo disting. tchr. So. Meth. U., 1987—; NSF scholar, 1969. Fellow Acad. Mgmt. (editor jour. 1979-81), Decision Scis. Intenat.; mem. Ea. Acad. Mgmt. (pres. 1971-72). Presbyterian. Office: So Meth U Cox Sch Bus 400 Fincher Bldg Dallas TX 75275

SLOCUM, OLIVER CONRAD, investment advisor, bank consultant; b. Echo, Minn., June 29, 1928; s. Charles Paul and Elsie Ruth (Johanssen) S.; m. Patricia M. Gregg, Oct. 14, 1978; children: Cynthia, Michael, John. BA in Govt. and Internat. Rels., Carleton Coll., 1952. Trainee Pillsbury Mills, Mpls., 1952-53; grocery products salesman Pillsbury Mills, Chillicothe, Mo., 1953-54; mcpl. bond salesman John Nuveen & Co., Chgo. and Detroit, 1954-59; pres., chmn. bd. Heber-Fugen-Wendin, Inc., Detroit, 1959-82; pres. SS&H Fin. Advisors, Birmingham, Mich., 1982—; investor rep. Mcpl. Securities Rulemaking, Washington, 1978-81; instr. Advanced Examiners Sch., Washington, 1966-76. Com. chmn. Oakland County Reps., Birmingham, 1968-72; mem. Beverly Hills Planning Commn., 1978-80; with U.S. Constabulary Occupation Force in Germany, 1947-48. With Ordnance Corps, U.S. Army, 1946-48. Recipient Service award No. Mich Sch. Banking, Marquette, 1966-81. Mem. Fin. Analysts Soc. Detroit, Soc. Mcpl. Analysts (pres. 1980-81), Investment counsel Assn. Am., Indianwood Golf and Country Club (Lake Orion, Mich.). Lutheran. Office: SS&H Fin Advisors 30800 Telegraph Rd S-2950 Birmingham MI 48010

SLOOK, GEORGE FRANCIS, financial executive; b. Phila., Aug. 14, 1946; s. Herbert F. and Eleanor L. (Barth) S.; m. Nancy Kathleen Krupsha, Sept. 23, 1972; children—Sally Ann, George Michael. B.S. in Bus. Adminstrn., Villanova U., 1968; M.B.A. in Fin., Widener U., 1982. Corp. auditor Sears, Roebuck & Co., Chgo., 1971-72, acct., N.Y.C., 1972-73, mechanization coordinator, Chgo., 1973-75, corp. acct., 1975-77; asst. treas. Sears Roebuck Acceptance Corp., Wilmington, Del., 1977-80, v.p., comptroller, 1980—. Republican precinct capt., Hoffman Estates, Ill., 1976; treas. Longview Farms Civic Assn., Wilmington, 1979-81; bd. dirs. Jr. Achievement, Delaware, 1985—; treas. 1986—. Served with U.S. Army, 1968-70. Mem. Fin. Execs. Inst. (dir. Phila. chpt. 1985, pres. Del. chpt. 1986), Nat. Assn. Accts. Roman Catholic. Office: Sears Roebuck Acceptance Corp PO Box 4680 Wilmington DE 19807 *

SLOSS, LYNES ROBINSON, infosystems executive; b. New Orleans, Dec. 18, 1953; s. Fred Maclin and Nina (O'Brien) S.; m. Eugenie Elizabeth Huger, Apr. 30, 1982; children: Joseph Merrick Jones, Alexander Dimitry. BA in Mgmt., Ga. Inst. Tech., 1977. Stockbroker Howard Weil, New Orleans, 1977-80; pres. Bellwether Tech. Corp., New Orleans, 1980—; bd. dirs. Audubon Computer Rentals, New Orleans, John A. Chauvin Seafood, New Orleans. Republican. Episcopalian. Office: Bellwether Tech Corp 203 Carondelet St Ste 250 New Orleans LA 70130

SLOTOROFF, JANICE BATES, marketing professional; b. Camden, N.J., Aug. 27, 1955; d. Warren Wesley and Bernice (Christopher) Bates; m. Jon William Slotoroff, Sept. 4, 1977 (div. Aug. 1984); 1 child, Jared Maxwell. Student, Atlantic Community Coll., Mays Landing, N.J., 1976; B in Nursing, Stockton State Coll., 1978. Surg. staff nurse Atlantic City Med. Ctr., 1976; maternal-child health specialist Atlantic County Health Dept., Mays Landing, 1978-79; rehab. specialist Cen. Rehab. Assn., Freehold, N.J., 1984-88; mktg. assoc., clin. evaluator New Medico Head Injury Systems, Lynn, Mass., 1988—. Apptd. Nat. Head Injury Found. Prevention Com., Metuchen, N.J., 1988—. Mem. N.J. State Nurses Assn. (pres. 1984, 2d v.p. 1981-86, mem. exec. bd. 1979-86, chmn. program planning com. 1981, apptd. interested nurses polit. action com., Princeton, 1987—), Assn. Rehab. Nurses (edu. com. 1988, chairperson mktg. sponsorship, mem. fund raising com. 1988, 89), Jersey Assn. Rehab. Profls. in Pvt. Sector, Sigma Theta Tau (program com. 1988—). Democrat. Roman Catholic. Home: 705 Maple Ave Northfield NJ 08225 Office: New Medico Combined Assocs 14 Central Ave Lynn MA 09101

SLOTTA, PETER LUIS, trade and finance company executive; b. Sao Paulo, Brazil, Jan. 8, 1942; came to U.S., 1956; s. Karl H. and Maja (Frenkel) S.; m. Karen Mallett, Apr. 15, 1971; children: James Edward, Katherine Ann. AB in Pub. and Internat. Affairs, Princeton U., 1964; MA, Johns Hopkins U., 1966; PhD in Internat. Relations, U. Pa., 1968. Treas., v.p. Star Steel Supply Co., Inc., Houston, 1969-71; trainee Swiss Bank Corp., Zurich, Switzerland and London, 1972-73, Schroder Wagg, London, 1973, Oppenheim Appel Dixon, N.Y.C., 1974, Universal Steel Co., Hallendale, Fla., 1974; treas. Pan Am. Trade Devel. Corp., N.Y.C., 1975—, v.p., 1978-83, sr. v.p., 1983-85, exec. v.p., 1985-86, pres., 1986—. Pres. Dobbs Ferry (N.Y.) Employment Service, 1977-79; dir. Dobbs Ferry Chamber Music Festival. Office: Pan Am Trade Devel Corp 2 Park Ave New York NY 10016

SLOVES, MARVIN, advertising agency executive; b. N.Y.C., Apr. 22, 1933; s. John H. and Evelyn S. (Wishan) S. AB, Brandeis U, 1955; postgrad., Oriental Inst., U. Chgo., 1955-61. Staff researcher Leo Burnett Co., Chgo., 1962; dir. rsch. Earle Ludgin Co., Chgo., 1963-64; account exec. Ted Bates Co., N.Y.C., 1964; account supr., v.p. Papert, Koenig, Lois, N.Y.C., 1965-67; pres., chief exec. officer Scali, McCabe, Sloves, Inc., N.Y.C., 1967-81, chmn., chief exec. officer, 1981—; bd. dirs. Horizons Internat. Foods Corp. Bd. dirs. Burden Ctr. for Aged, N.Y.C., Chamber Music Soc. Lincoln Ctr., N.Y.C., Santa Fe Chamber Music Festival, Santa Fe Opera. NEA fellow. Mem. Am. Assn. Advt. Agys. (bd. dirs. Ea. div.). Democrat. Jewish. Home: Bogtown House PO Box 50 North Salem NY 10560 Office: Scali McCabe Sloves Inc 800 Third Ave New York NY 10022 *

SLOVIKOWSKI, GERALD JUDE, engineering company executive; b. N.Y.C., Feb. 9, 1949; s. Felix J. and Wilhelmina S. BS in Mech. Engring. with honors, Pratt Inst., Bklyn., 1970; MBA magna cum laude, Wagner Coll., N.Y.C., 1975. Registered profl. engr., N.J. Project engr. Mobil Oil Corp., N.Y.C., 1970-72; project mgr. Am. Home Products, N.Y.C., 1972-74; ops. mgr. Continental Oil Corp., Houston, 1974-75, bus. devel. mgr., 1975-77; v.p. and gen. mgr. Herman, Sommer & Assocs., Newark, 1977-80; exec. v.p. and gen. mgr. Engineered Products Co., Inc., Oldbridge, N.J., 1980—; bd. dirs. Urban Assocs., Holmdel, N.J., Engineered Products Co., Perth Amboy, N.J., GS Indsl. Co., N.J.; prof. bus. adminstrn. Middlesex Coll., Edison, N.J., 1981—. Cons. Woodbridge Twp. Econ. Devel. Council, Woodbridge, N.J., 1980. Recipient Cons. Engrs. award N.Y. Cons. Engring. Assn., 1970, Dow Jones Fin. award Dow Jones Wall Street Jour., 1975. Mem. ASME, Am. Nuclear Soc. (assoc.), Am. Inst. Chem. Engrs. (assoc.), Tau Beta Pi, Pi Tau Sigma, Delta Mu Delta, Pi Mu Epsilon. Home: 166 Acorn Dr Clark NJ 07066

SLUDIKOFF, STANLEY ROBERT, publisher, writer; b. Bronx, N.Y., July 17, 1935; s. Harry and Lillie (Elberger) S.; m. Ann Paula Blumberg, June 30, 1972; children: Lisa Beth, Jaime Dawn, Bonnie Joy. B.Arch., Pratt Inst., 1957; grad. student, U. So. Calif., 1960-62. Lic. architect, real estate broker. Project planner Robert E. Alexander, F.A.I.A. & Assos., Los Angeles, 1965-66, Daniel, Mann, Johnson & Mendenhall (City and Regional Planning Cons.), Los Angeles, 1967-70; pres., publisher Gambling Times Inc., also Two Worlds Mgmt., Inc., Los Angeles, 1971—; v.p. Prima Quality Farms, Inc., P.R.; pres. Las Vegas TV Weekley, also Postal West, Las Vegas, 1975-79; founder Stanley Roberts Sch. Winning Blackjack, 1976; instr. city and regional planning program U. So. Calif., 1960-63. Author: (under pen name Stanley Roberts): Winning Blackjack, 1971, How to Win at Weekend Blackjack, 1973, Gambling Times Guide to Blackjack, 1983; author: The Beginner's Guide to Winning Blackjack, 1983, According to Gambling Times: The Rules of Casino Games, 1983, The Casino Gourmet, 6 vols., 1984, Casinos of the Caribbean, 1984; also monthly column, 1977—. Mem. Destination 90 Forum, Citizens Planning Group, San Fernando Valley, Calif., 1966-67. Served to lt. col. U.S. Army, now Res. ret. Recipient commendation from mayor Los Angeles for work on model cities funding, 1968. Mem. AIA, Am. Planning Assn., Am. Inst. Cert. Planners, Internat. Casino Assn. (sec. 1980—), Res. Officers Assn. (life), Mensa (life). Home: 17437 Tarzana St Encino CA 91316 Office: 16760 Stagg St #213 Van Nuys CA 91406

SLUSHER, LEWIS ELMER, JR., accounting consultant; b. Virginia Beach, Va., Mar. 20, 1957; s. Lewis Elmer and Nell Marie (Weeks) S. BS in Econs., Radford U., 1980, BBA, 1980, MBA, 1987. Adjuster loans United Va. Bank, Roanoke, 1981-87; cons. acctg. Va. Credit Union League, Lynchburg, Va., 1987—. Faculty teaching fellow Radford U., 1987. Mem. Inst. Cert. Mgmt. Accts. Club: Richmond Volleyball. Home: 8706 1 Beacontree Richmond VA 23229 Office: Va Credit Union League 1207 Fenwick Dr Lynchburg VA 24506

SLUSSER, EUGENE ALVIN, electronics manufacturing executive; b. Denver, Mar. 13, 1922; s. Jesse Alvin and Grace (Carter) S.; m. Anne L. Longley, Oct. 2, 1943; children: Robert, Jon, Carolyn. BS in Physics, U. Denver, 1947. Registered profl. engr., N.H. Staff mem. MIT Radiation Lab., Cambridge, 1942-45; project engr. Heiland Research Co., Denver, 1945-47; cons. Gen. Telephone System, N.Y.C., 1947-51; project engr. Airborne Inst. Lab., Mineola, N.Y., 1951-53; v.p. N.E. Electronics Corp., Concord, N.H., 1953-58; pres. Aerotronic Assocs., Inc., Contoocook, N.H., 1958-84, N.H. Automatic Equipment Corp., Concord, 1962—, E.A. Slusser & Assocs., Concord; bd. dirs. First Capital Bank. Patentee electronics field. Chmn. Hopkinton (N.H.) Water Bd., 1962-69, Hopkinton Planning Bd., 1971-77, Hopkinton Precinct Bd. Adjustment, 1977. Mem. Aircraft Owners and Pilots Assn. Lodge: Masons (32 degree). Home: RFD-3 Box 254 Hopkinton Village NH 03229 Office: 16 Centre St Concord NH 03301

SLUSSER, ROBERT WYMAN, aerospace company executive; b. Mineola, N.Y., May 10, 1938; s. John Leonard and Margaret McKenzie (Wyman) S.; BS, MIT, 1960; MBA, U. Pa., 1962; m. Linda Killeas, Aug. 3, 1968; children: Jonathan, Adam, Robert, Mariah. Assoc. adminstr.'s staff NASA Hdqrs., Washington, 1962-65; with Northrop Corp., Hawthorne, Calif., 1965—, adminstr. mktg. and planning dept., space labs., 1965-68, mgr. bus. and fin. Warnecke Electron Tubes Co. div., Chgo., 1968-71, controller Cobra Program Aircraft div., Hawthorne, 1971-72, mgr. bus. adminstrn. YF-17 Program, 1972-75, mgr. adminstrn. F-18/Cobra programs, also mgr. F-18 design to cost program, 1975-78, mgr. adminstrn. F-18L program, 1978-79, mgr. engring. adminstrn., 1980-82, acting v.p. engring., 1982, mgr. data processing, 1983-84, v.p. info. resources, 1985—; chief fin. officer, bd. dirs. So. Calif. Hist. Aviation Found., 1987—, We. Mus. Flight, 1987—; bd. dirs. PDES, Inc., 1988—. Grumman Aircraft Engring. scholar, 1956-60. Fellow AIAA (assoc.); mem. So. Calif. Soc. Info. Mgmt. Home: 7270 Berry Hill Dr Rancho Palos Verdes CA 90274 Office: Northrop Aircraft Div 1 Northrop Ave Hawthorne CA 90250

SLUSSER, WILLIAM PETER, investment banker; b. Oakland, Calif., June 20, 1929; s. Eugene and Thelma (Donovan) S.; m. Joanne Eleanor Briggs, June 20, 1953; children: Kathleen E., Martin E., Wendelin M., Caroline E., Sarah A. BA cum laude, Stanford U., 1951; MBA, Harvard U., 1953. Mgr. spl. situations dept. Dean Witter & Co., N.Y.C., 1955-60; partner, sr. v.p. in charge corp. fin. dept., 1960-75, also dir, mem. exec. com.; co-mgr. investment banking div., sr. v.p. Paine Webber, Inc., 1975-80; mng. dir. Paine Webber, Inc., N.Y.C., 1980-88; pres. Slusser Assocs., Inc., N.Y.C., 1988—; head merger and acquisition dept., underwriter or fin. cons. Square D. Co., Times Mirror Co., Ashland Oil, Inc., Ga. Pacific, TRW, Inc., Avon Products, TransAm. Realty Investors, Atex, Inc. subs. Eastman Kodak Co., Perini Corp., Downey Savs. & Loan, Booth Newspapers, Inc., Holly Hill Lumber Co., Stanhome, Inc., Santee Portland Cement Co., Grow Group, Dr. Pepper Co. of So. Calif., Gemini Computer Systems, London, De La Rue, P.L.C., London, VNU Inc., Haarlem, Netherlands, Bertlesmann Pub. Co., West Germany. Reading & Bates Offshore Drilling Co., Houghton Mifflin Co., Orion Research, Inc., Pacific Holding Co., also vice chmn., 1969-73; bd. dirs. Am. Global Lines, Inc.; founder original Stockholder Assn. Mortgage Cos. subs. Mfrs. Hanover Trust Co. Lectr. to profl. assns. Mem. Ends of the Earth; mem. bd. fin. advisors Columbia U. Bus. Sch., Calif. Senate Commn. on Corp. Governance. Served to 1st lt. USAF, 1953-55. Mem. Investment Assn. N.Y., Soc. Calif. Pioneers, Alpha Delta Phi (exec. council 1956-62, treas. 1961). Clubs: Knickerbocker, Downtown, Stanford Assos., Harvard (N.Y.C.); Lawrence Beach, Stanford of N.Y. Author numerous articles; contbr.; Handbook of Mergers, Acquisitions and Buyouts. Home: 901 Lexington Ave New York NY 10021 Home: Slusser Ranch Windsor CA 95492 Office: Slusser Assocs Inc 1 Citicorp Ctr 153 E 53d St Ste 5801 New York NY 10022

SLUTSKY, LEONARD ALAN, finance executive; b. N.Y.C., July 25, 1945; s. Hyman and Ruth (Neuman) S.; m. Sharlene Alexis Farber, Oct. 20, 1968; children: Jacquelyn Anne, Jason Ian, Adam Jeffrey. Student, U. Ariz., 1963-66. Chmn., pres., chief exec. officer Republic Pension Svc. Inc., Melville, N.Y., 1981-83; pres., chief exec. officer Am. Money Svc. Corp., N.Y.C., 1977—; chmn. bd. Peoples Nat. Bank of Rockland, N.Y., 1983-85, Millbrook Equity Corp., N.Y.C., 1985-86; chmn., chief exec. officer Republic Advisors, Inc., Lake Success, N.Y., 1981—; chmn. Am. Money Co., Inc., Lake Success, 1986-87; pres. Windsor Funding Corp., West Hills, N.Y., 1987—. Sgt. N.Y. N.G., 1966-71. Recipient Disting. Service award Rockland County, 1984, Com. Service award Dist. Atty. Rockland, 1984, Distinguished Service award 6th Congl. Dist., Washington, 1984, Yeshiva U., N.Y.C., 1984. Mem. Am. Soc. C.L.U. Republican. Jewish. Clubs: MHJC Men's, Plainview Soccer. Lodges: KC, KP, Lions. Home: 20 Equestrian Ct West Hills NY 11743 Office: Windsor Funding Corp 20 Equestrian West Hills NY 11743

SMAHA, JAMES, electrical components company executive; b. 1935. BS, U. Maine, 1954. With Fairchild Camera and Instrument Co., 1954-74; with Nat. Semiconductor Corp., Santa Clara, Calif., 1974—, now exec.

SMALBACH, DAVID HAROLD, insurance company executive; b. Cleve., July 28, 1935; s. Arthur Carl and Mary (Greenfield) S.; m. Carol Mindlin, Nov. 27, 1957 (div. 1965); children: Wayne, Neal; m. Barbara Schiller, Aug. 29, 1969. BA, Gettysburg Coll., 1957; MBA, NYU, 1965. Cert. fin. planner. Supr. data processing Bristol-Meyers, Hillside, N.J., 1957-63; dir. purchasing Barbizon, N.Y.C., 1963-72; asst. to pres. Piedmont, N.Y.C., 1972-73; inventory control mgr. Warnaco, N.Y.C., 1973-75; ins. and investment exec. C. M. Alliance, Garden City, N.Y., 1975—; lectr. in field. Trustee Rockville Ctr. Libr. Bd., 1980—; dir. Rockville Ctr. Home Rule Party, 1985—; co-chmn. Rockville Ctr. Bi-Centennial Festival Com., Rockville Ctr. 90th Anniversary Fair Com., 1983; founder, past treas. Rockville Ctr. Libr. Friends. Mem. Internat. Assn. Fin. PLanners, Nassau Life Underwriters Assn., Rockville Ctr. C. of C. (pres. 1984-86, Man of Yr. award 1988), Pi Lambda Sigma, TAm O'Shanter Country Club, Gleneagles Country Club, Kiwanis (pres., chmn. div. com. 1981-82). Republican. Jewish. Home: 10 Allen Rd Rockville Centre NY 11797

SMALE, JOHN GRAY, diversified industry executive; b. Listowel, Ont., Can., Aug. 1, 1927; s. Peter John and Vera Gladys (Gray) S.; m. Phyllis Anne Weaver, Sept. 2, 1950; children: John Gray, Catherine Anne, Lisa Beth, Peter McKee. BS, Miami U., Oxford, Ohio, 1949, LLD (hon.), 1979; LLD (hon.), Kenyon Coll., Gambier, Ohio, 1974; DSc (hon.), DePauw U., 1983; DCL (hon.), St. Augustine's Coll., 1985; LLD (hon.), Xavier U., 1986. With Vick Chem. Co., 1949-50, Bio-Research, Inc., N.Y.C., 1950-52; pres. Procter & Gamble Co., 1974-86, chief exec., 1981—, chmn. bd., 1986—, dir., 1972—; bd. dirs. Gen. Motors Corp., J.P. Morgan Guaranty Trust Co. Bd. dirs. United Negro Coll. Fund, United Way Am., Nat. Park Found.; bd. govs. The Nature Conservancy; mem. nat. adv. bd. Goodwill Industries Am., Inc.; emeritus trustee Kenyon Coll., Cin. Inst. Fine Arts. Served with USNR, 1945-46. Mem. Grocery Mfrs. Am. (bd. dirs.), Conf. Bd. (trustee), Bus. Council, Bus. Roundtable, Nat. Ctr. State Cts. (bus. and profl. friends com.), Internat. Life Scis. Inst. (CEO Council), Nutrition Found., Cin. Bus. Com. Clubs: Commercial, Commonwealth, Queen City, Cincinnati Country. Office: Procter & Gamble Co 1 Procter & Gamble Pla Cincinnati OH 45202

SMALHEISER, HARVEY, financial company executive, lawyer; b. N.Y.C., Jan. 6, 1942; s. Simon Smalheiser and Sylvia (Schindler) Smith. B.B.A., Baruch Sch. Bus., CCNY, 1962; J.D., Fordham U., 1965. Bar: N.Y.; C.P.A., N.J. Mem. tax staff Arthur Andersen & Co., Newark, 1965-70; tax mgr. Arthur Andersen & Co., N.Y.C., 1970-78; group dir.-corp. tax Ryder System, Inc., Miami, Fla., 1978-80, v.p.-corp. tax, 1980-85, sr. v.p.-corp. tax, 1985—, dir., 1981-82; chmn. Ryder System Fed. Credit Union, Miami, 1982—. Bd. dirs., treas., chmn. fin. com. Miami City Ballet, 1988—; bd. dirs. Informed Families of South Fla., Miami, 1984—. Mem. Am. Trucking Assn. (tax policy com. 1984—), Am. Trucking Assns. (chmn. taxation com. of nat. acctg. and fin. council 1982—, mem. exec. com. 1982—, pres. 1987-88) Am. Inst. C.P.A.s, N.J. Soc. C.P.A.s, Tax. Execs. Inst., N.Y. State Bar Assn., U.S. C. of C. (taxation com. 1984—), Miami C. of C. (subcom. arts festival 1985). Lodge: Rotary (pres. River Vale, N.J. 1977-78). Office: Ryder System Inc 3600 NW 82nd Ave Miami FL 33166

SMALL, ALBERT HARRISON, engineering company executive; b. Washington, Oct. 15, 1925; s. Albert and Lillian S.; BChemE., U. Va., 1946; student George Washington U. Law Sch., 1947-48, Am. U. Grad. Sch. Bus. Adminstrn., 1949-51; m. Shirley Schwalb, Sept. 14, 1952; children: Susan Carol, Albert H., James H. Founder, So. Engring. Corp., Washington, 1952—, pres., chief exec. officer, 1968—. Bd. dirs. Nat. Symphony Orch., Va. Engring. Found., U. Va. Served with USNR, 1943-46; bd. trustees Meridian House Internat., Folger Shakespeare Library Com. Mem. Nat. Assn. Real Estate Bds., Nat. Assn. Home Builders, Urban Land Inst. Republican. Clubs: Georgetown, Pisces, Harmonie, Army-Navy, Internat. Home: 7116 Glenbrook Rd Bethesda MD 20814 Office: 1050 Connecticut Ave NW Ste 444 Washington DC 20036

SMALL, GREGORY DAVID, motion picture executive; b. Boston, Nov. 4, 1957; s. Roger and Joan (Berland) S.; m. Adrienne Gail Lavine, Aug. 15, 1982. BA, Brown U., 1979; MBA, U. So. Calif., 1986. Producer Warner Amex QUBE TV, Columbus, Ohio, 1979-81; prodn. mgr. Mendelsohn & Adler Advt., San Francisco, 1981-82; v.p. Scheingarten & Assocs., San Francisco, 1982-84, Crawford-Lane Prodns., Sherman Oaks, Calif., 1986—. Author Hollywood Scriptletter, L.A., 1985-86; creator Latency, 1980. Democrat. Jewish. Office: Crawford-Lane Prodns 14101 Valleyheart Dr Ste 205 Sherman Oaks CA 91423

SMALL, REBECCA ELAINE, accountant; b. Meridian, Tex., Apr. 5, 1946; d. James Milford and Rosa Lee Elaine (Berry) Allen; m. Jay Austin Small, Sept. 16, 1964 (div.); children: Lashawn Renee, Jay Austin Jr.; m. Jerry Leon Cooper, Dec. 10, 1983 (div. Sept. 1985). Student Okla. Sch. Bus. and Banking, 1972; BS in Acctg. magna cum laude, Cen. State U., Edmond, Okla., 1977. Staff acct. Robert A. Mosley, CPA, Moore, Okla., 1972-74, Robert Stewart, CPA, Edmond, 1974-75, Lowder & Co., Oklahoma City, 1975-81; pvt. practice acctg., Oklahoma City, 1981—. Mem. Okla. Woman's Bus. Orgn. (chmn. 1982), Okla. Soc. CPA's, Am. Inst. CPA's, Am. Woman's Soc. CPA's, Nat. Assn. Accts. (hon.), Alpha Lambda Delta, Alpha Chi. Democrat. Avocations: writing poetry, interior decorating, horticulture.

SMALL, RICHARD DONALD, travel company executive; b. West Orange, N.J., May 24, 1929; s. Joseph George and Elizabeth (McGarry) S.; A.B. cum laude, U. Notre Dame, 1951; m. Arlene P. Small; children—Colleen P., Richard Donald, Joseph W., Mark G., Brian P. With Union-Camp Corp., N.Y.C., Chgo., 1952-62; pres. Alumni Holidays, Inc., 1962—, AHI Internat. Corp., Des Plaines, Ill., 1962—, All Horizons, Inc., 1982—; chmn. AHI, Inc., 1982—. Club: University (Chgo.). Home: 190 N Sheridan Rd Lake Forest IL 60045 also: 2202 Wailea Elua Wailea Maui HI 96753 Office: 1st Nat Bank Bldg 701 Lee St Des Plaines IL 60016

SMALL, WESLEY THOMAS, savings and loan executive; b. San Francisco, Aug. 10, 1943; s. Charles Havelock and Mary Adelaide (Rikeman) S.; standard diploma Inst. Fin. Edn., 1974, grad. diploma, 1974; grad. Sch. for Exec. Devel., 1976; m. Sally E. Stone, Sept. 25, 1971; children: Thomas W., Joseph A., Charles W., Kevin W. With Citizens Savs. & Loan Assn., Inc., Silver Spring, Md., 1961-79, br. coordinator, 1966-71, treas., 1967-71, v.p., 1972-77, sr. v.p., 1977-79; v.p. 1st Fed. Savs. & Loan Assn. Largo (Fla.), 1979-81, exec. v.p., 1981-84; founder, pres., chief exec. officer Madison Savs. & Loan Assn., Palm Harbor, Fla., 1984—, also bd. dirs.; founder Fla. DeNovo Savs. & Loan Exchange Group, Tampa, chmn. 1984-86. Bd. dirs. Suncoast YMCA, Clearwater, Fla., 1986-88; bd. dirs., treas., elder Countryside Christian Ctr., Clearwater. Mem. Inst. Fin. Edn. (former 2d v.p. chpt. 51, former 2d v.p. Eastern Seaboard Regional Conf.), Fin. Instn. Security Officers Assn. Pinellas County (dir.), Suncoast Soc. Savs. Officers, Fla. League Fin. Instns. (bd. dirs. 1988—). Home: 2630 Brewton Ct Clearwater FL 34621 Office: 2755 US 19 North Palm Harbor FL 34684

SMALLACOMBE, ROBERT JOSEPH, company executive; b. West Chazy, N.Y., May 26, 1933; s. Bert Henry and Flossie Jean (Relation) S.; m. Terry Mary Fitzpatrick, June 27, 1953; children: Daniel M., Melissa J., Margaret M., James F., Andrew B. BS, SUNY, Plattsburgh, 1960. Foreman composing room Plattsburgh Press-Rep., 1953-60; asst. mgr. prodn. Wall Street Jour. subs. Dow Jones & Co., Mass., Ill., 1960-64; dir. prodn. Washington Daily News, 1964-68; pres. MILGO/IDAB, Miami, Fla. and East Patterson, N.J., 1968-71, Tal-Star Computer Systems, Princeton Junction, N.J., 1971-79; pres., ptnr. Ferag, Inc., Bristol, Pa., 1979-80; pres., chmn. bd. Delta Data Systems Corp., Trevose, Pa., 1981-86; pres., founder Exec. Intervention, Inc., Pennington, N.J., 1986—; pres., chief exec. officer Applied Packaging Tech., Vineland, N.J., 1989—; pres., chief exec. officer Halco Packaging, Inc., Vineland, N.J., 1989—; bd. dirs. Emons Industries Inc., York, Pa., Quipp Inc., Miami, Fla., Tech. Mktg., Inc., Irvine, Calif. Trustee Am. Boychoir Sch., Princeton, N.J., 1979-80, Solebury (Pa.) Sch., 1985. Served with USMC, 1951-53, Korea. Mem. Nat. Assn. Corp. Dirs., World Bus. Council, Phila. Pres.'s Orgn., Am. Inst. Indsl. Engrs., Confrerie de la Chaine des Rotisseurs, Les Amis d'Escoffier. Republican. Roman Catholic. Clubs: Union League (Phila.), Hopewell (N.J.) Valley Country. Home: Stonecroft 321 Phillips Mill Rd New Hope PA 18938 Office: Exec Intervention Inc 65 S Main PO Box 732 Pennington NJ 08534

SMALLEY, KENNETH LEE, oil company executive; b. Custer City, Okla., Feb. 18, 1930; s. Richard Emory and Leila Floy (Ferguson) S.; m. Janet Marie Glasgow, Sept. 5, 1953; children—Susan Jill Smalley Arbour, Mary Kathleen, Lee Anne. B.S. in Engring., U. Okla., 1954. Pres. chems. Phillips Petroleum Europe-Africa, Brussels, 1972-77; mgr. splty. chems. Phillips Chem. Co., Bartlesville, Okla., 1977-79, v.p. petrochems., 1979-81; v.p. minerals Phillips Petroleum Co., Denver and Dallas, 1980-85; sr. v.p. Phillips Petroleum Co., Bartlesville, 1985—; bd. dirs. First Bancshares Inc., First Nat. Bak Bartlesville. Pres. bd. dirs. Internat. Sch., Brussels, 1974-76; bd. dirs. St. Joseph Hosp., Denver, 1982. Decorated Order of Leopold (Belgium). Mem. Natural Gas Processors Assn. (exec. com. 1985), Natural Gas Supply Assn. (exec. com. 1985), Western Regional Conf. (issues com. 1984), U. Okla. Alumni Assn. (bd. dirs. 1977-80). Club: Hillcrest Country (Bartlesville). Home: Denver Pl Bartlesville OK 74003 Office: Phillips Petroleum Co 17 Phillips Bldg Bartlesville OK 74004

SMALLRIDGE, JOHN DAVIN, JR., investment manager; b. Charleston, W.Va., Sept. 10, 1953; s. John Davin and Jane Miles (Giesen) S. BBA, Mid. Tenn. State U., 1977. Div. mgr. F&R Lazarus, Columbus, Ohio, 1977-82; chmn., pres. Smallridge Enterprises Inc., Charleston, 1982—; v.p. Hamilton Corp., Charleston, 1982—; v.p. SportMart, Inc., Charleston, 1982—, also bd. dirs.; bd. dirs. Liberty Bancshares, Montgomery, W.Va., The Steak Escape of Chattanooga, Inc., The Steak Escape of 5th Ave., Inc., The Steak Escape of Warner Centre, Inc., The Steak Escape of Ross Park, Inc., Silver Creek Properties, Inc., Slatyfork, W.Va.; pres., chief exec. officer The Steak Escape of Charleston, Inc., The Steak Escape of Kanawha City, Inc., The Steak Escape of East Towne, Inc., The Steak Escape of Nashville I, Inc. Mem. Old Charleston Task Force, 1987-88. Republican. Presbyterian. Home: 1527 Virginia St E Charleston WV 25311 Office: Smallridge Enterprises Inc 1013 Quarrier St Charleston WV 25301

SMALLWOOD, GLENN WALTER, JR., utility marketing executive; b. Jeffersonville, Ind., Oct. 12, 1956; s. Glenn Walter and Darlene Ruth (Zeller) S.; B.S. in Bus. Adminstrn., SE Mo. State U., 1978. Customer service advisor Union Electric Co., Mexico, Mo., 1979—; instr. Mexico Vo-Tech Sch., 1981; panelist on home design Mo. Extension Service, 1984. Coordinator local United Way, 1984; council mem. Great Rivers council Boy Scouts Am. Mem. Am. Mktg. Assn. (profl.), Nat. Eagle Scout Assn., Copper Dome Soc., Boy Scouts Am. Alumni Family, Mexico area C. of C., Semo U. Alumni Assn. Republican. Lodges: Optimist (cert. appreciation 1982, youth appreciation award 1974), Kiwanis (cert. appreciation 1984). Avocations: music, spectator sports, baseball, basketball, tennis. Office: Union Electric Co PO Box 38 Mexico MO 65265

SMALLWOOD, WALLACE NORMAN, management consultant; b. Rivers, Man., Can., Aug. 30, 1954; came to U.S., 1985; s. Kenneth Le Baron McLeod and Elizabeth Anne (Wardlaw) S.; m. Diana Elaine Williams, Apr. 22, 1978; children: Sarah, Emily, Rachael. BS, Brigham Young U., 1977, M in Organizational Behavior, 1979. Devel. mgr. Procter & Gamble Co., Oglethrorpe, Ga., 1979-80; orgn. effectiveness cons. Esso Resources, Calgary, Alta., Can., 1980-85; ptnr. Novations Group Inc., Provo, Utah, 1985—; adj. prof. Brigham Young U., Provo, 1985—; ptnr. Ctr. for Mng. Profl. Work, Orem, Utah, 1985-86. Contbr. articles to profl. jours. Mormon. Office: Novations Group Inc 226 West 2230 North Ste 201 Provo UT 84604

SMART, DAVID LOUIS, finance executive; b. Dallas, Jan. 29, 1941; s. John Paul and Faye (McDonald) S.; m. Janice Bremer, Jan. 26, 1963; children: Robert, Sharon. B.B.A. with honors, N. Tex. State U., 1963. Various positions, C.P.A. firms 1963-69; mem. corp. staff Tyler Corp., Dallas, 1970-72; asst. treas. Tyler Corp., 1976-78, treas., 1979—, v.p., 1985—; v.p., sec., dir. Smart & Young, Inc., Dallas, 1973-75. Mem. Am. Inst. C.P.A.s, Tex. Soc. C.P.A.s, Tax Execs. Inst. Republican. Baptist. Home: 1208 Clint Carrollton TX 75006 Office: Tyler Corp 3200 San Jacinto Tower Dallas TX 75201

SMART, JOHN ROBERT, telecommunications executive; b. Newark, Mar. 10, 1942; s. Russell Arthur and Esther (Burns) S.; m. Lynn Rand, May 22, 1965; children: Holly A., Andrew T. BS, Bucknell U., 1964; MS in Mgmt., MIT, 1977. Dir. corp. mktg. planning AT&T, Basking Ridge, N.J., 1981, asst. v.p. market planning, 1982, v.p. market mgmt. and ops., 1983; v.p market mgmt. AT&T Communications, Basking Ridge, 1983-84, v.p. bus. markets and services, 1984-86; v.p. mfg. AT&T Network Systems, Morristown, N.J., 1986-87; sr. v.p. bus. sales AT&T (End User Orgn.), Basking Ridge, 1987—. Bd. dirs. Monterey (Calif.) Peninsula Golf Found. Republican. Club: Roxiticus Golf (Mendham, N.J.). Office: AT&T 295 N Maple Ave Room 5305A3 Basking Ridge NJ 07920

SMART, PAUL M., utility company executive, lawyer; b. Middleport, Ohio, Jan. 6, 1929. A.B. summa cum laude, Capital U., 1952; J.D. summa cum laude, Ohio State U., 1953. Bar: Ohio 1953. Ptnr. Fuller & Henry, Toledo, 1959-84; v.p. Toledo Edison Co., 1974-78, sr. v.p., gen. counsel corp. devel., 1984-85, pres., chief oper. officer, 1985-88, vice-chmn., 1988—, also dir.; also exec. v.p. Centerior Energy Corp. Fellow Ohio State Bar Found.; mem. Am. Bar Found., Order of Coif, Phi Delta Phi. Office: Toledo Edison Co 300 Madison Ave Toledo OH 43652 *

SMART, STEPHEN BRUCE, JR., government official; b. N.Y.C., Feb. 7, 1923; s. Stephen Bruce and Beatrice (Cobb) S.; m. Edith Minturn Merrill, Sept. 10, 1949; children: Edith Minturn Smart Moore, William Candler, Charlotte Merrill Smart Rogan, Priscilla Smart Schwarzenbach. Student, Milton Acad.; A.B. cum laude, Harvard U., 1945; S.M., MIT, 1947. Sales engr. Permutit Co., N.Y., 1947-51; various sales, gen. mgmt. positions Continental Group, Inc. (formerly Continental Can Co.), N.Y.C., 1953—, v.p. Central metal div., 1962-65, v.p. marketing and corporate planning, 1965-67, v.p., asst. gen. mgr. paper operations, 1967-69, group v.p. paper operations, 1969-71, exec. v.p. paper operations, 1971-73, vice chmn. bd., 1973-75, pres., 1975-85, chmn., chief exec. officer, 1981-85; undersec. for internat. trade Dept. Commerce, Washington, 1985-88; cons. Dept. State, Washington, 1988—; bd. dirs. Chevron Corp. Served to 1st lt. AUS, 1943-46; C.E. 1951-53. Mem. Council Fgn. Relations, Conf. Bd., The Bus. Council, Sigma Xi. Clubs: Country of Fairfield (Conn.); Pequot Yacht, Links (N.Y.C.). Home: Rte #1 Box 38D Upperville VA 22176

SMELICK, ROBERT MALCOLM, investment banker; b. Phoenix, Mar. 27, 1942; s. Valentine and Mary Helen (McDonald) S.; m. Gail Paine Sterling, Dec. 10, 1979; children: Christopher Paine, Alexandra McBryde, Gillian Sterling. BA, Stanford U., 1964; MBA, Harvard U., 1968; postgrad. U. Melbourne (Australia), 1965-66. V.p. Kidder Peabody & Co., Inc., N.Y.C. and San Francisco, 1968-79; mng. dir. First Boston Corp., San Francisco, 1979-89; prin., founder Sterling Payot Co., San Francisco, 1989—; bd. dirs. King Broadcasting Corp., Seattle, Mayne Nickless Holdings. Republican. Episcopalian. Office: Sterling Payot Co One Montgomery St Telesis Tower Ste #110 San Francisco CA 94104

SMELTZ, RAYMON TECUMSEH, accounting firm executive; b. Spokane, Wash., Jan. 2, 1911; s. Earl Tecumseh and Amanda Rebecca (Link) S.; B.A., Wash. State U., M.A., 1933; postgrad. U. Wash., 1933-34, Columbia U., 1934-35; m. Ruth Dorcas Lewis, June 29, 1934; 1 son, Eric T. Acct. LeMater & Daniels, C.P.A.s, 1942-53, Smeltz & Schoeff, C.P.A.s, 1953-64, Smeltz, C.P.A., Pullman, Wash., 1964-75; partner Smeltz & Lamb, C.P.A.s, Pullman, 1975—; lectr. Wash. State U., 1946-75. Councilman, City of Pullman, 1949-53. Served to 1st lt. U.S. Army, 1943-46. Mem. Am. Inst. C.P.A.s, Wash. State Soc. C.P.A.s. Republican. Lodges: Rotary, Masons. Office: Smeltz & Lamb CPAs 204 Old National Bank Bldg Pullman WA 99163

SMERLING, JULIAN MELVIN, investment company executive; b. N.Y.C., July 27, 1928; s. Louis and Eva (Singer) S.; m. Barbara Albert, Sept. 8, 1962; 1 child, Fern Iris. B.B.A., CCNY, 1949. CPA, N.Y. With various acctg. firms, N.Y.C., 1949-57; v.p. The Dreyfus Corp., N.Y.C., 1958-75; sr. v.p. The Dreyfus Corp., 1975-81, vice-chmn., 1981—, also bd. dirs.; v.p., dir. Dreyfus Svc. Corp. (other subs.), 1968—; bd. dirs., sec. Dreyfus Med. Found.; bd. dirs. Nacolah Holding Corp., Old Greenwich, Conn. Mem. AICPA, N.Y. State Soc. CPA. Home: 84 Lotus Oval S Valley Stream NY 11581 Office: Dreyfus Corp 767 Fifth Ave 35th Fl New York NY 10153

SMETANA, LAWRENCE PAUL, corporate executive; b. Bridgeport, Conn., Jan. 8, 1944; s. Frank A. and Margaret Ann (Kasinak) S.; divorced; children: Paul F., Karen J.; m. Sheila M. Mello, Sept. 10, 1985. BS, U. Bridgeport, 1970; MBA, Fairleigh Dickenson U., 1980. Sales engr. Ingersoll-Rand Co., East Brunswick, N.J., 1970-72; mktg. mgr. Ingersoll-Rand Co., 1972-78; sales dir. Ingersoll-Rand Co., Woodcliff Lakes, N.J., 1978-80; mgr. sales and mktg. Raytheon Laser System, Burlington, Mass., 1982-84; exec. v.p. U.S. Ops. Schneeberger, Inc., Bedford, Mass., 1984—. Author: (handbook) Linear Bearing, 1987; contbr. articles to profl. jours. Mem. ASME, AM. Mktg. Assn. (Student of Yr. 1970), Chief Exec. Officers Club (Boston). Republican. Roman Catholic. Home: 4 Lothrop Circle Lexington MA 02173 Office: Schneeberger Inc 7 DeAngelo Dr Bedford MA 01730

SMIGROD, DANIEL LEE, marketing professional, consultant; b. N.Y.C., July 27, 1956; s. Seymour and Deane (Austin) S. Student, Northwestern U., Evanston, Ill., 1974-76; BA in Journalism, U. N.C., 1978. Dir. promotion Stas. WKIX and WYYD Radio, Raleigh, N.C., 1978-80, Sta. WHYI Radio, Miami, Fla., 1980-82; mgr. advt. and pub. rels. Knight-Ridder's Viewtron, Miami, 1982-86; dir. mktg. devel. program Sta. WTKR TV, Norfolk, Va., 1987; cons. mktg. communications N.Y.C., 1987—; speaker in field. Pub.: Knight-Ridder's Viewtron Mag. and Guide; contbr. articles and photgraphs to profl. publs. Mem. Newsletter Assn. Jewish. Home and Office: 22 Central Park S Ste 6C New York NY 10019

SMILEY, JOSEPH ELBERT, JR., evaluation engineer, librarian; b. Cin., Dec. 21, 1922; s. Joseph Elbert and Esther Marie (Lentz) S.; m. Leona Caroline Besenfelder, Aug. 23, 1953 (dec. Aug. 1986); 1 child, Mary Susan Smiley Liuzzi; m. Betty Concklin, May, 9, 1987. A.A., Edison Community Coll., 1978; B.A., U. S. Fla., 1981, M.A., 1983. Expediter VA, Miami, Fla., 1948-51, analyzer, 1953; evaluation engr. photographic equipment, CIA, Washington, 1953-75. Second v.p. pub. relations Country Club Estates Assn. Lehigh Acres, Inc., 1981-84, pres., 1984-86 ; coordinator, acting zone capt. Lehigh Acres Emergency Preparedness Com., 1983-84, chmn., 1984-86 . Served with U.S. Army, 1942-45, with USAF, 1951-52. Recipient commendation ribbon USAF, 1951; cert. of merit CIA, 1974, certs. of appreciation, 1975, 1981; letter of congratulations Gerald R. Ford, CIA, 1975. Mem. ALA, Fla. Library Assn., Internat. Platform Assn., Phi Theta Kappa, Kappa Delta Pi, Phi Kappa Phi, Beta Phi Mu. Republican. Roman Catholic. Club: KC. Home: 306 Dania St Lehigh Acres FL 33936

SMITH, ADAM See GOODMAN, GEORGE JEROME WALDO

SMITH, ALAN EDWARD, genetic research facility administrator; b. Fareham, Eng., Sept. 9, 1945; came to U.S., 1984; s. William George and Hilda Annie (Fidler) S.; m. Eva Ursula Paucha, Nov. 30, 1979 (dec. 1988); children: Stephen Edward, Alexandra Hannah. BA, U. Cambridge, 1967, PhD, 1970. Mem. sci. staff Imperial Cancer Rsch. Found., London, 1972-80; head biochemistry div. Nat. Inst. Med. Rsch. Mill Hill, London, 1980-84; v.p., sci. dir. Integrated Genetics, Inc., Farmington, Mass., 1984—. Home: 88 Cleveland Rd Wellesley MA 02181 Office: Integrated Genetics Inc 1 Mountain Rd Framington MA 01701

SMITH, ALBERT CROMWELL, JR., investments consultant; b. Norfolk, Va., Dec. 6, 1925; s. Albert Cromwell and Georgie (Foreman) S.; B.S. in Civil Engring., Va. Mil. Inst., 1949; M.S. in Govtl. Adminstrn., George Washington U., 1965; M.B.A., Pepperdine U., 1975; m. Laura Thaxton, Oct. 25, 1952; children—Albert, Elizabeth, Laura. Enlisted USMC, 1944, commd. 2d lt., 1949, advanced through grades to col., 1970; comdr. inf. platoons, companies, landing force; variously assigned staffs U.K. Joint Forces, U.S. Sec. Navy, Brit. Staff Coll., Marine Staff Coll.; adviser, analyst amphibious systems; ret., 1974; pres. A. Cromwell-Smith, Ltd., Charlottesville, Va., 1973, head broker, cons. A. Cromwell Smith, Investments, La Jolla and Coronado, Calif., 1975—. Bd. dirs. Republicans of La Jolla, 1975-76; vestryman St. Martin's Episcopal Ch., 1971-73. Decorated Legion of Merit with oak leaf cluster, Bronze Star medal with oak leaf cluster, Air medal with 2 oak leaf clusters, Purple Heart. Mem. ASCE, Nat., Calif. assns. Realtors, San Diego, Coronado bds. Realtors, Stockbrokers Soc., So. Calif. Options Soc., SAR, Mil. Order Purple Heart. Club: Kona Kai. Author: The Individual Investor in Tomorrow's Stock Market, 1977; The Little Guy's Stock Market Survival Guide, 1979; Wake Up Detroit! The EVs Are Coming, 1982; The Little Guy's Tax Survival Guide, 1984; The Little Guy's Sailboat Success Guide, 1986, The Little Guy's Business Success Guide, 1988; contbr. articles to civilian and mil. publs. Office: 1001 B Ave Ste 319/320 PO Box 192 Coronado CA 92118

SMITH, ALBERT KAY, engineer, mining company executive; b. Orange, N.J., Dec. 31, 1925; s. Albert K. and Anna D. (Hanser) S.; m. Betty E. Hanson, July 21, 1956; 1 child, Kara A. BS in Geol. Engring., U. Idaho. Registered profl. engr., Colo. Engr. indsl. div. Climax Molydenum Co., Colo., 1957-65, chief indsl. engr., 1965-70, supt. tunnel, 1970-75, chief engr., 1975-83; pres. Leadville Silver & Gold, Inc., 1980—; founder, pres., bd. dirs. Lake County TV/FM, Inc., 1956—. Founder, pres., bd. dirs. State Bd. Registration for Profl. Engrs. and Land Surveyors. Mem. AIME (past chmn.), Intermountain Sect. Vail Conf. (founder), Colo. Translator Assn. (founder, pres. 1961-87), Mt. Massive Golf Club (bd. dirs. 1978-80, pres. 1965-70). Home and Office: 1000 Mt View Dr PO Box 283 Leadville CO 80561

SMITH, ALEXANDER FORBES, III, engineering consulting firm executive; b. Reading, Pa., Feb. 7, 1929; s. Alexander Forbes and Ethyl Mohn (Wahl) S.; m. Mary Louise Taylor, Dec. 29, 1970; children: Sandra, Robin, Douglas, Steven. B.S. in M.E., Lehigh U., 1950, M.S. in M.E., 1951. Marine engr. U.S. Naval Boiler & Turbine Lab., Phila., 1951-54; mech. engr. Gilbert Assos., Inc., Reading, Pa., 1955-62, asst. to chief engr., 1962-68, project mgr., 1963-68, v.p. ops., 1968-70, v.p., gen. mgr., 1970-73, exec. v.p., 1973-77, group v.p., chief operating officer, 1977-78, pres., chief exec. officer, 1979—, chmn. bd., 1986—, also bd. dirs., 1970—; chmn. Gilbert/Commonwealth, Inc., 1984—, United Energy Services Corp., 1984—, Autodynamics, Inc., 1984—, GAI-Tonics Corp., 1980—, Resource Consultants Inc., 1988—. Patentee in field. Chmn. adv. bd. Berks Campus, Pa. State Univ., 1979-80; chmn. Berks County Bd. Assistance, 1966-67; trustee YMCA, 1979-86. Mem. ASME, NAM (past bd. dirs.), Pa. Soc. Profl. Engrs., C. of C. (past bd. dirs.), Pa. Bus. Roundtable, Tau Beta Pi, Omicron Delta Kappa, Pi Tau Sigma, Delta Tau Delta. Republican. Episcopalian. Home: Cricket Springs Box 182 Geigertown PA 19523 Office: Gilbert Assocs Inc PO Box 1498 Reading PA 19603

SMITH, ALEXANDER JOHN COURT, insurance executive; b. Glasgow, Scotland, Apr. 13, 1934; s. John Court and Mary Walker (Anderson) S.; m. Margaret Gillespie, Oct. 15, 1968. Student, Scottish schs. Actuarial trainee Scottish Mut. Ins. Co., Glasgow, 1957; asst. actuary Zurich Life Ins. Co., Toronto, Can., 1958-61; from actuary to exec. v.p. William M. Mercer Ltd., Toronto, 1961-74; sr. v.p., dir. Marsh & McLennan Inc., N.Y.C., 1974-78; pres. William M. Mercer, Inc., N.Y.C., 1974-82; group v.p. Marsh & McLennan Cos., Cons. and Fin. Services Group, N.Y.C., 1982-84; pres. Marsh & McLennan Cos., Cons. and Fin. Services Group, 1984-85; vice-chmn. Marsh & McLennan Cos., 1984-86, pres., 1986—; also dir. Marsh & McLennan Cos., Inc., N.Y.C. 1977—; trustee Employee Benefit Research Inst., 1979—. Fellow Faculty Actuaries Edinburgh, Can. Inst. Actuaries, Conf. Actuaries in Public Practice; asso. Soc. Actuaries; mem. Am. Acad. Actuaries, Internat. Congress Actuaries, Internat. Assn. Cons. Actuaries. Clubs: Racquet and Tennis (N.Y.C.); Royal Can. Yacht; Apawamis (Rye, N.Y.); Caledonian (London). Home: 630 Park Ave New York NY 10021 Office: Marsh & McLennan Cos Inc 1221 Ave of the Americas New York NY 10020

SMITH, ALVIN CLARENCE, textiles executive; b. Pickens, S.C., June 8, 1929; s. Ernest Benjamin and Loe (Pace) S.; m. Daisy Ruth Medlin, Aug. 5, 1951; children: Mike, Terry, Rick. BA, Furman U., 1950. Systems mgr. Bigelow Sanford, Greenville, S.C., 1965-80; mgr. data processing dept. World Carpet, Dalton, Ga., 1980-81; contingency coordinator J.P. Stevens & Co., Inc., Greenville, 1981—. 1st lt. U.S. Army, 1951-53, USAR, 1953-60. Mem. Assn. for Systems Mgmt. (pres. 1974-75, Outstanding Svc. award 1974, 75). Republican. Baptist. Home: 102 Pineview Dr Easley SC 29640

SMITH, ANDREW ALFRED, JR., urban planner; b. Lynchburg, Va., Oct. 3, 1947; s. Andrew Alfred and Josephine (Vaughan) S. BArch, Howard U., 1972; M in City Planning, MIT, 1980. Archtl. designer The Architects Collaborative Inc., Cambridge, Mass., 1972-76; archtl. coordinator Fay, Spofford & Thorndike Inc., Boston, 1977-79; city planner N.Y.C. Planning Commn., 1980—. Active Briarwood (N.Y.) Community Assn., 1985—, Cen. Queens YMCA, Jamaica, N.Y. HUD grantee, 1978-80. Mem. Am. Planning Assn., Inst. Urban Design, Nat. Assn. Housing and Redevelopment Officials, Urban Land Inst. (assoc.)., Howard U. Alumni Club L.I. (pres. St. Albans, N.Y. chpt. 1983-85). Democrat. Club: Nat. Travel (Floral Park, N.Y.). Home: 84-55 Daniels St Briarwood NY 11435 Office: NYC Planning Commn 22 Reade St New York NY 10007

SMITH, ANDREW VAUGHN, telephone company executive; b. Roseburg, Oreg., July 17, 1924; s. Andrew Britt and Ella Mae (Vaughn) S.; m. Dorothy LaVonne Crabtree, Apr. 25, 1943; children: Janet L., James A. B.S. in Elec. Engring, Oreg. State U., 1950. Registered profl. engr., Oreg. With Pacific N.W. Bell Telephone Co., 1951-88; asst. v.p. ops. Pacific N.W. Bell Telephone Co., Seattle, 1965; v.p., gen. mgr. Pacific N.W. Bell Telephone Co., Portland, Oreg., 1965-70; v.p. ops. Pacific N.W. Bell Telephone Co., Seattle, 1970-78, pres., 1978-88; pres. ops. U.S. West Communications, 1988-89; exec. v.p. U.S. West Inc., 1989—; bd dirs. U.S. Bancorp, Portland, Unigard Mut. and Unigard Ins. Cos., Univar Corp., Seattle, Cascade Natural Gas, Seattle, Airborne Freight Corp., Seattle, VWR Corp., Seattle, Aldus Corp., Seattle. Trustee Oreg. State U. Found., U. Wash. Grad. Sch. Bus., 1985; chmn. bd. trustees U. Wash. Grad. Sch. Bus., 1984-85; gen. chmn. United Way of King County, 1980-81; trustee Wash. State Internat. Trade Fair; mem. Seattle Urban League. Served with USNR, 1943-46. Mem. Seattle C. of C. (chmn. 1985-86). Episcopalian. Clubs: Harbor, Washington Athletic, Seattle Yacht, Rainier, Overlake Golf and Country, Arlington, Multnomah (Portland), Columbia Tower (Seattle). Lodge: Masons. Office: US West Inc 1600 Bell Pla Rm 1802 Seattle WA 98191

SMITH, BARBARA LOUISE, retail executive; b. Boone, Iowa, Jan. 1, 1943; d. Frederick O. and Ednamay (Schmidt) Erbe; m. Richard M. Smith, Jan. 24, 1965; children: Janet L., Richard M. II. BS, Iowa State U., 1964. Tchr. home econs. Dike (Iowa) Community Sch., 1965-66; v.p., chief exec. officer As You Like It Card and Gift Shops, various locations in Iowa, 1968—. Pres., Grundy Ctr. (Iowa) Sch. Bd., 1983-84, mem. 1980-86.; v.p., mem. bd. dirs. Grundy Ctr. Devel. Corp., 1982—. Republican. Presbyterian. Home: 1402 H Ave Grundy Center IA 50638 Office: As You Like It Card & Gift Shops Box 35 Grundy Center IA 50638

SMITH, BERNARD JOSEPH, civil engineer, consultant; b. Liverpool, Eng., Aug. 29, 1900; s. Thomas J. and Sarah Anne (Crum) S.; came to U.S., 1912, naturalized, 1930; student St. Edward's Coll., Liverpool, 1914-20; ed. Oxford U., Eng., 1918; B.Engring. with honors, U. Liverpool, 1923, M.Engring., 1926; m. Julia Susan Connolly, June 4, 1929; children—Bernard, Sarah Anne Kathleen, Maureen, Una, Aislin, Malachy, Joan, John. Pvt. tutor in math. and physics, Liverpool, 1923-24; field engr. Underpinning & Found. Co., N.Y.C., 1924; underground conduit engr. N.Y. and N.J. Bell Telephone Co., 1924-25, Ohio Bell Telephone Co., Toledo, 1925-26; asst. engr. to Alexander Potter, cons. engr. on water and sewerage systems, N.Y.

and N.J., 1926-30; design engr. Humble Oil & Refining Co., Baytown, Tex., 1930-32; city mgr. and engr. City of Baytown, 1932-33, cons. engr., 1933-34; engr. examiner Pub. Works Adminstrn., Ft. Worth, 1935-37; dir. research and personnel City of Ft. Worth, 1938-42; acting state dir. and state planning engr. Tex. Pub. Works Res., 1942; asst. regional dir. and regional economist Nat. Housing Agy., hdqrs. Dallas, 1942-46; cons. engr. on water systems and town planning, Dallas, 1946-65; cons. tides and water resources, San Francisco, 1965—, also Aptos, Calif.; water commr. Santa Cruz County, Calif.; planning engr. and chief San Francisco Bay sect. U.S. Corps of Engrs., 1957-65; lectr. urban devel. Tex. Christian U., Ft. Worth, 1939-43; guest lectr. on town devel. Ala. Poly. Inst., 1940; instr. econs. and engring. So. Meth. U., Dallas, 1943-53; guest panelist Ann. Radio Conf., U. Okla., Norman, 1946; speaker on econs. and town planning to various civic and bus. groups, 1939—; v.p. Southwestern States Water Co., 1949-51. Mem. bd. govs. Dallas Fed. Reference Exchange, 1943-46. Registered profl. engr., Calif., N.J., Tex.; registered pub. surveyor, Tex. Fellow ASCE (com. city planning tng. for civil engrs. 1942); mem. Am. Waterworks Assn., AAAS, Am., Western econ. assns., Assn. Evolutionary Econs., History of Econs. Soc., County Louth (Eire) Archeol. Soc., Irish Lit. and Hist. Soc. of San Francisco (pres. 1959-62), Sierra Club. Club: Commonwealth of Calif. Contbr. articles and reports on water systems, flood control, urban devel. and pollution to profl. publs. Home: 1446 Day Valley Rd Aptos CA 95003 Office: PO Box 663 Aptos CA 95003

SMITH, BERNARD JOSEPH CONNOLLY, civil engineer; b. Elizabeth, N.J., Mar. 11, 1930; s. Bernard Joseph and Julia Susan (Connolly) S.; B.S., U. Notre Dame, 1951; B.S. in Civil Engring., Tex. A&M U., 1957; M.B.A. in Fin., U. Calif.-Berkeley, 1976; m. Josephine Kerley, Dec. 20, 1971; children—Julia Susan Alice, Teresa Mary Josephine, Anne Marie Kathleen. Asst. Bernard J. Smith, cons. engr. office, Dallas, 1947-57; hydraulic engr. C.E., U.S. Army, San Francisco, 1957-59, St. Paul dist., 1959-60, Kansas City (Mo.) dist., 1960-63, Sacramento dist., 1963-65; engr. Fed. Energy Regulatory Commn., San Francisco Regional Office, 1965—. Served with U.S. Army, 1952-54. Registered profl. engr., Calif., Mo.; lic. real estate broker, Calif. Mem. ASCE (sec. power div. San Francisco sect. 1969), Soc. Am. Mil. Engrs. (treas. Kansas City post 1962), Am. Econ. Assn., Nat. Soc. Profl. Engrs., Res. Officers Assn. (chpt. pres. 1973). Club: Commonwealth of Calif. Home: 247 28th Ave San Francisco CA 94121 Office: Fed Energy Regulatory Commn 333 Market St San Francisco CA 94105

SMITH, BILLIE M., aircraft company executive; b. Littlefield, Tex., Sept. 4, 1933; s. James W. and Gracie Inez (Ratliff) S.; m. Faye Brewer, May 5, 1985. BS in Math. and Chemistry, Tex. A&I U., 1953. Project engr. Phillips Petroleum Co., McGregor, Tex., 1953-54, 55-58; project mgr., minuteman Thiokol Chem. Corp., Brigham City, Utah, 1958-60; program dir. Titan III United Tech. Corp., Sunnyvale, Calif., 1960-66; mgr. advanced launch systems LTV Aerospace and Def. Co., Mich., 1966-67, chief engr. systems integration, 1967-68, dep. program dir. Lance, 1968-69, v.p. Lance, 1970-72, v.p., gen. mgr., 1972-77; sr. v.p. advanced programs LTV Aerospace and Def. Co., Dallas, 1977-78, sr. v.p. Multiple Launch Rocket System program, 1978-83, sr. v.p., gen. mgr. MLRS div., 1983-85, exec. v.p., gen. missiles and advanced programs div., pres. aircraft products group, 1985—. Vice chmn. Dallas County U.S. Savs. Bond Campaign, Dallas, 1986-87, Tarrant County U.S. Savs. Bond Campaign, Ft. Worth, 1987. Served as sgt. U.S. Army, 1954-55. Recipient Outstanding Achievement award Missiles and Rockets Mag., 1965. Mem. Am. Def. Preparedness Assn., Assn. U.S. Army, AIAA, U.S. Field Artillery Assn., Navy League (life), Alphi Chi. Office: L2V Aircraft Products Group PO Box 655907 Dallas TX 75265-5907

SMITH, BRICE REYNOLDS, JR., engineering company executive; b. St. Louis; s. Brice Reynolds and Frances Matilda (Cook) S.; m. Jane Medart; children: Brice Reynolds III, Victoria D. Smith Trauscht, Hollis M. Smith Norman, Karen C., Todd E. B.C.E., U. Mo., Columbia, 1951; M.C.E., MIT, 1952; Cert. advanced mgmt. program, Harvard U., Hawaii, 1961. Registered profl. engr., D.C., Fla., Kans., Md., Mass., Mich., Mo., N.D., Ohio, Oreg., Tenn., Va., N.C. Resident engr. Sverdrup & Parcel, St. Louis, 1954-59, asst. to v.p. fgn. ops., 1959-64, treas., 1964-69, v.p., treas., 1970-75; exec. v.p. Sverdrup Corp., St. Louis, 1976-81, pres., 1982-86, pres., chief exec. officer, 1986-88, also bd. dirs., chmn. bd., pres., chief exec. officer, 1988—; dir. Boatmen's Trust Co., St. Louis; chmn. bd. dirs. Convention Plaza Redevel. Corp., St. Louis. Bd. dirs. Civic Progress, Inc., United Way of Greater St. Louis, Arts and Edn. Council Greater St. Louis, Boy Scouts Am. St. Louis Area Coun., . Served to 1st lt., USAF, 1952-54. Recipient Mo. Honor award for Disting. Service to Engring., U. Mo., 1979; Levee Stone award, Downtown St. Louis, Inc., 1982. Fellow Am. Cons. Engrs. Council; mem. ASCE, Cons. Engrs. Council Mo. (past pres.), Mo. Soc. Profl. Engrs., Nat. Soc. Profl. Engrs., The MOLES. Clubs: Bellerive Country, Log Cabin, Noonday, St. Louis (St. Louis). Office: Sverdrup Corp 801 N 11th St Saint Louis MO 63101

SMITH, CAROLINE MADDOX, economist, consultant; b. Norfolk, Va., Aug. 16, 1944; d. John Lucian and Louise (Outland) S.; m. John William Wilson, Mar. 27, 1980. BA, William & Mary Coll., 1967; MBA, Old Dominion U., 1969; PhD, U. Tex., 1974. Asst. prof. Va. Poly. Inst., Blacksburg, 1974-76; chief economist Tex. Pub. Utility Commn., Austin, 1976-78; economist, officer J.W. Wilson & Assocs., Inc., Washington, 1978—. Office: JW Wilson & Assocs Inc 2600 Virginia Ave NW Washington DC 20037

SMITH, CAROLYN SUE, oil company executive; b. Doeran, Ga., Feb. 17, 1944; d. James Washington and Corrie Irene (Hufstetler) Gunn; m. Jack Samuel Smith Sr., Apr. 3, 1942; children: Jack, Jill, Jody, John. Grad., Worth County High Sch., 1962. Lic. real estate. Program asst. USDA-ASCS Office, Moultrie, Ga., 1973-76; exec. Lubrico, Inc., Albany, Ga., 1977-83; owner, chief exec. officer S.E. Oil & Grease Co., Inc., Albany, 1983—. Mem. Women Bus. Owners, Nat. Lubricating Grease Inst., Am. Soc. Lubrication Engrs., Women In Constrn. Republican. Baptist. Lodge: Elks. Home: PO Box 4340 Albany GA 31706 Office: SE Oil & Grease Co Inc PO Box 4897 Albany GA 31706

SMITH, CARTER BLAKEMORE, broadcaster; b. San Francisco, Jan. 1, 1937; s. Donald V. and Charlotte M. (Nichols) S.; children: Carter Blakemore, Clayton M. AA, City Coll. San Francisco, 1958; BA, San Francisco State U., 1960; postgrad. N.Y. Inst. Finance, 1969-70; Assoc. in Fin. PLanning, Coll. for Fin. Planning, 1984. Announcer, Sta. KBLF, Red Bluff, Calif., 1954-56; personality Sta. KRE-KRE FM, Berkeley, Calif., 1958-63, Sta. KSFO, San Francisco, 1963-72, Sta. KNBR, San Francisco, 1972-83, Sta. KSFO, San Francisco, 1983-86, Sta. KFRC, San Francisco, 1986—; mem. faculty radio-TV dept. San Francisco State U., 1960-61. Mem. adv. bd. Little Jim Club Children's Hosp., 1968-71; bd. dirs. Marin County Humane Soc., 1968-73, San Francisco Zool. Soc., 1980—; trustee Family Service Agy. Marin, 1976-85; mem. alumni bd. Lowell High Sch. Recipient award San Francisco Press Club, 1965; named one of Outstanding Young Men in Am. U.S. Jaycees, 1972. Mem. Amateur Radio Relay League (life), Quarter Century Wireless Assn., Alpha Epsilon Rho. Office: Sta KFRC 500 Washington St San Francisco CA 94111

SMITH, CHARLES R., III, treasury manager; b. Ft. Riley, Kans., Oct. 3, 1956; s. Charles R. Jr. and Nancy H Smith; m. Laura Burrus, Mary 26, 1984; 1 child, Charles IV. BS in Civil Engring., Ga. Inst. Tech., 1978, MBA, 1982. Project engr. Marathon Oil Co, Houston, 1978-80; treas. analyst Scientific-Atlanta Inc., Atlanta, 1982-84, cash mgr., 1984—. Mem. Atlanta Treasury Mgmt. Assn. (pres. 1986-87), Nat. Corp. Cash Mgmt. Assn. Methodist. Office: Scientific-Atlanta Inc 1 Technology Park Norcross GA 30092

SMITH, CHESTER, broadcasting executive; b. Wade, Okla., Mar. 29, 1930; s. Louis L. and Effie (Brown) S.; m. Naomi L. Crenshaw, July 19, 1959; children: Lauri, Lorna, Roxanne. Country western performer on Capitol records, TV and radio, 1947-61; owner, mgr. Sta. KLOC, Ceres-Modesto, Calif., 1963-81, Sta. KCBA-TV, Salinas-Monterey, Calif., 1981-86; owner, ptnr. Sta. KCSO-TV, Modesto-Stockton-Sacramento, Sta. KREN-TV, Reno, Nev., Sta. KBCP-TV, Paradise-Chico, Calif., Sta. KO7TA-TV, Santa Maria, Calif., Sta. KO9UF-TV, Morro Bay, Calif., 1986—. Mem. Calif. Broadcasters Assn. Republican. Mem. Christian Ch. original rec. Wait A Little Longer Please Jesus; named to Country Music Hall of Fame, Nashville, 1955, Western Swing hall of Fame, Sacramento, 1988.

SMITH, DANIEL R., bank holding company executive; b. 1934. With First of Am. Bank of Mich., 1955-82, sr. v.p., 1971-77, pres., then pres., chief exec. officer, 1977-82; with First of Am. Bank Corp., Kalamazoo, 1972—, pres., 1982-85, chmn. bd., chief exec. officer, 1985—. Capt. USAR, 1955-64. Office: 1st Am Bank Corp 108 E Michigan Ave Kalamazoo MI 49007

SMITH, DARWIN EATNA, paper and consumer products manufacturing company executive, lawyer; b. Garrett, Ind., Apr. 16, 1926; s. K. Bryant and Hazel (Sherman) S.; m. Lois Claire Archbold, Aug. 19, 1950; children: Steven, Pamela, Valerie, Blair. B.S. in Bus. with distinction, Ind. U., 1950; LL.B. cum laude, Harvard, 1955. Bar: Ill. 1955, Wis. 1958. Assoc. atty. firm Sidley, Austin, Burgess & Smith, Chgo., 1955-58; With Kimberly-Clark Corp., Neenah, Wis., 1958—; gen. atty. Kimberly-Clark Corp., 1960—, v.p., 1962-67, v.p. finance and law, 1967-70, pres., 1970—, chmn., chief exec. officer, 1971—. Served with AUS, 1944-46. Office: Kimberly-Clark Corp APO Box 619100 Dallas TX 75261

SMITH, DARYL D., chemical company executive; b. Carlsbad, N.Mex., Dec. 28, 1940; s. Eldon C. Smith and Mace (Vaughter) Moreland; m. Marilyn Ingram Hall (div. 1986); children: Courtney, William Brian, Christopher Emery. BA, Dartmouth Coll., 1963; BEE, Thayer Sch. Engring., 1964; MBA, U. Pa. Mgr. planning Internat. Paper Co., N.Y.C., 1976-78; dir. fin. and planning E. Asiatic Co., N.Y.C., 1978-79; exec. v.p. Troy Chem. Corp., Newark, 1980-87, pres., 1987—, also bd. dirs. Bd. dirs. Theatre for New Audience, N.Y.C., 1988—. Capt. U.S. Army, 1975-77, Vietnam. Decorated Bronze Star. Republican. Episcopalian. Office: Troy Chem Corp 1 Ave L Newark NJ 07015

SMITH, DAVID CALLAWAY, accounting firm executive; b. Dallas, Aug. 28, 1941; s. Stanley W. and Julia M. (Callaway) S.; m. Marijane Dekema, May 5, 1961; children: Stephanie, Scott. BBA, Western Mich. U., 1964. Profl. staff, mgr. Peat Marwick Mitchell & Co., Chgo., 1964-71, ptnr., 1971-78; ptnr. in charge tax dept. Peat Marwick Mitchell & Co., Houston, 1978-87; vice-chmn. tax dept. KPMG Peat Marwick, N.Y.C., 1987—. Mem. AICPA, N.Y. State Soc. CPA's, Econ. Club of N.Y. Republican. Presbyterian. Office: KPMG Peat Marwick 767 Fifth Ave New York NY 10153

SMITH, DAVID EDWARD, business executive; b. Battle Creek, Mich., Sept. 16, 1939; s. Hebdin Leslie and Dureatha Rosella (Stephens) S.; m. Margaret Eugenia Clark, June 13, 1964; 1 child, Wendy Leigh. Student, Kellogg Community Coll., 1957-58; BS in Mech. Engring., Mich State U., 1962. Engr., scientist Douglas Aircraft Co., Santa Monica, Calif., 1962-63, McDonnell Douglas Astronautics Co., Cape Kennedy, Fla., 1963-78; broker salesman Cape Kennedy Realty, Inc., Cape Canaveral, Fla., 1978-87; pres., founder Cash Flow Seminars, Merritt Island, Fla., 1979—, Cash Flow Systems, Inc., Merritt Island, Fla., 1983—; lectr. numerous fin. convs. and orgns., including: Fla., Calif., Am. League Savs. Instns., Fin. Instns. Mktg. Assn., Acad. of Real Estate, Am. Congress on Real Estate; distbr. Hewlett Packard Corp., 1985-88; dir. comml. investment div. CKBOR, Merritt Island, 1978-79; mem. adv. bd., lectr. Fin Freedom Report, Salt Lake City, 1985—, Nat. Inst. Fin. Planning, Salt Lake City, 1985—; instr. Fla. Real Estate Commn., La. Real Estate Commn., Fla. Bd. Accountancy, Am. Inst. of Real Estate Appraisors. Author: Turbo-Diesel, The Time Value of Money, Creative Financing Techniques; contbr. numerous fin. articles to jours. and mags. Mem. Fla. Real Estate Exchangors, Internat. Platform Assn. Republican. Office: Cash Flow Seminars PO Box 540634 Merritt Island FL 32954-0634

SMITH, DAVID F., human resources executive; b. Providence, July 12, 1931; s. David F. and Mary A. (MacLeod) S.; m. Joan P. Boelens, Aug. 23, 1952 (div. 1980); children: Kathleen G., Cynthia J., David F. BS, Bryant Coll., 1956. With human resources dept. Korn Ferry Internat., N.Y.C. Sgt. U.S. Army, 1952-53, Korea. Decorated Purple Heart, Bronze Star, Silver Star, 1953. Home: 11 Fifth Ave New York NY 10003 Office: Korn Ferry Internat 237 Park Ave New York NY 10017

SMITH, DAVID KINGMAN, oil company executive; b. Malone, N.Y., June 5, 1928; s. Ernest DeAlton and Louisa Kingman (Bolster) S.; m. Lois Louise Wing, June 13, 1959; children: Mara Louise, David Andrew. BS in Engring., Princeton U., 1952. Registered profl. engr., Tex. Civil engr., supt. Raymont Internat. Inc., N.Y.C., 1952-55, asst. v.p., 1970-71, v.p., 1971-74; group v.p. Raymont Internat. Inc., Houston, 1974-80; mgr. Raymond-Brown and Root, Maracaibo, Venezuela, 1955-70; sr. engring. assoc. Exxon Prodn. Rsch. Co., Houston, 1980-81, supr., 1982—. Pres. Yorkshire Civic Assn., Houston, 1979-80, trustee, 1985—. With U.S. Army, 1946-48, PTO. Mem. ASCE, Soc. Petroleum Engrs. (treas. 1987-88), Nat. Soc. Profl. Engr., Men's Garden Club Houston, Tex. Soc. Profl. Engr., Am. Legion. Republican. Methodist. Home: 611 W Forest St Houston TX 77079 Office: Exxon Prodn Rsch Co PO Box 2189 Houston TX 77252-2189

SMITH, DAVID MICHAEL, financial executive; b. East Lansing, Mich., Mar. 15, 1949; s. Carl Bernard and Susanna Marie (Nelson) S.; m. Sandra Ann Smith, Aug. 13, 1977; children: David M. Jr., Nikolai Ryan. BS, U.S. Mil. Acad., 1971. Cert. fin. planner. Pvt. practice fin. planning Boeblingen, Fed. Republic Germany, 1977-80; pres. Intervest Internat. Inc., Boeblingen, 1980—; cons. IDS/Am. Express, Mpls., 1986-88. Capt. U.S. Army, 1971-77. Mem. Inst. Cert. Planners, Internat. Assn. for Fin. Planning (v.p. 1987—), Nat. Assn. Securities Dealers (registered prin.). Republican. Roman Catholic. Office: Intervest Internat Inc, Am Kaeppele 24, 7030 Boeblingen Federal Republic of Germany

SMITH, DELMONT KING, textile executive, consultant; b. Pocatello, Idaho, June 9, 1927; s. Leslie H. and Adelia A. (Loveland) S.; m. Velva Lee Stokes, Sept. 18, 1946; children: Linda L., Constance M., Dennis D., Shawna M., David M. BS, Utah State U., 1949, MS, 1955; PhD, Purdue U., 1954. Rsch. mgr. Rayonier, inc., Whippany, N.J., 1956-61; dir. woven products rsch. Chicopee (Mass.) Johnson and Johnson, 1961-70; dir. tech. planning Chicopee (Mass.) Johnson and Johnson, New Brunswick, N.J., 1970-85; cons. Mesa, Ariz., 1985—. Author chpts. in book; contbr. articles to profl. jours.; patentee in field. Served with USNR, 1945-46. Recipient Chmn. award INDA Assn. of Nonwovens Industry, 1977. Mormon. Home and Office: 3112 E Hampton Ave Mesa AZ 85204

SMITH, DENNIS CARL, plastics laboratory administrator; b. Monroeville, Ohio, Oct. 18, 1962; s. Adelbert Carl and Margaret Mary Smith; m. Danielle L. Love, Aug. 6, 1988. AAS in Plastics Tech., Shawnee State U., 1984; BS in Mfg. Tech., Bowling Green State U., 1987. Lab. technician PMS Consol. Inc., Norwalk, Ohio, 1982-83; rsch. and devel. technician A. Schulman, Inc., Bellevue, Ohio, 1984-87, lab. supr., 1987; lab. mgr. Bioplastics Co., Inc., North Ridgeville, Ohio, 1987—. Mem. Soc. Mfg. Engrs., Soc. Plastics Engrs. Home: 12 Ford Ave Norwalk OH 44857 Office: Bioplastics Co Inc North Ridgeville OH 44039

SMITH, DIMITRIE JAMES, SR., retail executive; b. New Orleans, Apr. 17, 1955; s. Herbert and Laura Lee (O'Quinn) S.; m. Linda Mae Wilkeason, Apr. 17, 1976 (div. Jan. 1981); children: Kimberly Ann, Dimitrie Jr. AA, Springfield Tech. Community Coll., 1975; BS in Archtl. Design, Coyahoga Coll., 1977; postgrad., U. Mass., 1986. Coordinator Milton Bradley Co., East Longmeadow, Mass., 1979-82; mktg. specialist TZ Assocs., West Springfield, Mass., 1985—; cons., 1985—; owner D.S. Systems, Springfield, 1987—; educator, tech. support Digital Equipment Corp., Springfield, 1983-88. Active Assn. for Childhood Edn. Internat. With USAF, 1979-81. Mem. Am. Soc. for Tng. and Devel., Am. Entrepreneurs' Assn., Assn. Supervision & Curriculum Devel. Republican. Baptist. Office: DS Systems PO Box 90574 HS Springfield MA 01139

SMITH, DONALD ANDREW, real estate development company executive; b. Phila., May 1, 1950; s. David James and Doris (Haines) S.; m. Melinda Ziegenfuss, Sept. 12, 1977; children: Andrew, Bradley. BA, U. N.C., 1972; MBA, Emory U., 1975; postgrad., Northwestern U., 1976. Assoc. officer Trust Co. Ga., Atlanta, 1974-76; sr. lending v.p. Continental Ill. Bank, Chgo., 1976-81; v.p. Jupiter Industries, Chgo., 1981—; pres. Jupiter Realty Corp., Chgo., 1986—, bd. dirs., 1985—; bd. dirs. Enterprise Savs. Bank, Chgo., Washington Capital Assocs. Bd. dirs. Evanston (Ill.) Inventure, 1985—. Mem. Urban Land Inst., Mid Day Club, Sheridan Shores Club. Republican. Office: Jupiter Realty Corp 919 N Michigan Ave Chicago IL 60611

SMITH, DONALD RAY, magazine dealer; b. Louisville, Dec. 12, 1934; s. Henry Bland and Margaret Frances (Corbett) S. Ed. pvt. schs., Louisville. Clerk Huber & Huber Motor Express, Louisville, 1951-52, Retail Credit Co., Louisville, 1952-53, Louisville & Nashville R.R., Louisville, 1953-65; owner, appraiser, cons. Don Smith's Nat. Geog. Mags., Louisville, 1969—. Author: (books) Nat. Geog. Mag. for Collectors, 1975, 3d ed., 1985, Gone With the Wagons, 1980; composer song, My Dreams Desire Another Way, 1968, poem, Calico Waltz, 1986, Beyond Repast, 1986, The Essence of Darkness, 1986, The Dominant Submissive, 1987, Agony'd Prelude, 1987, The Unmoving Distance, 1988; price guide booklet for collectors of Nat. Geographic mag.; also numerous pamphlets and articles on collecting mags. Democrat. Roman Catholic. Home and Office: 3930 Rankin St Louisville KY 40214

SMITH, DOUGLAS LARUE, marketing executive; b. Madison, Minn., July 25, 1917; s. Julius Waldo and Blanche (LaRue) S.; m. Jean Hefty, Feb. 8, 1941 (dec. 1979); children: Pamela Jean (Mrs. Robert Graham), and Gregory Douglas.; m. Annice Kerwin, Mar. 20, 1982. B.A., U. Minn., 1948. Employed with U.S. Gypsum Company, Chicago, Ill., 1938-42; account exec. Melamed-Hobbs, Inc. (advt.), Mpls., 1946-49; product mgr. Swift & Co., Chgo., 1949-53; account exec. Batten, Barton, Durstine & Osborn, 1953-55; advt. mgr. Johnson's Wax Co., Racine, Wis., 1955-56; dir. advt. and mktg. Johnson's Wax Co., 1956-64; sr. v.p. Lennen & Newell, Inc., N.Y.C., 1965-70; also dir., mem. exec. com.; sr. v.p. On-Line Decisions, Inc. (became Planmetrics, Inc. 1975), N.Y.C., 1970—; exec. v.p. Planmetrics, Inc., N.Y.C., 1981-88; lectr. and author, 1988—; chmn. bd. dirs. Assn. Nat. Advertisers, N.Y.C., 1965; bd. dirs. Advt. Fedn. Am., 1961—, Advt. Assn. West, 1962—. Author: Winged Foot Story, 1984. Mem. exec. com. Republican Party N.Y.C. Served to maj., inf. AUS, 1942-46, ETO. Decorated Bronze Star. Mem. Am. Assn. Advt. Agys. (gov. Eastern div.), Internat. Radio and Television Soc. (dir., treas.). Clubs: University (N.Y.C., Chgo.); Mid-Am. (Chgo.); Winged Foot Golf. Home: 249 E 48th St New York NY 10017 Office: 18 E 48th St New York NY 10017

SMITH, DWIGHT LEON, furniture company executive; b. Watervliet, Mich., June 4, 1946; s. Duard Lee and Lois Estelle (Lindsey) S.; m. Linda Carole Perry, July 16, 1967; children: Devin Lindsey, Jordan Paige. BA, Mich. State U., 1971. Buyer Nat. Standard Co., Niles, Mich., 1973-75; purchasing mgr. Rockwell Internat. Co., Galesburg, Ill., 1975-78; purchasing mgr., dir. mgmt. info. systems Beatrice Foods Corp., Skokie, Ill., 1978-84; procurement mgr. Multigraphics Corp., Mount Prospect, Ill., 1984-86; v.p. materials mgmt. Schnadig Corp., Chgo., 1986—. Mem. Am. Prodn. and Inventory Control Soc., Nat. Assn. Purchasing Mgrs.

SMITH, EDGAR NEWBOLD, investment executive; b. Phila., July 20, 1926; s. William Dulty and Portia Hulme (Black) S.; m. Margaret duPont, Sept. 30, 1950; children: Eleuthera Bradford, Stockton Newbold, Lewis du-Pont, Henry Belin duPont. BS, U.S. Naval Acad., 1948; MBA, U. Pa., 1956. Engr. E.I. duPont Nemours, Wilmington, Del., 1949-54; v.p. Laird & Co., N.Y.C., 1956-63, Laird, Bissell & Meeds, Wilmington, 1964-70, Drexel Firestone, Phila., 1970-72, Blue Bell (Pa.) Co., 1973-74; pres., founder E.N. Smith Co., Phila., 1974—; bd. dirs. Bell Co., West Chester, Pa. Author: Am. Naval Broadsidea, 1974, Down Denmark Strait, 1980. Trustee Phila. Maritime Mus., 1969—, Ch. Farm Sch., Exton, Pa., 1970—, Mystic Seaport, Conn., 1965-78, Pa. Hist. Soc., 1978-84. Lt. (j.g.) U.S. Navy, 1944-49. Mem. Explorers Club, Royal Cruising Club, Cruising Club of Am. (Blue Water medal 1977), New York Yacht Club. Republican. Episcopalian. Office: E N Smith Co Paoli PA 19301

SMITH, EDWIN LEON, retired credit manager; b. Burlington, Iowa, Mar. 17, 1924; s. Paul Smith and Gertrude Eldora (Hollenback) Rhoades; m. Norma Geraldine McGaffee, July 14, 1943; 1 child, Bradley Warren. BSBA, U. Redlands, 1980. Credit mgr. Reynolds Metals, Los Angeles, 1956-63, Hoffman Electronics, El Monte, Calif., 1965-70, Thomson-C.S.F. Components Corp., Woodland Hills, Calif., 1973-86. Pres. Woodland Townehome Owners' Assn., 1975, 85-86; landscape chmn. Dove Creek Condominium Assn. Served with USNR, 1942-45, PTO. Fellow Nat. Inst. Credit; mem. Soc. Profl. Credit Mgrs., Woodland Hills C. of C. Republican. Presbyterian. Home: 6225 104 Shoup Ave Woodland Hills CA 91367

SMITH, ELAINE ANN, financial executive; b. Galveston, Tex., Nov. 16, 1947; d. James Franklin and Louise Edna (Brown) Durst; m. James George Rhinehardt Smith; children: Stacy Smith Black, Patricia Kay Nelson Kantowski, Noel Kenneth Nelson, Richard Kevin Nelson. Student, Galveston Coll., 1980, Coll. Mainland, 1982, Tex. A&M U., 1985. Trust ops. officer Moody Nat. Bank, Galveston, 1970-81; mem. legal and tax staff Levy, Levy & Smith, Galveston, 1981-82; tax preparer Quinn-L Tax Svc. Inc., Shreveport, La., 1982-85; gen. ptnr. Taxsmith of Am. Inc., Galveston, 1985-86; pres. Taxsmith of Am. Inc., League City, Tex., 1986—. Mem. Am. Bus. Assn., Tex. Enrolled Agts. Soc., North Galveston County C. of C. Espicopalian. Office: Taxsmith of Am Inc 711 Bay Area Blvd Ste 610 Webster TX 77598

SMITH, ELIZABETH LANEY (BETH LANEY SMITH), advertising executive, public relations; b. Pageland, S.C.; d. Howard Gibson and Lona Agnes (Nicholson) Laney; divorced; 1 child, Edward Laney. AB cum laude, U. S.C., 1944. Editor After Hours for Am. Mission, Athens, Greece, 1948-49, Safari for C.E., Tripoli, Libya, 1951-52; account exec. Ayer & Gillett Advt., Charlotte, N.C., 1953-61; owner, operator Laney-Smith Inc., Charlotte, 1961—. Author: A Foundry, Vol. 1, 1977, A Centennial Celebration, 1989; editor: A History of the Early Years..., 1984; columnist The Dwelling Place, 1986. Mem. Nat. Trust Historic Preservation, Women in Communications, Nat. Home Fashions League (nat. sec. 1973-74), Advt. Club Charlotte (pres. 1961-62), Historic Preservation Found. N.C., Phi Beta Kappa. Republican.

SMITH, ELOUISE BEARD, restaurant owner; b. Richmond, Tex., Jan. 8, 1920; d. Lee Roy and Ruby Myrtle (Foy) Beard; m. Omar Smith, Nov. 27, 1940 (dec. July 1981); children: Mary Jean Smith Cherry, Terry Omar, Don Alan. Student, Tex. Womens U., 1937-39. Sec. First Nat. Bank, Rosenberg, Tex., 1939-41; owner Smith Dairy Queens, Bryan, Tex., 1947—. Author: The Haunted House, 1986; editor The College Widow, 1986. Omar and Elouise Beard Smith chair named in her honor Tex. A&M U., College Station, 1983, Elouise Beard Smith Human Performance Labs. named in her honor Tex. A&M U., 1984. Mem. AAUW. Republican. Baptist. Home: 411 Crescent Dr Bryan TX 77801 Office: Metro Ctr 3833 S Texas Ave Bryan TX 77802

SMITH, ERIC PARKMAN, retired railroad executive; b. Cambridge, Mass., Mar. 23, 1910; s. B. Farnham and Helen T. (Blanchard) S.; A.B., Harvard U., 1932, M.B.A., 1934. Staff fed. coordinator transp., Washington, 1934; with traffic and operating depts. N.Y. New Haven & Hartford R.R., Boston and New Haven, Conn., 1934-53; with Maine Central R.R., Portland, 1953-82, sec. adv. bd. retirement trust plan, 1958-82, asst. treas., dir. cost analysis, 1970-82. Trustee parish donations 1st Parish in Concord, Unitarian-Universalist Ch., 1960—. Mem. New Eng. R.R. Club (pres. 1973-74), Louisa May Alcott Meml. Assn. (dir. 1984—, treas. 1987—), The Thoreau Soc. (dir. 1987—, treas. 1987—). Author: Verses on an Icelandic Vacation, 1965; contbr. The Meeting House on the Green, 1985. Home and Office: 35 Academy Ln Concord MA 01742-2431

SMITH, FLOYD LESLIE, insurance company executive; b. Silver Creek, N.Y., Nov. 12, 1931; s. Harry Lee and Fanny Diem (Arnold) S.; m. Jane Katherine Elters, Feb. 18, 1956; children: Keith Arnold, Bruce Erik. A.B., Oberlin Coll., (Ohio), 1953; M.B.A., NYU, 1962. Investment trainee Mut. of N.Y., N.Y.C., 1953-64, dir. investments, 1964-66; asst. v.p. securities investment Mut. of. N.Y., N.Y.C., 1966-69; 2d v.p. securities investment Mut. of N.Y., N.Y.C., 1969-74, v.p. securities investment, 1974-78, sr. v.p., 1978-81, chief investment officer, 1981—, exec. v.p., 1983—; vice chmn., chief investment officer Mut. of N.Y., 1989—; trustee The Mut. Life Ins. Co. of N.Y., 1988—; also dir. numerous subs. Mut. of N.Y., N.Y.C.; trustee MONY Real Estate Investors, N.Y.C., 1981—, Mut. Life Ins. Co., N.Y.,

1988—. Trustee Friends Sem., N.Y.C., 1975-84, Village of Saltaire, 1984-87; mem. Saltaire (N.Y.) Zoning Bd. Appeals, 1982-84. Served with Signal Corps U.S. Army, 1954-56. Clubs: Ft. Worth Boat, Saltaire Yacht; Newport (R.I.) Reading Room; Metropolitan (N.Y.C.). Office: Mut Life Ins Co of NY 1740 Broadway at 55th St New York NY 10019

SMITH, FRANKLIN HOWARD, JR., lawyer; b. Indpls., Aug. 31, 1951; s. Franklin Howard and Marguerite (Barnes) S.; m. Julia Kay Steeb, June 5, 1976; children: Meredith, Franklin III, Andrew, Nathaniel, Amanda. Student, Ind. U., 1969-71; BS, U. Ariz., 1974; JD, Marquette U., 1974-77; MS, DePaul U., 1981. Bar: Wis. 1977, Mich. 1977, U.S. Dist. Ct. (ea. dist.) Wis. 1977, U.S. Dist. Ct. (we. dist.) Wis. 1977. Lawyer Butzbaugh & Ehrenberg, St. Joseph, Mich., 1977-79; tax mgr. Arthur Andersen & Co., Milw., 1979-83; dir. taxes Allen-Bradley Co., Milw., 1984-86; ptnr. Coopers & Lybrand, Milw., 1986-87; dir. taxes Johnson Controls, Inc., Milw., 1988—; instr. internat. bus. U. Wis., Milw. Mem. Internat. Fiscal Assn., ABA, Tax Execs. Inst., Wis. Inst. CPA's, Wis. Assn. Corporate Growth (v.p.). Episcopalian. Office: Johnson Controls Inc 575 N Green Bay Rd Milwaukee WI 53017

SMITH, FREDERICK WALLACE, transportation company executive; b. Marks, Miss., Aug. 11, 1944; s. Frederick W. Smith; m. Diane Davis. Grad., Yale U., 1966. Cert. comml. pilot. Owner Ark Aviation, 1969-71; founder, chmn. bd., chief exec. officer Fed. Express Corp., Memphis, 1972—, now also pres., dir. Served with USMC, 1966-70. Office: Fed Express Corp 2005 Corporate Ave Memphis TN 38132 •

SMITH, GEORGE EMMETT, lawyer, business executive; b. Glens Falls, N.Y., Aug. 2, 1928; s. George Lester and Julia Mae (O'Connell) S.; m. Therese Marie Deschambault, Dec. 28, 1950; children—Mark Christopher, Laura Ann, Claire Louise, Lydia Margaret. B.S. in Econs., Fordham U., 1953, J.D., 1956; M.A. in Econs., N.Y. U., 1959. Bar: N.Y. 1956, Tex. 1976. atty. Union Carbide Corp., N.Y.C., 1956-67; asst. sec., asst. gen. counsel Xerox Corp., Stamford, Conn., 1967-75; sr. v.p., gen. counsel, sec. LTV Corp., Dallas, 1975—. Trustee, Cath. Found. Served with Signal Corps, AUS, 1947-48. Mem. ABA (corporate bus. and banking sect. com. corporate law depts. 1977), N.Y. State, Dallas bar assns., State Bar Tex. (chmn. corporate Counsel Sect. 1984-85). Clubs: Bent Tree Country, Dallas. Home: 710 Park Ave New York NY 10021 Office: LTV Corp 299 Park Ave New York NY 10171

SMITH, GEORGE FOSTER, retired aerospace company executive; b. Franklin, Ind., May 9, 1922; s. John Earl and Ruth (Foster) S.; m. Jean Arthur Farnsworth, June 3, 1950; children—David Foster, Craig Farnsworth, Sharon Windsor. B.S. in Physics, Calif. Inst. Tech., 1944, M.S., 1948, Ph.D. magna cum laude (Standard Oil fellow 1949-50), 1952. Founding staff mem. Engring. Research Assos., St. Paul, 1946-48; teaching fellow, resident asso. Calif. Inst. Tech., 1948-52; mem. staff Hughes Research Labs., Malibu, Calif., 1952-87; asso. dir. Hughes Research Labs., 1962-69, dir., 1969-87; v.p. Hughes Aircraft Co., 1965-81, sr. v.p., 1981-87, mem. policy bd., 1966-87; adj. asso. prof. elec. engring. U. So. Calif., 1959-62; cons. Army Sci. Adv. Panel, 1975-78. Author; patentee in field. Adv. local Explorer post Boy Scouts Am., 1965-70; bd. mgrs. Westchester YMCA, 1974—, chmn., 1979-81; chmn. trustees Pacific Presbyn. Ch., Los Angeles, 1959-62. Served to lt. (j.g.) USNR, 1944-46. Fellow Am. Phys. Soc., IEEE (pres. Sorenson fellows 1972-73, Frederik Philips award 1988); mem. AAAS, Sierra Club, Sigma Xi, Tau Beta Pi (chpt. pres. 1957-58). Office: Hughes Aircraft Co Rsch Labs 3011 Malibu Canyon Rd Malibu CA 90265

SMITH, GEORGE HUDSON, banker, development company executive, medical services executive; b. Cleveland, Ala., Dec. 31, 1932; s. Leo Hobson and Ruby Betty (Horton) S.; B.A., Samford U., 1960, M.A., 1969; m. Janice Foster, June 4, 1955; 1 dau., Meghan. Announcer/sales Sta. WCRL, Oneonta, Ala., 1956-57; sales Sta. WAPI, Birmingham, Ala., 1957-58; prodn. Sta. WBRC-TV, Birmingham, 1958-60; dir. pub. relations, asso. prof. journalism Samford U., Birmingham, 1960-70; v.p. First Ala. Bank, Birmingham, 1970-74; sr. v.p. Bank of SE, Birmingham, 1974-77; partner GHS Devel. Corp., Birmingham, 1977-79; pres., cons., investor So. Med. Services, Inc., 1979-85. Bd. dirs. Birmingham Civic Ballet, 1972-78; active Birmingham Festival of Arts, 1965-72, Downtown Action Com., 1971-74, Operation New Birmingham, 1968-74. Served with AC, USN, 1954-56. Mem. Birmingham C. of C. (local ambassadors com.), Profl. Journalism Soc. (dir.), Birmingham Advt. Club (dir.), Bank Mktg. Assn., Birmingham Press Club (dir.), Ala. Pub. Relations Com. (dir.), ESOP Assn. Am. (nat. dir.). Clubs: Vestavia Country, Downtown, The Club. Author: The Life and Times of William James Samford, 1970. Home: 314 Vesclub Dr Birmingham AL 35216

SMITH, GEORGE S., JR., financial executive; b. Newark, Dec. 8, 1948; m. Pamela Smith. BS in Acctg., Hiram Scott Coll., Scott's Bluff, Nebr., 1971. Cash mgr. Diamondhead Corp., N.Y.C., 1971-75, Texasgulf Inc., N.Y.C., 1975-77; dir. fin. svcs. Viacom Internat. Inc., N.Y.C., 1977-79, dir. fin. planning, 1979-81, controller radio div., 1981-83, v.p. fin. and adminstrn. broadcast group, 1983-85, v.p., controller, 1985-87, sr. v.p., chief fin. officer, 1987—. Mem. Broadcast Fin. Mgmt. Assn. Office: Viacom Inc 1211 Ave of the Americas New York NY 10036

SMITH, GOFF, industrial equipment manufacturer; b. Jackson, Tenn., Oct. 7, 1916; s. Fred Thomas and Mabel (Goff) S.; m. Nancy Dall, Nov. 28, 1942 (dec. 1972); children: Goff Thomas, Susan Knight; m. Harriet Schneider Oliver, June 23, 1973. BSE, U. Mich., 1938, MBA, 1939; MS, MIT, 1953. Trainee Bucyrus Erie, South Milwaukee, Wis., 1939-40; mem. sales staff Amsted Industries, Chgo. and N.Y.C., 1946-55; subsidiary pres. Amsted Industries, Chgo., 1955-60, v.p., 1960-69, pres., dir., 1969-74, pres., chief exec. officer, dir., 1974-80, chmn., 1980-82; bd. dirs. Clark Equipment Co., South Bend, Ind., Cen. Ill. Pub. Svc., Springfield, Ill. Pres. Village of Winnetka, Ill., 1967-69; pres., bd. dirs. United Way Chgo., 1976-85; bd. dirs. Rehab. Inst., Chgo., Chgo. Theol. Sem. Maj. U.S. Army, 1940-46. Sloan Fellow MIT, 1952-53. Republican. Office: Amsted Industries 25 E Washington St Ste 1500 Chicago IL 60602

SMITH, GORDON RAY, utilities executive; b. San Francisco, Feb. 26, 1948; s. Margaret C. Orlando; m. Elizabeth Anne Rulfo, Sept. 26, 1981; children: Adam R., Alexandra R. BS in Fin., U. Calif., Berkeley, 1970; MBA in Fin., U. San Francisco, 1974. Fin. analyst Pacific Gas & Electric Co., San Francisco, 1970-76, sr. fin. analyst, 1976-78, dir., project financing, 1978-80, asst. treas., 1980-82, treas., 1982-83, v.p. fin., treas., 1983-87, v.p. fin. and rates, 1987—. Mem. Mayor's Fiscal Adv. Com., San Francisco, 1986, Investment Rev. Com., San Francisco Found., 1986. Mem. Fin. Officers No. Calif., Pacific Coast Electric Assn., Pacific Coast Gas Assn., Bankers Club San Francisco, Moraga Country Club. Office: Pacific Gas & Electric Co 77 Beale St San Francisco CA 94106

SMITH, GRACIE BERNON, dress designer, tailor; b. Hyden, Ky., Aug. 1, 1932; d. Joe and Eva Lee (Howard) Maggard; m. William Robert Smith, June 10, 1972; children by previous marriage: Donald Eugene Turpin, Jr., Daniel Edwin Turpin; stepchildren: Steven Carson Smith, Vicki Lynn Booth. Student Nat. Sch. Dress Design-Chgo., 1955-58; student in real estate Purdue U., 1973. Tailor Sovern Tailors, Lafayette, Ind., 1965-68; mgr. Millers Sportswear, Lafayette, 1968-70; with Benker Realty, Lafayette, 1973-75; service contract dept. head Montgomery Ward, Lafayette, 1975-77; alteration dept. head Montgomery Ward, 1977-80; owner, operator Bernon Custom Fashions, Lafayette, 1955—; cons. local 4-H Clubs, 1983—; local sales rep. Leiters Designer Fabrics, Kansas City, Mo., 1982-87; local sales mgr. House of Laird Fabrics, Lexington, Ky., 1985—. Com. mem. Tippecanoe County Fair, Lafayette, 1983-85. Fellow The Custom Tailors and Designers Assn. Am., Am. Bus. Womens Assn., mem. Nat. Assn. Female Execs. Baptist. Avocations: bowling; gardening; knitting; cooking; crocheting. Home and Office: 2350 N 23d St Lafayette IN 47904

SMITH, GREGORY L., financial executive; b. Xenia, Ohio, Sept. 25, 1953; s. Laurence Everett and Helen Zora (Pendell) S. BS, Wright State U., 1975; MBA, U. Dayton, 1984. CPA, Ohio. Supr. corp. tax The Duriron Co., Inc., Dayton, Ohio, 1977-80, tax mgr., 1980-85, asst. treas., 1985-87, treas., 1987—; treas., trustee Duriron Found., Dayton; treas., bd. dirs. Durco Fgn. Sales Corp., St. Thomas, V.I. Treas. Evangelical United Meth. Ch., Xenia, Ohio, 1979-80, Durco Polit. Action Com., Dayton, Ohio, 1980-85. Mem. Tax Execs. Inst., Ohio Soc. CPA's, Dayton Tax Profls. Assn., Beta Gamma Sigma. Club: Miami Twp. Optimist (v.p., bd. dirs. 1987-88). Home: 1044 Foxshire Pl Dayton OH 45458 Office: The Duriron Co Inc 425 N Findlay St Dayton OH 45404

SMITH, H. LAVERNE, motion picture distribution executive, accountant; b. Dallas, Aug. 16, 1927; d. John George and Mattie Pearl (Harmon) Hamilton; m. Charles Ray Smith, Feb. 23, 1946; children: Nancy Sharon Smith McDonald, Charles Marcus. Student, East Tex. State U., 1946-47, So. Meth. U., 1956-59, Southwest Christian Coll., 1961; intermittent student spl. interest courses, Dallas Community Coll., 1970—. Acct. Varo, Inc., Garland, Tex., 1960-72; pvt. practice acctg. Dallas, 1972-77; pres. Laurel Leaf, Inc., Dallas, 1977-84; gen. mgr. Day-Star, Inc., Jasper, Tex., 1977—; prodn. acct. Rosie Prodns. Assoc. Ltd., Dallas, 1985—; v.p., treas. La Rose Distrbn. Co., Dallas, 1986—. Recipient Wakan award Campfire Girls Am., 1960. Mem. Nat. Assn. Broadcast Employees and Technicians (treas., sec. 1976—), Am. Bus. Womens' Assn. (Dallas chpt. chairperson, Bus. Woman of Yr. award, 1975), Women of Motion Picture Industry, Women in Film (treas. 1985-86, pres. Tex. chph. 1986-87). Baptist. Home: PO Box 1987 Jasper TX 75951

SMITH, HAMILTON GEORGE, real estate development company executive; b. Jackson, Mich., Nov. 12, 1940; s. Hamilton Wood and Margaret Elizabeth (Seybold) S.; m. Karen Elizabeth Birlenbach, Aug. 27, 1966 (div. 1979); children: Mitchell Allan, Bradley Weston. BA in Econs., Stanford U., 1962; MBA in Fin., U. So. Calif., 1968; cert. acctg., UCLA, 1983. cert. fin. planner. Adminstrv. asst. City of L.A., L.A. Police Dept., 1966-68; mgr. fin. planning Avery Label Systems, Inc., Azusa, Calif., 1968-71; mgr. gen. and cost acctg. The Larwin Group, Inc., Encino, Calif., 1971-76; v.p., contr. Ticor Mortgage Ins. Co., L.A., 1976-81; v.p., contr. The Roberts Group, Inc., Simi Valley, Calif., 1981-85, chief fin. officer, 1985—; sr. v.p. fin. Genstar Mortgage Co., Glendale, Calif., 1985; pres. Lionsgate Fin. Group, Inc., Encino, 1987—. Sgt. U.S. Army, 1963-65. Mem. Internat. Assn. Fin. Planners, Inst. Cert. Fin. Planners, Nat. Assn. Enrolled Agts., Calif. Soc. Enrolled Agts, Nat. C. of C., Nat. Taxpayers Union. Republican. Episcopalian. Office: The Roberts Group Inc PO Box 1749 Wood Ranch 222 Country Club Dr Simi Valley CA 93065

SMITH, HERBERT FURRER, lawyer; b. Glendale, Calif., Aug. 4, 1938; s. Herbert Arthur and Thelma Caroline (Furrer) S.; m. Gisela Franziska Reer, Dec. 28, 1962; children: Herbert Walter, Heidi Franziska. BA, Stanford U., 1960; JD, U. Calif., San Francisco, 1963. Bar: Calif. 1964, Calif. Supreme Ct. 1964, Fed. Ct. Appeal (9th cir.) Calif. 1964, U.S. Supreme Ct. 1967. Counsel Weitkamp, Riddle & Bedrosian, Granada Hills, Calif., 1964-68; gen. counsel, sr. v.p., corp. sec. Avco Fin. Services Inc., Irvine, Calif., 1968—, also bd. dirs. With USAR, 1963-69. Mem. Am. Fin. Services Assn. (law com.), Calif. Bar Assn. Office: Avco Fin Svcs Inc 3349 Michelson Dr Irvine CA 92715

SMITH, HOMER GROVE, retired banker; b. Washington, Nov. 26, 1909; s. Homer Amos Arthur and Hazel (Grove) S., student Am. Inst. Banking, 1927-29; B.C.S., Benjamin Franklin U., 1931; summer study Pa. State U., 1933; m. Elsa Mildred Tavenner, Aug. 27, 1938; children—Linda, Carla (Mrs. Moxon), Greta (Mrs. Kotler), Martin. With Commn. Nat. Bank, Washington, 1927-30; installations Burroughs Adding Machine Co., 1930-31; staff accountant Haskins & Sells, Balt., 1931-34; land bank examiner FCA, Washington, 1934-36, various adminstrv. positions to asst. dep. prodn. Credit Commr., 1944, asst. dept. dir. Short Term Credit Services, 1953; dep. gov., dir. coop. Bank Service, 1954; pres. Central Bank for Coops., Washington, 1956-72, Denver, 1972-74; employed in Bangladesh by contractor to AID, 1976; leader Farm Credit Coop. mission to USSR, Europe, 1979. Mem. fiscal agy. com. Farm Credit Banks, 1964, 68-70, chmn., 1970. Presbyterian (elder). Club: Fossils. Lodge: Rotary. Author: The 13th Bank, A History of the Central Bank for Cooperatives, 1976, A Challenge to U.S. Agriculture - Building the Cooperative Production Credit System, 1987. Home: 4814 Wellington Dr Chevy Chase MD 20815

SMITH, HUGH ROBERTS HOVAL, lawyer; b. Chgo., Nov. 24, 1916; s. Hoval Arnold and Nina Cornelia (Roberts) S.; A.B., Yale U., 1939, LL.B., 1942; m. Marianne Morgan Moses, Nov. 7, 1942; children—Leslie, Lindsay, Morgan, Scott, Tilman. Admitted to D.C. bar, 1946, Md. bar, 1960; asso. firm Wilmer & Broun, Washington, 1946-50, mem. firm, 1950-62; mem. firm Wilmar, Cutler & Pickering, Washington, 1962-81, of counsel, 1982-84. Trustee Holton Arms Sch., Bethesda, Md., 1961—. Served to lt. USNR, 1942-46. Mem. Assn. Yale Alumni (gov. 1978-81). Clubs: Chevy Chase (Md.) (past pres.); Yale (pres. 1976), Lawyers (sec.-treas. 1972-81, pres. 1982-83), Barristers (past pres.); Met. (Washington). Home: 6803 Meadow Ln Chevy Chase MD 20815 Office: 2445 M St Washington DC 20037-1420

SMITH, JAMES F., oil industry executive; b. 1932; married. Student, St. Louis U.; grad., U. Tulsa, 1956. Various positions in oil industry 1951-72; with Tesoco Petroleum Corp., Houston, 1972-86; pres., chief ops. officer Crown Cen. Petroleum Corp., Balt., 1986—. Office: Crown Cen Petroleum Corp 1 N Charles St Box 1168 Baltimore MD 21203 •

SMITH, JAMES FORREST, natural gas company executive; b. Randolph, N.J., June 17, 1945; s. Herbert Eugene and Elizabeth J. (Radtke) S. BA in Geography, U. Denver, 1971. Lic. comml. pilot. Mgmt. trainee in textiles Deering Milliken, N.Y.C., 1971-72; lithography sales mgr. Young & Speedwell Inc., Hackensack, N.J., 1972-75; editor/pub. Ski Info, Forrest Publs. Inc., Morristown, N.J., 1975-79; pres. Terra Resources Inc., oil and gas exploration co., Morristown, 1979-83, James Forrest Smith Inc., Morristown, 1983-85, Oilsmith, Inc., Houston, 1985—. Mem. European div. Nat. Ski Patrol, 1967—. Served with U.S. Army, 1966-67. Recipient "I Dare You" award 4-H Club and N.J. Boy's State, 1962. Mem. Aircraft Owners and Pilots Assn. Home: 4212 San Felipe Apt #467 Houston TX 77027 Office: Oilsmith Inc 1101 Post Oak Blvd Suite 9591 Houston TX 77056

SMITH, JAMES FRANCIS, utilities executive; b. Saugus, Mass., May 15, 1936; s. James Gregory and Marion Irene (Huckins) S.; m. Margaret Ellen Frame, Nov. 30, 1963; children: Ellen Hawley Anne, James Gregory. AB, Bentley Coll., 1956. Security analyst Boston Safe Deposit & Trust Co., 1956-58; public acct. Robert C. O'Connell (CPA), Boston, 1958-60; controller Precision Microwave Co., Saugus, 1960-65; fin. v.p., dir. Bay State Gas Co., Exeter & Hampton Electric Co., Concord Electric Co., Fitchburg Gas & Electric Light Co., Boston, 1965-75; with Orange and Rockland Utilities, Inc., Pearl River, N.Y., 1965—; v.p. Orange and Rockland Utilities, Inc., Pearl River, 1969-75, exec. v.p., chief fin. officer, 1975-78, vice chmn. bd., 1978, chmn., 1979—, also dir.; mem. Mid Hudson regional bd. Bank of N.Y., N.Y. State Coun. on Fiscal and Econ. Priorities. Bd. dirs., exec. com. N.Y. State Com. for Jobs and Energy Independence; mem. energy com. Coalition of Northeast Govs.; bd. dirs. Bus. Coun. N.Y. State Inc., 1988; mem. N.Y. state Energy Rsch. and Devel. Authority, 1988; mem. gov.'s Mario Cuomo's Commn. on the Adirondacks in the 21st Century. Served with AUS, 1958-61. Mem. Am. Gas Assn., Edison Electric Inst., Commerce and Industry Assn. No. N.J. (bd. dirs.), Fin. Execs. Inst., Tuxedo Club, Met. Club, Capitol Hill Club. Home: Club House Rd Tuxedo Park NY 10987 Office: Orange & Rockland Utilities Inc 1 Blue Hill Pla Pearl River NY 10965

SMITH, JAMES HOWARD, accountant; b. Charleston, W.Va., Feb. 11, 1947; s. James Carlisle and Charlene Louise (Jones) S.; m. Kimberley Ann Johnson-Smith, Jan. 1, 1977; children: James Lloyd Woodward, Stephen Adam Carlisle. Student, Duke U., 1965-67, U. Tenn.-Nashville, summers 1970-72; BS, Belmont Coll., 1973; MBA, So. Ill. U., 1979. CPA, Tenn., D.C. Adminstr. Williams, Shields & Wildman, Attys., Nashville, 1973-75; tax law specialist IRS, Washington, 1975-77; supr. Ernst & Whinney, Washington, 1977-79; ptnr.-in-charge tax and fin. services Utility Group, Washington, 1979—. Speaker in field. Author: Federal Income Taxation of Rural Electric Cooperatives, 1982, Depreciation, Salvage, and Cost of Removal: A Critical Analysis, 1982. Mem. Boy Scouts Am., 1988—; treas. Waverly Hills Homeowners Assn., Arlington, Va., 1983, spokesman before county bd., 1983; treas. Animal Welfare League of Arlington (Va.), 1975-83, Animal Welfare Found. Arlington, 1983; v.p. Adam Walsh Child Resource Ctr. Greater Washington; bd. dirs. Missing Children of Greater Washington, 1985-88. Served with USN, 1967-70. Decorated with two Bronze Star medal with cluster, Purple Heart; recipient Spl. Achievement award U.S. Dept. Treasury, 1977. Fellow D.C. Inst. CPA's; mem. Am. Inst. CPA's, Tenn. Soc. CPA's, Nat. Assn. Accts. for Coops., Nat. Acctg. Assn., Duke U. Alumni Assn., So. Ill. U. Alumni Assn. Home: 3131 N Piedmont St Arlington VA 22207 Office: Ernst & Whinney Utility Group 1225 Connecticut Ave NW Washington DC 20036

SMITH, JAMES WILLIAMS, JR., association executive; b. Balt., Aug. 22, 1945; s. Smith James and Margie W. Dir. tng. Am. Assn. Congress Mgmt., Inc., Balt. Home and Office: Am Assn Congress Mgmt Inc 1428 N Fulton Ave Baltimore MD 21217

SMITH, JAY LAWRENCE, planning company executive; b. Detroit, June 10, 1954; s. Paul Edward Smith and Gloria D. Lawrence; m. Janice Irene Acheson, May 21, 1978; children: Kevin Hamilton, Travis Jay. Student, Oakland U., 1972-75. Cert. fin. planner. Asst. tng. dir. Equitable Cos., Troy, Mich., 1978-81; pres. JLS Fin. Planning Corp., Oxford, Mich., 1978—; adj. faculty Oakland U., Rochester, Mich., 1986-87; commentator TV show Your Money and You, 1987. Contbr. articles to profl. jours. Mem. Internat. Assn. Fin. Planning (v.p. 1985-87, bd. dirs. 1987—), Inst. Cert. Fin. Planners, Fin. Profl. Adv. Panel, Internat. Bd. Cert. Fin. Planners, Rotary Club (bd. dirs. 1984-86, treas. 1985-87). Republican. Methodist. Office: JLS Fin Planning Corp 28 S Washington St PO Box 4 Oxford MI 48051

SMITH, JIM, advertising executive; b. Liverpool, Eng., May 1, 1953; s. Jim and Lillian (McKay) S.; children: Gerry, Sally, Kitty. BA in English and English Lit., Oxford (Eng.) U., 1974. Sales exec. Thomson Regional Newspapers, London, 1975-76; account handler Young & Rubicam, London, 1976-84; mktg. dir. Ky. Fried Chicken, Eng., 1984-85; head client services WCRS, London, 1985-86, dep. mng. dir., 1986-87; exec. v.p. Della Femina, McNamee WCRS Inc., N.Y.C., 1987—. Mem. London Inst. Dirs., London Mktg. Soc. Home: 248 W 88th St New York NY 10024 Office: Della Femina McNamee WCRS Inc 350 Hudson St New York NY 10024

SMITH, JOHN A., charitable organization executive; b. Lebanon, Ky., Jan. 23, 1943; s. John Jr. and Halene C. (Burnett) S.; m. Doris Owens, Oct. 6, 1965 (div. Sept. 1979); children: Lesley, John, Lisa; m. Jean McAnulty, Dec. 5, 1981. BA, Bellarmine Coll., 1964; grad., Nat. Grad. Trust Sch., Northwestern U., 1975. Assoc. in trusts Dept. Treasury, Washington, 1968-70; v.p. Am. Fletcher Nat. Bank, Indpls., 1970-86; sr. v.p. United Way Cen. Ind., Indpls., 1986—. Co-chmn. United Negro Coll. Fund Telethon, Indpls., 1980—; treas. Nat. Mental Health Assn., 1985—, pres. Ind. chpt., 1985-86, pres. Marion County (Ind.) chpt. 1983-85; local organizing com. 1987 Pan Am. Games, Indpls., 1984—. Served to 1st lt. U.S. Army, 1964-68. Named Disting. Grad. Bellarmine Coll., Louisville, 1982, Citizen of Yr. Nat. Assn. Social Workers, Indpls., 1985, Vol. of Yr. United Way, Indpls., 1985; recipient Achievement in Fin. award Ctr. for Leadership Devel., Indpls., 1982. Mem. Midwest Pension Assn. (charter, chmn. Ind. chpt. 1982, recognition award 1982), Community Service Council (pres. 1984-86, recognition award 1982). Democrat. Roman Catholic. Club: Athletic (Indpls.). Office: United Way Cen Ind 1828 N Meridian St Indianapolis IN 46202

SMITH, JOHN BURNSIDE, transportation company executive; b. Indpls., 1931; m. Barbara J.; children: John S., Lynn B., Nancy L. Grad., U. Ind., 1957, postgrad. Sch. Bus. Adminstrn., 1958; LL.D. (hon.), Butler U., 1984. Pres., chmn., chief exec. officer, dir. Mayflower Group, Indpls.; dir. Citizens Gas & Coke Utility, Ind. Nat. Corp. Bd. govs. James Whitcomb Riley Assocs.; bd. dirs. Wholesale Club. Mem. Ind. State C. of C. (bd. dirs.). Office: Mayflower Group Inc PO Box 107 Indianapolis IN 46206-0107

SMITH, JOHN F., entrepreneur; b. Stamford, Conn., Mar. 4, 1965; s. William John and Dolores (Masson) S. Student, Fairfield U. Pres. Smith Enterprise Corp., New Canaan, Conn., 1987—. Mem. Nat. Rep. Sen. Com., 1986—. Roman Catholic. Home: 516 Weed St New Canaan CT 06840

SMITH, JOHN FRANCIS, JR., automobile company executive; b. Worcester, Mass., Apr. 6, 1938; s. John Francis and Eleanor C. (Sullivan) S.; children—Brian, Kevin. B.B.A., U. Mass., 1960; M.B.A., Boston U., 1965. Fisher Body div. mgr. Gen. Motors Corp., Framingham, Mass., 1961-73; asst. treas Gen. Motors Corp., N.Y.C., 1973-80; comptroller Gen. Motors Corp., Detroit, 1980-81, dir. worldwide product planning, 1981-84; pres., gen. mgr. Gen. Motors Can., Oshawa, Ont., Can., 1984-85; exec. v.p. Gen. Motors Europe, Glattbrugg, Switzerland, 1986-87, pres., 1987-88; exec. v.p. internat. ops. Gen. Motors Corp., Detroit, 1988—; Mem. chancellors adv. commn. U. Mass. Mem. Swiss-Am. S. of C. (bd. dirs. 1987), Beta Gamma Sigma. Roman Catholic. also: Gen Motors of Can Ltd, 215 William St E, Oshawa, ON Canada L1G 1K7

SMITH, JOHN J., manufacturing company executive; b. Woodland, Mich., Dec. 9, 1911; s. Owen Benjamin and Ethyl (Katherman) S.; m. Elinor S. Lamoreaux, Dec. 10, 1938. Student, Argubright Coll., 1929-31. C.P.A., 1940. Sr. partner Smith & Skutt (C.P.A.s), 1942-50; dir. Sparton Corp., now chmn.; chmn. (Sparton Can. Ltd.), London, Ont.; dir. Lake Odessa Machine Products, Inc., Mich., Kent Products, Inc., Grand Haven, City Bank Trust Co., Jackson., DU-WEL Metal Products. Mem. Chief Execs. Forum, Mich. Assn. C.P.A.s, Am. Inst. C.P.A.s. Club: Detroit Athletic (Detroit). Home: 1839 S Walmont Jackson MI 49203 Office: Sparton Corp 2400 E Ganson St Jackson MI 49202

SMITH, JOHN LYMAN, sales executive; b. Oakland, Calif., Jan. 13, 1946; s. Joseph Carol and Margaret Adele (Maloney) S.; m. Laura Reway Gebo, Dec. 30, 1988; children: Joshua, Jennifer, Nathan, Michael Stephen, Karen Stephen. BS in Forest Mgmt., Oreg. State U., 1968; MSBA, So. Oreg. State U., 1981. Forester U.S. Forest Svc., North Bend, Wash., 1973-76; timber sale contract adminstrn. specialist Indsl. Forestry Assn., Portland, Oreg., 1976-77; dist. forester Indsl. Forestry Assn., Medford, Oreg., 1977-79; timber mgr. Nikkel Corp., Central Point, Oreg., 1979-80; contract adminstr. Boise Cascade Corp., Medford, 1980; sec., mgr. So. Oreg. Timber Industries Assn., Medford, 1980-84; contract adminstr. Environ. Container Systems, Inc., Grants Pass, Oreg., 1984, program mgr., 1984-85, v.p. sales, 1985—. Bd. dirs. Medford Family YMCA, 1983-85; patroller Mt. Ashland (Oreg.) Ski Patrol, 1980—. Lt USNR, 1968-71. Republican. Mormon. Home: 2466 Springbrook Rd Medford OR 97504 Office: ECS Composites 3560 Rogue River Hwy Grants Pass OR 97526

SMITH, JOHN PRESTON, insurance company executive; b. Lynchburg, Va., Nov. 18, 1952; s. Robert Preston and Jean (Word) S.; m. Teresa Lipps, May 16, 1981; children: Allan Preston, Bryan Coleman, Laura Draper. BS in Commerce, U. Va., 1975. CPA, Va. Sr. auditor Richmond (Va.) Corp., 1975-79; assoc. controller Continental Fin. Svcs. Co., Richmond, 1979-85; controller Heritage Savs. Bank, Richmond, 1985-87; v.p., controller Liberty Life Ins. Co., Greenville, S.C., 1987—. Office: Liberty Life Ins Co 2000 Wade Hampton Blvd Greenville SC 29602

SMITH, K. CLAY, machinery transport company executive; b. New Orleans, Aug. 29, 1937; s. Kenneth Eugene and Yvonne (Roques) S.; m. JoAnne Underwood, Dec. 17, 1941; children: Elizabeth, K. Clay, Andrew. BBA, U. Notre Dame, 1960; JD, Georgetown U., 1964; DBA (hon.), Marian Coll., Indpls., 1988. Bar: Ind. 1964. Spl. agt. FBI, Los Angeles, 1964-68; assoc. Kightlinger, Gray, Indpls., 1968-71; pres., chief exec. officer Underwood Machinery Transport, Indpls., 1971—; bd. dirs. Bindley Western Industries, Indpls., Specialized Carriers. Chmn. lic. rev. bd., City of Indpls., 1974; mem. reciprocity com., State of Ind., 1988. Mem. Ind. Bar Assn., Indpls. Bar Assn., Am. Trucking Assn. (bd. dirs. 1980-88). Republican. Roman Catholic. Clubs: Indpls. Athletic (bd. dirs. 1981—), Highland Country, Skyline (Indpls.). Office: Underwood Cos 940 W Troy Ave Indianapolis IN 46225

SMITH, KIRK, investment executive, financial consultant; b. Ringgold, Ga., Aug. 20, 1952; m. Michelle Boudeaux, Aug. 22, 1979; children: Jessica, Tylor. B in Engring. Econ. Systems, Ga. Tech. U., 1974. Fin. cons. Merrill Lynch, El Paso, Tex., 1983-88; v.p., manager R.G. Dickinson and Co., El

Paso, 1988—. Dir. John Hancock Sun Bowl, El Paso, 1986, Am. Southwest Theater Co., Les Cruces, N.Mex., 1985—. Named Sportsman of Yr., Coronado Country Club, El Paso, 1987. Mem. Internat. Found. Employee Benefits, Internat. Assn. Fin. Planners. Office: R G Dickinson & Co 215 E Main St El Paso TX 79901

SMITH, LANTY L(LOYD), lawyer, textile manufacturing executive; b. Sherrodsville, Ohio, Dec. 11, 1942; s. Lloyd H. and Ellen Ruth (Newell) S.; m. Margaret Hays Chandler, June 11, 1966; children: Abigail Lamoreaux, Margaret Ellen, Amanda Prescott. BS with honors in Math., Wittenberg U., Springfield, Ohio, 1964; LLB with honors, Duke U., 1967. Bar: Ohio 1967. Assoc. Jones, Day, Cockley & Reavis, Cleve., 1967-68, 69-73; ptnr. Jones, Day, Reavis & Pogue, Cleve., 1974-77; exec. v.p., sr. gen. counsel Burlington Industries, Inc., Greensboro, N.C., 1977-86, pres., 1986-88; chmn., chief exec. officer Precision Fabrics Group Inc., Greensboro, 1988—; mem. bd. visitors Duke U. Sch. Law, U. N.C.-Greensboro Sch. Bus. and Econs., Guilford Coll., N.C. Agrl. and Tech. State U.; bd. dirs. First Union Corp., W.R. Bonsal Co., Wittenberg U., Cone Hosp. Bd. dirs. Greensboro Life-Care Retirement Community Inc., N.C. Inst. Politics; trustee Cove Hosp. With Office Gen. Counsel USN, 1968-69. Mem. ABA. Episcopalian. Home: 1401 Westridge Rd Greensboro NC 27410 Office: One Southern Life Ctr Ste 600 Greensboro NC 27401

SMITH, LAURA KNIGHT, accountant; b. Columbia, S.C., Aug. 4, 1962; d. George Ernest and Gail Ann (Wright) Knight; m. Albert Randolph Smith II, Dec. 1, 1984. BBA in Actg., U. S.C., 1983; student, Clemson U., 1980-81. CPA, S.C. Tax acct. Wilson Macewen and Co., Columbia, 1984-86; tax supr. Policy Mgmt. Systems Corp., Columbia, 1986—. Mem. AICPA, Profl. Women in Acctg. (v.p. 1987), S.C. Assn. CPAs, Columbia Running Club. Republican. Episcopalian. Office: Policy Mgmt Systems Corp 1 PMS Ctr Blythewood SC 29016

SMITH, LAUREN ASHLEY, lawyer, journalist, clergyman; b. Clinton, Iowa, Nov. 30, 1924; s. William Thomas Roy and Ethel (Cook) S.; m. Barbara Ann Mills, Aug. 22, 1947; children: Christopher A., Laura Nan Smith Pringle, William Thomas Roy II. BS, U. Minn., 1946, JD, 1949; postgrad., U. Chgo., 1943-49; MDiv, McCormick Theol. Sem., 1950. Bar: Colo. 1957, Iowa 1959, Ill. 1963, Minn. 1983, U.S. Supreme Ct. 1967; ordained to ministry Presbyn. Ch., 1950. Pastor Presbyn. Ch., Fredonia, Kans., 1950-52, Lamar, Colo., 1952-57; pastor Congl. Ch., Clinton, 1975-80; editor The Comml., Pine Bluff, Ark., 1957-58; pvt. practice Clinton, 1959—; internat. conferee Stanley Found., Warrenton, Va., 1963-72; legal observer USSR, 1978; co-sponsor All India Renewable Energy Conf., Bangaiore, 1971; law sch. conferee U. Minn., China, 1983. Author (jurisprudence treatise): Forma Dat Esse Rel, 1975; (monograph) First Strike Option, 1983; columnist Crow Call, 1968—; co-editor Press and News of India, 1978-82. Minister-at-large Presbyn. Ch., U.S.A., Iowa, 1987—; bd. dirs. Iowa div. UN Assn. U.S.A., Iowa City, 1970-85. Mem. St. Andrews Soc., Clinton County Bar Assn. (pres. 1968, Best in Iowa citation). Lodge: Rotary.

SMITH, LAURENCE ROGER, chamber of commerce executive; b. N.Y.C., Sept. 30, 1939; s. John and Edith (Haabestad) S.; m. Betty Ann Larsen, Oct. 9, 1965; children: Erik Lars, Alesa Ann. AAS, Staten Island Community Coll., 1962; BS, SUNY, Oswego, 1965; MBA, St. John's U., 1975. Dir. community devel. Staten Island (N.Y.) C. of C., 1965-77; exec. v.p., chief exec. officer Yonkers (N.Y.) C. of C., 1977-78; chief exec. officer Greater Lawrence (Mass.) C. of C., 1978—; dir., clk. Lawrence Downtown Parking Assocs., 1979—; dir., asst. treas. Greater Lawrence Revolving Loan Fund, 1979—. Chmn. Lower Merrimack Valley Pvt. Industry Council, Lawrence, 1981; treas. Lawrence YMCA, 1985; trustee Greater Lawrence Community Boating; bd. dirs. Greater Lawrence Red Cross; apptd. gov's working group on Youth Violence. Served with USCG, 1958-60. Recipient Pvt. Sector award Presdl. Commn., 1985, Flood Relief award ARC, 1987. Mem. Am. C. of C. Execs., New Eng. Assn. C. of C. Execs. (bd. dirs., sec., treas., 2d v.p., 1st. v.p., pres.), Mass. Assn. C. of C. Execs. (bd. dirs., sec., treas., 2d v.p., 1st. v.p., pres.). Democrat. Episcopalian. Home: 233 Osgood St North Andover MA 01845 Office: Greater Lawrence C of C 264 Essex St Lawrence MA 01840

SMITH, LAWRENCE HARTLEY, rubber company executive; b. Cornwall, N.Y., Nov. 16, 1934; s. Ernest and Nellie (Nunn) S.; m. Faye Irene Walraven, June 20, 1959; children: Karen Elaine, Douglas Gordon. B-SChemE, Rensselaer Poly. Inst., 1956. Chemist E.I. DuPont, Fairfield, Conn., 1959-65; sr. engr. E.I. DuPont, Old Hickory, Tenn., 1965-67; product sales mgr. Ohio Rubber, Stratford, Conn., 1967-72, mfg. mgr., 1972-73; gen mgr. Orcomatic Inc., Norwich, Conn., 1973-79, pres., 1979—. Adv. council Thames Valley Tech. Coll., Norwich, 1984—. Mem. Am. Soc. Chem. Engrs., Am. Chem. Soc., Conn. Rubber Group, R.I. Rubber Group, Am. Assn. Ind. Mgmt. (bd. dirs. 1987—), CBIA (adv. coun. 1988—). Republican.

SMITH, LESLIE JACK, management company executive; b. Calgary, Alta., Can., Apr. 15, 1939; m. Anita Eileen Nelligan, June 18, 1983; children: Carla Ann, Stephen Joel, Jason Edward. Chartered acct., Can. Audit supr. Thorne, Gunn, Helliwell & Christensen, Vancouver, B.C., 1963-65; v.p., fin. and chief fin. officer Westcoast Transmission Co., Ltd., Vancouver, 1965-81; exec. v.p. fin., chief fin. officer B.C. Resources Investment Corp., Vancouver, 1981-84, exec. v.p., chief oper. officer, 1985; pres., chief oper. officer Westar Group Ltd., Vancouver, 1986, dir., pres., chief exec. officer, 1986—; bd. dirs., chmn. Westar Mining Ltd., Vancouver, Westar Petroleum Ltd., Calgary, 1986—, Westar Timber Ltd., Vancouver, 1981—, Westshore Terminals Ltd., 1986; bd. dirs. Pegasus Gold, Inc. Trustee Discovery Found., Vancouver, 1983—; hon. bd. dirs. Vancouver Oral Ctr. for Deaf Children, 1970—. Mem. Inst. Chartered Accts. of B.C., Can. Inst. Chartered Accts.

SMITH, LINDLEY VAN, JR., bank executive; b. Newport, Ark., Jan. 8, 1951; s. Lindley Van and Elizabeth (Rossington) S.; m. Susan C. Padan; children: Elizabeth R., Jonathan L. BA, Westminster Coll., 1973; MBA, U. Mo., 1977. Collection officer Clarendon Industries, Kansas City, Kans., 1973-75; bank examiner Ark. State Bank Dept., Little Rock, 1976-79; exec. v.p. Bank of Tuckerman, Ark., 1979, pres., chief exec. officer, chmn., 1981—; pres., chmn. Rainbow Investment, Co., Inc., Tuckerman, 1986—; chmn. bd. Ark. Banking Schs., Little Rock, 1985-86. Mem. Dem. Cen. Com., Jackson County, Ark., 1980—, election commn., Jackson County; chmn. Tuckerman Indsl. Devel. Commn., 1985—; chmn. bd. Tuckerman United Meth. Ch., 1985-86; chmn. Ark. Emmaus Community. Mem. Ark. Bankers Assn. (treas., com. chmn. group 1), Ark. Ind. Bankers Assn. (bd. dirs., sec.). Methodist. Club: Newport Country (Ark.) (bd. mem., past pres.) Lodge: Rotary (bd. dirs. Newport club 1980-83), Tuckerman Service (pres. 1987-88). Home: 2405 Twin Oaks Jonesboro AR 72401 Office: Bank Tuckerman PO Box 700 Tuckerman AR 72473

SMITH, LONNIE MAX, diversified industries executive; b. Twin Falls, Idaho, July 28, 1944; s. Lonnie E. and Christie (Stuart) S.; m. Cheryl Diane Smith, June 10, 1968; children: Kristen, Maryam, Rebecca, Michael, Catherine. BSEE, Utah State U., 1967; MBA, Harvard U., 1974. Engr., mgr. field services, mgr. tech. services to asst. to v.p. plans and control IBM Corp., San Francisco, Palo Alto, Calif., and White Plains, N.Y., 1967-74; mgr., corp. strategy, then cons. Boston Cons. Group, 1974-76; exec. v.p. Am. Tourister, Inc., Warren, R.I., 1978-81; sr. v.p. corp. planning Hillenbrand Industries, Inc., Batesville, Ind., 1977-78, sr. exec. v.p., 1982—, also bd. dirs.; pres., chmn. bd. Hillenbrand Internat. Sales Corp.; v.p., bd. dirs. Forecorp, Inc., Batesville; bd. dirs. Hillenbrand Investment Adv. Corp., Batesville Casket Co., Batesville Internat. Corp., Hill-Rom Co., A.T. Retail, Inc., The Forethought Group, Inc., Hilico Life Ins. Co., Tudor Sq. Realty, Inc., Tudor Travel, all in Batesville; bd. dirs. Medeco Security Locks, Inc., Salem, Va., Support Systems Internat., Inc., Charleston, S.C., Lozier Corp., Omaha. Served to 1st lt. U.S. Army, 1969-72. Republican. Mormon. Office: Hillenbrand Industries Inc Hwy 46 Batesville IN 47006

SMITH, LOWELL DOUGLAS, insurance executive; b. Clinton, Mo., Mar. 17, 1945; s. C. Shobe and Waneta (Wallace) S.; m. Peggy Mills, Aug. 28, 1966 (div. Sept. 1976); children: Tracy, Kristin, Doug.; m. Jana Thomas, Nov. 2, 1984; 1 child, Rachel. BS, U. Mo., 1967. Dist. mgr. Federated Ins., Owatonna, Minn., 1967-69; mgr. Comml. Union Ins., Kansas City, Mo., 1969-71; co-owner Smiths Ins. Investments, Clinton, 1971-75; v.p. tng., dir. Miss. Educators Ins. Co., Jackson, 1975-79; co-owner Mid Am. Ins. Mgrs., Little Rock, 1979-80, Fed. So. Ins. Agy., McGeher, Ark., 1980-84; owner, chief exec. officer Cafeteria Plan Cons., Jackson, 1984—, Jackson Mgmt. Agy., 1985—; cons. Blue Cross/Blue Shield, Jackson, 1985-87; State of Miss. Ins., Jackson, 1986—. Republican. Methodist. Office: Cafeteria Plan Cons PO Box 97343 Jackson MS 39288

SMITH, MARIAN CHOU, publisher; b. Shanghai, Republic of China, Aug. 10, 1932; d. Victor and Sue (Chen) C.; m. Ward Durant Smith, Jan. 14, 1954 (dec. Feb. 1984); children: Philip, Deborah, Cathi. Student, U. Taiwan, Taipei, U. Mich., Taipei. Head bookkeeper Nowels Publs., Menlo Park, Calif., 1978-83, Sanborn Newspapers, San Carlos, Calif., 1983-85; pub. Shirjieh Pubs., Menlo Park, 1986—. Vol. Menlo Park Library, 1985-86. Republican. Episcopalian. Club: Ladera Oaks (Menlo Park). Home: 1060 Colby Ave Menlo Park CA 94025 Office: PO Box 259 Menlo Park CA 94026-0259

SMITH, MARK JOSEPH, accountant, financial planner. BBA in Acctg., U. Iowa, 1976. CPA, Colo. With Deloitte, Haskins, Sells, Colo., 1976-80, Affiliated Bankshares, Colo., 1980-84; owner M.J. Smith & Assocs. (formerly Advanced Fin. Strategies), Aurora, Colo., 1983—; tchr. income tax Bank Adminstrn. Inst. Mem. Inst. Cert. Fin. Planners, Internat. Assn. Fin. Planners, Am. Inst. for Pub. Accts., Colo. Soc. CPA's, Tax Execs. Inst. Office: 131 S Vaughn Way Ste 430 Aurora CO 80014

SMITH, MARSCHALL IMBODEN, lawyer; b. San Antonio, Oct. 3, 1944; s. Lowell B. and Jacqueline I. Smith; m. Elizabeth Braswell (div. 1973); m. Ann McNamara, June 3, 1976; children: Catherine, Elizabeth, Margaret, Austin, Lillian. AB, Princeton U., 1966; LLB, U. Va., 1973; MBA, U. Chgo., 1987. Bar: N.Y. 1974, Ill. 1981. Assoc. Debevoise & Plimpton, N.Y.C., 1973-75, Paul Weiss, Rifkind Wharton & Garrison, N.Y.C., 1975-81; atty. Baxter Travenol Labs., Deerfield, Ill., 1980-82; pres. Medcom Inc. subs. Baxter Internat. Inc., Deerfield, 1982-83, corp. counsel, 1983-85, asst. gen. counsel, 1985-87, assoc. gen. counsel, 1987—. Maj. USMC, 1966-73, Vietnam. Home: 308 Scott St Lake Forest IL 60045 Office: Baxter Healthcare Corp 1 Baxter Pkwy Deerfield IL 60015

SMITH, MARY CATHERINE, marketing executive; b. Shreveport, La., July 17, 1964; d. Mary Jane (Regnier) Lowry; m. David Oren Smith, July 25, 1987. BA, U. Miss., Oxford, 1986. Assignments editor, staff writer Daily Sentinel-Star, Grenada, Miss., 1987-88; dir. pub. relations and mktg. Grenada Lake Med. Ctr., 1988—. Mem. U. Miss. Alumni Assn., Phi Mu. Republican. Episcopalian. Home: 52 Walthall Grenada MS 38901 Office: Grenada Lake Med Ctr Grenada MS 38901

SMITH, MARY CHRISTINE, health science association adminstrator; b. Buffalo, Nov. 4, 1957; d. Neal Frederick and Geneve Christine (Hahin) S. BA, BS, SUNY, Buffalo, 1979; MBA, Canisisu Coll., 1985. Asst. dir. product mgmt. ARC Blood Svcs., Buffalo, 1979-82, dir. project mgmt., 1982—. Mem. ARC Product Mgmt. Adv. Com. Washington, 1984-87, chmn. 1986-87, St. Joseph Cathedral Choir, Buffalo, 1987—, cantor, 1987—, Ch. Musicians Guild, Buffalo Sabres Press Box Staff, Buffalo, 1978—; soloist Opera Sacra, Buffalo, 1986—. Mem. Am. Assn. Blood Banks, Nat. Pastoral Musicians Assn., Beta Gamma Sigma, Alpha Mu Alpha. Republican. Roman Catholic.

SMITH, MARY LOUISE, real estate broker/salesperson; b. Eldorado, Ill., May 29, 1935; d. Joseph Henry Smith and Opal Marie (Shelton) Hungerford; m. David Lee Smith, June 18, 1961; children: Ricky Eugene, Brenda Sue Smith Millsap. Student, So. Ill. U., 1954-56, 57-58. Cert. tchr., Mo.; cert. real estate broker/salesperson, Mo. With acctg. dept. Cen. Hardware Co., St. Louis, 1958-61; mgr. income tax office Tax Teller Inc., St. Louis, 1967-69, H&R Block Co., St. Louis, 1970-76; with acctg. dept. Weis Neumann Co., St. Louis, 1976-79; sales assoc. Century 21 Neubauer Realty, Inc., St. Louis, 1981-83, 88—, John R. Green Realtor, Inc., St. Louis, 1983-85; sales assoc. Century 21 Action Properties, St. Louis, 1985-86, real estate broker/salesperson, 1986-88; real estate broker/salesperson Century 21 Neubauer Realty, St. Louis, 1988—; substitute tchr., St. Louis Bd. Edn., 1967—. Children's dir. Lafayette Park Bapt. Ch., St. Louis, 1981—. Mem. St. Louis Metro Realtors Assn., Real Estate Bd. Met. St. Louis (mem. equal rights com.), Internat. Platform Assn., Nat. Assn. Realtors, Mo. Assn. Realtors. Home: 2627 Nebraska Saint Louis MO 63118

SMITH, MARY PERKINS, account analyst; b. Wytheville, Va., July 9, 1949; d. Cooper Kunkel Perkins and Mary Christian (Garth) Gentry; m. Roger Wayne Baiers, Sept. 7, 1968 (div. 1984); children: Christine Leigh, Brian Leslie. Student, LaSalle U., 1977, Rutledge Coll., 1987. Interior decorator Town Sq. Interiors, Radford, Va., 1978-81; mgr. Tupperware Home Parties, Roanoke, Va., 1981-86; patient account analyst Wesley Long Community Hosp., Greensboro, N.C., 1987—. Mem. Blue Ridge Jr. Womens Club (designer dist. crest 1973), Southwestern Va. Jr. Womens Club (designer dist. crest 1973). Presbyterian. Home: 3601 Normandy Rd Greensboro NC 27408 Office: Wesley Long Community Hosp Drawer X3 Greensboro NC 27402

SMITH, MONICA ELIZABETH, accountant; b. Columbia, S.C., Jan. 15, 1965; d. James Murray Jr. and Vera M. (Waters) S. BSBA, U. S.C., Aiken, 1987. Office mgr. Clearweave Hosiery Co., Saluda, S.C., 1983-85; sec., bookkeeper S.C. Aviation, Inc., Ninety Six, S.C., 1985-87; acct. Elliott, Davis & Co., Greenwood, S.C., 1987—. Baptist. Home: RR #1 Box 269 PO Box 26 Saluda SC 29138

SMITH, NANCY HOHENDORF, sales and marketing executive; b. Detroit, Jan. 30, 1943; d. Donald Gerald and Lucille Marie (Kopp) Hohendorf; m. Richard Harold Smith, Aug. 21, 1978 (div. Jan. 1984). BA, U. Detroit, 1965; MA, Wayne State U., 1969. Customer rep. Xerox Corp., Detroit, 1965-67; major account mktg. exec. Xerox Corp., Hartford, Conn., 1978-79, New Haven, Conn., 1979-80; state of N.Y. account exec. Xerox Corp., N.Y.C., 1981, N.Y. region mgr. customer support, 1982; N.Y. region sales ops. mgr. Xerox Corp., Greenwich, Conn., 1982; Ohio account exec. Xerox Corp., Columbus, 1983; new bus. sales mgr. Xerox Corp., Dayton, Ohio, 1983, major accounts sales mgr., 1984; info. systems sales and support mgr., quality specialist Xerox Corp., Detroit, 1985-87; mktg. rep. Univ. Microfilms subs. Xerox Corp., Ann Arbor, Mich., 1967-73, mktg. coordinator, 1973-74, mgr. dir. mktg., 1975-76; mgr. mktg. Univ. Microfilms subs. Xerox Corp., Can., 1976-77; new product launch mgr., ops. quality mgr. Xerox Corp., Detroit, 1988, dist. mktg. mgr., dist. quality mgr., 1989—. Mem. Detroit Inst. Arts. Named to Outstanding Young Women of Am., 1968, Outstanding Bus. Woman, Dayton C. of C., 1984. Mem. NAFE, Am. Mgmt. Assn., Detroit Inst. Arts, Women's Econ. Club of Detroit, Founder's Soc. Republican. Roman Catholic. Home: 23308 Reynard Dr Southfield MI 48034 Office: Xerox Corp 27710 Northwestern Hwy Ste 500 Southfield MI 48034

SMITH, NEIL ALLEN, manufacturing executive; b. Spokane, Wash., July 27, 1930; s. Allen William and Lorene Rachel (Widman) S.; m. Janet Dorothy Nelsen, June 19, 1955; children: Debra, Neil Jr., Todd Nelsen, Jeffrey William. BA in Edn., Cen. Wash. U., 1953. Territory salesman U.S. Rubber Co., Seattle, 1953-63; with Uniroyal, Inc., various locations, 1963-76; product mgr. Uniroyal, Inc., Washington, Ind., 1976-79; pres., chief exec. officer NASCO Industries, Inc., Washington, Ind., 1979—; adv. bd. twin Rivers Vocat. Area, 1982-85; mem. Ind. Econ. Devel. Council, 1987—. Pres. Washington (Ind.) Little League, 1977; campaign chmn. United Way, Daviess County (Ind.) 1980; chmn. Strategic Planning Task Force Group, 1987. Mem. Nat. Assn. Mfrs., Nat. Fedn. Ind. Bus., Daviess County C. of C. (pres. 1982, J.P. Hagel Service award 1984). Republican. Presbyterian. Clubs: Washington Country. Lodge: Kiwanis. Office: NASCO Industries Inc 3 NE 21st St Washington IN 47501

SMITH, NEWMAN DONALD, financial executive; b. Chesterville, Ont., Can., Dec. 26, 1936; s. Clarke Harold and Ethelwyn Irene (Cross) S.; chartered acct., 1961; certified mgmt. acct.; 1966; chartered Inst. of Secretaries, 1967; m. Mary Elizabeth Murdoch, June 27, 1964; children—Clarke Murdoch, Brian Newman. With Coopers & Lybrand Inc., Ottawa, Ont., 1955-62; sec.-treas. Deloro Smelting & Refining Co. Ltd., Ottawa, 1963-69, M.J. O'Brien Ltd., Ottawa, 1963-69; exec. v.p., sec. Andres Wines Ltd. and subs., Winona, Ont., 1969—, also dir.; dir. Les Vins Andres du Quebec Ltee., Peller Wines of Calif., Watleys Ltd., Superior Wines Ltd., Andres Wines (B.C.) Ltd., Andres Wines (Alta.) Ltd., Andres Wines Atlantic Ltd. Fellow Chartered Inst. of Secs.; mem. Fin. Execs. Inst., Chartered Accts., Hamilton Mgmt. Accts., Chartered Inst. Secs. Clubs: Hamilton Golf and Country, Hamilton. Home: PO Box 7185, Ancaster, ON Canada L9G 3L4 Office: PO Box 550, Winona, ON Canada L0R 2L0

SMITH, ORIN ROBERT, chemical company executive; b. Newark, Aug. 13, 1935; s. Sydney R. and Gladys Emmett (DeGroff) S.; m. Ann Raymond, July 11, 1964; children—Lindsay, Robin. B.A. in Econometrics, Brown U., 1957; M.B.A. in Mgmt., Seton Hall U., 1964. Various sales and mktg. mgmt. positions Allied Chem. Corp., Morristown, N.J., 1960-70; dir. sales and mktg. Richardson-Merrell Co., Phillipsburg, N.J., 1970-72; with M&T Chems., Greenwich, Conn., 1972-77, pres., 1974-77; with Engelhard Minerals & Chems. Corp., Menlo Park and Edison, N.J., 1977-81, corp. sr. v.p., 1978-81, pres. div. minerals and chems., 1978-81, pres., dir. various U.S. subs., 1979-81; exec. v.p., pres. div. minerals and chems. Engelhard Corp., Edison, 1981-84, pres., chief exec. officer, 1984—, also bd. dirs.; dir. Summit Trust Co., The Summit Bancorp., Vulcan Materials Co., N.J. Mfrs. Ins. Co. Past chmn. Ind. Coll. Fund N.J.; bd. overseers N.J. Inst. Tech.; vice chmn. Centenary Coll.; past dir.-at-large U. Maine Pulp and Paper Found.; mem. adv. com. Watchung Area council Boy Scouts Am.; bd. dirs. Welkind Rehab. Hosp. Served to lt. (j.g.) USN, 1957-60. Mem. Chem. Mfrs. Assn. (past bd. dirs.), N.J. C. of C. (bd. dirs.). Clubs: Economics, Union League (N.Y.C.); Essex Hunt (Peapack, N.J.); Roxiticus Golf (Mendham, N.J.). Home: Fox Chase Farm Gladstone NJ 07934 Office: Engelhard Corp Menlo Park CN 40 Edison NJ 08818 *

SMITH, PATRICIA LOUISE, financial planner; b. Pulaski, Va., Sept. 9, 1953; d. Everett Jr. and Vicie (Bowman) S. BS in Health and Phys. Edn., Wake Forest U., 1975; MEd in Adminstrn. and Supervision, N.C. State U., 1977. Personal and bus. fin. planner IDS Fin. Services Inc., Charlotte, N.C., 1982—; presenter exec. level seminars Mpls., 1988—. Chmn. Council on Status of Women, Catawba County, N.C., 1985-86; bd. dirs. Women's Resource Ctr., Hickory, N.C., 1986-88, presenter seminars, 1987—. Mem. Internat. Assn. for Fin. Planners, Inst. Cert. Fin. Planners (cert.). Office: IDS Fin Svcs Inc 6406 Carmel Rd Ste 304 Charlotte NC 28226

SMITH, PAUL JAMES, manufacturing company executive; b. Trumbull, Tex., July 16, 1932; s. Earl J. and Bessie K. (Pierce) S.; m. Barbara A. McConnell, Aug. 9, 1954; children: Marc, Cynthia. BSEE, U. Tex., 1959; postgrad., So. Meth. U., 1959-60. Mgr. mil. computer bus., consumer calculator bus., div. gen. mgr. digital systems Tex. Instruments, Dallas, 1959-75; dir. comml. electronics Martin Marietta Corp., Orlando, Fla., 1975-79; v.p., gen. mgr. semiconductor digital products div. Harris Corp., Melbourne, Fla., 1979-83; group v.p. line printer, then exec. v.p Dataproducts Corp., Woodland Hills, Calif., 1983-88; sr. v.p. Data Products div. Xidex/Anacomp Corp., Santa Clara, Calif., 1988—. Served with USN, 1953-55. Mem. IEEE, Machinery and Allied Products Inst., Mensa, Tau Beta Pi, Eta Kappa Nu. Office: 5302 Betsy Ross Dr Santa Clara CA 95050

SMITH, PAUL LESTER, photographic company executive; b. Columbus, Ohio, Oct. 7, 1935; s. Lester Wikel and Opal Mary (Spain) S.; m. Susan Virginia Wilson, June 14, 1958; children—Jennifer Louise, Paul Brian. B.A., Ohio Wesleyan U., 1957; M.B.A., Northwestern U., 1958. Various positions Eastman Kodak Co., Rochester, N.Y., 1958-82, v.p., 1982-83, sr. v.p. fin., 1983—; dir. Chase-Lincoln First Bank, N.A., Rochester, Merrill Lynch Mortgage Corp.; mem. Conf. Bd. Council Fin. Execs., 1986; mem. adv. com. Internat. Capital Markets of N.Y. Stock Exchange. Bd. dirs. Rochester Gen. Hosp., Rochester Area Hosp. Corp.; trustee Rochester Inst. Tech., 1986, Internat. Mus. Photography at George Eastman House, Rochester; bd. mng. dirs. Ind. Coll. Fund of N.Y., 1985; mem. chief fin. officers task force Pvt. Sector Council, 1986. Mem. Fin. Execs. Inst. Republican. Episcopalian. Club: Country (Rochester). Office: Eastman Kodak Co 343 State St Rochester NY 14650

SMITH, PETER BENNETT, banker; b. N.Y.C., Sept. 24, 1934; s. Richard Joyce and Sheila (Alexander) S.; B.A., Yale U., 1956; m. Elizabeth Weinberg, May 10, 1980; children—Marjorie, Alison, Peter, Michael, Madeleine, Hannah, Elizabeth. With J.P. Morgan & Co., 1958-59; with Morgan Guaranty Trust Co., N.Y.C., 1959—, sr. v.p. mgmt., 1976-79, exec. v.p., 1979-86; chmn. credit policy com., 1986—; mng. dir. Banco Frances del Rio de la Plata, Buenos Aires, Argentina, 1968-72, Bank Mees & Hope, Amsterdam, Netherlands, 1972-75; pres. Bank Morgan LaBouchere N.V., Amsterdam, 1976; trustee Canterbury Sch.; bd. dirs. Dravo Corp., N.Y.C. Ballet. Served to capt. USMCR, 1956-58. Mem. Assn. Res. City Bankers, Council on Fgn. Relations. Roman Catholic. Clubs: Economic, Yale (N.Y.C.); Rolling Rock, Sharon Country. Office: Morgan Guaranty Trust Co 23 Wall St New York NY 10015

SMITH, PETER JAY, insurance company executive, consultant; b. Englewood, N.J., Oct. 9, 1947; s. Seymour A. and Marjorie (Heft) S.; m. Dolores Mulhern, Aug. 17, 1984; children: Michael J., Douglas A., Brian D. BA, Syracuse U., 1970. CLU; chartered fin. cons. Ins. agt. N.Y.C., 1970—; prin. Peter J. Smith, CLU, Chartered Fin. Cons. & Assocs., N.Y.C., 1970—; pres. No. N.J. chpt. CLU, 1980-81. Pres. Dwight Englewood Sch. Alumni Assn., 1979-81, trustee 1978-81; exec. com. Young Men's div. Albert Einstein Coll. of Medicine, Bronx, N.Y., 1986. Recipient Vanguard award New Eng. Life, Boston, 1979, Flagship award New Eng. Life, 1983; named life mem. Hall of Fame, New Eng. Life, 1976. Mem. Assn. Advanced Life Underwriters, Million Dollar Round Table (qualifying, life mem.), Top of the Table, The Forum, The Am. Soc., Life Underwriters Assn. of N.Y.C., Passaic Bergen Life Underwriters Assn., Bergen County Estate Planners Assn. (bd. dirs.). Jewish. Clubs: Preakness Hills (bd. govs. 1985—); Wayne (N.J.) Country. Lodge: B'nai B'rith. Office: 1230 Ave of the Americas New York NY 10020 also: 2 University Pla Hackensack NJ 07601

SMITH, PETER WALKER, finance executive; b. Syracuse, N.Y., May 19, 1923; s. Stanley Sherwood and Elizabeth Wilkins (Young) S.; m. Lucile Elizabeth Edson, June 22, 1946; children: Andrew E., Laurie (Mrs. Samuel J. Falzone), Pamela C. (Mrs. Denison W. Schweppe, Jr.), Stanley E. B.Chem. Engring., Rensselaer Poly. Inst., 1947; M.B.A., Harvard U., 1948; LL.B., Cleve. Marshall Law Sch., 1955. Bar: Ohio 1955; Registered profl. engr., Ohio. Div. controller Raytheon Co., Lexington, Mass., 1958-66; v.p. finance, indsl. systems and equipment group Litton Industries Inc., Stamford, Conn., 1966-70; v.p. finance, treas. Copeland Corp., Sidney, Ohio, 1970-74; v.p. fin., treas., dir. Instrumentation Lab. Inc., Lexington, Mass., 1974-78; chief fin. officer, treas. Ionics, Inc., Watertown, Mass., 1978-80; v.p. fin., treas. Data Printer Corp., Malden, Mass., 1980-84, Orion Research Inc., Boston, 1984-87; pvt. practice cons. Concord, Mass., 1987—. Mem. fin. adv. bd., Northeastern U., Boston. Lt. AUS, 1943-46, 50-52. Mem. Fin. Execs. Inst., Am. Prodn. and Inventory Control Soc. (founding), Rensselaer Soc. Engrs., Sigma Xi, Tau Beta Pi. Home and Office: 155 Monument St Concord MA 01742

SMITH, PHILIP LAWTON, food company executive; b. LaGrange, Ga., Dec. 16, 1933; s. Hayden McKinley and Anne Mae (Slaughter) S.; m. Nancy Lou Fagan, Sept. 8, 1956; children: Kevin James, Stephen Eric, Scott Andrew. BBA with distinction, U. Mich., 1960, MBA with distinction, 1961. Account exec. Benton & Bowles, N.Y.C., 1961-65; v.p., account exec. Ted Bates, Inc., N.Y.C., 1965-66; product mgr. Gen. Foods Corp., White Plains, N.Y., 1966, product group mgr., 1966-69, mgr. advt. and merchandising Jell-O div., 1969-70, v.p. mktg. and devel., 1970-72, exec. v.p., 1972-73, mgr. strategic bus. unit, 1973-74, v.p., pres. pet foods div., 1974-77, v.p. U.S. grocery group, pres. Maxwell House div., 1977-79, exec. v.p. fin. and adminstrn., 1979-81, pres., chief operating officer, 1981-86, pres., chief exec. officer, 1987, chmn., 1987-88; chmn., chief exec. officer Pillsbury Co., Mpls., 1988—; bd. dirs. Philip Morris Cos. Inc., Whirlpool Corp., U.S. Trust Corp.; U.S. Trust Co. N.Y. Trustee Columbia Presbyn. Hosp. Office: Pillsbury Co 200 S 6th St Minneapolis MN 55402

SMITH, PHILLIP WOODY, sales executive; b. Graham, N.C., June 20, 1949; s. Walter Freeman and Mary Louise (Woody) S.; m. Virginia Jean Mahony, Sept. 25, 1982. BA in Econs., U. N.C., 1971. Sales rep. Stanley

Looms, N.Y.C., 1971-72, N. Erlanger Blungarl, N.Y.C., 1972-76; v.p. sales Tandler Textile, N.Y.C., 1976—. Republican. Presbyterian. Club: N.Y. Athletic. Home: 390 W End Ave New York NY 10024 Office: Tandler Textile 104 W 40th St New York NY 10018

SMITH, RAYMOND VICTOR, paper products manufacturing executive; b. Vancouver, B.C., Can., Apr. 28, 1926; s. Stanley Victor and Kathryn Stewart (Hunter) S.; m. Marilyn Joyce Meldrum, Oct. 17, 1947; children—Vicki, Kathi, Stan. Student, U. B.C., Banff Sch. Advanced Mgmt.; student Advanced Mgmt. Program, Harvard U. Trumpeter Dal Richards Band, 1942; ptnr. Warren McCuish Mens' Clothiers, 1947; sales rep. Vancouver Paper Box, 1949-54; with Home Oil Distbrs., 1954-57; with Kraft Paper & Board Sales, 1957-67, asst. mgr., 1961-65; newsprint rep. Powell River-Alberni Sales Corp., Pasadena, Calif., 1965-67; mgr. Powell River-Alberni Sales Corp., Pasadena, 1967-68; mgr. supply control and sales adminstrn. MacMillan Bloedel Ltd., Vancouver, 1968-70, gen. mgr., 1970-71, v.p. mktg. paper and pulp, 1971-73, v.p., gen. mgr. newsprint, 1973-77, group v.p. pulp and paper, 1977-79, sr. v.p. pulp and paper, 1979-80, pres., chief operating officer, 1980083, chief exec. officer, 1983—; bd. dirs. Fibres Internat., Inc., Noranda Forest; bd. govs. Bus. Council B.C.; co-chmn. Newsprint Info. Com. Served with Can. Army, 1944. Clubs: Terminal City, Capilano Golf and Country, Vancouver. Office: MacMillan Bloedel Ltd, 1075 W Georgia St, Vancouver, BC Canada V6E 3R9

SMITH, RAYMOND W., telecommunications company executive; b. 1937; married. B.S., Carnegie-Mellon U., 1959; M.B.A., U. Pitts., 1967. Dir. budget planning and analysis comptroller dept. AT&T, 1976-77; with Bell of Pa., Phila., 1959-75, 77-81; div. ops. mgr. Western area Bell Telephone Co. of Pa., Phila., 1973-74, asst. v.p. pub. relations, 1974-77, v.p., gen. mgr. Eastern region, 1977-81, v.p.-regulatory, 1981-83, pres., chief exec. officer, 1983-85, dir.; vice chmn., chief fin. officer, dir. parent co. Bell Atlantic Corp., Phila., 1985-88; v.p., chief operating officer Bell Atlantic Network Services, Arlington, Va., 1988—; pres., chief exec. officer Bell Atlantic Corp., Arlington, 1989—. Served with Signal Corps, U.S. Army, 1959-60. Office: Bell Atlantic Corp 1600 Market St Philadelphia PA 19103 *

SMITH, RICHARD ALAN, movie theater and soft drink bottling company executive; b. Boston, 1924; married. BS, Harvard U., 1946. With Smith Mgmt. Co., 1947—, pres., 1961-83; chmn. bd., chief exec. officer Gen. Cinema Corp., Boston, 1947—, dir.; dir. Liberty Mut. Ins. Co., 1st Nat. Boston Corp., Wang Labs. Inc. Office: Gen Cinema Corp 27 Boylston St Chestnut Hill MA 02167 *

SMITH, RICHARD HOWARD, banker; b. Tulare, Calif., Aug. 27, 1927; s. Howard Charles and Sue Elizabeth (Cheyne) S.; B.A., Principia Coll, 1958; LL.B., LaSalle U., 1975; postgrad. Sch. Banking U. Wash., 1970-72; m. Patricia Ann Howery, Mar. 12, 1950; children—Jeffrey Howard, Holly Lee, Gregory Scott, Deborah Elaine. Prin., Aurora Elementary Sch., Tulare, 1951-53; prin. Desert Sun Sch., Idyllwild, Calif., 1953-55; trust adminstr. trainee Bank of Am., San Diego, 1955-58, asst. trust officer, Ventura, Redlands, Riverside and Los Angeles, 1958-65; asst. trust officer Security Pacific Bank, Fresno, Calif., 1965-68; trust officer, 1968-72, v.p., mgr., 1972—; instr. San Bernardino Valley Coll., 1962—, Fresno City Coll., 1977—. Served with USN, 1945-46. Mem. Fresno, Bakersfield, Merced estate planning councils. Home: 3222 W Dovewood St Fresno CA 93711 Office: Security Pacific Corp 668 W Shaw Ste 199 Fresno CA 93704

SMITH, RICHARD JAMES, real estate company executive; b. Paterson, N.J., June 15, 1950; s. James John Richard Jr. and Audry Louise (Stalter) S.; m. Suzanne Marie Lukon, Aug. 7, 1971; children: James, Jessica. BBA, Ea. Mich. U., 1972. CPA, Mich. Acct. Coopers & Lybrand, Detroit, 1973-78; asst. contr. Taubman Co., Inc., Troy, Mich., 1978-81; contr. Taubman Co., Inc., Hayward, Calif., 1981-84; dir. fin. svcs. Taubman Co., Inc., Bloomfield Hills, Mich., 1984-85, corp. contr., 1985-87, contr., dir. devel. fin. svcs., 1987-88; sr. v.p., chief fin. officer Katersky Fin., Woodland Hills, Calif., 1988—. Mem. AICPA, Mich. Assn. CPAs. Office: Katersky Fin 21800 Oxnard St Ste 480 Woodland Hills CA 91367

SMITH, RICHARD JOSEPH, treasurer; b. Fremont, Ohio, Jan. 25, 1950; s. Gerard William and Phyllis Jean (Billow) S.; m. Luella Faye Gnepper, Sept. 18, 1971; children: Ryan Joseph, Erin Christine. BBA, Bowling Green State U., 1972. CPA, Ohio. Sr. acct. Peat, Marwick, Main Co., Toledo, 1972-75; treas., chief fin. officer The Cavalear Corp., Sylvania, Ohio, 1975—, also bd. dirs. Mem. pastor-parish relations com., adminstrv. bd. Collingwood United Meth. Ch., Toledo, 1974-78, fin. com., treas., 1976-78; adult Sunday Sch. tchr., mem. pastor-parish relations com. Grace United Meth. Ch., Perrysburg, 1982-83, chmn., 1983; auditor Perrysburg (Ohio) Alliance Ch., 1986-88, fellowship com., 1985-88, chmn., 1986-87, deacon, 1987-88, governing bd., 1988; bd. dirs. alumni bd. Bowling Green State U., 1982-84; bd. dirs., chmn. fin. com., planning com. Toledo Christian Schs., 1987-88. Served as cpl. U.S. Army, 1971. Recipient 4-H Danforth award Sandusky County (Ohio) 4-H Club, 1968; recipient Univ. Bookstore Scholarship, Bowling Green U., 1970-71. Mem. Am. Inst. CPA's, Ohio Soc. CPA's, Christian and Missionary Alliance, Beta Gamma Sigma. Republican. Clubs: Toledo, Falcon (Bowling Green, Ohio). Home: 25738 Brittany Rd Perrysburg OH 43551 Office: Cavalear Corp 6444 Monroe St Sylvania OH 43560

SMITH, ROBERT DRAKE, railroad company executive; b. Ft. Worth, Oct. 26, 1944; s. Kermit Rudebeck and Lynne Grace (Harris) S. B.A. with honors, U. Puget Sound, 1966; M.B.A., U. Pa., 1968. Planning analyst C. & N.W. Ry. Co., Chgo., 1968; supr. program planning C. & N.W. Ry. Co., 1969, mgr. program planning, 1970-73; corp. sec. Chgo. & North Western Transp. Co., 1973-82, v.p., corp. sec., 1982-84, sr. v.p. corp. communications, sec., 1985-86; sr. v.p. investor relations CNW Corp., Chgo., 1986—; dir. Des Moines & Central Iowa Ry., Ft. Dodge, Des Moines & So. Ry., Mpls. Indsl. Ry., Northwestern Communications Co., Ry. Transfer of Mpls., Oshkosh Transp. Co. Vol., Juvenile Ct. Cook County, 1970-78; dir. Gamma Reinsurance Co. Mem. governing bd. Chgo. Symphony. Mem. Am. Soc. Corp. Secs., Assn. Am. R.R.s, Nat. Investor Relations Inst., N.Y. Soc. Security Analysts, Chgo. Council Fgn. Relations, Wharton Sch. Alumni Assn. Clubs: Board Room, N.Y. Athletic Club, Metropolitan, Cliff Dwellers. Home: 1212 N Lake Shore Dr Apt 26BN Chicago IL 60610 Office: Chgo & Northwestern Corp Investor Rels 1 North Western Ctr Chicago IL 60606

SMITH, ROBERT ELLIS, parcel delivery company executive; b. Jersey City, Dec. 20, 1929; s. Hugh E. and Elizabeth L. (Free) S.; m. Marie Orr, Jan. 24, 1970. BS in Bus., Fairleigh Dickinson U., 1957. trustee United Parcel Service Found., 1986—. Sr. v.p. United Parcel Service, Greenwich, Conn., 1955—. Pres. River Vale (N.J.) Rep. Club, 1985—; mem. steering com. Nat. Ctr. for Small Communities, 1986—; chmn. bus. adv. council Transp. Ctr., Northwestern U., 1987—. With U.S. Army, 1951-53. Mem. U.S. C. of C. (services industry council 1986—). Office: United Parcel Svc Greenwich Office Park 5 Greenwich CT 06836

SMITH, ROBERT F., banker; b. Staten Island, N.Y., Oct. 11, 1932; s. Norman Stanley and Lida (Martin) S.; m. Miriam D. Smith; children—Brenda M., Robert F. BA, Bentley Coll., Boston, 1953; D Letters, St. Anselm Coll., 1986. Various positions Gen. Electric Co., 1953-77, staff exec., 1977-81; sr. v.p., treas. Am. Express Co., 1981; vice chmn., dir. Am. Express Bank Ltd. (formerly Am. Express Internat. Banking Corp.), N.Y.C., from 1981, vice chmn., co-chief operating officer, mem. Office of Chief Exec. Officer and Mgmt. Com., 1982-83, pres., chief operating officer, 1983-85, chmn. bd., chief exec. officer, 1985—. Office: Am Express Bank Ltd American Express Tower World Financial Ctr New York NY 10285

SMITH, ROBERT FRANCIS, transportation executive; b. Chgo., Oct. 5, 1943; s. Rudolph Louis and Marie Josephine (Klug) S.; m. Dorka Podmajersky, May 22, 1968 (div. May 1987); children: Wolfgang Sebastian, Dietrich Gustav, James Jeffrey, John Curtis, Edward Bradley. BS, W. Tex. State U., 1972, MS, 1974, MPA, 1978. CPA, registered med. technologist. Staff technician St. Anthony's Hosp., Amarillo, Tex., 1966-72, staff med. technologist, 1972-73, blood bank supr., 1973-78; staff acct. Cornell and Co., Amarillo, Tex., 1978-80, sr. acct., 1980-81, ptnr., 1982-87; treas. Jack B. Kelley, Inc., Amarillo, Tex., 1988—; bd. dirs. W. Tex. State U. Found. Patron Amarillo Little Theatre; com. chair Downtown Lions; mem. St. Joseph's Sch. Bd., 1984—, Middle Sch. Council, Diocese of Amarillo, 1986-88, incubator com. Amarillo C. of C. Served to sgt. USAF, 1964-68. Mem. Am. Inst. CPAs, Tex. Soc. CPAs, Panhandle Chpt. Tex. CPAs (com. chair 1981—), Beta Beta Beta. Clubs: Serra (dir. 1986—), Toastmasters (Toastmaster of the yr. 1987, Parliamentarian 1988, Disting. Toastmaster 1986). Office: Jack B Kelley Inc Rte 1 Box 4000 Amarillo TX 79106

SMITH, ROBERT MASON, b. Fort Sill, Okla., May 5, 1945; s. Arnold Mason and Lillyan (Scott) S.; m. Ramona Lynne Stukey, June 15, 1968; children—David, Angela. BA, Wichita State U., 1967; MA, Ohio U., 1968; PhD, Temple U., 1976. Debate coach Princeton U. (N.J.), 1971-73; dir. oral communication program Wichita (Kans.) State U., 1973-77, chmn. dept. speech communication, 1974-77, assoc. dean Coll. Liberal Arts and Scis., 1977-80, 81-87; dean sch. arts and scis. U. Tenn., Martin, 1987—, assoc. dean Univ. Coll. and Continuing Edn., 1981-85; spl. asst. U.S. Dept. HHS, Washington, 1980-81; cons. in field; chmn. corp. communication bd. Ea. Airlines, Miami, Fla., 1984-86. Contbr. articles to profl. jours. Bd. dirs. Sedgwick County unit Am. Heart Assn., 1982-85; mem. State Behavorial Sci. Regulatory Bd., Topeka, 1985-87; trustee Leasership Kans., Topeka, 1986-87; pres. Citizen Participation Coun., Wichita, 1981-85 ; chmn. Communications and Mktg. com. Sedgwick County United Way, 1986-87; bd. dirs. Wichita Festivals, Inc., 1985-87; chmn. pub. rels. United Way of Plains, Whichita, 1986-88. Recipient Univ. Leadership award Wichita State U., 1978; Excellence in Teaching award Coun. for Advancement and Support of Edn., 1984; HHS fellow, 1980. Mem. Am. Forensic Assn. (editorial bd. 1973-79), Kans. Speech Communication Assn. (Outstanding Coll. Speech Tchr. award 1977, pres. 1978), Assn. Communication Adminstrn. (chmn. profl. devel. com. 1980, pres. elect 1987), Internat. Communication Assn., Assn. for Communications (pres. 1988), Kans. Assn. Commerce and Industry (Kans. Leadership award, 1982), Phi Kappa Phi, Phi Eta Sigma, Delta Sigma Rho-Tau Kappa Alpha, Beta Theta Pi, Phi Theta Kappa, Rotary. Republican. Baptist. Avocations: model railroads, skiing, camping. Home: 168 Weldon Dr Martin TN 38237 Office: U Tenn Sch Arts and Scis Martin TN 38238

SMITH, ROBERT ROYCE, oil and gas operator, real estate developer, bank executive; b. Rule, Tex., July 19, 1928; s. Joseph Bunyan and Ima (Spurlin) S.; m. Claudia Townsend, Dec. 21, 1975; children: Rebecca, Kathy, Joey. BS, Tex. A&M U., 1949. Lab asst. Core Labs., Midland, Tex., 1953; landman Monsanto Co., Midland, 1953-58; landman Burford & Sams, Midland, 1958-60; ind. landman, Midland, 1960-77; exec. asst. Clayton W. Williams, Jr., Midland, 1977—; exec. v.p., dir. ClayDesta Corp., Midland, 1981—; dir., organizer ClayDesta Nat. Bank, 1982—, cons., 1983—; v.p., dir. ClayDesta Regional Med. Ctr., 1985—; ind. oil and gas producer; bd. govs. Plaza Club, Midland, 1983—. Served to 1st lt. U.S. Army, 1951-53. Mem. Tex. A&M U. Ex-Students Assn. Republican. Avocations: photography, golfing, fitness. Office: 6 Desta Dr Ste 3333 Midland TX 79705

SMITH, ROBERT WILLIAM, construction company executive; b. Phila., Nov. 2, 1943; s. William Riley and Erie (Kinser) S.; m. Judith Anne Bredesky, Oct. 3, 1964; children: Elyce Marie, Kristin Ann. Grad. high sch., Phila. Owner Smith Contracting, Phila., 1961-82; project mgr. Constrn. Coordinated Inc., Conshohocken, Pa., 1982-83; v.p. constrn. Conston Corp., Phila., 1984—, also corp. officer, 1986—; cons. R.J. Reynolds, Skolnik's. Mem. Shore Boating Club. Republican. Office: Conston Corp 3250 S 76th St Philadelphia PA 19036

SMITH, RODNEY MARTIN, retail executive; b. Keokuk, Iowa, Jan. 26, 1944; s. LeRoy Elmo and Kathleen English (Horn) S.; m. Phyllis Kay McElwain, Aug. 28, 1966; children: Scott Martin, Stacy Lynne, Leslie Kathleen. BS, NE Mo. State U., 1971. Sales rep. Xerox Corp., St. Louis, 1971-73; mgr. sales Am. Hosp. Supply Corp., Atlanta, 1973-76; mgr. sales Smith Bros. Farm Supply, Inc., Wyaconda, Mo., 1976-79, v.p., 1979-80, pres., 1980—. Dir. Mo. Agri. Industries Council, Jefferson City, 1983-85; committeeman Clark County Rep. Com., Kahoka, 1980—. Served with U.S. Army, 1968-69. Mem. Ducks Unltd. (zone chmn. 1985—, Conservation Service award 1985). Methodist. Lodge: Masons (master 1981-82). Home: PO Box 115 Wyaconda MO 63474 Office: Smith Bros Farm Supply Inc PO Box 146 Wyaconda MO 63474

SMITH, RODNEY WIKE, engineering company executive; b. Havre de Grace, Md., July 29, 1944; s. Marshall Thomas and Ellen Nora (Wike) S.; B.S., Va. Poly. Inst. and State U., 1972; m. Mary Katherine Trent, Dec. 20, 1967; children—Scott Walker, Craig Duncan. Project engr. Hercules, Inc., Radford, Va., 1967-72; planning engr. Va. state Water Control Bd., Richmond, 1972; project mgr. Cen. Shenandoah Planning Dist. Commn., Staunton, 1972-76; v.p., br. office mgr. Patton, Harris, Rust & Assocs., Bridgewater, Va., 1976-82, prin. in charge office Buchanan, W.Va., 1980-82; sr. v.p. Copper & Smith, P.C., Harrisonburg, Va., 1982-88; pres. R.W. Smith & Assocs., P.C., Staunton, Va., 1988—. Apptd. to Va. Resources Authority Citizens Adv. Comm., 1987—. Contbr. articles to profl. jours. Registered profl. engr., Va., W.Va. Named Exec. of Yr., Profl. Secs. Internat.; Cooper and Smith listed among fastest growing pvt. cos. by Inc. mag., 1987. Mem. Nat. Soc. Profl. Engrs., Water Pollution Control Fedn., Am. Water Works Assn., Nat. Water Well Assn. Republican. Lutheran. Home: Rte 5 Box 128 E Staunton VA 24401 Office: 1041 S High St Harrisonburg VA 22801

SMITH, ROGER BONHAM, automotive manufacturing executive; b. Columbus, Ohio, July 12, 1925; s. Emmet Quimby and Bess (Obetz) S.; m. Barbara Ann Rasch, June 7, 1954; children: Roger Bonham, Jennifer Anne, Victoria Belle, Drew Johnston. Student, U. Mich., 1942-44, B.B.A., 1947, M.B.A., 1949. With Gen. Motors, Detroit, 1949—; treas. Gen. Motors, 1970-71, v.p. charge fin. staff, 1971-73; v.p., group exec. in charge of non-automotive and def. group 1973-74, exec. v.p., 1974-80, vice chmn. fin. com., 1975-81, chmn., chief exec. officer, 1981—. Trustee Cranbrook Ednl. Community, Bloomfield Hills, Mich., Mich. Colls. Found., Detroit, Calif. Inst. Tech., Pasadena. Served with USNR, 1944-46. Mem. Bus. Council, Bus. Roundtable, Motor Vehicle Mfrs. Assn. (dir.). Clubs: Detroit, Detroit Athletic, Orchard Lake (Mich.) Country, Bloomfield Hills Country; Links (N.Y.C.). Office: Gen Motors Corp 3044 W Grand Blvd Detroit MI 48202

SMITH, ROGER T., financial planning company executive; b. Ft. Worth, Aug. 16, 1953; s. Thomas Floyd and Rose (O'Neal) S.; m. Betty Carol Nevling, Oct. 6, 1978; children: Shawn Christopher, Kristen Michelle. BA in Criminal Justice, Calif. State U., 1977; cert., Coll. Fin. Planning, Denver, 1987. Salesman Montgomery Ward and Co., Citrus Heights, Calif., 1976-80; dir. mktg. Larence McCarty and Assocs., Sacramento, 1980-81; pres. Smith Johnson Nix and Assocs., Sacramento, 1981—; bd. dirs. Qualified Investments, Sacramento; chmn. fin. planners br. Mgrs. Adv. Bd., Navato, Calif., 1983-87. Contbr. articles to profl. jours. Mem. com. Young Life, Sacramento, 1985-87; fund raiser United Way, 1986, Pub. TV Sta., Sacramento, 1988. Mem. Internat. Assn. for Fin. Planning (chmn. bd. 1987-88), Inst. Cert. Fin. Planners. Republican. Office: Smith Johnson Nix & Assocs 1860 Howe Ave Ste 360 Sacramento CA 95825

SMITH, RUSSELL FRANCIS, transportation executive; b. Washington, Mar. 26, 1944; s. Raymond Francis and Elma Gloria (Daugherty) S. Student East Carolina U., 1964, N.C. State U., 1964-65; BS with honors, U. Md.-Coll. Park, 1969, MBA, 1975. Exec. asst. mgr. Hotel Corp. Am. Internat. Inn and Mayflower Hotel, Washington, 1966-68; sr. venture capital cons. Initiative Investing Corp., Washington, 1968-69; pres., gen. mgr. Associated Trades Corp., Washington, 1970-74; cons. in fin., Greenbelt, Md., 1974-76; mng. cons. Bradford Nat. Corp., Washington, 1976-79; v.p. OAO Corp., Washington, 1979-81; ptnr. for fin. evaluation and ops. analysis Blake, Brunell, Lehmann & Co., Washington, 1981-86; v.p. mgmt. services adminstrn. United Airlines Services Corp., Lakewood, Colo., 1986—. Chmn. com. on wildlife Prince George Humane Soc., Hyattsville, Md., 1968-71, Soc. for Prevention Cruelty to Animals, Hyattsville. 1971-75. Served with U.S. Army, 1963-66. Decorated Silver Star medal, Bronze Star medal with V device, Purple Heart. Mem. Am. Fin. Assn., Ops. Research Soc. Am., Am. Acctg. Assn., N.Am. Soc. Corp. Planners, Internat. Assn. Math. Modeling, Assn. MBA Execs. (registered investment advisor), Beta Gamma Sigma, Beta Alpha Psi. Republican.

SMITH, RUSSELL WESLEY, management consultant, organizational development trainer; b. Penn Yan, N.Y., Jan. 23, 1947; s. Wesley Sanford and Gladys Klothe S.; m. Janice Larzelere, June 16, 1984; stepchildren—Gerald Allen, Christopher Michael. A.A.S., SUNY, 1973; B.S. cum laude, N.H. Coll., 1976. Project mgr. Robert Bell & Co., Balt., 1976-77; pres. Smith Klothe Asso., Warsaw, N.Y., 1983—; assoc. Resource Assos., Inc., Newmarket, N.H., 1979-84; assoc. Bus. Planning Group, Westport, Conn., 1985—; assoc. Cons. Capacities Group Inc., Cold Spring Harbor, N.Y., 1983—; assoc. Resource Mgmt. Group, Boston, 1984-85, Byrne Mgmt. Group, Inc., Medford, N.J., 1985—; cons. C. Todd, Inc., Haddenfield, N.J., 1978-79, Naus & Newlyn, Inc., Paoli, Pa., 1977-78. Served with Signal Corps, U.S. Army, 1966-68. Home and Office: Maple Winds 4768 Wilder Rd Warsaw NY 14569

SMITH, SCOTT ALAN, data processing and manufacturing management consultant; b. Buffalo, Aug. 31, 1957; s. Donald James and Geraldine (Manicki) S.; m. Rochelle Denise Rosenthal, May 25, 1985. BS in Computer Sci., Rensselaer Polytech. Inst., 1979. Analyst Arthur Andersen and Co., N.Y.C., 1979-80; sr. analyst Arthur Andersen and Co., Stamford, Conn., 1980-82; mgr. Arthur Andersen and Co., N.Y.C., 1982-86; sr. mgr. Arthur Andersen and Co., Rochester, N.Y., 1986—. Instr. Jr. Achievement, Rochester, 1987-88; vol. Meml. Art Gallery, Rochester, 1986—. Home: 300 Harbor Hill Rd Rochester NY 14617 Office: Arthur Andersen & Co 1 Marine Midland Pla Ste 1500 Rochester NY 14604

SMITH, SCOTT CLYBOURN, communications company executive; b. Evanston, Ill., Sept. 13, 1950; s. E. Sawyer and Jerolanne (Jones) S.; m. Martha Reilly, June 22, 1974; children—Carolyn Baldwin, Thomas Clybourn. B.A., Yale U., 1973; M.Mgmt., Northwestern U., 1976. Comml. banking officer No. Trust Co., Chgo., 1973-77; fin. planning mgr. Tribune Co., Chgo., 1977-79, asst. treas., 1979-81, treas., 1981-82, v.p., treas., 1982-84, v.p., controller, treas., 1984-85, v.p. fin., 1985—. Bd. dirs., YMCA of Met. Chgo., 1984. Episcopalian. Clubs: Glen View (Golf, Ill.); University (Chgo.); Yale (N.Y.C.). Office: Tribune Co 435 N Michigan Ave Chicago IL 60611

SMITH, SHERWOOD HUBBARD, JR., utilities executive; b. Jacksonville, Fla., Sept. 1, 1934; s. Sherwood Hubbard and Catherine Gertrude (Milliken) S.; m. Eva Hackney Hargrave, July 20, 1957; children: Marlin Hamilton, Cameron Hargrave, Eva Hackney. AB, U. N.C., 1956, JD, 1960. Bar: N.C. 1960. Assoc. Lassiter, Moore & Van Allen, Charlotte, 1960-62; ptnr. Joyner & Howison, Raleigh, 1963-65; assoc. gen. counsel Carolina Power & Light Co., Raleigh, 1965-70, sr. v.p., gen. counsel, 1971-74, exec. v.p., 1974-76, pres., 1976—, chmn., 1980—, also bd. dirs.; bd. dirs. Am. Nuclear Energy Council, 1980—, U.S. Council on Energy Awareness, 1st Wachovia Corp., Southeastern Electric Exchange, Hackney Bros. Body Co., Wilson, N.C., Wachovia Bank & Trust Co., Durham Life Ins. Co., Durham Corp.; bd. dirs. Edison Electric Inst., 1981—, chmn. bd., 1985-86; chmn., bd. dirs. Southeastern Electric Reliability Council, 1988—; mem. N.Y. Stock Exchange Listed Co. Adv. Com. Chmn. Raleigh Civic Ctr. Authority, 1973-77; vice chmn. Morehead Scholar Cen. Selection Com., U. N.C., 1970—; mem. Gov.'s Efficiency Study Commn., 1973, N.C. Council Mgmt. and Devel.; bd. dirs. Bus. Found. N.C., 1977—, sec., 1977-81, pres., 1981—; trustee Z. Smith Reynolds Found., 1978—; chmn., trustee Ind. Coll. Fund N.C., 1986-87; chmn. bd. dirs. N.C. Heart Assn., 1971-74; bd. dirs. United Fund Wake County; bd. dirs., exec. com. N.C. Citizens for Bus. and Industry, chmn. 1985-86; bd. dirs. Research Triangle Found. of N.C.; mem. com. U.S. World Energy Conf.; bd. dirs. Microelectronics Ctr. of N.C., 1980—; chmn. bd. trustees Rex Hosp.; mem. Pres.'s Coun. for Internat. Youth Exch., Kenan Inst.; trustee Com. for Econ. Devel. Inst. for Study of Pvt. Enterprise. Ensign USN, 1956-57. Mem. Electric Power Research Inst. (bd. dirs.), Greater Raleigh C. of C. (pres. 1979), Am. Nuclear Soc., U.S. C. of C. (energy com.), Phi Beta Kappa. Home: 408 Drummond Dr Raleigh NC 27609 Office: Carolina Power & Light Co 411 Fayetteville St Mall Raleigh NC 27602

SMITH, STANLEY VLADIMIR, economist, financial service company executive; b. Rhinelander, Wis., Nov. 16, 1946; s. Valy Zdenek and Sylvia (Cohen) S.; children: Cara, David. BS in Ops. Research, Cornell U., 1968; MBA, U. Chgo., 1972, postgrad., 1973. Lectr. U. Chgo., 1973; economist bd. govs. Fed. Res. System, Washington, 1973-74; staff economist First Nat. Bank of Chgo., 1974; assoc. December Group, Chgo., 1974-77; founding pres. Seaquest Internat., Chgo., 1977—; mgr., ptnr. Ibbotson Assocs., Chgo., 1981-85; pres. Corp. Fin. Group, Ltd., Chgo., 1981—; bd. dirs. Seaquest, Chgo.; expert econ. witness in field. Founding editor Stocks, Bonds, Bills and Inflation yearbook, 1984; also contbr. articles in field. Fellow Allied Chem., 1967, John McMullen Trust, 1969; grantee Ford Found., 1972, U.S. Fed. Res., 1973. Mem. Am. Econ. Assn., Am. Fin. Assn., Nat. Assn. Forensic Economists, Alpha Delta Phi. Republican. Office: Corp Fin Group 1165 N Clark St Ste 650 Chicago IL 60610

SMITH, STANTON THOMAS, insurance company data processing executive; b. Portland, Maine, Aug. 2, 1925; s. Cheever Stanton and Doris Faye (Ingersoll) S.; m. Betty Ann Brown, June 9, 1950; children: Stephen Neil, Gary Stanton, Rae Ellen. BA in Econs., Bates Coll., 1950. Adjuster super claims Liberty Mut. Ins. Co., Boston, 1950-60, methods analyst, 1960-68, methods mgr., 1968-72, asst. v.p. stats., 1972-80, v.p. data processing, 1980—. Served with U.S. Merchant Marine, 1945-46. Mem. Assn. for System Mgmt. (pres. Mayflower chpt. 1968-69). Office: Liberty Mut Ins Co 225 Borthwick Ave Portsmouth NH 03801

SMITH, STELLA ELIZABETH, multi-housing company executive; b. Springfield, Mo., July 6, 1931; d. Russell Lena and Oma Oble (Stockstill) Baber; m. Arthur A. Smith, May 30, 1952 (div. 1981); children: Michael A., Barbara A., James Edward, Cynthia Sue. Student St. Louis U., 1981-83. Office mgr. Consumers Warehouse Markets, Springfield, 1948-52; acctg. clk. Mathieson Chem. Corp., Little Rock, 1952-54; group leader McDonnell Aircraft Corp., St. Louis, 1954-59; office mgr. Arthur A. Smith, M.D., O'Fallon, Ill., 1968-74; pres., chief exec. officer Mantek, Inc., Springfield, 1981—. Bd. dirs. Signal Hill United Meth. Ch., Belleville, Ill., 1973-87. Mem. Nat. Assn. Women Bus. Owners, Nat. Assn. Female Execs., P.E.O. (treas. 1983-84, v.p. 1986-87, pres. 1987-89), Springfield Apt. Assn., Mo. Apt. Assn., Nat. Apt. Assn., St. Clair County LWV (bd. dirs. 1978-84), Women's Aux. Ill. Med. Soc. (bd. dirs. 1968-72), Women's Aux. St. Clair County Med. Soc. (safety chmn. 1963-69), Greater Springfield C. of C., St. Clair County Genealogy Soc. (charter 1977). Republican. Avocations: travel, theater, reading, collecting cook books. Home and Office: 7412 Williamsburg Colonial Ln Shrewsbury MO 63119

SMITH, STEVEN JAMES, insurance company executive; b. Ft Wayne, Ind., Jan. 25, 1945; s. Richard Hibbins and Helen Lucile (Coplen) S.; m. Carol Morrele, Feb. 19, 1972; children: Lucas, Tyler. AB, U. Mich., 1967; MBA, Harvard U., 1970. C.L.U. Asst. v.p. Lincoln Nat. Life Co., Ft. Wayne, Ind., 1970-75; v.p. Mut. Benefit Life Co., Kansas City, Mo., 1975-82; sr. v.p. Continental Ins. Co., N.Y.C., 1982-85; exec. v.p. Continental Ins. Co., N.Y.C., 1985—. Mem. Chatham Sch. Bd., 1988—; bd. dirs. Inroads Inc., 1987—, Inroads No. N.J., Newark, 1983—; pres. Learning exchange, Kansas City, Mo., 1980-82, Inroads/Kansas City, 1980-82; v.p. Pub. TV Nineteen Inc., Kansas City, 1979-81. Branstrom scholar; McAndless scholar. Mem. Am. Soc. CLUs. Home: 193 Noe Ave Chatham NJ 07928 Office: Continental Corp 180 Maiden Ln New York NY 10038

SMITH, STEVEN JEROME, home building company executive; b. Phila., Sept. 24, 1940; s. Clarence and Margaret (O'Conner) S.; m. Rebecca Reed, 1960; children: Scott, Jennifer. SB in Indsl. Mgmt., MIT, 1962. Various positions with Whirlpool, Benton Harbor, Mich., 1962-70, Engelhard Industries, Murray Hill, N.J., 1970-72; various positions with Ryan Homes Inc., Pitts., 1972-84, pres., chief operating officer, 1984-86, pres., chief exec. officer, 1986—; bd. dirs. NVRyan L.P., McLean, Va., Union Nat. Bank, Pitts. Mem. adv. bd. Salvation Army, Pitts., 1986—; agt. Class of 1962, Cambridge, Mass., 1962—; chmn. bd. trustees D.T. Watson Hosp., Sewickley, Pa., 1983—; bd. dirs. Pitts. Pub. Theater, 1986—. Recipient Corp. Leadership award MIT, 1985. Clubs: Allegheny Country, Edgeworth (Sewickley).

SMITH, STEVEN OWEN, mortgage company executive; b. San Angelo, Tex., July 16, 1956; s. Stanley Orton and Doris Claire (Allain) S.; m. Jeri

Deanne DeCuypere, May 18, 1985 (div. Feb. 1988). BA, U. West Fla., 1981. CPA, Fla. Mgr. McDonald's Corp., Ft. Walton Beach, Fla., 1974-81; staff acct. Touche Ross & Co., Jacksonville, Fla., 1982-83; internal auditor Tucker Holding Co., Jacksonville, 1983-85; asst. controller Tucker Bros., Inc., Jacksonville, 1985-86, v.p., controller, 1986—; also bd. dirs. Tucker Bros., Inc. Mem. Am. Inst. CPA's, Fla. Inst. CPA's. Roman Catholic. Home: 10835 Percheron Dr Jacksonville FL 32223 Office: Tucker Bros Inc 204 Pearl St Jacksonville FL 32202

SMITH, T. LAMAR, financial executive; b. Gadsden, Ala., July 26, 1956; s. George Allen and Jean (Waldrep) S.; m. Karen Parris, Jan. 1, 1978 (div.) 1978); m. Phyllis Thompson, Dec. 14, 1984. BS in Mgmt. and Fin., U. Ala., Birmingham, 1978. Cert. fin. planner. With Record Bar, Inc., Gadsden, 1978-84, Loveman Realty, Inc., Gadsden, 1984-85; fin. planner Investor Svcs. Co., Gadsden, 1985—. Fund raiser Boy Scouts Am., Anniston, Ala., 1985—. Mem. Inst. Cert. Fin. Planners, Gadsden C. of C., Kiwanis. Home: 701 Turrentine St Gadsden AL 35901

SMITH, TAD RANDOLPH, lawyer; b. El Paso, July 20, 1928; s. Eugene Rufus and Dorothy (Derrick) S.; m. JoAnn Wilson, Aug. 24, 1949; children: Laura, Derrick, Cameron Ann. BBA, U. Tex. 1952, LLB, 1951. Bar: Tex. 1951; assoc. firm Kemp, Smith, Duncan & Hammond, El Paso, 1951, partner, 1952—, mng. ptnr., 1975—; dir. El Paso Electric Co., M-Bank El Paso N.A., Property Trust Am.. El Paso Cert. Devel. Corp., El Paso Indsl. Devel. Corp. Active United Way of El Paso; chmn. El Paso County Reps., 1958-61, Tex. Rep. State Exec. Com., 1961-62; alt. del. Rep. Nat. Conv., 1952, 62, del., 1964; trustee Robert E. and Evelyn McKee Found. 1970—; mem. devel. bd. U. Tex. El Paso, 1973-81, v.p., 1975, chmn. 1976; dinner treas. Nat. Jewish Hosp. and Research Ctr., 1977, chmn. 1978, presenter of honoree, 1985; bd. dirs. Southwestern Children's Home, El Paso, 1959-78, Nat. Conf. Christians and Jews, 1965-76, chmn. 1968-69, adv. dir. 1976—, Renaissance 400, El Paso, 1982—. Named Outstanding Young Man El Paso, El Paso Jaycees, 1961; recipient Humanitarian award El Paso chpt. NCCJ, 1983. Fellow Tex. Bar Found.; mem. ABA, Tex. Bar Assn., El Paso Bar Assn. (pres. 1971-72), El Paso C. of C. (dir. 1979-82), Sigma Chi. Republican. Methodist. Home: 1202 Thunderbird El Paso TX 79912 Office: Kemp Smith Duncan & Hammond 221 N Kansas 2000 MBank Pla El Paso TX 79901

SMITH, THOMAS ARTHUR, utilities company executive, accountant; b. Frederick, Md., June 22, 1954; s. Jack A. and Mary Ann (Holter) S.; m. Katherine Sue Leamon, Nov. 8, 1986. BA, Catawba Coll., 1976; MS, Purdue U., 1978; MS in Indsl. Mgmt., Ga. Inst. Tech., 1980. CPA, Ga. Mgr. fin. services Oglethorpe Power Corp., Atlanta, 1979-82, mgr. fin. dept., 1983-86, v.p. fin., 1986—; mem. cash mgmt. task force DOE Nuclear Waste Fund, Washington, 1985-86. Vol. YMCA, Salisbury, N.C., 1973-76, West Lafayette, Ind., 1977-78. Fellow Ga. Soc. CPA's; mem. Am. Inst. CPA's, G&T Acctg. and Fin. Assn. Republican. Club: Yellow Jacket (Atlanta). Office: Oglethorpe Power Corp 2100 E Exchange Pl Tucker GA 30084

SMITH, THOMAS WINSTON, cotton marketing executive; b. Crosbyton, Tex., Mar. 16, 1935; s. Lance L. and Willie Mae (Little) S.; m. Patricia Mae Zachary, Dec. 13, 1958; children—Janna Olean, Thomas Mark. B.S., Tex. A&M U., 1957; P.M.D., Harvard U., 1964. Various positions Calcot Ltd., Bakersfield, Calif., 1957-77, exec. v.p., pres., 1977—; v.p. Amcot, Inc., Amcot Internat., Inc., Bakersfield, 1977—, also bd. dirs.; v.p. Nat. Cotton Coun., Memphis; bd. mgrs. N.Y. Cotton Exchange, N.Y.C. Bd. dir. Greater Bakersfield Meml. Hosp.; mem. pres.'s adv. commn. Calif. State Coll., Bakersfield. Mem. Rotary.

SMITH, TOM EUGENE, food retail executive; b. Salisbury, N.C., May 2, 1941; s. Ralph Eugene and Cora Belle (Ervin) S.; m. Martha Hatley; children: Leigh Ann, Nancy Thompson. AB in Bus. Adminstrn., Catawba Coll., 1964, LLD (hon.), 1986. With Del Monte Sales Co., 1964-67; account mgr. Del Monte Sales Co., Hickory, N.C., 1967-68; sales supr. Del Monte Sales Co., Charlotte, N.C., 1969-70; buyer Food Lion Stores, Inc., Salisbury, 1970-74, v.p. distbn., 1974-77, exec. v.p., 1977-81, pres., 1981—, chief exec. officer, 1986—, also bd. dirs.; chief exec. officer Food Lion Inc., Salisbury, 1986—; bd. dirs. N.C. Nat. Bank (chmn. bd. Salisbury chpt.), N.C. Food Dealers (pres. 1988). Trustee Catawba Coll., 1986—; bd. dirs. United Way, Salisbury, 1975-77. Recipient Martin Luther King Humanitarian award 1987, bronze and silver Chief Exec. Officer of Yr. awards Fin. World Mag., 1988. Mem. Nat. Assn. Retail Grocers, Sales Execs. Club (bd. dirs. 1974-79, pres. 1980), N.C. Food Dealers Assn. (bd. dirs. 1981—, 3d v.p. 1985, 2d v.p. 1986—), Am. Legion, C. of C. (bd. dirs. 1975-77). Republican. Lutheran. Club: Salisbury Country. Lodge: Rotary (bd. dirs. 1975-76). Office: Food Lion Inc Harrison Rd PO Box 1330 Salisbury NC 28144

SMITH, VANGY EDITH, accountant, consultant, writer, artist; b. Saskatoon, Sask., Can., Dec. 17, 1937; d. Wilhelm and Anne Ellen (Hartshorne) Gogel: m. Clifford Wilson, May 12, 1958 (de. Dec. 1978); children: Kenneth, Koral, Kevin, Korey, Kyle; m. Terrence Raymond Smith, Dec. 14, 1979. Student, Saskatoon Tech. Collegiate Inst., 1956, BBA, 1958, MBA, 1987, PhD in English with honors, 1988. Accounts payable clk. Maxwell Labs., Inc., San Diego, 1978; invoice clk. Davies Electric, Saskatoon, 1980-81; office mgr. Ladee Bug Ceramics, Saskatoon, 1981-87, Lazars Investments Corp., Eugene, Oreg., 1987; bookkeeper accounts payable Pop Geer, Eugene, Oreg., 1987; office mgr., bookkeeper Willamette Sprts Ctr. Inc., Eugene, Oreg., 1987—. Contbr. articles to scholarly jours. (recipient doctoral award 1987). Counselor Drug and Rehab. Ctr., Eugene, 1970-88; trustee Children's Farm Home, Corvallis, Oreg., 1989—. Recipient 3d and 4th place artists' awards Lane County Fair, 1987, 1st and 2d place awards Nat. Writing 1987, 88. Mem. Women's Christian Temperance Union (life, pres., state dir. projection methods 1987—, Appreciation award 1982, Presdl. award 1985), Found. for Christian Living, Lane County Council Orgns. (3d v.p. 1988—), Am. Soc. Writers, Beta Sigma Phi. Democrat. Home and Office: 1199 N Terry St Space 371 Eugene OR 97402

SMITH, WARD, manufacturing company executive, lawyer; b. Buffalo, Sept. 13, 1930; s. Andrew Leslie and Georgia (Ward) S.; m. Gretchen Keller Diefendorf, Oct. 29, 1960; children: Jennifer Hood, Meredith Ward, Jonathan Andrew, Sarah Katherine. Student, Georgetown U., 1948-49; AB, Harvard, 1952; JD, U. Buffalo, 1955. Bar: N.Y. 1955, Mass. 1962, Ohio 1977. Assoc. Lawler & Rockwood, N.Y.C., 1959-62; sec., gen. counsel Whitin Machine Works, Whitinsville, Mass., 1962-66; sec. White Consol. Industries, Inc., Cleve., 1966-69, v.p., 1967-69, sr. v.p., 1969-72, exec. v.p., 1972-76, pres., chief adminstrv. officer, 1976-84, pres., chief operating officer, 1984-86, pres., chief exec. officer, 1985-86, chmn., 1986; pres., chief exec. officer NACCO Industries, Inc., Cleve., 1986—, also chmn. bd.; bd. dirs. Soc. Bank and Soc. Corp., Sundstrand Corp., Rockford, Ill. Pres., trustee The Musical Arts Assn.; op. trustee The Cleve. Orch., Case Western Res. U., Cleve., others. Served to lt. USNR, 1955-59. Mem. ABA, N.Y. State Bar Assn. Clubs: Pepper Pike Country (Ohio); Union, Tavern (Cleve.). Home: 19701 N Park Blvd Shaker Heights OH 44122 Office: NACCO Industries Inc 12500 Shaker Blvd Cleveland OH 44120

SMITH, WARDELL CAESAR, personnel executive; b. Des Moines, Nov. 11, 1936; s. Robert Edward Smith and Grace Alice (Coyle) Rogers; m. Phyllis Anne Swink, Feb. 19, 1983; children: Corlis, Yvonne, Grayce, Caesar II, Robert, Michael Hubberd. BA, U. Nebr., Omaha, 1971. Enlisted U.S. Army, 1956, advanced through grades to maj., 1968; served in Vietna, ret., 1976; tng. assoc. Prin. Fin. Group, Des Moines, 1977-81, asst. tng. dir., 1981-86, dir. tng., 1986—. Democrat. Mem. Christian Church (Disciples of Christ). Home: 2525 Pine Circle Urbandale IA 50322 Office: Prin Fin Group 711 High St Des Moines IA 50309

SMITH, WARREN ALLEN, recording studio corporate executive; b. Minburn, Iowa, Oct. 27, 1921; s. Harry Clark and Ruth Marion (Miles) S.; BA, U. No. Iowa, 1948; MA, Columbia U., 1949. Chmn. dept. Eng., Bentley Sch., N.Y.C., 1949-54, New Canaan (Conn.) High Sch., 1954-86; pres., chmn. bd. Variety Sound Corp., N.Y.C., 1961—; pres. Afro-Carib Records, 1971—, Talent Mgmt., 1982—, pres. AAA Recording Studio, 1985—; pres. Variety Rec. Studio, 1988—; instr. Columbia U., 1961-62. Pres., Taursa Fund, 1971-73. Book rev. editor The Humanist, 1953-58; editor (jour.) Taking Stock, 1967—; contbr. book revs. Libr. Jour.; syndicated columnist Manhattan Scene in W.I. newspapers. Treas. Secular Humanist Soc. N.Y., 1988—. With AUS, 1940-44. Recipient Leavey award Freedoms Found. at Valley Forge, 1985. Mem. ASCAP, Mensa, Internat. Press Inst., Am. Unitarian Assn., Brit. Humanist Assn., Humanist Book Club (pres. 1957-62), Bertrand Russell Soc. (v.p. 1977-80, bd. dirs. 1977—), Mensa Investment Club (chmn. 1967, 73—). Signer Humanist Manifesto II, 1973. Avocation: teratology. Home: 1435 Bedford St Apt 10- Stamford CT 06905 Office: Variety Rec Studios 130 W 42nd St Rm 551 New York NY 10036

SMITH, WENDELL MURRAY, graphic arts control and equipment manufacturing company executive; b. Bklyn., May 15, 1935; s. J. Henry and Roberta (Foard) S.; m. Margaret McGregor, Aug. 24, 1957; children: Karen, Wendy, Kimberley, Kathryn, Jennifer. AB, Dartmouth Coll., 1957, MS in Engring., 1958. Devel. engr. Sikorsky Aircraft Co., Stratford, Conn., 1958-60; sales engr., mgr. Barnes Engring. Corp., Stamford, Conn., 1960-65; v.p. mktg. Baldwin-Gegenheimer Corp., Stamford, 1966-70, pres., chief exec. officer, 1971-79; pres. Polaris Corp., Stamford, 1980-84; pres., chmn. bd., chief exec. officer Baldwin Tech. Co., Inc., Rowayton, Conn., 1984—; bd. dirs. Reeves Communications Corp., N.Y.C., Totel Systems, Inc., Westford, Mass. Mem. ISAC 2, U.S. Dept. Commerce, Washington, 1986—; bd. dirs. Stamford Partnership Conn., 1978. Mem. Rsch. and Engring. Council (exec. v.p., pres.), Graphic Communications Am. (bd. dirs., vice chmn.), Soderstrom Soc. of Nat. Assn. Printers and Lithographers, Stamford Yacht Club, Royal Bermuda Yacht Club, Mid-Ocean Club. Republican. Methodist. Home: 3 Manor House, Smith's F107s Bermuda Office: Baldwin Tech Co Inc 65 Rowayton Ave Rowayton CT 06853

SMITH, WILFRED A., entrepreneur; b. N.Y.C., Aug. 9, 1968; s. Wilfred A. and Eva (Turner) S. Student, Tulane U., 1978-86, U. New Orleans, 1985-87, Princeton U., 1986—. V.p. Prodigy One Corp., New Orleans, 1978-80; pres. Prodigy Two Corp., Marrero, La., 1980-86, Human Devel., Marrero, 1987—; advisor Nationwide Credit Services, Metairie, La., 1987-88; exec. advisor Magnavox Corp., New Orleans, 1987-88; bd. dirs. The Omega Group, Dallas, 1983-86. Author: Adult Education, 1986, Lousiana: Renewing the Dream, 1987, Message from Oblivion, 1987; inventor 1 million bps modem, 1986. Supporter Council for Fiscal Reform, New Orleans, 1987—; campaigner Jesse Jackson's PUSH, 1984—, ACORN, New Orleans, 1986—. Recipient Promising Entrepreneur award Young Enterepreneurs Am., New Orleans, 1984, Am. Achievement award Borg-Warner, 1986. Mem. SIG Nat., Soc. Engrs., Soc. Black Engrs. Mem. Ch. of God. Clubs: Am. Mensa (New Orleans). Office: Human Devel 2577 Jarrot Dr Marerro LA 70073-0189

SMITH, WILLIAM ASHLEY, business executive, lawyer; b. Birmingham, Ala., Sept. 14, 1944; S. Robert Wesley and Nancy Victoria (Davis) S.; m. Blakeley Dean Dent, Sept. 2, 1967; children—William Ashley, Andrew Lindsey. B.A., U. Va., 1966; J.D., U. Ala., 1969. Bar: Ala. Atty. Sonat, Inc., Birmingham, Ala., 1970-73, asst. sec., 1973-79, asst. v.p., asst. sec., 1979-80, asst. v.p., asst. sec., assoc. gen. counsel, 1980-81, v.p., gen. counsel, sec., 1981-84, v.p., gen. counsel, 1984-87, sr. v.p., gen. counsel, 1987—. Asst. dist. commr. Boy Scouts Am., Birmingham, 1983; bd. dirs. Birmingham Music Club, 1984, Ala. Symphony Assn., Birmingham, 1985, Met. Arts Council, 1987-88. Mem. ABA, Ala. Bar Assn., Am. Assn. Corp. Counsel (bd. dirs. Ala. chpt. 1983—), Southeastern Law Inst. (planning com.). Episcopalian. Clubs: Country of Birmingham, Downtown, Jefferson.

SMITH, WILLIAM BRUCE, financial and investment planner; b. Whitinsville, Mass., Dec. 8, 1955; s. Lewis W. and Elinor G. (Wood) S.; m. Rebecca A. Nydam, Aug. 6, 1977; children: Benjamin, Alecia, Peter, Gabriel. BSBA, Bryant Coll., 1977; cert., Coll. Fin. Planning, Denver, 1988. Sales rep. Beecham Lab., Inc., Bristol, Tenn., 1978-80; fin. planner Paul Revere Cos., Worcester, Mass., 1980-81; fin. and investment planner First Worcester Fin./Grimes, Smith Fin. Group, Worcester, 1981—. Chmn. fin. com. Whitinsville Christian Sch., 1984-87. Mem. Internat. Assn. Fin. Planners, Coll. Fin. Planning. Delta Mu Delta. republican. Mem. Christian Ref. Ch. Home: 10 Williams St Uxbridge MA 01569 Office: Grimes Smith Fin Group 484 Main St 510 Worcester MA 01608

SMITH, WILLIAM DORSEY, industrial plastics company executive; b. Evansville, Ind., Oct. 27, 1949; s. William Glen and Mary Jane (Dorsey) S.; m. Marilyn Phyllis Belt, July 21, 1973; 1 child, Jennifer Lynn. BS in Bus., U. Evansville, 1971; MBA, Mich. State U., 1973; postgrad. in mgmt., Stanford U., 1985. Mgmt. intern Oldsmobile div. Gen. Motors Corp., Detroit, 1972; product mgr. Vick Chem. Co. div. Proctor & Gamble, N.Y.C., 1973-74; fin. mgr. Richardson-Merrell div. Vick Chem. Co. div. Proctor & Gamble, Wilton, Conn., 1974-75; gen. mgr. PVC Plastic Supply Co., Evansville, 1976-80, chief exec. officer, 1980—; cons., gen. mgr. Pegasus Group, Evansville, 1980—; mng. ptnr. Smith Properties, Evansville, 1982—. Mem. Nat. Assn. Plastic Distbrs. (bd. dirs.), Nat. Assn. Wholesale Distbrs. Office: PVC Plastics Co Inc PO Box 5029 Evansville IN 47716

SMITH, WILLIAM HERBERT, international development consultant; b. Cin., Nov. 11, 1943; s. James and Hilda Lee (Mitchell) W.; m. Betty Punim Kauga, May 13, 1983; children: Mario Demetrius, Hilda Marie. BS in Psychology, Xavier U., 1967; MEd, U. Mass., 1974; cert. Chinese Law, East China Normal U., Shanghai, 1983. Spl. asst. HEW, Washington, 1972-74; mgmt. analysis officer USPHS, Rockville, Md., 1974-75; sr. policy analyst U.S. Office Edn., Washington, 1975-76; mktg. rep. Data Mgmt. Systems Inc., Washington, 1976-77; mgr. program devel. Computer Scis. Corp., Falls Church, Va., 1977-80; prin. W.H. Smith & Assocs., Washington, 1980-81, Cin., 1987—; asst. sec. Dept. Prime Minister, Papua New Guinea, 1981-84; sr. project dir. Mgmt. Systems Internat., Cin., 1984-87; cons. Cin. Health Dept., 1985, Evanston Community Coun., Cin., 1986. Chmn. fin. Victory Neighborhood Svcs. Agy., Cin., 1984-86; mem. allocations com. United Way-Community Chest, Cin., 1985-86; chmn. Met. Bd. Social Concerns, Cin., 1985—; mem. steering comm. March of Dimes, Cin., 1986; sr. arbitrator Better Bus. Bur., Cin. Capt. USMC, 1967-69, Vietnam. Recipient Vol. award Mayor City of Cin., 1985; Univ. scholar Xavier U., 1967. Fellow Joint Ctr. Polit. Studies (assoc.); mem. Am. Arbitration Assn., Computer Support Assn., Soc. Internat. Devel. Methodist. Office: PO Box 6236 Cincinnati OH 45206

SMITH, WILLIAM HUGH, JR., brokerage house executive; b. Bklyn., July 22, 1935; s. William Hugh and Frances Norren (Magee) S.; m. Lorraine E. Fiore, June 10, 1958 (div. 1980); children: Christopher, Timothy, Lourdes Ann, Gregory; m. Nancy Ann Smith, Apr. 28, 1984. BS in Econs., Villanova U., 1957; MBA, Boston U., 1974. Internal auditor Am. Cyanamid, N.Y.C., 1961; builder, pres. Contemporary Devel. Corp., Cupsaw Lake, N.J., 1961-65; cons. Handle Brooks Co., Westwood, N.J., 1965-69; pres. Shareholder Svcs., Inc. (ValueLine), Boston, 1969-74; v.p. Bradford, Inc., Boston, 1974-79, Bank of New Eng., Boston, 1979-81; pres. Securities Fund Svcs., Inc., St. Petersburg, Fla., 1981-85; pres., bd. dirs. Pioneering Svcs. Corp., Boston, 1985—; bd. dirs. CMS Inc., Marshfield, Mass.; propr. Halcyon Hills Farm-Dairy, Andover, N.H., 1986—. Lt. USNR, 1957-61. Mem. Investment Co. Inst. (ops., broker-dealer adv. com. 1980). Home: 8 Browne St Brookline MA 02146 Office: Pioneering Svcs Corp 60 State St Boston MA 02109

SMITH, WILLIAM KENDALL, transportation executive; b. Oakland, Calif., Apr. 21, 1922; s. Earl B. and Lois (Loeffler) S.; m. Jean Lucille Taylor, May 23, 1949; children: Gregory, Lindsay, Christopher, Vincent. B.B.A., U. Minn., 1947; A.M.P., Harvard U., 1969. With Gen. Mills, Inc., 1948—; v.p. and dir. transp. Gen. Mills, Inc., Golden Valley, Minn., 1968-84; chmn. Lake States transp. unit Soo Line, Mpls., 1985-87; sr. exec. fellow U. Minn. Sch. Mgmt., Mpls., 1984—; mem. exec. com. Transp. Research Bd. NRC, 1974-80; dir. Nat. Indsl. Transp. League, Washington, 1974-84, Transp. Data Coordinating Com., 1970-84; chmn. U.S. Ry. Assn., 1977-80, dir., 1974-77. Mem. edit. rev. bd. Transp. Journal, 1980—. Bd. dirs. Family and Children Services, Mpls., 1977—; adv. com. Ctr. Transp. Studies MIT, 1980—. Served with U.S. Army, 1942-45. Recipient McCullough award Nat. Indsl. Transp. League, 1983, Scheleen award Am. Soc. Transp. and Logistics, 1984; Salzberg Meml. Lectr. Syracuse U., 1977. Mem. Am. Soc. Traffic and Transp. (Award of Excellence 1983), Nat. Council Phys. Distbn. Mgmt., Pvt. Truck Council Am., Transp. Research Bd., Ops. Research Soc. Am., Alpha Delta Phi, Beta Gamma Sigma. Clubs: Northwest Tennis & Racquet (St. Louis Park, Minn.); Hazeltine Nat. Golf (Chaska, Minn.). Home: 2439 Sherwood Hills Rd Minnetonka MN 55343 Office: U Minn Carlson Sch Mgmt Minneapolis MN 55455

SMITH, WILLIAM RICHARD, III, financial planner; b. Seymour, Ind., Oct. 24, 1946; s. William Richard Jr. and Dorothy (McNeil) S.; m. Susan Southwell, July 21, 1973; 1 child, Lane McNeil. BBA, Lenoir-Rhyne Coll., 1968; MBA, U. Ga., 1971. Chartered fin. cons., ChFC. Owner, fin. planner W. Richard Smith, CFP, Danville, Va., 1973-83; pres. Fin. Planning Resources, Inc., Richmond, Va., 1983—; sr. fin. planner Branch, Cabell & Co., Richmond, 1986; pres. 1st Va. Fin. Corp., Richmond, 1986-87; exec. v.p. Forcke, Smith & Assocs. Ltd., Richmond, 1987—. Pres. Estate Planning Council, Danville, 1974. Mem. Internat. Assn. Fin. Planning, Inst. Cert. Fin. Planners (bd. dirs. 1988), Am. Soc. CLU's and Chartered Fin. Cons., Westwood Raquet Club. Methodist. Home: 611 Westham Woods Dr Richmond VA 23229 Office: Forcke Smith & Assocs Ltd 728 E Main St Ste 608 Richmond VA 23219

SMITH, WILLIAM ROBERT, utility company executive; b. Mount Clemens, Mich., Nov. 11, 1916; s. Robert L. and Elsie (Chamberlain) S.; B.S., Detroit Inst. Tech., 1947; postgrad. Detroit Coll. Law, U. Mich. Grad. Sch. Bus. Adminstrn.; m. Ann Sheridan; children—William R., Laura A. Indsl. engr. Detroit Edison Co., 1934-60; mgr. econ. devel. East Ohio Gas Co., Cleve., 1960-80; mgr. nat. accounts Consol. Natural Gas Co., Cleve., 1980-85; dir. mktg., pres. Edison Polymer Innovation Corp. 1985-88; cons. Western Res. Econ. Devel. Coun., 1988—; pres. T.S.T. Corp. Trustee Cleve. Ballet; bd. dirs. Animal Protective League and Humane Soc. Served with USAAF, 1942-45. Registered profl. engr., Mich., Ohio. Fellow Am. Indsl. Devel. Council; mem. Ohio, Cleve. chambers commerce, Am. Inst. Corp. Asset Mgmt., Indsl. Devel. Research Council, Assn. Ohio Commodores, Delta Theta Tau. Presbyterian. Clubs: Mid-Day; Shaker Heights (Ohio) Country. Home: 27750 Fairmount Blvd Pepper Pike OH 44124 Office: Kent State U Coll Bus Adminstrn Goodyear Executive Office Kent OH 44242

SMITH, WILLIAM STANTON, accountant; b. Houston, Dec. 2, 1948; s. William Dorsett and Iona Nelle (Pierson) S.; m. Rosaline Buck Lewis, Feb. 24, 1979. BS in Econs., U. Pa., 1971; MBA in Fin. and Acctg., U. Tex., 1973. Staff acct. Coopers & Lubrand, N.Y.C., 1973-74; profl. staff recruiter Coopers & Lubrand, 1974-75, asst. personnel mgr., 1975-76, mgr. personnel and adminstrn. tax, 1976-78, group dir. recruiting, 1978-80; mgr. human resources and fin. Mobil Corp., N.Y.C., 1980-83; v.p. BFL Assocs., N.Y.C., 1983-84; dir. nat. tax human resources Price Waterhouse Co., N.Y.C., 1984—. Treas. Prospect Park Assn., White Plains, N.Y., 1986—. Mem. Human Resources Planning Soc., Am. Soc. Personnel Adminstrs., Am. Taxation Assn. (trustee 1985-87). Republican. Presbyterian. Home: 6 Winslow Rd White Plains NY 10606 Office: Price Waterhouse Co 1251 Ave of Americas New York NY 10020

SMITH, WINTHROP HIRAM, JR., financial services executive; b. N.Y.C., Aug. 5, 1949; s. Winthrop Hiram Sr. and Vivian Gordon (Brown) S.; m. Margaret Dunn, Aug. 7, 1971. BA, Amherst Coll., 1971; MBA, U. Pa., 1974. Investment banker Merrill Lynch, Pierce, Fenner & Smith, N.Y.C., 1974-77, mgr. fin. analysis, 1977-78, mgr. compensation and benefits, 1978-80, dir. human resources, 1980-82; sr. v.p., regional dir. Merrill Lynch, Pierce, Fenner & Smith, Washington, 1985—; dir. strategic devel. and mktg. Merrill Lynch Capital Markets, N.Y.C., 1982-84, dir. emerging investor svcs., 1984-85. Mem. Greenwich Country Club, F St. Club. Republican. Episcopalian. Office: Merrill Lynch Pierce Fenner & Smith Inc 1777 F St NW Washington DC 20006

SMITH, YOUNG MERRITT, JR., lawyer; b. Hickory, N.C., July 25, 1944; s. Young Merritt and Christine Ellen (White) S.; m. Louise Garner Price, Sept. 6, 1966 (div. Aug. 1974); 1 child, Patrick Adam; m. Charlie Mae Early, Nov. 19, 1977 (div. May 1985); m. Mary Gayle Jones, June 8, 1985. AB, U. N.C., 1966; JD, Duke U., 1969. Bar: N.C. 1969. Pres. The Litchfield Plantation Co., Pawleys Island, S.C., 1969-74, The Figure Eight Island Co., Wilmington, N.C., 1971-74; ptnr. Smith and Smith, Hickory, N.C., 1974—. Trustee Fund for Peace, N.Y.C., 1970-79, United Health Services N.C., Durham, 1971-73, N.C. Design Found., Raleigh, 1973-76. Mem. N.C. Bar Assn., Nat. Assn. Securities Dealers, Delta Kappa Epsilon. Democrat. Presbyterian. Office: Smith & Smith PO Drawer 1948 Hickory NC 28603

SMITHBURG, WILLIAM DEAN, food manufacturing company executive; b. Chgo., July 9, 1938; s. Pearl L. and Margaret L. (Savage) S.; m. Alberta Hap, May 25, 1963; children: Susan, Thomas. BS, DePaul U., 1960; MBA, Northwestern U., 1961. With Leo Burnett Co., Chgo., 1961-63, McCann-Erickson, Inc., Chgo., 1963-66; various positions Quaker Oats Co., Chgo., 1966-71, v.p., gen. mgr. cereals and mixers div., 1971-75, pres. food div., 1975-76, v.p. U.S. grocery products, 1976-79, pres., 1979-83, chief exec. officer, 1979—, chmn., 1983—, also bd. dirs. Served with USAR, 1959-60. Roman Catholic. Office: The Quaker Oats Co Quaker Tower 231 E Clark St Chicago IL 60610 *

SMOLENS, BRIAN, computer company marketing executive; b. Phila., Nov. 3, 1948; s. Martin T. and Beatrice (Greenwald) S.; m. Belinda R. Adams, May 27, 1978 (div. 1985). B.S., U. Pa., 1975, M.B.A., 1976. C.P.A., Md. Mgr. fin. reporting Walworth Anaconda, King of Prussia, Pa., 1978, Am. Standard Co., Hunt Valley, Md., 1978-80; fin. systems mktg. exec. STSC, Inc., Rockville, Md., 1980-83, Nat. Mgmt. Systems, Alexandria, Va., 1983-84; acct. systems mktg. exec. Entré Computers Ctrs., Vienna, Va., 1985-88; pvt. practice new direct mail concepts/media, McLean, 1988—. Designer computer system. Contbr. articles to profl. publs. Mem. No. Am. Soc. Corp. Planners, Wildwood Design Group (founder, pres.), Planners League (bd. dirs. 1982-83). Unitarian. Avocations: architecture; photography; deltiology. Home and Office: PO Box 3140 McLean VA 22103

SMOLENSKY, JEFFREY R., brokerage firm executive; b. Bklyn., Feb. 27, 1963; s. Samuel E. and Yetta (Distelman) S. Student, Pace U.; cert. in bus. and mktg., Murry Bergtraum Sch. of Bus. Cert. gemologist, 1981. Pres. Distelman, Inc., N.Y.C., 1976-89; pres., owner Diamond Works, Fla. and Israel, 1985-87; chief exec. officer Isreali Enterprises, U.S., Canada and Israel, 1988-89; sr. v.p. World Wide Holdings, Can. and Israel, 1988-89, Internat. Brokerage Inc., N.Y.C., Can., and Finland, 1989—. Fund raiser various N.Y. Jewish orgs., 1981—, N.Y.C. Opera Guild, 1984-85; v.p. Jewish Community Ctrs., 1983-86; hon. mem. Rep. Com. for V.p. Bush; mem. Re-elect Pres. Reagan; sustaining mem. Nat. Com., Washington, 1987—. Mem. Fla. Jewelers' Assn. (honor mem. 1981-83), Premium Mdse. Club (hon. 1984-85), Am. Mgmt. Assn., Sales and Mktg. Exec. of Greater N.Y., Incentive Mfrs. Reps. Assn., Rep. Club of Cedarhurst (trustee 1988-89). Republican. Jewish.

SMOLKA, WILLIAM PETER, marketing executive; b. N.Y.C., Feb. 8, 1944; s. M. H. and Marjory (Chankin) S.; BA in Psychology and Econs., Bucknell U., 1965; MBA in Mktg., Columbia U., 1967. Promotion mgr. Procter & Gamble, Cin., 1970-72, asst. brand mgr., 1972-73; mktg. mgr. Pillsbury Co., Mpls., 1973-77, group mktg. mgr. desserts and new products, 1977-79, dir. mktg., 1979-80; v.p. mktg. and sales Buitoni Foods, Hackensack, N.J., 1980-83; vice chmn. bd. Spencer Wood, Inc., N.Y.C., 1983-84; pres. Winston Stuart Assocs., Ltd., 1984—; owner, operator Winston Stuart Galleries, 1976-80. Mem. Republican County Com., N.Y.C., 1965-67; mem. Mpls. Symphony Com., 1974-79. Served to lt. j.g. USCG, 1967-70. Contbr. articles to various mags. Office: 2670 Nichols Canyon Rd Los Angeles CA 90046

SMOLLEN, LEONARD ELLIOTT, venture capitalist; b. N.Y.C., Jan. 1, 1930; s. Abner Charles and Madeleine (Ehrlich) S.; B.S., Carnegie Inst. Tech., 1951; M.S., Columbia U., 1952; M.E., Mass. Inst. Tech., 1962; m. Mindelle Deborah Hershberg, July 6, 1958; children: Rachel Anne, Jonathan Adam. Sr. engr. Sikorsky Aircraft, Bridgeport, Conn., 1953-57; engring. mgr. Allied Research Assos., Boston, 1957-61; tech. cons. Mitre Corp., Bedford, Mass., 1962-63; chief mech. engr. EG&G, Bedford, 1963-67, program mgr., 1967-69, dir. custom products and program mgmt., 1969-70; exec. v.p. Inst. for New Enterprise Devel., Belmont, Mass., 1971-77; exec. v.p. Venture Founders Corp., Waltham, Mass., 1976—; gen. ptnr. Venture Founders Capital, 1983-89; v.p. engr., treas. JIC Industries, Inc., Maiden, Mass., 1989—; lectr. Babson U.; research asso. Sloan Sch. Mgmt., MIT, 1970-71. Higgins fellow, 1952; Whitney fellow, 1960. Registered profl. engr., Conn., Mass. Mem. ASME. Club: Boston Yacht. Author: New Venture Creation: A Guide to Small Business Development, 1977; Source Guide for Borrowing

Capital, 1977. Home: 10 Central St Winchester MA 01890 Office: 1 Cranberry Hill Lexington MA

SMOOK, JOHN T., manufacturing company executive; b. Detroit, Oct. 28, 1927; s. Theo and Mary (O'Donnell) S.; student Westminster Coll., 1947-48, U. Utah, 1949-50; m. Hope van der Smissen, Jan. 21, 1951 (div.); children—Ted, Jim, Cindy, Pam, Pat, Jeannette; m. Barbara Quinn, Feb. 2, 1983. Founder, chief exec. officer Kosmo Corp., Glen Allen, Va., 1954—; founder, pres. Internat. Security Vault Systems Inc., Glen Allen, 1982—; sec. Mid-Atlantic Ins. Underwriters, Richmond, Va., 1981. Served with USN, 1946, U.S. Army, 1950-53. Mem. Va. Campground Owners Assn., Va. Mfg. Housing Assn., Clubs: Richmond Ski, Underseas Explorers. Home: Route 4 Box 250 Glen Allen VA 23060 Office: 24100 Washington Hwy Glen Allen VA 23060

SMOROL, ALBERT EDWARD, JR., construction executive; b. Syracuse, N.Y., Mar. 13, 1940; s. Albert E. and Isabel (Swietonowski) S.; m. Herta Maria Kluser-Lambelet, Apr. 12, 1969; children: Kristina Maria, Raissa Maria. BS in Pub. Acctg., Syracuse U., 1965. CPA, N.Y. Auditor Arthur Young & Co., N.Y.C., 1965-67, sr. auditor, 1967-70, acting mgr., 1970-71; dir. internal audit Turner Constrn. Co., N.Y.C., 1971-76; internat. controller Turner Internat. Industries Inc., N.Y.C., 1976-78; asst. treas. The Turner Corp., N.Y.C., 1978-85, treas., 1985—; bd. dirs. Hipp Waters Inc., Greenwich, Conn.; bd. advisors Berger Assocs., N.Y.C., 1984-86; bd. dirs., chmn. fin. com. Workers Compensation Research Inst., Cambridge, Mass., 1985—. Treas., bd. dirs. Friends North Castle Pub. Library, Armonk, N.Y., 1987; treas., trustee North Castle Hist. Soc., 1987. Served as staff sgt. USAR, 1971-77. Mem. Constrn. Fin. Mgmt. Assn. (v.p. N.Y. chpt., bd. dirs. 1987—), Nat. Assn. Corp. Treas., Fin. Exec. Inst., Am. Inst. CPA's, N.Y. State Soc. CPA's, Nat. Assn. Accts., Global Econ. Action Inst., Arthur Young Bus. Assn., Alpha Kappa Psi (master rituals Syracuse U. chpt. 1964-65), Beta Alpha Psi (hon.). Republican. Roman Catholic. Club: N.J. Lacrosse. Lodge: Lions (treas., bd. dirs. Armonk club 1985-87, Disting. Service award 1986). Home: 11 Laurel Hill Pl Armonk NY 10504 Office: The Turner Corp 633 3rd Ave New York NY 10017

SMURFIT, MICHAEL W. J., manufacturing company executive; b. 1936. With Jefferson Smurfit Group PLC, Dublin, Ireland, 1961—, pres., from 1966, now chmn., chief exec. officer; pres. Jefferson Smurfit Corp., Alton, Ill., 1979-82, now chief exec. officer, chmn. bd., 1982—. Office: Jefferson Smurfit Corp 401 Alton St Alton IL 62002 *

SMYTH, GLEN MILLER, management consultant; b. Abingdon, Va., July 26, 1929; s. Glen Miller and Kathleen (Dunn) S.; m. Cynthia Olson, Aug. 25, 1954 (div. 1967); children: Catherine Ellen, Glen Miller III, Allison; m. Lilian Castel Edgar, Oct. 31, 1968; children: Stephanie Castel, Kimberley Forsyth, Lindsay Dunn. BA, Yale U., 1951; MS in Psychology, Rutgers U., 1958. Mktg. rep. Wheeling Stamping Co., N.Y.C., 1953-56; personnel dir. Celanese Internat., N.Y.C., 1958-71; mgr. orgn. and Manpower Internat. and Can. group Gen. Electric Co., N.Y.C., 1971-73; sr. v.p. human resources Northwest Bancorp., Mpls., 1973-82; sr. v.p. Calif. Fed. Savs., L.A., 1983-85; v.p. Career Transition Group, L.A., 1985-87; pres. Fuchs, Cuthrell & Co., Inc., L.A., 1987—; leader seminars. Co-author: International Career Pathing, 1971; Contbr. articles to profl. jours. Chmn. nat. fgn. trade council Internat. Orgn. & Mgmt. Devel. Com., 1972—. Served with AUS, 1951-53. Mem. Am. Bankers Assn. (chmn. internat. personnel com., mem. adminstrv. and exec. coms.), Am. Psychol. Assn., Nat. Fgn. Trade Council (founder, past chmn., past. mem. exec. com. human resources, orgn. com. 1966—), Human Resources Planning Soc., Am. Soc. Personnel Adminstrn., Employment Mgmt. Assn., Jonathan Club, Yale Club of N.Y., Northranch Country Club, Phi Gamma Delta. Home: 1860 Mesa Ridge Ave Westlake Village CA 91362

SNARE, CARL LAWRENCE, JR., business executive; b. Chgo., Oct. 25, 1936; s. Carl Lawrence and Lillian Marie (Luoma) S.; B.B.A., Northwestern U., 1968; postgrad. Roosevelt U.; postgrad. in econs. San Francisco State U., 1976-77. Cert. fin. planner. Asst. sec., controller Bache Halsey Stuart & Shields Inc. (now Prudential Bache), Chgo., 1968-73; controller Innisfree Corp. div. Hyatt Corp., Burlingame, Calif., 1973-76; cash mgr. Portland (Oreg.) Gen. Electric Co., 1976-79; chief fin. officer, controller Vistar Fin. Inc., Marina del Rey, Calif., 1979-82; v.p., treas. Carson Estate Co., Rancho Dominguez, Calif., 1988—; pres. Snare Properties Co., Rialto, Calif., 1984—, Snare Fin. Services Corp., Rialto, 1985—; registered investment advisor. C.P.A., real estate broker, cert. fin. planner, Calif. Mem. Am. Inst. C.P.A.s, Calif. Soc. C.P.A.s, Internat. Assn. Fin. Planners, Am. Inst. Fin. Planners. Founder Cash Mgmt. Assn., Portland, Oreg. Home: 1131 Wisteria Ave Rialto CA 92376 Office: 17925 S Santa Fe Ave Rancho Dominguez CA 90221

SNAVELY, WILLIAM PENNINGTON, economics educator; b. Charlottesville, Va., Jan. 25, 1920; s. Tipton Ray and Nell (Aldred) S.; m. Alice Watts Pritchett, June 4, 1942; children: Nell Lee, William Pennington, Elizabeth Tipton. Student, Hampden-Sydney Coll., 1936-37; B.A. with honors, U. Va., 1940, M.A., 1941, Ph.D., 1950; postgrad. (Bennett Wood Green fellow), Harvard, 1946-47. Mem. faculty U. Conn., 1947-73, prof. econs., 1961-73, chmn. dept., 1966-72, economist econ. edn. workshop, summers 1954, 55, 56; prof. econs. George Mason U., 1973-86, chmn. dept., 1973-81; acting dean CAS, summer 1981, 85-86, assoc. dean, 1982-85; prof. econs. Liberty U., 1986—; cons. Ford Found., Jordan Devel. Bd., Amman, 1961-62, 64-65, Lebanese Ministry Planning, Beirut, 1964-65, Saudi Arabian Central Planning Orgn., Riyadh, 1964-65, Am. U. Beirut, 1969-70, Bahrain Ministry Fin. and Nat. Economy, 1974, 75, 76, U.N., Jordan Nat. Planning Council, Amman, 1972; mem. Danforth Workshop, summer 1966; mem. adv. com. Willimantic Trust Co., Conn., 1968-73; v.p. Contemporary Econs. & Bus. Assn., 1988—. Author: (with W.H. Carter) Intermediate Economic Analysis, 1961, Theory of Economic Systems, 1969, (with M.T. Sadik) Bahrain, Qatar and the United Arab Emirates, 1972; contbr. articles to jours.; articles Ency. Americana. Served to capt. AUS, 1942-46. Fellow Fund Advancement Edn. Harvard, 1951-52; faculty-bus. exchange fellow Chase Nat. Bank, N.Y.C., summer 1952; fellow Merrill Center Econs., summer 1957; Fulbright research fellow Rome, 1958-59. Mem. Am., So. econ. assns., Assn. Christian Economists, Assn. Comparative Econs., Va. Assn. Economists (pres. 1979-80), Phi Beta Kappa, Phi Kappa Phi. Home: 1551 Dairy Rd Charlottesville VA 22903

SNEAD, RICHARD THOMAS, restaurant company executive; b. Washington, Apr. 19, 1951; s. Walter Thomas and Ruth Claire (Reeves) S.; m. Marilyn Wolke; children: Richard Adam, Eric Thomas. BS in Engring., U. Tenn., 1973. Project mgr. First Fla. Bldg. Corp., Miami, 1974-78; constrn. mgr. Burger King Corp., San Francisco, 1978-79; nat. constrn. dir., Miami, 1979-81; dir. devel., Boston, 1981-84; regional v.p., Detroit, 1984-86; sr. v.p. devel., Miami, 1986-87, exec. v.p. devel., eastern div. mgr. (including responsibility for black minority affairs), 1987-88; pres. Burger King Internat. Div., 1988—. Republican. Home: 8090 SW 143 St Miami FL 33158 Office: Burger King Corp 7360 N Kendall Dr Miami FL 33156

SNEDEKER, SEDGWICK, lawyer; b. Bklyn., Apr. 11, 1909; s. Edwin Snedeker and Louise (Sedgwick) Atwater; m. Anne Carl Parke, June 28, 1940 (dec. 1961); children—Thomas S., William D., James P.; m. Elizabeth Gabrielle Naudin, Sept. 15, 1962; stepchildren—Nancy Seagren, Lynn, John F. Grad. Princeton U., 1933; LL.B., Columbia U., 1936. Bar: N.Y. 1938, U.S. Supreme Ct. 1945, U.S. Dist. Ct. (ea. dist.) N.Y. 1938. Trial asst. Holmes, Bernstein & O'Dwyer, Bklyn., 1937-39; trial atty. Leo T. Kisam, N.Y.C., 1939-42; trial atty. Snedeker & Snedeker, Bklyn., 1942-45, ptnr., 1945-50; banking and real estate atty. Shearman & Sterling, N.Y.C., 1950-74; counsel, trustee Bklyn. Savs. Bank. Pres. Cold Springs Harbor Civic Assn., 1940-45; treas. Holland Soc. N.Y.C., 1965-70. Republican. Episcopalian. Clubs: Piping Rock Locust Valley, Huntington Country, Princeton (N.Y.); Everglades, Beach (Palm Beach, Fla.); Tiger Inn (N.J.). Avocations: golf; gardening. Home: 369 S Lake Dr Palm Beach FL 33480 Office: 568 Cold Spring Rd Laurel Hollow Syosset NY 11791

SNEDEKER, THOMAS STEELE, bank executive; b. N.Y.C., Sept. 28, 1941; s. Sedgwick and Anne Carlle (Parke) S.; m. Marilee Eustis Eaves, July 20, 1968 (div. 1985); children: Anne Phyfe, Rebecca Tullis, Jennifer Eaves; m. Nancy Wells Crane, Aug. 14, 1987. BA, Trinity Coll., 1965; MBA, Tulane U., 1984. Asst. ofcl. Citibank, N.Y.C., 1965-68; ptnr. Kohlmeyer and Co., New Orleans, 1968-73; v.p. George Engine Co.Inc., Harvey, La., 1983-87, 1st Nat. Bank Commerce, New Orleans, 1987—. Bd. dirs., past pres. Jr. Achievement, New Orleans, 1969—. With U.S. Army, 1965-71. Mem. New Orleans C. of C. (bd. dirs. 1986-87), Westbank C. of C. (chmn. exec. com. 1985-86), New Orleans Lawn Tennis. Republican. Episcopalian. Home: 1725 Upperline St New Orleans LA 70115 Office: 1st Nat Bank Commerce PO Box 60279 New Orleans LA 70160

SNELL, JOHN NELSON, economist, gnosographer; b. Chgo., Apr. 24, 1929; s. Donald Wilson and Marian Hamilton (Gurley) S.; m. Ana Maria De Diego Jáuregui, Apr. 22, 1961; 1 child, Elena. BA in Liberal Arts, Amherst Coll., 1955; BS, MIT, 1955; MA in Planning Adminstrn. and Econs. and Engring., Antioch U., Yellow Springs, Ohio, 1977. Program economist U.S Agy. Internat. Devel., various locations, 1955-64; grad. researcher U. Chgo., 1965-66; chief program devel. Dept. Housing and Community Devel., Balt., 1967-76; chief economist Regional Planning Counc., Balt., 1977—; econ. forecaster Balt. Region Info. and Econ. Forecasts, 1982—. Designer graphic charts. With U.S. Army, 1952-54, Korea. Mem. Balt. Econ. Soc. (pres. 1981-82), Nat. Economists Club. Democrat. Roman Catholic. Home: 8418 Charles Valley Ct Towson MD 21204 Office: Regional Planning Coun 2225 N Charles St Baltimore MD 21218

SNELL, RICHARD, hotel company executive; b. Phoenix, Nov. 26, 1930; s. Frank L. and Elizabeth (Berlin) S.; m. Alice Cosette Wiley, Aug. 1, 1954. BA, Stanford U., 1952, JD, 1954. Bar: Ariz. Ptnr. firm Snell & Wilmer, Phoenix, 1956-81; pres., chmn., chief exec. officer Ramada Inc., Phoenix, 1981—; dir. Ariz. Public Service Co., Pinnacle West Capital Corp. Trustee Am. Grad. Sch. Internat. Mgmt., Phoenix; past pres. YMCA Met. Phoenix and Valley of Sun. Served with U.S. Army, 1954-56. Mem. ABA, Ariz. Bar Assn., Maricopa County Bar Assn. Republican. Lutheran. Clubs: Paradise Valley Country, John Gardiner's Tennis Ranch. Office: Ramada Inc 2390 E Camelback Rd Phoenix AZ 85016

SNELLING, GEORGE ARTHUR, banker; b. St. Petersburg, Fla., June 27, 1929; s. William Henry and Eula Hall S.; m. Carolyn Shiver, Mar. 3, 1963; children—George, John S. B.S.B.A., U. Fla., 1951. Partner Smoak, Davis, Nixon & Snelling, C.P.A.s, Jacksonville, Orlando, Fla., 1956-66; v.p. planning Barnett Banks of Fla., Jacksonville, 1966-76; exec. v.p. 1st Bancshares of Fla., Boca Raton, 1976-78; exec. v.p. Fla. Nat. Banks of Fla., Jacksonville, 1978-80; exec. v.p. corp. devel., chief fin. officer Sun Banks of Fla., Orlando, 1981-85; exec. v.p. corp. devel. SunTrust Banks, Inc., Atlanta, 1986—. Trustee Fla. So. U. Served with USAF, 1951-55. Mem. Am. Inst. C.P.A.s, Assn. Bank Holding Cos., Fla. Bankers Assn. Democrat. Methodist. Home: 2682 Varner Dr Atlanta GA 30345 Office: SunTrust Banks Inc 25 Park Pl NE Atlanta GA 30303 also: Sun Banks Inc 200 S Orange Ave Orlando FL 32801

SNELLING, HARRY NELSON, transportation company executive; b. Pasadena, Calif., Sept. 5, 1946; s. Glenn and Dorothy (Nelson) S.; m. Sandra Kaye Smith, June 1, 1985. BA in History, Calif. State U., L.A., 1972. Claims examiner Fremont Indemnity Co., L.A., 1974-76; asst. claims supr. Transport Indemnity Co., Burlingame, Calif., 1976-77; claims supr. Western Employers Ins. Co., San Bruno, Calif., 1977-79, Calif. Casualty Co., San Mateo, Calif., 1979-84, GAB Bus. Services, Inc., Sacramento, Calif., 1984-85; risk mgr. Fed. Express Corp., Memphis, 1985—. With U.S. Army, 1966-69, Vietnam. Mem. Risk and Ins. Mgmt. Soc., 7th Tenn. Cavalry (cpl. 1985—). Republican. Baptist. Office: Fed Express Corp 2007 Corporate Pla 3rd Fl Memphis TN 38132

SNELLING, RICHARD KELLY, telecommunications executive; b. St. Petersburg, Fla., Nov. 12, 1931; s. William Henry and Estelle Eula (Hall) S.; m. Barbara Mulligan; children: Richard K., Jr., Deborah Jane Doverspike, Laura Ann. B.S. in Indsl. Engring., U. Fla., 1955; postgrad. Clemson Coll., 1963-74. Registered profl. engr., Fla. Div. engr. So. Bell, Ft. Lauderdale, Fla., 1971-72, engring. dir., Atlanta, 1972-76, gen. plant mgr., 1976-78, v.p. Ga. network, 1978-79, v.p. network, 1979-82, exec. v.p. network, 1982—, also dir.; hon. dir. Ga. Engring. Found., Atlanta; mem. adv. council Southeastern Consortium Minorities in Engring. Active alumni U. Fla.; mem. Ga. Inst. Tech. Adv. Bd.; exec. com. Consumer Credit Counseling Service, Atlanta, 1984—; bd. dirs. Nat. Found. Consumer Credit. Served with USNR, 1950-58. Mem. IEEE, Nat. Soc. Profl. Engrs., Ga. Soc. Profl. Engrs. (sec. 1983). Clubs: Commerce, Peachtree World Champion Tennis. Office: So Bell Tel & Tel Co 675 W Peachtree St NE Rm 4516 Atlanta GA 30375

SNETZER, MICHAEL ALAN, multi-industry executive; b. Denver, May 26, 1940; s. Robert Ellis and Kathryn (Wake) S.; m. Peggy Ann Sparks, Jan., 1964 (div. 1973); children: Michael Ellis, Gregory Alan; m. Deborah Kay Gee, Mar. 15, 1975; 1 child, Robert Adam. BS, U. Ark., 1963; MBA, So. Meth. U., 1969. Indsl. engr. Collins Radio Co., Dallas, 1966-69; v.p. fin. UCCEL Corp., Dallas, 1969-77; v.p. fin. Contran Corp., Dallas, 1977-84, exec. v.p., 1984-87; pres. Valhi, Inc., Dallas, 1987—; bd. dirs. NL Industries, Inc., Houston, Baroid Corp., Houston, Amalgamated Sugar Co., Ogden, Utah; chmn., dir. Medford (Oreg.) Corp. wholly owned sub. Valhi Inc. Served to capt. U.S. Army, 1963-66, Vietnam. Recipient Bronze star. Mem. Univ. Club. Republican. Methodist. Home: 18722 Campbell Rd Dallas TX 75252 Office: Valhi Inc 3 Lincoln Ctr 5430 LBJ Frwy Dallas TX 75240

SNIDER, ANDREW J. (DREW SNIDER), publishing company executive; b. Greenwich, Conn., 1944. Grad., Western Ill. U., 1967. Pres. Standard Rate and Data Svc., Wilmette, Ill. Mem. Assn. Bus. Pubs., Mag. Pubs. Assn., Internat. Newspaper Advt. and Mktg. Execs. Assn. Office: SRDS 3004 Glenview Rd Wilmette IL 60091 *

SNIDER, HARLAN TANNER, manufacturing company executive; b. Owensboro, Ky., July 20, 1926; s. George William and Lydia (Tanner) S.; m. Helen Boswell, Mar. 7, 1953; children—William Jeffrey, Katherine Snider. B.A., Transylvania U., 1949. Territory salesman Sunray DX Corp., Owensboro, 1950-57; dist. sales mgr. Sunray DX Corp., Ind., 1958-63; div. mgr. Sunray DX Corp., Iowa, 1963-65; dir. mktg. services Sunray DX Corp., Tulsa, 1955-67; pres. Red Bar Chems., Tulsa, 1967-69; dir. petrochems. Sun Oil Co., Phila., 1969-71; v.p. mktg. Sun Oil Co., 1973-75; pres. Sunmark Industries, Phila., 1975-79; sr. v.p., external affairs Sun Co., Inc., Radnor, Pa., 1980-84; sr. v.p. planning pub. affairs Sun Co., Inc., 1984—. Served with USAF, 1944-46. Mem. Am. Petroleum Industry, 25 Yr. Club Petroleum Industry. Republican. Presbyterian. Clubs: Capitol Hill (Washington); Union League (Phila.); Aronimink Golf. Office: Sun Co Inc 100 Matsonford Rd Radnor PA 19087

SNIDER, JAMES RHODES, radiologist; b. Pawnee, Okla., May 16, 1931; s. John Henry and Gladys Opal (Rhodes) S.; B.S., U. Okla., 1953, M.D., 1956; m. Lynadell Vivion, Dec. 27, 1954; children—Jon, Jan. Intern, Edward Meyer Meml. Hosp., Buffalo, 1956-57; resident radiology U. Okla. Med. Center, 1959-62; radiologist Holt-Krock Clinic and Sparks Regional Med. Center, Ft. Smith, Ark., 1962—. Dir. Fairfield Community Land Co., Little Rock, 1968-87, Fairfield Communities, Inc., 1968-87. Mem. Ark. Bd. Pub. Welfare, 1969-71. Bd. dirs. U. Okla. Assn., 1967-70, U. Okla. Alumni Devel. Fund, 1970-74; bd. visitors U. Okla. Served to lt. comdr. USNR, 1957-62. Mem. Am. Coll. Radiology, Radiol. Soc. N.Am., Am. Roentgen Ray Soc., AMA, Phi Beta Kappa, Beta Theta Pi (trustee corp.), Alpha Epsilon Delta. Asso. editor Computerized Tomography, 1976-88. Home: 5814 Cliff Dr Fort Smith AR 72903 Office: 1500 Dodson St Fort Smith AR 72901

SNIDER, ROBERT LARRY, management consultant; b. Muskogee, Okla., Aug. 10, 1932; s. George Robert and Kathryn (Smiser) S.; m. Gerlene Rose Tipton, Nov. 26, 1953; children: Melody Kathryn Porter, Rebecca Lee. B.S. in Indsl. Engring., U. Houston, 1955, postgrad., 1956; postgrad., Pomona Coll., 1960. Instr. U. Houston Coll. Engring., 1955-56; sr. indsl. engr. Sheffield Steel Corp., Houston, 1955-59, Kaiser Steel Co., Fontana, Calif., 1959-60; cons. Arthur Young & Co., Los Angeles, 1960-61; mgmt. analyst Iranian Oil Exploration & Producing Co., Masjidi-Suliman, Iran, 1961-62; cons. 1962-65; v.p. operating methods div. Booz, Allen & Hamilton, Inc., Dallas, 1965-67; v.p., mng. officer internat. prodn. and inventory control div. Booz, Allen & Hamilton, Inc., 1967-69; prin., gen. cons. practice Peat Marwick Mitchell (C.P.A.s), Houston, 1969-71; exec. v.p. mfg. Sterling Electronics Corp., Houston, 1971-72, pres., chief operating officer, 1972-77; pres., chief exec. officer Rapoca Energy Corp., Cin., 1977-79; mng. partner, cons. Coopers & Lybrand, Southwest, Houston, 1979-81; mng. dir. Southwest region Korn Ferry Internat., Houston, 1981-86; ptnr.-in-charge mgmt. cons. Coopers & Lybrand, 1986—. Bd. dirs., exec. com. Houston Jr. Achievement; trustee, fin. com. Chapelwood Meth. Ch., chmn.-elect bd. trustees; trustee, mem. exec. com. Houston Grand Operation. Served with C.E. AUS, 1956. Recipient Outstanding Mil. Engr. award Soc. Mil. Engrs., 1955. Mem. Pres.'s Assn., Soc. Mining Engrs., Am. Mgmt. Assn., U. Houston Alumni Assn. (bd. dirs.), Phi Theta Kappa, Phi Kappa Phi. Clubs: Houston, Houstonian. Home: 11643 Green Bay Houston TX 77024 Office: Coopers & Lybrand Ste 4000 1100 Louisiana Houston TX 77002

SNIDE-VOLKER, CYNTHIA MARIE, university administrator, leadership consultant; b. Columbus, Ohio, Aug. 15, 1962; d. Richard Edward and Marilyn Jane (Morris) Snide; m. Stuart Edwin Volker, June 25, 1988. BA, Ohio State U., 1985; postgrad., U. S.C., 1987—. Model Izod-Lacoste, Columbus, 1980-84; asst. to pres. Ohio State U., Columbus, 1983-85; nat. leadership and ednl. cons. Alpha Xi Delta Nat. Fraternity, Indpls., 1985-86; dir. chpt. devel. Baldwin-Wallace Coll., Berea, Ohio, 1986-87; dir. leadership programs U. S.C., Columbia, 1987—; pvt. practice leadership cons., Columbia, S.C., 1985—; communications cons. U. S.C., 1987—. Bd. dirs. Maple Grove Ch., Columbus, 1982—, Sunday sch. tchr., 1981-86; coordinator Fun Run Am. Lung Assn., Columbia, 1988. Mem. S.C. Coll. Personnel Assn., Am. Coll. Personnel Assn., Nat. Assn. Student Personnel Adminstrs. Republican. Methodist. Home: 3121 Duncan St Columbia SC 29205

SNODGRASS, JEFFREY STEVEN, engineering business manager; b. Balt., Mar. 24, 1955; s. Charles Lee and Twila Elizabeth (Loudenslager) S.; m. Patricia Lou Donges, May 17, 1981; children: Grace Elizabeth, Philip Donges. BA, Miami U., Oxford, Ohio, 1977; MBA, Loyola Coll., Balt., 1987; postgrad., U. Md. Cons. Booz Allen and Hamilton, Washington, 1978-80; mgr., engr. Ori Intercon Corp., Columbia, Md., 1980-89; mgr. MIS Port of Balt., 1989—; cons. Micronet Assn., Balt. Author: Business Briefs, Topics for the Small Businessman, 1986. Recipient letter of merit Dept. Def., 1985, commendation Dept. Def., 1986. Mem. Am. Mktg. Soc., Engring. Soc. Balt. Home: 6639 Loch Hill Baltimore MD 21239

SNOOK, JOHN MCCLURE, telephone company executive; b. Toledo, May 31, 1917; s. Ward H. and Grace (McClure) S.; m. Marjorie Younce (dec.); student Ohio State U., 1936-43. Instr. history, fine arts and scis. Ohio State U., Columbus; exec. v.p. Gulf Telephone Co., Foley, Ala., 1955-71, pres., 1971—. Chmn., Baldwin Sesquicentennial, 1969; mem. Baldwin County Bicentennial Commn.; pageant chmn., dir. Ft. Morgan Bicentennial Program, 1976; mem. hon. staff Gov. Ala., 1967—; past pres. Friends of Library Assn.; asso. sponsor Gulf Shores Mardi Gras Assn. Hon. a.d.c. lt. col. Ala.; hon. Ala. state trooper; recipient Citizen of Year award Gulf Shores, 1956-57. Mem. Ala.-Miss. Ind. Telephone Assn. (past pres.), Nat. Rifle Assn. (life), Am. Ordnance Assn., South Baldwin C. of C., Delaware County, Baldwin County (pres.) hist. assns., Defiance and Williams' Hist. Soc., Am. Mus. Nat. History Assn., Nat. Hist. Soc., Nat. Wildlife Fedn., Clan McLeod Soc., Smithsonian Assn., Am. Heritage Soc., Nat. Fedn. Blind, Ohio State Alumni Assn., Ala. Ind. Telephone Assn., Telephone Pioneers, Ind. Pioneers. Clubs: Lions (past pres.), Kiwanis (past pres.; asst. chmn. ann. Christmas Party and Parade). Office: Gulf Tel Co PO Box 670 Foley AL 36535

SNOW, CLAUDE HENRY, JR., data processing executive, consultant; b. Lumberton, N.C., Feb. 25, 1954; s. Claude Henry and Vada Isabelle (Simpson) S.; m. Theresa Lee Gibson, Dec. 17, 1976 (div. Aug. 1981); m. Sarah Catherine Turnbull, Sept. 26, 1981. BA, U. N.C., 1976, MA, 1978. Communications systems rep. So. Bell Tel. & Tel., Charlotte, N.C., 1978-82; systems mgr. Sykes Datatronics, Atlanta, 1982-83; strategic planning mgr. Lockheed-Ga. Co., Marietta, 1983-86; regional mgr. communications Wang Labs., Atlanta, 1986-88, regional mgr. mktg., mfg., 1988—. Mem. Soc. Mfg. Engrs., Internat. Communications Assn., Nat. Mgmt. Assn. Data Processing Mgmt. Assn., U. N.C. Alumni Assn. (pres. Atlanta chpt. 1985, adv. bd. 1986—). Democrat. Episcopalian. Home: PO Box 88351 Atlanta GA 30356 Office: Wang Labs Inc 900 Ashwood Pkwy Atlanta GA 30338

SNOW, JOHN WILLIAM, railroad executive; b. Toledo, Aug. 2, 1939; s. William Dean and Catharine (Howard) S.; m. Fredrica Wheeler, June 11, 1964 (div. 1973); children: Bradley, Ian; m. Carolyn Kalk, Aug. 31, 1973; 1 child, Christopher. B.A., U. Toledo, 1962; Ph.D., U. Va., 1965; LL.B., George Washington U., 1967. Asst. prof. econs. U. Md., College Park, 1965-67; assoc. Wheeler & Wheeler, Washington, 1967-72; asst. gen. counsel Dept. Transp., Washington, 1972-73, asst. sec. for govtl. affairs, 1974-75, dep. under sec., 1975-76; dep. asst. sec. for policy U.S. Plans of Internal Affairs, Washington, 1973-74; adminstr. Nat. Hwy. Traffic Safety Adminstrn., Washington, 1976-77; v.p. govt. affairs Chessie System Inc., Washington, 1977-80; sr. v.p. corp. services CSX Corp., Richmond, Va., 1980-84, exec. v.p., 1984-85; pres., chief exec. officer Chessie System R.R.s, Balt., from 1985; pres., chief operating officer CSX Corp., Richmond, Va., 1988—, chief exec. officer, 1989—; adj. prof. law George Washington U., 1972-75; vis. prof. econs. U. Va., Charlottesville, spring 1977; vis. fellow Am. Enterprise Inst., Washington, spring 1977. Bd. dirs. Sch. Pub. Affairs, U. Md. Disting. fellow Yale U. Sch. Mgmt. Mem. ABA, D.C. Bar Assn., Va. Bar Assn. Episcopalian. Clubs: Chevy Chase, Metropolitan (Washington); Commonwealth, Country of Va. (Richmond). Office: CSX Corp PO Box C-32222 Richmond VA 23261 other: CSX Corp 1 James Ctr Richmond VA 23119 *

SNOW, WILLIAM CORY, human resources executive; b. Cambridge, Mass., Nov. 14, 1942; s. Cory and Constance Ruth (Culver) S.; m. Susanne Rebecca Gilmore, Sept. 25, 1966 (div. May 1980); children: Scott Culver, William Cory III. Student, Brown U., 1962; BA, Colby Coll., 1966; postgrad., Va. Commmonwealth U., 1971, U. So. Maine, 1975-79. Mgr. personnel Edwards Co., Pittsfield, Maine, 1967-68; supr. employment, safety & tng. Div. Ethyl Oxford Paper, Lawrence, Mass., 1968-71; adminstr. corp. personnel Ethyl Corp., Richmond, Va., 1971-72; mgr. indsl. relations Maremont Corp., Saco, Maine, 1972-74; mgr. personnel Fairchild Semi Conductor, South Portland, Maine, 1974-77; mgr. personnel div. Fairchild/A Schlumberger Co., South Portland, 1977-82; mgr. employee relations & employment L.L. Bean, Freeport, Maine, 1983-85; mgr. employee relations & devel. L.L. Bean, Freeport, 1985-89, dir. human resources ops., 1989—. Dir., corp. sec. Jr. Achievement S.W. Maine, Portland, 1985—; chmn. adv. bd. Dept. Edn. State Maine, Augusta, 1987—. Mem. Am. Soc. Personnel Adminstrn. (dir. 1974—), AIM Personnel Assocs. (pres. 1976-77), So. Maine Personnel Execs. Council (dir. 1975-86), Portland C. of C. (ecox. devel. com. 1987). Republican. Office: LL Bean Casco St Freeport ME 04033

SNOWDEN, DAVID EDWIN, financial planner; b. Birmingham, Ala., May 18, 1953; s. Joseph E. and Victoria G. (Gilbert) S.; m. Debbie Susan Bicknell, Aug. 6, 1976; children: Tiffany Lane, Sean Patrick. AA, Palm Beach Jr. Coll., 1973; BBA, Fla. Atlantic U., 1975. Cert. fin. planner, registered gen. securities rep.; CPA, Fla. Acct. William A. Stockton, CPA, West Palm Beach, Fla., 1975-78, Ernst and Whinney, West Palm Beach, 1978-81; controller PGA Nat., West Palm Beach, 1981-87; assoc. 1st Fin. Planners, Inc., Jupiter, Fla., 1988; prin. Martinelli, Snowden & Assocs. P.A., West Palm Beach, Fla., 1989—; part-time instr., Palm Beach Community Coll.; part-time counselor Small Bus. Devel. Ctr. Mem. AICPA, Fla. Inst. CPAs (mem. personal fin. planning com.), Inst. Cert. Fin. Planners, Internat. Assn. for Fin. Planning, Palm Beach-Martin County Estate Planning Council, North Palm Beaches C. of C. (mem. small bus. com.), Jupiter-Tequester C. of C. Democrat. Office: Martinelli Snowden & Assocs P A 12788 W Forest Hill Blvd Ste 2005 West Palm Beach FL 33414

SNOWDEN, GUY BERNHARD, manufacturing executive; b. Peeksill, N.Y., Sept. 11, 1945; s. Frederick and Grace (Martin) S.; divorced; children: Guy Jr., Sean, Heather, Aubrey; m. Diane Pailthorpe, 1987; 1 child, Stephanie. Student, Syracuse U., 1963-64, Pace U., 1966-67, Elizabethtown Coll., 1972. Systems analyst IBM Corp., Yorktown, N.Y., 1966-70; mgr. systems support Bunker Ramo Corp., N.Y.C., 1970-72; mgr. system design Systems Ops. Inc., Princeton, N.J., 1972-76; exec. v.p. Datatrol, Inc., Providence, 1976-80; chmn., chief exec. officer GTECH Corp., Providence, 1980—. Office: GTECH Corp 101 Dyer St Providence RI 02903

SNYDER, BARBARA KAREN, accountant; b. Far Rockaway, N.Y., Aug. 15, 1959; d. Gilbert W. and Carol (Cheifetz) Schneider. BA, U. Vt., 1982; cert., Catonsville Community Coll., 1983. CPA, Md. Tax acct. Ecalono & Co., Columbia, Md., 1984-85; assoc. acct. Cohen, Fisher & Assocs., Balt., 1985-86; tax supr. Coopers & Lybrand, Balt., 1986—. Mem. Am. Inst. CPA's, Md. Assn. CPA's, Internat. Assn. Fin. Planning. Home: PO Box 2374 Baltimore MD 21203-2374 Office: Coopers & Lybrand 217 E Redwood St Baltimore MD 21202

SNYDER, C. JACKSON, manufacturing company executive; b. Fairmont, W.Va., May 28, 1942; s. Carl J. and Margaret (Kerfoot) S.; m. Carolyn Gutbrod; children: Scott, Kevin, Elizabeth. BSME, W.Va. U., 1965; MBA, U. Pa., 1970. Engr. Owens-Ill. Inc., Lakeland, Fla., 1965-66, Charlotte, Mich., 1966-68; fin. analyst Owens-Corning Fiberglas, Toledo, Ohio, 1970-71, real estate mgr., 1971-72, mgr. fin. planning, 1972-74, mgr. cash mgmt., 1974-79, asst. treas., 1979—. Mem. Mayor's Fin. Adv. Com., Toledo, 1985. Mem. Toledo Cash Mgmt. Assn., Nat. Corp. Cash Mgmt. Assn. Office: Owens-Corning Fiberglas Corp Fiberglas Tower Toledo OH 43659

SNYDER, CLAIR ALLISON, banker; b. Reading, Pa., June 12, 1921; s. Augustus M. and Estella G. (Bright) S.; m. Jean Doris George, June 27, 1948; children: Joan Marie Snyder Ferguson, Jerry George. Student, W.Va. U., 1943-44, U. Mich., 1944-45. With Meridian Bancorp, Inc. and Meridian Bank, Reading, 1938-43, 46—; exec. v.p., gen. banking Meridian Bancorp, Inc. and Meridian Bank, 1973-78, exec. v.p., chmn. credit policy com., 1978-86; pvt. practice fin. cons. Reading, 1987—; chmn., pres. Pa. Devel. Credit Corp.; bd. dirs. Magnus Corp., York, Pa., Terre Hill (Pa.) Concrete Corp., Fiberstok Corp., Phila., Am. Beton Systems, Terrehill; asst. sec. Bi-Products, Inc., Upper Montclair, N.J. Bd. dirs. Pa. div. Am. Cancer Soc., 1965-87, chmn. bd. dirs., 1975-77; bd. dirs. Berks County (Pa.) unit Am. Cancer Soc., 1955—, pres. bd. dirs., 1964-66; pub. affairs adv. commn. Mid-Atlantic Legal Found.; chmn., Hope Lodge Com. Served with U.S. Army, 1943-46. Recipient Luther Halsey Gulick award Camp Fire Girls, 1966; div. Bronze medal Am. Cancer Soc., also Sword of Hope award. Mem. Am. Bankers Assn. (cert.), Pa. Bankers Assn. (group chmn. 1972-73), Robert Morris Assocs. (pres. 1972-73), Am. Legion (post comdr. 1948-49). Republican. Mem. United Churches of Christ. Clubs: Olde Point Golf and Country (Hampstead, N.Y.), Iris (Wyomissing), Moselem Springs Golf, Flying Hills Golf. Home: 92 Medinah Dr Flying Hills Reading PA 19607-3313 also: 616 Sawgrass Rd Olde Point Hampstead NC 28443 Office: 35 N 6th St Reading PA 19601

SNYDER, DONALD JAY, JR., lawyer; b. Mt. Pleasant, Pa., July 13, 1950; s. Donald J. Sr. and Mildred (Baumann) S.; m. Karen Foster, Feb. 7, 1976; children: Julie Elizabeth, Andrew Meade. BA, Washington & Jefferson Coll., 1972; JD, Dickinson Sch. of Law, 1975. Bar: Pa. 1975, U.S. Dist. Ct. (we. dist.) Pa. 1979, U.S. Dist. Ct. (mid. dist.) Pa. 1981, U.S. Ct. Appeals (3d cir.) 1982, D.C. 1985, U.S. Supreme Ct. 1981. Assoc. Costello & Berk, Greensburg, Pa., 1975-80, ptnr., 1980-88; ptnr. McDonald, Moore, Mason and Snyder, Latrobe, Pa., 1988—. Bd. dirs. Westmoreland-Fayette Hist. Soc., Scottdale, Pa., 1987—, Salvation Army, Greensburg, Pa., 1987—. Mem. ABA, Westmoreland County Bar Assn., Allegheny County Bar Assn., Pa. Bar Assn., D.C. Bar, Westmoreland Acad. of Trial Lawyers, Rotary. Republican. Methodist. Office: McDonald Moore Mason & Snyder 1005 Courtyard Pl PO Box 758 Latrobe PA 15650

SNYDER, EARL ALBIN, financial planner and consulant; b. Kokomo, Ind., Feb. 17, 1918; s. Earl A. and Fanny E. (Ford) S. AB, Ind. U., 1942, JD, 1947; LLM, Cath. U., 1953. Bar: Ind. 1947, Eng. 1958, D.C. 1961, ; cert. fin. planner; chartered fin. cons.; CLU; real property appraiser. Sole practice Crawfordsville, Ind., 1947-50; commd. capt. USAF, advanced though ranks to maj., served as judge advocate, 1950-65, ret., 1965; prof. law Howard U., Washington, 1965-66; legis. asst. U.S. Ho. of Reps., Washington, 1966-68; pres., owner Earl Snyder Assocs., Laurel, Md., 1968—; adj. faculty Coll. for Fin. Planning, Denver, 1986—, The Am. Coll., Bryn Mawr, Pa., 1987—, Inst. of Fin. Edn., Chgo., 1987—, Soc. of Real Estate Appraisers, Chgo., 1980—. Author: General Leemy's Circus, 1955, Every Serviceman's Lawyer, 1960, Before You Invest, 1981. Chmn. Midwest Young Reps., 1947. Mem. D.C. Bar Assn., Balt. Assn. for Fin. Planning (bd. dirs. 1986—), Soc. of Profl. Journalists of D.C. (bd. dirs. 1986—), Nat. Assn. Realtors, Am. Soc. of CLU's and Chartered Fin. Cons., Fin. Analysts Fedn. Office: 14909 Kalmia Dr Laurel MD 20207-3629

SNYDER, JAMES WILLIAM, JR., sales exec.; b. South Bend, Ind., Mar. 16, 1948; s. James William and Marjorie Jane (Blakeman) S.; BBA, Northwood Inst., 1970; postgrad. Oakland U., 1985; m. Sharon Ann Wallace, Aug. 22, 1970; children: Erin Elizabeth, Stephanie Wallace. Sales mktg. rep. Jim Snyder Sales Co., Grosse Pointe Woods, Mich., 1970-72, v.p., 1972-75, sr. v.p., treas., 1975—, dir., 1972—; v.p. sales and mktg., dir. Country Sales, Inc., 1983-85; v.p. Thomas S. Maentz, Inc., Troy, Mich., 1985-88; pres. Snyder & Assocs., East Detroit, 1988—. Bd. dirs. Northwood Inst. Alumni, chmn. Detroit chpt., Long Range Planning CSI, Inc.; active St. John Men's Hosp. Guild, 1971—, Grosse Pointe Woods Police and Fire Aux., 1971—. Mem. Am. Mgmt. Assn., Soc. Advanced Mgmt., Soc. Plastic Engrs., Am. Soc. Body Engrs., Founders Soc. Detroit Inst. Arts, Automotive Old Timers, Tau Kappa Epsilon, Rho Epsilon. Clubs: Detroit Athletic, Grosse Pointe Yacht, Grosse Pointe Crisis; Oakland Hills Golf; White Hall (Chgo.). Home: 522 Neff Ln Grosse Pointe MI 48230 Office: Snyder & Assocs 17200 E 10 Mile Rd East Detroit MI 48021

SNYDER, JED COBB, foreign affairs specialist; b. Phila., Mar. 24, 1955; s. David and Lynn Snyder; BA, Colby Coll., 1976; MA, U. Chgo., 1978, postgrad. Rsch. asst. U. Chgo., 1979; asst. researcher Pan Heuristics div. R&D Assocs., Marina del Rey, Calif., 1979-80, assoc. researcher, asst. div. mgr., 1980-81, cons. 1982-83; cons. Sci. Applications, Inc., 1979-81, Rand Corp., Santa Monica, Calif., 1979-81, Los Alamos Nat. Lab., 1984; sr. spl. asst. to dir. Bur. of Politico-Mil. Affairs, Dept. State, Washington, 1981-82; rsch. assoc. Internat. Security Studies Program, Woodrow Wilson Internat. Ctr. for Scholars, Smithsonian Instn., Washington, 1982-84; founder, chmn., dep. dir. Washington strategy seminar, 1984; dep. dir. nat. security studies Hudson Inst., 1984-87; sr. rsch. fellow Nat. Strategy Info. Ctr., 1988—; cons. Office of the Sec. Def., 1988; cons., 1984, Rand Corp., 1983—; John M. Olin fellow, 1987-88, Smith Richardson fellow, 1987-88; Herman Kahn fellow in nat. security studies, 1985-86, McArthur Sr. fellow, 1985-86; guest scholar Sch. Advanced Internat. Studies, Johns Hopkins U., Washington, 1982-83; guest scholar, profl. lectr., Washington, 1983-84; Inter-Univ. Seminar on Armed Forces and Soc. fellow, 1980; U. Chgo. fellow, 1979. Trustee Kents Hill (Maine) Sch. Mem. Internat. Inst. for Strategic Studies, Internat. Studies Assn., Coun. on European Studies, Mil. Ops. Rsch. Soc., U.S. Naval Inst., Fgn. Policy Rsch. Inst., AIAA, Am. Polit. Sci. Assn., Coun. on Fgn. Rels.. Contbr. articles on U.S. fgn. policy and mil. def. to profl. publs. Home: 2201 L St NW Apt 602 Washington DC 20037 Office: Nat Strategy Info Ctr 1730 Rhode Island Ave NW Ste 601 Washington DC 20037

SNYDER, JOSEPH JOHN, author, lecturer, historian; b. Washington, Aug. 27, 1946; s. Joseph John and Amy Josephine (Hamilton) S.; m. Sally Hale Walker, July 4, 1973; children: Lauren Elizabeth, Brian Joseph Seth. BA in Anthropology, George Washington U., 1968; MA in Anthropology, U. N.Mex., 1973. With U.S. CSC, Washington, 1974-77; editor, writer U.S. Nat. Park Service, Harpers Ferry, W.Va., 1977-81; cons. editor Early Man mag., Evanston, Ill., 1978-83; cons. editor Sea Power Mag., 1987—; freelance writer, 1981—; lectr. Maya archaeology Norwegian-Caribbean Lines, Miami, Fla., 1982; cons. mus. design. Chmn. parks com. Neighborhood Planning Adv. Group, Croydon Park, Rockville, Md., 1980-81; bd. dirs. Agrl. R & D Orgn, 1985—. Served with U.S. Army, 1970-71, Vietnam. Decorated Bronze Star. Mem. Soc. for History of Discoveries, Soc. Am. Archaeology, Council Md. Archaeology, Hakluyt Soc., Am. Com. to Advance Study of Petroglyphs and Pictographs (exec. sec. 1980—, editor Jour. Rock Art), Nat. Geog. Soc. (cons. 1987—), Nat. Ry. Hist. Soc. (editor, bd. dirs. Hagerstown, Md. chpt. 1988—). Democrat. Contbg. editor Sea Power Mag., Arlington, Va., 1986—; cons. editor jour. Archaeoastronomy, 1987—; contbr. articles to popular mags. Home and Office: 2008 Ashley Dr Shepherdstown WV 25443

SNYDER, JULIA ANN, international trade and coffee company executive; b. Springfield, Mo., May 17, 1950; d. Arthur Jennings and Catheryn Laverna (Gallion) Swain; m. Orville Edward Kelley, Dec. 29, 1968 (div. 1972); 1 child, Adam Wayne; m. Ronald Warren Synder, May 29, 1982. Cert. Graff Vocat. Tech. Ctr., 1974. Sales sec. Paul Mueller Co., Springfield, 1971-73; surg. technician Cox Med. Ctr., Springfield, 1974-76; corp. sec., dir. OR&D, Inc., Springfield, 1979—; v.p., dir. Hey Mon Coffee Ltd., Everton, Mo., 1984—. Active Nat. Republican Com., 1980, Rep. Presdl. Task Force, 1981. Recipient Medal of Merit, Rep. Presdl. Task Force, 1982; named One of Outstanding Young Women of Am., 1984. Mem. Nat. Assn. Female Execs., Am. Notary Assn., Am. Film Inst. Mem. Assembly of God Ch. Avocations: latch hooking, stitchery, collecting depression era glassware, writing poetry, walking. Office: Hey Mon Coffee Ltd 294A Coffee Ln Everton MO 65646

SNYDER, MARK JEFFREY, financial consultant, actuary; b. Bklyn., May 16, 1947; s. Milton A. and June (Freed) S.; m. Gloria Carol Beskin, May 31, 1969; children: Chad Alan, Heather Lynn. B of Engring. Sci., SUNY, Stony Brook, 1969. CLU; chartered fin. cons.; registered fin. planner. Ins. agt. Mass. Mut. Life Ins., Holbrook, N.Y., 1971-79; dist. mgr. Guardian Life Ins. Co., Port Jefferson, N.Y., 1979-81; v.p. pensions Exec. Planners, Ronkonkoma, N.Y., 1981-84; pres. CAS Adv. Services, Inc., Patchogue, N.Y., 1984—; mng. exec. Integrated Resources Equity Corp., Patchogue, 1986—; speaker in field. Moderator, host Moneywise, Brookhaven Cable TV, Port Jefferson Sta., N.Y., 1987-88; contbr. articles to profl. jours. Mem. South Setauket (N.Y.) Civic Assn., 1972—, Three Village Dem. Club, Setauket, 1984—; bd. dirs., chmn. pub. relations Suffolk Estate Planning Council, 1984-87; chmn. planned giving com. Suffolk County Council Boy Scouts Am., Medford, N.Y., 1985-87, mem. exec. bd., 1985—. Mem. Internat. Assn. Fin. Planners, Am. Soc. Pension Actuaries (assoc.), Am. Soc. CLU's and Chartered Fin. Cons. (v.p. pub. relations Suffolk chpt. 1986—), Registered Fin. Planners L.I. (bd. dirs., pres. 1986-87), Pension Forum of L.I. (bd. dirs., chmn. pub. relations 1986—). Democrat. Jewish. Club: Royal Racquet (Coram, N.Y.). Lodge: KP. Office: Integrated Resources Equity Corp 160 S Ocean Ave Ste 208 Patchogue NY 11772

SNYDER, ORVILLE WAYNE, clothing company executive; b. Independence, Mo., Nov. 27, 1947; s. Orville Nelson and Lena Ann (Winegar) S.; m. Wanda Sue Hendrix, May 27, 1967; children: Jeffrey Wayne, Brian Anthony, Darren Lee. AA in Bus. Data Processing, Longview Coll., 1974; BA in Bus. Data Processing, Avila U., 1977. With Unitog Co., Kansas City, Mo., 1965-66, 70-72, programming mgr., 1972-76, mgr. systems software and database adminstrn., 1976-79, mgr. programming and tech. support, 1978-79, v.p. mgmt. info. systems, 1984—, also dir. mgmt. info. systems. Served with U.S. Army, 1966-70. Mem. Assn. Systems Mgmt., Data Processing Mgmt. Assn., Kansas City C. of C. Office: Unitog Co 101 W 11th St Kansas City MO 64105

SNYDER, PETER LARSEN, public relations executive; b. Phila., Apr. 28, 1952; s. Philip Lerch and Adrienne Louise (Larsen) S.; m. Karen Suzanne Stachiw, June 1, 1973; children: P. Evan, Erik D. BS, Cornell U., 1975. Account exec. Gibbs & Soell Pub. Rels., N.Y.C., 1975-78; account assoc. Ruder & Finn Pub. Rels., N.Y.C., 1978-80; exec. v.p., mng. ptnr. Dorf & Stanton Communications, St. Louis, 1980—. Cons. Harbor Festival '78, N.Y.C., 1978, St. Louis Pub. Sch. Partnership program, 1985-87, St. Louis area ARC, 1987-88, Muscular Dystrophy Assn. St. Louis, 1988; bd. dirs., capital chmn. Rohan-Woods Sch., Warson Woods, Mo., 1986-88; bd. dirs. Kirkwood/Webster YMCA, Webster Groves, Mo., 1984-87. Mem. Nat. Agri-Mktg. Assn. (named Best of 1983), Cornell Club St. Louis (bd. dirs. 1988—), Media Club, Press Club St. Louis, Clayton (Mo.) Club, Round Table (Plymouth, Mich.). Episcopalian. Office: Dorf & Stanton Communications Inc 1221 Locust St Ste 555 Saint Louis MO 63103

SNYDER, RICHARD ALLEN, manufacturing executive, accountant, treasurer; b. St Paul, Minn., Jan. 9, 1940; s. Elmer F. and Margaret M. (Watzl) S.; m. Elizabeth A. Komor, Oct. 19, 1963; 1 child, Roxane L. BBA in Acctg., U. Minn., 1964. CPA, N.Y., Minn. Former ptnr. Deloitte, Haskins & Sells, N.Y.C., 1975-79; staff acct., audit mgr. Deloitte, Haskins & Sells, Mpls. and N.Y.C., 1964-74; chief auditor Dayton Hudson Corp., Mpls., 1979-81; chief fin. officer, treas., v.p. Tennant Co., 1981—. Staff sgt. U.S. Army N.G., USAF, 1963-69. Mem. AICPA, Minn. CPA Soc. (Harold Utley award 1966), Fin. Execs. Inst., Nat. Assn. Investor Rels. Home: 315 Mt Curve Blvd Saint Paul MN 55105 Office: Tennant Co PO Box 1452 Minneapolis MN 55440

SNYDER, RICHARD JOSEPH, lawyer; b. Boston, June 18, 1939; s. Harris H. and Ruth (Galner) S.; m. Joyce Marshall Aug. 19, 1962 (div.); children: Robert M., Lauren E., John K.; m. Susana Gohiman, Apr. 11, 1982; stepchildren: Joanna Maixner, Adriana Maixner. BS in Bus. Adminstrn. with honors, Babson Coll., 1960; JD with honors, Boston U., 1963; LLM, Georgetown U., 1966. Bar: Mass. 1963, U.S. Claims Ct., 1964, U.S. Tx Ct. 1966, U.S. Dist. Ct., 1967, U.S. Ct. Appeals (1st Cir.) 1968, U.S. Supreme Ct. 1968, Vt. 1988. Sr. trial atty. Dept. Justice, Washington, 1963-66; assoc. Epstein & Salloway, Boston, 1966-67, Cohn, REimer & Pollack (now Riemer & Braunstein), Boston, 1967-69; assoc. then ptnr. Widett & Widett (now Widett, Slater & Goldman), Boston, 1969-76; ptnr. Goldstein & Manello, Boston, 1976-88, chmn., 1988—; lectr. law Babson Coll., Wellesley, Mass., 1967-76. Contbr. Boston Law Rev., 1962; contbg. editor Direct Sales Mag., 1976-78. Bd. dirs. The Sunday Sch., Inc., 1974-85, pres., 1976-85: trustee Babson Coll., 1977—, mem. exec. com., 1979—, chmn., 1984—; mem. bus. and profl. leadership com. Boston Symphony Orch.; bd. dirs. Babson Recreation Ctr., chmn., 1987—, Mass. Corp. for Ednl. Telecommunications, 1985—, vice chmn., 1986—. Fellow Mass. Bar Found.; mem. ABA, Mass. Bar Assn., Vt. Bar Assn., Boston Bar Assn., Am. Bus. Law Assn. (chmn. real property com. 1976-77, pres. North Atlantic region 1976-77), Nat. Assn. Coll. and Univ. Attys., Mass. Conveyancers Assn., New Eng. Land Title Assn., Babson Coll. Alumni Assn. (pres. 1977-79). Clubs: Minuteman Yacht, Downtown. Home: 122 Bellevue St Newton MA 02158 Office: Goldstein & Manello 265 Franklin St 20th Fl Boston MA 02110

SNYDER, RICHARD LEE, tobacco company executive; b. Carlisle, Pa., June 24, 1940; s. Paul Bear and Mary (Fishburn) S.; m. Roberta Fitzgerald, Nov. 15, 1970. B.S. magna cum laude, Pa. State U., 1961. C.P.A., N.Y. With Coopers & Lybrand, N.Y.C., 1961-64; chief fin. officer Bell Equipment Corp., N.Y.C., 1964-71; treas. Wheelabrator-Frye, N.Y.C., 1971-73; v.p. fin. internat. Wheelabrator-Frye, 1973-75; v.p. fin. and adminstrn. Philip Morris USA, N.Y.C., 1975-79; corp. controller Philip Morris, Inc., N.Y.C., 1979-81; sr. v.p. adminstrn. Philip Morris Internat., 1981-83, exec. v.p., 1983-87; sr. v.p. human resources and adminstrn. Philip Morris Cos., 1987—. Treas. Sutton Area Community Assn., 1976-79; bd. dirs. Nat. Multiple Sclerosis Soc., 1981—. Served with U.S. Army, 1962. Recipient Alumni Achievement award Pa. State U., 1980. Mem. Nat. Assn. Accts., Fin. Execs. Inst., AICPA, Philippine Am. C. of C. (pres. 1986-87). Club: Sky (N.Y.C.). Office: Philip Morris Cos 120 Park Ave New York NY 10017

SNYDER, ROBERT MARTIN, consultant, retired government official; b. Lahmansville, W.Va., Sept. 6, 1912; s. Noah W. and Maggie M. (Varner) S.; m. Gail M. Hiser, Nov. 25, 1937; children—Rebecca J. (Mrs. Walbert Peters), Margaret A. (Mrs. John Bensenhaver), Shirley L. (Mrs. Jerry L. Williams), Robert Martin. B.S. in Agr, W.Va. U., 1937. Engaged in farming 1929-84; agrl. extension agt. Nicholas County, W.Va., 1937-41; adminstrn. commodity loans crop ins. and program performance AAA, Morgantown, W.Va., 1941-42; adminstrn. grain and oilseed program E central region AAA, U.S. Dept. Agr., 1942-47; asst. coordinator CCC, U.S. Dept. Agr., 1947-50, coordinator dairy, poultry, fruit and vegetable programs, 1950-52; chief agriculturist U.S. mission to Karachi, Pakistan FOA, 1952-54; counselor Am.embassy and dir. U.S. mission to Afghanistan, Kabul, Nairobi, Kenya, Uganda, Tanganyika and Zanzibar; councelor ICA, 1955-59; rep. ICA to, Brit. East AfricaKenya, Uganda, Tanganyika, Zanzibar, 1959-60; food and agr. officer West African countries of Ivory Coast, Upper Volta, Niger, Dahomey, 1961-62; acting dir. U.S. AID Mission, Ivory Coast, 1961-63; attache U.S. Embassy, food and agrl. officer, Ivory Coast, 1963; agr. adviser, area office rep. AID mission to, Rhodesia and Nyasaland, 1964; attache, AID affairs officer Malawi, Africa, 1964-68; cons. World Bank, IBRD, 1967; detail officer fgn. direct investments Dept. Commerce, 1968; AID affairs officers Washington, 1968-69; food and agr. officer U.S. AID, Amman, Jordan, 1969-70; planning adviser Ministry Natural Resources, Nigeria, 1970-72; cons. 1972—; Mem. del. Gen. Mem. Agreements Tariffs and Trade Conf., Torquay, Eng., 1951; mem. Mus. Commn., Library Commn. Served to lt. USNR, 1944-46, PTO. Recipient nat. 4-H alumni award Nat. 4-H Congress, Chgo., 1982, Disting. Alumnus award W.Va. Coll. Agriculture and Forestry, 1987. Mem. Fgn. Service Assn., Am. Legion, W.Va. U. Alumni Assn., Am. Acad. Polit. and Social Sci., Soc. Internat. Devel., Internat. Platform Assn., U.S. Nat. Trust for Historic Preservation, Nature Conservancy, Commn. on Aging, Alpha Zeta. Clubs: Masons, Kiwanis, Explorers. Home: Noah Snyder Farm Rte 1 Box 32 Lahmansville WV 26731

SNYDER, WILLARD BREIDENTHAL, lawyer; b. Kansas City, Kans., Dec. 18, 1940; s. N.E. and Ruth (Breidenthal) S.; m. Lieselotte Dieringer, Nov. 10, 1970 (dec. Nov. 1975); m. Christa Wittman, June 1, 1978; children: Kim Green, Jackie Green, Rolf. BA, U. Kans., 1962, JD, 1965; postgrad., Hague Acad. Internat. Law, The Netherlands, 1965-66, U. Dijon, France, 1966; grad., Command and Gen. Staff Coll., Ft. Leavenworth, Kans., 1977. Sole practice Kansas City, Kans., 1970-80, 85—; trust officer, corp. trust officer Security Nat. Bank., Kansas City, 1980-83, corp. sec., 1983-85; pres. Real Estate Corp. Inc., 1984—; bd. dirs. Providence St. Margaret Health Ctr., Kansas City, Kans.; adv. bd. dirs. United Mo. Bankshares, Kansas City; West German consul for Kans., Western Mo., 1972—. Mem. Platte Woods (Mo.) City Council, 1983-84; exec. bd. dirs. regional coun. Boy Scouts Am.; bd. dirs. Liberty Assn. Kansas City. U.S. Army, 1967-70; lt. col. Kans. Army N.G., 1984—. Decorated Commendation medal U.S. Army, 1970, Bundesverdienst Kreuz, 1982, Bundeswehr Kreuz (silver), 1987; named to Hon. Order Ky. Cols., 1988. Mem. Mo. Bar Assn., Kansas City Bar Assn., Kansas City Hosp. Attys., Kansas City Bd. Trade, Mil. Order of World Wars (chpt. comdr. 1983-84, regional comdr. 1987—), Nat. Eagle Scout Assn. Office: care Security Bank Kansas City PO Box 1297 Kansas City KS 66117

SNYDERMAN, RALPH, medical educator, physician; b. Bklyn., Mar. 13, 1940; m. Judith Ann Krebs, Nov. 18, 1967; 1 child, Theodore Benjamin. B.S., Washington Coll., Chestertown, Md., 1961; M.D., SUNY-Bklyn., 1965. Diplomate Am. Bd. Internal Medicine, Am. Bd. Allergy and Immunology. Med. intern Duke U. Hosp., Durham, N.C., 1965-66, med. resident, 1966-67, asst. prof. medicine and immunology, 1972-74, assoc. prof., 1974-77, chief, div. rheumatology and immunology, 1975-87, prof. medicine and immunology, 1980-84, Frederic M. Hanes prof. medicine, prof. immunology, 1984-87; surgeon USPHS, NIH, Bethesda, Md., 1967-69; sr. staff fellow Nat. Inst. Dental Research, NIH, Bethesda, Md., 1969-70, sr. investigator immunology sect. lab. microbiology and immunology, 1970-72; chief, div. rheumatology Durham VA Hosp., Bethesda, Md., 1972-75; v.p. med. rsch. and devel. Genentech, Inc., South San Francisco, Calif., 1987-88, sr. v.p. med. rsch. and devel., 1988—; adj. asst. prof. oral biology U. N.C. Sch. Dental Medicine, Chapel Hill, 1974-75; dir. Lab Immune Effector Function, Howard Hughes Med. Inst., Durham, 1977—; adj. prof. medicine U. Calif., San Francisco, 1987—. Editor: Contemporary Topics in Immunobiology, 1984, Medical Clinics of North American, 1985, Inflammation: Basic Concepts and Clinical Correlates, 1988; contbr. articles to profl. jours. Recipient Alexander von Humboldt award Fed. Republic Germany, 1985. Mem. Assn. Am. Physicians, Am. Assn. Immunologists, Am. Soc. Clin. Investigation, Am. Acad. Allergy, Am. Assn. Cancer Research, Am. Soc. Exptl. Pathology, Am. Fedn. Clin. Research, Am. Assn. Pathologists, Reticuloendothelial Soc., Am. Rheumatism Assn., Sigma Xi. Office: Genentech Inc VP Med Rsch & Devel 460 Point San Bruno Blvd South San Francisco CA 94080

SOAPER, ROBERT CALLAWAY, III, chemical company executive, independent oil producer; b. Henderson, Ky., June 6, 1932; s. Robert Callaway and Edith (Wilson) S.; m. Barbara Joan Shaver, Dec. 28, 1959; children—Susan Pringle, Robert Callaway IV. Student U. Ky., 1950-52, 56-57. With Soaper Oil Co., Henderson, 1960—, pres. 1965—; with Sinclair Oil Co., Henderson, 1960-65; pres., owner Soaper Chem. Co., Henderson, 1965-86; pres., chief exec. officer Vivo-Micro Inc., Henderson, 1988—. Served to 1st class petty officer USCG, 1952-56. Mem. Ind. Petroleum Assn. Am. (exec. com. 1980-82, 86-89, v.p. 1978-80, regional bd. dirs. 1983-85), Ky. Oil and Gas Assn. (pres. 1982-84), Ill. Oil and Gas Assn., Tenn. Oil and Gas Assn., Mich. Oil and Gas Assn., Indiana Oil and Gas Assn., Nat. Stripper Well Assn. (v.p. 1985—). Republican. Episcopalian. Office: Vivo-Micro Inc PO Box 215 Henderson KY 42420

SOARES DE MELLO, ADELINO JOSE RODRIGUES, mechanical engineer; b. Horta, Azores, Portugal, Oct. 3, 1931; s. Alfredo Luis and Hilda da Conceiç ã o (Rodrigues) S. de M.; Eng.Mec., Lisbon U., 1955; postgrad. Manchester (Eng.) Coll. Tech., 1956-57; m. Maria Odete Correia Baptista, Dec. 7, 1955; children—Joã o Carlos, Luis Miguel, Pedro Gonç alo. Mgr. mech. engrs. div. Profabril-Centro de Projectos, Sarl, Lisbon, 1958-68; dir. Tecnofabril-Industrias Mecanicas, Sarl, Lisbon, 1966-75; dir. Termec-Equipamentos Termicos de Coimbra, Lda, Portugal, 1968-71; mng. dir. Babcock & Wilcox Portuguesa, Sarl-Lisbon-Oporto, 1971-73; chmn. bd. dirs. Sorefame-Sociedades Reunidas de Fabricaç õ es Metalicas, Sarl, Amadora, Portugal, 1973-74; tech. rep. Brit. Ropeways Engring. Co., Ltd., Sevenoaks, Eng., Rio de Janeiro, 1975-78; dir. Smec-Ind. Metalo Mecanicas, Ltda., Botucatu S.P., Brazil, 1975-78, Costa Pinto J.A., Ltda., Botucatu S.P., 1975-78, Sociedade Indul. de Concentrados, Sarl-Azinhaga, Portugal, 1978-81, Mot Sistemas de Movimentaç ao e Transporte, Lda, Lisbon, 1978-81, Metalurgica Duarte Ferreira, Sarl-Tramagal, Portugal, RUF, Lda, Lisboa, Portugal; indsl. cons. Com. Electromech. Industry, Ministry of Industry, 1980-84. Met. Vickers Elec. Co. Ltd. grantee, 1955-58. Mem. Associaç ao Portuguesa dos Industriais de Tomate (hon. sec. 1980-82), Ordem dos Engenheiros. Roman Catholic. Clubs: Automovel de Portugal, Met. Vickers Overseas. Columnist econ. affairs newspapers, 1982-89; contbr. articles to profl. publs. Home: Rua Maria Veleda, Quinta da Luz Torre 2-10 C, 1500 Lisbon Portugal Office: Avenida 5 de Outubro 122 4, 1000 Lisbon Portugal

SOBELSOHN, RICHARD JON, school administrator; b. Kew Gardens, N.Y., Nov. 30, 1960; s. William and Hermine Sobelsohn. BA, Colgate U., 1982. Media planner Dancer Fitzgerald Sample, Inc., N.Y.C., 1981; dir. Sobelsohn Sch., N.Y.C., 1982—; pres., chief exec. officer Protape, Inc., N.Y.C., 1983—; pres. Three J's Travel Bur., Inc., N.Y.C., 1987—. Author: Termination of the Mandate and Defacto Recognition of the State of Israel, 1981. Aux. officer N.Y.C. Police Dept., 1981-84; mem. Kew Gardens Civic Assn., 1982—; dir. fire safety N.Y.C. Fire Dept., 1983-86; instr. CPR N.Y.C. chpt. ARC, 1980-86. Mem. Am. Acctg. Assn., Colgate U. Club of N.Y. (treas. 1982-84, v.p. 1984-88, pres. 1988—), Phi Alpha Theta. Democrat. Home: 235 W End Ave New York NY 10023 Office: Sobelsohn Sch 352 7th Ave New York NY 10001

SOBEY, DAVID F., food company executive; b. Stellarton, N.S., Can., Mar. 22, 1931; s. Frank Hoyse and Irene (MacDonald) S.; m. Faye B. Naugle, June 2, 1953; children—Paul David, Janis Irene Hames. With Sobeys Inc., Stellarton, N.S., Can., 1949—, store mgr., dir. merchandising and advt., v.p., exec. v.p., pres., dep. chmn., chief exec. officer, dir., 1981-85, chmn., chief exec. officer, dir., 1985—; bd. dirs. Empire Co. Ltd., Sobey Leased Properties Ltd., Atlantic Shipping Centres Ltd., Clover Group, Eastern Sign Print Ltd., Lumsden Brothers Ltd., Dominion Textile Inc., CHC Helicopters Corp., Evangeline Savs. & Mortgage Co., T.R.A. Foods Ltd., Provigo Inc., Hanaford Bros. Co., VS Services Ltd. Bd. dirs., Jr. Achievement Can., Retail Council of Can., Internat. Assn. Chain Stores-C.I.E.S.; mem. Halifax Bd. of Trade; bd. govs. St. Mary's U. Clubs: Royal N.S. Yacht Squadron; Halifax; City (New Glasgow). Office: Sobeys Inc, 115 King St, Stellarton, NS Canada B0K 1S0

SOBEY, DONALD RAE, real estate developer; b. New Glasgow, N.S., Can.; s. Frank Hoyse and Irene (MacDonald) S.; m. Elizabeth H. Purvis; children: Robert George Creighton, Irene Elizabeth, Kent Richard. B of Commerce, Queen's U. Bd. dirs. Sobey Leased Properties Ltd.; sec., now v.p. Foord Constrn. Ltd.; chmn. Empire Co. Ltd., 1985—, also bd. dirs.; pres. Halifax Devels. Ltd., 1972—; v.p. Empire Theatres Ltd.; mem. Cape Breton Adv. Com., Conf. Bd. Can.; chmn. bd. Maritime Telegraph and Telephone Co. Ltd.; bd. dirs. Atlantic Motors Ltd., Atlantic Shopping Centres Ltd., Atlantic Theatres Ltd., Crombie Ins. Ltd. U.K., Durham Leaseholds Ltd., I.C.G. Scotia Gas Ltd., Jannock Ltd., Lawton's Drug Stores Ltd., Provigo Inc., Tibbetts Paints Ltd., Toronto-Dominion Bank,

Wajax Ltd. Gov. Olympic Trust Can.; bd. govs. Dalhousie U.; patron 1986 World Congress on Edn. and Tech. Mem. Lloyd's of London (underwriting mem.), Internat. Assn. Students in Bus. and Econs. Office: Empire Co Ltd, 115 King St, Stellarton, NS Canada B0K 1S0

SOBLE, DAVID S., steel company executive; b. Chgo., July 3, 1943; s. Morris and Eleanor (Leishin) S.; m. Marica Greenstein, Aug. 5, 1966 (div. 1981); children: Michael, Jeffrey; m. Lee Ann Hoffman, Dec. 27, 1985; 1 child, Peggy Hoffman. BS in Econs., U. Pa., 1965. With sales dept. Lesso Steel Corp., Chgo., 1965-69, gen. mgr., 1969-71; v.p. sales Interstate Steel Co., Des Plaines, Ill., 1971-73, exec. v.p., 1973-75, pres., 1975—; chmn. govt. affairs Steel Service Ctr. Inst., Cleve., 1985—. Mem. Industry Sector Adv. com. Office: Interstate Steel Co 401 E Touhy Ave Des Plaines IL 60017

SOCHA, NANCY ANN, financial planner; b. Worcester, Mass., Jan. 13, 1955; d. Raymond Edward and Beatrice Marie (Campanile) Duquette; m. Louis Stanley Socha Jr., Apr. 15, 1978; children: Michael Eric, Michelle Lynn. BS, U. Mass., 1976. Cert. fin. planner. Lab. supr. Schuyler Hosp., Montour Falls, N.Y., 1978-83; pvt. practice fin. planning Corning, 1983—. Mem. Internat. Assn. Fin. Planners, Inst. Cert. Fin. Planners, Internat. Bd. Standards and Practices Cert. Fin. Planning. Roman Catholic. Home: 614 Beartown Rd Painted Post NY 14870 Office: 80 E Market St Ste 302 Corning NY 14830

SOCKWELL, OLIVER R., JR., financial services company executive; b. Washington, July 27, 1943; s. Oliver R. and Janette Muriel (Nealy) S.; m. Harriet Evelyne Riley, July 28, 1973; children—Kristine Evelyne, Brian Oliver, Jason Wendell. B.S., Howard U., 1965; M.B.A., Columbia U., 1972. Communications engr. N.Y. Telephone Co., N.Y.C., 1965-67; mktg. rep. IBM, Washington, 1967-70; investment banker Smith, Barney & Co., N.Y.C., 1972-74; v.p. mktg. Sallie Mae (Student Loan Mktg. Assn.), Washington, 1974-83, sr. v.p. ops., 1983-84, exec v.p. fin., adminstn. and planning, 1984-87; pres., chief exec. officer Coll. Constrn. Loan Ins. Assn. (Connie Lee), Washington, 1987—; bd. dirs. Connie Lee Ins. Co., Washington; bd. dirs. D.C. Govt. Retirement Bd., Washington, 1981-83. Trustee Wilberforce U., Ohio, 1983-87; mem. adv. bd. D.C. chpt. ARC, 1980; bd. dirs. Washington Project for the Arts, 1985-88, Washington Urban League, 1986—. Home: 1685 Myrtle St NW Washington DC 20012 Office: Connie Lee One Westin Ctr 2445 M St NW Washington DC 20007

SOCOL, SHELDON ELEAZER, university official; b. N.Y.C., July 10, 1936; s. Irving and Helen (Tuchman) S.; BA, Yeshiva U., 1958; JD, N.Y.U., 1963; m. Genia Ruth Prager, Dec. 26, 1959; children: Jeffrey, Steven, Sharon. Asst. bursar Yeshiva U., N.Y.C., 1958-60, assoc. bursar, 1960-62, dir. student fins., 1962-70, sec., 1970—, chief fiscal officer, 1971-72, v.p. bus. affairs, 1972—. Mem. N.Y. State Adv. Coun. on Fin. Assistance to Coll. Students, 1969-76; asst. dir. Tng. Inst. for Fin. Aid Officers, Hunter Coll., CUNY, 1970-71; presdl. adv. commn. Temple U., 1986; mem. N.Y.C. Regional Plan for Higher Edn. Regents Adv. Task Force, 1971-72. Pres., Minyon Park Estates, Inc. Mem. Nat. Assn. Coll. and Univ. Attys., NEA, N.Y. State, Met. N.Y.C. Fin. Aid Adminstrs. Assns., Ea. Assn. Student Financial Aid Officers, Am. Mgmt. Assn., Am. Assn. for Higher Edn., Nat. Assn. Coll. and Univ. Bus. Officers, Middle States Assn. Colls. (evaluation team commn. higher edn.), Soc. Coll. and Univ. Planning (U. Med. and Dentistry of N.J., 1985, Upstate Health Sci. Ctr., 1986, Carnegie-Mellon U., 1988), Albany Med. Ctr., 1989.

SODERLUND, PAMELA LYNNE, service industry executive; b. Moses Lake, Wash., Dec. 8, 1954; d. William Warren and Donna Jayne (Hawkins) Ruscher; m. Harry Richard Soderlund, July 20, 1974; children: Alisha, Jessica, David. Student, Green Mountain Coll., 1974. Sec. Halstead Dist., Somers, N.Y., 1972-74; sales clk. Abel's, Mt. Kisco, 1974; mgr., owner Housecleaning Bus., West County, N.Y., 1975—; clk. U.S. Post Office, 1979-86; mgr. sales Chain Reaction, Cross River, 1986-88. Methodist. Home and Office: Rt35 Box 419 Cross River NY 10518

SODERQUIST, DONALD G., retail executive; b. Chgo., 1934. BA, Wheaton Coll., 1955. Pres. Ben Franklin Stores div. City Products Co., 1963-80; sr. v.p. Wal-Mart Stores Inc., Rogers, Ark., 1980, formerly exec. v.p. ops. adminstrn., now vice-chmn., chief oper. officer, also bd. dirs.; bd. dirs. First Nat. Bank, Rogers. Office: Wal-Mart Stores Inc 702 SW 8th St Rogers AR 72756 *

SÖDERSTRÖM, HANS TSON, economist; b. Stockholm, Feb. 25, 1945; s. Torkel A.R. and Elisabet (Zielfelt) S.; Ekon dr. (Ph.D.), Stockholm Sch. Econs., 1974; (div. 1988); children—Christofer, Ebba, Marie. Sr. fellow Inst. Internat. Econ. Studies, U. Stockholm, 1971-84; assoc. dir., 1979-84; exec. dir. SNS-Ctr. for Bus. and Policy Studies, Stockholm, 1985—; vis. fellow public and internat. affairs Princeton U., 1975; vis. scholar Stanford U., 1976; vis. research prof., bd. govs. Fed. Res. System, 1976; expert Govt. Commns. on Exchange Control and Wage Earners Funds, 1979-81; mem. SNS Econ. Policy Group 1980-81, chmn., 1984—, Sven Hagströmer Fondkomm, 1988—; bd. dirs. SEB-Invest AB, 1980-85, Montagu Fondkomm, 1986-88. Mem. Jan Wallander Found. for Social Rsch., 1981—. Ford Found. research fellow, 1975-76. Recipient David Davidson prize in econs., 1971. Mem. Swedish Econ. Assn., Stockholm Stock Exchange, Swedish Shareholders Assn., Am. Econ. Assn., Liberal Econ. Club (chmn. 1984-85). Editor: Ekonomisk Debat, 1977-78, mem. editorial bd. 1979—, S-E Banken Quarterly Rev., 1983—; Author: Microdynamics of Production, 1974, Sweden-the Road to Stability, 1985, Getting Sweden Back to Work, 1986; contbr. articles to sci. jours. Home: Larsbergsvagen 27, Stocleholm, S 18138 Lidingö Sweden Office: SNS, Sköldungagatan 2, S-114 Stockholm 27, Sweden

SOFIA, CAROLYN MILDRED, financial analyst; b. Bklyn., Apr. 27, 1950; d. Gaspare Philip and Florence (Vollano) S.; m. Francis Napfel, Nov. 11, 1972 (div. Feb. 1975). BA in Humanities, Hofstra U., 1971. Assoc. editor Bank Systems & Equipment mag., N.Y.C., 1971-72; editor-in-chief Parkville Reporter, Balt., 1972-74; from assoc. research dir. to spl projects dir. The Value Line Investment Survey, N.Y.C., 1977—. Mem. Fin. Analysts Fedn., Internat. Women Writers Guild, N.Y. Soc. Security Analysts. Office: Value Line Inc 711 3d Ave New York NY 10017

SOFINOWSKI, JOHN ROBERT, mechanical engineer; b. Balt., May 24, 1950; s. John Joseph and Rita Maria (Fones) S.; m. Sandra Kathleen Shoap, June 29, 1974; children: Michael, Erin. BSME, U. Md., 1973; MS in Engring. Adminstrn., George Washington U., 1980. Patent researcher Mfrs. Aircraft Group, Arlington, Va., 1973-74; project engr. Ward Machinery Co., Cockysville, Md., 1974-82; supr. engring. Koppers Container Machinery, Glen Arm, Md., 1982-86; v.p. engring. United Container Machinery Group, Glen Arm, 1986—. Contbr. articles to profl. jours. Pres. Madonna Manor Improved Assn., Harford County, Md., 1982-84. Mem. Tech. Assn. of Pulp & Paper Industry (chmn. sub. com. 1984-85), ASME (com. officer 1974—). Democrat. Roman Catholic. Home: 2218 Nodleigh Terr Jarrettsville MD 21084 Office: United Container Machinery Group 5200 Glen Arm Rd Glen Arm MD 21057

SOGNEFEST, PETER WILLIAM, manufacturing company executive; b. Melrose Park, Ill., Feb. 4, 1941; s. Peter and Alvera E. Sognefest; m. Margaret Brunkow, Aug. 15, 1964; children: Scott, Brian, Jennifer. BSEE, U. Ill., 1964, MSEE, 1967. Elec. engr. Magnavox Corp., Urbana, Ill., 1964-67; sr. fellow, mgr. research, United Techs. fellow Mellon Inst., Pitts., 1967-71; gen. mgr. for semicondr. ops. United Techs., Pitts., 1971-77; v.p. indsl. electronics unit Motorola Inc., Schaumburg, Ill., 1977-84; pres., chief exec. officer Digital Appliance Controls, Inc., Hoffman Estates, Ill., 1984—, also bd. dirs.; bd. dirs. Two-Six Inc. Patentee in field. Pres. bd. deacons Presbyn. Ch., 1981-82, elder, 1988—. Mem. IEEE, U. Ill. Elec. Engring. Alumni Assn. (pres. 1986-87), Coves Property Owners Assn. (pres. 1982), Barrington Hills Country Club. Republican. Home: 4 Back Bay Rd Barrington IL 60010

SOHIGIAN, HARRY JAMES, stockbroker; b. Cambridge, Mass., Apr. 5, 1938; s. Harry James and Sylvia (Yaghjian) S.; student Northeastern U., 1956-58; BS in Bus. Adminstrn., Wayne State U., 1961; cert. N.Y. Inst. Fin., 1971; m. Emily N. Yagoobian, Apr. 30, 1966; children—James Paul, Tina Ann. Sales mgr. Lansing (Mich.) Candy & Cigar Co., 1961-71; salesman 1st Investor's Corp., N.Y.C., 1969-71; registered rep. William C. Roney & Co., Detroit, 1971-77; br. mgr., 1st v.p. Manley, Bennett, McDonald & Co., Lansing, 1977-84; registered rep., v.p. Thomson, McKinnon Securities Inc., Lansing, 1984-88; v.p. investments Prudential-Bache Securities Inc., Lansing, 1988—; coord. seminars in field of fin. Mem. Lansing Community Band, 1969-73; active membership drives Lansing YMCA. Mem. Internat. Assn. Fin. Planners. Republican. Mem. Armenian Apostolic Ch. Lodges: Masons, Knights of Vartan, Order of Ahepa, Lions. Office: Bus & Trade Ctr 1 Michigan Ave Ste 110 Lansing MI 48933

SOLAR, RICHARD LEON, banker; b. Boston, Aug. 15, 1939; s. Hervey L. and Mildred (Beckerman) S.; m. Stephanie Bennett; children: Andrew, Lisa. BA, Harvard U., 1961; MBA, Columbia U., 1963. Asst. v.p. Bankers Trust Co., N.Y.C., 1963-71; treas. Val D'Or Inds., N.Y.C., 1971-74, Diamondhead Corp., Mountainside, N.J., 1974, mng. dir., 1984—; sr. v.p. Bankers Trust Co., N.Y.C., 1975-84 ; chmn., dir. Bankers Trust Comml. Corp., 1983—. Mem. Nat. Comml. Fin. Assn. (chmn., dir.). Club: Wyantenuck Country (Great Barrington, Mass.), Explorers. Office: Bankers Trust Co 1775 Broadway New York NY 10016

SOLARI, LARRY THOMAS, manufacturing company executive; b. Stockton, Calif., July 30, 1942; s. John Fredrich and Elizabeth (Rubino) S.; m. Patricia Harlan, Feb. 5, 1966 (div. May 1978); m. Deirdre Duff, Apr. 9, 1980; children: Chris, Ryan, Erin, Brad. BS, San Jose State U., 1965, MBA, 1966. Mfg. trainee Owens Corning Fiberglas, Santa Clara, Calif., 1966-67; salesman Owens Corning Fiberglas, San Francisco, 1967-69; product mgr. Owens Corning Fiberglas, Toledo, 1970-73, mktg. mgr., 1974-78, gen. mgr., v.p., 1979-84, operating v.p., 1985-88, pres. constrn. products group, 1989—; mem. adv. bd. U. Toledo, 1983—, CAE Ltd., 1984-87, bd. dirs. Vitro Fibras, Mex.; pres. bd. dirs. Thermal Insulation Mfr. Assn. Chmn. bd. dirs. Jr. Achievement, Toledo, 1987—, pres. 1986. Served with U.S. Army, 1966-72. Named Outstanding Young Man in Am., 1971. Republican. Roman Catholic. . Home: 105 Secor Woods Ln Perrysburg OH 43551 Office: Owens Corning Fiberglas Corp Fiberglas Tower Toledo OH 43659

SOLBERG, NORMAN ROBERT, lawyer; b. Toledo, Aug. 28, 1939; s. Archie Norman and Margaret Jane (Olsen) S.; BA, Columbia Coll., 1961; LLB, Columbia U., 1964; postgrad. Parker Sch. Fgn. and Comparative Law, 1969; m. Susan Radcliffe Riley, Oct. 7, 1961; children: Eric Norman, Anne Olsen. Bar: N.Y. 1964, Mass. 1973, Mo. 1978, Ill. 1984. Assoc. firm Wickes, Riddell, Bloomer, Jacobi & McGuire, N.Y.C., 1964-69; sr. atty. The Gillette Co., Boston, 1969-75; asst. internat. counsel Monsanto Co., St. Louis, 1975-79; sr. staff coursel Household Internat. Inc., Prospect Heights, Ill., 1979-87; v.p., gen. counsel Alberto-Culver Co., Melrose Park, Ill., 1987—. Mem. Am. Bar Assn., Ill. Bar Assn., Chgo. Bar Assn. Republican. Lutheran. Home: 803 Bluff St Glencoe IL 60022 Office: Alberto-Culver Co 2525 Armitage Ave Melrose Park IL 60160

SOLE, CHRISTOPHER JOHN, marketing executive; b. London, Mar. 6, 1952; came to U.S., 1983; m. Susan Mary Hook; children: Lucy, Gemma. BS, U. Birmingham (Eng.), 1973; MBA, Stanford U., 1978. Brand mgr. Lever Bros. Ltd., London, 1973-76; bus. strategy cons. Boston Cons. Group, London, 1978-81; bus. planning mgr. Info. Tech. Ltd., Hemel Hempstead, Eng., 1981-82; bus. strategy cons. Bain & Co., Boston, 1982-84; v.p. mktg. D.A.S. Inc., Boston, 1984—. Harkness fellow, 1976-78. Mem. Am. Mktg. Assn., Am. Assn. for Artificial Intelligence, Instn. Mech. Engrs., Boston Computer Soc., Bus. Grads. Assn. Home: 125 W Concord St Boston MA 02118 Office: DAS Inc 11 Farnsworth St Boston MA 02210

SOLGANIK, MARVIN, real estate executive; b. Chgo., Nov. 7, 1930; s. Harry and Dora (Fastoff) S.; m. Judith Rosenberg, Sept. 11, 1960; children: Randall, Janet, Robert. B.B.A., Western Res. U., 1952. Real estate broker Cleve., 1950-65, Herbert Laronge Inc., Cleve., 1965-68; sr. v.p. real estate broker Revco D.S., Inc., Twinsburgh, Ohio, 1968—, corp. dir., 1974—; guest lectr. Cleve. State U., Case Western Res. U., Cuyahoga Community Coll., Cleve. Real Estate Bd. Vol. Jewish Welfare Fund, Shaker Heights, Ohio. Recipient Appreciation award Am. Soc. Real Estate Appraisers, Akron-Cleve. chpt., 1971. Mem. Nat. Assn. Corp. Real Estate Officers, Internat. Council Shopping Ctrs. Office: Revco DS Inc 1925 Enterprise Pkwy Twinsburg OH 44087

SOLHEIM, ALAN DALE, manufacturing executive; b. Seattle, Mar. 11, 1940; s. Karsten and Louise (Crozier) S.; m. Joan Elaine Chandler, Oct. 12, 1963; children: Allan Jr., Stacey, Karsten. Student, Phoenix Coll., 1961-62, Scottsdale Community Coll., 1980. Clerk U.S. Post Office, Redwood City, Calif., 1959; machinist Ampex, Redwood City, 1960; computer operator Gen. Electric Co., Phoenix, 1962-67; v.p. Karsten Mfg. Corp., Phoenix, 1967—. Bd. dirs. Ariz. Dist. Export Council, Phoenix, 1984—, Humana Hosp., Phoenix, 1985-87, World of Jr. Golf, Mesa, Ariz., 1979-87, Ariz. Fellowship Christian Athletes, 1988—; former deacon Paradise Valley Bapt. Ch., Phoenix. Served with USMCR, 1958-65. Mem. Ariz. World Trade Assn. (bd. dirs.), Nat. Golf Found. (sec., treas., bd. dirs.). Republican. Club: Moon Valley Country (bd. dirs.). Home: 1140 E Roberts Rd Phoenix AZ 85022 Office: Karsten Mfg Corp 2201 W Desert Cove Phoenix AZ 85029

SOLIDUM, ARLIN JAMES, sales executive; b. Honolulu, Nov. 25, 1955; s. James and Victoriana (Mayo) S.; m. Daren Gay Fung, June 17, 1978; children: Briana Lyn, Nashua James. Student, Foothill Coll., 1974; AA, Honolulu Community Coll., 1976. Sales rep. Bekins Internat., Honolulu, 1980-82, corp. sales rep., 1982-83; sales mgr. Bekins Moving & Storage, Honolulu, 1983—. Active panel I Aloha United Way, 1984—; agy. liason for Kalihi-Palama Health Clinic; mem. Hawaii Visitor's Bur.; campaign chmn. State House Reps., Ribellia, 1986; campaign steering com. for State Ho. Reps., Cam Cavasso, 1988. Mem. Hawaii C. of C., Am. Records Mgmt. Assn. (dir. 1983, treas. 1981-83). Republican. Club: St. Louis Alumni Assn. Home: 1122 Nanialii St Kailua HI 96734 Office: Bekins Moving & Storage 98-021 Kamehameha Hwy Aeia HI 96701

SOLIDUM, JAMES, finance and insurance counselor; b. Honolulu, Mar. 12, 1925; s. Narciso and Sergia (Yabo) S.; student U. Hawaii, 1949-50; m. Vickie Mayo, Aug. 14, 1954; children: Arlin James, Nathan Francis, Tobi John, Kamomi Teresa. BA, U. Oreg., 1953. Promotional salesman Tongg Pub. Co., 1953-54; editor Fil-Am. Tribune, 1954-55; master planning technician Fed. Civil Service, 1955-57; publs. editor Hawaii Sugar Planters Assn., 1957; field agt. Grand Pacific Life Ins. Co., 1957-59, home office asst., 1959-60, supr., 1960-62, asst. v.p., 1962-64; propr. J. Solidum & Assos., Honolulu, 1964—; pres. Fin. Devel. Inst., 1967—; v.p. Grand Pacific Life Ins. Co., 1983—; bd.dirs. Hawaii Econ. Devel. Corp., 1982—. Mem. adv. com. Honolulu dist. SBA, 1971-77; bd. advisors Philippine Consulate of Hawaii, 1959. Pres., Keolu Elementary P.T.A., 1960-62; mem. satisfaction com. Hawaii Visitors Bur., 1963-66; chmn. budget and rev. panel IV, Aloha United Fund, 1966-72, bd. dirs., 1971-77, 82—, chmn. bd., 1984; mem. mgmt. services com., 1977—, mem. central com., 1977—, chmn. budget and allocations com., 1982-84, ; chmn. Kamehameha Dist. finance com. Aloha council Boy Scouts Am., 1966; vice chmn. Businessmen's Cancer Crusade, 1965; chmn. Operation Bayanihan, Hawaii Immigration Task Force, 1970; participant Oahu Housing Workshop, State of Hawaii, Hawaii chpt. HUD, 1970; mem. task force on housing and transp. Alternative Econ. Futures for Hawaii, 1973; chmn. Bicentennial Filipiniana, 1976; chmn. SBA Bicentennial Com., 1976; campaign chmn. State Rep. Rudolph Pacarro, 1964-68; mem. exec. com. Campaign for Reelection U.S. Senator Hiram L. Fong, 1970, Gov. William Quinn for U.S. Senate, 1976; Republican candidate for Hawaii Ho. of Reps., 1972; mem. Rep. Citizens Task Force on Housing, 1973; trustee St. Louis Alumni Found., 1970—, Kuakini Med. Ctr., 1984-86, trustee Palama Settlement, 1975-82, v.p., 1976, treas., 1980-82; bd. mgrs. Windward YMCA, 1964-67; bd. advisers St. Louis High Sch., 1963-64; bd. govs. Goodwill Industries; bd. dirs. Children's Center, Inc., 1975-77, Hawaii Multi-Cultural Arts Ctr., 1977-81, treas., 1979; fin. chmn. St. Stephen's Parish Council, 1974—; bd. dirs. St. Louis Fine Arts Ctr. Served with AUS, 1945-47. C.L.U. Recipient Man of Year award Filipino C. of C., 1965; cert. of merit Aloha United Fund, 1971; Wisdom mag. honor award, 1974; Outstanding Alumnus honor medal St. Louis High Sch., 1976. Mem. C. of C. Hawaii (past v.p., dir.), Filipino C. of C. (past pres., com. chmn.), Am. Soc. C.L.U.'s, Honolulu Assn. Life Underwriters (past com. chmn., dir.), Hawaii Estate Planning Council, Hawaii Plantation Indsl. Editors Assn. (sec.-treas. 1957), St. Louis Alumni Assn. (pres. 1976, dir. 1964—), Phi Kappa Sigma. Republican. Roman Catholic. Home: 2622 Waolani Ave Honolulu HI 96817 Office: 1110 University Ave Honolulu HI 96826

SOLIS, LUIS, venture capitalist, investor, lawyer; b. Washington, Mar. 3, 1958; s. Matias and Natalia (Regil) S. BA, U. Pa., 1980; MBA, Stanford U., 1985, JD, 1986. Bar: Calif. Cons. Mgmt. Analysis Ctr., Washington, 1980-82; asst. to chief exec. officer Pizza Time Theatre, Sunnyvale, Calif., 1984; compt. Diasonics, Inc., Milpitas, Calif., 1985; assoc. McCown, De Leeuw & Co., Menlo Park, Calif., 1985-86, sr. assoc., 1987-88; mng. ptnr. First San Francisco Holdings, Ltd., Foster City, Calif., 1988—, chmn., 1989—; bd. dirs. MDV Holdings, Inc., Menlo Park, Snider Forest Products, Menlo Park; chmn. bd. dirs. Westward Ho Markets, L.A. Office: First San Francisco Holdings Ltd 909 E Hillsdale Blvd Ste 200 Foster City CA 94404

SOLLECITO, ROCCO MICHELE, construction company executive; b. N.Y.C., Apr. 30, 1957; s. Michele and Elena (Recine) S. BA, Iona Coll., 1979. Underwriter Comml. Union Ins. Co., White Plains, N.Y., 1979-82; sales producer Spadaccia & Ryan, Inc., Yonkers, N.Y., 1982-84; v.p., chief fin. officer SRM Constrn. Corp., Bronx, N.Y., 1984—; instr. adult edn. White Plains High Sch., 1980—; gen. studies Iona Coll., New Rochelle, N.Y., 1984. Republican. Roman Catholic. Office: SRM Constrn Corp 4557 Furman Ave Bronx NY 10470

SOLLOWAY, C. ROBERT, forest products company executive; b. Vancouver, B.C., Can., May 19, 1935; s. Harold Eugene and Elva Merle (McAllister) S.; m. Ila Noreen Kelly. B in Commerce, U. B.C., 1959, LLB, 1960. Bar: Can., 1961. Asst. to exec v.p., asst. to pres. West Coast Transmission Co. Ltd., Vancouver, 1962-68; corp. counsel, asst. sec. Weldwood Can. Ltd., Vancouver, 1968-73, gen. counsel, sec., 1973-75, v.p., gen. counsel, sec., 1975—. Mem. Law Soc. B.C., Can. Bar Assn., Vancouver Bar Assn. Anglican. Clubs: Vancouver; Vancouver Lawn Tennis and Badminton. Office: Weldwood of Can Ltd, 1055 W Hastings, PO Box 2179, Vancouver, BC Canada V6B 3V8

SOLOMON, ELLEN JOAN, management consultant; b. Orange, N.J., Aug. 26, 1943; d. Abram Shrier and Mildred Elizabeth (Berger) S. BA in Psychology, U. N.C., Chapel Hill, 1965; MS in human resource devel. Am. U., 1985. Contract writer Conn. Gen. Life Ins. Co., Bloomfield, 1965-66; mgmt. trainee, asst. buyer G. Fox & Co., Hartford, Conn., 1966-68; account exec. WLAE-FM, Hartford, 1968; sr. analyst Travelers Ins. Co., Hartford, 1968-70; job analyst Conn. Blue Cross, New Haven, 1970-71; sr. ops. auditor Govt. Employees Ins. Co., Washington, 1972-75; employee devel. specialist Employment Standards Adminstrn., U.S. Dept. Labor, Washington, 1975-81, mgmt. analyst, 1981-82, supervisory mgmt. analyst, 1982-87; mgmt. cons. State Maine, 1986-87; program designer, cons. Eastman Kodak Co., Rochester, N.Y., 1987-89, mgr., 1989—; conf. speaker; workshop leader; cons. Recipient spl. achievement award U.S. Dept. Labor, 1977, 78, 83, 85. Mem. Am. Soc. Tng. and Devel., OD Network, Gestalt Inst. Cleve., NOW, Rochester Women's Network, U. N.C. Alumni, Alpha Gamma Delta. Democrat. Jewish. Home: 67 Cornhill Pl Rochester NY 14608 Office: Eastman Kodak Co 343 State St Rochester NY 14650

SOLOMON, LEON J., investment merchant banker; b. Kansas City, Mo., Feb. 1, 1946; s. Maurice David and Betty (Mallin) S.; m. Carol Sue Miller, Dec. 13, 1970; children—; Aaron Justin, Gabriel Alan. Student, U. Mo., 1964-66; B.S., SUNY; postgrad. U. Ill.; M.B.A., Columbia Pacific U., Ph.D.; postgrad. Nova U., La. State U. Mgmt. services devel. Zale Jewelry Corp., Dallas, 1968-70; regional gen. mgr. Midwest div. retail ops. Gordon Jewelry Corp., Houston, 1970-75; exec. officer JMS Venture Capital Fund, Kansas City, Mo., 1975-80; mktg. dir., David R. Balogh, Inc., Fort Lauderdale, Fla., 1980-84; exec. v.p. Primary Care Systems, Inc., 1984—; mgmt. cons. L. Solomon and Assocs. Inc., 1981-88; chief acquisitions Xeneth-Fla. Holding Corp., 1988—. Bd. dirs. Broward Jewish Fedn.; bd. dirs. Jerusalem Mental Health Ctr.; sponsor Children Internat./Chile. Recipient Citizenship award B'nai B'rith; Leadership award Fla. Jewish Fedns.; Sales Devel. award Bulova Watch Corp., 1978; United Petro Corp.. Mem. Am. Mgmt. Assn., Sales Mktg. and Mgmt. Assn., Gemological Inst. Am., Nat. Assn. Appraisers, U.S. C. of C. (bd. dirs.), U.S. Jaycees (bd. dirs.). Republican. Jewish. Office: 301 Yamato Rd Ste 1199 Boca Raton FL 33431

SOLOMON, MAXIMILIAN, merchant banker; b. Cleve., Oct. 19, 1946; s. Harry and Betty (Gerhardt) S.; m. Phyllis Gordon, Aug. 18, 1974 (dec. 1979). BA, Ohio State U., 1969; postgrad. Stanford U., 1979. Dir. instl. adv. services Friedberg Merc. Group, Toronto, Ont., Can., 1978—; mng. dir. The First Toronto Merc. Corp., 1979—, The First Merc. Corp., Toronto, 1984—, The First Merc. Corp. of N.Y., N.Y.C., 1984-85 , The First Merc. Currency Corp., Toronto, 1987—, The First Merc. Global Corp., Toronto, 1987—; gen. ptnr. The First Merc. Partnership., Toronto, 1984—, The First Merc. Convertible Debenture Partnership., Toronto, 1986—, The First Merc. Global Partnership., Toronto, 1987—, The First Merc. Double Gold Plus Partnership I, Toronto, 1987—, The First Merc. Double Gold Plus Partnership I, Toronto, 1987—, The First Merc. Double Gold Plus Partnership II, Toronto, 1987—, The First Merc. Internat. Partnership, Toronto, 1988—, The First Merc. Am. Partnership, Toronto, 1988—; pres., chief exec. officer, dir. The First Merc. Currency Fund, Inc., Toronto, 1985—; pres., chmn. bd. govs. The Toronto Options and Futures Soc., 1984-85; dir. The First Gulf Currency Corp., Toronto. Co-author study on Argus Corp. for Royal Commn. on Corp. Concentration, 1975-77. Mem. Toronto Soc. Fin. Analysts, Fin. Analyst Fedn., Nat. Futures Assn., Futures Industry Assn., The Toronto Futures Exchange. Jewish. Home: 212 Strathallan Wood, Toronto, ON Canada M5N 1T4 Office: The First Mercantile Currency, Fund Inc, 347 Bay St, Toronto, ON Canada M5H 2R7

SOLOMON, NEAL EDWARD, management consultant; b. San Diego, Mar. 9, 1960; s. Donald Jay and Roberta Yvonne (Recht) S. BA, Reed Coll., Portland, Oreg., 1981; AM, U. Chgo, 1982. Pres., founder Calif. Legal Search, San Francisco, 1983—; founding mem. Nat. Assn. of Legal Search Cons., 1984—. Author: Social Theory, 1987. Mem. Ctr. for the Sudy of Dem. Institutions, Am. Philosophical Assn. Democrat. Home: 822 44th Ave San Francisco CA 94121

SOLOMON, PETER J., investment banker; b. N.Y.C., Sept. 17, 1938; s. Sidney L. and Jeannette (Rabb) S.; m. Linda Newman, Oct. 20, 1963; children—Joshua, Abigail, Kate. B.A. cum laude, Harvard U., 1960, M.B.A., 1963. Assoc. Lehman Brothers, N.Y.C., 1963-70, mng. dir., 1971-78; dep. mayor econ. policy and devel. City of N.Y., N.Y.C., 1978-80; chmn. Health Hosp. Corp., N.Y.C., 1979-80; counselor U.S. Treasury Dept., Washington, 1980; mng. dir., dir. Lehman Bros., N.Y.C., 1981-84; chmn. merger acquisition dept. Shearson Lehman Hutton, Inc., N.Y.C., 1984-87, vice chmn., 1985-88; chmn. Mcht. Banking Corp., N.Y.C., 1988—; bd. dirs. Culbro Corp., N.Y.C., Edison Bros. Stores Inc., St. Louis, Phillips-Van Heusen, N.Y.C., Century Communications, Inc., New Canaan, Conn., Chief Auto Parts, Inc., Dallas, Munro Muffler/Brake, Inc., Rochester, N.Y. Trustee Fedn. Jewish Philanthropies, N.Y.C., 1970-78, 81—; overseer Harvard U., Cambridge, Mass., 1982-88. Democrat. Jewish. Clubs: Harmonie, Grolier, Harvard (N.Y.C.); Century Country (Purchase, N.Y.). Office: Shearson Lehman Hutton Inc 200 Vesey New York NY 10285-1800

SOLOMON, PHYLLIS, personnel firm executive; b. N.Y.C., May 9, 1935; d. Herman Aaron and Sylvia (Haymes) Kanarick; m. Harvey Charles Solomon, Feb. 5, 1955 (div. Oct. 1976); children—Deborah, William, David. Sec. Scovill Mfg., Montclair, N.J., 1955-56; co-owner, officer mgr. Bloomfield Glass Co., N.J., 1962-75; office mgr. Am. Service, Inc., Bronx, N.Y., 1975-76, PDI, Englewood Cliffs, N.J., 1976-77; pres., owner V.I.P. Exec. Personnel, Englewood Cliffs, 1977—; founder, chief exec. officer Park Ave. Faces, Inc., 1981—, Phyllis Temps, Inc., Englewood Cliffs, N.J., 1983—; pres., owner V.I.P. Temps IV, Ramsey, N.J., 1987—; pres. V.I.P. Temps V, Nanuet, N.Y., 1988—. Pres. Women's Am. Orgn. Rehab. Tng., Verona, N.J., 1960-61. Fellow Healthcare Businesswomen's Assn.; mem. N.J. Assn. Personnel Counsellors (bd. dirs.), Pharm. Advt. Council, Nat. Assn. Female Execs., Englewood Cliffs C. of C., Fort Lee (N.J.) C. of C., Englewood Cliffs Rotary Club (sec.). Jewish. Rotary (pres., sec. 1987). Avocations: golf; tennis; music; reading. Office: VIP Exec Personnel 701 Palisade Ave Englewood Cliffs NJ 07632

SOLOMON, ZACHARY LEON, apparel manufacturing company executive; b. N.Y.C., July 22, 1934; s. Nathan and Rose Solomon; children—Lisa, Michael, Andrew; m. Susan Phillips. B.A., Bklyn. Coll., 1957; M.B.A., NYU, 1962. Div. mdse. mgr. Abraham & Strauss, Bklyn., 1957-72; v.p., gen. mdse. mgr. Apparel Buying Services, Secaucus, N.Y., 1972-73; sr. v.p., gen. mdse. mgr. May Co., Los Angeles, 1974-75; exec. v.p. The Emporium, San Francisco, 1976-77, pres., 1978-80; exec. v.p. May Co., Los Angeles, 1980-82; exec. v.p. Manhattan Industries, N.Y.C., 1983-87; pres. Ellen Tracy Co., N.Y.C., 1987—. Trustee Bklyn. Coll. Jewish. Office: Ellen Tracy Co 575 7th Ave New York NY 10018

SOLOW, ROBERT MERTON, economist, educator; b. Bklyn., Aug. 23, 1924; s. Milton Henry and Hannah Gertrude (Sarney) S.; m. Barbara Lewis, Aug. 19, 1945; children: John Lewis, Andrew Robert, Katherine. BA, Harvard U., 1947, MA, 1949, PhD, 1951; LLD, U. Chgo., 1967, Brown U., 1972, U. Warwick, 1976, Tulane U., 1983; DLitt, Williams Coll., 1974, Lehigh U., 1977, Wesleyan U., 1982; DSc (hon.), U. Paris, 1975, U. Geneva, 1982; D of Social Sci., Yale U., 1986; DSc, Bryant Coll., 1988. Mem. faculty MIT, 1949—, prof. econs., 1958—, Inst. prof., 1973—; sr. economist Council Econ. Advisers, 1961-62, cons., 1962-68; cons. RAND Corp., 1952-64; Marshall lectr., fellow commoner Peterhouse, U. Cambridge, Eng., 1963-64; Eastman vis. prof. Oxford U., 1968-69; overseas fellow Churchill Coll., Cambridge; sr. fellow Soc. Fellows Harvard U., 1975—; dir. Boston Fed. Res. Bank, 1975-80, chmn., 1979-80; mem. Pres.'s Commn. on Income Maintenance, 1968-70, Pres.'s Com. on Tech., Automation and Econ. Progress, 1964-65, Carnegie Commn. Sci., Tech. and Govt., 1988—. Author: Linear Programming and Economic Analysis, 1958, Capital Theory and the Rate of Return, 1963, The Sources of Unemployment in the United States, 1964, Growth Theory, 1970, Price Expectations and the Behavior of the Price Level, 1970. Bd. dirs., mem. exec. com. Nat. Bur. Econ. Research; trustee Inst. for Advanced Study, Princeton U., 1972-78. Served with AUS, 1942-45. Fellow Ctr. Advanced Study Behavioral Scis., 1957-58, trustee, 1982—; recipient David A. Wells prize Harvard U., 1951, Seidman award in Polit. Economy, 1983, Nobel prize in Econs., 1987. Fellow Am. Acad. Arts and Scis., Brit Acad. (corr.); mem. AAAS (v.p. 1970), Am. Philos. Soc., Nat. Acad. Scis. (council 1977-80), Acad. dei Lincei, Am. Econ. Soc. (exec. com. 1964-66, John Bates Clark medal 1961, v.p. 1968, pres. 1979), Econometric Soc. (pres. 1964, mem. exec. com.). Home: 528 Lewis Wharf Boston MA 02110 Office: MIT Dept Econs Cambridge MA 02139

SOLTIS, ROBERT ALAN, lawyer, photojournalist; b. Gary, Ind., Jan. 30, 1955; s. George William and Frances Marie (Jakob) S. AB (scholar), Ind. U., 1977; JD, DePaul U., 1982. Bar: Ill. 1982, Ind. 1982, U.S. Dist. Ct. (no. dist.) Ill. 1982, U.S. Dist. Ct. (no. and so. dists.) Ind. 1982, U.S. Ct. Apls. (7th cir.) 1983, U.S. Dist. Ct. Trial (no. dist.) Ill. 1984, Ind. Indsl. Bd. 1982; lic. instrument-rated pilot. Photographer Herald Newspapers, Merrillville, Ind., 1971-72; dep. coroner Lake County, Ind., 1972-78, spl. dep. sheriff, 1972-78; dep. coroner, Monroe County, Ind., 1975-76; area dir. Mayors Office of Urban Conservation, Gary, 1977-80; title examiner Law Bulld. Title Services, Chgo., 1980; field clm. rep. Employers Ins. of Wausau, River Forest, Ill., 1980-82; assoc. Perz & McGuire, P.C., Chgo., 1982-84, McKenna, Storer, Rowe, White & Farrug, Chgo., 1984—. Co-host twice weekly TV show: Cancer and You, Bloomington, Ind., 1975-76; contbr. articles in field of cancer; photographer Petersens Pro Football and Baseball; contbg. editor aviation law Midwest Flyer mag. Dir. pub. info. Am. Cancer Soc., Gary, 1977-79, Monroe County unit, 1975-76; pres. Gary Young Dems., 1977-78; precinct committeeman Dem. Party, Gary, 1978-82; bd. dirs. N.W. Ind. Urban League; chmn. Com. to Retain State Rep. William Drozda, 1978-82; mem., sponsor Beverly Art Ctr., Nat. Aviation Pub. Policy com.; vol. atty. S. Chgo. Legal Clinic, 1984—. Recipient Outstanding Reporter award Lake County Mar. of Dimes, 1973, Disting. Service award Am. Cancer Soc. Ind. Div., 1975-76; named Outstanding Young Man of Am., 1984. Mem. Ind. Bar Assn., Lawyer-Pilots Bar Assn., Aircraft Owners and Pilots Assn., Ill. Pilots Assn., Glen Park Jaycees (founder, charter pres. 1977), Nat. Press Photographers Assn., Dormitory Hang Glider Pilots Assn. (founder), Ind. U. Alumni Assn. (life), Slovak Club, Bus. Flyers Club. Roman Catholic. Avocations: flying, photography. Office: McKenna Storer Rowe White & Farrug 200 N LaSalle St #3000 Chicago IL 60601 also: 1109 E 45th Ave Gary IN 46409 also: Sportschrome 10 Brinkerhoff 2d Fl Palisades Park NJ 07650 also: Nawrocki Stock Photo 432 S Michigan Ave Ste 1632 Chicago IL 60604

SOMERS, HOWARD BARLOW, investment securities executive; b. Honolulu, Feb. 9, 1917; s. Harry Alfred and Edna Katherine (Barlow) S.; m. Catherine Josephine Lyon, Dec. 31, 1943; children: Linda Kae, Jo Anne Louise, Carol Lee, Debra Jean. Student, Lewis and Clark Coll., Northwestern Coll., Portland, Oreg. Registered investment securities broker. Registered rep. Camp & Co., Portland, 1937-42, 46-58, ptnr., 1958-61; ptnr. Lind, Somers, Collins, Inc., Portland, 1961-70; pres. Somers, Grove, Inc., Portland, 1970-75, chmn. bd., 1975-87; v.p. Murphey/Favre, Inc., Portland, 1987—; bd. dirs. Willamette View Manor, Inc., Portland, pres. (alternating terms)1981-84. dir. Portland Council Chs., 1955-60, pres. 1959, Ecumenical Ministries of Oreg., 1977-81, chmn. 1978-81, bd. dirs. 1977-81, 83—, Oreg. Colls. Found., Portland, 1962-64, Nat. Multiple Sclerosis Soc. bd. dirs. Oreg. chpt., 1980-84, Alcohol Rehab. Assn., Inc. bd. dirs., Portland, 1985—, Willamette View Found. bd. dirs., Portland, 1985—, Samaritan Counseling Ctr. bd. dirs., Portland, 1984—, Met. bd. dirs. YMCA, Portland, 1986-88, 89—, pres. 1954; panelist Am. Arbitartion Assn., 1988—; trustee Willamette U., 1966—; overseer Lewis and Clark Coll., 1966—; commr. Port of Portland Commn., 1960-70, pres. 1962, 65, Civic Auditorium Adv. Comm., Portland, 1974-77; treas., bd. dirs. Oreg. Council Chs., 1962; cons., bd. dirs. Meridian Park Hosp. Found., Tualatin, Oreg., 1987—; active Portland Met. Future Unltd., 1962-64, Portland C. of C., Oreg. Trade Misson to Japan, 1964, Council Fin. and Adminstrn., 1984-88, 88—. Chief petty officer USCG, 1942-46, PTO, comdr. USNR, 1948-65. Mem. Nat. Assn. Security Dealers, Investment Securities Dealers Assn., Kiwanis (pres. N.E. chpt. 1953, bd. dirs. Downtown chpt. 1987-89), Multnomah Athletic Club, Portland City Club. Republican. United Methodist. Home: 8265 SW Carmel Ct Portland OR 97204 Office: Murphey Favre Inc 900 SW 5th Ave Portland OR 97223

SOMERS, JAMES LAVAUGHN, tool manufacturing executive; b. Portland, Ind., Jan. 19, 1944; s. Ralph Lavaughn and Matilda Fay (Van Trees) S.; m. Carol Sue Zorn, Jan. 25, 1964; children: Michael, Jeffrey, Gregory, Daniel. BS, Purdue U., 1967, MS, 1968, PhD, 1972. Registered profl. engr., Wis. Material handling expediter Armstrong Cork Co., Dunkirk, Ind., 1963-65; prodn. control coordinator, prodn. control supr., sr. staff indsl. engr., mgr. materials mgmt. Collin's Radio Co., Cedar Rapids, Iowa, 1969-73; mgr. inventory mgmt., dir. phys. distbn., dir. mktg. planning, v.p. mktg. services, v.p. corp. quality, v.p. mfg. Snap-on Tools Corp., Kenosha, Wis., 1973—. Contbr. articles to profl. jours. Bd. dirs. Gateway Vocat., Tech. and Adult Edn. Dist., 1978-80, Gateway Tech. Inst. Found., 1980-86, exec. bd. Southeast Wis. council Boy Scouts Am.; bd. dirs. Kenosha Found. Mem. Council Logistics Mgmt., Am. Prodn. and Inventory Control Soc., Inst. Indsl. Engrs., Am. Soc. Quality Control, Sigma Xi, Alpha Pi Mu, Tau Beta Pi. Lutheran. Home: 8200 44th Ave Kenosha WI 53142 Office: Snap-on Tools Corp 2801 80th St Kenosha WI 53140

SOMERS, LOUIS ROBERT, retired food company executive; b. Pontiac, Mich., Aug. 8, 1926; s. Jay G. and Maggie (Gee) S.; m. Rynda Horinga, July 28, 1950; children: Linda, Laurie. B.S., Mich. State U., 1950. With Kellogg Co., Battle Creek, Mich., 1955-88; controller Kellogg Internat., 1967-70, 72-75; fin. dir. Kellogg Gt. Brit. Ltd., 1970-72; v.p. fin., treas. Kellogg Co., 1975-85, sr. v.p. fin., 1985-88; bd. dirs. Battle Creek Investors Growth Corp., William R. Biggs, Gilmore Assocs. Trustee Alma Coll., 1982—; bd. dirs. Mich. State U. Devel. Fund, 1983-88; bd. govs. ARC, 1985—, chmn. audit com. Served with USAF, 1951-55.

SOMERSET, HAROLD RICHARD, sugar company executive; b. Woodbury, Conn., Sept. 25, 1935; s. Harold Kitchener and Margaret Mary (Roche) S.; m. Marjory Deborah Ghiselin, June 22, 1957 (dec. Jan. 1984); children: Timothy Craig, Paul Alexander; m. Jean MacAlpine DesMarais, Jan. 2, 1985; stepchildren: Cheryl Lyn DesMarais, James Fenelon DesMarais. B.S., U.S. Naval Acad., 1957; B.C.E., Rensselaer Poly. Inst., Troy, N.Y., 1959; LL.B., Harvard U., 1967. Bar: Mass. 1967, Hawaii 1973. Commd. ensign U.S. Navy, 1957, advanced through grades to lt., 1961; service in U.S. and Hawaii; resigned 1964; with firm Goodwin, Procter & Hoar, Boston, 1967-72; corp. counsel Alexander & Baldwin, Inc., Honolulu, 1972-74, v.p., gen. counsel, 1974-78, group v.p.-sugar, 1978-79, exec. v.p.-agr., 1979-84; with Calif. & Hawaiian Sugar Co., San Francisco, 1984—, exec. v.p., chief operating officer, 1984-88, pres., chief exec. officer, 1988—, mem. exec. com., also bd. dirs. Mem. exec. bd. Bay Area Coun., San Francisco; bd. dirs., mem. exec. bd. Mt. Diablo coun. Boy Scouts Am. Home: 19 Donald Dr Orinda CA 94563 Office: Calif & Hawaiian Sugar Co PO Box 4126 Concord CA 94524-4127

SOMERVILL, CYNTHIA BELLE, corporate lawyer; b. Chgo., July 13, 1959; d. Robert Russell and Anne Currier (Dodge) S.; m. Terrance Alvan Noyes, Mar. 12, 1983; 1 child, Jonathan Currier. BA, Rice U., 1980; JD, U. Tex., 1983. Bar: Ga. 1983. Assoc. Ragsdale, Beals, Hooper & Seigler, Atlanta, 1983-85, Decker, Cooper & Hallman, Atlanta, 1985-86, Hurt, Richardson, Garner, Atlanta, 1986-87; corp. counsel Gerber Alley, Norcross, Ga., 1987—. Editor Tex. Internat. Law Jour., 1982-83; contbr. articles to profl. jours. Mem. Ga. Bar Assn. (computer law sect., sec. 1987-88, vice-chmn. 1988—), Computer Law Assn., Phi Delta Phi. Democrat. Episcopalian. Home: 572 Lakeshore Dr NE Atlanta GA 30307 Office: Gerber Alley & Assocs Inc 6575 The Corners Pkwy Norcross GA 30092

SOMERVILLE, WILLIAM GLASSELL, JR., lawyer; b. Memphis, July 27, 1933; s. William Glassell and Hilda (Deeth) S.; m. Mary Hateley Quincey, June 13, 1959 (div. Oct., 1985); children: William Glassell, John Quincey, Mary Campbell, Sarah Guerrant. AB, Princeton U., 1955; LLB, U. Va., 1961. Bar: Ala. 1961, U.S. Ct. Appeals (5th cir.) 1963, U.S. Supreme Ct. 1964, U.S. Ct. Appeals (8th cir.) 1968, U.S. Ct. Appeals (11th cir.) 1981. Law clk. to chief judge U.S. Dist. Ct. (no. dist.) Ala., 1961-63; assoc. Lange, Simpson, Robinson & Somerville, Birmingham, Ala., 1963-66, ptnr., 1966—; mem. supreme ct. adv. com. on rules of Ala. appellate procedure, 1972-77; mem. standing com. on Ala. rules of appellate procedure, 1979-86. Served with CIC U.S. Army, 1955-58. Mem. ABA, Ala. Bar Assn., Birmingham Bar Assn., Am. Judicature Soc., Ivy (Princeton), Birmingham Country Club, Rotary. Episcopalian. Office: FAB Bldg Ste 1700 Birmingham AL 35203

SOMMA, HENRY JEREMIAH, tool company executive; b. Waterbury, Conn., May 29, 1921; s. Gerard J. and Angelina S.; m. Mary Elizabeth Dileone, Sept. 8, 1947; children: Linda, Norma, Anita. Student, U. Hartford, 1981-82, U. N.H., 1978-79. Pres. Somma Tool Co. Inc., Waterbury, 1960—; sec., treas., bd. dirs. Centerbank, Waterbury, mem. adv. bd., 1987—. Coord. Reagan-Bush caompaign, Waterbury, 1984. Sgt. U.S. Army, 1944-46, ETO. Mem. Soc. Mfg. Engrs. (trustee 1985—, Honor award 1986). Roman Catholic. Home: 555 Riverside Dr Cheshire CT 06410-1816 Office: Somma Tool Co 109 Scott Rd Waterbury CT 06725

SOMMER, EMIL OTTO, III, financial executive; b. Bronxville, N.Y., July 9, 1947; s. Emil Otto and Elizabeth Arabell S.; B.A., Lafayette Coll., 1969; M.B.A., Cornell U., 1971; postgrad. George Washington U., 1973-74; m. Sandra Ann Kirk, May 18, 1974; children—April Ann, Eric Michael. Staff acct. Price Waterhouse & Co., N.Y.C., 1971, sr. acct., 1976-79, mgr., 1979; controller Transamerica ICS, Inc., N.Y.C., 1980—, v.p., 1982—, v.p. fin. and adminstrn., 1985-87; dir. of fin., chief fin. officer Paul, Weiss, Rifkind, Wharton & Garrison, 1987—. Served as 1st lt. Signal Corps, U.S. Army, 1972-74. Decorated Army Commendation medal, Joint Service Commendation medal. C.P.A., N.Y. Mem. Am. Inst. C.P.A.s, N.Y. State Soc. C.P.A.s (tech. com. fin. and leasing cos.), Am. Mgmt. Assn. Presbyterian. Club: Windmill. Home: 39 Evergreen Row Armonk NY 10504 Office: 1285 Ave of the Americas New York NY 10019

SOMMER, RICHARD BERNARD, banker; b. Waterloo, Ill., Feb. 22, 1940; s. Joseph A. and Octavia C. (Haberl) S.; m. Jane B. Beasley, July 14, 1960; children: Gregory J., Joan C. Masters, Gary W. BBA, U. Nebr., Omaha, 1971; postgrad., Northwestern U., 1978, U. Del., 1987. Enlisted USAF, 1959, advanced through grades to lt. col., 1968, aviation cadet, 1959-60, navigator, bombardier, 1960-65, fighter pilot, 1965-83, tng. pilot, 1967-68, instr. gunnery sch., 1969-70, ret., 1983; lab analyst Monsanto Co., Sauget Village, Ill., 1965-67; asst. cashier, trust officer First Nat. Bank, Columbia, Ill., 1971-75; trust officer So. Ill. Bank, Fairview Hieghts, Ill., 1976-78; v.p., trust officer The Bank of Edwardsville, Ill., 1979—. Mem. Ill. Bankers Assn. Trust Sch., Chgo. (bd. dirs. 1985—), Rotary. Roman Catholic. Home: 843 Amherst Place Edwardsville IL 62025 Office: The Bank of Edwardsville 330 W Vandalia St Edwardsville IL 62025

SOMMER, WAYNE CHARLES, savings and loan executive; b. N.Y.C., Oct. 8, 1957; s. Herbert Charles and Ann Agnes (Cronin) S. Jr.; m. Susan Claire Giordano, Sept. 10, 1983; 1 child, Rachel Claire. BS in Commerce, U. Va., 1980. CPA, Va. Asst. auditor Peat, Marwick, Mitchell & Co., Washington, 1980-81, staff auditor, 1981-82, sr. auditor, 1982-83; asst. controller Dominion Fed. Savs. and Loan, Tysons Corner, Va., 1983-84, controller, v.p., 1984-86, sr. v.p., fin., 1986—; bd. dirs. Appraisal Service Am., Tysons Corner, Va. Mem. Am. Inst. CPAs. Republican. Lutheran. Home: 10160 Yorktown Way Great Falls VA 22066 Office: Dominion Fed Savs & Loan 7799 Leesburg Pike Tysons Corner VA 22043

SOMMERS, LESLEY, financial planner, brokerage house executive; b. Oceanside, N.Y., Aug. 28, 1943; d. Harry Huberman; m. Ronald Sommers, Aug. 12, 1965; children: Stacey, Andrew, Barry. BA summa cum laude, Mich. State U., 1965. Cert. fin., estate and tax planner. V.p. Gary Goldberg & Co., Inc., Suffern, N.Y., 1981—; cons. Personal Finance and Ms. mags. Contbr. articles to profl. jours. V.p. Rockland Family Shelter, Spring Valley N.Y., 1975—, NOW, Spring Valley, 1979. Mem. Bus. and Profl. Women, Internat. Assn. Fin. Planners, Nat. Assn. Female Execs. Office: Gary Goldberg & Co Inc 75 Montebello Rd Suffern NY 10901

SOMNOLET, MICHEL PIERRE, cosmetics company financial executive; b. Chateaurenault, France, Feb. 6, 1940; came to U.S., 1969; s. Raoul Guillaume and Marthe Somnolet; B.Law, Paris Law Sch., 1963; M.B.A., Hautes Etudes Commerciales, Paris, 1964; m. Ghislaine Elizabeth Tenaille; children—Marc, Karine, Eric, Juliette. With L'Oreal, France, 1964-69, controller, 1969-74; v.p., treas. Cosmair, Inc.-U.S. Licensee of L'Oreal, Clark, N.J., 1974, sr. v.p. fin. and adminstrn., 1975-82, sr. v.p., gen. mgr. ops./fin., 1982-83, exec. v.p., 1983—, chief oper. officer, 1984—, also dir. Served to lt. col., armed forces, 1964—. Mem. French C. of C. in N.Y., French Res. Officers in U.S.A. (sec. 1978). Club: Paris-Am. Home: 824 Standish Ave Westfield NJ 07090 Office: Cosmair Inc 575 5th Ave New York NY 10017

SOMROCK, JOHN DOUGLAS, mobile communications executive; b. Ely, Minn., Aug. 10, 1942; s. John William and Margaret Ann (Seliga) S.; m. Barbara Ann Rien, Oct. 21, 1978; children: Jason, Jeffrey, Lindsay. BS in Chem. Engring., U. Minn., 1968. Engr. Minnegasco, Inc., Mpls., 1968-75, sr. engr. spl. projects, 1975-77, mgr. gas control, 1977-80, dir. supplemental energy supply, 1980-81, gen. mgr. Minn. alcohol producers, 1981-82, mgr. spl. projects, 1982, v.p. mktg. and sales, 1982-83, sr. v.p. ops. div., 1983-85, pres., chief operating officer, 1985-87; v.p. Diversified Energies, Inc., Mpls., 1983-85, sr. v.p., 1985—; pres., chief exec. officer E.F. Johnson Co. and EnScan, Inc., Eden Praire, Minn., 1987—; bd. dirs. Dyco Petroleum Corp., Minnegasco, Inc., Mpls. Bd. dirs. Viking Council Boy Scouts of Am., Mpls., 1986; bd. trustees Dunwoody Indsl. Inst., 1986; bd. dirs. Downtown Council of Mpls., 1987, E.F. Johnson Co., 1987—, EnScan, Inc. 1987—; chmn. bus. expansion com. Greater Mpls. C. of C., 1987. Mem. Am. Gas Assn. (chmn. mktg. sect. 1985-86, bd. dirs. 1986-87), Midwest Gas Assn. (bd. dirs. 1987). Republican. Roman Catholic. Clubs: Mpls., Mpls. Athletic, Interlachen Country (Mpls.). Office: E F Johnson Co 11095 Viking Dr Ste 220 Eden Prairie MN 55344

SONK, JOSEPH STANLEY, pharmaceutical company executive; b. Phila., Dec. 23, 1951; s. Stanley Lewis and Stella (Kogut) S.; m. Lynn Marie Lalli, July 8, 1978; 1 child, Gregory Christopher. AB, Rutgers U., Camden, N.J., 1973; PhD, Thomas Jefferson Med. Coll., Phila., 1978. Regional med. assoc. U.S. mktg. SK&F Labs., Phila., 1978-80, sales trainer U.S. mktg., 1980-81, adminstrv. mgr. pharmacology, research and devel., 1981-83, mgr. sci. adminstrn. biology, research and devel., 1983-84, mgr. exec. adminstrn., research and devel., 1984-85; dir. strategic planning U.S. E. R. Squibb & Sons, Princeton, N.J., 1985-86, dir. bus. devel., 1986—; cons. Med. U. Pa., Phila., 1984-85, Phila. Coll. Pharmacy and Sci., 1984-85. Fund raiser United Way, Phila., 1980-81; mem., sponsor Boy Scouts Am., Cherry Hill, N.J., 1982. Mem. Am. Soc. Microbiology, Am. Soc. Pharmacology Exptl. Therapeutics, N.Am. Soc. for Strategic Planning. Republican. Roman Catholic. Club: Square Circle Sportsmen (Gibbsboro, N.J.). Office: Squibb Mark Div ER Squibb PO Box 4000 Princeton NJ 08543-4000

SONNEBORN, KEVIN RICHARD, financial executive; b. San Francisco, Oct. 27, 1954; s. Robert Emerson and Ruth Carmen (Morales) S.; m. Teresa Elizabeth Frizzell, May 1, 1976; children: Ian Anders, Lael Elizabeth. BA in Econs., Seattle U., 1976; MBA in Fin., City U. Seattle, 1985. CPA, Wash. Acct. Rainier Bank, Seattle, 1984-85; chief acct. Rainier Realty Investors, Seattle, 1985-86; chief fin. officer Paris Am. Corp., Seattle, 1987—. Democrat. Roman Catholic. Office: Paris Am Corp 1158 Broadway Seattle WA 98122

SONNEBORN, RICHARD F., trust company executive; b. N.Y.C., May 28, 1918; s. Leo Breitenbach and Rose Pauline (Cronbach) S.; m. Elizabeth Brady Aufsesser, Oct. 11, 1945; children: James L., Thomas G., Elizabeth S. Hamel, Dirk. BS, U. Va., 1939. Trainee sales Goodall Co., Cin., 1939-42; asst. mgr. Sonneborn Bros., Dallas, 1942-49; pres., chief exec. officer Mohawk Brush Co., Albany, N.Y., 1949-75; 1st v.p. Fuller Brush Co., Hartford, Conn., 1975-78; chmn. bd. Key Trust Co., Albany, 1978—; bd. dirs., exec. com. Keycorp., Albany, KeyBank N.A., Albany. Pres. bd. Albany Boys Club, 1959-60; chmn. bd. Albany Med. Ctr. Hosp., 1976-80, 83-88, Albany Med. Ctr., 1983—; trustee Albany Acad. Girls, 1980—. Club: Ft. Orange (Albany). Office: Key Trust Co/Keycorp PO Box 88 Albany NY 12201-0088

SONNECKEN, EDWIN HERBERT, marketing consultant; b. New Haven, July 22, 1916; s. Ewald and Pauline (Halfmann) S.; m. Elizabeth Gregory, June 3, 1939; children: William H., Richard G., Paul D. B.S., Northwestern U., 1938; M.B.A., 1940. With Montgomery Ward & Co., Chgo., 1940-42; price adminstr. OPA, Chgo., 1943; mgr. sales B.F. Goodrich Co., Akron, Ohio, 1943-53; dir. planning Ford Motor Co., Dearborn, Mich., 1953-57; pres. Market Planning Corp., N.Y.C., 1957-61; from dir. corp. planning and research to v.p. corp. bus. planning Goodyear Tire & Rubber Co., 1961-80; chmn. Mktg. Sci. Inst., Cambridge, Mass., 1980-84; also trustee, chmn. research policy com. Mktg. Sci. Inst.; mgmt. cons., Akron, 1985—; Pres. Akron (Ohio) chpt. Am. Mktg. Assn., 1950; v.p. Detroit chpt., 1955, nat. v.p., dir., 1957, nat. pres., 1964-65. Pres. YMCA, Akron, 1978; chmn. trustees First Congl. Ch., Akron, 1985. Served with AUS, 1945-46. Mem. Am. Statis. Assn., Am. Assn. Pub. Opinion Research, Nat. Assn. Bus. Economists, Am. Mktg. Assn., Internat. Mktg. Fedn. (pres.), European Soc. for Opinion and Market Research, Beta Gamma Sigma, Portage Country (Akron). Home: 736 Hampton Ridge Dr Akron OH 44313

SONNICHSEN, DOROTHY GRIFFITH, corporation owner and executive; b. Ithaca, N.Y., May 25, 1942; d. Edward Stanley and Grace Louise (Kaltenbach) G.; m. Harold Eric Sonnichsen, Aug. 31, 1968; 1 child, Hans Matthew. Asst. mdse. mgr. Rothschild's Inc., Ithaca, 1964-67; asst. buyer Jordan Marsh Co., Boston, 1967-68; asst. mgr. service to investor program Arthur D. Little Inc., Cambridge, Mass., 1968-71; exec. v.p., owner Test Devices Inc., Stow and Hudson, Mass., 1971—; owner, treas. Griffith Balancing Machines Inc., Hudson, 1985—; prin. Griffith Co., Hudson, 1984—. Treas. Stow (Mass.) Rep. Town Com., 1978—, Stow Hist. Soc., 1979—; treas., trustee Randall Town Fund, 1980—, Randall Relief Fund, Stow, 1980—, Stow Conservation Trust, 1981—; bd. dirs. Stow Community Chest, 1983—. Mem. Assoc. Industries Mass., Stow Bus. Assn. (treas., bd. dirs. 1982-84). Club: Stow Garden (chmn. conservation 1983-85). Home: 101 Packard Rd Stow MA 01775 Office: Test Devices Inc 6 Loring St Hudson MA 01749

SONSTELIE, RICHARD ROBERT, utilities executive; b. Ottawa, Ont., Can., Mar. 31, 1945; s. Robert Daniel and Valerie Marjorie (St. Laurent) S.; m. Cynthia Louise Prussing, Sept. 19, 1970; children: Marit K., Jennifer A. BS, U.S. Mil. Acad., 1966; MS in Nuclear Engring., MIT, 1968; MBA, Harvard U., 1974. Commd. 2d lt. U.S. Army, 1966, advanced through grades to capt., served in Vietnam, 1966-72, resigned, 1972; staff mem., project mgr. Los Alamos (N.Mex.) Sci. Labs., 1969-72; with Puget Sound Power and Light Co., Bellevue, Wash., 1974-80, v.p. engring. and ops., 1980-83, sr. v.p. fin., 1983-85, exec. v.p., 1985-87, pres., 1987—, also bd. dirs. Mem. Mcpl. League, Wash. State Job Tng. Coordinating Council, Olympia, 1984-88; bd. dirs. Jr. Achievement of Greater Puget Sound, Seattle, 1985—, chmn., 1986-87; bd. dirs. Seattle Sci. Ctr., 1987—; bd. trustees Bellevue Community Coll., 1985—; civilian aide to sec. of army, 1987—; mem. Vietnam Vets. Leadership Program. Decorated Bronze Star. Mem. Edison Electric Inst., Seattle C. of C., West Point Soc. Puget Sound (pres.). Lodge: Rotary. Home: 5 Brook Bay Mercer Island WA 98040 Office: Puget Sound Power & Light Puget Power Bldg PO Box 97034 M/S 15 Bellevue WA 98009

SONTAG, PETER MICHAEL, travel services company executive; b. Vienna, Austria, Apr. 25, 1943; came to U.S., 1960; s. Otto Schiedeck and Maria Katharina (Schmidt) Cigalle; m. Eleanor Ann Alexander, Jan. 24, 1971; children: Alicia Alexandra, Julie Katherine. Diploma in hotel mgmt., Schule fuer Gastgewerbe, Viena, 1960; BS magna cum laude, West Liberty State Coll., 1969; MBA, Columbia U., 1971. Steel worker Weirton (W.Va.) Steel Co., 1965-69; fin. analyst Citicorp, N.Y.C., 1970-71; ops. staff exec. ITT, N.Y.C., 1971-73; asst. v.p. Sun Life Ins. Co. Am., Balt., 1974-75; exec. v.p. Travel Guide, Inc., Balt., 1975-76; pres. Travelwhirl, Inc., Balt., 1976-78, Gelco Travel Services, Mpls., 1978-83; chmn., chief exec. officer Sontag, Annis & Assocs., Washington, 1983-86, U.S. Travel Systems Inc., Washington, 1986—; prin. CORVES Cons., Inc., Rockville, Md., 1983-86; pub. Travel Bus. Mgr., 1983-86; speaker in field, 1983—. With Austrian Air Force, 1963-64. Named one of Twenty Five Most Influential Execs. in Travel Industry Travel Bus. News, 1985, 87; named Delta Sigma Pi scholar. Mem. Alpha Phi Sigma, Delta Mu Delta (charter), Lakewood Country Club. Republican. Office: US Travel Systems Inc 1401 Rockville Pike Ste 300 Rockville MD 20852

SÓNYI, WALTER HUGO, JR., human resource consultant; b. Pfarrkirchen, Fed. Republic of Germany, Apr. 1, 1947; came to U.S., 1951; s. Walter Hugo and Aranka (ûrge) S.; m. Theresia Laube, Oct. 31, 1980; children: Ernest Alexander, Andreas. BA, New Sch. for Social Rsch., 1970, BS, 1970; PhD (hon.), London Sch. for Social Rsch., 1970. Dir. Tubal, Inc., N.Y.C., 1970-74; v.p. Reed, Cuff & Assocs., N.Y.C., 1974-79; sr. mng. ptnr. Goodrich and Sherwood Co., Morristown, N.J., 1979—. Dir. Big Bros., N.Y.C., 1970-74. Mem. Human Resource Planning Soc., Am. Assn. Tng. and Devel., N.J. Bus. Industry Assn., Morristown C. of C., Venture Capital Club, Spring Brook Club, Fiddlers Elbow Club. Roman Catholic. Office: Goodrich & Sherwood Co 177 Madison Ave Morristown NJ 07960-1283

SOODER, KARL MICHAEL, beverage company executive; b. Miami, Fla., Jan. 31, 1943; s. Evald Karl and Janet Bernice (Selig) S.; m. Sandra Waters, Sept. 10, 1969 (div. June 1978); m. Heather Moreland Heinritz, Dec. 28, 1985; children: Damaris, Michael, Albert, Christopher. BA cum laude, U. Miami, 1967; MBA, Columbia U., 1972. Asst. dean of men U. Miami, Coral Gables, Fla., 1967; legis. asst. Congressman L.A. Bafalis, Miami, 1969-70; assoc. product mgr. Pepsi Co., Inc., Dallas, 1972-74; product mgr. Gillette Co., Boston, 1974-76; dir. mktg. William B. Reily & Co., New Orleans, 1976-81; v.p. mktg. Barq's Root Beer, New Orleans, 1981-85, Double-Cola Co., Chattanooga, 1985—; lectr. Amos Tuck Sch. Dartmouth Coll., Hanover, N.H., grad. sch. bus. U. Chgo., U. Tenn., Chattanooga; bd. dirs. Heartland Horticulture, Inc., Boise. Mem. Rep. Nat. Com., 1978—. Woodrow Wilson fellow, Princeton, N.J., 1967-69. Mem. Am. Mktg. Assn., Nat. Soft Drink Assn., Southside C. of C. (v.p. 1987, pres. 1989). Episcopalian. Club: Royal Palm Polo (Boca Raton, Fla.). Lodges: Masons, KT. Home: 3706 E Abercrombie Circle Chattanooga TN 37415 Office: Double-Cola Co 3350 Broad St Chattanooga TN 37408

SORCE, CHRISTOPHER NEAL, finance executive; b. Erie, Pa., Oct. 16, 1952; s. Joseph James and Mary Virginia (Neal) S. Student, Alliance Française, Paris, 1972; AS, Boston U., 1974, BA. Fin. planner IDS Fin. Svcs., Erie, 1976-85; assoc. mgr. IDS Fin. Svcs., Erie and Washington, 1986-87; div. mgr. IDS Fin. Svcs., Washington, 1987—. Chmn. Am. Express Philathropic Bd., Washington, 1987-88. Mem. Internat. Assn. Fin. Planners,

Inst. Cert. Fin. Planners. Clubs: University (Washington), Erie. Home: 4701 Connecticut Ave #401 Washington DC 20008 Office: IDS Fin Svcs 8405 Colesville Rd Ste 600 Silver Spring MD 20910

SORENSEN, DAVID PERRY, manufacturing research executive; b. Spring City, Utah, Nov. 1, 1930; s. David Leonard and Geneva (Benson) S.; m. Mary Lou Pritchett, Sept. 22, 1931; children: NaDene, Bradley. BS, U. Utah, 1952, PhD, 1955. Sr. chemist M.W. Kellogg Co., Jersey City, 1955-57, 3M, St. Paul, Minn., 1957-59; rsch. specialist 3M, St. Paul, 1959-61, supr., 1961-65; mgr. Imaging Rsch. Lab. div. 3M, St. Paul, 1965-67, dir., 1967-71, tech. dir. printing products div., 1971-81, dir. tech. analysis corp. tech. planning and coordination, 1981—. Inventor, holder 8 patents in field. Mem. Am. Chem. Soc., Am. Mgmt. Assn. (exec. com.), Rsch. and Engring. Council of Graphic Arts (exec. com.), Phi Beta Kappa, Phi Kappa Phi. Office: 3M 3M Ctr 225-3N-09 Saint Paul MN 55144

SORENTINO, RALPH JOSEPH, television executive; b. Flushing, N.Y., Nov. 26, 1961; s. Ralph Paul and Carol Ann (Bracchi) S. BA, Drew U., 1983. Rsch. analyst media div. A.C. Nielsen Co., N.Y.C., 1983-85, client svc. rep., 1985-86; rsch. mgr. A & E Cable Network, N.Y.C., 1987—. Active Christian Children's Fund, Richmond, Va., 1987—, World Wildlife Fund. Mem. Am. Mgmt. Assn., Cable TV Adminstrn. and Mktg. Soc., Nat. Conservation and Parks Assn. Republican. Roman Catholic. Office: A&E Cable Network 555 Fifth Ave New York NY 10017

SORG, EDMOND PAUL, controller; b. Huntington, N.Y., Dec. 3, 1951; s. Robert Lewis and Mabel Olga (Myhre) S.; m. Clare Ann Levine, Oct. 19, 1974; children: Erica Lauren, Aaron Keith, Ian Nathanial. AS, Dean Jr. Coll., 1971; BBA, Am. U., 1974. Adminstrv. asst. Am. Inst. for Rsch., Washington, 1972-75; mgmt. trainee Sorg Printing Co., Inc., N.Y.C., 1975-76, various positions, 1976-83, asst. treas., 1983-85, controller, 1985—. Active Cold Spring Hills Civic Assn. Mem. Young Printing Execs., Porsche Am. Club. Office: Sorg Inc 111 8th Ave New York NY 10011

SORKIN, BARRY GERALD, programming and computer systems executive; b. Memphis, May 10, 1941; s. Alfred and Rose Elizabeth Sorkin; B.S.E.E., U. Hartford, 1965; M.B.A. in Fin. Ops. Research, Adelphi U., 1970; m. Miriam Elaine Ungar, Sept. 9, 1973; children: Elliot Isaac, Rachel Naomi. Elec. engr. Grumman Aircraft, Bethpage, N.Y., 1964-67; elec. engr. Sperry Gyroscope Div., Sperry Rand, Gt. Neck, N.Y., 1967-70; systems analyst Greater N.Y. Ins. Group, N.Y.C., 1970-72; sr. applications analyst Equimatics, Fairfield, N.J., 1972-73; bus. systems specialist Gen. Reinsurance Corp., Greenwich, Conn., 1974-79; v.p. reins. systems A.I.G. Data Center, Inc., N.Y.C., 1979—. Adv., Jr. Achievement, 1976-78. Mem. IEEE, Jaycees (internal v.p. Ridgefield, membership chmn., state rep. 1975-79), Kappa Mu. Home: 10 Wildwood Rd Woodcliff Lake NJ 07675 Office: 70 Pine St New York NY 10270

SORKIN, CHARLES K., accountant; b. Basel, Switzerland, Sept. 22, 1907; s. Niklaus and Luise (Rinek) S.; m. Mathilde Burggraf, Jan. 16, 1934 (dec. Dec. 1982); 1 child, Charles Klaus. Student, U. Basel, U. Akron, Western Res. U. CPA. Various positions in banking, industry and commerce Switzerland and Germany, 1927-39; various positions Akron, Ohio, 1939-46; pvt. practice pub. acctg. Akron, 1946-62; mng. ptnr. Sorkin, Lawson & Parker, CPAs, 1962-70; cons. Sorkin. Lawson & Parker, CPAs, 1970-72. Treas. Greater Akron Musical Assn.; founding sponsor principal chair endowment, co-sponsor concertmaster chair Mathilde and Charles K. Sorkin Fund; vol. chess tchr. schs. and insts. Germany and U.S.; tournament dir. U.S. Chess Fedn.; bd. dirs. Note For Life; active fundraising United Fund, Red Cross, Hosps., Akron (Ohio) Symphony Orch.; founder West Akron Kiwanis Found; voluntary audits, United Fund Agys., Akron Art Inst. Mem. Am. Inst. CPAs, Ohio Soc. CPAs. Methodist. Clubs: Fairlawn Country, Akron Chess (Founder, honarary pres.), Sharon Golf. Lodges: Masons, Shriners, Kiwanis (past pres., West Akron club). Home: 100 Brookmont Rd Apt #245 Akron OH 44313

SORRELL, MARTIN STUART, marketing services executive; b. London, Feb. 14, 1945; s. Jack and Sally (Goldberg) S.; m. Sandra Carol Ann Finestone, Apr. 25, 1971; children: Mark, Robert, Jonathan. BA, Christ's Coll., Cambridge U., 1966, MA, 1970; MBA, Harvard U., 1968. Assoc., Glendinning Assocs., Westport, Conn., 1968; dir., v.p. Mark McCormack Orgn. London, 1969-72; dir. Pruway Investments Ltd., London, 1973-74, dir. James Gulliver Assocs., London, 1975-77; group fin. dir. Saatchi & Saatchi Co. P.L.C., London, 1977-86; dir. WPP Group P.L.C., 1985—; bd. dirs. Ind. Investment Co., 1987—; chmn. C.F. Doyle Ltd., 1987—. Fellow Inst. Dirs. Conservative. Jewish. Clubs: Reform (London); Harvard (London and N.Y.C.). Office: WPP Group PLC, 55 Lincoln's Inn Fields, London WC2A 3LJ, England also: Rasor Communications Inc 10 E 53rd St New York NY 10022

SOSNA, ROBERT WILLIAM, insurance executive; b. Phila., Nov. 18, 1941; s. Robert William and Catharine Anna (McGowan) S.; B.A., LaSalle Coll., 1963; postgrad. U. Mich., 1975, Xavier U.; m. Lyn T. Sulock, Oct. 24, 1964; children—Jackie, Kate, Kristen. Account underwriter Allstate Ins. Co., Valley Forge, Pa., 1964-70; sr. underwriter Fireman's Fund Ins. Cos., Phila., 1970-71, assoc. office mgr., 1971-73, personal lines mgr., 1973-75, sales mgr., 1975-77, adminstrv. exec., San Francisco, 1977-79, gen. mgr., resident v.p., Cin., 1979-80; ops. v.p. CG/Aetna Ins. Co., 1980-82, v.p. sales, field ops., 1982-84; pres., chief exec. officer Mktg. Mgmt. Inc. subs. Reliance Ins. Co., Pelham, Ala., 1984-88; sr. v.p. personnel div. Reliance Ins. Co., Phila., 1988—; pres. Reliance Mktg. Mgmt., Inc.; instr. Pa. State U., 1974-77. Mem. Montgomery Bus. Men's Assn. Republican. Roman Catholic. Clubs: Manufacturers Golf and Country; (Phila.), Union League (Phila.). Home: 1249 Forest Hill Dr Gwynedd Valley PA 19437 Office: Penn Ctr Plaza Philadelphia PA 19103

SOSS, JEFFREY HOWARD, banker, financial analyst; b. Derby, Conn., Apr. 24, 1964; s. Arthur and Ethel (Altes) S. BS in Acctg., Sacred Heart U., 1987. With LaFayette Bank & Trust Co., Bridgeport, Conn., 1986-87, fin. analyst, 1987, asst. treas., fin. analyst, 1987-88; pres., asst. controller, acctg. mgr. LaFayette Bank & Trust Co., Bridgeport, 1988—. Republican. Jewish. Home: 37-14 Balance Rock Rd Seymour CT 06483 Office: LaFayette Bank & Trust Co 1087 Broad St Bridgeport CT 06604

SOSTROM, SHIRLEY ANNE, organizational communications cons. co. exec., educator; b. Billings, Mont., Dec. 22, 1933; d. Jack Kenneth and Edith Ester (Bates) Thompson; student U. Wyo., 1951-59; B.Sc., No. Ill. U., 1966; M.A., Central State U., Ohio, 1970; Ph.D., Ohio State U., 1976; m. John Philip Sostrom, July 11, 1950; children—John David, Kristen Ingrid, Deena Rachael. Tchr. various high schs., Ohio, Mont., 1966-74; with Carroll Coll., Helena, Mont., 1972-74; lectr. linguistics and writing Sinclair Coll., 1976-78; program coordinator Sch. Public Adminstrn., Ohio State U., Columbus, 1978-80; lectr. English and journalism Muskingum Coll., 1980-81; pres. Sostrom Assocs., pub. relations cons., Columbus, 1979—; prin., dir. human resource services, officer The Sims Cons. Group, Lancaster, Ohio, 1983—; prof. Grad. Sch. Adminstrn., Capital U., Columbus, 1980-86; acting exec. dir. Internat. Materials Mgmt. Soc., Schaumburg, Ill., 1986-87; exec. dir. Health Care Mgmt. Soc., Columbus, 1988—. Mem. Women's Poetry Workshop, Am. Assn. for Tng. and Devel., Internat. Assn. Bus. Communicators, Am. Soc. Assn. Execs., Ohio State U. Alumni Assn., Phi Delta Kappa. Republican. Club: Zonta. Author chpts. and articles on pub. relations and bus.; contbr. poetry to mags. Home: 99 E Weber St Columbus OH 43202 Office: Sostrom Assocs PO Box 02266 Columbus OH 43209

SOTOS, HERCULES PETER, manufacturing company executive; b. Salonica, Greece, Apr. 14, 1933; came to U.S., 1946; s. Peter Hercules and Fotini (Drapelis) S.; m. Mary M. Yiotis, Mar. 9, 1959; children—Cynthia, Peter, Christina. B.S., NYU, 1962; grad. Advanced Mgmt. Program,, Harvard U., 1978. Dir. internat. fin. AMF, Inc., 1957-67; sr. fin. analyst W.R. Grace & Co., 1967-68; controller internat. div. Internat. Playtex, Inc., Stamford, Conn., 1968-70; corp. controller B.V.D. Internat. Playtex, Inc., 1970-71, v.p. fin., 1971-77, group v.p. fin. and adminstrn., 1977-80, exec. v.p. fin. and adminstr., 1980-85, pres., 1985; vice chmn. Internat. Playtex, Inc. (name change to Playtex, Inc.), 1986—; chief fin. officer Beatrice Consumer Products, 1985. Served with U.S. Army, 1953-55. Office: Playtex Inc 700 Fairfield Ave Stamford CT 06830 also: Beatrice Cos Inc 2 N LaSalle St Chicago IL 60602

SOUCY, KEVIN ALBERT, bank executive; b. Farmington, Maine, Jan. 15, 1955; s. Albert Ernest and Adeline Mae (Meader) S.; m. Linda Jean Dolloff, June 20, 1981; children: Andrew Kevin, Brice Patrick. BS, Bates Coll., 1977. Sales rep., agy. mgr. Met. Ins. Co., Augusta and Lewiston, Maine, 1977-81; trust devel. officer Depositors Co., Augusta, 1981-82, asst. v.p., pension trust officer, 1982-85; v.p., trust officer Indian Head Nat. Bank, Keene, N.H., 1985—; Contbr. articles to newspaper. Bd. dirs. Monadnock Area Pastoral Counselling, Keene, 1987—, Monadnock United Way, Keene, 1987—; mem. Conn. Valley Estate Planning Council, 1985—; mem. N.H. Employee Benefits Council. Mem. Rotary. Republican. Baptist. Home: 43 Evans Cir Keene NH 03431 Office: Indian Head Nat Bank Keene 20 Central Sq Keene NH 03431

SOUDER, ROBERT R., personnel director; b. Sellersville, Pa., Mar. 7, 1940; s. Robert and Francis S.; m. Joan A. Swartley, July 14, 1962; children: Jennifer, Amy. AB in English Lit., Colgate U., 1962. Personnel mgr. Acme Markets, Phila., 1962-69; sr. v.p. personnel Rite Aid Corp., Harrisburg, Pa., 1969—. Pres. Ams. for Competitive Enterprise, Harrisburg, 1988; bd. dirs. Family & Children's Services, Harrisburg, 1986-88; active United Way, Harrisburg, 1978-88. Office: Rite Aid Corp Box 3165 Harrisburg PA 17105

SOUDERS, DAVID S., electrical industry executive; b. Waynesboro, Pa., June 25, 1953; s. Paul Wilson and Mae Elizabeth (Nelson) S. BS in Physics, Juniata Coll., 1975. Asst. plant mgr. solar div. Champion, Waynesboro, 1977-79; owner United Enterprises, Waynesboro, 1979-81; ptnr. Wiring Harnesses, Inc., Waynesboro, 1981-83; owner SESCO Elec. Systems, Waynesboro, 1983—. Office: SESCO Div Souders Industries Inc 6524 Buchanan Tr E Waynesboro PA 17268

SOUDERS, WILLIAM FRANKLIN, office equipment executive; b. Detroit, July 14, 1928; s. Clifford E. and Julia (O'Brien) S.; m. Barbara L. Huskey, Nov. 25, 1950; children: Susan Lynn, Scott William, Sally Anne. B.A. in Econs., Lake Forest Coll., 1952. Various sales and mktg. positions A.B. Dick Co., Chgo., 1951-63; gen. mgr. subs. A.B. Dick Co., 1963-64; with Xerox Corp., from 1964; group v.p. Xerox Corp., Stamford, Conn., 1973-77; exec. v.p. ops. Xerox Corp., 1977-85; chmn., chief exec. officer Emery Air Freight Corp., Wilton, Conn., 1988—. Charter trustee, mem. exec. com. Lake Forest Coll.; bd. dirs. St. Joseph's Hosp., Stamford; bd. visitors U. Conn. Sch. Bus. Adminstrn. Served with parachute inf. U.S. Army, 1946-47. Clubs: Wee Burn Country, The Landmark, Conn. Golf, Oak Hill. Office: Emery Air Freight Corp Old Danbury Rd Wilton CT 06897 *

SOUKUP, ELOUISE MARILISS, controller; b. Hastings, Nebr., Oct. 15, 1926; d. Robert George and Gretchen Eloise (Guildner) Hoff; m. Leo Soukup Jr., Mar. 22, 1948; children: Leo, Mariliss Suzanne Soukup Erickson. Student, U. So. Calif., 1945-48; BA, U. Nebr., 1973. Co-owner, bus. mgr. Soukup Cleaners, Beatrice, Nebr., 1955—; controller C.D. Hoff, Inc., Hastings, Nebr., 1976—. Curator edn. Nebr. State Hist. Soc., Lincoln, 1974-77; vice-chmn. Gage County Rep. party, 1964; bd. dirs. Beatrice YWCA, 1965-67, Nebr. Gov.'s Commn. on Status of Women, 1977. Mem. Am. Hist. Assn., Internat. Fabricare Inst., Nebr. Writers Guild, AAUW, DAR, Women in Laundry and Drycleaning (internat. v.p. 1983-84), Internat. Drycleaning Congress (del. China Exchange 1983), Adams County Hist. Soc., Hastings Area C. of C., Lincoln U. Club, Lochland Country Club, Kappa Delta, Pi Alpha Theta. Home: RR 1 Box 22J Doniphan NE 68832 Office: 838 W 2d St PO Box 1141 Hastings NE 68901

SOULLIERE, JOHN HOLLIS, sales and marketing executive; b. Pawtucket, R.I., Apr. 7, 1945; s. Oscar Lucien and Yvette Henrietta (Fredette) S.; m. Catherine Ellen O'Malley, Aug. 17, 1968; children: Amy Beth, Gregory John, Jeremy John. BSME, Worcester Poly. Inst., 1967; MBA, Bryant Coll., 1974. Sales engr. Bailey Controls, N.Y.C., 1967-69; power industry specialist Foxboro (Mass.) Co., 1969-71; power sales engr. Foxboro (Mass.) Co., Wrentham, Mass., 1971-73, regional power mgr., 1973-75, regional sales mgr., 1975-77; mgr. industry sales Foxboro (Mass.) Co., Foxboro, 1977-81, mgr. wordwide industry sales and mktg., 1981-84; regional mgr. Foxboro (Mass.) Co., Cleve., 1984—. Bd. dirs. YMCA, North Attleboro, Mass., 1982-84, Hudson (Ohio) Youth Football Assn., 1985—. Mem. Instrument Soc. Am., ASME, Am. Mgmt. Assn., Hudson Boosters Club (v.p. 1987-88, pres. 1988-89), St. Mary's Men's Club. Roman Catholic. Home: 7686 Deerpath Tr Hudson OH 44236 Office: Foxboro Co 7123 Pearl Rd Middleburgh Heights OH 44130

SOURS, DWIGHT MATTHEW, state pollution control official; b. Balt., June 7, 1947; s. Leonard McKendra and Thelma Allene (Young) S.; m. Sandra Fay Good, Mar. 13, 1971; children: Kelly, Matthew, Aaron McKendra. Student, Ea. Mennonite Coll., 1965-67, James Madison U., 1968-69, Blue Ridge Community Coll., 1968-69. Research technician Va. Poly. Inst. and State U., Front Royal, 1969-73; engring. technician Va. Water Control Bd., Bridgewater, 1973-78, pollution control specialist, 1978—. County chmn. Inst. Cultural Affairs, 1976-79; pres. Stanley Elem. PTA, 1979-83; mem. Lord Fairfax Citizen Adv. Bd., Middletown, Va., 1979-80, Stanley area dr. recruitment com. Page Meml. Hosp., Luray, Va., 1986-87; mem. quality of life com. Page Valley Econ. Devel. Council, 1987; bd. dirs. Page County Unit Cystic Fibrosis Found., 1978-79, Am. Heart Assn., 1978-81. Recipient Pub. Service award Page County Edn. Assn., 1982, 83, Pub. Service award Stanley PTA, 1984, numerous awards local and state Jaycees, 1976-79, including named One of Outstanding Young Men of Am., 1977-81. Mem. Va. Govtl. Employees Assn., Stanley Jaycees. (county pres. Spl. Olympics 1975-79, county bd. dirs. 1979-81, area bd. dirs. 1975-79). Republican. Home: Rte 1 Box 544 Stanley VA 22851 Office: Va Water Control Bd PO Box 268 Bridgewater VA 22812

SOUTENDIJK, DIRK RUTGER, lawyer, corporate executive; b. Amsterdam, Netherlands, Apr. 13, 1938; came to U.S., 1946, naturalized, 1965; s. Louis Rutger Willem and Hermina C. (Schoonman) S.; m. Mary Tremaine, Dec. 22, 1961; children—Dirk Willem, Gregory Louis. B.A., Yale U., 1960; J.D., Columbia U., 1963. Bar: N.Y. 1966, Pa. 1975. Assoc., Shearman & Sterling, N.Y.C., 1963-68; laywer Westinghouse Electric Co., Pitts., 1968-77; gen. counsel Union Camp Corp., Wayne, N.J., 1977—, v.p. 1978—, sec. 1978—. Bd. dirs. Mid-Atlantic Legal Found., Phila., 1978—. Mem. ABA, Assn. of Bar of City of N.Y. Republican. Congregationalist. Club: Union League (N.Y.C.). Home: 52 Briarcliff Rd Mountain Lakes NJ 07046 Office: Union Camp Corp 1600 Valley Rd Wayne NJ 07470

SOUTHER, JEAN LORRAINE, accounting and management educator, accountant; b. North Weymouth, Mass.; d. Herbert Roy and Ruth Agnes (Perry) S. BSBA in Acctg., Northeastern U., 1960, MBA, 1968; EdD, U. Mass., 1986. Lic. pub. acct. From acct. to auditor to div. acctg. mgr. to systems mgr. to asst. to contr. Howard Johnson Co., Quincy, Mass., 1949-74; prof. Cape Cod Community Coll., Barnstable, Mass., 1974—; founding dir. Cape Cod Women's Credit Union, Barnstable. Editor: Basic Finance (Gitman), 1987. Chairwoman personnel bd. Town of Eastham, Mass., 1980-84, vice chairwoman fin. bd., 1986—. Recipient Merit award Town of Eastham, 1984. Mem. Am. Soc. Women Accts. (mem. editorial bd. 1980—), Assn. Systems Mgmt., Nat. Soc. Pub. Accts. Republican. Home: 50 Vandale Circle PO Box 326 Eastham MA 02642 Office: Cape Cod Community Coll Rte 1 321 W Barnstable MA 02668

SOUTHERN, RONALD DONALD, diversified corporation executive; b. Calgary, Alta., Can., July 25, 1930; s. Samuel Donald and Alexandra (Cuthill) S.; m. Margaret Visser, July 30, 1954; children: Nancy, Linda. B.Sc., U. Alta., Edmonton, 1953; LL.D. (hon.), U. Calgary, 1976. Pres., chief exec. officer Atco Ltd., Calgary, 1954-85, dep. chmn., chief exec. officer, 1985—; chmn., chief exec. officer Can. Utilities Ltd., Edmonton; hon. assoc. mem. Calgary Exhbn. and Stampede Bd.; gov. Olympic Trust Can.; bd. dirs. ATCO Ltd., B.C. Forest Products Ltd., Can. Airlines Internat., Can. Pacific Ltd., Can. Utilities Ltd., Easton United Securities Ltd., LaFarge Corp., Royal Ins. Ltd., Xerox of Can. Inc., Fletcher Challenge Ltd. Recipient Holland Trade award Govt. of The Netherlands, 1985, (with wife) Sportsmen of Yr. award Calgary Booster Club; named Businessman of Yr. U. Alta., 1986, to Order of Can., 1986. Mem. United Church of Can. Clubs: Calgary Petroleum, Earl Grey Golf, U. Calgary Chancellors. Home: 67 Massey Pl SW, Calgary, AB Canada T2V 2G7 also: Canadian Utilities Ltd, 10035 105 St, Edmonton, AB Canada T5J 2V6 also: Can Western Natural Gas Co Ltd, 909-11 Ave SW, Calgary, AB Canada T2R 1L8

SOUTHWARD, ROCK ALLEN, lawyer; b. Tiffin, Ohio, July 31, 1950; s. Stanton Clay and Dorothy Ann (Warfel) S. BS, Bowling Green State U., 1972; JD, U. Toledo, 1982. Counselor Non-Commn. Officers Assn., Colorado Springs, Colo., 1983; sole practice Columbus, Ohio, 1984-86; real estate specialist, U.S. Postal Service, San Bruno, Calif., 1986—. Scripps-Howard scholar, 1972. Mem. ABA, Ohio Bar Assn., Bar Assn. of San Francisco, Phi Alpha Delta, Rho Sigma Mu, Kappa Tau Alpha. Democrat. Methodist.

SOUTHWORTH, JAMES LEO, JR., electrician; b. Providence, Oct. 15, 1951; s. James Leo Sr. and Caterina Rose (Carbone) S.; m. Deborah Anne Brough, Oct. 20, 1979. AS, Community Coll. Air Force, 1985; BS in Indsl. Tech. magna cum laude, R.I. Coll., 1988. Electrician R.I. Hosp., Providence, 1974—. With R.I. Air N.G., 1970—. Roman Catholic. Home: 210 Hazleton St Cranston RI 02920 Office: RI Hosp 593 Eddy St Providence RI 02903

SOUTHWORTH, MARGARET MAY, financial executive; b. Oakland, Calif., July 22, 1945; d. Gordon B. and Margaret (Ward) Wright; m. Bradford Winslow Southworth, June 18, 1967; children: Barbara Anne, Laura Jayne. BA, U. Calif., Berkeley, 1967; cert. in teaching, Calif. State U., 1968; MA, Stanford U., 1974. Cert. fin. planner. Fin. planner Investors Diversified Services, Oak Park, Mich., 1978-80, Assoc. Fin. Planning Corp., Southfield, Mich., 1980-82; pres. Southworth & McFawn Adv. Corp., Troy, Mich., 1982—, Southworth & McFawn Inc., Troy, Mich., 1982—; adj. faculty mem. Coll. Fin. Planning, Denver, 1983-85; instr. Macomb Coll., Warren, Mich., 1983-86; cons. Allied Bendix Corp., Southfield, 1983-85, Detroit Free Press, Detroit News, 1988. Author: Money Moves: A Guide to Financial Fitness, 1986; author, producer TV series: Financial Planning with Experts, 1983. Mem. Inst. Cert. Fin. Planners, Internat. Assn. Fin. Planning, Registry Cert. Fin. Planners. Home: 190 Millrace Birmingham MI 48009 Office: Southworth & McFawn Adv Corp 803 W Big Beaver Suite 350 Troy MI 48084

SOUTTER, THOMAS D., lawyer; b. N.Y.C., Nov. 1, 1934; s. Thomas G. and Hildreth H. (Callanan) S.; m. Ginny Hovenden; children: Sam, Andy, Hadley. B.A., U. Va., 1955; LL.B., 1962; postgrad., Advanced Mgmt. Program, Harvard U., 1980. Bar: N.Y. State 1962, R.I. bar 1969. Atty. Breed, Abbott & Morgan, N.Y.C., 1962-68; with Textron Inc., Providence, 1968—; gen. counsel Textron Inc., 1972—, v.p., 1973-80, sr. v.p., 1980-85, exec. v.p., gen. counsel, 1985—; Mem. adv. bd. Internat. and Comparative Law Center, 1975—; bd. dirs. New Eng. Legal Found. Served to lt. USNR, 1955-59. Mem. Am., N.Y. State, R.I. bar assns., Internat. Bar Assn. Office: Textron Inc 40 Westminster St Providence RI 02903

SOUVEROFF, VERNON WILLIAM, JR., corporate executive, investor; b. Los Angeles, Aug. 12, 1934; s. Vernon William Sr. and Aileen (Young) S.; m. Aileen Patricia Robinson; children—Gail Kathleen, Michael William. B.S. in E.E., Stanford U., 1957; postgrad., Ohio State U., 1958-59. With Litton Industries, Beverly Hills, Calif., 1960-75; with ITT Corp., N.Y.C., 1975-87, corp. v.p., 1983-84, sr. v.p., 1984-87; pres. ITT Gilfillan, 1979-83; group exec. ITT Def. Space Group, 1983-84; dir. ITT Telecom and Electronics N.Am., 1984-86; pres., chief exec. officer ITT Def. Tech. Corp., 1986-87; bus. advisor, investor, corp. bd. dirs. 1987—; bd. dirs. Gilcron Corp., Avcron Corp.; mem. U.S. Def. Policy Adv. Com. on Trade, Washington, 1984-88; advisor-investor Venture Resources, Venture Capital, 1988—. Contbr. articles to profl. jours. Served as officer USAF, 1957-60. Recipient Exec. Salute award Los Angeles C. of C., 1981; Ring of Quality ITT Corp., 1983. Mem. IEEE, Nat. Contracts Mgmt. Assn., Electronics Industries Assn., Am. Def. Preparedness Assn., Nat. Security Indsl. Assn. Presbyterian. Club: Rancho Mirage Racquet (Calif.). Home: 75 Golden Meadow Ln Danville CA 94526

SOVEY, WILLIAM PIERRE, manufacturing company executive; b. Helen, Ga., Aug. 26, 1933; s. Louis Terrell and Kathryn Bell (White) S.; m. Kathryne Owen Doyle, Dec. 28, 1958; children: Margaret Elizabeth, John Todd. B.S.I.E., Ga. Inst. Tech., 1955; grad., Advanced Mgmt. Program, Harvard U., 1976. Gen. mgr. automotive div. Atwood Vacuum Machine Co., Rockford, Ill., 1963-68; v.p. internat. A.G. Spalding & Bros., Inc., Chicopee, Mass., 1968-71; pres. AMF Inc., Ft. Worth, 1971-77; corp. v.p., group exec. Indpls. products group AMF Inc., Stamford, Conn., 1977-79; pres., chief operating officer, dir. AMF Inc., White Plains, N.Y., 1982-85; pres., chief operating officer Newell Co., Freeport, Ill., 1986—, also bd. dirs. Served with USN, 1955-58. Home: 5349 Winding Creek Dr Rockford IL 61111 Office: Newell Co PO Box 117 Beloit WI 53511 *

SOVIERO, THOMAS TODD, securities analyst; b. Oyster Bay, N.Y., Oct. 26, 1963; s. John James and Mary Louise (Levi) S. BS, Boston Coll., 1985. Equity analyst Colonial Mgmt. Assn., Boston, 1985-86, corp. fin. analyst, 1987, mcpl. bond analyst, 1987-88; asst. v.p., high yield corp. bond analyst Crossland Savs., FSB, Bklyn., 1988—. Mem. United Shareholders Assn., Fin. Analyst Fedn., Boston Security Analyst Soc., Phi Beta Kappa, Beta Gamma Sigma, Alpha Sigma Nu. Republican. Roman Catholic. Home: 10 Brook Ave Huntington NY 11743 Office: Crossland Savs FSB 211 Montage St Brooklyn NY 11201

SOWA, FRANK XAVIER, entrepreneur, educator; b. Akron, Ohio, Aug. 9, 1957; s. William Walter and Olga Susan (DeMay) S. BA in English, Muskingum Coll., 1979. Reporter Dix Publs., Cambridge, Ohio, 1976-78; editor Messenger Newspapers, Akron, 1978-79; mgr. corp. communications Davy McKee Corp., Cleve., 1979-81; mgr. market communications Roadway Package System, Pitts., 1984-85; owner, chief exec. officer Xavier Communications, Pitts., 1982-87, The Xavier Group, Pitts., 1987—; cons. Community Coll. Allegheny City, Pitts., 1986—, instr. 1987—; instr. LaRoche Coll., Pitts., 1982-83, U. Akron, 1982. Author: Pittsburgh Reinvented, 1985, (software), Chronometics Modeller, 1987. Chmn. N.H. Civic-cultural Ctr., Pitts., 1987—; mem. U.S. Jaycees, Pitts., 1987—; adv. council Smaller Mfrs. Council, Pitts., 1984; sec., bd. dirs. Imaginarium Childrens Theatre, Pitts. 1985. Recipient Brownfield Pub. Svc., Pa. Jaycees, 1987. Mem. Pitts. Futures Inst. (chmn. 1988), World Future Soc., Nat. World Future Soc., Am. Entrepreneurs Soc., Congl. Inst. for Future. Democrat. Roman Catholic. Home: 740-16 Nineteen North Dr Pittsburgh PA 15237

SOWERS, ELIZABETH JANE, manufacturing executive; b. Washington, Feb. 3, 1962; d. Clarence Albert and Nancy Jane (Rexrode) S. BS in Rsch and Indsl. Engring. Ops., Cornell U., 1984. Process engr. Procter & Gamble Paper Products, Mehoopany, Pa., 1984-85, team mgr., 1985-87, process mgr., 1987—. Adviser Tunkhannock (Pa.) Jr. Achievement, 1984-86. Mem. Bus. and Profl. Women (mem. pub. rels. com. 1988—), Wyo. Valley Women's Network (program dir. 1986—), Spectrum (bd. dirs.). Methodist. Home: 60 E Harrison St Tunkhannock PA 18657 Office: Procter & Gamble PO Box 32 Mehoopany PA 18627

SOWERS, JOHN PHILLIP, aircraft manufacturing company executive, consultant; b. Los Angeles, Apr. 22, 1947; s. Norman Joseph and Cora Marie (Cirino) S.; m. Linda Joyce Boyer, Sept. 5, 1980; 1 stepchild, Alisa Joy Boyer. Student, U. Calif., Santa Cruz, 1965-67, U. Calif., Hong Kong, 1967-68; BA, UCLA, 1969; postgrad., U. B.C., 1969-71; cert., U. So. Calif., 1987. Indsl. security investigator U.S. Dept. of Def., Los Angeles, 1976-78; mgr. security and safety Raytheon Co., Santa Barbara, Calif., 1978-81; sr. safety adminstr. Santa Barbara Research Ctr. Hughes Aircraft Co., 1981-89; sr. environ. auditor Hughes Aircraft Co., Westchester, Calif., 1989—; mem. Hughes Aircraft Environ. Affairs Subcom., L.A., 1985—; owner, cons. Enviro-Tech, Santa Barbara, 1985—. Mem. Am. Soc. Safety Engrs., Santa Barbara C. of C. (hazardous waste subcom. 1985—).

SOWERS, WESLEY HOYT, lawyer, management consultant; b. Whiting, Ind., Aug. 26, 1905; s. Samuel Walter and Bertha E. (Spurrier) S.; m. Gladys Krueger, Jan. 21, 1929; children: Penny (Mrs. David Buxton), Wesley Hoyt. BS, Purdue U., 1926, MS, 1927; JD, DePaul U., 1941; grad., Advanced Mgmt. Program, Harvard, 1960. Bar: Ill. 1940; registered patent atty. and practitioner ICC. Chemist Shell Oil Co., East Chicago, Ind., 1927-29; sales engr. Nat. Lead Co., St. Louis, 1929-31; lab. supr. patent atty. Pure Oil Co., Chgo., 1932-42; v.p. Bay Chem. Co., New Orleans, 1942-50, Frontier Chem. Co., Wichita, Kans., 1950-57; pres. Frontier Chem. div. Vulcan Materials Co., 1957-65; exec. v.p., dir. Vulcan Materials Co., Birmingham, 1958-65; mgmt. counsel 1965—; former chmn. bd., dir. Archer Taylor Drug Co., Community Antenna TV Wichita, Inc.; dir. Coleman Co., Wichita, Gt. Lakes Chem. Co., West Lafayette, Ind., Huntsman Chem. Corp., Salt Lake City. Patentee in field. Past chmn. Met. Planning Commn., Wichita and Sedgwick County, 1958; commr. Kans. Econ. Devel. Bd.; chmn. Kansas Com. for Constitutional Revision, Sedgwick County U.S. Savs. Bonds Sales; past chmn. Kans. Radio Free Europe; past mem. adv. com. Kans. Geol. Survey; mem. Kans. Senate, 1970-81; former mem. engring. adv. council Sch. Engring. and Architecture, Kans. State U.; regent, trustee Wichita State U., HCA/Wesley Med. Ctr., Wichita; bd. dirs. Health Systems Agy. of Southeast Kans., Bd. of Health Sedgwick County, Inst. Logopedics, Quivira council Boy Scouts Am., YMCA, Health Systems Agy. S.E. Kans.; past trustee Midwest Research Inst.; mem. adv. bd. Kans. U. Bus. Sch.; chmn. Kans. Health Care Providers Malpractice Commn.; mem. Kans. Health Care Costs Commn., Kans. Health Coordinating Council, Wichita/Sedgwick County Bd. Health; mem. adv. com. Kans. Dept. Health and Environ. Mem. AAAS, Kans. C. of C. (past pres., past dir.), Wichita C. of C. (past pres. 1959, past dir., Uncommon Citizen award 1988), Kans. Assn. Commerce and Industry (past pres., dir.), Am. Chem. Soc., AAAS, Smithsonian Assocs., Soc. Chem. Industry, Ill. Bar Assn., Wichita Bar Assn., Phi Delta Theta. Lodge: Rotary. Home: 234 S Brookside Dr Wichita KS 67218 Office: 1010 Union Ctr Wichita KS 67202

SOWERWINE, ELBERT ORLA, JR., chemical engineer; b. Tooele, Utah, Mar. 15, 1915; s. Elbert Orla and Margaret Alice (Evans) S.; B. in Chemistry, Cornell U., 1937, Chem. Engr., 1938; m. Norma Borge; children—Sue-Ann Sowerwine Jacobson, Sandra Sowerwine Montgomery, Elbert Orla 3d, John Frederick, Avril Ruth Taylor, Albaro Francisco, Octavio Evans, Zaida Margaret. Analytical chemist Raritan Copper Works, Perth Amboy, N.J., summers 1936, 37; rsch. chem. engr. Socony-Vacuum Oil Co., Paulsboro, N.J., 1938-43; prodn. supr. Merck & Co., Elkton, Va., 1943-45; asst. plant mgr. U.S. Indsl. Chems. Co., Newark, 1945-48; project engr. and rsch. dir. Wigton-Abbott Corp., Newark, 1948-50, Cody, Wyo., 1950-55; cons. engring., planning, indsl. and community devel., resource evaluation and mgmt. Wapiti, Wyo., also C.Am., 1955-80. Commr. N.J., Boy Scouts Am., 1938-43; mem. Wapiti and Park County (Wyo.) Sch. Bds., 1954-58; bd. dirs. Mont. State Planning Commn., 1959-61; exec. bd. Mo. Basin Rsch. and Devel. Coun., 1959-61. Fellow Am. Inst. Chemists; mem. Am. Inst. Chem. Engrs., Am. Planning Assn., Nicaraguan Assn. Engrs. and Architects. Libertarian. Mem. Christian Ch. Researcher desulfurization of petroleum products, process control, alternate energy projects; patentee in petroleum and chem. processes and equipment. Home: Broken H Ranch Wapiti WY 82450 Office: Sowerwine Cons Wapiti WY 82450

SPACE, THEODORE MAXWELL, lawyer; b. Binghamton, N.Y., Apr. 3, 1938; s. Maxwell Evans and Dorothy Marie (Boone) S.; m. Susan Schultz, Aug. 18, 1962 (div. Apr. 1979); children: William Schuyler, Susanna. AB, Harvard U., 1960; LLB, Yale U., 1966. Bar: Conn., 1966. Assoc. Shipman and Goodwin, Hartford, Conn., 1966-71, ptnr., 1971-84, mng. ptnr., 1984-87, adminstv. ptnr., 1988—. Mem. Bloomfield (Conn.) Bd. Edn., 1973-85, chmn., 1975-85; treas. Citizens Scholarship Found., Bloomfield, 1971-73, bd. dirs. 1973—; mem. Bloomfield Human Relations Commn., 1973-75; mem. Bloomfield Town Democratic Com., 1976-83; corporator Hartford Pub. Library, 1976—. Served to lt. (j.g.), USNR, 1960-63. Mem. ABA, Conn. Bar Assn. (mem. exec. com. adminstrv. law sect. 1980—, intellectual property law sect. 1987—), Hartford County Bar Assn., Am. Law Inst., Nat. Health Lawyers Assn. Unitarian. Club: Hartford. Home: 59 Prospect St Bloomfield CT 06002 Office: Shipman & Goodwin 799 Main St Hartford CT 06103

SPADARO, DOUGLAS SEBASTIAN, banker, educator; b. Bklyn., July 20, 1956; s. John Michael and Margaret Teresa (Chesley) S.; m. Leah Russell, Sept. 21, 1986. Student, U. Oxford, 1977; BA in Econs., Roanoke Coll., 1978; MBA, U. Mich, 1980. Mgr. systems performance Am. Can Co., Greenwich, Conn., 1979-82; asset/liability mgmt. officer Dominion Bankshares Corp., Roanoke, Va., 1982-86; prof. bus. adminstrn. and computer info. systems Roanoke Coll., Salem, Va., 1986—; instr. FDIC, Arlington, Va., 1986—, cons. 1987—; cons. Community Banks SW Va., 1986—. Mem. Festival in Park, Roanoke, 1986—. Mem. Assn. for Systems Mgmt. (cert. systems profl.), Jefferson, Roanoke Country. Avocations: boating, fishing. Home: 1964 Laurel Mountain Dr Salem VA 24153 Office: Roanoke Coll Salem VA 24153

SPADEA, DOMINICK GEORGE, manufacturing executive; b. Camden, N.J., Dec. 13, 1945; s. Dominick and Mary (Ficchi) S.; m. Joan Poprycz, Aug. 6, 1966 (div. Nov. 1986); children: Dominick George Jr. (dec.), William, Thomas, John. Student, Temple U., 1963-71. Founder, chmn. Spadea Swiss Products Co., Westmont, N.J., 1974—, Hatton Industries, Westmont, 1979—; co-founder, chmn. Jersey Arms Works, Inc., Westmont, 1980—; founder, chmn. Spadea Mfg. Co., Dallas, 1980—, Avenger Systems Corp., Haddonfield, N.J., 1985—. Campaign coordinator for N.J. Gubernatorial Election Rep. Primary campaign state chmn. Conservative Caucus of N.J. Mem. Am. Def. Preparedness Assn., Nat. Screw Machine Products Assn. (bd. dirs. 1968-71), NRA. Republican. Roman Catholic. Home: 13 Circle Ln Cherry Hill NJ 08003 Office: Avenger Systems Corp 224 Highland Ave Westmont NJ 08108

SPAEH, WINFRIED HEINRICH, banker; b. Essen, Fed. Republic of Germany, Dec. 23, 1930; came to U.S., 1972; s. Josef and Anna (Belker) S.; Abitur, Gymnasium Essen-Werden, 1951; postgrad. Columbia U., 1961-62; m. Waltraut Schab, Aug. 15, 1964; children: Andrea, Olivier. With Dresdner Bank, Essen and Düsseldorf, 1951-60; with internat. banking div. Morgan Guaranty Trust Co. of N.Y., N.Y.C., 1961-66, v.p. German offices, Frankfurt, 1969, gen. mgr., 1972; exec. mgr. Dresdner Bank AG, Frankfurt/Main., 1975, dep. of mng. dirs., 1979-82, sr. officer, N.Y.C., 1982—; dir. Dresdner (SE Asia) Ltd., Singapore, 1978-80, Aseambankers Malaysia Berhad, Kuala Lumpur, 1977-80, P.T. Asian and Euro-Am. Capital Corp. Ltd., Jakarta, 1977-80. Mem. Deutsch-Australische Gesellschaft, Steuben-Schurz Gesellschaft, Nat. Planning Assn. (exec. com.), Contemporary Inst. German Studies (bd. dirs. 1983—), Bankers Assn. Fgn. Trade (internat. adv. council 1982—), German-Am. C. of C. (bd. dirs. 1985—). Clubs: Overseas Bankers (London); Munchener Herrenclub; Union Internat. (bd. dir. 1981—) (Frankfurt); Belle Haven (Greenwich, Conn.). Home: 18 Calhoun Dr Greenwich CT 06830 Office: Dresdner Bank AG 60 Broad St New York NY 10004 also: Juergen-Ponto-Platz 1, Frankfurt Federal Republic of Germany

SPAHIS, MIKE, chemical engineer; b. Wichita Falls, Tex., Dec. 30, 1958; s. Steve E. and Daisy (Katsidonis) S.; m. Joanna Kentes, Dec. 27, 1987. BS in Chemistry, Midwestern State U., 1981; MS in Chem. Engring., U. Tex., 1983. Process engr. Fina Oil and Chem. Co., Port Arthur, Tex., 1983-84; refinery adminstr. Fina Oil and Chem. Co., Dallas, 1984-86, supply analyst, 1986—. Author: Transition of Oxysulfides, 1983; contbr. articles to profl. jours. Pres. Holy Trinity Greek Orthodox Ch. Young Adults Group, Dallas, 1986, bd. dirs., 1987. Mem. Am. Soc. Chem. Engrs., Am. Chem. Soc., Phi Eta Sigma, Gamma Sigma Epsilon, Pi Sigma Pi. Republican. Home: 8653 Capri St Dallas TX 75238 Office: PO Box 2159 Dallas TX 75221

SPAIN, CATHERINE LAVIGNE, trade association administrator; b. Cohoes, N.Y., Sept. 16, 1951; d. Francis Joseph and Dorothy Mary (Jacon) Lavigne; m. James Andrew Spain, May 24, 1974; children: Mark Francis, Jacob Andrew. BA, SUNY, Albany, 1973, MA in Econs., 1975. Fiscal economist N.Y. State Assembly, Albany, 1975-77; research economist Govt. Fin. Officers Assn., Washington, 1977-80, asst. dir. research, 1980-82, dir. fed. liaison ctr., 1982—. Author: (with others) State and Local Government Finance and Financial Management: A Compendium of Current Research, 1978, State Roles in Local Government Financial Management: A Comparative Analysis, 1979, Financial Management Assistance Program Guidebooks, 1980-81, Financial Capability Guidebook, 1982, State Roles in Wastewater Treatment Financing, 1982; editor: (with others) Essays in Public Finance and Financial Management: State and Local Perspectives, 1980, Wastewater Utility Management Manual, 1981; contbr. articles to profl. jours. Recipient Bernard P. Friel medal for disting. service pub. fin. Nat. Assn. Bond Lawyers, 1986. Democrat. Roman Catholic. Office: Govt Fin Officers Assn 1750 K St NW Suite 200 Washington DC 20006

SPALDING, JAMES STUART, telecommunications company executive; b. Edinburgh, Scotland, Nov. 23, 1934; emigrated to Can., 1957, naturalized, 1962; Student, Edinburgh U., 1951-52, Glasgow U., 1953. Gen. mgr., dir. United Corps. Ltd., Montreal, Que., Can., 1970-72; pension fund mgr. BCE, Inc., Montreal, 1972-74, sr. asst. treas., 1974-76, treas., 1976-79, v.p., 1979-83, v.p. fin., 1983-84, exec. v.p. fin., 1984—; dir. Montreal Trust Co., Encor Energy Corp., BCE Devel. Corp., Trans Can. Pipelines, Union Bank Switzerland, Can., Maritime Telegraph & Telephone Co., Ltd., Kinburn Corp., Paperboard Industries Corp.; chmn. Bimcor Inc.; gov. Montreal Stock Exchange. Mem. Inst. Chartered Accountants Scotland, Order Chartered Accounts Que., Conf. Bd. Can., Council Fin. Execs., Fin. Execs. Inst. Can. (chmn.). Home: 54 Aberdeen Ave, Westmount, PQ Canada H3A 3H7

SPANGENBERGER, JOSEPH GEORGE, real estate broker; b. Newark, June 30, 1933; s. George Joseph and Gertrude A. (Farrell) S.; BA, Rutgers U., 1955; MBA, NYU, 1961; m. Mary Jacqmein, Sept. 14, 1957; children: Susan, Joseph, Kathryn, Elizabeth. Systems analyst Babcock & Wilcox, N.Y.C., 1957-59; retail rep., merchandising rep., real estate rep., regional real estate rep. Shell Oil Co., Newark, 1960-67; real estate rep., Tenafly, N.J., 1967-69; real estate broker, Cresskill, N.J., 1970—; adj. prof. bus. adminstrn. Bergen Community Coll., 1980—. Pres. Cresskill Rep. Club, 1988—, Cresskill County Com., 1988—; mem. Cresskill Bd. Edn., 1967-73; chmn. Cresskill Heart Fund, 1971; mem. N.J. Cultural Council, 1976—; bd. dirs. Cresskill-Alpine Little League, 1970—, N.J. Symphony, 1965-70; mem. alumni affairs com. Rutgers U.; pres. Cresskill Rep. Club, 1987—; com. man Bergen County, 1987—. Served with Signal Corps, AUS, 1955-57. Mem. Eastern Bergen County (sec. 1972-73), N.E. Bergen (sec. 1974-75, top selling awards 1975, 76, 77, 78, 79, chmn. to homeless 1989) multiple listing assns., Eastern Bergen County Bd. Realtors, Cresskill C. of C. (founder, charter mem., pres. 1981—), NYU Gad. Sch. Bus. Alumni Assn. (pres. no. N.J. chpt. 1985-87, bd. dirs., trustee 1987), Chi Psi. Roman Catholic. Lodges: K.C., Elks, Rotary (pres. Cresskill-Demarest club 1970-78). Office: 31 Union Ave Cresskill NJ 07626

SPANGLER, RONALD LEROY, television executive, aircraft distributor; b. York, Pa., Mar. 5, 1937; s. Ivan L. and Sevilla (Senft) S.; student U. Miami (Fla.), 1955-59; children—Kathleen, Ronald, Beth Anne. Radio announcer Sta. WSBA, York, 1955-57; TV producer-dir. Sta. WBAL-TV, Balt., 1959-65; pres., chmn. bd. LewRon Television, N.Y.C., 1965-74; now pres., chmn. bd. Spanair Inc., distbr. Rockwell Comdr. aircraft, Forest Hill, Md.; owner Prancing Horse Farm. Mem. Video Tape Producers Assn. N.Y., Rolls Royce Owners Club, Ferrari Clubs Am. Avocation: racing Ferrari automobiles. Home: PO Box 47 Bel Air MD 21014-0047

SPANIER, MAURY L(ESSER), aerospace industry executive, lawyer; b. N.Y.C., Aug. 13, 1916; s. Aaron and Elizabeth (Lesser) S.; m. Helen Green, July 9, 1941; children: David B., Jonathan G. BA, CCNY, 1936; LLB, Columbia, 1939. Bar: N.Y. 1939, U.S. Dist. Ct. 1941, U.S. Supreme Ct. 1947, U.S. Ct. Appeals 1951. Assoc. Hays, Podell & Shulman, N.Y.C., 1939-46; sr. ptnr. Hays, Porter, Spanier & Curtis and predecessors, 1946-79; chmn. exec. com. Baldwin Investment Co.; chmn. bd. dirs., chief exec. officer United Aircraft Products, Inc., Dayton, Ohio, 1971-86, now emeritus; gov. Am. Stock Exchange, 1981-87; chmn. Dextra Baldwin McGonagle Fedn., Inc., N.Y.C., 1967—. Editor: Columbia Law Rev., 1937-39. Trustee, mem. exec. com. Beth Israel Med. Ctr., N.Y.C., 1970—. Served with U.S. Army, 1942-46. Mem. ABA, Assn. Bar City N.Y., Columbia Law Alumni Assn. (bd. dirs. 1974-77), Phi Beta Kappa. Clubs: City Athletic (N.Y.C.); Maplewood (Hartsdale, N.Y.). Office: Dextra Baldwin McGonagle Fedn 445 Park Ave New York NY 10022

SPANN, GEORGE WILLIAM, management consultant; b. Cuthbert, Ga., July 21, 1946; s. Glinn Linwood and Mary Grace (Hiller) S.; B.S. in Physics with honors, Ga. Inst. Tech., 1968, M.S., 1970, M.S. in Indsl. Mgmt., 1973; m. Laura Jeanne Nason, June 10, 1967; children: Tanya Lynne, Stephen William. Engr., Martin Marietta Corp., Orlando, Fla., 1968-70; research scientist Engring. Expt. Sta., Ga. Inst. Tech., 1970-75; v.p., dir. Metrics, Inc., mgmt. and engring. cons., Atlanta, 1973-78, pres., dir., 1978—; v.p., dir. Exec. Data Systems, Inc., 1981—; mem. Ga. Energy Policy Council, Ga. Metrication Council, NASA applications survey group for Landsat follow-on; mem. com. on practical applications of remote sensing from space Space Applications Bd. Nat. Research Council; market research cons. NOAA, NASA, pvt. cos. Regents scholar, 1964. Mem. Am. Soc. Photogrammetry, Urban and Regional Info. Systems Assn., Atlanta Jaycees, Tau Beta Pi, Phi Kappa Phi, Sigma Pi Sigma. Author papers, reports. Home: 3475 Clubland Dr Marietta GA 30068 Office: 1845 The Exchange Ste 140 Atlanta GA 30339

SPANOS, ALEXANDER GUS, professional football team executive; b. Stockton, Calif., Sept. 28, 1923; m. Faye Spanos; children: Dean, Dea Spanos Economou, Alexis Spanos Ruhl, Michael. LLD (hon.), U. Pacific, 1984. Chmn. bd. dirs. A.G. Spanos constrn. Inc., Stockton, Calif., 1960—, A.G. Spanos Properties Inc., Stockton, Calif., 1960—, A.G. Spanos Mgmt. Inc., Stockton, Calif., 1967—, A.G. Spanos Enterprises Inc., Stockton, Calif., 1971—, A.G. Spanos Devel. Inc., Stockton, Calif., 1973—, A.G. Spanos Realty Inc., Stockton, Calif., 1978—, A.G. Spanos Jet Ctr. Inc., Stockton, Calif., 1980—, A.G.S. Fin. Corp., Stockton, Calif., 1980—; pres., chmn. bd. dirs. San Diego Chargers, 1984—. Former trustee Children's Hosp., San Francisco, San Francisco Fine Arts Mus.; trustee Eisenhower Med. Ctr., Rancho Mirage, Calif.; hon. regent U. Pacific, Stockton, 1972-82; gov. USO, , Washington, 1982—. Served with USAF, 1942-46. Recipient Albert Gallatin award Zurich-Am. Ins. Co., 1973, Horatio Alger award Horatio Alger Found., 1982, medal of Honor Statue of Liberty-Ellis Islan Found., 1982. Mem. Am. Hellenic Ednl. Progressive Assn., Calif. C. of C. (bd. dirs. 1980-85). Republican. Greek Orthodox. Office: San Diego Jack Murphy Stadium PO Box 20666 San Diego CA 92120 also: A G Spanos Constrn Co 1341 W Robinhood Dr Stockton CA 95207

SPARKS, BILLY SCHLEY, lawyer; b. Marshall, Mo., Oct. 1, 1923; s. John and Clarinda (Schley) S.; A.B., Harvard, 1945, LL.B., 1949; student Mass. Inst. Tech., 1943-44; m. Dorothy O. Stone, May 14, 1946; children—Stephen Stone, Susan Lee Sparks Raben, John David. Admitted to Mo. bar, 1949; partner Langworthy, Matz & Linde, Kansas City, Mo., 1949-62, firm Linde, Thomson, Fairchild Langworthy, Kohn & Van Dyke, 1962—. Mem. Mission (Kans.) Planning Council, 1954-63; mem. Kans. Civil Service Commn., 1975—. Mem. dist. 110 Sch. Bd., 1964-69, pres., 1967-69; mem. Dist. 512 Sch. Bd., 1969-73, pres., 1971-72; del. Dem. Nat. Conv., 1964; candidate for representative 10th Dist., Kans., 1956, 3d district, 1962; treas. Johnson County (Kans.) Dem. Central com., 1958-64. Served to lt. USAAF, 1944-46. Mem. Kansas City C. of C. (legis. com. 1956-82), Am., Kansas City bar assns., Mo. Bar, Law Assn. Kansas City, Harvard Law Sch. Assn. Mo. (past dir.), Nat. Assn. Sch. Bds. (mem. legislative com. 1968-73), St. Andrews Soc. Mem. Christian Ch. (trustee). Clubs: Harvard (v.p. 1953-54), The Kansas City (Kansas City, Mo.); Milburn Golf and Country. Home: 8517 W 90th Terr Shawnee Mission KS 66212 Office: City Center Sq 12th & Baltimore Sts Kansas City MO 64105

SPARKS, DAVID EMERSON, bank holding company executive; b. L.I., N.Y., May 7, 1944; m. Anne M. McLaughlin; children—Christopher Drew, Deborah Lee. B.A., Furman U., 1966; A.M.P., Harvard U., 1980. C.P.A. Coopers & Lybrand, 1969-73; chief fin. officer Provident Nat., 1973-81; exec. v.p. and chief fin. officer Provident Nat. Corp. Bank, 1981-83; treas. PNC Fin. Corp., 1983—. Mem. Am. Inst. C.P.A.s, Pa. Inst. C.P.A.s, Fin. Execs. Inst. Home: Lawrenceville NJ 08648 Office: Midlantic Corp Metro Park Pla PO Box 600 Edison NJ 08818

SPARKS, DICKINSON WHEELOCK, financial planner; b. Wessington, S.D., Aug. 13, 1933; s. Marvin Lee and Winona E. (Wheelock) S.; m. Patricia Lee Heinl, Mar. 15, 1952; children: Kim Lee, Cheryl Dee, Terry Anthony, Jon Dickinson. Grad. high sch., Fergus Falls, Minn. Cert. Fin. Planner. Locomotive fireman, engr. No. Pacific R.R., Staples, Minn., 1952-60; ins. agt. N.Y. Life Ins. Co., Staples, 1960-63; fin. planner Frank Russell Co., Tacoma, 1963-71, KMS Fin. Services, Lynnwood, Wash., 1971—; instr. fin. planning classes Everett Community Sch., 1979-82, 88, Edmonds Pub. Schs. Chmn. fin. com. Lake Tyee Camp Club, Concrete, Wash., 1983-86, mem. fin. com. 1987-88. Mem. Internat. Assn. Fin. Planners (charter, pres. 1970-72), Inst. Cert. Fin. Planners (pres. Puget Sound chpt. 1984-85, western Wash. chpt. bd. dirs, del. 1980-81, chmn. ethics com. 1978-80, bd. dirs. 1972-80), C. of C., Lynnwood Lions Club (pres. 1985), Elks,. Office: KMS Fin Svcs 3815 196th SW PO Box 2517 Ste 124 Lynnwood WA 98036

SPARKS, (LLOYD) MELVIN, appraiser; b. Putnam County, Mo., Sept. 12, 1921; s. Whitlow Vane and Anna Jane (Hart) S.; m. Naomi Nadine Wiles, Jan. 3, 1942; children: Beverly, Richard, Jill. Grad. high sch., Unionville, Mo. Farm operator Unionville, 1942-77; pres. Northeast Mo. Telephone Co., Green City, Mo., 1961-77; asst. cashier Farmers Bank, Unionville, 1967-77; appraiser Sparks Appraisal, Inc., Unionville, 1983—. Mem. school bd. Putnam County Rt. I, Unionville, 1967-72. Membership Quincy Chpt. Nat. Assn. Ind. Fee Appraisers. Republican. Mem. Ch. of Christ. Lodge: Rotary (pres. Unionville chpt. 1982-83). Home: Rt 2 Box 38 Unionville MO 63565 Office: Sparks Appraisals Inc Route 2 Box 38 Unionville MO 63565

SPARKS, O. V., accountant; b. Berea, Ky., June 15, 1951; s. Gene Edward and Patsy Ann (Arnett) S.; m. Dinah Sue Yost, July 26, 1975; children: Ryan Ashley, Erin Nicole. BS in Bus. and Acctg., Union Coll., Barbourville, Ky., 1974. Asst. comptroller So. Dollar Stores, Inc., Richmond, Ky., 1974-75; asst. office mgr. Jackson Co. Rural Electric Cooperative Corp, McKee, Ky., 1975-76; office mgr. Jackson Co. R.E.C.C., McKee, Ky., 1976-84, Nolin R.E.C.C., Elizabethtown, Ky., 1984—; chmn. supervisory com. Ky. Rural Cooperative Credit Union, 1988—. Pres. Jackson County Little League, McKee, 1975-80; external v.p. Jackson County Jaycees, 1976. Named Hon. Neb. Citizen, Gov. of Neb., 1976, Ky. Col., Gov. of Ky., 1984. Mem. Ky. Rural Elec. Accts. Assn. (sec. 1978-79, v.p. 1979-80, pres. 1980-81). Republican. Lodge: Kiwanis (sec., treas. 1975-80, v.p. 1980-81). Home: 1705 Lakewood Dr Elizabethtown KY 42701 Office: Nolin Rural Electric Coop Corp 612 E Dixie Ave Elizabethtown KY 42701

SPATAFORE, ANTHONY R., financial executive; b. Bklyn., Nov. 15, 1952; s. Anthony C. and Mercedes (Santiago) S.; Frances B. Berezuk, Aug. 28, 1976. Student, Bklyn. U.; Cert. Fin. Planning, Adelphi U., 1982. Registered fin. planner, ins. cons. Agt. Paul Revere Ins. Co., N.Y.C., 1974-76; ins. cons. M.O.N.Y., N.Y.C., 1976-79; fin. planner Home Life Ins. Co., N.Y.C., 1979-82; pres., fin. planner ARS Fin. Services, Inc., Valley Stream, N.Y., 1982—; advisor Securities and Exchange Com., Washington, 1983—. Mem. Internat. Assn. Registered Fin. Planners (bd. govs. 1987—), Internat. Assn. Fin. Planning, Inst. Cert. Fin. Planners (local bd. dirs. 1987—), Nat. Assn. Securities Dealers. Republican. Roman Catholic. Office: ARS Fin Services Inc 125 Franklin Ave Valley Stream NY 11580

SPAULDING, WILLIAM ROWE, investment consultant; b. Cambridge, Mass., Nov. 26, 1915; s. William Rowe and Jennie Jane (Gillam) S.; m. Gertrude Ellen Mowry, June 7, 1947; children: Edward Albert, William Mathews. BS, U. N.H., 1938; MBA, Harvard U., 1940. Trader, Kidder Peabody & Co., N.Y.C., 1940-41; asst. exec. v.p. Mut. Savs. Central Fund, Inc., Boston, 1946-58; v.p. Vance Sanders & Co., Boston, 1959-63; trustee Century Shares Trust, Boston, 1963-71, chmn., 1969-71; chmn. bd., chief exec. officer Wakefield Savs. Bank (Mass.), 1971-81, trustee, 1959-84; ind. dir., trustee Fidelity Group of Mut. Funds, Boston, 1972-87, active emeritus, 1988-89, ret., 1989. Trustee Wakefield YMCA, 1976—; trustee Melrose Wakefield Hosp., 1973-84; fin. v.p. Citizens Scholarship Found. Wakefield, 1962—; mem. ho. of dels. Mass. Easter Seal Soc.; trustee Laudholm Farm Trust, Wells Nat. Estuarine Research Res., 1983—, Internat. Exec. Svc. Corps, 1989—; mem. Wakefield Hist. Commn., 1984-86. Served with AUS, 1942-45, MTO, ETO, to lt. col. Mass. N.G., 1946-62. Decorated Bronze Star; Croix de Guerre (Belgium); named to Eagle Scout, Boy Scouts Am., 1928. Mem. Pres.'s Council U. N.H., Fin. Analysts Fedn., Phi Kappa Phi. Congregationalist. Club: Union of Boston. Home and Office: 35 Outlook Rd Wakefield MA 01880 also: Drakes Island PO Box 406 Wells ME 04090

SPEAKES, LARRY MELVIN, public relations executive, writer, consultant; b. Cleveland, Miss., Sept. 13, 1939; s. Harry Earl and Ethlyn Frances (Fincher) S.; m. Laura Christine Crawford, Nov. 3, 1968; children: Sondra LaNell, Barry Scott, Jeremy Stephen. Student, U. Miss., 1957-61; Litt. D. (hon.), Ind. Central U., 1982. News editor Oxford (Miss.) Eagle, 1961-62; news editor Bolivar Comml., Cleveland, 1962-63; mng. editor Bolivar Comml., 1965-66; dep. dir. Bolivar County Civil Def., 1963-65; gen. mgr. Progress Pubs., Leland, Miss., 1966-68; editor Leland Progress, Hollandale Herald, Bolivar County Democrat, Sunflower County News; press sec. U.S. Senator J.O. Eastland of Miss., 1968-74; staff asst. Exec. Office of Pres., Mar.-May 1974; press asst. to spl. counsel to Pres. May-Aug. 1974; asst. White House press sec., 1974-76, asst. press sec. to Pres., 1976-77; press sec. to Gerald R. Ford, 1977; v.p. Hill & Knowlton, Inc., internat. pub. relations and pub. affairs counsel, Washington, 1977-81; prin. dep. press sec. and asst. to Pres. of U.S., Washington, 1981-87; sr. v.p. Merrill Lynch & Co., Inc., N.Y.C., 1987-88. author: Speaking Out: The Reagan Presidency From Inside the White House. Recipient Presdl. Citizens medal, 1987; Gen. Excellence award Miss. Press Assn., 1968; Disting. Journalism Alumni award U. Miss., 1981, Hall of Fame, 1985; Silver Em Miss. Scholastic Press Assn., 1988; spl. achievement award Nat. Assn. Govt. Communicators, 1983. Mem. Sigma Delta Chi, Kappa Sigma (Man of Yr. award 1982), Lambda Sigma, Omicron Delta Kappa. Methodist. Home: 4800 Thiban Terr Annandale VA 22003

SPEARS, ALEXANDER WHITE, III, tobacco company executive; b. Grindstone, Pa., Sept. 29, 1932; s. Alexander White and Eva Marie (Elliott) S.; m. Shirley Pierce; 1 child, Craig Stewart. B.S., Allegheny Coll., Meadville, Pa., 1953; Ph.D., U. Buffalo, 1960. Research asso., then research fellow SUNY, Buffalo, 1956-58; instr. Millard Fillmore Coll., Buffalo, 1958-59; with Lorillard Corp., Greensboro, N.C., 1959—; v.p. research and devel. Lorillard Corp., 1971-74, sr. v.p. ops. and research, 1975-79, exec. v.p. ops. and research, 1979—; asst. prof. Greensboro div. Guilford Coll., 1961-65; bd. dirs. Greensboro Nat. Bank. Patentee in field; past editor: Tobacco Sci. Jour. Chmn. model sch. task force Greensboro Bd. Edn. and Greensboro C. of C., 1975, 86—; mem. N.C. Humanities Com., 1978-81; bd. dirs. United Way Greensboro, 1975, 79-85, Greensboro Devel. Corp., 1985—, Bus. Com. on Edn., 1985-86; chmn. Greensboro area United Negro Coll. Fund, 1982; chmn. Focus on Excellence campaign, bd. dirs. N.C. A&T U., 1983-86; bd. dirs. N.C. CItizens for Bus. and Industry, 1984-86, YMCA, 1989; adv. bd. U. N.C. Greensboro, 1988—; chmn. fund raiser campaign Greensboro Hist. Mus. Found., 1988—; bd. dirs. Ctr. Inter-Am. Rels., 1988—. Served with AUS, 1953-55. Recipient Distinguished Achievement award in tobacco sci. Philip Morris, 1970. Mem. AAAS, Am. Chem. Soc., Soc. Applied Spectroscopy, Plant Phenolic Group N.Am., Coblentz Soc., Am. Mgmt. Assn., N.Y. Acad. Scis., ASTM, Internat. Coop. Center Sci. Research Relative to Tobacco (sci. commn. 1972), Greensboro C. of C. (dir. 1974-75, 86, chmn. council edn. 1974, Nathanael Greene award 1975). Presbyterian. Office: Lorillard Inc 2525 E Market St PO Box 21688 Greensboro NC 27401 also: Loews Corp 1 Park Ave New York NY 10016-5896

SPECIAN, ROSEMARIE THERESE, pharmaceutical company executive; b. Somerville, N.J., Nov. 4, 1944; d. William Michael and Maryann (Dudek) Specian; m. Edward J. Sinusas, Jr. Dec. 28, 1985. B.S. in Home Econs. (Ella Mae Shellshy Holmes award), Albright Coll., Reading, Pa., 1966; M.S. in Human Behavior and Devel., Drexel U., Phila., 1971; M.B.A., Loyola-Marymount U., Los Angeles, 1980. Sales rep. Atlas Crown Brokerage, Los Angeles, 1973-75; regional rep. Reynolds Metals Co., Los Angeles, 1975-77; mktg. mgr. nat. accounts Glass Containers Corp., Anaheim, Calif., 1977-79; sr. package developer Lederle Labs., Pearl River, N.Y., 1980—. Recipient various sales awards. Mem. Am. Mktg. Assn., Packaging Inst., N.J. Mktg. Assn., N.J. Packaging Assn, AAUW. Home: 85 New Holland Village Nanuet NY 10954 Office: Lederle Labs N Middletown Rd Pearl River NY 10965

SPECTOR, EARL M., lawyer, retail executive; b. Cleve., Apr. 14, 1939; s. Philip and Lillian (Levine) S.; m. Sharon Selman, Sept. 9, 1963; children—Jeffrey Scott, Todd Michael, Halle Sarah. B.S., Ohio State U., Columbus, 1962, J.D., 1965. Sole practice Ohio, 1965-68, Arby's

Restaurants, Ohio, 1968-69; v.p. real estate Am. Snacks, Mass., 1969-71; pres. legal dept. Ames Dept. Stores, Inc., Conn., 1971—, v.p., sec., 1977, sr. v.p., 1983, exec. v.p., 1985. Home: 12 Merrywood Simsbury CT 06070 Office: Ames Dept Stores Inc 2418 Main St Rocky Hill CT 06067

SPECTOR, JACK, accountant; b. Phila., May 31, 1931; s. David and Gertrude (Weinman) S.; m. Harlene Sosnov, Sept. 14, 1952; children—Ellen Spector Wells, Susan Spector Rakusin, Andrea, Neil, Robert. B.S., Temple U., 1953; M.B.A., Rider Coll., 1971. C.P.A., Pa., N.Y., N.J. Ptnr. Friedman & Spector, C.P.A.s, Phila., 1959-65; bus. mgr. New Sch. Music Study, Princeton, N.J., 1965-69; mgr. S.D. Leidesdorf & Co., C.P.A.s, N.Y.C., 1969-71; controller Greater N.Y. Ins. Group, N.Y.C., 1971-73; vp. United Consol. Industries, Balt., 1973-81; owner, propr. Jack Spector C.P.A.s, Orangeburg, NY., 1981—; mem. faculty Ramapo Coll., 1981, Dominican Coll., 1981, Bergen Community Coll., 1981; seminar leader, lectr. various automotive assns. Contbr. articles to mags. Contbg. editor Jobber Retailer mag., 1983-84, Chilton's Motor Age mag., 1985—. Served with U.S. Army, 1953-55; Korea. Mem. Am. Inst. C.P.A.s, N.Y. State Soc. C.P.A.s, N.Y. and N.J. Automotive Wholesalers Assn. (seminar leader, lectr.), Nat. Soc. Pub. Accts. Home: 3 Dogwood Ln West Nyack NY 10994 Office: #1 Prel Pla Orangeburg NY 10962

SPEECH, ESTELLE GRACE, city manager; b. New Orleans, Feb. 6, 1951; d. Arthur and Mable Gladys (Lewis) Johnson; m. Charles Andrew Speech, June 25, 1983; children: Christopher A., Charles Arthur. BBA, Delgado Community Coll., 1983. Clk. safety and permits dept. City of New Orleans, 1973-75, account clk. police dept., 1975, clk. fin. dept., 1975-80, tax adminstr. fin. dept., 1980-86, instnl. bus. mgr. welfare dept., 1986—. Mem. Nat. Assn. Female Execs., La. Juvenile Detention Assn., City New Orleans Women Support Group. Democrat. Office: Youth Study Ctr Dept Welfare 1100 Milton St New Orleans LA 70122

SPEESE, DWAIN KEITH, marketing and financial professional; b. San Bernardino, Calif., Apr. 4, 1957; s. John Lyell and Ann Laura (Cunningham) S.; m. Alisa Maria Mannon, Aug. 31, 1985. BSBA, U. Nebr., 1980; MBA, DePaul U., 1986. Assoc. account rep. First Nat. Bank of Chgo., 1980-82; account rep. Rufenacht, Bromagen & Hertz, Chgo., 1982-83; mgmt. cons. Nat. Blvd. Bank, Chgo., 1984-85; mktg. dir. Gen. Electric Credit Corp., Chgo., 1985-88, The CIT Group, Park Ridge, Ill., 1988—. Bd. dirs. Kenwood-Oaklawn Devel. Orgn. Mem. Nat. Black MBA Assn., Chgo. C. of C. (speaker 1986). Baptist. Home: 1255 N Sandburg Terr #2011 Chicago IL 60610-2209 Office: The CIT Group 1400 Renaise Dr Ste 312 Park Ridge IL 60068

SPEIRS, DEREK JAMES, diversified corporation financial executive; b. Montreal, Que., Can., Dec. 21, 1933; s. James B. and Marie C. (Hunt) Speirs; m. Carol Alice Cumming, Dec. 8, 1967 (div. Feb. 1989); children: Lara Marie, Gregory Ross, Scott Lawrence Gorgon. B. Commerce with honors in Econs., McGill U., 1954, M.B.A., 1959. Chartered acct., Can., chartered corp. sec. Offshore assignments acct. Cyanamid of Can., Montreal, 1965-70; devel. dir. fine papers, corp. acctg. dir. Domtar, Inc., Montreal, 1970-72, dir. corp. devel., 1976-78, v.p. fin., corp. devel., 1978-89, sr. v.p. fin. and devel., 1989—; sr. v.p. fin. and devel., sec. Consoltex, Montreal, 1972-76, also dir., 1972-76. Mem. Can. Inst. Chartered Accts., Fin. Exec. Inst. (dir.), Soc. Prevention of Cruelty to Animals (bd. dirs.). Clubs: Lac Marois Country, St. James; Montreal Amateur Athletic Assn. Home: 365 Stanstead Ave, Ville Mont-Royal, Montreal, PQ Canada H3R 1X5 Office: Domtar Inc, PO Box 7210 Sta A, Montreal, PQ Canada H3C 3M1

SPELLMAN, DOUGLAS TOBY, advertising executive; b. Bronx, N.Y., May 12, 1942; s. Sydney M. and Leah B. (Rosenberg) S.; BS, Fairleigh Dickinson U., 1964; m. Ronni I. Epstein, Jan. 16, 1966 (div. Mar. 1985); children: Laurel Nicole, Daren Scott; m. Michelle Ward, Dec. 31, 1986. Media buyer Doyle, Dane, Bernbach, Inc., N.Y.C., 1964-66, Needham, Harper & Steers, Inc., N.Y.C., 1966; media supr. Ogilvy & Mather, Inc., N.Y.C., 1967-69; media dir. Sinay Advt., Los Angeles, 1969-70; chief ops. officer S.H.H. Creative Mktg., Inc., Los Angeles, 1969—; assoc. media dir. Warren, Mullen, Dolobowsky, Inc., N.Y.C., 1970—; dir. West Coast ops. Ed Libov Assocs., Inc., Los Angeles, 1970-71; media supr. Carson/Roberts Advt. div. Ogilvy & Mather, Inc., Los Angeles, 1971-72; assoc. media dir. Ogilvy & Mather, Inc., Los Angeles, 1972-73; media dir. Vitt Media Internat., Inc., Los Angeles, 1973-74; v.p., dir. West Coast ops. Ind. Media Services, Inc., Los Angeles, 1974-75; owner Douglas T. Spellman, Inc., Los Angeles, 1975-77, pres., chmn. bd., 1977-82; pres., chief operating officer Douglas T. Spellman Co. div. Ad Mktg., Inc., Los Angeles, 1982-85; pres., chief exec. officer, chmn. bd. Spellbound Prodns. and Spellman Media divs. Spellbound Communications, Inc., Los Angeles, 1984-86; gen. ptnr. Faso & Spellman, Los Angeles, 1984-86; chief operating officer, pres. Yacht Mgmt. Internat., Ltd., Los Angeles, 1984-86; v.p. media Snyder, Longino Advt. div. Snyder Advt., Los Angeles, 1985-86; advt./media cons., Los Angeles, 1986—; guest lectr. sch. bus UCLA, 1975, U. So. Calif., 1976. Served with U.S. Army Res. N.G., 1964-69. Mem. Aircraft Owners and Pilots Assn., Nat. Rifle Assn., Phi Zeta Kappa, Phi Omega Epsilon. Jewish. Clubs: Rolls Royce Owners, Mercedes Benz Am., Aston Martin Owners. Office: PO Box 180 Beverly Hills CA 90213

SPELLMAN, JOHN F., diversified products company executive; b. 1938; married. B.S., St. Peter's Coll., 1960. Audit mgr. Price Waterhouse & Co., 1968-69; asst. controller W.R. Grace & Co., N.Y.C., 1969-71, asst. corp. v.p., chief fin. officer consumer products group, 1971-74, corp. v.p., controller, 1974-78, exec. v.p., chief fin. officer, 1978—; also dir. W.R. Grace & Co., Inc., N.Y.C.; dir. Taco Villa, Inc. Mem. Am. Inst. CPAs, Fin. Exec. Inst. Club: Union League, Navesink Country. Office: W R Grace & Co Inc 1114 Ave of the Americas New York NY 10036

SPENCE, A. MICHAEL, economist; b. Montclair, N.J., 1943. BA, Princeton U., 1966; PhD, Harvard U., 1972; MA, Oxford U., 1968. Instr. Harvard U., 1971-72, prof. econs., 1976—, prof. bus. adminstrn., 1979—, dean faculty arts and scis., 1984—; instr. Stanford U., 1973-75; mem. econs. adv. panel NSF, 1977-79. Author: Market Signaling: Information Transfer in Hiring and Related Screening Processes, 1974; (with R.E. Caves and M.E. Porter) Competition in the Open Economy, 1980; mem. editorial bd. various jours. including Bell Jour. Econs., Jour. Econ. Theory, Pub. Policy. Rhodes scholar, 1966-68; recipient Galbraith Prize for Teaching Excellence, 1978, John Bates Clark Medal, Am. Econ. Assn., 1981. Office: Harvard U 5 University Hall Cambridge MA 02138

SPENCER, BILLIE JANE, lawyer; b. Caro, Mich., Sept. 16, 1949; d. William Norman and Jane Isabel (Putnam) S. AB in Econs., U. Miami, Coral Gables, Fla., 1971, LLM in Tax, 1980; JD, U. Fla., Gainesville, 1973; course cert. St. Catherine's Coll., Oxford U., 1973; grad. with highest distinction, Naval War Coll., Washington, 1988. Bar: Fla., Calif. Assoc. Frates Floyd, et. al., Miami, Fla., 1973-74; commd. lt. (j.g.) USNR, 1974, advanced through grades to comdr., 1988; judge advocate USNR, Subic Bay, Pensacola, 1975-78; sole practice San Francisco, and Stuart, Fla., 1978-85; asst. staff judge advocate USNR, Lemoore, Calif., 1982-83; DOD liaison USNR, Washington, 1985-88; civilian atty. USN, Mechanicsburg, Pa., 1988—; instr. econs. Fla. Inst. Tech., Jensen Beach, 1984-85; litigation cons. Castle & Cooke, Inc., San Francisco, 1979-83; clk. Ehrlichmann Watergate Trial team, Washington, 1974; del. state conf. on small bus., 1982. Mem. U.S. Naval Inst., Res. Officers Assn., The Navy League, Am. Mgmt. Assn. Republican. Unitarian. Home: 1441 Hillcrest Ct #202 Camp Hill PA 17011

SPENCER, EDSON WHITE, computer systems company executive; b. Chgo., June 4, 1926; s. William M. and Gertrude (White) S. Student, Princeton, 1943, Northwestern U., U. Mich., 1944; B.A., Williams Coll., 1948; M.A., Oxford (Eng.) U., 1950. With Sears, Roebuck & Co., Chgo., 1951-54, Honeywell, Inc., Mpls., 1954—; Far East regional mgr. Honeywell, Inc., Tokyo, 1959-65; corp. v.p. internal ops. Honeywell, Inc., Mpls., 1965-69, exec. v.p., 1969-74, pres., chief exec. officer, 1974-78, chief exec. officer, 1978-87, chmn. bd., 1978—. Mem. Phi Beta Kappa. Office: Honeywell Inc Honeywell Plaza Minneapolis MN 55408 *

SPENCER, JOHN-K JOSEPH, architect, real estate developer; b. Mahnomen, Minn., Nov. 21, 1938; s. Richard Delmar and Clara Josephine (von Rumreich) S.; m. Rebecca Fern Cholmondeley. Dec. 15, 1978; children: John Emerson, Sabrina Kaye Stasia, Jonathan Bernard Nathan. BS in Arch, U. Cin., 1962; M in City Planning, Harvard U., 1964. Registered architect, P.R., Kans., Ohio, Wis., Pa. Cons. Fomento Indsl., San Juan, P.R., 1964-66, Fomento Economico, San Juan, 1967-69; ptnr. Gaumann, Quinones, Spencer, San Juan, 1970-76; mgr., dir. Belcan Corp., Blue Ash, Ohio, 1976-81; v.p. A.M. Kinney, Inc. and Affiliates, Cin., 1981-83, Chas. V. Maescher & Co., Inc., Cin., 1983-88; ptnr. Dunn & Wendel, 1989—; mng. ptnr. Atlantes Devel. Co., 1988—; bd. dirs. Britannia, Inc., San Juan, The Allod Group; v.p. Envirotech, San Juan, 1969-87; rep. Constrn. Owners Assn. Tri-State Inc, 1988. Author: A Science and Technology Center for Puerto Rico, 1965, Comprehensive Tourism Plan for Puerto Rico; co-author: Tourism for Southwest, Puerto Rico. Rep. Intercommunity Cable Regulatory Commn. Southwest Ohio, Cin., 1985—; Laubach tutor, adult literacy program, No. Ky. Regional Library System, Covington, 1985-88; trustee Mental Health Services East, Inc., chmn. bd. 1988-89; active Walnut Hills Area Council Planning Task Force, 1986—. Mem. Soc. Mktg. Profl. Services (pres., chmn. edn. com. 1977-89), Assn. Gen. Contractors Am. (pres. econ. devel. com., Ohio chpt., 1984-88, constrn. mktg. com., Washington, 1985—), Cin. C. of C., Smale Commn. on Cin. Infrastructure (co-chmn. streets com. 1987-88), Mental Health Services East Inc., Industry Adv. Com., OMI Coll. Applied Sci. U. Cin. Republican. Roman Catholic. Club: Harvard (Cin.). Lodge: Rotary (chmn. dist. conf. 1986). Home: 7600 Graves Rd Indian Hill OH 45243 Office: Atlantes Devel Co Compton Sq Cincinnati OH 45231

SPENCER, MILTON HARRY, economics and finance educator; b. N.Y.C., Mar. 25, 1926; m. Roslyn Pernick; children: Darcy, Robin, Cathy. BS, NYU, 1949, MA, 1950; PhD, Cornell U., 1954. Instr. econs., fin. Queens Coll., N.Y.C., 1949-52; research asst. Cornell U., Ithaca, N.Y., 1952-54; economist Armour & Co., Chgo., 1954-55; assoc. prof. Wayne State U., Detroit, 1955-62, prof., 1962—; vis. prof. U. Hawaii, Honolulu, 1965-66; lectr., U.S., Australia, Europe, Asia, Africa, South Am.; cons. U.S. Dept. State, Washington, 1959—, govts. of Chile, Israel, England, France, Italy, Australia, Hong Kong, Japan, Republic of China. Author: Economic Thought, 1954, Managerial Economics, 3 edits., 1959-68, Comtemporary Economics, 7 edits., 1971-89; contbr. numerous articles to profl. jours. Served as cpl. U.S. Army, 1943-45. Recipient Disting. Service awards from U.S. Dept. State, Govts. of Chile, Israel, France, Spain, England, Italy, Belgium. Mem. Am. Econ. Assn., Am. Fin. Assn., Nat. Assn. Bus. Economists. Office: Wayne State U Sch Bus Adminstrn Detroit MI 48202

SPENCER, ROBERT HENRY, management consultant, educator; b. Washington, Mar. 11, 1950; s. John and Vesta (Palmer) McNeil; m. Mary Sue Thornberry, Apr. 4, 1970; children: Allison, Jason, Sarah, Justin. BS, Ind. U., 1982; MSA, Cen. Mich. U., 1989. Computer analyst Hardin Meml. Hosp., Elizabethtown, Ky., 1970-71; computer specialist U.S. Army Fin. Ctr., Indpls., 1974-80, U.S. Navy Edn. & Tng. Command, Pensacola, Fla., 1981-83; dir. Mgmt. Info. Systems, Saltmarsh, Cleaveland & Gund, Pensacola, 1984—; prof. U. W.Fla., 1986—. Active various civic and profl. orgns. With U.S. Army, 1972-74. Recipient Order Ky. Col. Mem. KC, Data Processing Mgmt. Assn., Nat. Assn. Realtors. Office: Saltmarsh Cleaveland & Gund 900 12th Ave Pensacola FL 32501

SPENCER, ROSE MARIE, accounting firm executive; b. Chgo., July 10, 1943; d. William and Katherine (Kristman) Schweitzer; divorced; children: Anna Marie, Tracy Neal, Jeffrey Earl, Stoney Alexander, Sunny Eric. Student, LaSalle Extension U., Chgo., 1966-69; BS, Cen. State U., Edmond. Okla., 1982. Pres. J & R Ranch, Inc., Yukon, Okla., 1972—, My-Co Acctg. Plus, Inc., Yukon, 1982—; v.p. Hillman's Taxidermy Studio, Inc., Yukon, 1976-82, Reliable Lawn Care, Inc., Yukon, 1982—; bd. dirs. South Tex. Electric, Houston, 1977-82, 33 Welding, Inc., Kingfisher, Okla., 1982—, B & B Air Express, Inc., Oklahoma City, 1984—; bd. dirs. Rowland Enterprises, Inc., Oklahoma City, Okla. Mem. Am. Bus. Women's Assn., Nat. Soc. Pub. Accts., Okla. Soc. Pub. Accts., Nat. Taxidermists Assn. Avocations: hunting, fishing, boating. Home: 819 Poplar Yukon OK 73099 Office: J&R Ranch Inc PO Box 850708 Yukon OK 73085

SPENCER, THOMAS MELVIN, III, food service executive; b. Richmond, Va., Feb. 16, 1949; s. Thos Melvin Jr. and Frances (Lawson) S.; m. Leslie Graham Murray, Sept. 14, 1984. AB, U. N.C., 1972. With fountain sales dept. Coca-Cola U.S.A., Atlanta, 1973-80; with Russell Pierce and Assocs., Richmond, Va., 1980-81; mgr. fountain sales div. Allegheny Pepsi, Richmond, Va., 1982; food service mgr. ops. Pep Com Industries, Inc., Durham, N.C., 1983—. Mem. Nat. Soft Drink Assn. Republican. Episcopalian. Home: 1115 Lakeside Dr Wilson NC 27893 Office: Pep Com Industries Inc 2717 Western Bypass Durham NC 27705

SPENCER, WILLIAM EDWIN, telephone company executive, engineer; b. Kansas City, Mo., Mar. 22, 1926; s. Erwin Blanc and Edith Marie (Peterson) S.; student U. Kansas City, 1942; A.S., Kansas City Jr. Coll., 1945; B.S. in E.E., U. Mo., 1948; postgrad. Iowa State U., 1969; m. Ferne Arlene Nieder, Nov. 14, 1952; children—Elizabeth Ann, Gary William, James Richard, Catherine Sue. With Southwestern Bell Telephone Co., Kansas City, Mo., 1948-50, Topeka, 1952-61, sr. engr., 1966-69, equipment maintenance engr., 1969-76, engring. ops. mgr., 1976-79, dist. mgr., 1979—; mem. tech. staff Bell Telephone Labs., N.Y.C., 1961-62, Holmdel, N.J., 1962-66; U.S. Senatorial Club, 1985—. Mem. Rep. Presdl. Task Force, 1984—. Served with AUS, 1950-52. Recipient best Kans. idea award Southwestern Bell Telephone Co., 1972, cert. of appreciation Kans. Miss Teen Pageant, 1984. Registered profl. engr., Kans. Mem. Kans. Engring. Soc., Nat. Soc. Profl. Engrs., IEEE, Topeka Engrs. Club (pres.), Telephone Pioneers Assn. (pres.), Nat. Geog. Soc., Kans. Hist. Soc., Am. Assn. Ret. Persons, U. Mo.-Columbia Alumni Assn., Nat. Travel Club. Republican. Patentee in field. Home: 3201 MacVicar Ct Topeka KS 66611 Office: 220 E 6th St Topeka KS 66603

SPERBER, PHILIP, lawyer, writer; b. N.Y.C., Feb. 29, 1944; s. Sol and Sally (Dolsky) S.; m. Doreen Faye Strachman, Dec. 27, 1969; children: Shoshana, Ryan, Sara, Jason. BS, N.J. Inst. Tech., 1965; JD, U. Md., 1969. Bar: Md., D.C., U.S. Ct. Appeals, U.S. Supreme Ct. Sales mgr. N.J. Electronics Corp., Kenilworth, N.J., 1965-68; ptnr. Blair, Olcutt, Sperber & Evans, Washington, 1968-71; v.p. Cavitron Corp., N.Y.C., 1971-77; group exec. Internat. Telephone & Telegraph Corp., Nutley, N.J., 1977-79; pres., dir. REFAC Internat., Ltd., N.Y.C., 1979—; pres. APRO Sci., Morristown, N.J., 1975—, PDS Industries, Convent Station, N.J., 1977—; chmn. The Negotiating Group, Morris Twp., N.J., 1975—; mng. ptnr. Bear Devel. Group, Livingston, N.J., 1985—. Author: Intellectual Property Management, 1974 (N.J. Writers Conf. Citation 1975), API Patent Manual, 1975, Ultrasonic Proceedings, 1976, Negotiating in Day-to-Day Business, 1976, Products Liability of Manufacturers: Prevention and Defense, 1977, The Science of Business Negotiation, 1979 (N.J. Writers Conf. Citation 1980), Corporation Law Department Manual, 1980 (N.J. Writers Conf. Citation 1981), Counseling Your Medical Device Client: Law, Business, Stategy, 1981, Failsafe Business Negotiating, 1983 (N.J. Writers Conf. Citation 1984), Closing the Deal, 1985 (N.J. Writers Conf. Citation 1986), The Attorney's Practice Guide to Negotiations, 1985 (N.J. Writers Conf. Citation 1987), Negotiator's Views on How to Avoid Nuclear War, 1986, International Transactions, 1987 (N.J. Writers Conf. Citation 1988), Bottom Line Negotiation and Scientific Persuasion, 1988, several others; over 90 pub. papers. Dir. N.J. Jaycees, Hillside, 1965-66, Md. Lions Internat., White Oak, 1970-71; pres. Runnymede Hills Civic Assn., Whippany, N.J., 1971-72, Consumer Clearinghouse, Morristown, N.J., 1977-78, Normandy Heights Civic Assn., Morris Twp.,N.J., 1986—; chmn., bd. trustees N.J. Literary Hall of Fame, Newark, 1986—; chmn. bd. trustees N.J. Inventors Congress and Hall of Fame, Newark, 1987—; v.p. Emmet Ave. Condominium Assn., Morris Twp., 1986—. Named one of Outstanding Young Men of Am. U.S. Jaycees, Tulsa, 1966; recipient Citation for Contbns. Am. Mktg. Assn., Newark, N.J., 1975, commendation for contbns. Am. Law Inst., Chgo., 1976, Plaque for Outstanding Performance Am. Mgmt. Assns., N.Y.C., 1978, Speaker Showcase award Internat. Platform Assn., Washington, 1983, Medal of Merit Pres. of U.S., Washington, 1987; decorated knight (hon.), Knights of Malta, Order of St. John of Jerusalem, 1986. Fellow N.J. Inst. Tech. (alumni assn. council chmn. 1986—, Outstanding Alumnus award 1981); mem. Health Industry Mfrs. Assn. (del. 1976-77), Licensing Execs. Soc. (trustee 1977-79), Ultrasonic Industry Assn. (v.p. 1975-77), Am. Soc. for Testing and Materials (sect. chmn. 1976-77), ABA (legis. com. chmn. 1975-80), Am. Biog. Inst. (bd. dirs. 1986—), N.J. State Bar Assn. (councilman 1977-80), Am. Arbitration Assn. (judge; Outstanding Service award 1977), Am. Acad. Negotiation and Diplomacy (pres. 1984-86), Am. Inst. Chem. Engrs. (mktg. div.), IEEE (sr.), Tau Beta Pi (Eminent Engr. award 1986). Republican. Jewish. Clubs: President's (Newark); Sales and Internat. Execs. (N.Y.C.). Home: 30 Normandy Heights Rd Convent Station NJ 07961 Office: REFAC Internat Ltd 100 E 42d St New York NY 10017

SPERLING, JOHN GLEN, education company executive; b. Willow Springs, Mo., Jan. 9, 1921; s. Leon Birchfield and Lena (McNama) S.; m. Virginia Vandergrift, June 1951 (div. 1965); 1 child, Peter Vandegrift. BA, Reed Coll., 1848; MA, U. Calif., 1952; PhD, U. Cambridge, Eng., 1955. Instr. U. Md., Europe, 1955-57; asst. professor Ohio State U., Columbus, 1957-76; prof. San Jose (Calif.) State U., 1960-72; pres. Inst. Profl. Devel., San Jose, 1972-76, U. Phoenix, 1976-80; pres., chief exec. officer Apollo Group Inc., Phoenix, 1980—. Co-author: Economic Concepts & Institutions, National Economic Policies, Communist Economies, Third World Economies, 1974-76, War Finance 1689-1714, New Cambridge Modern History, 1970; contbr. articles to profl. jours. Cons. Combating Juvenile Delinquency, Sunnyvale, Calif., 1972-75, Calif. Ctr. Community Schs., San Jose, 1971-73; active Open Space & Urban Devel. Commn., Santa Clara County, Calif., 1971-73. Recipient Ehrman Studentship, Kings Coll., Cambridge U., 1953-55, Acad. Freedom award Calif. Fedn. Tchrs., L.A., 1988. Mem. Plaza Club. Democrat. Home: 5932 E Mariposa Phoenix AZ 85018 Office: Apollo Group Inc 4615 E Elwood Phoenix AZ 85040

SPERO, FREDERICK HENRY, information systems specialist; b. Flushing, N.Y., Nov. 4, 1946; s. James Joseph and America (Valentini) S.; m. Rita Kehoe, Sept. 19, 1971; children: Patrick, Christopher. BA, Northeastern U., 1969. Analyst, asst. dist. mgr. ops. Dun & Bradstreet, Boston, 1969-72; dist. mgr. ops., sales trainee Dun & Bradstreet, Providence, 1972-75; area office mgr. Dun & Bradstreet, Springfield, Mass., 1975-76; div. sales mgr., nat. account mgr. Dun & Bradstreet, Boston, 1976-82; relationship mgr., dir. Dun & Bradstreet, N.Y.C., 1982—. Mem. Mktg. Scis. Inst. (mem. adv. com.). Home: 14 Earl Rd East Sandwich MA 02537 Office: Dun & Bradstreet Corp 299 Park Ave New York NY 10171 also: Dun & Bradstreet Info Group 1 Penn Pla Ste 4520 New York NY 10119

SPERO, JOAN EDELMAN, multi-service corporation executive; b. Davenport, Iowa, Oct. 2, 1944; d. Samuel and Sylvia (Halpern) Edelman; m. Carl Michael Spero, Nov. 9, 1969; children—Jason, Benjamin. Student, L'Inst. d'Etudes Politiques, Paris, 1964-65; B.A., U. Wis., 1966; M.A., Columbia U., 1968, Ph.D., 1973. Asst. prof. Columbia U., N.Y.C., 1973-79; ambassador of U.S. to UN Econ. and Social Council, N.Y.C., 1980-81; v.p. Am. Express Co., N.Y.C., 1981-83, sr. v.p. internat. corp. affairs, 1983—; dir. Hercules Inc., Wilmington, Del.; mem. council Japan-U.S. Businessmen's Council, Washington, 1983—; mem. Industry Sector Adv. Com., Washington, 1981—. Author: The Politics of International Economic Relations, 3rd edit., 1985, The Failure of the Franklin National Bank, 1980; contbr. articles to profl. jours. Bd. dirs. Internat. Peace Acad., 1983—; trustee Amherst Coll.; bd. dirs. French-Am. Found.; mem. adv. council Am. Ditchley Found. Named to Acad. of Women Achievers, YWCA, 1983; Woodrow Wilson fellow. Mem. Council on Fgn. Relations, Council of Am. Ambassadors, Phi Beta Kappa. Democrat. Jewish. Office: Am Express Co Am Express Tower World Fin Ctr New York NY 10004

SPERO, LESLIE WAYNE, linen service and distribution executive; b. Youngstown, Ohio, July 3, 1926; s. Harry and Sadie (Weiskopf) S.; m. Elaine Grossfield, Jan. 25, 1953; children: Rand Kevin, Laurie Diane. BA summa cum laude, UCLA, 1948; postgrad., Harvard U. Purchasing agt. United Service Co., Youngstown, 1948-53, v.p., dir., 1953-68, chmn., pres., 1968—; v.p., dir. United Paper Service Co., Youngstown, 1953-68, chmn., pres., 1968—; pres. TRSA, Hallendale, Fla., 1982-83; bd. dirs. Dollar Savs. and Trust, Youngstown. Past pres. Child Guidance Ctr., Jewish Federation Youngstown, Community Relations Council, Am. Jewish Com., Youngstown; past bd. dirs. Child and Adult Mental Health Ctr., March of Dimes Nat. Found., Youngstown, Friends Am. Art Butler Art Gallery, Jewish Community Ctr.; past chmn. Community Chest, March of Dimes Nat. Found., Com. Heritage Manor; past trustee Rodef Sholem Temple, Bellfaire Home for Exceptional Children, Cleve.; past commdr. U.S. Power Squadron, Youngstown; past mem. Am. Jewish Com., Young Leadership Cabinet Nat. United Jewish Appeal; bd. dirs. Heritage Manor Home for Aged. Served to lt. (j.g.) USN., 1944-47. Mem. MENSA, Youngstown C. of C., Gold Key, Phi Beta Kappa, Phi Eta Sigma. Clubs: Youngstown, Squaw Creek Country. Lodges: Rotary, Elks. Home: 2701 N Ocean Blvd Boca Raton FL 33431 Office: United Svc Co 350 N Ave Youngstown OH 44502

SPETRINO, RUSSELL JOHN, utility company executive, lawyer; b. Cleve., Apr. 22, 1926; s. John Anthony and Madeline S.; July 17, 1954 (dec.); children—Michael J., Ellen A. B.S., Ohio State U., 1950; LL.B., Western Res. U., 1954. Bar: Ohio 1954. Asst. atty. gen. Ohio, 1954-57; atty.-examiner Public Utilities Commn. of Ohio, Columbus, 1957-59; atty. Ohio Edison Co., Akron, 1959-69, sr. atty., 1970-73, gen. counsel, 1973-78, v.p., gen. counsel, 1978-87, exec. v.p., gen. counsel, 1987—. Served with inf. U.S. Army, 1944-46. Mem. Edison Electric Inst., Ohio Electric Utility Inst., Akron Bar Assn., Ohio Bar Assn., ABA, Fed. Energy Bar Assn. Republican. Episcopalian. Clubs: Portage Country, Akron City. Home: 867 Lafayette Dr Akron OH 44303 Office: Ohio Edison Co 76 S Main St Akron OH 44308

SPICAK, DORIS ELIZABETH, health services company executive; b. Balt., Sept. 6, 1943; d. Elwood Lee and Georgianna E. (Thomas) Fletcher; m. Marvin Ray Spicak, May 18, 1968; children: Charles Frank, Lisa Marie. Student, Towson State Coll., 1961-62, Balt. Jr. Coll., 1962-64; diploma in nursing, Sinai Sch. Nursing, Balt., 1965; AS, Bee County Coll., Beeville, Tex., 1976. RN, Md., Tex. Inservice dir. Meml. Hosp., Beeville, 1975-76, dir. nurses, 1980-81; dir. nurses Hillside Nursing Ctr., Beeville, 1978-80; dir. br. agy. Coastal Bend Home Health, Victoria, Tex., 1981-85; adminstr. Crossroads Home Health, Victoria, 1985—, pres. bd. dirs., 1985—; pres. bd. dirs. Crossroads Nursing Svc., Victoria, 1986—. Active John F. Kennedy Presdl. Campaign, Balt., 1960. 1st lt. U.S. Army, 1965-68, Vietnam. Mem. Tex. Assn. Home Health Agys. (medicare com. 1986—), Nat. Assn. for Home Care, Victoria C. of C. Democrat. Roman Catholic. Club: Coastal Plains Continuity of Care (Victoria) (treas. 1983-84). Home: 205 Kelly Crick Victoria TX 77904 Office: Crossroads Home Health 1501 E Mockingbird #403A Victoria TX 77904

SPICE, DENNIS DEAN, state university official, financial consultant; b. Rochester, Ind., Feb. 7, 1950; s. Donnelly Dean and Lorene (Rhodes) S.; m. Linda Kay Buehler, Oct. 1, 1971; children: Kristie Lorene, Danielle Deanne. AA, SUNY, Albany, 1974; BA, Eastern Ill. U., 1978; MBA, U. Ill., Urbana, 1985. Employee benefits mgr. Eastern Ill. U., Charleston, 1977-80; disbursements officer State Univs. Retirement System, Champaign, Ill., 1980-81, assoc. exec. dir. adminstrn., 1981—; pres., cons. Spice and Assocs., Champaign, 1984—; chmn. bd. U. Ill. Credit Union. Staff sgt. USMC, 1968-77; Vietnam. Mem. Nat. Conf. on Tchr. Retirement, Am. Soc. Pension Actuaries, Coll. and Univ. Pers. Assn. (bd. dirs. Ill. area), Govt. Fin. Offices Assn., Internat. Found. Employee Benefits Plans, Nat. Conf. Pub. Employee Retirement Systems, Pub. Retirement Info. Systems Group (bd. dirs.), Nat. Coun. Tchrs. Retirement, Champaign C. of C., Rotary. Republican. Home: Rural Rt 3 Box 39 Champaign IL 61821 Office: State Univs Retirement System 50 Gerty Dr Champaign IL 61820

SPIEGEL, ALLEN LEWIS, marketing executive; b. Bklyn., July 13, 1954; s. Robert Henry and Shirley (Laskin) S.; m. Sylvia Dolores Clark, Aug. 19, 1984. BA in Polit. Sci., Bklyn. Coll., 1975; MBA in Mktg. Mgmt., CUNY, 1983. Mktg. rep. Recognition Equipment Corp., N.Y.C., 1979-81; mem. staff Digital Equipment Corp., N.Y.C., 1981-87, sales mgr. dist. svcs., 1987—. Pvt. 1st class USMC, 1976. Home: 1428 Hylan Blvd Staten Island NY 10305 Office: Digital Equipment Corp 2 Penn Pla New York NY 10121

SPIEGEL, JOHN WILLIAM, bank executive; b. Indpls., Mar. 14, 1941; s. William Sordon and Elizabeth (Hall) S.; children: W. Robert, John F., Bradley H.; m. Elizabeth Devereux Morgan, Aug. 16, 1986; stepchildren: David P. Adams III, Morgan G. Adams, E. Devereux Adams. BA, Wabash Coll., 1963; MBA, Emory U., 1965. Research assoc. IMEDE (Mgmt. Inst.), Lausanne, Switzerland, 1965-66; mgmt. trainee Trust Co. Bank, Atlanta,

1966-67, bond portfolio mgr., 1967-72; data processing mgr. Trust Co. Ga., Atlanta, 1972-78, treas., 1978-85; exec. v.p., chief fin. officer Sun Trust Banks Inc., Atlanta, 1985—; former mem. taxation and payment systems coms. ABA; former instr. Morehouse Coll. and Banking Schs.; mem. exec. com. ABA Chief Fin. Officers Div., 1987-89. Mem. exec. com., bd. dirs. Alliance Theatre, Atlanta, 1985-88, High Mus. Art, Atlnata, 1985-89; pres. Young Audiences Atlanta Inc., 1982-84, bd. dirs., 1985, mem. adv. bd., 1986-89; pres. bd. visitors Grady Meml. Hosp., Atlanta, 1983-89; v.p. exec. bd. Atlanta Area council Boy Scouts Am., 1983-89; mem. adv. council Ga. State U. Sch. Accountancy, Atlanta, 1981-85, chmn. curriculum subcom., 1983-84; mem. exec. com., bd. dirs. Morehouse Sch. Medicine, 1984-88, chmn. fin. com., 1987-89; mem. Leadership Atlanta, 1976—; trustee, mem. exec. com., treas. Atlanta Arts Alliance, 1976-83, chmn. fin. com., 1984-89; chmn. fin. com., bd. dirs. Schenck Sch., Atlanta, 1986-88; exec. vice chmn. bd. trustees Holy Innocents Episcopal Sch., Atlanta, 1976-79; bd. dirs. Atlanta Opera, 1986-89, Emory U. Bus. Sch. Alumni Assn., Atlanta, 1985-88. Mem. Banking Adminstrn. Inst. (ops. and tech. com. chmn. 1987-89, banking services steering com. 1985-89, bd. dirs.), Fin. Execs. Inst., Atlanta C. of C. (pub. affairs coordinating com. 1984-87), Beta Gamma Sigma. Presbyterian. Club: Cherokee Town & Country (Atlanta). Home: 3043 Nancy Creek Rd Atlanta GA 30327 Office: SunTrust Banks Inc PO Box 4418 Atlanta GA 30302

SPIEGEL, SIEGMUND, architect; b. Gera, Germany, Nov. 13, 1919; s. Jakob and Sara (Precker) S.; ed. Coll. City N.Y., 1939-40, Columbia, 1945-50; m. Ruth Josias, Apr. 13, 1945; children—Sandra Renee, Deborah Joan. Came to U.S., 1938, naturalized, 1941. Draftsman, Mayer & Whittlesey, architects, N.Y.C., 1941-47, office mgr., 1947-55; pvt. practice architecture, East Meadow, N.Y., 1956—. Served with AUS, 1941-45; ETO. Decorated Purple Heart, Bronze Star, Croix de Guerre with palme (Belgium); recipient grand prize for instnl. bldgs. (for Syosset Hosp.), L.I. Assn., 1963; grand prize Human Resources Sch., 1966; grand prize Stony Brook Profl. Bldg., 1966; Beautification award, Town Hempstead, N.Y., 1969; Archi award for Harbour Club Apts., L.I. Assn., 1970, for Birchwood Blue Ridge Condominiums, 1974. Fellow Acad. Marketing Sci., L.I.U., 1971. Registered architect, N.Y., N.J., Mass., Md., Va., Pa., Conn., Ga., Vt., Tenn., N.H., Fla.; lic. profl. planner, N.J. Mem. AIA, N.Y. State Assn. Architects, East Meadow C. of C. (pres. 1966). Club: Kiwanis. Author: The Spiegel Plan. Contbr. articles to Progressive Architecture. Prin. works include: Syosset (N.Y.) Hosp., 1962; Reliance Fed. Savs. and Loan Assn. Bank, Queens, N.Y., 1961; Louden Hall Psychiat. Hosp., 1963; Human Resources Sch., Albertson, N.Y., 1964; Nassau Center for Emotionally Disturbed Children, 1968; Harbor Club Apt., Babylon, N.Y., 1968; Reliance Fed. Bank, Albertson, 1967; North Isle Club and Apt. Community, Coram, N.Y., 1972; County Fed. Savs. & Loan Assn., Commack, N.Y., 1972; Birchwood Glen Apt. Community, Holtsville, N.Y., 1972; Bayside Fed. Savs. & Loan Bank Plaza, Patchogue, N.Y., 1973; L.E. Woodward Sch. for Emotionally Disturbed Children, Freeport, N.Y., 1974, Birchwood Sagamore Hills, Blue Ridge and Bretton Woods Condominium Communities, Coram, N.Y., 1975, Maple Arms Condos, Westbury, N.Y., 1982, Dept. Pub. Works, Freeport, N.Y., Nuclear Molecular Resonance Bldg., 1983. Home: 1508 Hayes Ct East Meadow NY 11554 Office: 266 E Meadow East Meadow NY 11554

SPIEGEL, THOMAS, savings and loan association executive; b. 1946. With Columbia Savs. and Loan Assn., Beverly Hills, Calif., 1976—, pres., to 1988, chief exec. officer, also dir. Office: Columbia Savs & Loan Assn 8840 Wilshire Blvd Beverly Hills CA 90211 *

SPIELMAN, DAVID VERNON, insurance, finance and publications consultant; b. Humboldt, Iowa, Dec. 23, 1929; s. Elmo Bruce and Leona Belle (Blake) S.; m. Barbara Helen New, Nov. 24, 1956; children: Daniel Bruce, Linda Barbara. BA, U. Tex., 1966. Publs. engr. IBM Mil. Products, Kingston, N.Y., 1957-58; engring. writer Convair Astronautics div. Gen Dynamics Corp., San Diego, 1958-59; tech. publs. mgr. Ling-Temco Vought, Inc., Garland, Tex., 1960-62; tech. writer Ken Cook Pubs.-Tex. Co., Richardson, Tex., 1963-64; asst. coordinator Kuwait program U. Tex., Austin, 1964-66; ednl. writer Tex. Edn. Agy., Austin, 1966-74; real estate broker Dave Spielman Research Assocs., Austin, 1974—, ins. broker, 1974—; cons. Nat. Ctr. Vocat. Edn., Columbus, Ohio, 1974-75, Tex. State Auditor, Austin, 1976-77, U.S. Dept. Labor, Washington, 1975-78; exec. dir. Tex. Labor Ctr., Inc., 1978—. Counselor Distributive Edn. Clubs Am. Student Conf. Tex., Brenham, 1972; competition judge Tex. Carpenter's Apprentices, 1973-74; chpt. pres. Tex. Pub. Employees Assn., Austin, 1969-70; mem. Dem. Nat. Conv., 1988. Served to sgt. maj. U.S. Army, 1952-53, with USNR 1947-49, with Tex. N.G. 1949-50, cpl. USAF 1950-52. Recipient Outstanding Vocat. Edn. Contributor, Tex. House and Senate. Mem. Acctg. Computer Machinery Assn. (newsletter editor 1958-59), Soc. Tech Writers and Editors (chpt. pres. 1960-61), Soc. Tech. Writers and Pubs. (chpt. pres. 1961-62), Soc. Tech. Communications (membership chmn. 1983-84), Tex. State Tchrs. Assn., Delta Pi (local sec., treas.). Democrat. Presbyterian. Lodges: Masons. Home and Office: 3301 Perry Ln Austin TX 78731

SPIELVOGEL, CARL, marketing and advertising executive; b. N.Y.C., Dec. 27, 1928; s. Joseph and Sadie (Tellerman) S.; m. Barbara Lee Diamonstein, Oct. 27, 1981; children: David Joseph, Rachel Fay, Paul Abram. BBA, CUNY, 1956, LLD (hon.), 1984. Reporter, columnist N.Y. Times, 1950-60; with McCann-Erickson, Inc., Interpublic Group of Cos., Inc., N.Y.C., 1960-74; vice chmn., chmn. exec. com., dir. Interpublic Group of Cos., Inc., 1974-80; chmn., chief exec. officer Backer & Spielvogel, Inc., 1980-87; chief exec. officer, chmn. bd. dirs. Backer Spielvogel Bates Worldwide, Inc., N.Y.C., 1987—; dir. Manhattan Industries, Franklin Corp. Chmn. Com. in the Public Interest, 1975-79, Tri-State United Way, 1984; pres. bd. trustees Baruch Coll. Fund, 1979; mem. Bus. Com. Arts; pres. bd. trustees Baruch Coll. Fund, 1979; bd. dirs., mem. exec. com. Mt. Sinai Hosp., N.Y.C.; bd. dirs. N.Y. Council Humanities, N.Y. Philharmonic, 1987—, The Asian Soc., 1989—; exec. com. Bus. Mktg. Corp., N.Y.C.; chmn. com. div. WNET-Public Broadcasting; trustee, mem. exec. com., chmn. bus. com. Met. Mus. Art. Served with U.S. Army, 1953-55. Recipient Human Relations award Anti-Defamation League, 1972, Achievement award Sch. Bus. Alumni, CCNY, 1972, Citizens Union award, 1980; named Marketer of Yr. N.Y. chpt. Am. Mktg. Assn., 1982, Outstanding Exec. Crain's N.Y. Bus., 1987. Mem. Mcpl. Art Soc. Clubs: Princeton (N.Y.C.), Yale. Office: Backer Spielvogel Bates Worldwide Inc/ Chrysler Bldg 405 Lexington Ave New York NY 10174

SPIERS, RONALD IAN, diplomat; b. Orange, N.J., July 9, 1925; s. Thomas Hoskins and Blanca (De Ponthier) S.; m. Patience Baker, June 11, 1949; children: Deborah Wood, Peter, Martha, Sarah. BA, Dartmouth Coll., 1948; M in Pub. Affairs, Princeton U., 1950. With U.S. Atomic Energy Commn., 1950-54; officer-in-charge disarmament and arms control Dept. State, 1955-61; dir. NATO Affairs, 1962-66; polit. counselor London, 1966-69; dir. Bur. Politico-Mil. Affairs U.S. Dept. State, Washington, 1969-73; U.S. ambassador Nassau, Bahamas, 1973-74; dep. chief-of-mission Am. Embassy, London, 1974-77; U.S. ambassador Ankara, Turkey, 1977-80; dir. intelligence and research U.S. Dept. State, Washington, 1980-81; U.S. ambassador Islamabad, Pakistan, 1981-83; under-sec. for mgmt. U.S. Dept. State, Washington, 1983-89; career ambassador U.S. Fgn. Service, 1984. Served to lt. (j.g.) USN, 1943-46, PTO. Woodrow Wilson fellow Princeton U., 1948. Mem. Am. Fgn. Service Assn., Internat. Inst. Strategic Studies, Council on Fgn. Relations, Ditchley Found. Home: 2315 Kimbro St Alexandria VA 22307 Office: US Dept State 2201 C St NW Rm 7205 Washington DC 20520

SPIES, DONALD KERMIT, management consultant; b. Cleve., Apr. 15, 1935; s. George Donald and Lillian (Bindbeutel) S.; B.A., Case Western Res. U., 1960; student Columbia U., 1956-57; m. Carolyn Post, July 9, 1960; children—John, Robert, Richard, James. Asso., Towers, Perrin, Forster & Crosby, Dallas, 1964, cons., 1965, prin., 1971, mgr. Dallas cons. office, 1977, v.p., 1978—, regional mgr. S. Cent. Region, 1984—, corp. dir., 1985—; dir. group sales Gen. Life Ins. Co., Cleve., 1963-64; with Conn. Gen. Life, 1960-62, Bankers Life Co., 1962-63. Served with USCG, 1952-56. Mem. Am. Compensation Assn., S.W. Pension Conf. (founding chmn. 1974-78), Am. Assn. Pvt. Pension and Welfare Plans (regional chmn.), Internat. Assn. Mgmt. Cons. Methodist. Clubs: City, Northwood, Met. Soc. of Clubs, Bent Tree Country. Home: 6667 Crestway Ct Dallas TX 75230 Office: Lakeside Sq Bldg 12377 Merit Dr Ste 1200 Dallas TX 75251

SPIEVAK, WILLIAM WILSON, steel company official; b. Miami, Fla., Sept. 25, 1942; s. Paul A. and Rosaleen (Wilson) S.; m. Carolyn Joy Moore, Aug. 22, 1960; children: Elizabeth R., Stephanie J. BA, Miami U., Oxford, Ohio, 1964. Cert. compensation profl. Supr. personnel Federated Dept. Stores, Columbus, Ohio, 1964-65; recruiter Battelle Meml. Inst., Columbus, 1965-66, mgr. recruiting, 1966-68, compensation mgr., 1968-70, mgr. compensation and benefits, 1970-76; supt. compensation Wheeling Pitts. Steel Co., 1976-77; dir. compensation and benefits Ball Corp., Muncie, Ind., 1977—; dir. compensation com. Ball Meml. Hosp., Muncie, 1984—. Mem. Am. Compensation Assn. (bd. dirs. 1980-84, regional pres. 1980-81). Office: Ball Corp 345 S High St Muncie IN 47305

SPIGELMIRE, TIMOTHY CONNOR, international management consultant, executive search; b. Balt., May 20, 1946; s. Francis James and Eileen (Connor) S.; m. Patricia Meara, Sept. 7, 1968; children: Jennifer Anne, Christine Joy, Timothy Connor Jr., Andrew Connor, Patricia Coleen. BBA, Loyola Coll., 1968. V.p., dir. John S. Connor, Inc., 1968-85; founder, chief exec. officer Am. Heavy Lift Shipping Co., 1976-78; dir. bus. devel. Loss Mgmt., Inc., Balt., 1985-86; sr. assoc. Booz, Allen & Hamilton, Inc., Bethesda, Md., 1986—; consul Govt. of Denmark, 1982; bd. dirs. Balt. Oper. Sail. Asst. scoutmaster Boy Scouts Am., Balt., 1982. Mem. Propellar Club (Balt.). Republican. Roman Catholic. Office: Booz Allen & Hamilton 7515 Wisconsin Ave Bethesda MD 20814

SPIKERMAN, RICHARD C., banker; b. Monster, Netherlands, Dec. 19, 1940; came to U.S., 1965; s. Pieter Dirk and Geertruida A. (Middendorp) Spijkermans; m. Margaret Ann Seaman, Aug. 12, 1967; 1 child, Richard Charles. B.S. in Bus., Ind. U., Bloomington, 1970; Cert., Grad. Sch. Credit & Fin. Mgmt., London, 1980. Asst. v.p. Am. Fletcher, Indpls., 1968-76; v.p. Wells Fargo Bank, N.Y.C., 1976-79; exec. v.p. Republic Nat. Bank N.Y., N.Y.C., 1979—. Home: 144 Rotary Dr Summit NJ 07901 Office: Republic Nat Bank 452 Fifth Ave New York NY 10018

SPILMAN, RICHARD ALLEN, propane company executive; b. Neosho, Mo., Dec. 1, 1947; s. Charles F. and Floreine A. (Price) S.; m. Mary Ann Shadrix, Oct. 31, 1980; children: Tona Lassetter, Dusty. BSBA, U. Ark., 1969; MBA, Kennedy-Western U., 1989. Regional adminstrn. specialist NCR Corp., Dallas, 1969-70; corp. supr. Frozen Food Express, Dallas, 1970-73; gen. mgr. By-Lo Enterprises, Dallas, 1977-80; dist. mgr. Munford Inc., Atlanta, 1981-83; indsl. sales rep. A.P. Propane AmeriGas, Atlanta, 1983-85, area mgr., 1985—; founder Spilman Resources Unltd., 1988—. Lt. USMC, 1970. Mem. Nat. LP Gas Assn., Am. Mgmt. Assn. Republican. Methodist. Home: 4239 Laurel Brook Dr Smyrna GA 30082 Office: AP Propane AmeriGas PO Box 87516 Atlanta GA 30337

SPILMAN, ROBERT HENKEL, furniture company executive; b. Knoxville, Tenn., Sept. 27, 1927; s. Robert Redd and Lila (Henkel) S.; m. Martha Jane Bassett, Apr. 2, 1955; children—Robert Henkel Jr., Virginia Perrin, Vance Henkel. B.S., N.C. State U., 1950. With Cannon Mills, 1950-57; with Bassett Table Co., Va., 1957-60; dir. Bassett Furniture Industries Inc., 1960-66, exec. v.p., 1966, pres., 1966-82, chmn., pres., chief exec. officer, 1982—; officer, dir. Bassett Furniture Industries Inc.; bd. dirs. The Pittston Co., Greenwich, Conn., Blue Ridge Hardware Co., N.C. Nat. Bank Corp., Charlotte, Trinova Corp., Maumee, Ohio, Jefferson-Pilot Corp., Greensboro, N.C., Internat. Home Furnishings Ctr., High Point, N.C.; bd. govs. Dallas Market Ctr.; adv. bd. Liberty Mut. Ins. Co. Bd. visitors Va. Mil. Inst.; trustee Va. Found. Ind. Colls.; bd. dirs. Blue Ridge Airport Authority. Served to lt. U.S. Army, World War II and Korea. Recipient Best Chief Exec. Officer in Home Furnishing Industry award Wall Street Transcript, 1981, 82; named Humanitarian of Yr., City of Hope, 1982. Mem. Am. Furniture Mgrs. Assn. (James T. Ryan award 1984), So. Furniture Mfrs. Assn. (dir., past pres.), Furniture Factories Mktg. Assn. (past chmn., dir.), Va. Mfrs. Assn. (former mem. exec. com.). Episcopalian. Clubs: Bassett Country, Chatmoss Country, Hunting Hills Country, Brook, Commonwealth, Linville Golf, Sailfish of Fla; Waterfront Golf (Moneta, Va.); Grandfather Golf and Country (Linville, N.C.). Office: Bassett Furniture Industries Inc Main St PO Box 626 Bassett VA 24055

SPINATO, ANTHONY JOSEPH, healthcare executive; b. Easton, Pa., Nov. 11, 1933; s. Joseph and Lena (Ronco) S.; m. Margaret Anne O'Connell, Oct. 5, 1957; 1 child, Linda Marie. B.A., Pa. State U., 1955. Auditor, GAO, Washington, 1955-56; plant acct. Kleen Products Inc., Northwales, Pa., 1958-61; supr. project cost control Air Products & Chems., Inc., Allentown, Pa., 1961-67; contr. Sacred Heart Hosp., Allentown, 1967-69; v.p. fin. Community Gen. Hosp., Reading, Pa., 1969-85; dir. fin. Provincialate of Missionary Sisters of the Sacred Heart, Hyde Park, Pa., 1985—. Bd. dirs. Caron Rehab. Hosps., 1984—; treas., 1988—; treas. Nat. Coun. Alcoholism Berks County, 1981-83; trustee Berks Grand Opera, 1982; mem. adv. bd. Provincialite of Missionary Sisters of the Sacred Heart, Hyde Park, 1978-86. Served with AUS, 1956-58. Fellow Healthcare Fin. Mgmt. Assn. (pres. chpt. 1970-71, bd. dirs. 1971-74; William G. Follmer merit award 1972, Robert H. Reeves merit award 1981, Muncie Gold Merit award 1987), Nat. Assn. Accts. Democrat. Office: 51 Seminary Ave Hyde Park PA 19605

SPINKS, NELDA HUGHES, educator; b. Ruston, La., Sept. 3, 1928; d. Willie B. and Elizabeth Hughes; m. Wyman Allison Spinks, June 12, 1948; 1 son, Hugh Allison. BA, La. Tech. U.; MEd, U. Southwestern La.; Ed.D., La. State U. Cert. tchr., La. Instr. Acadia Baptist Acad., Eunice, La., 1954-63, Lafayette Parish Sch. Bd., 1963-67; asst. prof. U. Southwestern La., Lafayette, 1967-73, 75-87, assoc. prof., 1987—. Author: A Study of the Educational Needs of Potential Office Managers, 1974, (with others) Organizational Communication: A Practical Approach, 1987; guest editorial panelist Baptist Message newspaper, 1988—; panel of editors The State Bapt. Newspaper; contbr. articles to mags. Dir. Elizabeth Hughes Meml. Library, Bethel Bapt. Ch., Lafayette, 1987—. Recipient Postsecondary award Nat. Fed. Ind. Bus. Principles and Econs., 1987, career achievement award Connections, 1987; nominee Outstand Prof. award Amoco Found., 1987. Chmn., bd. dirs. U. Southwestern La. Bapt. Student Union; mem. dean's faculty adv. council U. Southwestern La., 1988—. Mem. Am. Bus. Communication Assn., Assn. Bus. Communication, S.W. Assn. Adminstrv. Services, Am. Mgmt. Assn. Nat. Collegiate Assn. for Secs. (sponsor), La. Assn. Bus. Educators (v.p. 1987-88, pres. 1989—), Nat. Fedn. Ind. Bus. (Outstanding Contributor award 1987), Lafayette C. of C. (edn. com. 1977), Kappa Delta Pi, Omicron Delta Epsilon, Delta Pi Epsilon (historian, editor newsletter 1987-88), Phi Delta Kappa, Phi Kappa Phi. Avocations: needlework, sports, reading. Home: 218 Brentwood Blvd Lafayette LA 70503 Office: U Southwestern La PO Box 41503 Lafayette LA 70504

SPINNER, LEE LOUIS, accountant; b. Hillsboro, Ill., Nov. 9, 1948; s. John Louis and Clara Mae (Brown) S. B.S. in Acctg., U. Ill., 1971, M.A.S. in Acctg., 1972; M.S. in Taxation, DePaul U., 1983. C.P.A., Ill. Sr. tax acct. Ernst & Whinney, Chgo., 1972-78; dir. tax returns and audits Sunbeam Corp., Chgo., 1978-82; dir. tax compliance Sara Lee Corp., Chgo., 1982-83; mgr. tax compliance AM Internat., Inc., Chgo., 1983-85; mgr. taxes Household Mfg., Inc., Prospect Heights, Ill., 1985—; instr. tax tng. program Ernst & Whinney, 1975-78. Tax advisor Sta. WIND, Call Your Acct., Chgo., 1977-78; sec. Grant Park Accts. Softball League, Chgo., 1976-77. Mem. Ill. C.P.A. Soc., Am. Inst. C.P.A.s. Democrat. Roman Catholic. Club: Top Social Athletic (Chgo.). Lodges: Moose, K.C. Home: 9332 Landings Ln Des Plaines IL 60016 Office: Household Mfg 2700 Sanders Rd Prospect Heights IL 60070

SPIRA, JOEL SOLON, electronics company executive; b. N.Y.C., Mar. 1, 1927; m. Ruth Rodale, Nov. 7, 1954; children: Susan, Lily, Juno. BS in Physics, Purdue U., 1948. Project engr. Reeves Instrument Corp., Paramus, N.J., 1952-59; prin. systems analyst ITT Communications Systems, Paramus, 1959-61; pres., dir. rsch. Lutron Electronics Co., Inc., Coopersburg, Pa., 1961—. Office: Lutron Electronics Co Inc PO Box 205 Coopersburg PA 18036

SPIRA, S. FRANKLIN, photographic and video accessories company executive; b. Vienna, Austria, Aug. 7, 1924; came to U.S., 1940, naturalized, 1945; s. Hans and Paula (Back) S.; m. Marilyn Hacker, Sept. 3, 1959; children: Jonathan Bruce, Greg Andrew. Student, CCNY, 1943-45. Pres. Spiratone, Inc., Flushing, N.Y., 1942-87, ret., 1987; mem. acquisitions com. and vis. com. Internat. Mus. Photography, George Eastman House, Rochester, N.Y.; dir. Photographic Art and Sci. Found. Hall of Fame, Oklahoma City; lectrs. at univs. and mus. on photo-history. Author: AP series on camera collecting; frequent contbr., editorial cons. History of Photography Jour.; has been profiled in N.Y. Times and photog. publs.; contbr. articles on history of photography, photographica to various publs. Fellow Am. Photog. Hist. Soc. N.Y.; mem. Soc. Motion Picture and TV Engrs., Soc. Photog. Adminstrs., Inc., Photog. Hist. Soc. New Eng., Photog. Hist. Soc. Calif., Deutsche Gesellschaft für Photographie (Germany), Club Daguerre (Germany), Gesellschaft der Freunde der Photographie und Ihrer Geschichte (Austria), Austrian Inst. N.Y. Jewish.

SPIRER, GARY STEVEN, investment banker, real estate finance and development; b. Rockaway Beach, N.Y., May 21, 1945; s. Leon and Gloria (Wagner) S.; m. Karen Hopē Welber, June 24, 1972; children: Alexandra, Danielle. BA, NYU, 1968; MBA, Columbia U., 1971. Analyst Lazard Freres, N.Y.C., 1971-72; pvt. practice real estate corp. fin. N.Y.C., Hartsdale, N.Y., 1973-78, Boca Raton, Fla., 1978-85; mng. dir., pres. G.S. Securities, Boca Raton, Fla., 1981-88; pres., mng. dir. Capital Hill Group, Boca Raton, 1988; pres. Capital Hill Investment Corp., N.Y.C., 1986—; cons. Buckeye Entertainment, Inc., N.Y.C., Filmstar Inc., N.Y.C., Los Angeles, 1986—; owner S.K. Techs. Mem. Phi Beta Kappa. Republican. Jewish. Office: Capital Hill Investment Corp 60 E 42d St Ste 2913 New York NY 10165

SPIRO, HERBERT TSVI, economist, educator; b. Hattingen, West Germany, Feb. 1, 1927; came to U.S., 1947; s. Georg Josef and Antoinette (Kaufmann) S.; m. Helen Goldstein, July 19, 1952; children: Valerie, Carolyn, Neal. BS, U. Pitts., 1952; MS, Carnegie Mellon U., 1953; PhD, UCLA, 1972. Engr. Ford Motor Co., Detroit, 1953-55; sr. analyst Tech. Operation Inc., Ft. Monroe, Va., 1957-58; mgr. Planning Research Corp., L.A., 1958-62, McDonnell Douglas Corp., Santa Monica, Calif., 1962-69; prof. fin. Calif. State U., Northridge, 1969-88; pres. Am. Valuation Group, Woodland Hill, Calif., 1985—. Author: Finance for the Nonfinancial Manager, 3d edit., 1988, Financial Planning for the Independent Professional, 1978; (with others) Automation and the Library of Congress, 1962. With U.S. Army, 1955-57. Mem. Am. Arbitration Assn., Am. Econ. Assn., Am. Soc. Appriasers (sr.). Home: 17516 Lemarsh Northridge CA 91325 Office: Am Valuation Group 20720 Ventura Blvd #260 Woodland Hills CA 91364

SPISAK-GAMBLE, ANTONINA STANISLAWA, recording company executive; b. Krakow, Poland, Feb. 22, 1946; came to U.S., 1974; d. Mieczyslaw Roman and Zofia Helena (Tworzydlo) Spisak; divorced; 1 child, Dominik M. M in Math., Yagellonian U., Krakow, 1968, PhD in Math., 1974. Asst. prof. math. Yagellonian U., 1968-74; lectr, Grinnell (Iowa) Coll., 1975-80, Tufts U., Medford, Mass., 1980-86; pres. Cathedral Prodns. Inc., Toronto, Can., 1987—; bd. dirs. Dorian Digital Recordings, Toronto, Can.; pres. Assn. of Friends of Papal Organ, Vienna, Austria, 1983—. Author, editor, translator numerous articles in profl. jours. Republican. Roman Catholic. Office: Cathedral Prodns Inc, 9 Humewood Dr Ste 26, Toronto, ON Canada M6C 1C9

SPITZ, ARNOLDT JOHN, corporate professional, consultant; b. Koenigsberg, East Prussia, Germany, Nov. 20, 1929; came to U.S., 1954; s. Josef and Edith (Simon) S; m. Eleanor Marie; children: Allyson, Neil, Nicholas, Francesa. MS, NYU, 1954; PhD, Ruprecht Karls U., Heidelberg, Fed. Republic Germany. Internat. economist Elektro Watt, Sindelfingen, Fed. Republic Germany, 1954-57, Arlen Industries, N.Y.C., 1957-66; sr. cons. and prof. Econ. Adv. Group Freiburg U., Fed. Republic Germany, 1966-70; exec. v.p. VAS Industries, Inc., NYC, 1970-74, Internat. Seaway Trading Corp., Mayfield Village, Ohio, 1974—; sr. cons. and pres. Campus bd., Kent State U., 1974—; sr. cons. Yonsei U., Seoul, Republic of Korea, 1982—; sr. cons. Beijing U., People's Republic of China, 1986—. Adv. Chardon (Ohio) Bd. Edn., 1987; dir. German-Am. Nat. Congress, Chgo., 1970-74. Recipient Spl. Recognition George Washington U., 1979. Mem. Nat. Assn. Accts., Nat. Assn. Bus. Economists, Am. Econ. Assn., Soc. Govt. Econs., Rep. Nat. Com. Roman Catholic. Home: 13046 Millstone Chardon OH 44024 Office: Internat Seaway Trading Corp 6680 Beta Dr Mayfield Village OH 44143

SPITZ, HUGO MAX, lawyer; b. Richmond, Va., Aug. 17, 1927, s. Jacob Gustav and Clara (Herzfeld) S.; m. Barbara Steinberg, June 22, 1952; children: Jack Gray, Jill Ann Levy, Sally. AA, U. Fla., 1948, BLaws, 1951, JD, 1967. Bar: Fla. 1951, S.C., 1955, U.S. Dist. Ct. (so. dist.) Fla. 1951, U.S. Dist. Ct. (ea. dist.) S.C. 1956, U.S. Ct. Appeals (4th cir.) 1957. Asst. atty. gen. State of Fla., Tallahassee, 1951; assoc. Williams, Salomon & Katz, Miami, Fla., 1951-54, Steinberg & Levkoff, Charleston, S.C., 1954-57; sr. ptnr. Steinberg, Spitz, Goldberg, Pearlman Holmes & White, Charleston, 1957—; lectr. S.C. Trial Lawyers Assn., Columbia, 1958—, S.C. U. Sch. Law, Columbia, 1975, S.C. Bar Assn., 1955—. Assoc. mcpl. judge Charleston, 1972-74, mcpl. judge, 1974-76; commr. Charleston County Substance Abuse Commn., 1976-79; bd. govs. S.C. Patient's Compensation Fund, Columbia, 1978-89; adv. mem., atty. S.C. Legis. Council for Workers' Compensation; chmn. bd. dirs. Franklin C. Fetter Health Ctr., Charleston, 1977-78; mem. S.C. Appellate Def. Commn., 1985-86; founding sponsor Civil Justice Found., 1986—; bd. dirs. Charleston Jewish Fedn., 1986—. Pres., Synagogue Emanu-El, 1969-71. Served with USN, 1945-46. Fellow S.C. Bar Assn., U. S.C. Ednl. Found; mem. ABA, Civil Justice Found., S.C. Law Inst., S.C. Trial Lawyers Assn. (pres. 1985-86), S.C. Claimants' Attys. for Worker's Compensation (exec. com. 1986), S.C. Worker's Compensation Ednl. Assn. (bd. dirs. 1978—), S.C. Law Inst., Am. Judicature Soc., N.Y. State Trial Lawyers Assn., Pa. Trial Lawyers Assn., Assn. Trial Lawyers Am. (mem. pres. council 1986—), Nat. Rehab. Assn., Nat. Orgn. Social Security Claimants' Reps. S.C. Bar (chmn. trial and appellate sect. 1982-83; ho. of dels. 1984-85), So. Assn. Workmen's Compensation Adminstrs., Nat. Inst. for Trial Advocacy (com. chmn. 1985). Democrat. Clubs: Hebrew Benevolent Soc. (pres. 1974-75), Jewish Community Ctr. (v.p. 1972-74) (Charleston). Home: 337 Confederate Circle Charleston SC 29407 Office: Steinberg Spitz Goldberg Pearlman Holmes & White PO Box 9 Charleston SC 29402-0009

SPITZ, RANDY JOSEPH, comptroller; b. Urbana, Ill., Aug. 26, 1958; s. Charles Samuel and Colleta Mary (Zwilling) S. BS in Acctg., U. Ill., 1981. CPA, Ill. Audit supr. Kesler & Co., Ltd., Urbana, 1981-86; comptroller Hicks Oils and Hicksgas Inc., Roberts, Ill., 1986—. Parade chmn. Champaign County Freedom Celebration com., Ill., 1986. Mem. Am. Inst. CPA's, Ill. CPA Soc., St. Joseph Jaycees (pres. 1982-83). Roman Catholic. Lodge: KC. Office: Hicks Oil & Hicksgas Inc 204 N Hwy 54 PO Box 98 Roberts IL 60962

SPITZER, PETER GEORGE, healthcare information systems executive; b. Oradea, Romania, July 16, 1956; came to U.S., 1969; m. Anne Taylor, 1985. BS in Bioelec. Engring., MIT, 1979, MS in Elec. Engring. and Computer Sci., 1980; MD cum laude, Harvard U., 1980; MBA, UCLA, 1986. Sr. systems analyst Nat. Cash Register Co., Los Angeles, 1977—; dir. pathology diagnosis registry Peter Brigham Hosps., Boston, 1978-80; research analyst Mass. Gen. Hosp., Boston, 1978-80; resident obstetrician, gynecologist UCLA Ctr. for Health Scis., Los Angeles, 1980-81; v.p. Am. Med. Internat., Info. Systems Group, Beverly Hills, Calif., 1981-87; chief info. officer Tex. Children's Hosp., Houston, 1988—; asst. research prof. pediatrics Baylor Coll. of Medicine, Houston, 1988—. Smith-Kline Found. fellow, 1978-80. Mem. IEEE, Am. Hosp. Assn., Am. Mgmt. Assn., Data Processing Mgmt. Assn., Am. Acad. Med. Dirs., Eta Kappa Nu, Sigma Xi. Office: Tex Children's Hosp 1020 Holcombe #420 Houston TX 77030

SPITZER, RANDAL EUGENE, financial consultant; b. Tacoma, May 20, 1952; s. LeRoy Earl and Corinne Hope (Aune) S.; m. Laurel Noreen Mosier, Oct. 20, 1972; children: Christof J., Heather N. BA in Edn., Pacific Luth. U., 1974. Cert. fin. planner. Tchr. choral music Totem Jr. High Sch., Federal Way, Wash., 1974-75, Colville (Wash.) High Sch., 1975-80, Shadle Park High Sch., Spokane, Wash., 1980-83; fin. cons. Century Cos. Am., Bremerton, Wash., 1983—; sec.-treas. Western Region Century Life, Waverly, Iowa, 1986—. Fin. columnist local newspaper, 1988—. Chmn.

membership com. Bremerton YMCA, 1986-87; chmn. fin. com., mem. council Elim Luth. Ch., Port Orchard, Wash., 1987—; guest vocalist Spokane and Bremerton Symphonies. Recipient Legacy award Kitsap Family YMCA, Bremerton, 1985. Mem. Inst. Cert. Fin. Planners, Olympic Peninsula Assn. Life Underwriters, Olympic Fin. Planners Assn. (pres. 1988), Bremerton C. of C. (chmn. edn. com. 1986—). Lodge: Kiwanis. Home: 3805 Beach Dr E Port Orchard WA 98366 Office: Century Cos Am 400 Warren Ave Suite 310 Bremerton WA 98310

SPIVACK, HENRY ARCHER, life insurance company executive; b. Bklyn., Apr. 15, 1919; s. Jacob and Pauline (Schwartz) S.; m. Sadie Babe Meiseles, Jan. 1, 1941; children: Ian Jeffrey, Paula Janis. Student CCNY, 1936-42; BBA, Am. Coll., Bryn Mawr, Pa., 1965. CLU. Comptroller Daniel Jones, Inc., N.Y.C., 1947-59; field underwriter Union Cen. Life Ins. Co., N.Y.C., 1959-79, mgr. programming dept., 1966-69, assoc. mgr., 1977-79; pension dir. Bleichroeder, Bing & Co., N.Y.C., 1975-77, sr. v.p. new confidence agy., 1979—; pension dir., employee benefit plan cons., pres. Profl. Benefit Planners Inc. N.J.; instr. N.Y. State Ins. Dept., C.W. Post Coll., L.I. U., N.Y. Ctr. for Fin. Studies; coordinator Ins. Dept. Yeshiva U., N.Y.; ins. courses instr.; also lectr., moderator. Contbr. articles to publs. Served with USN, 1943-46. Mem. Life Underwriters Assn. N.Y. (chmn. blood bank), Am. Soc. CLU's (past chmn. N.Y. chpt. pension sect., chmn. profl. liaison com.), Am. Soc. Pension Actuaries, Pensioneers at C.W. Post Coll., C.W. Post Coll. Tax Inst. and Fin. Planning Inst., Practising Law Inst., Internat. Assn. Fin. Planners, Internat. Assn. Registered Fin. Planners (cert.), Internat. Platform Assn., Greater N.Y. Brokers Assn. Lodge: K.P. (life; past dep. grand chancellor N.Y. state). Office: 2 Park Ave 3d Floor New York NY 10016

SPLAINE, ROBERT EMMET, audit manager, consultant; b. N.Y.C., Aug. 31, 1955; s. Robert Emmett and Madeline (Gusman) S.; m. Rita Ann Latz, June 20, 1982; 1 child, Robert. BS, Bryant Coll., 1977; MBA, Pace U., 1981. CPCU. Sr. acct. Continental Ins. Cos., N.Y.C., 1977-81; acct. Great Atlantic Ins. Co., N.Y.C., 1981-83; mgr. fin. reporting Ideal Mutual Ins. Co., N.Y.C., 1983-84; underwriting mgr. Delta Am. Re Ins. Co., Frankfort, Ky., 1984-87, Touche Ross, Newark, N.J., 1987—. Mem. N.Y. Soc. CPCU's. Office: Touche Ross Gateway One Newark NJ 07102

SPOLEY, RICHARD VLADIMIR, manufacturing company executive; b. Salem, Ohio, May 19, 1943; s. Richard Myron and Ruth Edith (Mohrmann) S.; m. Marie Spoley, July 20, 1977 (div.). Student pub. schs., Ordadell, N.J. With N.J. Bell Tel. Co., Newark, 1965-78; plan mgr. Tel Remanu Fracture Co. Am., Ridgway, Ill., 1978-82; product mgr. Tel & Data Systems, Chgo., 1982-84; regional sales mgr. San/Bar Corp., Irvine, Calif., 1984-87; v.p. sales Precision Components Co., Addison, Ill., 1987—. With U.S. Army, 1962-65. Mem. Tel. Pioneers, Assn. U.S. Army, Elks. Republican. Roman Catholic. Home: 5431 NE River Rd Chicago IL 60656

SPOLUM, ROBERT NIC, equipment company executive; b. Aberdeen, S.D., Jan. 8, 1931; s. Arthur and Marvelyn S.; m. Diane Spolum; children: Victoria Ann, Lynne Elizabeth. Student, Grinnell Coll., 1950-51; C.P.A., Acad. Accountancy, Mpls., 1952-53; A.M.P., Harvard U., 1983. Pub. acct. Broeker & Hendrickson of Mpls., 1953-63; comptroller, v.p. Melroe Co., Gwinner, N.D., 1963-70; v.p. Clark Equipment Co.; pres., gen. mgr. Melroe div. Clark Equipment Co., Fargo, N.D., 1971—; bd. dirs. Norwest Bank Fargo, Pioneer Mut. Life Ins. Co. Fargo. Dir. Theodore Roosevelt Medora Found.; mem. govs. mgmt. task force, govs. com. 100. Served with USN, 1949-50. Recipient Silver Knight of Mgmt. award Nat. Mgmt. Assn., 1985. Mem. N.D. Soc. CPAs, Minn. Soc. CPAs, Farm and Indsl. Equipment Inst. (past chmn., U.S. West N.D. adv. bd. 1988—), NAM (dir.), Greater N.D. Assn. (dir., Sci. and Industry award 1976, hon. chmn. Bus. Challange), Am. Legion, Fargo-Cass County Indsl. Devel. Assn. (dir.). Republican. Episcopalian. Club: Fargo Country (dir. 1979-82, pres. 1987). Lodge: Elks. Home: 818 Southwood Dr Fargo ND 58103 Office: Melroe Co 112 N University Dr Fargo ND 58102

SPONHOLZ, JOSEPH GERALD, banker; b. N.Y.C., Feb. 12, 1944; s. Otto George and Kathleen (O'Neill) S.; m. Jane Kathleen McAteer; children: Joseph Christian, Kathleen Jane. BA, Fordham U., 1966; MBA, NYU, 1968. Asst. v.p. Citibank, N.Y.C., 1970-74; ptnr. Booz, Allen & Hamilton, N.Y.C., 1974-81; exec. v.p. Chem. Bank, N.Y.C., 1981-85, chief tech. officer, 1986-88, chief fin. officer, 1988—. Served to 1st lt. U.S. Army, 1968-70. Home: 12 Powder Hill Saddle River NJ 07458 Office: Chem Bank 277 Park Ave New York NY 10172

SPONSKI, JOHN JEROME, financial services executive; b. Detroit, Oct. 21, 1939; s. John Frank and Jeanette Pauline (Nidzgurski) S.; m. Mary Lew Penn; children: Mary Lewellyn, Laura Jean, Samantha Ann. AB in English, Georgetown U., 1961; MBA in Mgmt., Mich. State U., 1973. Mgmt. trainee to v.p. Nat. Bank Detroit, 1967-79; sr. v.p. to exec. v.p. First and Mchts. Bank, Richmond, Va., 1980-83; corp. exec. officer Sovran Fin. Corp., Norfolk, Va., 1984—; bd. dirs. Fifth Fed. Reserve Com. Ops., Bank Adminstrn. Inst., Rolling Meadows, Ill. Contbr. articles to profl. jours., 1973-75. Bd. dirs., v.p. Va. Opera Assn., Norfolk, 1986-88. Served to capt. U.S. Army, 1961-66. Mem. Bank Adminstrn. Inst. (dir.-at-large), Am. Bankers Assn. (exec. com.). Republican. Roman Catholic. Office: Sovran Fin Corp 1 Comml Pl PO Box 600 Norfolk VA 23501

SPOONER, ROSALIND MORRI SPECTOR, retail executive; b. Coral Gables, Fla., Aug. 25, 1950; d. Martin Wilson and Dorothy Joy (Miller) Spector; m. Herbert Spooner, Dec. 7, 1975 (div. July 1985); 1 child, Marshall. BA, Washington U., St. Louis, 1972. With Spec's Music, Inc., Miami, Fla., 1972—, exec. v.p., 1981—. Mem. citizen's bd. U. Miami, 1986—; bd. dirs. Jewish Community Ctr., 1987—. Mem. Nat. Assn. Retail Mchts. Office: Spec's Music Inc 1666 NW 82d Ave Miami FL 33126

SPOOR, WILLIAM HOWARD, food company executive; b. Pueblo, Colo., Jan. 16, 1923; s. Charles Hinchman and Doris Field (Slaughter) S.; m. Janet Spain, Sept. 23, 1950; children—Melanie G., Cynthia F., William Lincoln. BA, Dartmouth Coll., 1949; postgrad., Denver U., 1949, Stanford U., 1965. Asst. sales mgr. N.Y. Export div. Pillsbury Co., 1949-53, mgr. N.Y. Office, 1953-62; v.p. export div. Pillsbury Co., Mpls., 1962-68; v.p., gen. mgr. internat. ops. Pillsbury Co., 1968-73, chmn. bd., chief exec. officer, 1973-85, chmn. emeritus, 1985-87, chmn. exec. com., 1987—, chmn., pres., chief exec. officer, 1988—, also bd. dirs.; dir. Berkley and Co., Inc.; mem. regional export expansion council Dept. Commerce, 1966-74; bd. dirs. Exec. Council Fgn. Diplomats, 1976-78. Exec. com. Minn. Hist. Soc., 1983, Minn. Orchestral Assn., United Negro Coll. Fund, 1973-75; chmn. Capitol City Renaissance Task Force, 1985; trustee Mpls. Found., 1985—; mem. sr. campaign cabinet Carlson Com. U. Minn., 1985—; corp. relations com. The Nature Conservancy, 1985; mem. Nat. Cambodia Crisis Com., Pres.' Pvt. Sector Dept. Transp. Task Force, 1982, Pres.' Pvt. Sector Survey on Cost Control, 1983; chmn. YWCA Tribute to Women in Internat. Industry. Served to 2d lt. inf. U.S. Army, 1943-46. Recipient Golden Plate award, Am. Acad. Achievement, Disting. Bus. Leadership award, St. Cloud State U., Miss. Valley World Trade award, Outstanding Achievement award, Dartmouth Coll., Horatio Alger award, 1986, Medal of Merit, U.S. Savs. Bond Program; honored with William H. Spoor Dialogues on Leadership, Dartmouth Coll. Mem. Grocery Mfrs. Am. (treas., bd. dirs. 1973-84), Nat. Fgn. Trade Council (dir. 1973-75), Minn. Hist. Soc. (bd. dirs.), Minn. Bus. Partnership. Clubs: River (N.Y.C.); Woodhill Country, Lafayette (Wayzata, Minn.); Minneapolis (bd. govs. 1985—), Tower (Mpls.); Delray (Fla.) Yacht, Gulf Stream Bath & Tennis, Gulf Stream Golf (Fla.); Old Baldy (Saratoga, Wyo.). Home: 622 W Ferndale Rd Wayzata MN 55391 Office: The Pillsbury Co Pillsbury Bldg 200 S 6th St Minneapolis MN 55402

SPORCK, CHARLES E., electronic products manufacturing company executive; b. 1928. B.S. in Mech. Engring., Cornell U. With semiconductor div. Fairchild Camera and Instrument Co., 1949-67; pres., chief exec. officer Nat. Semiconductor Corp., Santa Clara, Calif., 1967—, also dir. Office: Nat Semiconductor Corp 2900 Semiconductor Dr Santa Clara CA 95051 *

SPRADLIN, HAROLD WILLIAM, accounting professor; b. Chickasha, Okla., May 23, 1931; s. Clarence Lester and Malinda Mae (Ballard) S.; B.B.A., U. Okla., 1961; m. Norma Jean Schenk, Nov., 1951; children: Sandra Kay, Stacy Ann, Rebekah Lynn. Staff acct. Peat, Marwick, Mitchell & Co., Oklahoma City, 1961-65; pvt. practice acctg., Okla., 1965-74; instr. acctg. Oklahoma City U., 1974-75; sr. v.p., controller United Okla. Bank, Oklahoma City, 1975-80; v.p., treas. Midland Mortgage Co., Oklahoma City, 1980-83, Midland Fin. Co., Oklahoma City, 1983-84; prof. acctg. Oklahoma City U., 1984—; part-time instr. acctg. Oklahoma City U., 1966—. Served with AUS, 1952-54. Mem. Okla. Soc. C.P.A.s. Republican. Maranatha Ch. (deacon). Home: 8608 S Virginia Ave Oklahoma City OK 73159 Office: 2501 N Blackwelder Oklahoma City OK 73106

SPRAGUE, EVERETT RUSSELL, consumer products company executive; b. Inwood, N.Y., Aug. 9, 1915; s. Louie and Eva C. (Davison) S.; m. Karen Olson, Sept. 9, 1967; children—Dian Reed, Linda Kenney, Nancy Chouinard, Russell A. M.E., Stevens Inst. Tech., Hoboken, N.J., 1936, M.S., 1939; D.C.S. (hon.), Am. Internat. Coll., 1978; D. Engr. (hon.), Stevens Inst. Tech., 1988. With Tampax Inc. (named changed to Tambrands, Inc.), Lake Success, N.Y., 1939-88, pres., chief exec. officer, from 1976, chmn., 1981-88, hon. chmn., 1987—, also dir. Trustee, chmn. bd. dirs. Am. Internat. Coll., Springfield, Mass.; emeritus trustee Stevens Inst. Tech. Fellow Soc. Advancement Mgmt. (profl. mgr. citation Western Mass. chpt. 1960); mem. ASME, Phi Sigma Kappa, Tau Beta Pi. Lodges: Monson Rotary, Masons. Office: Tambrands Inc One Marcus Ave Lake Success NY 11042

SPRAGUE, JOHN LOUIS, management consultant; b. Boston, 1930; s. Robert Chapman and Florence Antoinette (van Zelm) S.; m. Mary-Jane Whitney, June 19, 1952; children—John Louis, William Whitney, Catherine van Zelm, David Hyatt. A.B., Princeton, 1952; Ph.D., Stanford, 1959. With Sprague Electric Co., North Adams, Mass., 1959-87; co-dir. engring. labs., sr. v.p. engring. Sprague Electric Co., 1964-65, v.p. research and devel., 1965-66, sr. v.p. semi-condr. div., 1967-76, pres., 1976-87, chief exec. officer, 1981-87; pres. John L. Sprague Assocs. Inc., 1988—; bd. dirs. Sprague Techs. Inc., Sipex Corp., State Mut. Cos. Chmn. Williamstown United Fund-ARC Campaign, 1961; trustee Pine Cobble Sch., 1978. Served to lt. (j.g.) USNR, 1952-55. Mem. IEEE, Electrochem. Soc., Am. Chem. Soc., Sci. Research Soc. Am., Confrerie des Chevaliers du Tastevin, Confrerie de la Chaine des Rotisseurs, Mayflower Hist. Soc., Sigma Xi, Phi Lambda Upsilon. Club: Princeton (N.Y.C.). Home: 124 Chestnut Circle Lincoln MA 01773 Office: John L Sprague Assocs Inc 1 Cranberry Hill Lexington MA 02173

SPRAGUE, MARION WRIGHT, financial consultant; b. Parkersburg, W.Va., Aug. 19, 1923; s. Marion Wesley and Frances (Shields) S.; m. Joyce Letbetter, Sept. 27, 1944 (div. Apr. 1974); children: Marion Wesley, Lee Scott, Laurence Wayne, Dee James; m. Rita Ann LoBianco, July 21, 1974. BBA with honors, Tex. Tech U., 1947; MBA, Northwestern U., 1949. CPA, Tex., Okla., N.Y.; lic. mortgage broker. Audit mgr. Arthur Andersen & Co., Houston, Oklahoma City, 1949-62; v.p., controller Avis, Inc., Mineola, N.Y., 1962-63; v.p. fin. Uni-Serv Corp., Great Neck, N.Y., 1963-68; pres., bd. dirs. Am. Express Credit Corp., Garden City, N.Y., 1966-71; pres., dir. Funding Systems Corp., N.Y.C., 1971-72; exec. v.p. United Electronics Inst., Pompano Beach, Fla., 1981-82; pres., owner Homeowners Funding Systems, Inc., Fort Lauderdale, Fla., 1978—. Bd. dirs. South Fla. Councils Boy Scouts Am., 1979—, previously active Nassau County (N.Y.) Council; chmn. Long Island div. Am. Cancer Society, 1977-78. Served with USN, 1943-46, PTO. Recipient Nat. Disting. Service award Nassau div. Am. Cancer Society, 1970, Silver Beaver award Boy Scouts Am., 1971. Mem. Am. Inst. CPA's, Nat. Assn. Mortgage Brokers, Fla. Assn. Mortgage Brokers (bd. dirs. 1984—, chpt. pres. 1985, Broker of Yr. 1985), Fin. Execs. Inst. (chpt. pres. 1973-74), Delta Sigma Pi (life). Republican. Methodist. Club: Marina Bay (Ft. Lauderdale). Home: 215 SE Third Ave Hallandale FL 33009 Office: Homeowners Funding Systems Inc 2175 State Rd 84 Fort Lauderdale FL 33312

SPRAGUE, PETER JULIAN, semiconductor and computer company executive; b. Detroit, Apr. 29, 1939; s. Julian K. and Helene (Coughlin) S.; m. Tjasa Krofta, Dec. 19, 1959; children: Carl, Steven, Kevin, Michael. Student, Yale U., 1961, MIT, 1961, Columbia U., 1962-66. Chmn. bd. dirs. Nat. Semiconductor Corp., Santa Clara, Calif.; bd. dirs. GEO Internat. Corp. Trustee Strang Clinic. Club: Yale. Home: 249 Undermountain Rd Lenox MA 01240 Office: Indata Corp 645 Fifth Ave 4th Fl New York NY 10022 also: Nat Semiconductor Corp PO Box 58090 Santa Clara CA 95052

SPRAGUE, ROBERTA JANE, accountant; b. Riverside, N.J., May 28, 1947; d. Robert L. Sprague and Doris Mae (Wiley) Dobry. AAS, Burlington County Coll., 1982; cert., Harris Sch. Bus., 1986, The Mgmt. Inst., 1988. Bookkeeper Bob White Flower Shop, Mt. Holly, N.J., 1968-72; office mgr. U.S. Supply Corp., Bristol, Penn., 1972-79; acct. Accountemps, Phila., 1980; controller, acct. H.A. Perotti, Inc., Bristol, 1981-85; acct. Winter Fruit, Inc., Phila., 1985-86; acct., adminstr. Paramount Fruit, Inc., Phila., 1987-88; gen. acct. Union Camp Corp., Trenton, N.J., 1988—. Fellow Nat. Notary Assn., Nat. Assn. Female Execs., Am. Soc. Profl. and Exec. Women, Accts. Pub Interest, Women in Mgmt., Execs. Club, Am. Soc. Women Accts.; mem. Nat. Assn. Accts. (dir. mem. relations 1987-88, v.p. communications and pub. relations, 1988-89, v.p. fin. and adminstrn., 1989-90, sec., 1989-90, dir. pub. relations 1988-89, acknowledgement of Continuing Edn. 1986-87, 87-88, Princeton chpt. Member of Yr. 1987-88), Data Processing Mgmt. Assn. (dir. publicity 1988-89), Big Brothers-Big Sisters (bd. dirs. 1988, 89, 90, fin. and fundraising com. 1988-89, 89-90, treas. 1989-90), Community Accts. (benefit dinner com. 1988-89), Phi Theta Kappa (treas. 1981-82). Baptist. Home: 45 Edgely Ln Willingboro NJ 08046 Office: Union Camp Corp 1400 E State St PO Box 2040 Trenton NJ 08609

SPRAGUE, WILLIAM WALLACE, JR., food company executive; b. Savannah, Ga., Nov. 11, 1926; s. William Wallace and Mary (Crowther) S.; m. Elizabeth Louise Carr, Oct. 3, 1953; children—Courtney, Lauren Duane, William Wallace III, Elizabeth Louise. B.S.M.E., Yale U., 1950. With Savannah Foods & Industries, Inc., 1952—, sr. v.p., 1961-62, v.p., 1962-72, pres., chief exec. officer, 1972—, also bd. dirs.; chmn. exec. com., bd. dirs. C&S Corp., Atlanta; bd. dirs. C&S Nat. Bank, Savannah, Everglades Sugar Refinery, Clewiston, Fla., Sunaid of Fla, Inc., Miami; chmn. bd. dirs. Mich. Sugar Co., Saginaw, Food Carrier, Inc., Savannah, Transales Corp., Savannah; bd. dirs., pres. Adeline Sugar Factory Co., Ltd., Savannah. Chmn. Southeastern Legal Found.; trustee Savannah Bus. Group, 1982-86; mem. steering com. United Way, Savannah; trustee Savannah Benevolent Assn. With USN, 1945-46. Named Sugar Man of Yr. and recipient Dyer Meml. award B.W. Dyer & Co., 1985; named Industrialist of Yr. Internat. Mgmt. Coun., 1988. Mem. World Sugar Rsch. Orgn. (chmn. 1982-85), Grocery Mfrs. Am. (bd. dirs.), The Sugar Assn. (bd. dirs.), NAM (bd. dirs.), Ga. Bus. and Industry Assn. (bd. govs.), Bus. Coun. Ga. (bd. govs.), Savannah C. of C. (bd. dirs.), Carolina Plantation Soc., St. Andrews Soc. Clubs: Oglethorpe, Century (Savannah). Office: Savannah Foods & Industries Inc PO Box 339 Savannah GA 31402

SPRANDEL, DENNIS STEUART, management consulting company executive; b. Little Falls, Minn., June 1, 1941; s. George Washington and Lucille Margaret (Steuart) S.; A.B., Albion Coll., 1963; M.Ed., U. Ariz., 1965; Ph.D., Mich. State U., 1973. Grad. teaching asst. U. Ariz., Tucson, 1964-65; dir. athletics, Owen Grad. Center Mich. State U., East Lansing, 1965-68; prof., dir. student teaching Mt. St. Mary's Coll., 1968-70; exec. dir. Mich. AAU, 1974-81, mem. numerous nat. coms., 1974-81; mem. U.S. Olympic Com., 1974-77; pres., chmn. bd. Am. Sports Mgmt., Ann Arbor, 1976—, Am. SportsVision, 1981—, Am. Sports Research, 1977—, Sprandel Group, 1984—; pres. Nat. Sports & Entertainment, Inc., 1984—, Sprandel Assocs., 1984—; bd. dirs. Nat. Golden Gloves, 1980—. bd. trustees, 1986, Port Huron TV Project, 1985—; pres. Detroit Golden Gloves Charities; pres. adminstrv. bd. Detroit Golden Gloves, 1985—; Bd. dirs. Mich. Sports Hall of Fame, 1976—; Cons. in field. Recipient Detroit Striders award, 1978; Emerald award, 1979; World TaeKwonDo award, 1979; Detroit Spl. Olympics award, 1978; Community Service award Mich. State U., 1985. Mem. Am. Soc. Assn. Execs., Nat. Assn. Phys. Edn. in Higher Edn., AAHPER, Nat. Recreation and Parks Assn., Internat. Boxing Fedn., N.Am. Boxing Fedn., U.S. Boxing Assn., World Boxing Assn., World Boxing Council, Nat. Assn. for Girls and Women in Sport, Psi Chi. Contbr. articles to profl. jours. Home: 5539 Geddes Rd Ann Arbor MI 48105 Office: 3001 State St Ste 10 Ann Arbor MI 48108

SPRANGER, HERMANN BRUNO, II, real estate developer; b. Springfield, Mich., Sept. 9, 1960; s. Hermann Bruno and Janet Arlene (Neusbaum) S. Receiving supr. Kendall Indsl. Supplies, 1980-83; driver U.P.S., 1983-86; owner, mgr. Classy Maids Inc., Springfield, 1986-88; salesman Ron Kuhn Real Estate, 1986—; pres. Baron Investments Inc., 1988—. Mem. Springfield Planning Commn., 1987—. Republican. Lutheran. Home: 282 N 20th St Springfield MI 49015 Office: Ron Kuhn Real Estate Co 110 S Woodrow St Battle Creek MI 49015

SPRATT, MARY CLARE, banker; b. Amboy, Ill., Mar. 23, 1942; d. William H. and Leone W. (Morrissey) Johnson; m. James E. Spratt, Apr. 20, 1963; children: Kimberley A., Robert H. Grad. high sch., Amboy. Sec. bd. dirs. Citizens 1st Nat. Bank, Princeton, Ill., 1976-87, v.p., v.p. investments, 1973—; sec. bd. dirs. Princeton Nat. Bancorp, Inc., 1982-87, v.p., 1987—; bd. dirs. Ohio (Ill.) Centennial Corp.; v.p. Gateway Ctr., Princeton. Dir. Ohio Growth Found., 1988; bd. dirs. CSS #17, 1979-86. Mem. Bur. County Profl. Women, Bur. Valley Country Club, Green River Country Club. Office: Citizens 1st Nat Bank 606 S Main St Princeton IL 61356

SPREIREGEN, PAUL DAVID, architect, planner, author; b. Boston, Dec. 12, 1931; s. Jacob Harold and Janet Elaine (Zisman) S.; m. Rose-Hélène Bester, Oct. 17, 1961. Grad., CIAM Sch., Venice, 1954, M.I.T., 1952-54, Rensselaer Poly. Inst., 1949-51, Boston Mus. Fine Arts Sch., 1946-49. Archtl. designer Studio Architetti BBPR, Milan, Italy, 1954, Uhlin & Malm, Stockholm, 1955; Skidmore Owings & Merrill Uhlin & Malm, N.Y.C., 1956; urban designer Adams Howard & Greeley, Boston, 1958-59, Downtown Progress, Washington, 1960-62; dir. urban design programs AIA, Washington, 1962-66; dir. architecture and environ. arts programs Nat. Endowment for Arts, Washington, 1966-70; architect, planner, author Washington, 1970—; mem. Fed. Commn. for Reconstrn. and Devel. Alaska, 1964; adv. Study of profl. Edn. of Landscape Architects, Ford Found., 1969-72; host weekly radio program Places for People Nat. Public Radio, 1972-84; tchr. Boston Archtl. Center, 1959, Yale U. Sch. Planning, 1966, Catholic U. Grad. Sch. Architecture and Planning, 1967, 77, U. Hawaii, 1968, U. Pa., 1968, U. Tenn., 1969, Harvard U., 1970, Ball State U., 1973-74, Emons Distinguished prof. architecture, 1973-74; profl. adviser Vietnam Vets. Meml. design Competition, Washington, 1981, adv. Intelsat HQ design competition, Washington, 1980; advisor Kent State U. Meml. Design Competition, 1985-86, AT&T/Bell Labs. Solid State Tech. Lab., Upper McCungie, Pa., 1982-83. Author: Urban Design: The Architecture of Towns and Cities, 1965 (also in Japanese and Spanish); (with H. Von. Hertzen) Building a New Town: The Story of Finland's New Garden City, Tapiola, 1971, Design Compeptitions, 1979, William Morgan, Architect, 1987; editor: The Modern Metropolis: Its Origins, Form, Characteristics, and Planning (Hans Blumenfeld), 1967, On the Art of Designing Cities: Selected Essays of Elbert Peets, 1968, Metropolis and Beyond: Selected Essays of Hans Blumnfeld, 1979. Mem. vis. com. on arts M.I.T., 1973-76. Served to 1st lt. C.E. U.S. Army, 1956-58. Waid Edn. Fund grantee, 1967; Innisfree Found. fellow, 1966; Fulbright fellow Italy, 1954-55. Fellow AIA (design citation Potomac chpt. 1974, Student medal 1954, chmn. com. design competitions 1977-84, chmn. com. regional devel. and natural resources 1970-74, com. urban design 1966-74), Am Inst. Interior Designers (hon.); mem. Am. Soc. Landscape Architects (Pres.'s award Potomac chpt. 1968), Am. Planning Assn. (Spl. award 1983). Address: Paul D Spreiregen FAIA 2215 Observatory Pl Washington DC 20007

SPREITZER, CYNTHIA ANN, computer programming professional; b. Chgo., July 16, 1953; d. John Herbert and Patricia Virginia (Tieman) S. BS in Math., Loyola U., Chgo., 1975. Cert. data processor, 1986. Sr. Arthur Andersen and Co., Chgo., 1975-80; lead analyst Larimer County, Ft. Collins, Colo., 1980—. Mem. Assn. Inst. Cert. Computer Profls., Computer Security Inst., Data Processing Mgmt. Assn. Roman Catholic. Home: 610 Grove Ct Loveland CO 80537 Office: Larimer County PO Box 1190 Fort Collins CO 80522

SPRING, JOHN BENHAM, car rental company executive; b. Nashua, N.H., Mar. 28, 1936; s. John D. and Ethel A. S.; m. Susan Kloster, Mar. 29, 1969; children: Jessica, Katherine, Elizabeth, Margaret. A.B., Dartmouth Coll., 1957, M.B.A., 1961. C.P.A., Calif., Mich., Minn., Ill. Mgr. Price Waterhouse & Co., San Francisco, 1961-70; mgr. fin. staff Ford Motor Co., Dearborn, Mich., 1970-74; group v.p. fin. and adminstrn. Nat. Car Rental System, Inc., subs. Household/Internat., Mpls., 1974-77; sr. v.p., chief fin. officer Household/Internat., Prospect Heights, Ill., 1977-83; exec. v.p., fin. Adminstrn. Nat. Car Rental System, Inc., subs. Household/Internat., Mpls., 1983-87; exec.v.p., chief fin. officer Nat. Car Rental System, Inc., Mpls., 1987—. Bd. govs./treas. Children's Theatre Co. Mpls. Served to capt. USMC, 1957-60. Mem. Fin. Execs. Inst. (com. on corp. fin.), Am. Inst. C.P.A.'s. Club: Econ. (Chgo.). Home: 100 SE 2d St #203 Minneapolis MN 55414 Office: Nat Car Rental System Inc 7700 France Ave S Minneapolis MN 55435

SPRINGER, ANDREW ALFRED, food exporter; b. London, England, Jan. 28, 1950; s. Maurice Barnet and Monica Springer; m. Judith Embledon, Apr. 1, 1973 (div. 1973); m. Rebecca Sissel, Dec. 18, 1979; children: Simon, Adam, Ashley. Student, Whittinghame Coll., Brighton, Eng. Salesman Tomato Importer S.A., London, 1966-69; corp v.p. Commn. Co., Inc., Seattle, 1969-78; pres., chief exec. officer Conco Trad Co., Seattle, 1978—; cons. Leegroc Co., Everett, Wash., 1978—; pres., bd. dirs. Shonelene Exch. Inc., Seattle, L.P. Martin Inc., Seattle. With USNR, 1973-78. Mem. Rotary. Republican. Jewish. Home: 15431 192nd Ct NE Woodinville WA 98072 Office: Conco Trad Co PO Box 630 Everett WA 98206

SPRINGER, DOUGLAS HYDE, food company executive, lawyer; b. Englewood, N.J., Jan. 31, 1927; s. Arthur Hyde and Melicent Katherine (Messenger) S.; m. Virginia Helen Chouinard, Nov. 23, 1949; children: Susan Compton, Debora Lee. Student, Wesleyan U., 1944-45; A.B., Yale U., 1947; LL.B., Columbia U., 1950. Bar: N.Y. 1950. Atty. Port of N.Y. Authority, 1950-52; legal counsel Worthington Corp., Harrison, N.J., 1953-61; asst. sec. Worthington Corp., 1956-61; asst. counsel Campbell Soup Co., Camden, N.J., 1961-65, asst. sec., 1965, spl. assignments, 1966, dir. spl. studies, corp. planning, 1966-69, dir. corp. planning frozen foods, 1969-70, asst. treas., 1970-71, treas., 1971-73, v.p. fin. planning, 1973-75, v.p., controller, 1975-78, v.p., treas., 1978-88, v.p. investment mgmt., 1988—; trustee Nexus Healthcare Corp.; mem. adv. bd. Pa. Liberty Mut. Ins. Co.; mem. Eastern regional adv. bd. Arkwright-Boston Mfrs. Mut. Ins. Co., 1971-89; exec. sec. Gov.'s Interstate Adv. Com., 1966; asst. to mem. Pres.'s Commn. on Postal Orgn., 1967-68; spl. asst. to chmn South Jersey Port Corp., 1969-71; mem. N.J. Econ. Devel. Council, 1972-76; mem. adv. council Tax Found. Trustee Nat. Food Processors Assn. Retirement Plan and Trust Indenture Fund, Perkins Center for Arts, 1979-88, Ind. Coll. Fund N.J., Burlington County Meml. Hosp.; mem. exec. bd., v.p. fin. Camden County council Boy Scouts Am. Served with USNR, 1944-46. Mem. ABA, Nat. Assn. Corp. Treas. (bd. dirs. 1982-88), Phila. Treas. Club, Grocery Mfrs. Assn. (econ. policy task force), Internat. Bus. Forum (bd. dirs. 1980-88), Phi Nu Theta, Phi Delta Phi. Republican. Club: Yale (Phila.). Home: 735 Mill St Moorestown NJ 08057 Office: Campbell Soup Co #3 Exec Campus 6th Fl W Rte 70 and Cuthbert Blvd Cherry Hill NJ 08002

SPRINGER, ERIC WINSTON, lawyer; b. N.Y.C., May 17, 1929; s. Owen Winston and Maida Christina (Stewart) S.; m. Cecile Marie Kennedy, Oct. 25, 1958; children: Brian, Christina. AB, Rutgers U., 1950; LLB, NYU, 1953. Bar: N.Y. 1953, Pa. 1975, U.S. Dist. Ct. (we. dist.) Pa. 1978. Law clk. to justice N.Y. State Supreme Ct., 1955-56; research assoc. U. Pitts., 1956-58, asst. prof. law, 1958-64, assoc. prof. law, 1965-68; dir. compliance EEOC, 1967; v.p., dir. Publs. Aspen Systems Corp., Pitts., 1968-71; ptnr. Horty, Springer & Mattern, Pitts., 1971-82, exec. v.p., 1982—; dir. Duquesne Light Co., Pitts. Author: Group Practice and the Law, 1969. Editor Nursing and the Law, 1970; Automated Medical Records and the Law, 1971; contbg. editor monthly newsletter Action-Kit for Hosp. Law, 1973—. Bd. dirs. Presbyn. Univ. Hosp., Pitts., 1966—, Cath. Health Corp., Omaha, 1988—, Hosp. Utilization Project., Pitts., 1975-86; mem. Pitts. Commn. on Human Relations, 1963-68, chmn., 1964-68. Fellow Am. Coll. Healthcare Execs. (hon.), Am. Pub. Health Assn.; mem. ABA, Nat. Bar Assn., Allegany County Bar Assn., Am. Acad. Hosp. Attys. (charter), Order of Coif. Democrat. Office: Horty Springer & Mattern PC 4614 5th Ave Pittsburgh PA 15213

SPRINGER, JOHN SHIPMAN, public relations executive; b. Rochester, N.Y., Apr. 25, 1916; s. Wilfred A. and Alice Jane (Grosjean) S.; m. June Alicia Reimer, June 3, 1953; children: Gary John, Alicia Ann, Cynthia Lynn. Student, U. Toronto, Ont., Can., 1935-37; Ph.B., Marquette U., 1939. Feature writer Rochester Democrat and Chronicle, 1940-41; head mag. publicity RKO Radio Pictures, N.Y.C., 1946-57, 20th Century-Fox Films, N.Y.C., 1957-59; v.p. Arthur Jacobs, Pub. Relations, 1959-60; ptnr. Jacobs & Springer (pub. relations), 1960-62; pres. John Springer Assos., Inc., N.Y.C., Los Angeles, London, Paris and Rome, 1964—. Author: All Talking! All Singing! All Dancing!, 1966, The Fondas, 1970, They Had Faces Then, 1975, Forgotten Films to Remember, 1980; contbr. to: Close Ups, Conversations with Joan Crawford; author mag. articles and newspaper features.; producer film segments Night of 100 Stars; producer/host stage-screen shows starring Bette Davis, Myrna Loy, Sylvia Sidney, Joan Crawford, Rosalind Russell, Debbie Reynolds, Joanne Woodward, Lana Turner, Henry Fonda, others in, N.Y.C., U.S. tour, Australia, Gt. Britain. Served with USAAF, 1942-45. Recipient Byline award Coll. Journalism, 1970, By-line award Marquette U., 1970. Democrat. Roman Catholic. Home and Office: 130 E 67th St New York NY 10021

SPRINGER, WAYNE GILBERT, computer leasing executive; b. El Paso, Tex., Oct. 6, 1951; s. Wayne Gill and Constance A. (Courtney) S.; m. Dianne Louise Slaydon, Jan. 3, 1981; children: Courtney Lee, Carol Jeanne, Kent Slaydon. BS in Engring., U.S. Mil. Acad., 1973; MBA, So. Meth. U., Dallas, 1979, MSCE, 1980. Registered profl. engr. Commd. 2d lt. U.S. Army, C.E., 1973, advanced through grades to capt., 1977, resigned, 1978; grad. sch. instr. So. Meth. U., 1978-80; engr. Fluor Corp., Irvine, Calif. and Houston, 1980-82; coord. project devel. United Energy Resources, Houston, 1982-83; pres., chief exec. officer Computer Leasing Exchange Corp., Houston, 1983—; founder Computer Helpline, Houston, 1984—; ptnr. Springer Cons., Houston and Whittier, Calif. 1980-86. Contbr. articles to profl. jours.; inventor mech. devices. Mem. Houston Conv. and Visitors coun., 1983—, First Congl. Ch. 1981—. Mem. MENSA, MIT Enterprise Forum, West Point Alumni Assn., Houston C. of C., West Houston C. of C., Houston Club, Nottingham Forest Club. Office: Computer Leasing Exch Corp 1003 Wirt Rd Ste 100 Houston TX 77055

SPRINGER, WILLIAM H., communications executive; b. Chgo., 1929; married. BA, Grinnell Coll., 1950; MS, MIT, 1968. With acctg. dept. AT&T, 1959-62; with Ill. Bell Telephone Co., Chgo., 1950-59, 62—, v.p. mktg., 1969-71, v.p. market planning, then v.p., comptroller, 1971-75, sec., v.p., comptroller, 1975-80, exec. v.p. fin., sec., 1980-83, sr. exec. v.p., treas., sec., 1983—; vice chmn., chief fin. officer Ameritech, Chgo., 1984-87, vice chmn., chief fin. and adminstrv. officer, 1987—, also bd. dirs. Office: Ameritech 30 S Wacker Dr Ste 3800 Chicago IL 60606

SPRINGSTEEN, DAVID FOLGER, financial consultant; b. N.Y.C., Mar. 29, 1932; s. Nelson J. and Gwendolyn (Folger) S.; BS, MIT, 1954; MBA, Harvard U., 1958; m. Nancy Neller, Oct. 22, 1955; children: Susan Jamieson, Linda Vanatta. Aero. rsch. scientist Lewis Flight Propulsion Lab. NASA, Cleve., 1955-57; with Chase Manhattan Bank, N.Y.C., 1958-71, asst. treas., 1961-64, 2d v.p., 1964-68, v.p. Energy div., 1969-71; v.p. corp. fin. Stone & Webster Securities Corp., 1971-74; v.p. corp. fin. E.F. Huttons & Co., Inc., N.Y.C., 1974-78; fin. cons., corp. fin. David F. Springsteen Co., Greenwich, Conn., 1978—. Served to lt. USAF, 1955-57. Mem. Holland Soc. Home: PO Box 248 Snow Hill Point Grantham NH 03753 Office: 205 Shore Rd Greenwich CT 06830

SPRINKEL, BERYL WAYNE, economist, consultant; b. Richmond, Mo., Nov. 20, 1923; s. Clarence and Emma (Schooley) S.; m. Barbara Angus Pipher; children: Gary L., Kevin G., Debra, Pamela. Student, N.W. Mo. State U., 1941-43, U. Oreg., 1943-44; BS, U. Mo., 1947; MBA, U. Chgo., 1948, PhD, 1952; LHD (hon.), DePaul U., 1975; LLD (hon.), St. Michael's Coll., 1981, U. Mo., 1985, U. Rochester, 1985, Govs. State U., 1988, U. Nebr., 1988; Doctor of Pub. Adminstrn., Marion Coll., 1988. Instr. econs. and fin. U. Mo., Columbia, 1948-49, U. Chgo., 1950-52; with Harris Trust & Savs. Bank, Chgo., 1952-81, v.p., economist, 1960-68, dir. rsch., 1963-69, sr. v.p., 1968-74, economist, 1968-81, exec. v.p., 1974-81; undersec. monetary affairs Dept. Treasury, Washington, 1981-85; chmn. Coun. Econ. Advisers, The White House, Washington, 1985-89, mem. Pres.'s Cabinet, 1987—; cons. Fed. Res. Bd., 1955-59, Bur. of Census, 1962-70, Joint Econ. Com. U.S. Congress, 1958, 62, 67, 71, Ho. of Reps. Banking and Currency Com., 1963, Senate Banking Com., 1975; mem. econ. adv. bd. to sec. commerce, 1967-68; bd. economists Time mag., 1968-80. Pres., Homewood-Flossmoor (Ill.) Community High Sch., 1959-60. Author: Money and Stock Prices, 1964, Money and Markets-A Monetarist View, 1971; co-author: Winning with Money, 1977;. With AUS, 1943-45. Recipient Hamilton Bolton award Fin. Analysts Assn., 1968. Fellow Nat. Assn. Bus. Economists; mem. Am. Econ. Assn., Nat. Assn. Bus. Economists, Beta Gamma Sigma. Home: 20140 St Andrews Dr Olympia Fields IL 60461 Office: 135 S LaSalle St Rm 2610 Chicago IL 60603

SPRITZER, SAMUEL LEWIS, financial executive; b. Bklyn., Sept. 15, 1954; s. Murray Graham and Sylvia (Lerner) S.; m. Stephanie Gaudio, Oct. 7, 1979; 1 chld, Michael Stephen. BBA in Acctg., Pace U., 1976. Auditor N.Y. State Dept. Law, N.Y.C., 1976-81; sr. acct. Covenant House, N.Y.C., 1981-82, mgr. gen. acctg., 1982-83, controller, 1983-88, dir. fin., treas., 1988—. Mem. Nat. Assn. Accts. Office: Covenant House 460 W 41st St New York NY 10036

SPRONG, GERALD RUDOLPH, banker; b. Rodman, Iowa, Oct. 16, 1933; s. Earl Frank and Minnie Viola (Schroeder) S.; m. Barbara J. Sprong, Oct. 7, 1956; children: Lisa Sprong Whitacre, Bradley N., Douglas R. BS in Edn., N.W. Mo. State U., 1956. CPA, Mo. Ptnr. Peat, Marwick, Mitchell & Co. CPA's, Kansas City, Mo., 1958-73; pres., chief exec. officer Ameribanc, Inc., St. Joseph, Mo., 1973—; also bd. dirs. Ameribanc, Inc.; bd. dirs. Am. Banke, St. Joseph, Kansas City, St. Louis, St. Joseph Light and Power. Bd. dirs. St. Joseph Devel. Corp., Sch. Dist. Found., United Way, Jr. Achievement, 1956—; trustee William Jewell Coll., Liberty, Mo., 1973-88; chmn., bd. dirs. Coordinating Bd. for Higher Edn., Jefferson City, Mo., 1980-86. 1st lt. USMC, 1955-58. Recipient awards Girl Scouts Am., N.Y.C., 1987—. Mem. Am. Inst. CPA's, St. Joseph C. of C. (bd. dirs.). Clubs: St. Joseph Country; River (Kansas City). Office: Ameribanc Inc 1 Robidoux Ctr Saint Joseph MO 64501

SPROUL, JOHN ALLAN, public utility executive; b. Oakland, Calif., Mar. 28, 1924; s. Robert Gordon and Ida Amelia (Wittschen) S.; m. Marjorie Ann Hauck, June 20, 1945; children: John Allan, Malcolm J., Richard O., Catherine E. A.B., U. Calif., Berkeley, 1947, LL.B., 1949. Bar: Calif. 1950. Atty. Pacific Gas & Electric Co., San Francisco, 1949-52, 56-62; sr. atty. Pacific Gas & Electric Co., 1962-70, asst. gen. counsel, 1970-71, v.p. gas supply, 1971-76, sr. v.p., 1976-77, exec. v.p., 1977-89, cons., 1989—; gen. counsel Pacific Gas Transmission Co., 1970-73, v.p., 1973-79, chmn. bd., 1979-89, also dir.; atty. Johnson & Stanton, San Francisco, 1952-56; bd. dirs. Alta. and So. Gas Co. Ltd., Alta. Natural Gas Co. Ltd., Oregon Steel Mills, Inc. Bd. dirs. Hastings Coll. of Law. Served to 1st lt. USAAF, 1943-46. Mem. Calif. Bar Assn., Am. Gas Assn., Pacific Coast Gas Assn. Clubs: Engineers, World Trade (San Francisco); Commonwealth, Bohemian, Pacific-Union, Orinda Country. Home: 8413 Buckingham Dr El Cerrito CA 94530 Office: Pacific Gas & Electric Co 77 Beale St San Francisco CA 94106

SPROUSE, JOHN ALWYN, retail executive; b. Tacoma, Nov. 23, 1908; s. Robert Allen and Jenne (Glaessel) S.; m. Mary Louise Burpee, Dec. 27, 1932 (div. June 1954); children—Lucy (Mrs. Clyde B. Fletcher), Robert Allen II, John Edward; m. Barbara Barker, May 22, 1955 (dec. July 1983). Student, U. Oreg., 1926-28. With Sprouse-Reitz Stores Inc., Portland, Oreg., 1928—, asst. to pres., 1945-61, pres., 1961-74, chmn. bd., 1974-86, hon. chmn., 1986—; Expert cons. to Q.M. Gen., 1943-45. Mem. U.S. Power Squadron, USCG Aux., Delta Upsilon. Clubs: Rotarian. (Portland), Yacht (Portland), Arlington (Portland), Multnomah (Portland). Office: Sprouse-Reitz Stores Inc PO Box 8996 1411 SW Morrison St Portland OR 97208-8996

SPROUSE, ROBERT ALLEN, II, retail chain store executive; b. Portland, Oreg., Dec. 25, 1935; s. John Alwyn and Mary.Louise (Burpee) S.; m. Frances Carolyn Russell, June 22, 1957. Student, Williams Coll., 1953-57. With Sprouse-Reitz Stores Inc., Portland, 1957—; buyer, sec. Sprouse-Reitz Stores Inc., 1963-69, v.p., 1969-73; pres. —, 1973—; chief exec. officer Sprouse-Reitz Stores Inc., 1986—; also bd. dirs. Active Jr. Achievement, Good Samaritan Hosp. Found. Mem. Chief Execs. Orgn., Portland Met. C. of C., Theta Delta Chi. Republican. Episcopalian. Clubs: Multnomah Athletic (Portland); Arlington. Lodge: Rotary. Office: Sprouse-Reitz Stores Inc PO Box 8996 Portland OR 97208-8996

SPRUNGER, RUSSELL ROBERT, software company marketing executive, consultant; b. Decatur, Ind., Jan. 21, 1953; s. Bruce William and Galen Arlene (Fox) S.; m. Debra Lynette Fields, Aug. 24, 1974 (div. May 1982); children: Brandon L., Brock R., Kimberly L.; m. Hope Frances Linklater, Feb. 8, 1986. BS in Math. and Physics summa cum laude, Lakeland Coll., 1975; MS in Computer Sci., Purdue U., 1978. Software engr. I Tektronix Inc., Beaverton, Oreg., 1978-80, software engr. II, 1980-81, sr. systems analyst, 1981; founder, sec. Graphic Software Systems, Beaverton, 1981—, v.p. engring., 1981-86, dir. mktg., 1987—; bd. dirs. Bevcon, Inc., Newberg, Oreg. Contbr. articles to profl. jours. Dir. choir 1st United Meth. Ch., Newberg, fin. chmn. 1987—. Mem. Assn. for Computing Machinery. Republican. Home: Rte 5 Box 140M Sherwood OR 97140

SPUNGIN, JOEL D., wholesale office supplies and equipment executive; b. 1937. With United Stationers Supply Co., Des Plaines, Ill., 1958—, exec. v.p., 1973-77, pres., chief operating officer, 1977-81; with United Stationers Inc., Des Plaines, 1981-87, pres., chief operating officer, 1987-88, vice chmn., chief exec. officer, 1988, chmn., chief exec. officer, 1989—. Office: United Stationers Inc 2200 E Golf Rd Des Plaines IL 60016

SPUNT, SHEPARD ARMIN, realty executive, management and financial consultant; b. Cambridge, Mass., Feb. 3, 1931; s. Harry and Naomi (Drooker) S.; B.S., U. Pa., 1952, M.B.A., 1956; m. Joan Murray Fooshee, Aug. 6, 1961 (dec. June 1969); children—Erica Frieda and Andrew Murray (twins). Owner, Colonial Realty Co., Brookline, Mass., 1953—, Cambridge, 1960—; sr. assoc. Gen. Solids Assocs., 1956—; chmn. bd. Gen. Solids Systems Corp., 1971-74; trustee Union Capital Trust, Boston; incorporator Liberty Bank & Trust Co., Boston. Chmn., Com. for Fair Urban Renewal Laws, Mass., 1965—; treas. Ten Men of Mass., 1980. Pres., New Eng. Council of Young Republicans, 1964-67, 69-71; vice chmn. Young Rep. Nat. Fedn., 1967-69, dir. region I, 1964-67, 69-71; mem. Brookline Republican Town Com., 1960—; del. Atlantic Conf. Young Polit. Leaders, Brussels, 1973; bd. dirs. Brookline Taxpayers Assn., 1964—, v.p., 1971-72, pres., 1972—. Registered profl. engr., Mass. Mem. Nat. Soc. Profl. Engrs., Rental Housing Assn., Greater Boston Real Estate Bd., Navy League, Boston Athenaeum, Copley Soc. Boston. Lodges: Masons, Shriners. Author: (with others) A Business Data Processing Service for Small Business Practitioners, 1956; A Business Data Processing Service for Medical Practitioners, 1956, rev. edit., 1959. Author, sponsor consumer protection and election law legislation Mass. Gen. Ct., 1969—. Patentee in field of automation, lasers, dielectric bonding. Home: 177 Reservoir Rd Chestnut Hill MA 02167 Office: 21 Elmer St Cambridge MA 02238-0172

SPURDLE, JOHN W., JR., banker; b. Orange, N.J., July 30, 1937; s. John William and Margaret (Lefferts) S.; m. Cynthia Warren Stauffer, Aug. 29, 1959; children—Sarah Stuart, Margaret Warren. B.A., Wesleyan; M.B.A., Harvard U. With Morgan Guaranty Trust Co., N.Y.C., 1961-64, asst. treas., 1964-68, v.p., 1968-77, sr. v.p., 1977-84, exec. v.p., 1984—. Office: Morgan Guaranty Trust Co 23 Wall St New York NY 10015

SQUAZZO, MILDRED KATHERINE (OETTING), corporate executive; b. Bklyn., Dec. 22; d. William John and Marie M. (Fromm) Oetting; student L.I. U. Sec.-treas., Stanley Engring., Inc. and v.p. Stanley Chems., Inc., 1960-68; founder, pres. Chem-Dynamics Corp., Scotch Plains, N.J., 1964-68; gen. adminstr., purchasing dir., Richardson Chem. Co., Metuchen, N.J., 1968-69; owner Berkeley Employment Agy. and Berkeley Temp. Help Service, Berkeley Heights, N.J., 1969—, Berkeley Employment Agy., Morristown, N.J., 1982, Bridgewater, N.J., 1987—; pres. M.K.S. Bus. Group, Inc., Berkeley Heights, 1980—; mgmt. cons.; personnel fin.; lectr. Served with Nurse Corps, U.S. Army, 1946-47. Mem. Nat. Bus. and Profl. Women's Club. Office: 312 Springfield Ave Berkeley Heights NJ 07922

SQUILLACE, ALEXANDER PAUL, investment advisor; b. Missoula, Mont., Feb. 25, 1945; s. Dominick Paul and Kathleen Marie S.; B.S. in Bus. Adminstrn., Ohio State U., 1967; m. Miriam Palmer Patterson, June 17, 1967; children—Sandra, Scott, Brian, Susan. Investment analyst Nationwide Ins. Cos., Columbus, Ohio, 1967-69; instl. bond rep. Hornblower & Weeks-Hemphill, Noyes, Columbus, 1969-71, mgr. fixed income securities, Indpls., 1971-74; v.p. United Nat. Bank-United Nat. Corp., Sioux Falls, S.D., 1974-79; pres. Investment Mgmt. Group, Sioux Falls, S.D., 1979-85, Farmers State Bank, Stickney, S.D., 1979-88, Bormann Ins. Agy., Stickney, 1979-88, Fin. Services Group Inc., 1984—; chmn. S.D. Investment Council, Postal Bus. Group Inc., 1986—; dir. Prairie States Ins. Co., 1988, Lemars Mutual Ins. Co., 1988, Western Warehouse, Inc.; instr. Am. Inst. Banking. Named hon. citizen of Indpls., 1974; chartered fin. analyst. Fellow Fin. Analysts Fedn.; mem. Am. Inst. Banking, S.D. Bankers Assn., S.D. Investment Soc., Twin Cities Soc. Security Analysts, Ohio State Alumni Assn. Home: 2009 E 52d St Sioux Falls SD 57103 Office: 100 South Dakota Ave Sioux Falls SD 57102

SQUIRES, JAMES RALPH, construction company executive; b. Dillon, S.C., Jan. 2, 1940; s. William Guilford and Ruby Alice (Whittington) S.; student public schs., Charlotte, N.C.; m. Ann Newton, Apr. 17, 1965; children—Samuel Guilford, James Drew. With Squires Constrn. Co., 1959-62; pres. SBS Builders, Inc., Charlotte, 1968-70; pres. Ralph Squires Homes, Charlotte, 1970-88, Squires & Assos., Realtors, 1975-88, JRS Enterprises, Inc., 1976-88, Squires Enterprises, Inc. Mem. Charlotte Tree Commn., 1977; bd. dirs. Athletic Found. U. N.C., Charlotte, 1979, Providence Day Sch., 1981-84, Better Bus. Bur., 1983; appointee pub. mem. N.C. State Bar; pres. Metrolina Home Owners, 1982, bd. dirs., 1983; bd. govs. Polit. Action Com for Building Industry; mem. Mercy Hosp., Charlotte, bd. visitors, 1986; mem. exec. council Boy Scouts Am. Mecklenburg County council, 1986; exec. council Muscular Dystrophy Assn., Charlotte, 1987. Recipient Profile award N.C. Blue Cross/Blue Shield, 1974, Albert Gallatin merit cert., 1974; named Charlotte Builder of Yr., 1977. Mem. Charlotte Homebuilders Assn. (pres. 1974), N.C. Home Builders Assn. (v.p. 1975), Nat. Homebuilders Assn., Charlotte Bd. Realtors, Carolina Ambassadors, Safari Club Internat. (Carolina chpt.). Republican. Baptist. Club: Charlotte Athletic, Piper Glen, Carmel Country. Home: 8811 Winged Bourne Charlotte NC 28210

STAAB, THOMAS EUGENE, chemist; b. Peoria, Ill., Jan. 26, 1941; s. Leo Reuben and Mary Blanche (Griffin) S.; BS in Chemistry, St. Louis U., 1963; m. Donna Marie Murnighan, May 30, 1967; children: Lynn Anne, Thomas Patrick. Research and devel. chemist for elastomers Victor Products div. Dana Corp., Chgo., 1963-65, application engr. for oil seals, 1965-67, application engring. supr. for oil seals, 1967-70, chief product engr. for oil seals, 1970-72, mgr. sales and engring., Ft. Wayne, Ind., 1972-73, chief product engr. for oil seals, Chgo., 1973-75, prodn. supr., 1975-77, materials engr. for gaskets, 1977-79, mgr. oil seal engring., Lisle, Ill., 1979-82, chief devel. engr. materials, 1982-83, mgr. materials devel., 1983-86, mgr. tech. services, 1986—. Alliance chief Y Indian Guides, 1975-76; mgr./coach Little League, 1978-81. Mem. Rubber Mfrs. Assn. (past chmn. oil seal tech. com.), Soc. Automotive Engrs. (past mem. adv. bd. of sealing com.), Am. Chem. Soc. Roman Catholic. Patentee hydrodynamic shaft seal, rotary shaft seals, antistick, non-liquid absorbing gasket. Home: 512 S Lincoln St Hinsdale IL 60521 Office: 1945 Ohio St Lisle IL 60532

STAAB, THOMAS ROBERT, textile company financial executive, controller; b. Beaver Falls, Pa., Apr. 23, 1942; s. Henry Louis and Margaret Constance (Clarke) S.; m. Angela Maria Simon, Aug. 5, 1965; children: Thomas II, Jennifer, Thea. BBA, U. Pitts., 1964, MBA, 1965. CPA, Pa. Sr. audit mgr. Price Waterhouse & Co., Pitts., 1970-77; practice fellow Fin. Acctg. Standards Bd., Stamford, Conn., 1978-80; sr. audit mgr. Price Waterhouse & Co., N.Y.C., 1981; controller Fieldcrest Cannon Inc., Eden, N.C., 1982—. Served to lt. USN, 1966-70. Mem. Am. Inst. CPA's, Pa. Inst. CPA's, N.C. Textile Mfrs. Assn., Am. Textile Mfrs. Inst. Republican. Roman Catholic. Home: PO Box 214 Rte 4 Reidsville NC 27320 Office: Fieldcrest Cannon Inc 326 E Stadium Dr Eden NC 27288

STACEY, NORMA ELAINE, farmer, civic worker; b. Roanoke, La., Sept. 13, 1925; d. August and Julie (Ravet) Trahan; m. Louis Brewer, June 10, 1949 (dec. 1978); children: Louis Timothy Brewer, John August Brewer; m. Truman Stacey, Feb. 2, 1980. BA, St. Mary's Dominican Coll., New Orleans, 1946. Acct. Cities Svc. Refining Corp., Lake Charles, La., 1946-49; sec. La. Tchrs. Retirement System, Baton Rouge, 1950-51; bus. mgr. Brewer Studios, Lake Charles, 1951-78; co-owner Ravet Estate, Bell City, La., 1958—, Trahan Farm, Lake Arthur, La., 1969—; co-owner Trahan Ins. Agy., Welsh, La., 1964-72, Trahan Estate, Fenton, La., 1969—. Mem. Lake Charles Messiah Chorus, 1946-52; choir singer Immaculate Conception Ch., 1946-52, chmn. landscaping com., 1975-82; chmn. scrapbook com., mem. ticket com. Lake Charles Community Concerts, 1955—; coordinator Art Assocs., Lake Charles, 1955-58; mem. ticket com. Lake Charles Symphony Auxiliary, 1957—, sec., 1960-61, treas., 1962-64; vol. librarian Landry Meml. High Sch., Lake Charles, 1963-68; active St. Patrick Hosp. Auxiliary, 1965—; sec. Gov. La.'s Program for Gifted Childern McNeese State U., Lake Charles, 1978-80; mem. scholarship com. McNeese State U. Found., 1979—; mem. com. on scouting, vol. sec. and receptionist, chmn. decorating com. Diocese of Lake Charles, 1980—, sec., 1980-84, mem. Companions of Honor, 1982—; mem. Cath. com. on scouting South Cen. Region, Lake Charles, 1981—, regional sec., 1985—; mem. emblems subcom. Nat. Cath. Com. on Scouting, Irving, Tex., 1981—; mem.-at-large Calcasieu Area council Boy Scouts Am., Lake Charles, 1980—; bd. dirs. Lake Charles Symphony Soc., 1981—, mem. pops com., 1981, membership co-chmn., 1982-83, chmn., 1983-84, program chmn., 1985—, mem. endowment com., 1987; patron La. Choral Found., Lake Charles, 1982—. Recipient Nat. Honors award Am. Guild Piano Competitions, 1943-45, Bronze Pelican Emblem award Nat. Cath. Com. on Scouting, 1984; named to Scouting Roll of Honor Diocese of Lake Charles, 1982; named Dame Equestrian Order of Holy Sepulchre of Jerusalem, 1982, Dame Comdr., 1987. Mem. AAUW (treas. pre-sch. program 1954-58), Am. Rose Soc., Lake Charles Rose Soc., Lake Charles Garden Club (treas. 1958-61, sec. 1962-64, chmn. telephone com. 1964-86, cert. Appreciation 1985), Les Etudientes Book Club, Pioneer Club, NCCJ (corr. sec. local chpt. 1988—). Democrat. Home and Office: 1802 2d Ave Lake Charles LA 70601

STACHNIK, RONALD ANTHONY, data processing executive; b. Detroit, Aug. 27, 1945; s. Anthony Clarence and Clara Marie (Pleva) S.; m. Diane Jean Carter, Apr. 17, 1971; children: Chad, Jennifer, Matthew, Joshua. BS, Eastern Mich. U., 1968. Research asst. U. Mich., Ann Arbor, 1968-69; computer programmer Buhr Machine Tool Corp., Ann Arbor, 1969-72; computer operator Coll. Am. Pathologists, Traverse City, Mich., 1972-74, asst. supr. computer ops., 1974-75, computer svcs. mgr., 1975-82, data processing svcs. mgr., 1982—. Mem. Kiwanis, K.C. Roman Catholic. Home: 3705 Randolph St Traverse City MI 49684 Office: Coll Am Pathologists Computer Ctr 13919 W Bay Shore Dr Traverse City MI 49684

STACHO, ZOLTAN ALADAR, construction and engineering company executive; b. Budapest, Hungary, Mar. 16, 1930; came to U.S., 1957; s. Aladar and Elizabeth (Balazs) S.; m. Maria E. Belatini, July 4, 1951; children: Dorika, Carla. MSCE, U. Tech. and Ec. Sci., Budapest, 1952. Registered profl. engr. Colo., Calif., Mass., Mich., Ga., N.Y., Pa. Chief engr. U.S. Army, Air Force Exchange, 1963-65; project mgr. PBQ&D, San Francisco, Boston, 1965-70; projects mgr. Kaiser Engrs., Inc., Oakland, Calif., 1970-78, v.p., 1978-84, group v.p., 1984-86, exec. v.p., 1986—, also bd. dirs. Contbr. articles to profl. jours. Mem. ASCE, Project Mgmt. Inst. Roman Catholic. Home: 1333 Jones St San Francisco CA 94109 Office: Kaiser Engineers Inc 1800 Harrison St Oakland CA 94623

STACHURA, JOHN ANDREW, JR., coal company executive; b. Waynesburg, Pa., Feb. 21, 1949; s. John Andrew and Mary (Lukaszczyk) S.; m. Sara Lee Gates, Sept. 15, 1973; children: Kristen, Andrew. BS in Bus. Mgmt., Ind. State U., 1972. With Peabody Coal Co., Universal, Ind., 1972-74, Amax Coal Co., Keensburg, Ill., 1974-75; instr. health and safety Amax Coal Co., Chandler, Ind., 1975-76, supr. health and safety, 1976-77; drilling and blasting foreman Amax Coal Co., Gillete, Wyo., 1977-78; v.p., gen. mgr. J&R Coal Co., Bicknell, Ind., 1978-86; supt. Undergroud Coal, Inc., Washington, Ind., 1987—; v.p. Wheatland (Ind.) Tire, Inc.; owner, mgr. K&R Real Estate, Vincennes, Ind.; bd. dirs. Am. Nat. Bank, Vincennes. Mem. IVV Tech. Coll. adv. bd., Terre Haute, Ind.; sponsor Boy Scouts Am., Vincennes, 1985, Children and Family Services, Vincennes, 1985. Named Eagle Scout Boy Scouts Am., 1962, to Hon. Order Ky. Cols., State of Ky., 1984, Sagamore of the Wabash State of Ind., 1989. Mem. Soc. Mining Engrs., Ind. Mining Inst. (pres., 1986), Ind. Coal Coun. (bd. dirs. 1980-88), INd. Mining and Tech. Soc., INd. Mining Bd. (bd. dirs. 1985-88). Republican. Roman Catholic. Clubs: Harmony Soc. (Vincennes); Bruceville (Ind.) Rod and Gun. Lodges: KC, Elks. Home: RR 6 Box 226 Vincennes IN 47591 Office: Underground Coal Inc PO Box 740 Washington IN 47501

STACK, DIANE VIRGINIA, medical center financial officer; b. Schenectady, N.Y., June 14, 1958; d. Albert Ross and Irene Anne (Lajeunesse) Musick; m. Robert Michael Stack, June 27, 1981; 1 child, Kelly Irene. BBA in Acctg., U. Mass., 1980. CPA, Mass. Staff acct. Stavisky, Shapiro & Whyte, Boston, 1980-84; asst. controller Joslin Diabetes Ctr., Boston, 1984-88; controller Marlborough (Mass.) Hosp., 1988—. Mem. Mass. Soc. CPA's, Hosp. Fin. Mgmt. Assn. Republican. Home: 106 Cherry St Framingham MA 01701 Office: Marlborough Hosp 57 Union St Marlborough MA 01752

STACK, ROBERT DOUGLAS, marketing communications executive; b. Las Vegas, Nev., Nov. 15, 1956; s. Benjamin J. and Doris J. (Rappaport) S. BS cum laude, Boston U., 1977. Salesman Stack's, N.Y.C., 1977-79; pres. Robert Stack Assocs., N.Y.C., 1979—; adj. faculty Mgmt. Inst. NYU, N.Y.C., 1987—. Mem. Pub. Relations Soc. (accredited, bd. dirs. N.Y. Chpt. 1987—, nat. accreditation bd. 1988—), Am. Mktg. Assn. (exec. com.), Nat. Acad. TV Arts and Scis., Internat. Radio and TV Soc., Old Oaks Country Club, Sigma Delta Chi. Office: 40 E 49th St New York NY 10017

STACK, STEPHEN S., manufacturing company executive; b. DuPont, Pa., Apr. 25, 1934; s. Steve and Sophie (Baranowski) Stasenko. BSME, Case Western Res. U., 1956; postgrad. Syracuse U. Registered profl. engr., Ill. Mech. engr. Kaiser Aluminum, Erie, Pa., 1956-58; instr. Gannon U., Erie, 1958-60, Syracuse (N.Y.) U., 1960-61; engring. supr. A. O. Smith Corp., Erie and Los Angeles, 1961-66; gen. mgr. Am. Elec. Fusion, Chgo., 1966-67; mgr. new products Maremont Corp., Chgo., 1967-69; dir. market planning Gulf and Western Ind., Bellwood, Ill., 1969-71; mgmt. and fin. cons. Stack & Assos., Chgo., 1971-76; pres. Seamcraft, Inc., Chgo., 1976—; mem. Ill. Legis. Small Bus. Conf., 1980, Gov.'s Small Bus. Adv. Commn., 1984—, Ill. State House Conf. on Small Bus., 1984, 86; mem. small adv. coun. Fed. Res. Bank of Chgo., 1989—; del. White House Conf. on Small Bus., 1986. Patentee in liquid control and metering fields. Active Sem. Townhouse Assn., Lincoln Park Conservation Assn., Sheffield Neighbors Assn. Recipient Am. Legion award, 1948, Case Western Res. U. Honor key, 1956, Eagle Scout award, 1949. Mem. Ill. Mfrs. Assn. (bd. dirs. 1986—), Small Mfrs. Action Council (vice chmn. 1986-87, chmn. 1988—), Mfrs. Polit. Action Com. (exec. com. 1987—), Am. Mgmt. Assn., U.S. Ind. Cellular Telephone Assn. (bd. dirs.), Pres.' Assn., Blue Key, Beta Theta Pi, Theta Tau, Pi Delta Epsilon. Clubs: Chgo. Execs., East Bank, Singapore (Mich.) Yacht, Fullerton Tennis (pres. 1971-79, treas. 1979-83, bd. dirs. 1983-86), Mid-Town Tennis, Lake Shore Ski (v.p. 1982). Office: 932 W Dakin St Chicago IL 60613

STACK, THOMAS MARSHALL, air freight company executive; b. New Milford, Conn., Sept. 14, 1953; s. Thomas Marshall III and Helen (McCahey) S. Student, Norwalk Community Coll., 1971-72; grad., Weaver Airline Sch., 1972. Mgr. Air Express Internat., Newark, 1974-76; dist. mgr. Air Express Internat., Memphis, 1976-78, Balt. and Washington, 1978-80; mgr. import sales Air Express Internat., London, 1980; dist. mgr. Air Express Internat., Boston, 1981-83, regional mgr., 1983-85; v.p. ops. Air Express Internat., Darien, Conn., 1985—. Mem. Nat. Customs Brokers and Forwarders Assn. Am. Office: Air Express Internat 120 Tokeneke Rd Darien CT 06820

STACY, DENNIS WILLIAM, architect; b. Council Bluffs, Iowa, Sept. 22, 1945; s. William L. and Mildred Glee (Carlsen) S.; BArch., Iowa State U., 1969; postgrad. U. Nebr., 1972. Registered architect, Iowa, Tex., Colo., Mo.; m. Judy Annette Long, Dec. 28, 1968; 1 child, Stephanie. Designer Troy &

Stalder Architects, Omaha, 1967, Architects Assocs., Des Moines, 1968-69, Logsdon & Voelter Architects, Temple, Tex., 1970; project architect Roger Schutte & Assos., Omaha, 1972-73; architect, assoc. Robert H. Burgin & Assocs., Coun. Bluffs, 1973-75, Neil Astle & Assocs., Omaha, 1975-78; owner, prin. Dennis W. Stacy, AIA, Architect, Glenwood, Iowa, 1978-81, Dallas, 1981—. Chmn., Glenwood Zoning Bd. Adjustment, 1979-81; chmn. Mills County Plant Iowa Program, 1979-81; mem. S.W. Iowa Citizen's Adv. Com., Iowa State Dept. Transp., 1977-81; regional screening chmn. Am. Field Svc. Internat./Intercultural Programs, 1974-79, Iowa-Nebr. rep., 1978-80. With U.S. Army, 1969-71. Decorated Nat. Def. Svc. medal, Vietnam Svc. medal, Vietnam Campaign medal, Army Commendation medal. Mem. AIA (AIA award 1981, chmn. Dallas profl. practice programs 1989), Nat. Coun. Archtl. Registration Bds., Dallas Mus. Fine Arts, Mus. Modern Art., The 500 Inc. (outstanding mem. 1985), Glenwood Optimist (Disting. Svc. award 1982, pres. 1980-81), Masons. Archtl. works include Davies Amphitheater, 1980, Addison Nat. Bank Bldg., 1985, The Colonnade Office Bldgs, 1985, LaFountain Ctr. Office Bldg., 1985, Merceded-Benz S.W. Parts Distribution Ctr., 1986, Fairview Recreation Complex, 1984, Computer Lang. Rsch. Corp. Learning Ctr., 1987., Villa Roma, 1988. Home: 4148 Cobblers Ln Dallas TX 78287 Office: 3939 Belt Line Rd Ste 222 Dallas TX 75244

STAFFORD, JOHN PETER, energy company executive; b. Elizabeth, N.J., Feb. 13, 1940; s. Leon John Suske and Petronella Martha (Kottage) S.; m. Susan Catherine Woolworth, Aug. 26, 1961; children—David Woolworth, Jeffrey John. B.B.A., Pace U., 1965; M.B.A., Harvard Bus. Sch., 1969; student Stevens Inst. Tech., 1958-60. C.P.A., N.Y. Auditor, sr. auditor Arthur Andersen & Co., N.Y.C., 1965-67, summer 1968; asst. to v.p. fin., chief fin. officer Argentina, internat. planning exec. S.C. Johnson & Son, Inc., Racine, Wis., 1969-70, 70-73, 73-76; controller, chief fin. officer Pharm. Group, G.D. Searle & Co., Skokie, Ill., 1976-78, 78-79, dir. audit, 1979-81; corp. controller DeKalb Corp., DeKalb, Ill., 1981-84, v.p. fin., treas., chief fin. officer, 1984-88; sr. v.p. Dekalb Energy Co., 1988—. Fund agt. Harvard Bus. Sch. Fund, Boston, 1984, sect. fund agt., 1980-83; alumni council Harvard Bus. Sch. Assn., 1983-86 . Mem. Am. Inst. C.P.A.s, N.Y. Soc. C.P.A.s. Club: Harvard Bus. Sch. Home: 960 Persimmon Ct Saint Charles IL 60174 Office: DeKalb Corp 3100 Sycamore Rd De Kalb IL 60115

STAFFORD, JOHN ROGERS, pharmaceutical and household products company executive; b. Harrisburg, Pa., Oct. 24, 1937; s. Paul Henry and Gladys Lee (Sharp) S.; m. Inge Paul, Aug. 22, 1959; children—Carolyn, Jennifer, Christina, Charlotte. A.B., Dickinson Coll., 1959; LL.B. with distinction, George Washington U., 1962. Bar: D.C. 1962. Assoc. Steptoe & Johnson, 1962-66; gen. atty. Hoffman-LaRoche, Nutley, N.J., 1966-67; group atty. Hoffman-LaRoche, 1967-70; gen. counsel Am. Home Products Corp., N.Y.C., 1970-74; v.p. Am. Home Products Corp., 1972-77, sr. v.p., 1977-80, exec. v.p., 1980-81, pres., 1981—, chmn., chief exec. officer, 1986—; dir. Mfrs. Hanover Corp., Met. Life Ins. Co.; bd. trustees The Presbyn. Hosp. in the city of N.Y. Mem. adv. bd. The Whole Theatre Co.; bd. dirs. Cen. Park Conservancy, Pharm. Mfgs. Assn.; bd. trustees U.S. Council for Internat. Bus., Presbyn. Hosp., N.Y.C. Recipient John Bell Larner 1st Scholar award George Washington U. Law Sch., 1962, Outstanding Achievement Alumnus award, 1981. Mem. Am. Bar Assn., D.C. Bar Assn., Nat. Assn. Mfrs. (bd. dirs.). Clubs: Sky (N.Y.C.); Essex Fells (N.J.) Country, Links (N.Y.C.). Office: Am Home Products Corp 685 3rd Ave New York NY 10017 *

STAFFORD, OLIVER MEAD, financial consultant; b. Yonkers, N.Y., Jan. 17, 1936; s. Frankland Fish and Hermine (Jisa) S.; m. Joy Allen, Apr. 14, 1972 (div.); children: Anne, Robert; m. Marcia Mae McDonald, Aug. 21, 1987. BA, Williams Coll., 1958. Registered investment advisor. Mktg. trainee Gen. Foods, White Plains, N.Y., 1958-59; gen. mgr. Mass. Mut. Life Ins. Co., Oakland, 1961-70; pres. Fin. Profiles Inc., Oakland, Calif., 1962-72, Meister and Stafford Inc., Larkspur, Calif., 1972-81; exec. v.p. AIS Fin. Svcs. Inc., Oakland, 1981—; mem. faculty Golden Gate U., San Francisco, 1979—, professorial lectr., 1981—; mem. adj. faculty Coll. for Fin. Planning, Denver, 1978—; adv. to Coll. on Nat. Testing Programs, Denver, 1984—; prof. JFK U., Orinda, Calif., 1985—; retirement planning advisor to various cos. Fundraiser YMCA, Oakland, Orinda, 1987. With U.S. Army, 1959-61. Mem. Internat. Assn. Fin. Planners (v.p. East By 1980—), East Bay Life Underwriters, Mt. Diablo Estate Planning Council, Inst. Cert. Fin. Planners (cert. fin. planner), Registry Fin. Planning Practioners, Racquetball Club, Lakeview Club, Rosicrucian Order (pres. 1986-88). Republican. Home: 649 Tahos Rd Orinda CA 94563 Office: AIS Fin Svcs Inc 300 Lakeside Dr Ste 1300 Oakland CA 94612

STAHL, JOEL SOL, plastic-chemical engineer; b. Youngstown, Ohio, June 10, 1918; s. John Charles and Anna (Nadler) S.; B. in Chem. Engring., Ohio State U., 1939; postgrad. Alexander Hamilton Inst., 1946-48; m. Jane Elizabeth Anglin, June 23, 1950; 1 child, John Arthur. With Ashland Oil & Refining Co. (Ky.), 1939-50, mgr. spl. products, 1946-50; pres. Cool Ray Co., Youngstown, 1950-51, Stahl Industries, Inc., Youngstown, 1951—, Stahl Internat., Inc., Youngstown, 1969—, Stahl Bldg. Systems, Inc., Youngstown, 1973—. Active Boardman Civic Assn., Boy Scouts Am., bd. mem. Ohio State U. Found., Community Chest, ARC; chair dean's exec. adv. bd. Coll. Engring. U. Cen. Fla. Named Ky. col., 1967. Mem. Regional Export Expansion Council, Soc. Plastics Engr., Soc. Plastics Industry, Internat. Platform Assn., Ohio Soc. N.Y., Citrus Club, Masons, Shriners, Rotary, Toastmasters (pres. 1949), Berlin Yacht (North Benton, O.), Circumnavigators. N.Y. Acad. Sci., Tau Kappa Epsilon, Phi Eta Sigma, Phi Lambda Upsilon. Republican. Chrisitan Scientist. Patentee insulated core walls, plastic plumbing wall. housing in continous process. Contbr. articles to profl. jours. Home: 530 E Central Blvd #1504 Orlando FL 32801 Office: 20 Federal Plaza W Ste 600 Youngstown OH 44503

STAHL, KEITH J., mgmt. cons.; b. Escanaba, Mich., Jan. 15, 1933; s. Walter and Doris Stahl; BBA, U. Wis., 1958; m. Nannita M. Ruggles, Aug. 31, 1957; children—Michael, Julie, Timothy. Sec., Gaarder & Miller, Inc., Madison, Wis., 1969-75, v.p., 1975-78, pres., 1978—. Treas., Kidney Found. Wis., 1972-74, chmn., 1974-76; mem. Dane County Mental Health Bd., 1978-81. With U.S. Army, 1953-54, Korea. Mem. Soc. Profl. Bus. Cons. (sec.-treas. 1973-75, cert.). Roman Catholic. Home: 3451 Le Flore Ct Verona WI 53593 Office: 5530 Medical Dr Madison WI 53719

STAHL, LOUIS EDMUND, retired food company executive; b. Boston, June 20, 1914; s. Harry G. and Esther S.; B.S., M.I.T., 1936; m. Dorothy Judith Tishler, Dec. 17, 1939; children—Lesley, Jeffrey. Tech. dir., pres. Stahl Finish Co., Peabody, Mass., 1936-65; pres. Stahl Finish div. Beatrice Foods, Inc., Wilmington, Mass., 1965-70, group mgr. chem. group, 1970-72, pres. Beatrice Chem. div., 1972-78, v.p. Beatrice Foods, Chgo., 1976-79; dir. Stahl Investment Corp., Shawmut Mchts. Bank, Salem, Mass. Mem. Corp. devel. com. M.I.T.; pres. Rehab. Center for Aged, Swampscott, 1968—. Mem. Am. Chem. Soc., Am. Leather Chemists Assn. Office: 160 Commonwealth Ave Boston MA 02116

STAHL, RONALD ALBERT, banker; b. St. Louis, Apr. 7, 1946; s. Albert Diel and Florence Marie (Mohlman) S.; m. Janice Lou Brunner, Aug. 24, 1968; children: David Eric, Brian Matthew, Michael Christopher. BSBA, U. Mo., 1969, MBA, 1970. Sr. planning analyst Pet Inc., St. Louis, 1973-79; v.p. strategic planning Mercantile Bancorp. (now Mercantile Bank N.A.), St. Louis, 1979-84, v.p., mgr. trust individual mktg., 1984-88, sr. v.p. trust individual svcs. and mktg., 1989—; instr. Cannon Fin. Inst., Athens, Ga., 1988—. Active on St. Louis U. Bequest and Gift Council, 1987—. Served to SP5 U.S. Army, 1971-73. Mem. Am. Inst. Banking (pres. 1987-88), Estate Planning Council. Republican. Presbyterian. Club: Mo. Athletic. Home: 14768 Dovershire Ct Chesterfield MO 63017 Office: Mercantile Bank NA 1 Mercantile Tower Saint Louis MO 63166

STAHL, ROY HOWARD, lawyer; b. Phila., May 7, 1952; s. Howard Charles and Elizabeth (Seitz) S.; m. Corinne Jarrett, Apr. 22, 1978; children: Benjamin Bradley, Alexander Roy. BA, Pa. State U., 1974; JD, Villanova Sch. Law, 1977. Bar: Pa. 1977. Asst. gen. counsel Gilbert Assocs., Inc., Reading, Pa., 1977-82; dir. group legal services Phila. Services Group, Bryn Mawr, Pa., 1982-84; corp. counsel Phila. Suburban Corp., Bryn Mawr, 1984-85, v.p. adminstrn., corp. counsel Phila. Sub. Corp., 1985-88, v.p., gen. counsel, 1988—. Pres. Ashbridge Homeowners Assn., Downingtown, Pa., 1984; v.p. Glen Craig Homeowners Assn., 1988. Fellow, Harry J. Loman Ins. Research Found., 1977. Mem. Montgomery County Bar Assn., Del. County Bar Assn., Phila. Bar Assn., Pa. Bar Assn., ABA. Office: Phila Suburban Corp 762 Lancaster Ave Bryn Mawr PA 19010

STAHR, ELVIS J(ACOB), JR., lawyer, conservationist, educator; b. Hickman, Ky., Mar. 9, 1916; s. Elvis and Mary Anne (McDaniel) S.; m. Dorothy Howland Berkfield, June 28, 1946; children: Stephanie Ann, Stuart Edward Winston, Bradford Lanier. AB, U. Ky., 1936; BA (Rhodes scholar), U. Oxford, Eng., 1938; BCL, 1939, MA, 1943; diploma in Chinese Lang., Yale U., 1943; LL.D., W.Va. Wesleyan Coll., Waynesburg Coll., 1959, Concord Coll., 1960, U. Md., U. Pitts., 1961, La. State U., Tex. Christian U., U. Ky., 1962, U. Notre Dame, 1964, Ind. State U., 1966, Brown U., 1967, Northwestern U., U. Fla., 1968, U. Tampa, 1972, Ind. U., 1976; D.Environ. Sci., Rollins Coll., 1973; Dr.Mil. Sci., Northeastern U., 1962; D.Pub. Adminstrn., Bethany Coll., 1962; D.H.L., DePauw U., 1963, Rose Poly Inst., 1965, Transylvania U., 1973; Litt.D., U. Cin., 1966, U. Maine, 1976; Pd.D., Culver-Stockton Coll., 1966; D.Sc., Norwich U., 1968, Hanover Coll., 1975. Bar: N.Y. State 1940, Ky. 1948, D.C. 1983, U.S. Supreme Ct. 1950. Practiced as assoc. Mudge, Stern, Williams & Tucker, N.Y.C., 1939-41; sr. assoc. Mudge, Stern, Williams & Tucker, 1946-47; assoc. prof. law U. Ky., 1947-48, prof. law, 1948-56; dean U. Ky. (Coll. Law), 1948-56, provost, 1954-56; exec. dir. Pres. Eisenhower's Com. on Edn. Beyond High Sch., 1956-57; vice chancellor professions U. Pitts., 1957-58; pres., prof. law W.Va. U., Morgantown, 1958-61; spl. asst. Sec. Army, Washington, 1951-52, cons., 1953; Sec. of the Army Dept. Def., Washington, 1961-62; pres., prof. law Ind. U., 1962-68; pres. Nat. Audubon Soc., N.Y.C., 1968-79; sr. counselor Nat. Audubon Soc., 1979-81, pres. emeritus, 1981—; ptnr. Chickering & Gregory, San Francisco, 1982-85; of counsel Chickering & Gregory P.C., San Francisco, 1986—; dir. Acacia Mut. Life Ins. Co., 1968-85; pres. Univ. Assos., Inc., 1981—; exec. v.p. Pub. Resource Found., 1982—; sr. assoc. Cassidy & Assocs., Inc., 1984—; chmn. Washington Conservation Roundtable, 1986-87; dir. Chase Manhattan Corp., 1976-79, Fed. Res. Bank Chgo., 1966-68, dep. chmn., 1967, 68; Mem. Constn. Rev. Commn. Ky., 1949-56, Ind., 1967-68; mem. U.S. del. UN Conf. on Human Environment, Stockholm, 1972, Joint U.S.-USSR Com. on Cooperation for Protection of Environment, 1973, Internat. Whaling Commn., London, 1975, 78; mem. U.S. Aviation Adv. Commn., 1970-73, Nat. Commn. for World Population Yr., 1974; nat. chmn. U.S.O., 1973-76; pub. mem. Nat. Petroleum Council, 1974-79; mem. Summit Conf. on Inflation, 1974. Author: (with others) Economics of Pollution, 1971. Mem. Nat. Commn. on Accrediting, 1963-68; trustee Transylvania U., 1969-76, mem. founders bd., 1978-80; pres. Midwestern Univs. Research Assn., 1963-66; incorporator Argonne Univs. Assn., 1965, trustee, 1965-67; trustee Univs. Research Assn., 1965, mem. council presidents, 1965-68, chmn., 1968; bd. dirs. Alliance To Save Energy, 1977-88, Resolve, 1977-81, Council Fin. Aid to Edn., 1966-69; chmn. higher edn. adv. com. Edn. Commn. States, 1966-68; mem. bd. Govtl. Affairs Inst., 1968-72, Pub. Adminstrn. Service, 1970-72, Inst. Services to Edn., 1965-67; chmn. Commn. on Fed. Relations, Am. Council on Edn., 1966-68; mem. exec. com. Nat. Assn. State Univs. and Land Grant Colls., 1965-68; mem. at-large bd. dirs. Am. Cancer Soc., 1970-76; trustee Com. Econ. Devel., 1964-82, hon. trustee, 1982—; mem. exec. bd. Nat. Assn. Ednl. Broadcasters, 1969-72; adv. council Electric Power Research Inst., 1973-77, Gas Research Inst., 1977-83, Population Inst., 1981—, FAIR, 1982—; mem. Govtl. Affairs Com. of Ind. Sector, 1980—; bd. dirs. Regional Plan Assn. Greater N.Y., 1970-75; evaluation panel Nat. Bur. Standards, 1975-77; adv. council Nat. Energy Project, Am. Enterprise Inst. Pub. Policy Research, 1974-76; chmn. Coalition Concerned Charities, 1972-78; mem. exec. bd. Am. Com. for Internat. Conservation, 1978-80; bd. dirs. World Environment Ctr., 1978-85, Environ. and Energy Study Inst., 1983—, Nat. Parks and Conservation Assn., 1988—, Nat. Water Alliance, 1983-86, Land Between The Lakes Assn., 1986-89. Served 2d lt. to lt. col., inf. AUS, North Africa and China, 1941-46. Decorated Spl. Breast Order of Yun Hui (2) Army Navy and Air Force medal 1st class (China); Bronze Star medal with oak leaf cluster (U.S.); Order of Grand Cross (Peru).; Recipient Algernon Sydney Sullivan medallion of N.Y. So. Soc., 1936; named One of Am.'s Ten Outstanding Young Men U.S. Jr. C. of C., 1948; Meritorious Civilian Service medal Dept. Army, 1953, Disting. Civilian Service medal Dept. Army, 1971; Disting. Service award U. Ky. Alumni Assn., 1961; Disting. Service award Res. Officers Assn. U.S., 1962, Kentuckian of Year award Ky. Press Assn., 1961 and WHAS (Louisville), 1968, Conservation Service award Dept. Interior, 1979, Conservation Achievement award Nat. Wildlife Fedn., 1978, Barbara Swain Award of Honor Natural Resources Council of Am., 1988; Sesquicentennial medal U. Mich., 1967, Centennial medal U. Ky., 1965; named Ky. Col. and gen.; La. and Neb. adm., Ind. Sagamore. Mem. Assn. U.S. Army (life, pres. 1965-68, chmn. council trustees 1969-74), Ind. Soc. of Chgo. (hon. life), Jr. C. of C. Internat. (hon. life senator), Assn. Am. Rhodes Scholars, ABA, Fed. Bar Assn., Kentuckians (pres. N.Y.C. 1976-79, life trustee), S.R., SAR, Ky. Bar Assn., D.C. Bar Assn., Ind. Bar Assn. (hon.), Disciples of Christ Hist. Soc. (life mem.), Order of Coif, Phi Beta Kappa, Sigma Chi (Balfour Nat. award 1936, Significant Sig 1961, dir. found. bd. 1974—, Order of Constantine 1981), Omicron Delta Kappa (dir. found. 1984—, Laurel Crown Circle award), Phi Delta Phi, Tau Kappa Alpha (Dist. Alumni award 1966), Merton Soc. (Oxford, Eng.); hon. mem. Blue Key, Beta Gamma Sigma, Alpha Kappa Psi, Kappa Kappa Psi. Presbyterian. Clubs: Army-Navy (Washington), City Tavern (Washington), Field (Greenwich); Pilgrims of U.S, Boone and Crockett. Home: Martin Dale Greenwich CT 06830 Office: Chickering & Gregory PC 1815 H St NW #600 Washington DC 20006

STAIR, CHARLES WILLIAM, service company executive; b. Ida Grove, Iowa, Oct. 21, 1940; s. Frderick Cleveland and Eunice (Carlson) S.; m. Patricia Ellen Gramley, June 15, 1963; children: Kerry John, Andrew Charles, Melissa Kathrine. BA, Wheaton Coll., 1963. Coordinating mgr. The ServiceMaster Co., Downers Grove, Ill., 1963-65, regional ops. mgr., 1966-68, area ops. mgr., 1969-70, div. v.p., 1971, exec. v.p., 1972-73, div. pres., 1974-75, group v.p. east group, 1976-77, group pres. east group, 1978-79, group pres. west group, 1980-82, group pres. cen. group, 1983-85, exec. v.p. healthcare/edn., 1986, exec. v.p., 1987—, also bd. dirs.; exec. chmn. bd. dirs. Tyndale House Pubs. Inc., Wheaton; bd. dirs. Healthcorp Affiliated, Naperville, Ill. Republican. Club: Chgo. Golf. Home: 25W 487 Plamondon Rd Wheaton IL 60187 Office: Servicemaster Industries Inc 2300 Warrenville Rd Downers Grove IL 60515

STALEY, DELBERT C., telecommunications executive; b. Hammond, Ind., Sept. 16, 1924; s. Eugene and Nellie (Downer) s.; m. Ingrid Andersen, Mar. 16, 1946; children—Crista Staley Ellis, Cynthia, Clifford, Corinn. Student, Rose Poly. Inst., Hammond, 1943-44; grad. advanced mgmt. program, Harvard U., 1962; D. Engring. (hon.), Rose Hulman Inst. Tech., 1981; LL.D., Skidmore Coll., 1983. With Ill. Bell Telephone, 1946-76, v.p. ops., 1972-76; pres. Ind. Bell, 1976-78; v.p. residence mktg. AT&T, 1978-79; pres. N.Y. Telephone, 1979-83, chmn. bd., chief exec. officer, 1983; chmn. bd. NYNEX Corp., White Plains, N.Y., 1983—, chief exec. officer, 1983-89, also dir.; dir. Dean Foods, Franklin Park, Ill., Ball Corp., Muncie, Ind., Bank N.Y., N.Y.C. Mem. com. econ. devel. Bus. Roundtable, Conf. Bd., N.Y.C. Partnership Inc.; mem. nat. bd. of govs. ARC, chmn., Greater N.Y.C.; vice chmn. United Way N.Y.C.; mem. United Way of Tri State. Served with U.S. Army, 1943-46, ETO. Recipient Puerto Rican Legal Def. and Edn. Fund award, 1981, Cleveland Dodge award YMCA Greater N.Y., 1983, New Yorker for N.Y. award Citizens Com. for N.Y., 1984, Leadership in Mgmt. award Pace U., 1988, Albert Schweitzer Leadership award Hugh O'Brian Youth Found., 1988, Hammond Achievement award The Hammond Hist. Soc., 1988, Gold Medal award USO, 1988. Mem. IEEE, Ind. Acad. (hon.), Telephone Pioneers Am. (pres. 1983-84). Presbyterian. Clubs: Westchester Country, Sky, Blind Brook, Exmoor, Royal Poinciana. Home: 100 Polly Park Rd Rye NY 10580 Office: Nynex Corp 1113 Westchester Ave White Plains NY 10604-3510 *

STALEY, ROBERT W., engineer, corporate executive; b. 1935. BSME, Cornell U., 1958, MBA, 1959. Dir. corp. devel. Trane Co., 1960-75; v.p. corp. tech. Emerson Electric Co., St. Louis, 1975-77, internat. v.p., 1977-78, chief fin. officer, sr. v.p. fin., 1978-81, sr. v.p., group v.p., 1981-83, exec. v.p., 1983-88, vice chmn., 1988—, also bd. dirs. Capt. U.S. Army, 1959-66. Office: Emerson Electric Co 8000 W Florissant Ave Saint Louis MO 63136 *

STALKER, SUZY WOOSTER, human resources executive; b. Atlanta, Oct. 12, 1948; d. George Edward Wooster and Mary Evelyn (Dayton) Schmidt; m. James Marion Stalker, Nov. 11, 1966; children: Marian Paige, Jason Alexander. Student, Ga. State U., 1981—. Tng. rep. Rich's, Atlanta, 1980-81, tng. supr., 1981-82, regional tng. coordinator, 1982-84, employee communications specialist, 1983-84; dir. human resources Home Fed. Savs. & Loan, Atlanta, 1984-85, v.p. human resources, 1985-88; v.p. personnel Gulf States Mortgage Co., Inc., Atlanta, 1988—. Editor Richbits, 1983-84. Leader Girl Scouts U.S., Austell, Ga., 1975-76; pres. Clarkdale Elem. PTA, Austell, 1975-76. Mem. Nat. Assn. for Female Execs., Inc., Ga. Exec. Women's Network. Avocations: sailing, cross-stitching, watercolors. Home: 4820 Glore Rd Mableton GA 30059

STALLINGS, KATHERINE RAE, financial services company executive; b. Rumson, N.J., Oct. 10, 1959; d. Charles Elias and Virginia Charlene (Bennett) S. BA, Trinity Coll., Hartford, Conn., 1981; postgrad., Columbia U., 1988—. Mgmt. assoc. Marine Midland Bank NA, N.Y.C., 1981-82, comml. banking rep., 1982-83; assoc. Integrated Resources Inc., N.Y.C., 1983-84, asst. treas., 1984-87, asst. v.p., 1987-89, v.p., 1989—. Class agt. Hotchkiss Sch. Alumni Assn., Lakeville, Conn., 1981-87. Mem. Women's Econ. Roundtable. Republican. Episcopalian. Office: Integrated Resources Inc 666 3d Ave 6th Fl New York NY 10017

STALLKAMP, WILLIAM J., banker, consultant; b. Quincy, Mass., May 20, 1939; m. Mary Lee Brady; children: Jonathan B., Christian B. BSBA, Miami U., Oxford, Ohio, 1961; postgrad., Carnegie-Mellon U., U. Pitts. Various positions Mellon Bank, Pitts., 1962-72, London, 1972-76; various v.p. positions Mellon Bank, Pitts., 1976-88; exec. v.p. mid. market banking Mellon Bank, Phila., 1988—; bd. dirs. Blue Cross Western Pa., Pitts., Yoder Bros., Ohio, Matthews Internat. Pitts. With USCG, 1961-67. Mem. Duquesne Club, Fox Chapel Golf Club. Republican. Roman Catholic. Home: 765 Newton Rd Villanova PA 19085

STALSBERG, GERALDINE MCEWEN, accountant; b. Springfield, Mo., May 10, 1936; d. Gerald Earl McEwen and Marie LaVerne (Pennington) Plautz; m. Bill Eugene Bottolfson, Mar. 10, 1956 (div. 1978); children: Bill Earl, Robert Edward, Brian Everett, Michelle Marie; m. Arvid Ray Stalsberg, Sept. 21, 1979; stepchildren: Angelite Renae, Neil Ray, Terry Jay. Diploma Hastings Beauty Acad., 1955; cert. in interior design, Cen. Tech. Community Coll., 1975; student Doane Coll., 1982; cert. computer programmer Lincoln Sch. Commerce, Nebr., 1984. Cosmetologist, Marinello Beauty Shop, Hastings, 1955-57; owner Nursery Sch. for Toddlers, 1958-67; acct. grain dept. Morrison-Quirk Elevator, Hastings, Nebr., 1968-69; acct., exec. sec., interior decorator Uerling's Home Furnishings, Hastings, 1970-79; acct., computer programmer, Lincoln Transp., Nebr., 1980-86, systems analyst, 1984-86; tax cons. H&R Block, Lincoln, 1983-86; pvt. practice acctg. and tax cons., 1987—; acct., systems analyst, computer programmer, tax cons., controller EBKO Industries, Hastings, 1988—. Emergency radio dispatcher Adams County Civil Def., Hastings, 1973-78; active YWCA, Girl Scouts USA, PTA, 4-H Clubs Am. Recipient Civic Achievement award City of Hastings, 1974. Mem. Nat. Assn. Govt. Employees, Bus. Profl. Women, Library Assn., Nat. Am. Mfrs. Assn., NAFE, Nat. Assn. Mfrs., Soroptimists Internat., Beta Sigma Phi (Woman of Yr. 1978, Order of Rose). Republican. Lutheran. Avocations: reading, bowling, fishing, swimming, jogging. Home: 414 W 14th St Hastings NE 68901 Office: PO Box 1123 Hastings NE 68902

STAMBERGER, EDWIN HENRY, farmer, civic leader; b. Mendota, Ill., Feb. 16, 1916; s. Edwin Nicolaus and Emilie Anna Marie (Yost) S.; m. Mabel Edith Gordon, Oct. 6, 1937; 1 child, Larry Allan. Farmer seed corn, livestock, machinery devel. Mendota, 1939—; bd. dirs. Mendota Coop. & Supply Co., 1949-67, pres., 1958-67. Mem. Mendota Luth. Ch. council, 1958-64, chmn. 1964, treas. northwest conf., 1966-68, trustee Bible camp; mem. Mendota Watershed Com., 1966-73, 77—, rev. and comment com. subregion and region Ill. Cen. Comprehensive Health Planning Agy., 1974-76; asst. in devel. Mendota Hosp., Mendota Lake; chmn. bldg. com. Mendota Luth. Home, 1972-73; bd. dirs. LaSalle County Mental Health Bd., 1969-74, U. Ill. County Extension, 1963-67, chmn. 1966-67; bd. dirs. Soil and Water Dist., 1968-73, vice chmn., 1971-73. Recipient Future Farmers Am. award. Mem. Am. Soc. Agrl. Engrs., Soil Soc. Am., Ill. Council Watersheds (founder), Smithsonian Inst., Mental Health Assn., People to People Internat., Internat. Platform Assn., Mendota C. of C. (Honor award 1974), Mendota Sportsman's Club, Loyal order of Moose, Odd Fellows, Lions (bd. dirs. Mendota chpt. 1965-67, Honor award 1981). Home and Office: Sabine Farm 4429 E 250th Rd Mendota IL 61342

STAMBOULIEH, NICHOLAS GABRIEL, real estate executive; b. Khartoum, Sudan, Sept. 4, 1915; came to U.S., 1976; s. Gabriel George and Catherine (Papadam) S.; m. Cleopatra Cassarkis, July 7, 1945; children: Mary Marsalis, George. Grad., Victoria Coll., Alexandria, Egypt; M in Mathematics, Oxford and Cambridge; cert. mathematics master, London U., 1963. Inspector, gen. sec. Alexandria Municipality, 1934-41; instr. mathematics pre-univ. level Victoria Coll., Alexandria, 1941-58, headmaster, 1956-58; gen. rep. for Sudan Stamboulieh Bros. Ltd. subs. Hartford Ins. Co., Khartoum, 1958-63; instr. mathematics Millfield Sch., Somerset, Eng., 1963-76; realtor, investment specialist Bice & Assocs., Houston, 1977—. concert pianist, 1937-58. Recipient Gold medal, 1934. Mem. Tex. Assn. Realtors, Tex. Investment Soc. Lodge: Masons (32 degree) (worshipful master), Armonia 12. Office: Bice & Assocs 11731 Jones Rd Houston TX 77070

STAMMEN, MARVIN JOSEPH, bank executive, agricultural company executive; b. Celina, Ohio, Oct. 19, 1946; s. Alfons John and Esther Marie (Rindler) S.; m. Mildred Ann Hoying, July 11, 1969; 1 child, Eric. BS, Ohio State U., 1969; MBA, Miami U., 1971. Officer State Bank & Trust Co., Defiance, Ohio, 1971-80; sr. v.p. State Bank & Trust Co., Defiance, 1981-82, exec. v.p., 1982-84, pres., 1984—. Bd. dirs. Wayne Industries Mental Health Workshop, Greenville, 1985; adv. bd. Darke County Airport, Greenville, 1985, Wayne Hosp., Greenville, 1986. Mem. Ohio Bankers Assn. (bd. dirs. 1984—), Community Bankers Assn. Ohio (bd. dirs. 1985—), Rotary, Elks. Republican. Roman Catholic. Home: 6546 Fairway Ct Greenville OH 45331 Office: 2d Nat Bank 4th & Broadway PO Box 130 Greenville OH 45331

STAMPER, MALCOLM THEODORE, aerospace company executive; b. Detroit, Apr. 4, 1925; s. Fred Theodore and Lucille (Cayce) S.; m. Marion Philbin Guinan, Feb. 25, 1946; children: Geoffrey, Kevin, Jamie, David, Mary, Anne. Student, U. Richmond, Va., 1943-44; B.E.E., Ga. Inst. Tech., 1946; postgrad., U. Mich., 1946-49. With Gen. Motors Corp., 1949-62; with Boeing Co., Seattle, 1962—; mgr. electronics ops., v.p., gen. mgr. turbine div. Boeing Co., 1964-66; v.p., gen. mgr. Boeing Co. (747 Airplane program), 1966-69, v.p., gen. mgr. comml. airplane group, 1969-71, corp. sr. v.p. ops., 1971-72; pres. Boeing Co., 1972-85, vice chmn., 1985—; bd. dirs. Travelers Ins. Cos., Nordstrom Co., Chrysler Corp.; trustee The Conf. Bd., 1988—. Chmn. Wash. State U.S. Treasury Savs. Bond Campaign, Boy Scouts Am. Devel. Fund State of Wash., Variety Club Handicapped Children Telethon.; candidate U.S. Ho. of Reps., Detroit, 1952; trustee Seattle Art Mus., Conference Bd., 1988; nat. bd. dirs. Smithsonian Assocs.; trustee The Conf. Bd., 1988. With USNR, 1943-46. Named Industrialist of Year, 1967; recipient Educator's Golden Key award, 1970, Elmer A. Sperry award, 1982, AIEE award, Ga. Inst. Tech. award, Sec. Dept. Health and Human Services award. Mem. Nat. Alliance Businessmen, Phi Gamma Delta. Office: Boeing Co 7755 E Marginal Way S Seattle WA 98108

STAMPS, GEORGE MORELAND, communications consultant; b. Kuling, Jiangxi, Peoples Republic of China, June 15, 1924; came to U.S., 1926 (parents Am. citizens); s. Drew Fletcher and Elizabeth Camilla (Belk) S.; m. Helen Leone Paty, Nov. 29, 1946; children: Margaret Evalyn, Robert Fletcher, Thomas Paty, John Belk. BS magna cum laude, Wake Forest U., 1947; MA in Physics, Columbia U., 1949; postgrad., Poly. Inst. Bklyn., 1950-52. Instr. physics and math. SUNY Maritime Coll., Bronx, 1949-51; asst. chief engr., dir. tech. sales Hogan Labs. Inc., N.Y.C., 1951-59; chief engr., asst. to pres. mktg. Telautograph Corp., Los Angeles, 1960-62; program mgr. Magnafax Program Magnavox Co., Torrance, Calif., 1963-65; mgr indsl. mktg. Magnavox Co., Urbana, Ill., 1965-71, mgr. bus. devel., 1971-73; corp. mgr. bus. devel. Xerox Corp., Stamford, Conn., 1973-76; pres. GMS Consulting, Westport, Conn., 1976-86, Oxford, Ga., 1986-89; expert witness on facsimile-visual scis. N.Y. Supreme Ct., 1982; chmn. numerous sci. and profl. confs. Contbr. over 35 articles on facsimile and telecommunication scis. to profl. jours. and govt. coms. Patentee in field. Del. Conn. Dem. Conv., Hartford, 1980; bd. dirs. Champaign-Urbana (Ill.) Symphony

Orch., 1968-72; bd. dirs. Newton County Red Cross, 1988. Served to first lt. USAAF, 1942-45, ETO, lt. col USAFR ret. Decorated Air medal with two oak leaf clusters. Mem. Electronics Industries Assn. (chmn. communications terminals and interfaces sect. 1963-73, founder TR-29 facsimile systems and equipment engring. com. 1961), IEEE, Computer Soc. of IEEE, Communications Soc. of IEEE (Ft. Wayne chpt. officer 1972-73), Geosci. and Remote Sensing Soc. of IEEE, Armed Forces Communications and Electronics Assn., Am. Phys. Soc., Phi Beta Kappa, Omicron Delta Kappa. Presbyterian. Home: 1280 Lake Stone Lea Dr PO Box 1299 Oxford GA 30267

STAMPS, THOMAS PATY, lawyer; b. Mineola, N.Y., May 10, 1952; s. George Moreland and Helen Leone (Paty) S.; m. Regina Ruth Thomas, May 23, 1981; children: Katherine Camilla, George Belk, Elizabeth Margaret. BA, U. Ill., 1973; postgrad. Emory U., 1975-76, JD, Wake Forest U., 1979. Bar: Ga. 1979, N.C. 1979. Personnel dir. Norman Jaspan, N.Y.C., 1973-74; assoc. Macey & Zusmann, Atlanta, 1979-81; owner Zusmann, Small, Stamps & White PC, Atlanta, 1981-85; cons. GMS Cons., Oxford, Ga., 1975—; ptnr. Destin Enterprises, Atlanta, 1983-85. Author: Study of a Student, 1973, History of Coca-Cola, 1976. Chmn. Summer Law Inst., Atlanta, 1981-85; mem. Dem. Party of Ga., Atlanta, 1983—; atty. Vol. Lawyers for Arts, Atlanta, 1981-85; panel mem. U.S. Bankruptcy Trustees No. Dist. Ga., 1982—; active High Mus. Art, 1986—, Atlanta Botanical Gardens, Campaign 88, Atlanta Symphony Orchestra, 1988, Ga. Legal History Found., 1988—; sec. Friends of Woodrow Wilson, 1988—. Recipient Service award Inst. Continuing Legal Edn., Athens, Ga., 1981, 86. Mem. ABA, Atlanta Bar Assn. (com. chmn. 1981-85), N.C. Bar Assn., Internat. Bar Assn., Hon. Order Ky. Cols., Atlanta Hist. Soc., Am. Bankruptcy Inst., Nat. Assn. Bankruptcy Trustees, Planetary Soc., Internat. Platform Assn., Phi Alpha Delta (justice, Atlanta 1982-83, emeritus 1983). Clubs: Lawyers, Sporting (Atlanta). Office: 460 E Paces Ferry Rd Atlanta GA 30305-3301

STANALAND, WILLIAM WHIT, JR., accountant; b. Benson Junction, Fla., Mar. 15, 1930; s. William Whit and Goldie (Merritt) S.; BS in Bus. Adminstrn., U. Fla., 1957, postgrad., 1959; postgrad. Rollins Coll., 1964; m. Norma Lee Ober, June 24, 1961; children—Sherry D., William Whit III, Terence B., Dana Lee; m. 2d, Sandra L. Swann, Dec. 1, 1971. Jr. acct. Pepsi Cola Bottling Co., 1957-58; acct. Wells, Laney, Earlich & Baer, 1958-59, A.J. Mixner, CPA, 1961-63; controller Halco Products, Inc., 1959-61; CPA, Orlando, Fla., 1963—. Lic. capt. U.S. Coast Guard. Served with USMC, 1948-52. CPA, Fla. Mem. Am., Fla. Insts. CPA's, Assn. Builders and Contractors, Associated Gen. Contractors of Mid-Fla., Mortgage Bankers Assn., Brevard Marine Assn., Cen. Fla. Tax Roundtable, Greater South Brevard C. of C. Clubs: Toastmasters; Coast (Melbourne); Eau Gallie Yacht. Lodge: Kiwanis. Home: 441 N Harbor City Blvd Unit C-20 Melbourne FL 32935 Office: 1600 Sarno Rd Ste 113 Melbourne FL 32935

STANDER, RICHARD RAMSAY, SR., civil engineer, construction executive; b. Mansfield, Ohio, Jan. 3, 1919; s. Carl H. and Eula (Ramsay) S.; m. Bette Penhorwood, Mar. 8, 1941; children: Richard Jr., William, Susan, Sally. BCE, Ohio State U., 1940. Registered profl. engr., Ohio. Gen. mgr. to chmn. Mansfield Asphalt Paving co., 1946—; chmn. The Rd. Info. Program, Washington, 1985-87. Mem. Ohio Transp. Rsch. Bd., Marysville, 1973-88, The State Underground Parking Commn., Columbus, Ohio, 1987—; candidate Ohio Senate Dist. 19, Columbus, 1986. Capt. U.S. Army, 1941-46. Recipient Centennial Alumnus award Ohio State U., 1970, Disting. Alumnus award Coll. Engring. Ohio State U., 1970, Rebuilding Am. award CIT Corp., 1986, ARTBA Nello Teer award, 1988. Fellow ASCE; mem. Nat. Soc. Profl. Engrs. (life), Assn. Asphalt Paving Techs. (life, bd. dirs. 1969), Soc. Am. Mil. Engrs., Transp. Rsch. Bd. (assoc.), Am. Rd. and Transp. Builders Assn. (chmn. 1978), Nat. Asphalt Pavement Assn. (pres. 1963-65), Elks, Westbrook Country Club (Mansfield, pres. 1953). Democrat. Presbyterian. Home: 500 Edgewood Rd Mansfield OH 44907 Office: Mansfield Asphalt Paving Co 153 Orange St Mansfield OH 44901

STANDISH, JOHN SPENCER, textile manufacturing company executive; b. Albany, N.Y., Apr. 17, 1925; s. John Carver and Florence (Spencer) S.; m. Elaine Joan Ritchie, Oct. 20, 1962 (div. 1984); children: John Carver, Christine Louise; m. Patricia Hunter, Nov. 9, 1985. BS, MIT, 1945. Asst. to prodn. mgr. Forstmann Woolen Co., Passaic, N.J., 1945-52; various positions Albany Internat. Corp., 1952-72, v.p., 1972-74, exec. v.p., 1974-76, vice chmn., 1976-84, chmn., 1984—; bd. dirs. Berkshire Life Ins. Co., Pittsfield, Mass., Key Bank N.A., Albany. Bd. dirs. Albany chpt. ARC, 1966—, chpt. chmn., 1971-74; bd. govs. ARC, Washington, 1980-86; bd. dirs. United Way of Northeastern N.Y., Albany, 1980—, pres., 1984-85; trustee Albany Med. Coll. and Ctr., 1984—; trustee Sienna Coll., Loudonville, N.Y., 1987; chmn. U. Albany Fund, 1982-87. Served to sgt. U.S. Army, 1945-46. Mem. Am. Mgmt. Assn., World Econ. Forum. Republican. Episcopalian. Clubs: Ft. Orange, Wolferts Roost Country (Albany); Schuyler Meadows Country (Loudonville). Home: 1 Schuyler Meadows Rd Loudonville NY 12211 Office: Albany Internat Corp PO Box 1907 Albany NY 12201

STANFIELD, JAMES NICKS, venture capitalist, broker; b. Roxboro, N.C., Dec. 6, 1938; s. Hillman B. Stanfield and Stella L. (Nicks) Bartlett; m. Beverly Kay Fischer, Sept. 7, 1963; children: Kelly Leigh, Kay Lynn. BBA, North Tex. State U., 1963. Asst. cashier First Nat. Bank, Dallas, 1964-66; v.p. First Nat. Bank, Corsicana, Tex., 1967, Rotan Mosle, Inc., Dallas, 1968-74, Eppler, Guerin & Turner, Inc., Dallas, 1975-76; chmn. bd. Metal Services, Inc., Dallas, 1973-79; pres. MSI Capital Corp., Dallas, 1976—; bd. dirs. Ennis (Tex.) Automotive Inc., Able Enterprises Inc., Ennis, Heads Up Techs. Inc., Dallas, Palindromic Systems Inc., Plano, Tex., MAPSCO Holdings, Inc., Dallas. Charter mem. bd. advisors Coll. Bus. Adminstrn. U. North Tex. Served with USAF, 1956-60. Mem. Nat. Venture Capital Assn., Tex. Venture Fourm, Dallas Venture Capital Forum. Republican. Methodist. Office: MSI Capital Corp 3103 Carlisle Dallas TX 75204

STANFIELD, VICKI ELAINE, hospital administrator; b. Takoma Park, Md., Apr. 12, 1955; d. James Barrington and Rosemary (Winebrenner) S. BS in Acct., Benjamin Franklin U., 1978; MBA, George Mason U. CPA, Va. Clk., asst. controller Psychiat. Inst. Am., Washington, 1976-82; controller, v.p. fin. Mental Health Mgmt., McLean, Va., 1982—. Republican.

STANFORD, MELVIN JOSEPH, university dean, management consultant; b. Logan, Utah, June 13, 1932; s. Joseph Sedley and Ida Pearl (Ivie) S.; m. Linda Barney, Sept. 2, 1960; children: Connie Stanford Tendick, Cheryl Stanford Bohn, Joseph, Theodore, Emily, Charlotte, Charles, Sarah. B.S. (First Security Found. scholar), Utah State U., 1957; M.B.A. (Donald Kirk David fellow), Harvard U., 1963; Ph.D., U. Ill., 1968. Asst. audit supr. Utah Tax Commn., 1958-61; acct. Haskins & Sells, C.P.A.s, Boston, 1961-62; acctg. staff analyst Arabian Am. Oil Co., Dhahran, Saudi Arabia, 1963-66; teaching and research asst. U. Ill., Urbana, 1966-68; mem. faculty Brigham Young U., Provo, Utah, 1968-82; dir. mgmt. devel. programs Brigham Young U., 1970-73, prof. bus. mgmt., 1974-82; dean Coll. Bus. Mankato (Minn.) State U., 1982—; bd. dirs. M.L. Bigelow, Inc.; cons. Strategic Planning; vis. prof. mgmt. Boston U., Europe, 1975-76. Author: New Enterprise Management, 1975, 82, Management Policy, 1979, 83; also articles, mgmt. cases. Founder Midwestern Jour. Bus. and Econs., 1985. Served with USAF, 1951-55; also Res. Named Amb. of City of Mankato, 1988. Mem. N. Am. Case Research Assn. (v.p. for research 1985-86, pres. 1987-88), Acad. Mgmt., Strategic Mgmt. Soc., SAR (pres. Utah 1978-79, nat. trustee 1979-80, Meritorious Service medal 1981), Kiwanis (bd. dirs. 1988—), Alpha Kappa Psi, Phi Kappa Phi. Mem. Ch. Jesus Christ Latter Day Saints. Home: 221 Crestwood Dr North Mankato MN 56001 Office: Mankato State U Coll Bus 120 MH Mankato MN 56001

STANFORD, THERESA A., investment officer; b. Atlanta, Nov. 16, 1953; d. Theodore Edward and Theresa (Charlot) Atkinson; m. Charlie Stanford, Aug. 13, 1977; children: Keisha Nichole, Jihan Patrice, Jarrett Kyle. BS in Acctg., Morris Brown Coll., 1975. Acctg. trainee Standard Oil, Louisville, 1975-76; staff acct. ITC, Atlanta, 1976-77; acct. City of Atlanta, 1977-79, fin. analyst, 1979-83, investment officer, 1983—. Mem. Nat. Assn. Securities Profls., Atlanta Assn. Women Securities. Office: City of Atlanta 68 Mitchell St 2d Fl Atlanta GA 30335

STANGELAND, LUDVIG BERNHARD, mechanical engineer, company executive; b. Bklyn., July 2, 1923; s. Ludvig E and Trine Louen) S.; m. Berit Heskestad, Aug. 23, 1947; 1 child, Geir. BSc in Mech. Engring. summa cum laude, U. N.H., 1949, MSc in Mech. Engring, 1950. Design engr. gas turbines Westinghouse Electric Corp., Lester, Pa., 1950-54; project engr. Exxon Corp. (formerly Esso Standard Oil Co.), Aruba, Netherlands Antilles, 1954-59; mgr. process engring. Norske Exxon (formerly Esso), Tonsberg, Norway, 1959-65; mgr. Valloy Refinery, 1965-68; chief engr., gen. prodn. mgr. Norsk Hydro AS, Karmoy, Norway, 1968—; chmn. bd. Skude Verft Skudenes, Norway, 1980—, br. office Rogalandsbanken, Haugesund, Norway, 1981—; bd. dirs. Saga Hotellene, Haugesund, Karmoy Industri. vice chmn. Karmoy Naeringsrad, 1974-80, Haugesund Industriforening, 1979-81; chmn. Industriens Kontakt/Samarbeidsorgan, Haugesund, 1975-81, Rogaland Industriforening, Stavanger, Norway, 1977-80. Mem. bd. advisors Haugesund Maritime Coll., 1989—. Recipient Participation Medal Norwegian Underground, 1943-45. Mem. Norwegian Soc. Grad. Engrs., Tau Beta Pi, Pi Mu Epsilon, Sigma Pi Sigma, Phi Kappa Phi, Theta Chi. Mem. Conservative Party. Lutheran. Lodge: Masons. Home: Stenderveien 37 5500, Haugesund Norway Office: Hydro Aluminum, N-4265, Havik Karmoy Norway

STANGELAND, TOR OSCAR, paper company executive; b. Quebec, Que., Can., June 13, 1929; s. Karl and Torborg Stangeland; m. Barbara Perry, Dec. 27, 1954; children—Lynne, Eric, Cara. B.A., McGill U., 1950, B.C.L. with honors, 1953. Bar: Que. 1954. Mem. legal dept. DuPont of Can. Ltd., 1955-58; asst. mgr. real estate and ins. Consol. Bathurst, Inc., Montreal, Que., 1958-59, asst. sec., mgr. real estate and ins., 1959-67, dir. employee and pub. relations, 1967-71, v.p. personnel, sec., 1971-76, exec. v.p. pulp and paper, 1976-82, pres., chief operating officer, 1982-88, chmn., chief exec. officer, 1988—, also bd. dirs., dir. several subs.; chmn., dir. CB Pak, Inc.; dir. Sceptre Resources Ltd., OE, Inc., Maritime Paper Products, Ltd., McMillan Bathurst, Inc., Domglas, Inc., Twinpak, Inc., Bridgewater Paper Co.; pres., dir. Unltd. Skills Inc. Gov. Conseil du Patronat du Que. Mem. Bar of Province of Que. Clubs: St. James, Mount Royal, Mount Bruno Country (Montreal). Home: 9 Rosemount Ave, Westmount, PQ Canada H3Y 3G6 Office: Consol-Bathurst Inc, PO Box 69, Montreal, PQ Canada H3C 2R5

STANGER, JOHN WILLIAM, finance company executive; b. Boston, Jan. 24, 1923; s. John Sawyer and Lenora (Leo) S.; m. Valerie Gudel, Apr. 14, 1951; 1 dau., Pamela Beth. Student, Boston U., 1941-43; A.B., Harvard U., 1947. With Gen. Electric Credit Corp. subs. Gen. Electric Co., N.Y.C., 1947-85; gen. mgr. comml. and indsl. fin. Gen. Electric Credit Corp., N.Y.C., 1960-62; v.p., gen. mgr. comml. and indsl. fin. Gen. Electric Credit Corp. subs. Gen. Electric Co., 1962-75, pres., gen. mgr., 1975-79, chief exec. officer, 1979-84, vice chmn., 1984-85, also dir.; chmn., dir. Signal Capital Corp., 1985—, Stanger, Miller Inc., 1985—; bd. dirs. Conn. Bank and Trust Co., Emery Air Freight Corp., GPA Inc., Sinclair and Valentine L.P., Curtis Industries, Inc., ATCO Products, Inc. Served to capt. USAAF, 1943-45, 51-53. Decorated D.F.C. Mem. Southwestern Area Commerce and Industry Assn. Conn. (past chmn., dir.), Elfun Soc. Republican. Clubs: Harvard Lower Fairfield, Greenwich Country, Sky, Jupiter Golf. Home: 72 Perkins Rd Greenwich CT 06830 Office: Century Plaza 100 Prospect St Stamford CT 06901

STANKARD, FRANCIS XAVIER, banker; b. N.Y.C., Jan. 13, 1932; s. John J. and Margaret (Daly) S.; m. Elsa C. Hoffmann, Apr. 19, 1959; children: Charles, Peter, John. BS cum laude, Coll. Holy Cross, 1953; grad. sr. internat. mgrs. program, Harvard U., Vevey, Switzerland, 1974. With Chase Manhattan Bank, N.Y.C., 1955—, asst. treas., 1959-62, asst. v.p., 1962-64, v.p., 1964-70, sr. v.p., 1970-75, exec. v.p., 1975-85; chmn. Chase Manhattan Capital Markets Corp., N.Y.C., 1985-87; exec. v.p. Chase Manhattan Corp., N.Y.C., 1987—; bd. dirs. Crown Cen. Petroleum Corp., Pvt. Export Fin Co.; trustee Conservation Internat., Police Athletic League, N.Y.C.; chmn. bd. trustees Christian Bros. Acad. Mem. pres.'s council Marymount Manhattan Coll.; trustee Coll. Holy Cross; mem. adv. council Fletcher Sch. Law and Diplomacy, Boston; trustee, treas. Asia Soc.; bd. dirs. Inst. for Health. Served to capt. USMC, 1953-55. Decorated Order Francisco de Miranda (Venezuela), commadeur Order Nacional (Guinea). Mem. Knights of Malta (Cross of Order of Merit), Coun. Fgn. Relations, N.Y.C. Roman Catholic. Clubs: Knickerbocker (N.Y.C.), Navisink Country (Middletown, N.J.). Home: 10 Autumn Ln Middletown NJ 07748 Office: Chase Manhattan Corp 1 Chase Manhattan Pla New York NY 10081

STANKE, HOWARD JOSEPH, banker, financial officer; b. Chgo., Aug. 12, 1948; s. Bruno Joseph and Helen (Netzel) S.; m. Kathleen Adaire Martin, Apr. 12, 1980; 1 son by previous marriage, David. B.S. in Fin., U. Ill.-Chgo., 1970. Auditor, Golf Mill State Bank, Niles, 1972-76; controller Roselle State Bank, Ill., 1976-78; sr. v.p. fin. Trans World Bank, Sherman Oaks, Calif., 1978—; chief fin. officer Trans World Bancorp, Sherman Oaks, 1982—; dir. So. Calif. chpt. of Bank Adminstrn. Inst., 1988—. Republican. Office: Trans World Bank 15233 Ventura Blvd Sherman Oaks CA 91403

STANLEY, JAMES RICHARD, lawyer; b. Williamsport, Pa., Oct. 23, 1931; s. Leslie Wright and Hazel (Stryker) S.; m. Darlene Foster, Nov. 18, 1961; children: Susan A., Sandra R., James F., Jeffrey W. BA, Pa. State U., 1953; JD, Dickinson Sch. Law, 1958. Bar: Pa. 1959, N.Y. 1963, U.S. Supreme Ct. 1967, Ill. 1983. Atty. Duquesne Light Co., Pitts., 1958-62, Hazeltine Corp., Little Neck, N.Y., 1962-64; div. counsel Sealtest Foods, Phila. and Schenectady, N.Y., 1964-71; dir. legal dept. Thiokol Corp., Newtown, Pa., 1971-82; assoc. gen. counsel specialty chems. group Morton Thiokol, Inc., Chgo., 1982-86, gen. counsel, 1986-87, v.p. legal affairs, gen. counsel, 1987—; mem. adv. bd. Northwestern U. Corp. Counsel Ctr., Chgo., 1986—. Served to 1st lt. U.S. Army, 1953-55. Mem. ABA (com. on corp. law depts. 1986—), Phila. Bar Assn., Ill. Bar Assn., Chgo. Bar Assn. Republican. Presbyterian. Clubs: Met., Tower (Chgo.). Office: Morton Thiokol Inc 110 N Wacker Dr Chicago IL 60606

STANLEY, LAURA JUDITH, financial executive; b. Boston, May 30, 1957; d. Joseph Richard and Rita Ann (Fay) Leonard; m. William Francis Stanley, Oct. 3, 1987. BS, North Adams State U., 1980. Coord. manufacture engring. Johnson & Johnson, Braintree, Mass., 1983-85; acct. Boston Cons. Group, 1985-86; office mgr. Profl. Mgmt. Svcs., Canton, Mass., 1986-88; fin. adminstr. LTX, Westwood, Mass., 1988—. Active town meeting Town of Milton, Mass., 1979-81. Roman Catholic. Home: 43 Springwood Ave Stoughton MA 02072

STANLEY, THOMAS BAHNSON, JR., investor; b. Martinsville, Va., Jan. 9, 1927; s. Thomas B. and Anne (Bassett) S.; m. Ruth Barnes, Sept. 10, 1949; children: Thomas Bahnson III, Susan Walker, Andrew. B.S. in C.E., Va. Mil. Inst., 1946; B.S.C., U. Va., 1948; grad., Advanced Mgmt. Program, Harvard U., 1970. With Stanley Furniture Co., Stanleytown, Va., 1948-79, dir., 1950-79, exec. v.p., 1952-62, pres., 1962-71, chmn., 1971-79; pres. Mead Interiors, Stanleytown, 1969-74; group v.p. Mead Corp., Dayton, Ohio, 1969-74; also dir. Mead Corp.; dir. Piedmont Bankgroup, Inc., Martinsville, Va., Stanley Land & Lumber Co., Drakes Branch, Va. Mem. Henry County Sch. Bd., 1957-80; chmn. bd. trustees Ferrum Coll., 1977-79. Mem. So. Furniture Mfrs. Assn. (dir., pres. 1966, chmn. 1967). Methodist. Lodge: Masons (32 deg.). Home: Land's End Hunter's Green Dr Stanleytown VA 24168 Office: PO Box 26 Stanleytown VA 24168

STANLEY, WALTER PAUL, sales executive; b. Hartsville, S.C., Feb. 24, 1955; s. Paul Murphy and Elsie Young (Neighbors) S.; m. Paulette Aspinall, April 27, 1985. BSEE, U. S.C., 1977. Proposition engr. Industry Control Dept. GE, Salem, Mass., 1977-78; customer svc. specialist Marine and Def. Facilities GE, New Orleans, 1978-80, sales engr., 1980-84; mgr. navy sales Turbine Bus. Ops. GE, Lynn, Mass., 1984-86; mgr. mil. sales Drive Systems Dept. GE, Salem, Va., 1986-89, mgr. govt. bus. sales, 1989—. Mem. Soc. Naval Architects and Marine Engrs., Am. Soc. Naval Engrs., Am. Def. Preparedness Agy., Nat. Contract Mgmt. Assn., Naval Submarine League, Gen. Electric Elfun Soc., Tech. Mktg. Soc. Am., Homeowner's Assn. (pres.). Republican. Baptist. Home: 7582 Boxwood Dr Roanoke VA 24018 Office: GE Drive Systems Dept 1501 Roanoke Blvd Salem MA 24153

STANN, JOHN ANTHONY, investment banker; b. San Francisco, Nov. 10, 1947; s. John Peter and Mary Jane (Erny) S.; m. Judith Darlene Knapp, Apr. 27, 1973; children: John Andrew, Theodore Joseph, Rebecca Marie. BA in Econs. and Math., U. Mo., 1969. Cost acct. Monsanto Co., St. Louis, 1971-73, acctg. supr., 1973-76; salesman Monsanto Co., Brighton, Mo., 1976-79; market mgr. Monsanto Co., St. Louis, 1979-81; mfr's. rep. Farbenfabriken, Bayer, Davos & Others, St. Louis, 1981-82; corp. valuations officer, v.p. A.G. Edwards & Sons, Inc., St. Louis, 1982—; investment banking advisor to numerous pvt. and pub. cos. Fund raiser Archdiocese of St. Louis, 1981-84, 87, YMCA, St. Louis, 1987; chmn. fin. com. St. Clare Parish, St. Louis, 1982-84; youth baseball mgr. Affton Athletic Assn., St. Louis, 1985-86; poll worker Danforth for Senate, St. Louis, 1982. Lt. USNR, 1969-71. Named Man of Yr. St. John's Men's Club, 1978. Mem. Inst. of Mgmt. Acctg., Country Hills Bath and Tennis Club. Republican. Roman Catholic. Home: 4862 Vermillion Saint Louis MO 63128 Office: AG Edwards & Sons Inc 1 N Jefferson Saint Louis MO 63103

STANSBURY, DENNIS NEAL, insurance executive; b. Washington, Ill., Feb. 17, 1944; s. Leslie Monroe and Norma Jean (Corder) S.; m. Barbara Ann Haselby, July 12, 1968; children: Kimberly Nicole, Dennis Haselby. BA, Purdue U., 1966. Cert. Life Underwriter, charterd fin. cons. Contract mgr. Carpetland, Lafayette, Ind., 1970-74; br. mgr. Met. Ins. Co., Logansport, Ind., 1974-85; regional dir. Jefferson-Pilot, Logansport, 1985—; cons. Barnabas Ent., Logansport, 1983—. Precinct committeeman Dem. Party, Harrison Twp., Ind., 1986-87; active fin. com. Jim Jontz for Congress, Logansport, 1986-88. Mem. Ind. Assn. Life Underwriters (pres. elect), Assn. Cert. Life Underwriters and Chartered Fin. Cons. (pres. 1986-87), Lions (pres. 1982-84), Elks. Democrat. Home: RR 2 Box 339 Lucerne IN 46947 Office: Stansbury Agy 200 Eel River Ave Logansport IN 46947

STANSELL, RONALD BRUCE, investment banker; b. Hammond, Ind., Apr. 9, 1945; s. Herman Bruce and Helen Rose Stansell; B.A., Wittenberg U., 1967; M.A., Miami U., Oxford, Ohio, 1969; m. Kathie Van Atta, Oct. 2, 1976; children—Kelsey, Kymberlie. Investment officer First Nat. Bank, Chgo., 1969-73; mgr. investments Chrysler Corp., Detroit, 1973; asst. v.p. A.G. Becker, Chgo., 1973-76; v.p. Blyth Eastman Dillon, Chgo., 1976-79; v.p. Dean Witter Reynolds Inc., Chgo., 1979-82; v.p. First Boston Corp., 1982-88; sr. v.p. Prudential-Bache Securities, Chgo., 1988—. Mem. Mettawa (Ill.) Zoning Bd., 1978-80; trustee Village of Mettawa, 1980-89, village treas., 1977-78. Served with USMCR, 1968-69. Named to Pres.'s Club, Blyth Eastman Dillon, 1977, 78, 79. Mem. Bond Club Chgo., Investment Analyst Soc., Fixed Income Group. Clubs: Exmoor Country, Bob O'Link Golf; John's Island Country; Grandfather Golf; LaSalle. Home: RR 1 Box 49 Old Sch Rd Mettawa IL 60048

STANTON, ERWIN S., industrial psychologist; b. Frankfurt-on-the-Main, Germany, May 23, 1930; s. Arthur and Erna Schoenfeld; m. Inge Josephine Marx, Dec. 26, 1954; children: Suzanne, Nancy. BA, Queens Coll., 1952; AM, NYU, 1953; PhD, Columbia U., 1958. Personnel mgr. Arwood Corp., N.Y.C., 1952-54; asst. personnel dir. United Mchts. and Mfrs. Inc., N.Y.C., 1954-65; pres. E.S. Stanton & Assoc., Inc., N.Y.C., 1965—; assoc. prof. Baruch Coll., N.Y.C., 1959-69; prof. St. John's U., N.Y.C., 1969—. Author: Successful Personnel Recruiting and Selection, 1977, Reality-Centered People Management, 1982. Active White House Conf. on Productivity, Washington, 1985. Recipient Author of Mem. Book of Yr. Am. Mgmt. Assn., 1982. mem. Am. Psychol. Assn., Acad. of Mgmt., Am. Soc. for Personnel Adminstrn. Republican. Office: ES Stanton & Assoc Inc PO Box 46 Wantagh NY 11793

STANTON, IVENS V., financial company executive; b. N.Y.C., Feb. 27, 1929; s. Harry and Yetta (Kalmowitz) S.; m. Joyce Needleman, Jan. 28, 1970; children: Marshall Scott, Alison Eve, Lynn Erica. BA, Syracuse U., 1954. Editor Simon & Schuster Co., N.Y.C., 1954-55; editor, bus.-fin. news dept. N.Y. Times, N.Y.C., 1955-62; fin. news dir. PR Newswire, N.Y.C., 1962-66; pres. Ivens Stanton Assocs. Inc., N.Y.C., 1966—; pres., bd. dirs. Wavehill Internat. Ventures, Inc.; chmn. bd. Personal Computer Rental Corp., Coral Gables, Fla.; pres., bd. dirs. PCR Internat., Inc., N.Y.C.; bd. dirs., treas. Sigma Med. Labs., Inc.; bd. dirs. Meridian Advt. Inc., Ivey Group Inc.; cons. fin., pub., mineral, mining, oil and gas firms. Contbr. articles to profl. jours. Served with Signal Corps, U.S. Army, 1951-53. Mem. Communications Alumni Soc. Syracuse U., Police Conf. N.Y. (hon.). Office: 25 W 45th St New York NY 10036

STANTON, MIRIAM RUTH ROSENTRATER, educator; b. Long Beach, Calif., Jan. 11, 1944; d. David Frederick and Olive Wanda (Walter) Rosentrater; m. Larry Robert Stanton, Aug. 21, 1965 (div. Jan. 1986); children: JoLynn Kay, David Clinton. BA with honors, LeTourneau Coll., 1967; postgrad., U. Tex., Tyler, 1987—. Cert. secondary tchr. in English, history, bus. Tchr. Pine Tree Jr. High Sch., Longview, Tex., 1985—. Mem. Ptnrs. in Edn., Longview, 1987—, Longview PTA, 1974—, pres. 1976-77, 82-83, coun. pres. 1978-80. Recipient Danforth award Tex. PTA, 1984; named life mem. Internat. Programs scholar U. Tex. 1988. Mem. Delta Kappa Gamma. Home: 2810 Emerald Dr Longview TX 75605 Office: PO Box 150181 Longview TX 75615

STANTON, PETER DIEUDONNE, insurance executive, investor; b. Newton, Mass., May 6, 1934; s. Frederick Everett and Hortense (Dievdonne) S.; m. Nancy Lee Moe, Dec. 20, 1958; children: Laura, Jeffrey, Bradley, Leah. BBA, U. Fla., 1958. Pres. Gateway Ins. Agy., Inc., Ft. Lauderdale, Fla., 1958—; bd. dirs. Ambassador Fin. Group, Inc., Tamarac, Fla., Fla. Fire & Casualty Ins. Co., Ft. Lauderdale. With U.S. Army, 1954-56. Republican. Office: Gateway Ins Agy Inc 2430 W Oakland Park Blvd Fort Lauderdale FL 33311

STANTON, WALTER OLIVER, electronics company executive; b. Canton, Ohio, Sept. 29, 1914; s. Bela Hayden and Edna (Keckley) S.; Elec. Engring., Wayne State U.; m. Mary Ann Wilcox; children—Sharon (Mrs. Robert Russell), Diana (Mrs. Grant Thornbrough), Pamela Stanton (Mrs. John O'Donnell). Pres. Pickering & Co., Inc., 1948—, Stanton Magnetics, Inc., 1966—, Pickering Impex S.A., Switzerland, Stanton Impex S.A. Fellow Audio Engring. Soc. (pres. 1957); mem. Newcomen Soc., Inst. Dirs. (London), Chief Exec.'s Forum. Home: 115 Lakeshore Dr North Palm Beach FL 33408 Office: Sunnyside Blvd Plainview NY 11803

STAPLEFORD, FREDERICK HAMILTON, distributing company executive; b. Phila., Jan. 19, 1945; s. Frederick Hamilton and Jane Reed (Limerick) S.; m. Laura Jean Stein, Nov. 1, 1980; children: John Townsend, Hunter Laurence. BA in Econs., Denison U., 1967; MS in Mgmt., U. Ark., 1972. Comml. officer Phila. Nat. Bank, 1972-75; asst. treas. Am. Medicorp., Bala Cynwyd, Pa., 1975-78; v.p. fiscal svcs. Universal Health Svcs., Gulph Mills, Pa., 1978-81; dir. devel. Ferguson Enterprises Inc, Newport News, Va., 1981—; bd. dirs. Mktg. Am. Inc., Williamsburg, Va. Bd. dirs. Newport News Clean Community Commn., 1985-86, Va. Living Mus., Newport News, 1986—; mem. budget com. Kingsmill Community Svc. Assn., 1988—. Capt. USAF, 1968-72. Mem. Hampton C. of C. (govt. affairs com. 1986—), James River Country Club, Kirksmill Golf Club. Republican. Episcopalian. Home: 21 Whittakers Mill Williamsburg VA 23185 Office: Ferguson Enterprises Inc 618 Bland Blvd Newport News VA 23602

STAPLES, BRUCE H., electrical engineer; b. Iowa City, July 17, 1958. BSEE, Iowa State U., 1981. Registered profl. engr., Wis. With Dairyland Power Coop., La Crosse, Wis., 1981—; supr. ops. Dairyland Power Coop., La Crosse, 1986—; bd. dirs. Dairyland Power Coop. Credit Union. Pres. Eng. Luth. Ch., 1986-89. Mem. IEEE, Wis. Soc. Profl. Engrs. (v.p. 1988-89, pres. 1989—), Etta Kappa Nu. Home: 1630 Barlow St La Crosse WI 54601 Office: Dairyland Power Coop PO Box 817 La Crosse WI 54602

STAPLES, DAVID GEORGE, import representative; b. Afton, Wyo., Sept. 1, 1955; s. George Emmett and Katherine Elna (Stanford) S.; m. Kathryn Sue Aneiro, Mar. 3, 1984; children: Laura Naomi, Rebekah Allene, Susannah Erika. BA in Journalism, Brigham Young U., 1981; MBA, Moorhead State U., 1987. Hist. editor Cass County Hist. Soc., West Fargo, N.D., 1975-76; missionary LDS Ch., Sendai, Japan, 1977-79; mgr. trainee Sav-On Drugs, Inc. (now Osco), Anaheim, Calif., 1981-82; ops. mgr. Cass County Hist. Soc., West Fargo, 1983-88; asst. to v.p./internat. div. Sony Plaza Co., Tokyo, 1988—. Editor: Rural Cass County: The Land and People, 1976, Joseph S. Stanford, 1981, My Highway in the Sky, 1984. Sec., treas. Fargo-Moorhead Area Attraction Assn., Heritage Edn. Commn., Moorhead, Minn. Home: Matsudo 2268-4, Matsudo-Shi, Chiba-Ken 271, Japan Office: Sony Plaza Co,

Ginza 6-8-5, Chuo-Ku, Tokyo 104, Japan also: RR 3 Box 72 Fargo ND 58103

STAPLES, LYLE NEWTON, lawyer; b. Radford, Va., Feb. 16, 1945; s. Lester Lyle and Velma Jean (King) S.; m. Christie Mercedes Carr, Feb. 1, 1971; children: Scott Andrew, John Randolph, Brian Matthew, Melissa Ann. BA, U. Md., 1967, JD, 1972; LLM in Taxation, Georgetown U., 1977. Bar: Md. 1973, U.S. Supreme Ct. 1978, U.S. Tax Ct. 1981, U.S. Dist. Ct. Md. 1981, U.S. Ct. Appeals (4th cir.) 1981. Tax law specialist IRS, Washington, 1972-77; assoc. Hessey & Hessey, Balt., 1978-82, Rosenstock, Burgee & Welty, Frederick, Md., 1982-84; sole practice, Hampstead, Md., 1984—; vis. asst. prof. Towson (Md.) State U., 1981-82. Active Carroll County (Md.) ARC, Hampstead Bus. Assn., Hampstead Elem. Sch. PTA, North Carroll Mid. Sch. PTO, Greenmount, Md., Balt. Council Fgn. Affairs, Inc. Served with U.S. Army, 1968-69, Vietnam. Mem. ABA, Md. Bar Assn. Democrat. Methodist. Home: 4304 Royal Ave Hampstead MD 21074 Office: 926 S Main St PO Box 205 Hampstead MD 21074

STAPLES, MICHAEL, medical industry executive; b. Redlands, Calif., Oct. 29, 1949; s. John and Cathrine Staples; children: Jon, Wendy. AA, City Coll. San Francisco, 1976, AS, 1979. Cert. radiation therapist. Head dept. biomed. engring. Oncological Services, Inc., Santa Rosa, Calif., 1979-81; pres. Accelerator Maintenance Systems, Santa Rosa, 1981-84, Radiotherapy Instruments, Santa Rosa, 1984—; bd. dirs. Oncological Resource Network, Sonoma, Calif. Contbr. articles to profl. jours. Served as sgt. USMC, 1966-70, Vietnam. Decorated Bronze Star. Mem. Am. Registry Radiologic Technologists, Calif. Radiol. Technologists, No. Calif. Soc. Radiation Therapy Technologists. Home and Office: 18370 Clayton Ave Sonoma CA 95476

STAPP, LARRY STEPHEN, banker; b. Corning, N.Y., Oct. 29, 1955; s. Lawrence Dale and Sarah (Greer) S.; m. Kelly Jeanne Fair, Dec. 31, 1977; children: Christy, Brady. BS, Tex. A&M U., 1978, MS in Fin., 1980; cert., Southwestern Grad. Sch. Banking, Dallas, 1987. Branch mgr. Fed. Land Bank, Huntsville, Tex., 1979-82; v.p. First State Bank Mathis, Tex., 1982—. Bd. dirs. Mathis Ind. Schs., 1987—, Mathis Ambulance Svcs., 1987—, Mathis Cubs & Library, 1985-87. Named Hon. Chpt. Farmer Future Farmers Am., 1986, Outstanding Agribus.man. Tex. Young Farmers, 1983. Mem. ABA (Young Bankers div.), Ind. Bankers Assn., Mathis C. of C. (pres. 1984-85), Kiwanis (pes. 1985-87). Republican. Baptist. Home: Rt 1 Box 172F Mathis TX 78368 Office: First State Bank Mathis 103 N Hwy 359 Mathis TX 78368

STARK, JEFFREY MICHAEL, financial company executive; b. Cleve., Aug. 11, 1947; s. Alvin Michael and Catherine Dorothy S.; m. Margaret Bennett, Apr. 15, 1984; 1 child, Catherine E. Student, U. Munich, 1967-68; BA, Muskingum Coll., 1969; MBA, Ind. U., 1972; cert., Coll. Fin. Planning, Denver, 1984. Sales rep. Xerox Co., Oakland, Calif., 1972-74; brokerage cons. Conn. Gen. Life Ins. Co., San Francisco, 1974-75; account exec. Equitec Securities Co., Lafayette, Calif., 1976-85; ptnr. Stark & Leitman, Lafayette, 1985—. Treas., bd. dirs. Calif. Grad. Sch. Family Psychology, San Rafael, 1984—. Mem. Internat. Assn. Fin. Planners, Inst. Cert. Fin. Planners, Walnut Creek C. of C. (chair bus. seminar com. 1988—, participant Leadership Program Contra Costa County), Securities Exch. Commn. (registered investment advisor), Nat. Assn. Securities Dealers (registered prin.). Republican. Office: Associated Planners Securities Corp 3730 Mt Diablo Blvd Ste 330 Lafayette CA 94949

STARK, MAURICE EDMUND, lawyer; b. Ft. Dodge, Iowa, Sept. 22, 1921; s. Max Martin and Lillian Veronica (O'Rourke) S.; m. Mary Murray, Dec. 27, 1952; children—Michelle, Diane, Stephen, Thomas, Julie, David. B.C.S., U. Iowa, 1942, J.D., 1949. Bar: Iowa 1949, U.S. Dist. Ct. (no. dist.) Iowa 1950, Tax Ct. U.S. 1951. Law clk. to judge U.S. Dist. Ct., 1949-50; spl. atty. criminal div. Dept. Justice, Washington, 1951; trial atty. Office Chief Counsel, IRS, N.Y.C., 1951, 53-55; mem. Stark, Crumley & Jacobs, Ft. Dodge, 1955—; mem. Fed. Tax Liaison Com. in Iowa, 1968—; mem. adv. group Commr. Internal Revenue, 1969-70; Iowa. mem. Midwest Region Liaison Com. with IRS, 1962-71, vice chmn., 1974-76, ABA rep., 1976-80. Sec. Trinity Regional Hosp. of Ft. Dodge, 1973-76, bd. dirs.; pres. Trinity Regional Hosp. Devel. Found., 1987-88. Served as lt., inf. U.S. Army, 1943-46, to capt., 1951-52. Decorated Bronze Star with Oak leaf cluster, Combat Infantry Badge with star; recipient Meritorious Pub. Service award Commr. Internal Revenue, 1971. Mem. Am. Judicature Soc., Am. Coll. Tax Counsel, Webster County Bar Assn. (treas. 1955-62, pres. 1976-77), Iowa State Bar Assn. (chmn. com. taxation 1967-69), ABA, Order Artus, Delta Theta Phi, Beta Gamma Sigma, Omicron Delta Kappa. Roman Catholic. Club: Rotary (pres. 1966-67). Notes editor Iowa Law Rev., 1948-49. Office: Stark Crumley & Jacobs Warden Pla Fort Dodge IA 50501

STARK, MAURICE GENE, research institute financial executive; b. Elyria, Ohio, Sept. 23, 1935; s. Maurice George and Florence Ann (Woiczikowski) S.; m. Judith Belle Martin, July 21, 1956; children: Susan, David, Daniel, Douglas, Dean. B.S., Ohio State U., 1957; cert. program for sr. execs., Sloan Sch. Mgmt., MIT, 1978. Supr., auditor Auditor Gen.'s Office, U.S. Air Force, Columbus, Ohio, 1961-65; mgr. corp. acctg. Battelle Meml. Inst., Columbus, Ohio, 1965-75; controller and dir. fin. Battelle Columbus div., Ohio, 1975-78; v.p.-treas. Battelle Meml. Inst. ., Columbus, 1978—; treas. Battelle Devel. Corp., Columbus, 1978—; bd. dirs., chmn. Research Ins. Co. Ltd., Hamilton, Bermuda, 1978—; treas., mem. Vorstand, Battelle-Institut e.V., Frankfurt, Fed. Republic Germany, 1978—; bd. dirs., sec. Tin Research Inst., Columbus, Ohio, 1982—; trustee The Sessions Group, Columbus. Trustee Central Ohio Transit Authority, Columbus, 1975—, Columbus Symphony Orch., 1983—, treas., 1984—. Served with USAF, 1958-61; served to capt. Res., 1961-63. Recipient Spl. Service award USAF, 1965. Mem. Fin. Execs. Inst. (dir. 1983-84), Treas. Club (dir. 1982-84), Columbus Council World Affairs. Lutheran. Club: Optimists (Columbus) (pres. 1975-76). Lodge: Rotary. Office: Battelle Meml Inst 505 King Ave Columbus OH 43201

STARK, STEVEN, electrical engineer, systems architect; b. N.Y.C., Aug. 4, 1943; s. Herman and Betty (Lazar) S.; m. Rita Ellen Sussman, Sept. 5, 1966; children: Darlena Bari, Tiffany Allysson, Ilana Valerie. BS in Physics, Bklyn. Coll., 1965; MS in Physics, NYU, 1967. Lab. specialist Ridgewood Jr. High Sch., N.Y.C., 1965-66; physicist Naval Applied Sci. Lab., N.Y.C., 1966-73; elec. engr. Naval Underwater Systems Ctr., New London, Conn., 1973-76, Naval Air Devel. Ctr., Warminster, Pa., 1976-82; elec. engr. Grumman Corp., Bethpage, N.Y., 1982—, program mgr. computer integrated tech. environ., 1986-87; co-founder, mgr.integration program Computer Integrated Enterprise, 1988—; owner, mgr. Stark Software, Richboro, Pa., 1980-85. Author: (software program) Time-Table, 1981, Design A Diet, 1988; inventor computer aided engring. system Advanced Virtual Architecture, 1984. Mem. Mensa.

STARKEY, RUSSELL BRUCE, JR., utility executive; b. Lumberport, W.Va., July 20, 1942; s. Russell Bruce and Dorotha Mable (Field) S.; m. Joan McClellan, May 27, 1966; children: Christine, Pamela, Joanne. BS, Miami U., Oxford, Ohio, 1964; grad. student U. New Haven, 1972-73, N.C. State U., 1974-75, U.S. Navy Schs., 1964-66, 68. Sr. engr., nuclear generation sect. Carolina Power & Light Co., Raleigh, N.C., 1973-74, sr. engr. ops. quality assurance, 1974, prin. engr., 1974-75, quality assurance supr. Brunswick Steam Electric Plant, Southport, N.C., 1975-76, supt. tech. and adminstrn., 1976, supt. ops. and maintenance, 1976-77, plant mgr. H.B. Robinson Steam Electric Plant, Hartsville, S.C., 1977-83, mgr. environ. services, Raleigh, 1984-85, mgr. nuclear safety and environ. services dept., 1985-88; mgr. Brunswick Nuclear Project Dept., 1988—; exec. dir. nuclear prodn. Pub. Service Ind., Jeffersonville, 1983-84. Served with USN, 1964-73. Mem. Am. Nuclear Soc., N.C. State Emergency Response Commn. (commr.), Rotary. Home: PO Box 306 Wilson's Mills NC 27593 Office: Brunswick Nuclear Project PO Box 1551 Raleigh NC 27602

STARKEY, WILLIAM EDWARD, telephone company executive; b. Ridley Park, Pa., Aug. 2, 1935; s. William Lester and Miriam Starkey; m. Barbara, June 20, 1959; children: William T., Michael M., Jennifer E. B.S. in Bus. Adminstrn, U. Del., 1957; M.S. in Bus. Adminstrn, St. Francis Coll., Ft. Wayne, Ind., 1964. Trainee Bell Telephone Co. of Pa., 1957, asst. dist. traffic mgr., 1959-64; traffic engr. Gen. Telephone Co., Ind., 1964; methods mgr. Gen. Telephone Co., 1965, gen. traffic adminstrn. mgr., 1965, gen. traffic engr. mgr., 1968; system traffic engr. mgr. GTE Service Corp., N.Y.C., 1969-71; traffic dir. Gen. Telephone Co. S.E., 1971-74, v.p. staff, 1974-76; operating v.p. Gen. Telephone Co. Pa., 1976-77, v.p. mktg. and customer service, 1977-78, regional v.p. mktg. and customer service N.E. region, 1979-80; v.p. regulatory affairs GTE Info. Svcs. Inc., Stamford, Conn., 1980-82; v.p. staff telephone ops. GTE Info. Svcs. Inc., 1982-85, pres., 1988—; pres. GTE Fla., Inc., Tampa, Fla., 1985-88. Boys basketball coach YMCA, 1971-78, bd. dirs., 1976-78; trustee The Fla. Orchestra, U. Tampa; chmn. bd. deacons 1st Presbyn. Ch., 1975; div. chmn. United Fund, 1962-64, 75-76, bd. dirs., exec. com. United Way of Greater Tampa, Hyde Park United Meth. Ch. Served with AUS, 1957-58, 60-61. Mem. Fla. C. of C. (bd. dirs.), Greater Tampa C. of C. (v.p.), Omicron Delta Kappa. Republican. Methodist. Office: GTE Info Svcs Inc PO Box 2924 Barnett Plaza 8th Fl Tampa FL 33601

STARKS, KIRK WILLIAM, real estate broker; b. Dodge City, Kans., Feb. 4, 1954; s. William Melvin and Dora Lee (Neidenthal) S.; m. Melissa Ann Payne, Apr. 25, 1987. B in Gen. Studies, U. Kans., 1977. Instr. Dodge City Community Coll., 1979; prin. The Doctors Office Pub, Dodge City, 1979-80; mgr. Starks-Henley Real Estate, Dodge City, 1977-83; mng. dir. Erle Rawlins Jr. Realtors, Inc., Dallas, 1983-88; v.p. real estate managed assets Deposit Ins. Bridge Bank, N.A., 1988—. Mem. Nat. Assn. Realtors, Greater Dallas Bd. Realtors, Tex. Assn. Realtors. Club: Dallas Gun.

STARKWEATHER, FREDERICK THOMAS, data processing executive; b. Sioux City, Iowa, Feb. 24, 1933; s. Fred Ervin and Gertrude Faye (Madden) S.; m. Margot Glassen, Nov. 19, 1959; children: Thomas Frederick, Jerry Russell, Michael Glassen. BA in Math. and Physics, U. Nebr., Omaha, 1955. Mathematician Flight Determination Lab., White Sands Missile Range, N.Mex., 1955-56; supervisory mathematician Analysis & Computation, White Sands Missile Range, N.Mex., 1956-81; chief Data Scis. Div. Nat. Range Ops., White Sands Missile Range, N.Mex., 1981—; Nat. council rep. Am. Def. Preparedness Assn., Washington, 1980—; pres. White Sands Pioneer Group, White Sands Missile Range, 1983-86; bd. dirs. Assn. U.S. Army, Washington. Author hist. and genealog. books; contbr. book reviews and articles to newspapers and mags. Chmn. El Paso (Tex.) City Planning Commn., 1980-84; bd. dirs. El Paso County Hist. Soc., 1983-87; mem. El Paso County Hist. Commn., 1983—. Served with USAR, 1955-63. Recipient Profl. Secs. Internat. Exec. of Yr. award, 1987; named Disting. Alumnus U. Nebr., Omaha, 1985; recipient Conquistador City of El Paso award, 1980; cited for Services to Mankind Sertoma, El Paso chpt., 1985. Mem. Fed. Mgrs. Assn. (bd. dirs.), Freedom Found. at Valley Forge (pres. El Paso chpt., George Washington Hon. medal 1982), El Paso C. of C. (assoc. dir. 1984—, bd. dirs.), Hon. Order Saint Barbara, U.S. Field Artillery Assn., Tau Kappa Epsilon (Hall of Fame 1986). Club: Toastmasters (dist. gov. 1970-71). Lodge: Masons. Home: 8010 Tonto Pl El Paso TX 79904 Office: Nat Range Ops Chief Data Scis Div White Sands Missile Range NM 88002

STARNER, CRAIG LESLIE, marketing executive; b. Chgo., Sept. 8, 1934; s. Morris Eugene and Beatrice Caroline (Thon) S.; student U. Miami, 1952-54; M.J.S., Northwestern U., 1956; children—Faith, Roni, Guy, Greta. Promotion mgr. Domestic Engring. Pub. Co., Cahner's Pub. Co., Chgo., 1956-60; promotion mgr. Look mag., Des Moines and N.Y.C., 1960-68; pres., owner Market Motivation, Inc., Sarasota, Fla., 1973-78; market/research analyst Manatee C. of C., Bradenton, Fla., 1978-81; mgmt. and econ. analyst Manatee County, Bradenton, Fla., 1981—. Cons., Manatee C. of C. and Econ. Devel. Council; advt. and mktg. cons. N.Y.C. Ad Agys.; dir. United Way. Recipient Mail Box award Direct Mail Advt. Assn., 1964, 65, 66, Apex award Am. Automobile Assn., 1977. Mem. Am. Mktg. Assn., Tampa Bay Regional Planning Council, Sigma Delta Chi, Alpha Tau Omega. Lodge: Kiwanis. Home: 5064 Live Oak Circle Bradenton FL 34207 Office: Bradenton Fin Ctr Suite 640 B Bradenton FL 34205

STARNES, WILLIAM HERBERT, JR., chemist, educator; b. Knoxville, Tenn., Dec. 2, 1934; s. William Herbert and Edna Margaret (Osborne) S.; m. Maria Sofia Molina, Mar. 4, 1986. BS with honors, Va. Poly Inst., 1955; PhD, Ga. Inst. Tech., 1960. Research chemist Esso Research & Engring. Co., Baytown, Tex., 1960-62, sr. research chemist, 1962-64, polymer additives sect. head, 1964-65, research specialist, 1965-67, research assoc., 1967-71; instr. and research assoc. dept. chemistry U. Tex., Austin, 1971-73; mem. tech. staff AT&T Bell Labs., Murray Hill, N.J., 1973-85; prof. chemistry Poly. U., Bklyn., 1985—, head dept. chemistry and life scis., 1985-88, assoc. dir. polymer durability ctr. 1987—; vis. scientist Tex. Acad. Scis., 1964-67; bd. doctoral thesis examiners Indian Inst. Tech., New Delhi, 1988, McGill U., Montreal, 1989; cons. numerous indsl. cos. Mem. adv. bd. and bd. reviewers Jour. Vinyl Tech., 1981-83. Contbr. articles to profl. jours., chpts. to books; patentee in field. NSF fellow 1958-60; recipient Profl. Progress award Soc. Profl. Chemists and Engrs. 1968, Disting. Tech. Staff award AT&T Bell Labs. 1982, Polymer Sci. Pioneer award Polymer News, 1988, Honor Scroll award N.J. Inst. Chemists, 1989; NSF grantee, Nat. Bur. Standards Ctr. for Fire Rsch. grantee . Fellow AAAS (Project 2061 1985-86, chmn. chemistry subpanel 1985-86, mem. panel on phys. scis. and engring., 1985-86), Am. Inst. Chemists (life); mem. Am. Chem. Soc. (bd. dirs. southeastern Tex. sect. 1970, speakers bur. div. polymer chemistry 1976—), N.Y. Acad. Scis. (life), Sigma Xi (M.A. Ferst award Ga. Inst. Tech. chpt. 1960), Phi Kappa Phi, Phi Lambda Upsilon (pres. Va. Poly. Inst. chpt. 1954-55). Current work: Degradation, stabilization, flammability, microstructures, and polymerization mechanisms of synthetic polymers, especially poly (vinyl chloride); free radical chemistry; carbon-13 nuclear magnetic resonance and organic synthesis. Subspecialties: Organic chemistry; Polymer chemistry. Office: Poly U Dept Chemistry & Life Scis 333 Jay St Brooklyn NY 11201

STARR, RICHARD DEAN, finance company executive; b. Springfield, Ohio, May 2, 1944; m. Judith Metzger, Apr. 2, 1977. BA, Ohio State U., 1967. Prin. RDS & Assocs., Bellevue, Wash., 1979—; pres., chief exec. officer Continental Am. Securities, Phoenix, 1982—, Long Beach (Calif.) Securities, 1983—, Trafalgar Securities Corp., L.A., 1984—; exec. v.p. FCA Mortgage Securities, L.A., 1984—; sr. v.p. Pacific First Fin. Corp., Seattle, 1986—, pres., 1986—. Bd. dirs. Bellevue Philharm. Orch., 1987—. Mem. Bank Securities Assn. (bd. dirs. San Francisco chpt. 1987—). Home: 13808 SE 51st Pl Bellevue WA 98006 Office: Pacific First Fin Corp 1145 Broadway Ste 1200 Tacoma WA 98402

STARR, ROSS MARC, economist, educator; b. Oak Ridge, Nov. 14, 1945; s. Chauncey and Doris E. S.; m. Susan S. Strauss, July 2, 1967; children: Daniel, Diana. B.S., Stanford U., 1966, Ph.D., 1972. Cons. Rand Corp., summers 1966, 67, Western Mgmt. Sci. Inst., Grad. Sch. Mgmt., UCLA, summers 1967, 71; Cowles Found. staff research economist Yale U., New Haven, 1970; faculty Yale U., 1970-74, assoc. prof. econs., 1974; assoc. prof. econs. U. Calif.-Davis, 1975-76, prof. econs., 1976-80; prof. econs. U. Calif.-San Diego, 1980—, chmn. dept., 1987—; vis. lectr. London Sch. Econs., 1973-74; vis. scholar U. Calif.-Berkeley, 1978-80; vis. lectr. Peoples U. of China, Beijing, 1987. Co-editor: Essays in Honor of Kenneth J. Arrow, 1986: v.1, Social Choice and Public Decision Making, v.2, Equilibrium Analysis, v.3, Uncertainty, Information and Communication, Gen. Equilibrium Models of Monetary Economies, 1989; contbr. articles to profl. jours. NDEA fellow, 1966-69; Yale jr. faculty fellow, 1973-74; Guggenheim fellow, 1978-79; NSF grantee, 1979-81, 83-85. Office: U Calif San Diego Dept Econs D-008 La Jolla CA 92093

STARR, SETH L., accountant; b. Bklyn., Oct. 23, 1959; s. Jack and Rivoli (Berlin) S. BS in Acctg., SUNY, Albany; MS in Taxation, Pace U. CPA, N.Y.; cert. fin. planner. Sr. auditor Ernst & Whinney, N.Y.C., 1981-84, tax mgr., 1986—; sr. auditor Manton, Gilbert & Levy, Rockville Centre, N.Y., 1985; mem. adj. faculty Coll. for Fin. Planning, Denver, 1987—. Lectr. Jr. Achievement, N.Y.C., 1984-85. Mem. AICPA, Inst. Cert. Fin. Planners, Internat. Assn. for Fin. Planning. Democrat. Jewish. Office: Ernst & Whinney 787 7th Ave New York NY 10019

STARR, STANLEY, retail executive, controller; b. N.Y.C., Oct. 2, 1941; s. Harry and Minnie (Kietz) S.; m. Arlene Baron, Aug. 3, 1969; children: Todd, Howard. BA in Acctg., Pace U., 1963. CPA, N.Y. Mgr. acctg. Korvettes Dept. Stores, N.Y.C., 1964-80, Mego Toy Co., N.Y.C., 1980-82; Mgr. acctg. Newmark and Lewis, Hicksville, N.Y., 1982-85, asst. controller, 1986—; controller Sleepy's Bedding, New Hyde Park, N.Y., 1985-86. Served with USAR, 1963-69. Mem. Knights of Pythias (treas. Appollo chpt. 1985—). Office: Newmark & Lewis Inc 595 S Broadway Hicksville NY 11801

STARR, WALTER DOUGLAS, JR., bank executive; b. Creswell, N.C., June 28, 1944; s. Walter Douglas Sr. and Ruth (Blanchard) S.; m. Linda Lauder, July 1, 1967; children: Matthew, Rachel. BS in Applied Math., N.C. State U., 1968; cert. in profl. banking, La. State U., 1977; cert. exec. program, U. N.C., 1980. Account rep. Wachovia Bank, Raleigh, N.C., 1968-69; asst. cashier Planters Nat. Bank, Rocky Mount, N.C., 1969—, asst. v.p., 1971-72, v.p., 1972-76; v.p., city exec. Planters Nat. Bank, Greenville, N.C., 1976-78, sr. v.p., regional exec., 1978-81; sr. v.p., regional exec. Planters Nat. Bank, Rocky Mount, N.C., 1981-85, exec. v.p., 1985-89, vice-chmn., 1989—. Pres. bd. advisors East Carolina U. Ctr. for Mgmt. Devel., Greenville, N.C., 1982; bd. dirs. Rocky Mount ARC, 1985—; bd. dirs. Rocky Mount Boys Club, 1984—, Full Gospel Bus. Men's Fellowship, Rocky Mt. Community Ministries, 1988. Mem. Atlantic States Bank Card (strategic planning com. 1984—), Greenville C. of C. (hon. life), Rocky Mt. C. of C. (bd. dirs. 1988), Benvenue Country Club. Lodge: Kiwanis. Home: 2725 Coleberry Tr Rocky Mount NC 27804 Office: Planters Nat Bank 131 N Church St Rocky Mount NC 27804

STARR, WARREN DAVID, accountant, lawyer; b. N.Y.C., June 18, 1939; s. Benjamin and Beatrice (Danson) S.; m. Janet Sheila Berger, Dec. 25, 1960; children—Mark, Wendy. B.S. in Acctg., Queens Coll., 1959; J.D., NYU, 1965. C.P.A., N.Y.; bar: N.Y. 1966. Acct., Herbert Strauss & Co., N.Y.C., 1960-62, David Sieger & Co., N.Y.C., 1962-64, Walter Leipzig, N.Y.C., 1964-67; sr. ptnr. Starr and Co. (formerly Leipzig & Starr, C.P.A.s), Great Neck, N.Y., 1967—; ptnr. Starr & Starr, attys., N.Y.C., 1971—; dir. Hudson Shipping Co., Inc., N.Y.C. Trustee Cow Bay Manpower, Port Washington, N.Y., 1977-78; fundraiser United Jewish Appeal, Sands Point, N.Y., 1981-83. NYU Law Sch. grantee, 1963-65. Mem. Am. Assn. Atty.-C.P.A.s, ABA, N.Y. State Bar Assn. (tax sect.), N.Y. State C.P.A. Soc., Queens Coll. Alumni Assn. (trustee 1984—). Democrat. Jewish. Avocations: rare book collector; travel; tennis. Office: Starr & Co 9 Park Pl Great Neck NY 11021 Office: 350 Park Ave New York NY 10022

STARRATT, LAWRENCE EVERETT, process control instrumentation company executive; b. Quincy, Mass., Sept. 11, 1937; s. Everett Otto and Priscilla (Guild) S.; m. Ellen Louise Smith, Nov. 7, 1959; children: Lynn, Laurie, Lawrence, Kim. Student, Northeastern U., 1959-60, Harvard U., 1964. Health physics technician E.G.&G, Mercury, Nev., 1958; clin. lab. technician L.A. Tumor Inst., 1959-60; health physics technician shipbuilding div. Bethlehem Steel Co., Quincy, 1960-62; asst. dir. health physics Harvard U., Cambridge, Mass., 1962-67; lab. technician Panametrics Inc., Waltham, Mass., 1967-71; gen. sales and mktg. mgr. Endress and Hauser, Maulberg, Fed. Republic of Germany and Greenwood, Ind., 1971-81; group mktg. mgr. Masoneilan/McGraw Edison, Norwood, Mass., 1981-84; pres. Eckardt Process Instrumentation Ltd., Stuttgart, Fed. Republic of Germany and Houston, 1984—. Contbr. articles to profl. jours. With USAF, 1955-58. Mem. Instrument Soc. Am. (sr., sr. lectr. 1970-87), K.C. Republican. Home: 2219 Sand Ct Richmond TX 77469 Office: Eckardt Process Instrumentation Ltd 11261 Richmond Ave Ste G-104 Houston TX 77082

STARRELS, RICKI SUE, real estate corporation officer; b. Henderson, Tex., Nov. 22, 1946; d. Irving and Miriam (Schachter) Gerger; m. John Murry Starrels, Dec. 24, 1974 (div. 1982). BA, Washington U., St. Louis, 1968; MA, George Washington U., 1976. Asst. v.p. Shannon and Luchs Co., Washington, 1981-84; v.p. Merrill Lynch Realty, Washington, 1984—. Mem. Washington Assn. Realtors (treas. 1987, v.p. 1988, pres. elect 1989), Nat. Assn. Realtors (vice-chmn. sub-com. 1988, bd. dirs. 1989). Jewish. Home: 2725 Connecticut Ave NW # 708 Washington DC 20008 Office: Merrill Lynch Realty 2305 Calvert St NW Washington DC 20008

STARRETT, CAM, personnel executive; b. Apr. 5, 1949; d. William Henry and Jeanne (Koop) Bocklage; m. Peter M. Starrett, June 14, 1986. BA in Polit. Sci., U. Cin., 1971. Sales specialist bookstore W.Va. U., Morgantown, 1971-74; dept. mgr. Filene's, Boston, 1974, asst. store mgr., 1975, buyer, 1976-77, store mgr., 1978-79, v.p. pers., 1980-85; sr. v.p. pers. Avon Products, Inc., N.Y.C., 1985-88; v.p. pers. and adminstrn. Maxwell Macmillan, N.Y.C., 1989—; bd. advisors Catalyst, N.Y.C., 1986-89. Contbr. articles to profl. jours. Bd. dirs. Tufts U. Women's Ctr., Boston, 1981-85, N.Y.C. Alcohol Coun., 1985-88. Mem. Conf. Bd. (advisor 1987-89), Human Resource Planning Soc. (bd. dirs. 1989). Office: Macmillan Inc 866 3rd Ave New York NY 10022

STASCH, RONALD WAYNE, company executive; b. Chgo., Jan. 12, 1936; s. Jess William and Mary M. (Hews) S.; m. Margo Jean Coffman, Oct. 11, 1958; children: David, Mark, Jill. BA, Wabash Coll., 1958. CPCU. Supr. mktg. Aetna Life & Casualty Co., Detroit, Chgo. and Milw., 1960-72; asst. ins. mgr. Budd Co., Troy, Mich., 1972-74; mgr. corp. risk Fed. Mogul Corp., Southfield, Mich., 1974—; instr. ins. Lawrence Inst. Tech.; bd. dirs. chmn. underwriting com. Corp. Officers and Dirs. Assurance Ltd., Bermuda, Mich. Contbr. articles to profl. jours. With U.S. Army, 1958-60. Mem. Assn. Ind. Colls. and Univs. Mich. (dir. workers compensation fund), Risk and Inst. Mgmt. Soc. (1st v.p. 1988—), Machinery and Allied Products Inst., Soc. CPCU. Republican. Home: 1767 Coventry Dr Troy MI 48083 Office: Fed-Mogul Corp PO Box 1966 Detroit MI 48235

STASKEWICZ, JACK J., automobile club exec.; b. Duryea, Pa., May 22, 1928; s. Felix and Florence (Jaworski) S.; B.S. in Bus. Mgmt., Am. Nat. U., 1982; m. Dolores F. Keiderling, Apr. 23, 1949; children—Robyn Sue, Scott John. Chief clk. AAA-N.J. Auto Club, Plainfield, 1948-51, rd. service mgr., safety dir. Central N.J., Trenton, 1951-55, br. mgr., Edison and New Brunswick, 1955-63, exec. v.p., gen. mgr., West Jersey, Phillipsburg, 1963—, sec., 1969—, pres., 1981—, also dir.; pres., gen. mgr. AAA-North Jersey Auto Club, Wayne, 1984—. Pres. Stony Brook PTA, North Plainfield, N.J., 1958-59; sec. Branchburg Twp. Taxpayers Assn., 1962; dir. Hunterdon County YMCA, 1970-72; pres. Hunterdon, Sussex and Warren Counties Safety Council, 1980-82; trustee Wayne Gen. Hosp., 1987—. Served with U.S. Navy, 1946-48. Mem. N.J. State AAA Assn. (pres. 1970, 78, 82, 87), AAA Clubs Under 50,000 Members (nat. pres. 1980-82), Am. Mgmt. Assn., N.J. Soc. Assn. Execs., Delaware Valley Wrestling Assn. (pres. 1978-79). Episcopalian. Clubs: N.J. Country, Oak Hill Golf (dir. 1965-68, Milford, N.J.); Phillipsburg Rotary (pres. 1968-69). Office: 418 Hamburg Turnpike Wayne NJ 07470

STASTNY, JOHN ANTON, real estate executive; b. Chgo., June 30, 1921; s. John Joseph and Bozena (Brezina) S.; m. Elizabeth Regina Ossowski, Jan. 2, 1943; children: Mary Elizabeth, John Bernard. Grad. high sch., Chgo. Owner, pres. Stastny Builders, Berwyn, Ill., 1945—; founder, pres. John A. Stastny & Co., Inc., Berwyn, 1954—, Care Ctr. Profls. Inc., Berwyn, 1961—, Fairview Health Care Ctr., Berwyn, 1964—, Fairfax Health Care Ctr., La Grange Pk., Ill., 1975—; chmn. bd. Mortgage Asset Mgmt. Assn., Berwyn, Ill., 1983—; pres., chief exec. officer Stastny Assocs., Berwyn; adv. bd. Fed. Nat. Mortgage Assn., Washington, 1971-73; chmn. bd. Fed. Home Loan Bank, Chgo., 1972-78. Contbr. articles to profl. jours.; co-founder (tech. jour.): Compendium of Multi-Family Housing, 1965. Bd. dirs. Avery Coonley Sch., Downers Grove, Ill., 1956-60, MacNeal Meml. Hosp., Berwyn, 1978—; founding gov. West Towns Community Nursing Service, Berwyn, 1968., Washington Sq. retirement housing, Hinsdale, Ill., 1986; elected del. Community Caucus, Hinsdale, Ill., 1955. Served with U.S. Army, 1942-43. Named Presdl. Appointee Constrn. Industry Collective Bargaining Com., Washington, 1969-71, advisor to U.S. Del. to Econ. Commn. for Europe, U.S. State Dept., Geneva, Switzerland, 1971; named to Housing Hall of Fame, Washington, 1980. Mem. Chgo. Home Builders Assn. (life mem., bd. dirs., pres. 1964-65, Award of Merit 1961), Nat. Assn. Home Builders (life bd. dirs., pres. 1971, numerous disting. service awards 1965-78), Nat. Housing Ctr. (gov., chmn. 1974), Lambda Alpha Internat. (key award 1964). Republican. Clubs: Mid America (Chgo.); Edgewood Valley Country (LaGrange, Ill.); Quail Creek Country (Naples, Fla.). Office: 3615 S Harlem Ave Berwyn IL 60402

STATLER, CHARLES WILLIAM, television advertising executive, sportscaster, consultant; b. Abilene, Tex., Oct. 3, 1956; s. Tivis Edward Jr. and Naomi (Favors) S.; m. Sherri Todd, July 23, 1983. Student, Cisco (Tex.) Jr. Coll., 1975-77, Tarleton State U., 1977, U. Md., Fed. Republic Germany,

1978-80, Abilene Christian U., 1986. Mgr. J.T. Morrow Texaco, Breckenridge, Tex., 1973-74; asst. mgr. Winn Dixie Supermarkets, Breckenridge and Granbury, Tex., 1974-78; sales mgr., news dir. Sta. KSTB-Radio, Breckenridge, 1981-83; sportscaster Sta. KROO-Radio, Breckenridge, 1984-87, Sta. KEAS-Radio, Eastland, Tex., 1986—, Abilene Christian Univ. Sports Network; sportswriter Abilene Reporter News, 1987—; advt. exec. Sta. KTAB-TV, Abilene, 1983—. Producer, writer news stories, commls., documentaries. Mem. fund raising bd. Ben Richey Boys Ranch, Abilene; bus. drive chmn. Taylor County Cancer Soc., Abilene, 1986; bd. dirs. Stephens County Red Cross, Breckenridge, 1981-83, Mend-A-Child, 1988; bd. mem. Hillcrest Ch. of Christ mktg. com., Abilene, 1983—. Served with U.S. Army, 1978-81. Mem. Abilene Advt. Fedn. (bd. dirs. 1983—), Abilene C. of C. (mil. affairs com. 1988—, vice chmn. Redcoats 1983—, chmn. 1988-89), TV Bur. of Advt., Abilene Fine Arts Mus., Patron 200 for the Arts, Hon. Commdr. 49th Test Squadron Dyess AFB, 1988. Democrat. Mem. Ch. of Christ. Lodge: Kiwanis (publicity chmn. Breckenridge club 1981-83). Office: Sta KTAB-TV PO Box 5676 Abilene TX 79605

STAUB, JERRY DAVIS, entrepreneur, consultant; b. Paragould, Ark., Oct. 25, 1936; s. Lorraine Gustav and Louise (Bingham) S.; m. Betty Carolyn Barnes, Jan. 5, 1960; children: Mary Louise, Janice Carolyn, Jonathan Davis, Stephen Patrick. Student, U. Mo., 1954-55; BS in Econs., Ark. State U., 1960. Clk. Security Bank and Trust Co., Paragould, 1958-59; claims adjustor Crawford and Co., Atlanta, 1960-62; claims mgr. Dairyland County Mut. Ins. Co., Austin, Tex., 1962-66; pres. Affable Fin., Co., Austin, 1966-68; chmn., pres. AVS Food Services, Inc., Austin, 1967—; pres. All Equipment Leasing, Austin, 1971—, Two State Vending, Texarkana, 1976—, Acme Food, Inc., Austin, 1978—, Affable Leasing, 1981—; v.p., bd. dirs. Available Fin., Austin, 1970—. Served with U.S. Army, 1956-58, Korea. Mem. Tex. Merchandising Vending Assn. (gov. 1975-79), Ark. Vending Assn., Nat. Automation Merchandisers Assn., Tex. Restaurant Assn., Nat. Coffee Service Assn., Tex. Good Rds./Transp. Assn., Austin C. of C. Republican. Episcopalian. Clubs: Onion Creek Country, The Austin, Metropolitan, Headliners. Home: 10917 Preston Trails Dr Austin TX 75747 Office: AVS Food Svcs Inc 611 Neches Austin TX 78747

STAUBLIN, JUDITH ANN, financial executive; b. Anderson, Ind., Jan. 17, 1936; d. Leslie Fred and Esta Virginia (Ringo) Wiley; student Ball State U., 1954-55, 69-70, Savs. and Loan Inst., 1962-67, U. Ga., 1974, Wright State U., 1975; children—Juli Jackson, Scott Jackson. Teller, Anderson Fed. Savs. and Loan Assn., Anderson, 1962-64, data processing mgr., 1965-70, loan officer, 1970-72, v.p. systems, 1972-74, fin. systems mktg., 1974-76; fin. dist. mgr. data centers div. NCR Corp., Atlanta, 1977-81, nat. sales mgr. EFT services Data Center Div., Dayton, Ohio, 1982-83; fin. dist. mgr. EFT and data services So. Thrift, Atlanta, 1983—. Active United Way. Mem. Am. Savs. and Loan Inst., Fin. Mgrs. Soc., Ga. Exec. Women's Network, Am. Soc. Profl. and Exec. Women, Anderson C. of C. Home: 6115 Woodmont Blvd Norcross GA 30092 Office: 5 Executive Dr NE Atlanta GA 30329

STAUFFER, THOMAS GEORGE, hotel executive; b. Akron, Ohio, Mar. 4, 1932; s. Caldwell E. and Rose C. (Ortscheidt) S.; m. Lois Campsey, June 18, 1960. B.S., Case Western Res. U., 1954. Pres. Stouffer Hotels; also dir., sr. v.p., chief fin. officer, real estate officer Stouffer Hotels, Solon, Ohio, 1954—. Recipient Legion of Honor, Order of DeMolay. Mem. Internat. Assn. Corp. Real Estate Execs., Am. Hotel and Motel Assn., Urban Land Inst., Nat. Restaurant Assn. (dir.), Sigma Chi (Significant Sigma Chi). Clubs: Cleve. Athletic, Clevelander, Rolling Rock, Hillbrook. Lodges: Masons; Shriners. Home: 1000 Estill Dr Lakewood OH 44107 Office: Stouffer Hotel Co 29800 Bainbridge Rd Solon OH 44139

STAUR, MARTIN JOHN, architect; b. Bridgeport, Conn., July 25, 1933; s. John and Julia Anna (Tudos) Staurovsky. Registered architect, Calif., N.Y., Conn., Ariz. Apprentice architect Anderson & Petrofsky, architects, Bridgeport, 1952-62; project architect A.J. Palmieri Co., Bridgeport, 1974-75, Bennett-Resnick Ptnrship, Westport, Conn. and Boston, 1976-78, Valus & Carpenter, Westport, 1979-80; architect Vineyard Realty Corp., White Plains, N.Y., 1980-83; prin. Martin J. Staur, AIA, Westport, 1983—; cons. architect Gassner Assocs., Westport, 1985—. Mem. AIA, Conn. Soc. Architects, Nat. Council Archl. Registration Bds. Republican. Roman Catholic. Avocations: building models; computers; gardening; sailing. Address: 11 Drumlin Rd Westport CT 06880

STAVELY, RICHARD WILLIAM, lawyer; b. Lyndon, Kans., May 14, 1927; s. A.K. and Bertha May (Patton) S.; m. Gladys Edith Voetmann, June 8, 1958; children: Jill Elizabeth, Jocelyn Carita. AB, U. Kans., 1950, LLB, 1954. Bar: Kans. 1954, U.S. Dist. Ct. Kans. 1954, U.S. Ct. Appeals (10th cir.) 1956. Assoc. Lilleston, Spradling, Gott & Stallwitz, Wichita, Kans., 1954-63; gen. counsel MISCO Industries, Inc., Wichita, 1964—, sec., 1966—, v.p., 1968—; co-trustee MISCO charitable trust. Editor: U. Kans. Law Rev., 1952-53. Mem. exec. com. Wichita area Devel. Inc., 1st v.p. 1982-83, pres. 1984-86, chmn. bd. dirs. 1986-88. With USNR, 1945-46. Fellow Kans. Bar Endowment; mem. ABA (chmn. div. jud. adminstrn. Kans. sect. 1958-68, Kans. rep. lawyers conf., 1979—), Kans. Bar Assn., Wichita Bar Assn. (chmn. pro-bono com. 1984—), Am. Judicature Soc., Wichita Corp. Counsel Soc. (pres. 1978-79), Am. Assn. Equipment Lessors (lawyers com. 1977-80, co-chmn. 1980), Wichita Club, Univ. Club, Phi Alpha Delta. Republican. Presbyterian. Home: 120 S Pinecrest Wichita KS 67218 Office: MISCO Industries Inc 257 N Broadway Rm 200 Wichita KS 67202

STAVROPOULOS, D(IONYSOS) JOHN, banker; b. Vicksburg, Miss., Jan. 19, 1933; s. John Dionysos and Olga (Balodemos) S.; m. Alexandra Gatzoyanni, Jan. 10, 1976; children: John, Theodore, Mark, Olga, Katerina. B.S., Miss. State U., 1955; M.B.A., Northwestern U., 1956. Chartered fin. analyst. With trust dept. First Nat. Bank of Chgo., 1956-69, internat. banking dept., 1970-76, sr. v.p. real estate dept., 1976-78, exec. v.p. comml. banking dept., 1979-80, chmn. credit strategy com., 1981—, chief credit officer, 1986—; v.p., dir. research Bache & Co., N.Y.C., 1969-70; instr. finance Northwestern U., 1962-68; dir. Central Ill. Public Service Co. Served with U.S. Army, 1951-53. Mem. Am. Bankers Assn., Assn. Res. City Bankers, Council Fgn. Relations (Chgo. com.), Robert Morris Assocs., (nat. dir.). Greek Orthodox. Clubs: Westmoreland Country; Economic (Chgo.). Office: First Chgo Corp 1 First National Pla Chicago IL 60670

STAWARZ, JEAN SHENOHA, public relations executive; b. Chgo., July 17, 1958; d. Raymond William and Adele Constance (Zitz) Shenoha; m. Steven Paul Stawarz, Aug. 16, 1981. BS in Advt. and Econs., U. Ill., 1980; MBA in Fin. Mgmt., Loyola U., Chgo., 1982. Sales mgr. Silver Funnel, San Francisco, 1982-83; account exec. Franson & Assocs., San Jose, Calif., 1983-84; investor relations analyst Daisy Systems Corp., Mountain View, Calif., 1984-86; dir. pub. and investor relations KSK Communications, Ltd., McLean, Va., 1986-88; owner The Corp. Communications Group, Bethesda, Md., 1988—. Contbr. articles to newspapers. Mem. Nat. Investor Relations Inst., Pub. Relations Soc. Am. (several awards).

STAWICKI, JOSEPH JOHN, JR., marketing executive; b. New Haven, Conn., Nov. 27, 1944; s. Joseph J. Sr. and Tonya (Bolash) S.; m. Barbara Jean Schneider, Jan. 19, 1968, children: Laura, Kevin, Dennis. BS, St. Joseph Coll., 1966; MBA, No. Ill. U., 1968. Investment adminstr. Phoenix Equity Planning Corp., Hartford, Conn., 1971-74; asst. prof. Cen. Conn. State U., New Britain, Conn., 1975-81; trade officer New Eng. Trade Assistance Ctr., Boston, 1981-83; dir. ops. Multimate Internat. Corp., East Hartford, Conn., 1983-84; pres. Mercor Resources Corp., Winsted, Conn., 1985—, also bd. dirs. Treas., bd. dirs. Winchester Area Homemaker Home Health Aide Service, Winsted, 1972-73; mem. Winchester Rep. Town Com., 1970—. Mem. FIABCI-USA, Internat. Real Estate Fedn. (pres. Conn. chpt.), Sigma Iota Epsilon, Elks. Roman Catholic. Home: RFD 3 Highland Lake W-1 Winchester CT 06098 Office: Mercor Resources Corp 135 W Wakefield Blvd Winsted CT 06098

STAWNYCHY, ZORIANA MARIA, financial executive; b. N.Y.C., May 31, 1953; d. Walter and Eugenia (Hanusczak) Salak; m. Yuri Andrij Stawnychy, Oct. 26, 1985. BA, Fordham U., 1975. Cert. fin. planner. Prodn. asst. Palmerton Pub. Co., N.Y.C., 1975-78; fin. planner Cigna, N.Y.C., 1978-83, 85—; mgr. Bruce Raines Assocs., N.Y.C., 1983-84; sr. fin. counselor Ind. Fin. Services, White Plains, N.Y., 1984-85. Mem. Internat. Assn. Fin. Planning, Inst. Cert. Fin. Planners.

STAYMATES, JAMES DUANE, financial planner; b. Wilkinsburg, Pa., May 27, 1950; s. Arthur Kissler and Maria (Hopf) S.; m. Saundra S. Stamboni, Aug. 13, 1978; children: Maria Danielle, James Bret. BSBA, Towson State U., 1973; cert., Coll. Fin. Planning, Denver, 1987. Purchasing agt. Fair Lanes Inc., Balt., 1973-76; dir. racquet sports Fair Lanes Inc., Chgo., 1976-79; owner, mgr. Staymates Fin. Concepts, Balt., 1979—; fin. advisor Tchrs. Assn. Baltimore County, 1981—; instr. Harford Community Coll., Bel Air, Md., 1979—, Towson State U., 1979—, Carroll County Bd. Edn., Westminster, Md., 1981—. Recipient Century Club award Oppenheimer Co., 1983, prodn. award for excellence Cardell & Assocs., 1983, Broker Dealer, 1984-86. Mem. Inst. Cert. Fin. Planners, Internat. Assn. Cert. Fin. Planners. Democrat. Office: 5506 Bortner Rd Upperco MD 21155

STEAD, JAMES JOSEPH, JR., securities company executive; b. Chgo., Sept. 13, 1930; s. James Joseph and Irene (Jennings) S.; m. Edith Pearson, Feb. 13, 1954; children: James, Diane, Robert, Caroline. BS, DePaul U., 1955, MBA, 1957. Asst. sec. C. F. Childs & Co., Chgo., 1955-62; exec. v.p., sec. Koenig, Keating & Stead, Inc., Chgo., 1962-66; 2d v.p., mgr. midwest municipal bond dept. Hayden, Stone Inc., Chgo., 1966-69; sr. v.p., nat. sales mgr. Ill. Co. Inc., 1969-70; mgr. instl. sales dept. Reynolds and Co., Chgo., 1970-72; partner Edwards & Hanly, 1972-74; v.p., instnl. sales mgr. Paine, Webber, Jackson & Curtis, 1974-76; v.p., regional instl. sales mgr. Reynolds Securities, Inc., 1976-78; sr. v.p., regional mgr. Oppenheimer & Co., Inc., 1978-88; sr. v.p., regional mgr. fixed income Tucker Anthony, 1988—; instr. Mcpl. Bond Sch., Chgo., 1967—. Served with AUS, 1951-53. Mem. Security Traders Assn. Chgo., Nat. Security Traders Assn., Am. Mgmt. Assn., Municipal Finance Forum Washington. Clubs: Executives, Union League, Municipal Bond, Bond (Chgo.); Olympia Fields Country (Ill.); Wall Street (N.Y.C.). Home: 20721 Brookwood Dr Olympia Fields IL 60461 Office: 1 S Wacker Dr Chicago IL 60606

STEAD, JERRE LEE, electronics company executive; b. Maquoketa, Iowa, Jan. 8, 1943; s. H. Victor and Anna Catherine (Grindrod) S.; m. Mary Joy Kloppenburg, Dec. 27, 1942; children: Joel A., Jay A. BBA, U. Iowa, 1965; student, Harvard U., 1982. Mgr. regional sales Honeywell Corp., Phila., 1971-73; dir. prodn. Mpls., 1974-75, dir. distbn., 1975-76, 87—; v.p. fin. and adminstrn. Brussels, 1977-81; chmn. Honeywell-Phillips Med. Electronics, Brussels, 1981-82; v.p. Mpls., 1982-86, gen. mgr., 1982-85, group exec., 1986; pres., chief operating officer Sq. D Co., Palatine, Ill., 1987-89, also bd. dirs., pres., chief exec. officer, chmn. bd., 1989—, also bd. dirs.; bd. dirs. Eljer Industries, Plano, TX, Elco Corp., Rockford, Ill., Bristol (Va.) Compressors, Trus Joint Corp., Boise, Idaho. Mem. Pres.' coun. Am. Lung Assn., N.Y.C., 1986—, The Wash. Ctr. Nat. Campaign Com.; bus. adv. com. N.C. A&T U.; trustee Coe Coll., Cedar Rapids, Iowa, 1987; adv. coun. Boy Scouts Am.; bd. trustees Internat. House U. Chgo. Mem. Nat. Elec. Mfrs. Assn. (bd. govs. 1984—), Nat. Assn. Elec. Distbrs. (edn. com.), Chgo. Com., Elec. Mfrs. Club, Harvard Bus. Sch. Club. Republican. Methodist. Office: Sq D Co 1415 S Roselle Rd Palatine IL 60067

STEADHAM, CHARLES VICTOR, JR., entertainment agent; b. Camp LeJune, N.C., Oct. 22, 1944; s. Charles Victor Sr. and Mary Alice (Adams) S. AA, U. Fla., 1964. Profl. musician various show bands, 1967-75; owner, agt. Blade Agy., Gainesville, Fla., 1975—. Contbr. articles to profl. jours. Mem. Orlando/Orange County (Fla.) Conv. and Visitors Bur., 1986—, Jacksonville (Fla.) Tourist and Conv. Bur., 1986—; grad. Leadership Gainesville XV, 1988. Recipient C. Shaw Founders award, 1988. Mem. Fla. C. of C., Country Music Assn. (assoc.), Nat. Assn. Campus Activities (assoc., bd. dirs. 1976-83, Founders award 1981, Entertainment Agy. of Yr. award 1983, 87), Am. Soc. Assn. Execs. (assoc.), Fla. Soc. Assn. Execs. (assoc.). Democrat. Office: Blade Agy PO Box 1556 Gainesville FL 32602

STEADMAN, RICHARD COOKE, retail corporate executive; b. Honolulu, Oct. 1, 1932; s. Alva Edgar and Martha (Cooke) S.; m. Jane Blaner Nuckolls, Aug. 20, 1955; children: Christopher M., Peter W., Lee H. AB, Yale U., 1955; MBA, Harvard U., 1957. Intelligence analyst U.S. Govt., Washington, 1957-59; assoc., ptnr. G.H. Walker & Co., N.Y.C., 1959-66; dep. asst. sec. def. E. Asia and Pacific affairs Dept. of Def., Washington, 1966-69; ptnr. J.H. Whitney & Co., N.Y.C., 1969-81; now chmn. Nat. Convenience Stores Inc., Houston, also bd. dirs.; bd. dirs. Storage Tech. Corp. Trustee Children's TV Workshop, N.Y.C.; co-chmn., trustee German Marshall Fund, Washington; chmn., chief transition Dept. Def., Carter-Mondale Adminstrn. Baker scholar, 1957. Mem. Council Fgn. Relations, Phi Beta Kappa. Democrat. Home: 59 Barrow St New York NY 10014 Office: Nat Convenience Stores Inc 100 Waugh Dr Houston TX 77007

STEARNS, H. KEITH, retail company executive; b. San Francisco, Nov. 19, 1935; s. Helen (Tomlinson) Wood; m. Dianne Ruth Synder, June 12, 1959; children: Doug, David. BS in Commerce, U. Santa Clara, 1957. Exhibits rep. Eastman Kodak Co., Anaheim, Calif., 1958-59; sales rep. Eastman Kodak Co., South Bend, Ind. and Mpls., 1959-65; sales promotion specialist Eastman Kodak Co., Chgo., 1965-67; sales promotion coordinator Eastman Kodak Co., Rochester, N.Y., 1967-71; dist. mgr. Eastman Kodak Co., San Francisco, 1971-80, Seattle, 1981-86; regional mgr. electronics Eastman Kodak Co., Whittier, Calif., 1986-87; dir. mktg. Eastman Kodak Co., Rochester, 1987; gen. mgr. sales Eastman Kodak Co., Dallas, 1987—. Cub master, scout master Boy Scouts Am., Calif. and Wash., 1974-86, mem. exec. com., 1974-86; bd. dirs. Sea Fair, Seattle, 1980-86. Served to capt. artillery U.S. Army, 1957-58. Mem. Photographic Mktg. Assn. Internat., Beta Gamma Sigma. Office: Eastman Kodak Co 5221 N O'Connor Blvd S-600 Irving TX 75039

STEARNS, JAMES GERRY, securities company executive; b. Lapine, Oreg., Jan. 29, 1922; s. Carey Summer and Betty (Hunt) S.; m. June Elizabeth Speer, Nov. 21, 1943; children: Robert Sumner, Katherine Inga, Gerry Marshall. Student, Oreg. State U. Supr. Modoc County (Calif.), Alturos, 1951-67; dir. Calif. Dept. Conservation, Sacremento, 1967-72; sec. Calif. Agr. and Services Agy., Sacremento, 1972-75; dir. office alcohol fuels U.S. Dept. Energy, Washington, 1981-82; chmn., chief exec. officer Securities Investor Protection Corp., Washington, 1982—. Republican. Lodges: Masons; Shriners. Office: Securities Investor Protection Corp 805 15th St NW Ste 800 Washington DC 20005

STEARNS, MILTON SPRAGUE, JR., financial executive; b. N.Y.C., June 3, 1923; s. Milton Sprague and Katherine (Stieglitz) S.; m. Virginia McCormick; children—Virginia Parker Stearns King, John Brackett, Barbara Ellison Stearns Terry, Kathryn Trowbridge Stearns Sergio, Elizabeth Sprague (dec.). Grad., Phillips Exeter Acad., 1942; B.S. cum laude, Harvard U., 1946, M.B.A., 1948. With The Fidelity Bank, Phila., 1948-72; group v.p. nat. lending div. The Fidelity Bank, 1960-72; pres. Charter Fin. Co., Phila., 1972—; chmn., chief exec. officer Judson Infrared, Inc., 1976-87; bd. dirs. The West Co., Phoenixville, Pa., Computer Chem. Systems Inc., Avondale, Pa. Trustee Franklin Inst., 1978—, Bryn Mawr Presbyn. Ch. Served with USNR, World War II; lt. (j.g.) Res. ret. Mem. Robert Morris Assocs. (pres. Phila. chpt. 1961-62). Clubs: Spee (Cambridge, Mass.); Merion Golf, Phila. Skating and Humane Soc., Racquet, Union League (Phila.); Delray Beach, Delray Beach Yacht, Country of Fla, Gulfstream Bath and Tennis, Pine Tree Golf. Home: 43 Righters Mill Rd Gladwyne PA 19035 Office: 1700 Market St Ste 2700 Philadelphia PA 19103

STEBBINS, GREGORY KELLOGG, treasurer; b. Lafayette, Ind., Jan. 10, 1951; s. Albert Kellogg and Nancy Ruth (Osborn) S. BS in Data Processing, Calif. Poly., Pomona, 1974; MBA, U. So. Calif., 1976; EdD, Pepperdine U., 1985. Account exec. Automatic Data Processing, Long Beach, Calif., 1977-78; salesman Grubb & Ellis, L.A., 1978-81; v.p. Grubb & Ellis, Beverly Hills, Calif., 1981-83; regional mgr. Hanes Co., Beverly Hills, 1983-85; treas. U. Santa Monica (name formerly Koh-E-Nor U.), L.A., 1983—. Mem. Am. Mgmt. Assn., Assn. MBA Execs., Organizational Devel. Network, The Planning Forum. Home: 3141 Mandeville Canyon Rd Los Angeles CA 90049 Office: U Santa Monica 2101 Wilshire Blvd Santa Monica CA 90403

STEBBINS, WILLIAM MORROW, insurance broker; b. Portland, Oreg., June 30, 1925; s. Liston Ash and Myra M. (Morrow) S.; student Linfield Coll., 1946-47, U. Oreg., 1947-48; B.S., Lewis and Clark Coll., 1949; m. Gloria Mae Russell, June 13, 1947; children—Janice Maureen (Mrs. D. Paul Zundel), Ronald William, Wendy Louise. Rep. State Mut. of Am.; ins. cons., broker to bus. and industry; pres. Bus. Ins. Service Corp., 1964-85; pres. Stebbins Fin. Inc., 1985—; part time faculty Portland State U., 1971—; fin. cons. for bus. and industry. Coach, Little League Baseball, 1964-66. Alumni dir. Lewis and Clark Coll. Fund Raising, 1961-62. Served with USNR, 1943-46, 50-52. Decorated Bronze Star with two oak leaf clusters; named Life Ins. Agt. of Yr., State of Oreg., 1965. Mem. Nat., Portland (past pres.) assns. life underwriters, Am. Soc. C.L.U.s (pres. 1984-85), Million Dollar Round Table (life). Clubs: Portland Agenda (past pres.), Masons, Lions (past pres.). Contbr. articles to profl. jours. Home: 13273 SW Bull Mountain Rd Tigard OR 97223 Office: Harrison Sq 1800 SW 1st St Ste 220 Portland OR 97201

STECK, BRIAN JASON, brokerage house executive; b. Montreal, Que., Can., Dec. 26, 1946; s. Edward and Lottie (Potofsky) S.; m. Ellen Weinstein, Aug. 22, 1968; 1 child, Stephen Mitchell. B in Commerce, Sir George Williams U., 1968; MBA, U. Pa., 1969. Research analyst Nesbitt Thomson, Inc., Montreal, 1969-72, assoc. mem. corp. fin., 1972-73, dir., v.p. research and instl. sales, 1974-77; pres. Nesbitt Thomson Bongard, Inc., Toronto, Ont., Can., 1978-80; pres., chief exec. officer Nesbitt Thomson Deacon, Inc., Toronto, 1980—; pres., chief exec. officer Fahnestock and Co., Inc., 1985-87; bd. dirs. BGR Precious Metals Inc. Bd. govs. North York Gen. Hosp., Toronto Arts Award Found. Mem. Toronto Soc. Fin. Analysts, Fin. Research Inst., Oakdale Golf and Country Club, Del-Aire Golf Club, Primrose Club, Cambridge Club. Office: Nesbitt Thomson Deacon Inc, 150 King St W, Toronto, ON Canada M5H 3W2

STEDRONSKY, FRANK, film, television executive; b. Oak Park, Ill., Mar. 29, 1935; s. Frank Joseph Stedronsky; m. Alice Frances Sarlin, June 15, 1957; children: Linda, Jon, Jill, Scott. Student, Lyons Township Jr. Coll., 1955; BA in Journalism, U. Iowa, 1957. Gen. ptnr. Motivation Enterprises, Palatine, Ill., 1978—, also bd. dirs.; pres. Motivation Media, Inc., Glenview, Ill., 1969—, also bd. dirs.; treas. Motivation Mktg., Inc., Glenview, 1979—, also bd. dirs.; pres. Photo Impressions, Inc., Glenview, 1980—, also bd. dirs.; chmn. Sound Impressions, Inc., Des Plaines, Ill., 1976—, also bd. dirs.; pres. Motivation Media Far East Co., Ltd., Tai Pei, Republic of China, 1986—, also bd. dirs.; pres. Teleslide, Inc., Glenview, 1986—, also bd. dirs.; bd. dirs. NBD Arlington Heights (Ill.) Bank. Writer, director, producer: (films) The Stencil, 1961 (Chris award Columbus Film Festival 1961), Modern Mimeographing, 1962 (1st Place award Nat. Visual Presentation Assn. 1962), The Master, 1963 (1st Place award Nat. Visual Presentation Assn. 1963), A Snow Job, 1970 (Bronze award Internat. Film Festival of N.Y. 1970). Pres. Va. Lake Homeowners Assn. Palatine, 1975-76; regional dir. Crusade of Mercy Niles, Ill., 1968; sustaining mem. Rep. Nat. Com. Washington, 1980-87; charter mem. Rep. Presdl. Task Force Washington, 1984-87; sponsor Nat. Rep. Congl. Com. Washington, 1985; bd. dirs. Clearbrook Center for Developmentally Disabled, Rolling Meadows, Ill., 1987—. Mem. Chgo. Audio Visual Producers Assn. (pres. 1983-86, disting. service award, 1986), Audio Visual Mgrs. Assn. (pres. 1968-69, pres. award 1969), U. of Iowa Alumni Assn. (life), Internat. Assn. for Multi-Image, Chgo. Film Video Council. Roman Catholic. Club: U.S. Senatorial (Washington). Home: 867 Virginia Lake Ct Palatine IL 60067 Office: Motivation Media Inc 1245 Milwaukee Ave Glenview IL 60025

STEEL, BETTI HEY, food service executive; b. N.Y.C., Oct. 27, 1955; d. Irving and Marilyn (Spiro) Hey; m. Laurence Steel, June 1, 1986; 1 child, Jesse Harrison. RN, Queensborough Community Coll., 1982; BS, Columbia U., 1983. Head instr. ABC Sch., N.Y.C., 1985-86; pres. Hang It Up, Inc., N.Y.C., 1986—. Patentee in field. Mem. Women's Econ. Round Table, N.Y. State Hospitality and Tourism Assn., Nat. Assn. Women Bus. Owners, Am. Women's Econ. Devel. Corp. Democrat. Jewish. Home: 407 Park Ave S New York NY 10016 Office: Hang It Up Inc 315 W 57th St New York NY 10019

STEEL, CHARLES LOWNDES, III, electric utility executive; b. Colon, Panama Canal Zone, Mar. 22, 1924; s. Charles and Katharine (Porter) S.; m. Janet Shearer Smith, Oct. 1, 1944; children: Charles Lowndes, Natalie, Christopher Allen. BS in Engring., U.S. Mil. Acad., 1944; MS, Harvard U., 1950; MS in Polit. Sci., George Washington U., 1961; postgrad., U.S. Army War Coll., 1961. Registered profl. engr., Mass., Ark. Commd. 2d lt. U.S. Army C.E., 1944; advanced through grades to col. 1966; nuclear weapons officer Manhatten Engring. Dist., Sandia Base, N.Mex., 1946-49; mem. faculty U.S. Army War Coll., 1961-64; spl. asst. to supreme comdr. SHAPE, Paris, 1964-66; ret. 1970; dir. pub. affairs Ark. Power & Light Co., Little Rock, 1970-75, v.p. pub. affairs, 1975-79, v.p., asst. to pres., 1979-81, sr. v.p., 1981-85, exec. v.p., 1985-88; ret. 1988. Mem. task force Presdl. Task Force on Nat. Water Policy, 1979-81; pres. Ark. Better Bus. Bur., 1977-78, Ark. Basin Assn., 1981—; bd. dirs. U.S. Indsl. Coun., 1972—; chmn. Ark. Nature Conservancy, 1983—; mem. Little Rock Port Authority, 1981—. Decorated Legion of Merit (3); decorated Joint Svc. Commendation medal; named Disting. Engr. Little Rock Dist. U.S. C.E., 1967—; decorated Disting. Svc. medal Korea. Mem. Ark. Fedn. Water & Air Users (pres. 1974, 75), Soc. Am. Mil Engrs. (pres.), Nat. Soc. Profl. Engrs., Ark. Soc. Profl. Engrs. Episcopalian. Home: 3409 Imperial Valley Dr Little Rock AR 72212 Office: Ark Power & Light Co PO Box 551 Little Rock AR 72203

STEELE, DONALD DICKINSON, public relations professional; b. Bozeman, Mont., Apr. 17, 1909; s. Fred M. and Cecille Roberta (Heywood) S.; student pub. and pvt. schs.; m. Evelyn Jane de Clairmont, May 8, 1932; 1 son, Donald de Clairmont. Founder, 1941, now chmn., pres. Steele Group, San Francisco; ptnr. IPR Group of Cos. Mem. Pub. Relations Soc. Am. (accredited), Pub. Rels. Round Table, Rotary, San Francisco Press, Olympic, Met., Shriners. Republican. Home: 201 Berkeley Way San Francisco CA 94131 Office: 703 Market St San Francisco CA 94103

STEELE, ELLEN LIVELY, business development executive, publishing executive; b. Fayette County, W.Va., Jan. 22, 1936; d. Alfred French and Sarah Ellen (Pritchard) L.; student N.Mex. State U., 1962-74; m. Henry Gilmer Steele, July 20, 1981; children: Gregory Benjamin Pake, Seana Ellen Pake. Civilian adminstrv. officer Dept. Army, White Sands Missile Range, N.Mex., 1962-67; mgr. Kelly Services Inc., Las Cruces, N.Mex., 1967-85; pres. Lively Enterprises, Inc., Las Cruces, 1967-76; sec., treas. Adam II, Ltd., Las Cruces, 1973-77; pres. Symposium Internat. Inc., Las Cruces, 1977-78, Asset & Resource Mgmt. Corp., Organ, N.Mex., 1978-83; lit. agt., prin. Ellen Lively Steele & Assocs., 1979—; mng. partner AVVA III, Las Cruces, 1981-82, Internat. Alliance Sports Ofcls., Las Cruces, 1982—; mng. ptnr. Steele Lehnert, 1986-88; pres., chief exec. officer Steele Svcs., Inc., Las Cruces, 1988—; ptnr., exec. producer Triple L Prodns., 1986—; chief exec. officer Nithra Corp., 1989—; dir. mktg. Los Cruces Conv. and Visitors Bur., 1984-85; dir. Santa Rosa Resources Corp., Denver; exec. GASCO Internat. Inc., Las Cruces, 1981-82; mem. N.Mex. State Senate, 1985-89, co-chmn. higher edn. reform com., 1985, 86, mem. interim coms., jud. com., edn. com., criminal justice com., Human Needs & Aids com., vice chmn. Children and FAmily Needs and Human Svcs., 1988; mem. nat. conf. state legislatures; N.Mex. Federated Rep. Women, Am. Legis. Exchange Commn.; mem. task force El Paso Electric Co. Rate Moderation; mem. firearms preemtion statute rev.; pres. N.Mex. Film Found., Inc., 1987-88. Served with USAF, 1954-57. Mem. Internat. Assn. Fin. Planners, Sales and Mktg. Execs. Internat., Am. Mgmt. Assn., DAR, La Croisee des Chemins Bruxelles, Belguim, Order Eastern Star, Picacho Hills Country (co-chmn. bd. dirs. 1980-84) (Las Cruces). Episcopalian. Home: PO Drawer 447 Organ NM 88052

STEELE, FRANK CHANNEL, sales executive; b. N.Y.C., Oct. 1, 1938; s. Ralph E. and Frances (Channell) S.; m. Karon Kay Kennelly, May 22, 1965; children: Darrin, Danielle. BA, U. Rochester, 1960. Sales rep. Scott Paper Co., Salt Lake City, 1964-66; adminstrv. asst. Scott Paper Co., Seattle, 1966-69, asst. dist. mgr., 1969-70; regional sales mgr. Airborne Freight Corp., Phila., 1970-72; regional mgr. Airborne Freight Corp., Boston, 1972-76; regional mgr. N.Y.C., 1976-78, regional mgr., v.p., 1978-80; v.p. sales Seattle, 1980-84, sr. v.p. sales, 1984—. 1st lt. USAF, 1960-63. Office: Airborne Freight Corp 3101 Western Ave Seattle WA 98111

STEELE, GEORGE PEABODY, marine transportation executive; b. San Francisco, July 27, 1924; s. James Mortimer and Erma (Garrett) S.; m. Elizabeth Yates Fahrion, July 11, 1944 (div. May 1988); children: Jane Yates Steele Mitchell, James Fahrion; m. Betty McDonnell, May 20, 1988. BS, U.S. Naval Acad., 1944. Commd. ensign USN, 1944, advanced through grades to vice adm., 1973; service aboard submarines in Pacific, World War

II; comdr. U.S.S. Hardhead, 1955-56; comdr. nuclear powered U.S.S. Seadragon (made 1st NW passage under ice to North Pole), 1959-61; comdr. Polaris missile sub U.S.S. Daniel Boone, 1963-66; head politico-mil. policy div. Europe/NATO br. Office Chief Naval Ops., 1966-68; comdr. Naval Forces, Korea, chief Naval adv. group, Korean Navy, comdr. Naval Component UN Command, 1968-70; comdr. Anti-Submarine Warfare Group 4, 1970-72; dep. asst. chief of staff Supreme Allied Comdr., Europe, SHAPE, Belgium, 1972-73; comdr. U.S. 7th Fleet, 1973-75; ret., 1975; exec. v.p., chief ops. officer Interocean Mgmt. Corp., Phila., 1976—, pres., 1978-85, chmn., chief exec. officer, 1981—; chmn. bd. dirs. Fgn. Policy Research Inst. Author: Seadragon, Northwest Under the Ice, 1962, (with H. Gimpel) Nuclear Submarine Skippers and What They Do, 1962, Vengeance in the Depths, 1963; contbr. articles to profl. publs. and newspapers. Decorated D.S.M., Legion of Merit with 4 gold stars, Navy Cross (Peru), Order of Rising Sun (Japan), Cloud and Banner (Republic China), Order Nat. Security of Merit (Republic Korea). Mem. Am. Bur. Shipping (bd. mgrs.), Am. Inst. Merchant Shipping (chmn. bd. dirs. 1986-87), U.S. Naval Inst. Episcopalian. Clubs: Univ., N.Y. Yacht; Union League (Phila.); Army-Navy, Army-Navy Country (Washington). Home: 225 S 18th St Apt 816 Philadelphia PA 19103 Office: Interocean Mgmt Corp Three Pkwy Ste 1300 Philadelphia PA 19102

STEELE, JAMES PATRICK, banking executive; b. Birmingham, Ala., June 2, 1939; s. James P. and Mary (Dunn) S.; m. Susan S. Steele, Feb. 26, 1976; children: James P., Philip. BA in Fin., U. Ga., 1962. Asst. br. mgr. 1st Nat. Bank Atlanta, 1964-67, main office credit officer, 1967-70, group head corp. accts., then credit officer internat., 1970-74, London rep., 1974-77, head overseas group, 1977-80, dep. mgr., internat., 1980-85; sr. v.p. Abu Dhabi Internat. Bank, Washington, 1985-86; exec. v.p. Abu Dhabi Internat. Bank, 1986—. Office: Abu Dhabi Internat Bank 1776 G St NW Ste 850 Washington DC 20006

STEELE, JOHN ROY, real estate broker; b. Detroit, Feb. 16, 1945; s. Wallace Lee Roy and Kay F. (Fitzpatrick) S.; B.A., Alma Coll., 1967; M.B.A., Central Mich. U., 1968; m. Beverly Louise Rauh, June 3, 1972; children—Josh Oliver, Matt Edward, Anne Elizabeth. Owner/broker Century 21 Steele, Realtors, Jackson, Calif., 1981—; partner/broker Century 21, Lewis-Steele, Realtors, Inc., Jackson and Truckee, Calif., 1976-81; v.p. Century 21 Foothill-Sierra council, 1987-88; dir. Amador Title Co., 1978-83, pres., 1978-79; ptnr. Computer World, Jackson, 1983-85. Bd. dirs. Trinity Episcopal Ch., Sutter Creek, Calif., 1978-79, 80-83, jr. warden, 1979; trustee Citizens for Progress, 1981-82; chmn. Amador County chpt. Easter Seals Telethon, 1985-88. pres. Amador Swim Team, 1986-87, 87-88; coach Mother Lode Youth Soccer League, 1984, 86; coach state finals Odyssey (Olympics) of the Mind, 1986, 87. Mem. Amador County Bd. Realtors (bd. dirs. 1974-82, profl. standards com. 1988, pres. 1978), Calif. Assn. Realtors (dir. 1978). Clubs: Friends of the Library, Toastmasters (charter mem. 1988). Office: PO Box 210 Jackson CA 95642

STEELE, SANDRA MARIE, small business owner; b. Newark, July 24, 1949; children: Gary, Gregory, Geoffrey. AS, Middlesex Coll., 1978; BS, N.H. Coll., 1987; cert. in Black Ministers Program, Hartford Sem., 1988. Sec. Wesleyan U., Middletown, Conn., 1969-75; word processing supr. CIGNA, Bloomfield, Conn., 1975-76; benefits cons. Aetna Life & Casualty, Hartford, Conn., 1976-88; owner 3-Dimensions, Upper Rm., S.M.S. Enterprises Inc., East Haddam, Conn., 1987—. Mem. Dem. Town Com., Middletown, 1985—; exec. com. Community Action for Greater Middletown, 1980—. Mem. Conn. Realtors Assn., Women in Leadership, U.S. C. of C., Women in Bus. Enterprise, NAACP. Democrat. Mem. Christian Ch. Office: 9 Goodspeed Landing East Haddam CT 06423

STEELE, WASHBURN WHITING, realtor, puppeteer; b. Mpls., Apr. 16, 1919; s. Harrison C. and Lydia Marie (Jepson) S.; m. Harriet Ann Rogers, Sept. 10, 1950; children: Lowell N., Quentin M., Miranda Lou. BA in Econs., Carleton Coll., 1940; postgrad. in civil engring. Iowa State Coll., 1941-42. Acctg. teller Steele State Bank, Cherokee, Iowa, 1946-51, farm mgr., agrl. loan officer, 1946-52; owner, operator Sioux River Ranch, Cherokee, 1953-69; owner, operator W.W. Steele Realty, Cherokee, 1969-89; co-owner Honeybee Nutrition, Cherokee, 1978-89. Mem. platform com. Republican Nat. Conv., Chgo., 1960; chmn. Cherokee County Rep. Com., Iowa, 1961; mem. Iowa Ho. of Reps., Des Moines, 1963-64. Served to lt. USNR, 1942-46; Cuba, PTO, comdr. USNR, ret. Mem. United Counties Bd. Realtors (past pres.), Am. Soc. Farm Mgrs. and Rural Appraisers, Am. Quarter Horse Assn. Mormon. Home: 2727 De Anza Rd Box M-20 San Diego CA 92109

STEELMAN, JEFFERY LAWRENCE, controller; b. Glen Ridge, N.J., Aug. 19, 1952; s. Merle Clark and Angela Marie (deKlyver) S.; m. Brenda Joyce Medlin, May 12, 1974; children: Erin, Andrew, Joel. BS in Acctg., Clemson U., 1974; postgrad., Furman U., 1976-77. CPA, S.C. Cost acct. Dow Badische, Anderson, S.C., 1974-76; supr. adminstrv. services Parke-Davis, Honea Path, S.C., 1976-79; fin. analyst Parke-Davis, Greenwood, S.C., 1979-82; mgr. fin. Profl. Med. Products, Greenwood, S.C., 1982-86; controller Kirschner Med. Products, Greenwood, S.C., 1986—. Treas. Pro-Family Forum, 1985-87, Billy Graham Films, 1987; budget analyst United Way, Greenwood, 1986—; exec. committeman Rep. Party; chmn. bd. Greenwood Crisis Pregnancy Ctr. Mem. Nat. Assn. Accts., Controller Council. Office: Kirschner Med Products Evans Pond Rd PO Box 488 Greenwood SC 29648

STEEN, FRANK HEIFNER, management executive; b. Greenwood, Miss., Sept. 4, 1946; s. Frank Heifner and Mae Camile (Townsed) S.; m. Gail Annette Titus, Jan. 8, 1972; children: Melynda Gayle, Frank H. III. Grad. high sch., Clarksdale, Miss. Various positions TGI Friday's Inc., 1970-77, dir. ops., 1973-75, v.p., 1975-77, sr. v.p., 1977-84, exec. v.p., 1984—. Office: TGI Fridays Inc 14665 Midway Rd Dallas TX 75080

STEEN, JAMES KENNETH, accountant, merchant banker; b. Whitehall, Wis., Nov. 17, 1940; s. Paul Waller and Dorothy Solsrud S.; divorced; children: Theodore James, Meredith Ellen. BS, Bradley U., 1962. CPA, N.Y. Supr. audit Ernst & Ernst, Chgo., 1965-72; dep. dir. Ins. Dept. State of Ill., Chgo. and Springfield, 1972-74; audit mgr. Coopers & Lybrand, N.Y.C., 1974-77; sr. v.p. Guy Carpenter, N.Y.C., 1977-88; merchant banker John Head & Ptnrs., N.Y.C., 1988—. Lt. USN, 1962-65. Mem. AICPA. Congregationalist.

STEEN, JOHN THOMAS, JR., lawyer; b. San Antonio, Dec. 27, 1949; s. John Thomas and Nell (Donnell) S.; m. Ida Louise Clement, May 12, 1979; children—John Thomas, Ida Louise Larkin, James Higbie Clement. A.B., Princeton U., 1971; J.D., U. Tex., 1974. Bar: Tex. 1974, U.S. Dist. Ct. (we. dist.) Tex. 1976. Assoc. firm Matthews & Branscomb, San Antonio, 1977-82; ptnr. firm Soules, Cliffe & Reed, San Antonio, 1982-83; sr. v.p., gen. counsel, dir. Commerce Savs. Assn., San Antonio, 1983-88; pvt. practice, San Antonio, 1988—; bd. dirs. North Frost Bank, San Antonio, 1982-84. Trustee San Antonio Acad., 1976-81, 87—; v.p. Bexar County Easter Seal Soc., San Antonio, 1976-77; trustee, vice chmn. San Antonio Community Coll. Dist., 1977-82; bd. dirs. Tex. Easter Seal Soc., Dallas, 1977-80, San Antonio Research and Planning Council, 1978-81, Community Guidance Ctr., 1983-84; vice-chmn. Leadership San Antonio, 1978-79; mem. Fiesta San Antonio Commn., 1982-83; Bexar County commr., San Antonio, 1982, Tex. Commn. on Economy and Efficiency in State Govt., 1985—; Coliseum Adv. Bd., 1985—; pres. San Antonio Performing Arts Assn., 1984-85; chmn. World Affairs Council San Antonio, 1984-86; trustee United Way San Antonio, 1985—; bd. dirs. Accord Med. Found., 1987—; mem. adv. bd. U. Tex., San Antonio, 1987—. Served to 1st lt. USAR, 1973-81. Fellow San Antonio Bar Found., Tex. Bar Found. (life); mem. Tex. Bar. Assn., Santa Gertrudis Breeders Internat., Tex. and Southwestern Cattle Raisers Assn., San Antonio Acad. Alumni Assn. (pres. 1976-77), Phi Delta Phi. Clubs: Ivy (Princeton, N.J.); San Antonio German (pres. 1982-83), Order of Alamo, Tex. Cavaliers, San Antonio Country, Argyle, Conopus, Princeton (San Antonio and South Tex.) (pres. 1980-81). Home: 207 Ridgemont Ave San Antonio TX 78209 Office: 300 Convent San Antonio TX 78205

STEER, DULANEY GORDON, lawyer; b. Ft. Worth, Mar. 2, 1956; s. Frederick Gordon and Florence (Dulaney) S.; m. Linda Carol Newman, Jan. 21, 1978; children: Melissa T., Michael F.N. BJ, U. Tex., 1977; JD, U. Okla., 1982. Bar: Okla. 1982, Tex. 1986. Mem. reporting staff Daily Texan, Austin, Tex., 1976-77, Tyler (Tex.) Courier-Times/Telegraph, 1977-79; assoc. Linn & Helms, Oklahoma City, 1982-86; bd. dirs. Kelly, Hart & Hallman, Ft. Worth, 1986—; speaker on continuing legal edn., Oklahoma City U., 1984-87. Contbr. Okla. Law Rev. Mem. Oklahoma City Lawyers' Tax Group (sec.-treas. 1985, program dir. 1986), State Bar Tex., Okla. Bar Assn., ABA, Order of Coif. Office: Kelly Hart Hallman PC 201 Main St Fort Worth TX 76102

STEFFENS, JAMES THOMAS, protective services official; b. Bound Brook, N.J., Nov. 24, 1939; s. Thomas George and Elsie (Taylor) S.; m. Evelyn Martha Schuz, Sept. 1, 1962 (div. Aug. 1982); children: Kristine Anne, Kimberli Joy; m. Wanda Carolyn Johnson, Sept. 10, 1982. BArch., Va. Tech. Inst., 1963, M in Urban and Regional Planning, 1963. Planner Hillsboroghy County Planning Commn., Tampa, Fla., 1963-67; project mgr. Candeub, Fleissig and Assocs., Newark, 1967-71; pres. James T. Steffens and Assocs., Tampa, 1971-74; dir. county planning Russell and Axon Engrs. Architects and Planners, Daytona Beach, Fla., 1974-82; chief adminstr. Oneco-Tallevast (Fla.) Fire Control Dist., 1982—. Pres. Lake Arrowhead Homeowners Assn., Denville, N.J., 1969-70, Dana Shores Civic Assn., Tampa, 1976-78. Recipient Resolution Merit Plant City Commn., 1967, Merit award Mayor and town coun. Town of Eatonville, 1982. Mem. Internat. Assn. Fire Chiefs (apparatus and equipment com. 1986—), Nat. Fire Protection Assn. (fire dept. equipment com. 1987—), Internat. Soc. Fire Svc. Instrs., Am. Inst. Cert. Planners, Manatee Kennel Club (pres. 1987-88). Democrat. Baptist. Home: 2515 55th Ave E Brandenton FL 34203 Office: Oneco Tallevast Fire Dept PO Box 731 Oneco FL 34264

STEFFENS, JOHN LAUNDON, brokerage house executive; b. Cleve., July 7, 1941; m. Louise Cullen, Nov. 25, 1967; children: Drew, Julie, Wesley. B in Econs., Dartmouth Coll., 1963. Various positions Merrill Lynch, 1963—, pres. consumer mkts., 1985—. Office: Merrill Lynch & Co Inc World Fin Ctr N Tower New York NY 10281

STEFFENS, LISA KAY, data processing executive; b. St. Cloud, Minn., Nov. 12, 1961; d. Edward Mathias and Anita Lorayne (Lauer) Medeck; m. Paul Edward Steffens, May 25, 1985. BS in Computer Sci., St. Cloud State U., 1984, BA in Maths., 1984. Programmer intern Fingerhut Corp., St. Cloud, 1984; sr. programmer, analyst Fingerhut Corp., Minnetonka, Minn., 1987—; programmer Cargill, Inc., Minnetonka, 1984-87. Home: 15301 McKenzie Blvd Minnetonka MN 55345 Office: Fingerhut Corp 4400 Baker Rd Minnetonka MN 55343

STEGEMEIER, RICHARD JOSEPH, oil company executive; b. Alton, Ill., Apr. 1, 1928; s. George Henry and Rose Ann (Smola) S.; m. Marjorie Ann Spess, Feb. 9, 1952; children: Richard Michael, David Scott, Laura Ann, Martha Louise. BS in Petroleum Engring., U. Mo., Rolla, 1950, cert. petroleum engr. (hon.), 1981; MS in Petroleum Engring., Tex. A&M U., 1951. Registered profl. engr., Calif. Various nat. and internat. positions with Unocal Corp. (formerly Union Oil Co.), Los Angeles, 1951—, v.p. sci. and tech. div., 1978-80, sr. v.p. corp. devel., 1980-85, pres., chief operating officer, 1985—, chief exec. officer, 1988—, also bd. dirs. Patentee in field. Pres. World Affairs Council of Orange County, 1980-81; chmn. Brea (Calif.) Blue Ribbon Com, 1979-80; mem. math sci.-engring. adv. council Calif. State U., Fullerton; mem. chem. adv. council Calif. State U., Long Beach; bd. dirs. YMCA, Los Angeles, Martin Luther Hosp. Med. Ctr. Fellow Tenn. Gas Transmissions Co., 1951; recipient Engring. Merit award Orange County Engring. Council, 1980, Outstanding Engr. Merit award, Inst. Advancement Engring., 1981. Mem. Am. Petroleum Inst., Soc. Petroleum Engrs (lectr. 1978). Republican. Roman Catholic. Club: California (Los Angeles). Office: Unocal Corp PO Box 7600 Los Angeles CA 90051 *

STEGMAN, CHARLES ALEXANDER (CHUCK ALEXANDER STEGMAN), marketing professional; b. Denver, Apr. 17, 1959; s. Harvey Eugene and Mary Martha (Newell) S. BSEE, U. Colo., 1981. Regional dir. Sigma Phi Epsilon, Richmond, Va., 1981-82, chpt. devel. dir., 1982-83; sales rep. Lanier/Harris, San Francisco, 1983, legal account rep., 1983-84; mktg. rep. Businessland, Oakland, Calif., 1984-86, sr. mktg. rep., 1986; mktg. mgr. of networks Businessland, San Jose, Calif., 1987-88, mgr. mktg. advanced systems div., 1988—; systems engring. instr. Businessland of San Jose, Calif., 1986-87. Co-chmn. Molinari for Mayor, 1987; active Dem. Party. Recipient numerous computer sales awards; named one of Outstanding Young Men of Am., 1985. Mem. Comstock Club, Commonwealth Club, Sigma Phi Epsilon. Roman Catholic. Home: 78 Buchanan St #302 San Francisco CA 94102 Office: Businessland 1001 Ridder Park Dr San Jose CA 95131

STEGMAYER, JOSEPH HENRY, steel company executive; b. Teaneck, N.J., Jan. 4, 1951; s. Arthur Harry and Alicia (Ward) S. BS, U. Louisville, 1973. Spl. projects Worthington Industries Inc., Columbus, Ohio, 1973-75, dir. investor relations, 1975-77, dir. corp. relations, 1977-80, v.p. corp. devel., 1980-82, v.p., chief fin. officer, 1982—, treas., 1983—, also bd. dirs.; v.p. JMAC Inc., Columbus, 1981—, bd. dirs.; bd. dirs. Clayton Homes Inc., Knoxville, Tenn., Cardinal Funds Inc., Columbus. Editor: We've Only Scratched the Surface, 1981. Chmn. YMCA, Columbus, 1981-82; pres. Columbus Zoo, 1986—; bd. dirs. Muskingum Coll., 1984—. Named Citizen of Yr., Columbus Jaycees, 1984; recipient Outstanding Achievement in Fin. award Phi Beta Kappa, 1984. Mem. Fin. Execs. Inst., Athletic Club, Columbus Maennerchor Club. Republican. Roman Catholic. Office: Worthington Industries Inc 1205 Dearborn Dr Columbus OH 43085

STEGMULLER, JOSEPH JAMES, consultant; b. Erbach, Germany, Sept. 9, 1939; came to U.S., 1949; s. Henry J. and Anna (Clausen) S.; m. Yvonne Harbeck, June 2, 1962 (div. 1979); children: Kurt, Heidi; m. Marisa L. Lelli, Sept. 29, 1979; 1 child, Paul. Student, Fordham U., 1967-68; BBA, Pacific Coll., 1970. Sr. auditor Moore-McCormack Lines, N.Y.C., 1958-68; mgr. claims and security Nat. Carloading, Inc., Chgo., 1969-73; dir. customer svc. Werner Continental, Roseville, Minn., 1973-78; dir. claims Cooper-Jarrett, Inc., Morristown, N.J., 1978-80; dir. Atlas Assocs., Jim Thorpe, Pa., 1980—. Author: Claim Prevention, 1970. Mem. Am. Soc. Indsl. Security, N.J. Bd. Realtors, Airplane Owners and Pilots Assn. Mormon. Office: Atlas Assocs Box 226 Jim Thorpe PA 18229

STEHMAN, BETTY KOHLS, data processing executive; b. Glencoe, Minn., Dec. 23, 1952; d. Clarence Otto and Pearl Amelia (Tuman) K.; m. Carl Knottwell Stehman, Feb. 12, 1984; 1 child, Sandra. BA, Winona State U., 1975. Cert. internal auditor. Acctg. mgr. Regan Mgmt., Bloomington, Minn., 1978-79; sr. internal auditor Bemis Co., Inc., Mpls., 1980; internal audit mgr. Hartzell Corp., St. Paul, 1980-82; controller Ragon Electronics, St. Paul, 1982-85; owner An Asst. to the Entrepreneur (formerly Interactive Bus. Systems), Eden Prairie, Minn., 1985-88, Wheaton, Md., 1988—; with Home Industries, 1987—; cons. in field. Chairperson Immanuel Lutheran Ch., Eden Prairie, 1981-84. Mem. Inst. Internal Auditors, Transamerican Mgmt. Assn. Republican.

STEIG, DONALD BARRY, management consultant; b. Bklyn., Dec. 27, 1933; s. Israel and Jean (Lerner) S.; m. Janet Barbara Feldman, Sept. 13, 1959; children: Jenifer Anne, Adam Brett, Jordan Scott. BS, MIT, 1955; MS, Columbia U., 1956. Systems analyst Curtiss-Wright Corp., Carlstadt, N.J., 1956-59; systems engr. IBM Corp., N.Y.C., 1959-61; dir. data processing Data Processing Systems, Inc., Rochester, N.Y., 1961-64; corp. systems cons. Celanese Corp., Newark, 1964-65; group mgr. systems devel. Hoffmann-LaRoche, Inc., Nutley, N.J., 1965-78; dir. mgmt. info. systems Pub. Clearing House, Port Washington, N.Y., 1978-82; v.p. info. svcs. Margrace Corp., Middlesex, N.J., 1982-85; pres. Practical Computer Solutions, Short Hills, N.J., 1985—; mem. adj. faculty Seton Hall U., South Orange, N.J., 1964-65, Rutgers U., New Brunswick, N.J., 1965-78, Adelphi U., Garden City, N.Y., 1980-82. Contbr. articles to profl. publs. Bd. dirs. Neighborhood Assn., Millburn, N.J., 1987—; regional chmn. MIT Ednl. Council, No. N.J., 1982—. With USN, 1958-59. Mem. Inst. Mgmt. Cons., Ind. Computer Cons. Assn. (bd. dirs. 1986-88), Soc. Info. Mgmt., Assn. Mng. Cons., Am. Arbitration Assn., MIT Club (No. N.J. chpt. pres. 1969-70). Jewish. Home and Office: Practical Computer Solutions 43 Mohawk Rd Short Hills NJ 07078

STEIGER, DALE ARLEN, publishing executivet; b. LaCrosse, Wis., May 14, 1928; s. Walter Elmer and Doris Adeline (Howe) S.; student U. Wis., LaCrosse, 1945-46, 48-49; BA, Chgo. Acad. Fine Arts, 1951; postgrad. Drake U., 1958-62, Iona Coll., 1968; m. Alyce Ann Dyrdahl, Oct. 8, 1949; children: Christine Ann, Marta Louise. Art dir. Trane Co., LaCrosse, 1955, Look mag., Des Moines, 1956, promotions mgr. Cowles Subscription div., 1957-67, exec. v.p. Cowles Communications subdiv., 1960-71; v.p. mktg., asso. pub. Curtis Publs. Co., N.Y.C., 1971-72; pres. Dale Steiger Assocs., N.Y.C., 1972—, Blue Ribbon Reading Svc., Rye, N.Y., 1979—; pres., pub. Videofinder mag., 1981—, Pulling mag., 1981—; pres. SUBCO, 1986; chmn. Hair and Beauty Inc.; pub. Hair and Beauty News, 1988—; lectr. direct mail and mktg. Served with AUS, 1946-48. Recipient Industry Achievement award Fulfillment Mgmt. Assn., 1979; Lee C. Williams award for outstanding contbns. to periodical pub. field, 1982. Mem. Mag. Publs. Assn., Audit Bur. Circulations, Fulfillment Mgmt. Assn. (pres., chmn. bd.), Nat. Soc. Art Dirs., VFW, Am. Legion, Cornell Club, Westchester Country Club. Republican. Presbyterian (elder). Author: (with others) The Handbook of Circulation Management, 1980. Office: 488 Madison Ave New York NY 10022

STEIN, ALLAN MARK, lawyer; b. Montreal, Quebec, Can., Oct. 18, 1951; came to U.S., 1977; s. Boris and Beatrice (Fishman) S. B in Commerce, Sir George Williams, 1972; BA, Loyola, Montreal, 1973; B in Civil Law, McGill U., 1976, LLB, 1977; JD, Nova U., 1979. Bar: Fla. 1979, U.S. Dist. Ct. (so. dist.) Fla. 1979, U.S. Ct. Appeals (5th cir.) 1980, U.S. Ct. Appeals (11th cir.) 1983. Assoc. Law Offices of Paul Landy Beiley, Miami, Fla., 1980, Heitner & Rosenfeld, Miami, 1980-85; ptnr. Rosenfeld & Stein, Miami, 1985—. Mem. North Dade Bar Assn. (bd. dirs. 1985—). Republican. Jewish. Office: Rosenfeld & Stein 18260 NE 19 Ave #202 North Miami Beach FL 33162

STEIN, ARTHUR WILLIAM, finance company officer; b. Wilkinsburg, Pa., Dec. 20, 1953; s. Arthur G. and Margaret (Stewart) S.; m. Stephanie Smith, Aug. 15, 1981; 1 child, Meredith T. AB, Princeton U., 1975; JD, U. Pitts., 1978; MS in Indsl. Adminstrn. with distinction, Carnegie-Mellon U., 1988. Bar: Pa. 1978, Fla. 1979, U.S. Dist. Ct. (we. dist.) Pa. 1978, U.S. Ct. Appeals (3rd cir.) 1981. Assoc. Stein & Winters, Pitts., 1978-81; atty. Duquesne Light Co., Pitts., 1981-84, atty., asst. sec., 1984-86, asst. treas. corp. fin., 1986-88, treas., 1988-89; v.p. Westinghouse Credit Corp., Pitts., 1989—. Mem. Fla. Bar Assn., Pa. Bar Assn., Allegheny County Bar Assn., Beta Gamma Sigma. Republican. Presbyterian. Club: River. Office: Westinghouse Credit Corp 301 Grant St 1 Oxford Centre Pittsburgh PA 15219

STEIN, CAREY M., lawyer; b. Chgo., July 15, 1947; s. Daniel and Shirley (Weinstein) S.; m. Seena R. Silverman, July 8, 1972; children: Allison, Amy. BS, So. Ill. U., 1970; JD, DePaul U., 1974. Bar: Ill. 1974, N.Y. 1988. Tax examiner IRS, Chgo., 1973-75; atty. Ill. Dept. Revenue, Chgo., 1975-77; asst. corp. counsel Hart, Schaffner & Marx, Chgo., 1977-83; Assoc. gen. counsel, asst. sec. Hartmarx Corp., Chgo., 1983-84, v.p., sec., gen. counsel, 1984—. Mem. exec. com., bd. dirs. Ctr. for Enriched Living, Deerfield, Ill., 1984—; adv. bd. Northwestern U. Corp. Counsel Ctr., Chgo., 1984—; exec. com., bd. dirs. Jewish Edn. Met. Chgo., 1987—, sec. treas. 1988—. Mem. ABA, Ill. Bar Assn., Chgo. Bar Assn., Am. Soc. Corp. Secs., Am. Apparel Mfrs. Assn. (legal com. 1985—). Am. Arbitration Assn. (adv. com., panel 1988—). Jewish. Office: Hartmarx Corp 101 N Wacker Dr Chicago IL 60606

STEIN, DAVID ALAN, distribution executive; b. Bklyn., Sept. 18, 1950; s. Arnold and Ruth (Bernholz) S.; m. Michelle Raum, May 4, 1980; children: Rebecca Simone, Daniel Alexander. BA in English, U. Rochester, 1972; MFA in Acting, Boston U., 1974. Founder, pres. Act One Office Supply, Inc., N.Y.C., 1980—. Actor McCarter Theater, Princeton, N.J., 1975, Am. Shakespeare Theater, Stratford, Conn., 1975. Mem. 42d St. Civic Assn., N.Y.C. Mem. Stationers Assn. N.Y., Stationers 12:30 Club. Democrat. Office: Act One Office Supply Inc 311 W 43d St New York NY 10036

STEIN, HOWARD, mutual fund executive; b. 1926. Student, Julliard Sch. Music, 1944-46. With Seaporcel Metals Inc., 1950-53, Bache & Co., 1953-55; asst., dir. Dreyfus Investment Mgmt. of Dreyfus and Co., also gen. partner, 1965—; v.p. Dreyfus Fund Inc., 1961-65, pres., chmn. bd., 1965—; pres., dir. Dreyfus Corp., 1965-70, chmn. bd., chief exec. officer, 1970—. Office: Dreyfus Corp 767 Fifth Ave 35th Fl New York NY 10153

STEIN, MARTIN MATTHEW, management consultant, research director; b. Bad Gastein, Austria, Feb. 21, 1946; s. Leon and Bess (Kicis) S.; came to U.S., 1949, naturalized, 1956; B.S. with high honors in Econs., U. Md., 1967, M.A. in Econs., 1975; D.E.S. avec la mention très bien in Ops. Research and Applied Math., U. Paris, 1976, D.Sc., 1978; children—Stephen, William, Joshua, Michelle, Jacqueline. Economist, U.S. Dept. Commerce and U.S. Dept. Transp., Washington, 1967-73, U.S. Dept. Interior, Washington, 1973; mgr. socio-econ. group Md. Dept. Transp., Balt., 1973-78; dir. automotive cons. dept. Abt Assocs., Inc., Cambridge, Mass., 1978—; sr. economist cons. Booz-Allen Hamilton; asst. prof. econs. Sch. Bus., U. Balt.; lectr. Johns Hopkins, Balt.; lectr. M.B.A. program Babson Coll., Wellesley, Mass.; v.p. Internat. Policy Inst., Washington; sr. tech. adv. energy and transport UN Dept. Tech. Cooperation and Devel., N.Y.C., UN Devel. Programme Ctr. for Water and Transport, UNCTAD, Geneva; adv. com. Def. Econ. Analysis Council, U.S. Dept. Def. Mem. retail trade study exec. com. Greater Balt. Com., 1976, Econ. Devel. Council, Regional Planning Council, 1977-78. Fellow Internat. Inst. Social Econs.; mem. Soc. Govt. Economists (award 1972; founder, pres., chmn. bd.), Soc. Automotive Analysts (pres., founder), Nat. Council Assns. for Policy Scis. (co-founder, v.p.), Balt. Econ. Soc. (founder, pres.), Am. Econ. Assn., Internat. Assn. Energy Economists, John Marshall Soc., U.S. C. of C. (coordinator coll. bus. symposium 1966), Internat. Inst. Forecasting, Transp. Research Bd., Transp. Research Forum, U. Md. Alumni Assn. (council, chpt. v.p., pres. 1973-77, Omicron Delta Epsilon, Delta Sigma Pi, Delta Nu Alpha. Research and cons. in transp. and automotive investment, pub. energy policy, socio-econ. impacts of tech. change, safety policy evaluation. Editor: Economic Development, The State and Local Government Perspective, 1976; contbr. articles to profl. jours.; speaker profl. confs. Home: 4801 Walkingfern Dr Rockville MD 20853 Office: 4250 Connecticut Ave NW Ste 500 Washington DC 20008

STEIN, MICHAEL KAY, financial investment company executive, consultant; b. Chgo., Sept. 14, 1933; s. Milton Jerome and Julia Yeta (Joseph) S.; m. Eunice Margaret Ogilvie, Nov. 28, 1957; children—Neil Brian, Douglas Milton, Katharine Diane. B.S., U.S. Mil. Acad., 1957; M.A., Am. U., 1967. Cert. fin. planner. Commd. 2d lt. U.S. Army, 1957, advanced through grades to lt. col., 1971; bus. mgr. High Country Furniture, Boulder, Colo., 1977-78; mgr. Boettcher & Co., Denver, 1978-82; pres. Fin. Planning & Mgmt., Boulder, 1982-88; regional dir. Fin. Network Investment Corp., Torrance, Calif., 1984—; advisor Advanced Pumping Systems, Lafayette, Colo., 1982—, Coll. Fin. Planning, Denver, 1982—. Advisor Boy Scouts Am.,Boulder, 1988; active Big Bros., Denver, 1988, Denver Mus. Art, 1988. Decorated Legion of Merit, Bronze Star. Mem. Internat. Assn. Fin. Planning (local v.p. 1982-84), Inst. Cert. Fin. Planners, Assn. Ret. Officers (v.p. 1985-87), Internat. Soc. Pre-Retirement Planners, Nat. Ctr. Fin. Edn. (advisor), Boulder C. of C., Toastmaster Internat. (pres. club 1981-82). Republican. Avocations: skiing, stamp collecting, woodworking. Office: Fin Planning & Mgmt 2995 Center Green Ct S Boulder CO 80301

STEIN, RICHARD ALLEN, real estate developer; b. Chgo., Jan. 16, 1939; s. Joseph and Selma (Strauss) S.; m. Carol Katzman, Oct. 1, 1967; children: Barbara, Katherine. BS in Hotel Adminstrn., Cornell U., 1961. Cert. property mgr. Ptnr., founder The Littlestone Co., Chgo., 1961-71; chmn., chief exec. officer Stein & Co., Chgo., 1971—; bd. dirs. Exch. Nat. Bank Chgo., Evanston/Northwestern U. Research Park, Ill., Navy Pier Devel. Authority; mem. adv. com. Civic Fedn. Chgo., 1985—; mem. Urban Land Inst., 1986—. Bd. dirs. Chgo. Urban League, 1987—, The Lambs, Inc., Libertyville, Ill., 1981—; trustee Ravinia Festival Assn., Highland Park, Ill., 1985—; bd. trustees St. Joseph's Coll., Renssaelaer, Ind., 1986—. Recipient Corp. Leadership award Hispanic Am. Constrn. Industry, 1988, Developer of Yr. award Black Contractors United, 1988, John Hyman Corp. award, 1988. Mem. Chgo. Real Estate Bd., Ill. Real Estate Bd., Nat. Assn.

Realtors, Met. Planning Coun., Lambda Alpha. Clubs: Met., Standard, Northmoor. Office: Stein & Co 208 S LaSalle St Ste 1630 Chicago IL 60604

STEIN, RICHARD PAUL, lawyer; b. New Albany, Ind., Sept. 2, 1925; s. William P. and Lillian M. (Russell) S.; m. Mary Charlotte Key, June 22, 1959; children: Richard Paul, William, Patricia. Student, Milligan (Tenn.) Coll., 1943-44, Duke, 1944-45; J.D., U. Louisville, 1950. Bar: Ind., 1950. With labor relations Goodyear Engring. Co., Charlestown, Ind., 1952-54; ptnr. Naville & Stein, New Albany, 1954-61; pros. atty. 52d Jud. Circuit Ind., 1956-61; U.S. atty. So. Dist. Ind., 1961-67; chmn. Pub. Service Commn. of Ind., 1967-70; legis. counsel Eli Lilly Co., Indpls., 1970-74; v.p. pub. affairs Pub. Service Co. Ind., 1974—; dir. Indpls. Indians; Co-counsel New Albany-Floyd County Bldg. Authority, 1960-62; mem. State Bd. Tax Commrs. Adv. Bd., Jud. Study Commn. Sec. New Albany Dist. Dem. Com., 1956-61; chmn. New Albany United Way, 1957. Served to lt. USNR, 1943-46, 50-51; lt. Res. Named Floyd County Young Man of Yr. Floyd County Jr. C. of C., 1955, Outstanding Young Man of Yr. New ALbany Jaycees, 1958. Mem. Ind. Bar Assn., Marion County Bar Assn., Ind. Prosecutors Assn. (pres. 1960-61), Ind. Electric Assn. (dir.), Am. Legion, Pi Kappa Alpha, Phi Alpha Delta. Roman Catholic. Clubs: Highland Country, Skyline. Lodge: K.C. Home: 5517 Surrey Hill Circle Indianapolis IN 46226

STEIN, ROBERT WILLIAM, actuary, accountant; b. Milw., Feb. 4, 1949; s. Herbert A. and Elizabeth (Greenman) S.; children: Paul, Jennifer; m. Christine Marie Denham, May 14, 1988. BBA, Drake U., 1971. CPA, N.Y. Cons. actuary Milliman & Robertson, Inc., Milw., 1971-74, Denver, 1974-80; sr. mgr. Ernst & Whinney, Denver, 1976-80; ptnr. Ernst & Whinney, Chgo., 1980-87, N.Y.C., 1987—. Author: Universal Life, 1980; contbr. articles on fin. mgmt. Fellow Soc. Actuaries; mem. Am. Acad. Actuaries, Am. Inst. CPAs. Office: Ernst & Whinney 787 7th Ave New York NY 10019

STEIN, SHELDON IRVIN, lawyer, investment banker; b. Bklyn., Aug. 11, 1953; s. Sidney and Esther (Gold) S.; m. Barbara Brickman, Aug. 18, 1974; children: Shane Randall, Kyle Noah, Reid Jordan. BA, Brandeis U., 1974; JD, Harvard U., 1977. Bar: Calif. 1977, Tex. 1978. Assoc. Fulop, Rolston, Burns & McKittrick, Beverly Hills, Calif., 1977-78; assoc. Hughes & Luce, Dallas, 1978-83, ptnr., 1983-86; mng. dir. s.w. corp. fin. Bear, Stearns & Co., Inc., Dallas, 1986—; bd. dirs. IMC Holdings, Inc., Ft. Worth, BSN Corp., Dallas. Mem. leadership cabinet United Jewish Appeal, N.Y., 1984-88; bd. dirs. Jewish Fedn. Dallas, 1985-88, Jewish Community Ctr. Dallas, 1985-87, Akiba Acad. Dallas, 1985—, Greenhill Sch. of Dallas, 1988—, Arthritis Found., 1988—. Mem. ABA, Tex. Bar Assn., Calif. Bar Assn., Phi Beta Kappa. Clubs: Columbian Country, Tower. Lodge: B'nai B'rith (bd. dirs. anti-defamation league Dallas 1983-87). Office: Bear Stearns & Co Inc 1601 Elm St Dallas TX 75201

STEINAU, RICHARD DAVID, lawn and pest control executive; b. Nashville, Apr. 5, 1947; s. Bert and Sarah (Strauss) S.; m. Valerie May, Dec. 31, 1982; children: Peter Emerson, Jay Royal. BFA, U. Cin., 1970. Pres. Univ. Mktg. Inc., Cin., 1970-71; gen. mgr. Ace Exterminating Co., Cin., 1972-75, pres., 1979—; pres. Greenlon Inc., Cin., 1974—. Trustee Ohio Pesticide Task Force, 1984-86; mem. Community Chest and Aging Allocation Svc. Com., Cin., 1985-886; nominating chair Cin. Local Devel. Co., 1987, 88; bd. dirs. Talbert House and Half Way House, Cin., 1975-76. Mem. Ohio Pesticide Applicators for Responsible Regulation (mem. bd. trustees 1984—), Structural Pesticide Applicators Assn. (founder, chmn. bd. 1986—), Profl. Lawn Care Assn. Am. (trustee 1987—), Greater Cin. Pest Control Assn. (v.p. 1974-86), Ohio Turf Found. (selection com. 1984-85). Home: 1826 Madison Rd Cincinnati OH 45206 Office: Greenlon Lawn Care 1920 Losantiville Ave Cincinnati OH 45237

STEINBACK, KENNETH B., computer sales company executive; b. St. Louis, Aug. 11, 1943; s. Sol Steinback and Dorothy (Millman) Steinback Vittert; m. Marilyn Ellen Dann, May 30, 1970; children: Susan Lynn, Robert Jay. BSBA, Washington U., 1966. Systems analyst McDonnel Douglas Automation Co., St. Louis, 1966-67; mktg. rep. Honeywell Info. Systems, St. Louis, 1970-72; dist. sales mgr. Fabri-Tek, Inc., St. Louis, 1972-73; v.p. Computer Sales Internat., Inc., St. Louis, 1973-77, exec. v.p., 1977-80, pres., chmn., 1980-84, chmn., chief exec. officer, 1984—; dir. Mark Twain Bank Frontenac, St. Louis. Bd. dirs. Shaare Emeth Temple, St. Louis, 1988—, Cen. Inst. for the Deaf, 1988—, Jewish Ctr. for the Aged, 1988—. 1st lt. U.S. Army, 1967-70. Mem. Am. Assn. Equipment Lessors, Computer Dealers and Lessors Assn. bd. dirs. 1982—, treas. 1984-86, chmn., chief exec. officer, 1988—).

STEINBACK, THOMAS R., food service corporate executive; b. Evansville, Ind., May 17, 1950; s. Edward Oscar and Thelma Jean (Ellison) S.; B.A., Ambassador Coll., Eng., 1972; postgrad. Miss. State U., 1974-75; M.B.A., Syracuse U., 1980. Cert. office automation profl.; m. Sherry Lynn Amos, Mar. 12, 1982; children: Lindsay Ann, Laura Jean, Chelsea Lynn. Exec. trainee Ambascol Corp., Eng., 1970-72; assoc. office mgr. Ambassador Coll., Pasadena, Calif., 1972-77; fin. loan counselor Syracuse (N.Y.) U., 1978-79; employee relations intern Gen. Electric Co., Syracuse, 1979, mgr. employee and community relations AEPD, Utica, 1979-82, mgr. communication programs-salaried relations AEPD, Syracuse, 1982-84; mgr. Profl. Relations Chgo. Pneumatic Tool Co., Utica, N.Y., 1984-87; corp. dir. human resources CIS Corp., Syracuse, 1987; pres. TRS Consulting, New Hartford, N.Y., 1987-88; pres., chief operating officer Rich Plan Food Corp., New Hartford, 1988—; adj. instr. AMA, Utica Coll., SUNY. Trustee ARC, Utica, 1980-82; chmn./trustee GE Employees Federated Service Fund, Utica, 1979-82; allstar mgr. New Hartford Lions Little League, 1982; pres. New Hartford ASA Girls Softball, 1984-85. Recipient Grad. Alumni award Syracuse U., 1980. Mem. Am. Soc. Personnel Adminstrs., Am. Mgmt. Assn., Assn. M.B.A. Execs., Assn. Meat Processors, Am. Frozen Food Inst., Direct Selling Assn. Office: 4981 Commercial Dr Yorkville NY 13495

STEINBERG, BURT, retail executive; b. N.Y.C., June 2, 1945; s. Harry and Etta (Lippman) S.; m. Francine Hershkowitz, Dec. 22, 1968; children: Michael, Jessica. BA, CCNY, 1968; MBA, Columbia U., 1970. Mdse. mgr. Abraham & Straus, Bklyn., 1972-77; sr. v.p. Brooks Fashion Stores, N.Y.C., 1977-82, Dress Barn Inc., Stamford, Conn., 1982—. Mem. Columbia Alumni Assn., Am. Mktg. Assn. Home: 6 Meridan Ln Nanuet NY 10954 Office: Dress Barn Inc 69 Jefferson St Stamford CT 06902

STEINBERG, DAVID ISAAC, economic development consultant; b. Cambridge, Mass., Nov. 26, 1928; s. Naaman and Miriam (Goldberg) S.; m. Isabel Maxwell, 1951 (div. 1962); 1 child, Christopher; m. Ann Myongsook Lee, May 15, 1964; children: Alexander L., Eric D. BA, Dartmouth Coll., 1950; MA, Harvard U., 1955; DLitt (hon.), Sungkunkwan U., Seoul, Republic of Korea. Analyst Nat. Security Council, Washington, 1951-53; program officer Asia Found., N.Y.C., 1956-58; asst. rep. Asia Found., Burma, 1958-62, Hong Kong, 1962-63; rep. Asia Found., Republic of Korea, 1963-68, Washington, 1968-69; cons., sr. fgn. service officer AID, Washington and Bangkok (Thailand), 1969-86; pres. Mansfield Ctr. for Pacific Affairs, Helena, Mont., 1986-87, cons., 1987—; pvt. cons., Washington, 1987—, World Bank, 1987—, The Asia Soc., 1988—; founding mem. Burma Studies Found., De Kalb, Ill., 1987. Author: Burma's Road toward Development, 1981, Burma, 1982, The Republic of Korea Economic Transformation and Social Change, 1988. 1st lt. U.S. Army, 1953-55. Fellow Lingnan U., Canton, China, 1948, Dartmouth Coll., 1950. Mem. Assn. Asian Studies, Oriental Ceramic Soc., Asia Devel. Roundtable (chmn. 1984-86, 87—), Cosmos Club. Home: 6207 Goodview St Bethesda MD 20817

STEINBERG, ELLIOT GERSHOM, lawyer; b. San Francisco, Oct. 15, 1937; William and Pauline (Finkelstein) S.; m. Sarah Jane Staats, Apr. 3, 1965 (div. 1973); children: John Michael, Aaron William, Scott Anthony; m. Janet Beth Goldberg, June 12, 1982. BA, U. Calif., Berkeley, 1960, JD, 1964. Bar: Calif. 1965, U.S. Dist. Ct. (no. dist.) Calif., U.S. Ct. Appeals (9th cir.); cert. specialist in taxation. Assoc. Thorne & Stanton, San Jose, Calif., 1965-66, ptnr., 1966-70; ptnr. Levenfeld & Kanter, San Francisco, 1970-79, Flynn & Steinberg, San Francisco, 1979-83; gen. ptnr. European Am. Securities Ventures L.P., San Francisco, 1984-85; v.p., gen. counsel Itel Corp., San Francisco, 1985—; cons. Itel Corp., 1985; bd. dirs. Kimco Mgmt. Co., San Francisco. Co-author: Closely Held Corporations, 1977, (book) Tax Reform Act of 1976, 1976, Income Taxation of Foreign Related Transactions, 1971; editor Jour. Taxation of Investments, 1984—. Chmn. bd. dirs. San Francisco Art Inst., 1982—; trustee Urban High Sch. of San Francisco, 1983—, Wright Inst., Berkeley, 1980-83. Served with USN, 1955-57. Mem. ABA, Calif. Bar Assn., Bar Assn. of San Francisco, Internat. Fiscal Assn. Democrat. Jewish. Clubs: Tiburon (Calif.) Peninsula, Bay (San Francisco), San Francisco Lawyers. Office: Itel Corp 909 Montgomery St Ste 600 San Francisco CA 94133

STEINBERG, IRWIN IRA, management consultant; b. Bklyn., Oct. 15, 1926; s. Samuel and Sophie (Emerman) S.; m. Mollie Deutsch, Mar. 11, 1951; children: Laurence D., Andrew B. BS, U.S. Mil. Acad., 1950; MBA, NYU, 1961. Commd. 2d lt. U.S. Army, 1950, advanced through grades to 1st lt., resigned; v.p. mgmt. Loral Corp., N.Y.C., 1960-70; pres., chief exec. officer Laurand Corp., N.Y.C., 1971-77, Gruma Corp., Los Angeles, 1978-82; sr. v.p., chief operating officer NTS, Calabasas, Calif., 1983-86; pres. The Steinberg Co., Encino, Calif., 1986—; adj. prof. bus. mgmt. Woodbury U., U. Redlands, 1988—. Recipient Gold Key Pub. Relations award N.Y. Pub. Relations Bd., 1966; named Man of Yr. Leather Industries Assn., 1973. Mem. IEEE, Am. Def. Preparedness Assn., West Point Soc. Los Angeles, Assn. Grads. U.S. Mil. Acad. Republican. Jewish. Home: 15610 Moorpark St Encino CA 91436 Office: 16000 Ventura Blvd #500 Encino CA 91436

STEINBERG, JOSEPH SAUL, investment company executive; b. Chgo., Feb. 5, 1944; s. Paul S. and Sylvia (Neikrug) S.; 1 child from previous marriage, Sarah Aliza; m. Diane L. Heidt, 1987. A.B., N.Y. U., 1966; M.B.A., Harvard U., 1970. Vol. Peace Corps, Kingston, Jamaica, 1966-68; v.p. Carl Marks & Co., Inc. (investment bankers), N.Y.C., 1970-78; pres. Leucadia Nat. Corp., N.Y.C., 1979—, also bd. dirs.; vice-chmn. Brae Corp., San Francisco, 1986—, also bd. dirs.; pres. Phlcorp, Inc., 1987—, also bd. dirs.; bd. dirs. Empire Ins. Group, Bolivian Power Co. Ltd. Clubs: Harvard, Nat. Arts (N.Y.C.). Office: Leucadia Nat Corp 315 Park Ave S New York NY 10010

STEINBERG, SHERIDAN L., corporate secretary; b. N.Y.C., July 17, 1943; s. Joseph and Annette (Ganson) S.; m. Diane Edelman, June 13, 1965; children: Ian Scott, Kevin Seth. BEE, Poly. Inst. N.Y., 1966, MS in Indsl. Mgmt., 1970. Engr. N.Y. Telephone Co., 1965-69; computer cons. Computer Tech., Inc., White Plains, N.Y., 1969-70; mgr. data processing and ops. Citibank, N.A., N.Y.C., 1970-79, dir. mktg. and advt., 1979-82, dir. pub. affairs, 1983-88, dir. corp. adminstrn., 1988—. Trustee Found. Am. Communications. Mem. IEEE, Pub. Relations Seminar, Wisemen. Jewish. Club: Atrium (N.Y.C.). Home: Mountainside Tr Peekskill NY 10566 Office: Citibank NA 399 Park Ave New York NY 10043

STEINBERG, SUSAN KIZER, pharmacist, consulting company executive; b. Bklyn., July 7, 1949; d. Rembert Samuel and Elizabeth (Bransford) Kizer; m. Ralf Gunther Steinberg, July 16, 1977; children: Gretel Susanne, Heidi Virginia. BS in Pharmacy with honors, U. S.C., 1972, MS in Pharmacy, 1975. Lic. pharmacist S.C., Ontario. Clin. pharmacist Sunnybrook Med. Ctr., Toronto, 1975-86; asst. prof. U. Toronto, 1975—; pres. Can. Pharmacy Cons. Inc., Toronto, 1985—. Author: Development of a Palliative Care Manual for Elderly Patients, 1984 (McNeil award). Mem. Am. Soc. Cons. Pharmacists, Am. Soc. Hosp. Pharmacists, Can. Soc. Hosp. Pharmacists, Can. Pharm. Assn., Can. Found. Pharmcy (dir. 1986—), Can. Assn. Women Bus. Owners, Rho Chi, Phi Beta Kappa, Lambda Kappa Sigma. Home and Office: 92 Ruscica Dr, Toronto, ON Canada M4A 1R4

STEINBRENNER, GEORGE EDWARD, marketing executive; b. Euclid, Ohio, June 7, 1947; s. Edward George and Easter L. (Sanger) S.; m. Grazyna Gockowski, July 31, 1971; children: Paul, Peter. BA, Wittenberg U., 1969. V.p. ESA Direct Mktg. Svcs. Inc. (formerly E.S. Advt. Services), Cleve., 1972-81, pres., 1982—; chmn. ESA Direct Mktg. Services Inc. (formerly E.S. Advt. Services), Cleve., 1987—; owner, pres. mgmt. program Harvard U., 1985; founding trustee, officer Historic Warehouse Dist. Devel. Corp., Cleve., 1977-84. Contbr. articles to profl. jour. Mem. Bus. Profl. Advt. Assn., Mail Advt. Svc. Assn. Internat., N.E. Ohio Direct Mail Mktg. Assn., Greater Cleve. Growth Assn., Coun. Smaller Enterprises (bd. dirs., mem. leadership coun. 1986—), Inc. 500 (steering com. 1988), Harvard Bus. Club Cleve. Home: 851 High St Bedford OH 44146 Office: ESA Direct Mktg Svcs Inc 1890 E 40th St Cleveland OH 44103

STEINER, JEFFREY JOSEF, industrial manufacturing company executive; b. Vienna, Austria, Apr. 3, 1937; came to U.S., 1958; s. Beno and Paula (Bornstein) S.; m. Linda Schaller, Mar. 6, 1976 (div. June 1983); children: Eric, Natalia, Thierry, Benjamin, Alexandra; m. Irja Bonnier, Mar. 19, 1987. Student textile design, U. London, 1956; student textile mfg., Bradford Inst. Tech., London, 1957. Mgmt. trainee Metals and Controls div. Tex. Instruments, Attleborough, Mass., 1958-59, mgr. internat., 1959-60; pres. Tex. Instruments, Argentina, Brazil, Mex., Switzerland, France, 1960-66, Burlington Tapis, Paris, 1967-72; chmn., pres. Cedec S.A. Engring. Co., Paris, 1973-84; chmn., chief exec. officer Banner Industries Inc., N.Y.C., 1985—; bd. dirs. Transcontinental Svcs. Group N.A., Copley Fund., Fall River, Mass., Franklin Corp., N.Y.C., Adrienarpel, Stone Savannah River Pulp and Paper Corp. Trustee Montefiore Med. Ctr., N.Y.C.; chmn. bd. trustees Haifa U. Mem. City Athletic Club, Racing Club, Polo Club. Jewish. Office: Banner Industries Inc 110 E 59th St New York NY 10022

STEINER, MARK HENRY, insurance company executive; b. Bluffton, Ohio, Sept. 3, 1952; s. Paul Andrew and Ruth Edna (Henry) S.; m. Ann Marie Rocke, July 11, 1981; children: Thomas Allen, Marie Elizabeth. BA, Taylor U., 1975; JD, Ind. U., 1979, MBA, 1979. Atty. Mut. Security Life Ins. Co., Ft. Wayne, Ind., 1979-81, sr. investment analyst, 1981-84; asst. v.p. fin. Brotherhood Mut. Ins. Co., Ft. Wayne, 1985—. Mem. ABA, Ind. State Bar Assn. (mem. group ins. programs com. 1986—), Fin. Execs. Inst. Mem. Missionary Ch. Lodge: Rotary. Home: 4715 Arlington Ave Fort Wayne IN 46807 Office: Brotherhood Mut Ins Co 6400 Brotherhood Way PO Box 2227 Fort Wayne IN 46801

STEINER, RICHARD RUSSELL, conglomerate executive; b. Chgo., Feb. 26, 1923; s. Frank Gardner and Ruth (Cowie) S.; m. Colleen M. Kearns, Dec. 6, 1949; children—Robert C., Kevin K., Sheila M. B.A., Dartmouth Coll., 1948. With Steiner Corp., Salt Lake City, 1948—; divisonal dir., v.p. Steiner Corp., 1951-59, pres., 1959—; dir. Am. Uniform Co. Served with USAAF, 1942-46. Decorated D.F.C. Mem. Phi Beta Kappa. Clubs: Alta, Salt Lake Country. Office: Steiner Corp 505 E S Temple St Salt Lake City UT 84102

STEINFALS, CHRISTIAN WERNER, hotel executive; b. Duesseldorf, W. Ger., Jan. 22, 1933; came to U.S., 1964; Ed., Duesseldorf Hotel and Gastronomic Sch., 1948-51. Cert. hotel adminstr. Banquet mgr. Hotel Sonesta, Hartford, Conn., 1964-68; food and beverage mgr. Euclid Charterhouse Hotel, Cleve., 1968-69, Kaanapali Beach Hotel, Maui, Hawaii, 1969-70; dir. food and beverage Carlton Tower Hotel, London, 1970-71; asst. gen. mgr. Sutton Pl. Hotel, Toronto, Ont., Can., 1971-72; gen. mgr. Bristol Pl. Hotel Group, Toronto, 1972-78; exec. v.p. ops. Resorts Internat. Hotel Casino, Atlantic City, 1978-86; dir. ops. AFRC Hotels Bavaria, Fed. Republic Germany, 1986-87; exec. v.p. pres. devel. The Bristol Group Park Plaza Hotel, Toronto, 1987—; mem. South Jersey Devel. Council. Mem. Am. Hotel and Motel Assn., Atlantic City Conv. Bur., Atlantic City Hotel Assn., Maitre de Table of Confrerie de la Chaine des Rotisseurs. Office: The Bristol Group, Park Plaza Hotel, 4 Avenue Rd, Toronto, ON Canada M5R 2E8

STEINFELD, MANFRED, furniture manufacturing executive; b. Josbach, Germany, Apr. 29, 1924; s. Abraham and Paula (Katten) S.; m. Fern Goldman, Nov. 13, 1949; children: Michael, Paul, Jill. Student U. Ill., 1942; BS in Commerce, Roosevelt U., 1948. Research analyst State of Ill., 1948-50; v.p. Shelby Williams Industries, Inc., Chgo., 1954-63, pres., 1964-72; chmn. bd., 1973—; dir. Amalgamated Trust & Savs. Bank. Mem. adv. bd. Sch. Human Ecology, U. Tenn., 1981-87, devel. council, 1982—; mem. adv. bd. dept. interior design Fla. Internat. U., 1981-85. Trustee Roosevelt U., Chgo.; past pres. Roosevelt U. Bus. Sch. Alumni Council; hon. governing mem. Art Inst. Chgo., mem. com. 20th century decorative art; dir. Jewish Fedn. Chgo.; gen. chmn. Jewish United Fund, 1987. Served to 1st lt. AUS, 1942-45, 50-52. Decorated Bronze Star, Purple Heart; named Small Bus. Man of Yr., Central Region, 1967; recipient Horatio Alger award of disting. Ams., 1981, Outstanding Bus. Leader award Northwood Inst., 1983. Mem. Beta Gamma Sigma. Clubs: Standard, Bryn Mawr Country (Chgo.); Tamarisk Country (Palm Springs, Calif.); Bocaire Country (Boca Raton, Fla.). Home: 1300 Lake Shore Dr Apt 34D Chicago IL 60610 Office: Mdse Mart Rm 1348 Chicago IL 60654 also: Shelby Williams Industries Inc 5303 E Tennesse Blvd Morristown TN 37814

STEINGRABER, FREDERICK GEORGE, management consultant; b. Mpls., July 7, 1938; s. Frederick F. and Evelyn (Luger) S.; m. Veronika Agnes Wagner, Aug. 9, 1974; children—Karla, Frederick. B.S., Ind. U., 1960; M.B.A., U. Chgo., 1964. Cert. mgmt. cons. Internat. banker Harris Trust, Chgo., 1960-61; with comml. loan and credit No. Trust Co., Chgo., 1963; assoc. A.T. Kearney, Chgo., 1964-69, prin., 1969-72, officer, ptnr., 1972—, pres., chief ops. officer, 1981, chief exec. officer, 1983—, chmn. bd., chief exec. officer, 1986—; mem. Inst. for Ill., 1986; bd. dirs. Maytag Corp., 1989—. Chief crusader United Way-Crusade of Mercy, Chgo., 1983-88, div. chmn., 1988; bd. dirs. Ill. Coalition, 1989; mem. pres. council, trustee Nat. Coll. of Edn., Chgo., 1984—; mem., vice chmn. dean's adv. council Ind. U., 1985—; mem. exec. edn. comm. and council of Grad. Sch. Bus. U. Chgo.; mem. Northwestern U. Assocs.; bd. dirs. Children's Meml. Hosp., Chgo., 1985—; exec. com. Mid-Am. Com., 1985—. Mem. Inst. Mgmt. Cons., Am. Mgmt. Assn., The Conf. Bd., Council Fgn. Relations, Ill. State C. of C. (bd. dirs. 1982-88, exec. com. 1984-88, chmn. Ill. Alliance for Econ. Initiatives), Exec. Club Chgo. (chmn. bd.), Acad. Alumni Fellows Ind. U. (award). Clubs: Chgo., Econ., Comml., Met., River (Chgo.); GlenView (Ill.). Home: 615 Warwick Rd Kenilworth IL 60043 Office: AT Kearney Inc 222 S Riverside Pla Chicago IL 60606

STEINHAUER, JOHN ROBERT, oil company refinery manager; b. Fresno, Calif., Nov. 1, 1946; s. Chester V. and Lois W. (Williams) S. BS ChemE, U. Calif., Davis, 1969. Tech. service engr. UOP Inc., Des Plaines, Ill., 1969-72, startup crew chief, 1973; tech. service supr. Hess Oil Virgin Islands Corp., St. Croix, 1974-79; project mgr. Amerada Hess Corp., Woodbridge, N.J., 1979-81, asst. dept. mgr., refinery engr., 1981-83; refinery mgr. Amerada Hess Corp., Purvis, Miss., 1983-87, Port Reading, N.J., 1987—. Mem. Nat. Assn. Corrosion Engrs. Office: Amerada Hess Corp 1 Hess Pla Woodbridge NJ 07095

STEINHAUSEN, THEODORE BEHN, JR., manufacturing executive; b. Rochester, N.Y., Dec. 21, 1942; s. Theodore B. and Jane (Wolcott) S.; m. Mary Jo Lucas, July 14, 1965; children: Amy, Ted. BA, Hobart Coll., 1965; MBA, U. Pa., 1967. With market research dept. Eastman Kodak Corp., Rochester, 1967-69, with sales, 1969-71, mktg. educator, 1971-73, with fin. dept., 1973-74, dir. mktg. edn., 1974-77; mktg. dir. Europe Eastman Kodak Corp., London, 1977-81; worldwide mktg. planner Eastman Kodak Corp., Rochester, 1981-83, mktg. planner for dental instruments, 1983-86, dir. dental markets, 1986—. Bd. dirs. Hillside Children's Ctr., Rochester, 1987-88; advisor Boy Scouts Am., Rochester, 1987-88; dir. Pittsford (N.Y.) Soccer Club, 1983—. Named Eagle Scout Boy Scouts Am., 1957. Mem. ADA, Am. Acad. Dental Radiology, Am. Mktg. Assn., ASTM. Republican. Presbyterian. Clubs: University; Ski Valley (Naples, N.Y.). Home: 6 Sugarwood Dr Pittsford NY 14534 Office: Eastman Kodak Corp 343 State St Rochester NY 14650

STEINHAUSER, JOHN WILLIAM, lawyer; b. Akron, Ohio, June 25, 1924; s. John Hugo and Francis Lillian (Pearson) S.; BSc in Bus. Adminstrn., Ohio State U., 1949; JD, U. Mich., 1950; m. Patricia E. Mooney, Dec. 1, 1956; children: John, Christian, Mark, Sharon. Bar: Colo. 1972, Mich. 1950. With Chrysler Corp., 1950-71, beginning as atty., successively dir. Latin Am., dir. export sales, gen. mgr. Africa-Far East, dir. Chrysler Internat., Geneva, dir. Africa-Far East, 1950-71; corp. atty., Denver, 1971—; founder, pres. Pearson Energy Corp., 1977, Sharon Energy, Ltd., Denver, 1980, also dir., 1971—. Sponsor Platte Valley Pony Club, Denver Symphony; active Colo. Rep. Party. With USNR, 1943-46. Mem. Colo. Bar Assn., Mich. Bar Assn., ABA, Soc. Internat. Law, Rocky Mountain Mineral Law Found., Cherry Hills Club, Naples Sailing & Yacht Club, Rotary (Denver). Home: 4210 S Dahlia St Englewood CO 80110 Office: Sharon Resources Inc 5340 S Quebec St Ste 220 Englewood CO 80111

STEINIG, STEPHEN NELSON, actuary, insurance company executive; b. Bklyn., Apr. 24, 1945; s. Maurice Harmund and Selma (Weitzner) S.; m. Renee E. Stern, June 25, 1967; children—Karen Elyse, Deborah Eve. A.B., Columbia Coll., 1965; M.S., Grad. Sch. Bus. Adminstrn., 1971. With N.Y. Life Ins. Co., N.Y.C., 1965—, 2d v.p., actuary, 1975-78, v.p., actuary, 1978-82, sr. v.p., 1982—. Fellow Soc. Actuaries; mem. Am. Acad. Actuaries, Phi Beta Kappa. Jewish. Office: NY Life Ins Co 51 Madison Ave New York NY 10010

STEINKE, RANDALL LEE, architect; b. Belvidere, Ill., Feb. 21, 1956; s. Richard Carl Jr. and Virginia Joyce (Smith) S. BArch., U. Ill., 1978, MArch., 1980. Registered architect, Ill., Colo. Architect Seigfreid, Johnson Edward AIA, Rockford, Ill., 1973-74, J. Robert Lofton & Assocs., Rockford, 1978-79, Metz, Train, Youngren Inc., Chgo., 1980-81, Davis & Assocs. Architects and Cons., Chgo., 1982-84, Pouw & Assocs. Inc., Denver, 1984-85, RMA Architects Alley Constrn., Denver, 1985-86; ptnr. Devel. Design Consortium, Denver, 1986—; vis. instr. Denver Tech. Coll., 1986-87. Author: (computer space program) Space Planning Package, 1983. Mem. task force Blueprint for Colo., Denver, 1987. Recipient Earl prize, U. Ill., 1978. Office: Devel Design Consortium 1999 Broadway Ste 3135 Denver CO 80202

STEINLAUF, MARVIN IRA, manufacturing company executive; b. Chgo., Apr. 22, 1938; s. David Steinlauf and Dorothy (Wenger) Estrin; m. Myrna Ruth Nathan, Oct. 26, 1958; children: Michael, Randy, Debbie. V.p. mdse. Health-a-Teria Co., Chgo., 1957-68; pres. Marvin Steinlauf & Assocs., Morton Grove, Ill., 1968—, All-Foam Products Co., Morton Grove, 1977—. Inventor, patentee poly foam cinder block, 1981, shopping list coupon organizer., 1982. Co-chmn. Chgo. Assn. Commerce and Industry Small Bus. Devel. Task Force, Chgo., 1985—; bd. dirs. Lathrop Chgo. Boys and Girls Club, 1985—; bd. dirs. Computer Task Force Chgo. Boys and Girls Clubs, 1987—; active Neediest Children's Fund, Chgo., 1978—; chmn. Jr. Achievement, Chgo., 1952-54. Served to sgt. U.S. Army, 1955-56. Mem. Nat. Housewares Mfrs. Assn., Ind. Bus. Assn. Ill., Houseware Club Chgo., Houseware Club Wis. Jewish. Lodge: B'nai Brith (sec. 1958-62). Home: 7632 W Church St Morton Grove IL 60053 Office: All Foam Products Co PO Box 128 Morton Grove IL 60053

STEINMETZ, MANNING LOUIS, III, investment broker; b. Glasgow, Mo., Aug. 17, 1942; s. Manning Louis and Stella Marie (Fehling) S.; B.S., N.E. Mo. State U., 1964; m. Karen Suzanne Cockriel, July 18, 1970; children—Melissa Leigh, Stephanie Monique, Suzanne Monique. Casualty ins. underwriter MFA Ins. Co., Columbia, Mo., 1965-67, systems analyst, 1967-70; systems analyst Kirksville (Mo.) Coll. Osteo. Medicine, 1970-72, dir. personnel, 1972-73, dir. devel., 1973-75; broker Edward D. Jones & Co., Maryland Heights, Mo., 1975-78, partner, 1978—; allied mem. N.Y. Stock Exchange; dir. S-J Capital Corp., Nooney Capital Corp. Served with U.S. Army, 1964-65. Mem. Nat. Assn. Security Dealers, Securities Industry Assn. (direct investment com.), Sigma Tau Gamma. Republican. Roman Catholic. Club: Bogey Hills Country. Lodges: Masons, Shriners. Home: 2928 W Adams St Saint Charles MO 63301 Office: Edward D Jones & Co 201 Progress Pkwy Maryland Heights MO 63043

STEINMETZ COSMIC, RACHEL ELA, communications executive; b. Haifa, Israel, Sept. 9, 1956; came to U.S., 1977; d. Wilhelm Steinmetz and Masha Pistiner; m. Richard Cosmic, Aug. 2, 1978 (div. Oct. 1986). Student, Tel Aviv U., 1973-75, Superior U. for Mktg., Caracas, Venezuela, 1975-77, San Francisco Art Inst., 1977-78; AA in Liberal Arts and Telecommunications, BA in Telecommunications and Cinema, Columbia Coll., 1981; M. in Communication Arts, Loyola Marymount U., Los Angeles, 1984; EdD, Pepperdine U., 1989. TV producer Tomorrow On Line Today, Los Angeles, 1983; promoter, co-producer Future World Expo 83, Los Angeles, 1983; exec. producer Cosmic Media Communications, Beverly Hills, Calif., 1983—; with media relations Hands Across Am., Los Angeles, 1986; chairperson Global News, Los Angeles, 1986—; promoter, co-producer Invention Conv., Los Angeles, 1987; owner, operator Cosmic Media Communications; founder Global News; dir. tech. TV Arts and Scis., Los Angeles, 1981—; tech. dir., co-producer video program Acad. TV Arts and Scis.; producer, dir., writer Elated Flame Prodns., San Francisco and Los Angeles, 1978—; pres. 13643 Victory Corp., Los Angeles, 1979-80. Author: (TV pilot) The Magic of Music, 1984, 88 (scholar 1984), (manuscript) Visual Communication Tarot Imagery, 1978 (honors award 1978); producer, dir. (short films) The Thirs Eye, Vampire Blast. Fund raiser Global News for orphaned children of Ecuador; liaison fund raising program Loyola Marymount U., Los Angeles; active donor research devel. program Los Angeles chpt. ARC. Scholar Loyola Marymount Univ., 1983-84. Mem. Am. Film Inst., Nichiren Shoshu Am. Home: Box 11253 Beverly Hills CA 90213-4253 Office: J Sent 9025 Wilshire Blvd Suite 307 Beverly Hills CA 90211

STELLING, THOMAS WAITE, medical products company executive; b. Columbus, Ohio, Jan. 12, 1960; s. Richard Davis and Marilyn Louise (Glenn) S. BA in Diplomacy and Foreign Affairs, Miami U., Oxford, Ohio, 1982. Sales rep. Time Distbn. Services, Roswell, Ga., 1982-83, Atlanta Med. Supply Co., Decatur, Ga., 1983-88; Southern ter. mgr. Incstar Corp., Stillwater, Minn., 1988; Fla. regional mgr. Southern Sales Assocs., Stone Mountain, Ga., 1988—. Home: 4588 Hickory Run Ct Acworth GA 30101 Office: Southern Sales Assocs 4301 Lizshire Ave Ste C 107 Orlando FL 32822 also: 4846 S Semoran Blvd Suite 1301 Orlando FL 32822

STELSON, HELEN MACLACHLAN, financial planner, tax consultant; b. Cambridge, Mass., Aug. 25, 1929; d. James Angell MacLachlan Sr. and Mary Jane (Carrier) Greve; m. Paul Hugh Stelson, Dec. 18, 1950 (div. 1970); children: Hugh Carrier, James MacLachlan, Fred Woolley, Ben Howard. AB, Wellesley Coll., 1951; MA, U. Tenn., 1966, MBA, 1984. Cert. fin. planner. Tax cons. H&R Block, Knoxville, Tenn., 1978, 886 tax, Oak Ridge, Tenn., 1979-84; prin. Helen Stelson Fin. Planning and Tax Services, Oak Ridge, 1984—. Founder, bd. dirs., sec.-treas. Oak Ridge Area Civil LIberties Union, 1968—; bd. dirs. ACLU, Tenn.; founder, treas. Girls Club Oak Ridge, 1976, Women's Ctr. Oak Ridge, 1976; founder, pres., treas. Oak Ridge Chpt. NOW, 1973. Mem. Inst. Cert. Fin. Planners, Nat. Assn. Enrolled Agts., Oak Ridge C. of C. (assoc., handicap access com. 1988), Oak Ridge Rowing Assn. (bd. dirs. 1985-87). Office: Helen Stelson Fin Planning Tax Svcs 886 W Outer Dr Oak Ridge TN 37830

STELZEL, WALTER TELL, JR., accountant, financial company executive; b. Chgo., Aug. 23, 1940; s. Walter Tell and Kathryn (Evans) S.; m. Sarah Rauen, Jan. 20, 1963; children: William, Susan, Michael. BSBA, Xavier U., 1962; MBA, U. Chgo., 1983. CPA, Ill. Sr. acct. Ernst & Ernst, 1962-69; contr. U.S. Reduction Co., 1969-74; asst. corp. contr. Am. Nat. Can. Co. (formerly Nat. Can. Corp.), Chgo., 1974-76, corp. contr., 1976-78, v.p., controller, 1978-81, v.p., asst. to pres., 1981-84, exec. v.p. fin., chief fin. officer, 1984-87, exec. v.p., chief fin. officer, treas., 1987—. 1st lt. U.S. Army, 1962-65, Germany. Office: Am Nat Can Co 8770 W Bryn Mawr Ave Chicago IL 60631

STELZNER, PAUL BURKE, recreation products executive; b. Iowa City, Iowa, Jan. 1, 1935; s. Glenn W. and Ruth (Schroder) S.; m. Martha Jane Schneeberger, Aug. 23, 1958; children: Martha Elizabeth Beuke and Barry Jane Lubbering. BS, Muskingum Coll., 1960; postgrad., Akron U., 1961-65. Tech. dir. Buckeye Fabric Finishing Co., Coshocton, Ohio, 1963-74; sec., sales mgr. Excello Fabric Finishers Inc., Coshocton, 1966-74; gen. mgr. Mineral Fiber Mfg. Corp., Coshocton, 1974-76; v.p., gen. mgr. Kellwood Co. Recreation Group, 1976-85; v.p. Am. Recreation Products, Inc., New Haven, Mo., 1985—. Pres. Coshocton County Young Rep. Club, 1960-62; mem. Coshocton County Rep. Exec. Com., 1960-62; pres. Coshocton Park Bd., 1972-76; mem. Coshocton City Planning Commn., 1972-76; chmn. indsl. div. United Fund, 1973; dist. commr. St. Louis Council Boy Scouts Am., 1977-79, pres. Gateway Amica, 1986-87. Served with USN, 1953-57. Mem. Am. Soc. Testing Materials, Indsl. Fabrics Assn. Internat. (assoc. dir. 1973-74, 82-88), Am. Assn. Textile Colorists and Chemists, Soc. Plastics Engrs. (sr.), Am. Legion. Presbyterian. Home: 1820 Wishwood Dr Washington MO 63090 Office: Am Recreation Prodns Inc 500 Orchard St New Haven MO 63068

STEMMER, WAYNE J., real estate and financial services company executive; b. Elizabeth, N.J., Oct. 29, 1942; s. Jay Stemmer; m. Barbara J. Mantz, Nov. 7, 1964; children: Wayne J. Jr., Traci. BA, Rutgers U., 1964. Gen. mgr. Citibank, Sydney, Australia, 1975-78; dir. Citicorp Real Estate Inc., Dallas and Houston, 1980-82; chief real estate investment officer Citibank N.A., N.Y.C., 1982-83; pres. Unicorp Am. Corp., N.Y.C., 1983—, also bd. dirs.; pres., chief operating officer The Lincoln Savs. Bank, N.Y.C., 1988—, also bd. dirs.; bd. dirs. Unicorp Can. Corp., Toronto; pres., chief oper. officer, dir. Lincoln Savs. Bank, N.Y.C. Served to capt. arty. U.S. Army, 1965-66. Mem. Internat. Council Shopping Ctrs., N.Y. Real Estate Bd., Soc. Real Estate Appraisers. Office: Unicorp Am Corp 99 Park Ave New York NY 10016

STEMMY, THOMAS JOSEPH, b. Shenandoah, Pa., July 29, 1938; s. Thomas W. and Jean C. (Shemansky) S.; m. Linda B. Cook, June 9, 1962; 1 child, Lynn Marie. BS in Econs., Villanova U., 1960; M. Mgmt. Sci., Nat. Grad. U., 1977. CPA, D.C. Fed. tax auditor IRS, Washington, 1960-63, rep. in pub. rels. programs, 1961-63; tax auditor U.S. Govt., Washington, 1963; acct., tax adviser T.J. Stemmy & Co., College Park, Md., 1963-73, acct., tax advisor, fin. planner Stemmy, Tidler & Morris, P.A., College Park, 1973—; instr. U . Md., College Park, 1973—, faculty coordinator U. Md.-Univ. Coll. Coop. Edn. Program, 1982—; instr. fed. taxation Prince George's Community Coll., 1974-76; dir. Lakewood Harbor Estates, Inc., Fredericksburg, Va. Campaign mgr. for Mayor of College Park, 1968; mem. Md. Crime Investigating Commn., 1976; treas. Prince Georges County Cleanup Com., 1967-72; pres. College Park Bd. of Trade, 1971; mem. Am. Security Coun., 1971; mem. Estate Planning Coun. Prince George's County, 1975; mem. Md. Ednl. Found., 1975-76; tchr. Confraternity Christian Doctrine, St. Matthias Ch.; basketball coach Lanham (Md.) Boys' Club, 1980. With AUSR, 1960-66. Recipient Key to the City of College Park, 1971. Mem. Md. Soc. CPAs, Md. State Sheriffs Assn., Md. State Toboggan Team Assn. (chmn. 1975), Am. Legion, Kiwanis, Elks, Gamma Phi. Republican. Roman Catholic. Avocations: golf, soccer. Home: 9532 Elvis Ln Seabrook MD 20801 Office: Stemy Tidler & Co 7525 Greenway Ctr Dr Greenbelt MD 20770

STEMPEL, ERNEST EDWARD, insurance executive; b. N.Y.C., May 10, 1916; s. Frederick Christian and Leah Lillian S.; m. Phyllis Brooks; children: Diana Brooks, Calvin Pinkcomb, Neil Frederick, Robert Russell. A.B., Manhattan Coll., 1938; LL.B., Fordham U., 1946; LL.M., NYU, 1949, D.J.S., 1951; LL.D. (hon.), Manhattan Coll., 1986. Bar: N.Y. 1946. With Am. Internat. Underwriters Corp., N.Y.C., 1938-53; v.p., dir. Am. Internat. Co. Ltd., Hamilton, Bermuda, 1953-63; chmn. bd. Am. Internat. Co. Ltd., 1963—; chmn., dir. Am. Internat. Assurance Co. (Bermuda) Ltd., Am. Internat. Reins. Co. Ltd., Bermuda; pres., dir. Am. Internat. Comml. Co., Inc., Bermuda; vice-chmn.-life, mem. exec. com., dir. Am. Internat. Group Inc.; dir. C.V. Starr & Co. Inc., N.Y.C.; pres., dir. Starr Internat. Co. Inc.; dir. Am. Life Ins. Co., Wilmington, Del., Am. Internat. Life Ins. Co., P.R., La Interamericana (S.A.), Mexico, Mt. Mansfield Co., Inc., Stowe, Vt., Seguros Venezuela (C.A.), Caracas; chmn., dir. Australian Am. Assurance Co., Ltd., Am. Internat. Assurance Co. Ltd., Hong Kong; chmn. bd., dir. Philippine Am. Ins. Cos., Manila; dir. Am. Internat. Underwriters (Latin Am.), Inc., Bermuda, Am. Internat. Underwriters Mediterranean, Inc., Bermuda; Del. Am. Life Ins. Co., Wilmington, Pacific Union Assurance Co., Calif., Underwriters Adjustment Co., Panama. Served to lt. (s.g.) USNR, 1942-46. Mem. Am. Bar Assn., N.Y. State Bar. Clubs: Marco Polo (N.Y.C.), Royal Bermuda Yacht (Bermuda), Mid-Ocean (Bermuda), Coral Beach (Bermuda), Riddell's Bay Golf and Country (Bermuda). Office: Am Internat Co Ltd, PO Box HM 152, Hamilton HM AX, Bermuda

STEMPEL, ROBERT C., automobile manufacturing company executive; b. 1933. BSME, Worcester Polytech. Inst., 1955, PhD, 1977; MBA, Mich. State U., 1970. Sr. detailer chassis design dept. Oldsmobile div. Gen. Motors Corp., Detroit, 1958-62, sr. designer, 1962-64, transmission design engr., 1964-69, motor engr., 1969-72, asst. chief engr., 1972-73, spl. asst. to pres., 1973-74, chief engines and components engr. Chevrolet div., 1974-75, dir. engring., 1975-78, corp. v.p. and gen. mgr. Pontiac div., 1978-80, corp. v.p. European passenger car ops., Fed. Republic Germany, 1980-82, corp. v.p., gen. mgr. Chevrolet div., 1982-84, corp. v.p., group exec. Buick-Oldsmobile-Cadillac Group, 1984-86, corp. exec. v.p. Worldwide Truck & Bus Group, Overseas Group, 1986-87, corp. pres., chief operating officer, 1987—. Served with U.S. Army, 1956-58. Office: GM Gen Motors Bldg 3044 W Grand Blvd Detroit MI 48202 *

STEP, EUGENE LEE, pharmaceutical company executive; b. Sioux City, Iowa, Feb. 19, 1929; s. Harry and Ann (Keiser) S.; m. Hannah Scheuermann, Dec. 27, 1953; children—Steven Harry, Michael David, Jonathan Allen. BA in Econs., U. Nebr., 1951; MS in Acctg. and Fin., U. Ill., 1952. With Eli Lilly Internat. Corp., London and Paris, 1964-69; dir. Elanco Internat. Eli Lilly Internat. Corp., Indpls., 1969-70, v.p. marketing, 1970-72, v.p. Europe, 1972; v.p. mktg. Eli Lilly and Co., Indpls., 1972-73, pres. pharm. div., 1973-86, exec. v.p., 1986—, also dir.; bd. dirs. Paul Harris Stores, Indpls., Vol. Hosps. of Am., Dallas. Served to 1st lt. U.S. Army, 1953-56. Mem. Pharm. Mfrs. Assn. (bd. dirs. 1980—). Home: 741 Round Hill Rd Indianapolis IN 46260

STEPAN, FRANK QUINN, chemical company executive; b. Chgo., Oct. 24, 1937; s. Alfred Charles and Mary Louise (Quinn) S.; m. Jean Finn, Aug. 23, 1958; children: Jeanne, Frank Quinn, Todd, Jennifer, Lisa, Colleen, Alfred, Richard. A.B., U. Notre Dame, 1959; M.B.A., U. Chgo., 1963. Salesman Indsl. Chems. div. Stepan Chem. Co., Northfield, Ill., 1961-63, mgr. internat. dept., 1964-66, v.p. corporate planning, 1967-69, v.p., gen. mgr., 1970-73, pres., 1974-84; pres., chmn., chief exec. officer Stepan Co., Northfield, Ill., 1984—, also bd. dirs. Mem. liberal arts council Notre Dame U., South Bend, Ind., 1972—; bd. dirs. Big Shoulders, Chgo. Served to 1st lt. AUS, 1959-61. Mem. Chem. Mfgs. Assn. (bd. dirs., 1987—), Chem. Industries Coun. Ill. (pres., bd. dirs. 1985—). Clubs: Economic (Chgo.), Exmoor Country (Highland Park, Ill.), Bob O'Link Golf (Highland Park), Harbour Ridge (Stuart, Fla.). Home: 200 Linden St Winnetka IL 60093 Office: Stepan Co Edens & Winnetka Rds Northfield IL 60093

STEPAN, PAUL HENRY, real estate executive; b. Chgo., July 1, 1943; s. Alfred Charles and Mary Louise (Quinn) S.; m. Ann Ruppe, June 12, 1965; children: Shannon, Paul Jr. BA, U. Notre Dame, 1965; MA, Oxford U., 1967; JD, U. Chgo., 1970. Ptnr. Mayer, Brown & Platt, Chgo., 1970-79; gen. ptnr. Stepan Venture, Chgo., 1972—; pres. Paul Stepan & Assocs., Chgo., 1985—, also bd. dirs.; mem. exec. com. Hyatt Regency Chgo., 1974-88; bd. dirs. Stepan Co., Northfield, Ill. Fin. chmn. Richard M. Daley Campaign Com., Cook County, Ill., 1979; chmn. Ill. pub. Action Fund, Ill., 1984; chmn. fin. Ill. Dem. Party, 1986—; bd. dirs. Erikson Inst., Ill., 1983; chmn. Club Wholesale, Inc.; mem. exec. com. Hyatt Rgency Chgo., 1974-88. Mem. ABA. Roman Catholic. Office: Paul Stepan & Assocs 218 N Jefferson Chicago IL 60606

STEPANIAN, IRA, banker; b. Cambridge, Mass., Nov. 14, 1936; s. Sarkis H. and Armenoohi (Kupelian) S.; m. Jacquelynne McLucas, Aug. 6, 1961; children: Philip, Alisa, Steven. B.A., Tufts U., 1958; M.B.A., Boston Coll., 1971. Credit investigator Dun & Bradstreet, Boston, 1958-59; research assoc. Ernst Assocs., Inc., Arlington, Mass., 1959-63; with First Nat. Bank Boston, 1963—, exec. v.p., 1980, vice chmn., 1981—, pres., 1983—; vice chmn. Bank of Boston Corp., 1981—, pres., 1983—, chief operating officer, dir., 1983-87, chief exec. officer, 1987—; bd. dirs. Liberty Mut. Ins. Co., Liberty Mut. Fire Ins. Co. Trustee Tufts U., Medford, Mass., 1981—, Boston Mus. Sci.; overseer Boston Mus. of Fine Arts, Boston Symphony; mem. corp. Mass. Gen. Hosp., Boston Mus. Sci. Mem. Assn. Res. City Bankers, Mass. Bankers Assn. (bd. dirs.), Greater Boston C. of C. (bd. dirs.). Office: Bank of Boston Corp 100 Federal St Boston MA 02110 *

STEPANSKI, ANTHONY FRANCIS, JR., computer company executive; b. Jersey City, N.J., June 29, 1941; s. Anthony Francis and Gertrude (Maykowski) S.; m. Jane Ellen Schuler, Sept. 5, 1965; children—Matthew A.W., Melinda Kate. B.A., Clark U., 1963. Sales rep. IBM Corp., N.Y.C., 1964-68; from sales rep. to sr. v.p. AGS Computers, Inc., N.Y.C. and Mountainside, N.J., 1968-82; exec. v.p. AGS Computers, Inc., Mountainside, 1982—; pres., chief exec. officer AGS Info. Services, Inc., Mountainside, 1986—; also bd. dirs. AGS Computers, Inc., Mountainside. Trustee Clark U., Worcester, Mass., 1987; bd. dirs. Westchester Artificial Kidney Ctr., Valhalla, N.Y., 1982, Westfield Symphony Orch., N.J., 1983. Served with USAR, 1965-66. Office: AGS Computers Inc 1139 Spruce Dr Mountainside NJ 07092

STEPHAN, BODO, manufacturing company executive; b. Berlin, Mar. 9, 1939; s. Hans-Werner and Ilse Charlotte (Kretschmann) S.; m. Ingrid-Maria Seeger, Apr. 1, 1942; children: Viola-Dorothee, Katharina-Marguerite. Doctor's degree, U. Cologne, Fed. Republic Germany, 1966. Admitted to Bar, Berlin. Asst. prof. U. Berlin and Cologne, 1963-69; head sales mgr. F. Meyer Steelworks, Dinslaken, Fed. Republic Germany, 1970-73; div. mgr. lighting technique AEG-Telefunken, Springe/Hannover, Fed. Republic Germany, 1974-80; sr. mgr. internat. div. AEG Cables, Moenchengladbach, 1980-82; chief exec. internat. ops. telecom, electronics Krone AG, Berlin, 1983-85, chief exec. corp. controlling, 1986-87; mng. dir., major stockholder Kluessendorf AGF, Berlin, 1988—; also bd. dirs. Kluessandorf AG, Berlin. Author: Rechtsschutzbeduerfuis, 1966; contbr. articles to profl. jours. Consul ad honorem of Ecuador to Berlin. Fellow Assn. of C. of C., Berlin Industrialists Club, German Soc. Internat. Affairs, German Electronical Assn., Controllers Assn. Lutheran. Clubs: Club des Affaires, Econ. Politics Discussion Circle. Lodge: Kiwanis. Office: Kluessendorf AG, Zitadellenweg 20 D-F, D-1000 Berlin 20, Federal Republic of Germany

STEPHAN, GEORGE PETER, electronic company executive; b. Milw., July 15, 1933; s. Peter George and Aphrodite (Moisakos) S.; m. Gesella Arolene (Hofmeister) Stephan, Nov. 5, 1955; children: Peter, Christopher, Paul, Cynthia. BS, U.Wis., 1954, LLB, 1958; M in Comparative Law, U. Chgo., 1960. Bar: Wis. 1958, N.Y. 1962. Assoc. lawyer Shearman & Sterling, N.Y.C., 1961-69; sec. Kollmorgen Corp., Simsbury, Conn., 1969-72; v.p., sec. gen. counsel Kollmorgen Corp., 1972-82, exec. v.p., 1982-84, vice chmn., 1984—, dir., 1982—, bd. dirs. Barr Labs., Inc. Trustee Hartwick Coll., 1977-87; bd. advisors Hartwick Humanities in Mgmt. Inst., 1987—. Served to 1st lt., U.S. Army, 1955-57. Fellow Ford Found., 1958-60; Fulbright fgn. scholar, 1959-60. Greek Orthodox. Home: 132 Westmont St West Hartford CT 06117 Office: Kollmorgen Corp 10 Mill Pond Ln Simsbury CT 06070 also: Kollmorgen Corp 66 Gate House Rd Stamford CT 06902

STEPHAN, INEZ VALLS, secretarial service company executive; b. Columbus, Ohio, Nov. 22, 1911; d. Rafael W. and Euphemia (Lloyd) Valls; 2 children. Student pub. schs., Cleveland Heights. Sec. Harlow Co., Coral Gables, Fla., 1959-63, U. Miami, Coral Gables, 1963-75; pres., owner Stephan Secretarial Coral Gables, 1975—; real estate salesperson Wirth Realty, Coral Gables, 1975—. Mem. Nat. Assn. Female Execs., Notary Pub. Assn., Coral Gables Bd. Realtors, Coral Gables C. of C. Republican. Roman Catholic. Avocations: swimming; playing bridge. Home: 8690 SW 74th Terr Miami FL 33143 Office: Stephan Secretarial Svc 3132-B Ponce de Leon Blvd Coral Gables FL 33134

STEPHANS, WILLIAM WALTER THOMAS, manufacturing and marketing company executive; b. Montevideo, Uruguay, Dec. 5, 1942; s. Walter T. and Grace (Clark) S.; m. Eva-Maria Barbara Reitmeier, Dec. 27, 1976; children: Kevin L.E., Lindsey E. BA, Harvard U., 1965, MBA, 1966. With TRW, 1966-84; fin. analyst Systems Group, Redondo Beach, Calif., 1966-68, lab. adminstr., 1968-69; sr. fin. analyst Automotive Internat., Cleve., 1969-70; asst. to mng. dir. Ehrenreich & Cie, Dusseldorf, Fed. Republic Germany, 1970-72; fin. dir. Repa GmbH, Aldorf, Fed. Republic Germany, 1972-79; controller Steering and Suspension div., Sterling Heights, Mich., 1979-80; asst. treas. TRW Inc., Cleve., 1980-84; with Scott Fetzer Co., Westlake, Ohio, 1984—, v.p., treas., 1984—, v.p., treas., controller, 1987—. Little League Baseball coach, Mentor, Ohio, 1987-88. Mem. Nat. Assn. Corp. Treas., Cleve. Treas. Club. Office: Scott Fetzer Co 28800 Clemens Rd Westlake OH 44145

STEPHEN, JOHN ERLE, lawyer, consultant; b. Eagle Lake, Tex., Sept. 24, 1918; s. John Earnest and Vida Thrall (Klein) S.; m. Gloria Yzaguirre, May 16, 1942; children: Vida Leslie Stephen Renzi, John Lauro Kurt. Student, U. Mex., 1937; JD, U. Tex., 1941; postgrad., Northwestern U., 1942, U.S. Naval Acad. Postgrad. Sch., 1944; cert. in internat. law, U.S. Naval War Coll., 1945, cert. in advanced internat. law, 1967. Bar: Tex. 1946, U.S. Ct. Appeals (D.C. cir.) 1949, U.S. Tax Ct. 1953, U.S. Supreme Ct. 1955, U.S. Dist. Ct. D.C. 1956, U.S. Ct. Appeals (2nd cir.) 1959, U.S. Ct. Appeals (7th cir.) 1964, U.S. Dist. Ct. (so. dist.) N.Y. 1964, D.C. 1972, U.S. dist. Ct. (no. dist.) Ill. 1974, U.S. Dist. Ct. (we. dist.) Wash. 1975, Mich. 1981, U.S. Dist. Ct. (we. dist.) Mich. 1981, U.S. Dist. Ct. (so. dist.) Tex. 1981. Gen. mgr., corp. counsel Sta. KOPY, Houston, 1946; gen. atty., exec. asst. to pres. Tex. Star Corp. and affiliated cos., Houston, 1947-50; ptnr. Hofheinz & Stephen, Houston, 1950-57; v.p., gen. counsel TV Broadcasting Co., Tex. Radio Corp., Gulf Coast Network, Houston, 1953-57; spl. counsel, exec. asst. Mayor, City of Houston, 1953-57; spl. counsel Houston C. of C., 1953-56; special counsel, exec. asst. to mayor City of Houston, 1953-56; v.p., gen. counsel Air Transp. Assn. Am., Washington, 1958-70, Amway Corp. and affiliated cos., Ada, Mich., 1971-82; counsellor, cons. Austin, Tex., 1983—; chief protocol City of Houston, 1953-56; advisor Consulates Gen. of Mex., San Antonio, Houston, New Orleans, Washington, 1956-66; adv. bd. Aviation Industry Employees Investment Fund, 1960-68, Jour. of Air Law and Commerce, 1966-72; vis. lectr. grad. sch. bus. Harvard U., Pacific Agribus. Conf., Southwestern Legal Found., Inter-Am. Law Conf.; bd. dirs. Tex. Transp. Inst.; legal advisor, del. U.S. Internat. Air-Rte. Dels. to U.K., France, Spain, Portugal, Belgium, the Netherlands, Japan, Rep. of Korea, Mex., Australia, Argentina, Soviet Union, and Brazil, 1960-70; hon. faculty mem. sch. of law U. Miami, 1968—; legal advisor, del. U.S. Diplomatic Dels. to Internat. Treaty Confs., Paris, London, Rome, Tokyo, Madrid, Bermuda, Guadalajara, Dakar, 1961-71; U.S. rep. Internat. Conf. on Aircraft Noise, London, 1967; legal advisor., del. U.S. Dels. to UN Specialized Orgns., Montreal, Geneva, 1964-71. Editor: Jour. Air Law & Commerce, 1966-72; author, editor in field. Bd. dirs. Houston Mus. Fine Arts, 1953-57, Contemporary Arts Assn., 1953-57, Tex. Transp. Inst., 1964-72; Comdr. line USNR, 1941-46, PTO and S.E. Asia; mem. staff Supreme Allied Command, NATO, 1952. Recipient Jesse L. Lasky award RKO-CBS, Hollywood, Calif., 1939, H.J. Lutcher Stark award U. Tex., 1940, 41, Walter Mack award Pepsico, U. Tex., 1941, Best U.S. Pub. Svc. Broadcast award CCNY, 1948. Mem. ABA (past chmn., mem. council, sect. public utility law, standing com. on aero. law), Am. Law Inst., World Peace Through Law Ctr. (past chmn. internat. aviation law com., Geneva hdqrs.), Fed. Bar Assn., D.C. Bar, State Bar Tex., State Bar Mich., Fed. Communications Bar Assn., Assn. ICC Practitioners, Am. Judicature Soc., Washington Fgn. Law Soc. (vis. lectr. 1967-68), Japanese Air Law Soc. (hon. mem. 1966—), Venezuela Air and Space Law Soc. (hon. mem. 1966—). Clubs: Internat., Explorers, Houston Polo, Lakeshore, Saddle and Cycle, Breakfast, Nat. Aviation, Execs., Ky. Cols. Home: 6904 Ligustrum Cove Austin TX 78750

STEPHENS, CHARLES MICHAEL, service executive; b. Wichita Falls, Tex., Feb. 4, 1949; s. Wilbur Wesley and Mildred Ruth (Smith) S.; m. Janet Kay Speare, Dec. 28, 1971; children: Kelley Michelle, Suzanne Janelle. BA, Okla. State U., 1971; postgrad., U. Okla., 1971-72. V.p. sales Arrowlite Industries, Tulsa, 1972-76; v.p., regional mgr. Top Value Motivation, Dayton, Ohio, 1976-86; v.p. S&H Motivation and Travel, Chgo., 1986—. Mem. Am. Mgmt. Assn., Motivation Round Table, Kappa Sigma, Cedar Ridge Country Club. Baptist. Home: 8124 S Quebec Tulsa OK 74137

STEPHENS, ELTON BRYSON, banker, service and manufacturing company executive; b. Clio, Ala., Aug. 4, 1911; s. James Nelson and Clara (Stuckey) S.; m. Alys Varian Robinson, Nov. 28, 1935; children: James Thomas, Jane Stephens Comer, Elton Bryson Jr., Dell Stephens Brooke. B.A., Birmingham-So. Coll., 1932, LL.D., 1977; LL.B., U. Ala., 1936; grad., Advanced Mgmt. Program, Harvard U., 1960. Bar: Ala. 1936. Regional dir. Keystone Readers Service, Birmingham, 1937-43; partner, then founder and pres. Mil. Service Co., Inc. (predecessor of EBSCO Industries, Inc.), Birmingham, 1943-58; founder EBSCO Industries, Inc., and affiliates, 1958; since pres., chmn. bd. EBSCO Industries, Inc., and affiliates, Birmingham; founder Bank of Southeast, Birmingham, 1970, co-organizer, 1971, dir., chmn. exec. com., 1977—; bd. dirs. R.A. Brown Ins. Agy. Ltd., 1966—; chmn. EBSCO Investment Service, Inc., 1959—, Canebsco Subscription Service, Toronto, Ont., Can., 1972—, Ala. Bancorp divs. The Citizens Bank Leeds, The Fort Deposit Bank; trustee EBSCO Employees Savs. & Profit Sharing Trust, 1958—; chmn., founder Highland Bank, 1988. Mem. fin. and investment com., past chmn. bd. trustees, chmn. exec. com. Birmingham-So. Coll.; trustee So. Research Inst.; former pres., chmn. bd. trustee Birmingham Met. YMCA; former chmn. Multi-State Transp. Systems Adv. Bd.; mem. bd., chmn. econ. pension com. Tenn.-Tombigbee Waterway Authority; mem. Ala. Election Law Commn.; exec. com. Future Farmers Am. Ala. Found.; founder Ala. 5%, Ala. 2% and Ala. 10% Clubs, United Art Fund/Met. Arts Council; mem. bd., permanent chmn. Nat. Workplace Giving program, Am. Council for the Arts. Elton B. Stephens Expressway named in his honor, 1970, Elton B. Stephens Library, Clio, 1979. Mem. Birmingham C. of C. (bd. dirs.) Alpha Tau Omega (past chmn. nat. found.), Omicron Delta Kappa, Phi Alpha Delta. Methodist. Clubs: Downtown (Birmingham), The Club (Birmingham), Birmingham Press (Birmingham), Relay House (Birmingham); Mountain Brook (Ala.) Country, Shades Valley Rotary (pres. 1979-80); Shades Valley Rotary (Homewood, Ala.) (Paul Harris fellow). Office: Ebsco Industries Inc Top of Oak Mountain Hwy Birmingham AL 35201

STEPHENS, JAMES M., federal agency administrator; b. Rochester, N.Y., Sept. 16, 1946; married; two children. AB, Wittenberg U., 1968; JD, Case Western Reserve U., 1971. Assoc. Roetzel and Ambress, Akron, Ohio, 1973-77; asst. minority labor counsel com. edn. and labor U.S. House Reps., 1977-81; majority labor counsel com. labor and human resources U.S. Senate, 1981-85; chmn. Nat. Labor Rels. Bd., Washington, 1985—. Office: NLRB 1717 Pennsylvania Ave NW Washington DC 20570 *

STEPHENS, LESTER JOHN, JR., corporate controller; b. N.Y.C., Sept. 14, 1943; s. Lester John and Margaret (Tableman) S.; m. Suzanne M. Ekkers. BBA in Acctg., Pace U., 1966, MBA in Fin., 1970; grad. cert. Stonier Sch., Rutgers U., 1973; grad. cert. Amos Tuck Sch., Dartmouth Coll., 1983. Various positions in acctg. and fin. Chase Manhattan Corp. and Chase Manhattan Bank, N.Y.C., 1966-74, v.p., dir. internat. acctg., 1974-77, v.p., dir. fin. projects, 1977-83, v.p., dir. fin. reporting, 1983-85, chief fin. officer, internat. sector, 1985-87, corp. controller, 1987—. Served as sgt. USNG, 1966-71. Mem. Bank Adminstrn. Inst. (acctg. and fin. commn. 1987). Clubs: Wall Street, Skytop. Office: Chase Manhattan Corp 33 Maiden Ln New York NY 10081

STEPHENS, MICHAEL JON, automobile industry executive; b. Alpena, Mich., Aug. 30, 1948; s. Byron L. and Jeanne E. (Hackett) S.; B.S. in Indsl. Engring., Gen. Motors Inst., 1972; M.B.A., Wayne State U., Detroit, 1976; m. Marise E. Mundwiler, Apr. 17, 1982. With Gen. Motors Corp., 1967-77, 79-81, sr. quality control engr., Detroit, 1973-77, sr. staff adminstr. corp. mktg. staff, 1979-81; mkt. planning analyst, Toyota Motor Sales USA, Torrance, Calif., 1977-78; nat. mktg. and product mgr., Brit. Leyland Inc., Leonia, N.J., 1978-79; mgr. sales and mktg., Pasha Group, San Francisco, 1981-82; exec. field cons. The Hdqrs. Co., 1982-84; mgr. advance product planning, Chrysler Corp., Detroit, 1984—. adj. prof. bus. Bergen (N.J.) Community Coll., 1978-79. Home: 31625 Auburn Birmingham MI 48009 Office: Chrysler Corp CIMS #415-03-10 PO Box 857 Detroit MI 48009

STEPHENS, SIDNEY DEE, chemical manufacturing company executive; b. St. Joseph, Mo., Apr. 26, 1945; s. Lindsay Caldwell and Edith Mae (Thompson) S.; m. Ellen Marie Boeh, June 15, 1968 (div. 1973); m. 2d, Elizabeth Ann Harris, Sept. 22, 1973; 1 child, Laura Nicole. B.S., Mo. Western State U., 1971; M.A., U. Houston, 1980. Assoc. urban planner Met. Planning Commn., St. Joseph, Mo., 1967-71; prodn. acctg. assoc. Quaker Oats Co., St. Joseph, 1971-72, office mgr., personnel rep., Rosemont, Ill., 1972-73, employee and community relations mgr., New Brunswick, N.J., 1973-75, Pasadena, Tex., 1975-80; site personnel mgr. ICI Americas, Inc., Pasadena, Tex., 1980—; pvt. practice mgmt. cons., Houston, 1981—. Contbr. articles to profl. jours. Served with USNR, 1963-65. Mem. Am. Soc. Personnel Adminstrs., Houston Personnel Assn. (community and govtl. affairs com. 1984-85, 85-86). Republican. Methodist. Home: 16446 Longvale Dr Houston TX 77059 Office: ICI Americas Inc 5757 Underwood Rd Pasadena TX 77507

STEPHENS, TAYLOR LANE, insurance company executive; b. Lawrence, Kans., Apr. 13, 1937; s. George Edward and Helen H. (Houghton) S.; m. Sheila Ruth Tomlin, Aug. 27, 1961; children: Shelley, Taylor. BS, U. Colo.,

1959. CLU, CPCU. Claims adjuster Farmers Ins. Group of Cos., Denver, 1960-62; dist. mgr. Farmers Ins. Group of Cos., Aurora, Colo., 1962—; bd. dirs. United Bank Aurora, United Bank Aurora South. Fellow Life Underwriter Tng. Council; mem. Soc. Chartered Property and Casualty Underwriters (pres. 1983-84), Am. Soc. Chartered Life Underwriters, Nat. Assn. LIfe Underwriters (pres. 1973-74, regional v.p. 1975-76). Republican. Lutheran. Lodge: Optimists (pres. 1968-69), Rotary. Office: Farmers Ins Group Co 12383 E Cornell Ave Aurora CO 80010

STEPHENS, WILLIAM THOMAS, mining and forest products company executive. married. BS, U. Ark., 1965, MS, 1966. Various mgmt. positions Manville Forest Products Corp., from 1963; asst. to pres., then sr. v.p., pres. forest products group Manville Corp., Denver, exec. v.p. fin. and adminstrn., from 1984, now pres., chief exec. officer. Office: Manville Corp Manville Pla 717 S 17th Denver CO 80202 also: Manville Corp PO Box 5108 Denver CO 80217

STEPHENSON, ARTHUR EMMET, JR., investment company executive, banker; b. Bastrop, La., Aug. 29, 1945; s. Arthur Emmet and Edith Louise (Mock) S.; m. Toni Lyn Edwards, June 17, 1967. B.S. in Fin. magna cum laude, La. State U., 1967; M.B.A. (Ralph Thomas Sayles fellow), Harvard U., 1969. Chartered fin. analyst. Adminstrv. aide to U.S. Sen. Russell Long of La., Washington, 1966; security analyst Fidelity Funds, Boston, 1968; chmn. bd., pres. Stephenson & Co., Denver, 1969—, Stephenson Mcht. Banking Inc., Circle Corp.; sr. ptnr. Stephenson Ventures, Stephenson Properties; chmn. bd. Charter Bank & Trust, Gen. Communications, Inc., Globescope Corp., Envirodata, Inc.; underwriting mem. Lloyd's of London; bd. dirs. Danaher Corp., River Oaks Industries, Inc., Signal Oilfield Svcs.; adv. bd. Thomas H. Lee Co. Fund, Capital Resource Ptnrs., L.P. Journ Bus. Venturing; pub. Denver Bus. Mag., Denver Mag., Devel. Sales Catalog, Colo. Book. Mem. assocs. council Templeton Coll. at Oxford U., Eng.; mem. nat. steering com. Norman Rockwell Mus., Stockbridge, Mass.; past mem. Colo. small bus. council; mem. adv. bd. NYU Ctr. for Entrepeneurial Studies; del. White House Conf. Small Bus. Mem. Harvard Bus. Sch. Assn. (internat. pres.), Young Pres.'s Orgn. (dir. Inland Empire chpt. 1987-89, membership chmn. 1987, sec., treas. 1988), Colo. Investment Advisers Assn. (treas., dir. 1975-76), Fin. Analysts Fedn., Denver Soc. Security Analysts (bd. dirs. 1975-77), Colo. Press Assn., Colo. Harvard Bus. Sch. Club (pres. 1979, chmn. 1980), Omicron Delta Kappa, Phi Kappa Phi, Beta Gamma Sigma, Kappa Sigma, Delta Sigma Pi. Clubs: Denver Press, Denver Petroleum, Met. Denver Exec. (pres. 1979-80, chmn. 1980-81); Thunderbird Country (Rancho Mirage, Calif.); Annabel's (London); Harvard of Boston; Harvard of N.Y., Harvard Bus. Sch. (N.Y.C., Boston, So. Calif., Orange County, Calif., Colo.); Jonathan (L.A.). Office: Stephenson & Co 100 Garfield St Denver CO 80206

STEPHENSON, HERMAN HOWARD, banker; b. Wichita, Kans., July 15, 1929; s. Herman Horace and Edith May (Wayland) S.; m. Virginia Anne Ross, Dec. 24, 1950; children: Ross Wayland, Neal Bevan, Jann Edith. BA, U. Mich., 1950; JD with distinction, U. Mo., Kansas City, 1958. Bar: Kans. 1958. Mem. fgn. dept. City Nat. Bank, Kansas City, Mo., 1952-54; asst. sec. City Bond & Mortgage Co., Kansas City, Mo., 1954-59; with Bank of Hawaii, Honolulu, 1959—, asst. cashier, 1960-62, v.p., 1962-68, sr. v.p., 1968-72, exec. v.p., 1972-80, pres., dir., 1980—; v.p., treas. Bancorp. Hawaii, Inc., Honolulu, 1978-80, pres., dir., 1980—; chmn., dir. Bancorp Life Ins. Co., Bancorp Bus. Systems of Hawaii, Inc.; v.p., chmn. bd. dirs. Bancorp Fin. of Hawaii, Inc.; chmn., dir. Bancorp Hawaii Small Bus. Investment Co., Inc., Bancorp Ins. Agy. of Hawaii, Inc.; vice chmn., dir. Hawaii Fin. Corp. (Hong Kong) Ltd., Hawaiian Trust Co., Ltd.; v.p. Bancorp Leasing of Hawaii, Inc. former trustee; chmn., Realty & Mortgage Investors of Pacific (RAMPAC); dir. Banque de Tahiti, Banque de Nouvell Caledonie, Bancorp Fin. of Hawaii-Guam, Inc., Bancorp Hawaii Service Corp., Investors Pacific Ltd., S.I.L., Inc., Bank of Hawaii Internat., N.Y., First Nat. Bank Ariz.; pres., treas., bd. dirs. Hawaiian Hong Kong Holdings, Ltd.; pres., bd. dirs. Bank of Hawaii Internat. Inc., Bankoh Adv. Corp., Bancorp Investment Adv. Services, Inc.; vice chmn., dir. BOH Investment Mgmt. Co., Ltd., Hong Kong. Chmn. urban renewal com. Oahu Devel. Conf., 1966-68, mem. comprehensive planning com., 1970-71; trustee, past pres. Tax Found. Hawaii; former trustee Hawaii Conf. Found., United Ch. of Christ; bd. dirs. Honolulu Symphony, Maunalani Hosp.; former chmn., bd. dirs. Aloha United Way; co-chmn. Ellison Onizuka Meml. Scholarship Fund Com.; v.p., treas., dir. Bancorp Hawaii Charitable Found.; mem. adv. group internat. arbitration; bd. regents U. Hawaii; mem. U. Hawaii Found. Served with U.S. Army, 1950-52. Mem. ABA, Am. Bankers Assn. (past chmn. exec. com. housing and real estate fin. div., dir. 1976-77, mem. governing council 1976-77, mem. govt. relations council Banking Leadership Conf.), Kans. Bar Assn., Mortgage Bankers Assn. Hawaii (past pres.), Hawaii Bankers Assn. (pres. 1984-85), U.S.-Japan Bus. Council, Pacific Asia Travel Assn., Navy League of U.S., Kappa Sigma, Pi Eta Sigma. Clubs: Rotary, Oahu Country, Pacific, Waialae. Office: Bancorp Hawaii Inc 111 S King St PO Box 2900 Fin Plaza of Pacific Honolulu HI 96813

STEPHENSON, HUGH LYNDON, financial services executive; b. Savannah, Ga., Jan. 7, 1958; s. Jack Lyndon and Winifred Hoskins (Harriss) S.; m. Amy Burnside Rhodes, July 21, 1984. Student, Oxford U., Eng., 1979; BA, U. of South, 1980; MBA, Ga. State U., 1983. Stockbroker Merrill Lynch, Atlanta, 1983-85; sr. v.p. Oppenheimer & Co., Atlanta, 1985—; cons., analyst various pvt. and civic orgns., Atlanta and southeast area. Bd. dirs. Big Bros. of Met. Atlanta, 1985—. Recipient Eagle Scout award, Boy Scouts Am., 1974. Mem. Internat. Assn. Fin. Planners, Coll. Fin. Planning, Stockbrokers Soc., Buckhead Bus. Assn., Atlanta Jr. C. of C. (bd. dirs.), Atlanta Alumni U. of South, Atlanta Alumni of Sigma Alpha Epsilon (pres., bd. dirs.), Soc. Mayflower Descendants. Republican. Episcopalian. Clubs: Cherokee Town, Buckhead, Amex (Atlanta); Capital City (Montgomery, Ala.), Heritage of YMCA (endowment com., bd. dirs.). Home: 145 The Prado Atlanta GA 30306 Office: Oppenheimer & Co Inc 7 Piedmont Ctr Suite 600 Atlanta GA 30305

STEPHENSON, IRENE HAMLEN, biorhythm analyst, consultant, editor, teacher; b. Chgo., Oct. 7, 1923; d. Charles Martin and Carolyn Hilda (Hilgers) Hamlin; m. Edgar B. Stephenson, Sr., Aug. 16, 1941 (div. 1946); 1 child, Edgar B. Author biorhythm compatibilities column Nat. Singles Register, Norwalk, Calif., 1979-81; instr. biorhythm Learning Tree Open U., Canoga Park, Calif., 1982-83; instr. biorhythm character analysis 1980—; instr. biorhythm compatibility, 1982—; owner, pres. matchmaking service Pen Pals Using Biorhythm, Chatsworth, Calif., 1979—; editor newsletter The Truth, 1979-85, Mini Examiner, Chatsworth, 1985—; researcher biorhythm character and compatibility, 1974—, selecting a mate, 1985—, biorhythm column True Psychic Inquirer, 1989—, True Astrology Forecast, 1989—; author: Learn Biorhythm Character Analysis, 1980; Do-It-Yourself Biorhythm Compatibilities, 1982; contbr. numerous articles to mags; frequent guests clubs, radio, TV. Office: Irene Hamlen Stephenson PO Box 3893 WW Chatsworth CA 91313

STEPHENSON, J. CLAYTON, chemical company executive; b. Pitts., July 12, 1932; s. Joseph Clayton and Helen Ruth (Hicks) S.; m. Sarah Helen Taylor, Dec. 5, 1959; children—Laurie Parker, Robert Willard. B.S. in Econs., Yale U., 1954. Pres. mining and metals div. Union Carbide Corp., N.Y.C., 1969-75; v.p. Union Carbide Corp., Geneva, 1975-79; sr. v.p. Union Carbide Corp., N.Y.C., 1979-82; exec. v.p., chief fin. officer Union Carbide Corp., Danbury, Conn., 1982-86; vice chmn. Union Carbide Corp., 1986—, also bd. dirs.; also bd. dirs. Union Carbide Canada Ltd., Toronto, Ont. Mem. Am. Mining Congress (bd. dirs. 1970-75). Clubs: Round Hill (Greenwich, Conn.). Office: Union Carbide Corp 39 Old Ridgebury Rd Danbury CT 06817

STEPHENSON, LINDA SUE, cosmetic company executive; b. Monroeville, Ind., June 30, 1939; d. LeRoy Lloyd and Edith Lillian (Marquardt) Koehlinger; m. Jack Lynn Stephenson, Dec. 31, 1961. Student modeling Ft. Wayne Finishing Sch., 1959, instr. cert., 1961. Bus. mgr. Ft. Wayne Finishing Sch., Ind., 1960-64; dir., tchr. Cameo Finishing Sch., Ft. Wayne, 1964-65; assoc. dir. Fashion Two Twenty, Decatur, Ind., 1969-71; dir. Marjo Cosmetics, Ft. Wayne, 1971-81; founder, dir. Cozme Cosmetics. Ft. Wayne, 1981—; founder, tchr. Image Projection Workshops, Ft. Wayne, 1981—; dir. Your Total Look, Ft. Wayne, Author: New Dimensions, 1982; Eyes on Ft. Wayne, 1983, also articles. 4-H leader 4-H Horse and Pony Club, Monroeville, Ind., 1962-75; foster parent Adams County Welfare, Decatur, Ind., 1969-73, Indian Program, Ft. Wayne, 1970-72; choral dir. Community Youth Choir, Monroeville, 1967-80, Methodist Men's Chorus, 1980-87. Named Equity Queen, Nat. Farmers Equity, 1960. Mem. Ft. Wayne Better Bus. Bur., Ft. Wayne Women's Bur., Women Bus. Owner's Assn., Nat. Hairdressers and Cosmetologists Assn., Ft. Wayne C. of C., Am. Women Entreprenuers. Avocations: physical fitness, music, bird watching, flower gardening. Home: RR 2 Monroeville IN 46773 Office: Cozme Cosmetics 5821 Decatur Rd Fort Wayne IN 46816

STEPHENSON, NED ELDON, real estate development company executive; b. Salt Lake City, Jan. 15, 1957; s. Robert Eldon and Frances Reeder (Call) S.; m. Lisa Bradley, Dec. 19, 1987, 1 child, David Bradley. BA in Fin., BA in Mgmt., U. Utah, 1982. Lic. real estate broker. Mgr. Peterson Devel. Co., Salt Lake City, 1978-82, v.p., 1982—; owner, pres. Stephenson Property Mgmt., Salt Lake City, 1982—, Ned Stephenson Devel., Salt Lake City, 1985—; v.p. sales and leasing Peterson Devel. Co.; ptnr., pres. Stephenson and Shaw Devel. Co., 1987—. Treas. U. Utah Student Assn., Salt Lake City, 1979-80; advisor Murray City (Utah) C. of C., 1985-87; del. Rep. Party Salt Lake County, 1984-85, State of Utah, 1986-87. Named one of Outstanding Young Men of Am., U.S. Jaycees, 1980. Mormon. Home: 730 Hilltop Rd Salt Lake City UT 84103 Office: Peterson Devel Co 220 S East Ste 300 Salt Lake City UT 84111

STEPHENSON, RICHARD KEITH, marketing professional; b. Miami, Fla., Dec. 25, 1925; s. Ellis H. and Blanche Lorraine (McKinley) S.; m. Marilyn Alice Posson, Sept. 15, 1951; 1 child, Keith Richard. BA, Drake U., 1950; MBA, U. Denver, 1955. Asst. mkt. research Bauer and Black Co., Chgo., 1950-51; engr. sales Aluminum Co. Am., Kansas City, Mo., 1955-56; mgr. mktg. promotion Sunbeam Corp., Chgo., 1956-58; mgr. adv. and pub. relations Sunbeam Equipment Corp., Meadville, Pa., 1958-83; mgr. mktg. communications SEGO/Warwick Corp., Meadville, 1983—. Pres. Council PTA, 1968-70; sec., trustee Spencer Hosp., 1972-76; chmn. chpt. ARC, 1985-87. Served to petty officer U.S. Navy, 1944-46, ETO; lt. U.S. Air Force, 1951-54. Named Outstanding Chmn. Yr. AAU Jr. Olympics, Western Pa., 1976, Boss Yr. Jaycees, 1971. Mem. Meadville Area C. of C. (fellow, pres. 1978-79), Pa. Med. Ctr. (corporate). Republican. Methodist. Lodge: Kiwanis (pres. 1982-83). Home: 348 Jefferson St Meadville PA 16335 Office: SECO/Warwick Corp 180 Mercer St Meadville PA 16335

STEPHENSON, WILLIAM BOYD, JR., life insurance executive; b. St. Louis, Feb. 27, 1933; s. William Boyd and Edna (Gore) S.; B.B.A., U. Okla., 1954; postgrad. Dartmouth Inst., 1984. Salesman, Pillsbury Co., Dallas, 1957-59; with Fidelity Union Life Ins. Co., Dallas, 1959-73, v.p., dir. coll. sales, 1962-67, exec. v.p., 1967-73; dir. coll. marketing Aetna Life & Casualty Co., Hartford, Conn., 1973-76, dir. individual ins. sales, 1976-78, regional v.p., 1978-85, v.p. mktg., 1986—. Bd. dirs., pres. Big Bros./Big Sisters Greater Hartford, Inc.; dir. Met. Hartford YMCA. Served as capt. USAF, 1954-57. C.L.U. Mem. Nat. Assn. Bus. Economists, Am. Soc. C.L.U.'s, Fin. Execs. Inst., Delta Upsilon, Beta Gamma Sigma. Clubs: Hartford, N.Y. Athletic. Home: 791 Prospect Ave West Hartford CT 06105 Office: Aetna Life & Casualty Co 151 Farmington Ave Hartford CT 06156

STEPLER, PAUL STONEHAM, manufacturing executive; b. Southington, Conn., Nov. 18, 1949; s. Wallace and Bernice Anita (Choquette) S. BBA, U. Conn., 1973. CPA, Conn., 1976. Staff acct. Albert Dudzik & Co., CPA's, Southington, 1973-75; sr. acct. Seward & Monde, Meriden, Conn., 1975-77; with Seal, Inc., Naugatuck, Conn., 1977—, corp. controller, 1981, v.p. fin., 1981-83, v.p. adminstrn. and fin., 1983-84, sr. v.p. adminstrn. and fin., 1984—; pres. Okay Industries, New Britain, Conn. Mem. Am. Inst. CPA;s, Conn. Soc. CPA;s, Am. Mgmt. Assn. Home: 49 Evelyn Dr Middlebury CT 06762 Office: Seal Inc 660 Spring St Naugatuck CT 06770

STERCK, GREGORY LEO, insurance company executive; b. Norwalk, Conn., Jan. 6, 1949; s. Frank Charles and Alice (McQuillan) S.; m. Betsy Lee Salmen, May 17, 1980. BBA, Loyola U., New Orleans, 1970, MBA, 1972. Sr. underwriter Aetna Life and Casualty Co., New Orleans, 1973-75; asst. v.p. George S. Kausler, Ltd., New Orleans, 1978; v.p. Underwriters Marine Services, New Orleans, 1978-82, pres., 1982-88, chmn., 1988—; bd. dirs. APS of La. Inc., APSIH Inc., N.Y., Ansbacher Ins. Holdings, PLC, London, Belgo Am. Underwriting Office, Brussels, Archives of La. Trade Labels, Slidell, La.; cons. various corps.; lectr. Tulane U. Sch. Law, Nat. River Acad., Ark. Patron Covington (La.) Jr. Service League, 1983—, Contemporary Arts Ctr., New Orleans, 1985—; mem. vis. com. Loyola U.; active various local civic assns. Mem. Am. Assn. MBA's, S.E. Admiralty Law Inst. Republican. Roman Catholic. Clubs: Beau Chene Golf and Racquet (Mandeville, La.), Internat. House, Plimsoll, World Trade (New Orleans). Club: Krewe of Bacchus (New Orleans).

STERLING, ROBERT LEE, JR., investment company executive; b. Cleve., June 12, 1933; s. Robert Lee and Kathryn (Durell) S.; student U. Edinburgh (Scotland), 1955; m. Deborah Platt, May 10, 1984; children: Robert Livingston, William Lee, Cameron Platt. BA, Brown U., 1956; MBA, Columbia U. Corp. research analyst Morgan Guaranty Trust, N.Y.C., 1962-63; asst. comptroller Western Hemisphere CPC Internat., N.Y.C., 1963-66; v.p. White, Weld & Co., Inc., N.Y.C., 1966-78; v.p. Merrill Lynch Asset Mgmt., 1978-80; v.p. Wood, Struthers & Winthrop Mgmt. Corp., N.Y.C., 1980-83; sr. v.p. Shearson/Am. Express Asset Mgmt., 1983-88; v.p. Chase Manhattan Bank, N.A., U.S. Pvt. Banking. Trustee, Lenox Hill Hosp., N.Y.C.; bd. dirs. Inst. Sports Medicine and Athletic Trauma; mem. adv. bd. Mus. Modern Art, Oxford U., Eng. Served to lt. USNR, 1956-60. Mem. New Eng. Soc. (past pres., J.P. Morgan medal), Nat. Trust Scotland (Edinburgh), St. Andrews Soc., St. Nicholas Soc., Pilgrims (v.p. N.Y. State chpt.), Soc. Cincinnati, Alpha Delta Phi, Alpha Kappa Psi. Clubs: Round Hill (Conn.); Downtown, Univ. (N.Y.C.); Edgartown (Mass.) Yacht. Home: 16 Pheasant Ln Greenwich CT 06830 Office: 1211 Ave of Americas New York NY 10036

STERN, ARLENE HELEN, human resources administrator; b. Bklyn., Nov. 7, 1950; d. Irving and Shirley Judith (Koretz) Stern. BS in Labor Relations, U. Bridgeport, 1971; postgrad. Pace U., 1972-75. Personnel asst. Pathmark, Woodbridge, N.J., 1971-72, regional personnel mgr., 1972-75, dir. human resource planning, 1975-77, dir. personnel and labor relations, Phila., 1977-81; v.p. human resources Howland-Steinbach-Hochschild's, White Plains, N.Y., 1981-85; sr. v.p. human resources and distbn. P.A. Bergner & Co., Milw., 1985—; mem. Frederick Atkins Personnel Adv. Bd., N.Y.C., 1981-86, chmn., 1984. Bd. dirs. Clavis Theatre, 1986—, women's div. Milw. Jewish Fedn., 1987—, Milw. Jewish Council, 1987—, Wis. State of Israel Bonds, 1988—. Mem. Am. Soc. Personnel Adminstrs., Am. Soc. Tng. and Devel. Home: 4800 N Lake Dr Whitefish Bay WI 53217

STERN, ARTHUR PAUL, electronics manufacturing company executive, electrical engineer; b. Budapest, Hungary, July 20, 1925; came to U.S., 1951, naturalized, 1956; s. Leon and Bertha (Frankfurter) S.; m. Edith M. Samuel; children: Daniel, Claude, Jacqueline. Diploma in Elec. Engring., Swiss Fed. Inst. Tech., Zurich, 1948; MSEE, Syracuse U., 1955. Mgr. electronic devices and applications lab. Gen. Electric Co., Syracuse, N.Y., 1957-61; dir. engring. Martin Marietta Corp., Balt., 1961-64; dir. ops. Bunker Ramo Corp., Canoga Park, Calif., 1964-66; v.p., gen. mgr. advanced products div. Magnavox, Torrance, Calif., 1966-79, pres. Magnavox Advanced Products and Systems Co., Torrance, 1980—; vice chmn., bd. dirs. Magnavox Govt. and Indsl. Electronics Co., Ft. Wayne, Ind.; non-resident staff mem. MIT, 1956-59; instr. Gen. Elec. Bus. Mgmt., 1955-57. Chmn. engring. div. United Jewish Appeal, Syracuse, 1955-57; mem. adv. bd. dept. elec. engring. U. Calif., Santa Barbara, 1980—; mem. Sch. Engring. Adv. and Devel. Council Calif. State U., Long Beach, 1985—. Co-author: Transistor Circuit Engineering, 1957, Handbook of Automation, Computation and Control, 1961; also articles; U.S., fgn. patentee in field. Fellow AAAS, IEEE (pres. 1975, bd. dirs., officer 1970-77, guest editor spl. issue IEEE Trans. on Circuit Theory 1956, invited guest editor spl. issue Procs. IEEE on Integrated Electronics 1964, Centennial medal 1984). Jewish. Office: Magnavox Advanced Products & Systems Co 2829 Maricopa St Torrance CA 90503

STERN, DAVID WILLIAM, retail executive; b. Providence, Oct. 7, 1960; s. Franklin Rutherford and Inger Marie (Flom) S.; m. JoAnn Juravich, June 4, 1988. BA, Syracuse U., 1982; postgrad., U. Denver, 1984. Sales rep. Am. Ski Assn., Denver, 1984-85, Zayre Corp., Syracuse, N.Y., 1985-86; sales mgr. USCS of N.Y., Syracuse, 1986-87; pres., chief exec. officer Fun Foods Fun, Inc., Syracuse, 1987—. 1st lt. USAF, 1982-84. Mem. Young Entrepreneurs Orgn., Chief Exec. Officers Club, Delta Kappa Epsilon. Home: 19 Tyler Ct Manlius NY 13104 Office: Fun Foods Fun Inc 720 University Ave Syracuse NY 13210

STERN, DOUGLAS DONALD, foundry company executive; b. New London, Wis., Apr. 29, 1939; s. Sylvester S. and Gretchen W. S.; divorced; children—Randal, Richard, Robert, Russell; m. Joy J. Schmitzer, Aug. 13, 1988. BS in Bus. and Math., U. Wis.-Oshkosh, 1962. With Navistar Foundry Co. (Wis.), 1962—, indsl. engr., 1962-65, dir. indsl. engring., 1965-73, gen. supt. Plant 3, 1973-83, plant mgr. Plant 2, 1983-88, mgr. ops., Waukesha Plant, 1988—; cons. FMC, Lenox; instr. Fox Valley Tech. Inst., Leach; dir. Dura Products. Coach. Neenah Baseball, 1976—, treas., 1976—; pres. Our Savior's Luth. Ch., 1971, treas. Found., 1983. Recipient Neenah Football Rocket award, 1981. Mem. Am. Foundrymen's Soc. (speaker's award 1976, pres. N.E. Wis. chpt.), Am. Inst. Indsl. Engrs. (past pres. and bd. dirs.), Nat. Foundry Assn. (indsl. engring. com.). Republican. Author student workbook: Operations Analysis, 1983. Home: 18000 NW 68 Ave Unit 214 Miami FL 33015 Office: 1401 Perkins Ave Waukesha WI 53186

STERN, DUKE NORDLINGER, lawyer, consultant; b. Chgo., Apr. 14, 1942. B.S. in Econs., U. Pa., 1963; postgrad. U. Va. Law Sch., 1964; J.D., Temple U., 1968; M.B.A., U. Mo., 1969; Ph.D., 1972. Admitted to Mo. bar, 1969, U.S. Supreme Ct., 1978. Cert. Assn. Exec. 1979, Systems Profl., 1984, Mgmt. Cons., 1985; dir. Center for Adminstrn. Legal Systems, Duquesne U., Pitts., 1974-75; exec. dir., gen. counsel W.Va. State Bar, Charleston, 1975-79; pres. Risk & Ins. Services Cons., Inc., St. Petersburg, Fla., 1979-80, Duke Nordlinger Stern & Assos., Inc., St. Petersburg, 1980—, Duke Nordlinger Stern and Assocs., Ltd., London, 1985—, Duke Nordlinger Stern and Assocs., Ltd., Barbados, 1986—, Bermuda, 1986—. Pres., W.Va. Legal Services Plan, Inc., 1978-79. Mem. Am. Soc. Assn. Execs. (cert.), Am. Arbitration Assn., Nat. Assn. Corp. Dirs., Am. Judicature Soc., ABA, Standard Com. on Lawyers' Profl. Liability, Assn for Systems Mgmy., Inst. Mgmt Cons. Author: An Attorney's Guide to Malpractice Liability, 1977, Case in Labor Law, 1977, An Accountant's Guide to Malpractice Liability, 1979, Avoiding Accountant's Malpractice Claims, 1982, Avoiding Legal Malpractice Claims, 1982; A Practical Guide to Preventing Legal Malpractice, 1983. Address: Duke Nordlinger Stern & Assocs Inc 1336 54th Ave NE Saint Petersburg FL 33703

STERN, GERALD M., lawyer, oil company executive; b. Chgo., Apr. 5, 1937; s. Lloyd and Fannye (Wener) S.; m. Linda Stone, Dec. 20, 1969; children: Eric, Jesse, Maia. B.S. in Econs., U. Pa., 1958; LL.B. cum laude, Harvard, 1961. Bar: D.C. 1961, U.S. Supreme Ct. 1971. Trial atty. civil rights div. U.S. Dept. Justice, 1961-64; assoc. firm Arnold & Porter, Washington, 1964-68; ptnr. Arnold & Porter, 1969-76; founding ptnr. Rogovin, Stern & Huge, Washington, 1976-81; exec. v.p., sr. gen. counsel Occidental Petroleum Corp., Washington, 1981-82, Los Angeles, 1982—; also bd. dirs.; bd. dirs. Occidental Petroleum Corp. Author: The Buffalo Creek Disaster, 1976; co-author: Southern Justice, 1965. Bd. dirs. Occidental Petroleum Corp., Facing History and Ourselves Nat. Found., Inc., Bet Tzedek. Mem. ABA. Office: Occidental Petroleum Corp 10889 Wilshire Blvd Los Angeles CA 90024

STERN, JAMES ANDREW, investment banker; b. N.Y.C., Oct. 1, 1950; s. Arthur and Lenore (Oppenheimer) S.; m. Jane Yusem, April 13, 1975; children: Peter, David. BS, Tufts U., 1972; MBA, Harvard U., 1974. Assoc. Lehman Bros. Kuhn Loeb (name now Shearson Lehman Hutton Inc.), N.Y.C., 1974-79, v.p., 1979-82, mng. dir., 1982—. Trustee Tufts U., Medford, Mass., 1982—. Clubs: Quaker Ridge Golf (Scarsdale, N.Y.), Beach Point (Mamaroneck, N.Y.). Office: Shearson Lehman Hutton Inc 200 Vesey St New York NY 10285

STERN, JONATHAN H., accountant; b. Bethesda, Md., Nov. 14, 1944; m. Isabel Ann Friedman; children: Heather, Andrew. BA, Bklyn. Coll., 1967; MBA, NYU, 1969. Sr. acct. Price Waterhouse, N.Y.C., 1972-74; v.p., controller Western Union Corp., Upper Saddle River, N.J., 1974—. V.p., treas. Woodcliff Lake (N.J.) Ednl. Found., 1985—. Mem. N.Y. State Soc. CPAs, Am. Inst. CPAs. Office: Western Union Corp 1 Lake St Saddle River NJ 07458

STERN, JOSEPH AARON, services contracting executive; b. N.Y.C., Apr. 24, 1927; s. Charles M. and Anna (Robinson) S.; m. Phyllis A. Swett, Aug. 26, 1950; children: Carole, Beth, Charles. BS in Food Tech., MIT, 1949, MS in Food Tech., 1950, PhD in Food Tech., 1953. Food technologist Davis Bros. Fisheries Inc., Gloucester, Mass., 1948-49; teaching and research asst. Dept. Food Tech. MIT, Cambridge, 1950-53; chief biochemistry unit, chief life scis. sect., mgr. interplanetary mission support and advanced exploration systems Boeing Co., Seattle, 1958-66; assoc. prof. U. Wash. Coll. of Fisheries, Seattle, 1963-68; asst. sect. mgr. Jet Propulsion Lab., Pasadena, Calif., 1966-69; pres. The Bionetics Corp., Hampton, Va., 1969—. Contbr. articles to profl. jours. Recipient cert. appreciation Viking Project Office, NASA, 1975, pub. svc. award NASA, 1977. Mem. Am. Inst. Biol. Sci., AIAA, Nat. Contract Mgmt. Assn., N.Y. Acad. Scis., Sigma Xi. Office: The Bionetics Corp 20 Research Dr Hampton VA 23666

STERN, LARRY N., actuary; b. St. Louis, June 8, 1949; s. J. Marvyn and Selma (Wolff) S.; children: Stacey, Adrienne. BS in Bus. with honors, Ind. U., 1971. Asst. actuary State Life Ins. Co., Indpls., 1971-81; assoc. actuary Durham Life Ins. Co., Raleigh, N.C., 1981-83; v.p., chief actuary United Presdl. Life Ins. Co., Kokomo, Ind., 1983-87; sr. v.p., chief actuary United Presdl. Life Ins. Co., Kokomo, 1987—. Contbr. articles to profl. jours. Mem. Soc. Actuaries (fellow), Am. Acad. Actuaries, Indpls. Actuary Club, Actuarial Club Ind.-Ohio-Ky. Home: 9365 Kungsholm Dr Apt C Indianapolis IN 46250 Office: United Presdl Life Ins Co PO Box 9006 Kokomo IN 46902

STERN, LEE EDWARD, communications company executive; b. Bethlehem, Pa., Sept. 16, 1936; s. Abraham and Rose S.; m. Phyllis Hanft, 1962. BA, Pa. State U., 1956, MA, 1958. Sr. writer Mobil Oil, N.Y.C., 1964-68; dir. corp. communications Eastern Airlines, N.Y.C., 1968-74; v.p. Mfrs. Hanover, N.Y.C., 1974-76; pres. Lee Edward Stern Communications, N.Y.C., 1976—; cons. Nat. Alliance Bus., Washington; art and entertainment critic Sta. WNYC, 1970-87. Author: The Motive Musical, 1970, Jeanette Mac Donald, 1972; editor: Leadership on the Job, 1973, Hanging Out a Shingle, 1988; contbr. articles to N.Y. Times. Home: Box 437 Dean Bridge Rd Somers NY 10589 Office: Lee Edward Stern 370 Lexington Ave New York NY 10017

STERN, MARC IRWIN, financial services executive; b. Vineland, N.J., Apr. 17, 1944; s. Albert B. and Sylvia (Goodman) S.; m. Eva Suzanne Kuhn, Aug. 14, 1966; children: Adam Bryan, Suzanne Rona. B.A. cum laude in Polit. Sci., Dickinson Coll., Carlisle, Pa., 1965; M.A., Columbia U., 1966, J.D. magna cum laude, 1969. Bar: N.Y. 1969, N.H. 1975. Law clk. U.S. Ct. Appeals 2d Circuit, 1969-70; assoc. Debevoise & Plimpton, 1970-74; v.p., gen. counsel Wheelabrator-Frye Inc., Hampton, N.H., 1974-80; sr. v.p. Wheelabrator-Frye Inc., 1980-83; sr. v.p. adminstrn. The Signal Cos., Inc., La Jolla, Calif., 1983-85, Allied-Signal Inc., Morristown, N.J., 1985-86; mng. dir., chief adminstrv. officer The Henley Group, Inc., N.Y.C. and La Jolla, 1986-88; pres. Broad, Inc., L.A., 1989—, also bd. dirs. Trustee Salk Inst. for Biol. Studies, La Jolla, San Diego Mus. of Art. Mem. ABA, Assn. Bar City N.Y., N.H. Bar Assn. Home: 2194 Century Woods Way Los Angeles CA 90067 Office: Broad Inc 11601 Wilshire Blvd Los Angeles CA 90025

STERN, MARIANNE, advertising agency executive; b. Elizabeth, N.J., July 17, 1950; d. Arthur Leo and Anne (De Paola) Monaghan; m. Manfred Joseph Stern, July 11, 1970 (div.); children: Kathryn Anne, Manfred Joseph III. Student, Montclair (N.J.) State Coll., 1970; BA in English summa cum laude, Kean Coll. of N.J., 1978. Copywriter Patrick J. Gallagher Advt., Westfield, N.J., 1978-79; media dir. Rapp Advt., Springfield, N.J., 1979-85; account exec. Spectrum advt., Springfield, 1985; pres., account exec. Whitney A. Morgan Advt., Montclair, 1985—; cons. Monadel, Inc., Rahway, N.J., 1985—; bd. dirs. Delatush Systems, Inc., Montclair. Mem. publicity com. 200 Club of Union County, N.J., 1978; pub. chmn. Boy Scouts Am. Union

County chpt., 1987. Mem. NAFE, Phi Kappa Phi, Lambda Alpha Sigma, Alpha Sigma Lambda. Office: Whitney A Morgan Advt 37 N Fullerton Ave Montclair NJ 07042

STERN, RICHARD DAVID, investment company executive; b. New Rochelle, N.Y., Nov. 5, 1936; s. Leo and Grace Marjorie (Phillips) S.; m. Phyllis Marlene Edelstein, Nov. 20, 1966; children: Marjorie Anne, Andrew Howard. AB, Princeton U., 1958; MBA, Harvard U., 1962. First v.p. Newburger, Loeb & Co., N.Y.C., 1962-74, also dir., 1962-74; sr. investment officer Central Trust Co., Cin., 1974-76, owner bus. valuation cons. co., 1976-78; v.p. Gt. Western Bank & Trust Co. (name now Citibank Ariz.), Phoenix, 1978-84; pres. Stern, Ludke & Co. (now named Stern Investment Mgmt. Co.), Phoenix, 1984—. Co-author: Air Cushion Vehicles, 1962. Trustee endowment trust Phoenix Chamber Music Soc., 1982—, v.p., 1986—; pres. Cen. Ariz. chpt. Arthritis Found., 1982-84, chmn. planned giving com., 1986—, mem. Nat. Planned giving com., 1987—; chmn. endowments and trusts com. Temple Beth Israel, Phoenix, 1980-83; mem. demographic survey com. Jewish Fedn. Greater Phoenix, 1982-84, mem. planning and budget com., 1983-84, investment com. Endowment Fund, 1984—, chmn. 1986-88; pres. Phoenix chpt. Am. Jewish Com., 1983-84, bd. dirs., 1980-84, mem. adv. bd., 1985—; bd. dirs. Asian Arts Council, Phoenix Art Mus., 1987—, treas. 1988-89, v.p., 1989—. Lt. comdr. USCGR, 1959. Mem. Phoenix Soc. Fin. Analysts (chmn. profl. conduct com. 1980-83, bd. dirs.), Anti-Defamation League of B'nai B'rith (dir. Cen. Ariz. chpt. 1986—, exec. bd. 1989—), University Club (Phoenix). Republican. Home: 6013 E Donna Circle Paradise Valley AZ 85253 Office: Stern Investment Mgmt Co 2035 N Central Ave Phoenix AZ 85004

STERN, STEVEN ALAN, investment banker; b. Chgo., Dec. 5, 1943; s. Sidney J. and Leona (Bernstein) S.; m. Helena Kerner, July 12, 1975; children: Jeremy, Jessica. AB, Brandeis U., 1965; postgrad. Columbia U. Grad. Sch. Bus., 1965-66. CPCU, Ill. Trust officer, First Nat. Bank Chgo., 1966-69; ptnr., Equicon, Inc., Chgo., 1970-74; coordinator Singer for Mayor, Chgo., 1974-75; mgr. underwriting policy CNA Ins., Chgo., 1976-79; project dir. Gov.'s Blue Ribbon Panel, Denver, 1979-81; dir. capital budget State of Colo., Denver, 1981-82; exec. dir. Ctr. Bus. and Econ. Forecasting, U. Denver, 1982-85; v.p. pub. finance, Kirchner, Moore & Co., Denver, 1986—; mem. adv. task force to capital devel. com. Colo. Gen. Assembly, 1985-87, chmn. adv. task force subcom. on privatization, 1986-87; mem. adv. council Colo. Advanced Tech. Inst., 1986—; guest lectr., 1982—; adv. task forces on capital budgeting, transp. Denver C. of C., 1980—. Speaker annual meetings Nat. Assn. State Mental Health Program Dirs., 1987—, Nat. Assn. State Mental Retardation Program Dirs., 1987, Nat. Assn. State Alcohol and Drug Abuse Dirs., 1988. Author: Colorado Capital Investment Budget, 1982; (with others) Colorado; Investing in the Future, 1981; editor: Techniques of Economic Research, 1981. Speaker, Adopt-A-Sch., Denver Pub. Schs., 1983, 86, numerous other orgns.; participant Leadership Denver, 1983-84; sec.-treas. Colo. Student Obligation Bond Authority, 1984-86, also bd. dirs.; bd. dirs. Circus Arts Found., 1985-86; chmn. devel. com. Stanley Brit. Primary Sch., Denver, 1984; mem. Denver Baseball Commn., 1987—; bd. dirs., chmn. corp. gifts Epilepsy Found. Chgo., 1977-79. Mem. Denver Zool. Soc., Denver Childrens Mus., Denver Mus. Natural Hist., Wilderness Soc., Brandeis U. Alumni Assn., NAACP (life), Colo. Mcpl. Bond Dealers Assn. (chmn. legis. affairs com. 1987), Denver C. of C. Democrat. Jewish. Office: Kirchner Moore & Co 717 17th St Ste 2700 Denver CO 80202

STERN, STEVEN LESLIE, lawyer; b. N.Y.C., Aug. 17, 1943; s. Fred D. and Erika (Sonder) S.; children: Jeffrey Michael, Jonathan Gary, Jennifer Rose. AB with great distinction, Stanford U., 1965; JD magna cum laude, Harvard U., 1968. Bar: Calif. 1969, D.C. 1985. Assoc. Irell & Manella, Los Angeles, 1968-70, Harris, Noble, McCormac and Uhler, Los Angeles, 1971; ptnr. McCormac, Davis, Punelli & Stern, Newport Beach, Calif., 1971-76; pvt. practice, Newport Beach, Calif., 1976-82; ptnr. McDermott & Trayner, Newport Beach, Calif., 1982-88, Corbett & Steelman, Irvine, Calif., 1989—; lectr. Orange County Bar Assn., Calif. Judge pro tem. Harbor Mcpl. Court, Newport Beach, 1978—. Served as 1st lt. U.S. Army, 1969. Mem. Orange County Bar Assn. (chmn. Health Care Law sect. 1984-85), Los Angeles County Bar Assn., D.C. Bar Assn., Calif. Soc. Health Care Attys., Dana West Yacht Club (judge adv. 1980-82), Balboa Ski Club (bd. dirs. 1975-76, 87). Democrat. Jewish. Office: Corbett & Steelman 18200 Von Karman Ave Ste 200 Irvine CA 92715

STERN, THEODORE, electric company executive; b. 1929; married. B-MechE, Pratt Inst., 1951; MS, NYU, 1956. With Westinghouse Electric Co., Pitts., 1958—, gen. mgr. pressurized water reactor systems div., 1966-71, gen. mgr. nuclear fuel div., 1971-72, v.p. than v.p. water reactor divs., 1972-74, exec. v.p. power generation, 1974-78, exec. v.p. nuclear energy systems, 1978—. Office: Westinghouse Electric Corp 6 Gateway Ctr Pittsburgh PA 15222 *

STERN, WALTER PHILLIPS, investment executive; b. N.Y.C., Sept. 26, 1928; s. Leo and Marjorie (Phillips) S.; m. Elizabeth May, Feb. 12, 1958; children: Sarah May, William May, David May. A.B., Williams Coll., 1950; M.B.A., Harvard U., 1952. With Lazard Freres & Co., N.Y.C., 1953-54; assoc. Burnham & Co., Inc. (now Drexel Burnham Lambert Group, Inc.), N.Y.C., 1954-60, partner, 1960-71, sr. exec. v.p., 1972-73; vice chmn., mng. dir. eastern ops. Capital Research Co., 1973—; chmn. bd. New Perspective Fund, Inc., 1973—, Fundamental Investors Inc., 1978—; chmn. Capital Research Internat., Capital Group Internat., Inc., EuroPacific Growth Fund Inc. 1984—; chmn. investment com. Emerging Markets Growth Fund; pres., dir. Income Fund Am., Inc., Growth Fund Am.; dir. Temple-Inland, Inc.; pub. bd. mem., Mcpl. Securities Rulemaking Bd. 1984-87; trustee Fin. Analysts Research Found.; chmn. bd. trustees Hudson Inst.; overseer Ctr. Naval Analysis; instr. NYU, 1956-62, 70-73. Contbr. articles to profl. jours. Chmn., fin. adv. com. Haddasah; chmn. investment com.. trustee Am. Jewish Com., bd. dirs. Westchester chpt.; gov. Anti-Defamation League; bd. dirs. Am. Friends of Tel Aviv U.; trustee Tel Aviv U.; trustee Jaffee Inst. for Strategic Studies, Tel Aviv; treas. Washington Inst. for Near East Policy; pres., bd. dirs. Research Project on Energy and Econ. Policy; chmn. Am. steering com. Freedom of Trade with Israel. Served as 1st lt. USAF, 1952-53. Mem. N.Y. Soc. Security Analysts (bd. dirs.), Fin. Analysts Fedn. (pres. 1971-72, bd. dirs.), Inst. Chartered Fin. Analysts (pres. 1976-77, dir.), Phi Beta Kappa. Jewish. Clubs: Board Room (N.Y.C.), Harvard (N.Y.C.), Williams (N.Y.C.), Economic (N.Y.C.); Sunningdale Country (Scarsdale N.Y.); California (Los Angeles). Home: 450 Ft Hill Rd Scarsdale NY 10583 Office: 280 Park Ave New York NY 10017 also: New Perspective Fund Inc 333 S Hope St Los Angeles CA 90071

STERN, WARREN CHARLES, pharmaceutical company executive; b. Bronx, N.Y., June 1, 1944; s. Julius and Eleanor (Fox) S.; m. Carol J. Hershkowitz, June 13, 1965; children: Andrew, Douglas, Gregory. BS, Bklyn. Coll., 1965; PhD, Ind. U., 1969. Postdoctoral fellow Boston State Hosp., 1969-70, Worcester Found, Shrewsbury, Mass., 1970-71; staff scientist Worcester Found, 1971-75; sr. scientist Squibb Inst. for Med. Res., Princeton, N.J., 1975-76; head clin. neuroscience Burroughs Wellcome Co., Research Triangle Park, N.C., 1976-83; dir. new products Burroughs Wellcome Co., 1983-85; pres., chief exec. officer, bd. dirs Pharmatec, Inc., Alachua, Fla., 1985—; bd. dirs. InnoVet, Inc., Boca Raton, Fla. Contbr. numerous articles to profl. jours.; patentee pharm. field. Recipient 1st prize for res. paper Am. Psychol. Assn., 1970. Mem. AAAS, Am. Soc. for Pharmacology and Exptl. Therapeutics, Soc. for Neurosci., Am. Soc. for Microbiology, Soc. for Clin. Pharmacology. Home: 4921 NW 19th Pl Gainesville FL 32606 Office: Pharmatec Inc PO Box 730 Alachua FL 32615

STERN, WAYNE BRIAN, investment company executive, management consultant; b. New Rochelle, N.Y., Jan. 8, 1948; s. Edward A. Stern and Gertrude (Eger) Lurie; m. Yvonne Eva Segelbaum, Sept. 1, 1968; children: Tiffany Joy, Colette Avi. BS in Aerospace Enging., U. Md., 1970; MBA in Fin. and Internat. Bus., U. Wash., 1977. Structures design engr. Pratt & Whitney Aircraft, West Palm Beach, Fla., 1970-72; control system engr., system cost analyst, mgr. internat. market research Boeing Co., Seattle, 1973-77; group mgr., v.p. planning and devel. W.R. Grace & Co., N.Y.C. and Troy, Mich., 1977-81; v.p., gen. mgr. Compo Industries, Inc., Cartersville, Ga., 1981-85; pres. Stern & Co., Atlanta, 1985—. Recipient Outstanding Research award AIAA, 1970. Mem. Am. Mgmt. Assn., Assn. Corp. Growth, Tau Beta Pi, Sigma Gamma Tau (past v.p.), Pi Mu Epsilon, Omicron Delta Kappa, Beta Gamma Sigma. Republican. Jewish. Home and Office: 745 Old Campus Tr Atlanta GA 30328

STERNE, SUSAN MAINS, financial analyst; b. N.Y.C., Feb. 28, 1946; d. William Donald and Florence (Sachse) Mains; B.B.A., U. Iowa, 1968; postgrad. N.Y. U., 1969; m. Lawrence Jon Sterne, Apr. 17, 1976; children—Christopher William Southern, Melissa Anne Southern, Marjorie Mains, Caroline Adams. Asst. economist Goldman Sachs & Co., N.Y.C., 1969-71; economist Cyrus S. Lawrence, Inc., N.Y.C., 1972-75, Faulkner Dawkins & Sullivan, N.Y.C., 1974-76; v.p., economist Salomon Bros., N.Y.C., 1976-79; pres. Econ. Analysis Assos., Stowe, Vt., 1979—; lectr. U. Mich. Annual Outlook Conf., 1979; lectr. New Sch., 1978, Mktg. and Media Workshop, 1983, Houston Bus. Forum, 1981, others; mem. econ. adv. bd. U.S. Dept. Commerce, 1978-79; NABE Annual Meeting, 1981, Wertheim Annual Consumer Conf., 1986-88, Grants Interest Rate Conf., 1988. Mem. Conf. Bus. Economists Bus. Econ. Issue Council, Nat. Assn. Bus. Economists, Fin. Analyst Fedn., N.Y. Soc. Security Analysts, Houston Soc. Security Analysts, 1988. Nat. Economists Club, Conf. Bus. Economists. Contbr. articles to profl. jours. Office: RD 2 Box 1080 Stowe VT 05672

STETSON, EUGENE WILLIAM, III, oil company executive; b. Norwalk, Conn., Mar. 31, 1951; s. Eugene William Jr. and Grace Jones (Richardson) S. AB, Harvard U., 1982, postgrad. in Sch. Arts and Scis., 1986. Assoc. exec. dir. Conn. River Watershed Coun., Easthampton, Mass., 1978-81; v.p. Fairhill Oil & Gas Corp. (Fairhill Oil Ltd.-Can.), N.Y.C., Calgary, Alta., Can., 1981-84; pres. Fairhill Oil & Gas Corp. (Fairhill Oil Ltd.-Can.), N.Y.C., Calgary, 1984—; bd. dir. Piedmont Fin. Co., Greensboro, N.C., 1978-80, Chisolm Mgmt. Corp., N.Y.C., 1983—; supr. Ottauguechee Conservation Dist., Woodstock, Vt., 1978-82; pres. Boatwright Found., N.Y.C., 1981—; exec. com. Simsbury, Conn., 1984-86; gov. Smith Richardson Found., N.Y., 1984—; trustee Proctor Acad., Andover, N.H., 1985—; cofounder River Watch Network, Montpelier, Vt., 1987—. Mem. Small Explorers and Producers Asssn. of Can., Harvard-Radcliffe Club Vt., Harvard Club N.Y.C., Hasty Pudding Club. Home: RR1 Box 167 Gully Rd Woodstock VT 05091 Office: Fairhill Oil Ltd, 2820 Bow Valley Sq IV, 250-6th Ave SW, Calgary, AB Canada T2P 3H7

STETTLER, JOHN EVERETT, pension fund administrator; b. Ashland, Ky., Dec. 7, 1942; s. Lloyd Everett and Alma Carolyn (Moritz) S.; m. Patricia Alice Frazier, Dec. 31, 1964; children: James Everette, Rebecca Ann, Joel Evan. BBA, Ea. Ky. U., 1967; MBA, U. Ky., 1969. Adminstrv. asst. Ashland Oil, Inc., Russell, Ky., 1969-72, asst. treas., 1973-75, asst. treas./mgr. pension fund investments, 1975-84; dir. employee benefit investments Ga.-Pacific Corp., Atlanta, 1984-85, dir. benefit investments/risk mgmt., 1986—. Mem. So. Pension Conf. Republican. Mem. Ch. of Christ. Home: 4523 Dartmoor Dr NE Marietta GA 30067 Office: Ga-Pacific Corp 133 Peachtree St NE Atlanta GA 30303

STEUDEL, HELMUT HENRY, structural engineer; b. Toledo, June 4, 1959; s. Joseph and Elizabeth (Hafner) S.; m. Madeline Dowdy, Oct. 22, 1983. BCE, Pa. State U., 1981. Registered profl. engr., Tex., Pa., N.Y. Engr. Brown & Root Inc., Houston, 1981-83, Gilbert Assocs. Inc., Reading, Pa., 1983-84, Lozier Architects, Engrs., Rochester, N.Y., 1984-88, Fluor Daniel, Rochester, 1988—. Mem. ASPE, Monroe Profl. Engrs. Soc. (bd. dirs. 1987—, chair scholarship com. 1987—), Chi Epsilon. Democrat. Baptist. Home: 95 Parkside Ave Rochester NY 14609 Office: Fluor Daniel 30 Corporate Woods Ste 100 Rochester NY 14623

STEUERT, DOUGLAS MICHAEL, financial executive; b. Oklahoma City, May 21, 1948; s. Douglas Anselm and Geraldine (Sparks) S.; m. Nancy Elizabeth Ridd, Aug. 22, 1970. BS in Physics, MS in Indsl. Mgmt., Carnegie-Mellon U., 1971. Staff asst. TRW, Inc., Cleve., 1971-73, mgr. fin. research and analysis, 1973-75, dir. fin. U.S., 1975-76; dir. fin. Europe TRW, Inc., Frankfurt, Fed. Republic Germany, 1976-79; asst. treas. internat. TRW, Inc., Cleve., 1979-81, sr. fin. dir. automotive worldwide sector, 1981-84, controller valve div., 1984-86; v.p., treas. GenCorp Inc., Akron, Ohio, 1986-87; v.p. fin. and planning GenCorp Inc., Fairlawn, Ohio, 1987—. Mem. Nat. Assn. Corp. Treas.; Fin. Execs. Inst. (nat. chpt., Northeast Ohio chpt., bd. dirs.), MAPI. Home: Riverview Rd Gates Mills OH 44040 Home: Riverview Rd Gates Mills OH 44040 Office: GenCorp Inc 175 Ghent Rd Fairlawn OH 44313-3300

STEVENS, ART, public relations company executive; b. N.Y.C., July 17, 1935; m. Eva Sandberg, Mar. 19, 1972. B.A., CCNY, 1957. Pub. relations dir. Prentice Hall, Inc., Englewood Cliffs, N.J.; account exec. William L. Safire Public Relations Inc., N.Y.C., 1966-69; v.p. William L. Safire Public Relations Inc., 1967-68, pres., 1968-69; pres. Lobsenz-Stevens Inc., N.Y.C., 1970—; instr. Fairleigh Dickinson U. Author: The Persuasion Explosion; weekly columnist Sanibel (Fla.) Island Reporter; contbr. articles to profl. jours. Bd. dirs. United Way of Putnam County, N.Y. Mem. Publicity Club N.Y. (Disting. Service award 1969), Public Relations Soc. Am. (chmn. ethics com. Counselors Acad. sect.). Club: Gipsy Trail (Carmel, N.Y.). Home: 201 E 21st St New York NY 10010 Office: Lobsenz-Stevens 460 Park Ave S New York NY 10016

STEVENS, CHANDLER HARRISON, communications executive, consultant; b. Trenton, N.J., Jan. 3, 1935; s. Chandler Harrison Sr. and Margaret (Cheyney) S.; m. Joann Gail Orcutt, Aug. 18, 1956; children: Emily Joan, Maria Lynn. BEE, Ga. Tech. Inst., 1956; PhD in Indsl. Econs., MIT, 1967. Data processing salesman IBM, Atlanta, 1956-57; mgmt. cons. C.W. Adams Assocs., Bedford, Mass., 1960-64; state legislator Mass. Ho. Reps., Boston, 1965-68; sci. dav. to Gov. of P.R. San Juan, 1969; sr. lectr. MIT Sloan Sch. Mgmt., Cambridge, 1970-71; Gilbreth prof. Rensselaer Poly. Inst., Troy, N.Y., 1971-74; sci. adv. to Mass. Legis. Boston, 1975-77; founder, pres. Participation Systems, Inc., 1970-84; chmn. Eventures, Ltd. (formerly PSI), Allentown, Pa., 1985-89, also bd. dirs.; vice-chmn. Network Techs., Internat. Ann Arbor, Mich., 1986-88; vis. scholar Cognitive Sci. and Machine Intelligence Lab. U. Mich., Ann Arbor. Designer computer software programs including Participate, 1982; developer various forms interactive media, graphics; contbr. articles to profl. jours. Chmn. bd. selectmen Bedford, 1962-65, Citizens For Mass., 1967; treas. Counc. For Constl. Reform in Mass., 1963. 1st lt. USAF, 1957-60. Recipient Outstanding Young Man award Bedford Jaycees, 1966; vis. fellow MIT Mgmt. 1990's Rsch. Program. Mem. Electronic Mail Assn., Electronic Networking Assn., Toastmasters (Ann Arbor club), Civic Theater Club. Democrat. Congregational. Home: 13 Southwick Ct Ann Arbor MI 48105-1409

STEVENS, CHESTER WAYNE, real estate executive; b. Milw., May 24, 1925; s. Daniel Augusta and Genevieve (Kingston) S.; m. Bernice Louise Limberg, Nov. 8, 1947; 1 child, Doreen Louise Scholtes. Student, Augustana Coll., 1944. Mgr. ops. Plankinton Bldg., Milw., 1962-72; v.p. 1st Wis. Devel. Corp., Milw., 1972-78; pres., chief exec. officer Stevens Carley Co., Milw., 1978-81, C.W. Stevens Co., Milw., 1981-85; v.p. Towne Realty Inc., Milw., 1985—; cons. Milw. Redevel., 1981-82, Milw. Ins., 1983. Served with USAAF, 1943-46. Mem. Bldg. Owners and Managers Assn. (pres. 1972-73, dir. exec. com. 1976-82), Inst. Real Estate Mgmt. (pres. 1982, Mgr. of Yr., 1981), Milw. Bd. Realtors. Democrat. Lutheran. Club: Lake Ripley Country. Home: N 4439 Friedel Cambridge WI 53253 Office: Towne Realty Inc 710 N Plankinton Ave Milwaukee WI 53203

STEVENS, CRAIG THOMAS, securities brokerage executive; b. Orlando, Fla., July 31, 1960; s. James Richard and Barbara Kiersten (Van Ackeran) S.; m. Jennifer Lynn Miller, Dec. 18, 1982; children: Kiersten Ann, Parker Thomas. BS in Fin., San Diego State U., 1982. Cert. fin. planner. Investment/compliance analyst Pvt. Ledger Fin. Svcs., San Diego, 1982-84; asst. v.p. Am. Diversified Equity Corp., Costa Mesa, Calif., 1984-85; v.p. IDM Securities Corp., Long Beach, Calif., 1985—. Mem. Calif. Assn. Broker/Dealers (v.p., bd. dirs. 1987), Real Estate Securities and Syndication Inst. (v.p., bd. govs. 1986—), Nat. Assn. Fin. Wholesalers, Internat. Assn. for Fin. Planning, Inst. Cert. Fin. Planners, Toastmasters (pres. Long Beach chpt. 1987—), Ctr. 500 Assocs. Republican. Methodist. Home: 12852 Charloma Dr Tustin CA 92680

STEVENS, DENNIS MAX, manufacturing and marketing company executive; b. Jersey City, Sept. 3, 1944; m. Susan Gail Brown, Mar. 15, 1969; children: Julie Ayn, Daniel Ross. BBA, Rutgers U., 1966; MA in Acctg., U. Mo., 1968. CPA, Mo. Staff Peat, Marwick, Mitchell and Co., St. Louis, 1968-80, ptnr., 1980-84; sr. v.p. and internal auditor Southwestern States Bankcard Assn., Dallas, 1985-86, sr. v.p. and chief fin. officer, 1986-89; corp. planner NCH Corp., Irving, Tex., 1989—. Contr. articles to profl. jours. Served to 1st lt. U.S. Army, 1969-70. Mem. Am. Inst. CPAs (electronic data processing auditing standards com. 1979-84), Beta Gamma Sigma, Beta Alpha Psi. Home: 2325 Fountain Head Dr Plano TX 75023 Office: NCH Corp 2727 Chemsearch Blvd Irving TX 75062

STEVENS, J. PAUL, entrepreneur; b. Detroit, July 1, 1942; s. Constantine Jerome Dziuk and Mary Magdalene Stepanski; m. Alice Eaton, Jan. 6, 1959. BA, U. Mich., Ann Arbor, 1963, Rider Coll., Lawrenceville, N.J., 1966, Mich. State U., East Lansing, 1967. Lic. real estate broker, Mich. Treas. Stepanski Holdings, Alpena, Mich., 1955-59, Eaton Holdings, Ottawa, Ont., Can., 1959-62, Bryant Holdings, Alanson, Mich., 1963-82; cons. I.P.C., N.Y.C., 1962—, J.P. Stevens & Co. Ltd., N.Y.C. and Lansing, Mich., 1955—, Pitcairn Holdings, Jenkinstown, Pa., 1955—. Author: The Secret of Federal Budget Balancing, 1982; How to Prepare for the Crash of 1992, 1984. Recipient Internat. Banking award World Internat. Bank, 1962; named Knight of the Fourth degree KC, 1980. Life mem. Mich. State Numismatic Soc. (bd. dirs. 1962). Club: Capitol City Coin (Lansing) (treas. 1955—). Lodge: KC. Home and Office: 315 W Allegan St PO Box 15 III Lansing MI 48901

STEVENS, LARRY LYNN, securities broker; b. Columbus, Kans., June 27, 1944; s. Ransome Edward and Ida Chrystine (Lasater) S.; m. Patricia Sue Kannady, Dec. 27, 1966 (div. Mar. 1986); children: Timothy Wayne, Mark Aaron, Jonathan, Andrew. BA, Okla. Bapt. U., 1966; MDiv, Southwestern Bapt. Theol. Sem., 1969. Ordained to ministry Bapt. Ch., 1968. Pastor Antioch Bapt. Ch., Lebanón, Mo., 1969-72, Mt. Sinai Ch., Clever, Mo., 1972-76; pastor 1st Bapt. Ch., Centerton, Ark., 1976-81, Dora, N.Mex., 1985; receiving mgr. Wal-Mart Stores, Yukon, Okla., 1981-82; chaplain Bapt. Med. Ctr., Oklahoma City, 1982-83; staff chaplain High Plains Bapt. Hosp., Amarillo, Tex., 1984; securities broker Penrod & Co., Nixa, Mo., 1986—. Contbr. articles to profl. jours. Bd. dirs. Ark. Bapt. State Conv., Little Rock, 1979-81. Mem. Assn. Clin. Pastoral Edn., Optimist Club (community chmn. Nixa chpt.). Office: Penrod & Co PO Box 679 Nixa MO 65714

STEVENS, LORELEI PATRICIA, brokerage company executive; b. Seattle, Aug. 15, 1950; d. Larry Lawrence Stevens and Patricia Daphne (Crosier) Krenik. BA, Anticoh U., 1988. Pres. Wall Street Brokers, Inc., Seattle, 1973—. Contbr. articles to profl. jours. Mem. Seattle Assn. Profl. Mktg Women. Office: Wall Street Brokers Inc 500 Wall St Ste 405 Seattle WA 98121-1577

STEVENS, MARTIN BRIAN, publisher; b. N.Y.C., Dec. 29, 1957; s. David Robert and Shirley (Marcus) S.; m. Sheri Doscher, Dec. 30, 1979. Grad. high sch. Advt. artist Unitron Pubs., N.Y.C., 1977, Westchester Publs., Elmsford, N.Y., 1978; pub. Marketers Forum, Centerport, N.Y., 1981—; pub. Can. Retailer, 1989, also eight bus. directories; rep. six bus. book pubs. Named Top Mail Order Dealer Nat. Mail Dealers Counsel, 1978. Mem. Mail Order Bus. Bd. (pres. 1978-80), Better Bus. Bur. Office: Marketers Forum 383 E Main St Centerport NY 11721

STEVENS, ROBERT EDWIN, insurance company executive; b. Hartford, Feb. 12, 1927; s. Horace and Anna E. (Lauritzen) S.; m. Betty L. Hippler, June 30, 1951; children—Paul, Lynn, Peter. B.A., Wesleyan U., 1949. Various positions bond and common stock divs. Conn. Mut. Life Ins. Co., Hartford, 1951-71; v.p., treas. Conn. Mut. Life Ins. Co., 1972-74, sr. v.p., 1974-76, exec. v.p., 1976—; pres. Conn. Mut. Investment Accounts, Inc.; bd. dirs. Liberty Bank for Savs., Middletown, Conn., Southport Fin. Corp., J.F. China Investment Co. Ltd. Bd. dirs. Hartford Hosp.; trustee Jacob L. and Lewis Fox Scholarship Found., Wesleyan U.; corporator Middlesex Meml. Hosp., Middletown, St. Francis Hosp., Hartford, Newington Children's Hosp. Served with USNR, World War II. Mem. Hartford Soc. Fin. Analysts (past pres.). Home: 46 Keighley Pond Rd PO Box 361 Cobalt CT 06414 Office: Conn Mut Life Ins 140 Garden St Hartford CT 06154

STEVENS, ROBERT GENE, banker; b. Marion, Ill., Jan. 4, 1930; s. Robert Bryan and Mae S.; children: David R., Craig R., Brian R. B.S., So. Ill. U., 1951; M.S., U. Ill., 1954, Ph.D., 1958; LL.D. hon., Mt. St. Joseph Coll., 1974. C.P.A, Ill. Auditor Arthur Andersen & Co., St. Louis, 1954-55; instr. acctg. U. Ill., Champaign Urbana, 1953-58; ptnr. Touche Ross & Co., N.Y.C., 1958-68; v.p. First Nat. City Bank, N.Y.C., 1968-70; pres., dir. Old Stone Bank, Providence, 1970-76; mng. trustee Old Stone Mortgage & Realty Trust, Providence, 1971-76; chmn., pres., chief exec. officer BancOhio Corp., Columbus, 1976-81; chmn., chief exec. officer BancOhio Nat. Bank, Columbus, 1979-81; pres., chief exec. officer First Am. Bancshares, Inc., Washington, 1982—; chmn. dir. First Am. Data Svcs., First Advantage Mortgage Corp.; dir. First Am. Bank, N.A. Washington, First Am. Bank N.Y., First Am. Internat. Bank Miami, Student Loan Mktg. Assn., Washington. Served to 1st lt. USAF, 1951-53. Mem. Phi Kappa Phi. Club: Metropolitan (Washington). Office: First Am Bancshares Inc 740 15th St NW Washington DC 20005

STEVENS, SHERRY N., credit officer; b. Corinth, Miss., Apr. 24, 1959; d. Noonan D. and Nadine (Lamberth) Nelson; m. Larry S. Stevens, May 8, 1982; 1 child, Tyler Patrick. BS in Acctg., Miss. U. for Women, Columbus, 1981. Auditor Touche Ross and Co., Jackson, Miss., 1981-82; internal auditor Pan Am. Life Ins., New Orleans, 1982-83; asst. loan officer Farm Credit Banks, New Orleans, 1983-84; loan officer Farm Credit Banks, Jackson, 1984-86, sr. loan officer, 1986-87, asst. v.p., 1987—. Republican. Methodist. Home: 3118 Tidewater Ln Madison MS 39110 Office: 1800 E County Line Rd Ridgeland MS 39157

STEVENS, WHITNEY, textile company executive; b. Plainfield, N.J., Nov. 26, 1926; s. Robert TenBroeck and Dorothy Goodwin (Whitney) S.; m. Helene Baldi, Nov. 1, 1961; children: Mark W., David W., J. Whitney. Student, Phillips Acad., 1940-44; B.A., Princeton U., 1947. With J.P. Stevens & Co., Inc., N.Y.C., 1948-89; v.p. J.P Stevens & Co., Inc., N.Y.C., 1958-64, exec. v.p., 1964-69, pres., 1969-79, chmn., chief exec. officer, 1980-89, also dir., mem. exec. com.; adv. bd. Chem. Bank, N.Y.C. Trustee St. Luke's/Roosevelt Hosp., N.Y.C.; Vice chmn. Citizens' Budget Commn. Served with USNR, 1944-46. Mem. Am. Textile Mfrs. Inst. Clubs: Links (N.Y.C.); Princeton (N.Y.); River. Office: J P Stevens & Co Inc 1185 Ave of Americas New York NY 10036 *

STEVENS, WILLIAM DAVID, oil company executive; b. Corpus Christi, Tex., Sept. 18, 1934; s. Walter Gerald and Amy (Grace) S.; m. Barbara Ann Duncan, Oct. 9, 1954; children: W. Scott, Robin, Suzanne, Kristen. BS in Natural Gas Enging., Tex. A&I U., 1958. With Exxon Co. U.S.A. (formerly Humble Oil & Refining Co. div. Exxon Corp.), 1958-73; exec. asst. to pres. Exxon Corp., N.Y.C., 1974, with corp. planning and producing, 1974-77, v.p. gas, 1977-78; v.p. upstream Esso Europe Inc., London, 1978-85, exec. v.p., 1985-86; exec. v.p. Exxon Co. U.S.A., Houston, 1986-88, pres., 1988—. Bd. dirs. Jr. Achievement, Stamford, Conn.; trustee United Way Tex. Gulf Coast; trustee Baylor U. Coll. Medicine. Mem. Am. Petroleum Inst. (bd. dirs.), Tex. Rsch. League (bd. dirs., exec. com.), Tex. Assn. Taxpayers (bd. dirs., mem. exec. com.), Greater Houston Ptnrship. (bd. dirs.). Office: Exxon Co USA 800 Bell St Houston TX 77002-7426

STEVENS, WILLIAM JOHN, management consultant, former association executive; b. Dusseldorf, Germany, Aug. 23, 1915; brought to U.S., 1923, naturalized, 1931; s. Peter and Margaret (Kaumanns) S.; student McCall Sch. Printing, 1933; student assn. mgmt. Northwestern U., 1947; m. Dorothy V. Santangini, Feb. 14, 1937 (dec.). With Ruttle, Shaw & Wetherill, Phila., 1931-34; partner New Era Printing Co., Phila., 1934-37; plant mgr. Marcus & Co., Phila., 1937-41; supt. Edward Stern & Co., Phila., 1941-46; exec. sec. Nat. Assn. Photo-Lithographers, N.Y.C., 1946-50, exec. v.p., 1961-64, pres., 1964-71; pres., chief operating officer NPEA Exhibits, Inc., 1971-80; owner Dorval Co., pub.; exec. sec. Met. Lithographers Assn., N.Y.C., 1946-50; asst. to v.p. Miehle Co., N.Y.C., 1950-56, mgr. Phila. dist., 1956-61; cons. Sales Devel. Inst., Phila., 1960—; mem. Am. Bd. Arbitration, 1962—; chmn. adv. commn. on graphic arts N.Y.C. Tech. Coll., 1972—; bus. adminstr. St.

Joseph's Parish, 1980-85 . Named Industry Man of Yr. Nat. Assn. Photo-Lithographers, 1954, Man of Yr., N.Y. Litho Guild, 1962; recipient B'nai B'rith award, 1968; N.Y. Navigators award, 1969; laureate N.Y. Printers Hall of Fame, 1980, NAPL-Soderstrom award, 1984, recipient Gold Founders medal N.Y.C. Tech. Coll., 1987, . Mem. Am. Soc. Assn. Execs., Graphic Arts Assn. Execs. (pres. 1969), Nat. Assn. Litho Clubs (founder, pres. 1947, Industry award 1947, 79, sec. 1964-71), N.Y. Club Printing House Craftsmen, Graphics Arts Tech. Found., Gamma Epsilon Tau. Clubs: Phila. Litho (pres. 1945); N.Y. Litho (N.Y.C.). Author: How To Prepare Copy for Offset Lithography, 1948, Building Construction and Floor Plans for Installing Web Offset Presses; contbr. articles to trade publs. Inventor Hiky-Picker, Quik-Match Color File for selection paint color samples, Stevens Foto Sizing System, Steve-O-Heat Printing Ink Dryer, "Travelr" security pocket, "Mar-Too-Nee" salad dressing. Home and Office: 7522 Hazelwood Circle Lake Worth FL 33467

STEVENS, WILLIAM TALBERT, finance company executive; b. Houston, Mar. 11, 1952; s. Talbert Maxton and Peggy Elizabeth (Cagle) S.; m. Christine Leslie Treml, May 24, 1975; 1 child, Anne Kathleen. BBA, Pacific Western U., 1988. Mgr. Capital Fin. Svcs., Akron, Ohio, 1975-80, Beneficial Mgmt., Columbus, Ohio, 1980-85; v.p. Mid Am. fed. Savs. and Loan, Columbus, 1985-87, Lender's Svc., Inc., Pitts., 1987—; Mem. faculty, bd, govs. Nat. Inst. Consumer Credit Mgmt. Marquette U., Milw., 1988—. Recipient Pres.'s Disting. Achievement Beneficial Mgmt., 1982, 83. Office: Lenders Svc Inc 113 Technology Dr Pittsburgh PA 15275

STEVENSON, BARBARA, construction cost analyst; b. Richmond, Tex., Aug. 30, 1954; d. Harry Jay and Markaleeta Bernice (Mathews) S. B of Environ. Design cum laude, Tex. A&M U., 1976, MArch in Bldg. Design, 1978. Drafting supr. store and facilities planning J.C. Penney Inc., Dallas, 1978-79; investment tax credit analyst Texas Instruments Corp., Dallas, 1979-83, constrn. analyst for corp. services control, 1987—; v.p. investment tax credits Arvizu Fin. Group, Dallas, 1983-86. Office: Tex Instruments 8330 LBJ Frwy Dallas TX 75243

STEVENSON, DENISE L., business executive, banking consultant; b. Washington, Sept. 18, 1946; d. Pierre and Alice (Mardrus) D'Auga; m. Walter Henry Stevenson, Oct. 17, 1970. AA, Montgomery Coll., 1967; BA in Econs./Bus. Mgmt., N.C. State U., 1983. Lic. ins. agt. Savs. counselor Perpetual Bldg. Assn. (now Perpetual Savs. Bank), Washington, 1968-70; regional asst. v.p. 1st Fed. Savs., Raleigh, N.C., 1971-83; pres., owner Diversified Learning Services, Raleigh, 1983—; instr. Inst. Fin. Edn., Raleigh, 1983—, Am. Inst. Banking, 1986; cert. leader Nat. Assn. Bank Women, 1987. Mem. Inst. Fin. Edn. (2d v.p. 1982-83), Am. Bus. Women's Assn. (woman of yr. award 1982), Nat. Assn. Female Execs., Nat. Assn. Bank Women (cert. leader 1987), Assn. Bank Trainers and Cons., Am. Soc. Tng. and Devel., Omicron Delta Epsilon. Clubs: Laurel Hills Women's (pres. 1974-75) (Raleigh). Avocation: fishing. Office: Diversified Learning Svcs PO Box 33231 Raleigh NC 27636

STEVENSON, EUGENE ANTHONY, food company executive; b. Niagara Falls, N.Y., Nov. 26, 1947; s. Anthony and Eugenia Anna Maria (Pavan) de Stefano; children—Gregory Dawson, Kathryn Dawson. B.A., Canisius Coll., Buffalo, 1969; M.A., Ind. U., 1971; postgrad. Suffolk U., 1977-78. Mgr. pub. relations Textron, Inc., Providence, 1976-78; dir. external communications Continental Group, N.Y.C., 1978-80; dir. fin. pub. relations R.J. Reynolds Industries, Winston-Salem, N.C., 1981-84; dir. corp. communications Reichhold Chems., Inc., White Plains, N.Y., 1984-88; v.p. external communications Kraft, Inc., Glenview, Ill., 1988—. Bd. dirs. Nat. Safety Council, Chgo., 1975-81. Am. Field Service scholar, Istanbul, Turkey, 1964; bd. trustees Arthur W. Page Soc., 1986—. Mem. Nat. Press Club, Pub. Relations Soc. Am., Nat. Investor Relations Inst., Overseas Press Club, Ill. State C. of C. (bd. dirs. 1988—).

STEVENSON, GERALD LEE, engineering contracting company executive; b. Salem, Ill., Jan. 16, 1937; s. Russell Claude and Oneta (Mills) S.; BSChemE., U. Mo., 1959, MSChemE, 1963, hon. profl. degree, 1981; student St. Louis U., 1959-61; postgrad. European Inst. Bus. Adminstrn., Harvard U., 1981; m. Eugenia Adele Bradford, Aug. 7, 1963; children—Lynne Anne, Laura Jean. Technologist, Shell Oil Co., Wood River, Ill., 1959-61; project/prodn. engr. Internat. Minerals, v.p. D.J. Stark Group of Cos., N.Y.C. and Toronto, Ont., 1967-70; sr. v.p. Davy McKee Corp., Cleve., 1970-84; group v.p. Eastern region Jacobs Engring. Group, Inc., Pasadena, Calif. and Lakeland, Fla., 1984—. Mem. budget com. Lakeland United Way, bd. dirs. 1988. Served with U.S. Army, 1960. NSF fellow, 1962; Monsanto Chem. Co. scholar, 1958. Mem. AIME, Am. Inst. Chem. Engrs. (sec. Lakeland 1967-68, exec. bd. dirs. ECC div. 1983-85), Am. Chem. Soc., Ont. Soc. Profl. Engrs., Fertiliser Soc., U. Mo.-Rolla alumni Assn (bd. dirs., v.p. 1977—), Alpha Chi Sigma, Tau Beta Pi. Republican. Episcopalian. Clubs: Lone Palm Golf, Imperial Lakes Golf, Lakeland Yacht and Country, Directors, Chagrin Valley Country. Avocations: golf, fishing. Home: State Rd 540-A Lakeland FL 33813 Office: Jacobs Engring Group Inc PO Box 2008 Lakeland FL 33806-2008

STEVENSON, JEFFREY TAYLOR, bank executive specializing in entertainment; b. N.Y.C., May 19, 1960; s. Lincoln Stevenson and Patricia (Cushman) Crouse. BA, Rutgers Coll., 1982. Assoc. Veronis, Suhler & Assocs., Inc., N.Y.C., 1982-83, v.p., 1983-84, exec. v.p., dir. corp. fin., 1984—; bd. dirs. CBH Holdings, Inc., Houston, 1988—, MCP, Inc., Mpls., 1988—. Club: Am. Yacht (Rye, N.Y.). Office: Veronis Suhler & Assocs 350 Park Ave New York NY 10022

STEVENSON, JOCKE SHELBY, lawyer; b. N.Y.C., June 12, 1934; s. Lincoln L. and Shirley (Grodnick) S.; m. Barbara Winokar, Oct. 7, 1970; 1 son, Marshall Lincoln. B.A., Yale U., 1956, J.D., 1959. Bar: N.Y. 1960, U.S. Dist. Ct. (ea. and so. dists.) N.Y. 1976, U.S. Ct. Internat. Trade 1978, U.S. Supreme Ct. 1981. Assoc. Marshall, Bratter, Greene, Allison & Tucker, N.Y.C., 1960-66; house counsel Burnham & Co., N.Y.C., 1966-70; sole practice, N.Y.C., 1971-77; ptnr. Hershcopf, Sloame & Stevenson, N.Y.C., 1978-80, Hershcopf, Stevenson, Tannenbaum & Glassman, N.Y.C., 1980—; adj. asst. prof. bus. law and polit. sci. Marymount Manhattan Coll., 1978-87; arbitrator N.Y.C. Small Claims Ct., 1977—, N.Y.C. Civil Ct., 1981—. Trustee Park Ave. Synagogue, N.Y.C. Mem. Assn. Bar City N.Y., N.Y. State Bar Assn. (com. on trusts and estates), ABA (com. sole practitioners and small firms). Clubs: Yale, University Glee (treas. 1987—) (N.Y.C.). Home: 400 E 85th St New York NY 10028 Office: 230 Park Ave Suite 3330 New York NY 10169

STEVENSON, RAY, private investor; b. Marion, Ohio, July 25, 1937; s. Ray and Hazel (Emmelhainz) S.; m. Patricia Parker, June 17, 1960 (div. 1979); children: Jeffrey Parker, Kirk Andrew; m. Ellyn Gareleck, Feb. 8, 1985. BS, Ohio State U., 1959, MBA, 1967. Asst. adminstr. Children's Hosp., Columbus, Ohio, 1963-67; adminstr. Martin Meml. Hosp., Mt. Vernon, Ohio, 1967-71; sr. v.p. Hosp. Affiliates, Nashville, 1971-77; exec. v.p. Charter Med. Corp., Macon, Ga., 1977-79, pres., 1979-85; pres. R.S. Operators Inc., Atlanta, 1985—, R.S. Investors Inc., Atlanta, 1985—; mem. adj. faculty Ohio State U., 1979-85; chmn. bd. dirs. World Link Corp., Atlanta, Filmworks Corp., Atlanta. Past chmn., bd. dirs. numerous hosps. and health-related orgns. Mem. Am. Coll. Hosp. Adminstrs., Am. Aquaculture Assn. (chmn.), Fedn. Am. Hosps. (bd. dirs. 1979-81), Nat. Assn. Psychiat. Hosps. Republican. Home: 1880 South Ocean Blvd Manalapan FL 33462 Office: RS Operators Inc 6487C Peachtree Indsl Blvd Atlanta GA 30360

STEVENSON, THOMAS HERBERT, management consultant, writer; b. Covington, Ohio, Oct. 16, 1951; s. Robert Louis and Dolly Eileen (Minnich) S.; m. Pamela F. Blythe, Mar. 10, 1979. BA, Wright State U., 1977. Teaching asst., research asst. Wright State U., 1975-77; teaching asst. Bowling Green State U., 1978; loan officer Western Ohio Nat. B Bank & Trust Co., 1979-80, asst. v.p. adminstrs., 1981-82, v.p. mgmt. services div., 1983-85; v.p., bank mgmt. cons. Young & Assocs., Inc., 1985-86, exec. v.p., 1987—; legis. impact analyst Community Bankers Ohio, 1985—, Community Bankers Ga., 1988—; mem. exec. com. Owl Electronic Banking Network, 1981-85; mem. adv. bd. Upper Valley Joint Vocat. Sch. for Fin. Instns., 1981-85. Author: Compliance for Community Banks, 1987, Compliance Deskbook, 1988, Internal Audit Systems for Community Banks, 1989, Truth in Lending for the Community Bank, 1989, Bank Protection for the Community Bank, 1989; contbr. articles to profl. jours. Served to cpl. USMC, 1972-73. Recipient George Washington medal of Honor Freedom's Found., 1974. Mem. Am. Inst. Banking (adv. bd. 1982-85), Community Bankers Assn. Ohio, Community Bankers Assn. Ga., Community Bankers Assn. Ill., World Future Soc. Republican. Mem. Ch. of Brethren. Club: Eagles. Home: 9020 W U S Hwy 36 Covington OH 45318 Office: 121 E Main St Kent OH 44240

STEVENSON, WALTER, ophthalmologist, treasurer; b. Rochester, Minn., Mar. 3, 1940; s. Walter Davis Jr. and Katharine (Gardner) S.; m. Darlene Gates, Dec. 23, 1965; children: Scott, Laura. BA, Williams Coll., 1962; MD, Washington U., St. Louis, 1966; postdoctoral, U. Pa., 1969-73. Bd. dirs. Physicians and Surgeons Clinic, Quincy, Ill., 1979-86, pres., 1983-86; treas. QP & S Clinic, Quincy, 1987—; bd. dirs. Mercantile Bank & Trust, Quincy. Bd. dirs., v.p. West Ctr. Ill. Health System Agy., Jacksonville, Ill., 1979-81. Lt. USN, 1967--69. Fellow Am. Acad. Ophthalmology; mem. AMA, Am. Soc. Cataract and Refractive Surgery, Quincy Country Club (pres. 1984-85). Office: QP&S Clinic 1101 Main Quincy IL 62301

STEWARD, CARLOS WARREN, arts administrator, filmmaker; b. Columbus, Ohio, June 25, 1950; s. Carl W. and Ethel Grace (Billingham) S.; m. Patricia Ruiz-Bayon (div. 1980); m. Deborah Hill; children: Stanton, Natasha. BFA, Fla. State U., 1972; MFA, U. Guanajuato, Mex., 1974. Instr. film, photo-silkscreening, scriptwriting U. Guanajuato, 1974-76; dir. pub. relations Escuela Ecuestre, Guanajuato, 1976-80; performer Franzini Family, Guanajuato, 1980-84; exec. dir. Oswego (N.Y.) Civic Arts Ctr., 1984—. Contbr. Practical Guide to Scriptwriting (D.V. Swain), 1980; editor (film) Mana, 1978 (1st place award 1979, 80); dir. Mateo, 1979 (award 1980); co-dir. History of Vaudeville, 1986. Dir. Oswego Art Guild, 1984—; pres. Arts in Oswego, 1984—; mem. adv. bd. Oswego County Arts, 1985—; v.p. Oswego Found. for the Performing Arts, 1985—; cultural chmn. Oswego Ptnrs. of the Ams., 1986—. Served with U.S. Dept. Def., 1980, 81, 83. Grantee Fla. State Arts Council, 1981, N.Y. State Council on the Arts, 1986-89;U. Guanajuato fellow, 1975-76. Mem. Soc. for the Preservation of Vaudeville (treas. 1984—). Home: PO Box 336 Fair Haven NY 13064 Office: Oswego Civic Arts Ctr PO Box 315 Oswego NY 13126

STEWARD, LEIGHTON, oil company executive; b. Fairfield, Tex., Dec. 1, 1934; s. Hugh Birt and Lucille (Riley) S.; m. Lynda Brady, June 6, 1959; children; Leighton Brady, Blake Worth. B.S. in Geology, So. Meth. U., 1958, M.S. in Geology, 1960. Chief explorations ops. Shell Oil Co., Houston, 1977-79; v.p. energy and minerals Burlington No. Inc., Billings, Mont., 1979-81; exec. v.p., chief ops. office Kilroy Co. of Tex., Houston, 1981-82; sr. v.p., then exec. v.p. La. Land & Exploration Co., New Orleans, 1982-84, pres., chief operating officer, 1985—, chmn., chief exec. officer, 1988—. Served to capt. USAF, 1959-62. Mem. Am. Assn. Petroleum Geologists, Am. Petroleum Inst. (bd. dirs. 1985-86), Mid Continent Oil and Gas Assn. Republican. Clubs: Metairie Country (La.); New Orleans Petroleum. *

STEWARD, PATRICIA ANN RUPERT, real estate executive, management consultant; b. Panama City, Panama, Apr. 20, 1945 (parents Am. citizens); d. Paul S. and Ernestina M. (Ward) Rupert; grad. Sch. of Mortgage Banking, Grad. Sch. of Mgmt., Northwestern U., 1979; m. Robert M. Levine, Oct. 28, 1978; children by previous marriage: Donald F. Steward, Christine Marie Steward. V.p. Assoc. Mortgage & Investment Co., Phoenix, 1969-71; v.p., br. mgr. Sun Country Funding Corp., Phoenix, 1971-72, Freese Mortgage Co., Phoenix, 1972-74, Utah Mortgage Loan Corp., Phoenix, 1974-81; pres. Elles Corp., 1982—, Elles Mgmt. Corp., 1987—, Elles Approvals Corp., 1987—; founder, The Elles Group, 1987; condr. numerous seminars on mortgage fin. State chmn. Ariz. Leukemia Dr., 1977-78, mem. exec. com., 1979-80; troop leader Cactus Pine council Girl Scouts U.S.A., 1979-80; bd. dirs. Nat. Mental Health Assn., 1986-87, Ariz. Mental Health Assn., pres., 1986-87, bd. dirs., treas. Maricopa Mental Health Assn., 1984-85, v.p., 1985-86, pres., 1986-87; apptd. by state supreme ct. to Ariz. Foster Care Rev. Bd., 1984—, chairperson Bd. 8, 1986-87. Recipient cert. of appreciation Multiple Listing Svc., Phoenix Bd. Realtors, 1975, Multiple Listing Service, Glendale Bd. Realtors, 1977. Lic. mortgage broker, Ariz. Mem. Ariz. Mortgage Bankers Assn. (dir. 1981-82, chmn. edn. com. 1981-82, founder continuing edn. seminar series 1981), Young Mortgage Bankers Assn. (chmn. exec. com. 1980-81), Cen. Ariz. Homebuilders Assn. Republican. Author: A Realtors Guide to Mortgage Lending, 1972. Office: Elles Corp 320 E McDowell Rd Ste 100 Phoenix AZ 85004

STEWART, ALAN, manufacturing engineer; b. London, Eng., May 10, 1937; came to U.S., 1949; s. Robert Dunn and Sarah Jane (Kelly) S.; m. Patty Jo Veselak, June 20, 1959 (div. 1974); children: Pamela Marie, Jill Anne; m. Katherine Anne Rose, July 19, 1974. BS, UCLA, 1960. Cert. mfg. engr. Engr. Norden Data Systems, Costa Mesa, Calif., 1960-61, Northrop Aircraft Corp., Fullerton, Calif., 1961, Coleman Systems Inc., Santa Ana, Calif., 1961-67; chief engr. Coleman Systems Inc., Irvine, Calif., 1967-71; pvt. practice Fayetteville, Ark., 1977-79; sr. engr. Rogers Tool Works Inc., Ark., 1979—. Patentee in field. Mem. Tau Beta Pi, Triangle. Republican. Home: Rte 9 Box 122 Fayetteville AR 72703 Office: Rogers Tool Works PO Box 9 Rogers AR 72756

STEWART, ARLENE JEAN GOLDEN, designer, stylist; b. Chgo., Nov. 26, 1943; d. Alexander Emerald and Nettie (Rosen) Golden; B.F.A. (Ill. state scholar), Sch. of Art Inst. Chgo., 1966; postgrad. Ox Bow Summer Sch. Painting, Saugatuck, Mich., 1966; m. Randall Edward Stewart, Nov. 6, 1970; 1 child, Alexis Anne. Designer, stylist Formica Corp., Cin., 1966-68; with Armstrong World Industries, Lancaster, Pa., 1968—, interior furnishings analyst, 1974-76, internat. staff project stylist, 1976-78, sr. stylist Corlon flooring, 1979-80, sr. exptl. project stylist, 1980—; exhibited textiles Art Inst. Chgo., 1966, Ox-Bow Gallery, Saugatuck, Mich., 1966. Home: 114 E Vine St Lancaster PA 17602 Office: Armstrong Tech Ctr 2500 Columbia Ave Lancaster PA 17604

STEWART, BYRAN JAMES, city official; b. Chgo., Jan. 18, 1956; s. Leonard and Ida Lillian (Robinson) S. AS, Triton Coll., 1977; BS, Eastern Ill. U., 1980. Cert. Ill. mcpl. treas. Freight analyst Mobil Oil Corp., Schaumburg, Ill., 1981-84; treas. Village of Maywood, Ill., 1985—. Authoized agt. Ill. Mcpl. Retirement Fund Village of Maywood; deacon Second Bapt. Ch., Maywood, 1986—; treas. Maywood Fest, 1986—, Maywood Firemen's and Police Pension Bds.; dir. Community Econ. Devel. Assn.-Food Program, Village of Maywood, 1985-86. Mem. Govt. Fin. Officers Assn., Ill. Mcpl. Treasury Assn. (bd. dirs. 1988—), Alpha Phi Alpha (treas. 1988), Delta Sigma Pi. Democrat. Baptist. Home: 200 S 20th Ave Maywood IL 60153 Office: Village of Maywood 115 South 5th Ave Maywood IL 60153

STEWART, CHARLES HENRY, JR., oil company executive; b. Houston, Mar. 25, 1929; s. Charles Henry and Gertrude Abby (Jordan) S.; m. Jean Donna Zienkiewicz, Feb. 21, 1953; children: Bill, Donna, Jennifer. BS in Petroleum Engring., U. Houston, 1957; BS in Math., So. Meth. U., 1963. Div. engr. Exxon USA, Tex. and La., 1957-62; sr. research engr. Shell Devel. Co., Houston and Dallas, 1963-72; sr. v.p. devel. H.J. Gruy & Assoc., Inc., Houston, 1972-82; v.p. engring. Swift Energy Co., Houston, 1983—. Office: Swift Energy Co 16825 Northchase Dr Ste 400 Houston TX 77060

STEWART, CLIFTON CYRUS, JR., oil company executive; b. Wynne, Ark., Oct. 29, 1943; s. Clifton C. and Ernestine Elizabeth (Summers) S.; m. Norma Elizabeth Golden, Dec. 26, 1963; children: Ashley, Coy, Amber, Sabrina, Marilee. BSME, U. Ark., 1966. Various engring. positions Exxon USA, Houston and Rosenberg, Tex., 1967-71; dist. prodn. mgr. Exxon USA, Baytown, Tex., 1971-72; dist. engring. mgr. Exxon USA, Andrews, Tex., 1972-74; dist. operating supt. Exxon USA, Kingsville, Tex., 1974-75; div. prodn. engr. Exxon USA, L.A., 1975-77; div. ops. mgr. Exxon USA, Midland, Tex., 1981-84; ops. mgr. Esso Expro U.K., London, 1977-79; mgr. corp. planning Esso Europe, Inc., London, 1979-81; v.p. prodn. and engring. Hamilton Oil Corp., Denver, 1984-88; v.p. tech. dept. Hamilton Bros. Oil & Gas, Ltd., London, 1988—. Chmn. United Way, Andrews, Tex. 1973. Mem. Am. Petroleum Inst., Soc. Petroleum Engrs., Denver Athletic Club, Champneys Club, Tau Beta Pi, Pi Tau Sigma, Theta Tau. Home: 9 Red Fox Ln Littleton CO 80127 Office: Hamilton Bros Oil & Gas Ltd, Devonshire House, Piccadilly, London W1X 6AU, England

STEWART, DAVID HAROLD, electronics company executive; b. Redding, Calif., Aug. 28, 1957; s. James Richard and Margaret Stewart; m. Nancy Trowbridge, June 27, 1987. BS in Engring., U. Calif.-Davis, 1980; MBA, U. Pa., 1986. Engr. Fluor Engrs., Irvine, Calif., 1980-84; product mgr. Hewlett Packard, Corvallis, Oreg., 1986—. Office: Hewlett Packard 1000 NE Circle Blvd Corvallis OR 97330

STEWART, DONALD CALDER, software company executive; b. Yonkers, N.Y., Aug. 7, 1932; s. Alexander William and Ruth (Kennedy) S.; m. Norma Dorothy Pfeiffer, Aug. 6, 1955; children: William, Anne. BSME, U. Rochester, 1954; MBA in Indsl. Adminstrn., Carnegie-Mellon U., 1959. CPA, Pa. Engr. GM, Rochester, N.Y., 1954-57; cons. Price Waterhouse, Pitts., 1959-65; v.p. corp. planning Contel, Bakersfield, Calif., 1965-76; staff exec. ITT Europe, Brussels, 1976-79; v.p. corp. devel. GE Calma, Santa Clara, Calif., 1979-83; exec. v.p., chief fin. officer Certel Inc., Fremont, Calif., 1983-85; pres., cons. Stewart Assocs., Los Gatos, 1985-88; v.p. fin., chief fin. officer Diversified Software Systems, Morgan Hill, 1988—; instr. U. Pitts., 1963-65; adj. prof. Boston U.-Brussels MBA Program, 1978-79. With U.S. Army, 1955-57. Mem. AICPA, IEEE, Nat. Assn. Accts. Home: 173 Altura Vista Los Gatos CA 95030 Office: Diversified Software System 18630 Sutter Blvd Morgan Hill CA 95037

STEWART, DONALD PAUL, insurance company executive; b. Memphis, Oct. 27, 1933; s. Carl W. and Josephine (McBride) S.; m. Patricia M. Patterson, Nov. 19, 1955 (dec. 1985); m. Constance J. Frick, Feb. 7, 1987; children: Robert Bloom, Vicki Harcourt. BS, Memphis State U., 1955. Br. claims mgr. Crawford & Co., Atlanta, Miami, Fla., Kansas City, Mo., Cheyenne, Wyo. and Davenport, Iowa, 1956-71; v.p. claims Universal Underwriters Ins. Co., Overland Park, Kans., 1972-88; mgr. area claim Dodson Ins. Group, Kansas City, Mo., 1988—. Mem. Wyo. Claims Assn. (pres. 1969), Kansas City Claims Mgrs. Coun. (pres. 1984), Kansas City Met. Anti Vehicle Crime Assn. (pres. 1987, chmn. bd. dirs. 1988—). Republican. Presbyterian. Office: Dodson Ins Group 9201 State Line Kansas City MO 64114

STEWART, E(DWARD) NICHOLSON, investment management executive; b. Bronxville, N.Y., Sept. 28, 1940; s. Edward Nicholson and Helen (Davis) S.; student Hamilton Coll., 1959-62; B.A., New Sch. Social Research, 1965; m. Mary Patricia Hunter, Aug. 8, 1964; children—Pamela Fowler, Wendy Hunter. Dir. membership Investment Co. Inst., N.Y.C., 1968; v.p. Lord, Abbett & Co., N.Y.C., 1969-74; pres. Trevor Stewart Burton & Jacobsen Inc., N.Y.C., 1974—. Trustee Hackley Sch., 1971-87, treas., 1972-87, v.p., 1980-87; pres. Hackley Alumni Assn., Inc., 1967-69. Mem. Am. Soc. Pension Actuaries (assoc.), Investment Assn. N.Y., 1975-84, USN League (Marine Corps com., N.Y. 1986—), Naval War Coll. Found. (assoc.), U.S. Naval Inst., Delta Kappa Epsilon. Republican. Clubs: Union League (bd. govs. 1985-87, vice chmn. 1987, pres. 1989—) (N.Y.C.); Pendennis (Louisville); Sleepy Hollow Country (Scarborough, N.Y.), Melrose (Daufuskie Island, S.C.). Co-founder, editor Hackley Rev., 1963-68. Home: 102 Crest Dr Tarrytown NY 10591 Office: 90 Park Ave New York NY 10016

STEWART, EDWARD WILLIAM, laboratory administrator; b. Cardiff, Md., Sept. 17, 1931; s. Edward William and Mary Eleanor (Williams) S.; m. Nancy Moore Stewart, June 12, 1954; children—Gail, William, Sandra. B.S. in Chemistry, Washington Coll., Chestertown, Md., 1952; M.S. in Metall. Engring, Lehigh U., Bethlehem, Pa., 1954. With E.I. duPont de Nemours & Co., Inc., 1954—; dist. mgr. E.I. duPont de Nemours & Co., Inc. (Pigments Dept.), New Eng., 1967-70, Chgo., 1970-73; dir. Chestnut Run Lab., Wilmington, Del., 1973-83, mktg. dir., 1983—. Served with AUS, 1956-57. Mem. Nat. Paint and Coatings Assn., Sigma Xi. Office: EI DuPont CAP Mktg Div Wilmington DE 19898

STEWART, FREDERICK A., medical electronics executive; b. Phila., May 30, 1952; s. Frederick Amon and Elizabeth (Bridges) S.; m. Margaret M. MacLeod, May 28, 1977; children: Katherine Alice, Ryan Frederick. Bio med. technician Beth Israel Hosp., Boston, 1972-73, Mass. Gen. Hosp., Boston, 1973-76; field engr. Physio-Control Corp., Boston, 1976-77; field supr. Physio-Control Corp., Cherry Hill, N.J., 1977-78; dist. mgr. Physio-Control Corp., Atlanta, 1978-80, regional mgr., 1980-85; mgr. ops. Physio-Control Corp., Redmond, Wash., 1985-86, mgr. nat. tech. service, 1986-87, dir. tech. services, 1987—. Mem. Assn. for Advancement of Med. Instrumentation, Nat. Assn. Field Service Mgrs. Office: Physio-Control Corp 11811 Willows Rd Redmond WA 98073

STEWART, GARY ALLEN, turf specialist; b. Youngstown, Ohio, Mar. 1, 1941; s. Raymond K. and Erna (Color) S.; m. Stephanie A. Stein, Apr. 26, 1965; children: Bradford Allan, Michael Chadwick. BS, Ohio State U., 1964. Tech. asst. Ohio Agri. Research and Devel. Ctr., Columbus, 1965-69; project leader O.M. Scott Co., Marysville, Ohio, 1969-72; rep. O.M. Scott Co., 1972-79; turf specialist Diamond Shamrock Corp., Cleve., 1979-86; pres. Turf & Nursery Supply, Inc., Canton, Ohio, 1986—. Mem. North Ohio PGMS, Pa. Turfgrass Council, North Ohio Golf Course Supt. Assn. (bd. dirs. 1973-75), Ohio Turfgrass Found. (trustee 1980-85, pres. 1985), Alpha Gamma Rho. Office: Turf & Nursery Supply Inc 3709 Columbus Rd NE Canton OH 44705

STEWART, GEORGE TAYLOR, insurance executive; b. N.Y.C., Dec. 29, 1924; s. Fargo Calvin and Berthe Adelle (Pelleton) S.; m. Bonnie Elizabeth Myers, Sept. 14, 1946; children: Diane Barbara Stewart Carrington, Susan Gail Stewart Dupuis. A.B., Wesleyan U., Conn., 1947. Analyst Geyer & Co., Inc., 1948-54, Shelby Cullom Davis & Co., 1954-56; v.p. Blyth & Co., Inc., N.Y.C., 1956-65; chmn., chief exec. officer 1st Colony Life Ins. Co., Lynchburg, Va., 1965—; dir. Media Gen., Crestar Fin. Corp., Am. Mayflower Life Ins. Co. N.Y., Ethyl Corp. Author: Investing in American Business, 1964. Pres. The Corp. for Jefferson's Poplar Forest; chmn. bd. trustees Lynchburg Coll., 1977—, Salvation Army; trustee Va. Found. for Indep. Colls. Served as ensign USN, 1943-46, PTO. Recipient Lynchburg Bi-Centennial award, 1976, Lynchburg Pro Opera Civica award, 1982, award Navy League, 1981, Outstanding Businessman award Lynchburg Coll. Bus. Sch., 1982. Mem. Lynchburg C. of C. (pres.), N.Y. Soc. Security Analysts. Republican. Presbyterian (elder). Clubs: Metropolitan (N.Y.C.), Drug and Chemical (N.Y.C.); California (Los Angeles); Boonsboro Country (Lynchburg) (bd. dirs.), Piedmont, Waterfront. Office: First Colony Life Ins Co PO Box 1280 Lynchburg VA 24505

STEWART, IRELAND J., auto parts manufacturing company executive; b. Belfast, No. Ireland, Dec. 17, 1934; came to U.S., 1966, naturalized, 1976; s. Irel and Margaret S. B.S. in Econs, Queen's U., Belfast, 1963; M.B.A. (scholarship 1967, fellowship 1968), U. Chgo., 1968. Asst. dean students Grad. Sch. Bus., U. Chgo., 1968-69; mgmt. cons. Boston Cons. Group, 1969-72; with Maremont Corp., Chgo., 1972—; v.p. internat. div. Maremont Corp., 1976-78, sr. v.p. internat., 1978-80, exec. v.p., 1980—; chmn. bd. Gabriel S. Africa Ltd.; pres. Gabriel Internat. Co.; sec. Gab. de Mex.; dir. Gabriel of India, Fric-Rot, S.A.I.C., Argentina, Gabriel Europe Inc., Van Der Hout & Assos., Can., Gabriel de Venezuela. Author papers in field. Mem. Am. Mgmt. Assn., Am. Arbitration Assn., Automotive Market Research Council (Spl. award 1976), Brit. Inst. Mgmt., Mid-west Planning Assn., Chgo. Assn. Commerce and Industry, Machinery and Equipment Mfrs. Assn., Internat. Bus. Council Mid-Am. (pres. 1984), Chgo. Council Fgn. Relations. Home: 552 Lincoln Ave Glencoe IL 60062 Office: Maremont Corp 250 E Kehoe Blvd Carol Stream IL 60188

STEWART, JAMES CHARLES, II, insurance agent; b. Spartanburg, S.C., Jan. 2, 1952; s. James Charles Sr. and Thelma (Robertson) S.; m. Nancy Eleanor Bates, Dec. 23, 1973; children: James Ryan, Matthew Daniel, Megan Eleanor. BS in Mktg., U. S.C., 1974; CLU, Am. Coll., Bryn Mawr, Pa., 1983. Mgr. I-26 Svc. Ctr., Woodruff, S.C., 1975; agt. Ind. Life Ins. Co., Jacksonville, Fla., 1975-84, N.Y. Life Ins. Co., N.Y.C., 1984—. Coach So. Spartanburg Youth Athletic Assn., Walnut Grove, S.C., 1984—, treas., 1986-87, pres. 1987-88; asst. chief Hobbysville Vol. Fire Dept., Woodruff, S.C., 1978; treas. Cavins (S.C.) Dem. precinct, 1978; campaign mgr. Stewart for Ho. of Reps. 1978, 80, co-campaign mgr. Hines for Senate, 1980. Named

Hon. Constable, S.C. Gov. Jim Edwards, 1975, S.C. Gov. R.W. Riley, 1979, S.C. Gov. Carrol A. Campbell, 1987; named Eagle Scout, Boy Scouts Am., 1967; named Div. Co-Winner, Grand Strand Fishing Rodeo, Myrtle Beach, S.C., 1987. Mem. Spartanburg Life Underwriters Assn. (pres. 1988-89), Life Ins. Leaders S.C., Am. Soc. CLU's, Nat. Assn. Life Underwriters, Gentlemen's Actuarial Soc. S.C. (charter mem.), U. S.C. Alumni Assn., Gamecock Club, Sand Hills Aero Club, Masons (Master Cavins-Wooodruff club 1983), Ruritan Clyhb (charter pres. 1988), Delta Sigma Pi, Sigma Pi Mu (various offices). Home: Fox Fire Apts 501 Camelot Dr #92 Spartanburg SC 29301 Office: NY Life Ins Co 156 Magnolia St Ste 5 Spartanburg SC 29301

STEWART, JAMES E., cement and concrete manufacturing company executive. Student, Shattuck Mil. Sch., Washington and Lee U., Pomona Coll. With Nat. Bldg. Ctrs., prior to 1971, Lone Star Industries Inc. (merged with Nat. Bldg. Ctrs.), Greenwich, Conn., 1971, 1971—, chmn. exec. com., 1971-73, chmn., chief exec. officer, 1973—, also bd. dirs.; former chmn. exec. com., vice chmn. Bangor Punta Corp. Served with U.S. Army, 1941-45. Office: Lone Star Industries Inc 1 Greenwich Pla Greenwich CT 06836 *

STEWART, JAMES GATHINGS, insurance company executive; b. Fort Wayne, Ind., Oct. 5, 1942; s. Gathings and Mary (Sieber) S.; m. Janet Kartalia, Feb. 19, 1966; children: John, David, Mitchell, Rebecca. B.A., DePauw U., 1964; M.A.S., U. Mich., 1965. Various fin. positions Conn. Gen. Life Ins. Co., Hartford, Conn., 1966-77; v.p. Conn. Gen. Life Ins. Co., 1977-82; exec. v.p., chief fin. officer CIGNA Corp., Phila., 1983—. Fellow Soc. Actuaries; mem. Am. Acad. Actuaries. Republican. Office: Cigna Corp One Logan Sq Philadelphia PA 19103

STEWART, JAMES MICHAEL, investment broker; b. Roswell, N.Mex., Aug. 11, 1952; s. Vernon Guy and Katherine Juanita (Steele) S.; m. Elaine Ann Faust, Sept. 29, 1984. BA, U. N.Mex., 1978. Ptnr. Doberman Films, Albuquerque, 1977-78; chmn. U. N.Mex. Film Commn., Albuquerque, 1977-79; pres. Union Cinema Co., Albuquerque, 1979-81; investment broker Am. Western, Albuquerque, 1981-82, Chesley & Dunn, Albuquerque, 1982-83, A.G. Edwards, Albuquerque, 1983—; cons. Z Bucks, Inc., Albuquerque, 1984—, Charto Graphics, Albuquerque, 1980—; bd. dirs. Union Cinema, Albuquerque. Producer, dir. Roswell Neon, 1979, (film) The Mirror, 1979. Mem. Nat. Assn. Securities Dealers (registered rep.), N.Y. Stock Exchange (registered rep.), Nob Hill Assn., U. N.Mex. Alumni Assn., Nat. Pub. Radio Support Assn. Club: A.G. Edwards Crest.

STEWART, J(AMES) TODD, financial executive; b. Las Vegas, Nev., Aug. 17, 1954; divorced; 1 child, Donald. BBA, U. Las Vegas, 1978. CPA, Nev. Acct. Kafoury, Armstrong & Co., Las Vegas, 1978-87; chief fin. officer Whiskey Pete's Casino, Inc., Jean, Nev., 1987—. Mem. AICPA, Nev. Soc. CPA's, Nat. Assn. Accts., Las Vegas C. of C. (bd. dirs. 1988—), Las Vegas Jaycees (pres. 1987-88). Home: PO Box 27314 Las Vegas NV 89126-1314 Office: Whiskey Pete's Casino PO Box 93718 Las Vegas NV 89193-3718

STEWART, JAMIE B., JR., banker; b. Elkhart, Kans., June 30, 1944; s. Jamie B. and Gudrun (Gudmundsdottir) S.; m. Deborah Clark, June 18, 1966; children: Rachel, Jamie III. BA, Dartmouth Coll., 1966; MBA, Harvard U., 1972; JD, Suffolk U., 1979. V.p. corp. fin. Bank Boston, 1972-85; exec. v.p. corp. banking Crocker Bank, San Francisco, 1985-86; sr. v.p. investment banking Bank Am., San Francisco, 1986-88; exec. v.p. corp. fin. Mellon Bank, Pitts., 1988—. Lt. USN, 1966-70. Office: Mellon Bank Corp One Mellon Bank Ctr Pittsburgh PA 15258

STEWART, JOHN MURRAY, banker; b. Summit, N.J., Apr. 2, 1943; s. Robert John Stewart and Mary Catherine (Grabhorn) Stewart Yoder; m. Sandra Meyers Frazier, Feb. 26, 1966; children: Jennifer Bricar, Catherine Dorothy. BA, U. Va., 1965; MBA, NYU, 1983. Trust officer, v.p. Bankers Trust Co., N.Y.C., 1965-82, Morgan Guaranty Trust Co., N.Y.C., 1982-83; mgr., pres., dir. Morgan Trust Co. Fla., Palm Beach, 1983—; bd. dirs. J.P. Morgan Pvt. Fin. Corp., Palm Beach. Campaign chmn. Palm Beach Community Chest, 1985, 86; vestryman Bethesda By the Sea Ch., Palm Beach, 1986—, treas., 1986-87. Mem. Fla. Bankers Assn. (chmn. trust bus. devel. com. 1989, planning commn.), N.Y. State Bankers Assn. (mem. trust bus. devel. com. 1978-82). Clubs: N.Y. Yacht (N.Y.C.); Palm Beach Sailing; Soc. Four Arts; Monmouth Boat (Red Bank, N.J.), Sailfish of Fla. (Palm Beach). Office: Morgan Trust Co Fla NA 350 Royal Palm Way Palm Beach FL 33480

STEWART, JOSEPH TURNER, JR., diversified company executive; b. N.Y.C., Apr. 30, 1929; s. Joseph Turner and Edna (Pride) S.; m. Carol Graham, Aug. 7, 1954; children—Lisa D., Alison D. S.B. with honors, U.S. Mcht. Marine Acad., 1951; M.B.A., Harvard U., 1954. Systems analyst Warner Lambert Co., Morris Plains, N.J., 1954-56; budget supr. internat. Warner Lambert Co., 1956-60, asst. div. controller consumer products group, 1960-62, div. controller group, 1962-66; dir. adminstrn. and fin. Warner Lambert Co. (Proprietary Drug div.), 1966; dir. Warner Lambert Co. (Lactona Products div.), 1967; controller Beech-Nut subs. Squibb Corp., N.Y.C., 1968; v.p. fin. Beech-Nut subs. Squibb Corp., 1968-71, v.p. planning, corp. staff parent corp., 1971-79, v.p. fin. and planning parent co., 1979-82, sr. v.p. corporate affairs, 1982—; also bd. dirs.; bd. dirs. Gen. Am. Investment Corp. Pres., mem. exec. council Harvard U. Bus. Sch. Assn., 1971-76, mem. vis. com. Bus. Sch., 1976-82; bd. dirs. CARE, 1977-80; trustee Tax Found., 1985; commr. N.J. State Commn. on Income and Expenditures, 1985-88; mem. adv. com. Grad. Sch. Indsl. Adminstrn. Carnegie Mellon U., 1986. John Hay Whitney Opportunity fellow, 1952-54; recipient Alumni Outstanding Profl. Achievement award U.S. Mcht. Marine Acad., 1971. Club: Harvard (N.Y.C.). Office: Squibb Corp PO Box 4000 Princeton NJ 08540

STEWART, JUDITH UNDERWOOD, securities analyst; b. Auburn, N.Y., Aug. 5, 1955; d. Martha (Davenport) Heard; m. Gordon Bennett Stewart III, June 13, 1981; 1 child, Gordon Bennett IV. BA, Wellesley Coll., 1977; student, MIT, 1975-77; MBA, Wharton Grad. Sch. Bus., 1979. Corp. fin. assoc. Shearson Loeb Rhoades Inc., N.Y.C., 1979-80; asst. treas. Chase Manhattan Bank, N.Y.C., 1980-83; mgr. Citicorp, N.Y.C., 1983-85; rating officer Standard & Poor's Corp., N.Y.C., 1985—. Contbr. writer: Standard & Poor's Structured Finance Criteria, 1988. Mem. Wharton Grad. Bus. Sch. Club N.Y., Jr. League City of N.Y. (chmn. provisional com. winter ball 1984, vice-chmn. and treas. career awareness com. 1985-87), Am. Cancer Soc. N.Y. Div. (jr. com. 1982), French Library (jr. com. 1978), Soc. Mayflower Descendants, Nat. Soc. Colonial Dames, DAR Mary Washington Coll. chpt., New Eng. Soc. City of N.Y., Princeton Club N.Y., Wellesley Coll. Club N.Y., U. Pa. Club N.Y.C.

STEWART, KEITH WALKER, infosystems specialist; b. Bluefield, W.Va., Oct. 21, 1950; s. Kemper Fergerson and Virginia (Hornbarger) S.; m. Cathryn Ann Canary, nov. 3, 1984; 1 child, Kevin Michael. BBA, Marshall U., 1973; MBA, Va. Poly. Inst. and State U., 1979. With IBM Corp., 1979—; field mgr. Nat. Svc. div. IBM Corp, Norfolk, Va., 1981-83, br. mgr., 1983-85; mgr. svc. bus. Nat. Svc. div. IBM Corp, McLean, Va., 1985-86, mgr. nat. accts., 1986-88, program mgr. strategy devel. and implementation Fed. Svc. Bus., 1988—. Rotary. Republican. Methodist. Home: 2 Symphony Woods Ct Silver Spring MD 20901

STEWART, MARY ANN, educator; b. Decherd, Tenn., Sept. 7, 1936; d. Joseph Francis and Mildred Edrice (Goodman) Knies; m. John Ebb Stewart, Aug. 23, 1969. BS in Bud. Edn., U. Tenn., 1972, MS in Edn., 1976. Cert. profl. sec. Adj. instr. U. Tenn., Chattanooga, 1975-76; assoc. prof. Chattanooga State Tech. Community Coll., 1976—, head bus. admstrn. dept., 1978-82; conductor seminars in field. Editor: Managing for Productivity, 1986. Assoc. probation officer Juvenile Ct., Chattanooga, 1970-72. Recipient Wall St. Jour. award, 1972, Nat. Bus. Edn. award, 1972. Mem. Tenn. Bus. Edn. Ass. (pres. 1982), So. Bus. Edn. Assn., Nat. Bus. Edn. Assn., Profl. Secs. Internat., U. Tenn. Alumni Assn. Avocations: travel, basketball, reading, walking.

STEWART, PAUL ARTHUR, pharmaceutical company executive; b. Greensburg, Ind., Sept. 28, 1955; s. John Arthur and Alberta Jeannette (Densford) S.; m. Susan Rhodes, Dec. 20, 1975; 1 child, John Rhodes; BS, Purdue U., 1976; MBA, Harvard Bus. Sch., 1987. Grad. asst. Purdue U., West Lafayette, Ind, 1977; asst. treas. Stewart Seeds, Inc., Greensburg, Ind., 1977-82, sec., treas., 1982-84; cons. The Boston Cons. Group, Inc., Chgo., 1986; founder, owner PASCO Group, mgmt. and computer cons., aircraft leasing, 1979-87; mgr. bus. planning-agrichems. Eli Lilly & Co., Indpls., 1987-88, dist. sales mgr. agrichems., 1989—. Mem. Greensburg-Decatur County Bd. of Airport Commrs., 1980-85, pres., 1980, 81, 83; mem. Decatur County Data Processing Bd., 1982-85. Mem. Alpha Gamma Rho. Republican. Presbyterian. Office: Eli Lilly & Co Lilly Corp Ctr Indianapolis IN 46285

STEWART, S. JAY, chemical company executive; b. Pineville, W.Va., Sept. 18, 1938; s. Virgil Harvey and Lena Rivers (Repair) S.; m. Judith Ann Daniels, June 3, 1961; children: Julie Annette, Jennifer Amy, Steven Jay. BS in Chem. Engring., U. Cin., 1961; MBA, W.Va. U., 1966. Various positions in engring., mfg., mktg. Monsanto Co., St. Louis, 1961-73; dir. mktg. Ventron Corp. subs. Morton Thiokol, Inc., Beverly, Mass., 1973-77, gen. mgr., 1977-79; pres. Dynachem Corp. subs. Morton Thiokol, Inc., Santa Ana, Calif., 1979-82; group v.p. Thiokol Corp., Newtown, Pa., 1982; group v.p. splty. chems. Morton Thiokol, Inc., Chgo., 1983-86, pres., chief oper. officer, 1986—, also bd. dirs. Mem. corp. adv. coun. Coll. Engring. Cin. U, 1988, Coun. Fgn. Rels. (Chgo com. Chgo. coun.), Anchor Cross Soc. Rush Presbyn.-St. Luke's Med. Ctr., 1987—, Charles McMicken Soc. U. Cin. Found., Northwestern U. Assocs., 1988—, Founders Coun. Field Mus. Nat. History, Chgo., 1987—; chmn. leadership group dept. orthopedic surgery Rush Presbyn.-St. Luke's Med. Ctr., 1987—; trustee Rush Presbyn.-St. Luke's Med. Ctr., Chgo., 1987—. Recipient Disting. Alumnus award U. Cin., 1984. Mem. Am. Chem. Soc., Am. Inst. Chem. Engrs., Chem. Mfrs. Assn. (bd. dirs. 1984-87), Comml. Devel. Assn., Assn. Governing Bds. Univs. and Colls. Republican. Methodist. Office: Morton Thiokol Inc 110 N Wacker Dr Chicago IL 60606

STEWART, STEPHEN THOMPSON, graphics company executive; b. N.Y.C., July 13, 1954; s. John Larry and Margaret (Thompson) S.; m. Jean Ann Valerio, Feb. 6, 1977; children; John Raymond, Scott Richard, Stephanie Jean. BBA, Bucknell U., 1976; Cert. of Mgmt.; spl. studies, Harvard U., 1984. Sales rep. Westvaco Corp., N.Y.C. and Chgo., 1976-78; sales rep., mgr. New Eng. region Lehigh Press Inc., Chgo., Boston, 1978-86; pres. Colotone Graphics, Inc., Branford, Conn., 1986-89; sr. v.p. Colotone, Inc., Branford, 1989—. Mem. Book Builders of Boston, Chgo. Book Clinic. Republican. Congregationalist. Home: 50 Randi Dr Madison CT 06443 Office: Colotone Inc 83 School Ground Rd Branford CT 06405

STEWART, TERRY LYNN, insurance broker; b. Sioux City, Iowa, Sept. 22, 1943; s. Fay P. and Clara (Morman) S.; m. Janice E. Rastede (div. 1977); children: Tammy L. Stewart Bogema, Dotty S.; m. Nancy L. Grubb, Apr. 5, 1986. BA, Ferris State U., 1969. Bookkeeper Bolstien Creative Printers, Sioux City, 1964-66; salesperson Ohio Nat. Life Ins. Co., S. Sioux City, Nebr., 1966-67, Employers Ins. Wausau, Jackson, Mich., 1969-72; salesperson, v.p. Hall and Kennedy Ins. Co., Jackson, Mich., 1972-84; pres., owner Stewart Ins. Agy., Inc., Kalamazoo, Mich., 1984—. Mem. Greater Kalamazoo Ind. Ins. Agents Assn. (pres. 1987—), Kalamazoo C. of C. Club: Kalamazoo Country. Lodge: Rotary. Office: Stewart Ins Agy Inc 616 W Centre Ave Portage MI 49081

STEWART-CLARKE, JOHN ERNEST, security company executive; b. Great Yarmouth, Norfolk, Eng., Dec. 30, 1928. Ed. Coll. Arts, Great Yarmouth, Coll. of Arts, Kidderminster, Ministry of Def., London, U. Bristol; M.A. in Human Resource Devel. Mgr., Gould Ltd., Norwich, Eng., 1945-49; prodn. exec. J. Corbett & Sons Ltd., Stourport, Eng., 1949-61; sales exec. Atkinsons Ltd., Bristol, 1961-70; cons. Securicor, London, 1970-80; dir. Security Tng. Ltd., Cheltenham, 1980-84; project exec., dir. Wirebird, Gloucester, Eng., 1984—; lectr. in aviation security, 1978—, Stroud (England) Coll. (formerly Mid Glos Tech. Coll.), 1987—; lectr. exec. protection, indsl. espionage prtotection, human resource and risk mgmt.; broadcaster bus. affairs, 1985—; dir. M.V.C., Gloucester, Stewart-Clarke Assocs., Gloucester, Alert Security Confs. Ltd., 1980-84, Marnat Mktg. Ltd., 1980-83; lectr. in human resource devel., bus. math., bus. law, fin. modelling; cons. P&M Office Equipment, Gloucester, 1984—. Contbr. articles to profl. jours. Chmn. Crime Prevention Panel, Gloucester, 1979—, Police and Community Com., Gloucester, 1982; vice chmn. Gloucester Conservative Assn., 1987—. Named Tng. Officer Grade A with honors, Rd. Transport Tng. Bd., London, 1978. Fellow Inst. Dirs., Inst. Indsl. Mgrs., Brit. Inst. Mgmt.; mem. Acad. Security Educators and Trainers (charter). Mem. Ch. of England. Clubs: Constitution (Bristol, Eng.); Conservative (Gloucester). Avocations: music; philately; ballroom dancing; writing. Home: The Willows, Crickley Hill Witcombe, Gloucestershire GL3 4UQ, England

STEYER, ROY HENRY, retired lawyer; b. Bklyn., July 1, 1918; s. Herman and Augusta (Simon) S.; m. Margaret Fahr, Feb. 21, 1953; children: Hume R., James P., Thomas F. A.B. with honors in Govt. and Gen. Studies, Cornell U., 1938; LL.B. cum laude, Yale U., 1941. Bar: N.Y. 1941, various fed. cts. from 1947, U.S. Supreme Ct. 1955. Assoc. firm Sullivan & Cromwell, N.Y.C., 1941-42, 46-52, ptnr., 1953-88, ret., 1988. Trustee N.Y.C. Sch. Vol. Program, 1974-78. Served to lt. USNR, 1943-46. Mem. Am. Coll. Trial Lawyers, ABA (chmn. com. on antitrust problems in internat. trade antitrust sect. 1959-62), N.Y. State Bar Assn., Assn. of Bar of City of N.Y. (chmn. com. on trade regulation 1962-64), Order of Coif, Century Assn., India House, Phi Beta Kappa, Phi Kappa Phi. Home: 112 E 74th St New York NY 10021

STIBBE, AUSTIN JULE, accountant; b. St. Paul, Mar. 29, 1930; s. Austin Julius and Agnes Dorothea (Delaney) S.; m. Mary Elizabeth King, May 29, 1952; children: Anne Marie, Craig Jule, David King, Karen Lee. BBA in Acctg., U. Minn., 1952. CPA, Minn., Wis. Tax acct. Ernst & Ernst, Mpls., 1955-60; corp. tax mgr. Econs. Lab., Inc., St. Paul, 1960-65; audit mgr. Coopers & Lybrand, Mpls., 1965-74; v.p. Wilkerson, Guthmann & Johnson, Ltd., St. Paul, 1974—. exec. officer Twin Cities Squadron, U.S. Naval Sea Cadet Corps, Mpls., 1974-80; bd. dirs., treas., mem. Twin Cities Council Navy League, 1970—, pres. 1979-81, treas. 1975-79, 81—; mem. adv. council to U. Minn. Dept. Acctg., Mpls., 1983-86; bd. dirs., chmn. audit com. St. Paul Area Council Chs., 1985-87; mem. adv. bd. Headwaters Soc., 1987-88. Lt. USN, 1952-55. Mem. Am. Inst. CPA's, Minn. Soc. CPA's, Nat. Assn. Accts., St. Paul Athletic Club, St. Paul Pool and Yacht Club, Masons (chmn. audit com. 1975-85), Rotary (asst. treas. 1986-87, treas. 1987-88). Republican. Presbyterian. Home: 1439 Cherry Hill Rd Mendota Heights MN 55118 Office: Wilkerson Guthmann & Johnson Ltd 1300 Norwest Ctr Saint Paul MN 55101

STICK, THOMAS HOWARD FITCHETT, architect; b. Balt., Feb. 28, 1938; s. Gordon M.F. and Anne Howard (Fitchett) S.; m. Rosalie Wade Reynolds, June 5, 1959 (div. Apr. 1982); children: H. Edward M., Alexander W., David F.; m. Joyce C. Yeargin, July 25, 1982 (div. 1989); stepchildren: Richard F. Carr Jr., Leah W. Carr, V. Maria Carr, John N. Carr; m. Alyce C. Cushing, 1989. BA in Psychology, Yale U., 1960; postgrad. Md. Inst., 1962, U. Pa. Grad. Sch. Architecture, 1964. Registered architect, Pa., Md., Del., N.J., Va., Maine, N.Y., D.C., Mass., N.H., N.C., Vt.; cert. recommendation Nat. Council Archtl. Registration Bds. Architect, Vincent G. Kling & Ptnrs., Phila., 1964-74, B.J. Hoffman & Assocs., Berwyn, Pa., 1974; ptnr. Grim & Stick, Ardmore, Pa., 1975-77; prin. Stick Assocs., Gladwyne, Pa., 1977-80; corp. architect Gino's Inc., King of Prussia, Pa., 1980-81; mgr. constrn. adminstrn. Ballinger Co., Phila., 1981-83; sr. constrn. claims cons. MDC Systems Corp., Phila., 1984-85; chief architect Day & Zimmermann Inc., Phila., 1985—, discipline mgr. 1987—; v.p. F-S Found., 1986—, also bd. dirs. Photographer in one-man show Eastern Camera Gallery, 1972. Mem. AIA, Pa. Soc. Architects, Bldg. Ofcls. and Code Adminstrs. Internat., Constrn. Specifications Inst., Nat. Fire Protection Assn., Soc. War of 1812 (sec. 1977-82), Soc. of Cincinnati, Soc. Colonial Wars, SR, Descs. of Lords of the Md. Manors, Mil. Order of Loyal Legion of U.S., Huguenot Soc., Am. Clan Gregor Soc., St. Andrew's Soc. of Balt., St. George's Soc. of Balt., Zeta Psi. Republican. Episcopalian. Clubs: Merion Cricket (Haverford, Pa.); Yale . Lodge: Sovereign Mil. Order of Temple of Jerusalem (comdr.), Sovereign Order of St. John of Jerusalem (Knight of Justice), Knights Malta. Home: 1501 Monticello Dr Gladwyne PA 19035 Office: Day & Zimmermann Inc 1818 Market St Philadelphia PA 19103

STICKEL, MONIKA MICHAELA, advertising manager; b. Sydney, N.Y., Jan. 11, 1961; d. Dieter Reinholt and Lilo (Heyer) S. BSBA in Philosophy, Lebanon Valley Coll., 1983. Asst. to mktg. dept. AT&T, Crystal City, Va., 1983; asst. to mktg. tng. mgrs. U.S. Lines, Inc., Cranford, N.J., 1984; cons. Am. Internat. Life Assurance Co. subs. Am. Internat. Group, N.Y.C., 1984-85, supr., 1985-86; competitive analyst advanced merchandising div. Mut. N.Y. Fin. Svcs., Teaneck, N.J., 1986-88; advt. mgr. Blue Cross and Blud Shield of N.J., 1988—.

STICKLER, PETER BLEIER, banker; b. Chgo., Nov. 6, 1952; s. Lawrence Reinstine and Eleanor Frances (Bleier) S.; m. Nancy Joan Buerckholtz, Sept. 11, 1982; 1 child, Michael Lawrence. BA in Econs., DePauw U., 1974; MBA, Emory U., 1976. Various positions Peat, Marwick, Mitchell, Chgo., 1976-82; chief acctg. officer UnibancTrust Co., Chgo., 1982-84, v.p., controller, 1984-85, v.p., cashier, 1985-87, treas., 1985—, sr. v.p., cashier, 1987—. Mem. Ill. Cert. Pub. Accts. Soc., Am. Inst. CPA's, Stanhope Square Condominium Assn. (treas. 1984-85), Beta Gamma Sigma. Republican. Club: Conquest Investment Ltd. (pres. 1986-87). Office: UnibanCorp Inc 223 S Wacker Dr Chicago IL 60606

STICKLEY, JOHN LEON, textile executive; b. Cambridge, Mass., Sept. 6, 1902; s. Leonard and Hanora Annie (Saint) S.; m. Jennie Williamson McMichael, Apr. 5, 1928; children: John Leon Jr., Georgiana Stickley Meginley, Nancy Virginia Stickley Grant. Student, Lowell Textile Inst., 1921-22. Asst. mgr. William Whitman Co., Inc., Charlotte, N.C., 1923-27, mgr. South and S.E. regions, 1927-48; pres. John L. Stickley & Co., Inc., Charlotte, 1948-68, chmn., 1968—; bd. dirs. Engraph, Inc., Atlanta, Rossville (Ga.) Mills, Inc., Camelot Industries, Charlotte, Chromatex, Inc., West Hazelton. Pres. Internat. Assn. Lions Clubs, Oakbrook, Ill., 1956-57. Served with Mass. N.G., 1921-23. Recipient medal of honor Republic of Chile, 1956, Man of Yr. award City of Charlotte, 1956, medal of honor Republic of Ecuador, 1957. Republican. Baptist. Clubs: Union League (N.Y.C.); Charlotte City, Myers Park (Charlotte). Lodges: Masons, Shriners. Home: 2270 Sharon Ln Charlotte NC 28211 Office: 5672 International Way Charlotte NC 28226

STICKNEY, ALBERT, III, banker; b. N.Y.C., Oct. 29, 1944; s. Albert and Eleanor Elizabeth (Herrick) S.; B.A., Harvard U., 1967; m. Susan Kent King, Apr. 27, 1974; children—Katharine Kent, Anna Noyes. Asst. treas. Chase Manhattan Bank, N.Y.C., 1973-75, 2d v.p., 1975-77; asst. v.p. Irving Trust Co., 1977, v.p., 1977-81; adminstrv. v.p., group head Marine Midland Bank, N.Y.C., 1982—. Served to lt. USNR, 1967-70. Mem. Ducks Unltd. (chmn. N.Y.C.). Clubs: Harvard, Anglers (N.Y.C.); Bedford Golf and Tennis, The Leash, Fishers Island Country, Hammonasset Fishing, Ducks Unltd. Home: West Ln Pound Ridge NY 10576 Office: 140 Broadway New York NY 10015

STIER, PATRICIA COOPER, oil and gas executive; b. Alexandria, La., Apr. 4, 1943; d. William Byron and Dorothy Vera (Dees) Cooper; m. Ronald Whitmore Stier, Nov. 20, 1970; 1 child, John Byron. BS in Math., Northwestern State U., Natchitoches, La., 1965. Systems analyst refining div. Exxon USA, Baton Rouge, 1966-70, process engr. refining div., 1971-72, systems supr. refining div., 1973-77, refinery energy coordinator refining div., 1978-79, computer ops. supr., 1980-83; project mgr. ICS dept. Exxon USA, Houston, 1984, supr. performance and planning ICS dept., 1984-86, head software/tech. support ICS dept., 1986, head applications tech services ICS dept., 1986—. Active Gov.'s Council on Energy Conservation, Baton Rouge, 1982-83, Mayor's Council on Transp., 1981-82; pres. Network, Baton Rouge, 1979-80, Nantucket Homeowners Assn., Houston, 1984—; com. mem. Westhaven Citizens Assn., Houston, 1986—; campaigner J. Bennett Johnston for U.S. Senator, La., 1976-83. Named finalist Outstanding Bus. Women of Yr., Baton Rouge, 1982. Mem. Assn. Computing Machinery, IEEE, Soc. Women Engrs. (charter mem. La. chpt.). Office: Exxon USA 800 Bell St Houston TX 77001

STIGLER, GEORGE JOSEPH, economist, educator; b. Renton, Wash., Jan. 17, 1911; s. Joseph and Elizabeth (Hungler) S.; m. Margaret Mack, Dec. 26, 1936 (dec. Aug. 1970); children: Stephen, David, Joseph. BBA, U. Wash., 1931; MBA, Northwestern U., 1932; PhD, U. Chgo., 1938; ScD, Carnegie Mellon U., 1973, U. Rochester, 1974, Helsinki Sch. Econs., 1976, Northwestern U., 1979; LLD, Brown U., 1980. Asst. prof. econs. Iowa State Coll., 1936-38; asst. prof. U. Minn., 1938-41, asso. prof., 1941-44, prof., 1944-46; prof. Brown U., 1946-47; prof. econs. Columbia, 1947-58; Walgreen prof. Am. instns. U. Chgo., 1958—, dir. ctr. study economy and the state, 1977—; lectr. London Sch. Econs., 1948; vice-chmn., bd. dir. Securities Investor Protection Corp., 1971-74; bd. dir. Chgo. Bd. Trade, 1980-83, Lynde and Harry Bradley Found., 1986—, Duff-Phelps Selected Utility Fund, 1987—. Author: Production and Distribution Theories, 1940, The Theory of Price, 1946, Trends in Output and Employment, 1947, Five Lectures on Economic Problems, 1949, (with K. Boulding) Readings in Price Theory, 1952, Trends in Employment in the Service Industries, 1956, (with D. Blank) Supply and Demand for Scientific Personnel, 1957, The Intellectual and the Market Place, 1964, 84, Essays in the History of Economics, 1965, The Organization of Industry, 1968, (with J.K. Kindahl) The Behavior of Industrial Prices, 1970, The Citizen and the State, 1975, The Economist as Preacher, 1982, The Essence of Stigler, 1986, Memoirs of an Unregulated Economist, 1988; Editor: Chgo. Studies in Political Economy, 1988; editor Jour. Polit. Economy, 1972—, Chicago Studies in Political Economy, 1988; contbr. articles to profl. jours. Mem. atty. gen.'s. com. for study anti-trust laws, 1954-55; mem. Blue Ribbon Def. Panel.; trustee Carleton Coll. Recipient Nobel prize in econs., 1982; Guggenheim fellow, 1955; fellow Ctr. for Advanced Study in Behavioral Scis., 1957-58; recipient Nat. Medal of Sci., 1987. Fellow Am. Acad. Arts and Scis., Am. Statis. Soc., Econometric Soc., Nat. Acad. Sci.; mem. Am. Econ. Assn. (pres. 1964), Royal Econ. Soc. Am. Philos. Soc., History of Econs. Soc. (pres. 1977), Mt. Pelerin Soc. (pres. 1977-78). Office: U Chgo GSB 1101 E 58th St Chicago IL 60637

STIGLITZ, JOSEPH EUGENE, economics educator; b. Gary, Ind., Feb. 9, 1943; s. Nathaniel David and Charlotte (Fishman) S.; m. Jane Hannaway, Dec. 23, 1978; children—Siobhan, Michael, Edward, Julia. B.A., Amherst Coll., Mass, 1964; D.H.L., Amherst Coll., 1974; Ph.D. in Econs., MIT, 1966; M.A. (hon.), Yale U., 1970. Prof. econs. Cowles Found., Yale U., New Haven, 1970-74; vis. fellow St. Catherine's Coll., Oxford, Eng., 1973-74; prof. econs. Stanford U., Calif., 1974-76, 88—; Oskar Morgenstern dist. fellow Inst. Advanced Studies Math., Princeton, N.J., 1978-79; Drummond prof. polit. economy Oxford U., Eng., 1976-79; prof. econs. Princeton U., 1979—; cons. World Bank, Washington, Bell Communications Research. Editor: Jour. Econ. Perspectives, 1986—, Mathematica; formerly co-editor: Jour. Pub. Econs.; Am. editor Rev. of Econ. Studies, 1968-76; assoc. editor Am. Econ. Rev., 1968-76, Energy Econs., Managerial and Decision Econs.; mem. editorial bd. World Bank Econ. Rev. Recipient John Bates Clark award Am. Econ. Assn., 1979; Guggenheim fellow, 1969-70. Fellow Econometric Soc. (council); mem. Am. Econ. Assn. (exec. com. 1982-84, v.p. 1985), Am. Acad. Arts and Scis. Home: 139 Broadmead Princeton NJ 08540

STILES, GAYNOR ALAN, health facility administrator, consultant; b. Springfield, Mo., July 23, 1960; s. Gaynor E. and Bess (Jones) S.; m. Shawn L. Anglin, Apr. 9, 1988. BBA in Gen. Bus. Adminstrn., Sam Houston State U., 1982. Pres., prin. GA Enterprises, Houston, 1979-81; v.p. Green Things, Inc., Houston, 1981-82; br. mgr. GELCO, Inc., Houston, 1982-84; mgr. adminstrv. svcs. Howard Hughes Med. Inst., San Diego, 1982—; cons., San Diego, 1982—. Active Rep. Nat. Com., Nob Hill Assn. Mem. Am. Mgmt. Assn., Biotech. Purchasing Mgmt. Assn. (sec.), Alpha Lambda Delta, Alpha Chi. Mem. Ch. of Christ. Office: Howard Hughes Med Inst 10010 N Torrey Pines Rd La Jolla CA 92037

STILES, MARY ANN, lawyer; b. Tampa, Fla., Nov. 16, 1944; d. Ralph A. and Bonnie (Smith) S. AA, Hills Community Coll., 1973; BS, Fla. State U., 1975; JD, Antioch Sch. Law, 1978. Bar: Fla. 1978. Legis. analyst Fla. Ho. of Reps., Tallahassee, 1973-74, 74-75; intern U.S. Senate, Washington, 1977; v.p., gen. counsel Associated Industries Fla., Tallahassee, 1978-84; assoc. Deschler, Reed & Crichfield, Boca Raton, Fla., 1980-81; founding ptnr. Stiles, Allen & Taylor, P.A., Tampa and Tallahassee, Fla., 1982—; bd. dirs. Univ. Community Physicians Assn., Tampa, Six Stars Devel. Corp., Tampa, Uniphy Corp., Tampa, Uniphy Diagnostics Inc., Tampa. Author: Workers'

Compensation Law Handbook. Bd. dirs., sec. Hillsborough Community Coll. Found., Tampa, 1985-87; bd. dirs. Hillsborough Area Regional Transit Authority, Tampa, 1986—; bd. dirs. Boys and Girls Club of Tampa, 1986—. Mem. ABA, Fla. Bar Assn., Hillsborough County Bar Assn., Hillsborough Assn. Women Lawyers, Fla. Assn. Women Lawyers, Fla. Women's Network, Athena Soc., Hillsborough County Seminole Boosters (past pres.). Democrat. Baptist. Club: Tiger Bay (Tampa) (pres.). Office: 315 Plant Ave Tampa FL 33606 also: 216 S Monroe Tallahassee FL 30302

STILES, THOMAS BEVERIDGE, II, investment banking executive; b. Easton, Pa., Oct. 4, 1940; s. Ezra Martin and Vivien (de Fay) S.; m. Elaine Ann Patyk, July 2, 1966 (div. Oct. 1980); children—Thomas Beveridge III, Jonathan Ezra; m. Barbara Toll Alexander, Mar. 7, 1981. B.A., Yale U., 1963; M.B.A., Harvard U., 1968. Vice pres. Laird, Inc., N.Y.C., 1968-73; sr. v.p., dir. Smith Barney Harris Upham and Co., Inc., N.Y.C., 1973-82; exec. v.p., dir. E.F. Hutton & Co. Inc., N.Y.C., 1982-87; chmn., chief exec. officer SLH Asset Mgmt. Co., N.Y.C., 1988—; dir., treas. Cedar Lawn Cemetery, Paterson, N.J., 1973—; dir. Bernstein Macauley, N.Y.C. Served to 1st lt. M.I., U.S. Army, 1963-66. Fellow Fin. Analysts Fedn.; mem. N.Y. Soc. Security Analysts. Republican. Presbyterian. Club: Spring Lake Bath and Tennis (N.J.). Office: SLH Asset Mgmt Co 31 W 52nd St New York NY 10019

STILL, HAROLD HENRY, JR., engineering company executive; b. Beggs, Okla., Sept. 17, 1925; s. Harold Henry and Hannah Jane (Blackburn) S.; student U. Calif., Santa Barbara, 1946-49, USC, 1949-50, UCLA, 1975-76. Sr. specification writer Welton Becket and Assocs., Los Angeles, Calif., 1968-71; dept. head Maxwell Starkman and Assos., Beverly Hills Architect, 1971-72; project mgr. May Dept. Stores Co., Los Angeles, 1972-74; sr. coordinator C.F. Braun and Co., Alhambra, Calif., 1975—, on leave, constrn. mgr. spl. project Runhau Evans Runhau Assocs., Riverside, Calif., 1978-79; architect, project adminstr. developing May Co. Dept. Store Complex for firm Leach Cleveland, Hyakawa, Barry & Assocs.; project mgr. constrn. Lyon Assocs., Inc.; pvt. cons. in constrn. practices, 1983—. Served with U.S. Army, 1943-45. Decorated Purple Heart. Mem. Construction Specifications Inst., ASTM. Republican. Congregationalist. Home: 503 Beverly Ave Paso Robles CA 93446

STILLMAN, ALFRED WILLIAM, JR., design/support engineer; b. Biloxi, Miss., Sept. 11, 1942; s. Alfred William and Marie Ann (Hengen) S.; AA, Am. River Coll., 1966; BSEE, Calif. Poly. State U., 1970, BS in Applied Math., 1970, MS in Applied Math., 1973; ME in Indsl. Engring., Tex. A. and M. U., 1976; postgrad. elec. engring. N.J. Inst. Tech., 1977; PhD in Mgmt., Calif. Coast U., 1984; children: Shannon Lynn, Laura Marie. Cert. profl. logistician, instr. Calif. Community Colls. Engring. intern U.S. Army Material Command, Texarkana, Tex., 1973-75, electronic systems staff maintenance engr., Ft. Monmouth, N.J., 1975-77, mil. tactical data system integrated logistics support mgr. Office of Project Mgr., ARTADS, Ft. Monmouth, 1977-78, tactical ADP ILS Mgr., ILS dir. CORADOM, Ft. Monmouth, 1978-79, engring. mgr. regional dist. office Office of Project Mgr., Firefinder, Hughes Aircraft Co., Fullerton, Calif., 1979-80; prof. systems acquisition mgmt. Dept. Def. Systems Mgmt. Coll., Ft. Belvoir, Va., 1980-82; integrated logistics support engring. specialist, advanced systems div. Northrop Corp., Pico Rivera, Calif., 1982-83; program mgmt. rep. space systems group Rockwell Internat., Downey, Calif., 1983-84; product assurance project engr. Space Sta. Systems div. Rockwell Internat., Downey, Calif., 1984-85; mgr. product support, 1985-86; sr. mgr. ILS, Amex Systems, Inc., Compton, Calif., 1986—; bd. dirs. ILS NavCom Def. Electronics Inc., El Monte, Calif.;pres. AWS Assocs. Calif., Inc., Huntington Beach, 1983—; corp. v.p., div. pres. HOPE Assocs., Inc., Huntington Beach, 1983—. With USAF, 1962-66. Mem. IEEE, Am. Mgmt. Assn., Am. Inst. Indsl. Engrs. (sr.) Soc. Logistics Engrs. (sr.), Am. Def. Preparedness Assn., Am. Security Council, Acacia, Tau Beta Pi. Presbyterian. Home: 10115 Valley Blvd Ste 263 El Monte CA 91731 Office: 4323 Arden Dr El Monte CA 91731

STILLMAN, ANNE WALKER, fashion designer; b. Amsterdam, The Netherlands, Apr. 15, 1951; came to U.S., 1953; d. Edmund and Mary (Gwathmey) S. Student Barnard Coll., 1968-72. Pres., designer Sofia & Anne, Ltd., Bethel, Ct. and N.Y.C., 1978—; designer Sofia & Anne Sportknit, 1983—, Sofia & Anne Children's Wear, 1985—, Go Cashmere for L'Zinger by Sofia & Anne, 1986. Office: Sofia & Anne 37 W 39th St New York NY 10018

STILLMAN, LARRY BARR, paper company executive, entrepeneur; b. Salt Lake City, Oct. 27, 1941; s. Tilden Barr and Lydia (Osguthorpe) S.; m. Mari Liane Wood, Nov. 20, 1968; children: Shaney, Tyler, Ashley, Allison, Cassidy, Blakely. BS, U. Utah, 1969. Pres., founder Apple Beer Corp., Salt Lake City, 1965—; group v.p. Dixon Paper Co., Denver, 1969—; pres. La Bathtique, Salt Lake City, 1971—; mng. gen. ptnr. Hexad Investment, Salt Lake City, 1980—; mem. adv. council Scott Paper Co., Phila., 1983—. Author: Women in Business, 1981. Mem. exec. com. Com. of 100, Salt Lake City. Recipient Silver Addy award Am. Advt. Fedn., 1984. Mem. Delta Sigma Pi (pres. 1968). Office: Dixon Paper Co 3700 W 1987 S Salt Lake City UT 84130

STILLMAN, STEPHANIE MATUSZ, computer contract company executive; b. Middlesex County, N.J., July 16, 1946; d. William Stephan Matusz and Mary Jane (Van Horn) Falger; m. Dennis Edison DeMercer, Aug. 22, 1970 (div. 1977); m. Richard Alan Stillman, May 10, 1980; 1 child, Taylor Edison. B.A., Moravian Coll., 1968. Tchr., Hawaii Edn. Dept., Kohala, 1968-71; acct. exec. with various ins. agys., N.J., 1975-79; div. mgr. E.T. Lyons & Assoc., New Brunswick, N.J., 1979-80; sr. personnel adminstr. Systemp, Inc., New Brunswick, 1980-84; br. mgr. Officeforce, Inc., Cedar Knolls, N.J., 1984; pres., chief exec. officer The Resource Group, Inc., Cambridge, Mass., 1985—. Bd. dirs., pres. Rutgers-Livingston Day Care Ctr., Piscataway, N.J., 1978-80. Mem. Cambridge C. of C., Smaller Bus. Assn. New Eng., Data Processing Mgmt. Assn., Assn. Women in Computing. Republican. Avocations: skiing; travel. Office: The Resource Group Inc PO Box 2327 Cambridge MA 02238

STILSON, ROBERT MINOTT, controller; b. Bridgeport, Conn., July 24, 1941; s. Minott A.O. and Mary Edith (Williams) S.; m. Susanne Whitaker, Nov. 29, 1969; children: Laura, David. BS in Indsl. Adminstrn., Yale U., 1964; MBA in Acctg., U. Bridgeport, 1975. CPA, Conn. Sr. acct. Coopers & Lybrand, New Haven, 1967-72; controller Broadstreet Communications, New Haven, 1972-74, Turnkey Systems, Norwalk, Conn., 1974-76, Paper Sales, Darien, Conn., 1976-78; audit mgr. Milton Friedberg Smith & Co., Bridgeport, 1978-82; co-owner Stern & Stern, CPA's, Bridgeport, 1982; controller, treas. Nutmeg Fin., Norwalk, 1982-85; controller Acctg. Mgmt. Co., N.Y.C., 1985—; pvt. practice acctg., Fairfield, Conn., 1972—. Mem. Rep. Town Meeting, Fiarfield, 1978-82, bd. fin., 1982-87. Lt. USN, 1964-67. Mem. Inst. CPA's. Republican. Congregationalist. Home: 103 Orchard Hill Dr Fairfield CT 06430 Office: Acctg Mgmt Co 667 Madison Ave New York NY 10021

STILWELL, JOHN PIERCE, II, financial planner, underwriter; b. Doylestown, Pa., May 26, 1927; s. Samuel B. Stilwell and Marjorie (Barbiere) Justice; m. Mary Angel, May 21, 1960; 1 child, Anne Bush. BBA, U. Ga., 1951; postgrad., George Washington U., 1952; grad., Am. Coll., Bryn Mawr, Pa., 1972, Coll. Fin. Planning, Denver, 1987. CLU, cert fin. planner. Field underwriter HL Fin. Group (formerly Home Life N.Y.), Orlando, Fla., 1963—. Contbr. articles to profl. jours. Treas. Orange County Rep. Exec. Com., 1968, Orange County unit Am. Cancer Soc., 1976, crusade chair, 1989; vice chmn. bd. trustees Orlando Gen. Hosp., 1980-83; vestryman Cathedral Ch. of St. Luke, Orlando, 1987—, Jr. warden, 1989—. Mem. Inst. Cert. Fin. Planners (nat. and regional v.p. 1981-85, polit. involvement chair 1988-89), Nat. Assn. Life Underwriters (co-chair host com. conv. 1987), Fla. Assn. Life Underwriters (sr. coun., bd. dirs.), Cen. Fla. Assn. Life Underwriters (pres. Orlando chpt. 1979-80), Nat. Assn. Security Dealers (registered rep. series 7 and 63), Marco Hunting and Fishing Club (pres. 1984-87), Toastmasters (pres. Orlando club 1968, 74, named Disting. Toastmaster 1971), Kiwanis (pres. Cen. Orlando club 1984-85), Civitan (v.p. Cen. Orlando club 1967). Home: 530 Central East Ave Ste 1201 Orlando FL 32801 Office: HL Fin Group 2301 Lucien Way Ste 285 Maitland FL 32751

STIMLEY, SHERMAN EDMOND, lawyer; b. Chgo., Aug. 2, 1944; s. Charles E. and Bernice (Allen) S.; m. Ruth Ann McGee, Aug. 2, 1968; children: Daryl, Courtland. BSCE, Kans. State U., 1967; JD, M of Pub. Policy, Harvard U., 1974. Tex. 1974. Chem. engr. Exxon, U.S.A., Houston, 1967-70; atty. Vinson & Elkins, Houston, 1974-84; sole practice Houston, 1985—. Adv. dir. Houston Symphony, 1982—; mem. com. Pres. Task Force Thurgood Marshall Sch., Houston, 1983—; bd. dirs. Buffalo Bayou Task Force, 1984—, Mcpl. Employees Pension System., 1988—. Mem. ABA, Nat. Bar Assn., Tex. Bar Assn., Houston Bar Assn., Nat Assn. Bond Lawyers, Govt. Fin. Officers Assn. Home: 7602 Hopewell Houston TX 77071 Office: 1980 Post Oak Blvd Ste 2200 Houston TX 77056

STIMPSON, JOHN H., insurance company executive; b. Milo, Maine, Nov. 7, 1926; s. Don H. and Dorrice A. (Clark) S.; m. Valerie B. Smith, June 13, 1953; children—Kevin, Karen, Kimberly. B.A., U. Maine, 1950; M.B.A., U. Pa., 1952. C.L.U. Exec. v.p. N.Y. Life Ins. Co., N.Y.C. Trustee Am. Coll., Bryn Mawr, Penn. Home: 42 W Clinton Ave Irvington-on-Hudson NY 10533 Office: NY Life Ins Co 51 Madison Ave New York NY 10010

STINE, ANNA MAE, publishing company executive; b. Monongahela, Pa., Sept. 6, 1938; d. Carlton Lee and Martha Regina (Graham) S.; B.S. in Edn., Calif. State Coll. (Pa.), 1959; elem. prin. cert. Duquesne U., 1962, masters in elem. edn., 1962; cert. reading specialist U. Pitts., 1963, postgrad., 1963-65. Tchr., student tchr. supr. Upper St. Clair Sch. Dist., Pitts., 1959-65; nat. lang. arts cons. Macmillan Pub. Co., N.Y.C., 1965-75, regional mgr., Riverside, N.J., 1975-78; v.p., nat. sales mgr.East, Macmillan Pub. Co., 1978—. Recipient Robert Hann award Macmillan Pub. Co., 1965, Donald McGrew award 1967, NJRA award, 1985. Mem. Internat. Reading Assn., NEA, Regional Edn. Service Agy., Keystone Reading Assn., Upper St. Clair Tchrs. Orgn. (pres.). Republican. Roman Catholic. Home: 215 Haddon Commons Haddonfield NJ 08033

STINE, JACK WILLIAM, utility company executive; b. Ft. Wayne, Ind., June 1, 1924; s. Kenneth Swaim and Ethel I. (Baxter) S.; m. Barbara L. Eversole, Apr. 15, 1950; children: Jean Trenam Stine Creasbaum, Thomas Kenneth. B.S.E.E., Purdue U., 1949; M.B.A., Northwestern U., 1956. Registered profl. engr., Ind. Vice pres. customer service, purchasing No. Ind. Pub. Service Co., Hammond, 1977-82, v.p. div. ops, 1982-85, sr. v.p., chief operating officer, 1985-87, exec. v.p., chief operating officer, 1987—; bd. dirs. First Bank of Whiting. Served with U.S. Army, 1943-45, ETO. Mem. Ind. Econ. Forum (pres. 1969), Ind. Gas Assn. (bd. dirs.), Ind. Electric Assn. (chmn. 1986-87). Republican. Presbyterian. Home: 1148 MacArthur Blvd Munster IN 46321 Office: No Ind Pub Svc Co 5265 Hohman Ave Hammond IN 46320

STINER, FREDERIC MATTHEW, JR., accounting educator, consultant; b. Balt., Apr. 4, 1946; s. Frederic Matthew and Bertha Moulton (Kidd) S.; m. Martha Susan Scharper, June 21, 1969; children—Frederic Matthew, John Alexander, James Michael, Katherine Elizabeth. M.S., U. Del., 1969; M.B.A., Marshall U., 1972; Ph.D., U. Nebr., 1976. C.P.A., W.Va. Staff acct. Goodman & Co., C.P.A.s, Norfolk, Va., 1973-74; sr. acct. Snyder, Grant, Muehling, C.P.A.s, Lincoln, Nebr., 1977-78; asst. prof. Iowa State U., Ames, 1978-79, U. Md., College Park, 1979-82; assoc. prof. acctg. U. Del., Newark, 1982—; cons. NSF, Washington, 1980-82. Contbr. articles to Jour. of Accountancy and other acad. and profl. jours.; editorial adv. bd. Jour. Accountancy, 1981-86. Mem. Am. Inst. C.P.A.s, W.Va. Soc. C.P.A.s Home: 109 Autumn Horseshoe Newark DE 19702 Office: U Del $S1Coll Bus and Econs Newark DE 19716

STINSON, DEANE BRIAN, auditor; b. Ottawa, Ont., Can., Nov. 12, 1930; s. Earl Minto and Clara Edna (Acres) S.; chartered acct. Inst. Chartered Accts. Ont., 1954; m. Patricia Ann Paynter, Aug. 25, 1956; children—Steven Wayne, Brian Richard, Andrew Alan. With Arthur A. Crawley & Co., Ottawa, 1949-54; staff chartered acct. Thorne, Ernst & Whinney, Sault Ste. Marie, Ont., 1958-59, audit partner, 1960-79, mng. ptnr., 1980-86, sr. exec. ptnr., 1986-88; ptnr. in charge Pannell Kerr MacGillivray, Sault Ste. Marie, Ont., 1988— ; mem. Ont. Regional Mgmt. Council, 1980-86, mng. ptnr. 1980-86; adv. bd. Guaranty Trust Co., 1975—; dir., pres. and chief exec. officer Sault Investments Ltd., Betwin Investments, Inc., Tille Investments Ltd., Tolstar Mgmt. Co., 1978-83; pres. and chief exec. officer Agate Venture (No. and Ea.) Inc., Venture Capital Corp.; mem. cultural task force Sault Ste. Marie, 1977-79. Fellow Inst. Chartered Accts. Ont.; mem. Can. Inst. Chartered Accts. (pres. chpt. 1965), Can. Tax Found. Progressive Conservative. Anglican. Club: Rotary (pres. 1978). Home: 15 Atlas Ave, Sault Ste Marie, ON Canada P6A 4Z2 Office: PO Box 1437, Sault Saint Marie, ON Canada P6A 6N2

STINSON, STANLEY THOMAS, systems engineer; b. Dothan, Ala., Dec. 17, 1961; s. Leonis and Betty Lois (Harrison) S.; m. Sharin B. Clark, Aug. 25, 1984; 1 child, Sarah Ashley. AS in Computer Sci., Enterprise State Jr. Coll., 1982; BSBA cum laude, Troy State U., 1984; MBA, Samford U., 1989. Fin. systems engr. NCR Corp., Birmingham, Ala., 1984-87; sr. systems specialist Systematics Inc., Birmingham, 1987-88, systems engr., 1988—. Mem. Am. Mgmt. Assn. (assoc.), Assn. MBA Execs., Am. Assn. Individual Investors, Gamma Beta Phi. Republican. Baptist. Home: 5132 Scenic View Dr Birmingham AL 35210 Office: Systematics Inc 2222 2nd Ave N Birmingham AL 35203

STINSON, WILLIAM W., transportation executive; b. Toronto, Ont., Can., Oct. 29, 1933; children: Janet, Margo, James. B.A., U. Toronto, 1954; diploma in bus. adminstrn., U. W. Ont., 1955. Various positions Can. Pacific Rail, Toronto, 1950-66, supt. Toronto div., 1966-69; asst. gen. mgr. ops. and maintenance Pacific Region Can. Pacific Rail, Vancouver, 1969-71; gen. mgr. ops. and maintenance Pacific Region Can. Pacific Ltd., Vancouver, 1971, gen. mgr. ops. and maintenance Eastern Region, 1972-74; asst. v.p. ops. and maintenance Can. Pacific Rail, Montreal, 1974-76; v.p. ops. and maintenance Can. Pacific Ltd., Montreal, 1976-79; exec. v.p. Can. Pacific Rail, Montreal, 1979-81; pres., dir. Can. Pacific Ltd., Montreal, 1981-85, pres., chief exec. officer, 1985—, chmn., pres., chief exec. officer, dir., 1989—; bd. dirs. Can. Pacific (Bermuda) Ltd, Can. Pacific Enterprises Ltd., Can. Pacific Express and Transport Ltd., Gen. Motors of Can. Ltd., Can. Pacific Forest Products Ltd., Can. Maritime Ltd., Harris Bankcorp Inc., Harris Trust and Savs. Bank, Marathon Realty Co. Ltd., Pan Can. Petroleum Ltd., Sun Life Assurance Co. Can., AMCA Internat. Corp., AMCA Internat. Ltd., Soo Line Corp, ROBCO Inc., Bank of Montreal, Laidlaw Transp. Ltd., PWA Corp. Mem. Mt. Royal Country Club, Mt. Bruno Country Club. Office: Can Pacific Ltd, PO Box 6042 Sta A, Montreal, PQ Canada H3C 3E4

STIPE, EDWIN, III, mechanical contracting company executive; b. Easton, Pa., Aug. 22, 1931; s. Edwin and Rose Mildred (Blackburn) S. AAS, SUNY-Farmingdale, 1958; m. Jean Elizabeth Boyer, Aug. 14, 1954; children: Daniel McMichael, Kelly Jean. Chief engr. Joseph E. Biro & Assocs., Easton, 1958-61; with ITT Nesbitt, 1961-72, br. mgr., Boston, 1967-70, N.Y.C., 1970-72; v.p. Byko-Stipe Assocs., Morristown, N.J., 1972-77; pres. Edwin Stipe, Inc., Easton, 1973—, Thermogetics, Inc., Morristown, 1977-80. Served with USN, 1951-55. Mem. ASHRAE, Assn. Energy Engrs. Lutheran. Clubs: Pomfret (Easton); Water Gap Country (Delaware Water Gap, Pa.); Harker's Hollow Golf (Belvedere, N.J.). Lodge: Kiwanis. Home: 1 Tanglewood Rd Easton PA 18042 Office: 420 W Lincoln St Easton PA 18042

STIREWALT, JOHN NEWMAN, coal company executive; b. Springfield, Ill., July 14, 1931; s. Newman Claude and Genevieve (Henton) S.; m. Joan Marie McCarthy, Dec. 26, 1957; children: Genevieve, Janice, James, Christopher. AB, U. Miami, 1953; grad. execs. program Carnegie-Mellon U. Grad. Sch. Indsl. Adminstrn., 1978. Salesman Kaiser Aluminum, Indpls., 1957-63; dist. sales mgr. Consol. Coal, Detroit, 1963-67, Cleve., 1967-73, gen. sales mgr., Detroit, 1973-76, asst. v.p., 1976-79; v.p. mktg. Youghiogheny and Ohio Coal Co., St. Clairsville, Ohio, 1979-81; v.p. mktg. Crown Coal and Coke Co., Pitts., 1981-85, Arch Mineral, 1985—; exec. reservist U.S. Dept. Interior emergency solid fuels adminstrn., 1971. Council chmn. Cub Scouts, Highland, Mich., 1976; mem. Mich. Energy Task Force, 1966; pres. bd. trustees Wheeling Country Day Sch., 1980-84; bd. trustees Wheeling Symphony. Served in U.S. Army, 1954-56. Mem. Sigma Chi. Presbyterian. Club: Bellerive Country. Home: 1009 Arlington Oaks Terr Chesterfield MO 63017 Office: Arch Mineral Corp Saint Louis MO 63102

STIRITZ, WILLIAM P., food company executive; b. Jasper, Ark., July 1, 1934; s. Paul and Dorothy (Bradley) S.; m. Susan Ekberg, Dec. 4, 1972; children—Bradley, Charlotte, Rebecca, Nicholas. B.S., Northwestern U., 1959; M.A., St. Louis U., 1968. Mem. mktg. mgmt. staff Pillsbury Co., Mpls., 1959-62; account mgmt. staff Gardner Advt. Co., St. Louis, 1963—; with Ralston Purina Co., St. Louis, 1963—; pres., chief exec. officer, chmn. Ralston Purina Co., 1981—; bd. dirs. Angelica Corp., Ball Corp., Boatmen's Bancshares, Inc., Gen. Am. Life Ins. Co., May Dept. Stores, S.C. Johnson & Son. Bd. dirs. Washington U., St. Louis. Served with USN, 1954-57. Mem. Grocery Mfrs. Assn. (dir.). Office: Ralston Purina Co Checkerboard Sq Saint Louis MO 63164

STITLEY, JAMES WALTER, JR., food manufacturing executive; b. York, Pa., May 23, 1944; s. James Walter and Geraldine Salome (Horn) S.; BS in Chemistry, Millersville U., 1970; m. Nancy Jane Miller, Dec. 29, 1972. Med. technician York Hosp., 1962-66; research biochemist Carter-Wallace, Inc., Cranbury, N.J., 1970-75; mgr. Ward Labs. div. Ward Foods, East Orange, N.J., 1975-77; mgr. tech. services Pepperidge Farm, Inc., Norwalk, Conn., 1977-86; dir. tech. devel. Am. Inst. Baking, Manhattan, Kans., 1986-88; dir. baking and cereal sci. research and biscuit product devel. internat., Campbell Soup Co., Camden, N.J., 1988—; cons. biochemistry and toxicology. Asst. scoutmaster Boy Scouts Am. Nominee Presidential Merit award Campbell Soup Co., 1982; mem. Am. Chem. Soc., Am. Mgmt. Assn., Am. Assn. Cereal Chemists, Am. Inst. Baking (ednl. adv. com. 1978—), Instrument Soc. Am. (asso. dir.-food industry liaison), AAAS, Am. Astron. Research Group, York Astron. Soc. (v.p. 1960). Contbr. articles to profl. jours.; patentee in field. Home: 13 Iredell Ln Mullica Hill NJ 08062 Office: Campbell Soup Co Campbell Pl Camden NJ 08103-1799

STITT, DAVID MOFFAT, finance company executive; b. Middletown, Ohio, July 12, 1942; s. Arthur Brown and Dorothy Brewster (Moffat) S.; divorced; children: C. Gregory, Tracy M., Christopher M., Jonathan D. BS in Fin., Miami U., Oxford, Ohio, 1980. CLU, chartered fin. cons. Exec. dir. Jr. Achievement, Middletown, 1969-78, Hamilton, Ohio, 1977-78; v.p., gen. mgr. Security Strassberger, Inc., Middletown, 1978-81; sr. v.p. Fin. Planning Cons., Inc., Middletown, 1981-87; fin. planner Gem Savs. Corp., Dayton, Ohio, 1987-88; dir. fin. planning Ptnrs. Capital, Centerville, Ohio, 1988—; Co-author (software): ProPlan. Author: Proplan, 1985, How to Select Hardware for Financial Planning, 1987. Pres. Middletown Young Reps., 1972; chmn. Concerned Citizens, Middletown, 1987. Mem. Internat. Assn. Fin. Planning (bd. dirs. Dayton chpt. 1983—), Inst. Cert. Fin. Planners, Fin. Forum., Am. Soc. CLU and Chartered Fin. Cons., Middletown Assn. Life Underwriters (pres. 1967-68), Masons, Shriners, Lions (pres. Middletown chpt. 1977, zone chmn. 1977-78, Guiding Lion award), KT, Middletown Club, High Twelve Club (Middletown, pres. 1985). Episcopalian. Home: 513 Orchard St Middletown OH 45044

STITT, DONALD PAUL, controller; b. Pitts., June 21, 1954; s. Edward Allan and Elizabeth Cecelia (Reismeyer) S. BBA in Acctg., Duquesne U., 1976. CPA, Pa. Acct. then audit mgr. Arthur Young and Co., Pitts., 1976-86; dir. acctg. then asst. controller Bradford (Pa.) Hosp., 1987, controller, 1987—. Mem. Am. Inst. CPA's, Pa. Inst. CPA's, Healthcare Fin. Mgmt. Assn. Republican. Presbyterian. Club: Penn Hills Country (Bradford). Home: 118 Congress St Apt B Bradford PA 16701-2260 Office: Bradford Hosp 116-156 Interstate Pkwy Bradford PA 16701

STIVERS, WILLIAM CHARLES, forest products company executive; b. Modesto, Calif., June 22, 1938; s. William P. and Helen Louise (Cummings) S.; m. Karen L. Gaspar, Aug. 6, 1961; children: William, Gregory, Michael, Kristy, Kelly, John, Jeffrey. B.A., Stanford, 1960; M.B.A., U. So. Calif., 1963; certificate, Pacific Coast Sch. Banking, 1969; grad., Advanced Mgmt. Program, Harvard U., 1977. Asst. cashier, asst. v.p., v.p. First Interstate Bank, San Francisco and Los Angeles, 1962-70; finance mgr. treas. dept. Weyerhaeuser Co., Tacoma, 1970; asst. treas. Weyerhaeuser Co., 1971, treas., 1972—, v.p., 1980—; treas. Weyerhaeuser Real Estate Co., 1970; dir. Protection Mut. Ins. Co., Park Ridge, Ill., Republic Fed. Savs. & Loan, GNA Corp., Gt. No. Ins. Annuity Corp.; dir., pres. S&S Land and Cattle Co. Trustee St. Francis Hosp., Tacoma; bd. dirs. Center Study Banking and Fin. Markets U. Wash., Seattle. Mem. Financial Execs. Inst.

STOBBS, JOHN PAUL, financial analyst; b. Alton, Ill., Mar. 26, 1955; s. William B. and Lena F. (Tillinghaust) S.; divorced; children: Atticus J., Thackeray L., August W. AA, Lewis and Clark Community Coll., Godfrey, Ill., 1976; BS in Acctg., So. Ill. U., 1979, MBA, 1988. CPA. Staff acct. C.J. Schlosser & Co., Alton, 1977-79, Arthur Andersen & Co., St. Louis, 1979-81; supr. taxes and property Olin Corp., East Alton, Ill., 1981-85, sr. internal auditor, 1985-87; dir., fin. analyst Stifel Fin. Corp., St. Louis, 1987—. Mem. Alton Little Theater. Mem. AICPA, Delta Sigma Pi. Office: Stifel Fin Corp 500 N Broadway Saint Louis MO 63102

STOCHEL, WALTER ROBERT, JR., small business owner; b. Plainfield, N.J., Dec. 18, 1959; s. Walter Robert and Louise Ann (Hollingshead) S. Student, Middlesex County Coll., Edison, N.J., 1985—. Prin. Walter Stochel Landscaping, Edison, 1977-85; equipment operator Hale-Built Constrn., Edison, 1983-86; pres. Victorian Plainfield Inc., Plainfield, N.J., 1985—; bd. dirs. Wild Things Inc., Plainfield. Copyright Victorian Plainfield, 1985. Vol. Dwyer for Congress, Edison, 1980, 82, 84, 86. Mem. Metuchen Regional Hist. Soc., Sons Am. Legion, Cen. Jersey C. of C. Office: Victorian Plainfield Inc PO Box 5021 Plainfield NJ 07061

STOCKDALE, GAYLE SUE, wholesale florist, ornamental horticulturalist; b. Crawfordsville, Ind., July 3, 1955; d. Robert Lavern and Faye Louise (Ball) S. Student St. Joseph's Coll., 1973-74, Purdue U., 1974; BS in Tech. Horticulture, Eastern Ky. U., 1977. Reclamation foreman South East Coal Co., Irvine, Ky., 1977-79; asst. mgr., landscape designer Evergreen Garden Ctr., Lexington, Ky., 1979-80; asst. mgr., landscape designer, head grower South Trail Garden Ctr., Ft. Myers, Fla., 1980-82; floral designer Flowers by Jean, Cape Coral, Fla., 1982-83; floral designer, landscape designer Bev's Greenhouse, Owenton, Ky., 1983-84; co-owner Royalty Wholesale, Lexington, 1984-87, Imperial Fowers and Gifts, Lexington, 1988—. Contbr. poetry to anthologies. Sponsor, Save the Children, Korea, 1986. Moose lodge scholar, 1973. Mem. Nat. Assn. Female Execs. Democrat. Roman Catholic. Avocations: reading, movies, exercise. Office: Imperial Flowers & Gifts 393 Waller Ave Lexington KY 40504

STOCKDALE, RONALD ALLEN, grocery company executive; b. Aplington, Iowa, Apr. 28, 1934; s. Carl Robert and Mildred Louise (Gerhardt) S.; m. Carol Ann Hermeier, Dec. 23, 1956; children—Bryan Ross, Russell Allen, Paul Roderick. B.S. in Commerce, State U. Iowa, 1958. C.P.A. Auditor Arthur Andersen & Co., Chgo., 1958-63; controller Super Food Services, Bellefontaine, Ohio, 1963-66, Mountain States Wholesale Co., Boise, Idaho, 1966-69; exec. v.p., sec. West Coast Grocery Co., Tacoma, 1969-82, pres., chief operating officer, 1982-87, chief exec. officer, 1988—; bd. dirs. Profit Sharing Council Am., Chgo., 1977-83. Trustee Humana Hosp.-Tacoma, 1985-87, San Francisco Theol. Sem., 1987—; mem. adv. bd. Sch. Bus. Adminstrn., Pacific Luth. U., 1986—. Served with U.S. Army, 1954-56. Mem. AICPA, Fin. Execs. Inst. Republican. Presbyterian. Home: 2720 Soundview Dr W Tacoma WA 98466 Office: W Coast Grocery Co PO Box 1834 Tacoma WA 98401

STOCKER, DONALD ALLAN, financial and real estate executive; b. L.A., May 13, 1958; s. Clement R. and Jane Elizabeth (Streur) S.; m. Catherine Trautt, Aug. 3, 1987. BBA, Calif. State U., Long Beach, 1980. Sales mgr. Ranch RV Sales, Irvine, Calif.; pres. Exec. Trust Deed Svcs., Fullerton, Calif.; v.p. Foreclosure Adminstrn., Inc., Fullerton; broker Marcus & Millichap, Sacramento, Calif. Mem. North Orange County Computer Club. Republican. Home: 10 Sand Pebble Ct Sacramento CA 95831 Office: Marcus & Millichap 1500 River Park Rd #100 Sacramento CA 95815

STOCKER, HAROLD LE ROY, marketing design company executive; b. Zion, Ill., Aug. 19, 1929; s. John Wesley Sr. and Emma Della (Robinson) S.; m. Marjorie Anne Maki, Aug. 22, 1956; children: Julie Ann, Jill Marie, Anna Lisa. Student, Denver U., 1952; grad., Am. Acad. Art, 1956; student, Inst. Design, Chgo., 1961, Art Inst. Chgo., 1962. Designer Fieldcrest Mills, Zion, 1948-51; graphics designer Montgomery Ward, Chgo., 1956-61, design supr., 1961-73, mgr. corp. design, 1974-84; pres. Stocker and Assocs., Chgo., 1984—; cons. Office of Mayor, Chgo., 1986-87. Creator newspaper feature Knowledge Knots, 1964-65. With USAF, 1951-54. Recipient Creative plaque Am. Hardware Mfrs. Assn., 1980, YMCA award 1983, Creative award Champion Paper Co., 1976, numerous others. Mem. Amb. Club (pres. 1966-69). Home: 3105 Emmaus Ave Zion IL 60099 Office: Stocker & Assocs 605 W Madison 3203-3 Chicago IL 60606

STOCKHAM, JAMES WALTER, steel company executive; b. Des Moines, Dec. 27, 1928; s. Dean Fortune and Gretchen Helene (Thompson) S.; B.A., Drake U., 1950; M.A., U. Chgo., 1955; m. Patricia Ann Doster, Mar. 28, 1952; children—Michael Bruce, Peter James. Merchandising and salesman Joseph T. Ryerson & Son, Inc., Chgo., 1955-57, operating supr., 1957-61, gen. supt. Los Angeles plant, 1961-69, plant supt. Chgo., 1969-70, plant engr., 1970-72, gen. supt., 1972-76, mgr. sheet and coil sales, 1976-77, gen. mgr. Dayton (Ohio) plant, 1977-79, gen. mgr. Pitts. plant, 1979-88, ret. Campaign and gen. chmn. Ryerson-Met. Crusade of Mercy, Chgo., 1972-74; mem. exec. com. exploring div. Boy Scouts Am., Chgo., 1972-76; bd. dirs. Boys Club, Carnegie, Pa., 1979-83, Chartiers Valley Indsl. and Comml. Devel. Authority, 1983—. Served with USAF, 1951-55. Mem. Steel Service Center Inst. (past pres. Pitts. chpt.). Clubs: Chartiers Country, Duquesne. Home: 305 Harvester Circle Pittsburgh PA 15241 Office: PO Box 1919 Pittsburgh PA 15230

STOCKLIN, ALMA KATHERINE, educational adminstrator; b. New London, Conn., May 9, 1926; d. Stephen Sullivan and Theresa Catherine (Flynn) Sheehan; m. Philip L. Stocklin, Jan. 28, 1950 (div. 1984); children: Brian, Christopher, Virginia Katherine, Walter, Stephen. Student, U. Conn., 1945-46, Conn. Coll., 1946; cert., Sch. Modern Photography, N.Y.C., 1948; AA, Charter Oak Coll., 1979; BA, Eastern Conn. State U., 1981. Advt. photographer Gen. Electric Co., Bridgeport, Conn., 1948-49; pub. rels. cons. Norwich and Groton, Conn., 1983-86; asst. to dean Eastern Conn. State U., Willimantic, 1986—; coordinator videotape courses for submarines, New London, 1984—. Mem. Norwich Harbor Day Com., 1982-83, Catchment area council Southeastern Conn. Mental Health, New London, 1985—, Norwich Regional Mental Health adv. bd., 1987—, Norwich State Hosp. adv. bd., 1987—; founder, chmn. Norwich Nuclear Freeze Com., 1982; bd. dirs. Eastern Conn. Symphony Orch., New London, 1984-87, Friends of Symphony, 1987—, Laurel Glen, Groton, 1984—; co-founder, bd. dirs. Newport Ch. Community Housing Corp., 1969-72; founder, chmn. Newport Holiday for Sr. Citizens Inc., 1971-72. Mem. Assn. Continuing Higher Edn., Conn. Assn. Continuing Edn. Democrat. Roman Catholic. Home: 74-3 Buddington Rd Groton CT 06340

STOCKMAN, DAVID ALLEN, former U.S. cabinet member, congressman, financier; b. Ft. Hood, Tex., Nov. 10, 1946; s. Allen and Carol (Bartz) S. BA in Am. History cum laude, Mich. State U., East Lansing, 1968; postgrad., Harvard U. Div. Sch., 1968-70; fellow, Inst. Politics, 1974. Spl. asst. to Congressman John Anderson, 1970-72; exec. dir. Republican Conf., Ho. of Reps., 1972-75; mem. 95th Congress from 4th Dist. Mich., Interstate and Fgn. Commerce Com., Adminstrn. Com.; chmn. Rep. Econ. Policy Task Force, 1977-81; dir. Office of Mgmt. and Budget, Washington, 1981-85; mng. dir. Salomon Bros., N.Y.C., 1985-88; gen. ptnr. The Blackstone Group, N.Y.C., 1988—; mng. ptnr. Stockman & Co., N.Y.C., 1988—; Mem. Nat. Commn. on Air Quality, 1978. Author: The Triumph of Politics: Why the Reagan Revolution Failed, 1986. Office: The Blackstone Group 345 Park Ave New York NY 10154

STOCKMAN, JOHN FREDERICK, lawyer, property management company executive; b. Fargo, N.D., Apr. 20, 1951; s. Jacque George and M. Louise (Aandahl) S.; m. Karen Kay Burkle, Nov. 27, 1974 (div. Dec. 1980); 1 child, Rebecca Louise; m. Mary Jo Williams, Dec. 27, 1986. BA, Concordia Coll., 1973; JD, Drake U., 1984. Bar: Minn. 1984, U.S. Dist. Ct. Minn. 1984. Spl. projects mgr. Met. Savs. and Loan, Fargo, N.D., 1974-75; broker, owner Stockman Investments, Fargo, 1975-84; owner, mgr. Stockman Properties, Fargo, 1975—; sole practice Mpls., 1984-87; assoc. Zimmerman and Reed, Mpls., 1987—; bd. dirs. Palace Supply Inc., Fargo, N.D., Art Ctr. Minn., Wayzata. Chmn. 44th Legis. Dist. Democrats, Fargo, 1976-78; mem. Fargo Planning and Zoning Commn., 1979-80; del. White House Conf. on Small Bus., 1980. Mem. ABA, Minn. Bar Assn., Inst. Property Mgmt., Am Agrl. Law Assn., Fargo Downtown Bus. Assn. (pres. 1978-79), Phi Alpha Delta. Lutheran. Lodge: Masons. Home: 204 Sunnyridge Ln Golden Valley MN 55422 Office: Zimmerman & Reed 580 Lumber Exchange Bldg Minneapolis MN 55402

STOCKSTILL, MICHAEL CHARLES, public affairs executive; b. Lynwood, Calif., Mar. 16, 1949; s. Charles Benton and Mary (Huff) S.; m. Margaret Stockstill, Oct. 9, 1971; children: Joyce Mason, Patrick. BA in Journalism, Humboldt St. U., Arcata, Calif., 1971. Intern Calif. St. Assembly, Sacramento, 1971-72; reporter, editor Laguna News Post, Laguna Beach, Calif., 1972-74, Irvine (Calif.) World News, 1974-76; editor KOCE-TV, Huntington Beach, Calif., 1976-78; mgr. pub. relations The Irvine Co., Newport, Calif., 1978—; mgr. govt. relations, dir., govt. relations, sr. dir. community affairs. Dir. Am. Youth Soccer Orgn., Irvine, 1988; fin. chmn. Boy Scouts Am., Irvine, 1986-87. Mem. Von Strobel Breakfast Soc. (pres. Orange County, Calif. chpt.). Democrat. Protestant. Office: The Irvine Co 550 Newport Ctr Dr Newport Beach CA 92658

STOCKTON, JOHN B., lawyer; b. London, Apr. 5, 1946; came to U.S., 1947; s. Philip B. and Zenobia (Forster-Brown) S.; m. Pamela Dwyer, Apr. 5, 1946; children: Nicholas, Hope. AB, Princeton (N.J.) U., 1968; JD, Columbia U., 1973. Assoc. Carter, Ledyard and Milburn, N.Y.C., 1973-81; v.p., gen. counsel Equilease Corp., N.Y.C., 1981-84, First Rock Fin. Corp., N.Y.C., 1984-86, Chrysler Capital Corp., Greenwich, Conn., 1986—. With U.S. Army, 1968-70, Vietnam. Office: Chrysler Capital Corp 51 Weaver St Greenwich CT 06836

STOCKWELL, OLIVER PERKINS, lawyer; b. East Baton Rouge, La., Aug. 11, 1907; s. William Richard and Lillie Belle (Dawson) S.; m. Roseina Katherine Holcombe, June 24, 1936; 1 child, Angell Roseina (Mrs. William C. Wright). LL.B., La. State U., 1932, J.D., 1968. Bar: La. 1932. Since practiced in Lake Charles; ptnr. firm Stockwell, Sievert, Viccellio, Clements & Shaddock (and predecessor firm), 1933—; Dir. Lakeside Nat. Bank of Lake Charles; past dir. Gulf States Utilities Co.; past mem. jud. council La. Supreme Ct.; past mem. La. Commn. on Law Enforcement and Adminstrn. Criminal Justice; referee bankruptcy U.S. Dist. Ct. (we. dist.) La., 1938-46. Contbr. to La. Law Rev. Pres. Lake Charles Centennial; bd. dirs., mem. exec. com. Council for a Better La., pres., 1972; past bd. dirs. Pub. Affairs Research Council La.; past bd. dirs. La. State U. Found.; past bd. suprs. La. State U., chmn., 1977-78, chmn. emeritus; past chmn. legal services adv. com. La. Joint Legis. Commn. on Intergovtl. Relations.; chmn. Paul H. Hebert Law Ctr. Council La. State U.; mem. Task Force on Excessive Govtl. Regulations. Served to lt. USNR, 1943-45. Research fellow Southwestern Legal Found. Fellow Am. Bar Found., Am. Coll. Trial Lawyers, Am. Coll. Probate Counsel; mem. Inter-Am. Bar Assn., Am. Judicature Soc., Internat. Bar Assn., ABA (past state chmn. jr. bar sect., mem. spl. com. adoption jud. conduct code;, chmn. La. membership com., sr. lawyers div.), La. Bar Assn. (past pres.), S.W. La. Bar Assn. (pres. 1942), Mid-Continent Oil and Gas Assn. (exec. com.), Comml. Law League, Internat. Assn. Ins. Counsel, Fedn. Ins. Counsel, Am. Law Inst. (life mem.), La. Law Inst. (past pres., chmn. mineral code com. 1986; chmn. 1987, chmn. emeritus, 1988), Lake Charles C. of C. (past pres., Civic award 1978), State Assn. Young Men's Bus. Clubs (past pres. Lake Charles), La. State U. Law Sch. Alumni Assn. (past pres.), Order of Coif, Henri Capitant, Lambda Alpha, Omicron Delta Kappa. Clubs: Kiwanis, Pioneer, City, Lake Charles Country, Boston of New Orleans, L of La. State U. (past pres.). Home: 205 Shell Beach Dr Lake Charles LA 70601 Office: $S11 Lakeside Pla Lake Charles LA 70601

STODDARD, NATHANIEL CLARK, manufacturing executive; b. Hartford, Conn., Jan. 22, 1945; s. Nathaniel Styles and Kathryn Roberta (Clark) S.; m. Kathryn Mallery Headley, Sept. 17, 1966; children: Kimberly Headley, John Clark. BA with honors, Denison U., 1966; MBA, U. Denver, 1972. Coordinator bus. planning and devel. Samsonite Corp., Denver, 1972-74; dir. planning consumer products div. Beatrice Foods Co., Chgo., 1974-75; v.p. mktg. service Charmglow Products div. Beatrice Foods Co., Bristol, Wis., 1975-76; v.p. mktg. Gerwin div. Leigh Products, Inc., Saranac, Mich., 1976-80; dir. mktg. consumer products div. Black & Decker, Inc., Easton, Md., 1980-82, v.p. mktg. household products group, 1982-84, v.p., gen. mgr. outdoor products div., 1984-85; v.p. sales, service, distbn. U.S. power tools group Black & Decker, Inc., Hunt Valley, Md., 1986-87, v.p., gen. mgr. U.S. service ops., 1987-89; pres., chief operating officer Garden Way, Inc., Troy, 1989—. Mem. adv. council Talbot County (Md.) Economic Devel. Commn., 1982-85; chmn. County/City Airport Study Group, Easton, 1983-84. Served to capt., pilot USAF, 1966-70. Mem. Am. Hardware Mfrs. Assoc., Hardware Mktg. Council, Home Ctr. Industry Council. Club: Young Execs. (v.p., pres. 1982), Hunt Valley (Md.) Golf, Chesapeake Bay Yacht, Easton. Office: Black & Decker Inc PO Box 564 Hampstead MD 21074

STODDARD, RICHARD ETHRIDGE, corporation executive, accountant, lawyer; b. Waterloo, Iowa, Nov. 23, 1950; s. Gilbert V. and Marian (Magner) S.; m. Kae Ethridge, May 12, 1979; children: Gregor, Abby. BBA summa cum laude, U. Iowa, 1972; JD, Georgetown U., 1976. Bar: Colo 1976; CPA, Iowa. Instr. U. Iowa, Iowa City, 1972-73, George Mason U., Fairfax, Va., 1975-76; fin. analyst Disclosure Inc., Silver Spring, Md., 1973-74; ptnr. Calkins Kramer Grimshaw and Harring, Denver, 1976-85; mng. dir. Roath and Brega, Denver, 1986-88; chief exec. officer, chmn. Kaiser Steel Resources Inc. (formerly Kaiser Steel Corp.), Rancho Cucamonga, Calif., 1988—; bd. dirs. Frontier Holdings Inc., Denver, 1985, Mine Reclamation Corp., San Diego, 1988—. Mem. Downtown Denver Inc., 1983-88. Mem. Denver C. of C., Glenmoor Country Club (Denver). Republican. Methodist. Office: Kaiser Steel Resources Inc 8300 Utica Ave #301 Rancho Cucamonga CA 91730

STODDARD, WILLIAM BERT, JR., economist; b. Carbondale, Pa., Oct. 6, 1926; s. William Bert and Emily (Trautwein) S.; student Lafayette Coll., 1944-45; B.S., N.Y. U., 1950, A.M., 1952; m. Carol Marie Swartz, Feb. 28, 1970; 1 dau., Emily Coleman. Asst. chief accountant, budget dir. Hendrick Mfg. Co., Carbondale, Pa., 1952-54, asst. dir. prodn., 1956-68, also dir.; credit corr. U.S. Gypsum Co., N.Y.C., 1954-56; investment counselor, Carbondale, 1968-73, Ridgefield, Conn., 1973—; dir. First Nat. Bank Carbondale, 1968-73; bd. dirs. Lackawanna County Mfrs. Assn., Scranton, Pa., 1960-73. Treas., trustee Aldrich Museum Contemporary Art, Ridgefield, 1976—; bd. dirs. Ridgefield Library and Hist. Assn., 1977-85, 87—; trustee Ridgefield Library Endowment Fund Trust, 1985—. Served with U.S. Army 1946-47. Mem. Nat. Assn. Accountants, Am. Def. Preparedness Assn., Phi Alpha Kappa, Phi Delta Theta. Republican. Methodist. Clubs: N.Y. U. (N.Y.C.); Waccabuc (N.Y.) Country. Home: 59 Bridle Tr Ridgefield CT 06877 Office: 23 Catoonah St Ridgefield CT 06877

STODDART, GEORGE ANDERSON, oil service company executive; b. Oyster Bay, N.Y., Sept. 16, 1933; s. Percival D. and Florence A. (Anderson) S.; m. Gail Miller, Dec. 6, 1958; children: Penelope G., Timothy M. BS, Yale U., 1956; postgrad., NYU, 1960-61. With Scudder Stevens & Clark, N.Y.C., 1960-73, ptnr., 1969-73; v.p. Thomson McKinnon, N.Y.C., 1973-75; asst. v.p. Gulf and Western, Inc., N.Y.C., 1975-77; with McDermott Internat., New Orleans, 1977—, v.p., 1982—. Mem. Chartered Fin. Analysts, N.Y. Soc. Security Analysts, Petroleum Investor Relations Assn., AIME. Republican. Episcopalian. Home: Rock Gate Farm Rd Mount Kisco NY 10549 Office: McDermott Internat Inc 245 Fifth Ave New York NY 10016

STOEBERL, GEORGE FRANK, professional association executive, consultant; b. Chgo., July 8, 1924; s. Frank and Wilhelmina (DeserHermayer) S.; m. Janet Ann Pearson, Aug. 20, 1949; children: Gary Joe, Catherine Ann. Student, Wis. State U., 1942-43, Lehigh U., 1944; AA, Spartan Coll., 1945. Resident mgr. Francis I. DuPont & Co., Phoenix, 1958-68; pres. Combined Fund Mgmt., Phoenix, 1968-72, Intermountain Petro, Phoenix, 1972-76, Guaranteed Mgmt. Corp., Phoenix, 1976-78; exec. dir. Am. Diabetes Assn., Phoenix, 1978—. With AUS, 1943-44. Republican. Congregationalist. Home: 68ll N 2d Pl Phoenix AZ 85012

STOECKERT, GEORGE IAN, service executive; b. Ft. Knox, Ky., Sept. 21, 1948; s. George I. and Shirley Ruth (Tonne) S.; m. Rebecca Horn Pope, Mar. 3, 1979; children: George Norford, Jane Gilbert. AB, U. Miami, 1970, MBA, 1972. Investment analyst trust investments dept. S.E. First Nat. Bank Miami, 1972-73; asst. to dir. investments, investment analyst S.E. Banks Trust Co., Miami, 1973-74; acquisition and merger analyst Ryder System, Inc., Miami, 1974, sr. fin. analyst, 1974-75, mgr. capital planning, 1975-76, mgr. long range and capital planning, 1976; dir. fin. planning Truckstop div. Ryder System, Inc., Nashville, 1976-77; dir. fin. planning Vehicle Leasing and Svcs. div. Ryder System, Inc., Miami, 1977-80, group dir. fin. planning Vehicle Leasing and Svcs. div., 1980-82, v.p. planning Vehicle Leasing and Svcs. div., 1982-83; v.p. fin., chief exec. officer Truckstop div. Ryder System, Inc., Nashville, 1983-84, pres. Fin. and Communication Svcs. div., 1984-86; sr. v.p. planning Ryder System, Inc., Miami, 1986, sr. v.p. corp. devel., 1986-88, pres., pres. Ins. Mgmt. Svcs. div., 1988—; bd. dirs. Access, Inc., Nashville, Capital Re Corp., N.Y.C. Trustee South Fla. Zool. Soc., Miami, 1987; bd. dirs. Nat. Found. for Advancement in Arts, 1988. 2d lt. inf., 1972. Mem. Greater Miami C. of C. (trustee 1988), Royal Palm Tennis Club. Home: 7371 SW 156th St Miami FL 33157 Office: Ryder System Ins Mgmt Svcs Div 8600 NW 36th St Miami FL 33166 Also: Ryder System Inc 3600 NW 82nd Ave Miami FL 33166

STOESS, BARRY WAYNE, construction material supply executive; b. Pewee Valley, Ky., Apr. 2, 1952; s. Clarence William and Dorothy Edna (Kilgus) S.; m. Barbara Lee Sammons, July 16, 1977; children: Jacquelyn Marie, Patrick Wayne. BS, Ea. Ky. U., 1975. With warehousing and distbn. Belknap, Inc., Louisville, 1975-76; sales rep. Bullitt Co. Stone, Shepherdsville, Ky., 1976-81; realtor assoc. Home Store, Crestwood, Ky., 1978—; mktg. rep. Roger's Group, Louisville, 1981-86, account mgr., 1987—. Mem. adminstrv. bd. Crestwood United Meth. Ch., 1978-88; coordinator United Meth. Youth Fellowship, Crestwood, 1978-86; bd. dirs. Briar Hill Taxing Dist., Crestwood, 1988—; mem. adv. bd. Met. United Way Oldham County, LaGrange, Ky., 1988—. Mem. Nat. Assn. Home Builders, Assoc. Gen. Contractors, Assoc. Builders and Contractors, Ky. Crushed Stone Assn., Nat. Stone Assn., Oldham C. of C., Kappa Alpha. Home: 7600 Cantrell Dr Crestwood KY 40014 Office: Rogers Group Inc 7700 Hwy 329 PO Box 237 Crestwood KY 40014

STOETZNER, ERIC WOLDEMAR, newspaper executive; b. Leipzig, Germany, Mar. 11, 1901; came to U.S. 1938, naturalized, 1944; s. Woldemar and Emma (Wolf) S.; student U. Leipzig, 1922; Dr. Econ. Sci., Frankfurt am Main, 1925; m. Fridel Henning-Gronau, Dec. 20, 1927 (dec. Sept. 1967); 1 chile, Renee. Advt. dir., bus. mgr., mem. bd. Frankfurter Zeitung, Germany, 1930-38; bus. mgr. mag. of Schurz Found., Phila., 1939-43; internat. analyst of pub. N.Y. Times, 1944-45, dir. fgn. bus. promotion, 1945-50, dir. fgn. advt., 1950-70, internat. cons., 1970—. Decorated Chevalier de l'ordre du Merite Comml. de la France; Officer's Cross, German Order of Merit, 1953; Grand Cross, German Order Merit, 1981, recipient hon. plaque City of Frankfurt, 1979, Disting. Internat. Recognition award Fellowship Former Overseas Residents, 1984; named Symbol of 1938 Frankfurter Allgemeine Zeitung in report, Four Dramatic Lives of a Frankfordian, 1983. Mem. Internat. Advt. Assn. (hon. life; v.p. 1956-59), Confrerie des Chevaliers du Tastevin. Quaker, Rotary (named Mr. Internationalist N.Y. chpt.). Subject of book by Horst Fischer: Werbung, Menschen, Politik: Die Stoetzner Story, 1986. Home: 376 Westover Rd Stamford CT 06902

STOFFERSON, TERRY LEE, financial officer; b. Omaha, Apr. 22, 1957; s. Dale Leslie and Alma Rose (Flores) S. BSBA, U. Nebr., Omaha, 1980. Auditor Alexander Grant & Co., CPA's, Omaha, 1979-81; budget mgr. Archbishop Bergan Mercy Hosp., Omaha, 1981-86; controller Lafayette (La.) Gen. Med. Ctr., 1986-87; chief fin. officer Opelousas (La.) Gen. Hosp., 1987—; cons. in field. Phila. Vol. Lawyers for the Arts. Mem. Healthcare Fin. Mgrs., Nat. Assn. Accts. (controller's council 1988), Nat. Health Lawyers Assn., Am. Hosp. Assn. Republican. Presbyterian. Lodge Optimist (pres., 1988). Office: Opelousas Gen Hosp 520 Prudhomme Ln Opelousas LA 70570

STOKELY, WILLIAM BURNETT, III, food products executive; b. L.A., Sept. 18, 1940; s. William Burnett and Tamara S.; m. Kay Haslett, July 25, 1962; children: William Burnett, Stacy Ivie, Shelley Kay, Clayton Frank. BS, U. Tenn. Chmn. bd., pres. The Stokely Co., Stokely Affiliated Fin. Enterprises, Inc., Knoxville, William B. Stokely Jr. Found. Inc., Knoxville; bd. dirs. Merchants Nat. Corp., Indpls., Merchants Nat. Bank &n Trust Co., Indpls., Industrias Portela, C. por A. Navarrete, Dominican Republic, Pvt. Investment Consortium Ltd., others. Mem. and past chmn. U. Tenn. Devel. Coun., Knoxville; bd. trustees Berry Coll., past chmn. bd. visitors; trustee Indpls. Mus. Art; chmn. bd. dirs. West Knoxville Bapt. Ch.; v.p. Crossroads Am. Coun., Boy Scouts Am.; chmn. Ind. Spl. Olympics. dir. Environ. Quality Control; chmn. U.S. Savs. Bonds Payroll Savs. Campaign Met. Indpls.; others. Mem. Young Pres.'s Orgn., Penrod Soc. Indpls. (past pres.), Skyline Club, Cherokee Country Club, Order of the Good Time Club, Melrose Club, U.S. C. of C. (past dir.), Econ. Club, Univ. Club, Crooked Stick golf Club, Penrod Soc. Indpls., Indpls. Athletic Club, Ind. C. of C. (past dir.), Newcomen Soc. N.Am., Kappa Sigma, Omicron Delta Kappa. Clubs: Econs. (Indpls.), Hundred (Indpls.), Univ. (Indpls.), Indpls. Athletic (Indpls.); Crooked Stick Golf (Carmel, Ind.), Cherokee Country (Knoxville), Club LeConte (Knoxville), Melrose (Daufuskie Island, S.C.). Office: Stokely Co 620 Campbell Station Rd Station West Ste Y Knoxville TN 37922

STOKES, BARBARA S., banker. Sec. J. P. Morgan & Co. Inc., New York, Morgan Guaranty Trust Co. N.Y., New York. Office: J P Morgan & Co Inc 23 Wall St New York NY 10015 *

STOKES, CHARLES EUGENE, JR., venture capitalist, wool merchant; b. Temple, Tex., Oct. 11, 1926; s. Charles Eugene and Esther Annette (Lawlis) S. BBA, U. Tex., 1948; MA, U. Tex., El Paso, 1968; PhD, Tulane U., 1974. Apprentice, then asst. buyer Conant & Co., Inc., Boston, 1946-48; wool buyer and dir. Stokes & Co., Ltd., Puno, Peru, 1949-55; pres., treas. Stokes Bros., Inc., New Braunfels, Tex., 1955-59; mng. ptnr. Stokes Bros. & Co., Peru, Uruguay and San Antonio, 1959—; wool mktg. and processing advisor Ministry Agr., La Paz, Bolivia, 1961-63. Fulbright fellow Tulane U., Bolivia and Brazil, 1970-71. Mem. Phi Alpha Theta. Republican. Methodist. Club: Union Puno, City Club of San Antonio. Home and Office: 8415 Fredericksburg Rd Suite 704 San Antonio TX 78229-3304

STOKES, EDMOND HAROLD, accounting firm executive; b. Atlanta, July 2, 1940; s. Edmond Harold and Bertha Aline (McCoy) S.; m. Juanita Laverne Summerlin, Jan. 26, 1963; children: Cynthia Anne, Michael Edmond, Michelle Elizabeth. BBA, Ga. State U., 1962. CPA, Ga. With Peat, Marwick, Mitchell & Co., Atlanta, 1962—; vice-chmn. southeast region Peat, Marwick, Main & Co., Atlanta, also bd. dirs. Chmn. bd. trustees Atlanta Leadership Found., Ga. State U. Alumni Assn., 1981-82; chmn. Ga. State U. Found., 1985-87; trustee Atlanta Arts Alliance, 1984—; bd. dirs. United Way Metro Atlanta, 1981-87, v.p. fin., 1982-83. Served as capt. U.S. Army, 1962-64. Named to Nat. Golden Key Honor Soc., 1983. Mem. Am. Inst. CPA's, Ga. Soc. CPA's, Nat. Assn. Accts. (pres. Atlanta chpt. 1976-77). Clubs: Cherokee Country, Commerce, Atlanta Bus. Roundtable. Office: Peat Marwick Main & Co 245 Peachtree Ctr Ave Ste 1900 Atlanta GA 30043

STOKES, PAUL ALLEN, air frieght company executive; b. San Bernardino, Calif., Aug. 12, 1927; s. James Allen and Vina Jane (Gaylor) S.; m. Rosetta Madeline Gorham, Oct. 18, 1955; children: Wendy Lee, Kerry Lee, Todd Allen. Student, U. Denver, 1949-52. Bookkeeper Denver Cen. Bank and Trust, 1950-51; ramp serviceman Flying Tigers, Los Angeles, 1951-52, supr., 1953-55, dir., 1959-72, gen. mgr. Japan, 1972-77, v.p. Asia, 1977-85, sr. v.p. Pacific div., 1985—; assoc. Air Cargo Inc., 1966-71. Served with USN, 1945-48. Mem.Air Transp. Assn. Am. (rep. 1965-72), Am. C. of C. Japan. Republican. Club: Tokyo Am. Lodge: Toastmasters. Home: Homat Iris Apt 101 Minato-ku, 6-5 Minami-Aoyama 3-chome, Tokyo Japan 107 Office: Flying Tiger Line Inc, 14-2 Nagata-cho 2-chome, Sanno Grand Bldg, Chivoda-ku Tokyo Japan 100

STOKES, THERESA EMMA (TERI STOKES), computer company executive; b. Boston, Apr. 9, 1943; d. Saverio L. and Mary Grace (Van Stratum) Santoro; m. Ivan L. Stokes, June 12, 1965 (div. 1977); children: Theresa-Ann, Eric M.; m. Peter R. Yensen, Apr. 30, 1982. BA in Biology, Boston U., 1965; cert. in chemistry and math, Wellesley (Mass.) Coll., 1970; MS in Applied Mgmt., Lesley Coll., 1987. Lic. med. technologist, (ASCP), Mass. Med. technologist Univ. and Hosp. Labs., 1966-82; sales mgr. Shaklee Products, Concord, Mass., 1972-76; lab. supr. Somerville Hosp. Bioran Med. Labs, Cambridge, Mass., 1976-77, dir. processing and communications, 1977-79; mgr. mktg. communications Digital Equipment Corp., Marlboro, Mass., 1979-81, specialist indsl. research and devel. bus. ops., 1981-83, mgr. internat. pharm. market, 1983-86, bus. mgr. life sci. and research Kodak corp. account team, 1986—. Contbr. articles to profl. jours.; speaker in field. Advisor Jr. Achievement, Marlboro, 1983-85. Mem. DAR, Drug Info. Assn., Assn. Official Analytical Chemists, N.Y. Acad. Scis., Tridelta. Office: Digital Equipment Corp 1250 Pittsford-Victor Rd PO Box 23227 Rochester NY 14692

STOLAR, HENRY SAMUEL, corporate lawyer; b. St. Louis, Oct. 29, 1939; s. William Allen and Pearl Minnette (Schukar) S.; m. Mary Goldstein, Aug. 26, 1962 (dec. Nov. 1987); children: Daniel Bruce, Susan Eileen. AB, Washington U., 1960; JD, Harvard U., 1963. Bar: Mo. 1963. Assoc. then ptnr. Hocker, Goodwin & MacGreevy, St. Louis, 1963-69; v.p., sec., gen. counsel LaBarge Inc., St. Louis, 1969-74; v.p., assoc. gen. counsel then sr. v.p., gen. counsel Maritz Inc., St. Louis, 1974—. Sec., bd. dirs. The New City Sch. Inc., St. Louis, 1968-75; mem. St. Louis Bd. Aldermen, 1969-73; mem. Freeholders City and County St. Louis, 1987-88. Mem. ABA, The Mo. Bar, Bar Assn. Met. St. Louis., Frontenac Racquet Club, Phi Beta Kappa. Home: 59 Kingsbury Pl Saint Louis MO 63112 Office: Maritz Inc 1375 N Highway Dr Fenton MO 63099

STOLL, ERIC D., consulting engineer; b. N.Y.C., Nov. 15, 1938; s. Duane C. and Bessie (Mosley) S.; B.E.E. magna cum laude, CCNY, 1961; M.E.E., N.Y. U., 1963, Ph.D. with honors, 1966, M.B.A., 1974. Mem. tech. staff Bell Telephone Labs., Murray Hill and Holmdel, N.J., 1961-68; program mgr. Bendix Corp. Nav. and Control Div., Teterboro, N.J., 1968-73; mgr. spl. programs ADT Security Systems Corp., N.Y.C., 1973-79; dir. engring. advanced tech. systems div. Austin Co., Fair Lawn, N.J., 1979-82; pres. Modulation Scis., Inc., Bklyn., 1982-85; owner Cons. Engring. Assocs., Teaneck, N.J., 1985—. Lic. profl. engr., N.Y., N.J. recipient Sandor I. Oesterreicher award Elec. Engring. Excellence, 1961, Founders Day award for outstanding scholarship N.Y.U., 1967. Fellow The Radio Club Am., Inc. (treas. 1987—); mem. IEEE, NSPE, N.J. Soc. Profl. Engrs., Bergen County Soc. Profl. Engrs. (v.p. 1986-87), Assn. Fed. Communications Cons. Engrs. (admissions com. 1986—), Inst. Mgmt. Scis. (pres. Met. N.Y. chpt. 1978-79, v.p. programs 1977-78), Tau Beta Pi, Eta Kappa Nu. Contbr. articles to profl. jours.; patentee in field. Home: 117 Hillside Ave Teaneck NJ 07666

STOLL, RICHARD EDMUND, manufacturing executive; b. Dayton, Ohio, Aug. 5, 1927; s. George Elmer and Mary Francis (Zimmerle) S.; m. Vera Mae Cohagen, Sept. 2, 1950; children: Richard Edmund, Linda Ann, Donna Gail. Student in mech. engring., MIT, 1945-47; MetE, Ohio State U., 1950. Registered profl. engr. Ill., Tex. Various staff and operating positions U.S. Steel Corp., Pitts., Chgo., Houston, 1952-78; gen. mgr. metall. services U.S. Steel Corp., Pitts., 1978-84, dir. quality mgmt. program and tech., 1983-84; corp. chief metallurgist Wheeling-Pitts. Steel Corp., Wheeling, W.Va., 1985-86, v.p., gen. mgr. flat rolled steel, 1986-87, v.p., gen. mgr., interim chief ops. officer, 1987-89, exec. v.p., 1989—; cons. McElrath & Assocs., Mpls., 1984; bd. dirs. Ohio Valley Industry and Bus. Devel. Corp., Wheeling. Contbr. articles to profl. jours.; patentee in field. Served with C.E., U.S. Army, 1950-52. Fellow Am. Soc. Metals (chmn. 1963); mem. Am. Iron and Steel Inst., Am. Inst. Mining and Metallurgy (Nat. Open Hearth award 1957, bd. dirs. 1961-68), Am. Inst. Steel Engrs., Am. Soc. Metals. Republican. Roman Catholic. Clubs: Wheeling Country, Ft. Henry, Duquesne, Laurel Valley. Home: 1490 Candlewood Dr Pittsburgh PA 15241 Office: Wheeling-Pitts Steel Corp 1134 Market St Wheeling WV 26003

STOLLE, RONALD HELLMUT, manufacturing executive; b. Chgo., Sept. 30, 1948; s. Hellmut Wilhelm and Eileen (Wray) S.; m. Marcia Ann Zieman Stolle, Apr. 25, 1970; children: Jeffrey Ronald, Jennifer Leigh. BA, Northeastern Ill. U., 1971; MBA, Loyola U., Chgo., 1976. Cert. cash mgr. Underwriter Rollins, Burdick, Hunter Co., Chgo., 1970-72; ins. analyst Interlake, Inc., Oakbrook, Ill., 1972-77; ins. mgr. Am. Air Filter Co., Louisville, 1977-78; dir. risk mgmt. Reliance Electric Co., Pepper Pike, Ohio, 1978-85, dir. risk mgmt., mgr. corp. cash, 1985-87, dir. treasury ops.,

1988—; dir. Wrenford Ins. Co. Ltd., Hamilton, Bermuda, 1979—, Vt. Res. Ins. Co., Burlington, 1986—. Editorial bd. Risk Management Mag., N.Y.C., 1982—. Rep. Nominee Ill. State Senate, 1976. Sgt. USAR, 1969-75. Named Outstanding Young Man Am., 1984. Mem. Nat. Corp. Cash Mgmt. Assn., Risk and Ins. Mgmt. Soc., Hudson (Ohio) Boosters Club. Republican. Lutheran. Home: 5801 Ogilby Dr Hudson OH 44236 Office: Reliance Electric Co 29325 Chagrin Blvd Cleveland OH 44122

STOLLENWERK, JOHN JOSEPH, shoe manufacturing company executive; b. Wauwatosa, Wis., Feb. 18, 1940; s. Roman Joseph and Marion Germain (Belongia) S.; m. JoEllen Koesterer, July 26, 1969; children: Susan, Philip, John, Joe, Daniel. BA, Marquette U., 1962, MA, 1966. Owner Commodities in Indsl. Products Internat. Ltd., Milw., 1970-80; pres., chief exec. officer Allen-Edmonds Shoe Corp., Port Washington, Wis., 1980—; bd. dirs. Koss Corp., The Milw. Co., Blood Ctr. of Southeastern Wis., Skylight Theater, Milw. World Trade Assn., Weasler Engring., Inc.; mem. Pres.'s Exec. Senate Marquette U., Dean's Adv. Council Marquette U. Active in Heart of Am. "Bill of Sail," Great Circus Parade, 1985-89, Communities against Pushers, Children's Hosp. Recipient Gov.'s Export award State of Wis., 1984; named Man of Yr., Harvard Bus. Club, 1985, Arthur Young Entrepreneur of Yr., 1986, Mfr. of Yr., Footwear News Mag., 1986, Mktg. Exec. of Yr., Sales and Mktg. Execs., Milw., 1987, Wis. Small Bus. Person of Yr., 1987 (nat. 1st runner up). Mem. Young Pres.s Orgn., Wis. Assn. Mfrs. and Commerce, World Trade Assn. (past bd. mem.), Footwear Industries Assn. (bd. dirs.), Nat. Inst. Am. Entrepreneurs, Men's Fashion Assn. Am., Port Washington C. of C. Roman Catholic. Clubs: University, Athletic (Milw.), South Shore Yacht. Office: Allen Edmonds 201 E Seven Hills Rd PO Box 998 Port Washington WI 53074-0998

STOLLEY, JAMES S., manufacturing executive; b. Peoria, Ill., Oct. 3, 1928; s. George Brockway and Stella (Sherman) S.; m. Margaret Moynahan, Feb. 14, 1953; children: Karen Stolley Drucker, James Jr., Elizabeth. BSME, MIT, 1952. With Procter & Gamble Co., Cin., 1952-55; engr., asst. supt. Beckett Paper Co., Hamilton, Ohio, 1955-62; with Hammermill Paper Co., Erie, Pa., 1963-80, sr. v.p., 1980—; bd. dirs. Gen. Telephone Co. of Ind. Corporator, trustee Hamot Med. Ctr., Erie; corporator St. Vincent Health Ctr., Erie; trustee Villa Maria Coll., Erie. With USN, 1946-48. Mem. Pa. C. of C. (bd. dirs.), Pa. Council on Econ. Edn. (bd. dirs.). Home: 4711 Wolf Rd Erie PA 16505 Office: Hammermill Paper Co East Lake Rd Erie PA 16533

STOLTE, LARRY GENE, computer processing company executive; b. Cedar Rapids, Iowa, Sept. 17, 1945; s. Ed August and Emma Wilhelmena (Tank) S.; B.B.A. with highest distinction (FS Services scholar), U. Iowa, 1971; m. Rebecca Jane Tappmeyer, June 13, 1970; children—Scott Edward, Ryan Gene. Tax and auditing acct. McGladrey Pullen & Co., Cedar Rapids, 1971-73; sr. v.p. TLS Co., Cedar Rapids, 1973—, also dir. Served to sgt. USMC, 1964-67. C.P.A., Iowa, Ill., Mo., Minn., Mich., Wis.; cert. mgmt. acct. Mem. Nat. Assn. Computerized Tax Processors (pres.), Nat. Assn. Accts., Am. Inst. C.P.A.'s, Am. Mgmt. Assn. Republican. Methodist. Home: 2107 Linmar Dr NE Cedar Rapids IA 52402-3736 Office: TLS Co 425 2nd St SE PO Box 1686 Cedar Rapids IA 52406

STOLTENBERG, BRUCE CARL, lawyer, financial planner; b. Mpls., May 21, 1950; s. Carl Henry and Jean (Shirley) S.; m. Robin Jean Miller, June 16, 1973; children: Jessica Marie, Kira Lea, Sean Paul. BS, Oreg. State U., 1971; JD, U. Oreg., 1974. Bar: Oreg. 1974. Sole practice law Corvallis, Oreg., 1974-78; owner, contractor Bethany Constrn. Co., Sandpoint, Idaho, 1978-80; owner, operator Bethany Ranch, Oakland, Oreg., 1980-82; rep. Fin. Network Investment Corp., Bellevue, Wash., 1982-86; owner, mgr. Bruce Stoltenberg JD, CFP, Issaquah, Wash., 1986—; pres. Adv. Assocs. NW, Inc., Bellevue, 1985-86; pub. Stoltenberg's Money Letter, 1987—. Mem. Internat. Assn. Fin. Planners (cert.), Estate Planning Coun. East King County, Issaquah C. of C. Republican. Presbyterian. Office: 2015 228th Ave SE Issaquah WA 98027

STOLTZ, CHARLES EDWARD, meat packing executive; b. Dubuque, Iowa, July 31, 1936; s. Edward and Bertha (Klingenberg) S.; m. Jean Wahlert, Aug. 20, 1964; children: Jennifer, Michael, John, Charles II. BS in Bus. Adminstrn., U. Dubuque, 1961; MA, U. Iowa, 1964. Salesman Am. Can Co., 1961-62; v.p. Dubuque Packing Co., 1965, exec. v.p., 1965-1977, pres., 1977-89, now also chief exec. officer, chmn., bus. cons., 1989—; dir. Dubuque Bank & Trust Co. Trustee U. Dubuque, United Fund, Boys Club. With USMC, 1956-58. Office: Dubuque Packing Co 7171 Mercy Rd Omaha NE 68106

STOMA, JOHN PATRICK, insurance company executive, lawyer; b. Logansport, Ind., Sept. 12, 1946; s. Alexander John and Mary Alice (Hennesey) S.; m. Karen Marie Cunningham, Dec. 27, 1947; 1 child, Mark Adam. BA, Purdue U., 1968; JD, Suffolk U., 1977. Bar: Mass. 1977. Group and pension rep. Union Mut., Boston, 1973-79; pension mgr. Union Mut., N.Y.C., 1979-84; v.p. group pensions Union Mut., Portland, Maine, 1984—. Capt. USAF, 1968-73. Mem. Life Office Mgmt. Assn. (com. mem.). Home: 19 Coveside Rd Cumberland Foreside ME 04110 Office: UNUM 2211 Congress St Portland ME 04122

STONE, ALAN, container company executive; b. Chgo., Feb. 5, 1928; s. Norman H. and Ida (Finkelstein) S.; children—Christie-Ann Stone Weiss, Joshua. B.S.E., U. Pa., 1951. Trainee, salesman Stone Container Corp., Chgo., 1951-53, dir. mktg. service, 1954-64, gen. mgr., regional mgr., 1964-72, sr. v.p. adminstrn., gen. mgr. energy div., 1972—, also dir.; pres. Atlanta and St. Andrews Bar Rwy. Co., Apache R.R. Pres. Jewish Vocat. Service, Chgo., 1975-77, Abbeville-Grimes R.R.; v.p. Sinai Temple, Chgo., 1977-84; vice chmn. Roycemore Sch., Evanston, Ill., 1982-87. Mem. Standard Club, Tavern Club, Bryn Mawr Country Club, Tamarisk Country Club, Long Boat Key Club, Beta Alpha Psi, Phi Eta Sigma, Zeta Beta Tau. Office: Stone Container Corp 150 N Michigan Ave Chicago IL 60601

STONE, ALAN JOHN, manufacturing company executive; b. Dansville, N.Y., Sept. 9, 1940; s. Guthrie Boyd and Doris Irene (Wolfanger) S.; B.S. in Mech. Engring., Rochester Inst. Tech., 1963; M.B.A., U. Pitts., 1964; m. Sandra Barber, Aug. 22, 1964; children—Teri, Timothy, Michael. Engring. aide Xerox Corp., Webster, N.Y., 1960-63; gen. mgr. plastic component div. Stone Conveyor Co., Inc., Honeoye, N.Y., 1964-67, v.p. sales, 1968; cofounder, chief exec. officer Stone Constrn. Equipment Inc., Honeoye, 1969-86, also cons., bd. dirs., 1969—; founder, pres., Canandaigua Apts. Inc. (N.Y.), 1968-83; pres. Wildtrak, Inc., 1983—; founder, mng. ptnr. Stone Properties, 1986—; v.p., dir., co-founder Baker Rental Service, Inc., 1973-76; dir. Accu Systems, Inc., 1980-84; mem. met. adv. bd. Chase Lincoln First Bank, 1981-84; bd. dirs. Canandaigua Nat. Bank & Trust Co., 1986—; mem. corp. bd. F.F. Thompson Hosp., 1987—. Mem. Town of Richmond (N.Y.) Planning Bd., 1970-75, chmn., 1970-71; mem. Honeoye Central Sch. Bd. Edn., 1971-76, pres., 1973-74; com. chmn. pack 10 Boy Scouts Am., 1975-77; mem. Ontario County Overall Econ. Devel. Com., 1976-81. Mem. Honeoye C. of C. (chmn. indsl. com. 1974-82), Constrn. Industry Mfrs. Assn. (exec. mem. new bus. challenges council 1980-83), Grand Slam Club, Safari Internat. Club, Found. N.Am. Wild Sheep, Honeoye Area Hist. Soc. (bicentennial com. 1989). Methodist. Patentee in field. Home and Office: 5170 County Rd 33 Honeoye NY 14471

STONE, CHARLES RAYMOND, financial and administrative consultant; b. Englewood, N.J., Sept. 19, 1932; s. Benjamin and Sally G. (Dorf) S.; m. Edna J. Wolfe, June 8, 1958; children: Robert L., Eric M., Julie E. BA, Rutgers U., 1954. CPA, N.J. Mem. staff Peat, Marwick, Mitchell & Co., N.Y.C., 1954-55; sr. acct. Wiley, Block & White, Paterson, N.J., 1955-60; v.p., treas., bd. dirs. Chemplast Inc., Wayne, N.J., 1960-87; dir. fin. and adminstrn., plastics div. Norton Co., Wayne, N.J., 1982-87; chief cons. C.R. Stone Assocs., West Caldwell, N.J., 1987—. Treas. The Bridge, Caldwell, N.J., 1983—. Sgt. U.S. Army. 1956-58. Mem. Am. Inst. CPAs, N.J. Soc. CPAs, Masons.

STONE, DONALD D., investment and sales executive; b. Chgo., June 25, 1924; s. Frank J. and Mary N. (Miller) Diamondstone; student U. Ill., 1942-43; B.S., DePaul U., 1949; m. Catherine Mauro, Dec. 20, 1970; 1 child, Jeffrey. Pres., Poster Bros., Inc., Chgo., 1950-71, Revere Leather Goods, Inc., Chgo., 1953-71; owner Don Stone Enterprises, Chgo., 1954—; v.p. Horton & Hubbard Mfg. Co., Inc. div. Brown Group, Nashua, N.H., 1969-71, Neevel Mfg. Co., Kansas City, Mo., 1969-71. Mem. adv. bd. San Diego Opera; founder Don Diego Meml. Scholarship Fund; mem. bd. overseers U. Calif., San Diego, chancellor's assoc.; mem. exec. bd. Chgo. Area council Boy Scouts of Am. Served with U.S. Army, 1943-46. Clubs: Bryn Mawr Country (Lincolnwood, Ill.) (dir.), Carlton, La Jolla Beach and Tennis, La Jolla Country, Del Mar Thoroughbred. Home: 8240 Caminito Maritimo La Jolla CA 92037

STONE, DONALD JAMES, retired retail executive; b. Cleve., Mar. 5, 1929; s. Sidney S. and Beatrice (Edelman) S.; m. Norma Fay Karchmer, Oct. 26, 1952; children—Michael, Lisa, Angela. B.B.A., U. Tex., Austin, 1949. With Foley's, Houston, 1949-75; v.p., gen. mdse. mgr. Foley's, 1960-75; chmn., chief exec. officer Sanger-Harris, Dallas, 1975-80; vice chmn. Federated Dept. Stores, Inc., Dallas and Cin., 1980-88; dir. M Corp., Bloom Agy., Dallas, XTEC Corp., Cin. Pres. Dallas Symphony Soc., 1980-82; chmn. exec. com. Dallas Ballet, 1979; bd. dirs. Dallas Mus. Fine Art, 1979-81; mem. adv. council Coll. Bus. Adminstrn., U. Tex., 1981—; bd. dirs. Cin. Ballet, 1982-87; bd. dirs. Cin. Symphony, 1983-88, pres., 1987; bd. overseers, bd. govs. Hebrew Union Coll. Mem. Dallas C. of C. (chmn. cultural com. 1979-81), Asso. Mdse. Corp . (dir., exec. com.), Hebrew Union Coll. (bd. govs., Cin. overseers). Democrat. Jewish. Home: 3601 Turtle Creek Dallas TX 75219 Office: 2001 Bryan Tower Ste 2855 Dallas TX 75201

STONE, DUDLEIGH CHAPIN, II, pharmaceutical company executive; b. N.Y.C., May 22, 1945; s. Dudleigh Chapin and Opal Odell (Hay) S.; m. Sallie Kasson Carter, May 29, 1971; children: Kasson Carter, Elizabeth Chapin. BS in Econs., Lehigh U., 1970, MBA in Fin., 1971; postgrad., NYU, 1972-73. CPA, N.Y. Acct. Price Waterhouse & Co., N.Y.C., 1971-75; sr. ops. auditor Pfizer Inc., N.Y.C., 1975-76, internal audit mgr., 1976-78, dir. corp. planning, 1983-88; v.p. planning projects Pfizer Internat. Inc., N.Y.C., 1988—; pres., gen. mgr. Pfizer Sri Lanka Ltd., Colombo, 1978-81, Pfizer Portugal, Coina, 1981-83; v.p. planning and projects Pfizer Internat., N.Y.C., 1983—. Served with U.S Army 1967-69, Vietnam. Mem. N.Y. State Inst. CPAs, Am. Inst. CPAs, The Planning Forum, Cotswold Assn. (bd. dirs. 1987—). Republican. Episcopalian. Home: 30 Hadden Rd Scarsdale NY 10583 Office: Pfizer Internat Inc 235 E 42d St New York NY 10017

STONE, ELHANAN COLEMAN, lawyer; b. Norwood, Mass., July 3, 1929; s. Moses J. and Miriam (Cushing) S.; children: Mark J., Peter B.; m. Miriam K. Wallace, July 2, 1987. A.B., Harvard U., 1952, LL.B., 1955. Bar: Mass. 1955, U.S. Dist. Ct. Mass 1957. Trial atty. Anti-Trust div. U.S. Dept. Justice, Washington, 1958-62; with Ted Bates Worldwide, Inc., N.Y.C., 1962-88; v.p., asst. gen. counsel, exec. v.p., gen. counsel Ted Bates N.Y., N.Y.C., 1976-88; counsel Hall, Dickler, Lawler, Kent and Friedman, N.Y.C., 1988—; instr. advt. law New Sch., N.Y.C.; co-chmn. advt. law workshop Practicing Law Inst. Chmn. zoning bd. appeals City of Stamford, Conn., 1971; mem. Stamford Bd. Edn., 1971-80, pres., 1972-73. Served with U.S. Army, 1955-57. Mem. Am. Bar Assn., Assn. Bar City N.Y., Am. Assn. Advt. Agencies (chmn. com. on advt. legal affairs 1973-79). Republican. Jewish. Club: Harvard of Fairfield County (bd. govs. 1972—, pres. 1971-72). Office: Hall Dickler Lawler Kent & Friedman 460 Park Ave New York NY 10022 also: Hall Dickler Lawler Kent & Feiedman 460 Park Ave New York NY 10022

STONE, GARY LEON, lawyer; b. Fruitridge, Calif., Oct. 29, 1941; s. Xerxes and Martha (Houts) S.; m. Lori Knoll, Aug. 17, 1985; children by a previous marriage: Diane Stone Bossert, Richard. BA in English, U. Calif., Berkeley, 1968; JD, Harvard U., 1972. Bar: Calif. 1972, U.S. Dist. Ct. (no. dist.) Calif., U.S. Ct. Appeals (9th cir.). Assoc. Petty, Andrews, Tufts & Jackson, San Francisco, 1972-75; counsel TRW Inc., Redondo Beach, Calif., 1975-80; sr. counsel Ralph M. Parsons Co., Pasadena, 1980-82, asst. gen. counsel, 1982-84; v.p., gen. counsel Parsons Corp., Pasadena, 1984—. Pres. Am. Cancer Soc., Northeast Los Angeles County. Mem. ABA, Los Angeles County Assn. Office: Parsons Corp 100 W Walnut St Pasadena CA 91124

STONE, HUBERT DEAN, editor, journalist; b. Maryville, Tenn., Sept. 23, 1924; s. Archie Hubert and Annie (Cupp) S.; student Maryville Coll., 1942-43; B.A., U. Okla., 1949; m. Agnes Shirley, Sept. 12, 1953 (dec. Mar. 1973); 1 son, Neal Anson. Sunday editor Maryville-Alcoa Daily Times, 1949; mng. editor Maryville-Alcoa Times, 1949-78, editor, 1978—; v.p. Maryville-Alcoa Newspapers, Inc., 1960—; pres. Stonecraft, 1954—. Vice chmn. Tenn. Great Smoky Mountain Park Commn., mem. mayor's adv. com. City of Maryville; mem. air service adv. com. Knoxville Met. Airport Authority; bd. dirs. United Fund of Blount County, 1961-63, 74-76, vice chmn. campaign, 1971-72, chmn. campaign, 1973, v.p., 1974, pres., 1975; vice chmn. bd. dirs. Maryville Utilities Bd.; photographer in field. Bd. dirs. Blount County Hist. Trust, Nat. Hillbilly Homecoming Assn., Friendsville Acad., 1968-73, Alkiwan Crafts, Inc., 1970-73, Middle E.Tenn. Regional Tourism Group; dir. Foothills Land Conservancy, Smoky Mountains Passion Play Assn.; mem. adv. com. Blount County Alternative Center for Learning; chmn. Blount County Long Range Planning for Sch. Facilities; mem. adv. bd. Harrison-Chilhowee Bapt. Acad, mem. Leadership Knoxville. Served from pvt. to staff sgt. AUS, 1943-45. Decorated Bronze Star; named Outstanding Sr. Man of Blount County, 1970, 77, Hon. Order Ky. Cols., Commonwealth of Ky. Mem. Profl. Photographers of Am., Internat. Post Card Distbrs. Assn., Great Smoky Mountains Natural History Assn., Ft. Loudoun Assn., Tenn. Jaycees (editor 1954-55, sec.-treas. 1955-56), Blount County Arts/ Crafts Guild, Jr. Chamber Internat. (senator) Maryville-Alcoa Jaycees (life mem., pres. 1953-54), Blount County (v.p. 1971, 76, pres. 1977), Townsend (dir. 1969-71, 83-85, pres. 1983) chambers commerce, Tenn. Associated Press News Execs. Assn. (v.p. 1973, pres. 1974), Asso. Press Mng. Editors Assn., Tenn. Profl. Photographers Assn., Am. Legion, V.F.W., Chilhowee Bapt. Assn. (chmn. history com.) U. Okla. Alumni Assn. (life mem., pres. East Tenn. chpt. 1954-55), Sigma Delta Chi (life, dir. E. Tenn. chpt.). Baptist (trustee, pres. bd. trustees, deacon, chmn. evangelism, finance, personnel coms.). Mason, Kiwanian (pres. Alcoa 1969-70); Club: Green Meadow Country. Contbr. articles to profl. pubs. Home: 1510 Scenic Dr Maryville TN 37801 Office: 307 E Harper Ave Maryville TN 37801

STONE, IRVING I., greeting card company executive; b. Cleve., Apr. 5, 1909; s. Jacob and Jennie (Canter) Sapirstein; m. Helen K. Sill, Dec. 12, 1976; children: Hensha (Mrs. Hirsch Gansbourg), Neil, Myrna (Mrs. Harold Tatar), Judith (Mrs. Morry Weiss). Student, Case-Western Res. U., Cleve. Inst. Art. With Am. Greetings Corp., Cleve., 1923—, pres., 1960-78, chmn. bd., 1978—, chief exec. officer, 1978-87, also chmn. exec. com. Chmn. bd. Hebrew Acad. Cleve.; bd. dirs. Cleve. Inst. Art, Young Israel of Cleve., Yeshiva U.; trustee Simon Wiesenthal Ctr. for Holocaust Studies; 1st v.p. Telshe Yeshiva; life mem. bd. dirs. Jewish Community Fedn. of Cleve.; v.p. Am. Assn. for Jewish Edn., Bur. Jewish Edn., Cleve., Am. Friends of Boys Town Jerusalem; founder Kiryat Telshe Stone, Israel. Office: Am Greetings Corp 10500 American Rd Cleveland OH 44144 *

STONE, J(AMES) CONLEY, oil pipeline company executive; b. Bassett, Va., Apr. 10, 1931; s. George F. and Cora B. (Turner) S.; m. Nancy J. Warren, Sept. 15, 1951; children: James Conley Jr., Karen L., Kathryn J. BS in Archtl. Engring., Va. Poly. Inst., 1959, MS in Archtl. Engring., 1960. Project engr. Baton Rouge refinery Esso, 1960-63, various mgmt. positions, 1963-69; tech. mgr. Humble Oil & Refining Co., Billings, Mont., 1969-70, ops. mgr., 1970-72; investment mgr. Humble Oil & Refining Co., Houston, 1972-74; ops. mgr. Baton Rouge refinery Exxon, 1974-76; joint interest mgr., v.p. ops. Exxon Pipeline Co., Houston, 1976-86; pres., chief exec. officer, chief operating officer Plantation Pipe Line Co., Atlanta, 1986—. Served to capt. USAF, 1950-54, Korea. Mem. Am. Petroleum Inst., Assn. Oil Pipe Lines (exec. com.). Republican. Office: Plantation Pipe Line Co 3390 Peachtree Rd NE Atlanta GA 30326

STONE, JOHN MORRIS, real estate executive, oil and gas executive; b. Little Rock, Aug. 17, 1948; s. John Madison and Dortha Dean (Hale) S.; m. Mary Banks Craton, Nov. 23, 1974. AA, Texarkana Community Coll., 1968; BBA in Personnel Mgmt., U. North Tex., 1970; postgrad. in law, So. Meth. U., 1970-71, MBA in Real Estate, 1972. Cert. property mgr. Mktg. dir. Lamm-Frates Co., Dallas, 1972-77; pres., owner John M. Stone Co., Dallas and Texarkana, Tex., 1972—; pres. John M. Stone Mgmt. Corp., Dallas, 1977—, Stone Equities Corp., Dallas, 1981—, Stone Fin. Corp., Dallas, 1981—; bd. councilors Comml.-Investment Real Estate, Chgo., 1978—. Mem. editorial adv. bd. SW Real Estate News, 1977—; contbr. articles to profl. jours. Bd. cons. polit. affairs Christian Life Com. Bapt. Gen. Tex., Dallas, 1972—; jr. bd. officer Park Cities Bapt. Ch., Dallas, 1974-77; pres. Sunday Sch. class asst. tchr. Park Cities Bapt. Ch., Dallas, 1988—. Named one of Outstanding Young Men of Am., 1979. Mem. Comml. Investment Real Estate Council, Inst. Real Estate Mgmt., Nat. Assn. Realtors (v.p., exec. com., sr. instr., nat. treas., chmn. designated courses com., budget com., investment r/e council, 1988). Democrat. Clubs: Petroleum. Summit (Longview). Office: John M Stone Co 6060 N Central Expwy Dallas TX 75206-5270

STONE, LAWRENCE, retail executive. Chmn. Sterns Dept. Store, Paramus, N.J. Office: Stern's Bergen Mall Shopping Ctr Rte 4 Paramus NJ 07652 also: Allied Stores Corp 1114 Ave of the Americas New York NY 10036§

STONE, MARY ALICE, house products company sales organizer; b. Savannah, Ga., Oct. 27, 1940; d. Melvin Theodore and Alice May (Shaw) Pearson; m. Thomas Lanier Stone, Aug. 14, 1960; children: Mary Elizabeth (dec.), Thomas Lanier, Jr., Michael A., Vicki Lynn. Bookkeeper, Radix Microelectronics, Tustin, Calif., 1967-69; owner Smart Set Bookkeeping-Employment Agy., Santa Ana, Calif., 1969-72; cons. Princess House Products, Havelock, N.C., 1973-74, unit organizer, 1974-77, area organizer, New Bern, N.C. and Ga., 1977-82, sr. area organizer, Marietta, Ga., 1982-88, divisional organizer, 1989—. Philanthropic chmn. Cystic Fibrosis Found., Tustin, Calif., 1971-72; vol. Craven Cherry Point Child Devel. Ctr., Havelock, 1972, Spl. Olympics, Marietta, 1983-84; choir dir. Christ Episc. Ch., Havelock, 1973; cookie chmn. Craven Country Council Girl Scouts U.S.; active Mother's March of Dimes. Recipient #1 Sr. Area award Princess House Field, 1980, #1 Cen. Unit award, 1985, #1 Sr. Area award, 1987, #1 Sr. Area award, 1988; named to Nat. Area Honor Roll Princess House Inc., 1986, 87, named to President's Honor Roll, 1987, 88. Mem. Nat. Female Execs. Assn., Am. Soc. Profl. Exec. Women, Beta Sigma Phi (Woman of Yr. Havelock chpt. 1973), Beta Sigma Phi Internat. (life, order of Rose Degree 1979). Avocations: Swimming; reading; dancing. Office: Princess House Products PO Box 965065 Marietta GA 30066

STONE, PETER GEORGE, lawyer, publishing company executive; b. N.Y.C., July 29, 1937; s. Leo and Anne S.; m. Rikke Linde, Dec. 26, 1974; children: Adam, Rachel. B.S. in Econs, Wharton Sch. Fin. and Commerce, U. Pa., 1959; J.D., Columbia U., 1962. Bar: N.Y. 1963. Asso. Ballon Stoll & Itzler, N.Y.C., 1963-65, Raphael, Searles & Vischi, N.Y.C., 1965-67; v.p., counsel Firedoor Corp. Am., N.Y.C., 1967-69; partner firm Cahill, Stone & Driscoll, N.Y.C., 1969-75; v.p. fin. and law, treas., gen. counsel Ottaway Newspapers, Inc., Campbell Hall, N.Y., 1975—; lectr. on media law Nat. Jud. Coll., U. Nev., Susquehanna U., Marshall U., Cabrillo Coll., Hartwick Coll., Bucknell U., U. N.C. Served with USAR, 1962-63. Mem. ABA (forum com. on communications law), N.Y. State Bar Assn. (cts. and community, pub. events and edn., pub. info. through TV coms. chmn. spl. com. media law), Wharton Bus. Club, N.Y. State Fair Trial Free Press Assn. (guidelines com.), Am. Newspaper Pubs. Assn., Am. Arbitration Assn., Internat. Newspaper Fin. Execs. Office: PO Box 401 Campbell Hall NY 10916

STONE, ROBERT RYRIE, financial executive; b. Toronto, Ont., Can., Mar. 25, 1943; s. Frank R. and Norah I. (Varey) S.; m. Jacqueline P. Cogan, July 8, 1966; children: Charlie, Tracy. B.Sc., U. Toronto, 1964. Chartered acct., Can Inst. Chartered Accts. Treas., dir. fin. Gt. No. Capital Corp., Toronto, 1969-73; various positions Cominco Ltd., Vancouver, B.C., Can., 1973-78, treas., 1978-80, v.p. fin., chief fin. officer, 1980—; mem. adv. bd. Allendale Ins.; bd. dirs. Cominco Am. Inc., Pine Point Mines Ltd., Exploracion Mineral Internat. Espana S.A. (Spain). Chmn. bd. Jr. Achievement B.C. Mem. B.C. Inst. Chartered Accts., Fin. Execs. Inst. (pres. 1983-84). Office: Cominco Ltd, 200 Granville St #2600, Vancouver, BC Canada V6C 2R2

STONE, ROGER WARREN, container company executive; b. Chgo., Feb. 16, 1935; s. Marvin N. and Anita (Masover) S.; m. Susan Kesert, Dec. 24, 1955; children: Karen, Lauren, Jennifer. B.S. in Econs, U. Pa., 1957. With Stone Container Corp., Chgo., 1957—; dir. Stone Container Corp., 1968-77, v.p., gen. mgr. container div., 1970-75, pres., chief operating officer, 1975-79, pres., chief exec. officer, 1979—, chmn. bd., chief exec. officer, 1983—; bd. dirs. First Chgo., Morton Thiokol, Inc., GTE Corp., Stamford, Conn., Am. Appraisal Assocs., McDonald's Corp. Former trustee Glenwood (Ill.) Sch. for Boys; trustee Chgo. Symphony Orch. Assn.; fellow Lake Forest (Ill.) Acad.; bd. overseers Wharton Sch., U. Pa., term trustee; pres. com. Smith Coll.; adv. council Kellog Sch. Mgmt. Northwestern U. Named Best or Top Chief Exec. Officer in firm's industry, Wall St. Transcript, 1981-86; recipient Top Chief Exec. Officer award in Forest & Paper Specialty Products Industry, Fin. World Mag., 1984. Mem. Am. Paper Inst. (chmn. bd. 1985-86), Chief Execs. Orgn., Corrugated Industry Devel. Corp. (former pres.), Inst. Paper Chemistry (trustee), The Chgo. Com., Mid-Am. Com., Chgo. Council Fgn. Relations. Republican. Clubs: Standard, Tavern, Comml., Econ. (Chgo.); Lake Shore Country (Glencoe, Ill.). Office: Stone Container Corp 150 N Michigan Ave Chicago IL 60601-7568

STONE, RONALD GLENN, insurance company executive; b. Washington, July 21, 1950; s. Max Raymond and Mildred Lenore (Olson) S. BBA, U. Miami, 1973. Agt. Equitable of Iowa, Coral Gables, Fla., 1974-78; pres. Comprehensive Pensions Corp., Coral Gables, Fla., 1978-85; chief exec. officer The Comprehensive Cos., Coral Gables, 1978—; trustee U. Miami, Coral Gables, 1981—. Chmn. Code Enforcement Bd., City of Coral Gables, 1981-87. Mem. U. Miami Nat. Alumni Assn. (pres. 1982-84, Alumnus of Yr. 1985), Coral Gables C. of C. (bd. dirs. 1978-84), Rotary. Republican. Episcopalian. Office: The Comprehensive Cos 100 Almeria Ave Ste 210 Coral Gables FL 33134

STONE, VIVIAN RENE, staff and facilities manager; b. Indpls., Dec. 21, 1957; d. Rhodell and Helena H. (Steidle) S. GED, George Washington, San Francisco, 1976. Cert. CPR, first aid instr. Asst. mgr. Hilton Hotel, San Francisco, 1978-83; dir. front office Meridien Hotel, San Francisco, 1983-84; ops. mgr. Sterns Law Firm, San Francisco, 1985-86; mem. exec. staff State Bar of Calif., San Francisco, 1986—. Mem. Assn. Legal Adminstrs., Assn. Law Office Services, Nat. Assn. Female Execs. Democrat. Roman Catholic. Club: Commonwealth of Calif. (San Francisco). Home: 2638 Clement St #1 San Francisco CA 94121 Office: State Bar Calif 555 Franklin St San Francisco CA 94102

STONE, WILLIAM EDWARD, association executive; b. Peoria, Ill., Aug. 13, 1945; s. Dean Proctor and Katherine (Jamison) S.; m. Deborah Ann Duncan; children: Jennifer, Allison. A.B., Stanford U., 1967, M.B.A., 1969. Asst. dean Stanford U., 1969-71, asst. to pres., 1971-77; exec. dir. Stanford Alumni Assn., 1977—; pres., dir. Alpine Chalet, Inc., Alpine Meadows, Calif., 1987—. Bd. dirs. North County YMCA, 1975-76; bd. dirs. and chmn. nominating com. faculty club Stanford U., 1979-81; trustee Watkins Discretionary Fund., 1979-82; community adv. bd. Resource Ctr. for Women; mem. adv. bd. Bing Nursery Sch. Recipient K.M. Cuthbertson award Stanford U., 1987. Mem. Stanford Hist. Soc., Stanford Assocs., Bay Area Profl. Women's Club. Democrat. Club: Stanford Faculty. Home: 1061 Cathcart Way Stanford CA 94305 Office: Stanford Alumni Assn Inc 416 Santa Teresa St Stanford CA 94305

STONECIPHER, HARRY C., manufacturing company executive. BS, Tenn. Polytech Inst., 1960. With GE, 1960-61, 62-86, Martin Aircraft Co., 1961-62; exec. v.p. Sundstrand Corp., 1987, pres., chief operating officer, 1987-88, pres., chief exec. officer, 1988—, also bd. dirs. Office: Sundstrand Corp 4751 Harrison Ave Box 7003 Rockford IL 61125 *

STONEHOUSE, JAMES ADAM, lawyer; b. Alameda, Calif., Nov. 10, 1937; s. Maurice Adam and Edna Sigrid (Thuesen) S.; m. Marilyn Jean Kotkas, Aug. 6, 1966; children: Julie Aileen, Stephen Adam. AB, U. Calif., Berkeley, 1961; JD, Hastings Coll. Law, U. Calif., San Francisco, 1965. Bar: Calif. 1966. Assoc. Hall, Henry, Oliver & McReavy, San Francisco, 1966-71; ptnr. firm Whitney, Hanson & Stonehouse, Alameda, 1971-77; pvt. practice,

Alameda, 1977-79; ptnr. firm Stonehouse & Silva, Alameda, 1979—; judge adv. Alameda council Navy League, 1978—. Founding dir. Alameda Clara Barton Found., 1977-80; mem. Oakland (Calif.) Marathon-Exec. Com., 1979; mem. exec. bd. Alameda council Boy Scouts Am., 1979—, pres., 1986-88, Lord Baden-Powell Merit award, 1988; mem. Nat. council Boy Scouts Am., 1986—; trustee Golden Gate Scouting, 1986—, treas. 1989—; bd. dirs. Lincoln Child Ctr. Found., 1981-87, pres., 1983-85. Named Boss of Yr. Alameda Jaycees, 1977; Coro Found. fellow in pub. affairs, 1961-62. Mem. ABA, State Bar Calif., Alameda County Bar (vice chmn. com. office econs., 1977-78). Republican. Roman Catholic. Club: Commonwealth. Lodges: Rotary (dir. club 1976-78), Elks (past exalted ruler, all state officer 1975-76, all dist. officer 1975-77, 78-79) (Alameda). Home: 2990 Northwood Dr Alameda CA 94501 Office: Stonehouse & Silva 512 Westline Dr Ste 300 Alameda CA 94501

STONEKING, CAROLE LYNNE, former association executive, therapist, educator, consultant; b. Detroit, Mar. 28, 1937; d. Robert Frank and Esther Freda (Meier) S. BS, Wayne State U., 1963, MA, 1972. Program dir. Oakland br. YWCA, Clawson, Mich., 1961-63; program dir. no. br. YWCA, Highland Park, Mich., 1964-67; ctr. dir. Macomb br. YWCA, Warren, Mich., 1968-74; exec. dir. YWCA, East Detroit, 1974-79, Jacksonville, Fla., 1979-85; exec. dir. YWCA of the Midlands, Columbia, S.C., 1985-88; pres. Designs to Accommodate Madame Execs. (DAME), Columbia, S.C., 1988—, Stress Mgmt. Inst. Massage Therapy, Columbia, 1988—. Chmn. legis. com., mem. steering com. United Way of Midlands, 1986-87; pres. Coalition to Take Back the Night, Columbia, 1987-88, v.p., 1989; com. mem. Respite Care Council on Aging, Columbia, 1987—. Recipient Cert. Appreciation Am. Patriotic Commn., Jacksonville, Fla., 1982. Mem. Nat. Assn. YWCA Execs., Mich. Recreation and Park Assn. (registered profl.), Network of Female Execs., Fla. Council for Profl. Fundraisers (bd. dirs. 1983-85), Greater Columbia C. of C. (bd. dirs. 1987—, chair wellness com. 1987, sec. 1988—), Greater Columbia chpt. NOW (v.p. 1987, pres. 1988—), Independent Bus. Women (Columbia chpt. treas. 1988), Columbia Network for Female Execs. (com. mem. 1986—, sec. 1988), Cities in Schs. (Columbia) (bd. trustees, 1988). Office: Designs to Accommodate Madame Execs (DAME) 1005 Jakcson Ave Columbia SC 29203 also: Stress Mgmt Inst Massage Therapy 1005 Jackson Ave Columbia SC 29203

STONEMAN, DOUGLAS GRAYSON, oil company executive; b. Ottawa, Ont., Can., May 21, 1931; s. John A. and Muriel L. (Grayson) S.; m. Barbara Joan Damery, Oct. 12, 1957; children: Sharon, Michael, William. BSCE, U. Man., Can., 1954. Registered profl. engr., Alta., Can. Gen. mgr. prodn. Shell Can. Ltd., Calgary, Alta., 1973-75, gen. mgr. pub. affairs, Toronto, Ont., 1975-77, gen. mgr. environ. and govt. affairs, 1977-78, v.p. devel., Calgary, 1978-82, sr. v.p. oil and gas, 1982-84, sr. vp. bus. devel., 1984-87, sr. v.p. ops. and mktg., 1987—; chmn. Sultran Ltd., Calgary, 1978-88, bd. dirs., 1978—; chmn. Pacific Coast Terminals, Vancouver, B.C., 1982-88, bd. dirs., 1982—. Recipient Gold medal U. Man., 1954. Mem. Assn. Profl. Engrs., Geologists and Geophysicists Alta. (membership chmn. 1975, young mem. task force 1979, admission requirements task force 1981), Can. Petroleum Assn. (chmn. bd. govs. 1986), Sulphur Inst. (chmn. 1986-88, bd. dirs. 1981—), Can. Energy Research Inst. (bd. dirs. 1981—), Calgary Petroleum Club, Canyon Meadows Golf Club. Office: Shell Can Ltd, 400 4th Ave SW, Calgary, AB Canada T2P 0J4

STONER, EDMUND CURTIS, JR., consulting engineer; b. Riverside, Calif., Oct. 20, 1903; s. Edmund Curtis and Margaret (Copley) S.; student Lafayette Coll., 1921-22; BSEE, Yale U., 1926; m. Margaret Dorman Hamilton, June 23, 1926 (dec. 1958); 1 child, Margaret Hamilton Schofield; m. Mary J. Garcia, 1960. Chief engr. ITT, Peru, Cuba and Spain, 1933-41; asst. v.p. Fed. Telephone & Radio, 1945-48; cons. engr. to minister of communications Govt. of Turkey, Ankara, 1948-51; chief engr. Gen. Telephone & Electronics Corp., Muskegon, Mich., 1954-58, chief engr., Tampa, Fla., 1958-65; engr. planning dir. Gen. Telephone Co. Fla., 1965-68; cons. engr., 1969—. Served to lt. col. USAAF, World War II (col. Res. ret.). Decorated Bronze Star; Mil. Order Brit. Empire. Mem. IEEE, Rochester, Muskegon, Tampa chambers commerce, Order of Daedalians, OX-5 Aviation Pioneers, Order of Quiet Birdmen, Phi Kappa Psi. Presbyn. Clubs: University (Tampa, Fla.); Yale (NYC). Home: 310 S Burlingame Ave Temple Terrace FL 33617

STONER, R(ICHARD) B(URKETT), manufacturing company executive, member of Democratic national committee; b. Ladoga, Ind., May 15, 1920; s. Edward Norris and Florence May (Burkett) S.; m. Virginia B. Austin, Feb. 22, 1942; children—Pamela T., Richard Burkett, Benjamin Austin, Janet Elizabeth, Rebecca Lee, Joanne Jeannea. B.S., Ind. U., 1941; J.D., Harvard U., 1947; LL.D., Butler U., 1975. With Cummins Engine Co., Inc., Columbus, Ind., 1947—, various adminstrv., exec. positions, 1947-66, exec. v.p., corporate gen. mgr., 1966-69, vice. chmn. bd., 1969—; del. Democratic Nat. Conv., 1956, 60, 64, 68, 72, 76, 80, 84, 88; Dem. nat. committeeman for Ind.; bd. dirs. Kirloskar Cummins Ltd., Am. United Life Ins. Co., Pub. Service Ind., Bank One Ind. Corp. Vice chmn. bd. dirs. Cummins Engine Found.; pres., bd. dirs. Irwin-Sweeney-Miller Found.; pres. bd. trustees Ind. U.; bd. dirs. Christian Found., Columbus. Served to capt. AUS, 1942-46. Mem. Ind. C. of C. (dir.). Office: Cummins Engine Co Inc Box 3005 MC-60909 Columbus IN 47202

STONG, JOHN ELLIOTT, retail electronics company executive; b. Elkater, Iowa, Sept. 20, 1921; s. Elliott Sheldon and Nora Elizabeth (Daly) S.; ed. U. Colo., 1943; m. Olive Miriam Foley, Dec. 11, 1943; children—Mary Mandelson, Jon, Miriam, Salesman, Purucker Music, Medford, Oreg., 1946-48, dept. mgr., 1949-56, store mgr., 1957, partner, 1958-61, owner, 1962-64; pres. Purucker Music Houses, Medford, 1965-67, Music West, Inc., Eugene, Oreg., 1968-70, Magnavox Centers, Medford, 1971—, Exec. Assist., Consultants Internat., 1972—. Served with USAF, 1943-45. Decorated Air medal. Mem. Nat. Assn. Music Mchts. (dir. 1969-72), Scull Mchts. Research Group (dir., chmn.). Republican. Roman Catholic. Home: 2120 Woodlawn St Medford OR 97501 Office: Cons Internat 117 N Central St Medford OR 97501

STOOKEY, JOHN HOYT, chemical company executive; b. N.Y.C., Jan. 29, 1930; s. Byron and Helen Phelps (Hoyt) S.; m. Katherine Elizabeth Emory, Sept. 3, 1954; children: Helen Hoyt, Laura Emory, Hunt Emory, Anson Greene Phelps. Student, Amherst Coll., 1952, Columbia U., 1955. Asst. v.p. S.Am. Gold & Platinum Co., N.Y.C., 1956-59; officer, dir. various pvt. corps. for Investor Syndicate, 1959-69; U.S. rep. Financiera Metropolitana S.A., N.Y.C., 1962-75, Pub. Works Bank of Mexican Fed. Govt., N.Y.C., 1964-75; pres. Wallace Clark, Inc., N.Y.C., 1970-75, also bd. dirs., 1962-80; pres. Nat. Distillers & Chem. Corp., N.Y.C., 1975-86, also bd. dirs., chmn., 1986—; bd. dirs. Riegel Textile Corp., Rexham Corp. Founder, pres. Berkshire Boy Choir, Inc., from 1967; pres. Canterbury Choral Soc., 1968; chmn. health manpower com. United Hosp. Fund, 1966-71; bd. dirs. Assn. For A Better N.Y., from 1976; trustee Boston Symphony Orch., from 1969, Northfield-Mt. Hermon Schs., 1974-79, Council of Ams., from 1977, Bio-Energy Council, from 1977, James Weldon Johnson Community Ctr., Inc., 1965-70, Oratorio Soc. N.Y., 1965-75, Kodaly Musical Tng. Inst., 1973-75; trustee Coll. for Human Services, from 1964, treas., 1964-75; trustee Stowe Sch., Inc., 1960-76, pres., 1960-73; mem. adv. bd. Grosvenor Neighborhood House, from 1970, Music in Old Deerfield, 1977. Mem. Council on Fgn. Relations, Alpha Pi Mu, Delta Kappa Epsilon. Clubs: Union, Down Town Assn., Pinnacle, Century Assn., Met. Opera, Pequot Yacht, Ctr. Harbor Yacht, Lenox, Weston Gun. Office: Nat Distillers & Chem Corp 99 Park Ave New York NY 10016 *

STOOLMAN, HERBERT LEONARD, public relations company executive; b. Newark, Apr. 6, 1917; s. Abe C. and Ida H. (Sinar) S.; A.B., Catawba Coll., 1937; B.S., Temple U., 1939; postgrad. Harvard U., 1938; m. Sarah Janice Cutler, Apr. 6, 1944; children—Cathy Lynn (Mrs. Richard Schwartz), Robert Henry. Pub., East Camden Newspapers, 1941-57; pres. Stoolman Assos., Camden, N.J., 1946—; dir. public relations Camden County, N.J., 1953-86. Mem. Camden County Econ. Devel. Commn., 1963—, Camden County Cultural and Heritage Commn., 1973—. Served with USAF, 1942-46. Recipient Nat. award Nat. Assn. Counties, 1969, 72, 78, 79; Nat. award Am. Indsl. Devel. Council, 1963. Mem. Am., N.J. hosps. public relations assns., S. Jersey, Phila. public relations assns., Am. Assn. County Public Relations Officers, N.J. Press Assn., Phila. Press Assn. Lodge: Lions (dir. pub. relations). Home: 6 S Mansfield Ave Margate NJ 08402 Office: 514 Cooper St Camden NJ 08102

STOOPS, BRADLEY NEIL, engineering company executive; b. Anderson, Ind., Feb. 25, 1951; s. Joseph Neil and Deloris Mae (Oesch) S.; m. Melaney Sue Jannelli, Oct. 27, 1979; children: Elizabeth Ann, Patrick Neil. BA, DePauw U., Greencastle, Ind., 1973; M in Internat. Mktg., Am. Grad. Sch. Internat. Mgmt., Glendale, Ariz., 1975; MSMechE, Cleve. State U., 1980. Analyst, supr. Premier Industries, Cleve., 1975-76; with mktg. B.F. Goodrich, Cleve., 1976-80; product mgr. Nordson Corp., Amherst, Ohio, 1980-84; gen. mgr. Otto Engring., Carpentersville, Ill., 1984-87; bus. mgr. Nordson Corp., Amherst, 1987—. Contbr. articles to profl. jours. Mem. ASME, Soc. Mfg. Engrs. Home: 28041 Lincoln Rd Bay Village OH 44140 Office: Nordson Corp 555 Jackson St Amherst OH 44001

STORER, TODD CLEMENT, retired petroleum engineer; b. Pueblo, Colo., Nov. 9, 1922; s. Todd C. and Esther Mathilda (Olson) S.; grad. in Petroleum Engring., Colo. Sch. Mines, 1947; m. Jessie Hope Dean, Oct. 24, 1944 (div. June 1978); children—Todd C., Nancy Storer Yang, Vivian Storer Shields; m. 2d Doris M. McKinney Perry; 1 stepson, James N. Perry. With Amoco Prodn. Co. and predecessors, Chgo., 1947-84, ret. as mgr. prodn. systems, 1984. Served with C.E., U.S. Army, 1943-46. Mem. Data Processing Mgmt. Assn., Soc. Petroleum Engrs. of AIME. Republican. Episcopalian. Contbr. articles to profl. jours. Home: 4031 S Birmingham Ave Tulsa OK 74105

STOREY, JOSEPH DALE, health administrator, accountant; b. Nashville, Sept. 14, 1962; s. Joseph Casville and Mary Rita (Sullivan) S.; m. Pamela Diane Fisher, May 16, 1987. BS in Acctg., Bus. Adminstr., Trevecca Nazarene Coll., 1985. Cost acct. Third Nat. Bank, Nashville, 1983-85; staff acct. Vanderbilt Plaza, Nashville, 1985-86; controller Signature Health Alliance, Nashville, 1986-87, v.p. fin., 1987—; exec. v.p., co-owner Innovative Concepts Nashville, 1987—; bd. dirs. Tenn. Pharmacy Care, Nashville. Mem. Nashville-Davidson County Young Reps. Assn.; v.p. Trevecca Athletic Booster Assn., bd. dirs., treas. Coll. Hill Ch. of the Nazarene. Mem. Am. Coll. Health Care Execs., Trevecca Circle Alumni Assn. Mem. Ch. of Nazarene. Home: 1133 Burlington Ct Antioch TN 37013 Office: Signature Health Alliance 28 White Bridge Rd #312 Nashville TN 37205

STORJOHANN, DARLYS WILLIAM, mortgage company executive; b. O'Neill, Nebr., Mar. 20, 1959; s. William James and Helen (Dohnal) S. Grad., Hume Fin., Century 21 Career Sch., Federated Tax Service; PhD, Clayton Theol. Inst.; BSBA, UCLA, 1987. Co-owner, mgr. World Western Farms, O'Neill, 1969—; pres. Tradefair Internat., Inc., Denver, 1977-83; pres., chief exec. officer World Western Investment Devel. Corp., North Hollywood, Calif., 1978—; ptnr. Greater Los Angeles First Mortgage Co., North Hollywood, 1983—; owner "That's Class" Limousine Service, West Hollywood, Calif., 1984—; tandem cons. AAA Mortgage Co., Ischua, N.Y., 1983-84; v.p. Fin. Digest Pub., West Hollywood, 1983—; pres., chief exec. officer Fin. Services Ednl. TV Network, North Hollywood, 1983-85—; chmn. bd. dirs. Calif. Life Mag., West Hollywood, 1978—; co-host Am. Congress on Real Estate, Burbank, Calif., 1985-88; owner Mountain States Constrn. Co., Mountain States Mining, Ltd., Mountain States Investment Co., Greater Nev. 1st Mortgage Co., Storjohann Farms, Asset One Mgmt. Co., World Wide Realty Corp. Author: Make Money Work for You, 1982; editor mag. Calif. Life, 1978-85, Mktg. Ideas Showcase, 1984. Chief exec. officer Fan Clubs of Am., Celebrity Concept Promotions, Sliver Screen Prodns., Hollywood Promotions, Miss Calif. Fan Club, Cindy Landis Fan Club, Flip Wilson Fan Club, Landis Promotions, Locklear Promotions, Heather Locklear Fan Club, Scott Baio Fan Club. Mem. World Mail Mktg. Assn. (pres., chief exec. officer, 1983—), Aircraft Owners and Pilots Assn., Nat. Assn. Fin. Cons., Nat. Notary Pub. Assn., Nat. Specialty Merchandisers Assn. Club: Eagle (Providence). Home: 279 S Beverly Dr Beverly Hills CA 90212 Office: Greater Los Angeles First Mortgage Co 12115 Magnolia Blvd Suite 137 North Hollywood CA 91607-2693

STORK, DONALD ARTHUR, advertising executive; b. Walsh, Ill., June 17, 1939; s. Arthur William and Katherine Frances (Young) S.; m. Joanna Gentry, June 9, 1962; 1 child, Brian Wesley. B.S., So. Ill. U., 1961; postgrad. St. Louis U., 1968-69. With Naegele Outdoor Advt., Mpls., St. Louis, 1961-63; account exec. Richard C. Lynch Advt., St. Louis, 1963-64; media exec. Gardner Advt. Co., St. Louis, 1964-69; v.p. mktg. Advanswers Media/Programming, Inc. div. Wells Rich Greene, N.Y.C., 1975-79, pres., 1979—; also sr. v.p. subs. ops. Gardner Advt. div. Wells Rich Greene, 1983-86, exec.v.p., 1986-88. Bd. dirs. Trailblazers, Inc., Belleville, Ill., 1976; pres. Signal Hill Sch. Assn. Parents Tchrs., Belleville, 1981; eucharistic minister Blessed Sacrament Parish, Belleville, 1983—. Recipient Journalism Alumnus of Yr. award So. Ill. U., 1971, Alumni Achievement award, 1983. Served to capt. USAFR, 1961-67. Mem. St. Louis Advt. Club, Mensa, Alpha Delta Sigma (Aid to Advt. Edn. award 1971). Clubs: Mo. Athletic (St. Louis); St. Clair Country (Belleville). Lodge: Elks. Home: 34 Symonds Dr Belleville IL 62223 Office: Advanswers Media/ Programming Inc 10 Broadway Saint Louis MO 63102

STORMONT, CLYDE JUNIOR, laboratory company executive; b. Viola, Wis., June 25, 1916; s. Clyde James and Lulu Elizabeth (Mathews) S.; m. Marguerite Butzen, Aug. 31, 1940; children: Bonnie Lu, Michael Clyde, Robert Thomas, Charles James, Janet Jean. BA in Zoology, U. Wis., 1938, PhD in Genetics, 1947. Instr., lectr. then asst. prof. U. Wis.-Madison, 1946-50; asst. prof. dept. vet. microbiology U. Calif.-Davis, 1950-54, assoc. prof., 1954-59, prof., 1959-73, prof. dept. reprodn., 1973-82, prof. emeritus, 1982—; chmn. Stormont Labs., Inc., Woodland, Calif., 1981—. Contbr. articles to profl. jours. Lt. (j.g.) USNR, 1944-46, PTO. Fulbright fellow, 1949-50, Ellen B. Scripps fellow, 1957-58, 64-65. Mem. AAAS, Am. Genetic Assn., Genetics Soc. Am., Nat. Buffalo Assn., N.Y. Acad. Sci., Am. Soc. Human Genetics, Soc. Exptl. Biology and Medicine, Internat. Soc. for Animal Genetics, Sigma Xi. Office: Stormont Labs Inc 1237 E Beamer St Suite D Woodland CA 95695

STORMS, CLIFFORD BEEKMAN, lawyer; b. Mount Vernon, N.Y., July 18, 1932; s. Harold Beekman and Gene (Pertak) S.; m. Barbara H. Grave, 1955 (div. 1975); m. Valeria N. Parker, July 12, 1975; children: Catherine Storms Fischer, Clifford Beekman. BA magna cum laude, Amherst Coll., 1954; LLB, Yale U., 1957. Bar: N.Y. 1957. Assoc. Breed, Abbott & Morgan, N.Y.C., 1957-64; with CPC Internat., Inc., Englewood Cliffs, N.J., 1964—; v.p. legal affairs CPC Internat., Inc., Englewood Cliffs, 1973-75, v.p., gen. counsel, 1975-88, sr. v.p., gen. counsel, 1988—. Trustee, mem. exec. com. Food and Drug Law Inst.; mem. adv. com. Parker Sch. Fgn. and Comparative Law, Columbia U.; bd. dirs. CPC Ednl. Found. Mem. ABA (com. on corp. law depts.), N.Y. State Bar Assn., Assn. Bar City N.Y. (sec., com. on corp. law depts. 1979-81), Assn. Gen. Counsel (exec. com. 1987—), Indian Harbor Yacht Club, Econ. Club. N.Y., Yale Club, Milbrook Cluk, Board Room Club, Phi Beta Kappa, Theta Delta Chi, Phi Alpha Delta. Home: 11 Serenity Ln Cos Cob CT 06807 Office: CPC Internat Inc Internat Plaza PO Box 8000 Englewood Cliffs NJ 07632

STORY, EDWARD T., JR., oil company executive; b. Hillsboro, Tex., Nov. 7, 1943; s. Edward T. and Mildred Mae (Holland) S.; BS in Acctg. cum laude, Trinity U., 1965; MBA, U. Tex., 1966; m. Josephine Vinson Story; children: Elisabeth Claire, Emily Catherine, Sara Marie. Fin. analyst Esso Eastern Inc., N.Y.C., 1966-68; acctg. mgr. Esso Thailand-Bangkok, 1968-70; asst. controller Esso Standard Sekiyu-Tokyo, Japan, 1970-73; controller Esso Asia Services, Inc., Singapore, 1973-75; refining controller Exxon Co., Houston, 1975-78, exploration and prodn. controller, 1978; v.p. fin., chief fin. officer Superior Oil, Houston, 1979-81; vice chmn. bd. Conquest Exploration Co., Houston, 1981—; dir. Conquest Exploration, Hi-Lo Automotive Inc., Banc Tex. Group Inc. Dir. Chrysalis Repertory Dance Co.; chmn., Yokohama Internat. Sch. Bd., 1972-73; treas. Superior Oil Polit. Action Com., 1980-81. Recipient Wall St. Jour. Scholastic Achievement award, 1965. Mem. Fin. Execs. Inst., Am. Petroleum Inst., Mid-Continent Oil and Gas Assn., Alpha Chi, Phi Kappa Phi, Beta Alpha Psi. Republican. Methodist. Club: Texas. Office: PO Box 4512 Houston TX 77210

STOTESBERY, WILLIAM DAVID, b. Pitts., Sept. 30, 1952; s. Thomas J. and Joan (Beegle) S. BA, Tex. Christian U., 1974; MA in Pub. Affairs, U. Tex., 1977. Sr. cons. Peat, Marwick & Mitchell, Austin, Tex., 1975-82; dir. govt., pub. affairs Microelectronics & Computer Tech. Corp., Austin, 1983-88; corp. v.p. Westmark Systems, Inc., Austin, Washington, 1988—; cons. , Austin, 1982-83, bd. dirs. MBank Arboretum; chmn. Tex. Tech. Industry Legis. Task Force, Austin, 1987—, Am. elect assocs. Tex. Govt. Affairs Coun., Austin, 1987—. Contbr. articles to profl. jours. Mem. Austin Community Devel. Commn., 1978-80; exec. com. Leadership Austin, 1986-87, chmn. 1979-80; curriculum chmn., 1983-84, chmn., 1986-87; bd. dirs. Austin Women's Ctr., 1983-86, pres., 1985-86, chmn. 1986-86. Named Rising Star of Tex Tex. Bus. Mag., 1985. Mem. IEEE, Austin C. of C. (bd. dirs. 1986-87, Sesquiscentennial gift com. 1984-88, Quality of Life award 1986). Office: Westmark Systems Inc 1911 Fort Myer Dr Ste 404 Arlington VA 22209

STOTLER, EDITH ANN, utilities executive; b. Champaign, Ill., Oct. 11, 1946; d. Kenneth Wagner and Mary (Odebrecht) S. Student, Mary Baldwin Coll., 1964-66; BA, U. Ill., 1968. Asst. v.p. Harris Trust and Savs. Bank, Chgo., 1969-83; mgr. Can. Imperial Bank of Commerce, Chgo., 1983, sr. mgr., 1983-85, asst. gen. mgr. group head, 1985-88, v.p., dir. utilities, 1988—; bd. dirs. Southeastern Mich. Gas Enterprises, Utilities Telecommunications Securities (past bd. dirs.). Bd. trustees Fourth Presbyn. Ch.; pres. U. Ill. Liberal Arts & Scis. Constituent Bd. Mem. U. Ill. Alumni Assn. (bd. dirs.), U. Ill. Pres.'s Coun., U. Ill. Found., Mid Am. Club, Champaign Country Club. Home: 900 N Lake Shore Dr Apt 2106 Chicago IL 60611

STOTT, CHARLES E., JR., metals and mining company executive. V.p. Amax Inc., Greenwich, Conn.; pres., chief exec. officer Amax Gold Inc., Golden, Colo.; pres. Amax Mineral Resources Co., Golden; chmn. bd. Canadian Resources, Inc., Toronto.

STOTT, JAMES CHARLES, chemical company executive; b. Portland, Oreg., Sept. 5, 1945; s. Walter Joseph and Rellalee (Gray) S.; m. Caroline Loveriane Barnes, Dec. 7, 1973; children: William Joseph, Maryann Lee. BBA, Portland State U., 1969. Ops. mgr. Pacific States Express, Inc., Portland, 1970-73; bus. mgr. Mogul Corp., Portland, 1974-80; v.p. Market Transport, Ltd., Portland, 1980-85; pres., founder, chmn. bd. dirs. Chem. Corp. Am., Portland, 1985—, also bd. dirs.; bd. dirs. Market Transport, Ltd., Portland; chmn. bd. dirs. Carolina Industries, Portland. Mem. TAPPI. Republican. Roman Catholic. Club: University (Portland). Home: 18321 Wood Thrush Circle Lake Oswego OR 97034 Office: Chem Corp Am 2525 SE Ninth Ave Portland OR 97202

STOTT, PETER WALTER, trucking company executive; b. Spokane, Wash., May 26, 1944; s. Walter Joseph and Rellalee (Gray) S. Student Portland State U., 1962-63, 65-68, U. Americas, Mexico City, 1964-65. Founder, chmn. bd. dirs. Market Transport Ltd., Portland, Oreg., 1969—; bd. dirs., officer United Express Ltd.; chmn. bd. dirs., chief exec. officer, prin. shareholder Crown Pacific, Ltd. Bd. dirs. Sunshine div. Portland Police Bur. Served with USAR, 1966-72. Mem. Nat. Football Found. and Hall of Fame, Oregon Sports Hall of Fame (bd. dirs.), Oreg. Trucking Assn., Western Hwy. Inst., Internat. Platform Assn. Republican. Roman Catholic. Clubs: Mazamas, Multnomah Athletic, Univ. Office: Market Transport Ltd 110 N Marine Dr Portland OR 97217

STOTTER, HARRY SHELTON, banker; b. N.Y.C., Aug. 28, 1928; s. Jack and Adele (Sgel) S.; m. Marilyn H. Knight, Nov. 7, 1954; children: Jeffrey Craig, Cheryl Dee. Student, L.I. U., 1948-49; JD, St. John's U., 1952; postgrad., N.Y. U. Law Sch., 1956-57. Bar: N.Y. 1952, N.J. 1974. Pvt. practice in N.Y.C., 1952-53, 54-56; atty. Dept. Def., 1953; with trust div. Bank of N.Y., 1956-63; exec. v.p., sr. mgmt. com. United Jersey Bank, Hackensack, 1963-84; v.p., div. exec. for trusts and estates mgmt. div. Chase Manhattan Bank, N.Y.C., 1984—; dir., vice chmn. Chase Manhattan Trust Co. Fla., Palm Beach, Fla.; mem. probate com. N.J. Supreme Ct. Jud. Conf. Former pres. bd. dirs. Bergen County council Girl Scouts U.S.A.; bd. dirs., pres., chief exec. officer Bergen County United Way; treas. 2d Century Fund, Hackensack Hosp.; bd. dirs. Holy Name Hosp., Teaneck, N.J. Served with USN, World War II; brig. gen. Army N.G. Mem. Am. Bankers Assn. (fed. legis. council), N.J. Bankers Assn. (exec. com. trust div., pres.), Am., N.J. bar assns., N.Y. Militia Assn., N.Y. County Lawyers Assn., Bergen County Bar Assn. (trustee, former chmn. probate and estate planning com.), Fed. Bar Assn.

STOTTER, JAMES, economist; b. Cleve., Feb. 13, 1941; s. Morton and Ruth (Biskind) S. BSBA, Miami U., Oxford, Ohio, 1965; MA in Econs., Case Western Res. U., 1972. Instr. Cleve. State U., 1966-72; bus. devel. coord. City of East Cleveland (Ohio), 1975-77; rsch. analyst Predicasts, Inc., Cleve., 1979-81; mgr. bus. devel. Greater Cleve. Growth Assn., 1979-81; prin. Busimetrics & Fry Cons., Cleve., 1981—; mem. adj. faculty various local colls., Cleve., 1973—. With U.S. Army, 1961-62. Mem. Nat. Assn. Bus. Economists, Am. Mktg. Assn., Coun. Smaller Enterprises, Cleve. C. of C. Home and Office: 3200 Warrensville Center Av Cleveland OH 44122

STOTTS, MARYJANE LANIER, financial executive; b. Gallipolis, Ohio, Dec. 19, 1948; d. Carl E. and Jane (Gardner) Lanier; 1 child, Kimberly Jane. BSBA, Ohio State U., 1973. Sales assoc. Drustar Unit Dose Systems, Grove City, Ohio, 1973-76; pub. rels. dir. Devel. Disabilities Coun., Columbus, Ohio, 1976-78; assoc. dir. Assn. for Retarded Citizens, Columbus, 1978-80; investment asst. Rockefeller & Co., N.Y.C., 1980-81; Midwest mgr. Juvenile Diabetes Found., N.Y.C., 1981-82; profl. svc. mgr. Touche Ross Internat., N.Y.C., 1982-86; fin. mgr. Fredericks Michael & Co., N.Y.C., 1986—. Author: Volunteer Training Manual on Leadership Skills, Resource and Organizational Development and Financial Forecasts, 1982. Mem. FAFE, Assn. Retarded Citizens. Home: 114 Orient Way Rutherford NJ 07070

STOUDENMIRE, WILLIAM WARD, lawyer; b. Charlotte, N.C., Apr. 8, 1944; s. Sterling F. and Betty Zane (Scott) S. BA in Polit. Sci., Furman U., 1966; JD, U. S.C., 1970. Bar: Ala. 1970, U.S. Dist. Ct. (so. dist.) Ala. 1970, U.S. Ct. Appeals (5th cir.) 1971, U.S. Supreme Ct. 1973, U.S. Tax Ct. 1982, U.S. Ct. Appeals (11th cir.) 1982, U.S. Ct. Appeals (D.C. cir.) 1982, D.C. 1982. Assoc. Pillans, Reams, Tappan, Wood, Roberts & Vollmer, 1970-74; jr. ptnr., 1974-78; sr. ptnr. Reams, Wood, Vollmer, Killion & Brooks, 1978-82, pvt. practice, Mobile, Ala., 1982—; legal rsch. asst. Select Com. on Crime, U.S. Ho. of Reps., 1969; mem. law day com. Ala. State Bar, 1975-78, chmn., 1978. Mem. Leadership Mobile Adv. Coun. on Govt., 1982; mem. transition adv. com. Ala. Gov.-Elect Guy Hunt, 1986; mem. Mobile County Rep. Exec. Com., 1976—, vice chmn., 1976-81, chmn., 1979-86; mem. Ala. Rep. Exec. Com., 1979-86, platform com., 1976, 78, co-chmn., 1978, vice-chmn., 1985-89; bd. trustees, sec. Wilmer Hall Episc. Diocese Children's Home, 1987-88, vice chmn., treas. 1988—. Served with USCGR, 1966-72. Mem. Mobile Bar Assn. (law day com. 1974-78, chmn. 1977, del. young lawyers sect. ABA conv. 1976, 77), ABA (internat. sect. human rights subcom. 1975—, chmn. 1976-79), Phi Delta Phi. Home: 212 C Nack Ln Mobile AL 36608 Office: 2864 Dauphin St Ste A Mobile AL 36606

STOUFFER, NANCY KATHLEEN, publishing company executive; b. Hershey, Pa., Feb. 14, 1951; d. William Lawrence Sweeny O'Brian and Edna Luttrell; m. David Joel Stouffer, July 19, 1980; children: Jennifer Belle, Vance David. Pres. Andé Pub. Co., Inc., Camp Hill, Pa., 1985-88; pres., chmn. The Book Cook Inc., Camp Hill, Pa., 1988—; v.p. R&D E.S.P. Inc., N.Y.C., 1989—; cons. Syn-Comm Group, Inc., N.Y.C., 1988—. Contbr. articles on dyslexia and learning disabilities to popular mags.; author children's books. Exec. researcher com. on advanced studies in learning disabilities Med. and Ednl. Profl., SPECTRA. Republican. Office: 3400 Trindle Rd Camp Hill PA 17011 Office: ESP Inc Penthouse 160 E 56th New York NY 10022

STOUT, CRISPIN GEOFFREY, business owner; b. Miami, Fla., Oct. 20, 1952; s. Donald P. and Joan S. (Bowers) S.; m. Sharon P. Monahan, Aug. 18, 1984; children: Christina Lynn, Nicole Danielle. BSBA, U. Fla., 1974; MBA, Pa. State U., 1976. Fin. analyst Ford Motor Co., Dearborn, Mich., 1976-78; mgr. fin. analysis Champion Home Builders, Dryden, Mich., 1978-79; gen. mgr. Neff Machinery, Inc., Miami, 1979-86; pres. Tampa Tractor Co., 1986—. Bd. dirs. Execs. Assn. Greater Miami, 1982-83; active U.S. Olympic Com. Fla. chpt., 1982; Orange Bowl Staging Com., Miami, 1981-84. Recipient Bronze Dealer Mark of Excellence award Deere and Co., 1987. Mem. Southeastern Dealers Club (bd. dirs. 1986-87, sec./treas. 1987-88).

Democrat. Roman Catholic. Home: 1627 Palmleaf Dr Brandon FL 33511 Office: Tampa Tractor Co 5102 N 56th St Tampa FL 33610

STOUT, DONALD EVERETT, real estate developer and appraiser; b. Dayton, Ohio, Mar. 16, 1926; s. Thorne Franklin and Lovella Marie (Sweeney) S.; B.S., Miami U., 1950; m. Gloria B. McCormick, Apr. 10, 1948; children—Holly Sue, Scott Kenneth. Mgr. comml.-indsl. div. G.P. Huffman Realty, Dayton, 1954-58; leasing agt., mgr. Park Plaza, Dayton, 1959-71; now pres. various real estate groups; developer 1st transp. center for trucking in Ohio; pres. The Falls Estates, Wright Gate Tech. Ctr., Edglo Land Recycle, pres. Donald E. Stout, Inc. Served with U.S. Army 1944-45, USN 1945-46. Named Outstanding Real Estate Salesman in Dayton, Dayton Area Bd. Realtors, in Ohio, Ohio Bd. Realtors, 1961. Lic. real estate broker, Ohio, U.S. Virgin Islands. Mem. Dayton Area Bd. Realtors (founder; 1st pres. salesman div.), Nat. Assn. Real Estate Bds., Soc. Real Estate Appraisers (sr. real estate analyst), Am. Inst. Real Estate Appraisers, , Soc. Indsl. Office Realtors, Res. Officers Assn., C. of C., Phi Delta Theta. Lodges: Masons (32 deg.), Shrine. Contbr. articles to profl. jours. Office: 531 Belmonte Park N Apt 1101 Dayton OH 45405-4749

STOUT, RICHARD ALFRED, insurance executive; b. Long Branch, N.J., Apr. 18, 1927; s. Jones Rutherford and Hannah (Bennett) S.; m. Nancy Anne Brasch, May 1, 1954; children: Richard E., William R., Susan P., David A. BBA, So. Meth. U., 1950. CLU, Pa. Sec. Continental Ins. Co., N.Y.C., 1953-70; v.p. Internat. Group Plans, Inc., Washington, 1970-77; chmn. ConsumersUnited Life Ins. Co., Washington, 1972-77; pres. Protectogon, Inc., Rockville, Md., 1978—. Office: Protectogon Inc 5836 Hubbard Dr Rockville MD 20852

STOVER, JAMES ROBERT, manufacturing company executive; b. Marion, Ind., 1927; married. BSME, Cath. U. Am., 1950; LLB, George Washington U., 1955. With legal dept. Eaton Corp., Cleve., 1955-63, with corp. engring., 1963-67, with engineered fasteners div., 1973-74, group v.p. indsl. and security products, 1974-77, exec. v.p. ops., 1977-78, vice chmn. and chief operating officer transp. products, 1978-79, pres. and chief operating officer, 1979-86, chmn. and chief exec. officer, 1986—, also bd. dirs.; bd. dirs. Nat. City Corp., Nat. City Bank, Ohio Bell Telephone Co., GenCorp. Bd. dirs. Greater Cleve. Growth Assn. Mem. Machinery and Allied Products Inst. (exec. com.), U.S. C. of C. (bd. dirs.). Office: Eaton Corp 1111 Superior Ave NE Cleveland OH 44114

STOVER, JERRY DOUGLAS, project manager; b. Cleveland, Tenn., June 28, 1955; s. Carl Lilburn Stover and Dixie (Hayes) Houck; m. Jama Gayle Sands, Mar. 21, 1987. BS in Acctg., Carson-Newman Coll., 1978. CPA. Auditor TVA, Casper, Wyo., 1979-82; auditor TVA, Knoxville, Tenn., 1982-86, auditor, journeyman, 1986-87, project mgr., 1987—. Fellow Am. Inst. CPA's; mem. Assn. Govt. Accts., Toastmasters Internat., Alpha Kappa Psi. Republican. Baptist. Home: 220 E Red Bud Dr Knoxville TN 37920

STOVER, MATTHEW JOSEPH, finance company executive; b. Palo Alto, Calif., May 5, 1955; s. Carl Frederick and Catherine (Swanson) S.; m. Elizabeth Biddle Richter, Apr. 27, 1985. BA, Yale U., 1976; postgrad., U. Va., 1987. Gen. mgr. K&S Assocs., Beltsville, Md., 1977-78; dir. outreach programs U.S. Office Personnel Mgmt., Washington, 1978-81; exec. asst. to chmn. Fed. Maritime Commn., Washington, 1981; exec. dir. STN Computer Services, Inc., Alexandria, Va., 1981-82; dir. corp. communications Norton Simon, Inc., N.Y.C., 1982-83; dist. mgr. corp. communications N.Y. Telephone Co., N.Y.C., 1983-86, dist. mgr. customer services, 1986-87; v.p. corp. communications Am. Express Co., N.Y.C., 1987—. Editor, pub.: (lit. mag.) Buffalo Stamps, 1971-74. Mem. Internat. Assn. Bus. Communicators, Am. Mgmt. Assn., Nat. Com. U.S.-China Relations, Pub. Relations Soc. Am. Club: Yale N.Y.C. Office: Am Express Co Am Express Tower World Fin Ctr New York NY 10285-4805

STOVER, WILLIAM RUFFNER, insurance company executive; b. Washington, Aug. 31, 1922; s. Daniel I. and Carrie E. (Brubaker) S.; m. Carolyn McKean, July 19, 1947; children—Deborah Ann Stover Bowgren, Wendi Lee Stover Mirretti, Sheree Kay. Student, Northwestern U., 1941-45. Sales rep. Old Republic Life Ins. Co., 1945-1949, v.p., 1949-60, sr. v.p., 1960-68, dir., 1961-68, pres., 1968-69; pres. Old Republic Internat. Corp., 1969—, chmn. bd., chief exec. officer, 1976—; dir. Old Republic Life N.Y., Old Republic Ins. Co., Internat. Bus. and Merc. Reassurance Co., Home Owners Life Ins. Co. and subs., Minn. Title Fin. Corp., Bitco Corp., Founders Title Group, Inc., Republic Mortgage Ins. Co. Republican. Home: 907 N Sheridan Rd Waukegan IL 60085 Office: Old Republic Internat Corp 307 N Michigan Ave Chicago IL 60601

STOWE, DAVID HENRY, JR., agricultural and industrial equipment company executive; b. Winston-Salem, N.C., May 11, 1936; s. David Henry and Mildred (Walker) S.; m. Lois Burrows, Nov. 28, 1959; children: Priscilla, David Henry. B.A. in Econs., Amherst Coll., 1958. Vice pres. First Nat. Bank Boston, 1961-68; mgr. Deere & Co., Moline, Ill., 1968-71; dir. Deere & Co., Moline, 1971-77, v.p., 1977-82, sr. v.p., 1982—, exec. v.p., 1987—, also bd. dirs.; dir. John Deere S.A., Mexico. Home: 4510 5th Ave Moline IL 61265 Office: Deere & Co John Deere Rd Moline IL 61265

STRACK, WILLIAM RICHARD, insurance company executive; b. N.Y.C., Feb. 3, 1936; s. William and Unity (Lockie) S.; m. Sheila Scanlon, July 9, 1960; children: Deborah, William, Tracy, Robert, Nancy, Karen. BS, NYU. CLU. Ins. agt. AETNA, N.Y.C., 1961-72, mgr. prodn., 1972-81; sr. v.p. U.S. Life Ins. Co., N.Y.C., 1982-85; pres., chief exec. officer All Am. Life Ins. Co. subs. of U.S. Life, Chgo., 1985—, also bd. dirs. Served to sgt. U.S. Army, 1954-57. Mem. Nat. Assn. Life Underwriters, N.Y.C. Life Underwriters, N.Y. Chpt. CLU's, Million Dollar Round Table. Republican. Roman Catholic. Home: 255 Board Walk Park Ridge IL 60068 Office: All Am Life Ins Co 8501 W Higgins Rd Chicago IL 60631

STRAIN, DOUGLAS CAMPBELL, precision instrument company executive; b. Spokane, Wash., Oct. 24, 1919; s. Clayton Preston and Edith (Crockatt) S.; m. Leila Cleo Karicofe, June 10, 1943; children: James Douglas, Barbara Joanne, Gordon Campbell. BSEE, Calif. Inst. Tech., 1948; PhD (hon.), Internat. Coll. of the Cayman Islands, 1979. Registered profl. engr., Oreg. Design engr. Nat. Tech. Labs. Beckman Instruments, South Pasadena, Calif., 1948-49; v.p. research and engring. Brown Electro Measurements Corp., Portland, Oreg., 1949-53; pres. Electro Sci. Industries, Inc., Portland, 1953-80, chmn. bd., 1953-85, vice chmn. bd., 1985—; pres. Sunset Sci. Park, Inc., Portland, 1963-70; bd. dirs. Org. Software Inc., Portland, U.S. Bancorp/U.S. Nat. Bank, Portland, Optical Data, Inc., Lattice, Portland, Oreg. Grad. Ctr.; bd. overseers The Org. Health Sci. U. Portland. Patentee optical and electronic devices. Chmn. Tri-County Colls. for Oreg.'s Future, 1964-68, treas., 1968—; mem. Gov.'s Adv. Council for Oreg. Tech. Services, 1966-70; chmn. adv. panel to electricity div. Nat. Bur. Standards, Nat. Acad. Sci., 1971-74; mem. nat. metric adv. panel Commerce Dept., 1969-70; trustee Internat. Coll. of Caymans, 1971—, Scis. of Tomorrow, Pacific U., past pres.; assoc. Calif. Inst. Tech., 1975—; chmn. Oreg. Alumni Fund, 1975—; bd. dirs. Vols. Internat. Tech. Assistance. Menninger Found. fellow; recipient Bausch and Lomb Sci. award, 1938, Reed Coll. award, 1975, Wildhack award Nat. Conf. Standards Labs., 1977. Fellow Instrument Soc. Am. (nat. pres. 1970-71); mem. IEEE (sr.), Sci. Apparatus Makers Assn. (chmn., indsl. instrument sect. 1966-68, bd. dirs. 1973-76), Nat. Mgmt. Assn. (pres. Portland chpt. 1956-57, v.p. West Coast 1962-63), AAAS, Western Electronic Mfrs. Assn. (bd. dirs. 1956-57), Nat. Soc. Profl. Engrs., Precision Mgmt. Assn. (sr.), Electron Microscope Soc. Am. Clubs: City (research bd.), Multnomah (Portland). Home: 1730 SW Harbor Way Riverplace Apt 601 Portland OR 97201 Office: Electro Scientific Industries Inc 13900 NW Science Park Dr Portland OR 97229

STRAIN, H. JAMES, oil company executive; b. Eston, Saskatchewan, Canada, Oct. 27, 1929; s. Hugh Carlyle and Susie Adeline (Carley) S.; children from previous marriage: Marilyn, Hugh, Sandra, Michael, Barbara; m. Laurene Susan Strain, Oct. 4, 1984. BSME, U. B.C., 1953. From engr. to dist. prodn. mgr. Gulf Oil Can., 1953-69; v.p. ops. Panarctic Oils, Ltd., Calgary, Alta., 1970-76; v.p. prodn. and drilling Dome Petroleum Ltd., Calgary, 1977-81, sr. v.p. drilling and heavy oil, 1982-83, sr. v.p. drilling and frontier, 1984—; mem. mgmt. com. Syncrude, Ft. McMurray, Alta., Can., 1982-84. Leader Boy Scouts Can., Regina, Sask., 1962-64; football coach, Estevan, Sask., 1967-68. Recipient Sproule Meml. Plaque for Disting. Achievement Can. Inst. Mining and Metall. Engrs., 1976. Mem. Assn. Profl. Engrs., Geologists and Geophysicists of Alta., Petroleum Club Calgary (various offices). Mem. Anglican Ch. Home: 327 Canter Place SW, Calgary, AB Canada T2W 3Z3 Office: Dome Petroleum Ltd, 333 7th Ave SW, Calgary, AB Canada T2P 2H8

STRAKA, LASZLO RICHARD, publishing company executive; b. Budapest, Hungary, June 22, 1934; came to U.S., 1950, naturalized, 1956; s. Richard J. and Elisabeth (Roeck) S.; m. Eva K. von Viczian, Jan. 20, 1962 (div. May 1981); children: Eva M., Monika E., Viktoria K. B.A. cum laude, NYU, 1959. Acct. Greatrex Ltd., N.Y.C., 1952-53; partner Hamber Co., accts., N.Y.C., 1953-79; with Pergamon Press, Inc., Elmsford, N.Y., 1954—, v.p., 1964-68, exec. v.p., treas., 1968-74, pres., 1974-75, 80-88, chmn. bd., 1975-77, 88—, vice chmn. bd., 1977-80, 88-89, also dir.; vice chmn. bd. Pergamon Books Ltd., Oxford, Eng., 1986-88; group v.p. Macmillan, Inc., N.Y.C., 1989—; treas. Brit. Book Centre, Inc., N.Y.C., 1956-67; pres. Pergamon Holding Corp., 1981—; chmn. bd. Microforms Internat. Inc., 1971—; dir. Pergamon Press GmbH, Frankfurt, Germany, Pergamon Press Can., Ltd., Toronto, Ont. Bd. dirs., sec. Szechenyi Istvan Soc., N.Y.C., 1967-80. Mem. Phi Beta Kappa. Club: K.C. Home: 80 Radnor Ave Croton-on-Hudson NY 10520 Office: Pergamon Press Inc Maxwell House Fairview Pk Elmsford NY 10523

STRANAHAN, ROBERT A., JR., manufacturing company executive; b. Toledo, 1915; married. With Champion Spark Plug Co., Toledo, 1935—, v.p., 1949-54, pres., 1954-85, chmn. bd., dir., 1962—, chief exec. officer, 1962-86; chmn. bd., dir. Baron Drawn Steel Corp., Anderson Co.; pres., dir. Hellertown Mfg., Iowa Industries, P B Mktg. Office: Champion Spark Plug Co 900 Upton Ave PO Box 910 Toledo OH 43661 *

STRANAHAN, ROBERT PAUL, JR., lawyer; b. Louisville, Oct. 29, 1929; s. Robert Paul and Anna May (Payne) S.; m. Louise Perry, May 12, 1956; children: Susan Dial, Robert Paul, Carol Payne. A.B., Princeton U., 1951; J.D., Harvard U., 1954. Bar: D.C. 1954, Md. 1964. Assoc. Wilmer & Broun, Washington, 1957-62; ptnr. Wilmer, Cutler & Pickering, Washington, 1963—; professorial lectr. Nat. Law Ctr., George Washington U., 1969-72. Served to 1st lt. USMCR, 1954-57. Mem. ABA, Fed. Bar Assn., D.C. Bar Assn. Clubs: Metropolitan (Washington), Gridiron (Washington); Chevy Chase (Md.). Home: 5316 Cardinal Ct Bethesda MD 20816 Home: 286 Beach Rd N Figure Eight Island Wilmington NC 28405 Office: Wilmer Cutler & Pickering 2445 M St NW Washington DC 20037

STRANEY, SHIRLEY GARTON, services administrator; b. Wilmerding, Pa., July 3, 1931; d. Harry Denelsbeck and Rosemary (Bridgeman) Garton. BS, Duquesne U., 1954; postgrad., Queens Coll., 1967-68; MPA, Baruch Coll., 1981; postgrad., NYU, 1981-86. Tchr. West Valley Pub. Schs., Pitts., 1960; compliance mgr. Bklyn. Home for Children, N.Y.C., 1984-85; dir. spl. projects Bklyn. Home for Children, 1985-86, fiscal dir., 1986—; mem. fiscal com. N.Y.C. Human Resources Adminstrn. Author: Church Archives, 1982; contbr. articles to profl. jours. Vol. Berger for Senate Campaign, Kew Gardens, N.Y., 1978, Bklyn. Hist. Soc. Mem. Am. Soc. Pub. Adminstrn., Coun. Profl. Genealogists, NAFE, N.Y. Geneal. and Biog. Soc. Home: 8336 Beverly Rd Kew Gardens NY 11415 Office: Forestdale 67-35 112th St Forest Hills NY 11375

STRANG, CHARLES DANIEL, marine engine manufacturing company executive; b. Bklyn., Apr. 12, 1921; s. Charles Daniel and Anna Lincoln (Endner) S. B.M.E., Poly. Inst. Bklyn., 1943. Mem. mech. engring. staff MIT, 1947-51; v.p. engring., exec. v.p. Kiekhaefer Corp. div. Brunswick Corp., Fond du Lac, Wis., 1951-64; v.p. marine engring. Outboard Marine Corp., Waukegan, Ill., 1966-68; exec. v.p. Outboard Marine Corp., 1968-74, pres., gen. mgr., 1974-80, pres., chief exec. officer, 1980-82, chmn. bd., chief exec. officer, 1982—, also dir. Patentee engine design and marine propulsion equipment; contbr. research papers to sci. publs. Bd. dirs. Poly. Inst. N.Y. Served with USAAF, 1944-47. Mem. Am. Power Boat Assn. (past pres.), Soc. Automotive Engrs., Union Internat. Motorboating (v.p.), Sigma Xi. Club: Waukegan Yacht. Home: 25679 W Florence Ave Antioch IL 60002 Office: Outboard Marine Corp 100 Sea Horse Dr Waukegan IL 60085

STRANGE, DONALD ERNEST, health care company executive; b. Ann Arbor, Mich., Aug. 13, 1944; s. Carl Britton and Donna Ernestine (Tenney) S.; BA, Mich. State U., 1966, MBA, 1968; m. Lyn Marie Purdy, Aug. 3, 1968; children: Laurel Lyn, Chadwick Donald. Asst. dir. Holland (Mich.) City Hosp., 1968-72, assoc. dir., 1972-74; exec. dir. Bascom Palmer Eye Inst./Anne Bates Leach Eye Hosp., U. Miami (Fla.), 1974-77; v.p. strategic planning and rsch. Hosp. Corp. Am., Nashville, 1977-80, group v.p., Boston, 1980-82, regional v.p., 1982-87; chmn., chief exec. officer HCA Healthcare Can. 1985-87; exec. v.p., pres. health care group Avon Products, Inc., 1987—; lectr. Duke U., 1980, Harvard U., 1982—; bd. dirs. Infusion Care, Mediplex Group, Genica Pharms. Corp., Greystone Therapeutics Corp., Sigecom. Mem. Investments Orange Nassau Adv. Bd., Boston Mus. Fine Arts Coun., Atlas Assocs. Adv. Bd. Mem. Internat. Hosp. Fedn., Am. Coll. Healthcare Execs., Fedn. Am. Hosps., Washington Bus. Group on Health. Republican. Episcopalian. Clubs: Harvard, Old Hickory Yacht, Capt. Harbor P.S. Author: Hospital Corporate Planning, 1981. Office: Avon Products 9 W 57th St New York NY 10019

STRASBERG, JEFFREY HOWARD, controller; b. Watertown, N.Y., Sept. 19, 1957; s. David and Evelyn (Nathanson) S.; m. Patricia Hernando, Oct. 14, 1980; children: Stephen, Matthew. BSBA in Acctg. with high honors, U. Fla., 1978. CPA, Oreg., Fla. Mgr. Price Waterhouse, Miami, Fla. and Portland, Oreg., 1978-84; asst. contr. NERCO, Inc., Portland, Oreg., 1984-87; contr. PacifiCorp Capital Inc., Reston, Va., 1988—. Mem. Nat. Assn. Accts. (bd. dirs. 1982-85), AICPA, Fin. Execs. Inst., Oreg. Soc. CPAs, Fla. Inst. CPAs. Office: PacifiCorp Capital Inc 1801 Robert Fulton Dr 3d fl Reston VA 22091-4347

STRASSER, RICHARD JOSEPH, JR., post office executive; b. N.Y.C., July 15, 1947; s. Richard Joseph Sr. and Lillian Mary (Murray) Strasser; m. Christine Therese Avery, Oct. 18, 1969; children: Richard, Mary Patricia, Therese, Clare, Meira. BA in Govt., Seton Hall U., 1969; M. in Pub. Admistrn., Am. U., 1983. Mgmt. intern U.S. Post Office, Washington, 1969-71; acting postmaster U.S. Post Office, Walnut Creek, Calif., 1972; mgr. mktg. U.S. Post Office Headquarters, Washington, 1973-80, dir. office of policy, 1981-86, asst. postmaster, 1987—; Mem. Corp. Planning 100, N.Y.C., 1986—. Soccer coach, Arlington, 1982-85. Roman Catholic. Office: US Postal Service 475 L'Enfant Plaza SW Rm 10601 Washington DC 20260-3700

STRASSHEIM, DALE STEPHEN, health care executive; b. Burlington, Iowa, Sept. 27, 1946; s. Fred George and Mary Eileen (Heiniger) S.; m. Carol Bea Rinkenberger, Aug. 3, 1968; children: Angela, Brian, Eric, Alison. AA, Burlington Community Coll., 1966; BBA, U. Iowa, 1968; MS in Healthcare Adminstrn., Trinity U., San Antonio, 1973. Adminstrv. resident Meth. Hosp. Ind., Indpls., 1971-72; adminstrv. asst. Elkhart (Ind.) Gen. Hosp., 1972-73, asst. adminstr., 1973-74, v.p., 1974-76, pres., 1976-86; pres. VHA North Cen., Minnetonka, Minn., 1986—; bd. dirs. Health Insights, Inc., Baton Rouge. Precinct chmn. Ind. Rep. Party, Minnetonka, 1988. Recipient Disting. Svc. award Elkhart Jaycees, 1978. Mem. Am. Coll. Health Execs. Apostolic Christian. Home: 15110 Woodruff Rd Wayzata MN 55391 Office: VHA North Cen Inc 9800 Bren Rd E Ste 444 Minnetonka MN 55343

STRATMAN, JOSEPH LEE, petroleum refining company executive, consultant, chemical engineer; b. Louisville, Oct. 15, 1924; s. Dominic Herman and Mary Ann (Wolf) S.; m. Elizabeth Jewell Doyle, July 1, 1950; children—Joseph Lee, Mary Elizabeth, Sharon Ann, Judith Ann. B.Chem. Engring., U. Louisville, 1947. Registered profl. engr., Tex. Chem. engr. Pan Am. Refining Corp. (doing bus. as Amoco Oil Co.), Texas City, Tex., 1947-55, operating supr., 1955-61; mgr. Texas City Refining, Inc., Texas City, Tex., 1961-69, v.p., 1969-80, sr. v.p., 1980—. Bd. dirs., mem. exec. com., treas., chmn. Galveston County ARC, 1966-73; bd. dirs., mem. exec. com., chmn. Texas City Jr. Achievement, 1966-73; treas. Texas City Refining Good Govt. Fund., 1983-88. Served with USNR, 1945-46. Mem. Am. Petroleum Inst., Nat. Petroleum Refiners Assn., Am. Inst. Chem. Engrs. Roman Catholic.

STRATTON, FREDERICK PRESCOTT, JR., manufacturing executive; b. Milw., May 25, 1939; married. B.S., Yale U.; M.B.A., Stanford U., 1963. With Arthur Andersen & Co., 1963-65, Robert W. Baird & Co., Inc., 1965-73; with Briggs & Stratton Corp., Wauwatosa, Wis., 1973—, asst. service mgr., 1973-75, asst. sales mgr., 1975-76, group sales and service adminstrn., 1976-77, v.p. adminstrn., 1977; formerly pres. Briggs & Stratton Corp., Wauwatosa, to 1987; chmn. bd., chief exec. officer Briggs & Stratton Corp., Wauwatosa, Wis., 1987—, chmn. bd. dirs.; bd. dirs. Marine Corp., Milw., Weyenberg Shoe Man Co., Milw. Office: Briggs & Stratton Corp 12301 W Wirth St Wauwatosa WI 53222 *

STRATTON, JOHN CARYL, real estate executive; b. Chgo., July 11, 1920; s. John Frederick Otto and Dorothy Marjorie (Young) S.; BS cum laude, Princeton, 1949; MBA, U. New Haven, 1980; m. Lucille Waterhouse Hall, Mar. 13, 1974; children by previous marriage: Caryl Stratton Killing, John Caryl II, Susan Hall Levy, Evelyn Hall Brenton, Kenneth Hall. Chief liaison engr., Avco Mfg. Co., Stratford, Conn., 1950-55; pres. Yankee Engring. Service, Roxbury Conn., 1955—; pres. Stratton Realty, Roxbury, Conn., 1965—; dir. Auto Swage Products Inc.; lectr. U. Conn., 1968-74, Western Conn. State U., 1975-80; spl. adviser U.S. Congl. Adv. Bd. Chmn. Zoning Commn. Newtown, 1971-77; mem. Republican Nat. Com., Rep. Presdl. Task Force. Served with USAF, 1942-46. Decorated D.F.C., Air medal with oak leaf cluster; recipient Presdl. Achievement award, 1981. Mem. AIAA, Internat. Real Estate Fedn., Nat. Real Estate Exchange, Internat. Platform Assn., Newtown Bd. Realtors (pres. 1974, dir. 1975-79), New Milford Bd. Realtors, Conn. Assn. Realtors (v.p. 1981), Nat. Assns. Realtors, Internat. Platform Assn., Realtors Nat. Mktg. Inst. (cert. real estate salesman, cert. real estate broker), Am. Assn. Individual Investors, Internat. Arabian Horse Assn., Arabian Horse Club Conn., Mensa. Sigma Xi. Republican. Congregationalist. Clubs: N.Y. Athletic, Princeton. Address: Squire Rd Roxbury CT 06783

STRATTON, WILLIAM RICHARD, utility executive; b. St. Paul, June 6, 1934; s. J.H. and Selby (Bryant) S.; m. Janet B., June 23, 1962 (dec. Apr. 1982); children: Elisa C., Ellen T.; m. Lois Haskell Lenderking, Nov. 25, 1983. A.B., Dartmouth Coll., 1955; LL.B., Harvard U., 1961; Stanford-Sloan fellow, Stanford U., 1970-71. Bar: D.C. 1961. Mem. firm Clark, Nevius & Stratton, Washington, 1965-70; cons. Nat. League Cities, Washington, 1971-72; exec. asst. to chmn. D.C. City Council, 1972-73; commr. D.C. Pub. Service Com., 1973-79; v.p. rates and revenue requirements Central and South West Services, Dallas, 1979-80; sr. v.p. fin. Pub. Service Co. Okla., Tulsa, 1980—, dir., 1981—. Contbr. articles to jours. in field. Served to lt. USN, 1955-58. Mem. D.C. Bar Assn. Republican. Office: Pub Service Co Okla 212 E 6th St Tulsa OK 74119

STRATTON-CROOKE, THOMAS EDWARD, investment banker; b. N.Y.C., June 28, 1933; s. Harold and Jeanne Mildred (Stifft) S.; m. Sally Jean Morse, Mar. 17, 1956 (div. 1976); children: Karen, John Ryland. Student, Hunter Coll., 1951-52; BS in Marine Engring. and Transp., U.S. Maritime Acad., 1952-56; student, Washington U., St. Louis, 1961; MBA in Internat. Mktg., Banking and Fin., NYU, 1967. Commd. ensign USN, 1956, advanced through grades to lt., 1965; with Goodyear Internat. Corp., Akron, Ohio, 1956-58, Esso Internat., N.Y.C., 1958-60, Continental Grain Co., N.Y.C., 1960-64; dir. charter contracts Conoco, Stamford, Conn., 1969-70; cons. A. T. Kearney, Cleve., 1970-81; investment banker E. F. Hutton, Cleve., 1981—; chmn. Indsl. Devel. Resch. Coun., Atlanta, 1970, Indsl. Devel. Resch. Coun., Snow Mass, Colo., 1971; lectr. bus. U. R.I., Kingston, 1968-70. Contbr. articles to profl. jours. Mem. Nat. Task Force Reps. for Pres. Reagan, Cleve., 1982—. Mem. Naval Res. Officers Assn., Great Lakes Hist. Soc., Soc. Naval Architects/Engrs., Navy League, Univ. Club, Circumnavigators, Internat. Shipmasters Assn., Propeller Club, Masons, Shriners. Office: AG Edwards and Sons Inc 1965 E 6th St Ste 150 Cleveland OH 44114-2214

STRAUS, IRVING LEHMAN, public relations executive; b. N.Y.C., Apr. 1, 1921; s. Nathan and Helen (Sachs) S.; m. Anna Straus, Jan. 27, 1977; children: Daniel, William. Student, Amherst Coll. (Mass.), 1939-41. Ptnr. Ralph E. Samuel & Co., N.Y.C., 1954-65; v.p. Energy Fund Inc., N.Y.C., 1958-65; pres., founder Straus Assocs., Inc., N.Y.C., 1965-80; ptnr. Fin. Rels. Board Inc., N.Y.C., 1980-88, sr. cons., 1986—; dir. Arnold Constable Corp., N.Y.C., 1979-88; chmn. bd. Straus Corp. Communications, N.Y.C., 1989—; Pres. Inst. Systems Corp., N.Y.C., 1983—; founder, pres. Westchester Aquarium, Inc., White Plains, N.Y., 1947-55; chmn. Intrepid Mus. Pilot's Assn., N.Y.C., 1985—. Served with U.S. Navy, 1942-45. Decorated Air medal; recipient Silver Anvil Pub. Relations Soc. Am., 1979. Mem. Am. Assn. Ind. Investors (adv. bd. 1980—). Office: Fin Relations Bd 675 Third Ave New York NY 10017

STRAUS, JERRY ALAN, management consultant; b. Steubenville, Ohio, Jan. 7, 1950; s. Thomas Gene and Natalie Rose (Ferrari) S.; m. Nancy Valerie Barst, Nov. 25, 1984; 1 child, Alexander John. BA, Bowling Green State U., 1972; MA, Boston U., 1974. Dir. Tanglewood Inst. Boston U., 1974-76; mgr. Werner Erhard & Assocs., San Francisco, 1976-78; asst. dir. Mass. Cultural Alliance, Boston, 1978-80; ptnr. Johnson & Straus, Boston, 1980-84; owner, v.p. JMW Cons. Inc., N.Y.C., 1984—; mem. affiliate council Transformational Techs. Inc., Greenbrae, Calif., 1987—. Composer concerto (Bowling Green State U. 1st prize 1971, 72). Bd. dirs. Theatre Dist. Devel. Boston, 1978, Resource Mgmt. Assn., 1980-81; mem. The Hunger Project, N.Y.C., 1977, patron Carnegie Hall, N.Y. Mem. N.Y. Athletic Club. Democrat. Presbyterian. Office: JMW Cons 12 E 41st St New York NY 10017

STRAUSS, ALBERT JAMES, consultant paper industry; b. Washington, Dec. 23, 1910; s. Albert A. and Lydia (Thompson) S.; A.B., George Washington U., 1935; m. Violet R. Haney, Nov. 27, 1935. Central purchasing agt. Hecht Co., Washington, 1947-49; purchasing agt. E.F. Drew, Boonton, N.J., 1949-52; v.p. purchasing and transp. Riegel Paper Corp., N.Y.C., 1952-72; v.p., dir. Riegel Products Corp., Milford, N.J., 1972-76; cons. to paper industry, 1976—. Mem. Am. Paper and Pulp Assn. (chmn. materials com. 1960-62), Lehigh Valley Purchasing Assn. (dir. 1958-59), Am. Mgmt. Assn., Nat. Assn. Purchasing Mgrs., Pulp Consumers Assn. (dir.). Contbr. articles to profl. jours. Clubs: Antique Automobile of Am., Williams, Rotary. Home: 930 Bobwhite Pl Harrisonburg VA 22801

STRAUSS, JAY JERALD, mortgage executive; b. Chgo., Jan. 30, 1936; s. Charles Chester and Annabelle Betty (Sternstein) S.; m. Nancy Lee Borak, July 2, 1957; children: Jill Ilene Jaffe, Lesli Ann Fleming, Abby Lynne. BS in Indsl. Engring., U. Ill., 1957. Various positions, then sr. v.p. Standard Securities and Mgmt., Chgo., 1960-67; from loan officer to pres. B.B. Cohen & Co., Chgo., 1967-78; pres., chief exec. officer The Abacus Group, Chgo., 1978-84; chmn., chief exec. officer Focus Fin. Group, Chgo., 1984-88; chmn. Regent Realty Group Inc., Chgo., 1988—; bd. dirs. Cen. Ariz. Bank, Chandler, 1983—; adv. bd. Skokie (Ill.) Fed. Savs., 1984—; trustee Duke Realty Investments, Indpls., 1986—. Bd. dirs. Am. Jewish Com., Chgo., 1986—. 1st lt. C.E., U.S. Army, 1957--59. Recipient Civic Achievement award Am. Jewish Com., Chgo., 1982, Disting. Alumni award U. Ill., Urbana, 1985. Fellow Nat. Soc. Real Estate Fin.; mem. Inst. Real Estate Mgmt., Ill. Mortgage Bankers Assn. (pres. 1976), Lambda Alpha. Club: Green Acres Country (Northbrook, Ill.) (v.p. 1986-88). Home: 1440 N State Pkwy Chicago IL 60610 Office: Regent Realty Group Inc 150 N Wacker Dr Chicago IL 60606

STRAUSS, MITCHELL LINDLEY, banker; b. Balt., Aug. 16, 1950; s. William Alfred and Amelia Ann (Pryor) S.; m. James Nelson Arbury, June 18, 1977; 1 child, Stuart William Arbury. BA, Lake Forest Coll., 1972; MBA, U. Conn., 1978. Analyst Conn. Bank & Trust, Hartford, 1978-79; analyst Riggs Nat. Bank, Washington, 1979-80, loan rev. officer, comml. banking officer, 1980-83, asst. v.p., 1983-84, v.p., 1984-87, sr. v.p., 1987—. Mem. Robert Morris Assn. Office: The Riggs Nat Bank Washington 808 17th St NW Washington DC 20006

STRAW, GARY ROBERT, service executive; b. Springfield, Vt., Mar. 19, 1951; s. Robert Archie and Muriel Gwendolyn (Mayette) S.; m. Diane Leslie Durnall, Mar. 17, 1979; children: Gary Robert II, Megan June. Student, Deerfield Acad., 1970; BS, U. Vt., 1974. Gen. mgr. Point Sebago Resort, Casco, Maine, 1974-80; gen. mgr Meramec Valley Resort, Cuba, Mo., 1980-81; gen. mgr., dir. sales and mktg. Lost Valley Lake Resort, Owensville, Mo., 1981-86; pres. Straw and Assocs., Inc., Port Clinton, Ohio, 1986—, Resort Mgmt., Inc., Youngstown, Ohio, 1989—, Straw & Assocs. Pa., Inc., Straw & Assocs. Wis., Inc., Port Clinton, 1987—, S and A Mktg., Port Clinton, 1987—, Straw & Assocs. of Ohio, Inc., Port Clinton, 1988—, Resort Mgmt. Inc., 1989, Straw-Roth-Fletcher Mgmt. Inc., Port Clinton, 1989—; guest speaker U. Vt., 1975-78, Coast To Coast, Inc., Marco Isle, Fla., 1987, Washington, 1987, Palm Springs, Calif., 1989; sales and mktg. mgr. Jellystone Pk., Milw., 1987-88, Tievoli Hills Resort, Clarksville, Mo., 1987, Erie Island Resort and Marina, Port Clinton, 1987—, Hunter's Sta., Tionesta, Pa., 1988, Hidden Cove Resort, Ashtabula, Ohio, 1989—, River Pines Resort, Parkman, Ohio, 1989—, Carey Sta., Greensboro, Ga., 1988; cons. Patten Corp. Mid-Atlantic, 1988—. Bd. dirs. El Vallejo Owners Assn., Washington, Mo., 1987-88. Recipient Five Star Mktg. award Direct Mail Svcs., 1983, Highest Sales Vol. award Leisure Systems, Inc., 1987, Coast to Coast Resorts, 1988. Mem. Ohio Residential and Resort Devel. Assn., Am. Residential and Resort Devel. Assn. (guest seminar speaker 1989), Coast to Coast, Inc. (guest speaker 1987-89, Dun and Bradstreet. Republican. Episcopalian. Club: Lost Valley Lake Resort Owners Camping (bd. dirs. 1982-86). Home: 4448D Marin Harbor Port Clinton OH 43452 Office: 4495 W Darr-Hopfinger Rd Port Clinton OH 43452

STRAWBRIDGE, G. STOCKTON, retail executive; b. 1913; married. With Strawbridge and Clothier, Phila., 1934—, v.p., 1948-51, exec. v.p., 1951-55, pres., 1955-67, chmn., chief exec. officer, 1967-79, chmn. exec. com., 1979—, also bd. dirs. Lt. comdr. USN, 1941-46. Office: Strawbridge & Clothier 801 Market St Philadelphia PA 19105 *

STRAWBRIDGE, PETER S., department store executive; b. Phila., 1938; married. B.A., Hamilton Coll., 1960. Exec. trainee Abraham & Straus, Bklyn., 1960-61; with Strawbridge & Clothier, Phila., 1961—, buyer men's sportswear, 1963-68; mgr. Neshaminy Br. Store-Strawbridge & Clothier, Phila., 1968-69; v.p., gen. mgr. Clover Store div. Strawbridge & Clothier, Phila., 1969-76, corp. exec. v.p. mdse. and publicity, 1976-79, pres., 1979—, dir.; bd. dirs. Associated Merchandising Corp., CoreStates Fin. Corp., Greater Phila. First Corp., PhilaPride, Inc. Mem. bd. mgrs. Pa. Hosp. Mem. Independence Hall Assn. (bd. dirs.). Office: Strawbridge & Clothier 801 Market St Philadelphia PA 19107

STRAWBRIDGE, STEVEN LOWRY, retail executive; b. Miami, Fla., Nov. 2, 1943; s. G. Stockton and Mary (Lowry) S.; m. Elizabeth Billings, May 4, 1968; children: Steven, Whitney, Allison. BA, Hobart Coll., 1966. Mgmt. trainee Bloomingdale's, N.Y.C., 1967-68; asst. dept. mgr. jr. dresses Strawbridge & Clothier, Phila., 1968-70, mgr. women's hosiery dept., 1970-73, mgr. men's mdse. div., 1976-82, v.p., treas., sec., 1982—, also bd. dirs.; mgr. br. store div. ready-to-wear mdse. Strawbridge & Clothier, Exton, Pa., 1973-74, mgr. store, 1974-76. Pres., bd. mgrs. Travelers Aid Soc., Phila., 1979; mem. adv. bd. Salvation Army, Phila, 1984; bd. dirs. Children's Hosp. Phila., 1986. Served with Army NG, 1966-72. Mem. Gladwyne Sports Assn. (v.p., treas). Republican. Episcopalian. Club: Merion Cricket (Pa.). Office: Strawbridge & Clothier 801 Market St Philadelphia PA 19107-3199

STRAZDINS, EDWARD, manufacturing consultant; b. More, Latvia, Sept. 19, 1918; s. Juris and Anna (Smits) S.; m. Vera Gosts (div. 1978); children: Baiba, Anne; m. Sally Bateman, June 21, 1986. Student, U. Latvia, Riga, 1939-43; MS, Technische Hochschule, Darmstadt, Germany, 1949; postgrad., Polymers Polytechnic Inst., 1953. Asst. supr. Baltic Pulp & Paper Mills, Sloka, Latvia, 1942-44; prin. research scientist Am. Cyanamid Co., Stamford, Conn., 1949-85; pvt. practice mfg. cons. Fairfield, Conn., 1985—. Contbr. chpt. to Naval Stores, 1988; contbr. articles to profl. jours; patentee in field. Chmn. Luth. Ch. Summer Camp, Elka Park, N.Y., 1965-70. Fellow TAPPI (Divisional award, Harris O. Ware prize); mem. Am. Chem. Soc.

STRECKER, IAN, oil service company executive; b. Nottingham, Eng., June 26, 1939; s. Charles and Freda Pauline (Abel) S.; m. Elaine Louise Noble, Sept. 17, 1965; children: Mark, Paul. BSc with honors, Bristol (Eng.) U., 1961. Div. mgr. Schlumberger Ltd., Tripoli, Libya, 1968-71; tech. mgr. Schlumberger Ea. Hemisphere, Paris, 1971-72; region mgr. Schlumberger West Africa, Lagos, Nigeria, 1972-75; v.p., gen. mgr. Schlumberger Europe, London, 1975-76; v.p. ops. Flopetrol Paris, 1976-78; pres. Dowell Schlumberger, Paris, 1978-80; v.p. ops. Schlumberger Well Services, Houston, 1980-82, pres., 1982-85; exec. v.p. Schlumberger Ltd., Houston, 1985—. Contbr. articles to profl. jours. Trustee U. Houston Found., 1983-87; bd. dirs. Jr. Achievement, 1985-87. Mem. Am. Petroleum Inst., Soc. Petroleum Engrs., Soc. Profl. Well Log Analysts, Nat. Ocean Industries Assn. (bd. dirs. 1985—). Club: Racquet (Houston). Office: Schlumberger Ltd 205 Industrial Rd Sugar Land TX 77478

STREET, CHRIS ROBERT, leasing company executive; b. Cuckfield, Sussex, Eng., Apr. 3, 1943; came to U.S., 1977; s. Harry James and Rose Maud Hilton; m. Dian Helfer, Aug. 29, 1981; children: Samantha, Tamara. Student, U. London, U. Southampton, Eng. Buyer Freeman's, London, 1965-67; chmn. North Midland (Eng.) Fin. Centre, 1968-77; pres. WWUSA, Inc., Encino, Calif., 1978-86, A.C. Leasing & Assocs., Inc., Van Nuys, Calif., 1985—; cons. Creative Force, Malibu, Calif., 1979-83. Patentee automatic confectionary dispenser, 1981. Republican. Episcopalian. Clubs: Lake Lindero Yacht (vice commodore, 1985), Lake Lindero Country (mem. world tennis bd. 1986—). Office: AC Leasing & Assocs Inc 14265 Oxnard St Van Nuys CA 91401

STREET, DAVID HARGETT, multi industry company executive; b. Oklahoma City, Dec. 4, 1943; s. Bob Allen and Elizabeth Anne (Hargett) S.; m. Betty Ann Nichols, Oct. 1, 1966; children: Elizabeth Ann, Randall Hargett, Jeffrey David. B.A. in English, U. Okla., 1965; M.B.A. in Fin, Wharton Grad. Sch., U. Pa., 1970. Vice pres. SEI Corp., 1970; v.p., prin. Street & Street, Inc., N.Y.C., 1970-74; v.p., mgr. San Francisco regional office First Nat. Bank Chicago, 1974-78; sr. v.p., chief fin. officer, treas. Bangor Punta Corp., Greenwich, Conn., 1978-84; v.p., treas. Penn Central Corp., Greenwich, Conn., 1984-86; v.p. fin. Penn Central Corp., Greenwich, 1986-87; sr. v.p. fin. Penn Central Corp., Cin., 1987—; bd. dirs. INFOTEC Devel. Corp., Costa Mesa, Calif.; mem. adv. bd. Mfrs. Hanover Trust Co., 1982-88. Vice chmn. bd., treas. Greenwich Acad. for Girls, 1984-87; chmn. bd., treas. Greenwich Acad., 1987-88. Served to 1st lt. M.I., U.S. Army, 1966-67. Mem. Greenwich Country Club, Bankers Club. Republican. Presbyterian. Home: 6475 Given Rd Cincinnati OH 45243 Office: Penn Cen Corp 1 E 4th St Cincinnati OH 45202

STREET, DOUGLAS DEAN, accountant; b. Vienna, Ill., Dec. 27, 1935; s. Logan and Mable Eliza (Richardson) S.; m. Lucy Ellen Brewer, July 3, 1957; children: Mark Dean, Matthew Douglas, Maureen Diane. AA, Longview Coll., 1975; BA, Park Coll., 1976; MBA, U. Mo., 1977. CPA, Mo., Kans. Enlisted as pvt. U.S. Marine Corps, 1953, advanced through grades to capt., 1969, ret., 1974; mgr. Ralph C. Johnson & Co., Kansas City, Mo., 1978-84, ptnr., 1984-86; owner Douglas D. Street CPA, Kansas City, 1986-87; ptnr. Bryant and Street, Kansas City, Kans. and Mo., 1987—. Mem. Am. Inst. CPA's, Mo. Soc. CPA's. Home: 10003 Beacon St Kansas City MO 64134 Office: 8040 Parallel Kansas City KS 66109

STREET, JAMES RICHARD, oil company executive; b. Detroit, June 10, 1937; s. James Albert and Charlotte Jean (Orions) S.; m. Judith Wicks, Aug. 2, 1975; children: Jon, Erik, Sharon, Kirsten, Karin. BSChemE., U. Mich., 1959, MSChemE., 1962, MS in Maths., 1962, PhDChemE., 1963. Engr. Shell Devel. Co., Emeryville, Calif., 1963-66, supr., 1966-67; mgr. tech. lab. Shell Chem. Co., Denver, 1967-69; process supt. Shell Chem. Co., Houston, 1969-71; dir. exploratory sci. Shell Devel. Co., Houston, 1971-72; dir. corp. research and devel. engring. Shell Oil Co., Houston, 1972-75, mgr. mfg. lubricants, 1975-77, mgr. bus. ctr., 1977-79, gen. mgr., 1979-80, v.p. corp. planning, 1980-81; pres. Shell Chem. Co., 1981-87, Shell Devel. Co., Houston, 1987—. Bd. dirs. Pub. Broadcasting System Channel-8, Houston, 1987—; mem. nat. adv. com. Coll. Engring. U. Mich.; mem. adv. com. ctr. for risk and decision processes U. Pa.; mem. adv. bd. Ctr. for History of Chemistry. Mem. Am. Inst. Chem. Engrs. (Robert L. Jacks Meml. award 1985), Soc. Chem. Industry (chmn. exec. com.), Century Club, Tex. Club. Office: Shell Devel Co PO Box 2463 Houston TX 77252

STREGE, DAVID GLENN, financial planner; b. Wickenberg, Ariz., Nov. 22, 1958; s. Glenn Harris and JoAnn L. (Beyer) S.; m. Jennifer Lynn Thompson, May 8, 1982; children: Erik C., Adrienne B. BSBA, Drake U., 1981. Cert. fin. planner; chartered fin. analyst. Personal fin. planner AID Fin. Planning Co., Des Moines, 1981-84; fin. planning rep. First Interstate Bank Des Moines, 1984-85; personal fin. planner Statesman Fin. Svc. Ctr., Des Moines, 1985-87; chief fin. planner Bryton Capital Mgmt., Inc., West Des Moines, Iowa, 1987—; mem. adj. faculty Coll. for Fin. Planning, 1984-87; speaker U.S. Cen. Edn., Des Moines, 1986—. Instr. Jr. Achievement, Des Moines, 1985; bd. dirs. Bus. Aid Soc. Polk County, 1984-87, Cornbelt Region USVBA, 1984-87. Fellow Fin. Analysts Fedn.; mem. Internat. Assn. for Fin. Planning (directory chmn. Des Moines chpt. 1982-85, v.p. memberships 1987-88, case study chmn. 1987-88), Des Moines C. of C. (chmn. Golden Circle games 1986-88), U.S. Volleyball Assn. (bd. dirs. Cornbelt region 1984-87), Des Moines Volleyball Club (pres. 1982-87). Lutheran. Office: Bryton Capital Mgmt Inc 2900 Westown Pkwy Ste D West Des Moines IA 50265

STREICH, ARTHUR HAROLD, financial services executive; b. Mpls., Apr. 22, 1925; s. Herman Henry and Rose (Anderson) S.; m. Arlene June Ostlund, Aug. 30, 1947; children: Jennifer Streich Hallam, Jack, Paula Jo. BA in Journalism, Macalester Coll., 1952. Ptnr., S&E Publs., St. Paul, 1952-55; asst. sec. Northwestern Lumbermans Assn., 1955-57; gen. mgr. Nat. Electronics Conf., 1957-59; pub. rels. exec. Mullen & Assos., Inc., Mpls., 1959-60; investment adviser Dempsey Tegeler & Co., Inc., Mpls., 1960-63; regional sales mgr. Dreyfus Corp., 1963-68; regional v.p. Anchor Corp., Chgo., 1968-69; regional v.p. wholesale sales and mgmt. Dreyfus Sales Corp., Chgo., 1969-72; regional v.p. Crosby Corp., Chgo., 1972-73; regional sales mgr. John Nuveen & Co., Chgo., 1973-74; owner Fin. Planning Svcs. Co., Wayzata, Minn., 1974-86; regional v.p. RNC Mut. Fund Group, Wayzata, 1986— Rep. candidate for mayor St. Paul, 1952. Served with USN, USMC, 1942-46. Mem. Nat. Assn. Security Dealers (registered prin.), Nat. Speakers Assn. Republican. Mem. Evang. Free Ch. Club: Toastmasters (Disting. Toastmaster). Address: 14431 Wellington Rd Wayzata MN 55391

STRENGER, CHRISTIAN H., brokerage house executive; b. 1943. Student, Cologne U., Fed. Republic of Germany. Sr. v.p. Deutsche Bank, Frankfort, Fed. Republic of Germany, 1972-82; gen. mge. Deutsch Bank A.G., London, 1982-85; pres., chief exec. officer, mng. dir. Deutsche Bank Capital Corp., N.Y.C., 1985—; bd. dirs. Deutsche Credit Corp., Deerfield, Ill. Office: Deutsche Bank Capital Corp 40 Wall St New York NY 10005 *

STRENGTH, ROBERT SAMUEL, manufacturing company executive; b. Tullos, La., May 14, 1929; s. Houston Orion and Gurcie Dean (Cousins) S.; B.S. in Indsl. Mgmt., Auburn U., 1956; m. Janis Lynette Grace, Sept. 12, 1954; children—Robert David (dec.), James Steven (dec.), Stewart Alan, James Houston (dec.). Engr., supr. plant safety Monsanto Co., 1956-74, engring. standards mgr. Corporate Fire Safety Center, St. Louis, 1974-78, mgr. product safety and acceptability Monsanto Polymer Products Co. (formerly Monsanto Plastics and Resins Co.), St. Louis, 1978-82, mgr. product safety, Monsanto Chem. Co., 1982-87; founder, pres. Product Safety Mgmt., Inc., 1987—. mem. com. on toxicity of materials used in rapid rail transit, NRC, 1984—. Pres. Greenwood (S.C.) Citizens Safety Council, 1966-68. Served with USAF, 1948-52. Recipient S. C. Outstanding Service to Safety award Nat. Safety Council, 1968; registered profl. engr., Calif.; cert. safety profl. Mem. Am. Soc. Safety Engrs., Nat. Safety Council (pres. textile sect. 1966), So. Bldg. Code Congress, Internat. Conf. of Bldg. Ofcls., Bldg. Ofcls. and Code Adminstrs. Internat., Nat. Fire Protection Assn., ASTM, Nat. Inst. Bldg. Scis., Plastic Pipe and Fittings Assn. ASHRAE, Soc. Plastics Ind. (chmn. coordinating com. on fire safety 1985—), Nat. Acad. Scis. Republican. Methodist. Club: Cherry Hills Country. Editor textile sect. newsletter Nat. Safety Council, 1961-62. Home and Office: 3371 Edgewater Dr Gulf Breeze FL 32562

STRENIO, ANDREW JOHN, JR., lawyer; b. Erie, Pa., Apr. 3, 1952; s. Andrew and Mary Coletta (Rodgers) S.; m. Judith Lee Ferington, Aug. 31, 1974; children: Elizabeth Ann, Andrew John III, Stephen Peter. AB, Princeton U., 1974; JD cum laude, M in Pub. Policy, Harvard U., 1978. Bar: D.C. 1978. Research assoc. Huron Inst., Cambridge, Mass., 1978-79; assoc. Wald, Harkrader & Ross, Washington, 1980; staff economist, atty. Pres.' Council of Econ. Advisers, Washington, 1980-81; asst. dir. regulatory evaluation, Bur. Consumer Protection FTC, Washington, 1982-84, commr., 1986—; commr. ICC, Washington, 1984-85. Author: The Testing Trap, 1981; contbr. articles to mags. Mem. ABA, D.C. Bar Assn. Democrat. Roman Catholic. Office: FTC Room 326 7th & Pennsylvania Aves NW Washington DC 20580

STRESEN-REUTER, FREDERICK ARTHUR, II, communications executive; b. Oak Park, Ill., July 31, 1942; s. Alfred Procter and Carol Frances (von Pohek) S.-R.; cert. in German, Salzburg (Austria) Summer Sch., 1963; BA, Lake Forest Coll., 1967. Mgr. advt. Stresen-Reuter Internat., Bensenville, Ill., 1965-70; mgr. animal products mktg. Internat. Minerals & Chem. Corp., Mundelein, Ill., 1971-79, dir. animal products mktg., 1979-87, dir. communications, 1987—; pres. Brit. Iron Ltd., Lake Forest, Ill., 1984-86; lectr. mktg. U. Ill., 1977, Am. Mgmt. Assn., 1978; cons. mktg. to numerous agrl. cos., 1973—. Trustee, governing mem. Libr. Internat. Rels., 1978, Chgo. Recipient cert. of excellence Chgo. 77 Vision Show, 1977; Silver Aggy award, 1977; spl. jury gold medal V.I., N.Y. Internat. film festival awards, 1977; CINE Golden Eagle, 1980, 88; Bronze medal N.Y. Internat. Film Festival, 1981, Silver medal, 1982; Silver Screen award U.S. Indsl. Film Festival, 1981. Mem. Nat. Feed Ingredients Assn. (chmn. publicity and publs. 1976), Nat. Agrl. Mktg. Assn. (numerous awards), Am. Feed Mfrs. Assn. (citation 1976, pub. rels. com., conv. com.), Mid-Am. Commodity Exch., 1984-86, USCG Aux., U.S. Naval Inst., Am. Film Inst., Bugatti Owners Club. Episcopalian. Club: Sloane (London). Contbr. articles to profl. jours. Home: Tryon Grove Farm 8914 Tryon Grove Rd Ringwood IL 60072 Office: Pitman-Moore Inc 421 E Hawley St Mundelein IL 60060

STREU, RAYMOND OLIVER, financial planner, securities executive; b. Hereford, Tex., July 7, 1931; s. William Urlin and Yetta May (Hackworth) s.; m. Joan Eliz Hardwick, Nov. 24, 1953 (div. Oct. 1963); children: William Raymond, Ronald Hardwick, Russell Francis; m. Wanda Mae Daves, Sept. 2, 1964; children: Rickey Lynn, Rodney Jack, Randall Oliver. BBA, Tex. Tech U., 1952. Co-owner Streu Hardware Co., Hereford, 1948-60; agt., broker Justice Real Estate, Hereford, 1960-62; pres. Mark IV Realtors, Hereford, 1962-73; rep. Waddell & Reed, Inc., Hereford, 1965-73, div. mgr., 1973-78; br. mgr. E.F. Hutton & Co., Amarillo, Tex., 1978-83; pres. Lusk & Streu Fin. Planners, Inc., Amarillo, 1983—. Leadership chmn. Llano Estacado coun. Boy Scouts Am., 1972-73. Lt. comdr. USNR, 1952-66. Mem. Internat. Assn. Fin. Planning (pres. local chpt. 1988—), Inst. Cert. Fin. Planners, High Plains Eye Bank (life), Jaycees, Lions (pres. Amarillo chpt. 1975-76). Republican. Presbyterian. Office: Lusk & Streu Fin Planners Inc 3414 Olsen Ste E Amarillo TX 79109

STRICKLAND, NANCY ARNETTE STANLEY, finance executive; b. Smithfield, N.C., Nov. 18, 1949; d. William Bennette and Lola (Holley) Stanley; m. Matthew Theodore Strickland, Dec. 20, 1975; 1 child, William Scott. BS in Math. Edn., N.C. State U., 1972; MBA, U. N.C., 1975. Tchr. math. Johnston County High Sch., Smithfield, N.C., 1972-73; office mgr. J.W. Simons, Raleigh, N.C., 1975-76; tchr. math. Cath. High Sch., Pensacola, Fla., 1976-79; fin. analyst Hardee's Food Systems, Inc., Rocky Mount, N.C., 1980-81, sr. fin. analyst, 1981-82, mgr. corp. analysis, 1982-83, dir. corp. planning, 1983-84, dir. fin. planning and analysis, 1984-86, corp. dir. fin., 1986—; mem. corp. contbns. com. Imasco U.S.A., Inc., Rocky Mount, 1984—, mem. exec. adv. bd., 1985—. Mem. Dental Aux., Rocky Mount, 1979—, Nash County Hist. Soc., 1982—, Friends of the Arts, Rocky Mount, 1983—, N.C. Mus. History Assocs., Raleigh, 1984—, Local Area Women's Network, Rocky Mount, 1984—; mem. budget and allocations com. Rocky Mount United Way, 1984-86; mem. exec. com. N.C. Young Dems., Raleigh, 1972-73; mem. fin. com. Rocky Mount Meth. Ch., 1985—. Mem. Nat. Assn. Female Execs., Pi Mu Epsilon, Phi Kappa Phi. Clubs: YWCA, Pilot (Rocky Mount) (v.p. 1984-85). Office: Hardee's Food Systems Inc 1233 N Church St Rocky Mount NC 27801

STRICKLAND, ROBERT, banker; b. Atlanta, May 20, 1927; s. Robert M. and Jessie (Dickey) S.; m. Telside Matthews, July 24, 1953; children: Robert Marion, Douglas Watson, William Logan, Walter Dickey. Grad., Marist Coll., 1944; BS, Davidson Coll., 1948; LLB, Atlanta Law Sch., 1953. With Trust Co. Ga., Atlanta, 1948-89, v.p., 1959-67, group v.p., 1967, sr. v.p., 1968-72, sr. exec. v.p., 1972-73, pres., 1973-89; chmn. bd. dirs. Trust Co. Bank, Atlanta, 1974—, pres. holding co., 1976—, chmn. bd. dirs. holding co., 1978—; chmn. bd. dirs., chief exec. officer SunTrust Banks, Inc., 1984—; bd. dirs., chmn. audit com. Equifax, Inc.; bd. dirs. Trust Co. Ga., Trust Co. Bank, Oxford Industries, Inc.; bd. dirs., mem. exec. com., chmn. audit com. Life Ins. Co. Ga.; bd. dirs. Ga. U.S. Corp., Investment Centre; bd. dirs., mem. exec. com. Ga. Power Co. Past pres. United Way Met. Atlanta, chmn. gen. campaign, 1972, chmn. fin. com., v.p. bd. dirs. Piedmont Hosp.; bd. dirs. Fulton County unit Ga. div. Am. Cancer Soc.; trustee emeritus Westminster Schs.; chmn. bd. trustees Emory U.; mem. chmns. council, past chmn. Cen. Atlanta Progress, Inc. Served with AUS, 1950-52. Mem. Assn. Res. City Bankers (bd. dirs.), Am. Bankers Assn. (past state v.p.), Ga. Bankers Assn. (past pres.), Atlanta C. of C. (pres. 1983), Atlanta Arts Alliance (past chmn. bd. dirs., trustee, exec. com.), Piedmont Driving Club (past pres.), Capital City Club, Commerce Club (pres. 1987, bd. dirs.), Peachtree Golf Club, Augusta Nat. Golf Club, Sigma Alpha Epsilon. Methodist. Home: 94 Brighton Rd NW Atlanta GA 30309 Office: SunTrust Banks Inc PO Box 4418 Atlanta GA 30302

STRICKLAND, ROBERT LOUIS, business executive; b. Florence, S.C., Mar. 3, 1931; s. Franz M. and Hazel (Eaddy) S.; m. Elizabeth Ann Miller, Feb. 2, 1952; children: Cynthia Anne, Robert Edson. AB, U. N.C., 1952; MBA with distinction, Harvard, 1957. With Lowe's Cos., Inc., North Wilkesboro, N.C., 1957—, sr. v.p., 1970-76, exec. v.p., 1976-78, chmn. bd., 1978—, mem. office pres., exec. com., 1970-78, also bd. dirs.; founder Sterling Advt., Ltd., 1966; v.p., mem. adminstrv. com. Lowe's Profit-Sharing Trust, 1961-87, chmn. ops. com., 1972-78; mem. mgmt. com. Lowe's ESOP plan, 1978; bd. dirs. Summit Communications, Atlanta; panelist investor relations field, 1972—; speaker, panelist employee stock ownership field, 1978—; speaker London Instnl. Investor Conf., 1980; speaker on investment relations, London, Edinburgh, Paris, Zurich, Frankfurt, Geneva, Vienna, Amsterdam, Brussels, Tokyo, Singapore, 1980—. Author: Lowe's Cybernetwork, 1969, Lowe's Living Legend, 1970, Ten Years of Growth, 1971, The Growth Continues, 1972, 73, 74, Lowe's Scoreboard, 1978, also articles. Mem. N.C. Ho. Reps., 1962-64, Rep. Senatorial Inner Circle, 1980—; mem. exec. com. N.C. Rep. Com., 1963-73; trustee U. N.C. Chapel Hill, 1987—; dir. U.S. Council of Better Bus. Burs., 1981-85; bd. dirs., v.p. Nat. Home Improvement Council, 1972-76; bd. dirs. N.C. Sch. Arts Found., 1975-79, N.C. Bd. Natural and Econ. Resources, 1975-76; bd. dirs., mem. govt. affairs com. Home Ctr. Inst.; trustee, sec. bd. Wilkes Community Coll., 1964-73; chmn., pres. bd. dirs. Do-It-Yourself Research Inst., 1981—; pres. Hardware Home Improvement Council City of Hope Nat. Med. Ctr., Los Angeles, 1987—. Served with USN, 1952-55, lt. Res. 1955-62. Named Wilkes County N.C. Young Man of Yr., Wilkes Jr. C. of C., 1962; recipient Bronze Oscar of Industry award Fin. World, 1969-74, 76-79, Silver Oscar of Industry award, 1970, 72-74, 76-79, Gold Oscar of Industry award as best of all industry, 1972, 87, Excellence award in corp. reporting Fin. Analysts Fedn., 1970, 72, 74, 81-82, cert. of Distinction Brand Names Found., 1970, Retailer of Yr. award, 1971, 73, Disting. Mcht. award, 1972, Spirit of Life award City of Hope, 1983. Mem. Nat. Assn. Over-the-Counter Cos. (bd. advisers 1973-77), Newcomen Soc., Employee Stock Ownership Assn. (pres. 1983-85, chmn. 1985-87), Scabbard and Blade, Phi Beta Kappa, Pi Kappa Alpha. Clubs: Twin City, Forsyth Country (Winston-Salem, N.C.); Hound Ears (Blowing Rock, N.C.); Roaring Gap (N.C.); Elk River (Banner Elk, N.C.). Home: 226 N Stratford Rd Winston-Salem NC 27104 Office: Lowe's Cos Inc PO Box 1111 Hwy 268 E North Wilkesboro NC 28656

STRICKLER, FRANK HUNTER, lawyer; b. Washington, Jan. 20, 1920; s. Charles Brennerman and Minnie (Hunter) S.; married; children: Nancy, Elizabeth Ann, Frank, Charles. LLB, George Washington U., 1941, JD, 1947. Bar: D.C. 1947, U.S. Ct. Appeals (D.C. cir.) 1947, U.S. Dist. Ct. D.C. 1947, U.S. Supreme Ct. 1953, U.S. Ct. Mil. Justice 1956, U.S. Ct. Appeals (4th cir.) 1964, U.S. Dist. Ct. Md. 1984, U.S. Tax Ct. 1984. Asst. U.S atty. Dept. of Justice, Washington, 1949-56; atty. Whiteford, Hart, Carmody and Wilson, Washington, 1956-85, Ober, Taylor, Grimes and Shriver, Washington, 1985; gen. counsel Washington Gas & Light Co., 1985—. Mem. ABA, Am. Coll. Trial Lawyers, D.C. Bar Assn., Md. Bar Assn. Republican. Presbyterian. Club: Congl. Country (Bethesda, Md.). Lodge: Kiwanis. Office: Washington Gas & Light Co 1100 H St NW Washington DC 20080

STRICKLER, IVAN, dairy products company executive; Pres., bd. dirs. Mid-Am. Dairymen, Inc., Springfield, Mo. Office: Mid-Am Dairymen Inc 3253 E Chestnut Expressway Springfield MO 65802 *

STRICKMAN, ARTHUR EDWIN, retired retail apparel executive; b. N.Y.C., July 12, 1924; s. Samuel W. and Lee (Light) S.; m. Rosemary C. Lawson, Sept. 13, 1947; children: Ellen Sue, Wendy Lee, Nancy Ann. B.A. in Bus. Adminstrn., Duke U., 1945. Exec. tng., asst. buyer Bloomingdales, 1946-47; sr. buyer Bond Stores, N.Y.C., 1948-50; pres. Sandra Post, N.Y.C., 1951-58; with Lerner Stores, N.Y.C., 1959-85; v.p. mdse. Lerner Stores, 1973-74, exec. v.p., 1975-81, pres., 1982-85, chmn. bd., chief exec. officer, 1982-85. Served as officer USN, 1942-46, PTO. Home: 136 Yale Dr Rancho Mirage CA 92270

STRIDER, DAVID LEE, banker; b. Balt., July 23, 1953; s. Robert L. and Evelyn (Martin) S. BSBA, Towson State U., 1977. Sales service mgr. Comml. Envelope Corp., Balt., 1976-77; with 1st Nat. Bank Md., Balt., 1977-88, v.p., div. head, 1985-88; v.p. Core States Fin. Corp., Phila., 1988—; mem. adv. group Visa U.S.A., San Mateo, Calif., 1981—, Internet, Inc., Reston, Va., 1986—. Bd. dirs. Better Bus. Bur., Balt., 1983—. Democrat. Presbyterian. Club: Hunt Valley Golf. Office: Core States Fin Corp 5th and Market Sts Philadelphia PA 19101

STRIDSBERG, ALBERT BORDEN, advertising specialist, editor; b. Wyoming, Ohio, July 22, 1929; s. Carl Alexander Herbert and Edith Vivian (Farley) S. BA with honors, Yale U., 1950; Diplome D'Etudes Franc., U. of Poitiers, Tours, France, 1951; postgrad., Am. U. Beirut, Lebanon, 1953-54; diploma, Direct Mktg. Inst. Copywriter Howard Swink Advt., Inc., Marion, Ohio, 1955-58; acct. supr. McCann-Erickson, Co., Brussels, 1958-60, J. Walter Thompson Co., Amsterdam, The Netherlands, 1960-63; asst. to internat. exec. v.p. J. Walter Thompson Co., N.Y.C., 1963-67, internat. cons. spl. projects, acquisitions and diversifications, 1969-73; cons., coordinator Internat. Markets Advt. Agy., Inc., N.Y., London, 1967-69; editor-in-chief Advt. World mag., N.Y.C., 1975-77; lectr. in mktg. NYU, N.Y.C., 1978-84; lectr. in advt. Marist Coll., Poughkeepsie, N.Y., 1984—; U.S. corr. Media Internat. Mag., London, 1984—, N.Y. features editor U.S. edit., 1987—; adj. assoc. prof. NYU, 1966-78; ind. cons., free lance writer on advt. and mktg. issues, N.Y.C., 1973—. Author: Effective Advertising Self-Regulation, 1974, Progress Toward Advertising Self-Regulation, 1976, Controversy Advertising, 1977, Advertising Self-Regulation, 1980; editor N.Y. features Media Internat. mag., 1988; actor with Tricolor Theatre, Washington, 1952-54, Arcadian Players, Beirut, 1953-54. Choir dir. Episcopal Chs., Beirut, Brussels. Served as cpl. U.S. Army, 1951-53. Fulbright fellow U.S. Dept. of State, U. Poitiers, 1950-51, Ford Found. fellow, Beirut, 1953-54. Mem. Internat. Advt. Assn. (cons., project coordinator 1974-80), Am. Mktg. Assn., Product Devel. and Mgmt. Assn., Advt. Research Found., Direct Mktg. Assn., Am. Acad. Advt. Democrat. Episcopalian. Clubs: Yale (N.Y.C.), Elizabethan (New Haven). Home and Office: Media Internat Mag 28 S Clover St Poughkeepsie NY 12601

STRIEDL, ROBERT GREGORY, real estate executive; b. N.Y.C., Aug. 7, 1945; s. Paul James and Rose Marie Striedl; m. Lois Elisa Maggiolo, June 8, 1968; children: Paul Louis, Karen Ann. Student, Queensboro Co., 1965-67, Queens Coll., 1968-73, Iowa State U., 1974. With N.Y. Telephone, N.Y.C., 1968-83; assoc. Nynex Materiel Enterprises, N.Y.C., 1984-85; v.p. fin. and adminstrn. Nynex Properties Co., N.Y.C., 1985—; bd. dirs. N.Y. Bldg. Congress; chmn, N.Y. Constrn. Users Council. Author: Codes and Regulation, 1982; (with others) Time is Money, 1978. Served with USNG, 1967-72.

Mem. Am. Soc. Quality Control. Republican. Roman Catholic. Club: Bethpage Golf. Home: 3859 Fulton Ave Seaford NY 11783 Office: Nynex Properties Co 21 Pennsylvania Plaza 17th Floor New York NY 10001

STRIEM, KAARL JAVIER, custom furniture manufacturer; b. Panama, Mar. 1, 1961; s. Haiman and Luz Gladys (Montero) S.; m. Mirna Mercedes Diaz de Striem, Nov. 1, 1985; 1 child, Jan Kaarl. BS, Ga. Inst. Tech., 1978. V.p. Tropicana Group, Panama, 1980-84; pres., gen. mgr. Karlestri S.A., Panama, 1984—; pres. Craftouch, Inc., Miami, Fla., 1987—; cons., Grupo Tropicana, 1980. negotiator Bilateral Treaties, Panama-Cen. Am., 1980; sub. dir. Users Assn. Colon Free Zone, Panama-Cen. Am., 1985-87. Mem. Assn. Furniture Mfrs. (dir. 1980), Chilean Indsl. Exposition, Brazilian Export Assn. Home: 14317 SW 62d St Miami FL 33183 Office: Craftouch Inc 9206 NW 106th St Medley FL 33178

STRIKE, GEORGE LOUIS, manufacturing company executive; b. Salt Lake City, July 27, 1930; s. Louis Nicholas and Christina (Chipian) S.; m. Susan Prewitt, Aug. 3, 1971; children: Tony, Christian, Jonathan. BBA, U. Utah, 1951. Pres. Am. Laundry Machinery Co., Cin., 1962-72, chmn., 1978—; chmn. Hess & Eisenhardt Co., Cin., 1973—, Martin Franchises Inc., Cin., 1978—; pres. Midway Investment Co., Denver, 1975—; bd. dirs. Peoples Bank, Denver; ptnr. Cin. Reds. Patentee textile processing technique. Past pres. Cin. Indsl. Inst.; past chmn. Cin. Com. Am. Farm Sch., Greece; past bd. dirs. Planned Parenthood-World Population, U.S., Children's Convalescent Hosp., Cin., WCET Ednl. TV Sta., Ohio Coll. Applied Sci.; bd. dirs., treas. Cin. Sci. Ctr. Mem. Newcomen Soc. N.Am., Nat. Assn. Mfrs. (past bd. dirs.), Greater Cin. C. of C. (past bd. dirs., 1st v.p.). Greek Orthodox. Clubs: Cin. Country, Queen City (Cin.). Office: 8959 Blue Ash Rd Cincinnati OH 45242

STROBBE, MICHAEL EMIEL, service executive; b. Ghent, Belgium, Sept. 5, 1924; came to U.S., 1946; s. Oscar A. and Johanna F. (Pirijns) S.; m. Hedwig Anna Kunkel, Sept. 4, 1959. BSBA, Boston U., 1950. Cert. hotel adminstr. Various staff positions Hilton Internat., Montreal, Que., Can. and Amsterdam, The Netherlands, 1957-63; mgr. Schine Hotels, Massena, N.Y., 1965-68; area supr. Esso Motor Hotels Europe, London, 1968-72; dir. devel. Sheraton Internat., Brussels, 1973-74; project mgr. Can. Pacific Hotels, Frankfurt, Fed. Republic Germany, 1975-77; owner, operator Flanders Inn, Massena, 1979-85; pres. Hospitality Mgmt. Svcs., Alburg, Vt., 1985—. Home and Office: Hospitality Mgmt Svcs RR 1 Box 130 Alburg VT 05440

STROBEL, MARTIN JACK, motor vehicle and industrial component manufacturing and distribution company executive; b. N.Y.C., July 4, 1940; s. Nathan and Clara (Sorgen) S.; m. Hadassah Orenstein, Aug. 15, 1965; children: Gil Michael, Karen Rachel. BA, Columbia U., 1962; JD, Cleve. Marshall Law Sch., 1966; completed advanced bus. mgmt. program, Harvard U., 1977. Bar: Ohio bar 1966. Counsel def. contract adminstrn. services region Def. Supply Agy., Cleve., 1966-68; with Dana Corp., Toledo, 1968—; gen. counsel Dana Corp., 1970—, dir. govt. relations, 1970-71, asst. sec., 1971—, v.p., 1976—, sec., 1982—. Mem. Am. Bar Assn., Fed. Bar Assn., Machinery and Allied Products Inst., Ohio Bar Assn., Toledo Bar Assn. Office: Dana Corp 4500 Dorr St PO Box 1000 Toledo OH 43697

STROBEL, NORMAN STEWART, corporate executive; b. Phila., Aug. 15, 1944; s. Norman Fredrick and Amy (Gault) S.; m. Diane Sweeney, Jan. 14, 1967; children: Steven, Lisa. BS in Acctg., Pa. State U., 1966; MBA in Info. Sci., Temple U., 1970. Mgr. Burroughs Corp., Detroit, 1970-78; v.p. Excelsior Truck Leasing, Conshohocken, Pa., 1978-84; pres. ETL Services, Conshohocken, Pa., 1984—, Franklin Corp., SBIC, Plymouth Meeting, Pa., 1987—; pres. bd. dirs. ETL Services, 1984—, Franklin Corp., SBIC, Plymouth Meeting; bd. dirs. SL Brown & Co., N.Y.C., Franklin Holding Corp., N.Y.C. Capt. U.S. Army, 1967-70. Mem. Union League Club, Whitemarsh Country Club. Republican. Office: Franklin Corp SBIC 610 N Germantown Pk Ste 461 Plymouth Meeting PA 19462

STROH, MICHAEL E., lawyer, manufacturing company executive; b. Milw., July 29, 1941; s. Donald Carl and Dorothy (Oeflein) S.; m. Mary Jo Remiker, June 28, 1969; children: Ann, Matthew, Katherine, Andrew. BA, Marquette U., 1963, JD, 1966. Bar: Wis. 1966, U.S. Dist. Ct. (ea. dist.) Wis. 1966. Spl. agt. FBI, Washington, 1966-69; program coord. Wis. Dept. Justice, Madison, 1969-70; dist. atty. Oneida County (Wis.), 1971-74; ptnr. Drager, O'Brien, Anderson, Eagle River, Wis., 1974-82; exec. v.p. Stroh Die Casting Co., Inc., Milw., 1982-83, pres., chief exec. officer, 1984—, bd. dirs., 1981—; bd. advisors Liberty Mut. Ins. Co., Boston, 1984—. Bd. advisors Wauwatosa (Wis.) Sch. Dist., 1986-88. Mem. Am. Die Cast Assn., N.Am. Die Cast Assn. (bd. dirs. 1985—, chmn. nat. affairs com.), Soc. Die Cast Engrs., Wis. Bar Assn., Assn. Trial Lawyers Am., Wis. Trial Lawyers Assn., Milw. Club. Republican. Office: Stroh Die Casting Co Inc 11123 W Burleigh Milwaukee WI 53222

STROHAN, JAMES MICHAEL, restaurant executive; b. North Battleford, Alta., Can., May 11, 1946; came to U.S., 1974; m. Marilyn Dawne Strohan, July 15, 1967; 1 child, Jeremy D. Chartered acct., U. Alta., Can., 1969. With Winspear Higgins et al (now Delatte Haskins & Sells), 1969-72, Pop Shoppes of Can., 1972-73, Pop Shoppes of Am., 1974-77; exec. v.p. Vicorp Restaurants, Inc., Denver, 1978—. Office: Vicorp Restaurants Inc 400 W 48th Ave Denver CO 80216

STROHM, RAYMOND WILLIAM, laboratory equipment company executive; b. Elgin, Ill., Sept. 14, 1924; s. Raympnd H. and Norma (Riggs) S.; BSBA, Northwestern U., 1948; m. Frances D. Plath, Sept. 1, 1946; children: Phillip A., David N., Meredith L., Ellen K. Pres., Pelam, Inc., Hinsdale, Ill., 1966-70, Gelman Instrument Co., Ann Arbor, Mich., 1971-74, Barnstead div. Sybron, Boston, 1974-78; group v.p. Sybron Corp., Rochester, N.Y., 1978-86; cons., pvt. investor, 1986—; bd. dirs. Orion Rsch., Boston, YSI, Inc., Yellow Springs, Ohio, Tecator, Inc., Herndon, Va., ALPKEM Co., Clackamus, Oreg., Promega Corp., Madison, Wis. Served with USAAC, 1942-46. Mem. Am. Chem. Soc., Assn. for Advancement of Med. Instrumentation, Parenteral Drug Assn., Northwestern Mgmt. Alumni Assn. Club, Bear's Paw Country Club.

STROKE, GEORGE WILHELM, physicist, educator; b. Zagreb, Yugoslavia, July 29, 1924; came to U.S., 1952, arrived in Fed. Republic of Germany, 1988; s. Elias and Edith Mechner (Silvers) S.; m. Masako Haraguchi, Feb. 5, 1973. B.Sc., U. Montpellier, France, 1942; Ing.Dipl., Inst. Optics, U. Paris, 1949; Dr. ès Sci. in Physics, Sorbonne U., Paris, 1960. Mem. research staff and def. research staff MIT, 1952-63, lectr. elec. engring., 1960-63; asst. research prof. physics Boston U., 1956-57; NATO research fellow U. Paris, 1959-60; prof. elec. engring., head electro-optical sci. labs. U. Mich., 1963-67; prof. elec. scis. and med. biophysics SUNY-Stony Brook, 1967-79; mem. corp. mgmt. staff Messerschmitt-Bolkow-Blohm GmbH, Munich, W. Ger., 1980-84, chief scientist space div., 1984-86, chief scientist, Corp. Hdqrs.-Devel., 1986—; vis. prof. Harvard U. Med. Sch., 1970-73, Tech. U. Munich, 1978—; adviser laser task force USAAF Systems Command, 1964; govt. sci. cons. U.S. and abroad, 1964—; cons. NASA Electronics Research Ctr., Cambridge, Mass., 1966—; mem. commn. I, Internat. Radio Sci. Union, Nat. Acad. Scis., 1965—; cons. Am. Cancer Soc., 1972—; mem. NSF blue ribbon task force on ultrasonic imaging, 1973-74; mem. U.S. Ho. of Reps. Select Com., photog. evidence panel on Pres. J. F. Kennedy's assasination, 1978-79. MBB Corp. mem. Max-Planck Soc., 1982—; bd. dirs. Max-Planck Soc. Inst. Quantum Optics, 1986—, NATO-AGARD study group on lasers, 1989. Recipient Humboldt prize, 1978. Fellow Optical Soc. Am., Am. Phys. Soc., IEEE. Contbr. articles to profl. jours. Author: An Introduction to Coherent Optics and Holography, 1966. Address: Messereschmitt-Bolkow-Blohm, GmbH Corp Hdqrs, Postfach 801169, D-8000 Munich 80, Federal Republic of Germany

STROLL, JOHN JAMES, management consultant; b. N.Y.C., Jan. 8, 1928; s. Joseph P. and Vivian (Casal) S.; m. Sheila Kaplan, June 25, 1955; children: Joseph, Jay, Betty. BS, Columbia Coll., N.Y.C., 1951, MS, 1953; MBA, Pace U., 1983. Registered pharmacist, N.Y. Mgr. Reilly's Pharmacy, Astoria, N.Y., 1951-54; salesperson Bendinger & Schesinger, Inc., N.Y.C., 1954-56, sales mgr., 1956-60; personnel cons. Careers Unltd., N.Y.C., 1960-62, Tech. Recruiting, N.Y.C., 1962-65; ptnr. St. George Pharmacy, N.Y.C., 1965-68; pres. J. Stroll Assoc., Inc., Westport, Conn., 1968—; chmn. Meditemps, Inc., N.Y.C., 1969—; ptnr. Sterling Devel., Westport, 1983—; co-owner 980 Post Rd. East Realty, Westport, 1983. Contbr. Rep. Party, 1988—. Mem. N.Y. Athletic Club. Office: J Stroll Assocs Inc 980 Post Rd E Westport CT 06880

STROM, MILTON GARY, lawyer; b. Rochester, N.Y., Dec. 5, 1942; s. Harold and Dolly (Isaacson) S.; m. Barbara A. Simon, Jan. 18, 1975; children: Carolyn, Michael, Jonathan. BS in Econs., U. Pa., 1964; JD, Cornell U., 1967. Bar: N.Y. 1968, U.S. Dist. Ct. (we. dist.) N.Y. 1968, U.S. Ct. Claims 1969, U.S. Ct. Mil. Appeals 1969, U.S. Ct. Appeals ((D.C. cir.) 1970, U.S. Supreme Ct. 1972, U.S. Dist. Ct. (so. dist.) N.Y. 1975. Atty. SEC, Washington, 1968-71; assoc. Skadden, Arps, Slate, Meagher & Flom, N.Y.C., 1971-77, ptnr., 1977—. Served with USCGR, 1967-68. Mem. ABA, N.Y. State Bar Assn. (corp. law sect.), Assn. of Bar of City of N.Y. Republican. Jewish. Club: Beach Point, Marco Polo. Office: Skadden Arps Slate Meagher & Flom 919 3d Ave New York NY 10022

STROMBOM, DAVID GLEN, architect; b. Pullman, Wash., Apr. 18, 1951; s. Donald A. and Dona S. (Bell) S.; m. Cathy J. Powers, June 17, 1972; 1 child, Paul Davis. Student, Whitman Coll., 1968-70; BS in Architecture, Wash. State U., 1973; MArch, Harvard U., 1977. Vol. U.S. Peace Corps, Marrakech, Morocco, 1973-75; designer Seattle, 1978-82; prin. Strombom Architects, Seattle, 1982—. Office: 1000 Lenora St Ste 404 Seattle WA 98121

STRONG, GEORGE GORDON, JR., litigation and management consultant; b. Toledo, Apr. 19, 1947; s. George Gordon and Jean Boyd (McDougall) S.; m. Annsley Palmer Chapman, Nov. 30, 1974; children: George III, Courtney, Meredith, Alexis. BA, Yale U., 1969; MBA, Harvard U., 1971; JD, U. San Diego, 1974. Bar: Calif. 1974, U.S. Dist. Ct. (cen. dist.) Calif. 1974; CPA, Calif., Hawaii, cert. mgmt. cons., U.S. customs house broker. Controller Vitredent Corp., Beverly Hills, Calif., 1974-76; sr. mgr. Price Waterhouse, Los Angeles, 1976-82, ptnr., 1987—; exec. v.p., chief operating officer Internat. Customs Service, Long Beach, Calif., 1982-84; chief fin. officer Uniform Software Systems, Santa Monica, Calif., 1984-85; exec. v.p. and chief operating officer Cipherlink Corp., 1986; pres. Woodleigh Lane, Inc., Flintridge, Calif., 1985-87; ptnr. Price Waterhouse, 1987—. Active Verdugo Hills Hosp. Adv. Council, Glendale, Calif., 1985. Mem. ABA, AICPA, Calif. State Bar Assn., Los Angeles County Bar Assn., Calif. Soc. CPA's, Inst. of Mgmt. Cons., Harvard Bus. Sch. Assn. So. Calif. (v.p. 1986-87, pres. 1988—), Harvard Club, Yale Club, Jonathan Club, Flint Canyon Tennis Club, Olympic Club, Annandale Golf Club, Coral Beach and Tennis Club. Republican. Presbyterian. Home: 4251 Woodleigh Ln Flintridge CA 91011 Office: 1880 Century Park E West Los Angeles CA 90067

STRONG, GEORGE WALTER, political consultant; b. Rapid City, S.D., June 8, 1937; s. Wesley Milo and Mariel Brown (Loomis) S. BS, S.D. State U., 1959; M in Pub. Adminstrn., U. Denver, 1963. Labor relations specialist AEC, Washington, 1963-69; asst. dir. Southwest Ctr. for Urban Research, Houston, 1969-73; exec. asst. Office of the Mayor, Houston, 1973-75; asst. to pres. for pub. policy Houston Natural Gas Corp., 1975-81; owner George Strong & Assocs., Houston, 1981—; gulf coast coordinator Gary Hart for Pres. Com., Tex., 1983-84; campaign mgr. Mike Andrews for Congress Com., Houston, 1980-82, Al Gore for Pres., 1987-88; campaign mgr., media cons. numerous Tex. polit. candidates. Campaign mgr., media cons. Harris County (Tex.) Dem. Party, 1981—. Served to Major U.S. Army, 1959-73. Mem. Houston C. of C. Methodist. Home and Office: 2242 Bartlett Houston TX 77098

STRONG, JOHN WILLIAM, medical products company executive, consultant; b. Elkhorn, Wis., Sept. 30, 1952; s. William J. and Betty J. (Dooley) S.; m. Christine Joyce, Sept. 8, 1984; children: Christopher, Jennifer. BBA, U. Wis., Eau Claire, 1974; MBA, De Paul U., 1981. Purchasing agt. Lakeland Hosp., Elkhorn, 1974-77; mgr. material St. Therese Hosp., Waukegan, Ill., 1977-80; chmn. div. Lutheran Gen. Hosp., Park Ridge, Ill., 1980-85; v.p. Parkside Assocs. Inc., Park Ridge, Ill., 1985—; pres. Health Care Materials Corp., Northbrook, Ill., 1985—; exec. com. bd. dirs. Hosp. Laundry Services, Chgo. Mem. editorial bd. Hosp. Purchasing News Mag., Northbrook, 1986—. Mem. Am. Soc. for Healthcare Material Mgmt., Am. Coll. Healthcare Execs. Republican. Roman Catholic. Home: 27094 W Kensington Ct Barrington IL 60010 Office: Health Care Materials Corp 2855 Shermer Rd Northbrook IL 60062

STROSS, HOWARD FRANCIS, marketing executive; b. Hammond, Ind., Oct. 23, 1948; s. Francis Howard and Julia (Bobalik) S.; m. Elizabeth Talbott Tewes, Oct. 18, 1975; 1 child, Alexander Talbott. BS, Purdue U., 1974. Engr. Chgo. Bridge and Iron, Kankakee, Ill., 1974-75; sales engr. Leeds & Northrup, South Holland, Ill., 1975-77; resident engr. Leeds & Northrup, Beaumont, Tex., 1977-78, dist. mgr. Beaumont, 1978-80; mgr. sales devel. Leeds & Northrup, Houston, 1980-81, area mgr. Houston, Baton Rouge, 1981-83; mgr. bus. devel. Leeds & Northrup Unit of Gen. Signal Corp., North Wales, Pa., 1983-86; dir. mktg. process control div. Honeywell Inc., Ft. Wash., 1986—; chmn. bd. Country Gardens Sch., East Rockhill, Pa., 1987—. Chmn. sch. bd. Country Gardens Sch., East Rockhill, Pa., 1987—. Republican. Home: 1429 Three Mile Run Rd Perkasie PA 18944 Office: Honeywell Inc 1100 Virginia Dr Fort Washington PA 19034-4360

STROUBE, WILLIAM BRYAN, JR., technical manager, chemist; b. Princeton, Ky., Oct. 29, 1951; s. William Bryan Sr. and Tillie Edna (Larkins) S.; m. Katharine Ann Kaiser, Dec. 30, 1973; children: Bryan Kaiser, Samuel James. BS in Chemistry, Murray State U., 1973; PhD in Chemistry, U. Ky., 1977; MBA in Fin., U. Md., 1986. Chemist Allied-Gen. Nuclear Svcs., Barnwell, S.C., 1978; post doctoral fellow FDA, Washington, 1978-79, rsch. chemist, 1979-86; group leader Bristol Myers Co., Evansville, Ind., 1986—; Contbr. articles to profl. jours. Mem. Am. Nuclear Soc. (chmn. biology and medicine div. 1985-86). Am. Chem. Soc., Assn. Offcl. Analytical Chemists (referee 1981-86). Democrat. Methodist. Office: Bristol Myers Co 2400 W Lloyd Expwy Evansville IN 47721

STROUCH, STANLEY I., insurance executive; b. Hartford, Conn., Oct. 25, 1940; s. Charles C. and Ida (Ziren) S.; m. Susan B. Strouch, Aug. 22, 1965; children: Michael, Lori, Marci. BS in Econs., U. Pa., 1963; LLB, Boston U., 1966, LLM In Taxation, 1969. Bar: Conn. 1966. Mem. dept. law New Eng. Life Ins. Co., Boston, 1966-71; dir. regional sales Aetna Life & Casualty Co., Hartford, 1971-74, gen. agt., 1974-83, gen. mgr., 1983-85, v.p., 1985-88; pres., chief exec. officer Hemisphere Life Ins. Co., Bridgeport, Conn., 1988—. V.p. Greater Bridgeport (Conn.) Jewish Community Ctr., 1980-87; bd. govs. Greater Bridgeport Jewish Fedn., 1983-87. Republican. Home: 325 Shetland Rd Fairfield CT 06430

STROUP, STANLEY STEPHENSON, lawyer; b. Los Angeles, Mar. 7, 1944; s. Francis Edwin and Marjory (Weimer) S.; m. Sylvia Douglass, June 15, 1968; children—Stacie, Stephen, Sarah. A.B., U. Ill., 1966; J.D., U. Mich., 1969. Bar: Calif., Ill., Minn. Atty. First Nat. Bank Chgo., 1969-80; chief legal officer Bank of Calif., San Francisco, 1980-84; sr. v.p., gen. counsel, sec. Norwest Corp., Mpls., 1984—; mem. adj. faculty Coll. Law, William Mitchell Coll., St. Paul, 1985—. Mem. ABA, Ill. Bar Assn., State Bar Calif., Minn. Bar Assn. Office: Norwest Corp Norwest Ctr Sixth and Marquette Sts Minneapolis MN 55479-1026

STROUT, ARTHUR EDWARDS, lawyer; b. Rockland, Maine, Sept. 6, 1935; s. Alfred Meserve and Olive (Edwards) S.; m. Anne Elisabeth Browning, May 3, 1960 (div. 1984); children: Alfred Browning, Charles Oliver. AB, Bowdoin Coll., 1957; LLB, Harvard U., 1960. Law clk. to presiding justice U.S. Ct. Appeals (9th cir.), San Francisco, 1960-61; trial atty. tax div. U.S. Dept. Justice, Washington, 1961-64; pvt. practice, Washington, 1964-71; sole practice Rockland, 1971—; bd. dirs Camden (Maine) Nat. Bank. Trustee Owls Head (Maine) Mus., Penobscot Bay Med. Ctr., Rockport, Maine, 1973-79. Mem. Maine Bar Assn., Maine Bd. Bar Examiners (chmn. 1983-87). Club: Camden Yacht. Home: 54 Meguuticook St Camden ME 04843 Office: Strout Payson et al 10 Masonic St PO Box 248 Rockland ME 04841

STRUBBE, JOHN LEWIS, retired food chain store executive; b. Cin., June 27, 1921; s. John August and Emma Katherine (Coleman) S.; m. Nancy Richards Baer, Sept. 16, 1950; children: William Burrows, Laura, John Charles, Mary. B.S. in Gen. Engring, U. Cin., 1947, J.D., 1948. Bar: Ohio 1948, U.S. Supreme Ct. 1960, U.S. Patent Office 1950. Assoc. Wood, Arey, Herron & Evans, Cin., 1948-50; with The Kroger Co., Cin., 1950-86, sec., 1959-65, gen. atty., 1956-62, v.p., 1961-77, group v.p., 1977-85, sr. v.p., 1985-86. Gen. chmn. United Appeal Greater Cin., 1967; mem. Food Industry Productivity Task Force, 1972; past pres. Dan Beard council Boy Scouts Am.; past pres. bd. trustees Community Chest and Council of Cin. Area; vice chmn., trustee Greater Cin. Found., James Gamble Inst. Med. Rsch.; v.p. devel. Cin. Ballet Co.; past trustee Meth. Union; vice chmn. U. Cin. Found.; bd. advisors to dean U. Cin. Coll. Bus. Adminstrn.; past chmn. bd. The Christ Hosp.; chmn. bd. Elizabeth Gamble Deaconess Home Assn. Served with USMCR, 1943-46, 50-52. Recipient U. Cin. Distinguished Alumnus award, chmn. award for devel. new food tech. Supermarket Inst., 1976, Brotherhood citation NCCJ, 1982; named Great Living Cincinnatian, Greater Cin. C. of C., 1986. Mem. Cincinnatus Assn. (past pres., dir.), Uniform Grocery Products Code Council (past chmn., pres.), Queen City Club, Commonwealth Club, Delta Tau Delta. Methodist. Home: 661 Chardonnay Ridge Cincinnati OH 45226

STRUDLER, ROBERT JACOB, real estate development executive; b. N.Y.C., Sept. 22, 1942; m. Ruth Honigman, Aug. 29, 1965; children: Seth, Keith, Craig. BS in Indsl. and Labor Relations, Cornell U., 1964; LLB, Columbia U., 1967. Bar: N.Y. 1967, Fla. 1973. Assoc. firms in N.Y.C., 1967-71; v.p., chmn. operating com. U.S. Home Corp., Clearwater, Fla., 1972-76, v.p. legal affairs, 1976-77, v.p. ops., 1977-79; sr. v.p. ops. U.S. Home Corp., Houston, 1979-81, sr. v.p. acquisitions, 1981-84, pres., chief operating officer, 1984-86, chmn., chief exec. officer, 1986—. Pres., trustee Sch. for Young Children U. St. Thomas. Mem. ABA, N.Y. State Bar Assn., Fla. Bar Assn., Cornell Real Estate Council. Home: 11110 Greenbay Rd Houston TX 77024 Office: US Home Corp 1800 W Loop S Houston TX 77027 *

STRUDWICK, MARTIN BARRY, financial executive; b. Balt., July 31, 1952; s. Robert Tilghman and Tressa (Barry) S.; m. Margaret Holz, May 16, 1987. BA, Emory U., 1976; MBA, U. Pa., 1980. Internat. banking officer Sun Trust Co. Bank, Atlanta, 1980-82; pres. Strudwick & Assocs., Inc., Balt., 1982—, LaserFax, Inc., Balt., 1985—; v.p. Md. Capital Mgmt., Inc., Balt., 1988—. Mem. Soc. Colonial Wars, Md. Club, Army/Navy Club, Old Line Crab and Pheasant Club (charitable fund raising). Office: Md Capital Mgmt 12 E Eager St Baltimore MD 21202

STRUEBING, ROBERT VIRGIL, retired oil company executive; b. Winfield, Kans., Nov. 8, 1919; s. Walter Charles and Jettie Marie (Hetherington) S.; m. Helen L. Harrington, Aug. 19, 1943; children: Gloria Struebing West, Steven R., William S. B.S. in Chem. Engring, U. Nebr., 1949. With Skelly Oil Co., El Dorado, Kans., 1949-76, refinery mgr., 1971-76; mgr. gas plants Getty Oil Co., Tulsa, 1977-80, v.p. mfg., 1980-85; sr. v.p. mfg. Getty Refining & Mktg. Co., Tulsa, 1980-85; ret. 1985. Mem. El Dorado Bd. Edn., 1965-75, pres., 1967-68. Served to capt. USAAF, 1940-45. Mem. Sigma Tau. Club: Cedar Ridge Country.

STRUL, GENE M., telecommunications company executive, former television news director; b. Bklyn., Mar. 25, 1927; s. Joseph and Sally (Chartoff) S.; student journalism U. Miami (Fla.), 1945-47; m. Shirley Dolly Silber, Aug. 7, 1949; children: Ricky, Gary, Eileen. News dir. Sta. WIOD AM-FM, Miami, 1947-56; assignment editor, producer Sta. WCKT-TV, Miami, 1956-57, news dir., 1957-79; dir. broadcast news Miami News, 1957; free-lance writer newspapers and mags.; cons. dept. communications U. Miami, 1979, acting dir. public relations, 1979-80; v.p. Hernstadt Broadcasting Corp., 1980-81; dir. corp. communications Burnup & Sims, 1981—. Communications dir. United Way of Dade County, 1981. Served with AUS, 1945. Recipient Peabody award, 1975; Preceptor award Broadcast Industry conf., San Francisco State U.; Abe Lincoln awards (2) So. Baptist Radio-TV Conf.; Nat. Headliners awards (5); led Stas. WCKT, WSVN to more than 200 awards for news, including 3 Peabody awards, Emmy award. Mem. Nat. Acad. Television Arts and Scis. (past gov. Miami chpt.), Radio-TV News Dirs. Assn., Fla. AP Broadcasters (past pres.), Greater Miami C. of C., Nat. Broadcast Editorial Assn., Sigma Delta Chi (2 nat. awards). Home: 145 SW 49th Ave Miami FL 33134

STRUTTON, LARRY D., newspaper executive; b. Colorado Springs, Colo., Sept. 12, 1940; s. Merril and Gladys (Sheldon) S.; m. Carolyn Ann Croak, Dec. 3, 1960; children—Gregory L., Kristen. A.A. in Electronics Engring., Emily Griffith Electronics Sch., 1968; B.S. in Bus. Mgmt. and Systems Mgmt., Met. State Coll., 1971; diploma in Advanced Mgmt. Program, Harvard U., 1988. Printer Gazette Telegraph, Colorado Springs, Colo., 1961-64; prodn. dir. Rocky Mountain News, Denver, 1964-80; exec. v.p. ops. and advt. Detroit Free Press, 1981-83; v.p. ops. Los Angeles Times, 1983-85, exec. v.p. ops., 1986—. Mem. adv. com. Rochester Inst. Tech., 1984—. Mem. Am. Newspaper Pubs. Assn. (chmn. 1987, chmn. TEC com. 1985-86), R&E Council (research and engring. council of the Graphic Arts Industry Inc.). Club: Lakeside Golf (Los Angeles). Home: 1214 Swarthmore Glendale CA 91206

STRUTTON, ROBERT JAMES, real estate sales representative; b. Jersey City, July 31, 1948; s. James V. and Eileen M. (Daly) S.; m. Marta I. Rivera, June 5, 1971 (div. Aug. 1977); m. Lucy M. Fidone, Sept. 29, 1978; children: Leslie Marissa, Michael A. AS in Criminal Justice, Brookdale Community Coll., 1977; cert., Grad. Realtor Inst., 1988; student, Jersey City State Coll., 1988—. Police officer Hazlet (N.J.) Police Dept., 1973—, detective, 1981-85; realtor assoc. Spindrift Gallery of Homes, Hazlet, 1986—; account rep. Met. Life Ins. Co., N.Y.C., 1987-88; realtor assoc. ERA Advantage Realty, Old Bridge, N.J., 1988—; tng. officer Hazlet Police Dept., 1980-84. Chmn. Youth Adv. Commn., Hazlet, 1980. Mem. Realtors Nat. Mktg. Inst., N.J. Assn. Realtors, Monmouth County Bd. Realtors (comml. investment/edn. coms.), Hazlet Patrolman'senevolent Assn. (sec. 1986-88). Democrat. Roman Catholic. Office: Spindrift Realty 3400 Highway 35 Hazlet NJ 07730

STRYCKER, WALTER PIERCE, venture capitalist, consultant; b. San Francisco, Oct. 23, 1928; s. Walter Pierce Strycker and Alice (Smith) Strycker Belisle; m. Constance de Curtoni, Sept. 4, 1953; children—Karen Ann, Jana Pierce. B.S., U. Calif., 1952. Mktg. mgr. IBM, N.Y.C., 1954-69; v.p., treas. Decimus Corp., San Francisco, 1969-72; ptnr. McCormick Strycker & Assocs., San Francisco, 1970—; v.p., treas. Wheelabrator Frye, Hampton, N.H., 1972-76; v.p. Delorean Motor Co., N.Y.C., 1978-79; pres. Assocs. Venture, San Francisco, 1978—; cons. Pullman Standard, Chgo., 1980-81, Signal Cos., 1982-87, Henley Group, 1986—; bd. dirs. Wheelabrator Environ. Systems Inc., SiFab Corp., Scotts Valley, Calif., Physis Corp., San Francisco. Bd. dirs. United Way, Pitts., 1974-77. With USAF, 1951-53. Mem. Air Pollution Control Assn., Nat. Assn. Small Bus. Investment Co., Western Pa. Econ. Devel. Assn., Phi Gamma Delta. Clubs: Duquesne (Pitts.). Home: 33 West Shore Rd Belvedere CA 94920 Office: Assocs Venture Capital 425 California St San Francisco CA 94104

STRYKER, STEVEN CHARLES, lawyer; b. Omaha, Oct. 26, 1944; s. James M. and Jean G. (Grannis) S.; m. Bryna Dee Litwin, Oct. 20, 1972; children: Ryan, Kevin, Gerrit, Courtney. BS, U. Iowa, 1967, JD with distinction, 1969; postgrad. Northwestern Grad. Sch. Bus., 1969-70; M in Taxation, DePaul U., 1971. Bar: Iowa 1969, Tex. 1986; CPA, Ill., Iowa. Sr. tax acct. Arthur Young & Co., Chgo., 1969-72; fed. tax mgr. Massey Ferguson, Des Moines, 1972-74; fed./state tax mgr. FMC Corp., Chgo., 1974-78; gen. tax atty. Shell Oil Co., Houston, 1978-81, asst. gen. tax counsel, 1981-83, gen. mgr., 1983-86, v.p., gen. tax counsel, 1986—. Mem. ABA, Texas Bar Assn., Iowa Bar Assn., Am. Inst. CPA's, Ill. Soc. CPA's, Iowa Soc. CPA's., Tax Execs. Inst., Am. Petroleum Inst. Republican. Home: 10819 Everwood St Houston TX 77024 Office: Shell Oil Co 1 Shell Plaza Ste 4570 Houston TX 77001

STRYKER, SUSAN MARIE, sales executive; b. Freeport, N.Y., July 6, 1955; d. Richard Lee and Dorothy (Malchiodi) Gleason; m. Andrew Roger Stryker, May 21, 1958. Student, U. S.C. Sales mgr. Adams Mark Hotels, Kansas City, Mo., 1982-85; nat. sales mgr. Adams Mark Hotels, N.Y.C., 1987-88; sales mgr. Trumbull Marriott, Conn., 1985-87; nat. accounts mgr. Westin Hotels & Resorts, N.Y.C., 1988—. Mem. Hotel Sales and Mktg. Assn., Meeting Planners Internat. Republican. Roman Catholic. Home:

55Mill Plain Rd #12-1 Danbury CT 06811 Office: Westin Hotels and Resorts Empire State Bldg Ste 350A New York NY 10118

STUART, ALICE MELISSA, lawyer; b. N.Y.C., Apr. 7, 1957; d. John Marberger and Marjorie Louise (Browne) S. BA, Ohio State U., 1977; JD, U. Chgo., 1980; LLM, NYU, 1982. Bar: N.Y. 1981, Ohio 1982, N.Y. 1982, U.S. Dist. Ct. (so. dist.) Ohio 1983, U.S. Dist. Ct. (so. and ea. dists.) N.Y. 1985. Assoc. Schwartz, Shapiro, Kelm & Warren, Columbus, Ohio, 1982-84, Paul, Weiss, Rifkind, Wharton & Garrison, N.Y.C., 1984-85, Kassel, Neuwirth & Geiger, N.Y.C., 1985-86, Phillips, Nizer, Benjamin, Krim & Ballon, N.Y.C., 1987—. Surrogate Speakers' Bur. Reagan-Bush Campaign, N.Y.C., 1984; mem. Lawyers for Bush-Quayle Campaign, N.Y.C., 1988. Mem. ABA, N.Y. State Bar Assn., Winston Churchill Meml. Library Soc., Jr. League, Phi Beta Kappa, Phi Kappa Phi, Alpha Lambda Delta. Republican. Presbyterian. Club: Women's Nat. Rep. (N.Y.C.). Office: Philips Nizer Benjamin Krim & Ballon 40 W 57th St New York NY 10019

STUART, EDWIN JAY, banker, educator; b. Belle Glade, Fla., Oct. 19, 1936; s. Clifford Lanier and P. Madrue (Enfinger) S.; m. Margaret J. Delano, Aug. 25, 1962; children: Cathy Lynn, Mary Elizabeth, Sharon Lee, Michael Edwin. BA in Polit. Sci. and History, U. Fla., 1959, JD, 1964, MBA in Econs., 1966; DBA in Fin. Mgmt., Fla. State U., 1976. Bar: Fla. 1966; cert. fin. planner; lic. securities dealer. Trust officer First Nat. Bank, Orlando, Fla., 1966-69; head trust dept. Nat. Bank Melbourne, Fla., 1969-73; instr. fin. Fla. State U., Tallahassee, 1973-76; prof. fin. U. Tex., Odessa, 1976-81; trust dept. exec. M Bank Odessa, 1981—; fin. cons. L & S Cons., Odessa, 1976—. Author: Energy Use in Florida, 1976. Home: 4648 Fountain Ln Odessa TX 79761 Office: M Bank Odessa Box 2632 Odessa TX 79760

STUART, GERARD WILLIAM, JR., corporate executive; b. Yuba City, Calif., July 28, 1939; s. Gerard William and Geneva Bernice (Stuke) S.; student Yuba Jr. Coll., 1957-59, Chico State Coll., 1959-60; A.B., U. Calif., Davis, 1962; M.L.S., U. Calif., Berkeley, 1963; m. Lenore Frances Loroña, 1981. Rare book librarian Cornell U., 1964-68; bibliographer of scholarly collections Huntington Library, San Marino, Calif., 1968-73, head acquisitions librarian, 1973-75; sec.-treas., dir. Ravenstree Corp., 1969-80, pres., chmn. bd., 1980—; pres., chmn. bd. William Penn Ltd., 1981—. Lilly fellow Ind. U., 1963-64. Mem. Bibliog. Soc. Am., Phi Beta Kappa, Alpha Gamma Sigma, Phi Kappa Phi. Clubs: Rolls-Royce Owners; Grolier (N.Y.C.); Zamorano (Los Angeles). Home: 500 E Country Club Dr Yuma AZ 85365 Office: 2424 W 5th St Yuma AZ 85364

STUART, JAMES MILTON, investment banking company executive, financial consultant; b. N.Y.C., Dec. 23, 1932; s. Milton M. and Elizabeth (Lowenstein) S.; m. Ellen Menke, Feb. 20, 1962 (dec. 1974); children: James M. Jr., John E., Mary E.; m. Eve Rosenbloom, Dec. 16, 1977; children: Nina L., Kara Stern, Edwin Stern, Amanda Stern. BA, Brown U., 1954; M in Bus., Columbia U., 1958. Ptnr. Stuart Bros., N.Y.C., 1966-85; owner, mgr. James M. Stuart, N.Y.C., 1985—; bd. dirs. Warner Computer Systems, Inc., Fairlawn J.J., Ketchum & Co., Inc., Clark, N.J., Wordtronics Corp., Prospect, N.J., Microbiol. Scis., Inc., Warwick, R.I. Trustee Hudson Guild, Inc., N.Y.C., 1971—, Am. Shakespeare Theater, Stratford, Conn., 1986-88; bd. govs. Pathways for Youth, N.Y.C., 1966—. gen. staff U.S. Army, 1954-56. Mem. Univ. Club, Harmonie Club (N.Y.C.). Office: 126 E 56th St New York NY 10022

STUART, JOAN MARTHA, association administrator; b. Huntington, N.Y., June 2, 1945; d. Ervin Wencil and Flora Janet (Applebaum) Stuart; student Boston U., 1963-67. Prodn. asst. Random House, N.Y.C., 1968-69; book designer Simon & Schuster, N.Y.C., 1969-71; feature writer Palm Beach Post, West Palm Beach, Fla., 1971-72; co-founder, communications dir. Stuart, Gleimer & Assocs., West Palm Beach, 1973-84, pres., 1982—; fin. devel. dir. YWCA Greater Atlanta, 1984-86, Ctr. for the Visually Impaired, Atlanta, 1986—; adj. prof. Kennesaw Coll. Mem. crusade com. Am. Cancer Soc. Bd., 1981—; bd. dirs. Theatre Arts Co., 1980-81; community services chmn., bd. dirs. B'nai B'rith Women, 1980-82; chmn. publicity Leukemia Soc. Atlanta Polo Benefit, 1983; com. chmn. Atlanta Zool. Beastly Feast Benefit, 1984; mem. Atlanta Symphony Assocs.; chmn. Salute to Women of Achievement, 1987-89. Recipient Nat. award B'nai B'rith Women, 1978, Regional award, 1979; cert. of merit Big Bros./Big Sisters, 1976. Mem. Nat. Soc. Fund Raising Execs., Ga. Exec. Women's Network, B'nai B'rith Women. Republican. Jewish. Contbr. articles to profl. jours. Office: Ctr for the Visually Impaired 763 Peachtree St NW Atlanta GA 30308

STUART, JOHN M., lawyer, author; b. N.Y.C., Apr. 3, 1927; s. Winchester and Maude Ruth (Marberger) S.; m. Marjorie Louise Browne, Dec. 11, 1954; children: Jane, Alice, Richard. BA, Columbia U., 1948, JD, 1951. Bar: N.Y. 1951, U.S. Supreme Ct. 1955. Assoc., Reid & Priest, N.Y.C., 1951-64, ptnr., 1965—; asst. sec. Minn. Power & Light Co., 1951-64. Recipient Internat. Brotherhood Magicians award, 1958-60, 1st prize in sci. fiction Phila. Writers Conf., 1958. Mem. ABA, N.Y. County Bar Assn., Sr. Republican. Presbyterian. Author: A Re-examination of the Replacement Fund, 1968; Avoiding Costly Bond Problems, 1980; (with Louis H. Willenken) Utility Mortgages Should be Reexamined, 1984; (with Majorie L. Stuart) (play) Make Me Disappear, 1969; (novel) You Don't Have to Slay a Dragon, 1976. Contbr. articles to mags. Magician, W. German TV magic spl., 1965; appeared in Spy at the Magic Show benefit for Project Hope, Manhasset, N.Y., 1967. Home: 31 Westgate Blvd Plandome NY 11030 Office: Reid & Priest 40 W 57th St New York NY 10019

STUART, THOMAS JOSEPH, manufacturing company executive; b. Detroit, July 22, 1935; s. Ray F. and Miriam S. (Smith) S.; m. Dorothy J. Kreiter, June 28, 1958; children: Michael, Thomas Joseph, Charles, Melissa. B.S., U. Detroit, 1957; postgrad., Harvard Sch. Bus., 1974. Agt., reviewer IRS, Detroit, 1957-65; tax mgr. McCord Corp., Detroit, 1965-68; asst. treas. McCord Corp., 1968-72, sec., 1972-78; asst. treas. Ex-Cello Corp., Troy, Mich., 1981, v.p., treas., 1981-87; v.p. fin. The Budd Co., Troy, 1987—. Mem. bus. adv. council U. Detroit. Mem. Bus./Edn. Alliance, Civic Inc. Roman Catholic. Club: Forest Lake Country. Lodge: Elks. Home: 2370 Valleyview Troy MI 48908 Office: Budd Co 3155 W Big Beaver Rd Box 2601 Troy MI 48084

STUBBLEFIELD, PAGE KINDRED, banker; b. Bloomington, Tex., Aug. 28, 1914; s. Edwin Page and Vinnye L. (Kindred) S.; m. Dorothea Mock, July 7, 1940; children—Edwin Mark, Bob Lynn. Student, Southwestern U., Georgetown, Tex., 1931; B.B.A., U. Tex., Austin, 1936. Mgr. Page Stubblefield Gen. Mdse., 1936-42; owner-operation P.K. Stubblefield Ins. Agy., 1946-51; asst. v.p. pub. relations Victoria (Tex.) Bank & Trust Co., 1951-52, v.p., 1952-58, sr. v.p., 1958-69, pres., 1969-81, chmn. bd., from 1977, vice chmn. bd., 1984-88; bd. dirs. Victoria Bankshares, Inc; devel. bd. U. Houston. Mem. adminstrv. bd. First United Meth. Ch. Victoria; hon. mem. U. Tex. Centennial Commn. Served with finance dept. USAAF, 1942-45. Mem. Am. Bankers Assn., Tex. Bankers Assn. Club: Plaza. Home: 2402 N DeLeon St Victoria TX 77901 Office: 120 Main Pl Ste 414 Victoria TX 77902

STUBBS, SUSAN LEE, mental health services administrator, psychotherapist; b. Boston, Oct. 23, 1946; d. Harold LeRoy and Lucille F. (Benedetti) S.; m. Barry Stuart Goldstein, Apr. 29, 1971; children—Robin Stubbs Goldstein, Rosemary Stubbs Goldstein. BA, Northeastern U., 1968; MSW, Fordham U., 1972. Lic. ind. clin. social worker. Social worker N.Y.C. Housing Authority, 1972-73; dir. learning ctr. Children's Aid Soc., N.Y.C., 1974-78; clin. supr. Gandara Mental Health Ctr., Springfield, Mass., 1978-80; asst. dir. Hampshire Assn. Mental Health, Northampton, Mass., 1980-81, exec. dir., 1982; exec. dir. Valley Programs, Northampton, 1983—; psychotherapist, Northampton, 1978—. Mem. Gov.'s Adv. Bd. Homelessness, 1984—, Mayor's Task Force Deinstitutionalization, 1982—. Mem. Nat. Assn. Social Workers, Mass. Coun. Human Svc. Providers, Mass. Coalition on Homelessness. Democrat. Home: 13 Trumbull Rd Northampton MA 01060 Office: Valley Programs Inc 98 Main St Northampton MA 01060

STUCKEY, MARION MELVIN, microtechnology investments executive; b. Oran, Mo., Sept. 22, 1938; s. Ray S. and Margaret L. (Beyer) S.; m. Lora Lee Stuckey, Oct. 6, 1963; children: Kimberly René, Cristen Michelle. BBA, So. Meth. U., 1961. Sales engr. Bell Helicopter, Dallas, 1961; with exec. mgmt. IBM Corp., 1963-76; pres. subs. Control Data Corp., Mpls., 1976-82; chmn. Micro Tech. Investments, Danville, Calif., 1982—. Author: (math. book) Spheroidal Wave Function, 1960, (children's books) Freed Seed, 1975. Office: Micro Tech Investments 46 Red Birch Ct Danville CA 94526

STUDT, STEVEN ALLEN, newspaper publisher; b. Iowa City, Nov. 19, 1941; s. Clarence Joseph and Cleo Mary (Slezak) S.; m. Ruth Anne Isaacs, Nov. 28, 1964; children: Mark Joseph, Karl Allen. BA, U. Iowa, 1964. Dist. mgr. Iowa City Press-Citizen, 1961-64; asst. circulation mgr. Reno (Nev.) Newspapers, 1967-71; circulation mgr. Ft. Collins Coloradoan, 1972-77; pres., publisher St. Cloud (Minn.) Daily Times, 1978-84; pres., pub. Great Falls (Mont.) Tribune, 1984—; v.p. regional newspapers Cowles Media Co., 1988—; bd. dirs. Norwest Bank, Great Falls. Bd. dirs. St. Cloud C. of C., 1981-83, Great Falls United Way, 1985—; chmn. Great Falls Econ. Devel. Coordinating Com., 1985—; v.p. Mont. Community Found., Helena, 1988. Capt. U.S. Army, 1965-66. Mem. Am. Newspaper Pubs. Assn., Soc. Profl. Journalists, Great Falls C. of C. (bd. dirs. 1985-88). Lutheran. Office: Great Falls Tribune 205 River Dr Great Falls MT 59403

STUECK, CLIFFORD F., air cargo transportation executive; b. N.Y.C., Feb. 28, 1932; s. Arthur Charles and Florence (Keenan) S.; m. Lois Elaine Hillicke, July 14, 1956; children: Eileen, Kathleen, John, Paul, Florence. BA in Econs., St. Johns Coll., 1958; MBA, U. Conn., 1970. Computer programmer Am. Locomotive Co., Schenectady, N.Y., 1958-59, Bridgeport (Conn.) Brass Co., 1959-62, Nat. Distillers Co., N.Y.C., 1962-63; systems engr. IBM Corp., Bridgeport, Conn., 1963-66; programming supr. Emery Air Freight Co., Wilton, Conn., 1966-74, v.p. data processing, 1974-82, v.p. mktg., 1982-86, sr. v.p. sales and service, 1986—. Served to 1st lt. U.S. Army, 1951-53. Office: Emery Air Freight Old Danbury Rd Wilton CT 06897

STUECK, WILLIAM NOBLE, small business owner; b. Elmhurst, Ill., May 20, 1939; s. Otto Theodore and Anna Elizabeth (Noble) S.; m. Martha Lee Hemphill Stueck, June 2, 1963; children: Matthew Noble, Erika Lee. BS, U. Kans., 1963. Owner, pres. Suburban Lawn & Garden, Inc., Overland Park, Kans., 1953—; chmn. bd. Mark Twain Bank South, Kansas City., Mo., 1984—. Bd. dirs. Ronald McDonald House, Kansas City; ambassador Am. Royal, Kansas City, 1983. Mem. Am. Assn. Nurserymen, Mission Valley Hunt Club (master 1986—), Leavenworth Hunt Club, Saddle & Sirloin Club. Home: 6701 W 167th St Stilwell KS 66085 Office: Suburban Lawn & Garden Inc 11900 Nall Overland Park KS 66209

STUHL, OSKAR PAUL, organic chemist; b. Wilhelmshaven, Germany, Dec. 23, 1949; s. Johannes Alexander and Johanna Wilhelmine (Hoelling) S.; Dipl. Chem., U. Duesseldorf, 1976, Dr.rer.nat., 1978. Tutor, Institut fuer Organische Chemie, U. Duesseldorf, 1975-76, sci. assoc., 1976-79; mgr. product devel. Drugofa GmbH, Cologne, W.Ger., 1980; mgr. sci. relations R.J. Reynolds Tobacco GmbH, Cologne, 1981-88, mgr. sci. svcs., 1989—; cons. in field. Mem. editorial bd. Beitraege zur Tabakforschung Internat. Mem. Duesseldorf Museums Verein, Verein der Freunde des Hetjens-Museums, Verein der Freunde und Foerderer der U. Duesseldorf, Verein der Freunde des Stadtmuseums Duesseldorf, Met. Mus. Art (N.Y.C.), Art Mus. Rheinlande und Westfalen, Gesellschaft der Freunde der Kurst SammLung NRW; Yesellschaft der Freunde und Foerderer der Univ. Duesseldorf; Verein zur Foerderung Deutsch-Japanischer Beziehungen. Mem. Gesellschaft Deutscher Chemiker, Gesellschaft Deutscher Naturforscher und Aerzte, Max-Planck-Gesellschaft, Am. Chem. Soc. (including various other divs.), Chem. Soc. Japan, Royal Soc. Chemistry, Am. Pharm. Assn. (Acad. Pharm. Research and Sci., AAAS, Am. Soc. Pharmacognosy, Fedn. Internat. Pharmaceutic, Christlich Demokratische Union, CDU-Wirtschaftsvereinigung. Roman Catholic. Clubs: Vereinigung AC Duesseldorf; PCL (London); KDStV Burgundia-Leipzig (Zu Duesseldorf) im CV, Golf Club Hilden. Contbr. articles to profl. jours. Home: Ander Thomaskirche 23, D 4000 Duesseldorf 30, Federal Republic of Germany Office: RJ Reynolds Tobacco GmbH, Maria-Ablass Platz 15, D 5000 Cologne 1, Federal Republic of Germany

STUHLREYER, PAUL AUGUSTUS, III, cultural organization administrator; b. Cin., Oct. 7, 1952; s. Paul Augustus Stuhlreyer Jr. and Genevieve Adams (Edwards) Hilmer; m. Janet Barbara Vidal, May 21, 1977; children: Hillary Brooke, Erica Adams, Ryan Edwards. BS, Miami U., Oxford, Ohio, 1974; MBA, U. Va., 1976. Dir. investor relations Baldwin-United Group, Cin., 1976-78; treas. Diem-Wing Paper Co., Cin., 1978-85; pvt. practice venture capitalist Cin., 1985-87; mng. dir. Cin. Opera Assn., 1987—; chmn. Uvonics Co. Inc., Columbus, Ohio, 1985—; adj. instr. Coll. of Mt. St. Joseph, Cin., 1981—. Mem. AMBA, Gyro Club Internat. Republican. Episcopalian. Club: Cin. Country. Home: 740 Crevelings Ln Cincinnati OH 45226 Office: 1241 Elm St Cincinnati OH 45210

STULTZ, ROBERT LEE, JR., marketing consultant; b. Washington, July 24, 1926; s. Robert Lee and Grace Dearborn (Spencer) S.; m. Patricia Elizabeth Miller, Nov. 24, 1948; children: Lynn, Robert, Richard, Sharon, Melanie. BA, W.Va. U., 1949. Group leader Union Carbide Corp., Charleston, W.Va., 1953-63; with Celanese Corp. and subs., N.Y.C. and Charlotte, N.C., 1963—; v.p. sales Celanese Corp., Charlotte, 1978-84, v.p. internat. bus., 1984-86; cons. Hoechst Celanese Corp., 1984—; bd. dirs. Nantong (Republic of China) Cellulose Fibers Co. Contbr. articles to profl. jours.; patentee in field. Mem. adv. bd. Bus. Sch. U. N.C., Charlotte, 1982—, Sch. for Internat. Studies, 1984—. With USN, 1944-46, PTO. Gen. Electric Sci. fellow, 1952. Mem. Carmel Country Club (bd. dirs. 1984-88), Tower Club. Home: 3801 Brinton Pl Charlotte NC 28226

STUMBO, RICHARD WILLIAM, JR., mining company financial executive; b. Atwood, Kans., Oct. 13, 1933; s. Richard William and W. Garnet (Crihfield) S.; m. Kathleen Ann Berry, Sept. 7, 1957; children: David, Elizabeth, Karen. BSCE, U. Wis., 1958; MBA in Acctg. and Fin., U. Pa., 1968; grad. advanced mgmt. program, Harvard U., 1983. Structural engr. and indsl. sales engr. Rilco div. Weyerhaeuser Co., St. Paul, 1958-60; div. engr., promotion dir. Plywood Fabricator Service, Chgo., 1961-63; div. v.p., gen. mgr., controller Berry Industries, Birmingham, Mich., 1963-67; new venture mgr. Conwed Corp., St. Paul, 1968-69; asst. v.p. fin. planning Burlington Northern Inc., St. Paul, 1969-71; div. controller Agrl. Equipment div. Allis-Chalmers Corp., Milw., 1971-74; v.p., sr.v.p. fin., corp. dir. Western Pacific R.R. Co., San Francisco, 1974-83; v.p. fin., chief fin. officer Homestake Mining Co., San Francisco, 1983—. With Signal Corps U.S. Army, 1954-56. Mem. Fin. Execs. Inst., Fin. Officers of No. Calif., Am. Mining Congress, Beta Gamma Sigma. Office: Homestake Mining Co 650 California St 9th Floor San Francisco CA 94108

STUMBRAS, JEROME MARTIN, lawn equipmemt company executive; b. Sheboygan, Wis., Sept. 23, 1933; m. Nancy C. Morgan, Apr. 9, 1954; children: Sheila, Teresa, Patrick, David, Sandra. BS in Mktg., Marquette U., 1956; MBA, U. Wis., Milw., 1980. Div. mgr compact tractor div. J.I. Case Co., Racine, Wis., 1964-71; sr. v.p. Gilson Bros. Co., Plymouth, Wis., 1971-82; group v.p. Roper Corp., Savannah, Ga., 1982-85; v.p. Outboard Marine Corp., Plymouth; div. gen. mgr. Lawn-Boy, Plymouth, 1985—. Capt. CE, U.S. Army, 1956-67. Mem. Outdoor Power Equipment Inst. (v.p. 1988—). Home: Rt 3 Mullet Ln Plymouth WI 53073 Office: Lawn-Boy Hwy 57 S PO Box 152 Plymouth WI 53073

STUMP, ROGER VINCENT, securities trading executive, accountant; b. Long Branch, N.J., July 23, 1946; s. James Dawson and Helene (Mitchell) S.; m. Arlene Lois Mahoney, Aug. 2, 1969; children: Scott W., Kyle A. BS, Fordham U., 1968. Sr. asst. acct. Deloitte, Haskins & Sells, N.Y.C., 1968-71; internal auditor White, Weld & Co., N.Y.C., 1971-72; mgr. acctg. J&W Seligman & Co., N.Y.C., 1972-80; sr. v.p., treas., chief fin. officer, chief operating officer Seligman Securities, Inc., N.Y.C., 1981—; mem. user com. ADP Brokerage Services Group, N.Y.C., 1984—. Treas. Shrewsbury (N.J.) Rep. Club, 1986—. Mem. K.C. (grand Knight 1985, navigator Bishop McFaul assembly 1988—). Roman Catholic. Office: Seligman Securities Inc 1 Bankers Trust Plaza New York NY 10006

STUMP, WILLIAM EDWARD, cemetery executive; b. Morgantown, W.Va., Sept. 2, 1928; s. Lee and Nellie Beatrice (Rowan) S.; m. Mary Frances Kirk, Oct. 26, 1951; children: Richard Michael, William Patrick, Lynn Stump Nicholson. BBA, W.Va. U., 1949. Salesman, sales mgr. Meml. Gardens Assn., Kansas City, Mo., 1952-54; sales mgr. Memory Gardens Mgmt. Corp., Indpls., 1954-59; v.p. Meml. Estates Mgmt. Corp., Parkersburg, W.Va., 1959-63; exec. v.p. Sunset Memory Gardens, Parkersburg, 1963-69; sales mgr. Roebuck, Wilson, & Lemming, Tiffin, Ohio, 1970-72; salesman Gibraltar Mausoleum Corp., Indpls., 1973-80; co-owner Resthaven & Mercer Memory Gardens, St. Marys, Ohio, 1977—; v.p. Heritage Cemetery Mgmt. Corp., Parkersburg, 1978—. Served to 1st lt. inf. U.S. Army, 1950-52. Mem. Am. Cemetery Assn., Ohio Cemetery Assn., W.Va. Cemetery Assn. (v.p. 1967-69). Home: 1811 23d St Parkersburg WV 26101 Office: Resthaven & Mercer Memory Gardens 138 1/2 E Spring St Saint Marys OH 45885

STUMPE, WARREN ROBERT, scientific, engineering and technical services company executive; b. Bronx, N.Y., July 15, 1925; s. William A. and Emma J. (Mann) S.; children: Jeffrey, Kathy, William. B.S., U.S. Mil. Acad., 1945; M.S., Cornell U., 1949; M.S. in Indsl. Engring, N.Y. U., 1965; grad., Command and Gen. Staff Coll., 1972, Army War Coll., 1976; Ph.D. (hon.), Milw. Sch. Engring., 1982. Registered profl. engr., N.Y., Fla., Wis. Commd. 2d lt., C.E. U.S. Army, 1945, advanced through grades to capt., 1954; with (65th Engr. Bn.), 1945-48; asst. prof. mechanics U.S. Mil. Acad., 1951-54; resigned 1954; from capt. to col. Res., 1958-79; dep. gen. mgr., gen. engring. div. AMF, Stamford, Conn., 1954-63; exec. v.p. Dortech, Inc., Stamford, 1963-69; dir. systems mgmt. group Mathews Conveyor div. REX, Darien, Conn., 1969-71; dir. research and devel. Rexnord, Inc., Milw., 1971-73, v.p. corp. research and tech., from 1973, v.p. bus. devel. sector, 1981-83, v.p., chief tech. officer, 1983-86; pres. Rexnord Techs., Milw., 1986-87; v.p. Radian Corp., Milw., 1987—; civilian aide to sec. army for State of Wis. 1981-85; mem. adv. bd. technology transfer program U. Wise-Whitewater. Contbr. articles to profl. jours. Founder, pres. No. Little League, Stamford, 1965-69; pres. Turn of River Jr. High Sh. PTA, 1967-68; vice chmn. for Wis. Dept. Def., Nat. Com. Employer Support Guard and Res.; bd. regents Milw. Sch. Engring.; mem. liaison coun. Coll. Engring., U. Wis., also mem. indsl. adv. coun.; mem. adv. coun. Marquette U.; mem. Wis. Gov.'s Task Force on Energy, Coun. Great Lakes Govs.' Regional Econ. Devel. Commn., 1987—; bd. dirs. MRA-Inst. Mgmt., Inc. Mem. Am. Water Pollution Control Fedn., Indsl. Research Inst. (pres., dir.), Wis. Assn. Research Mgrs. (founder), West Point Soc. N.Y. (career adv. bd.), West Point Soc. Wis., Tau Beta Pi, Phi Kappa Phi. Clubs: Wis., Ozaukee Country. Office: Radian Corp 5101 W Beloit Milwaukee WI 53214

STUPIN, SUSAN LEE, investment banker; b. Los Angeles, Sept. 14, 1954; d. Paul Alex and Elizabeth Lee (Williams) S.; m. Theodore Robert Gamble Jr., Mar. 3, 1984. AB cum laude, Princeton U., 1975; MBA, Harvard U., 1979. Rep. corp. bond sales Paine, Webber, Jackson & Curtis, N.Y.C., 1975-77; assoc. instl. fin. Eastdil Realty Inc., N.Y.C., 1979-83; assoc. real estate dept. Goldman, Sachs & Co., N.Y.C., 1983-85, v.p. real estate dept., 1985-88; prin. The Prescott Group Inc., N.Y.C., 1988—. Fellow Morgan Library; Bryant fellow Met. Mus. Art; exec. com., fund raiser Princeton Class of 1975. Mem. Urban Land Inst. (exec. group Comml. and Retail Devel. Council), Real Estate Bd. N.Y., Internat. Council Shopping Ctrs., Young Mortgage Bankers Assn., Doubles, N.Y. Jr. League, River Club, Harvard Club (N.Y.C., Boston). Republican. Episcopalian. Home: 860 United Nations Plaza New York NY 10017 Office: The Prescott Group Inc 767 Fifth Ave New York NY 10153

STURGEON, CHARLES EDWIN, corporate executive; b. Cherryvale, Kans., May 30, 1928; s. William Charles and Lucile Myrtle (Gill) S.; children by previous marriage: Carol Ann, John Randolph, Richard Steven; m. Karen R. Riggan, May 21, 1988. A.A., Independence Jr. Coll., 1948; B.S., U. Kans., 1951; postgrad., U. Tulsa Grad. Sch., 1953-56; grad., Advanced Mgmt. Program, Harvard Bus. Sch., 1977. Research engr. Standard Oil and Gas, Tulsa, 1953-56; production supr. Vulcan Materials Co., Wichita, Kans., 1956-62; maintenance supt. Vulcan Materials Co., 1962-64, mgr. tech. services, 1964-69; plant mgr. Vulcan Materials Co., Newark, N.J., 1970-71; gen. mktg. mgr., v.p. mktg. Vulcan Materials Co., Wichita, 1971-73; v.p. mfg. Vulcan Materials Co., Birmingham, Ala., 1974-77; pres. chem. div. Vulcan Materials Co., 1977-87, pres., sr. v.p., 1987—; bd. dirs. Metal Recovery Industries, Can. Adv. U. Kans. Sch. Chem. Engring. Served with U.S. Army, 1951-53. Mem. Am. Inst. Chem. Engrs., Nat. Mgmt. Assn., Chlorine Inst. (bd. dirs.), Chem. Mfg. Assn., Soc. Chem. Industries, Vestavia Country Club. Republican. Presbyterian. Office: Vulcan Materials Co PO Box 7497 Birmingham AL 35253

STURGES, JOHN SIEBRAND, consultant; b. Greenwich, Conn., Feb. 12, 1939; s. Harry Wilton and Elizabeth Helen (Niewenhous) S.; A.B., Harvard U., 1960; M.B.A., U. So. Calif., 1965; cert. EDP, N.Y.U., 1972; cert. exec. program. Grad. Sch. Bus., U. Mich., 1982; accredited Sr. Profl. in Human Resources, Personnel Accreditation Inst. 1986; cert. Life Office Mgmt. Assn., 1967; m. Anastasia Daphne Bakalis, May 6, 1967; children—Christina Aurora, Elizabeth Athena. With Equitable Life Assurance Soc. U.S., N.Y.C., 1965-79, mgr. systems devel., 1965-70, mgr. adminstrv. services, 1970-71, dir. compensation, 1971-75, v.p., personnel and adminstrv. services, 1975-79; sr. v.p. personnel Nat. Westminster Bank U.S.A., N.Y.C., 1979-82; corp. sr. v.p. adminstrn. and human resources Corroon and Black Corp., N.Y.C., 1982-84; mng. dir. human resources Marine Midland Bank, N.Y.C., 1984-87; mng. dir. Siebrand-Wilton Assocs., N.Y.C., 1986-87, pres., 1987—; adj. prof. Middlesex County Coll., 1987—. Lay reader St. Peters Episcopal Ch., Freehold, N.J., 1972—, vestryman, 1973—; bd. dirs. Freehold Area Hosp. Wellness Center, 1979—. Served to lt. USNR, 1960-65. Mem. Commerce Assocs., Soc. for Human Resource Mgmt. (dir. 1979—), Am. Compensation Assn., Human Resources Planning Soc., Adminstrv. Mgmt. Soc., Employment Mgmt. Assn., Monmouth-Ocean Devel. Coun. (dir. 1989—), Western Monmouth C. of C. (dir. 1989—), Beta Gamma Sigma (dir. N.Y. 1978—), Phi Kappa Phi. Republican. Clubs: India House, Harvard (N.Y.C., Princeton, N.J.). Office: Siebrand-Wilton Assocs Inc PO Box 2498 New York NY 10008-2498

STURMAN, JONATHAN MARK, coal and transportation services executive; b. Rochester, N.Y., Mar. 11, 1943; s. Leon H. and Florence (Silverman) S. AB, Dartmouth Coll., 1964; MBA, Harvard U., 1967. Security analyst Eaton & Howard, Inc., Boston, 1967-68; mgr. econ. and fin. analysis Eastern Gas & Fuel, Boston, 1968-73; mgr. fin. analysis Freeport Minerals Co., N.Y.C., 1973-79; v.p. fin. Freeport Chem. Co., Uncle Sam, La., 1979-83; sr. v.p. fin. Freeport Chem. Co., New Orleans, 1983-84; v.p. analysis and planning The Pittston Co., Greenwich, Conn., 1984-86, v.p., controller, 1986—. Served with USAR, 1964-70. Home: 23 Oakwood Dr Weston CT 06883 Office: The Pittston Co One Pickwick Plaza Greenwich CT 06830

STURTEVANT, RICHARD PEARCE, insurance consultant; b. Phila., Apr. 26, 1943; s. Hazen Kimbell Sturtevant and Lois (Armstrong) Edgerly; m. Phyllis Lanier, Oct. 10, 1970 (div. Apr. 1984); children: Kristen K., Hazen P.; m. Darlene May Achilli, Nov. 30, 1985. Student, Newtown (Mass.) Jr. Coll., 1967. CLU; chartered fin. cons., Pa. Asst. to pres. KSW Controls, Inc., Fairfield, Conn., 1969-70; prin. R.P. Sturtevant and Assocs., Rocky Hill, Conn., 1970-81; mgr. mkt. devel. Phoenix Mut. Life Ins., Hartford, Conn., 1981-83; asst. v.p. Fin. Data Planning Corp., Miami, Fla., 1983-84; dir. large corp. mktg. Mass. Mut. Life Ins., Springfield, 1984-86; v.p. Brown Bridgeman and Co. Inc., Hartford, 1986-87; pres., chief exec. officer Ultimate Benefits Corp., Cromwell, Conn., 1987—. Chairperson Jaycee's Spl. Olympics, Newington, Conn., 1975. Served with USAF, 1961-65. Recipient Gov.'s Civic award State of Conn., 1975. Republican.

STURZENEGGER, OTTO, chemical company executive; b. Zurich, Switzerland, Feb. 27, 1926; came to U.S., 1948; s. Otto and Julia (Oertle) S.; m. Gerd Wold, Oct. 19, 1957; children: Elsie, Thomas O. BS, Fed. Inst. Tech., Zurich, 1948; MS, Okla. State U., 1949, PhD, 1953; grad. advanced mgmt. program, Harvard U., 1969; LHD (hon.), Mercy Coll., Dobbs Ferry, N.Y., 1982. Asst. to pres. Geigy Chem. Corp., Ardsley, N.Y., 1960-63, pres. mfg.-engring. div., 1963-69, pres. agr. chem. div., 1969-70; pres., chief exec. officer Ciba-Geigy Corp., Ardsley, N.Y., 1970-78, chmn., chief exec. officer, 1978-86, chmn., 1978—; dir. Ciba-Geigy A.G., Basle, Switzerland, 1986—; bd. dirs. NCNB Corp., Charlotte, N.C., IBM World Trade Corp., Armonk, N.Y. Bd. dirs. United Way Tri-State, N.Y.C., 1974-75; bd. govs. Kennedy Ctr., Washington, 1981; mem. adv. coun. N.Y. Med. Coll.-Hosp. Found., Valhalla, 1983-86. Recipient Westchester Man of Yr. award Gannett Newspapers, 1982. Mem. Sigma Xi. Office: Ciba-Geigy Corp 444 Saw Mill River Rd Ardsley NY 10502

STUTTS, ELBERT HARRISON, financial executive; b.1947; s. Royal Armistead and Sallie Ann (Buie) S.; m. Evelyn Ruth Bailey; 1 child, Sharon Kay. B.S., Flora McDonald Coll., N.C., 1957; M.A., Am. Coll. Fin., Calif., 1982; M.Ed., St. Andrews U., N.C., 1968. Devel. exec. Boy Scouts Am., North Brunswick, N.J., 1973-78, assoc. regional dir., Sunnyvale, Calif., 1978-84, fin. edn. and devel., Las Colinas, Tex., 1984—, fin. mktg. cons., 1979—; pres. Am. Coll. Fin. Inc. of Calif. and Tex., 1981—. Author: Fund Raising Educational Systems, 1979. Mem. Council Advancement and Support of Edn., Am. Soc. Tng. and Devel., The Ind. Sector, Nat. Soc. Nonprofit Orgns. Republican. Presbyterian. Avocations: classical music, reading, writing. Home: 122 Surrey Ln Euless TX 76039

STYRSKY, DENNIS MARTAN, federal agency marketing administrator; b. Oak Park, Ill., Feb. 28, 1944; s. Jerry B. and Slavka M. (Martan) S.; m. Jerrolyn M. Vavricka, July 19, 1969 (div. May 1983); children: Jennifer B., Christopher J.; m. Donna Lee Letrich, Dec. 29, 1984. BS, U. N.Mex., 1971. Cert. contracting officer U.S. Govt. Cert. Program. Clk. VA, Hines, Ill., 1972, chief mktg. drugs, 1978—; trainee supply mgmt. VA, Chgo., 1972-74; specialist contract VA, Nashville, 1974-75, chief. inventory mgmt., 1975-76; asst. chief supply VA, Birmingham, Ala., 1976-78; co-chmn. Dept. Defense/VA/Pub. Health Service Procurement, Washington, 1979—; mem. VA Task Force Pres.'s Pvt. Sector Study on Cost Containment (Grace Commn.) Washington, 1985. Served as specialist 5th class U.S. Army, 1966-69. Mem. Am. Mgmt. Assn., Am. Mktg. Assn., Acad. Healthcare Services. Roman Catholic. Clubs: South Wilmington (Essex, Ill.), Sportsman's. Home: 8310 Regency Ct Willow Springs IL 60480

STYSLINGER, LEE JOSEPH, JR., manufacturing company executive; b. Birmingham, Ala., June 28, 1933; s. Lee Joseph and Margaret Mary (McFarl) S.; m. Catherine Patricia Smith, Apr. 30, 1960; children—Lee Joseph III, Jon Cecil, Mark Joseph. B.S., U. Ala., 1952. With Altec Industries, Inc. and predecessors, truck equipment mfrs., Birmingham, 1952—, pres., chief exec. officer, 1956—; dir. First Ala. Bank Birmingham, Complete Health Inc., First Ala. Bancshares, Ala. Mgmt. Improvement Program; bd. dirs. Diamond Head, Inc. Bd. dirs. Birmingham C. of C., Met. Devel. Bd. Birmingham, U. Ala. Birmingham Health Services Found., Birmingham Area Council Boy Scouts Am., St. Vincent's Found., Jr. Achievement of Greater Birmingham, Inc. Mem. NAM, Farm and Indsl. Equipment Inst., U.S. C. of C., Ala. Safety Council, U. Ala. Farrah Law Soc., Birmingham C. of C. (bd. dirs.), Bus. Council Ala. Roman Catholic. Clubs: Country of Birmingham, Mountain Brook, Shoal Creek, Willow Point Golf and Country. Lodge: Rotary. Home: 3260 E Briarcliff Rd Birmingham AL 35223 Office: 210 Inverness Center Dr Birmingham AL 35242

SUAO, ADRIANA CARTAYA, magazine publisher; b. Havana, Cuba, Jan. 20, 1946, came to U.S., 1962; d. Moises Gregorio and Acela Maria (Latour) Cartaya; m. Luis Suao, May 20, 1967; children—Tania Maria, Adriana Elena, Luisa Maria. Student Am. Dominican Acad., Cuba, 1962. Pub. relations staff Kenyon Wiles Advt. Agy., Miami, Fla., 1965, copy editor, 1965-69; gen. mgr., prodn. mgr. Internat. Constrn. Pub. Co., Inc., Miami, 1972—; pres. Cieco, Miami, 1977—; adminstr. BYS Tunnel Forms Co., Miami, 1983—. Republican. Roman Catholic. Avocations: yachting, fishing, cooking. Home: 1401 Lugo Ave Coral Gables FL 33156 Office: Internat Constrn Pub Inc Suite 110 9200 S Dadeland Blvd Miami FL 33156

SUBAK, JOHN THOMAS, chemical company executive; b. Trebic, Czechoslovakia, Apr. 19, 1929; came to U.S., 1941, naturalized, 1946; s. William John and Gerda Maria (Subakova) S.; m. Mary Corcoran, June 4, 1955; children—Jane, Kate, Thomas, Michael. BA summa cum laude, Yale U., 1950, LLB, 1956. Bar: Pa. 1956. From assoc. to ptnr. Dechert, Price & Rhoads, Phila., 1956-76, v.p., gen. counsel, 1976-77, group v.p., gen. counsel, 1977—, also bd. dirs.; dir., mem. exec. Milton Roy Co. Editor: The Bus. Lawyer, 1982-83. Bd. dirs. Am. Cancer Soc. Lt. (j.g.) USN, 1950-53. Mem. ABA (chmn. corp. and bus. law sect. 1984-85), Am. Law Inst. (council mem.), Chem. Mfrs. Assn. (gen. counsels group), Defender Assn. of Phila. (v.p., bd. dirs.). Democrat. Roman Catholic. Clubs: Merion Cricket, Phila., Down Town. Home: 214 Ivy Ln Haverford PA 19041 Office: Rohm & Haas Co Independence Mall W Philadelphia PA 19105

SUBLETTE, WILLIAM GORDON, personnel executive; b. Tyler, Tex., Nov. 23, 1939; s. Monroe Fields and Jessie Cleo (Ray) S.; m. Pamela Jean Miller, Sept. 3, 1977; 1 child, Brandon Miller. AA in Bus., Tyler Coll., 1959; BBA in Indsl. Mgmt., Lamar U., 1963; MBA in Mgmt., N. Texas State U., 1966. Profl. accredited exec. in personnel, cert. compensation profl. Mgr. salary control Collins Radio, Dallas, 1963-70; dir. compensation and mgmt. devel. GENESCO, Nashville, 1970-73; mgr. personnel practice Arthur Young & Co., Houston, 1973-75; mgr. corp. compensation Panhandle Eastern Corp., Houston, 1975-81; dir. compensation Occidental Chem., Houston, 1981-82; mng. prin. The Williams Group, Houston, 1982-88; v.p. human resources Enviro/Analysis Corp., Atlanta, 1988—; bd. dirs., William Sublette Enterprises, Inc., Houston, Chivoux, U.S.A., Inc., Houston.; mem. bus. coun. Ga. Mem. Am. Compensation Assn., Houston Compensation Assn., Am. Soc. Personnel Adminstrn., Acad. Polit. Sci., Houston West C. fo C. (chmn. internat. bus. com.), Sigma Chi. Republican. Mem. Ch. of Christ. Club: Toastmasters (Dallas, Nashville). Home: 8600 Woodledge Ln Roswell GA 30076

SUCCUSO, PETER JAMES, real estate company executive; b. Oceanside, N.Y., Oct. 14, 1950; s. Peter Joseph and Marjorie Ann (Ferraro) S.; m. Paulette M. Demers, Dec. 24, 1984. BA, Columbia U., 1971, MBA, 1975; BS, Columbia U. Sch. Engring., 1973. Asst. v.p. Citibank, NA, N.Y.C., 1975-79; exec. v.p. Property Resources Corp., N.Y.C., 1979-86; pres. Glickenhaus Realty, Inc., N.Y.C., 1986-88, Project Capitol Corp., N.Y.C., 1988—. Mem. Nat. Housing Rehab. Assn. (bd. dirs. 1981—). Home: 95 Horatio St Apt 625 New York NY 10014 Office: 777 Terrace Ave Hasbrouk Heights NJ 07604

SUCHER, CYNTHIA CLAYTON CRUMB, hospital marketing executive; b. Washington, Dec. 19, 1943; d. Francis Paul and Jewell Evangeline (Sheets) Crumb; m. Theodore Richard Sucher III, Sept. 7, 1961 (div. Dec. 1980); children: Theodore Richard IV, Evangeline Leigh Sucher Gabrielson; m. Carlton Wayne Vaught, Dec. 20, 1982; 1 child Clayton Wayne. Student, Stetson U., 1959-61; BA in Communications summa cum laude, U. Cen. Fla., 1975. Reporter, anchorwoman Sta. WFTV-TV, Orlando, Fla., 1974-76, exec. producer, 1977-78; news anchorman Sta. KWTX-TV, Waco, Tex., 1976-77; editor, pub. Dining Out mag., Orlando, 1978-80; pub. info. officer Fla. Dept. Health and Rehabilitative Svcs., Orlando, 1980-82; dir. media communication Orlando Regional Med. Ctr., 1982-85; asst. adminstr. Winter Park (Fla.) Meml. Hsop., 1985-86, v.p. mktg., 1986—; mentor Crummer Sch. Bus., Rollins Coll., Winter Park, 1987—. Producer/reporter radio documentary Ted Bundy series, 1980 (UPI award). Media coordinator Bill Frederick Campaign, Orlando, 1980; bd. dirs. Vol. Ctr. Cen. Fla., 1983-87; commr. Winter Park Sidewalk Art Festival, 1984—; mem. Orlando Mayor's Nominating Bd., 1987—; mem. pres.'s council advisors U. Cen. Fla., Orlando, 1987—. Recipient Healthcare Mktg. Report Merit award, 1986. Mem. Am. Mktg. Assn. (bd. dirs. Cen. Fla. chpt. 1987-88), Acad. Health Svcs. Mktg. (bd. dirs. 1988—), Soc. Profl. Journalists (pres. Cen. Fla. chpt. 1983), Fla. Exec. Women (pres. Orlando 1985-86), Town and Gown (council), Orlando C. of C. (chmn. community awards 1987), Winter Park C. of C. (bd. dirs. 1989—). Democrat. Methodist. Home: 8617 Amber Oak Ct Orlando FL 32817 Office: Winter Park Meml Hosp 200 N Lakemont Ave Winter Park FL 32792

SUCKOW, MARK WILLIAM, savings and loan executive; b. Des Moines, Jan. 12, 1957; s. Gordon William and Lola Pearl (Marlenee) S.; m. Milisa Gay Stuffings, July 12, 1986. BSBA, Washburn U., 1979. Cert. fin. planner. Loan officer Anchor Savs. Assn., Leawood, Kans., 1979-80; asst. br. mgr. Anchor Savs. Assn., Mission, Kans., 1980-81; br. mgr., asst. v.p. Anchor Savs. Assn., Shawnee, Kans., 1981-82; br. mgr., v.p. Anchor Savs. Assn., Lawrence, Kans., 1982-86; fin. planner Brad T. Miller & Assocs., Topeka, 1986-87; regional v.p. Columbia Savs., Overland Park, Kans., 1987—. Mem. Inst. Cert. Fin. Planners, Internat. Assn. Fin. Planning, Internat. Bd. Standards and Practices for Cert. Fin. Planners, Inc. Office: Columbia Savs 9901 Santa Fe Dr Overland Park KS 66212

SUDARSKY, JERRY M., industrialist; b. Russia, June 12, 1918; came to U.S., 1928, naturalized, 1934; s. Selig and Sara (Ars) S.; m. Mildred Axelrod, Aug. 31, 1947; children: Deborah, Donna. Student U. Iowa, 1936-39; B.S., Poly. U. Bklyn., 1942; D.Sc. (hon.), Poly. Inst. N.Y., 1976. Founder, chief exec. officer Bioferm Corp., Wasco, Calif., 1946-66; cons. to Govt. of Israel, 1966-67; founder, chmn. Israel Chems., Ltd., Tel Aviv, Israel, 1967-72; chmn. I.C. Internat. Cons., Tel Aviv, 1971-73; vice chmn., bd. dirs. Daylin, Inc., Los Angeles, 1972-76; pres., chmn. J.M.S. Assocs., Los Angeles, 1976-82; vice chmn. bd. Jacobs Engring. Group, Inc., Pasadena, Calif., 1982—. Patentee in field of indsl. microbiology. Bd. govs. Hebrew U., Jerusalem; trustee Polytechnic U. N.Y., 1976—; bd. dirs. Arthritis Found., L.A., 1989—. Served with USNR, 1943-46. Mem. AAAS, Am. Chem. Soc., Sigma Xi. Clubs: Brentwood Country (Los Angeles). Office: Jacobs Engring Group Inc 251 S Lake Ave Pasadena CA 91101

SUEDHOFF, CARL JOHN, JR., lawyer; b. Ft. Wayne, Ind., Apr. 22, 1925; s. Carl John and Helen (Lau) S.; m. Carol Mulqueeney, Apr. 10, 1954; children—Thomas Lau, Robert Marshall, Mark Mulqueeney. B.S., U. Pa., 1948; J.D., U. Mich., 1951. Bar: Ind. 1951, U.S. Dist. Ct. (no. and so. dists.) Ind. 1951, U.S. Ct. Appeals (7th cir.) 1957, U.S. Tax Ct. 1981. Assoc. mem. firm Hunt & Mountz, Ft. Wayne, 1951-54; ptnr. Hunt, Suedhoff, Borrorr & Eilbacher and predecessors, Ft. Wayne, 1955—; officer, dir. Inland Chem. Corp., Ft. Wayne, 1952-81; pres., dir. Lau Bldg. Co., Ft. Wayne, 1951-78, S.H.S. Realty Corp., Toledo, 1960-78; officer, dir. Inland Chem. P.R., Inc., San Juan, 1972-81, Northeast Cogen, Inc., others. Mem. Allen County Council, 1972-76, pres., 1974-76; mem. Allen County Tax Adjustment Bd., 1973-74, N.E. Ind. Regional Coordinating Council, 1975-76; bd. dirs. Ft. Wayne YMCA, 1961-63. Served with AUS, 1943-45. Mem. VFW (comdr. 1958-59), ABA, Ind. Bar Assn., Allen County Bar Assn., Beta Gamma Sigma, Phi Delta Phi, Psi Upsilon. Clubs: Univ. Mich. (pres. 1965-66), Friars, Ft. Wayne Country, Mad Anthony's. Office: 900 Paine Webber Bldg Fort Wayne IN 46802

SUGARMAN, HOWARD PAUL, real estate developer, lawyer; b. Balt., May 13, 1957; s. Morris and Sylvia (Cohen) S. BA with honors and distinction, Cornell U., 1979; JD with honors, George Washington U., 1983. Bar: Md. 1983. Assoc. Frank, Bernstein, Conaway & Goldman, Balt., 1982-84; pres. H.P. Sugarman Assocs., Inc., Lutherville, Md., 1984—. Mem. editorial bd. Jour. Internat. Law and Econs., 1981-82. Mem. young leadership coun. Assn. Jewish Charities, Balt., 1986-87, mem. advanced leadership devel. coun., 1987-88, mem. young exec. and profl. div. social com. Recipient Spl. Achievement award Social Security Adminstrn. Mem. Md. State Bar Assn. (young lawyers sect.), Greater Balt. Bd. Realtors, Home Builders Assn. Md., Zionist Orgn. Am., Am. Heart Assn., George Washington Alumni Assn., Cornell Club Md., Balt. Ski Club, Phi Beta Kappa, Zeta Beta Tau. Office: 5 Sugarvale Way Lutherville MD 21093

SUHRE, WALTER ANTHONY, JR., lawyer, brewery executive; b. Cin., Jan. 17, 1933; s. Walter A. and Elizabeth V. (Heimbuch) S.; m. Judy Lee Carrington, June 7, 1975. B.S. in Bus. Adminstrn., Northwestern U., 1956; LL.B. with honors, U. Cin., 1962. Bar: Ohio 1962, Mo. 1982. Assoc. Taft, Stettinius & Hollister, Cin., 1962-65; with Eagle-Picher Industries, Inc., Cin., 1965-82, gen. counsel, 1970-82; v.p., gen. counsel Anheuser-Busch Cos., Inc., St. Louis, 1982—. Served with USMC, 1956-59. Mem. ABA, Mo. Bar Assn. Republican. Presbyterian. Clubs: Queen City (Cin.), Old Warson Country (St. Louis). Home: 48 Woodcliffe Rd Saint Louis MO 63124 Office: Anheuser-Busch Cos Inc One Busch Pl Saint Louis MO 63118

SUKENIK, CHARLES M., investment banker; b. N.Y.C., Nov. 21, 1944; s. Sol and Melva (Factor) S.; m. Vivian Jansen, Feb. 14, 1974. BS, NYU, 1966, MBA, 1968. Analyst Pershing & Co., N.Y.C., 1968-71; mgr. pvt. placements Gen. Electric Investment Co., Stamford, Conn., 1971-82; mng. dir. Butler Capital Corp., N.Y.C., 1982—; dir. W.R. Holdings, N.Y.C., Sun Media, Cleve., Lancaster (Pa.) Press, Strine Printing, York, Pa. Mem. Nature Conservancy, Cen. Park Conservancy. Office: Butler Capital Corp 767 Fifth Ave New York NY 10153

SUKUN, ZIYA, business executive; b. Ankara, 1958; came to U.S., 1983; s. Fatima and Nacil. Diploma, Ankara Coll., 1977, Universita Italiana per Stranieri, Perugia, Italy, 1978; MFA, Accademia delle Belle Arti di Firenze, Florence, Italy, 1983. Reporter Adam mag., Istanbul, 1975; photo journalist Vog mag., Istanbul, 1979; fashion photo journalist Vizon mag., Istanbul, 1980-82, Conferme Moda mag., Florence, 1981-82, Neue Welt mag., Fed. Republic of Germany, 1982; pres. Ur-Khan Inc., Westport, Conn., 1983—; cons. Profesyonel Ltd. (Vizon show), Istanbul, 1986—, Ur-Khan SdF, Florence, 1982, Why Not model agy., Milan, 1979-81,. Republican. Home: PO Box 65 Westport CT 06881 Office: Ur-Khan Inc 250 Main St Box 5112 Westport CT 06881

SUKYS, JAMES JOSEPH, accountant; b. Cleve., Aug. 30, 1958; s. Vitus John and Catherine Louise (Corsi) S. BBA magna cum laude, U. Dayton, 1980. CPA, Ohio. Staff acct. Price Waterhouse, Cleve., 1980-84, tax cons., 1985-86; asst. mgr. fed. taxes AMCA Internat., Hanover, N.H., 1984-85; tax audit specialist Standard Oil Co., Cleve., 1986—, BP America Inc., Cleve., 1989—; fin. advisor Buckeye Evaluation and Tech. Inst., Cleve., 1985-86. Mem. Am. Inst. CPA's, Ohio Soc. CPA's, Nat. Assn. Accts., Nat. Inst. Accts. Roman Catholic. Office: BP America Inc 200 Public Sq Cleveland OH 44114

SULCER, FREDERICK DURHAM, advertising executive; b. Chgo., Aug. 28, 1930; s. Henry Durham and Charlotte (Thearle) S.; m. Dorothy Wright, May 2, 1953; children—Thomas W., Ginna M., David T. B.A., U. Chgo., 1949, M.B.A., 1963. Reporter UP Assn., Chgo., 1945-46; reporter AP, 1947; with Needham, Harper & Steers Advt., Chgo., 1947-78, dir., 1965-78, sr. account dir., 1965-66, mem. exec. com., 1966-78, exec. v.p., 1967, dir. N.Y. div., 1967-78; pres. N.Y. div. Needham, Harper & Steers Advt., 1974-75; chmn. bd. NH & S Internat., 1975-76; pres. Sulcer Communication Co., Inc., 1977-78; group exec., dir. Benton & Bowles (advt.), 1978-85; dir. D'Arcy Masius Benton & Bowles, advt., N.Y.C., 1985—. Served to capt. C.E. AUS, 1950-53. Mem. Am. Assn. Advt. Agys. (bd. govs. N.Y. chpt.), Internat. Advertisers Assn., Alpha Delta Phi. Home: 400 E 56th St Apt 6N New York NY 10022 Office: D'Arcy Masius Benton & Bowles Inc 909 3rd Ave New York NY 10022

SULEIMAN, SAMI KHALIL, financial planner, accountant; b. Palestine, Palestine, Mar. 27, 1947; came to U.S., 1969; s. Khalil A. and Hasna (Khatib) S.; m. Penelope Mitchell, Jan. 26, 1984; children: Nura, Ramzy. BS in Econs., U. Jordan, 1969; MBA in Internat. Fin., Stanford U., 1979. Sr. cons. Arthur Young and Co., N.Y.C., 1979-80; chief fin. officer Internat. Food Policy Inst., Washington, 1980-83; pres. Internat. Fin. Services, Washington, 1983—; fin. planner Home Life Ins. Co., N.Y.C., 1987—. Rockefeller Found. scholar, 1977. Mem. Nat. Soc. Pub. Accts., Nat. Assn. Security Dealers, Nat. Assn. Life Underwriters, Stanford Bus. Sch. Alumni Assn. (treas. 1985—), Assn. Arab-Am. Univ. Grads. (pres. 1983). Home: 6520 E Halbert St Bethesda MD 20817

SULGROVE, MICHELLE KUTRUMANES, accountant; b. Iowa City, Feb. 1, 1952; d. Constantine Peter and Mary (Prempas) K.; m. William Howard, May 8, 1976; children: Maria Jacqueline, Alexander Constantine. BS in Psychology, So. Ill. U., 1974; cert. in acctg., Ind. State U., 1986. CPA, Ind. Social worker Monroe County Community Action, Bloomington, Ind., 1974-76; tax preparer H&R Block Tax Svc., Bloomington, 1976-77; mgr. real estate office Bloomington Bldg. & Maintenance, 1977-79; tax assessor Cybernetic Svcs., Bloomington, 1978; chief adminstr. Reclamation Contractors, Bloomington, 1979-85; chief fin. officer Malltech Inc., Bloomington, 1986—. Vol. Synergy Group, Carbondale, Ill., 1972-74; pres. Sr. Citizens Nutrition Program, Bloomington, 1975-79; bd. dirs. Community Svc. Council, Bloomington, 1975-79. Office: Malltech Inc 1128 S Morton Bloomington IN 47401

SULICK, PETER, JR., broadcasting company executive; b. Paterson, N.J., Dec. 2, 1950; s. Peter Sr. and Margaret M.; m. Margaret Sarah Citarella, May 14, 1977; children: Paricia Anne, Peter III. BS, The Citadel, 1972; MBA, U. Mass., 1973. CPA, N.J. Acct. Arthur Andersen & Co., N.Y.C., 1973-78; asst. comptroller ITT, N.Y.C., 1978-82; v.p., chief fin. officer Intersoft Corp., N.Y.C., 1982-83; corp. controller Cablevision Systems Corp., Woodbury, N.Y., 1983-86; pres. Surburban Circle Communications, N.Y.C., 1985—; founder, chmn., chief exec. officer Independence Broadcasting Corp., N.Y.C., 1986—. bd. dirs. Kane Found., N.Y.C., 1985—. Mem. Nat. Assn. Broadcasters, AICPA, N.J. Soc. CPAs, Union League Club, Kane (Jr. warden 1988—), Masons. Home: 5 Bald Hill Pl Wilton CT 06897 Office: Independence Broadcasting 401 Merritt 7 Corp Park Norwalk CT 06856

SULIK, EDWIN (PETE), health care administrator; b. Bryan, Tex., Feb. 1, 1957; s. Edwin Peter and Bonny Jo (Robertson) S.; m. Kolleen Marie Stevens, Aug. 8, 1981; 1 child, Laine Sheridan. Student, Blinn Jr. Coll., 1977-78, U. Tex., 1977, Tex. A&M U., 1977-83, Ky. Western. U., currently. Lic. long term care adminstr. Sr. v.p. ops. Sherwood Health Care, Inc., Bryan, 1976—; sec.-treas. Sherwood Health Care, Inc., Lubbock, Tex., 1987—; pres. Three EPS, Inc., Bryan, 1987—; sec.-treas. B-CS Med. Supply Inc., Bryan, 1985. Mem. campaign com. for Sen. W.T. Moore, Bryan; participant state debate with Lt. Gov. Hobby, Austin, Tex., 1987. Mem. Am. Coll. Health Care Adminstrs., Am. Health Care Assn., Tex. Health Care Assn. (pres. Brazos Valley chpt. Long Term Adminstrs. 1986-87, legis. com. 1986-87, various other coms. 1987—), Nat. Fire Protection Assn.; chmn. of chpt. pres. council, State of Tex. Republican. Roman Catholic. Lodges: KC, Elks. Home: PO Box 3553 Bryan TX 77805-3553 Office: Sherwood Health Care Inc 1401 Memorial Dr Bryan TX 77802

SULIMIRSKI, WITOLD STANISLAW, banker; b. Lwow, Poland, May 18, 1933; came to U.S., 1957; s. Tadeusz and Olga (Lepkowska) S.; m. Teresa Maria Boniecka, Dec. 28, 1957; children—Elizabeth Sulimirski Blakeslee, Adam, Edward. B.A. with honors, Cambridge U., 1953, M.A., 1957. With Irving Trust Co., N.Y.C., 1957-89, exec. v.p., 1986-89; pres. Servus Assocs., Inc., N.Y.C., 1989—. Treas. Polish Inst. Arts and Scis., Inc., N.Y.C., 1976—; vice chmn. Kosciuscko Found., Inc., N.Y.C., 1983—; chmn. Polish Assistance, Inc., N.Y.C., 1984—; bd. dirs. Am.-Arab Affairs Council, Washington, 1984—, Nat. U.S.-Arab C. of C., Washington, 1987—. Roman Catholic. Club: Bronxville Field (N.Y.). Lodge: Knights of Malta. Office: Servus Assocs Inc 535 Fifth Ave Ste 2400 New York NY 10017

SULLIVAN, BARRY F., banker; b. Bronx, N.Y., Dec. 21, 1930; s. John J. and Marion V. (Dwyer) S.; m. Audrey M. Villeneuve, Apr. 14, 1956; children: Barry, Gerald P., Mariellen M., Scott J., John C. Student, Georgetown U., 1949-52; B.A., Columbia U., 1955; M.B.A., U. Chgo., 1957. Exec. v.p. Chase Manhattan Bank, N.Y.C., 1957-80; chmn., chief exec. officer 1st Chgo.-1st Nat. Bank Chgo., Chgo., 1980—; bd. dirs. Am. Nat. Corp., Fed. Reserve Bank. Dir. Econ. Devel. Commn., Chgo.; mem. Chgo. Urban League, Chgo. Central Area Com.; trustee Art Inst. Chgo., U. Chgo. Served with U.S. Army, 1952-54; Korea. Mem. Assn. Res. City Bankers, Trilateral Commn. Roman Catholic. *

SULLIVAN, BERNARD JAMES, accountant; b. Chgo., June 25, 1927; s. Bernard Hugh and Therese Sarah (Condon) S.; m. Joan Lois Costello, June 9, 1951; children: Therese Lynn Scanlan, Bernard J., Geralyn M. Snyder. BSC, Loyola U., Chgo., 1950. CPA, Ill. Staff Bansley and Kiener, Chgo., 1950-66, ptnr., 1966-82, mng. ptnr., 1982—; bd. dirs. Associated Acctg. Firms, Internat.; exec. com. Moore Stephens and Co., U.S.A., 1984—, Arbitrator Nat. Assn. Security Dealers. Served with USN, 1945-46. Mem. Am. Inst. CPA's, Ill. Soc. CPA's, Govt. Fin. Officer Assn., Internat. Found. Employee Benefit Plans, Delta Sigma Pi. Clubs: Beverly Country (Chgo.), Metropolitan (Chgo.). Lodges: Elks, K.C. Home: 2805 W 85th Place Chicago IL 60652 Office: Bansley and Kiener 300 W Washington Chicago IL 60606

SULLIVAN, DANIEL JOHN, information system executive; b. Butte, Mont., May 3, 1955; s. Daniel William and Mary Catherine (Evankovich) S.; children from previous marriage: Shannon Marie, Maureen Elizabeth. BS in Computer Sci., U. Mont. Programmer Mont. Power Co., Butte, 1977-79, sr. programmer, 1979-81, system analyst, 1981-83, mgr. application program, 1983-85, cons., 1983—, mem. design and rev. bd., 1983—, mgr. system plan and devel., 1985-86, mgr. computer and info. systems, 1986—. Canvasser United Way of Butte, 1984—, Heart Found, Butte, 1984-86, Boy Scouts Am., Butte, 1984; del. U. Mont., 1987; mem. Big Bros./Big Sisters, 1988—. Recipient Bronze award United Way, Butte, 1984. Mem. Mont. Data Processing Assn., Summit Valley Investment Club (presiding ptnr. 1985), Butte C. of C., Phi Kappa Psi, Grizzly Athletic Assn. Club, KC. Roman Catholic. Home: 2022 Wall St Butte MT 59701

SULLIVAN, DAVID STAFFORD, psychologist, publishing company executive, real estate developer; b. Oak Park, Ill., Dec. 11, 1943; s. Orville A. and Voris Allene (Stafford) S.; m. Sharon Eenigenburg, May 30, 1964; 1 child, David Jr. BA, No. Ill. U., 1965, MA, 1968, PhD, 1974. Assoc. prof. Wheaton (Ill.) Coll., 1967-73; clin. psychologist North Park Clinic, S.C., Park Ridge, Ill., 1973-82; pres. Brook Clinic, P.C., Oak Brook, Ill., 1982-87; gen. ptnr. Elgin Airport Property, Ltd., Wheaton, 1979—; pvt. practice clin. psychology Wheaton, 1987—; pres. Sullivan Pub. Co., Elmhurst, Ill., 1981—. Author: Thoroughbred Racing: Predicting the Outcome, 1973, Harness Racing: Predicting the Outcome, 1975, S/A Advanced Method, 1975; contbr. articles to profl.jours. and sports publs. Mem. Am. Psychol. Assn. (chmn. Ill. ethics com. 1985—). Office: 1127 Wheaton Oaks Ct 106 Wheaton IL 60187

SULLIVAN, EDWARD HOLDEN, JR., financial services executive; b. Shreveport, La., Oct. 5, 1941; s. Edward Holden and Florence (Tierney) S.; m. Lisa Rimer, June 24, 1977; 1 child, Shannon E. BS in Bus. Mgmt., LaSalle U., 1972. Pres., chief exec. officer Caballero Loan Svc., Inc., El Paso, Tex., 1966-74; dir. mktg. and advt. Richardson (Tex.) Savs. and Loan, 1974; mgr. regional sales and mktg. Depositors Portrait Svcs. Internat. div. Chromalloy Am. Corp., St. Louis, 1974-79; sales rep. Fla. Software Svcs., Altamonte Springs, 1979-80; dist. mgr. J.B. Steelman, Inc., Altamonte Springs, 1980-82; dir. sales Systematics, Inc., Little Rock, 1982-85; dir. nat. accounts UCCEL Corp., Dallas, 1985-86; div. mgr., chief exec. officer Security Pacific Fin. Systems, Phoenix, 1986-87; div. mgr. Security Pacific Info. Svcs. Corp., Denver, 1987-88; pres., chief exec. officer One Card Mktg., Inc., Culver City, Calif., 1988-89; pres. sales div. Dot Systems, Inc., Denver, 1989—. Recipient Community Svc. award Optimists, 1973. Mem. Am. Bankers Assn., Ind. Bankers of Am. (assoc.), Mortgage Bankers Assn., Bank of Adminstrn. Inst. (assoc.), Consumer Bankers Assn. (participating), U.S. Savs. League, Denver C. of C. Roman Catholic. Clubs: Memphis Petroleum; Greenwood Athletic (Englewood, Colo.); Glenmoor Country (Denver). Home: 5411 S Geneva St Englewood CO 80111 Office: Dot Systems Inc 10730 E Bethany Dr Ste 204 Aurora CO 80014

SULLIVAN, EDWARD JOSEPH, electrotype company executive; b. Concord, N.H., May 17, 1915; s. Edward J. and Ida (Packard) S.; student St. Anslem's Coll., 1935-36; m. Dorothea M. Ash, Sept. 30, 1944; children—James Ash, Maureen Packard. Treas., Merrimack Electrotyping Corp., 1950-55, pres., 1955—; treas. Sheraton Properties Corp., 1961—; exec. v.p. Blanchard Press Corp., 1968-69; pres. Tridel Housing Devels., 1970—, Ho-Tei Corp., St. Thomas, V.I.; dir. Concord Fed. Savs. Bank; pres. Allied Photo Engraving Corp., 1964. Mem. Concord Hosp. Corp., U.S. Commn. on Civil Rights; chmn. bldg. fund Carmelite Monastery, Concord, 1950, St. Peters Ch. for Bishop Brady High Sch. Bldg. Fund, 1961; citizens com. Concord Housing Authority; commr. Concord Urban Renewal Assn.; v.p., bd. dirs. Diocesan Bur. Housing, Inc., Manchester, N.H., 1975—; bd. dirs. Carpenter Center, Inc., Manchester, N.H., Concord chpt. ARC, Concord Hosp. Served with USNR, 1942-46. Mem. Internat. Assn. Electrotypers and Stereotypers Union, Internat. Assn. Electrotypers and Stereotypers, Inc., Am. Legion, Aircraft Owners and Pilots Assn., Audubon Soc. N.H., Printing Inst. Am., One Hundred Club N.H. Elk. Republican. Roman Catholic. Club: Serra (v.p.). Kiwanian, K.C. Home: 99 Manor Rd Concord NH 03303 Office: 99 Manor Rd Concord NH 03303

SULLIVAN, FRED R., business executive; b. Ft. Wayne, Ind., 1914; m. Judith Omanoff; children—Nancy, Judith, Fred Andrew. B.S., Rutgers U., 1938; M.B.A., N.Y. U., 1942; LL.D. (hon.), Washington and Jefferson Coll., 1974. Factory cost clk. Monroe Calculating Machine Co., 1934, advanced to pres., 1953; (co. merged with Litton Industries); sr. v.p. Litton, 1961-64; chief exec. officer, dir. Kidde Inc., 1963-88, pres., 1964-88, chmn., chief exec. officer, 1966; chmn. Interim Systems Corp., Clifton, N.J., 1988—; bd. dirs. Sequa Corp., N.Y.C., Midlantic Corp., Inc., Edison, N.J., Richton Internat. Corp., N.Y.C., The Home Group, Inc., Newark, Del., The Home Ins. Co., Manchester, N.H., Revlon, Inc., N.Y.C., Revlon Group, Inc., N.Y.C., Tyler Corp., Dallas, Internat. Am. Homes, Inc., Union, N.J., Kaisertech Ltd., Oakland, Calif. Trustee Lenox Hill Hosp., N.Y.C.; bd. dirs. emeritus Found. for Children with Learning Disabilities, N.Y.C., Fordham U., Bronx, N.Y. Office: Interim Systems Corp 4 Brighton Rd Clifton NJ 07015

SULLIVAN, JAMES JOSEPH, architect; b. Boston, Aug. 23, 1922; s. Gilbert and Ellen (Flaherty) S.; cert. Sch. Practical Arts, Boston, 1942, Art Students League, N.Y.C., 1947, Boston Archtl. Center, 1950-53; m. Mary Elizabeth Clarkson, Apr. 3, 1948; children—Mary Ellen Armold, Kathleen S. Picard, Michael J., Ann S. Harnett, Joseph C., James Joseph, Jr. Architect dist. public works U.S. Navy, Boston, 1952-58; asso. Cabot, Cabot & Forbes, Boston, 1958-63; dir. bldg. div. Charles A. Maguire & Assocs., Boston, 1963-66; pres., treas. Sullivan Design Group, Inc., Braintree, Mass., 1966—; instr. house constrn. adult edn. M.I.T., 1952-54; tchr. apprentice tng. program, Boston, 1956-60. Chmn. Bldg. Code Com., Braintree, 1970-72; mem. designer selection bd. Commonwealth of Mass., 1971-76, chmn., 1975-76; commr. Sewer Dept., Braintree, 1979—; pres. Sullivan Design Group, Inc., 1986-87. Served with USCGR, 1942-46. Recipient outstanding accomplishment awards Dept. Public Works, 1st Naval Dist. Hdqrs., Boston, 1957, 58. Mem. AIA, Boston Archtl. Center Alumni Assn., Mus. Fine Arts, Soc. Am. Mil. Engrs. Democrat. Roman Catholic. Clubs: Martha's Vineyard Art Assn., Cochato, Braintree, Chappaquiddick Beach, Quincy Neighborhood, Edgartown Yacht. Author: You and Your Architect, 1969, 73. Home: 53 Connell St Braintree MA 02184 Office: 44 Adams St Braintree MA 02184

SULLIVAN, JAMES KIRK, forest products company executive; b. Greenwood, S.C., Aug. 25, 1935; s. Daniel Jones and Addie (Brown) S.; m. Elizabeth Miller, June 18, 1960; children: Hal N., Kim J. BS in Chemistry, Clemson U., 1957, MS, 1964, PhD, 1966; PSE, MIT, 1975. Prodn. supr. FMC Corp., South Charleston, W.Va., 1957-62; tech. supt. FMC Corp., Pocatello, Idaho, 1966-69; mktg. mgr. FMC Corp., N.Y.C., 1969-70; v.p. govtl. and environ. affairs Boise Cascade Corp., Idaho, 1971—; dir. Key Bank Idaho. Contbr. articles to profl. jours.; patentee in field. Mem. Coll. of Forest and Recreation Resources com. Clemson U., Idaho Found. for Pvt. Enterprise and Econ. Edn., Idaho Rsch. Found., Inc., adv. com. Idaho Task Force on Higher Edn.; chmn. adv. bd. U. Idaho Coll. Engring., pub. affairs com. NAM; pres. Bishop Kelly Found.; chmn. centennial campaign U. Idaho; trustee Idaho Children's Emergency Fund, Bishop Kelly High Sch.; past chmn. Bronco Athletic Assn. 1st lt. U.S. Army, 1958-59. Mem. Am. Inst. Chem. Engrs., Am. Chem. Soc., Am. Inst. Chem. Engrs., Am. Paper Inst. (govtl. affairs com.), Bus. Week Found. (chmn. Bus. Week 1980), Bus. Roundtable (environ. com.), Idaho Assn. Commerce and Industry (bd. dirs.), C. of C. of U.S. (pub. affairs com.). Republican. Home: 5206 Sorrento Circle Boise ID 83704 Office: Boise Cascade Corp One Jefferson Sq Boise ID 83728

SULLIVAN, JAMES MICHAEL, credit union executive; b. Providence, Feb. 22, 1933; s. James Patrick and Mary Kathleyne (Neary) S.; m. Arlene Ann Vincent, Nov. 10, 1956; 1 child, Michael J. BS in Acctg., U. R.I., 1959, MBA, 1965. Gen. acct. Texas Instruments Inc., Attleboro, Mass., 1959-63, div. control analyst, 1963-67, div. acctg. mgr., 1967-71, group acctg. mgr., 1971-81, group audit mgr., 1981-82; pres., treas. Texas Instruments Fed. Credit Union, Attleboro, 1982—, also bd. dirs.; bd. dirs. Ea. Corp. Fed. Credit Union, Stoneham, Mass, Mass. Credit Union Nat. Assn., Southboro. Served with USN, 1951-55. Mem. Credit Union Exec. Soc. Democrat. Roman Catholic. Lodge: Elks (mem. local audit com. 1983—). Office: Texas Instruments Fed Credit Union 607 Pleasant St Attleboro MA 02703

SULLIVAN, JERRY STEPHEN, electronics company executive; b. Havre, Mont., July 17, 1945; s. Patrick Joseph and Evangeline (O'Neil) S.; m. Sharon Lee Horton, June 17, 1967; children: Garrett, Mindy, Darren. BS, U. Colo., 1967, MS, 1969, PhD, 1970; cert. in advanced mgmt., Harvard U. Bus. Sch., 1986. Tech. mgr. N.V. Philips Co., Eindhoven, The Netherlands, 1971-75; group dir. N.Am. Philips Corp., Briarcliff Manor, N.Y., 1975-80; dir. Tektronix, Beaverton, Oreg., 1981-83, div. gen. mgr., 1983-85, corp. dir., 1985-88; v.p. Microelectronics & Computer Tech. Corp., Austin, Tex., 1988—; bd. dirs. Sherpa Corp., San Jose, Calif.; mem. adv. bd. computer sci. Oreg. Grad. Ctr., Beaverton, 1981-83; mem. adv. bd. Ctr. Integrated Systems Stanford U., Palo Alto, Calif., 1982—. Mem. IEEE, Am. Phys. Soc., Assn. Computing Machinery, Am. Mgmt. Assn. Office: Microelectronics & Computer Tech Corp 3500 W Balcones Ctr Dr Austin TX 78759

SULLIVAN, JOHN ALAN, civil engineer, consultant; b. Calumet, Mich., Oct. 8, 1944; s. John Louis Paul and Hilma Aurora (Loukinen) S.; m. Helen Frances Carter, Apr. 10, 1965; children: John Arthur, Dolores Ruth, Roger Edward. AS in Civil Tech., Lansing Community Coll., 1965; BSCE, Wayne State U., 1970; postgrad., Mich. Tech. U., 1972. Registered profl. engr., Mich. Constrn. technician Mich. State Hwy. Dept., 1962-70; dir. pub. works City of Houghton, Mich., 1970-71; city mgr., engr. City of Hancock, Mich., 1971-74; exec. dir. Alexandria (Minn.) Lakes Area Sanitary Dist., 1974-78; engr., mgr. McCombs-Knutson Cons., Alexandria, 1978-79; dir. engring. U.P. Engring. & Archtl. Assocs., Houghton, 1979-83, v.p., 1983-87, pres., 1987—; ptnr. A/E Leasing Services, Norway, Mich., 1982—; bd. dirs. Baraga (Mich.) Motel Developers Inc. Mem. exec. com. Houghton county Reps., 1982—; bd. dirs. Stillwaters Community Elders Homes, Calumet, 1982-88. Mem. ASCE (br. sec. treas. 1984-88), Water Pollution Control Fedn., Alexandria Jaycees (bd. dirs. 1975-78, Disting. Service award 1977). Lutheran. Club: Kiwanis (pres. 1982-83) (Houghton). Home: 803 Lake Ave W Houghton MI 49931 Office: UP Engring & Archtl Assocs Inc 322 Shelden Ave Houghton MI 49931

SULLIVAN, JOHN HERBERT, insurance executive; b. Worcester, Mass., Aug. 8, 1937; s. Herbert Augustine and Mary Agnes (Hallisey) S. AB, U. Notre Dame, 1959; JD, Boston Coll., 1962. Bar: Mass. 1964; lic. ins. agent and broker, Mass., and 20 other states. V.p. Herbert A. Sullivan, Inc., Worcester, 1963-72; pres., chief exec. officer Herbert A. Sullivan, Inc., Waltham, Mass., 1972—, J. Herbert Sullivan Ins. Agy., Inc., Waltham, 1972—, Petroleum Ins. Agy., Inc., Waltham, 1972—, Cost Control Corp., Waltham, 1970—; underwriting mem. Lloyds of London, 1985—; mem. Intersure, Ltd., N.Y.C., 1970—. Western Mass. organizer Dem. Lt. Gov.'s campaign, Springfield, 1966; active Higgenson Soc. Boston Symphony Orch., Sorin Soc. U. Notre Dame, South Bend, Ind.; mem. bd. Catholic Charitable Bur. Archdiocese Boston; patron Boston Mus. Fine Arts. Mem. Nat. Assn. Casualty and Surety Agents, ABA, Mass. Bar Assn., Boston Bar Assn., Worcester County Bar Assn., Assn. Lloyd's Mems., Algonquin Club (Boston), Caledonian Club (London), Corinthian Yacht Club (Marblehead, Mass.), Club at World Trade Ctr. (N.Y.C.), Anabels Club (London), Plaza Club (Worcester). Republican. Roman Catholic. Home: Hi Forest Rim Noon Peak Rd Waterville Valley NH 03215 Office: Sullivan Risk Mgmt Group Watermill Ctr Fourth Fl 800 South St Waltham MA 02154

SULLIVAN, JOHN PHILLIP, bank executive; b. Portsmouth, Va., July 30, 1954; s. John L. Sullivan and Gloria Miller (Binzel) May; m. Lynn Kirkland, July, 1989. BS in Fin., Auburn U., 1976. Asst. v.p. Barnett Bank, Jacksonville, Fla., 1979-81, v.p., 1982-87, group v.p., 1987-89, area sr. v.p., 1989—; chmn. Barnett Minority Bus. Credit Com., Jacksonville, 1987—. Bd. dirs. YMCA Camp Imokolee, Jacksonville, 1986—, Vol. Jacksonville, 1985—; chmn. ARC Jacksonville Disaster Svcs., 1987—. Mem. Robert Morris Assn., Fla. Yacht Club, San Jose Country Club. Republican. Roman Catholic. Home: PO Box 472 Cocoa FL 32923 Office: Barnett Bank 100 Laura St Jacksonville FL 32202

SULLIVAN, JOHN VINCENT, life insurance company executive; b. Malden, Mass., Feb. 11, 1929; s. John Vincent and Jennie Helen (Marshall) S.; student Burdett Coll., 1947-49, Williams Coll., 1968; m. Mildred E. Goddard, Aug. 21, 1971; children—John, Patricia, Richard, Charles, Alyssa. Purchasing clk. City of Revere (Mass.), 1950; office mgr., bookkeeper Monroe Products, Chelsea, Mass., 1951; with John Hancock Mut. Life Ins. Co., Boston, 1951—, asso. controller, 1966-68, 2d v.p., 1969-74, v.p., 1975-81, sr. v.p., controller, 1982-87, ret., 1987 ; dir. John Hancock Variable Life Ins. Co.; adviser to Gov.'s Task force on Capital Formation for Econ. Devel., 1976-77. Chmn. fin. com. Town of Saugus (Mass.), 1963-65, treas. Saugus Housing Authority, 1962-64; pres. Saugus PTA, 1961-63. Mem. Life Ins. Assn. Mass. (treas. 1975—, mem. exec. com. 1975—, chmn. 1978-79), Mass. Taxpayers Found. (dir.), Blair Industry Tax Discussion Group, Am. Council Life Ins., Life Office Mgmt. Assn. (chmn. panel 1971), Am. Mgmt. Assn. (chmn. and panel mem. at seminar 1973). Home: 37 Lincoln Circle Andover MA 01810

SULLIVAN, JOSEPH ROBERT, financial service company executive, lawyer; b. Ridley Park, Pa., Jan. 11, 1931; s. Joseph Oswald and Catherine Patricia (McCallen) S.; m. Mary Patricia Gough, Aug. 14, 1954; children: Brian Patrick, Daniel Paul. Bar: Ind. 1963, Tex. 1977. Staff atty. Assocs. Corp. N. Am., South Bend, Ind., 1963, govt. relations counsel, 1964-66, asst. v.p. govt. affairs, 1966-72, v.p. govt. affairs, 1972-76; sr. v.p. govt. affairs Assocs. Corp. N. Am., Dallas, 1976—; pres. Tex. Cons. Fin. Assn., Austin, 1982-85; chmn. bd. Consumer Credit Ins. Assn., Chgo., 1986-87, pres., 1985-86. Served to 1st lt. USMC, 1950-57, Korea. Recipient Disting. Service award Am. Fin. Services Assn. Mem. ABA, Tex. Bar Assn., Ind. Bar Assn. Roman Catholic. Home: 1814 Burr Oak Arlington TX 76012 Office: Assocs Corp of N Am 250 E Carpenter Freeway Irving TX 75062

SULLIVAN, LAURA PATRICIA, insurance company executive, lawyer; b. Des Moines, Oct. 16, 1947; d. William and Patricia (Kautz) S. B.A., Cornell Coll., Iowa, 1971; J.D., Drake U., 1972. Bar: Iowa 1972. Various positions Ins. Dept. Iowa, Des Moines, 1972-75; various legal positions State Farm Mut. Auto Ins. Co., Bloomington, Ill., 1975-81, sec. and counsel, 1981-88; v.p., counsel and sec. State Farm Fire Mut. Auto Ins. Co., Bloomington, Ill., 1988—; v.p., sec., dir. State Farm Cos. Found., 1985—; v.p., counsel and sec. State Farm, Fire and Casualty Co., 1988—, State Farm Gen. Ins. Co., 1988—; sec. State Farm & Casualty Co., 1987-88, State Farm Gen. Ins. Co., 1987-88, State Farm Lloyd's Inc., 1987—. Trustee John M. Scott Indsl. Sch. Trust, Bloomington, 1983-86; bd. dirs. Scott Ctr., 1983-86, Bloomington-Normal Symphony, 1980-85; chmn. Ins. Inst. for Hwy. Safety, 1987-88. Mem. ABA, Iowa State Bar Assn., Am. Corp. Counsel Assn. Office: State Farm Mut Automobile Ins Co One State Farm Pla Bloomington IL 61710

SULLIVAN, MARCIA MARIE, chemical company executive; b. Milton, Mass., Apr. 22, 1957; d. Robert John and Barbara Lee (Hain) S. BA in Econs., Mt. Holyoke Coll., 1979. Mfg. supr. Rochester Products div. GM, Rochester, N.Y., 1979-81; order svc. supr. films div. Mobil Chem. Co., Rochester, 1981-83, customer svc. mgr., 1983-85, distbn. analyst, 1985-87; prodn. control mgr. Mobil Chem. Co., Stratford, Conn., 1987-89; distbn. mgr. Plasitc Packaging div. Mobil Chem. Co., Woodland, Calif., 1989—. Reading tutor Literacy Vols., Rochester, and New Haven, 1986-89. Democrat. Roman Catholic. Office: Mobil Chem Co PO Box 210 Woodland CA 95695

SULLIVAN, MICHAEL EVAN, investment and management company executive; b. Phila., Dec. 30, 1940; s. Albert and Ruth (Liebert) S.; BS, N.Mex. State U., 1966, MA (Ednl. Research Tng. Program fellow), 1967; BS, U. Tex., 1969; MBA, U. Houston, 1974; MS, U. So. Calif., 1976, MPA, 1977, PhD in Adminstrn., 1983; BS in Acctg., U. La Verne, 1981. Sr. adminstrv. and tech. analyst Houston Lighting & Power Co., 1969-74; electronics engr. U.S. Govt., Point Mugu, Calif., 1974-77; mem. tech. staff Hughes Aircraft Co., El Segundo, Calif., 1977-78; staff program adminstr. Ventura div. Northrop Corp., Newbury Park, Calif., 1978-79; div. head engring. div. Navastrogru, Point Mugu, 1979-82; br. head, div. head spl. programs Pacific Missile Test Ctr., (Calif.), 1983—; head operational systems integration office and assignments CNO-Dir. Research, Devel., and Acquisition in the Pentagon, Washington, 1987-88; pres., chmn. bd. Diversified Mgmt. Systems, Inc., Camarillo, Calif., 1978—. Author: The Management of Research, Development, Test and Evaluation Organizations; Organizational Behavior Characteristics of Supervisors-Public versus Private Sectors, Organizational Behavior Characteristics of Supervisors, Public versus Private Sectors; Self-Actualization in RDT & E Organizations; Self-Actualization in a Health Care Agency; others. V.p., bd. dirs. Ventura County Master Chorale and Opera Assn; bd. dirs. Southern Calif. Assn. of Pub. Adminstrn. (also mem. fin. com., programs com., student aid com.). Served with U.S. Army, 1958-62. Ednl. Research Info. Clearing House fellow, 1965-67. Mem. Am. Math. Soc., Math. Assn. Am., Am. Statis. Assn., IEEE, IEEE Engring. Mgmt. Soc., Am. Soc. Pub. Adminstrn., So. Calif. Assn. Pub. Adminstrn. (bd. dirs., various coms.), Am. Personnel and Guidance Assn., Fed. Mgrs. Assn., Am. Assn. Individual Investors, Mcpl. Mgmt. Assts. So. Calif., Acad. Polit. Sci., Assn. M.B.A. Execs., Phi Kappa Phi, Pi Gamma Mu. Home: PO Box 273 Port Hueneme CA 93041 Office: PO Box 447 Camarillo CA 93010

SULLIVAN, NEIL MAXWELL, oil and gas company executive; b. McKeesport, Pa., May 25, 1942; s. Thomas James and Jane Mason (Ginn) S.; m. Margaret Pedrick, Aug. 10, 1974; children: Margaret Blair, Mason Pedrick. BS, Dickinson Coll., 1970; postgrad., Tulane U., 1970-74. Exploration geologist Bass Enterprises, Midland, Tex., 1976-77; dist. geologist ATAPCO, Midland, 1977-78, Anadarko Prodn. Co., Midland, 1978-79, chief geologist, 1979-80, v.p. exploration, regional mgr., Houston, 1980-82; exploration ops. mgr. Valero Producing Co., San Antonio, 1982-85, v.p. exploration, New Orleans, 1985-87; pres. Bluebonnet Petroleum Co., New Orleans, 1987—; mem. Dept. Interior Outer Continental Shelf Com. adv. bd., 1985-87. Editor: Guadalupian Delaware Mountain Group of West Texas and Southeast New Mexico, 1979, Ancient Carbonate Reservoirs and Their Modern Analogs, 1977, Petroleum Exploration in Thrust Belts and Their Adjacent Forelands, 1976, Risk: Evaluation and Management, 1989. Bd. dirs. Permian Basin Grad. Ctr., Midland, 1979; com. chmn. Mus. of S.W., Midland, 1978. Served with USAF, 1964-68. Mem. Geol. Soc. Am., Am. Assn. Petroleum Geologists (cert. petroleum geologist), New Orleans Geol. Soc. (chmn. continuing edn. com. 1987—), South Tex. Geol. Soc. (nominating com. chmn. 1985), Soc. Econ. Paleontologists and Mineralogists (pres. Permian Basin sect. 1979), Am. Inst. Profl. Goelogists (cert. profl. geologist). Lodge: Elks. Home: 1738 Milan St New Orleans LA 70115

SULLIVAN, PATRICK SEAN, data processing executive; b. Fayetteville, N.C., Apr. 21, 1961; s. James and Diane (Dobson) S.; m. Denise Elliott, Mar. 7, 1987; 1 child, Sean. BA, San Jose State U., 1984. Editor Ceilidh, Inc., San Mateo, Calif., 1981—; book buyer Cen. Pk. Bookstore, San Mateo, 1981-86; supr. info. ctr. Franklin Resources, San Mateo, 1986—. Editor/pub. Literary Jour. Ceilidh, 1981—. Office: Franklin Resources 777 Mariners Island Blvd San Mateo CA 94404

SULLIVAN, ROGER CHARLES, JR., insurance executive; b. Denver, May 7, 1946; s. Roger C. and Eileen (Rohan) S.; divorced; 1 child, Roger C. III. BS in Bus., Colo. State U., 1969. From claim adjustor to supr. Liberty Mut. Ins., Chgo., 1969-73; corp. analyst., regional mgr. market facilities Res. Ins., Chgo., 1973-79; dir. claims adminstrn. Comml. Union Ins., Boston, 1979-84; v.p. claims Ga. Casualty Co., 1984-87, Atlanta Casualty Co., 1987—; Author of fraud profiles adopted by Ins. Crime Prevention Inst., 1981. V.p. Dunwoody Homeowner Assn., Atlanta, 1984. Mem. Southeastern Claim Execs. Assn., Atlanta Claims Assn., Atlanta Claims Mgrs. Assn. Republican. Presbyterian. Clubs: Mill Rock, River Bend (pres.), Cannongate (Atlanta). Office: Atlanta Casualty Co 3169 Holcomb Bridge Rd Norcross GA 30071

SULLIVAN, THOMAS CHRISTOPHER, coatings company executive; b. Cleve., July 8, 1937; s. Frank Charles and Margaret Mary (Wilhelmy) S.; m. Sandra Simmons, Mar. 12, 1960; children: Frank, Sean, Tommy, Danny, Kathleen, Julie. B.S., Miami U., Oxford, Ohio, 1959. Div. sales mgr. Republic Powdered Metals, Cleve., 1961-65; exec. v.p. Republic Powdered Metals, 1965-70; pres., chmn. bd. RPM, Inc., Medina, Ohio, 1971-78; chmn. bd. RPM, Inc., 1978—; dir. Pioneer Standard Electronics, Inc., Cleve., Nat. City Bank, Cleve. Bd. dirs. Culver Ednl. Found. Served to lt. (j.g.) USNR, 1959-60. Mem. Nat. Paint and Coatings Assn. (bd. dirs., exec. com.), Nat. Assn. Securities Dealers (bd. govs.). Roman Catholic. Office: 2628 Pearl Rd Medina OH 44256

SULLIVAN, THOMAS JOHN, communications company executive; b. Jersey City, N.J., Apr. 11, 1935; s. Patrick J. and Angel (Minihane) S.; m. Frances D. Gibbons, Oct. 28, 1961; children: Kelly Ann, Thomas J. B.S. in Acctg., St. Peter's Coll., 1957; J.D., Seton Hall U., 1969. With Merck & Co., Inc., Rahway, N.J., 1957-65; mgr. fin. systems McGraw-Hill Info. Systems Co., N.Y.C., 1965-67, budget dir., 1967-68; controller McGraw-Hill Info. Systems, 1968-71, sr. v.p. product devel., 1971-73; v.p. planning systems McGraw-Hill Inc., N.Y.C., 1973-76, v.p. fin. analysis, 1976-77, sr. v.p. corp. planning, 1977-83, sr. v.p. exec. asst. to pres., 1983-86, exec. v.p. adminstrn., 1986—; bd. dirs. McGraw-Hill Ryerson Ltd., Ont., Can. Mem. N.J. Bar Assn., ABA, Fin. Execs. Inst., Nat. Assn. Accts. Office: McGraw-Hill Inc 1221 Avenue of the Americas New York NY 10020

SULLIVAN, TIMOTHY BURNS, manufacturing executive; b. Providence, Apr. 7, 1940; s. Cornelius J. and Lorraine (Burns) S.; m. Louise Ryan, June 23, 1962; children: Cornelius, Mary Lou, Kathleen, Timothy Jr. BS in Bus., Holy Cross Coll., 1961; MBA, Northeastern U., 1970. Acct. bus. tng. program Gen. Electric Corp., Pittsfield, Mass., 1963-65; systems analyst Northrop Corp., Norwood, Mass., 1965-67, mgr. systems and programs, 1967-68; systems analyst L.G. Balfour Co., Attleboro, Mass., 1968-69, mgr. systems and program, 1969-70, dir. mgmt. info. systems, 1970-77, dir. adminstrv. services, 1977-78, v.p. adminstrv. services, 1978-80, v.p. corp. sec., 1980-83, v.p. new product devel., 1983-84, v.p., gen. mgr. ednl. products group, 1984—, also bd. dirs.; bd. dirs. Foxboro (Mass.) Fed. Savs. & Loan, Abington Mut. Ins. Co., Brockton, Ma.; vice chmn. Neponset Valley Health System, Norwood, 1988—, also bd. dirs.. Served as capt. U.S. Marines, 1961-63. Named Outstanding Young Leader Mass. Jaycees, 1975. Mem. Attleboro Area C. of C. (chmn. bd. 1982-83). Roman Catholic. Lodge: Lions (sec. Foxboro club 1983). Home: 15 Carmine Ave Foxboro MA 02035 Office: LG Balfour Co Inc 25 County St Attleboro MA 02703

SULLIVAN, TIMOTHY PATRICK, real estate developer; b. Phoenix, June 8, 1958; s. Jeremiah Joseph and Nancy Mignon (Otwell) S. BS in Animal Sci., Colo. State U., 1980; MBA, Ariz. State U., 1985. Lic. realtor, Ariz. Trust securities cashier The Ariz. Bank, Phoenix, 1980; owner Pronghorn Hereford Ranch, Ignacio, Colo., 1981—; assoc. J.J. Sullivan Realty, Scottsdale, Ariz., 1981-83; mng. ptnr. HKS Joint Venture Partnership, Scottsdale, 1983—; founder, corp. sec. Sullivan Devel. Corp., Scottsdale, 1983—. Alumni ambassador Colo. State U., Fort Collins; bd. dirs. Vol. Friends of Channel 8, Tempe, Ariz.; chmn. goodwill connections KAET-TV; chmn. mem. com. Cen. Ariz. ARC, 1986—; grad. Valley Leadership, Phoenix, 1988. Mem. Am. Hereford Assn., Colo. Hereford Assn., Alpha Zeta. Roman Catholic. Home: Pronghorn Hereford Ranch Ignacio CO 81137 Office: 4234 Winfield Scott Plaza Scottsdale AZ 85251

SULLIVAN, WILLIAM COURTNEY, communications executive; b. Webster Groves, Mo., Aug. 26, 1928; s. William J. and Corinne (Courtney) S.; m. Valerie Blaes, June 20, 1953; children: William C. Jr., Kathleen M., Margaret M. Stonecipher. Student, St. Louis U., 1946-49, J.D. cum laude, 1952. Atty. Southwestern Bell Telephone Co., St. Louis, 1956-58, atty. Mo.-Ill. area, 1958-64, gen. atty. Kans. area, 1964-70, gen. atty. Mo.-Ill., 1970-74, gen. solicitor Mo.-Ill., 1974-75, gen. solicitor gen. headquarters, 1975-84, v.p., assoc. gen. counsel, 1984—. Bd. dirs. Sea & Sky Found., Miami, 1985—, Town and Country Police Commn., Mo., 1986—. Capt. USAF, 1952-55. Mem. ABA, Mo. Bar. Assn., Kans. Bar Assn., St. Louis Bar Assn., Bellerive Country Club (St. Louis). Roman Catholic. Club: Bellerive Country (St. Louis). Office: Southwestern Bell Telephone Co 1010 Pine St Room 2305 Saint Louis MO 63101

SULLIVAN, WILLIAM ROBERT, investment banker; b. D.C., Apr. 28, 1947; s. William Gerald and Donna Marian (Martin) S.; m. Barbara Apple, Dec. 2, 1953. BS, U. Va., 1973, MBA, 1975. Assoc. Booz, Allen & Hamilton, N.Y.C., 1975-79; v.p. Am. Express Travel-Related Services Co., N.Y.C., 1979-84; sr. v.p. Shearson Lehman Hutton, N.Y.C., 1984-86; pres. Seaboard Investment Corp., Atlanta, 1986—.' Served to capt. U.S. Army, 1968-71, Vietnam. Mem. U. Va. Bus. Alumni (bd. dirs. 1975—). Office: Seaboard Investment Corp 3400 Peachtree Rd NE Suite 741 Atlanta GA 30326

SULZBERGER, ARTHUR OCHS, newspaper executive; b. N.Y.C., Feb. 5, 1926; s. Arthur Hays and Iphigene (Ochs) S.; m. Barbara Grant, July 2, 1948 (div. 1956); children—Arthur Ochs, Karen Alden; m. Carol Fox, Dec. 19, 1956; 1 dau., Cynthia Fox; adopted dau., Cathy. B.A., Columbia, 1951; LL.D., Dartmouth, 1964, Bard Coll., 1967; L.H.D., Montclair State Coll., 1972, Tufts U.; LLD (hon.), U. Scranton. With N.Y. Times Co., N.Y.C., 1951—; asst. treas. N.Y. Times Co., 1958-63, pres., pub., 1963—, also dir.; dir. Times Printing Co., Chattanooga. Trustee Columbia, Met. Mus. Art (chmn. bd. trustees, 1987—). Served to capt. USMCR, World War II, Korea. Mem. Bur. Newspaper Advt. (dir.), Newspaper Pubs. Assn., S.A.R. Clubs: Overseas Press (N.Y.C.), Explorers (N.Y.C.); Metropolitan (Washington); Century Country ((Purchase, N.Y.). Office: NY Times Co 229 W 43rd St New York NY 10036

SUMANTH, DAVID JONNAKOTY, engineering educator; b. Machilipatnam, India, Jan. 28, 1946; came to U.S., 1972; s. John Devraj and Nancy (David) Jonnakoty; m. Chaya J. Victor, June 26, 1974; children: John J., Paul J. B in Mech. Engring., Osmania U., Hyderabad, India, 1967, M in Mech. Engring., 1969; MS in Indsl. Engring., Ill. Inst. Tech., 1974, PhD in Indsl. Engring., 1979. Teaching/research asst. Ill. Inst. Tech., Chgo., 1973-78, instr., 1979; asst. prof. indsl. engring. U. Miami, Coral Gables, Fla., 1979-83, dir. productivity research group, 1979—, dir. grad. studies, 1980-83, assoc. prof., 1983-88, Coll. Engring. coordinator MBA/MSIE, 1984—; prof. U. Miami, Coral Gables, 1988—; productivity cons. in field. Author: Productivity Engineering and Management, 1984, also instr.'s manual; (script) Total Productivity Management, 1985; editor: Productivity Management Frontiers-I, 1985; contbr. articles to profl. jours. Recipient diploma of recognition U. Regiomontana, 1980, Monterrey Tech., 1981, cert. of recognition Assn. for Systems Mgmt., 1982, George Washington honor medal Freedoms Found., 1987; Eaton Honors Coll., U. Miami fellow, 1986. Sr. mem. Am. Inst. Indsl. Engrs. (pres. Miami chpt. 1982-83, bd. dirs. 1983-84, nat. asst. dir. productivity mgmt. 1984—, chairperson research com. 1987, Outstanding Indsl. Engr. of Yr. Miami chpt. 1983, 84), The Productivity Ctr. (trustee 1985—), Internat. Biog. Assn. (fellow 1989), Men of Achievement, Interna. Directory Disting. Leadership, Five Thousand Personalities of the World. Republican. Baptist. Office: U Miami Productivity Research Group Coral Gables FL 33124

SUMARNO, ISHAK, banker; b. Jakarta, Indonesia, May 13, 1943; s. Kang So Tan and It Nio Jo; m. Tjandra Grace Supratik, Apr. 24, 1975; children—Joyce, Allen. Dipl.-Ing., Stuttgart U., West Germany, 1970. Registered profl. engr., West Germany. Sub-mgr. Bank Buana Indonesia P.T., Jakarta, 1976-84, mgr., 1984—. Recipient Cert. Commendation award Bankers Trust Co., 1981, Meritorious Achievement award Bankers Trust Co., 1981, Cert. of Attendance award Bank of Am., 1982, Cert. of Completion award Bank of Am., 1985. Club: Hilton Exec. (Jakarta), Bankers (Indonesia). Avocations: reading; music. Office: Bank Buana Indonesia PT, Asemka 32-35, Jakarta 11110, Indonesia

SUMIDA, GERALD AQUINAS, lawyer; b. Hilo, Hawaii, June 19, 1944; s. Sadamu and Kimiyo (Miyahara) S.; m. Sylvia Whitehead, June 23, 1970. AB summa cum laude, Princeton U., 1966, cert. in pub. and internat. affairs, 1966; JD, Yale U., 1969. Bar: Hawaii 1970, U.S. Dist. Ct. Hawaii 1970, U.S. Ct. Appeals (9th cir.) 1970, U.S. Supreme Ct. 1981. Research assoc. Ctr. Internat. Studies, Princeton U., 1969; assoc. Carlsmith, Wichman, Case, Mukai & Ichiki, Honolulu, 1970-76, ptnr., 1976—; mem. cameras in courtroom evaluation com. Hawaii Supreme Ct., 1984—. Mem. sci. and statis. com. Western Pacific Fishery Mgmt. Council, 1979—; mem. study group on law of armed conflict and the law of the sea Comdr. in Chief Pacific, U.S. Navy, 1979-82; pres. Pacific and Asian Affairs Council Hawaii, 1982—, bd. govs., 1976—, Paul S. Bachman award, 1978; chmn. internat. com. Hawaii chpt. ARC, 1983—, bd. dirs., 1983; vice chmn. Honolulu Com. on Fgn. Relations, 1983—; pres., dir., founding mem. Hawaii Ocean Law Assn., 1978—; mem. Hawaii Adv. Group for Law of Sea Inst., 1977—; pres. Hawaii Inst. Continuing Legal Edn., 1979-83, dir., 1976—; pres., founding mem. Hawaii Council Legal Edn. for Youth, 1980-83, dir., 1983—; chmn. Hawaii Commn. on Yr. 2000, 1976-79; mem. Honolulu Community Media Council, exec. com., 1976-84, legal counsel, 1979-83; bd. dirs. Hawaii Imin Centennial Corp., 1983—, Hawaii Pub. Radio, 1983-88. Legal Aid Soc. Hawaii, 1984; mem. Pacific Alliance Trade and Devel., 1984—; founding gov. Ctr. Internat. Comml. Dispute Resolution, 1987—; exec. v.p., chmn.

rules and procedures, Pacific Rim Found., 1987—; exec. com. Pacific Islands Assn., 1988—. Recipient cert. of appreciation Gov. of Hawaii, 1979, resolutions of appreciation Hawaii Senate and Ho. of Reps., 1979; grantee Japan Found., 1979. Mem. ABA, Hawaii Bar Assn. (pres. young lawyers sect. 1974, v.p. 1984), Japan-Hawaii Lawyers Assn., Am. Soc. Internat. Law, Japan-Hawaii Lawyers Assn., Hawaii C. of C. (energy com. 1981-87, chmn. 1985-87), Am. Judicature Soc., AAAS, Asia Pacific Lawyers Assn., Phi Beta Kappa. Democrat. Clubs: Yale (N.Y.C.); Plaza (Honolulu); Colonial (Princeton). Author: (with others) Legal, Institutional and Financial Aspects of An Inter-Island Electrical Transmission Cable, 1984, Alternative Approaches to the Legal, Institutional and Financial Aspects of Developing an Inter-Island, Electrical Transmission Cable System, 1986; editor Hawaii Bar News, 1972-73; contbr. chpts. to books. Home: 1130 Wilder Ave #1401 Honolulu HI 96822 Office: Pacific Tower 1001 Bishop St Honolulu HI 96813 also: Carlsmith Wichman Case Mukai Ichiki 1001 Bishop St Pacific Tower Suite 2200 Honolulu HI 96813

SUMLIN, ROGER LEWIS, information systems executive; b. Freeport, Tex., Nov. 20, 1942; s. Lewis Henry and Nettie Moree (Brawner) S.; m. Margaret Nell Newby, Apr. 11, 1964 (div. 1977); children: David, Richard, Shea; m. Pamela Margaurite Longo, Nov. 25, 1977; 1 child, Sharon. BBA, North Tex. State U., 1965. Programmer Sears Roebuck & Co., Dallas, 1965-71; asst. mgr. data ctr. Sears Roebuck & Co., Kansas City, Mo., 1971-73; staff asst. Sears Roebuck & Co., Chgo., 1973-74, mgr. computer ops., 1974-78; dir. data ctr. Philip Morris U.S.A., Richmond, Va., 1978-80; mgr. data ctr. Schreiber Foods, Green Bay, Wis., 1980-82, Energy Res. Group, Wichita, Kans., 1982-86; mgr. info. services BHP Petroleum, Houston, 1986—; teaching fellow North Tex. State U., 1968-69. Author: (pamphlet) So This Is A Credit Union, 1968. Mem. Soc. Info. Mgmt., Pi Kappa Alpha (v.p. 1964). Office: BHP Petroleum 5847 San Felipe Suite 3600 Houston TX 77057

SUMMER, CHARLES EDGAR, business educator; b. Newton, Miss., June 13, 1923; s. Charles Edgar and Emily (O'Rourke) S.; m. Carol Carlisle, Feb. 21, 1968. B.A., Coll. William and Mary, 1948; M.B.A., U. Pa., 1949; Ph.D., Columbia, 1957. Dir. research Booz, Allen & Hamilton, N.Y.C., 1950-54; economist Texaco, Inc., N.Y.C., 1949-50; prof. bus. adminstrn. Columbia U., 1957-67, Institut pour L'Etude des Methodes de Direction de L'Enterprise, 1967-69, U. Wash., Seattle, 1969—; distinguished vis. prof. U. So. Calif., 1962; cons. corps., hosps. and trade assns. on orgn. and exec. devel.; cons. Seattle, 1969—. Author: The Managerial Mind, 1977, The Process of Management, 1972, Organizational Behavior, 1985, Strategic Behavior, 1980. Served as pilot USAAF, World War II. Fellow Acad. Mgmt. (pres. 1973, editorial bd. jour. 1960—); mem. Council Internat. Progress Mgmt. (bd. dirs. 1964—), Inst. Mgmt. Scis. Home: 2342 43d Ave E Seattle WA 98112 Office: U Wash Grad Sch Bus Adminstrn Seattle WA 98195

SUMMER, JAMES ROBERT, SR., real estate broker; b. Newberry, S.C., Jan. 27, 1913; s. Elbert Hugh and Vera Lucile Summer; m. Della LaVerne Walden (dec. Mar. 1972); children: J. Robert Jr., Carolyn LaVerne Brossy, John Michael; m. Ann Stewart, July, 1983. Student, Ga. Inst. Tech., 1942. Messenger Western Union Telegraph Co., Atlanta, 1930-33, service clk., 1933-36; with acctg. dept. Sinclair Refinery Co., Atlanta, 1936-49; sales rep. Sinclair Refinery Co., Albany, Ga., 1949-56; br. mgr. Sinclair Refinery Co., Savannah, Ga., 1957-59; asst. dist. mgr. Sinclair Refinery Co., Macon, Ga., 1959-60; asst. mgr. home office price control Sinclair Refinery Co., Atlanta, 1960-63, mgr. price control, 1963-73; v.p. Summer, Minter & Assocs., Atlanta, 1973-79; pres. Summer & Assocs., Atlanta, 1979-81; v.p. U.S. Mortgage and Investment Corp., Atlanta, 1981-84; pvt. practice real estate broker Atlanta, 1986—; mem. Oil Info. Com., Savannah, 1957-60. Trustee Rep. Presdl. Task Force, Atlanta, 1986-87. Served with USN, 1943-45. Mem. Am. Legion. Lutheran. Club: Sinclair. Lodge: Elks. Home: 2443 Cravey Dr NE Atlanta GA 30345 Office: 3179 Maple Dr NE Atlanta GA 30305

SUMMERFORD, SHERRY R., brokerage company executive; b. Hartselle, Ala., Jan. 21, 1948; d. James Benton and Lucy Ruby (Speakman) Roberts; m. Robert Copeland Summerford, Mar. 6, 1965 (dec. 1975); children: Cherie, Gina, Robin. Student, Calhoun Community Coll., Decatur, Ala., 1976-77. Collector Credit Bur. of Decatur (Ala.), 1976-78; collector, bookkeeper Wilson Equipment Co., Decatur, 1978; timekeeper Albert G. Smith Constrn. Co., Athens, Ala., 1978-79; bookkeeper, asst. mgr. Hogan's Ready Mix, Hartselle, Ala., 1979-82; rep. Dewline Trucking, Inc., Federalsburg, Md., 1982—; pres. Summerford & Summerford Enterprises Inc., Mgmt. Agy.-Environ., Decatur, 1987, SCL Warehouse Inc., Madison, Ala. mgr. Sheriff Buford Burgess polit. campaign, Decatur, 1980. Mem. Credit Women of Ala. (pres. 1977-78), Nat. Assn. Female Execs., Decatur C. of C., Nat. Fedn. Ind. Bus., Am. Legion Ladies Aux., North Ala. Traffic Club (v.p. 1988—), Tenn. Valley Traffic Club. Republican. Methodist. Office: SCL Warehouse Inc 9324 Hwy 20 W #19220 PO Box 655 Madison AL 35758

SUMMERS, ALFRED LAWRENCE, telecommunications executive; b. Sedalia, Mo., Jan. 10, 1950; s. Alfred Lawrence Sr. and Evelyn Martha (Fisher) S.; m. Linda Gayle Waite, July 21, 1979; children: David Lawrence, Karen Lynn. BS in Engring. Mgmt., U. Mo., Rolla, 1972; MBA, U. Minn., 1982; MPA, Park Coll., 1986. Mktg. rep. IBM Gen. Systems Div., Kansas City, Mo., 1976-79; ops. mgr. AT&T Communications, Mpls., 1979-81, nat. account mgr., 1981-84; mgr. regulatory relations AT&T Communications, Bismarck, N.D., 1984; mgr. mktg. United TeleSpectrum, Kansas City, 1984-85, mgr. external affairs, 1985-86; pres. Mid-Am. Cellular Telephone Co., Springfield, Mo., 1986—, also chmn. bd. dirs.; pres. Summers & Assocs. Cons., Overland Park, Kans., 1986. Served to 1st lt. U.S. Army, 1972-76, with Res. Mem. Am. Mgmt. Assn., Am. Mktg. Assn. (Exec.), Soc. Engring. Mgmt. (charter), Cellular Telephone Industry Assn., Telocator. Republican. Lodges: Kiwanis (Airport com. chmn. 1981, bd. dirs. 1982-83), Optimists, Rotary. Home: 3026 Impala Ct Springfield MO 65804 Office: Mid-Am Cellular Telephone Co 435 E Walnut Springfield MO 65806

SUMMERS, JAMES RICHARD, financial management consultant; b. Pomona, Calif., Aug. 15, 1962; s. Frank Gilbert Jr. and Shirley Lucille (Turner) S. BS in Acctg., Calif. Poly. State U., 1984. CPA, Calif.; cert. fin. planner. Acct. Deloitte Haskins & Sells, Los Angeles, 1983; small bus. cons., auditor Deloitte Haskins & Sells, Costa Mesa, Calif., 1984-85; mng. sr. Summers Accountancy Corp., Pomona, Calif., 1985-86; exec. v.p. Summers Accountancy Corp., Pomona and Rancho Cucamonga, Calif., 1987—; securities rep. John M. McGivney Securities, Inc., Rancho Cucamonga, Calif. 1986—. Mem. Am. Inst. CPA's, Calif. Soc. CPA's (chairperson personal fin. planning com. Citrus Belt chpt.), Nat. Eagle Scout Assn., Inst. Cert. Fin. Planners, L.A. Soc. Fin. Analysts Fedn., Rancho Cucamonga C. of C., Rancho Cucamonga Jaycees (charter treas., pres.), Pomona Jaycees (bd. dirs., Jaycee of month, Chmn. of Yr.), Delta Sigma Pi (v.p. 1983-84). Republican. Club: Rancho Cucamonga Bus. Network (pres. 1986-87). Lodge: Rotary. Home: 1646 N Palm Ave Upland CA 91786 Office: Summers Accountancy Corp 295 Pomona Mall West Pomona CA 91766

SUMMERS, JOHNNY STEVEN, county official, accountant; b. Orangeburg, S.C., Nov. 11, 1953; s. Johnny L. and Mary (Collier) S.; m. Barbara Berry, Aug. 6, 1976; children: Matthew, Somer Lynne. BS in Acctg., U. S.C., 1976. Acct. Palmetto Baking Co., Orangeburg, 1976-77; controller OCAB, Orangeburg, 1977-78; treas. County of Orangeburg, 1979—. Sec., treas. Branchville (S.C.) Jaycees, 1977-78; v.p. Orangeburg County Dem. Party, 1978-80; chmn. Raylrode Daze Festival, Branchville, 1981-82. Named one of Outstanding Young Men, S.C. Jaycees, 1983. Mem. S.C. Assn. Auditors and Treas. (v.p. 1985-86. pres. 1988—), S.C. Assn. CPA's. Democrat. Methodist. Home: Rt 1 Box 181-F Branchville SC 29432 Office: Orangeburg County Treas PO Box 1000 Orangeburg SC 29116

SUMMERS, SCOTT BROOKS, banker; b. Louisville, Sept. 12, 1948; s. Wilson and Marilyn (Merten) S. BA, Ohio U., 1972; cert. corp. banking mgmt., Northwestern U., 1986. Mgr. br. Valley Nat. Bank, Phoenix, 1973-78, credit analyst, supr., 1978-79, supr. credit tng., 1979-80, comml. credit officer, 1980-82, v.p., sr. comml. credit officer, 1982-85, v.p., mgr. comml. credit, 1985—, instr. credit, 1982—; cons. in field. Regional rep. No. Ariz. chpt. Am. Cancer Soc., 1978-79; bd. dirs. Ariz. Acad. Decathlon, Phoenix, 1987—. Mem. Robert Morris Assocs., YMCA, Civitan (officer Phoenix chpt. 1982—). Office: Valley Nat Bank PO Box 29528 Phoenix AZ 85038

SUMMERTON, JONATHAN EDWARD, retail executive; b. East Hartford, Conn., Feb. 19, 1946; s. Edward Joseph and Marguerite (Farmer) S.; m. Dorothy Joan Coverdale, Aug. 24, 1968; children: Shelly, Scott, Jason. BA in Econs., Swarthmore Coll., 1968; MBA, Stanford U., 1970. Exec. v.p. Am. Western Corp., Sioux Falls, S.D., 1973-87; pres., chief oper. officer Dakotah, Inc., Webster, S.D., 1987—, also bd. dirs. Lt. USN, 1970-73. Republican. Roman Catholic. Office: Dakotah Inc North Park Ln Webster SD 57274

SUMMERVILLE, JOYCE WILKINSON, cemetery executive; b. Charlotte, N.C., Nov. 20, 1933; d. Pierce Columbus and Mary Bell (Helms) Wilkinson; m. William Kelly Summerville, June 21, 1952; children: Michael Kelly, Craig Lewis, Emily Beth. Student, Brevard (N.C.) Coll., 1952-53. Lic. cemetarian, N.C. Asst. to dir. coll. extension N.C. State U., Raleigh, 1957-59; asst. to sales mgr. The Pure Oil Co., Charlotte, 1959-64; office mgr. The Forest Lawn Co., Charlotte, 1965-72; v.p., gen. mgr. The Forest Lawn Co., Matthews, N.C., 1972—. Editor, pub. (newsletter) Your North Carolina Cemeterian, 1981-85. Bd. dirs. Valleydale Sch., Charlotte, 1970-71; mem. N.C. Citizens Assembly, Charlotte, 1988; co-chmn. Dems. for Gov. Martin Com. Mem. N.C. Cemetery Assn. (bd. dirs. 1972-88, pres. 1986-87), So. Cemetery Assn., Matthews C. of C. (bd. dirs. 1984—, pres. 1986-87, Outstanding Membership Recruiter award 1984, Pres. Appreciation award 1985), Matthews Mcths. Assn. (bd. dirs. 1986-87). Democrat. Methodist. Home: 3709 Huntington Dr Matthews NC 28105

SUMRELL, GENE, research chemist; b. Apache, Ariz., Oct. 7, 1919; s. Joe B. and Dixie (Hughes) S.; B.A., Eastern N.Mex. U., 1942; B.S., U. N.Mex., 1947, M.S., 1948; Ph.D., U. Calif. at Berkeley, 1951. Asst. prof. chemistry Eastern N.Mex. U., 1951-53; sr. research chemist J. T. Baker Chem. Co., Phillipsburg, N.J., 1953-58; sr. organic chemist Southwest Research Inst., San Antonio, 1958-59; project leader Food Machinery & Chem. Corp., Balt., 1959-61; research sect. leader El Paso Natural Gas Products Co. (Tex.), 1961-64; project leader So. utilization research and devel. div. U.S. Dept. Agr., New Orleans, 1964-67, investigations head, 1967-73, research leader Oil Seed and Food Lab., So. Regional Research Center, 1973-84, collaborator, 1984—. Served from pvt. to staff sgt. AUS, 1942-46. Mem. Am. Chem. Soc., A.A.A.S., N.Y. Acad. Scis., Am. Inst. Chemists, Am. Oil Chemists Soc., Am. Assn. Textile Chemists and Colorists, Research Soc. Am., Phi Kappa Phi, Sigma Xi. Home: PO Box 24037 New Orleans LA 70184 Office: 1100 Robert E Lee Blvd New Orleans LA 70179

SUN, ROBERT ZU JEI, inventor, manufacturing company executive; b. Shanghai, July 5, 1948; s. David C.H. and Evelyn (Lee) S.; m. Nan Jennifer Ronis, Sept. 20, 1986; 1 child, Matthew Nyland. B.S., in Elec. Engring., U. Pa., 1970. Sr. project engr. Drexelbrook Engring. Co., Horsham, Pa., 1970-78; pres., chmn. bd. Suntex Internat., Inc., Easton, 1981—. Pres. Greater Easton Tech. Enterprise Ctr., Inc., 1986-87, Coalition of Religious and Civic Orgs., Easton, 1979-81. Inventor Mhing card game; patentee (4), the Twenty Four Game. Recipient 2 Excellence awards for Mhing pkg. Nat. Paperbox and Pkg. Assn., 1984-85. Office: 118 N 3d St Easton PA 18042

SUNDARAN, SOMA THAYYADATH, applications engineer; b. Calicut, Kerala, India, Mar. 2, 1940; came to U.S., 1971; s. Perachunni and Ammalu T.; m. Trinidad Raagas, Apr. 15, 1978. BS in Engring., Trivandrum Engring. Coll., India, 1962. Sales engr. Ketcham Pump Co., N.Y.C., 1971-77; applications engr. ITT-Flygt Corp., Norwalk, Conn., 1977-79; applications engr. ITT-Flygt Corp., Dallas, 1979-82, area mgr., 1982-86, asst. regional mgr., 1986—. Home: 2142 San Simeon Blvd Carrollton TX 75006 Office: ITT-Flygt Corp 2400 Tarpley Rd Carrollton TX 75006

SUNDBERG, EDWARD AUGUST, management consultant; b. Chgo., May 14, 1947; s. Edward B. and Ruth (Wildebush) S.; m. Leslie Dahn, June 17, 1972; children: Edward, Liisa, Lindsey, Lori. BS, U.S. Naval Acad., 1968; MBA, Boston U., 1974. Commd. ensign USN, 1968, served to lt., resigned, 1973; capt. USNR, Boston, 1973—; dir. sales Norlin Mus. Instruments, Lincolnwood, Ill., 1975-79; v.p. Burns Internat. Security Svc., Chgo., 1979-80; pres. Odgen Security, Inc., Boston, 1981-85, Blydenstein Willink, U.S.A., Inc., Boston, 1985-88; v.p. Blydenstein Willink, N.V., Enschede, The Netherlands, 1985-88; bd. dirs. ConsultAmerica, Inc., Boston; vis. prof. Boston U. Sch. Mgmt., 1984-85. Cubmaster Boy Scouts Am., Concord, Mass., 1984. Mem. Young Pres's. Orgn., Naval Res. Assn. (life), Res. Officers Assn., U.S. Naval Alumni Assn. (life), Boston U. Alumni Assn. (bd. dirs. MBA Alumni Bd. 1984-85). Office: PO Box 1253 Concord MA 01942

SUNDEL, HARVEY H., marketing research analyst and consultant; b. Bronx, NY, July 24, 1944; s. Louis and Pauline (Brotman) S. BBA, St. Mary's U., San Antonio, 1969, MBA, 1970; PhD, St. Louis U., 1974. Asst. dir. research Lone Star Brewery, San Antonio, 1970-71; cons. Tri-Mark, Inc., San Antonio, 1972-73; asst. prof. mktg. Lewis and Clark Coll., Godfrey, Ill., 1973-74; asst. prof. mktg. Met. State Coll., Denver, 1974-77, chmn., prof. mktg., 1977-86; pres. Sundel Research, Inc., Denver, 1976—; cons. Frederick Ross Co., Denver, 1979-84, U.S. West Direct, Denver, 1986—, Monsanto Chems. Co., St. Louis, 1985—, Mountain Bell, Denver, 1979-88, U.S. West Communications, Denver, 1988—, AT&T, 1986—, Holmdel, 1986—, Melco Industries, 1987—. Contbr. papers and proceedings to profl. jours. Com. mem. Mile High United Way, Denver, 1975-80. Jewish. Home: 1616 Glen Bar Dr Lakewood CO 80215 Office: Sundel Rsch Inc 1150 Delaware Denver CO 80204

SUNDERLAND, MARY COMPTON, portfolio manager, securities analyst; b. Chgo., Dec. 20, 1955; d. Thomas Elbert and Mary Louise (Allyn) S. BA, Northwestern U., 1978; MBA, Columbia U., 1980. Loan officer Bank of Paris, N.Y.C., 1980-81; fixed income analyst Prudential Ins. Co., Newark, N.Y., 1981-83; securities analyst Value Line, Inc., N.Y.C., 1985—; asst. portfolio mgr. Value Line Asset Mgmt., N.Y.C., 1987—. Mem. Columbia Alumni Club, Columbia Bus. Sch. Alumni Club. Republican. Episcopalian. Home: 49 Woodside Ave White Plains NY 10604 Office: Value Line Asset Mgmt 711 3d Ave New York NY 10016

SUNDERLAND, ROBERT, cement company executive; b. Omaha, Dec. 21, 1921; s. Paul and Avis Marie (Peters) S.; m. Terri Reed, Nov. 21, 1959; children—Sharon Marie, Lori Diane. B.S. in Bus. Adminstrn, Washington U., St. Louis, 1947; LL.D. (hon.), Bethany Coll., Lindsborg, Kans., 1980. With Ash Grove Cement Co., Overland Park, Kans., 1947—; sec., asst. treas. Ash Grove Cement Co., 1953-57, treas., 1957-61, v.p., treas., 1961-67, chmn. bd., 1967—; dir. Boatmen's First Nat. Bank, Boatmen's Bancshares, Inc., T.K. Communications, Inc. Trustee Lester T. Sunderland Found., Kansas City. Served with USAAF, 1942-46, Philippines. Mem. Greater Kansas City C. of C., University Club, Kansas City Club, Shadow Glen Golf Club, Sigma Chi. Republican. Presbyterian. Office: Ash Grove Cement Co 8900 Indian Creek Pkwy Ste 600 Overland Park KS 66210

SUNDERMAN, DUANE NEUMAN, chemist, research institute executive; b. Wadsworth, Ohio, July 14, 1928; s. Richard Benjamin and Carolyn (Neuman) S.; m. Joan Catherine Hoffman, Jan. 31, 1953; children: David, Christine, Richard. BA, U. Mich., 1949, MS, 1954, PhD in Chemistry, 1956. Researcher Battelle Meml. Inst., Columbus, Ohio, 1956-59; mgr. Battelle Meml. Inst., Columbus, 1959-69, assoc. dir., 1969-79, dir. internat. programs, 1979-84; sr. v.p. Midwest Rsch. Inst., Kansas City, Mo., 1984—; bd. dirs. Enzytec Corp., Kansas City. Contbr. numerous articles to profl. jours. Bd. dirs. Mid-Ohio chpt. ARC, 1982-83, U. Kansas City, 1985—, Mo. Corp. for Sci. and Tech., Jefferson City, 1986—. Mem. AAAS, Am. Chem. Soc., Am. Mgmt. Assn. Republican. Presbyterian. Office: Midwest Rsch Inst 425 Volker Blvd Kansas City MO 64110

SUNDT, PETER CHRISTIAN, instrument manufacturing company executive; b. London, July 28, 1925; came to U.S., 1926; s. Olaf Francis and Elizabeth (Lund) S.; m. Helen Elizabeth Guernseyl, 1951; children: Peter Christian Jr., Laurilla, Leslie. BSEE, Rice U., 1950. Engr. Hughes Aircraft Co., Culver City, Calif., 1950-53; v.p. Mandrel Industries, Houston, 1953-65; pres. Metrix Instrument Co., Houston, 1965—; bd. dirs. Tideland Signal Corp., Houston. Patentee in field. With USNR, 1943-46, PTO. Mem. Tejas Club (Houston). Republican. Episcopalian. Office: Metrix Instrument Co 1711 Townhurst Houston TX 77043

SUNDT, ROBERT STOUT, construction company executive; b. Phila., Nov. 23, 1926; s. Thoralf M. and Elinor S. Sundt; m. Frances Schmidt; children: Eric, Thea Cummins. Student, Swarthmore Coll., 1944, 46-47; BS, U. Ariz., 1950. With M.M. Sundt Constrn. Co., Tucson, 1948-83, div. mgr. bldg., 1965-75, exec. v.p. constrn. ops., 1975-79, pres., chief exec. officer, 1980-83; pres. Sundt Corp., Tucson, 1983—; bd. dirs. S.W. Gas Corp., Las Vegas. Mem. adv. bd. Constrn. Industry Pres. Forum, adv. com. Ariz. Coun. Econ. Edn. Tucson. Served with USN, 1944-46. Mem. Tucson Met. C. of C. (bd. dirs.), Am. Inst. Constructors, Cons. Constructors Coun. Am., Assoc. Gen. Contractors Am. (bd. dirs., past pres., bd. dirs. Ariz. Bldg. chpt.). Office: Sundt Corp 4101 E Irvington Rd Tucson AZ 85714

SUNG, C. B., multi-industry executive; b. Shanghai, China, Feb. 1, 1925; came to U.S., 1947; naturalized, 1954; s. Tsing-Ching and Hsu-Ying (Ma) S.; BS, Chiao-Tung U., China, 1945; MS, M.I.T., 1948; MBA, Harvard U., 1950; m. Beulah C.H. Kwok, June 4, 1953; children—Dean, Wingate. From engr. to dept. chief Nanking-Shanghai Ry. Systems Adminstrn., China, 1945-47; devel. engr. instrumentation Ruge-de Forest, Inc., 1950-52; engr. research labs. Bendix Corp., 1952-62, asst. gen. mgr., 1962-64, gen. mgr., dir., 1964-67, corporate v.p. engring. and research, Detroit, 1967-69, v.p., group exec. advanced tech. group, Southfield, Mich., 1969-72, v.p., group exec. advanced concepts group, 1972-74; pres., chief exec. officer CMA Inc., Cleve., 1974-78; chmn. bd. Airborne Mfg. Co., Elyria, Ohio, 1975-79; chief exec. officer Etec Corp., Hayward, Calif., 1977-79; pres., chief exec. officer Unison Pacific Corp., San Bruno, Calif.; chmn. bd. Cleve. Controls, Inc., 1978—, Unison Internat., 1982—, Optimum Control Corp., 1984—, Beckett Corp., 1987—, UniHorn Inc., 1988—; dir. Varo, Inc., Capital Investment of Hawaii, Communication Intelligence Corp.; cons. in field. Mem. vis. com. Engring. Coll. U. Mich., Carnegie-Mellon U., Oakland U., Am. Found. Traditional Chinese Medicine. Fellow Cleve. Mus. Art, Pacific Forum (bd. dirs.); mem. Soc. Automotive Engrs., Sigma Xi. Patentee in field. Office: 1200 Bayhill Dr Suite 300 San Bruno CA 94066

SUP, STUART ALLEN See ALLEN, STUART

SUPALLA, SHERYL K., restaurant owner, educator; b. Fairfield, Iowa, July 15, 1944; d. Glen Edward and Erma Eileen (Smutz) Dimmitt; m. Gary J. Supalla, July 31, 1967; children—Laura, Julia. B.S. in Elem. Edn. cum laude, Mo. Western State Coll., 1973. Life teaching cert., Mo. Elem. tchr. St. Joseph Sch. Dist., Mo., 1973-78, tchr. Buchanan County Children's Home, 1985—; elem. tchr. Park Hill Sch. Dist., Mo., 1978-80; owner Miller's Grill, St. Joseph, 1980—; owner Atchison Inn Family Restaurant, Kans., 1984-86. Fellow Mo. Restaurant Assn., Nat. Assn. Female Execs. Republican. Avocations: reading; travel; gardening. Office: Miller's Grill 3110 S 169 Hwy Saint Joseph MO 64503

SUPIN, CHARLES ROBERT, publishing company owner, consultant; b. Bklyn., Jan. 31, 1933; s. Louis Franklin and Eleanor (Evers) S.; m. Benita P. Percik, Dec. 27, 1959; children: Jeanne Leanora, Robert Wisdom. BA, Adelphi U., 1955; M in Divinty, Yale Div. Sch., 1960. Devel. officer Episcopal Ch. U.S.A., N.Y.C., 1966-74; pres., co-owner Sta. KUDO-FM, Las Vegas, 1975-80; broadcaster Sta. KLAS-TV, Sta. KDWN-AM, Sta. KNPR-FM, Las Vegas, 1978—; editor Vegas Mag., LA (Calif.) Herald Examiner, 1983-84, gen. mgr., 1984-86; pres., co-owner Nifty Nickel Pub. and Printing Co., Las Vegas, 1987—; communications cons. L.I. (N.Y.) Council of Chs., 1966-72. Author: Beyond Pledging, 1974; columnist LA Herald Examiner, 1983—; writer, producer 5 TV documentaries. Chmn. Program and Budget Commn., Diocese L.I., 1968-72; chmn. broadcast bd. Protestant council, City of N.Y., 1963-68; head writer Jerry Lewis Muscular Dystrophy Telethon, Las Vegas, 1986—; bd. dirs. Nev. Dance Theater, Las Vegas, 1984—, New West Stage Co., Las Vegas, 1986—. With USMC, 1955-57. Mem. Screen Actors Guild, Rockaway Hunt Club, Lawrence Beach Club. Republican. Episcopalian. Office: Silver State Merchandisers Inc 1934 E Sahara Ave Las Vegas NV 89104

SURDOVAL, DONALD JAMES, accounting and management consulting company executive; b. N.Y.C., Aug. 26, 1932; s. Donald J. and Catherine A. (Slevin) S.; m. Patricia Fitzpatrick, May 28, 1955; children: Donald, Lisa, John, Catherine, Brian. B.B.A., Manhattan Coll., 1954. C.P.A., N.Y., N.J. Mgr. Touche Ross & Co., 1956-63; treas. Mohican Corp., 1963-65; asst. controller, then v.p., controller Litton Industries, 1965-68; v.p., controller Norton Simon Inc., N.Y.C., 1968-81; owner Donald J. Surdoval, C.P.A. and Mgmt. Cons. Co., Waldwick, N.J., 1982—; dir. Fuller O'Brien Paint Co. Bd. dirs. Calvary Hosp., N.Y.C., Our Lady of Mercy Hosp. Served to 1st lt. USMCR, 1954-56. Mem. Fin. Execs. Inst. Club: Hackensack Golf. Home: 12 Warewoods Rd Saddle River NJ 07458 Office: 20 Franklin Turnpike Waldwick NJ 07463

SURDOVAL, LAWRENCE ANTHONY, JR., foundation administrator; b. Pitts., Sept. 10, 1930; s. Lawrence Anthony and Pearl (Elks) S.; m. Eileen Martha Bradford, July 10, 1950 (div. Sept. 1979); children: Nancy Jo, Robert James, Wayne Alan. BS in Acctg., Robert Morris Coll., 1954; BS in Econs., Duquesne U., 1962, MPF, 1972; MS, U. Pitts., 1974, postgrad., 1962. Acct. T. Mellon & Sons, Pitts., 1949-58; sec. Richard King Mellon Found., Pitts., 1959-71; treas. Alleghany Found., Pitts., 1972-78; adminstrv. officer, treas. Sarah Mellon Scaife Found., Pitts., 1971-76; pres. Philanthropic Cons., Inc., Farmington and Pitts., 1977—; pres. Nemacolin Inc., Farmington, 1979-81; lectr. in field. Bd. dirs., trustee Family and Children's Service, Pitts., 1965—; bd. visitors U. Pitts. Sch. Social Work, 1965—; bd. dirs. Pioneer Crafts Council, Uniontown, Pa., 1965—. Served with USMC, 1952-54. Republican. Clubs: Duquesne, Press (Pitts.). Home: RD #2 Box 463 Farmington PA 15437

SURRIDGE, ROBERT CALDWELL, III, lawyer; b. Los Angeles, June 3, 1951; s. Robert Caldwell and Margaret Cecilia (Fitzsimmons) S. B.A., San Diego State U., 1973; J.D., Western State U. Coll. Law, 1977. Bar: Calif. 1977, U.S. Dist. Ct. (so. dist.) Calif. 1977. Legal asst. to pres. HBJ Real Properties Corp., 1977; asst. counsel Sea World, Inc., Sea World, 1978-82; v.p., counsel, asst. sec. Arthur J. Wand Corp., Inc., Glendale, Calif., 1979—, also dir.; gen. counsel, sec. La Petite Acad., Inc., Kansas City, Mo., 1986—, gen. counsel, sec. Cencor, Inc., 1988—, Concorde Career Colls., Inc., 1988—, Concorde Career Inst., Inc., 1988—, Cen. Fin., Inc., 1988—, Kansas City, Mo.; trust officer employee benefits div. Calif. First Bank, Los Angeles 1982-85; trust officer employee benefits div. Home Fed. Savs. and Loan Assn., San Diego, 1985-86. Mem. maritime adv. com. Los Angeles City Council. Recipient Bancroft Whitney Am. Jurisprudence awards, 1974, 77. Mem. ABA, Los Angeles County Bar Assn., Los Angeles Barristers Club. Republican. Roman Catholic. Office: Cencor Inc 1100 Main St Ste 1050 Kansas City MO 64105

SUSLAK, HOWARD ROBINSON, investment banking executive; b. N.Y.C., Apr. 24, 1920; s. Sigmund and Estelle (Robinson) S.; m. Adele Barnett, June 19, 1949; children—Brian Edward, Neil Scott, Valerie Estelle, Pamela Simone. Grad., Juilliard Sch. Music, 1942; B.A. magna cum laude, NYU, 1942; M.B.A., Wharton Sch., U. Pa., 1943. Asst. to pres. E.R. Squibb & Sons, N.Y.C., 1945-46; v.p. Metacan Mfg. Co., Bklyn., 1946-47; with MacDonald & Co., N.Y.C., 1947—; mgr. MacDonald & Co., 1948; in charge offices MacDonald & Co., Chgo., Pitts., Boston, Detroit, 1949-54; gen. ptnr. MacDonald & Co., 1954—, v.p., 1956-58, exec. v.p., 1958-62, pres., 1962—; chmn., mng. dir. Indsl. Mgmt. Cons., Ltd., London, 1949—; dir. George Hopkinson, Ltd., Kaz Mfg. Co. Inc., Phi Beta Kappa Assocs. Mem. N.Y.C. Planning Commn., 1965-66; bd. dirs. Weizmann Inst. Sci., Opera Orch. N.Y., Sch. Weber Electronics. Served with U.S. Army, 1943-44. Mem. Am. Mgmt. Assn., Newcomen Soc. N.Am., Phi Beta Kappa Assocs. Clubs: Economics, Harmonie, Phi Beta Kappa Alumni (N.Y.C.); Royal Automobile (London); Royal Automobile Country (Epsom, Eng.); Windham Mountain Ski. Home: 303 E 57th St New York NY 10022 Office: Rockefeller Ctr 630 Fifth Ave Ste 2166 New York NY 10111

SUSNJARA, GARY M., advertising agency executive; b. N.Y.C., July 29, 1939; s. Michael J. Susnjara and Margaret (Coric) Lappin; m. Mary Angela Pellicane, Apr. 27, 1963; children: Stephanie, Rosemary. BA, Villanova U., 1961, MA, 1963. V.p. DFS Advt., N.Y.C., 1971-76, sr. v.p., 1976-81, pres. N.Y. div., 1981-84; pres., chief operating officer Saatchi & Saatchi DFS, Inc., N.Y.C., 1984—. Trustee Winthrope U. Hosp., Mineola, N.Y., 1986—; chmn. N.Y.C. Sport Commn. Found.; bd. dirs. Nat. Crime Prevention

Council, Washington, 1983—. Democrat. Roman Catholic. Home: 30 Sutton Pl N New York NY 10017 Office: Saatchi & Saatchi DFS Inc 375 Hudson St New York NY 10014

SUSSMAN, MARC MITCHELL, international business executive, management consultant; b. N.Y.C., Mar. 31, 1956; s. Max and Ruth (Lindner) S; m. Sharon Tracy, Apr. 9, 1988. B.A., George Washington U., 1978; M.P.A., NYU, 1980. Mem. nat. staff Carter/Mondale Campaign, Atlanta, 1976; intern The White House, Washington, 1977; internat. affairs analyst Chem. Bank, N.Y.C., 1980-82; pres., chief exec. officer Alpha Internat. Mgmt. Group, Ltd., N.Y.C., 1982—; dir. Mormac, N.Y.C. Fund raiser Mondale Presdl. Campaign, N.Y.C., 1981-84, Friends of Ed Koch, N.Y.C., 1981, Hubert H. Humphrey Cancer Research Ctr., Boston, 1984—, Hubert H. Humphrey Fund, 1986—, Humphrey Exploratory Com., 1987—, Humphrey for U.S. Sen., 1988. Mem. NYU Alumni Assn., Internat. Platform Assn. Jewish. Club: Nat. Tennis Assn. (N.Y.C.). Avocations: tennis, collecting tennis art. Office: Alpha Internat Mgmt Group Ltd 145 W 58th St New York NY 10019

SUTCLIFFE, ERIC, lawyer; b. Calif., Jan. 10, 1909; s. Thomas and Annie (Beare) S.; m. Joan Basché, Aug. 7, 1937; children: Victoria, Marcia, Thomas; m. Marie C. Paige, Nov. 1, 1975. AB, U. Calif. at Berkeley, 1929, LLB, 1932. Bar: Calif. 1932. Mem. firm Orrick, Herrington & Sutcliffe, San Francisco, 1943-85. Trustee San Francisco Law Library, 1988; bd. dirs. Merritt Peralta Found., 1988. Fellow Am. Bar Found; mem. ABA (chmn state regulation securities com. 1960-65), San Francisco Bar Assn. (chmn. corp. law com., 1964-65), San Francisco C. of C. (past treas., dir.), State Bar Calif., Pacific Union Club, Bohemian Club, Phi Gamma Delta, Phi Delta Phi, Order of Coif. Home: 260 King Ave Piedmont CA 94610 Office: 600 Montgomery St San Francisco CA 94111

SUTER, ALBERT EDWARD, manufacturing company executive; b. East Orange, N.J., Sept. 18, 1935; s. Joseph Vincent and Catherine (Clay) S.; m. Michaela Sams Suter, May 28, 1966; children: Christian C., Bradley J., Allison A. BME, Cornell U., 1957, MBA, 1959. Pres., chief exec. officer L.B. Knight & Assocs., Chgo., 1959-79; v.p. internat. Emerson Electric Co., St. Louis, 1979-80, pres. motor div., 1980-87, group v.p., 1981-83, exec. v.p., 1983-87, vice chmn., 1987; pres., chief operating officer, dir. Firestone Tire & Rubber Co., Akron, Ohio, 1987-88; pres., chief operating officer Whirlpool Corp., Benton Harbor, Mich., 1988—. Bd. dirs. Jr. Achievement Miss. Valley; chmn. Torch div. St. Louis chpt. United Way, 1982—. Republican. Episcopalian. Clubs: Chgo; Glenview Country (Chgo.); St. Louis; Old Warson Country (St. Louis). Office: Whirlpool Corp 2000 M-63 Benton Harbor MI 49022 *

SUTER, GEORGE AUGUST, management and marketing consultant; b. Zurich, Switzerland, July 22, 1934; came to U.S., 1972; s. Jakob G. and Ann (Hagi) S.; m. Annelise Grone, July 2, 1962 (div.); children: Jeannine H., Marcel D.; m. Elanore K. Kazusky, Feb. 14, 1981. Comml. Sci. degree, St. Michael Coll., Fribourg, Switzerland, 1954. V.p. mktg. Panteplast, Zurich, 1954-62; mktg. mgr. Semperit AG, Zurich, 1962-69; pres., chmn. bd. Suter Assocs., Inc., Zurich and Pitts., 1969-81; mgmt. cons., chmn., chief exec. officer Access Mgmt. Corp., Charlotte, N.C., 1981—; chief exec. officer, mgmt. cons., chmn. bd. dirs. FibreCem Corp., Charlotte; seminar leader U.S. Dept. Commerce, 1975, 77, 78, 79; presenter seminars to other orgns. Author: Jumping Import Barriers Alternative to Exporting, 1978, revised edit., 1984, You Open the Door, 1984. Bd. advisors Arthritis Found. N.C., also bd. dirs. Named Hon. Consul Switzerland, Berne, 1980. Mem. Am. Mgmt. Assn., Metrolina Trade Assn., Charlotte C. of C. (internat. trade com. 1986-87), Swiss Soc. (founding pres. 1986—), Swiss-Am. C. of C. (bd. advisors 1988—), Space Roundtable, Nat. Home Builders Assn. Club: Carmel Country (Charlotte). Lodge: Rotary (bd. dirs. Charlotte South club 1985-87). Office: Access Mgmt Corp 7 Woodlawn Green Charlotte NC 28217

SUTHERLAND, DONALD CLARE, chemical company executive; b. N.Y.C., Oct. 10, 1926; s. Judson Clare and Marie Helen (Gerstenberger) S.; m. Susan Isabel Faill, Aug. 22, 1953; children: John Clare, Sara Faill, Andrew Rankin. BS in Chem. Engring., Cornell U., 1949. With E.I. du Pont de Nemours & Co., 1950—; dir. electroni materials E.I. du Pont de Nemours & Co., Wilmington, Del., 1971-78, dir. clin. and instrument systems div., 1979-84, mng. dir. investor affairs, 1985—. Mem. Cornell Alumni Coun., Ithaca, N.Y., 1973—; chmn. adv. bd. Cornell Adult U., Ithaca, 1978-82. Mem. Semiconductor Equipment and Materials Inst. (bd. dirs. 1970-75), Internat. Soc. Hybrid Micro-electronics (pres. 1973-74, Daniel C. Hughes Meml. award 1974), Health Industries Mfrs. Assn. (bd. dirs. 1979-84), Greenville Country Club (pres. 1984-87). Home: 109 S Spring Valley Rd Wilmington DE 19807

SUTHERLAND, DONALD JAMES, investment company executive; b. Teaneck, N.J., Jan. 2, 1931; s. Conrad James and LaVinia Marie (Peters) S.; m. Denise Jackson, July 22, 1985; children: Paige, Donald, Shelley, Julie, Conor. A.B., Princeton U., 1953; M.B.A., Harvard U., 1958; LH.D (hon.), St. Michael's Coll., 1981. Regional sales mgr. Dahlstrom Corp., Jamestown, 1958-60; assoc. McKinsey & Co., N.Y.C., 1961-64; v.p. Laird, Inc., N.Y.C., 1965-67, New Court Securities Corp., N.Y.C., 1968-70; pres. Quincy Assocs., Inc., N.Y.C., 1970-75; pres., corp. gen. ptnr. Quincy Ptnrs., Glen Head, N.Y., 1975—; chmn. bd. Crane Hoist Engring. Corp., 1975-79, Am. Spring & Wire Splty. Co., Inc., 1977-82, Muehlhausen Bros. Spring & Mfg. Co., Inc., 1977-82, Lewis Spring & Mfg. Co., Inc., 1979-82, Ohio Locomotive Crane Co., Inc., 1981-86, Publix Shirt Co., L.P., 1979—, Will & Baumer, Inc., 1984—, Quincy Packaging Group, L.P., 1984—, Quincy Spring Group, Inc., 1986—, Quincy Techs., Inc., 1987—; PCI Group, Inc., 1987—, Water Products Co., 1988—; chmn. bd., pres. Ala. Metal Products Co., Inc., 1976-77; bd. dirs. Profit Systems, Inc. Contbr. articles to profl. jours. Trustee Sheltering Arms Children's Service, 1973-75, St. Michael's Coll., 1972-81, Cancer Research Inst., 1984—; trustee Joffrey Ballet, 1982—, pres., 1985-87; mem. vis. com. Fordham Bus. Sch., 1987—; mem. Nassau County (N.Y.) Planning Commn., 1965-68. Served to lt. (j.g.) USN, 1953-56. Democrat. Roman Catholic. Clubs: The Creek (gov. 1987—), Twenty Nine, Cap and Gown (trustee 1981—), The Links, Economic of N.Y.C. Office: PO Box 154 Glen Head NY 11545

SUTHERLAND, EARL CHRISTIAN, engineering executive; b. Detroit, July 23, 1923; s. Earl Jefferson and Mildred Fredricka (Schroeder) S.; m. Faith B. Maier, Aug. 12, 1946 (dec.); m. Marion Elizabeth Schultz; 1 child, Earl Maier. BS, Mich. Coll. Mining Tech., 1950, MS, 1950; MBA, Portland State U., 1974. Engr. IBM Corp., Endicott, N.Y., 1941-52; metallurgist Fansted Metall., N. Chgo., 1956; v.p. tech. Eriez S.A. Produtos Metall., Sao Paulo, Brazil, 1956-60; research scientist NASA Lewis Ctr., Cleve., 1960-62; mfg. mgr. Precision Castparts Corp., Portland, 1962-64; engring. mgr. Omark Industries, Milw., 1964-68; cons. engr. MEI Charlton, Inc., Portland, 1968-75; pres. Cellufibres Internat., Inc., Seattle, 1977—; cons. engr. Earl C. Sutherland & Assocs., 1975. Author: numerous books and articles. Served to col. U.S. Army, 1946-75, ret. Decorated Legion of Merit. Mem. Am. Cons. Engrs. Council, Cons. Engrs. Wash., Nat. Soc. Profl. Engrs., Am. Soc. Metals, AIME, Nat. Assn. Corrosion Engrs., Soc. Automotive Engrs. Baptist. Home: 2565 Dexter Ave N Seattle WA 98109-1913 Office: Earl C Sutherland & Assocs Eagle River AK 99577

SUTHERLAND, GEORGE LESLIE, retired chemical company executive; b. Dallas, Aug. 13, 1922; s. Leslie and Madge Alice (Henderson) S.; m. Mary Gail Hamilton, Sept. 9, 1961 (dec. Mar. 1984); children: Janet Leslie, Gail Irene, Elizabeth Hamilton; m. Carol Brenda Kaplan, Feb. 19, 1986. BA, U. Tex., Austin, 1943, MA, 1947, PhD, 1950. With Am. Cyanamid Co., various locations, 1951-87; asst. dir. research and devel. Princeton, N.J., 1969-70, dir. research and devel., agr. div., 1970-73; v.p. med. research and devel. Pearl River, N.Y., 1973—, dir. med. research div., 1978-86, dir. chem. research div., 1980-81; v.p. corp. research tech. Pearl River, 1986-87. Served with USN, 1944-46. Mem. Assn. Research Dirs. (pres. 1975-76), AAAS, Am. Chem. Soc., Royal Soc. Chemistry. Home: 42 Sky Meadow Rd Suffern NY 10901

SUTHERLAND, JEFFREY VICTOR, software development company executive; b. North Attleboro, Mass., June 20, 1941; s. Andrew Victor and Hazel Jean (Schofield) S.; m. Arline Conan, July 11, 1964; children: Andrew Victor II, Jeffrey Victor Jr. Student, Columbia U., 1959-60; BS in Engring., U.S. Mil. Acad., 1964; MS in Statistics, Stanford U., 1972; PhD in Biometrics, U. Colo., 1980. Commd. 2d lt. USAF, 1964, advanced through grades to capt., 1967, resigned, 1975, fighter, reconnaissance pilot, 1964-70, instr. math. at USAF acad., 1972-74, asst. prof. math., 1974-75; project dir. Co Regional Cancer Ctr., Denver, 1975-80; instr. biometrics U. Colo. Sch. Medicine, 1975-80; asst. prof., co-investigator U. Colo. Sch. Medicine, Denver, 1980-83, assoc. dir. Ctr. for Vitamins and Cancer Research, 1982-83; mgr. tech. applications Mid-Continent Computer Services, Englewood, Colo., 1983-84, v.p. electronic funds transfer div., 1985, v.p. advanced systems, 1986; v.p. product devel. Saddlebrook Corp., Cambridge, Mass., 1986-88; v.p. engring. Graphael, Inc., Waltham, Mass., 1989—; asst. prof. radiology, preventive medicine and biometrics U. Colo. Sch. Medicine, 1981-86; vice chmn. Rocky Flats Monitoring Com., 1980-85, chmn. subcom. on health and environment, 1983-84; mem. Rocky Flats Employees Health Assessment Group, 1976-80; cons. in field. Editorial cons. Differentiation, 1976-83, Internat. Jour. Epidemiology, 1978-83, Jour. Nat. Cancer Inst., 1978-81, Photochemistry and Photobiology, 1982-83; contbr. articles to profl. jours. Mem. steering com. Creative Initiative Found., Colo., 1972-85, chmn., 1975-82, 84-85; Rocky Mountain regional chmn. Beyond War Found., 1984-85, Boston regional chmn., 1986-87. Decorated D.F.C., 11 Air medals; Kellogg Nat. fellow, 1983-86; USAF Acad. fellow, 1970-72. Mem. Data Processing Mgmt. Assn., Am. Soc. Preventive Oncology, Am. Statis. Assn., N.Y. Acad. Scis., Alpha Iota Delta, Phi Kappa Phi. Democrat. Mem. Unitarian-Universalist Ch. Home: 34 Hancock St Boston MA 02114 Office: Graphael Inc 255 Bear Hill Rd Waltham MA 02154

SUTHERLAND, LEWIS FREDERICK, diversified services company executive; b. Charleston, W.Va., Jan. 1, 1952; s. Lewis Frederick and Dorothy Louise (Droddy) S.; m. Barbara Hall Hoover, Aug. 24, 1974; children—Matthew, Mark. B.S. in Physics, Duke U., 1973; M.B.A., U. Pitts., 1974. Credit trainee Chase Manhattan Bank, N.Y.C., 1974-76, asst. treas., 1976-78, 2nd v.p., 1978-80, v.p., 1980; asst. treas. ARA Services Inc., Phila., 1980-83, v.p., treas., 1983-87, v.p. corp. fin. and devel., 1987—. Com. mem. United Way Southeastern Pa., Phila.; trustee People's Light and Theatre Co. Named Treas. of Yr., Cash Flow mag., 1987. Mem. Fin. Execs. Inst., Beta Gamma Sigma. Club: Phila. Treas. (pres.). Office: ARA Svcs Inc 1101 Market St Philadelphia PA 19107

SUTTER, JAMES FRANCIS, aerospace company executive; b. Elizabeth, N.J., Apr. 5, 1937; s. Henry Gerard and Jane (Lynn) S.; m. Lynne Irene Matthews, June 7, 1960; children—John Brian, MaryBeth, Kevin, Kelly. B.S., U. Notre Dame, 1959; M.B.A., Marquette U., 1970. Cert. data processor; cert. in adminstrv. mgmt. Mgr. data processing Rexnord, Milw., 1961-66; mgr. data processing Iowa Beef Processors, Sioux City, Iowa, 1966-67; dir. mgmt. info. systems Xerox Corp., Stamford, Conn., 1967-83; v.p., gen. mgr. Rockwell Internat., Seal Beach, Calif., 1983—; dir. Infomart, Dallas; chmn. Tech. Council Am. Mgt. Assn. (v.p.), Pres.'s Council, LMU, U. Pitts.; mem. GSB adv. council. Committeeman, Boy Scouts Am., New Canaan, Conn., 1975-80. Served to lt. (j.g.) USN, 1959-61. Republican. Roman Catholic. Club: Lido Sailing (Newport Beach). Home: 25762 Highplains Terr Laguna Hills CA 92653 Office: Rockwell Internat PO Box 2515 Seal Beach CA 90740

SUTTER, WILLIAM PAUL, JR., venture capitalist; b. Chgo., July 23, 1957; s. William Paul and Helen (Stebbins) S.; m. Katherine Constance Adinamis, Aug. 28, 1982. BA cum laude with honors, Yale U., 1979; MBA, Stanford U., 1983. Analyst Smith Barney, Harris Upham & Co., Chgo., 1979-81, assoc., 1983-84; v.p. Mesirow Capital Markets, Inc., Chgo., 1984-87, sr. v.p., 1987—; bd. dirs. New West, Inc., Phoenix, Appliance Control Tech., Inc., Addison, Ill., Bell Helmets, Inc., Rantoul, Ill., Eurostyle, Ltd., Wheeling, Ill. Office: Mesirow Capital Markets Inc 350 N Clark St Chicago IL 60610

SUTTON, FREDERICK ISLER, JR., realtor; b. Greensboro, N.C., Sept. 13, 1916; s. Fred I. and Annie (Fry) S.; m. Helen Sykes Morrison, Mar. 18, 1941; children: Fred Isler III, Frank Morrison. Grad. Culver (Ind.) Mil. Acad., 1934; AB, U. N.C., 1939, student Law Sch., 1939-41. Lic. in real estate; cert. property mgr. Propr. Fred I. Sutton, Jr., realtor, Kinston, N.C., 1946—; comml. pilot, 1949—. Chmn. Kinston Parking Authority, Kinston Water Resources; pres. Lenoir County United Fund, 1969-70; trustee, dean U. N.C. Realtors Inst.; trustee Florence Crittenton Services; v.p. N.C. Real Estate Edn. Found.; deacon Presbyn. Ch. Served to lt. comdr. USNR, 1941-46. Named Kinston Realtor of Yr., 1963. Mem. Kinston Bd. Realtors (pres.), N.C. Bd. Realtors (v.p. 1957), N.C. Assn. Realtors (regional v.p., chmn. ednl. com., dir. Realtors Ednl. Found.), N.C. Assn. Real Estate Bds. (bd. dirs., v.p. 1958-60, 61, 63), Newcomen Soc., Am. Power Boat Assn. (7 Liter Hydroplane Nat. Champion 1951, Region 4 Champion 1976, 78-80, 82, Nat. High Point Champion 1982, Eastern Div. Champion 1982), U.S. Power Squadron (navigator, Kinston comdg. officer, adminstrv. officer dist. 27 1987), Kinston C. of C. (v.p.), SR. Lodges: Kiwanis (pres. Kinston chpt., bd. dirs.), Masons (32 deg.), Shriners, Elks. Home: 1101 N Queen St Kinston NC 28501 Office: Sutton Bldg PO Drawer 3309 Kinston NC 28501

SUTTON, JAMES ANDREW, diversified utility company executive; b. Gary, Ind., June 29, 1934; s. Winfield Alexander and Margaret (Aulwurm) S.; m. Beverly Joan McCorkle, Aug. 27, 1955; children—James II, Susan, Stephen, Scot. BS in Chem. Engring., Purdue U., 1957. V.P., gen. mgr./gas products Linde div. Union Carbide Corp., Danbury, Conn., 1978-82; sr. v.p. compressed gases UGI Corp., Valley Forge, Pa., 1982-84, exec. v.p., chief operating officer, 1984-85, pres., chief operating officer, 1985-86, pres., chief exec. officer, 1986—, also bd. dirs.; bd. dirs. Gilbert Assocs., Inc., Reading, Pa., Pa. Chamber Bus. and Industry, Penjerdel Council, Phila. Chmn. United Way, Del., Chester & Montgomery Cos., Pa., 1986—. Served to lt. U.S. Army, 1958. Mem. Compressed Gas Assn. (dir. 1978-84), Internat. Oxygen Mfrs. Assn., Greater Phila. C. of C. (bd. dirs.). Clubs: Phila. Country, Union League. Office: UGI Corp PO Box 858 Valley Forge PA 19482

SUTTON, JOSEPH RALPH, government contracts manager; b. Chgo., Mar. 4, 1952; s. Ralph Abraham and Rose (Ferdman) S.; m. Nancy Freedman, Feb. 24, 1980. BA, NYU, 1974, MA, 1976. Cert. assoc. contracts mgr. Law clk. Dinkes, Mandel & Dinkes, N.Y.C., 1974-76; document analyst Aspen Systems Corp., N.Y.C., 1977-78; paralegal specialist U.S. Dept. of Justice, Washington, 1978-81, Litigation Support Specialist, 1981-82, chief contracts and procurement, 1982—. Contbr. articles to newspapers, 1974. V.p. Darech Amuno Congregation, N.Y.C., 1977-78. Mem. Nat. Contract Mgmt. Assn., Nat. Capital Area Paralegal Assn., Kappa Tau Alpha. Democrat. Jewish. Home: 7546 Cross Gate Ln Alexandria VA 22310 Office: US Dept Justice Antitrust Div 1000 Constitution Ave Washington DC 20530

SUTTON, JUSTIN CORSER, JR., energy company executive; b. Lansing, Mich., May 11, 1949; s. Justin Corser Sr. and Barbara Jean (Barrett) S.; m. Patricia Ann Caldwell, Dec. 18, 1971; children: Corey, Marnie, Justin. BA, Albion Coll., 1971. Cost analyst Skylab Project Martin Marietta Co., Denver, 1971-75; pres. Ins. Petroleum Svcs., Denver, 1975-81, Asset Surety Corp., Denver, 1981-85; chmn. Rocky Mt. Energy Exchange, Denver, 1985—; cons. Natural Gas Mktg. Assn., Washington. Active fund raiser Denver Symphony Orch. Republican. Methodist. Home: 7094 S Madison Ct Littleton CO 80122

SUTTON, LEONARD VON BIBRA, lawyer; b. Colorado Springs, Colo., Dec. 21, 1914; s. Benjamin Edmund and Anne (von Bibra) S.; B.A., Colo. Coll., 1937; fellow Nat. Inst. Pub. Affairs, 1937-38; J.D., U. Denver, 1941; grad. Inf. Officers Sch., Ft. Benning, Ga., 1942; LLD (hon.) Colo. Coll., 1987, U. Denver, 1989. Bar: Colo. 1941, U.S. Supreme Ct., U.S. Tax Ct., Ct. of Claims, Customs Ct., U.S. Army Ct. Mil. Rev. Practiced law, Colorado Springs, 1941-42, 46-56; justice Colo. Supreme Ct., 1956-68, chief justice, 1960, 66; chmn. Fgn. Claims Settlement Commn. U.S., 1968-69; pvt. practice law, Denver and Washington, 1969—. Chmn. Colo. Statute Revision Com., 1964-67; del. various nat. and internat. bar assn. confs.; lectr.; past vice chmn. com. internat. cts. World Peace Through Law Commn.; past chmn. Colo. World Peace through Law Com., World Habeas Corpus Com.; hon. mem. N.J. World Trade Com., 1976—; mem. Colo. Democratic Central Com., 1948-56, mem. exec. com., 1948-58, chmn. rules com., 1955-56; del. Dem. Nat. Conv., 1952. Hon. trustee Inst. Internat. Edn., N.Y.C.; regent Dana Coll., Blair, Nebr., 1976-78; chmn. bd. govs. U. Denver, 1985—. Served from pvt. to capt., AUS, World War II. Recipient Grand Order of Merit Fed. Republic Germany, 1987. Mem. Colo. (Jr. Bar past chmn.), Internat., Inter-Am. (council), Am. (past chmn. com. on internat. cts., former mem. council sect. internat. law), Denver, D.C. bar assns., Mexican Acad. Internat. Law, Buenos Aires Bar Assn. (U.S. mem.), Am. Arbitration Assn., Can. Arbitration, Conciliation and Amicable Composition Cen., Inc. (internat. assoc.), Washington Fgn. Law Soc. (pres. 1970-71, now hon. mem.), Royal Danish Guards Assn. Calif., Consular Law Soc. N.Y. (hon.), Phi Delta Phi. Episcopalian. Clubs: Wyoming One Shot Antelope Past Shooter's (pres. 1985-86); Colo. Harvard Bus. Sch. (assoc.); Masons, Shriners; Garden of Gods, Kissing Camels (Colorado Springs); Cosmos (Washington). Author: Constitution of Mexico, 1973. Contbr. articles on law, jud. adminstrn. and internat. relations to jours. Home: 3131 E Alameda Ave Apt 1908 Denver CO 80209

SUTTON, THOMAS CARL, metal products manufacturing corporation executive; b. Longmont, Colo., Jan. 10, 1921; s. Carl and Alice J. (Hunter) S.; m. Jayne A. Harrington, June 22, 1946; children: Scott T., Leslie Lynn. B.B.A., U. Cin., 1948. With Dover Corp., N.Y.C., 1951—; pres. OPW div. Dover Corp., 1961-63, exec. v.p. corp., 1963-64, pres., chief exec. officer, 1964-71, chmn., chief exec. officer, 1971-81, chmn., 1981—, also dir.; dir. Dover Elevator Co., Dover Corp. (Can.), Ltd., Dover Internat., Inc., Alberta Oil Tool Co., Inc., F & M Schaefer Corp. Served to maj., pilot, USAAF, 1942-46. Decorated D.F.C. (2), Air medal (7). Clubs: Univ., Winged Foot Golf; Queen City (Cin.). Office: Dover Corp 277 Park Ave New York NY 10172 *

SUZUKI, GENGO, banker; b. Mino-Kamo City, Japan, Feb. 11, 1904; s. Seijiro Suzuki and Sumi Kani; grad. Taihoku Coll. Commerce, 1925; M.A. in Econs., U. Wis., 1927; m. Hide Motoda, Dec. 29, 1929 (dec. May 1975); children—Tsutomu, Sunao; m. 2d, Toshi Toki, July 7, 1976. Instr., then prof. econs. Taihoku Coll. Commerce, Taihoku, Taiwan, 1930-45; prof. econs. Taiwan Nat. U., 1945-48; dep. fin. commr. Ministry Fin., Japan, 1949-51, fin. commr., 1951-57; E.E. and M.P., fin. minister Japanese Embassy, Washington, 1957-60; exec. dir. IMF and IBRD, 1960-66; spl. asst. to minister fgn. affairs, minister fin., 1960-66; auditor Bank of Japan, Tokyo, 1966-70; chmn. Associated Japanese Bank (Internat.) Ltd., London, 1970-79, bd. counselor, 1979-87. Adv. bd. Mekong Com. ECAFE, UN, 1968-75; chief fin. mission on Ryukyus Island, 1968-69; vice chmn. Japanese com. bus. and industry adv. com. OECD, Paris, 1974-75; mem. European Atlantic Group, London, 1971-85. Mem. Internat. C. of C. (mem. council 1974-85, mem. commn. on ethical practices 1976-78). Trustee, Internat. Christian U., Tokyo, 1968—; bd. govs., Atlantic Inst. for Internat. Affairs, Paris, 1972—; councilor The Atlantic Council of U.S., 1986—; mem. joint com. on remunerations of exec. dirs. and their alternatives IMF-IBRD, 1977; trustee Rikkyo Sch. in Eng. Trust, Rudgwick, Eng., 1972—; bd. dirs. Per Jacobsson Found., Washington, 1970—; trustee ICU Cambridge House (Eng.), 1981—. Episcopalian. Clubs: Chevy Chase (Washington); Takanodai Country (ChibaKen, Japan); Royal Automobile (London and Epsom.). Home: 6301 Stevenson Ave Apt 717 Alexandria VA 22304 Home: 2-5-13 Nukui-Kitamachi, Koganei-Shi Tokyo 184, Japan

SUZUKI, HIROAKI, banker; b. May 1, 1942; came to U.S., 1981; s. Mastaka and Miye (Sato) S.; m. Setsuko Kaga, Apr. 6, 1975; children: Mayumi, Kaori, Hiroko. LLB, Kyoto U., 1965; postgrad. Adv. Mgmt., Harvard U., 1982. With Fuji Bank, Ltd., Tokyo and N.Y.C., 1965-81; sr. v.p. N.Y. subs. Fuji Bank and Trust Co., N.Y.C., 1982-84, exec. v.p., 1984-87, pres., chief exec. officer, 1987—. Mem. Canyon Club (Armonk, N.Y.). Office: Fuji Bank and Trust Co 1 World Trade Ctr 92d Fl New York NY 10048

SVEC, JANICE LYNN, military professional; b. Santa Anna, Calif., May 14, 1948; d. Leonard August Svec and Wanda Marcelle (Richards) McMillon; m. Lewis Eugene Humphrey, May 24, 1974 (div. 1977); 1 child, Jeromy Starbuck Svec. A.A. in Adminstrn. of Justice, Los Angeles Met. Community Coll., 1982; student criminal justice Thomas Edison State Coll., Trenton, 1985—. Adminstrv. supporter Naval Investigative Service, Subic Bay, Philippines, 1979-81; office supr. Naval Communication Ctr., Yokosuka, Japan, 1981-82; chief master at arms Naval Support Facility Security Dept., Diego Garcia, Brit. Indian Ocean Ter., 1982-83, U.S. Navy Drug Rehab. Ctr., San Diego, 1983-85; instr. U.S. Navy, Lakehurst, N.J., 1985-88, supr. Navy Support Office, 1988—. Roman Catholic. Avocations: body building; horseback riding. Home: 120 Village Way Crockett TX 75835 Office: PO Box 578 Lakehurst NJ 08733

SVENSON, CHARLES OSCAR, investment banker; b. Worcester, Mass., June 28, 1939; s. Sven Oscar and Edahjane (Castner) S.; m. Sara Ellen Simpson, Nov. 15, 1968; children: Alicia Lindall, Tait Oscar. A.B., Hamilton Coll., 1961; LL.B., Harvard U., 1964; LL.M., Bklyn. Law Sch., 1965. Bar: N.Y. 1965, U.S. Dist. Ct. (so. dist.) N.Y. 1965, U.S. Ct. Appeals (2d. cir.) 1965. Atty. Dewey, Ballantine, Bushby, Palmer & Wood, N.Y.C., 1964-68; v.p. Goldman Sachs & Co., N.Y.C., 1968-75; sr. v.p. Donaldson, Lufkin & Jenrette, N.Y.C, 1975—. Trustee Kirkland Coll., Clinton, N.Y., 1976-78; trustee Hamilton Coll., Clinton, 1979-83. Mem. ABA, N.Y. State Bar Assn., Asn. of Bar of City of N.Y. Clubs: Tuxedo (Tuxedo Park, N.Y.); Harvard (N.Y.C.). Home: 1185 Park Ave New York NY 10128 Office: Donaldson Lufkin & Jenrette 140 Broadway New York NY 10005

SVENTECK, DALE RICHARD, sales executive; b. Cleve., Jan. 4, 1951; s. Richard John and Julia (Gawry) S. BS in Aerospace Tech., Kent State U., 1973. Salesman Hilti, Inc., Akron, Ohio, 1976-79; sales mgr. Ohio and Pa. Hilti, Inc., 1980-82; br. mgr. Safway Steel Products Co., Cleve., 1982-84, Tampa, Fla., 1984-86; nat. sales mgr. Gunnebo Corp., Bristol Conn., 1986-88; v.p., gen. mgr. Uniset Corp., Indpls., 1989—. With USN, 1970-74. Mem. AIAA. Home: 4130 N Englewood Dr Indianapolis IN 46226 Office: Gunnebo Corp 293 Lake Ave Bristol CT 06010

SVEUM, PHILLIP ALLEN, investment and financial advisory company executive; b. Stoughton, Wis., May 27, 1954; s. Arthur Burns and Irene Theresa (Seamonson) S.; m. Susan Stangby, Feb. 4, 1956; children: Matthew, Kelsey. BS in Bus. and Real Estate, Ariz. State U., 1976. Cert. fin. planner; registered investment advisor. Ptnr. Coldwell Banker Sveum Realtors, Stoughton, 1977—; prin., owner Sveum Fin. Svcs., Inc., Madison, Wis., 1980—. Mem. Inst. Cert. Fin. Planners, Internat. Assn. Fin. Planning. Home: 1564 Black Oak Dr Stoughton WI 53598 Office: Sveum Fin Svcs Inc 2817 Fish Hatchery Rd Madison WI 53713

SWAIM, DAVID DEE, diversified company financial executive; b. Ft. Wayne, Ind., Aug. 12, 1947; s. Carl Edwin and Pauline E. (Johnson) S.; m. Barbara Lynn Strock, June 21, 1969; children: Emily Anne, Benjamin Dee, Thomas Ryan. BS in Acctg., Ind. U., 1969. Sr. auditor Price Waterhouse & Co., Indpls., 1970-76; controller VideoInd., Inc., Indpls., 1976-77; treas., chief fin. officer Bindley Western Industries, Inc., Indpls., 1977—, v.p., 1979—, sr. v.p., 1986—, also bd. dirs.; bd. dirs., officer all subs. of Bindley Western Industries, Inc.; bd. dirs. Travel Mat, Inc., Indpls. Mem. Am. Inst. CPAs, Ind. CPA Soc., Fin. Execs. Inst. Republican. Methodist. Lodge: Masons. Office: Bindley Western Industries Inc 4212 W 71st St PO Box 68450 Indianapolis IN 46268

SWAIM, JOHN FRANKLIN, physician, health care executive; b. Bloomingdale, Ind., Dec. 24, 1935; s. Max DeBaun and Edna Marie (Whitely) S.; m. Joan Dooley, Sept. 19, 1957 (div. Apr. 1979); children: John Franklin, Parke Allen, Pamela Ann; m. Peggy Lou Sankey, May 30, 1979; one child, Anne-Marie. BS cum laude, Ind. StateU., 1959; MD, Ind. U., Indpls., 1963. Diplomate Am. Bd. Family Practice. Med. dir. Parke Clinic, Rockville, Ind., 1969—; pres. Parke Investments Inc., Rockville, 1972—, Vermillion Health Care Corp., Clinton, Ind., 1977—; bd. dirs. Parke State Bank, Rockville. Author: One Year and Eternity, 1978; also contbr. articles to profl. jours. Coroner, Parke County, Ind., 1972-82. Served to capt. USAF, 1963-67, Vietnam. Decorated Bronze Star. Mem. Am. Acad. Family Physicians, AMA, Ind. State Med. Assn. (dist. pres. 1986—), Midwest Fin. Assn. Republican. Club: Hoosier Assocs. (Indpls.). Lodges: Elks, Masons, Shriners. Home and Office: Parke Clinic 503 Anderson St Rockville IN 47872

SWAIN, PHILIP RAYMOND, publishing company executive; b. Meriden, Conn., Nov. 30, 1929; s. Raymond Francis and Angela Catherine (Maslow) S. AB cum laude, Harvard U., 1950; MBA, Boston U. Tchr. Latin, Greek, pvt. schs., Cambridge and Still River, Mass., 1950-55; editor Ravengate Press, Cambridge, 1955-65, pres., 1965—. Mem. bd. advisers St. Benedict Acad., Still River. Mem. Book Builders of Boston. Roman Catholic. Club: Harvard. Author (as Philip Douglas): Saint of Philadelphia, The Life of Bishop John Neumann, 1977. Home: 56 Carpenter Ave Meriden CT 06450 Office: PO Box 103 Cambridge MA 02138

SWALES, MARLEE SANDRA, day care administrator; b. Oak Bluffs, Mass., Oct. 27, 1936; d. Warren Tillman and Enid Frances (Crozier) Hoffman; m. Bernard Pfau, Apr. 21, 1955 (div. 1968); children: Randolph Pfau, Ronald Pfau; m. Joseph Swales, Feb. 29, 1984. BS, U. Conn., 1971; cert. Tchrs. Coll., Columbia U., 1973; postgrad., St. Joseph Coll., 1976. Dir., owner Tom Thumb Day Care, Tolland, Conn., 1965-67; dir. Kiddie Korral Day Care, Manchester, Conn., 1967-71, Somers (Conn.) Presch., 1971-72; tchr. Head Start, Vernon, Conn., 1971; supervisory tchr. Amisted House-Day Care, Hartford, Conn., 1972-73; head tchr. St. Monica's Day Care, Hartford, 1973-74; dir. Creative Living & Learning, Enfield, Conn., 1974-77; adminstr., owner Creative Living & Learning, Enfield, 1982—; owner, dir. Creative Child Care, Vernon, 1977—; validator Nat. Acad. Early Childhood Programs, Washington, 1986—; ednl. cons. Red Balloon, Stafford, Conn., 1988—. Mem. Nat. Assn. for Edn. Young Children, Women's Forum (v.p.), Vernon C. of C. Home and office: 90 Grand Ave Vernon CT 06066

SWALES, ROBERT DAVID, insurance company executive, financial planner; b. Hamilton, Ohio, Jan. 2, 1948; s. Robert Lee and Freda Alene (Smith) S.; m. Caren Sue Johnson, June 15, 1974; 1 child, Whitney Dru. Student, Long Beach City Coll., 1967, U. Cin., 1973; Regis Coll., 1984. Pres. Republic Ind. Bank, Colorado Springs, 1977-82; v.p. Western Nat. Bank, Colorado Springs, 1982-83; broker Integrated Resources, Colorado Springs, 1983-86; pres. The Swales Agy., Colorado Springs, 1984—. Organizer Cystic Fibrosis Found., Colorado Springs. Served with USAF, 1967-71, ETO. Mem. Ind. Ins. Agts. Am., Nat. Assn. Fin. Planners, Nat. Assn. Securities Dealers. Republican. Lutheran. Lodge: Rotary (pres. Fountain Valley club 1981-82, pres. Rampart club 1984-85). Home: 814 Cresta Rd Colorado Springs CO 80906 Office: The Swales Agy PO Box 636 Colorado Springs CO 80901

SWALES, WILLIAM EDWARD, oil company executive; b. Parkersburg, W.Va., May 15, 1925; s. John Richard and Ellen (South) S.; m. Lydia Eugena Mills, Dec. 26, 1948; children: Joseph V., Susan Eugena, David Lee. BA in Geology, W.Va. U., 1949, MS in Geology, 1951; grad., advanced mgmt. program Stanford U., 1968; DSc (hon.), W.Va. U., 1986; LLD (hon.), Marietta Coll., 1986. With Marathon Oil Co. (subs. USX Corp.), Findlay, Ohio, 1954-70, 74-87, mgr. Western Hemisphere and Australia div., 1967-70; exec. v.p. Oasis Oil Co. of Libya Inc., Tripoli, 1970-72; exec. v.p. to pres. Oasis Oil Co., 1972-74; spl. asst. to sr. v.p. prodn., internat. Marathon Oil Co. (subs. USX Corp.), Findlay, Ohio, 1974, v.p. prodn., internat., 1974-77, sr. v.p. prodn., internat., 1977-82, also bd. dirs., chmn. bd., 1983-84, sr. v.p. exploration and prodn., 1983-84, pres., 1985-87, pres. Marathon Petroleum Co., 1982-83; vice-chmn. energy USX Corp., Pitts., 1987—, exec. dir.; bd. dirs. Tex. Oil & Gas Corp, Pitts. Nat. Bank, PNC Fin. Corp., Marathon Oil Co., 1982—; exec. v.p. Oasis Oil Co. of Libya, Inc., Tripoli, 1970-72, pres., 1972-74; exec. dir. USX Corp. Served with USN, 1943-45. Mem. Am. Petroleum Inst. (bd. dirs.), Am. Assn. Petroleum Geologists, Soc. Petroleum Engrs., Am. Geol. Inst., Nat. Petroleum Council, 25 Yr. Club Petroleum Industry. Clubs: Findlay Country, JDM Country, Laurel Valley Golf, Rolling Rock, Pitts. Field. Office: USX Corp 600 Grant St Pittsburgh PA 15219-4776

SWANBERG, CAROL JEAN, system administrator, analyst, programmer; b. N.Y.C., Oct. 28, 1961; d. Raymond J. and Florence J. (Pietrowski) S. BS, U. Pitts., 1983, postgrad. Adminstrv. specialist office admissions and student aid U. Pitts., 1984-85, system adminstr. Joseph M. Katz grad. sch. of bus., 1985—. Contbr. articles to profl. jours. Mem. Am. Mgmt. Assn., Internat. Platform Assn., Nat. Assn. Female Execs. Roman Catholic. Office: U Pitts Grad Sch Bus 315 Mervis Hall Pittsburgh PA 15260

SWANI, PARVESH, transportation company executive; b. Peshawar, North-West Frontier, Pakistan, Sept. 12, 1937; s. Girdhari Lal and Krishna Kumari (Bagga) S.; m. Sushma Khanna, Aug. 28, 1965; children: Sanjay, Rahul. BS, Allahabad (India) U., 1956, MS in Math., 1958; MBA, U. Pitts., 1970. CPA, Fla., CMA. Traffic and operating exec. Indian Railways, various locations, India, 1961-69; traffic planning engr. Pa. Dept. Transp., Harrisburg, 1970-71; sr. cost analyst Seaboard Coastline R.R., Jacksonville, Fla., 1971-74, mgr. econ. analysis, 1974-77; dir. econs. Family Lines Rail System, Jacksonville, 1977-82; asst. v.p. strategic planning and analysis Seaboard System R.R., Jacksonville, 1982-85, v.p. corp. planning and analysis, 1985-86; v.p. joint planning Chessie System R.R., Balt., 1985-86; v.p. fin. and planning Distbn. Services Group CSX Transp., Inc., Balt., 1986—; bd. dirs. Total Distrn. Services, Inc., Balt. Pres. India Cultural Soc. Jacksonville, 1975-76; mem. Nat. Aquarium Balt., 1987—; nat. assoc. Smithsonian Instn., 1986—. Mem. Am. Inst CPA's, Fla. Soc. CPA's, Am. Mgmt. Assn., Council Logistics Mgmt., Md. Acad. Scis., The Planning Forum, Center Club. Office: CSX Transp Inc 100 N Charles St Baltimore MD 21201

SWANSEN, RUSSELL WILLIAM, investor; b. Oak Park, Ill., Aug. 21, 1957; s. William Gustaf and Nancy Ellen (Thayer) S. BA in Econs., Gustavus Adolphus U., 1979; MBA, U. Minn., 1982. Mktg. rsch. analyst Munsingwear, Inc., Mpls., 1979-81; investment officer First Asset Mgmt., 1981-83; v.p., portfolio mgr. Washington Sq. Capital, 1983-86, First Bank System, 1986-87; sr. v.p. Washington Sq. Capital, Mpls., 1987-89, exec. v.p., 1989—. Mem. Mensa. Office: Washington Sq Capital PO Box 9402 512 Nicollet Mall Minneapolis MN 55440

SWANSON, BEVERLY JANE, records and information management executive; b. Willmar, Minn., Jan. 27, 1949; d. Vernon Leroy and Betty Arlene (Schockley) Fullerton; m. Roger William Swanson, Mar. 21, 1970; children: Tammy Marie, Randolph William. BS in Speech, Mankato (Minn.) State U., 1971. Mgmt. analyst, records mgr. Minn. Dept. Hwys., St. Paul, 1974-76; chief records mgr. Minn. Dept. Adminstrn., St. Paul, 1977-79; records mgr. City of Mpls., 1980—. Advisory bd. Minn. Hist. Soc., 1981-83. Named Outstanding Records Mgr. of Yr. IRM mag., 1979. Mem. Assn. Records Mgrs. and Adminstrs. (cert., v.p. region IV 1982-86, membership chmn., sec., treas., v.p., pres. Twin City chpt. 1973-79, mgr. mcpl. county govt. industry action com. 1987—, chair long range planning com. 1987—, parliamentarian Twin City chpt. 1987—, Chpt. Mem. of Yr. award 1980), Inst. Cert. Records Mgrs. and Adminstrs. Lutheran. Home: 7003 164th Ave NW Anoka MN 55303 Office: City of Mpls 300 City Hall Minneapolis MN 55415

SWANSON, CAROLEE GLORIA, commodities trader; b. Beverly, Mass., Oct. 16, 1947; d. Terrence Joseph and Edith Gloria (Swanson) Tavis; m. David Fosdahl, Mar. 24, 1974 (div.); 1 child, Heather Linea; m. Yuri Dadov, Nov. 26, 1986. Promotion asst. Ft. Lauderdale (Fla.) News, 1966-67; prodn. supr. Real Estate Computer Services, Pompano Beach, Fla., 1969-72; asst. graphics Fla. Living Mag., Ft. Lauderdale, 1972-75; supr. computer dept. Commerce Clearing House, Pompano Beach, 1980-82; dispatch asst. State Farm Ins., Ft. Lauderdale, 1982-86; ops. mgr. Norstar Brokerage, Ft. Lauderdale, 1986; asst. mgr. Prestige Investments, Ft. Lauderdale, 1986-87; office mgr. Berk Constrn., Ft. Lauderdale, 1987; asst. trader Multivest Inc., Ft. Lauderdale, 1987—. Author numerous poems. Mem. Internat. Platform Assn., Nat. Orgn. of Poetry for Women, Forresters. Democrat. Lutheran. Home: 220 NE 30th St Pompano Beach FL 33064

SWANSON, CHARLES RICHARD, accountant, oil and gas consultant; b. Tulsa, July 19, 1953; s. Donald Charles and Helen Kathryn (Smith) S.; m. Karen Marcelle Pfister, June 10, 1978; children—Kimberly Marcelle, Laura Kathryn, Philip Charles. BA, Tulane U., 1975, MBA, 1977. CPA, Tex.; cert. data processing. Staff auditor Ernst & Whinney, Houston, 1977-79; sr. auditor, 1979-81, oil and gas cons., 1981-84, sr. mgr. energy industry services, 1984-87; ptnr. Swanson Petroleum Enterprises, Houston, 1979-87; bd. dirs. Stratamodel, Inc., Houston, Swanson Geol. Services, Houston. Contbr. articles to profl. jours. Mem. Rep. Nat. Com., 1982. Teagle Found. scholar, 1971-75. Mem. Tulane Assn. Bus. Alumni (pres. 1982), Am. Inst. CPA's, Tex. Soc. CPA's, Petroleum Accts. Soc., Tex. Ind. Producers and Royalty Owners Assn., Ind. Petroleum Assn. Am., Houston Jaycees, Mensa, Delta Tau Delta (pres. 1971-75). Lutheran. Club: Krewe of Bacchus. Office: Ernst & Whinney 1900 Meidinger Tower Louisville KY 40202

SWANSON, DAVID HEATH, agricultural company executive; b. Aurora, Ill., Nov. 3, 1942; s. Neil H. and Helen J. (McKendry) S.; divorced; children: Benjamin Heath, Matthew Banford. B.A., Harvard U., 1964; M.A., U. Chgo., 1969. Account exec. 1st Nat. Bank Chgo., 1967-69; dep. mgr. Brown Bros. Harriman & Co., N.Y.C., 1969-72; asst. treas. Borden, Inc., N.Y.C., 1972-75; v.p., treas. Continental Grain Co., N.Y.C., 1975-77, v.p. chief fin. officer, 1977-79, gen. mgr. European div., 1979-81, exec. v.p. and gen. mgr. World Grain div., 1981-83, corp. sr. v.p., chief fin. and adminstrv. officer, 1983-86, group pres., 1985-86; pres., chief exec. officer Cen. Soya, Ft. Wayne, Ind., 1986—; adv. bd. U.S. Export-Import Bank, 1985-86; mem. Gov.'s Agrl. Bd. Ind. Bd. dirs. Internat. Policy Council on Agr. and Trade; mem. adv. bd. Purdue U. Agr. Sch. Mem. Council Fgn. Rels. (bd. dirs.), Ind. C. of C. (bd. dirs.), Ft. Wayne C. of C. (bd. dirs.), Ft. Wayne Hist. Soc. (bd. dirs.), Am. Alpine Club (bd. dirs.), Scottish Deerhound of Am. Club, Links Club N.Y.), Racquet and Tennis Club, (N.Y.), Ft. Wayne Country Club, Explorers Club (bd. dirs., sec., v.p.). Republican. Congregationalist. Office: Cen Soya Co Inc 1300 Ft Wayne Nat Bank Bldg Fort Wayne IN 46802

SWANSON, DAVID H(ENRY), economist, educator; b. Anoka, Minn., Nov. 1, 1930; s. Henry Otto and Louise Isabell (Holiday) S.; B.A., St. Cloud State Coll., 1953; M.A., U. Minn., 1955, PhD, Iowa State U., 1987; m. Suzanne Nash, Jan. 19, 1952; children—Matthew David, Christopher James. Economist area devel. dept. No. States Power Co., Mpls., 1955-56, staff asst., v.p. sales, 1956-57, economist indsl. devel. dept., 1957-63; dir. area devel. dept. Iowa So. Utilities Co., Centerville, 1963-67, dir. econ. devel. and research, 1967-70; dir. New Orleans Econ. Devel. Council, 1970-72; div. mgr. Kaiser Aetna Texas, New Orleans, 1972-73; dir. corp. research United Services Automobile Assn., San Antonio, 1973-76; pres. Lantern Corp., 1974-79; adminstr. bus. devel. State of Wis., Madison, 1976-78; dir. Center Indsl. Research and Service, Iowa State U., Ames, 1978-89, mem. mktg. faculty Coll. Bus. Adminstrn., 1979-85; dir. Iowa Devel. Commn., 1982-83; mem. adv. bd. Iowa Venture Capital Fund, 1985-88; dir. Applied Strategies Internat. Ltd., 1983-88; chief indsl. extension div. Ga. Inst. Tech., Atlanta, 1989—; chmn. Iowa Curriculum Assistance System, 1984-85. Mem. Iowa Airport Planning Council, 1968-70; mem. adv. council office Comprehensive Health Planning, 1967-70; mem. adv. council Ctr. Indsl. Research and Service, 1967-70, New Orleans Met. Area Com., 1972-73; mem. Iowa Dist. Export Council, 1978-88; mem. Atlanta Dist. Export Coun., 1989—; mem. region 7 adv. council SBA, 1978-88; dir. Mid-Continent R&D Council, 1980-84; chmn. Iowa del. White House Conf. on Small Bus., 1980; chmn. Gov.'s Task Force on High Tech., 1982-83; chmn. Iowa High Tech. Council, 1983-86; adv. com. U. New Orleans, 1971-73; county finance chmn. Republican Party, 1966-67; bd. dirs. Greater New Orleans Urban League, 1970-73, Indsl. Policy Council, 1984-88; mem. Iowa Gov.'s Export Council, 1984-89; v.p. Iowa Sister State Friendship Com., 1985-87, pres. 1988; Fed. lab. Consortium, 1985—. Served with USAF, 1951-52. C.P.C.U. Mem. Nat. Assn. Mgmt. Tech. Assistance Ctrs. (pres. 1985, bd. dirs. 1986—), Tech. Transfer Soc. (bd. dirs. 1984—, v.p. 1987—), Nat. Univ. Continuing Edn. Assn., Internat. Council Small Bus. Republican. Episcopalian. Clubs: Rotary (bd. dirs. 1986-88), Toastmasters (past pres.). Home: 3840 Savannah Sq W Atlanta GA 30340 Office: Ga Tech Rsch Inst Ga Inst Tech Atlanta GA 30332

SWANSON, HOWARD PAUL, airline executive; b. N.Y.C., May 7, 1926; s. Max and Gertrude (Handsman) S.; m. Sylvia Senturia, June 13, 1954; children—Linda, Richard. A.B., Bklyn. Coll., 1949; J.D., Harvard U., 1952. Bar: Ill. 1955. Tax acct. S.D. Leidesdorf & Co., Chgo., 1952-55; tax acct. U.S. Gypsum Co., Chgo., 1955-56; with M.W. Kellogg Co., N.Y.C., 1956-62; from asst. tax mgr. to tax mgr. 1956-60, asst. treas., mgr. tax. dept., 1960-62; dir. tax adminstrn. NBC, N.Y.C., 1962-63; treas. Trans World Airlines Inc., N.Y.C., 1963-66, v.p., treas., 1966-68; sr. v.p. fin. and legal Hudson Pulp & Paper Corp., N.Y.C., 1968-81; exec. v.p. fin. Braniff Internat., Dallas, 1981; pres. The Hampton Orgn., Boca Raton, Fla., 1981-83; v.p. fin., chief fin. officer Continental Airlines, Houston, 1983-84; vice chmn., dir. Continental Airlines Corp., Houston, 1984-88. Mem. Fin. Execs. Inst., ABA, Internat. Fiscal Assn. Clubs: Harvard (N.Y.C.); Tower (Fort Lauderdale, Fla.). Address: 9289 Pecky Cypress Ln Boca Raton FL 33428

SWANSON, RICHARD PAUL, busines educator; b. Kansas City, Mo., July 21, 1935; s. Geraldin (Rodd) Swanson Sirene; m. Joy Ann Hazard, July 23, 1955; children: Terry, Jeri, Denise, Richard Jr., William, Casey. BS, U. So. Miss., 1969; MBA, U. Nev., Las Vegas, 1972; diploma, Indsl. Coll. Armed Forces, 1974; D of Bus. Adminstrn, Internat. Grad. Sch., 1986. Enlisted USAF, 1954, advanced through grades to capt., 1972, ret., 1979; dean Phillips Coll., Gulfport, Miss., 1979-84, Brown-Mackie Coll., Salina, Kans., 1984-86; dir. Career Community Coll. Bus., New Orleans, 1986—. Bd. dirs. Gulfport Job Corps, 1981-84. Grantee Assn. Ind. Colls. and Schs., 1987; recipient Dana Hart award AICS, 1987. Mem. Nat. Bus. Edn. Assn., New Orleans C. of C., Pen & Sword. Republican. Roman Catholic. Club: Optimists. Lodge: Lions. Home: 429 Briargrove St Slidell LA 70458 Office: Career Community Coll Bus 7166 Crowder Blvd New Orleans LA 70127

SWANSON, ROBERT KILLEN, management consultant; b. Deadwood, S.D., Aug. 11, 1932; s. Robert Claude and Marie Elizabeth (Kersten) S.; m. Nancy Anne Oyaas, July 19, 1958; children: Cathryn Lynn, Robert Stuart, Bart Killen. B.A., U. S.D., 1954; postgrad., U. Melbourne, Australia, 1955. With Gen. Mills, Inc., Mpls., 1955-58, 71-79, v.p., 1971-73, group v.p., 1973-77, exec. v.p., 1977-79; with Marathon Oil Co., Findlay, Ohio, 1958-60; sr. v.p., dir. Needham, Harper & Steers, Inc., Chgo., 1961-69; joint mng. dir. S. H. Benson (Holdings) Ltd., Eng., 1969-71; pres., chief operating officer Greyhound Corp., Phoenix, 1980; chmn., chief exec. officer Del E. Webb Corp., Phoenix, 1981-87; chmn. RKS Inc., Phoenix, 1987—; bd. dirs. Grossman's, Inc., Conzept Internat. Trustee Scripps Clinic and Rsch. Found., Ariz. State U. Found.; bd. dirs. Phoenix Art Mus., Ariz. chpt. Am. Cancer Soc., Univ. S.D. Found. 2nd lt. U.S. Army, 1955. Fulbright scholar, 1954-55; Woodrow Wilson scholar. Mem. U.S. Coun. Fgn. Rels., U.K. Dirs. Inst., U.S. Internat. Scholars Assn. Episcopalian. Club: Phoenix Country. Lodge: Masons. Office: RKS Inc 3003 N Central Ave Ste 1800 Phoenix AZ 85012

SWANSON, THOMAS JOSEPH, mortgage company executive; b. Perry, Fla., July 16, 1928; s. Thomas Joseph and Isabelle (Biaza) S.; m. Marylee Young, Apr. 1, 1951. BA in Edn., Fla. State U., 1950; LLB, John Marshall Law Sch., 1957; cert. mortgage banking, Northwestern U., 1968. With claims div. Gen. Accident Fire and Life Assurance Co., Atlanta, 1955-58; v.p. quality control ops., SE regional office Fed. Nat. Mortgage Assn., Atlanta, 1958—. Mem. Atlanta Symphony Orchestra Guild, High Mus. of Art, Ga. Trust Hist. Preservation, Atlanta Steinway Soc. Mem. State Bar Assn. Ga. (real property law sect.), Mortgage Bankers Am., Mortgage Bankers Ga., Atlanta City Club, East Lake Country Club. Republican. Episcopalian. Home: 3982 Club Dr Atlanta GA 30319 Office: Fed Nat Mortgage Assn 950 E Paces Ferry Rd Atlanta GA 30326

SWARTHOUT, JOHN VANLEWEN, brokerage house professional; b. Tampa, Fla., July 18, 1945; s. John Max and Mary A. (Cianfoni) S.; m. Kathleen A. Deal, Aug. 19, 1984; 1 child; Jaime Michaela. Student, U. Washington, 1963-65, U. Utah, 1965; BA, Portland State U., 1967; MA, Ind. U., 1968. Cert. fin. planner; lic. securities broker, commodities broker. Instr. polit. sci. Tacoma Community Coll., 1968-73; mgmt. coordinator, personnel dir. Multnomah County, Portland, Oreg., 1973-75; indsl. engring. cons. Ritchie & Assoc., Los Angeles, 1976-77; personnel mgr. AAR Western Skyways, Troutdale, Oreg., 1977-80; stockbroker Kidder Peabody & Co., Portland, 1980-85, cons., 1985-88; equity mgr. ManEquity Inc., Portland, 1985-89; owner John Swarthout & Assocs., Investment Advisors, Portland, 1989—; instr., Portland State U., 1973-75. Bd. dirs. Am. Heritage Assn., Lake Oswego Oreg., 1984—. Nat. Def. Fgn. Lang. fellow U. Utah, 1965, NSF fellow Ind. U., 1967-68. Mem. Western Polit. Sci. Assn., Northwest Polit. Sci. Assn., Theta Delta Phi, Sigma Nu. Clubs: City, Willamette Athletic (Portland), Western Fitness and Racquet. Home and Office: 6970 SW Gable Pkwy Portland OR 97225

SWARTZ, JAMES RICHARD, investment company executive; b. Pitts., Oct. 4, 1942; s. Frank Thomas and Mary Elizabeth (Roth) S.; m. Susan Lee Shallcross, June 18, 1966; children: James Scott, Karin Lynn, Kristin Lee. AB, Harvard, 1964; MS in Indsl. Adminstrn., Carnegie-Mellon U., 1966. Asst. to v.p. mfg. Campbell Soup Co., Camden, N.J., 1966-68; sr. asso. Cresap, McCormick & Paget, N.Y.C., 1968-72; asst. v.p. G.H. Walker, Laird Inc., N.Y.C., 1972-74; v.p. Citicorp Venture Capital Ltd., N.Y.C., 1974-78; gen. partner Adler & Co., N.Y.C., 1978-83; mng. ptnr. Accel Ptnrs., 1983—; chmn. Patterson & Swartz, Inc., Princeton and San Francisco, 1983—; dir. Broadband Techs., Inc., Fleming Ventures, Netlink, Parallax Corp., Phys. Acoustics Corp., Sports Medicine Systems, Inc., Teleos Inc., WaferScale Integration, Inc.; chmn. Perceptron, Inc., pres. N.Y. Venture Forum, 1977-78. Mem. Nat. Venture Capital Assn. (chmn. bd. dir.). Republican. Clubs: Harvard (Boston, N.Y.C. and Princeton); Bd. Room, Racquet and Tennis (N.Y.C.); Nassau (N.J.); Boston. Home: 15 Hibben Rd Princeton NJ 08540 Office: One Palmer Sq Princeton NJ 08542

SWARTZ, WILLIAM JOHN, transportation resources company executive; b. Hutchinson, Kans., Nov. 6, 1934; s. George Glen and Helen Mae (Prather) S.; m. Dorothy Jean Parshall, June 5, 1956; children: John Christopher, Jeffrey Michael. BSME, Duke U., 1956; JD, George Washington U., 1961; MS in Mgmt. (Alfred P. Sloan fellow), MIT, 1967. With AT & SF Ry., 1961-78, 79—, asst. v.p. exec. dept., 1973-77, v.p. adminstrn., 1977-78, exec. v.p., 1979-83; exec. v.p. Santa Fe Industries, Chgo., 1978-79, pres., 1983—; vice chmn. Santa Fe So. Pacific, 1983—; pres. AT & SF Ry., 1983—. Bd. dirs. Chgo. Mus. Sci. and Industry. Served with USMC, 1956-59. Mem. Chgo. Assn. Commerce and Industry, Western Ry. Assn., Assn. Am. R.R. (bd. dirs.). Republican. Methodist. Clubs: Chgo. Athletic Assn., Mid-Am., Chgo. Home: 233 E Walton Pl Chicago IL 60611 Office: Atchison Topeka & Santa Fe Ry Co 80 E Jackson Blvd Chicago IL 60604

SWARZMAN, HERBERT GEORGE, investment banking executive; b. N.Y.C., May 29, 1937; s. Herman and Mollie (Mosberg) S.; m. Abby Levingson, Jan. 29, 1961 (div. May 1971); 1 child, David; m. Joyce Burick, Feb. 12, 1976; 1 child, Elizabeth Barbara. BA, Dartmouth Coll., 1958; LLB, Bklyn. Law Sch., 1960. Sales and mgmt. Dempsey-Tegeler Co., N.Y.C., 1961-62; with A.G. Becker & Co., N.Y.C., 1963-68; founder, mng. ptnr. Dryfoos & Co., N.Y.C., 1969-73; cons. security firms, 1974-75; founder, pres. Gulfcoast Cons. and Investors Corp., Tampa, Fla., 1976—; pres. Herand Inc., Real Estate Investments, Tampa, 1978—; chmn. N.Am. Steel Corp., Lakeland, Fla., 1979-82; pres. Gulf Coast Realty Investors, Inc., 1981—, West Coast Realty Mgmt. Inc., Tampa. Mem. fin. com. Horace Mann Elem. Sch., N.Y.C., 1971-72; chmn. N.Y.C. interviewing com. for applications for admission Dartmouth, 1965-75, dist. dir. enrollment for N.Y.C., 1974-75, chmn. reunion fund, 1974, pres. Class of 1958, 1974-79; co-chmn. basic gifts Tampa Jewish Fedn., 1977-78; treas. Dem. Com., N.Y.C., 1971-73; co-chmn. fin. Fla. for Reagan Campaign, 1980; del. Rep. Nat. Conv., 1980; spl. advisor on Jewish interests Rep. Party Fl., 1981-84; mem. adv. council SBA of Fla., 1981—; bd. dirs. Univ. Settlement, 1966-68; bd. dirs., treas. Tampa Jewish Fedn., v.p., 1984—; mem. ethics com. Fla. Bar Assn., 1983-87, ethics com. Meml. Hosp., Tampa, 1985—; bd. dirs. Menorah Home, 1987—, Anti-Defamation League, 1987—. Mem. Am.-Israel Pub. Affairs Com. (exec. com. 1981—), Dartmouth Alumni Assn. N.Y.C. (founder, pres. 1975-76). Clubs: Dartmouth (dir., bd. govs. 1974-75), Lawyers (N.Y.C.); Carrollwood Village Golf and Tennis. Home: 4214 Fairway Run Tampa FL 33624

SWASEY, CHESTER CLINTON, chemical company executive; b. N.Y.C., Oct. 5, 1943; s. Alton Raymond and Mildred (Van Alstyne) S.; m. Margret Ann Harrington, July 6, 1968; children: Alayne, Alexandra. BS in Chemistry, CCNY, 1965; MBA, Fairleigh Dickinson U., 1973. Research chemist St. Regis Paper Co., West Nyack, N.Y., 1967-71; mgr. quality assurance Rexene Polymers div. Dart Industries, Paramus, N.J., 1972-73; mgr. mktg. Sandoz Colors & Chems., East Hanover, N.J., 1973-81; pres. BK Ladenburg Corp., Cresskill, N.J., 1981—; bd. dirs. BK Ladenburg Corp., Cresskill. Contbr. articles on Polymer sci. to profl. jours. Patentee in field. Mem. bd. edn. Demarest, N.J., 1978-81, pres. 1981; vice chmn. Zoning Bd., Demarest, 1985-88; v.p. Nature Ctr., Demarest, 1985-88. 1st lt. U.S. Army, 1965-67, Vietnam. N.Y. State Regents scholar, 1961; recipient award TAPPI, 1970. Mem. Soc. Plastics Engrs. (dir. 1978-80), Am. Chem. Soc., Inst. Food Technologists. Republican. Presbyterian. Home: 35 County Rd Demarest NJ 07627 Office: BK-Ladenburg Corp 50 Spring St Cresskill NJ 07626

SWAYNE, CRAIG FRANKLYN, real estate holding company executive; b. San Francisco, June 4, 1954; s. Lloyd Jr. and Edith (Merrell) S. BBA, U. Denver, 1977. Ptnr. Combs Swayne & Valido, San Francisco, 1980-82; assoc. San Francisco Group, 1982-83; exec. v.p., bd. dirs. Vinex Imports Inc., San Francisco, 1977—; chief exec. officer, dir. San Francisco Warehouse Property Co., 1982—; cons. Urban Investment & Development Corp., Denver, 1977, Chappell & Co., San Francisco, 1984; bd. dirs., cons. Mi-Tech Co., Berkeley, Calif., 1982-84; bd. dirs. Timeless Travels, Inc., San Francisco. Mem. Am. Assn. Individual Investors, Inst. Econometric Research, Oceanic Soc., Master Mariners Benevolent Assn., Classic Sports Racing Assn. Clubs: Corinthian Yacht (Tiburon, Calif.), St. Francis Yacht (San Francisco). Office: San Francisco Warehouse Property Co 17 Osgood Pl San Francisco CA 94133

SWEARINGEN, JOHN ELDRED, business executive; b. Columbia, S.C., Sept. 7, 1918; s. John Eldred and Mary (Hough) S.; m. Bonnie L. Bolding, May 18, 1969; children by previous marriage: Marcia L. Swearingen Pfleeger, Sarah K. Swearingen Origer, Linda S. Swearingen Arnold. B.S., U. S.C., 1938, LL.D. (hon.), 1965; M.S., Carnegie-Mellon U., 1939, D.Eng. (hon.), 1981; hon. degrees from other colls. and univs. With Standard Oil Co. (Ind.), Whiting, Ind., 1939-83, chem. engr., 1939, various positions, 1939-53; v.p. prodn. Standard Oil Co. (Ind.), 1954-56, exec. v.p., 1956-58, pres., 1958-65, chief exec. officer, 1960-83, chmn. bd., 1965-83 (ret.); chmn., chief exec. officer Continental Ill. Corp., Chgo., 1984-87, chmn. exec. com., 1987-88, ret., 1988; dir. Lockheed Corp., Continental Ill. Corp., Continental Ill. Nat. Bank and Trust Co. Chgo., Sara Lee Corp., AON Corp.; chmn. Nat. Petroleum Council, 1974-76, Am. Petroleum Inst., 1978-79. Former dir. Am. Nat.Bank Chgo., 1957-60, 1st Nat. Bank Chgo. and 1st Chgo. Corp., 1960-73, Chase Manhattan Corp. and Chase Manhattan Bank N.A., 1960-84; mem. adv. bd. Hoover Instn. on War, Revolution and Peace, 1967—; trustee Carnegie Mellon U., 1960—, DePauw U., 1966-81, Chgo. Orchestral Assn., 1973-79; bd. dirs. McGraw Wildlife Found., 1964-75; bd. dirs. Automotive Safety Found., 1959-69, chmn., 1962-64; bd. dirs. Hwy Users Fedn. for Safety and Mobility, 1969-75; trustee Northwestern Meml. Hosp. Corp. (life); chmn. Nat. Petroleum Coun., 1974-76, Am. Petroleum Inst., 1978-79; pres. Boys and Girls Clubs Chgo., 1982-84, chmn. 1984-86. Recipient decorations from govts. of Iran, Italy, Egypt, Phillipines; recipient Washington award Western Soc. Engrs., 1981, Gold medal for disting. achievement Am. Petroleum Inst., 1983; Laureate, Nat. Bus. Hall of Fame, Jr. Achievement, 1984. Fellow Am. Inst. Chem. Engrs.; mem. Am. Inst. Mining, Metall. and Petroleum Engrs. (Charles F. Rand Meml. gold medal 1980), Am. Chem. Soc., Nat. Acad. Engring., Phi Beta Kappa, Sigma Xi, Omicron Delta Kappa, Tau Beta Pi. Clubs: Mid-Am., Chgo., Racquet (Chgo.); Links (N.Y.C.); Bohemian (San Francisco); Eldorado Country (Indian Wells, Calif.); Old Elm (Lake Forest, Ill.); Glen View (Golf, Ill.). Office: 200 E Randolph Dr Ste 6538 Chicago IL 60601

SWEAS, GERALD JOSEPH, financial executive; b. Chgo., Nov. 6, 1947; s. John and Helen (Wojnicki) S.; m. Sharleen Marie Barron, Nov. 9, 1947; children: Jason, Megan. BBA, Loyola U., Chgo., 1969; MBA, U. Wis., Madison, 1972. CPA, Ill. Audit mgr. Touche Ross & Co., Chgo., 1972-78; contr. Sargent-Welsh Sci. Co., Skokie, Ill., 1978-85; v.p. fin., chief fin. officer, treas. Sargent-Welsh Sci. Co., 1985—. Wtih U.S. Army, 1969-71, Vietnam. Mem. Fin. Execs. Inst., Am. Inst. CPA's, Ill. Inst. CPA's, Beta Gamma Sigma, Beta Alpha Psi, Economic Club, Chicago Soc. Club. Home: 511 Linden Ave Willmette IL 60091 Office: Sargent-Welch Sci Co 7300 N Linder Ave Skokie IL 60077

SWEATMAN, PHILLIP JAY, retail company executive, financial executive; b. Norfolk, Va., Sept. 23, 1955; s. Julius Caleb and Lucille (Nollet) S.;

m. Lynne Denise Baltic, June 27, 1980; children: Phillip Charles Julius, Adrienne Nicole.. BSBA in Econs., U. Denver, 1978; MBA in Fin., U. Pitts., 1982. Chartered fin. analyst. Asst. officer Mellon Bank Corp., Pitts., 1979-81, planning officer, 1983-84; fin. planning analyst Copperweld Corp., Pitts., 1981-83; bus. planning analyst Computer Sci. Corp., El Segundo, Calif., 1984-85, mgr. strategy and analysis, 1985-86; controller, asst. sec. CSC Comtec Inc., Farmington Hills, Mich., 1986-87; corp. controller Franks Nursery & Crafts Inc, Detroit, 1987—; founder, pres., chmn. P$L Computer Services Ltd., Pitts., 1983—. Recipient Univ. Honors Scholarship U. Denver, 1976-78. Mem. Fin. Analyst Soc. Detroit, Controllers Council, Nat. Assn. Accts. Republican. Roman Catholic. Lodge: Rotary. Home: 25612 Livingston Circle Farmington Hills MI 48331 Office: Frank's Nursery and Crafts Inc 6501 E Nevada Detroit MI 48234

SWEATT, JOHN W., insurance executive. s. John Eugene and Dorothy (Snyder) S.; m. Kathleen June Capurro, Dec. 26, 1947; children: Christine Burrows, Sherry Ober, John Richard. BS, UCLA, 1946; BA, U. Nev., 1947. Cert. ins. counselor. Treas. Am. Bapt. Fgn. Mission Soc., N.Y.C., 1947-48; underwriter, field rep. Continental Ins. Co., San Francisco, 1948-53; ins. dept. mgr. J.E. Sweatt Realty Co., Reno, 1953-57; founder, pres. Comstock Ins. Agys., Reno, 1957—. Pres. Am. Bapt. Chs. West, Oakland, Calif., 1985-86, No. Nev. Bd. Trade, Reno, 1973-74; bd. dirs. Am. Bapt. Chs. USA, Valley Forge, Pa., 1985—. Recipient Agt. of Yr. award Nat. Assn. Mut. Ins. Agts., 1975, Mr. Chmn. award Am. Assn. Mng. Gen. Agts. Las Vegas, 1983, Agt. of Yr. award Nat. Assn. Profl. Ins. Agts., San Francisco, 1984. Mem. Soc. Cert. Ins. Counselors, Nev. Ins. Edn. Found. (pres. 1985-86), Ins. Assn. Nev. (pres. 1973-75), Far West Conf. Surplus Lines Assn. (organizer, treas. 1970-71), Western Indsl. Club Nev., Reno Press Club, Masons. Republican. Office: Comstock Ins Agys 200 Kirman Ave Reno NV 89502

SWEEN, EARL A., food products executive; b. Mpls., Jan. 4, 1921; s. August E. and Florence E. Sween; student U. Minn., 1938-42; m. Shirley Ann Ogin, Feb. 14, 1942; children—Deborah Ann, Thomas Earl. Gen. mgr. Sween Bros. Dairy Farms, Inc., Chanhassen and Wayzata, Minn., 1938-53; rte. supr. Franklin Dairy Co., Mpls., 1953-55; propr., mgr. Stewart Sandwiches, Eden Prairie, Minn., 1955—, chmn. bd. dirs., 1978—; pres. Nat. Stewart Infrared Assn., Fontana, Wis., 1965-66. Mem. Republican Nat. Com.; sustaining mem. Boy Scouts Am. Clubs: Lafayette Country, Decathlon Athletic, Port Royal, Naples Sail and Yacht, Jesters. Lodges: Masons, Shriners. Home: 1400 Spyglass Ln Naples FL 33940 Office: 16101 W 78th St Eden Prairie MN 55344

SWEENEY, DANIEL BRYAN, JR., financial adviser, pension fund administrator; b. Providence, Oct. 23, 1946; s. Daniel Bryan Sr. and Clara Perene (Hodgdon) S.; m. Carol Jane Weir, June 18, 1966; children: Heather, Holly. AS in Electronic Engring., San Mateo Community Coll., 1969. CLU. Tax specialist Northwestern Nat. Life, Minn., 1974-81; pres. Dan Sweeney & Assocs., Inc., Bellevue, Wash., 1981—; pres., trustee Davis-Bacon Pension Adminstrn., Inc., Bellevue, 1987—. Author: Investment Planning Ideas, 1983. With USN, 1964-70. Mem. Internat. Assn. Fin. Planners, Eastside Estate Planning Coun., Masons, Elks. Office: Davis-Bacon Pension Adminstrn 11911 NE First St #102 Bellevue WA 98005

SWEENEY, ELIZABETH ANN, medical center executive; b. Birmingham, Ala., Nov. 9, 1946; d. Huretta and Elizabeth (Whisenant) Chappell; children: Wesley, Hugh Mitchell. BSN, U. Ala., 1973, MSN, 1975. Staff nurse VA Med. Ctr., Birmingham, 1972-74; asst. prof. nursing Sch. Nursing U. Ala., Birmingham, 1975-79; coordinator nursing services Cen. City Mental Health Ctr., Los Angeles, 1979-80; nurse educator VA Med. Ctr., Los Angeles, 1980—; asst. clin. prof. nursing Sch. Nursing U. Calif., Los Angeles, 1984—; dir. med. ctr. edn. and tng. Kaiser Permanente Med. Ctr., Bellflower, Calif., 1989—; Guest faculty mem. Stanford U., Palo Alto, Calif., 1984; mem. conf. faculty United Nurses Assn. Calif., 1982, 83, 87, Calif. Park and Recreation Soc. Conf., Sacramento, 1985, 86; Equal Employment Opportunity investigator VA, Washington, 1985—. Contbr. articles to profl. jours. Recipient Commendation for Superior Performance Fed. Exec. Bd., Los Angeles, 1984. Mem. Ala. Nurses Assn. (exec. bd. dirs. 1976-79), Am. Nurses Assn., Calif. Nurses Assn., Nat. Assn. Female Execs., Black Women's Network, Coun. Black Nurses. Office: Kaiser Permanente Med Ctr 9400 E Rosecrans Annex bldg Bellflower CA 90706

SWEENEY, GEORGE BERNARD, JR., broadcast executive, travel agency executive; b. Cleve., May 9, 1933; s. George Bernard and Ethel E. (Wise) S.; BS in Bus. Adminstrn., John Carroll U., 1955; MBA., U. Pa., 1957; m. Molly Jane O'Neill, July 13, 1963; children: Brian, Kelly, Mark, Kevin, Kim. With Exxon Corp., 1956-78, chmn., pres. Esso Pakistan Fertilizer Co., Karachi, 1969-74, v.p. Exxon Corp. and Exxon Chem. U.S.A., Houston, 1974-78; dir., prin. Chagrin Valley Co. Ltd., Cleve., 1977-81; dir. Nevamar Corp., Odenton, Md., Evergreen Capital Corp., Austin, Tex., Mapleleaf Capital Corp., Houston; chmn. bd. A/L Sports, Inc., Denver, 1979-83; bd. dirs. Resource Bank, Houston, 1985-87; pres., prin. Questers, Inc., Houston, 1979—; pres., prin. Stas. KMUV/KPHD, Conroe, Tex., 1984—, Sweeney Broadcasting Co., 1984—; pres., prin. Travel Network Sweeney Travel Quest Inc., 1987—. Bd. dirs., v.p. Houston Symphony, 1976—; trustee John Carroll U., Cleve., 1977—, Strake Jesuit Coll. Prep., Houston, 1979-85; trustee, chmn. bd. Trinity Coll., Washington, 1974-80; exec. bd. Wharton Grad. Sch., U. Pa., 1980-85; trustee, bd. dirs., exec. com. U. St. Thomas, Houston, 1982-88, chmn. pres.'s forum, 1988—; bd. dirs. Tex. Hunter-Jumper Assn., 1981-87; dir., v.p. Houston Hunter Jumper Charity Horse Show, 1983-88; chmn. "Friends of St. Francis" Franciscan Mission Service, Silver Springs, Md., 1987—, also bd. dirs. Served to 1st lt. Transp. Corps, U.S. Army, 1958. Recipient in Pakistan U.S. State Dept. citation of appreciation, 1974, John Carroll U. Centennial medal, 1986. Clubs: Houston, Houstonian Club. Lodge: Ancient Order of Hibernians. Home: Rt 1 Box 12 Macedonia Rd Hockley TX 77447-9712

SWEENEY, JAMES LEE, retired government official; b. Rocky River, Ohio, Mar. 23, 1930; s. John H. and Mary J. (Walkinshaw) S.; m. Marion J. Ridley, Oct. 4, 1958; children: John A., James L. BBA, Case-Western Res. U., 1959. Cost acct. AFB, Dayton, Ohio, 1959-62; acct. Def. Electronics Supply Center, Dayton, 1962-64, budget analyst, 1964-67, budget officer, 1967-74, supervisory budget analyst, 1974-82, supervisory mgmt. analyst, 1982, supervisory program analyst, 1983—; pres. 3001 Hoover Inc.; mem. tax adv. com. Dayton-Montgomery County, 1967-70. Bd. dirs. Dayton Human Relations Commn., 1970-74, Model Cities Housing Corp., 1972-74, M & M Broadcasting Co., Ohio Valley Broadcasting Co., 1979-81; vestryman, treas. St. Margaret's Episc. Ch. Served with U.S. Army, 1952-54. Recipient Public Service award Def. Electronics Supply Cen., 1972, Meritorious Civilian Service award, 1981, Unity award in Media, Lincoln U., 1982-83, Disting. Career award Def. Electonics Supply Ctr., 1986. Mem. Alpha Phi Alpha. Producer, commentator Spl. Community Report Sta. WHIO-TV, twice weekly 1970-76, daily, 1976—, producer, commentator Spotlight; spl. cons. Sta. WHIO-TV. Home: 743 Argonne Dr Dayton OH 45408

SWEENEY, JULIA, public relations executive; b. Ladonia, Tex., Feb. 2, 1927; d. Albert Earle and Julia (Nunn) S. Grad. Am. Acad., N.Y.C., 1946; student So. Meth. U., 1958-59. Asst. mgr. Ambrosia House, Milw., 1951-56; sec. Neiman-Marcus, Dallas, 1956-70, publicity dir., 1970-74; columnist, feature writer Dallas Times Herald, 1974-81; pres. Callas, Foster & Sweeney, Dallas, 1982—; bd. dirs. Fidelity Nat. Bank of Dallas. Bd. dirs. Boys' Clubs Dallas, Inc., No. Tex. chpt. Arthritis Found., N.E. Tex. chpt. Cystic Fibrosis Found.; trustee Protection of Animal World Soc.; mem. March of Dimes Women's Aux., Dallas Theater Ctr. Women's Com., Dallas Ballet Women's Com. Mem. Pub. Rels. Soc. of Am., Women in Communications, The Women's Found., Dallas C. of C., Dallas Symphony Orch. League, Dallas Mus. Art League, Dallas County Heritage Soc., Dallas Hist. Soc., Les Femmes Du Monde, Charter 100. Episcopalian. Office: Callas Foster & Sweeeney 2515 McKinney Ave Dallas TX 75201

SWEENEY, MARY CAROLYN, association executive; b. Balt.; d. Talmadge W. and Louella (Cox) Farmmer; m. William A. Sweeney, 1958; children: Diane, David. AS in Bus. Adminstrn., Del. Community Coll., 1979; B in Social Work, Widener U., 1982, BA in Psychology, 1982; MBA, Temple U., 1983. Property mgr., investment cons. Sweeney and Funderburg, Norwood, Pa., 1970—; owner, mgr. M.C. Sweeney & Co., Drexel Hill, Pa., 1970-75; adminstr. Children & Youth Services, Media, Pa., 1980-81, Del. County Services for the Aging, Media, 1982-83; dir. admissions and social services Chester (Pa.) Extended Care, 1983-84; dir. services Del. County Assn. for the Blind, Chester, 1984-87; exec. dir. Assn. for the Blind and Visually Impaired, Norristown, Pa., 1987—. Co-author: Death and Dying, 1983. Planner Greater Valley Forge C. of C., Norristown, 1987; coordinator United Way, Phila., 1984-87; active Del. County C. of C., 1984-87. Mem. Assn. for Edn. and Rehab. for the Blind and Visually Impaired, Am. Assn. for Univ. Women, Assn. for the Blind (bd. dirs.), Travel Aids for the Blind (chmn. fin. com., bd. dirs.), Southeastern Regional for the Death/Blind (adv. bd.), Council of and for the Blind (exec. bd.), Supportive Employment Assn. (adv. bd.), Pa. Council for the Blind, Mid-County Lions (v.p., 1987—). Home: 66 Winding Way Boothwyn PA 19061 Office: Assn for the Blind and Visually Impaired 704 W Marshall St Norristown PA 19401

SWEENEY, ROBERT JOHN, banking executive; b. San Antonio, Feb. 22, 1946; s. John Henry and Margaret Anne (Hauser) S.; m. Sandra Ann Dyer, June 9, 1973; children: Colin Edmond, Maureen Grayson, Megan Ann. BBA, St. Mary's U., San Antonio, 1968; postgrad., Southwest Grad. Sch. Banking, So. Meth. U., 1978, U. Okla., 1983-85. CPA, Tex. Staff acct. Price Waterhouse & Co., Houston, 1968-71; asst. controller Seiscom Delta, Houston, 1971-73; v.p., trust officer Tex. Comml. Bancshares Inc., Houston, 1973-79; exec. v.p. Tex. Am. Bank, Houston, 1979-86, pres., chief exec. officer Spring br., 1986-87, exec. v.p. Galleria NA, 1987—, also bd. dirs. Mem. sch. bd. St. Francis de Sales, Houston, 1987; vice chmn. bd. dirs. Downtown YMCA, Houston, 1986; trustee Mus. Art Am. West, Houston, 1987. Served with U.S. Army, 1968-74. Mem. Am. Inst. CPAs, Tex. Soc. CPAs (bd. dirs. 1985—), Houston Chpt. CPAs (v.p. 1982-83), Houston Estate and Fin. Forum (pres. 1986), Bldg. and Estate Planning Council (past pres.). Republican. Roman Catholic. Office: Tex Am Bank/Galleria NA 2800 Post Oak Houston TX 77056

SWEENEY, ROBERT JOSEPH, JR., retired oil executive; b. Montpelier, Vt., Oct. 23, 1927; s. Robert Joseph and Glenna Ethylin (Little) S.; m. Hazel Miller, Mar. 7, 1947; children: Robert Joseph, III, Theodore C., James Bradford. B.S., Auburn U., 1948; M.S., La. Tech. U., 1961. With Murphy Oil Corp., El Dorado, Ark., 1952-87; pres., chief operating officer Murphy Oil Corp., 1972-84, chief exec. officer, 1984-87; dir. Fed. Res. Bank St. Louis, 1983-88. Pres. El Dorado Boys Club, 1968, 74-78; trustee El Dorado YWCA, 1982-86. Served with USNR, 1945-46. Mem. AIME, Am. Petroleum Inst. (bd. dirs., exec. com.), Nat. Assn. Mfrs. (bd. dirs.).

SWEENEY, ROGER DAMIEN, manufacturing company executive; b. Pearl River, N.Y., Sept. 9, 1942; s. Roger Joseph and Gladys Georgette (DeLisle) S.; m. Barbara Adele Hessling, Sept. 4, 1965; children: Damien Joseph, Roger Anthony, Mark DeLisle. BSME, U.S. Naval Acad., 1964; MBA, Xavier U., 1972. Mfg. mgr. Procter and Gamble, Cin., 1969-70; plant engr. Signode Corp., Florence, Ky., 1970-73; mfg., distbg. mgr. Avon Products, Cin., 1973-77; con. McKinsey and Co., Cleve., 1977-81; product mgr. GE Co., Portsmouth, Va., 1981-83; pres. Hammerblow Corp., Wausau, Wis., 1983—; dir. Norac Corp., Wausau, 1987—. Pres. Wausau Symphony, Wausau, 1988—. Lt. comdr. USN, 1960-72. Republican. Roman Catholic. Home: 1002 Fulton St Wausau WI 54401 Office: The Hammerblow Corp 1000 First St Wausau WI 54401

SWEENEY, STEPHEN JOSEPH, electric utility company executive; b. Winthrop, Mass., Dec. 15, 1928; s. Stephen Joseph and Florence Fisher (Brown) S.; m. Genevieve Marie Barretta, May 17, 1952; children: Andrea Elizabeth, Paula Marie. B.A., Mt. St. Mary's Coll., Emmitsburg, Md., 1950; A.E.E., Northeastern U., 1957; P.M.D., Harvard U., 1963, A.M.P., 1979. Registered profl. engr., Mass. Dir. pub. affairs Boston Edison Co., 1974-76, v.p. ops., 1976-80, sr. v.p., 1980-83, exec. v.p., dir., 1983, pres., dir., 1983-84; pres., chief exec. officer, dir. Bank of Boston, 1984-86, chmn., pres., chief exec. officer, 1986—; dir. Liberty Mut. Ins. Co., Liberty Mut. Fire Ins. Co. Served as 1st lt. U.S. Army, 1950-53, Korea. Decorated Bronze Star. Democrat. Roman Catholic. Home: 7 Greenbrook Rd South Hamilton MA 01982 Office: Boston Edison Co 800 Boylston St Boston MA 02199

SWEET, JUDITH ELLEN, banker; b. Rouses Point, N.Y., July 16, 1939; d. Elwin Bernard and Anna Maud (Pratt) Clark; m. James Herbert Sweet, Dec. 28, 1968; children: Kara Lynn, Wendy Ann. BA, U. Ottawa, Ont., Can., 1967; BS in Bus. and Pub. Mgmt., SUNY, Utica, 1984; MS in Guidance, SUNY, Plattsburgh, 1970. Cert. fin. planner. Tchr. Assumption of Mary Sch., Redford, N.Y., 1960-63, St. Joseph's Sch., Brookfield, Conn., 1963-65, St. Mary Magdalene Sch., Oakville, Conn., 1965-66; tchr. French and English No. Adirondack Cen. Sch., Ellenburg, N.Y., 1966-70; substitute tchr. Chateaugay (N.Y.) Cen. Sch., 1971-74, Oneida (N.Y.) City Sch. Dist., 1979-84; fin. counselor The Savs. Bank of Utica, 1985-86, br. mgr., 1986-87; mgr. fin. services, v.p. SBU Ins. Agy., New Hartford, 1988—; facilitator fin. planning workshops The Savs. Bank of Utica, 1985-87; instr. fin. planning banker's course Am. Inst. Banking, Utica, 1987; speaker SUNY Coll. Tech., utica, 1987; adj. faculty Coll. Fin. Planning. Editor Seneca Smoke Signals, 1980-82; actress play: No Sex Please We're Bitish, 1979. counselor Franklin County Mental Health Svcs., Chateaugay, N.Y., 1971-73; zone chmn. Am. Heart Assn., Oneida, 1977; pres. PTO, Oneida, 1979-81, 1st v.p. 1977-79; 1st v.p. Oneida City Hosp. Aux., 1980-82; bus. canvasser Am. Cancer Soc., Oneida, 1980-82; parent rep. Oneida City Sch. dist., 1984-85, Regional Sch. for Excellence, Oneida-Tri County, 1985-86; bus. canvasser United Way, Utica, 1988. Named Booster of Yr., Seneca St. Sch. PTO, Oneida, 1986; recipient Silver Tray Oneida Silver Streaks, 1985. Mem. Inst. Cert. Fin. Planners, Internat. Assn. Fin. Planners (outreach coord. upstate N.Y. chpt., 1988—), Bus. & Profl. Women's Orgn. (2d v.p. 1987-88, New Careerist of Yr. 1986), Nat. Assn. Security Dealers (registered), SUNY Coll. Tech. Alumni Assn., Progress Lit. Club (rec. sec. 1980-82). Republican. Presbyterian. Clubs: Progress Literary (Oneida) (recording sec. 1982-84), Friends of the Library.

SWEET, MARC STEVEN, fin. exec.; b. Bklyn., Aug. 15, 1945; s. Edward I. and Bess G. (Freiman) S.; B.B.A. (trustees scholar), Pace Coll., 1967; postgrad. Columbia U. Sch. Bus., 1967-68; m. Naomi Charna Fishbein, Aug. 22, 1971; children—Erica Rebekah, Miriam Shoshana, Benjamin Lewis. Sr. staff auditor Arthur Young & Co., 1969-71; asst. corp. controller Liberty Fabrics of N.Y., Inc., 1971-72; corp. accounting mgr. Tetley Inc., 1972-75, corp. budget mgr., 1975-81; corp. controller, asst. sec. Jetro Holdings Inc. and subs., 1981-84; corp. controller Elmhurst Milk & Cream Co. Inc. and subs. and associated corps., 1984-86; chief fin. officer, controller, Modell Group, 1986—. Asst. scoutmaster Boy Scouts Am., 1963-66, mem. Flatbush dist. com., 1965-67, Eagle Scout, recipient Gold palm. C.P.A., N.Y. Texaco Co. scholar. Mem. Am. Inst. C.P.A.s, N.Y. State Soc. C.P.A.s, Scottish Deerhound Club Am. Home: 1282 E 29th St Brooklyn NY 11210

SWEET, ROBERT HENRY, manufacturing executive; b. Hartford, Conn., Aug. 6, 1925; s. William Henry and Frances May (Lawton) S.; m. Audrey Margery Smith; children: Robin Barclay, Margery Lawton, Christopher Leeds, Jonathan Wray; m. Heidi Travisen, Sept. 26, 1981. BS, Bryant Coll., 1949. With The Robbins Co., Attleboro, Mass., 1949—, pres., owner, 1966—. Home: 767 Fifth Ave New York NY 10153 Office: The Robbins Co O'Neil Blvd Attleboro MA 02703

SWEET, SHANE MICHAEL, oil company executive; b. Granville, N.Y., Mar. 2, 1960; s. Keith Edward and Frances (Gilbert) S.; m. Marianne E. Kennedy, Apr. 16, 1987; 1 stepchild, David Kennedy Cutler. Student, Rochester Inst. Tech., 1982. Asst. mgr. Johnson's Fuel Svc. Inc., Granville, N.Y., 1982-83; mgr. Johnson's Fuel Svc. Inc., Granville, 1983-84; gen. mgr. Johnson's Fuel Svc. Inc., Manchester, Vt., 1984-88; pres. Sweet Cons., 1988—; cons. nat. gas pipelines Vt. Oil Heat Inst., Ludlow, 1988—. Mem. adv. bd. Big Bros./Big Sisiters, Bennington, Vt. Mem. Manchester Area Personnel Assn. (founder), Granville C. of C. (v.p. 1983-84), Manchester C. of C., Rotary (sec. Manchester club.). Home: PO Box 232 Manchester VT 05254

SWEETLAND, DAVID LAWRENCE, engineering company executive; b. La Junta, Colo., Dec. 9, 1942; s. Paul C. and Eva F. (Hainline) S.; m. Diane M. Costanzo, July 21, 1968; children: Krista M., Douglas P. BSCE, Pa. State U., 1965, postgrad., 1970. Registered profl. engr., Pa.; registered land surveyor, Pa.; cert. sewage enforcement officer, Pa., sewage treatment plant operaotr, waterworks operator. Lt. (j.g.) coast and geoditic survey ESSA, Norfolk, Va., 1965-67; constrn. engr. Glenn O. Hawbaker, Inc., State College, Pa., 1968-70; pres., exec. mgr. Sweetland Engring. & Assocs., Inc., State College, 1970—; engr., cons. to 15 municipalities. Mem. adv. com. centre region Centre County Indsl. Devel. Corp., Patton Twp. Water Authority, 1981-85, Patton Twp. Home Rule Study Com., 1984-85. Recipient Outstanding Indsl. award Centre County Conservation Dist., 1986. Fellow Am. Congress on Surveying and Mapping (Cen. Pa. sect.); mem. Profl. Engrs. in Pvt. Practice, ASCE, Nat. Soc. Profl. Engrs., Pa. Soc. Profl. Engrs., Soc. Land Surveyors (past pres. Mid-State Pa. chpt.), Am. Pub. Works Assn., Am. Water Works Assn., State College Area C. of C., Lions (charter mem. Patton Twp. club). Office: Sweetland Engring & Assocs Inc 900 W College Ave State College PA 16801

SWEETS, SADIE ELIZABETH, financial executive; b. Butler, Mo., Jan. 27, 1963; d. Scott and Dolly Dimples (Sweets) Shockley. Office asst. Centralfed Mortgage Co. (name changed to Ameristar), San Diego, 1983-85; computer operator, loan processor Calif. Coast Mortgage, 1985; brokerage sec. Marcus & Millichap, 1985-86; loan processor, adminstrv. asst. Contempo Mortgage, Torrance, Calif., 1986; ptnr. Am. Fin., Torrance, 1986—; owner, pres. Acad. Fin. Resources, Torrance, 1988—. Mem. Nat. Assn. for Self-Employed, Entrepreneur Assn. Democrat. Methodist. Office: Am Fin 2309 Torrance Blvd #200 Torrance CA 90501

SWEGEL, JOHN FRANCIS, computer systems analyst, consultant; b. Forest City, Pa., Oct. 22, 1939. BS, Lehigh U., 1962; MBA, U. Md., 1970. Sr. systems analyst Marriott Corp., Washington, 1966-72, PepsiCo, Purchase, N.Y., 1972-74; regional support mgr. Informatics, Inc., River Edge, N.J., 1974-76; product mgr. Lockheed Electronics, Plainfield, N.Y., 1976-77; project leader Computer Horizons Corp., N.Y.C., 1977-80; project mgr. GE Info. Systems, Morristown, N.J., 1980-84; sr. systems analyst Monarch Systems Group, Springfield, Mass., 1984-87, Mass. Mut. Ins., Springfield, 1987—; adj. instr. Fisher Jr. Coll., Pittsfield, Mass., 1985-87, Berkshire Community Coll.; cons., owner Orchard St. Computing, Lee, Mass., 1987—. Vol. Royal Hart Election Com., Mt. Rainier, Md., 1967, Sun Citizens Com., Oak Ridge, N.J., 1982. Roman Catholic. Home: 106 Orchard St Lee MA 01238 Office: Mass Mut Ins 1295 State St Springfield MA 01111

SWEGER, JOHN BOULDIN, financial company executive; b. Quincy, Fla., Nov. 7, 1919; s. Roy Louis and Dicie (Bouldin) S.; m. Ruth Van Zyle, 1941 (div. 1946); 1 child, John B.; m. Gloria Patricia Burke, June 16, 1948; 1 child, Robert L. BA, U. Fla., 1941. Pres., Smith-Sweger Constrn. Co., Largo, Fla., 1948-75; chmn. Fortune Savs. Bank, Clearwater, Fla., 1982—, pres. 1983-84; chmn., pres. Fortune Fin. Group, Inc., Clearwater, 1984—. Former pres. Morton F. Plant Hosp. Assn., Clearwater, Fla., 1974-77; former trustee, 1970-83; trustee Human Services, Inc., Clearwater, 1984-85, Clearwater Neighborhood Housing Svcs., 1986—; bd. dirs. Arthritis Rsch. Inst., Clearwater, 1986—, Assn. fo Thrift Holding Cos., Washington, 1986—. Maj. U.S. Army, 1941-46, ETO. Democrat. Presbyterian. Avocation: ranching. Office: Fortune Fin Group Inc 2120 US Hwy 19 S Clearwater FL 34624

SWENSON, GARY LEE, investment banker; b. Kenmare, N.D., May 30, 1937; s. Orville K. and Lillian S. (Anderson) S.; m. Jannette E. Dye, July 27, 1963; children—Charlotte, Kimberly, Peter. B.S., U. Wis.-Madison, 1959, M.B.A., 1961. Instr. U. Wis.-Madison, 1960-61; with The First Boston Corp., N.Y.C., 1962—, mng. dir., 1972—. Trustee Greenwich Acad., Conn.; mem. Am. Enterprise Inst. for Pub. Policy Research, N.Y.C. Served to lt. U.S. Army, 1961-62. Mem. N.Y. Soc. Security Analysts, Am. Petroleum Inst. Clubs: Newcomen Soc., N.Y. Yacht, The Board Room, Landmark (N.Y.C.). Home: Pembroke Island Game Cock Rd Greenwich CT 06830 Office: The First Boston Corp 55 E 52nd St New York NY 10055

SWENTKOFSKE, MARVIN ROBERT, investment consulting company executive; b. Champion, Mich., Jan. 7, 1932; s. Carl Grover and Maybelle Marie (Dezotelle) S.; m. Eleanor Ann Montville, July 26, 1936; children: Sharon, Sandra, Mark, Susan, Matthew. BBA, Marquette U., 1955, MBA, 1959. V.p. Blunt Ellis & Loewi, Milw., 1959-72, Loomis Sayles & Co. Inc., Milw., 1972-81; pres. Seagate Capital Mgmt. Inc., Toledo, 1981-84; sr. v.p., chief investment officer First Wis. Trust Co., Milw., 1984-86; pres. Summit Investment Mgmt. Ltd., Milw., 1986—. Pres. sch. bd. St. Mary's, Elm Grove, Wis., 1978-81; pres. lay adv. bd. Divine Savior Holy Angels High Sch., Wauwatosa, Wis., 1965-68. Served with U.S. Army, 1955-57. Mem. Analysts Soc., Chartered Investment Counselors Soc., Marquette U. Bus. Adminstrn. Alumni Assn. (pres. 1968-69). Republican. Roman Catholic. Clubs: Univ., Bluemound Golf Country (Milw.). Lodge: KC. Office: Summit Investment Mgmt Ltd 2323 N Mayfair Rd Wauwatosa WI 53226

SWID, STEPHEN CLAAR, entertainment business executive; b. N.Y.C., Oct. 26, 1940; s. David and Selma (Claar) S.; m. Nan Goldman, Mar. 1, 1963; children: Robin, Scott, Jill. B.S., Ohio State U., 1962. Mgmt. trainee Alside Aluminum Co., Akron, Ohio, 1962-63; securities analyst Dreyfus Fund, N.Y.C., 1963-66; sr. investment officer Oppenheimer Fund, N.Y.C., 1966-67; gen. ptnr. City Assocs., 1967-69, Swid Investors, N.Y.C., 1970-78; co-chmn. bd. Gen. Felt Industries Inc., Saddle Brook, N.J., 1974-86, Knoll Internat., 1977-86; chmn. bd., chief exec. officer SBK Entertainment World, Inc., N.Y.C., 1986—; Chmn. Mcpl. Art Soc. N.Y.; trustee Solomon Guggenheim Found.; chmn. exec. com., chmn. exec. com., dir. East-West Security Studies; vis. com. 20th century art Met. Mus. Art; mem. nat. adv. bd. Am. Univ.; past trustee Horace Mann Sch., N.Y.C.; chmn. Jerusalem Coll. Tech.; former exec. v.p. bd. dirs. Lenox Sch. of N.Y. Office: SBK Entertainment World 1290 Avenue of the Americas New York NY 10104

SWIFT, AUBREY EARL, lawyer, petroleum engineer; b. Tulsa, Sept. 21, 1933; s. Virgil and Edith (Jackson) S.; m. Modell Paulding, Oct. 5, 1951 (div.); children: Terry Earl, Vannessa Suzanne; m. Glenda Kay Arnce, Apr. 8, 1978 (div.); 1 son, Nickolas Gorman. BS in Petroleum Engring., U. Okla., 1955; JD, S. Tex. Coll. Law, 1968; MBA, Pepperdine U., 1988. Bar: Tex. 1968, U.S. Supreme Ct. 1977. Petroleum engr. Humble Oil Co. div. Exxon, Houston, 1955-62; v.p. Mich.-Wis. Pipe Line, Houston, 1962-79, Am. Natural Gas Prodn., Houston, 1962-79; pres., chmn., chief exec. officer Swift Energy Co., Houston, 1979—; cons. Northwest Ala. Gas Dist., Hamilton, 1979—. Served to 1st lt. U.S. Army, 1956-57. Mem. Tex. Soc. Profl. Engrs., Soc. Petroleum Engrs. AIME, Order of Lytae, Tau Beta Pi. Presbyterian.

SWIFT, E. CLINTON, financial planner, lawyer; b. Providence, Sept. 8, 1945; s. Eugene Clinton Swift and Mary Simmons (Easton) Spence. A.B. cum laude, Brown U., 1967; J.D., U. Pa., 1971; cert. in fin. planning Coll. Fin. Planning, Denver, 1983. Bar: Pa. Assoc. counsel Phila. Nat. Bank, 1971-74; resident counsel, sec. MDC Corp., Cherry Hill, N.J., 1974-77; pres. PCM Assocs., Phila., 1977-81; fin. planner, v.p. investments A.G. Edwards & Sons, Hanover, N.H., 1981—; dir. Sands, Taylor & Wood Co., Norwich, Vt. Editor U. Pa. Law Rev., 1970-71. Mem. Inst. Cert. Fin. Planners, Internat. Assn. Fin. Planners. Clubs: Pine Valley Golf (N.J.); Hanover (N.H.) Country. Avocation: golf. Home: Box 248 Plainfield NH 03781 Office: A G Edwards & Sons Inc 73 S Main St Hanover NH 03755

SWIFT, ROBERT W., accounting executive; b. St. Louis, June 28, 1956; s. Harold and Edna Elizabeth (Thompson) S. BBA magna cum laude, U. Mo., St. Louis, 1974-77; MBA, Washington U., 1982. CPA, Mo.; cert. mgmt. acct. Consolidations acct. Wetterau, St. Louis, 1978-79; auditor Stone Carlie, CPA, St. Louis, 1979-80, Chromalloy Am., St. Louis, 1982-83; sr. auditor St. Joe Minerals, St. Louis, 1983-86, supr., 1985-86; acctg. mgr. Ralston Purina Corp., St. Louis, 1986-87; internat. cons. Cornelius & Co., St. Louis, 1988—; tax cons., auditor, St. Louis, 1982-86. Recipient scholarship U. Mo., 1974-77. Mem. Mo. Soc. CPA's, Univ. Mo. Alumni Assn. (budget com. 1986), Washington Univ. Alumni Assn. Home: 1379 Trampe Saint Louis MO 63138 Office: Cornelius & Co 7 Leaside Ct Saint Louis MO 63164

SWIFT, RONALD S., management consultant; b. N.Y.C., Mar. 3, 1945; s. Stephen K. and Rozsi (Lanyi) Pogany-Kerekes. BSBA, U. Nebr., 1968. Cert. systems profl. Fin. adminstr. several banks and brokerage firms, N.Y.C., 1963-66; brokerage adminstr. DeCoppet & Doremus, N.Y.C., 1964-66; personnel mgmt. U.S. Air Force-Aerospace Audio Visual Command, Orlando, Fla., 1966-68; fin. & personnel applications-software devel. U.S. Air

Force-Mil. Airlift Command, Scott AFB, Ill., 1968-70; systems engr. fin. and ins. industries IBM Data Processing div., St. Louis, 1970-77; info. systems mgmt. specialist IBM, Dallas, 1977-78; instr. Systems Sci. Inst. IBM, 1979-82; sr. planning and requirements adminstr. IBM Nat. Accts. Div. Hdqrs., Dallas, 1982-84; cons. support rep. IBM Exec. Briefing Ctr., Irving, Tex., 1984-88; office systems software product mgr. IBM Europe, 1988—. Contbr. numerous articles to profl. jours. Pres., chmn. Belleville (Ill.) Area Coll. Found., 1976-80; pres., chmn. bd. Belleville Ill. Jaycees, 1973-75; chmn. Sr. Citizens Programs Adv. Council, 1973-80; co-chmn. Bi-Centennial Commn., 1975-76. Named one of Outstanding Young Men of Am., 1979-82; recipient Dist. Service award Belleville Ill., 1975, Outstanding Young Man of Ill., 1977, RSVP and Belleville Area Coll., Outstanding Service award, Belleville, 1979. Mem. Data Processing Mgmt. Assn., Assn. of Systems Mgmt. Club: Richland Park Assn. Home: 525 Wentworth Dr Richardson TX 75081

SWIG, RICHARD LEWIS, JR., hotel executive; b. San Francisco, Aug. 26, 1951; s. Richard Lewis and Roselyne (Chroman) S.; m. Sari Lynn Gussman, Feb. 29, 1980; children: Benjamin, Adam. BA, Stanford U., 1972, cert. for Small Cos., 1983, cert. Mktg. Mgmt., 1987. Promotion mgr. H. R. Basford Co., San Francisco, 1969-73, CBS/Epic Records, San Francisco, 1973-75; N.E. regional promotion mgr. N.Y.C., 1975-76, dir. promotions, 1976-78; v.p. promotions MCA/Infinity Records, Los Angeles, 1978-80; v.p. mktg. and promotion Dreamland Records, Los Angeles, 1980-81; v.p. mktg. dir. Fairmont Hotel Mgmt. Co., San Francisco, 1981-86; pres. RSBA & Assocs., San Francisco, 1986—; bd. dirs. Fairmont Hotel Mgmt. Co., 1983. Vice chmn., trustee San Francisco Art Inst., 1986; trustee Friends of the Arts, San Francisco, 1987, San Francisco Girl's Chorus, 1988. Mem. Am. Mktg. Assn. Democrat. Jewish. Office: RSBA & Assocs 50 Francisco St Suite 255 San Francisco CA 94133

SWIHART, FRED JACOB, lawyer; b. Park Rapids, Minn., Aug. 19, 1919; s. Fred and Elizabeth Pauline (Judnitsch) S.; m. Edna Lillian Jensen, Sept. 30, 1950; 1 child; Frederick Jay. BA, U. Nebr., 1949, JD, 1954; M in Russian Lang., Middlebury Coll., 1950; grad., U.S. Army Command and Staff Coll., 1965. Bar: Nebr. 1954, U.S. Dist. Ct. Nebr. 1954, U.S. Ct. Appeals (8th cir.) 1977, U.S. Supreme Ct. 1972. Claims atty. Chgo. & Eastern Ill. R.R., 1954-56; atty. Assn. Amer. R.R.s, Chgo., 1956-60; assoc. Wagener & Marx, Lincoln, Nebr., 1960-61; prosecutor City of Lincoln, 1961-68; sole practice Lincoln, 1968—. Editor Law for the Aviator, 1969-71. Served to lt. col. U.S. Army, 1943-46, ETO, Korea, ret. col., USAR, 1979. Mem. ABA, Nebr. Bar Assn. Fed. Bar Assn., Assn. Trial Lawyers Am., Am. Judicature Soc., Aircraft Owners and Pilots Assn (legis. rep.), Nebr. Criminal Def. Attys. Assn., Nat. Assn. Criminal Def. Lawyers, Internat. Platform Assn., Nebr. Assn. Trial Lawyers, Nebr. Assn. Trial Attys., Nat. Assn. Criminal Def. Lawyers, Nat. Assn. for Uniformed Svcs., Res. Officers Assn., Nat. Assn. Legion of Honor, Internat. Footprint Assn., Am. Legion, Nebr. Navy (admiral). Republican. Presbyterian. Lodges: Masons (knight comdr. of ct. of honor 1983), Shriners (potentate 1983), The Cabiri. Home: 1610 Susan Circle Lincoln NE 68506 Office: 4435 O St Suite 130 Lincoln NE 68510

SWINDELLS, WILLIAM, JR., lumber and paper company executive; b. 1930; married. B.S., Stanford U., 1953. With Willamette Industries, Inc., Portland, Oreg., 1953—; sr. v.p. prodn., mktg. bldg. materials Willamette Industries, Inc., until 1978, exec. v.p., 1978-80, pres. forest products div., 1980-82, pres., chief exec. officer, 1982—, also dir., chmn., 1984—; dir. Oreg. Bank, Portland. Office: Willamette Industries Inc First Interstate Tower 1300 SW 5th Ave Portland OR 97201 *

SWINDLE, ORSON G., III, federal government official; b. Thomasville, Ga., Mar. 8, 1937; m.; 1 child. B.S., Ga. Inst. Tech., 1959; M.B.A., Fla. State U., 1975. Commd. U.S. Marine Corps, 1959, advanced through grades to lt. col.; fighter pilot U.S. Marine Corps, Southeast Asia; prisoner of war North Vietnam, 1966-73; fin. mgr. Marine Corps Logistics Base U.S. Marine Corps, Albany, Ga., 1975-79; ret. U.S. Marine Corps, 1979; Ga. state dir. FmHA, Dept. Agr., 1981-85; asst. sec. Econ. Devel. Adminstrn. Dept. Commerce, Washington, 1985—. Decorated Silver Star (2), Bronze Star (2), Legion of Merit (2), Purple Heart (2), 13 Air medals, numerous others. Office: US Dept Commerce 15th at Constitution Ave NW Washington DC 20230

SWINERTON, WILLIAM ARTHUR, building and construction company executive; b. San Francisco, Dec. 12, 1917; s. Alfred Bingham and Jane Thomas (Hotaling) S.; m. Mary Nichols Clark, June 5, 1943; children: Leslie Engelbrecht, Susan McBaine, James B., Sarah Blake. B.S., Yale, 1939; postgrad., Stanford, 1940. With Swinerton & Walberg Co., San Francisco, 1940-88, ret. Served with USMCR., 1940-46. Decorated Bronze Star. Clubs: Pacific Union, Burlingame Country. Home: PO Box 620265 Woodside CA 94062 Office: Swinerton & Walberg Co 100 Pine St San Francisco CA 94111

SWIRSKY, BENJAMIN, real estate developer. B.Commn., Dalhousie U., Halifax, N.S., Can., 1963; LL.B., Queen's U., Kingston, Ont., Can., 1969, F.C.A., 1965. Sr. tax ptnr. Peat, Marwick, Mitchell, Toronto, Ont., Can., 1969-79; pres., chief exec. officer Bramalea Ltd., Toronto, 1979—; bd. dirs. Slater Steels Corp., Four Seasons Hotels Inc., Consol. Talcorp Ltd., J.D.S. Investments Ltd. Clubs: Donalda (Don Mills, Ont.); Alpine Ski (Thornbury, Ont.), Maple Downs. Home: 33 Nomad Crescent, Don Mills, ON Canada M3B 1S5 Office: Bramalea Ltd, 1867 Yonge St, Toronto, ON Canada M4S 1Y5

SWITZER, RALPH JOSEPH, JR., diversified industry executive; b. New Rochelle, N.Y., July 1, 1930; s. Ralph Joseph and Kathleen Florence (Collins) S.; m. Gerd Hildegarde Wamnes, Feb. 7, 1954; children: Kurt Edmund, Gail Susan, Barbara Jean. BBA, Iona Coll., 1961; grad. advanced mgmt. program, Harvard U., 1976. With Abex Corp, N.Y.C., 1948-70; asst. treas. Whitman Corp. (formerly IC Industries), Chgo., 1970-73, dir. investments, 1973-81, asst. v.p., treas., 1981, v.p., treas., 1982-87, v.p. fin. ops., 1987-89, sr. v.p. fin. ops., 1989—. Mem. adv. bd. Ingalls Meml. Hosp. Devel. Found., Harvey, Ill., 1983—. With USN, 1951-55. Mem. Fin. Execs. Inst., Flossmoor Country Club, Plaza Club, Exec. Club.

SWOBODA, RALPH SANDE, credit union official, lawyer; b. Neenah, Wis., Oct. 4, 1948; s. Ralph F. and Sarah E. (Sande) S.; m. Susan Lucinda Bender, June 28, 1970; children: Katy, David. BA, U. Wis., 1970, JD, 1972. Bar: Wis. 1972. Law clk. to presiding justice Wis. Supreme Ct., Madison, 1972-73; assoc. Aberg, Bell, Blake & Metzner, Madison, 1973-75; v.p., gen. counsel ICU Svcs. Inc., Madison, 1975-83; exec. v.p., gen. counsel Credit Union Nat. Assn. and CUNA Svc. Group, Madison, 1983-86, exec. v.p., chief operating officer, 1983-87; pres., chief exec. officer Credit Union Nat. Assn. & Affiliates, Inc., Madison, 1987—. Mem. Wis. Bar Assn. Office: Credit Union Nat Assn PO Box 431 Madison WI 53701

SWOPE, SAMUEL DAVID, manufacturing executive; b. Gettysburg, Pa., Aug. 1, 1949; s. Samuel F. Jr. and Dorothy Louise (Zinn) S.; 1 child, Jessica Marie. AA in Bus. Adminstrn., Hagerstown (Md.) Jr. Coll., 1969; BA, Fla. Atlantic U., 1971; MSBA, U. Denver, 1976. Dir. personnel, indsl. relations JLG Industries, Inc., McConnellsburg, Pa., 1977-84; dir. human resources Environ. Air Control Inc., Hagerstown, 1984-85; v.p. human resources JLG Industries, Inc., McConnelsburg, 1985—. Co-chmn. Fulton County Pvt. Industry Council, 1987-88; vice chmn. PIC steering com. So. Alleghenies Planning Commn., 1987—. Mem. Cumberland Valley-Am. Soc. for Personnel Adminstrn. (pres. 1984, chair legislative com. 1987-88), Pa. C. of C. (chair employee benefits subcom., 1987—), Ind. Relations Commn. (exec. com., vice-chair designate). Republican. Office: JLG Industries Inc JLG Dr McConnellsburg PA 17233

SWORDS, HENRY LOGAN, II, retail executive; b. Ft. Worth, Oct. 5, 1948; s. H. Logan and Ruth C. (Riley) S.; m. Beverly Craig McFall, June 27, 1981; children: H. Logan III, Justin McFall, Jennifer Lauren. BA, Tex. Wesleyan Coll., 1971. Instr. Logan Swords Drum Studio, Ft. Worth, 1967-69; prin. Swords Drum Studio, Ft. Worth, 1969-73, Swords Music Co., Ft. Worth, 1973-85; pres. Swords Music Cos. Inc., Ft. Worth, 1985—. Actor: (extra, movie) Cotton Candy, 1978, Tough Enough, 1981, Dallas: The Early Years, 1985; drummer, leader Logan Swords & Co. Band. Met. chmn. Tex. Jaycees, Grand Prairie, Tex., 1982-83; bd. dirs., arbitrator Better Bus. Bur., Ft. Worth, 1984—; campaign worker Tarrant County Com. to re-elect Ronald Reagan, Ft. Worth, 1984. Recipient Pres. of Yr. Tex. Jaycees, Galveston, 1982. Mem. Nat. Fed. Ind. Bus., Nat. Assn. Music Mcht., Sales and Mktg. Execs. Ft Worth., Ft. Worth Jaycees (life, pres. 1981-82, Outstanding Recruiter 1982), Past Pres. Club of Ft. Worth Jaycees (v.p. 1986—). Methodist. Club: Rico Pronto Investment (pres. 1985-86). Home: 13 Legend Rd Fort Worth TX 76132 Office: Swords Music Cos Inc 4218 E Lancaster Fort Worth TX 76103

SWOYER, THOMAS MICHAEL, corporate professional; b. Phila., Jan. 14, 1947; s. Harry S. and Mary Elizabeth (Salisbury) S.; m. Katherine W. Swoyer, Nov., 1967; children: Thomas M. Jr., Patrick W., Sarah W. BA in Sci., U. Notre Dame, 1968; MA in Air and Ind. Hygiene, U. N.C., 1969; postgrad., Widener U., 1972-74. Controller Roy F. Weston, Inc., West Chester, Pa., 1972-80, v.p. mktg., 1980-83, pres., 1983—; adv. bd. dept. sci. U. Pa. With USN, 1969-72. Recipient Disting. Performance award Widener U. Sch. Mgmt., 1989. Mem. ASME (mem. indsl. adv. bd. 1987—), Profl. Svcs. Mgmt. Assn. (pres. 1980-81; founding mem. 1976-78), Water Resources Assn. (bd. dirs.). Office: Roy F Weston Inc Weston Way West Chester PA 19380

SYLAK, CHARLES JOHN, JR., holdings company executive; b. Rochester, Pa., May 15, 1950; s. Charles John and Josephine Lucille (Shutey) S. B.A. in Journalism and Mktg. Communications, Duquesne U., 1972. Pub. relations intern Magee-Women's Hosp., Univ. Health Center Pitts., 1971-72; personnel adminstr., elevator div. Westinghouse Electric Corp., Gettysburg, Pa., 1972-75, personnel staff asst., Buffalo divs., 1975-77; mgr. personnel and adminstrn. Shasta, Inc., Coraopolis, Pa., 1977-82, sec.-treas., 1978-82, v.p., 1982—; v.p., dir. Shasta-Ill., Inc., Madison, Shasta-East, Inc., Perth Amboy, N.J.; v.p. Shasta Holdings Co., dir. Shutey Assos., Inc., S&S Supply Co., Inc., Pitts.; cons. communications J&J Forging Co. Publicity chmn. United Way Adams County (Pa.), 1973; asst. campaign chmn. Easter Seal Soc. Adams County, 1974, campaign chmn., 1975; mem. personnel policies survey panel Bur. Nat. Affairs. Recipient Project PICA award United Way Buffalo and Erie County, 1977. Mem. Pitts. Personnel Assn., Am. Mgmt. Assn., Smaller Mfrs. Council Western Pa., Am. Compensation Assn., Urban League C. of C., Pitts. Symphony Soc. Democrat. Roman Catholic. Clubs: Bear Rocks Community, Seven Oaks Country, Isla Del Sol Golf and Racquet, Pawleys Plantation Golf and Country. Home: 511 Midway Dr Beaver PA 15009 Office: 1 Lewis Ave Coraopolis PA 15108

SYLK, LEONARD ALLEN, manufacturing company executive; b. Phila., Feb. 25, 1941; s. Harry S. and Gertrude (Bardy) S.; m. Barbara Ann Lovenduski, Dec. 1, 1975; 1 child, Tristan. BS in Econs., U. Pa., 1963; MBA, Columbia U., 1965. Cert. comml. property builder. Founder, pres. Material Fabrication Corp. (named changed to Shelter Systems Group Corp. 1987), Hainesport, N.J., 1965-88, chief exec. officer, chmn. bd., 1988—; bd. dirs. Hill Internat., Inc., Willingboro, N.J., Home Owners Warranty Corp., N.J., v.p., 1988—. Contbr. articles to industry publs. Chmn. ann. giving Friends Cen. Sch., Phila., 1983-86; co-chmn. ann. fund-raiser Pa. Hosp., Phila., 1987, Inst. for Contemporary Art, Phila, 1988; chmn. ann. awards dinner Jewish Nat. Fund, Phila., 1987. Mem. Nat. Assn. Homebuilders (com. chmn., nat. bd. dirs. 1984—), Wood Truss Coun. Am. (bd. dirs. 1983—, pres. 1987), Builders League South Jersey (v.p., bd. dirs. 1984—), Locust Club, Le Club (N.Y.C.), Masons. Republican. Home: RD #1 Mount Holly NJ 08060 Office: Shelter Systems Group Corp Park Ave Hainesport NJ 08036

SYLVAIN, KENNETH LIONEL, II, investment broker; b. Kittery, Me., Mar. 2, 1962; s. Kenneth Lionel and Leola Marie (Martin) S. Student, Duke U., 1980-82, U. Md., 1983-84, U. Coll., 1986. Adminstrv. asst. U. Coll., College Park, Md., 1983-84; supr. D.C. Dept. Recreation, Washington, 1984-85, tutor Neighborhood Art Acad., 1984-85; customer service rep. Equitable Bank N.A., Wheaton, Md., 1985-87; regional rep. First Investors Corp., Kensington, Md., 1987-88; asst. mgr. Baraka Art and Frame, Washington, 1988-89; mgr. Snow Goose Gallery, Washington, 1989—. Named Chpt. Mem. of Yr. Pan Hellenic Council, 1984; recipient Katherine Dullin Folger award Am. Cancer Soc., 1980; named one of Outstanding Young Men of Am., 1984. Mem. Nat. Assn. Securities Dealers, Alpha Phi Alpha. Democrat. Roman Catholic. Home: 7963 Riggs Rd #11 Adelphi MD 20783

SYLVESTER, RICHARD RUSSELL, strategic planning specialist; b. Newton, Iowa, Jan. 10, 1938; s. Leslie Gardner and Effie (Williams) S.; BA, UCLA, 1959; MBA, U. So. Calif., 1962; PhD (fellow), UCLA, 1970, postdoctoral scholar in Engring., 1971-74; J.D., Loyola U., 1981; m. Irene Elizabeth Lehman, Apr. 17, 1976; children—Bonnie Ann, Vicky Ellis, Juliesta Elaine. Designer corp. offices Gen. Motors Corp., Warren, Mich., 1958; sr. analyst Lockheed Aircraft Corp., Burbank, Calif., 1962-66; sr. planner corp. offices Hughes Aircraft Co., Culver City, Calif., 1966-68; sr. staff economist, staff mgr. TRW, Inc., Redondo Beach, Calif., 1969-70; pres. Def. Rsch. Co., 1970-81, Sylvester Consulting Group; pres. PhD Pub. Co., Sylvester Appraisal Co., 1970—; pres. U.S. Electropower Controls Corp., 1970-71; asst. prof. Calif. State U., 1970-73; mgr. corp. planning Brunswick Def./Celesco, Costa Mesa, Calif., 1973-75; staff specialist strategic planning Gen. Dynamics Corp., 1981-83; sr. staff specialist strategic planning Northrop Corp., 1983-89; cons. engring. and fin., L.A., 1970-73, 75-81; lectr. Northrop U., U. Calif., U. So. Calif., Loyola U., La Verne U., 1961-81; asst. prof. Calif. State U., 1970-73; asso. prof. Pepperdine U., 1975-76; co-founder Theta Cable TV, L.A., 1966-67. GM scholar, 1953-57, Ford Found. grantee, 1965, U.S. Fed. Govt. rsch. grantee, 1967-70. Mem. Beta Gamma Sigma, Alpha Kappa Psi. Author: Management Decisions and Actions, 2d edit., 1981; Investment Strategy, 1982; Tax Planning, 4th edit., 1980, Strategic Planning, 5th edit., 1986, Investment Planning and Tax Planning Software, 1983-86; contbr. tech. reports to profl. lit. Patentee in field. Home: 11606 Charnock Rd Los Angeles CA 90066

SYLVESTER, TERRY LEE, business manager; b. Cin., June 12, 1949; s. Wilbert Fairbanks and Jewell S.; B.S. in Bus. Accounting, Miami U., Oxford, Ohio, 1972; M.B.A. in Fin., Xavier U., Cin., 1983; m. Janet Lynn Brigger, Nov. 29, 1975; children—Carisa, Laura, Jason, Katherine. Staff accountant Alexander Grant & Co., C.P.A.'s, Cin., 1972; treas., controller Imperial Community Developers, Inc., Cin., subs. of Chelsea Moore Devel. Corp., 1972—; controller home bldg. div. Chelsea Moore Devel. Corp., 1978—; controller, chief fin. officer Armstrong Cos., apt. mgmt., 1978-79, Dorger Investments, Cin., 1979-81, Delta Mechanical Constructors, Inc., Fairfield, Ohio, 1981-83; bus. mgr. Oak Hills Local Schs., Cin., 1983-87; treas. Lockland City Schs., Cin., 1987—. Home: 31 Woodmont Ct Fairfield OH 45014 Office: 210 N Cooper Ave Cincinnati OH 45215

SYNK, JAMES ARTHUR, electronics company executive; b. Cleve., Dec. 20, 1934; s. John Bernard and Mary Rita (Mackin) S.; m. Mary Agnes Busemeyer, Dec. 29, 1956; children: David, Nancy, Peter. BS, U. Dayton, 1956. Sales engr. Superior Tool & Die Co., Cleve., 1960-62; systems analyst Cen. Nat. Bank, Cleve., 1962-64; sales trainee IBM Corp., Cleve., 1964-65; mgr. field sales, dir. Honeywell-Info.Systems, Ohio and Mich., 1965-73; dir. bus., market planning Honeywell-Info.Systems, Boston, 1973-75; sr. v.p. ADT Inc., N.Y.C., 1975-80; pres. Aritech Corp., Framingham, Mass., 1980—; chmn. Aritech Corp., Framingham, 1986—. Trustee Hospice at Home, Wayland, Mass., 1987. Capt. USMCR, 1956-59. Mem. Mass. High Tech. Coun., Am. Electronics Assn., Nat. Assn. Mfrs., C. of C. Republican. Roman Catholic. Office: Aritech Corp 25 Newbury St Framingham MA 01701

SYNNETT, ROBERT JOHN, construction executive; b. Poughkeepsie, N.Y., Jan. 20, 1958; s. William Thomas and Jean Gertrude (Dahlem) S.; m. Therese Frances Quinn, Oct. 24, 1981; children: Robert William, Conor Denis. BA, U. S.C., 1981. Personnel, safety mgr. M.B. Kahn Constrn. Co., Inc., Columbia, S.C., 1981-84, personnel, safety dir., 1984-87, asst. v.p., corp. sec., 1987-89, v.p., asst. corp. sec., 1989—. Vol. United Way of Midlands, Columbia, S.C., 1983-86. Mem. Am. Soc. Personnel Adminstrn., Columbia Personnel Assn.Assoc. Gen. Contractor's of Am., Inc. (active Carolina br. safety com. 1988, S.C. legis. com. 1988—). Home: 109 Chillingham Ct Irmo SC 29603 Office: M B Kahn Constrn Co Inc PO Box 1179 Columbia SC 29202

SYVERSON, THOMAS EDWARD, health care financial consultant; b. Benson, Minn., Dec. 30, 1960; s. Lavern Charles and Doris Elaine (Hogen) S. BA, Concordia Coll., 1983; MBA, U. Minn., 1987. CPA. Sales rep. NCR Corp., Mpls., 1983-84; acct. Midway Hosp., St. Paul, 1984-87; cons. Deloitte Haskins and Sells, Mpls., 1987—. Mem. Minn. Soc. CPA's. Office: Deloitte Haskins & Sells 4300 Norwest Ctr 90 S 7th St Minneapolis MN 55402

SZABO, ANDREW JOHN, brokerage house executive; b. Springville, N.Y., May 14, 1954; s. Lester John and Gloria (Parker) S. BA, SUNY, Binghamton, 1976; MA, Harvard U., 1979; JD, Yale U., 1984. Assoc. Shearson Lehman Bros., N.Y.C., 1984-85; assoc. Kidder, Peabody & Co., N.Y.C., 1985-86, asst. v.p., 1986-87, v.p., 1987-89, mem., 1989—. Home: 1019 Bloomfield St Hoboken NJ 07030 Office: Kidder Peabody & Co 10 Hanover Sq 18th Floor New York NY 10005

SZCZESNY, EDMUND JOHN, accountant; b. Natrona Heights, Pa., Apr. 12, 1954; s. Edmund J. and Harriet A. (Doyle) S.; m. Susan M. Leishman, Aug. 3, 1984. BS in Bus. Adminstrn., Duquesne U., 1976. CPA, Pa. Staff acct. Bluett & Bluett Acctg., Pitts., 1976-82; mgr. Carbis Walker & Assn., New Castle, Pa., 1982-86; controller Fed. Assurance Corp., New Castle, 1986—. Mem. Am. Inst. CPA's, Pa. Inst. CPA's, New Castle Jaycees (treas. 1984-85). Democrat. Roman Catholic. Home: 2924 Glenda Dr New Castle PA 16101 Office: East Mfg Corp 930-2 Cass St New Castle PA 16101

SZCZESNY, RONALD WILLIAM, lawyer; b. Detroit, Nov. 26, 1940; s. Raymond Joseph and Sophie (Welc) S.; m. Rosemary Edna West, Sept. 30, 1961 (div. 1973); children—Timothy, Laurie, Kristen; m. Susan Joy Feragne, May 25, 1985. B.A. in Chemistry, Wayne State U., 1963, J.D., 1972. Bar: Mich. 1975, U.S. Dist. Ct. (ea. dist.) Mich. 1975, U.S. Tax Ct. 1975, U.S. Supreme Ct. 1983, U.S. Ct. Appeals 1985. Research chemist Wyandotte Chems., Mich., 1961-64; exptl. chemist Cadillac Motor Car Co., Detroit, 1964-66, gen. supr. material lab., 1966-69; materials engr., 1969-72, staff analysis engr. Gen. Motors Co., Warren, Mich., 1972-77; assoc. firm Zeff and Zeff & Materna, Detroit, 1977—. Mem. ABA, Assn. Trial Lawyers Am., Mich. Trial Lawyers Assn., Detroit Bar Assn., N.Y. Trial Lawyers Assn., Soc. Automotive Engrs., Advocates Bar Assn., Tex. Trial Lawyers Assn., Internat. Assn. Arson Investigators. Republican. Roman Catholic. Club: President's (U. Mich., Ann Arbor). Home: 27333 Spring Arbor Dr Southfield MI 48076 Office: Zeff and Zeff & Materna 607 Shelby St Detroit MI 48226

SZE, CELESTINA KING, fashion garment executive; b. Shanghai, China, Apr. 20, 1938; d. Eugene C. and Ya-Yuan (Ling) King; m. Vincent Sze, Dec. 19, 1964; children: David, Joseph. BA, Providence Coll., Taichung, Taiwan, 1959; postgrad., Oreg. State U., 1964; cert., U. Nev., 1966. Teaching asst. Providenc Coll., 1959-64; mng. merchandiser Marlene Internat., Taipei, 1967-73; v.p. exports Chung-Hsin Textile Co. Ltd., Taipei, 1973-76; Far Ea. rep. Bronson Inc., Hong Kong, 1976-78; mng. dir. Slone (subs. Jay Jacobs, Inc.), Seattle, 1979, v.p., 1987—; mng. dir. Slone subs. Jay Jacobs, Inc., 1979, v.p., 1987. Home: 31626 37th Ave SW Federal Way WA 98023 Office: 1526 5th Ave Seattle WA 98101

SZORADI, CHARLES, architect; b. Matyasfold, Hungary, Nov. 2, 1923; came to U.S. 1957, naturalized, 1962; s. Nandor Stift and Margit (Tittl) S.; children: Charles Attila, Stephen Hill. Grad., Architecture Sch., Budapest Joseph Nador Inst. Tech., 1950. Registered architect, D.C., Md., Va., Pa. Architect, planner Hungarian Central Planning Office, 1950-56; architect Chatelain, Gauger & Nolan, Washington, 1957-60, Keyes, Lethbridge & Condon, Washington, 1962-68; architect, planner Doxiadis Assocs., Washington, 1968-71; chief architect Daniel, Mann, Johnson & Mendenhall, 1972; prin. Charles Szoradi, AIA, Architect and Planner, Washington, 1973—. Author: (with others) Encyclopedia of Architecture, Graphic Standards. Commr. DC Woodley Park, 1980-83. Served with Hungarian Army, 1944. Grantee Nat. Endowment for the Arts, 1974-75. Mem. AIA (juror Washington chpt. 1979, 84, First award for hist. preservation 1981), Am. Planning Assn. Home and Office: 128 G St SW Washington DC 20024

SZRAMA, LUCY THERESA, financial executive; b. Buffalo, Sept. 10, 1938; d. John Jerome and Victoria Appelonia (Gielinski) Mikulski; m. Bernard Leo Szrama, Aug. 9, 1958; children: Elaine Szrama Moore, Peter, James. With Erie County Dept. Health, Buffalo, 1956-61, Cheektowaga (N.Y.) Libr. Bd., 1966-73; CCD coord. Our Lady Help of Christians Parish, Cheektowaga, 1973-74; bus. mgr. R. Chmiel DDS, A. Shapiro DDS, Cheektowaga, 1974-84; reimbursement coord. Am. ContinueCare, Amherst, N.Y., 1984, Baxter, Amherst, 1985-88; reimbursement mgr. Caremark Homecare, Amherst, 1988—. cons. Maryvale Dist. on Bus. Reorgn., Cheektowaga, 1980. Mem. NAFE., Chapel Parents Guild (sec., B.S.A. counselor 1977-84, former pres., v.p., treas.), Cheektowaga Hist. Soc. (sec.), Polish Nat. Alliance. Office: Baxter Caremark 375 N French Rd Amherst NY 14120

SZUHY, LAWRENCE GREGORY, automotive company executive; b. Cleve., Aug. 10, 1942; s. Coleman Lawrence and Mary Margaret (Kemmeny) S.; m. Judith Mae Blair; children: Chris, Linda, Diana, Beth. BBA, Eastern Mich. U., 1965, MBA, 1969. Various mfg. mgmt. positions Ford Motor Co., 1964-72; from plant mgr. to v.p. mfg. ops. Arrow Automotive Industries Inc., Spartanburg, S.C., 1972-88; exec. v.p. Blue Chip Products, Inc., Fairless Hills, Pa., 1988—; instr. Schoolcraft Jr. Coll., Livonia, Mich., 1968-72, Rutledge Coll., 1973-74, U. S.C., Spartanburg, 1974-76. Bd. dirs. United Way, Spartanburg, 1987—, Spartanburg Devel. Assn., 1987—; chmn. Spartanburg Children's Shelter, 1987—. Mem. Automotive Parts Rebuilders Assn. (bd. dirs. 1979—, pres. 1986-87). Republican. Roman Catholic. Office: Blue Chip Products Inc One Newbold Rd Fairless Hills PA 19030

SZWALBENEST, BENEDYKT JAN, lawyer; b. Poland, June 13, 1955; s. Sidney and Janina (Bleishtif) S.; m. Shelley Joy Leibel, Nov. 8, 1981. BBA, Temple U., 1978, JD, 1981. Law clk. Fed. Deposit Ins. Corp., Washington, 1980; law clk. to presiding justice U.S. Dist. Ct. (ea. dist.) Pa., Phila., 1980-81; staff atty., regulatory specialist Fidelcor, Inc. and Fidelity Bank, Phila., 1981-86; regulations specialist sr. regulatory staff Fed. Res. Bank of N.Y., N.Y.C., 1986—. Author: Federal Bank Regulation, 1980. Mem. Commonwealth of Pa. Post-secondary Edn. Planning Commn., Harrisburg, 1977-79; trustee Pop Warners Little Scholars, Phila., 1981—. Recipient E. Gerald Corrigan Pres.'s Award for Excellence, 1988. Mem. ABA (nat. sec., treas. law student div. 1980-81, Silver Key award 1980, Gold Key award 1981), Am. Judicature Soc., Am. Bankers Assn. (cert. compliance specialist, lectr. 1984—), Temple U. Sch. Bus. Alumni Assn. (sec. 1982-84, v.p. 1984-86, pres. 1986—, bd. dirs. gen. alumni assn. 1986—), Tau Epsilon Rho, Omicron Delta Epsilon. Home: 1107 Bryn Mawr Ave Bala Cynwyd PA 19004 Office: Fed Res Bank of NY 33 Liberty St New York NY 10045

SZYMANSKI, ELEANORE KULAKOWSKI, financial planner; b. Chester, Pa., Dec. 19, 1938; d. James and Eleanor Veronica (Sczymczak) Kulakowski; m. Eugene Szymanski, Sept. 1, 1962. BS in Fin., Rider Coll., 1982, postgrad, 1983. Cert. fin. planner. V.p. adminstrn. Gund Investment Corp., Princeton, N.J., 1971-81; acct. Besselaar Assocs., Princeton, 1983-84, Princeton U., Princeton, 1984-86; fin. planner Eleanore K. Szymanski, Princeton, 1985—; chmn. Fin. Ind. Week Activities for Pub. Edn., 1985-88. Author: Age is Only a Number-Managing Your Money Throughout Changes in Life's Middle Years, 1987. Bd. dirs., v.p. Career Devel. Awards, Princeton, 1987-88; trustee United Way, Princeton, 1988—. Mem. Internat. Assn. Fin. Planning (pres. Princeton/Western N.H. chpt. 1987-88, dir. 1986-88, chairperson 1988-89), Nat. Assn. Accts., Inst. Cert. Fin. Planners (bd. dirs. Princeton chpt.), Mercer County Estate Planning Council, Fin. Mgmt. Assn., Princeton C. of C. Office: 601 Ewing St Ste C-8 Princeton NJ 08540

TABAKSBLAT, MORRIS, personal care products company executive; b. 1937; married. Student, Leiden Univ., The Netherlands. Chmn., chief exec. officer Chesebrough-Pond's, Inc., 1987-88; chmn., chief exec. officer Lever Bros., N.Y.C., 1988—, also bd. dirs. Office: Lever Bros 390 Park Ave New York NY 10022 *

TABATA, YUKIO, engineering researcher; b. Maizuru, Kyoto, Japan, Sept. 29, 1948; s. Denji and Kimie (Yamazoe) T.; m. Masayo Tsuneyama, Oct. 10, 1974; children: Kayoko, Kentaro. BS, Shizuoka U., Japan, 1971; MS,

Kanazawa U., Japan, 1974. With devel. dept. Ricoh Co., Ltd., Tokyo, 1974-79; with research ctr. Ricoh Reprographic Tech., Numazu, Shizuoka, Japan, 1979-86; assoc. research and devel engr. Ricoh Imaging Tech., Numazu, 1986—. Patentee electrical processes; inventor printing process. Co-founder Shizuoka U. Equestrian Club, 1970; mem. Good Will Guide, Tokyo, 1986—. Mem. Physical Soc. Japan, Inst. Image Electronics Engrs. Japan, Alumni Assn. Shizuoka U. Equestrian Club (chmn. 1975-83). Home: 49-8 Kamo, Mishima, Shizuoka 411, Japan Office: Ricoh Imaging Tech Rsch Ctr, 146-1 Nishisawada, Numazu, Shizuoka 410, Japan

TABET, CHAFIC ELIAS, construction company executive; b. Bcharri, Lebanon, July 3, 1955; s. Elias Dimitri and Helene Said (Daher) T. PhD, N.D. de Jamhour, Beirut, 1974; LLM, St. Joseph U., Beirut, 1978; diploma de juriste conseil d'Entreprise, diploma d'Etudes superieures specialisees, Jean Moulin U., Lyon, France, 1978-79. Mktg. officer K. Assouad Est., Beirut, 1977-78; lawyer P. Ghannam Law Office, Beirut, 1979-81; bus. law educator Belgium Ctr. for Comml. Specialized Studies, Beirut, 1979-81; legal adv. Archirodon Overseas Co. Ltd., Jeddah, Saudi Arabia, 1981-82; v.p., legal adminstrv. and internat. affairs Saudi Arabian Trading and Constrn. Co., Riyadh, 1982—. Mem. Beirut Bar Assn., Andjce Lyon. Office: Saudi Arabian Trading & Constrn Co, PO Box 346, 11411 Riyadh Saudi Arabia

TABISZEWSKI, EDWARD K(AZIMIERZ), consulting company executive; b. Warsaw, Poland, Jan. 19, 1927; s. Edward Michal and Kazimiera Maria (Zwierzynska) T.; m. Anna Maria Garbien, Aug. 26, 1948 (div. 1957); children—Maciej Andrzej, Jolanta Maria; m. Vreni Elisabeth Joerg, May 3, 1961; children—Mark George, Michael Andrew. M.A., Higher Sch. Commerce, Poland, 1949, M.B.A., Central Sch. Planning and Stats., Warsaw, 1952; M.Sc., Higher Sch. Econs., Cracow, Poland, 1956; postgrad. MIT, 1959-60. Dir. bus. devel. EAME, ITT (WD), Brussels, 1969-70, gen. mgr. Germany, Essen, Fed. Republic Germany, 1970-72; corp. dir. East-West devel. Borg Warner Corp., Brussels, 1973-82; v.p. European ops. Telephone Broadcasting Systems PLC, London, 1983; pres., chief exec. officer Bus. Devel. Cons. S.A., Montana, Switzerland, 1984—. Served to maj. Polish Underground Armed Forces (A.K.), 1942-45. Roman Catholic. Home: Residence du Rhone, CH-3962 Crans-Montana Switzerland Office: Bus Devel Cons SA, Residence du Rhone, CH-3962 Crans-Montana Switzerland

TABOR, CHARLES DWIGHT, JR., business educator; b. Fitzgerald, Ga., Apr. 19, 1937; s. Charles Dwight and Anna Belle (Little) T.; m. Wynn Hughes, 1959; children: Dwight III, Margaret, David. BS in Indsl. Engring., Ga. Inst. Tech., 1959; MBA, Ga. State U., 1966, PhD, 1970. With Southern Bell, Atlanta, 1962-66; educator Ga. State U., Atlanta, 1966—, chmn. MBA program, 1978-80, chmn. Decision Scis., 1984—; exec. dir. Alpha Iota Delta, Atlanta, 1985—. Contbr. articles to profl. jours. With USAF, 1959-62. Mem. Decision Scis. Inst. Office: Ga State Univ Atlanta GA 30303

TACKE, DAVID R., electrical systems company executive; b. St. Louis, 1922; married. MBA, Pepperdine U., 1973. Design and project engr. N.Am. Aviation, Inc., 1941-43; mgr. product engring., asst. dir. engring. LTV Temco Aerosystems div. Temco Aircraft Corp., 1946-65; with E-Systems Inc., 1965—; asst. gen. mgr. systems Garland div., Tex., 1965-67; v.p. systems Dallas, 1967-69; gen. mgr. Garland div., 1969-71, corp. v.p., 1969-77, pres., 1971-73; pres. elec. systems group Dallas, 1973-77, sr. v.p. elec. systems group, 1977-83, pres., chief operating officer, 1983-87, now chmn., chief exec. officer, 1987—, also bd. dirs. Served with U.S. Army, 1943-46. Office: E-Systems Inc PO Box 660248 Dallas TX 75266-0248 *

TAECKENS, DOUGLAS RICHARD, plastics manufacturing company executive; b. Flint, Mich., May 9, 1950; s. Richard Ernst and Shirley Joanne (Currie) T.; B.B.A., U. Mich., 1972, M.B.A., 1985. m. Pamela Kay Webb, Sept. 29, 1984; children—James, April. Mem. sales dept. Helmac Products Corp., Flint, 1972-74, Southwest regional mgr., Dallas, 1974-76, nat. sales mgr., Flint, 1976-78, v.p. sales and mktg., 1978—. Mem. Sales and Mktg. Execs. Club, Nat. Assn. Service Merchandising, Gen. Mdse. Distbrs. Council, U. Mich. Alumni Assn. Republican. Office: Helmac Products Corp PO Box 73 Flint MI 48501

TAETS, DENNIS RAY, marketing professional; b. Sheffield, Ill., Jan. 31, 1948; s. Marvin Edward and Mary Martha (Van Poucke) T.; m. Sharyn Constance Gillespie, Dec. 18, 1976; children: Jenifer, Jonathan, Michele. BS in Math. and Computer Sci., U. Ill., 1970; MBA, So. Ill. U., 1975. Forman Big Flats PLT Corning (N.Y.) Glass Works, 1976-78, planner, 1978-81, supr. customer svc. indsl. ceramics div., 1981-82, supr. customer svc. tech. ceramics div., 1982-85, supr. mktg. communications telecommunications products div., 1986-88, product mgr., 1988—. Mem. Am. Prodn. and Inventory Control Soc. (acting chair 1978-82). Roman Catholic. Home: 1578 Sing Sing Rd Horseheads NY 14845 Office: Corning Glass Works Telecommunications Products Div MP RO 03 Corning NY 14831

TAFEL, CHARLES B., sales executive; b. Lexington, Ky., Dec. 28, 1958; s. William D. and Mildred (Gill) T. BBA, U. Ky., 1981. Sales rep. Jarvis Corp., Atlanta, 1982-83, Burroughs Corp., Atlanta, 1984-85, BellSouth Mobility, Atlanta, 1985; sales mgr. BellSouth Mobility, Louisville, 1985-86, area mgr., 1986—; gen. mgr. Ky. BellSouth Mobility, Louisville, 1986—. Mem. Sales and Mktg. Execs. Louisville. Roman Catholic. Home: 410 Mocking Bird Valley Louisville KY 40207 Office: Bellsouth Mobility 6040 Dutchmans Ln Louisville KY 40205

TAFF, LINDA KAY, data processing executive; b. Bates, Ark., Aug. 27, 1945; d. Everett and Ruby E. (Winters) Sanders; m. Donald R. Knight, Aug. 3, 1963 (div. May 1970); children: Dianna, Scarlet; m. Glen D. Taff, Aug. 17, 1979. Cert. in Computer Sci., Tulsa Jr. Coll., 1982; student, Okla. U. Computer operator Unit Rig, Tulsa, 1971-73; programmer McMichaels, Tulsa, 1973-74; programmer analyst St. John Med. Ctr., Tulsa, 1974-80, system programmer, 1980-83, mgr. software system, 1983-87, asst. dir. mgmt. info. systems, 1987—. Mem. Guide, Commons, Nat. Assn. Female Execs., DOS Users Group (sec. 1982-83), Hi-Jinx Club (treas., sec. 1981-82, del. 1984-85), Toastmasters (adminstrv. v.p. 1988—, pres. 1989). Office: St John Med Ctr 1923 S Utica Ave Tulsa OK 74104

TAFT, DONALD ALLEN, publishing executive; b. Amityville, N.Y., Jan. 16, 1951; s. Nathaniel Copp and Norma (Nickerson) T.; m. Mary Biggins, Jan. 5, 1974; children: Benjamin, William, Nathaniel, Eleanor. BS, Worcester Poly. Inst., 1972; MBA, Harvard U., 1976. With Courier Corp., Lowell, Mass., 1978—, v.p., 1982—. 1st lt. U.S. Army, 1972-74. Office: Courier Corp 165 Jackson St Lowell MA 01852

TAFURI, SPENCER ANDREW, treasurer, insurance executive, municipal administrator, treasurer; b. N.Y.C., Aug. 2, 1952; s. Joseph Thomas and Barbara (Sarvi) T.; m. Wynne Kovall, Oct. 22, 1977; children: Joseph, Melanie, Scott. BA in History, Rutgers U., 1975; MEd, Paterson Coll., 1977; MBA in Fin., Rutgers U., 1978, MBA in Acctg., 1980. Council pres. Borough of Emerson, N.J., 1982-85; adminstr., treas. Borough of Little Ferry, N.J., 1982-86; treas. Borough of Riverdale, N.J., 1986; chief fiscal officer Bergen County Mcpl. Joint Ins. Fund, Park Ridge, N.J., 1985—; adminstr. Twp. Saddle Brook, 1987—; chmn. Bergen County Treas. Group, Pascack Valley, N.J., 1984; chief exec. officer Meadows Assocs., Middletown, Conn., 1985—. Trustee Bergen County Community Action Program, 1983-84, Hackensack-Meadowlands Mcpl. Com., Lyndhurst, N.J., 1984; aide Sen. Cardinale, Cresskill, N.J., 1983-85. Recipient Meritorious Service award Borough of Emerson, 1985. Fellow Assn. Govt. Accts.; mem. Mcpl. Fin. Officers Assn., Tax Collectors and Treas. Assn. N.J., N.J. Mcpl. Mgrs. Assn., Bergen County Mcpl. Mgrs. Assn., Saddle Brook C. of C. (trustee). Republican. Roman Catholic. Club: Emerson Rep. Lodge: Rotary (pres. Little Ferry/South Hackensack club 1984-86, Outstanding Service award 1984). Home: 16 Sycamore Ave Emerson NJ 07630 Office: 91 Newark-Pompton Turnpike Riverdale NJ 07457

TAGGART, DAVID MARSHALL, soft drink company executive; b. Wellington, Kans., May 24, 1951; s. James Howard and Dorothy Lenore (Trekell) T.; m. Ruth Lyon Berkelman, July 23, 1973; children: Kimberly Jean, John Marshall. AB cum laude, Princeton U., 1973; MBA, Harvard U., 1979. Internat. officer 1st Nat. Bank Boston, 1974-77; mgr. internat. fin. Continental Group Inc., N.Y.C., 1979-80; asst. treas. Coca-Cola Co., Atlanta, 1980—; seminar speaker Euromoney mag., 1987, Insight Ednl. Svcs., 1988. Co-recipient 2nd place fgn. exchange mgr. of yr. award Intermarket mag., 1988. Presbyterian. Home: 196 Old Rosser Rd Stone Mountain GA 30087 Office: Coc-Cola Co One Coca-Cola Plaza Atlanta GA 30313

TAGGART, ROBERT BURDETT, communications company executive; b. Paterson, N.J., Apr. 6, 1943; s. Robert Burdett and Marjorie Stewart (Wiley) T.; m. Donna Fay Bledsoe, Feb. 14, 1973; children—David Robert. B.S., Northwestern U., 1967, M.S., 1968; Engr., Stanford U. 1970. Engr., mgr. Hewlett-Packard, Palo Alto, Calif., 1970-78; mgr. mech. engring. Comprint, Inc., Mountain View, Calif., 1978-80; engr. Apple Computer, Cupertino, Calif., 1980-82; founder, chief exec. officer, Chaparral Communications, Inc., San Jose, Calif., 1980—. Contbr. articles to profl. publs.; patentee in field. Mem. Soc. for Pvt. and Comml. Earth Stas. (pioneer). Republican. Presbyterian. Home: 348 Ramona Rd Portola Valley CA 94025

TAGGART, SONDRA, financial planner, investment advisor; b. N.Y.C., July 22, 1934; d. Louis and Rose (Birnbaum) Hamov; children: Eric, Karen. BA, Hunter Coll., 1955. Cert. fin. planner, registered investment advisor; registered prin. Nat. Assn. Securities Dealers. Founder, dir. Copyright Service Bur., Ltd., N.Y.C., 1957-69; dir., officer Maclen Music, Inc., N.Y.C., 1964-69; pres. Westshore, Inc., pub. internat. bus. materials, Mill Valley, Calif., 1965-80; pres. securities broker dealer The Taggart Co. Ltd., 1981—; The Beatles, Ltd., 1964-69. Mem. Internat. Assn. Fin. Planners, Registry Fin. Planning Practitioners. Republican. Clubs: Bankers, Beverly Hills Country. Editor: The Red Tapes: Commentaries on Doing Business With The Russians and East Europeans, 1978. Office: 1875 Century Pk E #1400 Los Angeles CA 90067-2501

TAGLIAFERRI, LEE GENE, investment banker; b. Mahanoy City, Pa., Aug. 14, 1931; s. Charles and Adele (Cirilli) T.; B.S., U. Pa., 1957; M.B.A., U. Chgo., 1958; m. Maryellen Stanton, Apr. 29, 1962; children—Mark, John, Maryann. Div. comptroller Campbell Soup Co., Camden, N.J., 1958-60; securities analyst Merrill, Lynch, Pierce, Fenner & Smith, Inc., N.Y.C., 1960-62; asst. v.p. U.S. Trust Co. of N.Y., 1962-71; v.p. corporate finance div. Laidlaw & Co., Inc., N.Y.C., 1972-73; pres. Everest Corp., N.Y.C., 1973—; dir. Fairfield Communities Inc., UEC, Inc., LRA, Inc., Industrialized Bldg. Systems, Inc. Past pres. West Windsor Community Assn. Trustee Schuyler Hall, Columbia, Madison Sq. Boys Club. Served with AUS, 1953-55. K.C. Clubs: University of Pa., Princeton (N.Y.C.). Home: 77 Lillie St Princeton Junction NJ 08550 Office: 1 Penn Plaza New York NY 10001

TAIMA, FUAD KHAZAL, international financial executive; b. Baghdad, Iraq, Nov. 2, 1935; came to U.S., 1953; s. Kazal and Sharifa Taima; m. Rosemarie Walsh (div. 1968); children: Susan, Lyn, Junan, John, Merriam; m. Dorothy Draeger, June 13, 1970; 1 child, Leith. BS, U. Pa., 1958, MBA in Fin and Internat. Trade, 1960. Econ., polit. cons. Arab delegations UN, N.Y.C., 1960-68; dir. econs. cons. mid. east and N. Africa regions Crystal Mgmt. Services Inc., Beirut, 1968-71; Pres. Averroes, Inc., McLean, Va., 1971-88, Am. Iraqi Fin. & Trade Inc., McLean, Va., 1988—; cons. BDM, Inc., McLean, Va.; regional v.p. U.S. Arab C. of C., N.Y.C., 1977-82, bd. dirs., Washington, 1977-72; founder Mid Atlantic U.S. Arab C. of C.; co-founder Global Econ. Action Inst., Northern Va. Export-Import Trade Assn. (Internat. Trade Assn. No. Va.), Nat. Assn. Arab Am., Orgn. Arab Students. Authored several synopses on Arab funds in internat. project fin., 1982-84; contbr. articles to profl. jours. Mem. Shaybani Soc. Internat. Law, Mid. E. Inst., Soc. Internat. Devel., Washington Internat. Trad Assn., No. Va. Internat. Trade Assn., Les Ambassadeurs, London, U.K., Clermont Club, Assn. Arab Am. U. Grads. (v.p. 1968-70), Arab Am. Bankers Assn. Office: 8280 Greensboro Dr Ste 710 McLean VA 22102

TAINTOR, MELINDA MARY, financial planner; b. Port Jefferson, N.Y., Apr. 29, 1938; d. Charles Coal and Lucile (Points) T.; 1 child, Chris. BS, NYU, 1960, MA, 1965. Cert. elem. tchr., N.Y., fin. planner. Tchr. various locations, 1960-79; exec. dir. The Arts Pocket, Setauket, N.Y., 1974-79; owner Words Worth Svcs., Bellevue, Wash., 1979—; rep. Southmark Fin. Svcs., Bellevue, 1984-86, Investment Mgmt. & Rsch., Bellevue, 1986—; pvt. practice Bellevue, 1983—. Mem. ad hoc arts com. Suffolk County Legislature, 1971-78; sec., bd. dirs. The Hope Clinic, Bellevue, 1983-87. Mem. Inst. Cert. Fin. Planners, Internat. Assn. Fin. Planning (continuing edn. coordinator 1984-86). Office: 616 - 120th Ave NE Bellevue WA 98005

TAIT, FRANK CHRISTOPHER, computer company executive; b. Phila., Aug. 12, 1958; s. Francis Joseph and Patricia Lillian (Devlin) T.; m. Mary Angela Camille Sharkey, Nov. 13, 1982. BBA, Temple U., 1981. Sorter United Parcel Svc., Phila., 1977-79; office mgr. H & R Block, Phila., 1978-79; security officer John Wanamaker, Phila., 1979-80, sgt., 1980-81, spl. agt. in charge, 1981-82; site supr. Systems & Computer Tech., Malvern, Pa., 1983-84; user liaison Systems & Computer Tech., Malvern, 1984-85, mgr., 1985-87, dir. software devel., 1987—. V.p. Waynewood Commons Homeowners Assn., Wayne, Pa., 1986—. Mem. Nat. Rifle Assn. Republican. Office: Systems & Computer Tech 4 Country View Rd Malvern PA 19355

TAIT, JOHN EDWIN, insurance company executive; b. Moline, Ill., July 8, 1932; s. Edwin Marshall and Hazel Marie (Dodson) T.; m. Erlane Dorothy Dauffenbach, July 20, 1953; children: Michael, Robert, Kathryn. LL.B., U. Ill., 1961. V.p. mortgages Penn Mut. Life Ins. Co., Phila., 1975-79, v.p. investments, 1979-80, fin v.p., 1980-81, exec v.p., 1981-82, pres., chief operating officer, 1982-86, pres., chief exec. officer, 1987-88, chmn., chief exec. officer, 1988—; bd. dirs. Janney, Montgomery, Scott, Inc., Phila., Penn Mutual Life Ins. Co., Phila.; chmn. bd. Indepro Group. Bd. dirs. Drama Guild, 1982-86, YMCA, 1985—, Insurance Fedn. Penn., Mut. Life Insurance Tax Com., Phila Ranger Corps, Phila. Airport Adv. Com.; elder Bryn Mawr Presbyn. Ch., Pa., 1978, trustee, 1986. Served to maj. USAF, 1952-65, Korea; served to maj. Air Nat. Guard. Republican. Clubs: Philadelphia Country (Gladwyne, Pa.); Union League (Phila.). Office: Penn Mut Life Ins Co Independence Sq Philadelphia PA 19172

TAIT, STEWART RUSSELL, textile company executive; b. Phila., Nov. 24, 1945; s. Stewart Russell and Agnes (Allen) T.; m. Mary Colleen Terry, Dec. 15, 1968; children: Patricia Ann, Kelly Suzanne, Susan Kathleen. BS, Pa. State U., 1967. Regional sales mgr. Wyomissing Corp., N.Y.C., 1970-75; mktg. mgr. Wyomissing Corp., Reading, Pa., 1975-85; ptnr. Narrow Fabric Ind., Inc., Wyomissing, Pa., 1985—. Social dir. Maple Grove Raceway, Reading, 1984—. capt. Air NG, Pa. chpt., 1968-73. Recipient Amb. award Maple Grove Raceway, 1986, 87. Mem. Sales and Mktg. Execs. of Reading (pres. 1985-86, disting. sales award 1982). Republican. United Ch. Christ. Office: Narrow Fabric Industries Inc Box 6948 Wyomissing PA 19610

TAKACS, CHRISTINA SUZANNE, service manager; b. Indpls., July 15, 1953; d. George Burton and Mary Lou (Fletcher) Deaton; m. Louis John Takacs, July 9, 1976. Bookkeeper John Davis Men's Wear, Indpls., 1970-74; with Spalding Corp., Chicopee, Mass., 1975—; sr. customer svc. terr. mgr. Spalding Corp., Chicopee, Miss., 1987—. Mem. Nat. Assn. Female Execs. Democrat. Roman Catholic. Office: Spalding Corp 425 Meadow St Chicopee MA 01021

TAKACS, WENDY EMERY, economics educator; b. Wayne, N.J., Aug. 3, 1947; d. Wendell Sherwin and Louise Marie (Shay) Emery. BA, Douglass Coll., 1969; MA in Internat. Rels., John Hopkins U., 1971, MA in Econs., 1973, PhD in Econs., 1976. Rsch. asst. Pres.' Commn. on Internat. Trade and Investment Policy, Washington, 1970-71; economist Internat. Fin. Div. Bd. Govs. Fed. Res. System, Washington, 1975-76; asst. then assoc. prof. U. Md., Balt., 1976—; profl. lectr. John Hopkins SAIS, Washington, 1976—; rsch. fellow The Brookings Instn., Washington, 1973-74; vis. fellow dept. econs. U. Bristol, Eng., 1984-87, Inst. for Internat. Econs., Washington, 1986-87, Inst. for Internat. Econ. Studies, Stockholm, Sweden, 1987; cons. The World Bank, Washington, 1988—. Co-author Auction Quotas and U.S. Trade Policy, 1987; contbr. articles to profl. jours. Mem. Am. Econ. Assn., Can. Econ. Assn., Western Econ. Assn., Md. Combined Tng. Assn. (sec. 1980-82). Home: 11407 Frederick Rd Ellicott City MD 21043 Office: Dept Econs U Md Baltimore MD 21228

TAKAHASHI, KAZUO, architect; b. Maebashi-shi, Gunma-ken, Japan, June 28, 1951; s. Tyuuzi and Kikuno Takahashi; m. Fumiko Takahashi, Apr. 5, 1981; 1 child, Saito. BArch, Ashikaga Inst. Tech., Japan, 1974. Architect Ssekeikobo-K, Tokyo, 1976-78. Prin. works include Dohgi-House, 1981, K-House, 1982, Tomioka-Residence, 1985, Makiura-Residence, 1986. Home: 267 Rock-Machi, Maebashi-shi, Gunma-ken Japan Office: Kazu, 3-5-1-211 Kinuta, Setagaya-ku, Tokyo 157, Japan

TAKEHARA, DANIEL EIJI, investment company executive; b. Honolulu, Jan. 7, 1922; s. Toranoshin and Masayo (Mori) T.; m. Gladys Kimiko Kishinami, Aug. 25, 1949; children—Tyler, JoAnn. Student, U. Hawaii, 1939-46, Honolulu Bus. Coll., 1940-42, U.S. Army Intelligence Sch., 1944-46. Office mgr. Fed. Svcs. Fin., Honolulu, 1946-53; br. mgr. Budget Fin. Plan, Honolulu, 1953-57; ops. supr. First Hawaiian Bank, Honolulu, 1957-60; pres., chief exec. officer Investors Fin., Inc., Honolulu, 1960—, alsobd. dir. Mem. benefit, fund raising com. Kuakini Hosp., Honolulu, 1975-84, trustee; trustee Japanses Culture Ctr. of Hawaii. Master sgt. U.S. Army, 1944-46. Mem. Honolulu Japanese C. of C. (pres., exec. com.) Hawaii C. of C. (vice-chmn. 1987), Hawaii Fin. Svcs. Assn. (pres. 1985—, exec. com.), Japan-Am. Soc. (trustee). Budhist. Clubs: Honolulu Country; Mid-Pacific Country (Kailua Hawaii). Office: Investors Fin Inc 50 S Beretania St Ste 117-B Honolulu HI 96817

TALBERT, RAYMOND BRIAN, financial analyst; b. Pitts., July 17, 1943; s. Henry A. and Clara Baker (Wheelock) T.; children: Brian H., Daniel J. BS, Duquesne U., 1967; MBA, U. Pitts., 1970. Indsl. engr. Pitts. & Lake Erie R.R., 1967-70; sr. auditor Westinghouse Electric Corp., Pitts., 1970-73, cons. planning, 1973-76, cons. corp. devel., 1976-82; prin. R.B. Talbert & Assocs., Pitts., 1982-84; dir. bus. devel. Phillips Industries Inc., Dayton, Ohio, 1984-86; asst. v.p., regional mgr. Valuation Research Corp., Cin., 1986—. Republican. Office: Valuation Rsch Corp 120 W 5th St Cincinnati OH 45202

TALBOT, RODNEY GORDON, investment broker, consultant; b. Kansas City, Mo., Jan. 24, 1957; s. Kenneth Gordon and Phyllis Marie (Lehnert) T.; m. Joy E. Sipe, Dec. 27, 1986. BS in Fin., So. Ill. U., 1979. Chpt. services dir. Tau Kappa Epsilon Internat. Frat., Indpls., 1979-80; account exec. E. F. Hutton, Carmel, Ind., 1980-81, br. product mgr., cons. service dept., 1981-87; sr. investment exec. Moseley Securities Corp., Indianapolis, 1987-88, Prescott, Ball and Turben, Indianapolis, 1988—; instr. fin. Free U., Indpls., 1981-83, Learning Unlimited Indlps., 1983-84; investment com. Tau Kappa Epsilon Internat. Frat.; Indpls., 1982-86. Mem. Indpls. Corp. Basketball Classic, 1985; mem. Indpls. "500" Festival Assocs.; fin. mgr. Pan-Am. Games, 1987. Mem. Indpls. Ambassadors, Indpls. Bond Traders Club, Tau Kappa Epsilon Alumni Assn. (pres. 1986—, mem. investment com. 1982—, chmn. annual fund campaign), Hon. Order of Ky. Cols. Republican. Methodist. Club: Columbia. Lodge: Kiwanis, Sertoma. Home: 13109 Harrison Dr Carmel IN 46032 Office: Prescott Ball and Turben 135 N Pennsylvania St Ste 2060 Indianapolis IN 46204

TALLENT, ROBERT GLENN, chemical engineer, diving educator; b. Nashville, July 4, 1954; s. Glenn Oliver and Virginia Jo (Bell) T.; m. Sandra Marie McKenzie, Aug. 2, 1986; 1 child, Emily Suzanne. BE, Vanderbilt U., 1976. Cert. Scuba diving instr./trainer, emergency med. technician. Dir. tng. Am. Watersports Co., Oxon Hill, Md., 1980-83; chem. engr. Naval Sea Systems Command, Washington, 1980-87; pres. Caribbean Ventures, Alexandria, Va., 1984-88; dist. course dir. Profl. Assn. Diving Instrs., Va., Md., Del., Washington, 1984—; staff Am. Systems Corp., Chantilly, Va., 1988—. Author: Caribbean Ventures Dive Travel Notebook, 1986. Unit commr. Boy Scouts Am., Fairfax, Va., 1988. Lt. (j.g.) U.S. Navy, 1976-80. Mem. Nat. Eagle Scout Assn. (life), Just Clowning Around No. Va., Soc. Automotive Engrs., Undersea Med. Soc., Clowns of Am. Internat. Republican. Methodist. Home: 5504 Lakewhite Ct Fairfax VA 22032

TALLEY, MELVIN GARY, educational administrator; b. West Chester, Pa., Feb. 26, 1945; s. Melvin G. and Alberta M. (Faddis) T.; m. Jolene Keller (div.); children: Kristin Jolene, Mark Gary. BS, Pa. State U., 1967; D (hon.), Bristol (Tenn.) Coll., 1988. Registered rep. DeHaven & Townsend, Phila., 1967-68; dir. Brown Mackie Coll., Salina, Kans., 1968-72, pres., 1972—, also bd. dirs.; pres. Realty Mgmt. Investment Co., Salina, 1976—; advisor region VI HEW, 1976-86; adv. bd. U.S. Office Edn., 1988. Author: Reassessing Values in Postsecondary Edn., 1977. Bd. dirs. St. Francis Boys Home, Salina, 1975. Mem. Pvt. Edn. Research Council, Inner Circle, Assn. Ind. Colls. and Schs. (bd. dirs. Washington chpt. 1978). Home: 215 Greenway Rd Salina KS 67401 Office: Brown Mackie Coll 126 S Santa Fe Salina KS 67401

TALLEY, WILLIAM GILES, JR., container manufacturing company executive; b. Adel, Ga., Sept. 25, 1939; s. William Giles and Mary (McGlamry) T.; BSBA, U. S.C., 1961; m. Jacqueline Vickery, Apr. 14, 1962; children: William Giles, John Lindsey, Bronwyn Ashley. Mgmt. trainee Talley Veneer & Crate Co., Inc., Adel, 1961-62, plant mgr., salesman, Waynesboro, Ga., 1965-67; with Talley's Box Co., Leesburg, Fla., 1962-69, plant mgr., partner, 1967-69; gen. mgr. Growers Container Corp. Inc., Leesburg, 1969—; pres. Talley Acres, 1979—, pres. Talley Wood Products, Inc., 1985—; bd. dirs. Sun Bank N.A., Orlando, Fla. Past chmn. and bd. dirs. Leesburg Hosp. Assn. Served with USAAF, 1961. Mem. Leesburg C. of C. (dir.), Fla. Forestry Assn. (dir. 1977—), Elks, Kiwanis, Sigma Alpha Epsilon. Democrat. Methodist. Office: PO Box 817 Leesburg FL 32748

TALLICHET, JAN BOWEN, service executive; b. Dallas, Sept. 7, 1936; d. Gordon Dilworth and Mary Kate (Butcher) Bowen; m. Harry Eugene Evans, Sept. 25, 1954 (div. 1961); m. Julian Camille Tallichet Jr., June 3, 1967; children: Kimberly Elaine, Alan Keith, Mark Ashby, Camille Anne. Student, North Tex. State U., 1964-65. Owner, mgr. Evans Bus. Services, Dallas, 1962-67, Sanborn's Travel Ctr., San Antonio, 1967-84; group br. mgr. Sanborn's Travel, San Antonio, 1984-88; v.p. JJT Enterprises, Inc., 1985—, TW Industries, Inc., 1988—. Mem. Bandera Fine Arts Assn.; bd. dirs. Salvation Army Aux., San Antonio, 1975. Mem. Inst. Cert. Travel Agts. (cert.), Soc. Incentive Travel Execs., Am. Soc. Assn. Execs. (assoc.), Tex. Soc. Assn. Execs. (assoc.), San Antonio Women in Travel (1st v.p. 1983-84), Freedom's Found. of Valley Forge (life), Cowboy Capital Rodeo Assn. (bd. dirs. 1988—), Altrusa Club. Republican. Mem. Ch. of Christ. Clubs: Woman's of San Antonio (pres. 1974, 76), Opti-Mrs. of San Antonio (pres. 1972-73). Home: Enchanted River Estates Bandera TX 78003 Office: PO Box 2069 Bandera TX 78003

TALUCCI, SAMUEL JAMES, chemical company executive; b. Newark, Del., Feb. 13, 1929; s. Anthony and Josephine (Valocchi) T.; m. Charlotte Sisofo, Sept. 22, 1951 (dec. Oct. 1985); children: Samuel J., Charlene, Anthony, Catherine, Christina, Louisa; m. Louise Coulter, Oct. 1987. BS, U. Del., 1951. Resident mgr. Italian Subs. Rohm & Haas Co., Milan, 1956-58; gen. mgr. Italian Subs. Rohm & Haas Co., 1958-66; mng. dir. Brit. Subs. Rohm & Haas Co., London, 1966-68; dir. European ops. Rohm & Haas Co., Phila., 1968; asst. gen. mgr. Internat. div. Rohm & Haas Co., 1971, v.p. gen. mgr. Plastics div., 1974, v.p. corporate bus., group dir. agrl. and indsl. chems. Plastics div., 1975-83, regional dir. N.Am. region, 1983—; bd. mem. Rosemont Coll. Bd. dirs. Rosemont Coll. Mem. Nat. Assn. Agrl. Chems., Pa. Chamber Bus. & Industry (bd. dirs.). Address: Rohm and Haas Bldg Independence Mall W Philadelphia PA 19105

TAM, TSUN YAM, computer educator; b. Canton, China, May 16, 1949; came to U.S., 1955; s. Yan Soon and Man-Hok (Mok) T.; m. Patricia McDaniel Yacabacci, Dec. 11, 1983. B.S., NYU, 1974, M.A., 1978; student Cooper Union, 1968-71. Stuyvesant High Sch., N.Y.C., 1974-76; adj. asst. prof. NYU, 1974-76, asst. research scientist 1978-79, advisor, faculty, 1980-85; dir. info. systems Studley, Inc., N.Y.C., 1985—; instr. Inst. Audio Research, 1980-82; ptnr. chief engr. Ecompcon Ltd., Closter, N.J., 1983—; cons. Saab-Sania of Am., Orange, Conn., 1983-85; assoc., cons. engr. JBM Assocs., 1984—; cons. Regional Coll. Consortium, P.R., 1982; mem. com. N.Y. State Dept. Edn., 1976-79. Contbr. articles to profl. jours.; author: On the Upgrade 80-Micro; co-author: How To Work with Plastics and Equipment, 1974. Mem. Closter Nature Reserve (N.J.), 1983—. Hebrew Tech. Inst. scholar, 1972-74. Mem. IEEE, Assn. Computing Machinery, N.Y. Acad. Scis., Mensa, Leica Hist. Soc., AAAS, Phi Delta Kappa, Phi Kappa

Lambda, Epsilon Pi Tau. Republican. Home: PO Box 655 Closter NJ 07624 Office: Studley Inc 300 Park Ave New York NY 10022

TAMBERRINO, FRANK MICHAEL, county official; b. Wilmington, Del., May 3, 1955; s. Frank and Mary Pauline (Wilson) T.; m. Charlotte Jane Yates, June 4, 1982; 1 child, F. Michael. BA in Urban Affairs, Va. Poly. Inst. and State U., 1977, M in Urban Regional Planning, 1979. Grad. teaching asst. Va. Poly. Inst. and State U., Blacksburg, 1979; rsch. asst. R. Yearwood Enterprises, Blacksburg, 1979; sr. planner Pinellas County Planning Commn., Clearwater, Fla., 1979-83; exec. dir. com. of 100 Citrus County, Inverness, Fla., 1983-86; exec. dir. Citrus County Indsl. Devel. Authority, Crystal River, Fla., 1986—; Mem. Fla. Dept. Commerce Practitioners Adv. Com., 1988—. Contbr. articles to profl. jours. Mem. Citrus County Extension Svc. Adv. Com., Inverness, 1987—; bd. dirs. Crystal River chpt. Jr. Achievement, 1987., com. of 100 Citrus County, 1987—. Mem. Fla. Econ. Devel. Coun. (bd. dirs. 1988—, v.p. 1989—, Superior award 1987, 88), So. Indsl. Devel. Coun. (state dir. 1989—, Merit award 1986), Ducks Unltd. (chmn. Crystal River chpt. 1987—), Rotary (pres. Inverness chpt. 1987-88). Roman Catholic. Office: Citrus County Indsl Devel Authority PO Box 192 Crystal River FL 32629

TAMKIN, CURTIS SLOANE, real estate development company executive; b. Boston, Sept. 21, 1936; s. Hayward and Etta (Goldfarb) T.; B.A. in Econs., Stanford U., 1958; m. Priscilla Martin, Oct. 18, 1975; 1 son, Curtis Sloane. Vice pres., treas., dir. Hayward Tamkin & Co., Inc., mortgage bankers, Los Angeles, 1963-70; mng. ptnr. Property Devel. Co., Los Angeles, 1970-82; pres. The Tamkin Co., 1982—. Bd. govs. Music Center Los Angeles, 1974—; pres. Los Angeles Master Chorale Assn., 1974-78; mem. vis. com. Stanford U. Libraries, 1982-86; bd. dirs. Los Angeles Philharm. Assn., 1985—. Served to lt. (j.g.) USNR, 1960-63. Mem. Founders League of Los Angeles (pres.), Los Angeles Jr. C. of C. (dir. 1968-69). Republican. Clubs: Burlingame Country, Los Angeles, University. Office: 3600 Wilshire Blvd Los Angeles CA 90010

TAMMANY, ALBERT SQUIRE, III, savings and bank executive; b. Paget, Bermuda, Aug. 21, 1946; s. Albert Squire Jr. and Marion Genevieve (Galloway) T.; m. Teresa Reznor, Sept. 8, 1973. BA Stanford U., 1968; MBA, U. Pa., 1973. Budget and planning officer Tuskegee Inst., Ala., 1973-74; budget analyst controllers dept. Chase Manhattan Bank, N.Y.C., 1974-75; v.p., div. controller Wells Fargo Bank, San Francisco, 1975-78, v.p., retail group controller, 1978-79; v.p., controller Imperial Bank, Los Angeles, 1979-81, sr. v.p. fin., 1981-83; exec. v.p., First Network Savs. Bank, Los Angeles, 1983-87, pres., 1987—, also bd. dirs.; cons. Inst. for Services to Edn., Inc., 1973-74. Woodrow Wilson fellow U. Pa. Served with USMC, 1968-71. Wharton Pub. Policy fellow, 1972. Mem. Am. Bankers Assn. (trust ops. com.). Episcopalian. Clubs: Wharton, Stanford. Office: First Network Savs Bank 10100 Santa Monica Blvd Suite 500 Los Angeles CA 90067

TAMSETT, STEPHEN JAMES, hospital products executive; b. Herkimer, N.Y., May 31, 1946; s. Stephen and Josephine Marie (Servello) T.; A.B. in Biology, SUNY, 1966; B.S. in Microbiology, U. Ga., 1968; m. Susan Ott; children: Anne, Jay, Alison. Plant quality assurance mgr. C.R. Bard Inc., Covington, Ga., 1972-74, central quality assurance mgr., Murry Hill, N.J., 1974-76; corp. quality engr. Millipore Corp., Bedford, Mass., 1976-79; corp. quality assurance mgr. Kendall Co., Boston, 1979-86, corp. regulatory affairs mgr., 1986—. Mem. Am. Soc. Microbiology, Am. Soc. Quality Control, Am. Assn. Med. Instrumentation, Health Industry Mfrs. Assn. (group task force T.E.L.). Republican. Roman Catholic. Club: K.C. Office: Kendall Co 1 Federal St Boston MA 02101

TAN, JOHN K., chemical company executive, educator; b. Fukien, China, Sept. 23, 1934; s. E. Ching Lam and Goct Sia (Kua) T.; m. Lily Go Tan, Mar. 4, 1967; children—Carolyn G., Edward John G., Herbert Joseph G., Steven Julian G. B.S. in Chem. Engring., Mapua Inst. Tech., Manila, 1960; M.Engring., Yale U., 1964; postgrad. Stevens Inst. Tech., Hoboken, N.J., 1964-68. Chem. engr. Globe Paper Mills, Inc., Malabon, Rizal, Philippines, 1960-61; supr. Internat. Chem. Industries Inc., Guiguinto, Bulacan, Philippines, 1961-62; grad. research asst. dept. chem. engring. Yale U., New Haven, 1962-64; sr. research chem. engr. Research Ctr., research and devel. div. Lever Bros. Co., Unilever Ltd., U.S.A., Edgewater, H.J., 1964-65; prin. research chem. engr., 1965-68; tech. mgr., tech. asst. to pres. Internat. Chem. Industries Inc., Guiguinto, Bulacan, Philippines, 1968-70; tech. cons. Econ. Devel. Found., Inc., Makati, Rizal, Philippines, 1968-70; asst. gen. mgr., tech. dir. Philippines Fermentation Indsl. Corp., Guiguinto, Bulacan, Philippines, 1970-73; prof. dept. dept. chemistry and chem. engring. Grad. Sch. Chem. Engring., Mapua Inst. Tech., Intramuros, Manila, Philippines, 1968-79; pres., exec. v.p. Lakeview Garments, Inc., Taguig, Metro Manila, 1976-86, v.p., gen. mgr. Premier Steam Laundry, Inc., Taguig, 1978-85; gen. mgr., No. Chem. Sales Corp., Manila, Tex-Chem Mktg. Corp., Manila, 1972—; pres., chmn. bd. Bay Tank Yard, Inc., Manila, 1972—; exec. v.p., gen. mgr. Multi-Land Devel. Corp., Manila, 1972—; advisor Nat. Bd. Advisors, internat. div. Am. Biog. Inst., Raleigh, N.C. Pres., Philippine Assn. Chem. Suppliers, Inc., Makati, Metro-Manila, 1983—. Trustee Philippine Cultural High Sch.; pres. Mapua Inst. Tech. Chemistry and Chem. Engring. Alumni Assn.; trustee Prof. Lauro A. Limuaco Meml. Found. Conn. State Water Resources Commn. fellow Yale U., 1962-64; United Aircraft scholar Yale U., 1963-64; Univ. scholar Mapua Inst. Tech., Manila, 1955-60, Silver medalist in chem. engring., 1960; Internat. Biog. Assn. fellow, Cambridge, Eng., 1983—; named Outstanding Alumnus, Mapua Inst. Tech. Mem. Am. Inst. Chem. Engrs., Am. Chem. Soc., Yale Sci. and Engring. Assn., Sigma Xi, Eta Sigma Mu. Club: Yale of the Philippines. Home: 1973 Kasoy St, Dasmarinas Village, Makito Metro-Manila Philippines Office: No Chem Sales Corp, 950 Soler St, Binondo Manila Philippines

TAN, LIP-BU, venture capital executive; b. Kuala Lampur, Malaysia, Nov. 12, 1959; came to U.S., 1978; s. Keng-Lian Tan and Yeok-Choong Chew; m. Ysa Tan, Dec. 19, 1981. BS, Nanyang U., Singapore, 1978; MS, MIT, 1981; MBA, U. San Francisco, 1983. Registered profl. engr., Calif.; registered securities rep. Prin. engr. EDS Nuclear Co., San Francisco, 1980-81; lead engr. ECHO Energy Cons., Oakland, Calif., 1981-83; asst. v.p. Chappell & Co., San Francisco, 1982-84; gen. ptnr. Walden Group Venture Capital Funds, San Francisco, 1984—, Lateef Mgmt. Assocs., San Francisco, 1988—; pres., mng. ptnr. Walden Internat. Funds, San Francisco, 1984—; pres. Internat. Venture Capital Investment Corp., Taiwan, 1987—; pres., chief exec. officer Orient Capital and Tech. Corp., San Francisco, 1983—; mem. bus. adv. council U. San Francisco, 1987—; chmn., mng. dir. Pacven Investment Ltd., Singapore, 1988—; exec. dir. Penita Investments, Australia, 1987—; bd. dirs. Mouse System Corp., Santa Clara, Calif., F.P. Spl. Assets Ltd., Hong Kong, Rapro Tech., Fremont, Calif., Orchid Tech., Fremont, Raster Image Processing systems, Boulder, Denver, Eltech Electronics, Singapore. Mem. Western Assn. Venture Capitalists. Republican. Mem. Christian Ch. (Disciples of Christ). Office: Walden Group 750 Battery St 7th Floor San Francisco CA 94111

TANAKA, TOGO W(ILLIAM), financial executive; b. Portland, Oreg., Jan. 7, 1916; s. Masaharu and Katsu (Iwatate) T.; m. Jean Miho Wada, Nov. 14, 1940; children: Jeannine, Christine, Wesley. AB cum laude, UCLA, 1936. Editor Calif. Daily News, 1935-36, Los Angeles Japanese Daily News, 1936-41; documentary historian War Relocation Authority, 1942; staff mem. Am. Friends Service Com., Chgo., 1943-45; editor to head publs. div. Am. Tech. Soc., 1945-52; pub. Chgo. Pub. Corp., 1952-56; pub. School-Indsl. Press, Inc., Los Angeles, 1956-60; chmn. Gramercy Enterprises, Los Angeles; pres. T.W. Tanaka Co., Inc.; city commr. Community Redevel. Agy., Los Angeles, 1973-75; dir. Los Angeles Wholesale Produce Market Devel. Corp., 1979-89; Fed. Res. Bank, San Francisco, 1979-89; mem. adv. bd. Calif. First Bank, Los Angeles, 1976-78. Author: (with Frank K. Levin) English Composition and Rhetoric, 1948; (with Dr. Jean Bordeaux) How to Talk More Effectively, 1948; (with Alma Meland) Easy Pathways in English, 1949. Mem. citizens mgmt. rev. com. Los Angeles Unified Sch. Dist., 1976-77; adv. council to assessor Los Angeles County, 1981-84; bd. dirs. Goodwill Industries of So. Calif.; trustee Wilshire United Meth. Ch., 1976-78, Calif. Acad. Decathlon, 1978-81; bd. dirs. Meth. Hosp. So. Calif., ARC; adv. bd. Nat. Safety Council, Los Angeles, Visitors and Conv. Bur., 1984-88, Am. Heart Assn., 1984-88, New Bus. Achievement, Inc., YMCA Met. Los Angeles, Boy Scouts Am. Council, 1980-86; mem. adv. council Calif. World Trade Commn., 1986-87; Nat. Strategy Info. Ctr. N.Y., Internat. Aids Research Hosp. and Found. Recipient merit award Soc. Advancement Mgmt., 1950, mag. award Inst. Graphic Arts, 1953, 1st award Internat. Council Indsl. Editors, 1955, UNESCO Literacy award, 1974, Los Angeles Archbishop's Ecumenical award, 1986. Mem. Los Angeles Area C. of C. (dir. 1974-76), Japan-Am. Soc. So. Calif. (council 1960-78), Phi Beta Kappa, Pi Sigma Alpha, Pi Gamma Mu. Clubs: Petroleum, Lincoln. Lodges: Masons, Shriners, Rotary (dir., pres. Los Angeles club 1983-84). Home: 949 Malcolm Ave Los Angeles CA 90024 Office: 626 Wilshire Blvd Los Angeles CA 90017

TANARRO, FERNANDO MANUEL, financial consultant; b. La Coruña, Galicia, Spain, Feb. 11, 1933; s. Augusto Tanarro and Adela Nemiña. Degree in Econs., Cen. U., Barcelona, Spain, 1958; M in Taxation with honors, Inst. Católico de Adminstrn. e Industria, Madrid, 1964. Prof. U. Deusto, Bilbao-Vizcaya, Spain, 1969-71; ptnr. Price Waterhouse & Co., Barcelona-Catalunya, 1977—, Casals & Co., Barcelona-Catalunya, 1978—. Author: Investing in Spain, 1986; editor Exlusivas Económicas mag., 1987. Fellow Assn. Internal Accts., Assn. Authorized Pub. Accts., Inst. Taxation, Inst. Censores Cuentas; mem. Asociacion Española de Contabilidad y Adminstrn. de Empresas. Home: Casanova 59-61, 08011 Barcelona Spain Office: Price Waterhouse, Avenida de Roma 2 & 4, 08014 Barcelona Spain

TANENBAUM, MORRIS, telephone company executive; b. Huntington, W.Va., Nov. 10, 1928; s. Reuben S. and Mollie (Kadensky) T.; m. Charlotte Silver, June 4, 1950; children: Robin Sue, Michael Alan. B.A. in Chemistry, Johns Hopkins U., 1949; M.A. in Chemistry, Princeton U., 1950, Ph.D. in Phys. Chemistry, 1952. Mem. tech. staff Bell Telephone Labs., Murray Hill, N.J., 1952-55; dept. head Bell Telephone Labs. (Research div.), 1955-60; asst. dir. Metall. Research Lab., 1960-62, dir. solid state device lab., 1962-64, exec. v.p., 1975-76; also dir.; with Western Electric Co., N.Y.C., 1964-74; v.p. engring. Western Electric Co., 1971-72, v.p. transmission equipment, 1972-75; v.p. engring. and network services AT&T, Basking Ridge, N.J., 1976-78; pres. N.J. Bell Telephone Co., Newark, 1978-80; exec. v.p. AT&T, N.Y.C., 1980-84, 85-86, also vice chmn. bd., 1986—, chief fin. officer, 1988—; chmn., chief exec. officer AT&T Communications, 1984-85; dir. Am. Cyanamid Co., Cabot Corp., State Street Boston Corp. Patentee in field; contbr. numerous articles to profl. jours. Trustee, MIT, Battelle Meml. Inst., Brookings Instn., Johns Hopkins U., Ednl. Broadcasting Corp., N.Y. Philharm., Com. Econ. Devel., Nat. Action Council for Minorities in Engring. Fellow IEEE, Am. Phys. Soc.; mem. Nat. Acad. Engring., Am. Chem. Soc., AIME. Office: AT&T Co 550 Madison Ave Rm 3403 New York NY 10022 other: AT&T Techs Inc 1 Oak Way Berkeley Heights NJ 07922

TANGNEY, JOSEPH G., insurance executive; b. Boston, Dec. 7, 1944; m. Virginia Tangney (div.); children: Christopher, Patrick, Nicole; m. Janice L. Mackin; 1 child, Leah. AB in Econs., Providence Coll., 1966; JD, Boston Coll., 1969; cert. in advanced mgmt., Harvard U., 1982. Atty. Liberty Mut. Ins. Co., Boston, 1969-72, asst. counsel, 1972-78, counsel, 1978-80, v.p., asst. gen. counsel, 1980-83, v.p., mgr. gen. claims, 1983—. Mem. ABA, Arbitration Forums Inc., Ins. Crime Prevention Inst., Mass. and N.J. Guaranty Funds, Mass. Bar Assn., Boston Bar Assn.

TANGUAY, ANITA WALBURGA, real estate broker; b. Oberndorf, Fed. Republic of Germany, July 31, 1936; came to U.S., 1958, naturalized, 1968; d. Karl W. and Luise (Roescheisen) Ederle; m. Donald M. Tanguay, Jan. 21, 1958; children: Elizabeth Ivy, Aimee Marie. Student various schs., Oberndorf and Heidelberg, Fed. Republic of Germany; grad. in real estate, Middlesex (N.J.) Coll., 1981. Sales assoc. Lois Schneider Co., Summit, N.J., 1978-82; pres. Tanguay Assocs. Inc., Millburn, N.J., 1982—. Co-founder Hospice Overlook Hosp., Summit, 1978—, bd. dirs., 1980-84; mem. adv. bd. Summit Child Care Ctr. Recipient Women of Achievement award Greater Millburn (N.J.)/Short Hills (N.J.) Bus. and Profl. Women Inc., 1988. Mem. Bd. Realtors Maplewood Oranges (trustee), N.J. Assn. Realtors, Nat. Assn. Realtors, Comml. Indsl. Real Estate Women (exec. bd., treas. 1983—, pres.). Republican. Roman Catholic. Avocations: gardening, classical music. Home: 11 Ferndale Rd Short Hills NJ 07078 Office: 89 Millburn Ave Ste 101 Millburn NJ 07041

TANIGUCHI, RICHARD RYUZO, building supplies company executive; b. Eleele, Hawaii, Oct. 21, 1913; s. Tokuichi and Sana (Omaye) T.; B.A., U. Hawaii, 1936; m. Sumako Matsui, July 22, 1939; children—Grace Fujiyoshi, Susan Penisten. Acctg. clk. Bank of Hawaii, 1935-36; treas., gen. mgr. Hawaii Planing Mill, 1944-54; pres., gen. mgr. Hawaii Hardware Co., Ltd., Hilo, 1954—; pres., dir. Enterprises Hilo; v.p., dir. Hawaii Funeral Home. Chmn. Hawaii County CSC, 1950-56; vice chmn. Hawaii County Tidal Wave Adv. Com., 1961-68; vice chmn. Hawaii Council Tb and Health Assn., 1965; pres. Am. Cancer Soc., 1969-72, state bd. dirs., 1970-78; pres. Hilo Hongwanji Mission 1968-70, sr. adviser, 1972—; v.p. Hawaii State Hongwanji Mission, 1969—; mem. Hawaii Comprehensive Health Planning Com., 1970-72; gen. chmn. Kanyaku Imin Centennial Com., 1985. Named Hawaii Vol. of Year, Am. Cancer Soc., 1973, recipient Nat. award Am. Cancer Soc., 1978, Fifth Class Order of Sacred Treasure, Emperor of Japan, 1985. Mem. Am. Supply Assn., Nat. Plumbing Wholesalers Assn., Japanese C. of C. and Industry of Hawaii (pres. 1957), Hawaii (dir. 1958-59), Japanese (hon. dir.) chambers commerce, Hawaii Funeral Home (chmn. bd.), Hawaii Island Japanese Community Assn. (pres. 1983-85), Phi Kappa Phi, Pi Gamme Mu. Club: Waiakea. Lodge: Lions (treas., bd. dirs. 1956-60) Home: 572 Iwalani St Hilo HI 96720 Office: Hawaii Hardware Co 550 Kilauea Ave Hilo HI 96720

TANIS, JAMES NELSON, chemical company executive; b. Hackensack, N.J., May 22, 1944; s. Vernon Harold and Eleanore Elizabeth (Jones) T.; m. Sandra Jane Lashley, June 28, 1969; children: Tamara Jeane, Matthew James. BA, Marietta Coll., 1966; MBA, Fairleigh Dickinson U., 1969. Hall engr. Calgon Corp., Pitts., 1966-69; sales mgr. Olin Corp., Stamford, Conn., 1969-73; staff cons. E.I. duPont de Nemours Inc., Wilmington, Del., 1973-75; prin. cons. Drew Chem. Corp., Boonton, N.J., 1975-79; v.p., gen. mgr. The Perolin Co., Wilton, Conn., 1979-83; pres. Perolin-Bird Archer, Cobourgh, Ontario, Can., 1979-83; internat. mktg. mgr. Aquatec Quimica LTDA, Sal Paulo, Brazil, 1983-86; pres. LTAN Inc., Ridgefield, Conn., 1986-88; v.p., gen. mgr. Gen. Chem. Corp., Parsippany, N.J., 1988—. Author: Procedures of Indsl. Water Treatment, 1987. Mem. Nat. Assn. Corrosion Engrs., Am. Water Assn., Am. Pulp and Paper Industry. Office: Gen Chem Corp 90 E Halsey Rd Parsippany NJ 07054

TANKERSLEY, JAMES DANIEL, information systems executive; b. Clinton, Ky., June 6, 1952; s. Coy and Robbye Laverne (Williams) T.; m. Judy Faye Cagle, Nov. 6, 1975; children: Sabrina, Nickie, Lee. Cert. in data processing, So. Ohio Coll., 1971. Computer programmer Merit Clothing Co., Mayfield, Ky., 1972-75; programmer, analyst Comml. Data Processing Inc., Mayfield, 1975, Ingersol-Rand, Mayfield, 1975-77; programmer, analyst Comml. Systems Inc., Paducah, Ky., 1977-80, mgr. applications and techniques, 1980-84; mgr. systems Mednet Inc., Paducah, 1984-86; dir. tech. svcs. Appalachian Computer Svcs. Inc., London, Ky., 1986-87, exec. dir. mgmt., 1987—. Mem. exec. bd. dirs. Laurel County Ednl. Forum, London, 1987—. Mem. Am. Mgmt. Assn., West Ky. Bapt. Assn. (exec. bd. dirs. 1982-86). Democrat. Office: Appalachian Computer Svcs Inc Box 140 London KY 40741

TANNEBAUM, SAMUEL HUGO, accountant; b. Oklahoma City, Aug. 15, 1933; s. Simon L. and Eva (Kapp) T.; B.B.A. with spl. distinction, U. Okla., 1955; m. Nita Mae Levy, June 12, 1955; children: Joel L., Marilyn J. Staff acct. Alford, Meroney & Co., Dallas, 1955-61; pvt. practice acctg., Dallas, 1961-63; partner Tannebaum & Bindler, C.P.A.s, Dallas, 1963-67; mng. partner Tannebaum, Bindler & Lewis, C.P.A.s, Dallas, 1967-80, Tannebaum, Bindler & Co., C.P.A.s, Dallas, 1980-84; pres. Tannebaum Bindler & Co., P.C., 1984—; dir. Nat. Center Banks, Inc., 1983-86. Mem. adv. council Communities Found. Tex., 1987—; bd. dirs. Dallas Home and Hosp. for Jewish Aged, 1973-76; trustee Temple Emanu-El, Dallas, 1976-83, treas., 1980-82, v.p., 1982-83. Named C.P.A. of Yr., Dallas chpt. Tex. Soc. C.P.A.s, 1976; C.P.A., Tex., Okla. Mem. Am. Inst. C.P.A.s (council 1979-82), Tex. Soc. C.P.A.s (dir., past v.p., past chpt. pres.), Nat. Assn. Estate Planning Councils (dir. 1978-82, treas. 1982-83, v.p. 1983-84, pres. 1984-85), Dallas Estate Planning Council (past pres.). Clubs: Brookhaven Country, University. Home: 5820 Meletio Ln Dallas TX 75230 Office: 2323 Bryan St Suite 700 Lock Box 107 Dallas TX 75201

TANNEHILL, BOBBY EDWARD, technical training consultant; b. Marshalltown, Iowa, Apr. 20, 1952; s. Zelbert Hansel and Alice Genevieve (Brown) T.; m. Karla Ann Wall, May 1, 1971; children: David Edward, Amanda Dawn. BS, So. Ill. U., 1978; MEd, U. S.C., 1983. Instr. PWR simulator Gen. Physics Corp., Chattanooga, 1979-80; dir. tng. and tech. svcs. Gen. Physics Corp., Columbia, Md., 1988—; project mgr. V.C. Summer Nuclear Sta., Columbia, 1980-83; project mgr. Duane Arnold Energy Ctr., Cedar Rapids, Iowa, 1983-85, dir. tng. and tech. svcs. dept., 1985-88. With USN, 1971-79. Mem. Am. Nuclear Soc., Lions (pres. local club 1987-88). Office: Gen Physics Corp 6700 Alexander Bell Dr Columbia MD 21046

TANNENBERG, DIETER E. A., manufacturing and distributing company executive; b. Chevy Chase, Md., Nov. 24, 1932; s. E.A. Wilhelm and Margarete Elizabeth (Mundhenk) T.; m. Ruth Hansen, Feb. 6, 1956; 1 child, Diana Tannenberg Collingsworth Cann. BSME, Northwestern U., 1959. Registered profl. engr., N.Y., Conn., Ohio, Ill., Ind., Wis., N.J. Supervising engr. Flexonics div. Calumet & Hecla, Inc., Chgo., 1959-61, chief engr., 1961-63, program mgr. advanced space systems, 1963-65, dir. mfg. services, 1965-67; dir. mfg. engring. SCM Corp., Cortland, N.Y., 1967-69; tech. dir. internat. Singer Co., N.Y.C., 1969-71; v.p. ops. internat. div. Addressograph-Multigraph Corp., Cleve., 1971-74; mng. dir. Addressograph Multigraph GmbH, Frankfurt/Main, W. Ger., 1974-78; v.p., gen. mgr. Europe, Middle East, Africa AM Internat. Inc., Chgo., 1978-79; pres. AM Bruning div., 1979-82, AM Multigraphics Div., Mt. Prospect, Ill., 1982-86; corp. v.p. AM Internat., Inc., 1981-83, corp. sr. v.p., 1983-86; chmn. bd. dirs., pres., chief exec. officer Sargent-Welch Sci. Co., Skokie, Ill., 1986—; chmn. Am. Internat. GmbH, Frankfurt, 1977-86; bd. dirs. Artra Group, Inc. Contbr. chpts. to handbooks, articles to tech., trade mags.; patentee in machinery field. Served with M.I., U.S. Army, 1953-56. Named Man of Yr. Quick Print Mag., 1985. Mem. Assn. Reprodn. Materials Mfrs. (bd. dirs. 1979-82, v.p. 1980-82), Nat. Assn. Quick Printers (bd. dirs. 1982-84), Nat. Printing Equipment and Supplies Mfg. Assn. (bd. dirs. 1983-86, chmn. govt. affairs com. 1985-86), Computer and Bus. Equipment Mfg. Assn. (bd. dirs. 1983-86), Soc. Am. Value Engrs. (hon. v.p. 1985—), Value Found. (trustee 1985—), Chgo. Council Fgn. Relations, ASME, Nat. Soc. Profl. Engrs., Pi Tau Sigma. Club: Economic (Chgo.). Office: Sargent-Welch Sci Co 7400 N Linder Ave Skokie IL 60076

TANNER, JACQUI DIAN, chemist, information scientist; b. Indpls., Feb. 2, 1946; d. Richard O. and Norris (Shane) Tanner; divorced; children: Patrick Mahaffey, David Bridgeforth, Regina Easley, Darla Smith, Mark Young. BS, Marian Coll., 1970; MS, Ball State U., 1982. With Union Carbide, Indpls., 1965-68; with Eli Lilly & Co., Indpls., 1968-85, sr. patent specialist, 1978-85; with Ayerst Research Labs, Princeton, N.J., 1985-88; sr. info. scientist, head chem. and patent info. sect. Ortho Pharm. Co. (name now R.W. Johnson-Pharm. Rsch. Inst.), Raritan, N.J., 1988—. Bd. dirs., hosp. counselor Marion County Victims Advocates Program, 1978—; mem. youth adv. bd. Ctr. for Leadership Devel., 1979-85; mem. adv. bd. Walker Career Ctr., 1981-86; mem. Warren Twp. (Ind.) Sch. Improvement Council, 1980-86; mem. Warren Twp. curriculum study steering com., 1982-86; founder, exec. dir. Found. for the Success of Unwed Parents, 1986—. Mem. Am. Statis. Assn., Assn. Info. Mgrs., Am. Soc. Info. Sci., Spl. Library Assn., AAAS, N.Y. Acad. Sci., ALA, Am. Chem. Soc. Roman Catholic. Office: RW Johnson-Pharm Rsch Inst Rte 202 PO Box 300 Raritan NJ 08869-0602

TANOUS, PETER JOSEPH, banker; b. N.Y.C., May 21, 1938; s. Joseph Carrington and Rose Marie (Mokarzel) T.; BA in Econs., Georgetown U., 1960; m. Barbara Ann MacConnell, Aug. 18, 1962; children: Christopher, Helene, William. With Smith, Barney & Co., Inc. (now Smith Barney, Harris Upham & Co., Inc.), N.Y.C., 1963-78, 2d v.p., mgr. Paris office, 1967, v.p., 1968-78, resident European sales mgr., Paris, 1969-71, internat. sales mgr., N.Y.C., 1971-78, 1st v.p., 1975-78; chmn. bd. Petra Capital Corp., N.Y.C., 1978-81, now dir.; exec. v.p., Bank Audi (USA), N.Y.C., 1984—, dir. Bank Audi, Calif.; del. U.S.-Saudi Arabian Joint Econ. Commn. Bus. Dialogue; trustee Browning Sch., N.Y.C. Mem. internat. bd. advisers Ctr. Social Policy in Middle East Harvard U.; mem. adv. bd. Nat. Coun. U.S.-Arab Rels.; bd. dirs. Kahlil Gibran Centennial Found.; trustee The Fleming Sch., N.Y.C. 1st lt. AUS, 1961-63. Mem. Am. Geographical Soc. (councillor), Georgetown U. Alumni Assn. (gov. 1968-71), Georgetown Club France (pres. 1968-71). Roman Catholic. Clubs: Met. (N.Y.C.); Automobile de France (Paris). Author: The Earhart Mission, 1979; co-author: The Petrodollar Takeover, 1975, The Wheat Killing, 1979. Earhart Mission, 1979. Home: 136 E 64th St New York NY 10021 Office: 600 Fifth Ave New York NY 10020

TANSKY, BURTON, department store executive; b. 1938; married. BA, U. Pitts., 1960. With Kaufmann's, 1961-67; from asst. store mgr. to mgr. Filenes, Boston, 1967-71; mdse. mgr. Rikes, Dayton, Ohio, 1971-74; v.p. Forbes and Wallace, Springfield, Ohio, 1974, I. Magnin, San Francisco, 1974-77; from sr. v.p. to exec. v.p. Saks and Co., N.Y.C., 1977-80, pres., 1980—; also bd. dirs. Saks & Co., N.Y.C. Office: Saks & Co 611 Fifth Ave New York NY 10023 *

TANZER, JED SAMUEL, lawyer, financial consultant; b. Arverne, N.Y., Nov. 16, 1947; s. David and Mildred (Bondy) T.; B.S. with honors in Social Sci., SUNY, Oneonta, 1970; J.D. cum laude, Syracuse U., 1978, M.B.A., 1978; m. Sally Jane Ketcham, July 10, 1971. Tchr., union grievance chmn. Central Sch. Dist., Windsor, N.Y., 1970-75; research asst. Sch. Mgmt., Syracuse (N.Y.) U., 1977-78; admitted to N.Y. State bar, 1979, Fed. Dist. Ct. bar, 1979, U.S. Tax Ct. bar, 1979; sr. atty. Ayco/Am. Express Corp., Albany, N.Y., 1978-82, assoc. regional mgr., 1982-85, v.p., regional mgr., 1986—; regional v.p., 1988—; fin. cons., 1978—. Permanent teaching cert. N.Y. State; bd. dirs. Cobb Youth Chorus Ga., 1988—. Mem. Am. Bar Assn. (com. state and local taxation 1981-82), N.Y. State Bar Assn., Justinian Law Soc., Beta Gamma Sigma, Kappa Delta Pi. Home: 1113 Autumn Chase Ct Marietta GA 30064 Office: 2839 Paces Ferry Rd Suite 1250 Atlanta GA 30339

TAPP, LAWRENCE G., packaging and printing company executive; b. Thunder Bay, Ont., Can., Oct. 6, 1937; s. Grenville E. and Marguerite Tapp; m. Joanne Fuller, Jan. 3, 1959; children: John Grenville, Jill Mary Ellen. BA, McMaster U., Hamilton, Can.; Diploma in Bus. Adminstrn., U. Kans. Instr. mgmt. tng. Bell Can., Toronto, Ont., 1961; with labor rels. Ford Motor Co. of Can., Oakville, 1963-66; orgn. planner Gen. Foods, Toronto, 1966-67; dir. personnel orgn. planning Hallmark Cards, Toronto, 1967-69, assoc. dir. mfg., 1969-72, v.p. ops., bd. dirs., 1972-78; gen. mgr. Lawson Graphics Man., Winnipeg, 1978-79; div. mgr., bd. dirs. Lawson and Jones West, Winnipeg, 1979-80; exec. v.p., chief operating officer Lawson and Jones Ltd., London, Ont., 1980-82; pres., chief exec. officer Lawson and Jones Ltd., London, 1982-85, Lawson Mardon Group Ltd., London, 1985—; bd. dirs. Roman Corp. Ltd., Graphic ARts Tech. Found.; v.p. U.K. Inst. Packaging. Bd. govs. McMaster U., 1988—; chmn. Aquatic Trust of Can. Mem. Can. Amateur Swimming Assn. (past chmn., pres.), Aquatic Fedn. Can. (past chmn.), Can. Olympic Assn., Ont. Club. Conservative. Home: 2180 Marine Dr, Oakville, ON Canada L6L 5V2 Office: Lawson Mardon Group Ltd, 6711 Mississauga Rd, Mississauga, ON Canada L5N 2W3

TAPP, RONALD GENE, insurance company executive; b. Bloomington, Ind., July 15, 1941; s. Wayne E. and Golda G. Tapp; student Ind. U., 1959-63; m. Helen L. Black, Sept. 24, 1977; children—Rhonda Jean, Randy G., Rita Jean. Printer, Phoenix Newspapers, Inc., 1972-76; ins. agt. Am. Republic Ins. Co., Phoenix, 1976-77; ins. agt. Minn. Protective Life Ins. Co., Phoenix, 1977-78, gen. agt., 1978-82, Southwestern regional mgr., 1978-82; sec.-treas. Internat. Benefit Cons., Ltd., 1981—; mktg. dir. Lincoln Benefit Life, 1982—; regional mgr. Pan Am. Life Ins. Co., 1983-85; pres. Empire-Am. Ins. Cons., Ltd., 1982—, Empire-Am. Bonding, Inc., 1985—. Republican precinct committeeman, also state committeeman for dist. 19. Served with U.S. Army, 1964-65. Recipient various profl. awards, 1977-81. Mem. Ariz. Public Employees Assn. (assoc.), Profl. Bail-Agts. Ariz. (pres. 1987—), Bail-Agts. of the U.S. (pres.'s coun. 1987—). Home: 144 E Bluefield Phoenix AZ 85022 Office: 4215 N 16th St Suite 2 Phoenix AZ 85016

TAPPAN, DAVID S., JR., engineering, construction, natural resources management company executive; b. Hainan, People's Republic of China, May 27, 1922; m. Jeanne Boone. B.A., Swarthmore Coll., 1943; M.B.A., Stanford U., 1948. With sales and engring. dept. U.S. Steel Corp., 1948-52; adminstrv. asst. to v.p. of sales Fluor Corp., 1952-59, v.p. domestic sales,

1959-62, v.p. domestic and internat. sales, 1962-68, also. bd. dirs., sr. v.p., 1968-71; pres. Fluor Corp., Irvine, Calif., 1987-88; chmn., chief exec. officer, dir. Fluor Corp., Irvine, 1988—; pres. Fluor Engrs. & Constructors Inc. (now named Fluor Daniel Inc.), 1971-76, vice chmn. bd., 1976-82, pres., chief operating officer, 1982-84, chmn., chief exec. officer, from 1984; bd. dirs. Genentech Inc., Allianz Ins. Co., The Nat. Council for U.S.-China Trade Inc., Los Angeles-Guangzhou Sister City Assn., Nat. Energy Found.; bd. overseas exec. council on fgn. diplomats and adv. com. Export-Import Bank of U.S. Bd. dirs. Nat. Bus. Com. for Arts; chmn. Orange County Orgn.; councillor U. So. Calif. Sch. Bus. and Adminstrn., Stanford U. Grad. Sch. Bus. Served to lt. (j.g.) USNR, 1943-46. Mem. Am. Petroleum Inst., Los Angeles C. of C. (vice chmn., bd. dirs.). Office: Fluor Corp 3333 Michelson Dr Irvine CA 92730 *

TAPPIN, ANTHONY GERALD, marketing executive; b. London, July 17, 1925; came to U.S., 1940; naturalized, 1944; s. Edward Laurence Charles and Cecilia Mary (Seymour) T.; m. Nancy C. Harper, May 17, 1952; children: Cynthia Marie, Amy Elizabeth. AB, Cornell U., 1949; advanced mgmt. program, Harvard Bus. Sch., 1968. Asst. product mgr., chem. div. FMC Corp., N.Y.C., 1950; rep. FMC Corp., Washington, 1950-52; dist. sales mgr. FMC Corp., Cin., 1952-58, gen. sales mgr., 1958-67, dir. mktg., asst. div. mgr., 1967-70, dir. purchases, 1970-77, regional v.p., corp. exec. mktg., 1977-82, v.p. corp. exec. mktg., 1982—. Active United Fund, Crippled Children's Assn; pres., bd dirs. Saddle Brook Community Assn., 1985—. Served with inf. U.S. Army, 1944-46. Decorated Bronze star, Combat Inf. Badge. Mem. Am. Mgmt. Assoc. Mktg. Council, Nat. Assn. Mfrs. (dir. exec. com. 1985-87), Nat. Assn. Purchasing Mgmt. (cert. purchasing mgr.), Nat. Accounts Mgrs. Assn. (dir. 1978-82), Machine Allied Products Inst. (mktg. council), Racemics, Chem. Industries Council Ill. (dir. 1984—), Phi Gamma Delta. Roman Catholic. Clubs: Cornell Fairfield County (Conn.) (pres. 1972-73), Cornell of Chgo., Harvard Bus. Sch., Chicago, Mid-America (Chgo.); Country of Darien (Conn.); Capilano Golf and Country (Vancouver, B.C., Can.); Butterfield Country (Oak Brook, Ill.). Office: FMC Corp 200 E Randolph Dr Chicago IL 60601

TARALLO, ANGELO NICHOLAS, industrial gas and health care company executive, lawyer; b. Bklyn., May 3, 1940; s. Nicola and Josephine (Guariglia) T.; m. Patricia Klubnik, Nov. 21, 1964; 4 children. B.A., Columbia U., 1961, J.D., 1964; LL.M., NYU Law Sch., 1970. Bar: N.Y., N.J. Assoc. gen. counsel, mng. atty. The BOC Group, Inc., Murray Hill, N.J., 1977-78; asst. v.p. The BOC Group, Inc., Montvale, N.J., 1978-80, v.p. corp. activities, 1980-83, v.p. fin. and adminstrn., 1983-84, sr. v.p. fin. and adminstrn., 1984—; bd. dirs. Union Chelsea Nat. Bank, N.Y. Bd. dirs. United Way Bergen County, Paramus, N.J. Mem. ABA, N.Y. State Bar Assn., N.J. State Bar Assn., Fin. Execs. Inst. Roman Catholic. Office: BOC Group Inc 85 Chestnut Ridge Rd Montvale NJ 07645

TARANTINO, ANTHONY LOUIS, private investigator, investigation company executive; b. Brockton, Mass., Nov. 10, 1950; s. Louis Anthony and Louise Mary (Minerva) T.; m. Rose Masis Robbins, Jan 2, 1988. BA in Polit. Sci., L.I. U., 1975. Lic. pvt. investigator, N.Y., N.J. Investigator Intelligence Svcs., Inc., Hauppauge, N.Y., 1975-79, account exec., 1979-80, dir. protective svcs., 1980—, v.p., 1982—. Mem. Sigma Alpha Epsilon. Home: 75 Holiday Park Dr Centereach NY 11720 Office: Intelligence Svcs Inc 140 Adams Ave Ste 9 Hauppauge NY 11788

TARANTO, HARRI VITALI, management consultant; b. Istanbul, Turkey, Dec. 31, 1952; came to U.S., 1972; m. Ann L. Engelland, 1977; children: Nicholas, Simon. BS in Engring., Yale U., 1976; MBA, Columbia U., 1980. Analyst GTE, Stamford, Conn., 1976-78; sr. assoc. McKinsey and Co., N.Y.C., 1980-83; v.p., ptnr., bd. dirs. The Wilkerson Group, N.Y.C., 1983—. Office: The Wilkerson Group Inc 666 3d Ave New York NY 10017

TARBOX, FRANK KOLBE, insurance company executive; b. Mineola, N.Y., Feb. 27, 1923; s. John Preston and Mary (Kolbe) T.; m. Eleanor Borden, May 1, 1948; children: John Borden, Kathryn Ann. Student, Swarthmore Coll., 1940-42; A.B., U. Pa., 1947, LL.B., 1950. Pvt. practice law 1950-53, 55-60; asst. U.S. atty. Eastern Dist. Pa., 1953-55; v.p. adminstrn. Penn Mut. Life Ins. Co., Phila., 1960-71; pres. Penn Mut. Life Ins. Co., 1971-78, chief exec. officer, 1973-86, chmn. bd. dirs., 1979-87; bd. dirs. ARA Services, Inc., Quaker Chem. Co., Penn Mut. Life Ins. Co. With USNR, 1942-46. Office: Pa Mut Life Ins Co Independence Sq Philadelphia PA 19172

TARBOX, LAURA ANN, financial planner; b. Santa Monica, Calif., June 15, 1957; d. Charles Tarbox and Neta Mae (Kleaveland) Gagen. BA in English, UCLA, 1979. Cert. fin. planner. Ptnr. Gagen & Co., Tustin, Calif., 1980-85; owner Tarbox Equity, Costa Mesa, Calif., 1985—; instr. U. So. Calif.-Calif. Luth., Thousand Oaks, 1985—, U. Calif., Irvine, 1988—. Group leader Community Workshop-Youth at Risk, L.A., 1983-85; coord. Neighborhood Watch Program, Long Beach, Calif., 1984; participant Hunger Project, 1978—. Mem. AAUW (bd. dirs. 1985—), Inst. Cert. Fin. Planners (dir. 1986—, pres. Orange County 1988—), Internat. Assn. Fin. Planning, Soroptimist. Libertarian. Office: Tarbox Equity 3070 Bristol Ste 410 Costa Mesa CA 92626

TARGOFF, MICHAEL BART, defense corporation executive, lawyer; b. N.Y.C., July 20, 1944; s. Jerome H. and Tillie R. T.; m. Cheri Kamen, June 11, 1966; children: Ramie, Joshua, Jason, Hannah. AB, Brown U., 1966; JD cum laude, Columbia U., 1969. Bar: N.Y. 1969. Law clk. to presiding justice U.S. Dist. Ct. Mass., 1969-70; assoc. Willkie, Farr & Gallagher, N.Y.C., 1970-76; ptnr. Willkie, Fair & Gallagher, N.Y.C., 1976-80; gen. counsel, v.p. Savin Corp., Valhalla, N.Y., 1980-81; gen. counsel, v.p., sec. Loral Corp., N.Y.C., 1981—. Harlan Fiske Stone scholar, 1968-69. Mem. ABA, N.Y. State Bar Assn., Assn. of Bar of City of N.Y. Office: Loral Corp 600 Third Ave 36th Fl New York NY 10016

TARGOWSKI, ANDREW STANISLAW, computer educator, consultant; b. Warsaw, Poland, Oct. 9, 1937; came to U.S., 1980; s. Stanislaw Adam and Halina (Krzyzanska) T.; m. Alicja Kowalczyk, Jan. 22, 1966 (div. 1977); 1 child, Stanislaw; m. Irmina Dura, Mar. 11, 1978; children: Agnieszka, Kubas, John. MS in Indsl. Engring., MBA, Warsaw Poly., 1961, PhD in Computer Sci., 1968. Head dept. systems design Inst. Orgn. and Machinery Industry, Warsaw, 1961-64; pres. Warsaw Computer Svc. Ctr., 1965-71; sr. v.p. Bur. for Info. Tech., 1971-74; assoc. prof. Hamilton Coll., Clinton, N.Y., 1974-75; cons. Machinery Industry Ministry, Warsaw, 1976-79; prof. computer info. systems Western Mich. U., Kalamazoo, 1980-82, 85—; prof. Hofstra U., Hempstead, N.Y., 1982-84, Ea. Ky. U., Richmond, 1984-85; chmn., chief exec. officer Semantex, Systems Architects, Inc., 1988—. Author: Organization of Computer Centers, 1971, Informatics: A Key to Prosperity, 1971, Organization of Data Processing Process, 1975, Informatics, Models of Systems and Development, 1980, Red Fascism, 1982. Pres. Polish Tennis Assn., Warsaw, 1971-72; mem. planning com. Polish Study Ctr. Mem. Assn. Info. Resources Mgmt., Data Processing Mgmt. Assn., Assn. Computer Machinery, Assn. Bus Communication, Human Resources Mgmt. and Organizational Behavior, Polish Inst. Arts and Scis., U.S. Tennis Assn., Centre Courte Club. Roman Catholic. Home: 7682 Farmington Kalamazoo MI 49002 Office: Western Mich U Dept Bus Info Systems Kalamazoo MI 49008

TARLSON, NICK GLENN, financial advisor; b. Anchorage, May 31, 1955; s. Glenn Robert and Popi (Zafiri) T.; m. Mauna Anne Arnzen, Aug. 16, 1980; children: Claire, Diana, George. BBA, Seattle U., 1976. CPA, Calif., Wash., La. Mgr. Ernst & Whinney, San Francisco, 1976-83; v.p., sec., treas. Brayer Elec. Co., San Francisco, 1983-86; owner, mgr. Tarlson & Assoc., San Francisco, 1986—; bd. dirs. Brayer Electric Co., Brayer Lighting Co., San Francisco; pres.Jupiter Group, 1986-87, bd. dirs.; treas. Galacar & Co., 1987—, bd. dirs. Chmn. tax com. Bldg. Owners and Mgrs., San Francisco, 1985—; treas., trustee Opera West Found., San Francisco, 1986—. Republican. Greek Orthodox. Home: 73 Orange Larkspur CA 94939 Office: Tarlson & Assoc 444 Natoma St San Francisco CA 94103

TARNOFF, JEFFREY, investment advisor; b. N.Y.C., June 11, 1947; s. Edwin Max and Betty Fertig T.; m. Diane Winifred Seaman, Mar. 15, 1975; 1 child, Sarah W. BS cum laude, Lehigh U., 1969; MBA, U. Chgo., 1971. Securities analyst Equitable Life Assurance Soc. U.S., N.Y.C., 1971-73; investment officer Chase Investors Mgmt. Corp. N.Y., N.Y.C., 1973-76; v.p. Mfrs. Hanover Trust Co., N.Y.C., 1976-79; investment adv. Weiss, Peck & Greer, N.Y.C., 1979-81; exec. v.p., dir. ADV Fund Inc., N.Y.C., 1979-81; v.p. Verus Capital, 1981-83, v.p. Arnhold & S. Bleichroeder, Inc., 1981-83, Oppenheimer Capital Corp., 1983-86, sr. v.p., 1986—; pres. 470 West End Corp., 1982-84, 87—; bd. dirs., 1980—, treas., 1984, 87, 88—; trustee The Town Sch., Inc., 1988—. Mem. class gifts com., ann. giving fund, class agt. Lehigh U. Mem. Fin. Analysts Fedn., N.Y. Soc. Security Analysts, U. Chgo. Grad. Sch. Bus. Alumni Assn. (bd. dirs. 1984-87). Home: 470 West End Ave New York NY 10024 Office: Oppenheimer Capital Corp 200 Liberty St New York NY 10281

TARNOFF, JEROME, lawyer; b. Bklyn., June 22, 1931; s. Meyer and Anne (Soshnick) T.; children: Marcy Jane, Margery Lynne. AB, Syracuse U., 1952; JD, Columbia U., 1957. Bar: N.Y. 1957, Pa. 1983, U.S. Dist. Ct. (so. and ea. dists.) N.Y. 1960, U.S. Ct. Appeals (2d cir.) 1961. Ptnr., Sheldon and Tarnoff, N.Y.C., 1957-78, Feldesman, D'Atri, Tarnoff & Lubitz, N.Y.C., 1978, Baskin and Sears, P.C., N.Y.C., 1979-84, Baskin & Steingut P.C., 1984-85, Berger & Steingut, 1986—. Contbr. article to legal jour. Chmn. policy com. N.Y. Dem. Party, 1975-78, vice chmn. N.Y. County, 1978—, mem. nat. com., 1980-88; mem. Community Planning Bd. #8, 1966-75; bd. dirs. Grand St. Settlement, 1973—, Assoc. Y's of N.Y., 1972-88. With U.S. Army, 1952-54. Recipient Disting. Service award NAACP, 1975, cert. Achievement El Diario-La Prensa, 1977. Mem. ABA, Pa. State Bar, N.Y. State Bar Assn., Assn. of Bar of City of N.Y., N.Y. County Lawyers, Am. Arbitration Assn. (nat. panel arbitrators), Phi Alpha Delta, Hollywood Golf Club (Deal, N.J.), Audubon, Masons. Jewish. Avocation: golf. Home: 1735 York Ave New York NY 10128 Office: Berger & Steingut 600 Madison Ave New York NY 10022

TARR, CURTIS W., academic administrator; b. Stockton, Calif., Sept. 18, 1924; s. F.W. and Esther (Reed) T.; m. Elizabeth May Myers, 1955 (div. 1978); children: Pamela Elizabeth, Cynthia Leigh; m. Marilyn Van Stralen, 1979. B.A., Stanford U., 1948, Ph.D., 1962; M.B.A., Harvard U., 1950; L.H.D., Ripon Coll., 1965, Grinnell Coll., 1969, Lincoln Coll., 1980; LL.D., Lawrence U., 1974, Ill. Wesleyan U., 1980. Research asst., instr. Harvard U., 1950-52; v.p. Sierra Tractor & Equipment Co., Chico, Calif., 1952-58; staff mem. 2d Hoover Commn., 1954-55; asst. dir. summer session Stanford U., 1961-62, dir., 1962-63, asst. dean humanities and scis., 1962-63, lectr. bus. sch., 1962-63; pres. Lawrence U., Appleton, Wis., 1963-69; asst. sec. for manpower and res. affairs Air Force, 1969-70; dir. SSS, Washington, 1970-72; under sec. state for security assistance 1972-73, acting dep. under sec. state for mgmt., 1973; v.p. overseas devel. Deere & Co., Moline, Ill., 1973; v.p. parts distbn. and materials mgmt. Deere & Co., 1973-81, v.p. mgmt. devel., 1981-83; dean and prof. Johnson Grad. Sch. Mgmt. Cornell U., 1984—; trustee Inst. Paper Chemistry, 1963-69; dir. Banta Corp., Menasha, Wis., Intermet Corp., Atlanta, State Farm Mut. Ins. Co., Bloomington, Ill. Author: Private Soldier, 1976, By the Numbers, 1981. Chmn. Task Force on Govt. Orgn., Fin. and Tax Distbn. for State Wis., 1967-69; chmn. Def. Manpower Commn., 1974-76, Ill. State Scholarship Commn., 1978-79, Quad Cities Grad. Study Ctr., 1982-84, Republican candidate for Congress 2d Dist., Calif., 1958. Served with AUS, 1943-46, ETO. Recipient Exceptional Civilian Service medal Air Force Dept., 1970; Distinguished Service award SSS, 1975. Republican. Mem. United Ch. Christ. Clubs: University (Chgo.); Cosmos (Washington); University (N.Y.C.). Home: 529 Cayuga Heights Rd Ithaca NY 14850 Office: Cornell Univ Grad Sch Mgmt Ithaca NY 14853

TARR, KENNETH JAY, investment company executive; b. N.Y.C., Mar. 1, 1945; s. Julius and Alice (Tamres) T.; 1 child, Alexandra Jennifer. BA, U. Pa., 1967; MBA, Columbia U., 1971. With Chem. Bank, N.Y.C., 1971-73; asst. v.p. Standard and Poors/Inter Capital, N.Y.C., 1972-74; founder, mgr. S&P/Market Insights, N.Y.C., 1974-75; v.p. Kuhn Loeb and Co., N.Y.C., 1975-77; asst. v.p. Bessemer Trust Co., N.Y.C., 1977-80, v.p., 1980-82, sr. v.p., 1982—, dir. research, 1984. Mem. N.Y. Soc. Security Analysts. Clubs: N.Y. Yacht, Princeton (N.Y.C.). Office: Bessemer Trust Co 630 Fifth Ave New York NY 10111

TARR, ROBERT JOSEPH, JR., film company executive; b. Freeport, N.Y., Dec. 7, 1943; s. Robert Joseph and Janet Christman (Laughton) T.; m. Molly Worthington Upton, Feb. 28, 1970; children—William Upton, Robert Joseph, III, David Worthington. B.S., U.S. Naval Acad., 1966; M.B.A., Harvard U., 1973; M.A., Tufts U., 1976. Asst. v.p. corp. fin. Paine Webber Jackson Curtis, Boston, 1973-75; dir. corp. planning, then v.p., treas. Gen. Cinema Corp., Chestnut Hill, Mass., 1976-78, sr. v.p., 1978-83, exec. v.p., chief operating officer, 1983-85, pres., chief operating officer, 1985—, also dir.; pres., chief operating officer The Neiman-Marcus Group Inc., 1987—, also bd. dirs.; dir. Am. Retail Fedn. Bd. visitors Fletcher Sch. Law and Diplomacy; trustee Tenacre Country Day Sch. Served to lt. USN, 1966-71. Mem. Am. Retail Fedn. (dir.). Clubs: Newton Squash and Tennis; Quissett Yacht; Wellesley Country. Home: 40 White Oak Rd Wellesley MA 02181 Office: Gen Cinema Corp 27 Boylston St Chestnut Hill MA 02167 *

TARTE, CONRAD ANTHONY, financial executive; b. St. Albans, Vt., Nov. 29, 1953; s. Norman Eli and Martha (Rogers) T. AA in Bus., Champlain Coll., 1973; student, U. Conn., 1976. Sales mgr. Investor's Nat. Real Estate Co., Waterbury, Ct., 1976-79; supervising mgr. Comml. Investments Internat., Inc., Waterbury, 1979-84; dist. mgr. Waddell and Reed, Inc., Waterbury, 1982-87; mng. dir. Continental Nine Fin. Services, 1987—; advisor Sun Nat. Equity Investments I. Ltd. (ptnrship.), Waterbury, 1981-85; lectr. Soc. Mfg. Engrs., Conn. 1985, Am. Inst. Indsl. Engrs., 1985-86; instr., internat. lectr., presenter manuscript workshops Hartford Grad. Ctr., other Conn. Community Colls.; dir. Entrepreneurs Mgmt. Exch. Contbr. articles to profl. jours. Mem. ADA, Internat. Assn. Fin. Planners, Am. Assn. Individual Investors, Active Corps Execs., Waterbury C. of C., Conn. Assn. Real Estate Investors, Nat. Assn. Securities Brokers. Roman Catholic. Home: 173 Hillside Ave Waterbury CT 06710 Office: Comml Investments Internat Inc 173 Hillside Ave Waterbury CT 06702

TARTER, FRED BARRY, advertising executive; b. Bklyn., Aug. 16, 1943; s. Irving and Edna (Kupferberg) T.; m. Barbara Jane Smith, Apr. 12, 1969; children: Scott Andrew, Heather, Megan. BS, CCNY, 1966. Pres. Jamie Publs. Hootenanny Enterprises, Inc., 1962-65; mdse. dir. Longines Symphonette Soc., 1965-67; with Universal Communications, Inc., N.Y.C., 1967—, pres., chief exec. officer, 1969-74; exec. v.p. Deerfield Communications, Inc., N.Y.C., 1974-87, pres., chief exec. officer, 1977-88; pres. Deerfield Books, Inc., N.Y.C.; pub. S.E.W. mag., N.Y.C., 1977—; pres. The Rainbow Group Ltd., N.Y.C., 1988—; bd. dirs. Caribbean Internat. News Corp., Screenvision, Inc., Lakeside Group, Inc., Inc.; exec. producer Joanne Carson's VIP's, Miss American Teenager Pagent, 1972-73. Mem. Friars Club. Home: 9 Davis Dr Armonk NY 10504 Office: The Rainbow Group 210 E 39th St New York NY 10016

TASSONE, GELSOMINA (GESSIE), steel fabricating executive; b. N.Y.C., July 8, 1944; d. Enrico and A. Cira (Petriccione) Gargiulo; children: Ann Marie, Margaret, Theresa, Christine; m. Armando Tassone, Mar. 20, 1978. Student, Orange County Community Coll., 1975-79, Iona Coll., 1980—. Head bookkeeper Gargiulo Bros. Builders, N.Y.C., 1968-72; pres., owner A&T Iron Works, Inc., New Rochelle, N.Y., 1973—, Gessie Realty, New Rochelle, N.Y., 1980-86, Majestico Iron Works, Inc., N.Y.C., 1980—, A&G Distbg. of West, New Rochelle, 1987—, A&T Contractors Greater N.Y., N.Y.C., 1987—, Orsogril USA, Inc., N.Y.C., 1988—. Recipient Profl. Image award Contractors Council Greater N.Y.C., 1986; Named Businesswoman of Yr., Contractors Council Greater N.Y.C., 1985; company named a Successful Small Bus. Co., Westchester County C. of C./SBA, 1986-88; named N.Y. State Small Bus. Person of Yr., 1988. Mem. Am. Inst. Steel Constrn. Inc., Am. Welding Soc., Real Estate and Bldg. Servivces, Occupational Safety & Health Adminstrn., Assn. Bus. & Profl. Women in Constrn., Westchester Assn. Women Bus. Owners, The Am. Inst. (N.Y. chpt.). Office: A & T Iron Works Inc 25 Cliff St New Rochelle NY 10801

TATE, FRAN M., small business owner; b. Auburn, Wash., Oct. 5, 1929; dau. Frank Joseph and Theresa Mary (Bingesar) Pfulg; m. Rory Tate, Sept. 30, 1970 (div.); children—Michael C., Joseph M.; m. 2d, Juan Ramon Ramirez, Sept. 6, 1981 (div. May 1986). Student U. Wash. Gen. mgr., Sorensen Heating Co., Auburn, 1952-70; cons. Success Motivation Inst., Bellevue, Wash., 1970-72; field engr., draftsman, J. Dalton and Assocs., Point Barrow, Alaska, 1973-75; pres., owner Inupiat Water Delivery Co., Barrow, Alaska, 1977—; pres., owner Elephant Pot Sewage Haulers, Barrow, 1977—; pres., owner, operator Pepe's North of the Border Restaurant, Barrow, 1978—, pres., owner Tate Enterprises, Inc.; Burger Barn, Barrow, 1984—; disc jockey, Sta. KBRW, Barrow. Mem. Barrow Zoning commn. Recipient Boss of Yr. award Credit Women Internat., 1969; Outstanding Service award Barrow PTA; Alaska's Outstanding Women State Comm. for Status of Women, 1984. Mem. Barrow C. of C. (pres. 1989—, bd. dirs.), Blues Alley Music Soc., Nat. Geog. Soc., Smithsonian Instn., Jazz Heritage Found., Arctic Slope Scholarship Found., Nat. Assn. Female Execs. Roman Catholic. Club: Las Vegas Jazz.

TATE, PETER C., communications executive; b. Detroit, Feb. 26, 1952; s. George and Greta M. (Crick) T.; m. Denise Galluf, Mar. 17, 1978; 1 child, Alexandra Marie. BA in Communications, Mich. State U., 1976. Media planning supr. W.B. Doner Advt., Detroit, 1976-78, Kenyon & Eckhardt, Detroit, 1978-79, Wells, Rich and Greene, Inc., Detroit, 1979-81; regional sales mgr. Univision Spanish TV Network, Birmingham, Mich., 1981—; lectr. in field. Mem. AdCraft Club of Detroit. Office: Univision Spanish TV Network 30700 Telegraph #1550 Birmingham MI 48010

TATKEN, GRETA ELLEN, financial director, consultant; b. York, Pa., Apr. 16, 1951; d. Stanley Robert and Beverly (Coval) Kalish; m. Wayne Howard Tatken, Aug. 13, 1972 (div. Sept. 1982); children: Joshua, Todd. BS, Pa. State U., 1973. Claims corr. Blue Cross/Blue Shield Nat. Capitol Area, Washington, 1973-74, cons. various physicians, 1977-81; fin. dir. Va. Heart Surgery Assocs., P.C., Annandale, Va., 1981; info. cons. Am. Acad. Physicians Assts., Arlington, Va., 1986-87; cons. in field, Burke, Va., 1987—; fin. coord. heart transplant program Fairfax Hosp., Falls Church, Va., 1987. Mem. No. Va. Jewsih Community Ctr., Fairfax, 1986—. Mem. Am. Guild Patient Account Mgmt., Med. Group Mgmt. Assn. Democrat. Home: 10119 Walnut Wood Ct Burke VA 22015 Office: Virgina Heart Surgery Assocs PC 3301 Woodburn Rd Ste 301 Annandale VA 22003

TATMAN, RICHARD WAKEFIELD, manufacturing executive; b. Seattle, June 5, 1943; s. Esther Wakefield Tatman. AB, Whitman Coll., Walla Walla, Wash., 1965; MBA, Stanford U., 1967. Fin. analyst FMC Corp., San Jose, Calif., 1969-72; reports mgr. FMC Corp., Chgo., Ill., 1972-74; contr. agrl. machinery div. FMC Corp., Jonesboro, Ark., 1978-80; mgr. fin. analysis FMC Corp.- Chem. Group, Phila., 1974-76; materials mgr., contr., agrl. chem. div., FMC of Can. Ltd., Burlington, Ont., Can., 1976-78; v.p. fin. Baker Perkins, Inc., Saginaw, Mich., 1980-85; v.p., treas., sec., chief fin. officer Baker Perkins N.Am. Inc. subs. of APV, Saginaw, 1985-89; mem. bd. dirs. Baker Parkins No. Am. Inc. subs. of APV, Saginaw, 1988—; v.p. finance APV Crepaco, Inc., Lake Mills, Wis., 1989—; bd. dirs. APV Baker FM Inc., Raleigh, N.C. Treas. Boy Scouts of Am., Lake Huron Coun., Auburn, Mich. 1983-85, Investment Officer, 1985-87. Lt. USN, 1967-69, Vietnam. Mem. Stanford Bus. Sch. Alumni Assn., Whitman Coll. Alumni Assn. Presbyterian. Home: 5025 Sheybogan Ave #306 Madison WI 53705 Office: APV Crepaco Inc S CP Ave Lake Mills WI 53551

TATUM, DONN BENJAMIN, corporate executive, lawyer; b. L.A., Jan. 9, 1913; s. Frank D. and Terese (Murphy) T.; m. Vernette Ripley, Mar. 20, 1937; children: Frederic, Donn, Vernette, Forbes, Melantha. A.B. magna cum laude, Stanford U., 1934; postgrad., Loyola U., 1936-38; B.A., Oxford U., Eng., 1936; M.A., Oxford U., 1959; D.B.A., Woodbury Coll., 1953; LL.D. (hon.), Pepperdine U., 1977. Bar: Calif. 1938. Practice in Los Angeles, 1938-48; ptnr. Lillick, Geary, McHose & Adams, 1945-48; Pacific coast counsel RCA (and subs.'s), 1942-48; v.p., dir. Don Lee Cos., 1948-51; dir. TV Western div. ABC, 1951-54; v.p., mem. exec. com. Walt Disney Prodns. (now Walt Disney Co.), Burbank, Calif., 1956-67; dir. Walt Disney Prodns. (now Walt Disney Co.), 1956—, vice chmn., exec. v.p., 1967-68, pres., 1968-71, chief exec. officer, 1971-76, chmn. bd., 1971-80, chmn. exec. com., 1980-84; chmn. bd. Walt Disney World Co., 1971-80; bd. dirs. Western Digital Corp. Trustee New Economy Fund, Calif. Inst. Arts, Salk Inst., Morlborough Sch.; chmn. bd. John Tracy Clinic; bd. overseers Huntington Library. Mem. Acad. Motion Picture Arts and Scis., Acad. TV Arts and Scis., So. Calif. , Broadcast Pioneers. Lodge: The Knights of Malta. Home: 888 Napoli Dr Pacific Palisades CA 90272 Office: The Walt Disney Co 500 S Buena Vista St Burbank CA 91521

TATZ, PAUL H., real estate executive; b. Des Moines, June 24, 1935; s. Simon M. Tatz and Esther (Schumaker) Steele; m. Rochelle Sue Krantman, Feb. 26, 1981; children: John P., Jennifer A., Stephen C., Suzanne E. Student, U. Iowa, 1953, Drake U., 1956-59; LLB, Drake U., 1962. Bar: Iowa 1962, Ill. 1969, Mich. 1970, Calif. 1973. Sole pratice Des Moines, 1962-68; asst. atty. gen. State of Iowa, Des Moines, 1968; atty. Inland Steel Co., Chgo., 1968-70; sr. v.p. Wickes Corp., Mich., Ill. and Calif., 1970-76; sole practice Calif. and Iowa, 1976-82; asst. gen. counsel Del E. Webb Co., Phoenix, 1982-83; exec. v.p. Del E. Webb Devel. Co., Sun City West, Ariz., 1983-84, pres., chief operating officer, 1984-85; pres., chief exec. officer Del E. Webb Communities, Sun City West, 1985—. Mem. Ariz. Acad.-Ariz. Town Halls, Phoenix, 1985—, nat. bd. advisors U. Ariz., Tucson, 1987; assoc. mem. Urban Land Inst., Washington, 1985—; bd. dirs., vice chmn. Sun Health Corp., Sun City, 1986—. Served with AUS, 1954-56, Korea. Mem. Calif. Bar Assn., Ill. Bar Assn., Iowa Bar Assn., Mich. Bar Assn., Phoenix C. of C. (bd. dirs. 1987—), Econs. Club (dean's council 100, 1986—). Republican. Club: Arrowhead Country (Glendale, Ariz.). Office: Del Webb Corp 2231 E Camelback Rd Phoenix AZ 85016

TAUB, HENRY, retired computer services company executive; b. Paterson, N.J., Sept. 20, 1927; s. Morris and Sylvia (Sievitz) T.; m. Marilyn Adler, Sept. 13, 1958; children: Judith, Steven, Ira. B.S., N.Y. U., 1947. Pres. Automatic Data Processing, Inc., Clifton, N.J., 1949-69; chmn. bd. Automatic Data Processing, Inc., 1970-77, 82-86, chmn. exec. com., 1977—, hon. chmn. bd., 1986—; dir. Leumi Bank & Trust Co., N.Y.C., Rite Aid Corp., Hasbro, Inc.; past pres., hon. chmn. Joint Distbn. Com. Chmn., hon. pres. N.Y. chpt. Hemophilia Found., 1970-76; past vice-chmn. Nat. Hemophilia Found.; bd. dirs. Am. Friends Hebrew U.; trustee N.Y. U., Avi Chai Found.; bd. dirs. Interfaith Hunger Appeal, 1979—, N.Y. Shakespeare Festival, 1981—, Ch. United Israel Appeal, 1986—; bd. govs. Jewish Agy., 1981—; pres. Jewish Community Center of Palisades, 1980-84; chmn. Bus. Employment Found., Inc., 1980—. Mem. Am. Technion Soc. (vice chmn., internat. bd. govs.). Office: ADP Inc One ADP Blvd Roseland NJ 07068

TAUB, JESSE, oil company executive; b. Bronx, N.Y., July 25, 1923; s. Saul and Rae (Weinstock) T.; m. Shirley Jane Rippen, Aug. 3, 1952; children: Robert, Cathy. BS, Bradley U., 1950. Reporter Peoria (Ill.) Jour., 1947-50, N.Y. Jour. Commerce, 1950-52; account supr. Harshe-Rotman, N.Y.C., 1952-58, Fred Rosen Assn., N.Y.C., 1958-61; v.p., bd. dirs. John De Nigris Assocs., N.Y.C., 1961-75; v.p., asst. sec., bd. dirs. Macmillan Ring-Free Oil Co., Inc., N.Y.C., 1976—, sec., mem. exec. com., 1985—. Served with USN, 1942-45. Mem. Am. Petroleum Inst., Am. Soc. Corp. Secs., Nat. Assn. Corp. Dirs. Democrat. Clubs: Met.; Metuchen Golf and Country. Home: 10 Colonial Ct Edison NJ 08820

TAUB, RONALD H., merchandising executive; b. N.Y.C., July 16, 1929; s. Edward A. and Rose (Stoller) T.; m. Ethel Betty Flecker, June 1, 1952; children: Liba, Marcia, Zisl. BS in Bus. Edn., NYU, 1950; MS in Human Relations, Nat. Coll. Edn., 1982; LHD, Spertus Coll., Chgo., 1982. Chmn. Creative Displays, Inc., Chgo., 1957—. Inventor numerous display devices. Trustee Moriah Congregation, Deerfield, Ill., 1986—. Mem. Merchandising Execs. Club, Promotion Mktg. Assn. Am., Point of Purchase Advt. Assn. (guest speaker 1960—), Chgo. Advt. Club. Jewish. Clubs: Carlton, Internat. (Chgo.); Birchwood (Highland Park, Ill.). Home: 1154 Sheridan Rd Highland Park IL 60035

TAUBER, JOEL DAVID, manufacturing company executive; b. Detroit, June 28, 1935; s. Benjamin and Anne (Merliss) T.; m. Shelley Tauber; children: Julie, Ellen, Benjamin Brian, Melissa, Juliana. B.B.A., U. Mich., 1956, J.D., 1959, M.B.A., 1963. Bar: Mich. bar 1959. Pres. Key Internat. Mfg. Inc., Southfield, Mich., 1969-86; pres. Tauber Enterprises, 1986—; trustee Nat. Indsl. Group Pension Plan, 1980; bd. dirs. Fed. Home Loan Bank; chmn. bd. Key Mfg. Group iNc., Key Plastics Inc., S.G. Keywell Co. pres. Jewish Welfare Fedn., Detroit, 1983-86, chmn., 1986—; pres. Jewish

Community Ctr., 1978-80; vice-chmn. United Jewish Appeal, 1986—; bd. dirs. United Found., 1980—, v.p., 1986—; trustee Sinai Hosp., Detroit, 1980—; mem. Fed. Judges Selection Panel Ea. Dist. Mich., 1978; mem. U. Mich. Devel. Adv. Bd., 1986—; trustee Growth Fund, 1988—. Recipient Frank A. Wetsman Meml. Leadership award Jewish Welfare Fedn., 1970. Mem. Mich. Bar Assn., Detroit Bar Assn., World Bus. Council, Franklin Hills Country Club, Detroit Athletic Club, U. Mich. Alumni Club, U. Mich. Club., Pres. Club, U. Mich. Victors Club, Masons. Office: 27777 Franklin Rd Ste 1850 Southfield MI 48034

TAUBERT, FREDERICK WAYNE, oil company executive; b. Worcester, Mass., Feb. 15, 1933; s. Fredrick Otto and Florence (Ploch) T.; m. Sandra J. Taubert, Nov. 1, 1954 (div. 1972); m. Maureen A. Taubert, June 9, 1978; children: Martyn W., Debra L. BA, Worcester Jr. Coll., 1968; BS, Clark U., 1970. Service mgr. Central Oil Co., Worcester, 1958-60, sales, 1960-62; sales mgr. Union Oil Co., Boston, 1963-73, v.p. sales, 1973-79; sr. v.p., gen. mgr. New Eng., Inc., Boston, 1980; pres. The Belcher Co. of N.Y., Inc. and Belcher of New Eng., Inc., 1984—; now pres. Belcher New Eng., Inc.; dir. Better Home Heat Council, Boston, 1971-72, New Eng. Fuel Inst., 1976-83. Served with U.S. Army, 1954-56. Office: Belcher New Eng Inc 222 Lee Burbank Hwy Revere MA 02151

TAUBMAN, A. ALFRED, real estate developer; b. Pontiac, Mich., Jan. 31, 1925; s. Philip and Fannie Ester (Blustin) T.; m. Reva Kolodney, Dec. 1, 1949 (div. July 1977); children: Gayle Kalisman, Robert S., William S.; m. Judith Mazor, June 17, 1982. Student, U. Mich., 1945-47, Lawrence Inst. Tech., 1947-49; DArch (hon.), Lawrence Inst. Tech., 1985; D in Bus. (hon.), Eastern Mich. U., 1984. Chmn. The Taubman Co., Inc., Bloomfield Hills, Mich., 1950—; owner Woodward & Lothrop, Inc., Washington, 1984—; chmn. U. Pa.-Wharton Real Estate Ctr., Phila., Sotheby's Holdings, Inc., N.Y.C., 1983—; bd. dirs. Chase Manhattan Corp., N.Y.C., R.H. Macy, Inc., N.Y.C., 1986; chmn. A&W Restaurants, Inc., Livonia, Mich., 1982—, bd. dirs. Trustee Whitney Mus. Am. Art, N.Y.C., Founders Soc. Detroit Inst. Art, Harper-Grace Hosps., Detroit, Asia Soc., N.Y.C., White House Preservation Fund, Am. Assoc. Royal Acad. Arts Trusts, N.Y.C., Blenheim Found., N.Y.C.; adv. bd. United Found. Detroit, Wexner Ctr. for Visual Arts Ohio State U., U.S. Com. on Bicentennial of Constitution, U.S. Ct. Appeals (6th cir.); nat. chmn., trustee Archives Am. Art Smithsonian Inst., Washington; bd. dirs. Detroit Renaissance, Inc, Detroit Symphony Orch., Nat. Com. on U.S.-China Relations, N.Y.C., Friends of Art & Preservation in Embassies, Washington. Recipient Bus. Statesman award Harvard Bus. Sch. Club of Detroit, 1983, Sportsman of Yr. award United Found. Detroit, SE Mich. Chpt. March of Dimes Birth Defects, 1983; named Michiganian of Yr. The Detroit News, 1983. Mem. Urban Land Inst. (trustee), Nat. Realty Com. (bd. dirs.). Club: Econ. (Detroit) (bd. dirs.).

TAUSSIG, ANDREW RICHARD, investment banker; b. Abington, Pa., Aug. 27, 1951; s. Ralph J. and Sally G. T.; m. Susan Fierman, June 25, 1978. BA, Trinity Coll., 1973; JD, Georgetown Law Sch., 1976; MBA, Wharton Grad. Sch., 1978. Bar: Pa. 1976, N.Y. 1978. Corp. atty. Willkie, Farr & Gallagher, N.Y.C., 1978-82; investment banker, mng. dir. First Boston Corp., N.Y.C., 1982—, head retail investment banking, 1988—; bd. dirs. Big V. Supermarkets, Florida, N.Y., Pueblo Internat., Pompano, Fla., Connaught Tower Corp., N.Y.C. Office: The First Boston Corp Park Ave Plaza New York NY 10055

TAUSZ, JAMES WILLIAM, financial planning company executive; b. Hawarden, Iowa, Dec. 29, 1944; s. William H. and June L. (Finerity) T.; m. Judy Kay Ahders, Dec. 21, 1967; children: Jerrad Jay, Jodi Lynn, Jamie Jo. BA, Sioux Falls Coll., 1967; MS, S.D. State U., 1969. Cert. fin. planner. Tchr. Brandon Valley High Sch., S.D., 1966-68, Eagle Grove High Sch., Iowa, 1968-70; fin. planner Investors Diversified Svcs., Mpls., 1970-83; pres. Tausz Fin. Corp., Clarion, Iowa, 1970—; pres. Employers Svcs. Co., Clarion, 1971—, Med. Trust Adminstrs., Clarion, 1975—, Personal Fin. Planners, Clarion, 1983—, Progressive Employers Assn., Clarion, 1983—; pres., mng. exec. Integrated Resources Equity Corp., N.Y.C., 1983—, Nat. Ins. Mgmt., Pottsville, Pa., 1986—, Nat. Security Gen. Ins. Co., Pottsville, 1986—, Travel Connection, Inc., Clarion, Iowa, 1987—. Author: Should I Incorporate?, 1979. Bd. mem. Clarion Devel. Commn., 1973. Named Tchr. of Yr. Eagle Grove Chamber, 1970. Mem. Internat. Assn. Fin. Planners, Inst. Fin. Planning, Nat. Assn. Life Underwriters, Iowa Assn. Life Underwriters, Clarion C. of C., Rotary (pres. 1985-86). Home: 620 Birch Ln Clarion IA 50525 Office: Tausz Fin Corp 215 N Main St Clarion IA 50525

TAVAKOLI, AMIR, civil engineer, educator; b. Tehran, Iran, Sept. 19, 1957; came to U.S., 1975; s. Abbas and Roghieh (Shanizadeh-Asli) T.; (div. 1982); 1 child, Omid. BCE, U. Wash., 1978; MCE, Ga. Tech., 1979, MS in Indsl. Mgmt. and Fin., 1982, PhD in Civil Engring., 1983. Registered profl. engr., Mo.; cert. cost engr. Engr. civil design Planners and Engrs. Collaborative, Atlanta, 1981-83; asst. prof. constrn. So. Ill. U., Edwardsville, 1983-85; asst. prof. civil engring., coord. grad. program constrn. engring. and mgmt. Case Western Res. U., Cleve., 1985—; gen. mgr. Tavakoli & Assocs., Cleve., 1988—; cons. in field. Contbr. articles to profl. jours. Mem. Am. Assn. Cost Engrs. (pres. N.E. Ohio sect. 1988-89, v.p. 1987-88), Am. Soc. Civil Engrs., Am. Soc. Engring. Edn., Constrns. Fin. Mgmt. Assn., Project Mgmt. Inst. Office: Case Western Res U Dept Civil Engring Cleveland OH 44106 also: Tavakoli and Assocs PO Box 32518 Cleveland OH 44132

TAVEL, MARK KIVEY, investment company executive, economist; b. Cambridge, Mass., May 9, 1945; s. Bernard Benjamin and Elizabeth (Rogers) T.; m. Susana Sara Doño, Dec. 14, 1980; children: Sarah Emily, Rachel Florence, Amanda Victoria, Nathaniel Benjamin. BA cum laude, Harvard U., 1967; MBA, Columbia U., 1968. Pres. Value Line Leveraged Growth Investors Inc., 1975-88, Value Line Asset Mgmt. Co., 1978-88, Value Line Cash Fund, 1980-83, Value Line Tax Exempt Fund, 1981-83, Value Line Centurion Fund, 1984-88; exec. v.p. Value Line Inc., N.Y.C., 1983-88; chief investment officer Rothschild Asset Mgmt., N.Y.C., 1988—; also bd. dirs. Rothschild N.Am., N.Y.C. Pres. Epilepsy Inst., N.Y.C., 1980-86; treas. 110-118 Riverside Tenants Corp., 1981-86. Republican. Jewish. Club: Harvard (N.Y.C.). Home: 110 Riverside Dr New York NY 10024 Office: Rothschild Inc Rockefeller Pla New York NY 10020

TAVLIN, MICHAEL JOHN, telecommunications company executive; b. Lincoln, Nebr., Dec. 16, 1946. BEd, Oklahoma City U., 1970; JD, U. Nebr., 1973; LLM in Taxation, Washington U., St. Louis, 1977. Bar: Nebr. 1973, Mo. 1974. Ptnr. Nelson & Harding, Lincoln, 1973-79; sr. tax. mgr. Touche Ross & Co., Tulsa, 1979-84, Coopers & Lybrand, Tulsa, 1984-86; v.p., treas., sec. Lincoln Telecommunications Co., 1986—. Office: Lincoln Telecommunications Co 1440 M St Lincoln NE 68508

TAVROW, RICHARD LAWRENCE, lawyer, corporate executive; b. Syracuse, N.Y., Feb. 3, 1935; s. Harry and Ida Mary (Hodess) T.; m. Barbara J. Silver, Mar. 22, 1972; children—Joshua Michael, Sara Hallie. A.B. magna cum laude, Harvard U., 1957, LL.B., 1960, LL.M., 1961; postgrad., U. Copenhagen, 1961-62, U. Luxembourg, 1962. Bar: N.Y. bar 1961, U.S. Supreme Ct. bar 1969, Calif. bar 1978. Atty. W.R. Grace & Co., N.Y.C., 1962-66; asst. chief counsel Gen. Dynamics Corp., N.Y.C., 1966-68; chief counsel office of fgn. direct investments U.S. Dept. Commerce, Washington, 1969-71; ptnr. Schaeffer, Dale, Vogel & Tavrow, N.Y.C., 1971-75; v.p., sec., gen. counsel Prudential Lines, Inc., N.Y.C., 1975-78, also bd. dirs.; v.p., sec., gen. counsel Am. Pres. Lines, Ltd., Oakland, Calif., 1978-80, sr. v.p., sec., gen. counsel, 1982—, also bd. dirs.; sr. v.p., sec., gen. counsel Am. Pres. Cos., Ltd., Oakland, 1983—; also bd. dirs. Am. Pres. Cos., Ltd.; instr. Harvard Coll., 1959-61; lectr. Am. Mgmt. Assn., Practising Law Inst. Contbg. author: Private Investors Abroad - Problems and Solutions in International Business, 1970. Recipient Silver Medal award Dept. Commerce, 1970; Fulbright scholar, 1961-62. Mem. ABA, State Bar Calif., Internat. Bar Assn., Am. Soc. Internat. Law, Maritime Law Assn., San Francisco Bar Assn., Asia-Pacific Lawyers Assn., Transp. Lawyers Assn., Am. Steamship Owners Mut. Protection and Indemnity Assn. (dir.), Pacific Mcht. Shipping Assn. (dir., chmn. bd. dirs.), Am. Corp. Counsel Assn., Am. Soc. Corp. Secs. Inc., Assn. Transp. Practitioners, Harvard Law Sch. Assn., Navy League. Democrat. Jewish. Clubs: World Trade; Alpine Hills Swimming and Tennis; Lakeview (Oakland); Harvard (N.Y.C. and San Francisco); Concordia-Argonaut (San Francisco). Office: Am Pres Cos Ltd 1800 Harrison St Oakland CA 94612

TAWASHA, IBRAHIM YACOUB, business executive; b. Ramallah, Palestine, Dec. 13, 1924; came to U.S., 1947, naturalized, 1954; s. Y'coub Ghnaim and Jaleeleh S. (Rafeedy) T.; student Jerusalem Law Classes, 1941-45; J.D., King's Coll., London U., 1947; m. Leila T. Kash-shou, Oct. 12, 1958; children—Carolyn J., Jack I., Joseph G. Admitted to Temple bar, 1947; with Brit. Govt., Palestine Mandate, 1939-45, Saudi Embassy, 1947-50; self-employed businessman, 1953-68; dir. Western Region, Arab Info. Center, League of Arab States, San Francisco, 1969-74; pres. Arab-Am. Ventures, Inc., San Francisco, 1974—, chief exec. officer, 1974—; cons. to non-profit orgns.; lectr. on Arab history, culture and politics City Coll. San Francisco. Mem. exec. com. Republican Party of City and County of San Francisco, 1964-68; chmn. Arab-Am. Com., Finch for Senate Com., 1976, Arab-Am. Com., George Cory For Congress, 1976; trustee St. Nicholas Orthodox Ch., San Francisco. Served with U.S. Army, 1950-52. Named Hon. Citizen, State of Tenn., 1975, Ky. Col., 1976; recipient commendation Calif. Senate Rules Com., 1979. Mem. U.S.-Arab C. of C., Joint Mideast Bus. Conf. (adv. bd.), Nat. Assn. Arab Ams. (dir.), World Affairs Council No. Calif. Republican. Club: Commonwealth. Contbr. numerous articles on Arab-Israeli conflict to newspapers, mags. Home: 1990 18th Ave San Francisco CA 94116 Office: 155 Montgomery San Francisco CA 94104

TAYLOR, ADAM DAVID, real estate executive; b. N.Y.C., Mar. 31, 1917; s. William and Anne (Bernstein) T.; m. Sylvia Park, Oct. 15, 1941 (div. Apr. 1963); children: Hillary, Jeremy; m. Edna Deutsch, Jan. 28, 1964. B in Comml. Sci., NYU, 1941. Pres. Taylor Lumber Co., Inc., N.Y.C., 1936-63, Raje Realty, Inc., N.Y.C., 1955-63, Architects Svc. Ctr., Inc., N.Y.C., 1955-63, Bahama Properties, Inc., Miami, 1965-68; dir. sales Arlen Properties, Miami, 1968-72; owner Adam D. Taylor Real Estate, Miami, 1972—; pres. Dealers Supply, N.Y.C., 1955-63; mng. ptnr. Oak Plaza Assocs., Miami, 1985—, Pla. Ctr. Assocs., Miami, 1986—. Office: 12955 Bicayne Blvd Ste 304 North Miami FL 33181

TAYLOR, ALAN FREDERICK, pharmaceutical research corporation executive, physician, researcher; b. Spalding, Lincolnshire, Eng., Nov. 2, 1929; came to U.S., 1975, naturalized 1984; s. Jonathan Frederick and Irene Maud (Major) T.; m. Ann Joaquina Temple-Raston, July 9, 1955; children: Sarah Louise, Katherine Ann, Joanna Clare, Deborah Jane. M.B., Ch.B. with honors in Medicine, St. Andrews U., 1955; D.C.H., Royal Coll. Physicians, Eng., 1957. Resident, Dundee Royal Infirmary and Royal Postgrad. Med. Sch., Hammersmith Hosp., 1955-57; registrar in pediatrics and medicine Kingston Hosp., 1958-61; med. devel. dir. Organon Labs., London, 1961-71, mng. dir., 1971-73; mng. dir. Organon Internat., Oss, Holland, 1973-75; v.p. corp. devel. Organon Inc., West Orange, N.J., 1975-81; pres. Elan Pharm., Gainesville, Ga., 1981-84; corp. pres. Elan Corp., Athlone, Ireland, and Gainesville, Ga., 1984-85; ptnr. Devel. Southeast, Inc., 1985—; dir. Chateau Elan, Mulberry, Ga., 1982-85 ; mem. adv. bd. Seed Tech., Atlanta, 1984-86; pres. Cytrx Corp., 1986-88; mem. adv. bd. Integrated Healthcare Investments, Inc., 1987. Author: Alan Raston, various newspaper columns, med. and research articles in Brit. med. jours. Program chmn. Lanier Orch., Gainesville, 1983-86. Served as lt. Brit. Army, 1947-49, U.K., East Africa. Fellow Royal Soc. Medicine, Royal Hort. Soc.; mem. N.Y. Acad. Sci., Soc. for Study of Fertility, Shock Soc. Anglican. Clubs: Chattahoochee (Gainesville), Rotary. Home: 2421 Island Dr Gainesville GA 30501 Office: Devel SE Inc PO Box 2776 Gainesville GA 30503

TAYLOR, ALLAN RICHARD, banker; b. Prince Albert, Sask., Can., Sept. 14, 1932; s. Norman and Anna Lydia (Norbeck) T.; m. Shirley Irene Ruston, Oct. 5, 1957; children: Rodney Allan, Leslie Ann. LLD (hon), U. Regina, Sask., 1987, Concordia U., Montreal, Can., 1988. With Royal Bank of Can., Toronto, Ont., Can., 1949—, mgr. main br., 1971-74; dep. gen. mgr. internat. div. Royal Bank of Can., Montreal, 1974-77, sr. v.p. internat. div., 1977-78, exec. v.p., 1978-83; pres., chief operating officer, dir. Royal Bank of Can., Toronto, 1983-86, now chmn., chief exec. officer, dir.; bd. dirs. TransCan. Pipelines Ltd., Toronto, Can. Pacific Ltd., Gen. Motors Can. Ltd., Oshawa, Ont., Internat. Monetary Conf., Washington. Mem. adv. com. Sch. Bus. Adminstrn., U. Western Ont., London; bd. dirs. Corp.-Higher Edn. Forum; bd. trustees Queen's U., Kingston, Ont. Anglican. Clubs: Granite, Mississauga Golf & Country, National, Toronto, York (Toronto); Forest & Stream, Mount Royal, Royal Montreal Golf, St. James's (Montreal); Overseas Bankers' (London). Office: care Camille Laperrière, The Royal Bank of Can, Royal Bank Pla, Toronto, ON Canada M5J 2J5

TAYLOR, CARL LARSEN, lawyer; b. Honolulu, Apr. 9, 1937; s. William Henry and Dorothy (Gray) T.; m. Linda Ann Farrell, Aug. 3, 1963. AB, Harvard U., 1958, LLB, 1961. Bar: U.S. Ct. Appeals (D.C. cir.) 1965, U.S. Supreme Ct. 1969, U.S. Ct. Appeals (9th cir.) 1975, U.S. Ct. Appeals (2d cir., 4th cir.) 1977, U.S. Ct. Appeals (3d cir.) 1981, U.S. Ct. Appeals (7th cir.) 1982, U.S. Ct. Appeals (5th cir.) 1986, U.S. Ct. Appeals (10th cir.) 1987. Assoc. Hogan & Hartson, Washington, 1966-69, ptnr., 1978-80; gen. counsel Retail Clerks Internat. Assn., Washington, 1969-76; assoc. gen. counsel NLRB, Washington, 1976-78; ptnr. Kirkland & Ellis, Washington, 1980-87, Johnson & Gibbs, Washington, 1987—. Served to lt. (j.g.) USN, 1961-65. Mem. Barristers. Club: Belle Haven (Alexandria, Va.). Office: Johnson & Gibbs 1001 Pennsylvania Ave NW Ste 745 Washington DC 20004

TAYLOR, CHARLES EDWIN, financial planner; b. Flagstaff, Ariz., July 22, 1942; s. John Thomas and Helen Corene (Nieman) T.; m. Diana Romaine Rahe, July 10, 1964; children: Charles E. Jr., Samuel Rahe. BA in Psychology, Ariz. State U., 1964; CLU, Am. Coll., Bryn Mawr, Pa., 1974; cert. fin. planning, Coll. Fin. Planning, Denver, 1981. Spl. rep. Bus. Men's Assurance, Kansas City, Mo., 1969-75; ptnr., fin. planner Lincoln Tax Shelter and Fin. Planning, Prescott, Ariz., 1976-84; owner, fin. planner Taylor Fin. Planners and Assocs., Prescott, 1985—; mem. adj. faculty Coll. Fin. Planning, Denver, 1984—; instr. Nat. Ctr. Fin. Edn., San Diego, 1987—; mem. Fin. Planners Equity Corp.; adv. bd. Integrated Resources Equity Corp., N.Y.C., 1988; arbitrator Nat. Assn. Securities Dealers, Inc. Chmn. Conservative Bapt. Found. Ariz., Phoenix, 1983—; bd. dirs. Prescott Coll., 1988. 1st lt. U.S. Army, 1966-68, Vietnam. Mem. Inst. Cert. Fin. Planners, Internat. Assn. Fin. Planners, Nat. Assn. Life Underwriters, Prescott Estate Planning Council. Republican. Office: Taylor Fin Planners & Assocs 1202 Willow Creek Rd Prescott AZ 86301

TAYLOR, CHARLES WILLIAM, JR., county assistant supervisor; b. Moorefield, W.Va., Apr. 23, 1944; s. Charles William Taylor Sr. and Lillian Elizabeth (Miller) Shanholtzer; m. Diana Lee McDonald, June 27, 1966; children: Michelle Ann, Michael Allan. Student, Allegany Community Coll., 1980—. Cert. assessor and real estate cons. profl., Md. Stock clk. Joe's Food Market., Cumberland, Md., 1960-63; mech. draftsman Nat. Jet Drill Co., LaVale, Md., 1963-66; civil draftsman II City of Cumberland, 1966-70; assessor I, II, III, Dept. of Assessments and Taxation-Allegany County, Md., 1970-83, asst. county supr., 1983—. Copyright C&O canal barge model. Exec. bd. County United Way, Cumberland, 1985—; mem. Vocat.-Tech. Adv. Com. Allegany Community Coll., 1988—. Served to capt. USAF Aux., 1963-75. Mem. Md. Classified Employees Assn. (chpt. pres. 1979-81), Md. Assn. Assessing Officers (state editor 1979-85, v.p. 1985-86, pres. 1986-87), Northeastern Regional Assn. Assessing Officers (bd. dirs. 1986-87). Democrat. Lodge: Lions (pres., sec., dep. dist. gov. 22W 1986-87, zone chmn. 1988—). Home: 211 Allendale Ave LaVale MD 21502 Office: Allegany County Dept Assessments & Taxation State of Md PO Box 343 Cumberland MD 21501

TAYLOR, CLAUDE I., airlines executive; b. Salisbury, N.B., Can., May 20, 1925; s. Martin Luther and Essie (Troope) T.; m. Frances Bernice Watters, Nov. 4, 1947; children: Karen, Peter. Student, Robinson Bus. Coll., 1942; R.I.A., McGill U. Extension, 1953; D.C.L. (hon.), U. N.B.; LL.D. (hon.), McMaster U. With Air Can., 1949—, gen. mgr. comml. planning, 1962-64, gen. mgr. marketing services, 1964-70, v.p. strategic devel., 1970-71, v.p. govt. and industry affairs, 1971-73, v.p. pub. affairs, 1973-76, pres., chief exec. officer, 1976-84, chmn. bd., 1984—; chmn. exec. com. and council Gov. Gen.'s Can. Study Conf., 1987; chmn. bd. Internat. Aviation Mgmt. Tng. Inst.; dir. GPA Group LTD. Hon. dir. Aviation Hall of Fame, Can. Nat. Exhbn. Assn.; past pres. Boy Scouts Can.; life gov. Douglas Hosp. Corp.; gov. Montreal Gen. Hosp. Decorated comdr. Order St. John; officer Order Can.; recipient Gordon R. McGregor Meml. Trophy Royal Can. Air Force Assn., 1980, Excellence in Communications Leadership award Internat. Assn. Bus. Communicators, Merit award B'nai Brith Can., McGill Mgmt. Achievement award, Human Relations award Can. Council Christians and Jews, Gold Medal award Adminstrv. Mgmt. Soc., Tony Jannus award, 1988; named Nat. Transp. Person, 1987; inducted Can. Aviation Hall of Fame. Fellow Soc. Mgmt. Accts. Can., Inst. Transport; mem. Internat. Air Transport Assn. (mem. exec. com., pres. 1979), Profl. Corp. Indsl. Accts. Que., Order of Can. (officer), Beaver Club (Montreal), Toronto Club. Baptist. Clubs: Beaver, Mt. Stephen, Mt. Royal, Forest and Stream (Montreal); Rideau (Ottawa); Toronto. Office: Air Can, care Nicole Geoffrion, 500 René Levesque W, Montreal, PQ Canada H2Z 1X5 also: Air Canada Inc, 500 Dorchester 01700-2600, Montreal, PQ Canada H2Z 1X5

TAYLOR, CYRIL JULIAN HEBDEN, education association administrator, consultant; b. Leeds, Yorkshire, Eng., May 14, 1935; s. Cyril Eustace and Margaret Victoria (Hebden) T.; m. Judith Taylor, June 5, 1965; 1 child, Kirsten. MA, U. Cambridge, Eng., 1961; MBA, Harvard U., 1961. Brand mgr. Proctor & Gamble, Cin., 1961-64; founder, chmn. Am. Inst. for Fgn. Study, London, 1964—; advisor on city tech. colls. Sec. of State for Edn. and Sci., London 1987—. Author: No More Tick, 1974, The Elected Member's Guide to Reducing Public Expenditure, 1980, A Realistic Plan for London Transport, 1982, Reforming London's Government, 1984, Qualgoes Just Grow, 1985, London Presrv'd, 1985, Brining Acoountability Back to Local Government, 1985, Employment Examined: The Right Approach to More Jobs, 1986; (with others) The Guide to Study Abroad. Dep. leader The Conservative Group, 1977-86; active Greater London Council, 1977-86; pres. Ruislip/Northwood Conservative Assn., 1986; parliamentary Conservative candidate Keighley riding, 1974, Huddersfield East riding, 1974; chmn. City Tech. Colls. Trust, London, 1987—, Lexham Gardens Residents's Assn., 1986—; active Council Westfield Coll., 1983—, Council Royal Coll. Music, 1988—; bd. govs. Holland Park Comprehensive Sch., 1971-74. Served with inf. Brit. Army, 1954-56. Recipient Charles Bell scholarship London C. of C., 1961. Mem. Ctr. for Policy Studies (bd. dirs. 1984). Anglican. Clubs: Carlton, Chelsea Arts, Hurlingham (London). Office: Am Inst for Fgn Study, 37 Queens Gate, London SW7 5HR, England

TAYLOR, DAVID GEORGE, banker; b. Charlevoix, Mich., July 29, 1929; s. Frank Flagg and Bessie (Strayer) T.; m. Helen Alexander, Jan. 14, 1978; children: David, Amy, Jeanine. BS, Denison U., 1951; MBA, Northwestern U., 1953. With Continental Ill. Nat. Bank and Trust Co. Chicago, 1958-86, asst. cashier, 1961-64, 2d v.p., 1964-66, v.p., 1966-72, sr. v.p., 1972-74, exec. v.p., 1974-80, exec. v.p., treas., 1980-83, vice chmn., 1983-84, chmn., 1984; vice chmn. Irving Trust Co., N.Y.C., 1986-89; group exec. Chem. Bank, N.Y.C., 1989—. Mem. Dealer Bank Assn. Com. on Glass-Steagall Reform, 1985-86. Bd. dirs. Evanston Hosp., Glenbrook Hosp.; trustee Art Inst. Chgo., 1981-86 ; advisor J.L. Kellogg Grad. Sch. Mgmt., Northwestern U., 1984—. Served to lt. USN, 1953-56. Mem. Pub. Securities Assn. (bd. dirs. 1977-78, chmn. 1977, treas. 1978), Govt. and Fed. Agys. Securities Com. (chmn. bd. dirs. 1982-83), Assn. Res. City Bankers (asset/liability com/govt. relations com. 1983—). Republican. Presbyterian. Office: Chem Bank Global Securities & Fgn Exch Group 277 Park Ave 10th Fl New York NY 10172

TAYLOR, DOROTHY HARRIS, real estate broker; b. Richmond, Va., Nov. 3, 1931; d. Edgar Alan and Sadie (Wheeler) Harris; m. Gethsemane Jess Taylor (dec. Nov. 1964); children: Marlene J., Eric M., Andre E. Student, L.I. U., 1959, John J. Criminal Coll., 1974, Queen's Coll., 1983, 88—, residential properties cert., student St. John's U., 1984, 86. Lic. real estate broker. Toll collector Port of N.Y. Authority, N.Y.C., 1967-80, tolls dispatcher, 1967; sales exec. Flushing Tribune, 1979; real estate salesperson Parkfield Realty, Queens Village, N.Y., 1982-83, Arro of Queens, 1983-84; real estate broker Arro of Queens, Queens Village, 1984-85, residential appraiser, N.Y.C., 1986—. Active Nat. Arbor Day Found., North Shore Animal Shelter League; mem. com. for disabled children Queens Coll.; charter mem. Nat. Mus. Women in Arts; mem. Nat. Trust for Hist. Presentation, The Smithsonian Assocs. Mem. Nat. Assn. Female Execs. (network dir. 1983-84), Am. Assn. Ret. Persons, Nat. Assn. of Unknown Players for Film, TV, and Print Modeling Arts, Inc. (charter), Queen's Council on Arts, Am. Entrepreneurs' Assn., United Christian Evangelistic Assn. Democrat. Clubs: Dorcas Soc. (Bklyn.) (pres. 1957-58), Queens Coll. Women's. Lodges: Order Eastern Star, Heroines of Jericho, Lady of Knights. Avocations: gardening, crocheting, reading, contesting, interior decorating.

TAYLOR, ELIZABETH JANE, investment consultant, real estate company executive; b. Tiffin, Ohio, Oct. 27, 1941; d. Albert Joseph Lucas and Mary Jane Siebenaller-Swander; m. Gaylen Lloyd Taylor, July 11, 1977. Student, Heidelberg Coll., 1961, Austin Community Coll., Tex., 1983-84. Cons., Hypnosis Conn., Ohio and Tex., 1967—; dir. regional mktg. Sibrow, Inc., Ottawa, Can., 1981-83; realtor assoc. Alliance Sales, Austin, 1985-88; assoc. Broadway Comml. Investments, 1988—; prin., Taylor & Assocs., Internat. Mktg. & Bus. Devel., Hong Kong, U.S., 1980—; tchr. mktg. and bus. develop., 1980—. Author: profl. column Austin Women Mag., 1984-86; (poetry) Letters from Home, 1986. Vice pres. Am. Congress on Real Estate, 1982-83; arbitrator Better Bus. Bur., 1984—; mem. speakers bur. Austin Woman's Ctr., 1985-88; v.p. Austin World Affairs Council, 1984—; mem. adv. panel Austin Woman Mag., 1984-86. Nominated to Tex. Womens Hall of Fame, 1984. Mem. Nat. Assn. Female Execs. (network dir. 1980-88). Avocations: writing, behavior research. Home: 3406 Danville Dr Cedar Park TX 78613

TAYLOR, GEORGE ROBERT, retail executive; b. Wilmington, Ohio, June 15, 1948; s. Donald and Majorie Lewis (Fitts) T.; m. Joyce Ann Brown, Sept. 22, 1979; children: Rhonda, Lance, Kristin, Jordan. BA, MBA, Columbia Pacific U., 1985; postgrad., Kensington U., Glendale, Calif. Cert. paralegal. Regional credit mgr. Washington Industries, Nashville, 1967-76, asst. credit mgr., 1976-80; credit mgr. Better-Bilt Aluminum, Smyrna, Tenn., 1980-88; dir. credit and accounts recievable Hartmann Luggage Co., Lebanon, Tenn., 1988—. Author: Legal Considerations For Commercial Credit Managers, 1985, A Practical Study of Business Credit Management. bus. advisor Junior Achievement, Nashville, 1973; commr. Two Rivers Fall Softball League, Nashville, 1978. Recipient Honorable Mention Internat. Song Festival, L.A., 1980, Music City Song Festival, Nashville, 1985; named one of Days Sales Outstanding-Top 100 Credit Mgrs. Credit and Fin. Mgmt., N.Y.C., 1984, 85, 87. Fellow Nat. Inst. Credit; mem. Nat. Assn. Credit Mgmt. (accredited Bus. Credit Exec. 1986, cert. credit exec. 1988), Nashville Assn. Credit Mgmt. (bd. dirs., chmn. legis. com. 1979-80), Nat. Corp. Cash Mgmt. Assn. (cert. cash mgr. 1988). Home: 409 Morningview Dr Mount Juliet TN 37122 Office: Hartmann Luggage Co Lebanon TN 37087

TAYLOR, GRAHAM CHRISTOPHER, university administrator; b. Woodford, Essex, Eng., June 12, 1939; came to U.S., 1972; BS in Engring., Imperial Coll., London, 1960, Diploma of Membership in Coll. Sci. and Tech., 1963; MS in Mgmt., Loughborough (Eng.) U., 1970; PhD in Econs., Colo. Sch. Mines, 1978. Registered engr., Eng. Assoc. prof. U. Surrey, Guilford, Eng., 1961-69; process planner, cons. Atkins Planning, Epsom, Eng., 1970-72; research economist Denver Research Inst., 1972-75, 78-81; dir. research Colo. Energy Research Inst., Denver, 1981-84; dir. Rocky Mountin Trade Adutment Assistance Ctr. U. Colo., Boulder, 1984—; adj. prof. grad. sch. bus. U. Denver, 1981—; cons. in field; reviewer NSF, Washington, 1980-86. Contbr. articles to profl. jours. Fellow Colo. Engergy Research Inst., 1975-76; grantee U.S. EPA, 1976-78. Mem. Am. Mktg. Assn., Nat. Assn. Bus. Economists. Office: Rocky Mountain Trade Adjustment Assistance Ctr 3380 Mitchell Ln #102 Boulder CO 80301

TAYLOR, HARRY DANNER, telecommunications company executive; b. Savannah, Ga., Apr. 25, 1944; s. John Joseph and Elizabeth (Danner) T.; m. Dianne Coker, June 11, 1974 (div. 1986); children: Dana Taylor Tresenriter, James Brent, Harry Danner. BBA, Ga. State U., 1974. Lineman So. Bell, Atlanta, 1965-66, engr., 1966-67, 69-74, supervising engr., 1974-78, dist. engr., 1978-82, dist. mgr., 1982-85; ops. mgr. BellSouth Services, Atlanta, 1985-87; sr. v.p. mktg., gen. mgr. Telco Systems, Inc., Norwood, Mass., 1987—. Served with U.S. Army, 1967-69, Vietnam. Episcopalian. Home: 81 Carpenter St Foxboro MA 02035 Office: Telco Systems Inc 63 Nahatan St Norwood MA 02062

TAYLOR, HOWARD EARLE, banker; b. Columbus, Ga., Mar. 4, 1952; s. Thomas Earl and Beverly Nita (Smith) T.; m. Karen Harriet Muller, Jan. 12, 1980. BA, Furman U., 1974; postgrad. Ga. State U., 1976-78. Mktg. rep. First Nat. Bank, Columbus, Ga., 1974-76; asst. cashier Bank of the South, Atlanta, 1976-79; v.p. ops., dir. So. Ambulance Builders, Inc., LaGrange, Ga., 1979-83; cons. health care delivery systems, 1983-84; v.p. Viron Internat., Inc., 1981-83; chmn., pres. Thunderwood Corp., Thunderwood Holdings, Inc., 1985—, First Union Nat. Bank Ga., 1984—. Methodist. Home: RR 1 Box 315T West Point GA 31822 Office: 1st Union Nat Bank Columbus PO Box 40 Columbus GA 31993

TAYLOR, J(AMES) BENNETT, management consultant; b. Sarasota, Fla., June 15, 1943; s. Thurman Ralph and Lucille (Bennett) T. divorced; 1 child, Kelly Christine. BS in Advt., U. Fla., 1965. Dist. mgr. The Coca-Cola Co., Shreveport, La., 1966-68; allied product specialist Coca-Cola U.S.A., Dallas, 1968-70, dist. mgr., Cin., Indpls., 1970-75; v.p. Ott Rsch. and Devel., Miami, Fla., 1975-78; pres., chief exec. officer Exec. Group, Inc., Tampa, Fla., 1978—. Mem. Assn. Outplacement Cons. Firms, Rotary. Home: 855 N Village Dr 101 Saint Petersburg FL 33716

TAYLOR, JAMES BLACKSTONE, aviation company executive; b. N.Y.C., Dec. 14, 1921; s. James Blackstone Taylor, Jr. and Aileen (Sedgwick) Taylor Lippincott; m. Margaret Krout, May 3, 1947; children—James Blackstone IV, Ray K., Jane A., W. Thorne. Grad., Taft sch., Watertown, Conn. Pres. Upressitmetal Cap Corp., N.Y.C., 1948-59; v.p. Am. Flange, N.Y.C., 1959-62, Pan Am. World Airways, N.Y.C., 1962-69, Cessna Aircraft, Wichita, Kans., 1969-76; pres., chmn. bd. Canadair, Inc., Westport, Conn., 1976-85; pres., chief exec. officer, dir. Gates Learjet Corp., Tucson, 1985—. Served to lt. USNR, 1942-46. Recipient Runner Up award World Skeet Shooting Championship, 1962. Mem. Gathering of Eagles (Aviation Man of Yr. 1984), Nat. Aviation Club, Wing's Club (v.p., bd. dirs. 1965-67, 83-87). Republican. Episcopalian. Clubs: Country (Fairfield, Conn.); Skyline Country (Tucson); Clove Valley Rod and Gun (LaGrangeville, N.Y.) (bd. dirs. 1983-87). Home: 32 Regent's Park Westport CT 06880 Office: Gates Learjet Corp 1255 E Aero Park Blvd Tucson AZ 85706

TAYLOR, JAMES BOYD, management consultant; b. Owensboro, Ky., May 30, 1919; s. James Hays and Marie Bruce (Boyd) T.; student pub. schs. N.Y.C., Louisville and Owensboro; m. Anna Frances McCandless, May 24, 1943. With IRS, 1943-47; with Glenmore Distilleries Co., Owensboro, 1933-43, 47—, asst. v.p., 1955-64, v.p., gen. mgr., 1964-78; installation mgr. A.P.C. Skills Co., Palm Beach, Fla., 1978-80; dep. sec. public protection and regulation cabinet Commonwealth of Ky., 1980-81, dep. sec. Dept. Natural Resources and Environ. Protection, 1981-82, spl. adviser to gov., 1982-83; owner Leadership Devel. Co., Profiles of Ky., 1983—; mem. adv. coun. Naval Affairs; mem. adv. com. Louisville Dist. Small Bus. Assn.; pres. Govtl. Collections Inc., Owensboro, 1983-86; pres. Jabota Corp., Owensboro, 1986—; dir. Citizens State Bank, Owensboro. Mem. Adv. Council on Naval Affairs; mem. Louisville dist. adv. com. SBA. Trustee Brescia Coll., 1974-76; chmn. bd. Owensboro Daviess County Hosp., 1968-75, Tri State Health Council, 1972-75; mem. Green River Area Health Council, 1972-75. Chosen by U.S. Pres. to receive Loyalty award VFW, 1972. Mem. Owensboro Daviess County C. of C. (bd. dirs. 1967-69), Ky. C. of C., Distilled Spirits Inst. Presbyterian. Clubs: Campbell (Owensboro). Pioneer bulk gauging distilled spirits. Home: 1515 Dean Ave Owensboro KY 42301 Office: PO Box 2024 Owensboro KY 42302

TAYLOR, JAMES DAVID, health care executive; b. Pitts., Oct. 3, 1947; s. Howard Alvin and Florence Elizabeth (Dale) T.; m. Helen Blair, Apr. 14, 1973; children: Megan, Brian. BA, Westminster Coll., 1969; MBA, Duquesne U., 1972; MPH, U. Pitts., 1974. Fin. trainee Gen. Electric Co., Erie, Pa., 1969-70; adminstrv. trainee Presbyn. U. Hosp., Pitts., 1973; adminstrv. resident Montefiore Hosp., Pitts., 1973-74; mgr. Geisinger Med. Ctr., Danville, Pa., 1974-76, adminstrv. asst., 1976-78; asst. adminstr. Scott & White co., Temple, Tex., 1978-81, dir., 1982—; fellowship preceptor Scott & White, Temple, Tex., 1985—; chmn. Joint Am. Coll. of Health Care Execs. and Med. Group Mgmt. Nat. Com., Chgo. and Denver, 1986-87. Contbr. articles to profl. jours. Bd. dirs. Columbia-Montour Home Health, Bloomburg, Pa., 1976-78; chmn. Grace Sch., Temple, 1980-86; elder Grace Presbyn. Ch., Temple, 1985-87. Recipient Third Place Nat. award Health Industry Mfg. Assn., 1975. Fellow Am. Coll. Healthcare Execs., Am. Coll. Med. Group Adminstrs.; mem. Am. Mktg. Assn., Issues Mgmt Assn., Soc. Healthcare Planning/Mktg., Med. Group Mgmt. Assn. (chmn. Joint Am. Coll. Health Care Execs. and Med. Group Mgmt. Nat. Com., 1986-87), Am. Mktg. Assn., Beta Gamma Sigma, Omicron Delta Epsilon. Republican. Home: 3813 Buffalo Trail Temple TX 76504 Office: Scott & White 2401 S 31st St Temple TX 76508

TAYLOR, JAMES FRANCIS, marketing professional; b. Detroit, Sept. 5, 1951; s. Harold James and Mary Frances (Law) T.; m. Janet Elizabeth Joss, May 21, 1977; children: Jonathan Harold, Jessica Frances, Jenna Leigh, Jeanette Mary. BA in Polit. Sci., Mich. State U., 1976; postgrad., Thomas Cooley Law Sch., 1979. Product mgr. Gen. Aluminum Products, Charlotte, Mich., 1975-77; sales mgr. Empire Metal Products, Columbus, Ohio, 1978; bus. mgr. Law Offices of Paul Martin, Lansing, Mich., 1978-79; dir. mktg. and sales Feather-Lite Mfg. Co., Troy, Mich., 1979-81; v.p. mktg. and sales Innovative Products Corp., Madison Heights, Mich., 1981-82; pres. J.F. Taylor Assocs., Inc., Durham, N.C., 1982—. Mem. Mfr.'s Agts. Nat. Assn., Nat. Assn. Home Builders. Republican. Roman Catholic. Clubs: Univ. of Mich. State U. (East Lansing); Hope Valley Country, Univ. (Durham). Lodge: Rotary. Home: 4 Roswell Ct Durham NC 27707 Office: Univ Tower Suite 901 3101 Petty Rd Durham NC 27707

TAYLOR, JAMES WALTER, marketing professor; b. St. Cloud, Minn., Feb. 15, 1933; s. James T. and Nina C. Taylor; m. Joanne Syktte, Feb. 3, 1956; children: Theodore James, Samuel Bennett, Christopher John. BBA, U. Minn., 1957; MBA, NYU, 1960; DBA, U. So. Calif., 1975. Mgr. research div. Atlantic Refining, Phila., 1960-65; dir. new product devel. Hunt-Wesson Foods, Fullerton, Calif., 1965-72; prof. mktg. Calif. State U., Fullerton, 1972—; cons. Chint/Day Advt., 1982—, Smithkline Beckman Corp., Phila., 1972—, Govt. of Portugal, Lisbon, 1987—. Author: Profitable New Product Strategies, 1984, How To Create A Winning Business Plan, 1986, Competitive Marketing Strategies, 1986, The 101 Best Performing Companies In America, 1987, How to Write A Successful Advertising Plan, 1988, The Complete Manual for Developing Winning Strategic Plans, 1988, Every Manager's Survival Guide, 1989. Fulbright scholar Ministry of Industry, Lisbon, Portugal, 1986-87; recipient Merit award Calif. State U., 1986-89. Mem. North Am. Soc. Corp. Planners, Am. Mktg. Assn., Strategic Mgmt. Assn., Assn. for Consumer Research, Acad. Mktg. Sci. Home: 3190 Mountain View Dr Laguna Beach CA 92651 Office: Calif State U Dept of Mktg Nutwood at State College Fullerton CA 92634

TAYLOR, JULIAN HOWARD, metals company executive; b. Emporia, Kans., July 17, 1943; s. Robert Milton and LuVine Ella (Ballard) T. Student, Earlham Coll., Richmond, Ind., 1961-62; B.A., Emporia State U., (Kans.), 1965; Ph.D., Iowa State U., 1969. Economist Bank of Am., San Francisco, 1969-73; v.p., sr. economist Bank of Am., Los Angeles, 1973-75; chief economist Reynolds Metals Co., Richmond, Va., 1975-80, v.p., treas., 1980—. Mem. Internat. Sector Adv. Com., Washington, 1976-80; mem. adv. bd. econs. Gov. Va., 1978-81; bd. dirs. Goodwill of Richmond, 1980-84; chmn. econ. devel. Gov.'s Commn. on Future of Va., 1983. Mem. Nat. Assn. Corp. Treas. (founding dir. 1982—). Office: Reynolds Metals Co 6603 W Broad St Richmond VA 23261

TAYLOR, LARRY PHILLIP, telephone company executive; b. Greensboro, Ala., Jan. 28, 1948; s. Sam Jones Taylor and Mary Mildred (Johnson) Walker; m. Patricia Ann Corr, Dec. 16, 1967; children: Richard Scott, Jami Kathryn. BS, U. Ala., 1970. Personnel mgr. Sears, Roebuck & Co., Tuscaloosa, Ala., 1971-73; v.p., gen. mgr. Moundville (Ala.) Telephone Co., 1973—; pres. River Bend Cable Inc., Moundville, 1985—. Chmn. Downtown Revitalization Com., Moundville, 1988—; vice-chmn. Moundville United Way, 1988—. Mem. Ala. & Miss. Telephone Assn. (bd. dirs. 1987—), Am. Mgmt. Assn., Kiwanis. Republican. Baptist. Home: 3407 Firethorn Dr Tuscaloosa AL 35405 Office: Moundville Telephone Co Market St Moundville AL 35474

TAYLOR, LEE BERNARD, human resource executive; b. St. Clair Shores, Mich., July 13, 1956; s. Lee B. and Elizabeth A. (Tormondsen) T.; m. Cherie M. Purvis, June 6, 1981; children: Christopher G., Carrie E., Nicole Lee. BS, Western Mich. U., 1978, MA, 1980. Asst. plannerecon. devel. Monroe County (Mich.) Planning Dept., 1980-81, planner econ. devel., 1981-82; mktg. rep. CompHealth, Inc., Salt Lake City, 1982-83, dir. recruiting, 1983-84, dir. primary care div., 1985-86, v.p. specialties div., 1986-87; pres., chief exec. officer Group One Anesthesia (subs. CompHealth, Inc.), Salt Lake City, 1988—; mem. grad. sales class rev. panel Grad. Sch. Bus. Adminstrn., U. Utah, Salt Lake City, 1988—. Mem. Am. Mktg. Assn., Delta Tau Alpha. Roman Catholic. Home: 559 Ada Way Grand Rapids MI 49506 Office: Group One Anesthesia 155 South 300 West Ste 300 Salt Lake City UT 84101

TAYLOR, MARGARET TURNER, clothing designer, economist; b. Wilmington, N.C., May 7, 1944. A.B. in Econs., Smith Coll., 1966; M.A. in Econ. History, U. Pa., 1970, now Ph.D. candidate in City and Regionel Planning. Tchr. Jefferson Jr. High Sch., New Orleans, 1966-69; instr. econs. U. Tex.-El Paso, 1974-75; adj. prof. econs., Salisbury State Coll., (Md.), 1976-78; prin. mgr., designer Margaret Norriss, women's clothing, Salisbury, Md., 1980—; planner at Wharton Ctr. Applied Research, Phila., 1985-86; planning cons., freelance writer.

TAYLOR, MICHAEL DEAN, accountant; b. St. Louis, Jan. 1, 1947; s. Basil Dean and Cleo Mae (Scrivner) T.; m. Barbara Mary Lavallee, May 22, 1976; 1 child, Mary Catherine. BS, U. Md., 1975. CPA, Va. From jr. acct. to sr. acct. M.B. Hariton & Co., CPA's, Washington, 1975-79; dir. acctg. Fed. Home Loan Mortgage Corp., Washington, 1979-85; chief fin. officer Am. Lang. Acad., Rockville, Md., 1986-87; AMS systems mgr. Fed. Sav. Loan Ins. Corp., 1987-88. Dir. Couple to Couple League, Arlington, Va., 1980-86; del. Va. Rep. Party, Falls Church, 1983-86. Named one of Outstanding Young Men of Am., U.S. Jaycees, 1982.

TAYLOR, NATHALEE BRITTON, nutritionist; b. Lubbock, Tex., June 8, 1941; d. Nathaniel E. and Dessie Pauline (Moss) Britton; children by previous marriage: Clay H., Bret N. Courtney. BS in Home Econs., Tex. Tech U., 1963. Home economist Pioneer Gas, Lubbock, Tex., 1963-65; dietician Tex. Tech U., Lubbock, 1966-71; home economist South Plains Electric Co-op., Lubbock, 1986; mgr. quality control Rip Griffins Enterprises, Lubbock, Tex., 1987; sales rep. Time Chem., Lubbock, 1987—. Coauthor: (cookbook) From Our House to Yours, 1975; columnist: Lubbock Lights mag.; presenter TV show Southwestern Cooking Sta. KTXT. Bd. dirs. Am. Heart Assn., Lubbock, 1985-87; mem. Home Economist in Bus. (pres. Lubbock chpt., 1985); culinary co-chmn. Lubbock C. of C. Arts Festival, 1982, 83, 84. Named Lincoln County Fair Queen. Mem. Tech. Home Ec Alumns (sec./treas.), Am. Home Econs. Assn. (v.p., sec./treas.), Soroptomist (v.p. Lubbock club). Republican. Episcopalian. Office: Time Chem Inc 4607 27th St Lubbock TX 79410

TAYLOR, R. LEE, II, food products company executive; b. Memphis, 1941. BS, Princeton U., 1964. With Holly Farms Corp. (formerly The Fedral Co.), Memphis, 1966—, v.p., 1967-78, exec. v.p., 1978-80; pres. Holly Farms Corp. (formerly The Federal Co.), Memphis, 1980—, chief exec. officer, 1981—, dir. Office: Holly Farms Corp 1755-D Lynnfield PO Box 17236 Memphis TN 38187

TAYLOR, RICK JOSEPH, tax executive; b. Escanaba, Mich., Feb. 24, 1956; s. Harold J. and Helen J. BS in Acctg., U. Wis., Green Bay, 1979; MS in Taxation, U. Wis., Milw., 1985. CPA, Wis. Fin. acct. Shopko Stores, Green Bay, 1979-81; audit sr. Grant Thornton, Appleton, Wis., 1981-83; teaching asst. U. Wis., Milw., 1983-85; tax sr. Peat Marwick Main & Co., Milw., 1985-86, tax mgr., 1986-87; sr. tax mgr. Washington Nat. Tax Office Peat Marwick Main & Co., 1988—. Author: (with others) CPA's Guide to Financial and Estate Planning After the Tax Reform Act , Income Shifting After Tax Reform; (newspaper column) Smart Money, 1986-88; editor: (with others) Multistate Tax Almanac, 1986-89; mem. editorial bd. Jour. of State Taxation, 1983—. Recipient Meldman Case Weine award Meldman Case Weine, 1985; taxation scholar U. Wis. Milw., 1983-84. Mem. Am. Inst. CPA's (Elijah Watts Sells award 1982), Wis. Inst. CPA's, U. Wis.-Milw. Tax Assn. Roman Catholic. Home: 1123A Stuart St Arlington VA 22201 Office: Peat Marwick Main & Co 2001 M St NW Washington DC 20036

TAYLOR, ROBERT COLEMAN, chemical consultant; b. Abington, Pa., May 22, 1918; s. Thomas Houx and Edith Mae (Burns) T.; m. Anna Florence Ritter, June 8, 1940; children—Phyllis Anne Winsko, Gregory Robert. B.S. in Chem. Engring., Drexel U., 1940. Research chemist Atlantic Refining Co., Phila., 1940-46, analytical group leader, 1946-52, research chemist, 1952-54, group leader specialty chemicals Atlantic Richfield Co., Glenolden, Pa., 1956-78; head petroleum products Lion Oil Co., Monsanto, El Dorado, Ark., 1954-56; pvt. practice cons. chemicals, King of Prussia, Pa., 1978—; project mgr. MACH I Inc., King of Prussia, 1987—. Contbr. articles to profl. jours. Patentee in field. Mem. Am. Chem. Soc. (emeritus), Sigma Xi, Tau Beta Pi. Republican. Roman Catholic. Lodge: Artisan Order of Mutual Protection. Avocations: reading; gardening; travel. Home and Office: 963 Longview Rd King of Prussia PA 19406

TAYLOR, ROBERT JAMES, bank executive, accountant; b. Clayton, Mo., Mar. 16, 1943; s. James and Vernita (Dollar) T.; m. Janet Jeorgina Johnson, Nov. 14, 1975; children: Robert, Christopher, Bradley. BS, Washington U., St. Louis, Mo., 1966; M in Commerce, St. Louis U., 1969. CPA, Mo. Audit supr. Coopers & Lybrand, St. Louis, 1967-76; asst. controller Nat. Liberty Corp., Valley Forge, Pa., 1977-78; asst. v.p. Fed. Res. Bank of St. Louis, 1978—. Loan exec. United Way of Greater St. Louis, 1980; bd. dirs. Coll. Sch. of Webster Groves, Mo., 1982-85, treas. 1982-1985; mem. St. Louis County Welfare Adv. Bd., 1972-75, Friends St. Louis Art Mus., Mo. Bot. Garden, St. Louis Zoo Friends Assn., Rep. Pres. Task Force; mem. budget allocation com. United Way Child Care; bd. curators Lincoln U. Served with USCG, 1967-72. Mem. AICPA, Mo. Soc. CPAs, Nat. Assn. Black Accts. (pres. St. Louis chpt. 1976), Am. Inst. Banking (bd. dirs. St. Louis chpt. 1981-82), Nat. Arbor Day Found. Republican. Roman Catholic. Club: Washington Univ. Home: 15660 Sugar Ridge Ct Chesterfield MO 63017

TAYLOR, RONALD LESLIE, accounting educator; b. Phila., Jan. 12, 1946; s. Wade Eugene and May (Dassler) T.; m. Helen Mabel Snelgrove, June 5, 1966; children: Robert Leslie, Philip Stanley. BS, Bryan Coll., 1974; MBA, U. Tenn., 1975, DBA, 1978. Cert. N.Y., Tenn., S.C. Mgr. bookstore Elim Bible Inst., Lima, N.Y., 1966-69; acct. Pinecrest Bible Tng. Ctr., Salisbury Ctr., N.Y., 1970-72, asst. to pres., 1985; acct. Taxes and Money Mgmt., Dayton, Tenn., 1973; teaching asst. U. Tenn., Knoxville, 1974-78; asst. prof. U. S.C., Columbia, 1979-81, assoc. prof., 1982-84; prof. acctg. LeMoyne Coll., Syracuse, N.Y., 1986, prof., chmn. dept., 1987—; bd. adminstrs. Pinecrest Bible Tng. Ctr., Salisbury, 1975—, Elim Fellowship, Lima, 1979—; bd. dirs. Elim Bible Inst., Lima. Mem. Am. Acctg. Assn., Am. Taxation Assn., Beta Alpha Psi. Home: 4851 Westfield Dr Manilus NY 13104 Address: LeMoyne Coll Dept Acctg Syracuse NY 13214

TAYLOR, RONALD LEWIS, millwork company executive; b. Lancaster, Pa., July 1, 1938; s. William Lewis and Marion Hazel (Mendenhall) T.; m. Agnes Francine Luzius, May 6, 1967; children: Kelly Lyn, Kristen Leigh, Kevin Lewis. Student, Bloomsburg U., 1955-56, Franklin and Marshall U., 1958-61, Cen. Mich. U., evenings 1963-64. Salesman, Armstrong World Industries, Lancaster, Pa., 1956-66, Schultz, Snyder, & Steele, Lansing, Mich., 1967-70; regional mgr. Olympic Stain Co., Bellevue, Wash., 1970-73; gen. mgr. Ea. Stain Co., New Rochelle, N.Y., 1973-79; br. mgr. C.E. Morgan Co., Mechanicsburg, Pa., 1979-84; v.p. sales, mktg. Reeb Millwork Corp., Bethlehem, Pa., 1984-85, v.p., gen. mgr., 1985-86, dir., 1986—; v.p. gen. mgr. Reeb N.Y., 1987—. Dir. found. bd. Northampton City Community Coll., 1989. Paul Harris fellow Rotary Internat., 1985. Republican. Mem. Silver Creek Country Club (dir., v.p. 1988), Elks, Rotary. Avocations: golf, hockey, football, computers, bowling. Home: RD 4 50 Arden Ln Bethlehem PA 18015 Office: Reeb Millwork Corp PO Box 5332 600 Brighton St Ext Bethlehem PA 18015

TAYLOR, SCOTT L., property management executive; b. Seattle, Apr. 1, 1960; s. Peter Leslie and Margaret Ann (Dodd) T.; m. Lisa Christine Cole, June 30, 1984. BA, Wash. State U., 1982. CPA, Ariz.; lic. real estate broker, Ariz. Staff acct. Touche Ross & Co., Seattle, 1982-85; v.p. Goodman Mgmt. Group, Phoenix, 1985—. Office: Goodman Mgmt Group 1730 E Northern #122 Phoenix AZ 85020

TAYLOR, SCOTT MAXFIELD, department store executive; b. Evanston, Ill., Aug. 13, 1953; s. Brett Maxfield and Gretchen Pauline (Porter) T., Jr. BA, Coe Coll., 1975; M in Mgmt., Northwestern U., 1977; MSC, New Sem., 1985. Sales mgr. Daytons, Mpls., 1977-78, asst. buyer, 1978-79; store mgr. Brett's Dept. Store, Mankato, Minn., 1979-80, buyer jr. dept., 1981-83, v.p., 1981-87, div. mdse. mgr., 1984-85, gen. mdse. mgr., 1985—, pres., 1988—, also bd. dirs. Bd. dirs. Blue Earth County Hist. Soc., Mankato, 1984-87; bd. dirs. Mankato Area Conv. and Vis. Bur., 1985—, chmn., 1987-88; Presbyn. deacon, 1986-88, moderator 1987-88. George F. Baker scholar, 1975. Mem. Omicron Delta Epsilon, Kiwanis (bd. dirs. 1984—, pres. 1988-89). Avocation: curling. Home: Box 3642 Mankato MN 56002 Office: Brett's Dept Stores Box 609 Mankato MN 56002

TAYLOR, STEVEN DAVID, financial planner; b. Montclair, N.J., Jan. 1, 1960; s. Woodley David and Zenobia Jean (Davis) T. BA in Econs., Clark Coll., 1983; postgrad., Ohio State U., 1983-84. Cert. fin. planner. Fin. planner CWI Fin. and Estate Planning, Washington, 1984-87; pres., bd. dirs. TSM Group (formerly Taylor Fin. Services Corp.), Washington, 1987—; bd. dirs. Nat. Source of Solutions, Inc., Washington, E&L Enterprises, Washington. Mem. Internat. Assn. Fin. Planners, Inst. Cert. Fin. Planners, Toastmasters Internat. Mem. Prog. Party. Mem. Disciples of Christ. Clubs: Men of Union Temple (treas. 1988—), Tribe of Ujima (treas. 1988—) (Washington). Office: TSM Group Inc 2000 L St NW Suite 200 Washington DC 20036

TAYLOR, SUSAN MARTIN, university official; b. Atlanta, Sept. 5, 1956; d. Andrew Weldon and Sarah Evelyn (Jobson) Martin; m. James McDonald Smith, Sept. 7, 1974 (div. Sept. 1986); children: Lisa, Jason; m. Larry Hal Taylor, June 11, 1988; stepchildren: Sandra, Angela, Laura. BEd, U. Hawaii, 1978; MBA, U. West Fla., 1982. Tchr. bus. edn. Kamchamcha Schs., Honolulu, 1978-79, Newark (Ohio) Cath. High Sch., 1979-80; cons. Small Bus. Devel. Ctr. U. West Fla., Pensacola, 1981-82; fin. analyst div. econ. devel. Fla. Dept. Commerce, Tallahassee, 1984-86; office coord. Small Bus. Devel. Ctr. U. Ga., Gainesville, 1986-88; asst. dir. Small Bus. Devel. Ctr. U. Ga., Lawrenceville, 1988—; adj. instr. Brenau Coll., Gainesville, 1986—. Chmn. absentee ballots Tallahassee Rep. Women's Club, 1984-86. Mem. LWV (membership chmn. Gainesville, 1987-88), Am. Bus. Women's Assn. (program chmn. Tallahassee 1985-86, publicity chmn. Gainesville 1987), Atlanta Women's Network. Methodist. Home: 5010 Sunrise Ct Gainesville GA 30501 Office: U Ga Small Bus Devel Ctr 1250 Atkinson Rd Lawrenceville GA 30246

TAYLOR, TERRY, economist, financial executive; b. Detroit, Aug. 2, 1946; s. G. Manson and Beatrice (Herman) T.; m. Darlene Rose Babiarz, June 20, 1969; children: Jennifer, Jeffrey. BA in Econs., Wayne State U., 1971, MA in Econs. summa cum laude, 1979. Econ. analyst Comerica Inc., Detroit, 1976-83, chief economist, 1983—, officer, 1976—, asst. v.p., 1980-83, v.p., 1983-88, 1st v.p., mgr. funds mgmt. ops., 1988—; instr. econs. Wayne State U., Detroit, 1980-81. Contbr. articles to banking and investing publs. Mem. econ. adv. com. United Found., Detroit, 1985-87. With U.S. Army, 1965-67. Mem. Nat. Assn. Bus. Economists, Detroit Area Econ. Forum, Econs. Club (Detroit). Office: Comerica Inc 211 W Fort St Detroit MI 48275-1057

TAYLOR, THERESE ANNE, jet engine inspector; b. Grand Rapids, Mich., Apr. 5, 1962; d. James Everton and Anne Barbara (Bunway) Abrams. Grad. with Airframe and Powerplant Lic., 1986. Jet engine mechanic Lockheed Support Systems, Inc., Tucson, 1984-85; jet engine inspector Lockheed Support Systems, Inc., Balt., 1987—; jet engine mechanic Evergreen Air Ctr., Marana, Ariz., 1985-86; owner Enchanted Treasures, Balt., 1988—. With USAF, 1980-84. Home and Office: 30 Higan Ct Baltimore MD 21237

TAYLOR, THOMAS HUDSON, JR., import company executive; b. Somerville, Mass., June 8, 1920; s. Thomas Hudson and Virginia Gwendolyn (Wilson) T.; B.S. in Econs., Wharton Sch. Fin. and Commerce, U. Pa., 1947; m. Mary Jane Potter, Dec. 1, 1943; children—Thomas Hudson, III, James R., Jane, John E., Virginia. Acctg. exec. Collins & Aikman Corp., Phila., 1947-55, divisional controller automotive div., Albemarle, N.C., 1956-59, asst. dir. purchases, 1960-64; exec. v.p. Carolina Floral Imports, Inc., Gastonia, N.C., 1965-67, pres., treas., 1968—. County commr. Stanly County, Albemarle, N.C., 1962-66. Served to capt. USAAF, 1941-45. Decorated Air medal. Mem. Beta Theta Pi. Republican. Methodist. Clubs: Princeton, Gastonia City. Home: 4537 Forest Cove Rd Belmont NC 28012-8701 Office: Box 2201 Gastonia NC 28053

TAYLOR, VOLNEY, marketing company executive; b. Portsmouth, Ohio, Dec. 6, 1939; s. Lafayette and Martha Louise (Frederick) T.; m. Kathleen Ann MacMahon, May 17, 1969; children—Lafayette, Lloyd MacMahon, Kerry Erin, Frederick Daly. B.S. in Indsl. Engring, Ohio State U., 1962; M.B.A., Harvard U., 1966. Asso. mem. McKinsey & Co., Inc. (mgmt. cons.), N.Y.C., 1966-72; exec. v.p., dir. Funk & Wagnalls, Inc., N.Y.C., 1972-74; v.p. fin. Reuben H. Donnelley Co., N.Y.C., 1974-76; dir. corp. planning Dun & Bradstreet Corp., N.Y.C., 1976-77, v.p. corp. planning, 1977-78, corp. v.p., 1979-80, sr. v.p., 1980-82, exec. v.p., 1982—, also bd. dirs.; gen. mgr. Official Airline Guides, Oak Brook, Ill., 1978-79, also bd. dirs.; bd. dirs. Donnelley Info. Pub. Inc., Donnelley Directory Inc., Thomson Directories, The Reuben H. Donnelley Corp. Served to lt. (j.g.) USNR, 1962-64. Mem. Beta Theta Pi. Club: Harvard Bus. Sch. (N.Y.C.). Office: The Dun & Bradstreet Corp 299 Park Ave New York NY 10171

TAYLOR, WESLEY ALAN, accountant; b. Johnson City, Tenn., Oct. 27, 1958; s. Wesley Wentworth and Charlotte Marie (Holly) T. BS in Acctg., U. Tenn., 1980. CPA. Staff acct. Wesley W. Taylor CPA, P.C., 1980-85; sr. acct. Blackburn, Childers & Stegall, CPAs, Elizabethton, Tenn., 1985-88; acct., mgr. BCS & Co., CPAs, Briston, Tenn., 1988-89; pvt. practice, Elizabethton, 1989—. Auditor Miss Watauga Valley Pageant, 1985, 86, 87, 88, Miss Jonesboro Pageant, 1988. Mem. Am. Inst. CPA's. Tenn. Soc. CPA's, Johnson City Jaycees (mem. fin. com.). Republican. Home: PO Box 1435 Elizabethton TN 37644

TAYLOR, WILLIAM FREDERICK, advertising agency executive; b. Morristown, N.J., Aug. 14, 1956; s. Darel Frederick and Margaret Elizabeth (Mauger) T.; m. Karen Ann Deluca, July 16, 1983. BS in Criminology, Fla. State U., 1979; postgrad., Pace U., 1984-85. Casualty claims rep. Crawford and Co., Clifton, N.J., 1980-82; ins. analyst Colgate-Palmolive Co., N.Y.C., 1982-86; corp. risk mgr. Young & Rubicam, Inc., N.Y.C., 1986-87, dir. corp. ins., risk mgr., 1987—. Mem. Risk and Ins. Mgmt. Soc. (chmn. advt. agy. industry session 1986), Vt. Captive Ins. Assn., Captive Ins. Cos. Assn. Republican. Home: 56 Garden St Wood Ridge NJ 07075 Office: Young & Rubicam Inc 285 Madison Ave 22d Fl New York NY 10017

TAYLOR, WILLIAM JOHN, banker; b. N.Y.C., Oct. 12, 1951; s. William John and Edna May (Foulds) T.; m. Ninyupa Sairoong, Dec. 23, 1980; 1 child, Troy William. MS, Adelphi U., 1973, BBA, 1975. CPA, N.Y. Acct. Kenneth Leventhal & Co., Great Neck, N.Y., 1976-78; sr. mgr. Peat Marwick & Main, N.Y.C., 1978-86; sr. v.p., controller Crossland Savs. Fed. Savs. Bank, Bklyn., 1986—. Mem. Am. Inst. CPA's, N.Y. Soc. CPAs (com. on banking 1987-88), Fin. Execs. Inst., Mensa. Office: Crossland Savs FSB 211 Montague St Brooklyn NY 11201

TAYLOR, WILLIAM OSGOOD, newspaper executive; b. Boston, July 19, 1932; s. William Davis and Mary (Hammond) T.; m. Sally Coxe, June 20, 1959; children: William Davis II, Edmund C., Augustus R. B.A., Harvard U., 1954. With Globe Newspaper Co., Boston, 1956—; treas. Globe Newspaper Co., 1963—, bus. mgr., 1965-69, gen. mgr., 1969—, now chmn. bd., pub.; chmn. bd., dir. Affiliated Publs., Inc.; chmn. Am. Press Inst.; Pres. Cotting Sch. for Handicapped Children, 1973—; trustee Kennedy Library Found., Wellesley Coll., Trustees of Reservations; trustee New Eng. Aquarium. Served with U.S. Army, 1954-56. Office: Globe Newspaper Co 135 Morrissey Blvd Boston MA 02107

TAYLOR, WILLIAM ROBERT, software executive, educator; b. Pueblo, Colo., Aug. 22, 1954; s. Robert William Taylor and Martha E. Jefferson (Wold) Adams; m. Sharon Elaine Fisher, Aug. 28, 1983. BA in Environ. Biology, U. Colo., 1978; MBA in Resource Mgmt., U. Denver, 1983. Rsch. asst. Nat. Oceanic Atmospheric Adminstrn., Boulder, Colo., 1978-81; mgr. mktg. Johnson & Johnson Ultrasound, Denver, 1983-84; v.p., exec. dir. Colo. Mining Assn., 1984-85; pres. Softward Cons., 1985—; lectr. U. Colo., Boulder, 1976-77, Colo. and Wyo. Acad. Sci., Denver, 1977-78; chmn. pub. rels. Rocky Mountain Coal Inst., 1985; mem. adj. faculty U. Phoenix, Denver, 1986—. Mem. Colo. Microcomputers Mgrs. Assn. (pres.1985-87), SMART User Group (pres. 1984-85), DU Energy Mgmt. Assn. (pres. 1982-83). Home: 5735 W Atlantic Pl #303 Lakewood CO 80227 Office: Software Cons PO Box 36304 Lakewood CO 80227

TAYLOR, WILSON H., diversified financial company executive. Grad., Trinity Coll. With Conn. Gen., 1954-82, sr. v.p., chief fin. officer, 1980-82; v.p. Aetna Ins. Co., 1975; exec. v.p. Cigna Corp., Phila., 1982-88, pres. property casualty group, 1983-88, corp. vice-chmn., chief operating officer, 1988—, chief operating officer, 1988, pres., chief exec. officer, 1988—. Phi Beta Kappa. Office: Cigna Corp 1 Logan Sq Philadelphia PA 19103 *

TAYNTON, PAUL, engineer, real estate firm executive; b. Washington, Dec. 18, 1934; s. Mark and Ruth R. (Rosenthal) T.; m. Mary Hardig, June 2, 1979; children: Carol Wilson, Dienne Hetrick Louis, Vicki Hawkes, Anna Ruth, Brian Smith. BS in Aero. Engrng., Va. Poly. Inst., 1957; postgrad., U. Washington, 1958-59. Aerodynamicist Thieblot Aircraft Co., Bethesda, Md., 1957; flight test engr. Boeing Airplane Co., Seattle, 1957-58, design engr., 1958-60; aerodynamicist research Texaco Experiment, Inc., Richmond, Va., 1960-62, project engr., 1962-64; pres., mgr. Ruxville Corp., Richmond, 1964-72; field engr. Gee and Jensen, Engrs., West Palm Beach, Fla., 1973-74, project mgr., 1975-78; br. mgr. Gee and Jensen, Engrs., Lake Buena Vista, Fla., 1978-79; project mgr. Arvida Corp., Boca Raton, 1974-75; pres., mgr. Plan Developers, Inc., Kissimmee, Fla., 1979—; Configurator Original Swing-Wing Airplane, 1960; project officer Boron fiber program Boron Filament Devel., 1964. Co-author: Comprehensive Land Use Plan ITT Palm Coast, 1978; designer entertainment shopping complex, Old Town. Bd. dirs. Chesterfield Hosp. Corp., Richmond, 1965; pres. Clover Hill Ruritan, Richmond, 1964-66; mem. Fla. Econ. Devel. Council, 1985—. Mem. ASCE, ASME, NSPE, Fla. Engrng. Soc., Aircraft Owners and Pilot's Assn., U.S. Coast Guard Aux. (7th dist. Flotilla comdr. 1980-84), Kissimmee-Osceola Com. of 100. Republican. Methodist. Club: Toho Yacht (Kissimmee) (bd. dirs. 1983-84). Lodge: Rotary. Office: Plan Developers Inc 321 Church St Kissimmee FL 32741

TCHEREPNINE, PETER ALEXANDROVITCH, brokerage house executive; b. Paris, Jan. 21, 1939; came to U.S., 1951; s. Alexander and Ming (Lee) T.; m. Patricia Orssich, Mar. 18, 1967 (div. Apr. 1973); children: Alexander, Samantha; m. Jessica Elizabeth Harris, July 7, 1973. BA in Romance Lang. and Lit., Harvard U., 1960. Assoc. mgr. Loeb Rhoades & Co., N.Y.C., 1962-71, internat. inst. sales, 1972-73; mgr. internat. dept. Wood, Struthers & Winthrop, N.Y.C., 1973-74; v.p. mgr., internat. dept. Loeb Rhoades Hornblower, N.Y.C., 1974-80; exec. v.p. Loeb Ptnrs. Corp., N.Y.C., 1980—; bd. dirs. Am. Inst. Foreign Study, Inc., Greenwich, Conn. Bd. dirs., vice chmn. Am. Soc. for Prevention of Cruelty to Animals, N.Y., 1983—; trustee China Inst. in Am., N.Y., 1983—. Served to 1st lt. U.S. Army, 1960-62. Clubs: Racquet and Tennis (N.Y.C.), Down Town Assn. (N.Y.C.), Meshomack Fish and Game Preserve (Pine Plains, N.Y.), Millbrook (N.Y.) Polo, Gulfstream Polo, Millbrook Hunt. Home: RD 2 Box 87 Pine Plains NY 12567 Office: Loeb Ptnrs Corp 61 Broadway Rm 2450 New York NY 10006

TCHORYK, ROBERT CHARLES, oil company administrator; b. Johnstown, Pa., Jan. 14, 1956; s. Wasyl and Mary (Rudy) T. BA, Washington and Jefferson Coll., 1977; M of Accountancy, Bowling Green St. U., 1979. Sr. joint venture acct. Cities Service Co., Houston, 1979-83; sr. internat. acct. Ashland Oil Co., Houston, 1983-85; sr. administrator Sedco Forex-Schlumberger, Dallas, 1985-86; fin. analyst Continental Airlines, Inc., Houston, 1986-87; internat. contracts specialist Marathon Oil Co., Houston, 1987—. Home: 6722 Log Hollow Houston TX 77088-2122 Office: Marathon Oil Co 5555 San Felipe Houston TX 77056

TEAGUE, BURTON WILLIAM, management consultant, author; b. Portland, Oreg., Oct. 1, 1912; s. William Thomas and Bertie Mae (Bardo) T.; m. Sally Estes Reimer, July 30, 1938, children: Barbara Estes, Gregory Bardo. BA, Nichols Coll., 1933; JD, Ind. U., 1936. Bar: Ind. 1936. Spl. agt. F.B.I. U.S. Dept. Justice, Washington, 1942-46; supr. labor relations CalteX Petroleum, N.Y.C., 1946-67; pres. HI-ARC Corp., N.Y.C., 1968-72; sr. research assoc. The Conf. Bd., N.Y.C., 1970-77; pvt. practice mgmt. cons. Basking Ridge, N.J., 1977—; cons. The Conf. Bd., N.Y., 1967—, Right Assocs. Phila., 1982—. Contbr. articles to profl. jours. Pres. Northeast Assn., Montclair, N.J., 1955; chmn. bd. deacons Community Congl. Ch., Short Hills, N.J., 1968; treas. Neighborhood House (charity), Millburn, N.J., 1970. Mem. Soc. Former Spl. Agts. FBI, Nat. Assn. Fin. Cons., Internat. Assn. Fin. Planning. Clubs: Short Hills; Baltusrol (Springfield, N.J.). Home: 27 Dexter Dr N Basking Ridge NJ 07920

TEBBE, HORST, protective packaging manufacturing company executive; b. Hamburg, Federal Republic of Germany, Sept. 24, 1940; came to U.S., 1951; s. Wilhelm Tebbe and Erika (Helmuth) Apfelbaum; m. Shirley Ann Greene, July 26, 1964 (div. Apr. 1982); children: Nelson, Felice, Leslie. BSEE, Rensselaer Polytech. Inst., 1963; MSEE, U. Calif., 1965; PhD in Computer Sci., U. Pa., 1968. Mem. tech. staff Bell Telephone Labs., Holmdel, N.J., 1963-69; sr. mgr. Kraft Inc., Glenview, Ill., 1969-75; asst. sec. Gen. Reinsurance Corp., Stamford, Conn., 1975-76; dir. mgmt. info. systems Pepsi Cola div. PepsiCo. Inc., Purchase, N.Y., 1976-86; v.p. ops. Sealed Air Corp., Saddle Brook, N.J., 1986—; mem. info. systems exec. com. Grocery Mfrs. Am., Washington, 1981-85. Ford Found. fellow, 1966. Mem. IEEE, Old Greenwich Yacht Club. Office: Sealed Air Corp Park 80 Plaza East Saddle Brook NJ 07662

TEBOUL, ALBERT, nuclear power director; b. Oujda, Morocco, Sept. 28, 1936; s. Charles and Reine (Sayag) T.; m. Arlette Creps, Apr. 27, 1968. Supérieure, Ecole d'électricité et de mécanique industrielles, Paris, 1959; grad., INSEAD, Fontainebleau, France, 1984. Engr. Metafram-Pechiney, Paris, 1960; engr. sci. research Ecole Centrale, Paris, 1960-61; engr. Thomson/CSF, Dijon, France, 1961-62, Soc. de Fabrication d'Elements Catologues, Bollene, France, 1962-65; staff mgr. Soc. de Fabrication d'Elements Catalytiques, Bollene, France, 1970-80, gen. mgr., 1982-85; gen. mgr. Cle Industrielle de Combustible Atomique Fritté, Paris, 1965; pres. Bollene, 1982-86; project mgr. Chain Fabric & Cen Cadarache, France, 1968-70; pres. Sofretes. Mengin, Montargis, France, 1980-82; dir. Centre d'Etudes Nucleairs de la Vallé du Rhône, Com. l'Energie Atomique, Bagnols sur Cèze, France, 1985—; with pub. relations dept. dale Carnegie Assocs., Avignon, France, 1979; fin. mgr. CRC, Jouy. en Josas, France, 1983. Patentee in field. Conseiller mcpl. Mairie Lapalud, 1971, 77. Recipient decree Govt. of France, 1984, 86, decree Chambre de Commerce et de L'Industrie de Vaucluse, 1986, Chevaller de L'ordre Nat. Dumerite, 1987. Mem. Licensing Exec. Soc., Française de L'energie Nucléaire, Inginner Soc. Française. Lodge: Rotary (Bourg. St. Andéol-Viviers-Le Teil). Home: Rue Bourgades Hautes, 84840 Lapalud, Vaucluse France Office: Centre d'Etudes Nucleaires, la Vallee du Rhone BP 171, 30205 Bagnols-sur-Ceze France

TECKLENBURG, HARRY, pharmaceutical products executive; b. Seattle, Nov. 3, 1927; s. Harry and Frieda (Rasche) T.; m. Mary Louise Beaty, Sept. 1, 1951; children: Don, Bruce. B.S. in Chem. Engring., MIT, 1950; M.S. in Chem. Engring., U. Wash., 1952. With Procter & Gamble Co., Cin., 1952—; chem. engr., group leader, sect. leader. dir., mgr. research and devel. dept., v.p. research and devel. Procter & Gamble Co., 1952-76; sr. v.p. 1976—; gen. mgr. Norwich Div. N.Y., 1984—; rep. to Indsl. Research Inst., 1973-76. Mem. corp. devel. com. MIT, 1977-82; trustee Ohio Valley Goodwill Industries Rehab. Center, 1969-84, pres., 1974-82; bd. dirs. Goodwill Industries Am., 1978-84, vice chmn. bd., 1980-82, chmn. bd., 1982-84, dir. emeritus, 1984-87; mem. vis. com. dept. chem. engring. U. Wash., 1983; chmn. Goodwill Industries Internat. Fund, 1986. Served with AUS, 1946-48. Mem. Engring. Soc. Cin., Am. Inst. Chem. Engrs., Am. Chem. Soc., Pharms. Mfrs. Assn. (dir. 1984—), TAPPI, AAAS. Office: Norwich Eaton Pharms Inc Norwich NY 13815

TEDDER, JANE ANN, portfolio manager; b. Stillwater, Okla., Oct. 1, 1942; d. Robert M. and Guila M. (Harp) Pyle; children: Troy, Jay, Kira. B in Music Edn., Okla. State U., 1964; diploma in trust banking, Northwestern U., 1979; diploma in sr. mgmt. banking, Rutgers U., 1982. Asst. trust officer Douglas County Bank, Lawrence, Kans., 1975-76, trust officer, 1976-83, v.p., 1978-83; portfolio mgr. Security Mgmt. Co., Topeka, 1983—; vis. lectr. Kans. U., Lawrence, 1986-87. Trustee Plymouth Congl. Ch., Lawrence, 1981-83, moderator, 1984; dir. Ecumenical Christian Ministries Kans. U., Lawrence, 1984-88. Fellow Life Mgmt. Inst. Office: Security Mgmt Co 700 Harrison Topeka KS 66636

TEDERS, ELLA GROVE, financial planner; b. Brownsville, Tex., Oct. 8, 1931; d. Philip Wayne and Alberta Wilma (White) Grove; m. Kenneth Joseph Teders, July 14, 1951; children: Mark Alan, Clark Owen. Diploma in nursing, U. Okla., 1954, BS in Nursing, 1968. Registered nurse, investment advisor; cert. fin. planner. Nurse Enid (Okla.) State Sch., 1954; head nurse St. Mary's Hosp., Enid, 1955; pub. health nurse Payne Co. Health Dept., Stillwater, Okla., 1955-59; nursing service adminstr. Stillwater Health Ctr., 1959-68, Bass Meml. Bapt. Hosp., Enid, 1968-76; agt. Prudential Ins. Cos. Am., Enid, 1976—; owner, operator Ella Teders Fin. Services, Enid, 1977—; co-adminstr. Garfield County Eldercare, Enid, 1980—. Author: Nursing Service Procedures, 1966, 70. Mem. Civitan Internat. (bd. dirs. 1980-85), Altrusa Internat., Enid, 1988. Mem. Nat. Assn. Health Underwriters (bd. dirs. 1980-86, Leading Producers Roundtable 1980-87), Nat. Assn. Life Underwriters (local nat. committeeman 1985-88), Northwest Okla. Life Underwriters (pres. 1983-84, nat. committeeman 1985—), Internat. Assn Fin. Planners, Am. Assn. Individual Investors, AAUW,(Polished Diamond award 1986, Outstanding Woman Achievement in Bus. 1987), Mariners Club. Democrat. Presbyterian. Office: Ella Teders Fin Svcs 1820 W Garriott Enid OK 73702-3006

TEDESCO, ALBERT SEBASTIAN, communications executive; b. Mt. Vernon, N.Y., July 6, 1943; s. Pasquale Anthony and Marie (Rella) T. BA in Govt., Georgetown U., 1965; MA in Polit. Sci., Fordham U., 1966; MA in Communications, U. Pa., 1970. Instr. communications Drexel U., Phila., 1972-81; gen. mgr. Sta. WWSG-TV, Phila., 1981-85; gen. mgr. Pa. Pay TV, Phila., 1981-85, v.p., gen. mgr., 1985—; v.p., gen. mgr. Electronic Billboards Inc., Phila., 1985—; cons. U.S. Commn. Civil Rights, Washington, 1976, Channel 57 Corp., Phila., 1979-80. Author: (with Charles T. Meadow) Telecommunications for Management, 1985. Recipient Eastern Regional award Internat. TV Assn., 1978. Mem. Nat. Assn. TV Program Execs., Nat. Acad. TV Arts and Scis. Club: TV-Radio Advt. (Phila.). Office: Pa Pay TV 3600 Conshohocken Ave Philadelphia PA 19131

TEEL, RICHARD LARRY, climate control company executive; b. Elmore, Ala., Oct. 3, 1944; s. Marshall Byron and Olis (Mims) T.; m. Peggy Sanders, Dec. 20, 1964; children: Bart, Troy. BS, Auburn U., 1967. Owner, pres. Climate Control Equipment, Inc., Montgomery, Ala., 1972—. Bd. dirs., vice-chmn. Elmore County Bd. Edn., Wetumpka, Ala., 1980—; bd. dirs. Wetumpka YMCA, 1976—, Montgomery Area YMCA, 1984—. Mem. ASHRAE. Baptist. Home: 717 Harrogate Spring Rd Wetumpka AL 36092 Office: Climate Control Equipment Inc 536 George Todd Dr Montgomery AL 36117

TEEM, PAUL LLOYD, JR., savings and loan executive; b. Gastonia, N.C., Mar. 10, 1948; s. Paul Lloyd Sr. and Ruth Elaine (Bennett) T. BA, U. N.C., 1970; cert., Inst. Fin. Edn., 1984; diploma, Inst. Fin. Edn., Chgo., 1985, degree of distinction, 1989. Cert. tchr. N.C., consumer credit exec.; licensed real estate broker. V.p., sec. Gaston Fed. Savs. and Loan Assn., Gastonia, N.C., 1983—; sec., v.p., bd. dirs. Gaston Fin. Services, Inc., Gastonia, 1988—. Bd. dirs. Gastonia Mchts. Assn., Inc., 1981-83. Fellow Soc. Cert. Credit Execs.; mem. SAR, Phi Alpha Theta. Democrat. Episcopalian (lay reader). Lodges: Sons of Am. Revolution, Sons of Confederate Vets., Mil. Order of Stars and Bars, Masons (Disting. Service award 1987, Gold Honor award 1988, bd. dirs. 1981—), K.T., Shriner (32 degree). Home: 1208 Poston Circle Gastonia NC 28054-4634 Office: Gaston Fed Savs and Loan Assn 245 W Main Ave PO Box 2249 Gastonia NC 28053-2249

TEEPLE, RICHARD DUANE, lawyer; b. Portland, Ind., Oct. 31, 1942; s. Joseph Carlise and Sylvia Ann (Bailey) T.; m. Julie Favorite, June 5, 1965; children: Laura, Darin. BA, Purdue U., 1964; JD, U. Cin., 1967. Bar: Ohio 1967. Assoc. Wilke & Goering, Cin., 1967-72; atty. Gen. Motors Corp., Dayton, Ohio, 1972-77; gen. counsel Cooper Tire & Rubber Co., Findlay, Ohio, 1977—. Mem. advisory bd. Salvation Army, Findlay, 1982—. Mem. ABA, Ohio Bar Assn. (bd. govs. corp. counsel sect. 1984—), Findlay/Hancock Bar Assn., Am. Corp. Counsel Assn. Office: Cooper Tire & Rubber Co Lima and Western Aves Findlay OH 45840

TEER, HAROLD BENTON, JR., marketing educator and consultant; b. Eunice, La., June 12, 1945; s. Harold Benton and Kathryn (Weems) R.; m. Faye Peltier, Feb. 9, 1973. BSBA, Northwestern State U., 1969; MBA, Miss. Coll., Clinton, 1977; D in Bus. Adminstrn., La. Tech. U., 1985. Salesman Johnson & Johnson, Jackson, Miss., 1973-76; instr. Hinds Jr. Coll., Raymond, Miss., 1977-78, La. Tech. U., Ruston, 1978-81; prof. Fort Lewis Coll., Durango, Colo., 1981-86, James Madison U., Harrisonburg, Va., 1986—; vice chmn., bd. dirs. Durango Better Bus. Bur., 1984-86. Served as sgt. U.S. Army, 1967-71, Vietnam. Named one of Outstanding Young Men Am., Outstanding Faculty Member James Madison U., 1988-89. Mem. Am. Mktg. Assn., So. Mktg. Assn., Southwestern Mktg. Assn., Southwestern Small Bus. Assn., Mid-South Acad. Econs. and Fin., Acad. Mktg. Sci. Republican. Methodist. Home: Rt 11 Box 203 Harrisonburg VA 22801 Office: James Madison U Dept Mktg Harrisonburg VA 22807

TEERLINK, RICHARD FRANCIS, motor company executive; b. Chgo., Oct. 12, 1936; s. James and Martha (Vogel) T.; m. Ann L. Hofing, Apr. 23, 1960; children—John Robert, Leslie Ann, Victoria Lynn. B.S., Bradley U., 1961; M.B.A., U. Chgo., 1976. Sr. v.p. adminstrn. Union Special Corp., Chgo., 1971-78; v.p. fin. RTE Corp., Waukesha, Wis., 1978-80; sr. v.p., chief fin. officer Herman Miller, Inc., Zeeland, Mich., 1980-81; v.p., chief fin. officer Harley Davidson Motor Co., Inc., Milw., 1981—, also bd. dirs.; pres., chief exec. officer Harley Davidson Motorcycle, Inc., 1987—. Served with U.S. Army, 1955-58. Home: 1765 Wedgewood W Elm Grove WI 53122 Office: Harley-Davidson Inc 3700 W Juneau Ave Milwaukee WI 53208

TEETS, CHARLES EDWARD, financial executive; b. Terra Alta, W.Va., Feb. 11, 1947; s. Chester Carlton and Willye Katherine (Martin) T.; m. Judith Marlene Kildow, Dec. 19, 1970; children: Melissa Catherine, Brant Randolph. BS, Salisbury State Coll., 1973; MBA, So. Ill. U., 1980. Sr. cost acct. Perdue, Inc., Salisbury, Md., 1973-74; sect. chief acctg. terminal systems div. NCR, Millsboro, Del., 1974-76; contr. SPS Techs., Anasco, P.R., 1976-79; mgr. mfg. acctg. instrumentation div. Baxter Travenol Labs., Savage, Md., 1979-81; contr. Coated Abrasives N.Am. div. Standard Oil Co., Niagara Falls, N.Y., 1981-83; v.p., sec., treas. Carborundum Abrasives Co., Niagara Falls, 1983-86; v.p., chief fin. officer LeRoy (N.Y.) Industries, Inc., 1986—; mem. steering com. Treasury Mgmt. Inst., Holliston, Mass.; lectr. Cash Mgmt. Inst., Holliston, 1983—; bus. guest People's Republic China, Beijing, 1986, 87; mem. Korean trade mission Dept. State, Washington, 1987; del. U.S./People's Republic of China Joint Session on Industry, Trade and Econ. Devel., Beijing, 1988. Sgt. U.S. Army, 1967-70, Vietnam. Recipient Wall St. Jour. award Dow Jones Co., 1973. Mem. Am. Mgmt. Assn., Nat. Assn. Accts., Am. Prodn. and Inventory Control Soc., Assn. MBA Execs., Nat. Corp. Cash Mgmt. Assn., Am. C. of C. (Hongkong chpt.), Niagara Falls C. of C., Buffalo C. of C., Locust Hill Country Club, Beta Gamma Sigma. Republican. Methodist. Home: 4 Sutton Point Pittsford NY 14534 Office: LeRoy Industries Inc 7921 E Main Rd LeRoy NY 14482

TEETS, JOHN WILLIAM, diversifed company executive; b. Elgin, Ill., Sept. 15, 1933; s. John William and Maudie T.; m. Nancy Kerchenfaut, June 25, 1965; children: Jerri, Valerie Sue, Heide Jane, Suzanne. Student, U. Ill. Pres., ptnr. Winter Garden Restaurant, Inc., Carpenterville, Ill., 1957-63; v.p. Greyhound Food Mgmt. Co.; pres. Post Houses, Inc., and Horne's Enterprises, Chgo., 1964-68; pres., chief operating officer John R. Thompson Co., Chgo., 1968-71; pres., chief operating officer Restaurant div., also corp. v.p Canteen Corp., Chgo., 1971-74; exec. v.p., chief operating officer Bonanza Internat. Co., Dallas, 1974-76; chmn., chief exec. officer Greyhound Food Mgmt., Inc., Phoenix, 1976; group v.p. food service Greyhound Corp., Phoenix, 1976-81, group v.p. services group, 1980-81, vice chmn., 1980-82, chmn., chief exec. officer, 1981—, now also pres. and dir.; chmn., pres. Armour & Co., from 1981; chief exec. officer Dial Corp., Phoenix; chmn., chief exec. officer Greyhound Food Mgmt. Inc., Phoenix, 1982—; chmn. Greyhound Support Svcs. Inc., Phoenix; vice chmn. President's Conf. on Foodservice Industry; mem. adv. bd. Phoenix and Valley of Sun Conv. and Visitors Bur., 1979-82. Recipient Silver Plate award, Golden Plate award Internat. Foodservice Mfrs. Assn., 1980. Mem. Nat. Automatic Mdsg. Assn., Nat. Restaurant Assn., Nat. Inst. Foodservice Industry (trustee), Am. Mgmt. Assn., Christian Businessmen's Assn. (chmn. steering com. 1977), Nat. Speakers Assn. Club: Arizona. Office: The Greyhound Corp Greyhound Tower Sta 3103 Phoenix AZ 85077 *

TEICHER, ARTHUR MACE, personnel executive; b. N.Y.C., Dec. 17, 1946; s. Milton and Lilyan (Kaufman) T.; m. Marcia Fleschner, Nov. 23, 1974; 1 child, Craig Morgan. Student, U. Toledo, 1965-68, Long Island U., 1970-72. Mgmt. trainee Bank of N.Y., N.Y.C., 1970-72; agt. M & A Assocs., East Rutherford, N.J., 1972-73; sales rep. Fed. Express, N.Y.C., 1973-76; v.p., prin. Smith's 5th Ave., N.Y.C., 1976—. Asst. den leader, Boy Scouts Am., Westchester, N.Y., 1987—, chmn. pack com., 1987-88, Weblos den leader, 1988—; mem. Edgemont Commn. on Developing Capable Young People, Westchester, 1986—, Fort Hill Assn., Westchester, 1980—. Served in USNG, 1969. Mem. Am. Mktg. Assn. (membership chmn. 1982-84), Assn. Personnel Cons. N.Y., Nat. Assn. Personnel Cons. Clubs: U.S. Power Squadron (lt. 1985—), Castaways Yacht. Office: Smith's Fifth Ave Agy Inc 17 E 45th St New York NY 10017

TEICHER, MARCIA HARRIET, personnel consultant company executive; b. Bklyn., Mar. 31, 1947; d. Max and Bettina (Koerner) Fleschner; m. Arthur Mace Teicher, Nov. 23, 1974; 1 child, Craig Morgan. B.A., Queens Coll.-City U. N.Y., 1967. Sr. v.p., owner Smith's 5th Ave Agy., Inc., N.Y.C., 1965—; lectr. in field. Mem. Orgn. for Rehab. and Tng., Scarsdale, N.Y. Recipient Cert. Service award Lions Club, 1983. Mem. Advertising Women of N.Y., Assn. Personnel Cons. of N.Y. (cert., bd. dirs. 1979-80), N.Y. Chpt. of Am. Mktg. Assn. (bd. dirs. 1973—, Cert. award 1982, Cert. award 1984, publs. dir. 1984-85), Nat. Assn. Personnel Cons. Club: Castaways Yacht (New Rochelle). Avocations: boating; reading. Office: Smith's Fifth Ave Agy Inc 17 E 45th St New York NY 10017

TEICHGRAEBER, RICHARD KOENIG, oil company executive; b. Wichita, Kans., Nov. 9, 1928; s. William Emil and Mary Barbara (Heap) T.; m. Wanda Lee Leatherbury, 1949 (Div., 1949); 1 child, Ricella Kay Teichgraeber Rains; m. Helen Patricia Hughes, Mar. 26, 1950; children: Teresa Lynn Teichgraeber McClanahan, William Koenig, Arthur Cecil. Student, U. Okla., 1946-47. Owner Tye's Cafe, Severy, Madison and Hamilton, Kans., 1948-58, EDCO Drilling Co., Inc., Eldorado, Kans., 1956-74, Kans. Pump & Supply, Eldorado, 1968—, Internat. Petroleum Services, Inc., Eldorado, 1988—; bd. dirs., past pres., Internat. Trade Council, Manhattan, Kans., mem. adv. council, SBA, Wichita, 1988—. Bd. dirs. Kans. Tech. Enterprise Corp., Topeka, 1978-88; mem. Midian Shrine, Wichita, 1988—. Named Exporter of the Yr., Internat. Trade Inst., Kans. State U., 1977, Small Bus. Person of the Yr., Samll Bus. Adminstr., wichita, 1979; recipient Export Achievement award, World Trade Club, Wichita, 1978. Mem. Kans. C. of C., El Dorado C. of C., Eureka C. of C., Kans. Ind. Oil and Gas Assn., Assn. Oil Well Service Contractors, Internat. Assn. Drilling Contractors. Republican. Lutheran. Lodge: Elks. Home: Rural Rt 1 Eureka KS 67045 Office: Internat Petroleum Svcs Inc 635 Metcalf PO Box 471 El Dorado KS 67042

TELBERG, RURICK RICK, journalist; b. N.Y.C., Feb. 12, 1956; s. Val George and Lelia (Katine) T.; m. Doranne Phillips, Nov. 17, 1979; children: Devon Phillips, Katerina Elizabeth. AB in Journalism, NYU, 1978. Reporter Long Island Traveler-Watchman, Riverhead, N.Y., 1978-79; copy editor Beaumont (Tex.) Enterprise, 1979-81; fin. editor Nation's Restaurant News, N.Y.C., 1981-86, exec. editor, 1987—. Mem. Soc. Profl. Journalists, Deadline Club N.Y., N.Y. Fin Writers Assn. Home: 23 S Saxon Ave Bay Shore NY 11706

TELESCO, CHERYL SUE, small business owner; b. Stamford, Conn., Nov. 18, 1950; d. Irving Sidney and Arline Hannah (Shapiro) Libowitz; m. Daniel Angelo Telesco, Nov. 7, 1970 (div. 1978); children: Daniel, Christopher. Diploma, Claremont Sec. Sch., N.Y.C., 1969. Exec. sec. Clairol, Stamford, 1969-70; office mgr. Norwalk (Conn.) Jewish Community Ctr., 1980-85; prin. Telesco Sec. Svcs., Norwalk, 1985—. Treas. Women's Am. Orgn. for Rehab. through Tng., Norwalk, 1985, fundraising, 1986; treas. Cub Scouts, Norwalk, 1984; vol. Norwalk Jewish Community Ctr., 1985—, Alex Knopp for State Rep. Campaign; bd. dirs. Roton Sch. PTA, 1988—. Republican. Jewish. Home and Office: 1 Deerfield St Norwalk CT 06854

TELL, WILLIAM KIRN, JR., oil company executive, lawyer; b. Evanston, Ill., Feb. 27, 1934; s. William Kirn and Virginia (Snook) T.; m. Karen Nelson, July 16, 1960; children—Catherine, Caroline, William F. B.A. in Govt., Dartmouth Coll., 1956; J.D., U. Mich., 1959. Bar: N.Y. 1968. Atty. Texaco Inc., N.Y.C., 1968-70, asst. to v.p., gen. counsel, 1970, assoc. gen. counsel, 1970-73, asst. to chmn., 1973; v.p. Texaco Inc., Washington and N.Y.C., 1973-79, sr. v.p., 1979—; dir. Texaco Can. Mem. adv. bd. dirs. Met. Opera, N.Y.C., 1983—. Mem. Am. Petroleum Inst. (bd. dirs. 1980—). Clubs: Greenwich Country (Conn.); Congressional, Metropolitan (Washington). Home: 320 Old Church Rd Greenwich CT 06830 Office: Texaco Inc 200 Westchester Ave White Plains NY 10650

TELLE, CRAIG STEPHEN, educator; b. Clovis, N.Mex., Dec. 8, 1960; s. Byron J. Telle and Dorothy Lou (Shealley) Calley. BBA, Youngstown State U., 1982. CPA, Ohio. Internal auditor Ernst & Whinney, Cleve., 1983-84; staff acct. Unity Rubber Co., Newbury, Ohio, 1984-85; cons. O'Brien Office Products, Westerville, Ohio, 1985; unit controller Lancaster Colony Corp., Columbus, Ohio, 1985-86; controller Western Credit Union, Columbus, 1986-87; prof. acctg. Bradford Schs., Columbus, 1987—. Republican. Baptist. Home: 2069 Pinebrook Rd Columbus OH 43220 Office: Bradford Schs 6170 Busch Blvd Columbus OH 43228

TEMERLIN, J. LIENER, advertising agency executive; b. Ardmore, Okla., Mar. 27, 1928; s. Pincus and Julie (Kahn) T.; m. Karla Samuelsohn, July 23, 1950; children: Dana Temerlin Crawford, Lisa Temerlin Gottesman, Hayden Crawford, Sandy Gottesman. BFA, U. Okla., 1950. Editor Sponsor Mag., N.Y.C., 1950-51; copywriter Glenn Advt. Inc., Dallas, 1952-54, creative dir., 1954-70, chief operating officer, 1970-74; pres. Glenn, Bozell & Jacobs, Inc., Dallas, 1974-79; chmn. bd. dirs. Bozell & Jacobs Inc., 1979-85; chmn. bd. dirs. Bozell, Jacobs, Kenyon & Eckhardt, Irving, Tex., 1986-89, chmn., 1989—. Chmn bd. Dallas Symphony Assn., 1986-87, pres. bd. 1984-85; bd. dirs. So. Meth. U. Meadows Sch. for Arts, Dallas Citizens Council, 1984-86; trustee S.W. Med. Found., 1988-89, chair pub. affairs com.; mem. com. univ. devel. So. Meth. U., steering com. Susan G. Komen Found, 1989-91; mem. exec. com., bd. dirs. United Way Greater Dallas, Friends of John F. Kennedy Ctr. for Performing Arts, Blair House Restoration Com.; bd. dirs. Am. Film Inst., 1989, Bus. Commn. for the Arts, Dallas; chmn. grand opening fortnight Morton H. Meyerson Symphony Ctr, 1989. With U.S. Army, 1951-52, Korea. Decorated Bronze Star; recipient Brotherhood award NCCJ. Mem. Am. Assn. Advt. Agys. (chmn. S.W. council 1969-70, chmn. So. region), Dallas Advt. League (Bill D. Kerss award 1983).

TEMKIN, ROBERT HARVEY, accountant; b. Boston, Oct. 21, 1943; s. Max and Lillian (Giller) T.; m. Ellen Phyllis Band, Sept. 25, 1966; children—Aron, Rachel, Joshua. BBA, U. Mass., 1964. CPA, Mass., N.Y., Conn., Vt. With Arthur Young & Co., CPA's, 1964-72, 73—, ptnr., 1976—, nat. dir. auditing standards, 1980-88; controller SCA Services, Inc., Boston, 1972-73; mem. peer rev. com. SEC Practice Sect., Am. Inst. CPA's, 1982-84, auditing standards bd., 1984-88; adj. assoc. prof. NYU, 1982. Chmn. ad hoc com. low/moderate housing Town of Natick, Mass., 1972-73, mem. by-law revision com., 1972-73; mem. young leadership United Jewish Appeal, 1976-80; bd. dirs. Jewish Home for Elderly of Fairfield County, 1979—, pres., 1985-87; trustee Congregation Beth El, Norwalk, Conn., 1979—, pres., 1983-85, chmn. bd., 1986-87; mem. Bd. Edn., Weston, Conn., 1983-87; v.p. United Synagogue Am., chmn. audit com., mem. budget and fin. com.; mem. planning com. United Way Mass. Bay, bus adv. coun. U. Mass.; bd. dirs. Jr.

Achievement Stamford Area, 1978-80, spl. adv. nat. conf., 1967; trustee Am. Shakespeare Theatre/Conn. Ctr. for Performing Arts, 1981-84; v.p., mem. exec. com. United Synagogue Am., budget and fin. com., 1986—, chmn. audit com., 1987—, internat. v.p., 1988—, social and community services subcommittee Combined Jewish Philanthropies Greater Boston, 1988—; pres. Conn. Valley Region, United Synagogue Am., 1987-88; chmn. budget and fin. com. Synagogue Council Mass. Recipient Acctg. Alumni award U. Mass., 1978, Alumnus Award Sch. Mgmt. U. Mass., 1986. Mem. Am. Inst. C.P.A.s (staff dir. Commn. on Auditors Responsibilities 1976-78, mem. task force on auditor's report 1978-81, auditing standards bd. 1984-88), Mass. Soc. CPA's (Silver medal 1964), N.Y. State Soc. CPA's, Conn. Soc. CPA's., Greater Boston C. of C. (dir.). Club: Bay (Boston). Home: 1611 Commonwealth Ave West Newton MA 02165 Office: Arthur Young & Co One Boston Pl Boston MA 02109

TEMPEL, SHIRLEY KAREN, utility, industrial manufacturing company executive; b. Bloomington, Ill., Oct. 23, 1945; d. Ray V and Bertha M. (Schaefer) Johnson; m. Mahlon J. Tempel, June 8, 1963 (div. 1988); children: Kurt, Mark. BBA, St. Mary-of-the-Woods Coll., 1980. With mktg. adminstn. Gen. Electric Co., Ft. Wayne, Ind., 1973-83; distbn. sales mgr. McGraw-Edison div. Cooper Industries, Pitts., 1983-85; mgr. distbn., indsl. sales RTE Corp., Brookfield, Wis., 1985-86; mktg. mgr. RTE Corp., Pewaukee, Wis., 1986—. Recipient Women of Distinction award Waukesha YWCA, 1986, 87. Mem. Sales and Mktg. Execs. Milw., Pewaukee C. of C., Am. Legion Aux. Democrat. Home: 400-F Park Hill Dr Pewaukee WI 53072 Office: RTE Corp 1945 Hickory St Pewaukee WI 53072

TEMPLE, ARTHUR, investment company executive; b. Texarkana, Ark., Apr. 8, 1920; s. Arthur and Katherine (Sage) T.; m. Mary MacQuiston (div. 1963); children: Arthur III, Charlotte; m. Charlotte Dean, Sept. 4, 1963. Student U. Tex.-Austin, 1937-38; LLD (hon.), Pepperdine U., 1982. Bookkeeper, asst. mgr. retail yard Temple Lumber Yard, Lufkin, Tex., 1938-48; pres., chmn. bd. Temple Assocs., Inc., Diboll, Tex., 1941-70; exec. v.p. Temple Industries, Inc., Diboll, 1948-51, pres., chief exec. officer, 1951-75, chmn. bd., 1972-73; bd. dirs. Temple-Eastex Inc., 1973—, chmn. bd., 1975-83; chmn. planning and devel. com. Time Inc., 1973-81, group v.p., 1973-78, bd. dirs., exec. com., 1973—, vice chmn., 1978-83; chmn. bd. Exeter Investment Co., Lufkin, Tex., 1982-83; chmn. bd. Temple-Inland Inc., 1984—; bd. dirs., mem. exec. com. Republic Bank Corp., Dallas, 1976, Inland Container Corp., Ind., 1979; bd. dirs. Contractor's Supplies, Lufkin, Lufkin Block, E. Tex. Asphalt, Lufkin, Lumberman's Investment Corp., Austin, Sunbelt Ins. Co., Austin, Gt. Am. Res. Ins. Co., Dallas, Sabine Investment Co. of Tex., Inc., Diboll; chmn. bd. T&T Corp., Lufkin, Green Acres Convalescent Ctrs., Inc., Lufkin; adv. dir. Mason Best Co., Republic Bank of Lufkin, Pineland State Bank; ltd. ptnr. Dallas Cowboys Football Club, 1984—; pres., bd. dirs. Tex. Southeastern RR. Pres. Angelina County C. of C., 1950; active State Bd. Edn., 1949; bd. regents Lamar Tech. U., 1957; trustee Duke U., 1983, John E. Gray Inst., T.L.L. Temple Found.; bd. dirs. St. Michael Hosp. Found., Texarkana, 1984—, Nat. Park Found., 1984—. Recipient 1 of 5 Outstanding Young Men in Tex. award Tex. Jr. C. of C., 1948; Merit medal VFW, Forest Farmer Ann. award Forest Farmers Assn., 1965, Conservationist of Yr. award, 1977, East Texan of Yr. award Deep East Tex. Council Govts., 1983, Conservationist of Yr. award Safari Club Internat., 1983; named to Tex. Bus. Hall of Fame, 1983. Mem. Nat. Forest Products Assn. (past chmn., pres., bd. dirs.), Nat. Assn. Mfrs. (bd. dirs.), So. Forest Products Assn. (past chmn., pres.), Lumbermen's Assn. Tex. (past chmn., pres.), Am. Forest Products Assn. (trustee), Delta Kappa Epsilon. Club: Crown Colony Country (bd. dirs.). Office: Temple-Inland Inc PO Drawer N 303 S Temple Diboll TX 75941 *

TEMPLE, JOSEPH GEORGE, JR., chemical company executive; b. Bklyn., Aug. 29, 1929; s. Joseph George and Helen Frances (Beney) T.; m. Ann Elizabeth McFerran, June 21, 1952; children: Linda Jo, James, John. BSChemE, Purdue U., 1951, DEng (hon.), 1988. With Dow Chem. Co., Midland, Mich., 1951—, v.p. mktg., 1976-78, dir., 1979—; pres. Dow Chem. Latin Am., Coral Gables, Fla., 1978-80; group v.p. human health Dow Chem. Co., Cin., 1980-83; pres. Merrell Dow Pharmaceuticals Inc., Cin., 1983-87, chief exec. officer, chmn. bd. dirs., 1988—; bd. dirs. Chem. Bank and Trust Co.; trustee Com. for Economic Devel. Mem. pres.'s council Purdue U., 1978—; bd. fellows Saginaw Valley State U., 1987—. Recipient Disting. Engr. Alumni award Purdue U., 1978. Mem. Am. Inst. Chem. Engrs., Soc. Plastics Industry (bd. dirs.), Pharm. Mfrs. Assn. (bd. dirs.), Nat. Mgmt. Assn. (Silver Knight award 1976, Gold Knight award 1982). Episcopalian. Office: The Dow Chem Co 2030 Willard H Dow Ctr Midland MI 48674

TEMPLE, ROBERT WINFIELD, chemical company executive; b. New Albany, Ind., Feb. 25, 1934; s. Edgar Winfield and Kathryn (Rady) T.; m. Katrina Voorhis, Jan. 4, 1954 (div. Oct. 1970); children—James V., Robert K., Jennifer Anne; m. Katharine Ann Stobbs, Apr. 29, 1977 (div. June 1985); children—Andrew, Philip; m. Angela J., Aug. 5, 1986. B.S. in Chem. Engring., B.S. in Indsl. Mgmt., MIT, 1955; postgrad., Chem. Engring. Sch. MIT, 1955, Sch. Bus. Adminstrn. NYU, 1955-58, Mgmt. Devel. Program, Columbia U., 1966. Dist. sales mgr. ACF Industries, 1955-59; sr. staff cons. Arthur D. Little, Inc., 1959-64; dir. planning and devel. Am. Cryogenics, Inc., Atlanta, 1964-69; v.p. Williams Bros. Co., Atlanta, 1969-70; pres. Lang Engring., Coral Gables, Fla., 1970-74; pres. Western Process Co., Geneva and Houston, 1974—; head agribus., British-Am. Tobacco Co., London; dir. World Congress on Super Conductivity, Global Econ. Action Inst. Conf. on African Devel. Sunday sch. tchr.; chmn. MIT Enterprise Forum; bd. dirs. Dads Club Swim Team. Fellow Am. Inst. Chemists and Chem. Engrs.; mem. Am. Chem. Soc., Am. Mgmt. Assn., (seminar spkr.), Assn. Cons. Chemists and Chem. Engrs., Chem. Mktg. Research Assn., Internat. Food Technologists, MIT Alumni Assn. (past regional pres.), Cherokee Town and Country Club, Univ. Club. Presbyterian. Contbr. articles to profl. jours. Home: 14134 Bluebird Ln Houston TX 77079 Office: Western Process Co PO Box 19435 Houston TX 77224

TEMPLETON, JOHN MARKS, investment counsel, financial analyst; b. Winchester, Tenn., Nov. 29, 1912; s. Harvey Maxwell and Vella (Handly) T.; m. Judith Dudley Folk, Apr. 17, 1937 (dec. Feb. 1951); children: John Marks, Anne Dudley, Christopher Winston; m. Irene Reynolds Butler, Dec. 31, 1958. A.B., Yale U., 1934; M.A. (law) (Rhodes scholar), Balliol Coll., Oxford, Eng., 1936; LL.D. (hon.), Beaver Coll., 1968, Marquette U., 1980, Jamestown Coll., 1983, Maryville Coll., 1984; D.Litt. (hon.), Wilson Coll., 1974; D.D. (hon.), Buena Vista Coll., 1979; D.C.L. (hon.), U. of South, 1984. Chartered fin. analyst. Sec.-treas., v.p., dir. Nat. Geophys. Co., Dallas and N.Y.C., 1937-41; pres., dir. Templeton, Dobbrow & Vance, Inc., N.Y.C., 1941-65, Templeton Funds Inc., 1977—, Templeton Global Funds Inc., 1981—, Templeton Growth Fund Can., Ltd., Toronto, 1954-85, Templeton Emerging Markets Fund Inc., 1987—; chmn. Templeton Damroth Corp., 1959-62; v.p., dir. First Trust Bank Ltd., Bahamas, 1963—. Author: The Humble Approach, 1981; co-author: The Templeton Touch, 1985, The Templeton Plan, 1987; Contbr. to financial publs. Past pres. Lyford Cay (Bahamas) Property Owners Assn.; Chmn. YMCA Bergen County, 1952-54; dir., campaign chmn. Englewood Community Chest, 1953-54; trustee Englewood Hosp., 1953-56, Soc. for Promoting Christian Knowledge, 1984-87, Balliol Coll. Endowments (Oxford), Templeton Project Trust (Eng.), Am. European Community Assn.; chmn. bd. trustees Princeton Theol. Sem., 1967-73, 79-85; trustee Wilson Coll., 1941-73, Buena Vista Coll., 1981—, Templeton Found. Inc., 1952—, John Templeton Found. Inc., 1987—, council on theol. sems. United Presbyn. Ch. U.S.A., 1946-83; mem. Ctr. Theol. Inquiry, 1979—; mem. Commn. on Ecumenical Mission, 1961-70; bd. corporators Presbyn. Ministers Fund, Inc., 1960—; bd. visitors Harvard Div. Sch.; adv. bd. Harvard Ctr. for the study of World Religions; bd. mgrs. Am. Bible Soc.; mgmt. Council Templeton Coll. (Oxford); pres. Templeton Theol. Sem., Bahamas, 1984—; hon. rector Dubuque U. Recipient Churchman of the Yr. award Religious Heritage of Am., 1979, Ecumenical Patriarch's Hon. Order of Mt. Athos and Free Enterprise award Palm Beach Atlantic Coll., 1984, Internat. Churchman of the Yr., 1981. Mem. Soc. Security Analysts, World Bus. Council, Chief Execs. Orgn. (pres. 1968-69), Bahamas C. of C. (bd. dirs. 1976-79), Internat. Acad. Religious Scis., Mt. Pelerin Soc., Phi Beta Kappa., Zeta Psi. Clubs: Elihu, Elizabethan (New Haven); Yale, University (N.Y.C.); Rotary (Bahamas), Lyford Cay (dep. chmn. 1980-86) (Bahamas); Lansdowne, Royal Overseas League, Athenaeum (Eng.). Office: Box N7776, Nassau The Bahamas also: Templeton Growth Fund Inc, 14th St W PO Box 4070 Sta A, Toronto, ON Canada M5W 1M3

TEMPLETON, JOHN MARKS, JR., pediatric surgeon; b. N.Y.C. Feb. 19, 1940; s. John Marks and Judith Dudley (Folk) T.; BA, Yale Coll., 1962; MD, Harvard U., 1968; m. Josephine J. Gargiulo, Aug. 2, 1970; children—Heather Erin, Jennifer Ann. Intern, Med. Coll. Va., Richmond, 1968-69, resident, 1969; assoc. prof. pediatric surgery U. Pa. and Children's Hosp. of Pa., 1986—; assoc. prof., 1986—; chmn. bd. Templeton Growth Fund, Templeton World Fund, Templeton Income Funds, Templeton Global Funds, St. Petersburg, Fla., 1978—; bd. dirs. Templeton Emerging Market Fund, Templeton, Galbraith & Hansberger. Chmn. health and safety, exec. bd. Phila. coun. Boy Scouts Am.; Ea. Coll., Phila. Leadership Found., Nat. Recreation Found., Melmark Home; pres. Pa. div. Am. Trauma Soc. With M.C., USNR, 1975-77. Mem. ACS, Am. Pediatric Surg. Assn., AMA, Am. Assn. Pediatricians, Phila. Coll. Physicians. Republican. Evangelical. Club: Union League (Phila.), Merion Cricket (Haverford). Assoc. editor: Textbook of Pediatric Emergencies, 1988. Office: 4 King St West, Toronto, ON Canada M5W 1M3

TEN BROECK, DAVID LINCOLN, manufacturing executive; b. Hartford, Conn., Oct. 6, 1950; s. David Lincoln and Georgette Margret (Wellner) T.B.; m. Roberta Kaplohski, Oct. 5, 1975; children: David, Andrew, Julia Ann. BS, Nichols Coll., 1973. Lic. secondary tchr. Night mgr. restaurant div. Marriott Corp., Washington, 1973-76; supr. Beecham Products, Clifton, N.J., 1976-78, Standard Brands, Dayton, N.J., 1978-80, Nabisco Brands, Dayton, 1980-82; supr. prodn. Pfizer Inc., Leeming, Pacquin, and Parsippany, N.J., 1982—; supr. night ops. Pfizer Leeming/Paquin, Parsippany, N.J., 1986—. Comdr. USCG Aux., 1986. Mem. Am. Mgmt. Assn. Republican. Home: 8 Lenhome Dr Cranford NJ 07016 Office: Pfizer Inc Leeming Paquin 100 Jefferson Rd Parsippany NJ 07054

TENCH, THEODORE, investment management consultant; b. Clearwater, Fla., Jan. 12, 1952; s. William Ryan and Julia (Scaramanga) T.; m. Pamela Joy Rutenberg, Aug. 13, 1978; children: David Reuven, Jonathan William, Meir Avraham. AB in English Lit. summa cum laude, Bowdoin Coll., 1973. Registered investment adviser. Fgn. svc. officer Dept. State, Washington, 1978-80, Moscow, 1979; vice consul Dept. State, Jerusalem, 1976-78; account exec. Kidder Peabody & Co., Tampa, Fla., 1980-85; pres. Theodore Tench & Assocs., Clearwater, Fla., 1986—; bd. dirs. Rep. Bank, Clearwater. Patentee in field. Mem. Roebling Soc., Morton Plant Hosp., Clearwater, 1984—; treas. Jewish Fedn. Pinellas County, Clearwater, 1986-87; pres. Young Israel Clearwater, 1987—. Mem. Investment Mgrs. Cons. Assn. Republican. Office: Theodore Tench & Assocs 1250 Rogers St Ste D Clearwater FL 34616

TENENBAUM, BERNARD HIRSH, entrepreneur, educator; b. Long Beach, N.Y., Dec. 23, 1954; s. Abraham Benjamin and Helen Pearl (Wahrhaft) T. BA, Columbia Coll., 1976; postgrad., Stanford U., 1976-77; MBA, U. Pa., 1981. Mgr. Lido Beach (N.Y.) Hotel, 1976-77; gen. mgr. Sound Spectrum, Huntington, N.Y., 1977-78; dir. Small Bus. Ctr., Phila., 1980-84; asst. dir. Entre Ctr., Phila., 1984-85, assoc. dir., 1986-88; prof. entrepreneurial studies, dir. Fairleigh Dickinson U., Madison, N.J., 1988—; cons. Phila. Phillies, 1984-85; bd. dirs. Ogontz Ave Redevel. Corp., West Phila. Ptnrship. Del. Securities Exchange Commn. on Small Bus. Capital Formation, 1984-86; vice chmn. Small Bus. Devel. Ctr. adv. bd., Phila., 1983—; bd. dirs. Pvt. Industry Council, Phila., 1983—; chmn. Small Bus. Fair, Phila., 1983—. Mem. Phila. C. of C. (vice chmn. small bus. council, 1982-86, chmn. Small Bus. Council, 1986—), Venture Match of N.J., Inc., Venture Assn. N.J. (v.p.). Democrat. Jewish. Office: Rothman Inst Entrepreneurial Studies Fairleigh Dickinson U Madison NJ 07940

TENINGA, WALTER HENRY, retail executive; b. Chgo., Feb. 14, 1928; s. Cornelius and Emma (Huth) T.; m. Nancy Anne Neumann, Oct. 27, 1951; children: Laurie Wells Teninga Vyselaar, Robert Huth. BA, U. Mich., 1950; MBA, Mich. State U., 1971. Real estate broker Teninga & Co., Chgo., 1950-56; real estate rep. K Mart Corp., Detroit, 1956-61; mgr. Western region K Mart Corp., L.A., 1961-67; exec. v.p. K Mart Corp., Detroit, 1967-72, vice chmn., chief fin. and devel. officer, 1972-79; pres. Price Co. No. Calif., San Diego, 1982; pres., founder Warehouse Club, Chgo., 1982—; bd. dirs. Mich. Nat. Corp., Detroit, Orange Co., Inc., Lake Hamilton, Fla. Pres., bd. dirs. Boys and Girls Clubs Met. Detroit, 1974-80, bd. dirs., Chgo., 1980-87. With U.S. Army, 1946-47. Mem. Sigma Chi (Significant Sig award 1984). Republican. Episcopalian. Office: Warehouse Club Inc 7235 N Linder Skokie IL 60077

TEO, KIM-SEE, marketing professional; b. Batu Pahat, Johor, Malaysia, Sept. 3, 1948; s. Kah-Seng Teo and San-Eng Lim; m. Cheng- Kian, May 27, 1980. BS with honors, U. Malaysia, 1975; LLB, U. London, 1983; advanced diploma mktg., Inst. Mktg., Singapore, 1985. Process engr. Nat. Semiconductor, Singapore, 1975-78; sr. process engr. SGS-ATES Semiconductor, Singapore, 1978; prodn., quality engr. Hewlett-Packard, Singapore, 1978-81; regional sales mgr. Interconics Chgo., Singapore, 1981-84; area mgr. Bourns Asia Pacific, Singapore, 1984-87; v.p. Bourns Asia Pacific, Hong Kong, 1987—. Mem. IEEE, Inst. Mktg. Eng., Am. Mktg. Assn., Am. Soc. Internat. Law, Brit. Inst. Mgmt., Internat. Biog. Assn., Hong Kong Mgmt. Assn., Australian Mktg. Inst., Hong Kong Inst. Mktg., Mktg. Inst. Singapore. Home: 37 Barker Rd, 4-B The Peak, Hong Kong Hong Kong Office: Bourns Asia Pacific Inc, 18 Whitfield Rd 1401 Citicorp Bldg, Hong Kong Hong Kong

TERASKIEWICZ, EDWARD ARNOLD, international money broker; b. Bklyn., June 9, 1946; s. Edward A. and Anna A. (Romeo) T.; cert. Am. Inst. Banking, 1970; m. Geraldine Lucchesi, May 7, 1966; children—Marie Elena, Lisa. Money desk trader Citibank, N.Y.C., 1964-71; gen. partner Mabon Nugent & Co., N.Y.C., 1971-84; chmn. Fulton Prebon U.S.A., Inc., N.Y.C., 1984—; vice chmn. Internat. City Holdings PLC 34-40 Ludgate Hill, London, England, 1986—. Served with U.S. Army, 1965-68. Home: 114 Tillman St Staten Island NY 10314 Office: Fulton Prebon USA Inc 1 Exchange Plaza New York NY 10006

TERBELL, JOSEPH BODINE, retired steel company executive; b. Chgo., June 6, 1906; s. Joseph Bodine and Marie Gladys (Green) T.; m. Phoebe Logan, 1931 (div. 1935); m. Merna Pace, 1936 (div. 1952); m. Lilyann J. Place, Oct. 3, 1952 (div. 1969); children—Gladys, Susan, Joseph B. Jr., Lawrence R.; m. Mary Matthiessen, June 10, 1970. B.S., Yale U., 1928. Salesman, Am. Manganese Steel, 1928-40; v.p. Am. Brake Shoe Co., N.Y.C., 1940-58; pres. Joliette Steel Ltd., Montreal, Que., Can., 1946-58; dep. commr. N.Y. State Div. Housing and Urban Renewal, N.Y.C., 1959-64; chief castings br. Dept. Commerce, Washington, 1958-59. Charter mem. Republican. Presdl. Task Force, Washington, 1981—, mem. Rep. Nat. Com., 1983—; mem. U.S. Def. Com., Fairfax, Va., 1983—; sponsor GOPAC, Washington, 1974—. Mem. Delta Psi. Episcopalian. Club: Yale. Home: 500 Mine Hill Rd Fairfield CT 06430

TERBELL, THOMAS GREEN, JR., bank officer; b. N.Y.C., Oct. 22, 1938; s. Thomas Green Terbell and Louise (Boone) Peterson; m. Melinda Farris, June 17, 1960 (div. June 9, 1972); children: Elizabeth Louise, Alison Virginia, Jennifer Ellen; m. Yolanda Irene Mezey, June 10, 1972; children: Heather Irene, Thomas Green III. BA in Econs., Stanford U., 1960; MBA in Fin., Harvard U., 1962. Dir. mktg., co-owner Albin Enterprises, Inc. div. Jack Built Toys, Burbank, Calif., 1962-64; mgmt. trainee to asst. v.p. Security Pacific Bank, Los Angeles, 1964-69; acting dir. and then dir. Pasadena (Calif.) Art Mus., 1969-71; prin. Terbell Assocs., Pasadena, 1971-72; asst. v.p., then v.p. and gen. mgr. Security Pacific Nat. Bank, Los Angeles, Hong Kong, Tokyo, London, Chgo., San Francisco and Los An, geles, 1972—; mem. exec. com. Bank of Canton, Hong Kong, 1975-76; mem. No. Calif. exec. com. Security Pacific Nat. Bank, San Francisco, 1984-86. Trustee Pasadena Art Mus., 1968-71, Am. Sch. in Japan, 1976-80; treas. San Mateo County Jr. Hockey Club, 1986-87; alternate mem. Rep. State Cen. Com., 1966-68. Republican. Episcopalian. Clubs: American (Hong Kong), Valley Hunt (Pasadena). Office: Security Pacific Bank H12-60 333 S Hope St Los Angeles CA 90071

TERBRUEGGEN, THOMAS JOHN, oil company executive; b. Detroit, Aug. 5, 1948; s. Maurice F. and Catherine (Byrne) T.; m. Patricia M. Perkins, Apr. 29, 1978; children: Sarah A., Emily B., Paul C. BA, St. Edward's U., 1970. Sales rep. Met. Life Ins., Austin, Tex., 1970-71, Prudential Life Ins. Co. Am., Austin, 1971-73; account rep. Marsh & McLennan, New Orleans, 1974-76; offshore ins. mgr. Charter Co., Jacksonville, Fla., 1977-78, computer mgr., 1978-79, risk mgr., 1980-83, dir. risk mgmt., 1984—; bd. dirs., underwriter Corp. Ins. and Reins. Ltd., Hamilton, Bermuda, 1977-83, Cayman Overseas Reins. Assn. Ltd., Georgetown, Cayman Islands, 1980—. Mem. Reins. Mgmt. Soc. Episcopalian. Office: Charter Oil Co One Charter Pla Jacksonville FL 32202

TERRACCIANO, ANTHONY PATRICK, banker; b. Bayonne, N.J., Oct. 27, 1938; s. Patrick and Grace Terracciano; B.S. in Econs., St. Peter's Coll., Jersey City, 1960; M.A. in Philosophy, Fordham U., 1962; m. Rita Cuddy, Apr. 20, 1963; children—Laura, Karen, Kenneth. With Chase Manhattan Bank, N.Y.C., 1964-87, chief operating officer, exec. v.p. internat., 1974-76, 84-85, exec. v.p., treas., 1976-80, exec. v.p. ops., trust and systems dept., 1980-83, exec. v.p., chief fin. officer, 1983-84, vice chmn. global banking, 1985-87; pres. Mellon Bank Corp., Pitts., 1987—. Bd. dirs., treas. N.Y. Philharmonic; adv. council Grad. Bus. Sch. U. Chgo.; bd. dirs. Covenant House; nat. trustee Boys Clubs Am. Served to 1st lt. U.S. Army, 1962-64. Mem. Assn. Res. City Bankers, Council on Fgn. Relations, Nat. Italian Am. Found. Club: Columbus (N.Y.C.). Avocations: jazz, piano. Office: Mellon Bank Corp 1 Mellon Bank Ctr Rm 5200 500 Grant St Pittsburgh PA 15258-0001 *

TERRAGNO, PAUL JAMES, information industry executive; b. Ogden, Utah, May 17, 1938; s. Charles L. and Florence E. (Gabardi) T.; m. Nancy Robinson, Aug. 26, 1961; children—Thomas C., Paul A., Teresa A. B.A., U. Utah, 1960; M.S., U. Wyo., 1962. Vice pres. Westat, Inc., Rockville, Md., 1962-70; vice pres. Remac Information, Gaithersburg, Md., 1970-76; dir. U.S. Patent Office, Washington, 1976-80; v.p. Pergamon Internat., McLean, Va., 1980-84; pres. Pergamon InfoLine, McLean, Va., 1984-87, Pergamon ORBIT InfoLine, McLean, 1987—, Maxwell Online, Inc., 1989—; dir. Information on Demand, Berkeley, Calif., 1984—, Pergamon Orbit InfoLine, Ltd., London, 1984—, Pergabase, Inc., Gainesville, Fla., 1985—. Contbr. articles to various publs. Mem. Am. Soc. Info. Sci. Roman Catholic. Home: 10607 Vantage Ct Potomac MD 20854 Office: Pergamon ORBIT InfoLine Inc 8000 Westpark Dr McLean VA 22102

TERRELL, JANICE S., mortgage company executive; b. St. Louis, Mo., Oct. 13, 1948; d. William and Addie Marjorie Terrell. BS in Psychology, UCLA, 1980; A. in Fin. Mgmt., Chgo. Inst. Fin., 1985. Ops. supr. First Pacific Bank, Beverly Hills, Calif., 1979-83; br. supr. Mo. Savs., St. Louis, 1983-85; mortgage loan officer Germania Fin. Corp., St. Charles, Mo., 1985—; mortgage systems analyst Citicorp Mortgage, Inc., St. Louis, 1987. Mem. Bd. Realtors, St. Charles C. of C., St. Charles Home Builders Assn., Women's Council, Hist. Soc., St. Louis Charity Horse Show Assn., Horse Protection Assn. Republican. Methodist. Office: Germania Mortgage Corp 1523 Old Hwy 94 South Saint Charles MO 63303

TERRELL, MILES JEROME, small business owner; b. Hamilton, Ala., Nov. 10, 1955; s. Willie Gene and Lee Vera (Colburn) T.; m. Deborah Ann Brown, Apr. 6, 1985; 1 child, Whitney Je'nai. BSBA, Ala. A&M U., 1973-77. Credit analyst Dun & Bradstreet, Detroit, 1977-78; sales rep. Philip Morris USA, Detroit, 1978-83; asst. div. mgr. Philip Morris USA, Indpls., 1983-85, area mgr., 1985-86; div. mgr. Philip Morris USA, Schaumburg, Ill., 1986-88; owner, mgr. The Mktg. Edge, Hoffman Estates, Ill., 1988—. Mem. Kappa Alpha Psi. Democrat. Methodist. Home: 930 W Firestone Dr Hoffman Estates IL 60195

TERRY, CONRAD MARTIN, management reporting analyst; b. Washington, Aug. 11, 1947; s. Conrad Martin Sr. and Lois Viola (Nebblett) T.; m. Georgia Hamilton, Sept. 13, 1968; 1 child, Christopher Michael. BBA, U. D.C., 1978; M of Internat. Mgmt., Am. Grad. Sch. Internat. Mgmt., 1981; MBA, DePaul U., 1987. Loan officer The Export-Import Bank of U.S., Washington, 1978-80; account officer Continental Ill. Nat. Bank, Chgo., 1981-84; mgmt. info. analyst Sanwa Bus. Credit Corp., Chgo., 1985-88; adj. faculty Triton Comm. Coll., River Grove, Ill., 1983—; part-time prof. Roosevelt U., Chgo., 1983—. Advisor Jr. Achievement, Chgo., 1983; co-chmn. March of Dimes, 1988, Chgo. Region Youth Edn., com. workshop leader, Jobs for Youth/Chgo., 1987; treas., bd. dirs. Jazz Inst. Chgo. Served with USAF, 1965-73. Mem. VFW, Kappa Alpha Psi. Democrat. Baptist. Home and Office: 828 N Humphrey Oak Park IL 60302 Office: Sanwa Bus Credit Corp 1 S Wacker Dr Suite 3900 Chicago IL 60606

TERRY, EDMUND, entrepreneur; b. N.Y.C., July 1, 1942; s. Alfred and Mary (Juskiewicz) T.; m. Barbara Louise McGinnis, Aug. 15, 1964; children: Susan, Karen. BA in Econs. cum laude, Rutgers U., 1964; MBA, Harvard U., 1966; JD, Nova U., 1985. Bar: Fla. 1985. Owner, pres. Jaffe Stationers Inc., Miami, 1967-80, So. Wholesale Office Supplies Inc., Miami, 1970-80, Comml. Shopping Ctrs., various cities, U.S., 1980—; pres. Worldwide Properties, Boca Raton, Fla., 1980—; chmn. bd. dirs. 1st Nat. Bank Ind., Indpls., 1986—. Mem. ARC, 1966—, United Way, 1966—, Palm Beach Opera, 1966—. Mem. Royal Palm Improvement Assn. (bd. dirs. 1984), Soc. Advancement Mgmt., Acad. Fla. Trial Lawyers, Assn. Trial Lawyers Am., Fla. Bar Assn., Royal Palm Yacht Club (com. chmn.), Clumbia Club, Boca Raton Hotel and Club, Phi Beta Kappa, Tau Kappa Alpha, Alpha Chi Rho. Home: 429 Alexander Palm Rd Boca Raton FL 33432 Office: Worldwide Properties 429 Alexander Palm Rd Boca Raton FL 33432

TERRY, JOHN HART, lawyer, former utility company executive, former congressman; b. Syracuse, N.Y., Nov. 14, 1924; s. Frank and Saydee (Hart) T.; m. Catherine Jean Taylor Phelan, Apr. 15, 1950; children: Catherine Jean (Mrs. Richard Thompson), Lynn Marie (Mrs. Robert Tacher), Susan Louise (Mrs. Stanley Germain), Mary Carole (Mrs. Stephen Brady). B.A., U. Notre Dame, 1945; J.D., Syracuse U., 1948. Bar: N.Y. bar 1950, D.C. bar 1972. Asst. to partner Smith & Sovik, 1948-59; asst. sec. to Gov. State of N.Y., 1959-61; sr. partner firm Smith, Sovik, Terry, Kendrick, McAuliffe & Schwarzer, 1961-73; sr. v.p., gen. counsel, sec. Niagara Mohawk Power Corp., Syracuse, 1973-87; counsel Hiscock & Barclay, Syracuse, 1987—; mem. N.Y. State Assembly, 1962-70, 92d Congress from 34th N.Y. Dist., 1971-73; presdl. elector, 1972. State chmn. United Services Orgn., 1964-73; past pres. John Timothy Smith Found.; Founder, dir. Bishop Foery Found., Inc.; dir. St. Joseph's Hosp. Council; past pres. Lourdes Camp; bd. dirs. N.Y. State Traffic Council; nat. bd. dirs. Am. Cancer Soc.; trustee Maria Regina Coll.; mem. adv. council Syracuse U. Sch. Mgmt.; past pres. Cath. Youth Orgn.; bd. dirs. Syracuse Community Baseball Club. Served to 1st lt. AUS, 1943-46. Decorated Purple Heart, Bronze Star; named Young Man of Year Syracuse Jr. C. of C., 1958, Young Man of Yr. N.Y. State Jr. C. of C., 1959, Young Man of Yr. U. Notre Dame Club Cen. N.Y., 1959. Mem. ABA (utility law sect.), N.Y. State Bar Assn. (chmn. com. on public utility law), Onondaga County Bar Assn. (chmn. membership and legis. coms.), D.C. Bar Assn., County Officers Assn., Citizens Found., U. Notre Dame, Syracuse U. law assns., Am. Legion, VFW, DAV, 40 and 8, Mil. Order of Purple Heart. Roman Catholic. Clubs: Century, Bellevue Country, Capitol Hill (Washington), Vero Beach Country. Home: 25 Erregger Terr Syracuse NY 13224 Office: Hiscock & Barclay 500 Financial Plaza PO Box 4878 Syracuse NY 13221-4878

TERRY, RICHARD EDWARD, public utility holding company executive; b. Green Bay, Wis., July 7, 1937; s. Joseph Edward and Arleen (Agamet) T.; m. Catherine Lombardo, Nov. 19, 1966; children—Angela, Edward. BA, St. Norbert's Coll., West DePere, Wis., 1959; LLB, U. Wis., 1964; AMP, Harvard U., 1986. Bar: Ill. Assoc. Ross & Hardies, Chgo., 1964-72; atty. Peoples Energy Corp., Chgo., 1972-79, asst. gen. counsel, 1979-81, v.p., gen. counsel, 1981-84, exec. v.p., 1984-87, pres., chief operating officer, 1987—; v.p., gen. counsel subs. Peoples Gas, Light and Coke Co., Chgo., 1981-84, exec. v.p., 1984-87, pres., 1987—; bd. dirs. Peoples Energy Corp., Peoples Gas Light. Bd. dirs. Chgo. Assn. Commerce & Industry, 1988—, Boy Scouts Am., 1988—, Inst. Gas Tech., 1987—, Ill. Council on Econ. Edn., 1987—. Served to 1st lt. U.S. Army. 1959-61. Mem. ABA, Chgo. Bar Assn., Am. Gas Assn., Midwest Gas Assn., Univ. Club, Mid-Am. Club, Econ. Club, Comml. Club Chgo. Roman Catholic. Clubs: University, Mid-America, Economic (Chgo.). Office: Peoples Energy Corp 122 S Michigan Ave Chicago IL 60603

TERRY, WILLIAM MACK, investment banker; b. Oklahoma City, Sept. 2, 1943; s. O.A. and Helen (McConkey) T.; children: Paul Bryan, Rachel Lynn. BS, MIT, 1968, MS, 1968. Dir. mgmt. scis. Bank of Am., San Francisco,

1973-77, sr. v.p., dep. cashier, 1977-82, sr. v.p. product devel., 1982-84, dir. asset sales, 1984-86; chmn. Tavistock Capital Corp., San Francisco, 1986—. Pres. Dimensional Corp. Fin., 1988. Republican. Clubs: San Francisco Tennis, Bankers (San Francisco). Avocations: skiing, flying. Office: Tavistock Capital Corp 300 Montgomery Suite 1100 San Francisco CA 94104

TERZIAN, KARNIG YERVANT, civil engineer; b. Khartoum, Sudan, July 4, 1928; came to U.S.; s. Yeznig and Marie T.; m. Helen S., Dec. 21, 1958. B.A., B.S. in C.E., Am. U. Beirut, 1949; M.S. in C.E., U. Pa., 1954. Assoc., L. T. Beck & Assocs., 1956-60; prin. Urban Engineers, Inc., Phila., 1960—, now sr. v.p., sec.-treas., cons. major transp. projects in Pa., N.Y., N.J., Nigeria, Zaire. Bd. dirs. Armenian Sisters Acad., 1970-74. Mem. ASCE, ASTM, Prestressed Concrete Inst. Armenian Apostolic. Office: 300 N 3d St Philadelphia PA 19106

TESAR, GEORGE J(AROSLAV), marketing educator; b. Kladno, Czechoslovakia; s. Adolph Wenceslav and Bozena (Sip) T.; m. Catherine Tatiana Krno, June 20, 1964. BSME, Chgo. Tech. Coll., 1964; MBA, Mich. State U., 1967; PhD, U. Wis., 1975. Project engr. Uniroyal, Inc., Mishawaka, Ind., 1964-67; lectr. mktg. U. Wis., Madison, 1968-70; asst. prof. mktg. U. Wis., Whitewater, 1970-76, assoc. prof., 1978-81, prof., 1981—; asst. prof. Georgetown U., Washington, 1976-78; vis. prof. mktg. Helsinki (Finland) Sch. Econs., 1986—; Fulbright lectr. Council Internat. Exchange Scholars, Washington, 1979-80; dir. Persoft, Inc., Madison; cons. Wis. Dept. Devel., Madison, 1980-86, U.S. Dept. Energy, Washington, 1976-85, Ford Motor Co., Dearborn, Mich., 1980-83. Editor: Export Policy, 1982, Export Mgmt., 1982; co-author: the Electric Car, 1974; contbr. articles to profl. jours. Mem. gov.'s adv. com. Internat. Trade, 1983—. IREX rsch. grantee, 1980. Mem. Am. Mktg. Assn., Am. Econ. Assn., Acad. Internat. Bus., Product Devel. and Mgmt. Assn. (dir. 1988—), Beta Gamma Sigma. Democrat. Roman Catholic. Home: 4413 Woods End Madison WI 53711 Office: U Wis 800 W Main St Whitewater WI 53190

TESCHENDORF, LYNN, lawyer; b. Rhinelander, Wis., Aug. 24, 1951; d. Arno Erwin and Nancy Louise (Haddock) T. BA, U. Wix., 1973; JD, U. N.Mex., 1976. Bar: N.Mex. 1976, Colo. 1980, Calif. 1988. Gen. counsel N.Mex. Oil Commn., Santa Fe, 1976-79; compliance lawyer Consol. Oil & Gas Co., Denver, 1979-81; assoc. Fishman, Gersh & Bursieck, Denver, 1981-84; v.p., gen. counsel Angeles Corp., Denver, 1984-86; 1st v.p., corp. sec. Angeles Corp., Los Angeles, 1986-88; sr. v.p., gen. counsel, corp. sec. Morgan, Olmstead, Kennedy & Garder Inc., Los Angeles, 1988—. Mem. Los Angeles County Bar Assn., Am. Soc. Corp. Secs., Am. Corp. Counsel Assn., Phi Beta Kappa. Republican. Office: Morgan Olmstead Kennedy & Gardner 1000 Wilshire Blvd Los Angeles CA 90017

TESLER, LAWRENCE GORDON, computer company executive; b. N.Y.C., Apr. 24, 1945; s. Isidore and Muriel (Krechmer) T.; m. Shelagh Elisabeth Leuterio, Oct 4, 1964 (div. 1970); 1 child, Lisa Traci; m. Colleen Ann Barton, Feb. 17, 1987. BS in Math., Stanford U., 1965. Pres. Info. Processing Corp., Palo Alto, Calif., 1963-68; rsch. asst. Stanford U. Artificial Intelligence Lab., 1968-73; mem. rsch. staff Xerox Corp., Palo Alto, 1973-80; sect. mgr. Lisa div. Apple Computer, Inc., Cupertino, Calif., 1980-82, cons. engr., 1983-86, v.p. adv. tech., 1986—. Contbr. articles to profl. jours., various computer software. Bd. dirs. Peninsula Sch., Menlo Park, Calif., 1974-78. Mem. Assn. Computing Machinery (conf. co-chmn. 1987-88). Office: Apple Computer Inc 20525 Mariani Av Cupertino CA 95014

TESLER, MAX AARON, gastroenterologist, pharmaceutical company executive; b. N.Y.C., Jan. 29, 1931; s. James and Bertha (Snyder) T.; B.A., N. Y. U., 1951, M.D., 1955; m. Nancy Linda Blumenthal, Nov. 11, 1956; children—Kenneth, Robert, Douglas. Intern, Bellevue Hosp., N.Y.C., 1955-56, asst. resident, 1956-57, research fellow Cornell div., 1961-62; chief resident N.Y.U. Hosp., 1959-60; research Fellow Yale Med. Center, New Haven, 1960-61; practice medicine specializing in gastroenterology, N.Y.C., 1962—; chmn. bd. Biometric Testing Inc., 1970-79; pres., chmn. bd., chief exec. officer Pharma Control Corp., 1979—; bd. dirs. Synopse Telecommunications, Inc., Internat. Therapeutics Corp. Served to maj. USAF, 1957-59. Diplomate Am. Bd. Internal Medicine. Fellow Am. Coll. Gastroenterology; mem. Am. Gastroent. Assn., Am. Soc. Gastroenterol. Endoscopy, N.Y. Soc. Gastroenterology, N.Y. Soc. Gastroenterol. Endoscopy. Office: PharmaControl Corp 661 Palisade Englewood Cliffs NJ 07632

TESTA, DOUGLAS, biotechnology company executive; b. Concord, Mass., May 22, 1944; s. Morris and Alice (Crawford) T.; m. Rosemary Adorno, Aug. 20, 1966; children: Jonathan Douglas, Jaymes Andrew. AA, Queensborough Community Coll., 1965; BS, CCNY, 1967, MS in Edn., 1971, PhD, 1976. Cert. tchr. N.Y. Chmn. dept. biology N.Y.C. Pub. Schs., 1967-70; lect. Hunter Coll. CCNY, 1970-76; project leader Ortho Diagnostics, Inc., Raritan, N.J., 1979-80; asst. dir. biologics Hydron Labs., Inc., New Brunswick, N.J., 1980-84; exec. dir. research and devel. Interferon Scis., Inc., New Brunswick, N.J., 1981-84, v.p. research, 1984-87, v.p. research and devel., 1987—; adj. asst. prof. Hunter Coll. of CCNY, 1978-81; adj. assoc. prof. Rutgers U., New Brunswick, 1985—; advisor to molecular biology honors program L.I. U., Bklyn., Middlesex Community Coll., N.J., 1984-87. Contbr. articles to profl. jours.; patentee in field. V.p. Glen Eagles Homeowners Assn., Branchburg, M.J., 1984. Mem. Am. Soc. Biol. Chem., Am. Soc. Microbiology, Internat. Soc. for Hematology, Internat. Soc. for Interferon Research, N.Y. Acad. Scis., Sigma Xi, Phi Sigma. Office: Interferon Scis Inc 783 Jersey Ave New Brunswick NJ 08901

TESTA, STEPHEN MICHAEL, geologist, consultant; b. Fitchburg, Mass., July 17, 1951; s. Guiseppe Alfredo and Angelina Mary (Petitto) T.; m. Lydia Mae Payne, July 26, 1986; 1 child, Brant Ethan Gage. AA, Los Angeles Valley Jr. Coll., Van Nuys, 1971; BS in Geology, Calif. State U., Northridge, 1976, MS in Geology, 1978. Registered geologist, Calif., Oreg.; cert. profl. geol. scientist., Idaho, Alaska. Engring. geologist R.T. Frankian & Assocs., Burbank, Calif., 1976-78, Bechtel, Norwalk, Calif., 1978-80, Converse Cons., Seattle, 1980-82; sr. hydrogeologist Ecology Environment, Seattle, 1982-83; sr. geologist Dames & Moore, Seattle, 1983-86; v.p. west coast ops. Engring. Enterprises, Long Beach, Calif., 1986—. Editor: Geologic Field Guide to the Salton Basin, 1988, Environmental Concerns in the Petroleum Industry, 1989; contbr. numerous articles to profl. jours. Mem. Am. Inst. Profl. Geologists (profl. devel. com. 1986, continuing edn. com., program chmn., 1988—, Presidential Cert. of Merit, 1987), Geol. Soc. Am., Am. Assn. Petroleum Geologists, AAAS, Assn. Ground Water Scientists and Engrs., Assn. Engring. Geologists, Mineral. Soc. Can., Hazardous Materials Research Inst., Calif. Water Pollution Control Assn., Sigma Xi. Home: 29351 Kensington Dr Laguna Niguel CA 92677 Office: Engring Enterprises 21818 S Wilmington Ave Suite406 Long Beach CA 90816

TEW, E. JAMES, JR., electronics company executive; b. Dallas, July 7, 1933; s. Elmer James and Bessie Fay (Bennett) T; student Arlington State Jr. Coll., 1955-57; B.B.A. in Indsl. Mgmt., So. Meth. U., 1969; M.S. in Quality Systems, U. Dallas, 1972, M.B.A. in Mgmt., 1975, EdD in Adult Edn., Nova U., 1986, postdoctoral, 1986; Registered profl. engr., Calif. m. Barbara Dean Evans, Dec. 12, 1952; children—Teresa Annette, Linda Diane, Brian James. Mgr. quality assurance ops. and corp. reference standards lab. Tex. Instruments Inc., Dallas, 1957—, chmn. corp. metric implementation com., mem. credit com. Texins Credit Union; adj. faculty Richland Coll., Mountain View Coll. Precinct chmn., election judge, 1961-64, del. several county and state convs.; bus. computer info. systems adv. bd. U. North Tex., bd. dirs. ctr. for quality and productivity; bd. examiners Malcolm Baldrige Nat. Quality award, U.S. Dept. Commerce, Nat. Inst. Standard and Tech., 1988, 89. With U.S. Army, 1953-55. Decorated Army Commendation medal with oak leaf cluster. Fellow Am. Soc. Quality Control (cert. as quality and reliability engr., chmn. Dallas-Ft. Worth sect. 1974-75), U.S. Metric Assn. (cert., chmn. cert. bd. 1986-87); mem. Res. Officers Assn., Dallas C. of C. (chmn. world mfg. com. 1974-77, chmn. spl. task force career edn. adv. bd. 1973-74), Mensa, Sigma Iota Epsilon, Phi Delta Kappa. Baptist. Clubs: Texins Rod and Gun (pres. 1969-70), Texins Flying, Masons (32 deg.). Contbr. articles to profl. jours. Home: 10235 Mapleridge Dallas TX 75238-2256 Office: PO Box 655621 MS 3938 Dallas TX 75265

THACKER, SCOTT ARTHUR, financial manager; b. Cleve., Apr. 14, 1955; s. Claude Edward and Doris Ann (Mack) T. BS, Wake Forest U., 1977; MBA, U. Pa., 1986. CPA, Ohio. Acct. Arthur Andersen & Co., Cin., 1977-82; chief fin. officer Image Matrix Inc., Cin., 1982-84; assoc. corp. fin. AMR/Am. Airlines, Ft. Worth, 1986-87, assoc. mergers & acquisition, 1987-88, prin. real estate fin., 1988—. Mem. Am. Inst. CPA's, Theta Chi. Episcopalian. Office: Am Airlines Inc 4200 American Blvd 3H57 Fort Worth TX 76155

THAKOR, HAREN BHASKERRAO, manufacturing company executive; b. Ahmedabad, Gujarat, India, Dec. 12, 1938; came to U.S., 1960; s. Bhaskerrao Balvantrai and Kumud T.; m. Barbara Ann Martin, July 26, 1969; children: Manisha Ann, Sunil Haren. B.Civil Engring., Gujarat U., 1960; M.S. in Structural Engring., U. Ill., 1961; M.B.A., U. Calif.-Berkeley, 1965. Acct. Friden, Inc., San Leandroco, Calif., 1965-67; sr. acct. bus. product group Xerox, Rochester, N.Y., 1967-69; mgr. budget and planning Xerox, Chgo., 1969-70; sr. policy analyst Xerox, Stamford, Conn., 1970-72, mgr. intercompany pricing, 1972-74; dir. bus. planning, automotive div. Arvin Industries, Inc., Columbus, Ind., 1974-77, v.p. fin. automotive div., 1977-81, treas., 1981-82, v.p. fin., chief fin. officer, 1982—, also dir. Mem. Am. Inst. C.P.A.s, Ind. Assn. C.P.A.s. Hindu. Club: Harrison Lake Country. Home: 4351 Kennedy Ct Columbus IN 47203 Office: Arvin Industries Inc 1531 13th St Columbus IN 47201

THALER, RICHARD WINSTON, JR., investment banker; b. Boston, Apr. 9, 1951; s. Richard Winston and Victoria Louise (Sears) T.; m. Mary Alice Gast, June 28, 1980; children: Julia Davis, Sarah Sears. BA in Am. Polit. History cum laude, Princeton U., 1973; MBA, Harvard U., 1978. Salesman Media Networks, N.Y.C., 1973-74; banker Bank of Boston, Rio De Janeiro, Brazil, 1975-77; investment banker Shearson, Lehman, Hutton, N.Y.C., 1980—. Spl. Gifts Solicitor Princeton U. Annual Giving, N.Y.C., 1987-88, class agt. 1988—; trustee Daily Princetonian, 1989—. Recipient Menachen Begin award Young Princeton Male Alumni, N.Y.C., 1980. Mem. Princeton Alumni Schs. Com., Mass. Soc. Mayflower Descendants, Princeton Club, Siwanoy Country Club, University Cottage Club, Chequessett Country Club, Wellfleet Yacht Club. Democrat. Episcopalian. Home: 44 Edgewood Ln Bronxville NY 10708 Office: Shearson Lehman Hutton Am Express Tower World Fin Ctr New York NY 10285

THAMPI, MOHAN VARGHESE, environmental health and civil engineer; b. Kuching, Sarawak, Malaysia, Mar. 25, 1960; s. Padmanabha Ramachandran and Sosamma (Varghese) T. Gen. Cert. Edn., Cambridge U., 1976; B in Tech. with honors, Indian Inst. Tech., Kharagpur, India, 1983; MS in Engring., U. Tex., 1985. Assoc. engr. Brown & Caldwell, Dallas, 1985-87, 1987-88; design engr. Stottler Stagg & Assocs., Cape Canaveral, Fla., 1988—. Author: Ultraviolet Disinfection Studies in a Teflon-Tube Reactor, 1985; contbr. articles to profl. jours. Mem. NSPE, ASCE (assoc.), Internat. Assn. Water Pollution Research and Control, Am. Mensa, Am. Water Works Assn., Water Pollution Control Fedn., Am. Mgmt. Assn., U. Tex. Ex-Students Assn. Mar Thoma Syrian Christian. Office: Stottler Stagg & Assocs 8660 Astronaut Blvd Cape Canaveral FL 32920

THARP, CHARLES CHRISTOPHER, investment executive; b. Fairlawn, Ohio, July 18, 1950; s. Thomas Alva Tharp and Marmian Williams. BA with honors, Yale Coll., 1972; MA, Oxford U., 1975. Investment counselor Gen. Investment Funds (subs. Gen. Tire & Rubber Co., Washington, 1976-82; v.p. Gen. Investment Funds (subs. GenCorp., Inc.), Washington, 1982-83, 85—; dep. exec. dir. Pension Benefit Guaranty Corp., Washington, 1983-84, exec. dir., 1984-85; investment cons. Washington, 1985—; cons. investment com. Pension Benefit Guaranty Corp., Washington, 1985-86; mem. pension com. Am. Bur. Shipping, N.Y., 1983-84, 86—; chmn. fed. corp. com. Adminstrv. Conf. U.S., 1984-85; treas. Oberlin (Ohio) Coll., 1989—; bd. dirs. Sch., Coll. and Univ. Underwriters, Ltd., Hamilton, Bermuda, 1989—. Contbr. articles on pensions and investments to profl. jours. Mem. challenge grant com. NEH, Washington, 1982-84, Am. Council Young Polit. Leaders. Mem. Md. Hist. Soc. (library com. 1981—), Am. Council Young Polit. Leaders, Yale Alumni Sch. Com., City Tavern Club (Washington), Oxford and Cambridge Club (London), Yale Club (N.Y.C.), Elizabethan Club (New Haven, Conn.).

THAXTON, EVERETTE FREDERICK, lawyer; b. Charleston, W.Va., Jan. 11, 1938; s. Wilbur and Mildred F. (Gerwig) T.; m. Karen Caldwell, Dec. 29, 1967; children: James, LeeAnn, Emily. BA, U. Charleston, 1967; JD, W.Va. U., 1970. Bar: W.Va. 1970, Va. 1981, U.S. Ct. Appeals (fourth cir.) 1983. Cartographer, hwy. design technician W.Va. Dept. of Hwy., Charleston, 1961-63; dir. tax mapping W.Va. Tax Dept., Charleston, 1963-65; ptnr. Thaxton & Daniels, Charleston, 1970—. Served with USAF, 1955-61. Mem. ABA (various coms.), W.Va. Bar Assn., Assn. Trial Lawyers Am., W.VA. Trial Lawyers Assn., Am. Arbitration Assn. (panel arbitrators), Pi Gamma Mu, Aircraft Owners and Pilots Assn. Home: 502 Hillsdale Dr Charleston WV 25302 Office: Thaxton & Daniels 1115 Virginia St E Charleston WV 25301

THAYER, JAMES NORRIS, financial corporation executive; b. Janesville, Wis., July 9, 1926; s. James Norris and Hazel (VanWormer) T.; m. Sylvia Lucille Kittell, June 26, 1948; children: Scott Norris, Diane Marie, Bradley Raymond. B.S., UCLA, 1948. With Prudential Ins. Co. Am., 1948-55; with William R. Staats & Co., 1955-65, partner, 1960-65; sr. v.p. Glore Forgan-Wm. R. Staats Inc., 1965-67; treas. Lear Siegler, Inc., 1967—, v.p., 1969—, sec., 1972—, sr. v.p. fin., 1977-87; pres., chief exec. officer Gibraltar Fin. Corp., Beverly Hills, Calif., 1988—; bd. dirs. Bunker Hill Income Securities. Bd. dirs., treas. Hathaway Home Children, Highland Park, Calif., 1956-62. Served with USAAF, 1944-47. Mem. UCLA Alumni Assn. (pres. 1982-84), Delta Sigma Phi, Beta Gamma Sigma. Clubs: Bel Air Country, Regency (Los Angeles). Home: 305 S Camden Dr Beverly Hills CA 90212 Office: Gibraltar Fin Corp 9111 Wilshire Blvd Beverly Hills CA 90210

THAYER, RUSSELL, III, airlines executive; b. Phila., Dec. 5, 1922; s. Russell and Shelby Wentworth (Johnson) T.; m. Elizabeth Wright Mifflin, June 12, 1947; children: Elizabeth, Dixon, Shelby, Samuel, David. Student, St. George's Sch., 1937-42; A.B., Princeton U., 1949. Mgmt. trainee Eastern Air Lines, 1949-52; mgr. cargo sales and service Am. Airlines, Los Angeles, 1952-63; v.p. mktg. Seaboard World Airlines, N.Y.C., 1963-70; sr. v.p. Braniff Airways, Inc., Dallas, 1970-72; exec. v.p. Braniff Airways, Inc., 1972-77, pres., chief operating officer, 1977-80, vice chmn., 1981-82; dir. (Braniff Airways, Inc.), 1971-82; v.p. Pan Am. World Airways, Inc., N.Y.C., 1982-84, sr. v.p., 1984-88; sr. v.p. Airline Econs., Inc., Washington, 1988—, also bd. dirs.; dir. Ft. Worth Nat. Bank., 1977-82. Mem. Trinity Ch. Ushers Guild, Princeton, N.J., 1968—; Trustee Aviation Hall of Fame N.J. Served with USAAF, 1942-45, ETO. Decorated D.F.C., Air medal with 11 oak leaf clusters. Mem. Am. Aviation Hist. Soc., Air Force Assn., Exptl. Aircraft Assn., Nat. Aeros. Assn., Delta Psi. Clubs: Ivy (Princeton), Pretty Brook Tennis (Princeton); Bay Head (N.J.) Yacht; Princeton (N.Y.C.); Philadelphia. Home: 21 Lilac Ln Princeton NJ 08540 Office: Airline Econs Inc 1350 Connecticut Ave Ste 810 Washington DC 20036

THEISS, ELISABETH THORINGTON, real estate analyst; b. Montgomery, Ala., July 8, 1961; d. Robert Dinning and Winifred Ann (Pilcher) Thorington; m. Robert Mitchell Theiss, June 20, 1987. AB Econ., Duke U., 1983; MBA, U. Pa., 1987. Pub. fin. analyst Merrill Lynch Capital Markets, N.Y.C., 1983-85; summer intern Trammell Crow Co., Charlotte, N.C., 1986; real estate analyst Integrated Resources, N.Y.C., 1987—. Episcopalian. Office: Integrated Resources 666 3rd Ave New York NY 10017

THEOBALD, STANLEY CHRISTOPHER, finance director; b. Cleve., May 31, 1951; s. William Lindsey Theobald and Barbara Louise (Hoffman) Soos; m. Kathleen Ryan, Sept. 15, 1973; children: Meghan, Ryan. BBA, Kent State U., 1978. CPA. Mgr. acctg. Am. Soc. for Metals, Metals Park, Ohio, 1978-79, comptroller, 1979-81, asst. dir. fin., 1981-85; dir. fin. Am. Soc. for Metals Internat., Metals Park, Ohio, 1985—. Cons. Jr. Achievment, Chagrin Falls, Ohio, 1987—. Served as E4 USAF, 1971-75. Mem. Am. Inst. CPA's, Ohio Soc. CPA's, Nat. Assn. Accts., Am. Mgmt. Assn., Council Engring. Soc. Execs. Republican. Presbyterian. Office: MS Internat Rt 87 Metals Park OH 44073

THEOBALD, THOMAS CHARLES, banker; b. Cin., May 5, 1937; m. Gigi Mahon, Jan. 1987. AB in Econs., Coll. Holy Cross, 1958; MBA in Fin. with high distinction, Harvard U., 1960. With Citibank, N.A. div. Citicorp, 1960-87; vice-chmn. Citicorp, N.Y.C., 1982-87; chief exec. officer Continental Bank Corp., Chgo., 1987—; chmn. bd. dirs. Continental Bank N.A., Chgo., 1987—; bd. dirs. Xerox Corp. Vice-chmn. Overseers Com. to Visit Harvard Grad. Sch. Bus. Adminstrn., Coun. Found. for Child Devel.; bd. dirs. Chgo. Coun. on Fgn. Rels. Mem. Econ. Club Chgo. (bd. dirs.). Office: Continental Bank Corp 231 S LaSalle St Chicago IL 60697

THEODORE, GEORGE T., private investigator, investigation company executive; b. Elmhurst, Ill., July 7, 1940; s. Ted and Alice (Nicopoulos) T. Cert. genealogy, Elmhurst Coll., 1965; cert. electronics, Triton Coll., 1967, cert. locksmithing, 1969. Pres. Tracer's, Inc., Elmhurst, 1961—. Mem. Am. Security Council, Nat. Geneology Soc. Home: 197 Addison St Elmhurst IL 60126 Office: Tracers Inc 122 N York Rd Elmhurst IL 60126

THERIAULT, ALAN DAVID, investment company executive; b. Caribou, Maine, July 19, 1954; s. Lionel and Rita Irene (Damboise) T.; m. Wendy Sherman, July 29, 1979 (div. 1985); 1 child, Nathan. Student, U. Maine. Pres. First of Maine Cos., Portland, 1977-83; regional instl. rep. Drexel Burnham Lambert, Boston, 1980-83; sr. v.p. First of Maine Corp., Portland, 1983—; dir. various investment and service cos., New Eng. area; fin., investment cons. numerous credit unions, 1984—; bd. dirs. Credit Union Fin. Services, Portland. Mem. Nat. Assn. Securities Dealers, Maine Real Estate Commn. Home: 89 Spurwink Rd Scarborough ME 04074 Office: First of Maine Corp PO Box 1053 Portland ME 04104

THERRIEN, ROBERT WILFRID, contracting company executive; b. Manchester, N.H., Oct. 31, 1929; s. Alfred Wilfrid and Fedora Alma (Morin) T.; m. Beverly G. Ferron, Aug. 15, 1954; children: Robert Wilfrid, Clara Elena, David, Mary. BA, St. Anselm's Coll., Manchester, 1952; postgrad., Boston Coll., 1953. Pres. Al Melanson Co., Inc., Keene, N.H., 1953—, R&M Realty, Inc., Keene and Rutland, Vt., 1961—, Vt. Roofing Co., Inc., Rutlandand Bennington, 1962—, Tri-State Acoustical, Inc., Keene and Rutland, 1987—, N.E. Roofing Cons., Inc., Keene, 1980—, A.C. Hathorne Co., Inc., Burlington, Vt., 1983—. Bd. dirs. Monadnock Humane Soc., Keene, YMCA, Keene, Monadnock United Way; trustee N.H. Cath. Charities; mem. exec. bd. Daniel Webster council Boy Scouts Am., 1963 (recipient Silver Beaver award 1963). Mem. Nat. Roofing Contractors Assn. (nat. bd. dirs. 1980—), N.E. Roofing Contractors Assn. (bd. dirs. 1976—, pres. 1982-84, Clarence Carr award 1985), St. Anselm's Coll. Alumni Assn. (bd. dirs.), Rotary, Elks, Moose. Home: Sawyer Crossing Rd Swanzey NH 03431 Office: Al Melanson Co Inc 353 West St Keene NH 03431

THETFORD, RANDY ALAN, supermarket chain executive; b. El Paso, Tex., May 6, 1960; s. Roy Allison and Elizabeth Pauline (Qualls) T.; m. Anita Jane Ward, Sept. 8, 1984; 1 child, Allison Marie. AA, Dyersburg State Coll., 1980; BS, U. Tenn., Martin, 1983. CPA, Tenn. Coop. acct. Memphis Light Gas & Water, 1981-82; internal auditor Holiday Inns, Inc., Memphis, 1983-84, sr. acct., 1984-85; sr. acct. Embassy Suites, Dallas, 1985-86; contr. E.W. James & Sons, Inc., Union City, Tenn., 1986—. Tenn. CPA scholar, 1982-83. Mem. Nat. Assn. Accts., Union City Jaycees. Mem. Ch. of Christ. Home: 1012 Exchange St Union City TN 38261 Office: EW James & Sons Inc 1308-14 Nailling Dr Union City TN 38261

THIBODEAU, MICHAEL ALLEN, public utility executive, assistant treasurer; b. Presque Isle, Maine, Mar. 16, 1956; s. John Clayton and Marion Elizabeth (Butler) T.; m. Cynthia Mary Saucier, Aug. 24, 1984; 1 child, Emily Lauren. ABS in Acctg., North Maine Voc. Tech. Inst., 1977; BS in Acctg., Husson Coll., 1979. Pub. acct. Linwood Raymond, P.A., Presque Isle, 1979-81; staff acct. Maine Pub. Service Co., Presque Isle, 1981-83, rate analyst, 1983-85, mgr. rates and fin. planning, 1985-86, asst. treas., 1986—. Faculty adv. com. N. Maine Vocat. Tech. Inst.; mem. fin. com. St. Mary's; past treas., bd. dirs. Shelter for the Homeless Inc. Republican. Roman Catholic. Club: Toastmasters (Competent Toastmaster award 1985). Home: 103 Fleetwood St Presque Isle ME 04769 Office: Maine Pub Svc Co 209 State St Presque Isle ME 04769

THIBODEAUX, JOE N., retail administrator; b. New Orleans, La., May 14, 1953; s. Edna E. (Tucker) T.; divorced, 1978; children: Jeffery Michael, Debra Ann. Maintenance supr. Melvin Simon & Assocs., Springfield, Ill., 1978-80; energy mgmt. tech. So. region Melvin Simon & Assocs., Denton, Tex., 1980-84; cen. plant technician Melvin Simon & Assocs., San Antonio, 1984-86; ops. dir. Schroder Ctr. Mgmt., San Antonio, 1986—. Served with USN, 1971-75. Mem. Internat. Council of Shopping Ctrs., Bldg. Owners and Mgrs. Internat., San Antonio Assn. Bldg. Engrs. Office: McCreless Mall 1000 McCreless Mall San Antonio TX 78223

THIBODEAUX, MICHAEL JARED, lawyer, company executive, judge; b. Lake Charles, La., Nov. 3, 1942; s. Donald David and Ione Marie (Pizanie) Damanchyk; m. Nola Dean LeBlanc, Apr. 28, 1962 (div. 1976); children: Tina Marie, Milissa Jo; m. Barbara Lynn Ball, Mar. 13, 1982; children: Haley Elizabeth, Ashly Lynn. BA, McNeese State U., 1965; JD, South Tex. Coll. Law, 1970. Bar: Tex. 1970. Staff atty. Houston Legal Found., 1970-72; ptnr. Allen, Lykos & Thibodeaux, Houston, 1970-79; def. counsel Home Ins. Co., Houston, 1979-84; dir. risk mgmt. U.S. Home Corp., Houston, 1984—; instr. law Tex. So. U., 1975; instr. bus. law North Harris County Coll., Houston, 1978-81; presiding judge Hunters Creek Village, 1981—. Bd. dirs. Juvenile Justice, Inc., Houston, 1976-80, Neighborhood Justice, Inc., Houston, 1979-85, Concerned Teens, Inc., Houston, 1984—. With U.S. Army, 1965—; col. Res. Mem. Tex. Bar Assn., Risk and Ins. Mgmt. Soc. Office: US Home Corp PO Box 2863 Houston TX 77252-2863

THICKINS, GRAEME RICHARD, marketing consultant; b. Perth, Australia, Apr. 4, 1946; came to U.S., 1952; s. Richard Percy and Lucie Joy (McDiarmid) T.; m. Jane Elizabeth Bantle, Nov. 6, 1969; children: Jeffrey, Christopher, Sarah. AA, Austin State Jr. Coll., 1967; postgrad. U. Minn., 1967-70. Editor Data 100 Corp., Edina, Minn., 1970-72; pub. rels. and promotion writer, editor MTS Systems Corp., Eden Prairie, Minn., 1972-73; dir. pub. rels. svcs., writer, account exec. The Communication Coalition, Inc., Edina, 1973-74; free-lance writer, cons., Mpls., 1974-75; mktg. communications writer, asst. mgr. Medtronic, Inc., Mpls., 1975-77; mktg. svcs. mgr., communications mgr., Am. Med. Systems, Inc., Mpls., 1977-78; account exec. D'Arcy-MacManus & Masius, Twin Cities, Minn., 1978; cons. editorial svcs., corp. communications Control Data Corp., Mpls., 1978-79, mgr. editorial svcs., 1979, mgr. promotion lit., 1980, mgr. creative svcs., 1981, mgr. advt. and promotion, systems and svcs. co., 1982; cons. mktg., advt., direct mail, pub. rels., Mpls., 1975-82; founder, pres. GT&A, Inc., high tech. advt. and mktg. svcs., Mpls., 1982—; mem. Minn. High Tech. Coun. Bd. dirs. Cystic Fibrosis Found., Minn.; co-chairperson mktg. and communications 1986 Minn. Orch. Symphony Ball. Recipient numerous awards and certs. of excellence from various profl. assns. Mem. Advt. Fedn. of Minn., Midwest Direct Mktg. Assn., Direct Mktg. Assn., Am. Inst. Graphic Arts, Med. Alley Assn., Am. Mktg. Assn., Phi Gamma Delta. Clubs: Flagship Athletic (Eden Prairie). Avocations:tennis, swimming, surfing, skiing, cycling. Home: 8135 Kentucky Circle West Bloomington MN 55438 Office: 7625 Golden Triangle Dr Ste K Eden Prairie MN 55344

THIEBAUTH, BRUCE EDWARD, advertising executive; b. Bronxville, N.Y., Oct. 30, 1947; s. Bruce and Margaret Evelyn (Wiederhold) T.; m. Sherry Ann Proplesch, Aug. 31, 1968; 1 child, Bruce Revere. Student, Colby Coll., Waterville, Maine, 1965-66, Pace Coll., 1971; BA in Bus. Adminstrn. and Sociology magna cum laude, Bellevue Coll., 1972. Mgr. credit GE Credit Corp., Croton Falls, N.Y., 1971; mgr. ops. Bridal Publs., Inc., Omaha, 1972-73; regional mgr. Bridal Fair, Inc., Omaha, 1973-74, sales mgr., 1974-76, chmn. bd., pres., 1976—; bd. dirs. Multi-Media Group, Inc., Fair Communications, Inc. Pub., bd. dirs. Bridal Fair mag. With USAF, 1966-70, Vietnam. Recipient Nat. Def. Svc. medal, Somers (N.Y.) League Citizenship and Pub. Svc. award, 1965. Mem. Mag. Pubs. Assn., Nat. Assn. Broadcasters, Airline Passengers Assn., Bellevue Coll. Alumni Assn., Paso Fino Horse Assn. Republican. Congregationalist. Office: 9315 Binney St Omaha NE 68134

THIELE, WILLIAM EDWARD, insurance company executive; b. N.Y.C., Nov. 12, 1942; s. Elmer William and Ethel Mae (Stein) T.; m. Nancy June Watt, May 2, 1964; children: Christina, Jeanette, Amanda. BS, Queens (N.Y.) Coll., 1963. Trainee underwriter Phoenix Assurance, N.Y.C., 1963-68;

underwriter, asst. sec., asst. v.p., v.p., sr. v.p. Gen. Reinsurance Corp., Stamford, Conn., 1968-83; exec. v.p. Continental Corp., N.Y.C., 1983-88, sr. v.p., 1988—; chmn. Lombard Ins. Group, Hong Kong, 1984—; bd. dirs. Mcpl. Bond Investors Assurance, White Plains, N.Y., Associated Aviation Underwriters, Short Hills, N.J., Ins. Svcs. Office, N.Y.C., Continental Corp.; trustee Coll. of Ins.Queens Coll. Found. Contbr. articles to profl. jours. Republican. Methodist. Club: Milford (Conn.) Yacht. Office: Continental Corp 180 Maiden Ln New York NY 10038

THIELKE, MICHAEL MURRAY, transportation and cargo company executive; b. Evanston, Ill., Aug. 12, 1953; s. Eugene Anthony and Harriet Ann (Murray) T. BA, Knox Coll., 1975. Traffic mgr. APECO Corp., Evanston, 1975-76; export mgr. consumer products div. Rockwell Internat., Schaumburg, Ill., 1976-77; prin. M. Thielke & Assocs., Chgo., 1977-79; regional mgr. Harper Robinson & Co., Chgo., 1980-83; dir. internat. div. Interstate Internat. Inc., Washington, 1983—. Agt. Internat. Rep. Cooperation Fund, Washington, 1984, Rep. Inst. for Internat. Affairs, 1988. Mem. World Affairs Council, Internat. Platform Assn., World Trade Club of Washington, Household Goods Forwarders' Assn. Am. Republican. Roman Catholic. Home: 4740 Connecticut Ave NW Washington DC 20008 Office: Interstate Internat Inc 5801 Rolling Road Springfield VA 22152

THIGPEN, DANIEL CURRIE, office products company executive; b. Jacksonville, Fla., Feb. 14, 1948; s. John Jackson and Marie (Currie) T.; m. Elizabeth Merritt, Dec. 29, 1972 (div. Dec. 1987); children: Jonathan Daniel, Jackson David. AB, Mercer U., 1970; postgrad., U. Ga., 1974. Tchr. Griffin (Ga.) High Sch., 1970-73; mgr. circulation Athens (Ga.) Newspapers, Inc., 1973-79; dist. adminstr. Lanier Bus. Products, Charlotte, N.C., 1979-81, div. adminstr., 1981-82; regional adminstrv. mgr. Lanier Bus. Products, Washington, 1982-84; nat. adminstrv. mgr. Lanier Bus. Products, Atlanta, 1984-85, mgr. accounts receivable, 1985—. Mem. Assn. Record Mgrs. and Adminstrs. (Boss of Yr. 1987—). Republican. Baptist. Home: 4854 Woodhurst Way Stone Mountain GA 30088

THIMM, ROGER WALTER, accountant; b. Hartford, Wis., July 10, 1958; s. Walter J. and Helen (Wondra) T. BBA in Acctg., U. Wis., Milw., 1980, MBA, 1989. CPA, Wis. Acct. PDQ Corp., Madison, Wis., 1981-82, Conley, McDonald, Sprague & Co., Milw., 1982-84; dir. acctg. SBF Mgmt., Inc., Milw., 1984-87; controller Shadbolt & Boyd Co., Milw., 1987—. Mem. Am. Inst. CPA's, Wis. Inst. CPA's. Home: 409 Harrison Ave Hartford WI 53027 Office: Shadbolt & Boyd Co PO Box 2059 Milwaukee WI 53201

THIMON, JACQUES BERNARD, packaging company executive; b. St. Colombe, France, July 18, 1942; came to U.S., 1984; s. Michael and Marie (Masson) T.; m. Liliane Porret, Aug. 3, 1968; children: Florence, Cecile. ENP, La Martiniere, Lyon, France, 1962, BTS, 1964. Tech. v.p. Thimon Co., Aix-Les-Bains, France, 1963-83; dir. exports Soparind, Paris, 1983-84; exec. Newtec subs. Soparind, St. Louis, 1984—. Patentee shrink film package and stretch film package, numerous others. Bd. dirs. St. Louis-Lyon Sister City Program, 1988—. Mem. Food and Dairy Assn., Lions Club. Home: 12623 Tallow Hill Ln Saint Louis MO 63146 Office: Newtec 112 Weldon Pkwy Saint Louis MO 63043

THOBEN, KATHLEEN SALZIG, corporate secretary; b. Beacon, N.Y., Mar. 7, 1930; d. John Francis and Grace Marie (Higgins) Salzig; m. Alfred H. Thoben, Oct.26, 1957. Grad. high sch., Poughkeepsie, N.Y. Exec. sec. Cen. Hudson Gas & Elec. Corp., Poughkeepsie, 1952-71; exec. sec. Dutchess Bank & Trust Co., Poughkeepsie, 1971, corp. sec., 1978—. Mem. bd. trustees Elting Meml. Library, New Paltz, 1974-80. Mem. Nat. Assn. Bank Women. Democrat. Roman Catholic. Office: Dutchess Bank & Trust Co 285 Main Mall Poughkeepsie NY 12601

THOMA, CARL DEE, merchant banker; b. Roswell, N.Mex., Oct. 12, 1948; s. Edward C. and Imogene (Price) T.; m. Marilynn J. Thoma, Dec. 27, 1970; children: Margo, Mark. BS, Okla. State U., 1971; MBA, Stanford U., 1973. Asst. to pres. Az-Co Land & Cattle Co., Phoenix, 1973-74; acting head First Chgo. Investment Corp., 1974-80; ptnr. Golder, Thoma & Cressey, Chgo., 1980—; bd. dirs. Perkins Family Restaurants, Memphis, PageNet, Plano, Tex., Direct Mail Corp. of Am., St. Louis, Proxy Message Ctr., Dallas, Sullivan Graphics, Nashville. Office: Golder Thoma & Cressey 120 S LaSalle Ste 630 Chicago IL 60603

THOMA, KURT MICHAEL, designer, builder, photographer; b. Boston, Aug. 9, 1946; s. Kurt Richard and Janet (Holdsworth) T.; divorced; children by previous marriage—Heather Anne, Heidi. Student U. N.H., 1968. Clk., supr., asst. div. EDP coordinator, EDP coordinator, mut. funds div. 1st Nat. Bank Boston, 1968-69; v.p. cen. N.H. bldg. corp. Barry Dashner, Inc., 1969-72; field rep. Acorn Structures, Inc., 1972-75; v.p., treas. Design Structures Group, Inc., 1975-76; pres. Witthom Assocs., Inc., 1976-79; v.p. Confetti, Inc., 1978—; pres., treas., propr. Dessin Batir, Inc., Newport, R.I., 1979—. Served with U.S. Army N.G., 1966-72. Mem. Internat. and Am. Solar Energy Socs., Internat. Platform Assn. Republican. Christian Scientist. Avocations: writing, star class sailing, tennis, skiing, furniture design. Office: Dessin Batir Inc 12 Clarke St Newport RI 02840

THOMAS, ALAN, candy company executive; b. Evansburg, Pa., Jan. 1, 1923; s. William Roberts and Letta (Garrett) T.; student Rutgers U., 1941-42, 46-47; B.S., Pa. State U., 1949; M.S., U. Minn., 1950, Ph.D., 1954; m. Marguerite Atria, July 1, 1972; children—Garrett Lee, Michael Alan, Randall Stephen, Brett Eliot. Instr., Temple U., Phila., 1950-51, U. Minn., St. Paul, 1951-54; research asst. Bowman Dairy Co., Chgo., 1954-56; research project mgr. M&M Candies div. Mars, Inc., Hackettstown, N.J., 1956-60, product devel. mgr., 1961-64, chocolate research dir. 1964; v.p. research and devel. Mars Candies, Chgo., 1964-67; v.p. research and devel. M&M/Mars Div., Hackettstown, 1967-77, v.p. sci. affairs, 1977-78; gen. mgr. Ethel M, Las Vegas, 1978-83, cons., 1985; sr. cons. Knechtel Research Scis., Inc., Skokie, Ill., 1984; v.p. tech. Ferrara Pan Candy Co., Forest Park, Ill., 1986—. Chmn. industry council of industry liaison panel Food and Nutrition Bd., Nat. Acad. Scis./NRC, 1972-73; adv. U.S. del. Codex Alimentarius Com. on Cocoa and Chocolate Products, 1967-78. Served to 1st lt. inf. AUS, 1942-46. Recipient research award Nat. Confectioners Assn. U.S., 1971. Mem. AAAS, Grocery Mfrs. Am. (chmn. tech. com. 1975-76), Chocolate Mfrs. Assn. (chmn. FDA liaison com. 1975-77), Inst. Food Technologists, Am. Assn. Candy Technologists, Gamma Sigma Delta, Phi Kappa Phi. Home: 1625 Westwood Dr Las Vegas NV 89102 Office: Ferrara Pan Candy Co 7301 W Harrison St Forest Park IL 60130

THOMAS, ANTHONY GEORGE, golf company executive; b. New Bedford, Mass., Nov. 1, 1926; s. George and Mary (Peter) T.; m. Josephine Abraham, May 2, 1959; children: Matthew John, Jessica Lee, Andrew James. BS in Acctg. and Fin., Bryant Coll., 1950. With Aerovox Corp., New Bedford, 1951-65; with corp. div. Acushnet Co., New Bedford, 1965-81, div. controller Titleist Golf div., 1981-87, v.p., controller, 1988—. Chmn. Manhattan fundraiser Bishop Stang High Sch., Dartmouth, Mass., 1985, 86; mem. fin. bd. Our Lady of Purgatory Ch., New Bedford, 1986-88. With U.S. Army, 1945-46. Fellow Nat. Assn. Accts., Indsl. Mgmt. Club. Office: Titleist Golf Div Acushnet Co Box B 965 New Bedford MA 02741

THOMAS, BAILEY ALFRED, food company executive; b. Crisfield, Md.; s. Bailey and Mary H. (Hopkins) T.; children: Frank, John, Gregory Thomas. Assoc. Bus. Adminstrn., Balt. Coll. Commerce, 1952. With Libby, McNeill & Libby, 1950-51; then with Crosse & Blackwell Co., Balt.; now pres., chief operating officer McCormick & Co. Inc., Balt. Bd. govs. The Balt. Goodwill Industries Inc.; pres. Buddies Inc. Mem. Am. Spice Trade Assn. (past chmn. indsl. and food service com.), Inst. Food Technologists. Republican. Home: 12603 Mt Laurel Ct Reisterstown MD 21136 Office: McCormick & Co Inc 11350 McCormick Rd Hunt Valley MD 21031

THOMAS, BIDE LAKIN, utility executive; b. Mason City, Iowa, Aug. 14, 1935; s. Brice Lakin and Jane (Duffield) T.; children: Brice, Lorraine, Carolyn. BS in Indsl. Adminstrn., Yale U., 1957; MBA, Harvard U., 1959. With Commonwealth Edison Co., Chgo., 1959—, div. v.p., 1970-73, gen. div. mgr., 1973-75, v.p. div. ops., 1975-76, v.p. indsl. relations, 1976-80, exec. v.p., 1980-87, pres., 1987—; bd. dirs. Commonwealth Edison Co., No. Trust Corp., No. Trust Co., R.R. Donnelley & Sons Co. Trustee Rush-Presbyn.-St. Luke's Med. Ctr., DePaul U.; bd. dirs. Ravenswood Hosp. Med. Ctr., chmn., 1973-77; bd. mgrs. YMCA Met. Chgo., chmn., 1985-86; bd. dirs. Civic Fedn., Chgo. Crime Commn., Chgo.-Cities in Schs., Rush/Copley Health Care Systems Inc.; assoc. Northwestern U. Mem. Chgo. Club, Econ. Club of Chgo., Comml. Club. Office: Commonwealth Edison Co PO Box 767 1 First National Plaza Chicago IL 60690

THOMAS, CHARLES CARROLL, investment management executive; b. N.Y.C., Feb. 15, 1930; s. Charles Carroll and Miriam (Smith) T.; grad. Deerfield Acad., 1947; B.A., Yale U., 1951; m. Carolyn Rose Hirchert, June 16, 1951; children—Charles Carroll, Anne Hatheway, Megan Lloyd. Div. retail programs mgr. Mobil Oil Corp., Boston, 1953-63; exec. v.p. Lionel D. Edie & Co., N.Y.C., 1963-72; exec. v.p. Bank New Eng., Boston, 1972-76; v.p., dir. mktg. Loomis, Sayles & Co., Boston, 1976-85; pres. Concord Mgmt. Co., 1985—; co-pub. Cons. Compendium Inc., 1985—. Trustee, Deerfield Acad., 1975-78; trustee Babson Coll., 1976-82, 83—; trustee Cambridge Sch. of Weston (Mass.), 1976-82, New Eng. Home for Little Wanderers, 1983-86. Served with USAF, 1951-53. Mem. Assn. of Investment Mgmt. Sales Execs. (pres. 1980-81, dir. 1980-84), Air Force Assn. Republican. Congregationalist. Clubs: Yale of N.Y.C., Harvard of Boston. Home: 170 Barnes Hill Rd Concord MA 01742 Office: 33 Bedford St Concord MA 01742

THOMAS, CHRISTOPHER ROBERT, food products company executive; b. San Diego, Dec. 5, 1948; m. Christina Q. Thomas, Apr. 16, 1979. BSBA, U. So. Calif., 1977. CPA, Calif. Auditor Arthur Andersen & Co., Calif., 1977-84; v.p. fin., chief fin. officer Collins Foods Internat. Inc., L.A., 1984—. Sgt. USMC, 1967-70. Mem. AICPA, Calif. Soc. CPA's, Fin. Acctg. Found., Fin. Execs. Inst. Office: Collins Foods Internat Inc 12655 W Jefferson Blvd Los Angeles CA 90066

THOMAS, CLARENCE, government official; b. Savannah, Ga., June 23, 1948. BA, Holy Cross Coll., 1971; JD, Yale U., 1974. Bar: Mo., U.S. Ct. Appeals Mo. Asst. atty. gen. State of Mo., Jefferson City, 1974-77; atty. Monsanto Co., St. Louis, 1977-79; legis. asst. to Sen. John C. Danforth, Washington, 1979-81; asst. sec. for civil rights Dept. Edn., Washington, 1981-82; chmn. U.S. EEOC, Washington, 1982—. Office: EEOC 2401 E St NW Room 540 Washington DC 20507 *

THOMAS, CLAUDE ANDERSON, computer executive; b. Raleigh, N.C., Aug. 17, 1942; s. Claude A. and Marjorie (Lewis) T.; m. Theresa M. Holland, June 6, 1987; stepchildren: Francis, Carolyn. BChemE, Vanderbilt U., 1964; MBA in mktg., Wash. U., St. Louis, 1966. Systems engr. Electronic Data Systems, N.Y.C., 1970-73; v.p. Midwest Stock Exchange, Chgo., 1973-80; dir. fin. industry cons. services Coopers & Lybrand, Chgo., 1980-82; v.p. fin. industry mktg. Digital Equipment Corp., Andover, Mass., 1986—. Lt. U.S. Army, 1967-70, Pentagon. Mem. Tau Beta Pi, Beta Gamma Sigma. Home: 68 Pine Hill Ln Concord MA 01742

THOMAS, DANIEL FOLEY, telecommunications company executive; b. Washington, Aug. 24, 1950; s. Richard Kenneth and Margaret (Foley) T.; m. Barbara Jane Clark, June 30, 1973; 1 child, Alison Clark. BS in Acctg., Mt. St. Mary's Coll., 1972. CPA, Va. Auditor Deloitte, Haskins and Sells, Washington, 1972-74; various fin. positions Communications Satellite Corp., Washington, 1974-78, asst. treas., 1984-85, treas., 1986-87, controller, 1987-89; controller Comsat Telesystems, Washington, 1978-79; mgr. acctg. and taxes Satellite Bus. Systems, McLean, Va., 1979-81, treas., 1981-84; v.p. fin. Comsat Tech. Products, Inc., Washington, 1989—. Named One of Outstanding Young Men Am., 1981. Mem. AICPA, Va. Jaycees (life), Great Falls Jaycees (pres. 1978). Roman Catholic. Home: 708 Seneca Rd Great Falls VA 22066 Office: Communications Satellite Corp 950 L'Enfant Pla SW Washington DC 20024

THOMAS, DAVID ANSELL, retired university dean; b. Holliday, Tex., July 5, 1917; s. John Calvin Mitchell and Alice (Willet) T.; m. Mary Elizabeth Smith, May 18, 1946; 1 dau., Ann Elizabeth. B.A., Tex. Tech. Coll., 1937; M.B.A., Tex. Christian U., 1948; Ph.D., U. Mich., 1956. C.P.A., Tex. Accountant Texaco, Inc., 1937-42; asso. prof. Tex. Christian U., 1946-49; lectr. U. Mich., 1949-53; prof. accounting Cornell U., Ithaca, N.Y., 1953-84; asso. dean Cornell U. (Grad. Sch. Bus. and Pub. Adminstrn.), 1962-79, acting dean, 1979-81, dean, 1981-84. Author: Accelerated Amortization of Defense Facilities, 1958, Accounting for Home Builders, 1952; Contbr. numerous articles to publs.; Editor: Fed. Accountant, 1956-58. Pres. Exec. Investors, Inc.; exec. dir. Charles E. Merrill Family Found., 1954-57, Robert A. Magowan Found., 1957-60; adminstr. Charles E. Merrill Trust, 1957-81, Ithaca Growth Fund.; Bd. dirs. Ithaca Opera Assn., Cornell Student Agys. Served to capt. USAAF, 1942-46, PTO. Mem. Tex. Soc. C.P.A.'s, Nat. Assn. Accountants, Am. Accounting Assn., Phi Beta Kappa, Beta Alpha Psi. Clubs: Cornell of N.Y., University, Statler (pres., dir.). Home: 150 N Sunset Dr Ithaca NY 14850 Office: Samuel Curtis Johnson Grad Sch Mgmt Cornell U Ithaca NY 14853

THOMAS, DAVID LLOYD, textile manufacturing company executive; b. Atlanta, May 10, 1942; s. Elbert Lamar and Evelyn Grace (Combs) T.; m. Mary Jo Ann Matney, June 25, 1966; children: Christine, Michael. BSBA, U. N.C., 1964. CPA, N.C. Auditor Price Waterhouse, N.Y.C., 1964, Atlanta, 1969-70; div. controller Dart Industries, Atlanta, 1971; controller Ithaca Industries, Inc., Wilkesboro, N.C., 1971-82, sec.-treas., 1982—, chief fin. officer, 1983—, bd. dirs., 1988—. Sec. Wilkes Art Gallery, 1985-88, bd. dirs., 1985—. Capt. Med. Services Corps, U.S. Army, 1965-68. Fellow N.C. Assn. CPA's (sec. Catawba Valley chpt. 1982-83); mem. AICPA, Ga. Soc. CPA's, Nat. Assn. Accts., Fin. Execs. Inst., Wilkesboro C. of C. (bd. dirs. 1979-81, v.p. 1982, 86, trustee found. 1983—). Republican. Methodist. Lodge: Kiwanis (bd. dirs. North Wilkesboro 1984-85). Home: 6 Walnut Pl Wilkesboro NC 28697 Office: Ithaca Industries Inc Hwy 268 W Wilkesboro NC 28697

THOMAS, DEREK WILFRID, marketing executive; b. San Jose, Calif., Jan. 28, 1952; s. Michael Hall and Helen Mary (Gamble) T.; m. Lindy Lou Burdick, Oct. 1974 (div. Feb. 1983); m. Wilma Jean Boenker, Oct. 13, 1983. AS in English, Cen. Meth. Coll., 1973. Store mgr. various small retail stores, Columbia, Mo., 1972-77; gen. mgr. Lifestyles/Neenaco Cos., Columbia, 1977-80; internat. mgr. Internat. Jensen Inc., Chgo., 1980-85; pres. Boenker/Thomas Assocs. Inc., Glen Ellyn, Ill., 1985—; bd. dirs. Angstrom Assocs. USA Inc., Toronto, Canada, 1985-87, Venture Products, Ltd., Inglesham, U.K., 1988—. Mem. Midwest Soc. Profl. Cons., Pres.'s Club. Office: Boenker Thomas Assocs Inc 332 Oak St Glen Ellyn IL 60137

THOMAS, DEROY C., lawyer, business and insurance company executive; b. Utica, N.Y., Feb. 16, 1926. B.A., Iona Coll., 1949; LL.B., Fordham U., 1952. Bar: N.Y. 1952. Asst. prof. law Fordham U., N.Y.C., 1953-58; asst. counsel Assn. Casualty and Surety Cos., N.Y.C., 1959-64; with firm Watters & Donovan, 1964; with Hartford Fire Ins. Co. and subs. cos., Conn., 1964—; gen. counsel Hartford Fire Ins. Co. and subs. cos., 1966-69, v.p., 1968-69, sr. v.p., 1969-73; exec. v.p. Hartford Fire Ins. Co. and subs cos., 1973-76; pres., chief exec. officer Hartford Fire Ins. Co. and subs. cos., 1976-83, chmn., 1979—; exec. v.p. Hartford Accident & Indemnity Co., 1973-76, pres., 1976-83, chief exec. officer, 1978-83, chmn., 1979—, also dir.; exec. v.p. ITT Corp., N.Y.C., 1983-85, vice-chmn., 1985-88; pres., chief operating officer ITT Corp, 1988—; pres. ITT Diversified Services Corp., 1983—. Mem. ABA. Office: ITT Corp 320 Park Ave New York NY 10022 also: Hartford Life Ins Co Hartford Plaza Hartford CT 06115

THOMAS, SIR DONALD LLEWELLYN, banker; b. Niagara Falls, N.Y., Mar. 5, 1917; s. Phillip Charles and Dora Ellen (Redpath) T.; m. Lady Barbara Thomas, May 20, 1942; children—Donald Llewellyn, Rhys Evans. BBA magna cum laude, Niagara U.; postgrad. Stonier Grad. Sch. Banking, Rutgers U.; DCS (hon.), Niagara U., 1988. Treas. Niagara Falls Savs. Bank, 1945-54; v.p. No. Trust Co., Chgo., 1955-65; chmn., chief exec. officer Anchor Savs. Bank FSB, Hewlett, N.Y., 1966—, Thomas Property Corp., Marietta, Ga., 1970—, Anchor Mortgage Resources, Atlanta, 1980—, Anchor Mortgage Services, Wayne, N.J., 1983—; chmn. bd. Residential Funding Corp., Mpls., 1988—; mem. faculty Grad. Sch. Savs. Banking, Brown U., Stonier Sch. Banking, Rutgers U.; mem. thrift adv. bd. Fed. Res. Bank N.Y. Co-author: Commercial Bankers Handbook, Savings and Time Deposit Banking. Vice chmn. bd. trustees Lutheran Med. Ctr., N.Y.C.; past pres. Council of Chs. City of N.Y.; mem. council bd. guardians Soc. of Family of Man; past chmn. Community Preservation Corp. N.Y.C., bd. dirs., exec. com. Community Preservation Corp; chm. exec. com. Housing Mortgage Ptnrship Corp.; bd. dirs. Bklyn. Sunday Sch. Union, Bklyn. Philharm., N.Y. Gov.'s Com. for Aging. Decorated Knight of Malta; recipient Man of Yr. award Council of Chs., Bklyn. div., 1976, Indsl. Home for Blind, 1979, Sword of Hope-Am. Cancer Soc., 1980, Montauk Club, 1978, Citizens Recognition award Bklyn. YMCA, hon. Doctorate in Comml. Sci. Niagara U., 1988. Mem. Nat. Council Savs. Instns. (bd. dirs.), U.S. League Savs. Assns. (legis com.), Savs. Banks Assn. N.Y. State, Bklyn. C. of C. (bd. dirs.), NCCJ, Fed. Nat. Mortgage Assn. (adv. bd.). Republican. Clubs: Cherokee Town and Country (Atlanta); Cherry Valley (Garden City, N.Y.); Metropolitan, Marco Polo (N.Y.C.). Home: 1420 Broadway Hewlett NY 11557 Office: Anchor Savs Bank FSB 1420 Broadway Hewlett NY 11557

THOMAS, ELLEN MCVEIGH, human resources executive; b. Manchester, N.H., Aug. 14, 1952; d. John Joseph and Margaret Mary (Devan) McVeigh; m. Stephen David Thomas, Nov. 6, 1983. BS, St. Anselm Coll., 1974; MBA, Rivier Coll., 1989. Asst. dir. admissions Cath. Med. Ctr., Manchester, 1975-76, dir. admissions, 1976-77, adminstrv. coordinator, 1978-80, asst. dir. personnel, 1981-83, personnel mgr., 1983-85, dir. personnel, 1985-86, v.p. of human resources, 1986-89; v.p. of human resources Cen. Maine Healthcare Corp., Lewiston, Maine, 1989—; mgmt. cons. Porter-McGee, Manchester, 1983-85, Creative Entertainment Corp., Manchester, 1981—. Bd. dirs. Anselmian Summer Theatre, Manchester, 1973-76; bd. dirs. Big Bros./Big Sisters of Greater Manchester, 1987-89, N.H. Performing Arts Ctr., 1988-89. Mem. N.H. Soc. for Healthcare Personnel Adminstrn. (treas. 1983-84, v.p., 1984-85, pres. 1985-86), Manchester Soc. Personnel Adminstrs., N.H. Hosp. Assn. (council for mgmt. and recruitment task force 1984-88). Office: Cen Maine Med Ctr PO Box 4500 Lewiston ME 04240

THOMAS, FRANCIS DARRELL, oil compounder executive; b. Palestine, Ill., Feb. 11, 1928; s. Odin F. and Dorothy (Carrol) T.; m. Nancy Thomas; children: Steven, Bruce, Gail. BS, Butler U., 1951. Regional mgr. Sun Oil Co., Cin., 1955-72; pres. Keenan Oil Co., Cin., 1972-74; gen. mgr. Weatherator Engring. Co., Columbus, Ohio, 1975-76; pres. Nat. Oil Products div. Concord Industries, Inc., Hamilton, Ohio, 1976—. Served with USMC, 1946-47. Mem. Ind. Lubricant Mfrs. Assn., Assn. Petroleum Re-Refiners (past mem. nat. exec. com.), Am. Soc. Lubrication Engrs. (past chmn. Cin. sect.). Republican. Club: Clovernook Country. Lodges: Masons, Shriners. Office: 1000 Forest Ave Hamilton OH 45015

THOMAS, GARNETT JETT, accountant; b. Farmington, Ky., July 27, 1920; s. Pinkney Madison and Ethel (Drinkard) T.; m. Nell Penton, May 23, 1981; stepchildren: Vernon Bice, Michael Bice, Gena Bice. BS, Lambuth Coll., 1947; student, U. Notre Dame, 1943-44; MS, Miss. State U., 1949. Clk., acct. Ill. Cen. R.R., Paducah, Ky., 1941-42; mgr. Coll. Bookstore, Lambuth Coll., Jackson, Tenn., 1946-47; acct. Miss. Agrl. and Forestry Expt. Sta., Mississippi State, 1948-60, chief acct., 1960-75, adminstrv. officer and chief acct., 1975-85; mem. adv. bd. Nat. Bank of Commerce of Miss., 1974—; pres. Starkville (Miss.) PBR Corp., 1977-84; fin. adminstr. seed tech. research internat. programs, Brazil, India, Guatemala, Columbia, Thailand, Kenya, 1958-85; bd. dirs. Govt. Employees Credit Union, 1967-86, pres., 1969-73. Contbr. articles to profl. publs. Served with USN, 1942-46. Decorated Bronze Star with oak leaf cluster. Mem. Nat. Assn. Accts., Assn. Govt. Accts., Am. Assn. Accts., Acad. Acctg. Historians, So. Assn. Agrl. Scientists. Republican. Methodist. Lodge: Rotary (pres. 1959-60, dist. gov. dist. 682, 1977-78, adv. com. to pres. 1979-80, dist. chmn. Poloplus). Home: 114 Grand Ridge Dr Starkville MS 39759-4112

THOMAS, GARY LYNN, financial executive; b. Port Vue, Pa., May 15, 1942; s. Willis L. and Luella M. (Rorabaugh) T.; m. Sharen A. Gibbons, May 13, 1967; children—Gregory Scott, Tara Elizabeth. B.S. in Bus. Adminstrn, Pa. State U., 1964; grad., Sch. Bank Adminstrn., U. Wis., 1973. CPA, Pa. Sr. auditor Arthur Andersen & Co., Los Angeles and Pitts., 1964-69; v.p. and dep. comptroller Pitts. Nat. Bank, 1969-77; v.p. and treas. Md. Nat. Corp., Balt., 1977-80; v.p., mgr. corp. fin. div. Md. Nat. Bank, Balt.; exec. v.p. adminstrn. Peterson, Howell & Heather, Hunt Valley, Md., 1980-82; v.p. fin. Am. TeleServices, Inc., a Metromedia co., Balt., 1983-85; chief fin. officer First Cellular Group, Inc., Balt., 1985-88, Schelle, Warner, Murray & Thomas, Inc., Balt., 1988—; adj. instr. Sch. Bank Adminstrn., U. Wis., 1975-80; speaker 14th ann. Bank Tax Inst., 1978. Mem. adv. bd., fin. com. St. Joseph Hosp., Balt.; bd. dirs. industry luncheon club Towson State U. Served with USAR, 1968. Mem. Am. Inst. CPAs, Pa. Inst. CPAs, Md. Assn. CPAs (prior chmn. mems. in industry com.). Republican. Methodist. Home: 2211 Spring Lake Dr Timonium MD 21093 Office: 2212 Old Court Rd Baltimore MD 21208

THOMAS, GORDON ALEXANDER, retired baking company executive, lawyer; b. Newton Center, Mass., Jan. 19, 1928; s. Earle Lewis and Helen Westmoreland (Browder) T.; m. Doris Anita Aakervik, June 17, 1955; children—Krista Lynn, Alix Elizabeth. A.B., Dartmouth Coll., 1950; LL.B., Columbia U., 1953. Bar: N.Y. 1954, Calif. 1956. With firm Sage, Gray, Todd & Sims, N.Y.C., 1953-54; with Travelers Ins. Co., Los Angeles, 1954-58, Continental Baking Co., Rye, N.Y., 1958-87; v.p., gen. counsel Continental Baking Co., 1969-85; dir. Nat. Continental Corp., Kingston, Jamaica. Dist. chmn. Lewisboro (N.Y.) Town Republican Com., 1974-85; bd. dirs. Legal Aid Soc. Westchester County, 1978-88, Westchester County Assn., 1980-85. Served with AUS, 1945-47. Mem. ABA. Republican. Club: Wilson Cove Yacht. Home: Rural Route 4 Box 234 South Salem NY 10590

THOMAS, H. EMERSON, liquified petroleum and natural gas consulting company executive; b. Akron, N.Y., Nov. 24, 1902; s. James Robinson and Fannie Mae (Wilder) T.; m. Helen Mildred Hefferline, July 28, 1928; children: H. Emerson Jr., Gordon B. BA, Oklahoma City U., 1926. With Am. 1st Trust Co., Oklahoma City, 1927-29; eastern rep. Philgas Phillips Petroleum Co., N.Y.C., 1929-42; pres. Fuelite Natural Gas Corp., Lexington, Mass., 1935-54, Thomas Assocs., Inc., Westfield, N.J., 1942—, Thomas Cons. Co., Inc., Westfield, 1942—, Pa. & So. Gas Co. and 12 subs., Westfield, 1943-58, Suburban Fuel Tank Car Co., Westfield, 1943-87, Yankee Bottled Gas Co., Lexington, 1944-54, Continental Tank Car Co., Westfield, 1945—, Eastern Bottled Gas Co., Lexington, 1950-54; mng. ptnr. Thomas Bldg. Ltd., Westfield, 1966—; pres. Cowperthwaite Co., Westfield, 1969—; mng. ptnr. Hetsons Ltd., Westfield, 1976-87; bd. dirs. Cen. Jersey Bank & Trust Co., Freehold, N.J. Co-author: Butane-Propane Handbook, 1932, Industrial Fire Hazards Handbook, 1979; contbr. articles to industry mags. Pres., bd. dirs., trustee YMCA, Westfield, 1948-88; mayor, councilman Town of Westfield, 1950-61; bd. dirs. Children's Specialized Hosp., Mountainside, N.J., 1954-70; mem. N.J. Rep. Com., 1959-60. Recipient Citizenship award B'nai B'rith, 1984. Mem. Nat. LP Gas Assn. (Disting. Service award 1954), Nat. Propane Gas Assn. (bd. dirs. 1932—, pres. 1935-36, Disting Service award 1954), Compressed Gas Assn. (bd. dirs. 1930—, pres. 1943, 50 Yr. Service award 1982), Am. Gas Assn. (award of merit 1956), ASME, Soc. Fire Protection Engrs., Nat. Fire Protection Assn. (Disting. Service award 1982), Echo Lake Country Club (pres., bd. dirs. 1961-64), Rotary (Charles P. Bailey Humanitarian award 1988). Office: Thomas Cons Co Inc 200 North Ave E Westfield NJ 07091

THOMAS, JAMES RAYMOND, accountant; b. Aberdeen, Wash., Jan. 22, 1947; s. Haywood and Ada Elnora (Gerhardt) T.; m. Brenda Kay West, May 30, 1970 (div. Aug. 1981); children: Ronald James, Wendy Gayle; m. Mary Ann Williamson, Nov. 20, 1981. AA, Wharton (Tex.) County Jr. Coll., 1967; BBA, U. Houston, 1970. CPA, Tex. Staff acct. Ernst & Whinney, Houston, 1970-71; acct. C&K Petroleum, Inc., Houston, 1972-73; controller The Analysts, Inc., Houston, 1973; home builder Mountain Estates Constrn. Co., Cripple Creek, Colo., 1974-75; intermediate acct. Tenneco Realty, Inc., Houston, 1975-77; asst. controller Weingarten Realty, Inc., Houston, 1977-78; ptnr. Thomas Snyder MacAllister & Co., Pearland, Tex., 1978-86; pvt. practice acctg. Friendswood, Tex., 1986—. Contbr. articles to newspapers. Bd. dirs., treas. Tri-County YMCA, Pearland, sustaining mem., 1986-87; ambassador Pearland-Hobby C. of C., 1984-85, Friendswood C. of C., 1986-87; mem. founding bd. dirs. Pearland Multi-Services Ctr. United Way. Mem. Am. Inst. CPAs, Tex. Soc. CPAs, Houston Chpt. CPAs, Bass Busters of Houston, Rotary (bd. dirs. Pearland Club 1983-86, pres. 1986-87, dist. 589 com. mem. 1986-87, Paul Harris fellow 1987). Republican. Methodist.

Home: 10515 Sagewind Ln Houston TX 77089 Office: 211 E Parkwood Suite 210 Friendswood TX 77546

THOMAS, JIMMY LYNN, financial executive; b. Mayfield, Ky., Aug. 3, 1941; s. Alben Stanley and Emma Laura (Alexander) T.; m. Kristin H. Kent, Oct. 1986; children: James Nelson, Carter Danforth. BS, U. Ky., 1963; MBA, Columbia U., 1964. Fin. analyst Ford Motor Co., Detroit, 1964-66; asst. treas. Joel Dean Assocs., N.Y.C., 1966-67; asst. controller Trans World Airlines, N.Y.C., 1967-73; v.p. fin. svcs., treas. Gannett Co., Inc., Arlington, Va., 1973—; bd. dirs. Marine Midland Bank, Rochester, Charlevoix Paper Co., Arkwright Boston Mut. Ins. Co.-Atlantic Region, Brown Devel. Co., Newspaper Printing Corp., Pacific Media, Inc., Guam Publs., Gannett Supply Corp., Gannett Fla. Corp., Gannett Pacific Corp. Treas. Frank E. Gannett Found. Served with AUS, 1967-68. Ashland Oil Co. scholar, 1959-63, McKinsey scholar 1964; Samuel Bronfman fellow, 1963-64. Mem. U. Ky. Alumni Assn., Columbia U. Alumni Assn., Fin. Execs. Inst., Inst. Newspaper Controllers and Fin. Officers, Nat. Press Club bldg. (bd. dirs.), Country Club, Genessee Valley Club, Georgetown Club, Washington Golf and Country Club, Beta Gamma Sigma, Omicron Delta Kappa, Sigma Alpha Epsilon. Democrat. Mem. Christian Ch. (Disciples of Christ). Home: 100 Gibbon St Alexandria VA 22314 Office: Gannett Co Inc PO Box 7858 Washington DC 20044

THOMAS, JOEL JAMES, treasurer, accountant; b. South Pasadena, May 10, 1957; s. Keith Frederick and Avis LaVana (Crockett) T.; m. Michelle Deborah Roesler, July 15, 1984; 1 child, Graham. BS, Calif. State U., L.A., 1979; MBA, U. So. Calif., 1985. CPA, Calif. Auditor David McFadden, CPA, Pasadena, Calif., 1977-79; with audit and tax svc. Peat, Marwick, Mitchell & Co., L.A., 1979-83; asst. controller Community Bank, L.A., 1983-84; chief fin. officer Codecard, Inc., Irvine, Calif., 1984-86; treas. Associated Group Adminstrs., Newport Beach, Calif., 1985-86, Conversion Industries, Inc., Pasadena, 1986—; bd. dirs. Perennial Energy, Inc., West Plains, Md. Mem. Am. Inst. CPA's, Calif. Soc. CPA's. Office: Conversion Industries Inc 101 E Green St Ste 14 Pasadena CA 91105

THOMAS, JON CAYSON, financial advisor, real estate developer; b. St. Louis, June 22, 1947; s. Jefferson C. and Edna W. Thomas; B.S., U. Mo., 1971; M.B.A., So. Ill. U., 1978; m. Alma DeBasio, Aug. 31, 1968; children—Jennifer Anne, Jon Cayson, II. Div. mgr. pensions and mut. funds Safeco Securities Co./Safeco Life Ins. Co., St. Louis, 1970-74; v.p. fin. planning dept. A.G. Edwards & Sons, Inc., St. Louis, 1974-77; pres. Intermark Assets Group Inc., St. Louis, 1978—; v.p. Hammond Dist. Co., 1983—; chmn. Comml. Security BancShares, 1987—. Mem. Internat. Coun. of Shopping Ctrs., Internat. Assn. Fin. Planners, Inst. Cert. Fin. Planners, Beta Theta Pi. Office: Intermark Inc PO Box 31971 1655 Des Peres Rd Ste 325 Saint Louis MO 63131

THOMAS, LACY LLOYD, academic administrator; b. Memphis, Nov. 13, 1956; s. Albert L. and Lucille (McDaniel) T.; m. Margaret Allen, July 11, 1981; 1 child, Joshua L. BS in Acctg., Chgo. State U., 1978. CPA, Ill. Sr. asst. staff acct. Deloitte Haksins & Sells CPa's, Chgo., 1978-79; systems analyst Evang. Hosp. Assn., Oak Brook, Ill., 1980-81; project leader, sr. acctg. analyst Michael Reese Hosp. and Med. Ctr., Chgo., 1981-84; asst. v.p., controller Miles Sq. Health Ctr., Inc., Chgo., 1984-87; assoc. vice chancellor fin. City Colls. of Chgo., 1987—; adj. prof. acctg. Chgo. State U., 1987; bd. dirs. Specialty Care Devel. Corp., Ghog. Active Temple of Brotherly Love Community Ch. Mem. Ill. Soc. CPA's, Nat. Assn. Black Accts. (pres. 1980-82). Democrat. Office: City Colls of Chgo 226 W Jackson Chicago IL 60606

THOMAS, LEO, pension, insurance and executive compensation consultant; b. Los Angeles, July 5, 1947; s. Leonard and Rose (Morris) T.; m. Bernice Roberts, Aug. 19, 1969; 1 child, Tod. BA, Occidental Coll., Los Angeles, 1968. With pub. relations com. Dem. Party, Los Angeles, 1968-69; ins. agt. Prudential Co., Los Angeles, 1969-77; fin. estate mgr. Hansch Fin. Group, Los Angeles, 1970—; pres. Thomas Fin. and Ins. Services, Inc., Los Angeles, 1980—; cons. Fin. Adv. Clinic, Los Angeles, 1982-84, Fin. Digest, Los Angeles, 1983-88, Life Ins. Leaders Round Table, Los Angeles, 1984-86. Contbr. articles to profl. jours. Mem. Nat. Tax Limitation Com., Washington, 1982-85, So. Poverty Law Council, Atlanta, 1982-88; charter mem. Statue of Liberty-Ellis Island Found., 1984-88; past pres. Young Dems., 1967. Named Agt. of Yr., Los Angeles Life Underwriters, 1983, 84, 85. Mem. Internat. Assn. Fin. Planners, Am. Soc. CLU's, Internat. Forum, Top of the Table, First Fin. Resources Group. Jewish. Lodge: Kiwanis (bd. dirs. Los Angeles chpt. 1983-85). Office: Thomas Fin and Ins Svc Inc 5900 Wilshire 17 Los Angeles CA 90036

THOMAS, LEO J., manufacturing company executive; b. Grand Rapids, Mich., Oct. 30, 1936; s. Leo John and Christal (Dietrich) T.; m. Joanne Juliani, Dec. 27, 1958; children: Christopher, Gregory, Cynthia, Jeffrey. Student, Coll. St. Thomas, 1954-56; BS, U. Minn., 1958; MS, U. Ill., 1960, PhD, 1961. Research chemist Research Labs., Rochester, N.Y., 1961-67, head, 1967-70, asst. div. head color photography div., 1970-72, tech. asst. to dir., 1972-75, asst. dir., 1975-77, v.p., dir., 1977-78, sr. v.p., dir., 1978-84, 1984-85; gen. mgr. Life Scis., Rochester, N.Y., 1984-85, sr. v.p., gen. mgr., 1985—; bd. dirs. Rochester Telephone Corp., Norstar Bank, John Wiley and Sons Inc., N.Y.C.; vice-chmn. Sterling Drug Inc., chmn., 1988—. Mem. Nat. Acad. Engring., Am. Inst. Chem. Engrs., AAAS, NRC (bd. cooperative sci. and tech.), Rochester C. of C. Office: 90 Park Ave New York NY 10016 also: Sterling Drug Inc 90 Park Ave New York NY 10016

THOMAS, MARK ALAN, SR., financial consultant; b. Urania, La., July 24, 1955; s. Haze Wilson and Doris Grace (Sappington) T.; m. Martha McQuown Quinn, Jan. 12, 1980; children: Mark Alan Jr., Ellison Elizabeth. BA, La. State U., 1978; MBA in Fin., U. Southwestern La., 1985. Cert. fin. planner. Fin. cons. Horizon Fin. Planning, Lafayette, La., 1985—; mgr. money Internat. Money Mgmt. Group Inc., Lafayette, 1985—. Author: short story Answered Prayer, 1986. Mem. Internat. Assn. Fin. Planning, Inst. Cert. Fin. Planners, Greater Lafayette C. of C., Sigma Chi Alumni Assn. (treas. 1985). Democrat. Home: 200 Dryades Ln Lafayette LA 70503 Office: Horizon Fin Planning 141 Ridgeway Dr Lafayette LA 70503

THOMAS, MICHAEL ERIC, utility company executive; b. Portland, Maine, Sept. 30, 1959; s. Henry C. and Ingrid M. (Lind) T.; children: Krista, Erik, Allison. BA, Bowdoin Coll., 1981; MBA, U. So. Maine, 1988. Fin. trainee Cen. Maine Power, Augusta, 1981-82, fin. analyst, 1982-84, sr. fin. analyst, 1985-86, dir. treasury ops., 1986—; budget analyst G.H. Bass & Co./Cheseborough Ponds, Falmouth, Maine, 1984-85. Mem. Nat. Investor Relations Inst. Office: Cen Maine Power Edison Dr Augusta ME 04336

THOMAS, RICARDO D'WAYNE, financial services company executive; b. New Orleans, May 12, 1966; s. Leroy Henderson and Muriel (Ellis) T. BBA in Fin., Loyola U., 1988. Account exec. Pioneer Western Fin. Svc., Metairie, La., 1984-86, dist. v.p., 1986-87; pres., fin. cons. Thomas-Waddell & Assocs., Inc., Metairie, 1987—. Louis J. Twomey acad. scholar, 1984. Mem. Internat. Assn. Fin. Planning, Delta Sigma Pi, Masons. Democrat. Baptist. Office: Thomas-Waddell & Assocs Inc 3000 Kingman St Ste 208 Metairie LA 70006

THOMAS, RICHARD KING, correspondent; b. Detroit, Jan. 19, 1931; s. Charles Richard and Nellie Clare (Davis) T.; m. Sigrid Maria-Stella von Bremen; children: Karina, Stryk. BA in English Lit., U. Mich., 1952, postgrad., 1956-57; postgrad., U. Frankfurt/Main, Fed. Republic of Germany, 1955. Instr. English U. Mich., Ann Arbor, 1956-57; night mgr. Mich. UPI, Detroit, 1957-59; mem. pub. affairs. staff McGraw Hill Pub. Co., N.Y.C., 1959-60; fin. editor N.Y. Post, 1960-62; writer, editor Newsweek Mag., N.Y.C., 1962-70; chief econ. corr. Newsweek Mag., Washington, 1970—. Panelist various TV shows including Washington Week in Rev., Meet the Press, shows on Sta. WETA-TV, others. With U.S. Army, 1952-55. Poynter fellow Yale U., 1975. Mem. White House Corrs. Assn. Home: 9801 Sotweed Dr Potomac MD 20854 Office: Newsweek Inc 1750 Pennsylvania Ave NW Ste 1220 Washington DC 20006

THOMAS, RICHARD L., banker; b. Marion, Ohio, Jan. 11, 1931; s. Marvin C. and Irene (Harruff) T.; m. Helen Moore, June 17, 1953; children: Richard L., David Paul, Laura Sue. BA, Kenyon Coll., 1953; postgrad. (Fulbright scholar), U. Copenhagen, Denmark, 1954; MBA (George F. Baker scholar), Harvard U., 1958. With First Nat. Bank Chgo., 1958—, asst. v.p., 1962-63, v.p., 1963-65; v.p., gen. mgr. First Nat. Bank Chgo. (London (Eng.) br.), 1965-66; v.p. term loan div. First Nat. Bank Chgo. (London br.), 1968, vice-chmn. bd., 1973-75, pres., dir., 1975—; sr. v.p., gen. mgr. First Chgo. Corp., 1969-72, exec. v.p., 1972-73, vice chmn. bd., 1973-74, pres., 1974—, also dir., 1973-74; dir. CNA Fin. Corp., Sara Lee Corp., Chgo. Bd. Options Exchange. Trustee, past chmn. bd. trustees Kenyon Coll.; trustee Rush-Presbyn.-St. Luke's Med. Ctr.; trustee Northwestern U.; chmn. bd., Orchestral Assn. With AUS, 1954-56. Mem. Chgo. Coun. Fgn. Rels. (bd. dir.), Phi Beta Kappa, Beta Theta Pi. Clubs: Sunningdale Golf (London); Economic (past pres.), Commercial, Chicago, Casino, Mid-America (Chgo.); Indian Hill (Winnetka, Ill.); Old Elm (Ft. Sheridan, Ill.). Office: 1st Chgo Corp 1 1st Nat Plaza Chicago IL 60670 *

THOMAS, RICHARD STEPHEN, financial executive; b. Mason City, Iowa, June 5, 1949; s. H. Idris and Mildred (Keen) T.; m. Pamela Jane Chipka, Sept. 11, 1982. AA, No. Iowa Community Coll., 1969; BA, U. No. Iowa, 1971. Cost acct. Boise Cascade, Mason City, Iowa, 1971-72; cost acct. mgr. Boise Cascade, Shippensburg, Pa., 1973-74; staff acct. Grumman Corp., Williamsport, Pa., 1974-76; acctg. mgr. Pullman Power Products, Williamsport, 1976-79; treas, controller Schweizer Dipple Inc., Cleve., 1979-87; treas., corp. controller Langenau Mfg. Co., Cleve., 1987—, chief fin. officer, 1987—; sec.-treas. World Trade Wins Inc., Cleve., 1987—; bd. dirs. Dover Co., Westlake, Ohio, Langenau Mfg. Co., World Trade Wins Inc.; pres., chmn. bd. dirs. and chief exec. officer R.S. Thomas and Assocs. Mem. employer adv. com. Ohio Job Svc., Greater Cleve. Growth Assn. Mem. Nat. Assn. Accts. (controller's council, 1985—), Constrn. Fin. Mgmt. Assn., Am. Assn. Indsl. Investors, Am. Acctg. Assn. (profl. relations com. 1986-87), Westshore Businessman's Assn. (v.p.), Internat. Platform Assn., Nat. Assn. Corp. Dirs., Nat. Assn. Corp. Treas., Nat. Treas.'s Assn., Cleve. Treas.'s Assn., Ctr. Interdisciplinary Research Info. Systems (acct. research com., research assoc.), Porsche Club Am., Phi Beta Lambda. Republican. Lodges: Masons (local treas. 1984—), York Rite Bodies. Home: 22597 Locust Ln Rocky River OH 44116 Office: Langenau Mfg Co 7306 Madison Ave Cleveland OH 44102

THOMAS, ROBERT KNOLL, electrical products manufacturing company executive; b. Niagara Falls, Ont., Can., Sept. 16, 1933; came to U.S., 1979; s. Robert Samuel and Florence Lorinda (Lockhart) T.; m. Catherine Ann McLeod, Dec. 24, 1955; children: Kimberley Ann, Carey Lynn, Robert Scott, Thomas McLeod. Elec. degree, Ryerson Inst. Tech., 1953. Vice-pres. sales Allen-Bradley Can., Cambridge, Ont., 1971-73; exec. v.p., gen. mgr. Allen-Bradley Can., Cambrige, 1973-76; pres., chief exec. officer Allen-Bradley Can., Cambridge, 1976-79; corp. v.p., pres., gen. mgr. indsl. control div. Allen-Bradley Co., Milw., 1979-81, corp. exec. v.p., 1981—; dir. Rostone Can. Ltd., Elmira, Ont., 1974-77, Intergrated Power Systems Ltd., Houston, 1980-82, Allen-Bradley Can. Ltd., Cambridge, Ont., 1971—; chmn. bd. Allen-Bradley Co., Cambridge, Ont., 1981—; dir. AB Stromberg, Inc., AB Denso Co. Ltd., Tokyo. Bd. dirs. Canadian Games for Physically Disabled, Cambridge, 1976; chmn. Can-Amera Games, 1976-78; bd. dirs. ARC, Milw., 1981—, Wis. State Coun. Econ. Edn., 1982—. Mem. Canadian Mfg. Assn., Canadian Elec. Mfg. Assn., Nat. Elec. Mfg. Assn., Rotary. Presbyterian. Home: 9000 N WHite Oak Ln Apt 218 Milwaukee WI 53217 Office: Allen-Bradley Co 1201 S 2nd St Milwaukee WI 53204

THOMAS, ROBERT LEE, financial services company executive, consultant; b. San Antonio, Dec. 29, 1938; s. Lawrence Grant and Mabel Louise (Carlson) T.; m. Terry Eileen Morgan, Dec. 14, 1972; 1 child, Evan Grant. Cert., Am. Coll., 1984, 85, Coll. Fin. Planning, 1985. Various middle mgmt. positions Gen. Fin. Corp., Dallas, 1962-65; full charge mgmt. positions TransAm. Fin. Corp., Dallas, 1965-74; sr. agt. Am. Security Life, San Antonio, 1974-81; chmn., pres. Thomas Fin. Services, Inc., Dallas, 1981—; mem. adv. bd. Hatfield & Hatfield, Inc., Dallas, 1981—, Am. Security Life, 1977—, Cumberworth & Turner, Dallas, 1984—; frequent guest on internat. and nat. talk shows. Fin. profl. adv. panel mem. Digest of Financial Planning Ideas mag., 1984; designer, creator presentations in field; regular recorder pub. service and promotional messages for non-profit orgns.; co-host weekly radio program, 1986—; contbr. articles to profl. jours. Sheparding group leader Meadowview Ch. Christ, Mesquite, Tex., 1983—, bible class tchr., 1978—, deacon, 1987—; regular spokesman pub. service and promotional messages various civic orgns.; chmn. charity telethon Million Dollar Round Table. Recipient Lone Star Leader award Tex. Assn. Life Underwriters, 1982—, Nat. Sales Achievement award, Nat. Quality award Nat. Assn. Life Underwriters, 1976—. Fellow Life Underwriting Tng. Council; mem. Dallas Estate Planning Council, Dallas Assn. Life Underwriters (chmn. health com. 1979-80), Internat. Assn. Fin. Planning, Am. Soc. CLUs, Am. Inst. Cert. Fin. Planners, Am. Assn. Fin. Profls., Million Dollar Round Table (life), Tex. Assn. Life Underwriters (life, lone star leader award, 1982—), Nat. Assn. Life Underwriters (nat. sales achievement award, 1976—, nat. quality award, 1976—), Nat. Arbitration Panel Better Bus. Bur., Gen. Agents and Mgmt. Assn. (yearling achievement, 1975), Internat. Platform Assn. Republican. Club: Dallas Christian Men's. Lodge: Lions. Office: Thomas Fin Svcs Inc 9330 LBJ Suite 900 Dallas TX 75243

THOMAS, ROBERT LLOYD, manufacturing company executive; b. Atlanta, Aug. 1, 1941; s. Orville Kermit Smith and Ina Evelyn (Farris) Peterson; m. Karen Degenhardt, Dec. 4, 1960 (div. Apr. 1978); children: John Harding, Gregory James, Kristen Ann; m. Mary Ellen Seaman, May 2, 1981; children: Lindsey Marian, Mark Gordon. BA in History, Queens Coll., 1969. Asst. buyer J.C. Penney Co. Inc., N.Y.C., 1964-70; sales mgr. Avon Products Inc., Atlanta, 1970-72; pres. Saul Bros. & Co. Inc., Atlanta, 1973—. Bd. dirs. Murphey Candler Little League, Atlanta, 1972, also bd. trustees; bd. dirs. Leukemia Soc., Atlanta, 1988—; mem. Dekalb County Exec. Com. Rep. Party, Atlanta, 1970-74; delegate State Convention Rep. Party, Atlanta, 1972. Mem. South East Textile & Apparel Mfrs., U.S. Polo Assn., Atlanta Polo Club, Gulfstream Polo Club, West Palm Beach. Republican. Roman Catholic. Home: 4095 Big Creek Overlook Alpharetta GA 30201 Office: Saul Bros & Co Inc 820 Spring St NW Atlanta GA 30308

THOMAS, ROBERT MORTON, JR., lawyer; b. Kansas City, Kans., Jan. 1, 1941; s. Robert Morton Sr. and Arlowyne Edith (Arganbright) T.; m. Rebecca Ann Myers, Aug. 21, 1965; children: Brooke J., Austin B. BA, U. Kans., 1962; LLB, Harvard U., 1966. Bar: N.Y., U.S. Dist. Ct. (so. dist.) N.Y., U.S. Ct. Appeals (2nd cir.). Local govt. advisor Republic of Botswana, Gaborone, 1966; dist. officer Republic of Botswana, Serowe, 1967; dist. commr. Republic of Botswana, Maur, 1968; assoc. Sullivan & Cromwell, N.Y.C., 1969-75, ptnr., 1975—; ptnr.-in-charge Sullivan & Cromwell, London, 1979-82; mng. ptnr. gen. practice group Sullivan & Cromwell, N.Y.C., 1986—. Mem. ABA, N.Y. State Bar Assn., Assn. of Bar of City of New York, Internat. Bar Assn., India House, Buck's Club. Republican. Presbyterian. Office: Sullivan & Cromwell 125 Broad St New York NY 10004

THOMAS, ROBERT RAY, management consultant; b. Columbus, Ohio, Dec. 14, 1926; s. Robert Ray and Esther Susan (Wolfe) T.; B.S. in TV Engring., Am. Inst. of Tech., 1950; m. Ann Lee Estes, Nov. 24, 1973; children—Sandra Ann, Robert Ray; 1 dau. by previous marriage, Margo Lynne. Electronic engr. Oakton Engring. Co., Evanston, Ill., 1949-50, Stewart Warner Corp., Chgo., 1950-51, Gen. Transformer Co., Homewood, Ill., 1951-53; electronic sales engr. Electronic Components Inc., Chgo., 1953-54; gen. mgr. West Coast, Miller Calson Services, Los Angeles, 1954-55; sales engr. R. Edward Steem Co., Chgo., 1955-59; dist. sales mgr. Motorola Semiconductor div. Motorola, Inc., Chgo. and Dallas, 1959-61; pres., chmn. bd. Enterprises Ltd. Co., Inc., Dallas, 1961—, pres. subs. Robert R. Thomas Co., 1961—, Rep. Mgmt. & Mktg. Counselors, 1969—; pres. Press Insulator Co., 1978—; co-founder CH&T Transformers Inc., 1983—; owner, pres. Westwood Creations, Inc., 1986—. Served with USAAF, 1945-46. Named Boss of Year, Big D chpt. Am. Bus. Womens Assn., 1965, Super Salesman by Purchasing Mag., Oct. 1975. Mem. Mfrs. Electronic Reps. Assn. (dir. S.W. chpt. 1964-69, pres. S.W. chpt. 1968-69), Sales and Mktg. Execs. of Dallas pres. (1977-78), S.W. Found. for Free Enterprise in Dallas (pres. 1976-77). Baptist. Lodge: Masons (Shriner). Office: 4134 Billy Mitchell Dr Dallas TX 75244

THOMAS, ROLAND GLENN, planning consultant; b. Peachland, N.C., Sept. 26, 1939; s. Onas Hall and Susie Ann (Tucker) T.; m. Kathleen Gail Turner, June 23, 1984. Student, U. N.C., Charlotte, 1964-67. Printing clk. N.C. Nat. Bank div. Am. Trust Co., Charlotte, 1957-59; sales rep. McKesson & Robbins Drug Co., Charlotte, 1959-70; prin. R. G. Thomas Co., Charlotte, 1970-79; v.p., ptnr. Store Fixtures & Planning Inc., Charlotte, 1973—. Served with U.S. Army Res., 1961-66. Mem. S.C. Pharm. Assn. (pres. traveling mems. aux. 1987-88, bd. dirs.), N.C. Pharm Assn. (pres. traveling mems. aux. 1977-78), N.C. Mus. History (com. establishing 1925 pharmacy). Republican. Presbyterian. Office: Store Fixtures & Planning Inc 3555 Tryclan Dr Charlotte NC 28217

THOMAS, TERENCE KYNETT, data processing executive; b. Opelika, Ala., Nov. 21, 1963; s. Theodore Kynett and Henrietta (Lockett) T. BS, Auburn U., 1986. Pres. Maquiladora Software Engring., Las Cruces, N.Mex., 1987-88; systems analyst Cap Gemini Am., Houston, 1988—. Mem. Am. Mgmt. Assn., Kappa Lapha Psi, Kappa Alpha Psi. Home: 11000 Kinghurst Dr #133 Houston TX 77099 Office: CAP Gemini AM 1700 W Loop S Ste 1200 Houston TX 77027

THOMAS, TRACEY ALECIA, financial analyst; b. Rochester, N.Y., June 22, 1962; d. Stanley J. Thomas and Claire Jean (Burgess) Wheeler. BS in Indsl. Engring., U. Pitts., 1983; MBA, Columbia U., N.Y.C., 1986. Computer programmer Eastman Kodak Co., Rochester, 1978-82; fin. analyst Rochester Products div. of Gen. Motors, Rochester, 1986-88; sr. fin. analyst overseas ops. Gen. Motors Corp., Detroit, 1988—. Speaker Explorers Boy Scouts Program, 1988, PRISM, 1986; counselor Career Beginnings Program, 1988; role model Brainpower, 1988. Recipient of GM fellowship Gen. Motors Corp., 1985, COGME fellowship, COGME, 1984. Mem. Nat. Assn. Female Execs., Inst. Indsl. Engrs. Democrat. Baptist. Office: GM 3044 W Grand Blvd Room 12-158 Detroit MI 48202

THOMAS, W(ILLIAM) BRUCE, steel and oil and gas company executive; b. Ripley, Mich., Oct. 25, 1926; s. William and Ethel (Collins) T.; m. Phyllis Jeanne Smith, June 25, 1950; 1 son, Robert William. BA magna cum laude, Western Mich. U., 1950; JD with distinction, U. Mich., 1952; postgrad., Law Sch., NYU, 1953. Bar: Mich. 1952. With USX Corp. (formerly U.S. Steel) and subs., various locations, 1952—; tax atty. Oliver Iron Mining Div., Duluth, Minn., 1952-53; tax atty., tax supr., comptroller Orinoco Mining Co., N.Y.C. and Venezuela, 1953-64; v.p. taxes Orinoco Mining Co., N.Y.C., 1967-70, v.p., asst. treas., 1970-71, v.p., treas., 1971-75; vice chmn., chief fin. officer, dir. Orinoco Mining Co., Pitts., 1982—; dir. Mfrs. Hanover Corp., Marathon Oil Co., Mfrs. Hanover Trust Co., DCNY Corp., Discount Corp. N.Y., Tex. Oil & Gas Corp., Quantum Chem. Corp. Bd. dirs. Duquesne U., Allegheny Gen. Hosp.; trustee Tax Found., Inc.; chmn. bd. dirs. Pa. Economy League; trustee Kenyon Coll., Com. Econ. Devel., Penn's SW Assn. Served with USAAF, 1943-45. Mem. ABA, Mich. Bar Assn., Fin. Execs. Inst., Greater Pitts. C. of C., Order of Coif, Duquesne Club, Pitts. Club, Laurel Valley Golf Club, Rolling Rock Club, Allegheny Country Club, Sky Club, Links, Belleair Country Club, Phi Alpha Delta. Methodist. Office: USX Corp 600 Grant St Pittsburgh PA 15219 also: 767 Fifth Ave New York NY 10153

THOMAS, WILLIAM JOHN, management consultant; b. N.Y.C., Apr. 20, 1945; s. John Clayton and Frances Theresa (O'Shea) T.; 1 child by previous marriage, Rebecca; m. Anna Katherine Barton, May 17, 1977; children: Sarah, Caitlin. BA, Cath. U. Am., 1967; MA, U. Md., 1971. Tchr. St. John's High Sch., Washington, 1968-70; asst. prof. St. Mary's Coll., Balt., 1970-75; mgr. U. Md. Univ. Coll., College Park, 1975-81; mgmt. cons. in pvt. practice Columbia, Md., 1981—; cons. in field. Co-author: Working with Men's Groups, 1983; co-editor: Team Building: The Other Side of Engineering, 1985; contbr. articles to profl. jours. Chmn. Episcopal Diocese of Md. Christian edn. com., 1982-85, cong. del., 1987—. N.Y. State Regent's scholar, 1962; NDEA grad. fellow, U. Md., 1967; recipient Cert. of Merit, U.S. Gen. Acctg. Office, 1982. Fellow Consortium of Univs. of Washington Met. Area; mem. Mid-Atlantic Assn. for Tng. and Cons. Home and Office: 5138 Durham Rd W Columbia MD 21044

THOMAS-BRUMMÉ, MARTY, university director; b. Cedar Rapids, Iowa, Mar. 31, 1951; s. Carl Andre and Rose Emma (Woker) Brummé; m. Melissa Jane Thomas, Oct. 17, 1987. BS, Mansfield (Pa.) U., 1973; EdM, Millersville (Pa.) U., 1982. Tchr. Brussels Am. Schs., 1973-76; project officer Community Youth Support Scheme, Sterling, Australia, 1977-78; coach basketball devel. Whangarei (New Zealand) Basketball Assn., 1979; asst. dir. housing Elizabethtown (Pa.) Coll., 1982-85; asst. dir. residential life LaSalle U., Phila., 1985-88; asst. to dean of students Temple U., Phila., 1988—; cons. PEP Ctr. Temple U., Phila., 1987—. Conflict mediator Good Shepherd Neighborhood House, Phila., 1986—, Landlord and Tenant Ct., Phila., 1987—; leader Kensington Young Life, Phila., 1987—; com. chmn. The Chem. People, Elizabethtown, 1984-85. Mem. Mid-Atlantic Assn. Univ. and Coll. Housing Officers (chmn. edn. programs 1987), Nat. Assn. Student Pers. Adminstrs., Am. Coll. Pers. Assn., Internat. Brotherhood Magicians, Coll. Consortium on Drugs and Alcoholism (chmn. tng. seminars 1985). Office: Temple U Dean of Students Office 207 Mitten Hall Philadelphia PA 19122

THOMAS-HARLESTON, TONYA DELONNETTE, banking executive; b. Phila., July 25, 1961; d. Ellis Tony and Dolly Cleo (Lawson) Thomas; m. Farrell Ray Harleston, May 9, 1987; 1 child, Farrella Tiara. BS in Bus. Adminstrn., Morgan State U., 1984; postgrad., U. Md., 1985—. With Md. Nat. Bank, Balt., 1979—, ops. clk. III, 1984-86, asst. supr. II, 1986—. Trustees Mt. Zion United Meth. Ch., Balt., 1988, mem. fin. com., 1987; mem. com. to re-elect Barbara Mikulski, Balt., 1986. Mem. NAFE, Am. Prodn. and Inventory Control Soc. Democrat. Home: 3644 Forest Garden Ave Baltimore MD 21207 Office: 225 N Calvert St Baltimore MD 21202

THOMASSY, GEORGE ERNEST, III, venture capitalist; b. Hanover, Pa., Mar. 2, 1941; s. George E. and Gertrude (Hemler) T.; m. Carole Ann Jordison, June 12, 1976. BSEE, U. Detroit, 1964; JD, Columbia U., 1968, MBA, 1969. Mem. staff Arthur D. Little, Inc., Cambridge, Mass., 1969-72; ptnr. Becker Technol. Assocs., N.Y.C., 1972-75; dir. mergers and acquisitions Am. Can Co., Greenwich, Conn., 1975-79; gen. ptnr. Regional Fin. Enterprises, Inc., New Canaan, Conn., 1979—; dir. Comprehensive Addiction Systems, McLean, Va., Implant Tech., Inc., Secacus, N.J., Jem Brands, Inc, Greenwich, Conn., Mana, Inc., Ann Arbor, Mich., Renaissance Health Care, Inc., Atlanta, Access Med. System, Inc., Branford, Conn., Va., Trinity Living Ctrs., Inc., Williamsburg, Va. Bd. dirs. Westover Road Assn., Stamford, Conn., 1978—. Club: Greenwich (Conn.) Country, Dutchess Valley Rod and Gun. Office: Regional Fin Enterprises Inc 36 Grove St New Canaan CT 06840

THOMAZIN, GEORGE H., food distribution company executive; b. 1940. BA, U. Nebr., 1962. With Supermarket Interstate Inc., 1962-73, v.p.; divisional mgr. Super Valu Stores, 1973-83; sr. v.p. Wetterau Inc., from 1983, exec. v.p., also pres. food distbn. group, 1985-88, pres., chief operating officer, 1988—, also bd. dirs. Office: Wetterau Inc 8920 Pershall Rd Hazelwood MO 63042 *

THOMOPOULOS, ANTHONY D., motion picture company executive. m. Cristina Ferrare; 4 children. B.S. in Fgn. Service, Georgetown U. With NBC, 1959-64; dir. fgn. sales, then v.p., exec. v.p. Four Star Entertainment Corp., 1964-70; dir. programming Selectavision div. RCA, 1970-71; v.p. TV mktg. Tomorrow Entertainment, 1971-73; with ABC, N.Y.C., 1973-85, v.p. prime time programs entertainment div., 1973-74, v.p. prime time TV creative ops., 1974-75, v.p. spl. programs, 1975-76, v.p. TV div., 1976-78, pres. entertainment div., 1978-83, pres. Broadcast Group, 1983-85; pres. motion picture and TV groups United Artists Corp., Beverly Hills, Calif., 1985-86; chmn., chief exec. officer United Artists Pictures, Beverly Hills, 1986—. Office: United Artists Corp 450 Roxburry Dr Beverly Hills CA 90210

THOMPSEN, GAYLE SUSAN, accountant; b. Albuquerque, Sept. 29, 1953; d. Anderson Hassell and Sally Suzanne (Eckhart) Norton; m. Steven Roy Thompsen, June 25, 1978 (div. Oct. 1983); 1 child, Lisa Leigh; m. Steven Wayne Makowski, Nov. 21, 1987. B.B.A. in Acctg., Tex. Tech. U., 1975. C.P.A., Colo. Acct. Atlantic Richfield, Dallas, 1975-80; sr. cons. acct. Anaconda Minerals, Denver, 1980-81; supr. revenue Petro-Lewis Corp.,

Denver, 1981-85; mgr. acctg. U.S. West Info. Systems, Denver, 1985-86, mgr. fin. planning, 1986—. Mem. Beta Alpha Psi, Phi Kappa Phi, Pi Beta Phi (sec. 1974-75). Home: 3374 S Tulare Ct Denver CO 80231 Office: US West Bus Resources Inc 6892 S Yosemite B100 Englewood CO 80112

THOMPSON, ARNOLD WILBUR, airport architect; b. Chgo., Oct. 26, 1926; s. Oscar and Emma S. (Terkelsen) T.; student U. Wis., 1944, U. Ky., 1945; B.S. in Architecture, U. Ill., 1950; m. Marian Harding, Dec. 30, 1950; children—Keith Arnold, Bruce Windsor, Douglas Scott. Project planner U.S. Public Housing Adminstrn., Chgo., 1950-52; cons. Bldg. and Furnishings Service YMCA, Chgo., 1952-55; regional architect Am. Airlines, Chgo., 1955-60, chief architect, 1960-64; pres. Arnold Thompson Assocs., Inc., N.Y.C., 1964-72; v.p. Lester B. Knight & Assocs., Inc., Riverside, Conn., 1972-77; pres. Arnold W. Thompson, P.C., Airport Facilities Cons., Hawthorne, N.Y., 1978-82; chmn. chief exec. officer Thompson/Crenshaw Inc., Reston, Va., Los Angeles, Washington, London, Miami, Fla., Chgo., 1982-85; chmn. Thompson Cons. Internat., Briarcliff Manor, N.Y., Dallas, Los Angeles, Brussels, 1985—; chmn. bd. Potomac Assocs. Inc., Reston. Mem. New Castle Bd. Zoning Appeals, 1977-79; chmn. Chappaqua (N.Y.) Bd. Continuing Edn., 1980-86; bd. dirs. Bethel Nursing Home Corp., 1974-78. Served with U.S. Army, 1944-46. Registered profl. architect, N.Y., Conn., Fla., Ill., Ind., Ky., Mass., N.C., Pa., Va., Tex., also Nat. Council Archtl. Bds. Mem. AIA, ASCE, Am. Inst. Planners, Airport Cons. Council, Scarab. Congregationalist. Clubs: Wings (N.Y.C.); Whippoorwill (Armonk, N.Y.); Birchwood (Chappaqua). Office: Thompson Consultants Internat 575 N State Rd Briarcliff Manor NY 10510 also: 11733 Bowman Green Reston VA 22092 also: 452 NE 39th St Miami FL 33137 also: 8429 S Sepulveda Blvd Los Angeles CA 90065

THOMPSON, AUGUSTUS ROSCOE, JR., financial planner; b. Durham, N.C., July 29, 1949; s. Augustus R. Sr. and Lillian L. (Patterson) T. BS, N.C. State U., 1971; MS, Case Western Res. U., 1977. Cert. fin. planner. Systems engr. GE, Cin., 1977-78; sr. mem. staff Advanced Tech. Inc., Arlington, Va., 1979-86; pres. ART Fin. Svcs., Durham, 1986—. Bd. dirs. Auburn Village, 1982-86. HFS fellow Case Western Res. U., 1975-76; named Outstanding Young Man of Am., Jaycees, 1985. Mem. Internat. Assn. Fin. Planners, Inst. Cert. Fin. Planners, Durham C. of C. Office: ART Fin Svcs 1106 W Cornwallis Rd Ste 201 Durham NC 27705

THOMPSON, BARBARA JEAN, real estate sales associate; b. Redford, Mo., Dec. 2, 1943; d. Denver and Cliffie (Amsden) Pogue; m. Earl Eugene Thompson, June 8, 1968; children: Earl Eugene, Alan. Typist Merc. Commerce Nat. Bank, St. Louis, 1961-63; sec. RCA, Clayton, Mo., 1963-69, Williams Bros., Tulsa, 1975-78, Alternate Energy Systems, Inc., Tulsa, 1978-81; sales assoc. Merrill Lynch Realty, Tulsa, 1983—. Mem. Womens Coun. Realtors (chpt. pres. 1988). Republican. Methodist. Home: 7515 S Erie St Tulsa OK 74136

THOMPSON, BJORN J., food products company executive, mechanical engineer; b. Madison, Wis., June 9, 1934; s. Frederick and Marie (Olsen) T.; m. Gail Michele Olwell, July 27, 1957; children—Kai, Kristin, Kirk. B.S. in Mech. Engring., U. Wis., 1957; A.M.P., Harvard U., 1983. Registered profl. engr., Wis. Plant layout and materials handling supr. Madison plant OM Foods Corp., Wis., 1960-66; supr. Davenport plant Oscar Mayer Foods Corp., Iowa, 1966-67; corp. methods and planning coordinator Oscar Mayer Foods Corp., Madison, 1967-71, corp. facilities planning mgr., 1971-74, gen. mgr. facilities planning mgr., 1974-78, v.p. engring. devel., 1978-84; v.p. fresh meat ops. Oscar Mayer Foods Corp., 1984—, group v.p. tech. services, 1985—, sr. v.p. tech. services, 1987—, sr. v.p. strategic planning and bus. devel., 1988—. Trustee bd. Village of Maple Bluff, Wis., 1979-83. Served to lt. C.E., U.S. Army, 1957-59. Recipient Disting. Service citation U. Wis. Madison, 1984. Mem. Am. Material Handling Soc. (pres. 1964-65, bd. dirs. 1965-66), Inst. Indsl. Engrs. Clubs: Maple Bluff Country (bd. dirs. 1981-83, v.p. 1983—, pres. 1984), Madison. Office: Oscar Mayer Foods Corp PO Box 7188 Madison WI 53707

THOMPSON, BRUCE EDWARD, JR., corporate executive, former government official; b. Cleve., June 5, 1949; s. Bruce Edward and Mary Ruth (Miller) T.; m. Kathleen Ann Vaughn, May 27, 1972; children: Lesley, Bret. B.S.B.A. in Fin., Georgetown U., 1971. Sr. analyst Govt. Research Corp., Washington, 1971-74; legis. asst. U.S. Sen. William V. Roth Jr., 1974-81; dep. asst. sec. legis. affairs U.S. Treasury Dept., 1981-83, asst. sec. bus. and consumer affairs, 1983-84, asst. sec. legis. affairs, 1984-86; v.p., dir. govt. relations Merrill Lynch & Co., Inc., 1986—. Staff dir. fiscal and monetary affairs subcom. Republican Platform Com., 1980; adviser Pres. Reagan's Tax Policy Task Force; asst. Pres. Reagan's Transition Hqrs., 1980. Roman Catholic. Office: Merrill Lynch & Co Inc 1828 L St NW Washington DC 20036

THOMPSON, CHARLES EDWIN, import consultant and manufacturer; b. Chgo., July 1, 1938; s. J. Edwin and H. Loraine (Jirasek) T. BS in Bus., Loyola U., Chgo., 1960, postgrad., 1968; postgrad., Northwestern U., 1961-62. Sales agt. J. Hudson & Co., Birmingham, Eng., 1968—; pres. Thompson Corp., Oak Park, Ill., 1977—, Hiatt-Thompson Corp., Oak Park, Ill., 1984—, Impact Prodns., Albuquerque, 1988—; v.p. Refast Systems Corp., Palatine, Ill., 1988—; bd. dirs. Mktg. Matters Inc., Elk Grove Village, Ill.; v.p. REFAST Systems Corp. Inventor type of handcuffs. Bd. dirs. Marion Gardens Condominium Assn., Oak Park, 1987—. Served to 1st lt. U.S. Army, 1961-63. Mem. Fraternal Order Police (hon.). Office: PO Box 306 River Forest IL 60305

THOMPSON, CURTIS BROOKS, manufacturing company executive; b. Conway, Ark., Feb. 8, 1930; s. Curtis Barnabus and Clara Brooks (Terry) T.; m. Sally Talbert, Apr. 12, 1952; children—Cheryl, Nan, Gary. B.S.E.E., Purdue U., 1951, M.S.E.E., 1952. With Honeywell Inc., Mpls., 1952—; v.p.-ops. process control div. Honeywell Inc., Fort Washington, Pa., 1968-72; v.p. and gen. mgr. test instruments div. Honeywell Inc., Denver, 1972-76; v.p. corp. devel. Honeywell Inc., Mpls., 1976-79; v.p. indsl. products group Honeywell Inc., 1979-82, sr. corp. v.p., 1983-85, group v.p. components, 1986-88, sr. v.p. indsl., 1989—. Recipient Disting. Engring. Alumnus award Purdue U., 1981. Mem. IEEE, Instrument Soc. Am. Home: 4210 Chimo E Deephaven MN 55391 Office: Honeywell Inc Honeywell Plaza Minneapolis MN 55408

THOMPSON, DEAN ALLAN, cattleman; b. Peru, Ind., Jan. 29, 1934; s. Paul Franklin and Pauline St. Clair (Thrush) T. Student Purdue U., 1952-54. Mgr. Thompson Farms, breeders registered Hereford cattle, Peru, 1956-69; owner Thompson Farms, Wartrace, Tenn. and Peru, 1970-87, Dean Thompson Prodns., Wartrace, Wartrace Records; chmn. bd. Instant Copy and Printing, Inc., Monterrey, Calif., 1976-86, Trenton Energy Inc., 1977-83, Bloomfield, Ind.; v.p., dir. 5B Cattle Co., Twin Bridges, Mont., 1986-87; ptnr., Brann-Thompson Ltd.; internat. beef cattle judge; dir. Maine Manna, Gorham. Bd. dirs. Thrush-Thompson Found. (formerly H.A. Thrush Found.), Peru; trustee Middle Tenn. State U. Found., 1981-83, 85—, chmn. fin. com., 1982-83, 85-87, exec. com., 1983-89, sec. 1988, pres., 1989; precinct committeeman, chmn. Miami County (Ind.) Young Republican Com., 1962-67; elder Presbyn. Ch., 1986-88. With U.S. Army, 1955-56. Mem. Nat. Western (dir.), Ind. (dir. 1958-68, pres. 1960) Polled Hereford Assns., Ind. Cattleman's Assn. (founding dir.), Ind. Livestock Breeders Assn., Am. Hereford Assn. (v.p. pres.'s coun. 1981, pres. 1982), Tenn. Hereford Assn. (dir. 1977-81, v.p. 1979, pres. 1980-81), Toastmasters (pres., area gov.), Columbia Club. Home and Office: 900 19th Ave S #1201 Nashville TN 37212

THOMPSON, GEOFFREY ACHESON, banker; b. White Plains, N.Y., Oct. 26, 1940; s. Frederick D. and Julia (Acheson) T.; m. Claudia Geyer, June 18, 1966; 1 dau., Marina. B.A., Columbia U., 1963; M.B.A., Harvard U., 1967. Circulation dir. Newsweek Internat., N.Y.C., 1967-70; assoc. Warburg, Paribas Becker, N.Y.C., 1970-72; v.p. Citicorp-Citibank, N.Y.C., 1972-78, Gen. Electric Credit, Stamford, Conn., 1978-81; pres. Marine Midland Bank Inc., Buffalo, 1981—, chief operating officer, 1981-88, pres., also bd. dirs., 1986—, chief exec. officer, 1988—; bd. dirs. The Hong Kong and Shanghai Banking Corp., Nordeman, Grimm Inc., N.Y.C.; pres., chief exec. officer Marine Midland Bank, N.A. Nat. assoc. Boys Clubs of Am., 1978; deacon Madison Ave Presbyn. Ch., 1975; trustee Buffalo Gen. Hosp., 1985. Served to lt. USN, 1963-65. Democrat. Presbyterian. Clubs: Harvard, University, N.Y. Athletic; Buffalo. Home: 23 Rock Ln Guilford CT 06437 Office: Marine Midland Banks Inc Marine Midland Bldg 140 Broadway New York NY 10015 also: Marine Midland Banks Inc 1 Marine Midland Ctr 24th fl Buffalo NY 14240 *

THOMPSON, GERALD JORDAN, management consultant; b. Shreveport, La., Apr. 1, 1930; s. Raymon Hudgins and Helen Ashford (Robinson) T.; m. Ann Zuehl, Oct. 25, 1954; children: Daniel Jordan, Amy Denman Mangum, Raymon Hudgins. BS, U.S. Naval Acad., 1952; MBA, Stanford U., 1960. Commd. ensign USN, 1952, advanced through grades to rear adm., 1977; comdg. officer naval supply ctr. USN, Bremerton, Wash., 1974-76; dir. contracts div. Naval Sea Systems Command, Arlington, Va., 1977-79; dep. dir. Def. Logistics Agy., Alexandria, Va., 1979-81; ret. USN, 1981; ptnr. Coopers & Lybrand, Washington, 1982—. Decorated Legion of Merit. Fellow Nat. Contract Mgmt. Assn.; mem. U.S. C. of C. (coun. chmn. 1985-87), Navy League, Profl. Services Council. Republican. Methodist. Office: Coopers & Lybrand 1525 Wilson Blvd 8th Floor Arlington VA 22209 Also: Coopers & Lybrand 1800 M St NW Washington DC 20036

THOMPSON, JACK EDWARD, mining company executive; b. Central City, Nebr., Nov. 17, 1924; s. Ray Elbert and Bessie Fay (Davis) T.; m. Maria del Carmen Larrea, May 8, 1948; children: Jack Edward, Ray Anthony, Robert Davis. Student, Northwestern U., 1942-43, Colo. Sch. Mines, 1944-45. V.p. Cía. Química Comercial de Cuba S.A., 1946-60, Cía. de Fomento Químico S.A., 1946-60; with Newmont Mining Corp., N.Y.C., 1960-85; asst. to pres. Newmont Mining Corp., 1964-67, v.p., 1967-71, dir., 1969-86, exec. v.p., 1971-74, pres., 1974-85, vice chmn., 1985-86, cons., 1986—; dir. Peabody Coal Co., Peabody Holding Co., Newmont Oil Co.; Chmn. bd. trustees Minerals Industry Ednl. Found. Recipient Distinguished Achievement medal Colo. Sch. Mines, 1974. Mem. Mining Club N.Y. (former chmn. bd. govs.), AIME, Mining and Metall. Soc. Am., Mining Club of SW (bd. govs.). Clubs: Tucson Country; Mid Ocean (Bermuda). Office: Newmont Mining Corp 200 Park Ave 36th Fl New York NY 10166

THOMPSON, JAMES HOMER, insurance agent, educator; b. Henrietta, Tex., Sept. 11, 1926; s. James Hite and Virginia (Marberry) T.; student U. Okla., 1944-45; Ph.B., U. Chgo., 1947, M.B.A., 1950; M.S. in Fin. Services, Am. Coll., Bryn Mawr, Pa., 1980; m. Ilene Kriss, Mar. 17, 1979; children by previous marriage—Julie A., Laurie J. Dist. sales mgr. Studebaker Corp., South Bend, Ind., 1951-55; assoc. gen. agt. State Mut. Life Assurance Co. Am., Denver, 1955—; instr. U. Colo. 1964—; mem. bd. Nat. C.L.U. Inst. Recipient J. Stanley Edwards award Colo. Ins. Industry, 1985, Alumni Service Citation, U. Chgo., 1987; Inst. Mem. cabinet U. Chgo.; mem. Colo. Ins. Adv. Bd., 1980—. C.L.U., C.P.C.U. Bd. dirs. Adult Edn. Council of Met. Denver, 1977. Mem. Am. Soc. C.L.U.s (v.p. Rocky Mountain chpt. 1967, pres. 1968-69, regional v.p. 1972-73), Denver Assn. Life Underwriters (dir. 1963-66). Home: 180 Ivanhoe St Denver CO 80220 Office: 44 Cook St Denver CO 80206-5898

THOMPSON, JAMES RICHARD, communications executive; b. Marion, Ohio, June 6, 1933; s. Wallace Wait and Mabel Ann (Maloney) T.; BS in Indsl. Mgmt., U. Dayton, 1956; m. Ann Bacon Hallett, Sept. 7, 1973; children—J. Matthew, Mark A. Personnel asst. wage and salary Gen. Tel. Co. Ohio, Marion, 1957-59, personnel asst. communications and devel., 1959-61; mgmt. devel. adminstr. GTE Svc. Corp., N.Y.C., 1961-62, personnel mgr., 1962-66, personnel adminstr., 1966-67, dir. staffing coordination, Stamford, Conn., 1971-75; dir. personnel GTE Communications, Inc., N.Y.C., 1967-71; bd. dir. labor rels. and compensation Gen. Tel. Co. S.W., San Angelo, Tex., 1975-78, v.p. human resources, 1978-88; asst. v.p. employee rels. and orgn. devel. GTE Tel. Ops., 1989—; mem. Tex. Employment Law Coun., Tex. A&M U. System Human Resources Adv. Coun. Mem. Dallas Personnel Assn., Am. Soc. Personnel Adminstrn., Internat. Platform Assn. Republican. Home: 2707 Wooded Trail Ct Grapevine TX 76051 Office: Williams Sq 5205 N O'Connor Blvd Irving TX 75039

THOMPSON, JAMES WILLIAM, banker; b. Dunn, N.C., June 18, 1939; s. William J. and Lucy (Pope) T.; m. Meredith Cromartie, June 10, 1961; children—Ann, Lucy, Bill. B.S. in Bus. Adminstrn., U. N.C., 1961. Credit analyst NCNB Corp., Charlotte, N.C., 1963-68; v.p., bond dept. mgr. NCNB Corp., 1968-71, investment portfolio mgr., 1971-74, sr. v.p., funds mgmt. exec., 1974-77, exec. v.p., 1977-83, corp. exec. v.p., 1983-85, vice chmn. bd., 1985—; chmn. Southeastern Banking, Charlotte, 1988—; bd. dirs. Mercy Hosp. Holding Co. Inc., Charlotte. Pres. Mint Mus. Charlotte; bd. dirs. YMCA, Charlotte, Found. Carolinas, Research Triangle Found. With USAF, 1961-63. Mem. Res. City Bankers Assn., Charlotte C. of C. (bd. dirs.). Democrat. Methodist. Home: 629 Llewellyn Pl Charlotte NC 28207 Office: NCNB Corp 1 NCNB Pla Charlotte NC 28255

THOMPSON, JANE JOHNSON, retail executive; b. Charleston, W.Va., July 13, 1951; d. Robert Paul and Phyllis Jane (Judson) Johnson; m. t. Stephen Thompson, Aug. 28, 1976; children: Robert Baker, Catherine Brooke. BBA, U. Cin., 1977; MBA, Harvard Coll., 1978. Brand mgr. Procter & Gamble, Cin., 1973-77; prin., ptnr. McKinsey & Co., Inc., Chgo., 1978-88; v.p. Sears Specialty Merchandising div. Sears Roebuck & Co., Chgo., 1988—. Bd. dirs. Lincoln Park Zool. Soc. Aux. 1988—. Baker scholar Harvard U., 1978. Office: Sears Roebuck & Co Sears Tower 702SSM BSC 37-21 Chicago IL 60684

THOMPSON, JERE WILLIAM, retail food company executive; b. Dallas, Jan. 18, 1932; s. Joe C. and Margaret (Philp) T.; m. Peggy Dunlap, June 5, 1954; children: Michael, Jere W., Patrick, Deborah, Kimberly, Christopher, David. Grad. high sch., 1950; B.B.A., U. Tex., 1954. With Southland Corp., Dallas, 1954—; v.p. stores Southland Corp. (merged with Thompson Co. 1988), Dallas, 1962-73, exec. v.p., 1973-74, pres., 1974—, dir., 1962—, chief exec. officer, 1986—; bd. dirs. MCorp, Aris Corp. Bd. dirs. St. Paul Hosp. Found. Served to lt. (j.g.) USNR, 1954-56. Office: Southland Corp 2828 N Haskell Ave Dallas TX 75221

THOMPSON, JOHN CLAYTON, investment company executive; b. Richmond, Va., Sept. 8, 1941; s. Clayton Monroe and Mildred (Briggs) T.; m. Marie H. Thompson, June 20, 1978; children: John, Benjamin, Clayton. BA in History, U. Va., 1964. Supr. key accounts Dun & Bradstreet, Raleigh, N.C., 1964-67; registered rep., account exec. Wheat, First Securities Inc., Richmond, 1967-74; mgr. bank investment service United Va. Bank, Richmond, 1974-76; v.p., mgr. bond group Studley Shupert Co. Inc., Phila., 1976-79; v.p., mgr. fixed income Provident Nat. Bank, Phila., 1979-81; chief exec. officer, dir. fixed income policy, portfolio mgr. HT Investors Inc., Providence, R.I., 1981-82, 83-85; sr. v.p. trust div. R.I. Hosp. Trust Nat. Bank, 1981-82, 83-85; chmn., mng. dir. Va. Capital Mgmt. Corp., Richmond, 1985—; chmn. bd. dirs. Mariner Funds Services, Deerfield Beach, Fla., 1987—; chmn., mng. dir. Newport Adv. Group, Providence, 1985-87; chmn., pres. J.C. Thompson & Assocs. Inc., Marlton, N.J., 1982—; chmn. Instl. Capital Mgmt. Corp., Marlton, 1982—; chmn., pres. Va. Local Govt. Investment Fund; past pres., trustee Trinity Liquid Assets Trust, Oxford Cash Mgmt. Fund, Prime Cash Fund; chmn., pres. Ocean State Tax Exempt Fund; pres. Mariner Funds Trust. Mem. Market Technicians Assn. (Palm Beach chpt.), U. Va. Alumni Assn., Bull and Bear Club. Office: Mariner Funds Svcs 600 W Hillsboro Blvd Ste 300 Deerfield Beach FL 33441

THOMPSON, JUUL HAROLD, lawyer, educator; b. Chgo., May 3, 1945; s. Jules Harold and Ruth Edith (Pudark) T.; m. Elizabeth Jean Bohler, Sept. 20, 1975; children: Michael, Erin, David, Margaret, Joseph. BA in History, U. Chgo., 1967; JD, U. Ill., 1973. Bar: Ill. 1973. Asst. states atty. Kane County, Ill., 1974-76; ptnr. Beck and Thompson, Batavia, Ill., 1976-82; sole practice, Batavia, 1983—; counsel Batavia Council on Aging, 1979—; counsel, grant chmn. Batavia Social Services Com., 1983-86; counsel Programming for Low Income and Urban Services Community Service Agy., Batavia, 1978-86; local collection counsel Alcoa Bldg. Products, Security Pacific Fin. Corp., I.C. Collection Systems St. Paul; instr. law Elgin Community Coll., Ill., 1981-84, Harper Community Coll., Palatine, Ill., 1981-83, Waubonsee Community Coll., Sugar Grove, Ill., 1982, Person Wollinsky CPA Rev. Course, Downers Grove, Ill., 1984. Mem. Holy Cross Cath. Ch. Parish Council, 1985-86; pres. A.G.S. PTO, 1986-88. Served as 1st lt. U.S. Army, 1969-71, Vietnam. Decorated Bronze Star (2). Mem. VFW (Batavia comdr. 1979-80, trustee 1985-86), Holy Cross Players. Republican. Lodge: K.C. (4th degree). Avocations: reading, woodworking, writing. Home: 341 N Jefferson St Batavia IL 60510 Office: 150 W Houston St PO Box 543 Batavia IL 60510

THOMPSON, LEE BENNETT, lawyer; b. Miami, Indian Ter., Mar. 2, 1902; s. P.C. and Margerie Constance (Jackson) T.; m. Elaine Bizzell, Nov. 27, 1928; children: Lee Bennett, Ralph Gordon, Carolyn Elaine (Mrs. Don T. Zachritz). B.A., U. Okla., 1925, LL.B., 1927. Bar: Okla. 1927. Since practiced in Oklahoma City; spl. justice Okla. Supreme Ct., 1967-68; past sec., gen. counsel, dir. Mustang Fuel Corp. Past sec. Masonic Charity Found. Okla.; past chmn. Okla. County chpt. ARC, past chmn. resolutions com. nat. conv.; founding mem. Dean's Council, U. Okla. Coll. Law; past dir. Oklahoma City Symphony Orch., Oklahoma City Community Fund. Served to col. AUS, 1940-46. Decorated Legion of Merit; recipient Distinguished Service citation U. Okla., 1971; Rotary Found. Paul Harris fellow. Fellow Am. Bar Found. (past Okla. chmn.), Okla. Bar Found., Am. Coll. Trial Lawyers (past Okla. chmn.); mem. Oklahoma City C. of C. (past bd. dirs.), Oklahoma City Jr. C. of C. (past pres.), U.S. Jr. C. of C. (past dir., v.p.), ABA (del. 1972, past mem. com. law and nat. security, past mem. spl. com. on fed. ct. procedure), Okla. Bar Assn. (past mem. ho. dels., pres. 1972, Pres.'s award, profl. responsibility commn.), Oklahoma County Bar Assn. (past pres.), Jour. Record award), Okla. Bar Found. (trustee 1971-76, 81-84), U. Okla. Alumni Assn. (past mem. exec. com.), U. Okla. Meml. Student Union (past pres., Greek Alumnus of Yr. award 1982), Oklahoma City Zool. Soc. (past bd. dirs.), Am. Judicature Soc., Mil. Order World Wars, Mil. Order Carabao, Am. Legion, Masons (33 degree), Shriners, Jesters, Rotary (past pres., Paul Harris fellow), Univ. Club, Men's Dinner Club (past exec. com.), Oklahoma City Golf and Country Club, Beacon Club, Phi Beta Kappa (Phi Beta Kappa of Yr. 1982), Beta Theta Pi (past v.p., trustee). Democrat. Mem. First Christian Ch. (past deacon, life elder). Home: 539 NW 38th St Oklahoma City OK 73118 Office: 2120 First Nat Bldg Oklahoma City OK 73102

THOMPSON, LEROY, JR., army reserve officer, radio engineer; b. Tulsa, July 7, 1913; s. LeRoy and Mary (McMurrain) T.; B.S. in Elec. Engring., Ala. Poly Inst., 1936; m. Ola Dell Tedder, Dec. 31, 1941; 1 son, Bartow McMurrain. Commd. 2d lt. U.S. Army Res., 1935, advanced through grades to col., 1963; signal officer CCC, 1936-40; radio engr. Officer Hdqrs. 4th C A., 1941; with signal sect. Hdqrs. Western Def. command and 4th Army, San Francisco, 1942, comdg. officer 234th Signal Ops. Co., 1942; asst. chief, chief signal corps ROTC U. Calif., Berkeley, 1942-43; radio engring. officer O.C. SigO War Dept., Washington, 1943; radio engring officer Hdqrs. 3105th Signal Service Co. Hdqrs. CBI, New Delhi, 1944; signal officer Hdqrs. Northern Combat Area Command, Burma, 1944; signal officer Hdqrs. OSS Det 101, Burma, 1945; signal officer Hdqrs. OSS, China, 1945, radio engr., tech. liaison officer, Central Intelligence Group, CIA, 1945-50; chief radio br. Hdqrs. FEC, Tokyo, 1950-53, chief radio engring br. Signal C Plant Engring. Agy., 1953-55; radio cons. to asst. dir. def. research and engring. communications, 1960-62; ret., 1973; pvt. research and devel. on communication and related problems, 1963—; owner Thompson Research Exptl. Devel. Lab. Lic. profl. radio engr., Ga. Mem. IEEE (life sr.), Vet. Wireless Operators Assn., Am. Radio Relay League, Nat. Rifle Assn., Mil. Order World Wars, Res. Officers Assn., Am. Motorcycle Assn., Nat. Wildlife Fedn. Baptist. Home: 6450 Overlook Dr Alexandria VA 22312

THOMPSON, LILLIAN HURLBURT, communications company executive; b. Bennington, Vt., Apr. 27, 1947; d. Paul Rhodes and Evelyn Arlene (Lockhart) Hurlburt; m. Wayne Wray Thompson, June 28, 1969. BS, Skidmore Coll., 1969; MS, U. So. Miss., 1975. Communication cons. Southwestern Bell Telephone, San Antonio, 1978-80; acct. exec. C&P Telephone, Washington, 1980-82, Am. Bell, Washington, 1983; staff mgr. AT&T Info. Systems, Rosslyn, Va., 1984; mgr. sales intermediary mktg. dept. Bell Atlantic Corp., Silver Spring, Md., 1984-89, mgr. product line mgmt. dept., 1089—. Home: 9203 St Marks Pl Fairfax VA 22031 Office: Bell Atlantic 13100 Columbia Pike Silver Spring MD 20904

THOMPSON, MELISSA ANN, entrepreneur; b. Astoria, Oreg., Sept. 14, 1950; d. Bernard Eugene and Evelyn Elaine (May) T.; m. William Leslie Harrington, June 3, 1972 (div. Mar. 1987); children: Elaine Leslie Ione, Thomas Jefferson Eugene. BA, U. Wash., 1972. Legis. dir. NOW, Washington, 1976-77; Wash. rep. Population Resource Ctr., Washington, 1977-78; mgr. Feminist Fed. Credit Union, Seattle, 1979-81; exec. dir. Associated Women Contractors, Seattle, 1981-82; ops. mgr. KAPA, Inc., Seattle, 1983; pres. MTA Services, Seattle, 1984—. Treas. N.W. Women's Law Ctr., Seattle, 1981-83; endorsement chmn. Wash. State Women Polit. Caucus, Seattle, 1981; chmn. King County Women's Polit. Caucus, Seattle, 1982-84; chair adv. com. to city council mem. Virginia Galle, 1986-89. Mem. Associated Builders and Contractors (bd. dirs. 1985-87), Associated Women Contractors (treas. 1985), Wash. Assn. Temporary Service (sec. 1985), Women Constrn. Owners and Execs., Women's Managerial and Profl. Network, Sea-First Bus. and Profl. Women (treas. 1982-83), Seattle Women Bus. Owners, Nat. Assn. Female Execs. Avocations: reading, women's rights, politics. Office: MTA Svcs Inc PO Box 9634 Seattle WA 98109

THOMPSON, PETER CAMPBELL, investment counselor; b. Newton, Mass., Mar. 18, 1933; m. Joan Jackson, Sept. 8, 1962; children: Christopher, Andrew. AB, Dartmouth Coll., 1955. With Bank of Boston, 1957-66; investment counselor David L. Babson & Co., Cambridge, Mass., 1966-83, pres., investment counselor, 1983—. Mem. The Trustees of Reservations, Beverly, Mass., 1985—. Mem. Boston Security Analysts Soc. Office: David L Babson & Co Inc One Memorial Dr Cambridge MA 02142

THOMPSON, PETER RUSSELL, retired construction and development company executive; b. N.Y.C., Dec. 12, 1921; s. Alfred Peter and Edythe Morris (Helfenstein) Swoyer; m. Elizabeth Smith Park, Oct. 23, 1948 (dec. 1971); children—Sharon F., Peter Russell, Elizabeth Park; m. Elizabeth Ann Edwards, Jan. 28, 1973. B.E. in C.E., Yale U., 1947. Engr., Gulf Oil Corp., N.Y.C., 1947-49, Gilbane Bldg. Co., Providence, 1949-52; sales engr. Masonite Corp., Providence, 1952-53; regional sales mgr. Nat. Homes Corp., Lafayette, Ind., 1953-58; exec. v.p. Inland Homes Corp., Piqua, Ohio, 1958-61; chief exec. officer, pres. Mid-Continent Properties, Inc., Piqua, 1962-86; chmn., Piqua Planning Commn., 1967-74; bd. dirs. Fifth Third Bank of Miami Valley, N.A.; mem. Ohio Housing Devel. Bd., 1971-74; mem. adv. com. on truth in lending to Bd. Govs., FRS, 1971-76; trustee Miami Valley Health Systems Agy., 1980; trustee Upper Valley Med. Ctr., Dettmer Hosp., Piqua Meml. Med. Ctr., Stouder Hosp., Dittmer Hosp. Found., Med-Terra, Inc., UVMC Nursing Care, Inc.; trustee, past bd. dirs. Piqua YMCA; past pres., bd. dirs. Piqua United Fund. Served to lt. AUS, 1943-46; ETO. Decorated Air medal; recipient Man of Yr. awards Piqua Jaycees, Piqua C. of C. Mem. Nat. Assn. Home Builders (dir. 1965-78), Ohio Home Builders Assn. (trustee, past pres.), Miami County Home Builders Assn. (life dir., past pres.), Piqua C. of C. (past pres., past dir.). Republican. Episcopalian. Clubs: Piqua Country (past pres., dir.), Rotary (past pres., dir.), Yale of Dayton. Office: 322 W Water St PO Box 1659 Piqua OH 45356

THOMPSON, RICHARD STEPHEN, management consultant; b. Des Moines, Oct. 14, 1931; s. Richard Stephen and Mary Ellen (Dailey) T.; m. Nancy Ann Jensen, Apr. 17, 1954; children—Traci Nan, Gregory Christian, Jonathan Richard. B.S.C., State U. Iowa, 1953; M.B.A., Ind. U., 1960. Regional dir. Bristol Meyers Co., N.Y.C., 1969-75; regional dir. Warner Lambert Co., Morris Plains, N.J., 1975-78; exec. v.p. Milton Bradley Co., Milton Bradley Internat., Inc., Springfield, Mass., 1979-83, pres., 1983-84; sr. v.p. internat., dir. Hasbro, Inc., Pawtucket, R.I., 1984-89, mgmt. cons., 1989—. Served to 1st lt. USAF, 1954-55. Republican. Clubs: Chatham Beach Tennis (Mass.); Pilgrims (London and N.Y.); American (London).

THOMPSON, ROBERT EUGENE, employment agency executive; b. Pitts., Dec. 4, 1942; s. John Thomas and Mary (Bell) T.; m. Julie Anne Wollerman; children: Amy, Robby, Regina. BS in Acctg., Ind. U., 1970. Divisional controller Montgomery Ward Inc., Chgo., 1971-81; v.p. Kelly Services Inc., Troy, Mich., 1982-88, sr. v.p., group exec., 1989—; bd. dirs. J. Thompson & Assocs., Huntington Beach, Calif., 1980—. Home: 71 S Berkshire Rd Bloomfield Hills MI 48013 Office: Kelly Svcs Inc 999 W Big Beaver Rd Troy MI 48084

THOMPSON, ROBERTA ANN (BOBBI), small business owner; b. Dayton, Ohio, Oct. 15, 1946; d. Robert Alvin and Lois G. (Hockett) Netzley; m. David Vornholt, Sept. 1966 (div. 1972); 1 child Pamele J.; m. William Lee, Mar. 17, 1972 (div. Jan. 1988). Student, Ohio State U., 1964-66. Pres., owner Aviation Sales, Inc., Vandalia and Miamisburg, Ohio, 1986—; v.p. Argo Comml. Ventures, Inc., Dayton, Ohio, 1988—; chief exec. officer, pres. Condor Aviation Enterprises, Dayton, 1988—. Feature writer Times Publ. mag. Mem. Rep. Nat. Com.; cand. Montgomery County Commr.; trustee, treas. United Cerebral Palsy; bd. dirs. Wright B. Flyer, v.p., hon. aviator, 1985, Women's Air and Space Mus., Nat. Aviation Hall Fame. Mem. Nat. Assn. Female Execs., U.S. C. of C., Ohio C. of C. (task force mem. internat. tort, civil legis., ins. protection, bd. dirs.), Aircraft Owners and Pilots Assn., Dayton Entrepreneurs Bus. Round Table, Nat. Fedn. Ind. Bus. (hon.), Nat. Air Transp. Assn. (trustee, chmn. 1986 awards com.), Dayton Area C. of C. (chmn. transp. com., legis. and govtl. affairs transp. com., program com., bd. dirs.), Ohio Small Bus. Council (bd. dirs., nat. delegate to White House Conf., U.S. chamber dir.), South Metro Dayton Area C. of C. (pres. elect). Republican. Clubs: 500, Aero (Washington); Dayton Airport Mgmt. Office: Argo Comml Ventures Inc 2541 Far Hills Ave Suite 202 Dayton OH 45419

THOMPSON, ROBIN JOHN MURRAY, marketing and communications consultant; b. Southsea, Hants, Eng., Jan. 29, 1934; came to U.S., 1979; s. John William and Lorna (Murray) T.; m. Jacqueline Hyde, Oct. 24, 1969; 1 child, Miranda Hyde. BA with honors, Cambridge U., 1957. Mktg. mgr. Shell Co., Melbourne, Australia, 1960-62; mktg. dir. Murphy Oil, London, 1962-64; mgmt. cons. McKinsey and Co., London, 1964-67, Hamburg, Federal Republic Ger., 1967-70; mgmt. cons. Viscose Group, London, 1970-74; chief exec. officer Allied Internat. Designers, London, 1974-79; v.p. mktg. Landor Assocs, N.Y.C., 1979-85; prin. Anspach Grossman Portugal, Inc., N.Y.C., 1985-87; v.p., cons. Lippincott & Margulies, N.Y.C., 1988—; bd. dirs., treas. 245 E 72d St. Coop. Assn., N.Y.C., 1987—. Lt. British Army, 1952-54. Mem. Royal Soc. Arts London, Lotos Club (dir., N.Y.C.). Home: 245 E 72d St New York NY 10021 Office: Lippincott & Margulies 499 Park Ave New York NY 10022

THOMPSON, TERENCE WILLIAM, lawyer; b. Moberly, Mo., July 3, 1952; s. Donald Gene and Carolyn (Stringer) T.; m. Caryn Elizabeth Hildebrand, Aug. 30, 1975; children: Cory Elizabeth, Christopher William. BA in Govt. with honors and high distinction, U. Ariz., 1974; JD, Harvard U., 1977. Bar: Ariz. 1977, U.S. Dist. Ct. Ariz. 1977, U.S. Tax Ct. 1979. Assoc. Brown & Bain P.A., Phoenix, 1977—; legis. aide Rep. Richard Burgess, Ariz. Ho. of Reps., 1974; mem. bus. adv. bd. Citibank Ariz. (formerly Great Western Bank & Trust, Phoenix), 1985-86. Mem. staff Harvard Law Record, 1974-75; rsch. editor Harvard Internat. Law Jour. , 1976; contbr. articles to profl. jours. Mem. Phoenix Mayor's Youth Adv. Bd. 1968-70, Phoenix Internat. Active 20-30 Club, 1978-81, sec. 1978-80, Valley Leadership, Phoenix, 1983-84, citizens task force future financing needs City of Phoenix, 1985-86; deacon Shepherd of Hills Congl. Ch, Phoenix, 1984-85; pres. Maricopa County Young Dems., 1982-83, Ariz. Young Dems., 1983-84, sec. 1981-82, v.p. 1982-83; exec. dir. Young Dems. Am., 1985, mem. exec. com. 1983-85; sec. Ariz. Dem. Com., 1984-87; bd. dirs. City Phoenix Mcpl. Ctr. Corp., 1987—, sec., 1987—. Fellow Ariz. Bar Found. (securities council/law sect. 1988—, vice chmn. internat. law sect. 1978); mem. ABA, State Bar Ariz. (vice chmn. internat. law sect. 1978, vice chmn. securities council/law sect. 1988—), Maricopa County Bar Assn., Nat. Assn. Bond Lawyers, Am. Acad. Hosp. Attys., Blue Key, Phi Beta Kappa, Phi Kappa Phi, Phi Eta Sigma. Home: 202 W Lawrence Rd Phoenix AZ 85013 Office: Brown & Bain PA PO Box 400 Phoenix AZ 85001

THOMPSON, THOMAS RONALD, manufacturing company executive; b. Gilman, Iowa, May 31, 1927; s. Thomas R. and Sarah Elizabeth (Westerfield) T.; B.A., U. Iowa, 1950; m. Evelyn M. Muckler, June 8, 1945; children—Thomas, Craig, Jann, Jill, Lori. With Lennox Industries Inc., Marshalltown, Iowa, 1950—, cost acct., 1950-52, asst. office mgr., 1952-53, office mgr., 1964-64, div. controller, 1964-76, v.p., gen. mgr. Midwest Div., 1976—; dir. Fidelity Brenton Bank, Marshalltown. Pres. Marshalltown Indsl. Bur., 1977-80; dir. Iowa Valley Community Coll., 1966-71, pres., 1969-71; vice chmn. United Way Drive, 1976, chmn., 1982, bd. dirs. United Way, 1974-81; bd. dirs. Marshalltown Area Community Hosp.; pres., 1988, bd. dirs., 1986-87; mem. nat. leadership com. Wartburg Coll.; chmn. Iowa Coll. Found., Marshalltown; endorsement chmn. Quakerdale Ptnrs. in Caring. Served with U.S. Army, 1945-46. Mem. Nat. Mgmt. Assn. (exec. adv. com. 1979—, silver knight award for mgmt., 1971), Iowa Mfrs. Assn., Rotary (dir. Marshalltown). Republican. Congregationalist. Home: 1406 S 12th St Marshalltown IA 50158 Office: 200 S 12th Ave Marshalltown IA 50158

THOMPSON, TREVÁ LEVI, bank executive, management consultant; b. Jamaica, Apr. 29, 1951; arrived in Eng., 1956; came to U.S., 1973; s. Jacob U. and Lucille U. (Gregory) T.; m. Glora E. Watson, Aug. 9, 1975; children: Marland S., Marc A., Donnamarie A. Systems engr. IBM, Birmingham, Eng., 1969-73; dir. mgmt. info. services GAB Bus. Services, N.Y.C., 1973-76; sr. v.p. TAS Mgmt. Cons., N.Y.C., 1976-80; v.p. Citibank/Citicorp, N.Y.C., 1981-88, Citicorp, N.Y.C., 1983—; bd. dirs. Aaroncorp, N.Y.C., Beautycare Corp, Ft. Lauderdale, Fla., Absolute, Ft. Lauderdale. Author: Information Processing Job Descriptions, 1980, USAM Performance and System Fine-Tuning, 1981. Bd. dirs., fund-raiser Africa-Am. United Hosp. Fund, Bklyn. Mem. Tampa Palms Golf and Country Club. Home: 10672 NW 17th Ct Coral Springs FL 33071 Office: Citicorp/Citibank 399 Park Ave New York NY 10043

THOMSEN, THOMAS RICHARD, communications company executive; b. Avoca, Iowa, July 29, 1935; s. Howard August and Edna Mary (Walker) T.; m. Raylene Alice Tomes, Sept. 1, 1956; children: Jeffrey, Cathy. BSME, U. Nebr., 1958; MS, MIT, 1973. Engr. Western Electric Co., Omaha, 1957-64; mgr. Western Electric Co., Columbus, Ohio, 1964-72; v.p. Bell Sales West Western Electric Co., Morristown, N.J., 1979-80; asst. v.p. ops. staff AT&T, Basking Ridge, N.J., 1980-82; exec. v.p. Western Electric Corp., N.Y.C., 1982—; pres. AT&T Tech. Systems, Berkeley Heights, N.J., 1982—; bd. dirs. AT&T Credit Corp., Sandia Corp., Albuquerque. Trustee Rensselaer Poly. Inst. Mem. Telephone Pioneers Am. (former pres.), Pi Tau Sigma, Sigma Tau. Republican. Presbyterian. Club: Windows on the World. Home: 4 Powderhorn Dr Kinnelon NJ 07405 Office: AT&T Tech Systems 1 Oak Way Berkeley Heights NJ 07922

THOMSON, ALEXANDER BENNETT, JR., certified financial planner, tax and management consultant; b. Wyandotte, Mich., Sept. 1, 1954; s. Alexander Bennett and Norma Lee (Fields) T.; m. Rita Elizondo, May 8, 1982; 1 child, Luis Joaquin Elizondo. Student Eastern Mich. U., 1972-74, Kalamazoo Coll. 1975-77; M.A., Antioch Sch. Law, 1983; Cert. fin. planner. Pres. Thomson & Assocs., Ltd., Washington, 1977—; budget dir. The White House Conf. on Small Bus., 1979; asst. treas. Kennedy for Pres. Com. 1980, nat. scheduler, Geraldine A. Ferraro, 1984. Mem. Inst. Certified Fin. Planners, Internat. Assn. Fin. Planners, ABA, Am. Mgmt. Assn., Nat. Assn. Life Underwriters, Nat. Assn. Tax Practitioners, Nat. Assn. Security Dealers. Democrat.

THOMSON, BARBARA JEANNE, purchasing executive; b. Cardiff, Calif., Feb. 10, 1929; d. Zack Rowden and Zula Mae (Tuckness) Taylor; m. Robert Allyn San Clemente, Feb. 8, 1946 (div. Aug. 1954); children—Robert Allyn Jr., Frances Irene, Michael George; m. Seeth Lyle Thomson, Aug. 7, 1954; 1 child, David Seeth. Grad. high sch., Encinitas, Calif. Various positions Gen. Dynamics Convair, San Diego, 1957-73; purchasing agt. Systems, Sci. & Software, San Diego, 1973-78; sr. buyer Gen. Dynamics Electronics, San Diego, 1978-80; sr. buyer LSI Products div. TRW, San Diego, 1980-84, purchasing mgr., 1984—. Named Employee of Yr., Gen. Dynamics Electronics, San Diego, 1978. Mem. Ry. Hist. Soc. (sec. San Diego 1957-60), Pacific Beach Model R.R. Club (sec. 1955-65), Nat. Assn. Female Execs., Nat. Mgmt. Assn., San Diego Hospice Assn. Democrat. Avocations: model railroading; photography; baseball; football. Home: 3204 McGraw St San Diego CA 92117 Office: TRW LSI Products Div 4243 Campus Point Ct San Diego CA 92121

THOMSON, RICHARD HARVEY, financial executive; b. Jersey City, July 6, 1959; s. Wallace H. and Lucille Rita (Giuttari) T. BBA magna cum laude, Temple U., 1983. Cash mgr. Damson Oil Corp., N.Y.C., 1983-84, asst. treas., 1984-86; mgr. fin. svcs. Butler Internat., Inc., Montvale, N.J., 1986-87; asst. treas. Sanofi, Inc., N.Y.C., 1987—. Mem. Nat. Corp. Cash Mgmt. Assn. (cert. cash mgr.). Home: 122 Riverview Ave North Arlington NJ 07032 Office: Sanofi Inc 101 Park Ave 24th Fl New York NY 10178

THOMSON, ROBERT HENNESSEY, manufacturing executive; b. Amesbury, Mass., July 28, 1933; s. Robert H. and Mary Catherine (Hennessey) T.; m. Suzanne Louise Locher, Aug. 26, 1957; children: Robert H. Jr., Karen Cantor, David L., Peter J., Christine. BSBA, Seton Hall U., 1957. Salesman Constrn. Specialties Inc., Cranford, N.J., 1957-59, product mgr., 1959-61, v.p., gen. mgr., Toronto office, 1961-68, v.p., gen. mgr., 1969-73, exec. v.p., 1973-75, pres., chief exec. officer, 1975—, also bd. dirs. Served with USMC, 1953-55, Korea. Mem. The Pres. Assn. of Am. Mgmt. Assn. Republican. Roman Catholic. Home: 112 Colchester Rd New Providence NJ 07974 Office: Constrn Specialties Inc 55 Winans Ave Cranford NJ 07016

THOMSON, ROBERT JAMES, natural gas distribution company executive; b. Detroit, Dec. 16, 1927; s. Harold E.J. and Irene L. (Silsbee) T.; m. Doris L. Mullen, Sept. 19, 1953; children—Gregory R., Susan C., Jeffrey S., Arthur J. A.B., Mich. State U., 1951, M.B.A., 1967. C.P.A., Mich. Mgr. Arthur Andersen & Co., Detroit, 1951-58; v.p. Southeastern Mich. Gas Co., Port Huron, 1961-71, pres., 1971-84, chmn. bd., chief exec. officer, 1984-86; pres., chmn. bd., chief exec. officer Southeastern Mich. Gas Enterprise, Inc., Port Huron, 1987—; dir. Mich. Nat. Bank-Port Huron. Trustee Community Found. St. Clair County, 1972—, pres., 1981-83; bd. dirs. Indsl. Devel. Corp., Port Huron, 1972-86, pres., 1976-78; trustee Port Huron Hosp., 1981—, vice chmn., 1985—; trustee Blue Water Health Services Corp., 1981—, vice chmn., 1981—; trustee Marion Manor Nursing Home, 1987—. Served with USN, 1946-47, PTO. Mem. Am. Gas Assn., Am. Mgmt. Assn., Mich. State C. of C. (bd. dirs. 1982-88), Mich. Utilities Assn. (bd. dirs., treas. 1983-85). Clubs: Renaissance, Detroit (Detroit); Port Huron Golf; Port Huron Yacht; Mich. State U. AMP. Home: 3355 Lomar Dr Port Huron MI 48060 Office: Southeastern Mich Gas Enterprises Inc 405 Water St Port Huron MI 48060

THOMSON, THOMAS HAROLD, petroleum executive; b. Winnipeg, Man., Can., Feb. 12, 1935; s. Harold W. and Mary Hislop (Lees) T. B in Applied Sci. (Engring.), U. Toronto, 1957; MBA, Harvard U., 1959. Sr. analyst mktg. Imperial Oil Ltd., Montreal, Que., Can., 1959; various downstream positions Imperial Oil Ltd., Toronto, Vancouver, 1959-74, sr. v.p., 1980-84, also dir.; exec. v.p. Home Oil Distbrs., Vancouver, 1974-75; with Exxon Corp., N.Y.C., 1975-76; pres., chief operating officer, dir. Suncor Inc., 1985-86, pres., chief exec. officer, dir., 1986—; bd. dirs. Electrohome Ltd. Trustee, treas. Hillcrest Hosp., Toronto, 1978-86; trustee United Way Greater Toronto, 1979-83; campaign chmn. Cystic Fibrosis Found., 1986. Mem. Assn. Profl. Engrs. Ont., Am. Petroleum Inst. Clubs: Rosedale Golf and Country, York, Muskoka Lakes Country, Toronto Badminton and Racquet, Granite; Harvard (Toronto) (dir. 1983-86). Office: Suncor Inc, 36 York Mills Rd, North York, ON Canada M2P 2C5

THORBECKE, WILLEM HENRY, international company executive, consultant; b. Paris, July 4, 1924; s. Willem Johan Rudolf and Madelaine (Salisbury) T.; m. Sonya Stokowski, June 8, 1946; children—Noel Evangeline, Johan Rudolf, Willem Leif, Christine Louise, B.S. in Engring., MIT, 1948, B.S. in Bus. Adminstrn., 1948. Exec., Royal Dutch Shell, N.Y.C., London, Tokyo, 1948-60, Mobil Corp., N.Y.C., 1960-69; cons. various cos., N.Y.C., Chgo., Houston, Tokyo, Taipei, Manila, Bangkok, Singapore, Paris, others, 1969-75; pres. Dravo Internat., Pitts., 1975-82, W.H. Thorbecke Assocs., Sewickley, Pa., 1982—; chmn., chief exec. officer Energy Support Services Inc., Sewickley, 1982—; chmn. ESSI Internat. Ltd., London; dir. G.F. Corp., Youngstown, Ohio, 1983—. Dir. World Affairs Council, Pitts., 1978—; chmn. MIT Enterprise Forum, Pitts., 1987—. Served to flight lt. RAF, 1942-46, ETO. Decorated D.F.C., RAF; named tri-state area Entrepreneur of Yr. Venture Mag., 1987. Mem. Am. Mgmt. Assn. (internat. council 1977-83), Nat. Assn. Corp. Dirs. Republican. Episcopalian. Clubs: Duquesne (Pitts.), Haagse (The Netherlands). Home: Deer Haven Farm Stonedale Rd Sewickley PA 15143 Office: Energy Support Svcs Inc 600 Commerce Dr Coraopolis PA 15108

THORN, BRIAN EARL, retail company division operations supervisor; b. Tucson, Oct. 30, 1955; s. Charles Walter and Jacquelyn Grace (Sloat) T.; m. Mary L. Ayala, Nov. 23, 1979 (div. 1981); m. Brenda Anne Benson, Dec. 28, 1983; 1 child, Justin. Grad. high sch., Tucson. Crew chief McDonald's restaurant, Tucson, 1972-74; sales clerk Save-Co, Tucson, 1974-77; security supr. HRT Industries, Tucson, 1977-82; salesman Zodys div. Circuit City, Albuquerque, 1982-84; store mgr. Zodys div. Circuit City, Las Vegas, Nev., 1984-86; sales mgr. Superstore div. Circuit City, El Toro, Calif., 1986; ops. mgr. Circuit City, Huntington Beach, Calif., 1986-87; No. Calif. div. ops. supr. Circuit City, 1987—. Republican. Presbyterian.

THORNBURG, FREDERICK FLETCHER, diversified business executive, lawyer; b. South Bend, Ind., Feb. 10, 1940; s. James F. and Margaret R. (Major) T.; children: James Brian, Charles Kevin, Christian Sean, Christopher Herndon; m. Patricia J. Malloy, Dec. 4, 1981. AB, DePaul U., 1963; postgrad., U. Notre Dame, 1965; JD magna cum laude, Ind. U., 1968. Bar: Ind. 1968, U.S. Tax Ct. 1970, U.S. Ct. Appeals (7th cir.) 1970, U.S. Supreme Ct. 1971. Tchr., coach U.S. Peace Corps, Colombia, 1963-65; law clk. to presiding justice U.S. Ct. Appeals (7th cir.), 1968-69; assoc. Thornburg, McGill, Deahl, Harman, Carey & Murray, South Bend, 1969-75, ptnr., 1975-80; v.p. systems and svcs. group Wackenhut Internat. Inc., Coral Gables, Fla., 1981-82, sr. v.p. adminstrn., 1982-86, pres., 1982-83, exec. v.p. 1986-88; pres. Wackenhut Support Svcs., Inc., Wackenhut Svcs., Inc.; v.p., legal counsel St. Thomas U., 1988—; adj. prof. bus. law St. Mary's Coll., 1975-78; vice-chmn., pvt. sec. adv. coun. Fla. Sec. of State, 1986-88; bd. dirs. M.F. Parker Fund, 1985—; assoc. editor in chief: Ind. Law Jour., 1967-68; contbr. articles to legal jours. Bd. dirs. YMCA, Channel 34, Symphony Orch. Assn. Grantee Fulbright scholar, Halleck scholar. Mem. ABA, Ind. Bar Assn., Dade County Corp. Counsel Assn., Order of Coif, Greater Miami C. of C. (bd. trustees), Phi Delta Phi, Alpha Delta Sigma. Clubs: Doral Country, Biltmore, City Club of Miami. Lodge: Rotary. Office: 10005 NW 52 Terr 16400 NW 32 Ave Miami FL 33178

THORNBURG, RONALD RAY, municipal official; b. Beloit, Kans., Mar. 30, 1948; s. Raymond J. and Ardyce Mae (Wilson) T.; m. Lori Ann Moorhous, May, 1988; children by previous marriage: Belinda, Alan. Student, Ft. Hays State U., 1966-67; Diploma in Acctg., Barnes Bus. Sch., Denver, 1970. Cert. mcpl. clk. Asst. office mgr., buyer Fredricks Fabrics, Inc., Denver, 1968-71; asst. city clk. City of Dodge City (Kans.), 1971-72, computer programmer, 1972-76, fin. dir., 1977—; state rep. Govt. Fin. Officers Assn., Dodge City. Author: (with others) Systems That Work, 1983. Bd. dirs. Kans. Intergovtl. Risk Mgmt. Agy., Topeka. Mem. League of Kans. Mcpls. (mem. taxation and fin. com.), Internat. Inst. Mcpl. Clks., Kans. Mcpl. Fin. Officers Assn. (sec.). Club: Ducks Unlimited (Dodge City). Lodge: St. Bernard (chpt. 222). Home: 300 Plaza Dodge City KS 67801 Office: City of Dodge City Office of Fin Dir 705 First Ave Dodge City KS 67801

THORNDYKE, LLOYD MILTON, computer company executive; b. Edgerton, Minn., May 28, 1927; s. W. Keith and Grace A. Thorndyke; m. Jo Ann M. Thompson, July 23, 1949; children: Lloyd, Keith. B.S. in Physics, Hamline U., St. Paul, 1950. Engr. A.B. McMahon Co., St. Paul, 1950-54; engr., mgr. Sperry Univac Co., St. Paul, 1954-60; with Control Data Corp., Mpls., 1960-83; v.p., chief engr. peripheral equipment MPI div. Control Data Corp., 1973-75, sr. v.p. computer systems, 1975-77, sr. v.p. tech. and supercomputers, 1977-83; chmn., pres., chief exec. officer ETA Systems Inc., 1983-88, chmn., 1988—. Trustee Hamline U. Served with USNR, 1945-46. Mem. IEEE, Am. Assn. Engring. Socs. (Chmn. award 1988), Air Force Assn., Am. Legion. Methodist. Office: 1450 Energy Park Dr Saint Paul MN 55108

THORNE, EDWARD DAVID, retired administrative analyst; b. Los Angeles, Apr. 19, 1926; s. Harry Morris and Adelaide Marie (Kanne) T.; m. Mary Therese Gleason, May 30, 1952 (div. 1956); m. Chrystel Irene Pugh, July 2, 1960 (dec. Feb. 1982); children: Richard, Steven. BBA in Fin., Loyola U., Los Angeles, 1963. Credit reporter Dun & Bradstreet, 1952-53; asst. mgr. Seaboard Fin., 1953-56; prodn. planner Hannon Engring., 1962-64; service parts mgr. Picker K-Ray Corp., 1964-68; adminstrv. analyst City of Santa Monica, Calif., 1969-84; v.p. Fed. Credit Union, Santa Monica, 1975, chmn. credit union., 1972-74; treas. City Employees, City of Santa Monica, 1977, 80, 82-83; pres. City of Santa Monica, 1981, 84. Roman Catholic. Lodge: Optimists. Home: PO Box 1139 Sugarloaf CA 92386

THORNTON, DEAN DICKSON, airplane company executive; b. Yakima, Wash., Jan. 5, 1929; s. Dean Stoker and Elva Maud (Dickson) T.; m. Joan Madison, Aug. 25, 1956 (div. Apr. 1978); children—Steven, Jane Thornton; m. Mary Shultz, Nov. 25, 1981; children—Volney, Scott, Peter, Todd Richmond. B.S. in Bus., U. Idaho, 1952. C.P.A., Wash. Acct. Touche, Ross & Co., Seattle, 1954-63; treas., controller Boeing Co., Seattle, 1963-70; various exec. positions Boeing Co., 1974-85; pres. Boeing Comml. Airplane Co., 1985—; sr. v.p. Wyly Co., Dallas, 1970-74; bd. dirs. Seafirst Corp, Prin. Fin. Group. Bd. dirs. YMCA, Seattle, 1966-68, Jr. Achievement, Seattle, 1966-68; chmn. Wash. Council on Internat. Trade, Seattle, 1984-87. Served to 1st lt. USAF, 1952-54. Named to U. Idaho Alumni Hall of Fame. Mem. Phi Gamma Delta. Republican. Presbyterian. Clubs: Rainier, Seattle Tennis, Seattle Yacht, Conquistadores de Cielo. Home: 1602-34 Ct W Seattle WA 98199 Office: Boeing Co PO Box 3707 Seattle WA 98124

THORNTON, GERARD FRANCIS, proprietary school executive; b. Flushing, N.Y., Nov. 23, 1947; s. Joseph Francis and Marion Elizabeth (Horan) T.; m. Anne Marie O'Reilly, May 1, 1970; children: Michelle, Brian. BS, N.Y. Inst. Tech., 1969. Supr. services dept. Allstate Ins. Co., Huntington, N.Y., 1970-74, div. supr. services dept., 1974-78; sch. mgr. Wilfred Am. Ednl. Corp., Jamaica, N.Y., 1978-80; regional mgr. Wilfred Am. Ednl. Corp., Chgo., 1980-83, regional v.p., 1983-87; exec. v.p. Wilfred Am. Ednl. Corp., N.Y.C., 1987—. With U.S. Army, 1969-70. Mem. N.Y. State Career Schs. Assn., Teaching Edn. Council, Ill. Assn. Coll. and Schs. Republican. Roman Catholic. Office: Wilfred Am Ednl Corp 1657 Broadway New York NY 10019

THORNTON, GERARD MATTHEW, real estate executive; b. N.Y.C., Apr. 23, 1938; s. Thomas Kelly and Nora Margaret (Burke) T.; m. Lynn Soerensen, Sept. 22, 1962; children: Laura Ann, Matthew Burke, Roseanne, Frederick Thomas. BS, Fordham U., 1959. With Aetna Ins. Co., 1961-63, Chase Manhattan Bank, N.Y.C., 1963-65; purchasing agt. Atlantic Richfield Co., N.Y.C., 1965-69; dir. purchasing Rockefeller Center Mgmt. Corp., 1969—. Mem. Devel. Commn. W. Windsor (N.J.) Twp. Served with AUS, 1959-65. Mem. Purchasing Mgmt. Assn. N.Y. (bd. dirs. 1976-78, 2d v.p. 1987, 1st v.p. 1988—), Am. Arbitration Assn. (arbitrator 1970—), Nat. Assn. Purchasing Mgmt., Fordham U. Alumni Assn. Office: 1230 Ave of Americas New York NY 10020

THORNTON, JOHN T., corporate financial executive; b. N.Y.C., Oct. 22, 1937; s. John T. and Catherine (Burke) T.; m. Patricia C. Robertson; children: Kevin, Brian, Vincent, Elizabeth, Monica. BBA, St. John's U., 1959, JD, 1972. Bar: N.Y.; CPA. Auditor Peat, Marwick, Mitchell & Co., N.Y.C., 1961-67; asst. controller Texasgulf Inc., Stamford, Conn., 1967-81, v.p., controller, 1981-84; sr. v.p., controller Norwest Corp., Mpls., 1984-87, exec. v.p., chief fin. officer, 1987—. Office: Norwest Ctr 6th and Marquette Minneapolis MN 55479-1052

THORNTON, JOHN VINCENT, lawyer; b. N.Y.C., Jan. 13, 1924; s. Thomas Francis and Elizabeth Rose (McCullough) T.; m. Edna Grace Lawson, June 28, 1952; children: John, Nancy, Sarah, Amy, Laura. BS, St. John's U., 1944; JD, Yale U., 1948; LLD (hon.), N.Y. Law Sch., 1969. Bar: N.Y. 1948. Assoc. in law Columbia U., 1948-49; assoc. Skadden Arps, 1949; law clk. to assoc. judge N.Y. Ct. of Appeals, 1950-52; ptnr. Whitman & Ransom, N.Y.C., 1952-69, of counsel, 1989—; asst. gen. counsel Consol. Edison Co. N.Y. Inc., 1969, v.p., 1970-73, v.p., treas., 1973-76, sr. v.p. fin., 1976-79, exec. v.p. fin., 1979-80, sr. exec. v.p., 1980-84, vice chmn., 1984-89; exec. v.p. Columbia U., N.Y.C., 1989—; treas. Empire State Electric Energy Research Corp., 1975-78; bd. dirs. Consol. Edison Co., Am. Savs. Bank, Pub. Utilities Reports, Inc., chmn., 1986-89; bd. dirs. Nuclear Electric Ins. Ltd., chmn., 1986-89; adj. prof. law NYU Sch. Law, 1949-66; Lubin lectr. Pace U., 1982; adj. prof. law, assoc. dean N.Y. Law Sch., 1964-69, v.p., 1969-73, chmn., 1973-85, hon. chmn., 1985—; asst. in econs. Yale U., 1946-48; instr. econs. Albertus Magnus Coll., 1946-48; assoc. dir. USPHS Study on Heart Disease and the Law, 1958-61; counsel judiciary com. N.Y. State Constl. Conv., 1967; mem. Bd. Edn., Bronxville, N.Y., 1970-76, pres. bd., 1972-74. Contbg. editor: Ann. Survey of Am. Law, 1950-60, Ann. Survey of N.Y. Law, 1950-60, Jour. Occupational Medicine, 1964-67, Pub. Utilities Fortnightly, 1969—. Bd. dirs., sec. Hall of Sci. N.Y.C., 1968-76; trustee Pace U., N.Y. Bot. Garden, N.Y.C. Citizen's Budget Commn., com. and fund for modern cts.; bd. visitors City Coll. of CUNY, 1976-82; mem. bd. advisers Dickinson Coll., chmn., 1979-81, trustee, 1979-89; mem. pres.'s adv. council NYU Sch. Social Work, 1969-75; mem. Can.-Am. Com., 1980-85. Lt. (j.g.) USNR, 1944-46, PTO. Mem. ABA, Edison Electric Inst. (fin. com.), Am. Gas Assn. (fin. com.), Order of Coif, Phi Delta Phi. Home: 55 Prescott Ave Bronxville NY 10708 Office: Columbia U 311 Low Libr New York NY 10027

THORNTON, ROBERT RICHARD, lawyer; b. Jersey City, Oct. 16, 1926; s. Arthur A. and Sabina V. (Williams) T.; m. Dorothy M. McGuire, Sept. 10, 1966; children: Matthew, Nicholas, Jennifer, Julia. AB, Georgetown U., 1950; LLB, Columbia U., 1953. Bar: N.Y. 1953, Ill. 1970. Assoc. Dorr, Hand & Dawson, N.Y.C., 1953-63, Mudge, Rose, Guthrie & Alexander, N.Y.C., 1963-70; gen. atty. Caterpillar Inc. (formerly Caterpillar Tractor Co.), Peoria, Ill., 1970-74, assoc. counsel, 1974-83, gen. counsel, sec., 1983—. Mem. ABA, Ill. State Bar Assn., Peoria County Bar Assn., Assn. Bar City of N.Y. Republican. Roman Catholic. Club: Country of Peoria. Home: 3715 Linden Ln Peoria IL 61614 Office: Caterpillar Inc 100 NE Adams St Peoria IL 61629-7310

THORP, JAMES DAVID, venture capitalist; b. Oskaloosa, Iowa, Jan. 23, 1959; s. Vern Emmett Thorp and Barbara Ann (Small) Southworth; m. Lisa Maureen Kenyon, Mar. 21, 1987; 1 child, Heather. AA in Agr., Econs., Acctg., Miami Okla. A&M, 1979; BS in Bus. Adminstrn., Acctg., Okla. State U., 1981; MBA in Fin., U. Pa., 1983. Assoc. R.W. Allsop & Assocs. (now called Allsop Venture Ptnrs.), Cedar Rapids, Iowa, 1983-87, prin., 1987—; bd. dirs. Ind. Railroad Co., Indpls., INterconnect Systems Inc., L.A., N.y. Alarm, Inc., Marion, Iowa. Active in Entrepreneurs' Network, Cedar Rapids. Mem. Nat. Assn. Small Bus. Investment Cos., Nat. Venture Capital Assn. Home: 3403 C Ave Ext Marion IA 52302 Office: Allsop Venture Ptnrs 2750 1st Ave NE Cedar Rapids IA 52402

THORPE, JAMES ALFRED, utilities executive; b. Fall River, Mass., Apr. 19, 1929; s. James and Charlotte Ann (Brearley) T.; m. Maxine Elva Thompson, Mar. 4, 1950; children: James Alfred, Peter R., David T., Carol L., Mark W. B.S., Northeastern U., 1951. Asst. supt. prodn. Fall River Gas Co., 1951-55; chief engr. Lake Shore Gas Co., Ashtabula, Ohio, 1955-57; cons. Stone & Webster Mgmt. Corp., 1958-67; pres. Wash. Natural Gas Co., Seattle, 1967; chmn., chief exec. officer Wash. Natural Gas Co., 1980—; dir. Sea First Corp., Unigard Ins. Group. Bd. dirs. Salvation Army; trustee U. Puget Sound. Mem. Am. Gas Assn., Pacific Coast Gas Assn. (pres. 1977-78). Methodist. Clubs: Rainier (Seattle), Wash. Athletic (Seattle), Rotary (Seattle). Home: 11160 SE 59th St Bellevue WA 98006 Office: Washington Energy Co 815 Mercer St Box 1869 Seattle WA 98111

THORSEN, NANCY DAIN, real estate broker; b. Edwardsville, Ill., June 23, 1944; d. Clifford Earl and Suzanne Eleanor (Kribs) Dain; m. David Massie, 1968 (div. 1975); i dau., Suzanne Dain Massie; m. James Hugh Thorsen, May 30, 1980. B.Sc. in Mktg., So. Ill. U., 1968, M.Sc. in Bus. Edn., 1975; grad. Realtor Inst., Idaho, 1983. Cert. resdl. and investment specialist. Personnel officer J.H. Little & Co. Ltd., London, 1969-72; instr. in bus. edn. Spl. Sch. Dist. St. Louis, 1974-77; mgr. mktg./ops. Isis Foods, Inc., St. Louis, 1978-80; asst. mgr. store Stix, Baer & Fuller, St. Louis, 1980; assoc. broker Century 21 Sayer Realty, Inc., Idaho Falls, Idaho, 1981-88, RE/MAX Homestead, Inc., 1989— . Bd. dirs. Idaho Vol., Boise, 1981-84, Idaho Falls Symphony, 1982; pres. Friends of Idaho Falls Library, 1981-83; chmn. Idaho Falls Mayor's Com. for Vol. Coordination, 1981-84. Recipient Idaho Gov.'s award, 1982, cert. appreciation City of Idaho Falls/Mayor Campbell, 1982, 87, Century 21 Gold Assoc. award, 1987, 88; named to Two Million Dollar Club, Three Million Dollar Club, 1987, 88 ; named Top Investment Sales Person for Eastern Idaho, 1985, No. 1 Century 21 Agt. in Idaho, 1986, 87, 88. Mem. Idaho Falls Bd. Realtors (chmn. orientation 1982-83, chmn. edn. 1983), So. Ill. U. Alumni Assn., Idaho Fallls C. of C. Clubs:

Newcomers, Civitan (Idaho Falls) (Civitan of Yr. 1986, 87, pres. 1988—). Office: RE/MAX Homestead Inc 1301 E 17th St Ste 1 Idaho Falls ID 83404

THORSON, MILTON ZENAS, paint and varnish company executive; b. Thorsby, Ala., Oct. 26, 1902; s. Theodore T. and Emma (Hokanson) T.; student Am. Inst. Banking, extension courses U. So. Calif.; Degree in Bus. (hon.); m. 3d, Helen Lob, Aug. 31, 1978. Chief teller Tenn. Valley Bank, Decatur, Ala., 1919-28; teller Security First Nat. Bank, Los Angeles, 1928-29; with Red Spot Paint & Varnish Co., Inc., Evansville, Ind., 1929-60, chmn. exec. bd., dir., 1961-79; chmn. exec. bd. Owensboro Paint & Glass Co. (Ky.); ; former mem. Regional Export Expansion Council, U.S. Dept. Commerce. Mem. Audubon Soc., Nat. Paint and Coatings Assn. (hon.), Soc. Plastic Engrs. (Plastic Industry Pioneer). Republican. Club: President's of U. Evansville (life). Contbr. tech. articles profl. jours. Home: Box 418 Evansville IN 47703 also: 527 Harbor Dr Key Biscayne FL 33149 Office: 110 Main St Evansville IN 47701

THRASHER, RICHARD DEVERE, JR., economic development executive, consultant; b. Windsor, Ont., Can., Nov. 10, 1947; came to U.S., 1967; s. Richard Devere Sr. and Norma Jeanne (Whittal) T.; m. Gail Cathryn Erickson, june 28, 1969; children: Richard Devere III, Tia Lee. BS, U. Wis., 1971. Tchr. Hermantown (Minn.) Community Sch., 1972-76; instr. Indianhead Tech. Inst., Superior, Wis., 1976-77; exec. dir. Econ. Devel. Assn., Inc., 1977-80; pres., chief exec. officer Econ. Devel. Corp., New Castle, Ind., 1980-86, Lakeland, Fla., 1986—, Salt Lake City, 1988—; cons. in field. Author: (monograph) Industrial Parks, 1982. Bd. dirs. Cert. Econ. Devel. Bd., Chgo., 1982—, Gov.'s Econ. Devel. Com., Indpls., 1984-86. Mem. Am. Econ. Devel. Council (bd. dirs. 1987—), Nat. Council on Urban Econ. Devel., Indsl. Devel. Rsch. Council, So. Indsl. Devel. Council, Fla. Econ. Devel. Council. Home: 8426 S Azul Way Sandy UT 84093 Office: Utah Econ Devel Corp 175 East 400 South Salt Lake City UT 84093

THRASHER, SCOTT ROBERT, sales executive; b. Ft. Madison, Iowa, June 14, 1955; s. Robert Eugene and Joan Louise (Petersen) T.; m. Kristine Therese Dougall, Mar. 10, 1979; children: Molly, Robert. BS in Mktg., U. Mo., 1977. Sales trainee Toastmaster, Columbia, Mo., 1977; sales rep. Toastmaster, Des Moines, 1978; dist. mgr. Toastmaster, Milw., Chgo., 1979-82; regional mgr. Toastmaster, Chgo., 1982-84; dir. sales Toastmaster, Columbia, Mo., 1984-86, v.p. sales, 1986—. Named Eagle Scout Boy Scouts Am., 1971. Mem. Houseware Club of Chgo., Kappa Sigma (alumni advisor Beta Gamma chpt. 1986—). Office: Toastmaster 1801 N Stadium Columbia MO 65203

THRO, ARLIN BROOKER, corporate speechwriter; b. Rockford, Ill., May 9, 1940; s. Arlin Eugene and Mavis Brown (Green) T.; m. Elaine Marie Broydrick, June 19, 1965. AB magna cum laude, Harvard U., 1962; MA, U. Calif., Berkeley, 1967; PhD, U. Calif., 1974. Asst. prof. English U. Va., Charlottesville, 1971-74; instr. composition Calif. State U., Northridge, 1975-76; instr. lit. UCLA, 1976; instr. composition Santa Monica (Calif.) Coll., 1976-77; speechwriter, mgr. publs. Whittaker Corp., L.A., 1977-83; exec. speechwriter Allied Signal, Inc., Morristown, N.J., 1983—. Contbr. articles to profl. jours. Lt. USNR, 1962-65. U. Calif. fellow, 1968-70. Home: 54 Fairmont Ave Morristown NJ 07960 Office: Allied Signal Inc Columbia Rd Morristown NJ 07960

THRYFT, ANN R., marketing communications writer, editor; b. San Francisco, Dec. 22, 1950; d. William Boyd and Margaret Evelyn (Wilson) T.; m. Alfred Stephens Nelson, May 15, 1971 (div. 1983); m. Mark J. Tussman, Mar. 2, 1985 (div. 1988). BA in Anthropology, Stanford U., 1976. Cert. bus. communicator U.S.A. Mktg. communications specialist Franklin Electric, Sunnyvale, Calif., 1981-82; advt. specialist Lear Siegler Inc., Menlo Park, Calif., 1982-83; mktg. communications mgr. Buscom Systems, Santa Clara, Calif., 1983-84; corp. communications mgr. Nat. Tech. Systems, Calabasas, Calif., 1985-86; mktg. communications mgr. Forth, Inc., Manhattan Beach, Calif., 1986-88; cons. in field, 1989—. Contbr. articles to profl. jours. Rep., sec. Los Trancos Woods Community (Calif.) Assn., 1978-79, pres., 1979-80. Mem. Bus.-Profl. Advt. Assn. (bd. dirs. L.A. chpt.), Stanford Alumni Assn., Publicity Club L.A., Phi Beta Kappa. Avocations: historical research, research history of religions, poetry, writing fiction.

THULIN, LARS UNO, banker; b. Uddevalla, Sweden, Mar. 25, 1939; came to Norway, 1939; s. Haakon Erling and Signe Ingeborg (Thulin) Hansen; m. Anne Skard, Oct. 7, 1977. M.Sc., Norwegian Inst. Tech., 1965, Dr.Ing., 1970. Lectr., scientist U. Trondheim, 1965-70, dep. dean univ. planning unit, 1970-74; mng. dir. Norwegian Agy. Devel. Aid, Trondheim, 1974-75; undersec. Ministry Research and Edn., Oslo, 1975-76; undersec. Ministry Industry and Energy Oslo, 1976-77; exec. v.p. Den Norske Creditbank, Oslo, 1977—, mng. dir. den Norske Creditbank Plc., London, 1987—; exec. v.p., head internat. div. Den Norske Creditbank, Oslo, 1989—; chmn. bd. Ctr. for Indsl. Research, Oslo. Decorated Gt. Cross of Merit (Fed. Republic of Germany). Fellow Inst Petroleum U.K. Office: Den Norske Creditbank, Kirkegt 21, 1 Oslo Norway

THUMS, CHARLES WILLIAM, designer, consultant; b. Manitowoc, Wis., Sept. 5, 1945; s. Earl Oscar and Helen Margaret (Rusch) T. B. in Arch., Ariz. State U., 1972. Ptnr., Grafic, Tempe, Ariz., 1967-70; founder, prin. I-Squared Environ. Cons., Tempe, Ariz., 1970-78; designer and cons. design morphology, procedural programming and algorithms, 1978—. Author: (with Jonathan Craig Thums) Tempe's Grand Hotel, 1973, The Rossen House, 1975; (with Daniel Peter Aiello) Shelter and Culture, 1976; contbg. author: Tombstone Planning Guide, 5 vols., 1974. Office: PO Box 3126 Tempe AZ 85280-3126

THUNE, DALE GENE, financial executive, appraiser; b. Toronto, S.D., Apr. 19, 1935; s. Carl E. and Julia (Gorder) T.; m. Lorna Gail Pierce, Dec. 21, 1958; children: Diana Carol, Cynthia Ann. BS, Calif. State U., 1964; cert., UCLA, 1969. Sr. real estate appraiser County of Los Angeles, 1964-73; v.p. property and sales tax Carter Hawley Hale Stores Inc., Los Angeles, 1973—. Sgt. USMC, 1953-57. Named to Hon. Order Ky. Cols., 1982. Mem. Inst. Property Taxation (cert. property mem., salestax mem., bd. dirs. 1978—, pres. 1986-87), Internat. Assn. Assessing Officers (Outstanding Subscribing Mem. 1986), Am. Soc. Appraisers (sr. mem.), Soc. Auditor Appraisers, Los Angeles Assessors Adv. Com., Retail Mchts. Calif. State Tax Commn., Los Angeles Taxpayers Assn. (chmn. 1987-88). Republican. Lutheran. Clubs: Jonathan (Los Angeles); Ironwood Country (Palm Desert, Calif.). Lodges: Rotary, Masons. Office: Carter Hawley Hale Stores Inc 550 S Flower St Los Angeles CA 90071

THURBER, CLEVELAND, JR., trust banker; b. Detroit, Aug. 2, 1925; s. Cleveland and Marie Louise (Palms) T.; m. Elizabeth-Mary Hamilton, June 22, 1946; children: Cleveland III, Elizabeth King Thurber Crawford, David. Student, Purdue U.; B.A., Williams Coll., 1948. Asst. trust officer Comerica Bank-Detroit, 1958-61, trust officer, 1961-63, v.p., 1963-69, sr. v.p., 1969-81, exec. v.p., chief trust officer, 1981—. Pres. Friends of Grosse Pointe Pub. Library, 1971-72, Mich. Heart Assn., 1969-74; sec. United Community Services, 1968-70; Bd. dirs. Cottage Hosp., United Found., Mich. Humane Soc., Elmwood Cemetery, Ctr. for Creative Studies, Wm. L. Clements Library, Ann Arbor. Served with USMCR, 1943-46. Clubs: Detroit (Detroit) (past pres.), Yondotega (Detroit), Country (Detroit). Home: 34 Edgemere Rd Grosse Pointe Farms MI 48236 Office: Comerica Inc 211 W Fort St Detroit MI 48275

THURMAN, RALPH HOLLOWAY, pharmaceutical company executive; b. Chgo., July 28, 1949; s. Joseph Ralph and Jean (Holloway) T.; m. Karen Ann Eisenhart, Mar. 14, 1980; children: Kelly Ann, Kaitlin Leigh, Kyle Joseph. BA, Va. Poly. Inst., 1971; MA, Webster U., 1974; postgrad., USAF Air Command and Staff Coll., 1974. Dir. orgn. Exxon Corp., N.Y.C., 1976-82; dir. personnel Pepsico Internat., Purchase, N.Y., 1982-84; sr. v.p. Datapoint Corp., San Antonio, 1984-85, Rorer Group, Inc., Ft. Washington, Pa., 1985—; cons. on resource mgmt. Contbr. articles to profl. publs. Bd. dirs. Jr. Achievement SW, San Antonio, 1984, Phila. Bus. Attraction Commn., 1987—, Univ. City Sci. Ctr., Phila., 1987—; mem. Greater Phila. Econ. Devel. Coal., 1987—. Capt. USAF, 1971-76, Vietnam. Home: 142 Three Ponds Ln Malvern PA 19355 Office: Rorer Group Inc 500 Virginia Dr Fort Washington PA 19034

THURMON, JACK JEWEL, financial services executive; b. Kilgore, Tex., Aug. 14, 1944; s. Merida Eldridge and Agnes (Jones) T.; BS in Indsl. Engring., So. Meth. U., 1967; MBA, Harvard U., 1969; m. Barbara Fern Henson, July 1, 1966; children: J. Gregory, J. Clarke, J. Douglas. Pres., Rimcor, Inc., Houston, 1969-71, Houston Mut. Agy., Inc., 1972-85, Jojoba Mgmt., Inc., Houston, 1982-88. sr. v.p. Crump Co. Houston, 1985-87; chmn. Strictly Petites, Inc., Kilgore, Tex., 1987—; trustee Kilgore Ind. Sch. Dist. Served with USAR, 1969-75. Republican. Home: 3000 Houston Kilgore TX 75662 Office: 500 E Main Kilgore TX 75662

THURMOND, GERALD PITTMAN, lawyer; b. Madison, Ga., Aug. 20, 1936; s. Gilbert Duard and Viola Elnora (Pittman) T.; m. Ann Sexton, May 21, 1960; children: Gerald Pittman, William R., Susan A. BBA, U. Ga., 1958, JD cum laude, 1964; LLM in Taxation, Georgetown U., 1981. Bar: Ga. 1963, Pa. 1970, D.C. 1976, U.S. Dist. (no. dist.) Ga., U.S. Dist. Ct. (we. dist.) Pa., U.S. Ct. Appeals (5th dist.), U.S. Supreme Ct. Atty. Troutman, Sams, Schroder & Lockerman, Atlanta, 1964-68; staff atty., gen. counsel Gulf Oil Corp., Pitts., 1963-73, asst. to chmn. bd., pres. and exec. v.p.'s, 1973, adminstrv. v.p., 1974-75, Washington counsel, 1975-83, sr. counsel, 1983-85, corp. asst. sec., corp. affairs, Chevron Corp., 1985-87, asst. gen. counsel natural gas, 1987—. Gulf Oil Co. employee chmn. United Fund of Houston, 1975. Served to 1st lt. AUS, 1958-60. Mem. ABA, D.C. Bar Assn., Ga. Bar Assn., Allegheny County Bar Assn., Ga. State Soc. (bd. dirs.), Houston C. of C., U.S. C. of C. (council on antitrust policy), NAM (com. on corp. governance and competition, com. on regulatory reform), Phi Kappa Phi. Episcopalian. Club: Commercial (San Francisco), Houston Ctr. Home: 1 E Broad Oaks Ln Houston TX 77056 Office: 1301 McKinney Ste 2200 Houston TX 77010

THURSTON, ERNEST ALBERT, data processing executive; b. Plainfield, N.J., Aug. 31, 1946; s. Ernest Albert and Florence E. (Hann) Thurkauf; 1 child, Meda. BA in Physics, Harvard U., 1968. Computer analyst Bio-Dynamics, Inc., Cambridge, Mass., 1968-72; co-dir. Earthworm, Inc., Boston, 1973-78; project supr. Vista, Asheville, N.C., 1979-81; dir. tng. Computerland of Asheville, N.C., 1982-83; cons. in data processing Asheville, 1983-85; ptnr. Skyline Computer Assocs., Asheville, 1985-87; pres. The Meda Corp., Asheville, 1987—. Campaign cons. Clarke for Congress, Asheville, 1986-88, Buncombe Co. Dem. Party, 1988. Democrat. Office: The Meda Corp 19 Panola Asheville NC 28801

THURSTON, FRED STONE, printing company executive; b. Oak Park, Ill., Apr. 1, 1931; s. Fred Stone and Marie (Stemen) T.; m. E. Marie Young, Apr. 20, 1983; children: Fredric Kent, Bruce Edward, Crystal Marie. Student, Ea. Ill. State Coll., 1948-50; BA, N.Mex. Highlands U., 1954; postgrad. exec. program, U. Chgo., 1975-76. Cert. forms cons. Asst. plant mgr. UARCO, Inc., Watseka, Ill., 1955-63; asst. to pres. Joe Daley & Sons, Inc., Los Angeles, 1963-64; div. mgr. manifold forms Diamond Internat.W.G.A.D., San Francisco, 1964-66; gen. mgr. Uniform Printing & Supply div. Courier Corp., Chgo., 1965-69; dir. mfg. Bus. Forms div. Control Data Corp., Phila., 1969-70; pres., gen. mgr. Printing Services, Inc. div. Am. Standard Co., Detroit, 1970-71; exec. v.p., gen. mgr. Workman Bus. Forms div. John Blair & Co., Chgo., 1971-72; exec. v.p., dir. mktg., 1972-86; exec. v.p. mktg. and sales Forms Corp. Am. div. Nodaway Valley Co., Spring Grove, Ill., 1986—. V.p. Iroquois County (Ill.) Young Reps., 1960-61. Served to capt. AUS, 1951-53, USAR, 1953-64. Mem. Mensa, Sigma Tau Gamma. Home: 27 Russet Way Palatine IL 60067 Office: PO Box 278 3106 Rt 12 Spring Grove IL 60081

THURSTON, RAY R., courier company executive; b. Los Angeles, Jan. 17, 1947; s. Nelson R. Thurston and Lillian (Arnold) Chapman; m. Amy Leusette Luther, May 12, 1984.u. BA, Utah State U., 1971. Chief mng. officer Rocket Messenger Service, Los Angeles, 1971-72, chief exec. officer, 1972-76; chief exec. officer Sonicair Courier Co., Scottsdale, Ariz., 1976—; founder, dir., v.p., pres. Air Courier Conf. Am., 1977—; owner Bloody Mary's Restraunt, Bora Bora, Tahitti. Served with U.S. Army, 1966-68. Named one of 500 Fastest Growing Cos. INC Mag., 1982-84, one of 100 Largest Cos., Ariz. Trend Mag., 1985-86. Mem. Young Pres.'s Orgn., Calif. Trucking Assn. Republican. Club: Via Portola (San Juan Capistrano).

THYGERSON, KENNETH JAMES, finance company executive; b. Chgo., Oct. 1, 1945; s. R. James and Doris L. (Niemann) T.; m. Darlene Kay Vernon, May 24, 1967; children: Keith David, Kent James. B.S., Northwestern U., 1967, Ph.D., 1972. Staff v.p., chief economist U.S. League Savs. Assns., Chgo., 1970-81; exec. v.p. Western Fed. Savs. Colo., Denver, 1981-82; pres., chief exec. officer Fed. Home Loan Mortgage Corp., Washington, 1982-85, Imperial Corp. Am., San Diego, 1985—; vice chmn., dir. Imperial Corp. Am., 1985—; dir. Shelter Am. Corp., 1981-82, W. Am. Mortgage, 1981-82, Instl. Investors, Inc., 1981-82, Western Service Agy., Inc., 1981-82, (all Denver), Midwest Conf., Inc., Chgo., 1976-79; cons. U.S. Gypsum Corp., Chgo., 1967-69. Co-author: Homeownership: Coping with Inflation, 1980, Homeownership: Realizing the American Dream, 1978, Mortgage Portfolio Management, 1978, Tax Management for Savings and Loan Executives, 1977. Mem. council Trinity Lutheran Ch., Evanston, Ill., 1974-77. Served to 1st lt. USAR, 1970-75. NDEA fellow, 1967-70. Mem. Am. Real Estate and Urban Econs. Assn. (dir. 1977-80), Chgo. Am. Statis. Assn. (pres. 1976). Club: Cosmos (Washington). Office: Imperial Corp Am 8787 Complex Dr PO Box 23036 San Diego CA 92123 also: Am Savs Assn of Kansas 201 N Main St Wichita KS 67202

TIBBETTS, HUBERT M., food products company executive; b. 1924. Grad., Harvard. With Lever Bros. Co., 1950-57, Salada Foods Co., 1957-60, Lennen & Newell, 1960-62; pres. Borden Foods div. Borden Inc., 1962-69; exec. v.p. Thomas J. Lipton, Inc., 1969, now pres., chief exec. officer, also dir. Office: Thomas J Lipton Inc 800 Sylvan Ave Englewood Cliffs NJ 07632 *

TICE, CHRISTIAN SHAWN, financial planning executive, educator; b. Chgo.; s. Leroy E. and Julia Tice. BA, U. Calif., Berkeley, 1975; cert., Coll. for Fin. Planning, Denver, 1983. Pres. Alliance for Profl. Planning, Santa Clara, Calif., 1983—; instr. Mission Coll., Santa Clara, 1982—. Mem. Inst. Cert. Fin. Planners, Internat. Assn. Registered Fin. Planners, Internat. Assn. for Fin. Planning. Office: Pvt Ledger Fin Svcs 5450 Thornwood Dr Ste H San Jose CA 95123

TICKETT, DEBORAH LANEY, insurance company executive; b. Jacksonville, Fla., May 18, 1951; d. Charles T. Jr. and Isabelle Lee (Capers) Laney; m. Kenneth Tickett, Mar. 15, 1969; children—Kenneth II, Steven Lee. Student Pinellas Vocat. Tech. Inst., Tampa U.; lic. ins. agent. Sec. Laney & Assocs., Clearwater, Fla., 1974-75, bookkeeper, 1975-77, ins. agent, 1977—, asst. mgr., 1977-79, v.p., mgr., 1979-85, pres., owner, 1986—; sec./treas., majority ptnr. Debco Electric, Inc. Tchr. Episc. Ch. of Good Samaritan, 1972-79, counselor youth group, 1975-79. Mem. Ind. Ins. Agts. Am., Ins. Women St. Petersburg, Nat. Assn. Female Execs., Fla. Assn. Ins. Agts., Clearwater C. of C., Beta Sigma Phi (v.p.). Democrat. Episcopalian. Avocations: design, decorating. Office: Laney & Assocs 514 N Ft Harrison Ave PO Box 1508 Clearwater FL 33517

TIEFEL, WILLIAM REGINALD, hotel company executive; b. Rochester, N.Y., Mar. 30, 1934; s. William Reginald and Mary Hazel (Cross) T.; m. Vada Morell, Dec. 30, 1985. Student, Williams Coll., 1952-54; B.A. with honors, Mich. State U., 1956; postgrad., Harvard Bus. Sch. Gen. mgr. Marriott Hotels, Arlington, Va., 1964-65, Saddle Brook, N.J., 1966-69, Newton, Mass., 1969-71; regional v.p. Marriott Hotels, Washington, 1971-80; corp. v.p. Marriott Corp., Washington, 1976—; exec. v.p. Marriott Hotels and Resorts, 1980-88, pres., 1988—. Bd. visitors Valley Forge Mil. Acad. and Jr. Coll., 1976-79, chmn., 1979, trustee, 1982-88; chmn. Campaign for Valley Forge, 1985—. Served with U.S. Army, 1956. Recipient Distinguished Alumni award, 1977. Mem. Hotel Assn. Va. (dir. 1964-65), Hotel Assn. N.J. (dir. 1966-69), Hotel Assn. Mass. (dir. 1969-71). Republican. Roman Catholic. Home: 2426 Wyoming Ave NW Washington DC 20008 Office: Marriott Corp 1 Marriott Dr Washington DC 20058

TIERNEY, JOHN PATRICK, automotive company financial executive; b. Detroit, Aug. 31, 1931; s. John William and Mary Margaret (Rogers) T.; Dec. 26, 1955; children: Christine, Deanna. B.S. in Acctg. cum laude, U. Detroit, 1955. C.P.A., Mich. Staff acct. Touche Ross, Detroit, 1958-63; dir., profit planning and fin. analysis Am. Motors, Southfield, Mich., 1968-70, asst. controller, 1970-72, corp. dir. fin. services staff, 1972-77, v.p., treas., 1977-82, v.p. fin. staff, controller, 1982-86, v.p. chief fin. officer, 1986-87; chmn. Chrysler Fin. Corp., Troy, Mich., 1987—. Trustee Siena Heights Coll., Adrian, Mich., 1980—. Served to capt. USAF, 1955-58. Mem. Fin. Exec. Inst., Am. Inst. C.P.A.s, Mich. Assn. C.P.A.s. Club: Detroit. Home: 3688 Quail Hollow Bloomfield Hills MI 48013 Office: Chrysler Fin Corp 901 Wilshire Troy MI 48084

TIETBOHL, JON ALAN, investment banker; b. Reading, Pa., Jan. 2, 1959; s. Ralph Harry and Susan Rachel (Foltz) T.; m. Elizabeth Ann Davis, Mar. 12, 1988. BS, Susquehanna U., 1981; MBA, U. Pa., 1985. Assoc. Eppler, Guerin and Turner Inc., Dallas, 1981-83, Bear Stearns and Co., N.Y.C., 1984; v.p. fin. Parkemore Corp., Phila., 1985-86; v.p. Tucker, Anthony and R.L. Day Inc. subs. John Hancock Mut. Lif. Ins. Co., N.Y.C., 1986—. Bd. dirs. Assts. to Homeless of N.Y., 1988. Univ. scholar Susquehanna U., 1981; Univ. fellow U. Pa., 1983. Republican. Lutheran. Club: Wharton. Office: Tucker Anthony and RL Day Inc 120 Broadway Suite 3146 New York NY 10271

TIGER, HYMAN SIDNEY, microwave engineer; b. Bklyn., Aug. 17, 1918; s. Samuel and Mary (Banis) T.; student RCA Inst., 1950; B.E.E., Bklyn. Poly. Inst., 1957; m. Shirley Bezoza, Jan. 11, 1957; children—Neil, Abbe. Engr., Narda Microwave Corp., L.I., N.Y., 1955-57, Airborne Instruments Lab., L.I., 1957-60, Loral Electronics Corp., 1960-63, Blass Antenna Corp., N.Y.C., 1963-65, Honeywell Radiation Center, Boston, 1965-66, RCA Aerospace Div., Burlington, Mass., 1966-68; chief engr. Diamond Antenna & Microwave Corp., Winchester, Mass., 1968-77; with Weinschel Engring. Co., Inc., Gaithersburg, Md., 1977-78, Maury Microwave Corp., Cucamonga, Calif., 1978-79, Microwave Assocs., Burlington, Mass., 1979-81, Diamond Antenna & Microwave Corp., 1981—. Served with Signal Corps, AUS, 1941-45; ETO. Decorated Bronze Star with 3 oak leaf clusters; lic. profl. engr., Mass. Mem. N.Y. Acad. Scis., IEEE, AAAS, Profl. Group Microwave Theory and Techniques. Office: 2 Colony Rd Woburn MA 01801

TIGER, PHILLIP EDWARD, brokerage house executive; b. Bklyn., May 4, 1940; s. William and Belle (Sisserman) T.; m. Sylvia Bellerman, Oct. 7, 1967 (div. 1984); 1 child, Jahn Stefan. BS in Mining and Geology, Colo. Sch. Mines, 1961; MSME, U. Hartford, 1970. Cert. commodity trading advisor. Prodn. foreman Alpha Metals, Inc., Jersey City, N.J., 1961-68; sr. mfg. engr. Hamilton Standard div. United Techs., Windsor Locks, Conn., 1968-70; project engr. cities svc. div. United Techs., Reston, Va., 1970-72; account exec. H.S. Kipnis & Co., Washington, 1972-73; v.p. Conti Commodity Svcs., Washington, 1973-83, Shearson, Lehman, Hutton, Washington, 1983—; editor, chief exec. officer Tiger on Spreads, McLean, Va., 1981—; speaker in field. Co-author: Commodity Research Bureau Yearbook, 1987, Trading Strategies, 1987; editorial rev. bd.: Commodities mag., 1978; contbr. articles to profl. jour. Mem. Nat. Futures Assn. Home: 2245 N Quincy St Arlington VA 22207 Office: Shearson Lehman Hutton 1825 I St NW Washington DC 20006

TIGHE, GERALD GEORGE, diversified holdings corporation executive; b. Bronx, N.Y., Sept. 9, 1935; s. Patrick Francis and Mary Josephine (Friel) T.; m. Catherine Harris, Aug. 24, 1959; children: Denise Sinclair, James, Brian, Sean, David. BS in acctg., Seton Hall U., 1966, JD, 1971. Bar: N.J. 1971. Treas. Wagner Electric Corp., Parsippany, N.J., 1961-85; v.p. legal and tax FL Industries, Livingston, N.J., 1985—, FL Aerospace Corp., Livingston, 1986—; sr. v.p., legal and tax, sec., treas. Lear Siegler Diversified Holdings Corp., Livingston, 1987—. Mem. Tax Execs. Inst., ABA, N.J. Bar Assn., Fin. Exec. Inst. Republican. Roman Catholic. Home: 19 Meyer Rd Edison NJ 08817 Office: FL Industries Corp 220 S Orange Livingston NJ 07039

TIGHT, DEXTER CORWIN, lawyer; b. San Francisco, Sept. 14, 1924; s. Dexter Junkins and Marie (Corwin) T.; m. Elizabeth Callander, Apr. 20, 1951; children: Dexter C. Jr., Kathryn Marie Gerstein, Steven M., David C. BA, Denison U., 1948; JD, Yale U., 1951. Bar: Calif. 1951. Assoc. Pillsbury, Madison & Sutro, San Francisco, 1953-60; gen. atty. W.P. Fuller & Co., San Francisco, 1960-61; gen. counsel Schlage Lock Co., San Francisco, 1961-77; dir. govt. affairs Crown Zellerbach, San Francisco, 1977-78; sr. v.p., gen. counsel The Gap Inc., San Bruno, Calif., 1978—; bd. dirs. Shaw-Clayton Plastics, San Rafael, Calif., Granite Rock Co., Watsonville, Calif., X-L Mfg. Co., Chico, Calif. Bd. dirs. San Francisco Boy's and Girl's Club, Am. Cancer Soc.; trustee Denison U., 1978. 1st lt. U.S. Army, 1943-45, 51-52. Mem. ABA, Calif. Bar Assn., San Francisco Bar Assn. (chmn. various coms.), Commonwealth Club Calif. (past bd. dirs.), Menlo Country Club, Bohemian Club (San Francisco), Guardsmen Club (1st v.p. 1961), Phi Beta Kappa. Republican. Presbyterian. Home: 2744 Steiner St San Francisco CA 94123 Office: The Gap Inc 900 Cherry Ave San Bruno CA 94066

TILDEN, CHARLES RIPLEY, manufacturing company executive; b. Evanston, Ill., Oct. 27, 1953; s. Averill Baylies and Elizabeth Ann (Pomeroy) T.; m. Elizabeth Behr, Oct. 22, 1977; children: Matthew, Emily, Michael. BA, DePauw U., 1975; MBA, U Chgo., 1982. Mgr. news svc. Montgomery Ward & Co., Chgo., 1975-78; dir. communications A.T. Kearney Co., Chgo., 1978-83; dir. ctr. for entrepreneurship, lectr. communications Depauw U., Greencastle, Ind., 1983-85; dir. communications DiversiTech Gen., Akron, Ohio, 1985-88; v.p. communications GenCorp, Inc., Fairlawn, Ohio, 1988—. Trustee Akron Zool. Pk., 1986-89; chmn. promotions com. United Way Summit County, Akron, 1987; vestryman St. John's Episcopal Ch., Cuyahoga Falls, Ohio, 1988—. Mem. Pub. Relations Soc. Am., Akron Press Club, Cleve. Press Club, Cascade Club, Fairlawn Country Club. Office: GenCorp Inc 175 Ghent Rd Fairlawn OH 44313-3300

TILGHMAN, RICHARD GRANVILLE, banker; b. Norfolk, Va., Sept. 18, 1940; s. Henry Granville and Frances (Fulghum) T.; m. Alice Creech, June 28, 1969; children—Elizabeth Arrington, Caroline Harrison. B.A., U. Va., 1963. Asst. cashier United Va. Bank-Seaboard Nat., Norfolk, Va., 1968-70, asst. v.p., 1970-72; pres., chief adminstrv. officer United Va. Bank, Richmond, 1978-80; asst. v.p. United Va. Mortgage Corp., Norfolk, Va., 1972, v.p., 1972-73, pres., chief exec. officer, 1974-76; pres., chief exec. officer United Va. Leasing Corp., Richmond, Va., 1973-74; sr. v.p. bank related United Va. Bankshares, Inc., Richmond, 1976-78, exec. v.p. corp. banking, 1980-84, vice chmn., 1984-85; pres., chief exec. officer United Va. Bankshares, Inc., now Crestar Fin. Corp., Richmond, 1985—, chmn., 1986—; bd. dirs. dir. Chesapeake Corp., Richmond, 1986—; chmn. Va. Public Bldg. Authority, Richmond, 1982-87. Chmn. bd. dirs. Richmond Symphony, Va., 1984-85; bd. dirs. Sheltering Arms Hosp., Richmond, 1985—, Va. Mus. Found., 1986—; mem. Va. Literacy Found. Bd.,1986—; trustee Randolph-Macon Coll., 1985—, Richmond Renaissance, 1986—. Served to 1st lt. U.S. Army, 1963-66. Mem. Assn. Reserve City Bankers, Am. Bankers Assn., Am. Inst. Bankers, Va. Bankers Assn., Robert Morris Assocs., Assn. Bank Holding Cos. Episcopalian. Clubs: Commonwealth, Country of Va. Office: Crestar Fin Corp 919 E Main St PO Box 26665 Richmond VA 23261-6665

TILLEY, C. RONALD, gas company executive; b. Welch, W.Va., Oct. 20, 1935; s. Clarence D. and Mildred R. (Carnes) T.; m. Janice E. Tilley, Aug. 24, 1956; children: Christopher R., Cory G., Beth Ann. B.S. in Acctg., Concord Coll., 1957. Clk. rate dept. United Fuel Gas Co., Charleston, W.Va., 1957-62, rate analyst, 1962-64; engr. rate dept. Columbia Gas Service Corp., N.Y.C., 1964-71; mgr. rate dept. Columbia Gas Service Corp., Columbus, Ohio, 1971-73; dir. rate dept. Columbia Gas Service Corp., Charleston, 1973-75; v.p. corp. Columbia Gas Service Corp., Washington, 1975-80; v.p. rate Columbia Gas Service Corp., Wilmington, Del., 1980-82; sr. v.p. Columbia Gas Distbn. Cos., Columbus, 1982-85, pres., 1985-87, chmn., chief exec. officer, 1987—; Bd. dirs. BancOhio Nat. Bank. Mem. bd. trustees Columbus Symphony Orch., 1988—; bd. dirs. United Negro Coll. Fund, 1987—. Served with U.S. Army, 1958-60. Mem. Columbus Area C. of C. (bd. dirs. 1987—). Republican. Office: Columbia Gas Distbn Cos 200 Civic Center Dr Columbus OH 43215

TILLINGHAST, JOHN AVERY, technology company executive; b. N.Y.C., Apr. 30, 1927; s. Charles C. and Dorothy J. (Rollhaus) T.; m. Mabel Healy, Sept. 11, 1948; children: Katherine Brickley, Susan Trainor, Abigail Ryan. BS in Mech. Engring., Columbia U., 1948, MS, 1949. Registered profl. engr., Ky., Ind., Mich., N.Y., Ohio, Va., W.Va., N.H. With Am. Elec. Power Service Corp., N.Y.C., 1949-79, exec. v.p. engring. and constrn., 1967-72, sr. exec. v.p., vice chmn. engring. and constrn., 1972-79; sr. v.p. tech. Wheelabrator-Frye Inc., Hampton, N.H., 1979-83, Signal Advanced Tech. Group, The Signal Cos., Hampton, N.H., 1983-85; sr. v.p. Allied-Signal Internat., Hampton, 1985-86, Sci. Applications Internat. Corp., San Diego, 1986-88; pres. TILTEC, Portsmouth, N.H, 1987—. Patentee generating unit control system. Elder Reformed Ch., 1976-79. Served with USN, 1944-46. Fellow ASME; mem. Nat. Acad. Engring. (chmn. energy engring. bd.), IEEE, Sigma Xi, Tau Beta Pi. Office: TILTEC 20 Ladd St Portsmouth NH 03801

TILTON, WEBSTER, JR., general contractor; b. St. Louis, Sept. 11, 1922; s. Webster and Eleanor (Dozier) T.; student St. Marks Prep. Sch., 1936-40, Pawling Prep. Sch., 1940-42; master brewers degree, U.S. Brewers Acad., 1949; m. Grace Drew Wilson, Feb. 14, 1948 (div. Oct. 1959); 1 son, Webster III; m. 2d, Nancy McBlair Payne, Jan. 5, 1963. Asst. brewing technologist F&M Schaffer Brewing Co., Bklyn., 1948-52; factory sales rep. Cole Steel Equipment Co., N.Y.C., 1957-68; dist. sales mgr. Scantlin Electronics, Inc., Washington, 1968-70; sales rep. Comml. Washer & Dryer Sales Co., Washington, 1970-72; propr. Webster Tilton, Jr., contractor, Washington, 1972-86. Served from cadet to chief mate Mcht. Marine Res.-USNR, 1942-45. Episcopalian. Home: RD #2 Box 634 Cooperstown NY 13326

TILVES, MARIA PILAR, organization official; b. N.Y.C., Sept. 6, 1964; d. Jose and Josephine (Alonso) T. BA, NYU, 1986. Staff asst. U.S.-USSR Trade and Econ. Council, N.Y.C., 1986-87; asst. to pres. Council on Fgn. Relations, N.Y.C., 1987—. Democrat. Roman Catholic. Home: 290 9th Ave Apt 15B New York NY 10001 Office: 58 E 68th St New York NY 10021

TIMBLIN, STANLEY WALTER, manufacturing executive; b. Butler, Pa., Feb. 16, 1937; s. William Cecil and Beulah (Rankin) T.; m. Mary Evelyn Cabe, June 7, 1959; children: Stephen Douglas, Jeffrey William, Dianne Elizabeth. BSEE, N.C. State U., 1960; M in Engring. Adminstrn., George Washington U., 1967. Registered profl. engr., Md. Quality control engr. Westinghouse Electric, Balt., 1960-64, test engring. supr., 1965-68, mgr. product reliability, 1968-70; corp. quality staff Westinghouse Electric, Pitts., 1970-71, engring. mgr. consumer services, 1971-73; pres., owner Tim-Tech Controls, Greensboro, N.C., 1973—. Contbr. numerous articles on quality control, 1965-71; patentee bldg. automation controls, refrigeration and security controls. Mem. IEEE, ASHRAE, Assn. Energy Engrs. Republican. Presbyterian. Club: Greensboro Engrs. Home: 4 Forest Hill Ct Greensboro NC 27410 Office: Tim Tech Controls Co 1109 S Chapman St Greensboro NC 27403

TIMBOE, TODD JEFFREY, accountant; b. Great Falls, Mont., May 31, 1960; s. Harlan Eugene and Barbara Helen (Trent) T.; m. KellyLee Marie Peabody, June 1, 1985 (div. Aug. 1987); children: Shawn Todd, Matthew Harlan (dec.). Student, Phoenix Jr. Coll., 1978-80; BSBA, U. Mont., 1983. Staff acct. Douglas Wilson & Co. CPA's, Great Falls, 1983-86; supr. Joseph Eve & Co. CPA's, Great Falls, 1986—. Treas. Mont. chpt. Mutiple Sclerosis Soc., Great Falls, 1985-86, vice-chmn., 1986-87, chmn. bd. dirs., 1987—. Mem. AICPA, Mont. Soc. CPA's, Great Falls Chpt. CPA's, Meadow Lark Country, Universal Sports and Cts., Great Falls Quarterbacks's Club, Inc. (sec., treas. 1986—). Home: 102 21st Ave NW Great Falls MT 59404 Office: Joseph Eve & Co CPAs Strain Bldg Ste 414 Great Falls MT 59401

TIMKEN, W. ROBERT, JR., manufacturing company executive; b. 1938; married. B.A., Stanford U., 1960; M.B.A., Harvard U., 1962. With Timken Co. (formerly The Timken Roller Bearing Co.), Canton, Ohio, 1962—, asst. v.p. sales, 1964-65, dir. corp. devel., 1965-68, v.p., 1968-73, vice-chmn. bd., chmn. fin. com., 1973-75, chmn. bd., chmn. fin. com., 1975—, chmn. exec. com., 1983—, also dir. Office: The Timken Co 1835 Dueber Ave SW Canton OH 44706 *

TIMLIN, MICHAEL JOSEPH, III, sales and marketing executive; b. Chgo., Aug. 27, 1958; s. Michael Joseph Jr. and Anne (Mancini) T.; Lisa A. Deverse, July 16, 1983 (div. Dec. 1987). BS, U.S. Mil. Acad., 1980; MS in Mech. Engring., Stanford U., 1981. Sales engr. Internat. Microcircuits, Santa Clara, Calif., 1985-86, product mktg. mgr., 1986-87, dir. mktg. and sales, 1987-88; field sales engr. Advanced Micro Devices, San Jose, Calif., 1988—. Capt. U.S. Army, 1980-85. Hertz Found. fellow Fannie and John Hertz Found., Livermore, Calif., 1980. Republican. Roman Catholic. Home: 3770 Flora Vista #903 Santa Clara CA 95051 Office: Advanced Micro Devices 1751 Fox Dr Suite 29000 San Jose CA 95131

TIMM, ALBERT LEONARD, management executive; b. Bronx, N.Y., July 12, 1929; s. Charles John and Margaret (Hanson) T.; m. Ursula Rippholz, June 24, 1961; children: Scott A. and Brian R. (twins). B in Marine Engring., N.Y. State Maritime Acad., 1951; MBA, NYU, 1963; postgrad. in mgmt. Harvard U. Sch. Bus., 1978, Rensselaer Poly. Inst., 1967. Lic. gen. contractor, real estate broker. Field service engr., dist. sales mgr., then Eastern regional sales mgr. A.M. Byers subs. Gen. Tire & Rubber Co., N.Y.C., 1956-64; sr. mktg. analyst, market research mgr., mktg. mgr. subs. level, then mgr. mktg., acquisitions and long range planning indsl. group Combustion Engring. Inc., Hartford, Conn., 1964-69; v.p. E.S. Moorhead & Assos. Inc., Ft. Lauderdale, Fla., 1969-70; v.p. mktg. Sunair Electronics, Ft. Lauderdale, 1970-71; v.p. mktg. and planning C.E. Morgan Inc. div. Combustion Engring. Inc., Miami, Fla., 1972-83; fin. cons. Merrill, Lynch, Pierce, Fenner & Smith, Ft. Lauderdale, 1983-85; property mgr. 1st Am. Bank, Lake Worth, Fla., 1985-87; pres. Eagle Precision Co., Ft. Lauderdale, 1987—; assoc. prof. mktg. Ft. Lauderdale U., also Embry Riddle Grad. Sch. at Biscayne Coll., Nova U., Broward Community Coll. Served to lt. USN, 1952-53, Korea. Mem. Am. Mktg. Assn., Soc. Naval Architects and Marine Engrs. Lodge: Lions. Home: 649 Ixora Ln Plantation FL 33317

TIMMERMAN, LEON BERNARD, pump industry consultant; b. Buffalo, Aug. 20, 1924; s. Leon D. and Julia (Schlau) T.; m. Kathryn Wagner, Feb. 26, 1924; children: Kathryn Timmerman Susak, Carol Timmerman Yorty. BSME, Purdue U., 1949; grad. bus. mgmt. program, Harvard U., 1970. Lic. profl. engr., N.Y. With Buffalo Pumps, 1949-87; engr., sales mgr. various locations, 1949-80; nat. sales and mktg. mgr. North Tonawanda, N.Y., 1981-87; pres., cons. to pump and related industries CP Cons. Svcs., Williamsville, N.Y., 1987—; com. chmn. Hydraulic Inst., 1961-78, v.p., 1978-79, pres., 1979-80, chmn. exec. com., 1980-81, Europump rep. 1978-81. Contbr. articles to profl. jours. Served with Signal Corps U.S. Army, 1945-48, PTO. Recipient numerous Salesman of Yr. awards Buffalo Pumps Inc. 1955-70. Mem. Tech. Assn. Pulp and Paper Industry, Scalp & Blade. Republican. Presbyterian. Club: Brookfield Country. Office: CP Cons Svcs 41 Carriage Circle Williamsville NY 14221

TIMMERMAN, WILLIAM B., utilities company financial executive; b. Columbia, S.C., Nov. 12, 1946; s. William Bledsoe and Helen (Speissegger) T.; m. Janet Russell, Sept. 15, 1971; children: William III, Catherine Lucille. BA in Pub. Acctg., Duke U., 1968. CPA, N.C. Auditor Arthur Andersen & Co., Charlotte, N.C., 1968-78; sr. v.p. Carolina Energies, Inc., Columbia, 1978-82; v.p. S.C. Electric & Gas Co., Columbia, 1982-83, v.p., group exec., 1983-84; chief fin. officer, sr. v.p. Scana Corp., Columbia, 1984—; exec. adv. com. Edison Electric Inst.; acctg. and fin. exec. com. Southeastern Electric Exchange; owner, dir. Pearson Yacht Corp., Portsmouth, R.I. Trustee United Way of Midlands, Columbia, 1985—; vice chmn. fin. ARC, Columbia, 1986—; adv. bd. Sch. Bus. U. S.C., 1985—. Served with USN, 1968-72. Office: Scana Corp 1426 Main St Suite 100 Columbia SC 29202

TIMMINS, E. SCOTT, management consultant; b. Phila., Dec. 15, 1960; s. Edward John and Carolyn Wells (Bond) T. BA, Skidmore Coll., 1982; MBA, Babson Coll., 1987. Mktg. dir. Wintz Assoc., Morristown, N.J., 1982-85; brand mgr. Pepsi-Cola Internat., Nicosia, Cyprus, 1986; gen. mgr. New Eng. Window Designs, Inc., Hingham, Mass., 1986-87; mgmt. cons. Orgnl. Dynamics, Inc., Burlington, Mass., 1987—. Charles Merill scholar Skidmore Coll., 1978-79. Mem. Am. Soc. Quality Control. Home: 25 E Concord St Boston MA 02118 Office: Orgnl Dynamics Inc 25 Mall Rd Burlington MA 01803

TIMMONS, GORDON DAVID, economics educator; b. Elbert, Tex., May 21, 1919; s. Walter James and Ella Mae (McCarson) T.; m. Jean Betty Kulhanek, Feb. 11, 1947; children: Kathy, Linda, Scott, Jim, Tamara, Dallas, Timothy, Kelly, Susanna. Student, U. Tex., 1937-40, U. Mont., 1961-64; BS, Utah State U., 1955; MS, Mont. State U., 1958. Enlisted USAF, 1939, advanced through grades to col., ret., 1961; instr. Columbia Basin Coll., Pasco, Wash., 1966-86; pres. Assn. Higher Edn., 1969-72. Decorated Legion of Merit, Croix de Guerre (France). Mem. Northwest Econ. Conf. Democrat. Home and Office: Star Rt Box 39-A Olney TX 76374

TIMMONS, JEFFREY CLARK, finance executive, accountant, consultant; b. Columbus, Ohio, Nov. 14, 1959; s. Robert Lacey Timmons and Jane Anne (Dodge) Kenan. BA, BS, Otterbein Coll., 1981; MBA, Ohio State U., 1983. CPA, Ohio; cert. managerial acct. Staff acct. Dale R. Saylor, CPA, Dublin, Ohio, 1980-83; pvt. practice cons. Columbus, Ohio, 1983-84; treas., chief fin. officer Great Am. Fun Corp., Columbus, 1984—; mgmt. rep. to bd. dirs. Great Am. Fun Corp., Columbus, 1985—; cons. computer programming, Columbus, 1984—. Mem. Am. Inst. CPA's, Ohio Soc. CPA's, Nat. Assn. Accts., Phi Eta Sigma. Clubs: Columbus Ski. Home: 1461 Runaway Bay Dr Apt 1-D Columbus OH 43204 Office: Great Am Fun Corp 3656 Paragon Dr Columbus OH 43228

TIMMRECK, JOE EDWARD, data processor; b. Longview, Wash., Oct. 8, 1950; s. Carmin C. and Betty (Snyder) T.; m. Janet Clipp; 1 dau., Jennifer. A.A. in Computer Sci., Lower Columbia Coll., 1970; student Weber State Coll., 1971-74. Engr. technician Ultrasystems, Ogden, Utah, 1973-75; system programmer St. Benedict's Hosp., Ogden, 1975-77; system analyst Jackson County (Oreg.), 1978-79; data processing mgr. Medford (Oreg.) Sch. Dist. 549C, 1979-83; writer, bus. cons. The Key Found., Point Roberts, Wash., 1987—. Founder, pres. Human Potentials Unltd., Medford, 1981-87; pub. The Obelisk, Medford, 1982-87. Mem. Am. Mgmt. Assn., Oreg. Assn. Ednl. Data Systems. Home and Office: 1905 Province Rd Point Roberts WA 98281

TIMMS, LEONARD JOSEPH, JR., gas company executive; b. Pitts., Dec. 10, 1936; s. Leonard Joseph Sr. and Dorthea W. (Abernethy) T.; m. Annabel Phillips, Apr. 1, 1959; children: Cynthia, Rebecca, Sarah. BCE, MIT, 1958; BS in Bus. and Econs., Salem Coll., 1975. Pipeline engr. Williams Bros., Tulsa, 1958-61; planning engr. No. Natural Gas, Omaha, 1961-63; sr. engr. CNG Transmission Corp. (name formerly Consol. Gas Transmission), Clarksburg, W.Va., 1963-70, asst. chief engr., 1970-72, mgr. computer services, 1972-75, chief engr., 1975-80, v.p. engring. and ops. services, 1980-84, sr. v.p. ops., 1984-86, pres., 1986—, also bd. dirs., 1983—; bd. dirs. Empire Nat. Bank, United Hosp. Ctr. Served to capt. USAR. Mem. ASCE, NSPE, Am. Gas Assn., So. Gas Assn. (bd. dirs.). Republican. Presbyterian. Lodge: Lions (pres. Clarksburg chpt. 1979-80). Home: 801 Worthington Dr Bridgeport WV 26330

TINKER, DEBRA ANN, health facility administrator; b. Cleve., June 27, 1951; d. Keith Donald and Rita Patricia (Rowinski) T.; m. Charles Earl Enos, Aug. 6, 1983; children: Christopher Tinker Enos, Matthew Tinker Enos. BS in Edn. cum laude, Ohio U., 1973; MA in Clin. and Community Psychology, Chapman Coll., 1988. Tchr. English, remedial reading Northmont Jr. High Sch., Clayton, Ohio, 1973-76; dance instr. Schehera's Studio, Dayton, Ohio, 1974-76; substitute tchr. Knox County Schs., Mt. Vernon, Ohio, 1976; tchr. English, remedial reading Ohio Youth Commn., Massillon, Ohio, 1977; coordinator spl. needs program Knox County Joint Vocat. Sch., Mt. Vernon, 1977-82; life ins. sales Belding and Assocs., Mt. Vernon, 1980-82; student control officer Naval Air Tng. Unit, Sacramento, 1982-85; dir. Navy Counseling and Assistance Ctr., Charleston, S.C., 1985-88; chief counseling svcs. Navy Family Svc. Ctr., Charleston, 1988—. Leader Girl Scouts Am., Dayton, Ohio counsel, 1975-76, mem., cons. North Charleston, S.C., 1987—; exec. producer Mt. Vernon AWARE, 1977-81; mem. Navy Family Advocacy Support Team, Charleston, 1985—, Navy Alcohol and Drug Adv. Council, Charleston, 1985-88, chairwoman, 1988; bd. dirs. Exchange Club Ctr. for the Prevention of Child Abuse, Charleston, 1987-88, adv. com. Promulgation Child Abuse & Neglect Definitions, 1989. Served to lt. USNR, 1982—. Mem. Am. Psychol. Assn. (assoc. 1989—), Charleston Women Officer's Assn., S.C. Mental Health Counselors' Assn., Soc. Mayflower Descendants, Mensa, Kappa Delta Pi. Independent. Lutheran. Home: 202 Brailsford Rd Summerville SC 29485 Office: Navy Family Svc Ctr Naval Base Code N52 Charleston SC 29408-5100

TINKOFF, BERNARD, accountant; b. N.Y.C., Dec. 10, 1933; s. Richard and Anna (Condiotti) T.; m. Norma L. DeCastro, Feb. 10, 1952; children: Glen, Wendy, Adam. BBA, CCNY, 1958. CPA, Fla., N.Y., Iowa. Staff acct. Coopers and Lybrand, N.Y.C., 1957-70, ptnr., 1970-72; mng. ptnr. Coopers and Lybrand, Long Island, N.Y., 1972-79, Des Moines, 1979-83; ptnr. Coopers and Lybrand, Miami, Fla., 1983-86; mng. ptnr. Coopers and Lybrand, West Palm Beach, Fla., 1986—. Bd. dirs., treas. Palm Beach Devel. Bd., Palm Beach County, Fla, 1986—, Ctr. for Family Services of Palm Beach County, 1986—; mem. adv. bd. World Tech. Ctr. Fla., Miami, 1987—; bd. dirs. Jr. Achievement, Palm Beach County, 1987—. Served as cpl. U.S. Army, 1950-52. Mem. Am. Inst. CPA's, Fla. Soc. CPA's, Broadcast Fin. Mgmt. Assn., Mcpl. Fin. Officers Assn. Office: Coopers and Lybrand 1675 Palm Beach Lakes Blvd West Palm Beach FL 33401

TINNEY, DEE MELVIN, marketing executive; b. Muskegon, Mich., Oct. 11, 1940; s. Rodney Melvin Tinney and Katherine Elisabeth (Hollowell) Kunkle; m. Linda Texie Heilig, Apr. 21, 1964; children: Robin E., Christine A. Grad. high sch., Muskegon, Mich.; diploma, McDonald's Mgmt. Sch., 1966; cert.fin. mgmt., Wharton Sch. U. Pa., 1986; cert., U. Denver. Registered fin. broker. Gen. mgr. Millman Braodcasting, St. Petersburg, Fla., 1970-76; pres. Media 1, Inc., Eau Claire, Wis., 1976-81; dir. new bus. Eau Claire Press Co., 1979-81; mgr. new bus. devel. ATC, Englewood, Colo., 1981-86; dir. mktg. SISCOM, Boulder, Colo., 1986-87; mktg. mgr. Digital Equipment Corp., Merrimack, N.H., 1987—. Author: How to Start Your Own Ad Agency, 1979; pub. newsletter, Advertising Ideas, 1978; inventor Still Frame Ad Machine, 1982; contbr. articles in field. Home: 168 S Merrimack Rd Hollis NH 03049

TINNEY, RICHARD D., forest products executive; b. Everett, Wash., Apr. 19, 1939; s. William Abner and Helen (Cane) T.; m. Carol J. Zalenski; children: Meagan Helen, Michael Donavan. Student, Oreg. State U., 1957-58; BS in Forest Mgmt., U. Wash., 1967. Asst. gen. mgr. Pubs. Paper Co., Oregon City, Oreg., 1969-73; v.p., gen. mgr. West Coast Lumber Mills, Tacoma, 1974-78, Plum Creek, Inc., Seattle, 1978-83; asst. to pres. Bohemia, Inc., Eugene, Oreg., 1983-84, exec. v.p., 1984-87, pres., chief exec. officer, 1987—. Mem. adv. com. Sacred Heart Hosp., Portland, Oreg., 1987—. Lt. U.S. Army, 1958-62. Mem. Assn. Oreg. Industries (bd. dirs. 1987—), Lumbermen's Underwriting Alliance (mem. adv. com. 1987—), Oreg. Forest Industries (mem. exec. com. 1987—), Town Club, Arlington Club (Portland). Democrat. Office: Bohemia Inc PO Box 1819 2280 Oakmont Way Eugene OR 97401

TINSLEY, THOMAS VINCENT, JR., accounting company executive; b. Wilkes-Barre, Pa., Oct. 16, 1940; s. Thomas Vincent and Mary Clare (Green) T.; B.S. in Acctg., U. Scranton, 1963; grad. in programming Electronic Computer Programming Inst., 1966; m. Katherine Alice Swan, Oct. 15, 1966; children: Sara Elisabeth, Tracy Swan. Jr. acct. Peat, Marwick, Mitchell & Co., Balt., 1963-64; accounts receivable mgr., import acctg. mgr. Aimcee Wholesale Corp., N.Y.C., 1964-65; sr. acct. Richards, Ganly, Fries & Preusch, N.Y.C., 1965-66, Morris J. Weinstein, Groothius & Co., N.Y.C., 1966-69; supr. Brach Lane Hariton & Hirshberg, N.Y.C., 1969-70; owner mgr. Thomas V. Tinsley, Jr., C.P.A., Wilkes Barre, Pa. and N.Y.C., 1970-78; sr. partner Tinsley & Co., C.P.A.s, Wilkes-Barre and N.Y.C., 1978-83; pres. Tinsley & Co. P.C., Wilkes-Barre, Pa. and N.Y.C., 1984—; notary public, Luzerne County, Pa.; mem. faculty bank Found. for Acctg. Edn. Mem. Fairview Twp. Planning Commn., 1979-89, Fairview Twp. Zoning and Hearing Bd., 1979—. Served with USMCR, 1960-66. C.P.A., N.Y., Pa., N.J. Mem. Am. Arbitration Assn., Am., Pa. insts. C.P.A.s, Acctg. Research Assn., N.J., N.Y. State socs. C.P.A.s, Nat. Rifle Assn., U. Scranton Nat. Alumni Soc. (bd. govs. 1979—), Luzerne County Law Enforcement Officers and Assocs. Democrat. Roman Catholic. Clubs: Valley Country, N.Y. Athletic, World Trade Center, Union League (N.Y.C.); Nuangola Rod and Gun; West Side Tennis. Lodge: K.C. Home: Box 366 White Birch Ln Glen Summit Mountaintop PA 18707 Office: 10 W Northampton St Suite 500 Wilkes-Barre PA 18707

TINSTMAN, DALE CLINTON, investment company executive, lawyer; b. Chester, Nebr., May 19, 1919; s. Elizabeth (Gretzinger) T.; married; children: Thomas C., Nancy Remington, Jane Kramer. BSBA, U. Nebr., 1941, JD, 1947. Bar: Nebr. Asst. sec., asst. mgr. investment dept. 1st Trust Co. Lincoln, Nebr., 1947-58; v.p., asst. treas. Securities Acceptance Corp., Omaha, 1958-60; fin. v.p., treas. Cen. Nat. Ins. Group of Omaha, 1958-60; pres., treas. Tinstman & Co., Inc., Lincoln, 1960-61; exec. v.p. 1st Mid-Am., Inc., Lincoln, 1961-68, pres., 1968-74, chmn. bd., 1974, fin. cons., 1974-76; pres., mem. exec. com., bd. dirs. Iowa Beef Processors, Inc. (now IBP, Inc.), Dakota City, Nebr., 1976-77; vice chmn., chmn. fin. com., mem. exec. com. Iowa Beef Processors, Inc. (now IBP, Inc.), Dakota City, 1977-81, co-chmn. bd., chmn. fin. com., bd. dirs., 1981-83; chmn., bd. dirs. Eaton Tinstman Druliner, Inc., Lincoln, 1983—; bd. dirs. FirsTier, Inc., Mall Corp., Nebr. Broiler Co., Inc., Nat. Dynamics Corp. Past chmn. Nebr. Investment Council; mem. Nebr. Investment Fin. Auth.; trustee U. Nebr. Found. Inst., Livestock Merchandising Council; elder Westminster Presbyn. Ch., Lincoln; former bd. dirs. and officer Lincoln Community Chest; past mem. exec. com. Cornhusker council Boy Scouts Am. With USAAF, WWII; with USAF, Korea; col. Res. ret. Mem. Nebr. Bar Assn., Nebr. Securities Assn., Nat. Ind. Meat Packers Assn. (bd. dirs.), Nebr. Diplomats, Newcomen Soc. N.Am., Omaha-Lincoln Soc. Fin. Analysts, Lincoln C. of C. (past bd. dirs., officer), Am. Legion, N.G. Assn. Nebr. (past pres.), Linclon Country Club, Firethorn Country Club, Nebr. Country Club, Phi Delta Phi, Alpha Sigma. Office: Eaton Tinstman Druliner Inc 1712 FirsTier Bank Bldg Lincoln NE 68508

TIPPER, HARRY, III, reinsurance company executive; b. Somerville, N.J., Oct. 15, 1949; s. Harry Jr. and Marjorie Hyde (Burns) T.; m. Kathleen Suzanne McQueen, Aug. 28, 1970; children: Bradley Stockton, Russell Winston. BA, Cornell U., 1971; MBA, NYU, 1980. Underwriting cons. Nat. Council on Compensation Ins., N.Y.C., 1973-75; asst. sec. Gen. Reins. Corp., N.Y.C., 1975-79; asst. v.p. Gen. Reins. Corp., Greenwich, Conn., 1979-84; 2d v.p. Gen. Reins. Corp., Stamford, Conn., 1984—. Bd. dirs. Wilton (Conn.) Soccer Assn., 1986—, v.p., 1987—. Mem. Self-Ins. Inst. Am., NYU Grad. Sch. Bus. Adminstrn. Alumni Assn. (bd. dirs. 1984-87, treas. 1985-87), N.Y. Athletic Club, Aspetuck Valley Country Club. Office: Genesis Underwriting Mgmt Co PO Box 10352 Stamford CT 06904-2352

TIPPETS, DENNIS WILCOCK, mineral exploration executive, state legislator; b. Wheatland, Wyo., Dec. 30, 1938; s. Neff H. and Elizabeth (Wilcock) T.; m. Dianne Elizabeth Barkley, June 11, 1961; children: Lynn Elizabeth, Kevin Craig, Bruce Barkley. BA, U. Colo., 1962. Personnel adminstr. Lamb-Grays Harbor Co. Inc., Hoquiam, Wash., 1965-67; mgmt. cons. Roy Jorgenson Assoc., Gaithersburg, Md., 1967-71; v.p. Stylhomes Inc., Riverton, Wyo., 1971-76; pres. Tippets Appraisal Service, Riverton, 1976-80; chmn. bd., pres., chief exec. officer Minex Resources Inc., Riverton, 1980—; bd. dirs. Methanol Prodn. Corp., Denver; comdg. officer U.S. Naval Res. Surface Div. 13-9, Aberdeen, Wash., 1966-67. State rep. Wyo. Ho. of Reps., Cheyenne, 1985—; chmn., mem. Riverton Sch. Bd., 1975-81; pres., bd. dirs. Idea Inc., Riverton, 1986-88; v.p. Fremont County Rep. Party, Lander, Wyo., 1978-80. Served to lt. USNR. Named Most Effective Freshman Legislator, Wyo. Capital Press Corp., Cheyenne, 1985. Mem. Am. Inst. Real Estate Appraisers (residential mem., chmn. Sci. & Tech. Com.), Nat. Conf. State Legislatures, Am. Mining Congress, Rocky Mountain Oil & Gas Assn., Am. Legion (trustee Riverton post 1987-89). Republican. Mormon. Lodge: Rotary (pres. Riverton club 1978). Home: 1614 Gannett Dr Riverton WY 82501 Office: Minex Resources Inc 205 S Broadway Riverton WY 82501

TIPPETT, WILLIS PAUL, JR., textile company executive; b. Cin., Dec. 27, 1932; s. Willis Paul and Edna Marie (Conn) T.; m. Carlotta Prichard, Jan. 24, 1959; children: Willis Paul III, Holly. A.B., Wabash Coll., 1953. Brand mgr., advt. supr. Procter & Gamble Co., Cin., 1958-64; advt. and sales promotion mgr. Ford Motor Co., Dearborn, Mich., 1964-65; gen. mktg. mgr. Ford Motor Co., 1965-69; advt. mgr. Ford Motor Co. (Ford div.), 1969-70, advt. and sales promotion mgr., 1970-72; v.p. product and mktg. Philco-Ford Corp., Phila., 1972-73; dir. sales and mktg. Ford of Europe, Inc., Brentwood, Essex, Eng., 1973-75; pres., dir. STP Corp., Ft. Lauderdale, Fla., 1975-76; exec. v.p., dir. Singer Co., N.Y.C., 1976-78; pres., chief operating officer, dir. Am. Motors Corp., Southfield, Mich., 1978-82; chmn., chief exec. officer Am. Motors Corp., Southfield, 1982-85; pres. Springs Industries, Inc., Ft. Mill, S.C., 1985—; bd. dirs. Springs Industries, Inc., Barry Wright Corp. Mem. bus. com. Met. Mus. Art. Served with USN, 1953-58. Club: Univ. (N.Y.C.). Office: Springs Industries Inc 205 N White St Fort Mill SC 29715

TIPTON, GARY LEE, personal services company executive; b. Salem, Oreg., July 3, 1941; s. James Rains and Dorothy Velma (Dierks) T.; BS, Oreg. Coll. Edn., 1964. Credit rep. Standard Oil Co. Calif., Portland, Oreg., 1964-67; credit mgr. Uniroyal Inc., Dallas, 1967-68; partner, mgr. bus. Tipton Barbers, Portland, 1968—. Mem. Rep. Nat. Com., 1980—, Sen. Howard Baker's Presdl. Steering Com., 1980; apptd. Deputy Dir. Gen., Internat. Biog. Ctr., Cambridge, England, 1987—; mem. U.S. Congl. adv. bd. Am. Security Council, 1984-88. Recipient Key to Internat. Biog. Cen., Cambridge, U.K., 1983, World Culture prize Accademia Italia, 1984, Presdl. Achievement award, 1982, cert. disting. contbn. Sunset High Sch. Dad's Club, 1972, 73. Fellow Internat. Biog. Assn. (life, Key award 1983) (U.K.); mem. Sunset Mchts. Assn. (co-founder, treas. 1974-79, pres. 1982-83), Internat. Platform Assn., Smithsonian Assocs., Council on Fgn. Relations (vice chmn. steering com. Portland 1983-84, chmn. Portland com. on fgn. relations 1984-86), UN Assn. (steering com. UN day 1985). Office: Tipton Barbers 1085 NW Murray Rd Portland OR 97229

TIRINO, PHILIP JOSEPH, accountant; b. N.Y.C., Feb. 12, 1940; s. Philip Vincent and Louise Ann (Lanza) T.; m. Joan M. Marino, 1979; children—Philip Jr., Bart Scott, David. B.B.A. in Bus. Acctg., Hofstra U., 1962. C.P.A., N.Y. Auditor N.Y. State Dept. Fin., N.Y.C., 1962-65; acct., auditor various publ. acctg. firms, N.Y.C., 1964-69; controller Berman Leasing Co., Englewood, N.J., 1969-73, Bank of Calif., Stanford, Conn., 1973-74, Chase Manhattan Bank, N.Y.C., 1975-78, Bankers Trust Co., N.Y.C., 1978-83; speaker Found. Acctg. Edn., N.Y.C., 1977—, Am. Assn. Equipment Lessors, Washington, 1977-82, World Trade Inst., 1980. Contbr. articles to profl. jours. Tax planner Taxpayer's Assn., Nanuet, N.Y., 1981; budget officer Clarkstown Suprs. Office, New City, N.Y., 1984. Mem. Am. Inst. C.P.A.s, N.Y. State Soc. C.P.A.s (com. fin. leasing 1977-80, fin. acctg. standards com., 1980-83, 85-87). Republican. Roman Catholic. Lodge: Rotary, W. Nyack, NY. Home: 16 Maple Ave West Nyack NY 10994 Office: NE Fin Systems 14 Maple Ave West Nyack NY 10994

TISCH, ANDREW HERBERT, watch company executive; b. Asbury Park, N.J., Aug. 14, 1949; s. Laurence Alan and Wilma Zelda (Stein) T.; divorced; children: Alexander, Lacey. B.S., Cornell U., Ithaca, N.Y., 1971; M.B.A., Harvard U., 1977. Brand mgr. Lorillard Co., N.Y.C., 1971-75; mgr. operational analysis Loews Corp., N.Y.C., 1977-79, v.p., 1985—; pres. Bulova Corp., Woodside, N.Y., 1980—, also bd. dirs.; bd. dirs. Wyndham Foods, Inc., Loews Corp., Gordon Jewelry Corp., Lorillard Corp. Contbr. articles to profl. jours. Mem. fgn. affairs com. Am. Jewish Com., N.Y.C., 1983—; bd. dirs. Outward Bound, Inc., Greenwich, Conn., 1983-88; trustee Central Synagogue, NYC, 1984—; gen. chmn. United Jewish Appeal Fedn. of Jewish Philanthropies N.Y., vice chmn. United Jewish Appeal, chmn. Prime Minister's Council, 1987—; bd. dirs. N.Y. Shakespeare Festival, 1987—, Children's Hearing Inst., 1988. Mem. 24 Karat Club of N.Y., Jewelry Industry Council, Am. Watch Assn. (1st v.p.), Jewelers Vigilance Com. (bd. dirs.), Jewelers Security Alliance. Clubs: Century Country (Purchase, N.Y.); Harmonie (N.Y.C.), Plumb (N.Y.). Office: Bulova Corp 1 Bulova Ave Woodside NY 11377

TISCH, LAURENCE ALAN, diversified corporation executive; b. N.Y.C., Mar. 15, 1923; s. Al and Sadye (Brenner) T.; m. Wilma Stein, Oct. 31, 1948; children: Andrew, Daniel, James, Thomas. B.Sc. cum laude, N.Y. U., 1942; M.A. in Indsl. Engring, U. Pa., 1943; student, Harvard Law Sch., 1946. Pres. Tisch Hotels, Inc., N.Y.C., 1946—; chmn. exec. com. Loews Theaters, Inc. (co. name changed to Loews Corp.), N.Y.C., 1959-65, chmn. bd., 1960—, pres., 1965-69, chief exec. officer, 1969—; chmn. CBS Inc., N.Y.C., 1986-87, chief exec. officer, 1986—; pres., chief exec. officer, dir. CBS Inc.,

New York, 1987—; chmn. CNA Fin. Corp. (subs. Loews Corp.), Chgo.; chmn. bd. CNA; dir. Automatic Data Processing Corp., Columbia Broadcasting System. Trustee, chmn. bd. N.Y. U.; trustee Legal Aid Soc., Met. Mus. Art, N.Y. Pub. Library, Carnegie Corp.; trustee-at-large Fedn. Jewish Philanthropies N.Y. Home: Island Dr N Manursing Island Rye NY 10580 Office: CBS Inc 51 W 52nd St New York NY 10019 *

TISCH, PRESTON ROBERT, finance executive; b. Bklyn., Apr. 29, 1926; s. Abraham Solomon and Sayde (Brenner) T.; m. Joan Hyman, Mar. 14, 1948; children: Steven E., Laurie M., Jonathan M. Student, Bucknell U., 1943-44; B.A., U. Mich., 1948. Pres., co-chief exec. officer, chmn. exec. com., dir. Loews Corp., N.Y.C.; Postmaster Gen. U.S. Postal Svc., Washington, 1986-88. Chmn. emeritus N.Y. Conv. and Visitors Bur., Nat. Democratic Conv., 1976-80; trustee NYU, mem. Quadrennial Commn. Exec., Legis. and Jud. Saleries, 1988—; mem. Travel and Tourism Adv. Bd. of Dept. of Commerce, Gov.'s Bus. Adv. Council for N.Y. State. Served with AUS, 1943-44. Mem. Sales & Mktg. Execs. Greater N.Y. (bd. trustees), Harrison Club, Rye Racquet Club, Century Country Club, Sigma Alpha Mu. Office: Loews Corp 667 Madison Ave New York NY 10021

TISCHLER, LEWIS PAUL, financial consultant; b. Catskill, N.Y., July 16, 1947; s. Morris and Sylvia (Lieber) T.; m. Binnie Davidson, May 27, 1972; children: Wendy Frances, Brian Howard. BSBA, SUNY, Albany, 1969. Apprentice Iron Worker Local 12, Albany, 1969-73; with Nat. Comml. Bank & Trust Co., 1973-79, regional credit officer, 1977-79; dir. Nat. Devel. Coun., N.Y.C., 1979-85; cons. Tischler Fin. Svcs., Columbiaville, N.Y., 1983—. Trustee Congregation Anshe Emeth, Hudson, N.Y., 1983-85, 2d v.p., 1987, treas., 1988. With USAR, 1969-75. Mem. Mensa, Delta Sigma Pi. Office: Tischler Fin Svcs PO Box 23 Columbiaville NY 12050

TISDALE, STUART WILLIAMS, holding company executive; b. Leominster, Mass., Aug. 15, 1928; s. Malcolm and Ruth (Williams) T.; m. Ann Howard, Dec. 7, 1967; children: Stuart, Walter, Malcolm, Andrew, Ward; stepchildren: Peter, Scott, Bruce. B.A., Yale U., 1951. Pres. Southworth Machine Co., Portland, Maine, 1954-65; pres. climate control div. Singer Co., N.Y.C., 1965-74; exec. v.p. Dover Corp., N.Y.C., 1974-76; chmn. STA-RITE Industries, Inc., Milw., 1976—; pres., chief exec. officer, dir. WICOR, Inc., Milw., 1984—; chmn., chief exec. officer, dir. Wis. Gas Co., Milw., 1986—; bd. dirs. Marshall and Isley Bank, Marshall & Ilsley Corp., Twin Disc Inc., Modine Mfg. Co. Bd. dirs. Columbia Hosp., Milw. Met. YMCA. Served with USN, 1952-54. Office: Wicor Inc 777 E Wisconsin Ave Milwaukee WI 53202

TITE, RALPH WILLIAM, JR., auditor; b. Cleveland Heights, Ohio, Apr. 27, 1961; s. Ralph William and Julia Francis (Gleason) T.; m. Theresa Helene Reed, June 24, 1989. BA in Acctg., Loyola U., Chgo., 1983. CPA. Staff acct. Ernst and Whinney, Chgo., 1983-84, experienced staff, 1984-85, sr. staff, 1985-87, mgr., 1987-88, consulting mgr., 1988; audit mgr. Arthur Young and Co., Chgo., 1987—. Mem. AICPA, Ill. CPA Soc. (savs. and loan com.). Roman Catholic. Office: Arthur Young & Co One IBM Plaza Chicago IL 60611

TITER, JEFFRY LEE, financial adviser; b. Springfield, Ohio, Dec. 25, 1957; s. Howard Neal Sr. and Mary Frances (Clark) T.; m. Diane Lynn Kennedy, Sept. 15, 1984; 1 child, Elizabeth. BA, Wright State U., 1981; cert., Coll. for Fin. Planning, Denver, 1984; Cert. in Fin. Planning, Coll. Fin. Planning, Denver, 1984. Asst. treas. and bd. dirs. TC Industries, Springfield, 1978—; fin. planner Benefit Communication Services, New Carlisle, Ohio, 1981-83; v.p. and fin. planner Fin. Focus, Dayton, 1983-86; fin. adviser Prudential-Bache, Dayton, 1986—. Mem. Internat. Assn. Fin. Planning, Inst. Cert. Fin. Planners, Wright State U. Alumni Assn. (benefits com., Outstanding Service award 1987), Xenia (Ohio) Area C. of C., Optimists. Republican. Lutheran. Office: Prudential-Bache Securities 130 W 2d St Ste 1720 Dayton OH 45402

TIZZIO, THOMAS RALPH, brokerage executive; b. Elmont, N.Y., Jan. 9, 1938; s. Anthony Thomas and Ann Marie (Paschal) T.; m. Mary Ann Gentile, Aug. 26, 1962; children: Anthony, Vincent, Thomas. B.B.A., Bklyn. Coll., 1962. Underwriter W.J. Roberts & Co., N.Y.C., 1958-65; sr. underwriter Atlantic Mut. Ins. Co., N.Y.C., 1965-67; sr. v.p. Am. Home Assurance Co., N.Y.C., 1967-77; exec. v.p. Transatlantic Reins. Co., N.Y.C., 1977-79, pres., 1979-82, also bd. dirs.; sr. v.p. Am. Internat. Group, N.Y.C., 1982—, now pres. Brokerage div.; exec. v.p. Am. Internat. Group-Brokerage, N.Y.C. Club: N.Y. Mariners. Office: Am Internat Group Inc 70 Pine St New York NY 10270

TOBIAS, RANDALL L., communication company executive; b. Lafayette, Ind., Mar. 20, 1942; m. Marilyn Jane Salyer, Sept. 2, 1966; children—Paige Noelle, Todd Christopher. B.S. in Mktg., Ind. U., 1964. Numerous positions Ind. Bell, 1964-81; v.p. residence mktg. sales and service AT&T, 1981-82, pres. Am. Bell Consumer Products, 1983, pres. Consumer Products, 1983-84, sr. v.p., 1984-85; corp. exec. v.p. AT&T, N.Y.C., 1985-86, vice chmn. bd., 1986—, also chmn. bd. dirs.; bd.dirs. AT&T Co., Eli Lilly and Co., Indpls.; mem. Bretton Woods Com., Washington; mem. dean's adv. council Grad. Sch. Bus. Ind. U., Bloomington; trustee Drew U., Madison, N.J., Duke U., Durham, N.C. Chmn. nat. campaign Ind. U. Annual Fund Drive, 1984-85. Served to 1st lt. U.S. Army, 1964-66. Mem. Ind. U. Alumni Assn., Well House Soc., Ind. U. Varsity Club Hoosier Hundred, Blue Key, Theta Chi. Clubs: Roxiticus Country (Mendham, N.J.). Office: AT&T 550 Madison Ave New York NY 10022 *

TOBIN, CHARLES JAMES, cartographer, publisher; b. Langford, S.D., Nov. 29, 1927; s. Charles James and Genevieve (Gianella) T.; m. Harryette Cora Strain, June 4, 1954; children: Carmal, Patricia, Susan, Kathleen. Student, No. State Coll., Aberdeen, S.D., 1947-49. Sales mgr. Thomas Nelson Co., Fergus Falls, Minn., 1960-65; founder, pres. Midland Atlas Co. Inc., Milbank, S.D., 1965—; pres. Tobin Broadcasting Co., Inc. (formerly Midland Communications, Inc.), Milbank, S.D., 1987—; bd. dirs. Midland Communications, Milbank. Served with U.S. Army, 1950-52. Mem. Nat. Assn. Publishers (past. bd. dirs.), Elks, Kiwanis (bd. dirs. Milbank 1974-78). Republican. Methodist. Home: 1102 S Viola St Milbank SD 57252 Office: Midland Atlas Co PO Box 283 101 N Main Milbank SD 57252

TOBIN, JAMES, economics educator; b. Champaign, Ill., Mar. 5, 1918; s. Louis Michael and Margaret (Edgerton) T.; m. Elizabeth Fay Ringo, Sept. 14, 1946; children: Margaret Ringo, Louis Michael, Hugh Ringo, Roger Gill. AB summa cum laude, Harvard U., 1939, MA, 1940, PhD, 1947; LLD (hon.), Syracuse U., 1967, U. Ill., 1969, Dartmouth Coll., 1970, Swarthmore Coll., 1980, New Sch. Social Research, 1982, NYU, 1982, Bates Coll., 1982; LHD (hon.), Hofstra U., 1983; LLD (hon.), U. Hartford, 1984, Colgate U., 1984; D in Econs. (hon.), New U. Lisbon, 1980; LLD (hon.), U. New Haven, 1986; LHD (hon.), Hofstra U., 1983, Gustavus Adolphus Coll., 1986; D in Social Scis. honoris causa, U. Helsinki, 1986. Assoc. economist OPA, WPB, Washington, 1941-42; teaching fellow econs. Harvard U., Cambridge, Mass., 1946-47, with Soc. Fellows, 1947-50; assoc. prof. econs. Yale U., New Haven, 1950-55, prof. emeritus, 1955—, Sterling prof. econs., 1957—, prof. emeritus, 1988—; mem. Council Econ. Advisers, 1961-62, Nat. Acad. Scis. Author: National Economic Policy, 1966, Essays in Economics-Macroeconomics, vol. 1, 1972, The New Economics One Decade Older, 1974, Consumption and Econometrics, vol. 2, 1975, Asset Accumulation and Economic Activity, 1980, Theory and Policy, Vol. 3, 1982, Policies for Prosperity, 1987. Served to lt. USNR, 1942-46. Recipient Nobel prize in econs., 1981; Social Sci. Research Council faculty fellow, 1951-54. Fellow Am. Acad. Arts and Scis., Econometric Soc. (pres. 1958), Am. Statis. Assn., Brit. Acad. (corr.); mem. Am. Philos. Soc., Am. Econ. Assn. (John Bates Clark medal 1955, v.p. 1964, pres. 1971), Acad. Scis. Portugal (fgn. assoc.), Phi Beta Kappa. Home: 117 Alden Ave New Haven CT 06515 Office: Yale U Dept Econs PO Box 2125 New Haven CT 06520

TOBIN, JAMES MICHAEL, lawyer; b. Santa Monica, Calif., Sept. 27, 1948; s. James Joseph and Glada Marie (Meisner) T.; m. Kathleen Marie Espy, Sept. 14, 1985. BA with honors, U. Calif., Riverside, 1970; JD, Georgetown U., 1974. Bar: Calif. 1974, Mich. 1987. From atty. to gen. atty. So. Pacific Co., San Francisco, 1975-82; v.p. regulatory affairs So. Pacific Communications Co., Washington, 1982-83; v.p., gen. counsel Lexitel Corp., Washington, 1983-85; v.p., gen. counsel, sec. ALC Communications Corp., Birmingham, Mich., 1985-87, sr. v.p., gen. counsel, sec., 1987-88; of counsel Morrison & Foerster, San Francisco, 1988—; bd. dirs. Allnet Communication Services Inc., Birmingham. Mem. ABA, Calif. Bar Assn., Mich. Bar Assn., Fed. Communications Bar Assn., Am. Soc. Corp. Secs., Competetive Telecommunications Assn. (bd. dirs. 1986—, vice chmn.). Republican. Unitarian. Home: 2739 Ottawa St San Francisco CA 94123 Office: Morrison & Foerster 345 California St San Francisco CA 94104

TOBIN, JAMES ROBERT, hospital supply company executive; b. Lima, Ohio, Aug. 12, 1944; s. J. Robert and Doris L. (Hunt) T.; m. Janet Trafton, Dec. 30, 1971; children: James Robert III, Amanda Trafton. BA in Govt., Harvard U., 1966, MBA, 1968. Fin. analyst Baxter Internat., Inc., Deerfield, Ill., 1972-73, internat. contr., 1973-75; mng. dir. Japan Baxter Internat., Inc., Tokyo, 1975-77; mng. dir. Spain Baxter Internat., Inc., Valencia, 1977-80; pres. parenteral products Baxter Internat., Inc., Deerfield, 1981-84, group v.p., 1984-88, exec. v.p., 1988—; bd. dirs. Lakeland Health Svcs., Highland Park Hosp., DNA, Inc. Lt. USN, 1968-72. Republican. Home: 53 Canterbury Ln Lincolnshire IL 60069 Office: Baxter Internat Inc 1 Baxter Pkwy Deerfield IL 60015

TOBIN, PETER J., financial executive; b. N.Y.C., Mar. 3, 1944; s. Patrick J. and Kathleen A. (Sweetnam) T.; m. Mary P. Gamble, June 25, 1966; children—Kristin, Peter G. B.B.A., St. John's U., N.Y.C., 1965. C.P.A. Mgr. Peat, Marwick Mitchell, N.Y.C., 1965-72; supr., controller Mfgrs. Hanover Corp., N.Y.C., 1972-85; exec. v.p., chief fin. officer Mfrs. Hanover Corp., 1985—. Mem. Am. Inst. C.P.A.s, N.Y. State Soc. C.P.A.s, Fin. Execs. Inst. (bd. dirs. N.Y. chpt. 1979-82), Bank Adminstrn. Inst. Republican. Roman Catholic. Office: Mfrs Hanover Corp 270 Park Ave New York NY 10017

TOBIN, WALLACE EMMETT, III, paper manufacturing executive; b. N.Y.C., July 23, 1937; s. Wallace Emmett Sr. and Elizabeth (Lovell) T.; m. Eva Britt Dysthe; children by previous marriage: Briggs Lovell, Ashley Manchester, Bliss Radcliffe. BA, Yale U., 1959; MA, Cambridge U., 1961; MBA, U. New Haven, 1980. Dir. devel. Yale U., New Haven, 1967-74; pres. Acigraf Internat. Corp., Branford, Conn., 1974-81; v.p. planning and devel. Dead River Corp., Portland, Maine, 1981-84; sr. v.p. Brant-Allen Industries, Greenwich, Conn., 1984—; mem. adv. bd. Conn. Bank & Trust, Greenwich, 1985—. Author: Mariner's Pocket Companion; contbr. articles to profl. jours. Mem. Sailing Edn. Assn. Corp., Woods Hole, Mass., 1972—, Fales com. U.S. Naval Acad., Annapolis, Md., 1977—; asst. treas. Am. Friends of Cambridge U., Washington, 1975—; v.p., treas. Colony Found., New Haven, 1975—. Officer USN, 1961-67. Named Mellon Found. fellow, 1959-61. Mem. Am. Paper Inst., N.Y. Yacht Club, Cruising Club Am., Royal Ocean Racing Club, Indian Harbor Yacht Club, Storm Trysail Club, Off Soundings Club. Office: Brant Allen Industries 80 Field POint Rd Greenwich CT 06836

TOBIN, WILLIAM THOMAS, retail executive; b. Cleve., May 31, 1931; s. Paul William and Ellen Louise (Fenlon) T.; m. Mary Ellen Fawcett, May 22, 1976; children: William Thomas, Bradford Fenlon. B.A., Yale U., 1949-53. With M. O'Neil Co., Akron, Ohio, 1953-73; exec. v.p. M. O'Neil Co., 1973-75, pres., 1975-79; pres., chief exec. officer Kaufmann's, Pitts., 1979—. Episcopalian. Clubs: Yale (N.Y.C.); Portage Country, Rolling Rock, Duquesne, Fox Chapel Golf, Pittsburgh Golf, Rivers. Office: Kaufmann's 400 5th Ave Pittsburgh PA 15219

TOBLER, D. LEE, chemical and aerospace company executive; b. Provo, Utah, July 25, 1933; s. Donald and Louise Harriet (Shoell) T.; m. H. Darlene Thueson, Nov. 21, 1956; children—Lisa, Julianne, Curtis, Craig, Denise, Bradley. B.A. in Fin. and Econs., Brigham Young U., 1957; M.B.A. in Fin., Northwestern U., 1958. Mgr. planning and econs. Exxon, N.Y.C., 1958-72; v.p., treas. Aetna Life & Casualty, Hartford, Conn., 1972-81; group v.p., chief fin. officer Zapata Corp., Houston, 1981-84; exec. v.p., chief fin. officer B.F. Goodrich Co., Akron, Ohio, 1985—; also bd. dirs. B.F. Goodrich Co., Akron. Pres. Literacy Vols. of Conn., Hartford, 1973-81; mem. exec. bd. Sam Houston Area council Boy Scouts Am., 1984. Republican. Mormon. Club: Portage Country (Akron). Home: 1005 Robinwood Hills Dr Akron OH 44313 Office: B F Goodrich Co 3925 Embassy Pkwy Akron OH 44313-1799

TODD, BILL FRANKLIN, marketing professional; b. Washington, Nov. 11, 1955; s. John Donald and Lilliam (Moriarty) T. BS, Translyvania U., 1979. Mgr. nat accounts Comfort Inns-Quality Inns, various, 1981-82, dir. nat. sales, 1982-85, dir. mktg., 1985—. Mem. Soc. Travel Agts. in Govt., Am. Soc. on Aging, Am. Bus. Assn., Chevy Chase Men's Club (gen. mgr. 1977—). Home: 4998 Battery Ln Bethesda MD 20814 Office: Quality Internat 10750 Columbia Pike Silver Spring MD 20901

TODD, BOSWORTH MOSS, JR., investment counselor; b. Frankfort, Ky., Mar. 1, 1930; s. Bosworth Moss and Mary Jouett (Rodman) T.; m. Joan Yandell Henning, June 4, 1955; children: Samuel B., David Yandell, James Rodman. BS, U. Ky., 1952; MBA, Harvard U., 1954. Chartered fin. analyst, investment counselor. Vice pres. Ky. Trust Co., Louisville, 1958-67; pres. Todd-Boston Co., Louisville, 1967-79; pres. Todd Investment Advisors, Louisville, 1979—; mem. The Boston Company Investment Policy Com., 1977, 79; dir. Cumberland Savs. & Loan, Louisville, 1983—. Contbg. editor Business First Weekly, 1984-85. Treas., Schizophrenia Research Found., Louisville, 1983-85, Schizophrenia Found. Ky., Inc., Louisville, 1982—; dir., sec. Nat. Alliance for Research on Schizophrenia and Depression; founding chmn. St. Francis Sch., Goshen, Ky., 1965-73. Served to capt. USAF, 1954-56. Mem. Investment Counsel Assn., N.Y. Soc. Security Analysts, Louisville Soc. Fin. Analysts. Republican. Episcopalian. Clubs: Pendennis, Juniper (Louisville). Home: 452 Swing Lane Louisville KY 40207 Office: Todd Investment Advisors 3160 First National Tower Louisville KY 40202

TODD, CHARLES IRWIN, stockbroker; b. Denver, Mar. 24, 1956; s. Charles Irwin and Betty Jo (Pahmeier) T.; m. Tamara Jo Byrd, June 24, 1976; children: Jana Nicole, Brianne Elizabeth. AS, Vincennes U., 1976; BS, Ind. U., 1979. Lic. ins. agt., broker. Sr. v.p. Dean Witter Reynolds, Cape Coral, Fla., 1980—. Mem. Inst. of Cert. Fin. Planners (bd. dirs. S.W. Fla. chpt. 1987-88, cert. fin. planner), Lee County Stockbrokers Assn., Big Cypress Porsche Club. Office: Dean Witter Reynolds 523 Cape Coral Pkwy E Cape Coral FL 33904

TODD, DAVID LEE, finance company executive; b. Long Beach, Calif., Nov. 12, 1950; s. Leonard Chrisman and Vivian E. T.; m. Raquel Todd, Dec. 29, 1973. BA, Yale U., 1971; MBA, U. So. Calif., 1982. Sr. economist CalFed Inc., L.A., 1982-84; div. planner Great Western Bank, Beverly Hills, Calif., 1984-87; dir. corp. planning Great Western Fin. Corp., Beverly Hills, 1987—. Democrat. Unitarian. Office: Gt Western Fin Corp 8484 Wilshire Blvd Beverly Hills CA 90211

TODD, GORDON C., insurance company executive; b. Chasm-Falls, N.Y., July 30, 1934; s. Carl A. and Neola M. (Childs) T.; m. Eleanor J. Holden, Aug. 17, 1958; children: Stephen G., Sharon E. BS, Syracuse U., 1960. Dist. mgr. Travelers Ins. Co., Hartford, Conn., 1960-80; pres. Burns, Brooks & McNeil, Torrington, Conn., 1980—; mem. agts. adv. counc. Cigna Co., Hartford, Royal Co., Hartford, The Hartford; mem. corp. mktg. presdl. adv. counc. Middleses Mut., Middleton, Conn. 1988—. Bd. trustees Salvation Army, Torrington, 1981-83, Master Sch., Simsbury, Conn., 1978-80. With U.S. Army, 1954-56. Mem. Ind. Ins. Agts. (pres. 1984-86), Profl. Ins. Agts., Ins. Mktg. Inst. Am., C. of C. (amb. 1981-88), Rotary. Home: 1 Whynwood Rd Simsbury CT 06070 Office: Burns Brooks McNeil 187 Church St PO Box 717 Torrington CT 06790

TODD, HARRY WILLIAMS, aircraft propulsion system company executive; b. Oak Park, Ill., 1922. BSME, U. So. Calif., 1947, BS, 1948, MBA, 1950. With Rockwell Internat., Pitts., 1946-76, former v.p. ops.; pres., chmn., chief exec. officer, bd. dirs. The L.E. Myers Co., Pitts., 1976-80; with Rohr Industries, Inc., Chula Vista, Calif., 1980—, pres., chief operating officer, 1980-82, pres., chief exec. officer, chmn., 1982—, now chmn., chief exec. officer, 1989—, also bd. dirs.; bd. dirs. Pacific Scientific, Helmnich & Payne. Served with U.S. Army, 1944-46. Office: Rohr Industries Inc PO Box 878 Chula Vista CA 92012 *

TODD, JAMES AVERILL, JR., steel company executive; b. Beckley, W.Va., July 31, 1928; s. James A. Sr. and Effie (Whisman) T.; m. Mary Margaret Barlow; children: Candace Todd Ewert, Mark A., Jennifer E. BS in Mining Engring., W.Va. U., 1950. With sales and mktg. dept. E.I. Du Pont de Nemours & Co., 1951-75; v.p. mktg. Atlas Powder Co., 1975-77; pres. United Affiliates Corp., Dallas, 1977-80; chmn., chief exec. officer Birmingham (Ala.) Bolt Co., 1980-84; pres., chief exec. officer Birmingham Steel Corp., 1984—; bd. dirs. SouthTrust Bank of Ala. Chmn. Exploring div. Birmingham council Boy Scouts Am., 1985-86, also mem. exec. com. Mem. Am. Mining Congress (bd. govs.), Inst. Scrap Iron and Steel, N.Y. Mining Club. Clubs: The Club, Shoal Creek, Downtown (Birmingham). Lodge: Rotary. Office: Birmingham Steel Corp 3000 Riverchase Galleria Suite 1000 Birmingham AL 35244

TODD, STEPHAN K., lawyer; b. Evansville, Ind., Dec. 22, 1945; s. Rayburn W. and Juanita E. (Schmitt) T.; children from previous marriage: Whitney, Jason. BS, Ohio State U., 1967; JD, Valparaiso U., 1970; LLM, U. Va., 1976. Bar: Ind. 1970, Pa. 1977, Ill. 1986, U.S. Supreme Ct. Atty., officer U.S. Army, 1970-76; atty. U.S. Steel Corp., Pitts., 1976-82; gen. atty. U.S. Steel Corp., Pitts., Chgo., 1982-86; sr. gen. atty. USX Corp., Chgo., 1986—. Served with USAR, 1967—. Mem. ABA, Chgo. Bar Assn. Office: USX Corp 600 Grant St Pittsburgh PA 15230

TODD, ZANE GREY, utility executive; b. Hanson, Ky., Feb. 3, 1924; s. Marshall Elvin and Kate (McCormick) T.; m. Marysnow Stone, Feb. 8, 1950 (dec. 1983); m. Frances Z. Anderson, Jan. 6, 1984. Student, Evansville Coll., 1947-49; BS summa cum laude, Purdue U., 1951, DEng (hon.), 1979; postgrad., U. Mich., 1965. Fingerprint classifier FBI, 1942-43; electric system planning engr. Indpls. Power & Light Co., 1951-56, spl. assignments supr., 1956-60, head elec. system planning, 1960-65, head substation design div., 1965-68, head distbn. engring. dept., 1968-70, asst. to v.p., 1970-72, v.p., 1972-74, exec. v.p., 1974-75, pres., 1975-81, chmn., 1976—, chief exec. officer, 1981—; chmn., pres. IPALCO Enterprises, Inc., Indpls., 1983—; chmn. bd., chief exec. officer Mid-Am. Capital Resources, Inc. subs. IPALCO Enterprises, Inc., Indpls., 1984—; gen. mgr. Mooresville Pub. Service Co., Inc., Ind., 1956-60; bd. dirs. Mchts. Nat. Bank, Mchts. Nat. Corp., Am. States Ins. Co., Environ. Quality Control, Inc.; chmn. 500 Festival Assocs., Inc., pres., 1987; dir. Indpls. Pvt. Industry Council. Originator probability analysis of power system reliability; contbr. articles to tech. jours. and mags. Mem. adv. bd. St. Vincent Hosp.; bd. dirs. Commn. for Downtown, YMCA Found., Crime Stoppers Cen. Ind., Corp. Community Council, Indpls. Ctr. for Advanced Research; mem. adv. council, trustee Christian Theol. Sem.; chmn. bd. trustees Ind. Cen. U. (now U. Indpls.); bd. govs. Associated Colls. of Ind.; chmn. U.S. Savs. Bond program State of Ind.; mem. Conf. Bd., Nat. and Greater Indpls. adv. bds. Salvation Army; mem. adv. bd. Clowes Hall. Sgt. AUS, 1943-47. Named Disting. Engring. Alumnus, Purdue U., 1976, Knight of Malta, Order of St. John of Jerusalem, 1986. Fellow IEEE (past chmn. power system engring. com.); mem. ASME, NSPE, NAM (bd. dirs.), Am. Mgmt. Assn. (gen. mgmt. council), Power Engring. Soc., Ind. Electric Assn. (bd. dirs., past chmn.), Edison Electric Inst. (bd. dirs.), Ind. Fiscal Policy Inst. (bd. govs.), Ind. C. of C. (bd. dirs.), Indpls. C. of C. (bd. dirs.), Mooresville C. of C. (past pres.), Newcomen Soc. (chmn. Ind.), Eta Kappa Nu, Tau Beta Pi. Clubs: Columbia, Indpls. Athletic (past bd. dirs.), Meridian Hills Country (bd. dirs.), Skyline (bd. govs.). Lodges: Rotary, Lions (past pres.). Home: 7645 Randue Ct Indianapolis IN 46278 Office: Indpls Power & Light Co 25 Monument Circle Indianapolis IN 46206

TOEVS, ALDEN LOUIS, mortgage researcher; b. American Falls, Idaho, Jan. 25, 1949; s. Alden Louis and Wilma Christen (Coffee) T.; m. Coralie Norwood Sickels, July 20, 1974. BS, Lewis and Clark Coll., 1971; PhD, Tuland U., 1975. NSF fellow MIT Energy Lab., Boston, 1975-76; prof. econs. La. State U., Baton Rouge, 1976-77, U. Oreg., Eugene, 1978-83; dir. mortgage research Morgan Stanley and Co., N.Y.C., 1983—; vis. scholar Fed. Home Loan Bank, San Francisco, 1983, Fed. Reserve Bank, 1982; dir. capital market research U. Oreg., Eugene, 1982-83. Author: Innovations in Bond Portfolio Management, 1983; editor, bd. dirs. Fin. Analysts Jour., 1983—, Jour. Portfolio Mgmt., 1984—; contbr. articles. Recipient Graham and Dodd scroll Fin. Analysts Fed., 1983. Office: Morgan Stanley and Co 1251 Ave of the Americas New York NY 10020

TOFIAS, ALLAN, accountant; b. Boston, Apr. 13, 1930; s. George I. and Anna (Seidel) T.; m. Arlene Shube, Aug. 30, 1981; children: Bradley Neil, Laura Jean Silver. BA, Colgate U., 1951; MBA, Harvard U., 1956. CPA, Mass. Sr. acct. Peat, Marwick, Mitchell & Co., Boston, 1956-60; mng. ptnr. Tofias, Fleishman, Shapiro, & Co. P.C., Boston, 1960—. Mem. town meeting Town of Brookline (Mass.), 1970-77, mem. fin. adv. bd., 1975-81; mem. New Eng. Bapt. Health Care Corp., 1985—; bd. dirs. West Newton YMCA, 1986—, Boston Aid for Blind, 1988—, also mem. exec. com. Lt. (j.g.) USNR, 1951-54. Mem. Am. Inst. CPAs, Mass. Soc. CPA's (bd. dirs.), Nat. CPA Group (exec. com. 1983-88, vice chmn. 1985-88), N.Eng.-Israel C. of C. (mem. exec. com.). Clubs: Wightman Tennis (Weston, Mass.) (treas. 1974-76); Newton Squash and Tennis (Mass.) (bd. dirs. 1966—). Lodge: Moses Michael Hays. Home: 59 Monadnock Rd Wellesley MA 02181 Office: Tofias Fleishman Shapiro & Co PC 205 Broadway Cambridge MA 02139

TOFOLO, MICHAEL D., consumer products industry executive; b. Utica, N.Y., Sept. 13, 1942; s. Joseph M. and Anna M. (Stocco) T.; m. Gloria D. LaPolla; children: David M., Raymond M. BS in Bus. Econs., Syracuse U., 1965. Cert. profl. materials mgr. Mgr. confections planning Beech-Nut Lifesavers, Inc., Cahajoharie, N.Y., 1965-68; asst. prodn. mgr. thru group prodn. mgr. Hammermill Paper Co., Erie, Pa., 1968-73; mgr. materials planning Amway Corp., Ada, Mich., 1973-78, mgr. internat. inventory, 1978-80, dir. internat. distbn., 1980-83, dir. materials mgmt., 1983—; asst. prof. bus. Aquinas Coll., Grand Rapids, Mich., 1976—; guest lectr. phys. ditbrn. Cen. Mich. U., 1986, 88. Mem. social commn. St. Roberts of Newminster Ch., Ada, 1977-78; active United Fund, Grand Rapids, 1987. Mem. Council of Logistics Mgmt. (sec. 1977-78), Am. Prodn. and Inventory Control Soc. (mem. acad. liaison com.), Internat. Materials Mgmt. Soc. Republican. Roman Catholic. Home: 7327 Oliver Woods Dr SE Grand Rapids MI 49506-9707 Office: 7575 E Fulton St Ada MI 49301

TOFTNER, RICHARD ORVILLE, engineering executive; b. Warren, Minn., Mar. 5, 1935; s. Orville Gayhart and Cora Evelyn (Anderson) T.; BA, U. Minn., 1966; MBA, Xavier U., 1970; m. Jeanne Bredine, June 26, 1960; children: Douglas, Scott, Kristine, Kimberly, Brian. Sr. economist Federated Dept. Stores, Inc., Cin., 1967-68; dep. dir. EPA, Washington and Cin., 1968-73; mgmt. cons. environ. affairs, products and mktg., 1973-74; prin. PEDCo Environ., Cin., 1974-80; trustee PEDCo trusts, 1974-80; pres. ROTA Mgmt., Inc., Cin., 1980-82; gen. mgr. CECOS, 1982-85, cons., 1985—; v.p. Smith, Stevens & Young, 1985-88; real estate developer, 1980—; adj. prof. U. Cin.; pres., chief exec. officer Toxitrol Internat., Inc., 1988—; lectr. Grad. fellowship rev. panel Office of Edn., 1978—; advisor, cabinet-level task force Office of Gov. of P.R., 1973; bd. dirs. EnviroAudit Svcs. Inc.; subcom. Nat. Safety Council, 1972; nominee commr. PUCO, Ohio; chmn. Cin. City Waste Task Force, 1987-88. Served with AUS, 1954-57. Mem. Engring. Soc. Cin., Cin. C. of C., Columbia Club, Bankers Club. Republican. Lutheran. Contbr. articles on mgmt. planning and environ. to periodicals, chpts. to books; developer Toxitrol. Home: 9175 Yellowwood Dr Cincinnati OH 45251 Office: 4700 Ashwood Dr Suite 100 Cincinnati OH 45241

TOFTNESS, CECIL GILLMAN, lawyer, consultant; b. Glasgow, Mont., Sept. 13, 1920; s. Anton Bernt and Nettie (Pedersen) T.; m. Chloe Catherine Vincent, Sept. 8, 1951. A.A., San Diego Jr. Coll., 1943; student Purdue U., Northwestern U.; B.S., UCLA, 1947; J.D., Southwestern U., 1953. Bar: Calif. 1954, U.S. Dist. Ct. (so. dist.) Calif. 1954, U.S. Supreme Ct. 1979. Sole practice, Palos Verdes Estates, Calif., 1954—; dir., pres., chmn. bd. Fisherman & Mchts. Bank, San Pedro, Calif., 1963-67; dir., v.p. Palos Verdes Estates Bd. Realtors, 1964-65. Chmn. Capital Campaign Fund, Richstone Charity, Hawthorne, Calif., 1983. Served to lt. (j.g.) USN, 1938-46, ETO, PTO. Named Man of Yr., Glasgow, 1984. Mem. South Bay Bar Assn., Southwestern Law Sch. Alumni Assn. (class rep. 1980—), Internat. Physicians for the Prevention of Nuclear War (del. 7th World Congress,

1987), Themis Soc.-Southwestern Law Sch., Schumacher Founder's Circle-Southwestern Law Sch. (charter). Democrat. Lutheran. Lodges: Kiwanis (sec.-treas. 1955-83, v.p., pres., bd. dirs.), Masons, K.T. Participant Soc. Expedition thur the N.W. Passage. Home: 2229 Via Acalones Palos Verdes Estates CA 90274 Office: 2516 Via Tejon Palos Verdes Estates CA 90274

TOKAR, EDWARD THOMAS, JR., manufacturing company executive; b. Passaic, N.J., June 12, 1947; s. Edward Thomas Sr. and Helen (Fabian) T.; m. Frances Deland, Sept. 30, 1972; 1 child, Adam Edward. BS with high honors, U. Md., 1969; MBA, Coll. William and Mary, 1971; postgrad., George Washington U., 1972. CPA, N.J., Washington. Audit, cons. Touche Ross & Co., Washington, 1970-73; mgr. fin. div. Nat. Rural Electric Coop. Assn., Washington, 1973-77; v.p. investments Allied-Signal Inc., Morristown, N.J., 1977—; bd. dirs. Sentinel Group Inc., Stamford, Conn.; Allen Value Ptnrs., Noel Group Inc.; bd. advisers Saugatuck Capital Co., Stamford, Regional Fin. Enterprises, Stamford; mem. pension adv. com. N.Y. Stock Exchange, N.Y.C. Trustee Newark Boys Chorus Sch., 1980-84; mem. investment adv. com. Paterson Diocese Roman Catholic Ch., Clifton, N.J.; dir. Trinity Living Ctrs. Mem. Nat. Econs. Club., Am. Inst. CPAs, Sentinel Pension Inst. (bd. advisers), Investment Tech. Symposium, Morris County C. of C., Fin. Exec. Inst. Nome: 8 Sweetbriar Rd Summit NJ 07901 Office: Allied-Signal Inc PO Box 1219R Morristown NJ 07960

TOLAN, DAVID J., life insurance corporation executive; b. Detroit, Dec. 27, 1927; s. Joseph James and Helen Barbara (Blahnik) T.; m. Roseann Biwer, Feb. 15, 1958; children: Joseph, David, Julie. AB, Haverford Coll.; JD, U. Mich.; MS, Am. Coll. Bar: Wis.; CLU. Pvt. practice atty. Milw., 1952-57; agt. Northwestern Mut. Ins. Co., Milw., 1957—; prin. Tolan & Schueller Ltd., Milw., 1959-82; pres. Tolan & Schueller Assocs. Ltd (formerly Tolan MacNeil & Schueller Ltd.), Milw., 1982—; lectr. Am. Inst. CPA's, Am. Soc. CLU's, Wis. Bar Assn., 1975—. Contbr. articles to profl. jours. Pres. Young Reps. Milw. County, 1961; bd. dirs. United Performing Arts Fund, Milw., 1966; pres., dir. Bel Canto Chorus, Milw., 1960—; scoutmaster Boy Scouts Am., 1975-77; mem. com. for future Milw., 1988. Served with U.S. Army, 1954-57. Mem. Am. Soc. CLU's, Assn. Advanced Life Underwriters. Republican. Roman Catholic. Clubs: University (Milw.); Western Racquet (Elm Grove, Wis.). Home: 2620 Woodbridge Rd Brookfield WI 53005 Office: Tolan Schueller and Assocs 770 N Jefferson St Milwaukee WI 53202

TOLAN, DAVID JOSEPH, transportation executive; b. N.Y.C., Jan. 25, 1933. BS in Marine Transp., SUNY-Maritime Coll., Bronx, 1955. Deck mcht. marine officer Alcoa Steamship Co., Bklyn., 1955-61; with Sea-Land Service (name now Sea-Land Corp.), 1961—; group v.p. Ams. Sea-Land Service (name now Sea-Land Corp.), Edison, N.J., 1984-85, sr. v.p. labor relations, 1985—; bd. dirs. Shipping Industry Mutual Assurance Soc., Vt. Industry Mutual Assurance Soc. Mem. Am. Maritime Assn. (pres. 1985—), Carriers Container Council, Inc. (chmn. 1985—), Transp. Inst. (bd. dirs. 1985—), N.Y. Shipping Assn., Inc. (bd. dirs. 1985—), Pacific Maritime Assn. (exec. com. 1985—). Office: Sea-Land Svc Inc PO Box 800 Iselin NJ 08830

TOLBERT, RICHARD VACANERAT, financial advisor; b. Monrovia, Liberia, Apr. 12, 1950; s. Frank E. and Clara (Tay) T.; m. Celestine S. Watts, June 26, 1982; children: Rita, Renee, Sekou. BA cum laude in Econs., Harvard U., 1972; JD, Columbia U., 1975. Bar: Montserrado County, Liberia. V.p. Mesurado Corp., Monrovia, 1975-80; atty. Merrill Lynch, N.Y.C., 1980-82; internat. investment advisor, 1982-89; v.p. Merrill Lynch Internat., N.Y.C., 1989—; bd. dirs. Liberia Petroleum Co., Liberia Hotels, Inc., Unipac Liberia Ltd, Sierra Fishing Co. Baptist. Club: Harvard Fly. Avocations: tennis, fencing, African history and economic development. Office: Merrill Lynch Internat 200 Park Ave 37th Fl New York NY 10166

TOLCHINSKY, PAUL DEAN, organizational psychologist; b. Cleve., Sept. 30, 1946; s. Sanford M. and Frances (Klein) T.; m. Kathy D.; children: Heidi E., Dana M. BA, Bowling Green State U., 1971; PhD in Orgnl. Behavior, Purdue U., 1978. Mgmt. trainer Detroit Bank and Trust Co., 1971-73; tng. and devel. mgr. Babcock & Wilcox Co., Barberton, Ohio, 1973-75; internal cons. Gen. Foods, Inc., West Lafayette, Ind., 1975-77; prof. Fla. State U., Tallahassee, 1978-79, U. Akron, Ohio, 1979-81; prin. Performance Devel. Assocs., Cleve., 1981—; adj. prof. Bowling Green State U., 1981-82. Contbr. numerous articles to profl. jours. Sgt. in U.S. Army, 1966-69, Vietnam. Mem. Am. Psychol. Assn., Cert. Cons. Internat., Acad. Mgmt., Vietnam Vets Am., Jewish War Vets. Democrat.

TOLL, MAYNARD JOY, JR., investment banker; b. Los Angeles, Feb. 5, 1942; s. Maynard Joy and Ethel (Coleman) T.; m. Kathryn Wiseman, Sept. 12, 1964; children: Ian Wolcott, Adam Donahue. BA, Stanford U., 1963; MA, Johns Hopkins U., 1965, PhD, 1970. Asst. prof., asst. dean faculty U. Mass., Boston, 1968-71; legis. and adminstrv. asst. Sen. Edmund Muskie, Washington, 1971-75; from asst. v.p. to mng. dir. First Boston Corp., N.Y.C., 1975—. Active Council Fgn. Relations, N.Y.C. Democrat. Episcopalian. Clubs: Links; Vineyard Haven (Mass.) Yacht; Anglers N.Y. Home: 171 W 71st #7-A New York NY 10023

TOLLEFSON, JOHN OLIVER, management educator, university dean, consultant; b. Lane County, nr. Eugene, Oreg., Mar. 24, 1937; s. George Theodore Morris and Ona Belle (Simpson) T.; m. Nona Aileen Falmlen, Aug. 27, 1961; children: John F., William G., Elizabeth C. B.S. in Forest Engring., Oreg. State U., 1958; M.S. in Indsl. Mgmt., Purdue U., 1960, Ph D. in Econs., 1966. Logging engr. Internat. Paper Co., Vaughn, Oreg., 1958-59; asst. prof. grad. sch. bus. Tulane U., New Orleans, 1963-67; asst. prof. sch. bus. U. Kans., Lawrence, 1967-70, assoc. prof., 1970-74, prof., 1974—, assoc. dean Sch. Bus., 1974-81, dean, 1981—; bd. dirs. Security Cash Fund, Topeka, Security Tax Exempt Fund, Security Investment Fund, Kantronics, Douglas County Bank, Lawrence; adv. dir. Kans. Pub. Service, Lawrence, 1986—; mem. tech. adv. com. assessment sales ratio study State of Kans., 1974—. Contbr. articles to profl. jours. Mem. bd. govs. Lawrence Meml. Hosp. Endowment Assn., Lawrence, 1982—. Mem. Am. Assembly of Collegiate Schs. Bus. (co-chmn. ann. meeting program 1983), Am. Mktg. Assn., Decision Scis. Inst., Inst. Mgmt. Scis., AAUP, Lawrence C. of C. (bd. dirs. 1982-85). Office: Univ of Kans Bus Sch Lawrence KS 66045

TOLLENAERE, LAWRENCE ROBERT, industrial products company executive; b. Berwyn, Ill., Nov. 19, 1922; s. Cyrille and Modesta (Van Damme) T.; m. Mary Elizabeth Hansen, Aug. 14, 1948; children: Elizabeth, Homer, Stephanie, Caswell, Mary Jennifer. BS in Engring., Iowa State U., 1944, MS in Engring., 1949; MBA, U. So. Calif., 1969; LLD (hon.), Claremont Grad. Sch., 1977. Specification engr. Alumninum Co. Am., Huntington Park, Calif., 1946-47; asst. prof. indsl. engring. Iowa State U., Ames, 1947-50; sales rep. Am. Pipe and Constrn. Co. (name changed to AMERON 1969), South Gate, Calif., 1950-53; spl. rep. Am. Pipe and Constrn. Co. (name changed to AMERON 1969), S.Am., 1953-54; 2d v.p., div. mgr. Colombian div. Am. Pipe and Constrn. Co. (name changed to AMERON 1969), Bogota, S.Am., 1955-57; div. mgr., v.p. Am. Pipe and Constrn. Co. (name changed to AMERON 1969), Calif., 1957-63; v.p. concrete pipe ops. Am. Pipe and Constrn. Co. (name changed to AMERON 1969), Monterey Park, Calif., 1963-65, pres. corp. hdqrs., 1965-67; pres., chief exec. officer Ameron Inc., Monterey Park, Calif., 1967—, also bd. dirs.; bd. dirs. Avery Internat., Pasadena, Calif., Newhall Land and Farming Co., Valencia, Calif., Pacific Mut. Life Ins. Co., Newport Beach, Calif., The Parsons Corp., Pasadena. Trustee The Huntington Library, Art Gallery and Bot. Gardens; mem. bd. fellows Claremont U. Ctr.; bd. gov.'s Iowa State U. Found. Mem. Merchants and Mfrs. Assn. (past chmn. bd. dirs.), Nat. Assn. Mfrs., Soc. Advancement Mgmt., AMA Pres. Assn., Newcomen Soc. N.Am., Calif. C. of C. (bd. dirs. 1977—), Alpha Tau Omega. Republican. Clubs: California (bd. dirs.), Jonathan, Pauma Valley Country, San Gabriel Country, Bohemian, San Francisco, Commanderie de Bordeaux, Los Angeles, Los Angeles Confrerie des Chevaliers du Tastevin, Twilight, Lincoln, Beavers (past. pres., hon. dir.), Valley of Montecito (Santa Barbara, Calif.). Home: 1400 Milan Ave South Pasadena CA 91030 Office: Ameron Inc 4700 Ramona Blvd Monterey Park CA 91754

TOLLER, WILLIAM ROBERT, chemical and oil company executive; b. Ft. Smith, Ark., Aug. 10, 1930; s. Audly Sr. and Martha (Anderson) T.; m. Jo Ella Perry, June 13, 1959; children: William R. Jr., Michelle D., Gregory A. BBA, U. Ark., 1956; postgrad., Stamford U., 1971. Various positions Conoco Inc., Okla., Tex. and Colo., 1955-77; v.p. fin. and adminstrn. Continental Carbon Co., Houston, 1977-81, pres., chief exec. officer, 1981-84; v.p., gen. mgr. Concarb div. Witco Corp., Houston, 1984-86; dir., exec. v.p. Witco Corp., N.Y.C., 1986—. Mem. Republican Nat. Com., Washington, 1988-89. Mem. Am. Chem. Soc., Am. Petroleum Inst., Fin. Execs. Inst. Presbyterian. Home: 102 Windsor Circle Washington Township NJ 07675 Office: Witco Corp 520 Madison Ave New York NY 10022-4236

TOLLESON, FREDERIC LEROY, corporate financial executive; b. San Antonio, Oct. 29, 1932; s. Fred L. and Della Leila (Howard) T.; m. Betty Sue Thornberry, June 11, 1955; children: Frederic Lawrence, William Glenn, Joseph Alan. BS in Engring., U.S. Naval Acad., 1955; MBA in Fin. Mgmt., George Washington U., 1967. Commd. 2d lt. USMC, 1955, advanced through grades to col., 1975, ret., 1981; spl. asst. to Asst. Sec., Dept. of Navy, Washington, 1975-76; asst. head budget USMC, Washington, 1976-78; comptroller USMC, Camp Lejeune, N.C., 1978-79, commdg. officer 6th Regiment, 1980-81; mgmt. cons. Tolleson Assocs., Annandale, Va., 1981-83; ops. analyst SAIC, Vienna, Va., 1983-84; v.p. corp. fin. The Douglas-Michaels Corp., Spingfield, Va., 1984—; lectr. Leadership and Mgmt. Motivation, 1985—, bd. dirs. Marine Fed. Credit Union, Camp Lejeune, 1978-79. Scoutmaster Boy Scouts Am., Pa., Va., N.C., 1975—; coach youth football, 1969-78. Decorated Silver Star, Bronze Star with v device, Legion of Merit; recipient Rep. of Vietnam Cross of Gallantry with Silver Star. Mem. U.S. Naval Inst. (life), Retired Officers Assn. (life), Marine Corps Assn., Marine Corps League. Club: Army Navy Country (Arlington, Va.). Home: 9610 Burnt Oak Dr Fairfax Station VA 22039

TOLLETT, GLENNA BELLE, accountant, mobile home park operator; b. Graham, Ariz., Dec. 17, 1913; d. Charles Harry and Myrtle (Stapley) Spafford; m. John W. Tollett, Nov. 28, 1928; 1 child, Jackie J., 1 adopted child, Beverly Mae Malgren. Bus. cert., Lamson Coll. Office mgr, Hurley Meat Packing Co., Phoenix, 1938-42; co-owner, sec., treas. A.B.C. Enterprises, Inc., Seattle, 1942—; ptnr. Bella Investment Co., Seattle, 1962—, Four Square Investment Co., Seattle, 1969—, Warehouses Ltd., Seattle, 1970—, Tri State Partnership, Wash., Idaho, Tex., 1972—; pres. Halycon Mobile Home Park, Inc., Seattle, 1979—; co-owner, operator Martha Lake Mobile Home Park, Lynwood, Wash., 1962-73. Mem. com. Wash. Planning and Community Affairs Agy., Olympia, 1981-82, Wash. Mfg. Housing Assn. Relations Com., Olympia, 1980-84; appointed by Gov. Wash. to Mobile Home and RV Adv. Bd., 1973-79. Named to RV/Mobile Home Hall of Fame, 1980. Mem. Wash. Mobile Park Owners Assn. (legisl. chmn., lobbyist 1976-85, cons. 1984, pres. 1978-79, exec. dir. 1976-84, This is Your Life award 1979), Wash. Soc. of Assn. Execs. (Exec. Dir. Service award 1983), Mobile Home Old Timers Assn., Mobile Home Owners of Am. (sec. 1972-76, Appreciation award 1976), Nat Fire Protection Assn. (com. 1979-86), Aurora Pkwy. North C. of C.)sec. 1976-80), Fremont C. of C. Republican. Mormon. Home: 18261 Springdale Ct NW Seattle WA 98177 Office: ABC Enterprises Inc 3524 Stone Way N Seattle WA 98103

TOLLETT, LELAND EDWARD, food company executive; b. Nashville, Ark., Jan. 21, 1937; s. Vergil E. and Gladys V. (Sturgis) T.; m. Betty Ruth Blew, June 2, 1961; children—Terri Lynn, Gary Dwayne. B.S.A., U. Ark., 1958, M.S.A., 1959. Dir. Research Tyson Foods, Inc., Springdale, Ark., 1959-64, gen mgr. prodn., 1965-66, v.p. prodn., 1966-80, chief operating officer, 1981-83, pres., chief operating officer, 1984—, also dir. Served with USAF, 1961-62. Mem. Nat. Broiler Council (bd. dirs. 1979—). Home: 2801 S Johnson Rd Springdale AR 72764 Office: Tyson Foods Inc 2210 W Oaklawn Dr Springdale AR 72764 *

TOLLEY, JERRY RUSSELL, clinical laboratory executive; b. Goldsboro, N.C., Nov. 6, 1942; s. Elva Russell Tolley and Clara (Smith) Tolley-Bunch; m. Joan Morrison, June 8, 1965; children: Jerry R. Jr., Justin Clay. BS, East Carolina U., 1965, MEd, 1966; EdD, U. N.C., Greensboro, 1982; postgrad., Duke U., Dartmouth Coll., Vanderbilt U. Tchr., coach Fayetteville (N.C.) Sr. High Sch., 1966; asst. football coach, head track and tennis coach Elon Coll., N.C., 1967-77, head football coach, 1977-81, dir. athletic sholarship fund, 1982, dir. corp. and ann. resources, 1983, coordinator Pride II Capital Campaign, 1984, assoc. dir. devel., 1985; asst. v.p. tng., career devel. and recruitment Roche Biomed. Labs. Inc., Burlington, N.C., 1986—; cons. AKD Prodns., Roanoke, Va., 1982—; bd. trustees Pop Warner Football League Am., 1987. Author: Intercollegiate History of Athletics and Elon College, 1982, American Football Coaches Guidebook to Championship Football Drills, 1985; contbg. author: 101 Winning Plays, 1977; mem. editorial bd. Growing-Up mag., Greensboro, 1986—; contbr. articles to profl. jours. Treas. Town of Elon Coll., 1984-87, mayor protem, 1988; convenor City County Govt. Assn. Alamance County, N.C., 1986—; mem. exec. bd. Cherokee council Boy Scouts Am., 1986. Named one of Outstanding Young Men Am., 1980; recipient Dwight D. Eisenhower award Nat. Football Hall of Fame, 1980, 81; named Nat. Football Coach of Yr., Nat. Assn. Intercollegiate Athletics, 1980; named to Elon Coll. Sports Hall of Fame. Mem. Am. Football Coaches Assn., Phi Delta Kappa, Sigma Delta Psi. Lodge: Rotary. Home: 209 Courtland Dr Box 463 Elon College NC 27244 Office: Roche Biomedical Labs Inc 430 Spring St Burlington NC 27215

TOLMIE, DONALD MCEACHERN, lawyer; b. Moline, Ill., June 21, 1928; s. Ronald Charles and Margaret Blaine (Kerr) T.; m. Joann Phillis Swanson, Aug. 15, 1953; children; David M., John K., Paul N. AB, Augustana Coll., 1950; JD, U. Ill., 1953. Bar: Ill. 1953, Va. 1968. Atty. Pa. R.R., Chgo., 1953-60; asst. gen. soliciter Pa. R.R., Phila., 1961-67; gen. atty. Norfolk & Western, Roanoke, Va., 1968, gen. soliciter, 1968-75, gen. counsel, 1975-82; gen. counsel Norfolk (Va.) So. Corp., 1982, v.p., gen. counsel, 1983—; bd. dirs. Trailer Train Co., Chgo. Mem. ABA, Va. Bar Assn., Norfolk and Portsmouth Bar Assn., U.S. Supreme Ct. Bar Assn. Lutheran. Clubs: Harbor, Norfolk Yacht and Country, Cedar Point. Home: 912 Hanover Ave Norfolk VA 23508 Office: Norfolk So Corp 3 Commercial Pl Norfolk VA 23510-2191

TOM, PING, trading company executive, lawyer; b. Chgo., Apr. 15, 1935; s. Y. Chan and Lillian (Goo) T.; m. Valerie Ching Oct. 11, 1958; children—Darryl, Curtis. B.A. in Econs., Northwestern U., 1956, J.D., 1958. Bar: Ill. 1958. Vice pres. Chinese Noodle Mfg., Chgo., 1958-66; v.p. Chinese Trading Co., Chgo., 1966-72, pres., 1972—; pres. Lekel Pail Co., Chgo., 1980—, Mah Chena Corp., Chgo., 1980—, Griesbaum Meat Co., Chgo., 1981—; bd. dirs. Madison Fin. Co. holding corp. Madison Nat. Bank, Niles, Ill., 1st Nat. Bank, Wheeling, Ill.; prin. Chgo.-United; legal advisor Chinese Benevolent Assn., Chgo. Pres. Chinese Am. Civic Council, Chgo., 1973; trustee Hull House Assn., Chgo.; bd. dirs. South Side Planning Bd., Chgo.; bd. dirs. exec. com Chgo.'s Sister City Commn; mem. Chgo.'s World's Fair Corp., State of Ill. Devel. Fin. Authority; mem. bd. of advisors Mercy Hosp., Chinese Am. Service League; chmn. Chinatown Parking Corp.; pres. Chinese-Am. Devel. Corp.; mem. bldg. jury Chgo. Cen. Library Design. Mem. Chinatown C. of C. (pres. 1983). Club: Econ., Exec. (Chgo.); Park Ridge Country. Home: 6945 Lexington Ln Niles IL 60648 Office: Chinese Trading Co 2263 Wentworth Ave Chicago IL 60616

TOMASH, ERWIN, retired computer equipment company executive; b. St. Paul, Nov. 17, 1921; s. Noah and Milka (Ehrlich) T.; m. Adelle Ruben, July 31, 1943; children—Judith Freya Tomash Diffenbaugh, Barbara Ann. B.S., U. Minn., 1943; M.S., U. Md., 1950. Instr. elec. engring. U. Minn., 1946; assoc. dir. computer devel. Univac div. Remington Rand Corp., St. Paul, 1947-51; dir. West Coast ops. Univac div. Sperry Rand Corp., L.A., 1953-55; pres. Telemeter Magnetics, Inc., L.A., 1956-60; v.p. Ampex Corp., L.A., 1961; founder, pres. Dataproducts Corp., L.A., 1962-71; chmn. bd. Dataproducts Corp., 1971-80, chmn. exec. com., 1980—; chmn. Tomash Cons., Inc., cons. to high tech. industry; chmn. bd. Tomash Pubs., pubs. computer and physics works, Newport Corp., Fountain Valley, Calif.; dir. L.A. Ednl. Partnership, Supershuttle Internat., Inc., L.A.. Founder, chmn. bd. trustees Charles Babbage Found., U. Minn.; dir. and nat. gov. Coro Found., L.A..; trustee Computer Mus., Boston. Served to capt. Signal Corps AUS, 1943-46. Decorated Bronze Star. Mem. IEEE (sr.), Assn. Computing Machinery, Am. Soc. for Technion (exec. v.p., dir.). Home: 110 S Rockingham Ave Los Angeles CA 90049 Office: Dataproducts Corp 6200 Canooga Ave Woodland Hills CA 91365

TOMASKO, MARK DANIEL, lawyer; b. N.Y.C., June 22, 1948; s. Daniel Paul and Ruth (Syckelmoore) T.; m. Nancy Ruth Norton, Nov. 16, 1985. BA, Yale U., 1970; JD, U. Pa., 1973. Bar: N.Y. 1974. Assoc. atty. Chadbourne, Parke, Whiteside & Wolf, N.Y.C., 1973-78; corp. counsel Singer Co., N.Y.C. and Stamford, Conn., 1978-83, group counsel, Stamford, 1983-86; v.p., gen. counsel, sec. Esselte Bus. Systems Inc., Garden City, N.Y., 1986—. Mem. ABA, Assn. Bar City of N.Y., Am. Soc. Corp. Secs., Am. Corp. Counsel Assn., Univ. Club, Grolier Club. Office: Esselte Bus Systems Inc 71 Clinton Rd Garden City NY 11530

TOMBET, ANDRE, lawyer; b. Geneva, Mar. 2, 1927; s. Adolphe and Alice-Helene (Meyer) T.; LL.B., U. Geneva, 1950; postgrad. Sch. Law, London U., 1951; LL.M., Yale U., 1954; m. Dorothea von Bradsky, Sept. 7, 1957; children—Ariane, Alain. Admitted to Geneva bar, 1952; asso. firm White & Case, N.Y.C., 1954-56; individual practice law, Geneva, 1961—; legal adv. permanent dels. to UN, Geneva and fgn. cos.; dir. Swiss Deposit and Creditbank, 1984—; vice-chmn. bd. Hotel and Country Club Le Mirador, 1971—. Trustee Martin Bodmer Found., 1980—; pres. Igor Carl Faberge Found., 1983. Capt., mil. justice, 1968-80. Sterling fellow, 1953. Mem. Swiss Fedn. Lawyers, Geneva Law Soc., Internat. Bar Assn., Geneva Bar Assn. (mem. council 1984—), Internat. Assn. for Protection Indsl. Property, Swiss Soc. Bibliophiles, Internat. Assn. Bibliophiles (mem. council 1986), Soc. Geneva State Archives (mem. com. 1970—, v.p. 1983—). Clubs: Cercle De La Terrasse, Golf (com. 1983—), Am. Internat. (v.p. 1983-84, mem. exec. com. 1983—) (Geneva); Le Mirador Country (gov.); Yale (N.Y.C.). Home: 12 Chemin du Nant d'Argent, 1223 Cologny Switzerland Office: Rue du Marche 7, 1211 Geneva 3, Switzerland

TOMCZAK, CHRISTINA MARY, banker; b. Yonkers, N.Y., Sept. 24, 1946; d. Henry Peter and Jane Mary (Brzozowski) T. BS, Fla. State U., 1968. Sr. examiner Fed. Res. Bank Atlanta, 1968-77; sr. v.p. Great Am. Banks Inc., Miami, Fla., 1977-83; v.p. Barnett Banks Inc., Jacksonville, Fla., 1983—. Mem. Gamma Sigma Sigma (bd. dirs. 1969—). Republican. Roman Catholic. Home: 1574 Palm Ave Jacksonville FL 32207 Office: Barnett Banks Inc 100 Laura St Jacksonville FL 32202

TOMICH, LILLIAN, lawyer; b. Los Angeles, Mar. 28, 1935; d. Peter S. and Yovanka P. (Ivanovic) T. AA, Pasadena City Coll., 1954; BA in Polit. Sci., UCLA, 1956, cert. secondary teaching, 1957, MA, 1958; JD, U. So. Calif., 1961. Bar: Calif. Sole practice, 1961-66; house counsel Mfrs. Bank, Los Angeles, 1966; ptnr. Hurley, Shaw & Tomich, San Marino, Calif., 1968-76; assoc. Driscoll & Tomich, San Marino, 1976—; dir. Continental Culture Specialists Inc., Glendale, Calif. Trustee, St. Sava Serbian Orthodox Ch., San Gabriel, Calif. Charles Fletcher Scott fellow, 1957; U. So. Calif. Law Sch. scholar, 1958. Mem. ABA, Calif. Bar Assn., Los Angeles County Bar Assn., Women Lawyers Assn., UCLA Alumni Assn., Town Hall and World Affairs Council, Order Mast and Dagger, Iota Tau Tau, Alpha Gamma Sigma. Office: 2297 Huntington Dr San Marino CA 91108

TOMLINSON, JOHN MICHAEL, financial, acquisitions executive; b. Detroit, Apr. 9, 1949; s. James Patrick and Joy Henrietta (Benesh) T.; m. Carole Elizabeth Smith, April 15, 1978; children: Jack, Clarke. BBA magna cum laude, Georgetown U., 1971; MBA, Harvard U., 1974. CPA, N.Y. Sr. asst. Deloitte, Haskins, Sells, Miami, Fla., 1974-76; fin. analyst Gulf & Western, N.Y.C., 1977-79; group controller, asst. treas. Hanson Industries, Iselin, N.J., 1979-84; dir. bus. planning and devel. Lear Siegler/SLI, Stamford, Conn., 1984-88; sr. v.p., chief fin. officer Alliance Internat. Group, Norcross, Ga., 1988—; bd. govs. Am. League For Exports and Security Assistance, 1986-88. Mem. N.Y. State Soc. CPA's, Harvard Bus. Sch. Club of N.Y. (officer 1983), Nat. Assn. Corp. Dirs. (adv. bd. N.Y. chpt.). Democrat. Roman Catholic. Club: Noe (Chatham, N.J.); Harvard (N.Y.C.). Office: Alliance Internat Group PO Box 920488 Norcross GA 30092

TOMLINSON, JOSEPH ERNEST, manufacturing company executive; b. Sycamore, Ill., Apr. 22, 1939; s. Bernie Gilbert and Elizabeth Lowe (Hoffman) T.; m. Judith Ann Worst, Sept. 20, 1969; children: Mark Joseph, Amy Ann. BS in Acctg., U. Ill., 1962. CPA. Staff acct. Price Waterhouse and Co., Chgo., 1962-65, sr. acct., 1965-69; audit mgr. Price Waterhouse and Co., Indpls., 1969-74; corp. controller Inland Container Corp., Indpls., 1974-82, v.p., treas., controller, 1982—. Congl. chmn. Carmel Luth. Ch., Ind., 1983-86, v.p., 1988—. Served with Ill. N.G., 1963-69. Mem. Fin. Execs. Inst. (treas. Indpls. chpt. 1986-87, sec. 1987-88, 2d v.p. 1988-89, 1st v.p. 1989—). Republican. Club: Crooked Stick Golf. Home: 2063 St Andrews Circle Carmel IN 46032 Office: Inland Container Corp PO Box 925 Indianapolis IN 46206

TOMLINSON, ROBERT JOHN, energy industry legal executive; b. Detroit, May 4, 1936; s. Harry John and Helen Adele (Strauss) T.; m. Margaret Armstrong, June 9, 1962 (div. 1977); 1 child, Justin Hudspeth. BA in Econs., U. Mich., 1958; JD, Wayne State U., 1961. Bar: Mich. 1962, Wash. 1972. Internat. atty. Parke Davis & Co., Detroit, 1962-68; assoc. Heritier & Abbott, Detroit, 1969-70; atty. Mich. Consol. Gas Co., Detroit, 1970-72; sr. v.p. legal Wash. Energy Co. & Wash. Nat. Gas Co., Seattle, 1972—, pres. thermal efficiency, 1988—; bd. dirs. Mercer Ins. Co., Hamilton, Bermuda. Mem. ABA, Am. Soc. Corp. Secs. (pres. n.w. region 1978-79), Pacific Coast Gas Assn. (legal adv. com. 1977—, legal sect. chmn. 1977, 78, 80, 85), N.W. Gas Assn., Chi Phi. Clubs: Bellevue Athletic (Wash.); Seattle Athletic. Home: 6321 Seaview Ave NW Seattle WA 98107 Office: Washington Energy Co 815 Mercer St Seattle WA 98109

TOMLINSON, WILLIAM HOLMES, management educator, retired army officer, b. Thornton, Ark., Apr. 12, 1922; s. Hugh Oscar and Lucy Gray (Holmes) T.; m. Dorothy Payne, June 10, 1947 (dec.); children: Jane Axtell, Lucy Gray, William Payne; m. Florence Mood Smith, May 1, 1969 (div.); m. Suzanne Scollard Gill, Mar. 16, 1977. BS, U.S. Mil. Acad., 1943; grad. Air Command Staff Coll., 1958; MBA, U. Ala., 1960; MS in Internat. Affairs, George Washington U., 1966; grad. U.S. Army War Coll., 1966; grad. Indsl. Coll. Armed Forces; PhD in Bus. Adminstrn., Am. U., 1974; postgrad. Advanced Mgmt. Program, Harvard U., 1968, 69; BAS, U. N. Fla., 1988. Commd. 2d lt. U.S. Army, 1943, advanced through grades to col., field arty., 1966; service in Philippines 246 Field Atry. Bn. Americal div, Japan; aide de camp, comdg. gen. 8th Army, 1945-48; mem. Office of Undersec. Army, Pentagon, Washington, 1961-64; comdr. 2d Bn., 8th Arty. and 7th Div. Arty., S. Korea, 1964-65; faculty Indsl. Coll. Armed Forces, Ft. McNair, Washington, 1966-72, ret., 1973; faculty U. North Fla., Jacksonville, 1972—, assoc. prof. mgmt., 1976—; vis. prof. U. Glasgow, Scotland, fall 1987; mem. Nat. Def. Exec. Res., Fed. Emergency Mgmt. Agy., 1976—. Decorated Bronze Star, Legion of Merit, Philippine Liberation medal, Japanese Occupation medal; recipient Freedom Found. award, 1973, Sr. Profl. in Human Resources. Mem. Acad. Mgmt., Am. Soc. Personnel Adminstrn., Indsl. Rels. Rsch. Assn., Acad. Internat. Bus., European Internat. Bus. Assn., Co. Mil. Historians, Nat. Eagle Scout Assn., Nat. Employee Services Assn. (pres. 1987-88), Co. Mil. Historians, West Point Soc. N. Fla. (pres. 1976), Mil. Order Stars and Bars (Fl. state comdr.), Army Navy Club, Fla. Yacht Club, Masons (32d degree), Shriners, Rotary, Beta Gamma Sigma (pres. 1988), Kappa Alpha. Presbyterian (elder). Contbr. articles to profl. jours. and books. Home: 1890 Shadowlawn Jacksonville FL 32205 Office: U North Fla Dept Mgmt 4567 S St Johns Bluff Rd Jacksonville FL 32216

TOMPKINS, DONALD ROBERT, telephone company executive; b. Port Chester, N.Y., June 9, 1941; s. Reed Pershing and Lucille Marion (Radcliffe) T.; AAS, Western Conn. State Univ., 1974; postgrad. Fairleigh Dickinson U., 1977-79; m. Cherylee Ganzenmuller; children: Brian Dale, Kathleen Kim, Colleen Joy. Engring. supr. AT&T Long Lines, White Plains, N.Y., 1968, ops. supr., 1968-71, ops. cutover chmn., 1971-73, ops. cutover chmn., Bridgeport, Conn., 1973-75, ops. mgr., White Plains, 1975-77, industry mgr. sales, Newark, 1977-78, nat. account mgr. sales, White Plains, 1978-80, dist. mktg. mgr. sales, 1980-83; nat. account mgr. Am. Bell Inc., White Plains, N.Y., 1983-84, sr. nat. account mgr. AT&T Info. Systems, 1984-85, mktg. mgr., 1986-87, nat. account mgr., Pitts., 1987—. Com. chmn. Fairfield County coun. Boy Scouts Am., 1965-70, scoutmaster, 1970-78; sch. supt. Meth. Ch., Danbury, Conn., 1965-72; mem. steering com. March of Dimes, Pitts., 1988; bd. dirs. Civic Light Opera, Pitts., 1989. Served with U.S. Navy, 1960-64. Recipient Partners in Profit award, 1980, Play to Win award, 1981, Sales Mgr. of Yr. award, 1982; Pacesetter Leadership award, 1983, Bravo Zulu award, 1983, others; named to AT&T Achievers Club, 1982-87. Mem.

Telelphone Pioneers, City Club (Pitts.) Mktg. Execs., Internat. Platform Assn., City Club, Green Mountain Hiking Club. Republican. Methodist (lay speaker). Home: 2532 Lindenwood Dr Wexford PA 15090 Office: AT&T 600 Grant St Room 3650 Pittsburgh PA 15219 other: 600 Grant St Rm 3650 Pittsburgh PA 15219

TOMPKINS, JAMES MCLANE, insurance company executive, government adviser; b. Balt., Jan. 1, 1913; s. John Almy and Frederica (McLane) T.; m. Barbara Miller, Nov. 22, 1965. Grad, Phillips Acad., 1931; B.A., Yale, 1935, M.A. (Pierson Coll. fellow 1940-43), 1943; certificate grad. study labor relations, N.Y. U. Research fellow Yale, 1937-40; dir. Bur. Mil. Service and Information, Yale and Dept. Def., 1940-43; dir. exec. placement, asst. chmn. bd. Vick Chem. Co., N.Y.C., 1943-48; with C.V. Starr & Co., Inc., N.Y.C., 1948—; v.p. public affairs C.V. Starr & Co., Inc., 1968—, cons., 1979—, also dir.; dir. Am. Internat. Underwriters Overseas, TAM Sigorta, Turkey; chmn. AIU Pakistan, Vt. Accident Ins. Co. Int., Uganda Am. Ins. Co., AIU Mediterranean, Inc.; vice chmn. bd. Am. Life Ins. Co., Wilmington, Del.; adviser WGM FOG, Norfolk, Va., 1988. Mem. U.S. delegation UN Conf. Trade and Devel., 1968—; adviser U.S. delegation OECD, 1969—; mem. U.S. Maritime Transport Com.; mem. U.S. del. London Diplomatic Conf. Maritime Claims, 1976, Geneva Conf. Multi Modal Transport, 1975, 77, 78, 79; spl. rep. internat. affairs Internat. Ins. Adv. Council, 1967—; pres. James M. Tompkins Co., 1987—; adv. bd. Sta. WMFOG, 1987—; Trustee Asia Soc., Samuel Goodyear Scholarship Fund (Yale); chmn. Eisenhower Fellowship Com., Pakistan, 1955-60; mem. Yale Alumni Bd. Recipient Spl. Cert. of Appreciation Internat. Ins. Adv. Council, 1981-82, Grand Cross Knights Holy Sepulchre. Mem. Yale Alumni Assn. (pres. New Canaan chpt., Yale Class 1935 Alumni Fund rep.), Co. Mil. Historians, Miniature Figure Collectors Am., Alpha Sigma Phi (past nat. trustee). Clubs: Yale (N.Y.C.), India House (N.Y.C.), Sky (N.Y.C.); American (London); Sind (Karachi, Pakistan). Home: Inshallah Dunrovin Wilton Creek Rd Hartfield VA 23071 Office: Am Internat Bldg 40 Pine St New York NY 10270

TONER, JOSEPH EDWARD, III, utility marketing executive, sales consultant; b. Phila., Jan. 19, 1948; s. Joseph Edward Jr. and Dorothy Mae (Miller) T.; m. Gail Louise Oehme, Feb. 18, 1967; children: Cathy, Joseph E. IV. BA in Humanities, La Salle Coll., Phila., 1974. Retail industry analyst AT&T, Morristown, N.J., 1974-75; retail market mgr. Bell of Pa., Phila., 1975-77, retail industry mgr., 1977-80, staff mgr. cert. bd., 1980-81; sales mgr. Bell of Pa., King of Prussia, 1981-84; dist. staff mgr. tactical staff Bell of Pa., Phila., 1984-87; dir. telemktg. Bell of Pa., Bala Cynwyd, 1987—; chmn. supervisory com. Phila. Telco Credit Union, 1971-72; pres. Sales Track, Inc., Richboro, Pa., 1985—. Mem. Phila. Republican Com., 1975-79; bd. dirs. Philadelphia County Bd. Assistance, 1981-84, Manor Jr. Coll., Jenkintown, Pa., 1988—; mem. Northampton Twp. Planning Commn., 1984-88; instr. Pa. Game Commn., 1986—. With USN, 1966-72. Mem. Sales and Mktg. Execs. Phila. (edn. com., outstanding contbn. award 1987), NRA (life). Methodist. Home: 14 E Pickering Bend Richboro PA 18954 Office: AT&T One Presidential Blvd 204 Bala-Cynwyd PA 19004

TONGUE, PAUL GRAHAM, financial executive; b. Phila., Dec. 30, 1932; s. George Paul and Florence Amelia (Kogel) T.; m. Marjorie Joan Meyers, May 26, 1954; children: Suzanne Marjorie, Douglas Paul. BS in Commerce, Drexel U., 1957; MBA, NYU, 1965. With Chase Manhattan Bank, N.Y.C., 1957-87; dir. Plus Systems Inc., Denver. Pres. Our Saviour Luth. Ch., Manhasset, N.Y., 1984; bd. dirs. Nassau Symphony Orch. Served with U.S. Army, 1954-55. Mem. Nassau Country Club (trustee).

TONNA, ARTHUR J., brewery company executive; b. San Francisco, Jan. 15, 1927; s. Emmanule and Carrie (Cilia) T.; m. Barbara Haverty, Apr. 27, 1946 (div. 1966); children—Jeanette, Patricia Tonna Cuthbert, Valerie Tonna Ariazza, Kenneth. Vice pres. Maier Brewing Co., Los Angeles, 1965-71; from v.p. to sr. v.p. Falstaff Brewing, St. Louis, 1971-76; exec. v.p. G. Heileman, LaCrosse, Wis., 1976-78, Joseph Schlitz, Milw., 1978-82, The Stroh Brewery Co., Detroit, 1982—. Patentee in field. Mem. Master Brewers Assn. Ams., Brewers, Beverage and Packaging Assn. (life; pres. Los Angeles chpt. 1965-70). Republican. Roman Catholic. Club: Renaissance Ctr. (Detroit). Home: 60 Fordcroft Rd Grosse Pointe Shores MI 48236 Office: Stroh Brewery Co 100 River Pl Detroit MI 48207

TOOHER, JAMES MARSHALL, energy company executive; b. Schenectady, N.Y., Aug. 9, 1931; s. James Leslie and Margaret (Marshall) T.; m. Barbara Mason, Aug. 2, 1952; children: Allison, Judith. BBA, Lehigh U., 1952. From salesman to v.p. eastern region AM Internat. Inc., Cleve., 1953-81; sr. v.p. Mohawk Data Scis., Inc., Parsippany, N.J., 1981-83, Cogenic Energy Systems, Inc., N.Y.C., 1983—. Served to capt. USAF, 1952-53. Mem. Assn. Energy and Engrs., Am. Gas Assn., Am. Cogeneration Assn. (bd. dirs.). Republican. Presbyterian. Club: Canoe Brook (Summit, N.J.). Lodges: Shrines, Masons. Home: 34 Van Houton Ave Chatham NJ 07928 Office: Cogenic Energy Systems Inc 76 Madison Ave New York NY 10016

TOOHEY, EDWARD JOSEPH, financial services company executive; b. Jersey City, Jan. 15, 1930; s. John Joseph and Estelle Anita (Hudson) T.; B.A., Yale U., 1953; m. Ruth Phyllis Scheidecker, Mar. 13, 1948; 1 dau., Phyllis Karen. With Merrill Lynch, Pierce, Fenner & Smith, Inc., N.Y.C., 1956—, mgmt. devel. program exec., 1966-68, v.p. resident mgr., N.Y.C., 1968-77, Washington, 1977-80, v.p., regional dir., N.Y.C., 1980—; dir. Bunbury Co., N.Y.C. Trustee Windham Found., Grafton, Vt., 1978—; vice chmn. Peddie Sch., Hightstown, N.J., 1981—, trustee, 1976—; bd. dirs. N.Y.C. Ballet, 1983—. Served to maj. USMC, 1953-55. Clubs: Canoe Brook Country (Summit, N.J.); Yale, Sky (N.Y.C.); Univ., Georgetown (Washington). Home: One Gracie Terr New York NY 10028 Office: 330 Madison Ave New York NY 10017

TOOHIG, MICHAEL FRANCIS, telecommunications executive; b. Lawrence, Mass., Dec. 9, 1924. BS in Physics, Boston Coll., 1949, MS in Physics, 1951. V.p., dir. engring. Electro Optical div. ITT, Roanoke, Va., 1972-79, pres., gen. mgr., 1979-82, v.p., dir. strategic planning, 1982-84; v.p. strategic planning/internat. mktg. Hekimian Labs., Inc., Gaithersburg, Md., 1984—; mem. Open System Interface, Network Mgmt. Patentee in field. Served with U.S. Army, 1943-46, ETO. Mem. Night Vision Mfrs. Assn. (1st pres. 1980-82, founder, organizer), Open System Interface/Network Mgmt. Forum (industry group coord.). Home: 6619 Brawner St McLean VA 22101 Office: Hekimian Labs Inc 9298 Gaither Rd Gaithersburg MD 20877

TOOKER, GARY LAMARR, electronics company executive; b. Shelby, Ohio, May 25, 1939; s. William Henry and Frances Ione (Melick) T.; m. Diane Rae Kreider, Aug. 4, 1962; children: Lisa, Michael. B.S.E.E., Ariz. State U., 1962. With Motorola Inc., Phoenix, 1962—, v.p., gen. mgr. internat. semicondr. div., 1980-81, v.p., gen. mgr. semicondr. products sector, 1981-82, sr. v.p., gen. mgr. semicondr. products sector, 1982-83; exec. v.p., gen. mgr. semicondr. products sector Motorola Inc., 1983-86; sr. exec. v.p., chief corp. staff officer Motorola Inc., Schaumburg, Ill., 1986-87, sr. exec. v.p., chief operating officer, 1988—; also bd. dirs.; mem. engring. adv. council Ariz. State U., Tempe, 1982-86. Bd. dirs. Scottsdale, Ariz. Boys Club, 1980-86, Jr. Achievement Chgo., 1988—; chief crusader, major corp. group United Way, Chgo., 1988—. Named Outstanding Alumni of Yr., Ariz. State U., 1983. Mem. IEEE, Am. Mgmt. Assn., Semicondr. Industry Assn. (dir. 1981-86, chmn. bd. 1983-86), Ariz. Assn. Industries (dir. 1981-86), Am. Electronics Assn. (bd. dirs. 1988—). Republican. Club: Economic of Chgo. Office: Motorola Inc 1303 E Algonquin Rd Schaumburg IL 60196

TOOLE, ROBERT F., personnel administrator; b. Syracuse, N.Y., Mar. 9, 1941; s. John Crawford and Kathryn (Lynn) T.; m. Patricia A. Hensel, Sept. 16, 1963; 1 child, Robert F. BBA, Lemoyne Coll., Syracuse, 1962. With Social Security Adminstrn., 1962-67; sales rep. Sandoz Pharmacy, 1967-73; from employee benefit analyst to v.p. human resources of services and parts div. Carrier Corp., 1973-86; v.p. fin. and adminstr. POMCO, 1986-87; founder, pres. R.F. Toole Assocs., Ltd., East Syracuse, N.Y., 1987—. Bd. dirs. Boys Club, Syracuse, 1979—; mem. Health Systems Agy., Chips-Health Planning Council; chmn. employee benefits com. Diocese of Syracuse; trustee, mem. exec. com. Loretto Geriatric Ctr. Served with USAR, 1963—, comdr., 1983—. Mem. Mfrs. Assn. Cen. N.Y., N.Y. Bus. Council, Nat. Assn. Mfrs., N.Y. State Health Care Fin. Council. Republican. Roman Cathlic. Club: Cavalry (dir., treas.). Home: 6 Edgewood Pkwy Fayeteville NY 13066 Office: RF Toole Assocs Ltd 6309 Fly Rd PO Box 426 East Syracuse NY 13057

TOOLEY, WILLIAM LANDER, real estate development company executive; b. El Paso, Tex., Apr. 23, 1934; s. William Lander and Virginia Mary (Ryan) T.; m. Reva Berger, Mar. 5, 1966; children: William Ryan, Patrick Boyer, James Eugene. BA, Stanford U., 1956; MBA, Harvard U., 1960. Treas., mgr. Pickwick Hotel Co., San Diego, 1960-63, David H. Murdock Devel. Co., Phoenix, 1963-67; ptnr. Ketchum, Peck & Tooley, L.A., 1967-74; chmn. Tooley & Co., investment builders, L.A., 1974--;; bd. dirs. Fed. Res. Bank San Francisco; dir. Nat. Realty Com., Washington, 1975--. Trustee Loyola Marymount U., L.A., 1975-82, bd. regents, 1982--, mem. task force, 1988--; bd. dirs. Internat. Leadership Ctr., Dallas, 1988--. Lt. (j.g.) USNR, 1956-58. Mem. Urban Land Inst., Calif. Club, Calif. Yacht Club, Lambda Alpha. Office: 3303 Wilshire Blvd Los Angeles CA 90010

TOOT, JOSEPH F., JR., bearing manufacturing company executive; b. 1935; married. A.B., Princeton U., 1957; postgrad., Harvard U. Grad. Sch. Bus. Adminstrn., 1961. With Timken Co., Canton, Ohio, 1962—; dep. mgr. Timken (France) Co., 1965-67; v.p. internat. div. Timken Co., Canton, 1967-68, corp. v.p., then exec. v.p., 1968-79, pres., 1979—, also bd. dirs.; bd. dirs. Rockwell Internat. Office: The Timken Co 1835 Dueber Ave SW Canton OH 44706

TOPE, DWIGHT HAROLD, management consultant; b. Grand Junction, Colo., Aug. 29, 1918; s. Richard E. and Elizabeth (Jones) T.; m. Carolyn Stagg, Apr. 29, 1949; children: Stephen R., Chris L. AS, Mesa Coll., 1940; student, George Washington U. Staff adjuster Fire Cos. Adjustment Bur., Denver, Albuquerque, 1946-48; br. mgr. Gen. Adjustment Bur., Deming, N.Mex., 1948-50; spl. agt. Cliff Kealey State Agy., Albuquerque, 1950-56; pres. Dwight Tope State Agy., Inc., Albuquerque, 1956-84, also chmn. bd., sr. cons., 1985-87. Mem. adv. bd. Salvation Army, Albuquerque, 1974—, Meals on Wheels, 1987—; past chmn. bd., pres. Presbyn. Heart Inst., Albuquerque, 1977—. Maj. Coast Arty. Anti-Aircraft, 1941-45. Mem. N. Mex. Ins. Assn. (past chmn.), Ins. Info. Inst. (past chmn.), N. Mex. Surplus Lines Assn. (past pres.), Air Force Assn., Assn. of U.S. Army, Am. Legion, Rotary, Masons, Shriners, Elks, Albuquerque Country Club, Petroleum Club. Republican. Home: 1812 Stanford Dr NE Albuquerque NM 87106 Office: 8100 Mountain Rd NE Ste 203F Albuquerque NM 87110

TOPFER, MORTON LOUIS, communications company executive; b. Bklyn., Sept. 18, 1936; s. Abraham and Sadie (Rindner) T.; m. Arlene Siegel, June 6, 1959 (div.); children: Bonnie, Jacqueline, Alan, Richard. B.S. in Physics, Bklyn. Coll., 1959; M.S., Poly. Inst. Bklyn., 1962. Engr. Elec. Tran, N.J., 1959-61; physicist Kollsman Inst., Elmhurst, N.Y., 1961-62; mgr. RCA, Princeton, N.J., 1962-69; v.p. Kulite Semiconductor, Ridgefield, N.J., 1969-71; sr. v.p., group gen. mgr. Motorola, Inc., Schaumburg, Ill., 1971—. Author: Thick Film Microelectronics, 1971. Mem. South Fla. Coordinating Council, 1979-82; mem. United Way of Broward County, 1979-81, Discovery Center, Fla., 1979-81. Mem. IEEE, Internat. Soc. Hybrid Microelectronics (Dan Hughes award 1977). Jewish. Home: The Landmark Northfield IL 60093 Office: Motorola Inc 1301 E Algonquin Rd Schaumburg IL 60196

TOPHAM, VERL REED, utility company executive; b. Paragonah, Utah, Aug. 25, 1934; s. Angus Reed and Louesa (Wilcock) T.; m. Darlene Sharp, Aug. 9, 1956 (dec. July 1961); m. Joyce Moss, Aug. 2, 1962; children: Lisa, Reed, Maria. BSL, U. Utah, 1955, JD, 1960. Bar: Utah, 1960. Ptnr. Stewart, Topham & Harding, Salt Lake City, 1961-69; asst. atty. gen. State of Utah, Salt Lake City, 1969-72; atty. Utah Power & Light Co., Salt Lake City, 1972—, asst. corp. sec., 1974-80, assoc. gen. counsel, 1980-81, v.p., chief fin. officer, 1981-84, sr. v.p., chief fin. officer, comml. mgr., 1984—, also bd. dirs. Mem. Utah Coordinating Council on Natural resources, Salt Lake City, 1965-67; mem. Utah Constl. Revision Commn., 1969-77; bd. dirs. ARC, Salt Lake City, 1987—. Served to capt. USAF, 1956-59. Mem. ABA, Utah State Bar (chmn. energy and natural resources sect. 1983—), Salt Lake County Bar, Utah Fin. and Acctg. Forum, Salt Lake C. of C. (bd. dirs. 1986—). Mormon. Office: Utah Power & Light Co 1407 W North Temple Salt Lake City UT 84140

TOPOR, ROBERT ALBIN, automotive company executive; b. Hartford, Conn., Sept. 22, 1947; s. Albin S. and Wanda (Wezowic) T.; m. katherine V., June 3, 1978; children: Sarah, Jason. BBA, Western New Eng. Coll., 1969; MBA, Babson Coll., 1971. Zone mgr. Ford div. Ford Motor Co., Falls Church, Va., 1975-78, distbn. mgr., 1978-79, merchandising mgr. Lincoln Mercury div., 1979-80; dealer sales planning mgr. Toyota Motor Sales in USA, Torrance, Calif., 1980-84; asst. regional sales mgr. Nissan Motor Corp. in USA, Jacksonville, Fla., 1984-86; nat. dealer planning mgr. Nissan Motor Corp. in USA, Carson, Calif., 1986-87, nat. sales planning and analysis mgr., 1987-88, nat. fleet and leasing adminstrn. mgr., 1988—. With U.S. Army, 1969-71. Mem. Deerwood Club (Jacksonville), Beta Gamma. Republican. Home: 5714 West View Dr Orange CA 92669 Office: Nissan Motor Corp 18501 S Figueroa St Carson CA 90248

TOPPEL, HAROLD H., diversified company executive; b. Franklin, N.J., 1924; B.A., U. Ill., 1948; married. Salesman, Lever Bros. Co., 1944, Food Fair Corp. and Penn Fruit Co., Inc., 1945-50; pres. Nat. Grocery Co., Metuchen, N.J., 1950-54; chmn. bd., chief exec. officer Pueblo Internat., Inc., formerly Pueblo Supermarkets, Inc., 1955—. Office: Pueblo Internat Inc 1300 NW 22nd St Pompano Beach FL 33069

TOPPING, JAMES FRANCIS, computer company executive; b. Elmira, N.Y., Nov. 25, 1931; s. Glenn B. and Eleanor E. (New) T.; m. Lura Lea Williams, July 7, 1955; children: Thomas N., Peter C., Christopher M. BS in Engring., U.S. Naval Acad., 1954; MS in Indsl. Mgmt., Purdue U., 1961; grad. with honors, Naval War Coll., 1968. Commd. ensign USN, 1954, advanced through grades to capt., 1975, ret., 1977; v.p. CACI Internat. Inc., Arlington, Va., 1979-81, sr. v.p., 1981-83, exec. v.p., 1983-86, oper. div. pres., 1986—. Mem. Belle Haven Country Club. Home: 612 S Lee St Alexandria VA 22314 Office: Caci Internat Inc 1815 N Fort Myer Dr Arlington VA 22209

TORAN, TERENCE WILLIAM, financial executive; b. Bklyn., June 27, 1948; s. William Paul and Helen K. T.; m. Catherine Anne Zaums, 1980; children: Paul, Nicholas, Michael. BSE, Princeton U., 1970; MBA, Dartmouth Coll., 1975. Assoc. Gulf Oil Co., Pitts., 1975-77; cons. Booz Allen & Hamilton, N.Y.C., 1978-80; dir. strategy Borg Warner Corp., Parsippany, N.J., 1980-82; dir. planning and bus. devel. Uniroyal, Inc., Middlebury, Conn., 1983-85; asst. controller Marriott Corp., Washington, 1986-88, v.p. fin., sr. living div., 1988—. Lt. USNR, 1970-73, comdr., 1975—. Mem. Navy League, Smithsonian Inst., Naval Inst., Naval Res. Assn. Office: Marriott Corp 1 Marriott Dr Dept 83170 Washington DC 20058

TORBERT, CARL ALLEN, JR., natural resources company executive; b. Mobile, Ala., Dec. 3, 1935; s. Carl Allen and Mary Hughes T.; m. Betty Reed, Sept. 8, 1962; 1 child, Mary Shannon. B.S. in Commerce, Spring Hill Coll., 1958. Pres. Dravo Natural Resources Co., Mobile, Ala., 1984—; sr. v.p. Dravo Corp., Pitts., 1984-88, pres., 1988—; also bd. dirs. Dravo Corp. Dir. Bus. Council Ala., 1984. Served to capt. U.S. Army, 1958-66. Roman Catholic. Office: Dravo Corp 1 Oliver Pla Pittsburgh PA 15222

TORCIVIA, BENEDICT J., SR., construction company executive; b. Passaic, N.J., Sept. 8, 1929; s. Joseph and Felicia (Latteri) T.; m. Elvira Venneri, June 20, 1953; children—Benedict J., Joseph A. B.S. in Archtl. Engring., Catholic U. Am., 1951. Registered profl. engr., N.H. Estimator, project mgr. Arthur Venneri Co., Westfield, N.J., 1951-60, v.p., asst. to pres., 1960-63, pres., 1963-65; pres., treas. Torcon, Inc., Westfield, N.J., 1965-84, pres., treas., chief exec. officer, 1984—; dir. Crestmont Fed. Savs. and Loan. Trustee bd. overseers N.J. Inst. Tech., Newark, 1980—; trustee Found. U. Medicine and Dentistry N.J., Newark, 1985-88; regent St. Peter's Coll., Jersey City, 1972-80 No. N.J. Area chmn. U.S. Olympic Com., 1984—; exec. com. March of Dimes, Monmouth County, N.J., 1985, N.J. unit NCCJ, 1985; trustee Kidney Fund of N.J., Union County, 1980-85, The Pingry Sch. Recipient Ann. Alumni Achievement in Engring. award Cath. U. Am., Washington, 1978; named Constrn. Man of Yr., N.J. Ready Mixed Concrete Assn., 1981, Gen. Contractor of Yr. N.J. chpt. Am. Subcontractors Assn., 1974, 82. Mem. Constrn. Congress (pres. 1983-85), Union County Bldg. Contractors Assn. (pres. 1975-83), Am. Concrete Inst., Bldg. Contractors Assn. N.J. (pres. 1981-82), N.J. Alliance for Action (trustee 1980—), Navesink Country Club, Jupiter Hills Club. Roman Catholic. Office: Torcon Inc PO Box 609 214 E Grove St Westfield NJ 07091

TORCIVIA, BENEDICT JOSEPH, JR., construction company executive; b. Buffalo, July 5, 1957; s. Benedict Joseph and Elvira (Venneri) T.; m. Judith Anne Hlavenka, May 2, 1981; children: Benedict III, Brian, Christopher. BS in Bus., Lehigh U., 1979; lic. in real estate, Union Coll., 1980. Lic. in real estate. Exec. v.p., chief oper. officer Torcon, Inc., Westfield, N.J., 1979—, exec. v.p., 1979—. Bd. dirs. N.J. Alliance for Action. Mem. Bldg. Contractors Assn. N.J. (trustee), Constrn. Mgmt. Com., Associated Gen. Contractors of Am. (com. mem.), Waterfront Invest (bd. advisors), Navesink Country (Middletown, N.J.). Roman Catholic. Office: Torcon Inc 214 E Grove St Westfield NJ 07091

TORCIVIA, JOSEPH ARTHUR, construction company executive; b. Plainfield, N.J., Sept. 16, 1959; s. Benedict J. Sr. and Elvira (Venneri) T.; m. Bonnie Lewis, Aug. 18, 1984; 1 child, Joseph A., Jr. BS in Fin., Lehigh U., 1981; JD, Seton Hall U., 1985. Assoc. Crummy, Del Deo, Dolan, Griffinger & Vecchione, Newark, 1985-86; exec. v.p. Torcon, Inc., Westfield, N.J., 1986—. Mem. corp. fundraising com. U.S. Olympics, Basking Ridge, N.J., 1986—. Mem. ABA, ASA Packer Soc. Roman Catholic. Clubs: Navesink (Middletown, N.J.); Suburban (Union, N.J.). Office: Torcon Inc 214 E Grove St Box 609 Westfield NJ 07091

TORELL, JOHN RAYMOND, III, banker; b. Hartford, Conn., July 10, 1939; s. Raymond John and Gertrude May (Bent) T.; m. Anne A. Keller, Feb. 17, 1962; children: John Raymond, Anne Elizabeth, Susan Allgood. BA, Princeton U., 1961. With Mfrs. Hanover Trust Co., N.Y.C., 1961—, asst. sec., 1964-67, asst. v.p., 1967-70, v.p. nat. div., 1970, v.p. credit dept., 1970-71, v.p. corp. planning, 1971-72, sr. v.p. planning, mktg. and spl. products, 1973-75, sr. v.p., dep. gen. mgr. retail banking, 1975-76, exec. v.p. met. div., 1976-78, vice chmn., dir., 1978-82, pres., dir., 1982-88; exec. vice chmn., dir. Mfrs. Hanover Corp. (parent), N.Y.C., from 1982, pres., until 1988; chmn., chief exec. officer Calfed Inc., Los Angeles, Ca., 1988—; chmn. Calif. Fed. Savs. and Loan, Los Angeles, Ca., 1988—; dir. Am. Home Products, N.Y. Telephone, Reins Corp., Econ. Captial Corp., N.Y.C. Bd. dirs. Juilliard Mus. Found. Served with USN, 1962. Republican. Clubs: Blind Brook, Siwanoy Country, Bronxville Field. Home: 16 Birchbrook Rd Bronxville NY 10708 Office: Calfed 5670 Wilshire Blvd Los Angeles CA 90036 *

TORGERSON, LARRY KEITH, lawyer; b. Albert Lea, Minn., Aug. 25, 1935; s. Fritz G. and Lu (Hillman) T. BA, Drake U., 1958, MA, 1960, LLB, 1963, JD, 1968; MA, Iowa U., 1962; cert., The Hague (The Netherlands) Acad. Internat. Law, 1965, 69; LLM, U. Minn., 1969, Columbia U., 1971, U. Mo., 1976; PMD, Harvard U., 1973, EdM, 1974. Bar: Minn. 1964, Wis. 1970, Iowa 1970, U.S. Tax Ct. 1971, U.S. Supreme Ct. 1972, U.S. Dist. Ct. Minn. 1964, U.S. Dist. Ct. (no. dist.) Iowa 1971, U.S. Dist. Ct. (ea. dist.) Wis. 1981, U.S. Ct. Appeals (8th cir.) 1981. Asst. corp. counsel 1st Bank Stock Corp., Mpls., 1963-67; v.p., trust officer Nat. City Bank, Mpls., 1967-69; sr. mem. Torgerson Law Firm, Northwood, Iowa, 1969-87; trustee, gen. counsel Torgerson Farms, Northwood, 1977—, Redbirch Farms, Kensett, Iowa, 1987—, Sunburst Farms, Grafton, Iowa, 1987—, Gold Dust Farms, Bolan, Iowa, 1988—; chmn., gen. counsel Internat. Investments, Mpls., 1983—, Transoceanic, Mpls., 1987—; pres., gen. counsel Torgerson Investments, Northwood, 1984—, Torgerson Properties, Northwood, 1987—. Mem. ABA, Am. Judicature Soc., Iowa Bar Assn., Minn. Bar Assn., Wis Bar Assn., Mensa, Psi Chi, Circle K, Phi Alpha Delta, Omicron Delta Kappa, Pi Kappa Delta, Alpha Tau Omega, Pi Delta Epsilon, Alpha Kappa Delta. Lutheran.

TORIGIAN, PUZANT CROSSLEY, pharmaceutical company executive; b. Istanbul, Turkey, Sept. 21, 1922; s. John and Shakeh (Yaver) T.; BS in Pharm., Columbia U., 1949; postgrad. N.Y.U.; D.Sc. (hon.), U. Ea. Fla., 1971; m. Joanne Curatolo, Mar. 28, 1971; children—Christine, John, Michael. Staff, Torigian Labs. Inc., Queens Village, N.Y., 1939-50, sales mgr., 1955-58, pres., 1976-84; staff, Lloyd Chemists, Jamaica, N.Y., 1951-53; pres. Crossley Pharms. Corp., Queens Village, 1953-55; asst. to pres. Marvin R. Thompson Inc., Stamford, Conn., pres., 1958-59; ops. mgr. J.B. Williams Co., N.Y.C., 1959-60; pres. Tobison Personnel Agy., N.Y.C., 1960-64; pres. Bravo Smokes Inc., Hereford, Tex., 1964-74; plant mgr. Sterling Drugs Internat., Kuala Lumpur, Malaysia, 1974-76; pres. Challenger Industries, Fort Lee, N.J., 1978-87; pres. Anoush Parfumerie, Ft. Lee, 1978—; mng. dir. Found. for Alternative Research, Inc., 1985—; pres., chmn. bd. dirs. Safer Smokes, Inc., Fort Lee, 1986—. Served with USNR, 1942-46, PTO. Decorated knight comdr. Order St. George of Corinthia. Mem. Columbia U. Coll. Pharmacy Alumni Assn. (pres. 1963-64, editor Graduate 1956-63, Lion award, Disting. Service award), Fedn. Alumni Assns. Columbia U. (trustee 1960-64), Am. Pharm. Assn., Am. Soc. Parenteral and Enteric Nutrition, Parenteral Drug Assn., N.Y. Acad. Scis., Internat. Soc. Pharm. Engrs. (charter), AAAS, Kappa Psi (nat. historian 1961-63). Mem. Armenian Apostolic Ch. Author: How to Give Up Tobacco, 1971; 4 patents in field. Home: 2 Horizon Rd Fort Lee NJ 07024 Office: Challenger Industries PO Box 401 Fort Lee NJ 07024-0401

TORISKY, DONALD DAVID, financial executive; b. Pitts., Aug. 20, 1938; s. Charles A. and Cecilia G. (Blahut) T.; m. Patricia A. Sucs, June 2, 1962; children: Shawn, Kristina. Cert. in advanced mgmt. program, Harvard U., 1978. Salesman Sears Roebuck & Co., 1958-60, 84 Lumber Co., 1960-62; regional rep. sales securities Wadell & Reed, 1962; with Borg-Warner Acceptance Corp., Chgo., 1962—, group v.p., 1976-79, exec. v.p., 1979-80, pres. consumer div., 1980-83, pres., chief exec. officer, 1983-87; v.p. Borg-Warner Corp., Chgo., 1986-87; exec. v.p. Transamerica Fin. Corp., Los Angeles, 1987—; pres., chief exec. officer Transam. Comml. Fin. Corp., 1987—; exec. v.p. Transam. Fin. Group, 1987—, also bd. dirs.; trustee Northwest Community Hosp., Arlington Heights, Ill., 1978—; bd. dirs. Nat. Bank Detroit. Sgt. USMC, 1956-58. Democrat. Roman Catholic. Club: Harvard (Chgo. and N.Y.C.). Office: Transamerica Comml Fin Corp 225 N Michigan Ave Chicago IL 60601

TORNEDEN, ROGER L(EE), insurance executive; b. Lawrence, Kans., Feb. 2, 1944; s. William E. and Lelia M. (Kindred) T.; B.S. in Indsl. Mgmt., U. Kans., 1966, M.S. in Ops. Research, 1967; Ph.D. in Internat. Bus., N.Y. U. 1974; m. Lisa Meredith Ross, Dec. 18, 1982; children: Jennifer, Stephanie. Corp. planning analyst ARCO, N.Y.C., 1967-69; sr. fin. analyst J.C. Penney, N.Y.C., 1969-72, dir. ops. analysis Sarma-Penney, Brussels, 1972-74, Japan project dir., Kobe, 1974-77, dir. internat. devel., N.Y.C., 1977-81, dir. econ. affairs, N.Y.C., 1982-87; sr. v.p. worldwide mktg. Am. Internat. Group, N.Y.C., 1988—; asst. prof. mktg. Baruch Coll., 1978-84; bd. dirs. Lenox Manor Owners, Inc.; internat. cons. disposal fgn. ops.; bd. dirs. Am. C. of C. in Japan, 1976-77; bd. dirs. YMCA of Greater N.Y., 1988—. Served with USNR, 1961-65. Recipient Outstanding Performance award Bd. Govs. Am. C. of C. in Japan, 1977; Commodity Trader of Yr. award Internat. Moneyline, 1984. Mem. Nat. Retail Mgmt. Assn. (internat. com.), Soc. Applied Econs., Japan Soc. Republican. Lutheran. Author: Foreign Disinvestments by U.S. Multinational Corporations, 1975; contbr. articles to profl. jours. Home: 176 E 77th New York NY 10021 Office: Am Internat Group 70 Pine St New York NY 10270

TORNETTA, PAUL, publishing company executive; b. N.Y.C., Feb. 6, 1927; s. Paul Salvator and Regina (Cahill) T.; m. Phyllis Rosalind Biegun, Nov. 1, 1952; children: Linda, Paul III. BS, Bklyn. Poly. Inst., 1960. Nat. sales mgr. Crowell Collier Pubs., N.Y.C., 1964-67; v.p., asst. to pres. Berkeley Pub. Co., N.Y.C., 1967-70; exec. v.p., dir. mktg. Pinnacle Books, N.Y.C., 1970-76; exec. v.p., gen. mgr. Trans-High Corp., N.Y.C., 1976-78; pres., pub. Laurant Pub. Co., N.Y.C., 1978-86; pres. Nubind Graphics, Ltd., N.Y.C., 1986—. Served with USAF, 1945-47. Home: 15 Laurel Hall Rd Crugers NY 10520

TORRES, CYNTHIA ANN, banker; b. Glendale, Calif., Sept. 24, 1958; d. Adolph and Ruth Ann (Smith) T.; m. Michael Victor Gisser, Mar. 11, 1989. AB, Harvard U., 1980, MBA, 1984. Research assoc. Bain & Co.,

Boston, 1980-82; assoc. Goldman, Sachs & Co., N.Y.C., 1984-88, v.p., 1988; v.p. First Interstate Bancorp, L.A., 1989—. Mem. judiciary rev. bd. Bus. Sch. Harvard U., Boston, 1983-84. Rockefeller Found. scholar, 1976; Harvard U. Ctr. for Internat. Affairs fellow, 1979-80; recipient Leadership award Johnson and Johnson, 1980; by Council for Opportunity in Grad. Mgmt. Edn. fellow, 1982-84. Mem. Acad. Polit. Sci., L.A. World Affairs Council, Harvard Club of So. Calif. (mem. schs. com. 1988—). Office: First Interstate Bancorp 707 Wilshire Blvd Los Angeles CA 90017

TORRES, GUIDO ADOLFO, water treatment company executive; b. Esmeraldas, Ecuador, Aug. 29, 1938; s. Carlos M. and Nora I. (Andrade) T.; m. Lupe N. Duran, Aug. 29, 1964; children: Guido, Alex, Juan Jose. B of Chem. Engring, Cen. U. Ecuador, 1967. Chief of study group Indsl. Devel. Ctr. Ecuador, Quito, 1965-69, tech. asst. to exec. dir., 1969-70; researcher Frakes Water Treatment Plant, Luverne, Minn., 1970-71; researcher Andean Water Treatment Soc. Anonima, Quito, 1972-84, gen. mgr., 1984-85, pres., 1985—. Author: Industrial Water Treatment; contbr. articles on water treatment to jours.; developer water treatment chems., equipment. Fellow Chem. Engring Coll. Ecuador (pres. 1976); mem. Am. Inst. Chem. Engrs., Am. Water Works Assn., Quito Indsl. Chamber, Quito C. of C., Quito Small Industry Chamber. Club: Castillo Amaguana. Home: 261 Miravalle, Quito Pichincha, Ecuador Office: Andean Water Treatment Soc, Belgica 161 PO Box 3297, Quito Pichincha, Ecuador

TORRES, SUNNY, relief agency administrator; b. Thomaston, Maine, Oct. 4, 1939; d. Wilbert and Bertha (Kent) Mull; m. Edward Torres, July 11, 1959; children: Debra, Dale, David. BS, Bridgewater Coll., 1974; MEd, R.I. Coll., 1980; postgrad., U. So. Maine, 1980—. Spl. edn. specialist L.G. Nourse Sch., Norton, Mass., 1974-80; dir. spl. edn. Sch. dist. 39, Sumner, Maine, 1980-81; instr., cons. U. So. Maine, Gorham, 1981-85; dir. spl. edn. Sch. Union 29, Poland, Maine, 1982-83; pres., dir. Therapy Edn. Assn., North Conway, N.H., 1983-86; headmaster Elan Sch., Poland Spring, Maine, 1986—; owner, dir. Profl. Health Care Services, Naples, Maine, 1987—; ednl. supr., Jackson Brook Inst., Portland, Maine, 1988—; ednl. cons., U. So. Maine, 1980—. Mem. Nat. Assn. Female Execs. Home: PO Box 334 Naples ME 04055

TORREY, RICHARD FRANK, utility executive; b. Saratoga Springs, N.Y., Dec. 31, 1926; s. Reginald Frank and Marian (Currey) T.; BA cum laude, Syracuse U., 1951; m. Betty Louise Stetson, July 2, 1949; children: Patricia Ann Torrey Simpkins, Carol Louise Torrey Kress, Barbara Jean Torrey Friedman. News reporter Syracuse (N.Y.) Post Standard, 1947-51; pub. relations account exec., Syracuse, 1951-53; home sec. 35th Congl. Dist., Syracuse, 1952-53; exec. sec. to mayor Syracuse, 1954-58; dir. area devel. Niagara Mohawk Power Corp., Syracuse, 1958-66, comml. v.p. Western div., Buffalo, 1966-68, adminstrv. v.p., 1968-72, v.p., gen. mgr., 1972-76, sr. v.p., Syracuse, 1976-88, ret., 1988; pres. Canadian Niagara Power Co. Ltd., 1968-88, dir. 1968—; pres., dir. Caragh Investments Ltd., 1981-85; pres. Opinac Investments Ltd., 1982-88, bd. dirs. 1982—; pres. Opinac Energy Ltd. (Calgary, Ala.) 1983-88, bd. dirs. 1983—; dir. Utilities Mut. Ins. Co., 1968-87, Syracuse Savs. Bank, 1962-68, 76-87, Liberty Nat. Bank, 1968-76, Buffalo Savs. BAnk, 1970-76, Norstar Bancorp., Albany, 1973-88 . Pres., Syracuse USO, 1959-61, mem. nat. council 1959-62, 68-72; co-chmn. Central N.Y. Interim Council Regional Planning, 1965-66; gen. chmn. Dunbar-Huntington Bldg. Fund, Syracuse, 1963; state campaign chmn. N.Y. Job Devel. Authority, 1961; gen. chmn. United Way of Buffalo and Erie County, 1971; mem. Syracuse U. Corporate Adv. Council, 1972-76. Trustee Elmcrest Children's Center, 1962-63, Camp Good Will, Syracuse, 1964-66, Syracuse Area Council Chs., 1959-64; bd. dirs. United Way Buffalo and Erie County, 1967-76, Greater Buffalo Devel. Found., Kenmore Mercy Hosp., 1970-76, Crouse Irving Meml. Hosp. Found., 1978—, Nat. Kidney Found., 1987—. Served with Air Corps, U.S. Army, 1944-47. Recipient Syracuse Young Man of Yr. award, 1962; Outstanding Citizen award Buffalo Evening News, 1973. Mem. N.Y. State Assn. Indsl. Devel. Agys. (pres. 1959-62), Empire State (v.p., dir. 1963-80), Buffalo Area (v.p. 1968-72, dir. 1968-76, pres. 1972-73, chmn. bd. 1973-74, named Man of Yr. 1974) chambers commerce, Associated Industries of N.Y. (dir. 1978-80), Bus. Council of N.Y. (dir. 1980-82), Mfrs. Assn. Central N.Y. (dir. 1977-88), Delta Upsilon, Sigma Delta Chi. Mem. Dewitt Community Ch. Clubs: Buffalo (past 2d v.p., dir.), Syracuse Century (gov. 1980-83), Onondaga Golf, Plantation Golf and Country (Venice, Fla.), Automobile of Western N.Y. (dir., v.p. 1971, pres. 1973). Home and Office: 248 Cerromar Way Venice FL 34293

TORREY, TERESA MCGUINNESS, insurance company executive; b. Ithaca, N.Y., Sept. 26, 1946; d. James Lawrence and Helen (Hautala) McGuinness; m. Preston Allan Torrey, Oct. 2, 1971. BA, Albertus Magnus Coll., 1968; MBA, U. Conn., 1976. Rsch. asst. The Travelers, Hartford, Conn., 1968-72, asst. dir. urban affairs, 1972-76, account exec. surety bond div., 1976-79, fin. analyst, 1979-81, investment mgr., 1981-84, investment officer, 1984-87, 2d v.p. pvt. placements, 1987—. Chmn. investment com. YWCA, Hartford, 1987—. Recipient Nat. Observer Student Achievement award Dow Jones Co., 1976. Mem. Greater Hartford C. of C. (women execs. com.), Hartford Club, Beta Gamma Sigma. Roman Catholic. Home: 664 New Rd Avon CT 06001 Office: The Travelers 1 Tower Sq Hartford CT 06183

TOSTENRUD, DONALD BOYD, banker; b. Estherville, Iowa, Mar. 24, 1925; s. O.M. and Irene (Connell) T.; m. Arlene Girg, Jan. 12, 1950; children: Eric, Amy. B.B.A., U. Minn., 1948; grad., Rutgers U. Grad. Sch. Banking, 1957. Nat. bank examiner Mpls., 1948-57; v.p. First Nat. Bank Black Hills, Rapid City, S.D., 1958-59; with Ariz. Bank, Phoenix, 1959—, exec. v.p., 1967-69, sr. exec. v.p., 1969-71, pres., 1971-78, chmn. bd., chief exec. officer, 1978-87, chmn. bd., chmn. exec. com., 1987-88, chmn. emeritus, chmn. exec. com., 1988—; pres. COMPAS 6; bd. dirs. Samcor, Security Pacific Nat. Bank & Corp. Trustee Phoenix Art Mus., pres., 1980-82; bd. fellows Center for Creative Photography, U. Ariz., Tucson; trustee Grand Central Art Galleries, Inc., N.Y.C., Am. Grad. Sch. Internat. Mgmt., Ariz. Heart Inst., Scottsdale Artists Sch. Inc. Served with AUS, 1943-45. Mem. Ariz. Commn. on Arts, Western Art Assos., Tucson C. of C. (past pres.), Ariz. Bankers Assn. (dir., past pres.), Am. Bankers Assn. (governing council, past dir.). Home: 3059 E Marshall Phoenix AZ 85016 Office: Ariz Bancwest Corp 101 N 1st Ave Phoenix AZ 85003

TOSUNLAR, AKIF ZAFER, small business owner, computer systems dealer; b. Istanbul, Turkey, Dec. 17, 1950; s. Huseyin Behcet and Melahat (Saygel) T.; m. Julia Claire Parker-Jones, July, 3, 1973; children: Lara Claire Filiz, Olivia Yeliz. Student, Bosphorus U., 1971-73, 74-75. Mgr. ops. Tourism Transport, Ltd., Istanbul, 1969-73; sr. cons. Anglo-World Travel, Ltd., Bournemouth, Eng., 1976-80; mng. dir. Euro Package Tours, Ltd., Bournemouth, 1980-87; owner Silversands Computers, Poole, Eng., 1987—. Mem. Tourism Soc. Muslim.

TOTH, DENNIS JOHN, real estate developer; b. Passaic, N.J., June 29, 1946; s. Joseph and Anna (Malick) T; m. Suzi Kay Rines, Nov.25, 1978; 1 child, Lisa Anna. BA, Randolph-Macon Coll., 1968. Tchr. Warwick (Va.) High Sch., 1968-70; sales mgr. Sea Land Service Inc., Boston, 1971-87; pvt. practice real estate devel. Norwell, Mass., 1986—; mng. ptnr. T&S Realty, Norwell, 1983—, Windemere Castle Ptnrs., Norwell, 1986—, Meadow Ridge Ptnrs., Mt. Freedom, N.J., 1989—; pres. Container Storage Co., Accord Mass., 1987—, Empire cons. Group, Accord, 1983—; prtn. Lakeside Properties, Lake Hopatcong, N.J., 1986—, Family Realty, Landing, N.J., 1985—; bd. dirs. Suja Corp., Hanover, Mass., Glasser, N.J., Properties Mgmt. Corp. Active So. Shore Natural Sci. Ctr., Norwell, 1985—, Nat. Trust for Hist. Preservation, Washington, 1987—, Norwell Hist. Soc., 1987—. Mem. Nat. Assn. Realtors, Fgn. Commerce Club New Eng., Plymouth County Bd. Realtors, Boston Traffic Assn. Home: 114 Hemlock Dr Norwell MA 02061 Office: Glasser Properties Mgmt Corp PO Box 158 Accord MA 02018

TOTH, STEPHEN MICHAEL, electronics specialist; b. Columbus, Ohio, July 12, 1946; s. Stephen Charles and Marian June (Hamilton) T.; m. Loreen Ann Bromeling, May 6, 1965 (div. 1974); children: Kathleen Marie, Stephen Charles. Tech. degree, Gt. Lakes Naval Tng. Ctr., 1965; EE, Capitol Radio Engring. Inst., Washington, 1971. Cert. electronics technician, engring. technician. Navigational aids technician USN, Meridian, Miss., 1966-68; radar supr. USN, Sangley Point, Philippines, 1968-71; navigtional aids supr. USN, Lemoore, Calif., 1971-75; communications technician County of Tulare, Visalia, Calif., 1975-77, communications supr., 1977-79; communications technician Tidewater Communications and Elec. Corp., Virginia Beach, Va., 1979-85, shop mgr., 1985—; communications cons. City of Virginia Beach, 1985-87; control system cons. USN, 1983, alarm system cons., 1986. Inventor security alarm system, 1971, portable telephone system, 1979. Asst. cub master Cub Scouts Am., Virginia Beach, 1980-85, sponsor, 1985—; dir. Tidewater Soap Box Derby, Inc., Virginia Beach, 1982-87 (nat. cert. of appreciation, 1983, 84). Mem. Nat. Assn. Bus. and Ednl. Radio, Am. Philatelic Soc., Smithsonian Inst. Republican. Lutheran. Club: Foresters (chief ranger, 1982-84, pub. relations officer 1987—, Forester of Yr., 1983). Home: 736 Lincoln Ave Virginia Beach VA 23452 Office: Tidewater Communications Corp 216 N Witchduck Virginia Beach VA 23462

TOTLIS, GUST JOHN, banking executive; b. Highwood, Ill., May 15, 1939; s. John Chris and Agape (Galelis) T.; m. Joyce Elaine Edholm, June 5, 1960; children: Kenneth Chris, Charles Gust. BA, Lake Forest Coll., 1962; MBA, U. Chgo., 1964. Fin. planning mgr. Gen. Foods Corp., Battle Creek, Mich., 1964-68; fin. analyst Irving Trust Co., N.Y.C., 1968-69, asst. sec., 1969-71, asst. v.p., 1971-72, v.p., 1972-75; corp. controller Irving Bank Corp., N.Y.C., 1975-82; exec. v.p., chief fin. officer Fidelity Union Bancorp, Newark, 1982-85, Star Banc Corp (formerly First Nat. Cin. Corp.), Cin., 1985—; also bd. dirs. Star Banc Corp (formerly First Nat. Cin. Corp.); bd. dirs. Miami Valley Ins. Co., Cin., 1st Nat. Bldg. Corp., Cin. Adv. bd. dirs. Salvation Army, Cin., 1987—; bd. dirs. Cin. Chamber Orch., May Festival Assn. Mem. Fin. Execs. Inst., Am. Inst. Banking, Bank Adminstrn. Inst. Presbyterian. Clubs: University, Bankers, Kenwood Country (Cin.). Home: 5450 Waring Dr Indian Hill OH 45243

TOTMAN, PATRICK STEVEN, lawyer, retail executive; b. Stockton, Calif., Sept. 29, 1944; s. Mervyn Willis and Margaret Elizabeth (McDow) T.; m. Rosemarie Bachle, Aug. 27, 1966 (div. Jan. 1989); children—Michael, Jarrod. A.B., U. San Francisco, 1966, J.D., 1969. Bar: Calif. Atty. Safeway Stores, Inc., Oakland, Calif., 1969-72, asst. v.p., 1973-79, v.p., 1979-83, sr. v.p. treasury, 1983—; seminar leader NYU, 1983-84. Mem. ABA, Calif. Bar Assn., Nat. Assn. Corp. Retail Execs., Internat. Council Shopping Ctrs. Roman Catholic. Office: Safeway Stores Inc 201 4th St Oakland CA 94660

TOURE, MOHAMED ALI, professional society administrator; b. Dakar, Senegal, Feb. 20, 1949; s. Moustapha and Rouguietou (Diallo) T.; m. Mariame Tiam, Nov. 30, 1976; children: Rouguietou, Moustapha, Said Nour, Mohamed Fadel, Bineta. Maths. Baccalauract, Lycee Blaise Diagne, Dakar, 1967; Electricity-Mechanics Engr. diploma, Ecole Speciale de Mecanique et Electricité, Sudria, Paris, 1975. Dep. head of staff Senelec Power Authority, Dakar, Senegal, 1975-79, head of staff (research), 1979; gen. mgr. Sinaes, Dakar, 1980-86; mem. profl. staff Islamic Found. Sci., Tech. and Devel., 1986—. Recipient Internat. Africa award, 1980, 85. Muslim. Avocations: public relations, foreign languages, civilizations, philology. Home: Bopp rue 1 No 103, Dakar Senegal Office: IFSTAD, PO Box 9833, Jeddah 21423, Saudi Arabia

TOVEY, JOSEPH, investment banker; b. Tel Aviv, Israel, Nov. 5, 1938; came to U.S., 1940, naturalized, 1947; s. Samuel and Rachel (Weiman) T.; B.S. summa cum laude, Bklyn. Coll., 1959; M.B.A., N.Y.U., 1961, Ph.D., 1969; m. Anita Beverly Losice, Feb. 20, 1961; children—David, Debra, Nissan Chaim, Seth Reuven, Shayna Nava. Staff acct. Machtiger, Green & Co., N.Y.C., 1959-60, Loeb & Troper, N.Y.C., 1960-61; tax researcher Lybrand, Ross Bros. & Montgomery, 1961-63; planning asso. Mobil Oil Corp., N.Y.C., 1963-67; asst. v.p. A.G. Becker & Co., N.Y.C., 1967-70; asso. Roth, Gerard & Co., N.Y.C., 1970-73; v.p. Faulkner, Dawkins & Sullivan Inc., 1973-76; v.p. Shields Model Roland, Inc., N.Y.C., 1976-77; partner Tovey & Co., N.Y.C., 1977—; pres. Joint Trading Ltd., 1977-83, Tovey & Co., Inc., 1978—, Midwood Petroleum Corp., 1980—, Joint Trading (Del.) Ltd., 1984—; chmn. Midwood Asset Mgmt. Co., Inc., 1985—. Mem. exec. bd. Agudath Israel Am., 1963-67. C.P.A., N.Y. Mem. Newcomen Soc. N.Am., Am. Fin. Assn., Am. Inst. C.P.A.s, Fgn. Policy Assn., N.Y.U. Alumni Assn., Bklyn. Coll. Alumni in Fin. Jewish religion. Club: N.Y. Univ. (N.Y.C.). Author: (with H.C. Smith) Federal Tax Treatment of Bad Debts and Worthless Securities, 1964. Asso. editor Tax Letter, 1961-66. Contbr. articles to profl. jours. Home: 1170 E 19th St Brooklyn NY 11230 Office: 40 Wall St New York NY 10005

TOWER, HORACE LINWOOD, III, consumer products company executive; b. New Haven, July 16, 1932; s. Horace Linwood, Jr. and Madeline Elizabeth (Davin) T.; m. Elizabeth Wright, Dec. 29, 1956; children—Cynthia, William, John. B.A., Cornell U., 1955, M.B.A., 1960; DHL (hon.), Westfield (Mass.) State Coll., 1984. Br. mgr. Procter & Gamble Corp., Cin., 1960-62; mgmt. cons. Booz, Allen & Hamilton, N.Y.C., 1962-63; product mgr. Gen. Foods Corp., White Plains, N.Y., 1963-67; advt. and merchandising mgr. Gen. Foods Corp., 1967-69, dir. corporate devel., 1969-71; exec. v.p. Gen. Foods Corp. (Maxwell House div.), 1971-73, pres. div., 1973-78, v.p. parent corp., 1978—; pres., chmn. bd., chief exec. officer Stanhome Inc.; dir. Bank of New Eng.-West, Tambrands, Inc. Mem. Cornell Fund, Cornell Sch. Bus. Adv. Council. Served to capt. USAF, 1956-59. Mem. Cornell Coun., Air Force Assn., Sabre Pilots Assn., Pi Kappa Phi, Sigma Gamma Epsilon. Clubs: Colony (Springfield, Mass.); Suffield (Conn.) Country, Suffield Paddle; Fox Hollow (Suffield); Thimble Island Sailing and Lit. Soc, Stoney Creek Boating. Office: Stanhome Inc 333 Western Ave Westfield MA 01085

TOWER, PETER, brokerage house executive; b. Niagara Falls, N.Y., May 29, 1921; s. Clarence Eugene and Mabel Barret (Paterson) T.; m. Elizabeth Nelson Clarke, Aug. 29, 1942; children: Mollie Paterson Byrnes, Cynthia Clarke Doyle. Student, Cornell U., 1939-41. Clk. C.J. Tower and Sons, Niagara Falls, 1946-49, ptnr., 1949-56; v.p. C.J. Tower and Sons, Inc., Niagara Falls and Buffalo, 1956-63; pres. C.J. Tower and Sons, Inc., eastern U.S., 1963-87, C.J. Tower, Inc., eastern U.S., 1988—; vice-chmn. upstate N.Y. dist. export coun. U.S. Dept. Commerce, 1978—; mem. adv. com. on comml. ops. of U.S. customs Treasury Dept., 1988—; bd. dirs. Mfrs. and Traders Trust Co., First Empire State Corp. Office: CJ Tower Inc 128 Dearborn St Buffalo NY 14207-3198

TOWER, RAYMOND CAMILLE, manufacturing company executive; b. N.Y.C., Feb. 20, 1925; s. Raymond C. and Elinor (Donovan) T.; m. Jaclyn Bauerline, Feb. 7, 1948; children: Raymond, Patricia, Christopher, Robert, Mary, Michael, Victoria. B.S., Yale U., 1945; postgrad., Advanced Mgmt. Program, Harvard U. Research chemist Westvaco Chlorine Products Corp., Carteret, N.J., 1946-48; v.p., gen. mgr. Organic Chem. div. Westvaco Chlorine Products Corp., 1964-67, exec. v.p., mgr. chem. group, 1967-77; pres., chief operating officer FMC Corp., Chgo., 1977—; bd. dirs. FMC Corp.; chmn., chief exec. officer FMC Gold Co., 1987-89, bd. dirs.; dir. Morton Thiokol Inc., Household Internat., Inland Steel Co. Trustee Ill. Inst. Tech.; bd. govs. IIT Research Inst.; vice chmn. Evanston (Ill.) Hosp. Corp. Served to lt. USNR, 1943-46, 51-53. Mem. Chem. Mfrs. Assn., Machinery and Allied Products Inst. (exec. com.), Aerospace Industries Assn. Am., Chgo. Assn. Commerce and Industry (dir.), Chgo. Council Fgn. Relations (Chgo. com.), Alpha Chi Sigma. Clubs: Chicago, Commercial, Economic, Mid-Am. Glen View. Office: FMC Corp 200 E Randolph Dr Chicago IL 60601

TOWERS, ROBERT, service executive; b. N.Y.C., Feb. 24, 1947; s. Albert and Ronnie Torriani; m. June 25, 1970; 1 child, Brian. BBA in Acctg., St. Francis Coll., Bklyn., 1968; MS in Acctg., L.I.U., 1972. Acct. Keller & Steinmiller CPA's, N.Y.C., 1968-69; div. controller CBS, Inc., N.Y.C., 1969-72; controller B. Lippman Inc., N.Y.C., 1972-74; exec. v.p., chief fin. officer Blanchard Mgmt. Corp., N.Y.C., 1974-82; exec. Rivers Food, Moonachie, N.J., 1982-83; v.p., treas., dir. ARK Restaurants, N.Y.C., 1983—. Home: 124 MacKenzie St Brooklyn NY 11235-2304 Office: ARK Restaurants Corp 158 W 29th St New York NY 10001

TOWEY, J. DESMOND, financial company executive; b. N.Y.C., Oct. 8, 1937; s. James A. and Nora (Sheridan) T.; m. Marianne Marrin, June 1, 1967 (div. 1979); children: Emmett, Justin, Siobhan. BA in Classical Langs., Cath. U., Washington, 1960; MA in Classical Langs., Manhattan Coll., 1967; MBA in Mktg., Fordham U., 1977. Chmn. dept. classical langs. Bros. of the Christian Schs., N.Y.C., 1960-67; media buyer Ogilvy & Mather, N.Y.C., 1967-68; account exec. SSC&B and J. Walter Thompson, N.Y.C., 1968-72; registered rep. Walston & Co., N.Y.C., 1972-73; registered investment advisor First Ecumenical Fund, N.Y.C., 1973-75; mng. dir. Kehoe, White, Towey & Savage, Inc., N.Y.C., 1975-85; pres. J. Desmond Towey & Assocs., Inc., N.Y.C., 1985—; adj. prof. New Sch. for Social Research, 1980-84; chmn. bd. dirs. The Grapevine, Inc., N.Y.C., 1984—. Named to Cardinals Com. of Laity, N.Y. Archdiocese, 1986. Mem. Nat. Investor Relations Inst. (bd. dirs. 1984—, v.p. 1987, bd. dirs. N.Y. chpt. 1980—, pres. 1985-86), Investment Tech. Assn., Phi Beta Kappa. Roman Catholic. Home: 115 E 86th St New York NY 10028

TOWEY, ROBERT, pharmaceutical company executive; b. Newark, Feb. 20, 1949; s. oswald Joseph and Bertha Ann (Rinderer) T.; m. Maureen Savage, Aug. 14, 1971; children: Jeffrey, Jarid. BS in Acctg., Fairleigh Dickinson U., 1971. CPA, N.J. Mem. audit staff Coopers & Lybrand Co., Newark, 1971-73, audit supr., 1973-74; auditor Hoffmann-LaRoche, Nutley, N.J., 1975-76; mgr. acctg. policies Hoffmann-LaRoche, Nutley, 1976-78, dir. corp. acctg., 1978-86; contr. Roche Diagnostic Systems, Nutley, 1986-87, v.p. fin., 1987—; asst. prof. Fairleigh Dickinson U., Rutherford, N.J., 1976-81. Mem. fin. com. St. Thomas The Apostle Ch., Bloomfield, N.J., treas., 1986-87; advancement chmn. Bloomfield area Boy Scouts Am. Mem. Am. Inst. CPAs, N.J. Soc. CPAs, Nat. Assn. Accts. Home: 8 Carolyn Ct East Hanover NJ 07936

TOWNLEY, RALPH, author, government consultant; b. Horncastle, Lincolnshire, Eng., Oct. 13, 1923; came to U.S., 1952; s. Francis Harry and May Elizabeth (Poucher) T.; m. Jozy Smith, Aug. 22, 1949 (div. Dec. 1982); children: Christopher Harry, Miranda Jane; m. Phyllis Joy Leonard, Dec. 31, 1982. Student, U. Nottingham, Eng., 1947-49, London Sch. Econs., 1950-51. Profl. officer UN, N.Y.C., Geneva, Switzerland, Nairobi, Kenya, 1951-84, dir., 1972-84; sr. cons. UN, world wide, 1984—. Author: (with others) The Development of International Institutions, 1967, The United Nations: A View From Within, 1968, (with B.B. Waddy) A Word Before You Go, 1981, The Brides of Enderby, 1988; translator (play) Madam, I'm Adam, 1983. Mem. Soc. Friends. Clubs: UN Judo (pres. 1980-87), Century (N.Y.); Muthaiga (Nairobi). Home and Office: 51 Main St Marion MA 02738

TOWNSEND, CELIA VICTORIA See GIBBONS, MRS. JOHN SHELDON

TOWNSEND, EARL CUNNINGHAM, JR., lawyer, author; b. Indpls., Nov. 9, 1914; s. Earl Cunningham and Besse (Kuhn) T.; m. Emily Macnab, Apr. 3, 1947 (dec. Mar. 1988); children: Starr (Mrs. John R. Laughlin), Vicki M. (Mrs. Christopher Katterjohn), Julia E. (Mrs. Edward Goodrich Dunn Jr.), Earl Cunningham III, Clyde G. Student, De Pauw U., 1932-34; AB, U. Mich., 1936, JD, 1939. Bar: Ind. 1939, Mich. 1973, U.S. Supreme Ct. 1973, U.S. Ct. Appeals (4th, 5th, 6th, 7th cirs.), U.S. Dist. Ct. (no. and so. dists.) Ind., U.S. Dist. Ct. (ea. dist.) Va., U.S. Dist. Ct. (ea. dist.) Mich. Sr. ptnr. Townsend & Townsend, Indpls., 1940-64, Townsend, Hovde & Townsend, Indpls., 1964-84, Townsend, Yosha & Cline, Indpls., 1984—; dep. prosecutor, Marion County, Ind., 1942-44; radio-TV announcer WIRE, WFBM, WFBM-TV, Indpls., 1940-49, 1st TV announcer Indpls. 500 mile race, 1949, 50; Big Ten basketball referee, 1940-47; lectr. trial tactics U. Notre Dame, Ind. U., U. Mich., 1968-79; chmn. faculty seminar on personal injury trials Ind. U. Sch. Law, U. Notre Dame Sch. Law, Valparaiso Sch. Law, 1981; mem. Com. to Revise Ind. Supreme Ct. Pattern Jury Instructions, 1975-83; lectr. Trial Lawyers 30 Yrs. Inst., 1986. Author: Birdstones of the North American Indian, 1959; contbr. articles to legal and archeol. jours. Recipient Ind. Univ. Writers Conf. award, 1960; Hanson H. Anderson medal of honor Arsenal Tech. Schs., Indpls., 1971; named to Council Sagamores of Wabash, 1969, Hon. Ky. Col., 1986; Rector scholar, 1934; Ind. Basketball Hall of Fame; hon. chief Black River-Swan Creek Saginaw-Chippewa Indian tribe, 1971. Fellow Internat. Acad. Trial Lawyers, Internat. Soc. Barristers; mem. ABA, Assn. Trial Lawyers Am. (v.p.), Ind. State Bar Assn. (Golden Career award 1989), Ind. Trial Lawyers Assn. (pres. 1965), Am. Bd. Trial Advs. (pres., diplomate, pres. Coll. of Fellows 1984-88), Key Biscayne Yacht Club, Columbia Club, Indpls. Athletic Club, Masons, Shriners. Republican. Methodist. Home: 5008 N Meridian St Indianapolis IN 46208

TOWNSEND, HAROLD GUYON, JR., publishing company executive; b. Chgo., Apr. 11, 1924; s. Harold Guyon and Anne Louise (Robb) T.; A.B., Cornell U., 1948; m. Margaret Jeanne Keller, July 28, 1951; children—Jessica, Julie, Harold Guyon III. Advt. salesman Chgo. Tribune, 1948-51; gen. mgr. Keller-Heartt Co., Clarendon Hills, Ill., 1951-62; pub. Santa Clara (Calif.) Jour., 1962-64; pres., pub. Dispatch-Tribune newspaper Townsend Communications, Inc., Kansas City, Mo., 1964—; dir. United Mo. City Bank. Chmn., Suburban Newspaper Research Commn., 1974—; dir. Certified Audit Bur. of Circulation, 1968-72. del. Rep. Nat. Conv., 1960; chmn. Mission Hills Rep. Com., 1966-77; bd. dirs. Kansas City Jr. Achievement, 1966-68, Kansas City council Girl Scouts U.S.A., 1969-71, Kansas City council Boy Scouts Am., 1974, Kansas City chpt. ARC, 1973-79, Kansas City Starlight Theater, Clay County (Mo.) Indsl. Commn.; treas., trustee Park Coll., Parkville, Mo., 1970-78. Mem. adv. com. North Kansas City Hosp.; bd. dirs. Taxpayers Research of Mo., 1978—, Nelson Gallery Friends of Art, 1980-85. Served with inf. AUS, World War II. Mem. Kansas City Advt. and Sales Club, Kansas City Press Club, Suburban Press Found. (pres. 1969-71), Suburban Newspapers Am. (pres. 1976-77), Kansas City Printing Industries Assn. (pres., dir.), Printing Industries of Am. (pres. non-heatset web sect. 1980-82), North Kansas City C. of C. (dir., pres. 1964-70), Univ. Assocs. (treas. 1977-80), Sigma Delta Chi, Pi Delta Epsilon, Phi Kappa Psi. Clubs: University (treas. 1977); Indian Hills Country; Hinsdale (Ill.) Golf; Mission Valley Country, Field (Sarasota, Fla.). Home: 829 W 54th Terr Kansas City MO 64112 Office: 7007 NE Parvin Rd Kansas City MO 64117

TOWNSEND, IRENE FOGLEMAN, accountant, tax analyst; b. Birmingham, Ala., May 29, 1932; d. James Woods and Virginia (Martin) Fogleman; m. Kenneth Ross Townsend, Mar. 18, 1951; children: Marietta Irene, Martha Shapard, Kenneth Ross Jr., Elizabeth Buchanan. BSBA, East Carolina U., 1980. Acct. Norwood P. Whitehurst & Assocs., Greenville, N.C., 1981-86; sr. tax analyst Psychiat. Inst. Am., Washington, 1986—. Fellow AICPA, N.C. Assn. CPA's, D.C. Inst. CPA's; mem. DAR, N.C. Soc. Daughters of the Colonial Wars, Colonial Dames 17th Century. Democrat. Episcopalian (lay reader, chalice bearer). Home: PO Box 466 Vanceboro NC 28586 Office: Psychiat Inst Am 1010 Wisconsin Ave NW Suite 900 Washington DC 20007

TOWNSEND, J. RUSSELL, JR., insurance executive; b. Cedar Rapids, Iowa, Nov. 21, 1910; s. J. Russell and Mabel (Ferguson) T.; B.S., Butler U., 1931; M.B.A., U. Pa., 1933; m. Virginia Holt, Aug. 1, 1938; 1 son, John Holt. CLU, registered health underwriter. Field asst. Equitable Life Ins. Co. Iowa, 1933-50, gen. agt., 1950-69, gen. agt. emeritus, 1969—; mng. asso. J. Russell Townsend & Assos., 1969—; assoc. prof. emeritus bus. adminstrn. Butler U., Indpls., 1982; cons. Ind. Dept. Ins., 1948-50; mem. Ind. Ho. of Reps., 1946-48, Ind. Senate, 1956-64; lectr., writer ins. field. Chmn. Indpls. Bicentennial Com., 1975-76; pres. Indpls. Jaycees, 1940. Served with USNR, 1942-46; lt. comdr. Res. ret. Recipient 25-year teaching award Am. Coll. C.L.U.s, 1960; Alumni Achievement award Butler U., 1979. Mem. Indpls. chpt. C.L.U.s (past pres.), Ind. Life Underwriters Assn. (past v.p.), Ret. Officers Assn. (past pres. Indpls. chpt.), Ind. Soc. Assn. Execs., Naval Res. Assn., Navy League U.S., Am. Soc. C.L.U.'s, AAUP, Am. Soc. Risk and Ins., Ind. Acad. Sci., Sales and Marketing Execs. Council, U.S. Naval Inst., Phi Delta Theta (past pres. Indpls. alumni club). Republican. Presbyterian. Clubs: Columbia, Meridian Hills Country, Indpls. Literary, Kiwanis (dir. Ind. Found., lt. gov. Ind. dist. internat. 1975-76), Indpls. Press, Ft. Harrison Officers, Masons, Sojourners (Indpls); Army and Navy (Washington); Crystal Downs Country (Frankfort, Mich.) (past pres.); U. Pa. Faculty. Contbr. articles to trade mags. Home: 8244 N Pennsylvania St Indianapolis IN 46240 Office: 906 Investors Trust Bldg 107 N Pennsylvania St Indianapolis IN 46204

TOWNSEND, M. WILBUR, manufacturing company executive; b. Oyster Bay, N.Y., Jan. 17, 1912; s. Maurice West and Alberta (Say) T.; m. Barbara White Hayden, Oct. 1, 1938; children—Barrett Say, Philip Hayden. A.B., Wesleyan U., Middletown, Conn., 1934. With Handy & Harman, N.Y.C., 1946—; exec. v.p. Handy & Harman, 1961-64, pres., 1964-79, chmn. bd.,

1967-87, chmn. emeritus, cons., 1988—; past pres. 24 Karat Club, N.Y.C. Mem. Community Ch. Club, Board Room Inc. Office: Handy & Harman 850 3d Ave New York NY 10022

TOWNSEND, NATHANIEL, JR., transportation company executive; b. Seattle, Oct. 29, 1953; s. Nathaniel Sr. and Lucie Ann (Davis) T. BS in Math. and Econs., Settle Pacific U., 1976; MBA, Wash. State U., 1978. Asst. buyer Boeing Comml. Airplane Co., Seattle, 1978-79; system analyst Service Bur. Corp., Seattle, 1979; v.p. Faber Enterprises Inc., Canoga Park, Calif., 1979—.

TOWNSEND, SUSAN ELAINE, social service institute administrator, hostage survival consultant; b. Phila., Sept. 5, 1946; d. William Harrison and Eleanor Irene (Fox) Rogers; m. John Holt Townsend, May 1, 1976. BS in Secondary Edn., West Chester State U., 1968; MBA, Nat. U., 1978; PhD in Human Behavior, La Jolla U., 1984. Biology tchr. Methacton Sch. Dist., Fairview Village, Pa., 1968-70; bus. mgr., analyst profl. La Jolla Research Corp., San Diego, 1977-79; pastoral asst. Christ Ctr. Bible Therapy, San Diego, 1980-82, also bd. dirs.; v.p., pub. relations World Outreach Ctr. of Faith, San Diego, 1981-82, also bd. dirs.; owner, pres., cons. Townsend Research Inst., San Diego, 1983—; teaching assoc. La Jolla U. Continuing Edn., 1985-86. Author: Hostage Survival-Resisting the Dynamics of Captivity, 1983; contbr. articles to profl. jours. Religious vol. Met. Correctional Ctr., San Diego, 1983—, San Diego County Jail Ministries, 1978—. Served to comdr. USN, 1970-76, USNR, 1976—. Mem. Naval Res. Assn. (life), Res. Officers Assn. (Outstanding Jr. Officer of Yr. Calif. chpt. 1982), Navy League U.S. (life), West Chester U. Alumni Assn., Nat. U. Alumni Assn. (life), La Jolla U. Alumni Assn., Gen. Fedn. Women's Clubs (pres. Peninsula club 1983-85, pres. Parliamentary law club 1984-86, Past Pres.' Assn.), Calif. Fedn. Women's Clubs (v.p.-at-large San Diego dist. 25 1982-84). Office: 1060 Alexandria Dr San Diego CA 92107

TOWNSEND, T(HEODORE) PETER, oil company executive; b. St. Paul, Jan. 5, 1937; m. Joanna Lerner; children: Pamela, John. BS, Yale U.; MBA, U. Chgo. With Exxon Corp. (formerly Standard Oil Co), N.J., 1962—; dep. mgr. pub. affairs Exxon Corp. (formerly Standard Oil Co)., N.Y.C., 1985-86; various positions Esso Eastern, Inc. subs. Exxon Corp., N.Y.C., also India, 1965-70; mgr. corp. and internat. fin. Standard Oil N.J. div. Exxon Corp., N.Y.C., 1970-73; treas. Esso Europe, Inc. subs. Exxon Corp., London, 1973-80; exec. dir. Esso UK plc subs. Exxon Corp., London, 1980-85; mgr. corp. and pub. affairs Exxon Co. Internat. div. Exxom Corp., Florham Park, N.J., 1986-87; asst. treas. Exxon Corp., N.Y.C., 1987—. Office: Exxon Corp 1251 Avenue of the Americas New York NY 10020

TOWNSEND, TOM DAVID, sales executive; b. Marquette, Mich., Oct. 28, 1952; s. Rubin and Shirley Ann (Deegan) T.; m. Bettye Wilson Stutts; Apr. 15, 1981. Assoc's. degree, Grand Rapids (Mich.) Jr. Coll., 1972; BS, Cen. Mich. U., 1974. Adminstrv. asst. Kent County Parks Assn., Grand Rapids, 1975-77; ctr. dir. Fulton County Recreation Dept., Atlanta, 1977-79; sales rep. John H. Harland Co., Atlanta, 1979-81; sales rep. Rand McNally & Co., Atlanta, 1981-85, ea. region sales mgr., 1985-86, nat. sales mgr., 1986-88; mgr. nat. sales Direct Mktg. of Nat. Computer Print, Inc., Calif., 1989—. Mem. Atlanta C. of C. Republican. Presbyterian. Clubs: So. Sailing, Atlanta Ski.

TOWSON, SHELDON KERRUISH, JR., material handling, manufacturing company executive; b. Cleve., June 15, 1927; s. Sheldon Kerruish and Gertrude Charlotte (Moeller) T.; m. Anne Gardner Wofford, Mar. 1952; children: Carol, Jane, Elizabeth, Katherine. BA, Amherst Coll., 1950; MBA, Harvard U., 1952. Adminstrv. asst. Allegheny-Ludlum Steel Co., Pitts., 1952-55; asst. to pres. Elwell-Parker Electric Co., Cleve., 1956-58, v.p., 1958-61, pres., chief exec. officer, 1961—; bd. dirs. Elwell-Parker Electric Co., Cleve., Elwell-Parker, Inc., Detroit, Y-Mut., Ins., Ltd., Hamilton, Bermuda. Trustee, mem. exec. com. Cleve. YMCA, 1975—; bd. dirs. Goodwill Industries, Cleve., 1978-87. Mem. Material Handling Inst. (pres. 1966, bd. dirs.), Indsl. Truck Assn. (pres. 1972, bd. dirs.), Union Club, Univ. Club (past bd. dirs.). Republican. Episcopalian. Office: Elwell-Parker Electric Co 4205 St Clair Ave Cleveland OH 44103

TOYOMURA, DENNIS TAKESHI, architect; b. Honolulu, July 6, 1926; s. Sansuke Fujimoto and Take (Sata) T.; m. Akiko Charlotte Nakamura, May 27, 1949; children—Wayne J., Gerald F., Amy J., Lyle D. BS in Archtl. Engring., Chgo. Tech. Coll., 1949; cert., U. Ill., Chgo., 1950, 53, 54; student, Ill. Inst. Tech., Chgo., 1953-54; cert., U. Hawaii-Dept. Def., Honolulu, 1966-67, 73. Lic. architect, Ill., Hawaii; lic. real estate broker, Ill. Designer, draftsman James M. Turner, Architect, Hammond, Ind., 1950-51, Wimberly and Cook, Honolulu, 1952, Gregg, Briggs & Foley, Architects, Chgo., 1952-54; architect Holabird, Root & Burgee, Architects, Chgo., 1954-55, Loebl, Schlossman & Bennett, Architects, Chgo., 1955-62; prin. Dennis T. Toyomura, AIA, Architect, Honolulu, 1963-83, Dennis T. Toyomura, FAIA, Architect, Honolulu, 1983—; fallout shelter analyst Dept. Def., 1967—; cert. analyst multi-distaster design, Dept. Def., 1973; cert. value engr. NAVFACENGCOM, Gen. Svc. Adminstrn, U.S.A., 1988; cons. Honolulu Redevel. Agy., City and County of Honolulu, 1967-71; sec., dir. Maiko of Hawaii, Honolulu, 1972-74; bd. dirs. Pacific Canal Hawaii; mem. steering com. IX world conf. World Futures Studies Fedn., U. Hawaii, 1986; conf. organizer pub. forum 10th Hawaii Conf. in High Energy Physics, U. Hawaii, 1985; mem. Hawaii State Found. on Culture and the Arts, 1982-86; mem. Gov.'s Com. on Hawaii Econ. Future, 1984; archtl. mem. Bd. Registration for Profl. Engrs., Architects, Land Surveyors and Landscape Architects, State of Hawaii, 1974-82, sec. 1980, vice chmn. 1981, chmn., 1982; mem. Nat. Council Engring. Examiners, 1975-82; mem. Nat. Council Archtl. Registration Bds., Western region del. 1975-82, nat. del. 1976-82; appointments Research Corp. U. Hawaii, 1986—. Ecclesiastical del. commr. state assembly, Synod of Ill., United Presbyn. Ch. U.S.A., 1958, alt. del. commr. nat. gen. assembly, 1958, del. commr. Los Angeles presbytery, 1965; bd. session 2d Presbyn. Ch., Chgo., 1956-62, trustee, 1958-62; trustee 1st Presbyn. Ch., Honolulu, 1964-66, 69-72, sec., 1965, bd. sessions, 1964-72, 74-79; founding assoc. Hawaii Loa Coll., Kaneohe, 1964; mem. adv. commn. drafting tech. Leeward Community Coll., U. Hawaii, 1965—; bd. dirs. Lyon Arboretum Assn., U. Hawaii, 1976-77, treas., 1976. Served with U.S. Army, 1945-46. Recipient cert. appreciation Leeward Community Coll./U. Hawaii, 1971-86, Human Resources of U.S.A. award Am. Bicentennial Research Inst., 1973; Outstanding Citizen Recognition award Cons. Engrs. Council Hawaii, 1975; Cert. Appreciation, Gov. of Hawaii, 1982, 86, commendation, 1983; resolution and cert. commendation Hawaii Ho. of Reps. and Senate, 1983. Fellow AIA (Coll. Fellows 1983, bd. dirs. Hawaii Soc. 1973-74, treas. 1975, Pres.'s Mahalo award 1981); life mem. AAAS, Acad. Polit. Sci., Am. Acad. Polit. and Social Scis., N.Y. Acad. Scis., Chgo. Art Inst., Chgo. Natural History Mus., Honolulu Acad. Arts, Nat. Geog. Soc.; mem. Council Ednl. Facility Planners Internat. (bd. govs. N.W. region 1980-86), Bldg. Research Inst. (adv. bd. of Nat. Acad. Sci.), Ill. Assn. Professions, ASTM, Constrn. Specifications Inst., Constrn. Industry Legis. Orgn. (bd. dirs. 1973-81, 83—, treas. 1976-77), Japan-Am. Soc., Hawaii State C. of C. (bd. dirs. 1984-87), U. Hawaii Kokua O'Hui, O'Nahe Popo (bd. dirs. 1984—), Hawaii-Pacific Rim Soc. (bd. trustees 1988—), Alpha Lambda Rho, Kappa Sigma Kappa, Pres. Club Hawaii Loa Coll., Pres. Club U. Hawaii. Clubs: Malolo Mariners (purser 1964, skipper 1965) (Honolulu); U. Hawaii Pres.', Hawaii Loa Coll. Pres.'. Home: 2602 Manoa Rd Honolulu HI 96822 Office: Dennis T Toyomura FAIA Architect 1370 Kapiolani Blvd Honolulu HI 96814

TOZZI, RICHARD RAYMOND, oil and gas company executive; b. N.Y.C., June 27, 1941; s. Aurelio and Margaret (Tassille) T.; m. Sharon L. Roberts, Aug. 17, 1961 (div. June 1981); children: Dina Michelle, Anna Maria, Donna Rene; m. Brenda Lee Hallberg, Jan. 29, 1982; 1 child, Burton Anthony. BS in Acctg., Cen. State U., Edmond, Okla., 1969. CPA, Okla. Ctr. mgr. Univ. Computing Co., Oklahoma City, 1965-70; mgr. Arthur Young & Co., Oklahoma City, 1970-79; pres. Aftak, Columbus, Okla., 1979-81; treas. Alpha Energy, Oklahoma City, 1981; v.p. fin. Adams Exploration Co., Tulsa, 1981-84, Ward Petroleum Corp., Enid, Okla., 1984—. With U.S. Army, 1960-62. Named Boss of Yr. Am. Bus. Women's Club, 1987. Mem. Petroleum Accts. Assn., Cash Mgmt. Assn., Okla. Inst. CPA's, AICPA, Grand Nat. Quail Club, Ducks Unltd. Club. Home: 3540 Chickadee Ln Enid OK 73703 Office: Ward Petroleum Corp PO Box 1187 Enid OK 73702

TRACE, WILLIAM FREDERICK, credit company executive; b. Meadville, Pa., June 30, 1928; s. James Bennett and Marion Rebecca (Ewing) T.; B.A., Allegheny Coll., 1953; m. Helen Irene Britton, Sept. 25, 1946; children—Karen Rylander, Kim Reynolds, Gary B. Treasury rep. Westinghouse Electric Corp., Pitts. and Chgo., 1953-61; regional mgr. Westinghouse Credit Corp., Chgo., 1961-69; regional v.p. 1st Mortgage Adv. Corp., South Bend, Ind., 1969-71, sr. v.p., Miami Beach, Fla., 1971-73; chmn. bd., pres. USI Credit Corp., Los Angeles and N.Y.C., 1973-83; v.p. Westinghouse Credit Corp., Darien, Conn., 1983-86; sr. v.p., mgr. comml. mortgage dept. Yankee Bank, Boston, 1986-87; v.p., mgr. real estate group Signal Capital Corp., Hampton, N.H., 1987—. Past deacon Calvary Bapt. Ch., Darien, Conn. Served with U.S. Army, 1946-48, 50-51. Clubs: Ipswich (Mass.) Country; Shore Haven Golf (Norwalk, Conn.). Home: 67 Clark Rd Ipswich MA 01938 Office: Signal Capital Corp Liberty Ln Hampton NH 03842

TRACEY, RUSSELL LEE, financial planner; b. Kansas City, Kans., Feb. 16, 1932; s. Walter Samuel and Alice Marie T.; m. Arline V. Gorton, Aug. 30, 1953; children: Diane Renee, Stephen Gorton, Mark Christopher. BA, Loma Linda U., 1966. Founder, pres. Chartered Investment Advisors, Inc., 1968—; lectr. in field; bd. dirs. Inland Empire Chpt. Served with USMC, 1950-54. Mem. Inst. Cert. Fin. Planners, Am. Soc. Pension Actuaries (assoc.). Republican. Home: 11555 Norwood Ave Riverside CA 92505 Office: 11498 Pierce St Riverside CA 92505

TRACHSEL, WILLIAM HENRY, corporate counsel; b. El Paso, Tex., Apr. 20, 1943. BS in Aerospace Engring., U. Fla., 1965; JD, U. Conn., 1971. Bar: Conn. 1971. With United Tech. Corp., Hartford, Conn., 1965-86, v.p., dep. gen. counsel, 1986—. Mem. ABA, Am. Corp. Counsel Assn. (bd. dirs. Hartford chpt.). Office: United Tech Corp United Tech Bldg Hartford CT 06101

TRACHTENBERG, MATTHEW J., bank holding company executive; b. N.Y.C., June 20, 1953; s. Mark Trachtenberg and Joanne Horne. BA magna cum laude, NYU, 1974; JD, Bklyn. Law Sch., 1977; MBA in Fin., Fordham U., 1982. Bar: N.Y. 1977. Mgmt. trainee Mfrs. Hanover Trust Co., N.Y.C., 1977-78, credit analyst, 1978-79, corp. banking rep., 1979-80, asst. sec., 1980-82, asst. v.p., 1982, v.p., 1982—, corp. sec., 1987—; v.p., corp. sec. Mfrs. Hanover Corp., N.Y.C., 1987—; bd. dirs. Mfrs. Hanover Found., 1987—. N.Y. State Regents scholar. Mem. N.Y. State Bar Assn., Am. Soc. Corp. Secs., Phi Beta Kappa, Pi Sigma Alpha. Office: Mfrs Hanover Corp 270 Park Ave New York NY 10017

TRACY, DAVID M., textile manufacturing company executive; b. 1924; m. Barbara Weisberg, 1982; children: Kellie Charlotte, Brendan Charles; children by previous marriage: Maureen Judith, Shawn Christopher. B.S., Brown U., 1944; M.B.A., Harvard U., 1948. With Fieldcrest Mills, Inc., Eden, N.C., 1948-81, former pres.; vice-chmn. J.P. Stevens & Co., Inc., N.Y.C., 1981—, vice chmn. exec. com., 1987—, also bd. dirs. Served to lt. USN, 1940-55. Mem. Am. Textile Mfrs. Assn. (chmn. consumer affairs). Office: J P Stevens & Co Inc 1185 Ave of the Americas New York NY 10036

TRACY, EUGENE ARTHUR, utility executive; b. Oak Park, Ill., Dec. 14, 1927; s. Arthur Huntington and Emily Margaret (Groff) T.; m. Irene Walburga Kacin, June 30, 1951; children: Glen Eugene, Diane Emily Tracy Champion, Janet Freda Tracy Bootz. BSBA, Northwestern U., 1951; MBA, DePaul U., Chgo., 1958. With Peoples Gas Light & Coke Co., Chgo., 1951—, pres., 1977-84, chmn., chief exec. officer, 1981—, also dir.; pres. North Shore Gas Co., Waukegan, Ill., 1977-84; chmn., chief exec. officer North Shore Gas Co., Waukegan, 1981—, also dir.; chmn., chief exec. officer Peoples Energy Corp., Chgo., 1981—, pres., 1981-84, also dir.; bd. dirs. La Salle Nat. Bank, Chgo., Assoc. Electric and Gas Ins. Svcs. Inc. Trustee Taxpayers Fedn. Ill., 1973-77; bd. dirs. Civic Fedn. Chgo., 1966-77; bd. dirs. Cen. YMCA Community Coll., Chgo., 1971—, treas., 1972-77, chmn. bd., 1977-79; treas. St. David's Episcopal Ch., Glenview, Ill., 1970-79; bd. dirs. Jr. Achievement, Chgo., 1978-88, Chgo. Assn. Commerce and Industry, 1979-84; trustee Mus. Sci. and Industry, 1981—, DePaul U., 1982—; bd. dirs. United Way of Chgo., 1983—, vice chmn., 1986-87, chmn., 1987—; bd. dirs. Met. Crusade of Mercy, Chgo., 1986—, dir. NCCJ, Chgo., 1986—, Protestant Found., 1987-88, Chgo. Cen. Area Com., 1983—, v.p., 1985-86; co-chmn. Chgo. United, 1984-86, Chgo. Equity Fund, 1987-88. With U.S. Army, 1946-47. Mem. Am. Gas Assn. (dir. 1981-85, vice chmn. 1986-87, chmn. 1988—), Midwest Gas Assn. (dir. 1979—, chmn. 1985-86), Inst. Gas. Tech. (trustee 1978-88, chmn. 1985-86), Econ. Club, Univ. Club, Chgo. Club, Comml. Club, Sunset Ridge Club, Mid-Am. Club, Pine Tree Golf Club. Office: Peoples Energy Corp 122 S Michigan Ave Chicago IL 60603

TRACY, MARGARET LYNNE, financial planner; b. Chgo., Sept. 24, 1955; d. Leo P. and Eleanor (Jankowski) Karolewski; m. Richard J. Tracy, Oct. 24, 1981; 1 child, Christopher. BA, Mundelein Coll., 1977; MBA, Loyola U., Chgo., 1981. Acct. Walter E. Heller & Co., Chgo., 1974-82; investment advisor Insight Fin. Planning, Barrington, Ill., 1982-84, Strategic Fin. Cons., Bensenville, Ill., 1984-86; owner Priority Planning, Wheaton, Ill., 1986—; adj. faculty Coll. Fin. Planning, Denver, 1984—. Mem. Internat. Assn. Fin. Planning, Inst. Cert. Fin. Planners, Nat. Assn. Tax Practitioners, Registry Fin. Planning Practitioners. Office: Priority Planning 520 W Roosevelt Rd #301 Wheaton IL 60187

TRACY, RICHARD LOUIS, mortgage company executive; b. Brookline, Mass., Sept. 24, 1949; s. Richard Louis Sr. and Mary Elizabeth (Blinn) T.; m. Nancy Ann Toth, Sept. 30, 1972; children: Richard Louis III, Sean R., Shannon Lynn. BA, John Carroll U., 1972. Field rep Conn. State Lottery, Newington, 1972-77; real estate assoc. Century 21, Chamberlin, West Haven, Conn., 1977-79; account exec. Lomas & Nettleton, New Haven, 1979-80; mortgage loan rep. McCue Mortgage, New Britain, Conn., 1980-84; v.p. sales McCue Mortgage, New Britain, 1984—. Fire commr. West Shore Fire Dist., West Haven, 1986—. Democrat. Roman Catholic. Home: 85 Honeypot Rd West Haven CT 06516

TRAESTER, JAMES EDWARD, accountant; b. New Haven; s. Lewis Robert and Frances (Wright) T.; m. Gail Ann Liefeld, Oct. 1, 1983; 1 child, Christopher. BS, Providence Coll., 1977; M in Profl. Studies, Quinnipiac Coll., 1984. CPA, Conn. Asst. controller Yale Coop. Corp., New Haven, 1978-80; mgr. Anquillare Saas Lipnicki & Co., CPA's, West Haven, Conn., 1980—; adj. prof. So. Conn. State U., New Haven, 1985-86. Mem. AICPA, Conn. Soc. CPA's. Office: Anquillare Saas Lipnicki & Co CPAs PO Box 308 98 Elm St West Haven CT 06516

TRAHAN, MARGARET FRITCHEY, co-owner wholesale food distributing company; b. Harrisburg, Pa., May 3, 1934; d. John Augustus and Dorotha Amy (Warren) Fritchey; m. Henry Voltaire Trahan, Jr., Sept. 29, 1956; children—Henry Voltaire III, Randall Scott. B.S. in Bus. Edn., Cedar Crest Coll., 1955; B.E. in Curriculum & Instrn., Fla. Atlantic U., 1971. Corr. course writer Acad. Health Scis., U.S. Army, San Antonio, 1976-77, team chief, individual analysis and design. br., 1977-80, dep. chief individual tng. analysis and design br., 1980-81; satellite TV program dir. U.S. Army Health Services Command, San Antonio, 1981-84; chief individual tng. in forces br. Acad. of Health Scis., U.S. Army, San Antonio, 1984-85; co-owner, operator Circle T Farms, San Antonio, 1985—. Vol. worker Army Community Services, 1966-67, ARC, 1966-74; pres. sr. state officer club, sr. 1st v.p. Tex. soc. Children of the Am. Revolution, 1979-81, sr. nat. v.p. south central region, 1978-80, sr. nat. historian, nat. conv. vice chmn., 1980-82, hon. sr. nat. v.p. nat. soc., 1982-85, sr. Nat. Officers' Club, 1977—; sr. organizing pres. Rio Grande Soc., 1988—, Denny Anderson Soc., 1976-78. Recipient Outstanding Performance award Acad. of Health Scis. and Sec. of Army, 1958, 79, 80; commendation cert. ARC, 1967, U.S. Army Community Services, 1974, Nat. Soc. Children Am. Revolution, 1980, Spl. Act award Acad. Health Scis. U.S. Army, 1977; Exceptional Performance award U.S. Army Health Services Command and Acad. of Health Scis., 1981, 83, 84; Comdr.'s award for civilian service Dept. Army, 1985; named one of Notable Women of Tex., 1983-84. Mem. AAUW, Fed. Ednl. Tech. Assn., Assn. Edn. and Communication Tech., Armed Forces Pub. Affairs Council, Nat. Assn. Female Execs., Am. Mgmt. Assn., Hilton Sea Island Tower Assn. (v.p., bd. govs. 1987—), DAR (rec. sec. Alamo chpt. 1975-76), DuBois-Hite chapter (correspondent, sec. 1989—), Radisson Sea Island Tower Assn. (v.p. 1989—, bd. govs.). Republican. Lutheran. Club: U.S. Army Theater Support Communications Officers Wives (pres. 1968-69), Sr. Nat. Officers'. Lodge: Ladies of the Shrine. Avocations: tennis, seashells, swimming, knitting, latchhook. Home: PO Box 2576 South Padre Island TX 78597-2576 Office: Circle T Farms 9322 Oak Downs San Antonio TX 78230

TRAICOFF, SANDRA M., financial company executive; b. O'Neill, Nebr., Aug. 31, 1944; d. Theodore Edwin and Ella Pauline (Fuhrer) Rustemeyer; m. Chris J. Traicoff, Feb. 17, 1973. B.A. in Polit. Sci. and Asian Studies, U. Kans., 1967; M.A. in L.S., U. Ill., 1970; J.D., DePaul U., 1978. Bar: Ill. 1978. Asst. reference and documents librarian U. Ill. Law Library, Urbana, 1970-73; assoc. librarian, head pub. services DePaul U. Law Library, Chgo., 1973-77; loan rev. officer Comml. Nat. Bank of Peoria (Ill.), 1978-82; corp. sec. Midwest Fin. Group, Inc., Peoria, 1982-86; v.p., sec. and gen. counsel Midwest Fin. Group, Inc., 1986—; lectr., cons. Comml. Nat. Mgmt. Cons. Co., Peoria, 1979-82; lectr. Grad. Sch. Library Scis., U. Chgo., 1975-77. Bd. dirs. Heart of Ill. Big Bros./Big Sisters, Peoria, 1981—, pres. bd., 1981-82; bd. dirs., mem. coms. YWCA, Peoria, 1981—, bd. dirs. 1986—, v.p., 1987—. Regents scholar U. Colo., Boulder, 1962, Univ. Fellow U. Ill., Urbana, 1968. Mem. ABA, Ill. Bar Assn., Peoria County Bar Assn., Women in Mgmt., Beta Phi Mu. Home: 912 Shoreline St Dunlap IL 61525 Office: Midwest Fin Group Inc 301 SW Adams St Peoria IL 61631

TRAINOR, DAVID BRUCE, business executive; b. Phila., Feb. 28, 1942; s. John F. and Gertrude (Rhoads) T.; m. Kathleen McNichol, June 11, 1976; children: David B., Daniel H., Elizabeth K., John F. BA, LaSalle Coll., 1964; postgrad. Temple U. and U. Pa., 1964-65. Account exec. Butcher & Sherrerd, Phila., 1965-69; pres. Tax Shelter Advisory Service Inc., Narberth, Pa., 1970-73; pres., chmn. World Resources Corp., Radnor, Pa., 1973-84; pres., chmn. Omni-Exploration, Inc., Radnor, 1974-84; mng. dir. Knightsbridge Ptnrs., Blue Bell, Pa., 1984; now pres. Spectrum Staffing, Inc., Newton Sq., Pa., 1988—. Republican. Roman Catholic. Clubs: Union League, Aronimink Golf. Office: Spectrum Staffing Inc PO Box 143 Newtown Square PA 19073

TRAMONTANO, JOHN PATRICK, JR., electrical products company executive; b. N.Y.C., Nov. 4, 1941; s. John Patrick and Jean (Franco) T.; B.E.E., Manhattan Coll., 1963; m. Mary Louise Mellow, Apr. 24, 1965; children—John, Craig, Tracy. Standards engr. Con. Edison, N.Y.C., 1963-66; product engr. Burndy Corp., Norwalk, Conn., 1966-71, product mgr., 1971-77, dir. mktg., 1977-78; v.p. sales and mktg. Teledyne Penn-Union, Edinboro, Pa., 1978-83, pres., 1983—. Pres., Norwalk Young Republicans, 1974-75; mem. Rep. Town Com., Norwalk, 1976-77; vice chmn. Norwalk Planning and Zoning Com., 1976-77; pres. Little League Baseball, Fairview-Tri-Boro, Pa., 1979; mem. adv. bd. Edinboro U. Pa., 1984—; bd. incorporators Millcreek Community Hosp., 1989—; bd. dirs. Blue Cross Western Pa., 1989—; mem. capital campaign cabinet Edinboro U. Pa., 1986—; mem. adv. bd. Marine Bank, Edinboro, 1987—. Mem. IEEE, Nat. Elec. Mfrs. Assn. (chmn. elec. connector sect. 1981-82), Am. Mgmt. Assn., Sales and Mktg. Execs. Erie, Mfrs. Assn. Northwest (bd. govs. 1987—, mem. Pa. exec. bd., 1988—). Republican. Roman Catholic. Contbr. articles to various publs. Home: 6357 Longwood Dr Erie PA 16505 Office: 229 Waterford St Edinboro PA 16412

TRAN, CHRISTINE THIEN-HUONG, international consulting firm executive; b. Hanoi, Socialist Republic of Vietnam, Feb. 15, 1958; d. Mai D. and Toan (Pham) T. BBA in Acctg., St. Mary's Coll., 1979. Acct. Price Waterhouse, Washington, 1980-83; ptnr. Diversified Bus. Cons., McLean, Va., 1983-85; v.p. WJS, Inc., McLean, 1985-88, Pan Asia Resources, Ltd., Hong Kong, 1988—; pub. rels. cons. Nat. Maintenance Svcs., Inc., McLean; bd. dirs. Cafe Francais, Inc., McLean. Mem. Nat. Assn. Accts., Am. Mktg. Assn., NAFE.

TRANQUILLO, MARY DORA, organization development educator; b. Pitts., Apr. 14, 1943; d. Guy and Dora (Grossi) Caranfa; m. Joseph Anthony Tranquillo. BFA, Pratt Inst., 1965; MA, NYU, 1971; PhD, Union Grad. Sch., 1987. Distbr. Koscot Kosmetics, Conn. and Fla., 1970-71; tchr. Horace Mann Jr. High Sch., Brandon, Fla., 1971-72, Plant City (Fla.) High Sch., 1972-74; prof. St. Petersburg Jr. Coll., Clearwater, Fla., 1974—; pres. Productivity Improvement, Safety Harbor, Fla., 1987—; cons. St. Petersburg Jr. Coll., Clearwater, 1988—, Rutenberg Corp., 1988, Pixie Playmates, Clearwater, 1987—. Author: Styles of Fashion, 1984. Recipient Outsanding Svc. award DECA. Mem. Am. Soc. Tng., Orgn. Devel. Inst., Orgn. Devel. Network, Am. Psychol. Assn., Soc. Psychologists in Mgmt., Married Couples Club (host). Home: 34 Turnstone Dr Safety Harbor FL 34695 Office: St Petersburg Jr Coll 2465 Drew St Clearwater FL 34625

TRAPOLIN, FRANK WINTER, insurance executive; b. New Orleans, Jan. 29, 1913; s. John Baptiste and Florence Bertha (Winter) T.; BS in Econs., Loyola U. of South, New Orleans, 1935; m. Thelma Mae Mouledoux, Oct. 27, 1937; children: Timothy, Patricia Couret, Jane Oaksmith, Anne Britt. Agt., Godchaux & Mayer, New Orleans, 1935-42, 46-51; pres. Trapolin-Couret Ins. Agy., Inc., New Orleans, 1953—; mem. faculty Loyola U.; ins. cons. Former pres. Cath. Human Relations Commn. Greater New Orleans, Associated Cath. Charities New Orleans, Maryland Dr. Homeowners Assn., Loyola U. Alumni Assn.; former chmn. adv. bd. New Orleans Juvenile Cts., Ursuline Nuns New Orleans; former scoutmaster Boy Scouts Am.; former v.p. Community Relations Council Greater New Orleans, New Orleans Jr. C.of C., La. Interch. Conf.; former trustee United Fund Greater New Orleans Area; tng. officer 8th Coast Guard Dist. Aux.; former mem. adv. bd. Coll. Bus. Adminstrn., Loyola U., Mother-house of Sisters of Holy Family; former bd. dirs. St. John Berchman Orphanage, New Orleans Interfaith Conf., St. Elizabeth's Home for Girls, Cath. Book Store Found., Manresa Retreat House; adv. bd. New Orleans Track Club; founder, Serra Run for Vocations. Served with USN, 1942-46, 51-53, with Res., ret. Recipient Merit cert. City of New Orleans, 1972; Order of St. Louis. Mem. La. Assn. Ins. Agts., Nat. Assn. Ins. Agts., New Orleans Ins. Exchange, Navy League, Mil. Order World Wars, Greater New Orleans Exec. Assn. (pres. 1985, named Exec. of the Year 1985), New Orleans Photog. Soc., Sierra Club, Blue Key. Democrat. Roman Catholic. Clubs: Sertoma (pres. New Orleans 1955-56), Serra (pres. New Orleans 1973-74), Internat. House, New Orleans Track, New Orleans Yacht, Pass Christian Yacht. Lodge: KC (4 deg.). Patentee gunnery, tng. and machinery devices for USN. Home: 119 Audubon Blvd New Orleans LA 70118-5538 Office: Trapolin-Couret Agy 837 Gravier St Suite 1212 New Orleans LA 70112-1514

TRAUB, MARVIN STUART, department store executive; b. N.Y.C., Apr. 14, 1925; s. Sam D. and Bea (Bruckman) T.; m. Lee Laufer, Sept. 2, 1948; children: Andrew D., James S., Peggy Ann. B.A. magna cum laude, Harvard U., 1947, M.B.A., 1949. Trainee Macy's, N.Y.C., 1947; assoc. buyer Alexander's, N.Y.C., 1949; with Bloomingdale Bros., N.Y.C., 1950—, asst. to v.p., 1950-51, mgr. hosier dept., 1951-52, asst. to chmn., 1952-53, mgr. rug dept., 1953-54, div. mgr. mdse., 1956-60, v.p. mdse., 1960-62, exec. v.p., gen. mgr. mdse., 1962-69, pres., from 1969, chmn., chief exec. officer, 1978—. Mem. Mayor's Com. in the Pub. Interest, 1975; trustee, mem. bd. Hosp. Joint Diseases and Med. Center; mem. vis. com. Tobe-Coburn Sch. for Fashion Careers; bd. dirs. Am. Health Found., Ednl. Found. of Fashion Inst. Tech.; trustee Nat. Jewish Hosp., Denver; mem. vis. com. Costume Inst., Met. Mus. Art; mem. adv. council vol. Urban Consulting Program, Harvard Bus. Sch. Club of N.Y. Served with AUS, 1942-46. Decorated Purple Heart. Recipient Chevalier de la Legion d'honneur, France, 1987, Commendatore de la Republica, Italy, 1985. Clubs: Sunningdale Country; Harvard (N.Y.C.). Office: Bloomingdale's 59th St & Lexington New York NY 10022

TRAUTMAN, WILLIAM E., investment banker; b. Bklyn., June 7, 1938; s. Frank Joseph and Francis Pauline (Herdez) T.; m. Catherine Shelton Forester, Sept. 2, 1962; children: Mark F., Charles Eric. BA in Acctg., Birmingham So. Coll., 1962; MBA in Fin., U. Ala., 1964. Instr. acctg. U. Ala., Tuscaloosa, 1962-64; mgr. fin. program Litton Industries, Pascagoula, Miss., 1967-70; fin. exec. McLean Securities, N.Y.C., 1970-74; v.p., gen. mgr. Mideast Seatrain Lines Inc., London, 1974-78; pres. Maric Assocs., Morristown, N.J., 1978-82; exec. v.p. Moore & Schley Securities, N.Y.C., 1982—; bd. dirs. Dionics Inc., Garden City, N.Y., Gamma Biols. Inc., Houston. Crusade chmn., bd. dirs. Am. Cancer Soc., Morristown, 1986—. Named Vol. of Yr. Am. Cancer Soc., Morristown, 1987. Mem. Securities Industry Assn. (com. corp. fin. 1987—), Magnet Group, Spring Brook Country Club. Office: Moore & Schley Securities Corp 45 Broadway New York NY 10006

TRAVERS, JUDITH LYNNETTE, human resource executive; b. Buffalo, Feb. 25, 1950; d. Harold Elwin and Dorothy (Helsel) Howes; m. David Jon Travers, Oct. 21, 1972; 1 child, Heather Lynne. BA in Psychology, Barrington Coll., 1972; cert. in paralegal course, St. Mary's Coll., Moraga, Calif., 1983; postgrad., Southland U., 1982-84. Exec. sec. Sherman C. Weeks, P.A., Derry, N.H., 1973-75; legal asst. Mason-McDuffie Co., Berkeley, Calif., 1975-82; paralegal asst. Blum, Kay, Merkle & Kauftheil, Oakland, Calif., 1982-83; exec. v.p. Western Med. Personnel Inc., Concord, Calif., 1983—; pres. All Ages Sitters Agy., Concord, 1986—. Vocalist record album The Loved Ones, 1978. Vol. local Congl. campaign, 1980, Circle of Friends, Children's Hosp. No. Calif., Oakland, 1987—; mem. Alameda County Sheriff's Mounted Posse, 1989, Contra Costa Child Abuse Prevention Coun., 1989. Mem. NAFE, Am. Assn. Respiratory Therapy, Calif. Soc. Respiratory Care, Am. Mgmt. Assn., Gospel Music Assn., Palomino Horse Breeders Am., DAR, Barrington Oratorio Soc., Commonwealth Club Calif., Nat. Trust Hist. Preservation, Alpha Theta Sigma. Republican. Baptist. Home: 3900 Brown Rd Oakley CA 94561 Office: Western Med Pers Inc 1820 Galindo St Ste 225 Concord CA 94520

TRAVERS, OLIVER S., JR., manufacturing company executive; b. Balt., 1926; married. Grad., U. Md., 1949. With Nat. Dairies, 1950-52; with Schenuit Industries, 1953-80, v.p., 1953-63, pres., 1963-80; chmn., pres., chief exec. officer Allegheny Internat. Inc., 1986—. With USN, 1944-46. Office: Allegheny Internat Inc 2 Oliver Pla PO Box 456 Pittsburgh PA 15230 *

TRAVIS, ANDREW DAVID, lawyer; b. Washington, Mar. 23, 1944; s. Don Carlos Jr. and Nevenna (Tsanoff) T. BA, Rice U., 1966; JD, U. Tex., 1969. Bar: Tex. 1969. Sole practice Houston, 1971-75; atty. Allright Auto Parks Inc., Houston, 1975-82, v.p., legal counsel, 1982—. Mem. ABA, Tex. Bar Assn., Houston Bar Assn. Home: 307 Timber Terr Houston TX 77024 Office: Allright Auto Parks Inc 1919 Smith St Suite 1200 Houston TX 77002

TRAVIS, ANITA HARTMAN, state official; b. Frankfort, Ky., Jan. 26, 1944; d. Howard Fredrick and Rosalie (Page) Hartman; m. Zane Grey Travis, July 22, 1961 (div. July 1981); children: Deborah Grey, Kevin Thomas, Gwendolyn Louise. Cert., Capitol Bus. Sch., Frankfort, 1959; student, Ky. State U., 1971-78, 87—. Pub. health rep. consumer health protection div. Ky. Dept. for Health Svcs., Frankfort, 1978-80, adminstrv. supr. sanitation programs info. system, 1980-82, unit supr. environ. health data unit, 1982-84, supr. data info sect., 1984-86, mgr. info. and support br. food and sanitation div., 1987—; mem. planning com. statewide regional health confs., 1986, 87, 88; mem. Computer Network Steering Com., Frankfort, 1986—; mem. processing steering com. Cabinet for Human Resources Data, Frankfort, 1986-87; mem. local health dept. funding formula study group Ky. Dept. Health Svcs., 1988—. Editor Ky. Sanitarian's and Fieldmen Jour., 1978-80; contbr. articles to profl. jours. Mem. Ky. Pub. Health Assn. (nomination and election chmn. 1987), Ky. Assn. Milk, Food and Environ. Sanitarians (sec., treas., chmn., mem. various coms., Environ. Svc. award 1986), Assn. Food and Drug Ofcls. So. States, Ten-Ure Club. Democrat. Baptist. Home: 191 Travis Rd Frankfort KY 40601 Office: Ky Dept for Health Svcs Info and Support Br 275 E Main St Frankfort KY 40621

TRAVIS, JILL HELENE, bank executive; b. Detroit, Aug. 12, 1948; d. Norton Martin and Margaret Dorothy (Gerge) Schuknecht; m. James Ernest Travis, Jan. 29, 1972. BSBA, Valparaiso U., 1970; MBA, Wayne State U., 1976; postgrad., U. Colo., 1978-86, B in Mcpl. Adminstrn., 1986; cert., Coll. Fin. Planning, 1988. Writer, editor Rakco Creative Services, Royal Oak, Mich., 1970-71; dir. fashion merchandising Lear Siegler Inc., 1971-72, dir. placement edn. div., 1972-74; asst. research dir. Detroit Bus. Inst./Detroit Inst. Tech., 1974-76; v.p. Liberty State Bank and Trust, Troy, Mich., 1977—. Author, editor: The Cost-Benefit Aspects of Co-Operative Education, 1976. Mem. adv. bd. Birmingham (Mich.) Community Women's Ctr., Inc., 1986—. Grad. Profl. scholar Wayne State U., 1975-76. Mem. Inst. Cert. Fin. Planners, Internat. Assn. Fin. Plannning, Bank Mktg. Assn., Nat. Assn. Bank Women, Oakland County C. of C., Women's Econ. Club Detroit. Republican. Lutheran. Office: Liberty State Bank and Trust 801 W Big Beaver Troy MI 48048

TRAVIS, LAWRENCE ALLAN, accountant; b. Bloomington, Ill., Sept. 17, 1942; s. Willard Burns and Florence May (Harvey) T.; m. Katy Quinones, Apr. 4, 1965 (div. Feb. 1978); children: Lawrence A. Jr., Matthew B. BS in Bus. Edn., Ill. State U., 1968; MA in Pub. Adminstrn., Sangamon State U., Springfield, Ill., 1976. CPA, Ill. Staff acct. Alexander Grant & Co., Chgo., 1969; internal auditor State Farm Ins., Bloomington, 1969-73; dep. dir. Ill. Dept. Ins., Springfield, 1973-74; mgr. auditing Ill. Auditor Gen., Springfield, 1974-81; pres. Lawrence Travis & Co., P.C., CPA's, Virden, Bloomington and Springfield, Ill., 1979—; also bd. dirs. Lawrence Travis & Co., P.C., Virden, Bloomington and Springfield; v.p. Virden Broadcasting Corp., 1986—, also bd. dirs.; pres., bd. dirs. Travco, Inc., Virden, 1985—; v.p., bd. dirs. Miller Communications, Inc., Virden, 1987—, Carlinville Broadcasting Corp., 1988—. Mem. Ill. Common Cause, Springfield. Mem. Am. Inst. CPA's, Assn. Govt. Accts., Ill. CPA Soc. (legis. contact 1981—), Internat. Platform Assn. Democrat. Roman Catholic. Home: 2409 Idlewild Dr Springfield IL 62704 Office: Lawrence Travis & Co P C The Mall Virden IL 62690

TRAVIS, ROBIN, computer conversion specialist, author: b. Bklyn., Dec. 20, 1949; d. Elias and Fay Travis; m. Jeffrey Sanchez Hinkle, Dec. 9, 1972; 1 child, Jesse Robin. BA, Hunter Coll., 1971; MA, CUNY, 1974. Chief exec. officer Travis, Campbell, Fisher & Assocs. (formerly TLC Computer Services), 1976-84, sr. tech. ptnr., 1984-88; mktg. communications specialist Hamilton-Avnet Corp., Los Angeles, 1988; with Travis, Campbell, Fisher East, Rochester, N.Y., 1988—; cons. Calif. Bd. Realtors, 1988; registered expert Tech. Adv. Svc. for Attys. Author: (novels) China Train, 1979, Entering the Middle Kingdom, 1981, (play) Red Flannel Murders, 1980, Selling Computers, 1987; contbr. articles to bus. sect. local newspaper, Calif. Banker Mag., others; appeared on local TV show, co-host computer show radio sta. KIEV. Mem. Nat. Assn. for Exec. Females, Ind. Assn. Computer Cons., Nat. Assn. Women Bus. Owners, Smithsonian Inst., Los Angeles Mus. Contemporary Art.

TRAVIS, SUSAN KATHRYN, real estate broker; b. Charleston, W.Va., Aug. 31, 1940; d. James Edward and Iva Catherine (Mangus) Roberts; m. Ray Ransleur Collins, Apr. 15, 1960 (dec. May 1964); children: Cary Calvin, Camala Kathryn; m. Burr James Travis, Oct. 8, 1966 (div. Oct. 1979); children: Tammi Jill, Terry James (twins). Student, Gulf Pk. Coll., Gulfport, Miss., 1957-58, Coll. Conservatory Music, Cin., 1958-59. Dir. rental svcs. Nat. Computerized Property Mgmt. Inc., Cin., 1970-75; real estate broker First Comml. Realty Inc., Florence, Ky., 1978—; prin. First Comml. Realty Inc., Florence, 1978—; cons. market analysis and concept E.W. Richmond Retirement Ctr. and Nursing Home, Owensboro, Ky., 1985-86. Founder Tri-State rehabilitation and counciling program Kids Helping Kids, 1980, sec. 1980-88, chmn. fund raising 1987—, trustee, 1987; appointee Gov.'s Drug Abuse Bd. Trustees for Commonwealth of Ky., Frankfort, 1983; mem. Internat. Econ. Devel., Louisville, 1987, ACT for Covington, Ky., 1988, Govt. Affairs Council, No. Ky., 1988; initiated House Bill No. 26 in Gen. Assembly in Commonwealth of Ky., 1982. Named Outstanding Woman Mo., Women's World News, No. Ky., 1981. Mem. No. Ky. C. of C., Small Bus. Council (steering com. 1982), Econ. Devel. Bus. and Industry (com. mem. 1988), Greater Cin. C. of C. Democrat. Home: 1082 Cayton Rd Florence KY 41042 Office: First Comml Realty 8172 Mall Road Ctr Ste 239 Florence KY 41042

TREADWAY, JAMES, JR., securites company executive, lawyer, former government official; b. Anderson, S.C., May 21, 1943; s. James C. and Maxine (Hall) T.; m. Susan Pepper Davis, Sept. 6, 1969; children: Elizabeth Pepper Hall, Caroline Worrell Harper. A.B., U. Ga., 1964; JD summa cum laude, Washington and Lee U., 1967. Bar: Ga. 1967, Mass. 1968, D.C. 1970. Assoc. Candler, Cox, McClain & Andrews, Atlanta, 1967-68; assoc. Gadsby & Hannah, Boston and Washington, 1968-72; ptnr. Dickstein, Shapiro & Morin, Washington, 1972-82; commr. SEC, Washington, 1982-85; ptnr. Baker & Botts, Washington, 1985-87; exec. v.p. Paine Webber Inc., N.Y.C., 1987—; chmn. Nat. Commn. on Fraudulent Fin. Reporting, 1985-87. Mem. Mass. Bar Assn., Ga. Bar Assn., D.C. Bar Assn., Order of Coif, Chevy Chase Club, City Tavern Club, Univ. Club, City Club, Tennis Club, Phi Beta Kappa, Omicron Delta Kappa, Omicron Delta Epsilon. Republican. Episcopalian. Clubs: Chevy Chase (Md.); City Tavern, University, City (all Washington). Home: Laurel Ledge Farm Croton Lake Rd RD #4 Mount Kisco NY 10549 Office: Paine Webber Group Inc 1285 Ave of the Americas New York NY 10019

TREECE, CHARLES DOUGLAS, insurance sales executive; b. Springfield, Mo., Nov. 19, 1946; s. Denver Douglas and Nettie Fay (May) T.; m. Deborah Lynn Causey, Dec. 3, 1982 (div. 1986); 1 child, Steven Douglas; m. Laura Lynn Marsh, June 12, 1987. Student, U. Ark., 1964-66. Mgmt. trainee Household Fin. Corp., Springfield, 1967-68; salesman Fidelity Union Life Ins. Co., Springfield, 1968-71, 74-76; data processing mgr. Heritage Pub. Co., Sherwood, Ark., 1976-88; salesman Met. Life Ins. Co., North Little Rock, Ark., 1988—. Mem. Aircraft Owners and Pilots Assn., Rotary. Republican. Methodist. Office: Met Life Ins Co 5601 JFK Blvd Ste 201 North Little Rock AR 72116

TREES, JOHN SIMMONS, insurance company executive; b. Evanston, Ill., Mar. 26, 1932; s. Harry A. and Eleanor Irene (Smith) T.; m. Dianne Schneider, Oct. 16, 1954; children: Julie Watumull, Michael, Nancy Vogt. B.A., DePauw U., Greencastle, Ind., 1954. V.p. pricing Allstate Ins. Co., Northbrook, Ill., 1973-78, group v.p. personal lines, 1978-80, sr. v.p. personal property and casualty lines, 1980-82, sr. v.p. corp. planning, 1982-84, v.p. controller, 1985—; dir. Hwy. Loss Data Inst., Washington, 1972—, Ins. Statis. Service, Des Plaines, Ill., 1978—, All Industry Reserach Adv. Council, Oak Brook, Ill., 1977—; mem. Nat. Hwy. Safety Adv. Commn., Washington, 1981-84, Ins. Inst. for Hwy. Safety, 1987—. Mem. Lake Bluff Bd. Appeals, Ill., 1971-78, Lake Bluff Sch. Bd., 1964-71. Served to 1st lt. SAC, USAF, 1954-57. Mem. Casualty Acturial Soc. (assoc. mem.), Am. Acad. Actuarial. Presbyterian. Home: 1384 Arcady Lake Forest IL 60045 Office: Allstate Ins Co Allstate Plaza Northbrook IL 60062

TREFFTZS, KENNETH LEWIS, business and finance educator; b. Sparta, Ill., Dec. 28, 1911; s. John Sydney and Dorothy Nora (Wright) T.; m. Ellen Lois Ryniker, Aug. 7, 1937; children: Jeffrey Lewis, Ellen Sterling. B.S., U. Ill., 1936, M.S., 1937, Ph.D., 1939. Asst. economist, com. on bank research Ill. Bankers Assn., 1937-39; instr. Carnegie Inst. Tech., 1939-41; asst. prof. fin. U. So. Calif., Los Angeles, 1941-45; assoc. prof. U. So. Calif., 1945-50, prof., 1951-82, prof. emeritus, 1982—, disting. prof. emeritus, 1988—, head dept. fin., 1945-57, head dept. fin. and real estate, 1959-66, chmn. dept. fin. and bus. econs., 1966-71; vis. assoc. prof. UCLA, 1948; vis. assoc. prof. sch. bus. adminstrn. U. Wash., 1949-50; instr. Pacific Coast Banking Sch., Seattle, summer, 1949; conf. dir. Ann. Inst. Fin., So. Calif., 1962, 63, 64; chmn., dir. Fund of Am., Inc., Provident Fund for Income, Inc., Am. Capital Comstock Fund, Inc., Am. Capital Corp. Bond Fund, Inc., Am. Capital Enterprise Fund, Inc., Am. Capital Govt. Securities, Inc., Am. Gen. Money Market Accumulation Fund, Inc., Am. Gen. High Yield Accumulation Fund, Inc., Am. Capital Mcpl. Bond Fund, Inc., Am. Capital Prime Series Inc., Am. Capital Pace Fund, Inc., Am. Capital Res. Fund, Inc., Am. Capital Venture Fund, Inc., Am. Capital Over-the-Counter Securities, Inc., Am. Capital Harbor Fund, Am. Capital High Yield Investments, Inc.; dir. Source Capital, Inc., MGM/UA Communications Co., Inc., FPA Perennial Fund, Inc., FPA New Income Inc., Fremont Gen. Corp., FPA Capital Fund, Inc., Pacific Horizon Fund, Inc. (govt. money market portfolio, money market portfolio, high yield bond portfolio, aggressive growth portfolio), Pacific Horizon Calif. Tax Exempt Bond Portfolio ; trustee, chmn. Am. Calif. Tax-Exempt Trust, Am. Capital Fed. Mortgage Trust, Am. Capital Govt. Money Mkt. Trust, Am. Capital Life Investment Trust, Am. Capital Tax-Exempt Trust; trustee The Horizon Funds (Horizon Prime Fund, Treasury Fund. Tax-Exempt Money Fund, Intermediate Govt. Fund, Intermediate Tax-Exempt Fund); cons. (under AID) U. Karachi, Pakistan, 1962. Author: Mathematics of Banking and Finance, 1944, (with E.J. Hills) Mathematics of Business and Accounting, 1947, Mathematics of Business, Accounting and Finance, 1956, What Put the Stock Market Where It Is; Contbr. articles to profl. jours. Recipient Dean's award Grad. Sch. Bus., U. So. Calif., 1963; Teaching Excellence award U. So. Calif., 1974-75; Assos. award for excellence in teaching, 1977. Mem. Am. Econ. Assn., Western Econ. Assn. (pres. 1955-56), Western Fin. Assn. (pres. 1965-66), Am. Fin. Assn. (v.p. 1946-48), Beta Gamma Sigma, Phi Kappa Phi, Rho Epsilon, Omicron Delta Epsilon, Lambda Alpha, Beta Alpha Psi, Alpha Kappa Psi. Address: Am Capital Comstock Fund Inc 2800 Post Oak Blvd Houston TX 77056 *

TREGENZA, NORMAN HUGHSON, investment banker; b. Morristown, N.J., Feb. 1, 1937; s. Norman J. and Marion Esther (Hughson) T.; B.A., St. Lawrence U., 1959; M.B.A., N.Y. U., 1963; m. Alyce Virginia Bruene, Aug. 27, 1966; children—Norman Arthur, Suzanne Carol. Sr. investment officer Tchrs. Ins. & Annuity Assn., N.Y.C., 1960-71; sr. v.p. Republic Funding Corp., N.Y.C., 1971-82; pres. Convent Capital Corp., 1982—; co-founder, dir. Tempo Enterprises, Inc., Tulsa; chmn. Tellus, Inc., N.Y.C. Chmn. stewardship com. Presbyn. Ch., Morristown, N.J., 1978, ruling elder, 1979, pres. bd. trustees, 1982; trustee St. Lawrence U., Canton, N.Y., Gill/St. Bernards Sch. (hon.), The Morris Mus., Morristown, N.J. Mem. St. Lawrence U. Alumni Assn. N.J. (pres. 1970-72). Club: Baltusrol Golf. Home and Office: White Gates Kitchell Rd Convent Station NJ 07961

TREGURTHA, PAUL RICHARD, marine transportation company executive; b. Orange, N.J., 1935; married. BSME, Cornell U., 1958; MBA, Harvard U., 1963. V.p., controller Brown & Sharpe Mfg. Co., 1969-71; v.p. fin. Moore-McCormack Resources, Inc., Stamford, Conn., 1971-73, exec. v.p. fin., 1973-78, pres., chief operating officer, from 1978, pres., chief exec. officer, chmn., 1987-88; chmn. Mormac Marine Group, Inc., Stamford, 1988—; bd. dirs. Shawmut Nat. Corp., Brown & Sharpe Mfg. Co. Served to 1st lt. USAF, 1958-61. Mem. Tchrs. Ins. and Annuity Assn. (trustee). Office: Mormac Marine Group Inc Three Landmark Sq Stamford CT 06901

TREINAVICZ, KATHRYN MARY, software engineer; b. Brockton, Mass., Nov. 25, 1957; d. Ralph Clement and Frances Elizabeth (O'Leary) T. BS, Salem State Coll., Mass., 1980. Tchr., Brockton Pub. Schs., 1980-81; instr. Quincy CETA Inc., Mass., 1981-82; programmer Systems Architects Inc., Randolph, Mass., 1982, programmer analyst, Dayton, Ohio, 1982-84; sr. programmer analyst System Devel. Corp., Dayton, 1984-86; project mgr. Unysis Inc., Dayton, 1986-87; software engr. Systems and Applied Scis. Corp., 1987-89, project mgr. Atlantic Rsch. Corp., Fairborn, Ohio, 1989—. Mem. NAFE. Democrat. Roman Catholic. Avocations: Steven King novels, needlepoint, knitting, crocheting.

TREMBLAY, DONNA MAY, real estate corporation officer; b. Marlboro, Mass., May 20, 1951; d. Roland Francis and Beatrice Edith (Lemon) T. BS, N.H. Coll., 1986. Lic. real estate broker, N.N. Owner, publisher Women For Women Weekly, Exeter, N.H., 1977-81; gen. mgr. Advantage Mobile Home Brokers, Lebanon, Maine, 1984-86, Am. Mobile Home Brokers, Hampton, N.H., 1981-84; pres. Images Mobile Modular Concepts Inc., Greenland, N.H., 1986-88; realtor Seacoast Bd. of Realtors, Hampton, N.H., 1987—. Editor: They Paved The Way, 1980. Named Young Career Woman, Nat. Fedn. of Bus. and Profl. Woman, 1980. Mem. Nat. Home Builders Assn., Nat. Fedn. of Ind. Bus. Democrat. Roman Catholic. Office: Images Mobile Modular Concepts Inc Rt 101 Box 700 Greenland NH 03840

TREMBLAY, ROGER LEON, publisher; b. Lowell, Mass., Mar. 25, 1948; s. Armand Louis and Germaine Bella (Dubois) T.; m. Judy Arlene DeBlaay, Sept. 2, 1971; 1 child, Darren. BA, Mich. State U., 1970, MA, 1971. Advt. sales rep. Wall St. Jour., Cleve., 1971-74; regional advt. mgr. So. Living Mag., Dallas, 1974-82; advt. dir., assoc. pub. Tex. Monthly, Austin, 1982-87; pub., v.p. Chgo. Mag., 1987—. Contbr. articles to profl. jours.; chmn. Mag. Day in Tex. com., 1981; mem. mktg. com. Mag. Pubs., N.Y.C., 1983. Mem. Advt. Council Am., Am. Mktg. Assn. (Dallas/Ft. Worth chpt. v.p. 1972), Mag. Advt. Sales Assn. (founder, pres. 1976), City and Regional Mag. Assn. (pres., bd. dirs. 1984). Roman Catholic. Home: 74 E Westminster St Lake Forest IL 60045 Office: Chgo Mag 414 N Orleans St 800 Chicago IL 60610

TRENNEPOHL, GARY LEE, finance educator; b. Detroit, Dec. 6, 1946; s. Leo Donald and Wilma Mae (Tiensvold) T.; m. Sandra K. Yeager, June 9, 1968; children: Paige E., Adrienne A. BS, U. Tulsa, 1968; MBA, Utah State U., 1971; PhD, Tex. Tech U., 1976. Asst. prof. aero. studies Tex. Tech U., Lubbock, 1972-74; asst. prof. fin. Ariz. State U., Tempe, 1977-80, assoc. prof., 1980-82; prof. U. Mo., Columbia, 1982-86, dir. Sch. Bus., 1984-86; prof. fin. Tex. A&M U., College Station, 1986—, head dept., 1986—. Author: An Introduction to Financial Management, 1984; assoc. editor Jour. Fin. Research, 1983—; contbr. articles to profl. jours. Capt. USAF, 1968-72. Decorated Commendation medal with oak leaf cluster, Vietnam Svc. medal. Mem. Fin. Mgmt. Assn. (bd. dirs. 1987-88, v.p. 1987—), So. Fin. Assn., Southwestern Fin. Assn. (bd. dirs. 1983-84, pres. 1986), Midwest Fin. Assn. (bd. dirs. 1985—). Republican. Lutheran. Home: 2010 Pebblestone College Station TX 77840 Office: Tex A&M U Coll Bus College Station TX 77843

TRENT, JOHN EDWARD, automobile company executive; b. Irvington, N.J., June 22, 1956; s. Earl David and Lola Trent. BA, Hampton U., 1979; MBA, U. Pitts., 1985. Lic. real estate salesman, N.J. Rsch. asst. CIBA-Geiby Corp., Summit, N.J., 1980-81; clin. technologist Metpath Inc., Teterboro, N.J., 1981-82; sales rep. Eli Lilly and Co., Indpls., 1983-86; field sales mgr. Ford Motor Co., Indpls., 1987—. Minority fellow U. Pitts., 1983. Mem. Am. Mgmt. Assn., Nat. Black MBA Assn. Office: Ford Motor Co 6900 English Ave Indianapolis IN 46206

TRENT, RICHARD O(WEN), financial executive; b. Ft. Worth, Nov. 13, 1920. Student U. Okla., 1940-47; grad. Inst. Life Ins. Mktg., So. Meth. U., 1948. Agt., Mass. Mut. Life Ins. Co., Oklahoma City, 1946-55; founder Mid-Am. Life Ins. Co., Oklahoma City, 1955, pres., chmn. bd., 1955-65, pres. Richard O. Trent and Assocs., Inc., Oklahoma City, 1965—, chmn. Sales, Mergers and Acquisitions-Worldwide, 1966—; dir. Okla. Mut. Investors, Inc.; past pres., chmn. bd. Liberty Investment Corp.; v.p., dir. Lee Realty Corp.; past v.p., dir. Cleary Petroleum Corp.; pres. Southwest Mut. Casualty Co. Served to lt. col. USAF, 1942-66. Decorated Air Medal, Purple Heart, D.F.C. Mem. Oklahoma City C. of C., YMCA, Okla. Econ. Club, Nat. Assn. Life Underwriters (life mem. Million Dollar Round Table), Am. Legion. Presbyterian. Clubs: Men's Dinner, Oklahoma City Golf and Country. Lodges: Masons, Shrine, Jesters. Office: 7201 Classen Blvd Suite 202 Oklahoma City OK 73116

TRESCA, PAUL JOSEPH, clothing manufacturing company executive; b. Phila., Nov. 11, 1945; s. William Arthur and Rose Marie (Smargisso) T.; m. Carol Ann Malandra, Sept. 23, 1967; children: Melina Rose, Frank Paul. AA, St. Joseph's U., Phila., 1974, BA, 1975. Personnel mgr. John Wanamaker, Phila., 1969-73; corp. dir. of personnel Penn Jersey Auto Stores, Phila., 1973-76; corp. mgr. employee relations Walworth Co., Valley Forge, Pa., 1976-78; asst. supt. personnel services Sch. Dist. Upper Darby (Pa.), 1978-80; dir. corp. resources After Six, Inc., Phila., 1980—; advisor career devel. program Pa. Correctional Inst., Muncy, 1985—. Co-founder Larkin Knoll Civic Assn., Boothwyn, Pa., 1972; bd. dirs. Campfire Program, Phila., 1988—. Served with U.S. Army, 1967-69, Vietnam. Mem. Am. Soc. Personnel Adminstrs. Democrat. Roman Catholic. Home: 4535 Bethel Rd Boothwyn PA 19061 Office: After Six Inc G St and Hunting Park Ave Philadelphia PA 19124

TRESKA, CLAYTON LEONARD, metal distribution executive, consultant; b. Cleve, Apr. 20, 1945; s. Edward James and Eleanore Matilda (Lang) T.; m. Alice Villarreal, Mar. 12, 1976; children: Julie Christen, Clayton Matthew. Buyer Builders Structural Steel, Cleve., 1961-63, territorial salesman, 1963-65; v.p., co-founder Bessemer Steel Co., Cleve., 1965-68; chief exec. officer, founder Clayton Steel Co., Cleve, Charlotte, N.C., Houston, and Chgo., 1969-77, Kodiak Steel Co., Cleve., 1977-83; dir., gen. mgr. Olympic Steel Co., St. Simons, Ga., Birmingham, Ala. and Charlotte, N.C., 1983—. Mem. SSCI, ASTM, NTEA, Am. Iron and Steel Inst. Roman Catholic. Club: Island (St. Simons). Office: Olympic Steel So 312 Plantation Chase Saint Simons GA 31522

TRESTYN, PHILIP, accountant; b. Poland, Sept. 10, 1919; came to U.S., 1927; s. Harry and Esther (Kelmanowitz) T.; m. Mildred Silverberg, May 24, 1942; children: Alan, Beverly, Cary. BBA, CCNY, 1940. CPA, N.Y. Ptnr. Herman Seidman & Co., N.Y.C., 1943-51, Root and Trestyn, N.Y.C., 1952-57; sr. ptnr. Trestyn & Rabin, N.Y.C., 1957-76, Trestyn, Trestyn & Pugsley, N.Y.C., 1977—. Mem. Am. Inst. CPA's, N.Y. State Soc. CPA's. Democrat. Jewish. Home: 192-10 48th Ave Flushing NY 11365 Office: Trestyn Trestyn & Pugsley 1450 Broadway New York NY 10018

TRETTER, JAMES RAY, pharmaceutical company executive; b. Boone, Iowa, June 7, 1933; s. Raymond J. and Freda E. (Ohge) T.; m. Neltje Van Loon; 1 child, Elsa. BS in Chemistry, Loras Coll., 1956; PhD in Chemistry, U. Berkeley, 1960. Chemist Pfizer, Inc., Groton, Conn., 1960-72, dir. med. chem. dept., 1972-74, dir. chem. process research, 1975-77, exec. dir. devel. research, 1977-80; v.p. research and devel. William H. Rorer, Inc., 1980-86; pres. cen. research Rorer Group, Inc., Horsham, Pa., 1986—. Office: Rorer Group Inc 800 Business Center Dr Horsham PA 19044 also: Rorer Group Inc 500 Virginia Dr Fort Washington PA 19034 *

TREU, JESSE ISAIAH, venture capitalist; b. N.Y.C., Apr. 10, 1947. BS, Rensselaer Poly. Inst., 1968; MS, Princeton U., 1971, PhD, 1973. Physicist, liaison sci. components, materials group Gen. Electric Co., Schenectady, N.Y., 1973-77; tech. dir. Technicon Corp., Tarrytown, N.Y., 1977-82; v.p. Channing Weinberg-CW Ventures, N.Y.C., 1982-85; gen. ptnr. Domain Assocs., Princeton, N.J., 1986—. Office: Domain Assocs 1 Palmer Sq Princeton NJ 09542

TREUHOLD, CHARLES RICHARD, investment banker; b. Bklyn., May 24, 1930; s. Eugene and Selma (Straus) T.; m. Kerstin Margareta Nevrell, July 28, 1956; 1 child, Robert Charles. BA, Yale U., 1952; postgrad., U. Paris, 1955-56. Syndicate assoc. Lehman Bros., N.Y.C., 1956-61; syndicate mgr. Paribas Corp., N.Y.C., 1961-66; sr. v.p., syndicate mgr. Arnhold & S. Bleichroeder, Inc., N.Y.C., 1966—. Editor: Bawl St. Jour., 1977, 88. Lt. (j.g.) USN, 1952-55). Mem. Assn. Internat. Bond Dealers (bd. dirs. 1979-86), Bond Club N.Y. (gov. 1988—), City Midday Club. Home: 200 E 66th St New York NY 10021 Office: Arnhold & S Bleichroeder Inc 45 Broadway New York NY 10006

TREVITHICK, RONALD JAMES, financial planner; b. Portland, Oreg., Sept. 13, 1944; s. Clifford Vincent and Amy Lois (Turner) T.; m. Delberta Russell, Sept. 11, 1965; children: Pamela, Carmen, Marla, Sheryl. BBA U. Wash., 1966. CPA, Alaska, N.C., Va., La. Mem. audit staff Ernst & Ernst, Anchorage, 1966, 68-70; pvt. practice acctg., Fairbanks, Alaska, 1970-73; with Touche Ross & Co., Anchorage, 1973-78, audit ptnr., 1976-78; exec. v.p., treas., bd. dirs. Veco Internat., Inc., 1978-82; pres., bd. dirs. Petroleum Contractors Ltd., 1980-82; bd. dirs. P.S. Contractors A/S, Norcon, Inc., OFC of Alaska, Inc., V.E. Systems Services, Inc., Veco Turbo Services, Inc., Veco Drilling, Inc., Vemar, Inc., 1978-82; with Coopers & Lybrand, Anchorage, 1982-85; field underwriter, registered rep. New York Life Ins., 1985—; instr. acctg. U. Alaska, 1971-72; lectr. acctg. and taxation Am. Coll. Life Underwriters, 1972, instr. adv. sales Life Underwriters Tng. Coun., 1988-89; bd. dirs. Aetna Devel. Corp., 1985-86. Div. chmn. United Way, 1975-76, YMCA, 1979; bd. dirs., fin. chmn. Anchorage Arts Council, 1975-78, Am. Diabetes Assn., Alaska affiliate, 1985—, chmn. 1988-89, Am. Heart Assn., Alaska affiliate, 1986-87. With U.S. Army, 1967-68. Mem. AICPA, Alaska Soc. CPAs, Petroleum Accts. Soc. (bd. dirs. Alaska 1976; nat. tax com. 1978-80), Fin. Execs. Inst. (pres. Alaska chpt. 1981-83), Internat. Assn. Fin. Planners, Am. Soc. CLUs, Nat. Assn. Life Underwriters, So. Alaska Assn. Life Underwriters, Alaska Assn. Life Underwriters (sec., treas. 1987—), Million Dollar Roundtable, Rotary, Beta Alpha Psi. Clubs: Alaska Goldstrikers Soccer; Petroleum; Rainier. Home: 4421 E Huffman Rd Anchorage AK 99516 Office: 1400 W Benson Blvd Anchorage AK 99503

TREVOR, BRONSON, economist; b. N.Y.C., Nov. 12, 1910; s. John Bond and Caroline Murray (Wilmerding) T.; A.B., Columbia Coll., 1931; m. Eleanor Darlington Fisher, Nov. 8, 1946; children—Eleanor, Bronson, Caroline. Own bus., 1931—; dir., asst. sec. Northwestern Terminal R.R., 1952-58; chmn. bd. Texinia Corp.,. Former dir. chmn. fin. com. Gen. Hosp. of Saranac Lake mem. Council for Agrl. and Chemurgic Research, Am. Forestry Assn. Mem. Republican County Com. of N.Y. County, 1937-39; leader in primary election campaigns N.Y. County, 1937, 38, 39 to free local Rep. party orgn. from leftwing affiliations; mem. Nat. Rep. Club. Served with U.S. Army, 1942, World War II. Mem. S.A.R., Soc. Colonial Wars.

Clubs: Union, Knickerbocker, Racquet and Tennis, Piping Rock. Author: (pamphlet) The United States Gold Purchase Program, 1941; also numerous articles on econ. subjects. Home: Paul Smith's NY 12970 Office: POB 182 Oyster Bay NY 11771

TREYBIG, JAMES G., computer company executive; b. 1940. Mkgt. mgr. Hewlett-Packard Co., 1968-72; with Kleiner and Perkins, 1972-74; with Tandem Computer Inc., Cupertino, Calif., 1974—, now pres., chief exec. officer, dir. Office: Tandem Computers Inc 19333 Vallco Pkwy Cupertino CA 95014 *

TRIBBLE, RICHARD WALTER, brokerage executive; b. San Diego, Oct. 19, 1948; s. Walter Perrin and Catherine Janet (Miller) T.; m. Joan Catherine Sliter, June 26, 1980. BS, U. Ala., Tuscaloosa, 1968; student, Gulf Coast Sch. Drilling Practices, U. Southwestern La., 1977. Stockbroker Shearson, Am. Express, Washington, 1971-76; ind. oil and gas investment sales, Falls Church, Va., 1976-77; pres. Monroe & Keusink, Inc., Falls Church and Columbus, Ohio, 1977-87; institutional investment officer FCA AssetMgmt., 1983-85; fin. cons. Merrill Lynch Pierce, Fenner & Smith, Inc., Phoenix, 1987-89, cert. fin. mgr, fin. cons., 1989—. Served with USMC, 1969-70. Mem. Renaissance Athletic Club. Republican. Methodist. Office: 2929 E Camelback Rd Phoenix AZ 85016

TRICE, WILLIAM HENRY, paper company executive; b. Geneva, N.Y., Apr. 4, 1933; s. Clyde H. T.; m. Sandra Clayton, July 16, 1955; children—Russell, Amy. B.S. in Forestry, State U. N.Y., 1955; M.S., Inst. Paper Chemistry, Appleton, Wis., 1960, Ph.D., 1963. With Union Camp Corp., 1963—, tech. dir. bleached div., 1972-74; v.p., corp. tech. dir. research and devel. Union Camp Corp., Wayne, N.J., 1974-79; sr. v.p. tech. Union Camp Corp., 1979-85, exec. v.p., 1985—. Trustee, pres. Western Mich. U.-Paper Tech. Found.; mem. adv. com. So. Forest Research Center N.C. State U.; pres. Syracuse Pulp and Paper Found. Served with USAF, 1955-57. Fellow TAAPI (bd. dirs. 1978-81), Indsl. Research Inst. (alt. rep.), Inst. Paper Chemistry (bd. trustees), Inst. Paper Chemistry (exec. commn. alumni assn.). Home: 6 Hanover Rd Mountain Lakes NJ 07046 Office: Union Camp Corp 1600 Valley Rd Wayne NJ 07470

TRIEN, JAY WILLIAM, accountant; b. Hillside, N.J., May 1, 1940; s. Louis Trien and Beatrice (Haines) Garfield; m. Ildiko Eva Brayer, Aug. 5, 1973; 1 child, Ooana Louise. BS in Econs., U. Pa., 1962; JD, Rutgers U., 1966; cert. in exec. edn., Harvard U., 1985. Bar: N.J. 1966; CPA, N.Y., N.J. Prin. Trien & Trien, Newark, N.J., 1968-70; ptnr. Weiner & Co., N.Y.C. and Morristown, N.J., 1970—; mng. ptnr. Weiner and Co., Morristown, 1986—. Pres. United Cerebral Palsy, East Orange, N.J., 1973-75; pres., bd. dirs., treas. THE BRIDGE, Caldwell, N.J., 1975—; treas. Jewish News, E. Orange, 1983-85; adv. com. mem. Sta. WNET, Newark, 1982—; bd. govs. Newark Acad., Livingston, N.J., 1980-84. Mem. Am. Inst. CPA's, N.J. Soc. CPA's, N.Y. State Soc. CPA's, N.J. Bar Assn. Clubs: Green Brook Country (Caldwell, N.J.), Morristown; Harvard (Boston), Princeton (N.Y.C.). Home: 1 Old Mill Rd North Caldwell NJ 07006 Office: Weiner & Co CN 1982 177 Madison Ave Morristown NJ 07960

TRIGG, PAUL REGINALD, JR., lawyer; b. Lewistown, Mont., Mar. 25, 1913; s. Paul Reginald and Opal Stella (Fay) T.; m. Helen Ruth Leake, Dec. 25, 1938; children: Paul Reginald III, Mary Adra. BA, Grinnell Coll., 1935; JD, U. Mich., 1938. Bar: Mich. 1938. Practiced law in Detroit; ptnr. Dykema, Gossett, Spencer, Goodnow & Trigg (and predecessor), 1938—; chmn. exec. com., dir. Dallas Corp.; bd. dirs. Alma Piston Co., Crowley Milner & Co. Mem. ABA, Mich. Bar Assn., Detroit Bar Assn. Clubs: Detroit, Detroit Country, Yondotega. Office: Dallas Corp 6750 LBJ Freeway Dallas TX 75240

TRIGG, SHARI JENELL, broadcasting executive; b. Lawton, Okla., Sept. 21, 1957; d. Jasper Alphonso and Aurora Lou (Cooke) T. BS, Northwestern U., 1978. Asst. mgr. The Ltd., Chgo., 1978; advt. asst. Bentley, Barnes & Lynn Advt., Chgo., 1978-79; account mgmt. trainee Leo Burnett Advt., Chgo., 1979-80, WMAQ-TV, Chgo., 1980-88; acct. exec. Sta. Fox 32/WFLD-TV, Chgo., 1988—; sales account exec. Sta. WMAQ-TV, Chgo., 1980—; spl. events com. mem. Broadcast Advt. Club Chgo., 1981—, also bd. dirs. Mem. employer adv. bd. Project Skil-Disadvantaged Youth Employment Service, Chgo., 1982-83, chair adv. bd., 1983—, pres. employer aux. bd., 1982-86; co-chmn. Friends of the El-Commuter Group, Chgo., 1978; trustee Lawrence Hall Sch. for Boys, 1985-86. Recipient Outstanding Leadership award YWCA Met. Chgo., 1982, named Outstanding Achiever of Industry, 1983, One of Outstanding Young Women of Am, 1984. Mem. NAFE, Chgo. Urban League, Delta Sigma Theta, Inc. (mem planning com. 75th anniversary celebration, nat. mktg. rep. 1987—, nat. info. and communications com. 1988—), NBC Variety Soc. (com. chmn. 1983). Democrat. Unitarian. Office: Fox 32/WFLD-TV Sales 205 N Michigan Ave Chicago IL 60601

TRIMBLE, MATTHEW ALAN, electrical engineer; b. Harrisburg, Pa., Oct. 11, 1949; s. Lloyd Emerson and Melicent Margaret (Dick) T.; m. Ruth Marie Krysher, June 20, 1970; children: Mark, Jonathan, Matthew David, Michael. Grad., high sch., Dillsburg, Pa. Registered electrician, Pa. Electrician York Shipley Inc., Pa., 1970-72; electrician, owner Strinestown Electric Service, Manchester, Pa., 1972-76, Carlisle, Pa., 1986—; instrument technician Commonwealth of Pa., Harrisburg, 1976-79; bldg. maintenance supr. United Telephone Co. Pa., Carlisle, 1979-80; nuclear instrument and control techician Job Shopper Cos., 1980-86; extensive study in energy mgmt. lighting tech.; with Combustion Enging., Winsor, Conn., 1981; indsl. field engr. Midland Nuclear Plant-Consumers Power, 1982. Vol. firefighter Borough of Carlisle, 1980—, Strinestown Community Fire Co., Manchester, 1970-79. Republican. Mem. Assembly of God. Ch. Clubs: South Mountain (pres. 1975-76), Citizens Radio Service Inc. (sec. 1968-69, 78-79). Home and Office: 264 Henderson Ave Carlisle PA 17013-2016

TRIMBLE, PAUL JOSEPH, lawyer; b. Springfield, Mass., Oct. 9, 1930; s. Peter Paul and Bernnese (Myrick) T.; children—Troy, Derrick. B.A., Am. Internat. U., Springfield, Mass., 1952; LL.B., U. Tex., Austin, 1955. Bar: Calif., Tex., Ill., Alaska. Counsel Mobil Oil Corp., Joliet, Ill., 1964-72; assoc. counsel Fluor Corp., Irvine, Calif., 1972-73, corp. counsel, 1973-74, sr. corp. counsel, 1974, asst. gen. counsel, 1974-80, gen. counsel, 1980-82, sr. v.p., gen. counsel, 1982—, sr. v.p. law, gen. counsel, 1984—. Mem. ABA, Calif. Bar Assn., Tex. Bar Assn., Ill. Bar Assn., Alaska Bar Assn. Republican.

TRIMBLE, THOMAS JAMES, utility company executive; b. Carters Creek, Tenn., Sept. 3, 1931; s. John Elijah and Mittie (Rountree) T.; m. Glenna Kay Jones, Sept. 3, 1957; children: James Jefferson, Julie Kay. BA, David Lipscomb Coll., 1953; JD, Vanderbilt U., 1956; LLM, NYU, 1959. Bar: Tenn. 1956, Ariz. 1961, U.S. Dist. Ct. Ariz. 1961, U.S. Dist. Ct. D.C. 1963, U.S. Ct. Appeals (10th cir.) 1971, U.S. Supreme Ct. 1972, U.S. Ct. Appeals (9th cir.) 1975. From assoc. to ptnr. Jennings, Strouss & Salmon, Phoenix, 1960-85, mng. ptnr., 1985-87; sr. v.p., gen. counsel S.W. Gas Corp., Las Vegas, Nev., 1987—. Mem. editorial bd. Vanderbilt U. Law Rev., 1954-56. Mem. Pepperdine U. Bd. Regents, Malibu, Calif., 1981—, sec., mem. exec. com., 1982—; mem. bd. visitors Pepperdine Sch. Law, Malibu; pres. Big Sisters Ariz., Phoenix, 1975, bd. dirs., 1970-76; chmn. Sunnydale Children's Home, Phoenix, 1966-69, bd. dirs., 1965-75; pres. Clearwater Hills Improvement Assn., Phoenix, 1977-79, bd. dirs., 1975-80; trustee Nev. Sch. of Arts, 1988—. Served to 1st lt. JAGC, USAF, 1957-60. Fellow Ariz. Bar Found. (founding); mem. ABA, Ariz. Bar Assn. (editorial bd. Jour. 1975-80), Am. Gas Assn. (legal sect. mng. com.), Pacific Coast Gas Assn. (legal adv. com. 1987—), Energy Ins. Mut. Ltd. (bd. dirs. 1988—), Order of Coif, Phi Delta Phi. Republican. Mem. Ch. Christ. Club: Spanish Trail Country (Las Vegas). Lodge: Kiwanis (pres. Phoenix 1972-73). Home: 5104 S Turnberry Ln Las Vegas NV 89113 Office: SW Gas Corp PO Box 98510 5241 Spring Mountain Rd Las Vegas NV 89193-8510

TRINER, ALMA, public relation executive; b. N.Y.C., Feb. 17, 1925; d. Abraham and Frances (Tennenbaum) T.; children: Susan, Kim. BA, Bklyn. Coll., 1944. With Daniel J. Edelman, Inc., Chgo., N.Y.C., 1953-62; dir. pub. relations, gen. pub. Macmillan, Inc., N.Y.C., 1963-67, asst. v.p. corp. pub. relations, 1967-74; v.p. pub. relations Arthur D. Little, Inc., Cambridge, Mass., 1975-88; mng. dir. Corporate Initiatives, Boston, 1988—; br. dirs. The Marcomm Group; mem. adv. bd. Pub. Relations News, N.Y.C., 1982—. Bd. dirs. Nat. Hair Techs.; trustee Endicott Coll., Beverly, Mass., 1982—; mem. adv. bd. Ft. Point Arts Community, Boston, 1988—. Recipient Matrix award Women in Communications, Boston, 1981. Mem. Pub. Relations Soc. Am., Pub. Affairs Council. Office: Corp Initiatives 66 Long Wharf St Boston MA 02110

TRINGALE, ANTHONY ROSARIO, insurance executive; b. Syracuse, N.Y., Apr. 20, 1942; s. Anthony and Susan Marie (Cerio) T.; B.S.F.S., Georgetown U., 1967; CLU, Am. Coll. Life Underwriters, 1973; children: Anthony William, Michael Paul, Mark David, Amber Marie. Cert. mktg. exec. Office mgr. trainee N.Y. Life Ins. Co. No. Va., 1965-66, office mgr. Fairfax, 1966, field underwriter, 1966-68, asst. mgr., 1968-73, mgmt. asst., home office, N.Y.C., 1973, gen. mgr. Pitts. gen. office, 1973-76; gen. mgr. Acacia Mut. Life Ins. Co., Annandale, Va., 1976-83; fin. and ins. planner, mgmt. and mktg. cons., 1983-86; pres. Ins. Cons. Group (iCG), Annandale, 1986—; pres., Acacia Prodn. Clubs, 1984, 86; field rep. to mktg. com. Acacia Mut. Life, 1983-86; lectr. estate and employee and exec. fringe benefit plans and retirement programs, bus. ins. and communications; mem. steering com. Entrepreneurship Forum, Washington, 1982—; nat. adv. bd. The Entrepreneurship Inst., Columbus, Ohio, 1985—. Trustee SME-I Accreditation Inst., Memphis State U.; chmn. mktg. edn. adv. bd. Commonwealth of Va., 1988—; liaison rep. Am. Soc. CLU's, Bryn Mawr, Pa.; bd. dirs., exec. com. No. Va. Community Found.; founding vice chmn. Fairfax Orgn. Christians/Jews United in Service (FOCUS); arbitrator Fairfax County Dept. Consumer Affairs; lector, extraordinary minister Nat. Shrine of Immaculate Conception; past chmn. planned giving com. ARC; v.p. bd. dirs., exec. com. Jeane Dixon's Children to Children Found.; chmn. VIP panel United Cerebral Palsy campaign, 1978-89, bd. dirs. 1985—, v.p. exec. com. 1988—, D.C.and No. Va.; mem. bd. mktg. and distributive edn. Fairfax County Schs. (past chmn.), 1978—; vice chmn. adv. bd. Fairfax County Vocat. Edn., 1978-88. Mem. No. Va. Soc. CLUs (past pres.), Am. Soc. CLU's (liaison team rep.), No. Va. Assn. Life Underwriters (treas. 1972), Assn. Advanced Life Underwriting, Sales and Mktg. Execs. Met. Washington (pres. 1979-80, exec. com. 1982-84, bd. dirs. 1989—), Nat. Assn. Life Underwriters (nat. mgmt. award Gen. Agts. and Mgrs. Conf., 1976-83; exec. com. 1984-85, life, qualifying) No. Va. Estate Planning Council (exec. com. 1985—, 1st v.p. 1988—), Internat. Platform Assn. (trustee, bd. govs.), No. Va. Gen. Agts. and Mgrs. Assn. (pres. 1980-81, dir. 1982-83), Greater Washington Assn. Health Underwriters, Fairfax County C. of C. (small bus. com., bd. dirs.), Annandale C. of C., Sales and Mktg. Execs. Internat. (area dir., internat. dir. 1982-84, regional v.p. 1984-85, sr. v.p. 1986-87, trustee), Nat. Italian Am. Found, Council of 1000, Venture Clinic No. Va. Roman Catholic (lector, instr.). Contbr. articles in field of personal and business fin. strategies to Md. Bus. Observer; local radio host Current Edition Sta. WGMS-FM. Office: Ins Cons Group 7700 Little River Turnpike Suite 222 Annandale VA 22003

TRINH, Q. BINH, electronic executive; b. Bui-Chu, Vietnam, Apr. 25, 1944; came to U.S., 1967; s. Don and Ry (Pham) T.; m. Thanh K. Tran; 1 child, Josephine. LLB, Saigon U., Rep. of Vietnam, 1966; MBA, U. Wis., 1970; MSc, U. B.C., 1973. Dir. corp. planning Fed. Industries & Subs., Winnipeg, Man., Can., 1974-82; v.p. fin. Codart Com. Inc., Novato, Calif., 1982-83; v.p. Bailard, Biehl & Kaiser Inc., San Mateo, Calif., 1983-84; v.p. fin., dir. Sigma Designs Inc., Fremont, Calif., 1984—. Mem. Fin. Exec. Inst. Home: 604 San Nicholas Ln Foster City CA 94404 Office: Sigma Designs Inc 46501 Landing Pkwy Fremont CA 94538

TRIPP, THOMAS NEAL, lawyer, political consultant; b. Evanston, Ill., June 19, 1942; s. Gerald Frederick and Kathryn Ann (Siebold) T.; m. Ellen Marie Larrimer, Apr. 16, 1966; children: David Larrimer, Bradford Douglas, Corinne Catherine. BA cum laude, Mich. State U., 1964; JD, George Washington U., 1967. Bar: Ohio 1967, U.S. Ct. Mil. Appeals 1968, U.S. Supreme Ct. 1968. Sole practice, Columbus, Ohio, 1969—; real estate developer, Columbus, 1969—; chmn. bd. Black Sheep Enterprises, Columbus, 1969—; polit. cons. Keene, Shirley & Assocs., Washington, 1986—; vice chmn. bd. Sun Valley-Elkhorn Assn., Idaho, 1983-85, chmn. 1986—; vice chmn. Sawtooth Sports, Ketchum, Idaho, 1983-85; legal counsel Wallace F. Ackley Co., Columbus, 1973—; bd. dirs. KWRP Broadcasting Corp., 1986—; presiding judge Ohio Mock Trial Competition, 1986—; bd. dirs. U.S. Master's Swimming, Ohio. Trustee Americans for Responsible Govt., Washington, GOPAC; mem. Peace Corps Adv. Council, 1981-85; mem. U.S. Commn. on Trade Policy and Negotiations, 1985-88; campaign mgr., fin. chmn. Charles Rockwell Saxbe, Ohio Ho. of Reps., 1974, 76, 78, 80; campaign mgr. George Bush for Pres., 1980, nat. dep. field dir., 1980; mem. alumni admissions council Mich. State U., 1984—; regional co-chmn. Reagan-Bush, 1984, mem. nat. fin. com., 1984; mem. Victory '84 fin. com.; mem. Victory '88 fin. com. Bush-Quayle; co-chmn. Ohio Lawyers for Bush/Quayle, 1988; Rep. candidate 2d U.S. Congl. Dist., Idaho, 1988. Served to capt. U.S. Army, 1967-69. Fellow Pi Sigma Alpha; mem. Vietnam Vet. Am., Phi Delta Phi. Republican. Avocations: swimming, tennis, skiing, writing, political essays. Home: 5420 Clark State Rd Gahanna OH 43230-1956

TRIPP, WILLIAM KARL, marketing executive; b. Pottsville, Pa., Apr. 13, 1948; s. Albert William and Phyllis Louise (Klingeman) T.; m. Nancy Diane Rassiga, July 12, 1975. BS in Econs., U. Pa., 1970; postgrad., U. Mass., 1971-75. Project dir. Simmons Market Research Bur., N.Y.C., 1977-80; account exec. NFO Research, Inc., N.Y.C., 1980-81; project supr. NPD Research, Inc., Port Washington, N.Y., 1981-83; v.p. Opinion Research Corp., Princeton, N.J., 1983-85, Decision-Making Info. Co., McLean, Va., 1985-86; mng. dir. Data and Mgmt. Counsel, Inc., McLean and Bala Cynwyd, Pa., 1986—. Bd. dirs., mem. exec. com. Entrepreneurs' Forum Phila., 1987—. Mem. Am. Assn. Pub. Opinion Research, Am. Sociol. Assn., Am. Mktg. Assn., World Affairs Council D.C. Clubs: Princeton, U. Pa. (N.Y.C.) (bd. govs. 1980—). Office: Data and Mgmt Counsel Inc 110 Montgomery Ave Bala-Cynwyd PA 19004

TRIPPE, CHARLES WHITE, financial and development executive; b. N.Y.C., Jan. 30, 1935; s. Juan Terry and Elizabeth (Stettinius) T.; m. Pamela Reid; children: Charles Jr., James R., Elizabeth, Carie. BS in Engring., Yale U., 1957; MBA, Harvard U., 1959. V.p. fin. Intercontinental Hotels, N.Y.C., 1962-66; v.p., treas. Pan Am, N.Y.C., 1966-69, v.p. planning, 1969-71; v.p. corp. devel. Pan Am., N.Y.C., 1971-77; v.p. planning Bell & Howell, Chgo., 1978-85; ptnr. and founder Trippe & Co., Greenwich, Conn., 1985—; chmn. AmPro Corp., Liberia Devel. Corp., The Liberia Co.; pres. Bermuda Properties, Ltd. Club: Links (N.Y.C.), Round Hill (Greenwich).

TRISCHLER, FLOYD D., real estate executive, consultant; b. Pitts., Aug. 31, 1929; s. Edward C. and Margaret (Sirlin) T.; m. Gloria N. Fusting, June 30, 1951; children: Thomas J., John D., Annette M., Nannette L., Rene L., Denise M. BS, U. Pitts., 1951; postgrad. San Diego State U., 1953-56, postgrad. in bus. adminstrn., 1963-69. Cert. master real estate cons. Program dir. Whittaker Corp., San Diego, 1963-71; exec. v.p. Turner Devel., Indpls., 1971-73; pres. Guadalupe Developers, Inc., Indpls., 1973-78; pres. Iroquois Realty, Inc., Indpls., 1978—, also dir; cons. NASA, Huntsville, Ala., 1963-69, Rincon Indian Reservation, Escondido, Calif., 1969-71, Promotora Ritco Alpemex, Cancun, Mex., 1985, Sistema Promos, Cancun, 1987. Author publs. Patentee in polymer chemistry. Vol. Central State Hosp., Indpls., 1984—; notary pub., Indpls., 1980—; mem. Scottish Rite Chorus; mem. nat. publicity com. Nat. Pow-wow VII, 1987. Mem. Nat. Assn. Home Builders, Indpls. Builders Assn., Indpls Bd. Realtors, Ind. Bd. Realtors, Nat. Assn. Real Estate Cons., Midwest Cherokee Alliance, VFW. Republican. Roman Catholic. Lodges: Masons, Tecumpseh. Home: 8249 Filly Ln Plainfield IN 46168 Office: Iroquois Realty Inc 8249 Filly Ln Plainfield IN 46168

TRISKO, THOMAS, health care executive; b. Mpls., Jan. 24, 1945; s. Edward Carl and Adaline Gracia (Schneider) T. BA, St. John's U., Collegeville, Minn., 1963-67; student, Georgetown U., 1967-68; MA, U. Minn., 1971. Asst. prof. St. John's U., Collegeville, Minn., 1968-69; research analyst State of Minn. and U.S. Govt., St. Paul and Washington, 1967-72; strategic planning mgr. Dayton Hudson Corp., Mpls., 1972-75; planning and govt. affairs dir. Medtronic Inc., St. Anthony, Minn., 1975-78; fin. planning dir. Pickwick div. Am. Can Co., St. Louis Park, Minn., 1978-80; fin. dir. The Home Ins. Co., Edina, Minn., 1980-83; chief fin. officer Crest View Luth. Home, Mpls., 1985-88; pres. TeleHealth, Inc., Mpls., 1988—; pres. Strategy Assoc. Inc., Mpls., 1975—. Contbr. article in book Micropolis in Transition, 1968. State cen. com., 1986-88, conv. del., precinct capt. Dem. Farm Labor Party, St. Paul, 1970—; community faculty, bd. mem. Minn. Metro State U., St. Paul. 1971—; pres., treas. Calhoun Isles Home Owners Assn., Mpls., 1983—. Mem. Health Care Fin. Mgmt. Assn., Nat. Assn. Accts. Dem. Farmer Labor. Roman Catholic. Clubs: Gamma (bd. dirs.), Calhoun Beach. Home: 3120 Dean Ct Minneapolis MN 55416 Office: TeleHealth Inc 1516 W Lake St Suite 103 Minneapolis MN 55408

TRIVEDI, BAL C., financial consultant; b. Mahuva, Gujarat, India, Mar. 23, 1943; s. Chhotalal J. and Bhanuben Trivedi; m. Urmila B., Jan. 19, 1969; 1 child, Shilpa B. BSc, St. Xavier's Coll., 1961; BSME, Bihar Inst. Tech., Sindri, India, 1965; MSME, U. Houston, 1976, MBA in Fin., 1978. Registered profl. engr., Tex.; registered securities prin. Engring. supr. Bechtel Power Corp., Houston, 1974-77, 79-84; sr. engr. Brown & Root Corp., Houston, 1977-79; fin. cons. Merrill Lynch, Houston, 1984-85, First Met. Fin. Services, Houston, 1985—; chmn. Mech. Engring. Soc., Binar Inst. Tech., 1965; pres. NDT Corp., Houston, 1981-83, Metropolis, Inc., Houston, 1984—. Mem. Nat. Productivity Council, Bombay, 1967-70. Mem. ASME, NSPE, Nat. Assn. Realtors, Nat. Assn. Securities Dealers. Hindu. Home: 3919 Mayfield Oaks Ln Houston TX 77088 Office: First Met Fin Svcs 6420 Hillcroft St Houston TX 77081

TRIVELPIECE, CRAIG EVAN, computer electronics executive; b. Pasadena, Calif., Apr. 23, 1957; s. Alvin William and Shirley Ann T. Student, Calif. Inst. Tech., 1974-75; BA in Physics, U. Md., 1979. Scientist Maxwell Labs, San Diego, 1979-81; design engr. Rockwell Internat., Costa Mesa, Calif., 1981-83; mgr. engring. Tex. Instruments, Irvine, Calif., 1983-84; owner, mgr. CST Engings Inc., Irvine, 1984—; cons. Payview Ltd., Hong Kong, 1985—. Co-inventor: Video Scrambling System, 1985. Republican. Home: 3715 W Balboa Ave Newport Beach CA 92663 Office: CST Engring Inc 2070 Business Center Dr #200 Irvine CA 92715

TROAN, JOHN TRYGVE, lawyer, accountant; b. Mpls., Nov. 6, 1932; s. Trygve and Blanche Maggie (Goff) T.; m. Janet Lillian Cook, March 21, 1953; 2 children: Gordon Trygve, Janine Henderson. BSL, U. Minn., 1959, JD, 1961; PhD, John Marshall U., Chgo., 1963. Bar: Minn. 1961, U.S. Supreme Ct. 1970. Prosecutor, criminal tax div. U.S. Govt., 1961-68; atty. Troan Law Firm, Coon Rapids, Minn., 1968-71; tax atty., chief exec. officer Five Star Enterprises, Inc., Phoenix, 1971—; arbitrator Phoenix Better Bus. Bur., 1981—. Contbr. articles to profl. jours. Commr. Coon Rapids Planning and Zoning Commn., 1965-69; mem. Village Planning Com., Phoenix, 1974—; mem. State Dem. Cen. Com., Minn. and Ariz., 1968—; mem. ct. discipline Evang. Luth. Ch. in Am., Grand Canyon Synod. Served to lt. col. USAF, 1951-55. Mem. Nat. Assn. Tax Consultors, Phoenix C. of C., Internat. Jaycees (senator Minn. and Ariz. 1966—), Am. Legion. Democrat. Lutheran. Office: Five Star Enterprises Inc 10635 N 19th Ave Phoenix AZ 85029

TROEGER, CURTIS RALPH, advertising executive; b. St. Louis, Jan. 24, 1931; s. Alfred Donald and Bernice Elizabeth (Kleisley) T.; m. Joyce Earline Thurmon, 1953; children: Melody Beth, Susan Elaine, Curtis Ralph Jr., Elizabeth Ann. BA, Culver-Stockton Coll., Canton, Mo., 1953; postgrad., Pace U., 1966-67. Credit mgr. Chase Manhattan Bank, N.Y.C., 1955-56; advt. sales rep. N.Y. Times, 1956-61, resort and travel mgr., 1961-65, radio and TV advt. mgr., 1965-69, fin. advt. mgr., 1970-71; v.p. Doremus & Co., N.Y.C., 1971-74, sr. v.p., 1974-82, exec. v.p., 1982-85, pres., 1985-86, chmn., chief exec. officer, 1986—. Served as cpl. U.S. Army, 1953-55. Mem. Fin. Communications Soc. (pres.), Advt. Club N.Y. Republican. Episcopalian. Clubs: Downtown Assn., Bond of N.Y. Home: 135 Oenoke Ridge New Canaan CT 06840 Office: Doremus & Co 120 Broadway New York NY 10271 *

TROIANO, ROBERT JOSEPH, JR., banker; b. N.Y.C., Feb. 13, 1953; s. Robert Sr. and Elizabeth (Nims) T.; m. Sharon Linda Handy; children: Chauncey, Keely. BA, Brown U., 1975; MBA, Stanford U., 1978. CPA, Calif., N.Y. Auditor Touche Ross And Co., San Francisco, 1978-81; investor relations mgr. Marine Midland Banks Inc., N.Y.C., 1982—, capital planning mgr., 1984—, portfolio mgr., 1985—; pres. Tri-Log Properties, N.Y.C., 1986—. Mem. Stanford Black Alumni Assn. Home: 423 Grand Blvd Westbury NY 11590

TROILO, JOSEPH CARMEN, supermarket executive; b. Phila., Mar. 7, 1934; s. Joseph and Susie (Maiuri) T.; m. Anita Costanzo, Sept. 15, 1956; children—Lisa, Vicki, Marc. Student, U. Pa., 1960. C.P.A., Pa. Controller Foodarama Supermarkets Inc., Freehold, N.J., 1968, v.p. fin., 1974, sr. v.p. fin., 1984-88, treas., 1988—. Served with AUS, 1954-56. Mem. Am., Pa. insts. C.P.A.'s. Home: 3542 Windmill Circle Huntingdon Valley PA 19006 Office: Foodarama Supermarkets Inc PO Box 592 303 W Main St Freehold NJ 07728

TROJAN, VERA MARIA, banker; b. N.Y.C., Sept. 5, 1960; d. Myroslaw and Nadia (Perehiwsky) T. AB in Econs., Princeton U., 1982; MBA, Harvard U., 1987. Econs. educator U. East Asia, Macau, 1982-83; analyst First Boston Corp./CSFB, N.Y.C., 1983-85; asst. to Robert V. Roosa Brown Brothers Harrimant & Co., N.Y.C., 1987—. Contbr. articles to profl. jours. Office: Brown Bros Harriman & Co 59 Wall St New York NY 10005

TROLIO, WILLIAM MICHAEL, health care executive, educator; b. Amsterdam, N.Y., July 12, 1947; s. Morino Fiorello and Jeanne Estelle (Lawrence) T.; m. Judith Mary Starr, Sept. 27, 1969; children: Kristen Marie, Matthew Lawrence. A in Applied Sci., Hudson Valley Community Coll., Troy, N.Y., 1968; BS, SUNY, Albany, 1972; MBA, Northland U., Toronto, Ont., 1983. Lic. clin. lab. scientist. Med. technician Faxton Hosp., Utica, N.Y., 1968-69; mktg. devel. specialist Gen. Electric Co., Milw., 1969-74; mktg. devel mgr. Bio Data Corp., Hatboro, Pa., 1974-79; lab. mgr. Cen. Maine Med. Ctr., Lewiston, 1979-80; gen. mgr. lab. services Mary Imogene Basset Hosp., Cooperstown, N.Y., 1980—; adj. clin. prof. med. tech. Utica Coll., Syracuse U., 1980—; adj. clin. faculty Broome County Community Coll., Binghamton, N.Y., 1984—. Editor; Cen. N.Y. Clin. Lab. Assn. bull., 1984-88; contbr. articles to profl. jours. Asst. leader Weblo's Boy Scouts Am. Fellow Bus. Adminstrn. Can. Sch. Mgmt., 1983. Mem. North Eastern N.Y. Hosp. Assn., Hosp. Assn. of N.Y. (rep.), Clin. Lab. Mgmt. Assn. (chpt. pres 1987—, legis. liaison bd. 1984), Iroquois Hosp. Consortium (various coms. 1985—), Am. Soc. Clinical Pathologists (assoc.), Mid Atlantic Health Cong., CSM Alumni Club. Republican. Roman Catholic. Clubs: MIB Investment (Cooperstown). Home: Rd 1 Box 23D Fly Creek NY 13337 Office: Mary Imogene Basset Hosp One Atwell Rd Cooperstown NY 13326

TROM, BRADLEY L., insurance company representative; b. Austin, Minn., Nov. 30, 1955; s. Lowell Irving and Evelyn Grace (Gross) T. Grad. high sch., Blooming Prairie, Minn. Agt. Nat. Farmers Unio Ins. Cos., Rochester, Minn., 1978—; owner Stockbury (Am. Eagle Gold and Silver Bullion Coins), Rochester, Minn., 1985—. Author: The Collie Fanciers Handbook, 1984; editor The Collie Fanciers Nat. Pedigree Directory of Stud Dogs and Brood Matrons, 1983. Mem. Am. Assn. of Crop Insurers, Minn. Farmers Union, Olmsted County Farmers Union (pres. 1988—), Rochester Coin and Stamp Club (treas. 1987—), Rochester Kennel Club (show chmn. 1982—), Collie Club of Am. Home: PO Box 5789 Rochester MN 55903-5789 Office: Nat Farmers Union Ins Cos 2409 52 N W Frontage Rd Ste 1307 Rochester MN 55901-8313

TROMBLEY, JOSEPH EDWARD, insurance company executive, underwriter, financial planner; b. Hartford, Conn., Aug. 15, 1935; s. Joseph Lawrence and Helen Agnes (Crowley) T.; m. Claire Marie Jenkins, Sept. 20, 1958; children: Patricia A. Trombley Barone, Kevin C. BS, U. Conn., 1957. CLU; chartered fin. cons. Sales rep. Met. Life & Affiliated Co., Bridgeport, Conn., 1960-63; asst. mgr. Met. Life & Affiliated Co., Nyack, N.Y., 1963-66; field trainer Met. Life & Affiliated Co., Albany, N.Y., 1966-68, advance underwriting adviser, 1968-69; mgr. Met. Life & Affiliated Co., Glens Falls, N.Y., 1969—; instr. Successful Money Mgmt. Seminars, Glens Falls, 1987—. Bd. dirs. Adirondack chpt. ARC, Glens Falls, 1982—; mem. adv. bd. N.Y. State Dept. Ins., Albany, 1985—. 1st lt. U.S. Army, 1958-60. Mem. Tri-County Life Underwriters (bd. dirs. 1969—, Man of Yr. 1983), Am. Soc.

CLUs, (Northeastern chpt.), Estate Planning Coun. Northeastern N.Y., Rotary (bd. dirs. Glens Falls chpt. 1982-85). Avocations: golf, woodworking, antiques, traveling. Office: Met Life Ins Co 420 Glen St PO Box 788 Glens Falls NY 12801

TRONE, DONALD BURNELL, investment company executive; b. Gettysburg, Pa., Jan. 22, 1954; s. Donald Burnell and Mary Ann (Moreau) T.; m. Virginia Christman; children: Tara C., Donald Timothy. BS in Govt., USCG Acad., 1977; MS in Fin. Svcs., Am. Coll., Bryn Mawr, Pa., 1989. Lic. real estate and stock broker. Commd. ens. USCG, 1977, advanced through ranks to lt. comdr., 1988; fin. planner Fla. Fin. Advisers, Tampa, 1987; sr v.p. Investment Adv. Svcs. of Raymond James, St. Petersburg, Fla., 1987—. Actor, pilot (film) Cocoon, 1985. Recipient Sikorsky Heroism award United Techs., 1981. Mem. Internat. Bd. Cert. Fin. Planners (dir. 1987—), Nat. Assn. Realtors, Nat. Assn. Security Dealers. Republican. Episcopalian. Home: 2620 Lakeside Circle Palm Harbor FL 34684 Office: Investment Adv Svcs PO Box 14508 880 Carillon Pkwy Saint Petersburg FL 33716

TRONNIER, BILL FREEMAN, insurance company executive; b. McAlester, Okla., Oct. 20, 1935; s. William Monroe and Jessie (Newman) T.; m. Marie E. Janda, Mar. 27, 1957 (div. 1986); m. Randi Susan Weir, Nov. 7, 1987; children: Kenneth Freeman, Monique Elise, Nathan Wade. AA, Wesleyan coll., 1970; BBA, U. Tulsa, 1973. Asst. dir. Phillips Petroleum co., Bartlesville, Okla., 1971-79; v.p. Parker Drilling Co., Tulsa, 1979-86; v.p., mng. dir. Casuarina Ltd., Bermuda, 1981-86; pres., chief exec. officer Rock Island Internat. Ltd., Bermuda, 1982-86; v.p. energy div. Alexander & Alexander Tex. Inc., Dallas, 1986-89; v.p. Marsh & McLennan, Inc., Tulsa, 1989—; bd. dirs., chmn. adv. and underwriting com. Wrenford Ins. Ltd., Bermuda, 1981-86; bd. dirs. Petroleum Ins. Conf., N. Tex. U.; lectr., cons. in field. Mem. Okla. Soc. Ins. Mgmt. (mem. nat. Risk Ins. Mgmt. Soc. editorial adv. bd. 1979-86, pres., bd. dirs.). Office: Marsh & McLennan Inc 1579 E 21st St Tulsa OK 74114

TRONSRUE, GEORGE MARION, JR., financial counselor; b. St. Paul, Minn., July 15, 1930; s. George M. and Ruth (Cote) T.; m. Florence Kubicki, Jan. 22, 1954; children: Barbara, George M. III, Karin. BS, U.S. Mil. Acad., 1952; MPA, Princeton U., 1966. Cert. fin. planner. Comd. 2d lt. U.S. Army, 1952, advanced through grades to col., retired, 1977; account exec. Dean Witter Reynolds, Inc., San Diego, 1978-85; fin. cons. CIGNA Individual Fin. Service Co., 1985-87; owner, fin. counselor Tronsrue & Assocs., San Diego, 1987—. Contbr. articles to profl. jours. Bd. dirs. San Diego County Coun. Boy Scouts Am., 1979-87; elder Presby. Ch. U.S.A., 1983—. Decorated Silver Star. Mem. Internat. Assn. Fin. Planning (v.p. San Diego chpt. 1987-88), Inst. Cert. Fin. Planners. Republican. Office: Tronsrue & Assocs 4370 LaJolla Village Dr #400 San Diego CA 92122

TROSINO, VINCENT JOSEPH, insurance company executive; b. Upland, Pa., Nov. 19, 1940; s. Sylvester N. and Stella Trosino; m. Patricia Ann Gibney, June 18, 1960; children: Laura, Valerie, Vincent Jr. BS in Psychology, Villanova U., 1962; MS in Psychology, Ill. State U., 1973. Ops. supr. State Farm Mut. Auto Ins. Co., Springfield, Pa., 1962-67; personnel mgr. State Farm Mut. Auto Ins. Co., Bloomington, Ill., 1970-72, dir. personnel, 1972-74, corp. v.p., 1986-87, exec. v.p., 1987—, also bd. dirs.; div. mgr. State Farm Mut. Auto Ins. Co., Costa Mesa, Calif., 1974-75, dep. regional v.p., 1976-80; regional v.p. State Farm Mut. Auto Ins. Co., Wayne, N.J., 1981-85; bd. dirs. State Farm Fire & Casualty Co., State Farm Life Ins. Co., State Farm Internat. Services, State Farm Investment Mgmt. Corp., all Bloomington. Bd. dirs. Chilton Hosp., Pompton Lakes, N.J., 1982-85, Jr. Achievement, McLean County, Ill., 1971, McLean County Law and Justice Com., 1970, McLean County Alcohol and Drug Assistance Corp., 1970-74. Mem. N.J. Ins. News Service (pres. 1984-85, bd. dirs.), N.J. Joint Underwriting Assn. (bd. dirs. 1982-85). Office: State Farm Ins Cos 1 State Farm Plaza Bloomington IL 61710

TROTTER, SHIRLEY ANN, computer specialist, educator; b. Oklahoma City, Nov. 30, 1934; d. Charles George and Bessie Lee (Armstrong) Huber; BS in Bus. Edn., Oklahoma City U., 1961, MA in Teaching Math., 1973; m. George Monroe Hilton Trotter, Jr., Oct. 11, 1980; children: Darrell Lynn, Darren Lee Smith; stepchildren: David, Paige. Tchr. math. and bus., Putnam City Schs., Oklahoma City, 1961, 69-79; adminstrv. asst. Nat. Assn. Mature People, Oklahoma City, 1979; instr. FAA, Oklahoma, 1979-81; co-founder, pres. DocuWrite, Inc., Bethany, Okla., 1981-83; CBT analyst First Data Mgmt. Co., Oklahoma City, 1981-83; mgr. Interactive Product Devel., Advanced Systems, Inc., Arlington Heights, Ill., 1983-84; computer specialist, analyst Computer Data Systems Inc., Rockville, Md., 1984-85, Office of Naval Reserach, Arlington, Va., 1985, Booz, Allen & Hamilton, Inc., Arlington, 1985-87, Applied Sci. Assocs., Inc. Landover, Md., 1987-88; asst. dir. of spl. programs, U. Md. Univ. Coll., 1988-89; cons. in field, College Park, 1989—; adj. faculty El Reno (Okla.) Jr. Coll., Okla. State U. Tech. Inst. Mem. alumni bd. Oklahoma City U., 1963-64; past pres. The Lakes Property Owners; active Presbyn. Ch. of Absecon, N.J. Mem. Assn. Devel. Computer-Based Instructional Systems, Am. Soc. Tng. and Devel., Balt.-Washington Instructional Systems Educators Assn., Am. Evaluation Assn., Mensa, Beta Gamma. Democrat. Home and Office: 120 S Concord Terr Absecon NJ 08201

TROUBH, RAYMOND STANLEY, financial consultant; b. Portland, Maine, May 3, 1926; s. Maurice J. and Sadye (Brickman) T.; m. Jean Troubh, May 28, 1971; children: Amy, John. AB, Bowdoin Coll., Brunswick, Maine, 1949; LLB, Yale U., 1952. Lawyer Sullivan & Cromwell, N.Y.C., 1954-58; investment banker Lazard, Freres & Co., N.Y.C., 1958-73; fin. cons. Troubh & Co., N.Y.C., 1974—; bd. dirs. Applied Power Inc., Becton, Dickinson & Co., Manville Inc., Warner Communications Inc. Mem. Bd. Overseers Bowdoin Coll. Mem. Legal Aid Soc. Office: 10 Rockefeller Plaza New York NY 10020

TROUPE, TERRY LEE, holding company banker; b. Ephrata, Pa., Apr. 17, 1947; s. Jacob I. and Mary J. (Shober) T.; m. Judy A. Hagy, May 28, 1966; children—Todd L., Brenda R. B.S., Pa. State U. C.P.A., Conn. Auditor Arthur Andersen & Co., Hartford, Conn., 1969-73; exec. v.p., chief fin. officer Am. Bank and Trust Co. Pa., Reading, 1973-85; vice chmn., chief fin. officer Meridian Bancorp, Inc., Reading, 1985—; dir., chmn. Meridian Funding Corp., Reading, Pa.; bd. dirs. Meridian Mortgage Corp., Devon, Pa., Meridian Title Ins. Co., Reading, Am. Title Ins. Co., Miami Fla., Meridian Del. Investment, Inc. Bd. dirs. Reading Hosp. & Med. Ctr; mem. adv. bd. Pa. State U. Mem. Am. Inst. C.P.A.s, Bank Adminstrn. Inst. (rep.), Fin. Execs. Inst., Am. Inst. Banking, Pa. Bankers Assn. (legis. policy com., chmn. agy. relations com.). Republican. Mem. United Ch. of Christ. Office: Meridian Bancorp Inc 35 N 6th St PO Box 1102 Reading PA 19603

TROUTMAN, WILLIAM M., cement and concrete company executive; b. 1940; married. BS, Cornell U., 1962; JD, U. Mich., 1965. With Medusa Corp., 1961-83, former pres.; exec. v.p. domestic ops. Lone Star Industries Inc., Greenwich, Conn., 1983-86, pres., chief operating officer, 1986—, also dir. Office: Lone Star Industries Inc 1 Greenwich Pla Box 5050 Greenwich CT 06836 *

TROWBRIDGE, ALEXANDER BUEL, JR., trade association executive; b. Englewood, N.J., Dec. 12, 1929; s. Alexander Buel and Julie (Chamberlain) T.; m. Eleanor Hutzler, Apr. 18, 1981; children by previous marriage: Stephen C., Corrin S., Kimberly. Grad., Phillips Acad., Andover, Mass., 1947; AB cum laude, Princeton U., 1951; LLD (hon.), D'Youville Coll., 1967, Hofstra U., 1968, Hobart Coll. and William Smith Coll., 1975. With Calif. Tex. Oil Co., 1954-59; ops. mgr. Esso Standard Oil S.A. Ltd., Panama C.Z., 1959-61; div. mgr. Esso Standard Oil S.A. Ltd., El Salvador, 1961-63; pres., mgr. div. Esso Standard Oil Co., P.R., 1963-65; asst. sec. commerce for domestic and internat. bus. U.S., 1965-67; sec. of commerce 1967-68; pres., chief exec. officer Am. Mgmt. Assn., N.Y.C., 1968-70; pres. The Conf. Bd., Inc., N.Y.C., 1970-76; vice chmn. bd. Allied Chem. Corp., 1976-80; bd. dirs. Nat. Assn. Mfrs., Washington, 1978—, pres., 1980—; bd dirs. New Eng. Mut. Life Ins. Co., PHH Corp., Waste Mgmt., Inc., Rouse Co., Sun Resorts Ltd. N.V., Warburg Pincus Counsellors Funds. Trustee Phillips Acad., Andover, Mass.; bd. dirs. Enterprise Found.; mem. Pres.'s Task Force on Pvt. Sector Initiatives, Pres.'s Commn. on Social Security, 1982; mem. Nat. Commn. on Exec. Legis. and Jud. Salaries, 1985. Served with USMCR, 1951-53; maj. Res. Decorated Bronze Star with combat V; recipient Arthur Flemming award, 1966, Pres.'s E cert. for export service, 1968, Bryce Harlow award for Bus.-Govt. Relations. Mem. Coun. Fgn. Rels., Met. Club, Georgetown City Club, Links, Univ. Club. Home: 1823 23d St NW Washington DC 20008 Office: Nat Assn Mfrs 1331 Pennsylvania Ave NW Ste 1500 Washington DC 20004

TROWBRIDGE, AMELIA ANN, real estate company executive; b. Birmingham, Ala., July 24, 1945; d. William Clinton and Dicie Ozella (Black) Barton; m. John Charles Crow, July 27, 1967 (div. Apr. 1977); m. Charles Arthur Trowbridge, Mar. 1, 1981. BS, Auburn U., 1967. Econ. analyst Urban Cons., Montgomery, Ala., 1967-69; mgr. Paraphenalia, Atlanta, 1969-71; sales assoc. Harry Norman Realtors, Atlanta, 1972-74, dir. client rels., 1979-81; sales mgr. Coldwell Banker, Atlanta, 1975-79; dir. broker svcs. Hometrend, Denver, 1983—, sec., treas., 1984—; treas. C.I. Devel., Denver, 1987—. Vol., mem. guild Denver Symphony, 1981-85, Denver chpt. Juvenile Diabetes Found., 1985-88; vol. Opera Colo., Denver, 1985; bd. dirs. Temple Emanuel Restoration, Denver, 1985-88. Mem. Nat. Assn. Realtors, Denver Bd. Realtors, Am. Mgmt. Assn. Republican. Methodist. Home: 7151 Apache Dr Sedalia CO 80135 Office: Hometrend 3600 S Beeler St Ste 300 Denver CO 80237

TROWBRIDGE, KEITH WAYNE, business owner, consultant; b. Sarnia, Ont., Can., Mar. 6, 1937; s. Albert Bernard and Dorothy Jean (Kemsley) T.; m. Doris Millicent Gillespie, June 20, 1981; children: Michael, David. BS, Bowling Green U., 1961; MBA, Bowling Green State U., 1966; PhD, U. Mich., 1971. Dir. instl. research Bowling Green (Ohio) State U., 1963-68; assoc. U. Mich., Ann Arbor, 1968-69; asst. to pres. Fla. Internat. U., Miami, 1969-73; pres. Captran, Sanibel, Fla., 1974-86; owner Vacation Shoppe, Sanibel, 1982—; cons. Time Share, Ft. Myers, Fla., 1984—. Author: Resort Time Share, 1981, Real Estate Broker's Guide to Time Sharing, 1984. Named Alumnus of Yr., Bowling Green State U., 1981. Mem. Alpha Tau Omega. Republican. Lodge: Kiwanis (pres. Sanibel chpt.). Home: 1270 Bay Dr Sanibel Island FL 33957

TROXELL, REBECCA LYNNE, information systems professional; b. Winston-Salem, N.C., July 23, 1959; d. John Cline and Elevee Era (Ammons) T. BS, U. N.C., 1983. Cert. info. systems profl. Instr. Guilford Tech. Community Coll., Jamestown, N.C., 1982; info. system staff AT&T Tech., Greensboro, N.C., 1983—. Mem. N.C. Clogging Coun., Inc., treas. 1988—, Nat. Clogging Hoedown Coun. Mem. Nat. Assn. Female Execs., Quill & Scroll, Am. Clogging Hall fo Fame, Clog Leaders Orgn. Am., N.C. Clogging Council. Republican. Club: Deep River Cloggers (dir. 1987—).

TROYER, ALVAH FORREST, seed corn company executive, plant breeder; b. LaFontaine, Ind., May 30, 1929; s. Alvah Forrest and Lottie (Waggoner) T.; m. Joyce Ann Wigner, Sept. 22, 1950; children: Anne, Barbara, Catherine, Daniel. B.S., Purdue U., 1954; M.S., U. Ill., 1956; Ph.D., U. Minn., 1964. Research assoc. U. Ill., Urbana, 1955-56; research fellow U. Minn., St. Paul, 1956-58; research sta. mgr. Pioneer Hi-Bred Internat., Inc., Mankato, Minn., 1958-65, research coordinator, 1965-77; dir. research and devel. Pfizer Genetics, St. Louis, 1977-81, v.p. and dir. research and devel., 1981-82; v.p. research and devel. De Kalb-Pfizer Genetics, Ill., 1982—; researcher corn breeding, econ. botany, increasing genetic diversity. Contbr. articles to numerous publs.; developer of popular corn inbreds and hybrids. Served with U.S. Army, 1951-53, Korea. Fellow AAAS, Am. Soc. Agronomy, Crop Sci. Soc. Am.; mem. Am. Genetic Assn., Genetic Soc. Am., N.Y. Acad. Sci., CAST, Sigma Xi, Gamma Sigma Delta, Alpha Zeta, Lambda Chi Alpha, Gamma Alpha, VFW. Methodist. Lodge: Masons. Home: 611 Joanne Ln De Kalb IL 60115 Office: DeKalb-Pfizer Genetics 3100 Sycamore Rd De Kalb IL 60115

TRUBECK, WILLIAM LEWIS, air transportation company executive; b. Chgo., July 5, 1946; s. G. William and Priscilla Jeanne (Nelson) T.; m. Judith Carpenter Williams, Aug. 17, 1969; 1 child, William Andrew. BA, Monmouth Coll., Ill., 1968; MBA, U. Conn., 1976. Fin. sales mgr. Ford Motor Credit Co., Walnut Creek, Calif. and Stamford, Conn., 1971-74; v.p. Aetna Bus. Credit (Barclays Am. Corp.), East Hartford, Conn., 1974-81; corp. v.p., treas. Armco Inc., Middletown, Ohio and Parsippany, N.J., 1981-89; exec. v.p. fin. and chief fin. officer Northwest Airlines Inc. and NWA Inc., St. Paul, 1989—. Served to capt. C.E., U.S. Army, 1968-70, Vietnam. Mem. Fin. Execs. Inst., Nat. Assn. Corp. Treas., Blue Key, Pi Gamma Mu. Republican. Presbyterian. Office: NW Airlines Inc Mpls-St Paul Internat Airport Saint Paul MN 55111

TRUCKSESS, JAMES MORGAN, JR., real estate finance company executive; b. Phila., Nov. 29, 1931; s. James Morgan and Anna Cecilia (Patton) T.; m. Susan Stanley Power, Dec. 17, 1960; children: Lisa Von, Eric Morgan, Kristen Von, Jeffrey Morgan. BS, Temple U., 1953; postgrad., NYU, 1956-60. Mortgage loan rep. Equitable Life Assurance, N.Y.C., 1955-62; sr. v.p. Tchr.'s Ins. and Annuity Assn., N.Y.C., 1962-75, CitiBank, N.Y.C., 1975-82; exec. v.p. Merrill Lynch Pierce Fenner & Smith, N.Y.C., 1982-83; pres. Real Estate Advisors Ltd., N.Y.C., 1983—; bd. dirs. Park Ave Savs. & Loan Assn., N.Y.C., 1988—. Mem. REal Estate Bd. N.Y. Mortgage Bankers, Urban Land Inst., Nat. Assn. Indsl. Office Parks. Republican. Presbyterian.

TRUDEL, JOHN DAVIS, electronics company executive; b. Trenton, N.J., Aug. 1, 1942; s. LeRoy Renee and Elizabeth Etta (Reading) T. BEE cum laude, Ga. Inst. Tech., 1964; MEE, Kans. State U., 1966. Research and devel. project engr. Collins Radio Co., Richardson, Tex., 1966-67; sr. engr. Sanders Assocs., Inc., Nashua, N.H., 1967-68; sr. electronic system engr. LTV Electrosystems, Inc., Greenville, Tex., 1968-69; sr. engr. Collins Radio Co., Richardson, 1969-70; project engr. F & M Systems, Co., Dallas, 1970-71; pres. Sci. System Tech., Inc., Richardson, 1971-74; product mgr. portable oscilloscopes Tektronix, Inc., Beaverton, Oreg., 1974-82, mgr. application mktg. Lab. Instrument div., 1983-84; v.p. mktg. Cable Bus. Systems Corp., Beaverton, 1982-83; mktg. mgr. Tektronix Labs., 1984-87, gen. mgr. new products team, 1988—. Primary author of MAGIC, gen. purpose microwave computer-aided design program; contbr. articles to profl. jours. Mem. nat. adv. bd. Am. Security Council, 1974—. Recipient Scholastic award Lambda Chi Alpha, 1963-64; Western Electric scholar, State of N.J. scholar, McLendon scholar; NDEA Grad. fellow. Mem. IEEE, Assn. Old Crows, Am. Mktg. Assn., Nat. Avionics Soc., Automatic R.F. Techniques Group, Am. Electronics Assn., Aircraft Owners and Pilots Assn., Tau Beta Pi, Eta Kappa Nu. Roman Catholic. Office: Tektronix Labs MS 50-230 PO Box 500 Beaverton OR 97077

TRUE, PALMER DEXTER, software company executive; b. Orange, N.J., Mar. 6, 1933; s. Howard Dexter and Ruth Callender (McMurtrie) T.; m. Norma Jean Dempsey, Aug. 22, 1954 (div. 1979); children: Ellen Elizabeth, Bruce Dexter, Brian Palmer; m. Jean Rice, Sept. 9, 1984. BS, Northwestern U., 1954, MBA, 1957. Various positions Corning (N.Y.) Glass Works, 1957-67; mgr. prodn. planning Polaroid Corp., Cambridge, Mass., 1967-69, prodn. control mgr., 1969-73, prodn. mgr., 1973-77; v.p., gen. mgr. Hendrix Electronics, Manchester, N.H., 1977-78; dir. distbn. Instrumentation Lab., Lexington, Mass., 1978-79, dir. ops., 1979-82; v.p. ops. Lotus Devel. Corp., Cambridge, 1983—. Sgt. U.S. Army, 1954-56. Methodist. Home: 1572 Massachusettes Ave Cambridge MA 02138 Office: Lotus Devel Corp 55 Cambridge Pkwy Cambridge MA 02142

TRUEBLOOD, GENE EDWARD, insurance company executive; b. Anderson, Ind., July 25, 1951; s. Harold Edward Trueblood and Phyllis Jean (Gowen) Crabill; divorced: 1 child, Aaron Edward. BA in Econs., Ind. U., 1973, MBA in Fin., 1982. Securities analyst Indpls. Life Ins. Co., 1973-83, mgr. securities, 1983-87, v.p. securities, 1987—; v.p. Indpls. Life Investment Mgmt., Inc., 1986—. Pres. Rise Learning Ctr., PTA, Indpls., 1987-88. Fellow Inst. Chartered Fin. Analysts, Fin. Analysts Fedn. (del. 1986-88); mem. Indpls. Soc. Fin. Analysts (bd. dirs. 1985—, pres. 1986-87). Home: 510 Griffin Rd Indianapolis IN 46227 Office: Indpls Life Ins Co 2960 N Meridian St Indianapolis IN 46208

TRUELL, GEORGE ANDREW, personnel administrator; b. Westfield, N.Y., Aug. 31, 1959; s. George Foster and Patricia Angeline (Stitt) T.; m. Rebecca Jean Hohenstein, June 1, 1985; children: Alexander Jay, John Andrew. BS in Indsl. Rels., Purdue U., 1981. Personnel advisor Consumers Power Co., Flint, Mich., 1981-83; sr. staff asst. Amstar Corp., Bklyn., 1983-85; employment mgr. Frito-Lay, Inc., Overland Park, Kans., 1983-86; supr. personnel adminstrn. Playtex Family Products, Inc., Dover, Del., 1987—. Citizens adv. bd. mem. Pyschotherapy and Tng. Ctr., Flint, 1983. Mem. Am. Soc. Personnel Adminstrs., Alpha Epsilon Pi (scribe 1980-81). Home: 212 N Governors Ave Dover DE 19901 Office: Playtex Family Products Inc PO Box 7016 Dover DE 19901

TRUESCHLER, BERNARD CHARLES, utility executive; b. Balt., Jan. 3, 1923; s. Philip Joseph and Gertrude Cecilia (Carey) T.; m. Helen Rita Golley, Nov. 19, 1956; children: John G., Jeanne C., Paul C., Mary K. B.A. in Chemistry, Johns Hopkins U., 1947; LL.B., U. Md., 1952. With Balt. Gas & Electric Co., 1948-88, v.p. gas ops., 1971-74, pres., 1974—, chmn. bd., 1980-88, also dir.; bd. dirs. Signet Banking Corp., Johns Hopkins U., Fidelity & Deposit Co. Md., Bank of Va. Bd. dirs. Bus. and Industry Polit. Action Com., Southeastern Electric Exchange, St. Joseph Hosp., Balt. Symphony Orch.; trustee Council Econ. Edn. in Md., Md. Hist. Soc., Community Found. Greater Balt.; chmn. Md. Bus. Roundtable. Served with AUS, 1944-46. Mem. Am. Gas Assn., Kappa Alpha. Republican. Roman Catholic. Clubs: Balt. Country (Balt.), Center (Balt.) (gov.). Office: Baltimore Gas & Electric Co Gas Building 19th Floor PO Box 1475 Baltimore MD 21203

TRUITT, KENNETH RAY, hospital administrator; b. Greensboro, N.C., Feb. 21, 1945; s. Marvin Lee Truitt and Edna Lindsey (Sheffield) Brower; m. Linda Alice Morrison, 1965 (div. 1973); children: Maria Paige, Lisa Christine; m. Victoria Ruth Mize, Aug. 23, 1975. BS in Math., U. N.C., 1970; MS in Indsl. Engring., U. Mo., 1972. Lab. technician Pitts. Testing Lab., Greensboro, 1963-65; indsl. insulation estimator Starr-Davis Co., Greensboro, 1965-66; cons. indsl. engring. dept. Cone Mills Corp., Greensboro, 1968-70; grad. teaching asst. U. Mo., Columbia, 1970-71; dir. mgmt. engring. Med. Ctr., Columbia, 1971-74; dir. mgmt. svcs. Med. Coll. Va., Richmond, 1974-75; dir. mgmt. engring. Bethany Med. Ctr., Kansas City, 1975-78, v.p. mgmt. svcs., 1978-86, v.p. planning, mktg., 1986—. Planning commr. City of Lake Quivira (Kans.). Mendenhall scholar U. N.C., 1970. Mem. Am. Mktg. Assn., Soc. Hosp. Planning and Mktg., Hosp. Info. Mgmt. Systems Soc., Inst. Indsl. Engrs. (assoc. dir. confs. 1979-80, pres. health svcs. div. 1981-82), Phi Beta Kappa, Pi Mu Epsilon, Alpha Pi Mu, Quivira Lake Country Club. Office: Bethany Med Ctr 51 N 12th St Kansas City KS 66102

TRULIO, DONNA MARIE, advertising executive; b. Boston, Sept. 3, 1958; d. Joseph and Patricia (O'Leary) T. BBA, Johnson State Coll., 1980. Lic. real estate salesman, Mass. Acctg. asst. Quinn & Johnson, Boston, 1980-83, asst. traffic mgr., 1983-85; sr. traffic mgr. Ingalls Quinn & Johnson, Boston, 1985-87, traffic supr., dept. head, 1987-88; traffic supr. Heller Breene Advt. and Design, Boston, 1988—. Home: 100 Washington St #18 Quincy MA 02169 Office: Heller Breene Advt. & Design 101 Arch St Boston MA 02110

TRUMBULL, STEPHEN MICHAEL, operations executive; b. Columbus, Ohio, Sept. 18, 1954; s. Clyde Austin and Patricia Ann (Ranck) T. MusB in Voice Performance and Choral Edn., DePauw U., Greencastle, Ind., 1977; postgrad., Ohio State U., 1982-85. Cert. profl. music educator, Ohio; cert. broker/dealer. Dir. vocal music Columbus City Schs., 1978-87; pres., owner Columbus Music Studios, 1984—; pres. The Trumbull Pub. Co., Washington, 1986—, Stephen M. Trumbull, Inc., Columbus, 1986—, Goldmark Securities Corp., Columbus, 1987—; exec. v.p. Hamilton Capital Corp., Columbus, 1988—, also bd. dirs., corp. v.p., sec., bd. dirs., 1987—; v.p. Hamilton Mktg. Corp., Columbus, 1988—, Kaiser Enterprises, Columbus, 1988—; pres. Shelter One Group Corp., Columbus, 1988—, also bd. dirs.; soloist First Community Ch., Columbus, 1982—; mktg. cons. Beckenhorst Press, Inc., Columbus, 1986-87. Adv. Lambda Chi Alpha, Ohio State U., 1982-87, chmn. alumni adv. bd., 1982-87; pres. Friends of Neoteric Dance Theatre, Columbus, 1986—; coordinator nat. co. competition Jr. Achievement Nat. Conf., Bloomington, Ind., 1985—; bd. dirs. Neoteric Dance Theatre, 1986—; mem. bus./mktg. com. Jr. Achievement Cen. Ohio Inc., 1987—; cons. The Source Group, Toronto, 1986—. Named Outstanding Alumni, Lambda Chi Alpha, 1984. Mem. Columbus Edn. Assn. Lodge: Optimist. Home: 119 E Willow St Columbus OH 43206 Office: 663 Park Meadow Ste D Westerville OH 43081

TRUMKA, RICHARD LOUIS, labor leader, lawyer; b. Waynesburg, Pa., July 24, 1949; s. Frank Richard and Eola Elizabeth (Bertugli) T.; m. Barbara Vidovich, Nov. 27, 1982; 1 child, Richard L. BS, Pa. State U., 1971; JD, Villanova U., 1974. Bar: U.S. Dist. Ct. (D.C.) 1974, U.S. Ct. Appeals (3d, 4th and D.C. cirs.) 1975, U.S. Supreme Ct. 1979. Atty. United Mine Workers Am., Washington, 1974-77, 78-79, internat. pres., 1982—; miner, operator Jones & Laughlin Steel, Nemacolin, Pa., 1977-78, 79-81; internat. exec. bd. Dist. 4 United Mine Workers Am., Masontown, Pa., 1981-82; bd. dirs. Am. Coal Found.; mem. Nat. Coal Council, 1985. Trustee Pa. State U. Democrat. Roman Catholic. Office: United Mine Workers Am 900 15th St NW Washington DC 20005

TRUMP, DONALD JOHN, real estate executive, casino owner; b. N.Y.C., 1946; s. Fred C. and Mary T.; m. Ivana Zelnicek, 1977; children: Donald Jr., Ivanka, Eric. Student, Fordham U.; BA, Wharton Sch. Fin., U. Pa., 1968. Pres. Trump Orgn., N.Y.C.; owner Trump Enterprises Inc., N.Y.C., The Trump Corp., N.Y.C., Trump Devel. Co., N.Y.C., Wembly Realty Inc., Park South Co., Land Corp. of Calif., Plaza Hotel, Trump Tower, Trump Plaza, Trump Parc, Trump Palace, all N.Y.C.; chmn., owner Trump Shuttle (formerly Ea. Air Shuttle); owner Trump Plaza, Trump Castle, Trump Taj Mahal, casinos, hotels, Atlantic City, Trump Plaza of the Palm Beaches, Fla., West Side Rail Yards to be devel. as Trump City, N.Y.C. Author: The Art of the Deal, 1987. Co-chmn. N.Y. Vietnam Vets. Meml. Fund; founding mem. constrn. com. Cathedral of St. John the Divine; mem. N.Y. Citizens Tax Council, Fifth Ave Assn., Realty Found. of N.Y., Met. Mus. of Art's Real Estate Council; bd. dirs. Police Athletic League; mem. adv. bd. Lenox Hill Hosp., United Cerebral Palsy; spl. advisor to Pres.'s Council on Physical Fitness and Sports; mem. N.Y. Sportsplex Commn.; bd. of overseers Wharton Sch.; mem. adv. bd. Wharton Real Estate Ctr.; bd. dirs. Fred C. Trump Found.; chmn. N.Y. citizens com. 78th Ann. NAACP Conv., 1987. Recipient Entrepreneur of Yr. award Wharton Entrepreneurial Club, 1984; inducted Wharton Hall of Fame. Office: Resorts Internat Inc 915 NE 125th St North Miami FL 33161

TRUMP, JOHN ROBERT, advertising executive; b. Evanston, Ill., Dec. 6, 1956; s. Robert Misel and Rosemary Utterback (DeLee) T. BBA, Washington and Lee U., Lexington, Va., 1979; M in Bus. with highest honors, Am. Grad. Sch. Internat. Mgmt., 1983. Brand asst. Procter & Gamble, Cin., 1979-80; account exec. Bozell & Jacobs, Phoenix, 1981-83, Foote, Cone, and Belding, L.A., 1983-88; advt. cons. Chgo., 1987—. Sustaining member Rep. Nat. Com., Washington, 1986. Mem. L.A. Ad Club, Ariz. Club (Phoenix/Scottsdale), Glen View Club (Golf, Ill.). Episcopalian. Home: 2618 Sheridan Rd Evanston IL 60201

TRUNCALE, JOSEPH PAUL, association executive; b. Newark, Nov. 4, 1955; s. Alfred F. and Jewel A. (Malizia) T.; m. Karen Anello, Mar. 24, 1985; 1 child, Alfred Alexander. BS, Monmouth Coll., 1977; MS, Rutgers U., 1983. Dir. communications and svcs. N.J.Assn. Realtors, Edison, 1977-83; mgr. programs Metal Powder Industry Fedn., Princeton, N.J., 1983-84; sr. staff dir. Nat. Assn. Printers and Lithographers, Teaneck, N.J., 1984—. Active state polit. campaigns. Mem. Am. Soc. Assn. Execs., N.J. Soc. Assn. Execs. (bd. dirs. 1987—). Republican. Roman Catholic. Office: Nat Assn Printers and Lithographers 780 Palisade Ave Teaneck NJ 07666

TRURAN, WILLIAM R., electrical engineer; b. Franklin, N.J., Feb. 14, 1951; s. Wilfred Hardy and Stella Eva (Hall) T.; m. Virginia Lynn Johnson, Aug. 18, 1979; children: Michael, Wendy. BSEE, U. Tenn., 1972; MBA, Fairleigh Dickinson U., 1981; PhD in Mgmt., Rutgers U., 1984. Registered profl. engr., Ind., N.J., N.Y., Calif., Fla. Design engr. Gordos Corp., Bloomfield, N.J., 1972-73; project engr. Edwards Engring., Pompton Plains, N.J., 1973-78; sr. engr. Apollo Tech., Whippany, N.J., 1978-81; elec. product mgr. Dodge-Newark, Fairfield, N.J., 1981—; pres. Trupower Engring., Sparta, N.J., 1984—; cons. in field. Contbr. articles to profl. jours. Republican. Episcopalian. Home and Office: 37 Rainbow Trail Sparta NJ 07871

TRUSKEY, DENNIS R., human resources director; b. Neptune, N.J., Jan. 3, 1958; s. George Leonard and Elizabeth Patricia T.; m. Rona Burnbaum, Sept. 17, 1988. BA, George Washington U., 1981, MA, 1985, EDS, 1987. Supr. personnel Preston, Thorgrinson, Ellis, & Holman, Washington, 1982-83; resident dir. Office Housing and Residence George Washington U., Washington, 1983-86; human resources mgmt. specialist Office Orgn. and Human Devel. U.S. Gen. Acctg. Office, Washington, 1986-88; human resources cordinator Future Enterprises Inc., Washington, 1988—. Mem. Am. Assocs. Coonsety and Devel., Am. Soc. Personnel Adminstrs., Amnesty Internat. Office: Future Enterprises Inc 1331 Pennsylvania Ave NW Washington DC 20004

TRUSLOW, ROBERT GURDON, banker; b. Summit, N.J., Mar. 23, 1936; s. William Auchincloss and Frances (Ray) T.; m. Sarah Anne Truslow, Mar. 9, 1968; children: Anne, Thomas. BA in History, Yale U., 1958; MBA, Columbia U., 1964. Asst. cashier Citibank, N.A., N.Y.C., 1964-68; mgr. Dennison Mfg. Co., Framingham, Mass., 1969-73; sr. v.p. Fleet Nat. Bank, Providence, 1973-83; ptnr. Kaufman & Co., Boston, 1983-85; pres. U.S. Trust Co., Boston, 1985—. Bd. dirs. Boys and Girls Clubs Boston, 1988—. Lt. USN, 1958-62. Mem. Robert Morris Assocs., Mass. Bankers Assn. (merger-conversion com.), Union Club (Boston) (bd. govs. 1987—). Home: 27 Farm Rd Sherborn MA 01770 Office: US Trust Co 40 Court St Boston MA 02108

TRUTTER, JOHN THOMAS, consulting company executive; b. Springfield, Ill., Apr. 18, 1920; s. Frank Louis and Frances (Mischler) T.; m. Edith English Woods II, June 17, 1950; children: Edith English II, Jonathan Woods. BA, U. Ill., 1942; postgrad., Northwestern U., 1947-50, U. Chgo., 1947-50; LHD (hon.), Lincoln Coll., 1986. Various positions Ill. Bell, Chgo., 1946-58, gen. traffic mgr., from asst. v.p. of pub. relations to gen. N. Suburban mgr., 1958-69, v.p. pub. relations, 1969-71, v.p. operator services, 1971-80, v.p. community affairs, 1980-85; mem. personnel staff AT&T, N.Y.C., 1955-57; pres. John T. Trutter Co., Inc., Chgo., 1985—; pres., chief exec. officer Chgo. Conv. and Visitors Bur., 1985-88; pres. Chgo. Tourism Council, 1988—; bd. dirs. NBD Bank, Evanston; mem. adv. bd. Alford and Assocs., Chgo., 1984—, Chgo. Apparel Industry Assn., 1987—; v.p. Chgo. Apparel Industry Found., 1988—. Co-author: Handling Barriers in Communication, 1957, The Governor Takes a Bride, 1977. Past pres. Hull House Assn.; chmn. United Cerebral Palsy Assn. Greater Chgo., v.p. nat. bd.; bd. dirs. Chgo. Crime Commn., Abraham Lincoln Assn., Lyric Opera Chgo.; v.p. English Speaking Union; chmn. bd. dirs. City Colls. Chgo. Found.; past chmn. Childrens Home and Aid Soc.; v.p. PruCare HMO, 1982-88; bd. dirs. Upper Ill. Valley Assn., vice chmn., 1988—; bd. dirs. Greater State St. Coun., 1988—; treas. Chgo. United, 1970-85; mem. Ill. Econ. Devel. Commn., 1985, Commn. on Improvement Cook County Circuit Ct. System, 1985—, Civic Com. for Domestic Relations Ct. Div., 1986—; past presiding co-chmn. NCCJ; bd. dirs. Ill. Humane Soc. Found.; chancellor Lincoln Acad. Ill., 1985—; numerous others; bd. govs. Northwestern U. Library Council, 1984—; trustee Lincoln (Ill.) Coll., 1987—, Mundelein Coll., 1988—; mem. State Ill. Assembly Sch. Problems Council, 1985—, spl. commn. on adminstrn. of justice in Cook County, 1986—; adv. bd. Art Resources in Teaching, 1987—, Dana Thomas House Found., 1988—. Served to lt. col. U.S. Army. Decorated Legion of Merit; recipient Outstanding Leadership award Chgo. West Project, 1985, Laureate award Lincoln Acad. Ill., 1980, Outstanding Civic Leader award Am. Soc. Fundraisers, Humanitarian of Yr. award, New Directions award SSMC, 1987. Mem. Pub. Relations Soc. Am., Sangamon County Hist. Soc. (founder, past pres.), Ill. State Hist. Soc. (pres. 1985-87), U. Ill. Alumni Assn. (bd. dirs. 1988—), Alpha Sigma Phi, Phi Delta Phi. Clubs: Tavern, Economic, Mid-America, City (v.p.). Home: 630 Clinton Pl Evanston IL 60201 Office: 225 W Randolph St Chicago IL 60606

TRYBER, THOMAS ANTHONY, JR., manufacturing company executive; b. Rapid City, S.D., May 18, 1943; s. Thomas A. and Rose Mary Tryber; student pub. schs., Racine, Wis; m. Kathleen M. Kober, May 25, 1963. Supr. cost and budgets J.I. Case, Racine, 1971-74, mgr. cost and budget control, 1974-77, fin. systems analyst, Wichita, Kans., 1977-78, mgr. systems and data processing, 1978-81; mgr. systems and data processing Steffens Dairy Foods Co., Inc., Wichita, Kans., 1982-87; system mgr. Hay & Forage Industries, 1988—. Mem. Data Processing Mgmt. Assn., Am. Prodn. Inventory Control Soc. Home: 2528 Milro Wichita KS 67204-2353 Office: Hay & Forage Industries PO Box 4000 Hesston KS 67062-2094

TRZCINSKI, RONALD E., mattress and bedding company executive; b. 1944; married. MBA, Univ. Va., 1971. Pres., dir. Ohio Mattress Co., Cleve.; v.p. Ohio Sealy Mattress Mfg. Co., Cleve., 1975-77, exec. v.p., from 1977, now pres., chief operating officer. Office: Ohio Mattress Co 1300 E 9th St Cleveland OH 44114 *

TRZNADEL, FRANK DWIGHT, JR., leasing company executive; b. Chgo., Feb. 7, 1942; s. Frank G. and Lorraine (Pachter) T.; children—Kelly Ann, Daniel Adam, C. Marc. B.S. in Bus. and Econs., Ill. Inst. Tech., 1968; M.S. in Taxation, De Paul U., 1974. C.P.A., Ill. Prodn. control exec. Anchor Coupling Co., Libertyville, Ill., 1961-67; asst. treas. J.B. Carroll, Chgo., 1967-68; tax exec. N.W. Industries, Chgo., 1968-72; sr. v.p. fin., treas. Comdisco, Inc., Rosemont, Ill., 1972-83, also dir.; sr. v.p. Comdisco, Inc., 1976-87; pres. Comdisco Investment Group, Inc., Rosemont, 1987—. Fellow Am. Inst. C.P.A.s, Ill. Soc. C.P.A.s. Republican. Roman Catholic. Office: Comdisco Investment Group 6111 N River Rd Rosemont IL 60018

TSAI, GERALD, JR., financial services corporation executive; b. Shanghai, China, Mar. 10, 1929; came to U.S., 1947, naturalized, 1954; s. Gerald and Ruth (Lea) T.; m. Cynthia Ekberg, Oct. 31, 1987; children: Gerald Van, Veronica Lee, Christopher. BA, MA in Econs., Boston U., 1949. Security analyst Bache & Co., N.Y.C., 1951-52; with Fidelity Mgmt. & Research Co., Boston, 1952-65; v.p. Fidelity Mgmt. & Research Co., 1960-63, dir., 1961-65, exec. v.p., 1963-65; chmn. Tsai Mgmt. & Research Corp., N.Y.C., 1965-68; exec. v.p., dir. CNA Fin. Corp., N.Y.C., 1968-73; chmn. bd., chief exec. officer Associated Madison Cos., Inc., 1978-86; dir. Am. Can Co. (now Primerica), 1982—, exec. v.p., 1982-83, vice chmn., 1983-86, chief exec. officer, 1986-88, pres., 1987-88; chmn., chief exec. officer Primerica, 1987-88. Office: Associated Madison Cos Inc 200 Park Ave New York NY 10166 also: Primerica Corp American Ln Greenwich CT 06836 *

TSCHAPPAT, DOUGLAS WILSON, utility executive; b. Martins Ferry, Ohio, Dec. 30, 1927; s. Charles Wesley and Bertha Mae (Anshutz) T.; m. Ellen L. Phillips, Feb. 6, 1949; children—Kay Tschappat Chamberlain, Karen Tschappat Gerber. B.S. in Mech. Engring, Chgo. Tech. Coll., 1951; A.M.P., Harvard U., 1983. Fireman B.&O. R.R., Lorain, Ohio, 1948-51; with Ohio Edison Co., 1951—; v.p., then sr. v.p. Ohio Edison Co., Akron, 1976-80; exec. v.p., chief operating officer, dir. Ohio Edison Co., 1980—; dir. Pa. Power Co., New Castle.; dir. Ohio Valley Electric Corp., Columbus, Ind.-Ky. Electric Corp.; mem. exec. bd. E. Cen. Area Reliability, Canton, Ohio, 1980—. Served with USN, 1946-48. Mem. ASME, IEEE, Am. Nuclear Soc., Atomic Indsl. Forum, Assn. Devel. Inland Navigation in Am.'s Ohio Valley (bd. dirs. 1986—). Clubs: Cascade, Portage Country, Akron City. Office: Ohio Edison Co 76 S Main St Akron OH 44308

TSE, STEPHEN YUNG NIEN, insurance executive; b. Shanghai, China, Feb. 14, 1931; came to U.S., 1949; s. Koong Kai Tse and Teh-Ying Koo Tse; student Ripon Coll., 1951-52; BBA, U. Wis., Madison, 1955; m. Margaret Miray Lock, Sept. 7, 1957; children: Chida, Chiming, Chiyung, Chikai. V.p. investments Am. Internat. Assurance Co., Hong Kong, 1962-64, fin. v.p., 1964-70; v.p. fgn. investments Am. Internat. Group, Inc., N.Y.C., 1971-82, sr. v.p., 1982—; pres., chief exec. officer AIG Assocs., 1986—; bd. dirs. Am. Internat. Assurance Co., Transatlantic Fund, Am. Internat. Underwriters, Ltd., Equitable Investment Co., Hong Kong Carpet Mfrs. Ltd., Worldwide Looms, Ltd., AIG Realty Inc., C.V. Starr & Co., Inc. Mem. Sky Club, Club at the World Trade Ctr., India House Club, Hong Kong Country CLub, Am. Club of Hong Kong, Royal Hong Kong Golf Club, Singapore Country Club, Beta Theta Pi. Office: Am Internat Group Inc 70 Pine St New York NY 10270

TSENG, HOWARD SHIH CHANG, business and economics educator, investment company executive; b. Tainan, Taiwan, Jan. 14, 1935; came to U.S., 1963; s. Picheng and Chaoliu (Wang) T.; m. Evelina M. Young, Dec. 25, 1965; 1 child, Elaine Evelina. BA, Nat. Taiwan U., Taipei, 1957, MA, 1963; PhD, U. Okla., 1972. Chief economist Cooperative Bank Taiwan, Taipei, 1959-61; dir. tax services Bur. Taxation, Govt. Taiwan, Republic China, Taipei, 1961-63; prof. bus. and econs. Catawba Coll., Salisbury, N.C., 1971—; pres. Am. Prudential Investments, Salisbury, 1981—; adj. prof., cons. Columbia Pacific U., San Rafael, Calif., 1981—. Author: Investments, 1982; contbr. articles to profl. jours. Coordinator, supporter study mathematically precocious youth Johns Hopkins U., Balt., 1982—; ptnr. World Vision, Caluf., 1986—. Academic research grantee Academia Sinica, Taipei, 1962; Ford Found. fellow, Taipei, 1963. Mem. Am. Assn. Univ. Profs., Eastern Econ. Assn., Am. Econ. Assn., Am. Assn. Individual Investors, Taiwan Investment (organizer 1986—). Club: National Travel. Home: 316 Bethel Dr Salisbury NC 28144 Office: Catawba Coll W Innes St Salisbury NC 28144

TSEU, FRED K., insurance company executive; b. Hunan, Peoples Republic of China, Nov. 19, 1923; came to U.S., 1930; s. Joseph Y. and Lillian (Choy) T.; m. Alice Y. Chu Tseu, Dec. 16, 1946 (div. Mar. 1958); 1 child, Eygenia; m. Edna K. Loo, Apr. 8, 1959; children: Steven F., Deborah M., Lori A. Chartered life underwriter. Sales agt. Security Life and Accident Co., Denver, 1947-53; asst. mgr. ins. sales Fin. Security Life, Honolulu, 1953-54; br. mgr. ins. sales Standard Ins. Co., Portland, Oreg., 1954-55; pres, mgr. ins. sales Guardian of Hawaii, Ltd., Honolulu, 1955—. St. chmn. com. Life Underwriters Polit. Action, 1978—; commr. neighborhood Boy Scouts Am., 1956; youth counselor YMCA, 1959-60; vol. solicitor Am. Heart Assn., ARC, 1950—; team leader Aloha United Way, 1968-80. With USN, 1942-45, WWII, 1950-51, Korea. Decorated Pacific Theatre medal, Am. Def. medal, Victory medal. Mem. Honolulu Assn. Life Underwriters (chmn. mem. com. 1949, legis. com. 1950), Wast Honolulu Assn. of Life Underwriters (chmn. 1976-78), Gen. Agt. and Mgr. Assn. (mem. com. 1985), Am. Soc. CLU's, Assn. Ind. Brokerage Agys. Republican. Home: 530 Ulukou St Kailua HI 96734 Office: Guardian of Hawaii Ltd 850 Richards St Ste 504 Honolulu HI 96813

TSOTSOROS, STATHIS, economist, management executive; b. Nafpactos, Greece, Apr. 22, 1949; s. Nicolaos and Julia (Mandelos) T.; m. Helen Harissis, Feb. 24, 1974; children: Nicolaos, Dimitris. MS in Elec. Engring., Nat. Tech. U., Athens, 1972; BS in Econs., U. Athens, 1978; PhD in Econs., Pantios Sch. Polit. Scis., AThens, 1982. Registered profl. engr. Dist. engr. Pub. Power Corp., Arcadia, Greece, 1974-75, head tech. sector, 1975-76; dist. dir. Pub. Power Corp., Arcadia-Argolis, 1976-81; dir. by gov. Pub. Power Corp., Athens, 1983-84; cons. Ministry of Energy, Greece, 1981-83; v.p. and governing council in charge Econ. Affairs Fin. and Mining Trust, Athens, 1984-85; v.p. and mng. dir. Bus. Reconstrn. Orgn., Athens, 1984-86; v.p. exec. com., dir. gen. Orgn. for Planning and Environ. Protection of Athens, 1986-88; cons. Hellenic Agy. for Local Govt. and Devel., Athens, 1987-88, feasibility studies and property value, ops. assessment, for indsl. enterprises, 1988—; chmn. 5-yr. plan formulation com. Ministry of Energy and Natural Resources, Greece, 1982-87, chmn. 5-yr. plan formultation com. of Ministry of Nat. Economy, Attica Region, 1988—; guest researcher evolution of Greek Indsl. Enterprises, Ctr. for Neohellenic Rsch. Nat. Rsch. Found., 1987—. Author: Economic and Social Mechanisms in the Highland Regions (1715-1828), Problematic (financially unstable) Industrial Enterprises and Public Law N. 1386/83; contbr. articles to profl. jours. Cpl. Army, Greece, 1972-73. Grantee Comml. Bank of Greece, 1984, Nat. Bank of Greece, 1987. Mem. Panhellenic Soc. Mech. and Elec. Engrs., Tech. Chamber of Greece, Econ. Chamber of Greece. Hellenic Socialist Party. Greek Orthodox. Home: 47 Ventouri St, 15562 Cholargos, Athens Greece Office: OPEPA, 30 Fokionos Negri, 11361 Athens Greece

TSUCHIYA, MASAHIRO, computer company executive; b. Kobe, Japan, May 23, 1948; s. Kiyoshi and Shizuko (Saito) T. BS, Konan U., Kobe, 1965; PhD, U. Tex., 1972. Prof. computer sci. Northwestern U., Evanston, Ill., 1973-74; prof. U. Calif., Irvine, 1974-76, U. Hawaii at Manoa, Honolulu, 1976-79; pres. Computer Progress Unltd., Honolulu, 1977-80; mgr. Def. Systems Group TRW, Inc., Redondo Beach, Calif., 1980-87; pres. Sypex Internat. Co., Kailua, Hawaii, 1986—. Contbr. over 30 articles to profl. jours. Mem. Computer Soc. of IEEE (sr.). Home and Office: PO Box 1199 Manhattan Beach CA 90266-8199

TSUKIOKA, MITSUKO (HSIU-JEN LIU), commercial firm executive; b. Taipai, Taiwan, Republic of China, Mar. 22, 1940; came to Japan, 1965.; s. Tien and Shao (Lin) Liu; m. Yasunori Matsumura, Sept. 24, 1959; children: Lie-Jun, Kan-Li, Lie-Shin, Chien-Chia. BBA, Lincoln U., San Francisco, 1984. With Japan Showa Kosan Co., Ltd., Tokyo, 1966-73, Sanshi Co., Ltd., Tokyo, 1973-80; pres. So An Co., Ltd., Taipei, Taiwan, 1979—, Sanwa Shoji Co., Ltd., Tokyo, 1980—; exec. Pres. Ent. Corp., 1975—, Ky. Fried Chicken, Taiwan, 1980—, Chain Store Corp., 1979—; pres. Leisure Corp., 1989—. Fellow World Scout Found., Geneva. Recipient 30th Anniversary medal and Letter of Appreciation, Magistrate of Nan-Tao Prefecture, Taiwan, 1981, Social Service Silver medal, Minister of Interior, Taiwan, 1982, Hua-Hsia medal, Pres. of Republic of China, 1987; The Baden-Powell World fellow World Scout Found., 1985. Home: Sanwa Bldg 4th Floor, 4-21-4 Ryohgoku, Sumida-ku, Tokyo 130, Japan Office: Sanwa Shoji Co Ltd, 1-20-1 Shinkawa, Chuo-ku, Tokyo 104, Japan

TUBBS, RICHARD HOLMES, JR., bank executive, educator; b. Providence, May 31, 1946; s. Richard Holmes and Patricia Honor (Hynes) T.; m. Carolyn Ann Smiles, Sept. 2, 1967 (div. Apr. 1985); children: Richard Holmes III, Nicole Marie; m. Kay Ann Krusemark, May 25, 1985. AB in English, Coll. of the Holy Cross, 1967. Asst. v.p. Citizens Savs. & Loan, Silver Spring, Md., 1972-76; dir. pub. affairs Internat. Snowmobile Industry Assn., Washington, 1976-77; asst. v.p. mktg. Equitable Savs. and Loan, Wheaton, Md., 1978-80; v.p. Providence Savs. and Loan, Vienna, Va., 1981—; adj. prof. Montgomery Coll., Rockville, Md., 1976-84; instr. Inst. of Fin. Edn., Chgo., 1977-84. Co-author: Management Issues, 1985; speaker seminars; contbr. articles to profl. jours. Pres., bd. deacons Vienna Presbyn. Ch., 1985-86, elected ruling elder, 1986—; founder, dir. Have a Heart campaign, 1984-89, pres., 1989—. Recipient World award for mktg. excellence Fin. Instn. Mktg. Assn., 1974. Mem. Inst. Fin. Edn. (v.p. 1982-84, pres. 1984-85, Writers Excellence award, 1983, 84). Republican. Home: 19843 Bazzellton Pl Gaithersburg MD 20879 Office: Providence Savs & Loan Assn 527 Maple Ave E Vienna VA 22180

TUCHSCHER, ARLEEN, public relations executive, public speaker; b. San Mateo, Calif., Sept. 24, 1938; d. Fayette A. and Mercedes (Castelleon) Carlin; children: Monica, Tom, Terrese, Denise, Alena. BBA, Nat. U., 1983, M. in Telecommunications, 1984. Polit. cons. San Deigo, Calif., 1974-81; bus. owner San Deigo, 1976-81; instr. seminars various instts., 1979—; dir promotion F. Lee Bailey Moot Ct. Competitions, San Diego, 1982-83. Contbr. articles to profl. jours. Fundraiser polit. and charitable orgns., San Diego, 1976-80. Mem. San Diego Pub. Relations, San Diego Press. Republican. Roman Catholic. Home: 3375 Herman Ave San Diego CA 92104 Office: Nat U 4141 Camino Del Rio San Diego CA 92108

TUCK, MURRAY, accountant, insurance company executive; b. Bklyn., Nov. 12, 1920; s. Samuel and Rose (Green) T.; grad. with honors Pace Inst. Sch. Acctg., N.Y.C., 1945; student Pace Inst. Ins., 1949-50; m. Leah Samuels, Aug. 6, 1971; 1 child by previous marriage, Susan (Mrs. R. Greenbaum), stepchildren—Edward Schultz, Charlotte (Mrs. K. Hoek), Larry Schultz. Jr. Acct., Morris Traum & Co., C.P.A.s, Bklyn., 1938-39; jr. acct. Mathew Weiss & Co., C.P.A.s, Bklyn., 1939-40, supervising sr. acct., 1940-45; asst. dept. head internal audit dept. United Mchts. and Mfrs., Inc., N.Y.C., 1945-52; comptroller TransRadio Press Service, Inc., N.Y.C., 1952-57, Bus. Factors, Inc., N.Y.C., 1957-62; pvt. practice acctg., Farmingdale, N.Y., 1950—; prin. Murray Tuck, ins. broker, Farmingdale, 1950—; ins. cons. Assn. for Help of Retarded Children, Inc., Nassau, N.Y., 1965—, Suffolk, N.Y., 1967—; mem. C.W. Post Coll. Fin. Planning Inst., 1980. Pres., Farmingdale Sr. High Sch. PTA, 1963-65; chmn. Farmingdale Community Scholarship Fund, 1962-67; sec., v.p. Group for Childrens Welfare, Central Islip, N.Y., 1961-65; treas. Farmingdale Little League Assn., 1956—; treas. Farmingdale Youth Council, Inc., 1956—; founder and donor Farmingdale Community award, 1962-65, Farmingdale Fireman award, 1962-65; co-committeeman Farmingdale Salvation Army, 1960-61; mem. Farmingdale Adult Edn. Adv. Com., 1955-60; mem. Farmingdale Police Aux., 1960-70; air raid warden, Farmingdale, 1944-50; notary pub. N.Y., 1960; Republican committeeman, Farmingdale, 1966-76; bd. dirs. Advancement for Commerce and Industry, Inc., pres., 1971-73, bd. dirs., 1974-78. Recipient Farmingdale Classroom Tchrs. Honor award 1963, cert. of appreciation Farmingdale CAP, 1964, Disting. Service plaque Advancement for Commerce and Industry, 1972, 74, cert. of service Farmingdale Youth Council, 1964, cert. of merit N.Y. Gov. Rockefeller. 1961, Village of Farmingdale, 1981; Citizen of Yr. award Kiwanis-Lions-Rotary Club, 1981, Congress U.S. Proclamation, 1981, Oyster Bay citation, 1980, 81, numerous other awards for community service; accredited in accountancy and taxation Nat. Accreditation Council; enrolled to practice with U.S. Treasury Dept. Mem. Nat. Soc. Pub. Accts., Nat. Assn. Ins. Agts., Empire State Accts. Assn., C.W. Post Coll. Tax Practicioners Forum, Nat. Assn. Enrolled Agts. Jewish. Editor: ARC Lamplighter, 1965-69; contbr. numerous articles on ins. and taxes to various publs. Home and Office: 670 Conklin St Farmingdale NY 11735

TUCK, ROBERT GRANT, JR., business executive; b. Brawley, Calif., Sept. 26, 1943; s. Robert Grant Sr. and Dorothy T.; m. Yvette R. Olsen, Aug. 16, 1963; children: Robert Grant III, Shila Renee. Student mgmt., U. Calif., Riverside, 1979-82, Antelope Valley Jr. Coll., Lancaster, Calif., 1986-88. Linen div. mgr. Lancaster (Calif.) Indsl. Laundry, 1970-78; sales mgr. Mission Linen Supplies, Lancaster, 1978-80, gen. mgr., 1980-85; controller High Desert Charter, Lancaster, 1985-87; gen. mgr. High Desert Mortgage, Lancaster, 1986-87; owner, operator R.G. Tuck Enterprises, Lancaster, 1987—. Contbr. sales articles to bus. jour. Recipient Service awards Cystic Fibrosis Found., Lancaster, 1982-84, 23d Olympics, Los Angeles., 1984. Republican. Lodges: Eagle (local bd. dirs. 1982-84), Kiwanis (local treas. 1987-88, bd. dirs. 1982-87). Home: 1141 W Pillsbury Lancaster CA 93534 Office: RG Tuck Enterprises 6201 East Ave G-8 Lancaster CA 93535

TUCKER, AVIS GREEN, utility company executive; b. 1915; widow. AB, U. Mo., 1937. With UtiliCorp United Inc. (formerly Mo. Pub. Svc.), Kansas City, 1973—, chmn., 1982—, bd. dirs. Office: Utilicorp United Inc 911 Main Suite 2000 Kansas City MO 64105 *

TUCKER, DON EUGENE, lawyer; b. Rockbridge, Ohio, Feb. 3, 1928; s. Beryl Hollis and Ruth (Primmer) T.; m. Elizabeth Jane Parke, Aug. 2, 1950; children: Janet Elizabeth, Kerry Jane, Richard Parke. B.A., Aurora Coll., 1951; LL.B., Yale, 1956. Bar: Ohio 1956. Since practiced in Youngstown, Ohio; asso. Manchester, Bennett, Powers & Ullman, 1956-62, ptnr., 1962-73, of counsel, 1973-87; gen. counsel Comml. Intertech Corp., Youngstown, 1973-75, v.p., gen. counsel, 1975-83, also dir., sr. v.p., gen. counsel, 1983-87, sr. v.p., 1987—; instr. Am. Inst. Banking, 1964, 66; dir. Union Nat. Bank Youngstown., Bank One of Eastern Ohio. Solicitor Village of Poland, Ohio, 1961-63; Former chmn. bd., pres., trustee United Cerebral Palsy Assn., Youngstown and Mahoning County; trustee Mahoning County Tb and Health Assn., Indsl. Info. Inst.; former pres., trustee Eastern Ohio Lung Assn.; trustee, pres. Butler Inst. Am. Art. Served with USMCR, 1946-48, 51-53. Mem. ABA, Ohio Bar Assn., Mahoning County Bar Assn. (pres. 1972, trustee 1970-73), Youngstown Area C. of C. (chmn. bd. dirs. 1979). Methodist. Home: 7850 W Garfield Rd Salem OH 44460 Office: Comml Intertech Corp 1775 Logan Ave Youngstown OH 44501

TUCKER, GEORGE MAXWELL, SR., building maintenance company executive; b. Bainbridge, Ga., Jan. 17, 1950; s. John Pierce, Sr., and Isabel (Slade) T.; A.B. in Polit. Sci. and Christianity, Mercer U., 1972, postgrad. Sch. Theology, 1972-74; m. Janet Almand, July 18, 1981; children: George Jr., Michael Almand, Kelly Marie. Mem. high sch. ministry team and exec. staff Internat. Devel. Campaign and spl. field rep. for pres. Campus Crusade for Christ Internat., San Bernardino, Calif., 1972-77; dir. pub. relations, acting adminstr., Shepherd Prodns., Inc., Denver, 1977-78; personnel mgr. Riverside Mfg. Co., Moultrie, Ga., 1978; sales mgr. Western U.S., Plains Mfg. Co., Sidney, Nebr., 1978-79; asst. to pres. for spl. projects Campus Crusade for Christ, Internat., San Bernardino, Calif., 1979-80, asso. staff exec. ministries, 1980-86; owner, gen. mgr. Environ. Control Bldg. Maintenance Co., Chamblee, Ga., 1980—, also Environment Control of Cobb County, Ga., 1983-85; pres., chief exec. officer Environment Control of Atlanta, Inc., Bldg. Maintenance Cos., 1984—; elder Presbyn. Ch. Recipient Youth Leadership award, Elks Club, 1968. Mem. Christian Conciliation Services of Atlanta, Inc. (bd. dirs. 1983-87), East Coast Mgmt. Assn. Environment Control Bldg. Maintenance Cos. (sec./treas.), Alpha Tau Omega. Co-author: A Resource Manual for Church Youth Workers, 1976. Home: Atlanta GA Office: PO Box 81145 Atlanta GA 30366-1145

TUCKER, HOWARD MCKELDIN, investment banker, consultant; b. Washington, Apr. 1, 1930; s. Howard Newell and Bessie Draper (McKeldin) T.; B.A., U. Va., 1954; postgrad. NYU Grad. Sch. Bus. Adminstrn., 1956; m. Julia Spencer Merrell, Feb. 1, 1952; children—Deborah, Mark, Alexander, H. David; m. 2d, Megan Evans, Aug. 17, 1979. Investment research J.P. Morgan & Co., N.Y.C., 1954-59; pension investment dept. Morgan Guaranty Trust Co., N.Y.C., 1959-61; registered rep.-analyst Mackall & Coe, Washington, 1962-69; dir. internat. dept., analyst Legg Mason Wood Walker & Co., Washington, 1969-79; with Govt. Research Corp./Nat. Jour., 1979-82, Potomac Asset Mgmt., 1982—; cons. Washington Analysis Corp., 1985—; dir. Monarch Enterprises, Inc., Uniflight, Inc.; Sci. Mgmt. Assocs., Inc., Jeffrey Bigelow Assocs.; mem. task force on balance-of-payments U.S. Dept. Treasury, 1967—; co-organizer U.S.-Ger. Parliamentary Exchange, 1980-82; observer OECD, 1980-82; spl. overseas visitor Australian Govt., 1982. Author: Literature in Medicine; writer London Investment Jour.; contbr. articles to fin. jours. Trustee Nat. Cathedrala Sch. for Girls, 1972-78; chmn. missionary devel. fund Episcopal Diocese of D.C., 1974; vestryman Christ Episcopal Ch., Georgetown, 1962-65; del. Va. Republican Conv., 1968; co-dir. Andover-Exeter Washington Intern Program, 1976-86; mem., trustee Washington Cathedral chpt., 1966-72; patron West Europe program Woodrow Wilson Ctr., 1985—. Served with USNR, 1950-56. Chartered fin. analyst. Mem. Washington Soc. Investment Analysts, Fin. Analysts Fedn., Nat. Economists Club, Cogswell Soc. Clubs: Naval and Mil. (London), Nat. Press, A.K.C., B.O.M.C., Georgetown Visitation Tennis, Saints and Sinners. Home: 2038 18th St NW Washington DC 20009 Office: 5247 Wisconsin Ave NW Suite 5 Washington DC 20015

TUCKER, JOHN EDWARD, architect, consultant; b. Austin, Tex., Sept. 6, 1955; s. Oliver Truman and Jewel (Rogers) T.; m. Patricia Ann Holliman, Mar 8, 1974; children: Jessica, Jathan, Joshua. BS in Architecture, U. Tex., Arlington, 1978. Project architect Oliver T. Tucker, Architect & Engr. Co., Irving, Tex., 1976-86; corp. pres. Ott: Tucker, Architects & Assocs., Inc., Irving, 1986—; cons. Dallas Ind. Sch. Dist., 1985—. Prin. works include Nimitz High Sch. Library, Irving, Lee Britain Elem. Sch., Irving. Home: 420 Southlake Park Rd W Southlake TX 76092 Office: Ott: Tucker Architects & Assocs Inc 2001 W Irving Blvd Irving TX 75061

TUCKER, KEITH E., pension fund executive, portfolio manager; b. N.Y.C., Jan. 31, 1933; s. Frederick Randall and Eula (Edwards) T.; m. Lindsey Ann Sale, July 7, 1936 (div. May 1977); children: Bruce Douglas, Craig Randall, Janis Lynne; m. Mary Ethel Willoschat, Aug. 31, 1937. BS in Commerce and Fin., Bucknell U., 1955; postgrad., NYU, 1958-60. Comml. banker Irving Trust Co., N.Y.C., 1957-63; fin. analyst Met. Life Ins. Co., N.Y.C., 1963-68; portfolio mgr. J. Aron & Co., N.Y.C., 1969, Shawmut Trust Co., Boston, 1970-71, Hartford (Conn.) Nat. Bank, 1971-73; portfolio mgr., sr. investment officer E.I. DuPont de Nemours & Co., Wilmington, Del., 1973—; bd. dirs. EQK Realty I, Bala Cynwyd, Pa. Mem. exec. bd. 1st Ch. Christ Scientist, Newark, Del., 1987. Served with U.S. Army, 1955-57. Office: E I du Pont de Nemours & Co 1007 Market St Wilmington DE 19898

TUCKER, L. WAYNE, banker; b. Dallas, Oct. 17, 1962; s. Larry Wayne and Frances (Michaels) T. BS in Bus. Adminstrn., Baylor U., 1985, MBA, 1986. Adminstrv. asst. Thermalloy Inc., Dallas, 1975-84; pres. Wayne Tucker Cos., Dallas, 1983-86; sr. analyst Tex. Commerce Bank, Austin, 1986-88, metro. banking officer, 1988—. Dir., treas. Mike Tucker Ministeries, St. Joseph, Tenn., 1987—; del. County Rep. Caucus, Austin, 1988. Mem. Fin. Mgmt. Assn., Austin Symphony Sq., Sigma Chi (sec. 1984-86, advisor 1987—, pres. 1989—). Baptist. Club: Austin Baylor. Home: 3816 S Lamar #1505 Austin TX 78704 Office: Tex Commerce Bank 700 Lavaca Austin TX 78789

TUCKER, LARRY REID, county official; b. Longview, Tex., Nov. 25, 1948; s. Tracy G. and Dorothy M. (Reid) T.; m. Sue E. Dresher, Dec. 18, 1971; children: Courtney, Melissa, Sean. BS in Acctg., U. Kans., 1972. Acct. Fox, Westheimer & Co., Topeka, 1972-78, Main, Hurdmand, CPA, Wichita, Kans., 1978-79, Diehl, Fletcher, Banwart CPA, Chanute, Kans., 1979-80, Robert Spielman, CPA, Lyons, Kans., 1980-84, Pierce, Faris & Co., CPA, Hutchinson, Kans., 1984-86; county treas. Reno County, Hutchinson, 1987—. Mem. Hutchinson Area Youth Council; sec. Reno County Dem. Party; treas. Reno County Spl. Olympics, Hutchinson. Mem. Kans. Soc. CPA's, Am. Inst. CPA's, Kans. Treas. Assn. Democrat. Club: Kiwanis (chpt. pres. 1985-86, internat. gov.-elect). Office: Reno County Treas 206 W 1st Hutchinson KS 67501

TUCKER, MARSHALL DANIEL, retail company executive, accountant; b. Dresden, Tenn., Mar. 30, 1932; s. Marshall Jackson and Julia Isabell (Travis) T.; m. Gloria Shelwitt, Aug. 27, 1957; children: Susan, Karen, Mark. BA, U. Tenn., 1954. Corp. fin. analyst Mead Corp., Dayton, Ohio, 1966-70, asst. treas., 1977-79; dir. planning Mead Interiors, Dayton, 1971-74; controller Mead Corp.-Stanley, Stanleytown, Va., 1975-76; v.p., chief fin. officer McJunkin Corp., Charleston, W.Va., 1979-84, Dixon Paper Co., Denver, 1984—. Bd. dirs., treas. Charleston Symphony Orch. Served with U.S. Army, 1956-57. Mem. Fin. Exec. Inst. Lodge: Rotary. Home: 5528 S Iris St Littleton CO 80123 Office: Dixon Paper Co 410 Raritan Way Denver CO 80244

TUCKER, MORRISON GRAHAM, banker; b. Lincoln, Nebr., May 24, 1911; s. Charles Andrew and Olive Myrtle (Graham) T.; m. Gladys Mae Hartz, Nov. 25, 1944; children: Suzanne, John Graham. AB, Dartmouth Coll., 1932. Asst. nat. bank examiner U.S. Treasury Dept., 1932-36; fed. bank examiner 1936-38; asst. chief div. exam. Fed. Deposit Ins. Corp., 1939-42; banking adviser to pres. of Philippines, 1944-47; mgr. Latin Am. interests Rockefeller family, 1947-51; chmn. exec. com. Liberty Nat. Bank & Trust Co., Oklahoma City, 1951-69; owner Morrison G. Tucker & Co. (banking and investments); bd. dirs. First Security Bank & Trust Co., Trust Co. of Okla., United Del City Bank, Southwestern Bank & Trust Co., Will Rogers Bank & Trust Co.; bd. dirs. S.W. Title & Trust Co., Oklahoma City. Bd. dirs. Frontiers of Sci. Found.; trustee Oklahoma City U.; pres. alumni council Dartmouth Coll., 1965-66. Served as lt. (j.g.) USNR, 1941-44. Elected to Okla. Hall of Fame, 1978. Mem. Okla. Bankers Assn. (pres. 1974-75). Episcopalian. Clubs: Metropolitan (Washington); University (N.Y.C.); Oklahoma City Golf and Country, Petroleum, Men's Dinner (Oklahoma City). Home: 2403 NW Grand Blvd Oklahoma City OK 73116

TUCKER, RAY MOSS, agricultural products cooperative executive. BS, U. Ky. Pres. Dairymen Inc., Louisville, also bd. dirs. Office: Dairymen Inc 10140 Linn Station Rd Louisville KY 40223 *

TUCKER, RICHARD FRANK, petroleum company executive; b. N.Y.C., Dec. 25, 1926; s. Frank W. and Marion (Ohm) T.; m. Genevieve P. Martinson, Oct. 13, 1951. B.Chem. Engring., Cornell U., 1950. With Esso Standard Oil Co., 1950-55; with Caltex Oil Co., 1955-61; with Mobil Corp., 1961—, vice chmn. bd., 1986—; pres., chief operating officer Mobil Oil Corp., 1986—; dir. Nova Pharm. Corp., Perkin Elmer Corp., U.S. Trust, Am. Petroleum Inst. Trustee Cornell U.; mem. bd. overseers Cornell U. Med. Sch.; bd. dirs. N.Y.C. Partnership. Served with USN, 1945-46. Mem. Nat. Acad. Engring., Council Fgn. Relations. Clubs: Cornell, Sky (N.Y.C.). Office: Mobil Corp 150 E 42d St New York NY 10017

TUCKER, THOMAS HOWARD, lawyer; b. Providence, Nov. 20, 1939; s. Donald Pitkin and Mary Louise (Moss) T.; m. Elizabeth Ann Corrigan, Sept. 25, 1982; children: Michael Austin, William Denison. BA, Yale Coll., 1961; JD, Harvard U., 1968. Bar: Colo. 1968. D.C. 1974, Mass. 1976. Assoc. Akolt, Shepherd, Dick & Rovira, Denver, 1968-70; staff atty. OEO, Washington, 1970, spl. counsel, 1971; asst. to dir. Office Legal Svcs., Washington, 1970-71; asst. to gen. counsel Fed. Trade Commn., Washington, 1971-73, asst. gen. counsel, 1973-75, asst. to chmn., 1976; assoc. Burlingham & Sawyer, 1976-78; ptnr. Sawyer, Burlingham & Tucker, Boston, 1979-84; prin. McGowan, Engel, Tucker & Garrett, Boston, 1984—; adj. counsel N.Y. Stock Exch., 1988—; arbitrator Nat. Assn. Securities Dealers, 1988—. Mem. Conservation Commn. Acton, Mass., 1978; mem. fin. com. Scituate, 1984-86; bd. dirs. Young Reps., Denver, 1969-70, World Affairs Coun. Boston, 1981-83. Lt. (j.g.) USNR, 1962-65. Mem. Mass. Bar Assn., Boston Bar Assn. Episcopalian. Office: McGowan Engel Tucker & Garrett 211 Congress St Boston MA 02110

TUCKER, THOMAS PEARCE, JR., manufacturing company executive; b. Abington, Pa., Apr. 21, 1953; s. Thomas P. and Dorothy (Zimmerman) T.; m. Carol Caldwell, May 13, 1978. BS in Mktg., Pa. State U., 1975. Mgr. territory Burroughs Corp., Williamsport, Pa., 1976-78; account mgr. Burroughs Corp., Harrisburg, Pa., 1978-80; product mgr. Burroughs Corp., King of Prussia, Pa., 1980-81, mgr. dist. sales, 1981-82; account exec. Wang Labs., Phila., 1982-83, mgr. mktg., 1983, br. mgr., 1983-84; mgr. nat. account mktg. Wang Labs., Lowell, Mass., 1984-85; dist. mgr. Recognition Equipment Inc., Malvern, Pa., 1985—. Vol. Big Brothers and Big Sisters, Phoenixville, Pa., 1982—; bd. dirs. Phoenixville YMCA, 1983—. Republican. Presbyterian. Club: Softball (Phoenixville) (mgr. 1982—). Home: 47 Devyn Dr Chester Springs PA 19425 Office: Recognition Equipment 200 Lindenwood Dr Malvern PA 19355

TUCKER, THOMAS RANDALL, public relations executive; b. Indpls., Aug. 6, 1931; s. Ovie Allen and Oris Aleen (Robertson) T.; A.B., Franklin Coll., 1953; m. Evelyn Marie Armuth, Aug. 9, 1953; children—Grant, Roger, Richard. Grad. asst. U. Minn., 1953-54; dir. admissions, registrar Franklin Coll., 1954-57; with Cummins Engine Co., Inc., Columbus, Ind., 1957; dir. pub. relations, 1968—. Mem. Bd. Sch. Trustees Bartholomew County, Ind., 1966-72, pres., 1968-69; mem. Ind. State Bd. Edn., 1977—; treas. Bartholomew County Rep. Cen. Com., 1960-80; mem. Columbus Area Visitor Info. and Promotion Commn.; chmn. Columbus 2000; trustee, chmn. ednl. policy com. of bd. trustees Franklin Coll.; bd. dirs. The Hoosier Salon. Mem. Pub. Relations Soc. Am., Columbus (Ind.) C. of C. (Community Service award 1986), Kappa Tau Alpha, Phi Delta Theta, Sigma Delta Chi. Lutheran. Lodge: Rotary. Home: 4380 N Riverside Dr Columbus IN 47203 Office: Box 3005 Columbus IN 47202

TUFF, TIMOTHY C., metal company executive. Pres. Alcan Aluminum Corp., Cleve. Office: Alcan Aluminum Corp 100 Erieview Pla Cleveland OH 44114 *

TUFTS, DAVID ALBERT, JR., securities company executive; b. Winchester, Mass., Sept. 9, 1945; s. David Albert and Florence Ida (Watters) T.; m. Jocelyne Maggiar-Nash, Aug. 21, 1971; children: Stephanie Elizabeth, Natalie Alexandra. BA, Hobart Coll., 1967. Dir. sales Kennedy Ctr. for Performing Arts, Washington, 1970-71; mgr. Merrill Lynch, Washington, 1971-81; asst. mgr. Oppenheimer & Co., N.Y.C., 1981-84, mng. dir., 1984—; mem. mgmt. com. Oppenheimer & Co., N.Y.C., 1986—. Bd. dirs. Brunswick Sch., Greenwich, Conn., 1986—, alumni council Hobart Coll., Geneva, N.Y., 1985—. Served to lt. USN, 1968, Vietnam. Mem. Kappa Alpha. Republican. Congregational. Clubs: Rocky Point (Greenwich); U. (Washington). Home: 37 Lockwood Dr Old Greenwich CT 06870 Office: Oppenheimer & Co Inc World Fin Ctr New York NY 10081

TUĞCU, NEJAT, tourism and hotel company executive, information systems expert; b. Antalya, Turkey, Mar. 27, 1945; s. Cavit Fikri and Ayse (Sapci) T.; m. Seyhan Kozanoğlu, May 26, 1976. BS in CE magna cum laude, Robert Coll., Istanbul, Turkey, 1967; MS in Structures, Cornell U., 1969, PhD in Structures and Theoretical and Applied Mechanics, 1970. Data processing and sr. systems analyst Geiger-Berger Cons., N.Y.C., 1970-72; dep. gen. mgr. computer ctr. Boğazici U., Istanbul, 1972-75, asst. prof. computer sci., 1975-80; dep. gen. mgr. Hisarbank, Istanbul, 1980-83; sr. comml. project mgr. Intes Constrn. and Contracting, Inc., Istanbul, 1983-86; exec. Seven Hills Internat. Tourism, Hotel and Trade, Inc., Istanbul, 1986—; ptnr., prin. Infotek Enformasyon Sistem A.S., Istanbul, 1980-87. Co-editor Master Plan for Istanbul and Marmara Ports, 1974. Fellow Cornell U., 1967-68. Islam. Lodge: Rotary (sec. Istanbul-Findikli chpt. 1982-83, v.p. 1983-84, pres. 1984-85. Home: Mirgün-Istinye Cad, 67 Park Apt Emirgan, Istanbul 80850, Turkey Office: Seven Hills Internat Tourism Hotel & Trade Inc, Gaziumurpasa Cad 38/6, Bimar Plaza Balmumcu, Istanbul 80700, Turkey

TULGA, LOUIS CREIGHTON, real estate corporation officer; b. North Platte, Nebr., Jan. 23, 1933; s. Chester Earl and Edna Marie (Main) T.; m. Lois Jean Olsen, Jan. 22, 1955; children: Brian, Louise, Renee. BA, Wheaton Coll., 1957, MA, 1961; PhD, Ohio State U., 1967. Asst. prof. U. N.Mex., Albuquerque, 1967-71; assoc. prof. Ind. U., Pa., 1971-72; real estate assoc. Sunland Realty, Albuquerque, 1972-76; pres., assoc. Nationwide Realty, Albuquerque, 1977—; pres. Nationwide Profl. Svcs., Albuquerque, 1986—. Mem. Realtors Assn. N.Mex. (1st v.p. 1987, treas. 1986-87, pres. elect 1988—), Albuquerque Bd. Realtors (3d v.p. 1985-86), Cert. Comml. Investment Brokers (pres. N.Mex. chpt. 1985-86), Kiwanis, Toastmasters. Democrat. Home: 10600 Cielito Lindo NE Albuquerque NM 87111 Office: Nationwide Realty Inc 3200 Carlisle NE Albuquerque NM 87110

TULL, ROBERT WHITE, JR., financial planner; b. Wilmington, Del., Oct. 25, 1958; s. Robert White and Lillie Mae (Parks) T.; m. Cathy Lynn Climpson, Mar. 13, 1982; 1 child, Andrew Robert. Student, Okla. State U., 1977-78; BS in Bus., Oral Roberts U., 1981; MBA, U. Houston, 1982. Cert. fin. planner. Teller First Nat. Bank Jenks, Okla., 1979; mktg. asst. IBM, Tulsa, 1980-81; credit analyst intern First Nat. Bank Tulsa, 1981; area dir. fin. planning dept. Christian Broadcasting Network, Virginia Beach, Va., 1983-85; fin. planner Innovative Fin. Concepts, Virginia Beach, 1985—. Precinct rep. Virginia Beach Rep. City Com., 1986—. Mem. Inst. Cert. Fin. Planners, Internat. Assn. Fin. Planners (v.p. programs 1987—), Oral Roberts U. Alumni Assn. (acting pres. Hampton Rds. chpt. 1987—), Rotary. (Lindhaven club). Mem. Assembly of God Ch. Home: 4237 Derby Wharf Dr Virginia Beach VA 23456 Office: Innovative Fin Concepts Inc 6037 Providence Rd Ste 2 Virginia Beach VA 23464

TULLER, WENDY JUDGE, educational foundation administrator; b. Cranston, R.I., Dec. 17, 1943; d. Alfred Carmen and Anna Louise (Waterman) Judge. A.B., Brown U., 1965; M.L.S., U. R.I., 1969. Librarian, Providence Public Schs., 1965-69; mgr. various locations Xerox Corp., 1969-75; mgr. Carter Hawley Hale Stores, Inc., Los Angeles, 1976; cons. Sibson & Co., Inc., Princeton, N.J., 1976-78; coordinator Atlantic Richfield Co., Los Angeles, 1978-87; pres. Found. for Ednl. Excellence, 1987—. Mem. Am. Soc. Personnel Adminstrn., Am. Soc. Tng. and Devel., Internat. Assn. Personnel Women, AAUW (v.p. local chpt. 1979-80). Club: Los Angeles Athletic. Home: 222 S Figueroa St Los Angeles CA 90012

TULLY, DANIEL P., investment company executive; b. 1932; married. BBA, St. Johns U., 1953. With Merrill Lynch, Pierce, Fenner & Smith, Inc., N.Y.C., 1955—, acct. clerk, 1955-59, acct. exec. trainee, 1959-63, asst. to mgr. Stamford, Conn. office, 1963-70, mgr., 1970-71, v.p., 1971-79, dir. individual sales, 1976-79, exec. v.p., 1979-82, pres. individual services group, 1982-84, pres. consumer mktg., from 1984, now chmn., pres., dir.; with Merrill Lynch & Co. (parent), N.Y.C., 1955—, former exec. v.p., now pres., chief operating officer, dir. Served U.S. Army, 1953-55. Office: Merrill Lynch & Co Inc 1 Liberty Pla 165 Broadway New York NY 10080 also: Merrill Lynch & Co Inc World Fin Ctr N Tower 32rd Fl New York NY 10281 *

TULLY, HERBERT BULLARD, corporate executive; b. Glen Ridge, N.J., Sept. 3, 1943; s. Richard Golfe and Marie Foster (Towne) T.; m. Nancy Dee Zook, Dec. 22, 1967; children: Kimberly, Christine, Gregory. BS, U. Calif., Berkeley, 1967. Mem. fin. mgmt. staff Gen. Electric Co., San Jose, Calif., 1967-70; mem. corp. audit staff Gen. Electric Co., Schenectady, N.J., 1970-73; mgr. acct. dept. Gen. Electric Co., San Leandro, Calif., 1973-75; mgr. audit dept. Am. Express Co., Fireman's Fund, San Francisco, 1975-77; asst. controller Fireman's Fund Ins. Co., San Francisco, 1977-81; controller Wilbur-Ellis Co., San Francisco, 1981-86, asst. treas., 1986-89, treas., 1989—; bd. dirs. Overseas Cos., San Francisco. Home: 7 Spring Rd PO Box 1735 Ross CA 94957

TULLY, THOMAS ALOIS, building materials executive, consultant; b. Dubuque, Iowa, Nov. 11, 1940; s. Thomas Aloysius and Marjorie Mae (Fosselman) T.; m. Joan Vonnetta Dubay, Nov. 30, 1963; children: Thomas Paul, Maureen Elizabeth. BA, Loras Coll., 1962; postgrad., Georgetown U., 1963-66; MPA, Harvard U., 1968. Mgmt. trainee Office of Sec. Def., Washington, 1962-63, fgn. affairs officer, 1963-70; v.p. Dubuque Lumber Co., 1970-84, pres., 1984—; part-time instr. Divine Word Coll., 1971, Loras Coll., 1972, Clarke Coll., 1987—. Mem. Dubuque Human Rights Commn., 1974-75, chmn., 1975; city councilman, Dubuque, 1975-79; bd. dirs. League Iowa Municipalites, 1977-79; mayor City of Dubuque, 1978; vice chmn. Iowa Temporary State Land Pres. Policy Com., 1978-79; pres. N.E. Iowa Regional Coordinating Council, 1985—, East Cen. Intergovtl. Assn. Bus. Growth, Inc., 1987—; bd. dirs. Pvt. Industry Council of Dubuque and Delaware Counties, Inc., 1983-86; trustee Divine Word Coll., 1986—; pres. Barn Community Theatre, 1988-89. Recipient Meritorious Civilian Svc. award Sec. of Def., 1970, Gov.'s Vol. award, 1989. Mem. Iowa Lumbermens Assn. (pres. 1984, chmn. legis. com. 1985—), Northwestern Lumbermen Assn. (bd. dirs. 1984-87, 2d v.p. 1988—), Nat. Lumber and Bldg. Material Dealers Assn. (exec. com. 1988—). Democrat. Roman Catholic. Club: Thunder Hills Country. Home: 838 Stoneridge Pl Dubuque IA 52001 Office: Dubuque Lumber Co 2655 Lincoln Ave Dubuque IA 52001

TUMAS, MARC LIONEL, communications systems manufacturing executive; b. Lowell, Mass., Dec. 11, 1943; s. Lionel Joseph and Jeanne Simone (Heroux) T.; B.S. in Engring., U.S. Mil. Acad., 1966; M.B.A., Harvard U., 1973. Fin. systems analyst Hewlett Packard Co., Waltham, Mass., 1973-76, div. controller, Andover, Mass., 1976-83; v.p. fin. and adminstrn., treas., and chief fin. officer Applitek Corp., 1983—; lectr. Merrimack Coll. Served with U.S. Army, 1966-71. Decorated Bronze Star medal with one oak leaf cluster. Mem. Am. Mgmt. Assn. Republican. Roman Catholic. Club: Harvard Bus. Sch. Club of Boston. Office: 107 Audubon Rd Suite 5 Wakefield MA 01880

TUMMINELLO, STEPHEN CHARLES, electronic parts manufacturing company executive; b. Paterson, N.J., Nov. 7, 1936. Grad., Fairleigh Dickinson U., 1958. Former pres. N.Am. Philips Lighting Corp.; exec. v.p., former v.p., group exec. N.Am. Philips Corp., 1984—. Office: N Am Philips Corp 100 E 42nd St New York NY 10017 *

TUMPERI, JOHN ROBERT, consulting and leadership training executive; b. Lake Linden, Mich., Feb. 25, 1930; s. Isaac Herman and Lydia Catherine (Wesala) T.; B.S. in Mech. Engring., U.S. Mil. Acad., 1953; m. Barbara Ann Krieger, Feb. 25, 1954; children—Laura, Eric, Scott. With Gen. Electric Co., various locations, 1957-72, mgr. mfg., King of Prussia, Pa., 1972-75; v.p. ops. Esterline Angus, Indpls., 1975-77; pres. Indsl. Timer Co., Parsippany, N.J., 1977-78; v.p. ops. Yokogawa Corp. Am., Shenandoah, Ga., 1979-83; pres. K&T Mgmt. Systems, 1984—; bd. dirs. C&S Bank. Dist. chmn. McIntosh council Boy Scouts Am., 1980-82. Served with AUS, 1953-56. Registered profl. engr., Ohio. Mem. Newnan-Coweta C. of C. (bd. dirs. 1982-85). Republican. Methodist. Clubs: Kiwanis (pres. 1969), Rotary (bd. dirs. Newnan club 1981-83, sec.-treas. elect 1983). Home and Office: 103 Greenville St Newnan GA 30263

TUNDIDOR, BERT A., banker; b. Matanzas, Cuba, Feb. 28, 1952; came to U.S., 1961; s. Theodore and Bertha (Taranov) T.; m. Grizzell Penichet, Nov. 24, 1972; children: Victoria Marie, Alec-Nicholas, Daniel Abram. AA, Miami-Dade Community Coll., 1973; BBA, U. Miami, 1976. Br. v.p. First Nationwide Savs. Bank, Miami Beach, Fla., 1979-82; v.p. corp. lending officer Amerifirst Bank, Miami, 1982-86; 1st v.p., from asst. chmn, to chmn. Peoples First Nat. Bancshares, Miami, 1986-88; regional v.p. Centrust Savs. Bank, Miami, 1988—. Mem. Br. Mgrs. Soc., Kiwanis. Roman Catholic. Home: 8465 SW 151 St Miami FL 33158 Office: Centrust Savs Bank 101 Flagler St Miami FL 33131

TUNG, PAUL PING-YU, trade company executive; b. Xian, China, Mar. 6, 1943; came to U.S, 1965; naturalized, 1978; s. Shou-Hsun and Yee-Shing (Pi) T.; m. Chiang-Ying Mei, Dec. 9, 1972; children: Yong-Jin Marshall Tung, Elsa Mei Tung. BS in Engring., Nat. Taiwan U., Taipei, 1964; MS in Engring., UCLA, 1967, MBA, 1982, PhD in Engring., 1971. Mem. tech. staff Rockwell Internat., L.A., 1971-78, Jet Propulsion Lab., Pasadena, Calif., 1978-81; v.p. mktg. Global Machinery Corp., Compton, Calif., 1982-83; pres. Eastern Materials, Inc., L.A., 1983—. Editor: Fracture and Failure: Analyses, Mechanisms and Applications, 1981. Mem. ASTM, Am. Soc. Metals, Assn. Iron and Steel Engrs., Wire Assn. Internat., Chinese-Am. Assn. Scientists and Engrs. in So. Calif., Beta Gamma Sigma. Home: 1031 Camino Magenta Thousand Oaks CA 91360 Office: Eastern Materials Inc 6033 W Century Blvd 4th Fl Los Angeles CA 90045

TUNG, ROSALIE LAM, b. Shanghai, China, Dec. 2, 1948; came to U.S., 1975; d. Andrew Yan-Fu and Pauline Wai-Kam (Cheung) Lam; BA (Univ. scholar), York U., 1972; MBA, U. B.C., 1974, PhD in Bus. Adminstrn. (Univ. fellow, Seagram Bus. fellow, H.R. MacMillan Family fellow), 1977; m. Byron Poon-Yan Tung, June 17, 1972; 1 dau., Michele Christine. Lectr. diploma div. U. B.C., 1975, lectr. exec. devel. program, 1975; prof. mgmt. grad. sch. mgmt. U. Oreg., Eugene, 1977-80; prof. U. Pa. , Phila. 1981-86; prof., dir. internat. bus. ctr. U. Wis., Milw. , 1986—; vis. scholar U. Manchester (Eng.) Inst. Sci. and Tech., 1980; vis. prof. UCLA, 1981, Harvard U., 1988; Wis. disting. prof. U. Wis. System, 1989—. Mem. Acad. Internat. Bus. (mem. exec. bd., treas. 1985-86), Acad. Mgmt. (bd. govs. 1987—),Internat. Assn. Applied Psychology, Am. Arbitration Assn. (comml. panel arbitrators). Author: Management Paractices in China, 1980, U.S.-China Trade Negotiations, 1982, Chinese Industrial Society After Mao, 1982, Business Negotiations with the Japanese, 1984, Key to Japan's Economic Strength: Human Power, 1984, The New Expatriates: Managing Human Resources Abroad, 1988; editor: Strategic Management in the U.S. and Japan, 1987. Oppehheimer Bros. Found. fellow, 1973-74, U. B.C. fellow, 1974-75, H.R. MacMillan Found. fellow, 1975-77; named Wis. Disting. Prof., 1988. Roman Cathlic. Avocation: creative writing. Home: PO Box 17441 Milwaukee WI 53217 Office: U Wis Sch Bus PO Box 742 Milwaukee WI 53217

TUOHEY, CONRAD GRAVIER, lawyer; b. N.Y.C., Dec. 27, 1933; s. James L. and Rose (Gravier) T.; BA, George Washington U., 1957; JD, U. Mich., 1960; m. Judith Octavia Jeeves, July 7, 1956; children: Octavia Jeeves, Heather Gravier, Meighan Judith, Caragh Rose. Admitted to Calif. bar, 1962, N.Y. bar, 1980, D.C. bar, 1980; sr. mem. firm Tuohey & Prasse; dir. Fed. Home Loan Bank, San Francisco, 1980-83; legal cons., counsel Calif. State Senate, 1981—; counsel Senate Select Com. on the Pacific Rim, 1986-87. Mem. citizens adv. bd. Orange County Transit Com., 1966-68; pres. Calif. Alliance Partners for Progress, 1969-72, Friends of Calif. State U. at Fullerton, 1969-71; mem. InterAm. bd. Partners Alliance for Progress, 1969-72, nat. bd. dirs., 1970-72. Served with AUS, 1951-54. Decorated Combat Infantryman's Badge, Korean Service medal with 3 battle stars; named Outstanding Young Man of Yr., Fullerton Jr. C. of C., 1967. Mem. State Bar Calif., ABA (internat., corp., banking and bus. law sects.), Los Angeles Bar Assn., Orange County Bar Assn. chmn. environ. law sect.), D.C. Bar Assn., N.Y. Bar Assn., Kent Inn of Phi Delta Phi, Phi Sigma Kappa. Home: 24762 Red Lodge Pl Laguna Hills CA 92653 Office: 1200 N Main St Ste 800 Santa Ana CA 92701

TURBERG, PHILLIP ALBERT, consulting executive, actuary; b. Rochester, N.Y., May 30, 1928; s. Garson and Esther (Goldstein) T.; m. Katherine Ramsay Parsons; children: Charlotte, Thomas, Susan, James. Student, U. Rochester, 1947-49; BA, Syracuse U., 1951. Actuarial asst. N.Y. Life Ins. Co., N.Y.C., 1951-58; assoc. actuary Life Ins. Co. N. Am., Phila., 1958-63; dir. Peat Marwick Main & Co., N.Y.C., 1963—; mem. adv. bd. E. Noyes Inc, Swarthmore, Pa.; bd. dirs. Hay Group, Phila., Advanta, Inc. (formerly TSO Fin. Inc.), Willow Grove, Pa., Employee Benefit Research Inst., Unity Mutual Life Ins. Co, Syracuse, N.Y. Served with U.S. Army, 1945-47, PTO. Fellow Soc. Actuaries,; mem. Am. Acad. Actuaries, Internat. Assn. Cons. Actuaries. Democrat. Club: Union League (Phila.). Home: PO Box 87 Wallingford PA 19086 Office: Huggins Fin Svcs Inc 229 S 18th St Philadelphia PA 19103

TUREEN, THOMAS NORTON, lawyer; b. St. Louis, Dec. 15, 1943; s. Bernard Henry and Rose Lorraine (Dansker) T.; m. Susan Albright, June 15, 1968; children: Phoebe Albright, Rufus Louis. BA, Princeton U., 1966; JD, Goerge Washington U., 1969. Bar: Maine 1969, D.C. 1971, U.S. Dist. Ct. D.C. 1974, U.S. Dist. Ct. (we. dist.) N.Y. 1975, U.S. Ct. Appeals (1st cir.) 1975, U.S. Ct. Appeals (D.C. cir.) 1976, U.S. Supreme Ct. 1980. Directing atty., Indian legal services unit Pine Tree Legal Assistance Inc., Calais, Maine, 1969-72; of counsel Native Americans Rights Fund, Calais, 1972-80; ptnr. Tureen & Margolin, Portland, Maine, 1981—; chmn. Tribal Assets Mgmt., Portland, 1983—. Trustee Susan Curtis Found., Portland, 1983. Club: Cumberland (Portland). Home: Old Mill Box 216 Limerick ME 04048 Office: Tureen & Margolin 178 Middle St Portland ME 04101

TURILLO, MICHAEL JOSEPH, JR., management consultant; b. Hartford, Conn., Aug. 22, 1947; s. Michael Joseph and Alice (Vargas) T.; m. Deborah Sherburne; children—Stephanie, Christopher. B.S., Providence Coll., 1969; M.B.A., Syracuse U., 1972; M.S., U. Mass., 1973. Cons. Peat, Marwick, Mitchell & Co. (name changed to Peat, Marwick Main & Co.), Boston, 1974-77; mgr. Peat, Marwick, Mitchell & Co., Boston, 1977-82, ptnr., 1982—, nat. cons. practice dir. for fin. service cos., 1985—; chmn. Internat. Mgmt. Cons. Practice Com. on Banking and Fin., 1986—. Com. mem. United Way, Boston, 1981-83; trustee Elliot Montessori, South Natick, Mass., 1984-85; dir. Greater Boston council Boy Scouts Am., 1988—. Served to capt. U.S. Army, 1969-71, Vietnam. Decorated Bronze Star. Mem. Bank Mktg. Assn., Assn. Planning Execs., Assn. Corp. Planners, Beta Gamma Sigma. Roman Catholic. Home: 47 S Street South Natick MA 01760 Office: Peat Marwick Main & Co One Boston Pl Boston MA 02108

TURK, JOHN W., JR., retired utility company executive; b. Clarksville, Tex., Apr. 3, 1924; s. John W. and Elena (DuPriest) T.; m. Anne Dean, Jan. 5, 1945. B.S.M.E., U. Tex., 1949; grad. advanced mgmt. program, Harvard U., 1982. With Southwestern Electric Power Co., Shreveport, La., 1949-88, supr. power, 1971-75, v.p., 1975-83, pres., chief exec. officer, 1983-88; ret. Southwestern Electric Power Co., Shreveport, 1988; dir. Tex. Commerce Bank, Longview. Served to capt. USMC, 1942-46; PTO. Mem. ASME. Methodist. Clubs: Pinecrest Country (bd. dirs., pres.) Summit (gov.) (Longview, Tex.). Office: Southwestern Electric Power Co 428 Travis St PO Box 21106 Shreveport LA 71156

TURK, MARTIN ERWIN, real estate developer; b. Balt., Sept. 5, 1945; s. Jerome and Shirley (Amorky) T.; m. Mary Agnes Lovinski, Nov. 24, 1980. B.A., U. Md., 1970. Sales mgr. Cavalier Formals, Alexandria, Va., 1971-77; salesman Lewis & Silverman Realty, Burke, Va., 1977-78; comml. mgr. White House Real Estate, Annandale, Va., 1978-84; pres. New Homes Realty, Inc., Falls Church, Va., 1984—, Nat. Greetings Corp., Falls Church, 1985-87, Nat. Equity and Devel. Co., Falls Church, 1987—; cons. Woodward & Lothrop, Washington 1985-87. Mem. No. Va. Bd. Realtors (Top Producer award 1981, 83), No. Va. Builders Assn., Optimist (pres. 1981). Avocation: tennis, ballroom dancing. Home: 4500 Park Rd Alexandria VA 22312 Office: 6500 Arlington Blvd Falls Church VA 22042

TURK, MILAN JOSEPH, chemical company executive; b. Baton Rouge, Nov. 25, 1938; s. Frank P. and Zdenka (Cop) T.; m. Margot Genre, Sept. 10, 1937; children: Milan J. Jr., Margot C., Richard P. BS in Chem. Engring., La. State U., 1960, MBA, 1962; grad. advanced mgmt. program, Harvard U., 1985. Asst. to v.p. mfg. Consol. Chem. Co., Houston, 1965-67; with Stauffer Chem. Co. div. Chesebrough-Pond's Inc., 1967-85; asst. to v.p. corp. planning Stauffer Chem. Co. div. Chesebrough-Pond's Inc., N.Y.C., 1967-69; adminstr. fin. ind. chem. div. Stauffer Chem. Co. div. Chesebrough-Pond's Inc., 1969-72; sr. bus. analyst corp. planning Stauffer Chem. Co. div. Chesebrough-Pond's Inc., Westport, Conn., 1972-73; dir. ops. Latin Am. div. Stauffer Chem. Co. div. Chesebrough-Pond's Inc., 1973, gen. mgr. Latin Am. div., 1973-75; dep. gen. mgr. Europe div. Stauffer Chem. Co. div. Chesebrough-Pond's Inc., Geneva, 1975-76, v.p., gen. mgr. Europe div., 1976-80; v.p. spl. projects Stauffer Chem. Co. div. Chesebrough-Pond's Inc., Westport, 1980-81; v.p., gen. mgr. food ingredients div. Stauffer Chem. Co. div. Chesebrough-Pond's Inc., 1981-82, group v.p. agr./food products, 1982-85; pres. agr. products div., corp. v.p. Chesebrough-Pond's Inc., Westport, Conn., 1985-88; corp. v.p. Chesebrough-Pond's Inc., Westport, 1985-88; exec. v.p., mem. exec. com. Mobay Corp., Pitts., 1988—, also bd. dirs. Mem. Am. Inst. Chem. Engring., Soc. Chem. Ind., Nat. Agrl. Chem. Assn.

(bd. dirs. 1986—, exec. com. 1986—). Republican. Roman Catholic. Club: Patterson (Fairfield, Conn.). Home: 1085 Burr St Fairfield CT 06430 *

TURK, S. MAYNARD, lawyer, business executive; b. Roanoke County, Va., Oct. 14, 1925; s. James Alexander and Geneva (Richardson) T.; m. Patricia A. Tucker, June 1, 1957; children—Heather F., William A., Thomas M.T. B.A. in Econs., Roanoke Coll., 1949; LL.B., Washington and Lee U., 1952. Bar: Va. 1951, Del. 1961, U.S. Patent and Trademark Office 1975. With Hercules Inc., 1954—; sr. counsel Hercules Inc., Wilmington, Del., 1966-70, sr. patent counsel, 1972, dir. patent dept., 1972-76, gen. counsel, 1976—, sec., 1980-82, v.p., 1982—, also bd. dirs.; bar examiner State of Del. Bd. Examiners, 1987—. Bd. overseers Del. Law Sch., Widener U., 1977-87. Mem. Assn. Gen. Counsel, ABA, Phila. Patent Law Assn., Mfg. Chemists Assn. (legal adv. com.), Atlantic Legal Found. (bd. dirs.), Southwestern Legal Found. (adv. bd.), Licensing Execs. Soc., N.A.M., Assn. Corp. Patent Counsel (emeritus), Nat. Security Indsl. Assn. Home: PO Box 3958 Greenville DE 19807 Office: Hercules Inc Law Dept 1313 N Market St Wilmington DE 19894

TURLEY, KEITH L., holding company executive; b. Mesa, Ariz., June 16, 1923; s. Ora Elmer and Zella Exa (Thurman) T.; m. Dorothy Rae Welton, Sept. 2, 1950; children: Sue Ann, Cinda Jane, Nancy Lynn, Robert. B.A., Ariz. State U., 1948. With Central Ariz. Light & Power Co., Phoenix, 1948-51, Stanolind Oil & Gas Co., Okla., 1951; with Ariz. Pub. Service Co., Phoenix, 1952-87, v.p. marketing, 1967-69, exec. v.p. customer services, 1969-72, exec. v.p., gen. mgr., dir., 1972-73, pres., chief exec. officer, 1974-81, pres., chmn. bd., 1981-82, chief exec. officer, 1982-87, chmn. bd., 1982—; chief exec. officer Pinnacle West Capital Corp., Phoenix, 1987—. Dir. Central Ariz. Project, 1971—; chmn. Phoenix Commn. on Housing, 1972; trustee Heard Mus.; bd. dirs. Sun Angel Found. Lt. (j.g.) USNR, 1943-47. Recipient Alumni Service award Ariz. State U., 1971. Mem. Edison Electric Inst. (dir.), Ariz. State U. Alumni Assn. (pres. 1966), Paradise Valley Country Club. Office: Pinnacle W Capital Corp PO Box 52132 Phoenix AZ 85072-2132

TURLEY, STEWART, retail company executive; b. Mt. Sterling, Ky., July 20, 1934; s. R. Joe and Mavis S. T.; children: Carol, Karen. Student, Rollins Coll., 1952-53, U. Ky., 1953-55. Plant mgr. Crown Cork & Seal Co., Orlando, Fla., Phila., 1955-66; mgr. non-drug ops., dir. corporate employee relations and spl. services Jack Eckerd Corp., Clearwater, Fla., 1966-68, v.p., 1968-71, sr. v.p., 1971-74, dir., 1971—, pres., chief exec. officer, 1974—, chmn. bd., 1975—; bd. dirs. United Telecommunications, Inc., Barnett Banks, Inc., Springs Industries, Inc. Trustee Eckerd Coll., St. Petersburg, US Ski Ednl. Fedn. Mem. Fla. Council Econ. Edn. (bd. dirs.), Nat. Assn. Chain Drug Stores (bd. dirs., chmn. bd. 1978-79, 88-89), Am. Retail Fedn. (dir.), Fla. Council of 100 (bd. dirs.), Bus. Roundtable, World Bus. Council, Inc., Chief Execs. Orgn., Inc., Pinellas Suncoast C. of C. (trustee), Kappa Alpha. Clubs: Carlouel Yacht (Clearwater); Belleair Country. Home: Clearwater FL 34616 Office: Jack Eckerd Corp 8333 Bryan Dairy Rd PO Box 4689 Clearwater FL 34618

TURNBULL, ADAM MICHAEL GORDON, financial executive, accountant; b. Dumfries, Scotland, Dec. 29, 1935; emigrated to Canada, 1977; s. Robert Wilson and Catherine Russell (Strang) T.; m. Karen Margaret Walker, June 12, 1965; children: Candida Louise, Andrew Robert. M.A., Edinburgh U., 1956, LL.B., 1958. Chartered acct., Scotland. With Price Waterhouse Co., Paris, 1960-62, U.S. Time Corp., France and U.S., 1962-64; group chief secondant Formica Internat. Ltd., London, 1965-70; group fin. dir. Donald Macpherson Group Ltd., London, 1970-77; controller, asst. treas. Indal Ltd., Weston, Ont., Can., 1978-81; controller Indal Inc., Weston, Ont., Can., 1978-81; v.p., treas. Indal Ltd., Weston, Ont., Can., 1981—. Mem. Inst. Chartered Accts. Scotland. Home: 2610 Hammond Rd, Mississauga, ON Canada L5K 2M4 Office: Indal Ltd, 4000 Weston Blvd, Weston, ON Canada M9L 2W8

TURNER, CAL, JR., discount stores executive. married. BA cum laude, Vanderbilt U., 1962. With Dollar Gen. Corp., Scottsville, Ky., 1965—, v.p., 1966-67, exec. v.p., 1967-77, pres., 1977—, also dir., chief exec. officer. Served with USN, 1962-65. Office: Dollar Gen Corp 1 Burton Hills Blvd Ste 210 Nashville TN 37215 *

TURNER, CAL (H. CALISTER), SR., discount stores executive. married. With Neely Harwell Co., 1931-36; operated Retail Goods Store, 1936-39; with Dollar Gen. Corp., Scottsville, Ky., from 1939, now chmn. bd., dir. Office: Dollar Gen Corp 427 Beech St Scottsville KY 42164 *

TURNER, CARL JEANE, electronics engineer, international business development executive; b. Sevierville, Tenn., July 27, 1933; s. Kenneth Albert and Lenna Faye (Christopher) T.; m. Flossie Pearl Ingram, Dec. 11, 1954; children: Marcia, Kenneth, Theresa, Christopher, Robin. BEd, BSEE, MBA, PhD, Columbia Pacific U. Active duty in USAF, 1950, advanced through grades with service in Korea and Vietnam, ret. 1972; with Itek Corp., 1972-77, 78-81, sr. engr./analyst, chief instr. E-Systems, Inc., Greenville, Tex., 1977-78; gen. mgr. Optical Systems div. Itek Internat. Corp., Athens, Greece, 1978-79, gen. mgr. German Programs Applied Tech. div. Itek Internat. Corp., Ulm, Fed. Republic of Germany, 1979-81, mgr. program planning and control, internat. ops. Applied Tech. div., Sunnyvale, Calif., 1981; mgr. export mktg. GTE Corp., Systems Group, Western Div., Mountain View, Calif., 1981-83; pres. C.J. Turner and Assocs., Co., 1983; internat. sales mgr. Probe Systems, Inc., 1983-84; dir. internat. mktg. Gen. Instrument Corp., Govt. Systems div., Hicksville, N.Y., 1984—; named to Order of Seasoned Weasels. Author, editor electronic warfare mgmt. courses and internat. bus. books. Recipient George Washington Honor medal Freedoms Found., 1965, Presdl. Achievement award, 1982, Pres.'s Medal of Merit, 1982. Mem. IEEE, Assn. Old Crows, Air Force Assn., Am. Entrepreneurs Assn., Armed Forces Communications and Electronics Assn., Nat. Assn. Professions. Republican. Baptist. Address: 51 Harbor Park Dr Centerport NY 11721-1640

TURNER, CHERI ANNE, financial executive; b. Spring City, Pa., Apr. 7, 1949; d. Harold William and Evelyn Virginia (Wagner) T. Student Syracuse U., 1967-69; Cert. Fin. Paraplanner, Coll. Fin. Planning, Denver, 1986. Pub. relations mediator Don Poindexter & Assocs., St. Petersburg, Fla., 1969-72; exec. sec. Honeywell Inc., Largo, Fla., 1972-75; sec., design coordinator SCM Design Ctr., Syracuse, N.Y., 1975-76; personnel dir. Jay Galbraith's Penthouse, St. Petersburg, 1977-79; cert. fin. paraplanner R. A. Siebern & Assocs., St. Petersburg, 1982-87, pres. C.A. Turner Services Inc., 1987— ; real estate sales rep. Corwin Realty Inc., St. Petersburg 1988—; registered rep. gen. securities Mut. Benefit Fin. Service Co. Inc., Tampa, Fla., 1985—; music dir. Capt. Anderson Cruises, Clearwater, Fla., 1982-88; pres. CA Turner Services, Inc., Clearwater, Fla., 1987; pvt. practice music tchr., Largo, 1964—. Composer, illustrator children's music book: Ditties for Kiddies, 1980. Mem. Nat. Assn. Female Execs., Inst. Cert. Fin. Planners (soc. adminstr. 1988—), Am. Soc. Notaries, Hospitality Industry Assn. Inc., Nat. Assn. Security Dealers, Internat. Assn. Reg. Fin. Planners, U.S. Figure Skating Assn. (preliminary test judge 1975—), Sun Coast Figure Skating Club. Avocations: figure skating, music, fishing, gemology, rock hounding. Office: CA Turner Svcs Inc 4161 103d Ave N Clearwater FL 34622

TURNER, EUGENE ANDREW, manufacturing executive; b. Bridgeton, N.J., Aug. 7, 1928; s. Benjamin Homer and Pearl Irene (Wolbert) T.; m. Paula Ann Webb, 1987; children from previous marriage, Mary Ann, John-Reed. Student, Mich. State U., 1966, Columbia U., 1980. With Owens Ill., 1950-73, regional mgr. West Coast, 1970-73; v.p. adminstrn. Midland Glass Co., Cliffwood, N.J., 1973-76, pres., chief operating officer, 1981-82, also bd. dirs.; v.p., gen. mgr. Anchor Hocking Corp., Lancaster, Ohio, 1976-81; dir. ops. Theo Chem Labs, Tampa, Fla., 1988; mng. cons. 1987-88. Mem. Harbor Island Club, Yacht Club, Seaview Country Club, Navesink Country Club. Home: 2411 Carolina Ave Tampa FL 33629 Office: Theo Chem Labs 7373 Roulett Pic Dr Tampa FL 33610

TURNER, FRANK ALLEN, manufacturing company executive; b. Burlington, Iowa, July 22, 1922; s. John Giles and Sabine (Allen) T.; m. Mary Beth Bludworth, Oct. 25, 1946; children: Susan Kathleen Danner, Timothy Allen. Student, U. So. Calif., 1942-43. Driver, sales Pennzoil Products Co., Colton, Calif., 1946-50; dealer, sales Pennzoil Products Co., Los Angeles, 1950-60; br. mgr. Pennzoil Products Co., Denver, 1960-64, div. mgr., 1964-66, regional v.p., 1966-76; v.p. nat. sales Pennzoil Products Co., Los Angeles, 1976-81; v.p. motor oil div. Pennzoil Products Co., Houston, 1982-84, exec. v.p. automotive prodn., 1984-85, pres., 1985—. Mem. bd. zoning Manhattan Beach (Calif.) City Council, 1958-69. Served to lt. USAF, 1942-46, Korea. Republican. Lodges: Sertoma (pres. Denver club 1962-64), Masons. Office: Pennzoil Products Tech Div 1520 Lake Front Circle PO Box 7569 The Woodlands TX 77387

TURNER, FRED LAMAR, accountant; b. LaGrange, Ga., Oct. 8, 1949; s. John Cletus and Dean (Norris) T.; m. Mary Katherine Daws, Sept. 27, 1969; children: Jessica, Jennifer, Judson. AA in Electronics, Troup Tech. Sch., LaGrange, 1969; BA, Columbus (Ga.) Coll., 1973; M in Taxation, Ga. State U., 1979, JD, 1986. CPA, Ga. Elec. installer N. Electric Co., Orlando, Fla., 1969-70; instr. La Grange (Ga.) Coll., 1979-81; pres., treas. La Grange Motor Hotel, 1978-85; prin., owner J.K. Boatwright & Co., PC, La Grange, 1973—; also bd. dirs. J.K. Boatwright & Co., La Grange; bd. dirs. LaGrange Motor Hotel, Revolving Loan Fund, LaGrange. Bd. dirs. Troup County Cert. Devel. Corp., 1982—, Troup County Planning Commn.; trustee Callaway Found., Inc., Clark Holder Clinic Ednl. Found., treas., bd. dirs. Chattahoochee Valley Art Assn., LaGrange, 1982—. Named Acct. Advocate of Yr. for Ga. SBA, Atlanta, 1986. Mem. Am. Inst. CPA's (tax div.), Ga. Soc. CPA's, LaGrange C. of C. (bd. dirs., treas., pres. 1988). Baptist. Lodge: Rotary (bd. dirs., treas. LaGrange chpt. 1984—). Home: 903 Whitaker Rd La Grange GA 30240 Office: J K Boatwright Co PC 17 1/2 N LaFayette Sq La Grange GA 30240

TURNER, HENRY BROWN, finance executive; b. N.Y.C., Sept. 3, 1936; s. Henry Brown III and Gertrude (Adams) T.; m. Sarah Jean Thomas, June 7, 1958 (div.); children: Laura Eleanor, Steven Bristow, Nancy Carolyn. A.B., Duke U., 1958; M.B.A., Harvard U., 1962. Controller Fin. Corp. of Ariz., Phoenix, 1962-64; treas., dir. corporate planning Star-Kist Foods, Terminal Island, Calif., 1964-67; dir., 1st v.p. Mitchum, Jones & Templeton, Los Angeles, 1967-73; asst. sec. Dept. Commerce, Washington, 1973-74; v.p. fin. N-Ren Corp., Cin., 1975-76; v.p. Oppenheimer & Co., N.Y.C., 1976-78; exec. v.p., mng. dir. corporate fin. Shearson Hayden Stone Inc., N.Y.C., 1978-79; sr. mng. dir. Ardshiel Inc., 1980-81, pres., 1981—; bd. dirs. Info. Techs., Inc., MacDonald & Co., Pembrook Mgmt. Co., Golden State Vinters Inc., Swanson Co. Sponsor Jr. Achievement, 1964-67. Served to lt. USNR, 1958-60. Coll. Men's Club scholar Westfield, N.J., 1954-55. Mem. Fed. Govt. Accountants Assn. (hon.), Duke Washington Club, Omicron Delta Kappa. Home: 1100 Park Ave Apt 8A New York NY 10028 Office: Ardshiel 230 Park Ave New York NY 10169

TURNER, JOE STEWART, electrical engineer; b. Sherman, Tex., 1909; s. Ethelbert and Annie Lee (Stewart) T.; m. Vivian Dybwad, Jan. 7, 1932; children: Jo Ann (Mrs. Lawrence Albert Westhaver), Robert Roger. Grad. Chgo. Radio and T.V. Inst., 1932; BA with honors, U. Tex., 1934. Elec. engr. Cooney Mining Co., Glenwood, N.M., 1934-35, Internat. Milling Co., Greenville, Tex., engr., sect. supr. CAA, Ft. Worth, and Washington, 1936-47, supt. Pacific area communications, Honolulu, 1948-52; chief radar div. FAA, Washington, 1953-59; project dir. systems div. dir. Collins Radio Co., Dallas, 1960-65; supr. cost control and new tech. reporting Bendix Launch Support, Kennedy Space Center, Fla., 1966-73; research and devel. on alt. energy sources, Titusville, Fla., 1974—. Author: DOD/Commerce Joint Use of Radar Agreement, 1958, Airport Surface Detection Equipment, 1959, Perfomance Standards for Communications Systems, 1960; patentee in field. Coach, Annandale (Va.) Swim Team, 1956; bd. dirs. Annandale Recreation Center, 1956; charter mem. Republican Presdl. Task Force. Served with AUS, 1943-44. Named Bendix/NASA launch honoree, Nov. 1973, Man of Month, Dec. 1973; honored by astronauts for work on Apollo program; Dept. Energy research grantee, 1981; recipient award Best Cost Control Program, Launch Support div. Bendix Corp., 1977, Letter of Commendation, Civil Aeronautics Adminstrn., 1958, Launch Support div. Bendix Corp., 1968. Mem. IEEE (sr.; chmn. Pacific sect. 1951), Bendix Mgmt. Club, Soc. Airway Pioneers (life), Planetary Soc. Home: 2825-614 S Washington Ave Titusville FL 32780

TURNER, JOHN W., paper manufacturing company executive; b. 1936; married. Student, Coll. Wooster; BS, U.S. Naval Acad., 1959; MBA, U. Pitts., 1977. Commd. 2d lt. USN, 1959, resigned, 1964; with Kimberly-Clark Corp., 1964-71; product mgr. Appleton (Wis.) Papers, Inc., 1971-72, mgr. Spring Mill, 1972-79, gen. mgr. eastern area, 1979-81, v.p. mfg. ops., 1981-84, sr. v.p. mktg., 1984-85, pres., chief operating officer, 1985-86, chief exec. officer, chmn. bd. dirs., 1986—. Office: Appleton Papers Inc 825 E Wisconsin Ave Appleton WI 54912

TURNER, JOHN WALTER, investor; b. Cleve., June 4, 1923; s. John H. and Dessa (Walter) T.; m. Marion T. Taylor, Feb. 3, 1945; 1 child, Leslie Ann. Student, N.Mex. Mil. Inst., 1942-43, U. N.Mex., 1943-44. With Davis, Skaggs & Co. investment bankers, San Francisco, 1946-49; S.W. rep. Axe Securities Corp., 1949-52; founder, pres., chmn. bd. Eppler Guerin & Turner, Inc., 1952-73; pres. N.Y. Stock Exch., Dallas, 1952-65, chmn. bd., 1965-73; bd. dirs. United N.Mex. Fin. Corp., El Chico, Inc., 1st So. Trust Co., Banctec, Inc., Dallas, Comml. Metals Col, Computer Lang. Rsch., Inc., Highland Park Cafeterias, Inc., Fin. Securities Advs., Inc., Nashville; adv. dir. Hayward, Inc., Dallas; past gov. Am. Stock Exchange, Midwest Stock Exch., Vicorp Restaurants, Denver, Golden Era Svcs., Inc., Houston; past chmn. Tex. State Securities. Trustee St. Vincent Hosp., Santa Fe, N.Mex.; bd. dirs. Santa Fe Community Found., Santa Fe Inst. Fine Arts. With USNR, 1943-46, PTO. Mem. Ind. Petroleum Assn. Am., N.MEx. Rsch. and Devel. Inst. (bus. adv. group), Am. Brahman Breeders Assn., Dallas Security Dealers Assn., Inst. Bus. Appraisers, Nat. Assn. Corp. DIrs., N.Mex. Mil. Inst. Alumni Assn., Sigma Chi (life), Chuck Wagon Trial Riders N.Mex. Club, Dallas Country Club, Dallas Petroleum Club, Kiva Club. Clubs: Dallas Petroleum, Dallas Country, Kiva of New Mexico. Home: RR 9 PO Box 62T Santa Fe NM 87505 Office: 2001 Bryan Tower Ste 2874 Dallas TX 75201

TURNER, JOSEPH CRAWFORD, operations manager; b. Winston-Salem, N.C., Apr. 26, 1955; s. William Francis and Notre Joan (Meadows) T.; m. Rhia Annette Nunnally, July 19, 1980. AA in Sci., Haywood Tech. Coll., 1975. Research technician Minerals Research Lab, Asheville, N.C., 1977-79; quality control supr. Internat. Minerals Chems. Corp., Green Mountain, N.C., 1979-80, plant supt., 1980-82, plant mgr., 1982-86; ops. mgr. Applied Indsl. Materials Corp., Green Mountain, N.C., 1986—. Mem. Soc. Mining Engrs. Baptist. Home: 4 Fern Cove Rd Asheville NC 28804 Office: Applied Indsl Materials Corp Drawer N Green Mountain NC 28740

TURNER, JOSEPH LEWIS, JR., utility company executive; b. Coatesville, Pa., Nov. 20, 1936; s. Joseph L. Sr. and Mildred (Myers) T.; m. Patricia Dinsdale, Jan. 21, 1961; children: David L., Robin P. BA in English, Williams Coll., 1959. Gen. mgr. U.S. Steel Corp., Pitts., 1960-78; pres. Marmon/Keystone Corp., Butler, Pa., 1978-79; v.p. Fluor Corp., Irvine, Calif., 1979-84, Hydril Co., Houston, 1984-86; v.p., gen. mgr. No. Ind. Pub. Svc. Co., Hammond, 1986—. Bd. dirs. Hospice N.W. Ind., Hammond, 1986—, BEV-PAC, Monticello, Ind.; bd. dirs., chmn. lake area United Way. Sgt. U.S. Army, 1960-66. Mem. Am. Iron and Steel Inst., Am. Gas Assn., Electric Power Rsch. Inst., Gas Rsch. Inst., Edison Electric Inst. Home: 8620 Baring Ave Munster IN 46321 Office: No Ind Pub Svc Co 5265 Hohman Ave Hammond IN 46320

TURNER, LA FERRIA MARIA, tax consultant; b. Chgo., Oct. 7, 1962; d. James and Irma (Thomas) T. Data processor Acad. Gen. Dentistry, Chgo., 1986-87; exec. officer adminstr. Alpha Kappa Alpha, Chgo., 1986; computer cons. Ellis & Ellis Realty, Chgo., 1987; tax cons. IRS, Chgo., 1987—. Fellow NAFE, Am. Soc. Women Accts., Am. Mgmt. Assn., Nat. Coun. on Pay Equity, Assn. Info. Systems Profls. Democrat. Home: 8011 S Union Ave #G Chicago IL 60620 Office: IRS 230 S Dearborn Ave Chicago IL 60604

TURNER, LISA PHILLIPS, data processing executive; b. Waltham, Mass., Apr. 10, 1951; d. James Sinclair and Virginia (Heathcote) T. BA in Edn. and Philosophy magna cum laude, Washington Coll., Chestertown, Md., 1974; AS in Electronics Tech., Palm Beach Jr. Coll., 1982; MBA, Nova U., 1986, DSc, 1989. Cert. personnel adminstr., quality engr., human resource professional. Founder, pres. Turner's Bicycle Svc., Inc., Delray Beach, Fla., 1975-80; electronics engr., quality engr. Audio Engring. and Video Arts, Boca Raton, 1980-81; tech. writing instr. Palm Beach Jr. Coll., Lake Worth, Fla., 1981-82; adminstr. tng. and devel. Mitel Inc., Boca Raton, 1982-88; mgr. communications and employee relations Modular Computer Systems, Inc., Ft. Lauderdale, Fla., 1988—. Mem. Am. Soc. for Personnel Adminstrn., Am. Soc. Tng. and Devel., Internat. Assn. Quality Circles, Am. Soc. Quality Control, USCG Aux., Am. Acad. Mgmt. Home: 2027 SW 12th Ct Delray Beach FL 33445 Office: Modular Computer Systems Inc PO Box 6099 Fort Lauderdale FL 33340

TURNER, MARY LOUISE, bank supervisor; b. Glens Falls, N.Y., June 24, 1954; d. Gilmore Eldridge and Joan (Ringrose) T. AAS, Adriondack Community Coll., Glens Falls, 1974. Computer operator Glens Falls Nat. Bank & Trust Co., 1974—; refreshment mgr. Lake George Opera Festival, Glens Falls, summer 1974. Author: (novel) Today Begins Tomorrow, 1986; (poetry) Why Me, 1983, Auf Wiedersehen, 1988, Jealousy (poetry), 1988, You've Got To Be Kidding (poetry), 1988, What If Time Stood Still (poetry), 1989. Republican. Home: Box 113 Schuylerville Rd Gansevoort NY 12831

TURNER, PAUL F., biomedical company executive; b. Salt Lake City, Apr. 19, 1947; s. Frank Paul and Needra (Fullmer) T.; m. Judith Marie Hilton, May 23, 1968; children; Paul Scott, Lisa Marie. BSEE, U. Utah, 1971, MSEE, 1983. Project engr. U. Utah., Salt Lake City, 1970-71; systems engr. Sperry Univac, Salt Lake City, 1971-78; sr. scientist, staff engr. BSD Med. Corp., Salt Lake City, 1978-86, sr. v.p. rsch., 1986—; sponsor, coord. rsch. clinic U. Utah, 1987—. Contbr. articles to profl. jours.; patentee in field. Missionary LDS Ch., Alta., Can., 1966-68, bishopric counselor, North Salt Lake, Utah, 1979-82, high counsel 1982-88; asst. dist. coord. Boy Scouts Am., Davis County, utah, 1982-86. NIH grantee, 1985—. Mem. IEEE, N.Am. Hyperthermia Group, Bioelectromagnetics Soc. Home: 762 Lacey Way North Salt Lake UT 84054 Office: BSD Med Corp 420 Way Salt Lake City UT 84108

TURNER, RALPH (CHIP) WILSON, JR., broadcasting executive, clergyman; b. Shreveport, La., Jan. 18, 1948; s. Ralph W. and Gladys Pearl (Ma Gouirk) T.; m. Sandra Elaine Aymond, May 23, 1970; children: Christopher Layne, Cory Wilson. BA cum laude in Speech Edn., La. Coll., 1970; MRE, New Orleans Bapt. Theol. Sem., 1973. Ordained to ministry Bapt. Ch., as deacon, 1972. Assoc. pastor and minister edn. 1st Bapt. Ch., Farmerville, La., 1968-71, 1st Bapt. Ch., Summit, Miss., 1971-73, 1st Bapt. Ch., Slidell, La., 1973-75, 1st Bapt. Ch., Port Arthur, Tex., 1975-76; minister edn. and bus. adminstr. 1st Bapt. Ch., Beaumont, Tex., 1976-79; assoc. dir. missions, teaching and tng. Greater New Orleans Bapt. Assn., 1979-81; dir. media services dept. La. Bapt. Conv., 1981—, also state dir. The ACTS Satellite Network, 1983—; state coordinator Bapt. Telecommunication Network, 1983—; guest faculty New Orleans Bapt. Theol. Sem., 1979-80, 84, 87; Sunday sch. dir. St. Tammany Bapt. Assn., Slidell, 1973-75; ch. tng. dir. Concord Bapt. Assn., Farmerville, 1970-71; mem. Commn. for Ch. and Youth Agy. Relationships (nat. pres. 1988-90, founding editor nat. newsletter Youthscope 1985—); mem. state editorial panel Bapt. Message, 1988—; Merit badge counselor, exec. bds. New Orleans Area, Three Rivers and Attakapas councils Boy Scouts Am., 1973—, relationships v.p., 1983—, Nat. Religious Relationships Com., 1988, Nat. Relationships Standing Com., 1989—, Nat. Duty to God Task Force, 1988-89, Nat. Values Emphasis Task Force, chmn. 1989—, So. Pub. Rels. Fedn.; dist. rep. Nat. Eagle Scout Assn., 1975-79, participant Nat. Boy Scout Teleconf., 1988; faculty mem. Bapt. Week at Philmont Scout Ranch, 1978, 80, 88, dir. Protestant Wk. Philmont Ranch, 1987, 88; coord. Chaplain for Nat. Jamboree, 1985, 85, 89; mem. Nat. Protestant Com., 1980— ; deacon Calvary Bapt. Ch., Alexandria, 1987, assoc. chmn., 1988, La. Baptist Message Guest Editorial Panel, 1988—. Recipient Alexandria (La.) Civitan Citizenship award, 1969, 70; Silver Beaver award Boy Scouts Am., 1982; Good Shepherd award Nat. Assn. Baptists for Scouting, 1980; Nat. God and Service recognition (Protestant), 1986; Bronze Pelican award Cath. Com. on Scouting, 1986, Nat. Promotion award ACTS Network, 1986, 87. Mem. Nat. Assn. of Ch. Bus. Adminstrs., Pub. Relations Assn. La., La. Bapt. Religious Edn. Assn., Bapt. Public Relations Assn., Met. Assn. of Religious Edn. Dirs., So. Bapt. Religious Edn. Assn., Golden Triangle Religious Edn. Assn., Nat. Audio-Visual Assn., Tex. Bapt. Public Relations Assn., So. Pub. Relations Fedn., La. Cable TV Assn. (assoc.), Southwestern Bapt. Religious Edn. Assn., Nat. Assn. Local Ch. Communicators (charter), Assn. Bapt. for Scouting (nat. bd. 1978—), Internat. TV Assn., Assn. for Ednl. Communications and Tech., La. Assn. for Ednl. Communications and Tech., Internat. Platform Assn., Nat. Assn. Local Cable Programmers, Am. Assn. Media Specialists, Assn. State ACTS Dirs. (founder, chmn., 1st pres. 1986-88, 88-89), Young Men's Bus. League of Beaumont, Alpha Phi Omega (life mem.; chpt. founder). Republican. Lodges: Lions, Rotary (newsletter editor 1976, chorister 1976). Author: Training Sunday School Workers, 1982; How To Use Audiovisuals; The Church Video Answerbook: A Nontechnical Guide for Ministers and Lay Persons, 1986; contbr. articles to religious, adminstrv. and scouting publs. Avocations: writing, computers, photography. Office: LBC Media Svcs 1250 MacArthur Dr PO Box 311 Alexandria LA 71309

TURNER, RICHARD ARLEN, financial executive; b. Lynchburg, Ohio, Feb. 5, 1934; s. Issac Hamilton and Cleo (Wood) T.; m. Marilyn June Rose, Aug. 30, 1959; children— Kimberly Ann, David Arlen. BS, Miami U., 1960, postgrad., 1962-63. CPA, Ohio, Calif. Mgr. Deloitte Haskins & Sells, Dayton, Ohio, San Francisco and Caracas, Venezuela, 1960-73; sec.-treas. Grihalva Chevrolet, San Diego, 1973-74; cons. various cos., San Diego and Phoenix, 1975-76; v.p. fin. Pepper Industries, San Diego, 1976-80; v.p. fin. Ernst Enterprises, Inc., Dayton, Ohio, 1980-86; pres. H.R. Large & Assocs., Inc., San Diego, 1986—; v.p. fin. Sail Am. Found. (name changed to Am.'s Cup Organizing Com., 1988—; ptnr., co-founder Corp. Mgmt. Specialists, San Diego, 1988—; chief fin officer High Ground Assocs., San Diego, 1988—. dir. Dolly Toy Co., Tipp City, Ohio, R & R Constrn. Co., Union, Ohio; fin. cons. Kuhns Tool Co., Brookville, Ohio, 1983-86. Bd. dirs. Grace Brethern Community Ch., Union, 1984-86. Served with USAF, 1952-56. Mem. AICPA, Nat. Ready Mixed Concrete Assn. (fin. mgmt. com.), Ohio Ready Mixed Concrete Assn. (treas. 1984-86), Rotary, Optimist (treas. 1974-75). Republican. Home: 803 Concerto Glen Escondido CA 92025 Office: Am's Cup Organizing Com 1660 Hotel Circle N Ste 710 San Diego CA 92108 Also: Sail America Found 1904 Hotel Circle N San Diego CA 92108

TURNER, RODERICK L., consumer packaged products manufacturing company executive; b. Mineola, N.Y., June 1, 1931; s. Claude E. and Eulalia (Rodriguez) T.; m. Teresa C. Vadetaire, May, 1957; children—R. Bradford, Melissa A. B.A., Cornell U., 1952. Vice-pres. Benton & Bowles, Inc., N.Y.C., 1958-63; group product mgr. personal products div. Colgate-Palmolive Co., N.Y.C., 1963-67; group product mgr. household products div. Colgate-Palmolive Co., 1967-68; pres., gen. mgr. Colgate Canadian Co., 1969-72, v.p. mktg. services div., 1973; corp. v.p., gen. mgr. Western hemisphere div. Colgate-Palmolive Co., 1974-76, gen. mgr. European div., 1977-78, group v.p., internat. ops., 1979-81, exec. v.p., 1981-85, sr. exec. v.p., 1985—. Served to 1st lt. AUS, 1952-54, Korea. Office: Colgate-Palmolive Co 300 Park Ave New York NY 10022

TURNER, ROSS JAMES, investment corporation executive; b. Winnipeg, Man., Can., May 1, 1930; s. James Valentine and Gretta H. (Ross) T.; children: Ralph, Rick, Tracy Lee. U. Man. Extension, 1951, Banff Sch. Advanced Mgmt., 1956. Various sr. operating and mgmt. positions Genstar Corp., San Francisco, 1961-76, chmn./pres., chief exec. officer, 1976-86, also bd. dirs.; chmn. Genstar Investment Corp., San Francisco, 1986—; chmn., bd. dirs. Rio Algom Ltd., Gt. West Life Assurance Co., Fed. Industries Ltd.; bd. dirs. Blue Shield of Calif., Guy F. Atkinson Co. of Calif., Oxford Properties Can. Ltd., Western Corp. Enterprises Inc. Vice chmn. bd. dirs. YMCA, San Francisco; mem. Bay Area Internat. Forum. Fellow Soc. Mgmt. Accts. Can.; mem. San Francisco C. of C. (past chmn., dir.), Toronto Club, Vancouver Club, World Trade Club, Pacific Union Club, Rancho Santa Fe Golf Club, Peninsula Golf and Country Club. Office: Genstar Investment Corp 801 Montgomery San Francisco CA 94133

TURNER, STANSFIELD, former government official, lecturer, writer; b. Chgo., Dec. 1, 1923; s. Oliver Stansfield and Wilhelmina Josephine (Wagner)

T.; m. Eli Karin Gilbert, Mar. 16. 1985. Student, Amherst Coll., 1941-43, DCL, 1975; BS, U.S. Naval Acad., 1946; MA (Rhodes scholar), Oxford U., 1950; LHD, Sierra Nev. Coll., 1984; HumD, Roger Williams Coll., 1975; DSc in Edn, Bryant Coll., 1977; LLD, Salve Regina Coll., 1977, The Citadel, 1980, Pace U., 1980. Ensign USN, 1946, advanced through grades to adm., 1975, ret., 1979; served primarily in destroyer; commd. U.S.S. Horne, guided missile cruiser, 1967-68; comdr. in Vietnam conflic; aide to sec. Navy, 1968-70; comdr. carrier task group 6th Fleet, 1970-71; dir. systems analysis div. Office Chief Naval Ops., Navy Dept., Washington, 1971-72; pres. Naval War Coll., Newport, R.I., 1972-74; comdr. U.S. Second Fleet, 1974-75; comdr.-in-chief Allied Forces So. Europe, NATO, 1975-77; dir. CIA, Washington, 1977-81. Author: Secrecy and Democracy, 1985. Decorated Nat. Security medal, Legion of Merit, Bronze Star. Home and Office: 1320 Skipwith Rd McLean VA 22101

TURNER, STEVE, discount store executive. Exec. v.p., chief oper. officer Dollar Gen. Corp., Ky. Office: Dollar Gen Corp 427 Beech St Scottsville KY 42164 *

TURNER, STEVEN WILSON, mortgage broker, consultant; b. Fillmore, Utah, July 20, 1959; s. Sanford (Jack) and Alta Margaret (Wilson) T. BA in Econs., U. Utah, 1986. Mktg. asst. Comphealth, Salt Lake City, 1983-85; fin. cons. Peak Fin., Inc., Bountiful, Utah, 1985—. Served to 2d lt. U.S. Army, 1985-86. Republican. Mormon. Club: Inter Broth of Magicians (Ohio). Office: Peak Fin Inc 845 S Main #102A Bountiful UT 84010

TURNER, TED (ROBERT EDWARD TURNER, III), broadcasting and sports executive, yachtsman; b. Nov. 19, 1938; m. Judy Nye (div.); children: Laura Lee, Robert Edward IV; m. Jane Shirley Smith, 1964 (div.); children: Rhett, Beau, Jennie. Ed., Brown U. Gen. mgr. Turner Advt., Macon, Ga., 1960-63; pres., chief exec. officer various Turner Cos., Atlanta, 1963-70; chmn. bd., pres. Turner Broadcasting System, Inc.; pres. Atlanta Braves, 1976—; chmn. bd. Atlanta Hawks, 1977—; sponsor, creator The Goodwill Games, Moscow, 1986. Won America's Cup in his yacht Courageous, 1977; named Yachtsman of Yr. 4 times. Office: care Atlanta Braves 100 International Blvd PO Box 105366 Atlanta GA 30348-5366 also: Turner Broadcasting System Inc One CNN Ctr Box 105366 Atlanta GA 30308 *

TURNER, WILLIAM COCHRANE, international management consultant; b. Red Oak, Iowa, May 27, 1929; s. James Lyman and Josephine (Cochrane) T.; m. Cynthia Dunbar, July 16, 1955; children: Scott Christopher, Craig Dunbar, Douglas Gordon. BS, Northwestern U., 1952. Pres., chmn. bd. dirs. Western Mgmt. Cons., Inc., Phoenix, 1955-74, Western Mgmt. Cons. Europe, S.A., Brussels, 1968-74; U.S. ambassador, permanent rep. OECD, Paris, 1974-77, vice chmn. exec. com., 1976-77, U.S. rep. Energy Policy Com., 1976-77; mem. U.S. dels. internat. meetings, 1974-77, western internat. trade group U.S. Dept. Commerce, 1972-74; chmn. Argyle Atlantic Corp., Phoenix, 1977—; chmn. European adv. council, 1981-88, Asia Pacific adv. council AT&T Internat., 1981-88; mem. European adv. council IBM World Trade Europe, Africa, Mid. East Corp., 1977-80; mem. Asia Pacific adv. council Am. Can Co., 1981-85, Gen. Electric of Brazil adv. council Gen. Electric Co., Coral Gables, Fla., 1979-81, Caterpillar of Brazil adv. council Caterpillar Tractor Co., Peoria, Ill., 1979-84, Caterpillar Asia Pacific Adv. Council, 1984—, U.S. adv. com. Trade Negotiations, 1982-84; bd. dirs. Goodyear Tire & Rubber Co., Akron, Ohio, 1978—, Salomon Inc., N.Y.C., 1980—, Atlantic Inst. Found., Inc., 1984—, mem. internat. adv. council Avon Products, Inc., N.Y.C., 1985—; mem. Spencer Stuart adv. council Spencer Stuart and Assocs., N.Y.C., 1984—; chmn., mem. internat. adv. council Advanced Semiconductor Materials Internat. NV., Bilthoven, The Netherlands, 1985-88; bd. dirs. The Atlantic Council of the U.S., Washington, 1977—; co-chmn. internat. adv. bd. Univ. of Nations, Pacific & Asia Christian U., Kona, Hawaii, 1985—; bd. dirs. World Wildlife Fund/U.S., 1983—, The Conservation Found., 1985—; bd. govs. Joseph H. Lauder Inst. Mgmt. and Internat. Studies, U. Pa., 1983—; trustee Heard Mus., Phoenix, 1983-86, mem. adv. bd., 1986—; trustee Am. Grad. Sch. Internat. Mgmt., 1972—, chmn. bd. trustees, 1987—; bd. govs. Atlantic Inst. Internat. Affairs, Paris, 1977-88; adv. bd. Ctr. Strategic and Internat. Studies, Georgetown U., 1977-81; mem. European Community-U.S. Businessmen's Council, 1978-79; bd. govs. Am. Hosp. of Paris, 1974-77; trustee Nat. Symphony Orch. Assn., Washington, 1973-83, Am. Sch., Paris, 1976-77, Orme Sch., Mayer, Ariz., 1970-74, Phoenix Country Day Sch., 1971-74; mem. nat. councils Salk Inst., 1978-82; mem. U.S. Adv. Com. Internat. Edn. and Cultural Affairs, 1969-74; nat. rev. bd. Ctr. Cultural and Tech. Interchange between East and West, 1970-74; mem. vestry Am. Cathedral, Paris, 1976-77; pres., bd. dirs. Phoenix Symphony Assn., 1969-70; chmn. Ariz. Joint Econ. Devel. Com., 1967-68; exec. com., bd. dirs. Ariz. Dept. Econ. Planning and Devel., 1968-70; chmn. bd. Ariz. Crippled Children's Services, 1964-65; treas. Ariz. Rep. Com., 1956-57; chmn. Ariz. Young Rep. League, 1955-56. Recipient East-West Ctr. Disting. Service award, 1977. Mem. U.S. Council Internat. Bus. (trustee, exec. com.), Council Fgn. Relations, Council of Am. Ambassadors, U.S.-Japan Bus. Council, Nat. Adv. Council on Bus. Edn., Council Internat. Edn. Exchange, Phoenix 40, Met. Club, Links Club (N.Y.C.), Plaza Club (Phoenix), Paradise Valley (Ariz.) Country Club, Bucks Club (London). Episcopalian. Office: 4350 E Camelback Rd Suite 240-B Phoenix AZ 85018

TURNER, WILLIAM HUTCHINS, banker; b. Paterson, N.J., Mar. 25, 1940; s. William Hutchins and Margaret (Gray) T.; m. Judith Clarke, July 28, 1962; children—Christopher, Andrew. B.A., Trinity Coll., 1962; M.B.A., NYU, 1966; AMP, Harvard U., 1986. Credit officer Chem Bank, N.Y.C., 1962-71; v.p. Chem. Bank, N.Y.C., 1971-77, sr. v.p., 1977-82, exec. v.p., 1982-86, group exec., 1987—; chmn. N.Y. Bd. Trade, N.Y.C., 1983-86; dir. N.Y.C. Housing Partnership. Trustee Mcpl. Art Soc., N.Y.C., 1984-86; treas. Internat. Coll., Beirut, 1975-86, chmn. 1986—; v.p. fin. Adult Sch. Montclair, N.J., 1974—; bd. dirs. UN Assn. of U.S.A., 1986—, Regional Plan Assn., 1986—; mem. adv. bd. Queens Coll., 1986—. Clubs: Montclair Golf; Farmington Country (Charlottesville, Va.). Home: 384 Upper Mountain Ave Upper Montclair NJ 07043 Office: Chem Banking Corp 277 Park Ave New York NY 10172 *

TURNER, WILLIAM J., data processing company executive; b. 1944; married. Grad., U. Maine, 1965; MBA, Northeastern U., 1969. With Digital Equipment Co., 1973-80, Tex. Instruments, 1980-83; pres. Automatic Data Processing, Inc., Roseland, N.J., 1983—, also bd. dirs. Office: ADP Inc 1 Automatic Data Processing Blvd Roseland NJ 07068 *

TURNER, WILLIAM THOMAS, JR., oil and gas industry executive; b. Bastrop, La., Nov. 8, 1928; s. William Thomas and Annie (Aden) T.; m. Sara Kathryn Miller, Dec. 4, 1954 (dec. May 1967); children: Jeffrey Stephen, Lisa Kathryn Swanton, Christopher William; m. Colleen Street, June 14, 1968; 1 child, Felicia Street. BSChemE, La. Tech. U., 1948; MSChemE, Ill. Inst. Tech., 1951. Registered profl. engr. Sr. engr. Tex. Gas Transmission Corp., Owensboro, Ky., 1950-52, sr. rsch. engr., 1952-60, dir. planning, 1960-67, asst. to v.p. engring., 1967-75, v.p. engring., 1975-85; sr. v.p. devel. Tex. Gas Transmission Corp., Owensboro, 1985—; pres. Tex. Gas Engring. Inc., Owensboro, 1985—, Tex. Gas Alaska Inc., Owensboro, 1986—; bd. dirs. Yukon Pacific Corp., Anchorage. With U.S. Army, 1950-52. Mem. ASME, Nat. Soc. Profl. Engrs., La. Engring. Soc., Internat. Gas Union, Investigators Club. Republican. Methodist. Home: 4113 Mason Woods Ln Owensboro KY 42301 Office: Tex Gas Transmission Corp 3800 Frederica St Owensboro KY 42301

TURNEY, HOWARD RAY, inventor, personal security company executive; b. Ft. Thomas, Ariz., June 24, 1931; s. Raymond and Grace (Caswell) T.; m. Helen Hogue (div.); children: Jo Ann, Susie Turney Bryant; m. Dedra LaPage, Sept. 5, 1977. With various restaurant cos. 1950-64; food packaging and chem. cos. Los Angeles, 1964-66; exec. v.p. Nat. PAX, Inc., Los Angeles, 1966-70; semi-ret. in investments and real estate Greenville, Tex., 1970-75; pres. VISTA Internat. Inc., Addison, Ill., 1975-77; chmn., pres. Shrimp Systems Internat. Inc., Park Forest South, Ill., 1977-80; chmn. bd. Electric Systems Internat. Inc., Lombard, Ill., 1977-80, Power Resource Systems Tex. Ltd., Houston, 1980-83, Systems Internat., Houston, 1983-87, MAYDAY USA, Inc., Houston, 1987—. Inventor MAYDAY system, intensive shrimp growing system, food products/consumer items. Mem. Internat. Cogeneration Soc., World Mariculture Soc., Am. Mensa. Office: MAYDAY USA Inc 2525 McAllister Rd Houston TX 77092

TURNHEIM, PALMER, financial consultant, banker; b. S.I., N.Y., June 30, 1921; s. Gustav and Helga (Hansen) T.; m. Gloria Freer, June 6, 1948; 1 dau., Joy Karen. B.S. magna cum laude, N.Y. U., 1960; 4 year diploma, Am. Inst. Banking, 1947; grad., Stonier Grad. Sch. Banking, Rutgers U., 1958, Advanced Mgmt. Program, Harvard, 1962. Asst. mgr. credit dept. Chase Nat. Bank, 1951-55, asst. treas., 1955; asst. v.p. Chase Manhattan Bank, N.Y.C., 1956-61; v.p. Chase Manhattan Bank, 1961-71, sr. v.p., 1971-86; sr. v.p. Chase Manhattan Capital Markets Corp.; instr. mgmt. decision lab. Grad. Sch. Bus. Adminstrn. NYU, 1986—; v.p. and treas. Chasex Assocs. Inc. Author: International Finance Corporation, 1958. Nat. pres. United Cerebral Palsy Assns., Inc., 1967-70; dir. United Cerebral Palsy Research and Ednl. Found.; Mem. U.S. govt. com. on cash mgmt. Gen. Services Adminstrn., Washington, Am. Bankers Assn. task force advising Dept. Energy on gasoline rationing, 1979-81; Bd. dirs. Fund for Theol. Edn., 1957-84, N.Y. Inst. Credit, 1971-84. Served with USAAF, 1942-46. Mem. N.Y. State Bankers Assn. (dir. 1972-75), N.Y.U. Sch. Commerce Alumni Assn. (pres. 1982-83), N.Y.U. Alumni Fedn. (v.p., dir., mem. coun.), Am. Legion, Beta Gamma Sigma, Phi Alpha Kappa. Lutheran. Clubs: Harvard Bus. Sch., Union League, NYU Fin. (pres., dir. 1982-83); Internat. (Washington). Home: 23 Oak Ln Mountain Lakes NJ 07046

TURNOY, BERNARD IVAN, insurance broker; b. Chgo., Nov. 8, 1954; s. Herbert Samuel and Jule H. (Young) T. BA in Polit. Sci., The Am. U., Washington, 1976; postgrad. in Legal Studies, Cambridge U., Eng., 1977-79. Lic. ins. agt., Ill. Field rep. The Mutual Life Ins. Co. N.Y., Chgo., 1980-85; chief exec. officer Bernard I. Turnoy & Assocs., Chgo., 1986—; mktg. cons. The Mut. Life Ins. Co. N.Y., 1984. Mem. Chgo. Council on Fgn. Relations, English Speaking Union, Chgo.; issues coordinator Congl. Campaign 10th Congrl. Dist., 1979. Mem. Nat. Assn. Life Underwriters (Nat. Sales Achievement award 1985, Health Ins. Quality award 1988), Chgo. Assn. Life Underwriters, Life Ins. Mktg. and Rsch. Assn. (Nat. Quality award 1984), United Oxford and Cambridge Club. Office: 1631 N Halsted St Chicago IL 60614

TURSSO, DENNIS JOSEPH, business executive; b. St. Paul, Apr. 13, 1939; s. Joseph Bias and Cecelia Beatrice (Solheid) T.; m. Sharon Ann Benike, June 6, 1964 (div. 1975); 1 child, Jason Bradford; m. Jacqueline Mary Hoffmann, Oct. 19, 1977; children: Shannon and Missey Michele (twins). Student U. Minn., 1959-61. Sales mgr. Sten-C-Labl Inc., St. Paul, 1958-65; salesman Dymo Industries, Berkeley, Calif., 1965-68; with Dawson Patterson, St. Paul, 1968—; pres., chief exec. officer Tursso Cos. holding co., St. Paul, 1980—; dir. Printing Inds. of Minn.; chmn. Venture Capital Fund St. Paul Port Authority; bd. dirs. Summit Nat. Bank, St. Paul, Blackourn Co., Shamrock Inc., Omaha. Advisor SBA, St. Paul, 1981-83, Norwest Nat. Bank St. Paul; bd. dirs. Childrens' Home Soc. St. Paul. Recipient Star Club sales awards Dymo Industries, 1966, 67. Mem. Nat. Fed. Ind. Bus., Soc. Packaging Engrs., St. Paul C. of C. (cert. of merit, Outstanding Businessman 1987), St. Paul Athletic Club, St. Paul Club, University Club, Minnesota Club, Decathlon, Pool and Yacht Club, Town and Country Club. Address: Tursso Cos 223 Plato Blvd E Saint Paul MN 55107 Office: Tursso Co Plant 3540 Midway Blvd Fort Dodge IA 50501

TUSCHMAN, JAMES MARSHALL, lawyer; b. Toledo, Nov. 28, 1941; s. Chester and Harriet (Harris) T.; m. Ina S. Cheloff, Sept. 2, 1967; children: Chad Michael, Jon Stephen, Sari Anne. BS in Bus., Miami U., Oxford, Ohio, 1963; JD, Ohio State U., 1966. Bar: Ohio 1966. Assoc. Shumaker, Loop & Kendrick, Toledo, 1966-84, ptnr. 1970-84; co-founder, sr. prin., chief operating officer Jacobson Maynard Tuschman & Kalur, Toledo, Cleve., Cin., Columbus, Youngstown and Dayton, Ohio, Charleston, W.Va. and Louisville, 1984—, mem. mgmt. com., v.p. and asst. mng. dir.; chmn. bd., sec. Tuschman Steel Co., Toledo, 1969-76; vice chmn. bd. Kripke Tuschman Industries, Inc., 1977-85, dir. 1977-86; chmn. bd., sec. Toledo Steel Supply Co., 1969-86; ptnr. Starr Ave. Co., Toledo, 1969-86; bd. dirs., asst. gen. counsel PIE Mut. Ins. Co., Cleve.; bd. dirs. Capital Holdings Inc., Toledo, Capital Bank, Toledo. Trustee, chmn. fin. com., treas. Maumee Valley Country Day Sch.; past trustee, v.p., treas. Temple B'nai Israel. Mem. ABA, Ohio Bar Assn., Toledo Bar Assn., Def. Research and Trial Lawyers Assn., Zeta Beta Tau, Phi Delta Phi. Club: Toledo. Home: 2579 Olde Brookside Rd Toledo OH 43615 Office: 4 Sea Gate Ste 901 Toledo OH 43604

TUSIANI, MICHAEL DANTE, ship and cargo broker, consultant; b. N.Y.C., Aug. 23, 1948; s. Michele and Maria (Pisone) T.; B.A., L.I.U., 1969; M.A., Fordham U., 1970; m. Beatrice A. Cicio, July 11, 1971; children—Michael, Paula, Pamela. With Zapata Naess Shipping Co. Ltd., N.Y.C., 1970-73; with Poten & Partners, Inc., N.Y.C., 1970—, chief operating officer, 1980-83, chmn., chief exec. officer, 1983—; chmn. Poten & Partners Ltd. (Bermuda); mem. faculty Fordham U., 1971-75. Served with USAR, 1970-71. Mem. Am. Econ. Assn., Nat. Assn. Bus. Economists, Am. Fin. Assn. Clubs: Metropolitan (N.Y.C.). Author articles in field.

TUSZYNSKI, DANIEL J., JR., sales and marketing executive; b. Erie, Pa., Aug. 22, 1947; s. Daniel and Dorothy (Tlyman) T. AA, L.A. City Coll., 1973; BS, Calif. State U., 1975; MBA, Gannon U., 1979. Indsl. engr. Gen. Electric Co., Erie, Pa., 1965-75; sales mgr. Burroughs Corp., Culver City, Calif., 1975-76, Gen. Electric Co., Erie, 1976-81; dir. sales, mktg. Peerless Mfg. Co., Inc, Dallas, 1981-85; v.p. sales, mktg. Consumat Systems, Inc., Richmond, Va., 1985-88; v.p. mktg. Sutton Holding Co., Richmond, 1988-89. Author: (manual) Peerless Air Inlet Systems, 1984. 1st lt. USNG, 1968-75. Mem. Am. Mktg. Assn., Assn. MBA Execs. Roman Catholic. Home: 2911 Linderwood Dr Mechanicsville VA 23111 Office: W B Goode Co Inc 1000 Jefferson Davis Hwy Richmond VA 23224

TUTELMAN, JACKI DEENA, textile company executive, consultant; b. Roslyn, N.Y., Nov. 14, 1954; d. Paul and Elaine (Kligman) T. BS in Mass Communications, Emerson Coll., Boston, 1976. Group buyer European and Am. designer collections for women Bloomingdale's, 1976-86; v.p. Jakob Schlaepfer, Inc., St. Gallen, Switzerland, N.Y.C., 1986—. Mem. Fashion Group, Emerson Coll. Alumni Assn.

TUTHILL, WALTER WARREN, retail executive; b. Madison, N.J., Nov. 28, 1941; s. Walter Warren and Elizabeth Emma (Kniskern) T.; m. Barbara Ann Stephens, Apr. 22, 1967. BSBA, U. N.C., 1964. CPA, N.Y., N.J., N.C.; cert. info systems auditor, cert. internal auditor. Sr. mgr. Price Waterhouse, N.Y.C., 1964-77; dir. internal audit Carter Hawley Hale Stores Inc., Los Angeles, 1977-82, gen. auditor, 1982-85, v.p., 1985—; lectr. in field. Contbr. articles to profl. jours. Pres. Twin W Rescue Squad, Princeton Junction, N.J., 1976-77. Mem. Am. Inst. CPA's, N.Y. State Soc. CPA's, Am. Statis. Assn., Am. Acctg. Assn., Inst. Internal Auditors, Nat. Retail Mchts. Assn. (chmn. bd. internal audit group 1982-84, bd. dirs.), L.A. Athletic Club. Office: Carter Hawley Hale Stores Inc 550 S Flower St Los Angeles CA 90071

TUTT, FRED DAVID, insurance executive; b. N.Y.C., Jan. 4, 1946; s. Wilson Fred and Bertha Florene (Davis) T.; m. Gloria Jean Rutherford, Nov. 27, 1964; children: David Wayne, Danny Ray, Darryl Wilson. Grad., Arkansas High Sch., Texarkana, 1964. Adminstrv. v.p. Nat. Found. Life Ins., Oklahoma City, 1966-78; dir. corp. devel. Am. Liberty Fin. Corp., Baton Rouge, 1978-80; pres., chief exec. officer So. Capitol Enterprises, Baton Rouge, 1980—; v.p. La. Cajun Specialties, 1989—; pres. Ins. Mgmt. and Assocs. La., 1989—; mem. exec. bd. dirs. Acadia State Bank; millionaire bd. dirs. Capitol Am. Life Ins. fin. supporter Spl. Olympics, Baton Rouge, 1986-87. Mem. Baton Rouge C. of C. Republican. Baptist. Office: So Capitol Enterprises 10915 Perkins Rd Baton Rouge LA 70810

TUTTLE, DONNA FRAME, government official; b. Los Angeles, Apr. 21, 1947; d. Les Frame and Marilyn (Dunton) Simpson; m. Robert Holmes Tuttle, Mar. 25, 1972; children—Tiffany Noel, Alexandra Christina. B.A. in History, U. So. Calif., 1969; Edn. credential, UCLA, 1970. Tchr. Los Angeles City Schs., 1970-75; nat. chmn. Youth for Reagan-Bush Campaign, Los Angeles, 1980; under sec. for travel and tourism U.S. Dept. Commerce, Washington, 1983-88; dep. sec. U.S. Dept. Commerce, 1988—. Bd. dirs. Coro Found., Los Angeles, 1978—, John F. Kennedy Ctr., Washington, 1982. Recipient Travel Woman of Yr. award Travel Industry of Am., 1984; Travel Leader of Yr. award Nat. Tour Assn., 1984; Golden Wheel award Am. Bus. Assn., 1984; Travel South Leader of Yr. award Travel South USA, 1985. Republican. Office: US Travel and Tourism Adminstrn US Dept Commerce Rm 1865 Washington DC 20230

TUTTLE, EDWIN ELLSWORTH, chemical company executive; b. Syracuse, N.Y., Apr. 24, 1927; s. John Ross and Celia (Boyington) T. B.S., Haverford Coll., 1949; M.B.A., Harvard U., 1951. Apptd. asst. to pres. Pennwalt Corp., Phila., 1957, v.p., treas., 1965-70, v.p. finance, 1971-72, group v.p. chems., 1972-74, exec. v.p. adminstrn., 1974-76, pres., 1976-77, vice chmn., 1977-78, chmn., chief exec. officer, 1978—; bd. dirs. 1st Pa. Corp., 1st Pa. Bank N.A., Westmoreland Coal, Gen. Accident Ins. Co. Am., Fidelity Mut. Life Ins. Co. Bd. dirs. Urban Affairs Partnership, Greater Phila. First Corp., Pa. Bus. Roundtable, Met. Phila. Family YMCA's; chmn. bd. Pa. Ballet; mem. corp. Haverford Coll. Mem. Pa. Chamber Bus. and Industry (bd. dirs.). Home: 514 Pine St Philadelphia PA 19106 Office: Pennwalt Corp Pennwalt Bldg 3 Parkway Philadelphia PA 19102

TUTTLE, JANET SOLTIS, computer company executive; b. Bridgeport, Conn., Nov. 5, 1943; d. Michael and Jennie Agnes (Leko) Soltis; m. David Dustin Tuttle, Oct. 7, 1972 (div. 1988). BS in Math., Bates Coll., 1965; MBA in Mktg. and Ops. Research, Columbia U., 1967. With corp. staff IBM Corp., Armonk, N.Y., 1966; systems engr. IBM Corp., N.Y.C., 1967-69; mktg. rep. to Harvard U. IBM Corp., Cambridge, Mass., 1969-72; asst. to dir. info. processing svcs. MIT, Cambridge, Mass., 1972-75; mng. dir. Tuttle Family Trust, Cambridge, Mass., 1975-81; VAX product mktg. mgr., then sr. product mgr. Digital Equipment Corp., Marlborough, Mass., 1981-86, artificial intelligence market conditioning mgr., 1986-87, fin. systems group market conditioning mgr., 1987—; Speaker in field. Appeared in Disney channel documentary film Silver Men, 1987. Chmn. Concord Coun. Boston Symphony Orch., assoc. assn. vols., supporter Tanglewood scholarship programs, capt. Centennial Major Gifts campaign; active guild bd. Opera Co. Boston, patron Fledrmaus Ball; life mem., chmn. Emerson Hosp. Aux.; active ladies assn. bd. Concord Antiquarian Mus., bd. advisors Mus. Sci. and Boston and Sci. Mus. Exhibit Collaborative, Garden Club Concord; life mem. Harwich Hist. Assn., Mus. Fine Arts Boston, Friends Loch Lomond, Nat. Trust for Scotland; mem. fin. com. Trinitarian Congl. Ch.; trustee, life mem. Women's Ednl. and Indsl. Union; bd. dirs., life mem. Hannah Duston Garrison House Assn. Fellow Internat. Biog. Ctr. (life); mem. Am. Assn. Artificial Intelligence, Am. Biog. Inst. Rsch. Assn. (dep. gov., hon. advisor, nat. rsch. bd. advisors), Bates Coll. Class 1965 (reunion chmn., com. chmn. 25th reunion major gifts), Columbia U. Grad. Sch. Bus. Alumni Assn. (nat. chmn. membership), Columbia Bus. Club Boston (founding dir., bd. dirs.), Columbia Club New Eng. (founding dir.), Columbia Club N.Y., Concord Country Club, Harvard Club, Stone Horse Yacht Club, Women's City Club (com. membership), Royal Scottish Automobile Club, Mass. Hort. Soc., So. Mass. Yacht Racing Assn. Home: 77 Francis Ave Cambridge MA 02138 Office: Digital Equipment Corp 397 Williams St Marlborough MA 01749

TUTTLE, ROBERT D., manufacturing and distributing company executive; b. 1925; married. BS, Northwestern U., 1951; MBA, U. Chgo., 1960. With H.M. Harper Co., 1951-60, mgr. mktg.; sr. cons. Booz, Allen & Hamilton, 1960-62; vice chmn. bd., exec. v.p. ops. Ill. Tool Works, 1962-80; pres., chief operating officer Sealed Power Corp., 1980-84, pres., chief exec. officer, 1984-85, chmn., chief exec. officer, 1985—, also bd. dirs. Served to 2d lt. USAF, 1943-46. Named Industrialist of Yr. Mich.'s Impression 5 Sci. Mus., Lansing. Office: SPX Corp 100 Terrace Pla Muskegon MI 49443

TUZ, PETER WILLIAM, financial analyst; b. Derby, Conn., Mar. 27, 1982; m. Nancy S. Tuz, Mar. 27, 1982; children: Courtney, Isabel. BA, Ripon Coll., 1976; MA, U. Mo., 1978; MBA, Tulane U., 1984. Columnist AP, Jefferson City, Mo., 1978-79; reporter St. Louis Bus. Jour., 1980-82; fin. analyst Robert Siegel and Assocs., New Orleans, 1984-85, Howard, Weil, Labouisse and Friedrichs, New Orleans, 1986—. Mem. New Orleans Fin. Analysts. Office: Howard Weil Labouisse and Friedrichs 1100 Poydras St New Orleans LA 70163

TWEED, JOHN LOUIS, investments executive, small business owner; b. Neptune, N.J., Sept. 27, 1947; s. Harry Scullion and Mary Jane (Manniello) T.; m. Joan Marie Parente, Sept. 12, 1970 (div. Apr. 1989); children: Jennifer F., Christin A., Jonathan M. AA in Bus. Adminstrn., Ocean County Coll., Toms River, N.J., 1978. Notary pub. Br. mgr. Retail Delivery Service, Paterson, N.J., 1969-75; pres., chief exec. officer Ambicab, Inc., Toms River, 1975-85; proprietor Bob's Auto Wax Shop, Asbury Park, N.J., 1985-87; mng. ptnr. Investment Enterprises, Toms River, N.J., 1984-86; v.p. strategic planning Multi-Care Emergency Med. Service, Matawan, 1986-89; founder Formal Limousine Service Inc., Toms River, 1988—; v.p. Double Messenger Svc., Inc., Aberdeen, Md. Sec. Toms River Hawks Soccer Club, 1985-86, v.p., 1986-88; founding mem., bd. dirs. Toms River (select) Soccer Assn., 1987-89; mem. Dover Twp. Dem. Club. Served to sgt. USAF, 1965-69. Mem. Am. Ambulance Assn. (dir. at large 1982-87), Med. Transp. Assn. N.J. (pres. 1978-84, exec. dir. 1985—), Am. Entrepreneur's Assn. Roman Catholic. Lodge: Kiwanis (bd. dirs. Toms River club 1982-83). Home and Office: 1962 Lakewood Rd Toms River NJ 08755-1292

TWEEL, NICHOLAS J(OHN), free-lance financial analyst; b. Huntington, W.Va., May 5, 1916; s. John William and Anna (Thabit) T.; m. Vivienne Joy Chapman, Sept. 13, 1942; children: Joyce Gail Tweel Lewis, Nina Lynn Tweel Wood. Grad. high sch., Huntington; student, Marshall U., 1934-36. Clk. U.S. Post Office Dept., Huntington, 1935-42; prin. Mayflower Distbrs., Huntington, 1946-49, Ceredo (W.Va.) Drive-In Theater, 1949-52, Waterford Park Race Track, Pitts., 1952-55; co-owner Tanforan Race Track, San Francisco, 1955-61; prin. Charlestown (W.Va.) Race Track, 1960-63; co-owner Holiday Inns, Huntington and Ft. Lauderdale, 1969-81; prin. River Downs Race Track, Cin., 1973-77; freelance fin. analyst N.Y.C., Beverly Hills, Ft. Lauderdale, 1961; prin. Gen. Mgmt. Co, N.Y.C., Beverly Hills, Ft. Lauderdale, 1961; prin. motion picture industry Emprise Pictures Inc., Beverly Hills, Calif. Patentee in field. Served to capt. US Army, 1942-46. Mem. Am. Legion. Democrat. Episcopalian. Clubs: Army & Navy; Army Officers; N.Y. Athletic; N.Y.A.C. Yacht; Coral Ridge Country; Lago Mar Beach & Tennis. Lodges: Knights of Malta, Elks, Masons, Shriners. Home and Office: 150 Central Park S New York NY 10019

TWELLS, JOHN LAWRENCE, manufacturing and distributing company executive; b. Flint, Mich., Feb., 1934; s. Robert and Margaret Shaw (MacKillop) T.; m. Mary Jane Jentzen, Nov. 1961; children: Linda, John Lawrence, Robert William. BBA, U. Toledo, 1957; postgrad., Marquette U., 1975; MBA, Columbia Pacific U., 1981, DBA, 1983. Lab., terr. mgr., nat. accounts rep. Motorcraft/Autolite div. Ford Motor Co., Dearborn, Mich., 1950-63; dist. mgr., regional sales mgr. MOPAR div. Chrysler Corp., Detroit, 1963-67; asst. gen. mgr. NAPA Genuine Parts Co., Atlanta, 1967-68; gen. mgr. John MacKillop and Co., Inc., Poland, Ohio, 1968—; parts mktg. mgr. Dresser Industries, Waukesha (Wis.) Engine div. 1973-76; mgr. replacement and OEM parts profit ctr. Baker Material Handling Corp., 1976-78; gen. sales mgr. Amweld Bldg. Products Inc., Garretsville, Ohio, 1978-82, asst. gen. mgr., 1982, gen. mgr., 1983-87; pres., chief exec. officer Mesker Door Co., St. Louis, 1987—; lectr. in field. Contbr. articles on microfiche, inventory control, personnel selection, motivation and evaluation to profl. jours. Deacon Immanuel Presbyn. Ch., Milw., 1974-76. Served with U.S. Army, 1957-59. Recipient Disting. Mktg. award Sales and Mktg. mag., 1980. Mem. Am. Prodn. and Inventory Control Soc., Constrn. Specifications Inst., Sales and Mktg. Execs. Internat., Am. Inst. Indsl. Engrs., Am. Def. Preparedness Assn., Am. Legion, VFW, Tau Kappa Epsilon. Republican. Lodge: Rotary. Home: 8996 Sherwood Dr NE Warren OH 44484 Office: PO Box 5214 Poland OH 44514

TWITCHELL, CHRISTINA MARIE, bank executive; b. Cambridge, Mass., Sept. 24, 1953; d. John Bernard and Dorothy Marie (Tobin) Clune; m. Henry David Twitchell, May 13, 1978; children: Stephanie Marie, Justin David. BS in Edn., Northeastern U., 1976. Bookkeeper accounts payable Women's Ednl. and Indsl. Union, Boston, 1976-78; floater Exeter (N.H.) Banking Co., 1978-79; asst. mgr. savs. dept. Exeter, 1979-81; customer svc. rep. Seabrook (N.H.) Bank and Trust Co., 1981-83, customer svc. officer, 1985-86, asst. v.p., 1986-87, v.p., 1987—. Vol. My Greatest Dream, Seabrook, 1985. Mem. Am. Inst. Banking (bd. dirs. 1985-88, gov., v.p. mktg. 1985-86, editor newsletter 1986-88), Hampton Area C. of C. Roman

Catholic. Office: Seabrook Bank and Trust Co 369 Lafayette Rd Hampton NH 03842

TWOMEY, JOSEPH GERALD, lawyer, aerospace executive; b. Boston, Sept. 9, 1926; s. Jeremiah James and Catherine (McPherson) T.; m. Eve Fatzinick, Nov. 3, 1956; children: Brendan, Denise, Lisa, Brian, Leslie. A.B. cum laude, Boston Coll., 1948, LL.B., 1951. Bar: Mass. 1951, Calif. 1964. Atty. Office of Quartermaster Gen., Washington, 1951-61; chief trial atty. Def. Logistics Agy., Washington, 1961-62; counsel Def. Industry Supply Ctr., Phila., 1962-63; assoc. counsel, then chief counsel Lockheed Missiles & Space Co., Sunnyvale, Calif., 1963-77; v.p., chief counsel Lockheed Corp., Burbank, 1977-83, v.p., gen. counsel, 1983—. Served with AUS, 1944-46. Mem. ABA, Fed. Bar Assn., State Bar Calif., Los Angeles County Bar Assn. (exec. com., sec. corp. law dept. 1982-83), Aerospace Corp. (counsel conf.), Machinery and Allied Products Inst. (law counsel), Nat. Contract Mgmt. Assn., Woodland Hills Country Club. Roman Catholic. Office: Lockheed Corp 4500 Park Granada Blvd Calabasas CA 91399

TWYMAN, JACK, wholesale grocery company executive, management services company executive.; b. May 11, 1934; married. Ed., U. Cin. Basketball player Cin. Royals, 1955-67; announcer ABC, 1967-72; vice-chmn. Super Food Services, Inc., Dayton, Ohio, from 1972, formerly pres., chief operating officer, now chmn., chief exec. officer. Office: Super Food Svcs Inc 3185 Elbee Rd Dayton OH 45439 *

TYLER, ORAN BUELL, fiber company executive; b. Schulenburg, Tex., Oct. 15, 1929; s. Oran Buell Tyler Sr. and Alma Isobel (Greenshield) Ramsey; m. Kay Margaret Sullivan, Apr. 19, 1953; children: Lawrence Sullivan (dec.), Hugh Richard, Thomas Oran. AA, Del Mar Coll., 1949; BS, Corpus Christi State U., 1951. Quality control supr. A&M Karagheusian, Albany, Ga., 1954-56; prodn. control supr. A&M Karagheusian, Albany, 1956-58, asst. plan mgr., 1962-64; devel. engr. tufted carpet A&M Karagheusian, Freehold, N.J., 1958-62; supr. carpet testing and evaluation Monsanto Chem. Co., Decatur, Ala., 1964-70; mgr. carpet tech. Monsanto Chem. Co., Decatur, 1970—; speaker in field. 1st lt. U.S. Army, 1951-53, Korea. Mem. Am. Soc. for Testing and Materials, Carpet and Rug Inst. (chmn. performance standards com.). Republican. Methodist. Club: Exchange (Decatur) (pres. 1987). Home: 908 Way Thru the Woods SW Decatur AL 35603 Office: Monsanto Chem Co Courtland Rd Decatur AL 35601

TYMOCZKO, WALTER MICHAEL, housewares manufacturing company financial executive; b. New Kensington, Pa., Dec. 16, 1950; s. Walter John and Florence Beatrice (Telford) T.; m. Wendy Louise Lloyd, Aug. 18, 1972; children—Matthew, Megan. B.S. in Econs., U. Pa., 1972; M.B.A., Duquesne U., 1983. Various fin. and acctg. positions Gen. Electric Co., Phila., 1972-77; mgr. acctg. Action Industries Inc., Cheswick, Pa., 1977-79, v.p., corp. controller, 1979-85; v.p. and chief operating officer Action Internat. Ltd. div. Action Industries, Cheswick, 1985—, sr. v.p., 1987—. Mem. Nat. Assn. Accts., Fin. Execs. Inst., Beta Gamma Sigma. Democrat. Presbyterian. Home: 417 Maplevale Dr Pittsburgh PA 15236 Office: Action Industries Inc 460 Nixon Rd Cheswick PA 15024

TYNDALL, GENE RAMON, management consultant; b. Washington, May 30, 1939; s. Francis M. and Virginia (Creech) T.; m. Shirley V. Friedman, Oct. 6, 1962; children: Traci, Susan. BS, U. Md., 1962; MBA, George Washington U., 1966, DBA, 1969. Systems analyst Gen. Research Corp., McLean, Va., 1966-69; sr. cons. Temple, Barker & Sloane, Inc., Boston, 1969-73; dir. planning U.S. Dept. Trans., Washington, 1973-78; ptnr. Ernst & Whinney, Washington, 1978—. Author: Strategic Marketing Plan, 1985, Distribution Accounting Control, 1983, 2d edit., 1985, Corporate Profitability and Logistics, 1987; logistics columnist Jour. Cost Mgmt., 1986—, Mktg. News, 1988—. Served to lt. USN, 1962-66. Mem. Nat. Assn. Accts., Council Logistics Mgmt. Republican. Office: Ernst & Whinney 1225 Connecticut Ave NW Suite 700 Washington DC 20036

TYNDALL, MARSHALL CLAY, JR., banker; b. Wilmington, Del., Feb. 20, 1943; s. Marshall Clay Sr. and Dorothy Mabel (Batten) T.; m. Bonnie Gay Blankenburg, June 19, 1965; children: Steven Marshall, Michael Edward, Julie Anne. BS, U. Del., 1965, MBA, 1975. With First Pa. Bank, Phila., 1965-73; sr. mktg. officer First Pa. Bank, 1971-73; v.p., dir. mktg. Tex. Commerce Bank, Houston, 1973-76; sr. v.p. Tex. Commerce Bank, 1976—; sr. v.p., dir. mktg. Tex. Commerce Bancshares, Inc., Houston, 1976-82, exec. v.p. mktg., 1982—; bd. dir. Tex. Commerce Bank-Lubbock, Tex. Commerce Bank-River Oaks, Houston. Bd. dirs. Bluebonnet Bowl Assn., Greater Houston Conv. and Visitors Coun.; exec. com. Houston Grand Opera. Mem. Bank Mktg. Assn. (bd. dir. 1977-80), Houston C. of C. Methodist. Office: Tex Commerce Bank NA 712 Main St PO Box 2558 Houston TX 77252

TYNES, THOMAS HUBBARD, accountant; b. Guntersville, Ala., Sept. 4, 1962; s. Hubbard Armstrong and Virginia Allene (Jacobs) T. BBA summa cum laude, Auburn U., 1983. CPA, Ala. Audit staff Coopers & Lybrand, Birmingham, Ala., 1984-85, audit sr., 1986-87, audit supr., 1987—. Mem. Racerunners Ministry, 1987—. Mem. Nat. Assn. Accts. (bd. dirs.), Ala. Soc. CPA's (Acctg. Achievement award 1984), Birmingham Jaycees (fin. v.p. 1988-89), Phi Kappa Phi, Beta Alpha Psi, Beta Gamma Sigma. Republican. Baptist. Home: 3228 Georgetown Pl Birmingham AL 35216 Office: Coopers & Lybrand 1500 Financial Ctr Birmingham AL 35203

TYPERMASS, ARTHUR G., insurance company executive; b. N.Y.C., May 15, 1937; s. Carl and Estelle (McClain) T.; m. Joan L. ALspach, May 16, 1964; children: Laurie, David. A.B., Wesleyan U.-Middletown, Conn., 1957; M.B.A., Columbia U., 1959. Chartered fin. analyst. Fin. analyst Met. Life Ins. Co., N.Y.C., 1960-67, loan officer, 1967-71, v.p., 1971-80, v.p., treas., 1980-83, sr. v.p., treas., 1983—. Bd. trustees YWCA Retirement Plan, 1979—; bd. dirs., treas. Met. Life Found., 1976—. Mem. N.Y. Soc. Security Analysts, Inst. Chartered Fin. Analysts. Office: Met Life Ins Co 1 Madison Ave New York NY 10010

TYRAN, GARRY K., banker; b. Washington, Feb. 25, 1953; s. Benjamin and Jeanne Marie (Deckman) T.; m. Page West Allner, June 26, 1982; children: Keith, West. BA, Stanford U., 1975; MBA, UCLA, 1982. Rep. Fahran Overseas, Ltd., Burlingame, Calif., 1976-77; with Tarfa Comml. and Indsl. Co., Riyadh, Saudi Arabia, 1977-79; mgmt. asst. Fahran Overseas, Ltd., Ashland, Ore., 1979-80; economist Dept. Energy, Washington, 1980; v.p. Bank Am., Houston, 1982—. Mem. Kappa Sigma, Stanford Alumni Assn. Methodist. Home: 2611 Thelma Dr Houston TX 77009 Office: Bank Am 500 Dallas St Ste 3100 Houston TX 77002

TYREE, LEWIS, JR., retired compressed gas company executive, inventor; b. Lexington, Va., July 25, 1922; s. Lewis Sr. and Winifred (West) T.; m. Dorothy A. Hinchcliff, Aug. 21, 1948; children: Elizabeth Hinchcliff, Lewis III, Dorothy Scott. Student, Washington & Lee U., 1939-40; BS, MIT, 1947. Cryogenic engr. Joy Mfg. Co., Michigan City, Ind., 1947-49; v.p. Hinchcliff Motor Service, Chgo., 1949-53; cons. engr. Cryogenic Products, Chgo., 1953-76, Liquid Carbonic Corp., Chgo., 1960-76; exec. v.p. Liquid Carbonic Industries, Chgo., 1976-87; bd. dirs. Liquid Carbonic Industries, Chgo. Patentee in cryogenics. Served to 1st lt. U.S. Army, 1943-46, PTO. Mem. ASME, Am. Soc. Heating, Refrigeration, and Air Conditioning Engring. Republican. Episcopalian. Clubs: Hinsdale Golf, Lexington Golf and Country. Office: Liquid Carbonic Industries 135 S La Salle St Chicago IL 60603

TYSALL, JOHN ROBERT, oil company executive; b. London, Feb. 9, 1938; came to Can., 1963; s. Frank John and Lillian Doris (Hornby) T.; m. Wendy Doris Cottrell, Dec. 30, 1984; children: Innis, David. BA in Econs., York U., Toronto, Ont., Can., 1969; MSc in Econs., London Sch. Econs., 1971; M.B.A., U. Chgo., 1974. Sr. economist Ministry of Treasury, Govt. of Ont., Toronto, Ont., Can., 1974-76; v.p. McLeod Young Weir, Toronto, 1976-79; dir. treasury Gulf Can. Ltd., Toronto, 1979-82, treas., officer, 1982-85, v.p., treas., 1985—; v.p., treas. Gulf Can. Resources Ltd., Toronto, 1986—, GW Utilities Ltd.; treas. Consumers Gas Co. Ltd., 1989—; bd. dirs. Maple Ins. Ltd., Hamilton, Bermuda. Mem. Fin. Execs. Inst. Can., Soc. Internat. Treas. Office: Gulf Can Resources Ltd, 2 First Canadian Pl, Box 20, Ste 2700, Toronto, ON Canada M5X 1B5

TYSIAC, LAWRENCE LEON, engineering executive, consultant; b. Buffalo, Dec. 31, 1953; s. Boleslaus Chester and Regina Rose (Grenda) T.; m. Eleonora Kazimiera Szostak, Apr. 29, 1985; children: Jimmy Lawrence, Cassie-Marie Regina, Stephanie Lynn. BCE, U. Detroit, 1976, MCE, 1978. Registered profl. engr., Ariz., Nev., Utah. Asst. engr. DeLeuw-Cather Corp., Buffalo, 1974-76; staff engr. City of Flagstaff, Ariz., 1978-80; project mgr. PRC Engring., Phoenix, 1980-84; chief engr. Anderson-Nichols Corp., Phoenix, 1984-86; v.p. A-N West, Inc., Phoenix, 1986—. Mem. Glendale (Ariz.) Archtl. Control Com., 1987—; dist. rep. Santa Maria Homeowners Assn., Glendale. Mem. Soc. Am. Mil. Engrs., ASCE. Republican. Roman Catholic. Home: 5320 W Cochise Dr Glendale AZ 85302 Office: A-N West Inc 7600 N 15th St Phoenix AZ 85020

TYSON, CYNTHIA HALDENBY, college administrator; b. Scunthorpe, Lincolnshire, Eng., July 2, 1937; came to U.S., 1959; d. Frederick and Florence Edna (Stacey) Haldenby; children: Marcus James, Alexandra Elizabeth. BA, U. Leeds, Eng., 1958, MA, 1959, PhD, 1971. Lectr. Brit. Council, Leeds, 1959; faculty U. Tenn., Knoxville, 1959-60, Seton Hall U., South Orange, N.J., 1963-69; faculty, v.p. Queens Coll., Charlotte, N.C., 1969-85; pres. Mary Baldwin Coll., Staunton, Va., 1985—; bd. dirs. Am. Frontier Culture Edn., Staunton, 1986—; commr. Am. Council on Edn./Commn. on Higher Edn. and Adult Learner, Washington, 1981—. Contbr. articles to profl. jours. Commr. Va. Internat. Trade Commn., Richmond, 1987—; trustee Woodrow Wilson Birthplace Found., Staunton, 1985—; bd. dirs. United Way, Staunton, 1986—. Fulbright scholar, 1959; Ford Found. grantee Harvard U., 1981; Shell Oil scholar Harvard U., 1982. Fellow Soc. for Values in Higher Edn.; mem. Am. Mgmt. Assn. (council ops. enterprise 1985—), So. Assn. Colls. for Women (pres. 1980-81). Republican. Presbyterian. Office: Mary Baldwin Coll Staunton VA 24401

TYSON, DONALD JOHN, food company executive; b. Olathe, Kans., Apr. 21, 1930; s. John W. and Mildred (Ernst) T.; m. Twilla Jean Tyson, Aug. 24, 1952; children: John H., Cheryl J., Carla A. Student, U. Ark. Plant mgr. Tyson Foods, Inc., Springdale, Ark., 1951-55, pres., 1955-67, chmn., chief exec. officer, 1967—, also dir. Lodge: Elks. Home: 2210 Oak Lawn Dr Springdale AR 72764 Office: Tyson Foods Inc 2210 W Oaklawn Dr Springdale AR 72764

TYSON, FREDERICK CARROLL, JR., financial analyst; b. Lockport, N.Y., Aug. 14, 1944; s. Frederick Carroll and Mildred Lizetta (Jost) T.; m. Jeanne Daly, Sept. 28, 1968 (div. 1978); m. Judith Dorothea Stancill, Sept. 1, 1978; children: Timothy Neuman, Kathleen Neuman, William Neuman. BA, Antioch Coll., 1968; MBA, Loyola Coll., 1982. CPA, Md. Acct. Peat, Marwick, Mitchell & Co., Balt., 1968-76; contr. Union Meml. Hosp., Balt., 1976-82; pvt. practice acctg. Lutherville, Md., 1982—; prin. PSA Equities Inc., Lutherville, 1985—; mem. partnership com., planning com. PSA Fin. Inc., Lutherville, 1985—, chmn. fin. planning com., 1985-87. Treas. Fellowship of Lights, Balt., 1972-75, pres., 1975-76; trustee Friends Sch. Balt., 1981-87. Mem. AICPA, Md. Assn. CPA's, Internat. assn. for Fin. Planning, Inst. Cert. Fin. Planners. Republican. Presbyterian. Home: 10914 Gateview Rd Cockeysville MD 21030 Office: PSA Fin Inc 1304 Bellona Ave Lutherville MD 21093

TYSON, GEORGE JAMES, biotechnology company executive; b. Watertown, Wis., Sept. 20, 1931; s. George Elmer and Norma Ann (Goelte) T.; m. Ruth Ann McKay, Sept. 20, 1987; children: Susan, Theresa, George M., Gerald, Mary Debera. Degree, Madison Sci. Dist., 1984. Self-employed farmer Watertown, 1945-69; real estate sales rep. Empire Realty, Madison, Wis., 1969-70; owner, sales rep. Futura Realty, Madison, 1970-73; pres. T&J Constrn. Co., Adams, Wis., 1974-76; sales mgr. Sandwater Equipment Co., Westfield, Wis., 1977-78; mgr. rsch. and devel. Biohol Devel. Co., Madison, 1979-82; pres., dir. Food & Energy Breakthru, Inc., Madison, 1982—, Xylan, Inc., Madison, 1985—; chief exec. officer, chmn. bd. Fiber Farms, Inc., Madison, 1987—; cons. Madison area Tech. Coll., 1987—. Patentee in field. Mgr. Watertown Jr. Baseball League, 1950-54; leader Watertown 4-H Club, 1954-58. Wis. Dept. Devel. grantee, 1987. Mem. William F. Renk Corn Growers Assn., Nat. Farmers Orgn. (nat. bd. dirs., state sec. 1961-62). Office: Xylan Inc 505 Science Dr Madison WI 53713

TYSON, PATTI BIRGE, lawyer; b. Sherman, Tex., Oct. 3, 1939; d. John Sinclair and Evelyn (Wolverton) Birge; m. Bruce Spivey, Dec. 20, 1987. AB, U. Tex.; JD, George Washington U. Asst. to dir. of peer review HEW, Washington, 1973-75; adminstrv. asst. to U.S. Rep. Gillis Long Washington, 1975-76; chief counsel, staff dir. sub-com. on rules and procedures House Com. on Rules, Washington, 1976-79, chief counsel, staff dir. sub-com. on legis. process, 1979-83; exec. asst. to sec. health and human services Washington, 1983-85; mem. U.S. Postal Rate Commn., Washington, 1985—; asst. to vice-chmn. Equal Employment Opportunity Commn, Washington, 1968; exec. asst. to Rep. Margaret M. Heckler, 1968-72, Joe Pool 1964-68; adv. council Fogarty Internat. Ctr. NIH, Bethesda, Md., 1985-88. Pres. Tex. State Soc., Washington, 1985-86; bd. trustees St. John's Child Devel. Ctr., Washington, 1986-88; mem. Liberal Arts Found., Austin, Tex.; adv. council U. Tex. 1987—; adv. commn. Congressional Asst. Program, Conf. Bd., Washington, 1986—. Mem. State Bar Assn. Tex., D.C. Bar Assn., Nat. Assn. Regulatory Utility Commnrs., Nat. Women's Econ. Alliance (exec. adv. com. 1985—). Democrat. Club: Charter 100 (Washington). Office: Postal Rate Commn Office of Chmn 1333 H St NW Ste 300 Washington DC 20268

TYSON, THEODORE ROBERT, management consultant; b. N.Y.C., Sept. 10, 1926; s. Charles Randolph and Irene M. (Jansen) T.; student UCLA, 1946-49; m. Patricia Tyson; children: Lawrence, Christopher, Randall. Regional sales mgr. Am. Hosp. Supply Corp., N.Y.C., 1959-65; v.p. mktg. Standard Sci., N.J., 1965-69; corp. v.p. mktg. Telco Mktg. Services Inc., Chgo., 1969-75; health care industry cons. Britt and Frerichs, Chgo., 1975-78; mktg. cons. health care bus. orgns. Tyson Cons. Group, Inc., Buffalo Grove, Ill., 1978—; cons. health care, bus. orgns., 1975—. pres. Tyson Cons. Group. Served with USNR, 1944-46. Republican. Contbr. articles to profl. jours. Home: 612 White Pine Rd Buffalo Grove IL 60089

TZAMOS, JAMES MICHAEL, service executive; b. Boston, Jan. 22, 1943; s. Nickolas and Anne (Dooley) T.; m. Jeaann Neville, July 8, 1968; children: Jennifer, Lisa, Michael. AA, Valley Forge Jr. Coll., 1963; BSBA, Suffolk U., 1967, MBA, 1978. Dir. personnel Howard Johnson Co., Brockton, Mass., 1967-72, Brockton Hosp., 1972-79; asst. dir. St. Elizabeth Hosp., Boston, 1979-83; dir. human resources Quincy (Mass.) Hosp., 1983-86; pres. Internat. Productivity Mgmt. Centre, Duxbury, Mass., 1986—; prof. Anna Maria Coll., Paxton, Mass., 1978—, Stonehill Coll., Easton, Mass., 1979—. Author: Practitioners Approach to Productivity Management, 1987. Mem. Internat. MBA Assn. (pres. 1987-88). Office: Internat Productivity Mgmt Ctr 322 Standish St Duxbury MA 02332

UBA, JUDE EBERE, economic and industrial development company executive; b. London, Oct. 2, 1960; came to U.S., 1981; s. Andrew and Juliana U. BA in Polit. Sci., Econs., Baker U., 1984. Ind. writer City News Svc., Houston, 1984, Hwang & Assocs., Houston, 1984; mgr. Bei Noy Investments, Houston, 1984-86; pres., chief exec. officer U-Jude & Assocs., Houston, 1986—. Author: Love in Africa, 1988, A Mind with Love, 1987, Taking Profit, A Guide to Africa's Market Place, 1989. Recipient achievement award Rotary Club, 1983. Mem. Inst. Profl. Mgrs., Am. Mgmt. Assn., Am. Soc. Internat. Law, Houston C. of C. (internat. bus. com., govt. rels. com.), Am. Assn. Polit. Cons., Internat. Social Sci. Honor Soc., Am. Intenat. Devel. Alliance (bd. dirs.), Mus. Fine Arts, Club 21 (pres. 1988—), Houston Forum Club, Pi Gamma Mu. Roman Catholic. Home: 6633 W Airport #1406 Houston TX 77035 Office: U-Jude Corp 10700 Richmond Ave Ste 271 Houston TX 77042

UCHTMAN, CHARLES CONRAD, JR., small business owner; b. Chgo., Dec. 12, 1961; s. Charles Conrad Sr. and Ruth Scudder (Cameron) U. AA in Bus., Manatee Coll., 1985. Printer/etcher Card-O-Link, Evanston, Ill., 1977-78; night mgr. Card-O-Link, Evanston, 1978-81; waiter Sandbar Restaurant, Anna Maria, Fla., 1981-84; mgr. plant Card-O-Link, Evanston, 1985-87; owner, pres. Wippin Awards, Evanston, 1987—. Mem. Cen. Assn. Prof. Engravers (nominator 1986—), Trophy Dealers & Mfg. Assn., Evanston C. of C. Presbyterian. Office: Wippin Awards 922 Noyes Evanston IL 60201

UDCOFF, GEORGE JOSEPH, financial executive; b. Bklyn., Dec. 26, 1946. BS in Acctg., CUNY, 1968. Staff acct. Deloitte, Haskins & Sells, N.Y.C., 1968-74, mgr., 1974-77; mgr. Deloitte, Haskins & Sells, Bergen County, N.J., 1977-80; contr. Cabot Mineral Resources, N.Y.C., 1981-83; v.p. fin. Metallurg, Inc., N.Y.C., 1983—. Mem. Am. Inst. CPA's, N.J. Soc. CPA's. Office: Metallurg Inc 25 East 39th St New York NY 10016

UDELL, JON GERALD, business educator, executive; b. Columbus, Wis., June 22, 1935; s. Roy Grant and Jessie M. (Foster) U.; m. Susan Smykla, June 12, 1960; children—Jon Jr., Roy Steven, Susan Elizabeth, Bruce Foster, Alan Joseph, Kenneth Grant. BBA, U. Wis., 1957, MBA, 1958, PhD, 1961. Instr., asst. prof., assoc. prof. U. Wis.-Madison, 1959-68, prof. bus., 1968—, assoc. dir. and dir. Bur. Bus. Research and Service, 1963-75, assoc. dir. Univ-Industry Research Program, 1967-77, Irwin Maier prof. bus., 1975—; chmn. bd. Fed. Home Loan Bank of Chgo., 1982—; econ. cons. Am. Newspaper Pubs. Assn., 1964—, Wis. Builders Assn., 1985—; bd. dirs. Research Products Corp., Madison, Wis. Electric Power Co., Milw., Wis. Energy Corp., Milw. Author: Successful Marketing Strategies in American Industry, 1972; The Economics of the American Newspaper, 1978; Reporting on Business and the Economy, 1981; Marketing in An Age of Change, 1981. Pres. Consumer Adv. Council, State of Wis., 1973-74; mem. Gov.'s Council of Econ. Devel., Wis., 1967-73; v.p. Madison C. of C., 1976; elder, deacon Presbyn. Ch. Recipient Gov.'s citation for svc., 1969, 71, Sidney S. Goldish award, 1973; named Wisconsinite of Yr. Wis. State C. of C., 1973, Mktg. Man of Yr. So. Wis. chpt. Am. Mktg. Assn., 1976, Robert A. Jerred Distng. Service award U. Wis., Madison, 1986. Mem. Am. Mktg. Assn., Bus.-Edn. Coordinating Council (pres. 1979-80, bd. dirs. 1975—), Wis. for Research (bd. dirs. 1979-87), Wis. Assn. Mfrs. and Commerce (trustee Bus. World 1981—), Assn. Pvt. Enterprise Edn. (bd. dirs. 1978-79, 86—), Wis. Alumni Assn., Faculty Roundtable Club (chmn. 1970-71), Rotary. Home: 5210 Barton Rd Madison WI 53711 Office: U Wis Sch Bus 1155 Observatory Dr Madison WI 53706

UDOUJ, HERMAN J., diversified industries company executive; b. 1917. With Riverside Furniture Corp., 1946—, now chmn. bd. dirs.; with Twin Rivers Corp. (now Ark. Best Corp.), 1946—, formerly v.p. furniture mfg. ops. now vice-chmn. bd. dirs.; vice-chmn. Ark. Best Corp., Ft. Smith. Office: Ark Best Corp 1000 S 21st St Fort Smith AR 72901 *

UDWADIA, FIRDAUS ERACH, engineering educator, consultant; b. Bombay, Aug. 28, 1947; came to U.S., 1968.; s. Erach Rustam and Perin P. (Lentin) U.; m. Farida Gagrat, Jan. 6, 1977; children: Shanaira, Zubin. BS, Indian Inst. Tech., Bombay, 1968; MS, Calif. Inst. Tech., 1969, PhD, 1972; MBA, U. So. Calif., 1985. Mem. faculty Calif. Inst. Tech., Pasadena, 1972-74; asst. prof. engring. U. So. Calif., Los Angeles, 1974-77, assoc. prof., 1977-83, prof. mech. engring., civil engring. and bus. adminstrn., 1983-86; prof. engring, bus. adminstrn. U. So. Calif., 1986—; also bd. dirs. Structural Identification Computing Facility U. So. Calif.; cons. Jet Propulsion Lab., Pasadena, Calif., 1978—, Argonne Nat. Lab., Chgo., 1982-83, Air Force Rocket Lab., Edwards AFB, Calif., 1984—. Contbr. articles to profl. jours. Bd. dirs. Crisis Mgmt. Ctr., U. So. Calif. NSF grantee, 1976—. Mem. AIAA, ASCE, Am. Acad. Mechanics, Soc. Indsl. and Applied Math., Seismological Soc. Am., Sigma Xi (Earthquake Engring. Research Inst., 1971, 74, 84). Home: 2100 S Santa Anita Arcadia CA 91006 Office: U So Calif University Park 364 DRB Los Angeles CA 90089-1114

UDY, EARL BRENT, oil company executive; b. Preston, Idaho, June 26, 1940; s. Earl M. and Velda Irene (Anderson) U.; m. Linda Ann Stephens, July 20, 1961; children: Tauna, Clain, Rick, Nicole, Rebecca. Tech. degree, Ida State U., 1961; student, Brigham Young U., current. Furniture salesman Blacker Appliance & Furniture, Burley, Ida, 1960-62; owner, dairy farmer Malta, Ida, 1962-72; ins. agt., asst. mgr. Farm Bur. Ins. Co., Burley, 1972-81; ins. agt., owner 1982-85; gen. mgr. Peterson Oil Co., Provo, Utah, 1985—. Mayor City of Malta, Ida, 1978-85; mem. bd. Cassis Meml. Hosp., Burley, 1982-85; vol. fireman Raft River Fire Dept., Malta, 1964-85. Recipient Prodn. award, Northwestern Nat., 1982; mem. Life Hall of Fame, Western Farm Bur., Denver, 1981; Triple Crown Producer, Ida Farm Bur., 1980-81. Mem. C. of C., Raft River Alumni Assn., (pres. 1973-76). Republican. Mem. Ch. of Jesus Christ of Latter Day Saints. Home: 1958 Spring Oaks Dr Springville UT 84663 Office: Peterson Oil Co Provo UT 84603

UEBERROTH, JOHN, travel company executive; b. Phila., 1943. Student, U. Calif., Berkeley, U. So. Calif. Formerly pres. Ask Mr. Foster Travel, Encino, Calif.; formerly v.p. TCU Travel Corp.; now pres., chief operating officer 1st travel Corp., Van Nuys, Calif.; also v.p. Carlson Cos. Inc., Mpls.; also pres. Carlson Travel Group, Mpls. Office: First Travel Corp 7833 Haskell Ave Van Nuys CA 91406 also: Carlson Cos Inc 12755 State Hwy 55 Minneapolis MN 55441 *

UEDA, NOBUYA, architect, educator; b. Himeji, Hygo, Japan, July 26, 1940; s. Nobuo and Kunie (Hirose) U.; m. Tomoko Murakami. MArch, Kyoto U., Japan, 1965, U. Calif., Berkeley, 1967. Lic. 1st class architect, Japan. Chief architect Nikken Sekkel Ltd., Osaka, Japan, 1965—; jr. architect Skidmore, Owings and Merrill, San Francisco, 1967-68; asst. prof. Okla. State U., Stillwater, Okla., 1970-71; lectr. Akashi (Japan) Technol. Coll., 1984—; archtl. advisor World Bank, Seoul, South Korea and Washington, 1977-78, FAO UN, Bangkok and Rome, 1976-76. Author: Designing Wholesale Markets for Asian Cities, 1975. Fulbright grantee, 1966. Mem. Japan Inst. Architects (profl.), Archtl. Inst. Japan, Archtl. Assn. Japan. Home: 3-2-13 Sakasedai, 665 Takarazuka Japan Office: Nikken Sekkel Ltd, 5-21-1 Koraibashi, Higashi-ku, Osaka 541, Japan

UELNER, ROY WALTER, agricultural equipment executive; b. Dubuque, Iowa, Aug. 24, 1935; s. Felix Hugo and Susan M. (Phillipp) U.; m. Sandra S. Hammerand, Dec. 13, 1958; children: Steven Roy, Scott Michael. B.S. in Indsl. Engring, Iowa State U., 1957. Various mfg. engring. and mgmt. positions Allen-Bradley, Inc., Milw., 1957-64; with Allis-Chalmers Corp., 1964-85; indsl. engr. agrl. equipment div. Allis-Chalmers Corp., La Crosse, Wis., 1964-65; gen. plant mgr. Allis-Chalmers Corp., 1965-68; gen. mgr. (Independence (Mo.) plant), 1968-70; mgr. combine operation Independence, 1970-72; mgr. sales and mktg. agrl. equipment div., Milw., 1971-72; gen. mgr. sales and mktg. agrl. equipment div., 1972-73, v.p., 1973, group exec. and v.p. agrl. equipment group, 1974-76; pres. agrl. equipment div., 1976-85; pres., chief exec. officer Deutz-Allis Corp., West Allis, Wis., 1985—. Served with U.S. Army, 1958. Mem. Farm and Indsl. Equipment Inst. (past chmn.), Am. Soc. Agrl. Engrs., Tau Beta Pi, Phi Kappa Phi. Office: Deutz Allis Corp 1135 S 70th St West Allis WI 53214

UEMATSU, YOSHIAKI, investment company executive; b. Kyoto, Japan, Aug. 30, 1957; came to U.S., 1975; s. Yoshihisa and Toshiko (Kawai) U.; m. Debra Faye Notowitz, Dec. 8, 1985. BSBA, U. Denver, 1984. Translator Welborn, Dufford, Brown & Tooley, Denver, 1985; sr. acct. Peat, Marwick, Main & Co., N.Y.C., 1985-87; v.p. Daiwa Internat. Capital Mgmt. Corp., N.Y.C., 1987—. Office: Daiwa Internat Capital Mktg Corp 1 World Fin Ctr 200 Liberty St New York NY 10281

UFEMA, JOHN WILLIAM, physician, medical equipment company executive; b. Johnstown, Pa., July 31, 1946; s. George and Loretta Cecilia (Bent) U.; m. Mary Jo Federici, June 21, 1980; 1 child, Anthony M. Oliver. Student, Johns Hopkins U., 1964-67; MD, Emory U., 1971; MBA, Nova U. Adminstrn. Studies Ctr., 1987. Cert. in Diagnostic Radiology, 1975. Intern in internal medicine Emory affiliated hosps., 1971-72, resident in diagnostic radiology, 1972-75; attending physician Ponce de Leon Infirmary, Atlanta, 1972-75; clin. assoc. Emory U., Atlanta, 1976; attending radiologist Diagnostic Clinic, Largo, Fla., 1977-80; pres., chmn. Med. Imaging Services, Port Charlotte, Fla., 1980-88; mng. gen. ptnr. Ufema Capital Equipment Leasing, Port Charlotte, 1984—; med. dir. Palm Harbor (Fla.) Imaging, 1988—; pres. Physician's Reference Lab. Charlotte County, 1987-88. Contbr. numerous articles to profl. jours. Mem. Soc. for Entertainment and Arts Devel., Port Charlotte, 1984-88. Maj. USAF, 1975-77. Mem. AMA (Physicians' Recognition award in Continuing Med. Edn.), Am. Coll. Radiology, Radiol. Soc. N.Am., Fla. Radiol. Soc., Soc. Nuclear Medicine, Fla. Med. Assn., Pinellas County Med. Soc., Am. Mgmt. Assn., Mensa, Nat. Rifle Assn. (life). Republican. Roman Catholic. Office: 2595 State Rd 584 Suite T Palm Harbor FL 34684

UFFNER, MICHAEL S., retail automotive executive; b. Phila., July 18, 1945; s. Ray and Shirley A. (Block) U.; m. Marilyn A. Ursomarso; 1 child, Lauren R. BA, MA, U. Pa., 1971. V.p. Union Park Pontiac, BMW, Honda, Wilmington, Del., 1972-82; pres. Del. Motor Sales Inc., Wilmington, 1982—; mem. manpower tng. adv. com. Gen. Motors Corp., pres.' dealer adv. council, 1985. Bd. dirs. Del. chpt. Am. Heart Assn., 1981—, pres., 1985-86, chmn., 1986-87. Recipient various sales awards. Mem. Cadillac Motor Car div. Nat. Dealer Council, Am. Heart Assn. (v.p., bd. dirs. Nat. Ctr., 1987—), Am. Econ Assn., Am. Mgmt. Assn., Tavistock Civic Assn. (pres. 1976-77), U. Pa. Alumni Assn. (v.p. Del. chpt. 1978-80, pres. 1980-81). Clubs: Rodney Square, University, Whist, U. Pa. Faculty, Concord Country. Office: 1606 Pennsylvania Ave Wilmington DE 19806

UFHEIL, JOHN LLOYD, manufacturing company executive; b. Pekin, Ill., Sept. 3, 1933; s. Albert Adolph and Leora Ellen (Flathers) U.; m. Rosemary Margaret Sell, Feb. 8, 1958; children—Tracey Ellen, John Thomas, Patricia Anne. B.S., Bradley U., 1958. With Baxter Travenol, 1959-75; with Bard, Inc., 1975-76, Litton, Inc., 1976-77; group v.p., then sr. v.p. Mallinckrodt, Inc., St. Louis, from 1977, now exec. v.p., Chief operating officer, also dir. Fund drive capt. Children's Hosp., St. Louis, 1981; mem. adv. council Deaconess Hosp., St. Louis, 1983—; bd. dirs. Met. St. Louis YMCA, Boys Club St. Louis; assoc. trustee Bradley U., Peoria, Ill.; Endowment Fund Chmn. Boys Club of St. Louis. Served with U.S. Army, 1953-55. Mem. Health Industry Mfg. Assn. (bd. dirs.). Republican. Lutheran. Clubs: Bellerive Country, St. Louis. Office: Mallinckrodt Inc 675 McDonnell Blvd PO Box 5840 Saint Louis MO 63134 *

UGGLA, JOHAN FREDRIK, gourmet food products executive; b. Gothenburg, Bohuslán, Sweden, Oct. 7, 1962; s. Claes Lennart Uggla and Britta (Engberg) Engberg. Grad. high sch., Conn. Carpenter Classic Constrn., Stamford, Conn., 1980-82; with Amtemp, Greenwich, Conn., 1981-82; various positions Scandia Seafood Inc., Norwalk, Conn., 1983-85; gen. mgr., ptnr. Scandia Seafood Inc., Norwalk, 1985—, chmn. Home: 9 A Van Buskirk Ave Stamford CT 06902 Office: Scandia Seafood Inc 35 Lexington Ave Norwalk CT 06854

UGLOW, WILLIAM GARY, sales and marketing executive; b. Sacramento, Oct. 6, 1947; s. Ray D. Jr. and Geraldine (Mathis) U.; m. Kathleen Joan Sriver, Feb. 23, 1969 (div. 1983); 1 child, Todd Anthony; m. Michelle Newman, June 23, 1984. AA, Palm Beach Jr. Coll., 1967; BA, Fla. Atlantic U., Boca Raton, 1970, MBA, 1971. Dir. Disney Merchandise The Walt Disney Co., Burbank, Calif., 1971-79; dir. retail sales The Akron, Los Angeles, 1979-80; v.p. Royal Orleans, New Orleans, 1980-83; gen. mgr., v.p. gift div. Tomy Corp., Carson, Calif., 1983-86; pres. Internat. Creative Co., Cerritos, Calif., 1986-88; sr. v.p. Collins Co., Inc., Irvine, Calif., 1988—. Producer of catalogues The Heirloom Tradition, 1986, 87, Royal Orleans, 1985. Mem. Am. Assn. Prof. Cons. Republican. Office: Collins Co Inc 14101 Alton Pkwy Irvine CA 92718

UHL, CHARLES DANIEL, JR., marketing executive; b. Anaconda, Mont., Dec. 13, 1938; s. Charles Daniel Sr. and Mayme Patti Uhl; m. Vera Ruggles, Jan. 20, 1959; children: Kimberly Ann, Kenneth D., Angela L. BA, Mont. State Coll., 1960. Sales mgr. Reiters Marina, Billings, Mont., 1964-74; v.p. Alphenhaus Sports Motors, Great Falls, Mont., 1974-79, Avitel, Inc., Great Falls, 1979-84; nat. sales mgr. M/A-Com, Hickory, N.C., 1984-86, Gen. Instrument Corp., San Diego, 1986—; v.p. Nat. Satellite Distbrs., 1980-81. With USN, 1956-58. Republican. Roman Catholic. Office: Gen Instrument Corp 6262 Lusk Blvd San Diego CA 92121

UHL, GEORGE DAVID, utilities executive; b. Woodside, N.Y., June 23, 1934; s. Edward J. and Marie E. (Schultz) U.; m. Carole A. Ambrose, Dec. 29, 1961; children: Diana Lee, Deborah Anne, Dawn Elizabeth, George Douglas, Dana Carole. BS, U. Conn., 1962. Staff auditor Price Waterhouse & Co., Hartford, Conn., 1962-64; fin. analyst Hartford Electric Light Co., Wethersfield, Conn., 1964-66; internal auditor Northeast Utilities, Berlin, Conn., 1966-69, fin. asst., 1969-72, asst. controller, 1972-79, assoc. controller, 1979-81; controller Northeast Utilities, Rocky Hill, Conn., 1981-86, v.p., controller, 1986—; treas. Northeast Power Coordinating Council, N.Y.C., 1984—. Bd. dirs. Literacy Vol. Am., Hartford, 1987; treas. St. Marks, Storrs, Conn.,1964-69; coach Little League Basketball, Glastonbury, Conn., 1971-74. Named Top Acctg. Student, Conn. Soc. CPA's, 1962. Mem. Fin. Execs. Inst., Edison Electric Inst. Republican. Episcopalian. Club: Glastonbury (Conn.) Tennis. Office: NE Utilities 100 Corp Pl Rocky Hill CT 06067

UHL, THOMAS EDWARD, bank executive; b. Cin., Nov. 1, 1961; s. Thomas John and Alice Virginia (Rogers) U.; m. Mary Terese Spraul, June 15, 1985. BBA, U. Cin., 1985; postgrad., Xavier U., 1986—. Lic. real estate agt., Ohio. Sales rep. Cin. Microwave, Inc., 1981-85; sales assoc. Cin. Environs Corp., 1985-86; trust property adminstr. Fifth Third Bancorp, Cin., 1986—. Intern Cin. Bus. Com., 1984; bus. cons. Jr. Achievement, Cin., 1988. Mem. Cin. Homebuilders, Cin. Apt. Assn., Cin. Sales and Mktg. Coun., Mortgage Bankers Assn., Builder and Mgrs. Assn., Sigma Chi, St. Xavier Boosters Club. Office: Fifth Third Bancorp 38 Fountain Sq Plaza Cincinnati OH 45202

UKROPINA, JAMES ROBERT, energy company executive, lawyer; b. Fresno, Calif., Sept. 10, 1937; s. Robert J. and Persida (Angelich) U.; m. Priscilla Lois Brandenburg, June 16, 1962; children—Michael Steven, David Robert, Mark Gregory. A.B., Stanford U., 1959, M.B.A., 1961; LL.B., U. So. Calif., 1965. Bar: Calif. 1966, D.C. 1980. Assoc. firm O'Melveny & Myers, Los Angeles, 1965-72; partner O'Melveny & Myers, 1972-80; exec. v.p., gen. counsel Santa Fe Internat. Corp., Alhambra, Calif., 1980-84, dir., 1981-86; exec. v.p., gen. counsel Pacific Enterprises, Los Angeles, 1984-86, pres., dir., 1986—; bd. dirs. Security Pacific Corp., Lockheed Corp., Pacific Mut. Life Ins. Co.; lectr. in field. Editor-in-chief: So. Calif. Law Rev, 1964-65. Trustee Occidental Coll.; mem. adv. council Stanford Bus. Sch.; mem. Calif. Econ. Devel. Corp. Bd. Served with USAF, 1961-62. Mem. Am. Bar Assn., Calif. Bar Assn., Los Angeles County Bar Assn., Beta Theta Pi. Club: Calif. Office: Pacific Enterprises 801 S Grand Ave Los Angeles CA 90017

ULAKOVICH, RONALD STEPHEN, real estate developer; b. Youngstown, Ohio, Nov. 17, 1942; s. Stephen G. and Anne (Petretich) U. B.S., Indsl. Engring. Coll., 1967; M.S., Method Engring., Ill. Inst. Tech., 1969. Methods engr. Supreme Products, Chgo., 1964-66; pres. Contract Chair, 1966-70; v.p. sales Amrep Corp., Rosemont, Ill., 1970-73; pres. Condo Assoc., Ltd., Arlington Heights, Ill., 1973—, Am. Resorts Internat. Ltd., 1983. Named Employee of Yr., 1965; recipient Nat. Home Builders Grand award, 1977, Million Dollar Circle award Chgo. Tribune, 1978, Cert. of Recognition award Congressional Com., 1982, Cert. of Merit award Pres. Reagan's Task Force, 1984; named to Ky. Col.State of Ky., 1982. Mem. Am. Assn. Investors, Apt. Owners Assn., Real Estate Soc. of Syndicators and Investors, Am. Resort and Resdl. Devel. Assn. Roman Catholic. Avocations: auto racing, golf. Home: 510 Van Buren St East Dundee IL 60118

ULBRICH, SCOTT CARL, banker; b. Lake Forest, Ill., Oct. 27, 1954; s. Carl Herman and Elizabeth (Sanders) U.; m. Susanne Scherkl, Aug. 2l, 1976; l child, Eric Scott. BS, Utah State U., 1976; MS, Colo. State U., 1980. Fin. analyst Norwest Bank Mpls., 1978-80, acctg. officer, 1980-82, asst. v.p., 1982-84; v.p. lst Security Corp., Salt Lake City, 1984-86, sr. v.p., 1986—; mem. faculty Sch. Bank Adminstrn., Madison, Wis., 1987—. Contbr. chpt. to book. Mem. Am. Bankers Assn., Bank Adminstrn. Inst. Republican. Episcopalian. Office: lst Security Corp 6l S Main St Salt Lake City UT 84130

ULIN, PETER A., investment executive; b. Boston, Dec. 20, 1930; s. Benjamin and Rebecca (Cantarow) U.; m. Bonnie Handmaker, Aug. 24, 1958; children: Daniel, Jennifer. AB, Harvard U., 1953; postgrad., Columbia U., 1954. V.p. investment banking Hornblower-Weeks, Boston, 1964-67, F.I. du Pont Co., Boston, 1967-70; owner Peter Ulin Co., Boston, 1970-80; v.p., dir. corp. fin. E.F. Hutton Co., Boston, 1980-84; mng. dir. Ulin, Morton, Bradley & Welling, Inc., Boston, 1984—. Trustee Beth Israel Hosp., Boston, 1966—, Combined Jewish Philanthropies, Boston, 1966—, Harvard Hillel, Cambridge, Mass., 1976—. With U.S. Army, 1954-56. Office: Ulin Morton Bradley & Welling Inc 75 Federal St Boston MA 02110

ULLERY, JAMES KARL, credit manager, legal assistant; b. Syracuse, N.Y., Feb. 12, 1953; s. Robert James and Ursula Margaret (Kampe) U.; m. Launa Elva Garrett, Oct. 8, 1976; children: Scott Garrett, Amanda Rachael. BA, Simpson Coll., 1974; cert., Am. Inst. Paralegal Studies, 1983; postgrad., Russell Sage Coll., 1986; cert. credit research, Mid-Career Sch., 1986. Cert. credit specialist. Officer, br. mgr. Mfrs. Hanover, Albany, N.Y., 1973-77; ops. mgr. P.E.C. Industries, Inc., Schenectady, N.Y., 1977-79; adminstrv. mgr. Photo Fantasy Portrait Studios, Latham, N.Y., 1970-80; account mgr. Raymar Recoveries, Albany, 1981; credit mgr., legal asst. Albany Ladder Co., Inc., 1981—; speaker, seminar leader various nat. and local trade assns. Contbr. articles to profl. jours. Mem. Citizens for Am., Albany and Washington, 1984-85, Make N.Y. State #1, Albany, 1984; bd. dirs. Capital City Rescue Mission, Albany, 1980-82; advisor for ch. youth group, 1981—. Recipient Citizenship award Syracuse (N.Y.) U., 1971, History award Kiwanis, Latham, 1971. Mem. N.Y. Inst. Credit (adv. bd. 1983—), Credit Research Found. (apptd. trustee 1988), Credit Mgmt. Assn. Eastern N.Y. (bd. dirs.), Constrn. and Elec. Wholesale Credit Interchange Group (pres., founder), Hudson-Mohawk Tng. and Devel. Assn., Plumbing Suppliers Credit Interchange Group (founding mem.). Republican. Methodist. Lodge: Elks. Home: 966 Inman Rd Schenectady NY 12309 Office: Albany Ladder Co Inc 1586-90 Central Ave Albany NY 12205-2494

ULLMAN, MARIE, manufacturing company executive; b. Linlithgo, N.Y., Mar. 19, 1914; d. Max and Sarah (Jaffe) Michaelson; R.N., Bklyn. Hosp., 1935; m. Robert Ullman, Aug. 15, 1935. Pres., sec.-treas. Ullman Devices Corp., Ridgefield, Conn., 1938—; dir. State Nat. Bank Conn., Ridgefield. Mem. C. of C. Ridgefield, Bklyn. Hosp. Nurses Alumnae. Home: 43 Chestnut Hill Rd Wilton CT 06897 Office: PO Box 398 Ridgefield CT 06877

ULLO, NICHOLAS MATTHEW, artist, advertising executive; b. N.Y.C., June 4, 1951; s. Matthew and Muriel (DeMonte) U. BA, CCNY, 1975. Artist Imperial Gold Products, Queens, N.Y., 1975-76; art dir. Ries, Cappiello & Colwell, N.Y.C., 1976-78; pres. 21st Century Advt., 1978-80; advt. dir. Jersey Bus. Rev., Ramsey, N.J., 1980-81; advt. mgr. Greenwald Industries, Bklyn., 1981—. Exhibited painting and sculpture Winter Gallery, N.Y.C., 1975, Rhona Sande Gallery, N.Y.C., 1976, Galerie Naifs Et Primitifs, N.Y.C, 1986, 89, Nat. Art Club's Gregg Gallery, N.Y.C., 1986, Galerie Timothy Roberts, Montréal, Can., 1987, 88, 89 Recipient Prof. Florian G. Kraner Meml. award CCNY Alumni Assn. Mem. Alliance Francaise of N.Y., Ctr. for Def. Info. Office: 1340 Metropolitan Ave Brooklyn NY 11237

ULRICH, DAVID ANTHONY, financial executive; b. Milw., Apr. 28, 1927; s. Gerald Maurice and Margaret Johanna (Schmitt) U.; m. Agatha Theresa Bauer, Jan. 28, 1950; children—Kathleen Lynn, Thomas George, Marilyn Therese, David Anthony Jr. Student, Marquette U., 1947-52. Ptnr. Hy-View Mobile Homes, Oak Creek, Wis., 1952-83; chmn., pres., chief exec. officer Tri City Shopping Ctr., Oak Creek, 1959—, Tri City Bankshares Corp., 1963—, N.D.C., Inc., Oak Creek, 1974—; chmn., chief exec. officer Mega Marts, Inc., 1987—; pres. Oak Creek Indsl. Devel. Corp., 1971-74; pres., trustee Roundy's Inc., Milw., 1986—, bd. dirs., 1972-74; dir. Ninth Regional Nat. Bank Adv. Bd., Mpls., 1974-76. treas., bd. dirs. St. Charles Boys Home, Milw., 1975—; gen. chmn. Pius XI Decade of Excellence Fund Dr., Milw., 1979; bd. dirs. Oak Creek Police and Fire Commn., 1983-85. Served as pfc. Q.M.C., U.S. Army, 1946-47; ETO. Recipient 1st ann. Outstanding Alumni award Pius XI High Sch., Milw., 1982. Mem. Wis. Retail Hardware Assn. (bd. dirs. Stevens Point 1968-79, pres. 1976), Wis. C. of C. (bd. dirs. 1964-68, Citizen of Yr. 1981). Democrat. Roman Catholic. Lodge: Kiwanis (bd. dirs. 1964-70). Office: Tri City Bankshare Corp 6400 S 27th St Oak Creek WI 53154

ULRICH, JERRY NEIL, microcomputer company executive; b. Toledo, Nov. 19, 1954; s. Laurence Alfred and Sarah (Hill) U.; m. Ilona Ostertag, Aug. 2, 1980. BS, Ohio State U., 1975. Mem. audit staff, then sr. audit mgr. Arthur Young & Co., Costa Mesa, Calif., 1976-84; contr. AST Rsch., Inc., Irvine, Calif., 1984-86, v.p. fin., 1986—, treas., 1988—. Mem. Am. Electronics Assn., Fin. Execs. Inst., Orange County Fin. Soc. Home: 8 Cobblestone Ct Laguna Niguel CA 92677 Office: AST Rsch Inc 2121 Alton Ave Irvine CA 92714

ULRICH, MAX MARSH, executive search consultant; b. Kokomo, Ind., Mar. 21, 1925; s. Max Dan and Esther Stone (Marsh) U.; m. Mary Ellen Fisher, Sept. 12, 1950; children—Max Dwight, Jeanne Nanette; m. Geraldine A. Kidd, Jan. 25, 1973; 1 child, Amanda Marsh. B.S., U.S. Mil. Acad., 1946; M.S. in Civil Engring, Mass. Inst. Tech., 1951. Comd. 2d lt. C.E. U.S. Army, 1946, advanced through grades to capt., 1950; resigned 1954; asst. to mng. dir. Edison Electric Inst., 1954-58; with Consol. Edison Co., N.Y.C., 1958-71; asst. v.p. Consol. Edison Co., 1962-63, v.p. charge advt. and pub. relations, 1963-67, v.p. customer service, 1968-69, v.p. Bklyn. div., 1969-71; prin., dir. Ward Howell Internat. Inc., N.Y.C., 1971-74; pres., chief exec. officer Ward Howell Internat. Inc., 1974-84, chmn., chief exec. officer, 1984-88; pres. Ward Howell Internat. Group, Inc., 1988—. Mem. Sigma Xi. Home: 2 Kingswood Dr Orangeburg NY 10962 Office: Ward Howell Internat Inc 99 Park Ave New York NY 10016

ULRICH, PAUL GRAHAM, lawyer, author, editor; b. Spokane, Nov. 29, 1938; s. Donald Gunn and Kathryn (Vandercook) U.; m. Kathleen Nelson Smith, July 30, 1982; children—Kathleen Elizabeth, Marilee Rae, Michael Graham. B.A. with high honors, U. Mont., 1961; J.D., Stanford U., 1964. Bar: Calif. 1965, Ariz. 1966, U.S. Supreme Ct. 1969, U.S. Ct. Appeals (9th cir.) 1965. Law clk. judge U.S. Ct. Appeals, 9th Circuit, San Francisco, 1964-65; assoc. firm Lewis and Roca, Phoenix, 1965-70; ptnr. Lewis and Roca, 1970-85; pres. Paul G. Ulrich PC, Phoenix, 1985—; owner Pathway Enterprises, 1985—; judge pro tem Ariz. Ct. Appeals Div. 1, Phoenix, 1986; instr. Thunderbird Grad. Sch. Internat. Mgmt., 1968-69, Ariz. State U., Coll. Law, 1970-73, 78, Scottsdale Community Coll., 1975-77, also continuing legal edn. seminars. Author: Applying Management and Motivation Concepts to Law Offices, 1985; editor, contbr.: Arizona Appellate Handbook, 1978—; Working with Legal Assistants, 1980, 81; Future Directions for Law Office Management, 1982; People in the Law Office, 1985-86; contbg. editor Law Office Economics and Management, 1984—; contbr. numerous articles to profl. jours. Mem. Ariz. Supreme Ct. Task Force on Ct. Orgn. and Adminstrn., 1988—; bd. visitors Stanford U. Law Sch., 1974-77. Served with U.S. Army, 1956. Recipient continuing legal edn. award State Bar Ariz., 1978, 86, Harrison Tweed Spl. Merit award Am. Law Inst./ABA, 1987. Fellow Ariz. Bar Found. (founding 1985—); mem. ABA (chmn. selection and utilization of staff personnel com., econs. of law sect. 1979-81, mem. standing com. legal assts. 1982-86, co-chmn. joint project on appellate handbooks 1983-85, co-chmn. fed. appellate handbook project 1985-88, chmn. com. on liaison with non-lawyer orgns. Econs. of Law Practice sect. 1985-86), Ariz. Bar Assn. (chmn. econs. of law practice com. 1980-81, co-chmn. lower ct. improvement com. 1982-85, co-chmn. Ariz. Appellate handbook project 1976—), Maricopa County Bar Assn., Calif. Bar Assn., Am. Law Inst., Am. Judicature Soc. (Spl. Merit Citation 1987), Phi Kappa Phi, Phi Alpha Delta, Sigma Phi Epsilon. Republican. Presbyterian. Home: 107 E El Caminito Rd Phoenix AZ 85020 Office: 3030 N Central Ave Suite 1000 Phoenix AZ 85012

ULRICH, ROBERT GARDNER, retail food chain executive; b. Evanston, Ill., May 6, 1935; s. Charles Clemens and Nell Clare (Stanley) U.; m. Diane Mary Granzin, June 6, 1964; children—Robert Jeffrey, Laura Elizabeth, Meredith Christine. LL.B. (Law Rev. key), Marquette U., Milw., 1960. Bar: Wis. bar 1960, Ill. bar 1960, N.Y. bar 1981. Law clk. to fed. dist. judge Milw., 1961-62; atty. S.C. Johnson & Son, Inc., Racine, Wis., 1962-65, Motorola, Inc., Franklin Park, Ill., 1965-68; atty., then asst. gen. counsel Jewel Cos., Inc., Melrose Park, Ill., 1968-75; v.p., gen. counsel Gt. Atlantic & Pacific Tea Co., Inc., Montvale, N.J., 1975—; sr. v.p., gen. counsel Gt. Atlantic & Pacific Tea Co., Inc., 1981—. Mem. Am. Bar Assn., N.Y. State Bar Assn. Home: 500 Weymouth Dr Wyckoff NJ 07481 Office: Great Atlantic & Pacific Tea Co Inc 2 Paragon Dr Montvale NJ 07645

UMBEL, RUTH MARIE, restaurant executive; b. Friendsville, Md., Oct. 7, 1942; d. Wilbur Arthur and Leona Catherine (Friend) Winebaugh; m. Hugh Denzil Umbel, July 9, 1960 (div. Sept. 1974); children: Sherry Lynne, Jeffrey Dean, Jonathan Scott. BS in Social Sci., Frostburg State Coll., 1976. Saleswoman Avon Cosmetics, Silver Spring, Md., 1964-70; retail clk. Grand Union Co., Bethesda, Md., 1964-66; telephone operator C & P Telephone Co., Silver Spring, 1966-68; bookkeeper Exxon Co., College Park, Md., 1966-73; receptionist, mgr. Point View Inn, McHenry, Md., 1973-76; tchr. Garrett County Bd. Edn., Oakland, Md., 1976-81; recreational dir. Wisp Entertainment and Red Run Lodge, Oakland, 1976-81; account exec. Hilton Hotels, Columbia, Md., 1981-82; owner, mgr. Red Run Restaurant Inc., Oakland, 1982—. V.p. Oakland Rep. Women's Club, 1987. Mem. Garrett County Beverage Assn. (sec.-treas.), Nat. Restaurant Assn., Deep Creek Bus. Assn., Am. Orgn. Profl. Women, NAFE. Home and Office: Rte 5 Box 268 Oakland MD 21550

UMEGAKI, HARUKI, insurance company executive, architect, city planner; b. Kawasaki, Kanagawa, Japan, Mar. 29, 1951; s. Yoichiro and Tatsuko (Iwaya) U. Student, Toyo (Isaka) U.; BS in Engring., Yokohama Nat. U., Japan, 1973. Asst. Dai-ichi Mut. Life Ins. Co., Tokyo, 1973-78, mgr., 1978—. Recipient Bldg. Constructor Soc. prize for the Toshiba Bldg., 1985. Mem. Archtl. Inst. Japan. Home: 1-1-7 Moto-Akasaka Minato-ku, Tokyo 107, Japan Office: Dai-ichi Mut Life Ins Co, 1-13-1 Yuraku-cho Chiyoda-ku, Tokyo 100, Japan

UMHOLTZ, CLYDE ALLAN, financial analyst; b. Du Quoin, Ill., Dec. 20, 1947; s. Frederick Louis and Opal Kathleen (Beard) U. BS, U. Ill., 1969; postgrad. U. Ark., 1969-70; MS, U. Miss., 1972; MBA, Memphis State U., 1983, PhD, 1986. Chartered fin. analyst; cert. systems profl.; registered profl. engr.; cert. in data processing. Supr. quality control Champion Internat. Corp., Oxford, Miss., 1971-72; mgr. div. quality control Cook Industries, Memphis, 1973; engring. planner Northwest Industries and subsidiaries, Memphis, 1974-75; long range planning and analysis, W.R. Grace & Co. and subsidiaries, Memphis, 1975-78, mgr. planning and analysis Center Nuclear Studies, Memphis State U., 1979-83; data processing mgr. Shelby County Govt., 1983-87, deputy adminstr., 1987—; adj. prof. U. Tenn.-Memphis, 1985—; ptnr. Custom Data Systems Inc., Memphis, 1987—, Western Techs. Inc., Memphis, 1988—; cons. in field. Contbr. articles to profl. publs; inventor angle trisector, 1966; researcher energy considerations of Haber cycle, 1969, comprehensive bus. and fin. studies of sulfur, sulfuric acid, and phosphate industries, 1975-78, cost and materials sci. studies for nuclear industry, 1979-80, studies of distillation with vapor recompression, 1983, studies of prototyping in devel. computerized fin., systems, 1985-86, Context Analysis in System Design, 1987. Active presdl. election campaigns, 1968, 72, 80, 84, 88, mayoral campaign Memphis, 1975, 83, 87, Mid-South Billy Graham Crusade, 1978. Recipient Oratorical award Optimist Club, 1963, Leadership and Human Relations award Dale Carnegie Inst., 1977; NSF fellow, 1970-72. Mem. Memphis Jaycees, AAAS, U. Ill. Alumni Assn., U. Miss. Alumni Assn., Memphis State U. Alumni Assn., Am. Mgmt. Assn., Am. Rose Soc., Am. Inst. Chem. Engrs., Fin. Execs. Inst., Am. Chem. Soc., Assn. MBA Execs., Data Processing Mgmt. Assn., Planning Execs. Inst., Internat. Platform Assn. Baptist. Clubs: Admirals, Exec. of Memphis, Petroleum of Memphis. Lodge: Order of De Molay. Home: 3580 Hanna Dr Memphis TN 38128

UMSTED, LOUIS FRANKLIN, manufacturing executive; b. Phila., Oct. 31, 1928; s. Louis Franklin and Alyce Benson (Rutherford) U.; m. Peggy J. Hatmaker, Aug. 6, 1955; children: Nancy Sullivan, Eric Umsted, Jennifer McKinley. BA, U. Washington, 1951. Sales rep. Nat. Can Corp., San Francisco, 1958-62, dist. sales mgr., 1962-68; gen. sales mgr. Nat. Can Corp., Chgo., 1968-71, v.p. sales and mktg., 1971-77, sr. v.p. sales and mktg., 1977-83, exec. v.p. sales and mktg., 1983-86, vice-chmn., 1986-88; vice-chmn. corp. mktg. Am. Nat. Can Co., Chgo., 1988—; also bd. dirs.; bd. dirs. Barry-Wehmiller Co., St. Louis, 1980—; mem. standing com. Can Mfrs. Inst., Washington, 1982—. bd. dirs., chmn. compensation com. King Bruwaert House, Hinsdale, Ill., 1987. Lt. (j.g.) USNAC, 1951-55. Mem. Hinsdale Golf Club. Republican. Mem. Evangelical Covenant Ch. Office: Am Nat Can Corp 8770 W Bryn Mawr Ave Chicago IL 60631

UNDERHILL, JAMES FELTON, manufacturing executive; b. May 27, 1955; m. Teresa L. Pauley, Sept. 13, 1980; children: David G., John F. BS in Acctg. and Econs., Lehigh U., 1977. CPA, N.Y., W.Va. Staff acct. Main Hurdman & Cranston, CPA's, N.Y.C., 1977-79, supervising sr. acct., 1979-80; corp. acctg. supr. McJunkin Corp., Charleston, W.Va., 1980-83, corp. acctg. mgr., 1983-84, asst. controller, 1984-85, controller, 1985—, v.p., 1987—. Mem. Am. Inst. CPA's, W.Va. Soc. CPA's. Office: McJunkin Corp 835 Hillcrest Dr Charleston WV 25311

UNDERKOFLER, JAMES RUSSELL, utility executive; b. Baraboo, Wis., Oct. 25, 1923; s. Ray Carr and Margaret (Thompson) U.; married; children: James H., Thomas R., R. Craig, Kevin S., Cynthia M. LL.B., U. Wis., 1950. With Wis. Power and Light Co., Madison, 1941—, pres., chief exec. officer, 1968-82, chmn. bd., pres., chief exec. officer, 1982-87, chmn. bd., chief exec. officer, 1987-88; pres., chief exec. officer South Beloit Water, Gas & Electric Co., Wis., 1987—; pres., chmn., chief exec. officer WPL Holdings, Inc., Madison, 1988—; chmn. Heartland Devel. Corp., 1988—; dir. First Wis. Nat. Bank, Madison, Am. Family Mut. Ins. Co., Madison, H.C. Prange Co., Sheboygan, Wis., Firstar (formerly First Wis. Corp.); mem. bd. visitors U. Wis. Sch. Bus., 1987—. Pres. United Way Madison, 1971, Electric Utilities Research Found., 1970—; bd. visitors U. Wis. Sch. Bus., 1987—. Served with inf. AUS, 1943-46. Decorated Purple Heart. Mem. Edison Elec. Inst. (bd. dirs. 1978-85, 1986—), Wis. Utilities Assn. (pres. 1972-73, chmn. 1973-74, bd. dirs. 1975-88), Wis. Bar Assn., Wis. C. of C. (bd. dirs. 1970-74, 89—), U.S. C. of C., Wis. Electric Utilities Research Found. (bd. dirs. 1968—), Competitive Wis. (bd. dirs. 1981-88), Forward Wis., Inc. (bd. dirs. 1983—), Meriter Health Services, Inc. (bd. dirs. 1983—), Assn. Edison Illuminating Cos. (bd. dirs. 1988—), Madison Club (bd. dirs. 1970-72), Rotary (bd. dirs. Madison chpt. 1970-72, 87—). Lutheran. Office: Wis Power & Light Co 222 W Washington Ave PO Box 192 Madison WI 53701-0192

UNDERWEISER, IRWIN PHILIP, mining company executive, lawyer; b. N.Y.C., Jan. 3, 1929; s. Harry and Edith (Gladstein) U.; m. Beatrice J. Kortchmar, Aug. 17, 1959; children: Rosanne, Marian, Jeffrey. B.A., CCNY, 1950; LL.B., Fordham U., 1954; LL.M., NYU, 1961. Bar: N.Y. 1954. With firm Scribner & Miller, N.Y.C., 1951-54, 56-62; partner firm Feuerstein & Underweiser, 1962-73, Underweiser & Fuchs, 1973-77, Underweiser & Underweiser, 1977—; v.p., sec. Sunshine Mining Co., Kellogg, Idaho, 1965-70, chmn. bd., 1970-78, pres., 1971-74, 77, v.p., 1977-83; vice chmn., dir. Underwriters Bank and Trust Co., N.Y.C., 1969-73; dir. Anchor Post Products, Inc. Bd. dirs. Silver Inst. Inc.; gen. counsel, mem. bus. council Friends City Center Music and Drama, N.Y.C., 1966-67; pres. W. Quaker Ridge Assn., 1969-70; treas. Scarsdale Neighborhood Assn. Presidents, 1970-71. Served with AUS, 1954-56. Mem. Am., N.Y. State bar assns., Bar Assn. City N.Y., Phi Beta Kappa, Phi Alpha Theta. Home: 7 Rural Dr Scarsdale NY 10583 Office: 405 Park Ave New York NY 10022

UNDERWOOD, HARRY BURNHAM, II, corporation financial executive, accountant; b. Easton, Pa., Jan. 6, 1943; s. Harry Burnham and Edythe (Walters) U.; m. Nancy Chostner, Nov. 23, 1963; children: Cheryl, Cathy. BA, Davidson Coll., 1964; MBA, U. N.C., 1966. CPA, N.C. Sr. auditor Haskins & Sells, Charlotte, N.C., 1968-72; controller Chadbourn, Inc., Charlotte, 1972-73, Rose's Store, Inc., Henderson, N.C., 1973-78; v.p., treas. Best Products Co., Inc., Richmond, Va., 1978-81; v.p., treas. Lowe's Cos., Inc., North Wilkesboro, N.C., 1981-84, sr. v.p., treas., chief fin. officer, 1985—. Pres. United Way, Wilkes County, N.C., 1986-87. Served to 1st lt. U.S. Army, 1966-68. Fellow Am. Inst. CPA's, Fin. Exec. Inst. Presbyterian. Lodge: Rotary (pres. N. Wilkesboro 1985-86). Home: 367 Pine Valley Rd Winston-Salem NC 27104 Office: Lowe's Cos Inc Hwy 268 East North Wilkesboro NC 28656

UNDERWOOD, NANCY MAE, occupational health and safety consultant; b. Vancouver, Wash., Dec. 29, 1944; d. Robert Izea and Jennie Mae (McWhorter) Espie; B.S. in Occupational Health and Safety, Calif. State U., 1974, now post grad.; cert. of proficiency-engring./occupational safety and health, Travelers Ins. Co., 1975, Textron, Inc., 1977; postgrad. U. San Francisco, 1978-81; 1 dau., Apryl. Safety engr. Travelers Ins. Co., Los Angeles, 1975-76; tchr. Los Angeles City Unified Sch. System, 1976; mgr. safety Hydraulic research subs. Textron, Inc., Valencia, Calif., 1977-78; mgr.

safety Northrop Aircraft Group, Hawthorne, Calif., 1978—, now with Underwood Loss Control, Lynwood, ; operator Nancy's Safety Tng. and Cons. firm. Recipient Performance "78" Monthly Cost Reduction/Recognition award, Northrop Aircraft Corp., 1978. Mem. Nat. Safety Council, Am. Soc. Safety Engrs., Am. Indsl. Hygiene Assn., Intersafe Safety Soc., Nat. Assn. Female Execs., Am. Soc. Profl. and Exec. Women, Calif. State Univ. Alumni Assn., Am. Mgmt. Assn. Christian Scientist; Clubs: Wilshire; Tiffanys Social; Eastern Star; Daughters of Isis Court. Office: Underwood Loss Control Inc 3516 E Century Blvd Ste 10 Lynwood CA 90262

UNDERWOOD, ROBERT CLAY, oil and gas company executive; b. Lockney, Tex., June 7, 1912; m. Jane Adams, Dec. 16, 1933; children: Lynn Moran, Robert Lee II, Mary Underwood Hill. Student, Washington and Lee U.; BS in Bus. Adminstrn., U. Oklahoma; grad., Army Indsl. Coll., Washington. Bookkeeper City Nat. Bank, Wichita Falls, Tex., 1933; proration clerk R.R. Commn. Tex., 1933-34; oil and gas reporter Ft. Worth Star-Telegram, 1933-34; asst. to exec. v.p. N. Tex. Oil and Gas Assn., Wichita Falls, 1934-35; bus. mgr. Wichita Falls Clinic-Hosp., 1935-38; organizer, mng. ptnr. Underwood Oil Co., 1938-48; co-owner Undrey Engine and Pump Co., Oklahoma City, Nortex Engine and Equipment Co., Wichita Falls; pres., chmn. bd. dirs. Underwood Oil Co. Inc., Wichita Falls, chief exec. officer, chmn. bd. dirs.; v.p. domestic and fgn. projects Internat. Quasar Inc.; bd. dirs. Employers Nat. Life Ins. Co., Dallas, Knight Oil Resources (bd. dirs.). Charter mem. Rep. Senatorial Inner Circle, U.S. Senatorial Club; co-founder Rep. Presdl. Task Force; mem. Nat. Conservative Pol. Action Com., exec. adv. bd. Trust for Senate Leadership; bd. govs. Coun. for Nat. Policy; bd. dirs. Glaucoma Rsch. and Edn. Found. Inc.; past bd. dirs. Wichita Falls Community Chest, Wichita Falls YMCA; mem. Tex. State Bd. of Edn., 1953-56, past chmn. legis. and budget coms., past chmn. permanent sch. fund; past chmn. bd. regents Midwestern U., citizens adv. com. City Wichita Falls. Major USAF, 1942-46. Mem. N. Tex. Oil and Gas Assn. (pres. 1950-52, exec. com., bd. dirs.), Tex. Employers Ins. Assn. (bd. dirs.), Internat. Coun. Forum (bd. govs.). Methodist. Home: #4A Newcomb Terr Wichita Falls TX 76308 Work: Oil and Gas Bldg Ste 420 Wichita Falls TX 76301

UNDERWOOD, ROBERT LEIGH, venture capitalist; b. Paducah, Ky., Dec. 31, 1944; s. Robert Humphreys and Nancy Wells (Jessup) U.; BS with gt. distinction (Alcoa scholar), Stanford U., 1965, MS (NASA fellow), 1966, PhD (NSF fellow), 1968; MBA, U. Santa Clara, 1970; m. Susan Lynn Doscher, May 22, 1976; children: Elizabeth Leigh, Dana Whitney, George Gregory. Research scientist, project leader Lockheed Missiles & Space Co., Sunnyvale, Calif., 1967-71; spl. asst. for engring. scis. Office Sec., Dept. Transp., Washington, 1971-73; sr. mgmt. assoc. Office Mgmt. and Budget, Exec. Office Pres., 1973; with TRW Inc., Los Angeles, 1973-79, dir. retail nat. accounts, 1977-78, dir. product planning and devel., 1978-79; pres., chief exec. officer OMEX, Santa Clara, Calif., 1980-82; v.p. Heizer Corp., Chgo., 1979-85; v.p. No. Trust Co., pres. No. Capital Corp., Chgo., 1985-86; mng. ptnr. ISSS Ventures, 1986-88; sr. v.p. N.Am. Bus. Devel. Co., Chgo., 1988—; dir. various portfolio cos.; mem. adv. com. indsl. sci. and tech. innovation NSF. Mem. AIAA, IEEE, Sigma Xi, Phi Beta Kappa, Tau Beta Pi, Beta Gamma Sigma. Elder, Presbyterian Ch., 1978-79. Clubs: Union League Chgo.; Manasquan River Yacht (Brielle, N.J.); Indian Hill (Winnetka, Ill.). Contbr. articles to profl. jours. Home: 59 Woodley Rd Winnetka IL 60093 Office: 135 S LaSalle St Chicago IL 60603

UNFRIED, STEPHEN MITCHELL, investment banker; b. Summit, N.J., Jan. 3, 1943; s. Everett Eugene and Ruth Vivien (Miller) U.; m. Amy Dietrich Bright, June 8, 1968; children—Lydia Dietrich, Thomas Mitchell, Juliet Bright. A.B. in Econs., Princeton U., 1965; LL.B., Yale U., 1969, M.A. in Econs., 1969. Bar: N.Y. 1969. Mng. dir. The First Boston Corp., N.Y.C., 1969—. Office: The First Boston Corp Park Ave Plaza New York NY 10055

UNGER, LARRY DAVID, bank executive; b. Balt., Mar. 26, 1948; s. Sam and Esther (Drapkin) U.; m. Sherry Lynn King, June 16, 1968; children: Michael, Karen, Robert. BS in Fin., U. Balt., 1973; grad., Stonier Grad. Sch. Banking, 1988. Exec. v.p. Md. Nat. Leasing Corp., Towson, 1974-84; pres. Atlantic Leasing & Fin., Inc., Balt., 1984—; exec. v.p. Bank of Balt., 1987—. Mem. U. Balt. Alumni Assn. (bd. govs. 1986—). Republican.

UNGER, PAUL TEMPLE, executive search firm, consultant; b. N.Y.C., June 9, 1942; s. Samuel Unger and Estelle (Temple) Unger Slater; m. Patricia Ann Coffin, Feb. 4, 1967 (div. June 1977); children—Kimberly Anne, David Temple; m. Susan Jean McCarthy, Oct. 1, 1983; 1 child, Samantha Leigh. BS, Upsala Coll., 1966; MBA, Case Western Res. U., 1969. Personnel recruiter RCA, Harrison, N.J., 1966-67; personnel mgr. Parker Hannifin Corp., Cleve., 1967-69; dir. indsl. rels. Indian Head, Inc., Dallas, Pa., 1969-72; dir. indsl. rels., gen. mgr. Macke Co., Cheverly, Md., 1972-76; pres. P.T. Unger Assocs., Washington, 1976—; chmn. Florington Group, Inc., Washington, 1980—. Mem. Soc. Satellite Profls. (pres. Mid-Atlantic charter 1987-88), Armed Forces Communications and Electronics Assn., Old Crows, Security Affairs Support Assn. Republican. Jewish. Home: 1550 McLean Commons Ct McLean VA 22101 Office: P T Unger Assocs 8605 Westwood Ctr Dr #501 Vienna VA 22180

UNGVARY, SUSAN, accountant; b. N.Y.C., Feb. 2, 1959. BA, Clark U., 1978; MBA, Babson Coll., 1980. CPA, N.Y. Ptnr. Max Felberbaum & Co. CPA's, Bayside, N.Y., 1981-84; mgr. fin. reporting Showtime/The Movie Channel, Inc., N.Y.C., 1984-86; bus. mgr. USA Weekend, N.Y.C., 1986-87; controller Gannett Nat. Newspaper Sales, N.Y.C., 1987-88, Rough Trade Records, Inc., N.Y.C., 1988—. Mem. Am. Inst. CPA's, N.Y. State Soc. CPA's. Home: 185 W End Ave Apt 27J New York NY 10023 Office: Rough Trade Records Inc 611 Broadway Ste 311 New York NY 10022

UNNO, KENZO, architect; b. Tokyo, Apr. 1, 1949; s. Shiro and Yoshi (Kubota) U.; m. Masako Takayama, Aug. 31, 1984; children: Haruka, Genyo. B of Engring., Sci. U. Tokyo, 1974. Various archtl. and constrn. positions Tokyo, 1974-80; owner Umi Kenchikuka Kobo Co., Ltd., Toyko, 1980—. Contbr. articles to profl. jours. Recipient Japan Pvt. House Architecture prize and various design awards. Mem. Tokyo Soc. Architects and Bldg. Engrs., Shimoda Yacht Owner's Club. Buddhist. Home and Office: 11-19 Higashi-komatsugawa, 4-chome, Edogawa-Ku, Tokyo 132, Japan

UNO, ANNE QUAN, financial planner, tax consultant; b. Ukiah, Calif., Feb. 27, 1942; d. Dock and Chew (Ying) Quan; m. Tadao Uno, June ll, 1967; children: Kiri, Marili. BS, UCLA, 1964; MEd, Tex. A&M U., 1972; cert., Coll. Fin. Planning, Denver, 1983. Tchr. Waco (Tex.) Ind. Sch. Dist., 1969-76; rep. Investors Diversified, Mpls., 1977-79, Cardell & Assocs., Morristown, N.J., 1979-8l, Lowry Fin., West Palm Beach, Fla., 1982—; fin. planner Fin. Assocs., Arlington, Va., 1982—. Author: Aesthetic Activities for Exceptional Children, 1975. Mem. Nat. Assn. Investors Corp. (chmn. Met. Washington coun. 1987—), Internat. Assn. Fin. Planners, Inst. Cert. Fin. Planners, Nat. Soc. Tax Profls., Am. Assn. Individual Investors, Orgn. Pan Asian Am. Women, Hui 5 Club. Office: Fin Assocs 933 N Kenmore St Ste 217 Arlington VA 22201

UNRUH, JAMES ARLEN, business machines company executive; b. Goodrich, N.D., Mar. 22, 1941; m. Candice Leigh Voight, Apr. 28, 1984; children: Jeffrey A., Julie A. BSBA, Jamestown Coll., 1963; MBA, U. Denver, 1964. Dir. corp. planning and analysis Fairchild Camera & Instrument, Calif., 1974-76, v.p. treasury and corp. devel., 1976-79, v.p. fin., 1979-80; v.p. fin. Memorex Corp., Santa Clara, Calif., 1980-82; v.p. fin. Burroughs Corp. (now known as Unisys Corp.), Detroit, 1982-84, sr. v.p. fin., 1984-86, exec. v.p. fin., 1986, exec. v.p., 1986—, also bd. dirs. Mem. Fin. Execs. Inst. Home: 208 Rose Ln Haverford PA 19041 Office: Unisys Corp PO Box 500 Blue Bell PA 19424

UNVERFERTH, RICHARD ARTHUR, farm equipment manufacturing company executive; b. Kalida, Ohio, Sept. 4, 1923; s. Lawrence G. and Lorreta (Quinn) U.; m. Glaydy Marie Pugh, July 7, 1951; children: Steven, Joseph, James, Mark, Jeffrey, Lawrence, David, Chad. Grad., Kalida High Sch. Ptnr. Unverferth Mfg. Co., Kalida, 1948-60, owner, 1960-64, pres., 1964—; pres. Unverferth Farms Inc., Kalida, 1964—; pres. Unferferth Leasing, Inc., 1964—, Hammer & Gump Corp., Kalida, 1966—, McCordy Mfg. Co., Ada, Ohio, 1971-86; pres., chmn. Health Care Facilities, Inc., Lima, Ohio, 1969—; bd. dirs. BankOne Lima, Health Care Riet, Toledo. Pres. Kalida Athletic Assn., 1951-52; chmn. St. Michael Fin. Com., Kalida, 1971-81; bd. dirs. St. Rita Hosp., Lima. Served with USN, 1943-48, PTO. Mem. Farm Equipment Mfrs. Assn. (pres. 1987—), Shawnee Country Club, Country Acres Kalida Club, Elks, Lions. Roman Catholic. Home: Box 157 Kalida OH 45853 Office: Unverferth Mfg Co 224 West Kalida OH 45853

UPADRASHTA, KAMESWARA RAO, chemical engineering educator; b. Jangaon, Andhra Pradesh, India; came to U.S., 1982; s. Venkatarama Sastry and Anantha Lakshmi (Godavarthi) U.; m. Radhika Konduru; children: Pradyumna, Pradipta. B.Tech., Osmania U., India, 1966; M.Tech., Osmania U., 1968; PhD in Chem. Engring., Indian Inst. Tech., Madras, 1979. Research scholar dept. chem. engring. Indian Inst. Tech., Madras, 1969-72; sr. sci. officer chem. engring. edn. devel. ctr. Indian Inst. Tech., 1972-82; postdoctoral fellow dept. metall. engring. U. Utah, Salt Lake City, 1982-84; asst. research prof. dept. metall. engring. U. Utah, 1984-86; assoc. prof. dept. chem. processing engring. U. Minn., Duluth, 1986—; cons. in field. Editor: Manual of Chem. Tech., 1975-79 (4 vols.); patentee in field; contbr. articles to profl. jours. NSF grantee, 1986; Pa. Electric Co. grantee, 1986; United Coal Co. Research Corp. grantee, 1985, others. Mem. Fine Particle Soc., Soc. Mining Engrs. of AIME, Am. Inst. Chem. Engrs. Home: 1716 Morningside Ave Duluth MN 55803 Office: U Minn Dept Chem Processing Engring Duluth MN 55812

UPSHAW, LISA GAYE, systems analyst; b. Alamogordo, N.Mex., June 27, 1959; d. James Leroy Upshaw and Margaret (Shackelford) Carrell; m. Michael J. Zamora, Nov. 3, 1976 (div. July 1983); 1 child, Jeremy Brandon; m. Eddie Gonzalez, Mar. 19, 1984. BS in Bus. Computer Systems, U. N.Mex., 1983. Govt. and large account system analyst Office Systems, Alburquerque, 1982-84; sr. system analyst, nat. accounts mgr. Bell Atlantic/CompuShop, Houston, 1984-88; nat. account mgr. CompuCom Systems, Inc., Houston, 1988—; cons. Bell Atlantic Pres.' Club, Dallas, 1986-87, 88, Bell Atlantic Leaders Club, 1986, 87; mem. CompuCom Pres.'s Coun., 1988. Chmn. publicity Ronald McDonald House, Alburquerque, 1982, chairwoman spl. events, 1983; chairwoman Rep. Vol. Community, Houston, 1986; sponsor Houston Ballet, Theatre of Arts, Fundraising Heart Assn. Mem. Nat. Assn. Female Execs. (network dir. 1987-88), Assn. Info. System Profls., Houston Areal League Personal Computer Specialists, NOW, VFW. Home: 17731 December Pine PO Box 11211 Spring TX 77391-1211 Office: CompuCom Systems Inc 4111 Directors Row Houston TX 77092

UPSON, STUART BARNARD, advertising agency executive; b. Cin., Apr. 14, 1925; s. Mark and Alice (Barnard) U.; m. Barbara Jussen, Nov. 2, 1946; children—Marguerite Nichols, Anne Marcus, Stuart Barnard. B.S., Yale U., 1945. With Dancer, Fitzgerald, Sample, Inc., N.Y.C., 1946—, sr. v.p., 1963-66, exec. v.p., 1966-67, pres., 1967-74, chmn., 1974-86; chmn. DFS-Dorland, N.Y.C., 1986-87, Saatchi & Saatchi DFS Inc., N.Y.C., 1987—; bd. dirs. Manhattan Life Ins. Co. Bd. dirs. Fresh Air Fund, N.Y.; vice chmn. Advt. Council. Served with USNR, 1943-46. Mem. St. Elmo Soc. Clubs: Wee Burn Country (Darien); Sky (N.Y.C.); Blind Brook, Pine Valley Golf. Home: 68 Stephen Mather Rd Darien CT 06820 Office: Saatchi & Saatchi DFS Inc 375 Hudson St New York NY 10014

UPTON, HUGH DOUGLAS, real estate developer; b. Royal Oak, Mich., Apr. 29, 1934; s. William Earl and Raymoth Francis (Ashworth) U.; m. Rosemary Jane Mason, May 10, 1952; children: Stephen Douglas, Christen Carol Upton Lundy. Student, Detroit Bus. Inst., 1951-52. Auditor, teller Wayne Oakland Bank, Royal Oak, Mich., 1955-57; motel owner, operator Upton Inns, Inc., Royal Oak, 1957—; real estate developer, pres. Outrigger Beach Club, Ormond Beach, Fla., 1981—; pres. Chapin, Broad, Upton, Novi, Mich., 1978—, Host Inn Harmony, Inc., Royal Oak, 1973—. Bd. dirs. Salvation Army Bd., Royal Oak, 1980-81. Served with US. Army, 1953-55. Fla. Hotel/Motel Assn., Mich. Lodging Assn., Greater Royal Oak C. of C. Home: 1420 N Atlantic Ave Suite 803 Daytona Beach FL 32018 Office: Outrigger Beach Club 215 S Atlantic Ave Ormond Beach FL 32074

UPTON, MARK R., land development company executive; b. Rochester, Mich., Oct. 24, 1957; s. J. Terry and Beverly Carol (Milton) U.; m. Barbara Jean Naugle, July 31, 1982; children: Jon Steven, Laura Jean. BS, Mich. State U., 1979. Intern Ryan Homes Inc., Warren, Ohio, 1978; asst. supt. Ryan Homes Inc., Toledo, 1979-80; sales rep. Ryan Homes Inc., Akron, Ohio, 1980-82; supt. Ryan Homes Inc., Columbus, Ohio, 1982-83; market coordinator Ryan Homes Inc., Cin., 1983-84; v.p., div. mgr. UDC-Universal Devel. L.P., Tempe, Ariz., 1984-85; sr. v.p., regional mgr. UDC-Universal Devel. L.P., Charlotte, N.C., 1985—. Republican. Congregationalist. Home: 6801 Fairview Rd Charlotte NC 28210 Office: UDC-Universal Devel LP 4965 Liechalet Blvd Boynton Beach FL 33437

URBACH, SUSAN KAY, small business development administrator; b. York, Nebr., June 30, 1956; d. James Floyd and Mary Jane (Schwab) U. B. Mus., Oklahoma City U., 1978, M in Mus., 1980. Comml. loan asst., sec. Citizens Loan Nat. Bank, Oklahoma City, 1983-86; loan svc. asst. SBA, Oklahoma City, 1986-88; dir. Small Bus. Devel. Ctr., Edmond, Okla., 1988—; mem. adv. bd. Okla. Home Based Bus. Assn.; mem. steering com. Gov.'s Conf. on Small Bus. Editor: (songbook) Sigma Alpha Iota Songbook Supplement vols. I and II, 1981, 84. Mem., choir dir. Chapel-Tinker AFB, Midwest City, Okla., 1982-88, St. Francis Assisi Cath. Ch., Oklahoma City, 1988—. Mem. Edmond C. of C., Okla. C. of C. (mem. small bus. fin. subcom.), Sigma Alpha Iota. Republican. Roman Catholic. Home: 2012 NW 19th St Oklahoma City OK 73106 Office: Cen State U Small Bus Ctr 100 N University Dr Edmond OK 73034

URBAHNS, FRANKLIN ALLEN, investment executive; b. Rushville, Ind., July 13, 1941; s. John Bruce and Marthena (Bitner) U.; m. Marsha Joan Bowman, June 21, 1969; children: Anne Elizabeth, Allen Franklin. BS, Ind. U., 1963. Mem. staff Weyerhauser Co., Chgo., 1966-68, Time Container Corp., Chgo., 1968-69; Dupont, Glore, Forgan Time Container Corp., 1969-70; v.p. Wood, Struthers & Winthrop, 1970-77; sr. v.p. Moseley Securities, 1977-81; sr. v.p. investments Gruntal & Co., 1988—. Precinct capt. New Trier Republican Orgn., Kenilworth, Ill.; chief fin. officer USO Ill., Chgo. 1st lt. USMC, 1963-66, Vietnam. Mem. Ind. Soc. Chgo. (past pres.), Westmoreland Country Club (Glenview, Ill.), Mich. Shores (Wilmette, Ill.). Office: Gruntal & Co 235 S LaSalle St Chicago IL 60603

URBAN, GILBERT WILLIAM, banker; b. Silver Lake, Minn., Oct. 20, 1928; s. William and Alice (Polak) U.; m. Elvera Mattson, Feb. 23, 1954; children: Lisa Alice Marie, Leann Kay. BBA, U. Minn., 1949. Sr. acct. Price Waterhouse and Co., Chgo., 1949-50; chief acct. Calif. Bank, L.A., 1950-51; asst. contr. 1st Nat. Bank, Mpls., 1951-63, contr., 1963-69; v.p., cashier La. Nat. Bank, Baton Rouge, 1969-73, v.p. corp. planning, 1973-84, v.p. assets and liabilities, 1984-86; sr. v.p. fin. policy Premier Bancorp Inc., Baton Rouge, 1986—; instr. evening sch. U. Minn., 1956-69, La. State U., 1970—; instr. Nat. Assn. Bank Auditors and Contrs. Sch. U. Wis., 1960-63, sect. leader, 1963-69; chmn. dept. controllership Bank Adminstrn. Inst., 1970—; course coord. Banking Sch. of South, 1970, 79—. Mem. Beta Alpha Psi, Alpha Kappa Psi. Lutheran. Office: Premier Bancorp Inc PO Box 1522 Baton Rouge LA 70821

URBAN, THOMAS N., agricultural products company executive; b. 1934; married. MBA, Harvard U., 1960. Began at Pioneer Hi-Bred Internat., Inc., Des Moines, 1960, now chmn., pres., also bd. dirs. Office: Pioneer Hi-Bred Internat Inc 700 Capital Sq 400 Locust St Des Moines IA 50309 •

URBAN, WARD ALINGTON WICKWIRE, banker; b. Buffalo, Mar. 14, 1960; s. Henry Z. and Ruth W. Urban. BA in Econs. cum laude, Hamilton Coll., 1982; MBA, Dartmouth Coll., 1988. Asst. treas. The Bank of N.Y., N.Y.C., 1982-86; assoc. Citibank N.A., N.Y.C., 1988—. Republican. Episcopalian. Home: 150 W 79th St Apt 2C New York NY 10024 Office: Citibank NA 399 Park Ave New York NY 10043

URBANOWSKI, JOHN RICHARD, lighting systems company official; b. Jamaica, N.Y., May 31, 1947; s. John Casimir and Alfreda (Dabrowski) U.; m. Linda Holmes, Dec. 17, 1967 (div. June 1973); 1 child, Richard. BA, U. South Fla., 1968. Ptnr. Freeman Assocs., Ft. Lauderdale, Fla., 1972-76; sales engr. Holophane Lighting Co., Portland, Oreg., 1977—. Author computer program Microlux, 1984. With USN, 1969-72. Mem. Illuminating Engring. Soc. (bd. dirs. 1981-86, pres. 1983-84), Holophane Lighting Co. Dir's Club. Methodist. Office: Holophane Lighting Co 34 NW First Ave #203 Portland OR 97209

URBIK, JEROME ANTHONY, financial services executive; b. Chgo., Oct. 30, 1929; s. Anthony Frank and Sophie Elizabeth (Stripeikis) U.; married, 1956; children: Laura M., Michael A., Anthony J., Mary L., John T. BA in Philosophy, St. Mary's Coll., Techny, Ill., 1953; Grad., Am. Coll., 1970. CLU, chartered fin. cons. Field underwriter MONY Fin. Svcs., Chgo., 1955-59; merchandising specialist Mut. of N.Y., N.Y.C., 1959; pvt. practice brokerage cons. Northfield, Ill., 1960-64; chief exec. officer Hinsdale (Ill.) Assocs. Fin. Svcs. Corp., 1964—; v.p. Interstate Coll. Personology, San Diego, 1982-87. Contbr. articles on industry to profl. mem. editorial bd. Leaders Mag., 1981—. Mem. adv. council congressman Henry Hyde, Nat. Rep. Com., Washington; mem. fin. com. Judy Koehler senate campaign, Hinsdale; mem. Small Bus. Devel. Ctr., Lewis U., Lockport, Ill.; mem. Legatus (Cath. chief exec. officer's) Bd., bd. dirs. United Rep. Fund, 1987—, Chgo. Osteopathic Health Systems, 1989—; bd. advisors Lewis U., Lockport, Ill., 1987—. Named Small Bus. Acct. of Yr. for State of Ill. SBA, 1987. Mem. Am. Soc. CLU's (bd. dirs. 1970—), Gen. Agts. Mgrs. Conf. (pres. 1967-68), Nat. Assn. Life Underwriters, Chgo. Orchestral Assn., Chgo. Lyric Opera. Roman Catholic. Home: 474 E South St Elmhurst IL 60126 Office: Hinsdale Assocs Fin Svc Corp 119 E Ogden Hinsdale IL 60521

URCIOLO, JOHN RAPHAEL, II, real estate developer, real estate and finance educator; b. Washington, July 29, 1947; s. Joseph John and Phillie Marie (Petrone) U.; m. Jean Marie Manning, Jan. 2, 1972. BBA, Am. U., 1969, postgrad. real estate, 1970, MS, 1971. Cert. real estate broker, appraiser. Researcher Homer Hoyt Inst., Washington, 1967-69; economist Nat. Assn. Home Builders, Washington, 1971-75; adj. prof. U. Md., College Park, 1972-79; property mgr. Urciolo Realty Co., Washington, 1976-79; comml. broker Urciolo & Urciolo, Washington, 1980-82; real estate developer Urciolo & Urciolo, Takoma Park, Md., 1982—; lectr., assoc. prof. Montgomery Coll., Rockville, Md., 1971-72; assoc. prof. U. Md., 1972-79, Am. U., Washington, 1980—; cons. Montgomery County Govt., Rockville, 1980-81, Nat. Ski Area Assn., Hartford, 1978-79; court expert Superior Ct. for D.C., Civil and Criminal divs.; lectr. to various organs. Author: Real Estate Manual, 1976; co-author: The White Book of Ski Ateas (U.S. and Canada), 1977, 3d edit., 1979, Industry Edition-The White Book, 1978, The Housing Fact Book, 1976, Housing Component Costs, 1975, 2d edit., 1976, Material Usage in Housing, 1970; co-editor: Labor Wage Rate Bulletin, 1976. Fellow Urban Mass Transp. Assn., 1969, Am. U., 1970; Soc. Real Estate Appraisers scholar, 1968. Mem. Cert. Real Estate Appraisers, Am. Planning Assn., Am. Univ. Real Estate Assn. (charter mem., v.p. edn., v.p. award 1983), Am. Assn. Univ. Profs., Ea. Ski Writers Assn. (com. mem.), Rho Epsilon (editor newsletter 1969). Republican. Roman Catholic. Office: Urciolo & Urciolo 6935 Laurel Ave Ste 100 Takoma Park MD 20912

URCIUOLI, J. ARTHUR, investment banker; b. Syracuse, N.Y., Nov. 13, 1937; s. Joseph R. and Nicoletta Anne (Phillips) U.; m. Margaret Jane Forelli, Aug. 13, 1966; children: Karen Sloan, Christian J.A. B.S., St. Lawrence U., 1959; J.D., Georgetown U., 1966; grad. Advanced Mgmt. Program, Harvard Bus. Sch., 1982. Bar: N.Y. 1966. Atty. Brown, Wood, Fuller, Caldwell & Ivey, N.Y.C., 1966-69; internat. investment banker, dir. internat. fin. Merrill Lynch, N.Y.C., Paris, 1970-78; pres. Merrill Lynch Internat., 1978-82; chmn. Merrill Lynch Internat. Bank, London; dir. banking div. Merrill Lynch Capital Markets, 1980-84; dir. Merrill Lynch Bus. Fin. Services, Merrill Lynch Co., 1984—. Contbr. articles to profl. jours. Trustee St. Lawrence U., 1976—; bd. dirs. United Way, Greenwich, Conn., 1978-81. Served to capt. USMC, 1959-63. Mem. Securities Industry Assn. (chmn. sales and mktg. com. 1987-89). Republican. Congregationalist. Clubs: River, Univ. (N.Y.C.); N.Y. Yacht, Riverside (Conn.) Yacht; Rocky Point (Old Greenwich, Conn.). Office: Merrill Lynch Pierce Fenner & Smith Inc 717 5th Ave New York NY 10022

URFER, RICHARD PETERSON, investment banking executive; b. Spring Green, Wis., June 28, 1936; s. Walter Chester and Alice Mae (Peterson) U.; m. Cynthia Leigh Vaughan, June 22, 1968; children: Jocelyn Leigh, Gilbert Fielding, Courtney Vaughan. BS, U. Wis., 1958; MBA, Harvard U., 1964. Assoc. Morgan Stanley & Co., N.Y.C., 1964-67; pres., chief exec. officer Diebold Computer Leasing, Jersey City, 1967-69; dir. fgn. direct investments Dept. Commerce, Washington, 1969-71; sr. v.p., dir. Blyth Eastman Dillon, N.Y.C., 1972-74, Atlantic Capital Corp., N.Y.C., 1974-82; chief operating officer Chase Manhattan Capital Markets Corp., N.Y.C., 1982-88; mng. dir. R.P. Urfer & Co., N.Y.C., 1988—; bd. dirs. Riverbend Internat. Corp., Sanger, Calif., Syracuse Supply Co. Served to lt. U.S. Army, 1959-60. Mem. Nat. Council-Salk Inst., Council Fgn. Relations. Republican. Episcopalian. Clubs: Seal Harber Yacht (commodore 1987—), Union, India House, Morris County Golf, Essex Hunt. Home: Willowbrook Farm Blue Mill Rd Morristown NJ 07960 Office: R P Urfer & Co Inc 20 Exchange Pl New York NY 10005

URI, GEORGE WOLFSOHN, accountant; b. San Francisco, Dec. 8, 1920; s. George Washington and Ruby (Wolfsohn) U.; m. Pamela Dorothy O'Keefe, May 15, 1961. A.B., Stanford U., 1941, I.A., 1943, M.B.A., 1946; postgrad., U. Leeds, Eng., 1945. C.P.A., Calif.; Chartered Fin. Cons.; Cert. Fin. Planner. Mem. acctg., econs. and stats. depts. Shell Oil Co., Inc., San Francisco, 1946-48; ptnr. Irelan, Uri, Mayer & Sheppie, San Francisco; pres. F. Uri & Co., Inc., Athos Corp., Irelan Accountancy Corp.; instr. acctg. and econs. Golden Gate Coll., 1949-50. Contbr. articles to profl. jours. Chmn. San Rafael Redevel. Adv. Com., 1977-78, mem., 1978—; bd. dirs. San Francisco Planning and Urban Renewal Assn., 1958-60. Served with AUS, 1942-46, to col. Res. (ret.). Recipient Key Man award San Francisco Jr. C. of C.; Meritorious Service medal Sec. of Army, 1978. Mem. AICPA, Inst. Mgmt. Scis. (treas. No. Calif. chpt. 1961-62), Calif. Soc. CPA's (sec.-treas. San Francisco chpt. 1956-57, dir. 1961-63, state dir. 1964-66, mem. Forbes medal com. 1968-69, chmn. 1969-71), Am. Econs. Assn., Nat. Assn. Accts., San Francisco Estate Planning Council (dir. 1965-68), Am. Statis. Assn., Am. Soc. Mil. Comptrollers, Execs. Assn. San Francisco (pres. 1965-66), Inst. Cert. Mgmt. Accts. (cert. mgmt. acctg., Disting. Performance cert. 1978), Inst. Cert. Fin. Planners, Am. Soc. CLUs and Chartered Fin. Cons., Am. Soc. Mil. Comptrollers. Clubs: Engrs. San Francisco, Commonwealth, Stanford, Rafael Racquet; Army and Navy (Washington). Home: 11 McNear Dr San Rafael CA 94901 Office: Suite 2000 100 Pine St San Francisco CA 94111

URICH, JOSEPH MICHAEL, computer education founder; b. Boston, Mar. 14, 1947; s. William James and Josephine Teresa (Roche) U.; m. Janet R. Rocklin, Feb. 21, 1981 (div. Dec. 1987); 1 child, Joseph William. Ethics officer Hubbard Coll. of Improvement, Clearwater, Fla., 1985-88; pres. Applied Scholastics, Malden, Mass., 1982—; v.p. 8C Cons., Clearwater; exec. dir. Bernstein McCaffrey & Lee, Inc., Clearwater. With U.S. Army, 1968-71. Mem. Internat. Assn. Scientologists. Republican. Home: PO Box 1841 Clearwater FL 34617-1841 Office: Computer Establishment Orgn 1248 Rogers St #J Clearwater FL 34616

URKOWITZ, MICHAEL, banker; b. Bronx, N.Y., June 18, 1943; s. David and Esther (Levy) U.; m. Eleanor Naomi Dreazen, July 2, 1966; children—Brian, Denise. B.Engring., CCNY, 1965, M.M.E., 1967. Project engr. Lunar Module program Grumman Corp., Bethpage, N.Y., 1964-72; asst. to dep. commr. for housing code compliance, project mgr. City of N.Y., 1972-74; 2d v.p. Chase Manhattan Bank, N.Y.C., 1974-77, v.p. group exec. ops. dept., money transfer group, 1977-80, sr. v.p., 1980—, group exec. internat. bank services, 1981-82, product and prodn. risk mgmt. exec., 1982-85, exec. v.p., corp. ops. and systems exec., 1985-87, service product sector exec., 1987—; lectr. CCNY, 1967-68. Contbg. author: Thermal Control and Radiation, 1972. Mem. Tau Beta Pi, Pi Tau Sigma. Office: Chase Manhattan Corp 1 Chase Manhattan Pla 13th Fl New York NY 10081

URQUHART, STEPHEN E., lawyer; b. Quincy, Mass., Mar. 2, 1949; s. Raymond Miles and M. Eileen (MacDonald) U.; m. Katherine Driscoll, Mar. 15, 1970; 1 child, Stephen M. AB, Boston Coll., 1976, JD, 1979. Bar: Mass. 1979, U.S. Dist. Ct. Mass. 1980. Legis. aide Mass. Ho. of Reps.,

Boston, 1976; counsel B.C. Legal Assistance Bur., Waltham, Mass., 1976-79; assoc. Law Offices of Robert J. Ladd (formerly Law Offices of Roland I. Wood), North Andover, Mass., 1980-88, Law Offices Nicholas Macaronis, Lowell, Mass., 1988—. Precinct capt. Edward M. Kennedy for Senator, Mass. 1979-80; campaign worker various Dem. candidates. Recipient cert. of merit United World Federalists, 1974. Mem. ABA, Mass. Bar Assn., Mass. Acad. Trial Attys., Am. Arbitration Assn., Internat. Platform Assn., Am. Trial Lawyers Assn., Phi Beta Kappa. Methodist. Club: Clan Urquhart (Va.). Home: PO Box 610 Danville NH 03819 Office: 9 Central St Lowell MA 01852

URRY, JAMES DALE, banker; b. Ogden, Utah, Nov. 12, 1947; s. William C. and Fae (East) U.; m. Vickie Taylor Aug. 20, 1971; children: Jennifer, Justin, Kamilyn, Kraig, Kristin, KariAnn. BA, Weber State Coll., 1973. Mgr. Dial Fin. Co., Ogden, Utah, 1973-78; asst. mgr. consumer loans First Security Bank of Utah, N.A., Ogden, 1978-79, asst. mgr. 12th st. office, 1980-81, mgr. consumer loans, 1981-82, North Ogden br. mgr., 1982-86, asst. v.p., South Ogden area mgr., 1986-87, asst. v.p., mgr. consumer loans, 1987—. Mem. planning com. North Ogden City, 1981, city councilman, 1983; mem. Robert Morris Assoc. With USAR, 1970-76. Mem. Weber State Coll. Alumni Bd., Ogden Breakfast Exchange, Rotary. Avocations: softball, basketball, gardening, horses. Home: 1615 N Mountain Rd North Ogden UT 84404

URSIN, BJARNE ELLING, manufacturing company executive; b. Bridgeport, Conn., Aug. 8, 1930; s. Bjarne and Esther (Schiott) U.; student Oberlin Coll., 1949-51; BS in Physics, MIT, 1957; m. Mary Elizabeth Locke, July 26, 1969; children: Stephanie, Lara, Matthew, Jonathan, Teri, Kristian. Project engr. Raytheon, Andover, Mass., 1957-60; prin. investigator Gen. Dynamics, San Diego, 1960-62; sr. scientist Philco-Ford, Newport Beach, Calif., 1962-67; with McDonnell Douglas Corp., Huntington Beach, Calif., 1967-76, sr. ops. project mgr., mgr. mfg., 1967-76; prodn. mgr. Eldec Corp., Lynnwood, Wash., 1976-78; v.p. mfg. TCS Inc., Redmond, Wash., 1978-80; dir. new bus. Data I/O Corp., Redmond, 1980-82; prodn. mgr. Atex Inc., A Kodak Co., 1982-83; quality assurance systems mgr. Boeing Electronics Co., Seattle, 1983—; assoc. Coldwell Banker Co., 1981-83, Wallace and Wheeler Realty, 1984—; owner Westechnology, Bellevue, Wash., 1980—; co-owner Lighthouse Interiors, 1982—; community chmn. City of Huntington Beach, 1975-76. Served with AUS, 1951-53, Korea. Recipient NASA Team award Saturn/Apollo, 1975, Nasa Design VIP award Skylab, 1976, Cert. Appreciation, McDonnell Douglas, 1976. Mem. Am. Assn. Physics Tchrs., AIAA, AAAS, U.S. Internat. Sailing Assn., Am. Mgmt. Assn. Republican. Roman Catholic. Clubs: Bahia Corinthian Yacht (dir. 1972-76, rear commodore 1974, vice commodore 1975, commodore 1976) (Corona Del Mar); Royal Norwegian Yacht (Oslo); Balboa Bay; Seattle Yacht, U.S. Power Squadron, MIT of Puget Sound (dir. 1979—). Home: 9520 SE 61st Pl Mercer Island WA 98040 Office: PO Box 596 Mercer Island WA 98040 Office: PO Box 6968 Bellevue WA 98008

URSTADT, CHARLES DEANE, real estate and publishing executive; b. N.Y.C., June 13, 1959; s. Charles Jordan and Elinor McClure (Funk) U.; m. Lynn Caroline Jackson, May 19, 1984. BA cum laude, NYU, 1982. News reporter Sta. WNYC-TV, N.Y.C., 1979-80; adminstrv. asst. Mayor's Press Office, City of N.Y., 1980-81; asst. v.p. Urstadt Property Co. Inc. (formerly Pearce, Urstadt, Mayer & Greer, Inc.), 1981-84, v.p., mem. exec. com., 1984-86, sr. v.p., sec., 1986—; pub., editor-in-chief N.Y. Constrn. News, 1984—. Chmn. Young Reps. of Bronxville, 1984-85; Village Rep. Campaign Com. of Bronxville, N.Y., 1984-85, Young People for O'Rourke Campaign, 1986; mem. adv. bd. Community Housing Improvement Program, Inc., 1987—; treas., bd. dirs. N.Y. Bldg. Congress; bd. dirs. 61 E. 86th St. Owners Corp., 1987—, Forum 500 (N.Y. Rep. State Com.), 1987—, The Ensemble Studio Theater, 1988—, East Side Assn., 1988—. Mem. Bldg. Contractors Assn., Nat. Assn. Home Builders, Fairfield County Home Builders Assn., L.I. Builders Inst., Rockland County Builders Assn., Assoc. Builders and Owners of Greater N.Y., Builders Inst., N.Y. Bldg. Congress (bd. dirs. 1988—), Urban Land Inst. Clubs: Nat. Realty, Links. Office: 200 Madison Ave Rm 2112 New York NY 10016 also: Office No 3 2 Park Pl Bronxville NY 10708

URSTADT, CHARLES JORDAN, real estate executive; b. N.Y.C., Oct. 27, 1928; s. Charles G. and Claire C. (Jordan) U.; m. Elinor McClure Funk, Mar. 23, 1957; children: Charles Deane, Catherine Cary. BA, Dartmouth Coll., 1949, MBA, 1951; LLB, Cornell U., 1953. Bar: N.Y. Assoc., Nevius Brett & Kellogg, N.Y.C., 1953-58; asst. sec. Webb & Knapp, Inc., N.Y.C., 1958-63; v.p., sec., counsel Alcoa Residences, Inc., N.Y.C., 1963-67; commr. N.Y. State Div. Housing and Community Renewal, N.Y.C., 1967-73 ; chmn., Battery Park City Authority, N.Y.C., 1968-78; chmn. bd., pres., dir. Urstadt Property Co. Inc. (formerly Pearce, Urstadt, Mayer & Greer, Inc.), N.Y.C., 1979—; trustee HRE Properties (formerly Hubbard Real Estate Investments), N.Y.C., 1975—, chmn., 1986—; trustee Tchrs. Ins. and Annuity Corp., 1985—; bd. dirs. Lawrence Investing Co., Inc., Bronxville, N.Y. Trustee, Pace U., 1973—; mem. fin. com. N.Y. Rep. State Com., 1981—, del. Rep. Nat. Conv., 1988; mem. Gov.'s Task Force on N.Y. Housing, 1988—; bd. dirs. N.Y.C. Partnership, Inc., 1984—; chmn. N.Y. State Statue of Liberty Celebration Found., 1983-84, N.Y. State Housing Fin. Agy., 1969, Tri-State Regional Planning Commn., 1969-70; mem. Pres.'s Commn. on Housing, 1981-82, others. Lt. USNR, 1954-56. Recipient Good Scouting award Boy Scouts Am., 1973; Urban Leadership award NYU Real Estate Inst., 1979; Man of Yr. award Realty Found. N.Y., 1979. Gov. Real Estate Bd. N.Y., Assoc. Builders and Owners Greater N.Y. (dir. 1979—), N.Y. Bldg. Congress (bd. govs. 1973—). Mem. Nat. Soc. Real Estate Fin., Maritime Assn. Port of N.Y./N.J. Mem. Reformed Church. Clubs: Links, Union League (N.Y.C.); Siwanoy Country (Bronxville); Bohemian (San Francisco). Home: 6 Beechwood Rd Bronxville NY 10708 Office: 200 Madison Ave Rm 2112 New York NY 10016

USDAN, JAMES MORRIS, health care executive; b. Englewood, N.J., Nov. 3, 1949; s. Leo Judah and Selma (Goldfein) U.; m. Vinette Ann Carknard, June 8, 1980. AB, Havard U., 1971. Gen. mgr. Some Place Else Restaurant, Schuylerville, N.Y., 1972-77; v.p. Meth. Hosp., Houston, 1977-83, Health Resource Corp. Am., Houston, 1983-84; pres., chief exec. officer Behavioral Health Systems, Houston, 1984-87; exec. v.p., chief operating officer Rehab. Hosp. Services Corp., Camp Hill, Pa., 1987-88; pres., chief exec. officer Am. Transitional Care, Inc., Houston, 1987—; cons. Rehab. Care Corp., St. Louis, 1978-88. Mem. Houston Philosophical Soc., Harvard Club. Home: 15119 Quail Rock Creek Houston TX 77095 Office: Am Transitional Care Inc 14550 Torrey Chase Blvd #450 Houston TX 77014

USLAN, SEYMOUR STEPHEN, financial executive; b. Irvington, N.J., May 30, 1928; s. Maxwell Ellex and Rebecca (Sprotz) U.; m. Barbara Judith Swartz, Dec. 27, 1953; children: Jeffrey Fred, Glen David. AA, Los Angeles City Coll., 1947; BA, Calif. State U.-Los Angeles, 1953, MA, 1955; PhD, UCLA, 1960. Human factors scientist Hughes Aircraft Co., Culver City, Calif., 1952-60; dir. tng. Litton Industries, Beverly Hills, Calif., 1960-66, v.p., 1966-68; sr. v.p. Mentec Corp., Los Angeles, 1968-72; pres. Human Potential Devel. Corp., Los Angeles, 1972-82; prof. sch. bus. Pepperdine U., Los Angeles, 1972-84; pres. Husan Med. Systems, Dallas, 1984-86; exec. v.p. OneCard Internat., Inc., Los Angeles, 1986—, also dir.; cons. Bur. Mines, OSHA, EPA, other agys., Washington, 1972-83; invited witness U.S. Cong. Com. on Edn., Washington, 1965; speaker at profl. confs. and on t.v. programs. Contbr. articles to profl. jours. Served with U.S. Army, 1950-52. Recipient Cert. of Accomplishment, Calif. Legis., 1965; named hon. Ky. Col., 1968. Republican. Home: 2243 Westshore Ln Westlake Village CA 91361 Office: OneCard Internat Inc 6120 Bristol Pkwy Culver City CA 90230

USUI, LESLIE RAYMOND, clothing executive; b. Wahiawa, Hawaii, Feb. 2, 1946; s. Raymond Isao and Joyce Mitsuyo (Muramoto) U.; m. Annie On Nor Hom, Oct. 23, 1980; 1 child, Atisha. BA in Zool., U. Hawaii, 1969, MA in Edn., 1972. Cert. tchr., Hawaii. Flight steward United Airlines, Honolulu, 1970; spl. tutor Dept. Edn., 1971-73; v.p. Satyuga, Inc., Honolulu, 1974-80; pres. Satyuga, Inc., 1980—; also bd. dirs.; cons. Hawaii Fashion Guild, 1978-79. Composer: Song to Chenrayzee, Song to Karmapa. Cofounder, bd. dirs. Kagyu Thegchen Ling Meditation Ctr., 1974—, Maitreya Inst., 1983-86; bd. dirs. Palpung Found., 1984-88, U.S. Senatorial Bus. Adv. Bd., Washington, 1988. Mem. Hawaii Bus. League, Nat. Fedn. Ind. Bus. Republican. Buddhist. Home: 1417 Laamia Pl Honolulu HI 96821 Office: Satyuga Inc 248 Mokauea St Honolulu HI 96819

UTLEY, EDWIN EMERY, utility company executive; b. Wadesboro, N.C., Apr. 10, 1924; s. Edwin Emery and Stella (Ray) U.; m. Hellon Norma Lawrence, Mar. 1, 1947; children: Nancy Utley Hutchins, Sharon Utley Weigle, James, Douglas. Student, N.C. State U., 1941-42, Louisburg Coll., 1946-47. With Carolina Power & Light Co., Raleigh, 1951—, v.p., sr. v.p., until 1980, sr. exec. v.p. power supply and engring and constrn., 1980—, dir.; dir. Leslie Coal Mining Co., Cleve., McInnes Coal Mining Co., Cleve. Served with USN, 1943-46, PTO. Mem. ASME (chmn. eastern sect. 1962), N.C. Soc. Engrs. (dir. 1981-82), Am. Nuclear Soc., Nat. Soc. Profl. Engrs. (sr. assoc. mem.), Profl. Engrs. N.C. (sr. assoc.). Democrat. Methodist. Office: Carolina Power & Light Co 411 Fayetteville St Raleigh NC 27602 *

UTSEY, JOHN BLAINE, retail store executive; b. Kilgore, Tex., Dec. 19, 1938; s. John Henry and Gertrude Pauline (Hensley) U.; m. Lavelle Watkins, June 4, 1960; children: John David, Jennifer Lynn. B.B.A. (scholar), Baylor U., 1960; M.S. (scholar), N.Y. U., 1961. With Foley's Dept. Store, Houston, 1961—; chmn., chief exec. officer Foley's Dept. Store, 1987—; dir. Asso. Merchandising Corp.; bd. dirs. Federated Dept. Stores Found. Bd. dirs. Tex. Research League, United Way of Tex. Gulf Coast. Mem. Greater Houston Conv. and Visitors Council (bd. dirs.). Baptist. Clubs: Heritage, Forum. Office: Foley's Dept Store 1110 Main St Houston TX 77001

UVEGES, GEORGE, medical equipment company executive; b. Cleve., Jan. 2, 1948; s. George and Irene (Merker) U.; m. Reneé Butler, July 30, 1971; children: Tom, Paul. BBA, Cleve. State U., 1970; MBA, Baldwin-Wallace U., 1978. CPA, Ohio. Sr. audit mgr. Ernst & Whinney, Cleve., 1971-85; treas., corp. controller Invacare Corp., Elyria, Ohio, 1985—. With U.S. Army, 1970-71. Mem. Fin. Execs. Inst., Treas. Club, Am. Inst. CPA's, Ohio Soc. CPA's, Cleve. State U. Alumni Assn. (pres. 1984-85). Republican. Roman Catholic. Office: Invacare Corp 899 Cleveland St Elyria OH 44036

UVENA, FRANK JOHN, printing company executive; b. Ernest, Pa., Feb. 2, 1934; s. Nicholas and Margaret Jean (Clary) U.; m. Helena Toivola, Aug. 13, 1960; children—Lisa, Michael, Geoffrey, Steven. A.B., Ohio U., Athens, 1959; LL.B., Ohio State U., Columbus, 1963. Bar: Ill bar 1963. Assoc. firm McDermott, Will & Emery, Chgo., 1963-68; atty. R.R. Donnelley & Sons, Chgo., 1968-75, v.p., gen. counsel, 1975-84, sr. v.p. law and corp. staffs, 1984—. Mem. Chgo. Crime Commn., 1975; commr. Ill. Guardianship and Advocacy Commn., 1984; bd. dirs. United Charities Chgo. With AUS, 1954-56. Mem. Am. Bar Assn., Ill. Bar Assn., Chgo. Bar Assn. Club: Union League (Chgo.). Office: R R Donnelley & Sons Co 2223 Martin Luther King Dr Chicago IL 60616

VACHON, BARBARA L., manufacturing executive; b. Healdsburg, Calif., Jan. 3, 1956; d. Floyd Franklin and Susan Clementine (Waldrop) Ambrose; m. Andre G. Vachon, Jan. 5, 1974 (div. 1981); children: Paris Andrea, Maris Ola. LLD, Portland U., 1983. home health exec. Ambulatory Svcs. of Oreg., Canby, 1981-83; assoc. E.M. Kruse Atty.-at-Law, Santa Ana, Calif., 1984-85; v.p. G.S.E. Inc., Dana Point, Calif., 1985-88. Creator data processing programs; mem. Pres.'s Coun. on Aging, Portland, 1981. Mem. Nat. Assn. Female Execs. Democrat. Lutheran. Home: PO Box 3068 Corona CA 91718 Office: ACO Enterprises 104 N School St Corona CA 91720

VACHON, REGINALD IRENEE, engineer; b. Norfolk, Va., Jan. 29, 1937; s. Rene Albert Vachon and Regina (Galvin) Radcliffe; student U.S. Naval Acad., 1954-55; B.M.E., Auburn U., 1958, M.S., 1960; Ph.D., Okla. State U., 1963; LL.B., Jones Law Sch., 1969; m. Mary Eleanor Grigg, Jan. 16, 1960; children—Reginald Irenee, Eleanor Marie. Engr., Hayes Internat., 1958; instr., research asst. Auburn U., 1958-60, research asso., 1961, asso. prof., 1963-78; research and devel. engr. E.I. DuPont, 1960; aerospace engr., technologist NASA Marshall Space Flight Center, summers, 1964, 65; pres. Vachon Nix & Assocs., 1977—, VNA Systems Inc., 1982—; chmn. bd. Optimal Systems Internat., Inc., 1969—; chief operating officer Thacker Constrn. Co., Thacker Orgn. Inc., 1981—; admitted to Ala. bar, 1971. Served with U.S. Army, 1960-61. Registered profl. engr., Ala., Ga., Miss., La., Wis., Tex. Fellow ASME; mem. Am. Inst. Aeros. and Astronautics, Nat. Soc. Profl. Engrs., Ala. Bar Assn., Am. Bar Assn. Roman Catholic. Club: Cosmos (Washington). Contbr. articles to profl. jours.; patentee in field. Home: 1414 Epping Forest Atlanta GA 30319 Office: PO Box 467069 Atlanta GA 30346

VAGELOS, PINDAROS ROY, pharmaceutical company executive; b. Westfield, N.J., Oct. 8, 1929; s. Roy John and Marianthi (Lambrinides) V.; m. Diana Touliatos, July 10, 1955; children: Randall, Cynthia, Andrew, Ellen. A.B., U. Pa., 1950; M.D., Columbia U., 1954; D.Sc. (hon.), Washington U., 1980, Brown U., 1982, U. Medicine and Dentistry of N.J., 1984. Intern medicine Mass. Gen. Hosp., 1954-55, asst. resident medicine, 1955-56; surgeon Lab. Cellular Physiology, NIH, 1956-59; surgeon Lab. Biochemistry, 1959-64, head sect. comparative biochemistry, 1964-66; prof. biochemistry, chmn. dept. biol. chemistry Washington U. Sch. Medicine, St. Louis, 1966-75; dir. div. biology and biomed. scis. Washington U. Sch. Medicine, 1973-75; sr. v.p. research Merck, Sharp & Dohme Research Labs., Rahway, N.J., 1975-76, pres., 1976-84; corp. sr. v.p. Merck & Co., Inc., Rahway, N.J., 1982-84, also bd. dirs., 1984—, exec. v.p., 1984-85, pres., chief exec. officer, 1985-86; chmn., pres., chief exec. officer Merck & Co., Inc., 1986—; mem. molecular biology study sect. NIH, 1967-71, mem. physiol. chemistry study sect., 1973-75; mem. commn. on human resources NRC, 1973-76, Inst. Medicine, Nat. Acad. Scis., 1974—; chmn. sci. adv. bd. N.J. Ctr. for Advancement of Biotech. and Medicine, 1985—; bd. dirs. TRW, Inc., 1987—, Prudential Ins. Co. Mem. editorial bds. jours. in field. Trustee U. Pa., 1988-89, Rockefeller U., 1976—, Danforth Found., 1978—, Ptnrship. for N.J., 1989—; mem. Bus. Coun., 1987—. Recipient N.J. Sci./Tech. Medal Rsch. and Devel. Coun. N.J., 1983. Mem. Am. Chem. Soc. (award enzyme chemistry 1967), Am. Soc. Biol. Chemists, Nat. Acad. Scis., Am. Acad. Arts and Scis., Bus. Roundtable (policy com. 1987—), Nat. Acad. Scis., Am. Acad. Arts and Scis. Home: 10 Canterbury Ln Watchung NJ 07060 Office: Merck & Co Inc PO Box 2000 126 E Lincoln Ave Rahway NJ 07065

VAHSHOLTZ, ROBERT JOHN, manufacturing executive; b. Emporia, Kans., Oct. 5, 1935; s. Fred Richard and Merle Evelyn (Butler) V.; m. Marjorie Alice Otte, Aug. 21, 1955; children: Jon K., Kim J. Student, Kans. State U., 1953-54; BFA, Art Ctr. Coll. Design, Los Angeles, 1957. Designer Kaiser Aluminum Corp., Oakland, Calif., 1957-58; sr. designer Richardson Homes Corp., Elkhart, Ind., 1960-66; exec. v.p. Slayter Assocs., Inc., Elkhart, 1966-71; sr. designer Multicon Properties, Inc., Delaware, Ohio, 1971-72; owner RJV Indsl. Design, Elkhart, 1972-74; v.p., planning Norcom Homes Ltd., Mississauga, Ont., Can., 1974-81; sr. v.p. planning Fed. Industries, Ltd., Winnipeg, Man., Can., 1981—; mem. adv. bd. Royal City Realty Ltd. Served with U.S. Army, 1958-60. Home: 866 Pine View Dr Arroyo Grande CA 93420 Office: Fed Industries Ltd, 2400 One Lombard Pl, Winnipeg, MB Canada R3B 0X3

VAIL, FREDERICK SCOTT, record company executive; b. San Francisco, Mar. 24, 1944; s. Morgan Willard and Doris Louise (Jacobus) V.; m. Brenda Joyce Howard, June 18, 1972 (div. 1977). Student, Calif. State U., Sacramento, 1962-64, Indsl. Coll. of the Armed Forces, 1963, Vol. State Community Coll., Nashville, 1980-81. Radio announcer, program dir. Stas. KXOA-FM and KJML-FM, Sacramento, 1958-62; pres. Frederick Vail Prodns., Sacramento and Hollywood, Calif., 1962-66; producer Teen-Age Fair, Inc., Hollywood, 1966-68, nat. sales mgr., 1968-69; mgr. The Beach Boys, Hollywood, 1969-71; promotion mgr. Capital Records, Inc., Hollywood, 1972-73; pres., cons. Frederick Vail and Assocs., Nashville, 1974-80; pres., gen. mgr. Treasure Isle Rec. Studios, Inc., Nashville, 1980—; cons. promotion and mktg. Waylon Jennings, Glaser Bros., Nashville, 1974-75, GRT Records, Inc., 1976-78, RSO Records, Hollywood, 1978-79; lectr. Vanderbilt U., Belmont Coll., Mid. Tenn. State U., Vol. State Col., Nashville, 1981. Contbr. articles to several books. Life mem. Rep. Nat. Com., Washington, 1984—, Conservative Caucus, Washington, 1982—; Rep. nominee U.S. Ho. of Reps., 1986; aide-de-camp Gov.'s staff State of Tenn., 1986. Recipient seven gold records, two platinum records Rec. Industry Assn. Am., 1980-88. Mem. Country Music Assn., Acad. Country Music, NARAS (v.p., bd. govs. 1981-83). Presbyterian. Office: Treasure Isle Rec Studios Inc 2808 Azalea Pl Nashville TN 37204

VAIL, JOE FRANKLIN, marketing company executive; b. Indpls., Mar. 24, 1928; s. Frank Albert and Trixie May (Hawley) V.; m. Margaret Louise Warne, Nov. 24, 1984; 1 son, Kevin Joe. BS, Purdue U., 1951. Treas., Apex Corp., Indpls., 1953-60; owner, operator Bus. Service Co., Indpls., 1961-63; partner Pulse Publs., Indpls., 1963-64; pres. Unique, Inc., Indpls., 1965-70; owner, operator Mid-Am. Advt. Co., Indpls., 1970-73; pres. Mid-Am. Mktg., Inc., Indpls., 1973—; editor, pub. Land Opportunity Rev., 1970—, Internat. Employment Opportunities Digest, 1970—. Mem. Chgo. Assn. Direct Mktg., Nat. Fedn. Ind. Bus., Indpls. C. of C. Am. Bus. Club. Clubs: John Purdue, Masons. Author: Keys to Wealth, 1971; Your Fortune in Mail Order, 1972; How to Get Out of Debt and Live Like a Millionaire, 1977; Money-Where It Is and How To Get It, 1981. Home: 8228 E 13th St Indianapolis IN 46219 Office: 7149 Southeastern Ave Indianapolis IN 46239

VAINSTEIN, GUSTAVO ALFREDO, television executive; b. Buenos Aires, Dec. 9, 1949; arrived in France, 1976; s. Carlos and Dora (Wainer) V. M in Sociology, U. Buenos Aires, 1972; M in Communication, U. Paris, 1978. Dir. local TV programming La Pampa, Argentina, 1974-75; programmer Radio Nacional, Buenos Aires, 1975-76; instr. Inst. Nat. de L'Audiovisuel, Paris, 1977-83, mgr. mktg., 1983-87; mgr. mktg., dir. programs Region Cable, Lille and Nice, France, 1987—; cons. Instituto Interamericano De Ciencias Agricolas, Argentina, 1976, UNESCO, France, 1980. Writer (radio program) Conquest of Future, 1974. Home: 138 Blvd Auriol, 75013 Paris France Office: Region Cable, 43 Mal Lattre de Tassienr, 59350 Saint Andre France

VAITL, WILLIAM LUDWIG, treasurer; b. Milw., Feb. 10, 1934; s. Ludwig and Julianna (Schmuck) V.; m. Barbara Lenore Pitt, July 28, 1956; children: Laura, Amy, Valerie. BS, U. Wis., 1956. Supr. Gen. Mill Inc., Mpls., 1958-61, mgr., 1961-62; various mgmt. positions Allis-Chalmers Corp., Milw., 1962-74, asst. treas., 1974-88, treas. Reorgn. Trust, 1989—. Active Brookfield (Wis.) Lutheran Ch., 1963—. Served with U.S. Army, 1956-58. Home: 4180 Cherokee Dr Brookfield WI 53005

VALCOURT, BERNARD, lawyer, Canadian government official; b. St. Quentina de Restigouche, N.B., Can., Feb. 18, 1952; s. Bertin and Gerladine (Allain) V.; children: Annie, Edith. Student, U. N.B. Lawye; mem. Ho. of Commons, 1984; formerly parliamentary sec. Ministry State for Sci. and Tech. and Ministry Revenue; minister state for small bus. and tourism 1986—, minister state for Indian affairs and no. devel., 1987-89; mem. Privy Council, 1986—; minister state consumer and corp. affairs. 1989—. Mem. ABA, N.B. Bar Assn. Progressive Conservative. Roman Catholic. Office: House of Commons, Parliament Bldgs, Ottawa, ON Canada K1A 0A6 *

VALDESALICE, JAMES KERRY, service company executive; b. Cleve., Dec. 4, 1939; s. James B. and Harriet (Jane) V.; m. Claire Louise Nelson, June 21, 1969; children: James, Kerry. BS, Carnegie-Mellon U., 1962; post-grad., Duquesne U., 1969-70. Substitute tchr. Pitts. Pub. Schs., 1971-72, Greensburg and Hempfield (Pa.) Pub. Schs., 1976-78; with Hogan's Carpet Cleaning, Greensburg, 1978-81; owner, operator Valdesalice Quality Cleaning Service, Greensburg, 1981—. Mem. council Boy Scouts Am., Greensburg, 1988. Mem. Tri-State Carpet Cleaners Assn. Democrat. Roman Catholic. Office: Valdesalice Quality Cleaning 540 Harrison Ave Greensburg PA 15601

VALDEZ, JOSEPH, real estate broker, consultant; b. Los Angeles, Dec. 26, 1942; s. Joseph Angel and Rebecca (Cohen) V.; m. Ann Robinson. Student, U. San Francisco, 1983-85. Cert. real estate broker, Calif. Sales mgr. Valco Enterprises, Los Angeles, 1973-80; cons., sales mgr. Canyon Country Estates, Sherman Oaks, Calif., 1981-84; owner Valdez Realty, Los Angeles, 1984—; loan cons. to builders and div. developers, owners of sub-divs.. Photographer for profl. mag. and various newspapers. Mem. Conservative Dem. Com., Los Angeles, 1973—; vol. Proposition 13, Los Angeles, 1974-78. Served with USN, 1960-64. Mem. San Fernando Valley (Calif.) Bd. Realtors, Los Angeles Bd. Realtors, Nat. Rifle Assn., Calif. Rifle and Pistol Assn., Inc. Club: Los Angeles Athletic. Home and Office: 1357 Elysian Park Dr Los Angeles CA 90026

VALENTINE, HERMAN EDWARD, computer company executive; b. Norfolk, Va., June 26, 1937; s. Frank and Alice Mae (Heigh) V.; m. Dorothy Jones, Nov. 27, 1958; children: Herman Edward, Bryce Thomas. BS in Bus. Adminstrn., Norfolk State Coll., 1967; postgrad., Am. U., 1968; grad. student, Coll. William and Mary. Asst. bus. mgr. grad. sch. Dept. Agr., 1967, exec. officer grad. sch., 1967-68; bus. mgr. Norfolk State Coll., 1968; pres. Systems Mgmt. Am. Corp., Norfolk, 1969—, now also chmn. Star amb. City Norfolk; adv. coun. of the Va. Stage Co.; bd. dir. Cooperating Hampton Rds. Orgn. for Minorities in Engring., Operation Smile, Greater Norfolk Corp.; pres.'s coun. Old Dominion U.; adv. bd. Tidewater Vets. Meml. Project; active BOD, Push Internat. Trade Bur., Tidewater Regional Miority Purchasing Coun. Named Entrepreneur of Yr. Dept. Commerce Minority Bus. Devel. Agy., Supplier of Yr. Nat. Minority Supplier Devel. Council, 1987, Outstanding Businessperson of Yr. Va. Black Pres.'s Roundtable Assn.; recipient Presdl. Citation, 1984, Cert. of Merit City of Chg., 1985, Presdl. Citation Nat. Assn. Equal Opportunity in Higher Edn., 1981, McDonald's Hampton Roads Black Achievement award United Negro Coll. Fund., 1986, Disting. Svc. award Va. State Conf. NAACP, 1985, Citizen of Yr. award William A. Hunton YMCA, 1986, Nat. Bus. Leadership award Tidewater Minority Purchasing Coun., 1984, Meritorious Svc. award United Negro Coll. Fund., 1982, Outstanding Community Svc. award Va. State Conf. NAACP, 1984, Delicados, Inc. award, 1986, Colgate Whitehead Darden award, U. Va., 1987, cert. recognition Lt. Gov. Commonwealth of Va., 1987. Mem. Am. Mgmt. Assn., Tidewater Regional Polit. Assn. (founder, chmn.), Air Traffic Control Assn., Soc. Logistics Engrs., Armed Forced Communication and Electronics Assn. Office: Systems Mgmt Am Corp 254 Monticello Ave Norfolk VA 23510

VALENZUELA, DEBRA GUADALUPE, utility company executive; b. San Antonio, Mar. 7, 1957; d. Isaac Rosales and Jesusa (Escobar) V. BBA, St. Mary's U., San Antonio, 1979. Personnel asst. Union Camp Corp., San Antonio, 1979-82; benefits adminstr. City Water Bd., San Antonio, 1982-85, personnel and safety specialist, 1985—; bd. dirs. San Antonio Water Bd. Fed. Credit Union. Mem. Am. Water Works Assn., Nat. Assn. Female Execs., Nat. Notary Assn. Democrat. Roman Catholic. Office: City Water Bd PO Box 2449 1001 E Market San Antonio TX 78298

VALENZUELA, PABLO DE TARSO, biotechnology company executive, researcher; b. Santiago, Chile, June 13, 1941; came to U.S., 1967; s. Fernando and Carmen (Valdes) V.; children—Fernando, Andres, Javier, Francisca. Biochemist, U. Chile, 1966; Ph.D. in Chemistry, Northwestern U., 1970. Prof. biochemistry Catholic U., Santiago, 1972-75; assoc. prof. biochemistry and biophysics U. Calif.-San Francisco, 1977-81; v.p. research Chiron Corp., Emeryville, Calif., 1981—; adj. prof. biochemistry Cath. U., Santiago, 1976—. NIH fellow, 1975. Mem. Am. Soc. Biol. Chemists, Chilean Biochem. Soc., Chilean Biol. Soc. Home: 455 Upper Terr #3 San Francisco CA 94117 Office: Chiron Corp 4560 Horton Emeryville CA 94608

VALERIO, MARK LUKE, automobile executive; b. N.Y.C., Jan. 7, 1954; s. Aronzo A. and Imelda Theresa (Bell) V. BA, Marquette U., 1976. Consumer relations rep. Chevrolet Motor div. GM, Tarrytown, N.Y., 1977-78, area service mgr., 1978-81; dist. sales mgr. GM, Phila., 1982-84; mgr. communication services GM, Detroit, 1985; asst. br. mgr. Motors Holding div. GM, Detroit and Denver, 1986; br. mgr. Motors Holding div. GM, Charlotte, N.C., 1986—; bd. dirs. Motors Holding Investments, Va., N.C., S.C., Fla. Active with Statue of Liberty/Ellis Island Commn., N.Y.C., 1986. Roman Catholic. Club: Westchester Country (Rye, N.Y.). Office: GM Motors Holding Div 6525 Morrison Blvd #510 Charlotte NC 28211

VALERO, RON, cosmetic company executive; b. Jerusalem, Jan. 7, 1945; came to U.S., 1987; s. Ahron and Miriam (Shaposhnick) V. BSc, Bologna Med. Sch., 1973; BA, Jerusalem U., 1977. Dir. sales S. Valero Ltd., Jerusalem, 1980-84; v.p. S. Valero Ltd., London, 1984-88; exec. v.p., chief exec. officer Biofase Corp., N.Y.C., 1988—. Served to maj. Israeli Def. Forces, 1964-67. Home: 201 E 86th St New York NY 10028 Office: Biofase Corp 116 E 68th St New York NY 10021

VALESKY, SUSAN JEANNE, accountant; b. St. Petersburg, Fla., June 5, 1956; d. Charles Bernard Valesky and Jeanne (Schulz) Morgan. BS in Merchandising, Fla. State U., 1978; BA in Acctg., U. South Fla., 1983. CPA, Fla. Mgmt. trainee Burdines, Miami, Fla., 1978-79; store mgr. Nomalus Inc. subs. Levi Strauss, San Francisco, 1979; prin. Susan J. Valesky, P.A., St. Petersburg, 1980—. Bd. dirs. Windward Pointe Condominiums Inc., St. Petersburg, 1983-85. Mem. Fla. Inst. CPA's. Democrat. Office: Susan J Valesky PA 9152 Seminole Blvd Seminole FL 34642

VALHOULI, ARCHIMEDES N., accountant; b. Grevena, Macedonia, Greece, Apr. 23, 1935; came to U.S., 1951; naturalized, 1957.; s. Nicholas and Koula (Ntavara) V.; m. Maria Kallikatsos, June 22, 1969; children: Costa, Christina. BBA, Suffolk U., 1961, MBA, 1963; MS in Taxation, Bentley Coll., 1983, postgrad., 1984-86. CPA, Mass. Controller Am. Biltrite Co., Garfield, N.J., 1963-71; pvt. practice acctg. Haverhill, Mass., 1971—. Fellow Am. Inst. CPA's, Mass. Soc. CPA's; mem. Nat. Assn. Accts., Merrimack Valley Assn. Accts. Home: 56 Hoyt Rd Bradford MA 01830 Office: 259 S Main St Bradford MA 01830

VALIMAHOMED, SALIM AKBARALI, investment banker; b. Uganda, Nov. 25, 1948; came to U.S., 1967; s. Akbarali V. and Roshankhanoo (Jamal-Merali) Vaiya; m. Maurisse Taylor Gray, Apr. 24, 1982; 1 child, Zahra. BSCE, U. R.I., 1971; MHA, Duke U., 1974; MS in Mgmt., Stanford U., 1978. Assoc. Booz Allen & Hamilton, N.Y.C., 1974-79; v.p., ptnr. Kidder, Peabody & Co., N.Y.C., 1980-86; pres. Longview Inc., N.Y.C., 1986—. Prin. investigator NIH report: Supply/Demand for Hemophilia Products in U.S., 1978. Chmn. Nat. Com. Aga Khan Found. U.S., Washington, 1984-87. Mem. Internat. Hosp. Fedn., Asia Soc., Inst. Stategic Planning. Club: Union League (N.Y.C.). Home: 2 Heywood Rd Pelham Manor NY 10803 Office: Longview Inc 157 E 57th St New York NY 10022

VALLEE, JACQUES FABRICE, venture capital investor; b. Pontoise, France, Sept. 24, 1939; came to U.S., 1962; s. Gabriel and Madeleine (Passavant) V.; m. Janine M. Saley, Oct. 19, 1960; children: Olivier, Catherine. BS in Math., U. Paris Sorbonne, 1959; MS in Astrophysics, U. Lille, France, 1961; PhD in Computer Sci., Northwestern U., 1967. Sr. software specialist RCA Corp., Cherry Hill, N.J., 1969-70; mgr. infosystems Stanford U., Palo Alto, Calif., 1970-71; research engr. SRI Internat., Menlo Park, Calif., 1971-72; sr. research fellow Inst. for Future, Menlo Park, 1972-76; chmn. Infomedia Corp., Palo Alto, 1976-81; v.p. Sofinnova, Inc., San Francisco, 1982-86; pres. Eurolink Internat., San Francisco, 1987—; dir. Photonetics, Inc., Marly, France. Author: Computer Message Systems, 1984, Dimensions, 1988. Recipient Jules Verne prize Hachette Pubs., Paris, 1961. Mem. Soc. Sci. Exploration. Office: Eurolink Internat 2882 Sand Hill Rd Ste 220 Menlo Park CA 94025

VALLERIE, PAUL JOSEPH, aerospace company executive; b. Norwalk, Conn., June 21, 1937; s. Eugene Michael and Lillian Wilhemina (Kuntz) V.; m. Kathryn Ann Knutson, Aug. 19, 1967; children: Paul Joseph Jr., Tonya Rene. Student, U. Conn., 1955-56; BS, USAF Acad., 1960; MS, Tex. Tech U., 1966; MBA, N.Mex. Highlands U., 1983. Commd. USAF, 1960, advanced through grades to lt. col., 1977; staff officer USAF, Pentagon, Washington, 1969-74; dept. comdr. maintenance USAF, 321 Strategic Missile Wing, Grand Forks, N.D., 1974-76; br. chief, lt. col. USAF Hqdrs. SAC/Plans, Omaha, 1976-79; dir., lt. col. USAF Dir. Aero Studies, Albuquerque, 1979-84; retired USAF, 1984; mgr. aerospace engring. Boeing Aerospace Co., Seattle, 1984-86; mktg. research Boeing Electronic Co., 1986—; cons. Project Vanguard, Andrews AFB, Md., 1979-84; co chmn. space based laser programs Rand Corp., 1982-84; air force rep. Office Sec. Defense/Employee Support Guard, Albuquerque, 1982-84. Pres. Bellevue, Nebr. Soccer Club, 1977-79; div. rep. Boeing Employees Good Neighbor Fund/United Way Drive, Seattle, 1985; council mem. Holy Cross Luth. Ch., Bellevue, Wash., 1986. Named Mgr. of Yr., N.Mex. Fed. Exec. Bd., 1982. Mem. Boeing Mgmt. Assn., Air Force Assn., USAF Acad. Assn. Graduates (life), Phi Kappa Phi. Republican. Club: SKIBAC. Office: Boeing Aerospace Co PO Box 3999 M/S 9N-35 Seattle WA 98124

VAN, PETER, lawyer; b. Boston, Sept. 7, 1936; s. Frank Lewis and Ruth (Spevack) V.; m. Judith Ellen Hershman, June 19, 1958; children—Jami Lynne, Robert Charles. B.A., Dartmouth, 1958; LL.D., Boston Coll., 1961. Bar: Mass. 1962. Assoc. Brown, Rudnick, Freed and Gesmer, Boston, 1961-63; assoc. Fine and Ambrogne, Boston, 1963-65; ptnr., 1966-73, sr. ptnr., 1973—. Clubs: Pine Brook Country (Weston), Mason (Boston). Office: Exchange Pl 27th Floor Boston MA 02109

VAN ALSTYNE, VANCE BROWNELL, arbitration management consultant; b. Rochester, N.Y., Feb. 3, 1924; s. Guy Brownell and Jessie Cary Van A.; B.A., U. Rochester, 1948; LL.B., Blackstone Coll. Law, 1964; m. Jane Kotary, Aug. 12, 1950; children—Cary B., Stacey E. Research asst. Gilbert Assos., Inc., N.Y.C., 1950-56; corp. sec., v.p., dir. R.C. Simpson & Staff, Inc., Newark and Ridgewood, N.J., 1956-74, pres., dir. R.C. Simpson, Inc., Ridgewood, 1975—. Served to 2d lt. USAF, 1943-45. Decorated Air medal. Mem. Am. Mgmt. Assn., Indsl. Relations Research Assn., Am. Arbitration Assn., Internat., Swiss-Icelandic Salmon Assns. Home: 175 Brush Hill Rd Kinnelon NJ 07405 Office: United Jersey Bank Bldg PO Box 567 Ridgewood NJ 07451

VAN AMBURG, WILLIAM FRED, broadcasting executive; b. Oakland, Calif., Apr. 9, 1955; s. Fred L. and Lois Marilyn (Jurgens) V.; m. Jo Nugent, Jan. 31, 1981. BA in Anthropology, U. Calif., Berkeley, 1977. Anchorman, reporter Sta. KALX, Berkeley, 1976-77; assignment editor Sta. KGTV-TV, San Diego, 1978-79; reporter Sta. KATU-TV, Portland, Oreg., 1979-80; reporter/anchorperson Sta. KABC-TV, Los Angeles, 1980-83; reporter/anchorperson Sta. KGO-TV, San Francisco, 1984, East Bay news bur. chief, 1984-87; pres., owner BVA Independent Productions, Point Richmond, Calif., 1987—; producer, cons. VA Enterprises, Inc., El Cerrito, Calif., 1983—. Recipient Merit award Sigma Delta Chi, 1981, Best Feature Reporting San Fernando Valley Press Club, 1983, Best News Reporting Radio and TV News Dirs. Assn., 1984, Assistance to Children award Missing Children's Project, Oakland, Calif., 1986. Mem. AFTRA. Democrat. Office: BVA Independent Prodns 427 Washington Ave Point Richmond CA 94801

VAN AMRINGE, JON ERIC, financial executive; b. Nashua, N.H., Nov. 28, 1948; s. Hollis Helton and Marjorie Louise (Gustafson) Van A. BA, Yale U., 1970; MBA, Harvard U., 1978. Asst. treas. Morgan Guaranty Trust Co., N.Y.C., 1978-80; sr. v.p., treas. Air Internat., Inc., Erie, Pa., 1981; cons., ptnr. Van Amringe & Conner, Erie, 1982-83; sr. v.p., chief fin. officer, chief operating officer Spectrum Control, Inc., Erie, 1982—; adj. prof. Gannon U., Erie. Served to lt. comdr. USN, 1970-76. Mem. Fin. Execs. Inst., Nat. Assn. Amateur Oarsmen, Yale Club, Perry's Landing Yacht Club. Democrat. Office: Spectrum Control Inc 2185 W 8th St Erie PA 16505-4747

VAN ANDEL, BETTY JEAN, household products company executive; b. Mich., Dec. 14, 1921; d. Anthony and Daisy (Van Dyk) Hoekstra; A.B., Calvin Coll., 1943; m. Jay Van Andel, Aug. 16, 1952; children—Nan Elizabeth, Stephen Alan, David Lee, Barbara Ann. Elementary sch. tchr., Grand Rapids, Mich., 1943-45; service rep. and supr. Mich. Bell Telephone Co., Grand Rapids, 1945-52; bd. dirs. Amway Corp., Grand Rapids, 1972—. Treas., LWV, 1957-60; chmn. Eagle Forum, Mich., 1975—; bd. dirs. Christian Sch. Ednl. Found., Pine Rest Christian Hosp., Grand Rapids Opera, 1982, exec. com. Mem. Nat. Trust Hist. Preservation, St. Cecelia Music Soc., Smithsonian Assos. Republican. Club: Women's City of Grand Rapids. Home: 7186 Windy Hill Rd SE Grand Rapids MI 49506 Office: PO Box 172 Ada MI 49301

VAN ANDEL, JAY, home and personal products company executive; b. Grand Rapids, Mich., June 3, 1924; s. James and Nella (Vanderwoude) Van A.; m. Betty J. Hoekstra, Aug. 16, 1952; children—Nan, Stephen, David, Barbara. Student, Pratt Jr. Coll., 1945, Calvin Coll., 1942, 46, Yale, 1943-44; DBA (hon.), No. Mich. U., 1976, Western Mich. U., 1979; LLD (hon.), Ferris State Coll., 1977. Formerly engaged in aviation, restaurant and mail order businesses; co-founder, chmn. bd. Amway Corp., Ada, Mich.; chmn. bd. Amway Internat., Amway Mgmt. Co. (Amway Hotel Properties), Nutrilite Products, Inc.; bd. dirs. Mich. Nat. Bank, Lansing, Van Andel & Flikkema Motor Sales, Grand Rapids. Mem. adv. council Nat. 4H Found.; trustee Ferguson Hosp., Grand Rapids, Hillsdale (Mich.) Coll., Citizens Research Council Mich.; chmn. bd. dirs. Jamestown Found., Washington; bd. dirs. Hudson Inst., Indpls., Nat. Endowment for Democracy, Washington, Gerald K. Ford Found., Washington, Ctr. for Internat. Pvt. Enterprise, Washington, Heritage Found., Washington; pres. Van Andel Found.; Served to 1st lt. USAAF, 1943-46. Knighted Grand Officer Order of Orange-Nassau, The Netherlands; recipient Disting. Alumni award Calvin Coll., 1976, Golden Plate award Am. Acad. Acievement, Gt.Living Am. award and Bus. & Profl. Leader of Yr. award Religious Heritage Am., George Washington Medal of Honor Freedom Found., Gold medals Netherland Soc. of Phila. and N.Y.C., Disting. Citizen award Northwood Inst., Patron award Mich. Found. for Arts, 1982. Mem. Direct Selling Assn. (bd. dirs., named to Hall of Fame), U.S. C. of C. (past chmn. bd.), Mensa, Omicron Delta Kappa. Mem. Christian Reformed Ch. (elder). Clubs: Penisular, Cascade Hills, Lotus; Capitol Hill (Washington); Macatawa Bay Yacht (Holland, Mich.); La Mirador (Switzerland). Home: 7186 Windy Hill Rd Grand Rapids MI 49506 Office: Amway Corp 7575 E Fulton Rd SE Ada MI 49355

VANASEK, JAMES GEORGE, commercial banker; b. Chgo., Jan. 20, 1944; s. James Harold and Virginia Edna (Von Asch) V.; m. Deborah Ann Zaccagnini, Nov. 28, 1975. AB, Ind. U., 1966; MBA, Penn State U., 1968. Sr. v.p. Pitts. Nat. Bank, 1968-79, Banc Ohio Nat. Bank, Columbus, 1979-84; exec. v.p. First Interstate Bank of Ariz., Phoenix, 1984—; bd. dirs. Robert Morris Assocs., Phoenix, Assn. for Corporate Growth, Phoenix. Sgt. U.S. Army Res., 1968-74. Mem. Phi Beta Kappa. Republican. Home: 13720 N 85th Pl Scottsdale AZ 85260 Office: 1st Interstate Bank Ariz NA 1st Interstate Bank Pla 100 W Washington St Phoenix AZ 85038-9743

VAN AUKEN, ROBERT HANLON, manufacturing executive; b. Detroit, Aug. 30, 1940; s. Robert Danforth and Ruth Bowen (Cutler) Van A.; m. Beverly Gayle Graves, Oct. 27, 1965; 1 child, Angela. BS, U. Okla., 1963. Dept. head Corning Glass Works, Louisville, 1972-74; prodn. supt. Corning Glass Works, Pascagoula, Miss., 1974-76; plant mgr. Flo-Con Systems Inc., Forest, Miss., 1977-78; gen. mgr. Flo-Con Systems Inc., Champaign, Ill., 1978-80, v.p. mfg., 1980—. Mem. Am. Mgmt. Assn., Am. Soc. for Quality Control, Am. Prodn. and Inventory Control Soc. Republican. Clubs: Running (bd. dirs. 1986), Second Wind (Champaign). Lodge: Masons. Home: 1906 Barberry Circle Champaign IL 61821 Office: Flo-Con Systems 1404 Newton Dr Champaign IL 61821

VAN BAAK, ANTHONY EDWARD, resort executive, accountant; b. Shanghai, China, Mar. 26, 1949; came to U.S., 1949; s. Edward Anthony and Frances Ruth (Ribbens) Van B.; BA in History, Calvin Coll., 1970; postgrad. Western Mich. U., 1970-71; m. Arlene Florence Dewey, Aug. 7, 1982; children: Edward Anthony, Florence Ribbens, Rachel Dewey. Pres., stockholder The Entertainment Store, Inc., Steamboat Springs, Colo., 1976-83; asst. controller LTV Corp., 1971-76, Utah Internat., Craig, Colo., 1976-77; controller Mountain Resorts, Steamboat Springs, 1978-80, Steamboat Resorts, 1980—; owner Resort Group Ltd., Inc., 1983—; condominium and computer cons., 1977—. Republican. Mem. Christian Reformed Ch. Home: PO Box 1809 65 Park Ave Steamboat Springs CO 80477

VAN BEURDEN, WILLIAM JOSEPH, insurance services executive; b. Kalidjati, Indonesia, July 21, 1941; s. Cornelius Wilhelmus and Maria Arnolda (Teurlings) Van B.; came to U.S., 1957, naturalized, 1962; BS in Polit. Econs., Calif. State U., 1964; m. Lise Marie Tremblay, Oct. 1, 1966; children: Erik, Christian. Casualty underwriter Aetna Life & Casualty Co., San Francisco, 1964-67; v.p. Wigh & Assocs., Kingsburg, Calif., 1967-75, pres. Van Beurden & Assocs. Ins. Svcs., Inc., Kingsburg, 1975—;; pres. Bonaire Leasing; bd. dirs. Nat. Am. Ins. Co., 1987—; chmn. Greenwich Group, 1989—. With USAR, 1964-70. Mem. Am. Mgmt. Assn., Ind. Agts. Assn., Calif. Trucking Assn. Republican. Roman Catholic. Office: Van Beurden & Assocs Inc 1615 Draper St Kingsburg CA 93631

VAN BOSCH, JOHN EDWARD, engineering manager; b. Harvard, Ill., Nov. 4, 1960; s. James M. and Jean C. (Baumgartner) Van B. BS in Indsl. Engring., U. Wis., 1982; MBA, Pepperdine U., 1986. Registered profl. engr., Calif.; registered indsl. engr., Calif. Mgr. indsl. engring. Vitro Labs., Oxnard, Calif., 1982-84; mgr. facility and indsl. engring. Spectramed, Inc., Oxnard, Calif., 1984-87; v.p., chief operating officer HML Med. Inc., Irvine, Calif., 1987—. Sr. mem. IIE, Am. Prodn. and Inventory Control Soc.

VAN BOXTEL, DIANE LYNN, financial services executive; b. Green Bay, Wis., July 24, 1952; d. Sylvester Robert and Dolores Mae (Arnoldussen) V.B.; m. Russell G. Tapley, Apr. 11, 1984. Student, Santa Rosa (Calif.) Jr. Coll., 1975-80, Golden Gate U., San Francisco, 1981-84. Cert. fin. planner; lic. property and casualty, Wis. Adminstrv. asst. First Nat. Bank, Seymour, Wis., 1970-72; various positions Wells Fargo Bank, Novato, Calif., 1973-80; regional mktg. mgr. Wells Fargo Bank, San Francisco, 1980-82, dir. of tng., 1982-84; relationship banking mgr. First Interstate Bank, Koehler, Wis., 1984—; dir. corp. sales Valley Bancorp., Appleton, Wis., 1985—. Mem. editorial adv. bd. Northwestern Fin. Rev. Mag.; contbr. articles to profl. jours. Adviser Jr. Achievement, 1973-78. Mem. Nat. Assn. Bank Women (group sec., treas. 1979-80, group v.p. 1980-81, group pres. 1981-82, nat. dir. 1987-88, chairperson various coms.), Calif. Bankers Assn. (legis. relations com. 1983-84), Wis. Bankers Assn. (faculty mem. personal banking sch. 1987), Greater Green Bay Area C. of C. (mktg. com. and taxpayers assn. 1987), Internat. Assn. for Fin. Planning (bd. dirs. 1987, chairperson fin. planning symposium 1988-89), Inst. Cert. Fin. Planners (program chair, bd. dirs.), Am. Soc. for Tng. and Devel. Home: 2851 S Fox Run Circle Green Bay WI 54302 Office: Valley Bancorp 100 W Lawrence St Appleton WI 54912

VAN BRUWAENE, RAYMOND T., air freight company executive; b. 1938; married;. Student, Bradley U. Formerly div. mgr. Consol. Freight; dir. ground services Airborne Freight Corp., 1972-73, v.p. then exec. v.p., 1973—. Office: Airborne Freight Corp PO Box 662 Seattle WA 98111 *

VAN BULCK, HENDRIKUS EUGENIUS, accountant; b. Beek en Donk, The Netherlands, Dec. 13, 1950; came to U.S., 1972; s. Marcellus Maria and Josephina Theodora (Koelman) Van B.; m. Margaret West, Aug. 7, 1976; children: Marcel Allen, Sydney Josette. Grad., Nijenrode, The Netherlands, 1972; MBA, U. Ga., 1974, PhD in Bus. Adminstrn., 1979. CPA, S.C. Instr. U. S.C., Sumter, 1975-77; asst. prof. Clemson (S.C.) U., 1977-80; chmn. dept., assoc. prof. St. Andrew's Presbyn. Coll., Laurinburg, N.C., 1980-83; staff acct. L. Allen West, CPA, Sumter, 1983-84; ptnr. West & Van Bulck, CPAs, Sumter, 1984-88, Van Bluck & Co. CPAs, Sumter, 1989—; part time instr. U. S.C., Sumter, 1983—; cons. in field. Contbr. articles to profl. jours. Chmn. Make-a-Wish Found., Midlands, S.C., 1983—. Recipient Mktg. award Netherlands Ctr. of Dirs., 1972. Mem. Sumter Estate Planning Council, Am. Inst. CPA's, Nat. Assn. Estate Planning Councils, Beta Gamma Sigma. Presbyterian. Home: 234 Haynsworth PO Box 1327 Sumter SC 29151-1327 Office: Van Bulck & Co CPAs 15 Broad St Sumter SC 29151-1327

VAN BULCK, MARGARET WEST, accountant, financial planner, educator; b. Chgo., Nov. 25, 1955; d. Lee Allen and Margaret Ellen (Sauls) West; m. Hendrikus E.J.M.L. van Bulck, Aug. 7, 1976; children: Marcel Allen, Sydney Josette. BS in Mktg., U. S.C., 1978; MA in Econs., Clemson U., 1981. CPA, S.C. Econs. instr. St. Andrews Presbyn. Coll., Laurinburg, N.C., 1980-82; staff acct. L. Allen West, CPA, Sumter, S.C., 1982-84; ptnr. West & van Bulck, CPA's, Sumter, 1984-88, Van Bulck & Co., CPA's, Sumter, 1989—; part time instr. U. S.C., Sumter, 1985-87. Contbr. articles to profl. jours. Treas. Make-A-Wish Found., Sumter, 1985-87, chmn. 1987—; edn. found. chmn. Laurinburg/Scotland County chpt. AAUW, 1981-83; treas. Friends Sumter County Library, 1986—, Women of Ch., 1987—; mem. Jr. Welfare League, Sumter; Circle Bible Leader. Recipient Sirrine Found. award, Clemson U., 1978, 79; grantee U.S. Dept. Labor, 1979-80. Mem. Am. Inst. CPA's, S.C. Assn. CPA's, Internat. Assn. Fin. Planning, Sumter Estate Planning Council (past treas.), Omicron Delta Epsilon. Presbyterian. Home: 234 Haynsworth St PO Box 1327 Sumter SC 29151-1327 Office: Van Bulck & Co CPAs PO Box 1327 Sumter SC 29151-1327

VAN CASPEL, VENITA WALKER, financial planner; b. Sweetwater, Okla.; d. Leonard Rankin and Ella Belle (Jarnagin) Walker. Student, Duke, 1944-46; B.A., U. Colo., 1948, postgrad., 1949-51; postgrad., N.Y. Inst. Fin., 1962. Cert. fin. planner. Stockbroker Rauscher Pierce & Co., Houston, 1962-65, A.G. Edwards & Sons, Houston, 1965-68; founder, pres., owner Van Caspel & Co., Inc., Houston, 1968—, Van Caspel Wealth Mgmt.; owner, mgr. Van Caspel Planning Service, Van Caspel Advt. Agy.; sr. v.p. investments Raymond James and Assocs.; owner Diamond V Ranch; dir. MBank; Moderator PBS TV show The Money Makers and Profiles of Success, 1980; 1st women mem. Pacific Stock Exchange. Author: Money Dynamics, 1975, Dear Investor; The New Money Dynamics, 1978, Money Dynamics for the 1980's, 1980, The Power of Money Dynamics, Money Dynamics for the New Economy, Money Dynamics for the 1990's; editor: Money Dynamics Letter; columnist The Sat. Evening Post. Bd. dirs. Boy Scouts Am., Horatio Alger Assn., Robert Schuller Ministries. Recipient Matrix award Theta Sigma Phi, 1969, Horatio Alger award for Disting. Americans, 1982, Disting. Woman's medal Northwood Inst., 1986, George Norlin award U. Colo. Alumni Assn., 1987. Mem. Internat. Assn. Fin. Planners, Inst. Cert. Fin. Planners, Phi Gamma Mu, Phi Beta Kappa. Methodist. Office: Raymond James & Assocs Inc 5051 Westheimer 1440 Post Oak Tower Houston TX 77056

VANCE, CYRUS ROBERTS, lawyer, former government official; b. Clarksburg, W.Va., Mar. 27, 1917; s. John Carl and Amy (Roberts) V.; m. Grace Elsie Sloane, Feb. 15, 1947; children: Elsie Nicoll, Amy Sloane, Grace Roberts, Camilla, Cyrus Roberts. Student, Kent Sch.; B.A., Yale U., 1939, LL.B., 1942, LL.D. (hon.), 1968; LL.D. (hon.), Marshall U., 1963, Trinity Coll., 1968, W.Va. U., 1969, Bowling Green U., 1969, Salem Coll., 1970, Brandeis U., 1971, Amherst Coll., 1974, W.Va. Wesleyan U., 1974, Harvard U., 1981, Colgate U., 1981, Gen. Theol. Sem., 1981, Williams Coll., 1981, Notre Dame U., 1982, Mt. Holyoke Coll., 1982. Bar: N.Y. State 1947, U.S. Supreme Ct. 1970. Asst. to pres. Mead Corp., 1946-47; assoc. firm Simpson Thacher & Bartlett, N.Y.C., 1947-56; partner firm Simpson Thacher & Bartlett, 1956-61, 67-77, 80—; gen. counsel Dept. Def., 1961-62; sec. of army 1962-63, dep. sec. def., 1964-67; spl. rep. of Pres. Cyprus, 1967, Korea, 1968; U.S. negotiator Paris Peace Conf. on Vietnam, 1968-69; sec. state 1977-80; spl. counsel preparedness investigating subcom. Senate Armed Services Com., 1957-60; cons. counsel Spl. Com. on Space and Astronautics, U.S. Senate, 1958; chmn. com. on adjudication of claims Adminstrv. Conf. U.S.; mem. Com. To Investigate Alleged Police Corruption in N.Y.C., 1970-72; chmn. UN Devel. Corp., 1976; mem. Ind. Com. on Disarmament and Security Issues; bd. dirs. Gen. Dynamics Corp., Mfrs. Hanover Trust Co., N.Y. Times; chmn. Fed/ Res. Bank of N.Y. Trustee Yale Corp., 1968-78, 80-87; trustee Rockefeller Found., 1970-77, 80-82, chmn., 1975-77; trustee Mayo Found.; chmn. Am. Ditchley Found., 1981—. Lt. USNR, 1942-46. Recipient Medal of Freedom, 1969. Fellow Am. Coll. Trial Lawyers; mem. ABA, Assn. Bar City N.Y. (pres. 1974-76), Council on Fgn. Relations (dir., vice chmn. 1985-87), Japan Soc. (chmn. 1985—). Office: Simpson Thacher & Bartlett 425 Lexington Ave New York NY 10017-3909

VANCE, JAMES, manufacturing company executive; b. Cleve., May 20, 1930; m. Dolores Bernadette Doyle, July 6, 1957; 1 child, James J. BA cum laude, Baldwin Wallace Coll., 1955; JD magna cum laude, Cleve. State U., 1960. Bar: Oct. 1960. Asst. treas., asst. to v.p. fin. and adminstrn., financial analyst Rep. Steel Corp., 1956-68; treas. Addressograph & Multigraph Corp., Cleve., 1968-72; v.p. fin. Cin. Milacron Inc., 1972-77; vice chmn., dir. Dayton-Walther Corp., 1977-87; sr. v.p., gen. counsel, sr. bus. advisor Varity Corp., Toronto, 1987-88, sr. v.p., chief fin. officer, chief legal officer, 1988—; bd. dir. Citation Cos., Amertool Corp., Gen. Automation, Min-Cer (S.A.), Mexico, Dwisa of Paris, Dayton-Est of Vesoul, Fiday of Asnieres, France; lectr. bus. law Baldwin Wallace Coll., 1961-63. Vice chmn. United Appeal, 1959; mem. Citizens League Cleve., 1960—; mem. fin. com. YMCA, 1961—; mem. Greater Cleve. Growth Center, 1963—; Vice chmn. fin. com. Cuyahoga Rep. Com., 1968-69. With AUS, 1951-52. Decorated Bronze Star. Mem. Cleve. Soc. Security Analysts, Am., Ohio Bar Assn., Fin. Execs. Inst., Am. Ordnance Assn., Nat. Machine Tool Builders Assn., Machinery and Allied Products Inst., Am. Mgmt. Assn., Cin. Indsl. Inst., Ohio C. of C., Alpha Tau Omega, Delta Theta Phi, Cleve. Club, Treas.' Club (bd. dir.). Club: Cleve. Treasurers (dir.). Home: 6600 Wyman Ln Cincinnati OH 45243 Office: Varity Corp, 595 Bay St, Toronto, ON Canada M5G 2C3

VANCE-GILBERT, CAROLE AMY, insurance company executive; b. Hartford, Conn., Sept. 22, 1942; d. Lester George Harding and Violet Edla Peterson; m. Bruce Gilbert, Feb. 1988. Instr., Inst. Computer Mgmt. div. Litton Industries, 1967-69; mgr. computer ops., dir. ednl. seminars Computer Mgmt. Inst., Detroit, 1969-73; mgr. computer ops. Shatterproof Glass Corp., Detroit, 1973-75; with City Nat. Bank, Detroit, 1975-79, asst. v.p., 1979; sec., dir. research tech. Hartford (Conn.) Ins. Group, 1979-86; ptnr. Vance Communications Ltd., Glastonbury, Conn., 1986—. Mem. Assn. Systems Mgmt. Republican. Episcopalian. Home: 96A Lakeside Dr Lebanon CT 06249

VAN CLEAVE, PETER, underwriting and foundation consultant; b. Evanston, Ill., May 18, 1927; s. Wallace and Katherine M. (Ziesing) Van C.; m. Barbara Adams, Dec. 30, 1960; 1 child, Claire. B.S., Northwestern U., 1949. Prodn. mgr. F.L. Jacobs Co., Traverse City, Mich., 1949-50; asst. to ambassador U.S. embassy, Rio de Janeiro, Brazil, 1953-55; with James S. Kemper & Co., Chgo., 1955-83, vice chmn., 1965-83; pres. Peter Van Cleave & Assocs., Inc., Chgo., 1983—; prin. Donor's Mgmt. Services; underwriting mem. Lloyds of London, Trustee Newberry Library, Chgo.; bd. dirs. Lyric Opera, Chgo. Served with U.S. Army, 1950-52. Mem. Nat. Assn. Security Dealers, Northwestern U. Alumni Assn. (past pres.). Republican. Clubs: Chicago; Bohemian (San Francisco); University, Glen View (Chgo.); The Casino. Home: 71 E Bellevue Pl Chicago IL 60611 Office: 35 E Wacker Dr Chicago IL 60601

VANDELL, KERRY DEAN, real estate educator; b. Biloxi, Miss., Jan. 8, 1947; s. Benedict S. and Eleanor Ruby (Lenhart) V.; m. Deborah Ann Lowe, May 16, 1971; children: Colin Buckner, Ashley Elizabeth. BA, Rice U., 1970, MME, 1970; M in Civil Planning, Harvard U., 1973; PhD, MIT, 1977. Assoc. reservoir engr. Exxon Co. USA, Houston, 1970-71; asst. prof. real estate and urban land econs. So. Meth. U., Dallas, 1977-81, assoc. prof., 1981-85, prof. and chmn., 1986—; vis. assoc. prof. urban design Harvard U., Cambridge, 1985-86; vis. prof. real estate and urban land econs. U. Calif. Berkeley, 1988—; mem. real estate adv. bd. Salomon Bros., N.Y.C., 1988—; cons. in field. Contbr. articles to profl. jours.; editorial bd. Am. Real Estate and Urban Econs. Assn. Jour., 1983—. Mem. housing task force Cen. Dallas Assn., 1987—; mem. Dallas Alliance, 1978-80. Homer Hoyt Inst. fellow, 1988; NSF fellow, 1971-74; Charles Abrams fellow, 1975-76, others. Mem. Am. Real Estate and Urban Econs. Assn. (dir. 1983—), Fin. Mgmt. Assn., Real Estate Fin. Execs. Assn. Episcopalian. Home: 18910 Mahogany Trail Dallas TX 75252 Office: So Meth U Edwin L Cox Sch Bus Dallas TX 75275

VANDENBERGHE, RONALD GUSTAVE, accountant, real estate developer; b. Oakland, Calif., July 1, 1937; s. Anselm Henri and Margaret B. (Bygum) V.; B.A. with honors, San Jose State Coll., 1959; postgrad. U. Calif. at Berkeley Extension, 1959-60, Golden Gate Coll., 1961-63; CPA, Calif.; m. Patricia W. Dufour, Aug. 18, 1957; children: Camille, Mark, Matthew. Real estate investor, pres. VandenBerghe Fin. Corp., Pleasanton, Calif., 1964—. Instr. accounting U. Cal., Berkeley, 1963-70; CPA, Pleasanton, 1963—. Served with USAF. Mem. Calif. Soc. CPAs. Republican. Presbyterian. Mason (Shriner). Home: PO Box 803 Danville CA 94526 Office: 20 Happy Valley Rd Pleasanton CA 94566

VANDENBURGH, ROY NATHAN, management consultant; b. Johnstown, N.Y., May 14, 1928; s. Roswell Peter and Ethel Lambert (Moffitt) V.; m. Elizabeth Potts, Aug. 20, 1949; children: David Roy, Terry Ross, Arthur Scott. BS, SUNY, 1949. Tchr. Harford (Pa.) Sr. High Sch., 1949-50; sr. planner IBM, Charlotte, N.C., 1949-87; cons. VanDenburgh Cons. Svcs., Charlotte, N.C., 1987—. Deacon Bible Bapt. Ch., Charlotte, 1982-84, chmn., 1985-87, 89—; leader 4H Club, Forest Lake, Pa., 1960-75; chmn., deacon Forest Lake Bapt. Ch., 1957-67. Mem. Recognition Technologies Users Assn. (bd. dirs. 1982-86, Recognition of Svc. 1978-88), Am. Nat. Standards Inst. (chmn. check standards com. 1986—, Recognition of Svc. 1986). Republican. Home: 6301 Welford Rd Charlotte NC 28211

VANDERBEEK, ROBERT EASTON, insurance company executive; b. Somerville, N.J., Feb. 11, 1928; s. Horace A. and Katherine (Abbey) V.; m. Nancy Pratt, Sept. 20, 1958; children: Abbey Lee, Amy Pratt. BS, Cornell U., 1952. Spl. group rep. Conn. Gen. Ins. Co., Washington, 1952-56; zone group mgr. Nationwide Ins. Co., Columbus, Ohio, 1956-60; pres. League Life Ins. Co., Southfield, Mich., 1960—; sr. v.p., div. mgr. CUNA Mut. Ins. Group, Madison, Wis., 1983—; mem. Ins. Devel. Bur., 1965; past chmn. Internat. Coop. Ins. Fedn.; bd. dirs. Nat. Coop. Bus. Assn., Washington; adv. com. automobile ins. study U.S. Dept. Transp., 1970-72. Cons. U.S. AID; mem. Mich. Gov's. Ins. Task Force, 1987—, elected ofcls. compensation com. City of Detroit, 1985—; bd. dirs. YMCA Met. Detroit, 1986—. Sgt. U.S. Army, 1946-48. Mem. Mich. Actuarial Soc. (pres. 1963-65), Am. Risk & Ins. Assn. (bd. dirs. 1970-74), Life Assn. Mich. (pres. 1970-76). Democrat. Unitarian. Home: 8162 E Jefferson St Detroit MI 48214 Office: League Ins Cos 15600 Providence Dr Southfield MI 48075

VANDER HEIDE, G. PETER, architect; b. Grand Rapids, Mich., Jan. 29, 1947; s. Peter and La Verne (Van Bree) V.H.; m. Donna J. Boynton, July 1, 1966 (div. Sept. 1978); children: Jeanne Marie, Judith Gale; m. Rena E. Cellini, May 20, 1983. BArch, U. Mich., 1971, MBA, 1977. Registered architect, Mich., Pa. Architect Unistrut Corp., Wayne, Mich., 1970-75; mgr. MERO div. Unistrut div. GTE Products Co., Wayne, 1975-80; v.p., treas. Curtis Cox Kennerly, Phila., 1980—. Co-author 1988 ACEC/PSMA/AIA Incentive Compensation Survey of Design Professional Services Firms, 1988. Mem. AIA (treas. Phila. chpt. 1985-88), Soc. Mktg. Profl. Services, Profl. Services Mgmt. Assn. (nat. v.p. profl. devel. 1987, chmn. exec. com. Phila. chpt. 1986, 87, pres.-elect. 1988, pres. 1989). Clubs: U. Mich. of Greater Phila. (bd. govs. 1984-87, v.p. 1988), Delaware Valley Sail (Phila.) (sec. 1987, treas. 1988); Wissahickon Ski (Conshohocken, Pa.), Vesper Club (Phila.). Office: Curtis Cox Kennerly 327 N 17th St Philadelphia PA 19103

VANDERLAAN, RICHARD B., marketing company executive; b. Grand Rapids, Mich., Sept. 2, 1931; s. Sieger B. and Helen (Kerr) V.; cert. liberal arts Grand Rapids Jr. Coll., 1952; cert. mech. engring. U. Mich., 1955; cert. indsl. engring. Mich. State U., 1960; cert. Harvard Bus. Sch., 1970; m. Sally E. Conroy, Mar. 26, 1982; children—Sheryl Vanderlaan, Pamella Vanderlaan DeVos, Brenda Vanderlaan Thompson. Tool engr. Four Square Mfg. Co., Grand Rapids, 1950-60; sales engr. Ametek, Lansdale, Pa., 1960-63; br. mgr. J.N. Fauver Co., Grand Rapids, 1964-68; v.p. Fauver Co. subs. Sun Oil Co., Grand Rapids 1968-76, exec. v.p., 1976-80; pres. House of Printers, Inc., 1980-82, also dir.; pres. Richard Vanderlaan Assocs., 1982—. Named eagle scout Boy Scouts Am. Mem. Mfrs. Agts. Nat. Assn., Soc. Automotive Engrs. Republican. Clubs: Birmingham Country, Oakland Hills Country, Economic of Detroit, Detroit Athletic. Avocations: golf, tennis. Office: 22157 Metamora Dr Birmingham MI 48010

VANDERLINDEN, CAMILLA DENICE DUNN, quality assurance development and management executive, educator; b. Dayton, July 21, 1950; d. Joseph Stanley and Virginia Danley (Martin) Dunn; m. David Henry VanderLinden; Oct. 10, 1980; 1 child, Michael Christopher. Student, U. de Valencia, Spain, 1969; BA in Spanish and Secondary Edn., U. Utah, 1972, MS in Human Resource Econs., 1985. Asst. dir. Davis County Community Action Program, Farmington, Utah, 1973-76; dir. South County Community Action, Midvale, Utah, 1976-79; supr. customer service Ideal Nat. Life Ins. Co., Salt Lake City, 1979-80; mgr. customer service Utah Farm Bur. Mutual Ins., Salt Lake City, 1980-82; quality assurance analyst Am. Express Co., Salt Lake City, 1983-86, quality assurance and human resource specialist, 1986-88; mgr. quality assurance & engring. Am. Express Co., Denver, 1988—; adj. faculty Westminster Coll., Salt Lake City, 1987-88. Vol. translator Latin Am. community. Republican. Office: Am Express Info Svcs Co Integrated Payments Systems Div 181 Inverness Dr W Englewood CO 80112-3100

VANDERPOOL, ROBERT LEE, JR., banker; b. Galveston, Tex., Nov. 10, 1918; s. R.L. and Felicia (Hussey) V.; m. Mildred Frances Loscalzo, Sept. 23, 1946; children: Janet Ann Vanderpool Haedicke, Robert Lee III. Student, Tex. A&M U., 1935-36; B.B.A., Tulane U., 1941. V.p., dir. Citizens State Bank, Dickinson, Tex., 1946-50; v.p., dir. Ouachita Nat. Bank, Monroe, La., 1951, pres., dir., 1952-85, chmn. bd., 1985-88; chmn. exec. com., dir. La. Bancshares, Inc., Baton Rouge, 1985—. Past pres., bd. dirs. Monroe C. of C., La., 1953; past chmn. ARC fund campaign, Ouachita Parish, 1954, United Givers Fund, 1960; past pres. N.E. La. U. Found., Monroe, 1980. Recipient David C. Silverstein Citizens of Yr. Monroe C. of C., 1975. Mem. La. Bankers Assn. (past pres.), Am. Bankers Assn. Episcopalian. Clubs: Bayour DeSiard Country (Monroe, La.) (past pres.); Lotus (Monroe, La.); Plimsoll (New Orleans).

VANDERPOOL, WARD MELVIN, management and marketing consultant; b. Oakland, Mo., Jan. 20, 1917; s. Oscar B. and Clara (McGuire) V.; m. Lee Kendall, July 7, 1935. MEE, Tulane U. V.p. charge sales Van Lang Brokerage, Los Angeles, 1934-38; mgr. agrl. div. Dayton Rubber Co., Chgo., 1939-48; pres., gen. mgr. Vee Mac Co., Rockford, Ill., 1948—; pres., dir. Zipout, Inc., Rockford, 1951—, Wife Save Products, Inc., 1959—; chmn. bd. Zipout Internat., Kenvan Inc., 1952—, Shevan Corp., 1951—, Atlas Internat. Corp.; pres. Global Enterprises Ltd., Global Assos. Ltd.; chmn. bd. dirs. Am. Atlas Corp., Merzat Industries Ltd.; trustee Ice Crafter Trust, 1949—; bd. dirs. Atlas Chem. Internat. Ltd., Kenlee Internat., Ltd., Shrimp Tool Internat. Ltd.; mem. Toronto Bd. Trade; chmn. bd. dirs. Am. Atlas Corp., Am. Packaging Corp. Mem. adv. bd. Nat. Security Council, congl. adv. com. Heritage Found.; mem. Rep. Nat. Com., Presdl. Task Force, Congrl. Adv. Com. Hon. mem. Internat. Swimming Hall of Fame. Mem. Nat. (dir. at large), Rock River (past pres.) sales execs., Sales and Mktg. Execs. Internat. (dir.), Am. Mgmt. Assn., Rockford Engring. Soc., Am. Tool Engrs., Internat. Acad. Aquatic Art (dir.), Am. Inst. Mgmt. (pres. council), Am. Ordnance Assn., Internat. Platform Assn., Heritage Found., Ill. C. of C. Clubs: Jesters, Elks, Rockford Swim, Forest Hills Country, Exec., Elmcrest Country, Pyramid, Dolphin, Marlin, Univ. Lodges: Masons, Shriners. Home: 374 Parkland Dr SE Cedar Rapids IA 52403 also: 40 Richview Rd #308, Toronto, ON Canada M9A 5C1 Office: Box 242A Auburn St Rd Rockford IL 61103 also: 111 Richmond St W, Suite #318, Toronto, ON Canada M5H 1T1

VANDER PUTTEN, LEROY ANDREW, insurance company executive; b. Appleton, Wis., Aug. 20, 1934; s. Theo S. and Lorraine M. (Quella) Vander P.; m. Evon Marie Schumacher, July 3, 1956; children: Suzanna, Dale, Lisa, Carole, Kim. BS in Math. and Psychology, Wis. State U., 1961; Advanced Mgmt. Program, Harvard U., 1983-84. Asst. sec. EDP research Aetna Life & Casualty, Hartford, Conn., 1968-69, asst. cashier, 1969-74, dir. investment planning, 1974-79, asst. v.p. investment planning, 1979-81, v.p. investment planning, 1981-82, v.p. corp. fin., 1982-86, v.p. and deputy treas., 1986-87, chmn., pres., chief exec. officer ERIC Reins Co., Simsbury, Conn., 1987—; chmn., chief exec. officer Exec. RE, Inc., Simsbury, Conn., 1987—, also bd. dirs., 1986—; adv. bd. Conn. Nat. Bank, 1988—; Chmn. South Windsor Econ. Devel. Com., Conn., 1977; trustee Talcott Mountain Sci. Ctr., Avon, Conn. Recipient Distinguished Alumni award U. Wis., 1987—. With USCG, 1952-56. Mem. Fin. Exec. Inst., Am. Council Life Ins. Cos. (chmn. investment reporting sub-com. 1982-83), AMP 91 Assocs. of Boston (treas. 1982—). Republican. Roman Catholic. Avocations: sailing, sports car restoration, canoeing. Office: RE Exec Inc 82 Hopmeadow St PO Box 129 Simsbury CT 06070

VANDERSLICE, THOMAS AQUINAS, electrical manufacturing company executive; b. Phila., Jan. 8, 1932; s. Joseph R. and Mae (Daly) V.; m. Margaret Hurley, June 9, 1956; children: Thomas Aquinas, Paul Thomas Aquinas, John Thomas Aquinas, Peter Thomas Aquinas. B.S. in Chemistry and Philosophy, Boston Coll., 1953; Ph.D. in Chemistry and Physics, Catholic U. Am., 1956. With Gen. Electric Co., Fairfield, Conn., from 1956, gen. mgr. electronic components bus. div., 1970-72, v.p., from 1970, group exec. spl. systems and products group, 1972-77; sr. v.p., sector exec. Gen. Electric Co. (Power Systems Sector), Fairfield, Conn., 1977-79, exec. v.p., sector exec., 1979-84; chief operating officer, dir. Gen. Telephone & Electronics Corp., Stamford, Conn., 1979-83; chmn., chief exec. officer Apollo Computer, Inc., Chelmsford, Mass., 1984—, also bd. dirs.; dir. Texaco Inc., Bank of Boston Corp., Computer Consoles Inc. Patentee low pressure gas measurements and analysis, gas surface interactions and elec. discharges; co-author: Ultra High Vacuum and Its Applications, 1963; reviser: Scientific Foundations of Vacuum Technique, 1960; contbr. to profl. jours. Chmn. bd. trustees Boston Coll., Com. Econ. Devel.; steering com. Econ. Policy Council UNA. Fulbright scholar, 1953-56; recipient Golden Plate award Acad. Achievement, 1963; Bicentennial medallion Boston Coll., 1976. Mem. Nat. Acad. Engring., Conn. Acad. Sci. and Engring., Am. Vacuum Soc., ASTM, Am. Chem. Soc., Am. Inst. Physics, Sigma Xi, Tau Beta Pi, Alpha Sigma Nu, Sigma Pi Sigma. Clubs: Conn. Golf (Easton, Conn.); Patterson (Fairfield). Office: Apollo Computer Inc 330 Billerica Rd Chelmsford MA 01821

VANDER VENNET, GEORGE WILLIAM, JR., lawyer, trust banker; b. Davenport, Iowa, July 20, 1937; s. George William and Eleanor Katherine (Volz) Vander V.; m. Ann Marie Meagher, Sept. 21, 1963; children: George William III, Elizabeth, Mary, Claire, John. BA, U. Notre Dame, 1959, LLB, 1962. Bar: Ill. 1962, Iowa 1962. Assoc. G.W. Vander Vennet, Davenport, 1962; mgmt. trainee 1st Nat. Bank Chgo., 1963, from trust officer to v.p., 1965-81; exec. v.p., trust officer UnibancTrust Co. (formerly Sears Bank & Trust Co.), Chgo., 1981—. Mem. fin. com. St. Francis Xavier Ch., Wilmette, Ill., 1984—; chmn. bd. dirs. Regina Dominican High Sch., Wilmette, 1986—. Mem. Ill. Bar Assn., Chgo. Bar Assn., Met. Club, Michigan Shores Club. Republican. Roman Catholic. Home: 915 Ashland Wilmette IL 60091 Office: UnibancTrust Co 233 S Wacker Dr Chicago IL 60606

VAN DOREN, DONALD HUIZINGA, communications executive; b. Detroit, Apr. 23, 1942; s. James Huizinga and Cornelia (Thompson) Van D.; m. Emily Watson, June 20, 1964; children: Linda, David. BA, Yale U., 1964; MBA with distinction, U. Mich., 1970. Salesperson, quality coordinator Scott Paper Co., Phila., 1964-68; exec. v.p. R. Shriver Assocs., Parsippany, N.J., 1970-78; pres., founder Cabot Cons. Group, Washington, 1978-80; chmn., founder, chief exec. officer Vanguard Communications Corp., Morris Plains, N.J., 1980—; Frequent lectr. in field. Contbr. articles to profl. jours. Home: 10 Farview Ave Randolph NJ 07869 Office: Vanguard Communications Corp 100 American Rd Morris Plains NJ 07950

VAN DYKE, JOSEPH GARY OWEN, computer consulting executive; b. N.Y.C., Dec. 21, 1939; s. Donald Wood and Gladys Ann (Tague) Van D.; m. Lynne Diane Lammers; June 25, 1966; children: Alison Baird, Jeremy Wood, Matthew Kerr. BA, Rutgers U., 1961; postgrad., R.I. Sch. of Design, 1962, Am. U., 1964-67. Computer programmer System Devel. Corp., Paramus, N.J., 1962-64; sect. head computer tech. div. System Devel. Corp., Falls Church, Va., 1964-67; project mgr. Informatics Inc., Bethesda, Md., 1967-70; dept. dir. Informatics Inc., Rockville, Md., 1970-74, v.p., gen. mgr., 1974-78; owner, pres. J G Van Dyke and Assoc., Inc., Bethesda, 1978—; chmn. bd., chief exec. officer The Outreach Group, Inc., 1987—. Bd. dirs. Westbrook Sch., Bethesda, 1981-82, St. Columba's Ch., Washington, 1980-84; founder Computer Edn. Workshop, Bethesda, 1981; coach MSI soccer, Bethesda, 1979—. Mem. Inst. Elec. Engring. Democrat. Episcopalian. Home: 5117 Dalecarlia Dr Bethesda MD 20816 Office: 6701 Rockledge Dr 250 Bethesda MD 20817

VAN DYKE, WILLIAM GRANT, manufacturing company executive; b. Mpls., June 30, 1945; s. Russell Lawrence and Carolyn (Grant) Van D.; m. Karin Van Dyke; children: Carolyn Julie, Colin Grant. B.A. in Econs., U. Minn., 1967, M.B.A., 1976. Vice pres., chief fin. officer Northland Aluminum Co., Mpls., 1977-78; controller Donaldson Co., Inc., Mpls., 1978-80, v.p. controller, 1980-82, v.p. chief fin. officer, 1982-84, v.p., gen. mgr. indsl., 1984—. Served to lt. U.S. Army, 1968-70; Vietnam. Mem. Fin. Execs. Inst., Kappa Sigma Alumni Assn. Office: Donaldson Co Inc 1400 W 94th St Minneapolis MN 55431

VAN EKRIS, ANTHONIE CORNELIS, trading corporation executive; b. Rotterdam Netherlands, June 3, 1934; came to U.S., 1963; s. Cornelis and Evertje (Mulder) van E.; m. Heather Frances Button, Sept. 7, 1960; children: Anthonie Cornelis, Marijke Karin. Trainee Van Rees, Ltd., Rotterdam, 1952-57; mgr. African Coffee Trading Ops., Mombasa, E. Africa, 1957-63, Ralli Trading Co., N.Y.C., 1963-67; pres. Van Ekris & Stoett, Ltd., N.Y.C., 1967-70; pres., dir. Ralli-Am. Ltd., N.Y.C., 1970-72; pres. Kay Corp. (now Balfour Maclaine Corp.), N.Y.C., 1972—, chief exec. officer, chmn., 1988—, also bd. dirs.; chmn. Kay Jewelers, Inc., Balfour, Maclaine Internat. Ltd., Van Ekris & Stoett, Inc., Marcus & Co., Inc. Served with Royal Dutch Navy, 1951-53. also: Balfour Maclaine Corp Wall Street Pla New York NY 10005 Address: Hilltop Pl Rye NY 10580 *

VAN GIFFEN, REITZE, oilseed processing company executive; b. Haarlen, Netherlands, Oct. 28, 1937; came to U.S., 1980; s. Klaas and Johanna (Visser) Van G.; m. Anne Marie De Graaf, Oct. 21, 1967; children: Maaike J., Nicolien H., Anne E. BA in Agronomy, Leeuwarden U. With Cargill, Inc., 1961—; comml. dir. oilseeds div. Cargill, Inc., Amsterdam, Netherlands, 1971-74, account mgr., 1974-76, asst. gen. mgr., 1976-80; asst. v.p. internat. oilseeds processing div. —, Mpls., 1980-83, v.p., 1983-86, pres., 1986—; bd. dirs. Dutch Feeding Stuffs Produce Bd., The Hague, Netherlands, 1977-80; mem. adv. com. Internat. Assn. Seed Crushers, London, 1984—. Chmn. Dinner at Your Door, Netherlands, 1977-80. With Netherlands Armed Forces, 1959-61. Mem. Netherlands Oils and Fats Trade Orgn. (bd. dirs. 1975-80), Netherlands Crushers Assn. (bd. dirs., vice chmn. 1977-80), Internat. Oilseeds Assn. (consultative com. 1977-80), Netherlands-Am. Assn. Minn. (vice chmn. 1983-85). Mem. Dutch Conservative Party. Presbyterian. Office: Cargill Inc PO Box 9300 Minneapolis MN 55421

VAN GILDER, DEREK ROBERT, lawyer, engineer; b. San Antonio, Feb. 26, 1950; s. Robert Ellis and Genevieve Delphine (Hutter) Van G.; m. Charlene Frances Madison, Jan. 21, 1984. Student, U.S. Mil. Acad., 1969-71; BS in Civil Engring., U. Tex., 1974, JD, 1981; MBA, U. Houston, 1976. Bar: Tex. 1981, U.S. Ct. Appeals (9th cir.) 1982, Calif. 1982, U.S. Dist. Ct. (cen. dist.) Calif. 1982, U.S. Dist. Ct. (ea. and so. dists.) Tex. 1982, U.S. Ct. Appeals (5th cir.) 1982, U.S. Dist. Ct. (we. dist.) Tex. 1983, U.S. Dist. Ct. (no. dist.) Tex. 1988, U.S. Supreme Ct. 1988; registered profl. engr. Tex., La., N.M., Calif. Engr. various engring cos., Houston, Longview and Austin, Tex., 1974-81; assoc. Thelen, Marrin, Johnson & Bridges, Los Angeles, 1981-82, Bean & Manning, Houston, 1982-85; pvt. practice Houston, 1985-86, Van Gilder & Assocs., Houston, 1986-88; ptnr. Van Gilder & Alenik, Houston, 1988—; instr. Houston Community Coll., 1981—. Mem. ABA, Houston Bar Assn., Coll. The State Bar Tex., Am. Arbitration Assn. (panel arbitrators), Houston Med.-Legal Soc., Nat. Soc. Profl. Engrs., Def. Rsch. Inst., Tex. Assn. Def. Counsel, Tex. Soc. Profl. Engrs. Republican. Roman Catholic. Club: Houston City. Office: 11 Greenway Plaza Suite 2222 Houston TX 77046

VAN GORDER, JOHN FREDERIC, lawyer; b. Jacksonville, Fla., Mar. 22, 1943; s. Harold Burton and Charlotte Louise (Anderson) Van G.; grad. Dover (Eng.) Coll., 1961; A.B., Dartmouth Coll., 1965; postgrad. Air Force Inst. Tech., 1967-68; M.S. in Adminstrn., George Washington U., 1973; postgrad. U. Va., Coll. William and Mary, Cath. U. Am., Northeastern U., Babson Coll.; J.D., Fordham U. Sch. Law, 1981; m. Sandra Joan Hagen, June 4, 1977; children: Alyssa Jane, Kathryn Ann. Bar: N.J. 1981, N.Y. 1983, U.S. Supreme Ct. 1989. Weapons controller Aerospace Def. Command, Ft. Lee, Va., 1965-67; buyer electronics systems div. Air Force Systems Command, Bedford, Mass., 1968-69; project mgr. research and devel. Hdqrs. U.S. Air Force, Washington, 1969-73, br. chief personnel, 1973-74; Presdl. social aide The White House, Washington, 1971-74; asso. Louis C. Kramp & Assos., Washington, 1975; program officer J.M. Found., N.Y.C., 1975-81; assoc. firm Winne, Banta & Rizzi Esqs., Hackensack, N.J., 1981-83; asst. sec., program adminstr. Glenmeade Trust Co., Phila., 1983-86; exec. dir. Leon Lowenstein Found., 1986—; mem. Tabernacle Twp. Planning Bd., 1985-88, Tabernacle Bd. Edn., 1988—, Tabernacle Rep. Club, 1983—; atty. Rent Leveling Bd., Borough of Bergenfield (N.J.), 1983. Chmn. N.Y.C. steering com. Nat. Congress on Volunteerism and Citizenship, 1976; mem. exec. com. Mayor's Vol. Action Council, 1977-78; bd. govs. N.Y. Jaycees Found., 1978-79; bd. govs., 4th v.p. First Assembly Dist. Republican Club, 1977-82; vestryman All Saints Episc. Ch., Bergenfeld, N.J., 1982-83; Jr.Warden, 1987-88, sr. warden, 1989—, vestryman, lay reader St. Peter's Episc. Ch., 1985—, . Served to capt. USAF, 1965-74; lt. col. Res., 1974—. Named Outstanding Young Man of Va., 1975, USAF Res. Officer of Yr., 1985. Mem. Internat. (senator; v.p. 1975; rep. to UN 1976), U.S. (nat. v.p. 1973-74), D.C. (pres. 1972-73) N.Y.C. (bd. govs. 1978-79) Jaycees, S.A.R., Soc. Mayflower Descs., ABA, N.J. Bar Assn., N.Y. Bar Assn., Student Bar Assn. (class pres. 1978-81), Alpha Delta Phi. Republican. Episcopalian. Clubs:Toastmasters (local pres. 1969-70, area gov. 1970-71); Lodges: Lions (pres. Medford Twp. club 1985-86, co-chmn. Charity Ball 1987), Masons. Home: 23 Sleepy Hollow Dr Tabernacle NJ 08088 Office: 126 E 56th St New York NY 10022

VAN GORP, GARY WAYNE, clergyman; b. Reasnor, Iowa, July 16, 1953; s. Laverne Leroy and Emma Jean (Meyers) Van G.; m. Marietta Louise Burns, Dec. 29, 1972; children: Caleb Aaron, Kari Beth, Micah Alan, Faith Elise. Diploma in Pastoral Studies, Bible and Doctrine, Berean Coll., 1975; BS in Pastoral Studies, Religious Edn., North Cen. Bible Coll., Mpls., 1978; Diploma in profl. office mgmt., Alexandria (Minn.) Tech. Sch., 1984. Ordained to ministry Assemblies of God Ch., 1981. Pastor Verndale (Minn.) Assembly of God Ch., 1979-82; asst. mgr., caretaker Lake Geneva Bible Camp, Alexandria, 1982-83; christian edn. and outreach pastor Alexandria Assembly of God Ch., 1983-84; pastor, adminstrv. asst. Allison Park (Pa.) Assembly of God Ch., 1984—. Treas. The DoorWay, Pitts., 1988—. Mem. Nat. Assn. Ch. Bus. Adminstrs. (pres. Pitts. chpt. 1987-89). Home: 5260 Turner Rd Gibsonia PA 15044 Office: Allison Park Assembly of God Ch 2326 Duncan Ave Allison Park PA 15101

VAN GUNDY, GREGORY FRANK, lawyer; b. Columbus, Ohio, Oct. 24, 1945; s. Paul Arden and Edna Marie (Sanders) Van G.; m. Lisa Tamara Langer. B.A., Ohio State U., Columbus, 1966, J.D., 1969. Bar: N.Y. bar 1971. Asso. atty. firm Willkie Farr & Gallagher, N.Y.C., 1970-74; v.p. legal, sec. Marsh & McLennan Cos., Inc., N.Y.C., 1974-79; v.p., sec., gen. counsel Marsh & McLennan Cos., Inc., 1979—. Mem. ABA, Phi Beta Kappa. Roman Catholic. Club: University (N.Y.C.). Home: 232 Fox Meadow Rd Scarsdale NY 10583 Office: Marsh & McLennan Cos Inc 1221 Ave of the Americas New York NY 10020

VAN HAGEN, JAN KAROL, electrical equipment company executive; b. Eau Claire, Wis., Nov. 11, 1937; s. Henry Joseph and Elsie Marie (Hagenstad) Van H.; m. Kathryn Frances Fults, July 11, 1938; children: Mark A., David M., Kathryn T. Student, U. Wis., Eau Claire, 1956-58; BSME, U. Wis., 1961. Various mktg. positions Trane Co., La Crosse, Wis., 1961-69; mgr. group sales, mng. dir Trane Ltd. subs. Trane Co., La Crosse, 1969-72, v.p., gen. mgr. process div., 1972-73; exec. v.p. internat., v.p. corp. projects A.B. Chance div. Emerson Electric Co., Centralia, Mo., 1977-78; pres., group v.p. White Rodgers div. Emerson Electric Co., St. Louis, 1978-84, exec. v.p., pres., 1984-85, v.p. internat. parent co., 1978, exec. v.p., 1984-88, vice chmn., 1988—, also bd. dirs. Mem. Bellerive Country Club. Republican. Mem. Ch. of Christ. Office: Emerson Electric Co 8000 W Florissant Ave Saint Louis MO 63136

VAN HEMERT, JUDY, manufacturing executive; b. Dallas, Feb. 8, 1947; d. Marion Everett and Thelma Rhea (Robinson) Van H.; children: Christopher Martin, Matthew Everett. BA, Vanderbilt U., Nashville, 1969; cert. lang. therapist Scottish Rite Hosp., Dallas, 1971. Cert. secondary tchr., Tex., cert. Lang. therapist. Lang. therapist Scottish Rite Hosp., Dallas, 1970-72, The Winston Sch., Dallas, 1975-82; mktg., purchasing S.V. Mfg., Richardson, Tex., 1982-84; pres. Bullet Electronics, Rockwall, Tex., 1984—; owner C-Power, Inc. Elder Presbyn. Ch. Named Miss Park Cities. Mem. Assn. Women Entrepreneurs of Dallas, Nat. Assn. Women Bus. Owners, Small Bus. Owners, Tex. Bus. Coun., Rockwall C. of C. (exec. bd. dirs.), Soroptimist Internat. Republican. Avocations: golf, tennis. Office: C-Power Products Inc 2007 Industrial Ln Rockwall TX 75087

VAN HORN, VERNE HILE, III, retail executive; b. Tulsa, July 27, 1938; s. Verne Hile and Vonnie Hoffman (King) Van H.; m. Anne Burkhalter; children: Tracy, Melissa, David, William. Student, U. Okla., 1957; B.S. in Bus., U. Tulsa, 1962. Salesman, Phillips Petroleum Co., Dallas, 1963-66; with Nat. Convenience Stores Inc., Houston, 1966—; v.p. stores div. Nat. Convenience Stores Inc., 1971-75, exec. v.p., 1975, pres., dir., 1975—, also chief exec. officer.; bd. dirs. 1st City Bank of Houston, Tex. Research League. Chmn. Houston Parks Bd.; bd. chmn. United Way of Tex. Gulf Coast; bd. dirs. Houston Symphony Orchestra, Sam Houston area councul Boy Scouts Am. Houston Ballet, Houston Better Bus. Bur. Mem. Tex. Assn. Taxpayers (bd. dirs.), Am. Leadership Forum (bd. dirs.), Forum Club of Houston (bd. dirs.), Young Pres.'s Assn. Republican. Office: Nat Convenience Stores Inc 100 Waugh Dr Houston TX 77007

VAN HOUTEN, PETER SAMUEL, data processing executive; b. Pocatello, Idaho, Aug. 8, 1958; s. N. Gene and Blossom Ann (Carlson) Van H.; m. Kay Denise Anderson, June 4, 1983; children: Andijoy, Kristopher. BA, Concordia Coll., Portland, Oreg., 1980; MBA, U. Portland, 1987. Mgr. computer ops. Computer Mgmt. Svc., Inc., Portland, 1980-86; systems mgr. Mentor Graphics Corp., Beaverton, Oreg., 1986—; adj. prof. Concordia Coll., Portland, 1987—. Commr. Boy Scouts Am., Portland, 1980-83; big brother Beaverton Youth Svcs., 1983-88; adviser Beaverton Jr. Achievement, 1986-87. Mem. Assn. Systems Mgrs., Computer Ops. Mgmt. Assn. (bd. dirs., sec. 1987-88, pres. 1988—), Data Processing Mgrs. Assn. Republican. Office: Mentor Graphics Corp 8500 SW Creekside Pl Beaverton OR 97005-7191

VAN LANDINGHAM, LEANDER SHELTON, JR., lawyer; b. Memphis, July 15, 1925; s. Leander Shelton Van L.; m. Henrietta Adena Stapf, July 5, 1959; children—Ann Henrietta, Leander Shelton III. B.S. in Chemistry, U. N.C., 1948, M.A. in Organic Chemistry, 1949; J.D., Georgetown U., 1955. Bar: D.C. 1955, Md. 1963, Va. 1976. Patent adviser Dept. Navy, Washington, 1953-55; sole practice comml. law and patent, trademark and copyright law, Washington met. area, 1955—. Served to lt. USNR, 1943-46, 51-53. Mem. Am. Chem. Soc., Sci. Assn., Fed. Bar Assn., ABA, D.C. Bar Assn., Va. Bar Assn., Md. Bar Assn., Am. Patent Law Assn., Am. Judicature Soc., Sigma Xi, Phi Alpha Delta. Home: 10726 Stanmore Dr Potomac MD 20854 Office: 2001 Jefferson Davis Hwy Arlington VA 22202

VAN LEUVEN, ROBERT JOSEPH, lawyer; b. Detroit, Apr. 17, 1931; s. Joseph Francis and Olive (Stowell) Van L.; student Albion Coll., 1949-51; B.A. with distinction Wayne State U., 1953; J.D., U. Mich., 1957; m. Holly Goodhue Porter, Dec. 31, 1976; children—Joseph Michael, Douglas Robert, Julie Margaret. Bar: Mich. 1957. Since practiced in Muskegon, Mich.; ptnr. Hathaway, Latimer, Clink & Robb, 1957-68, McCroskey, Libner & Van Leuven, 1968-81, Libner, Van Leuven & Kortering, 1982—; past mem. council negligence law sect. State Bar Mich. Bd. dirs. Muskegon Children's Home, 1965-75. Served with AUS 1953-55. Fellow Mich. Bar Found., Mich. Trial Lawyers Assn., Am. Coll. Trial Lawyers; mem. Assn. Trial Lawyers Am., Delta Sigma Phi. Club: Muskegon Country. Home: 966 Mona Brook Muskegon MI 49445 Office: Hackley Bank Muskegon Mall Muskegon MI 49443

VANMEER, MARY ANN, publisher, writer, researcher; b. Mt. Clemens, Mich., Nov. 22; d. Leo Harold and Rose Emma (Gulden) VanM.; stepmother Ruth (Meek) VanM. Student Mich. State U., 1965-66, 67-68, Sorbonne U., Paris, 1968; BA in Edn., U. Fla., 1970. Pres. VanMeer Tutoring and Translating, N.Y.C., 1970-72; freelance writer, 1973-79; pres. VanMeer Publs., Inc., Clearwater, Fla., 1980—, VanMeer Media Advt., Inc., Clearwater, 1980—; exec. dir., founder Nat. Ctrs. for Health and Med. Info., Inc., Clearwater, 1982—; pres. Health and Med. Trends, Inc. 1987—. Author: Traveling with Your Dog, U.S.A., 1976, How to Set Up A Home Typing Business, 1978, Freelance Photographer's Handbook, 1979; See America Free, 1981, Free Campgrounds, U.S.A., 1982, Free Attractions, U.S.A., 1982, VanMeer's Guide to Free Attractions, U.S.A., 1984, VanMeer's Guide to Free Campgrounds, 1984, DUI Survival Manual, 1987, The How to Get Publicity for Your Business Handbook, 1987; pub. Nat. Health and Med. Trends Mag., 1986—. Pub. info. chairperson, bd. dirs. Pinellas County chpt. Am. Cancer Soc., Clearwater, 1983-84, 86-88. Mem. Am. Booksellers Assn., PACT (Performing Arts, Concert, and Theatre), Author's Guild. Office: VanMeer Publs Inc PO Box 2138 Clearwater FL 34617 also: Health and Med Trends Inc PO Box 2138 Clearwater FL 34617

VAN METER, JAMES COMBS, forest products company executive; b. Lexington, Ky., Apr. 15, 1938; m. Mary Bailey Fitts, Nov. 28, 1957; children—Solomon L., Ben H., John M. Student, Phillips Exeter Acad., N.H., 1956; M.S. in Math., U. Ky., 1963. Instr. U. Ky., Lexington, 1963; instr.

Centre Coll., Danville, Ky., 1963-65; Danforth tchr. Washington U., St. Louis, 1966-67; various positions to adminstrv. v.p. Ashland Oil, Inc., Ky., 1968-81; chief fin. officer, exec. v.p.-fin and adminstrn. Cities Service Co., Tulsa, 1981-83; chief fin. officer, exec. v.p.-fin. Ga.-Pacific Corp., Atlanta, 1983—. Bd. dirs. High Mus. Art, Atlanta, 1984; mem. adv. council Ga. State U., Atlanta, 1984; trustee Centre Coll., Danville, Ky., 1985—; bd. visitors Berry Coll., Mt. Berry, Ga., 1985—. Mem. Fin. Execs. Inst. Office: Ga-Pacific Corp 133 Peachtree St NE Atlanta GA 30303 *

VANNAERSSEN, HENRI JOHAN (HANS), software company executive; b. Antofagasta, Chile, July 12, 1943; came to U.S., 1944; s. Eduard J. and Anna W. (Dehaan) V.; m. Margaret Mitchell Moore, Nov. 13, 1972; children: Eric Hans, Michelle Allison. BA, Park Coll., 1965; MBA, NYU, 1971. Cert. in data processing. Computer/analyst programmer Burroughs Bus. & Mgmt. Software Systems, Detroit, 1973-76; mgr. software devel. Burroughs Program Products div., Irvine, Calif., 1976-80; mgr. mktg. support Burroughs-China, Beijing, 1980-82; mgr. software and services Burroughs Far East, Hong Kong, 1982-86; gen. mgr. Burroughs-Cyberware, Singapore, 1986-88; dir. product devel., info. and productivity systems Unisys Corp., Bluebell, Pa., 1988—; lectr. Burroughs Corp., worldwide. Mem. Am. Bus. Council, Singapore, 1986-88. Served to 1st lt. U.S. Army, 1966-69, Vietnam. Decorated Bronze Star. Mem. Singapore Fedn. Computer Industry. Office: Unisys Corp MS B260 PO Box 500 Bluebell PA 19424

VANORA, JEROME PATRICK, lawyer; b. N.Y.C., Dec. 18, 1941; s. Jerome Anthony and Mary (Fitzpatrick) V.; m. Marianne Elizabeth Hartmann, Oct. 12, 1968; children—Judith, Kimberly. B.A., Queens Coll., 1963; LL.B., St. John's U., 1966. Bar: N.Y. 1967. Atty. N.Y. Dept. of State, Corp. Bur., Albany, 1967-70, sr. atty. div. human rights, N.Y.C., 1970-81, assoc. atty. div. housing community renewal, N.Y.C., 1981— chief of hearings bur. (chief adminstrv. law judge) office of rent adminstrn., div. housing and community renewal, N.Y.C., 1984—; asst. counsel Nassau county rent Guidelines Bd., 1982-86; lectr. (twice yearly) L.I. U., Greenvale, N.Y., 1984-85 . Recipient Am. Jurisprudence prize Lawyers' Coop. Pub. Co., Mem. Nat. Assn. Adminstrv. Law Judges, Queens County Bar Assn., Phi Beta Kappa. Republican. Roman Catholic. Home: 1100 Delmar Ave Franklin Square NY 11010 Office: NY State Div Housing and Community Renewal Gertz Plaza 92-31 Union Hall St Jamaica NY 11431

VAN PELT, PETER JOHNSON, manufacturing executive; b. Rockville Center, N.Y., June 13, 1937; s. Arthur Johnson and Annebelle (Gilbert) Van P.; m. Louise Ellen Smith, Aug. 20, 1960; 1 child, Craig Johnson. Student, Santa Monica (Calif.) Community Coll. Mgr. Singer Co., Herkimer, N.Y., 1963-67; sales rep. Sta. WALY-FM, Herkimer, 1967-69; mgr. Sta. WLFH-FM, Little Falls, 1969-74; v.p. Moval Mgmt. Corp., Herkimer, N.Y., 1974-76; sales rep. Library Bur., Inc., Herkimer, 1976-80, Ea. regional sales mgr., 1980-81, nat. sales mgr., 1981-83, v.p. nat. sales, 1983-85, v.p. mktg., 1985-87, pres., chief operating officer, 1987-89, pres., chief exec. officer, 1989—, also bd. dirs. Bd. dirs. Herkimer County Area Devel. Corp., Mohawk, N.Y., 1987. Served with USAF, 1957-62. Mem. Herkimer Businessmen's Assn. Republican. Lodges: Lions (v.p. Herkimer chpt. 1986—), Kiwanis, Elks, KC. Office: Library Bur Inc 801 Park Ave Herkimer NY 13350

VAN ROOSEN, DONALD COLLETT, chemical equipment company executive; b. Boston, Aug. 11, 1923; s. Hugo and Ellen Margaret (Halck) Van R.; m. Nancy Johnston Crough, June 10, 1950 (div. Nov. 1980); children: Christine, Laurie Ellen, Hugh; m. Marcia Hunnefield, Oct. 17, 1982. BA, Harvard U., 1949. Dist. mgr. Hercules Gasket & Rubber Co., Buffalo, 1953-56; div. mgr., dir. market rsch. Gaulin Corp., Everett, Mass., 1956-70; dir. mktg. Columbia Precision Corp., Wilmington, Mass., 1971-73; dir. internat. mktg. Applicon, Inc., Burlington, Mass., 1973-75; div. mgr. Comstock & Wescott, Cambridge, Mass., 1975-77; ptnr. Group IV Capital Investments, Inc., Burlington, 1980-82; v.p. mktg. Silane Corp., Ashland, Mass., 1982-88; dir. mktg., homogenizer div. Union Pump Co., North Andover, Mass., 1989—; mem. Hydraulic Inst., N.Y.C., 1956-70. Pres. Minuteman coun. Boy Scouts Am., Stoneham, Mass., 1970-75, v.p. New Eng. area Boy Scouts Am., Boston, 1983—, mem. N.E. Regional Com.; mem. allocations com. United Way of Mass. Bay, Boston, 1984—. Served with U.S. Army, 1943-45, ETO. Decorated Silver Star, Bronze Star with cluster, Purple Heart with 3 clusters, Croix de Guerre (France). Mem. Am. Inst. Chem. Engrs. (reciprocating pump specification com. 1965-70), Am. Mgmt. Assn. (dir. program 1968-70), Nat. Order Battlefield Commns., Harvard Club, Appalachian Mountain Club, Pi-Eta Speakers Club. Republican. Home: 35 Eastbluff Rd Ashland MA 01721 Office: Union Pump Co 334 Clark St North Andover MA 01845

VAN SANT, DANIEL MILTON, lawyer; b. Little Sandy, Ky., Jan. 9, 1924; s. Vernon Vaughn and Jessie Milton (Jones) Van S.; m. Mildred Frances Blair, June 3, 1945; children: Dorothy Little, Michael, Judith Ogles, Robert, Richard. BS, U. Ky., 1947; MBA, Case Western Res. U., 1951; JD, Nashville Sch. Law, 1983. Bar: Tenn., 1983; CPA, Tenn. Mem. staff Ernst & Ernst, Cleve., 1947-57; mgr. Ernst & Ernst, Nashville, 1957-62; mng. ptnr. Ernst & Whinney, Nashville, 1962-81; registered rep. Paine Webber, Nashville, 1982-83; prof. Middle Tenn. State U., Murfreesboro, 1982-83; v.p. Health Industries Am., Nashville, 1983-84; ptnr. firm Bradley & Van Sant, Nashville, 1985—; bd. dirs. Rogers Mfg. Co. Inc., Nashville, Union Planters Nat. Bank, Nashville, Healthmaster, Nashville, Clini-Therm Corp, Dallas; prof. acctg. Middle Tenn. State U., Murfreesboro, 1982-83; chmn. Tenn. Bd. Accountancy, 1975-77. Mem. Employee Benefit Bd., Nashville, 1982—, treas., 1972—. Served to 1st lt. U.S. Army, 1943-45, ETO. Mem. ABA, Nashville Bar Assn., Am. Inst. CPAs, Tenn. Soc. CPAs (past pres. Nashville chpt.) Nat. Assn. Accts. (past pres. Nashville chpt.). Clubs: Hillwood Country (treas.), Nashville City (pres.). Lodge: Masons. Home: 96 Jamestown Park Nashville TN 37205 Office: Bradley & Van Sant 315 Deaderick St Nashville TN 37238

VAN SANT, ROBERT WILLIAM, heavy manufacturing company executive; b. Iowa Falls, Aug. 19, 1938; s. Oscar and Muriel (Mullane) Van S.; m. Marilyn J. Noonan, May 31, 1981; children: William, Kathy, David, Susan, Jeff. BSMechE, U. Iowa, 1966, MSMechE, 1967. With Deere & Co., 1957-83; gen. mgr. Waterloo, Iowa, 1975-80; dir. Moline, Ill., 1980-81; v.p. Deere & Co., Moline, Ill., 1981-83; pres. Cessna Aircraft Co., Wichita, Kans., 1983-87; pres., chief op. officer Blount, Inc., Montgomery, Ala., 1987—; bd. dirs. NAM, Lukens Inc. Trustee Machinery and Allied Products Inst. Home: 3284 Bankhead Ave Montgomery AL 36106

VAN SCHAICK, ANTHONY GERARD, aerospace executive; b. N.Y.C., Oct. 11, 1945; s. Gerrit Wessel and Dorothy Angell (Cameron) Van S.; m. Patricia Kay Parks, Aug. 28, 1980; children: Christopher, Jeffrey, Stephen. BA, Yale U., 1967; MBA, Stanford U., 1972. V.p. Citibank, N.A., N.Y.C., 1973-78; exec. v.p. Lockheed Fin. Corp., Burbank, Calif., 1978-81; asst. treas. Lockheed Corp., Burbank, 1984-85; v.p., treas. Lockheed Corp., Calabasas, Calif., 1985—; bd. dirs. Lockheed Fed. Credit Union; mem. western adv. bd. Allendale Ins. Bd. dirs., treas. YMCA Met. L.A., 1986—; ptrustee Pacific Am. Fund. Lt. USN, 1967-70. Republican. Office: Lockheed Corp 4500 Park Granada Blvd Calabasas CA 91399

VANSICKLE, BARBARA JEAN, coordinator of computer services; b. Parkersburg, W.Va., Oct. 18, 1948; d. Robert Syrl and Evelyn June (Anderson) McGraw; m. John Vernon Morrison Jr., Oct. 7, 1968 (dec. June 1981); children: John Vernon III, Deborah Margarette; m. Danny Ray Vansickle, Oct. 1, 1983. AS, Shawnee State Community Coll., 1984; student, Ohio U., 1985, Wilmington Coll., 1988. Keypunch operator Columbus (Ohio) Mut. Life Ins. Co., 1966-67, Steele Data Processing, Washington Court House, Ohio, 1971-74; data entry operator F&R Lazarus, Columbus, 1978-79; clk. III Parker Hannifin Corp., Waverly, Ohio, 1979-80; computer programmer Shawnee State U., Portsmouth, Ohio, 1981-88; coord. computer svcs. Wilmington (Ohio) Coll., 1988—; instr. part-time Southeastern Bus. Coll., Portsmouth, 1982-83. Mem. Valley High Sch. PTA, Lucasville, Ohio, 1982-85; pres. Valley High Sch. Band Boosters, 1986-87, v.p., 1985-86. Mem. Data Processing Mgmt. Spl. Interest Group for Edn., Data Processing Mgmt. Assn., Digital Equip. Corp. Users Soc. (assoc.). Republican. Home: 132 Ludovic St Wilmington OH 45177 Office: Wilmington Coll Pyle Ctr Box 1204 Wilmington OH 45177

VAN SICKLE, PAUL BRUNTON, financial executive; b. Toronto, Ont., Can., Sept. 17, 1939; came to U.S., 1967; s. Percy Orton Van Sickle and Audrey Winefred (Dandie) Palmquist; m. Christine Cornfoot, Sept. 9, 1967 (div. July 1985); children: Giles, Kirsten. Grad. advanced mgmt. program, Harvard U., 1986. Canadian chartered acct. V.p. Fin. Rexcel, Ludlow, Mass., 1973-76, Specialty Products Sector, LaGrange, Ga., 1976-77; v.p. Thompson Industries, Phoenix, 1977-79, exec. v.p., 1979-81; controller Home & comml. Products Group, Northbrook, Ill., 1981-82, Duracell, Inc., Danbury, Conn., 1982-83; sr. v.p. fin. Hobart Corp., Troy, Ohio, 1983-85; v.p., controller Dart & Kraft, Inc., Northbrook, Ill., 1986; v.p., controller Premark Internat., Deerfield, Ill., 1986-88, v.p. control and info. systems, 1988-89; v.p., chief fin. officer Tupperware, Orlando, Fla., 1989—. Office: Premark Internat 1717 Deerfield Rd Deerfield IL 60015 also: Tupperware Orlando FL

VAN SLYCK, PHILIP, public relations executive; b. New Orleans, Jan. 10, 1920; s. Philip Noyes and Edith Gabriel (Conley) van S.; m. Aug. 10, 1945 (div. 1952); children: Phyllis Elizabeth, Peter Wilson. AB with honors, U. Calif., Berkeley, 1941. Advt. mgr. Standard Optical Co., Salt Lake City, 1946-48; pres. Philip van Slyck & Assocs., San Francisco, 1948-53; sec. gen. Jaycees Internat., Miami Beach, Fla., 1953-55; editor Fgn. Policy Assn., N.Y.C., 1955-62; ptnr. Allen Murden Inc., N.Y.C., 1962-66; pres., chief exec. officer Philip van Slyck Inc., N.Y.C., 1966—. Author: Peace: Control National Power, 1963, Strategies for 1980's, 1981; contbg. editor: Gallatin Ann. Internat. Bus., 1963; contbr. articles to profl. jours. Sec., chmn. exec. com. Freedom House and Willkie Meml., N.Y.C., 1966—; treas., mem. fin. com. Internat. Inst. in Spain Found., 1975—; trustee Japan-Am. Social Svc. Inc., 1982—. Capt. AUS, 1941-46, PTO. Democrat. Home: 126 S Oxford St Brooklyn NY 11217 Office: 271 Madison Ave Ste 808 New York NY 10016

VANTREASE, ALICE TWIGGS, marketing executive; b. Augusta, Ga., Mar. 29, 1943; d. Samuel Warren and Harriett Alice (Wright) Twiggs; m. John Mulford Marks, July 8, 1964 (div. Oct. 1972); children: John Mulford, Sarah Elizabeth; m. James David Vantrease, May 9, 1980 (div. Mar. 1988). Student Winthrop Coll., 1961-62, Augusta Coll., 1962-64. Sales staff Chalker Publ. Co., Waynesboro, Ga., 1972-74; with Creative Displays, Inc., Tuscaloosa, Ala., 1974-78; sales mgr. GMC Bdcasting, Chattanooga, 1978-80; corporate sales, mktg. dir. Creative Displays Inc., Augusta, 1980-83; pres. Creative Mktg. Services, Augusta, 1983—. Bd. dirs. Better Bus. Bur., 1987-89; pres. Good Luck Found., 1988—. Mem. Outdoor Advt. Suppliers Assn. (v.p. 1984-87, pres. 1987-88, editor newspaper 1985-88), Nat. Speakers Assn., Am. Mgmt. Assn., Am. Assn. Coop Advt. Profls., Outdoor Advt. Assn. Am. Instr. Episcopalian. Avocations: painting, writing. Home: 2927 Lake Forest Dr Augusta GA 30909 Office: Creative Mktg 825 Russell St Augusta GA 30914-2247

VAN TUYLE, ROBERT WOODING, health care facilities company executive; b. Manchester, Ill., 1912. Student, Univ of Cincinnati, MIT. Chmn., chief exec. officer Beverly Enterprises, Pasadena, Calif.; dir. Jacobs Engring. Group, Inc., Alpha Microsystems. Office: Beverly Enterprises Inc 99 S Oakland Ave Pasadena CA 91101 *

VAN VLECK, JAMES, forest products company executive; b. Oklahoma City, May 10, 1930; s. Charles Lewis and Lula Grace (Mahanke) Van V.; m. Joan Ellen Amery, July 19, 1952; children: Susan Lynn Van Vleck Patton, Betsy Lee Van Vleck Aliffi. BA, Principia Coll., 1952; MBA, Harvard U., 1956. Pres. Stanley Furniture Co. div. Mead Corp., Stanleytown, Va., 1970-72; gen. v.p. Mead Interiors div. Mead Corp., Stanleytown, 1972-76; gen. v.p. corp. staff Mead Corp., Dayton, Ohio, 1976-82, gen. v.p. indsl. products, 1982-84, v.p. operational planning, 1984-86, sr. v.p. internat., pres. pulp affiliates, 1987—; bd. dirs. Moto Photo, Dayton, 1981—. bd. dirs. Greater Dayton Pvt. Industry Coun., 1982-85, City-Wide Devel. Corp., Dayton, 1985—, Performing Arts Fund, Dayton, 1979-86, United Way of Dayton, 1983-84, State Job Tng. Coordinating Coun., Columbus, Ohio, 1983-88, New Futures Initiative of Dayton, 1987—. Served to sgt. U.S. Army, 1952-54. Named Bus. Vol. of Yr. Nat. Alliance Bus's., Washington, 1985. Mem. Dayton Area C. of C. (bd. dirs 1988—). Home: 120 Grandon Rd Dayton OH 45419 Office: Mead Corp Courthouse Pla NE Dayton OH 45463

VAN VORST, ROBERT LEO, pipeline service company analyst; b. Helena, Mont., July 3, 1940; s. Robert Van Vorst and Mary Elizabeth (Murphy) Brown; m. Lorraine Grunwald, Nov. 22, 1963; step-children: Don E. Stobaugh Jr., Jerry Del Stobaugh; children: Timothy Scott, Bobbi Lorraine, Ti. Student, Tex. Weslyan Coll., 1968, Anchorage Community Coll., 1979-80, 81, Alaska Pacific U., 1982-83, Clayton U., 1982-88. Tech. rev. and spares analyst LTV Aerospace, Inc., Grand Prairie, Tex., 1968-70; sr. logistics coord. Aerospatiale Helicopter Co. (formerly Vought Helicopter), Grand Prairie, 1970-75; chief logistics coord. Internat. Air Transport, Anchorage, 1975-77; purchasing agt. Alyeska Pipeline Svc. Co., Anchorage, 1977-80, supr. inventory control, 1980-81, sr. tech. analyst, 1981—. With USAF, 1959-68. Mem. Soc. Logistics Engrs. (sr. Alaska bd. dirs. 1983—). Roman Catholic. Home: 8300 Resurrection Dr Anchorage AK 99504 Office: Alyeska Pipeline Svc Co 1835 S Bragaw St Anchorage AK 99512

VAN WACHEM, LODEWIJK CHRISTIAAN, petroleum company executive; b. Pangkalan Brandan, The Netherland East Indies, July 31, 1931; m. Elisabeth G. Cristofoli, 1958; 3 children. Student Tech. U., Delft, The Netherlands. With Bataafsche Petroleum Maatschappij, The Hague, The Netherlands, 1953; mech. engr. Cia Shell de Venezuela, 1954-63; chief engr. Shell-BP Petroleum Devel. Co. Nigeria, 1963-66, mgr. engr., 1966-67, chmn., mng. dir., 1972-76; head tech. adminstrn. Brunei Shell Petroleum Co. Ltd., 1967-69, tech. dir., 1969-71; head production div. Shell Internat. Petroleum Maatschappij, The Hague, 1971-72, coordinator exploration and production, 1976-79; mng. dir. Royal Dutch Petroleum Co., until 1982, pres., 1982—; mem. presidium bd. dirs. Shell Petroleum N.V.; mng. dir. Shell Petroleum Co. Ltd., 1977; chmn. Shell Oil Co. USA; bd. dirs. Shell Can.; chmn. joint com. mng. dirs. Royal Dutch/Shell Group, 1985—. Recipient K.B.E., 1988, Knight Order Netherlands Lion, 1981. Office: Shell Oil Co 1 Shell Pla Houston TX 77252 also: Royal Dutch/Shell Group Cos, 30 2596 HR Carel van Bylandtlaan, Hague Netherlands

VAN WAGNER, BRUCE, telecommunications equipment distribution company executive; b. 1925. Student, Harvard U.; AB, U. N.C., 1945, BS, 1947. Various positions to v.p. Anaconda Wire and Cable Co., 1947-64; v.p. Am. Enka Corp., 1964-68; v.p. ops. then exec. v.p. Anixter Bros. Inc., 1968—, now chmn. exec. com. Served to lt. j.g. USN, 1942-46. Office: Anixter Bros Inc 4711 Golf Rd Skokie IL 60076

VAN WINKLE, WILLIAM, financial planner; b. Englewood, N.J., July 3, 1934; s. Marshall Jr. and Helen (Wescott) V.; m. Beverly Elsie Peterson, Sept. 9, 1956; children: Stuart Wilson, Ainsley Ann, Carrie Lee. BS in Mech. Engring. and Bus. Adminstrn., Lehigh U., 1957. Cert. fin. planner, CLU. Ops. mgr., plant engr. Procter and Gamble, N.Y., Ga., Kans., Calif., Ohio, 1957-67; ops. mgr. Sheffield Chem. div. Kraftco, Union, N.J., 1967-71; dir. mfg. USA C.R. Bard, Inc., Murray Hill, N.J., 1971-74; v.p. Estey Corp., Eatontown, N.J., 1974-79; pres. Van Winkle Assocs., Tinton Falls, N.J., 1979—. Host, producer: (cable TV program) Insurance Matters, 1980—; contbr. articles to profl. jours. Bd. dirs. Monmouth Office Social Svcs., Red Bank, N.J., 1985—; trustee Greater Red Bank YMCA, 1986—; pres., trustee Brookdale Community Coll. Found., Lincroft, N.J., 1985—. Mem. Inst. Cert. Fin. Planners, Internat. Assn. Fin. Planning (bd. dirs. 1984-86, cen. N.J. chpt.), Am. Soc. CLU & ChFC (bd. dirs. 1986—, cen. N.J. chpt.), Nat. Assn. Life Underwriters (nat. quality award 1983—), Monmouth Assn. Life Underwriters (pres. 1982-83), Cen. N.J Estate Planning Coun., Million Dollar Round Table (dir., speaker liaison, gen. sessions 1987-88), Navesink Countrt Club (Middletown, N.J.), Holland Soc. N.Y. Club, Shrewsbury Sailing and Yacht Club (Oceanport, N.J., commodore 1972-73), N. J. Yacht Racing Assn. (Beach Haven, commodore 1984-85). Republican. Episcopalian. Home: 41 Breezy Point Little Silver NJ 07739 Office: Van Winkle Assocs 776 Shrewsbury Ave Tinton Falls NJ 07724

VAN ZEE, DOUGLAS WAYNE, food company executive; b. Platte, S.D., Jan. 16, 1959; s. Marvin and Darlene (Breukelman) Van Z.; m. Brenda DeLange, June 3, 1978; children: Chelsea Dawn, Preston Douglas, Megan Renae. Grad. high sch., New Holland, S.D. Owner Canton (S.D.) Food Ctr., Inc., 1977—. Office: Canton Food Ctr Inc 715 E 5th Canton SD 57013

VARDA, KAREN A., federal agency administrator; b. Terre Haute, Ind., Oct. 15, 1961; d. Peter Richard and Mary Ann (Gourdouze) V. BS, Ind. State U., 1982, postgrad., 1982—. CPA, Ind. Staff acct. Valley Fed. Savings Bank, Terre Haute, 1981-84; agt. IRS, Indpls., 1984—; instr. corp. tax IRS, Indpls., Cin., 1987; instr. Income Tax Sch. Purdue U., 1986. Coach sports Nat. Youth St. Luke's Ch., Indpls., 1987—, Tabernacle Recreational Ministry, Indpls., 1987—. Mem. Fed. Exec. Assn., Am. Soc. Women Accts. (bd. dirs. 1986-87), Ind. Soc. CPA's (Hispanic program mgr.'s subcom). Roman Catholic. Home: 8408 Devonshire Ct Indianapolis IN 46260

VARET, MICHAEL A., lawyer; b. N.Y.C., Mar. 9, 1942; s. Guster V. and Frances B. (Goldberg) V.; m. Elizabeth R. Varet, June 3, 1973; 3 children. BS in Econs., U. Pa., 1962; LLB, Yale U., 1965. Mem. Milgrim Thomajan & Lee P.C., N.Y.C., 1982—. Trustee Montefiore Med. Ctr., Bronx, N.Y., 1980—; bd. dirs. Sem. Library Corp. Jewish Theol. Sem., N.Y.C., 1983—, United Jewish Appeal-Fedn. Jewish Philanthropies of Greater N.Y., Inc., 1979-86, Mosholu Preservation Corp., Bronx, 1982—; bd. overseers Jewish Theol. Sem., 1982—, Jewish Publ. Soc. of Am., 1986—; mem. exec. com. Montefiore Med. Ctr., 1985—; mem. Coun. of Overseers United Jewish Appeal Fedn. of Jewish Philanthropies of Greater N.Y., Inc., 1986—. Served with USAR, 1966-72. Mem. ABA, N.Y. State Bar Assn., Assn. Bar City N.Y. (bd. dirs., exec. com. 1971-75), Internat. Fiscal Assn., Internat. Tax Planning Assn., Yale Club. Democrat. Jewish. Office: Milgrim Thomajan & Lee PC 53 Wall St New York NY 10005

VARGAS, AL GARCIA, marketing executive; b. Fresno, Calif., Apr. 21, 1943; s. Aurelio Villegas and Anita (Garcia) V.; m. Luci Guerrero Cruz, Sept. 22, 1968; children: Sylvia, Al Jr., George. AA, Fresno City Coll., 1974; BS in Bus. Adminstrn., Calif. State U., Fresno, 1977. Acctg. clerk Anderson/Clayton, Fresno, 1968-70; constrn. salesman Wilson Constrn., Fresno, 1974-76; bldg. contractor Vargas Homes, Fresno, 1981-82; mktg. exec. Econ. Opportunity Commns. Fresno County, 1983—. Recipient Ambassador award Calif.-Nev. Weatherization Bd., Sacramento, 1985, Superior Performance award, Fresno County EOC Weatherization Project, 1985. Republican. Mem. Assemby of God Ch. Home: 6643 Latonia PO Box 751 Laton CA 93242 Office: Fresno County EOC 3120 W Nielsen Suite 102 Fresno CA 93706

VARGAS, FERNANDO RODOLFO, recording studio executive; b. San Jose, Costa Rica, Sept. 22, 1928; came to U.S., 1946; s. Elias and Elena (Zamora) V.; student, RCA Inst., 1954. Engr. Audiosonic Rec., N.Y.C., 1953-61; exec. dir. Variety Sound Corp., N.Y.C., 1961-88; co-owner, engr. Variety Rec. Studio, 1961-88; v.p. AAA Record Plating, N.Y.C., 1986-88; co-owner AAA Rec. Studio, 1980-88. Avocations: electrical engineering, astronomy. Office: Variety Rec Studio 130 W 42d St #551 New York NY 10036

VARGO, GEORGE FRANCIS, JR., electrical engineer, electronics company executive; b. Hamtramck, Mich., June 19, 1942; s. George Francis Vargo and Josephine (Kadlubowski) Vettese; m. Linda Darlene Myers, May 21, 1966; children: Marjorie Ann, Mary Kathleen, Dawn Michele, David Andrew, Daniel Michael. BEE, U. Detroit, 1972. Registered profl. engr., Mich., Wash. Project engr. Nucleus Corp., Madison Heights, Mich., 1971-73, chief engr., 1973-75; v.p. engring. Computer Engring., Inc., Farmington Hills, Mich., 1975-76; chief engr. Vega Servo Control, Inc., Troy, Mich., 1976-78; contract engr. Mid-Columbia Engring. Co., Richland, Wash., 1978-80; prin. engr. Westinghouse Hanford Co., Richland, 1980-84; v.p. engring. Electronic Systems Tech., Inc., Kennewick, Wash., 1985—. Patentee wireless computer modem. With USN, 1961-67. Mem. Nat. Soc. Profl. Engrs., Wash. Soc. Profl. Engrs., Tri-City R/C Modellers Club (pres. Richland chpt. 1983-84). Roman Catholic. Home: 219 Indian Ct Richland WA 99352 Office: Electronic SystemsTech Inc 1031 N Kellogg St Kennewick WA 99336

VARNEDOE, HEETH, III, food products company executive; b. 1937; married. Grad., U. Ga., 1959. With Flowers Industries Inc., 1959—, pres. baked foods div., 1976-83, exec. v.p. ops., from 1983, now pres., also dir. Office: Flowers Industries Inc US Hwy 19 PO Box 1338 Thomasville GA 31799 *

VARNER, CHARLEEN LAVERNE MCCLANAHAN (MRS. ROBERT B. VARNER), educator, administrator, nutritionist; b. Alba, Mo., Aug. 28, 1931; d. Roy Calvin and Lela Ruhama (Smith) McClanahan; student Joplin (Mo.) Jr. Coll., 1949-51; B.S. in Edn., Kans. State Coll. Pittsburg, 1953; M.S., U. Ark., 1958; Ph.D., Tex. Woman's U. 1966; postgrad. Mich. State U., summer, 1955, U. Mo., summer 1962; m. Robert Bernard Varner, July 4, 1953. Apprentice county home agt. U. Mo., summer 1952; tchr. Ferry Pass Sch., Escambia County, Fla., 1953-54; tchr. biology, home econs. Joplin Sr. High Sch., 1954-59; instr. home econs. Kans. State Coll., Pittsburg, 1959-63; lectr. foods, nutrition Coll. Household Arts and Scis., Tex. Woman's U., 1963-64, research asst. NASA grant, 1964-66; asso. prof. home econs. Central Mo. State U., Warrensburg, 1966-70, adviser to Colhecon, 1966-70, adviser to Alpha Sigma Alpha, 1967-70, 72, mem. bd. advisers Honors Group, 1967-70; prof., head dept. home econs. Kans. State Tchrs. Coll., Emporia, 1970-73; prof., chmn. dept. home econs. Benedictine Coll., Atchison, Kans., 1973-74; prof., chmn. dept. home econs. Baker U., Baldwin City, Kans., 1974-75; owner, operator Diet-Con Dietary Cons. Enterprises, cons. dietitian, 1973—. Mem. Joplin Little Theater, 1956-60. Mem. NEA, Mo., Kans. state tchrs. assns., AAUW, Am., Mo., Kans. dietetics assns., Am., Mo., Kans. home econs. assns., Mo. Acad. Scis., AAUP, U. Ark. Alumni Assn., Alumni Assn. Kans. State Coll. of Pittsburg, Am. Vocat. Assn., Assn. Edn. Young Children, Sigma Xi, Beta Sigma Phi, Beta Beta Beta, Alpha Sigma Alpha, Delta Kappa Gamma, Kappa Kappa Iota, Phi Upsilon Omicron. Methodist (organist). Home: Main PO Box 1009 Topeka KS 66601

VARNER, DAVID EUGENE, energy company executive, lawyer; b. Dallas, Oct. 9, 1937; s. E.C. and D. Evelyn (Bauguss) V.; m. Joan Paula Oransky, Aug. 13, 1963; children—Michael A., Kevin E., Cheryl L. B.A., So. Meth. U., Dallas, 1958, J.D., 1961. Bar: Tex. 1961, Fla. 1974, Okla., 1977, U.S. Supreme Ct. 1978. Assoc. Eldridge, Goggans, Davidson & Silverberg, Dallas, 1962-65; atty., asst. sec. Redman Industries, Inc., Dallas, 1965-66; assoc. gen. atty. Tex. Instruments, Inc., Dallas, 1966-73; sr. atty., asst. sec. Fla. Gas Co., Winter Park, 1973-76; v.p., gen. counsel, sec. Facet Enterprises, Inc., Tulsa, 1976-78, Summa Corp., Las Vegas, Nev., 1978-82; sr. v.p., gen. counsel, sec. Transco Energy Co., Houston, 1982—; dir. Transcontinental Gas Pipe Line Corp.; mem. royalty mgmt. adv. com. Minerals Mgmt. Service, Dept. Energy. Mng. editor Southwestern Law Jour., 1960-61. Mem. ABA, NAS (commn. phys. scis., math. and resources), NRC (commn. phys. scis., math. and resources), Fed. Energy Bar Assn., Houston Bar Assn., Tex. Bar Assn., Okla. Bar, Fla. Bar., Am. Soc. Corp. Secs., Nat. Assn. Corp. Dirs. Home: 13415 Perthshire Houston TX 77079 Office: Transco Energy Co 2800 Post Oak Blvd Houston TX 77056

VARNER, ROBERT BERNARD, educator, counselor; b. Ellsworth, Kans., May 31, 1930; s. Bernard Lafayette and Leota (Campbell) V.; B.S., Kans. State U., Pittsburg, 1952; M.S., U. Ark., 1959; postgrad. Mich. State U., summer 1955, U. Mo., summer 1962, (grantee) U. Kans., 1972-73; m. Charleen LaVerne McClanahan, July 4, 1953. Athletic coach, social sci. tchr. Joplin (Mo.) Sr. High Sch., 1956-63; head social sci. dept. R.L. Turner High Sch., Carrollton, Tex., 1963-66; asst. athletic coach, jr. high sch. social sci. tchr. Warrensburg, Mo., 1966-70; coach, social sci. tchr., Emporia, Kans., 1970-72; asst. cottage dir., counselor Topeka Youth Ctr., 1973—; substitute tchr. Topeka Pub. Schs., 1974—. Recreation dir. Carrollton-Farmers Branch (Tex.) Recreation Center, 1964-66; city recreation dir., Warrensburg, Mo., 1966-68. Served with USN, 1953-54. Mem. NEA, Kans. State U.-Pittsburg Alumni Assn., U. Ark. Alumni Assn., Phi Delta Kappa, Sigma Tau Gamma. Democrat. Methodist. Club: Elks. Address: Main PO Box 1009 Topeka KS 66601

VARNER, STERLING VERL, oil company executive; b. Ranger, Tex., Dec. 20, 1919; s. George Virgle and Christina Ellen (Shafer) V.; m. Paula Jean Kennedy, Nov. 17, 1945; children—Jane Ann, Richard Alan. Student, Murray State Sch. Agr., 1940, Wichita State U., 1949. With Kerr-McGee, Inc., 1941-45, Koch Industries, Inc., Wichita, Kans., 1945—; pres., chief operating officer Koch Industries, Inc., 1974-86, vice chmn., 1987—, also bd. dirs. Bd. dirs. NCCJ. Mem. Assn. Oil Pipelines, Petroleum Industry 25

Year Club (bd. govs.), Nat. Petroleum Refiners Assn. Mem. Church of Christ. Clubs: Wichita, Crestview Country. Home: 1515 Linden Ct Wichita KS 67206 Office: Koch Industries Inc PO Box 2256 Wichita KS 67201

VARRELMANN, ROBERT GALE, architect; b. Los Angeles, Aug. 5, 1947; s. Gale L. and Jane E. (Weller) V.; m. Diane Slibsager, Sept. 8, 1968; children: Erik Steven, Sheri Louise, Jason Robert. BArch, Calif. Poly., 1971. Registered architect, Calif. Draftsman/designer James Dodd & Assoc., Sacramento, 1973-74, Churchill-Zlatunich Architects, San Jose, Calif., 1974, Hawley-Stowers & Assocs., San Jose, 1975, Higgins & Root Architects, Los Gatos, Calif., 1975-76, The Griffin/Joyce Assoc., San Jose, 1976, Oscar E. Sohns Arch., Los Gatos, 1976-79; owner/prin. Varrelmann Design, San Jose, 1979—. Mem. Better Bus. Bur.; mgr. little league, 1980-83, 87-88; coach San Jose Girls Soccer, 1982-83; active Cub Scouts, 1982, 87, 88. Served to Capt., U.S. Army, 1971-73. Recipient Cert. of Appreciation Future Bus. Leaders of Am., 1982, 85, Cert. of Appreciation Seicho-No-Ie Truth of Life Ctr., San Jose, 1982. Mem. AIA, Better Bus. Bur., Valle del Sur Art Guild, Morgan Hill Art Guild (Artist of Yr. 1977). Republican. Methodist.

VARRENTI, ADAM, JR., financial executive; b. Phila., Apr. 9, 1949; s. Adam Sr. and Yolanda (Messina) V.; m. Diane Maria Squillace; children: Jocelyn, Adam III, Melissa, Andrew. BS in Acctg., Villanova U., 1971; cert. CLU, Am. Coll., 1981, cert. chartered fin. cons., 1985. Registered fin. planner. Pres. Diversified Fin. Group, West Chester, Pa., 1981—; bd. dirs. Equipment Leasing Corp. Am., Bala Cynwyd, Pa., Guthrie Landscaping Co. Inc., Elwyn, Pa. Named Man of Yr. Phila. Gen. Agts. and Mgrs. Assn., 1978. Mem. Internat. Assn. Registered Fin. Planners, Nat. Assn. Security Dealers (registered rep.), Am. Soc. CLU's, Am. Soc. Chartered Fin. Cons., Nat. Assn. Accts., Nat. Assn. Life Underwriters, Pa. Assn. Life Underwriters, Chester County Life Underwriters (pres. 1988-89), Million Dollar Round Table (1st v.p. Brandywine Pa. chpt., 1988-89, pres. 1989-90). Lodge: Lions (Brandywine, Pa. chpt.).

VASQUEZ, JESUS ANGULO, financial executive; b. San Antonio, Mar. 15, 1955; s. Jesus G. and Trinidad (Angulo) V. BBA, U. Tex., 1977. CPA, Tex. Internal auditor Harte-Hanks Communications, San Antonio, 1977-79; group controller San Diego Group, 1979-80; group controller, fin. dir. Ga. group, Carrollton, 1980-85; fin. dir. Abilene (Tex.) Reporter-News, 1985—. Mem. Nat. Assn. Accts. (pres. 1988-89), Tex. Soc. CPA's, Internat. Newspaper Fin. Execs., Abilene Jaycees (bd. dirs. 1986-87). Roman Catholic. Office: Abilene Reporter News 100 Block Cypress St Abilene TX 79601

VASSEL, TOMMIE ALONZO, accountant, educator; b. New Orleans, Dec. 2, 1956; s. Juanita (Brock) V. BA in Acctg., Dillard U., 1978. Asst. sr. acct. Deloitte Haskins & Sells CPA's, New Orleans, 1978-81; acct. cost and internal control Mobil Oil Co., New Orleans, 1981; mgr. tax and audit Montegut & Rabb, CPA's, New Orleans, 1981-83; ptnr. Vassel & Co., CPA's, New Orleans, 1983—; prof. acctg. So. U. New Orleans, 1985—. Mem. audit com. United Way, New Orleans, 1985—, allocations com. 1985—; bd. dirs. Sta. WRBH for Blind and Print Handicapped, 1987—, vol. reader; v.p. St. Augustine Ch. Parish council, 1988. Mem. Am. Inst. CPA's, Nat. Assn. Black Accts., La. Soc. CPA's (New Orleans chpt. chmn. acctg. career promotion com. 1987-88), Dillard U. Alumni Assn. (pres.). Democrat. Roman Catholic. Home: 1139 Marais St New Orleans LA 70116-2325

VASS-SKOOG, CATHY ELIZABETH, financial executive; b. Roanoke, Va., July 23, 1952; d. Dennis Shelby and Faye Myrtle (Hanks) Vass; m. Douglas Albert Skoog, Apr. 10, 1982; children: David August, Shelby Amanda. BS, U. Richmond, 1973; MBA, U. Va., 1979; postgrad., Coll. for Fin. Planning, Denver, 1984-85. Cert. fin. planner. Exec. asst. A.B. Brannock Ltd., Raleigh, N.C., 1974-76; dir. acctg., staff research and planning Commonwealth Computer Advisers, Richmond, Va., 1977; fin. analyst, supr. Celanese Corp., Charlotte, N.C., 1979-84; prin., fin. planner Winston-Salem, Charlotte, 1985—. Mem. Inst. Cert. Fin. Planners, Internat. Assn. Fin. Planners. Democrat. Methodist.

VASTINE, WILLIAM JOHN, marketing executive, consultant; b. Cin., Sept. 24, 1939; s. Gilbert Franklyn and Alma Goldie (Meyers) V.; m. Elaine Carolyn Mumper, Apr. 26, 1963; children: Konnie E., Kathe E., Scott W., Todd W. BS, Ohio State U., 1960, MS, 1963, PhD, 1966. Asst. prof. to assoc. prof. agr. econs. N.Mex. State U., Las Cruces, 1966-72; assoc. prof. Texas A&M U., College Station, 1972-79; v.p. mktg. southwest div. McLane Co., Temple, Tex., 1979-81, mgr. corp. mktg., 1981-83; exec. v.p. Rubber Roofing Co., Brownsville, Tex., 1983-84; pres. Vastine & Assocs., Arlington, Tex., 1984—; owner Group 7, Raleigh, N.C., 1984—; sr. mktg. cons. Market Max Inc., Manchester, Mass., 1987—; cons. Nat. Am. Wholesale Grocers Assn., Food Mktg. Inst., Nat. Grocery Assn., Nat. Assn. Tobacco Distbrs., Internat. Assn. Refrigerated Warehouses, McLane Co., Temple, 1984—. Author (with others) Introduction Agricultural Economics and Agricultural Business, 1971; contbr. articles to profl. jours. Pres. Martin High Sch. Soccer Boosters, Arlington, 1986-87; del. Tarrant County Rep. Com., 1986; sponsor various local charities. Mem. Food Distbn. Research Soc. (bd. dirs. 1973-76, 87—, v.p. 1973-75, pres. 1975-76), Am. Agr. Econ. Assn., Western Agr. Econ. Assn., So. Agr. Econ. Assn., Nat. Trade Orgn., Tex. Trade Orgn. Republican. Methodist. Home: 3208 Heritage Ct Arlington TX 76016 Office: William J Vastine & Assocs PO Box 170174 Arlington TX 76003

VAUGHAN, CLEFTON DURELL, oil company executive; b. McComb, Miss., July 29, 1941; s. John Alexander and Elma Virginia (Humphreys) V.; m. Mary Robertha Persons, Sept. 3, 1961; children: Clayton, Allison, Paul, Carness, Clefton. BS, U. So. Miss., 1963. With Murphy Oil Corp., El Dorado, Ark., 1963-69, London, 1969-81; sr. v.p. Murphy Eastern Oil Co., London, 1981-84; sr. v.p. Murphy Oil U.S.A., Inc., El Dorado, 1984-88, pres., 1988—, also bd. dirs. Bd. dirs. El Dorado Civitan Club, 1963-69, 1st United Meth. Ch., El Dorado, 1984-88; chmn. Am. Ch. in London, 1982. Mem. Am. Petroleum Inst., El Dorado C. of C. (bd. dirs. 1988). Club: El Dorado Golf and Country. Home: 2004 W Elm El Dorado AR 71730 Office: Murphy Oil USA Inc 200 Peach St El Dorado AR 71730

VAUGHAN, DAVID JOHN, distribution company executive; b. Detroit, July 17, 1924; s. David Evans and Erma Mildred V.; A.B., U. Ill., 1950; postgrad. U. Chgo., U. Mo.; m. Anne McKeown Miles, Aug. 21, 1975; children by previous marriage—David John, Melissa Ann, Julia Crawford McLaughlin. Chemist, Midland Electric Colleries, 1950-52; pres. Varrco Distbg. Co., Peoria, Ill., 1953—; prin. David J. Vaughan, investment adv., Peoria, 1970—; investment adviser Fundamentalist Fund; instr. Carl Sandburg Coll., Peoria, 1968—; advisor Leelanau Found., Leelanau Meml. Found. Served to lt. USAAF, 1942-46, USAF, 1951-52; Korea. Registered investment adv. Mem. Alpha Tau Omega, Phi Eta Sigma, Phi Alpha Delta. Republican. Presbyterian. Clubs: Peoria Country, Northport Point (Mich.); Peoria Skeet, Racquet, Naples (Fla.). Lodges: Masons, Shriners, Jesters. Home: 4510 N Miller Ave Peoria IL 61614 Office: 4617 N Prospect Rd Peoria Heights IL 61614

VAUGHAN, DENNIS RALSTEN, JR., lawyer; b. Charleston, W.Va., Mar. 1, 1941; s. Dennis Ralsten and Evelyn (Cooligan) V.; m. Diane Tamplin, Aug. 24, 1963; children: Lara Nicole, Shawn Dennis. AB, Morris Harvey Coll., 1963; JD, U. Cin., 1966; postgrad., U. Pitts., 1967. Bar: W.Va. Asst. atty. gen. State of W.Va., Charleston, 1967-72, spl. asst. atty. gen., 1972-82, 85—; ptnr. Watt, Kessinger, McKittrick & Vaughan, St. Albans, W.Va., 1972-75, McKittrick & Vaughan, St. Albans, 1975-84, Lovett, Vaughan & Cooper, Charleston, 1984-88, Vaughan & Withrow, Charleston, 1988—; bd. dirs. Evergreen Fed. Savs. Bank, Charleston, Citizens Nat. Bank St. Albans; pres., bd. dirs. Kanawha Title Ins. Agy., Inc., Charleston; sec./treas., Cent. Distbg. Co., Inc., Charleston; bd. dirs. Ran-Dot Devel. Co., Scott Depot, W.Va. Author: Model Code Of Ordinance for West Virginia Towns and Cities, 1977. Bd. dirs. Buckskin council Boy Scouts Am., 1978-80, W.Va. Mcpl. League Ins. Trust Fund, Charleston, 1984—. Mem. Nat. Assn. Bond Lawyers, W.Va. State Bar Assn., W.Va. Bar Assn., Kanawha County Bar Assn., Pi Gamma Mu, Edgewood Country Club, Charleston Tennis Club. Republican. Presbyterian. Home: 2 Dunlevy Rd Charleston WV 25314 Office: Vaughan & Withrow Capitol Centre 232 Capitol St Ste 200 Charleston WV 25301

VAUGHAN, ELIZABETH CROWNHART, management consultant, book editor; b. Madison, Wis., Jan. 9, 1929; d. Jesse George and Hildegarde Lucretia (Wooll) Crownhart; m. Thomas James Vaughan, June 16, 1951; children: Meagan, Margot, Stephen, Cameron. BA, U. Wis., 1950; MA, Portland State U., 1970. Script writer Wis. Pub. Broadcasting, Madison, 1950-52; women's program dir. KEX Westinghouse Broadcasting, Portland, Oreg., 1954-56; sec., treas. Salar Enterprises, Ltd., Portland, 1968-86, pres., 1987—; bd. dirs. First Interstate Bank of Oreg., Portland, mem. exec. com., 1987—, chmn. audit and examining, 1983—; bd. dirs. Nordstrom, Inc., Seattle, chmn. compensation com., 1977—. Translator, editor: Explorations of Kamchatka, 1972, Colonial Russian America, 1976, End of Russian America, 1979, Russia's Conquest of Siberia and the North Pacific, 3 vols., 1984-88; contbr. articles to profl. jours. With Russian desk Oreg. Hist. Soc., Portland, 1972-78, fgn. archives coord., 1978—; bd. dirs. Oreg. Ind. Coll. Found., Portland, 1983—, Chamber Music Northwest, Portland, 1983-85; exec. dir. N. Pacific Studies Ctr., Oreg. Hist. Soc., 1988—. Recipient Aubrey Watzek award Lewis and Clark Coll., 1975. Fellow Royal Geog. Soc. London; mem. Capital Funds Com., Oreg. Pub. Broadcasting, Am. Assn. Advancement of Slavic Studies, Western Slavic Assn., No. Am. Falconry Assn., Am. Com. on East-West Accord, Phi Kappa Phi, Town Club, Univ. Club. Clubs: Town, University (Portland). Office: 1230 SW Park Ave Portland OR 97205

VAUGHAN, HERBERT WILEY, lawyer; b. Brookline, Mass, June 1, 1920; s. David D. and Elzie G. (Wiley) V.; m. Ann Graustein, June 28, 1941. Student U. Chgo., 1937-38; SB cum laude, Harvard U., 1941, LLB, 1948. Bar: Mass. 1948. Assoc. Hale and Dorr, Boston, 1948-54, jr. ptnr., 1954-56, sr. ptnr., 1956-82, co-mng. ptnr., 1976-80; pres. Herbert W. Vaughan, P.C., sr. ptnr. Hale and Dorr, 1982—. Fellow Am. Bar Found. (life); mem. Am. Law Inst., Am. Coll. Mortgage Attys., Am. Coll. Real Estate Attys., ABA, Mass. Bar Assn., Boston Bar Assn., Internat. Bar Assn.; chmn. The Trustees of Reservations; mem. bd. trustees, Am. Friends of New Coll. (Oxford Univ.); Clubs: Bay, Badminton and Tennis, Union (Boston), Boston Econ.; Longwood Cricket (Brookline, Mass.).

VAUGHAN, MICHAEL J., trust company executive; b. New York, Jan. 26, 1942; s. Michael J. and Florence Vaughan; m. Sherree R., June 26, 1965; children: Gary R., Andrew M. AA, Santa Ana Coll., 1962; BA in Psychology, Calif. State U., Fullerton, 1964; postgrad., U. So. Calif., 1966-67; M in Banking Trust, U. Wash., 1973. Lic. real estate, Calif. V.p. Union Bank, Los Angeles, 1965-74, Lloyds Bank, Santa Ana, Calif., 1974-79; pres. M.J. Vaughan & Co. Inc., Santa Ana, 1979-83; sr. v.p. Valencia Bank, Newport Beach, Calif., 1983-85; thesis reviewer Pacific Coast Banking Sch., Seattle, 1973-77. Mem. Orange County Estate Planning Council, Orange County Trust Officers Assn., Internat. Assn. Fin. Planners, Internat. Found. of Employee Benefit Plans, Western Pension Conf., Am. Soc. of Pension Actuaries, U. So. Calif. Alumni. Republican. Lutheran. Clubs: Hoag Hosp. 552, Pacific (Newport Beach), Los Angeles City, USC-Cardinal & Gold, USC-The Com. Home: 2317 N Linwood Santa Ana CA 92701 Office: Imperial Trust Co 201 N Figueroa St Suite 610 Los Angeles CA 90012

VAUGHAN, OLIVE ELIZABETH, marketing and industrial specialist, educator; b. Bridgeport, Conn., Oct. 23, 1925; d. Joseph Jackson and Olive Elizabeth (Sears) V. BA, Mt. Holyoke Coll., 1947, MA, 1949; PhD in Econs., Columbia U., 1973. Price economist U.S. Bur. Labor Stats., N.Y.C., 1949-50; econ. researcher, chief price sect. The Conf. Bd., N.Y.C., 1951-58; research analyst Gen. Electric Co., N.Y.C., 1958-66; asst. prof. C.W. Post Coll., Greenvale, N.Y., 1967-73, Fordham U., Bronx, N.Y., 1973-76; staff specialist, planning So. New Eng. Telephone, New Haven, Conn., 1977—; planning cons. Gen. Electric Co. N.Y.C., 1973-74. Contbr. articles to bus. publs. Mem. Nat. Assn. Bus. Economists, Am. Econ. Assn., Am. Mktg. Assn., Am. Statis. Assn. Office: S New Eng Telephone 195 Church St 5th Fl New Haven CT 06506

VAUGHAN, RICHARD ALLEN, life insurance underwriter; b. Sherman, Tex., July 18, 1946; s. John W. and Margaret Ann (Fires) V.; m. Terence Hall Thompson, Jan. 12, 1968; children—Shannon, Elizabeth, Todd. Student U. Tex., 1964-68; BBA North Tex. State U., 1969. CLU. Mgr., Vaughan Dept. Stores, Sherman, 1968-73; assoc. Fallon Co., Sherman, 1973-76; sr. assoc. Fallon & Vaughan, CLUs, Sherman, 1976-87, A.G. Edwards & Sons Inc., 1987—; founder, dir. Consol. Printing, Inc.; instr. Life Underwriter Tng. Council, Washington. Bd. dirs. Grayson County (Tex.) chpt. Am. Cancer Soc., 1973-77, pres., 1976-77; bd. dirs. Salvation Army, 1975-77; mem. Sherman City Council, 1977-79. Qualifying and life named Agt. of Yr., Indpls. Life Ins. Co., 1975. Mem. Am. Soc. CLUs, Nat. Assn. Life Underwriters, Life Underwriters Assn. (bd. dirs.), Tex. Assn. Life Underwriters, Assn. for Advanced Life Underwriting, Mensa, Intertel, Greater Sherman C. of C. (bd dirs. 1985-88), Sigma Alpha Epsilon. Baptist. Office: AG Edwards & Sons Inc PO Box 3104 Sherman TX 75090

VAUGHAN, ROBERT TIMOTHY, real estate broker; b. West Palm Beach, Fla., Jan. 13, 1956; s. Richard Stetson and Katherine (Johnson) V.; m. Emily McFadden Evarts, Oct. 8, 1983; children: Maxwell Evarts, Katherine Danielle. Property mgr. Moana Corp., Park City, Utah, 1977-79; constrn. finisher John Price Group, Park City, 1979-81; real estate broker Mansell & Assocs., Park City, 1981-84; securities and real estate broker Coleman Land & Investment Co., Park City, 1984-85; comml. real estate broker Coldwell Banker, Torrance, Calif., 1985—. Chmn. Park City 4th July Parade and Picnic, 1983, Park City Ann. Winter Carnival, 1984; v.p. Park City Men's Coalition, 1984. Mem. Assn. Indsl. Realtors, Toastmasters. Republican. Office: Coldwell Banker 950 W 190th St Ste 100 Torrance CA 90502

VAUGHAN, TIMOTHY MICHAEL, oil production company executive; b. Woodward, Okla., Dec. 6, 1946; s. Donald Delroy and Boydine Duer (Quiring) V.; B.S. in Bus. Adminstrn., U. Kans., 1968, M.S. in Acctg., 1971; m. Susan Kay Addis, Sept. 14, 1974 (div. 1984); 1 child, Icer. Mem. staff Deere & Co., Moline, Ill., 1967-69; staff acct. Farrow, Stone & Blubaugh C.P.A.s, Wichita, Kans., 1971-75; controller Addis Oil Ops., Wichita, 1975-82, gen. mgr., 1982-87 ; controller Barco Supply Co., Wichita 1975-82, gen. mgr. 1982-87 , pres., Wolland, Inc., Wichita, 1986—. ptnr. Pishny Vaughan & Durler, Wichita, 1988—. Treas., bd. dirs. Starkey Devel. Center for Retarded, Inc. 1974-75; treas., bd. dirs. Heritage Homeowners Assn., Inc., 1986—; instr.Webster U., 1989—. v.p. Episcopal Young Churchmen. C.P.A. Kans. Mem. Am. Inst. C.P.A.s, Kans. Soc. C.P.A.s, Petroleum Accts. Soc. Kans., Phi Kappa Psi. Republican. Clubs: Wichita Country, Porsche of Am., Sports Car Am. Office: PO Box 8198 Wichita KS 67208

VAUGHAN, WALTER JAMES, hunting preserves owner; b. Thomasville, Ga., July 11, 1940; s. Walter James and Sarah Virginia (Maybin) V.; m. Miriam Helen Chastain, Feb. 5, 1973 (div.); children: Gregory, Alice Paige; m. Mary Elizabeth Franklin, Dec. 5, 1976; children: Catherine, Jon Allen. Student, Middle Ga. Coll., 1958-59, Valdosta St, 1959. Pres. Vaughans Sporting Goods, Inc., Thomasville, Ga., 1959-67, Outdoor Svcs., Thomasville, 1967-70, Southeastern Maintenance, Thomasville, 1970-86, Foxfire Hunting Preserve, Inc., Thomasville, 1986—; cons. Hunting & Wildlife Industry, 1986—; speaker wildlife mgmt., 1987—. Dir. Thomasville Youth Ctr., 1961-63, Deep South Fair Assn., Thomasville, 1963-65. Mem. Wildlife Harvest Assn., Thomasville Retail Merchants Assn. (pres.), Thomasville Exchange Club, Thomasville C. of C. Republican. Methodist. Home: Rt 1 Box 101 Boston GA 31626 Office: Foxfire Hunting Preserve PO Box 26 Thomasville GA 31799

VAUGHAN, WAYLAND EDWARD, marketing educator; b. Boston, July 18, 1934; s. Wayland Farries and Clara (Colton) V.; m. Barbara Ann Badoian, Apr. 26, 1959; children: Wayland Edward, Richard Martin, Robert Peter, John Michael. BA, Brown U., 1955; MBA, Rutgers U., 1969; postgrad., Kent State U., 1977—. Midwest sales rep. Nashua (N.H.) Corp., 1957-59; eastern sales and mktg mgr. Daniels Mfg. Co., Rhinelander, Wis., 1959-69; regional sales mgr. Metal Edge Industries, Barrington, N.J., 1969-71; owner, pres. Village Ice Cream Shoppe, Edinboro, Pa., 1971-84; asst. prof. Westminster Coll., New Wilmington, Pa., 1978-79; adj. assoc. prof. Alliance Coll., Cambridge Springs, Pa., 1984-86; asst. prof. Slippery Rock (Pa.) U., 1979—; instr. Edinboro U., 1974-76, Kent State U., Ohio, 1977-78; mktg. cons. Ctr. Econ. and Community Devel., Slippery Rock, 1987-88; research supr. Slippery Rock U. Grad. Sch., 1986-88. Reviewer manuscripts Merrill Pub. Co., Columbus, Ohio, 1987; contbr. articles to profl. jours. Youth hockey coach Princeton, N.J., Crawford County, Meadville, Pa., 1965-84; ice hockey coach Slippery Rock U., 1979—. Mem. Am. Mktg. Assn. (Outstanding Service award 1987), East Econ. Assn., Am. Hockey Coaches Assn., Delta Upsilon. Republican. Baptist. Lodge: Lions(treas. 1974-76). Home: 117 S Skytop Dr Edinboro PA 16412 Office: Slippery Rock U 313 G Eisenberg St Slippery Rock PA 16057

VAUGHAN-RICHARDS, ALAN, architect; b. Maidenhead, England, May 10, 1925; s. Arthur and Elizabeth Grace (Hamer) Richards; m. Gladys Ayo Vaughan, Apr. 2, 1959; children: Elizabeth Remi, Arthur Deinde, Vanessa Apinke, Kenneth Olufemi. Diploma in Arch., Poly. London, 1950; Diploma in Tropical Arch., Archtl. Assn. London, 1955. Architect Iraq Devel. Bd., Baghdad, 1952-54; assoc. Architects Co.-Partnership, Lagos & London, 1955-61; prin. Alan Vaughan-Richards Architects, Lagos, Nigeria, 1961-71; dir. Ibru, Vaughan-Richards & Assocs., Lagos, 1971—; external examiner Ahmadu Bello Univ., Zaria, Nigeria, supr. Univ. Lagos Arch. Dept.; dir. Alagbon Gallery of Fine Art. Co-author: Building Lagos, 1977; editor: W.A. Builder & Architect, 1969; contbr. articles to profl. jours.; master planner U. Benin, U. Lagos Akoka and Abeokuta campuses; designer sci. faculty complex Sports Centre and Senor Staff Residences Univ. Benin, Benin Teaching Hosp., Accident Centre Gen. Practice Clinic and residences, temp campus Idi-Araba, vice-chancellor's lodge and professorial residences Law Faculty Complex, student hostels and Sports Centre Univ. Lagos, Bendel State Govt. Secretariate Benin City, Murtala Muhammed Civic Centre, TV Prodn. Centre, offices, factories, residences. Fellow Royal Inst. Brit. Architects; mem. Nigerian Inst. Architects, Lagos Hist. Monuments Preservation Com. Avocations: swimming; reading; writing; carpentry. Home: 12 James George St, PO Box 2458, Lagos Nigeria Office: Ibru Vaughan-Richards & Assocs, 225 Apapa Rd PO Box 2458, Lagos Nigeria

VAUGHN, DONALD CHARLES, international engineering and construction company executive; b. McPherson, Kans., Mar. 21, 1936; s. Vernon (dec.) and Ramona Vaughn; m. Moira Lynch Provan; children: James, Sandra Vaughn Cornwell, Connie Vaughn Ohman. BSCE, Va. Poly. Inst., 1958. Registered profl. engr., Tex. Field engr. The M.W. Kellogg Co., Houston, 1958-59, from constrn. supt. to pres., 1961-83; pres. The M.W. Kellog Co., Houston, 1983—; exec. v.p. ops. Rust Internat. Corp., Birmingham, Ala., 1982-83; pres. M.W. Kellogg Constructors, Inc., Houston, 1980-82; chmn. adv. com. Eximbank, Export-Import Bank of the U.S. Mem. Cultural Arts Coun. of Houston, Va. Poly. Inst. Com. for Excellence. Mem. Tex. Engring. Soc., Turkish-U.S. Bus. Coun. (former chmn.), India-U.S. Bus. Coun., Greater Houston C. of C. (sr. rep.), Tex. Research League (sr. rep.), U.S. C. of C. (internat. policy com.), 25 Yr. Club Petroleum Industry, Houston World Trade Assn., Nat. Constructors Assn. (past mem. adv. bd., chmn., vice chmn.), Chi Epsilon. Clubs: Houston City, Va. Polytech 100. Office: M W Kellogg Co 3 Greenway Pla E Houston TX 77046-0395

VAUGHN, FRANK EDWARD, JR., corporate executive; b. Phila., May 20, 1929; s. Frank Edward and Sarah Marie (Heller) V.; m. Nancy Gale Boebel, Aug. 1, 1953 (dec. 1975); children: Susan Vaughn Weir, Elizabeth A., Jennifer L.; m. Carol Lynne Krider, May 21, 1983. BA in Econs., U. Pa., 1951; MBA, Ind. U., 1956. Mgr. indsl. relations and personnel The Hoover Co., North Canton, Ohio, 1967-72, v.p. adminstrv. services, 1972-83, sr. v.p. U.S. ops., 1983-86, sr. v.p., 1986-88; exec. v.p. Hoover Worldwide Corp., North Canton, 1986-88; chmn. Rowenta-Werke GmbH, Offenbach, Fed. Republic Germany, 1986—, Hoover plc, London, 1987—; exec. v.p. and pres. appliance group Chgo. Pacific Corp., Chgo., 1988—; bd. dirs. Hoover Can. Inc., Burlington, Ont., Hoover Mexicana S.A. de C.V., Mexico City, Juver Indsl. S.A. de C.V., Juarez, Mex. Mem. Stark County (Ohio) Bluecoats, 1988—; trustee Aultman Hosp., Canton, 1988—, Canton Art Inst. 1987. Mem. Univ. Club Chgo., Congress Lake Country Club. Republican. Lutheran. Office: Chgo Pacific Corp 55 E Monroe St 30th Fl Chicago IL 60603

VAUGHN, JOHN VERNON, banker, industrialist; b. Grand Junction, Colo., June 24, 1909; s. John S. and Alice Ann (Baylis) V.; m. Dorothy May Pickrell, Oct. 12, 1934; children: Dorothy (Mrs. Richard H. Stone), John Spencer. A.B., UCLA, 1932. Br. mgr. Nat. Lead Co., 1932-37; sales mgr. Sillers Paint & Varnish Co., 1937-46, pres., gen. mgr., dir., 1946-58; pres., chmn. Dartell Labs., Inc., 1959-70; vice chmn. bd. Crocker Nat. Bank and Crocker Nat. Corp., San Francisco, 1970-75; dir. Crocker Nat. Bank and Crocker Nat. Corp., 1969-85; hon. dir. Crocker Nat. Bank; cons. Coopers & Lybrand, 1975-85; chmn. bd. Recon Optical, Inc.; dir. Trust Services Am., Forest Lawn Corp., Am. Security & Fidelity Corp.; IT Corp. Chmn. San Marino Recreation Commn., 1956-58, La. Better Bus. Bur., 1959-61, Invest-in-Am., 1970-73; chmn. citizen's adv. Council Pub. Transp., 1965-67; commr. Los Angeles Coliseum Commn., 1971-74; trustee Calif. Mus. Found., 1968-79; bd. dirs. Orthopaedic Hosp., 1965-87, pres., 1974-78, chmn. bd., 1978-79; bd. dirs. YMCA, Los Angeles, 1965-77, Central City Assn., So. Calif. Visitors Council, 1970-76, NCCJ, Calif. Museum Sci. and Industry, United Way of Los Angeles, Am. Heart Assn.; mem. Los Angeles Adv. Bd., Friends of Claremont Coll., 1973-78, Los Angeles Beautiful, 1972-74; regent U. Calif., 1958-59; hon. trustee UCLA Found., 1967—, Forest Lawn Meml. Park, 1968—, Claremont Men's Coll., 1970-71, Pepperdine U., 1972—; regent, mem. bd. visitors Grad. Sch. Bus. Adminstrn. UCLA, 1971-85; mem. Chancellor's Assocs., Calif. State Univs. and Colls. Recipient Distinguished Service award U. Calif. at Los Angeles, 1965; Outstanding Community Service award, 1970; Alumnus of Year award, 1971; Brotherhood award NCCJ, 1971; Los Angeles Jaycees award merit, 1972; Most Distinguished Citizen Los Angeles Realty Bd., 1972; other honors. Mem. Los Angeles Area C. of C. (bd. dirs. 1961, pres. 1969, chmn. 1970), World Affairs Council (chpt. v.p., treas. 1970-85, hon. dir. 1985—), Iranian-Am. Chamber Industry and Commerce (pres. 1971-79), Paint, Varnish and Lacquer Assn. (past nat. v.p., past chpt. pres.), Town Hall Calif. (dir. 1973-75), Young Pres.'s Orgn., Beta Theta Pi (pres. 1960). Presbyn. Clubs: Mason, Jonathan (pres. 1964), Los Angeles Country, California, Los Angeles (dir. 1979-85); San Gabriel (Calif.); Country (dir. 1964-68); Pasadena Athletic. Lodge: Internat. Order St. Hubertus. Home: 454 S Orange Grove Blvd Pasadena CA 91105 Office: 225 S Lake Ave Pasadena CA 91101

VAUGHN, MARY PATRICIA, financial planner; b. N.Y.C., Aug. 22, 1961; d. James Augustin and Mary Ellen (Burns) Oakes; m. Bruce David Vaughn, Sept. 19, 1987. BS, Marymount Coll. of Va., 1983. Cert. fin. planner. Fin. casewriter McLean (Va.) Fin. Group, 1983-84; dept. mgr., v.p. McLean Fin. Planning Corp., 1984—. Mem. Internat. Assn. Fin. Planners, Internat. Assn. Cert. Fin. Planners. Republican. Roman Catholic. Home: 1809 Olney Rd Falls Church VA 22043 Office: McLean Fin Planning Corp 1313 Dolley Madison Blvd Ste 304 McLean VA 22101

VAUPEN, BURTON, film industry executive; b. N.Y.C., Apr. 28, 1930; s. Alex and Betty (Stimell) V.; m. Frederika Manios, 1971; children: Robert, Susan, Pamela, Jill; 1 stepson, Paul. B.S., Columbia U., 1952; M.A., Columbia Tchrs. Coll., 1954. Asst. dir. NBC, N.Y.C., 1953-54; researcher Benton & Bowles Advt., N.Y.C., 1954-56; with Young & Rubicam Inc., 1956—; mgr. adminstrn. Young & Rubicam Inc., San Francisco, 1958-69; sr. v.p., dir. domestic bus. affairs Young & Rubicam Inc., N.Y.C., 1969-79; sr. v.p., treas. Young & Rubicam Inc., 1979-80; sr. v.p. fin. and adminstrn. Y&R Affiliates, Inc. div., 1979-80; corp. sr. v.p., sec. dir. Young & Rubicam Australia Pty. Ltd., 1980-82; exec. v.p., chief fin. officer, sec., treas Young & Rubicam/Dentsu Inc., 1982-85; exec. v.p., chief fin. and adminstrv. officer Kenyon & Eckhardt, Inc., 1985-86; sr. v.p. adminstrn. Lorimar Telepictures, Inc., 1986—. Mem. Fin. Execs. Inst. Home: Beverly Hills CA 90212 also: Saddle River NJ 07458 Office: Lorimar Telepictures Corp 10202 W Washington Blvd Culver City CA 90232

VAZQUEZ, FRANK, software company executive; b. N.Y.C., Aug. 29, 1940; s. Frank and Carlota (Rodriguez) V.; m. Lillian C. Marini, Feb. 17, 1960; children: Frank R., Sandra A. BS, Columbia U., 1960-64. Corp. cons. ITT, Mexico City, 1968-71; dir. ops. Levi Strauss Mexico, Mexico City, 1971-76; dir. sales Coopervision Pharms., San German, P.R., 1976-80; cons. Booz, Allen, Hamilton, N.Y.C., 1980-82; v.p., gen. mgr. TeleSales Tech., Houston, 1982-84; v.p. Trinity Computing Co., Houston, 1984—. Bd. dirs. Jr. Achievement, Mayaguez, P.R., 1977-79. Office: Trinity Computing Systems Inc 11 Greenway Plaza Suite 1212 Houston TX 77046

VAZQUEZ, RENE, marketing executive; b. San German, P.R., July 19, 1934; s. Enrique and Maria (Valle) V.; m. Elsie Long, Mar. 10, 1956; 1 child, Jared Andrew. Student, Gilead Missionary Coll., 1957-58. Ordained to ministry Gilead Missionary Coll. Religious educator Watchtower Bible and Tract Soc., N.Y.C., 1957-69; export agt. Paper Corp. U.S., N.Y.C., 1969-71; pres. REJ Enterprises, N.Y.C., 1972—; master coordinator sales Shaklee Corp., N.Y.C., 1987—. Editor: Nutrition Counselor Letter. Mem. Nutritionists Inst. Am. Republican. Home: 25-61 90th St East Elmhurst NY 11369 Office: REJ Enterprises 67 08A Roosevelt Ave Suite 201 Woodside NY 11377

VEBLEN, THOMAS CLAYTON, management consultant; b. Hallock, Minn., Dec. 17, 1929; s. Edgar R. and Hattie (Lundgren) V.; m. Susan Alma Beaver, Sept. 1, 1950 (div. 1971); children: Kari Christen, Erik Rodli, Mark Andrew, Sara Catherine; m. Linda Joyce Eaton, Aug. 30, 1975; 1 child, Kristen Kirby. Student, U. Calif., Santa Barbara, 1950-51; BS, Cal. Poly. U., 1953; MS, Oreg. State U., 1955. Corp. v.p. Cargill, Inc., Wayzata, Minn., 1955-75; spl. asst. Sec. Interior, Washington, 1965; dir. food, agriculture SRI Internat., Menlo Park, Calif., 1975-80; pres. Food System Assocs., Inc., Washington, 1980—, also bd. dirs.; Mem. CMC Inst. Mgmt. Cons., 1988—. Author: The U.S. Food System, 1978; editor Food System Update, 1986—. Treas., bd. dirs. White House Fellows Assn., Washington, 1985; chmn., trustee Freedom from Hunger Found., Davis, Calif., 1986-89; bd. dirs. Patterson Sch., U. Ky., Lexington, 1986—, Internat. Devel. Conf., 1986—. Recipient Presdl. Appointment White House Fellows Commn., Washington, 1965, Disting. Alumnus award Calif. Poly. U., San Luis Obispo, 1977. Mem. Inst. Food Technologists, The Nature Conservancy. Episcopalian. Office: Food System Assocs Inc 1054 31st St NW Washington DC 20007

VECCI, RAYMOND JOSEPH, airline executive; b. N.Y.C., Jan. 22, 1943; s. Romeo John and Mary (Fabretti) V.; m. Helen Cecelia Clampett, Sept. 3, 1967; children: Brian John, Damon Jay. BBA, CCNY, 1965; MBA, NYU, 1967. Adminstrv. asst. Internat. Air Transport Assn., N.Y.C., 1961-66; econ. analyst United Airlines, Chgo., 1967-74; asst. v.p. planning and regulatory affairs Alaska Airlines Inc., Seattle, 1975-76, staff v.p. planning and regulatory affairs, 1976-79, staff v.p. planning, 1979, v.p. planning, 1979-85, exec. v.p., chief operating officer, 1986—. Served with U.S. Army, 1968-69, Vietnam. Decorated Bronze Star. Roman Catholic. Office: Alaska Airlines Inc 19300 Pacific Hwy S Seattle WA 98188 *

VECELLIO, LEO ARTHUR, JR., construction company executive; b. Beckley, W.Va., Oct. 26, 1946; s. Leo Arthur and Evelyn (Pais) V.; m. Kathryn Grace Cottrill, Nov. 29, 1975; children: Christopher Scott, Michael Andrew. BCE, Va. Poly. Inst. and State U., 1968; MCE, Ga. Inst. Tech., 1969. Sr. v.p. Vecellio & Grogan, Inc., Beckley, 1973—; pres. Vecellio Contracting Corp. and subs., West Palm Beach, Fla., 1982—; bd. dirs. Gulf Nat. Bank, Sophia, W.Va., Raleigh County Nat. Bank, Beckley. Chmn. bd. dirs., mem. Econ. Council of Palm Beach County, Fla., 1985—, chmn.-elect 1987, chmn., 1989; gov. Northwood Inst., West Palm Beach, 1985—; organizer, trustee Beckley Area Found., 1985; v.p., trustee Vecellio Family Found., Beckley, 1972—; mem. Mini-Grace Commn., Fla. Coun. of 100, 1989—; commn. dir., v.p. Criminal Justice Commn. Served as capt. USAF, 1969-73. Republican. Roman Catholic. Clubs: Mayacoo Lakes Country (West Palm Beach), Adios Golf (Coconut Creek, Fla.), Jupiter Hills (Fla.), Lost Tree. Home: 771 Village Rd North Palm Beach FL 33408 Office: Vecellio Contracting Corp PO Box 15065 West Palm Beach FL 33416

VED, CHANDRAKANT, computer consulting company executive; b. Bombay, Dec. 5, 1943; came to U.S., 1967; s. Mulji Manilal and Godavari V.; m. Shobha, Dec. 16, 1972; children: Gunj, Nipa, Reena. BMetE, U. Poona, India, 1966; BSME, Wash. State U., 1969; cert. in data processing, Loop Jr. Coll., Chgo., 1974; MBA, Roosevelt U., Chgo., 1979. Systems programmer REA Express, Chgo., 1972-75; data base adminstr. Montgomery Ward, Chgo., 1975-77; project mgr. Consumer Systems Services Group, Oak Brook, Ill., 1977-81; sr. cons., site mgr. Applied Info. Devel., Oak Brook, 1981-84; sr. cons. Knauer Cons., San Francisco, 1984-85; owner, prin. Lily Computer Cons., Rowland Hts., Calif., 1985—. Office: Lily Computer Cons 19314 E Oakview Ln Rowland Heights CA 91748

VEITCH, BOYER LEWIS, printing company executive; b. Phila., Oct. 20, 1930; s. Samuel Lewis and Agnes May (Bell) V.; A.B., Lafayette Coll., 1953; postgrad. Wharton Evening Sch. Acctg. and Fin., U. Pa., 1957-59; m. Emmeline Barbara Smith, Nov. 22, 1952; children—William S., Nancy B., Thomas C. Advt. dir. Ware Bros. Co., Phila., 1956-62, v.p., 1962-69; salesman Zabel Bros. Co., Phila., 1969-75; chmn., pres. Veitch Printing Corp., Lancaster, Pa., 1975—. Trustee Lafayette Coll., Easton, Pa., 1981-86, 87—; vice chmn. coll. relations com., chmn. ann. fund, 1982-86, mem. fin. com., 1987—; bd. dirs., 1st v.p. Boys' and Girl's Club, Lancaster, 1980—; dir.Boy's Club Lancaster Found., Gt. Valley Civic Assn., 1969-79; trustee Fulton Opera House Found., 1985—, treas., 1985—; chmn. citizens for Schulze Com., Pa. 5th Congressional Dist., 1972-78; vestryman, sr. Warden St. Peter's Ch. of Gt. Valley, 1972-78. Served with CIC, U.S. Army, 1954-56. Recipient Bronze Hope Chest award Nat. Multiple Sclerosis Soc., 1982. Mem. Printing Industries Am., Graphic Arts Assn. (dir. 1980—, 1st vice chmn. 1986—), Susquehanna Litho Club (dir. 1976-80, pres. 1979-80), Lancaster Assn. Commerce and Industry, Aircraft Owners and Pilots Assn., SAR, Lafayette Coll. Alumni Assn. (dir. 1974-78, pres. 1978-80), NAM, Pa. Economy League, Nat. Fedn. Ind. Bus., Phi Kappa Psi (past pres. and dir. chpt. alumni assn.). Republican. Episcopalian. Lodge: Rotary. Clubs: Hamilton, Wash Day, Lancaster Country, Dawtaw Country, Avalon Yacht, Lancaster Aero. Home: 264 Little Creek Rd Lancaster PA 17601 also: 65 E 17th St Avalon NJ 08202 Office: Veitch Printing Corp 1740 Hempstead Rd Lancaster PA 17601

VEITH, ROBERT JOSEPH, insurance consultant, financial planner; b. Norfolk, Va., Mar. 3, 1955; s. Arthur Paul and Lita (Panella) V.; m. Susan L. Felton, June 30, 1979 (div. Jan. 1984); 1 child, Adam F. AAS in Mgmt., Tidewater Community Coll., 1975; BS in Fin., St. Leo (Fla.) Coll., 1978. Co-owner Veith & Spindel Assocs., Virginia Beach, Va., 1978—. Bd. dirs. Tidewater Rape Info. Services, Norfolk, 1982-84, Am. Lung Assn., Norfolk, 1985-86. Mem. Internat. Assn. Registered Fin. Planners, Nat. Assn. Life Underwriters, Internat. Assn. Fin. Planners (named to Million Dollar Round Table, Nat. Quality award, Health Ins. Quality award), Kiwanis (bd. dirs. 1984—, Internat. Fellow award 1984, George F. Hixson award 1985, Disting. Pres. award 1987). Roman Catholic. Office: Veith & Spindel Assocs 397 Little Neck Rd Ste 222 Virginia Beach VA 23452

VELARDE, ROBERT M., nursing, hospital administrator, educator; b. Tampa, Fla., Oct. 28, 1950; s. Jesus Manuel and Angela (Velasco) V. AS in Nursing, Hillsborough Community Coll., Tampa, 1972; BS in Nursing, Samford U., 1975; M.Pub.Adminstrn., Golden Gate U., 1980. RN, Fla., Ala.; cert. in nursing adminstrn. advanced Am. Nurses Assn.; cert. surg. technologist Assn. Surg. Technologists. Surg. technologist attendant Centro Espanol Hosp., Tampa, 1965-72, nursing supr., 1972-74, asst. adminstr. patient services, 1975-85, adminstr., chief exec. officer, 1985-87; charge nurse emergency room Brookwood Med. Ctr., Birmingham, Ala., 1974-75; health occupations instr. Armwood High Sch., Seffner, Fla., 1988—; mem. blue ribbon task force to Fla. Bd. Nursing, 1982-83; mem. adv. bd. Fla. Nursing News. Active Tampa ARC. Recipient award from bd. dirs. Centro Espanol Hosp., 1977; Contbns. to Nursing award Minority Nurses Assn., 1979. Mem. Hillsborough County Vocat. Assn., Nursing Educators Assn. Tampa, Health Occupations Students Am., Am. Orgn. Nurse Execs., Tampa Bay Orgn. Nurse Execs., Am. Nurses Assn., Fla. Nurses Assn., Nurses House, Inc., Sigma Theta Tau (chpt. v.p. 1983-84). Democrat. Methodist. Home: 2618 W Saint John St Tampa FL 33607

VELLA, RUTH ANN, real estate executive; b. West Chester, Pa., Aug. 18, 1942; d. Eric and Carmella Tanberg; children: Michele Francette Vella, Nicole Renae Vella. Grad., Realtor's Inst. Real estate sales assoc. Reeve Realty, Wilmington, Del., 1966-72; owner, realtor Heritage Realty, Wilmington, 1972—; instr. sales Wilmington Coll., 1978-85; mem. faculty Del. State Coll., 1979—; instr. Realtor's Inst., dean, 1983; asst. dean, 1983—. Speaker at seminars on Non Verbal Sales Strategies, Retaining Training and Managing Real Estate Agents, LIstings, Making Housing Decisions, Coping with Business and Personal Stress, The Professional Woman, Closing Techniques, Co-Broker Etiquette. Mem. New Castle County Bd. Realtors (dir. 1983-86, edn. com.), Womens Coun. Realtors (past state pres., gov.), Nat. Assn. Realtors (nat. speaker, energy conservation instr., Cert. Real Estate Broker instr.), Ind. Fee Appraisers Assn., Newark Profl. Womens Assn., Del. Assn. Realtors (edn. com. 1986—), Realtor's Mktg. Inst. (various coms., instr. leadership, mgmt. courses). Roman Catholic. Office: Heritage Realty Inc 4631 Ogletown-Stanton Rd Ste 500E Newark DE 19713

VELSINK, WILLEM BERNHARD, electronics company executive; b. The Netherlands, 1938; came to U.S., 1961; m. Evelyn Velsink. BSEE, Hogere Tech. Sch., 1962. Engr. Tektronix Inc., Beaverton, Oreg., 1962-70, mgr. engring., 1970-72, v.p. labs., 1972-80, v.p. tech. group, 1980-82, group v.p. instruments and tech., 1982-84, exec. v.p., 1984-88; v.p. Microwave Group, Beaverton, Oreg., 1988—. Office: Tektronix Inc PO Box 500 Beaverton OR 97077

VENDITTO, JAMES JOSEPH, chemical engineer; b. Dobbs Ferry, N.Y., Nov. 13, 1951; s. Vincenzio Rocco and Maria Nichola (Cassetti) V.; children: Vincent James, Joseph Ryan. BSChemE, U. Okla., 1973. Registered profl. engr., Tex. Engr.-in-tng., Victoria, Tex., 1973-74; field engr. Halliburton Services, Alice, Tex., 1974-75, dist. engr., Mission, Tex., 1975-77, regional svc. sales engr., New Orleans, 1977-80, asst. div. engr., Corpus Christi, Tex., 1980-83, supt. stimulation dept., 1983, div. engr., 1983-88, rsch. engring. advisor, 1988—; cons. in field; researcher high temperature fracturing fluids, chem. stimulation S. Tex. sandstones. Devel. new API cementing temperatures and new refracturing tech. for oil and gas industry; contbr. articles to profl. jours. Active United Way; coach Little League and soccer. Mem. Am. Inst. Chem. Engrs., Soc. Petroleum Engrs., AIME, Am. Petroleum Inst., Internat. Platform Assn., Nat. Soc. Profl. Engrs., Tex. Soc. Profl. Engrs., Pharoh Country Club, KC. Republican. Roman Catholic. Home: 421 S 27th Apt E3 Duncan OK 73533 Office: PO Box 1431 Duncan OK 73536-0420

VENIT, WILLIAM BENNETT, electrical products company executive, consultant; b. Chgo., May 28, 1931; s. George Bernard and Ida (Schaffel) V.; m. Nancy Jean Carlson, Jan. 28, 1956; children: Steven Louis, Aprilann. Student U. Ill., Champaign, 1949. Sales mgr. Coronet, Inc., Chgo., 1952-63, pres., chmn. bd. dirs., 1963-74; pres., chmn. bd. dirs. Roma Wire Inc., Chgo., 1971-74; chmn. bd. dirs. Swing Time #2, 1988—; pres. Wm. Allen Inc., Chgo., 1972-74, Wraprama Inc., 1989—; pres., chmn. bd. dirs. William Lamp Co., Inc., William Wire Co., Inc., 1974-76; chmn. bd. dirs. MSWV, Inc., 1981—, pres. bd. dirs. 1985—; pres. Trio Steel Inc., Chgo., 1987; spl. cons. Robert Shields Co., Pasadena, Calif.; cons. Nu Style Lamp Shade. Patentee Printed-Cir., 1964. With QMC AUS, 1949-52. Mem. Mfr. Agt. Club, Chgo. Lamp and Shade Inst. (bd. dirs.). Avocation: bicycling. Home: 323 Suwanee Ave Sarasota FL 34243 Office: Swing Time Inc 5512 W Lawrence Ave Chicago IL 60630 also: 323 Suwanee Ave Sarasota FL 33508

VENNARD, DAVID LEIGH, manufacturing company executive; b. Westerly, R.I., Feb. 26, 1945; s. Robert Joseph and Adele Catherine (Bianchi) V.; BA, Tufts U., 1967; 1 child by previous marriage, Christopher; m. Elaine H. Hudack, Sept. 24, 1988. With Celanese Corp., Chatham, N.J., 1970-78, distbn. supr. Plastics div., 1972-74, internat. distbn. mgr., 1974-78; with Becton Dickinson & Co.,Franklin Lakes, N.J., 1978-81, mgr. distbn. services Internat. div., 1981-85; dir. Internat. Sales div.; with M&M/Mars Co., Hackettstown, N.J., mgr. phys. distbn., 1985-87, dir. customer rels., 1988—. Mem Morristown Bd. Adjustment, 1979—. Served to lt. (j.g.) USN, 1967-70. Mem. Coun. of Logistics Mgmt., Warehouse Edn. and Research Council, Am. Prodn. and Inventory Control Soc., Internat. Trade Roundtable (chmn., dir. 1984-85). Home: 33 Hill St Morristown NJ 07960 Office: M&M/Mars Co Hackettstown NJ 07852

VENO, GLEN COREY, management consultant; b. Montreal, Que., Can., Sept. 5, 1951; came to U.S., 1953; s. Corey Elroy and Elsie Milly (Munro) V. BS in Aviation Tech. and Mgmt., Western Mich. U., 1976. Cert. mgmt. cons. Project mgr. The ASIST Corp., Oak Park, Mich., 1978-83; mgr. tech. support J.B. Systems, Inc., Woodland Hills, Calif., 1984-85; mgr. cons. svcs. Mgmt. Tech., Inc., Troy, Mich., 1985-88; v.p. Mgmt. Support Svcs., Inc., Southfield, Mich., 1989—. With U.S. Army, 1969-72, Vietnam. Recipient Cert. Appreciation U. Wis.-Extension Dept. Engring. and Applied Sci., 1984. Mem. Inst. Mgmt. Cons. (sec./treas. Detroit chpt.), Soc. Mfg. Engrs. (sr.), Am. Prodn. and Inventory Control Soc., Inst. Indsl. Engrs., Project Mgmt. Inst., Am. Mgmt. Assn., VFW (life). Home: 6397 Kinyon Rd Brighton MI 48116 Office: PO Box 605 Brighton MI 48116

VENTRES, ROMEO JOHN, manufacturing company executive; b. Boston, Nov. 2, 1924; s. Christy and Marzia (Giammarco) V.; m. Norma Louise Chapman, July 10, 1948; children: Judith Ventres Thompson, Jane, Mary, Patricia, Katherine, Michael, Peter. B.S. in Chem. Engring., Worcester Poly. Inst., 1948. Lic. profl. engr., Mass. Jr. engr. Atlantic Refining Co., Phila., 1948-55, group leader, 1955; oil indsl. engr. Govt. Refineries Adminstrn., Baghdad, Iraq, 1955-57; asst. chief engr. Borden Chem. Div. Borden Inc., Leominster, Mass., 1957, chief engr., 1958, ops. mgr., 1961, gen. mgr., 1966, div. v.p., 1968-72, group v.p., 1972-74; exec. v.p. Haven Industries, Phila., 1974-79; group v.p. Borden Chem. div. Borden Inc., Columbus, Ohio, 1979-83, div. pres., 1983-85; pres. Borden Inc., N.Y.C., 1985—, chief exec. officer, 1986—, chmn., 1987—; bd. dirs. Banc One Corp., Marsh and McLennan Cos. Inc., Schering-Plough Corp., Grocery Mfrs. Am. Trustee at St. Clare's Hosp., N.Y.C.; mem. adv. coun. PHilips U.S. Served with USN, 1944-46, PTO. Mem. Grocery Mfrs. Am. (bd. dirs.). Republican. Roman Catholic. Office: Borden Inc 277 Park Ave New York NY 10172

VENTRY, CATHERINE VALERIE, lawyer; b. Bronxville, N.Y., Feb. 19, 1949; d. Victor and Catherine Regina (Dillon) V. AB in Logic and Philosophy, Vassar Coll., 1971; postgrad., Boston U., 1972; JD, N.Y. Law Sch., 1978. Bar: N.Y. 1979, U.S. Dist. Ct. (so. and ea. dists.) N.Y. 1979. Adj. asst. prof. John Jay Coll. of Criminal Justice, N.Y.C., 1978-80; adj. asst. prof. bus. law Coll. Mount St. Vincent Lehman Coll., N.Y.C., 1978-82; staff atty. City of N.Y. Dept. Housing Preservation and Devel. Litigation Bureau, N.Y.C., 1981-84; sole practice Congers, N.Y., 1984—; Tax editor Prentice-Hall Pub. Co., Englewood Cliffs, N.J., 1980-81. Mem. N.Y. State Bar, Rockland County Women's Bar, Rockland County Bar Assn., MENSA. Office: 376 Washington St Newburgh NY 12550

VENTURINI, MARTIN JOHN, convenience store company executive; b. Chgo., June 19, 1948; s. Herman and Dorothy Ann (Wisniewski) V.; m. Judith Diane Koss, Nov. 1, 1975 (div. Apr. 1986); children: Michael, Laura. AA, Wright City Coll., 1968; BA, Northeastern U., 1971. Store mgr. White Hen Pantry, Elmhurst, Ill., 1972-74, store counselor, 1974-77, specialist advt., 1977-80, mgr. sales promotions, 1980-83; assoc. dir. regional devel. Convenient Food Mart, Chgo., 1983-84; nat. mktg. dir. Convenient Food Mart, Rosemont, Ill., 1984-85, v.p. mktg., 1985-87, sr. v.p. mktg., 1987, sr. v.p. regional devel., 1988, pres., 1988—. Mem. Chgo. Crime Commn. Republican. Roman Catholic. Office: Convenient Food Mart Inc 9701 W Higgins Rosemont IL 60018

VERARDO, DENZIL, state park system administrator; b. Watsonville, Calif., Mar. 24, 1948; s. Riccardo and Florence (Cook) V.; m. Jennie Dennis, Aug. 21, 1971; 1 child, Mark. BA, U. Calif., Santa Cruz, 1970; MA, Calif. State U., 1971; PhD, Columbia Pacific U., 1982. Cert. community coll. tchr., Calif. Ranger Calif. Dept. Parks and Recreation, Big Basin Redwoods, 1971-76; mgr. Calif. Dept. Parks and Recreation, Napa Valley, 1976-78; adminstrv. officer Calif. Dept. Parks and Recreation, Santa Rosa, 1978-79; tng. coordinator Asilomar, 1979-83; mgr. visitor services, cen. coast region services Calistoga (Calif.) Park and Recreation Commn., 1978-79. Author: Big Basin, 1973; author (with J. Verardo) Napa Valley, 1986, Santa Cruz County, 1987, In the Valley of Bottled Poetry, 1985, others. Sponsor Sempervivens Fund, Los Altos, Calif., 1974—; founding dir. Santa Cruz Mts. Natural History Assn., Felton, Calif., 1973-74, Napa Valley Natural History Assn., St. Helena, Calif., 1977-78; del. 1st Pacific Environ. Conf., Nagoya, Japan, 1987; vice chmn. Am.-Japanese Pacific Environ. Forum, 1987—; bd. dirs. Napa County Hist. Soc., 1977-79, Monterey County Hist. Soc., 1988, Castroville Artichoke Festival, 1984-87. Recipient Gov.'s Safety award State of Calif., 1987; research grantee Sourisseau Acad. History, 1982. Mem. Monterey Indsl. Safety Soc. (bd. dirs. 1984-87), Monterey County Hist. Soc. Soc., Calif State Park Rangers Assn. (pres. 1977-82), World Wildlife Fund. Democrat. Roman Catholic. Home: 10899 Palm St Castroville CA 95012 Office: State Dept Parks and Recreation 2211 Garden Rd Monterey CA 93940

VERDI, NEJAT HASAN, financial executive; b. Istanbul, Turkey, Feb. 14, 1913; s. Fazil Ibrahim and Fatma (Nigar) V.; M.Comml.Sci., Comml. Acad., Calw, Germany, 1933; m. Liselotte Annemarie Auer, Apr. 1, 1950; children—Aylin, Murat, Nilufer. Partner Verdi Ticaret ve Sanayi A.S., Istanbul, Turkey, 1927—, chmn. bd., also chmn. bd. subs., 1950—; bd. dirs. Finans Bank A.S., Istanbul. Bd. dirs. Am. Hosp., Istanbul, 1967-81; chmn. Am. Hosp. and Nursing Sch. Com., 1967-81. Named Hon. Ambassador of New Orleans, in Istanbul, 1957. Mem. Middle East Assn., Turkish-Am. Businessmen's Assn. (bd. dirs.). Clubs: Propeller of N.Y. (pres. 1952-60), Moda Yacht, Golf. Home: Husrev Gerede Cadd 75/7, Zorlu Apartman Teskiviye, 80200 Istanbul Turkey Office: Verdi Ticaret ve Sanayi, Cumh Cadd 26/A, Pegasus Evi Harbiye, 80200 Istanbul Turkey

VERDIER, QUENTIN ROOSEVELT, personnel consultant; b. Mancelona, Mich., Mar. 19, 1921; s. John Walter and Louise (Hills) V.; m. Margaret Elizabeth Wells, Nov. 13, 1943; children: Margaret Louise, Quentin Wells, Nanette Marie Bloom. AB in Pub. Adminstrn., Kalamazoo Coll., 1943, MA in Pub. Adminstrn., 1947; postgrad., Am. U., 1948-51; PhD in Human Resource Devel., Columbia Pacific U., 1985. Cert. employment cons., personnel cons., forensic vocat. expert; lic. employment agt., Wis. Asst. personnel officer U.S. Savs. Bonds div. U.S. Treasury Dept., Washington, 1951-58; div. chief office of personnel Internat. Coop. Adminstrn./Agy. for Internat. Devel., Washington State Dept., 1959-63; dep. chief pub. adminstrn. div. U.S. Ops. Mission/Agy. for Internat. Devel., Saigon, South Vietnam, 1963-65; asst. dir. tng. Inst. Govt. Affairs U. Wis. Extension, Madison, 1966-67; pres., chief ops. officer AvailAbility of Madison, Inc., 1967—, also chmn. bd. dirs.; mem. adv. panel Nat. Forensic Ctr., Princeton, 1983—; intern Group XIII, Nat. Inst. Pub. Affairs, 1948-49. Author City Employee Handbook-Better Pub. Service, 1947; editor hist. pamphlet series Understanding Backgrounds, 1964; contbr. articles to profl. jours. Bd. dirs. Capital Community Citizen's Assn., Madison, 1967; pres. Country Heights Homeowners Assn., Oregon, 1969. Served with U.S. Army Air Corps, 1943-46. Decorated Republic of Vietnam Merit medal 1st class, 1965; recipient Wm G. Howard prize in polit. sci., 1946, Suggestion awards U.S. Treasury Dept., 1949; Upjohn fellow Kalamazoo Coll., 1946-47. Mem. Nat. Assn. Personnel Cons., Am. Soc. Personnel Adminstrn., Wis. Assn. Personnel Cons., Am. Arbitration Assn. (arbitrator, mem. panel Chgo. regional office), U.S.A. Tug-of-War Assn. (sec., parliamentarian 1978), Am. Assn. Ret. Persons, Nat. Forensic Ctr., Wis. Acad. Scis., Arts and Letters, Nat. Geographic Soc., Smithsonian Instn., Nat. Assn. Retired Credit Union People, Internat. Platform Assn., Internat. Exec. Service Corps, Friendship Force. Clubs: Fox Run Health, Toastmasters (dist. 36 gov.). Lodges: Masons (32 degree), Rotary (Internat. New Club award 1988-89).

VERDIER, STEPHEN JOHN, lawyer; b. Grand Rapids, Mich., Aug. 22, 1950; s. Robert Martin and Beatrice (O'Connor) V.; m. Donna Daniels, June 17, 1972; children: James Martin, Mary Caitlin. BS, Am. U., 1972; JD, Cath. U. Am., 1976. Bar: D.C. 1976. Of counsel com. banking U.S. Ho. of Reps., Washington, 1976-83; sr. legis. counsel Ind. Bankers Assn. Am., Washington, 1983—. Contbr. articles to profl. jours. Democrat. Roman Catholic. Office: Ind Bankers Assn Am 1 Thomas Circle Washington DC 20005

VERDUIN, BERT M., real estate executive; b. Benton, Ark., Feb. 9, 1947; d. Elvis Lee and Helen Lee (McBride) Moses; m. Michael Hankins, May 23, 1970; children—Valerie Ann, Clinton Logan. A.A.S., Brookhaven Coll., 1982. Acct., Realty Devel. Corp., Dallas, 1970-77; owner, mgr. Tax Service, Dallas, 1977-83; sr. v.p., controller Realty Devel. Corp., Dallas, 1983-87; pres. Strobe Mgmt. Services, Inc., Dallas, 1987—. Republican. Mem. Ch. of Christ. Avocations: reading; crafts.

VEREEN, WILLIAM JEROME, uniform manufacturing company executive; b. Moultrie, Ga., Sept. 7, 1940; s. William Coachman and Mary Elizabeth (Bunn) V.; m. Lula Evelyn King, June 9, 1963; children—Elizabeth King, William Coachman. B.S. in Indsl. Mgmt, Ga. Inst. Tech., 1963. With Riverside Mfg. Co., Moultrie, 1967—; v.p., then exec. v.p. Riverside Mfg. Co., 1970-77, pres., 1977-84, pres., treas., chief exec. officer, 1984—; also dir.; v.p., dir. Moultrie Cotton Mills, 1969—; exec. v.p. Riverside Industries, Inc., Moultrie, 1973-77; pres. Riverside Industries, Inc., 1977-84, chief exec. officer, 1984—, also dir.; v.p., dir. Riverside Uniform Rentals, Inc., Moultrie, 1971-80, pres., 1980-84, chief exec. officer, dir., 1984—; pres. Riverside Mfg. Co. (Ireland) Ltd., 1977—, Right Image Corp.; pres. Riverside Mfg. Co. GmbH, Rep. of Germany, 1979—, chief exec. officer, dir. 1984; pres., treas., chief exec. officer G.A. Rivers Corp., 1984—, Riverside Mfg. Co. (U.K.) Ltd., 1985—; bd. dirs. Ga. Power Co.; advisor textile and apparel tariffs and quotas U.S. Dept. State Bd; bd. dirs. U.S. Bus. and Indsl. Council, C&S Nat. Bank of Colquitt County. Bd. dirs. Moultrie-Colquitt County (Ga.) Devel. Authority, 1973—, Moultrie-Colquitt County United Givers, 1968-75, Moultrie YMCA, 1968—, Colquitt County Cancer Soc., 1969-73; trustee Community Welfare Assn. Moultrie, 1970—, Pineland Sch., Moultrie, 1971—, Leadership Ga., 1972—, Ga. Council Econ. Edn.; trustee Am. Apparel Edn. Found. Served to capt. USMCR, 1963-67. Decorated Bronze Star, Purple Heart. Mem. Internat. Apparel Fedn. (bd. dirs. exec. com.), Am. Apparel Mfrs. Assn. (dir., exec. com., edn. found. com., 2d vice-chmn., now 1st vice-chmn.), Nat. Assn. Uniform Mfrs. and Distbrs. (dir.), Young Presidents Orgn., Am. Apparel Edn. Found. (v.p., trustee), Sigma Alpha Epislon. Presbyterian (chmn. bd. deacons). Clubs: Elks, Kiwanis. Home: 21 Dogwood Circle Moultrie GA 31768 Office: PO Box 460 Moultrie GA 31768

VEREKETIS, CONSTANTIN KIMON, gas distribution company executive; b. Smyrna, Oct. 27, 1908; s. Kimon Constantin and Maria (Psychopoulou) V.; M.Law, Law U. Bucharest, Romania, 1940; m. Smaragda Kalassounda, June 2, 1963 (dec. 1983). With Concordia SA Petroleum Co. (Petrofina group), Ploesti and Bucarest, Romania, 1930-58; supply mgr. Greek State Refinery, Athens, 1958-60; with Petrogaz, Athens, 1960-83, dir., gen. mgr., 1965—, mng. dir., pres., 1984—; pres. Kosmogaz, Athens, 1980—, Mercantile SA, Athens, 1972—, Pyrogaz SA, Athens, 1968—, Petronaus, Athens, 1968—, Drago Fina, S.A., Athens, 1960—, Betofil SA, Athens, 1978-85; v.p. FINA Petroleum Co., Athens, 1978-86; pres. Greek Gas Distbn. Industries, Athens, 1972-86, hon. pres. 1986. Author: (novel) Marilena; also short stories and plays Served with arty., 1940-41. Mem. Assn. Greek Industries. Greek Orthodox. Clubs: Yacht of Greece; Athens; Tennis; Automobil. Lodge: Rotary (gov. 1982-83). Home: 7 Semitelou, 115 28 Athens Greece Office: 57 Acadimias St, 106 79 Athens Greece

VER HAGEN, JAN KAROL, electrical manufacturing company executive; b. Eau Claire, Wis., Nov. 11, 1937; s. Henry Joseph and Elsie Marie (Hagenstad) Ver H.; m. Kathryn Frances Fults; m. June 25, 1960; children: Mark A., David M., Kathryn T. Student, U. Wis., Eau Claire, 1956-58; BSME, U. Wis., Madison, 1961. Capital goods mktg. Trane Co., La Crosse, Wis., 1961-69, group sales mgr., mng. dir. Trane Ltd., 1969-72, v.p., gen. mgr. process div. (heat transfer), 1972-73, v.p., gen. mgr. internat. div., 1973-77; exec. v.p. internat., v.p. corp. projects A.B. Chance div. Emerson Electric, Centralia, Mo., 1977-78; v.p. internat. Emerson Electric Co., St. Louis, 1978; pres., group v.p. White-Rodgers div. Emerson Electric Co., St. Louis, 1978-84, exec. v.p., pres., 1984-85; exec. v.p. Emerson Electric Co., St. Louis, 1985-86, exec. v.p. corp., chmn. electronics and space div., 1986-87, exec. v.p., corp. dir., 1987-88, vice chmn., dir., 1988—. Republican. Mem. United Ch. Christ. Clubs: St. Louis, Bellerive Country (St. Louis), Firestone Country (Akron). Office: Emerson Electric Co 8000 W Florissant Ave Saint Louis MO 63136

VERITY, C. WILLIAM, JR., federal official; b. Middletown, Ohio, Jan. 26, 1917; m. Margaret Wymond; 3 children. BA, Yale U., 1939. Various mgmt. positions 1940-65; pres., chief exec. officer Armco Inc., Middletown, 1965-71, 72-82; chmn. U.S. C. of C., 1980-81, Presdl. Task Force on Pvt. Initiatives, Washington, 1981-83; co-chmn. U.S.-U.S.S.R. Trade and Econ. Council, 1977-84; mem. Presdl. Adv. Council on Pvt. Sector Initiatives, 1983—; sec. Dept. of Commerce, Washington, 1987—. Served with USN, 1942-46.

VERMEER, RICHARD DOUGLAS, investment banking executive; b. Bronxville, N.Y., July 2, 1938; s. Albert Casey and Helen (Valentine Casey) V.; m. Grace Dorothy Ferguson, May 22, 1960; children—Carin Dawn,

Catherine Jeanne, Robert Brooke. B.S., Fairleigh Dickinson U., 1960; M.B.A., Lehigh U., 1967; postgrad. Corp. Fin. Mgmt. Program, Harvard U., 1983. Dir. fin. systems TWA, N.Y.C., 1967-71; dir. MIS Kaufman & Broad, Los Angeles, 1971-74, group controller, 1974-76; from asst. to pres. to v.p., controller Global Marine Inc., Los Angeles, 1976-82; v.p. control and adminstrn. Global Marine Inc., Houston, 1982-84, sr. v.p., 1984-86; exec. v.p. Printon, Kane Corp., Short Hills, N.J., 1986-87; v.p., chief fin. officer, treas., sec. Stars To Go, Inc., Los Angeles, Calif., 1987—. Recipient award Am. Legion, 1956; award Am. Mktg. Assn., 1960. Mem. Fin. Exec. Inst. (com. Nat. Mgmt. Info. Systems), Jonathan Club (Los Angeles), Club at Falcon Point (Houston). Home: 11401 Bolas St Los Angeles CA 90049 Office: Stars To Go Inc 4751 Wilshire Blvd Los Angeles CA 90010

VERMEULEN, JOHN PETER, buisness owner, horticulturist; b. Mineola, N.Y., May 27, 1919; s. John and Johanna (van den Hoorn) V.; m. Edith Lorna Newman, Feb. 9, 1946; children: Barbara Lee, Nancy Jo, James Peter, Wendy Jane, Jeffrey Paul. Cert., Brownes Bus. Sch., Jamaica, N.Y., 1937; student, Cornell U., 1939. Apprentice R. I. Nurseries, Newport, R.I., 1939-41; asst. mgr. John Vermeulen & Son, Inc., Carle Place, N.Y. and Neshanic Station, N.J., 1946-63, pres., mgr., 1963-85, pres., chmn. bd., 1985—; mem. N.J. State Bd. Agriculture, Trenton, 1977-81, v.p. 1981; bd. mgrs. Cook Coll./NJAES, Rutgers U. 1962-70, 1985-88, pres., 1967-68. Mem. Branchburg Twp. Sch. Bd., 1957-61, v.p., 1961; sec., treas. indsl. commn. Branchburg twp., 1956-64; mem. Somerset County Bd. Argl., 1964—, pres. 1977-79, Somerset County Agrl. Devel. Bd., Somerville, N.J., 1984—, vice chmn., 1988—, N.J. Rural Adv. Council, Trenton, 1984—; chmn. Somerset County Ams. for Robertson, Neshanic Station, 1988; founder Jesus Said Found. Capt. U.S. Army, 1941-46, USAR 1946-70. Recipient Citation N.J. Agrl. Experiment Station, 1980, Svc. award Arthur West Dist., 1986, Citation Disting. Svc. N.J. Dept. Agrl. Mem. N.J. Assn. Nurserymen (pes. 1961-62, citation 1979), Internat. Plant Propogators Soc. (pres. 1968-69), Eastern Region Internat. Plant Soc. (pres. 1965-66, award of merit 1981). Republican. Office: John Vermeulen & Son PO Box 600 Woodfern Rd Neshanic Station NJ 08853

VERMILYA, DALE NELSON, financial analyst; b. Columbus, Ohio, June 15, 1959; s. Ray Nelson and Linda Jo (Way) V.; m. Ellen Kathryn Von Hagen, Nov. 3, 1984; children: Christopher Dale, Samara Lyn. BBA, U. Akron, 1981. CPA, Ky., Ohio, Mich. Sr. auditor Ashland Oil Inc., Ky., 1981-84; advanced auditor Owens-Corning Fiberglass corp., Toledo, 1984-87; sr. fin. analyst Monroe (Mich.) Auto Equipment Co., 1987-88, sr. cost analyst, 1988-89, mgr., mfg. accounting, 1989—. Mem. Am. Inst. CPAs, Ohio Soc. CPAs, Beta Alpha Psi., Beta Gamma Sigma. Democrat. Roman Catholic. Home: 3520 Scarsborough toledo OH 43615 Office: Monroe Auto Equipment Co One International Dr Monroe MI 48161

VERNEY, RICHARD GREVILLE, paper company executive; b. Providence, Aug. 24, 1946; s. Gilbert and Virginia Ruth (Piggott) V.; m. Dorothy Howard, Aug. 26, 1967; children: Virginia F., Elizabeth I., Heather B., Eric G. AB, Brown U., 1968. Mgmt. trainee Monadnock Paper Mills, Bennington, N.H., 1969-70, asst. gen. mgr., 1970, exec. v.p., 1970-76, pres., 1977-85, chmn., chief exec. officer, 1978—. Mem. exec. com. Crotched Mt. Found., Greenfield, N.H., 1974-87, trustee, 1974—; trustee St. George's Sch., Newport, R.I., 1978—, chmn., 1985-89. Mem. Am. Paper Inst. (chmn. splty. packaging and indsl. div. 1984-85, chmn. exec. bd. API-pulp consumers div. 1980-82, chmn. cover and text exec. com. 1989—), Sales Assn. Paper Industry, Boston Paper Trade Assn. (pres. 1985-86). Republican. Episcopalian. Clubs: Algonquin (Boston); Nantucket Yacht (Mass.); N.Y. Yacht (N.Y.C.). Home: The Verney Farm Bennington NH 03442 Office: Monadnock Paper Mills Inc Antrim Rd Bennington NH 03442

VERNI, RALPH FRANCIS, financial executive; b. N.Y.C., Jan. 26, 1943; s. Ralph and Marguerite (DiPalma) V.; m. Kathleen Margaret O'Malley, Apr. 22, 1978; children: Michele, Lisa, Rachel, Kevin. BA in Math., Colgate U., 1964; MBA, Columbia U., 1966; advanced profl. cert. fin., NYU Sch. Bus., 1977. Chartered fin. analyst. Mgmt. sci. analyst Equitable Life, N.Y.C., 1966-69, dir. mgmt. sci., 1969-72, asst. v.p. investment research, 1972-77, v.p. pvt. placements, 1977-81, sr. v.p. bonds, 1981-82; pres. inst. investment group The New Eng., Boston, 1982—, also bd. dirs., chmn. fin. com.; chmn., chief exec. officer New Eng. Securities, Boston, NE Cash Mgmt. Trust, NE Bond Income Fund, Inc., NE Zenith Fund, Inc., NE Tax Exempt Income Fund, Inc., NE Tax Exempt Money Market Trust, NE Variable Annuity Fund I, NE Equity Income Fund, Inc., NE Growth Fund, Inc., NE Retirement Equity Fund, Inc., NE Govt. Securities Fund; chmn. bd. Investment Trust Boston Funds, Copley Real Estate Advisors, Back Bay Advisors, Inc., Marlborough Capital Advisors, Inc., GRENEL Fin. Corp., Conn. Nat., Inc.; bd. dirs. Loomis, Sayles & Co., Inc., New Eng. Variable Life Ins. Co., New Eng. Pension and Annuity Co., New Eng. Gen. Life Ins. Co., Copley Properties, Inc.; mem. adv. com. MIT Ctr. for Real Estate Devel. Contbr. articles to profl. jours. Trustee, mem. audit com. Mass. Eye and Ear Infirmary; mem. exec. com. Boston Mpl. Rsch. Bur. Mem. Am. Fin. Assn., Fin. Analysts Fedn., N.Y. Soc. Security Analysts, Inst. Chartered Fin. Analysts. Unitarian. Home: 123 Belcher Dr Sudbury MA 01776 Office: New Eng Mut Life Ins Co 501 Boylston St Boston MA 02117

VERNON, BRIAN ELLIOT, real estate executive; b. Montebello, Calif., Mar. 18, 1953; s. William Thomas and Natalie Margaret (Prentice) V.; m. Janet Bishop, Aug. 16, 1975; children: Brian Elliot Jr., Vanessa Lyn. BS, SUNY, 1975; postgrad., Suffolk Community Coll., 1976. Property adminstr. Chase Manhattan Bank N.A., N.Y.C., 1976-78; real estate mgmt. officer Marine Midland Bank N.A., N.Y.C., 1978-81; v.p. property acquisitions Pan Am Properties, Inc. and Buckingham Holdings, Inc., N.Y.C., 1981—; bd. dirs. Pan Am. Mgmt., Inc., N.Y.C. Webelos leader Boy Scouts Am., Huntington, N.Y., 1988, asst. scoutmaster troop 12, 1989—; asst. coach St. Patrick's Baseball League, Huntington, 1988. Mem. Real Estate Bd. N.Y. Methodist. Home: 141 Clinton Ave Huntington NY 11743 Office: Pan Am Properties Inc 521 Fifth Ave Ste 1407 New York NY 10175

VERNON, CARL ATLEE, JR., retired wholesale food distributor executive; b. Topeka, Aug. 15, 1926; s. Carl Atlee and Capitola May (Jarboe) V.; m. Marion Leila Colton, May 7, 1950; children—Mary Catherine, Matthew Fowler, Susan Elizabeth. B.S., Yale U., 1947. Merchandising mgr. Fleming Cos., Topeka, 1957-61, dir. merchandising, 1961-66, dir. info. services, 1966-72, v.p. info. services, 1972-74, v.p. regional systems, 1974-79; sr. v.p. mktg. services Fleming Cos., Oklahoma City, 1979-88. Chmn. Shawnee County chpt. ARC, Topeka, Kans., 1957-58. Served to ensign USNR, 1944-46. Republican. Episcopalian.

VERNON, WILLIAM FREDERICK, JR., advertising company executive; b. Newton, Iowa, Nov. 17, 1931; s. William Frederick Sr. and Marjorie (Herrick) V.; m. Marilyn Mathieson, Dec. 26, 1954; children: William F. III, Christopher Paul, Cameron Matheison, Stephanie Herrick. Student, Trinity Coll., 1950-52, U. Iowa, 1952-54. With Vernon Co., Newton, 1956—, exec. v.p. ops., 1966-69, pres., 1969-74, pres., chmn. bd. dirs., 1974-87, chmn. bd. dirs., chief exec. officer, 1987—; dir. Norwest Bank of Des Moines. Mem. U.S. Olympic com., Gov.'s Blue Ribbon Nat. Guard com., 1975, nom. com. Iowa Arts Council, 1985, Gov.'s Humane Svcs. Leadership Roundtable, 1984—; trustee, past chmn. Progress Industries, Civic Ctr. Greater Des Moines; trustee Lake Forest (Ill.) Acad.; mem. adv. council Mid-Iowa council Boy Scouts Am., U.S. Olympic State Games com., 1988—; past pres. Jasper County ARC, Newton YMCA; mem. corp. cabinet Am. Heart Assn.; chmn. Iowa State Games, 1985—; civilian aide to sec. Army, State of Iowa, 1978-82. With U.S. Army, 1954-56. Named Man of the Year Newton Jr. C. of C., 1963, Iowa Manof the Month Iowa Bus. and Industry Mag., 1975, Joseph M. Segal Specialty Advt. Man of the Year award Counselor Mag., 1987. Mem. Specialty Advt. Assn. Internat. (past chmn., Hall of Fame 1985), Iowa Assn. Bus. and Industry (past chmn.), Newton C. of C. (recipient Community Disting. Svc. award 1982, past. bd. dirs.), World Bus. Council, Chief Execs. Orgn., Def. Orientation Conf. Assn., Inc., Wokanda County Club, Des Moines Embassy Club, People to People Sports Club, Newton Country Club (bd. dirs.), Contrerie de la Chaine Des Ritissers Club. Republican. Presbyterian. Home: 300 W 14th St Newton IA 50208 Office: Vernon Co 604 W 4th St N Newton IA 50208

VERONESI, UMBERTO, surgeon; b. Milan, Italy, Nov. 28, 1925; m. Susy Razon, Apr. 13, 1961; children—Paolo, Marco, Alberto, Pietro, Giulia, Silvia. Grad. Milan U., 1951. Dir. gen. Nat. Cancer Inst., Milan, 1975—; prof. pathology Perugia U. (Italy), from 1957; prof. surgery Milan U., from 1961; chmn. Melanoma Group, WHO, Milan, 1967. Author: Surgical Anatomy, 1961; Clinical Oncology, 1973, Europe Textbook om Surgical Oncology, 1989; dir. Jour. Clin. and Exptl. Oncology. Recipient Nat. award Am. Cancer Soc., 1977, Gold medal Italian Ministry Health, 1978, Lucy Wortham James Clin. Research award Soc. Surg. Oncology, 1982. Mem. Internat. Union Against Cancer (pres. 1978-82), European Orgn. for Research in Cancer Treatment (pres. 1985). Office: Istituto Nazionale Tumori, Via Venezian 1, 20133 Milan Italy

VERRECCHIA, ALFRED J., toy company executive; b. 1943. Asst. controller Hasbro Inc., 1965-70, controller, 1970-74, treas., 1974—, v.p., 1980—, then sr. v.p. fin., then exec. v.p. fin. and adminstrn., pres. mfg. svcs. div., exec. v.p., 1989—. Office: Hasbro Inc 1027 Newport Ave Pawtucket RI 02862-0200

VERRILL, CHARLES HAMILTON, corporation executive; b. Buhl, Minn., Oct. 8, 1928; s. Charles Edwin and Nettie Mae (Hamilton) V.; m. Peggy Ann Anderson, Jan. 9, 1953; children: Charles, Scott, Todd. MBA, Columbia Pacific U., 1986. Licensed gen. contractor. Ops. mgr. Frieden Calculator, Arcadia, Calif., 1967-69; plant mgr. Astro Seal Inc., Su El Monte, Calif., 1969-71; ops. mgr. Am. Standard Inc., Monrovia, Calif., 1971-75; v.p. ESP Co., Covina, Calif., 1975-76; pres. Comml. Interiors, Creative Innovations, Tri-Country Svcs. Corp., Upland, Calif., 1976-86; chmn. bd. Humantics Corp., Studio City, Calif., 1986—. Patentee in field. Sgt. U.S. Army, 1950-52, Korea. Mem. Inst. of Human Engring. Scis. (bd. dirs. 1988), Nat. Narcotics Edn. Assn. (bd. dirs. 1960), Elks. Home: 833 W 10th St Claremont CA 91711

VERRILL, CHARLES OWEN, JR., lawyer; b. Biddeford, Maine, Sept. 30, 1937; s. Charles Owen and Elizabeth (Handy) V.; m. Mary Ann Blanchard, Aug. 13, 1960; children: Martha Anne, Edward Blanchard, Ethan Christopher, Elizabeth Handy, Matthew Lawton, Peter Goldthwait. AB, Tufts U., 1959; LLB, Duke U., 1962. Bar: D.C. 1962. Assoc. Weaver & Glassie, 1962-64; assoc. Barco, Cook, Patton & Blow, 1964-66, ptnr., 1967; ptnr. Patton, Boggs & Blow, 1967-84, Wiley, Rein and Fielding, Washington, 1984—; lectr. law sch. Duke U., 1970-73; adj. prof. internat. trade law ctr. Georgetown U., Washington, 1978—; conf. chmn. The Future of the Internat. Steel Industry, Bellagio, Italy, 1984, 87, 88, The U.S. Agenda for the Uruguay Round, Airlie House, Warenton, Va., 1986, The Polish Joint Venture Law, Cracow, Poland, 1987, Internat. Steel Industry II, Bellagio, 1987. Local dir. Tufts U. Ann. Fund, 1965-69; mem. Duke Law Alumni Coun., 1972-75; trustee Internat. Law Inst., 1981—, chmn. bd. trustees, 1983-87. Mem. ABA, D.C. Bar Assn., Order of Coif, Theta Delta Chi, Phi Delta Phi, Met. Club (Washington), Chevy Chase Club (Md.), Tarratine Club (Dark Harbor, Maine). Home: 8205 Dunsinane Ct McLean VA 22101 Office: 1776 K St NW Washington DC 20006

VERRONE, PATRIC MILLER, lawyer, writer; b. Glendale, N.Y.C., Sept. 29, 1959; s. Pat and Edna (Miller) V. BA, Harvard U., 1981; JD, Boston Coll., 1984. Bar: Fla. 1984, U.S. Dist. Ct. (mid. dist.) Fla. 1984, Calif. 1988. Assoc. Allen, Knudsen, Swartz, DeBoest, Rhoads & Edwards, Ft. Myers, Fla., 1984-86; writer The Tonight Show, Burbank, Calif., 1987—; counsel Fla. Motion Picture and TV Assn., Ft. Myers, 1985-86. Editor Harvard Lampoon, 1978-84, Boston Coll. Law Rev., 1983-84, editor Fla. Bar Jour., 1987-88; contbr. articles to profl. jours. Mem. ABA, Assn. Trial Lawyers Am., Fla. Bar, Writers Guild of Am. West (mem. acad. liaison com. 1988—), Harvard Club Lee County (v.p. 1985-86), Harvard Club So. Calif.. Republican. Roman Catholic. Home and Office: 6466 Odin St Hollywood CA 90068

VERSEMAN, ERIC WAYNE, securities firm executive; b. Odessa, Tex., Aug. 21, 1957; s. C.S. and Lillian E. (Mezo) V.; m. Cia Anne Houghland, Oct. 13, 1984. Student, U. Mo., 1975-76; BBA, Lincoln U., 1982. Cert. fin. planner. Staff Luth. Altenheim Soc., St. Louis, 1983-84; dir. devel. Am. Capital Equities Inc., St. Louis, 1984-85, v.p., 1985—. Mem. Nat. Assn. Compliance Profls., Internat. Assn. Fin. Planners, Inst. Cert. Fin. Planners, Columbia Alumni Assn. (dir. 1985—), Beta Sigma Psi (bd. dirs. ednl. found. 1984—). Republican. Lutheran. Office: Am Capital Equities Inc 111 W Port Plaza Ste 900 Saint Louis MO 63146

VERZONE, RONALD D., insurance brokerage executive, investment advisor; b. Boston, July 17, 1947; s. Peter H. and Helen B. (McLeavy) V. BS, U. Hartford, 1970. Pres. Bay State Talent, Inc., Springfield, Mass., 1970-76; owner Ronald Verzone & Assocs., 1975-83; exec. v.p. United Underwriters, Inc., Exeter, N.H., 1983—. Mem. SUB Ctr., Inc., Pioneer Valley Estate Planning Coun. Staff sgt. U.S. Army, 1968-70. Mem. Internat. Assn. Fin. Planners, Nat. Life Underwriters Assn., N.H. Assn. Life Underwriters, Nat. Assn. Ind. Life Brokerage Agys. Home: 12 Chase Rd Newton NH 03858 Office: United Underwriters Inc 6 Chestnut St Exeter NH 03833

VESCOVI, SELVI, pharmaceutical company executive; b. N.Y.C., June 14, 1930; s. Antonio and Desolina V.; BS, Coll. William and Mary, 1951; m. Elma Pasquinelli, Oct. 17, 1954; children: Mark, James, Anne. Salesman, Upjohn Co., N.Y.C., 1954-59, sales supr.,1959-62, product mgr. U.S. domestic pharm. dir., 1962-65, mgr. mktg. planning internat. div., 1965-71, v.p. Europe, 1971-74, group v.p. Europe, 1975-77, exec. v.p. Upjohn Internat., Inc., Kalamazoo, Mich., 1978-85, pres., gen. mgr., 1975-88, v.p. parent co., 1978-88; adj. prof. mgmt. Western Mich. U., Kalamazoo, 1988-89; bd. dirs. Carrington Labs. 2d lt. M.C., U.S. Army, 1951-53. Mem. Internat. Pharm. Mfrs. Assn., Park Club (Kalamazoo), NYAC (N.Y.). Republican. Roman Catholic. Office: Upjon Internat Co 7000 Portage Rd Kalamazoo MI 49001

VESELY, ALEXANDER, civil engineer; b. Ladmovce, Czechoslovakia, Dec. 7, 1926; came to U.S., 1949; s. Joseph and Margaret (Lefkovitz) V.; m. Harriet Lee Roth, Aug. 11, 1957; 1 child, David Seth. BSCE, Carnegie Mellon U., 1952; postgrad. John Marshall Law Sch., 1955; MSCE, Ill. Inst. Tech., 1957. Registered profl. engr., Ind., W.Va.; registered land surveyor, Ind. Staff engr., Amoco Oil Co., Whiting, Ind., 1952-62; mgr. engring. Borg Warner Chem. Co., Washington, W.Va., 1962-77; assoc. engr. Mobil Rsch. & Devel. Corp., Princeton, N.J., 1977-83; cons. engr. D.G. Peterson & Assocs. Inc., Greenfield, Mass., 1983—; prin. Alexander Vesely & Assocs, 1983-87; assoc. prof. Community Coll., Parkersburg, W.Va., 1965-67; chmn. Engrs. Week Com., Parkersburg, 1973. Pres. B'nai Israel Congregation, Parkersburg, 1976; bd. dirs. Bros. of Israel Congregation, Trenton, N.J., 1978-83. Served with U.S. Army, 1952-54. Carnegie Mellon U. scholar, 1950-52. Mem. Nat. Soc. Profl. Engrs. (pres. Parkersburg chpt. 1973-74), Am. Inst. Plant Engrs., ASCE, Scrabble Club, Chess Club, Bridge Club, Tau Beta Pi (life). Republican. Jewish. Avocations: ping-pong, tennis, swimming. Home and Office: 48 Hillcrest Dr Northampton MA 01060

VESTAL, GEORGE ALEXANDER, plastics company executive; b. Fayetteville, N.C., Dec. 4, 1927; s. Herman L. and Blanche M. (Martin) V.; m. Lura Janice Williford, Oct. 8, 1950. B.S. in Bus. Adminstrn, U. N.C., 1956. With Union Carbide Corp., 1956—; gen. mgr. prodn. Union Carbide Corp., Cartersville, Ga., 1967-68; engring. prodn. mgr. Union Carbide Corp., N.Y.C., 1968-74; gen. mgr. internat. ops. Union Carbide Corp., 1974-75, dir. mktg., 1975-79, gen. mgr. home products, 1979-81, v.p., gen. mgr. home products, home and automotive div., 1981-87; exec. v.p. home products First Brands Corp., Danbury, Conn., 1987—. Served with U.S. Navy, 1945-46. Republican. Baptist. Home: 5 Mine Hill Rd West Redding CT 06896 Office: First Brands Corp 83 Wooster Heights Rd Box 1911 Danbury CT 06810 *

VESTAL, ROBERT, III, public relations and publishing executive; b. Elyria, Ohio, July 7, 1933; s. Robert and Frances Alma (Whiteley) V.; divorced; children: Paul, Debra, Janice, William. BA, U. Denver, 1957. Editor Shell Oil Co., Denver, 1957-62; pub. relations rep. AT&T, N.Y.C. and Denver, 1962-67; chief of communications Colo.-Wyo. Regional Med. Program, 1967-68; pub. relations mgr. Hamilton Mgmt. Corp., Denver, 1968-69; mgr. communications dept., Denver C. of C., 1969-72; acct. exec., Botsford-Ketchum Co., Denver, 1972-74; pub. relations dir. The Potato Bd., Denver, 1974-80; v.p. advt., pub. relations Fuller & Co., Denver, 1981-87; pres., Vestal Communications, 1986—. Mem. Denver Bd. Realtors, Denver Press Club, Denver Advt. Club. Avocations: golf, travel, photography, shortwave radio.

VESTERFELT, COLIN EDWARD ANSON, investment executive, consultant; b. Belleville, Ont., Can., May 23, 1947; came to U.S., 1965; s. James Peter and Evelyn Elizabeth (Anson) V.; m. Rondee Allene Holmes, Jan. 31, 1969; children—Kirste, Ian, Carly, Devra, C. Christian, Candice, Jamie. B.S., Brigham Young U., 1969, M.A., 1974, M.B.A., 1981; postgrad. U. Utah, Salt Lake City, 1978-79. Cert. psychologist, Alta. Counselor, Glenwood State Hosp., Iowa, 1971-73; counselor Latter Day Saints Social Services, Calgary, Alta., Can., 1973-74; program adminstr., psychologist Alta. Mental Health, Medicine Hat, Alta., 1974-78; pres. Can Am Assocs., Orem, Utah, 1978—; sr. fin. advisor Music Tchrs. Supply, Omaha, 1978—; supr. new product devel. and fin. analysis Timp Industries, Pleasant Grove, Utah, 1982-83. Author: (with Karen Ireland) Five Year Projection for Handicapped, 1978. Contbr. articles to profl. jours. Mem. exec. bd., treas. Alta. Union of Provincial Employees, Edmonton, 1976-78; co-chmn. Joint Consultation Com., chmn. Profl. Affairs Com., Province of Alta., Edmonton, 1976-78; council chmn. Boy Scouts Am., Orem, 1984—. Skagg's scholar, 1980; Exxon scholar, 1981; Grad. Sch. Mgmt. scholar Brigham Young U., 1982. Mem. Am. Assn. Mental Deficiency, Psychologists Assn. Alta., Canadian Psychol. Assn., Am. Psychol. Assn., Brigham Young U. Mgmt. Soc. Mormon. Home: 227 W 2000 N Orem UT 84057

VETTER, MARY MARGARET (PEGGY), investment manager financial consultant; b. Richmond, Va., June 7, 1945; d. Robert Joseph and Miriam Thomas V.; B.A., Cath. U. Am., 1967; M.B.A. with distinction, N.Y.U., 1978; m. Dimitri Yannacopoulos, May 24, 1980. Asst. to controller N.C. Trading Co., N.Y.C., 1972-74; asst. controller Shaheen Natural Resources Inc., N.Y.C., 1974-76; fin. coordinator mining div. Nat. Bulk Carriers, Inc., N.Y.C., 1976-77; corp. cons. mktg. and strategic planning Gen. Electric Co., Bridgeport, Conn., 1978-80; v.p., internat. mktg. strategy Bankers Trust Co., N.Y.C., 1980-83; fin. cons. Shearson Lehman/Am. Express, Stamford, Conn., 1984—. Bd. dirs. South Central Conn. Emergency Med. Services Council. Named Woman of Yr., N.Y.U. Alumnae Assn., 1978. Mem. Fin. Women's Assn. N.Y., Women in Mgmt., Beta Gamma Sigma. Republican. Roman Catholic. Home: 11 Don Bob Rd Stamford CT 06903 Office: 5 High Ridge Park Stamford CT 06905

VIA, THOMAS HENRY, manufacturing engineer; b. Martinsville, Va., Sept. 12, 1959; s. Henry E. and Margaret (Dandridge) V. AS in Welding and Machine Tool, Solano Community Coll., 1980; AAS in Aircraft Maintenance and Metallurgy, Community Coll. Air Force, 1982; BS in Indsl. Tech., So. Ill. U., 1982; MBA, Golden Gate U., 1984. Cert. mfg. engr. in robotics and mfg. systems mgmt. Ironworker, welder Viking Steel Co., Anaheim, Calif., 1982-83; electromechanical technician Tegal Corp., Novato, Calif., 1984-85; jet mechanic, thermal sprayer United Airlines, San Francisco, 1985—; mfg. engr., cons. Via Tech., Fairfield, Calif., 1985—; instr. Solano Coll., Suisun, Calif., 1982—; prof. engring. So. Ill. U., Carbondale, 1986; chmn. Robotics Automated Instructional Network, Dearborn, Mich., 1987—. Patentee in field. Advisor 4H Clubs, Collinsville, Va., 1985. With USAF, 1977-81, USAF Reserve, 1981—. Mem. Nat. Soc. Profl. Engrs., Am. Welding Soc. (thermal spray and robotics com. 1987—), Soc. Mfg. Engrs. (mem. Robotics Internat. tech. council 1987—, CASA/SME tech. coun.), Robotics Industries Assn. (human interface com. 1986—), Automated Vision Assn. (sensor interface com. 1986—), ASM Internat. (thermal com. 1988—), Air Force Assn. Office: Via Tech PO Box 2868 Fairfield CA 94533-0286

VIALARDI, ENZO JOSEPH, publishing company executive; b. N.Y.C., Nov. 22, 1936; s. Ottavio and Maria (Bertagnolio) V.; m. Barbette Joyce Pollack, Aug. 10, 1969; children: Robert, Suzanne. BBA, Iona Coll., 1959. CPA, N.Y. Acct. Deloitte, Haskins & Sells, N.Y.C., 1959-66; div. v.p., controller PepsiCo Inc., Purchase, N.Y., 1966-72; v.p., treas. Revlon Inc., N.Y.C., 1972-84; exec. v.p., chief operating officer Simon & Schuster, N.Y.C., 1984—. Served with USAR, 1959-65. Office: Simon & Schuster Inc 1230 Avenue of the Americas New York NY 10020

VIART, GUY PASCAL, export manager; b. Arras, France, May 16, 1957; s. Micheline and Denis (Brasseur) V.; m. Brigitte Marie Theret, Aug. 19, 1977; children—Marc, Sophie. Baccalaureat with Honors, Lycee Robespierre, France, 1975; D. in Engring., Enstimd, France, 1975; grad. in Bus. Mgmt. Bus. Inst. Lille, 1986; grad. in Human Anatomy, Pitie-Salpetriere Hosp., Paris, 1986 . Research & Devel. mgr. FICAL, Loison/Lens, France, 1980-83, export mgr., 1983-85, project mgr. in production restructuration, USINOR Wire Group, 1985-86; tech. mgr. SOFAMOR, Berck/mer., France, 1986—; auditor internat. orgn. OIPEEC, 1981-85; tchr. biomaterials, U. Medcine of Lille, France, 1986—; Author: (Invention) New Wire Galvanization, 1982; New Rope Design, 1983, New internal fixator for spine, 1987, New table for spinal surgery, 1988. Town councillor, Capelle-Fermont Pas De Calais, 1983. Mem. Departmental Council Confederation Gen. Des Cadres, Cotrel-Dubousset (mem. tech. documentation resp 1987), Sand Yachting (adminstrv. mgr. French fedn. 1987). Roman Catholic. Home: CD 49, 62690 Capelle-Fermont France Office: SOFAMOR BP 139, 62604 Berck-mer France

VICE, JON EARL, hospital executive; b. Fairfield, Ala., July 1, 1947; s. Jon Walker Vice and Martha Ann (Lee) Cain; m. Sara Rose Romano Marino, July 26, 1967 (div. Feb. 1975); children: Jon E. Jr., Lisa Ann; m. Joanne Katherine Richter, June 28, 1975; children: Jeffrey Walker, Jessica Lynn. BS, U. Ala., Tuscaloosa, 1970; MS, U. Ala., Birmingham, 1974. Asst. to adminstr. Children's Hosp. Ala., Birmingham, 1971-72, adminstr., chief operating officer, 1977-79; assoc. adminstr. Children's Hosp. Med. Ctr., Cin., 1972-76; exec. v.p., chief operating officer Children's Hosp. Wis., Milw., 1979-84, pres., chief exec. officer, 1984—; mem. exec. com., bd. dirs. Milw. Regional Med. Ctr., Milw., 1985—; bd. dirs. Child Health Corp. Am., Kansas City, Mo.; pres., bd. dirs. Total Care Health Plan (HMO), Milw., 1985-87. Named Outstandng Alumnus Grad. Program in Health Adminstrn., U. Ala.-Birmingham Alumni Assn., 1987. Mem. Am. Coll. Healthcare Execs., Nat. Assn. Childrens Hosps. (exec. council, bd. dirs. 1986—, chmn.-elect), Westmoor Country Club, University Club. Presbyterian. Office: Children's Hosp Wis PO Box 1997 Milwaukee WI 53201

VICK, AUSTIN LAFAYETTE, civil engineer; b. Cedervale, N.Mex., Jan. 28, 1929; s. Louis Lafayette and Mota Imon (Austin) V.; BSCE, N.Mex. State U., 1950, MSCE, 1961; m. Norine E. Melton, July 18, 1948; children: Larry A., Margaret J., David A. Commd. 2d lt. USAF, 1950, advanced through grades to capt., 1959, ret., 1970; ordnance engr. Ballistics Rsch. Lab., White Sands Proving Ground, Las Cruces, N.Mex., 1950-51, civil engr., 1951-55, gen. engr. White Sands Missile Range, 1957-73, phys. scientist adminstr., 1955-57, 73—; owner A.V. Constrn., Las Cruces, 1979—; realtor Campbell Agy., Las Cruces, 1979-84; cons. instrumentation systems, ops. maintenance and mgmt., 1984—; pres., treas. Survey Tech., Inc., 1985—; cons. in field, Las Cruces, 1984—. Mem. outstanding alumni awards com. N.Mex. State U., 1980. Recipient Outstanding Performance award Dept. Army, White Sands Missile Range, 1972, Spl. Act awards, 1967, 71, 75. Mem. Mil. Ops. Research Soc. (chmn. logistics group 1968-69), Am. Def. Preparedness Assn. (pres. 1970-72), Assn. U.S. Army (v.p. 1970-71), Am. Soc. Photogrametry, Am. Astronautical Soc. (sr. mem.), N.Mex. State U. Acad. Civil Engring. Contbr. articles to profl. jours. Home and Office: 4568 Spanish Dagger Las Cruces NM 88001

VICK, BUD LAWRENCE, accountant, consultant; b. Murray, Ky., Feb. 3, 1947; s. Ernest R. and Louise (Lawrence) V.; m. Susan Frances Klaff, Sept. 7, 1969; 1 child, Andrew W. BS, Washington U., St. Louis, 1969, MBA, 1970. CPA, Mo., N.J. Staff acct. Peat Marwick Main & Co., Kansas City, Mo., 1970-74, mgr., 1974-81, ptnr. in charge mid. market practice, 1981-88; nat. ptnr. in charge profl. devel. Peat Marwick Main & Co., Montvale, N.J., 1988—. Contbr. articles to profl. jours. Vice chmn. Friends Nelson-Atkins Mus. Art, Kansas City, 1983—; bd. of govs. Am. Royal Horse Show, Kansas City, 1981—; mem. Kansas City Tomorrow Civic Leadership, 1986—; bd. dirs., treas. Kansas City Neighborhood Alliance, 1986—. Mem. Mo. Soc. CPAs (vice chmn. acctg. procedure com. 1981-82, mem. state coun. 1975-81, chmn. careers com. 1982-84, chmn. ethics com. 1986-87), Kansas City Entrepreneurs Exch. (bd. advisors 1988—), Silicon Prairie Tech. Assn. (founding mem. 1986), Carriage Club, Kansas City Athletic Club, Apple Ridge Country Club, Omicron Delta Kappa. Home: 4 Collette Dr Ramsey

NJ 07446 Office: Peat Marwick Main & Co 3 Chestnut Ridge Rd Montvale NJ 07645

VICKERS, DAVID LEROY, materials executive; b. Detroit, Jan. 15, 1942; s. Vay Aldon and Vada Ann (Gaw) V.; m. Tomiye Tado, Apr. 22, 1961; children: David L. Jr., Steven T. BS in Indsl. Tech., Tenn Tech. U., 1967; MBA, Calif. State U., Long Beach, 1972. Chief indsl. engr. Pacific Tube Co., Commerce, Calif., 1967-73; dir. mfg. Ameron Inc., Monterey Park, Calif., 1973-84; exec. v.p. H.G. Fenton Material Co., San Diego, 1984—; bd. dirs. Pre-Mixed Concrete Co., San Diego, Sorrento Ready Mix Co., San Diego, A-1 Soils Co., San Diego, East County Materials, Inc.; officer Western Salt Co., San Diego; instr. U. of Hawaii, Honolulu, 1976-79, Loyola Marymount U., L.A., 1970-74. Bd. dirs. Mission Valley YMCA, San Diego, 1985-88. With USN, 1959-63. Mem. Inst. Indsl. Engrs. (sr.), So. Calif. Work Simplification Assn. (bd. dirs., pres. 1968-74), The Execs. Assn. (bd. dirs. San Diego chpt.), San Diego Employers Assn. (bd. dirs., pres. 1988—). Republican. Methodist. Office: HG Fenton Material Co 7220 Trade St Ste 300 San Diego CA 92112

VICKERS, NAOMI R., real estate executive; b. Anderson, Ind., Mar. 25, 1917; d. Floyd Leroy and Gertrude Marie (Richards) Stamm; m. Robert Ross Vickers (dec.); children—Robert V. Vickers, Richard R. Vickers, Philip L. Vickers, Denise (Mrs. Jack L. Healey). Sec., treas. Vickers Fine Homes, Anderson, 1951—, Vickers Apts., 1956—; sec., treas. Comml. Bldgs., 1958—. Mem. Toy Collectors Am. (antique toy train collector). Mem. Order Eastern Star, White Shrine, Madison County Shrine. Home: 2003 E 7th St Anderson IN 46012 Office: 724 Alhambra Dr Anderson IN 46012

VICKERY, GARY A., accountant; b. Gadsden, Ala., Sept. 26, 1942; s. Al Burns and Alice Ruth (Williams) V. BBA in Acctg., Ga. State U., 1968, M of Taxation, 1980. CPA, Ga. Acct. Coca-Cola Co., Atlanta, 1966-77; plant acct. Mead Packaging, Atlanta, 1971-77; auditor Post, Parr & Co., Atlanta, 1977-80; tax acct. Stewart & Assocs., Inc., Atlanta, 1980-85; tax mgr. Lanier Bus. Products, Inc., Atlanta, 1985—; instr. acctg. Ga. State U., Atlanta, 1987—. Mem. Nat. Assn. Accts. (dir. meeting 1986, dir. employment 1987, student affiliate 1989), Ga. Soc. CPA's, Atlanta Tax Club (sec. 1988, treas. 1989). Home: 2341 Dunwoody Crossing Atlanta GA 30338 Office: Lanier Bus Products Inc 1700 Chantilly Dr Atlanta GA 30324

VICKERY, JOHN DAVID, JR., lawyer. real estate company executive; b. Central, S.C., July 18, 1926; s. J.D. Vickery Sr. and Sadie (Stewart) V.; m. Martha Roper, 1948; children: John David III, Eugene, Sarah Martha, Susan. Student, Clemson U., 1943-46; LLB, U. S.C., 1950, JD, 1970. Bar S.C. Supreme Ct. 1950; ordained deacon First Bapt. Ch., Pickens, S.C., 1959. Enlisted USN Air Force, 1944, advanced through ranks to capt., resigned, 1956; broker-dealer INA Security Corp.; chmn. bd. dirs. Vickery Leaseholds Internat., Inc.; prin., ins. broker Vickery Ins. Agy.; prin., realty broker Pickens County Realty Co.; v.p. Vickery Corp. Sunday sch. tchr., tng. union dir., Pickens First Bapt. Ch., 1955—; trustee S.C. Bapt. Found., 1959—, pres. 1970, chmn. bd. trustees, 1981; trustee Long Creek Christian Acad., Oconee County, S.C., 1957-62; chmn. bd. trustees Pickens-Twelve Mile Bapt. Assn., 1970-73; del. So. Bapt. Conv., 1968, mem. stewardship commn., 1974-82; mem. S.C. House Reps., 1948-50, U.S. Postal Service Adv. Council, 1974-75; chmn. Pickens County United Fund Drive campaign, 1958, Pickens county Easter Seals campaign, 1960; past pres. Pickens Sch. PTO; mem. Pickens County Bd. Edn., 1964-71; sec., mem. S.C. Water Authority Bd. Pickens County, 1971-73. Mem. Masons, Shriners, Rotary Club. Home and Office: Vickery Office 102 Court St Pickens SC 29671

VIDETTO, SUSAN ANNE, marketing executive; b. Cin., Aug. 20, 1959; d. Donald Arthur and Mildred Dolores (Lowes) V. BA in Polit. Sci., Indiana U. of Pa., 1981; MS in Urban and Environ. Engring., Rensselaer Poly. Inst., 1982. Community relations dir. Federated Stores Realty, Hackensack, N.J., 1982-83; mktg. dir. Pyramid Cos., Kingston, N.Y., 1983-84, spl. project mgr., Syracuse, N.Y., 1984-86, dir. pub. relations, 1986-87; dir. mktg. The Cedarwood Cos., Akron, Ohio, 1987—. Solicitor Am. Heart Assn., North East, Pa., 1977-81; chmn. Upstate N.Y. Kids Say No, 1987. Mem. Internat. Council Shopping Ctrs., Nat. Assn. Indsl. and Office Parks, Akron C. of C., Pi Gamma Mu (pres. 1981), Syracuse Ski Hawks, Syracuse Updowntowners, Crestdale Garden Club. Republican. Avocations: classical piano. Home: 4508 Yorkdale Dr Stow OH 44224 Office: Cedarwood Cos 1765 Merriman Rd Akron OH 44313

VIE, RICHARD CARL, insurance company executive; b. St. Louis, Sept. 26, 1937; s. George William and Geraldine (Bell) V.; m. Joan Kay Wilschetz, June 4, 1960; children—Laura, Mark, Todd, Amy, Paul, Sarah. Student, St. Louis U., U. Mo. Agt. Reliable Life Ins. Co., St. Louis, 1962-63; from asst. v.p. to sr. v.p. Reliable Life Ins. Co., 1964-79; pres. Old Reliable Fire Ins. Co., St. Louis, 1972-79, Commonwealth Life Ins. Co., St. Louis, 1979-82, United Ins. Co. Am., Chgo., 1983—; mem. devel. com. Concordia Coll. Bd. dirs. Grand Ctr. Assn., St. Louis, 1982, St. Louis U. Corp., 1982; trustee Lutheran Assn. Higher Edn., St. Louis, 1982; chmn. Trinity Ch. Bldg. Fund Drive. Served to lt. USN, 1958-62. Home: 6286 Timberview Lisle IL 60532 Office: United Ins Co Am One E Wacker Dr Chicago IL 60601

VIEHE, KARL WILLIAM, educator, consulting firm executive; b. Allentown, Pa., Aug. 12, 1943; s. John Sage and Margaret (Higgs) V. MA in Econs., Am. U., 1968, JD, Howard U., 1981; MLT, Georgetown U., 1982. Bar: D.C., U.S. Ct. of Internat. Trade, U.S. Tax Ct., U.S. Ct. Appeals (4th, fed. and D.C. cirs.), U.S. Supreme Ct. Tchr. math. and Russian St. Alban's Sch., Washington, 1967-68; pres., chief exec. officer Investment Futures Group, Washington, 1968—; assoc. prof. math. and stats., U. D.C., Washington, 1970—; chmn. bd. dirs. Nat. Ednl. Trust, Washington, 1971—; internat. advt. dir. Washingtonian Mag., 1972-75; adj. prof. grad. sch. bus. Am. U., Washington, 1972—; assoc. prof. law, chmn. mgmt. program Fla. Inst. Tech., 1983-85; of counsel Ebert & Bowytz, 1983—; ptnr. Tighe, Curhan & Viehe, Washington, 1983—. adj. prof. grad. sch. bus. adminstrn. George Washington U., 1986—, Am. U., 1972—; vis. prof. Internat. Devel. Law Inst., Rome, 1987—. Creator numerous speeches, symposia and seminars; contbr. articles to profl. jours. Mem. Am. Econ. Assn., Am. Fin. Assn., ABA, D.C. Bar Assn., Am. Arbitration Assn. (comml. panel, internat. panel). Avocations: painting, piano, photography, tennis, golf. Home: 4397 Embassy Park Dr NW Washington DC 20016 Office: Tighe Curhan & Viehe 1750 Pennsylvania Ave NW Washington DC 20006

VIEMEISTER, PETER EMMONS, business executive; b. Mineola, N.Y., Feb. 15, 1929; s. August Louis and Janet (Emmons) V.; B.M.E. (Grumman scholar), Rensselaer Poly. Inst., 1950; S.M. (Sloan Fellow), Mass. Inst. Tech., 1969; m. Suzanne Neelands, 1951 (div. 1965); children—Clay N., Read L., Susan B., Katherine A.; m. 2d, Cynthia Lee Grubbs, 1983; 1 child, Benjamin T. With Lippincott & Margulies, N.Y.C., 1945; with Grumman Aircraft, Bethpage, N.Y., 1946-57, mgr. bus. planning, 1960-65, asst. to pres. and chmn. bd., 1965-69; pres. Grumman Data Systems Corp., Bethpage, 1969-73; chmn. bd. Computility, Inc., Boston, 1971-73; v.p. Grumman Corp., 1973-79; dir. Grumman Allied Industries, 1975-79, Paumonack Leasing Corp., 1976-79; adj. assoc. prof. Dowling Coll., 1972-73. Chmn. Empire State Coll. Found., 1975-78; trustee Huntington (Dist. 3) Public Schs., 1964-66; bd. dirs. Energy Research Inst. S.C., 1977-81; treas. Bedford Meml. Found., 1982—; chmn. Bedford City/County Mus., 1983—; trustee Lynchburg Coll., 1984—; adv. com. Inst. Energy Analysis, Oak Ridge, 1980-84. Mem. Sigma Xi, Tau Beta Pi. Author: The Lightning Book, 1961; Psychosystems, 1973. Inventor behavior simulator. Office: Solaridge Bedford VA 24523

VIENER, JOHN DAVID, lawyer; b. Richmond, Va., Oct. 18, 1939; s. Reuben and Thelma (Kurtz) V.; m. Karin Erika Bauer, Apr. 7, 1969; children: John David Jr., Katherine Bauer. BA, Yale U., 1961; JD, Harvard U., 1964. Bar: N.Y. State 1965, U.S. Supreme Ct. 1970, U.S. Dist. Ct. (so. dist.) N.Y. 1974, U.S. Tax Ct. 1975. Assoc. Satterlee, Warfield & Stephens, N.Y.C., 1964-69; sole practice N.Y.C., 1969-76; founder, bd. dirs., gen. counsel Foxfire Fund Inc., 1968-88; sr. ptnr. Christy & Viener, N.Y.C., 1976—; gen. counsel, bd. dirs. Landmark Communities, Inc., 1970—, NF&M Internat., Inc., 1976—, Singer Fund, Inc., 1979—; gen. counsel Nat. Cancer Found. Cancer Care, 1982-85, Am. Continental Properties Group, 1978—, Troster, Singer & Co., 1970-77; bd. dirs. Gen. Financiere Immob. et Commer. S.A., 1985—; spl. counsel fin. instns., investment banking and securities concerns; real estate and tax advisor to fgn. instns. Mem. ABA, N.Y. State Bar Assn., Assn. Bar City N.Y. Clubs: Harmonie (N.Y.C.); Manursing Island (Rye, N.Y.). Home: 45 E 62d St New York NY 10021 also: The Parsonage Washington CT 06793 Office: Christy & Viener 620 Fifth Ave New York NY 10020

VIERMETZ, KURT F., banker; b. Augsburg, Bavaria, Germany, Apr. 27, 1939; came to U.S., 1985; s. Alfons and Claire (Bruck) V.; m. Felicitas Kempe, May, 1966; 1 child, Maximilian. Grad., Heilig Kreuz Coll., Germany, 1957. With Morgan Guaranty Trust Co. of N.Y., Frankfurt, Fed. Republic Germany, 1966-69; asst. v.p. Morgan Guaranty Trust Co. of N.Y., Frankfurt, 1969-71; v.p. Morgan Guaranty Trust Co. of N.Y., Paris, 1971-82; sr. v.p. for Central Europe Morgan Guaranty Trust Co. of N.Y., N.Y.C., 1982-85, dir., 1985—; gen. mgr. Saudi Internat. Bank, London, 1975-77. Author books and articles on internat. fin. to profl. publs. Mem. Am. C. of C. in Germany. Roman Catholic. Home: 30 Island Dr Rye NY 10580 Office: Morgan Guaranty Trust Co NY 23 Wall St New York NY 10015

VIETS, RICHARD NOYES, international consultant, former foreign service officer; b. Burlington, Vt., Nov. 10, 1930; s. John Bartlett and Natalie (Noyes) V.; m. Marina Leonarda Woroniecka, May 28, 1959; children: Alexandra, Katrina, Marynka. AB, U. Vt., 1955, LLD (hon.), 1986; post-grad., Harvard U., 1980. Jr. officer U.S. Info. Agy., various locations, 1955-57; asst. trade fair mgr. Dept Commerce Office Internat. Trade Fairs, 1957-60; with Bur. Labor Statistics, 1962; fgn. service officer Dept. State, Bucharest, Romania, Tel Aviv and India, 1962-79; ambassador to Tanzania, 1979-81, Jordan, 1981-84; career minister 1984-88; pres. Aspen Hill Enterprises Ltd., Washington, 1988—. With U.S. Army, 1950-52. Mem. Met. Club (Washington), Turf Club, Atheaneum Club (London). Office: Aspen Hill Enterprises 900 17th St NW Ste 400 Washington DC 20006

VIETS, ROBERT O., utilities executive; b. Girard, Kans., Dec. 8, 1943; s. Willard O. and Caroline L. (Bollwinkel) V.; m. Karen M. Kreiter, June 13, 1980. BA in Econs., Washburn U., 1965; JD, Washington U., 1969. CPA; Bar: Kans., Mo., Ill. Auditor Arthur Andersen & Co., Chgo., 1969-73; mgr. spl. studies Cen. Ill. Light Co., Peoria, 1973-76, mgr. rates and regulatory affairs, 1976-80, asst. v.p., regulatory affairs, 1980-81, v.p. fin. services, 1981-83, v.p. fin. group, 1983-86; sr. v.p. Cilcorp, Inc. and Cen. Ill. Light Co., Peoria, 1986-88, pres., chief exec. officer, chmn. bd., 1988—; bd. dirs. Comml. Nat. Bank Peoria, Lincoln Office Supply, Inc., Randolph and Assocs. Inc., Peoria, TS Communications, Inc., Springfield, Ill., Agrl. Research and Devel., Peoria. Bd. dirs. Heart of Ill. United Way; bd. dirs., pres. Peoria Goodwill Industries; bd. dirs., v.p. W.D. Boyce council Boy Scouts Am. Mem. ABA, Ill. Bar Assn., Peoria County Bar Assn., Am. Inst. CPA's, Ill. Soc. CPA's. Republican. Lutheran. Lodge: Rotary (bd. dirs. 1985—, pres. 1986-87). Home: 305 W Wolf Rd Peoria IL 61614 Office: CILCORP Inc 300 Liberty St Peoria IL 61602

VIGNOLA, ANDREW MICHAEL, SR., systems management executive; b. N.Y.C., Sept. 6, 1938; s. Michael John and Mary Elizabeth (Romano) V.; student in Bus. Adminstrn., Coll. City N.Y., 1956-59; m. Barbara Francis Hummel, Aug. 22, 1959; children—Ellen Ann, Andrew Michael, Robert Eugene. Programmer trainee Citibank, N.Y.C., 1959-60; programmer analyst Soc. for Savs., Hartford, Conn., 1960-63; mgr. on-line data center NCR Corp., Boston, 1963-67; cons., sr. partner Computer Assistance, Inc., Hartford, 1967-72; v.p., info. systems svc. div. Soc. for Savs., Hartford, 1972-80; pres. Solar Srvcs., Inc. subs. Soc. for Savs., 1977-80; sr. v.p., info. svcs. dir. Dime Savs. Bank, N.Y.C., 1980-83; v.p. Info. Svcs. Group, Advest Inc., Hartford, Conn., 1983-85; pres. Cosine Inc., Meriden, Conn., 1985—; mem. faculty Conn. Savs. Sch. Fin. and Mgmt.; lectr. in field. Mem. Data Processing Mgmt. Assn. (pres., chmn. bd. Hartford chpt. 1976-77). Contbr. articles to profl. jours. Inventor of banking brokerage interfact. Home: 161 N Timber Ln Cheshire CT 06410 Office: Cosine Inc 180 Research Pkwy Meriden CT 06450

VIGNOLA, LEONARD, management consultant, investment banker; b. Orange, N.J., Aug. 8, 1830; s. Leonard Sr. and Evelyn (Foertsch) V.; m. Dorothea Maude Costello, Sept. 5, 1953 (div. Aug. 1975); children: Mark, Eric, Chad, Cort, Noel, Adam, Dawn. BS in Fin., Northwestern U., 1951; MBA, Case Western Res. U., 1959. Controller U.S. Steel Corp., Cleve., 1951-59; prin. Cresap, McCormick & Paget-Checchi & Co., N.Y.C., 1959-64; dir. corp. planning Crucible Steel, Pitts., 1964-65; dir. internal cons. PepsiCo, N.Y.C., 1965-70; v.p. Alan Patricof & Assocs., N.Y.C., 1970-71; pres. Automated Ticket Systems, N.Y.C., 1971-73; v.p. Marwit Capital, Stamford, Conn., 1974-75; mng. dir. Beacon Ptnrs., Stamford, 1975—; v.p., bd. dirs. Venture Assn. N.J., Morristown, 1984—; bd. dir. Bridgeport (Conn.) Venture Group Accts. for Pub. Interest, N.Y.C. Author: Strategic Divestment, 1974, (with others) Handbook on Local Government Productivity, 1980. Chmn. Stamford Bd. Fin., 1977-79, Stamford Transit Dist., 1980-85, Stamford Small Bus. Council, 1984-85; candidate for mayor City of Stamford, 1987; bd. dirs. New Eng. Lynch Operetta. Mem. Planning Forum Nat. Assn. Bus. Economists, Conn. Venture Group, Nat. Assn. Small Bus., Investment Corpus, Mensa. Republican. Club: Republican Foroum (Stamford) (bd. dirs. 1984—). Home: 71 Strawberry Hill Ave #614 Stamford CT 06902 Office: Beacon Ptnrs 71 Strawberry Hill Ave Stamford CT 06902

VIGODA, DAVID, financial executive; b. Bklyn., May 18, 1946; s. William Vigoda and Anita (Rinzberg) Shapiro; m. Elizabeth Platt Eson, June 22, 1969; 1 child, Benjamin William. BA, U. Chgo., 1968. Cert. fin. planner; chartered fin. analyst. Gen. mgr. Cold Mountain Pottery, Albany, N.Y., 1974-84; pres. Assoc. Investment Mgmt., Albany, N.Y., 1984-88; mgr. fin. planning Bollam Sheedy Torani & Co., Albany, 1989—. Author newspaper column: Money Talks, 1987—; commentator radio program: Dialog 81, 1987—. Mem. urgent action network Amnesty Internat., 1984—; coach Bethlehem Soccer Club, Delmar, N.Y., 1985—; mem. investment com. Bethlehem Bd. Edn., 1984-85. Mem. Inst. Chartered Fin. Analysts, Inst. Cert. Fin. Planners (mem. com. 1986—), Internat. Assn. Fin. Planning, Capital Dist. Soc. Inst., Cert. Fin. Planners (pres. 1985-88, chmn. 1988—). Office: Bollam Sheedy Torani & Co 26 Computer Dr W Albany NY 12205

VILA, ANDREW CLINCHY, accountant; b. Phila., Oct. 11, 1957; s. Joseph Sala and Jean (Clinchy) V.; m. Nancy Jo Romantini, Aug. 3, 1985. BBA, U. Wis., 1980; postgrad., U. Wis., Milw., 1984—. CPA, Wis. Staff acct. Payco Am. Corp., Brookfield, Wis., 1980-85; sr. tax acct. Applied Power, Inc., Butler, Wis., 1985—. Recipient Bus. Edn. Recognition award Glendale (Wis.) Women's Club, 1976. Mem. Beta Alpha Psi. Republican. Episcopalian. Home: 2113 E Jarvis St Milwaukee WI 53211 Office: Applied Power Inc 13000 W Silver Spring Dr Butler WI 53007

VILGRAIN, PIERRE E., company executive; b. Nancy, France, June 7, 1922; s. Robert M. and Lucile Edith (Joucla-Pelous) V.; m. Micheline H. Jeannequin, Mar. 11, 1947; children: Francois, Marie-Edith Vilgrain Rey-Jouvin, Edouard, Elizabeth. Ed. St. Lawrence Coll., Instn. Frilley. Pres., Grande Semoulerie De L'Quest a Gond Pontouvre (France), adminstr., sr. v.p. Grands Moulins De Paris; dir. Compagnie Francaise Commerciale et Financiere; dir., pres. Sofida France, Sofida Belgium, S.A. Cerealis Geneve, Vie De France Corp. USA. Decorated Croix-de-Guerre (France); recipient Presdl. Citation (U.S.A.). Clubs: Automobile de France, Yacht de France, Cercle du Bois de Boulogne, St-Cloud Country (pres.). Office: Grands Moulins De Paris, 15 rue Croix-des-Petits-Champs, 75001 Paris France

VILLA, NANCY STELL, information systems consultant; b. Milw., Dec. 1, 1959; d. Thomas Patrick and Hilary Susan (Ambrose) S. BS in Bus. Adminstrn., Marquette U., 1982. Dist. tng. mgr. Computer Craft, San Antonio, 1983-85, major account rep., 1985-86; cons. The Stell Group, San Antonio, 1986—; researcher SW research Inst., San Antonio, 1985—. Republican. Roman Catholic. Home and Office: 5762 Hawaiian Sun San Antonio TX 78244

VILLAMIL, JOSE ANTONIO, bank executive; b. Havana, Cuba, Aug. 23, 1946; s. Jose Antonio and Maria Luz (Quinones-Monteagudo) V.; 1 child from previous marriage, Ana Maria; m. Maria E. Alejo, July 16, 1988. BS in Econs., La. State U., 1968, MA in Econs., 1971, postgrad., 1972-73. Economist U.S. Dept. Treasury, Washington, 1974-75; internat. economist Continental Ill. Nat. Bank, Chgo., 1975-78; v.p., economist Crocker Bank, San Francisco, 1978-81; sr. v.p., chief economist Southeast Bank, N.A., Miami, Fla., 1981—; Bd. economists The Miami Herald, 1985—; chmn. research council Fla. Internat. U., Miami, 1983—; mem. Gov. of Fla. Council of Econ. Advisors, 1987—. Contbr. articles to books, profl. jours. and newspapers. Bd. dirs. Miami-Dade Community Coll., 1985—; vice-chmn. Fla. Council on Econ. Edn., 1988—. Mem. Nat. Assn. Bus. Economists (forecasting panel 1984—), Fla. Exporters and Importers Assn (econ. advisor 1981—), Nat. Assn. Credit Mgrs. (econ. advisor 1985), Am. Club. Democrat. Roman Catholic. Office: SE Bank One Southeast Financial Ctr Miami FL 33131

VILLANI, KEVIN EMIL, banker; b. Boston, Apr. 16, 1948; s. Edmund Vincent and Alice Louise (Maloof) V.; m. Jane Elizabeth Flynn, Dec. 23, 1967; children: David, Brian, Patrick. BS in Math., U. Mass., 1970; MA in Econs., Purdue U., 1971, PhD in Econs. and Fin., 1974. Dep. asst. sec., chief economist HUD, Washington, 1979-82; sr. v.p., chief economist Fed. Home Loan Mortgage Corp., Washington, 1982-85; fin. officer Imperial Corp. Am., San Diego, 1985—. Author approx. 100 books and articles; editor-in-chief (mag.) Secondary Mortgage Markets, 1983-85; co-editor (mag.) Housing Fin. Rev. Recipient service awards, HUD, 1979-82. Mem. Am. Real Estate & Urban Econs. Assn. (program chmn. 198-84, 1st v.p. 1985, pres-elect, bd. dirs. 1985,), Am. Econ. Assn., Am. Fin. Assn., Krannert Alumni Assn. Office: Imperial Corp Am 9275 Skypark Ct PO Box 23036 San Diego CA 92123 also: Imperial Savs & Loan Assn 8787 Complex Dr San Diego CA 92123-0036

VINCENT, BRUCE HAVIRD, investment banker, oil and gas company executive; b. Laramie, Wyo., Nov. 7, 1947; s. Dale Leon and Mildred Sara (Havird) V.; m. Pamela Jean Benson, Dec. 20, 1968 (div. May 1986); children: Jennifer Jean, Bryce Havird. BBA, Duke U., 1969; MBA in Fin., U. Houston, 1976. Asst. v.p. First City Nat. Bank, Houston, 1975-77, v.p., group mgr. energy dept., 1977-80; exec. v.p., chief operating officer, bd. dirs. Peninsula Resources Corp., Corpus Christi, Tex., 1980-82; ptnr. investment banking Johnson & Vincent, Houston, 1982-85; pres., chief exec. officer Tangent Oil and Gas, Inc., Houston, 1985-86; exec. v.p., chief operating officer, chief fin. officer Energy Assets Internat. Corp., Houston, 1986-88; pres. Vincent & Co., 1988—. Served to lt. USN, 1969-72. Mem. Ind. Petroleum Assn. of Am., Tex. Mid-Continent Oil and Gas Assn., Tex. Ind. Producers and Royalty Owners Assn., Internat. Assn. Fin. Planning. Republican. Episcopalian. Home: 5292 Memorial Ste M8 Houston TX 77007

VINCENT, NORMAN L., insurance company executive; b. Milw., July 21, 1933; s. Victor V. Vincent and Hilda I. (Boedecker) Vincent Patlow; m. Arlene Page, Jan. 31, 1953 (div. 1978); children: J. Todd, Meg; m. Donna Jean Doll, Aug. 8, 1980. B.S., U. Wis., 1957; M.S., Purdue U., 1958, Ph.D., 1960. Diplomate Am. Bd. Profl. Psychology; registered psychologist., Ill., C.P.C.U., C.L.U. Supr. agy. research State Farm Ins. Cos., Bloomington, Ill., 1960-63, dir. agy. research., 1963-66, asst. v.p. agy., 1966-69, asst. v.p. exec., 1969-70, v.p. data processing, 1970—. Pres. Bloomington Bd. Edn., 1974-77; bd. dirs. YMCA, Bloomington, 1971-85. Served with M.I. U.S. Army, 1953-55. Mem. AAAS. Home: 304 N Perrin Ave Bloomington IL 61701 Office: State Farm Mut Automobile Ins Co One State Farm Plaza Bloomington IL 61710

VINCENT, THOMAS JAMES, retired manufacturing company executive; b. Balt., Mar. 17, 1934; s. Thomas Alonzo and Helen Geraldine (Cloman) V.; divorced; children: Wayne S., Robin K. MS, MIT, 1968. Div. gen. mgr. Fairchild Industries, St. Augustine, Fla., 1969-72; pres. T.J. Vincent Properties Ltd., St. Augustine, 1972-75, Pacific Concrete & Rock Co., Honolulu, 1975-77, Ramsey Engring. Co., St. Paul, 1977-80, Kobe Inc., Los Angeles, 1980-84, Milchem Inc., Houston, 1984-85; pres. York (Pa.) Internat. Corp., 1985-88, also bd. dirs., cons. Author: Fairplan, 1962. Named one of Outstanding Young Men in Am., Jaycees, 1965; Alfred P. Sloan fellow MIT, 1967; recipient Research for Progress Achievement award, 1972. Home and Office: 225 Overbrook Dr Casselberry FL 32707

VINCO, JAMES RAY, transportation executive; b. Oakland, Calif., Aug. 16, 1938; s. James Samuel and Pauline Gertrude (Isabel) V.; m. Margaret J. Sheridan, Oct. 27, 1968; children: Andrea, Michael, Paul. BS, U. Calif., 1960. Asst. treas. Western Temporary Svcs., Walnut Creek, Calif., 1966-69; treas. Flying Tiger Line Inc., L.A., 1969-77, Shaklee Corp., San Francisco, 1977-83; v.p. fin., chief fin. officer Alaska Air Group/Alaska Airlines, Seattle, 1983—, also bd. dirs. With U.S. Army, 1960-61. Mem. Fin. Execs. Inst. Office: Alaska Airlines Inc PO Box 68900 Seattle WA 98168

VINES, HENRY ELLSWORTH, III, controller, wood product executive, computer and tax consultant; b. Chgo., Apr. 17, 1950; s. Henry Ellsworth and Verle (Low) V.; m. Ethel Melton (div. 1977); 1 child, Tiffany Layne; m. Cindy Lou Rich, Jan. 5, 1985; 1 child, Sasha Teresa Root. BS, Menlo Sch. Bus. Adminstrn., 1972; MBA, Golden Gate Grad. Sch., 1985; CFP, Coll. Fin. Planning, Denver, 1987; postgrad., William F. Taft Law Sch., 1989—. CPA. Asst. controller Legallet Tanning, San Francisco, 1973-79; auditor Martin Schoonover & Paddock, Orange, Calif., 1980-82; tax mgr. Helsley Mulcahy & Fesler, Santa Ana, Calif., 1982-85; controller Biz Group, Fullerton, Calif., 1985—; chief fin. officer Precision Concepts, Anaheim, Calif., 1987—; pvt. practice in tax preparation Orange, Calif., 1985—, pvt. practice in computer consulting, 1985—. Contbr. articles in field. Mem. Am. Inst. CPA's, Calif. Inst. CPA's. Republican. Clubs: Foster City Tennis (pres. 1977), San Mateo Tennis (pres. 1978). Home: 401 W La Veta #192 Orange CA 92667 Office: Biz & Assocs 2100 E Valencia #D Fullerton CA 92731

VINGO, JAMES RAY, transportation executive; b. Oakland, Calif., Aug. 16, 1938; s. James Samuel and Pauline G. (Isbell) V.; m. Margaret Joanna Sheridan, Oct. 16, 1968; children: Andrea, Michael, Paul. BBA, U. Calif., Berkeley, 1960. Underwriter Calif. Compensation Fund, San Francisco, 1960-63, Fireman's Fund, San Jose, Calif., 1963-66; asst. treas. Western Temporary Services, San Francisco, 1966-68; casualty mgr. CNA Ins. Group, San Francisco, 1968-69; treas. Flying Tiger Line, Los Angeles, 1969-77, Shaklee Corp., San Francisco, 1977-83; v.p. fin. and chief fin. officer Alaska Airlines, Inc., Seattle, 1983—; v.p. fin. and chief fin. officer Alaska Air Group, Seattle, 1983—, also bd. dirs.; bd. dirs. Horizon Air Industries, Seattle. Served with U.S. Army, 1960-61. Mem. Fin. Execs. Inst. Office: Alaska Air Group Inc 19415 Pacific Hwy S Box 68947 Seattle WA 98168

VINOPAL, TIMOTHY JOHN, aerospace engineer; b. Rice Lake, Wis., Mar. 15, 1959; s. Emanuel J. and Margaret R. (LePlant) V.; m. Evelyn Struck, June 6, 1987. BSME, Rensselaer Polytechnic Inst., 1981; postgrad. in astronautics, U. Wash., 1982-85. Registered profl. engr. Mechanism designer Digital Equipment Corp., Maynard, Mass., 1979; thermodynamicist Cons. Engrs., Mpls., 1980; flight performance analyst Swissair, Zurich, Switzerland, 1981; designer space sta. Boeing Aerospace, Seattle, 1981-82, dep. study mgr. manned planetary transp., 1982-83, study mgr. upper stage, 1983-85; lead designer space sta. lab. Boeing Aerospace, Huntsville, Ala., 1985-87; systems launch vehicles upper stages configurator Boeing Aerospace, Seattle, 1987, study mgr. upper stage, 1989—. Author: Aeroassist Orbital Transfer Technologies, 1985; editor: Closed Cycle Life Support Systems, 1983, 84; contbr. articles to profl. jours. Active Habitat for Humanity, Seattle, 1988—. Fellow Space Studies Inst.; mem. Am. Inst. Aeronautics and Astronautics (pub. policy dir. 1988—, young mems. com. 1985—, space transp. com. 1989—); Am. Soc. Mech. Engrs., Nat. Space Soc. (local pres. 1980-82). Home: 4658 Eastern Ave N Seattle WA 98103 Office: Boeing Aerospace Seattle WA 98124

VINSON, BERNARD L., temporary personnel services executive; b. N.Y.C., July 31, 1919; s. I. Edward and Eva (Levin) V.; m. Gloria Ann Konowitch, Oct. 17, 1948; children: Marsha Lynn, Edward B. BA, U. Mich., 1940, MA, 1941. Asst. to v.p. sales M. Lowenstein & Sons, N.Y.C., 1946-48; pres. The Original Tempo Services Corp., East Meadow, N.Y., 1949—. Pres. Nassau County Conv. & Visitors Bur., Mineola, N.Y., 1978, chmn. 1979—; mem. bd. Hofstra U., 1975—. Lt. comdr. USN, 1941-46. Mem. L.I. Mid-Suffolk Bus. Assn. (pres. 1986—). Republican. Jewish. Clubs: Chairmen's (Mineola); Princeton, U. Mich. (N.Y.C.); Govs. (W. Palm Beach, Fla.), Hofstra. U. (Hempstead, N.Y.). Lodges: Masons, Shriners,

Elks. Home: 100 Bayview Ave Great Neck NY 11021 Office: The Original Tempo Svcs Corp 1900 Hempstead Turnpike East Meadow NY 11554

VINSON, JAMES A., real estate corporation officer; b. Jersey City, 1945. Grad., U. Pa., 1967. Now pres., dir. Merrill Lynch div. Hubbard, Inc., N.Y.C., chief oper. officer. Office: Merrill Lynch Hubbard Inc 2 Broadway New York NY 10004 *

VIRIYARUNGSARIT, SANTI, editor, publisher, columnist; b. Nakornpathom, Thailand, Aug. 1, 1946; s. Su and Ungmui V.; m. Sumolkree Chandra Kunjara, Nov. 13, 1975; children—Tanit, Pakanee and Parita (twins), Kawin. B. in Pub. Relations, Chulalongkorn U., 1973. Polit. news editor Thairath Daily, Bangkok, Thailand, 1972-76, social editor, 1976—; mng. dir. Media Associated, Bangkok, 1981—; cons. pub. relations Maboonkrong Complex, Bangkok, 1983-87. Editor: Computer Dictionary, 1984, 25 Thai Millionaire Life, 1984; exec. editor: (jour.) Money and Banking, 1982; (mag.) Modern Office, 1984. Chmn. pub. relations com. Thairath Found., Bangkok, 1983—; mem. bd. com. Communication Arts Alumni Chulalongkorn U., Bangkok, 1984-85; bd. dirs. Prommit Hosp., Bangkok, 1984—, Ramathibodi Found., Ramthibodi Hosp., 1987—. Decorated comdr. 2nd and 3d class Most Exalted Order of White Elephant; knight comdr. 2d class Most Noble Order Crown of Thailand. Mem. Journalist Assn. Thailand, Reporter Assn. Thailand, Polo Club. Avocations: tennis; swimming; reading. Home: 42/38 Sci Chokchairuammit, Vipavadeerungsit Rd, Bangkok 10900, Thailand Office: Media Associated Co Ltd, 42/37 Soi Chokchairuammit, Vipavadeerungsit Rd, Bangkok 10900, Thailand

VIRTUE, VIRGINIA MAY, real estate broker; b. Berlin, N.J., Aug. 17, 1926; d. Carl and Gertrude (Heinecke) Fabrizio; m. Harlan N. Virtue, Apr. 10, 1948; children: Wanda, Penny, Melodie. Cert. real estat broker. Mgr. Fine Arts Silver & China Co., Wilmington, Del., 1945-68; sales assoc. J.P. Stoltz Realtor, Wilmington, Del., 1968-75; pres. V Virtue, Inc., Wilmington, 1975—; bd. dirs. First State Bank, Wilmington. Chmn. ladies activities Immanuel Bapt. Ch., Wilmington, 1965-80; mem. legis. com. State Assn. Realtors, Dover, Del., 1980-88. Named Realtor of Yr. New Castle County Assn. of Realtors, 1978. Mem. Nat. Assn. Realtors (coord. fed. dist. Del. chpt.) 1984-86), Del. Assn. Realtors (bd. dirs. 1978-88), New Castle County Assn. Realtors, Realtors Nat. Mktg. Inst. Home: 49 Michangelo Ct RD #6 Hockessin DE 19707 Office: V Virtue Inc 26 Honeysuckle Dr Wilmington DE 19804

VISCARDI, PETER G., manufacturing and service company executive; b. N.Y.C., Dec. 28, 1947; s. Peter and Louise (Johnson) V.; m. Margaret E. McGowan, Sept. 11, 1971; children: Margaret, Peter. BA, Hunter Coll., 1970. CPCU. Ins. mgr. Jaffie Contracting Co., Inc., N.Y.C., 1971-73; ins. adminstr. Otis Elevator Co., N.Y.C., 1973, supr. ins. adminstrn., 1974; dir. adminstrn. Finsure div. Studebaker-Worthington, Inc., N.Y.C., 1975-78, corp. risk mgr./exec. v.p., chief operating officer, 1978-80; mgr. corp. ins. Am. Brands, Inc., N.Y.C., 1980-81, mgr. corp. ins. and real estate, 1981-87; dir. corp. ins. Am. Brands, Inc., Old Greenwich, Conn., 1987—; bd. dirs., v.p. 1700 Ins. Co., Ltd., 1986—; alt. bd. dirs. CODA, Ltd. Mem. editorial adv. bd. Risk and Benefits mag. Mem. Soc. CPCU, Risk and Ins. Mgmt. Soc., Nat. Fire Protection Assn. Office: Am Brands Inc 1700 E Putnam Ave Old Greenwich CT 06870

VISCUSI, W. KIP, economics educator; b. Trenton, N.J., Oct. 3, 1949; s. William Edward and Evelyn (Martin) V.; m. Catherine Makdisi, Sep. 26, 1972; children: Kira Margaret, Michael Kip. AB summa cum laude, Harvard U., 1971, MPP, 1973, AM, 1974, PhD, 1976. Prof. econs. Northwestern U., Evanston, Ill., 1976-80, 85-88; dep. dir. White House Council on Wage and Price Stability, Washington, 1979-81; prof. econs. Duke U., Durham, N.C., 1981-85; research prof. econs. U. Chgo., 1985-86; research assoc. Nat. Bur. Econ. Research, 1978—, Nat. Commn. for Employment Policy, 1981; mem. EPA Sci. Adv. Bd., 1986—, Nat. Acad. Sci. Panel, 1978-79; cons. U.S. Gen. Acctg. Office, 1981-85, Dept. of Justice, 1986-87, U.S. Office of Mgmt. and Budget, 1983; assoc. reporter Am. Law Inst., 1986—. Author: Employment Hazards, 1979 (Wells prize 1977), Risk by Choice, 1983, Regulating Consumer Porduct Safety, 1984, Learning About Risk, 1987; editor Jour. of Risk and Uncertainty; contbg. editor Regulation Mag.; assoc. editor Internat. Rev. of Law and Econs. Mem. Am. Econ. Assn. Roman Catholic. Home: 2419 Sedgefield Dr Chapel Hill NC 27514 Office: Duke U Dept Econs Durham NC 27706

VISH, DONALD H., lawyer; b. Ft. Benning, Ga., Jan. 18, 1945; s. D.H. Jr. and Dorris (Parrish) V.; m. Catherine Hamilton, Aug. 20, 1966 (div. 1986); children: Donald Hamilton, Daphne Mershon. BA in English, Bellarmine Coll., 1968; JD cum laude, U. Louisville, 1971. Bar: Ky. 1971, Fla. 1972, U.S. Ct. Appeals (6th cir.) 1974. Sec., gen. counsel Gen. Energy Corp., Lexington, Ky., 1978-83; ptnr. firm Wyatt, Tarrant & Combs, Lexington, 1980-88, Frost & Jacobs, Lexington, 1988—; assoc. prof. Coll. of Law, U. Ky., Lexington, part-time 1977-80, adj. assoc. prof. mineral law, 1979-85. Contbr. to legal ency. American Law of Mining, 2d edit., 1984; co-editor, contbr. Coal Law and Regulation, 1983. Trustee Sayre Sch., Lexington, 1980-88, chmn. bd., 1986-88; coun. Blue Grass Boy Scouts Am., Lexington. Fellow Am. Bar Found.; mem. Am. Law Inst., Ea. Mineral Law Found. (trustee 1979—, exec. com. 1979-82, chmn. coal subcom. 1984-85), Am. Judicature Soc., Fla. Bar Assn., Ky. Bar Assn. (ethics com. 1983-85), ABA (chmn. coal com., nat. resources sec.) , Am. Soc. Corp. Secs., English-Speaking Union., Bluegrass Charity Ball Assn. , Pendennis Club, Keeneland Club, Lexington Club. Republican. Episcopalian. Home: 1788 Moreland Dr Lexington KY 40502 Office: Frost & Jacobs 1100 Vine Center Tower Lexington KY 40507

VISKOVICH, FRED JOHN, information technology consultant; b. Passaic, N.J., Mar. 30, 1950; s. Fred Methodius and Elizabeth Margaret (Kovalchik) V.; m. Cynara Bernadette Himes; children: Frederick, Charles, Cynara, Robert, William. BA, Rutgers U., 1973; MA, U. Dayton, 1975. Data coordinator Walworth-Aloyco, Linden, N.J., 1975-76; programmer, analyst County of Lehigh, Allentown, Pa., 1976-77; dir. Dept. Treasury State of Pa., Harrisburg, 1977-83, Coopers & Lybrand, Phila., 1983—. Contbr. articles to profl. jours. Roman Catholic. Home: 1198 Quarry Commons Dr Yardley PA 19067 Office: Coopers & Lybrand 2400 Eleven Penn Ctr Philadelphia PA 19103

VITALE, FRANCIS XAVIER, JR., communications executive; b. Bklyn., June 16, 1944; s. Francis Xavier and Laura Ann (Lucente) V.; m. Sandra Kaye Hager, Sept. 16, 1967 (div. May 1979); m. Linda Lucie Evans, Oct. 18, 1986. AS in Electrical Engring., Spring Garden Coll., 1964; BS in Mktg., Del. Valley Coll., 1972; MBA, Temple U., 1976. Communications assoc. ITT Corp., N.Y.C., 1967-71; mgr. press rels. Leeds & Northrup Co., North Wales, Pa., 1971-76; v.p. corp. rels. Narco Sci. Inc., Ft. Washington, Pa., 1976-81; cons. fin. and corp. communications Phila., 1981-83; v.p. investor rels. and corp. communications Engelhard Corp., Edison, N.J., 1983—. Mem. exec. legis. affairs com. Health Industry Mfrs. Assn., Washington, 1979-81. Served with USAF, 1965-67. Mem. Nat. Investor Relations Inst. (chpt. pres. 1980-81), Chem. Mfrs. Assn. Roman Catholic. Office: Engelhard Corp Menlo Park CN40 Edison NJ 08818

VITANZA, ROBERT DOMINIC, personnel consultant; b. Bronx, Dec. 20, 1955; s. Basilio and Joan (Gaul) V.; m. Anne Beaupre Dubuque, Jan. 30, 1982. BA, Niagara (N.Y.) U., 1978. Recruiter Hipp Waters, Inc., Greenwich, Conn., 1979-84; exec. recruiter, owner Licari & Vitanza Assoc., Inc., Rye, N.Y., 1984—. guest speaker R.I. Personnel Assn. Conf., Providence, 1982. Mem. Nat. Assn. Personnel Cons. (guest speaker 1981). Republican. Roman Catholic. Home: 99 Sherman Turnpike Redding CT 06896 Office: Licari & Vitanza Assoc Inc 16 Elm Pl Rye NY 10580

VITKOWSKY, VINCENT JOSEPH, lawyer; b. Newark, Oct. 3, 1955; s. Boniface and Rosemary (Ofack) V.; m. Mary Gunzburg, May 16, 1981; 1 child, Vincent Jr. BA, Northwestern U., 1977; JD, Cornell U., 1980. Bar: N.Y. 1981, N.Y. Dist. Ct. (so. and ea. dists.) N.Y. 1981. Assoc. Hart and Hume, N.Y.C., 1980-84, Kroll, Tract, Harnett, Pomerantz & Cameron, N.Y.C., 1984-86, Finley, Kumble, Wagner, Heine, Underberg, Manley, Meyerson & Casey, N.Y.C., 1987; of counsel Nixon, Hargrave, Devans & Doyle, N.Y.C., 1988—; lectr. industry and bar groups. Contbr. articles to profl. jours. Mem. ABA, Assn. Bar of City of N.Y., Internat. Bar Assn., Lawyers Alliance for Nuclear Arms Control, Internat. Amigo of Orgn. Am. States, Arms Control Assn. Democrat. Club: Cornell (N.Y.C.). Home: 24 Radio Pl No 25 Stamford CT 06906 Office: Nixon Hargrave Devans & Doyle 30 Rockefeller Plaza New York NY 10112 also: One Thomas Circle Washington DC 20005

VITT, DAVID AARON, medical manufacturing company executive; b. Phila., Aug. 3, 1938; s. Nathan and Flora B.; m. Renee Lee Salkever, Oct. 20, 1963; children: Nadine Lori, Jeffrey Richard. BS, Temple U., 1961. Sales engr. Picker X-Ray Corp., Phila., 1961-65; sales engr. Midwest Am., Chgo., 1965-67, product mgr., 1967-68, product mgr. regional sales, 1968-70; dir. mktg. Valtronic & Living Wills, Bronx, N.Y., 1970-74; v.p. Siemens Med. Systems Inc., gen. mgr. dental div., Iselin, N.J., 1974-86, past corp. v.p.; chief exec. officer, pres. Pelton & Crane, Charlotte, N.C., 1986—; industry rep. to Am. Nat. Standards Inst.; mem. exec. com. Jr. Achievement, Charlotte. Bd. dirs. Am. Fund for Dental Health; apptd. mem. Charlotte Mecklenburg Community Relations Com.; mem. bd. visitors, bd. vis. U. N.C., Charlotte; Jr. Achievement exec com. mem., officer. Served in USAR, 1961-68. Mem. Am. Mgmt. Assn. (bd. dirs. N.J. chpt.), Am. Mktg. Assn., Am. Dental Trade Assn. (bd. dirs.), Dental Mfrs. Am. (past pres.), Am. Acad. Dental Radiology, Charlotte C. of C. (bd. advisors), Acad. Gen. Dentists (bd. mem. found.), Masons (32 deg.), Shriners. Republican. Office: Pelton and Crane PO Box 241147 200 Clanton Rd Charlotte NC 28224

VITT, SAM B., independent media service executive; b. Greensboro, N.C., Oct. 23, 1926; s. Bruno Caesar and Gray (Bradshaw) V.; m. Marie Foster, Oct. 30, 1955; children: Joanne Louise, Michael Bradshaw, Mark Thomas. A.B., Dartmouth Coll., 1950. Exec. asst. TV film CBS, N.Y.C., 1950-52; broadcast media buyer Benton & Bowles, Inc., N.Y.C., 1952-54, Biow Co., N.Y.C., 1954-55; asso. account exec. Biow Co., 1955-56; broadcast media buyer Doherty, Clifford, Steers & Shenfield, Inc., N.Y.C., 1956-57; media supr. Doherty, Clifford, Steers & Shenfield, Inc., 1958-59, v.p. media supr., 1960, v.p., asso. media dir., 1960, v.p., media dir., 1960-63, v.p. in charge media and broadcast programming, 1963-64; v.p., exec. dir. media-program dept. Ted Bates & Co., Inc., N.Y.C., 1964-66; sr. v.p., exec. dir. media-program dept. Ted Bates & Co., Inc., 1966-69; dir. Advt. Info. Services, Inc., 1964-65; founder, pres. Vitt Media Internat., Inc., N.Y.C., 1969-81, chmn., chief exec. officer, 1982—; advt. dir. Banking Law Jour., 1955-69; lectr. in field, 1967—; lectr. advt. media NYU, 1973, 74, Am. Mgmt. Assn., 1974, 75, Assn. Nat. Advertisers, 1967, 69, 70, Advt. Age Media Workshop, 1975. Media columnist: Madison Ave, 1963-68; editorial cons.: Media/Scope, 1968-69; contbg. editor: Handbook of Advertising Management, 1970; contbr. to: Advertising Procedure, 1969, rev. edit., 1973, 5th, 6th, 7th edits., 1977, Exploring Advertising, 1970; contbr. editor to Nation's Bus., Broadcasting, Variety, Anny, TV/Radio Age, Sponsor, Printer's Ink; producer rec. album The Body in the Seine; cover story guest editor: Media Decisions, 1967. Dir. N.Y.C. Comml. Devel. Corp., 1966-69; mem. com. Nat. UN Day Com., 1973, vice chmn., 1974, assoc. chmn., 1975, co-chmn., 1976-77; bd. dirs. UN Assn. Am., 1977; bd. dirs., chmn. Research Inst. Hearing and Balance Disorders Ltd., 1979—; mem. Pres. Reagan's Joint Presdl., Congl. Steering Com., 1982; mem. advt. adv. com. The Acting Com., 1984; chmn. radio-TV reps. div. Greater N.Y. Fund, 1962, chmn. consumer pub. div., 1963; bd. govs. N.Y. Young Rep. Club, 1957-58; editor Directory, 1956-57. Lt. (j.g.) USN, 1944-46. Recipient Media award sta. WRAP, Norfolk, Va., 1962, award of Merit Greater N.Y. Fund, 1963, Gold Key Advt. Leadership award Sta. Reps. Assn., 1967, ann. honors Ad Daily, 1967, certificate of merit Media/Scope, 1967, 1969 Creative Pub. Statement Concerning Advt. award; named one of 10 Best Dressed Men in Advt. Community Gentlemen's Quar., 1979. Mem. Am. Assn. Advt. Agys. (broadcast media com. dir. corr. 1958-63, media operating com. on consumer mags. 1964-65), Internat. Radio and TV Soc. (timebuying and selling seminar com. dir. 1961-62), Internat. Radio and TV Found. (faculty semina 1974), Nat. Acad. Arts Sci. (mem. com. dir.), Media Dirs. Council, Sigma Alpha Epsilon. Presbyterian. Clubs: Manor Park Beach (Larchmont, N.Y.); N.Y. Athletic (N.Y.C.); Roxbury Run (Denver, N.Y.). Home: 3 Roosevelt Ave Larchmont NY 10538 Office: Vitt Media Internat Inc 1114 Avenue of the Americas New York NY 10036

VITTY, RODERIC BEMIS, financial planning executive; b. St. Johnsbury, Vt., July 28, 1933; s. Clarence Lucian and Leota (Cobleigh) V.; m. Patricia Lyster, June 21, 1986; children: Roderic G., Virginia A., David P., Suzanne L., Leigh P. BS, U.S. Mil. Acad., 1955; MS in Fin. Services, Am. Coll., Bryn Mawr, Pa., 1977, MS in Mgmt., 1987; exec. mgmt. program, Columbia U., 1986. CLU; chartered fin. cons.; cert. fin. planner. With Conn. Gen. Life Ins. Co. (now CIGNA-Individual Fin. Services), 1960—, mgr. br. office, Cherry Hill, N.J., 1968—, Greater Phila. office, 1981—, mktg. gen. mgr., 1983-85, gen. mgr., regional v.p., 1985—. Served with inf. U.S. Army, 1955-59, Pa. N.G., 1961-68. Recipient GAMC Master Agy. Builder award, 1982-88, Nat. Mgmt awards 17, 1972-88; Outstanding Agy. awards Cigna, 9. Mem. West Point Soc. Phila. (bd. govs., pres. 1969-71), Nat. Assn. Life Underwriters, South Jersey Fin. Planning Council, Internat. Assn. Fin. Planners, Am. Soc. CLU's (South Jersey chpt.), So. N.J. Gen. Agts. and Mgrs. Assn. (pres. 1979-80, regional v.p. GAMC 1986—), Assn. Grads. U.S. Mil. Acad., Army Athletic Assn. Presbyterian. Clubs: Sunnybrook Swim, Cherry Hill Raquet, Riverton Country, Quechee (Vt.), Safari Internat., Chevalier du Tastevin, Union League Phila. Lodges: Masons (32 deg.), Shriners, K.T. Home: 570 New Albany Rd Moorestown NJ 08057 Office: CIGNA-Individual Fin Svcs 1800 Chapel Ave W Ste 300 Cherry Hill NJ 08002

VITULLO, ANTHONY JOSEPH, controller; b. Phila., July 18, 1948; s. Gennaro Anthony and Anna Theresa (Lariccia) V.; m. Marlene L. Cilibeti, June 20, 1970; children: Anthony J. Jr., Michael A. BS in Acctg., St. Joseph's U., Phila., 1970; MBA, St. Joseph's U., 1986. CPA, Pa., N.J. Sr. acct. Laventhol and Horwath, Phila., 1970-73; dir. internal audit Nat. Student Mktg. Corp., Chgo., 1973-75; v.p. fin. Capital Equipment Leasing Corp., Phila., 1975-80, Geriatric and Med. Ctrs. Inc., Phila., 1980-81, Horsham Psychiatric Group Inc., Ambler, Pa., 1981-83; pvt. practice Medford, N.J., 1983-86; controller, chief fin. officer Vineland (N.J.) Transit Mix Concrete Co. Inc., 1986—. Mem. St. Mary of the Lakes Parish fin. com., Medford, Medford Cub Scout Pack com.; coach Lenape Youth Athletic Assn., Medford; pres. Woodridge Homeowners's Assn., 1983-85. Fellow N.J. Soc. CPAs; mem. AICPA, Pa. Inst. CPAs. Roman Catholic. Office: Vineland Transit Mix Concrete Co Inc Vineland NJ 08360

VIVERITO, MARGARET JOSEPHINE, safety and health administration executive; b. East Orange, N.J., Feb. 14, 1945; d. William George and Stella Antoinette (Vuono) Lazarus; m. Paul Lawrence Viverito, Apr. 17, 1971. BA in Nursing, Fairleigh Dickinson U., 1967. Regional coordinator Vt. Profl. Standards Rev. Orgn., South Burlington, 1976-81; occupational health supr. Erving Paper Mill, Brattleboro, Vt., 1981-85; co-owner, fin. officer Gallery Craft, West Townshend, Vt., 1974—; product quality specialist Strathmore Paper Co., Westfield, Mass., 1985-88, mgr. safety and health adminstr. Facilitator Quality Program, 1988—. Ambulance attendant Grace Cottage Hosp., Townshend, Vt., 1984-86; ARC instr., Windham County, Vt., 1984—. Served to 1st lt. USAR, 1984—. Mem. Am. Soc. for Quality Control (officer Western Mass. sect. 1985, chairperson 1989—), Nat. Assn. Female Execs., Res. Officers Assn. Republican. Roman Catholic. Home: Rural Rt 1 Box 218 West Townshend VT 05359 Office: Strathmore Paper Co S Broad St Westfield MA 01085

VIZCAINO, HENRY P., mining engineer, consultant; b. Hurley, N.Mex., Aug. 28, 1918; s. Emilio D. and Petra (Perea) V.; m. Esther B. Lopez, Sept. 16, 1941; children: Maria Elena, Rick, Arthur, Carlos. BS in Engring., Nat. U., Mexico City, 1941; BS in Geology, U. N.Mex., 1954. Registered profl. engr. With Financiera Minera S.A., Mexico City, 1942-47; gen. mgr. Minas Mexicanas S.A., Torreon, Mex., 1947-51; exploration engr. Kerr McGee Corp., Okla., 1955-69; cons. Albuquerque, 1969-75, 84—; regional geologist Bendix Field Engring., Austin, Tex., 1976-79; staff geo-scientist Bendix Field Engring., Grand Junction, Colo., 1979-81; sr. geologist Hunt Oil Co., Dallas, 1981-84. Contbr. articles to profl. publs. Mem. Rotary, Elks. Republican. Congregationalist. Home and Office: 20 Canoncito Vista Tijeras NM 87059

VLASIC, ROBERT JOSEPH, food company executive; b. Detroit, Mar. 9, 1926; m. Nancy Rita Reuter; children: James, William, Richard, Michael, Paul. B.S., U. Mich., 1949. Chmn. Vlasic Foods, Inc., West Bloomfield, Mich., 1963-88; chmn. Campbell Soup Co., Camden, N.J.; bd. dirs. Mich. Nat. Corp., Farmington Hills, Reynolds Metals Co., Richmond, Va. Trustee Henry Ford Health Care Corp., Detroit, 1977; vice chmn. bd. trustees Cranbrook Ednl. Community, Bloomfield Hills, 1979. Home: 1910 Rathmor Rd Bloomfield Hills MI 48013 Office: Vlasic Foods Inc 710 North Woodward Bloomfield Hills MI 48013

VLIET, ELIZABETH LEE WADKINS, psychiatrist and neurologist, healthcare related company executive; b. Richmond, Va., July 12, 1946; d. James T. and Virginia (Hutchinson) Wadkins; m. Gordon C. Vliet, July 13, 1968. BS, Coll. William and Mary, 1968, MEd, 1974; MD, Ea. Va. Med. Sch., 1978. Diplomate Am. Bd. Psychiatry and Neurology. Tchr. Williamsburg (Va.) James City County, 1968-74; dir. alumni activities Coll. William and Mary, Williamsburg, 1974-75; resident Johns Hopkins Hosp., Balt., 1979-82; asst. prof. U. Kans. Sch. Medicine, Wichita, 1982-83; asst. prof. depts. psychiatry, family medicine Ea. Va. Med. Sch., Norfolk, 1983—; pres. Health Strategies Inc., Norfolk, 1984—. Mem. AMA, Am. Psychiatric Assn., So. Med. Assn., Am. Med. Women's Assn., Womens Forum. Republican. Presbyterian. Clubs: Town Point, Greenbrier Country (Norfolk). Home: 7613 Leafwood Dr Norfolk VA 23518 Office: Health Strategies Inc 330 W Brambleton #2104 Norfolk VA 23510

VOECKS, DANIEL MICHAEL, insurance company executive; b. Waverly, Iowa, July 4, 1934; s. Walter George and Lucille (Schornhorst) V.; m. Karen Ann Jenson, Sept. 5, 1958; children: Elizabeth Ann, Daniel Michael Jr. BA, U. Wis., 1958. Trainee Homesteaders Life Co., Des Moines, 1960, advisor to pres. and chief exec. officer, 1960—. Pres. Iowa Spl. Olympics., 1987-88. Mem. Des Moines Soc. Fin. Analysts. Republican. Lutheran. Home: 2880 Grand Ave #307 Des Moines IA 50312 Office: Homesteaders Life Co 2141 Grand Ave Des Moines IA 50312

VOELKER, HAROLD FRANK, credit union executive, financial consultant; b. Detroit, Oct. 7, 1940; s. Franz Xavier and Eva (Willman) V.; m. Nancy Naomia Wolfe, Nov. 25, 1966; children: Lois Ann, Eva Marie, M. Katherine, H. Frank. BS in Acctg., U. Detroit, 1963. Corp. examiner Calif. Dept. Corps., LA, 1963-68; treas., gen. mgr. Sterling Van Dyke Credit Union, Sterling Heights, Mich., 1968—. Pub. edn. officer, U.S. Coast Guard Aux., Calif., 1983-86. Mem. Mich. Assn. Credit Unions (pres. 1973-78, sec. 1978—), Consumer Credit Assn., Delta Sigma Pi. Episcopalian. Home: 1027 Bedford St Grosse Pointe Park MI 48230 Office: Sterling Van Dyke Credit Union 39139 Mound Rd Sterling Heights MI 48310

VOELPEL, LAWRENCE WILLIAM, savings and loan executive; b. Pontiac, Mich., Nov. 22, 1950; s. John F. and Eileen G. (Capel) V.; m. Mary Jo Kosinski, Mar. 14, 1975; children: John Edward and Nicholas James (twins). BS in Mgmt., Oakland U., 1976; grad., Savs. and Loan Inst., 1978. Br. mgr. trainee 1st Fed. Savs Bank & Trust, Pontiac, 1972-74, asst. treas., 1974-76, asst. v.p. comml. loans, 1976-79; mktg. rep. Collateral Control, St. Paul, 1979-81; comml. loan officer Mich. Nat. Bank, Brighton, 1981-84; asst. v.p. Franklin Savs & Loan Assn., Southfield, Mich., 1984-85, v.p., 1985-87, sr. v.p., 1987—; bd. dirs. Tranex Fin., Birmingham, Mich. Chmn. tickets Oakland County coun. Boy Scouts Am., 1980; chmn. ticket sales Mich. Gov.'s Election Com., 1984. Recipient cert. Navy League U.S., 1980. Mem. Builders Assn. Southeastern Mich., Oakland County Bd. Realtors, Southfield Mortgage Bankers Assn., Oakland County C. of C., Elks. Republican. Roman Catholic. Home: 3175 Wynns Ct Metamore MI 48455 Office: Franklin Savs & Loan Assn PO Box 5006 Southfield MI 48006

VOEPEL, KARL HEINZ, chemical company executive; b. Badwildungen, Germany, May 2, 1931; came to U.S., 1974; s. Heinrich and Minna (Meister) V.; m. Renate C. Klingenburg, May 22, 1958; children: Kai, Christina, Jens. PhD in Chemistry, U. Of Marburg, Hesse, Germany, 1960. Prodn. mgr. Bayer AG, Leverkusen, Fed. Republic Germany, 1960-74; v.p., gen. mgr. Mobay, Kansas City, Mo., 1974-84; exec. v.p. Miles Inc., Elkhart, Ind., 1984-87, exec. v.p. tech., 1987—. Patentee in petro chem. and pesticide chemistry. Mem. Kansas City Civic Council, 1978-84, United Way Met. Found., Kansas City, 1980-84, Crime Commn., Kansas City, 1978-82, 4-H Club. Mem. Midwest Research Inst. (adv. council 1980), Nat. Agrl. Chems. Assn. (bd. dirs. 1977-84, vice chmn. 1984-85). Club: Knollwood Country. Office: Miles Inc 1127 Myrtle St PO Box 40 Elkhart IN 46515

VOET, PAUL C., specialty chemical executive; b. Cin., July 7, 1946; s. Leo C. and Claire G. (Burdick) V.; m. Judy A. Gates, Aug. 24, 1968; children—Jefrey, Jeannette, Jamie, Jodie. B.A., U. Cin., 1968; M.B.A., U. Pa., 1970. Asst. to pres. KDI Corp., Cin., 1970; asst. to pres. Chemed Corp., 1970-72; v.p. Vestal Labs. div. Chemed, St. Louis, 1972-74, exec. v.p., 1974-76, pres., 1976-80; exec. v.p., chief operating officer Chemed Corp., Cin., 1986-88, vice chmn., 1988—; chief exec. officer, also bd. dirs. Nat. Sanitary Supply Co.; dir. Omnicare, Inc., Cin., Roto Rooter Corp., Cin. Mem. Pres.'s adv. council St. Louis U., 1979. Mem. Am. Mgmt. Assn. (pres.'s council), Phi Beta Kappa, Beta Gamma Sigma, Omicron Delta Epsilon, Phi Alpha Theta, Phi Eta Sigma. Home: 8180 Graves Rd Cincinnati OH 45243 Office: Chemed Corp DuBois Tower Cincinnati OH 45202

VOGEL, CARL EDWARD, property administration executive; b. Chgo., Oct. 21, 1919; s. Eugene E. and Madeline (Keim) V.; student Wilson Jr. Coll., Chgo., 1937-39, Northwestern U., 1940-41; m. Frances Stevens Terrell, Mar. 17, 1945; children—Cynthia, Susan, Meredith, Kirkland. With Nat. Bur. Property Adminstrn., Inc., Chgo., 1939—, chmn. bd., exec. v.p., 1958-63, chmn. bd., pres., 1963—; chmn., bd., pres. Kirkland Corp., Chgo., 1969—. Active in local fund-raising drives. Served to 1st lt. USAAF, 1942-46. Mem. Chgo. Assn. Commerce and Industry, Nat. Assn. Rev. Appraisers, Internat. Assn. Assessing Officers, Nat. Tax Assn., Inst. Property Taxation. Clubs: Mid-America (Chgo.); North Shore Country (Glenview). Home: 720 Glenayre Dr Glenview IL 60025 Office: 1824 Prudential Plaza Chicago IL 60601

VOGEL, HOWARD MICHAEL, lawyer; b. Phila., June 8, 1947; s. Edward Nathan and Sara C. (Harris) V. BS summa cum laude, U. Fla., 1970; postgrad., Stanford U., 1973-74, U. Geneva, Switzerland, 1974-75; JD, U. Calif., Berkeley, 1975. Bar: Fla. 1977, D.C. 1980, U.S. Supreme Ct. 1980. Legal officer Internat. Commn. on Jurists, Geneva, 1974-75; assoc. Brobeck, Phleger & Harrison, San Francisco, 1975-76; gen. counsel, fin. advisor Nationwide Chems., Ft. Lauderdale, Fla., 1978-82; sole practice Miami, Fla., 1982—. Author: Racial Discrimination and Repression in Southern Rhodesia, 1975, Universal Human Rights: Do They Exist in Rhodesia?, 1975. Ford Found. fellow, DuPont fellow; United Nations scholar, Dinkelspiel legal scholar. Mem. ABA, Internat. Bar Assn., Assn. Trial Lawyers Am., Internat. and Comparative Law Soc. (chmn.), Phi Beta Kappa, Kappa Tau Alpha, Tau Delta Tau. Home: 536 Shasta Way Mill Valley CA 94941 Other: 2602 Nassau Bend #C-2 Coconut Creek FL 33066

VOGEL, HOWARD STANLEY, lawyer; b. N.Y.C., Jan. 21, 1934; s. Moe and Sylvia (Miller) V.; m. Judith Anne Gelb, June 30, 1962; 1 son, Michael S. B.A., Bklyn. Coll., 1954; J.D., Columbia U., 1957; LL.M. in Corp. Law, NYU, 1969. Bar: N.Y. 1957, U.S. Supreme Ct. 1964. Assoc. Whitman & Ransom, N.Y.C., 1961-66; with Texaco Inc., 1966—, gen. atty., 1970-73, assoc. gen. counsel, 1973-81, gen. counsel Texaco Philanthropic Found. Inc., 1979-82, gen. counsel Jefferson Chem. Co., Texaco Chems. Can. Inc., 1973-82, assoc. gen. tax counsel, White Plains, N.Y., 1981—. Pres., dir. 169 E. 69th Corp., 1981—. Served to 1st lt. JAGC, U.S. Army, 1958-60. Mem. ABA, Assn. Bar City N.Y., Fed. Bar Council, Assn. Ex-Mems. of Squadron A (N.Y.C.). Club: Princeton (N.Y.C.). Home: 169 E 69th St Apt 9-D New York NY 10021 Office: 2000 Westchester Ave White Plains NY 10650

VOGEL, JOHN DENNING, financial services manager; b. Harrisburg, Pa., July 23, 1946; s. Harry Denning Jr. and Helen M. (Beasom) V.; m. Katherine Laura Maloney, Mar. 29, 1969; children: Kelly, Heather. BA in History and Polit. Sci., Elizabethtown Coll., 1968. Asst. dept. mgr. Chevrolet Motor Div., Harrisburg, 1968-73; sales mgr. Scott Murphey Chevrolet, Lancaster, Pa., 1973-76; sales rep. Paul Revere Cos., Harrisburg, 1976-77; asst. mgr. cen. Pa., The Travelers, Harrisburg, 1977-78, fin. services mgr. cen. Pa.,,

1978-81; fin. services mgr. N.H. and Vt., The Travelers, Bedford, N.H., 1981-87; fin. services mgr., equities mgr. The Travelers, Charleston, W.Va., 1987—; bd. dirs. Pa. Motor Truck Assn., Lancaster, 1973-74, Solid Fuel Adv. Council, Manchester, N.H., 1982-85. Chmn. Perry County Young Reps., Pa., 1978-79; borough councilman Duncannon (Pa.) Borough, 1978-82, pres. council, 1980-82, Rep. committeeman, 1969-81. Served with USAR. Lodge: Lions (v.p. Duncannon club 1971-73). Home: 963 Ridgemont Rd Charleston WV 25314

VOGEL, ROBERT, real estate developer; b. Hamburg, Fed. Republic Germany, June 8, 1919; s. Max P. and Anna M. (Freudendahl) V.; children: Tom, Jicky. Student, Hamburg High Sch. Mng. dir. Handesgesellschaft MbH, Hamburg, 1943—; gen. ptnr. Robert Vogel Kommanditges, Hamburg, 1955—, Anna M.M. Vogel Kommanditgesellschaft; mng. dir. Avis Immobilien GmbH, Hamburg, 1982—, Uccello Immobilien GmbH, Hamburg, 1982. Pres. Liberal party, Hamburg, 1987—; mem. parliament Hamburg, 1987—. Decorated chevalier Ordre de la Couronne (Belgium). Clubs: Überseeclub, Norddt Regattaverein, Anglo-German. Office: Esplanade, 37 Hamburg 36, Federal Republic of Germany

VOGEL, STEVE GREGORY, controller; b. Lawrence, Kans., Sept. 11, 1951; s. John Joseph and Anne Meredith (Beardsworth) V.; m. Denise Linda Doller, 1984. BA in Psychology, Lehigh U., 1973, MBA in Fin., 1974. CPA, Pa., Ohio. Fin. analyst Ford Motor Co., Pennsauton, N.J., 1974-76; plant controller Corning (N.Y.) Glass Works, 1976-79; controller Ryder System, Inc., Buffalo, 1979-81, group controller, Detroit, 1981-82; div. planning Ryder Systems, Inc., Bloomfield Hills, Mich., 1982-83; group controller Guardian Ind., Inc., Upper Sandusky, Ohio, 1983-85; dir. fin., chief fin. officer Llodio, Spain, 1985-86, acting chief fin. officer, Detroit, 1986-87; v.p. fin. Bush Industries Inc., Jamestown, N.Y., 1987—; v.p. fin. and adminstrn., chief fin. officer Nastec Corp., Southfield, Mich., 1988—; teaching asst. Dale Carnegie, Buffalo, 1981-82. Recipient James Clark Hayden award Lehigh U., Bethlehem, Pa., 1971, 72, 73. Mem. Mich. Soc. CPAs, Ohio Soc. CPAs, Nat. Assn. Accts., Fin. Execs. Inst., Mensa. Republican. Roman Catholic. Home: 20243 Evergreen Meadows Rd Southfield MI 48076 Office: Nastec Corp 24681 Northwestern Hwy Southfield MI 48075

VOGEL, WERNER PAUL, retired machine company executive; b. Louisville, June 15, 1923; s. Werner George and Emma (Bartman) V.; B. Mech. Engring., U. Louisville, 1950; m. Helen Louise Knapp, Oct. 2, 1954. With Henry Vogt Machine Co., Louisville, 1942—, asst. plant supt., 1957-60, plant supt., 1961-73, v.p., 1974-86. Trustee, City of Strathmoor Village, Ky., 1959-61; clk. City of Glenview Manor, Ky., 1967-73, trustee, 1974-75, treas. 1986—; bd. dirs. Louisville Protestant Altenheim, 1979—, pres., 198—. Served with USAAF, 1944-46. Mem. ASME, Am. Welding Soc., Am. Def. Preparedness Assn., Tau Beta Pi, Sigma Tau. Republican. Methodist. Home: 29 Glenwood Rd Louisville KY 40222

VOGELSANG, WILLIAM ROBERT, utilities company executive; b. Cleve., July 7, 1925. BS, Kent State U., 1949; student, Case-Western Res. U., 1971. Corp. sec. Cleve. Electric Illuminating Co., 1949-74; v.p. fin. services San Diego Gas & Electric Co., 1974-77; with Cen. Ill. Lighting Co., Peoria, 1977—, treas., asst. v.p. fin., 1977-78, v.p., treas., 1978-80, v.p. fin., 1980-81, sr. v.p. fin., 1981-82, exec. v.p. fin., 1982-84, pres., chief operating officer, 1984-85, pres., chief exec. officer, from 1985; now chmn. CILCorp Inc., Peoria. Served with USAAF, 1943-46. Office: CILCORP Inc 300 Liberty St Peoria IL 61602 •

VOGELSTEIN, JOHN L., venture capitalist; b. N.Y.C., Dec. 9, 1934; s. Hans A. and Ruth E. (Krieger) V.; m. Jacqueline C. Wolf, Sept. 5, 1957 (div. Sept. 1983); children: Hans A. II, Andrew W.; m. Lee Gibouleau, Dec. 29, 1983. Grad., The Taft Sch., 1952; student, Harvard U., 1954. Assoc. Lazard Freres & Co., N.Y.C., 1954-64, ptnr., 1964-66; v.p. E.M. Warburg, Pincus & Co., Inc., N.Y.C., 1967-70, exec. v.p., 1970-82, vice chmn., 1982—; bd. dirs. Mattel, Inc., Hawthorne, Calif., Ingersoll Newspapers, Inc., Princeton, N.J., Allstar Inns G.P. Inc., Santa Barbara, Calif., Ingersoll Publs. Ltd., London, Community Newspapers Inc., Princeton, JPT Holdings Inc., N.Y.C. Trustee The Taft Sch., Watertown, Conn., 1982—, Prep for Prep, N.Y.C., 1983—. Home: 270 Cantitoe St Bedford Hills NY 10507 Office: EM Warburg Pincus & Co Inc 466 Lexington Ave New York NY 10017

VOHRA, SAROJ KUMAR, instrument company executive; b. Chakwal, India, May 16, 1947; s. Sohan Dutta and Shanty (Malhotra) V.; m. Elly Yermian, Dec. 27, 1975. B.Sc. with honors, Panjab U., 1969, M.Sc. with honors, 1970; Ph.D., Temple U., 1978. Postdoctoral fellow Temple U., Phila., 1977-78; research assoc., vis. prof. chemistry Fels Cancer Inst., Phila., 1978-79; applications scientist EG&G Princeton Applied Research, N.J., 1979-81; product specialist IBM Instruments, Inc., Danbury, Conn., 1981-82, mgr. gen. instruments tech. support, 1982-84, ultraviolet/visible products mgr., optical spectrophotometry tech. support mgr., 1985-87, sr. scientist, 1987— . Contbr. articles to profl. jours. Editor, cultural soc. India Assn., Phila. chpt., 1974-75. Recipient nat. trainee award in cancer research NIH, 1979. Mem. Am. Chem. Soc., Sigma Xi. Democrat. Avocations: writing poems; skating; travelling; helping people.

VOIGT, JOHN JACOB, telecommunications executive; b. Atlantic City, Apr. 2, 1942; s. Jacob Joseph and Mary Margret (Camp) V.; grad. Lawrenceville Sch., 1960; student U. Pitts., 1960-61; B.S. in Econs., Wharton Sch. Fin. and Commerce U. Pa., 1963, postgrad., 1964; m. Glenna Fitzsimons, Sept. 22, 1961; children—Bridget Glenna, John Jacob Jr. Pres., Nat. Accessories Co., Phila., 1970—; chmn. ICCI, ICCI Europe Ltd., Brussels, The Dynoptics Corp., Lausanne, Switzerland, 1984—, also bd. dirs.; pres., treas., dir. The Inteleplex Corp.; pres. Howard Butcher Trading Corp., Phila., 1976—; chmn. IMS Corp., Geneva, Switzerland, 1987—; dir. Atlantic Metal Finishing Co., Butcher Foods Inc., Cont. Quality Industries, IHESA, San Pedro Sula, Honduras, Sterling Group Ltd., London, Torreya Fin. Corp., Palm Beach, Fla.; cons. Compagnie Generale d'Electricite, Paris, Matra Group, Paris; v.p. Iben Petterson A/S, Copenhagen. Bd. govs. Betty Bacharach Hosp., 1976—; mem. vestry, sr. warden Ch. of Epiphany, Ventnor, N.J., 1975—. Republican. Clubs: Union League Phila., Princeton N.Y.C.; Atlantic City Country; Seaview Country; Ocean City Yacht; U. Pa. (N.Y.C.). Lodges: Order of St. John Jerusalem, Knights of Malta. Home: 2215 Burroughs Ave Linwood NJ 08221 Office: 30 Ave Van Bever, Brussels 1180, Belgium

VOJTECKY, MARK ANTHONY, health educator; b. Natrona Heights, Pa., June 18, 1958; s. Joseph Stephen and Margaret Mary (Hrnciar) V.; m. Shirley Ann Harold, May 28, 1983. BS, Pa. State U., 1980, MS, 1985; MPH, U. Pitts., 1986. Rsch. assoc. U. Pitts., 1986-87; dir. health edn. Western Res. Care System, Youngstown, Ohio, 1987—; health educator Pa. State U., Pitts., 1986-88. Planner AIDS Task Force Edn., Youngstown, 1987, Hypertension Task Force, Youngstown, 1987; vol. ARC, Youngstown, 1988. Capt. USMC, 1981-87. Named Outstanding Young Am., 1987. Fellow Soc. Pub. Health Edn. (state coordinator interest group 1987—); mem. Am. Pub. Health Assn., Pa. Pub. Health Assn., Ohio Pub. Health Assn., Internat. Brotherhood Magicians. Republican. Roman Catholic. Home: 211 Frontenac Rd Kensington PA 15068 Office: Western Res Care System 345 Oak Hill Ave Youngstown OH 44501

VOLCKER, PAUL A., economist; b. Cape May, N.J., Sept. 5, 1927; s. Paul A. and Alma Louise (Klippel) V.; m. Barbara Marie Bahnson, Sept. 11, 1954; children: Janice, James. AB summa cum laude, Princeton U., 1949, LLD (hon.), 1982; MA, Harvard U., 1951, LLD (hon.), 1985. Economist Fed. Res. Bank N.Y., 1952-57; pres. Fed. Res. Bank of N.Y., 1975-79; economist Chase Manhattan Bank, N.Y.C., 1957-61, v.p., dir. planning, 1965-68; with Dept. Treasury, Washington, 1961-65, 69-74, dep. under sec. monetary affairs, 1963-65, under sec., 1969-74; chmn. bd. govs. Fed. Res. Bd., Washington, 1979-87; chmn. James D. Wolfensohn Co., N.Y.C., 1988—; prof. Woodrow Wilson Sch. of Pub. and Internat. Affairs, 1988. Sr. fellow Woodrow Wilson Sch. Pub. and Internat. Affairs, 1974-75.

VOLCKHAUSEN, WILLIAM ALEXANDER, lawyer, banker; b. N.Y.C., Mar. 13, 1937; s. William Louis and Jessie (Rankin) V.; m. Grace Lyu, Aug. 2, 1968; children: Sharon, Alexander. AB, Princeton U., 1959; AM, U. Calif., Berkeley, 1963; JD, Harvard U., 1966. Bar: N.Y. 1967. Program officer Asia Found., N.Y.C. and San Francisco, 1966-69; mng. atty. Moblzn. for Youth Legal Services, N.Y., 1969-73; dep. supt., gen. counsel N.Y. State Banking Dept., N.Y.C., 1973-79; spl. counsel Hughes Hubbard & Reed, N.Y.C., 1979-80; exec. v.p., counsel, sec. The Dime Savs. Bank of N.Y. Fed. Savs. Bank, N.Y.C., 1980—; adj. prof. Cardozo Sch. Law Yeshiva U., N.Y.C., 1980—. Bd. dirs. Berkeley Carroll St. Sch., Bklyn., 1974-82, pres., 1975-76; bd. dirs. Asian-Am. Legal Def. Fund, N.Y.C., 1981-86, H.E.L.P., 1986—, Carroll Gardens Neighborhood Assn., 1988—. Mem. ABA, Assn. of Bar of City of N.Y., N.Y. County Bar Assn., Nassau County Bar Assn. Democrat. Club: Princeton (N.Y.C.). Home: 262 President St Brooklyn NY 11231 Office: Dime Savs Bank EAB Pla 9th Fl Uniondale NY 11556-0129

VOLLSTEDT, STEVE, controller, chief accountant; b. Danville, Ill.; s. Richard Wayne Vollstedt and Doris Marie (Laird) Ivey; m. Cathy L. Mason, Aug. 10, 1974; children: Trevor, Raimey. BS in Acctg. summa cum laude, U. Ariz., 1977. CPA, Nev., Ariz. Staff acct. Ernst & Whinney CPAs, Tucson, 1978-79; sr. internal auditor Newmont Mining Corp., Tucson, 1979-82; project acct. Newmont Gold Co., Carlin, Nev., 1982-85, controller, chief acctg. officer, 1985—. Served with U.S. Army, 1970-73, Vietnam. Republican. Office: Newmont Gold Co PO Box 669 Carlin NV 89822-0669

VOLLUM, ROBERT BOONE, management consultant; b. Abington, Pa., Sept. 13, 1933; s. Charles Milton and Marion (Yocum) V.; m. Gayle Lorraine Timmerman, July 8, 1956; children: Robert Boone III, Jeffrey Charles. BS in Engring. and Sci., U.S. Naval Acad., 1955. Sr. cons., group leader Stevenson, Jordan & Harrison, Inc., N.Y.C., 1959-65; asst. to pres., plant supt. W.L. Gore & Assocs., Inc., Newark, Del., 1965-69; gen. mgr. Philmont Pressed Steel subs. Gulf & Western Industries, Inc., Bethayres, Pa., 1969-72, Air Shields div. Narco Sci. Industries, Inc., Hatboro, Pa., 1972-75; pres. ADvanced Airflow Tech., Inc., Warminster, Pa., 1975-76, R.B. Vollum & Assocs., Huntingdon Valley, Pa., 1986—; prin. mfg. cons. Sperry Corp., Blue Bell, Pa., 1976-89; dir. cons. Creative Output, Inc., Milford, Conn., 1984-86; speaker in field. Contbr. articles to profl. jours. Bd. dirs. Upper Moreland Little League, 1965-76. Served to lt. USN, 1955-59. Fellow Am. Prodn. and Inventory Control Soc. (chpt. pres. 1984-85); mem. soc. Mfg. Engrs (sr. mem.), Computer and Automated Systems Assn. (sr. mem.). Republican. Episcopalian. Home: 2045 Overlook Ave Willow Grove PA 19090 Office: PO Box 206 Huntingdon Valley PA 19006

VOLNEY, TAYLOR, financial executive; b. Portsmouth, Ohio, Dec. 6, 1939; s. Lafayette and Martha Louise (Frederick) T.; m. Kathleen Ann MacMahon, May 17, 1969; children: Lafayette, Lloyd MacMahon, Kerry Erin, Frederick Daly. BS in Indsl. Engring., Ohio State U., 1962; MBA, Harvard U., 1966. Assoc. McKinsey & Co., N.Y.C., 1966-72; exec. v.p. Funk & Wagnalls, N.Y.C., 1972-74; v.p. fin. Reuben H. Donnelley, N.Y.C., 1974-76; dir. corp. planning Dun & Bradstreet Corp., N.Y.C., 1976, v.p. corp. planning, 1977-78; gen. mgr. Transp. Guides div., Ofcl. Airline Guides div. Dun & Bradstreet Corp., Oak Brook, Ill., 1978; corp. v.p. Dun & Bradstreet Corp., N.Y.C., 1979-80, sr. v.p., 1980-8l, exec. v.p., 1982—, also bd. dirs. Lt. (j.g.) USNR, 1962-64. Office: Dun & Bradstreet Corp 299 Park Ave New York NY 10171

VOLPI, WALTER MARK, lawyer, diversified company executive; b. N.Y.C., Oct. 4, 1946; s. Walter Joseph and Arlene (Bryant) V.; m. Diana De Rosa, Dec. 13, 1969; 1 son, Mark Joseph. B.A., St. John's U., 1968, J.D., 1974. Bar: N.Y. 1975. Law clk. chief judge N.Y. Ct. Appeals, 1974-76; assoc. Cleary, Gottlieb, Steen & Hamilton, N.Y.C., 1976-80; v.p., gen. counsel Macmillan, Inc., N.Y.C., 1980-85; sec., assoc. gen. counsel Lever Bros., N.Y.C., 1985-86, v.p., sec., gen. counsel, 1986—. Served to 1st lt. U.S. Army, 1969-71. Mem. ABA, N.Y. State Bar Assn., Am. Law Inst., Bar Assn. City N.Y. Office: Lever Bros 390 Park Ave New York NY 10022

VONA, CARMINE, banker; b. Quindici, Italy, April 6, 1938; came to U.S., 1966, naturalized, 1972; s. Salvatore and Luisa (Volino) V.; m. Carmela Josephine Pacia, July 22, 1967; children—Salvatore, Joseph C. Doctorate in Physics, U. Naples, Italy, 1962. Asst. prof. physics U. Naples, 1962-63; computer analyst Italsider, Genova, Italy, 1963-66; prof. physics U. Natal, Brazil, 1966; sr. cons. Computer Usage Co., N.Y.C., 1967-69; sr. v.p. Bankers Trust Co., N.Y.C., 1969—. Editor: Automation in the Bank of the Future, 1980. Office: Bankers Trust Co 280 Park Ave New York NY 10017 •

VON CLEMM, MICHAEL, financial executive; b. N.Y.C., Mar. 18, 1935; m. Louisa Hunnewell, 1956; children: Stefanie Claire, Charlotte Hunnewell. B.A. cum laude, Harvard U., 1956; M.Litt., Oxford U., 1959; Ph.D., 1962. Staff reporter Boston Globe, 1958-59; mgr. First Nat. City Bank, N.Y.C., London, 1962-67; asst. prof. Harvard Bus. Sch., Boston, 1967-71; mng. dir., chmn. dept. White Weld & Co. Ltd., London, 1971-78; chmn. Credit Suisse First Boston Ltd., London, 1978-86; chmn. Roux Restaurants Ltd., London; chmn. Merrill Lynch Capital Markets, 1986—; dir. La Tante Claire Ltd., London; hon. treas., trustee British Mus. Devel. Trust, London; v.p. mgmt. com. City of London Archaeol. Trust; mem. adv. council Japan-U.S. Econ. Relations; mem. nat. com. Tanglewood Music Ctr., Boston; mem. Vis. Com. Harvard U. Grad. Sch. Design and vis. com. on univ. resources, Harvard, Court Mary Rose, mem. com. on univ. resources, Korea Bus. Council (founder, mem.), adv. bd. Royal Acad. Trust, mem. Corp. Mass. Gen. Hosp.; Episcopalian. Clubs: Brook (N.Y.C.); White's (London), Boodles. Office: Merrill Lynch Capital Markets World Fin Ctr 250 Vesey St New York NY 10281-1220

VON DER ESCH, HANS ULRIK, lawyer; b. Nurnberg, Germany, Jan. 27, 1928; s. Hans Joachim and Kerstin Marianne (Sandstedt) von der E.; m. Marianne Hedvig Margaretha Celsing, Aug. 23, 1975; children: Ulrik, Fredrik; 1 child by previous marriage: Alexandra Louise. MBA U. Gothenburg, 1951; LLB, U. Stockholm, 1954. Bar: Sweden 1966. With Dist. Ct. Service, Nykoping and Stockholm, 1954-57; pres.'s asst. Bonniergroup, Stockholm, Hamburg, Geneva and N.Y.C., 1957-63, atty., Stockholm, 1963-66; sole practice, Stockholm, 1966—; ptnr. Advokatfirman Landahl, 1972—; chmn., dir. numerous Swedish and fgn. cos. Served with Swedish Army, 1946-48. Decorated Swedish Sign of Distinction; Finnish Golden Order of Merit; Norwegian Badge of Honor; Knight of the Order of St. John in Sweden. Mem. ABA, Swedish Lawyers Assn. (dir. 1974-79, del. 1979-88), Swedish Army and Air Force Res. Officers League (pres. 1975-78), Swedish Parachute Assn. (pres. 1966-68), Royal Swedish Aero Club (bd. dirs. 1966-78, gen. counsel 1967-78, v.p. 1983-88), Internat. Bar Assn., Internat. Fiscal Assn., Lawyer-Pilots Bar Assn. Club: Nya Saellskapet (Stockholm). Mem. Swedish Ch. Contbr. articles on aviation. Holder world class record Class C light aircraft 1000-1750 kgs, piston engine, speed record over recognized course: Sal (Rep. of Cape Verde-Funchal) (Madeira) 224.06 km/hr. Home: 25 Strandvägen, 11456 Stockholm Sweden Office: Cardellgatan 1, PO Box 5209, 102 45 Stockholm Sweden

VONDEROHE, RONALD R., accountant; b. Norfolk, Nebr., Oct. 11, 1947; s. Ruben W. and Ruby E. (Blank) V.; m. Karolyn K. (Knoepfel), June 29, 1969; children: Marcus J., Michael R., Jodi L. A in Bus., Grand Island Sch. Bus., 1967; BS, Kearney State Coll., 1971. Programmer, systems analyst First Nat. Bank, Grand Island, 1967-69; acct., systems analyst Contryman & Assoc., CPA's, Grand Island, 1969-72; div. controller Chief Industries, Inc., Grand Island, 1972-75; acct., sec., treas. Mid-Continent Enterprises, Grand Island, 1975-80; acct. T.F.S., Inc., Grand Island, 1981-82, Town & Country Realty, Grand Island, 1982-85; prin. Vonderohe Bus. Services, St. Paul, Nebr., 1985—. Republican. Lutheran. Lodges: Rotary (bd. dirs.), Sertoma (past pres., past sec., past chmn. bd. dirs.). Office: Vonderohe Bus Svcs 801 7th St Saint Paul NE 68873

VONDRASEK, FRANK CHARLES, JR., utilities executive; b. Omaha, Oct. 1, 1928; s. Frank Charles Sr. and Lillian Constance (Schoessler) V.; m. Charleen McMamus (dec. 1960); children: Steven, Mark, Roger; m. Irene Alice Leach, Dec. 9, 1961; children: Marlyn, Madilyn, Larry. BSEE, Iowa State Coll., 1949; MBA, Creighton U., 1965. Registered profl. engr., Nebr., Wis. With Omaha Pub. Power Dist., 1949-70; with Madison (Wis.) Gas & Elec. Co., 1970-87, pres., chief operating officer, 1988—. Bd. dirs. ARC Dane County, Madison, 1983—. Served to 1st lt. Signal Corps, 1951-53. Mem. IEEE, Nat. Soc. Profl. Engrs, Rotary, Masons, Shriners. Methodist. Office: Madison Gas & Electric Co 133 S Blair St PO Box 1231 Madison WI 53701-1231

VON DREHLE, RAMON ARNOLD, lawyer; b. St. Louis, Mar. 12, 1930; s. Arnold Henry and Sylvia E. (Ahrens) Von D.; m. Gillian Margaret Turner, Sept. 13, 1980; children by previous marriage: Carin L., Lisa A., Courtney A. B.S., Washington U., St. Louis, 1952; LL.B., U. Tex., Austin, 1957; postgrad, Parker Sch. Internat. Law, Columbia U., 1965. Bar: Tex. 1956, Mich. 1957, U.S. Supreme Ct. 1981. Sr. atty. Ford Motor Co., Dearborn, Mich., 1957-67; assoc. counsel Ford of Europe, Inc., Brentwood, Essex, Eng., 1967-75; v.p., gen. counsel Ford of Europe, Inc., 1975-79; v.p. legal Ford Motor Credit Co., Dearborn, 1979-87; v.p., gen. counsel Am. Road Ins. Co., Dearborn, 1979-87; exec. dir. legal affairs Ford Fin. Services Group, Dearborn, 1987—. Article editor: Tex. Law Rev, 1956-57. Trustee Birmingham Unitarian Ch., 1966-67. Served to 1st lt. AUS, 1952-54, Korea. Mem. ABA, Mich. Bar Assn., Tex. Bar Assn., Internat. Bar Assn., Am. Fin. Services Assn. (dir. 1981—), Fin. Services Council (dir. 1987—), Washington U. Alumni Club Detroit (past pres.), Order of Coif, Tau Beta Pi, Omicron Delta Kappa. Mem. Christ Ch. Clubs: Renaissance (Detroit); Les Ambassadeurs (London); Confrérie des Chevaliers du Tastevin (France). Office: Ford Motor Co American Rd Dearborn MI 48121

VON ELSNER, RENEE MAE, insurance agent; b. Hilo, Hawaii, Aug. 12, 1932; d. Shigeru and Sui Ean (Pang Ching) Kobayashi; m. Glenn W. Bitle, Sept. 3, 1954 (div. Oct. 1980); children: Dean Kalani, Deanna Kalua, Glenn Kunani; m. Don Von Elsner, Apr. 5, 1986. Student, U. Hawaii, 1974. CLU; cert. fin. planner. Mgr. Guzz Glenns, Inc., Hilo, 1970-79, Allied Foods Corp., Kona, Hawaii, 1979-84; ins. agt. Continental Ins. Agy., Hilo, 1985—; registered rep. CNA Investors Services, Inc., Hilo, 1987—; Mem. Mgmt. Adv. State Hosps., Hawaii, 1978-86; mem. New Horizons Fair Housing Task Force, County Hawaii, 1986—; v.p. KIAA Credit Union, Hilo, 1977-78, pres., 1978. Pres. Kanoelehua Indsl. Assn., Hilo, 1975; chmn. United Way, Kona, Hawaii, 1983; chmn. Petition for New Hilo Hosp., 1977; fin. chmn. Spl. Olympics, West Hawaii, 1983. Named Life Agt. of Yr., Continental Ins. Agy., Hawaii, 1987. Mem. Inst. Cert. Fin. Planners, Big Island Life Underwriters Assn. (sec. 1987-88), Hawaii C. of C. (dir. 1980). Club: Civitan (pres. 1983-84, editor newsletter 1983). Home: 2405 Kalanianaole Ave Hilo HI 96720 Office: Continental Ins Agy Inc 688 Kinoole St Suite 121 Hilo HI 96720

VON FELDT, FRANCIS JAMES, physician, corporate medical specialist; b. Austin, Minn., Dec. 3, 1940; s. John Leo and Rose Louise (Bedard) Von F.; m. Audrey Ann Youso, Apr. 4, 1964; children: Christine Louise, Matthew James, Luke Donald. BS, St. Thomas Coll., St. Paul, 1964; MD, Med. Coll. Wis., 1968; MPH, U. Minn., 1977. Diplomate Am. Bd. Preventive Medicine, Occupational and Aerospace Medicine. Resident in internal medicine Mayo Clinic, Rochester, Minn., 1972-73; asst. regional flight surgeon FAA, FArmington, Minn., 1973-77; dir. med. svcs. Prudential Ins. Co., Mpls., 1977-79; asst. med. dir. 3M Corp., St. Paul, 1980-83; regional med. dir. Unocal, Schaumburg, Ill., 1983-84; corp. med. dir. Paccar Inc., Bellevue, Wash., 1984—. Maj. USAF, 1969-72; lt. col. USARNG, 1969-83. Fellow Am. Coll. Occupational Medicine; mem. AMA, King County Med. Soc., Am. Publ. Health Assn., Can. Occupational Med. Assn., Aerospace Med. Assn. (past), Assn. Life Ins. Med. Dir. Assn. (past). Home: 13817 180th Ave NE Redmond WA 98052 Office: Paccar Inc 777 106th Ave NE Bellevue WA 98004

VON HARZ, JAMES LYONS, communications executive; b. Palatine, Ill., Feb. 9, 1915; s. Benjamin Carl and Honore Regina (Lyons) von H.; m. Mary Jane Patterson, Oct. 31, 1938; children: John T., Patricia Christine, Rosanne D., Mary Jane, Kathleen Ann, Sheila Marie. B.S.M.E., Purdue U., 1938. Exec. v.p. Oak Mfg. Co., Crystal Lake, Ill., 1941-62; v.p. Waller Corp., Crystal Lake, 1962-63; gen. mgr. Internat. Resistor Corp.-TRW, Burlington, Iowa, 1963-68; group exec. v.p. Transitron Electronic Corp., Wakefield, Mass., 1968-71; pres. ITT Cannon Electric, Santa Ana, Calif., 1971-75; v.p. ITT; group gen. mgr. ITT Components Group-N.Am. ITT Cannon Electric, Fountain Valley, Calif., 1974-83; v.p., exec. rep. ITT Corp., N.Y.C., 1983-84; cons. ITT Corp., 1984—. Recipient Achievement award Delta Tau Delta. Mem. Am. Electronics Assn. (chmn. Orange County council 1973), Nat. Alliance Bus. (chmn. region IX 1973-76), Winter Conv. Aerospace and Electronic Systems (gen. chmn. 1976), C. of C. Clubs: Balboa Bay, Kiwanis, K.C. Office: 1485 Daleway Costa Mesa CA 92628

VON HORN, KNUT RAOUL LEOPOLD ROBERT, agriculturist, former government official; b. Stockholm, Nov. 28, 1907; s. Robert and Elizabeth (Bohnstedt) von H.: student U. Cambridge, 1927; B.A., U. Stockholm, 1930, LL.B., 1934; m. Birgitta von Horn, June 1, 1940; children—Johan, Edward, Michaela. Sec., Swedish State Commn. of Trade, 1939-41; chief sec. Ministry Supply, 1942-46, Ministry Commerce, 1946-48; mem. State-Commn. Agr., 1950-56; chmn. Swedish State Seed Testing Sta., 1959-74, Gullspang Power AB, 1973-81; chamberlain at Royal Ct., 1946; dep.-marshall Diplomatic Corp., 1950-59; first surveyor at Royal Ct., 1956; Swedish del. internat. econ. confs. GATT, ECE, 1946-55; bd. dirs. Korsnas-Marma AB, Investment AB Kinnevik, AB Swedish Lithographic Industries, 1949-86. Mem. Royal Swedish Acad. Agr. and Forestry (chmn. 1972-75), Swedish Milling Assn. (chmn. 1973-80). Office: Hjelmarsnas, S71592 Stora Melloesa Sweden

VON KALBEN, REIMAR RUDOLF ERNST, refrigeration company executive; b. Vienau, Fed. Republic of Germany, Feb. 26, 1931; came to U.S., 1959; s. Heinrich Detlof and Johanna (Krog) von K.; m. Dagmar Kaehler, Nov. 14, 1964; children: Stephan, Gytha. Student, Verwactungs Akademie, Nuernberg, Fed. Republic of Germany, 1953. Master electrician, Colo. State Dept. Regulatory Agys. Frequency conversion specialist Can. Comstock, St. Catherines, Ont., Can., 1956-59; founder, owner, pres. Allied Refrigeration & Electric, Inc., Pueblo, Colo., 1959—. Pres. Pueblo Symphony, 1975-76; Ward 3 Councilman City of Pueblo, 1983-86; bd. dirs. Pueblo Ballet, 1983-88; treas. Pueblo Girls' Club, 1984—. Mem. Refrigeration Svc. Engrs. Soc. (pres. 1968-69, v.p. 1988—), Optimist Club, German Club of Pueblo, Elks, Shriners. Democrat. Presbyterian. Home: 2311 S Prairie Ave Pueblo CO 81005 Office: Allied Refrigeration & Electric Inc 2313 S Prairie Ave Pueblo CO 81005

VON LINSOWE, MARINA D., systems analyst; b. Indpls., July 21, 1952; d. Carl Victor and Dorothy Mae (Quinn) von Linsowe; m. Russell W. Kidd, Mar. 21, 1982; 1 dau., Kira Christina von Linsowe. Student Am. River Coll., Portland State U. Verbal operator Credit Bur. Metro, San Jose, Calif. and Portland, Oreg., 1970-72; computer clk. Security Pacific Bank, San Jose, 1972-73; proof operator Crocker Bank, Seaside, Calif., 1973-74; proof supr. Great Western Bank, Portland, 1974-75; bookkeeper The Clothes Horse, Portland, 1976-78; computer operator Harsh Investment Co., Portland, 1978-79; data processing mgr. Portland Fish Co., 1979-81; data processing mgr. J & W Sci. Inc., Rancho Cordova, Calif., 1981-83; search and recruit specialist, data processing mgr. Re:Search Exec. Recruiters, Sacramento, Calif., 1983; sr. systems cons. Unisys Corp. (formerly Burroughs), 1983—; mfg. specialist, computer conversion cons., Portland, Oreg. First violinist Am. River Orch. Recipient Bank of Am. Music award, 1970. Mem. NAFE, Am. Prodn. and Inventory Control Soc., Am. Mgrs. Assn., MENSA, Data Processing Mgmt. Assn. Republican. Lutheran. Home: 4 SW Touchstone Dr Lake Oswego OR 97035

VON PISCHKE, JOHN D., development banker; b. East Cleveland, Ohio, Apr. 11, 1940; s. John LeRoy and Edna Elizabeth (Kolb) Von P.; m. Gretel Langford, July 15, 1967; children: John Makonnen, Leslie Alexander. BA, Coll. Wooster, 1962; MBA, Columbia U., 1964; PhD, U. Glasgow, Scotland, 1977. Credit trainee Chase Manhattan Bank, N.Y.C., 1967-69; asst. treas. Chase Manhattan Bank, London, also Monrovia, Liberia, 1972-75; vis. research assoc. Inst. for Devel. Studies, U. Nairobi, Kenya, 1972-75; ind. cons. Nairobi and Glasgow, Scotland, 1971-76; fin. analyst World Bank, Washington, 1976-81, sr. fin. analyst, 1981—; sec. Bank-Fund Staff Fed. Credit Union, Washington, 1983—. Sr. editor, contbr.: Rural Financial Markets in Low-Income Countries, 1983; co-editor, contbr.: Undermining Rural Development with Cheap Credit, 1984, Credito Agricola y Desarrollo Rural: La Nueva Vision, 1987. Treas., Reston (Va.) Commuter Bus, Inc., 1980-83. Office: World Bank 1818 H St NW Washington DC 20433

VON SCHUBERT, ANDREAS, wine and agricultural executive; b. Berlin, June 23, 1922; s. Carl and Renata (Harrach) von S.; student State Vocat. Inst., Trier, 1947-49, Nat. Viniculture Inst., Geisenheim, 1949-57; m. Gloria Horstmann, Mar. 15, 1951; children—Ellinor, Carl, Andrea. Owner estate

Maximin Grünhaus, Trier, 1952—; pres. Assn. Shareholders Steel Works, Dillingen-Saar, 1950—; fin. com. Steel Worls Dillinger Hütte, 1960—; supervisory bd. Saar Industrie Bank, Neunkirchen, 1965—; mng. com. State Labor Office and Chamber Agr. Rheinland Pfalz, 1960—; mem. Dist. Assembly Trier, 1952-72; lay assessor Ct. of Aldermen, Trier, 1975-84; trustee State Vocat. Inst. Viniculture, Trier, 1950—; adv. bd. Port Authority Trier. Served with German Army, 1941. Decorated knight Order St. John; Paul Harris fellow Rotary Internat., 1974. Mem. Winegrower and Farmers Assn. Rheinland Pfalz, Agrl. Profl. Assn. Rhine, Fed. Union Agrl. Grads. (mng. com.), German Agrl. Soc. (wine commn.), German French Soc. Trier (pres. 1961—), Soc. Christian Jewish Coop., Chamber Music Assn. Mem. consistory Protestant Ch. Rhineland; mem. synod Protestant Ch. Germany. Club: Trier Rotary (pres. 1965-66). Address: GRünhaus bei, D5501 Trier Federal Republic of Germany

VONTOBEL, PAUL, hardware company executive. Chmn. Hardware Wholesaler Inc., Ft. Wayne, Ind., also bd. dirs. Office: Hardware Wholesalers Inc PO Box 868 Fort Wayne IN 46801 *

VON WINCKLER, BEVERLY ANN PURNELL, personnel consultant; b. Joliet, Ill., Feb. 16, 1935; d. Edwin Dodd and Viola U. (Nelson) Purnell; m. David F. von Winckler, Sr., Oct. 26, 1957 (div. Aug. 1985); 1 child, David Franz. Student Joliet Jr. Coll., 1953-55, Brenau Coll., Ga., 1956-57. Sec. Office of Govt. P.R., Chgo., 1973-76; sales rep. Standard Register Co., Schiller Park, Ill., 1976-77; dir. devel. Irish Found., Chgo., 1978-79; pres. BEverly von Winckler & Assocs., Inc. div. Von Winckler Temporaries, Chgo., 1980—; lectr. Northwestern U. Program on Women, 1983—; prin. Hispanic-Am. Film Festival, Chgo., 1979; panelist Mundelein Coll., Chgo., 1985; lectr. Midwest Women's Ctr., 1985; guest various local TV shows. Vol., Sta. WTTW-TV, 1966-72, Chgo. Internat. Film Festival, 1964-85; bd. dirs. Evanston (Ill.)-North Shore YWCA; pub. relations dir. Democratic mayoral campaign, Evanston, 1981; docent Evanston Hist. Soc., 1988. Recipient Service award Chgo. Internat. Film Festival, 1964. Mem. Evanston Jr. Women's Club, Alpha Delta Pi. Avocation: wood crafts. Home: 1018 Lee St Evanston IL 60202 Office: 105 W Madison St #1600 Chicago IL 60602

VOORHIES, KENNETH OWEN, civil engineer; b. Kingsport, Tenn., Apr. 29, 1949; s. Edwin Springer and Marjorie (Childress) V.; m. Cynthia Lynn Boni, Nov. 25, 1977; children: James Michael, Amy Katherine. BCE, Ga. Inst. Tech., 1972, MSCE, 1973. Registered profl. engr., Ga., Tenn. Transp. engr. Bechtel Inc., San Francisco, 1973-75; pron. transp. planner Atlanta Regional Commn., 1976-81; chief transp. planner The RBA Group, Atlanta, 1982-83, dir. Ga. ops., 1983—. Mem. ASCE, Inst. Transp. Engrs., Transp. Rsch. Bd. Presbyterian. Office: The RBA Group 1375 Peachtree St NE Ste 690 Atlanta GA 30309

VORBRICH, LYNN KARL, lawyer, utility executive; b. Iowa City, Feb. 12, 1939; s. William August and Anna Margaretha (Seibert) V.; m. Ann McGregor Wriight, Feb. 27, 1959; children: Sally, Andrew, Peter, David. BS Indsl. Adminstrn., Iowa State U., 1960; JD, U. Iowa, 1962. Bar: Iowa 1962, Ill. 1962. Assoc. Seyforth, Shaw, Fairweather & Geraldson, Chgo., 1962-64; assoc., ptnr. Dickinson, Thruckmorton, Parker, et al, Des Moines, 1964-69; asst. counsel The Bankers Life Co., Des Moines, 1969-73; assoc. counsel Iowa Power & Light Co., Des Moines, 1973-76, assoc. gen. counsel, 1976-78, sec., assoc. gen. counsel, 1978-79, sr. v.p., 1985, exec. v.p., 1986—; sec., gen. counsel Iowa Resources Inc. and Iowa Power & Light Co., 1979-83, v.p., gen. counsel, sec., 1983-85; exec. v.p. Iowa Resources, Inc., 1987—; bd. dirs. Bankers Trust Co., Des Moines, 1986—. Mem. adv. com. Iowa State Boys Tng. Sch., Eldora, Iowa, 1987—, legis. study com. on Juvenile Justice, 1989—; dean's adv. council Iowa State U. Coll. of Bus. Adminstrn., Ames, 1987—; pres. bd. Polk County Legal Aid Soc., 1970, Iowa Children's and Family Services, 1970, 78, Planned Parenthood of Mid-Iowa, 1983, Des Moines Area Community Coll. Found., 1986-87; chmn. Des Moines Human Rights Commn., 1970; bd. dirs. Golden Circle Incubator bd., Golden Circle Labor-Mgmt. Commn., Ankeny, Iowa, 1988—, Civic Music Assn., Des Moines, 1986-87; Bur. Econ. Devel. Named Outstanding Young Alumnus Iowa State U., 1973. Mem. ABA, Iowa Bar Assn., Des Moines Club (trustee 1982). Republican. United Church of Christ. Office: Iowa Power & Light Co 823 Walnut PO Box 657 Des Moines IA 50303

VORHOLT, JEFFREY JOSEPH, lawyer, telecommunications company executive; b. Cin., Feb. 20, 1953; s. Edward C. and Rita L. (Kinross) V.; m. Marcia Anne Meyer, Apr. 30, 1976; children: Kimberly Anne, Gregory Michael. BBA cum laude, U. Cin., 1976; MBA, Xavier U., Cin., 1978; JD, Chase Law Sch., 1983. Bar: Ohio, 1983; CPA, Ohio. Sec., treas. Cin. Bell Info. Systems, Inc., 1983-84, v.p., chief fin. officer, 1984-88, also bd. dirs.; v.p., controller Cin. Bell, Inc., 1988—. Voting mem. Cin. Playhouse, 1985—; mem. fin. planning com. ARC, Cin., 1986—. Mem. ABA, Am. Inst. CPA's, Nat. Assn. Accts. (controllers council 1987—), Ohio Bar Assn., Aircraft Owners and Pilots Assn., Cin. Hist. Soc. Club: Bankers (Cin.) (adv. bd. 1986—). Office: Cin Bell Inc 201 E 4th St Cincinnati OH 45201

VORIS, WILLIAM, educational administrator; b. Neoga, Ill., Mar. 20, 1924; s. Louis K. and Faye (Hancock) V.; m. Mavis Marie Myre, Mar. 20, 1949; children: Charles William II, Michael K. BS, U. So. Calif., 1947, MBA, 1948; PhD, Ohio State U., 1951; LLD, Sung Kyun Kwan U. (Korea), 1972, Eastern Ill. U., 1976. Teaching asst. Ohio State U., Columbus, 1948-50; prof. mgmt. Wash. State U., Pullman, 1950-52; prof., head dept. mgmt. Los Angeles State Coll., 1952-58, 60-63; dean Coll. Bus. and Pub. Adminstrn., U. Ariz., Tucson, 1963-71; pres. Am. Grad. Sch. Internat. Mgmt., Glendale, Ariz., 1971—. Ford Found. research grantee Los Angeles State Coll., 1956; prof. U. Tehran (Iran), 1958-59; Ford Found. fellow Carnegie Inst. Tech., Pitts., 1961; prof. Am. U., Beirut, Lebanon, 1961, 62; cons. Hughes Aircraft Co., Los Angeles, Rheem Mfg. Co., Los Angeles, Northrop Aircraft Co., Palmdale, Calif., Harwood Co., Alhambra, Calif., ICA, Govt. Iran. Served with USNR, 1942-45. Fellow Acad. Mgmt.; mem. Ariz. Acad., Beta Gamma Sigma, Alpha Kappa Psi, Phi Delta Theta. Author: Production Control, Text and Cases, 1956, 3d edit., 1966; Management of Production, 1960. Research in indsl. future of Iran, mgmt. devel. in Middle East. Home: Thunderbird Campus Glendale AZ 85306

VOROS, GERALD JOHN, advertising executive; b. Milw., May 13, 1930; s. Thomas Louis and Theresa Johanna (Huebler) V.; m. Carla Marie Olson, Nov. 22, 1958; children: Bergen, John, Marta, Andrew, Matthew. PhB, Marquette U., 1951; postgrad., U. Utah, 1956-57. Reporter Blackfoot (Idaho) Daily Bull., 1953-54, Longview (Wash.) Daily News, 1954-56, Salt Lake Tribune, 1956-57, 58-61, Milw. Jour., 1957-58; writer E. & J. Gallo Winery, 1961; v.p., gen. mgr. William Kostka & Assos., Denver, 1961-64; account supr. N.W. Ayer & Sons, Inc., Chgo., 1964-66; account exec. Ketchum MacLeod & Grove Public Rels., Pitts., 1982—, dir. pub. rels., 1969-77, exec. v.p., 1977-79, pres., 1979-82; pres., chief oper. officer Ketchum Communications, Inc., Pitts., 1982—; bd. dirs. Ketchum Group Holdings Inc., Ketchum Communications Inc., Pitts. Co-editor: (book) What Happens in Public Relations, 1982. Vice chmn. World Affairs Coun. of Pitts.; v.p. Cath. Charities of Pitts. Diocese, 1987—; mem. exec. com. Nat. Coun. Boy Scouts Am., 1982—, chmn. mktg. com., 1987—; cilivian aide to sec. U.S. Army, Pitts., 1982—; bd. dirs. Pitts. Children's Mus., 1982—, Allegheny Trails Coun., Pitts., 1987—, Western Pa. Hist. Soc., Pitts., 1987—; trustee The Carnegie Inst., Pitts., 1987—. With USMCR, 1953-64, Korea. Recipient Byline award Marquette U., Milw., 1987. Mem. Public Rels. Soc. Am. (accredited, bd. dirs. 1982-84, mem. Counselors Acad., various nat. and local offices), Soc. Profl. Journalists, Duquense (Pitts.). Roman Catholic. Home: 146 N Bellefield #701 Pittsburgh PA 15213 Office: Ketchum Communications Inc Six PPG Pl Pittsburgh PA 15222

VORREITER, PATRICIA JOAN, lawyer; b. Savanna, Ill., July 5, 1940; d. Harry and Florence K. (Fitzpatrick) Wolfe; m. John Vorreiter, Dec. 28, 1962; children: Janelle, Riane, Loren. BA, Colo. State U., 1962; JD, Santa Clara (Calif.) U., 1980. Bar: Calif. 1980, U.S. Dist. Ct. (no. dist.) Calif. 1980. Assoc. Mackey & Friedland, San Jose, Calif., 1980-81; sole parctice Sunnyvale, Calif., 1981—. Elder Sunnyvale Presbyn. Ch., 1988—, deacon, 1984-86; v.p., bd. dirs. Life's Garden Inc., Sunnyvale, 1986—; bd. dirs. Condo Assn., Sunnyvale, 1986—. Mem. ABA, Calif. Bar Assn., Santa Clara Bar Assn. (family law com. 1987), Sunnyvale-Cupertino Bar Assn. (lawyer referral com. 1986-88, bd. dirs. 1988—). Democrat. Home: 937 Aster Ct Sunnyvale CA 94086 Office: 333 W Maude Suite 201 Sunnyvale CA 94086

VORSE, JERRY DAVID, civic organization executive; b. Erie, Pa., Nov. 9, 1953; s. Clarence Harry and Winifred Elaine (Giddings) V.; m. Sandra McClelland, July 5, 1980; 1 child, Linda Marie. BBA, Kent State U., 1975. Dist. exec. Johnny Appleseed Council Boy Scouts Am., Mansfield, Ohio, 1976-79; dir. devel. Greater N.Y. Council Boy Scouts Am., N.Y.C., 1979-82; dir. devel. Columbia Presbyn. Med. Ctr., N.Y.C., 1982-83; dir. ann. giving Fordham U., N.Y.C., 1983-84; fin. dir. Bergen Council Boy Scouts Am., River Edge, N.J., 1984—; bd. dirs. N.Y. Soc. Fund Raising Execs., 1982-84. Mem. N.J. Soc. Fund Raising Execs., Phi Epsilon Kappa. Republican. Presbyterian. Lodges: Rotary (pres. Shelby, Ohio club 1979), Kiwanis (pres. Crestline, Ohio club 1978-79). Home: 94 Eastern Way Rutherford NJ 07070 Office: Boy Scouts Am Bergen Council 1060 Main St River Edge NJ 07661

VORYS, ARTHUR ISAIAH, lawyer; b. Columbus, Ohio, June 16, 1923; s. Webb Isaiah and Adeline (Werner) V.; m. Lucia Rogers, July 16, 1949 (div. 1980); children: Caroline S., Adeline Vorys Cranson, Lucy Vorys Noll, Webb I.; m. Ann Harris, Dec. 13, 1980. BA, Williams Coll., 1945; LLB, JD, Ohio State U., 1949. Bar: Ohio 1949. From assoc. to ptnr. Vorys, Sater, Seymour & Pease, Columbus, 1949—; sr. ptnr. Vorys, Sater, Seymour & Pease, 1982—; bd. dirs. Corroon & Black Corp., First Equity Life Ins. Co., N.Am. Nat. Corp., Ohio Casualty Corp., Ohio Casualty Ins. Co., Ohio Life Ins. Co., Ohio Security Ins. Co., Pan-Western Life Ins. Co., Shelby Ins. Co., Vorys Bros., Inc., Wendy's Internat., Inc., other corps.; supt. of ins., Ohio, 1957-59. Trustee, past pres. Children's Hosp., Greenlawn Cemetery Assn., Griffith Found. for Ins. Edn., Internat. Ins. Soc.; trustee, former chmn. Ohio State U. Hosps.; regent Capital U.; del. Rep. Nat. Conv., 1968, 72. Lt. USMCR, World War II. Decorated Purple Heart. Fellow Ohio State Bar, Columbus Bar Assns.; mem. ABA, Am. Judicature Soc., Phi Delta Phi., Chi Psi. Clubs: Rocky Fork Headley Hunt, Rocky Fork Hunt and Country (Gahanna); Columbus Athletic, Capital. Home: 5826 Havens Corners Rd Gahanna OH 43230 Office: Vorys Sater Seymour & Pease 52 E Gay St PO Box 1008 Columbus OH 43216

VOS, HUBERT DANIEL, private investor; b. Paris, Aug. 2, 1933; s. Marius and Aline (Porge) V.; m. Susan Hill, Apr. 18, 1958; children: Wendy, James. BA, Institut d'Etudes Politiques, U. Paris, 1954; M in Pub. Adminstrn., Princeton U., 1956. Internal auditor Internat. Packers Ltd., 1957-61, dir. fin., 1962-64; asst. to contr. Monsanto Co., 1964-66, contr. internat. div., 1966-69; v.p. planning and fin. Smith Kline Corp., 1969-72; sr. v.p. fin. Comml. Credit Co., Balt., 1972-74; sr. v.p. fin. and adminstrn., dir. Norton Simon Inc., N.Y.C., 1974-79; sr. v.p. fin., dir. Becton Dickinson and Co., Paramus, N.J., 1979-83; pres. Stonington Capital Corp., Santa Barbara, Calif., 1984—; bd. dirs. Rowe Price New Era Fund Inc., New Horizons Fund Inc., Equity Income Fund Inc., Capital Appreciation Fund Inc., Sci. and Tech. Fund, Inc., Small Capital Value Fund, Inc.; mem. adv. bd. Genetic Systems Diagnostic Ptnrs., Seattle; bd. dirs. Kilovac Corp., Carpinteria, Calif. Pres. Santa Barbara Scholarship Found., past bd. dirs. Mem. Am. Mgmt. Assn. (gen. mgmt. coun.), Surg. Eye Expdns. Internat (bd. dirs.). Clubs: Princeton of N.Y; Univ., Santa Barbara, La Cumbre Golf and Country (Santa Barbara). Home: 800 Via Hierba Santa Barbara CA 93110 Office: 1231 State St Ste 210 Santa Barbara CA 93101

VOSBURGH, WILLIAM GEORGE, hobby and craft shop owner; b. Flint, Mich., May 30, 1925; s. Merle Joseph and Eda (Morgen) V.; m. June 15, 1946 (dec. Sept. 1987); children: William George Jr., Robert, Susan, Bruce, John, Nancy. PhD in Organic Chemistry, U. Del., 1956. Chemist E.I. Du Pont de Nemours and Co., Wilmington, Del., 1950-51, rsch. chemist, 1951-71, sr. rsch. chemist, 1971-82; owner, mgr. Vosburgh's Hobby and Craft Shops, West Chester, Pa., 1959-86, V.H.C. Corp., West Chester, Pa., 1986—. With AUS, 1943-48, PTO. Office: VHC Corp 43 W Gay St West Chester PA 19380

VOSO, DEBORAH ELIZABETH, financial planning executive; b. Camden, N.J., Mar. 29, 1950; d. H. David and Elizabeth Ann (Lesicko) Rau; m. Richard F. Voso, Oct. 2, 1971; children: Jennifer, Lisa. AA, Frederick Community Coll., 1979; BA, Shepherd Coll., 1983. Cert. fin. planner. Fin. planner Fin. Mgmt. Resources, Churchton, Md., 1983-84, Investment Mgmt. and Research, Greenbelt, Md., 1984-85, Capital Fin. Group, Silver Spring, Md., 1985-86; pres. Voso Assocs., Frederick, Md., 1986—; lectr. Frederick County Adult Edn., 1987—, Frederick Community Coll., 1987—. Bd. dirs. Heartly House, Frederick, 1987—; chmn. Frederick County Women's Fair, Bus. Women's exhibits, 1986-88; treas. Frederick County Women's Ctr. Council, 1986-88. Mem. Frederick Community Coll. Alumni Assn. (pres. 1988), Internat. Assn. Fin. Planners, Inst. Cert. Fin. Planners, Surburban Md. Life Underwriters Assn. (bd. dirs. 1986, chmn. pub. service com. 1986-87, chmn. pub. relations 1987-88). Republican. Methodist. Lodges: Rotary, Toastmasters. Home: 9005 Mountainberry Circle Frederick MD 21701 Office: Voso Assocs 220 W Patrick St Frederick MD 21701

VOSS, WILLIAM CHARLES, oil company executive; b. Buffalo, Sept. 22, 1937; s. William T. and Dorathea S. (Grotke) V.; m. Marilyn Erickson, Sept. 6, 1958; children: William, John, Douglas. AB with honors, Harvard U., 1959, MBA with honors, 1961. With Northwestern Refining Co., St. Paul Park, 1961-70; v.p. adminstrn. Northwestern Refining Co., 1969-71; with Ashland Oil Inc., Ky., 1971—, v.p., 1973-79, adminstrv. v.p., 1979-80, sr. v.p., group operating officer, 1980—; pres. Ashland-Warren Inc., 1979-83, APAC, Inc., 1980-82, 83-86. Mem. Am. Petroleum Inst., Ind. Petroleum Assn. Am., Am. Chem. Soc. Republican. Home: 8930 Ridgemont Dr Atlanta GA 30350 Office: Ashland Oil Inc 3340 Peachtree Rd NE Atlanta GA 30326

VOWELL, JEFF D., consulting company executive; b. Hobbs, N.Mex., Apr. 19, 1952; s. Jeff D. and Dolly Jo (White) V.; m. Carol Ann Setaro, Mar. 17, 1974; children: Daniel Patrick, Christopher Brian. BS, SUNY, Albany, 1976; MBA, Pacific Western U., 1987. Data base cons. various orgns., 1976-79; data base adminstr. Greyhound Corp., Phoenix, 1979-80; sr. systems engr. Amdahl Corp., Tempe, Ariz., 1980-82; mgr. systems quality Avco-Lycoming, Stratford, Conn., 1982-83; engr. account systems IBM, Boston, 1983-84; mgr. systems Litton Itek Optical Systems, Lexington, Mass., 1984-85; owner Vowell Systems Group, Middletown, N.J., 1985-87; v.p. FSS Cons. Co., N.Y.C., 1987—. Author: Implementation and Usage of DB2, 1987; developer Relationally Integrated Design Devel. and Control System software; contbr. articles to profl. jours. Pres. Sierra Vista Jaycees, Ariz., 1975-76; regional dir. Minn. Jaycees, 1977-78; v.p. Ariz. Jaycees, 1979-81; cubmaster pack 242 Boy Scouts Am., Middletown, N.J., 1986—. Served with U.S. Army, 1970-76. Recipient Outstanding Performance in Electronic Data Processing award Am. Soc. Mil. Comptrollers, 1975, Keyman award U.S. Jaycees, 1976; named one of 3 Outstanding Young Men of Ariz., Ariz. Jaycees, 1976. Mem. Mass. Jaycees (v.p. 1984-85). Home: 398 Harmony Rd Middletown NJ 07748 Office: FSS Cons Co 1180 Avenue of the Americas New York NY 10036

VREELAND, ELEANOR P., publishing company executive. BS, Queens Coll., 1952; MBA, NYU, 1958. With Peck & Peck, 1947-58; pub. relations dir. Bklyn. Pub. Library, 1960-65; v.p., treas., cons. St. John's Library Cons., Inc., 1965-67; advt. and publicity dir. Frances Denny, 1967-68; product mgr. Macmillan Library Services, 1960-69; dir. mktg. Strechert-Hayner, 1971-79; pres., chief exec. officer Katharine Gibbs Schs., 1981—; with Macmillan, Inc., N.Y.C., 1971—, v.p., 1981—. Office: Macmillan Inc 866 3rd Ave New York NY 10022 *

VREELAND, JAMES ALBERT, financial executive; b. East Orange, N.J., June 23, 1927; s. Albert L. and Helen (Aeschbach) V.; student Stevens Inst. Tech., 1947-50; B.B.A., Upsala Coll., 1952; grad. Exec. Mgmt. Program, N.Y.U., 1964; M.B.A. magna cum laude, Fairleigh Dickinson U., 1972; m. Laura Price, June 10, 1949 (div. Nov. 1970); children—Elizabeth Ann, Stephen, Keith; m. 2d, Joyce Kessel, Dec. 10, 1977. Supr. chem. div. Celanese Corp., Newark, 1952-55; div. controller Kelsey-Hayes Co., Clark, 1955-59; asst. corp. comptroller Ametek, Inc., Newark, 1959-61; controller Graver Water Conditioning Co. div. Trans Union Corp., Union, N.J., 1961-70, v.p., 1970-72, v.p., controller Unitech Co. div., 1968-72; v.p., treas. Cascade Industries, Inc., Edison, N.J., 1972-75; sr. v.p. fin. Belco Pollution Control Corp., Parsippany, N.J., 1975—, dir., 1981—. Mem. Short Hills-Millburn Republican Club, 1953-62; fund drive dir. fin. com. Rahway YMCA, 1954-56, Overlook Hosp., 1959-60, Knollwood Assn., 1959-61; mem. adv. com. Somerset Coll., 1969-75; mem. steering com. Human Resources Inst., U. Mich., 1972-77; pres. bd. trustees Marcus L. Ward Home, N.J., 1986—. Served with USNR, 1945-47; officer mil. intelligence CIC, 1955-61. Public acct., N.J. Mem. Nat. CIC Assn., Nat. Rifle Assn. (life), Mil. Order World Wars (regional comdr., life), Union C. of C. (industry com. 1968-72), Am. Mgmt. Assn. (chmn., speaker seminars), Fin. Execs. Inst. (past pres. N.J. chpt. 1974, vice chmn. conf. 1977), Holland Soc. N.Y., Delta Mu Delta. Clubs: Masons (KT). Gardeners Bay Country. Home: 23 Fairbanks Ln Basking Ridge NJ 07920 Office: 8 Peach Tree Hill Rd Livingston NJ 07039

VRETTOS, WILLIAM C., mining executive; b. Chgo., Feb. 7, 1947; s. Milton J. and Florence Mae (Gillies) V.; m. Nancy L. Strange, June 27, 1970; children: Elizabeth, Jessica, Nicholas, Andrew. BS in Mktg., Ea. Ill. U., 1968. Mgr. indsl. engring. Continental Can Co., Portage, Ind., 1969-75; regional indsl. engr. Continental Can Co., Elk Grove Village, Ill., 1976-79; plant supt. Continental Can Co., Lima, Ohio, 1979-81; gen. supt. ops. U.S. Fuel Co., Hiawatha, Utah, 1981—; chmn. acad. adv. council mining edn., Coll. Ea. Utah, Price, 1982-88. Mem. city planning and zoning commn., City of Wellington, Utah, 1982-83; chmn. Econ. Devel. Com., Carbon County, Utah; bd. dirs. United Way Carbon County, 1982-83. Recipient Am. Spirit of Honor Medal, U.S. Army, 1969. Mem. Carbon County C. of C. (bd. dirs. 1985-87). Home: 2272 Mt View Circle Wellington UT 84542 Office: US Fuel Co PO Box A Hiawatha UT 84527

VROOMAN, ROBERT STEVEN, entertainment executive; b. Seattle, May 5, 1951; s. Robert Glen and Josephine A. (Spaccarotelli) V.; m. Judith Ann Meadows, Jan. 6, 1980. Assocs. in Applied Sci., Green River Coll., 1971; B in Bus., U. Wash., 1973. Dir. transportation Med. Investment Corp., Mpls., 1973-74; unit contr. Holiday on Ice, 1974-76; adminstrv. mgr. Seattle Mariners Baseball Club, 1976-78; v.p. adminstrn. and mktg. Fidelity Ln. Cos., 1978-85; exec. v.p. Vrooman Entertainment Group, Bellevue, Wash., 1986—; cons. in field. Mem. Assn. Profl. Baseball Players, Internat. Assn. Auditorium Mgrs., Puget Sound Assn. Sports Writers and Broadcasters. Republican. Roman Catholic. Home: 6153 144th Pl SE Bellevue WA 98006 Office: Vrooman Entertainment Group 123 Boylston Ave E Seattle WA 98102

VU, JEAN-PIERRE, consultant; b. Thai Binh, Vietnam, Aug. 11, 1934; s. Xan Ngo Vu and Hoang T. Nguyen; m. Josephine Brece, Oct. 1, 1960; children: Cecile, Denis A., Catherine. BS in Agrl., U. Wis., 1958, MS in Agrl. Econs., 1959; MBA, Internat. U., Manila, 1982, PhD, 1983. Coop. expert Nat. Agrl. Credit Office, Saigon, Vietnam, 1959-61; asst. to retail mgr. Standard Vacuum Oil Co., Saigon, 1961-62; asst. planning mgr. Esso Standard Eastern, Saigon, 1966-71; project economist Asian Devel. Bank, Manila, 1971-79, sr. project economist, 1979-83, sr. cons. services specialist, 1983—. Spl. minister of Eucharist. Served to lt. Republic Vietnam Army, 1962-66. Roman Catholic. Home: 26 Jackson St, Greenhills W, San Juan 1500, Philippines

VUCHETICH, MARY KATHLEEN, gas company executive; b. Green Bay, Wis., July 29, 1948; d. Austin Hillary and Alice Mae (Zegers) Koeppel; m. Dennis Lee Wieck, Apr. 2, 1972. BS, U. Wis., 1970; MBA, DePaul U., 1977. Tchr. Luxembourg (Wis.) Sch. Dist., 1970-72; cash mgmt. analyst Brunswick Corp., Chgo., 1972-74, acquisition analyst, 1974-77; mgr. GATX Corp., Chgo., 1977-81; asst. v.p. MidCon Corp., Chgo., 1981-86; v.p. Consol. Nat. Gas Co., Pitts., 1986—. Recipient Award of Excellence, Fin. Analyst Fedn., 1980, 84, Leadership award YMCA, Chgo., 1985. Mem. Am. Gas Assn. (chmn. investor relations subcom. 1985-87), Petroleum Investor Relations Assn., Nat. Investor Relations Inst. (sec. 1984-85), Nat. Trust Historic Preservation, Frank Lloyd Wright Home and Studio Found. (vol. 1985-86). Office: Consol Nat Gas Co CNG Tower Pittsburgh PA 15222-3199

VUKOVIC, DRAGO VUKO, electronic engineer; b. Dubrovnik, Yugoslavia, Sept. 9, 1934; s. Vuko and Katica (Simunovic) V.; m. Marija Kakarigji, May 15, 1956; children—Katija, Snjezana, Sanja. Diploma engr., Faculty of Electrotehnics, Zagreb, 1961; M.S., Faculty of Econs., Zagreb, 1977. Supervising engr. Elektrojug, Dubrovnik, Yugoslavia, 1961-62; lighting designer Arhitekt, Dubrovnik, 1963-64; designer, supr. Biro za izgradnju, Dubrovnik, 1964-71, mng. dir., 1971-74; leader architect team Atelier LAPAD, Dubrovnik, 1974—; tchr., head electrotechnical div. Nautical Coll., Dubrovnik, 1963-67; cons. engr. Dubrovnik, Cavtat, Dubrovnik, 1968-75; collaborator Faculty of Architecture, Zagreb, 1974—. Contbr. in field. Served to capt. Yugoslavian Air Force, 1962-63. Recipient Town Planning & Architecture award Yugoslav Competition Com., Titograd, 1978; Plaque Assn. Visual Artists and Applied Arts of Croatia, 1982. Mem. Assn. Visual Artists of Applied Arts of Croatia, Soc. Ind. Geodesists, Civil Engrs. and Architects. Clubs: Radio Club (Dubrovnik); Am. Radio Relay League Inc, Am. Biog. Inst. Research Assn. Office: Atelier LAPAD, L Rogovskog 10, 50000 Dubrovnik Yugoslavia

VYTAL, JAMES ALFRED, printing company executive; b. Newton, Mass., Mar. 30, 1936; s. Alfred E. and Gertrude M. (Barlow) V.; student Boston U. evening div., 1954-60; m. Barbara A. Frost, June 14, 1957; children—Barry J., Karen L. Production mgr. Houghton Mifflin Co., Boston, 1966-73; v.p. mfg. Scott, Foresman & Co., Glenview, Ill., 1973-78; v.p., mid-Atlantic regional mgr. Banta Co., Menasha, Wis., and N.Y.C., 1978-81; v.p. mktg. and sales The Village Press, Inc., Concord, N.H.; pres. J & B Graphics. Mem. Assn. Am. Pubs., Printing Industries of New Eng. Republican. Clubs: N.Y. Athletic, Mason.

WABLER, ROBERT CHARLES, II, retail and distribution executive; b. Dayton, Ohio, Dec. 14, 1948; s. Robert Charles Sr. and Eileen Marie (Langen) W.; m. Linda Adele Rayburn; 1 child, Robert Charles III. BS in Acctg. cum laude, U. Dayton, 1971; MS in Acctg. magna cum laude, U. Ga., 1976. Sr. auditor Touche Ross and Co., Dayton, 1971-73; internal auditor So. Company Services, Atlanta, 1974-75; acctg. mgr. Rich's div. Federated Dept. Stores, Atlanta, 1976-77; dir. auditing Munford, Inc., Atlanta, 1977-81, v.p., controller, 1982-83, v.p. fin. analyses, 1983-86; v.p. adminstrn. World Bazaar div. Munford, Inc., Atlanta, 1981-82, sr. v.p. fin., 1986-89; v.p., chief fin. officer The Athlete's Foot Group, Inc., Atlanta, 1989—. Mem. Am. Inst. CPA's, Ga. Soc. CPA's, Inst. Internal Auditors, Assn. Systems Mgmt., EDP Auditor Assn. (bd. dirs. 1978-79). Home: 7171 Twin Branch Ct Atlanta GA 30328 Office: The Athlete's Foot Group Inc 3735 Atlanta Industrial Pkwy Atlanta GA 30331

WACHENHEIM, EDGAR, III, investment management executive; b. N.Y.C., Oct. 14, 1937; s. Edgar Jr. and Elizabeth (Lewis) W.; m. Sue Wallach, June 6, 1963; children: Lance, Kim, Chris, Amy. BA, Williams Coll., 1959; MBA, Harvard U., 1966. Securities analyst Goldman, Sachs & Co., N.Y.C., 1966-69; mng. dir. Cen. Nat. Gottesman Inc., N.Y.C., 1969-88; chmn., chief exec. officer Greenhaven Assocs., Inc., N.Y.C., 1988—; bd. dirs. Cen. Corp., N.Y.C., Sejak, N.Y.C., Cen. Nat. Gottesman. Inc., N.Y.C. Trustee Arthur Ross Found., N.Y.C., 1978—; chmn. investment com., trustee UJA Fedn. Jewish Philanthropies, N.Y.C., 1985—; mem. fin. com., trustee Rye Country Day Sch., N.Y., 1985—; bd. dirs. Miriam and Ira D. Wallach Found. Mem. N.Y. Soc. Security Analysts, Beach Point Club, Harvard Club, Century Country Club. Office: Greenhaven Assocs Inc 100 Park Ave New York NY 10017

WACHNER, LINDA JOY, apparel marketing and manufacturing executive; b. N.Y.C., Feb. 3, 1946; d. Herman and Shirley W.; m. Seymour Applebaum, Dec. 21, 1973 (dec., 1983). BS in Econs. and Bus., U. Buffalo, 1966. Buyer Foley's Federated Dept. Store, Houston, 1968-69; sr. buyer R.H. Macy's, N.Y.C., 1969-74; v.p. Warner div. Warnaco, Bridgeport, Conn., 1974-77; v.p. corp. mktg. Caron Internat., N.Y.C., 1977-79; pres. U.S. div. Max Factor & Co., Hollywood, Calif., 1979-82, pres., chief ops. officer, 1982-83; pres., chief exec. officer Max Factor & Co. Worldwide, 1983-84; mng. dir. Adler & Shaykin, N.Y.C., 1984-86; owner, pres., chief exec. officer Warnaco Inc., N.Y.C., 1986—; bd. dirs. Standard Brands Paints, Reebok Internat.; mem. bus. adv. council City of Los Angeles, U. So. Calif. Sch. Bus. Adminstrn.; mem., chmn. trade promotion U.S.-Philippines Bus. Com. Presdl. appointee Adv. Com. for Trade Negotiations; trustee Martha Graham Ctr. Contemporary Dance, Inc.; mem. bd. trustees U. Buffalo Found. Recipient Silver Achievement award Los Angeles YWCA; named Outstanding Woman in Bus., Women's Equity Action League, 1980, Woman of Yr., MS. Mag.,

1986; honoree Nat. Women's Forum, 1986. Mem. Young Pres.'s Orgn., Com. of 200, Am. Mgmt. Assn., Am. Apparel Mktg. Assn. (bd. dirs.), Los Angeles C. of C. (bd. dirs.). Republican. Jewish. Office: Warnaco Inc 90 Park Ave New York NY 10016 also: Warnaco Inc 11111 Santa Monica Blvd Los Angeles CA 90025

WACHSMAN, GIL, communications company executive. Pres. Child World, Inc., Avon, Mass. Office: Lieberman Enterprises Inc 9549 Penn Ave Minneapolis MN 55431

WACHTEL, BONNIE KIM, investment banker, securities analyst; b. Washington, July 18, 1955; d. Sidney B. and Irma S. (Schocken) W. BA, U. Chgo., 1977, MBA, 1978; JD, U. Va., 1980. Bar: N.Y. 1982, D.C. 1984. Assoc. Weil, Gotshal & Manges, N.Y.C., 1980-84; v.p., gen. counsel Wachtel & Co. Inc., Washington, 1984—. Home: 1171 Massachusetts Ave NW Washington DC 20036 Office: Wachtel & Co Inc 1101 14th St NW Washington DC 20005

WACHTEL, S. ERIC, business executive; b. N.Y.C., May 14, 1942; m. D. Lynn Wachtel, Nov. 29, 1969; 1 child, Sarah Elisabeth. BA, U. Mo., 1964. Asst. dir. Am. Stock Exchange, N.Y.C., 1964-67; dir. personnel, adminstr. Aucholiss, Parker & Redpath, N.Y.C., 1967-71; v.p. Gulf & Western Industries, Inc., N.Y.C., 1972-79; pres. Wachtel & Assocs. Ltd., N.Y.C., 1980-85; pres., chmn. bd. Medphone Corp., Paramus, N.J., 1986—, bd. dirs., 1985—. Author: How To Hold on to Your Job, 1983. Mem. Centre Club (Tampa, Fla.). Office: Medphone Corp The Atrium E 80 Rte 4 Paramus NJ 07652-2647

WACHTELL, THOMAS, petroleum company executive, lawyer; b. Crestwood, N.Y., Mar. 27, 1928; s. Theodore and Carolyn (Satz) W.; grad. Choate Sch., 1946; B.S., Syracuse U., 1950; LL.B., Cornell U., 1958; m. Esther Carole Pickard, Jan. 27, 1957; children—Roger Bruce, Wendy Ann, Peter James. Bar: N.Y. 1958. Assoc. Livingston, Wachtell & Co., C.P.A.s, N.Y.C., 1958-60; pres. Allied Homeowners Assn., Inc., White Plains, N.Y., 1960-63, pres. Gen. Factoring Co., White Plains, N.Y., 1960-63; exec. asst. to pres. Occidental Petroleum Corp., Los Angeles, 1963-65, v.p., exec. asst., chmn. bd., 1965-72, exec. v.p., 1972-73, officer, dir. numerous subs.; pres. Hydrocarbon Resources Corp., 1973-81; chmn. Oriental Petroleum Corp., 1982—; exec. v.p. Frontier Oil and Refining Co., Denver, 1985-87, also bd. dirs.; chmn. bd. Frontier Oil Internat., 1985-87; pres., chief exec. officer, dir. NMR Ctrs., Inc., 1982-83; pres., dir. Cayman Petroleum Corp., 1974-75, Ridgecrest Energy Corp., 1979; dir. Tanglewood Consol. Resources, 1982-84. Panelist, lectr. Nat. Indsl. Conf. Bd.; bd. govs. The Los Angeles Music Center, 1973—; chmn., chief exec. officer, bd. dirs. Los Angeles Music Center Opera Assn., 1972—, chmn., chief exec. officer, 1981—; trustee Good Hope Med. Found., Los Angeles, 1974—. Served to lt. Office Naval Intelligence, USNR, 1952-56. Mem. Am. Mgmt. Assn., Los Angeles World Affairs Council, Choate Alumni Assn. So. Cal. (chmn. 1969—), Confrerie des Chevaliers du Tastevin, Beta Theta Pi, Phi Delta Phi.

WACHTER, MICHAEL L., economics educator; b. N.Y.C., Mar. 12, 1943; s. Abraham and Florence W.; m. Susan M. Jaffe, June 23, 1968; children: Jessica, Jonathan. B.S., Cornell U., 1964; M.A., Harvard U., 1967, Ph.D., 1970. Asst. prof. econs. U. Pa., Phila., 1969-73, assoc. prof., 1973-76, prof. econs., law and mgmt., 1976—, dir. Inst. for Law and Econs., 1984—; sr. advisor Brookings Instn., Washington, 1976—; commr. Minimum Wage Study Commn., Washington, 1978-81; cons. U.S. Postal Svc., 1980—. Editor: Removing Obstacles to Economic Growth, 1984, Toward a New U.S. Industrial Policy, 1982; contbr. articles to profl. jours. NIH grantee, 1981-83; NSF grantee, 1974-77; 20th Century Fund grantee, 1978-82; Gen. Electric Found. grantee, 1980-83. Mem. Am. Econ. Assn., Econometric Soc., Indsl. Relations Research Assn. Office: U Pa Law Sch Inst for Law & Econs Philadelphia PA 19104

WACKENHUT, GEORGE RUSSELL, security services executive; b. Phila., Sept. 3, 1919; s. William Henry and Frances (Hogan) W.; m. Ruth Johann Bell, Apr. 8, 1944; children—Janis Lynn Wackenhut Ward, Richard Russell. Student, U. Pa. Wharton Evening Sch., 1937-38, State Tchrs. Coll., West Chester, Pa., 1938-41; B.S., U. Hawaii, 1943; postgrad., Temple U., 1946; M.Ed., Johns Hopkins U., 1949. Ops. edn. profl. program tchrs. tng. Johns Hopkins U., 1946-50; civilian cons. recreational sports br. Office Spl. Services, U.S. Army, Washington, 1950-51; spl. agt. FBI, 1951-54; dir. personnel, security and safety Giffin Industries, Inc., Miami, Fla., 1954; pres., chmn. bd. Spl. Agt. Investigators, Inc., Spl. Agts. Security Guards, Inc., Security Services Corp. (all Miami), 1954-58; pres., chmn. bd., dir. Wackenhut Corp., Coral Gables, Fla., 1958-86, chmn. bd., chief exec. officer, 1986—; pres., chmn. bd., dir. Wackenhut Systems Corp., Titania Advt., Inc., Wackenhut of Alaska, Inc., Wackenhut Services, Inc.; chmn. bd., dir. Wackenhut Advanced Techs. Corp., Stellar Systems, Inc., Am. Guard and Alert, Inc., Wackenhut Internat., Inc.; dir. Wackenhut of Can., Ltd., Wackenhut de Guatemala (S.A.), Wackenhut U.K. Ltd., Wackenhut Dominicana (S.A.), Wackenhut del Ecuador (S.A.), Wackenhut Keibi, K.K.-Japan, Titania Ins. Co., Ltd., SSJ Med. Devel., Inc., Miami, Fla., Servicios Profesionales de Proteccion y Seguridad, S.A. de C.V., Mex., 1980-86; chmn. bd. dirs. Wackenhut Electronic Systems Corp., Wackenhut Internat. Trading Corp., Wackenhut of North Africa, Inc., Wackenhut Support Services, Inc.; mem. Dean's Adv. Bd. U. Miami Sch. Bus. Mem. law enforcement council Nat. Council Crime and Delinquency, 1971-73; Bd. dirs. Heart Assn. of Greater Miami, 1965-66, Gov.'s War on Crime, Fla., 1967-70, SSJ Med. Devel., Inc., Miami, Fla.; bd. visitors U.S. Army M.P. Sch., 1972-74; mem. Small Bus. Adminstrn. REgion IV, Miami Adv. Council, 1983—. Served with U.S. Army, 1941-45. Recipient George Washington Honor medal Freedom's Found. at Valley Forge, Vigilant Patriot award All Ams. Conf. to Combat Communism; named Chief Exec. Officer of the Yr., Fin. World Mag., 1987, Disting. Alumnus U. Hawaii, West Chester U. Mem. Soc. Former Spl. Agts. FBI, Inc., Am. Soc. for Indsl. Security, Cert. Protection Profl., AIM (pres.'s council 1964-66). Christian Scientist. Clubs: Ocean Reef (Key Largo, Fla.), Biltmore Bus. (Coral Gables, Fla.). Home: 20 Casuarina Concourse Gables Estates Coral Gables FL 33143 Office: Wackenhut Corp 1500 San Remo Ave Coral Gables FL 33146

WACKENHUT, JOYCE, advertising executive; b. Chgo., May 31, 1945; d. William Henry and Mary Francis (Boyd) W.; m. Charles Norman Hilbert, Oct. 13, 1984. Student, U. Ill., 1963-65; BA, Hunter Coll., N.Y.C., 1977; MA, CUNY, 1984, PhD in Psychology, 1987. Asst. prodn. application specialist Service Bureau Corp., N.Y.C., 1967-68; project coordinator TeleSession Corp., N.Y.C., 1972-74; adminstr. psychology dept. Post Grad. Ctr. Mental Health, N.Y.C., 1974-76; research asst. Grad. Sch. and Univ. Ctr. City Univ. of N.Y., 1977-83; program evaluator Ctr. Advanced Study in Edn., N.Y.C., 1979; indsl. mktg. specialist Yankelovich, Skelly and White, N.Y.C., 1983-85; advt. research specialist Young and Rubicam, N.Y.C., 1985—; cons. Hillebrandt Cons., Inc., ARAWAK Cons. Group, Ctr. for the Advancement of Edn. Contbr. numerous articles to profl. jours. Mem. Am. Mktg. Assn., APA, Met. N.Y. Assn. for Applied Psychology, The N.Y. Acad. Scis., The Art Students League. Home: 685 West End Ave New York NY 10025 Office: Young & Rubicam 285 Madison Ave New York NY 10017

WACKENHUT, RICHARD RUSSELL, security company executive; b. Balt., Nov. 11, 1947; s. George Russell and Ruth Johann (Bell) W.; m. Mariane Hutson Ball, Mar. 13, 1971; children: Jennifer Anne, Lisa Renee, Ashley Elizabeth, Lauren Hutson. BA in Polit. Sci., The Citadel Mil. Coll., 1969; grad. bus. sch. advanced mgmt. program, Harvard U., 1987. With Wackenhut Corp., Coral Gables, Fla. and Columbia, S.C., 1973—; v.p. ops. Wackenhut Corp., Coral Gables, 1981-82, sr. v.p. domestic ops., 1982-83, sr. v.p. ops., 1983-86, pres., chief operating officer, 1986—, also bd. dirs. various subs. Republican. Christian Scientist. Clubs: Ocean Reef (Key Largo, Fla.); Seabrook Island (S.C.); Biltmore (Coral Gables). Office: Wackenhut Corp 1500 San Remo Ave Coral Gables FL 33146

WACKER, FREDERICK GLADE, JR., manufacturing company executive; b. Chgo., July 10, 1918; s. Frederick Glade and Grace Cook (Jennings) W.; m. Ursula Comandatore, Apr. 26, 1958; children: Frederick Glade III, Wendy, Joseph Comandatore. BA, Yale U., 1940; student, Gen. Motors Inst. Tech., 1940-42. With AC Spark Plug div. Gen. Motors Corp., 1940-43, efficiency engr., 1941-43; with Ammco Tools, Inc., North Chicago, Ill., 1947-87, pres., 1948-87, chmn. bd., 1948-87; founder, pres., chmn. bd. Liquid Controls Corp., North Chicago, 1954-87, chmn. bd., 1954—; chmn. bd. Liquid Controls Europe, Zurich, Switzerland, 1985-87; ltd. ptnr. Francis I. DuPont & Co., N.Y.C., 1954-70; mem. exec. coun. Conf. Bd., 1971—. Condr. Freddie Wacker and His Orch., 1955-69, orch. has appeared on TV and radio, recs. for Dolphin and Cadet records. Bd. govs. United Rep. Fund Ill.; trustee Lake Forest Acad., 1956-71, Warren Wilson Coll., 1973-81, Chgo. chpt. Multiple Sclerosis Soc.; bd. govs. Lyric Opera Chgo., 1963-66; bd. advisers Nat. Schs. Com., 1966-88; mem. adv. coun. Trinity Evang. Div. Sch., 1977—; bd. dirs., vice chmn. Rockford Inst., 1983-87; bd. govs. GMI Engring. and Mgmt. Inst., 1983—; bd. regents Milw. Sch. Engring., 1981—. Lt. (j.g.) USNR, 1943-45. Mem. Chief Execs. Forum, Young Pres. Orgn. (chmn. Chgo. chpt. 1965-66), Sports Car Club Am. (pres. 1952-53), Ill. Mfrs. Assn. (bd. dirs. 1966—, chmn. bd. 1975), Chgo. Pres. Orgn. (pres. 1972-73), Automotive Hall of Fame (life, dir. 1976-88, v.p. 1980-81, sec. 1981-88), Soc. Automotive Engrs., World Bus. Coun., Waukegan C. of C. (dir. 1965-68), Chgo. Fedn. Musicians (life), Am. Motorcycle Assn. (life), Racquet Club (pres. 1960-61), Shoreacres Club, Onwentsia Club, Vintage Club. Presbyterian. Home: 1600 Green Bay Rd Lake Bluff IL 60044 Office: Wacker Park North Chicago IL 60064

WACKER, MARGARET MORRISSEY, communications executive; b. Washington, Dec. 12, 1951; d. Warren Ernest Clyde and Ann Romeyn (MacMillan) W. BA, Carnegie Mellon U., 1974. Promotion specialist Millipore Corp., Bedford, Mass., 1974-77, corp. communications mgr., 1982—, dir. communications Lab. Products div., 1981-82; dir. advt. IVAC div. Eli Lilly Co., San Diego, 1977-79, dist. sales mgr., L.A., 1979-80; bus. unit mgr. Sage div. Orion Rsch., Cambridge, Mass., 1980-81; counselor to handicapped individuals in bus. Mem. Internat. Assn. Bus. Communicators, Boston Computer Soc. Democrat. Episcopalian. Avocations: painting, sewing. Home: The Brook House Atrium 99 Pond Ave Unit 322D Brookline MA 02146 Office: Millipore Corp 80 Ashby Rd Bedford MA 01730

WADA, OSAMU, computer company executive; b. Tokyo, Mar. 16, 1948; came to U.S., 1985; s. Hiroshi and Kinuko (Ono) W.; m. Moriko Iwamura, Apr. 3, 1978; children: Tomoko, Keiko, Kyouko, Aiko. BS, Keio U., 1970, MS, 1972. Sr. engr. Fujitsu Ltd., Kawasaki, Japan, 1972-85; dir. Fujitsu Am. Inc., San Jose, Calif., 1985--; cons. SuperMedia, Tokyo, 1983--. Patentee in computer field. Mem. Assn. for Computing Machinery, Japan Info. Processing Soc., Japan Office Automation Soc. (chief editorial staff). Home: 12186 Woodside Dr Saratoga CA 95070 Office: Fujitsu Am Inc 3055 Orchard Dr San Jose CA 95134

WADDELL, JOHN COMER, electronics distribution company executive; b. Bridgeport, Conn., Sept. 10, 1937; s. John and Dorothy Margot (Comer) W. B.A., Yale U., 1959; M.B.A., Harvard U., 1965. Assoc. R.W. Pressprich & Co., N.Y.C., 1965-68; ptnr. Glenn, Green & Waddell, N.Y.C., 1968-80; exec. v.p. Arrow Electronics, Inc., Melville, N.Y., 1969-80; chmn. bd. Arrow Electronics, Inc., 1980—. Served with U.S. Navy, 1960-63. Home: 12 E 12th St New York NY 10003

WADE, BROOKE NELSON, diversified energy and chemicals company executive, accountant; b. Edmonton, Atla., Can., Sept. 19, 1953; s. Walter Brooke and Mollie (Nelson) W.; m. Annette Patricia Roberge, May, 28, 1983 (div. 1982); children: Kristin, Robert. B of Commerce, U. Calgary, 1975, CA, 1977. Chartered acct., 1977. Acct. Thorne Riddell, Calgary, 1975-78; gen. mgr. E.O. Parry Group, Drumheller, Atla., 1978-80; pres. Val Air Aviation, Ltd., Drumheller, 1980-82; controller Ocelot Industries, Ltd., Calgary, 1983-85, v.p. spl. projects, 1985-87, v.p. fin., 1987, pres., 1987—; bd. dirs. Pelorus Nav. Systems, Calgary, Confidata, Calgary, No. Reef, Calgary, Ocelot Industries, Ltd., Calgary. Chmn. bd. Vocat. Tng. Centre for Handicapped, Drumheller, 1979-82. Mem. Drumheller C. of C. (pres. 1981), Can. Inst. Chartered Accts., Inst. Chartered Accts. Alta., Inst. Chartered Accts. Man., Drumheller Falcons Hockey Club (chmn. bd.). Office: Ocelot Industries Ltd, 2400 400 3 Ave SW, Calgary, AB Canada T2P 4H2

WADE, CHRISTINE BLAIR, food company executive, writer; b. Palmetto, Ga., Sept. 20, 1943; d. Harvey Leonard and Winnie Mae (Turpen) Blair; m. Howard Alexander Wade, July 27, 1961 (div. Aug. 1979); children: Sharon Lynne, Donnie Brian. Student, Clayton State Coll., 1984; exec. devel. cert., Dale Carnegie, Smyrna, Ga., 1986. Sec. to gen. mgr. Dixie Frozen Foods, Inc., Peachtree City, Ga., 1961-64, office supr., 1964-67, corp. officer, asst. sec., 1967-69; dir. gen. acctg. Hi-Brand Foods, Peachtree City, 1967-78, dir. adminstrn., 1978-83, v.p. adminstrn., 1983-87, div. v.p. info. systems, 1987—; speaker Peachtree City Elem. Sch., 1980, West Ga. Coll., 1987. Author numerous poems. Mem. com. Adopt-A-Sch. Fed. Program, Fayette County, Ga., 1986-87; pres. McIntosh Pilot Club, 1989, mem. media com. McIntosh High Sch. PTC, 1988; vice chmn. adv. com. Fayette County United Way, mem. dist. admissions com. Mem. Dale Carnegie Inst. (participant, exec. image, Best Presentation award 1986), Common (IBM User's Group), Fayette County C. of C. (pub. relations rep. 1987, chmn. pub. relations 1988, econ. devel. com., nominating com. for new dirs., bd. dirs. 1988-90). Democrat. Baptist. Clubs: Pilot Internat., McIntosh Pilot (Peachtree City) (charter, officer). Home: PO Box 2167 Peachtree City GA 30269 Office: Hi-Brand Foods PO Box 2048 Peachtree City GA 30269

WADE, JAMES MICHAEL, treasurer; b. Fremont, Ohio, July 30, 1943; s. William M. and Jeanne (Freeh) W.; m. Jacqueline Quatman, Oct. 31, 1964; children: Wendy, Amy, James. BA in Fin., St. Joseph's U., Rensselaer, Ind., 1965. Mktg. rep. IBM Corp., Lima, Ohio, 1965-67; systems analyst Johnson Controls, Inc., Milw., 1967-73, mgr. fin. planning, 1973-76, controller, 1976-83, treas., 1983—; bd. dirs. Teloc, Van Nuys, Calif. Treas. Wis. chpt. Arthritis Found, 1984—. Home: 525 Adelmann G Brookfield WI 53005 Office: Johnson Controls Inc 5757 N Green Bay Ave Box 591 Milwaukee WI 53209

WADE, MICHAEL ROBERT ALEXANDER, Asian marketing specialist; b. N.Y.C., June 29, 1945; s. Burton Jean and Celia (Handleman) W.; student U. Rennes, France, 1964; AB, U. Chgo., 1967; postgrad. in pub. adminstrn., Am. U., 1967-71; MBA in Fin., N.Y. U., 1975; m. Carole Kay West, Aug. 25, 1974. Program analyst, mgmt. intern HUD, 1967-71; dep. dir. Mgmt. Communications and Briefing Center, U.S. Price Commn., 1972; asst. exec. sec. policy coordination U.S. Cost of Living Council, 1973-74; asso. dir. U.S. Indochina Refugee Program, 1975-76; pres. China Trade Devel. Corp. of Chgo., 1977—: participant with W.R. Grace & Co. in Okla. oil and gas prodn. Recipient Meritorious Service award Exec. Office of the Pres., 1972, Disting. Service award U.S. Cost of Living Council, 1974. Mem. Soc. Contemporary Art, Internat. Bus. Council MidAm. (bd. dirs.). Office: China Trade Devel Corp 2049 Century Park East Suite 416 Los Angeles CA 90067

WADE, ORMAND JOSEPH, utility company executive; b. Key West, Fla., Apr. 12, 1939; s. Charles H. and Jean (Calhoun) W.; m. Miriam Knapp, June 11, 1960; children: Charles S., Valerie A. BS, U. Maine, 1961; MS, MIT, 1973. With AT&T Long Lines, 1961-81; staff supr., asst. v.p. personnel dept. AT&T Long Lines, N.Y.C., 1964-66, network service mgr. ops. staff dept., 1970-71; dist. plant supr. AT&T Long Lines, Balt., 1966-68; engring. mgr. engring. dept. AT&T Long Lines, White Plains, N.Y., 1968-70; div. ops. mgr. ops. staff dept. AT&T Long Lines, Washington, 1971-73, area chief engr. engirng. dept., 1973-78; v.p. staff AT&T Long Lines, Bedminster, N.J., 1978-79; v.p. central region network ops. AT&T Long lines, Chgo., 1979-81; exec. v.p. Ill. Bell Telephone Co., Chgo., 1981-82, pres., 1982-87, also bd. dirs.; pres. Ameritech Bell Group, Chgo., 1987—; bd. dirs. Harris Bankcorp., Inc., Chgo., Harris Trust & Savs. Bank, Chgo., Dearborn Park Corp., Chgo. Bd. dirs. United Way-Crusade of Mercy, Chgo., 1982—; bd. mgrs. YMCA Met. Chgo., 1982—; trustee Ill. Inst. Tech., 1982—, Northwestern Meml. Hosp., Chgo., 1983—; mem. Ill. Gov.'s Task Force on Pvt. Sector Initiatives, 1983, Ill. Savs. Bond Com., 1983. Sloan fellow, 1972. Clubs: Econ. (Chgo.), Chgo. Office: Ameritech Bell Group 30 S Wacker Dr 38th Floor Chicago IL 60606 •

WADE, SUZANNE, systems analyst; b. Chgo., Dec. 29, 1938; d. Edward Peter and Dorothy Rose Traxel; m. Robert Gerald Wade (div. Feb. 1980); children: Peter John, Robert Gerald Jr., Suzette Marie, Francesca Louise, Elizabeth Rose. AA, Orange Coast Coll., 1980; BA, Calif. State U., Fullerton, 1985. Analyst data info. Motorola, Mesa, Ariz., 1972-75; planner prodn. Ford Aerospace, Newport Beach, Calif., 1975-79; supr. prodn. control Shiley, Inc., Irvine, Calif., 1979-81; mgr. bus. systems Hughes Aircraft Co., Fullerton, 1981-85; systems specialist Long Beach, Calif., 1985—; lectr. to clubs, classes Calif. State U., Fullerton, 1984-85. Author: (manual) Data Services, 1985; columnist, 1984-85. Mem. Am. Prodn. and Inventory Control Soc., Nat. Assn. Female Execs., Los Angeles Aerospace and Def. Spl. Interests Group (steering com., publicity chmn. 1987—, editor LA-ADSIG's Digest). Methodist. Club: Toastmasters (Long Beach) (treas. 1986—). Home: 2299 Legion Dr Apt #402 Signal Hill CA 90806

WADE, THOMAS EARL, data processing executive, educator; b. Birmingham, Ala., Dec. 14, 1945. BA, Calif. State U., Los Angeles, 1977; MA, Pepperdine U., 1979; PhD, Columbia U., 1981; MPA, U. Phoenix, 1985. Cert. coll.-level educator, Calif. Sr. mktg. cons. Radio Shack Corp., L.A., 1982-84; site mgr. Electronic Data Systems, L.A., 1983-85; project mgr. Systems Corp., L.A., 1985-87; pres. CPR, L.A., 1987—; adj. prof. Am. Coll. of the Applied Arts, L.A., 1983—, U. of Phoenix L.A., 1985—, Union Inst. Advanced Studies, L.A., 1986-87; adj. faculty mem. U. Exptl. Colls. and Univs., L.A., 1988—; dir. client rels. L.A. Bus. Digest mag. Contbr. articles to profl. jours. Served with U.S. Army, 1966-70. Club: Torrance Gymnastics. Office: CPR 2265 Westwood Blvd #917 Los Angeles CA 90064

WADLEY, M. RICHARD, consumer products executive; b. Lehi, Utah, Sept. 3, 1942; s. Merlyn R. and Verla Ann (Ball) W.; m. Kathleen Frandsen, Mar. 25, 1965 (div. Aug. 1984); children: Lisa Kathleen, Staci Lin, Eric Richard. BS, Brigham Young U., 1967; MBA, Northwestern U., 1968. Brand asst. packaged soap and detergent div. Procter & Gamble Co., Cin., 1968-69, asst. brand mgr. packaged soap and detergent div., 1970-71, brand mgr. Dawn detergent, 1972-73, copy supr. packaged soap and detergent div., 1974-75, brand mgr. Tide detergent, 1975-77, assoc. advt. mgr. packaged soap and detergent div., 1977-81; corp. product dir. Hallmark Cards, Inc., Kansas City, Mo., 1982-83, corp. product dir. Ambassador Cards div., 1983-85; v.p., gen. mgr. feminine protection div. Tambrands Inc., Lake Success, N.Y., 1986-88; pres. dairy/cheese div. Bongrain, Inc., N.Y.C., 1988—. Bd. dirs. L.I. Friends of the Arts, 1986-88. Served with Ohio N.G., 1960-67. Recipient scholarship Northwestern U., 1967-68; named An Outstanding Sr. Grad. Coll. Bus. Brigham Young U., 1967. Mem. Brigham Young U. Alumni Assn. (bd. dirs. 1984-85), Beta Gamma Sigma. Republican. Office: Bongrain Inc 32 Derby Rd Port Washington NY 11050 also: Bongrain Inc 23 E 73d St New York NY 10021

WADMAN, WILLIAM WOOD, III, health physicist, consulting company executive, consultant; b. Oakland, Calif., Nov. 13, 1936; s. William Wood, Jr., and Lula Fae (Raisner) W.; M.A., U. Calif., Irvine, 1978; children—Roxanne Alyce Wadman Hubbing, Raymond Alan (dec.), Theresa Hope Wadman Foster; m. Barbara Jean Wadman; stepchildren: Denise Ellen Varine, Brian Ronald Varine. Radiation safety specialist, accelerator health physicist U. Calif. Lawrence Berkeley Lab., 1957-68; campus radiation safety officer U. Calif., Irvine, 1968-79; dir. ops., radiation safety officer Radiation Sterilizers, Inc., Tustin, Calif., 1979-80; prin., pres. Wm. Wadman & Assocs. Inc., 1980—; pres. Intracoastal Marine Enterprises Ltd., Martinez, Calif.; mem. team No. 1, health physics appraisal program NRC, 1980-81; cons. health physicist to industry; lectr. dept. community and environ. medicine U. Calif., Irvine, 1979-80, Orange Coast Coll. Active Cub Scouts; chief umpire Mission Viejo Little League, 1973. Served with USNR, 1955-63. Recipient award for profl. achievement U. Calif. Alumni Assn., 1972, Outstanding Performance award U. Calif., Irvine, 1973. Mem. Health Physics Soc. (treas. 1979-81, editor proc. 11th symposium, pres. So. Calif. chpt. 1977, Professionalism award 1975), Internat. Radiation Protection Assn. (U.S. del. 4th Congress 1977), Am. Nuclear Soc., Am. Public Health Assn. (chmn. program 1978, chmn. radiol. health sect. 1979-80), Campus Radiation Safety Officers (chmn. 1975, editor proc. 5th conf. 1975), ASTM. Club: UCI Univ. (dir. 1976, sec. 1977, treas. 1978). Contbr. articles to tech. jours. Home: 3687 Red Cedar Way Lake Oswego OR 97035

WADSWORTH, DAWN, finance executive; b. Ogden, Utah, Mar. 13, 1955; d. Don Joseph and Ardiena Joy (Doezie) W. BS in Acctg., U. Colo., 1977. CPA, Colo., Calif. Audit mgr., sr. staff acct. Arthur Andersen & Co., Denver, 1977-82, tax mgr., 1982-85; tax mgr. Arthur Andersen & Co., Los Angeles, 1985-87; v.p. fin., adminstrn. Modern Videofilm, Inc., Hollywood, Calif., 1987—. asst. treas.Paramount Theater Revitalization, Denver, 1984-85; active Music Ctr., Los Angeles, 1986. Mem. Am. Inst. CPA'S, Fin. and Adminstrv. Execs. in Entertainment Industry, Calif. Soc. CPA's (Gold Key award Colo. Soc. 1977). Office: Modern Videofilm Inc 7165 Sunset Blvd Hollywood CA 90046

WADSWORTH, DEAN AAROE, investment executive; b. Schenectady, N.Y., Mar. 29, 1954; s. Gordon William and Jean (Aaroe) W.; m. Susan Hill, Apr. 29, 1978; children: Meredith, Sarah, Gordon. BS, Old Dominion U., 1976. Cert. fin. planner, Coll. Fin. Planning. Marine biologist Va. Inst. Marine Sci., Gloucester Point, 1976-79; advt. mgr. Atlantic Publs., Accomac, Va., 1979-81; investment exec. Paine Webber Inc., Roanoke, Va., 1981—. Mem. adv. bd. Presbyn. Childrens Home, Va., 1986-87; elder First Presbyn. Ch., Roanoke, 1988—, numerous other coms. Mem. Inst. Cert. Fin. Planners, Roanoke Valley C. of C., Rotary (youth svc. com. 1986-88). Home: 1650 Center Hill Dr Roanoke VA 24015 Office: Paine Webber 600 Colonial Pl Roanoke VA 24011

WADSWORTH, DYER SEYMOUR, lawyer, business executive; b. N.Y.C., June 16, 1936; s. Seymour and Phoebe Armistead (Helmer) W.; m. Beverley Allen Dunn Barringer, Feb. 2, 1963; children: Sophia, Jennifer. B.A., Yale U., 1959; J.D., Harvard U., 1962. Bar: N.Y. 1963, Pa. 1979. Asso. Humes, Andrews & Botzow, N.Y.C., 1962-64; with Inco Ltd. (and its U.S. subs.), N.Y.C., 1964—; v.p., chief legal officer, sec., dir. Inco U.S., Inc., N.Y.C., 1982—; asst. gen. counsel Inco Ltd.; v.p., chief legal officer, sec., bd. dirs. Internat. Nickel Inc., Saddle Brook, N.J.; v.p., dir. Inco Securities Corp., N.Y.C.; chief legal officer, sec., dir. Inco Alloys Internat., Inc., Huntington, W.Va.; v.p., dir. Cass County Iron Co., Atlanta, Tex.; v.p., sec., dir. Am. Copper & Nickel Co., Inc., Golden, Colo.; v.p., dir. Internat. Metals Reclamation Co., Inc., Ellwood City, Pa.; sec., dir. LaQue Ctr. Corrosion Tech., Wrightsville Beach, N.C.; v.p., dir. Barringer Crater Co., Flagstaff, Ariz.; sec., bd. dirs. Baseline Fin. Services, Inc., Morristown, N.J., 1984-88; pres., dir. Amsterdam Nursing Home Corp., N.Y.C., 1986—. Assoc. counsel The Sailors Snug Harbor, Sea Level, N.C., 1987—; trustee, past treas. Isaac Tuttle Fund for the Aged, N.Y.C. Mem. ABA, N.Y. State Bar Assn., Pa. Bar Assn., Assn. of Bar of City of N.Y., Meteoritical Soc. Clubs: Down Town Assn., Union, Pilgrims (N.Y.C.). Home: 215 E 48th St New York NY 10017 Office: Inco US Inc 1 New York Pla New York NY 10004

WAGATSUMA, BERT MAMORU, accountant; b. Hilo, Hawaii, Feb. 11, 1955; s. Shinichi and Kikue (Arai) W. BBA, U. Hawaii, 1977. CPA, Hawaii. Staff auditor U.S. Army Audit Agy., Ft. Lewis, Wash., 1978-79; mem. staff Thayer & Matsushita, Kahului, Maui, Hawaii, 1979-80; sr.-in-charge Lester Witte & Co., Honolulu, 1980-81; mgr. Thayer & Assocs., Kahului, 1981-83; controller Fuku Constrn., Wailuku, 1983, Build N Grow, Hilo, 1983; owner Bert M. Wagatsuma CPA, Hilo, 1983—. Advisor Jr. Achievement, 1988-89; mem. acctg. adv. com. Maui Community Coll., 1981-83; asst. treas. Dem. Party, 1984—; treas. Friends for Wayne Metcalf, Hilo, 1986—. Mem. AICPA, Hawaii Soc. CPAs, Hawaii Assn. Pub. Accts., Hawaii State Bd. Pub. Accountancy, Lehua Jaycees (exec. v.p. 1986-87, treas. 1985-86, pres. 1987-88), Univ. Hawaii Alumni Assn. (treas. 1986—), Hilo High Sch. Alumni Assn. (auditor 1986—, jr. achievement advisor 1988). Democrat. Home: PO Box 1676 Hilo HI 96721

WAGEMAKER, DAVID ISAAC, human resources developement executive; b. Grand Rapids, Mich., Feb. 10, 1949; s. Raymond Ogden and Inez Loraine W.; m. Sharon Williams, Jan. 30, 1977. BA in Philosophy, Grand Valley State U., 1971. Owner Edn. Ctr., Grand Rapids, 1970-72; apiarist Bee Haven Honey, Grand Rapids, 1970-72; cons. Am. Leadership Coll., Washington, 1972-78, Wagemaker Co., Honolulu, 1978-80; edn. cons. Batten, Batten, Hudson & Swab, Inc., San Diego, 1980-81, m., 1981; securities broker, ins. agt. The Equitable Assurance Co., San Diego, 1982; assoc. cons. Pacific S.W. Airlines, San Diego, 1982-83; organizational devel. adminstr. Hughes Aircraft Co., El Segundo, Calif., 1983—; v.p. Wagemaker, Inc., Grand Rapids, 1984—; sr. cons. Nat. Mgmt. Inst., Flower Mound, Tex., 1985—; mgmt. cons. Mgmt. Devel. Ctr., San Diego State U., 1980—;

seminarist Penton Learning, Inc., N.Y.C., 1982—; pres. Par Golf Co., Redondo Beach, Calif., 1984—. Co-author: Build A Better You Starting Now, 1982; author: (cassette program) Effective Time Management, 1979, (with others) How to Organize Yourself to Win, 1988. Fellow Acad. Mgmt.; mem. Sigma Chi, Zeta Nu (pres. 1968-70), Hughes Golf Club (El Segundo). Republican. Congregationalist. Home: 2226 Bataan Rd Redondo Beach CA 90278

WAGENER, RICHARD HARRY, investment advisor, financial planner; b. Balt., Aug. 9, 1949; s. William James and Florine Mildred (Burns) W.; m. Julianna Marlene Wagener, Sept. 23, 1972; children: Jennifer Lauren, Amanda Rae. BS, W.Va. U., 1971; cert., Coll. for Fin. Planning, Denver, 1982. CLU; chartered fin. cons., cert. fin. planner. Profl. baseball player N.Y. Mets., Flushing, 1971-73; dist. mgr. Investors Diversified Svcs., Towson, Md., 1974-76; propr., owner Fin. Planning Svcs., Ellicott City, Md., 1976-79; chmn. bd., v.p. Consol. Fin. Svcs., Inc., Greenbelt, Md., 1979-86; pres. Fin. 1st Advisors, Inc., Columbia, Md., 1986—. Named One of Top 200 Fin. Planners, Money mag., 1987. Mem. Internat. Assn. for Fin. Planning, Inst. Cert. Fin. Planners, Am. Soc. CLU, Balt. Assn. for Fin. Planning (pres. 1985-86, chmn. bd. 1986-87, v.p. legis. 1987—). Republican. Roman Catholic. Office: Fin 1st Advisors Inc 9861 Broken Lane Pkwy 255 Columbia MD 21046

WAGG, TIMOTHY JOHN, pulp and paper company executive; b. Gullane, Scotland, Aug. 15, 1934; emigrated to Can., 1952; s. Kenneth A. and Katherine R. (Horlick) W.; m. Susan Waterous, June 18, 1960; children: Alexandra, Geoffrey. B.Eng.(Civil), McGill U., 1957; M.B.A., Harvard U., 1961. With Stone & Webster Engring., Toronto, Ont., Can., 1957-58, Boston, 1958-59; with Canadian Ingersoll-Rand, Montreal and Sherbrooke, Que., Can., 1961-66; v.p. adminstrn. Consol.-Bathurst Inc., Montreal, 1966—; dir. Central Sprinkler Corp., Lansdale, Pa. Club: University (Montreal). Home: 426 Berwick Ave, Montreal, PQ Canada H3R 1Z9 Office: Consol-Bathurst Inc, 800 Dorchester Blvd W, Montreal, PQ Canada H3B 1Y9

WAGNER, ALVIN LOUIS, JR., professional real estate appraiser, consultant; b. Chgo., Dec. 19, 1939; s. Alvin Louis and Esther Jane (Wheeler) W.; student U. Ill., 1958-59; B.A., Drake U., 1962; postgrad. Real Estate Inst., Chgo., 1960-65; m. Susan Carole Fahey, Aug. 14, 1965; children: Alvin Louis III, Robert Percy. Asst. appraiser Oak Park (Ill.) Fed. Savings & Loan Co., 1955-60; v.p. real estate sales A. L. Wagner & Co., Flossmoor, Ill., 1961-63; real estate loan officer, chief appraiser Beverly Bank, Chgo., 1963-67; asso. real estate appraiser C. A. Bruckner & Assos., Chgo., 1967-70; founder, profl. real estate appraiser and cons. A. L. Wagner & Co., Flossmoor, 1970—. Mem. faculty Am. Inst. Real Estate Appraisers, Chgo., 1974—; instr. real estate appraising Prairie State Coll., Chicago Heights, Ill., 1970—; mem. adv. com. Real Estate Sch., 1972—; community prof. Gov.'s State U., 1977—, founding mem. real estate adv. bd. Mem. Rich Township (Ill.) Personal Services Commn., 1973—; v.p., drive chmn. Flossmoor Community Chest, Crusade of Mercy, 1974-75, pres., 1975-76. Auditor, Rich Township, 1973-77. Governing bd. Glenwood (Ill.) Sch. for Boys, 1973—; chmn. bus. edn. occupational adv. com. Homewood-Flossmoor High Sch., 1977; pres. South Suburban Focus Council; mem. South Suburban Mayors and Mgrs. Bus. and Industry Adv. Council, Flossmore Econ. Devel. Commn.; bd. dirs. Prairie State Coll. Found., 1985—; treas. U.S. Dept. Housing & Urban Devel. South Suburban Community Housing Resources BD., 1981—; assoc. mem. Employee Relocation Council. Mem. Am. Inst. Real Estate Appraisers (mem. governing council 1974-75, Profl. Recognition award 1977), Soc. Real Estate Appraisers (nat. pub. relations com., vice chmn. 1985—), Real Estate Educators Assn., South Suburban Assn. Commerce and Industry, Chgo. Assn. Commerce and Industry, Chgo., Homewood-Flossmoor real estate bds., Nat., Ill. assns. realtors, Homewood-Flossmoor Jaycees, Phi Delta Theta (pres. chpt. 1960), Chgo. Phi Delta Theta Alumni Club (pres.), Omega Tau Rho, Lambda Alpha. Clubs: Flossmoor Country, Variety, Rotary, Masons. Mem. editorial bd. Appraisal Jour., 1975—; contbr. articles to real estate jours., also Mobility mag., Mcpl. Econ. Devel. Home: 927 Park Dr Flossmoor IL 60422 Office: 2709 Flossmoor Rd Flossmoor IL 60422

WAGNER, BRUCE STANLEY, advertising agency executive; b. San Diego, Aug. 1, 1943; s. Robert Sheldon and Janet (Lowther) W.; m. Elizabeth Pearsall Winslow, Oct. 4, 1975; children: Sage Elizabeth, Alexander Winslow. B.A., Dartmouth Coll., 1965; M.B.A., U. Pa, 1985. Sr. v.p. Grey Advt., Inc., N.Y.C., 1967-81; exec. v.p., chief operating officer Campaign '76 Media Communications, Inc., Washington, 1975-76; exec. v.p. Ross Roy, Inc., Bloomfield Hills, Mich., 1981; also bd. dirs. Ross Roy, Inc., Detroit. Mem. Am. Assn. Advt. Agys. (bd. govs. cen. region 1988—, bd. govs., chmn. Mich. coun. 1985-86), Wharton Alumni Assn. (exec. com. 1981-85, chmn. 1983-85). Clubs: Wharton of Mich. (bd. dirs. 1985—); Detroit Athletic; Orchard Lake Country (Mich.), Birmingham Athletic (Mich.). Home: 975 Arlington Rd Birmingham MI 48009 Office: Ross Roy Inc 100 Bloomfield Hills Pkwy Bloomfield Hills MI 48013

WAGNER, DAVID JAMES, banker; b. Cin., Mar. 15, 1954; s. George A. and Mary (Tyssowski) W.; m. Kay A. Ambrosius, Dec. 27, 1975. BA, Ind. U., 1975, MBA, 1976. Chmn., pres., chief exec. officer Old Kent Bank of Grand Haven (Mich.), 1983-85; exec. v.p. Old Kent Bank and Trust Co., Grand Rapids, Mich., 1983-85, pres., 1986—. Office: Old Kent Bank & Trust Co One Vandenberg Ctr Grand Rapids MI 49503

WAGNER, DONALD ROGER, real estate corporation executive, owner; b. Mpls., Sept. 21, 1926; s. Louis and Bertha Lorraine (Meili) W.; m. Marjorie Lou Johnson, Jan. 21, 1961; children: Kristen Ann, Jill Lea. BBA, U. Minn., 1948; postgrad., Am. Coll., 1974. CLU; lic. real estate broker, Fla. Mgr. consumer products A-D-M Co., Mpls., 1948-58; v.p. Spring Co., Mpls., 1958-63; nat. promotion dir. G.A.C., Miami, Fla., 1963-68; ins. assoc. First Fin., Miami, 1968-78; v.p., gen. mgr. Gulfstream Realty Co., Hollywood, Fla., 1978-82; mgr. sales Royal Palm Beach (Fla.) Realty, Inc., 1982-86, owner, pres., 1986—. Mem. hon. com. Multiple Sclerosis Soc., Ft. Lauderdale, Fla., 1985-86. Served as 2nd lt. USAFR, 1950-51. Recipient Edn. Trophy award Sales and Mktg. Execs. Club, Mpls., 1963. Mem. West Palm Beach Bd. Realtors (pub. relations chmn. 1985-87, Realtor Assoc. of Yr. 1985), C. of C. Palm Beaches (communications com.), Palms West C. of C. (communications com.), F.A.R. Speakers Bur., Nat. Speakers Assn., Pi Sigma Epsilon. Home: 5641 Washington St Hollywood FL 33023

WAGNER, DOROTHY MARIE, court reporting service executive; b. Milw., June 8, 1924; d. Theodore Anthony and Leona Helen (Ullrich) Wagner; grad. Milw. Bus. U., 1944; student Marquette U., U. Wis., Milw. Stenographer, legal sec., Milw., 1942-44; hearing reporter Wis. Workmen's Compensation Dept., 1944-48; ofcl. reporter to judge Circuit Ct., Milw., 1952-53; owner, operator ct. reporting service Dorothy M. Wagner & Assocs., Milw., 1948—; guest lectr. ct. reporting Madison Area Tech. Coll., 1981—. Recipient Gregg Diamond medal Gregg Pub. Co., 1950. Mem. Nat. (registered profl. reporter, certificate of proficiency), Wis. shorthand reporters assns., Am. Legion Aux., Met. Milw. Assn. Commerce. Roman Catholic. Home: 214 Williamsburg Dr Thiensville WI 53092 Office: 135 Wells St Suite 400 Milwaukee WI 53203

WAGNER, GARY R., sales executive; b. Jersey City, N.J., Mar. 8, 1951; s. John L. and Marion E. (Kante) W. BE, Miami U., Oxford, Ohio, 1973; MA, Columbia U., N.Y., 1975. Producer, writer, performer self-employed, N.Y.C., 1973-80; salesperson Phoenix Mutual Life Ins. Co., Dayton, Ohio, 1980-83, Computerland, Totowa, N.J., 1983-84; v.p. Compu-Sales Corp., Hawthorne, N.J., 1984-86, Scientific Devices Inc., Teaneck, N.J., 1986—; pres. Now Cons., Washington Twp., N.J., 1984—; v.p. J.C.G. Devel., 1987—. Leader Bergen County Boy Scouts Am., Washington Twp., N.J., 1988. Office: Sci Devices 1415 Queen Anne Rd Teaneck NJ 07666

WAGNER, JUDITH BENITA, hospitality services executive; b. Phila., Oct. 6, 1931; d. Walter D. and Leah (Jaffe) Cherry; m. Seymour Wagner, June 22, 1952; children: Robin E., Alicia S. BA, U. Pa., 1973. V.p. Internat. House, Phila., 1973-81; exec. dir. Hospitality Phila. Style, 1982-84; pres. Access Phila., Inc., 1984—. Mem. community adv. bd. WHYY, Phila., 1983—, Benjamin Franklin Bridge Lighting Commn., 1988—; bd. dirs. Philapride, 1986—, Friends of Rittenhouse Sq., Phila., 1983—. Mem. Meeting Planners Internat., Phila. C. of C. Club: Cosmopolitan. Office: Access Phila Inc 250 S 18th St Philadelphia PA 19103

WAGNER, JUDITH BUCK, investment firm executive; b. Altoona, Pa. Sept. 25, 1943; d. Harry Bud and Mary Elizabeth (Rhodes) B.; m. Joseph E. Wagner, Mar. 15, 1980; 1 child, Elizabeth. BA in History, U. Wash., 1965; grad. N.Y. Inst. Fin., 1968. Chartered fin. analyst; registered Am. Stock Exchange; registered N.Y. Stock Exchange; registered investment advisor. Security analyst Morgan, Olmstead, Kennedy & Gardner, L.A., 1968-71; rsch. cons., St. Louis, 1971-72; security analyst Boettcher & Co., Denver, 1972-75; pres. Wagner Investment Counsel, 1975-84; chmn. Wagner & Hamil, Inc., Denver, 1983—; chmn., bd. dirs. The Women's Bank, N.A., Denver, 1977—, organizational group pres., 1975-77; chmn. Equitable Bankshares Colo., Inc., Denver, 1980—; bd. dirs. Equitable Bank of Littleton, 1983-88, pres., 1985; bd. dirs. Colo. Growth Capital, 1979-82; lectr. Denver U., Metro State, 1975-80. Author: Woman and Money series Colo. Woman Mag., 1976; moderator 'Catch 2' Sta. KWGN-TV, 1978-79. Pres. Big Sisters Colo., Denver, 1977-82, bd. dirs., 1973—; bd. fellows U. Denver, 1985—; bd. dirs. Red Cross, 1980, Assn. Children's Hosp., 1985, Colo. Health Facilities Authority, 1978-84, Jr. League Community Adv. Com., 1979—, Brother's Redevel., Inc., 1979-80; mem. Hist. Paramount Found., 1984, Denver Pub. Sch. Career Edn. Project, 1972; mem. investment com. YWCA, 1976-88; mem. adv. com. Girl Scouts U.s.; mem. agy. rels. com. Mile High United Way, 1978-81, chmn. United Way Venture Grant com., 1980-81; fin. chmn. Schoettler for State Treas., 1986; bd. dirs. Downtown Denver Inc., 1988—; bd. dirs., v.p., treas. The Women's Found. Colo., 1987—. Recipient Making It award Cosmopolitan Mag., 1977, Women on the Go award, Savvy mag., 1983, Minouri Yasoni award, 1986, Salute Spl. Honoree award, Big Sisters, 1987; named one of the Outstanding Young Women in Am., 1979; recipient Woman Who Makes A Difference award Internat. Women's Forum, 1987. Fellow Fin. Analysts Fedn.; mem. Women's Forum of Colo. (pres. 1979), Women's Found. Colo., Inc. (bd. dirs. 1986—), Denver Soc. Security Analysts (bd. dirs. 1976-83, v.p. 1980-81, pres. 1981-82), Leadership Denver (Outstanding Alumna award 1987), Pi Beta Phi (pres. U. Wash. chpt. 1964-65). Office: Wagner & Hamil Inc 410 17th St #840 Denver CO 80202

WAGNER, MICHAEL GRAFTON, investor, corporation executive; b. Greenville, Ohio, May 31, 1935; BA, Vanderbilt U., 1957; With Henny Penny Corp., Eaton, Ohio, 1957-76, sales, 1957-60, dir. advt., 1960-63, dir. mktg., 1963-68, pres., chief exec. officer, 1968-76, also of Henny Penny, Ltd., Toronto, Ont., Can.; pvt. investor, 1976—; pres. Schaefer Corp., Madison, Ala., 1979-81; cons., pvt. investor Rair Systems Inc., Nashville, 1985-87. Area chmn. Vanderbilt U. Endowment Fund, Nashville, 1961-66, 70-74; fin. chmn. Tenn. Republican Com., 1977-78. Mem. Nat. Commadore Club, Alpha Tau Omega. Episcopalian (sec., treas., warden 1969-71). Home: PO Box 237 Gallatin TN 37066-0238

WAGNER, NORMAN PAUL, utility company executive; b. Newark, Mar. 25, 1924; s. Julius and Gertrude (Burke) W.; m. Gwendolyn Marshall, June 3, 1950; children: Norman Paul, Neil, Carol, Elizabeth, Lisa. B.S.M.E., Clemson U., 1949. Prodn. control engr. Babcock & Wilcox, Barberton, Ohio, 1951-62; works and project mgr. Babcock & Wilcox, Mount Vernon, Ind., 1962-68; mem. staff ops. and mktg. So. Ind. Gas & Electric Co., Evansville, 1968-77, exec. v.p., 1977-79, pres., chief operating officer, 1980-81, pres., chief exec. officer, dir., chmn. exec. com., 1982—, chmn. bd., 1986—; dir. Citizens Nat. Bancshares, Evansville, Ohio Valley Electric Corp.-Ind.-Ky. Electric Corp., Columbus, Deaconess Hosp. Service Corp., Evansville, Community Natural Gas, Mt. Carmel, Ill., Internat. Steel Co., Evansville; dir., past pres. East Cen. Nuclear Group; exec. bd. East Cen. Area Reliability Council. Campaign chmn. United Way of Southwestern Ind., Evansville, 1983-84; co-chmn. Hoosiers for Econ. Devel. Com., Indpls.; dir., past pres. Evansville Indsl. Found., past pres. Tri-State Health Planning, Evansville. Served as flight engr. USAF, 1943-46. Mem. ASME, Ind. Gas Assn. (bd. dirs., vice chmn.), Ind. Electric Assn. (bd. dirs., past chmn.), Edison Electric Inst. (bd. dirs.), U. Evansville Alumni Assn. (bd. trustees), Met. Evansville C. of C. (chmn. 1984-85), Ind. C. of C. (bd. dirs.). Clubs: Evansville Country (bd. dirs., v.p. local chpt.); Petroleum (Evansville); Columbia (Indpls.). Home: 315 Charmwood Ct Evansville IN 47715 Office: So Ind Gas & Electric Co 20-24 NW 4th St Evansville IN 47741

WAGNER, RALPH ALBERT, accountant; b. Lafayette, Ind., Nov. 8, 1945; s. Raymond Francis and Nellie Marie (Vehnekamp) W.; m. Ellen Elizabeth White, Feb. 27, 1965; children: Michelle Renee, Beth Ellen, Michael Francis. BS in Acctg., Ball State U., 1967. CPA, Ill., Ind., N.Y. Sr. acct. Deloitte Haskins & Sells, Indpls., 1967-73; mgr. Deloitte Haskins & Sells, Dayton, Ohio, 1973-76, N.Y.C., 1976-79; dir. internal control A.E. Staley Mfg. Co., Decatur, Ill., 1979-82, controller, 1982-85; asst. controller Staley Continental, Inc., Rolling Meadows, Ill., 1985-88; pvt. practice, Rolling Meadows, 1988—; bd. dirs. Genencor, Inc., San Francisco. Bd. dirs. Jr. Achievement, Decatur, 1982-85. Mem. AICPA, Ill. Soc. CPAs, Jaycees (bd. dirs. 1973-76, Key Man award 1975, 76), Wynstone Golf Club (Barrington, Ill.), Haig Pt. Club (Daufuskie Island, S.C.), High Point Club. Republican. Roman Catholic. Home and Office: 207 E Lake Shore Dr Barrington IL 60010

WAGNER, ROGER PHILIP, hotel executive; b. Billings, Mont., July 13, 1947; s. Joseph Philip and Rosa Wilhelmena (Eisenman) W.; m. Patricia Ann Dively, Dec. 29, 1973 (div. Mar. 1979); m. Catherine Jean Brooks, Nov. 28, 1980; children: Michelle, Jeffrey, Joseph. Student, U. Idaho; BS in Hotel Adminstrn., U. Nev., Las Vegas. Asst. hotel mgr. Sands Hotel & Casino, Las Vegas, 1970-73, asst. gen. mgr., 1976-77, exec. v.p., 1978-81; hotel mgr. Dunes Hotel & Casino, Las Vegas, 1973-74, Frontier Hotel & Casino, Las Vegas, 1974-76; exec. v.p. MGM Grand Hotel, Reno, Nev., 1977-78; v.p., gen. mgr. Edgewater Hotel & Casino, Laughlin, Nev., 1981-83; pres. Claridge Hotel & Casino Corp., Atlantic City, N.J., 1983—, also bd. dirs. Campaign dir. Atlantic County chpt. United Way, Atlantic City, 1986-87; hon. trustee So. Jersey Regional Theater, Sommers Point, N.J., 1986-87; trustee So. Jersey Conf. Christians and Jews, Atlantic City, 1987—. Mem. Hotel Sales and Mgmt. Assn., MGM Employees Credit Union (founder, v.p. 1977-78), SYMMA Employees Credit Union (founder, v.p., sec. 1975-77), Elks. Republican. Methodist. Office: Claridge Hotel & Casino Boardwalk at Park Pl Atlantic City NJ 08401

WAGNER, STEVEN MARC, finance company executive; b. Houston, Apr. 25, 1954; s. George and Betty Lee (Sand) W.; divorced; 1 child, Genesis Elan; m. Annette Marie Garcia, Aug. 29, 1981; 1 child, Nicole Renee. B Liberal Arts, U. Tex., 1976. Bus. cons. Hosp. Affiliates Internat., Dallas, 1976-81; bus. dir. HCA Vista Hills Med. Ctr., El Paso, Tex., 1981-83; corp. bus. dir. Republic Health Corp., Dallas, 1983-86; v.p. Reliant Fin. Corp., Dallas, 1986—; cons. Am. Healthcare Mgmt., Dallas, 1986—; bd. dirs. Fast Times Automotive, Inc., Plano, Tex.; pres, chief exec. officer The Basic Group, Inc., Dallas, 1988—. Contbr. articles to profl. jours. Mem. Am. Guild Patient Account Mgmt. (cert. patient account mgr., v.p. 1981-83, Host award 1983), Nat. Assn. Hosp. Admitting Mgrs. (accredited), Nat. Assn. Securities Dealers (lic.), PTO Plano, Plano YMCA. Home: 7913 Sloan Circle Plano TX 75023 Office: Reliant Fin Corp 3939 Beltline Rd #400 Dallas TX 75244

WAGNER, THOMAS JOHN, automotive executive; b. Peoria, Ill., July 28, 1938; s. Nicholas and Margaret (Sullivan) W.; m. Louise Mary Bombinski, Sept. 4, 1971; children: Susan Noelle, Julie Nicole. BS in Econs., Bradley U., 1960; postgrad., U. Mich., 1963-64; MBA, Marquette U., 1968. Sales tng. mgr. Ford div. Ford Motor Co., Dearborn, Mich., 1972-74; asst. dist. sales mgr. Ford div. Ford Motor Co., Mpls., 1974-76; dist. sales mgr. Ford div. Ford Motor Co., Louisville, 1976-77, Washington, 1977-78, Los Angeles, 1979-80; regional sales mgr. cen. Ford div. Kansas City, Mo., 1980-83; gen. mktg. mgr. Ford div. Detroit, 1983-85; v.p., gen. mgr. Lincoln-Mercury div. Ford Motor Co., Detroit, 1985-88, v.p., gen. mgr. Ford div., 1988—; mem. adv. bd. Ford Exec. Devel. Ctr., Detroit, 1988—. Trustee Bradley U., Peoria, Ill., 1986—; chmn. div. sustaining membership campaign Boy Scouts Am., Detroit, 1988; active Ford Community Relations Coms., Louisville, Washington, Los Angeles, Kansas City. 1st lt. USAF, 1960-63. Recipient Disting. Alumni award Bradley U., 1987. Mem. Adcraft Club Detroit, Automotive Hall of Fame, Forest Lake Country Club (Bloomfield Hills, Mich.), Renaissance Club (Detroit). Roman Catholic. Office: Ford Motor Co Ford div 300 Renaissance Ctr PO Box 43301 Suite 3700 Detroit MI 48243

WAGONER, THOMAS PATRICK, financial planning executive; b. Milw., Mar. 17, 1958; s. Edmund L. and Joan L. (Steinhagen) W.; m. Diana G. Roy, Sept. 21, 1984; 1 child, Katherine M. BS, Miami U., Oxford, Ohio, 1980; postgrad., Dayton U., 1983. Cert. fin. planner. Purchasing agt. Am. Electric Power, Columbus, Ohio, 1980-82; fin. planner IDS, Columbus, 1982-83; pres. Accelerated Fin. Planning, Columbus, 1983—; tchr. Bishop Watterson High Sch., Columbus, 1988; with Money Matters radio show Sta. WSNY, Columbus, 1986-87. Mem. Internat. Assn. Fin. Planners, Cert. Fin. Planners, Columbus Life Underwriters. Republican. Roman Catholic. Office: Accelerated Fin Planning 853 S High St Columbus OH 43206

WAGSTAFF, THOMAS WALTON, lawyer, banker; b. Kansas City, Mo., June 2, 1946; s. Robert Wilson and Katherine (Hall) W.; m. Starr Smith, May 26, 1972; children: Thomas Lynwood, Elizabeth Jane, Aimee Hall. BA, Williams Coll., 1968; JD, U. Kans., 1972. Bar: Mo. 1972. Ptnr. Blackwell, Sanders, Matheny, Weary & Lombardi, Kansas City, Mo., 1972—; judge Mission Hills (Kans.) Mcpl. Ct., 1979-88; vice chmn. Kans. Nat. Bank, Prairie Village, 1980—, also bd. dirs.; bd. dirs. Kans. Nat. Bank, Prairie Village, KNB Banashares, Inc., Prairie Village. Bd. dirs. Crippled Childrens Nursery Sch., Kansas City, 1980-85, St. Luke's Hosp., Kansas City, 1986—. Mem. Kansas City Bar Assn. (chmn. med. legal relations com.), Kansas City Country Club (sec., bd. dirs. 1984-87), River Club (bd. dirs. 1987—). Republican. Episcopalian. Home: 6540 Wenonga Mission Hills KS 66208 Office: Blackwell Sanders Matheny Weary & Lombardi 2300 Main St PO Box 419777 Kansas City MO 64141-6777

WAHL, PAUL, publisher, author; b. Union City, N.J., Jan. 17, 1922; s. Frank Joseph and Anne (Frechen) W. Grad. high sch., Bogota, N.J. Acct. Am. Cyanamid Co., N.Y.C., 1943-44, Wright Aero. Corp., Paterson, N.J., 1944-46; ptnr. Wahl Arms Co., Bogota, N.J., 1948-68; propr. Wahl Co., Bogota, N.J., 1962-68; ptnr. Frank J. Wahl Co., Bogota, N.J., 1969—; pres. Paul Wahl Corp., Bogota, N.J., 1986—. Author: Gun Traders Guide, 1953-78, Arms Trade Yearbook, 1955, 56, Single Lens Reflex Guide, 1959, Subminiature Technique, 1960, Press/View Camera Technique, 1962, The Candid Photographer, 1963, Carbine Handbook, 1964, (with D.R. Toppel) The Gatling Gun, 1965, Big Gun Catalog, 1988; cons. editor Popular Sci. mag., 1976-80; contbr. feature articles to other major nat. mags.; designer Gatling Gun Centennial medal, 1961, Grant and Lee Commemorative medals, 1962. Mem. Authors League Am., Am. Soc. Mag. Photographers, Authors Guild, Nat. Writers Union, Am. Def. Preparedness Assn., Nat. Rifle Assn., Soc. Photographic Scientists and Engrs., Internat. Motor Press Assn. Club: Nat. Press. Office: Paul Wahl Corp PO Box 500 Bogota NJ 07603-0500

WAHLBERG, ALLEN HENRY, construction executive; b. Stockholm, Sweden, May 12, 1933; s. Allan H. and Oda J. Wahlberg; m. Barbara Bogert, June 16, 1962; children: Susan, Andrew. BS, MIT, 1956. Cost engr. Turner Constrn. Co., N.Y.C., 1966-69, chief cost engr., 1969-70, asst. treas., 1970-73, controller, 1973—, v.p., 1980—, chief fin. officer, 1985—; pres., treas. The Turner Constrn. Co. Found., N.Y.C., 1980—. Mem. City Council and Planning Bd., Ho-Ho-Kus, N.J. Served with U.S. Army C.E., 1957-59. Mem. Fin. Execs. Inst., Am. Mgmt. Assn., The Conf. Bd., Nat. Assn. Accts., MIT Alumni Ctr. N.Y. Republican. Clubs: Barnegat Light Yacht (Harvey Cedars, N.J.) (commodore 1987-88); Ridgewood (N.J.) Country. Office: The Turner Corp 633 Third Ave New York NY 10017

WAHLBERG, RAYMOND E., academic administrator; b. Isle, Minn., Dec. 11, 1930; s. Clinton E. and Alma J. (Grant) W.; m. Marilyn Ann Pearson, March 18, 1950; children: Randall, Bradley, Thomas, John Kathryn. Degree in Bus. Adminstrn., U. Minn., 1954; JD, William Mitchell Coll., St. Paul, 1958. Bar: Minn. Acct. Investors Diversified Services, Mpls., 1954-56; asst. comptroller Elec. Machinery Mfg. Co., Mpls., 1956-58; credit mgr. Land-O-Nod Co., Mpls., 1958-59, Waldorf Paper Co., St. Paul, 1959-62; bus. mgr. Internat. Housing Corp., Mpls., 1962-63; sole practice Kenyon, Minn., 1963-78; dir. planned giving St. Olaf Coll., Northfield, Minn., 1978-84; v.p., treas. Luther Coll., Decorah, Iowa, 1984—; bd. dirs. Assn. Luth. Devel. Exec., Chgo.; lectr. Continuing Legal Edn., Minn. Contbr. articles to profl. jours., newspapers, mags. Bd. dirs. Minn. State Sch. Bd. Assn., St. Peter, 1975-79, Am. Heart Assn., Decorah, 1987—; chmn. SE Minn. Sch. Planning Task Force, Rochester, 1977-80, Bd. Edn., Kenyon, 1972-78. Served as sgt. USMC, 1951-52. Mem. Nat. Assn. Colls., Univ. Bus. Offices. Republican. Lodges: Rotary, Lions. Home: 1213 Skyline Dr Decorah IA 52101 Office: Luther Coll 700 College Dr Decorah IA 52101

WAHLEN, EDWIN ALFRED, JR., merchant banker; b. Gary, Ind., Nov. 17, 1947; s. Edwin Alfred and Alice Elizabeth (Condit) W.; m. Catherine Francis Willard Jan. 7, 1978. BS in Indsl. Mgmt., Ga. Inst. Tech., 1970; MBA, U. N.C., 1972. Chartered fin. analyst. Assoc. investment banking Interstate Securities Corp., Charlotte, N.C., 1972-73; loan officer First Nat. Bank Chgo., Atlanta, 1973-77; sr. v.p. investment banking Dean Witter Reynolds, Inc., Atlanta, 1977-85; mng. dir. Cravey, Green & Wahlen, Inc., Atlanta, 1985—; Bd. dirs. CGW Holdings, Inc., Atlanta, Picture Classified Network, Atlanta. Bd. dirs. Met. Atlanta Am. Diabetes Assn. Mem. Atlanta Venture Forum, U. N.C. Bus. Sch. Club Atlanta (pres. 1982-83), Ravinia Club, Atlanta Club. Office: Cravey Green & Wahlen Inc 5600 Glenridge Dr Suite 350 Atlanta GA 30342

WAINBERG, ALAN, footwear company executive; b. Zelechow, Poland, June 25, 1937; came to U.S., 1949; s. Jaime M. and Pearl (Boruchowicz) W.; m. Karen Sue Schneider, July 31, 1966; children: David, Laura, Daniel. BS in Indsl. Engring., U. Miami, 1964; MS, NYU, 1965. Indsl. engr. U.S. Naval Propellant Plant, Indian Head, Md., 1964; sr. cons., mgr. Arthur Andersen & Co., N.Y.C., 1965-70; sr. cons. Alexander Grant & Co., Miami, 1970-71; sr. v.p., sec., treas., dir. Suave Shoe Corp., Miami, 1971-75, 78-84; group v.p. G.H. Bass & Co., Falmouth, Maine, 1984-86, pres., 1986—; owner, cons., pres. Mgmt. Cons. Services, Miami, 1975-77; dir., pres. Damaron Investment Services, Miami, 1975-78; vis. com. Coll. Engring. U. Miami. Mem. Footwear Industries Am. (mem. tech. steering com., chmn. new tech. com., 1981, bd. dirs. 1986—), U. Miami Coll. Engring. Alumni Assn. (bd. dirs., officer). Office: GH Bass & Co 360 Rt #1 Falmouth ME 04105

WAINESS, MARCIA WATSON, legal administrator; b. Bklyn., Dec. 17, 1949; d. Stanley and Seena (Klein) Watson; m. Steven Richard Wainess, Aug. 7, 1975. Student, UCLA, 1967-71, 80-81, Grad. Sch. Mgmt. Exec. Program, 1987-88, grad. Grad. Sch. Mgmt. Exec. Program, 1988. Office mgr., paralegal Lewis, Marenstein & Kadar, Los Angeles, 1977-81; office mgr. Rosenfeld, Meyer & Susman, Beverly Hills, Calif., 1981-83; adminstr. Rudin, Richman & Appel, Beverly Hills, 1983; dir. adminstrn. Kadison, Pfaelzer, Los Angeles, 1983-87; exec. dir. Richards, Watson and Gershon, Los Angeles, 1987—; faculty mem. UCLA Legal Mgmt. & Adminstrn. Program, 1983, U. So. Calif. Paralegal Program, Los Angeles, 1985; mem. adv. bd. atty. asst. tng. program, UCLA, 1984—. Mem. ABA (chmn. Displaywrite Users Group 1986, legal tech. adv. council litigation support working group 1986-87), State Bar Calif., Los Angeles County Bar Assn. (exec. com. law office mgmt. sect.), Assn. Profl. Law Firm Mgrs., Assn. Legal Adminstrs. (asst. regional v.p. Calif. 1987-88, regional v.p. 1988-89, pres. Beverly Hills chpt. 1985-86, membership chmn. 1984-85, chmn. new adminstrn. sect. 1982-84). Office: Richards Watson and Gershon 333 S Hope St 38th Floor Los Angeles CA 90071

WAINIO, MARK ERNEST, loss control specialist; b. Virginia, Minn., Apr. 18, 1953. BA, Gustavus Adolphus Coll., 1975. Cert. safety profl., assoc. loss control mgmt., assoc. risk mgmt., CPCU. Carpenter ABI Contracting Inc., Virginia, 1975-77; co-owner Mesabi Builders, Albuquerque and Eveleth, Minn., 1977-79; sr. engring. rep. Aetna Life & Casualty, Albuquerque, 1979-86; loss control specialist CNA Ins. Cos., Albuquerque, 1986—. Mem. Am. Soc. Safety Engrs., CPCU. Home: 5525 Sonata Dr NE Albuquerque NM 87111 Office: CNA Ins Companies 8500 Menaul NE Albuquerque NM 87112

WAINWRIGHT, PAT LEE, computer company executive; b. Montclair, N.J., Jan. 5, 1948; d. Thomas C.H. and Susan (Lum) L.; m. Lee Wainwright, June 14, 1970 (div. 1987); children: Randall Lee, Jenna Christine; m. James Stefanou, Oct. 7, 1988. AB, Barnard Coll., 1967; MS, Pa. State U., 1970. Editor Bioscis. Info. Svcs., Phila., 1970-78; sec., treas. Dynamic Horizon Visuals, Inc., Langhorne, Pa., 1977-88; pres., cons. Broad Street Computers, Bethlehem, Pa., 1987—. Den leader Boy Scouts Am., Bethlehem, 1987-88. Republican. Lutheran. Home: 1802 Barrett Dr Bethlehem PA 18017 Office: Broad Street Computers 441 E Broad St Bethlehem PA 18018

WAIT, CHARLES VALENTINE, bank executive; b. Albany, N.Y., May 28, 1951; s. Newman Edward Jr. and Jane Caroline (Adams) W.; m. Candace Ellin Hollar, May 27, 1978; children: Charles Valentine Jr., Christopher David, Alexandra Dallas Wait. BA, Cornell U., 1973; cert. in banking, Rutgers U., 1980. Asst. v.p. The Adirondack Trust Co., Saratoga Springs, N.Y., 1974, treas., 1978-81, sec., treas., 1981-84, pres., 1984—, also bd. dirs.; bd. dirs. Fin. Computer Ctr. of Ea. N.Y., Burnt Hills. Trustee Skidmore Coll., Saratoga Springs, 1984—, Nat. Mus. of Dance, Saratoga Springs, 1987—, N.Y. Racing Assn., N.Y.C., Nat. Mus. of Racing, 1988—; chmn. Saratoga Springs City Ctr. Authority, 1983—; treas. Saratoga Performing Arts Ctr., 1987—. Recipient Pvt. Sector Initiative award Pres. Ronald Reagan, 1984. Mem. Ind. Bankers Assn. of N.Y. State (bd. dirs., sec. 1986-87), N.Y. State Bankers Assn. (bd. dirs. 1987), N.Y. State Bankers Retirement System (trustee 1987), Am. Inst. Banking (Counsel of Yr. 1976). Republican. Lodges: Rotary, Elks. Home: 658 N Broadway Saratoga Springs NY 12866 Office: The Adirondack Trust Co 473 Broadway Saratoga Springs NY 12866

WAITE, DARVIN DANNY, accountant; b. Holdenville, Okla.; s. Delmer Charles and Lorraine (Young) W. BSBA, U. Ark., 1954. CPA, Ill. Auditor USDA, N.Y.C., New Orleans, 1963-69; auditor commodity exchange authority USDA, Chgo., 1969-75; sr. auditor U.S. Commodity Futures Trading Commn., Chgo., 1975—. With U.S. Army, 1948-51, Ark. Air N.G., 1954-56, USAFR, 1956-62. Mem. Am. Inst. CPA's, Assn. Govt. Accts. (Chgo. chpt.), Ill. CPA Soc., Chgo. Met. CPA. Chpt. Republican. Lutheran. Home: 101 Wallace St Bartlett IL 60103 Office: US Commodity Futures Trading Commn Sears Tower Chicago IL 60606

WAITNEIGHT, STEPHEN K., finance company executive; b. Phila., Aug. 27, 1944; s. James Goodwynn and Fanny Neiman (Midgley) W.; m. Gloria Dawn Gerbitz, Aug. 23, 1969; children: Courtney Dawn, Brent Stephen. BS in Bus. Mgmt. and Econs., David Lipscomb Coll., 1968. V.p., dir. sales, mktg. and personnel, controller DeHaven & Townsend, Crouter & Bodine, Phila., 1968-77; 1st v.p., mgr. br. office Janney Montgomery Scott, Inc., Cherry Hill, N.J., 1977—. With U.S. Army, 1968. Mem. Internat. Assn. Fin. Planning, Investment Assn. Phila. Office: Janney Montgomery Scott Inc 1909 E Marlton Pike Cherry Hill NJ 08003

WAKEFIELD, STEPHEN ALAN, lawyer; b. Olney, Ill., Oct. 18, 1940; s. George William and Blanche Lucille (Sheesley) W.; children from previous marriage: Melissa, Tracy, Stephen, Jr.; m. Patricia Ann McGuire, Nov. 29, 1980; 1 child, Mark. LL.B., U. Tex., Austin, 1965. Bar: Tex. 1965. Assoc. Baker & Botts, Houston, 1965-70, ptnr., 1974-84, sr. ptnr., chmn. energy dept., 1986—; atty. Federal Power Commn., Washington, 1970-72; asst. sec. energy and minerals Dept. Interior, Washington, 1973-74; asst. adminstr. Fed. Energy Office, Washington, 1973-74; vice chmn., gen. counsel United Energy Resources, Inc., Houston, 1985-86; pres. United Gas Pipe Line Co., Houston, 1985-86; exec. v.p. MidCon Corp., 1985-86. Mem. ABA, Tex. Bar Assn., Fed. Energy Bar Assn., Houston Bar Assn. Republican. Episcopalian. Clubs: River Oaks Country, Ramada (Houston). Home: 16 West Ln Houston TX 77019 Office: Baker & Botts 3000 One Shell Plaza Houston TX 77002

WAKEFIELD, THOMAS DORR, financial executive; b. Milw., Apr. 20, 1951; s. John Dorr and Martha (McGonagle) W.; m. Victoria Wakefield, Nov. 25, 1978. BA, U. Denver, 1973; MA in Internat. Bus., Am. Grad. Sch. Internat. Mgmt., 1976. Cert. fin. planner. Fin. planner Assoc. Planners Securities Corp., Walnut Creek, Calif., 1983-84, IDS Am. Express, Milw. and Danville, Calif., 1984-86; staff fin. planner, coordinator security products Equitable Fin. Cos., Milw., 1986—; adj. faculty Coll. for Fin. Planning. Mem. Internat. Assns. Fin. Planners, Inst. Cert. Fin. jPlanners, Estate Planning Council, Nat. Assn. Life Underwriters. Club: Milw. Curling (Mequon, Wis.). Office: Equitable Fin Cos 322 E Michigan St 5th Floor Milwaukee WI 53202

WAKELY, MICHAEL LEE, financial planner; b. San Antonio, Apr. 20, 1957; s. Thomas J. and Ann (Edwards) W.; m. Jane Ellen McConnell, Sept. 5, 1981. BBA, U. Tex., 1978. V.p. fin. Regis Pub. Co., San Antonio, 1978-82; chief fin. officer Watex Corp., San Antonio, 1982-86; account mgr. Acacia Fin. Group, San Antonio, 1986—. Mem. Inst. Cert. Fin. Planners. Republican. Roman Catholic. Home: 813 Garraty St San Antonio TX 78209 Office: Acadia Fin Group 7550 IH 10 W Ste 1000 San Antonio TX 78229

WAKEMAN, FRED JOSEPH, paper company executive; b. St. Louis, Mar. 19, 1928; s. Fred Otis and Blossom Marie W.; m. Carol Ann Muraski, Sept. 15, 1958; children: Julie, Jennifer, John, Jill. B.Sc., St. Norbert Coll., 1950; postgrad., U. Wis., 1952-53. With Green Bay Packaging Inc., Wis., 1953—; v.p., regional mgr. Green Bay Packaging Inc., 1973-77, exec. v.p. converting ops., 1977; bd. dirs. Associated Kellogg Bank, Internat. Corrugated Packaging Found. Served with U.S. Army, 1950-52. Decorated Purple Heart, Bronze Star. Mem. Nat. Fibre Box Assn. (exec. bd.), Am. Paper Inst., Am. Mgmt. Assn., TAPPI, Internat. Corrugated Case Assn. (bd. dirs.), AICC. Clubs: Alpine Country, Oneida Golf and Riding. Lodge: Rotary. Office: Green Bay Packaging Inc PO Box 19017 Green Bay WI 54307

WALCOTT, JOHN L., journalist; b. Paterson, N.J., Aug. 29, 1949; s. Henry Richards Jr. and Katharine McCauley (Fearing) W.; m. Nancy Bittles, Aug. 11, 1973; children: Jennifer James, Allison Tierney. BA, Williams Coll., Williamstown, Mass., 1971. Reporter The Ridgewood (N.J.) News, 1972, The Bergen Record, Hackensack, N.J., 1972-75; Washington correspondent The Bergen Record, Washington, 1975-77; Washington correspondent Newsweek Mag., Washington, 1977-81, chief diplomatic correspondent, 1981-86; nat. security correspondent The Wall Street Journal, Washington, 1986—; U.S. Rep. U.N. Conf. on Media, Igls, Austria, 1983; mem. seminar Georgetown U. Sch. Fgn. Svc. Leadership, Washington, 1985. Co-author: (with David C. Martin) Best Laid Plans: The Inside Story of America's War Against Terrorism, 1988. Named Disting. Friend Georgetown U. Sch. Fgn. Svc., 1985—; recipient Edward Weintal prize Georgetown U., 1988, Edwin M. Hood award Nat. Press Club, 1983, Overseas Press Club award, 1983, 84, Newspaper Guild of N.Y. award, 1985. Mem. Overseas Writers Club (pres. 1986-88), White House Correspondents Assn., Sigma Delta Chi. Presbyterian. Office: Wall St Jour 1025 Connecticut Ave NW Washington DC 20036

WALD, BERNARD JOSEPH, lawyer; b. Bklyn., Sept. 14, 1932; s. Max and Ruth (Mencher) W.; m. Francine Joy Weintraub, Feb. 2, 1964; children—David Evan, Kevin Mitchell. B.B.A. magna cum laude, CCNY; J.D. cum laude, NYU, 1955. Bar: N.Y. 1955, U.S. Dist. Ct. (so. dist.) N.Y. 1960, U.S. Dist. Ct. (ea. dist.) N.Y. 1960, U.S. Ct. Appeals (2d cir.) 1960, U.S. Supreme Ct. 1971. Mem. Herzfeld & Rubin, P.C. and predecessor firms, N.Y.C., 1955—. Mem. ABA, N.Y. State Bar Assn., Assn. Bar City N.Y., N.Y. County Lawyers Assn. Office: 40 Wall St New York NY 10005

WALDECK, JOHN WALTER, JR., lawyer; b. Cleve., May 3, 1949; s. John Walter Sr. and Marjorie Ruth (Palenschat) W.; m. Cheryl Gene Cutter, Sept. 10, 1977; children: John III, Matthew, Rebecca. BS, John Carroll U., 1973; JD, Cleve. State U., 1977. Product applications chemist Synthetic Products Co., Cleve., 1969-76; assoc. Arter & Hadden, Cleve., 1977-85, ptnr., 1986-88; ptnr. Porter, Wright, Morris and Arthur, Cleve., 1988—. Chmn. Bainbridge Twp. Bd. Zoning Appeals, Chagrin Falls, Ohio, 1984—; trustee Greater Cleve. chpt. Lupus Found. Am., Cleve., 1978—, sec., 1979-86; bd. dirs. Geauga County Mental Health Bd., Chardon, Ohio, 1988—. Mem. ABA (real property sect.), Ohio State Bar Assn. (real property sect.), Greater Cleve. Bar Assn. (real property sect.). Democrat. Roman Catholic. Club: 13th St. Racquet. Home: 18814 Rivers Edge Dr W Chagrin Falls OH 44022 Office: Porter Wright Morris & Arthur 1700 Huntington Bldg Cleveland OH 44115

WALDEN, ROBERT E., JR., broadcast executive; b. Selfridge AFB, Mich., Oct. 4, 1954; s. Robert Edison Sr. and Ethel Lee (Bazar) W. BA, U. Toledo, 1977; MA, Bowling Green State U., 1980. Lic. FCC 3d class radiotelephone operator with endorsement. Vol. prodn. asst. Sta. KDET-FM (name now Sta. WKDT-FM), West Point, N.Y., 1972-73; vol. announcer, disc jockey Sta. WERC-FM, Toledo, 1974-75; announcer, disc jockey Sta. WKLR-FM, Toledo, 1976-77; sr. fl. dir. Sta. WTOL-TV, Toledo, 1977-78; intern Sta. WBGU-TV, Bowling Green, 1980; prodn. asst., assoc. producer Sta. WQED-TV, Pitts., 1980-82; freelance producer, dir., writer, cons. 1982-84; producer, dir. Sta. WGTE-TV, Toledo, 1984; photographer, videographer Associated Cataract and Laser Surgeons, Inc., Toledo, 1985; supr. TV/audio prodns. dept. Med. Coll. Ohio, Toledo, 1986—; producer, instr., vis. artist, writer Ethnic Cultural Arts Program, Bowling Green State U., 1983; media design prodn. cons. Riverside Hosp., Toledo, 1985. Writer, producer, dir. Maddox & Company, Pitts., 1982; writer Behind the Scenes: A Recent Killing, San Juan, P.R., 1982-83; writer, editor Incest: A Family Affair, Toledo, 1983. With USAR, 1972-73. March of Dimes grantee for videotape series, 1988. Mem. Internat. TV Assn. (sec., bd. dirs. Toledo chpt. 1988), Assn. Biomedical Communication Dirs., Kappa Alpha Psi (v.p. Toledo undergrad. chpt. 1974-75). Office: Med Coll Ohio Prodns Dept PO Box 10008 Toledo OH 43699-0008

WALDREP, GEORGE C., JR., textile company executive; b. 1939. BS, Clemson U., 1964. Mfg. mgmt. trainee Burlington Industries, Greensboro, N.C., 1962-64, dep. mgr. mfg. plant, 1964-70, supr. mfg. plant, 1970-71, plant mgr., 1971-77, group mfg. mgr., 1977-80, div. mfg. mgr., 1980-85, group v.p. mfg., from 1985, now exec. v.p. Office: Burlington Industries Inc 3330 W Friendly Ave Greensboro NC 27410 *

WALDRON, ALBERT DOUGLAS, accountant; b. Rockville Centre, N.Y., Oct. 21, 1949; s. Stoddard Stone and Mary Bush (Moncure) W. BS in Acctg. and Bus. Adminstrn., U. San Diego, 1967-71; MPA, Ga. State U., 1987. Jr. auditor County of San Diego, 1971-73, asst. acct., 1973-75; sec.-treas. P.N.R., Inc., San Diego, 1975-79; supr. acctg. The Toronto Dominion Bank, San Francisco, 1979-83; mgr. acctg. and adminstrn. The Toronto Dominion Bank, Atlanta, 1983-85, mgr. subs. acctg., 1985-87; bd. dirs., v.p. Toronto Dominion Holdings, Inc., Atlanta, 1985-87; bd. dirs., sec.-treas. Toronto Dominion Investments, Inc., Del., 1984-87; v.p., sec., treas., bd. dirs.Indian Creek Drive Corp., Fla., 1982-87, NE 48 St. Corp., 1984-87, Jefferson Corp., Mich., 1985-87, Medallion Bay Corp., Fla., 1985-87, Helios Holdings, Inc., 1985-87; sec. Toronto Dominion, Inc., Atlanta, 1985-87; N.Y.C. br. mgr. fin. acctg. Toronto-Dominion Bank, Inc., 1988—. Republican. Roman Catholic. Office: Toronto Dominion Bank 42 Wall St 8th fl New York NY 10005

WALDRON, HICKS BENJAMIN, retired cosmetics company executive; b. Amsterdam, N.Y., Oct. 31, 1923; s. Hicks Benjamin and Dorothy (Clearwater) W.; m. Evelyn Rumstay; 1 child, Janet Waldron Ambrose. Student, Green Mountain Jr. Coll., 1941-42, U. Mich., 1943; BS, U. Minn., 1944. With Gen. Electric Co., 1946-73, v.p., group exec. consumer products group, 1971-73; pres., chief executive officer Heublein, Inc., Farmington, Conn., 1973-82; exec. v.p. R.J. Reynolds Industries, Inc., Winston-Salem, N.C., 1982-83; pres. Avon Products, Inc., N.Y.C., 1982-85, chmn., chief exec. officer, 1983-89; bd. dirs. CIGNA, Atlantic Richfield Co., Ryder Systems Co., Ryder System, Inc., Hewlett-Packard; mem. listed co. adv. com. N.Y. Stock Exchange. bd. dirs Jr. Achievement, United Way; trustee Green Mountain Coll.; bd. dirs. Boys Clubs Am., Cen. Park Conservancy; adv. bd. Salvation Army of Greater N.Y. Served to ensign USNR, 1944-46. Mem. Fgn. Policy Assn. (bd. govs.), Phi Gamma Delta. Episcopalian. Clubs: Hartford Golf, Country of Farmington. Office: Avon Products Inc 9 W 57th St New York NY 10019 *

WALENDOWSKI, GEORGE JERRY, business management specialist, accounting educator; b. Han-Minden, W.Ger., Mar. 25, 1947; came to U.S., 1949; s. Stefan and Eugenia (Lewandowska) W. A.A., Los Angeles City Coll., 1968; BS, Calif. State U.-Los Angeles, 1970, MBA, 1972. Cert. community coll. instr. acctg. and mgmt., Calif. Acct., Unocal (formerly Union Oil Co. Calif.), Los Angeles, 1972-76, data control supr., 1976-78, acctg. analyst, 1978-79; sr. fin. analyst Hughes Aircraft Co., El Segundo, Calif., 1979-83, fin. planning specialist, 1983-86; instr. bus. math. Los Angeles City Coll., 1976-80, instr. acctg., 1980—, mem. acctg. adv. com., 1984, 87; bus. mgmt. specialist, 1986—. Mem. commn. Republican Pres. Task Force, 1986. Contbr. articles to profl. jours. Softball co-organizer Precious Blood Ch., Los Angeles, 1979. Recipient Outstanding Achievement awards, 1980, 87, cert. of merit Rep. Presdl. Task Force Presdl. Commn., 1986, Superior Performance award Hughes Aircraft Co., 1987. Mem. Acad. Mgmt., Am. Acctg. Assn., Nat. Assn. Accts. (Robert Half Author's trophy Los Angeles chpt. 1980, cert. of appreciation 1980, 83, mem. Author's Circle 1980), Planning Forum (recognition award Los Angeles chpt. 1983), Am. Econ. Assn., World Inst. Achievement, Beta Gamma Sigma. Republican. Roman Catholic. Home: 426 N Citrus Ave Los Angeles CA 90036 Office: Hughes Aircraft Co 2141 E Rosecrans El Segundo CA 90245

WALGREEN, CHARLES RUDOLPH, III, retail store executive; b. Chgo., Nov. 11, 1935; s. Charles Rudolph and Mary Ann (Leslie) W.; m. Kathleen Bonsignore Allen, Jan. 23, 1977; children: Charles Richard, Tad Alexander, Kevin Patrick, Leslie Ray, Chris Patrick; stepchildren—Carleton A. Allen Jr., Jorie L. Allen. B.S. in Pharmacy, U. Mich., 1958. With Walgreen Co., Chgo., 1952—; adminstrv. asst. to v.p. store ops. Walgreen Co., 1965-66, dist. mgr., 1967-68, regional dir., 1968-69, v.p., 1969, pres., 1969-75, chmn., 1976—, also dir. Mem. bus. adv. council Chgo. Urban League.; bd. dirs. Jr. Achievement Chgo. Mem. Am. Found. Pharm. Edn. (bd. dirs.), Nat. Assn. Chain Drug Stores (bd. dirs.), Ill. Retail Mchts. Assn. (bd. dirs. 1966—), Am. Pharm. Assn., Ill. Pharm. Assn., Delta Sigma Phi. Clubs: Economic, Commercial (Chgo.); Great Lakes Cruising; Yacht and Country (Stuart, Fla.); Exmoor Country (Highland Park, Ill.); Key Largo Anglers (Fla.). Office: Walgreen Co 200 Wilmot Rd Deerfield IL 60015

WALIGORA, JAMES, financial services consultant; b. Harvey, Ill., Sept. 30, 1954; s. John Joseph and Lucille Patricia (Gargala) W.; m. Cheryl L. Stewart. AA, Thornton Community Coll., 1976; BS in Acctg. and Fin., U. Ala., Birmingham, 1978. CPA, Ala. Sr. acct. Ernst & Whinney, Birmingham, Ala., 1978-81; dir. internal auditing Motion Industries Inc., Birmingham, 1981-82; registered rep. DeRand Investment Corp., Arlington, Va., 1983-85; pvt. practice CPA Birmingham, 1982-86; pres. Equity Ptnrs. Inc., Birmingham, 1986-87, James Waligora Assocs., Birmingham, 1987—. Mem. Birmingham Mus. Art, 1985, Big Bros. Birmingham, 1979-86; pres. Greater Birmingham Arts Alliance, 1985. Mem. Am. Inst. CPA's, Ala. Soc. CPA's, Internat. Assn. Fin. Planning (treas. Ala. chpt. 1986). Lodge: Civitan Internat. (charter mem. local club 1983, pres. 1986, award 1987). Home: 1131 11th Pl S Birmingham AL 35205 Office: 300 Century Park S Suite 204 Birmingham AL 35226

WALKER, BETTY STEELE, utility company executive; b. Newtown, Pa., Oct. 24, 1955; d. George Robert and Olive May (Smith) Steele; m. James P. Walker, Oct. 1, 1988. Student, Phoenix Coll., 1974-75, Bucks County Community Coll., 1980. Mgr. order entry Lemmon Co., Sellersville, Pa., 1975-80; programmer/analyst Granite Data Co., Jenkintown, Pa., 1980-81; project leader Compute-R-Systems, Whitemarsh, Pa., 1981-83; supr. tech. svcs. Lee County Electric Corp., North Ft. Myers, Fla., 1983—. Contbr. articles and cartoons to profl. jours. Mem. NAFE, Digital Equipment Corp. Users Soc., Toastmasters. Home: 706 SW 35th Terr Cape Coral FL 33914 Office: Lee County Elec Corp 4980 Bayline Dr North Fort Myers FL 33917

WALKER, BILLY J., financial services company executive; b. Mar. 4, 1931. Student, Jacksonville U.; AMP, Harvard U.; grad., Sch. Banking of the South, La. State U. With Atlantic Nat. Bank of Jacksonville, 1948—, pres., chief exec. officer, 1974-75; pres., chief exec. officer Atlantic Bancorporation, from 1976; vice chmn. First Union Corp. (merger Atlantic Bancorp.); now chmn., chief exec. officer First Union Nat. Bank of Fla. Bd. dirs. North Fla. Council, Boy Scouts of Am.; pres., bd. dirs. Tournament Players Championship Charities; mem. fin. and exec. com. St. Luke's Hosp.; vice chmn., trustee, exec. com. bd. dirs. Jacksonville U.; mem. Fla. Council of 100, Coll. Bus. Adminstrn. U. Fla., Bus. Adv. Council U. Fla. Served with U.S. Army, 1953-55. Recipient Brotherhood award NCCJ. Office: 1st Union Nat Bank Fla PO Box 2080 Jacksonville FL 32231-0010

WALKER, BLAIR KENDALL, savings and loan association executive; b. Riverside, Calif., Dec. 25, 1962; s. Timothy Peter and Moira K. (Porter) W. BA in Econs., Whittier Coll., 1985; grad., IBM Mktg. Sch., San Francisco, 1985. Sales rep. ADB Bus. Systems Inc., L.A., 1985-86; account exec. Columbia Savings and Loan Assn., L.A., 1987—. Republican. Home: 1309 S Bundy Apt 8 Los Angeles CA 90049 Office: Columbia Savs and Loan 11999 San Vicente Blvd Los Angeles CA 90049

WALKER, BROOKS, JR., retired leasing company executive; b. Oakland, Calif., Apr. 28, 1928; s. Brooks and Marjory (Walker) W.; m. Margaret Myles Kirby, May 21, 1955 (dec. May 18, 1981); children: Kirby, Brooks III, Leslie; m. Danielle Musulin Carlisle, Jan. 4, 1985. B.A., U. Calif.-Berkeley, 1950; M.B.A. in Finance, Harvard U., 1957. Financial analyst Shasta Forest Corp., San Francisco, 1956; with U.S. Leasing Internat., Inc., San Francisco, 1957-87, asst. to treas., asst. to pres., treas., v.p. and treas., sr. v.p., dir., 1957-63, pres., 1963-69, chmn. bd., 1969-87; mng. gen. partner Ala Moana Hawaii Properties; dir. The Gap Stores, Inc., Pope & Talbot, Inc., Di Giorgio Corp. Chmn. bd. San Francisco Mus. Modern Art; bd. dirs. San Francisco Opera Assn., Pacific Legal Found., Smith Kettlewell Eye Research Found.; trustee Santa Catalina Sch. Served to lt. (j.g.) USNR, 1951-55. Mem. Delta Kappa Epsilon.

WALKER, CARLA SUE, audit supervisor; b. Brownwood, Tex., Sept. 9, 1958; d. Ralph Carlton and Jackie Nell (Sparks) W. BBA in Acctg., Angelo State U., 1980. CPA, Tex. Auditor Office of Compt. of Pub. Accounts, Austin, Tex., 1980-81, Dallas, 1981-82, Odessa, Tex., 1981-86; audit supr. Office of Compt. of Pub. Accounts, Waco, Tex., 1986, Dallas, 1986—. Vol. Lit. Vols. of Am., Dallas, 1988—. Mem. Tex. Soc. CPA's (Dallas chpt.), Angelo State U. Ex-students Assn. Office: Compt of Pub Accounts 9241 LBJ Frwy Ste 200 Dallas TX 75243

WALKER, CHARLES ARTHUR, JR., financial executive; b. Aldrich, Ala., Oct. 19, 1927; s. Charles Arthur and Ruth Acenath (Jones) W.; m. Marjorie Lou Ardis, July 25, 1953; children: Cynthia Ardis, Bradford Charles. BS in Acctg., U. Ill., 1951. Acct. Armstrong World Industries, Inc. (formerly Armstrong Cork Co.), Pitts., Lancaster, Pa., Braintree, Mass., 1951-55; asst. treas., gen. credit mgr. Armstrong World Industries, Inc., Lancaster, 1963-67; sr. asst. treas. Armstrong World Industries, Inc., 1968-74, v.p., treas., 1974—; controller, asst. treas. Deltox Rug Co., Oshkosh, Wis., 1955-61, v.p., treas., 1961-63. Treas., trustee James Buchanan Found., Lancaster; trustee First Presbyn. Ch., Lancaster; active United Way Lancaster County, 1975-87. Served with USNR, 1946-47. Recipient Benjamin Rush award for vol. work with United Way Lancaster City and County Med. Soc., 1985. Mem. Nat. Assn. Corp. Treas., Del. Valley Fin. Execs. Group, U. Ill. Alumni Assn., Alpha Kappa Psi, Alpha Sigma Phi. Republican. Presbyterian. Clubs: Lancaster Country, Farmington Country. Office: Armstrong World Industries Inc PO Box 3001 Lancaster PA 17604

WALKER, CHARLES ROBERT, JR., financial executive; b. Milw., Sept. 20, 1930; s. Charles Robert and Florence Caroline (Jahn) W.; m. Mona Jean Reehl, May 21, 1956 (div. Jan. 1980); children: Kenneth C., Kathleen A.; m. Carollee Josephine Doerr, July 13, 1980. BS in Acctg., Marquette U., 1954. Semi sr. acct. Arthur Andersen and Co., Milw., 1954-57; budget dir. Milprint, Inc., Milw., 1957-59; asst. controller Jack Winter, Inc., Milw., 1959-64; budget dir. Oshkosh Truck Corp., Wis., 1965-69, controller, 1969-72, asst. treas., controller, 1972—. Mem. Pub. Expenditures Survey, Oshkosh chpt., 1972-76; treas., bd dirs. Oshkosh YMCA, 1976-85. Served with U.S. Army Nat. Guard, 1947-62. Mem. Fin. Execs. Inst. (pres. N.E. Wis. chpt. 1980-81), Nat. Assn. Accts., YMCA Men's Club (pres. 1970-71), Kiwanis (sec. 1973-79). Republican. Congregationalist. Office: Oshkosh Truck Corp 2307 Oregon St Oshkosh WI 54901

WALKER, CLAYTON EUGENE, grain company executive, farmer; b. Dresden, Kans., Feb. 21, 1915; s. Henry L. and Ruby (Harold) W.; m. Pearl Maxine Herrick, Aug. 21, 1946 (dec. 1983); m. Loreta Louise Yorgensen, Aug. 7, 1985; step children: Ann Reinert, Sandra Bartley, Patricia Whitley, Peggy Mendoza, Michael Nebel, Mark Nebel, Nanette Kraus. Farmer Dresden, 1935-37; grain trucker A.R. Broyles Trucking Co., Greeley, Colo., 1939-42; ind. grain trucker Greeley, 1946-48; owner, mgr. elevator grain bus. Simpson, Mankato, Kans., 1948-54; pres. Walker Grain Co., Burr Oak, 1953—; farmer, Burr Oak, Kans., 1956—. Staff sgt. USAAF, 1942-46, PTO. Mem. Nat. Grain and Feed Assn., Kans. Grain and Feed Dealers, Nat. Cattlemen's Assn. (charter), VFW, Elks. Republican. Methodist. Address: 1414 Jackson St Burr Oak KS 66936

WALKER, CYNTHIA HELEN, medical records company executive; b. Springfield, Mo., July 28, 1941; d. Maurice Jesse and Helen Pauline (Newton) LeFors; childern: Lori, Johney, Tim, Chris. BS in Health Info. Mgmt., Stephens Coll., 1984; MEd, Drury Coll., 1988. Registered record adminstr. Cons. Americana-Fremont Nursing Home, Springfield, Mo., 1982—; dir. med. records Lester E. Cox Med. Ctr. South, Springfield, Mo., 1979—; adj. faculty mem. Stephens Coll. Columbia, Mo., 1985—. Author course module Management of Health Information Centers, 1987. Mem. Am. Med. Records Assn. Republican. Club: Pilot Orgn. Home: 3661 S Blackburn Ct Springfield MO 65807

WALKER, DALE RUSH, banker; b. High Point, N.C., Jan. 14, 1943; s. Raymond Lowe and Virginia (Rush) W.; m. Maedell Goodson, Aug. 13, 1966 (div. Oct. 1987); children—Virginia Ashley, Whitney Beaumont. B.S. in Math., Wake Forest U., 1965; M.B.A., U. N.C., 1967. Asst. cashier Citibank, N.Y.C., 1967-70; sr. v.p. Union Bank, San Francisco, 1970-75, regional v.p., 1975-78; regional v.p. Union Bank, Oakland, Calif., 1978-80; chief mktg. officer Wells Fargo Leasing, San Francisco, 1980-81; exec. v.p. real estate industries group Wells Fargo Bank, San Francisco, 1981—; chmn. bd. Wells Fargo Leasing Corp.; dir. Wells Fargo Realty Advisors, Inc., Wells Fargo Capital Markets, Inc., Wells Fargo Realty Fin., San Francisco, 1983—, Ctr. for Re and Urban Econs., Berkeley, Calif., 1984. Chmn. United Way Campaign Wells Fargo & Co., San Francisco, 1983-84; bd. dirs. Pacific Vision Found. Mem. Urban Land Inst. Democrat. Methodist. Club: University (San Francisco) (v.p. 1977-78). Home: 455 Vallejo #203 San Francisco CA 94133 Office: Wells Fargo Bank 464 California St San Francisco CA 94163

WALKER, DANIEL CHARLES, distribution company executive; b. Grand Rapids, Mich., Feb. 2, 1948; s. Harvey Leonard Finkler and Joan (Walker) Burton; m. Thaila Renae Koning, Sept. 8, 1984; children: Gentry Leigh, Kaley Renae. BBA, Davenport Coll., Grand Rapids, 1977. Supr. warehousing Amway Corp., Ada, Mich., 1969-74, supr. planning and scheduling, 1974-77, rep. sales, 1977-80, sr. rep. sales, 1980-84; owner small bus. 1984-86; v.p. ops. Empire Distbrs., Inc., Grandville, Mich., 1986-88, sr. v.p. ops., 1988—. Chmn. area devel. Holland (Mich.) C. of C., 1985-86; chmn. mayor's traffic task force City of Holland, 1986. Served with U.S. Army, 1966-68. Congregationalist. Home: 458 W Lakewood Blvd Holland MI 49424 Office: Empire Distbrs Inc 2971 Franklin SW Grandville MI 49468

WALKER, DAVID ALLEN, technology company executive; b. L.A., July 19, 1956; s. Steven and Florence (Rothman) W.; m. Linda Ann DeHart, Mar. 5, 1983. BS in Engring., UCLA, 1978; MBA in Fin. and Mktg., U. Chgo., 1982. Team mgr. Procter & Gamble Paper Products Co., Oxnard, Calif., 1978-80; sr. financial analyst Dataproducts Corp., Woodland Hills, Calif., 1982-83; mgr. bus. planning and fin. Burroughs Corp., Camarillo, Calif., 1983-85; dir. corp. financial planning MICOM Systems, Inc., Simi Valley, Calif., 1985-89; ptnr. DeHart Walker Enterprises, Agoura Hills, Calif., 1986—; v.p. fin. and adminstrn. CT&T Systems, Inc., Chatsworth, Calif., 1989—. Mem. ASME, UCLA Alumni Assn., U. Chgo. Alumni Assn., Tau Beta Pi. Republican. Jewish. Home: 5908 Carell Ave Agoura Hills CA 91301

WALKER, DAVID MICHAEL, federal government official; b. Birmingham, Ala., Oct. 2, 1951; s. David Sellers and Dorothy Ann (West) W.; m. Mary Carmel Etheredge, June 12, 1971; children: Carol Marie, James Andrew. BS in Acctg., Jacksonville U., 1973. CPA, Fla., Tex. Sr. auditor Price Waterhouse & Co. and Coopers & Lybrand, Jacksonville, Fla., 1973-76; dir. personnel Coopers & Lybrand, Atlanta and Houston, 1976-79; Ea. regional mgr. Source Services Corp., Washington, 1979-83; acting exec. dir. and dep. exec. dir. Pension Benefit Guaranty Corp., Washington, 1983-85; dep. asst. sec. U.S. Dept. of Labor, Washington, 1985-87, asst. sec., 1987—. Contbr. articles to profl. jours. Active United Fund. Mem. Am. Inst. CPA's, Nat. Assn. Accts., D.C. Inst. CPA's , Tex. Soc. CPA's, Fla. Inst. CPA's, U.S. Jaycees (past v.p., dir., treas.). Republican. Methodist. Lodge: Kiwanis (Atlanta, past v.p., dir.). Home: 1429 Ironwood Dr McLean VA 22101 Office: US Dept Labor 200 Constitution Ave NW #S2524 Washington DC 20210

WALKER, DENNIS WILLIAM, sales executive; b. Memphis, Mar. 20, 1948; s. Dennis William and Marjorie (Moseley) W.; m. Cynthia R. Higgins, Mar. 24, 1970; children: Dennis W., Robert Christian. BA, Memphis State U., 1970, MA, 1972, MBA, 1984. Asst. to pres. Raifords, Inc., Memphis, 1969-73; account exec. The Herbst Corp., Little Rock, 1973-81, Stride Rite Footwear, Inc., Cambridge, Mass., 1981-86; regional mgr., v.p. field sales, dir. mktg. The Rockport Co., Marlboro, Mass., 1986—. Served as capt. USAF, 1969-72. Mem. Assn. Fashion Services (chmn. children's footwear com. 1986), Nat. Shoe Retailers (children's style com. 1985-86), Shriners, Masons, Scottish Rite, Omicron Delta Kappa, Beta Gamma Sigma, Pi Delta Epsilon, Alpha Epsilon Rho, Phi Mu Alpha, Lambda Chi alpha. Republican. Roman Catholic. Home: 8993 Cairn Ridge Dr Germantown TN 38138 Office: The Rockport Co 72 Howe St Marlborough MA 01752

WALKER, DONNA HENRY, securities executive; b. Atlanta, Feb. 9, 1954; d. Robert Edward and Evelyn Pauline (Smith) Henry; m. Robert Martin Walker, May 20, 1977; children—Robert Brandon and Matthew Lee (twins). B.A., So. Methodist U., 1976, M.B.A., 1977. Asst. securities officer Southwestern Life Ins. Co., Dallas, 1977-80; convertible securities trader Bass Bros., Ft. Worth, 1980-84; v.p. convertible arbitrage Paine Webber, Inc., N.Y.C., 1984-86; ltd. ptnr. Schwarzman Ptnrs., Greenwich, Conn., 1986—. Sponsor, The 500 Inc. Mem. Fin. Analysts Fedn., Jr. League of Stamford-Norwalk, Inst. Chartered Fin. Analysts. Republican. Methodist. Home: 76 Noroton Ave Darien CT 06820 Office: 475 Steamboat Rd Greenwich CT 06830

WALKER, ESPER LAFAYETTE, JR., civil engineer; b. Decatur, Tex., Sept. 22, 1930; s. Esper Lafayette and Ruth (Mauldin) W.; B.S., Tex. A&M U., 1953; B.H.T., Yale U., 1958; m. Sara Lynn Dunlap, Oct. 2, 1955; children—William David, Annette Ruth. Design engr. Tex. Hwy. Dept., Austin, 1956-57; dir. Dept. Traffic Engring., High Point, N.C., 1958-63; v.p. Wilbur Smith & Assos., Houston, 1963-—. Pres. Meadow Wood PTA, 1976-77; chmn. Pack 902 com. Sam Houston council Boy Scouts Am., 1973-74, treas. Troop 904 com., 1976-80; treas. Stratford High Band, 1981-82, bd. dirs., 1980-82; baseball team mgr. Spring Br. Sports Assn., 1975-77; mem. adminstrv. bd. Meml. Drive Meth. Ch., 1971-77, 83-88, bldg. com., 1974-82, fin. com., 1975-77, 83-85, trustee, 1983-87. Served to 1st lt. C.E., AUS, 1953-56. Recipient Key Man award High Point Jaycees, 1962. Registered profl. engr., Tex., S.C., Colo., Ark., Wis., La., Okla., N.Mex., Wyo. Mem. Nat., Tex. socs. profl. engrs., High Point Jaycees (dir.), Tex. A&M U. Alumni Assn. (ctr. urban affairs council 1985—, vice chmn. 1988), Houston C. of C. (chmn. transit com. 1975-79), Inst. Transp. Engrs. (pres. So. sect. 1963). Clubs: Warwick, Summit, Plaza. Home: 14216 Kellywood Ln Houston TX 77079 Office: 908 Town and Country Blvd Ste 400 Houston TX 77024

WALKER, EVELYN, retired educational TV executive; b. Birmingham, Ala.; d. Preston Lucas and Mattie (Williams) W.; AB, Huntingdon Coll., 1927, student Cornell U., 1927-29, spl. courses U. Ill., 1955, MA, U. Ala., 1963; LHD, 1974. Speech instr. Phillips High Sch., Birmingham, 1930-34; head speech dept. Ramsay High Sch., Birmingham, 1934-52; chmn. radio and TV, Birmingham Pub. Schs., 1944-75, head instructional TV programming services, 1969-75; Miss Ann, broadcaster children's daily radio program, Birmingham, 1946-57; producer Our Am. Heritage radio series, 1944-54; TV staff producer programs shown daily Ala. Pub. TV Network, 1954-75; past cons. Gov.'s Ednl. TV Legislative Study Com., 1953; nat. del. Asian-Am. Women Broadcasters Conf., 1966; past chmn. Creative TV-Radio Writing Competition. Mem. emerita Nat. Def. Adv. Com. on Women in Services; past TV-radio co-chmn. Gov.'s Adv. Bd. Safety Com.; past TV chmn. Festival of Arts; past audio-visual chmn. Ala. Congress, also past mem. Birmingham council P.T.A.; media chmn. Gov.'s Commn. on Yr. of the Child; bd. dirs. Women's Army Corps Found. Recipient Alumnae Achievement award Huntingdon Coll., 1958; Tops in Our Town award Birmingham News, 1957; Air Force Recruiting plaque, 1961; Spl. Bowl award for promoting arts through Ednl. TV., 1962; citation 4th Army Corps., 1962; cert. of appreciation Ala. Multiple Sclerosis Soc., 1962; Freedoms Found. at Valley Forge Educator's medal award, 1963; Top TV award A.R.C., 1964; Ala. Woman of Achievement award, 1964; Bronze plaque Ala. Dist. Exchange Clubs, 1969; cert. of appreciation Birmingham Bd. Edn., 1975; Obelisk award Children's Theatre, 1976; 20-Yr. Service award Ala. Ednl. TV Commn.; key to city of Birmingham, 1966; named Woman of Yr., Birmingham, 1965; named Ala. Woman of Yr., Progressive Farmer mag., 1966; hon. col. Ala. Militia. Mem. Am. Assn. Ret. Persons, Ala. Assn. Ret. Tchrs., Huntingdon Coll. Alumnae Assn. (former internat. pres.), Former Am. Women in Radio and TV, Ala. Hist. Assn., Arlington Hist. Assn. (dir., pres. 1981-83), Magna Charta Dames (past state sec.-treas.), DAR (former pub. relations com. Ala., TV chmn., state program chmn. 1979-85, state chmn. Seimes Microfilm com. 1985-88, state chmn. Motion Picture, Radio TV com. 1988—), Colonial Dames 17th Century (chmn. pub. relations com.), U.S. Daus. 1812 (past state TV chmn.), Daus. Am. Colonists (past 2d v.p. local chpt., state chmn. TV and radio), Ams. Royal Descent, Royal Order Garter, Plantagenets Soc. Am., Salvation Army Women's Aux., Symphony Aux., Humane Soc. Aux., Eagle Forum, Nat. League Am. Pen Women, Com. of 100 Women (bd. dirs.), Royal Order Crown, Women in Communications (past local pres., nat. headliner 1965), English Speaking Union, Birmingham-Jefferson Hist. Soc., Delta Delta Delta (mem. Golden Circle), Ladies Golf Assn. Methodist. Clubs: Downtown, Birmingham Country, The Club. Home: 744 Euclid Ave Mountain Brook Birmingham AL 35213

WALKER, FRANCIS CHARLES, consulting industrial psychologist; b. Knox County, Ill., Feb. 1, 1926; s. Ivan Banks and Hazel Anna (Weiler) W.; m. Donna Jean Bender, Sept. 1, 1946; children: Gregory C., Taffy Leigh. BA in Humanities with honors, Bradley U., 1949, MA in Psychology, 1950. Lic. psychologist, Fla.; cert. rehab. counselor, Fla.; diplomate Am. Bd. Vocat. Experts. Personnel counselor Caterpillar Tractor Co., Inc., Peoria, Ill., 1950-55; indsl. psychologist Byron Harless and Assocs., Inc., Tampa, 1955; indsl. relations cons. Sangamo Elec. Co., Inc., Springfield, Ill., 1955-60; sec., dir. adminstrv. services Byron Harless, Schaffer, Reid Assocs., Inc., Tampa, 1960-69; v.p. Rutenberg Homes, Inc., Belleair Bluffs, Fla., 1969-70, cons., 1970-71; pres. Frank Walker Assocs., Inc., Tampa, 1970—. Contbr. articles to profl. jours. Past clk. of session treas. Bayshore Presbyn. Ch., Tampa. Served with USAF, 1944-46. Mem. Internat. Assn. Applied Psychology, Am. Psychol. Assn., Southeastern Psychol. Assn., Fla. Psychol. Assn. (past pres., chapter rep.), Nat. Mgmt. Assn., Tampa Bay Psychol. Assn. (past pres.), Nat. Rehab. Assn., Nat. Rehab. Counseling Assn., Greater Tampa C. of C. (past chmn. law enforcement com., chmn. Small Bus. Council 1988-89). Republican. Clubs: Exchange, University (Tampa). Avocations: photography; bicycling; reading. Home: 215 S Hesperides Tampa FL 33609 Office: Frank Walker Assocs Inc 1300 N Westshore Blvd Ste 140 Tampa FL 33607

WALKER, FRANCIS JOSEPH, lawyer; b. Tacoma, Aug. 5, 1922; s. John McSweeney and Sarah Veronica (Meechan) W.; m. Julia Corinne O'Brien, Jan. 27, 1951; children—Vincent Paul, Monica Irene Hylton, Jill Marie Nudell, John Michael, Michael Joseph, Thomas More. B.A., St. Martin's Coll., 1947; J.D., U. Wash., 1950. Bar: Wash. Asst. atty. gen. State of Wash., 1950-51; sole practice, Olympia, Wash., 1951—; gen. counsel Wash. Cath. Conf., 1967-76. Served to lt. (j.g.) USNR, 1943-46; PTO. Home: 2723 Hillside Dr Olympia WA 98501 Office: 203 E 4th Ave Ste 301 Olympia WA 98501

WALKER, GRACE BAIR, tax consultant; b. Natrona Heights, Pa., Oct. 1, 1926; d. Maurice C. and Rhoda (Culbert) Bair; m. William E. Walker, Dec. 27, 1945; children: Holly Elizabeth, Laurie VanTine, Scott E. Grad. high sch., Natrona Heights. Asst. X-ray technician Alcoa, New Kensington, Pa., 1944-46; geophysics asst. Gulf Rsch., Harmarville, Pa., 1948-52; tax preparer H & R Block, 1976-82, Beneficial Fin., 1983; tax cons. Walkers Tax Svc., 1984—. vol. Ally Valley Hosp., Natrona Heights, 1985—, Meals on Wheels; elder, deacon Natrona Heights Presbyn. Ch., 1980-85. Mem. Nat. Assn. Enrolled Agts., Nat. Assn. Tax Preparers. Republican. Home and Office: 116 Ekastown Rd Sarver PA 16055

WALKER, HAROLD OSMONDE, newspaper and television executive; b. Bronxville, N.Y., Aug. 1, 1928; s. Harold Osmonde and Marie Louise (Clinch) Walker; m. Dorothy Jean Tollifson, Aug. 21, 1954; children: Pamela Gardner, Richard Talbot. AB, Harvard U., 1953, MBA, 1962. Asst. contr. Copley Press, Inc., La Jolla, Calif., 1962-66, dir. corp. planning, 1974-76, v.p., 1976-78, v.p. mktg., planning, rsch., 1978—; sec. Copley Internat. Corp., La Jolla, Calif., 1965-66, treas., 1967-69, v.p., 1966-69, 71-74; v.p. Copley/Colony (Cablevision) Inc., Providence, 1984—; pres., treas. Emerald Baseball, Inc., Eugene, Oreg., 1979-82; asst. sec. Ivac Corp., San Diego, 1968-70, v.p. 1968, exec. v.p. 1969-70; sec. Spasors Electronics Corp., San Diego, 1964-65, treas. 1964-68, v.p. 1965-68. Contbr. articles to profl. jours. Sgt. U.S. Army, 1946-49; capt. USAF, 1953-60. Mem. Internat. Newspaper Fin. Execs., Nat. Assn. Bus. Economists, Harvard Bus. Sch. Assn. of San Diego (pres. 1965-66), San Diego Press Club, Harvard Club of San Diego, La Jolla Beach and Tennis Club. Republican. Home: 5528 Via Callado La Jolla CA 92037 Office: Copley Newspapers 7776 Ivanhoe Ave La Jolla CA 92037

WALKER, HENRY ALEXANDER, JR., diversified corporation executive; b. Honolulu, Mar. 5, 1922; s. H. Alexander and Una (Craig) W.; m. Nancy Johnston, Mar. 10, 1946; children: Henry Alexander III, Susan Walker Kowen. Student, Harvard U., 1940-42, Columbia U., 1946-47. With AMFAC, Inc., Honolulu, 1947—, v.p., ops., 1966, exec. v.p., 1966-67, pres., 1967-74, chief exec. officer, chmn. bd., 1974-78, chmn., chief exec. officer, pres., 1978-83, chmn., 1983—, chief exec. officer, 1987—; bd. dirs. Hawaiian Telephone Co., Gulf Westerns, Inc. Bd. dirs. Hawaii Maritime Ctr., Straub Found., East-West Ctr. Found., Aloha United Way; mem. adv. bd. U. Hawaii Coll. Bus. Adminstrn.; mem. dean's adv. bd. Chaminade U. Sch. Bus. Served with USNR, 1944-46. Mem. Hawaiian Sugar Planters Assn. Clubs: Pacific Union (San Francisco); Phoenix S.K, Massachusetts, Harvard (N.Y.C.); Pacific, Waialae Country, Oahu Country (Honolulu). Office: Amfac JMB Realty Corp 700 Bishop St Honolulu HI 96801 also: Amfac Inc 44 Montgomery St San Francisco CA 94104 *

WALKER, JAMES ANDREW, aluminum company executive; b. Toronto, Ont., Can., Mar. 23, 1925; came to U.S., 1960; s. Wilson Gordon and Florence Owena (Godfrey) W.; m. Elizabeth Jennette McDonald, Sept. 20, 1967; children—Scott Robert, John Gordon, Susan Elizabeth. BAS in Civil Engring., U. Toronto, 1951. Constrn. engr. Aluminum Co. Can., Montreal, Que., 1951-53; salesman Alcan Aluminum, Toronto, Can., 1953-60, N.Y.C., 60-63; sales mgr. Amax Aluminum Co., N.Y.C., 1963-67; res. mgr. Ugine-Kuhlman (Paris), N.Y.C., 1967-70; sales mgr. Noranda Aluminum Inc., Westport, Conn. and New Madrid, Mo., 1970-79, v.p. sales, Cleve., 1979—. bd. dir. U.S. Reduction Co., Marnor, Inc., Excel Extrucation, Inc., Aluminum Extruder Coun. Area capt. United Fund, Westport, 1974-75. Republican. Clubs: Nutmeg Curling (gov. 1974-76) (Darien, Conn.); Met. (N.Y.C.), Chagrin Valley Country. Office: Noranda Aluminum Inc 30100 Chargin Blvd Ste 100 Cleveland OH 44124

WALKER, JAMES ETHAND, truck leasing company executive; b. Huntsville, Ala., Oct. 3, 1946; m. Julia Patricia O'Doherty. BS in Fin., U. Ala., 1972; MBA, W.Va. U., 1976. Team mgr. Ryder Truck Lines, various locations, 1972-80; sales mgr. Ryder System, Miami, Fla., 1980-82; regional mgr. Ryder System, Boston, 1982-85; gen. mgr. Lily Truck Leasing, Inc., Boston, 1985-86, v.p., gen. mgr., 1986-88; pres. Lily Transport, Inc., Boston, 1988—; acquisition cons. Barnes Enterprises, houston, 1987-88. Mem. Coun. Logistics Mgmt., Congregators Club (Boston). Republican. Congregationalist. Office: Lily Transport Inc 1280 Soldiers Field Rd Boston MA 02135

WALKER, JAMES SILAS, college president; b. LaFollette, Tenn., Aug. 21, 1933; s. John Charles and Ruth Constance (Yeagle) W.; m. Nadine Leas Mortenson, May 28, 1954; children—Steven J., David K., Bradley P., Scott C. B.A., U. Ariz., 1954; B.Div., McCormick Theol. Sem., 1956; postgrad. U. Basel, Switzerland, 1956-57; Ph.D., Claremont Coll., 1963. Ordained to ministry Presbyterian Ch., 1956. Asst. paster Central Presbyn. Ch., Denver, 1957-60; prof. Huron Coll., S.D., 1963-66; prof. Hastings (Nebr.) Coll., 1966-75, dir. devel., 1975-79, dean, 1979-83; pres. Jamestown Coll., N.D., 1983—; adj. faculty mem. Luther Northwestern Theol. Sem., St. Paul, 1984—. Author: Theology of Karl Barth, 1963. Bd. dirs. Salvation Army, Jamestown. Rotary Internat. Found. fellow, 1956-57; Nat. Def. Title IV grantee, 1960-63. Mem. Assn. Presbyn. Colls. and Univs., Presbytery of No. Plains, Rotary (dist. 563 gov. 1978-79). Republican. Avocations: travel, hunting, photography. Office: Jamestown Coll Office of the Pres Box 6080 Jamestown ND 58401

WALKER, JAMES WILLIAM, JR., lawyer; b. Birmingham, Ala., Aug. 19, 1927; s. James William and Eva Victoria (Harris) W.; m. Eileen Newton, Apr. 30, 1949; children: James William III, Michael, Lee, Helen, Caroline. AB, Birmingham So. Coll., 1949; JD, Emory U., 1953. Bar: Ga. 1954, D.C. 1966. With Merrill Lynch, Fenner & Smith, N.Y.C., 1954-67; exec. v.p. Am. Stock Exchange, N.Y.C., 1968-74, Securities Industry Assn., Washington, 1974-77; exec. asst. to chmn. bd. INA Corp., Phila., 1977-78, sr. v.p., 1978-79, exec. v.p., 1979-80, exec. v.p., gen. counsel, 1980-82; exec. v.p., gen. counsel CIGNA Corp., Phila., 1982—. Mem. Emory U. Law Sch. Coun.; bd. trustees Phila. Mus. Art. Capt. U.S. Army, 1946-48, Res. 1948—. Mem. ABA, Am. Law Inst., Union League Club. Office: Cigna Corp One Logan Sq Philadelphia PA 19103

WALKER, JEFFREY CLEMENS, venture capitalist; b. Knoxville, Tenn., Sept. 22, 1955; s. William Clemens and Joyce Hazel (Harkins) W.; m. Suzanne Marie Connelly, Apr. 27, 1984; 1 child, Courtney. BS, U. Va., 1977; MBA, Harvard U., 1981. CPA, Tex. Sr. auditor, cons. Arthur Young & Co., Houston, 1977-79; assoc. Chem. Bank, N.Y.C., 1981-82, project mgr., 1982-83, v.p., 1983-86; mng. gen. ptnr. Chem. Ventures Ptnrs., N.Y.C., 1986—; bd. dirs. Funk & Wagnalls & Co., N.J., Gymboree Corp., Burlingame Calif., Smartnames Corp., Waltham, Mass., In-Store Advt., N.Y.C., The Geneva Cos., Costa Mesa, Calif., Eric Chandler Holding Corp., San Diego, PTN Holding Corp., N.Y.C., Proxy Message Ctrs., Dallas, Exeter Capital, N.Y.C., Riordan Freeman & Spogli Fund, L.A. Mem. Nat. Venture Capital Assn., Nat. Assn. Small Bus. Investment Cos., Am. Inst. CPA's. Beta Gamma Sigma. Republican. Unitarian. Clubs: Harvard, Harvard Bus. sch. (bd. dirs. 1988—, sec.1984—) (N.Y.C.). Home: 16 Hearthstone Ln Wilton CT 06897 Office: Chem Ventures Ptnrs 277 Park Ave 11th Floor New York NY 10172

WALKER, JORDAN CLYDE, SR., lawyer, real estate executive; b. Clearfield, Utah, July 18, 1927; s. Clarence Clyde and Verlina June (Jordan) W.; m. Viola Dale Stoner, Mar. 15, 1947 (div. Nov. 1964); children: Jordan Clyde Jr., Pamela Jean, Olivia June, Aaron Kim (dec.); m. Maxine M. Armstrong, Aug. 4, 1967; children: Karen Joann, Mark Allen, Leslie Susan. JD, McGeorge Sch. Law, Sacramento, 1975. Bar: Calif. 1976. Mgr. sales Gen. Foods Corp., Sacramento, 1949-58; sales rep. Smith-Klein & French, Sacramento, 1959-63; ind. real estate salesman and developer, Sacramento, 1963-75; ptnr. Walker & Crawford, Sacramento, 1976—; owner, mgr. Walker & Assocs., Sacramento, 1979—; v.p., sec. Jordan Devel. Co., Inc., Sacramento, 1975—. Rep. fundraiser, Sacramento, 1980-87. Served with USN, 1945-46, PTO. Mem. Phi Alpha Delta. Mormon. Club: Sutter (Sacramento). Avocations: fly fishing, horseback riding, duck hunting. Office: Walker & Crawford 3600 American River Dr Suite 145 Sacramento CA 95864

WALKER, K. GRAHAME, manufacturing company executive; b. West Bridgford, Nottinghamshire, Eng., June 19, 1937; came to U.S., 1979; s. John P. and Lilian (Wright) W.; m. Robina Mairy Bendell, Aug. 20, 1959 (div. 1979); children: Belinda Sharon, Victoria Jane; m. Shirley Dean Allison, Dec. 6, 1980. Student, Merchant Taylors' Sch., 1948-55; grad., Britannia Royal Naval Coll., 1955-57, Royal Naval Engring. Coll., 1959-62. Mktg. exec. Rank Orgn., Eng., 1962-65; mng. dir. Hysol Sterling Ltd., Eng., 1965-74, Dexter GmbH, Fed. Republic Germany, 1974-79; pres. Hysol div. Dexter Corp., Industry, Calif., 1979-85; pres. specialty chems. and services group Dexter Corp., Windsor Locks, Conn., 1985-88, pres., 1988—. Bd. dirs. Greater Hartford chpt. ARC, 1986—, Barnes Group Inc., Bristol, 1988—, New Eng. Air Mus., Windsor Locks, 1988—. Served to lt. Royal Navy, 1955-62. Clubs: Hartford; Golf Club Avon (Conn.). Office: Dexter Corp 1 Elm St Windsor Locks CT 06096

WALKER, MICHAEL ARTHUR, accountant; b. N.Y.C., Aug. 22, 1936; s. Arthur B. and Alva (Strausburg) W.; m. Ann Hirshburg, Aug. 30, 1958; children: Debbie, Karen. BS, Pa. State U., 1958. CPA, Pa., N.Y., N.J., Fla. Mgr. Price Waterhouse & Co., Pitts. and N.Y.C., 1958-71; ptnr. Mann Judd Landau, N.Y.C., 1971-89, Touche Ross & Co., N.Y.C., 1989—; adj. prof. CUNY. Mem. Citizens Budget Adv. Com., Maplewood, N.Y., 1981-87. Served to 2nd lt. U.S. Army, 1958-59. Mem. Am. Inst. CPA's chmn. quality rev. exec. com.), N.Y. State Soc. CPA's (bd. dirs.), N.J. Soc. CPA's, Nat. Assn. Accts., Accts. Club Am. Democrat. Jewish. Home: 12 Village Green Ct South Orange NJ 07079 Office: Mann Judd Landau 230 Park Ave New York NY 10169

WALKER, MOIRA KAYE, sales executive; b. Riverside, Calif., Aug. 2, 1940; d. Frank Leroy and Arline Rufina (Roach) Porter; m. Timothy P. Walker, Aug. 30, 1958 (div. 1964); children: Brian A., Benjamin D., Blair K., Beth E. Student, Riverside City Coll., 1973. With Bank of Am., Riverside, 1965-68, Abitibi Corp., Cucamonga, Calif., 1968-70, Lily div. Owens-Illinois, Riverside, 1970-73; salesperson Lily div. Owens-Illinois, Houston, 1973-77; salesperson Kent H. Landsberg div. Sunclipse, Montebello, Calif., 1977-83, sales mgr., 1983-85; v.p., sales mgr. Kent H. Landsberg div. Sunclipse, Riverside, 1985—. Mem. Nat. Assn. Female Execs., Women in Paper (treas. 1978-84). Lutheran. Office: Kent H Landsberg div Sunclipse 1180 Spring St Riverside CA 92507

WALKER, P(ERCIVAL) DUANE, health care industry infomation systems executive, consultant; b. McKeesport, Pa., June 5, 1931; s. Percy Theodore and Bertha I. (Westerberg) W.; B.S., Pa. State U., 1953; M.B.A., N.Y. U., 1969; m. Doris Jane McClymont, Dec. 12, 1959; children—Jeannine Cherie, Andrea Lee, Edward Duane. Systems engr. IBM Corp., Pitts., 1955-58; cons. corporate controller's staff Westinghouse Elec. Co., Pitts., 1958-59; mgr. mgmt. adv. services Price Waterhouse & Co., Pitts., 1959-62; successively mgr. market analysis-programming systems, mgr. info. systems planning and arch., mgr. bus. systems planning IBM Corp., Poughkeepsie and White Plains, N.Y., 1962-74; sr. v.p. mgmt. systems Humana, Inc., Louisville, 1974-82; founder, pres. PDW, Inc., 1982-84; founder, chmn. bd., chief exec. officer Internat. Med. Exchange, 1984-87; founder Dewey Walker & Assocs., 1987—; mem. adv. com. First Profl. Bank Los Angeles; dir. Gateway Med. Systems, Inc., Atlanta; dir., chmn. compensation com. Kurfees Coatings, Inc., Louisville; lectr., speaker univs., nat. profl. soc. meetings. Pa. State v.p. Jaycees, 1957; chmn. Hire the Physically Handicapped, 1957, Fund for the Arts, Louisville, 1976; dir. Jr. Achievement; mem. athletic com. Ky. Country Day Sch.; mem. Louisville Schs. and Bus. Coordinating Council, 1979-80; mem. Leadership Louisville, 1979-80; com. vice chmn. Boy Scouts Am., 1981. Named a Disting. Alumni Pa. State U.; named one of 87 People to Watch in 1987 by Louisville Mag. Mem. Soc. Mgmt. Info. Systems, Am. Inst. Indsl. Engrs., Kappa Delta Rho. Presbyterian. Clubs: Penn State Alumni, Penn State of Ky., Nittany Lions, Pitts. Playhouse, N.Y. U., Harmony Landing Country, Jefferson (Louisville). Home: 1309 N Buckeye Ln Goshen KY 40026 Office: Internat Med Exch 9000 Wessex Pl Suite 201 Louisville KY 40222

WALKER, RAY STARKEY, coal company executive; b. Bigler, Pa., Mar. 13, 1912; s. Chester Arthur and Gertrude Elizabeth (Confer) W.; m. Louise A. Saupp, Mar. 11, 1940; children: James Chester, Charles Alan, Susan Louise, Lenore Anne. BA in Commerce and Fin., Pa. State U., 1935. Pres., founder Bradford Coal Co., Bigler, 1935-75, chief exec. officer, 1975-88; pres. Manor Mining and Contracting, Bigler, 1949-75, Laddie Coal & Mining Co., Scott County, Tenn., 1953-66; pres. C.A. Walker Lumber & Supply, Bigler, 1972-75, chief exec. officer, 1975-88; pres. Bradford-Am. Internat., Bigler, 1972-75; bd. dirs. Clearfield (Pa.) Bank & Trust Co. Mem. Rep. fin. com. for Pa., Harrisburg, 1980-88; exec. bd. mem. Bucktail council Boy Scouts Am., DuBois, Pa., 1955-75; chmn. troop com. Boy Scouts Am., Bigler, 1957-75. Recipient 1952 Pa. Week award Commonwealth of Pa., Silver Beaver award Boy Scouts Am., 1965. Mem. Pa. Soc., Am. Mining Congress, N.Y. Coal Trade. Club: Gateway Investment (DuBois). Lodge: Rotary. Office: Bradford Coal Co 1101 Main St PO Box 368 Bigler PA 16825

WALKER, RAYMOND FRANCIS, business and financial consulting company executive; b. Medicine Lake, Mont., Nov. 9, 1914; s. Dennis Owen and Rose (Long) W.; m. Patricia K. Blakey, May 15, 1951; children: Richard A., Mark D., Maxie R. Forest, Victoria L. Le Huray, Suzanne J. Buhl, Tracy A. Grad. pub. schs.; student, Edison Vocat. Sch., 1935-39. Truck mgr. Pacific Food Products, Seattle, 1939-42; machinist Todd Shipyard, Seattle, 1943-45; owner Delbridge Auto Sales, Seattle, 1945-48; pres. Pacific Coast Acceptance Corp., 1949-60; v.p. West Coast Mortgage, Seattle, 1960-67, United Equities Corp., Seattle, 1965-69; pres. Income Mgmt. Corp., Seattle, 1970—; v.p. Internat. Mint and Foundry, Redmond, Wash., 1983—; cons. Life Ins. Co. Am., Bellevue, Wash., 1982-87, Consumer Loan Service, Lynwood Wash., 1980—; dir., cons., v.p. fin. Am. Campgrounds, Bellevue, 1971-74; cons., bd. dirs. Straits Forest Products, Inc., Port Angeles, Wash. Mem. Nat. Assn. Security Dealers. Methodist. Lodge: Elks. Home: 777 W Sequim Bay Rd Sequim WA 98382

WALKER, RICHARD DAVID, pipeline executive; b. Sault Ste. Marie, Ont., Can., Feb. 21, 1932; s. Wilfred and Daisy Jane (Dale) W.; children: David, Richard, Michael, Gregory, Ann. BASc, U. Toronto, 1954; M in Advanced Mgmt. Program, Harvard U., 1979. With TransCan. Pipelines, Toronto, 1972—; v.p. ops. 1972-74, v.p. engring. and ops., 1974-77, v.p. gas transmission, 1977-80, sr. v.p. mktg., 1980-83, sr. v.p., chief operating officer pipelines, 1984-87; chief exec. officer IPEL KOPP Internat. Inc. (subs. TransCan Pipelines), 1987—. Fellow Inst. Gas Engrs.; mem. Can. Gas Assn. (chmn. 1987-88), Assn. Profl. Engrs. Ont., Inst. Engrs. Australia. Office: TransCan Pipelines Ltd, PO Box 54 Commerce Ct W, Toronto, ON Canada M5L 1C2

WALKER, RONALD F., corporate executive; b. Cin., Apr. 9, 1938; married. BBA, U. Cin., 1961. Vice pres. Kroger Co., Cin., 1962-72; with Am. Fin. Corp., Cin., 1972—, exec. v.p., 1978-84, pres., chief operating officer, dir., 1984—; exec. v.p. Gt. Am. Ins., Cin., 1972-80, pres., 1980—, vice chmn., 1986—; pres., chief operating officer, dir. United Brands Co., N.Y.C.; pres., chief operating officer Penn Cen. Corp., 1987—; also bd. dirs.; bd. dirs. United Brands, Cin., Am. Fin. Enterprises, Cin., Sprague Techs., Inc., Gt. Am. Communications Co., Republic Am. Corp. Office: Gt Am Ins Co PO Box 2575 Cincinnati OH 45201 also: Am Fin Corp 1 E 4th St Cincinnati OH 45202

WALKER, SALLY BARBARA, glass company executive; b. Bellerose, N.Y., Nov. 21, 1921; d. Lambert Roger and Edith Demerest (Parkhouse) W.; diploma Cathedral Sch. St. Mary, 1939; A.A., Finch Jr. Coll., 1941. Tchr. interior design Finch Coll., 1941-42; draftsman AT&T, 1942-43; with Steuben Glass Co., N.Y.C., 1943—, exec. v.p., 1959-62, exec. v.p. ops., 1962-78, exec. v.p. ops. and sales, 1978-83, exec. v.p., 1983—. Mem. Fifth Ave. Assn. Republican. Episcopalian. Clubs: Rockaway Hunting, Lawrence Beach, U.S. Lawn Tennis, Colony, English-Speaking Union. Home: 116 E 66th St New York NY 10021 Office: 715 Fifth Ave New York NY 10022

WALKER, THERESE MAUREEN, mortgage banking executive; b. Hawthorne, Calif., July 27, 1951. BBA, Portland State U., 1973, MBA, 1981. Project liason student housing rsch. study Portland State U. and Oreg. State Bd. Higher Edn., 1973-75; credit and collection mgr. Securities-Intermountain, Inc., Portland, 1976-80; asst. v.p., income property loan officer First Security Realty Services (West), Portland, 1981-84; v.p., mgr. CrossLand Mortgage Corp., Lake Oswego, Oreg., 1985—. Mem. credit com. Securities-Intermountain, Inc. Fed. Credit Union, 1982-83, chmn. credit com., 1984, pres., 1985; vol. Oreg. Rep. Party, 1983-84; vol. ann. fund dr. Portland State U. Found., 1986, campaign co-chmn., 1987-88. Mem. Portland C. of C., Oreg. Mortgage Bankers Assn. Am., Portland State U. Alumni Assn., Nat. Assn. Indsl. and Office Pks., Internat. Club, Griffith Pk. Athletic Club. Republican. Episcopalian. Office: CrossLand Mortgage Corp 5285 SW Meadows Rd Ste 296 Lake Oswego OR 97035

WALKER, THOMAS COLE, telephone company executive; b. Indpls., Sept. 14, 1929; s. Frank Dilling and Dorothy Mae (Cole) W.; m. Dorothy Henson, June 15, 1952; children: David, Karen, Michael, Linda. B.A. in Econs., DePauw U., 1951. Various ops. positions Ind. Bell Telephone Co., Indpls., 1951-74, v.p. mktg., rates and revenue requirements, 1974-78, v.p. bus., 1978-80, v.p., chief fin. officer, 1980-83, exec. v.p., chief fin. officer, 1983—; dir. Ind. Bell Telephone Co., Indpls; bd. dirs. Associated Ins. Cos. (formerly Blue Cross-Blue Shield), Indpls., Bison Money Market Fund, Indpls. Mem. Greater Indpls. Community Health Initiative, 1983; bd. dirs. 500 Festival Assocs. Mem. Fin. Execs. Inst., Econ. Club Indpls., Indpls. C. of C., Salvation Army (adv. bd). Methodist. Clubs: Indpls. Athletic, Columbia, Skyline. Lodge: Rotary. Office: Ind Bell Telephone Co Inc 240 N Meridan St Indianapolis IN 46204

WALKER, WALTER WAYNE, retail management executive; b. Rosiclare, Ill., Dec. 27, 1938; s. Walter Perkins W. and Rachel (Denton) Scott; m. Marilyn Janice Ashford, Feb. 13, 1960; children: Kimberly Kay, Mark Wayne. BS, So. Ill. U., 1960. Mgr. office and credit Firestone Tire & Rubber Co., Kokomo, Ind., 1960-61; coord. mdse. Interstate Dept. Stores, N.Y.C. and Evansville, Ind., 1961-74; pres., chief exec. officer S.W. Anderson Co., Inc., Owensboro, Ky., 1974—. Pacesetter chmn., bd. dirs. United Way Owensboro, 1978-82; pres., bd. dirs. Downtown Owensboro, Inc., 1979—. Named to Alumni Hall Fame Coll. Bus. Adminstrn. So. Ill. U., 1988. Mem. Nat. Retail Mchts. Assn., Ky. C. of C., Owensboro C. of C., Nat. Fedn. Ind. Bus., Ky. Retail Fedn. (bd. dirs. 1985—), Downtown Bus. and Profl. Assn. (past pres., bd. dirs.), Masons, Shriners, Lions. Republican. Presbyterian. Home: 2221 Sheffield Ct Owensboro KY 42301 Office: SW Anderson Co Inc 122 E 2d St Owensboro KY 42301

WALKER, WELMON (RUSTY), JR., publisher, consultant; b. Chgo., Dec. 28, 1947; s. Welmon Sr. and Mary Ann (Befford) W.; m. Nedra Kay Carlson, Dec. 30, 1972; children: Welmon III, Whitney O. Student, U. Alaska, 1970-74; AA, Tanana Valley Community Coll., 1984; BS, U. of the State of N.Y., 1985. Gen. mgr. Sta. KMPS (name now Sta. KSUA-FM), Fairbanks, Alaska, 1971-74; duty dir. Sta. KUAC-TV, Fairbanks, 1973-74; staff photographer Sta. KFAR-TV, Fairbanks, 1974-75; bus. mgr. Nat. Painting Corp., Fairbanks, 1975-76; instr. Fairbanks Native Assn., 1975-76; asst. mgr. Wometco-Lathrop Co., Fairbanks, 1978-79; pres. That New Pub. Co., Fairbanks, 1977—, pub. seminar dir., 1986-88; instr. U. Alaska, Fairbanks, 1979-80. Author: Alaska Corp Manual, 1977, Publishing Manual, 1987; contbr. articles to profl. jours. Dir. Lost Lake Camp, Midnight Sun Council Boy Scouts Am., 1986-87, bd. dirs., 1978—; pres., bd. dirs. Fairbanks Youth Svcs., Inc., 1979—; dir. Bapt. Tng. Union, St. John Bapt. Ch., Fairbanks, 1969; student affairs chmn. univ. assembly U. Alaska, 1971-74. With U.S. Army, 1968-70. Mem. Com. Small Mag. Editors and Publishers, Star Fleet Club (lt. comdr. 1983—). Office: That New Pub Co 1525 Eielson St Fairbanks AK 99701

WALKER, WENDY DIANA KNIGHT, insurance company specialist; b. Elizabeth, N.J., Nov. 11, 1961; d. William Henry Jr. and Catherine Lillian (Fulton) Knight; m. George Russell Walker, Jr., Oct. 25, 1986. Student, U. Warwick, Eng., 1981-82; BA, Duke U., 1983. Lic. real estate agent. Underwriter Chubb & Son, Inc., N.Y.C., 1983-86; sr. underwriter Atlantic Mut. Ins. Cos., N.Y.C., 1986-87, producer specialist, 1987-88, underwriting supr., 1988; asst. brokerage mgr. Continental Ins. Cos. Nat. Brokerage Svcs. div., N.Y.C., 1988—; tchr. internship program Howard U., N.Y.C., 1986. Active St. John's Choir. Mem. Nat. Assn. Realtors, Assn. Profl. Ins. Women, NAFE, Oranges/Maplewood Bd. Realtors. Democrat. Episcopalian. Home: 486 Valley Rd West Orange NJ 07052 Office: The Continental Corp 180 Maiden Ln New York NY 10038

WALKER, WILLIAM JAMES, corporate executive, controller; b. Farmersville, Tex., Jan. 11, 1935; s. William James and Beatrice (Kelly) W.; m. Janet Ivy Burton, Oct. 6, 1972; 1 child, H. Michael. BS in Bus., Stetson U., 1957; MBA, Syracuse U., 1971. CPA, Fla. Ptnr. Cochrane & Co., CPA's, Palm Beach, Fla., 1957-65; commd. 2d lt. U.S. Army, various locations, 1965, advanced through grades to lt. col., controller career program, 1968; served with res. U.S. Army, 1957-64, 75-85, on active duty, 1965-75, retired, 1985; div. adminstr. Arabian Am. Oil Co., Houston and Dhahran, Saudi Arabia, 1975-84; controller Gen. Dynamics, Abilene, Tex., 1984-87; v.p., gen. mgr. Hughes Aircraft Ms Inc., Forest, Miss., 1987—; sec., treas. Art Internat., Inc., Jackson, Miss. and Houston, 1979-84. Contbr. articles to profl. jours. Chmn. Fiesta del Sol, Lake Worth, Fla., 1960. Recipient Key Man award Fla. Jr. C. of C., 1962-63. Republican. Episcopalian. Lodge: Rotary. Home: 57 Oak Crest Brandon MS 39042 Office: Hughes Aircraft Ms Inc Rural Rt 5 Box 9 Forest MS 39074

WALL, BRIAN RAYMOND, forest economist, policy analyst, consultant; b. Tacoma, Wash., Jan. 26, 1940; s. Raymond Perry and Mildred Beryl (Pickert) W.; m. Joan Marie Nero, Sept. 1, 1962; children: Torden Erik, Kirsten Noel. BS, U. Wash., 1962; MF, Yale U., 1964. Forestry asst. Weyerhaeuser Timber Co., Klamath Falls, Oreg., 1960; inventory forester West Tacoma Newsprint, 1961-62; timber sale compliance forester Dept. Nat. Resources, Kelso, Wash., 1963; rsch. forest economist Pacific N.W. Rsch. Sta., USDA Forest Svc., Portland, Oreg., 1964-88, cons. 1989—; co-founder, bd. dirs. Cordero Youth Care Ctr., 1970-81; owner Brian R. Wall Images and Communications; cons. to govt. agys., Congress univs., industry; freelance photographer. Co-author: An Analysis of the Timber Situation in the United States, 1982; contbr. articles, reports to profl. publs., newspapers. Interviewed and cited by nat. and regional news media. Recipient Cert. of Merit U.S. Dept. Agr. Forest Service, 1982. Mem. Soc. Am. Foresters (chmn. Portland chpt. 1973, Forester of Yr. 1975), Conf. of Western Forest Economists Inc. (founder, bd. dirs. 1988—, treas. 1982-87), Portland Photographic Forum, Zeta Psi. Home and Office: 7155 SW Alden St Portland OR 97223

WALL, EDWARD MILLARD, environmental consulting executive; b. Newburyport, Mass., Dec. 17, 1929; s. Millard Edward and Edith Noyes (Carter) W.; m. Jean Titus, Jan. 27, 1951; children: Karen, Kenneth, Kathryn. BSME, Tufts U., 1951; MBA, Xavier U., 1962. Tech. service engr. Goodyear Tire, Akron, Ohio, 1951-53; mgr. engine test facilities Gen. Electric, Cin., 1956-62; mgr. mfg. Williams Mfg., Portsmouth, Ohio, 1962-74; sr. project mgr. N-Ren Corp., Cin., 1975-78; v.p. mfg. Nelson Electric, Tulsa, 1979-88; chief exec. officer Techrad Environ. Services, Oklahoma City, 1988—, also chmn. bd. dirs. Mem. Vo-Tech Edn. Adv. Com., Tulsa, 1982-88. Lt.(j.g.) USNR, 1953-56. Mem. Am. Prodn. and Inventory Control Soc. (cert.), ASME, Am. Mgmt. Assn. Republican. Presbyterian. Lodges: Rotary, Masons. Home: 9017 E 68 St Tulsa OK 74133 Office: Techrad Environ Svcs Inc 4619 N Santa Fe Oklahoma City OK 73118

WALL, M. DANNY, federal agency administrator. BArch, N.D. State U., 1963. Exec. dir. Urban Renewal Agy., Fargo, N.D., 1964-71, Salt Lake City Redevel. Agy., 1971-75; dir. legis. Office U.S. Senator Jake Garn, Washington, 1975-78; minority staff dir. Senate Com. for Banking, Housing and Urban Affairs, Washington, 1979-80, staff dir., 1980-86, Rep. staff dir., 1987; chmn. Fed. Home Loan Bank Bd., Washington, 1987—. Office: Fed Home Loan Bank Bd 1700 G St NW Washington DC 20552 *

WALL, MARK EMANUEL, banker, engineer, consultant; b. N.Y.C., Mar. 12, 1937; s. Jacob Bernard and Eva (Goldstein) W.; m. Diane Nachbar, Dec. 15, 1962; children—Michael Edward, Stephen Philip. BEE cum laude, City Colls.-N.Y., 1957; M. Engring., Moore Sch., 1962; postgrad. N.Y.U., 1962-68. Registered profl. engr., N.J., N.Y. With tech. staff RCA Labs., Astro-Elec. Div., Princeton, N.J., 1957-62; dir. research and devel. Computer Scis. Corp., Paramus, N.J., 1962-75; pres. Tech. Fin. Services, Fair Lawn, N.J., 1975-80; dir. digital systems Western Union Telegraph Co., Upper Saddle River, N.J., 1977-81; v.p. Chase Manhattan Bank N.A., N.Y.C., 1981-87, sci. and tech. Nynex Corp., White Plains, N.Y., 1987—; vis. assoc. prof. Stevens Inst. Tech., Hoboken, N.J., 1979-81; adv. bd. Bramson ORT Inst., N.Y.C., 1980-84. Contbr. articles on engineering to jours. Trustee Radburn Assn., Fair Lawn, 1981-85, pres. bd. trustees, 1985. Mem. IEEE, Eta Kappa Nu. Office: Nynex Corp 500 Westchester Ave White Plains NY 10604

WALL, SONJA ELOISE, nurse, nursing service company executive; b. Santa Cruz, Calif., Mar. 28, 1938; d. Ray Theothornton and Reva Mattie (Wingo) W.; m. Edward Gleason Holmes, Aug. 1959 (div. Jan. 1968); children: Deborah Lynn, Lance Edward; m. John Aspesi, Sept. 1969 (div. 1977); children: Sabrina Jean, Daniel John; m. Kenneth Talbot LaBoube, Nov. 1, 1978; 1 child, Tiffany Amber. BA, San Jose Jr. Coll., 1959; BS, Madonna Coll., 1967; studnet, U. Mich., 1968-70. RN, Calif., Mich., Colo. Staff nurse Santa Clara Valley Med. Ctr., San Jose, Calif., 1959-67, U. Mich. Hosp., Ann Arbor, 1967-73, Porter and Swedish Med. hosp., Denver, 1973-77, Laurel Grove Hosp., Castro Valley, Calif., 1977-79, Advent Hosp., Ukiah, Calif., 1984-86; motel owner LaBoube Enterprises, Fairfield, Point Arena, Willits, Calif., 1979—; staff nurse Northridge Hosp., L.A., 1986-87, Folsom State Prison, Calif., 1987; co-owner, mgr. nursing registry Around the Clock Nursing Svc., Ukiah, 1985—; RN Kaiser Permanente Hosp., Sacramento, 1986—. Contbr. articles to various publs. Asst. leader Coloma 4-H, 1987, 88. Mem. Am. Heart Assn. (CPR trainer, recipient awards), Am. Assn. Critical Care Nurses, Calif. Bd. RNs, Calif. Nursing Rev., Calif. Critical Care Nurses, Am. Motel Assn. (beautification and remodeling award 1985), Am. Miniature Horse Assn. (winner nat. grand championship 1981, 82, 83), Cameron Park Country Club. Republican. Episcopalian. Home and Office: Around the Clock Nursing Svc PO Box 543 Coloma CA 95613

WALL, STEPHEN JAMES, management consultant; b. Wallasy, U.K., Aug. 25, 1947; came to U.S., 1955, naturalized, 1966; s. John and Margaret M. (Dixon) W.; B.A., SUNY, 1969; M.A. in Psychology, U. Akron, 1971; M.A. in Indsl./Organizational Psychology, N.Y. U., 1980; m. Margaret Mary King, Aug. 26, 1978; 1 child, Alissa Gabrielle. With Human Resources Lab., AT&T, N.Y.C., 1972-73, personnel supr., mgmt. selection and devel. research, 1973-75; profl. devel. assoc. Union Carbide Corp., N.Y.C., 1975-76, mgr. profl. devel., 1976-77, dir. corp. mgmt. devel., 1977-82, dir. employee relations and adminstrn., 1983-84; pres. Manus Assocs., N.Y.C., 1985—. Mem. Ctr. Creative Leadership (editorial rev. bd.). Contbr. articles to profl. jours. Home: 1465 E Putnam Ave #633 Old Greenwich CT 06870 Office: 175 Fifth Ave Ste 712 New York NY 10010

WALL, WILLIAM J., insurance executive; b. Bklyn., May 17, 1940; s. William John and Dorothy (O'Meara) W.; m. Mary Ann Sgrignvoli, Oct. 10, 1970; children: William, Rosemary. BA, Cathedral Coll., 1961; STB, Cath. U., 1965; JD, Bklyn. Coll., 1974. Bar: N.Y., 1974. Atty. Wilson Elser Edelman & Dicker, N.Y.C., 1975-79; pres. Atlanta Group, Inc., 1979-86; exec. v.p. Shand, Morahan & Co., Evanston, Ill., 1986—. Mem. N.Y.C. Bar Assn. Democrat. Roman Catholic. Clubs: North Shore Country (Glenview, Ill.), Dunwoody Country (Ga.). Office: Shand Morahan & Co Inc Shand Morahan Pl Evanston IL 60201

WALLACE, DAVID WILLIAM, financial executive; b. N.Y.C., Feb. 23, 1924; s. Fergus Ferguson and Isabelle Taylor (Wilson) W.; m. Jean Ives McLean, June 20, 1953; children: Mary H., Anne S. BS, Yale U., 1948; JD, Harvard U., 1951. Bar: N.Y. 1952, U.S. Supreme Ct. 1976. Assoc. White & Case, N.Y.C., 1951-54; gen. counsel Alleghany Corp., 1954, sec.-treas., 1954-56, v.p., 1956-58, exec. v.p., 1958-59; exec. v.p. chmn. exec. com. United Brands Corp., until 1967; dir., pres. Bangor Punta Corp., 1967-84, chief exec. officer, 1969-84, chmn. bd., 1973-84; chmn. bd., chief exec. officer Todd Shipyards, 1987—; chmn. bd. Nat. Securities & Rsch. Corp., 1988—; mem. Lloyds of London, 1975—; chmn. bd. FECO Engring. Systems, Nat. Securities & Rsch. Corp; dir., mem. exec. com., chmn. audit com. Lone Star Industries, Inc.; bd. dirs. Emigrant Savs. Bank, BV Capital Corp., UMC Electronics Co., Hoover Group Inc., Zurn Industries, Putnam Trust Co. Pres., trustee Robert R. Young Found.; bd. govs. N.Y. Hosp.; vice chmn. bd. trustees, mem. pres.'s com. Smith Coll. 1st lt., inf. U.S. Army, 1943-46. Mem. St. Andrew's Soc. N.Y., Brook Club, Yale Club, Econ. Club, Greenwich Country Club, Sky Club. Presbyterian. Home: Deer Park Greenwich CT 06830 Office: 2 Greenwich Pla Ste 100 Greenwich CT 06830

WALLACE, GARY CHRISTOPHER, accountant; b. Kansas City, Mo., May 31, 1954; s. Sherman Thomas and Elizabeth (Larsen) W.; m. Deborah Lynn Hallen, Sept. 6, 1975; children: Ryan, Elizabeth, Alexander, Andrew. BBA, Calif. State U., 1975. CPA, Calif. Ptnr. Peat Marwick Main & Co., Oakland, Calif., 1975—, KPMG Peat Marwick, N.Y.C. Bd. dirs. Calif. State Affiliates, Hayward. Mem. AICPA, Nat. Assn. Accts., Nat. Vehicle Leasers Assn., Nat. Soc. Accts. for Coops., Golden Gate Retail Fin. Execs., Blackhawk Club, Delta Sigma Phi, Beta Alpha Psi. Democrat. Presbyterian. Home: 3430 Silver Maple Dr Danville CA 94526 Office: Peat Marwick Main & Co One Kaiser Pla Oakland CA 94612

WALLACE, JOHN T., marketing professional, industrial motion control systems executive; b. Waterbury, Conn., Mar. 19, 1941; s. William Joseph and Eva (Talbot) W.; m. Jean M. Rosenbeck, Oct. 6, 1962; children: Michael, Peter, David, Brian. ASET, U. Hartford, 1962; student, Boston Coll., U. Conn., N.H. Coll., 1980. Mgr. customer svc., sales engr. Gen. Time Corp., Torrington, Conn., 1962-69; mgr. product mktg. Superior Elec. Co., Bristol, Conn., 1969-81; v.p. sales and mktg. B&B Motor & Control Corp., L.I., N.Y., 1981—; instr. Waterbury State Tech. Coll., 1985—. Author: Design Engineering Guide to Stepping Motors, 1979, Home Fire Safety, 1981. Mem. Bd. Police Study, Harwinton, 1984-86; mem., driver Harwinton Ambulance Assn., 1984—; chief Torringford Vol. Fire Dept., 1968-78, chmn., commr., 1978-82. Mem. Electronic Industries Assn., Robbins & Myers Distbr. Council. Office: B&B Motor & Control Corp 60 Apple Hill Commons Burlington CT 06013

WALLACE, KEITH G., mining company executive; b. 1926. BS, Stanford U., 1949. With Bradley Mining Co., 1950-56; asst. mgr., staff engr. Utah Internat. Inc., San Francisco, 1956-58, asst. to v.p., 1958-61, dir. mining services, 1961-66, mgr. ops., Blackwater, Australia, 1966-69, v.p., mgr. Australian ops., 1969-74, sr. v.p. Australian div., from 1974, now exec. v.p.; also pres. Utah Devel. Co. Served with USAF, 1944-45. Office: BHP-Utah Minerals Internat Inc 550 Califonia St San Francisco CA 94104 *

WALLACE, LEONARD OTTO, manufacturing company executive; b. Superior, Wis., Dec. 29, 1940; s. George W. and Agnes Olivia (Touve) W.; m. Kenni Caye, Oct. 30, 1959 (div. 1969); children: George, Wendy, Mindy. With Powertec Inc., Chatsworth, Calif., 1966-72; pres., co-founder Power-One Inc., Camarillo, Calif., 1972-79; pres., founder Condor D.C. Power Inc., Oxnard, Calif., 1979—.

WALLACE, MARTHA REDFIELD, management consultant; b. Omaha, Dec. 27, 1927; d. Ralph J. and Lois (Thompson) Redfield. BA, Wellesley Coll., 1949; MA in Internat. Fin., Tufts U., 1950; LittD (hon.), Converse Coll., 1975; LLD (hon.), Occidental Coll., 1975, Pace U., 1975, Manhattan Coll., 1977. Instr. in econs., asst. to dean Fletcher Sch. Econs., Tufts U., 1950-51; economist Dept. State, Washington, 1951-53; with RCA Internat., 1954-55; mem. editorial staff Fortune mag., 1955-57; with IBM, 1960-61; asst. dir. corp. devel. Time, Inc., 1963-67; dir., bd. dirs. Henry Luce Found., Inc., N.Y.C., 1967-83; pres. Redfield Assocs., N.Y.C., 1983—; bd. dirs. Am. Express Co., Bristol-Myers Co.; bd. dirs. N.Y. Stock Exchange, 1977-83, mem. surveillance com., 1985—; mem. Conf. Bd., 1974—, Nat. Com. on U.S.-China Relations, 1975—, Temporary Commn. on City Fins., 1975-77, Brit.-N.Am. Com., 1976—, Trilateral Commn., 1978-84; chmn., trustee Trust for Cultural Resources of City N.Y., 1977-81; mem. Adv. Com. on Adminstrn. of Justice, 1981-82; mem. social services vis. com. dept. polit. sci. MIT, 1986-88; mem. vis. com. dept. social scis. U. Chgo., 1980-84; treas. Nat. Com. for United States-China Relations, 1987—; mem. adv. com. Fletcher Sch. Law and Diplomacy, Tufts U.; mem. Sr. Bus. Adv. Council, Pres.'s Council and Adv. Group. Trustee Williams Coll., 1974-86, trustee emeritus, 1986—, citizens budget commn., 1976—, Internat. House, Greater N.Y. Councils, Boy Scouts Am.; bd. dirs. Am. Council on Germany, Greater N.Y. Fund/United Way, 1974-86, Legal Aid Soc., Regional Plan Assn., 1985-88, Citizens Crime Commn. N.Y.C., Inc., 1983—, N.Y.C. Partnership, 1980-85, Council Fgn. Relations, Inc., 1972-82; chmn. N.Y. Rhodes Scholars Selection Com., 1983-86, membership council Whitney Mus.; mem. Bretton Woods Com., 1987; bd. visitors Fletcher Sch. Law and Diplomacy, 1987—, mem. Wilson Council of Wilson Ctr., Washington. Wellesley Coll. Durant scholar, 1949. Mem. Am. Judicature Soc. (bd. dirs. 1978—, v.p., exec. com. 1978-81, chmn. 1981-83), Council on Founds. (bd. dirs. 1971-77), Found. Ctr. (bd. dirs. 1971-77), Japan Soc. (bd. dirs. 1975—, chmn. 75th Anniversary Fund 1982-83), Am. Council on Germany (bd. dirs. 1980—), World Resources Inst., Asia Soc. (mem. pres.'s council, mem. Asian agenda adv. group), N.Y. Racing Assn. (bd. dirs. 1976—), Acad. Polit. Scis., Saratoga Reading Rooms, Inc., Fairbank Ctr. for East Asian Studies, Phi Beta Kappa Assocs., Phi Beta Kappa. Clubs: River, Bd. Room, Economic, Wellesley. Home and Office: 435 E 52d St New York NY 10022

WALLACE, MARY ANN, development company executive; b. Reno County, Kans., Feb. 19, 1939; d. Ivan Lewis and Vina Sue (Smith) Newell; m. Alexander Wallace III, Feb. 17, 1968 (div. June 1982); 1 child, Alexander IV. BS, Wichita State U., 1961. Property mgr. 650 S. Grand Bldg. Co., Los Angeles, 1961-68; v.p. Milner Devel., Santa Monica, Calif., 1981-83; chief fin. officer Milner Devel., Los Angeles, 1983—; cons. Kitty Prodns., Los Angeles, 1978—; cons., v.p. Am. Mut. Prodns., Redlands, Calif., 1975—. V.p. Sister Servants of Mary Guild, Los Angeles, 1970-77; treas. Hosp. of Good Samaritan Aux., Los Angeles, 1969-75; press sec. Orphanage Guild Jrs., Los Angeles, 1974. Named Downtown Working Angel, Downtown Businessmen's Assn., Best Fund Raiser, Sister Servants of Mary Guild, 1974-76. Mem. Los Angeles World Affairs Council, Los Angeles Women in Bus., Nat. Art Assn. Republican. Roman Catholic. Club: Los Angeles Country (Beverly Hills, Calif.).

WALLACE, MATTHEW WALKER, entrepreneur; b. Salt Lake City, Jan. 7, 1924; s. John McChrystal and Glenn (Walker) W.; m. Constance Cone, June 22, 1954 (dec. May 1980); children—Matthew, Anne; m. Susan Struggles, July 11, 1981. B.A., Stanford U., 1947; M.C.P., MIT, 1950. Prin. planner Boston City Planning Bd., 1950-53; v.p. Nat. Planning and Research, Inc., Boston, 1953-55; pres. Wallace-McConaughy Corp., Salt Lake City, 1955-69; pres. Ariz. Ranch & Metals Co., Salt Lake City, 1969-84; chmn. Wallace Assocs., Inc., Salt Lake City, 1969—; dir. 1st Interstate Bank, Salt Lake City, 1956—, dir. Arnold Machinery Co., 1988—, dir. Roosevelt Hot Springs Corp., 1978—; mem. adv. bd. Mountain Bell Telephone Co., Salt Lake City, 1975-85. Pres., Downtown Planning Assn., Salt Lake City, 1970; chmn. Utah State Arts Council, Salt Lake City, 1977; mem. Humanities and Scis. Council, Stanford U., also mem. athletic bd.; mem. nat. adv. bd. Coll. Bus., U. Utah; chmn. endowment com. Utah Symphony Orch. Lt. (j.g.) USN, 1944-46; PTO. Recipient Contbn. award Downtown Planning Assn., 1977. Mem. Am. Inst. Cert. Planners (charter), Alta Club (dir.), Cottonwood Club (pres. 1959-63), Salt Lake Country Club (dir.) Club, Masons, Phi Kappa Phi. Home: 2510 Walker Ln Salt Lake City UT 84117 Office: Wallace Assocs Inc 165 S Main St Salt Lake City UT 84111

WALLACE, MINOR GORDON, JR., architect, landscape architect, mayor; b. Texarkana, Tex., Oct. 30, 1936; s. Minor Gordon and Dessie (Bledsoe) W.; children: Rayma, Minor Gordon III. BA, U. Ark., 1961, BArch., 1961. Project architect Bruce R. Anderson, Architect, Little Rock, 1964-67; univ. architect U. Ark., Fayetteville, 1968—; prin. Minor G. Wallace, Jr., Architect, 1969—, Wallace & Estes, Architects, Fayetteville, 1978-80; dir. facilities planning and constrn. U. Ark. System, Fayetteville, 1968-81, dir. facilities planning, 1981-84, asst. v.p. facilities planning, 1984—; cons. ednl. planning, architecture. Alderman, City of Prairie Grove, (Ark.), 1981-83, mayor, 1983-86; chmn. bd. dirs. Northwest Ark. Arts and Crafts Guild, 1977-79; bd. dirs. Northwest Ark. Cultural Center, 1978—, acting pres., 1981-84, pres., 1984—; pres. D & W Devel. Co., Inc., 1985—; ptnr. Country Inn Restaurants and Antiques, 1985—. Campus landscaping Pine Bluff and Fayetteville campuses U. Ark., 1977-78, indoor tennis ctr., Fayetteville campus, 1979-80, also botany greenhouse and sports arena, Ch. for Fayetteville Christian Fellowship, 1987. Mem. AIA, Am. Soc. Landscape Architects, Council Ednl. Planners, Soc. Coll. and Univ. Planning, Nat. Trust Hist. Preservation, Assn. Univ. Architects, Am. Planning Assn. Democrat. Unitarian. Home: PO Box 586 Prairie Grove AR 72753 Office: PO Box 1384 Fayetteville AR 72702

WALLACE, ROANNE, hosiery company executive; b. Greenwood, Miss., Dec. 18, 1949; d. Robert Carter and Lois Anne (Vick) W. BM, U. Tenn., 1971; MA, U. N.C., 1976; MBA, Wake Forest U., 1982. Exec. dir. Am. Bd. Clin. Chemistry, Winston-Salem, N.C., 1977-78; administrv. officer Winston-Salem/Forsyth County Office Emergency Mgmt., 1978-79, sr. asst. dir., 1979-82; with L'eggs Products, Inc. div. Sara Lee, Winston-Salem, 1982—, product mgr., 1986-88, mktg. dir., 1988—. Mem. adv. coun. Winston-Salem/Forsyth County Office of Emergency Mgmt. Mem. Am. Mgmt. Assn., Winston-Salem Sales and Mktg. Execs. Home: 803 Devon Ct Winston-Salem NC 27104 Office: L'eggs Products Inc PO Box 2495 Winston-Salem NC 27102

WALLACE, ROBERT FERGUS, banker; b. Bklyn., Oct. 5, 1934; s. Fergus F. and Isabelle (Wilson) W.; m. Florence Faminow, Dec. 18, 1959; children: Douglas, Barbara. BA, Colgate U., 1956. Comml. loan officer Chem. Bank, N.Y.C., 1956-68; chmn. First Interstate Bank, Portland, Oreg., 1968-81; pres. Nat. Westminster Bank U.S.A., N.Y.C., 1982—. Bd. dirs. N.Y.C. Opera Co., 1986—. Served to lt. USN, 1957-60. Mem. Assn. Res. City Banks, Downtown-Lower Manhattan Assn. (treas. 1988). Republican. Presbyterian. Club: Econ. of N.Y. Office: Nat Westminster Bank USA 175 Water St New York NY 10038

WALLACE, ROBERT GEORGE, retired construction company executive, civil engineer; b. Flagstaff, Ariz., Apr. 30, 1928; s. William Robert Francis and Maeclaire (Wright) W.; m. Gloria Mae Reid, Oct. 29, 1960. B.S.C.E., U. Ariz., Tucson, 1953. Registered profl. civil engr. Pres. Wallace & Royden Equipment Co., Phoenix, 1956-67; v.p. Royden Constrn. Co., Phoenix, 1953-67; v.p. The Tanner Cos., Phoenix, 1967-81, exec. v.p., 1971-82, pres., 1982-88, also dir.; bd. dirs. Assn. Gen. Contractors, 1973-80, The Road Info. Program, 1978-82, The Beavers, 1982—, Western Force, 1972-78, Kasler Corp. Served with USN, 1946-48; PTO. Recipient award of Disting. Service Ariz. Assoc. Gen. Contractors, 1967; Disting. Citizen award U. Ariz. Engring. Coll., 1983. Mem. Rancho Santa Fe Country Club, Plaza Club (Phoenix), Masons (32nd degree). Republican. Episcopalian. Home: 17461 Avenida De Acacias PO Box 494 Rancho Santa Fe CA 92067

WALLACE, ROBERT GLENN, petroleum company executive; b. Webb City, Okla., Oct. 8, 1926; s. Glenn McKinsey and Sarah Elizabeth Wallace; m. Kelmor Wallace, Oct. 9, 1954; 1 child, John. B.S.Ch.E., Tex. A&M U., 1950; grad., Advanced Mgmt. Program, Harvard U.-U. Hawaii, 1972. Registered profl. engr., Okla. Mgr. internat. sales and devel. Phillips Petroleum Co., 1970-71; pres. Sealright Co., Inc., Kansas City, Mo., 1972-73; v.p. plastics Phillips Petroleum Co., Bartlesville, Okla., 1974-78; sr. v.p. Phillips Petroleum Co., 1978-80, exec. v.p., 1980-88; pres. Phillips 66 Co., ret. 1988; cons. IBM, 1988—, ChemShare, 1988—; dir. Phillips Chem Co., CBI Industries, Inc., Valmont Industries Inc. Devel. council Tex. A.&M. Coll. Bus. Adminstrn., Tex. A&M Coll. Engring. Served with USNR, 1944-46. Mem. Am. Petroleum Inst., 25 Yr. Club of Petroleum Industry, Ctr. for Free Enterprise. Republican. Home: 1912 Polaris Dr Bartlesville OK 74006 Office: Price Tower Annex Bartlesville OK 74004

WALLACE, ROBERT POPE, investment company executive, lawyer; b. Dallas, Oct. 15, 1925; s. William Farrier and Mary Ethel (Pope) W.; m. Anne Drought, Nov. 7, 1953; children: Anne Farrier Wallace Morris, David Richard. AA, Schreiner Inst., 1943; LLB, U. Tex., Austin, 1948; postdoctoral, U. Pa., 1952; cert. in banking, Rutgers U., 1958. Bar: Tex., U.S. Supreme Ct. Pres. United Savs. Assn., Corpus Christi, Tex., 1952-77, chmn. bd. dirs., 1977-80; pres. Fin. Life Ins., Houston, 1977-81; v.p. fin., dir. Southwestern Group Investors, Houston, 1977-81; chmn. bd. dirs. South Tex. Pub. Broadcasting, Corpus Christi, 1980-87; gen. ptnr. Gen. Trading Co. Ltd., Corpus Christi, 1981—. Author: The Bank Officer As Director of Customer Corporations, 1958, Higher Education in South Texas: The Next Twenty Five Years, 1963. Chmn. United Way, Corpus Christi, 1954, Corpus Christi Symphony, 1953-55, Art Mus. South Tex., Corpus Christi, 1958-60, 72-74, Corpus Christi Guidance Ctr. With USAAF, 1943-45, with USNR, 1943—. Mem. Tex. Bar Assn. Episcopalian. Clubs: Corpus Christi Yacht, Corpus Christi Country; Corpus Christi Town, The Argyle, San Antonio Country. Home: 4442 Ocean Dr Corpus Christi TX 78412 Office: Gen Trading Co Ltd PO Box 416 Corpus Christi TX 78403

WALLACE, ROBERT THOMAS, coal industry executive; b. N.Y.C., Aug. 13, 1932; s. George Dudley and Frances (Rienecker) W.; m. Mildred Murphy, Dec. 26, 1959; children: Jonathan, Matthew, Joseph, Robert. BS in Commerce, U. Notre Dame, 1954; PMD, Harvard U., 1961. Mgr. contracts planning RCA Def. Systems, Morristown, N.J., 1957-67; dir. mktg. ops. Computer Scis. Corp., Falls Church, Va., 1967-73; v.p. mng. dir. Computer Scis. Corp., Tehran, Iran, 1977; sr. mgmt. assoc. U.S. Office Mgmt. and Budget, Washington, 1973-74; dep. under sec. HUD, Washington, 1974-77; v.p. corp. planning Peabody Coal Co., St. Louis, 1977-82, Peabody Holding Co., Inc., St. Louis, 1983-84, 1984-88, sr. v.p. corp. devel., 1988—; bd. dirs. Peabody Australia, Ltd., Brisbane, Peabody Coal U.K., Ltd., London, Midco Supply & Equipment, St. Louis, Mid-Continent Barge Lines Inc., St. Louis. Trustee St. Louis Art Mus., St. Louis, 1987—. 1st lt. USAF, 1955-57. Republican. Roman Catholic. Office: Peabody Holding Co Inc 301 N Memorial Dr Saint Louis MO 63102

WALLACE, WILLIAM FARRIER, JR., lawyer, banker; b. Dallas, Apr. 2, 1918; s. William Farrier and Mary Ethel (Pope) W.; m. Ruth Saunders, Aug. 2, 1956. Student U. Tex., 1935-41. Bar: Tex. 1941. Sole practice, Corpus Christi, Tex., 1941, 44—; chmn. bd. dirs. First State Bank, Bishop, Tex., 1964—; pres. WONDOB, Corpus Christi, 1965—. Founder, chmn. bd. dirs. Exec. Audial Rehab. Soc., Corpus Christi, 1966—. Served to 2d lt. AUS, 1941-44. Named Handicapped Texan of Yr., 1961; recipient Pres.'s Citation for Aid to Handicapped, 1961. Mem. Tex. Bar Assn., Corpus Christi C. of C., Tex. Bankers Assn., Independent Bankers Assn. Tex., Tex. Assn. Bank Counsel (charter mem.), Southwest Legal Found. Oil and Gas Inst. (founding mem.). Episcopalian. Clubs: Corpus Christi Town, Corpus Christi Country, Dallas Petroleum. Lodge: Rotary. Home: 4767 Ocean Dr Corpus Christi TX 78412 Office: 500 American Bank Tower Corpus Christi TX 78403

WALLACE, WILLIAM RAY, fabricated steel manufacturing company executive; b. Shreveport, La., Mar. 25, 1923; s. Jason Mohoney and Mattie Evelyn (Adair) W.; m. Minyone Milligan Rose, Oct. 5, 1966; children: Jayne Cecile Rose McDearman, Susan Rose O'Brien, H. Robert Rose; children by previous marriage: Patrick Scott, Michael B., Timothy, Shelly. BS in Engring., La. Tech., 1944. Field engr. Austin Bridge Co., Dallas, 1944-45; core analyst Core Labs., Bakersfield, Calif., 1945-46; chief engr., then sec.-treas., exec. v.p. Trinity Industries, Inc., Dallas, 1946-58, pres., chief exec. officer, 1958—, also bd. dirs.; bd. dirs. Lomas & Nettleton Fin. Corp., Tex. Employers Ins. Assn., ENSERCH Corp. Methodist. Office: Trinity Industries Inc 2525 Stemmons Frwy PO Box 10587 Dallas TX 75207

WALLACH, PHILIP, real estate development executive; b. N.Y.C., May 29, 1928; s. Morris and Lillian (Levy) W.; m. Florence O'Neil, Apr. 8, 1951; children—Ruth, Sandra, Louis, David. B.S., U.S. Mcht. Marine Acad., 1950; postgrad., N.C. State Grad. Sch. Engring., N.Y. U. Grad. Sch. Bus. Sales mgr. Nordberg Mfg. Co., 1955-67; v.p. mktg., pres. Engine div. Fairbanks Morse subs. Colt Industries, Inc., N.Y.C., 1967-71; corporate v.p. Colt Industries, Inc., 1971; pres. Colt Industries Internat., Inc.; exec. v.p. U.S. Industries, Stamford, Conn., 1982-84; pres., prin. Philip Wallach Assocs., South Norwalk, Conn., 1984—; pres. Guilman Inc., South Norwalk, Conn., 1984—. Served to lt. USNR. Recipient Outstanding Profl. Achievement award U.S. Mcht. Marine Acad., Marine Man of the Yr. award. Mem. Am. Soc. Naval Engrs., Soc. Naval Architects and Marine Engrs. Club: Economic (N.Y.C.). Home: 1450 Bldv Stamford CT 06902

WALLACH, PHILIP C(HARLES), public relations executive; b. N.Y.C., Nov. 17, 1914; s. Edgar Smith and Rix (Roth) W.; m. Magdalena Charlotta Falkenberg, Mar. 14, 1950. Student, NYU. Editor, writer Hearst Publs., N.Y.C., 1938-42; editor Shell Oil Co., N.Y.C., 1943-46; editor, dir. pub. relations W.R. Grace & Co., N.Y.C., 1946-54; dir. pub. relations and advt. H.K. Porter & Co., N.Y.C., 1954-58; pres. Wallach Assocs., Inc., N.Y.C., 1958-85; v.p. investor relations Occidental Petroleum Co., Los Angeles, 1985—; v.p. Occidental Internat. Corp., New York, 1987—. Pres. St. Paul Guild, N.Y.C., 1959-68, dir., 1964-72; pres. Catholic. Inst. of Press, N.Y.C., 1959-61, 61-63, 63-65; co-founder Air Force Assn., Washington, 1946; nat. committeeman Republican party, N.Y., 1945-60; mem. Repub. Nat. Com., Greenwich, Conn., 1982—; dir., mem. exec. com. U.S. Pakistan Econ. Council. Served with USAF, 1942-43. Mem. Pan Am. Soc., English Speaking Union, Bolivian Soc., Peruvian Soc., Chilean Soc. Home: 84 Lower Cross Rd Greenwich CT 06831 Office: Occidental Internat Corp 1230 Ave of Americas New York NY 10020 *

WALLENBERG, SCOTT ALAN, sales marketing executive; b. Ripon, Wis., June 2, 1958; s. Frank A. and Nancy E. (Schorb) W.; m. Debra K. Kengott, July 11, 1981; 1 child, Daniel A. BS in Chemistry and Biochemistry, U. Ill., 1980; MBA, DePaul U., 1980—. Chemist aerospace div. DeSoto, Inc., Des Plaines, Ill., 1980-83; tech. rep. def. div. Enterprise Chem. Coatings Co., Wheeling, Ill., 1983-86; tech. rep., sales mgr. def. div. Valspar Corp., Wheeling, 1986—. Patentee in field. Mem. Am. Chem. Soc., Soc. Mfg. Engrs., Nat. Assn. Corrosion Engrs. Republican. Episcopalian. Home: 26W103 Grand Ct Wheaton IL 60187

WALLER, SETH, corporate lawyer; b. 1933. BA, CUNY, 1954; JD, Harvard U. Law Sch., 1957. Pvt. practice 1957-61; house counsel Joe Lowe Corp., 1961-65; gen. counsel DCA Industries, 1965-70; v.p. sec. Matsushita Electric Corp. of Am., Secaucus, N.J., 1970—. Office: Matsushita Electric Corp Am One Panasonic Way Secaucus NJ 07094

WALLER, WILLIAM STREET, JR., bank executive; b. Schenectady, N.Y., May 8, 1955; s. William Street and Elizabeth Willard (Reid) W.; m. Carol Elaine Rankie, Apr. 13, 1985; children: Nancy Lee, Douglas Alan, William Street III, Katherine Lonsdale. BA in Econs., Cornell U., 1977; MBA in Fin., U. Calif., Berkeley, 1979. Asst. sec. Chem. Bank, N.Y.C., 1980-83; v.p. Lloyds Internat. Corp., N.Y.C., 1983—. Episcopalian. Office: Lloyds Internat Corp 199 Water St 8th Floor New York NY 10038

WALLGREN, SVEN EINAR, manufacturing company executive; b. Ystad, Sweden, Sept. 17, 1929; s. Sven F. and Anna-Lisa (Bjurstrom) W.; m. Lena Sandlund, June 16, 1956 (dec.); children: Henrik, Johan, Britta, Per. MBA Stockholm Sch. Econs., 1953. Sales mgr. packing machines AB Akerlund & Rausing, 1958; mng. dir. Akerlund & Rausing Verpackung GmbH, Fed. Republic Germany, 1960-68; dir. match div. Swedish Match, 1968-73; exec. v.p. Esselte AB, Stockholm, 1973-74, pres., chief exec. officer, 1974-89; dir. Esselte Bus. Systems Inc., Skandinavisha-Enskilda Banken, 1983—, Tarkett AB, 1984, Swedish Match AB, 1984, Stockholm Stock Exchange, 1985, AB Marabov, 1988—. Fellow Royal Acad. Engring. Scis.; mem. Confedn. Swedish Industry (dir., chmn. 1983-85), Internat. C. of C., Swedish-Am. C. of C., Swedish-Finnish C. of C., Deutsch-Schwedishe C. of C., Swedish Industry and Commerce Trust Fund. Club: Stockholm Merchants' (chmn.). Home: Slalomvagen 3, S 133 36 Saltsjobaden Sweden Office: Esselte Bus Systems Inc 71 Clinton Rd Garden City NY 11530

WALLING, DAVID PERCY, retail sales corporation executive; b. St. Thomas, Ont., Can., Mar. 15, 1932; came to U.S., 1958; s. Percy William and Edith Beulah (Brown) W.; m. Elizabeth Anne Corbett, July 4, 1958; 1 dau., Linda. B.A., U. Western Ont., London, Can., 1955; M.B.A., Mich. State U., 1976. With S.S. Kresge, Detroit, 1958-80, mgr. property acctg., 1965-67, chief acct., 1967-73, asst. controller, 1973-76, v.p. acctg., 1976-80; v.p. corp. acctg. and reporting K-Mart, Troy, Mich., 1980-87, v.p. acctg. and adminstrn., 1987—. Mem. Fin. Execs. Inst., Nat. Assn. Accts., Planning Execs. Inst., Nat. Retail Mchts. Assn. Home: 1457 Ardmoor St Birmingham MI 48010 Office: K Mart Corp 3100 Big Beaver Troy MI 48084

WALLIS, MARIJAYNE, controller, accountant; b. Carbondale, Pa., May 31, 1957; d. William Carl and Jeanne Ann (McDonnell) Sears; m. George Joseph Wallis Jr., Oct. 13, 1984; children: Lauren Michelle, Katlyn Marie. BS in Acctg., Bloomsburg (Pa.) State Coll., 1979; MBA in Fin., U. Scranton, 1983; Cert. in Controllership, Sch. for Bank Adminstrn., 1988. CPA, Pa. Acct. Summit Elec. Corp., Carbondale, 1979-80; from staff acct. to asst. contr. fin. Northeastern Bank, 1980-89; contr. Wallis Electric Co., Carbondale, Pa., 1989—; bd. dirs. Employment Opportunity Tng. Ctr., 1988. Mem. Nat. Assn. Banking Women, Nat. Assn. Accts. (sec. 1982-83, treas. 1983-84, pres. 1984-85), Am. Inst. Banking. Republican. Roman Catholic. Home: 130 S Church St Carbondale PA 18407

WALLIS, W(ILSON) ALLEN, economist, educator, statistician; b. Phila., Nov. 5, 1912; s. Wilson Dallam and Grace Steele (Allen) W.; m. Anne Armstrong, Oct. 5, 1935; children: Nancy Wallis Ingling, Virginia Wallis Cates. A.B., U. Minn., 1932, postgrad., 1932-33; postgrad. fellow, U. Chgo., 1933-35, Columbia U., 1935-36; D.Sc., Hobart and William Smith Colls., 1973; LL.D., Roberts Wesleyan Coll., 1973, U. Rochester, 1984; L.H.D., Grove City Coll., 1975. Economist, Nat. Resources Com., 1935-37; instr. econs. Yale U., 1937-38; asst., later assoc. prof. econs. Stanford U., 1938-46; Carnegie research assoc. Nat. Bur. Econ. Research, 1939-40, 41; dir. war rsch. Statis. Research Group, Columbia U., 1942-46; prof. stats. and econs. U. Chgo., 1946-62, chmn. dept. stats., 1949-57, dean Grad. Sch. Bus., 1956-62; pres. (later chancellor), trustee U. Rochester, N.Y., also prof. econs. and stats., 1962-82; under sec. for econ. affairs U.S. Dept. State, Washington, 1982—; staff Ford Found., 1953-54; fellow Ctr. for Advanced Study in Behavioral Scis., 1956-57. mem. math. div. NRC, 1958-60; dir. Nat. Bur. Econ. Research, 1953-74; spl. asst. Pres. Eisenhower, 1959-61; pres. Nat. Commn. Study of Nursing and Nursing Edn., 1967-70; chmn. Commn. Presdl. Scholars, 1969-78; mem. Pres.'s Commn. all All-Vol. Armed Force, 1969-70; chmn. Pres.'s Commn. Fed. Stats., 1970-71; mem. Nat. Council Ednl. Research, 1973-75; chmn. Adv. Council Social Security, 1974-75; bd. dirs. Corp. Pub. Broadcasting, 1975-78, chmn., 1977-78; former dir. Trans Union Corp., Esmark Inc., Lincoln 1st Bank Rochester, Eastman Kodak Co., Bausch and Lomb, Inc., Macmillan, Inc., Met. Life Ins. Co., Standard Oil Co., Rochester Telephone Corp. Author: (with others) Consumer Expenditures in the United States, 1939, A Significance Test for Time Series and Other Ordered Observations, 1941, Techniques of Statistical Analysis, 1947, Sampling Inspection, 1948, Sequential Analysis of Statistical Data: Applications, 1945, Acceptance Sampling, 1950, Statistics: A New Approach, 1956, The Nature of Statistics, 1962, Welfare Programs: An Economic Appraisal, 1968, An Overgoverned Society, 1976; co-compiler: The Ethics of Competition and Other Essays by Frank H. Knight, 1935; chmn. editorial adv. bd.: Internat. Ency. Social Scis., 1960-68; contbr. articles to profl. jours. Trustee, Tax Found., chmn. bd., 1972-75; trustee Robert A. Taft Inst. Govt., 1973-77; bd. overseers Hoover Instn. War, Revolution and Peace, 1972-78; trustee Eisenhower Coll., 1969-79, Nat. Opinion Research Center, 1957-62, 64-68, Com. Econ. Devel., 1965-71, Colgate Rochester Div. Sch., Center Govtl. Research, Inc., Internat. Mus. Photography at George Eastman House. Rsch scholar Am. Enterprise Inst., 1989—. Fellow Am. Soc. Quality Control, Inst. Math. Stats., Am. Statis. Assn. (editor Jour. 1950-59, pres. 1965), Am. Acad. Arts and Scis.; mem. Am. Econ. Assn. (exec. com. 1962-64), Rochester C. of C. (trustee 1963-68, 70-75), Mont Pelerin Soc. (treas. 1949-54), Phi Beta Kappa, Chi Phi, Beta Gamma Sigma. Clubs: Cosmos (Washington); Bohemian (San Francisco); Genesee Valley; Country (Rochester); Pundit, Fortnightly. Office: Am Enterprise Inst 1150 17th St NW Washington DC 20005

WALLMAN, CHARLES JAMES, historian; b. Kiel, Wis., Feb. 19, 1924; s. Charles A. and Mary Ann (Loftus) W.; student Marquette U., 1942-43, Tex. Coll. Mines, 1943-44; B.B.A., U. Wis., 1949; m. Charline Marie Moore, June 14, 1952; children—Stephen, Jeffrey, Susan, Patricia, Andrew. Sales promotion mgr. Brandt, Inc., Watertown, Wis., 1949-65, v.p., 1960-70, exec. v.p., 1970-80, v.p. corp. devel., 1980-83, past dir.; written formal paper to the inst. "The 48ers of Watertown", presented orally at Symposium U. Wis.-Madison (Inst. for German-Am. Studies), 1986, written formal paper "Business, Industry and the German Press in Early Watertown, Wis., 1853-65", presented orally at symposium U. Wis.-Madison Inst. for German-Am. Studies, 1987; guest speaker dept. German, U. Wis.-Madison, 1987. Former mem. exec. bd. Potawatomi council Boy Scouts Am., also former v.p. council; former bd. dirs., pres. Earl and Eugenia Quirk Found., Inc. Trustee, Joe Davies Scholarship Found.; bd. dirs., exec. com. mem. Watertown Meml. Hosp. Served with armored inf. AUS, 1943-45; ETO. Decorated Bronze Star. Mem. Am. Legion, E. Central Golf Assn. (past pres.), Wis. Alumni Assn. (local past pres.), 12th Armored Div. Assn., Watertown Hist. Soc. (bd. dirs.), Am. Ex-Prisoners of War, Inc., Phi Delta Theta. Republican. Roman Catholic. Club: Watertown County (past dir.). Lodges: Rotary (former bd. dirs.), Elks (past officer). Author: Edward J. Brandt, Inventor, 1984. Home: 7 Oakridge Ct Watertown WI 53094

WALLRAFF, BARBARA JEAN, magazine editor, writer; b. Tucson, Mar. 1, 1953; d. Charles Frederick and Evelyn Pauline (Bartels) W. BA in Polit. Sci. and Philosophy, Antioch Coll., 1972. Sect. editor Boston Phoenix, 1979-83; assoc. editor The Atlantic Monthly, Boston, 1983-89, sr. editor, 1989—; freelance writer, 1978—. Office: Atlantic Monthly 745 Boylston St Boston MA 02116

WALLSTRÖM, WESLEY DONALD, banker; b. Turlock, Calif., Oct. 4, 1929; s. Emil Reinhold and Edith Katherine (Lindberg) W.; student Modesto Jr. Coll., 1955-64; certificate Pacific Coast Banking Sch., U. Wash., 1974; m. Marilyn Irene Hallmark, May 12, 1951; children: Marc Gordon, Wendy Diane. Bookkeeper, teller First Nat. Bank, Turlock, 1947-50; v.p. Gordon Hallmark, Inc., Turlock, 1950-53; asst. cashier United Calif. Bank, Turlock, 1953-68, regional v.p., Fresno, 1968-72, v.p., mgr., Turlock, 1972-76; founding pres., dir. Golden Valley Bank, Turlock, 1976-84; pres. Wallström & Co., 1985—. Campaign chmn. United Crusade, Turlock, 1971; chmn., founding dir. Covenant Village, retirement home, Turlock, 1973—, treas. Covenant Retirement Communities West; founding pres. Turlock Regional Arts Coun., 1974, dir., 1975-76. Served with U.S. N.G., 1948-56. Mem. Nat. Soc. Accts. for Coops., Ind. Bankers No. Calif., Am. Bankers Assn., U.S. Yacht Racing Union, No. Calif. Golf Assn., Turlock C. of C. (dir. 1973-75), Stanislaus Sailing Soc. (commodore 1980-81), Turlock Golf and Country Club (pres. 1975-76, v.p., 1977, dir. 1977, 83), Masons, Rotary. Republican. Mem. Covenant Ch. Home: 1720 Hammond Dr Turlock CA 95380 Office: Wallstrom & Co 2925 Niagara Turlock CA 95380

WALSH, CHARLES RICHARD, banker; b. Bklyn., Jan. 30, 1939; s. Charles John and Anna Ellen Walsh; B.S., Fordham U., 1960; M.B.A., St. John's U., 1966; D of Comml. Scis. (hon.), St. John's U., 1985; m. Marie Anne Goulden, June 24, 1961; children—Kevin C., Brian R., Gregory M. Credit and collection mgr. Texaco Inc., N.Y.C., 1961-67; mgr. credit research Trans World Airlines, N.Y.C., 1967-71; dir. br. ops. Avon Products Inc., N.Y.C., 1971-74; exec. v.p. Mfrs. Hanover Trust Co., Hicksville, N.Y., 1974—; dir., former chmn. bd. dirs. Eastern States Monetary Services, Lake Success, N.Y., 1978-88; pres., chief exec. officer, dir. The Bankcard Assn., Hicksville, N.Y., 1988— . Sustaining mem. Republican Nat. Com., 1978—; mem. St. John's U. Adv. Bd., 1982—. Served with USAR, 1960, 61-62. Recipient Disting. Service award St. John's U., 1985. Cert. Soc. Cert. Consumer Credit Execs. Mem. N.Y. State Bankers Assn. (former dir., mem. gov. council, chmn. consumer banking div.), Am. Bankers Assn. (chmn. bank card div., mem. exec. com., former mem. communications council and chmn. edn. com.), Am. Mgmt. Assn., N.Y. Credit and Fin. Mgmt. Assn., Beta Gamma Sigma, Omicron Delta Epsilon. Republican. Clubs: Forest Estates (Oyster Bay, N.Y.). Home: 9 Blueberry Ln Oyster Bay NY 11771 Office: 100 Duffy Ave Hicksville NY 11801

WALSH, DANIEL JOSEPH, accountant; b. N.Y.C., July 11, 1955; s. Daniel Joseph and Geraldine Mary (Ryan) W. BA, Queen's Coll., 1977; MBA, St. John's U., 1983. CPA, N.Y. Staff acct. Merrill Lynch, N.Y.C., 1977-78; auditor-in-charge U.S. Dept. Def., Garden City, N.Y., 1978-86; govt. affairs advisor Loral Corp., N.Y.C., 1986-87; mgr. govt. cons. Price Waterhouse & Co., Jericho, N.Y., 1987—. Mem. Am. Inst. CPA's, N.Y. State Soc. CPA's, Assn. MBA Execs., Assn. Govt. Accts., Nat. Contract Mgmt. Assn., Nat. Security Indsl. Assn. Office: Price Waterhouse & Co 100 Jericho Quadrangle Jericho NY 11753

WALSH, DONALD FRANCIS, information services executive; b. Newport, R.I., Apr. 24, 1932; s. Frank C. and Kathryn (Ring) W.; m. Pauline C. Loftus, Apr. 23, 1955; children: Sheila, Mary, Michael, Anne, Patrick, John. BBA, Bryant Coll., 1951. With Equifax Svcs. Inc., 1953-73, 1977—; gen. mgr. Equifax Svcs. Inc., Palm Beach, Fla., Newark, Phila., 1953-70; asst. v.p. Equifax Svcs. Inc., Atlanta, 1970-73, exec. v.p. automation, 1981-84, exec. v.p., gen. mgr., 1984-86, pres., chief operating officer, 1986—, sr. v.p., 1987—; v.p. Credit Bur., Inc., Atlanta, 1973-77; pres. Data Flo-Equifax, Atlanta, 1977-81; mem. Home Office Life Underwriters, 1984. Pres. Pvt. Industry Coun., Atlanta, 1985-87; bd. dirs. Better Bus. Bur., Atlanta, 1986-89; trustees Lit. Action, Inc., Atlanta, 1988—. Served with U.S. Army, 1951-53. D.F. Walsh Day proclaimed by City of Atlanta, 1987; selected Disting. Alumnus Bryant Coll., 1988. Mem. Assn. Data Processing Svc. Orgns., Internat. Ins. Soc., Kiwanis. Roman Catholic. Home: 543 Heyward Circle Marietta GA 30064 Office: Equifax Svcs Inc 1600 Peachtree St NW PO Box 4081 Atlanta GA 30302

WALSH, EDWARD PATRICK, wood products company executive; b. Québec, Que., Can., Sept. 7, 1924; s. Edward Michael and Clara (Bussière) W.; m. Rowena Mercer, Oct. 16, 1951; children: Ann, Brian, Rosemary, Maureen, Robert. B in Chem. Engring., McGill U., Montréal, Que., 1946. Devel. engr. Can. Industries Ltd., Shawinigan Falls and Cornwall, Ont., Can., 1946-47; asst. control supt. Anglo Nfld. Devel. Co. Ltd., Grand Falls, Can., 1947-51; successively control supt., groundwood supt. and gen. supt. Anglo Can. Pulp & Paper Mill, Que., 1952-62; gen. mgr. Gaspesia Pulp & Paper Co. Ltd., Chandler, Que., 1962-67; pres., chief exec. officer Donohue Inc., Québec, 1967-88; chmn. Donohue Malbaie Inc., 1988—; chmn., chief exec. officer, bd. dirs. Donohue Charlevoix Inc.; pres., bd. dirs. Donohue St.-Félicien Inc., Donohue Normick Inc. Chmn. steering com. Forest Sector Adv. Council. Mem. Can. Pulp and Paper Assn. (bd. dirs., chmn. 1979), Que. Forest Industries Assn. (bd. dirs.), Profl. Engrs. Que., Engring. Inst. Can. Roman Catholic. Clubs: Garrison (Québec); Mount Royal (Montréal). Home: 1264 des Gouverneurs, Sillery, PQ Canada G1T 2G1 Office: Donohue Inc, 1150 Claire-Fontaine, Quebec, PQ Canada G1R 5G4 *

WALSH, FRANCIS XAVIER, marketing and sales executive; b. Jersey City, Mar. 24, 1927; s. William J. and Agatha (Encowsky) W.; m. Gloria C. Bonomo, May 13, 1950; children: Kenneth X., Brian X. BS in Pharmacy, Rutgers U., 1950. Sales rep. E.R. Squibb & Sons, Princeton, N.J., 1952-59, sales tng. assoc., 1959-66; sales tng. and devel. mgr. Warren-Teed Pharms, Inc., Columbus, Ohio, 1966-68, dir. manpower devel., 1969; sales mgr. Consol. Biomed. Labs. subs. Rohm & Haas, Columbus, 1969-70, dir. mktg., 1970-78, v.p. sales, 1978-81, bd. dirs., 1975-81, sales and mktg. tng. cons. parent co., after 1981; dir. sales and mktg. MDS Health Group, Inc., 1984-88; now v.p. sales and mktg. Biosonics, Inc.; prin. Frank X. Walsh Assocs. Recipient Alumnus of Yr. award Rutgers Coll. Pharmacy, 1966. Served with USN, 1945-46, 51-52. Named to Hon. Order Ky. Colonels. Mem. Am. Soc. Tng. and Devel. (chmn. sales tng. div. 1970), Rutgers Coll. Pharmacy Alumni Assn. (pres. 1964-65), Rutgers U. Alumni Assn. (bd. govs. 1964, 65), N.J. Pharm. Assn. Roman Catholic. Club: Atlantic City Yacht. Lodge: Rotary. Office: 14000 D Commerce Pkwy Mount Laurel NJ 08054

WALSH, JAMES MICHAEL, investment banker; b. Newark, Sept. 27, 1947; s. Charles Michael and Mary Ellen (Bowman) W.; m. Mary Anne Mullroney, June 21, 1969; children: Christopher, Kathryn, Michael, Elizabeth. BS in Physics, Stevens Inst. Tech., 1969, MS in Physics, 1971; MBA, Columbia U., 1972. Asst. treas. Bank N.Y., N.Y.C., 1972-76; mng. dir. 1st Boston Corp., N.Y.C., 1976-84, Tokyo, 1984—; exec. dir. Credit Suisse 1st Boston Ltd., London, 1983—. Mem. Am. C. of C. in Japan (chmn. fin. svcs. com. 1984—), Tokyo Club, Edgartown (Mass.) Yacht Club, N.Y. Athletic Club. Home: 3-3-15 Minami Azabu Minato-ku, Tokyo 106, Japan Office: CS First Boston (Japan) Ltd, Asahi Seimei Hibiya Bldg, 1-5-1 Yurakucho Chiyoda-ku, Tokyo 100, Japan

WALSH, JAMES PATRICK, JR., insurance consultant, actuary; b. Ft. Thomas, Ky., Mar. 7, 1910; s. James Patrick and Minnie Louise (Cooper) W.; m. Evelyn Mary Sullivan, May 20, 1939. Comml. engr. degree, U. Cin., 1933. Acct. Firestone Tire & Rubber Co., also Gen. Motors Corp., 1933-36; rep. ARC, 1937, A.F.L., 1938-39; dir. Ohio Div. Minimum Wages, Columbus, 1939-42; asst. sec.-treas. union label trades dept. A.F.L., Washington, 1946-53; v.p. Pension and Group Cons., Inc., Cin., 1953—; Mem. Pres.'s Commn. Jud. and Congl. Salaries, 1953, Ohio Gov.'s Commn. Employment of Negro, 1940, Hamilton (O.) County Welfare Bd., 1955—, council long term illness and rehab. Cin. Pub. Health Fedn., 1957-68. Bd. dirs. U. Cin., 1959-67; mem. Library Guild of U. Cin.; bd. govs. St. Xavier High Sch., Cin.; trustee Brown Found., Newman Cath. Center, Cin.; mem. Green Twp. Civic Club.; Archives Assoc. Lt. col. AUS, 1942-46; col. Res. ret. Decorated Legion of Merit, Commendation ribbon with two oak leaf clusters; named Ky. col., 1958, Ky. adm., 1968, Ohio commodore, 1985; recipient Disting. Alumni award U. Cin., 1969, Disting. Alumni award Covington Latin Sch., 1983, Insignis award St. Xavier High Sch., 1973, Americanism award Am. Legion, Kevin Barry award Ancient Order of Hiberians. Fellow Am. Soc. Pension Actuaries; mem. Am. Arbitration Assn. (nat. community disputes panel, employee benefit claims panel), Marine Corps Res. Officers Assn., Naval Res. Assn., Res. Officers Assn., Am. Legion, Q.M. Assn., VFW, Am. Mil. Retiree Assn., Nat. Assn. Uniform Services, English Speaking Union, Ohio Ret. Officers Assn. (past pres. council), Ret. Officers Assn. (past pres. Cin. chpt. 1973-74), Amvets, Air Force Assn., Ret. Officers Assn. (nat. bd. dirs. 1983-88), Marine Corps League, Nat. Football Found. and Hall of Fame, Am. Fedn. State, County and Employees Union, Naval Order, Internat. Alliance Theatrical Stage Employees (past sgt. at arms), Internat. Hodcarriers, Bldg. and Common Laborers Union, Ins. Workers Internat. Union, Office Employees Internat. Union, Cooks and Pastry Cooks Local, Friendly Sons St. Patrick (past pres.), Covington Latin Sch. Alumni Assn. (past pres.), Soc. for Advancement Mgmt., Defense Supply Assn., Ancient Order Hibernians (past pres.), Assn. U.S. Army (trustee), Am. Ordnance Assn., Soc. Am. Mil. Engrs., Order of Alhambra, Internat. Assn. Health Underwriters, Allied Constrn. Industries, Navy League, Scabbard and Blade, Nat. Council of Cath. Men, Indsl. Relations Research Assn., Green Twp. Rep. Club, Rep. Nat. Com. (life), United Food and Comml. Workers Union, Cursillo, U Cats, Nat. Travel Club, Zoo Soc. of Cin., Seneca County Geneal. Soc., Men of Milford, Cin. Hist. Soc., Intraveler Club, Mil. Order of World Wars, Fraternal Order of Police, Germania Soc., High Frontier, Mature Outlook, Ret. Officers Club. Cen. Ohio, Buckeye State Sheriffs Assn., Butterfield Sr. Citizens Ctr., Nat. Geog. Soc., Millcreek Valley Assn., Alpha Kappa Psi. Republican. Roman Catholic. Clubs: C. Cin. (past pres.), Queen City, American Irish, Insiders, Touchdown, Blue Liners, Roundtable, Scuttlebuts, Newman, Bankers, Mil. (Cin.). Lodges: K.C. (4 deg.), Elks. Home: 5563 Julmar Dr Cincinnati OH 45238 Office: 309 Vine St Room 200 Cincinnati OH 45202

WALSH, JOHN BRONSON (J.B.), lawyer; b. Buffalo, Feb. 20, 1927; s. John A. and Alice (Condon) W.; m. Barbara Ashford, May 20, 1966; 1 child, Martha. AB, Canisius Coll., 1950; JD, Georgetown U., 1952. Bar: N.Y. 1953, U.S. Supreme Ct. 1958, U.S. Ct. Internat. Trade 1969, U.S. Ct. Customs and Patent Appeals 1973. Trial atty. Garvey & Conway, N.Y.C., 1953-54; vol. atty. Nativity Mission, N.Y.C., 1953-54; ptnr. Jaeckle, Fleischmann, Kelly, Swart & Augspurger, Buffalo, 1955-60; pvt. practice Buffalo, 1960-75; ptnr. Jaeckle, Fleischmann & Mugel, Buffalo, 1976-80, Walsh & Cleary, P.C., Buffalo, 1980—; trial counsel antitrust div. Dept. Justice, Washington, 1960-61; spl. counsel on disciplinary procedures N.Y. Supreme Ct., 1960-76; appointee legal disciplinary coordinating com. State of N.Y., 1971; legis. counsel, spl. counsel to mayor Buffalo, 1969-75; counsel to sheriff Erie County, 1969-72; legis counsel Niagara Frontier Transp. Authority; cons. Norfolk So. R.R., Ecology and Environment on Govtl. Affairs; guest lectr. univs. and profl. groups. Author: (TV series) The Law and You (Freedom Found. award, ABA award, Internat. Police Assn. award). Past pres. Ashford Hollow Found. Visual and Performing Arts; past trustee Dollar Bills, Inc.; past co-producer Grand Island Playhouse and Players. With U.S. Army, 1945-46. Recipient Gold Key Buffalo Jr. C. of C., 1962, award Freedom Found., 1966. Fellow Am. Bar Found.; mem. ABA (del. internat. conf. Brussels 1963, Mexico City 1964, Lausanne, Switzerland 1964, merit award com. 1961-68, crime prevention and control com. 1968-70), N.Y. Trial Lawyers Assn., Am. Immigration Lawyers Assn., Am. Judicature Soc., N.Y. State Bar Assn. (past sec.), Buffalo Bar Assn., Nat. Pub. Employer Labor Relations Assn., Am. League, Capital Hill Club of Buffalo, Am. Assn. Airport Execs., N.Y. State Bus. Council (environ. law subcom., chmn. subcom.), Erie County Bar Assn., Buffalo Irish Club (bd. dirs.), Buffalo Athletic Club (past bd. dirs., past v.p.), Buffalo Canoe Club, Buffalo City Club, Ft. Orange of Albany Club, KC, Knights of Equity, Leoknights. Roman Catholic. Home: 193 Depew Ave Buffalo NY 14214 Office: Walsh & Cleary 210 Ellicott Sq Bldg Buffalo NY 14203

WALSH, JOHN ROBERT, manufacturing company executive; b. Boston, Apr. 17, 1930; s. Edward Robert and Alice Imelda (McMahon) W.; m.

Christiane Bernadette Septier, Feb. 25, 1955; children—Mary Anne, John Robert, Marie-Noelle, Thomas M. B.S. in Engring, M.I.T., 1953, postgrad. in process metallurgy, 1953. Registered prof. engr., Mass. Sr. partner Stephenson Walsh & Assos. (cons. engrs.), Paris, 1958-61; with Borg-Warner Corp. (and sub's.), 1961-86; v.p. internat. ops. Borg-Warner Corp. (York div.), Pa., 1967-68; pres. Borg-Warner Corp. (York Europe div.), Geneva and Brussels, 1969-77, Borg-Warner Corp. (York Internat. div.), 1978-85, York Air Conditioning and Refrigeration Inc., 1986—; v.p., gen. mgr. Applied Systems Worldwide York Internat. Corp., sr. v.p.; chmn. mgmt. com., dir. Brown Boveri-York Kalte-Und Klimatechnik GmbH, Ger.; chmn. bd., dir. Aircondi and Refri A.G., Zug, Switzerland; joint mng. dir., dir. York Internat. Ltd., U.K.; dir. Le Froid Industriel York (S.A.), France, York Air Conditioning and Refrigeration Inc., U.S.A; dir. York Aire (S.A.), Mexico, Recold S.A. De C.V., Mexico, Refrigeracion York (S.A.), Venezuela, McFarland Co., Harrisburg, Pa., OYL Condair Sdn. Bhd., Maylasia, Saudi (Arabia) Air Conditioning Co., MARCO, Saudi, Arabia, MIRACO, Egypt. Served to 1st lt. C.E. U.S. Army, 1954-58. Mem. Am. Mgmt. Assn. (pres's. council), Machinery and Allied Products Inst. (internat. ops. council). Republican. Roman Catholic. Clubs: Country of York, Lafayette, Rose Tree Fox Hunting. Home: 1100 Grantley Rd York PA 17403 Office: York Internat Corp PO Box 1592 York PA 17405

WALSH, JOSEPH PATRICK, JR., investment advisor, small business owner; b. Lawrence, Mass., May 8, 1952; s. Joseph Patrick and Eileen Catherine (Hannagan) W.; m. Michele La Roche, Dec. 18, 1976; children: Joseph Patrick III, Katherine, Michael, Thomas. BS in Mgmt., No. Ill. U., 1974, MBA in Fin., 1986. Registered real estate broker, investment advisor, ins. agt.; cert. fin. planner. Owner J.P. Hannagan's Restaurant, DeKalb, Ill., 1975—, Midwest Bus. Assocs., DeKalb, 1984-85; pres. J.P. Walsh & Assocs., DeKalb, 1985—; mem. adj. faculty Coll. Fin. Planning, 1986. Mem. Inst. Cert. Fin. Planners, Internat. Assn. Cert. Fin. Planners, Nat. Assn. Securities Dealers, Mutual Service Corp., Inst. Chartered Fin. Analysts, Am. Bus. Clubs, Sycamore (Ill.) Jaycees. Office: JP Walsh & Assocs 1215 Blackhawk De Kalb IL 60115

WALSH, JULIA MONTGOMERY, investment banking executive; b. Akron, Ohio, Mar. 29, 1923; d. Edward A. and Catherine Skurkay Curry; m. John G. Montgomery, Apr. 7, 1948 (dec. 1957); children: John, Stephen, Michael, Mark; m. Thomas M. Walsh, May 18, 1963; 1 child, Margaret; stepchildren: Mary F., Patrick J., Kathleen Carr, Thomas D., Joan Cassedy, Daniel, Ann Walton; BBA magna cum laude, Kent State U., 1945, LLD, 1967; postgrad. Harvard U., 1962; LLD Smith Coll., 1983. Dir. Fulbright Program, Ankara, Turkey; personnel officer Am. Consulate Gen., Munich, Fed. Republic of Germany; sr. v.p., registered rep. Ferris & Co., 1955-74; vice chmn. Ferris & Co., Inc., 1974-77; chmn. Julia M. Walsh & Sons, Inc., Washington, 1977-83; mng. dir. Julia M. Walsh & Sons (div. Tucker Anthony & R.L. Day, Inc.), Washington, 1984—; bd. dirs. Pitney Bowes, Stamford, Conn.; mem. Investment Banking Adv. Com. Am. Stock Exchange, former gov. and exchange ofcl.; trustee Dole Commn.; mem., dir. exec. com. Greater Washington Bd. of Trade; panelist TV program Wall Street Week. Bd. dirs. Nat. Bd. of Shrine of Immaculate Conception, Neighborhood Econ. Devel. Corp. D.C.; trustee Kent State U. Found., Nat. Assn. Bank Women, Mount St. Mary's Coll., Emmitsburg, Md., S.I.A. Inst., Wharton Bus. Sch. U. Pa.; past trustee Georgetown U.; mem. adv. bd. First Am. Bank; former trustee Simmons Coll., Boston. Roman Catholic. Office: Tucker Anthony & RL Day Inc 1050 Connecticut Ave #490 Washington DC 20036

WALSH, KATHRYN ANN, information systems specialist, librarian; b. Bay Shore, N.Y., Aug. 1, 1950; d. James R. and Virginia G. (Cloos) W.; m. Wesley A. Romansky, Oct. 9, 1978; children: Carter, Alexander. BA, SUNY, Buffalo, 1973; MLS, U. Chgo., 1977. Reference librarian biomed. library UCLA, 1976-79; info. scientist Purdue Frederick Co., Norwalk, Conn., 1979-83, librarian, 1983-86, mgr. library svcs., 1986—; co-owner Somerset Books, Greenwich, Conn., 1980—. Trustee Patchogue (N.Y.) Pub. Library, 1974-76. Mem. Spl. Libraries Assn. (bull. editor 1987—). Democrat. Office: Purdue Frederick Co 100 Connecticut Ave Norwalk CT 06856

WALSH, MICHAEL H., business executive; b. Binghamton, N.Y., July 8, 1942. B.A. in Econs., Stanford U., 1964; J.D., Yale U., 1969. Bar: Calif. 1970. Asst. dir. admissions Stanford U., 1964-65; White House fellow U.S. Dept. Agr., 1965-66; sr. staff atty. Defenders Inc., San Diego, 1969-72; mem. firm Sheela, Lightner, Hughes, Castro & Walsh, San Diego, 1972-77; U.S. atty. for Calif. 1978-80; exec. v.p. ops. and internat. Cummins Engine Co., Inc., Columbus, Ind., 1980-86; chmn., chief exec. officer Union Pacific R.R. Co., Omaha, Nebr., 1986—. Contbr. articles to profl. jours. Trustee Stanford U. Mem. San Diego County Bar Assn., State Bar Calif. Office: Union Pacific RR 1416 Dodge St Omaha NE 68179

WALSH, RICHARD TROY, business executive; b. Saginaw, Mich., July 5, 1935; s. Richard Troy and Christina (Mayan) W.; m. Marianne Hogan, Sept. 12, 1959; children—Susan C., Richard T., Kathleen A., Michael P., Daniel J., Patrick H., Margaret M., Timothy W. B.S. magna cum laude in Acctg., U. Notre Dame, 1957. With Touche Ross & Co., Detroit, 1957-62, supr. 1962-64, mgr., 1964-66, ptnr., 1966-73; sec.-treas. Core Industries, Bloomfield Hills, Mich., 1973-82, v.p. fin., 1982-86, also dir., pres., 1986—; dir. Mich. Nat. Corp., Farmington Hills. Mem. adv. bd. Walsh Coll., Troy, Mich., 1975—, trustee, 1985—. Recipient Haskins & Sells Found. award U. Notre Dame, 1957. Mem. Am. Inst. C.P.A.s, Mich. Assn. C.P.A.s, Fin. Execs. Inst. (dir., pres. Detroit chpt. 1985-86). Republican. Roman Catholic. Clubs: Birmingham Athletic; Detroit Golf, Detroit Athletic; Notre Dame. Office: Core Industries Inc 500 N Woodward Bloomfield Hills MI 48013

WALSH, ROBERT ANTHONY, lawyer; b. Boston, Aug. 26, 1938; s. Frank and Emily Angelica (Bissitt) W.; m. Angela Rosalie Barile, Aug. 3, 1966; children: Maria, Robert II, Amy. SB, MIT, 1960; MS, Fla. Inst. Tech., 1967; JD, Suffolk U., 1971. Bar: Mass. 1971, Ill. 1976, U.S. Dist. Ct. Mass. 1972, U.S. Patent Office 1972, Can. Patent Office 1973, U.S. Supreme Ct. 1976, U.S. Ct. Appeals (Fed. cir.) 1982, U.S. Ct. Mil. Appeals 1983; registered profl. engr., Mass. Patent trainee, engr. Avco Research Lab., Everett, Mass., 1968-72; patent atty. GTE Labs., Waltham, Mass., 1972-73; group patent counsel Bell & Howell Co., Chgo., 1973-78; patent counsel ITT E. Coast Patents, Nutley, N.J., 1978-80, patent counsel internat., 1980-82; dir. internat. patents ITT Corp., N.Y.C., 1986-87; gen. patent counsel ITT Def. Tech. Corp., Nutley, 1987-89; chief patent counsel Allied-Signal Aerospace Co., Phoenix, 1989—; ednl. counselor admissions MIT, Northern, N.J., 1978—. Mem. Lakeland Hills YMCA, Mountain Lakes, N.J., Served to col. USAF, 1961-64, with Res. 1960—. Mem. ABA (co-chmn. subcom. PTC sect. 105), Tri-State USAFR Lawyers Assn. (meritorious achievement award 1980), Internat. Patent Club (pres. 1988—), Am. Patent Law Assn., Chgo. Patent Law Assn., Air Force Assn., Res. Officers Assn., N.J. Patent Law Assn., Sigma Xi. Roman Catholic. Lodge: K.C. Home: 39 Arden Rd Mountain Lakes NJ 07046 Office: Allied Signal Aerospace Co Patent Dept 111 S 34th St Phoenix AZ 85010

WALSH, ROBERT FRANCIS, oil company executive; b. N.Y.C., Sept. 8, 1930; s. Robert F. and Marie R. (Schultz) W.; m. Carol A. Teston; children: Robert F., Brian D., Michael K., Maureen A., Christopher D., Julie M., Kathy M. BS ChemE, MIT, 1952, MS ChemE, 1953. Refinery planner ea. div. Chevron Oil, Perth Amboy, N.J., 1955-63, econ. analyst ea. div., 1963-66; supply coordinator Standard Oil Co. Calif. (later Chevron), San Francisco, 1966-71; traffic mgr. Chevron Shipping Co., San Francisco, 1971-74; v.p. Standard Oil div. Chevron Oil, Louisville, 1974-76; v.p. supply Chevron U.S.A. Inc., San Francisco, 1977-86; pres. Chevron Internat. Oil Co. Inc., San Francisco, 1986—. Served to lt. U.S. Army, 1953-55. Club: World Trade (San Francisco). Office: Chevron Internat Oil Co Inc 555 Market St 9th Floor San Francisco CA 94105

WALSH, THOMAS GERARD, actuary; b. N.Y.C., Jan. 14, 1942; s. Martin Joseph and Margaret Ellen (Moyles) W.; children: Brian, Kristen, Meghan, Jacqueline. B.S., Manhattan Coll. Exec. v.p. Tchr. Ins. & Annuity Am./CREF, N.Y.C. Fellow Soc. Actuaries. Office: Tchrs Ins & Annuity Assn Am 730 3rd Ave New York NY 10017

WALSH, VINCENT ARTHUR, brokerage operations; b. Rockville Centre, N.Y., May 14, 1951; s. James J. and Arleen (Anderson) W.; m. Susan Glaser, Oct. 9, 1983. BBA, U. Notre Dame, 1973; MBA, Columbia U., 1980. CPA, N.Y. Registered fin./ops. prin. underwriter Am. Internat. Group, N.Y.C., 1977-78; project mgr. Citibank, N.A., N.Y.C., 1979-80; ops. specialist Gen. Electric Credit Corp., Stamford, Conn., 1980-82; mgr. fin. & adminstrn. Morgan Stanley & Co., N.Y.C., 1982-85; sr. v.p. ops. Instinet Corp., N.Y.C., 1985—. Lt. with USN, 1973-77. Mem. Securities Industry Assn. Ops. Com., Internat. Ops. Assn. (chmn. symposium com. 1985—), Nat. Assn. Security Dealers (registered). Roman Catholic. Office: Instinet Corp 757 Third Ave New York NY 10017

WALSH, WILLIAM DESMOND, private investor; b. N.Y.C., Aug. 4, 1930; s. William J. and Catherine Grace (Desmond) W.; m. Mary Jane Gordon, Apr. 5, 1951; children: Deborah, Caroline, Michael, Suzanne, Tara Jane, Peter. B.A., Fordham U., 1951; LL.B., Harvard, 1955. Bar: N.Y. State bar 1955. Asst. U.S. atty. So. dist. N.Y., N.Y.C., 1955-58; counsel N.Y. Commn. Investigation, N.Y.C., 1958-61; mgmt. cons. McKinsey & Co., N.Y.C., 1961-67; sr. v.p. Arcata Corp., Menlo Park, Calif., 1967-82; gen. ptnr. Sequoia Assocs., 1982—; pres., chief exec. officer Atacra Liquidating Trust, 1982-88; chmn. bd. dirs. Pacific Fruit Growers-Packers Inc., Wenatchee, Wash., Sequoia Pacific Systems, Exeter, Calif., Timberjack Holding Inc., Woodstock, Ont., Can., Newell Mfg. Co., Lowell, Mich., Champion Rd. Machinery Ltd., Goderich, Ont.; bd. dirs. Thortec Internat., Inc., San Mateo, Calif., Nat. Edn. Corp. of Irvine, Calif., Traditional Industries Inc., Westlake Village, Calif. Mem. bd. visitors sch. bus. Georgetown U., U. So. Calif. Mem. ABA, N.Y. State Bar Assn. Clubs: Harvard (N.Y.C. and San Francisco). Home: 279 Park Ln Atherton CA 94025 Office: 3000 Sand Hill Rd Bldg 2 Suite 140 Menlo Park CA 94025

WALSHE, PATRICK JOSEPH, lawyer, consultant; b. Washington, Sept. 14, 1947; s. Helen Agnes (Fury) W.; m. Mary Ellen Gall, Dec. 27, 1969; children: Beth, Kate, Megan. BA, Wheeling Coll., 1969; JD, Georgetown U., 1973. Bar: Md. Assoc. Wheeler & Korpeck, Silver Spring, Md., 1974-75; tax law specialist IRS, Washington, 1975-78; assoc. Feder & Gordon, Washington, 1978-82; ptnr. Coopers & Lybrand, Washington, 1982—. Co-author: Guide to Tax Strategic Planning, 1988; contbr. Compensation and Benefits Jour., 1986-88. Counselor Parole and Probation Bd. Md., Montgomery County, 1974-75. Mem. Assn. Pvt. Pension and Welfare Plans (chmn. com. 1988—), ERISA (mem. industry com.), Psi Chi. Republican. Roman Catholic. Office: Coopers & Lybrand 1800 M St NW Washington DC 20036

WALTEMEYER, ROBERT VICTOR, soft drink company executive; b. Dallastown, Pa., June 8, 1934; s. Howard James and Helen Susan (Siltzer) W.; m. Gloria Jane Hoover, Mar. 28, 1956. B.S. Chem. Engring., Pa. State Univ., 1956; M.S. Chem. Engring., Northwestern Univ., 1958. Planning engr., process engr., pilot plant engr. Esso Research & Engring., N.J., 1957-62; sr. engr. Esso Standard-East, N.Y., 1962-64; ops. analysis engr. Esso Standard Refining, India, 1964-65, tech. and ops. supt. Esso Standard, Malaysia, 1965-68; ops. supt. spl. projects The Coca-Cola Co., Kenya & Atlanta, 1968-69, group mgr. engring. techs., 1969-72, dept. mgr. corp. engring., 1972-76, v.p. engring., 1975-78, v.p., mgr. corp. tech. div., 1978-79, sr. v.p. tech., 1979—, sr. v.p. Coca-Cola Export Corp., Atlanta, 1981—. Mem. nat. adv. bd., 1982-88, mem. mgmt. adv. council Ga. Inst. Tech., Atlanta, 1980-84; mem. Met. Atlanta adv. bd. Salvation Army, 1985—; mem. alumni council Pa. State U., 1985-86; v.p. Atlanta Council Boy Scouts Am., 1985—; bd. dirs. Sci. and Tech. Mus. Atlanta. Alumni fellow Pa. State Univ.; recipient Dist. Alumnus award Pa. State U. Mem. Nat. Soc. profl. Engrs. (Order of Engr. 1975, Ga. Engr. of Yr. 1986), Am. Mgmt. Assn., Am. Inst. Chem. Engrs., Ga. Soc. Profl. Engrs., Tau Beta Pi, Sigma Tau, Phi Lambda Upsilon. Republican. Clubs: Capital City, Commerce (Atlanta). Office: The Coca-Cola Co One Coca-Cola Pla NW PO Drawer 1734 Atlanta GA 30301

WALTER, JAMES W., construction materials company executive; b. Lewes, Del., 1922; m. Monica Saraw, 1946; children: James W., Robert. Ptnr., Walter Constrn. Co. 1948-55; chmn. bd., dir. Walter Inds. Inc. (formerly Jim Walter Corp.), Tampa, Fla., 1955—; dir. Walter E. Heller Internat. Corp., Gen. Telephone & Electronics Co., Biejerinvest, Sweden. Served USN, 1942-46. Office: Walter Industries 1500 N Dale Mabry Hwy Tampa FL 33607 *

WALTER, JOHN ROBERT, printing company executive; b. Pitts., Jan. 20, 1947; s. Jack and Helen (Sech) W.; m. Carol Ann Kost, Sept. 6, 1969; children: Lindsay, Ashley. BBA, Miami U., Oxford, Ohio, 1969. With R.R. Donnelley & Sons Co., Chgo., 1969—, various sales positions, 1969-77, v.p. sales, 1977-81, sr. v.p. sales, 1981-83, dir. mfg. div., 1983-85, group pres., 1985-86, exec. v.p., 1986-87, pres., 1987—; bd. dirs. Evanston (Ill.) Hosp.; mem. bus. adv. com. Miami U., 1987—. Bd. dir. Jr. Achievement Chgo.; trustee Glenwood (Ill.) Sch. for Boys, 1987—, DePaul U. Mem. Ill. Mfrs. Assn. (bd. dirs. 1987—). Republican. Congregationalist. Clubs: Chgo., Economic (Chgo.).

WALTER, KENNETH GEORGE, printing company executive; b. Bklyn., Nov. 8, 1942; s. Nicholas Conrad and Mildred Christine (Weiser) W.; AAS, Delhi Tech. Coll., 1963; m. Norma Mischler, Nov. 23, 1963; children: Christian, Kevin. Purchasing agt. Chemicolloid Labs., Inc., Garden City Park, N.Y., 1963-71; purchasing agt. Del-Met Corp., Walton, N.Y., 1971-72, dir. purchasing, 1972-83, dir. ops., 1983-84; dir. internat. sourcing, 1984-85; gen. mgr. Reporter Co., Walton, 1985-88, v.p. 1988—; lead time panel mem. Purchasing mag., 1975-85. Commr. Franklin-Treadwell Fire Dist., 1974-77; chief Treadwell Volunteer Fire Dept., 1978-82, pres., 1982-84, 1st asst. chief, 1985—; hunter tng. instr. N.Y. State Dept. Environ. Conservation, 1964-85; bd. dirs. Treadwell TV Cable, 1978—; mem. Delhi Tech. Coll. Assembly, 1981-85, Oneonta Daily Star Reader Bd., 1985, pvt. industry council youth bd., 1987—; mediator N.Y. State, 1987; bd. dirs. Walton Youth Employment Co., 1987, Del. County Dispute Resolution Ctr., 1987—; project bus. cons. Jr. Achievement, 1989—. Recipient Purchasing Mag. Value Improvement award, 1977. Mem. Nat. Assn. Purchasing Mgmt. (internat. group adv. council 1984-85), Purchasing Mgmt. Assn. of So. Tier-East N.Y., Am. Soc. Metals, Nat. Assn. Printers and Lithographers. Lodge: Masons. Home: PO Box 268 Treadwell NY 13846 Office: Reporter Co Inc 181 Delaware St Walton NY 13856

WALTER, ROBERT D., wholesale pharmaceutical distribution executive; b. 1945. BMechE, Ohio U., 1967; MBA, Harvard U., 1970. With Cardinal Foods Inc. (acquired by Roundy's Inc. 1988), Dublin, Ohio, 1971-88; chief exec. officer, chmn. bd. Cardinal Distbn. Inc., Dublin, 1979—. Office: Cardinal Distbn Inc 655 Metro Pl S Dublin OH 43017 *

WALTERS, BARBARA R., sociologist, consultant; b. Vincennes, Ind., Sept. 21, 1948; d. Eugene and Juanita (Eubanks) Wl; m. Martin Brown Berry, Sept. 29, 1979 (div. 1985); m. Thomas J. J. Altizer, June 10, 1987. BA, Vanderbilt U., 1970; MA, SUNY, Stony Brook, 1974; PhD, SUNY, 1978. Vis. asst. prof. Coll. William and Mary, Williamsburg, Va., 1974-75; vis. instr. Vanderbilt U., Nashville, 1975-76; rsch. assoc. SUNY, Stony Brook, 1976-77; dir. human rsch. Farm Fresh Supermarkets, Norfolk, Va., 1977-82; v.p. adminstrn. Farm Fresh Supermarkets, 1982-84, v.p. strategic planning, 1984-85; gen. mgr. Va. Opera, Norfolk, 1985-86; cons. L.I. Rsch. Inst., Islip, N.Y., 1975-76, Nat. Grocers Assn., Reston, Va., 1987; bd. dirs. Star Food Mart, Norfolk, 1987—. Bd. dirs. Jr. Achievement, Norfolk, 1982-85, Va. Opera, Norfolk, 1983—; trustee City Retirement System, Norfolk, 1983-84; coun. mem. Coun. Health Regulatory Bds., Richmond, Va., 1985—. NIMH trainee, 1971-74, Ctr. Lit. and Culture Rsch. fellow, Paris, 1972-73; recipient Rsch. Svc. award NIH, 1976-77. Mem. Am. Sociol. Assn., So. Sociol. Soc. Democrat. Episcopalian. Home: 1848 Fendall Ave Charlottesville VA 22903

WALTERS, BETTE JEAN, lawyer; b. Norristown, Pa., Sept. 5, 1946. BA, U. Pitts., 1967; JD, Temple U., 1970, LLM in Taxation, 1974. Bar: Pa. 1970, U.S. Dist. Ct. (ea. dist.) Pa. 1971. Law clk., assoc. William R. Cooper, Lansdale, Pa., 1969-72; spl. asst. to pub. defender Montgomery County (Pa.), 1973; pvt. practice North Wales, Pa., 1972-73; assoc. counsel Alco Standard Corp., Valley Forge, Pa., 1973-79, group counsel mfg., 1979-83; v.p., gen. counsel, sec. Alco Industries, Inc., Valley Forge, 1983—. Mem. ABA, Pa. Bar Assn., Montgomery County Bar Assn., Am. Soc. Corp. Secs., Am. Corp. Counsel Assn., DAR (chpt. rec. sec. 1982-83). Republican. Office: Alco Industries Inc PO Box 937 Valley Forge PA 19482

WALTERS, DENNIS GEORGE, automotive company executive; b. Brockton, Mass., Jan. 28, 1945; s. George Joseph and Laverne Theresa (Olson) W.; m. Catherine Hazel Drysdale, Aug. 20, 1966; children: Lisa Mary, Dennis George, Justin Christopher. BS in Chemistry, Stonehill Coll., 1966; MBA, N.H. Coll., 1985. Cert. quality engr. Tchr. Marshfield (Mass.) Sch. System, 1966; chemist Bostik Corp., Middleton, Mass., 1967-72; quality engr. Bailey Corp., Seabrook, N.H., 1972-74, mgr. engring., 1974-76, mgr. quality and engring., 1976-80, dir. quality control, 1980-83, dir. mfg., 1983-85, sr. v.p. ops., 1985—; cons., quality specialist, Danvers, Mass., 1982—; pres. Bailey Fed. Credit Union, 1984—. Mem. steering com. PTA Against Drug Abuse, Middleton, Mass., 1968; mgr. Youth Little League, Danvers, 1980-84; mem. Growth Opportunity Alliance of Greater Lawrence. Mem. Am. Soc. Quality Control, Am. Mgmt. Assn., Boston Rubber Group. Roman Catholic. Home: PO Box 2157 Seabrook NH 03874 Office: Bailey Corp 700 Lafayette Rd Seabrook NH 03874

WALTERS, HARRY N., manufacturing company executive; b. Fostoria, Ohio, July 4, 1936; s. Harry and Orpha (Hockensmith) W.; m. Illa F. Bernhausen, July 14, 1962; children: Brad, Kelly. BS, U.S. Mil. Acad., 1959. Commd. lt. U.S. Army, 1959, advanced through grades to 1st lt., resigned, 1963; mgmt. positions various cos., 1963-76; pres., chief exec. officer Potsdam (N.Y.) Paper Corp., 1977-81; asst. sec. Army for Manpower and Res. Affairs Washington, 1981-82; adminstr. VA, Washington, 1982-86; pres. Gt. Lakes Carbon Corp., Briarcliff Manor, N.Y.; bd. dirs. Gibson Greeting Cards Inc. Adv. bd. Potsdam Coll. Found., Inc.; mem. Pres.' Council on Phys. Fitness and Sports; bd. govs. USO, Nat. Handicapped Ski Assn. Served with USAR, 1963-69. Recipient Disting. Service award Dept. Def. Mem. West Point Soc. N.Y. (bd. govs.), Assn. U.S. Army, Paralyzed Vets. Am. (life, hon.), AMVETS (life), Am. Legion. Republican. Episcopalian. Clubs: Sleepy Hollow (Scarborough, N.Y.); Burning Tree (Bethesda, Md.); Army & Navy (Washington). Office: Gt Lakes Carbon Corp 320 Old Briarcliff Rd Briarcliff Manor NY 10510

WALTERS, JAY B., banker; b. Bourbonnais, Ill, Jan. 13, 1946; s. Jack B. and Elaine V. (Frette) W.; m. Monique P. Pagano, Jan. 31, 1970; children: Danielle, Aaron, Anique. B.A., U. Ill., Champaign, 1968; M.B.A., U. Mo., Columbia, 1970. With Harris Bank & Trust, Chgo., 1970-81, mgr. cons. group, 1980-81; investment banker E.F. Hutton & Co., Chgo., 1981; exec. v.p. Sears Bank & Trust, Chgo., 1981-83; pres., chief exec. officer First Bank Milw., 1983-86; exec. v.p. First Bank System, 1987—; pres. corp. banking First Bank Nat. Assn., 1988—; mem. Greater Milw. Com., 1984—, Wis. Bankers Assn. Task Force on Interstate Acquisition of Banks/Madison, 1984-86, State of Wis. Legis. Council, 1984, Marquette U. Sch. Bus. Adv. Council, 1984—; bd. advisors Banking Research Ctr., Northwestern U., 1982—; lectr. Fed. Res. Bd. Sr. Examiner Tng., 1980—. Mem. adv. council U. Wis.-Milw. Sch. Bus.; mem. lay adv. bd. St. Mary's Hosp., Milw. Mem. Bank Adminstrn. Inst. (bd. dirs. region 5 1985—), Young Pres.'s Orgn., Assn. Res. City Bankers. Office: First Bank System Inc 300 First Bank Pl E Minneapolis MN 55480

WALTERS, MICHAEL W., soft drink company executive; b. Pitts., Dec. 20, 1946; s. George William and Jean A. (Fritz) W.; m. Joan Shirkey, Dec. 13, 1969; children: Carolyn, Meredith. Ptnr. Langston Assocs., Atlanta, 1971-72; sr. fin. analyst The Coca-Cola Co., Atlanta, 1972-76, asst. to chief fin. officer, 1976-79, mgr. domestic employee benefits, 1979-82, dir. corp. employee benefits, 1982-85, asst. v.p., dir. corp. employee benefits, 1985—; pres. So. Pension Conf., 1987; mem. Am. Pension Conf., 1982—. Bd. dirs. Planned Parenthood of Atlanta, 1986—. Mem. Am. Compensation Assn. (nat. bd. dirs. 1987-89), Atlanta Healthcare Alliance (bd. dirs. 1985—), Council on Employee Benefits. Office: The Coca-Cola Co One Coca-Cola Plaza Atlanta GA 30313

WALTERS, PETER INGRAM, petroleum company executive; b. Birmingham, Eng., Mar. 11, 1931; s. Stephen and Edna F. (Redgate) W.; m. Patricia Anne Tulloch, 1960; 3 children. Student King Edward's Sch., Birmingham, Eng.; B.Com., U. Birmingham, D in Social Sci. (hon.), 1986. Joined Brit. Petroleum, 1954, v.p. BP N.Am., 1965-67, gen. mgr. supply and devel., 1969-70, regional dir. Western Hemisphere, 1971-72; dir. BP Trading Ltd., 1971-73, BP Chems. Internat., 1972, chmn., 1981; dep. chmn. The Brit. Petroleum Co. Ltd., 1980-81, mng. dir., 1973—; chmn. BP Am. Inc., N.Y.C.; v.p. Gen. Council of Brit. Shipping, 1974-76, pres., 1977-78; dir. Post Office, 1978-79, Nat. Westminister Bank. Created Knight, 1984; decorated comdr. Order of Leopold (Belgium), 1984. Mem. Soc. Chem. Industry (pres. 1978-80), Inst. Manpower Studies (pres. 1980-86). Office: British Petroleum Co Ltd, Britannic House, Moor Ln, London EC2 9BU, England *

WALTERS, SUE FOX, businesswoman, corporate executive; b. Louisville, June 9, 1941; d. Thomas Burke and Reva (Crick) Fox; m. Hugh Alexander Walters; children: Thomas Wade, Susan Alexandra Walters Ebling. Student, N.C. State U., Ky. Wesleyan Coll. Acct., legal worker for various fin. instns. and firms; ct. adminstr. 45th Jud. Cir. Ct. Ky.; v.p., treas. Alexander and Assocs., CATV cons. firm, Greenville, Ky.; corp. adminstr. pub. corp., Bellevue, Wash. Pres., Jr. Woman's Club Greenville, 1964-65, Woman's Club Greenville, 1976-78; vice gov. 2d dist. Ky. Fedn. Women's Clubs, 1980. Mem. Epsilon Sigma Omicron. Avocations: design, antiques, dogs, flying. Home: 746 S Church St Paris TX 75460 Office: 2570 Culbertson St Paris TX 75460

WALTHALL, BENNIE HARRELL, geologist; b. Sayre, Ark., Mar. 12, 1925; s. Charles Clayton and Blanche Jewel (Hooks) W.; student So. Ark. U., 1942-44, 46-47; B.S., U. Tulsa, 1949, M.S., 1963; Ph.D., Columbia U., 1966; postgrad Grad. Sch. Bus. U. Tulsa, 1966; m. Marisa Mathilde Oggeri, Apr. 25, 1955; 1 dau., Dany Charmaine. Geol. draftsman, Sinclair Petroleum Co., 1949-51; jr. geophysicst Rogers Geophysical Co., Ethiopia, Tex. and Somalia, 1951-54; geologist, Sinclair Somal Corp., Somalia, 1954-59; geologist Sinclair Colombia Oil, Colombia, 1959-61; with Sinclair Oil & Gas, Tulsa, 1961-63; geologist Sinclair Oil & Gas Co., Alaska and Can., 1966-67; geologist Aramco, Saudi Arabia and London, 1968-78, sr. staff geologist, sr. edn. adv., 1978—; dir., pres. Watha;; Bros. Investments. Served with AUS, 1944-46. Mem. Arabian Philatelic Assn. (treas. 1979, 81-82, pres. 1984-85), Arabian Natural History Soc. (pres. 1980-81), Geol. Soc. Am., Am. Assn. Petroleum Geologists, Can. Soc. Petroleum Geologists, Geol. Soc. London, Sigma Xi. Republican. Address: Box 2194 Aramco, Dhahran Saudi Arabia

WALTHER, GARY D., retail company executive; b. Canton, Ohio, July 7, 1955; s. Carl Arthur and Evelyn Jane (Cartwright) W.; m. Sherree Ann Lipsey, Sept. 10, 1977; children: Ashley Lenore, Gregory Cameron. BS, Ohio State U., 1976. CPA, Tex. Audit mgr. Arthur Andersen & Co., Houston, 1976-85; dir. internal audit Gordon Jewelry Corp., Houston, 1985-86, controller, 1986—. Mem. Am. Inst. CPAs, Tex. Soc. CPAs, Houston Chpt. CPAs. Clubs: Houston, Champions Golf. Office: Gordon Jewelry Corp 820 Fannin Houston TX 77002

WALTHER, JOHN HENRY, banker; b. Hartford, Conn., June 13, 1935; m. Pamela Ball; children: John, Jerome, Joshua. BA in Econs., Wesleyan U., 1957. Pres. N.J. Nat. Bank, Pennington, 1972-76, chief exec. officer, 1976-87, chmn., 1976—; vice-chmn. CoreStates Fin. Corp., Phila., 1986—; chmn. bd. dirs. N.J. Bankers Assn., Princeton, 1980-81; bd. dirs. Am. Bankers Assn., Washington, 1983-84, Fed. Reserve Bank Phila., 1984-86; bd. dirs., mem. exec. com. Assn. Bank Holding Cos., 1985-87. Office: CoreStates Fin Corp PO Box 7618 Philadelphia PA 19101

WALTON, GORDON, III, electrical engineer; b. New Haven, June 14, 1955; s. Gordon and Patricia Marie (Jackson) W.; m. Rhonda Kay Moore, May 29, 1982; children: Don Raymond Carlson, Kristen Ashley Walton. BSEE, Worcester Poly. Inst., 1977; MSEE, Northwestern U., 1978. Design engr. Tex. Instruments, Houston, 1978-82; mem. tech. staff/sect. mgr. The Analytic Sci. Corp., Reading, Mass., 1982—. Contbr. articles to profl. jours. Mem. Civil Air Patrol, yalesville Conn., 1971-72. Mem. IEEE, Tau Beta Pi, Eta Kappa Nu. Home: 99 Nashua Rd Windham NH 03087 Office: The Analytic Sci Corp 55 Walkers Brook Dr Reading MA 01867

WALTON, JOHN SHEPPARD, diversified business executive; b. Toronto, Ont., Can., Dec. 7, 1930; s. John Ruskin and Doris Armstrong (Sheppard) W.; m. Joan Patricia Watson; children: Ross, Stuart. Student, Ridley Coll., St. Catherines, Ont., 1949; B.C.E., McGill U., 1953; postgrad., U. Western Ont., London, 1965. Gen. mgr. Atlas Titanium, Ltd., Welland, Ont., 1963-65; mgr. mktg. Atlas Steels Co., Welland, 1965-70; exec. v.p., chief operating officer, dir. Can. Liquid Air, Ltd., Montreal, Que., 1970-76; chief exec. officer, dir. Amalgamated Metal Corp., London, 1977-79; chief exec. officer Cia Estanifera do Brasil, Rio Janiero, 1979-82; exec. v.p., dir. Westmin Resources, Ltd., Calgary, Alta., Can., 1982—; chief exec. officer, then pres. Placer Devel. Ltd. (now Placer Dome Inc.), Vancouver, B.C., Can., 1985-88; chmn. Placer Pacific Ltd., Kidston Gold Mines Ltd., Sydney, Australia, Prairie Producing Co., Houston; bd. dirs. Equity Silver Mines Ltd., Gibraltar Mines Ltd., Vancouver, Can. Imperial Bank of Commerce, Toronto. Progressive. Anglican. Clubs: Victorial Golf, Royal Montreal Golf; Mid-Ocean (Bermuda); Ranchmen's (Calgary). Office: 1600-1055 Dunsmuir St, PO Box 49330, Bentall Postal Sta, Vancouver, BC Canada V7X 1P1 *

WALTON, JON DAVID, lawyer; b. Clairton, Pa., Sept. 18, 1942; s. Thomas Edward and Matilda Lucy (Sunday) W.; m. Carol Jeanne Rowland, Sept. 15, 1964; children: David Edward, Diane Elizabeth. BS, Purdue U., 1964; JD, Valparaiso U., 1969. Bar: Pa. 1969. Atty. U.S. Steel Corp. (now USX Corp.), Pitts., 1969-73; asst. gen. counsel Harbison-Walker Refractories, Pitts., 1973-75; gen. counsel Harbison-Walker Refractories, 1975-81, v.p., gen. counsel, 1981-83; regional gen. counsel Dresser Industries., Inc., Pitts., 1983-86; gen. counsel, sec. Allegheny Ludlum Corp., Pitts., 1986—. Mem. Allegheny County Rep. fin. com., Pitts. 1986—. Mem. ABA, Pa. Bar Assn., Allegheny County Bar Assn., Licensing Exec. Soc., Am. Soc. Corp. Secs., Am. Corp. Counsel Assn., Duquesne Club (Pitts.), Valley Brook Country Club (Peters Twp., Pa.). Home: 137 Hoodridge Dr Pittsburgh PA 15228 Office: Allegheny Ludlum Corp 1000 6th PPG Pl Pittsburgh PA 15222-5479

WALTON, JONATHAN TAYLOR, banker; b. Evanston, Ill., Mar. 28, 1930; s. Howard Roberts and Louise (Ryther) W.; m. Salome Edgeworth, Nov. 27, 1954; children—Jonathan Taylor, Katherine Edgeworth Walton Day, Lucy Downes Walton Mooney, Andrew Roberts. B.A., Dartmouth Coll., 1952, M.B.A., 1953. Analyst trainee Nat. Bank of Detroit, 1956-59, asst. cashier, 1959-62, asst. v.p., 1962-64, v.p., 1964-72, sr. v.p., 1972-79, exec. v.p., 1979—; exec. v.p. NBD Bancorp, Inc., 1982—. Chmn. Greater Detroit Area Health Council, 1977; trustee W.K. Kellogg Found., Battle Creek, Mich., 1980, ARC Endowment Fund, Washington, 1986, Community Found. Southeastern Mich., Detroit, 1988; bd. dirs. Detroit Symphony Orch., 1982; trustee Community Found. for S.E. Mich., 1988. Mem. Assn. Res. City Bankers. Home: 40 Oldbrook Ln Grosse Pointe Farms MI 48236 Office: NBD Bancorp Inc 611 Woodward Ave Detroit MI 48226

WALTON, JOSEPH CARROLL, finance company executive; b. Frankfurt, Fed. Republic Germany, Nov. 23, 1955; (parents Am. citizens); s. James Mellon and Ellen Marie (Carroll) W.; m. Molly Erwin, Mar. 23, 1985. BA in Eng. Lit., Williams Coll., 1979; MBA, U. Tex., 1983. Dist. mgr. Sand Springs, Inc.,, Williamstown, Mass., 1978-79; asst. to chmn. MCO Resources Corp., Austin, Tex., 1981; corp. issue analysis intern Gulf Oil Corp., Pitts., 1981; asst. to pres. William B. Wilson Co., San Antonio, 1982; bank credit dept. trainee MBank Houston, 1983-84, fin. analyst treasury group, 1984-85, treasury officer, 1985; banking officer MBank Houston, Houston, 1985-86; asst. to pres. MCorp., 1986-87; investment analyst The Arnold Corp., 1987-88; v.p. MMC Group Inc., Pitts., 1988—. Bd. dirs. Charity Players, Houston, 1987-88; mem. Gov.'s Task Force on Bus. Devel. and Job Creation, 1986—. Recipient Outstanding Advisor award Jr. Achievement, 1984. Clubs: Rolling Rock (Ligonier, Pa.); Beaumaris Yacht (Ont., Can.). Office: MMC Group Ste 3725 One Oliver Plaza Pittsburgh PA 15222

WALTON, PAUL A., banker. Sr. v.p. Chem. Bank, N.Y.C. Office: Chem Bank 277 Park Ave New York NY 10172 *

WALTON, S. ROBSON, discount department store chain executive; b. 1945; s. Sam Moore W.; married. Grad., Columbia U., 1969. Formerly with Conner, Winters, Ballaine, Barry & McGowen; with Wal-Mart Stores Inc., Bentonville, Ark., 1969—, sr. v.p., 1978-82, also bd. dirs., vice chmn. bd., 1982—. Office: Wal-Mart Stores Inc 702 SW 8th St Bentonville AR 72712 *

WALTON, SAM MOORE, discount retail chain executive; b. Kingfisher, Okla., 1920; m. Helen Walton; 4 children. BA, U. Mo., 1940. With J. C. Penney Co., Des Moines, 1938-42; franchise owner, operator Ben Franklin Stores, 1945-62; co-founder Wal-Mart Stores, Bentonville, Ark., 1962—, chmn., chief exec. officer, 1974—, chief exec. officer, 1974-88, also bd. dirs. Served with U.S. Army, 1942-45. Office: Wal-Mart Stores Inc 702 SW 8th St Bentonville AR 72716 *

WALTON, VALLI YVONNE, financial services company consultant; b. Bronx, N.Y., May 24, 1950; d. William Jackson Sr. and Addie Ruby (Scott) Foy; m. Haywood Walton Sr., May 23, 1981. BA magna cum laude, Barrington Coll., 1971; postgrad., New Sch. for Social Rsch., 1975; cert. small bus. mgmt., NYU, 1976; MA in Liberal Studies, SUNY, Stony Brook, 1980; postgrad., Rutgers U., 1980. Approver group health benefits Metro. Life Ins. Co., Hauppauge, N.Y., 1971-73; account analyst, sales agt., publs. specialist group benefits dept. Equitable Life Assurance Soc. of the U.S., N.Y.C., 1973-76, litigations specialist, 1980-82; supr. major med. and death benefits Program Planners Ins. Cons., N.Y.C., 1976-77; group health and disability benefits specialist Operating Engrs. Local 825 Welfare Fund, Newark, N.J., 1977-80; various positions to mgr. assn. claims svcs. MONY Fin. Svcs., Purchase, 1982—; assoc. mem. Practising Law Inst., N.Y.C., 1985—. Mem. Nat. Com. to Preserve Social Security and Medicare, Rep. Nat. Com., Washington, 1986; dir. Bklyn. Dist. Children, Christian Edn. Durham A.M.E. Zion Ch., 1972. With USAR, 1974-76. Mem. NAFE (certificate 1987), N.Y. Acad. Scis. (assoc.). Home: 1 Fordham Hill Oval Bronx NY 10468 Office: MONY Fin Svcs 4 Manhattanville Rd Purchase NY 10577

WALTON, WILLIAM ROBERT, college administrator; b. Macon, Ga., Aug. 28, 1949; s. Swift Jessie and LouVenia Mattie (Helms) W.; m. Cynthia Bonell Pollock, Dec. 14, 1969; children: David Anthony, Kelly Melissa. Student, Marsh-Draughon Bus. Coll., 1968; BBA, Ga. State U., 1972, M Pub. Adminstrn., 1977. treas. bd. trustees, Roanoke Coll. Salem, 1983—; trustee June Cheelsman Unitrust, Salem, 1984—, Lois C. Fisher Unitrust, Salem, 1984—, Harold W. Harris Unitrust, Salem, 1983—, James W. Sieg Annuity Trust, Salem, 1984—, T.B. & R.E. Meador Annuity Trust, Salem, 1985—. Acct. K.L. Kemp, Atlanta, 1968-72, Berman Mills & Co., Atlanta, 1972; internal auditor U. Ga. System, Atlanta, 1972-74, asst. dir. budgets, 1974-78; dir. bus. and fin. Ft. Valley (Ga.) State Coll., 1978-82; v.p. bus. affairs Roanoke Coll., Salem, Va., 1982—. Pres. West Salem PTA, 1985-87. Mem. Nat Assn. Coll. and Univ. Bus. Officers, So. Assn. Coll. and Univ. Bus. Officers, Luth. Coll. Bus. Officers, Coll. and Univ. Personnel Assn., Assn. Phys. Plant Adminstrs., Salem/Roanoke County C. of C. Lodge: Rotary (bd. dirs. Salem club 1985—). Home: 413 High St Salem VA 24143 Office: Roanoke Coll Salem VA 24153

WALTRIP, WILLIAM HUGH, transportation corporation executive; b. East St. Louis, Ill., Sept. 18, 1937; s. Remis Porter and Rachel (Smith) W.; m. Donna Rackleff, Dec. 6, 1957; children: Karen Waltrip Bennewitz, Janie Dee. Student, Okla. U., 1955-57. Dir. planning Eastern Airlines, Miami, Fla., 1967-72; pres., chief operating officer Pan Am. World Airlines, N.Y.C., 1972-82; pres., chief exec. officer Purolator, Inc., Piscataway, N.J., 1982-85; pres., chief operating officer IU Internat. Corp., Phila., 1985—, also bd. dirs.; bd. dirs. Tchrs. Ins. and Annuity Assn., N.Y.C., 1978—, Fidelity Union Bancorp., Newark, 1983, Bausch & Lomb, Rochester, 1985—, Thomas & Betts Corp., Raritan, N.J., 1983—, Environ Services, Inc., 1987—. Trustee Nat. Ctr. Econ. Edn. Elem. Sch. Children, Cambridge, Mass., 1980-83, Marine Corps Command and Staff Coll. Found., 1984—; bd. dirs. Pa. Ballet Assn., 1986—. Served with USMC, 1957. Republican. Congregationalist. Clubs: Sky, Wings (N.Y.C.); Burning Tree (Washington); Racquet (Phila.); Conquistatores del Cielo (Santa Barbara, Calif.). Home: 327 Grays Ln Haverford PA 19041 Office: IU Internat Corp 1500 Walnut St Philadelphia PA 19102 *

WALTZ, GERALD DONN, utility engineering executive; b. Terre Haute, Ind., Feb. 5, 1939; s. George Donald and Ava Lee (Hortin) W.; m. Vicki Lyn Broyles, Apr. 8, 1961; children: Sheryl, Elizabeth, Gregory, Dawn, Angela. B.S. in Elec. Engring., Rose-Hulman Inst. Tech., 1960; M.B.A., Butler U., 1970. Protective relay engr. Indpls. Power and Light Co., 1960-71, dir. elec. system planning dept., 1971-75, chief elec. engr., 1975-78, asst. v.p. engring. and constrn., 1978-79, v.p. engring. and constrn., 1979-81, sr v.p. engring. and constrn., 1981-86, sr. v.p. engring. and ops., 1986—. Bd. dirs., chmn. Westview Hosp. Mem. IEEE (past chmn. Cen. Ind. sect.), ASME, Indpls. Sci. and Engring. Found., Air Pollution Control Assn., NSPE, Ind. Bd. Registration for Profl. Engr. and Land Surveyors (past chmn.), Nat. Council Engring. Educators, Electric Power Research Inst. (past chmn. coal combustion systems div. adv. com., research adv. com.), Nat. Coal Council, Sagamore of the Wabash, Alpha Tau Omega. Republican. Lutheran. Clubs: Indpls. Athletic, Country of Indpls; Columbia (Indpls.). Lodge: Rotary (bd. dirs. Indpls. club). Office: Indpls Power & Light Co 25 Monument Circle Indianapolis IN 46204

WALZ, EARL LAWRENCE, medical association adminstrator; b. Covington, Ky., Jan. 17, 1952; s. Earl Robert and Lillian B. (Taylor) W.; m. Georgiana Gryst, June 5, 1987. BS, Northern Ky. U., 1976; MBA, Xavier U., 1988. Lab. technologist MECS P.S.C, Edgewood, Ky., 1972-76, dir. sales/mktg. rep., 1977-81, dir. sales and mktg., 1981-83, asst. adminstr., 1983-84, adminstr., 1984—. Author numerous presentations, publications and abstracts. Mem. Med. Group Mgmt. Assn., Ky. Med. Group Mgmt. Assn., Am. Acad. Med. Adminstrs. (cert.), Am. Assn. Blood Banks (Outstanding Donor Recruiter award 1983), Am. Assn. Donor Recruitment Profls., Ohio Assn. Blood Banks, Alumni Assn. Northern Ky. U., Alumni Assn. Xavier U., Rotary. Home: 1707 Cherokee Dr Fort Wright KY 41011 Office: MECS P.S.C 20 Medical Village Dr Edgewood KY 41017

WAMBOLT, THOMAS EUGENE, financial consultant; b. Scottsbluff, Nebr., Aug. 9, 1938; s. Andrew, Jr. and Anne (Altergott) W.; B.S., Met. State Coll., Denver, 1976; m. Linda E. Shifflett, Oct. 31, 1967; 1 son, Richard Duane King. Pres. Universal Imports Co., Westminster, Colo., 1967-71; printer Rocky Mountain News, Denver, 1967-78; propr., accountant Thomas E. Wambolt Co., Arvada, Colo., 1974-77, fin. adviser, 1977—. Baptist. Address: 6035 Garrison St Arvada CO 80004

WAMPLER, BARBARA BEDFORD, entrepreneur; b. New Bedford, Mass., July 23, 1932; d. William and Mary (Fitzpatrick) Bedford; m. John H. Wampler, Oct. 21, 1950; children: John H. Jr., William C., James B., Robert T. AS, Tunxis Community Coll., 1975. Lic. real estate agt., Mass. Counselor Wampler Counseling Rehab. Services, Farmington, Conn., 1975-85; owner, mgr. Wampler Mktg., Farmington, 1980-84, Earth Campgrounds I and II, Otis, Mass., 1984—; pres., mgr. Earth Works (name now Earth Enterprises), Otis, Mass., 1984—; founder, pres. Advt. Matters, Otis, 1989—; v.p. Mastery Books, Otis, 1989—. Contbr. articles to profl. jours. Dir. music First Congl. Ch., Otis. Faculty scholar U. Hartford, 1976. Mem. Bus. Mgrs. Assn., Nat. Campground Owners Assn., Mass. Assn. of Campground Owners. Home and Office: Earth Enterprises PO Box 690 Rte 8 Otis MA 01253

WAMPOLD, EDWARD L., healthcare company executive; b. Montgomery, Ala., Feb. 25, 1928; s. Edward L. Wampold and Caroline Virginia (Gilmer) Weldon; m. Diane Eve Woodcock, July 2, 1960; children: Troy Curtis, Tracy Dane. BS, Auburn U., 1953; postgrad., Syracuse U., 1967-68, Columbia U., 1970. Sales rep. Ortho Pharm. and Diagnostic Co., Ft. Lauderdale, Fla., 1953-67; div. mgr. Ortho Diagnostics, Inc., Atlanta, 1963-69; regional mgr. Ortho Diagnostics, Inc., Raritan, N.J., 1969, nat. sales mgr., 1969-73; gen. mgr. Ortho Diagnostics, Inc., Arlington, Tex., 1973-74; exec. v.p. Biol. Corp. Am., Valley Forge, Pa., 1975-78; v.p. sales and mktg. Geometric Data, SmithKline, Valley Forge, 1979-80; group v.p. Cooper Biomed., Inc., Malvern, Pa., 1981-85; pres., chief exec. officer Technimed Corp., Ft. Lauderdale, 1985-89; panel mem. AIDS, ethics and blood supply Am. Blood Commn. and Hastings Inst., Washington, 1984-85. Bd. dirs. Warren (N.J.) Bd. Health, 1971-73, Bus. Devel. and Tng. Ctr., Great Valley, Pa., 1982-83, Am. Blood Commn., 1982-86; mem. exec. com. Valley Forge Jr. High Sch., 1977-78. With U.S. Army, 1946-47, 50-52. Mem. Am. Chem. Soc., Am. Assn. Blood Banks, Am. Blood Resource Assn. (bd. dirs. 1982-86). Republican. Presbyterian. Home: 3130 Via Napoli Deerfield Beach FL 33442

WAN, SHAO-HONG, marketing executive; b. Chongqing, Sichuan, China, Jan. 6, 1946; s. Dingguo and Juanru (Shen) W.; m. Hua-Hua Xie, Aug. 15, 1976; 1 child, Qifu. BS, Tsinghua U., Beijing, 1968; MS, Stanford U., 1983, PhD, 1988. Engr. Weifun (Republic of China) Computer Co., 1968-76, Research Inst. Automation, Beijing, 1976-80, Systems Control Inc., Palo Alto, Calif., 1981-87; v.p. Nampac Inc., Montreal, Que., Can., 1988—; internat. advisor Visidata Corp., Fremont, Calif., 1984-85; mktg. cons. Bldg. Product Can., Lachine, Que., 1986-87; advisor China Venturetech Investment Corp., Beijing, 1986-88. Contbr. articles to profl. jours. Mem. Ops. Research Soc. Am. Office: Nampac Inc, 5165 Sherbrooke W, Ste 300, Montreal, PQ Canada H4A 1T6

WAND, RICHARD WALTON, paper company executive; b. Shelbyville, Ind., Sept. 20, 1939; s. J. Harold and Josephine Katharine (Harvey) W.; m. Sharon Brierly, June 21, 1964; children: Brian James, Katharine. BS in Mech. Engring., Purdue U., 1961; MBA, Ind. U., 1964. Project engr. Combustion Engring., Inc., 1961-63; mgr. tech. ops. Aerospace Research Applications Ctr., Ind. U., 1963-65; with Bergstrom Paper Co., Neenah, Wis., 1965-80, adminstrv. v.p., 1972-79, exec. v.p. ops., 1979-80; v.p. adminstrn. P.H. Glatfelter Co., Spring Grove, Pa., 1980—; bd. dirs. Ecusta Australia Ltd. Contbg. editor: Infosystems Mag., 1972-73. Bd. dirs. Jr. Achievement York County, Pa., York Found., Strand Capitol Performing Arts Ctr. Mem. Am. Paper Inst. (Chmn. deinking mills sect., chmn., dir. pulp consumers bd.), Syracuse Pulp and Paper Found. (dir., v.p.), Solid Waste Council, Beta Theta Pi. Republican. Presbyterian. Home: 45 E Springettsbury Ave York PA 17403 Office: PH Glatfelter Co 228 S Main St Spring Grove PA 17362

WANDER, JOHN MICHAEL, financial printing executive; b. N.Y.C., Oct. 15, 1948; s. Nathaniel and Bridget (Tunney) W.; m. Melanie Carvill, June 20, 1981 (dec. July 1983); children: Gillian, Piers; m. Alix Anne Masson, Sept. 29, 1985; children: Charlotte, Penelope. BA magna cum laude, NYU, 1971; MA in English, SUNY, Stony Brook, 1972, PhD in Am. Studies, 1977. Copywriter N.Y. Rev. Books, 1974; script cons. N.Y. Shakespeare Festival Lincoln Ctr., 1975; arts editor Westchester Eagle, Bronxville, N.Y., 1976; theatre critic Alexandria (Va.) Times, 1976; dir. mktg. Walter de Gruyter, Berlin, 1977-79; dir. Aldine Pub. Div., Hawthorne, N.Y., 1979-81; asst. to chmn. Intergraphic Tech./Bowne, Spring Valley, N.Y., 1981-83, v.p. sales and mktg., 84-87; v.p. internat. markets Aztech Fin. Printers, N.Y.C., 1987-88; mng. dir. Internat. Document Systems, 1989—; publ. panelist NEH, 1981; lectr. Book Builders Boston, 1982; dir. graphics lab. U. Balt., 1982, prof. publs design, 1982-83. Mem. Am. Graphics Assn., Typographers Assn. N.Y., Assn. Graphic Arts, Phi Beta Kappa. Clubs: University (Dublin); Soc. des Chasseurs de Gibier De L'eau; Internat. Press; Overseas Press.

WANDERS, HANS WALTER, banker; b. Aachen, Germany, Apr. 3, 1925; came to U.S., 1929, naturalized, 1943; s. Herbert and Anna Maria (Kusters) W.; m. Elizabeth Knox Kimball, Apr. 2, 1949; children: Crayton Kimball, David Gillette. B.S., Yale, 1947; postgrad., Rutgers U. Grad Sch. Banking, 1961-64. With Gen. Electric Co., 1947-48, Libbey-Owens-Ford Glass Co., 1948-53, Allied Chem. Co., 1953-55, McKinsey & Co., 1955-57; from asst. cashier to v.p. No. Trust Co., Chgo., 1957-65; v.p. Nat. Blvd. Bank, Chgo., 1965-66, pres., 1966-70; exec. v.p. Wachovia Bank & Trust Co., N.A., Winston-Salem, N.C., 1970-74, pres., 1977-85, vice chmn., 1985—, also bd. dirs.; pres. Wachovia Corp., Winston-Salem, 1974-76, 85-87, chmn., 1977-85, vice chmn., 1987—, also bd. dirs.; pres., chief exec. officer 1st Wachovia Corp. Services, Inc., Winston-Salem, 1986-88, ret., 1988; mem. com. on bank relationships Council on Founds., Inc., 1973-74; mem. exec. com. Pres.' Pvt. Sector Survey on Cost Control, 1982-84; v.p., bd. dirs. Winton Mineral Co. Chmn. Winston-Salem Found. Com., 1981-82; bd. dirs. N.C. Textile Found., N.C. Engring. Found., Inc.; trustee, mem. exec. com. Salem Coll. and Acad., Tax. Found., 1982—, vice chmn., 1984-86, chmn., 1986—; bd. visitors Fuqua Sch. Bus., Duke U.; mem. nat. corps. com. United Negro Coll. Fund; trustee, mem. exec. com. Salem Acad. and Coll. Served to lt. USNR, 1943-46, 51-53. Mem. Am. Bankers Assn. (chmn. mktg. div. 1979-80, dir. 1971-73), Assn. Res. City Bankers, Conf. Bd. (So. regional adv. council), Assn. Bank Holding Cos. (bd. dirs., exec. com. 1981-83), Newcomen Soc. in N.Am. Clubs: Chgo., Commonwealth (Chgo.); Piedmont, Old Town (Winston-Salem); Roaring Gap (N.C.); Yale (N.Y.C.). Home: 10 Graylyn Pl Winston-Salem NC 27106 Office: 1st Wachovia Corp PO Box 3099 Winston-Salem NC 27150

WANG, AN, office automation systems company executive; b. Shanghai, China, Feb. 7, 1920; came to U.S., 1945, naturalized, 1955; s. Yin Lu and Zen Wan (Chien) W.; m. Lorraine Chiu, July 10, 1949; children: Frederick A., Courtney S., Juliette L. B.S., Chiao Tung U., 1940; M.S., Harvard U., 1946, Ph.D., 1948; D.Sc. (hon.), Lowell Inst. Tech, 1971; D.Comml. Sci. (hon.), Suffolk U., 1980; D.Sc. (hon.), Southeastern Mass. U., 1981; D.Engring. (hon.), Poly Inst. N.Y., 1982; D.Sc. (hon.), Syracuse U., 1982; LL.D. (hon.), Emmanuel Coll., 1982; D.Sc. in Bus. Adminstrn. (hon.), Bryant Coll., 1982; L.H.D. (hon.), Fairleigh Dickinson U., 1982; D.Bus. Econs. (hon.), Tufts U., 1982; D.Sc. (hon.), U. Hartford, 1983; LL.D. (hon.), Boston Coll., 1983; D of Univ. (hon.), U. Stirling, Scotland, 1983; D.Sc. (hon.), Northeastern U., 1984; D.Engring. Sci., Merrimack Coll., 1984; D.Sc. (hon.), Brown U., 1985; D.Sc., U. Mass., Amherst, 1986; D of Engring. (hon.), Worcester Poly. Inst., 1987; LL.D, Harvard U., 1987; DSc (hon.), Boston U., 1988; D Engring. (hon.), Rensselaer Poly. Inst., 1988; HHD (hon.), N.E. Sch. Law, 1988; DSc (hon.), Williams Coll., 1988, Chiao Tung U., 1988. Tchr. Chiao-Tung U., China, 1940-41; engr. Central Radio Works, China, 1941-45, Chinese Govt. Supply Agy., Ottawa, Ont., Can., 1946-47; research fellow Harvard, 1948-51; owner Wang Labs., Cambridge, Mass., 1951-55; chmn. bd., chief exec. officer, dir. Wang Labs., Inc., Lowell, Mass., 1955—. Patentee in field. Trustee Northeastern U., Mus. Sci. Fellow IEEE, Am. Acad. Arts and Scis.; mem. Nat. Acad. Engring., Sigma Xi. Office: Wang Labs Inc 1 Industrial Ave Lowell MA 01851

WANG, CHEN CHI, electronics company executive, real estate executive, finance company executive, food products executive; b. Taipei, Taiwan, China, Aug. 10, 1932; came to U.S., 1959, naturalized, 1970; s. Chin-Ting and Chen-Kim (Chen) W.; m. Victoria Rebisoff, Mar. 5, 1965; children: Katherine Kim, Gregory Chen, John Christopher, Michael Edward. B.A., Nat. Taiwan U., 1955; B.S.E.E., San Jose State U., 1965; M.B.A., U. Calif., Berkeley, 1961. With IBM Corp., San Jose, Calif., 1965-72; founder, chief exec. officer Electronics Internat. Co., Santa Clara, Calif., 1968-72, owner, gen. mgr., 1972-81, reorganized as EIC Group, 1982, now chmn. bd. and pres.; dir. Systek Electronics Corp., Santa Clara, 1970-73; founder, sr. partner Wang Enterprises, Santa Clara, 1974—; founder, sr. partner Hanson & Wang Devel. Co., Woodside, Calif., 1977-85; chmn. bd. Golden Alpha Enterprises, Foster City, Calif., 1979—; mng. ptnr. Woodside Acres-Las Pulgas Estate, Woodside, 1980-85; founder, sr. ptnr. DeVine & Wang, Oakland, Calif., 1977-83; Van Heal & Wang, West Village, Calif., 1981-82; founder, chmn. bd. EIC Fin. Corp., Redwood City, Calif., 1985—; chmn. bd. Maritek Corp., Corpus Christi, Tex., 1988—. Served to 2d lt., Nationalist Chinese Army, 1955-56. Mem. Internat. Platform Assn., Tau Beta Pi. Mem. Christian Ch. Author: Monetary and Banking System of Taiwan, 1955; The Small Car Market in the U.S., 1961. Home: 195 Brookwood Rd Woodside CA 94062 Office: EIC Fin Corp 2055 Woodside Rd Suite 100 Redwood City CA 94061

WANG, FREDERICK ANDREW, computer company executive; b. Boston, Sept. 12, 1950; s. An and Lorraine (Chiu) W.; m. Laurel A. O'Connor, Oct. 5, 1985; 1 child, Katharine O'Connor. BS in Applied Math., Brown U., 1972; cert. in mgmt. devel., Harvard U., 1978. Programmer Wang Labs. Inc., Lowell, Mass., 1972-74, telecommunications specialist, 1974-76, dir. office systems mktg., 1976-78, v.p. office systems mktg., 1978-80, sr. v.p. rsch. and devel., 1980-83, exec. v.p., chief devel. officer, 1983-84, treas., exec. v.p., 1984-86, treas., 1986-87, pres., 1986—, chief operating officer, 1987, also bd. dirs. Corporator Mus. of Sci., Boston; trustee New Eng. Med. Ctr., Wang Ctr. Performing Arts, Brown U.; vice-chmn. John F. Kennedy Libr.; trustee and overseer Mus. Fine Arts, Boston. Office: Wang Labs Inc 1 Industrial Ave Lowell MA 01851

WANG, STEPHEN, oil company executive; b. Havana, Cuba, Dec. 19, 1947; came to U.S., 1952, naturalized, 1962; s. Lincoln and Grace (Chiang) W.; A.B., Columbia Coll., 1968; B.S., Columbia U., 1970, M.B.A., 1971; m. Dulia Prima Co, Sept. 15, 1979; 1 child, Michael Clifton. Pres., Dining Systems, Inc., N.Y.C., 1973-76; dir. supply Buckeye Petrofuels Co., Radnor, Pa., 1976-79; v.p. Am. Refining Co., Villanova, Pa., 1979-83; v.p. Phoenix Petroleum Co., King of Prussia, Pa., 1983—. Mem. petroleum adv. bd. N.Y. Mercantile Exchange, 1980—. Mem. Oil Traders Assn. Republican. Office: Phoenix Petroleum Co King Prussia Bus Ctr 1009 W 9th Ave King of Prussia PA 19406

WANGLER, WILLIAM CLARENCE, insurance company executive; b. Buffalo, Dec. 7, 1929; s. Emil A. and Viola M. (Roesser) W.; m. Carol B. Sullivan, Aug. 17, 1957; children: Jeffrey W., Eric J. BS, SUNY, Cortland, 1951. Claims adjuster Liberty Mut. Ins. Co., Buffalo, 1954-60; claims supr. Liberty Mut. Ins. Co., Miami, Fla., 1960-65; home office examiner Liberty Mut. Ins. Co., Boston, 1965-68; asst. claims mgr. Liberty Mut. Ins. Co., Cleve., 1968-69; claims mgr. Liberty Mut. Ins. Co., Cleve, 1969-73; div. claims service mgr. Liberty Mut. Ins. Co., Pitts., 1973-79, div. claims mgr., 1979-86; v.p. asst. gen. claims mgr. adminstrn. Liberty Mut. Ins. Co., Boston, 1986—; pres. Claims Mgrs. Counsel, Cleve., 1970; chmn. Nationwide Intercompany Arbitration, Cleve., 1969-70. Loaned exec. Mass. Bay United Way, Boston, 1964; account exec. Pitts. United Way, 1985-86. Served to capt. USMC, 1951-54. Republican. Roman Catholic. Home: 64 Trout Farm Ln Duxbury MA 02332 Office: Liberty Mut Ins Co 175 Berkeley St Boston MA 02117

WANTUCH, ERNEST, electronics executive; b. Vienna, Austria, Feb. 1, 1926; s. Richard and Margaret (Chlamtatsch) W.; m. Vivian Mendel, July 2, 1987; children: Elizabeth, Peter; m. Eve Fechner, Dec. 4, 1976 (div. 1985). BA, NYU, 1945, PhD, 1950; PhD, Fordham U., 1976. Dir. engring. Airtron div. Litton Industries, Morris Plains, N.J., 1956-65; prof. Fairleigh Dickinson U., Teaneck, N.J., 1965-88; dir. engring. Premier Microwave, Port Chester, N.Y., 1970—; cons. MIT Lincoln Labs., Lexington, Mass., 1965-67, Westinghouse Electric, Balt., 1965-68, Solitron Microwave, N.Y.C., 1968-70. Inventor, patentee in field; contbr. articles to sci. jours. Office: Premier Microwave 33 New Broad St Port Chester NY 10573

WARACH, BERNARD, social agency administrator; b. N.Y.C., Feb. 10, 1921; s. Joseph and Frances (Farber) W.; m. Shirley Wagner, May 5, 1950 (widowed May 1974); children: Joshua David, Jonathan Brian, Beth Ellen; m. Marie Sieff, May 30, 1976. BS, CCNY, 1940; MSW, U. Pitts., 1942. Field rep. agrl. mktg. adminstrn. USDA, Washington, 1942-44; adminstr. United Nations Relief and Rehab. Adminstrn., Fed. Republic Germany Office, 1944-48; asst. dir. Irene Kaufman Settlement House, Pitts., 1948-52; from asst. dir. to exec. dir. Jewish Assn. Neighborhood Ctrs., N.Y.C., 1952-58; gen. dir. Associated YM & YWHA's of Greater N.Y., N.Y.C., 1958-68; exec. dir. Jewish Assn. of Services for Aged and Subs. Corps., N.Y.C., 1968—. Author: The Older Americans Survival Guide, 1981; also articles. Fellow Gerontol. Soc. Am., Nat. Assn. Social Workers, Nat. Assn. Jewish Ctr. Workers, Phi Beta Kappa. Office: Jewish Assn Svcs for Aged 40 W 68th St New York NY 10023

WARBURTON, RALPH JOSEPH, architect, engineer, planner, educator; b. Kansas City, Mo., Sept. 5, 1935; s. Ralph Gray and Emma Frieda (Niemann) W.; m. Carol Ruth Hychka, June 14, 1958; children: John Geoffrey, Joy Frances. B.Arch., MIT, 1958; M.Arch., Yale U., 1959, M.C.P., 1960. Registered architect, Colo., Fla., N.J., Md., Ill., N.Y., Va., D.C.; registered profl. engr., Fla., N.J., N.Y.; registered community planner, Mich., N.J. With various archtl. planning and engring. firms Kansas City, Mo., 1952-55, Boston, 1956-68, N.Y.C., 1959-62, Chgo., 1962-64; assoc. chief planning Skidmore, Owings & Merrill, Chgo., 1964-66; spl. asst. for urban design HUD, Washington, 1966-72, cons., 1972-77; prof. architecture, archtl. engring. and planning U. Miami, Coral Gables, Fla., 1972—, chmn. dept. architecture, archtl. engring. and planning, 1972-75, assoc. dean engring. and environ. design, 1973-74; adviser govt. Iran, 1970; advisor govt. France, 1973, govt. Ecuador, 1974; cons. in field, 1972—, lectr., critic design juror in field, 1965—; mem. chmn. Coral Gables Bd. Architects, 1980-82. Assoc.

author: Man-Made America: Chaos or Control, 1963; editor: New Concepts in Urban Transportation, 1968, Housing Systems Proposals for Operation Breakthrough, 1970, Focus on Furniture, 1971, National Community Art Competition, 1971, Defining Critical Environmental Areas, 1974; contbg. editor: Progressive Architecture, 1974-84; editorial adv. bd.: Jour. Am. Planning Assn., 1983-88, Planning for Higher Edn., 1986—; contbr. numerous articles to profl. jours.; mem. adv. panel, Industrialization Forum Quar., 1969-79. Mem. Met. Housing and Planning Council, Chgo., 1965-67; mem. exec. com. Yale U. Arts Assn., 1965-70; pres. Yale U. Planning Alumni Assn., 1983—; mem. ednl. adv. com. Fla. Bd. Architecture, 1975. Recipient W.E. Parsons medal Yale U., 1960; recipient Spl. Achievement award HUD, 1972, commendation Fla. Bd. Architecture, 1974, Fla. Trust Historic Preservation award, 1983, Group Achievement award NASA, 1976; Skidmore, Owings & Merrill traveling fellow MIT, 1958; vis. fellow Inst. Architecture and Urban Studies, N.Y.C., 1972-74; NSF grantee, 1980-82. Fellow AIA (nat. housing. com. 1968-72, nat. regional devel. and natural resources com. 1974-75, nat. systems devel. com. 1972-73, nat. urban design com. 1968-73, bd. dirs. Fla. S. chpt. 1974-75), ASCE, Fla. Engring. Soc.; mem. Am. Inst. Cert. Planners (exec. com. dept. environ. planning 1973-74), Am. Soc. Engring. Edn. (chmn. archtl. engring. div. 1975-76), Nat. Soc. Profl. Engrs., Nat. Sculpture Soc. (allied profl. mem.), Nat. Trust Hist. Preservation (principles and guidelines com. 1967), Am. Soc. Landscape Architects (hon.) (chmn. design awards jury 1971, 1972), Am. Planning Assn. (Fla. chpt. award excellence 1983), Internat. Fedn. Housing and Planning, Am. Soc. Interior Designers (hon.), Greater Miami C. of C. (chmn. new neighborhoods action com. 1973-74), Omicron Delta Kappa, Sigma Xi, Tau Beta Pi. Club: Cosmos (Washington). Home: 6910 Veronese St Coral Gables FL 33146 Office: 420 S Dixie Hwy Coral Gables FL 33146 also: U Miami Sch Architecture Coral Gables FL 33124

WARD, ANTHONY GILES, management consultant; b. Bloomington, Ill., July 16, 1938; s. William V. and Leone J. (Costigan) W.; BS in Polit. Sci., Loyola U., Chgo., 1961; postgrad. Sch. Bus., U. Chgo., 1967-68; m. Diane J. Anstett, Jan. 9, 1965; children—Joseph M., Daniel S., Kevin P., Christopher B. Mgmt. asst., sales asst., sales mgr., group sales mgr., mktg. mgr. data communications, Ill. Bell, Chgo., 1965-69; cons. Fry Cons., Chgo., 1969-72; cons., assoc., mng. assoc. Booz, Allen & Hamilton, Chgo., 1972-78; v.p. Space/Mgmt. Programs, Chgo., 1978-83; sr. v.p. trading floor ops. Chgo. Merc. Exchange, 1983-88; pres. Internat. Trading Places Inc., 1989—, A.G. Ward & Assocs., 1989—; sr. v.p. Tellefsen Cons. Group, 1989—. Served with U.S. Army, 1962-64. Mem. Futures Industry Assn., Midwest Telecommunications Assn., Inst. Mgmt. Cons., River Club, University Club (Chgo.). Roman Catholic. Home: 1231 Lake St Libertyville IL 60048 Office: 507 N Milwaukee Ave Libertyville IL 60048 also: 19 Rector St Ste 1708 New York NY 10006

WARD, CHESTER VIRGIL, banker; b. Wood River, Ill., Dec. 2, 1949; s. Martin Wesley and Bernadine Fay (Behrer) W.; m. Melinda Jo Temperly, Oct. 6, 1973; 1 child, Meredith. Student Bradley U., 1968-69; AA, Columbia Coll., 1984; BA magna cum laude, Columbia Coll., 1986. Mgr., Household Internat., Kansas City, Mo., 1971-76; asst. v.p. So. Ill. Bank, Fairview Heights, Ill., 1976-78; v.p. Bethalto Nat. Bank (Ill.) 1978-84; exec. v.p., chief exec. officer Cen. Bank of Glen Carbon, Ill., 1984-87, dir., 1985-87; area pres., chief exec. officer, bd. dirs. Landmark Bank of Alton, Ill., 1987—, Landmark Bank of Troy, 1987—, Landmark Bank of Madison County, 1987—; bd. dirs. Landmark Bank of Ill., Landmark Bank of Edgemont, Landmark Bank of Carbondale, Landmark Bank of St. Clair County, 1987—; bd. dirs. Alton Growth Assn. Bd. dirs. Piasa Bird coun. Boy Scouts Am., 1980—, Bethalto Hist. Soc., 1980-83, Easter Seal Soc., Alton, Ill., 1983; adv. bd. dirs. Lewis & Clark Community Coll., 1987—; mem. Glen Carbon Econ. Commn., 1985. Named Outstanding Young Man in Ill., Ill. Jaycees, 1982, Outstanding Young Man Am., U.S. Jaycees, 1983. Mem. Am. Inst. Banking (cert. 1979, 80), Ill. bankers Assn. (cert. 1980, 81, 83), So. Ill. Bank Officers, Bethalto C. of C. (dir. 1978-79, pres. 1979), Wood River C. of C. (dir. 1980-83, pres. 1982), Metro East C. of C. (dir. 1981-82), Edwardsville C. of C. (bd. dirs. 1985), Phi Theta Kappa. Methodist. Lodge: Rotary (bd. dirs. 1978-83, pres. 1982-83, gov's aide 1986, Bethalto). Home: 4424 Thatcher Alton IL 62002 Office: Landmark Bank 2850 Adams Pkwy Alton IL 62002

WARD, DIANE KOROSY, lawyer; b. Cleve., Oct. 17, 1939; d. Theodore Louis and Edith (Bogar) Korosy; m. S. Mortimer Ward IV, July 2, 1960 (div. 1978); children: Christopher LaBruce, Samantha Martha; m. R. Michael Walters, June 30, 1979. AB, Heidelberg Coll., 1961; JD, U. San Diego, 1975. Bar: Calif. 1977, U.S. Dist. Ct. (so. dist.) Calif. 1977. Ptnr. Ward & Howell, San Diego, 1978-79, Walters, Howell & Ward, A.P.C., San Diego, 1979-81; mng. ptnr. Walters & Ward, A.P.C., San Diego, 1981— ; dir., v.p. Oak Broadcasting Systems, Inc., 1982-83; dir. Elisabeth Kubler-Ross Ctr., Inc., 1983-85; sheriff Ranchos del Norte Corral of Westerners, 1985-87; trustee San Diego Community Defenders, Inc., 1986-88. Pres. bd. dirs. Green Valley Civic Assn., 1979-80; trustee Palomar-Pomerado Hosp. Found., chmn. deFerred giving Found., 1985-89; v.p. Endowment Devel., 1989—; trustee Episc. Diocese of San Diego. Mem. ABA, Rancho Bernardo Bar Assn. (chmn. 1982-83), Lawyers Club San Diego, Profl. and Exec. Women of the Ranch (founder, pres. 1982—), San Diego Golden Eagle Club, Soroptimist Internat. (pres. chpt. 1979-80), Phi Delta Phi. Republican. Episcopalian. Home: 16503 Avenida Florencia Poway CA 92064 Office: Walters & Ward 11665 Avena Pl Ste 203 San Diego CA 92128

WARD, FRANCIS XAVIER, retail executive; b. St. Louis, Oct. 18, 1955; s. Maurice H. and Marcella E. (Robert) W.; m. Judy Ann Mc Lallen, Mar. 30, 1985; 1 child, Stephen Clinton. BA, St. Louis U., 1978, MBA, 1981. Asst. reporting mgr. May Dept. Stores, St. Louis, 1981-82, treasury analyst, 1982-84, mgr. treasury, 1984-85, dir. strategic planning, 1985-86, asst. treas., 1986—. Roman Catholic. Office: May Dept Stores 611 Olive St Saint Louis MO 63101

WARD, FRANK BENJAMIN, corporate executive; b. Nashville, Tenn., June 9, 1947; s. Eugene Charles and Helen Felicita (McDonald) W.; m. Linda Ann Newman, Oct. 1, 1977. BS, U. Ala., Tuscaloosa, 1969, MA, 1971. Exec. asst. Am. Nat. Bank, Chattanooga, 1971; mktg. rep. Wilson Learning Corp., Mpls., 1972-76, v.p. banking div., 1976-78, v.p. eastern region, 1978-81; pres., chief exec. officer Corp. Performance Systems, Boston, 1981—; cons., Citibank, N.Y.C., AT&T, Morristown, N.J., 1st Nat. Bank Chgo., Wang, Harris Trust, Credit Suisse First Boston, Chem. Bank, Bankers Trust Co., Shearson Lehman Bros., Nat. Westminster Bank; adviser Marquis Who's Who, Chgo., 1984—; lectr. on tactical planning, mktg. of corp. fin. and capital markets U.Va. Contbr. articles to profl. jours. Club: Downtown Athletic (N.Y.C.). Office: Corp Performance Systems 727 Atlantic Ave Boston MA 02111

WARD, JAMES ALTO, III, financial executive; b. New Orleans, May 28, 1951; s. James Alto and Audrey Charbonnet W.; B.S. in Bus. Adminstrn., Samford U., 1973, M.B.A., 1975; Cert. mgmt. acct. m. Sara Beth Kirkland, July 28, 1979; children—Sara Elizabeth, Jessica Kirkland, Linda Patricia. Trust adminstr. First Nat. Bank of Birmingham (Ala.), 1975; pension cons. Compensation Programs, Inc., Harrison, N.Y., 1976; internat. fin. and adminstrn. coordinator C.A.R.S. Inc., Birmingham, 1976-79; legal and fin. mgr., mini-computer div. Dyatron Corp., Birmingham, 1979-82, controller, fin. systems div., 1982-83; fin. mgmt. cons. Ernst and Whinney, Atlanta, 1983—. Mem. The Planning Forum (Atlanta chpt.), Pi Gamma Mu, Alpha Kappa Psi, Sigma Chi. Home: 2841 Clearbrook Dr NE Marietta GA 30068 Office: Ernst & Whinney 225 Peachtree St NE Ste 1800 Atlanta GA 30303

WARD, JEFFREY BLAIR, SR., manufacturing company executive; b. Morristown, N.J., June 17, 1951; s. Karl Hughes and Gwendoline Phyllis (Kobke) W.; m. Carol Ann Habegger, Feb. 15, 1975; children: Lauren Elizabeth, Jeffrey Blair Jr., Zachary Alexander. BA, Taylor U., 1973; MBA, Temple U., 1986. Supr. prodn. Continu-forms, Inc., Lansdale, Pa., 1973-75, mgr. plant, 1975-78; v.p. mfg. Kulpsville, Pa., 1978-82, pres., 1982—, also chmn. bd.; lectr. in field; bd. dirs. Form-Set, Inc., Kulpsville. Chmn. bd. deacons Ch. of Open Door, Ft. Washington, Pa., 1982-85, sec. search com., 1986. Recipient Graphic Excellence award Fox River Paper Co., 1987. Mem. Internat. Bus. Forms Ind. (chair com. 1986-88, long range planning com. 1988—, ann. meeting com. 1988—). Republican. Club: Indian Valley Country (Telford, Pa.). Office: Continu-forms Inc 1500 Gehman Rd Kulpsville PA 19443

WARD, LANE DENNIS, management consultant, business executive; b. Salt Lake City, Apr. 22, 1948; s. Orville Milton and Mildred (Tyler) W.; m. Julie Glazier, Nov. 22, 1971; children: Glazier, Johnathan, Joseph, Christian, Julane. BA, Brigham Young U., 1972, M Edn. Adminstrn., 1976, EdD, 1979, postgrad., 1981-82. Cert. educator, Utah. Cross-cultural trainer Lang. Tng. Ctr., Provo, Utah, 1969-72; educator Latter-Day Saints Edn. System, Salt Lake City, 1972-78; asst. dir. tng. Brigham Young U., Provo, 1978-80, assoc. dir. rsch. and devel., 1980-83, exec. asst. to pres., dir. planning and devel., 1983-86; pres. L. Ward & Co., Orem, Utah, 1982—; assoc. dir. planning and internat. svcs. World Hdqrs. Latter Day Saints Ch., Salt Lake City, 1986-87; gen. mgr. Shipley Assocs., Bountiful, Utah, 1987-88; v.p. ops. Dynix, Inc., Orem, 1989—. Contbr. articles to profl. jours. Mem. nat. nominating com. Human Resource Devel. Hall of Fame, N.Y.C., 1984—. Mem. Am. Mgmt. Assn. Republican. Mormon. Home: 1043 N 750 W Orem UT 84057 Office: Dynix Inc 151 E 1700 S Provo UT 84601

WARD, LLEWELLYN O(RCUTT), III, oil producer; b. Oklahoma City, July 24, 1930; s. Llewellyn Orcutt II and Addie (Reisdorph) W.; m. Myra Beth Gungoll, Oct. 29, 1955: children: Casidy Ann, William Carlton. Student, Okla. Mil. Acad. Jr. Coll., 1948-50; BS, Okla. U., 1953. Registered profl. engr., Okla. Dist. engr. Delhi-Taylor Oil Corp., Tulsa, 1955-56; ptnr. Ward-Gungoll Oil Investments, Enid, Okla., 1956—; owner L.O. Ward Oil Ops., Enid, 1963—; v.p. 1420 Lahoma Rd. Inc., Enid, 1967—, also bd. dirs.; mem. Okla. Gov.'s Adv. Council on Energy; rep. to Interstate Oil Compact Commn.; bd. dirs. Community Bank and Trust Co. Enid. Chmn. Indsl. Devel. Commn., Enid, 1968—; active YMCA; mem. bd. visitors Coll. Engring., U. Okla.; mem. adv. council Sch. Bus., trustee Phillips U., Enid, Univ. Bd., Pepperdine, Calif.; Okla. chmn. U.S. Olympic Com., 1986—; chmn. bd. Okla. Polit. Action Com., 1974—, Bass Hosp.; Rep. chmn. Garfield County, 1967-69; Rep. nat. committeeman from Okla.; bd. dirs. Enid Indsl. Devel. Found., Pepperdine (Calif.) U.; trustee Phillips U., Enid. Served with C.E., U.S. Army, 1953-55. Named to Order of Ky. Cols. Mem. Am. Inst. Mining and Metall. Engrs., Ind. Petroleum Assn. Am. (area v.p., bd. dirs.), Okla. Ind. Petroleum Assn. (pres., bd. dirs.), Nat. Petroleum Council, Enid C. of C. (v.p., then pres.), Alpha Tau Omega. Methodist. Clubs: Toastmasters (pres. Enid chpt. 1966), Am. Bus. (pres. 1964). Lodges: Masons, Shriners, Rotary. Home: 900 Brookside Dr Enid OK 73701 Office: 502 S Fillmore Enid OK 73701

WARD, MILTON HAWKINS, mining company executive; b. Bessemer, Ala., Aug. 1, 1932; s. William Howard and Mae (Smith) W.; m. Adele Randle, June 30, 1952; children: Jeffrey Randle, Lisa Adele. BS, U. Ala., 1955, MS, 1981; MBA, U. N.Mex., 1974. Registered profl. engr., Tex., Ala. Supr., engr. Magma Copper Co., San Manuel, Ariz., 1955-60; gen. supt. Kerr-McGee Corp., Grants, N.Mex., 1960-66; gen. mgr. Homestake Mining Co., Grants, 1966-70; v.p. ops. Ranchers Exploration & Devel. Corp., Albuquerque, 1970-74; pres., bd. dirs. Freeeport Minerals Co., N.Y.C., 1974-85; pres., chief operating officer Freeport-McMoRan, Inc., New Orleans, 1985—, also bd. dirs.; bd. dirs. Freeport-McMoRan Inc. Contbr. articles to profl. jours. Bd. dirs. Mineral Info. Inst., Denver, 1983—; bd. dirs. New Orleans Mus. Art, New Orleans Symphony Orch., Children's Hosp., New Orleans, YMCA, New Orleans; mem. Pres.'s Cabinet U. Ala. Mem. NSPE, Am. Mining Congress, Am. Inst. Indsl. Engrs., Mining and Metall. Soc. Am. (pres. 1981-83), Mining Club (v.p., gov. 1979—). Republican. Presbyterian. Clubs: City, New Orleans Country; Univ. (N.Y.C.). Office: Freeport-McMoRan Inc PO Box 61119 New Orleans LA 70161 *

WARD, NELSON, printing company executive; b. Lubbock, Tex., Aug. 16, 1941; s. Daniel Z. and Irma (Struve) W.; m. Jenifer Milller, Feb. 14, 1980. BBA, Tex. Tech. U., 1965. CPA, Tex. Auditor Peat, Marwick, Mitchell & Co., Dallas, 1966-71; v.p., treas., sec. Ennis (Tex.) Bus. Forms, Inc., 1971-79; pres. Tested Advt. Techniques, Inc., Louisville, 1980—. With USN, 1959-63. Mem. Direct Mktg. Assn., Louisville Direct Mktg. Assn., Louisville Sales and Mktg. Execs., Tex. State Soc. CPAs, Am. Inst. CPAs. Republican. Methodist. Office: Tested Advt Techniques Inc 1160 Industrial Blvd Louisville KY 40219

WARD, NICHOLAS DONNELL, lawyer; b. N.Y.C., July 30, 1941; s. Francis Xavier and Sarah Delamater (Donnell) W.; m. Elizabeth Reed Lowman, Sept. 6, 1968 (dec.); m. Virginia Ann McArthur, June 7, 1985. BA, Columbia Coll., 1963; LLB, Georgetown U., 1966. Bar: D.C. 1967, U.S. Supreme Ct. 1977. Assoc. Hamilton & Hamilton, Washington, 1967-72, ptnr., 1973-85; ptnr. Muir & Ward, Chartered, 1986-87, Noterman and Ward, Washington, 1987—; instr. paralegal progams U. Md., College Park, 1975-77, Georgetown U., Washington, 1977; mem. adv. com. on Superior Ct. rules of probate and fiduciary procedure, Superior Ct. of D.C., 1975—, cons. Register of Wills, 1987-88, rules cons., 1988—; mem. Jud. Conf., D.C., 1981—, D.C. Cir., 1981, 84, 85; mem. faculty Mus. Mgmt. Inst., Berkeley, Calif., 1979-86; adj. prof. Sch. Law Cath. U., 1986-88. Editor legal form book: Will and Testamentary Trust Forms, 1974 (2d edit. 1982 ABA Spl. Recognition award 1982); state editor Wilkins' Drafting Wills and Trust Agreements, D.C. Supplement; contbr. articles to profl. jours.; performer and author phonograph record: The Roast Beef of Old England, Come Dance With Me In Ireland. Trustee Benjamin Franklin U., Washington, 1976-79; ann. corp. mem. Children's Hosp. of D.C., Washington, 1971-81; trustee Conf. Meml. Assn., Inc., Washington, 1975-77; comdr. Mil. and Hospitaller Order of Saint Lazarus of Jerusalem, 1977—; Receiver Commandery of the Atlantic, 1987—; pres. gen. Gen. Soc. of War of 1812, 1984-87; gen. sec. Gen. Soc. SR, 1976-85; gov. gen. Hereditary Order of Descendants of Col. Govs., 1983-85; gov. Soc. of Col. Wars in D.C., 1982-84; mem. steering com. Friends of Music at Smithsonian, 1986—. Staff sgt. USAR, 1966-72. Fellow Am. Coll. Probate Counsel (state chmn. 1987—); mem. Bar Assn. of D.C. (bd. dirs. 1979-81, treas. 1982-85, Marvin E. Preis award 1980), D.C. Estate Planning Coun. (bd. dir. 1985-87, membership com. 1983-86), ABA (real property, probate and trust law sect., chmn. com. on charitable instns. 1985—, state reporter on current probate and trust law decisions 1983—; planning com. and faculty Am. Law Inst. continuing legal edn. program, legal problems of mus. adminstn. 1975—), Selden Soc., Am. Soc. for Legal History, Associated Musicians of Greater N.Y., Am. Fedn. Musicians, D.C. Jaycees (bd. dir. Downtown chpt. 1971-72, legal counsel, 1972-74), D.C. Bar (trustee client's security fund 1981-1990, chmn. 1983—, chmn. sect. 8, estates, trust and probate sect. 1984-86), Nat. Assn. of Coll. and Univ. Attys. (sec.-treas. 1979-86, chmn. sect. on univ. mus. and collections 1981-86), Am. Counsel Assn. (sec.-treas. 1987—), Alpha Delta Phi, Cosmos Club (bd. mgmt. 1984-86, 87-90, sec. 1986-87), Met. Club, City Tavern Club, Union (bd. mgrs. 1985—)., St. Nicholas Soc. of City N.Y. Club (bd. mgrs. 1985—), Barristers, Phi Delta Phi (pres. Barrister Inn 1977-78). Episcopalian. Home: 3040 O St NW Washington DC 20007-3107 Office: Noterman and Ward 1616 H St NW Washington DC 20006-4995

WARD, ROBERT ALLEN, corporate executive; b. Greensboro, N.C., Aug. 2, 1940; m. Margaret Cude; children: David, Robert Jr. BSBA, East Carolina U., 1962; cert. for postgrad. exec. program, U. N.C., 1976. CPA, N.C. Staff acct. A.M. Pullen & Co., Raleigh, N.C., 1962-65; acctg. mgr. Stedman Mfg. Co., Asheboro, N.C., 1965-67; v.p., treas. Universal Textured Yarns, Mebane, N.C., 1967-71; exec. v.p. fin. and adminstrn. Unifi Inc., Greensboro, 1971—, also bd. dirs. Mem. bd. visitors Elon (N.C.) Coll., 1987—; fellow bus. adv. coun. sch. bus. East Carolina U., Greenville, N.C., mem. ecec. com. Pirate Club, bd. dirs. Named Disting. Alumni East Carolina U., 1988. Mem. AICPA, Fin. Execs. Inst. (pres. 1987-88), N.C. Assn. CPA's, Rotary (fellow). Office: Unifi Inc PO Box 19109 Greensboro NC 27419

WARD, ROBERT THOMAS, sales executive, mayor; b. Milwaukee, Sept. 3, 1944; s. Robert and Eleanor (O'Connor) W.; m. Rosemarie Bendel, Nov. 16, 1968; children: Meghan, Justin. Grad., St. Joseph's Coll., 1966. Salesman, account exec. Internat. Paper, Milw.; mgr. nat. accounts Continental Group, Stamford, Conn., 1980-85, Gaylord Container, Milw., 1985—. Alderman City of Cedarburg, Wis., 1982-85, common council pres. 1983-84, mayor, 1985-86; founder, pres. Cedarburg Centennial Corp., 1985; pres. Cedarburg Youth Soccer, 1986-87; mem. Cedarburg Planning Commn., 1989—. Recipient City of Cedarburg Citation for Civic Contributions, 1986. Mem. Cedarburg C. of C. Roman Catholic. Lodge: Rotary (bd. dirs. Cedarburg-Grafton club, 1981-88; State of Wis. Meritorious Service citation 1986). Home: W53 N884 Castle Ct Cedarburg WI 53012

WARD, SAMUEL JOSEPH, JR., public relations executive, banker; b. Savannah, Ga., Jan. 7, 1928; s. Samuel Joseph and Frankie Ward; m. Barbara Sue McDuffee, June 27, 1951; children: Samuel J. III, Raymond Curtis, Dana Reginald, James Grady, Robert Edwin, Glenn William. AS, Armstrong Coll., 1948; BS, Ga. Inst. Tech., 1951; cert., Indsl. Coll. Armed Forces, 1975. Commd. USAF, 1951; advanced through grades to col. USAFR, 1981, ret., 1981; asst. mgr. Savannah C. of C., 1954-60; asst. to chmn. Savannah Gas Co., 1960-66; v.p. First Nat. Bank, Atlanta, 1966-72, Signet Bank/Va. & Signet Banking Corp., Richmond, Va., 1972—. Bd. dirs. Urban League, Richmond, 1988—. Recipient Silver Beaver award Boy Scouts Am., 1986, Cross of Mil. Service, United Daughters of Confederacy, 1986. Mem. Va. Bankers Assn. (chmn. pub. relations and mktg., bd. dirs. 1987), Pub. Relations Soc. Am., Bank Mktg. Assn., Nat. Press Club, Richmond C. of C. (bd. dirs. 1983-85), Va. C. of C. (bd. dirs., chmn. edn. com. 1984-86), Nat. Conf. Religious Freedom (chmn. 1986), Ga. Tech. Alumni (pres. 1982-84), Savannah & Ga. Jaycees (Outstanding Young Man of Yr. 1965). Republican. Presbyterian. Club: Bull and Bear (bd. dirs. 1984-87, v.p. 1987—) (Richmond). Home: 13924 Pagehurst Terr Midlothian VA 23113 Office: Signet Banking Corp 7 N Eighth St Richmond VA 23219

WARD, THOMAS JEROME, manufacturing company executive; b. New Kensington, Pa., May 6, 1936; s. Richard Thomas and Renatha Ann (Hruscienski) W.; m. Lindley Ann Bennett, Aug. 20, 1960; children: Christine Lester, Janice, Thomas, James, Jeffrey, Matthew. BS, Duquesne U., 1958; JD, Villanova U., 1961. Tax atty. Westinghouse Electric Corp., Pitts., 1961-65; successively atty., sr. atty., asst. gen. atty. Rockwell Mfg. Co., Pitts., 1965-71, mgr. corp. devel., 1971-73; v.p., gen. counsel, sec. Disston Inc., Pitts., 1973-78; ptnr. Meyer, Darragh, Buckler, Bebenek & Eck, Pitts., 1978-84; v.p. fin. and law, gen. counsel, sec. Dravo Corp., Pitts., 1984-87, sr. v.p. fin. and adminstrn., 1987-88, exec. v.p., 1988—. Editor Villanova Law Rev., 1960-61. Bd. dirs., past pres. Cath. Charities of Pitts.; bd. advisors Duquesne U. Sch. Bus. and Adminstrn., Pitts.; mem. Century Club Disting. Alumni, Duquesne U. Mem. ABA, Pa. Bar Assn., Allegheny County Bar Assn., Machinery & Allied Products Inst. (legal council), Am. Soc. Corp. Secs. Democrat. Roman Catholic. Club: Duquesne. Office: Dravo Corp 1 Oliver Pla Pittsburgh PA 15222

WARD, WILLIAM LOUIS, finance executive, business owner; b. Pitts., Aug. 1, 1929; s. William Edward and Mary Agnes (Bigenwald) W.; m. Florence May Falkenhagen, Feb. 26, 1952; children: Carol, Joanne, William, Cynthia, Thomas. BBA, Duquesne U., 1951, postgrad., 1954-55; cert. in advanced mgmt., Harvard U., 1972. Treasury rep. Westinghouse Electric Corp., N.Y.C., 1953-61; sales mgr. Westinghouse Credit Corp., Pitts., 1961-63, regional mgr., 1963-68, v.p. indsl. div., 1968-72, sr. v.p. real estate and comml. lending, 1972-79, sr. v.p., chief operating officer, 1979-80; pres. Ward Fin. Co., Pitts., 1980—. 1st lt. USAF, 1951-53. Republican. Roman Catholic. Office: Ward Fin Co Manor Oak II Ste 304 Pittsburgh PA 15220

WARDEBERG, GEORGE E., household appliances manufacturing company executive; b. Barnesville, Minn., 1935; married. B.A., Mich. State U., 1957. With Whirlpool Corp., Benton Harbor, Mich., 1957—, mgmt. trainee St. Joseph Div., 1957-61, mgr. quality control Clyde div., 1961-66, dir. personnel parent co., 1966-70, dir. floor care products and sales to Sears St. Paul div., dir. mfg. material control parent co., 1970-78, mgr. St. Paul div., 1978-80, div. v.p. St. Paul div., 1980-81, v.p. sales to Sears, 1981-83, exec. v.p. sales to Sears, 1983-84, exec. v.p. internat. div., 1984-85, vice chmn., chief operating officer, 1985—, also bd. dirs.; bd. dirs. Inglis Ltd.; mem. GMI Engring. & Mgmt. Inst. Office: Whirlpool Corp 2000 M63 N Benton Harbor MI 49022

WARDELL, CHARLES WILLARD BENNETT, III, corporate executive; b. N.Y.C., Apr. 27, 1945; s. Charles Willard Bennett Jr. and Elsa (Adam) W.; m. Cathie Bush, June 19, 1971; children: Charles W.B. Wardell IV, Diana D. AB with honors, Harvard U., 1973. Staff asst. to Pres. The White House, Washington, 1973-74, dep. spl. asst. to Pres., 1974-75; dep. asst. Dept. State, Washington, 1975-77; exec. asst. to chief exec. officer Am. Express Co., 1977-79, v.p. internat. dollar card, 1979-80, v.p., gen. mgr. Mid. East, 1981-82; chief exec. officer Highstoy, 1981-82; sr. v.p., chief operating officer pvt. banking Am. Express Bank, N.Y.C.; sr. v.p. The Travelers Corp., Hartford, Conn. Mem. U.S. Com. Present Danger, Washington, 1982; trustee Phelps-Stokes Fund, N.Y.C, 1986—, Clarkson Coll., Potsdam, N.Y., 1988. Lt. U.S. Army, 1966-69, Vietnam. Decorated Bronze Star with V device., 1968. Mem. Links Club N.Y.C., Cold Spring Harbor Beach Club. Republican. Home: 5H Talcott Ridge Rd Farmington CT 06032 Office: Travelers Corp 1 Tower Sq Hartford CT 06183

WARDELL, DAVID JOSEPH, travel industry consultant; b. Portland, Oreg., Feb. 4, 1956; s. Joseph Lindsay and Alice Freda (Salvisburg) W.; m. Lydia Wilhelm. Owner The Book House, Portland, 1974-76; agt., account exec. Gateway Travel, Portland, 1976-83; v.p. tech. services Sontag, Annis & Assocs., Inc., Rockville, Md., 1984-87; v.p. product devel. Citicorp Info Mgmt. Services, Rockville, 1987—; cons. software and travel. Pub., editor: (newletter) Automation Guidelines, 1982-84; columnist: (trade jour.) Travel Weekly, 1985—; contbr. articles to profl. jours. Mem. IEEE, Soc. Travel and Tourism Educators, Am. Assn. for Artificial Intelligence, Travel Agts. Computer Soc. Republican. Mormon. Home: PO Box 1746 Vienna VA 22180 Office: Citicorp Info Mgmt Svcs 600 E Jefferson St Ste 300 Rockville MD 20852

WARE, BARBARA LEE, real estate broker; b. Cin., July 26, 1947. Diploma real estate, Grad. Realtors Inst. Sec. Sunland Tng. Ctr., Ft. Myers, Fla., 1965-67, Lee County Bank, Ft. Myers, 1967-69; with First Nat. Bank, Ft. Myers, 1973-74; realtor assoc. U.S. Homes Realty, Inc., 1974, Rutenberg Realty, Ft. Myers, 1974-75, Rinehart Realty, Ft. Myers, 1975-79; realtor Barbara L. Ware Realty, Inc., Ft. Myers, 1979—; mortgage broker Ft. Myers Mortgage Brokers, Inc., 1984—; Contbr. articles to profl. jours. Real estate columnist Spotlight newspaper, 1987—; writer, editor, pub. program book for S.W. Fla. Championship Rodeo, 1987—. Pres. Suburban East Bus. and Profl. Assn., Ft. Myers, 1985-86, v.p. 1987, pres. 1988; mem. Lee County Concerned Citizens, Ft. Myers, 1985—, Lee County Sheriff Possettes, 1986—, announcer Gymkana Horse Shows, 1987—; mgr. horse barn S.W. Fla. Fair for 4-H, Lee County, 1986—; active Riverdale High Sch. Parents Guidance Council, 1987—; coordinator, exec. dir. Suburban East Country Music Family Fun Day, 1985, 86, 87, Jody Rogers Country Christmas for Kids, 1985, 86, 87; exec. dir. Lee County Country Christmas for Kids, 1988; rep. East Lee County Civic Assn., 1988; mem. CDP Census Study for Fla. Southwest Regional Planning Coun., Russell Park Community Assn., 1988, 89, Ft. Myers Assn. Realtor Million Dollar Club, 1988; notary, 1971—. Recipient Lee Grows award Lee County Commn., 1989. Mem. Nat. Assn. Realtors, Fla. Assn. Realtors (dean Grad. Realtors Inst., 1989, mem. Diamond Pin Club, hon. soc.), Ft. Myers Bd. Realtors (profl. standards com. 1983-84, chmn. membership 1985, vice chmn. edn. 1985, fin. com., bd. dirs. 1985-86), Fla. Notary Pub. Assn., Ft. Myers C. of C., Mores Shores Mcht. Assn. (pres. 1985), Antique Automobile Club of Am. and Edison. Republican. Methodist. Office: Barbara L Ware Realty Inc 4841 Palm Beach Blvd Fort Myers FL 33905

WARE, PAUL ALAN, infant products company executive; b. Oak Ridge, Tenn., May 5, 1946; s. Paul and Anna Ruth (Kelley) W.; m. Carol Susan Katz, Jan. 7, 1972; children: Erik Michael, Jennifer Lyn. BS in Indsl. Mgmt., MIT, 1968; MS in Engring. Mgmt., Northeastern U., Boston, 1977; MBA, Boston U., 1984. Indsl. engr. Brewer-Titchener Co., Cortland, N.Y., 1968; engr. Polaroid Corp., Waltham, Mass., 1971-74, supr., 1974-76; sr. engr. Polaroid Corp., Norwood, Mass., 1976-83, prin. engr., 1983-85; v.p. quality assurance Kiddie Products Inc., Avon, Mass., 1985—; cons. prin. Quality Dimensions, Stoughton, Mass., 1985—; cons. ptnr. Quality Directions, Stoughton, 1982—. Contbr. articles to profl. jours. Served to 1st lt. U.S. Army, 1968-71. Fellow Am. Soc. Quality Control (cert. quality engr. 1977, instr. 1980—, regional dir. 1983-85, 88—, v.p. 1985-86); mem. ASTM, Theta Delta Chi. Home: 34 McNamara St Stoughton MA 02072 Office: Kiddie Products Inc One Kiddie Dr Avon MA 02322

WARING, VIRGINIA, publisher, musician; b. Dinuba, Calif., Oct. 18, 1915; d. M. Rene and Elma (Merritt) Clotfelter; m. Livingston Hawley Gearhart, Feb. 28, 1940 (div. 1953); 1 child, Paul Alexander; m. Frederic Malcolm Waring, Dec. 2, 1954; 1 child, Malcolm Merritt. BA and MusB, Mills Coll., 1937; piano student of Robert Casadesus, Paris, 1937-39. Mem. 2-piano team Morley & Gearhart, 1940-53; owner Interior Design Assocs., East Stroudsburg, Pa., 1962-68; creative costume designer Fred Waring's Pennsylvanians, 1969-83, asst. condr. and mistress of ceremonies, 1980-83; chmn. bd. Fred Waring Enterprises, Delaware Water Gap; pres., owner Shawnee Press, Inc., Delaware Water Gap, Pa., 1983—; artistic dir. Fred Waring U.S. Chorus, Pa. State U., 1985. Rec. artist (Morley and Gearhart) 4 Two-Piano Record Albums (Columbia Records and Omni Sound). Founding bd. dirs. Child Help U.S.A., 1965—; pres. bd. trustees Joanna Hodges Piano Competition, Palm Desert, Calif., 1983, 84, 85; bd. dirs. Palm Valley Sch., Palm Springs, Calif., 1967, 68, 69; founding bd. dirs. Pocono Arts Ctr., Stroudsburg, Pa., 1965-75. Mills Coll. scholar, 1934, 35, 36, 37; Fleischman Trustee Fund scholar, 1937-39. Mem. Am. Soc. Interior Designers, Music Pubs., Ch. Music Pubs. Assn., ASCAP. Republican. Avocations: needlework, reading, tennis, golf. Home: The Gatehouse Shawnee-on-Delaware PA 18356 Office: Shawnee Press 1 Waring Dr Delaware Water Gap PA 18327

WARLICK, DEE FOLDS, healthcare facility administrator; b. Monroe, La., Mar. 29, 1959; d. Lenard T. and Mona Alice (poole) Folds; m. Anderson Charles Warlick III, Aug. 10, 1979; children: Christina Len, Bradley Steven. BBA in Acctg., NE La. U., 1980. CPA, La. Acct. Ouachita Parish Policy Jury, Monroe, 1981; sr. fin. examiner Blue Cross/Blue Shield La., Monroe, 1981-87; chief fin. officer St. Francis Med. Ctr., Monroe, 1987—. Mem. Healthcare Fin. Mgmt. Assn., La. Hosp. Assn., La. Hosp. Assn. (NE dist.). Office: St Francis Med Ctr 309 Jackson St Monroe LA 71201

WARMACK, KEVIN LAVON, securities examiner; b. Chgo., Dec. 20, 1956; s. Kenneth Lowe and Jacqueline (Elliott) W.; m. Delma Lee LaSane, Nove. 27, 1957; children: Delma, Kevin II, Nadia, Marcus. AB, Ripon coll., 1979; student, Keller Grad. Sch. Mgmt., 1979-82. Asst. supr. Mayer, Brown & Platt, Chgo., 1981-83; legal asst. Arnstein, Gluck & Lehr, Chgo., 1983-85, Hisaw & Schultz, Chgo., 1985-86, McSherry & Gray, Chgo., 1986-87, Santa Fe So. Pacific R.R., Chgo., 1987-88; compliance examiner Nat. Assn. Securities Dealers, Chgo., 1988—. Poll watcher Com. to Elect Harold Washington, Chgo., 1983. Mem. Nat. Black MBA Assn. (com. chair 1987-88), Am. Mgmt. Assn. Democrat. Episcopalian. Home: 7364 N Winchester Chicago IL 60626 Office: Nat Assn Securities Dealers 3 First National Plaza Chicago IL 60602

WARMAN, C. DALE, retail company executive; b. Springfield, Conn., July 4, 1929; s. William Thomas and Ella (Nagel) W.; m. Marilyn Trudgeon, Feb. 14, 1950; children: Douglas, Sharon, Ronald. Student, Warner Pacific Coll., Portland State U. With Fred Meyer, Inc., Portland, Oreg., 1949-72, 75—, mdse. mgr., supr. mktg., until 1975, exec. v.p. mktg., 1975—, pres. food group; exec. v.p. Allied Supermarkets, Detroit, 1973-75. Trustee Warner Pacific Coll.; chmn. United Way. Republican. Mem. Ch. of God. Club: Toastmasters. Office: Fred Meyer Inc 3800 SE 22d St Portland OR 97202 *

WARNER, BRADFORD ARNOLD, JR., investment executive; b. N.Y.C., Oct. 7, 1938; s. Bradford Arnold Sr. and Nancy (Hill) W.; m. Pamela Claire Glasier, Aug. 3, 1963 (div. Oct. 1976); children: Elizabeth, Claire; m. Patricia Jean Beard, Oct. 29, 1976. BA, Yale U., 1960; MBA, Columbia U., 1965. Asst. to treas. Dunn & Bradstreet Inc., N.Y.C., 1965-68; sr. bus. analyst ITT, N.Y.C., 1968-69; v.p. Schroder Capital Corp. div. Real Estate Corp., N.Y.C., 1969-76; investment officer Internat. Fin. Corp., Washington, 1976-78; v.p., bd. dirs. Am. Express Bank div. Amity Bank Ltd., N.Y.C. and London, 1978-82; exec. v.p., bd.dirs. Guinness Marton Inc., N.Y.C., 1982-86; sr. v.p. EuroPtnrs. Securities Corp., N.Y.C., 1986-88, CL Globel Ptnrs. Securities Corp. (successor to EuroPtnrs. Securities Corp.), N.Y.C., 1988—; allied mem. N.Y. Stock Exchange, 1986—. Lt. U.S. Navy, 1960-64. Mem. Heights Casino Club. Office: CL Global Ptnrs Securities Corp 95 Wall St New York NY 10005

WARNER, CECIL RANDOLPH, JR., lawyer; b. Fort Smith, Ark., Jan. 13, 1929; s. Cecil Randolph and Reba (Cheeves) W.; m. Susan Curry, Dec. 10, 1955 (div. 1982); children—Susan Rutledge, Rebecca Jane, Cecil Randolph III, Matthew Holmes Preston, Katherine Mary; m. Barbara Ragsdale, May 26, 1983. B.A. magna cum laude, U. Ark., 1950; LL.B. magna cum laude, Harvard U., 1953, Sheldon fellow, 1953-54. Bar: Ark. 1953. Practiced in Fort Smith, 1954—; partner firm Warner & Smith (and predecessor), 1954—; pres., chief exec. officer Fairfield Communities, Inc., 1973-81, chmn., chief exec. officer, 1981-85, chmn., pres., chief exec. officer, 1985—; dir. Mid-Am. Industries, Inc., Wortz Co., 1st Comml. Corp.; Instr. U. Ark. Sch. Law, 1954, 56; vice chmn. Ark. Constl. Revision Study Commn., 1967; v.p. 7th Ark. Constl. Conv., 1969-70. Scoutmaster troop 23 Boy Scouts Am., Fort Smith, 1955-58; commr. Ark. State Police Commn., 1970; bd. dirs. St. Vincent Infirmary Found., Ctrs. for Youth and Family, Ark. Symphony. Fellow Am. Bar Found., Ark. Bar Found.; mem. Am. Law Inst., ABA, Ark. Bar Assn. (past chmn. exec. com., past chmn. young lawyers sect.), Sebastian County Bar Assn., Fifty for the Future, Phi Beta Kappa, Phi Eta Sigma, Omicron Delta Kappa, Sigma Alpha Epsilon. Methodist. Office: Fairfield Communities Inc 2800 Cantrell Rd Little Rock AR 72203

WARNER, DARRELL G., petroleum company executive. Pres. Exxon Pipeline Co., Houston. Office: Exxon Pipeline Co 800 Bell Ave Houston TX 77002 *

WARNER, RICHARD ALAN, banker; b. Davenport, Iowa, Feb. 1, 1936; s. Charles C. and Audrey (Huson) W. B.S., Fla. State U., 1960. Public info. and employee communications mgr. Gen. Telephone Co. Fla., Tampa, 1961-67; exec. asst. to Gov. of Fla., Tallahassee, 1967-71; v.p. public relations Gen. Acceptance Corp., Miami, Fla., 1971-75; mem. public relations staff Eastern Airlines, Miami, 1975-77; with Security Pacific Nat. Bank, Los Angeles, 1978—; sr. v.p. public relations Security Pacific Nat. Bank, 1978-85, exec. v.p. corp. relations, 1985—. Office: Security Pacific Nat Bank PO Box 2097 Terminal Annex Los Angeles CA 90051

WARNER, ROLLIN MILES, JR., economics educator, financial planner, real estate broker; b. Evanston, Ill., Dec. 25, 1930; s. Rollin Miles Warner Sr. and Julia Herndon (Polk) Clarkson. BA, Yale U., 1953; cert. in law, Harvard U., 1956; MBA, Stanford U., 1960; cert. in edn., U. San Francisco, 1974. Asst. to v.p. fin. Stanford U., 1960-63; instr. econs. Town Sch., San Francisco, 1963-70; dean Town Sch., 1975—; prin. Mt. Tauralpais, Ross, Calif., 1972-74; dir. devel. Katharine Branson Sch., 1974-75; cons. Educators Collaborative, San Anselmo, Calif., 1983—, Nat. Ctr. for Fin. Edn., San Francisco, 1986—. Author: America, 1986, Europe, 1986, Africa, Asia, Russia, 1986, Greece, Rome, 1981. Scoutmaster to dist. commr. Boy Scouts Am., San Francisco, 1956—. Recipient Silver Beaver award Boy Scouts Am., 1986. Mem. Inst. Cert. Fin. Planners, Internat. Assn. for Fin. Planning, Manteca Bd. Realtors, Ind. Schs. Bus. Mgrs. Assn., Am. Econs. Assn., University (San Francisco), Grolier (N.Y.C.), San Francisco Yacht (Belvedere, Calif.), Old Oundelian (London). Office: Town Sch 2720 Jackson St San Francisco CA 94115

WARNOCK, JOHN JOSEPH JR., investment company executive; b. Hazlet, N.J., Sept. 29, 1955; s. John Joseph and Ann Margaret (Donovan) W.; m. Kathleen Mary Catrambone, Oct. 4, 1980; 1 child, Kaitlin Therese. BS, Villanova U., 1977. CPA, Pa. Acct., mgr. Arthur Andersen & Co., Phila., 1977-85; v.p. corp. fin. W.H. Newbold's Son & Co., Inc., Phila., 1985—; bd. dirs. World Affairs Council of Phila. Mem. Delaware Valley Venture Orgn., Assn. Corp. Growth, Racquet Club, Waynesborough Country Club. Republican. Roman Catholic. Office: WH Newbold's Son & Co Inc 1500 Walnut St Philadelphia PA 19102

WARREN, ALEX MCLEAN, JR., automotive executive; b. Augusta, Ga., Aug. 4, 1940; s. Alex McLean and Bessie Clay (Farris) W.; m. Barbara Howell, Feb. 16, 1963 (div.); children: Elizabeth Clay, Brian Lee; m. Virginia A. Fitzgerald, Jan. 3, 1980. B.A., U. Ky., 1962, LL.B., 1965; M.B.A., U. Chgo., 1979. Bar: Ky. 1965, Pa. 1969. Labor atty. U.S. Steel Corp., Pitts., 1968-72; dir. indsl. relations Rockwell Internat. Graphics Group, Chgo., 1972-75, dir. personnel, 1975-77; corp. dir. human resources Allegheyn Internat. Chemetron Group, Chgo., 1977-80; v.p. human resources Leaseway Transp. Corp., Cleve., 1980-83, sr. v.p. adminstrn., 1983-86; sr. v.p. adminstrn. Toyota Motor Mfg. USA, Lexington, Ky., 1986—. Trustee Greater Cleve. Jr. Achievement, 1982-86; task force Greater Cleve. Growth Assn., 1983-86, Ky. Econ. Devel. Corp., 1987—; bd. dirs. United Way Bluegrass, 1987—, Cleve. 500 Found., Fund for the Arts, 1988—, Opera House Fund, 1988—; founder, co-chmn., bd. dirs. Blugrass Tomorrow, 1988—. Served to capt. USAF, 1965-68. Mem. Lexington C. of C. (bd. dirs. 1988—), Georgetown C. of C. Republican. Presbyterian. Club: Chagrin Valley Country (Ohio). Home: 890 McMeekin Pl Lexington KY 40502 Office: Toyota Mfg USA Inc 1001 Cherry Blossom Way Georgetown KY 40324

WARREN, JEAN ELIZABETH, hospital executive; b. Phila., May 17, 1930; d. William Lawrence and Julia Evelyn (Bell) Hall; m. George Howard Warren, Mar. 4, 1949 (div. Apr. 1962); children—Bruce Eric, Adrienne Lynn. Student York Coll., 1977; Managerial Studies cert., Hofstra-Cornell Univs., 1979. Telephone operator N.Y. Telephone Co., Bklyn., 1952-61; telephone operator N.Y.C. Health and Hosp. Corp., Jamaica, N.Y., 1961-67, clinic supr., 1967-69, adminstrv. asst., 1969-74, acting asst. dir. grants, N.Y.C., 1974-76, Women, Infants and Children's program dir., Jamaica, 1976—; mem. health adv. bd. South Jamaica Ctr. for Children and Parents, 1978—. Recipient Significant Service award South Jamaica Ctr. for Children, 1978, 80, 84, 87, 88, Merit cert. N.Y. State Assembly, 1982; mem. Internat. Platform Assn., nutrition com. Queens Interfaith Network, Cen. Queens Task Force for the Homeless; Recognition award Queens Hosp. Ctr., 1982, 86, 87. Mem. Nat. Assn. Female Execs., N.Y. State Women Infant Children's Assn., Queens Zeta Amicae of Zeta Phi Beta (Amica of Yr. 1988). Democrat. Lutheran. Avocations: travel; cooking; sewing; swimming. Office: Queens Hosp Ctr Women Infants & Children Program 114-02 Guy R Brewer Blvd Jamaica NY 11434

WARREN, JOHN A., utility company executive; b. 1925; married. BS, Vanderbilt U., 1948. V.p. Goodwin Engrs., Inc., Birmingham, Ala., 1948-57; vice chmn., pres., chief operating officer Carolina Energies, Inc., Columbia, S.C., 1957-82; pres., chief operating officer S.C. Electric and Gas Co., Columbia, 1982-85, now chmn., chief exec. officer; pres., chief oper. officer Scana Corp., Columbia, 1982-85, vice chmn., chief exec. officer, 1985—, now chmn., chief exec. officer, also bd. dirs. Served with air corps USN. Office: SCANA Corp 1426 Main St Columbia SC 29226 *

WARREN, JOHN MARK, manufacturing executive; b. Wilmington, N.Y., Jan. 5, 1911; s. Frank and Mary (Haselton) W.; m. Nina Mason Koller, Oct. 22, 1938; 1 child, Nina Marie Warren Lancaster. Student, East Nazerene Coll., Wollaston, Mass., 1930-34; corr. cert., Inst. Applied Scis., Chgo., 1936-37. Mktg. profl. F.E. Mason Sons, Batavia, N.Y., 1936-37; driver Greyhound Bus Co., Phila., 1938-45; supt. Dr. Rodger W. Mann, Jeffersonville, Vt., 1947-48; mktg. profl. Rhea Lightning Rod Co., Trenton, N.J., 1948-49; pres. Warren Lightning Rod Co., Collingswood, N.J., 1950—; orignator, sponsor bus. forum Eastern Nazarene Coll., 1973—. Mem. Eastern Nazarene Coll. Alumni Assn. (pres. 1961-63, chmn. pres.' council 1965-67, named Alumnus of Yr. 1980). Republican. Methodist. Office: Warren Lightning Rod Co 2 Richey Ave Collinswood NJ 08107

WARREN, LAWRENCE DALE, insurance and trade companies executive; b. Scottsburg, Ind., Jan. 4, 1944; s. Lionel G. and Edna Marie (Hollin) W.; student Purdue U., 1961-65; m. Esther Sibal, Aug. 7, 1976; children—Alana Kay, Douglas Dale, Kirsten, Kourtney. Owner, pres. Products Unltd., Inc., Houston, 1967-69; ter. mgr. W. R. Grace & Co., Houston, 1970-76; owner L. Warren & Co., Houston, 1965—; owner, pres. Warren Internat., Inc., 1976—, pres. Ledak, Inc., 1984—; dir. Delta Gulf Industries, Houston, Continental Casing Inc. Mem. Producers Council, Inc. (pres. 1975-76), Constrn. Specifications Inst. (membership chmn. 1973-74), Million Dollar Round Table, Internat. Platform. Assn. Republican. Methodist. Home: 506 Magic Oaks Dr Spring TX 77388 Office: 5616 Spring-Cypress Rd Spring TX 77379

WARREN, PETER BEACH, economist; b. Washington, Oct. 9, 1922; s. Robert Beach and Mildred (Fisk) W.; m. Larissa Bonfante, Sept. 2, 1950 (div. 1962); 1 child, Alexandra; m. Ana Lillian Columna, Nov. 10, 1962. Econ. cons. USAID, Conakry, Guinea, 1962-64, Port-au-Prince, Haiti, 1981; econ. cons. Ford Found., Riyadh, Saudi Arabia, 1966; econ. cons. World Bank, Port-au-Prince, Haiti, 1975-76, Cairo, 1977-79; econ. cons. UN Devel. Program, Libreville, Gabon, 1979-81, Kingston, Jamaica, 1983; econ. cons. African Devel. Bank, Abidjan, Ivory Coast, 1986. Contbr. articles to profl. jours. Mem. planning bd. City of Roosevelt, N.J., 1974; active local civic affairs, Roosevelt, 1984—. Fulbright grantee, 1950. Democrat. Presbyterian. Home and Office: WEI 56 Pine Dr Roosevelt NJ 08555

WARREN, ROBERT A., electronics company executive; b. 1922; married. BS, U. Ill., 1948. With Cleve. Electric Illuminating Co., 1952; mgr. systems and procedures Harris-Seybold Co., 1952-54; with Premier Indsl. Corp., Cleve., 1954—, pres., 1970-87, now vice-chmn., 1987—, also bd. dirs. Office: Premier Indsl Corp 4500 Euclid Ave Cleveland OH 44103 *

WARREN, ROGER FREDERICK, manufacturing company executive; b. London, Apr. 26, 1941; came to U.S., 1977; s. George Frederick and Ivy Mabel (Locke) W.; m. Lucille Mary Theriault, June 2, 1966; children: Michael, Andrew. BS in Econs., U. Hull, Eng. Dir. new product devel. Gen. Foods Corp., Toronto, Ont., Can., 1965-77; dir. mktg. services Swift and Co., Chgo., 1977-78, v.p. internat. mktg., 1978-80, v.p., gen. mgr., 1980-85; exec. v.p., gen. mgr. Rayovac Corp., Madison, Wis., 1986—. Republican. Office: Rayovac Corp 601 Rayovac Dr Box 4960 Madison WI 53711

WARREN, RUSSELL JAMES, finance company executive, consultant; b. Cleve., July 28, 1938; s. Harold Fulton and Agnes Elmina (Hawkswell) W.; BS, Case Western Res. U., 1960; MBA, Harvard U., 1962. CPA, Ohio; m. Doris Helen Kenyeres, June 6, 1964. With Ernst & Whinney, Cleve., 1962-87, ptnr. in charge merger and acquisition svcs., 1976-87; pres. The TransAction Group, 1987—. Co-author: Implementing Mergers and Acquisitions in the Fin. Svcs. Industry, 1985; assoc. editor Jour. Corp. Growth, 1986-87, mem. editorial bd., 1988; contbg. editor Jour. Buyouts and Acquisitions, 1984-86; contbg. author venture capital financing study conducted in five selected countries for Asian Devel. Bank, Malaysia, Indonesia, Pakistan, Sri Lanka, Thailand, 1986. Trustee, Case Western Res. U., 1980—, Fairmount Prebyn. Ch., 1987—; dir. Univ. Tech., Inc.; bd. dirs. zoning appeals City of Lyndhurst, 1978—, chmn., 1980-82. Mem. Am. Inst. CPA's, Ohio Soc. CPA's, Assn. for Corp. Growth (bd. dirs intenrat. orgn. 1988, v.p. Cleve. chpt. 1983-86, pres. 1986-87), Cleve. Com. on Fgn. Rels. , Cleve. World Trade Assn., Newcomen Soc. Clubs: Mayfield Country, Catawba Island (Port Clinton, Ohio), Cleve. Athletic; Harvard (N.Y.C.); Put-in-Bay (Ohio) Yacht. Lodge: Jesters. Office: The TransAction Group 1666 Hanna Bldg Cleveland OH 44115-2001

WARREN, SUSAN, budget analyst; b. Montgomery, Ala., Oct. 31, 1948; d. James Stephen and Pearl Aquilla (Jones) Mangum; m. Bobby C. Warren, Aug. 13, 1977; children: Erica S., Bobbina C. BS, Ala. State U., 1971; postgrad., U. Md., 1973, 83, George Washington U., 1974, Johns Hopkins U., 1974. Cert. tchr., real estate agt. Md. claims authorizer HEW and Social Security, Balt., 1971-76; ops. analyst HHS, Social Security Adminstrn., Savannah, Ga., 1976-77; claims rep. Social Security Adminstrn., Columbus, Ga., 1977-80, HHS, Griffin, Ga., 1980-83; instr. Augsburg (Fed. Republic Germany) Edn. Ctr., 1983-84, Augsburg Am. High Sch., 1984-85; instr. European div. U. Md., Augsburg, 1984, Ala. State U., Montgomery, 1986; civilian employee U.S. Army, 1986—; budget analyst U.S. Army, Atlanta, 1987—. Mem. Internat. Tng. in Communication Club (2d v.p. Atlanta chpt. 1987—), NAACP, Am. Soc. Mil. Comptrollers, Alpha Kappa Alpha. Office: Hdqrs FORSCOM FC J8-PB-RPA Fort McPherson GA 30330

WARREN, TAMARA MARI, publishing executive; b. San Gabriel, Calif., Dec. 24, 1959; d. Allen Edward and Tana Mari W. BS, U. So. Calif., 1981. Mgr. Am. Teaching Aids, Covina, Calif., 1981-85; nat. sales mgr. Am. Teaching Aids, Covina, 1986-88, v.p., 1988—. Mem. L.A. World Affairs Council, 1985-88. Mem. Nat. Sch. Supply and Equipment Assn. (chmn. young execs. 1985-86), Pasadena Jr. C. of C., U. So. Calif. Assocs., Alpha Omicron Pi Alumni (pres. 1981-85). Republican. Jewish. Home: 630 Orange Grove Ave South Pasadena CA 91030 Office: 980 W San Bernardino Rd Covina CA 91722

WARREN, WILLIAM CLEMENTS, lawyer, educator; b. Paris, Tex., Feb. 3, 1909; s. Archibald Levy and Elma (Clements) W.; m. Diana June Peel Willock, Jan. 13, 1945; children—Robert Peel, Larissa Eve, William Liversidge. A.B., U. Tex., 1930, A.M., 1931; LL.B., Harvard U., 1935; LL.D. (hon.), L.I. U., 1955, Columbia U., 1981; Dr. rer. pol., U. Basle, 1965. Bar: Ohio 1937, N.Y. 1952, D.C. 1959. Assoc. Davis, Polk & Wardwell, N.Y.C., 1935-37; assoc. Holiday, Grossman & McAfee, Cleve., 1937-42; assoc. Milbank, Tweed, Hadley & McCloy, N.Y.C., 1942-47; prof. law Western Res. U., Cleve., 1937-42; mem. faculty Columbia Law Sch., N.Y.C., 1946-82, Kent prof. law, 1959-77, Kent prof. emeritus, 1977—, dean, 1952-70, dean emeritus, 1970—; ptnr. Roberts & Holland, N.Y.C., 1957—; dir. Guardian Life Ins. Co. Am., Sandoz, Inc., Sandoz United States, Inc., Sterling Nat. Bank & Trust Co. N.Y.C., CSS Industries, Aston-Martin LaGonda Group, Aladan Corp.; mem. N.Am. adv. bd. Swissair. Served as lt. col. U.S. Army, 1943-46. Decorated Bronze Star (2), Legion of Merit; comdr. Order of the Crown (Italy); recipient Medal for execellence Columbia Law Sch. Alumni Assn., 1969. Mem. ABA, Am. Judicature Soc., Am. Law Inst., Assn. of Bar of City of N.Y., N.Y. County Lawyers Assn., N.Y. State Bar Assn., Inst. Internat. Edn. (trustee), Order Moral Scis. (fgn. corr.), Accademia delle Scienze dell' Instituto di Bologna (fgn. corr. mem.; Order Moral Scis. 1971). Presbyterian. Clubs: Broad Street, Century Assn., Cosmos, Links, Metropolitan, Univ. Co-author: U.S. Income Taxation of Foreign Corporations and Nonresident Aliens, 1966; Cases and Materials on Accounting and the Law, 1978; Cases and Materials on Federal Wealth Transfer Taxation, 1982; Cases and Materials on Federal Income Taxation, Vol. I, 1972, supplement, 1983, Vol. II, 1980; pres., dir. Columbia Law Rev. Office: Roberts & Holland 30 Rockefeller Plaza New York NY 10112

WARREN, WILLIAM MICHAEL, JR., utilities company executive; b. Bryan, Tex., June 8, 1947; s. William Michael and Rebecca Carolyn (Glass) W.; m. Anne Candler McLeod, June 5, 1968; children: William Powers, Laura Anne, Amy Lynn. BA, Auburn U., 1968; JD, Duke U., 1971. Bar: Ala. 1971. Assoc. Bradley, Arant, Rose & White, Birmingham, Ala., 1971-77, ptnr., 1977-83; v.p., gen. counsel Ala. Gas Corp., Birmingham, 1983-84, pres., chief operating officer, 1984—; exec. v.p. Energen Corp., Birmingham, 1987—; bd. dirs. AmSouth Bank Birmingham N.A., Energen Corp., Ala. Gas Corp. Contbr. articles to periodicals. Bd. dirs. Ala. Symphony Orch., Birmingham, 1985—; trustee Truman Pierce Inst., Auburn, Ala., 1986—; vice chmn. Leadership Birmingham Alumni Assn., 1987. Served to 1st lt. USAF, 1971-72. Mem. ABA, Am. Gas Assn., So. Gas Assn., Birmingham Area C. of C. (bd. dirs. 1986—), Relay House (bd. dirs. 1987). Democrat. Methodist. Lodge: Rotary. Home: 3533 Mill Springs Rd Birmingham AL 35223 Office: Ala Gas Corp 2101 6th Ave Birmingham AL 35203

WARRICK, WILLIAM W., banker. V.p. corp. audit Am. Express Co., N.Y.C. Office: Am Express Co Am Express Tower World Fin Ctr New York NY 10004 *

WARTELL, WARREN MICHAEL, marketing professional; b. Bklyn., Apr. 28, 1946; s. George and Edna W.; m. Joan Lyons, Dec. 25, 1975; children: Phillip, Dean. B in Indsl. Design, Pratt Inst., 1965; BA, CUNY, 1969; MBA, Wagner Grad. Sch. Bus., 1977. Mgr. bus. devel., adminstrv. mgr., then exec. asst. to pres. Vimar Bus. Systems, N.Y.C., 1969-75; adminstr., med. services div. Itel Corp., Port Washington, N.Y., 1977-79; with Lumex, Inc., Bay Shore, N.Y., 1979—; mktg. Lumex, Inc., 1983-86, mgr. market planning, devel., 1986—; speaker in field. Co-editor, adviser Gadget Book: Ingenious Devices, 1985. Bd. dirs. Community Programs L.I., Dix Hill, N.Y., 1984—; mem. adv. bd. Adelphi U. , Garden City, N.Y., 1986. Mem. Electronic Industries Assn. (adviser 1984—), Internat. Assn. Gerontol. Entrepreneurs, Am. Mktg. Assn., Nat. Assn. Sr. Living Industries, Rehab. Engring. Soc. N. Am., Am. Acad. Med. Adminstrs., Health Industry Mfrs. Assn., Nat. Assn. Retail Druggists. Home: 61 Hooper St Port Jefferson NY 11776 Office: Lumex Inc 100 Spence St Bay Shore NY 11706

WARTH, PHILLIP ROGER, foundation administrator; b. Balt., June 5, 1947; Philip Roger and Agnes (Schuster) W.; m. Jeanne Marie Pickert, Aug. 10, 1968; children: Celia Lea, Jason Charles. BS, U. Dayton, Ohio, 1969; M in Cert. Planning, Ohio State U., 1971. Dir. Greenville (S.C.) County Planning Com., 1971-75; exec. dir. Greenville Redevel. Authority, 1976-85; interim exec. dir. Greenville Mus. of Art, 1982-83; pres., chief exec. offficer Second Harvest Nat. Foodbank Network, Chgo., 1985—; adj. prof. econs. Furnam U., Greenville, 1976-78; lectr. Clemson U., 1974-82. Editor fin. newsletter The Greystone Letter, 1986. Bd. dirs. Chgo. Commons, 1988—, Food Research & Action Ctr., Washington, 1987—; gubenatorial appointee, S.C. Election Law Study Com., Columbia, S.C., 1980. Recipient Order of the Palmetto, Gov. Richard Riley, Columbia, S.C., 1985. Mem. Am. Soc. Planning Ofcls. Roman Catholic. Club: Union League (Chgo.). Home: 2752 Eastwood Ave Evanston IL 60201 Office: Second Harvest Nat Foodbank Network 343 W Dearborn Suite 410 Chicago IL 60604

WARTHEN, JOHN EDWARD, construction, leasing and finance executive; b. Cedar City, Utah, May 8, 1922; s. Mark Tew and Emma (Simkins) W.; student Branch Agrl. Coll. So. Utah, Cedar City, 1940-41; m. Norma Jane Hansen, June 22, 1943; children—Russel Edward, John Merrill, Judith Lally, Linda Fahringer, Carla Jean Thompson, Lauri Janette Sherratt. Pres., mgr. St. George Service, Inc. (Utah), 1945-61, Warthen Constrn. Co., Las Vegas, 1961—, Warthen Buick, 1961—; pres., gen. mgr. Diversified Investment & Leasing Corp., Las Vegas. Councilman, City of St. George, 1950-54. Trustee, treas. Latter Day Saint Br. Geneal. Library, Las Vegas, 1964-76 ; co-founder Ctr. for Internat. Security Studies; past dist. dir. Freeman Inst.; past nat. dir. Liberty Amendment Com.; past chmn. Citizens for Pvt. Enterprise, Las Vegas; mem. Council Inter-Am. Security, Americanism Ednl. League; past fin. chmn. Boy Scouts Am.; past state chmn. Nev. Dealer Election Action Com.; mem. Nev. Devel. Authority, Pres.'s Club Brigham Young U. Mem. Ludwig Von Misses Inst. Econs. (charter), SAR (Good Citizenship award nat. soc.). Mormon (bishop 1957-61). Clubs: Rotary, Kiwanis. Home: 2475 E Viking St Las Vegas NV 89121 Office: 3025 E Sahara Ave Las Vegas NV 89104

WARWICK, ROBERT FRANKLIN, accountant; b. Wilmington, N.C., May 26, 1936; s. James Franklin and Virginia (Cayce) W.; m. Catherine Herring, Sept. 11, 1955; children: Carol Diane, Steven James. Student, Wilmington Coll., 1955; BBA, U. N.C., 1958. CPA, N.C. Staff acct. C.S. Lowrimore & Co., Wilmington, 1958-62; ptnr. Lowrimore, Warwick & Co., Wilmington, 1962-73, mng. ptnr., 1973—. Bd. dirs. East Carolina U. Med. Sch. Found., Greenville, N.C., 1979—, U. N.C. Wilmington Found., 1981—; pres. Wilmington C. of C., 1981, Wilmington Indsl. Devel., 1982-83. Mem. Am. Inst. CPA's, N.C. Assn. CPA's, Nat. Acctg. Assn., Associated Regional Acctg. Firms (chmn. 1988—). Rebublican. Presbyterian. Clubs: Cape Fear (Wilmington) (bd. dirs., pres. 1978-86), Cape Fear Country. Home: Wilmington NC 28402 Office: Lowrimore Warwick & Co PO Box 661 110 Grace St Wilmington NC 28402

WASCHKA, RONALD WILLIAM, independent oil and gas producer; b. Memphis, Sept. 2, 1932; s. Frederick William and Hazel Celeste (Guidroz) W.; B.A., U. Miss., 1960; M.A., Memphis State U., 1970, Ph.D., 1977; m. Patricia Janet Sinclair Hanney, July 27, 1963; children—Michael, John, Anne Marie, Helen Marissa. Service asst. Memphis State U., 1970, teaching asst., 1972-75; with Legis. Reference Service, Library of Congress, Washington, 1955; founder, owner Ronald Co., Inc., Memphis, 1963-81; ind. oil and gas producer, Germantown, Tenn., then Ft. Worth, 1972—. Com. mem. Boy Scouts Am., Germantown, 1975-81. Served with USAF, 1955-59, Tenn. Air N.G., 1963-69. Mem. Res. Officers Assn., Am. Petroleum Inst., Ind. Producers Assn. Am., Am. Econ. History Assn., Am. Hist. Assn., Orgn. Am. Historians, So. Hist. Assn. Republican. Roman Catholic. Clubs: Petroleum (Ft. Worth); Padre Isles Country (Corpus Christi); Sturgeon Bay Yacht (Wis.); Summit. Lodge: Rotary (Paul Harris fellow 1985). Died Feb. 6, 1987. Home: 2108 Oak Knoll Dr Colleyville TX 76034 Office: 210 W 6th St Suite 1202 Fort Worth TX 76102

WASHBURN, CHARLES WAYNE, transportation company executive; b. Brookfield, Mo., June 13, 1946; c. Gerald L. and Hazel L. (McCollum) W.;

m. Linda E. Stanturf, Aug. 18, 1972; children: Scott A., Monica L. BBA, U. Mo., 1968. CPA, Mo. Staff auditor U.S. Dept. Treasury, St. Louis, 1968; staff acct. Harden, Cummins, Moss & Miller, Chillicothe, Mo., 1970-72; asst. controller Marshfield Homes, Inc., Chillicothe, 1972-74; controller McCarty Truck Line, Inc., 1974-75; treas. Churchill Truck Lines, Inc., Chillicothe, 1975—; treas. employee polit. action com., 1982—. Treas. Chillicothe Park Bd., 1981—. With U.S. Army, 1968-70. Mem. Am. Inst. CPA's, Am. Legion, Masons. Republican. Baptist. Office: Churchill Truck Lines Inc PO Box 250 Chillicothe MO 64601

WASHBURN, JERRY MARTIN, accountant, information systems company executive; b. Powell, Wyo., Dec. 31, 1943; s. Roland and Lavon (Martin) W.; divorced; children: Garth, Gavin, Kristina. BS in Acctg. Brigham Young U., 1969. CPA, Wash., Idaho, Oreg. Staff acct. Arthur Andersen & Co., Seattle, 1969-70, sr. auditor, Boise, Idaho, 1971-73, audit mgr., Boise and Portland, Oreg., 1976-79; v.p. controller Washburn Musicland, Inc., Phoenix, 1980-82; mgr., ptnr. Washburn Enterprises, Phoenix, 1977—; pres. Total Info. Systems, Inc., Phoenix, 1984—; founding dir. Internat. and Commerce Bank, Phoenix, 1985-86. Mem. Inst. Internal Auditors (pres. Boise chpt. 1974, bd. dirs. Boise and Portland chpts. 1975-77), Am. Mgmt. Soc., Am. Inst. CPAs, Wash. Soc. CPAs, Idaho Soc. CPAs. Republican. Office: Total Info Systems Inc 4201 N 24th St Suite 150 Phoenix AZ 85016

WASHBURN, JOEL TRENT, editor; b. McKenzie, Tenn., Jan. 26, 1957; s. James Loyd and Ramona (Kemp) W.; m. Teresa Brawner, Apr. 18, 1981; 1 child, Brittany. BBA, Union U., 1979. Mng. editor The McKenzie (Tenn.) Banner Newspaper, 1981—; chmn. bd. Associated Pubs., Inc., Huntington, Tenn., 1986—. Mem. McKenzie Jaycees (pres. 1980). Lodge: Lions (treas. McKenzie club 1984-85, pres. 83-84). Home: PO Box 125 McKenzie TN 38201 Office: The McKenzie Banner PO Box 100 McKenzie TN 38201

WASHBURN, JOHN ROSSER, entrepreneur; b. Hopewell, Va., July 24, 1943; s. Winthrop Doane and Mary Virginia (Overstreet) W.; m. Judith Ann Rosen, May 16, 1971 (div. Feb. 1982); m. Tana Jean Demro, July 9, 1982; children: Eric Joseph Harrison, Amanda Ashley. Student Louisburg Jr. Coll., 1963, Va. Commonwealth U., 1963-64, U. Richmond Extension, 1967-69, Williams Coll., 1985, Stanford U., 1986-87. Asst. mgr. Liberty Loan Corp., Richmond, Va., 1965-67; loan interviewer Cen. Fidelity Bank, Richmond, 1967-69; regional credit/sales supr. Moores Bldg. Supplies, Inc., Roanoke, Va., 1969-74; corp. credit mgr. Owens & Minor, Inc., Richmond, 1974—; fin., investment cons. JA-GO Enterprises, Richmond, 1982—, Washburn Enterprises, 1984—; instr., lectr. investment, fin., credit mgmt., 1970—; sec.-treas. Multi-Enterprises, Inc., 1988—. Active Nat. Rep. Congl. Com., 1980—, YMCA, 1979—, Am. Mus. Nat. History, 1982—, U.S. Def. Com., 1981—; mem. Credit Rsch. Found. Mem. Internat. Platform Assn., Nat. Assn. Credit Mgmt. (Appreciation cert for outstanding svc. 1980-81, pres. Cen. Va. sect. 1979-80, chmn. legis. com. 1977-79, dir. 1983—), Am. Mgmt. Assn., Nat. Wildlife Fedn. Congressional Club, Hopewell Yacht Clut, Moose. Episcopalian. Office: Owens & Minor Inc 2727 Enterprise Pkwy Richmond VA 23229

WASHBURN, STEWART, management consultant; b. Boston, July 24, 1923; s. Charles Parker and Mary Ethel (Stewart) W. AB, St. John's Coll., 1951. Cert. mgmt. cons. Sr. engr. to asst. dir. indsl. hygiene Nat. Safety Council, Chgo., 1951-54; mng. dir. Stewart A. Washburn & Co., Inc., N.Y.C., 1954-62; ptnr. Porter Henry & Co., Inc., N.Y.C., 1962-77; pvt. practice cons. Lakeville, Mass., 1977—. Author: Measuring Sales Effectiveness and Productivity, 1983, Successful Pricing, 1985, Finding and Launching Successful New Products, 1985, Managing the Market Functions, 1988; co-founder, practice devel. editor: Jour. Mgmt. Cons., 1982—. Actice various mcpl. offices and coms. With U.S. Army, 1943-46. Recipient Silver medal Internat. Film Festival, 1968, 69. Mem. Inst. Mgmt. Cons. (founding mem., chpt. pres. 1984-87), Am. Arbitration Assn. (mem. comml. panel). Home and Office: Off Old Main St East Lakeville MA 02347

WASMUTH, DUANE LEE, corporate executive, consultant; b. Midland, Mich., Jan. 2, 1939; s. Ralph and Midge Winefred (Mathewson) w.; m. Gwendolyn Beatrice McKay, Aug. 10, 1963; children: Lisa Anne, Jeffrey Duane. BSME, U. Mich., 1962, MS in Indsl. Engring., 1963, MBA, 1964. Supt. mfg. Chevrolet div. Gen. Motors Corp., Detroit, 1964-70; v.p. mfg. Rectrans Inc., Brighton, Mich., 1970-71; pres. Internat. Husky Inc., Bloomfield Hills, Mich., 1971-77; group v.p. Key Internat. Inc., Southfield, Mich., 1977-79; pres. vehicle group IC Industries Inc, Chgo., 1980-83, Amerind Inc., Chgo., 1983-86; exec. v.p. CCC Info. Services Inc., Chgo., 1986—; bd. dirs. GMW Fin. Services Inc., GIS Info. Systems Inc., v.p., 1987—; cons. Anographics Corp., Chgo., 1986—. Mem. Hundred Club of Cook County, Chgo., 1981—, U. Mich. Pres. Club, Ann Arbor, 1977—, U. Mich. Victors Club, Ann Arbor, 1977—, Chgo. Econ. Club, 1981—. Regents Alumni scholar U. Mich., 1957; Indsl. Engring. fellow Inst. Labor and Indsl. Reins., 1962. Mem. Exmoor Country Club, Ocean Reef Club, Health and Tennis Club. Home: 811 N Sheridan Rd Lake Forest IL 60045 Office: CCC Info Svcs Inc 640 N La Salle St Chicago IL 60610

WASSERLEIN, JOHN HENRY, paper manufacturing company executive; b. Evergreen Park, Ill., July 25, 1941; s. Henry George and Dorothy (Brink) W.; children: John Henry, Heather, Deborah. S.B. in M.E., MIT, 1963; grad Program Mgmt. Devel., Harvard U., 1971. With Scott Paper Co., 1963-69, mgr. engring. research and devel., 1969-83; v.p., gen. mgr. splty. paperboard div. Boise Cascade Corp., Brattleboro, Vt., 1983—, v.p., gen. mgr. Pub. Packaging Paper div., 1983—; v.p., dir. Boise Cascade Can Ltd., 1983—; pres. Missisquoi Assocs., 1982—, Sheldon Springs Power Co., 1982—, Brownville Power Co., 1982—, Beaver Falls Power Co, 1982—. Patentee winding apparatus. Served to capt. C.E. AUS, 1964-66. Recipient Monongahela Forestry Leadership award, 1977. Mem. Am. Mgmt. Assn., TAPPI, Paper Industry Mgmt. Assn., ASME, Fourdinier Kraft Bd. Group (bd. dirs.), Am. Paper Inst., Nat. Rifle Assn., Internat. Bicycle Touring Soc., Mensa, Pi Tau Sigma, Chi Phi. Republican. Congregationalist. Office: Boise Cascade Corp One Jefferson Sq Boise ID 83728

WASSERMAN, BERNARD, engineering executive; b. Hamilton, Ont., Can., June 12, 1925; came to U.S., 1947; m. Joan B. Baucum, Dec. 28, 1973; children: Katherine, Deborah, Henry, Jan, Kyle. B of Applied Sci., U. Toronto, Can., 1947; MS, MIT, 1949. Instr. U. Wis., Madison, 1949-51; sr. engr. Sylvania Inc., Buffalo, 1952-56; program mgr. Bell Aero Systems, Buffalo, 1956-61; chief engr. Epsco Inc., Westwood, Mass., 1961-64; program mgr. Avco Systems Div., Wilmington, Mass., 1964-68; program dir. Avco Everett Research Labs., Everett, Mass., 1968-75; mgr. systems engring. Am. Sci. and Engring., Cambridge, Mass., 1975-77; program dir. Dynatrend Inc., Woburn, Mass., 1977-83; v.p. engring. Textron Def. Systems, Wilmington, 1983—. Inventor in field. Mem. Wayland (Mass.) Conservation Commn., 1966, industry task force Cen. New Eng. Coll., 1986-88. Mem. IEEE (sr.), Tech. Mktg. Soc. Am., Am. Mgmt. Assn., Am. Def. Preparedness Assn., Nat. Wildlife Fedn., Profl. Engrs. Ont., Sigma Xi (assoc.), Eta Kappa Nu. Republican. Jewish. Club: U.S. Senatorial. Home: 37 Moonpenny Dr Boxford MA 01921 also: Sint Maarten Netherlands Antilles Office: Textron Def Systems 201 Lowell St Wilmington MA 01887

WASSERMAN, BERT W., communications and publishing company executive. With office of pres. Warner Communications Inc., N.Y.C. Office: Warner Communications Inc 75 Rockefeller Pla New York NY 10019 *

WASSERMAN, LEONARD MARTIN, lawyer; b. Wilmington, Del., Mar. 6, 1946; s, Isaac Ephraim and Elizabeth (Winkler) W.; m. Miryam Rivka Weiser, June 16, 1968; children: Abigail Eva, Gabriel Zachary. BS, Columbia U., 1968; JD, Bklyn Law Sch., 1972. Bar: N.Y. 1973, U.S. Dist. Ct. (so. dist., ea. dist.) N.Y. 1974. Jr. project coord. N.Y.C. Housing Devel. Adminstrn., 1968-69; law clk. to presiding judge U.S. Dist. Ct. (so. dist.) N.Y., 1972-73; assoc. Stroock & Stroock & Lavan, N.Y.C., 1973-77, Herrick & Feinstein, N.Y.C., 1977-80; assoc. regional counsel U.S. Gen. Services, N.Y.C., 1980-81; assoc. counsel N.Y. State Mortgage Loan Enforcement & Adminstrn. Corp., N.Y.C., 1981-83; successively dep. gen. counsel, dep. chief econ. devel. div. N.Y.C. Law Dept., 1984-85, chief econ. devel. div., 1985—; bd. dirs. N.Y.C. Indsl. Devel. Agy., N.Y.C. Pub. Devel. Corp. BD. dirs. Hebrew Immigrant Aid Soc., N.Y.C., 1976—; trustee, v.p. Congregation B'nai Israel Anshei Emes, Bklyn., 1980—. Mem. ABA, N.Y. State Bar Assn., Assn. of Bar of City of N.Y. Democrat. Office: NYC Law Dept 100 Church St New York NY 10007

WASSERMAN, LEW R., film, recording, publishing company executive; b. Cleve., Mar. 15, 1913; m. Edith T. Beckerman, July 5, 1936; 1 dau., Lynne Kay. D (hon.), Brandeis U., NYU. Nat. dir. advt. and publicity Music Corp. Am., 1936-38, v.p., 1938-39, became v.p. charge motion picture div., 1940; now chmn., chief exec. officer, dir., mem. exec. com. MCA, Inc., also chmn. bd., chief exec. officer, dir. subsidiary corps.; dir. Am. Airlines; chmn. emeritus Assn. Motion Picture and TV Producers. Trustee John F. Kennedy Library, John F. Kennedy Center Performing Arts, Calif. Inst. Tech., Jules Stein Eye Inst., Carter Presdl. Ctr., Lyndon Baines Johnson Found.; pres. Hollywood Canteen Found.; chmn. Research to Prevent Blindness Found.; hon. chmn. bd. Center Theatre Group Los Angeles Music Center; bd. dirs. Amateur Athletic Found. of Los Angeles (chmn. fin. com.), Los Angeles Music Ctr. Found.; bd. gov.'s Ronald Reagan Presdl. Found. Recipient Jean Hersholt Humanitarian award Acad. Motion Picture Arts and Scis., 1973. Democrat. Office: MCA Inc 100 Universal City Plaza Universal City CA 91608 *

WASSERMAN, RODGER DEAN, transportation-computer systems consulting company executive; b. Detroit, Jan. 14, 1946; s. Alvin and Edith Lorraine (Kavieff) W.; M.A., Mich. State U., 1968; m. Aug. 3, 1969; children: Amy Briar, Kurt Nicholas, Songwriter, pub. Charrington Music Co., Detroit and Notable Music, Inc., N.Y., 1967-69; v.p. Allied Indsl. Contractors, Inc., Detroit, 1969-72; pres. Abacus Corp., Detroit, 1972—; pres. Am. Delivery System, Detroit, Am. Distbn. Systems, Detroit; dir. Allied Delivery System, Detroit, Rodger Wasserman & Partners, Detroit; chmn. Distbn. Logistics Inst., Detroit; cons. computerization and design transp. systems Gen. Motors Parts div. Upjohn Co., Signal Delivery. Contbr. articles to profl. jours. Jewish. Club: Bloomfield Open Hunt. Designed and developed one of first mini-computer bus. systems in U.S., 1972, first computer system capable performing 100% freight routing, billing, and control, 1974, first commercially feasible computerization of freight rating, 1976, developed/introduced first totally computerized nat. distbn. system, 1986, 88, 89. Home: 3951 Shellmarr Bloomfield Hills MI 48013

WASSERSTEIN, BRUCE, investment banker; b. N.Y.C., Dec. 25, 1947; s. Morris and Lola Wasserstein; m. Christine Parrott; children: Pamela, Ben, Alex. BA with honors, U. Mich., 1967; MBA with high distinction, Harvard U., 1971, JD cum laude, 1971; diploma in law, Cambridge U., 1972. Assoc. Cravath, Swaine & Moore, N.Y.C., 1972-77; mng. dir. The First Boston Corp., N.Y.C., 1977—; pres. Wasserstein, Perella and Co., NYC, 1988—. Author: Corporate Finance Law. Trustee Dalton Sch. Mem. Council on Fgn. Relations. Democrat. Office: Wasserstein Perella & Co 31 W 52nd St 7th Floor New York NY 10019

WASSINK, JAMES MICHAEL, management information systems executive; b. Batavia, N.Y., Nov. 6, 1946; s. Robert G. and Mary E. (Dunn) W.; m. Sheila L. Widgay, July 6, 1985. Supr. Erie Boces #1, Lancaster, N.Y., 1968-79; mgr. mgmt. info. systems Wegmans Food Market, Rochester, N.Y., 1979—. Sgt. USAF, 1964-68, ETO.

WATANABE, KOUICHI, pharmacologist, educator; b. Manchuria, Japan, Aug. 26, 1942; s. Tetsuya and Mine W.; children—Toshikazu, Yoshihiro, Motohiro. B.S., Tokyo Coll. Pharmacy, 1966; M.S., Osaka U., 1968; Ph.D., 1971; LPIBA, 1986; DSc (hon.) Internat. U. Found., 1987. Vis. fellow reprodn. research br. Nat. Inst. Child Health and Devel., NIH, Bethesda, Md., 1971-73; vis. scientist dept. pharmacology Coll. Medicine, Howard U., Washington, 1973-75, asst. prof., 1975-83; asst. prof. pharmacology U. Hawaii, 1983—; mgr. Fiujimoto Diagnostics Inc., Osaka, Japan. Contbr. articles to sci. jours. Am. Cancer Soc. grantee, 1980-81. Mem. Am. Soc. Pharmacology and Exptl. Therapeutics, N.Y. Acad. Scis., Am. Soc. Hypertension (charter). Subspecialties: Chemotherapy; Molecular pharmacology. Current work: Mechanism of action of various antineoplastic agts. on calmodulin. Vinca alkaloids found to be calmodulin inhibitors. Suggested that amounts of calmodulin or its binding proteins may be endogenous regulators of antineoplastic action or transport of these drugs. Home: 8-2-10 Minamirin-Kan, Yamato-City, Kanagawa 242, Japan Office: TKK Internat Div Taiyo Keiei Kanri Co Ltd, 1-22-27, Taiyo BLD, Hyakunincho, Shinjuku-ku, Tokyo Japan

WATCHORN, WILLIAM ERNEST, diversified management executive; b. Toronto, Ont., Can., Aug. 8, 1943; s. Roy Elgin and Josephine (Swyryda) W.; m. Maureen Emmett, Dec. 28, 1967; 1 child, Meghan. Degree in Acctg., Queen's U., Toronto, 1967. Mgr. fin. planning Found. Group of Cos., Toronto, 1968-72; controller Selkirk Holdings, Ltd., Toronto, 1972-75; corp. contr. Torstar Corp., Toronto, 1975-78; v.p. fin. Canwest Capital Corp., Winnipeg, Man., 1978-82; exec. v.p. Kaiser Resources Ltd., Vancouver, B.C., 1982; sr. v.p., chief fin. officer Fed. Industries Ltd., Winnipeg, 1982-88; pres., chief exec. officer Fed. Industries Indsl. Group, Winnipeg, 1989—, also bd. dirs.; bd. dirs. Delhi Industries Holdings Ltd., Heron Cable Industries Ltd., Hull-Thomson Ltd., Milltronics Ltd., Neo Industries Inc., Neolor S.Am. Vice-chmn. bd. govs. Balmoral Hall Sch., Winnipeg; chmn. Winnipeg Bus. Devel. Corp.; vice-chair Western Regional Com. C.D. Howe Inst., Toronto; bd. dirs. adv. bd. Manitoba Small Bus. Growth Fund. Mem. Can. Inst. Chartered Accts., Man. Inst. Chartered Accts., B.C. Inst. Chartered Accts., Ont. Inst. Chartered Accts., Winnipeg C. of C. (v.p.), Carleton Club, Winter Club. Mem. Conservative Party. Home: 6453 Southboine Dr, Winnipeg, MB Canada R3R 0B7 Office: Fed Industries Indsl Group, 1210 One Lombard Place, Winnipeg, MB Canada R3B 0X3

WATERBURY, JACKSON DEWITT, marketing executive; b. Evanston, Ill., Feb. 4, 1937; s. Jackson D. and Eleanor (Barrows) W.; m. Suzanne Butler, Aug. 27, 1958 (div. Jan. 1970); children: Jackson D. III, Arthur Barrows; m. Lynn Hardin, Mar. 17, 1971 (div. July 1984); 1 child, Timothy Bradford; m. Carolyn Jenkins, Sept. 20, 1986; 1 child, Kathryn Britt. AB, Brown U., 1959. Account exec. D'Arcy Advt. Co., St. Louis, 1958-63, Batz-Hodgson-Neuwoehner, Inc., St. Louis, 1963-66; exec. v.p., sec. Lynch, Phillips & Waterbury, Inc., St. Louis, 1966-68; pres. Jackson Waterbury & Co., St. Louis, 1968-73; v.p., ptnr. Vinyard & Lee & Ptnrs., 1973-74; pres. Waterbury Inc., 1975-80, Bright Ideas, Inc., 1977-80; v.p./group supr. Batz-Hodgson-Neuwoehner, St. Louis, 1980-81; sr. v.p. Fawcett McDermott Cavanagh, Honolulu, 1981-82; prin. Waterbury Cons., 1982-88; sr. v.p. planning & research Kenrick Advt., Inc., St. Louis, 1984-86; chmn. Pocket Guide Publs., Inc., Denver, 1986—; chmn. Mountain Sports Sales, Inc., Denver, 1986—; v.p., group supr. Kerlick, Switzer & Johnson, Inc., St. Louis, 1987-88; chmn., chief exec. officer Keystone Group, St. Louis, 1988—; chmn. publicity U.S. Golf Assn. Open Championship, 1964; bd. dirs. River Cities Broadcasting Corp., Belleville, Ill., 1986—, Mo. Motorcycle Assn., 1972-75, Strathalbyn Farms Club, 1971-79, 1986—, Alice Blake Realtors, 1971-79, Arimo Distbrs., 1967-75, Children's Christmas Fund. Football coach Mo. High Sch. All-Stars, 1966-67, St. Louis U., 1968-70; vice chmn. bd. dirs. Hawaii Soccer Assn., 1981-83. Mem. Ducks Unltd., Am. Motorcycle Assn., St. Louis Advt. Producers Assn. (steering com., negotiating com. 1977-80), Beta Theta Pi. Episcopalian. Clubs: Racquet, Strathalbyn Farms (bd. dirs.). Home: 118 N Bemiston Saint Louis MO 63105 Office: Keystone Group 10 S Brentwood Blvd Saint Louis MO 63105

WATERFIELD, RANDOLPH HEARST, JR., accountant; b. Drexel Hill, Pa., Dec. 19, 1931; s. Randolph H. and Clara N. (Pontius) W.; m. Elizabeth Geistweit, Jan. 21, 1956; children: Adam D., Ellen. BS in Bus. Adminstrn., Drexel U., 1955. CPA, Pa. Staff acct. Arthur Young & Co., Phila., 1955-62, audit mgr., 1962-66, audit prin., 1966-68, ptnr., 1968-75; dir. east region acctg. and auditing Arthur Young & Co., N.Y.C. and Washington, 1975-85; office mng. ptnr. Arthur Young & Co., Washington, 1985-89, sr. ptnr., 1989—. Contbr. articles to profl. jours. Trustee Drexel U., Phila., 1983—; bd. dirs. Greater Washington Bd. Trade, 1988; corp. sponsors com. Washington Performing Arts Soc., Washington, 1987—. Mem. Am. Inst. CPA's (chmn. ins. co. com. 1973-76, chmn. com. relations with actuaries 1976-79), Dist. Columbia Inst. CPA's, Nat. Assn. Accts., Univ. Club, Washington Golf and Country Club, Pisces Club. Republican. Episcopal. Home: 8400 Sparger St McLean VA 22102 Office: Arthur Young & Co 3000 K St NW Washington DC 20007

WATERMAN, JOSEPH FRANCIS, corporate executive; b. Phila., Nov. 11, 1951; s. Joseph F. and Claire Marie (Halpin) W.; m. Jo-el Borden, June 1, 1974; children: Joseph, Christine, Kevin, Timothy. BS in Acctg., St. Francis Coll., Loretto, Pa., 1973. CPA, Pa. Staff to sr. acct. Touche Ross and Co., Phila., 1973-77; supr. fin. rep. IU Internat., Phila., 1977-79; fin. project mgr. Safeguard Scientifics Inc., King of Prussia, Pa., 1979-81, asst. controller, 1981-84; mgr. corp. devel. Safeguard Scientifics Inc., King of Prussia, 1984-86, v.p. corp. devel., 1986—; v.p., treas. MVIC/CompuCom Systems, Cherry Hill, N.J., 1986-89; bd. dirs. MVIC/CompuCom Systems, Cherry Hill, 1987—; bd. dirs. DDI Fin. Systems, Wayne, Pa. Mem. AICPA, Aronimink Golf Club. Office: Safeguard Scientifics Inc 630 Park Ave King of Prussia PA 19312

WATERS, DAVID MICHAEL, real estate finance executive; b. Springfield, Mass., Oct. 13, 1942; s. John Francis and Mary Agnes (Cavanaugh) W. BA in English, Am. Internat. Coll., 1965. Assoc. dir. real estate investment Mass. Mut. Life Ins. Co., Springfield, 1968-80; div. v.p. Barclays Am./Bus. Credit Inc., East Hartford, Conn., 1980-82, v.p. real estate financing activity, 1982-84, sr. v.p. real estate ops., 1984-86, pres. real estate div., 1986—; sr. v.p. Barclay's Am. Corp., Charlotte, N.C., 1986—; chmn. real estate adv. com. Barclays Bank PLC, N.Y.C., 1987—. Contbr. articles to profl. publs. Lt. (j.g.) USNR, 1965-68, Vietnam. Mem. Mortgage Bankers Assn. Am. (income property com.), Urban Land Inst., Internat. Coun. Shopping Ctrs. Republican. Roman Catholic. Home: 385 Nassau Dr Springfield MA 01129 Office: Barclays Am Bus Credit Inc 111 Founders Plaza East Hartford CT 06108

WATERS, DAVID ROGERS, retail executive; b. Akron, Ohio, Apr. 27, 1932; s. Herbert H. and Winifred Elsie (Kearns) W.; m. Barbara West; children: Ann S., David Rogers, Thomas J., Peter M., Christopher C., Elizabeth E., Jeffrey P. BS in Econs., U. Pa., 1954. Trainee, asst. to controller W.R. Grace & Co., N.Y.C., 1954-55; buyer M. O'Neil Co., Akron, 1957-62; div. mdse. mgr. May-Cohens, Jacksonville, Fla., 1962-66, Rich's, Atlanta, 1967; pres., gen. mdse. mgr. DePinna, N.Y.C., 1967-69; gen. mdse. mgr., then pres. Garfinckel's, Washington, 1969-73; pres. Garfinckel, Brooks Bros., Miller & Rhoads, Inc., Washington, 1972-76, pres., chief exec. officer, 1976-81; chmn., dir. Frederick Atkins, Inc., 1980-81; exec. v.p., mem. mgmt. policy com., pres. Splty Retailing Group Gen Mills., Inc., 1985-88; chmn., dir., chief exec. officer Joseph A. Bank Clothiers, Inc., Owings Mills, Md., 1988—; cons. DLJ Capital Corp., 1984—; 1st vice chmn. Nat. Retail Mchts. Assn., 1980-81; dir. Babbage's, Inc., Findings, Inc. Served with U.S. Army, 1955-57. Office: Joseph A Bank Clothiers Inc 25 Crossroads Dr Owings Mills MD 21117

WATERS, LAWRENCE ELLIOT, brokerage house executive; b. Boston, May 2, 1939; s. Max and Florence (Barkin) W.; m. Jane Ellen Lowe, Dec. 28, 1965; children: Teri Ellen, Wendy Sue. BS, U.S. Mil. Acad., West Point, 1962. Commd. 2d lt. U.S. Army, 1962, advanced through grades to capt., 1968, retired, 1968; stockbroker, v.p. Wheat First Securities, Norfolk, Va., 1968-77; stockbroker, 1st v.p. Investment Corp. Va., Norfolk, 1977—. Author monthly newsletter Waters Bits and Pieces, 1985. Trustee Va. Stage Co., Norfolk, 1985—. Named one of Outstanding Young Men of Am. Home: 1600 Bay Point Dr Virginia Beach VA 23454 Office: Investment Corp Va 2400 Dominion Tower 999 Waterside Dr Norfolk VA 23510

WATERS, ROLLIE ODELL, consulting company executive; b. Charleston, S.C., Oct. 14, 1942; s. Rollie Robert and Mary Olivia (Brown) W.; m. Nancy Yvonne Chapman, May 3, 1975; children—Wendie Kay, Lauren Olivia. A.A., Spartanburg Coll., 1968; B.S., U. S.C., 1969; M.B.A., Pepperdine U., 1980. Supr. communications and spl. activities Owens-Corning Fiberglas, Aiken, S.C., 1970-71, asst. personnel dir., Fairburn, Ga., 1971-72; personnel dir. Meisel Photochrome Corp., Atlanta, 1972-73, dir. corp. personnel, Dallas, 1973-76, asst. v.p., dir. human resources, after 1976; co-founder, sr. ptnr. chief exec. officer Waters, Trego & Davis, Dallas, 1976-88; owner The Waters Cons. Group, 1988—, now div. Lane, Gorman, Trubitt & Co.; publicity dir., program dir. 35th and 36th North Tex. Personnel Confs.; guest lectr. Lorch Found., London, Calif. Inst. Tech., U. Md., Am. Mgmt. Assn. So. Methodist U. Contbr. articles to profl. jours. Served with USAF, 1962-66. Mem. Am. Soc. Personnel Adminstrn. (nat. compensation and benefits com.), Dallas Personnel Assn. (v.p. membership 1977-78), Am. Mgmt. Assn., Am. Compensation Assn., Am. Soc. for Tng. and Devel., Mensa, Psi Chi, Phi Theta Kappa, Omicron Delta Kappa, Beta Phi Gamma. Home: 278 Creekwood Lancaster TX 75146 Office: 3500 Maple Ave Suite 1200 LB6 Dallas TX 75219

WATERS, VIVIAN BURGESS, distributor executive; b. Oakdale, Calif., Jan. 26, 1934. Pres. BA Custom Pin and Pathe Inc., St. Charles, Mo., 1988—, B A Specialty Advertising, St. Charles, Mo., 1988—. Mem. Nat. Assn. Women Bus. Owners (bd. dirs. 1987-88, polit. action com. 1987-88, com. liaison, 1987-88), Greater St. Louis 99's (pres./chmn. 1987-88). Office: 605 Kipling Way Saint Charles MO 63303

WATERS, WAYNE ARTHUR, conference and travel service agency executive; b. Ft. Wayne, Ind., Mar. 9, 1929; s. Roy Edwin and Mary Catherine (Housel) W. m. Helen Marie Gump, Nov. 18, 1950; children: Bradley Wayne, Jeffry Scott, Ann Kathryn. Owner, mgr. Grain and Dairy Farm, Ft. Wayne, 1947-54; auto salesman Haynes & Potter, Auburn, Ind., 1956-58; asst. v.p. Lincoln Nat. Life, Ft. Wayne, 1958-83; pres. Conf. and Travel Services Inc., Ft. Wayne, 1983—; bd. dirs. Meeting World, 1979-81, 87. Contbr. articles to Best Ins. Guide, Meetings and Conventions, Green Book of Convention Planning, Ins. Conf. Planners Mag., others. With U.S. Army, 1954-56. Fellow Internat. Biog. Assn.; named Boss of Yr. Am. Bus. Women. Assn., 1972, Boss of the Yr. Ft. Wayne Jaycees, 1987. Mem. Soc. Co. Meeting Planners (bd. dirs. 1973-74, pres. 1975-76, Leadership award 1974), Ins. Conf. Planners (bd. dirs. 1979-81, pres. 1982), Am. Soc. Travel Agts., Soc. Incentive Travel Execs., Cruise Line Internat. Assn., Meeting Planners Internat., Internat. Platform Assn., The Travel Council, Ft. Wayne C. of C. (air service council 1984—, Small Bus. Person of May 1984), Ind. C. of C., Ft. Wayne Air Svc. Council, Small Bus. Council. Republican. Mem. Ch. of the Brethren. Clubs: Orchard Ridge Country (Ft. Wayne), Summit. Office: Conf and Travel Svcs Inc 1300 S Clinton Ste One Fort Wayne IN 46802

WATERS, WILLIAM ERNEST, microelectronics executive; b. Toronto, Ont., Can., Aug. 18, 1928; s. Charles Lacy and Margaret (Boulden) W.; B.A.Sc., U. Toronto, 1950; m. Evelyn Elizabeth Phillips, Jan. 18, 1952; children—Kenneth Geoffrey, Brian Gregory, Kimberly William. Gen. mgr. Hoskins Alloys of Can. Ltd., Toronto, 1953-59; pres. Waters Metal Products Ltd., Toronto, 1960—, Waters Metal Products, Inc., Buffalo, 1960-69, Watmet Inc., Niagara Falls, N.Y., 1968—, Microtectonics, Inc., Buffalo, 1968-71. Served with RCAF, 1946-52. Mem. Engring. Inst. Can., Ont. Assn. Profl. Engrs., Canadian Soc. for Elec. Engring., Internat. Soc. Hybrid Microelectronics, Mfrs. Agts. Nat. Assn. (dir. 1973-77), Beta Theta Pi. Clubs: Niagara Falls Golf and Country, Port Colborne, Rotary. Home: 5060 Woodland Dr Lewiston NY 14092

WATERSTON, JAMES RUFUS, banker. B.B.A., U. Mich., 1963, M.B.A. with distinction, 1964. C.P.A., Ill. Mem. audit staff Arthur Andersen & Co. (C.P.A.'s), Chgo., 1964-68; with Comerica Inc. also Comerica Bank—Detroit, 1968—, vice chmn., 1981—, also dir. Bd. dirs. Met. Detroit YMCA, Indsl. Tech. Inst., Met. Ctr. High Tech. Mem. Am. Inst. C.P.A.s, Robert Morris Assocs., Assn. Res. City Bankers, Mich. Assn. C.P.A.'s, Nat. Assn. Accountants. Office: Comerica Inc 211 W Fort St Detroit MI 48275

WATKINS, DEAN ALLEN, electronics executive, educator; b. Omaha, Oct. 23, 1922; s. Ernest E. and Pauline (Simpson) W.; m. Bessie Ena Hansen, June 28, 1944; children—Clark Lynn, Alan Scott, Eric Ross. B.S., Iowa State Coll., 1944; M.S., Calif. Inst. Tech., 1947; Ph.D., Stanford, 1951. Engr. Collins Radio Co., 1947-48; mem. staff Los Alamos Lab., 1948-49; tech. staff Hughes Research Labs., 1951-53; asso. prof. elec. engring. Stanford, 1953-56; prof., dir. Electron Devices Lab., 1956-64, lectr. elec. engring., 1964-70; co-founder, pres., chief exec. officer, dir. Watkins Johnson Co., Palo Alto, Calif., 1957-67; chmn., chief exec. officer, dir. Watkins Johnson Co., 1967-80, chmn., dir., 1980—; cons. Dept. Def., 1956-66; mem. White House Sci. Coun., 1988—. Patentee in field; contbr. articles to profl. jours. Legis. chmn., dir. San Mateo County Sch. Bds. Assn., 1959-69; gov. San Francisco Bay Area Council, 1966-75; Republican precinct capt. Portola

Valley, 1964; vice chmn. San Mateo County Finance Com., 1967-69; mem. Calif. Rep. Central Com., 1964-68; trustee Stanford, 1966-69; regent U. Calif., 1969—, chmn., 1972-74; mem. governing bd. Sequoia Union High Sch. Dist., 1964-68, chmn., 1967-68; mem. governing bd. Portola Valley Sch. Dist., 1958-66; mem. bd. overseers Hoover Instn. on War, Revolution and Peace, Stanford, 1969—, chmn., 1971-73, 85-86; adv. policy commn. Santa Clara County Jr. Achievement; trustee Nat. Security Indsl. Assn., 1965-78. Served from pvt. to 1st lt. C.E., O.R.C. AUS, 1943-46. Fellow IEEE (7th region Achievement award 1957, Frederik Philips award 1981), AAAS; mem. Am. Phys. Soc., Am. Mgmt. Assn., Western Electronic Mfrs. Assn. (chmn. San Francisco council 1967, v.p., dir.), Calif. C. of C. (dir. 1965—, treas. 1978, pres. 1981), Nat. Acad. Engring., Mounted Patrol San Mateo County (spl. dep. sheriff 1960-70), San Mateo County Horsemen's Assn., San Benito County Farm Bur., Calif. Cattlemen's Assn., Delta Upsilon. Clubs: Palo Alto (Palo Alto), University (Palo Alto); Shack Riders (San Mateo County); Commonwealth (San Francisco); Rancheros Visitadores. Office: Watkins-Johnson Co 3333 Hillview Ave Palo Alto CA 94304

WATKINS, DELMAR HARRELL, oil and gas company executive; real estate agent, rancher; b. Heavner, Okla., June 1, 1930; s. Delmar and Lucelle (Culbertson) W.; m. Sandra Beth Brown, Mar. 18, 1955; children—Joe Harrell, Mike Delmar. Student, Wayne U., 1950-51, Okla. A&M U., 1952-53, North Tex. State U., 1953-55. Rep., NCR, Amarillo, Tex., 1955-62; owner, operator 22 Gibson Discount Stores, hdqrs. Pampa, Tex., 1962-81; pres. The Sandra Corp., Pampa, 1962—; oil and gas producer WBD Oil & Gas Co., Pampa, 1976—. Served to staff sgt. USAF, 1948-51, Korea. Republican. Methodist. Lodge: Masons. Office: Sandra Corp PO Box 2474 822 E Foster St Pampa TX 79066

WATKINS, FELIX SCOTT, printing company executive; b. Sutton, W.Va., Nov. 27, 1946; s. Felix Sutton and Helena Sara (Cogar) W.; student W.Va. Inst. Tech.; m. Vivian L. Watkins, June 20, 1970; children—Jeffrey Scott, Jamie Leigh. Salesman, Kingsport Press (Tenn.), 1971-73; sales mgr. George Banta Co., N.Y.C., 1973-74; production mgr. Fuller Typesetting, Phila., 1974-75; account exec. Rocappi, Pennsauken, N.J., 1975-78; pres. Photo Data, Inc., Washington, 1978—. Founding mem. Print Polit. Action Com. Mem. Washington Club Printing House Craftsmen, Washington Printing Guild (dir. masters printers div.), Printing Industries of Met. Washington (chmn. govt. affairs com.), Printing Industries of Am. (mem. Chmn.'s Club). Home: 9521 Orion Ct Burke VA 22015 Office: 12104-J Indian Creek Ct Beltsville MD 20705

WATKINS, HAYS THOMAS, railroad executive; b. Fern Creek, Ky., Jan. 26, 1926; s. Hays Thomas Sr. and Minnie Catherine (Whiteley) W.; m. Betty Jean Wright, Apr. 15, 1950; 1 son, Hays Thomas III. BS in Acctg., Western Ky. U., 1947; MBA, Northwestern U., 1948; LLD (hon.), Baldwin Wallace Coll., 1975, Alderson Broaddus Coll., 1980, Coll. of William and Mary, 1982, Va. Union U., 1987. C.P.A. With C. & O. Ry. Cleve., 1949-80, v.p. fin., 1964-67, v.p. adminstrv. group, 1967-71, pres., chief exec. officer, 1971-73, chmn. bd., chief exec. officer, 1973-80; with B. & O. R.R., 1964-80, v.p. finance, 1964-71, pres., chief exec. officer, 1971-73, vice chmn. bd., chief exec. officer, 1973-80; chmn., chief exec. officer Chessie System, Inc., 1973-80; pres. and co-chief exec. officer CSX Corp. (merger of Chessie System, Inc. and Seaboard Coast Line Industries, Inc.), Richmond, Va., 1980-82, chmn. bd., chief exec. officer, 1982—; bd. dirs. Black & Decker Mfg. Co., Westinghouse Electric Corp., Signet Banking Co., Richmond, Fredericksburg & Potomac R.R.; chmn. Ctr. for Inovative Tech., Va., 1987. Vice rector bd. visitors Coll. William and Mary, 1984-87, rector, 1987—; trustee Johns Hopkins U. Mus. Arts Assn. (Cleve. Orch.), Richmond Symphony Orch; mem. Va. Bus. Council. Served with AUS, 1945-47. Named Man of Yr., Modern R.R. mag., 1984; recipient Excellence in Mgmt. award Industry Week mag., 1982. Mem. Nat. Assn. Accts., Am. Inst. C.P.A.'s. Clubs: Commonwealth (Richmond, Va.); Country of Va. (Richmond). Home: 22 Lower Tuckahoe Rd W Richmond VA 23233 Office: CSX Corp PO Box C-32222 Richmond VA 23219

WATKINS, JAMES DAVID, food products executive; b. Rochester, Minn., Sept. 17, 1947; s. John Frederick and Lillian Kay (Johnson) W.; m. Elizabeth Smith Cieslowski; children: James David Jr., Joseph John. BA, U. Minn., 1969—. Venture mgr. Pillsbury, Mpls., 1971-78; chief exec. officer Golden Valley Microwave Foods, Mpls., 1978—; bd. dirs. Country Lake Foods, Mpls. Bd. dirs. Big Brothers/Big Sisters, 1987. Home: 18591 Mushtown Rd Prior Lake MN 55372 Office: Golden Valley Microwave Foods 7450 Metro Blvd Edina MN 55435

WATKINS, JERRY WEST, oil company executive, lawyer; b. Vernon, Tex., Dec. 10, 1931; s. Terrell Clark and Daisy (West) W.; m. Elizabeth Jill Cole, Sept. 3, 1955. Student, Hendrix Coll., 1949-50, La. Poly. Inst., 1950-51; JD, U. Ark., 1954. Bar: Ark. 1954. Law clk. Supreme Ct. Ark., Little Rock, 1954-55; with Murphy Oil Corp., El Dorado, Ark., 1955—, sec., gen. atty., 1966-71, sec., gen. counsel, 1971-88, v.p., dir., 1975-88, exec. v.p., 1988—, also dir.; bd. dirs. Ocean Drilling and Exploration Co., New Orleans, First Fin. Fed. Savs. and Loan Assn., El Dorado; mem. Ark. Bd. Law Examiners, 1969-74. Trustee Ark. State U., 1982-87; bd. dirs. Barton Library Bd., El Dorado, Ark., 1966—, South Ark. Arts Ctr., El Dorado, 1979-82, 85-88, Warner Brown Hosp., El Dorado, 1984-87, South Ark. Med. Systems, 1987—. Mem. ABA, Ark. Bar Assn., Union County Bar Assn., Am. Petroleum Inst. Home: 111 Watkins Dr El Dorado AR 71730 Office: Murphy Oil Corp 200 Peach St El Dorado AR 71730

WATKINS, JOHN CHESTER ANDERSON, newspaper publisher; b. Corpus Christi, Tex., Oct. 2, 1912; s. Dudley Warren and Ruth (Woodruff) W.; m. Helen Danforth, Nov. 20, 1943 (div. 1959); children: Fanchon Metcalf, Robert Danforth, Stephen Danforth, Jane Pierce; m. Izetta Jewel Smith, Feb., 1960. Litt.D., Bryant Coll.; D.J., Roger Williams Coll., 1983. Reporter, makeup editor, aviation editor Dayton (Ohio) Jour. and Herald, 1934-35; reporter, aviation editor, mil. corr. Balt. Sun, 1935-41; asst. to pub., assoc. pub. Providence Jour.-Bull., 1945-54, pub., 1954-79; chmn. Providence Jour. Co., 1961-85, chmn. emeritus, 1985—; chmn. bd. dirs. Copley/Colony Inc., Calif.; also bd. dirs. Colony Communications; pres. Interam. Press Assn., 1971-72; also mem. adv. council. Served as fighter pilot USAAF, 1941-45; ops. officer 325th Fighter Group MTO. Decorated D.F.C., Air medal with 9 oak leaf clusters; knight comdr. Order of Merit Italy), R.I. Heritage Hall of Fame. Fellow New Eng. Acad. Journalists (Yankee Quill award); mem. Air Force Assn., Am. Soc. Newspaper Editors, New Eng. Daily Newspaper Assn. (pres. 1966-68). Clubs: Army-Navy Country (Washington); Hope, Agawam Hunt (Providence); Cruising Am; N.Y. Yacht (N.Y.C.); Spouting Rock Beach Assn., Ida Lewis Yacht (Newport, R.I.); La Jolla (Calif.) Beach and Tennis. Home: PO Box 1085 Providence RI 02901 Office: Providence Jour Co 75 Fountain St Providence RI 02902

WATKINS, VINCENT GATES, supermarket executive; b. Wichita, Kans., Nov. 27, 1945; s. Joseph Wade and Martha Geneve (Gates) W.; m. Josephine Anna Prickett, July 6, 1968 (div. 1985); children—Paul Clayton, Jason Wade, Vernon Curtis; m. Ann Bridger, Apr. 30, 1988; 1 child, Kenneth Marshall Moffitt. B.S. in Real Estate and Urban Devel., Am. U., 1973; M.B.A., Wake Forest U., 1976. Mortgage loan officer Better Homes Realty, Arlington, Va., 1969-72, Carey Winston Co., McLean, Va., 1972-73; real estate officer, property mgr. NCNB Nat. Bank, Charlotte, N.C., 1973-77; v.p. spl. projects and devel. Food Lion, Inc., Salisbury, N.C., 1977—; pres. In Good Spirits, Ltd., Little River and Columbia, S.C. mem. bus. adv. council East Carolina U., Greenville, N.C., 1984—; dive control specialist Scuba Schs. Internat., Fort Collins, Colo., 1984. Mem. Civitan, Am. Soc. Tng. and Devel., Am. Mgmt. Assn., Food Mktg. Inst. (govt. relations council), N.C. Retail Merchants Assn. (bd. dirs.), Les Amies du Vin. Methodist. Clubs: Tower (Charlotte), High Rock Ski (Salisbury). Avocations: scuba diving; racketball; snow and water skiing; cooking; carpentry. Home: 10 Waters Edge Salisbury NC 28144 Office: Food Lion Inc PO Box 1330 Salisbury NC 28144

WATLINGTON, JOSEPH, JR., insurance broker; b. Phila., Aug. 22, 1924; s. Joseph and Susie (Banks) W.; BA, Temple U., 1947. Lic. ins. broker, N.J., Md., Va., D.C.; accredited ins. adviser Ins. Inst. Am.; m. Marion Spencer, July 9, 1949; children: Joseph Richard, Leigh Ellen. Visitor, Pa. Dept. Pub. Assistance, Phila., 1947-48; sales agt. N.C. Mut. Life Ins. Co., Phila., 1948; with Watlington & Cooper, Inc., Phila., 1948—, pres., 1967—; chmn. Nat. Urban Ins. Co., 1971-74; broker First Pa. Bank Ins.; cons. Sch. Dist. Phila., others; instr. Community Coll. Phila., 1972; mem. ins. adv. com. City of Phila., 1980—; chmn. adv. com. Office of Employment and Tng., City of Phila., 1970-73; mem. risk mgmt. adv. com. Southeastern Pa. Transp. Authority; bd. dirs. Vision Svc. Plan Pa.; chmn. Phila. Facilities Mgmt. Corp. for Phila. Gas Works. V.p. Afro-Am. Hist. and Cultural '76 Bicentennial Corp. Phila., 1975-77. Bd. dirs., pres. Lighthouse, 1971-72; bd. dirs. Urban Studies Ctr., LaSalle Coll., 1969-72, Nat. Bonding Svc. Found., 1969-75, Upward Exec. Tng. Inst., 1969, Phila. Conv. and Visitors Bur., 1982-86, Pub. Interest Law Ctr. of Phila.; vice-chmn. fin. com. Goode for Mayor Com., 1982; trustee W. Kuhn Day Camp Coll. Settlement Phila.; pres. Black Unitarian-Universalist Caucus Delaware Valley, 1970-71; chmn. the Citizens, 1972-80; chmn. Phila. Allied Action Commn., 1976-79; bd. dirs., treas. Edn. to Work Coun., 1979-85. With AUS, 1943-45. Recipient Disting. Sales award Sales Mktg. Execs. of Phila., 1980; Mem. Nat. Assn. Ins. Agts., Pa. Assn. Ins. Agts., Profl. Ins. Agts. Assn., Minority Ins. Agts. of Phila., Urban Ins. Com. of Phila., Greater Phila. C. of C. (dir.), Ins. Soc. Phila. (bd. dirs. 1979-84), Alpha Phi Alpha. Unitarian Universalist (past trustee, ann. fund chmn.). Clubs: The Racquet Club, The Engrs. Club. Home: 6447 Magnolia St Philadelphia PA 19119 Office: 1315 Walnut St Ste 700 Philadelphia PA 19107

WATROUS, PHILIP JORDAN, financial executive; b. Chgo., Apr. 16, 1933; s. Robert Morgan and Blanche (Greene) W.; m. Ann Elizabeth Merchant, Sept. 30, 1955 (div. Jan. 1965); children: Deborah Greene, Wendy Watrous Smith; m. Linda Louise Lenz, Jan. 2, 1982. BS, Yale U., 1958. V.p., sec., treas. Kenton Corp., N.Y.C., 1969-79; pres. P.J. Watrous & Co., Inc., N.Y.C., 1979—; v.p., sec., treas. Internat. Inst. for Med. Scis., N.Y.C., 1980-82, Medizone Internat., Inc., N.Y.C., 1986—; v.p., sec. Trans-Resources, Inc., N.Y.C., 1986—. Cpl. U.S. Army, 1953-55. Mem. Yale Club of N.Y.C. Republican. Episcopalian. Home: 20 W 84th St New York NY 10024 Office: PJ Watrous & Co Inc 685 Fifth Ave 14th Fl New York NY 10022

WATSON, BEN CHARLES, research and development executive; b. Mobile, Ala., Oct. 3, 1944; s. Ben and Bessie (Turner) W.; m. Mae Johnson, Jan. 31, 1970. B.S., Morehouse Coll., 1967; M.S., Ill. Inst. Tech., 1974, M.B.A., 1978; Ph.D., N.D. State U., 1981. Chemist applied research dept. Sherwin-Williams Co., Chgo., 1968, sr. chemist, 1968-71, group supr., 1971-74, sect. supr., project coordinator, 1974-77; mgr. applied research Sherwin-Williams, Chgo., 1977-79; tech. dir. Chem. Coatings div. Sherwin-Williams Co., Chgo., 1981-82, v.p., tech. dir., 1982—. Mem. Young Businessmen's Assn., Chgo., 1975-76; mem. Community Devel. Com., 1976. Recipient Outstanding Scientist Yr. award State of Ga., 1966, Roon award Fedn. Socs. for Coatings Tech., 1982. Mem. Am. Chem. Soc., Electrochem. Soc., Chgo. Soc. for Coatings Tech., AAAS, Nat. Assn. Corrosion Engrs. Home: 5201 S Cornell Ave Chicago IL 60615-4202 Office: Sherwin Williams Co 11541 S Champlain Ave Chicago IL 60628

WATSON, SIR BRUCE DUNSTAN, mining company executive; b. Stanthorpe, Queensland, Australia, Aug. 1, 1928; s. James Harvey and Edith Mary (Crawford) W.; m. June, Dec. 30, 1952; three children. B.Elec. Engring., U. Queensland, 1949, B. Commerce, 1957. Engr., Tasmanian Hydro Electricity Comm., 1950-54, Townsville Regional Electricity Bd., 1954-56; with M.I.M. Holdings Group Cos., 1956—, engr. Copper Refineries Pty., Ltd., Townsville, 1956-69, Mount Isa Mines, Ltd., 1970-73, group indsl. relations mgr. M.I.M. Group, Brisbane, Queensland, 1974-75; 1st gen. mgr. Agnew Mining Co., Western Australia, 1975-77; dir. M.I.M. Holdings Ltd., Brisbane, 1977, mng. dir., 1980, mng. dir., chief exec. officer, 1981-83, chmn., chief exec. officer, 1983—; Nat. Australia Bank Ltd. Bd. dirs. Australian Adminstrv. Staff Coll.; dir. ASARCO Inc. Named knight bachelor in Queen's birthday honours, 1985. Mem. Australia Mining Industry Council, supervisory bd. Metallgesellschdtt AG. Lodge: Lions. Office: MIM Holding Ltd, GPO Box 1433, Brisbane Queensland 4001, Australia

WATSON, CARL BENNETT, JR., securities corporation, realty corporation executive; b. Cheraw, S.C., Jan. 16, 1933; s. Carl Bennett and Victoria (Hathcock) W.; m. Lilian Singleton Twitty, June 9, 1962; children—Victoria Coker, Carl Bennett III, Lilian Singleton. B.A., U. S.C., 1955, J.D., 1958. Loan officer Wachovia Bank, Winston-Salem, 1958-64; nat. div. loan officer N.C. Nat. Bank, Charlotte, N.C., 1964-67; dir. fgn. investment State of S.C., Columbia, 1967-72; sr. v.p. Interstate Securities Corp., Charlotte, 1972—, also dir.; pres. ISC Realty, Charlotte, 1978—, also dir.; guest lectr. U. S.C. Bus. Sch., Columbia, 1975. Vice chmn. S.C. Gov.'s Econ. Task Force, Columbia, 1972-75; bd. visitors, alumni council U. S.C., 1981—. Recipient Contbn. to Fgn. Trade and Investment Service awards U.S. Dept. Commerce, 1969, 71, 72; decorated Order of Palmetto, State of S.C., 1972. Mem. Internat. Assn. Fin. Planners, Securities Industry Assn. (mcpl. fin. com. 1975—), S.C. Indsl. Developers Assn., N.C. Indsl. Developers Assn., N.C. Citizens Assn., Charlotte C. of C., Newcomen Soc. Clubs: Charlotte City; Palmetto (Columbia). Office: Interstate Securites Corp 2700 NCNB Plaza Charlotte NC 28280

WATSON, CAROL, accountant; b. Nagoya, Japan, Apr. 10, 1957; (parents Am. citizens); d. Crestle and Annie Lee (Brown) W. Student, U. Md., 1975-77, Prince Georges Community Coll., 1979; BS, Bowie (Md.) State Coll., 1981. Operating acct. Maritime Adminstrn., Washington, 1981-85; supervisory cost acct. Dept. Transp., Office of Sec. of Transp., Washington, 1985-87; operating acct. spl. programs and analysis sect. U.S. Dept. Treasury, Washington, 1987, operating acct. U.S. Mint, 1987—; tax cons. H&R Block, Washington, 1982-84. tutor Hine Jr. High Sch., Washington, 1985-86; citizen ambassador All China Women's Fedn., Boise, 1987. Served with USAFR, 1985—. Named Outstanding Airman of Yr. 459th Mil. Airlift Wing, Andrews AFB, 1987. Mem. Nat. Assn. Female Execs., Assn. for Profl. And Exec. Women. Democrat. Home: 117 Panorama Dr Oxon Hill MD 20745 Office: Benchmark Communications Mgmt 2164 Wisconsin Ave NW Washington DC 20007

WATSON, DAVID COLQUITT, electrical engineer, educator b. Linden, Tex., Feb. 9, 1936; s. Colvin Colquitt and Nelena Gertrude (Keasler) W.; m. Flora Janet Thayn, Nov. 10, 1959; children: Flora Janeen, Melanie Beth, Lorrie Gaylene, Cheralyn Gail, Nathan David, Amy Melissa, Brian Colvin. BSEE, U. Utah, 1964, PhD in Elec. Engring. (NASA fellow), 1968. Electronic technician Hercules Powder Co., Magna, Utah, 1961-62; research fellow U. Utah, 1964-65, research asst. microwave devices and phys. electronics lab., 1964-68; sr. mem. tech. staff ESL, Inc., Sunnyvale, Calif., 1968-78, head dept. Communications, 1969-70; sr. engring. specialist Probe Systems, Inc., Sunnyvale, 1978-79; sr. mem. tech. staff ARGO Systems, Inc., Sunnyvale, 1979—; mem. faculty U. Santa Clara, 1978-81, San Jose State U., 1981—. Contbr. articles to IEEE Transactions, 1965-78; co-inventor cyclotron-wave rectifier; inventor gradient descrambler. Served with USAF, 1956-60. Mem. IEEE, Phi Kappa Phi, Tau Beta Pi, Eta Kappa Nu. Mormon. Office: Argo Systems Inc 884 Hermosa Ct Sunnyvale CA 94086

WATSON, DOUGLAS GEORGE, pharmaceutical company executive; b. Dunfermline, Scotland, Mar. 16, 1945; came to U.S., 1981; s. David Henderson and Margaret Huntly Paxton (Smith) W.; m. Linda Worswick, Aug. 26, 1967; children: Andrew, Heather. BA in Math., Cambridge U., 1966, MA in Math., 1970. With ops. research, corp. planning Ciba-Geigy Ltd., Manchester, Eng., 1966-72; rep. U.K. internat. acctg. team Ciba-Geigy AG, Basle, Switzerland, 1972-73; mgr. acctg. devel. and investment appraisal Ciba-Geigy Ltd., London, 1973-76; mgmt. acct. Ciba-Geigy ADP Ltd., Manchester, 1976-78; personal asst. to chmn. Ciba-Geigy AG, Basle, 1978-81; sr. v.p. planning and adminstrv. pharm. div. Ciba-Geigy Corp., Summit, N.J., 1981-83, sr. v.p. planning and bus. devel. pharm. div., 1983-86, corp. v.p., pres. pharm. div., 1986—; bd. dirs. Summit Bancorp. Mem. Pharm. Mfrs. Assn. (bd. dirs.), Chartered Inst. Mgmt. Accts. (assoc.), Ops. Research Soc., N.J. Partnership. Office: Ciba-Geigy Corp Pharms Div 556 Morris Ave Summit NJ 07901

WATSON, EDWARD, electric utility executive; b. Wichita Falls, Tex., Aug. 27, 1934; s. Samuel Edward and Dillie Ima (Thompson) W.; m. Martha Nann Lambert, May 31, 1953; children: Laura, Karan, Jeffrey. A. in EE, Arlington State U., 1955. Engring. asst. TU Elect., Wichita Falls, 1952-56, chief dispatcher, 1956-60; sales rep. TU Elect., Midland, Tex., 1960-64; mgr. TU Elect., Andrews, Tex., 1964-66, Odessa, Tex., 1966-72; div. mgr. TU Elect., Wichita Falls, 1972-76; v.p. TU Elect., Ft. Worth, Tex., 1976-85; sr. v.p. TU Elect., Dallas, 1985—; also bd. dirs. TU Elect., 1987—; chmn., dir. Industrial Found., 1963, 71. Mem. House Select com. on Statewide Energy Plan, Austin, 1988; bd. regents, Midwestern State U., 1986—. Named Outstanding Young Man Odessa Jaycees, 1972. Mem. Tex. Rsch. League (bd. dirs. 1987—), Assn. Elec. Cos. of Tex. (bd. dirs. 1988—), Tex. Assn. Taxpayers (bd. dirs. 1988—). Methodist. Office: Tex Utilities Electric Co 2001 Bryan Tower Dallas TX 75201

WATSON, FORREST ALBERT, lawyer, bank executive; b. Atlanta, May 7, 1951; s. Forrest Albert and Virginia Doris (Ritch) W.; m. Marlys Wise, Oct. 16, 1982; 1 child, Annaliese Marie Elizabeth. AB, Emory U., 1973; JD, U. Ga., 1975; postgrad., Mercer U., 1979-80, U. London, 1988—. Bar: Ga. 1975, U.S. Dist. Ct. (mid. dist.) Ga. 1976, U.S. Tax Ct. 1976, U.S. Ct. Appeals (5th cir.) 1977, U.S. Supreme Ct. 1980; cert. data processor. Assoc. Banks, Smith & Lambdin, Barnesville, Ga., 1976-78; ptnr. Watson & Lindsey, Barnesville, 1978-82; gen. counsel United Bank Corp., Barnesville, 1981—, v.p., chief exec. officer, 1982—; gen. counsel Lamar State Bank, Barnesville, 1976-84, judge Small Claims Ct. Lamar County, Ga., 1976, City Ct. Milner, Ga., 1977; lectr. IBM, 1984-85; atty. City of Meansville, Ga., 1976, City of Milner, 1977. Assoc. editor Ga. Jour. Internat. Law, 1975. Gen. counsel Lamar County Devel. Authority, Barnesville, 1977; bd. dirs. Legaline Inc., Atlanta, 1983-85. Mem. ABA, Ga. Bar Assn., Cir. Ct. Bar Assn., Flint Cir. Bar Assn., Ga. Rural Health Assn. (trustee 1981-82), Southeast Bank Card Assn. (mem. operating com. 1986—). Lutheran. Home: PO Box 347 Barnesville Rd Zebulon GA 30295 Office: United Bank Corp 314 Thomaston St Barnesville GA 30204

WATSON, HOWARD LEE, senior consultant; b. Louisville, July 16, 1927; s. Clarence James and Annie (Lynch) W.; B.S., U. Louisville, 1949; m. Lorraine Virginia Wagner, Dec. 31, 1948; children—Connie Ann, Sandra Lee, Marc Alan, Gregory Thomas, Barbara Lynn. Registered profl. engr., Fla., Ky., Ohio, N.J. Plant engr. Nat. Carbide, Louisville and Calvert City, Ky., 1949-56; utilities project engr. Gen. Electric Co., Evendale, Ohio, 1956-57; ops. mgr. Air Products & Chems., Inc., Calvert City, Ky., 1957-71, plant mgr., 1971-73, group prodn. mgr., Allentown, Pa., 1973-77, tech. mgr.-emulsions, 1978-81, mgr. mfg. services, 1981-86, cons. Watson Engring., Inc., Palm Harbor, Fla., 1986—. Served with USNR, 1945-46. Mem. Am. Inst. Chem. Engrs. (chpt. pres. 1963). Republican. Methodist. Club: Rotary (pres. 1973). Home: 2601 Landing Way Palm Harbor FL 34684 Office: 2750 Alt 19 N Palm Harbor Ct Palm Harbor FL 33563

WATSON, JOHN LAWRENCE, III, investment trader; b. Rome, Ga., Jan. 14, 1932; s. John Lawrence and Mary (Cowen) W.; m. Dorothy Palmer Mclanahan, Aug. 9, 1958; children: Mary Palmer Watson Gard, Valerie Catherine Watson Bilbrough, John Lawrence IV. B.S., Auburn U., 1954. Trader-over the counter J.C. Bradford & Co., Atlanta, 1957-58; with Robinson Humphrey & Co., Atlanta, 1958-64, dept. head-over the counter, 1964-74, dir. equity trading, 1974-83, dir. capital markets, 1983-85; pres. Security Traders Assn., N.Y.C., 1985—. Mem. bd. visitors Babcock Sch. Mgmt. Wake Forest U.; past chmn. Parent's Council Wofford Coll.; trustee Pace Acad. Served to 1st lt. U.S. Army, 1954-56. Named Man of Yr., Over the Counter Rev. mag. Mem. Security Traders Assn., Nat. Assn. Securities Dealers (dist. chmn. 1982, bd. govs. 1983-85). Presbyterian. Clubs: Capital City, Piedmont Driving (Atlanta); Ponte Vedra, Saw Grass Country (Ponte Vedra, Fla.); University (N.Y.). Home: 115 Central Park West New York NY 10023 Office: Security Traders Assn One World Trade Ctr Suite 4511 New York NY 10048

WATSON, PETER DEKKER, land management company executive; b. Haverford, Pa., Oct. 17, 1924; s. Frank Dekker and Amey Brown (Eaton) W.; m. Elizabeth Ehm; children: Margaret Dunnell, Charles Eaton. BS, Harvard U., 1948; student, Harvard U. Med. Sch., 1950-52; postgrad., Boston U., 1955-60. Research asst. U. Rochester (N.Y.) Med. Sch., 1943-45; prin. investigator the pain project Harvard U. Med. Sch., Boston, 1952-62; pres. Vermont Devel. Corp., Boston, 1958-62, Evergreen Farms, Inc., Greensboro, Vt., 1958-62, Hazen Road Inn, Greensboro, 1958-70, Gibou Valley Corp., Greensboro, 1962-87, Peter D. Watson Agy., Inc., Greensboro, 1970—. Editor: History of Greensboro, Vt., 1987; contbr. articles to profl. jours. Served with Civilian Pub. Service, 1942-45. Mem. Society of Friends. Home and Office: PO Box 95 Greensboro VT 05841

WATSON, RAYMOND LESLIE, architect; b. Seattle, Oct. 4, 1926; s. Leslie Alexander and Olive (Lorentzen) W.; m. Elsa Constance Coito, Sept. 18, 1954; children: Kathy Ann, Bryan Frederich, Lisa Marie, David John. B.A., U. Calif.-Berkeley, 1951, M.A., 1953. Architect firm Donald Haines & Assos., San Francisco, 1955-60; mgr. planning The Irvine Co., Newport Beach, Calif., 1960-64, v.p. planning, 1964-66, sr. v.p. land devel., 1966-70, exec. v.p., 1970-73, pres., 1973-77; pres., partner Newport Devel. Co., 1977-83; chmn. bd. The Walt Disney Co., 1983-84, chmn. exec. com., 1984—; vice chmn. bd. The Irvine Co., 1986—; vice chmn. The Irvine Co., 1986—; dir. Disney Corp., Mitchell Energy and Devel. Co., Pacific Mut. Life Ins. Co., The Irvine Co.; Regent's prof. U. Calif.-Irvine, 1985-86. Served with USAAF, 1944-45. Fellow AIA. Home: 2501 Alta Vista Dr Newport Beach CA 92660 Office: The Walt Disney Co 500 S Buena Vista St Burbank CA 91521

WATSON, RICHARD PRATHER, lawyer, small business consultant; b. Westfield, Ill., Apr. 18, 1938; s. Jesse L. and Ardie E. (Prather) W.; m. Rena Jo Stegner, Feb. 14, 1938; children: Richard Gregg, Steven T., Rachel Marie. BS in Acctg., Eastern Ill. U., Charleston, 1950; MS, Butler U., 1953; JD, Ind. U., 1957; cert. acctg., Fin. Sch. U.S.A.; grad., Gen. Motors Inst. Jr. Exec. Tng. Program. Bar: Ind., U.S. Dist. Ct. (so. dist.) Ind., U.S. Ct. Appeals (7th cir.) 1957, U.S. Ct. of Claims 1963. Evaluator dept. safety responsiblity State of Ill., Springfield, 1950; instr. acctg. U.S. Army Fin. Ctr., Ft. Harrison, Ind., 1953; dept. foreman Delco-Remy div. Gen. Motors Co., Anderson, Ind., 1953-57; adminstrv. asst. Ind. Toll Rd. Commn., Indpls., 1954-57; chief hearing judge Pub. Service Commn. Ind., Indpls., 1958-62; corp. counsel Ind. Sec. of State, Indpls., 1962-64; ptnr. Carvey, Watson & McNevin, Indpls.; sr. assoc. Watson & Rochford, Indpls.; pvt. practice cons. to small bus. Indpls., 1981-87; pvt. practice Watson & Leatherbury, Indpls., 1987—; small business and corp. owner, chief exec. officer Watson Mgmt. Corp., Watson Shopping Ctr., The Village Inn, Grandma's Italian Kitchen, Italian/Italian, Inc.; former owner State House Deli, State House Inn, Earline's Cocktail Lounge; cons. to numerous cos.; lectr. in fin. and small bus. Chmn. civilian bd. Indpls. Police Motorcycle Drill Team; mem. Indpls. Mus. Art; bd. dirs. Indpls. Vets. Day Council, Northeastwood Football Assn., Avocat Nat. La Societte des 40 Hommes et 8 Chevaux; chmn., bd. dirs. Avalon Hills Civic Assn. Mem. ABA, Ind. State Bar Assn., Indpls. Bar Assn., Am. Judicature Soc., Assn. Trial Lawyers Am., Ind. Trial Lawyers Assn., Am. Assn. Hosp. Attys., Ind. Assn. Hosp. Attys., Am. Legion, Ind. U. Alumni Assn., Nat. C. of C., Fraternal Order of Police, Nat. Boxcar Assn. Republican. Methodist. Clubs: Morse-Indpls. Yacht (past commodore); Indpls. Athletic, Athenaeum Turners, Ind. U. Men's; Ind. Soc. (Chgo.). Office: Watson & Leatherbury 730 Century Bldg 36 S Pennsylvania St Indianapolis IN 46204

WATSON, ROBERT LESLIE, SR., food products executive; b. Homboldt, Tenn., Dec. 5, 1949; s. Marcus and Francis (Mayes) W.; m. Dorothy J. Short, Aug. 18, 1973; children: Cherika Nataye, Robert L. Jr. Assoc. in Radiology, Kellogg Community Coll., 1974; BS, Western Mich. U., 1978; M magna cum laude, Polytechnique Inst. N.Y., 1983, PhD. With Gen Foods Corp., various locations, 1975—; tech. asst. to engring. and mfg. Gen Foods Corp., Saratoga Springs, N.Y., 1978-79; buyer Gen Foods Corp., White Plains, N.Y., 1981-83; mgr. Gen Foods Corp., White Plains, 1983—. Active Valhalla Sch. Bd., N.Y., 1983—. Baptist. Home: 351 Parkway Homes Rd White Plains NY 10603

WATSON, ROSS OLIVER, chemical company executive; b. Charlotte, N.C., May 19, 1924; s. Ross Oliver Watson and Elizabeth (Barber) Young; m. Nella Little Wilson, June 12, 1949; children: Mary Beth, Nancy Little. BS in Chem. Engring., MIT, 1949. Registered profl. engr., Del. Asst. plant mgr. Hercules Inc., Parlin, N.J., 1962-63; plant mgr. Covington, Va., 1963-65; asst. gen. mgr. Wilmington, Del., 1970-73, gen. mgr., 1973-74, asst. gen. mgr., 1974-78, dir. prodn. control, 1978-81, controller, 1981-83, v.p., 1983—; pres. Hystron Fibers, Spartanburg, S.C., 1965-70. Active Wilmington Med. Ctr., 1979—. Served as sgt. U.S. Army, 1943-46. Office: Hercules Inc 1313 Market St Hercules Plaza Wilmington DE 19894

WATSON, STEWART CHARLES, construction company executive; b. Brock, Sask., Can., Sept. 17, 1922; s. Samuel Henry and Elva Jane (St. John) W.; student U. Buffalo; m. Irene Lillian Ahrens, Aug. 4, 1943; children: Judith Gail (Mrs. David Stafford), Wendy Carolyn (Mrs. Rocco Amuso), Ronald James. With Acme Steel & Malleable Iron Works, Buffalo, 1940-42; with Acme Hwy. Products, Buffalo, 1946-69, internat. mktg. mgr., 1955-69; pres. Watson-Bowman Assocs., Inc., Buffalo, 1970—, pres., Kinematics, 1984—. chmn. bd. Air Stewart Inc.; Internat. lectr. on kinetics of civil engrng. structures; mem. U.S. Transp. Rsch. Bd.; bd. dirs. Internat. Bridge of Peace for Bering Strait Crossing. Served with AUS, 1943-45; ETO. Fellow Am. Concrete Inst. (dir. 1984—, Delmar Bloehm award 1984, Charles S. Whitney Medal 1987, hon. mem.); mem. ASTM, Nat. Acad. Sci. Mason (32 deg., Shriner). Home: 272 Lake Shore Rd, Fort Erie, ON Canada L2A 1B3

WATSON, SYLVIA FRANCES, commercial painting company executive; b. Parkersburg, W.Va., Feb. 3, 1950; d. Thomas Elias and Alice (Michael) Coram; m. Leonard Grant Watson, Sept. 11, 1971; children—Janica, Sonya, Brian. A.A., W.Va. U., 1969; B.A., Marietta Coll., 1971; postgrad. Our Lady of the Lake, San Antonio, 1972-73; cert. constrn. drawings and quantity survey Columbus Tech. Inst., 1980. Teaching cert., Ohio, Tex. Asst. mgr. Truly Yours Gift Shop, Parkersburg, W.Va., 1969-70; intern social worker W.Va. Dept. Welfare, Parkersburg, summer 1970; tchr. art San Antonio Sch. Dist., 1971-74; co-founder, v.p. New Day Painting, Inc., Columbus, Ohio, 1974—, co-founder, coordinator painting apprenticeship tng., 1983—. Mem. Our Lady of Peace Sch. Com. for St. Stephen's Community Ctr. Recipient merit award San Antonio Sch. Dist., 1972, 73, 74; SBA bus. devel. grantee, 1983; recipient Best of Show award, painting and sculpture W.Va. U., Parkersburg, 1973. Mem. NAFE, Women's Aux. Assoc. Builders and Contractors (bd. dirs. 1980-82), Assoc. Builders and Contractors (dirs. bus. devel. com. cen. Ohio chpt. 1986), Builders Exchange of cen. Ohio, Women's Bus. Bd., Associated Builders and Contractors (chairwoman community involvement com.), Ohio Ctr. for the Dance (bd. dirs. 1987—), Nat. Assn. Minority Contractors. Roman Catholic. Avocations: art, reading; gardening. Office: New Day Painting Inc 1373 E Main St Columbus OH 43205

WATSON, WILLIAM DOWNING, JR., economist, educator; b. Durango, Colo., Aug. 9, 1938; s. William Downing and Carrie Elizabeth (Bailey) Blanchard; m. Dolores Marie Boisclair, Sept. 7, 1968; children—Kelli, Adam, Seth. B.A. in Math., No. Colo. U., 1964; M.A. in Econs., Syracuse U., 1965; Ph.D. in Econs., U. Minn., 1970. Asst. prof. Wash. State U., Pullman, 1971-72; economist EPA-Washington, 1972-73; sr. fellow Resources for the Future, Washington, 1973-78; adj. prof. Va. Poly. Inst. and State U., Falls Ch., 1981—; economist U.S. Geol. Survey, Reston, Va., 1978—; staff economist dirs. office U.S. Geol. Survey, Reston, 1984—. Author: To Choose a Future, 1980; contbr. articles to profl. jours. Served with U.S. Army, 1956-59. Earhart fellow, U. Minn., 1967; Resources for the Future Dissertation fellow, Washington, 1969. Mem. Am. Econs. Assn., Internat. Assn. Energy Economists, Assn. Environ. and Resource Economists. Avocations: tennis; hiking; skiing. Home: 1927 Upper Lake Dr Reston VA 22091

WATT, BARBARA ANN, retail store executive; b. Chgo., Oct. 9, 1939; divorced; children: William Jr., Michael, Lorna, Rodney, Roxanne. BS, Northwestern U., 1985; postgrad., Keller Grad. Sch. Bus. Mgmt., 1985—. Community vocat. instr. New Horizons, Inc., Pontiac, Mich., 1979-81; vocat. specialist Northwest Suburban Mental Health Ctr. Consortium, Des Plaines, Ill., 1981-83, Orchard Mental Health Ctr., Skokie, Ill., 1981—; sec., treas. Bess Hardware and Sports Store, Northfield, Ill., 1983—; instr. Adult Devel. Ctr., Scotts Bluff, Neb., 1979. Mem. LWV (bd. dirs., edn. chmn. 1971-73), Options, Inc. (charter bd. dirs. 1972-73), Brown County Community Council on Alcoholism (bd. dirs. 1976-78), Brown County 51:42 Bd. Planning Commn., United Way of Brown County (community action chmn.). Home: 710 Green Bay Rd Winnetka IL 60093 Office: Bess Hardware & Sports 785 Golf Rd Des Plaines IL 60016

WATT, CHARLES VANCE, healthcare executive, consultant; b. Wilmington, Del., Aug. 7, 1934; s. Henry Vance and Nancy Paule (Beck) W.; m. Diana Mae Bates, Apr. 3, 1964; children: Steven Vance, Kristin Marie. AA, St. Petersburg (Fla.) Jr. Coll., 1957; BS, U. Fla., 1959; postgrad., Case Western Res. U., 1959-60. Mgr. lab. contract dept. Am. Hosp. Supply corp., Edison, N.J., 1960-69; dir. sales and mktg. Alberene Stone div. Ga. Marble, Schuyler, Va., 1969-72; pres. Watt Assocs., Charlotte, N.C., 1972-79; dir. planned giving Open Doors With Bro. Andrew, Greensboro, N.C., 1979-82, The Salvation Army, Oklahoma City, 1982-84; pres. Devel. Resource Group, Edmond, Okla., 1984-86; pres. devel. and mktg. Elyria (Ohio) United Meth. Home, 1986—; bd. dirs. Reconciliation Ministries, Inc., Elyria, 1986—. Mem. com. on Gift Annuities; cons. United Cerebral Palsy, Okla. City, 1984-86, Edmond Youth Coun., 1985-86, Drug Rehab. Program, Okla. City, 1985-86; pres. Edmond Crimestoppers Assn., 1985-86; chmn. bd. Labor/Mgmt. Prayer Ministry, Elyria, 1987—; bd. dirs. Lorain County Arts Coun., Elyria, 1988—; adv. bd. The Salvation Army, Elyria, 1988—. With USN, 1952-55. Named to Hon. Order Ky. Cols., 1982. Mem. Nat. Soc. Fund Raising Execs. (pres. Okla. chpt. 1985-86), Nat. Assn. for Hosp. Devel., Ohio Coun. Fund Raising Execs., Assn. Ohio Philanthropic Homes and Housing for the Aging, Am. Assn. Fund Raising Counsel, Nat. Planned Giving Assn. (chartered), Christian Legel Soc. (assoc. mem.), Rotary. Home: 769 Bedford Ave Elyria OH 44035 Office: Devel Resource Group 769 Bedford Ave Elyria OH 44035

WATT, EUAN HARVIE, insurance broker; b. Edinburgh, Scotland, Dec. 24, 1942; came to U.S., 1985; s. George and Bettie (Taylor) H-W.; m. Olivia Mason Smith, Mar. 11, 1967 (div.); children: Katrina, Jennie. Grad. high sch., Eng. Broker Sedgwick Group, London, 1962-77; dir. Sedgwick Internat., London, 1977-80, U.K., 1980-85; exec. v.p. Sedgwick Internat. Mktg. Svcs., Inc., N.Y.C., 1985—. Mem. Royal and Ancient Golf Club (St. Andrews, Scotland), Muirfield Club (Scotland), Deepdale Golf Club (N.Y.). Conservative. Presbyterian. Home: 333 E 56th St New York NY 10022 Office: Sedgwick Internat Svcs Inc 130 John St New York NY 10038

WATTS, CAROLE JAYNE, real estate broker, interior designer; b. Orange, N.J., Jan. 6, 1938; d. William John and Irene Elizabeth (Kiss) Matzek; m. John E. Watts, Sept. 28, 1963 (div. 1979); children: Colleen Lee, Kelley Jayne, John Craig; m. George Durnell Jr., Nov. 15, 1986. Student, Coll. William and Mary, 1958, Sch. Interior Design, Ft. Lauderdale, Fla., 1970, Marymont Coll., Boca Raton, Fla., 1971, Bert Rogers Sch. Real Estate, 1972, Sam Brown Sch. Real Estate, Tom Bermingham Sch. Real Estate. Lic. real estate broker, Fla. Pres. Jupiter Island Interiors, Hobe Sound, Fla., 1972—; pres., chmn. bd. dirs. Jupiter Island and Hobe Sound Properties, Inc., Hobe Sound, Fla., 1972—. Contbr. articles in field to local newspapers. Active Hobe Sound Civic Group. Mem. Nat. Assn. Realtors, Nat. Multiple Listing Assn., Womens Council Realtors (pres. 1974), Jupiter Island Assn., Jupiter C. of C., Hobe Sound C. of C., Stuart C. of C, Jupiter Bd. Realtors, Hobe Sound Bd. Realtors, Stuart Bd. Realtors, Fla. Assn. Realtors. Republican. Catholic. Home: 120 N Beach Rd Hobe Sound FL 33455 Office: Jupiter Island and Hobe Sound PropertiesInc 11770 A1A-SE Dixie PO Box 1083 Hobe Sound FL 33455

WATTS, DAVE HENRY, corporate executive; b. Montgomery, Ala., Jan. 18, 1932; s. Lawson Tate and Annie (Sherman) W.; m. Eleanor Lewis, Nov. 5, 1950; children—Anne Watts Durham, Martha Watts Keens, Susan Watts Balla. Student, U. Ala., 1950, U. Va., 1962; B.B.A., George Washington U., 1968, M.B.A., 1970, D.B.A., 1974. Constrn. clk. So. Ry., Birmingham, Ala., 1950-51, safety supr., various other positions, 1951-77; v.p. personnel So. Ry., Washington, 1977-82; v.p. personnel and corp. devel. Norfolk So. Corp., Va., 1982-85, exec. v.p. planning and devel., 1985-86, exec. v.p. mktg., 1986—; lectr. George Washington U., 1974—. Contbr. articles to pubs. in field. Mem. Old Dominion U. Research Found. Bd., Va. Internat. Trade Commn., Va. Opera Bd., Norfolk Airport Authority Bd. of Commrs., Future of Hampton Roads, Inc. Mem. Nat. Freight Transp. Assn., Am. Soc. Transp. and Logistics, Nat. Indsl. Transp. League (presdl. adv. com. Project 2000). Methodist. Clubs: Washington Golf & Country (Arlington, Va.); Princess Anne Country, Cavalier Golf & Yacht (Virginia Beach, Va.); Town Pt. (Norfolk, Va.). Office: Norfolk So Corp Three Commercial Place Norfolk VA 23510-2191

WATTS, JAMES CLAYTON, mining company executive; b. Salt Lake City, Oct. 5, 1951; s. Arthur James and Sarah (Clayton) W.; m. Phyllis LaVaughn Dettor, Nov. 26, 1977; children: Andrew C., Emmeline, Elizabeth, Nathanael. BS in Metall. Engring., U. Utah, 1974; MBA with honors, U. Phoenix, 1983. Sr. tech. systems analyst Cities Service Co., Cranbury, N.J., 1974-77; project mgr. Cities Service Co., Tulsa, 1977-79; planning dir. Cities Service Co., Miami, Ariz., 1979-81, asst. supt., 1981-82; systems mgr. Pinto Valley Copper Co., Miami, 1982-84; dir. info. services Inspiration Consol. Copper Co., Claypool, Ariz., 1984-87, dir. fin. analysis and planning, 1987-88; supr. adminstrv. svcs. Cyprus Miami Mining Corp., Claypool, 1988—. Author: (with others) Grinding Process Control, 1979. Scoutmaster Boy Scouts Am., Globe, Ariz., 1980—. With Utah N.G. and USAR, 1970-76. Mem. AIME, Soc. Mining Engrs., Data Processing Mgmt. Assn. (CDP, CSP). Mem. LDS Ch. Office: Cyprus Miami Mining Corp PO Box 4444 Claypool AZ 85532

WATTS, JEFFREY ALAN, venture capitalist; b. Pontiac, Mich., Sept. 28, 1950; s. Harold Maurice and Jeanne Lucille (Helgeson) W.; m. Linda Ginsburg, Sept. 2, 1978; 1 child, Robert. BS in Cellular Biology, U. Mich., 1972, MBA in Fin. and Acctg., 1975. CPA, Calif., Ill., chartered fin. analyst. Acct., sr. cons. Arthur Andersen & Co., Chgo., 1975-78; loan officer No. Trust & Co., Chgo., 1978-82; sr. investment officer Union Venture Corp., Los Angeles, 1982-86, v.p., 1986-87, pres., 1987—; bd. dirs. Bipolar Integrated Tech., Portland, Oreg., Carlyle Systems, Emeryville, Calif. Mem. AICPA, Nat. Assn. Small Bus. Investment Cos. (bd. govs. 1986—, mem. exec. com. 1987-88), Western Regional Assn. Small Bus. Investment Cos. (pres. 1986), Fin. Analysts Fedn., Calif. Soc. CPA's, Ill. Assn. CPA's, Los Angeles Soc. Fin. Analysts. Avocations: skiing, scuba diving, swimming, golf. Office: Union Venture Corp 445 S Figueroa St Los Angeles CA 90071

WATTS, ROBERT GLENN, pharmaceutical manufacturing company executive; b. Norton, Va., Apr. 28, 1933; s. Clifford Amburgey and Stella Lee (Cornette) W.; m. Doris Juanita Slaughter, Aug. 29, 1953 (dec. 1980); children—Cynthia L. Watts Akers, Robert Glenn, Kelly L.; m. Sara Lowry Childrey, Aug. 20, 1982; stepchildren—J. Eric Alexander, Matthew R. Alexander. B.A., U. Richmond, 1959. Dir. ops. A.H. Robins Co., Inc., Richmond, Va., 1967-71, asst. v.p., 1971-73, v.p., 1973-75, sr. v.p., 1975-79, exec. v.p., 1979—; dir. A.H. Robins Mfg. Co., San Juan, P.R., Lee Labs., Petersburg, Va., Action Savs. Bank, Richmond. Bd. dirs. United Way, Richmond, 1982—; Pvt. Industry Council, Richmond, 1983—; sec. YMCA, Richmond, 1984—. Served with USN, 1952-56. Mem. Met. Richmond C. of C. (chmn. 1985-86). Presbyterian. Clubs: Bull and Bear, Hermitage Country. Home: 2409 Islandview Dr Richmond VA 23233 Office: A H Robins Co Inc 1407 Cummings Dr Richmond VA 23220

WATTS, ROSS LESLIE, educator, accounting consultant; b. Hamilton, Australia, Nov. 10, 1942; came to U.S., 1966; s. Leslie R. and Elsie B. (Horadam) W.; B. Commerce with honors (Commonwealth Govt. scholar 1960-65), U. Newcastle (Australia), 1966; M.B.A. (Ford Found. fellow 1967-68), U. Chgo., 1968, Ph.D., 1971; m. Helen Clare Firkin, Jan. 15, 1966; children—Andrew David, James Michael. Audit clk. Forsythe & Co., Newcastle, Australia, 1960-64, acct., 1964-66; instr. Grad. Sch. Bus., U. Chgo., 1969-70; asst. prof. Simon Sch. Mgmt., U. Rochester (N.Y.), 1971-78, assoc. prof., 1978-84, prof., 1984-86, Rochester Telphone Corp. prof. 1986—; prof. commerce U. Newcastle, 1974-76; cons. to bus. firms, 1972—. Recipient Notable Contbn. award Am. Inst. C.P.A.s, 1979, 80. Mem. Am. Acctg. Assn., Am. Fin. Assn., Inst. Chartered Accts. in Australia. Contbr. articles on acctg. research to profl. jours.; asso. editor Jour. Acctg. Research, 1972-78, Jour. Fin. Econs., 1974—, Australian Jour. Mgmt., 1976-81; co-editor Jour. Acctg. and Econs., 1979—; mem. adv. bd. Midland Corp. Fin. Jour., 1983-88, Continental Bank Jour. of Applied Corp. Fin., 1988—; mem. editorial bd. Contemporary Acctg. Research, 1983-85. Recipient Acctg. award, Alpha Kappa Psi Found. Home: 17 Burncoat Way Pittsford NY 14534 Office: U Rochester Simon Sch Mgmt Wilson Blvd Rochester NY 14627

WATZ, MARTIN CHARLES, brewery executive; b. St. Louis, Oct. 31, 1938; s. George Michael and Caroline Theresa (Doggendorf) W.; m. Deborah Jurgan; children: Pamela, Kathlene, Karen. BS in Chemistry and Biology, SE Mo. State U., 1961; postgrad. Washington U., 1966-67. Safety engr. McDonnell-Douglas, 1962-64; sr. brewing chemist Anheuser-Busch, Inc., St. Louis, 1965-68, asst. brewmaster, Columbus, Ohio, 1968-79, sr. asst. brewmaster, St. Louis, 1979-82, resident brewmaster, Baldwinsville, N.Y., 1982-84, Williamsburg, Va., 1984-87; v.p. Anheuser-Busch Indsl. Products Corp., St. Louis, 1987-88, dir. brewing ops., 1988—. Served with USAF, 1962-65. Mem. Master Brewers Assn. Am. (v.p.), Am. Soc. Brewing Chemists, Internat. Food Tech. Assocs. Patentee in field. Home: 12503 W Watson Rd Sunset Hills MO 63127 Office: Anheuser-Busch Indsl Products Corp 1 Busch Pl Saint Louis MO 63118

WAUGH, ROBERT JAMES, corporate professional; b. Toronto, Ont., Can., May 8, 1934; s. James and Eleanor Curtis (Rogan) W.; m. Patricia Susan Fleming, Jan. 15, 1966 (div. Oct. 1973); m. Doris Janet Whitnable, Dec. 22, 1973. BS, U. Toronto, 1956; MBA, Harvard U., 1961. Registered profl. engr., Ont. Asst. supt. Hawaiian Dredging, Honolulu, 1961-62; field engr. Bechtel Corp., San Francisco, 1962-63; mgr. contracts Del E. Webb Co. Inc., Phoenix, Ariz., 1963-64; sr. dir. McKinsey & Co., Inc., N.Y.C., 1964-84; exec. v.p., sector pres. aerospace/aviation UNC Inc., Annapolis, Md., 1985—; bd. dirs. Clear Lake Land Co., Gouverneur, N.Y. Served with Royal Can. Air Force, 1956-59. Office: UNC Inc 175 Admiral Cochrane Dr Annapolis MD 21401 *

WAVLE, JAMES EDWARD, JR., pharmaceutical company executive; b. N.Y.C., July 19, 1942; s. James Edward and Florence Marie (Kehoe) W.; m. Marcianne Elizabeth Mitiguy, Aug. 21, 1965; children: James Edward, William Patrick, Robert Thomas, Stephanie Elizabeth. B.A., Adelphi U., 1964; J.D., Georgetown U., 1967; LL.M., N.Y. U., 1968. Bar: N.Y. bar 1967. With Warner-Lambert Co., Morris Plains, N.J., 1968-87; internat. counsel Warner-Lambert Co., 1971-74, assoc. gen. counsel, 1974-77, v.p., gen. counsel, 1977-80, sr. v.p., gen. counsel, 1980-81; corp. sr. v.p. and pres. Parke-Davis Group, 1982-87; pres., chief operating officer Centocor Inc., Malvern, Pa., 1987—, also bd. dirs. Mem. Am. Bar Assn., Internat. Lightning Class Assn. Clubs: Lake Mohawk Country and Golf, Stamford Yacht. Office: Centocor Inc 244 Great Valley Pkwy Malvern PA 19355

WAWRZYNIAK, STEPHEN DAVID, manufacturing company executive; b. St. Joseph, Mo., Oct. 21, 1949; s. Michael Joseph and Kathryn Maxine (Cook) W.; B.B.A., Mo. Western State Coll., 1973, B.S. in Psychology, 1973; m. Melneta Elizabeth Maschek, June 25, 1975; children—Shannon, Tammy, Lisa, Karrie. Quality control insp. Carnation Co., St. Joseph, 1973-74, plant sanitarian, plant safety coordinator, 1974-76; exec. dir. quality control Doane Products, Joplin, Mo., 1976-82; exec. dir. tech. services, 1982-84; v.p. tech. services, 1984—. Served with U.S. Army, 1969-70. Lic. and cert. comml. pesticide applicator Mo., Iowa, Calif., Va., AL. Mem. Am. Soc. Quality Control (sr.mem., section chmn. 1980-81, reg. councilor adminstr. applications div. 1984-85), Inst. Food Technologists (profl. mem.), Am. Soc. Animal Sci., Am. Oil Chemists Soc., Am. Assn. Cereal Chemists, Pet Food Inst., Nat. Environ. Health Assn., Assn. Am. Feed Control Ofcls., Ducks Unltd., Mo. Pest Control Assn., Joplin, Mo. Sr. Volunteer Program (bd. dir. ombudsman program), Nat. Rifle Assn. Republican. Baptist. Clubs: Joplin Rifle and Pistol; Masons, Shriners. Home: 2602 S Kingdale Joplin MO 64804-1343 Office: PO Box 879 Joplin MO 64801

WAX, EDWARD L., advertising executive; b. 1937; 2 children: Elizabeth, Alex. BS, Northeastern U., 1959; MBA, U. Pa., 1961. With E.I. DuPont de Nemours, 1955-63; account exec. Compton Advertising, N.Y.C., 1963-68; gen. mgr. Ace Compton Manila, Philippines, 1968-72; sr. v.p. Compton Advertising, N.Y.C., 1972-77; pres. Saatchi & Saatchi Compton Inc. (now Saatchi & Saatchi DFS Compton Inc.), N.Y.C., 1983-88, chief exec. officer, 1983-87, 1988—, co-chief exec. officer, 1987-88, chmn., 1988—, also bd. dirs.; pres., chief operating officer Richard K. Manoff Inc., later Geers Gross Advertising, 1977-81; exec. v.p. Wells Rich Greene, Inc., 1981-82. Served to capt. signal corps U.S. Army, 1965-67. Office: Saatchi & Saatchi DFS Compton 375 Hudson St New York NY 10014 *

WAX, GEORGE LOUIS, lawyer; b. New Orleans, Dec. 6, 1928; s. John Edward and Theresa (Schaff) W.; LL.B., Loyola U. of South, 1952, B.C.S., 1960; m. Patricia Ann Delaney, Feb. 20, 1965; children—Louis Jude, Joann Olga, Therese Marie. Admitted to La. bar, 1952, practiced in New Orleans, 1954—. Served with USNR, 1952-54. Mem. Am., La., New Orleans bar assns., Am. Legion. Roman Catholic. Kiwanian. Clubs: New Orleans Athletic, Suburban Gun and Rod, Pendennis. Home: 6001 Charlotte Dr New Orleans LA 70122 Office: Nat Bank Commerce New Orleans LA 70112

WAX, RANDALL PAUL, graphic designer, small business owner; b. Fremont, Ohio, Sept. 29, 1951; s. Dale Clifford and Maxine LaVerne (Sharpe) W.; m. Patricia Ann Miller, Aug/ 9, 1975; children: Amanda Nicole, Megan Renee. BFA, Columbus Coll. Art and Design, 1973. Designer Nat. Ctr. Vocat. Edn. of Ohio State U., Columbus, 1973-74; art dir. Sta. WDHO-TV, Toledo, 1974-76, Mlicki Design, Columbus, 1976-80; prin. Wax Design Assocs., Columbus, 1980—. Treas. Univ. View Civic Assn., Columbus, 1983, pres., 1984. Mem. Columbus Soc. Communicating Arts (show chmn. 1979, v.p. 1981, pres. 1982). Republican. Methodist. Office: Wax Design Assocs 2015 5th Ave Columbus OH 43212

WAXLAX, LORNE R., manufacturing company executive; b. Two Harbors, Minn., Sept. 15, 1933; s. Rudolph A. and Ebba (Bergren) W.; m. Jacqueline Jean Semerad, July 16, 1959; children—John, Carol, Paul. B.B.A., U. Minn., 1955; M.B.A., Northwestern U., 1967. C.P.A., Ill. Chmn., pres. Braun Espanola S.A., Barcelona, Spain, 1971-76; group gen. mgr. Braun AG, Kronberg, Fed. Republic of Germany, 1976-80; chmn. mgmt. bd. Braun AG, Kronberg, W.Ger., 1980-85; v.p. Gillette Co., Boston, 1983-85, exec. v.p., 1985—; mem. adv. bd. Deutsche Bank, Frankfurt, Fed. Republic Germany, 1980—; mem. adminstrv. bd. BHF Bank, Frankfurt, 1980—. Served with U.S. Army, 1957-58. Disting. scholar Northwestern U., 1967. Mem. Nat. Assn. Mfrs. (bd. dirs.), Beta Gamma Sigma. Clubs: Kronberg Golf and Land, Brae Burn Country; Algonquin of Boston. Office: The Gillette Co Prudential Tower Bldg Boston MA 02199 *

WAY, CAROL JANE, non-profit organization administrator; b. Providence, Jan. 24, 1940; d. Wilfred Bartholomew and Lillian Elizabeth (Tainsh) Martineau; m. Paul Howard Way, June 28, 1958 (div. 1986); children: Laura L. Way Jordahl, P. Craig, Victoria L. Way Hermansen, J. Brent. EdB, R.I. Coll., 1960; postgrad., U. R.I., 1960; MPA, Mankato (Minn.) State U., 1978; postgrad., Universidad Internacional, Mexico City, 1985. Cert. in secondary edn.; lic. in real estate. Tchr. pub. secondary schs. Scotia, N.Y., 1962-64, 67-68, Schenectady, N.Y., 1968-69; reporter, freelance writer The Long Islander newspaper, Huntington, N.Y., 1969-71; tchr. pub. secondary schs. Avon, Conn., 1971-72; asst. to dir. Ret. Sr. Vol. program, Hartford, Conn., 1972-73; dir. pub. info. Mankato Schs., 1974-78; tchr. pub. secondary schs. Fairfield, Conn., 1979-80; assoc. dir. YWCA of Greater Bridgeport, Conn., 1980-81; dir. alumni relations Sacred Heart U., Fairfield, 1982-84; exec. dir. Westport (Conn.) C. of C., 1986-88, West Hartford (Conn.) C. of C., 1988—; bd. dirs. Child Guidance Ctr. of Greater Bridgeport, 1986—; participant English Inst. SUNY chpt. N.Y. State Tchrs. Assn., 1964. Contbr. articles to mags. and newspapers. Lt. gov. R.I. Girls' State, Providence, 1955; mem. Housewives for Rockefeller and Schenectady Reps., 1964; registered lobbyist various non-partisan groups, Minn. and Washington, 1975-78; chairwoman Blue Earth County (Minn.) Reps., 1975-78; town com. Fairfield Reps., 1980-83; bd. dirs. YMCA of West Hartford. Mem. Nat. Assn. Bus. Economists, Nat. Assn. Female Execs., AAUW (life, bd. dirs. 1963-81, nat. legis. com. 1976-78, 80-83), Women in the Arts (charter), Fairfield Network Exec. Women, Women in Mgmt., Farmington Woods Country Club. Episcopalian. Lodge: Rotary. Home: 48 Gate Ridge Rd Fairfield CT 06432 Office: West Hartford C of C 948 Farmington Ave West Hartford CT 06107

WAY, PHILIP KEITH, industrial relations specialist, human resources management; b. London, Feb. 25, 1956; s. Keith Stanley and Bess (Lauder) W. BA in Econ., Cambridge (Eng.) U., 1976; MA in Indsl. Relations, U. Warwick, Coventry, Eng., 1977, PhD in Indsl. Relations, 1986. Research officer Nuffield Coll., Oxford (Eng.) U., 1977-79; asst. prof. U. Cin., 1985—; vis. fellow Harvard U., Cambridge, Mass., 1982-85; cons. in field. Contbr. articles to profl. jours. Frank Knox Meml. fellow, 1982-83. Mem. Indsl. Relations Rsch. Assn. (bd. govs. Greater Cin. chpt.), Acad. of Mgmt., Greater Cin. Human Resources Assn. Office: U Cin Dept Econ Cincinnati OH 45221-0371

WAYLAND, WILLIAM FRANCIS, diversified manufacturing company executive; b. Woonsocket, R.I., July 10, 1935; s. William F. and Cora (Dew) W.; m. Patricia Ann Whalen, Nov. 5, 1960; children: M. Scott, Pamela M., Catherine E. AB in Polit. Sci., Providence Coll., 1958; postgrad. in indsl. relations, U. Mich., 1964-65. Indsl. relations Chrysler Corp., 1961-75; dir. indsl. relations Schering Plough Corp., Kenilworth, N.J., 1975-77; v.p. adminstrn. A. Johnson & Co. Inc., N.Y.C., 1977-85; sr. v.p. human resources Textron Inc., Providence, 1985—. Bd. dirs. Providence Coll. Corp., 1985—, Roger William Gen. Hosp. Corp., Providence, 1986—. Served to 1st lt. U.S. Army, 1959-61. Recipient Personal Achievement award Providence Coll., 1984. Mem. Am. Soc. for Personnel Adminstrn. (human resources strategies and issues council 1985—), Human Resources Planning Soc., Providence Coll. Alumni Assn. (bd. dirs. 1985—). Roman Catholic. Club: Canoe Brook Country (Summit, N.J.). Office: Textron Inc 40 Westminster St Providence RI 02903

WAYMAN, ROBERT PAUL, electronics company executive; b. Chgo., July 5, 1945; s. Lowell Roger and Dorothy Emma (Francke) W.; m. Susan O. Humphrey; children: Jennifer, Allison, Grant, Kirsten, Clayton. BS in Sci. Engring., Northwestern U., 1967, MBA, 1969. Cost acct. Hewlett-Packard Co., Loveland, Calif., 1969-71, mgr. cost accounts, 1971-73, div. controller, 1973-76; instrument group controller Palo Alto, Calif., 1976-83, corp. controller, 1983-84, chief fin. officer, 1984—. Mem. Fin. Execs. Inst., Council Fin. Execs. Office: Hewlett-Packard Co 3000 Hanover St Palo Alto CA 94304

WAYNE, THOMAS FRANCIS, financial executive; b. Elmira, N.Y., Dec. 21, 1954; s. William Anthony and Rita (Dailey) W.; m. Bonnie Amoroso, Aug. 12, 1978; children: Tiffany Theresa, Taryn Elizabeth. BS, Elmira Coll., 1977. Cert. fin. planner. Fin. planner IDS Fin. Svcs., Inc., Syracuse, N.Y., 1981-84, dist. mgr., 1984-86; regional mgr. tng. IDS Fin. Svcs., Inc., Mpls., 1986-87, regional dir. field mgmt. systems, 1987-88; div. mgr. IDS Fin. Svcs., Inc., Albany, N.Y., 1988—. Treas., bd. dirs. Am. Cancer Soc., Cortland, N.Y., 1985-86; coach youth soccer YMCA, Pittsford, N.Y., 1988. Mem. Internat. Assn. Fin. Planners, Inst. Cert. Fin. Planners. Republican. Roman Catholic. Home: 15 Judith Dr Clifton Park NY 12065 Office: 421 Newkarner Rd Albany NY 12205

WAYNS, ARLENE MORRIS, elderly service corporation executive; b. Phila., Jan. 22, 1947; d. Leroy and Helen (Morris) Lewis; m. Eugene Preston Wayns, Oct. 16, 1965 (dec. Sept. 1977); children—Kevin, Verland, Eugene. B.A., Temple U., 1978. Asst. mgr. Ctr. of Social Policy and Community Devel., Temple U., Phila., 1978-81; mgr. Stephen Smith Towers Apts. for the Elderly, Phila., 1981-85, exec. dir., 1985—; realtor assoc. Wilson & Wilson Assocs., Phila., 1983-86, Green Valley Realty, 1987—; mem. cons. Stephen Smith Home for the Aged, Phila., 1985—; lectr. in field. Election judge City of Phila., 1975-76. Recipient Outstanding Achievement award Southeastern Penna Transp. Assn., 1987, Pub. Media Salutation S.E.P.T.A. Mem. Phila. Assn. Housing Mfrs. for the Elderly (pres. 1983—), Pa. Assn. Non-profit Homes for the Aging, (com. 1984—), Am. Assn. Housing for the Aging, Inst. Real Estate Mgmt. Avocations: aerobics; tennis; theater. Home: 1714 E Tulpehocken St Philadelphia PA 19138 Office: Stephen Smith Towers Apts for Elderly Inc 1030 Belmonmt Ave Philadelphia PA 19104

WEADOCK, DANIEL P., corporate executive; b. N.Y.C., June 21, 1939; m. Florence Towey, Oct. 5, 1961; children: Daniel, Bryan, Kevin, Ann, Kathleen. B.S. in Fin, Fordham U., 1967. With central bookkeeping Chase Manhattan Bank, 1957-61; with ITT, 1961—, spl. asst. to office of pres., 1969-75; dir. ops. ITT Africa and Middle East, Brussels, 1975-79; pres. ITT Africa and Middle East, 1979; v.p. ITT, 1979-83; pres. ITT Europe Inc.,

Brussels, 1983—; exec. v.p. ITT, 1983—, group exec.-Europe; pres. ITT-Europe, Inc.; chmn., pres., chief exec. officer ITT Communications and Information Services, Secaucus, N.J., 1988—. Office: ITT World Hdqrs 320 Park Ave New York NY 10022

WEARE, ASHLEY, banker; b. Boston, Mar. 22, 1927; s. John and Helene W.; m. Marguerite Trocmé, Apr. 15, 1955; children—Isabelle, Cynthia, Christopher, Betsey Ann. AB, Harvard U., 1952, MBA, 1954. Contr. Bankers Trust Co., N.Y.C., 1966-72; contr. Bankers Trust N.Y. Corp., 1972, asst. to chmn., 1972-87, sr. v.p. corp. fin. and investor rels., 1978—. With USNR, 1945-46. Mem. Nat. Investor Rels. Inst., Investor Rels. Assn. (pres.), Bank Adminstrn. Inst., Fin. Execs. Inst. Home: 275 W 96th St Apt 21G New York NY 10025 Office: Bankers Trust Co 280 Park Ave New York NY 10017

WEATHERBEE, LINDA, insurance executive; b. Decatur, Ill., July 20, 1956; d. Carl and V. Lucile (Westwood) W. BA magna cum laude, James Millikin U., 1977; postgrad., Ill. State U., 1981-82. CLU, chartered fin. cons. Fin. analyst State Farm Life Ins., Bloomington, Ill., 1979-82; supr. State Farm Life Ins., Austin, Tex., 1982-86; asst. supt. State Farm Life Ins., Salem, Oreg., 1986—. Cellist Decatur Civic Orch., 1973-75; ch. pianist, 1975-77, youth advisor Cen. Ill, 1979-81; Rep. vol., Bloomington, 1982; tutor adult edn. program Chemeketa Community Coll., Salem, 1986, 87; tchr. high sch. religion course, Salem, 1987—. Fellow Life Mgmt. Inst.; mem. Adminstrv. Mgmt. Soc., Life Office mgmt. Assn., Williamette Soc. CLU and Chrtered Fin. Cons. (bd. dirs. 1987—), Am. Horse Show Assn., N.W. Horse Council (Oreg.), Am. Bus. Women's Assn. (Townlake chpter Austin, Tex. 1984-86), Nat. Assn. Female Execs., Phi Kappa Phi. Mem. LDS Church. Office: State Farm Ins 4600 25th Ave NE Salem OR 97313

WEATHERHEAD, ALBERT JOHN, III, business executive; b. Cleve., Feb. 17, 1925; s. Albert J. and Dorothy (Jones) W.; m. Celia Scott, Jan. 1, 1975; children: Dwight S., Michael H., Mary H. AB, Harvard U., 1950, postgrad., 1951. Prodn. mgr. Yale & Towne, Stamford, Conn., 1951-54, Blaw-Knox, Pitts., 1954-56; plant mgr. Weatherhead Co., Cleve., 1957-59, gen. mgr., 1959-61, v.p., gen. mgr., 1962-66, gen. sales mgr., 1962-63, v.p. mfg., 1964-66; v.p., dir. Weatherhead Co. of Can., Ltd. 1960-63, pres., chief exec. officer, dir., 1964-66; treas. Weatherchem Corp., 1971-82, pres., dir., 1971—; pres. Weatherhead Industries, 1987—, also bd. dirs., 1987—; bd. dirs. Weatherhead Co., Protane Corp., L.P.G. Leasing Corp., Leasepac Corp., Leasepac Can., Ltd., Creative Resources, Inc. Author: The New Age of Business, 1965. Mem. Harvard U. com. on univ. resources; trustee Case Western Res. U., mem. resources com., council on research involving human subjects, trustee Michelson-Morley Centennial Celebration; mem. Univ. Sch. alumni council, trustee Univ. Sch., hon. trustee for life Univ. Sch., Cleve., 1988—; trustee, adv. bd. Egyptian Studies Assn., U. S.C.; mem. vis. com. Ohio U., Athens; v.p. nat. adv. com. Rollins Coll., Winter Park, Fla.; adv. trustee Pinecrest Sch., Ft. Lauderdale, Fla.; mem. capital campaign steering com. Laurel Sch.; trustee Vocat. Guidance and Rehab. Services, Hwy. Safety Found., Arthritis Found.; v.p. Weatherhead Found.; bd. dirs. New Directions Inc., Glenwillow, Ohio; col. CAF. Served with USAAF, 1943-46. Mem. Am. Newcomen Soc., Beta Gamma Sigma (hon.). Clubs: Union (Cleve.); Country (Shaker Heights, Ohio); Ottawa Shooting (Freemont, Ohio); Ocean (Delray, Fla.); Everglades (Palm Beach, Fla); Codrington (Oxford, Eng.). Home: 19601 Shelburne Rd Shaker Heights OH 44118 Office: 25700 Science Park Dr Beachwood OH 44122

WEATHERLY, EUGENE MITCHELL, human resources executive; b. Nacogdoches, Tex., Jan. 24, 1948; s. Eugene M. Sr. and E. Maurine (Hutson) W.; m. Nancy Elaine Spencer, Feb. 27, 1971 (div. 1981); m. Theresa Margaret Mitzel, Jan. 21, 1983; children: Edward Mitchell, Cara Virginia. BS in Econs., Stephen F. Austin U., 1970. Dir. pers. Henry S. Miller Realtors Inc., Dallas, 1973-74; regional mgr. human resources Fleming Cos. Inc., Houston and Topeka, 1974-79; various numan rels. mgmt. positions Frito-Lay Inc., Dallas, 1979-85; sr. mgr., cons. Ernst & Whinney, Dallas, 1985; v.p. human resources Pier 1 Imports Inc., Ft. Worth, 1985—. Bd. dirs. Downtown Ft. Worth Inc., 1987—, Neighborhood Devel. Coun., Ft. Worth, 1986—, Dallas SER-Jobs for Progress Inc., 1984-86. 1st lt. U.S. Army, 1970-73, Vietnam. Decorated Bronze Star, 10 Air medals. Mem. Am. Soc. Pers. Adminstrs. (bd. dirs. Tex. coun. 1985—), Ft. Worth C. of C. (bd. dirs. Cen. Bus. dist. coun. 1986—), Stephen F. Austin Alumni Assn. (pres. 1973-75, bd. dirs. 1975-80), City Club Ft. Worth, Elks. Home: 2920 Scarborough Ln Colleyville TX 76034 Office: Pier 1 Imports Inc PO 961020 Fort Worth TX 76161-0020

WEATHERSTONE, DENNIS, trust company executive; b. London, Nov. 29, 1930; s. Henry Philip and Gladys (Hart) W.; m. Marion Blunsum, Apr. 4, 1959; children—Hazel, Cheryl, Gretel, Richard Paul. Student, Northwestern Poly., London, 1946-49. Sr. v.p. Morgan Guaranty Trust Co. N.Y., N.Y.C., 1972-77, exec. v.p., 1977-79, treas., 1977-79, vice chmn., 1979-80, chmn. exec. com., 1980-86; pres. Morgan Guaranty Trust Co. N.Y. (name changed to J.P. Morgan & Co., Inc.), N.Y.C., 1987—; bd. dirs. Gen. Motors Corp. Mem. Assn. Reserve City Bankers. Office: J P Morgan & Co Inc 23 Wall St New York NY 10015

WEAVER, CHARLES LYNDELL, JR., architect; b. Canonsburg, Pa., July 5, 1945; s. Charles Lyndell and Georgia Lavelle (Gardner) W.; m. Ruth Marguerite Uxa, Feb. 27, 1982; children: Charles Lyndell III, John Francis. BArch, Pa. State U., 1969; cert. in assoc. studies U. Florence (Italy), 1968. Registered architect, Pa., Md., Mo., Va., Ky. With Celento & Edson, Canonsburg, Pa., part-time 1966-71; project architect Meyers & D'Aleo, Balt., 1971-76, corp. dir., v.p., 1974-76; ptnr. Borrow Assocs.-Developers, Balt., 1976-79, Crowley/Weaver Constrn. Mgmt., Balt., 1976-79; pvt. practice architecture, Balt., 1976-79; cons., project mgr. U. Md., College Park, 1979-80; corp. cons. architect Bank Bldg. & Equipment Corp., Am., St. Louis, 1980-83; dir. archtl. and engring. svcs. Ladue Bldg. & Engring. Inc., St. Louis, 1983-84; v.p., sec. Graphic Products Corp.; pres. CWCM Inc. Internat., 1987—; project dir. Sverdrop Corp., 1989—; vis. Alpha Rho Chi lectr. Pa. State U., 1983; vis. lectr. Washington U. Lindenwood Coll., 1987; panel mem. Assn. Univ. Architects Conv., 1983. Project bus. cons. Jr. Achievement, 1982-85; mem. cluster com., advisor Explorer Program, 1982-85. Recipient 5 brochure and graphic awards Nat. Assn. Indsl. Artists, 1973; 1st award Profl. Builder/Am. Plywood Assn., 1974; Honor award Balt. chpt. AIA, 1974; Better Homes and Gardens award Sensible Growth, Nat. Assn. Home Builders, 1975; winner Ridgely's Delight Competition, Balt., 1976. Mem. BBC Credit Union (bd. dirs. 1983-85), Vitruvius Alumni Assn., Penn State Alumni Assn., Alpha Rho Chi (nat. treas. 1980-82). Home and Office: 1318 Shenandoah Saint Louis MO 63104

WEAVER, CHARLES RICHARD, household products company executive; b. Kingman, Ind., Sept. 16, 1928; s. Atha Lavern and Jennie Mildred (Best) W.; m. Phyllis Jane Plaster, Sept. 30, 1950 (div. 1982); children—Wendy, Cynthia, Daniel; m. Donna Lee Lambert, Nov. 21, 1982. B.S., Purdue U., 1950. Sales trainee Faultless Caster Co., Evansville, Ind., 1950-51; product mgr. Westinghouse Corp., Pitts., 1951-53; brand mgr. Procter & Gamble Corp., Cin., 1953-59; mgr. spl. products div. Procter & Gamble Corp., Italy, 1963-66; mktg. mgr. Clorox Co., Oakland, Calif., 1959-62, advt. mgr., 1966-69, v.p., 1969-81, advt. mgr., 1969-82, pres., chief operating officer, 1982-85, pres., chief exec. officer, 1985-86, chmn., chief exec. officer, 1986—. Served with USMC, 1946-47. Office: Clorox Co 1221 Broadway Oakland CA 94612

WEAVER, DONNA RAE, college administrator; b. Chgo., Oct. 15, 1945; d. Albert Louis and Gloria Elaine (Graffis) Florence; m. Clifford L. Weaver, Aug. 20, 1966; 1 child, Megan Rae. BS in Edn., No. Ill. U., 1966, EdD, 1977; MEd, De Paul U., 1974. Tchr. H.L. Richards High Sch., Oak Lawn, Ill., 1966-71, Sawyer Coll. Bus., Evanston, Ill., 1971-72; asst. prof. Oakton Community Coll., Morton Grove, Ill., 1972-75; vis. prof. U. Ill., Chgo., 1977-78; dir. devel. Mallinckrodt Coll., Wilmette, Ill., 1978-80, dean, 1980-83; assoc. v.p. Nat. Coll. Edn., Chgo., 1983—, dean dept. applied behavioral scis., 1985-89, dean Sch. Mgmt. and Bus., 1989—; cons. Nancy Lovely and Assocs., Wilmette, 1981-84, North Cen. Assn., Chgo., 1982—. Contbr. articles to Am. Vocat. Jour., Ill. Bus. Edn. Assn. Monograph, Nat. Coll. Edn.'s ABS Rev. Mem. Ill. Quality of Work Life Council, 1987—, New Trier Twp. Health and Human Services Adv. Bd., Winnetka, Ill., 1985-88; bd. dirs. Open Lands Project, 1985-87, Kenilworth Village House, 1986-87. Recipient Achievement award Women in Mgmt., 1981; Am. Bd. Master Educators charter disting. fellow, 1986. Mem. Nat. Bus. Edn. Assn., Delta Pi Epsilon (past pres.). Office: Nat Coll Edn 18 S Michigan Ave Chicago IL 60603

WEAVER, ELIZABETH, financial service marketing executive; b. N.Y.C., Apr. 29, 1958; d. Leonard Joseph and Marie (Kelly) W.; m. Charles Theodore Sporing, Nov. 14, 1982. BA, Marist Coll., 1980; MBA, Adelphi U., 1986. Asst. mktg. Shearson Loeb Rhoades, N.Y.C., 1980-81; asst. v.p. mktg. E. F. Hutton, Garden City, N.Y., 1981-87; v.p. mktg. Shearson Lehman Hutton, 1987—. Mem. Newcomer's Assn., Rockville Ctr., N.Y., 1982. Mem. Nat. Assn. Female Execs. Republican. Roman Catholic. Avocations: cross-country skiing, all-terrain vehicle riding. Office: Shearson Lehman Hutton 2 World Trade Ctr New York NY 10048

WEAVER, MARGUERITE MCKINNIE (PEGGY), plantation owner; b. Jackson, Tenn., June 7, 1925; d. Franklin Allen and Mary Alice (Caradine) McKinnie; children: Lynn Weaver Hermann, Thomas Jackson Weaver III, Franklin A. McKinnie Weaver. Student, U. Colo., 1943-45, Am. Acad. Dramatic Arts, 1945-46, S. Meisner's Profl. Classes, 1949. Actress theatrical cos., Can., New Eng., N.Y.C., 1946-52; mem. staff Mus. Modern Art, N.Y.C., 1949-50; editor radio/TV Sta. WTJS-AM-FM, Jackson Sun Newspaper, 1952-55; columnist Bolivar (Tenn.) Bulletin-Times; owner Heritage Plantation, Hickory Valley, Tenn. Chmn. Ho. of Reps. of Old Line Dist. Hardeman Countyy, Tenn., 1985—; founder, hon. bd. dirs. Paris-Henry County (Tenn.) Arts Council, 1965—; charter mem. adv. bd. Tenn. Arts Commn., Nashville, 1967-74, Tenn. Performing Arts Ctr., Nashville, 1972—; chmn. Tenn. Library Assn., Nashville, 1973-74; regional chmn. Opera Memphis, 1979—; patron Met. Opera Nat. Council, N.Y.C., 1980—. Mem. Am. Women in Radio and TV, Internat. Platform Assn., DAR. Methodist. Clubs: Jackson Golf and Country, English Speaking Union, Summit (Memphis). Avocations: horseback riding, travel, theatre, visiting art museums, golf. Home: Heritage Hall Heritage Farms Hickory Valley TN 38042

WEAVER, MARILYN ROSADO, financial executive; b. Camden, N.J., Sept. 30, 1944; d. Joaquin Victor Rosado and Isabel (E'del) Kelley; m. John L. Weaver, June 20, 1964; children: John, Cindy, Sherry. AS in Acctg., St. Joseph's U., 1985. Staff acct. Campbell Chevrolet, Runnemede, N.J., 1961-62; supr. banking dept. RCA Service Co., Cherry Hill, N.J., 1963-65; pres., cons. J&L Acctg. Services, Cherry Hill, 1966-77; from staff acct. to v.p. fin. Learn Inc., Mt. Laurel, N.J., 1978-86; pres., cons. J&L Computer Services, Cherry Hill, 1986—; cons. J&L Computer Services, Cherry Hill, 1983-87. Mem. Nat. Assn. Accts. (v.p. edn., devel. dir.), Nat. Assn. Female Execs., Controllers Council.

WEAVER, RONALD LEE, lawyer; b. Winston-Salem, N.C., June 8, 1949; s. Robert Lee and Laura (Reich) W.; m. Jacquelyn Kay Witt, June 12, 1971; children: Lara Alison, Ronald Lee. AB, U. N.C.-Chapel Hill, 1971; JD cum laude, Harvard U., 1974. Bar: Fla. Mem. Carlton, Fields, Ward, Emmanuel, Smith & Cutler, Tampa, Fla., 1974-79; ptnr. Stearns, Weaver Miller Weissler, Alhadeff & Sitterson, Tampa, 1979-81, mng. ptnr. 1981—; bd. dirs. Majestic Towers, Pasadena and Tampa, St. Joseph's Hosp. Chmn. Am. Heart Assn., Tampa, 1983, patron's com. ARC Ball, Deacons First Bapt. Ch. Tampa,mem. Fla. Homebuilders Assn., Nat Homebuilders Assn.; bd. fellows U. Tampa (program chmn.); bd. dirs. Nat. Assn. of Indsl. and Office Parks (gov. affairs com. 1985, Pres. award Outstanding Svc. 1986), St. Joseph's Hosp. 1st. lt. USAF, 1971-81. Mem. ABA (chmn. real estate matters subcomm., real property section, chmn. real estate fin. subcom. comml. fin. svcs. com.), Hillsborough County Bar Assn. (program chmn. 1980), Tampa C. of C. (chmn. cultural affairs, bd. govs. 1983); bd. dirs. Nat. Assn. Corp. Real Estate Execs. (lectr.), Phi Beta Kappa, Phi Eta Sigma. Clubs: Harvard, Centre, Tampa, University, Palma Ceia Country (Tampa). Author: Florida and Federal Banking, 1981; Commercial Real Estate Acquisition, 1983; presented over 100 seminars on real estate and real estate law. Home: 4304 W Azeele Tampa FL 33609 Office: Stearns Weaver Miller Alhadeff & Sitterson One Tampa City Ctr Ste 3300 Tampa FL 33602

WEAVER, SAMUEL CLYDE, financial analyst; b. Bethlehem, Pa., Sept. 18, 1953; s. Henry and Naomi L. (Kramer) W.; m. Kerry Diane Landes, June 22, 1974; children: Derek S., Justin S., Kristine D. BS, Lehigh U., 1975, MBA, 1978, PhD, 1985. Project leader Blue Cross Lehigh Valley, Allentown, Pa., 1975-77, fin. analyst, 1977-78; sr. fin. analyst Hershey (Pa.) Foods Corp., 1978-81, fin. cons., 1981-84, mgr. corp. fin. analysis, 1984—; asst. prof. Elizabethtown (Pa.) Coll., 1981-84; adj. prof. Lehigh U., Bethlehem, 1986—, Moravian Coll., Bethlehem, 1987, Phila. Textile Sch., 1985; presenter at seminars and profl. meetings. Asst. coach Hershey Youth Soccer Assn., 1987-88, Hershey Youth Hockey Assn., 1988, Hershey Little League, 1988. Mem. Fin. Mgmt. Assn. (bd. dirs. 1988—), Inst. Mgmt. Accts., Am. Fin. Assn., Ea. Fin. Assn., Southwestern Fin. Assn. Democrat. Mem. Church of the Brethren. Home: 245 E Granada Ave Hershey PA 17033 Office: Hershey Foods Corp 14 E Chocolate Ave Hershey PA 17033

WEAVER, WILLIAM CLAIR, JR., human resources development executive; b. Indiana, Pa., Apr. 11, 1936; s. William Clair and Zaida (Bley) W.; m. Janet Marcelle Boyd, Sept. 18, 1963 (div. 1978); 1 child, William Michael; m. Donna June Hubbuch, Feb. 10, 1984. B Aero Engring., Rensselaer Poly. Inst., 1958; MBA, Washington U., ST. Louis, 1971; postgrad., Rutgers U. Registered profl. engr. Engr. aerodynamics N.Am. Aviation, Los Angeles, 1959-60; engr. flight test ops. Boeing/Vertol, Phila., 1963-66; engr. flight test project Lockhead Electronics, Plainfield, N.J., 1966-69; project engr. advanced systems, sr. staff engr. Emerson Electric Co., St. Louis, 1969-72; pres. Achievement Assocs., Inc., St. Louis, 1972—; founder, charter mem. Catalyst, 1978—; speaker in field. Contbr. articles to profl. jours. 1965-71; author: Winning Selling, 1983, Winning Manager, 1988. Mem. adv. com. Boy Scouts Am., Bridgeton, Mo., 1974. Served to capt. USAF, 1960-63. Mem. Nat. Soc. Profl. Engrs.,Am. Soc. Bus. and Mgmt. Cons., Am. Ordnance Soc., Am. Inst. Aeronautics and Astrounautics, Assn. MBA Execs., Air Force Assn., Am. Helicopter Soc., St. Louis C. of C., Mensa, Beta Gamma Sigma. Republican. Lutheran. Home and Office: 13018 Ray Trog Ct Saint Louis MO 63146

WEBB, ALAN WHITNEY, advertising agency executive; b. Needham, Mass., May 13, 1939; s. Kenneth Whitney and Lois Francis (Wry) W.; m. Jane Liechty, Apr. 6, 1963; children: Andrew Stuart, Alexandra Elizabeth. BA, Tufts U., 1962. Copywriter J. Walter Thompson Co., N.Y.C., 1963-65; copy supr. J. Walter Thompson Co., Tokyo, 1965-67; copy group head J. Walter Thompson Co., N.Y.C., 1967-71; creative dir. J. Walter Thompson Co., Amsterdam, The Netherlands, 1971-74; creative supr. J. Walter Thompson Co., N.Y.C., 1974-79; creative group head J. Walter Thompson Co., Chgo., 1979-85, exec. creative dir., 1985-87, gen. mgr., 1987-88, vice chmn., 1988—; also bd. dirs. J. Walter Thompson Co. With U.S. Army, 1962-63. Recipient Effie awards Am. Mktg. Assn., various awards Am. Advt. Fedn., Internat. Film and TV Festival, Cannes Film Festival. Mem. Chgo. Advt. Club. Home: 1139 Ridge Ave Evanston IL 60201 Office: J Walter Thompson Co 900 N Michigan Ave Chicago IL 60611

WEBB, GEORGE HENRY, material handling company executive; b. Detroit, Feb. 26, 1920; s. Jervis Bennett and Maurene Mae (Campbell) W.; m. Barbara L. McCain, Sept. 16, 1944; children: Barbara Alice, Dianne Maurene, Ann Marie, Patricia May. BS in Mech. Engring., U. Mich., 1942. Engr. Jervis B. Webb Co., Detroit, 1942-53, treas., automotive sales engr., 1953-62, dir., 1951—, v.p., 1962-65, dir., sec., 1954—, exec. v.p., gen. mgr., 1965-88, pres., 1988—. Bd. dirs., trustee Evans Scholars Found., Chgo., 1970. Mem. ASME, Soc. Automotive Engrs. Clubs: Avondale Golf; Golf Assn. Mich. (pres. 1969-70); The Hundred; Detroit Athletic; Bloomfield HLS, Orchard Lake Golf, Springs. Lodge: Ashlar. Office: Jervis B Webb Co 1 Webb Dr Farmington Hills MI 48018

WEBB, JAMES NEIL, contract engineering company executive; b. Maryville, Tenn., Sept. 6, 1947; s. Harley Jr. and Beulah Ann (Webb) W.; m. Paulette Gail Roberts, June 2, 1968; children: James Robert, Elizabeth Gail. BS in Metall. Engring., U. Tenn., 1970; postgrad., Ill. Community Coll., 1972-74, Bradley U., 1974-75. Research asst. in metall. engring., coordinator Metall. Lab. U. Tenn., Knoxville, 1969-70; metall. and chem. engr. Caterpillar Tractor Co., East Peoria, Ill., 1970-74; welding and metall. engr. Caterpillar Tractor Co., Mossville, Ill., 1975-76; quality engr. Caterpillar Tractor Co., Davenport, Iowa, 1977-83; mgr. quality control Russelloy Foundry, Inc., Durant, Iowa, 1984-85; cons. quality engr. Par Services/Copeland Corp., Hartselle, Ala., 1986; contract materials engr. Butler Service Group/USBI-BPC, Huntsville, Ala., 1986-87; pres. PG Enterprises, Inc., Marysville, Tenn., 1987; contract metall. engr. Kirk-Mayer/Morton Thiokol, Huntsville, 1987—. Asst. dist. commr., asst. scoutmaster, com. chmn. Boy Scouts Am., Davenport, 1977-85; pres. North Little League, Davenport, 1977-81; v.p. Davenport Youth Baseball Assn., 1978-82; sec. Ridgeview Dad's Club, Davenport, 1979-85. Recipient Woodbadge Beads Boy Scouts Am., 1980, Dist. award of merit Illowa council Boy Scouts Am., 1985; coop. scholar Aluminum Co. Am., 1966-69. Mem. Am. Soc. for Metals Internat., Am. Welding Soc., Soc. Mfg. Engrs. (sr. mem.), Metall. Soc., Am. Soc. for Quality Control, NRA (instr.). Republican. Baptist. Home and Office: 329 Teleford St Alcoa TN 37701

WEBB, ROBERT DONALD, JR., financial executive; b. Chgo., Apr. 23, 1943; s. Robert D. and Marjorie (Hoffman) W.; m. Linda Dale Wasserman, June 25, 1967; children: Lauren, Robyn. BSBA, No. Ill. U., 1965. C.P.A., Ill. From auditor to audit mgr. Arthur Andersen & Co., Chgo., 1965-78; dir. corp. fin. CF Industries, Inc., Long Grove, Ill., 1978-79, corp. controller, 1980-87, v.p. planning and control, 1987—; v.p. fin. Valley Nitrogen Producers, Fresno, Calif., 1979-80. Served as staff sgt. USAFR, 1965-71. Named Outstanding Acctg. Alumnus, No. Ill. U., 1982. Mem. Fin. Execs. Inst., Am. Inst. CPA's, Ill. Soc. CPA's, Beta Alpha Psi (Gamma Pi chpt.). Lutheran. Office: CF Industries Inc Salem Lake Dr Long Grove IL 60047

WEBB, THOMAS IRWIN, JR., lawyer; b. Toledo, Sept. 16, 1948; s. Thomas Irwin and Marcia Davis (Winters) W.; m. Polly S. DeWitt, Oct. 11, 1986; 1 child, Elisabeth Hurst. BA, Williams Coll., 1970; postgrad. Boston U., 1970-71; JD, Case Western Res. U., 1973. Bar: Ohio. Assoc. Shumaker, Loop & Kendrick, Toledo, 1973-79, ptnr., 1979—; dir. Comml. Aluminum Cookware Co., Yark Oldsmobile, Inc. Council mem. Village of Ottawa Hills, Ohio, 1978-85, planning commn., 1978-85, chmn. fin. com., 1978-82; adv. bd. Ohio Div. Securities, 1979—; bd. dirs. Kiwanis Youth Found. of Toledo, Inc., Toledo Area Regional Transit Authority, 1989—. Mem. ABA, Ohio Bar Assn. (corp. law com. 1989—), Toledo Bar Assn., Northwestern Ohio Alumni Assn. of Williams Coll. (pres. 1974-83), Nat. Assn. Bond Lawyers, Healthcare Fin. Mgmt. Assn., Toledo-Rowing Found. (trustee 1985—), Order of Coif. Republican. Episcopalian. Clubs: Crystal Downs Country, Toledo Country, The Toledo (trustee 1984—, pres. 1987—); Williams Club of N.Y. Office: Shumaker Loop & Kendrick 1000 Jackson Toledo OH 43624

WEBBER, MICHAEL DAVID, mgmt. cons.; b. Enid, Okla., May 27, 1940; s. Mike E. and Lorine L. (Loomis) W.; BBA, U. Okla., 1962; MBA (fellow), U. Pa., 1964; m. Janet Joyce Dodson, June 30, 1962; children: Michael David, Meredith. Vice pres. A.T. Kearney, Inc., Chgo., 1967-77; pres., dir. Kearney Mgmt. Cons., Ltd., Toronto, Ont., Can., 1975-77; sr. v.p. Booz-Allen & Hamilton, Inc., N.Y.C., 1977-87, Diebold Group, N.Y.C, 1987—. Served to 1st lt. USAF, 1964-67. Cert. mgmt. cons. Inst. Mgmt. Cons. U.S. and Ont. Mem. Inst. Mgmt. Scis., Ops. Research Soc. Am. Clubs: Greenwich Country; Milbrook Country; Internat. (Chgo.); Union League (N.Y.C.); Garden of Gods (Colorado Springs, Colo.); Boca Raton (Fla.). Contbr. articles to profl. jours. Home: 18 Woodside Dr Greenwich CT 06830 Office: Diebold Group Inc 475 Park Ave S New York NY 10016

WEBER, BARBARA M., sales executive; b. Oneonta, N.Y., Apr. 27, 1945; d. Peter J. and Helen (Bettiol) Macaluso; m. Peter Biddle Weber, July 29, 1972 (div. July 1988). Student, SUNY, Cortland, 1963-67; AAS in Merchandising and Retail Mgmt., SUNY, Mohawk Valley. Service cons. N.Y. Telephone, Albany, N.Y., 1966-68; sr. service advisor N.Y. Telephone, Albany, 1970-73; data communications instr. AT & T, nationwide, 1968-70; equipment mgr. Rushmore & Weber, Albany, 1978-82; v.p. ops. Rushmore & Weber, 1983—, gen. mgr., v.p., 1987-88, pres., chief exec. officer, 1988, also bd. dirs. Republican. Roman Catholic. Club: Schuyler Meadows Country. Home: PO Box 236 Newtonville NY 12128 Office: Rushmore & Weber Inc 277 Wolf Rd PO Box 757 Latham NY 12110

WEBER, D(AVID) M(ALCOLM), controller, accountant; b. Zanesville, Ohio, Nov. 19, 1948; s. Philip Theodore and Bernice Lucille (Harmon) W.; m. Deborah Rae Thompson, May 18, 1974; children: Dustin, Kyle, Amber. BS in Math., Ohio U., 1971. Tax agt. Ohio Dept. Taxation, Columbus, 1972-81; corp. treas. The Roekel Co., Zanesville, 1981—, also bd. dirs. Fin. chmn. Boy Scouts Am., Zanesville, 1986—. Mem. Nat. Assn. Accts. Democrat. Presbyterian. Lodges: Kiwanis, Elks. Office: The Roekel Co 36 S 2d St Zanesville OH 43701

WEBER, DONALD W., telephone company executive; b. Turtle Creek, Pa., Oct. 4, 1936; s. James J. and Hazel (Frederick) W.; m. Rose Mary Gaugler, Apr. 4, 1964; children: Jennifer A., Steven D., Christopher J. BSBA, Duquesne U., 1961. Sr. acct. Arthur Andersen & Co., Pitts., 1961-64; controller Contel Corp. (formerly Continental Telephone Co. then Continental Telecom Inc.), Dryden, N.Y., 1964-65; controller NE div. Contel Corp., Syracuse, N.Y., 1965-69; corp. controller telephones Contel Corp., St. Louis, 1969-70; v.p. telephone acctg. Contel Corp., Bakersfield, Calif., 1970-72; v.p. ea. region Contel Corp., Dulles, Va., 1972-75; v.p. revenue requirements Contel Corp., Bakersfield, 1975-76; v.p. telephone ops. Contel Corp., Atlanta, 1976-82, exec. v.p. telephone ops., 1982-87, pres., chief exec. officer, 1987—; also bd. dirs. Bd. dirs. Atlanta Auditory Edn. Ctr., 1987, Atlanta Sci. and Tech. Mus., 1988. With US Army, 1954-57. Mem. U.S. Telephone Assn. (bd. dirs. 1981-88). Republican. Roman Catholic. Clubs: Dunwoody Country (Ga.); Ashford (Atlanta). Office: Contel Corp PO Box 105194 Atlanta GA 30348

WEBER, EDWARD P. JR., steel company executive; b. Lorain, Ohio, July 26, 1937; s. Edward P. and Elizabeth (Chrustic) W.; m. Sheila J. Gethin, Dec. 15, 1962; children: Edward P. III, David E., Kristen E., Joseph M. BS in Commerce, Ohio U., 1959; JD, Case Western Reserve U., Cleve., 1964. Bar: Ill. 1966, Ohio 1967, Colo. 1964. Assoc. Hodges, Silverstein, Hodges and Harrington, Denver, 1964-67; lawyer United Air Lines, Inc., Chgo., 1967-68; assoc. gen. counsel Rep. Steel Corp., Cleve., 1968-84; asst. group counsel LTV Steel Co., Inc., Cleve., 1984-85; ptnr., shareholder Black, McCuskey, Souers and Arbaugh, Canton, Ohio, 1985-86; v.p., gen. counsel, sec. Acme Steel Co., Chgo., 1986—; bd. dirs. Olga Coal Co., Tilden Iron Mining Co., Universal Tool and Stamping Co., Inc. Pres., Aurora Rep. Com., 1972-76; mem. exec. com. Portage County Ohio Rep. Com., 1976-84; mem. Hoffman Estates Sch. Dist. Bd., Ill., 1967-68. Mem. ABA, Ill. Bar Assn., Ohio Bar Assn., Cleve. Bar Assn., Am. Iron and Steel Inst., Briar Ridge Country Club. Office: Acme Steel Co 13500 S Perry Ave Chicago IL 60627-1182

WEBER, GEORGE RICHARD, accountant, author; b. The Dalles, Oreg., Feb. 7, 1929; s. Richard Merle and Maud (Winchell) W.; B.S., Oreg. State U., 1950; M.B.A., U. Oreg., 1962; m. Nadine Hanson, Oct. 12, 1957; children—Elizabeth Ann Weber Katooli, Karen Louise Weber Zaro, Linda Marie. Sr. trainee U.S. Nat. Bank of Portland (Oreg.), 1950-51; jr. acct. Ben Musa, C.P.A., The Dalles, 1954; tax and audit asst. Price Waterhouse, Portland, 1955-59; sr. acct. Burton M. Smith, C.P.A., Portland, 1959-62; pvt. C.P.A. practice, Portland, 1962—; lectr. acctg. Portland State Coll.; expert witness fin. and tax matters. Sec.-treas. Mt. Hood Kiwanis Camp, Inc., 1965. Exec. counselor SBA; mem. fin. com., powerlifting team U.S. Powerlifting Fedn., 1984, ambassador People to People, China, 1987. Served with AUS, 1951-53. Decorated Bronze Star; C.P.A., Oreg. Mem. Am. Inst. C.P.A.s, Internat. Platform Assn. Portland (com. fgn. rels. 1985—). Oreg. City Traditional Jazz Soc., Order of the Holy Cross Jerusalem, Order St. Stephen the Martyr, Order St. Gregory the Illuminator, Knightly Assn. St. George the Martyr., World Literary Acad., Portland C.S. Lewis Soc., Beta Alpha Psi, Pi Kappa Alpha. Republican. Lutheran. Clubs: Kiwanis, Portland Track, City (Portland); Multnomah Athletic; Sunrise Toastmasters. Author: Small Business Long-term Finance, 1962, A History of the Coroner and Medical Examiner Offices, 1963. Contbr. to profl. publs. and poetry jours. Home: 2603 NE 32d Ave Portland OR 97212 Office: 4380 SW Macadam Suite 400 Portland OR 97201

WEBER, HARRY VANCE, financial aid consultant; b. Louisville, Dec. 18, 1937; s. Harry Volz and Martha (Pace) W.; m. Sandra Whitt, Aug. 12, 1962;

children: John Burnett, Joel Vance. BA, Morehead State U., 1961, MA, 1962; LittD (hon.), Steed Coll., 1983. Instr. Western High Sch., Louisville, 1962-65; guidance dir. Sullivan Bus. Coll., Louisville, 1964-68, v.p., 1968-71; exec. dir. Spencerian Coll., Louisville, 1971-78; exec. v.p. Edn. Unltd., Inc., Louisville, 1978-83; v.p. Branell Coll., Nashville, 1983-84; pres., bd. dirs. Fin. Aid Cons. & Tng., Boca Raton, Fla., 1984—, Fin. Aid Mgmt. for Edn., Ft. Lauderdale, Fla., 1984—; bd. dirs. FAME Brokerage Inc., Ft. Lauderdale; pres. Southeastern Assn. Bus. Colls. Found. for Advancement Career Planning, Louisville, 1980-83; bd. dirs. Found. for Advancement Vocat. Research, Washington, 1978-84. Author: Financial Aid for Students, 1973—; numerous articles in work force publs. Mem. exec. council Pvt. Industry Council, Louisville, 1980-83; mem. exec. bd. local council Boy Scouts Am., 1981-83, dist. chmn. 1982-83, scout leader mem. troop com., 1985—. Served with U.S. Army, 1955-56. Mem. Assn. Ind. Colls. and Schs. (bd. dirs. 1978-81, treas. 1982-85, Mem. of Yr. award 1983), Morehead State U. Alumni Assn. (v.p. 1965-68). Republican. Home: 4641 NW 28th Way Boca Raton FL 33434 Office: Fin Aid Mgmt for Edn 5301 N Dixie Hwy Fort Lauderdale FL 33334

WEBER, JAMES STUART, management educator; b. Sayre, Pa., Apr. 8, 1947; s. Arthur William and Margaret (Jensen) W. BA in Math., Northwestern U., 1971; AM in Math., Loyola U., Chgo., 1973; MS in Stats., U. Ill., Chgo., 1975, PhD in Policy Analysis, 1981. Teaching asst. dept. math. and polit. sci. U. Ill., Chgo., 1977-81; vis. asst. prof. dept. mgmt. Roosevelt U., Chgo., 1981-82, dir. MS in Info. Systems Mgmt. program, 1982-86, asst. prof. dept. mgmt., 1982-88; v.p. , asst. prof. dept. econs. Loyola U., Chgo., 1989—. Co-editor: Business & Society, 1984-85; proceedings editor Structured Techniques Assn., 1986—, Structured Devel. Forum, 1987; contbr. to profl. jours. Block capt. Waukegan (Ill.) Neighborhood Watch Program, 1982-85; mem. Waukegan Downtown Assn., 1986—. Mem. Ops. Rsch. Soc. Am. (full), London Math. Soc., Regional Sci. Assn., Acad. Mgmt., Am. Math. Soc., Am. Statis. Assn., Hill Sch. Alumni Assn., Northwestern U. Club, RROC. Republican. Episcopalian. Home: 4282 Adeline Ct Gurnee IL 60031-2031

WEBER, JOSEPH BRADLEY, sales executive, lawyer; b. Chgo., Dec. 18, 1959; s. Joseph Adam and Doris Jean (Peterson) W.; m. Shelia Diane Alford, July 2, 1988. BBA, Ariz. State U., 1982; JD, Cooley Law Sch., 1985. Bar: Ill. 1986. Atty. Cook County Cir. Ct., Chgo., 1986-87; regional sales mgr. Weber Marking Systems Inc., Arlington Heights, Ill., 1987—. Mem. ABA, Ill. Bar Assn., Chgo. Bar Assn. Office: Weber Marking Systems Inc 1420 Valwood Pkwy Ste 160 Carrollton TX 75006

WEBER, MAX O., glass fiber products manufacturing company executive; b. 1929. Sr. v.p. Owens Corning Fiberglass Corp., Toledo, Ohio, 1955-88; pres. constrn. products group Owens Corning Fiberglass Corp., to 1988, now pres., 1988—. Office: Owens-Corning Fiberglas Corp Fiberglas Tower Toledo OH 43659 *

WEBER, MILAN GEORGE, retired army officer, management consultant; b. Milw., Oct. 15, 1908; s. Adam George and Frances (Lehrbaumer) W.; B.S., U.S. Mil. Acad., 1931; grad. Coast Arty. and Air Def. Sch., 1938, Nat. War Coll., 1952; m. Mary Agnes Keller, Sept. 2, 1931; 1 son, Milan George. Commd. 2d lt. U.S. Army, 1931, advanced through grades to col., 1944; various army command and staff exec. positions, Philippine Islands, 1932-36, Hawaii, 1938-41, Ft. Monroe, Va., 1936-38; anti-aircraft exec., hdqrs. 3d and 9th armies, U.S., Europe, 1943-45; mem. Gen. Patton's staff, 1944, War Dept. Gen. Staff, 1945-48; mil. adviser to Argentine govt., 1949-51; global strategic planner Joint Chiefs of Staff, 1952-54; comdr. Missile Defense of Norfolk and Hampton Roads, 1954-55; chief of staff advisory group, Japan, 1955-58; dept. comdr. Air Def. Region, Ft. Meade, Md., 1958-60, ret., 1960; mgr. electronic counter measures Loral Electronics Corp., N.Y.C., 1960-62; product mgr. electronic counter measures Hallicrafters Corp. (name changed to Northrop Corp.), Chgo., 1962-64; partner Weber Assos., Mgmt. Cons., Deerfield, Ill., 1964-69; pres. dir. Milan G. Weber Associates, Inc., Deerfield, 1969—; mgmt. cons. to various bus. firms, 1964—; acquisitions and mergers cons. to various corps., 1969—. Chmn. Great Lakes Ecology Assn. Ill., 1974—; chmn. Citizens Com. Honesty in Govt., 1969—; mem. Ill. Drivers Safety Adv. Com., 1975—, Deerfield Library Bd., 1976—, Deerfield Caucus Com., 1978—, Deerfield Energy Adv. Council, 1981—. Decorated Legion of Merit, Bronze Star, Commendation medal with oak leaf cluster. Mem. Assn. Old Crows, West Point Soc. Chgo., Internat. Platform Assn., Assn. Grads. U.S. Mil. Acad., Electronic Counter Measures Assn., Great Lakes Ecology Assn. of the Mil. Clubs: Army Navy, Army Navy Country. Contbr. articles on anti-aircraft arty., air def. and mil. strategy to profl. publs. author of joint strategic capabilities plan; author weekly column on environment, 1977—. Home: 611 Colwyn Terr Deerfield IL 60015 Office: PO Box 81 Deerfield IL 60015

WEBER, WILLIAM P., electronics company executive; b. 1940; married. BS, Lamar U., 1962; MS, So. Meth. U., 1966. With Tex. Instruments, Inc., Dallas, 1962—, mgr. assembly and test equipment group, 1965-70, mfr. mgr. electro-optics div. equipment group, 1970-71, mgr. ops. digital systems, 1971-75, asst. v.p., mgr. missile div. equipment group, 1975-79, 1979-80, mgr. Lewisville site, 1979-80, v.p., mgr. electro optics div., 1980-81, mgr. Forest Ln. site, 1980-81, v.p., mgr. equipment group, 1981-82, v.p. and pres. defense systems and electronics group, 1982-84, exec. v.p., mgr. corp. devel., 1984-87, exec. v.p., pres. semiconductor group, 1987—, also bd. dirs. Office: Tex Instruments Inc PO Box 655012 MS73 Dallas TX 75265

WEBSTER, DANIEL JAMES, JR., manufacturing executive; b. Pitts., July 5, 1947; s. Daniel J. and Dorothea A.M. (Englisby) W.; m. Carol Ann Plankenhorn, Aug. 24, 1968; children: Gregory, Kimberly. BS, Clarkson U., 1969; MBA, SUNY, Albany, 1975. Asst. to corp. controller Rotron, Inc., Woodstock, N.Y., 1973-74, div. controller, 1974-75; mgr. material control comml. div. EG&G Rotron, Woodstock, 1975-77, mgr. mktg. custom div., 1977-83; gen. mgr. EG&G Chandler Engring., Tulsa, 1983-87, exec. v.p., div. gen. mgr., 1987—; chmn., supr. comm., treas. Rotron Employee Fed. Credit Union; lectr. in field. Contbr. articles to profl. jours. Served to lt. USNR, 1969-72. Recipient Gov. Award for Excellence in Exporting, Tulsa, 1985; Edn. award Am. Product and Inventory Control Systems, 1976. Mem. Instrument Soc. Am. Republican. Methodist. Office: EG&G Engring 7707 E 38th St Tulsa OK 74145

WEBSTER, DAVID ANDREW, underwriter; b. Ambler, Pa., Oct. 16, 1952; s. William and Betty Juel (Davies) W.; m. Deborah Lynn Smith, June 22, 1973; children: Michael David, Mark Thomas. BBA, Drexel U., 1974; M in Fin. Svcs., Am. Coll., 1986. CLU; chartered fin. cons. Sales rep. ins. Phila., 1974-79, Warren & Welch Co., King of Prussia, Pa., 1979-85, Compensation Mgmt. Inc., King of Prussia, 1985—. Coach, bd. dirs. Warrington Soccer Club, 1988, Warrington Little League Baseball, 1988, 89. Mem. Phila. Assn. Life Underwriters, Am. Soc. CLU's, Yacht Club of Stone Harbor, Upper Moreland Swim Club. Methodist. Home: 2414 Fairway Terr Warrington PA 18976 Office: Compensation Mgmt Inc Irwin Bldg 460 N Gulph Rd PO Box 1562 King of Prussia PA 19406

WEBSTER, FREDERICK ELMER, JR., marketing educator, consultant; b. Auburn, N.Y., Oct. 22, 1937; s. Frederick Elmer and Evelyn May (Dudden) W.; m. Mary Alice Powers, Dec. 27, 1957; children: Lynn Marie, Mark Andrew, Lisa Ann. AB, Dartmouth Coll., 1959, MBA, 1960; PhD, Stanford U., 1964; AM (hon.), Dartmouth Coll., 1974. Asst. prof. mktg. Columbia U., N.Y.C., 1964-65; from asst. prof. to prof. bus. adminstrn. Dartmouth Coll., Hanover, N.H., 1965-79; assoc. dean Amos Tuck Sch. Dartmouth Coll., Hanover, 1976-83, E.B. Osborn prof. mktg., 1979—; vis. prof. Internat. Mgmt. Inst., Geneva, 1970-88; vis. prof. bus. sch. Harvard U., Boston, 1987-89; exec. dir. Mktg. Sci. Inst., Cambridge, Mass., 1987-89; bd. dirs. Whitney Blake Co. Vt., Bellows Falls, 1987—; cons. CPM Inc., Claremont, N.H., 1983—, Traditional Living Inc., Hanover, 1973—. Author: Marketing Communications, 1968, Social Aspects of Marketing, 1974, Marketing for Managers, 1974, Industrial Marketing Strategy, 1979, 2d edit., 1984 Marketing Management Casebook, 1980, 4th edit., 1984, Field Sales Management, 1983; editor: Ronald Series on Marketing Management, 1975—; editorial bd., sect. editor: Jour. Mktg, 1968—, Mktg. Letters, 1989—; contbr. article to profl. jours. Trustee Alice Peck Day Meml. Hosp., Lebanon, N.H., 1970-87; bd. overseers Hanover Inn, N.H., 1985—; firefighter Town of Hanover, 1970—, mem. fin. com., 1973-78, chmn. com., 1977-78; bd. dirs., v.p. Vt. Pub. Radio, 1978—; mem. fin. com. Dresden Sch. Dist., Hanover, 1973-78, chmn., 1976-77; vestryman St. Thomas Episcopal Ch., Hanover, 1967-70, 75-78; mem. missions com. Episcopal Diocese N.H., Concord, 1988—. Gulf Oil fellow, 1959-60, U.S. Steel Found. fellow, 1961-63, Nat. Assn. Purchasing Agts. Doctoral fellow, 1963-64. Mem. Am. Mktg. Assn. (dir. 1972-74), Assn. for Consumer Rsch., Inst. Mgmt. Scis., Norford Lake Club. Republican. Episcopalian. Home: Deer Run Farm Stevens Rd RFD1 Box 396 Lebanon NH 03766 Office: Dartmouth Coll Amos Tuck Sch Bus Adminstrn Hanover NH 03755

WEBSTER, GEORGE DRURY, lawyer; b. Jacksonville, Fla., Feb. 8, 1921; s. George D. and Mary Gaines (Walker) W.; m. Ann Kilpatrick; children: Aen Walker, George Drury, Hugh Kilpatrick. B.A., Maryville Coll., 1941, LL.D. (hon.), 1984; LL.B., Harvard U., 1948. Bar: Tenn. 1948, D.C. 1952, Md. 1976. Atty. tax div. Dept. Justice, 1949-51; sr. partner Webster, Chamberlain & Bean, Washington; lectr. numerous tax. insts. Author: Business and Professional Political Action Committees, 1979, The Law of Associations, 1988. Trustee U.S. Naval Acad. Found., Annapolis, Md.; spl. U.S. ambassador, 1972. Served to lt. USNR, 1942-46. Mem. Am. Law Inst., Am. Bar Assn. Clubs: Chevy Chase (Md.); Metropolitan (Washington); Racquet and Tennis (N.Y.C.). Home: 5305 Cardinal Ct Bethesda MD 20816 also: Webster Angus Farms Rogersville TN 37857 Office: Webster Chamberlain & Bean 1747 Pennsylvania Ave NW Washington DC 20006

WEBSTER, JAMES COLIN EDEN, oil company executive; b. Rangoon, Burma, Mar. 5, 1936; came to U.S., 1986; m. Susan Gorton Scarff, Sept. 13, 1965; children: Vanessa, Alexander, Benedict. BA, Trinity Coll., 1959, MA, 1967. With British Petroleum, London, 1959-85; pres. British Petroleum N.Am., N.Y.C., 1986; exec. v.p. British Petroleum Am., Cleve., 1987—, Standard Oil Co., Cleve., 1986-87. Office: BP Am Inc 200 Public Sq Cleveland OH 44114

WEBSTER, JOHN KIMBALL, investment executive; b. N.Y.C., June 7, 1934; s. Reginald Nathaniel and Lillian (McDonald) W.; m. Katherine Taylor Mulligan, Jan. 28, 1967; children: John McDonald, Katherine Kimball. B.A., Yale U., 1956; postgrad., Wharton Sch., U. Pa., 1957-58. With Dominick & Dominick, N.Y.C., 1961-73; v.p. Dominick & Dominick, 1968-73; v.p., sec. Dominick Fund, Inc., also Barclay Growth Fund, N.Y.C., 1971-73; v.p. Dominick Mgmt. Corp., N.Y.C., 1971-73, Monumental Capital Mgmt., Inc., Balt., 1974-75, Bernstein-Macaulay, Inc., N.Y.C., 1975-78; v.p., dir. Penmark Investments, Inc., Chgo., 1978-79; sr. v.p. Penmark Investments, Inc., 1979-80, exec. v.p., 1980-84; exec. v.p. Trust Banking Group, Sun Banks, Inc., 1984-85, MPT Assocs., 1986—; mem. no-load com. Investment Co. Inst., Washington, 1971-73; exec. com. No Load Mut. Fund Assn., N.Y.C., 1971-73; treas. No Load Mut. Fund Assn., 1972-73. Chmn. Nat. Telethon com. Lawrenceville Sch., 1986-89; vice chmn. Parents Fund Trinity Coll., Conn., 1987—. Served to capt. USAF, 1958-61. Episcopalian. Clubs: Church (N.Y.C.), Yale (N.Y.C.), Rumson (N.J.) Country, Seabright (N.J.) Lawn Tennis, Baltasrol Golf. Home: 255 Oak Ridge Ave Summit NJ 07901 Office: MPT Assocs 630 Fifth Ave Ste 2670 New York NY 10111

WEBSTER, LOIS SHAND, information resources executive; b. Springfield, Ill., Sept. 25, 1929; d. Richings James and C. Odell (Gilbert) S.; m. Terrance Ellis Webster, Feb. 12, 1954 (dec. July 1985); children: Terrance Richings, Bruce Douglas, Andrew Michael. BA, Millikin U., 1951; cert. in library tech., Coll. Du Page County, Glen Ellyn, Ill., 1974; postgrad. library sci., No. Ill. U., 1977-82. Mgr. info. resources Am. Nuclear Soc., La Grange Park, Ill., 1973—. Contbr. articles and book chpts. to profl. publs. Field dir. Springfield council Girl Scouts U.S., 1951-54; library advisor Du Page County council Girl Scouts U.S., 1973-74. Mem. Am. Soc. for Info. Sci., Spl. Libraries Assn. (chair div. 1985-86, chair bylaws com. 1987—), Council Engring. and Sci. Soc. Execs., Met. Chgo. Library Assembly (bd. dirs. 1982-85). Republican. Home: 560 Dorset Ave Glen Ellyn IL 60137 Office: Am Nuclear Soc 555 N Kensington Ave La Grange Park IL 60525

WEBSTER, SHARON B., economist; b. Wildwood, Fla., Aug. 23, 1937; d. James McWilliams and Marion (Hallbrook) Boen; BA in Polit. Sci., Econs. and Psychology, U. Fla., 1959; postgrad. (vis. doctoral fellow), Princeton U., 1964-65; PhD, U. Va., 1965. . Asst. prof. No. Mich. U., Marquette, 1962-64, U. Md., 1964-66, Hollins Coll., Roanoke, Va., 1966-71; prof. Fed. Exec. Inst., Charlottesville, Va., 1971-72; internat. program mgr. Dept. Treasury, Washington, 1972-74; economist Econs., Statistics and Coop. Svc., U.S. Dept. Agr., Washington, 1974-79; mem. Presdl. Commn. for Exec. Exchange, 1979-80; dir. internat. econs. Occidental Petroleum Corp., L.A., 1980-83; investment banker, account exec. Johnston, Lemon and Co., Inc., Washington, 1983-88; fin. cons. Shearson Lehman Hutton, 1988—. Mem. adv. bd. Pres.'s Carribbean Basin Initiative, 1982; chmn. bd. dirs. NATA, Inc.; bd. dirs. GENTA, Inc., NABE; pres., chief exec. officer A.A. Global; bd. advisors Sintal Communications USA, Inc., Internat. Trade Council, Patterson Sch. Diplomacy and Internat. Commerce, U. Ky., Consumer Health and Svcs. of Am., Inc. Contbr. articles to profl. jours. Recipient Presdl. award Pvt. Sector Initiative, 1982; NDEA fellow. Mem. AAUP, Internat. Policy Inst. (v.p. 1977—), Internat. Assn. Energy Economists, Am. Assn. Agrl. Economists, Am. Polit. Sci. Assn., Nat. Assn. Bus. Economists, Internat. Studies Assn., Soc. Internat. Devel., Nat. Council Career Women, Washington Soc. Money Mgrs., Assn. Polit. Risk Analysts, Pres.'s Exec. Exchange Assn., Fed. Exec. Inst. Alumni Assn., Capital Speakers Club, Army Navy Club, Internat. Club. Home: The Winthrop #602 1727 Massachusetts Ave NW Washington DC 20036-2159 Office: Shearson Lehman Hutton 217 E Redwood St Suite 2100 Baltimore MD 21202 Other: Washington United States

WEBSTER, WAYNE RICHARD, financial executive; b. Portland, Maine, July 10, 1943; s. George Pennell and Dorothy Margaret (Marston) W.;m. Pamela Louise Hollywood, Aug. 22, 1964; children: Andrea, David, Peter. Acct., Northeastern Bus. Coll., Portland, 1964; BS in Bus., U. So. Maine, 1977. Exec. trainee, computer programmer Canal Nat. Bank, Portland, 1964-67, asst. internal auditor, 1967-69; mgr. acctg. Sanders Assocs., South Portland, Maine, 1969-70; external auditor Blue Cross-Blue Shield Maine, Portland, 1970-73, internal auditor, 1973-74, asst. to v.p. fin., 1974-78, dir. gen. acctg., 1978-81, v.p. fin., 1981-88, sr. v.p. corp. resources, 1988—; bd. dirs. Health Maint. Orgn. - Maine, Portland, 1986-88; trustee Blue Cross-Blue Shield Retirement Plan, Portland, 1985-88; treas. Carepac Maine, Portland, 1986-88; chmn. audit com. Blue Cross-Blue Shield Credit Union, Portland, 1973-79. Mem. Coastal Water Access Study Com., Cumberland, Maine, 1979; mem. recreation com. Town of Cumberland, 1978, town councilor, 1981. Served with Maine Air Nat. Guard, 1964-70. Mem. Nat. Assn. Accts. (dir. 1978-79), Healthcare Fin. Mgmt. Assn., Fin. Execs. Inst. (mem. adv. bd. 1986—), Inst. Internal Auditors (v.p. 1973-74). Republican. Roman Catholic. Clubs: Val Halla Golf Assn. (Cumberland) (pres. 1979-81); Purpoodcock (Cape Elizabeth, Maine), Cumberland (Portland). Home: 10 Carriage Rd Cumberland Foreside ME 04110 Office: Blue Cross Blue Shield Maine 110 Free St Portland ME 04101

WECK, KRISTIN WILLA, savings and loan association executive; b. Elgin, Ill., Nov. 5, 1959; d. John Francis and Florence Elaine (Ebel) W. BBA, Augustana Coll., Rock Island, Ill., 1981. Lic. real estate salesman, Ill. Intern with investment banking group First Chgo. Bank, London, 1980; intern Prudential-Bache Co., Ft. Lauderdale, Fla., 1981; residential appraiser Fox Valley Appraisal Counselors, Ltd., West Dundee, Ill., 1982-84; asst. real estate loan officer First Nat. Bank, Barrington, Ill., 1982-84; savs. and loan field examiner III Fed. Home Loan Bank, Chgo., 1984—. V.p. Brandywine Condo Assn., Crystal Lake, Ill., 1983. Recipient Outstanding Achievement award Fed. Home Loan Bank Bd., 1985. Mem. Soc. Real Estate Appraisers (candidate). Republican. Lutheran. Home: 435A Brandy Dr Crystal Lake IL 60014 Office: Fed Home Loan Bank 111 E Wacker Dr Suite 800 Chicago IL 60601-4360

WECKER, IRWIN R., business executive, professional engineer; b. Bklyn., Aug. 21, 1935; s. Morris and Eva (Kolodny) W.; m. Harriet Lederman, July 9, 1960; children: Jeffrey Scott, Rita Lynn. BEE, CCNY, 1958; MBA, Baruch Coll., 1964; cert. in advanced exec. mgmt., U. Pa., 1984. Registered profl. engr., N.Y., N.J., Mass., Fla. Sales application engr. Bailey Meter Co., Cleve., 1958-63; sr. instrument engr. Amstar Corp., N.Y.C., 1963-73; mgr., continuing edn. Stone & Webster Engring. Corp., N.Y.C., 1973-76, mgr. marketing, 1976-79; dir. corp. tng. and devel. EBASCO Services Inc., N.Y.C., 1979-87; dir. human resources and adminstrn. ea. group hdqrs. Sverdrup Corp., White Plains, N.Y., 1987—; adj. prof. Fairleigh Dickinson U., Teaneck, N.J., 1972-73; vis. lectr. Wharton Sch., U. Pa., 1982-83, CUNY PhD Mgmt. Program, 1986—. Contbr. articles to profl. jours. Adv. council U. of State of N.Y., Albany, 1980-86, bd. of regents, 1980-86; pres. Fieldstondale Mut. Housing Corp., Riverdale, N.Y., 1983-85, Hunters Run Homeowners Assn., Dobbs Ferry, N.Y., 1987—; mem. tech. council N.Y. Inst. Tech., Westbury, L.I., 1983-86; bd. visitors PhD mgmt. program, CUNY, 1985-86. Recipient Disting. Service award Fieldstondale Mut. Housing Corp., 1985. Mem. ASME, Inst. of Mgmt. Studies (adv. council 1982-86), Am. Mgmt. Assn. Home: 301 Hunters Run Dobbs Ferry NY 10522 Office: Sverdrup Corp One North Lexington Ave White Plains NY 10601

WEDDING, CHARLES RANDOLPH, architect; b. St. Petersburg, Fla., Nov. 16, 1934; s. Charles Reid and L. Marion (Whitaker) W.; m. Audrey Whitsel, Aug. 18, 1956 (div. Apr. 1979); children: Daryl L., Douglas R., Dorian B.; m. Vonnie Sue Hayes, June 22, 1984; stepchildren: Stephanie M., Brian E. BArch, U. Fla., 1957. Registered architect, Fla., Ga., N.C., S.C., Del., Va., Tex., Ill., Ind., Kans., La., Mo., Okla., Tenn. Architect in tng. Harvard & Jolly AIA, St. Petersburg, 1957-60; architect, prin., pres. Wedding & Assocs., St. Petersburg, 1960—. Mayor City of St. Petersburg, 1973-75; past chmn. Pinellas County Com. of 100, Bldg. Dept. Survey Team, City of St. Petersburg; trustee All Children's Hosp., 1968-70; sect. leader St. Petersburg United Fund, 1965-70; mem. city council Action Team for Pier Redevel., 1967-68; mem. exec. com. Goals for City of St. Petersburg, 1970-72; den. leader Weblos, Boy Scouts Am., 1971-72; chmn., trustee Canterbury Sch. YMCA, 1968-72; mem. adv. com. Tomlinson Vocat. Sch., 1969-79; past trustee Mus. Fine Arts; past bd. dirs. Neighborly Ctr., Jr. Achievement Pinellas County. Served to 1st lt. U.S. Army, 1958-60. Fellow AIA (5 Silver Spike awards, Merit of Honor, Medal of Honor); mem. Am. Soc. Landscape Architects, St. Petersburg Assn. Architects (past. pres.), Fla. Assn. Architects (8 Merit Design awards). Republican. Episcopalian. Clubs: Suncoasters; St. Petersburg Yacht. Avocations: sailing, hunting, golfing, tennis. Home: 1310 45th Ave N Saint Petersburg FL 33703 Office: Wedding & Assocs Inc 360 Central Ave Saint Petersburg FL 33701

WEDDLE, STEPHEN SHIELDS, manufacturing company executive; b. Boston, Nov. 9, 1938; s. Harold Mansfield and Esther Letha (Bales) W.; m. Meredith Baldwin, June 10, 1961; children: Christopher, Timothy, Justin, Jamien. A.B., Harvard, 1960; LL.B., Columbia, 1963. Bar: N.Y. 1966, Conn. 1989. Lectr. in law (supported by Ford Found. Project for Staffing African Instns. for Legal Edn. and Research) Ahmadu Bello U., Zaria, Nigeria, 1963-65; assoc. firm Debevoise & Plimpton, N.Y.C., 1965-71; corporate counsel Technicon Corp., Tarrytown, N.Y., 1971-74; sec. Technicon Corp., 1972-78, sr. v.p., gen. counsel, 1974-78; v.p., gen. counsel, sec. Stanley Works, New Britain, Conn., 1978—. Mem. Assn. Bar City N.Y. (sec. com. on fgn. and comparative law 1968-70), Am., Conn., N.Y. bar assns., Am. Soc. Corp. Secs., Am. Corp. Counsel Assn. Office: Stanley Works PO Box 7000 New Britain CT 06050

WEDEMEYER, RITA KAY, investment executive; b. Greencastle, Ind., Sept. 7, 1961; d. Earl Eugene and Phyllis Jean (Nelson) Clodfelter; divorced, 1984; 1 child, Kyle Nelson. Grad. high sch. Cert. fin. planner. Teller Lafayette (Ind.) Bank and Trust Co., 1981, investment clk., 1981-84, investment mgr. trust dept., 1984-87, investment officer, 1987—. Home: 511 N 27th St Lafayette IN 47904 Office: Lafayette Bank & Trust Co 133 N 4th St Lafayette IN 47901

WEEDEN, WALTER WARDWELL, JR., transportation executive; b. Boston, Apr. 8, 1932; s. Walter W. and Greta Linnea (Anderson) W.; m. Shirley May Colburn, June 12, 1954; children: Jeffrey, Valerie, Heather. BS in Indsl. Engring., Northeastern U., Boston, 1955. Dist. sales mgr. Gen. Electric Co., Chgo., 1972-75, western regional sales mgr., 1978-79; program mgr. Gen. Electric Co., Erie, Pa., 1975-78; dir. mktg. and sales Servo Corp. Am., Hicksville, N.Y., 1979-81, v.p. mktg. and sales, 1981-83, sr. v.p. transp. div., 1983—; bd. dirs., past pres., 1st v.p. Ry. System Suppliers, Inc. Served as 1st lt. U.S. Army, 1955. Mem. Ry. Progress Inst. Republican. Methodist. Club: Ctr. Port Yacht (N.Y.) (chmn. hosp. commn. 1983-85). Home: 52 Wagon Wheel Ct Dix Hills NY 11746 Office: Servo Corp Am 111 New South Rd Hicksville NY 11802

WEEKLY, JOHN WILLIAM, insurance company executive; b. Sioux City, Iowa, June 21, 1931; s. John E. Weekly and Alyce Beatrice (Preble) Nichols; m. Bette Lou Thomas, Dec. 31, 1949; children: John William Jr., Thomas Patrick, Michael Craig, James Mathew, Daniel Kevin. Grad. high sch., Omaha. V.p. First Data Resources, Inc., Omaha, 1969-74; v.p. Mut. United Omaha Ins. Co., Omaha, 1974-81, sr. exec. v.p., 1981-87; pres., chief operating officer Mut. of Omaha Ins. Co., 1987—, bd. dirs.; bd. dirs. United of Omaha Ins. Co., Companion Life Ins. Co., Kirkpatrick, Pettis, Smith, Polian, Inc., Conservative Savs. Bank. Bd. dirs. Salvation Army, Omaha, 1984—, United Way of Midlands, 1987—, Bellevue (Nebr.) Coll., 1986—; active Archbishop's Com. for Ednl. Devel., 1988—. Club: Omaha Country (treas. 1986—). Office: Mut of Omaha Ins Co Mutual of Omaha Pla Omaha NE 68175

WEEKS, MRS. ANDI EMERSON See EMERSON, ANDI

WEEKS, CHARLES R., bank executive; b. Lansing, Mich., Apr. 23, 1934; s. John Eastman and Thelma (Pobanz) W.; m. Judith Elaine Adams, June 27, 1959; 1 child, Christopher James. BBA in Mgmt., Mich. State U., 1961. With Nat. Bank Detroit, 1961-73; various positions to exec. v.p. So. Ohio Bank, Cin., 1973-75; various positions to pres. Union Commerce Bank, Cleve., 1975-78; pres., bd. dirs. Union Commerce Corp., Cleve., 1978-82; pres., chief exec. officer, bd. dirs. Citizens Comml. & Savs. Bank (now Citizens Banking Corp.), Flint, Mich., 1982-87; pres., chief exec. officer Citizens Comml. & Savs. Bank (now Citizens Banking Corp.), Flint, 1982—; also bd. dirs. Citizens Comml. & Savs. Bank (now Citizens Banking Corp.); vice chmn. Citizens Comml. & Savs. Bank; bd. dirs. 2nd Nat. Corp., 2nd Nat. Bank Saginaw. Bd. dirs. Flint Exec. Service Corps; trustee Urban Coalition Greater Flint; pres. bd. trustees Women's Hosp. Assn.; trustee Flint Inst. Music; sponser Coll. and Cultural Devel. Fund; treas. 100 Club Flint; active Citizens Adv. Council U. Mich., Flint; pres.-elect Tall Pine Council Boy Scouts Am. Mem. Am. Bankers Assn. (Gov. Relations Council), Mich. Bankers Assn. (1st v.p., pres.-elect, 1988), Am. Inst. Banking. Lodge: Rotary (Flint). Office: Citizens Banking Corp 1 Citizens Banking Ctr Flint MI 48502

WEEKS, E. WAYNE, JR., telecommunications company executive. Pres. network system AT&T Techs. Inc., Berkeley Heights, N.J., also bd. dirs.; bd. dirs. Summit (N.J.) Trust Co. Office: AT&T 550 Madison Ave New York NY 10022 *

WEEKS, GARY LEE, electronic company executive, applications engineer; b. Ithaca, N.Y., July 4, 1949; s. John A. and Esther (Bulmore) W.; m. Frieda M. Weston, Sept. 10, 1983; children: Heather, Nathan. BS in Edn., SUNY, Oswego, 1972. Mng. ptnr. Last Week Music, B.M.I., Syracuse, N.Y., 1973-82; applications engr. SSAC Inc., Liverpool, N.Y., 1982-83; mgr. regional sales SSAC Inc., Liverpool, 1983-84, mgr. nat. sales, 1984—. Composer popular, rock and children's songs, 1972-82. Mem. Refrigeration Svc. Engrs. Soc. Mem. Covenant Ch. Office: SSAC Inc 8220 Loop Rd Box 1000 Baldwinsville NY 13027

WEEKS, ROBERT GRAY, oil, chemicals, minerals and real estate executive; b. Camden, N.J., July 14, 1936; s. Richard William Jr. and Catharine Gray (Bray) W.; m. Nancy Rae Shupe, Dec. 15, 1956; children: Jayne, James, John. BS, Drexel U., 1958. Engr. U.S. Refining, N.J., Tex. and N.Y., 1954-69; asst. mgr. planning U.S. Mktg., Mass., Vt. and N.Y., 1969-74; various planning and fin. assignments positions Mktg. and Refining div. Mid. East Transp. Supply, N.Y.C., 1974-80; exec. v.p. Mktg. and Refining div. Mid. East Transp. Supply, Fairfax, Va., 1980-86; pres. Mobil Chem. Co., Stamford, Conn., 1986-88; sr. v.p. Mobil Corp, N.Y.C., 1988—; bd. dirs. Sovran Fin. Corp, Norfolk, Va., Mobil Corp., N.Y.C. 1st lt. U.S. Army, 1958-59. Mem. Am. Petroleum Inst. (bd. dirs. 1987—), Chem. Mfrs. Assn. (bd. dirs. 1986—), NATAS (bd. dirs. internat. counc. 1988—), Va. Found.

Ind. Colls. (trustee 1988—), Mansion Club (Phoenix), Washington Golf and Country Club (Arlington, Va.), Camelback Golf Club (Scottsdale, Ariz.), Desert Mountain Golf Club (Scottsdale), Stratton Club (Bondville, Vt.). Republican. Congregationalist. Office: Mobil Corp 150 E 42d St New York NY 10017

WEEKS, ROBERT WALKER, lawyer, manufacturing company executive; b. Rock Island, Ill., Aug. 14, 1926; s. Harold Parker and Miriam (Walker) W.; m. Phyllis Anne Grams, July 24, 1948; children: Susan Carol, Katharine Ann, Nancy Jane. B.S. in Naval Sci, Purdue U., 1947, B.S. in Mech. Engring, 1948; J.D., Northwestern U., 1951. Bar: Ill. 1951. With law dept. Deere & Co., Moline, Ill., 1951—; gen. counsel Deere & Co., 1969—, v.p., 1977—; dir. John Deere Credit Co., John Deere Ins. Group, John Deere Leasing Co., Iowa-Ill. Gas and Electric Co. Trustee Ill. Wesleyan U. Served with USNR, 1944-46. Mem. ABA, Ill. Bar Assn. Home: 60 Hawthorne Rd Rock Island IL 61201 Office: Deere & Co John Deere Rd Moline IL 61265

WEFER, DONALD PETERS, lawyer; b. Bronxville, N.Y., Oct. 23, 1933; s. A. Ralph C. and Margaret E. (Peters) W.; m. Janet G. Schade, July 12, 1958; children: Douglas P., Ellen G., Amy L. BA, U. Rochester, 1954; LLB, Yale U., 1960. Bar: N.Y. 1960. Law clk. to presiding justice U.S. Dist. Ct. Conn., New Haven, 1960-61; assoc. Simpson, Thacher & Bartlett, N.Y.C., 1961-70, ptnr., 1970-80; v.p. legal dept. Assn. Metals and Minerals, White Plains, N.Y., 1980—; bd. dirs. Christiania Gen. Ins. Corp. N.Y., Tarrytown. Lt. (j.g.) USN, 1955-58. Mem. Port Washington (N.Y.) Yacht Club (commodore 1981-82). Home: 117 Country Club Dr Port Washington NY 11050 Office: Assn Metals and Minerals 3 N Corporate Park Dr White Plains NY 10604

WEGENSTEIN, MARTIN WILLI, electric company executive; b. Zurich, Switzerland, May 23, 1950; came to U.S., 1976; s. Willi Otto and Doris (Maya) W.; m. Jill Schneier, June 3, 1979; children: Danielle Maya, Michelle Andrea. Diploma in math., Swiss Fed. Inst. Tech., 1976; MS in Computer Sci., Union Coll., 1977. Research asst. Swiss Fed. Inst. Tech., Zurich, 1976.; ops. analyst Emerson Electric Co., St. Louis, 1977-78, corp. hardware specialist, 1978-80, mgr. corp. data planning, 1980-81; dir. systems planning Skil Corp. subs., Chgo., 1981-82; dir. systems and planning Skil Netherland BV, Breda, 1982-85; dir. corp. mgmt. info. systems parent co. Emerson Electric Co., St. Louis, 1985—; dir. systems and planning Skil Netherlands B.V., Breda, 1982-85; chmn. European meeting Round Table, Breda, 1984-85. Office: Emerson Electric Co 8000 W Florissant Ave Saint Louis MO 63136

WEGMULLER, HUGO WERNER, electrical engineer; b. Gland, Vaud, Switzerland, Mar. 18, 1935; came to U.S., 1986; s. Werner and Erna (Schwegler) W.; m. Annie Charlotte Elise Charbonnier, Nov. 4, 1963; children: Jean-Philippe, Jacques. BEE, Coll. Engring., Geneva, 1955. Mng. dir. South African subs. French GE, Paris, 1964-78; pres. Elmaco Internat. S.A., Panama City, Panama, 1979—; also bd. dirs. Elmaco Internat. S.Am., Panama City, Panama; pres. Canutel Industries, H&A Trading, Canutel Cons. Svcs., Wegmuller Internat. Holdings Inc., Alta., Can., 1981—, also bd. dirs., 1981—; pres. Canutel USA Inc., Canutel Berrien Inc., Cirtec Systems Inc., Berrien Springs, Mich., 1986—, 1986. Office: Canutel Berrien Inc 4445-1 E Shawnee Rd Berrien Springs MI 49103

WEICHMANN, CRAIG THOMAS, financial company executive; b. Chgo., Oct. 11, 1950; s. Carlyle Thomas and Lois Ann (Kragh) W.; m. Karen Anne Siebenhausen, May 5, 1973; children: Joelle Aarland, Karena Jordan, Kristianna Joy, Craig Trevor. BS with distinction, So. Meth. U., 1972; MBA, U. Va., 1975. Chartered fin. analyst. Rsch. asst. Eppler, Guerin & Turner, Dallas, 1972-73, Tayloe Murphy Inst., Charlottesville, Va., 1974-75; rsch. asst. Holiday Corp., Memphis, 1975-76, dir. investor relations, 1976-79; rsch. analyst Morgan Keegan & Co., Memphis, 1979—; mng. dir. Morgan, Keegan & Co., Memphis, 1986—. Past deacon, First Evang. Ch., Memphis. Mem. Memphis Soc. Security Analysts (pres. 1988—), Rotary, Beta Theta Pi (treas. 1971-72). Republican. Home: 7446 Pyron Oaks Cove Germantown TN 38138 Office: Morgan Keegan & Co 50 N Front St Memphis TN 38103

WEIDA, LEWIS DIXON, marketing analyst/consultant; b. Moran, Ind., Apr. 23, 1924; s. Charles Ray and Luella Mildred (Dixon) W.; student Kenyon Coll., 1943, Purdue U., 1946; B.S., Ind. U., 1948; M.S., Columbia U., 1950. Mgr. statis. analysis unit Gen. Motors Acceptance Corp., N.Y.C., 1949-55; asst. to exec. v.p. Am. Express Co., 1955-82. Served with USAAF, 1943-46; PTO. Mem. Internat. Platform Assn. Democrat. Club: Masons. Home: 25 Tudor City Pl New York NY 10017

WEIDENBAUM, MURRAY LEW, economics educator; b. Bronx, N.Y., Feb. 10, 1927; s. David and Rose (Warshaw) W.; m. Phyllis Green, June 13, 1954; children: Susan, James, Laurie. B.B.A., CCNY, 1948; M.A., Columbia U., 1949; M.P.A. (Banbury fellow), Princeton U., 1954; Ph.D., Princeton, 1958; LL.D., Baruch Coll., 1981, U. Evansville, 1983. Fiscal economist Bur. Budget, Washington, 1949-57; corp. economist Boeing Co., Seattle, 1958-62; sr. economist Stanford Research Inst., Palo Alto, Calif., 1962-63; mem. faculty Washington U., St. Louis, 1964—; prof., chmn. dept. econs. Washington U., 1966-69, Mallinckrodt prof., 1971—, dir. Ctr. for Study Am. Bus., 1975-81, 82—; asst. sec. econ. policy Treasury Dept., 1969-71; chmn. Council of Econ. Advs., 1981-82; Chmn. research adv. com. St. Louis Regional Indsl. Devel. Corp., 1965-69; exec. sec. Pres.'s Com. Econ. Impact of Def. and Disarmament, 1964; mem. U.S. Financial Investment Adv. Panel, 1970-72; cons. (various firms and insts.). Author: Federal Budgeting, 1964, Modern Public Sector, 1969, Economics of Peacetime Defense, 1974, Economic Impact of the Vietnam War, 1967, Government-Mandated Price Increases, 1975, Business, Government, and the Public, 1989, The Future of Business Regulation, 1980, Rendezvous With Reality: The American Economy After Reagan, 1988; Editorial bd.: Publius, 1971—, Jour. Econ. Issues, 1972-75, Challenge, 1974-81, 83—. Served with AUS, 1945. Recipient Alexander Hamilton medal Treasury Dept., 1971, Distinguished Writer award Georgetown U., 1971, award for disting. teaching Freedoms Found., 1980; named to Free Market Hall of Fame, 1983. Fellow Nat. Assn. Bus. Economists, Am. Inst. Aeros. and Astronautics (asso.), City Coll. Alumni Assn. (Townsend Harris medal 1969), Assn. for Pvt. Enterprise Edn. (Adam Smith award 1986). Club: Cosmos. Office: Washington U Ctr Study Am Bus Campus Box 1208 Saint Louis MO 63130

WEIERMAN, ROBERT CHRISTIAN, manufacturing company executive, mechanical engineer; b. San Francisco, Oct. 25, 1945; s. Wallace Stanley Weierman and Jean Marian (Lowe) Durant; m. Joanne Marie Bystrom, June 29, 1969; children: William, Anna, Jacob, Benjamin, Jared, Emily, Thomas. BSME, Calif. State U., L.A., 1972. Rsch. engr. Escoa Finture Corp., Alhambra, Calif., 1972-74; chief engr. Escoa Finture Corp., Pryor, Okla., 1974-85; gen. mgr. Escoa div. Fintube Corp., Pryor, 1985—. Author: Fintube Engineering Manual, 1979; contbr. articles to profl. jours. Mem. Osage Sch. Bd. Edn., Pryor, 1982-88; former scoutmaster troop 82, Boy Scouts Am., Pryor. Mem. ASME. Republican. Mormon. Home: Rte 1 Box 143 Pryor OK 74361 Office: Fintube Corp Escoa Div PO Box 399 Pryor OK 74362

WEIGEL, ELSIE DIVEN, publishing executive, writer, editor; b. Phila., May 31, 1948; d. William Bleakley Diven and Elsie May (Betts) Darling; m. John C. Weigel, Dec. 19, 1970 (div. 1979); 1 Child, Kimberly Joy. BA, Am. U., 1970. Editorial asst. Water Pollution Control Fedn., Alexandria, Va., 1970-72; Asst dir. publs. Am. Speech, Hearing, and Lang. Assn., Rockville, Md., 1972-78; editor-in-chief Potato Chip/Snack Food Assn., Alexandria, 1978-79; dir. publs. Nat. Soc. Pub. Accts., Alexandria, 1979-80; editorial project dir. Energy Info. Adminstrn. U.S. Dept Energy, Washington, 1980—. Editor newsletter Rittenhouse Family Assn.; contbr. articles to profl. jours. Mem. Life Skills Ctr. (bd. dirs. 1987—), Washington. Mem. Nat. Assn. Govt. Communicatiors (Blue Pencil award), Nat. Assn Female Execs., Sigma Delta Chi. Home: 8303 Pondside Terr Alexandria VA 22309 Office: US Dept Energy 1000 Independence Ave Washington DC 20003

WEIL, DAVID S., plastics manufacturing executive; b. Germany, Apr. 6, 1925; came to U.S., 1943; s. William and Martha Weil; m. Grace K. Weil, Mar. 20, 1949; children: Aryeh L., Esther R. Weil Sturm. BA, CCNY, 1949. Pres., chief exec. officer Ampacet Corp., Mt. Vernon, N.Y., 1958—. Sgt. U.S. Army, 1943-46, CBI. Decorated Bronze Star. Mem. Soc. Plastics Engrs. (Internat. Excellence award 1986), Soc. Plastics Industry (bd. dirs. 1983-86). Office: Ampacet Corp 250 S Terrace Ave Mount Vernon NY 10550 *

WEIL, DENIE SANDISON, foundation administrator; b. St. Louis, Mar. 16, 1931; d. James Calvin and Eliza (Tillman) Sandison; m. Frank A. Weil, Feb. 11, 1951; children: Deborah, Amanda, Sandison, William. AB, Radcliffe Coll., 1954. Dep. dir. rsch. Vera Inst., N.Y.C., 1974-77; program officer German Marshall Fund U.S., Washington, 1977-82; writer, cons. 1983-85; pres. Citizens' Participation Project, Washington, 1986—; bd. dirs. Fiduciary Trust Co. Internat., N.Y.C., Banner Life Ins. Co., Rockville, Md. Contbr. articles on career mgmt. to Working Women. Trustee, v.p. Irvington Inst. Med. Rsch., N.Y.C., 1958-77, Abbott House, Irvington, N.Y., 1965-75, Jewish Assn. for Svcs. for Aged, N.Y.C., 1969-77; trustee Arena Stage, Washington, 1984—, Radcliffe Coll., Cambridge, Mass., 1972-83; bd. overseers Harvard U., Cambridge, 1981-87. Mem. Harvard Club (N.Y.C., bd. mgrs. 1987—), Cosmopolitan Club (N.Y.C.). Democrat. Home: 1516 28th St Washington DC 20007 Office: Citizens Participation Proj 2000 P St NW Ste 508 Washington DC 20036

WEIL, ERNST, oil industry executive. Chmn., chief exec. officer Phibro Energy Inc., Greenwich, Conn. Office: Phibro Energy Inc 600 Steamboat Rd Greenwich CT 06830 also: Salomon Inc 1221 Ave of the Americas New York NY 10020 *

WEILL, PATRICIA GENE, controller; b. N.Y.C., June 30, 1939; d. Harold and Lisbeth (Goldmann) W.; m. Richard Alan Rosenthal, June 10, 1962 (div. 1985); children: Pamela Gail, Mark Carroll. BS in Publications, Simmons Coll., 1961; postgrad., Northeastern U., 1981-82; Cert. in Acctg., Bentley Coll., 1987. Assoc. editor various TV and fan mags., N.Y.C., 1961-62; free-lance writer N.Y.C., N.J. and Mass., 1962-78; asst. to mgr. credit/receivables Dodge Chem. Co., Cambridge, Mass., 1980-83; asst. controller Edward R. Marden Corp., Allston, Mass., 1983-86; controller Aarlan, Inc., Cambridge, 1986-87; asst. controller SDK Healthcare Info. Systems, Boston, 1987—. Vol. tutor Adult Literacy Program, Brighton, Mass., 1988—; pres., bd. mgrs. condominium assn., 1987—. Mem. Mensa. Office: SDK Healthcare Info Systems 1550 Soldiersfield Rd Boston MA 02135

WEILL, SANFORD I., banker; b. N.Y.C., Mar. 16, 1933; s. Max and Etta (Kalika) W.; m. Joan Mosher, June 20, 1955; children: Marc P., Jessica M. B.A., Cornell U., 1955, student Grad. Sch. Bus. and Pub. Adminstrn., 1954-55. Chmn. bd., chief exec. officer Carter, Berlind & Weill (name changed to CBWL-Hayden, Stone, Inc. 1970, to Hayden Stone, Inc. 1972, to Shearson Hayden Stone 1974, to Shearson Loeb Rh, N.Y.C., 1960-84; dir., chmn. exec. com. Carter, Berlind & Weill (name changed to CBWL-Hayden, Stone, Inc. 1970, to Hayden Stone, Inc. 1972, to Shearson Hayden Stone 1974, to Shearson Loeb Rh, 1981-83, pres., 1983-85; chmn. Fireman's Fund, 1984-85; past pres., chmn. exec. com., mem. fin. com. Am. Express Co., until 1989; chmn., chief exec. officer Primerica Corp., Greenwich, Conn., 1989—; dir. IDS Mutual Funds Group; vice chmn. adv. council The Johnson Grad. Sch. of Mgmt.; founder Acad. of Fin. Mem. bd. overseers Cornell Med. Coll.; trustee Carnegie Hall (co-chmn. steering com. Campaign for Carnegie Hall); mem. bus. com. Mus. of Modern Art. Mem. N.Y. Soc. Security Analysts. Clubs: Cornell (N.Y.C.), Century Country (Purchase, N.Y.), Harmonie (N.Y.C.). Office: Primerica Corp 1 American Ln Greenwich CT 06836 *

WEILLER, PAUL ANNIK, diversified company executive; b. Neuilly/Seine, France, July 28, 1933; s. Paul Louis Weiller and Aliki (Diplarakos) Russell; m. Olimpia Emanuela Torlonia, June 26, 1965; children—Beatrice, Sibilla, Cosima, Domitilla. Baccaraureat, Ecole des Roches, France, 1951; B.Sc. in Mech. Engring., MIT, 1956. Shareholders rep. IMOSTAB Group, Dusseldorf, W.Ger., 1965—. Vice pres. Wallerstein Found., Ares, France, 1969—; vice pres., treas. Paul Louis Weiller Found., Geneva, 1975—. Served to lt. French Air Force, 1957-59. Decorated Croix Valeur Militaire. Greek Orthodox. Club: Traveller's (Paris). Home: 19 Quai Des Bergues, 1211 Geneva Switzerland Office: IMOGEST SA, 47 rue Vieille du Temple, Paris France

WEIMER, PETER DWIGHT, mediator, lawyer; b. Grand Rapids, Mich., Oct. 14, 1938; s. Glen E. and Clarabel (Kauffman) W.; children: Melanie, Kim. BA, Bridgewater Coll., 1962; JD, Howard U., 1969. Assoc. counsel Loporto & Weimer Ltd., Manassas, Va., 1970-75; chief counsel Weimer & Cheatle Ltd., Manassas, 1975-79, Peter D. Weimer, P.C., Manassas, 1979-82; pres., mediator Mediation Ltd., Manassas, 1981—; pres. Citation Properties, Inc., Manassas, 1971—; pres. Preferred Rsch. of No. Va., Inc., 1985—. Address: PO Box 1616 Manassas VA 22110

WEIN, PHILIP STEPHEN, accounting company executive; b. N.Y.C., Oct. 10, 1942; s. Arthur and Ruth (Monter) W.; m. Susan Moore, Aug. 8, 1973; 1 child, Agatha Susan. BBA, U. Toledo, 1963; MS in Indsl. Engring., Ohio State U., 1965. Asst. to treas. Perfect Chem. and Film, N.Y.C., 1965-68; dir. systems devel. N.Am. consumer products Singer Co., Syosset, N.Y., 1968-71; dir. mgmt. info. systems Burger King div. Pillsbury, Miami, Fla., 1971-74; dir. info. systems Thriftimart Corp., L.A., 1974-78; ptnr. mgmt. cons. svc. Coopers & Lybrand, L.A., 1978—. Contbr. articles to profl. jours. Mem. ops. com. L.A. March of Dimes, 1986—, Conejo Make A Wish Found., Thousand Oaks, Calif., 1986—. Mem. Inst. Cert. Computer Profls., Am. Soc. Ind. Security, Am. Inst. Ind. Engrs., Oasis Country Club, L.A. Athletic Club, Calif. Yacht Club, Sunset Hills Country Club. Office: Coopers & Lybrand 1000 W Sixth St Los Angeles CA 90017

WEINBACH, ARTHUR FREDERIC, computing services company executive; b. Waterbury, Conn., May 3, 1943; s. Max and Winifred (Eckstein) W.; m. Joanne Kaplan, Nov. 20, 1970; children: Michael Scott, Jonathan David. BS in Econs., U. Pa., 1965, MS in Acctg., 1966. CPA. Various positions with Touche Ross & Co., N.Y.C., 1966-75; ptnr. Touche Ross & Co., Stamford, Conn., 1976-79; v.p. Automatic Data Processing, Inc., Roseland, N.J., 1980-81; v.p. fin. Automatic Data Processing, Inc., Clifton, N.J., 1981-82, sr. v.p. adminstrn. and fin., 1982—; also bd. dirs. Automatic Data Processing, Inc., Clifton. Editor mag. sect. Conn. CPA Mag., 1978-79. Chmn. task force Stamford Area Commerce and Industry Assn., 1979. Mem. AICPA (minority recruitment-equal opportunity com. 1975-76), Conn. Soc. CPAs (chmn. auditing standards com. 1978-79), Fin. Exec. Inst. Jewish. Home: 372 Long Hill Dr Short Hills NJ 07078 Office: ADP Inc One ADP Blvd Roseland NJ 07068

WEINBACH, LAWRENCE ALLEN, accountant; b. Bklyn., Jan. 8, 1940; s. Max N. and Winifred H. (Eckstein) W.; m. Patricia Leiter, Dec. 25, 1961; children: Wendy, Peter, Daniel. B.S. in Econs, Wharton Sch., U. Pa., 1961. CPA, Conn., N.Y., other states. With Arthur Andersen & Co. (CPA's), N.Y.C., 1961—; mng. partner Arthur Andersen & Co. (CPA's), Stamford, Conn., 1974-80; ptnr.-in-charge N.Y. acctg. and audit practice Arthur Andersen & Co., N.Y.C., 1980-83, mng. ptnr. N.Y. and N.Y. Met. area, 1983-87, mem. bd. ptnrs., 1984—, chmn. bd. ptnrs., 1986-87, mng. ptnr., chief oper. officer, 1987-89, chief exec. officer, 1989—; exec. com. Stamford Commerce and Industry Assn., 1978-80, bd. dirs., 1976-80. Chmn. bd. Hartman Regional Theatre, Stamford, 1977-78, bd. dirs., 1976-80; bd. incorporators Stamford Hosp., 1976-84; bd. dirs. United Way Stamford, 1976-78, Phoenix House Inc., 1984—, Council on Fgn. Relations, 1986—; trustee Carnegie Hall, 1985—; mem. adv. bd. Wharton Sch., U. Pa., 1988—. Mem. AICPA, N.Y. Soc. CPA's, Conn. Soc. CPA's, Beta Gamma Sigma, Beta Alpha Psi. Republican. Clubs: Conn. Golf, Birchwood Country, Harmonie, University, Board Room. Office: Arthur Andersen & Co 1345 Ave of the Americas New York NY 10105 also: Arthur Andersen & Co 69 W Washington Chicago IL 60602

WEINBERG, BARBARA BICKERSTAFFE, municipal official, real estate executive; b. Boston; d. Herbert Powers and Florence (Jameson) Bickerstaffe; m. Stanley Weinberg, Nov. 21, 1959; children: Leslie Jeanne, Susan Elizabeth. BS, Boston U., 1958; postgrad. U. Conn., 1969-70, U. Hartford; grad. Conn. Realtors Inst., 1973. Broker, owner B/W Realty, Inc. doing bus. as Re/Max East of the River, Manchester, 1972-87 ; mem. Manchester City Council, 1979— (state coordinator Friendship Force 1983-87, state dir. 1987—); dep. mayor City of Manchester (Conn.), 1981-83, mayor, 1983-87. Asst. state coordinator Carter Presdl. Primary, 1976; chmn. Com. for 51.3% Conn. presdl. campaign, 1976; bd. dirs. Friendship Force, Atlanta, also state dir., 1977; mem. Winograd Commn., Democratic Nat. Com., 1977-78, Mid-Term Conf., 1978; alt. del. Conn. State Dem. Conv., 1980; del. Dem. Nat. Conv., 1980; bd. dirs. Town Council, Manchester, 1979—, chmn. Housing Com., 1981—; bd. dirs. Manchester United Way, East of the River Tourism Dist. Charles Kettering fellow, 1981-83. Mem. Nat. Assn. Realtors, Women's Council Realtors (past pres. chpt.; service award), Conn. Assn. Realtors, Greater Hartford Bd. Realtors, Greater Hartford Multiple Listing Corp., Manchester Bd. Realtors (dir.; Realtor of Yr. 1981), Manchester Multiple Listing Corp. (dir.), Greater Manchester C. of C. Democrat. Methodist. Home: 157 Pitkin St Manchester CT 06040 Office: Re/Max East of River 297 E Center St Manchester CT 06040

WEINBERG, HAROLD, civil engineer, educator; b. Bklyn., Oct. 28, 1934; s. Isaac and Rae (Metzger) W.; m. Dorothy Waters, May 27, 1956; children—Miriam, Elaine, Alan. BCE in Civil Engring., Cooper Union, 1956; MCE, Bklyn. Poly. Inst., 1960. Registered profl. engr., N.Y., N.J., Pa., Fla. Civil engr. Hewitt-Robins, N.Y.C., 1956-58, N.Y.C. Transit Authority, Bklyn., 1958-69; pres. Weinberg, Kirshenbaum & Tambasco, Architects and Engrs., Bklyn., 1969-85; pres. Harold Weinberg, P.E., Cons. Engr., 1986—; adj. lectr. N.Y.C. Tech. Coll. Civil & Constrn.; adj. asst. prof. fire sci. div. grad. sch. John Jay Coll. Tech. Pres. Hebrew Alliance of Brighton Synagogue, Bklyn., 1974-83; mem. exec. bd. Manhattan Beach Community Group, Bklyn., 1970—, Bklyn. Community Bd. 15, 1975-87. Mem. NSPE. Democrat. Jewish. Avocations: chess; music; reading; sports. Home: 723 Hampton Ave Brooklyn NY 11235

WEINBERG, JOHN LIVINGSTON, investment banker; b. N.Y.C., Jan. 5, 1925; s. Sidney James and Helen (Livingston) W.; m. Sue Ann Gotshal, Dec. 6, 1952; children: Ann K. (dec.), John, Jean. A.B. cum laude, Princeton U., 1948; M.B.A., Harvard U., 1950. With Goldman, Sachs & Co., N.Y.C., 1950—, partner, 1956-76, sr. ptnr., 1976—, co-chmn. mgmt. com., 1976-84, chmn. mgmt. com., 1984—; bd. dirs. B.F. Goodrich Co., Knight-Ridder, Inc., Seagram Co. Ltd., Capital Holding Corp., E.I. du Pont de Nemours & Co.; mem. Conf. Bd., N.Y.C. Ptnrship., Inc. Bd. govs., mem. exec. com. N.Y. Hosp.; mem. adv. Council Stanford U. Bus. Sch.; charter trustee Princeton U. Served to 2d lt. USMCR, 1942-46; capt. 1951-52. Mem. Chgo. Bd. Trade, Coun. on Fgn. Relations, Japan Soc. (bd. dirs.), The Bus. Council. Clubs: Blind Brook, Century Country. Office: Goldman Sachs & Co 85 Broad St New York NY 10004

WEINBERG, NORMA PASEKOFF, communications executive; b. Pitts., July 19, 1941; d. Herbert Jack and Helen Barbara (Hersh) Pasekoff; m. J. Morris Weinberg, Dec. 16, 1962; children: Adam, Erin. BSE, Ohio State U., 1963; MS, Emerson Coll., 1969; postgrad., NYU, 1986-87. Dir. mktg. communications Fibronics Ltd., Haifa, Israel, 1978-82; dir. corp. communications, investor relations Fibronics Internat., Inc., Hyannis, Mass., 1983—; investor relations cons., Mass., 1987—; corp. communications cons., 1987-88. Recipient Nicholson award Fin. World, 1986, Mead award Fin. World, 1986. Mem. Nat. Investor Relations Inst. (mem. nat. adv. com.), Pub. Relations Soc. Am., Hyannis C. of C. Office: Fibronics Internat Inc Independence Park Communications Way Hyannis MA 02601-1892

WEINBERGER, LEON JOSEPH, insurance company executive; b. Leroy, Wis., Nov. 15, 1931; s. James J. and Marie Ann (Bauer) W.; m. Janet M. Hietbrink, Mar. 28, 1977; children: Alan, Carol, Eric, Janet, Randal, Kelly, John. Student, St. Norbert Coll., 1949-50; BBA, U. Wis., 1957; postgrad., Harvard U., 1975. Staff acct. Peat, Marwick, Mitchell & Co., Milw., 1957-61; controller Lake to Lake Dairy Co., Sheboygan, Wis., 1961-67; exec. v.p. Sentry Ins. Co., Stevens Point, Wis., 1967-79; v.p. Nationwide Ins., Columbus, Ohio, 1980-85; pres., chief exec. officer Wausau (Wis.) Ins. Cos., 1985—, also bd. dirs. Served with U.S. Army, 1952-54. Mem. Am. Inst. CPA's. Office: Wausau Ins Cos 2000 Westwood Dr Wausau WI 54401

WEINBLATT, RICHARD B., public relations executive; b. N.Y.C., Aug. 4, 1962; s. Myron Benjamin and Annie R. (Weitz) W. BS, Guilford Coll., Greensboro, N.C., 1986. Chmn. CEN Group, Inc., N.Y.C., 1984-86; pres. CEN Communications, Inc., Monmouth Junction, N.J., 1986—. Mem. Nat. Assn. Rising Communicators (pres., bd. dirs. 1985—), Assn. Collegiate Entrepreneurs, Internat. Radio and TV Soc., Ctr. Entrepreneurial Mgmt., Am. Film Inst., Princeton C. of C., N.J. Communications and Mktg. Assn. Office: CEN Communications Inc 42 Arrowwood Ln Monmouth Junction NJ 08852-2018

WEINER, DEBORAH ANNE, advertising executive; b. Cleve., July 14, 1964; d. Richard and Jacqueline Doris (Houtkin) W. BA in Journalism, Ohio State U., 1987. Acct. exec. Baron Advt., Inc., Cleve., 1987—. Vol. Cystic Fibrosis Found., Columbus, 1984-87, assoc. bd. mem., Cleve., 1987—. mem. Young Bus. Prof. Cleve. Jewish Community Ctr., Cleve. Advt. Club. Office: Baron Advt 1422 Euclid Ave Ste #645 Cleveland OH 44115

WEINER, JOEL DAVID, food products executive; b. Chgo., Aug. 27, 1936; m. Judith L. Metzger; children: Beth, David. BBA, Northwestern U. Dir. new products and household div. Alberto-Culver Co., Melrose Park, Ill., 1963-66; group mktg. mgr. Bristol Myers Co., N.Y.C., 1966-74; v.p. new products Carter Wallace Co., N.Y.C., 1974-78; exec. v.p. Joseph E. Seagram Corp., N.Y.C., 1979-84; exec. v.p. corp. mktg. Kraft, Inc., Glenview, Ill., 1984-87, sr. v.p. corp. mktg., 1987—. Office: Kraft Inc Kraft Court Glenview IL 60025

WEINGARTNER, HARRY, investment house executive, financial planner; b. Cin., Sept. 23, 1936; s. Harry Anselm and Dorothy Ruth (Lederle) W.; m. Betty Jane Tschohl, June 27, 1970; children: David Allen, Stephen Andrew, Susan Ann. BSME, U. Ky, 1958; MBA, U. Mich., 1963. Sales specialist then sales engr. Gen. Electric Co., 1964-68; mgr. market sales Honeywell Corp., Mpls., 1968-69, specialist market rsch., 1969-70; dist. mgr. Am. Appraisal Co., Mpls., 1971-74; stockbroker Dain Bosworth, Inc., Edina, Minn., 1975-88, assoc. v.p., 1988—. Dist. v.p. Edina Reps., 1973. Lt., USN, 1958-61. Mem. Nat. Assn. Accts. (v.p. 1973-74), Twin Cities Cert. Fin. Planners, Sales and Mktg. Execs., Minnetonka Power Squadron (chmn. audit com. 1986—). Roman Catholic. Home: 7137 Glouchester Ave Edina MN 55435

WEINGROW, HOWARD L., financial executive, investor; b. N.Y.C., Dec. 6, 1922; s. Nathan and Anna (Mintzes) W.; m. Muriel Corrine Franzblau, Nov. 24, 1946; children: Terry Vaccaro, Caron Abby Haim. Owner Legion Fluorescent Corp., N.Y.C., 1946-56; ptnr. Hechler & Weingrow, Inc., N.Y.C., 1956-58, Hechler, Lifton & Weingrow, Inc., N.Y.C., 1958-60; exec. v.p. Tanscontinental Investing Corp., N.Y.C., 1960-67; pres. Tanscontinental Investing Corp., 1967-70; prin. Lifton & Weingrow, N.Y.C., 1970—; co-chmn. Marcade Group, Inc., N.Y.C., 1986—; treas. Preferred Health Care, N.Y.C., 1984—, Four Winds, Inc., N.Y.C., 1982—. Treas. Dem. Nat. Com., Washington, 1970-72; dep. fin. chmn. Pres. Carter, Washington, 1980; trustee Hofstra U., Hempstead, N.Y., 1973-76, James S. Brady Presdl. Found., 1982, Nassau County Mus. Fine Arts, 1988—; bd. govs. Hofstra Law Sch., 1977-79; trustee L.I. Jewish Children's Hosp., Lake Success, N.Y., 1986—, Am. Jewish Congression, 1988—; advisor to Pres. Lyndon Johnson, Office of Econ. Opportunities, Washington; fin. advisor to the Govt. of Grenada and the Office of the Prime Min. Garry, 1977-78; founder Howard and Muriel Weingrow Collection of Avant Garde Arts and Lit., Hofstra U. Library, 1972. With USAF, 1942-45, Europe. Decorated Air medal, Disting. Flying Cross, Presdl. Citation; recipient of Hofstra U. Presdl. medal. Office: Marcade Group 805 Third Ave New York NY 10022

WEINHARDT, W. JOHN, wire manufacturing company executive; b. East Liverpool, Ohio, Nov. 23, 1950; s. William T. and Yvonne (Golding) W.; m. Mary Ann Donovan, Aug. 11, 1979; children: Kelly Marie, Christopher Thomas, Linda Maureen, Taylor Donovan. BS in Mech. Engring., Rose Hulman Inst., 1972; MS in Indsl. Adminstrn., Purdue U., 1973. Mfg. supt. Automotive Div. Bendix Corp., St. Joseph, Mich., 1976-77, project engr., 1977; product mgr. mktg. Automotive Div. Bendix Corp., South Bend, Ind., 1977-78, dir. internat. bus., 1978-79, worldwide dir. bus. devel., 1979-81; group dir. bus. strategy Allied Automotive, Southfield, Mich., 1981-83, worldwide dir. anti-skid, 1983-84; v.p., gen. mgr. Allied Automotive Bendix

Wire Div., Toledo, 1984-86; pres., chief exec. officer Prestolite Wire Corp., Farmington Hills, Mich., 1986—. Mem. Nat. Elec. Mfrs. Assn. (bd. dirs. wire and cable div. 1985—, chmn. high-temperature sect.), Soc. Automotive Engrs., Young Pres.'s Orgn., Detroit Inst. Arts, Founder's Soc. Episcopalian. Office: Prestolite Wire Corp 32871 Middlebelt Rd Farmington Hills MI 48018

WEINIG, ROBERT WALTER, holding company executive; b. Columbus, Ohio, Aug. 3, 1930; s. Robert F. and Catherine H. (Walter) W.; m. Virginia Doree, Aug. 16, 1958; children: Katrina, Stephen, Cynthia. BA, Dartmouth Coll., 1952; MBA, Amos Tuck Sch. Bus. Adminstrn., 1955. Chartered fin. analyst. Engaged in comml. banking Chgo., 1955-57, in mcpl. fin., 1957-59; asst. v.p. Duff & Phelps, Inc., Chgo., 1959-66; spl. asst. to pres. Ea. Gas & Fuel Assocs., Boston, 1966-67, controller, 1967-69, v.p., 1969-70, sr. v.p. fin., 1970-77, sr. v.p. fin. and adminstrn., 1977-79, exec. v.p., chief adminstrv. officer, 1979-83, exec. v.p. marine and utility ops., 1983-85, exec. v.p., chief operating officer, 1985, pres., chief exec. officer, 1987—; bd. dirs. Peabody Holding Co., Inc., Shawmut Bank, N.Am. Served to 2d lt. AUS, 1952-54. Mem. Fin. Analysts Fedn. Office: Ea Gas & Fuel Assocs 9 Riverside Rd Weston MA 02193

WEINMAN, ROBERTA SUE, marketing and financial communications consultant; b. Bennington, Vt., Sept. 22, 1945. BA, U. Calif., Berkeley, 1967; MA, Stanford U., 1975; MBA, Pepperdine U., 1982. Tech. editor SRI Internat., Menlo Park, Calif.; adminstr. consumer affairs Fed. Home Loan Bank, San Francisco, 1977-79; legal research asst. Townsend and Townsend, San Francisco, 1979-80; pvt. practice mktg. and fin. communications cons. Palo Alto, Calif., 1981—. Editor, writer, developer various mktg., pub. relations and fin. documents, primarily for high-tech. industry profl. jours. Home and Office: 129 Churchill Ave Palo Alto CA 94301

WEINMANN, RONALD VINCENT, business educator; b. Harvey, N.D., Apr. 14, 1945; s. Vincent R. and Adeline C. (Muscha) W.; m. Loretta Jane Schmaltz, Dec. 28, 1973; children: Shannon, Shane, Shawn. AA, N.D. State Sch. Sci., 1971; BS, N.D. State U., 1974; MS in Adminstrn., Cen. Mich. U., 1988. Asst. mgr. Pierce Co., Fargo, N.D., 1974-76; spl. agt. Lincoln Nat. Life Ins. Co., Fargo, 1976-78; buyer Crane Johnson Co., West Fargo, N.D., 1978-79; small bus. mgmt. instr., coordinator small bus. mgmt. Lake Region Community Coll., Devil's Lake, N.D., 1979—; cons. SBA. Contbr. articles to profl. jours. Pub. relations dir., past dist. commr. Boy Scouts Am., 1980—; commr. Devil's Lake Park Bd., 1986, Ramsey County Fair Bd., 1987. Served with USAF, 1967-69. Decorated Air Force Commendation medal; recipient Dist. award of Merit, Boy Scouts Am., 1984. Mem. N.D. Assn. Small Bus. Mgmt. Instrs. (past pres.), Nat. Assn. Small Bus. Mgmt. Instrs. (past editor), Devil's Lake C. of C. (bd. dirs.), Jaycees (past state officer, mem. internat. senate), N.D. Assn. Acctg. Instrs., VFW. Roman Catholic. Lodge: Eagles. Home: 1207 2d Ave W Devils Lake ND 58301 Office: Lake Region Community Coll Devils Lake ND 58301

WEINRAUB, ALAN PAUL, lawyer, insurance executive; b. N.Y.C., Jan. 9, 1947; s. Irving Robert and Doris Gloria (Marx) W.; m. Amalia Leser Slatkin, Nov. 23, 1983; children: William, Lilach, Lior. BA, Franklin and Marshall Coll., 1968; JD, Syracuse U., 1972. Bar: N.J. 1972, N.Y. 1976. Assoc. Winne and Banta, Hackensack, N.J., 1972-73, Cole and Dietz, N.Y.C., 1973; asst. counsel Gen. Signal Corp., N.Y.C., 1974-77; pvt. practice N.Y.C. and Westwood, N.J., 1977-82; pres. Palacio and Weinraub, Inc., Miami, Fla., 1982—; pres. Inter-Atlantic Ins. Svcs., Miami and Chatsworth, Calif., 1988—; chmn. Inter-Atlantic Group, 1988—. Exec. editor Syracuse Jour. Internat. Law, 1971-72. Mem. Fla. Victory Com. (Republican), Miami, 1987—. Mem. ABA, N.Y. Bar Assn., Assn. of Bar of City of N.Y., N.J. Bar Assn. Jewish. Lodge: Masons. Home: 3700 Pine Tree Dr Miami Beach FL 33140 Office: Palacio and Weinraub Inc 7699 Biscayne Blvd Miami FL 33138

WEINROTH, ABE, real estate broker; b. Bklyn., Nov. 18, 1912; s. Israel and Gussie (Gellman) W.; m. Eleanor Eisen, Dec. 25, 1948; children: Marc Steven, Patti Ann. Student, Dana Coll., 1930-31. Operator Cen. Bus Terminal, Trenton, N.J., 1931-41; realtor Weinroth Realty Co., Mercer County, N.J., 1947-87; mem. adv. bd. Carteret Savs., Lawrenceville, N.J., 1983-86. Served to 1st lt. USAF, 1942-45. Mem. Mercer County Bd. Realtors (pres. 1958-59). Republican. Club: Green Acres Country (Lawrenceville), (bd. dirs. 1978-80). Office: Weinroth Realty Co PO Box 6508 Lawrenceville NJ 08648

WEINSTEIN, MARK MICHAEL, lawyer; b. N.Y.C., Apr. 20, 1942; s. Nathan and Caroline (Levine) W.; m. Adrienne Peni Kuba, Aug. 15, 1965; children: Samantha Beth, Caleb Jonathan. AB, Columbia Coll., 1964; LLB, U. Penn., 1968. Assoc. Paul Weiss, Rifkind, Wharton and Garrison, N.Y.C., 1968-76; asst. v.p., dep. gen. counsel Warner Communications Inc., N.Y.C., 1976-78, v.p., 1978-85; v.p., gen. counsel Viacom Internat. Inc., N.Y.C., 1985-87, sr. v.p., gen. counsel and sec., 1987—. Office: Viacom Internat Inc 1211 Avenue of the Americas 28th Floor New York NY 10036

WEINSTEIN, MARTIN, aerospace manufacturing executive, materials scientist; b. Bklyn., Mar. 3, 1936; s. Benjamin and Dora (Lemo) W.; m. Sandra Rebecca Yaffie, June 5, 1961; children: Hilary Ann, Sarah Elizabeth, Joshua Aaron. BS in Metals Engring., Rensselaer Poly. Inst., 1957; MS, MIT, 1960, PhD, 1961. Mgr. materials sci. Tycolabs, Waltham, Mass., 1961-68; tech. dir. turbine support div. Chromalloy Am. Corp., San Antonio, 1968-71, v.p., asst. gen. mgr., 1971-74, pres. 1975-79; pres. Chromalloy Compressor Techs., San Antonio, 1979-82; group pres. Chromalloy Gas Turbine, San Antonio, 1982-87, chmn., chief exec. officer, N.Y.C., 1986—; supervisory mng. dir. Turbine Support Europe, Tilburg, Netherlands, 1975—; dir. Internat. Coating Co., Tokyo, Japan, Heurchrome, Paris, Malichaud Orleans, Frances. Bd. dirs. Jewish Fedn., 1981-85, Chamber Players of San Antonio, 1979-82, NCCJ, 1982-85. Recipient Turner Meml. award Electrochem. Soc., 1963; Achievement award NASA, 1965; Am. Iron and Steel Inst. fellow, 1960. Mem. Am. Soc. Metals, Am. Inst. Metall. Engrs., N.Y. Acad. Sci., Sigma Xi. Patentee diffusion coating of jet engine materials. Contbr. articles to profl. jours. Home: 111 Sheffield Pl San Antonio TX 78213 Office: Chromalloy Gas Turbine Corp 200 Park Ave New York NY 10166

WEINSTOCK, GEORGE DAVID, financial company executive; b. Vienna, Austria, Jan. 31, 1937; came to U.S., 1940; s. Paul and Ernestine Esther (Stark) W.; m. Lorna Smith, July 17, 1965; children: Pamela Ellen, Andrea Joan. AB, Columbia U., 1958, BSEE, 1959, MS, 1962; cert., Coll. for Fin. Planning, Denver, 1985. Sr. engr. ITT, Nutley, N.J., 1959-61; sr. mem. tech. staff RCA, N.Y.C., 1961-65; project dir. Computer Scis. Co., Paramus, N.J., 1965-69; v.p., dir., sec. Ultimacc Systems, Inc., Maywood, N.J., 1969-78; v.p. Satnick Devel. Group, Hoboken, N.J., 1978-84; sr. v.p. Knitwaves, Inc., Moonachie, N.J., 1984-85; chmn. bd. Bancroft Group, Inc., Paramus, 1985-87; dir. fin. planning The Equitable, Paramus, 1987—. Author: System 360/DOS Operation, 1971. Com. mem. United Jewish Community Bergen County, 1988. Mem. Inst. for Cert. Fin. Planners, Nat. Assn. Accts., IEEE. Jewish. Home: 64 Ellsworth Terr Glen Rock NJ 07452 Office: The Equitable East 80 Rt 4 Paramus NJ 07652

WEIR, ALEXANDER, JR., utility consultant; b. Crossett, Ark., Dec. 19, 1922; s. Alexander and Mary Eloise (Field) W.; m. Florence Forschner, Dec. 28, 1946; children—Alexander III, Carol Jean, Bruce Richard. B.S. in Chem. Engring., U. Ark., 1943; M.Ch.E., Poly Inst. Bklyn., 1946; Ph.D., U. Mich., 1954; cert., U. So. Calif. Grad. Sch. Bus. Adminstrn., 1968. Analyst, chemist Am. Cyanimid and Chem. Corp., summers 1941, 42; chem. engr. Am. Cyanimid Co., Stanford Research Labs., 1943-47; with U. Mich., 1948-58; research assoc., project supr. Engring. Research Inst., U. Mich., 1948-57; lectr. chem. and metall. engring. dept. U. Mich., 1954-56, asst. prof., 1956-58; cons. Ramo-Wooldridge Corp., Los Angeles, 1956-57, mem. tech. staff, sect. head, asst. mgr., 1957-60, incharge Atlas Missile Captive test program, 1956-60; various tech. adv. positions Northrop Corp. Corp. Office, Beverly Hills, Calif., 1960-70; prin. scientist for air quality So. Calif. Edison Co., Los Angeles, 1970-76, mgr. chem. systems research and devel., 1976-86, chief research scientist, 1986-88; utility cons. Playa del Rey, Calif., 1988—; rep. Am. Rocket Soc. to Detroit Nuclear Council, 1954-57; chmn. session on chem. reactions Nuclear Sci. and Engring. Congress, Cleve., 1955; U.S. del. AGARD (NATO) Combustion Colloquium, Liege, Belgium, 1955; Western U.S. rep. task force on environ. research and devel. goals Electric Research Council, 1971; electric utility advisor Electric Power Research Inst., 1974-78, 84-87; industry advisor Dept. Chemistry and Biochemistry Calif. State U., Los Angeles, 1981—. Author: Two and Three Dimensional Flow of Air through Square-Edged Sonic Orifices, 1954; (with R.B. Morrison and T.C. Anderson) Notes on Combustion, 1955; also tech. papers. Inventer Weir power plant stack scrubber. Bd. govs., past pres. Civic Union Playa del Rey, chmn. sch., police and fire, nominating, civil def., army liaison coms; mem. Senate, Westchester YMCA, chmn. Dads sponsoring com., active fundraising; chmn. nominating com. Paseco del Rey Sch. PTA, 1961; mem. Los Angeles Mayors Community Adv. Com.; asst. chmn. advancement com., merit badge dean Cantinella dist. Los Angeles Area council Boy Scouts Am. Mem. Am. Geophys. Union, Navy League U.S. (v.p. Palos Verdes Peninsula council 1961-62), N.Y. Acad. Scis., Sci. Research Soc. Am., Am. Chem. Soc., Am. Inst. Chem. Engrs., AAAS, Combustion Inst., Air Pollution Control Assn., U.S. Power Squadron, Sigma Xi, Phi Kappa Phi, Phi Lambda Upsilon, Alpha Chi Sigma, Lambda Chi Alpha. Club: Santa Monica Yacht. Office: 8229 Billowvista Dr Playa del Rey CA 90293

WEIR, ELLIOTT HENRY, JR., health care executive; b. Meridian, Miss., Sept. 11, 1946; s. Elliott H. Sr. and Margaret (Cunningham) W.; m. Anna Katharine Wilson, Dec. 21, 1967; children: Ashley, Elliott III. BS, Miss. State U., 1968. Various positions IBM Corp., Huntsville, Ala., and Atlanta, 1968-71; chief fin. officer hosp. div. Charter Med. Corp., Macon, Ga., 1971-78; asst. exec. dir. Forrest Gen. Hosp., Hattiesburg, Mass., 1978-80; exec. v.p. Healthcare Internat., Austin, Tex., 1980—, also bd. dirs.; pres. HealthVest Real Estate Trust, 1986—, also bd. dirs.; bd. dirs. Healthcare Internat.; pres. Continental Health Services, Atlanta, 1978-80. Mem. Am. Coll. Health Care Execs., Hosp. Fin. Mgmt. Assn. Presbyterian. Office: Healthcare Internat Inc 9737 Great Hills Trail PO Box 4008 Austin TX 78765

WEIS, KONRAD MAX, chemical company executive; b. Leipzig, Germany, Oct. 10, 1928; came to U.S., 1971, naturalized, 1985; s. Alfred and Margarete (Leipoldt) W.; m. Gisela Lueg, Aug. 3, 1956; children—Alfred, Bettina. Ph.D., U. Bonn, 1955. Joined Bayer AG, Leverkusen, Fed. Republic Germany, 1956, mgmt./exec. positions, 1961-74; pres., chief exec. officer Mobay Corp. subs. Bayer AG, Pitts., 1974-81, chmn., pres., chief exec. officer, 1981-86; pres., chief exec. officer, chmn. bd. Bayer USA Inc., Pitts., 1986—; chmn. Agfa Corp., Miles Inc., Mobay Corp.; bd. dirs. Cyclops Industries, Inc., Dravo Corp., PNC Fin. Corp., Pitts. Nat. Bank. Mem. exec. com., life trustee Carnegie-Mellon U., 1981—; life trustee The Carnegie, Pitts., 1984—; trustee, bd. dirs. Presbyn.-Univ. Hosp., Pitts., 1986—, Phipps Conservatory, 1987—; v.p. Allegheny Conf. on Community Devel., 1983—; mem. policy com. Pa. Bus. Roundtable, 1983—; exec. com. Soc. Chem. Ind.; bd. dirs. Pitts. Symphony Soc., 1987—; trustee Penn's Southwest Assn., 1976—; bd. dirs., mem. exec. com. Regional Indsl. Devel. Corp. Southwestern Pa., 1986—; bd. dirs. Pitts. High Tech. Council, 1987—. Mem. Chem. Mfrs. Assn. (dir., exec. com. 1985-88), German Am. C. of C. (dir. 1981-88), World Affairs Council Pitts. (dir. 1983—). Clubs: Links (N.Y.C.); Pitts. Golf, Duquesne (Pitts.); Fox Chapel (Pa.) Golf; Rolling Rock Country (Ligonier, Pa.). Office: Bayer USA Inc 1 Mellon Ctr 500 Grant St Pittsburgh PA 15219-2502

WEISBERG, DAVID CHARLES, lawyer; b. N.Y.C., June 25, 1938; s. Leonard Joseph and Rae M. (Kimberg) W.; m. Linda Gail Kerman, Aug. 27, 1975; children: Leonard Jay, Risa Beth. AB, U. Mich., 1958; LLB, Harvard U., 1961. Bar: N.Y. 1962, U.S. Dist. Ct. (so. and ea. dists.) N.Y. 1965, U.S. Supreme Ct. 1970. Assoc. firm Dreyer & Traub, Bklyn., 1962, Lee Franklin, Mineola, N.Y., 1962-65; pvt. practice, Patchogue, N.Y., 1965-67, 77-80; ptnr. Bass & Weisberg, Patchogue, 1967-77, Davidow, Davidow, Russo & Weisberg, Patchogue, 1981-82, Davidow, Davidow, Weisberg & Wismann, 1982-87, Davidow, Davidow, Wismann & Levy, 1987-88, Davidow, Davidow & Wismann, 1988—; assoc. justice and justice Village of Patchogue, 1968-70, village atty., 1970-85; spl. asst. dist. atty. Suffolk County, Patchogue, 1970-85; assoc. estate tax atty., appraiser N.Y. State Dept. Taxation and Fin., Hauppauge, N.Y., 1975-85; lectr. estate tax Suffolk County Acad. Law, 1976-84. Law chmn. Suffolk County Dem. Com., N.Y., 1975-85; bd. dirs. Temple Beth El of Patchogue. With USAR, 1961-62. Mem. Assn. Trial Lawyers Am., N.Y. State Trial Lawyers Assn., Nassau-Suffolk Trial Lawyers Sect., N.Y. State Bar Assn., Suffolk County Bar Assn., Lions (pres. Medford 1978-79, 2d v.p. 1984-85), Masons. Avocations: bicycling, skiing, backpacking. Office: Davidow Davidow & Wismann 110 N Ocean Ave Patchogue NY 11772

WEISBROD, KEN (JOSEPH LOUIS), marketing professional; b. Los Angeles, July 31, 1957; s. Louis Isadore and Dolores Joan (Adamczyk) W. Cert., Gemological Inst. Am, 1988. Jewelry designer House of Time Jewelers, Granada Hills, Calif., 1968-79; pres. Ken Weisbrod Prodns., Inc., Chatsworth, Calif., 1979-85; v.p. The Ramolap Co., Chatsworth, 1985—; dir. prodn. Katherine's of Broadway Market, Chatsworth, 1987—. Designer jewelry for numerous art exhibits, 1969-75. Mem. Mfg. Jewelers and Silversmiths Am., Calif. Jewelers Assn. Democrat. Roman Catholic. Office: Ramolap Co PO Box 5359 Chatsworth CA 91313-5359

WEISENBERG, DIANE RUTH, financial consultant, accountant; b. Bklyn., May 16, 1947; d. Irving and Rose (Greenberg) W. B.B.A., CUNY, 1969. Staff acct. Peat, Marwick, Mitchell & Co., N.Y.C., 1969-70; asst. controller Hawley Coal Mining Corp., N.Y.C., 1970-78; mgr. fixed assets NBC, Inc., N.Y.C., 1979-80; divisional controller Sentry Refining Co., Inc., N.Y.C., 1980-84; pvt. practice Diane R. Weisenberg & Assocs., N.Y.C., 1984—. Home: 432 Park Ave S Rm 1501 New York NY 10016

WEISENBERGER, DOUGLAS JAMES, financial planner. s. James Marcus and Audrey Ann (Pelowski) W.; m. Kimberlie Ann Meyer, Aug. 28, 1982. BBA in Mktg., U. Wis., Eau Claire, 1979; MBA in Fin., U. Wis., 1980. Cert. fin. planner; chartered fin. cons. Sr. assoc. Resource Fin. Group, Madison, Wis., 1981—. Mem. Internat. Assn. Fin. Planning, Inst. Cert. Fin. Planners, Nat. Assn. Life Underwriters, Nat. Assn. Health Underwriters. Republican. Roman Catholic. Office: Resource Fin Group 2901 W Beltline Hwy Ste 310 Madison WI 53713

WEISENFELD, PAULETTE WENDY, cosmetic company executive; b. N.Y.C., Nov. 26, 1955; d. Arnold and Eliette W. BA, Northwestern U., 1976. Asst. buyer China dept. Bloomingdale's, N.Y.C., 1977-78; dept. mgr. tabletop Bloomingdale's, Chestnut Hill, Mass., 1978-79; assoc. buyer crystal dept. Bloomingdale's, N.Y.C., 1979-81, closet shop/notion buyer, 1981, women's fragrance buyer, 1981-83, cosmetics and treatment buyer, 1983-84; mgr. sales promotion and spl. events. Biotherm/Cosmair, N.Y.C., 1984-85; v.p. mktg. Jean Patou Inc., N.Y.C., 1985—. Mem. adv. bd. N.Y. Woman mag., 1986—. Co-chmn. internat. com. for scents of time exhbn. Frangrance Found., N.Y.C., 1986-87; vo. Dorot, N.Y.C., 1988; mem. jr. com. Mus. Natural History, 1988. Mem. Cosmetic Exec. Women, Fashion Group. Democrat. Jewish. Home: 212 E 48th St New York NY 10017

WEISER, NORMAN MYRON, retail executive; b. Cin., July 10, 1931; s. Isadore and Helen (Rubinowitz) W.; m. Margo Groetzinger, Feb. 28, 1954; children: Jeffrey, Cynthia. BBA, U. Cin., 1954. Mgr. systems and programming Shillito's div. Federated Dept. Stores, Cin., 1964-68, corp. v.p. systems R & D, 1978-83; v.p. M.I.S., Cin., 1969-72, v.p., treas., 1972-78; asst. contr. Abercrombie & Fitch, N.Y.C., 1968-69; v.p. M.I.S., Morse Shoe Inc., Canton, Mass., 1983—; cons. in field. Author: Information Week, 1987, Retail Control, 1986. V.p. ops., bd. dirs. Old Colony Coun. Boy Scouts Am., 1984—. With U.S. Army, 1954-56. Recipient Silver Beaver award Boy Scouts Am., 1974. Mem. Nat. Retail Merchants Assn. (bd. dirs. 1981-88, 1st v.p. systems div. 1986-88). Republican. Jewish. Home: 49 Bishop Rd Sharon MA 02067 Office: Morse Shoe Inc 555 Turnpike St Canton MA 02021

WEISER, NORMAN SIDNEY, publishing executive; b. Mpls., Oct. 1, 1919; s. Simon and Rosa (Davidson) W.; m. Ruth Miller, Mar. 23, 1943 (dec. July 1986); children: Judith Ann, Richard Alan. BA, Northwestern U., 1939. Reporter Radio Daily, 1938-42; reporter, editor Billboard Mag., 1947-52; pub. Down Beat Mag., 1952-59; v.p. United Artists, 1959-62, 64-68, 20th Century Fox, 1962-64; v.p., dir. (European ops. Paramount Music Div.), 1968-69; v.p., gen. mgr. Chappell Music Co., N.Y.C., 1969-73; pres. Chappell Music Co., 1973-77; sr. v.p., dir. Polygram Corp. U.S.; mem. mgmt. com., v.p. Internat. Polygram Pub. Div.; pres. Sesac, Inc., 1978-81; v.p., gen. mgr. Largo Music Corp., 1981-85; chmn. bd., chief exec. officer WMC Entertainment Corp., 1985; chmn. Am. Acad. of Comedy Hall of Fame, N.Y.C., 1987—. Author: Writers' Radio Theater, 1940, Writers' Radio-TV Theater, 1942, Under The Big Top, 1947, History AAF, World War II, 1947; lyricist 40 songs. Bd. dirs. Parkinson Found.; mem. corp., bd. dirs. UNICEF. Served to capt. USAAF, 1943-47. Decorated Purple Heart, Commendation medal Sec. War; recipient Ben Gurion award, 1975. Mem. ASCAP (dir.), Nat. Music Pubs'. Assn. (v.p., dir.), Country Music Assn. (chmn. bd.). Club: Friars. Lodge: B'nai Brith. Home and Office: 58 W 58th St Apt 14E New York NY 10019

WEISMAN, LORENZO DAVID, investment banker; b. Guatemala, Apr. 22, 1945; came to U.S., 1957; s. Eduardo Tobias and Suzanne (Loeb) W.; m. Danielle Maysonnave, June 22, 1971; children—Melissa Anne, Alexia Maria, Thomas Alexander. B.A. in History and Lit. cum laude, Harvard U., 1966; postgrad., Conservatoire Nat. D'Art Dramatique, Paris, 1966-71; M.B.A. in Fin., Columbia U., 1973. V.p. Dillon, Read & Co., Inc., N.Y.C., 1977-80, sr. v.p., 1980-82; mng. dir. Dillon, Read & Co., Inc., London, 1982—; pres. Dillon Read Ltd., London, 1980—, 1984—; dir. The France Fund, Inc., N.Y.C., Cofir (Spain) S.A., Madrid, Dillon, REad & Co., Inc., N.Y.C., Dillon, Read Ltd., London. Clubs: Travelers (Paris); Rac (London). also: Sagaponack Rd Bridgehampton NY 11932

WEISMAN, MICHAEL HENRY, railroad executive; b. Detroit, Mar. 12, 1929; s. George and Stella Louise (Busekrus) W.; m. Nancy Joan Samp, Oct. 7, 1961; children: Susan M., Christopher M. BA in Physics and Math, Washington U., 1950. Various positions Mo. Pacific R.R., St. Louis, 1950-57; cost acct. Detroit, Toledo & Ironton R.R., Dearborn, Mich., 1957-61, asst. comptroller, 1962-74, treas., 1975-80; dir. cost analysis Grand Trunk Western R.R., Detroit, 1981—; cons. Ann Arbor R.R., Detroit, 1976-85. Co-author: Economic Costing of Railroad Operations, 1960, A Guide to Railroad Cost Analysis, 1964. 2d lt. U.S. Army, 1951. Mem. Planning Forum, Assn. Am. R.R.'s (acctg. div.). Republican. Lutheran. Home: 16843 Shrewsbury Ct Livonia MI 48154 Office: Grand Trunk Western RR 1333 Brewery Pk Blvd Detroit MI 48207

WEISMAN, ROBERT HAROLD, investment banker; b. N.Y.C., Sept. 9, 1941; s. Harold M. and Carol (Van Wezel) W; m. Aline J. Massey Sept. 3, 1966 (div. 1970); m. Annette F. Gallagher, Feb. 24, 1979; children: Samantha, Patrick. BA with honors, Cornell U., 1963; JD, Harvard U., 1966. Bar: N.Y. 1968. Assoc. Milbank, Tweed, Hadley & McCloy, N.Y.C., 1968-69; exec. v.p. Intercontinental Energy Corp., Denver, 1970-80; sr. v.p. Dain Bosworth, Inc., Mpls., 1981-87; mng. dir. First Bank System (merger Merchant Bank), Mpls., 1987—; bd. dirs. Ports of Call, Denver, Le Peep Restaurants Inc., N.Y.C. Fulbright grantee, 1966-67. Republican. Jewish. Club: Harvard (N.Y.C.). Office: FBS Merchant Banking Group 150 S Fifth St Minneapolis MN 55480

WEISMANTEL, GREGORY NELSON, food products company executive; b. Houston, Sept. 8, 1940; s. Leo Joseph and Ellen Elizabeth (Zudis) W.; m. Marilyn Ann Fanger, June 18, 1966; children: Guy Gregory, Christopher Gregory, Andrea Rose. BA, U. Notre Dame, 1962; MBA, Loyola U., Chgo., 1979. Dist. mgr. Gen. Foods Corp., White Plains, N.Y., 1975-80; pres., chief exec. officer Manor House Foods, Inc., Addison, Ill., 1980-82, Weismantel & Assocs., Downers Grove, Ill., 1982-84; v.p. perishable div. Profl. Marketers, Inc., Lombard, Ill., 1984-86, group v.p. sales and mktg. services, dir. corporate strategy, 1986-87; v.p. mng. prin. Louis A. Allen Assoc. Inc., Palo Alto, Calif., 1987-89; pres., chief exec. officer Productivity Systems, Ltd., St. Charles, Ill., 1989—; bd. dirs. Epicurean Foods, Ltd., Chgo.; cons. in field. Chmn. fin. St. Edward's High Sch. Jubilee, Elgin, Ill., 1982-85; bd. dirs. Dist. 301 Sch. Bd., Burlington, Ill., 1980-84, St. Edward's Found., Elgin, 1982—. Served to capt. U.S. Army, 1962-66. Mem. Grocery Mfg. Sales Execs., Chgo. C. of C. (small bus. com.). Roman Catholic. Clubs: Merchandising Execs., Food Products, Am. Mktg. (Chgo.).

WEISS, ARMAND BERL, economist; b. Richmond, Va., Apr. 2, 1931; s. Maurice Herbert and Henrietta (Shapiro) W.; BS in Econs., Wharton Sch. Fin., U. Pa., 1953, MBA, 1954; D.B.A., George Washington U., 1971; m. Judith Bernstein, May 18, 1957; children: Jo Ann Michele, Rhett Louis. Cert. assn. exec. Officer, U.S. Navy, 1954-65; spl. asst. to auditor gen. Dept. Navy, 1964-65; sr. economist Center for Naval Analyses, Arlington, Va., 1965-68; project dir. Logistics Mgmt. Inst., Washington, 1968-74; dir. systems integration Fed. Energy Adminstrn., Washington, 1974-76; sr. economist Nat. Commn. Supplies and Shortages, 1976-77; tech. asst. to v.p. System Planning Corp., 1977-78; pres., chmn. bd. Assns. Internat., Inc., 1978—; chmn. bd. dirs., chief fin. officer Rail digital Corp., 1988—; v.p., treas. Tech. Frontiers, Inc., 1978-80; sr. v.p. Weiss Pub. Co., Inc., Richmond, Va., 1960—; v.p. Condo News Internat., Inc., 1981; v.p., bd. dirs. Leaders Digest Inc., 1987-88; sec., bd. dirs. Mgmt. Svcs. Internat. Inc., 1987—; adj. prof. Am. U., 1979-80, 89—; vis. lectr. George Washington U., 1971; assoc. prof. George Mason U., 1984; chmn. U.S. del., session chmn. NATO Symposium on Cost-Benefit Analysis, The Hague, Netherlands, 1969, NATO Conf. on Operational Rsch. in Indsl. Systems, St. Louis, France, 1970; pres. Nat. Council Assns. Policy Scis., 1971-77; chmn. adv. group Def. Econ. Adv. Council, 1970-74; resident assoc. Smithsonian Instn., 1973—; expert cons. Dept. State, GAO; undercover agt. FBI, 3 yrs. Del. Pres.'s Mid-Century White House Conf. on Children and Youth, 1950; scoutmaster Japan, U.S., leader World Jamborees, France, Can., U.S.A., 1945-61; U.S. del. Internat. Conf. on Ops. Rsch., Dublin, Ireland, 1972; organizing com. Internat. Cost-Effectiveness Symposium, Washington, 1970; speaker Internat. Conf. Inst. Mgmt. Scis., Tel Aviv, 1973, del., Mexico City, 1967. Mem. bus. com. Nat. Symphony Orch., 1968-70, Washington Performing Arts Soc., 1974—; bus. mgr. Nat. Lyric Opera Co., 1983—; mem. mktg. com. Fairfax Symphony Orch., 1984—; exec. com. Mid Atlantic council Union Am. Hebrew Congregations, 1970-79, treas., 1974-79, mem. nat. MUM com., 1974-79; mem. dist. com. Boy Scouts Am., 1972-75; bd. dirs. Nat. Council Career Women, 1975-79. Fellow AAAS, Washington Acad. Scis. (gov. 1981-88, v.p. 1987-88); mem. Ops. Research Soc. Am. (chmn. meetings com. 1969-71; chmn. cost-effectiveness sect. 1969-70), Washington Ops. Research/Mgmt. Sci. Council (editor newsletter 1969—, sec. 1971-72, pres. 1973-74, trustee 1975-77, bus. mgr. 1976—), Internat. Inst. Strategic Studies (London), Am. Soc. Assn. Execs. (membership com. 1981-82, cert.), Inst. for Mgmt. Sci., Am. Econ. Assn., Wharton Grad. Sch. Alumni Assn. (exec. com. 1970-73), Am. Acad. Polit. and Social Sci., Nat. Eagle Scout Assn., Am. Legion, Navy League of the U.S., Greater Wash. Soc. Assn. Execs., Fairfax County C. of C., Vienna, Va. C. of C., Alumni Assn. George Washington U. (governing bd. 1974-82, chmn. univ. publs. com. 1976-78, Alumni Service award 1980), Alumni Assn. George Washington U. Sch. Govt. and Bus. Adminstrn. (exec. v.p. 1977-78, pres. 1978-79), George Washington U. Doctoral Assn. (sr. v.p. 1968-69). Jewish (pres. temple 1970-72). Club: Wharton Grad. Sch. Washington (sec. 1967-69, pres. 1969-70). Co-editor: Systems Analysis for Social Problems, 1970, The Relevance of Economic Analysis to Decision Making in the Department of Defense, 1972, Toward More Effective Public Programs: The Role of Analysis and Evaluation, 1975. Editor: Cost-Effectiveness Newsletter, 1966-70, Operations Research/Systems Analysis Today, 1971-73, Operation Research/Mgmt. Sci. Today, 1974-87; Feedback, 1979—, Condo World, 1981; assoc. editor Ops. Research, 1971-75; publisher: IEEE Scanner, 1983—, Spl. and Individual Needs Tech. (SAINT) Newsletter, 1987-88, Jour. Parametrics, 1984-88. Home: 6516 Truman Ln Falls Church VA 22043

WEISS, FRED GEOFFREY, pharmaceutical company executive; b. N.Y.C., Aug. 31, 1941; s. Reuben and Rose (Youngstien) W.; m. Amy Susan Cooperman, Sept. 4, 1965; children: Daniel Carl, Aaron Marc, Alisha Rachael. Student, London Sch. Econs., 1960-61; BS, U. Pa., 1963; MBA, U. Chgo., 1967. Various fin. positions Exxon Corp., N.Y.C., Houston, Hong Kong, Tokyo, 1968-79; with Warner-Lambert, A.T. Internat., Morris Plains, N.J., 1979-80, Vice pres., treas., 1981-83, v.p., treas., 1981-83, v.p. planning, investments and devel., 1983—; pres. Med-Teck Ventures, Morris Plains, 1983—; mem. adv. bd. T. Rowe Price Venture Capital Fund, Balt., 1986—, Massey Burch Venture Investors, 1987—, adv. com. N.Y. Stock Exchange Pension Mgrs, 1988—; bd. dirs. FEI-Com. Pension Investments Employee Benefit Assets, N Y.C, chmn. fees and commns. subcoms., 1988—. Bd. dirs. Nat. Soc. to Prevent Blindness N.J., 1988—. Mem. Nat. Assn. for Corp. Growth, Fin. Execs. Inst., Short Hills (N.J.) Racquet Club, Polo Club (Boca

Raton, Fla.). Home: 55 Highland Ave Short Hills NJ 07078 Office: Warner Lambert Co 201 Tabor Rd Morris Plains NJ 08950

WEISS, GARY, financial writer, editor; b. N.Y.C., Mar. 3, 1954; s. Samuel R. and Adele (Sidelman) W.; m. Patricia Anne Sierman, Dec. 15, 1982. BA, CCNY, 1975; MS, Northwestern U., 1976. Reporter Hartford (Conn.) Courant, 1976-81; corr. States News Svc., Washington, 1981; reporter Network News, Inc., Washington, 1981, bus. editor, 1981-83; staff writer Barron's, N.Y.C., 1984-86; staff editor Bus. Week, N.Y.C., 1986-87, assoc., editor markets and investments, 1989—. Recipient Deadline Club award Sigma Delta Chi, 1989. Mem. Phi Beta Kappa. Office: Bus Week 1221 Ave of Americas New York NY 10020

WEISS, JOAN RUTH, educator; b. Phila., Feb. 14, 1953; d. Fred and Sara (Ginsberg) Cantor; m. Fredric K. Weiss, Oct. 13, 1953; 1 child, Saul Aaron. BS, Pa. State U., 1974; MA in Teaching and Bus. Edn., Trenton State Coll., 1988. Retail buyer Lit Bros., Phila., 1974-77; real estate saleswoman Korman Corp., Trevose, Pa., 1980-81; retail mgr. Macy's (formerly Bambergers), Langhorne, Pa., 1981-83; prof.mktg. & retailing Buck's Community Coll., Newtown, Pa., 1983—, chairwoman Curricular Revision Com., 1987-88. V.p. Women's Am. Orgn. Rehab. and Tng., Richboro, Pa., 1985-87, Ohev Shalom Sisterhood, 1986—. Mem. Fashion Group Phila., Delta Pi Epsilon. Republican. Office: Bucks County Community Coll Swamp Rd Newtown PA 18940

WEISS, LAWRENCE ROBERT, investment banking executive; b. Pasadena, Mar. 8, 1937; s. Joseph B. and Elsie (Shaw) W.; BS in Applied Physics, UCLA, 1959; MS in Mgmt. Sci., U. So. Calif., 1974; m. Elaine Saxon, June 23, 1963; children: Jeffrey Arthur, Jason Ashley. Electronic systems engr., N.Am. Aviation, Inc., Los Angeles, 1960-62, Litton Systems, Inc., 1962-63; group head Hughes Aircraft Co., Culver City, Calif., 1963-67, group head, sales rep., br. sales mgr., 1967-70; with Sci. Data Systems, Systems Engring. Labs., Gen. Automation, Inc., Interdata Corp., Applied Digital Data Systems, Inc., 1973-80; co-founder, chmn., pres. Health-tronics Labs. Inc., Rochester, N.Y., 1970-72, Cal-trend Personality Systems, Inc., Los Angeles, 1973-85; co-founder, chmn. bd., v.p. Evolution Computer Systems Corp., (name changed to Evolution Techs., Inc. 1981), Irvine, Calif., 1980-82; co-founder, chmn., pres. Capital Tech. Group Inc., Irvine, 1981-83; co-founder, pres. Tek-Net Funding Corp., Irvine, 1984-85; fin. cons. Shearson Lehman Bros., Inc., Orange, Calif., 1985-86; v.p. investments Drexel Burnham Lambert Inc., Newport Beach, Calif., 1986-87; chmn. Covest Holdings, Inc., 1987-88; v.p. Wedbush-Morgan Securities, Inc., Newport Beach, 1988—. Mem. Planetary Soc., U.S. Naval Inst., Am. Def. Preparedness Assn., Mensa. Home: 22706 Islamare Ln El Toro CA 92630 Office: Wedbush-Morgan Securities Inc 620 Newport Ctr Dr Ste 610 Newport Beach CA 92660

WEISS, LEWIS STEPHEN, pharmaceutical executive; b. N.Y.C., June 5, 1934; s. Moe and Rose (Kiel) W.; m. Linda Sharon Freid, Jan 8, 1967; 1 child, Scott Jeffrey. BS in Pharmacy, L.I. U., 1956. Exec. v.p. Nysco Labs. div. Revlon Health Care, N.Y.C., 1962-77, Rexall Drug Co., St. Louis, 1977-81; v.p. pharms. ICC Industries, N.Y.C., 1981-84; pres. L.S. Weis & Co., Inc., N.Y.C., 1984—; bd. dirs. Zenith Labs., Montvale, N.J., Medigum Corp. Contbr. articles to profl. jours. Mem. Nat. Assn. Pharm. Mfrs., Aircraft Owners and Pilots Assn., Drug, Chem. and Allied Trades Assn., Pvt. Label Mfrs. Assn. (founding, bd. dirs. 1979—), Delta Sigma Theta (pres. 1955-56). Jewish. Club: Concord Squash (N.Y.C.) (bd. dirs. 1987—). Home: 315 E 68th St New York NY 10021

WEISS, MORRY, greeting card company executive; b. Czechoslovakia, 1940; m. Judith Stone. Grad., Wayne State U. Salesman, field mgr. Am. Greetings Corp., Cleve., 1961-66, advt. mgr., 1966-68, v.p., 1969-73, group v.p. mktg. and sales, 1973-78, formerly chief operating officer, from 1978, pres., 1978—, also bd. dirs., chief exec. officer, 1987—. Office: Am Greetings Corp 10500 American Rd Cleveland OH 44144 *

WEISS, PETER H., business consultant; b. N.Y.C., Oct. 12, 1956; s. Edward and Janis (Silbert) W. AB cum laude, Princeton U., 1979; MBA, Harvard U., 1984. Gen. mgr. Paprikas Weiss Importer, N.Y.C., 1979-80; fin. analyst Warburg Paribas Becker, N.Y.C., 1980-82; asst. to pres. Barnes Drill Co., Rockford, Ill., 1983-84; v.p. Trump Group, N.Y.C., 1984-86; pres. P. Weiss & Co., Inc., Seattle, 1986—, Call Carpet, Inc., Seattle, 1987—; bd. dirs. Gerbeaud, Inc., N.Y.C.; cons. Alatus Projects Corp., Vancouver, B.C., Can., 1987—. Mem. regional adv. bd. AntiDefamation League Pacific N.W. Office: P Weiss & Co 2917 1st Ave S Seattle WA 98134

WEISS, ROBERT MARK, bank executive; b. Jamestown, N.D., June 6, 1950; s. Herman and Donna (Ovind) W.; m. Jean Schoene, Aug. 31, 1974; children: Jennifer, Stephanie. AA, N.Mex. Inst., 1970; BA, U. N.D., 1972; MBA, Rutgers U., 1984. Ops. officer First Bank of Grand Forks, N.D., 1970-72; bank examiner First Bank Systems, Mpls., 1972-74; comml. loan officer First Bank of Southdale, Edina, Minn., 1974-75, The Bank-Wayzata, Minn., 1976-78; v.p. The Bank-Wayzata, Wayzata, 1978-79, v.p. loan adminstr., 1979-81; pres., chief exec. officer The Bank Excelsior, Minn., 1982—, also bd. dirs.; bd. dirs. Wayzata Mortgage Co., Plymouth, Minn., Info. Svcs., Inc., Plymouth. Rep. council United Way, Mpls., 1987-88; pres. Mount Calvary Luth. Ch., Excelsior, 1986; bd. dirs., pres. Excelsior C. of C., 1986. Mem. Better Bus. Bus., Lafayette Club (Minnetonka Br.), Flagship Athletic Club. Republican. Office: The Bank Excelsior 411 Water St Excelsior MN 55331

WEISS, ROBERT STEPHEN, medical manufacturing company financial executive; b. Honesdale, Pa., Oct. 25, 1946; s. Stephen John and Anna Blanche (Lescinski) W.; B.S. in Acctg. cum laude, U. Scranton, 1968; m. Marilyn Annette Chesick, Oct. 29, 1970; children—Christopher Robert, Kim Marie, Douglas Paul. Supr., Peat, Marwick, Mitchell & Co., N.Y.C., 1971-76; asst. corp. controller Cooper Labs., Inc., Parsippany, N.J., 1977-78, v.p./corp. controller, Palo Alto, Calif., 1981-83; v.p., corp. controller The Cooper Cos., Inc. (formerly CooperVision, Inc.), Palo Alto, Calif., 1984— ; v.p. fin./controller CooperVision Pharms., Mountain View, Calif., 1979. Served with U.S. Army, 1969-70. Decorated Bronze Star with oak leaf cluster, Army Commendation medal; C.P.A., N.Y. State. Mem. N.Y. State Soc. C.P.A.s., Am. Inst. C.P.A.s. Republican. Roman Catholic. Home: 446 Arlington Ct Pleasanton CA 94566 Office: The Cooper Cos Inc 3145 Porter Dr Palo Alto CA 94304

WEISS, ROBIN JOANNA, county official, urban planner; b. Bayside, N.Y., Dec. 18, 1955; d. Robert Neil and Rose Amelia (Aronson) Kase; m. Stanley Herbert Weiss, July 12, 1981; children: Madeline Joy, Jeremy Michael.. Student, Dartmouth Coll., 1976; BA, Smith Coll., 1977; M in City and Regional Planning, Harvard U., 1979. Community devel. asst. N.Y. State Div. Housing and Community Renewal, N.Y.C., 1979-81; cons. Community Housing Resources Bd., Rockville, Md., 1983-84; assoc. for program planning and rsch. OWD Enterprises, Washington, 1984; devel. program specialist Housing Opportunities Commn., Kensington, Md., 1984-86; community assistance planner No. Va. Planning Dist. Commn., Annandale, 1986-87; sr. planner Essex County Div. Housing and Community Devel., Cedar Grove, N.J., 1988—. Chmn. Rockville (Md.) Landlord Tenant Commn., 1984-87. Mem. Nat. Assn. Housing and Redevel. Ofcls., Washington Jewish Geneal. Soc. (coord. membership 1982-87), LWV. Democrat. Office: 42 Ridge Dr Livingston NJ 07039

WEISS, SAMUAL, hotel and restaurant company executive; b. Rock Springs, Wyo., Dec. 25, 1924; s. Morris and Alta Weiss; m. Barbara R. Coggan; children: Cathy, Marcy, Karen. BA cum laude, U. Mich., 1948; LLB, Harvard U., 1951. Asst. v.p. Cuneo Press, Inc., Chgo., 1951-68; exec. v.p., treas., dir. Holly's Inc., Grand Rapids, Mich., 1968-87; exec. v.p., dir. Holly Enterprises, Inc., Grand Rapids, 1969-87, Holly Grills of Ind., South Bend, 1970-87, Fare Devel. Corp., Grand Rapids, 1974-87. Co-chmn. U.S. Olympic com. Mich., 1976-80; bd. control Intercollegiate Athletics U. Mich., 1982—. Served to 2d lt. USAAF, 1942-46. Mem. Nat. Assn. Corp. Real Estate Execs. (founding), Nat. Restaurant Assn., U. Mich. Alumni Assn. (dir.), Peninsular Club. Home: 3645 Oak Terrace Ct SE Grand Rapids MI 49508 Office: Holly "S" Inc PO Box 9260 255 Colrain St SW Grand Rapids MI 49509

WEISS, SAMUEL SCOTT, textile company executive; b. Salinas, Kans., Jan. 28, 1954; s. Jay Kenneth and Joan Burke (Tutin); m. Judith Mollie Garb, May 7, 1978; children: Schuyler Sussman, Bryony Tutin. AB, Harvard U., 1976; MS, Columbia Bus. Sch., 1982. Buyer Lord and Taylor, N.Y.C., 1976-79; brand mng. Springs Industries, N.Y.C., 1979-83; mng. dir. Springs Ltd., London, 1984-87; dir. of devel. Springs Industries, N.Y.C., 1987-88; v.p. Doblin Fabrics, N.Y.C., 1988—. Mem. Inst. of Mktg., Harvard Club. Office: Doblin Fabrics 41 Madison Ave New York NY 10010

WEISS, WILLIAM LEE, communications executive; b. Big Run, Pa., May 21, 1929; s. Harry W. and Dorothy Jane (McKee) W.; m. Josephine Elizabeth Berry, June 3, 1951; children: Susan Leigh Weiss Miller, David William, Steven Paul. B.S. in Indsl. Engring, Pa. State U., 1951. With Bell Telephone Co. of Pa., 1951, 1953-76; v.p. staff Bell Telephone Co. of Pa., Phila., 1973-74; v.p., gen. mgr. Bell Telephone Co. of Pa. (western area), 1974-76; v.p. ops. Wis. Telephone Co., Milw., 1976-78; pres. Ind. Bell Telephone Co., Indpls., 1978-81; also dir. Ind. Bell Telephone Co.; pres. Ill. Bell Telephone Co., Chgo., 1981, chmn., 1982-83; chmn., chief exec. officer Ameritech, Chgo., 1983—, also bd. dirs.; bd. dirs. Abbott Labs., Chgo., Continental Ill. Nat. Bank, Chgo., Continental Ill. Corp., The Quaker Oats Co., Chgo., USG Corp., Chgo. Bd. dirs. Chgo. Council on Fgn. Relations, chmn. corp. service com., 1988; Lyric Opera of Chgo.; trustee Mus. Sci. and Industry, 1982, Northwestern U., 1982, Orchestral Assn., Chgo., 1982, Com. for Econ. Devel.; chmn. Info. Industry Council; mem. Bus. Roundtable; mem. adv. council J.L. Kellogg Grad. Sch. Mgmt., Northwestern U.; mem. Bus. Com. for the Arts. Served with USAF, 1951-53. Mem. Commercial Club, Chgo. Club, Econ. Club, Mid-Am. Club (Chgo.), Glenview (Ill.) Club, Old Emns Country Club of N.C., Tau Beta Pi, Phi Delta Theta.

WEISSMAN, NORMAN, public relations executive; b. Newark, Apr. 12, 1925; s. Julius and Lenora (Schimmel) W.; m. Sheila Holtz, Dec. 12, 1950 (div. Dec. 1973); 1 son, Lee; m. Natalie Ruvell, Aug. 31, 1984. BA in English, Rutgers U., 1949; MA in Journalism, U. Wis., 1951. Asst. editor McGraw Hill Pub. Co., Inc., 1951-54; sec. to dept. Dept. Air Pollution Control, N.Y.C., 1954-56; account exec. Ruder & Finn, N.Y.C., 1956-59; v.p. Ruder & Finn, 1959-62, sr. v.p., 1962-68, pres., 1968-85, vice-chmn., 1983-85; vice-chmn. G.C.I. Group, Inc., N.Y.C., 1986—. Served with USN, 1943-46. Mem. Phi Beta Kappa, Sigma Delta Chi, Advt. Women N.Y. (hon.). Lodge: Rotary. Home: 162 E 93rd St New York NY 10128 Office: G.C.I. Group Inc 777 Third Ave New York NY 10017

WEISSMAN, ROBERT EVAN, financial information company executive; b. New Haven, May 22, 1940; s. Samuel and Lillian (Warren) W.; m. Janet Johl, Aug. 27, 1960; children—Gregory, Christopher, Michael. B.S. in Bus. Adminstrn., Babson Coll., Wellesley, Mass., 1964. Exec. v.p. Redifusion, Inc., Saugus, Mass, 1972-73; dir. corp. devel. Nat. CSS, Wilton, Conn., 1973-74, chmn., 1975-81; exec. v.p. Dun & Bradstreet Corp., N.Y.C., 1981-84, pres., chief operating officer, 1985—. Mem. Assn. Data Processing Service Orgns. (chmn. 1981), Young Pres.'s Orgn., IEEE, Soc. Mfg. Engrs. (sr.), Nat. Assn. Accts. Office: Dun & Bradstreet Corp 299 Park Ave New York NY 10171

WEISWASSER, STEPHEN ANTHONY, lawyer; b. Detroit, Nov. 21, 1940; s. Avery and Eleanor (Sherman) W.; m. July 3, 1962 (div. 1985); children: Jonathan, Gayle; m. Andrea Timko, Apr. 19, 1986. BA, Wayne State U., 1962; student, Johns Hopkins U., 1962-63; JD, Harvard U., 1966. Bar: D.C. 1967, U.S. Supreme Ct. 1970. Law clk. to chief judge U.S. Ct. Appeals, Washington, 1966-67; assoc. Wilmer, Cutler and Pickering, Washington, 1967-74, ptnr., 1974-86; sr. v.p., gen. counsel Capital Cities/ABC, Inc., N.Y.C., 1986—. Trustee Arena Stage, Washington, 1982-86, Nat. Capital Region NCCJ, Washington, 1984-86. Mem. ABA, Fed. Communications Bar Assn. Jewish. Home: 2 Quincy St Chevy Chase MD 20815 Office: Capital Cities/ABC Inc 77 West 66th St New York NY 10023

WEISZ, WILLIAM JULIUS, electronics company executive; b. Chgo., Jan. 8, 1927; m. Barbara Becker, Dec. 25, 1947; children: George, Terri, David. B.S. in Elec. Engring, MIT, 1948; D.B.A. (hon.), St. Ambrose Coll., 1976. With Motorola, Inc., Chgo., 1948—; exec. v.p. Motorola, Inc., 1969-70, pres., 1970-80, chief operating officer, 1972-86, vice chmn., 1980—, chief exec. officer, 1986-87, also dir.; Pres. Motorola Communications Internat., 1966-69; Motorola Communications and Electronics, Inc., 1966-69; dir. (Motorola Israel.); Mem. exec. com. land mobile adv. com. to FCC. Com. chmn. Cub Scout pack Evanston council Boy Scouts Am., 1960-62; Trustee MIT, 1975-85; mem. exec. com. Land Mobile Adv. Com. to FCC. Served with USNR, 1945-46. Recipient award of merit Nat. Electronics Conf., 1970; Freedom Found. of Valley Forge award, 1974; MIT Corp. Leadership award, 1976. Fellow IEEE (past nat. chmn. vehicular communications group); mem. Electronic Industries Assn. (past chmn., bd. govs. past chmn. indsl. elec. div., medal of honor 1981), Bus. Roundtable, Sigma Xi, Tau Beta Pi, Eta Kappa Nu, Pi Lambda Phi. Clubs: Economic, Commercial, MIT (Chgo.) (bd. dirs.). Office: Motorola Inc 1303 E Algonquin Rd Schaumburg IL 60196 *

WEITHAS, WILLIAM VINCENT, advertising agency executive; b. Jamaica, N.Y., May 10, 1929; s. William and Margaret (Beese) W.; m. Mary Eileen Livingston, Sept. 1, 1956; children—Suzann Weithas Cahill, Bill, John, Jeremy, Claudia. B.S., Seton Hall U., 1951. Salesman Nabisco Co., 1951; v.p., account supr. Batten, Barton, Durstine & Osborn, Inc., N.Y.C., 1952-66; advt. mgr. P. Ballantine & Sons, N.Y.C., 1966-67, v.p., dir. mktg. services, 1967-68; v.p. SSC&B, Inc., N.Y.C., 1968-72, exec. v.p., 1972-79, pres., chief operating officer, 1979-81, chmn., chief exec. officer, 1981-83; vice chmn. SSC&B: Lintas Internat., London, 1981-82, chmn., chief exec., 1982-85; chmn., chief exec. officer SSC&B: Lintas Worldwide, N.Y.C. and London, 1985—; dir. Interpub. Group Cos., Inc., N.Y.C.; dir. The Advt. Council, 1986—. Mem. N.Y. State Gov.'s Bus. Adv. Bd., 1986—. Mem. Am. Assn. Advt. Agys. (vice chmn. 1987—, chmn. 1988—, dir.-at-large 1983-85, ops. com. 1984-85), Nat. Advt. Rev. Coun., Navesink Country Club, Madison Sq. Garden Club. Office: Lintas Worldwide 1 Dag Hammarskjold Pla New York NY 10017 also: Lintas House, 15-19 New Fetter Ln, London EC4P 4EU, England

WEITZEL, JOHN ANTHONY, insurance executive; b. Springfield, Ohio, Dec. 1, 1945; s. Paul J. and Marie S. (Eifert) W.; m. Pamela Jean Messer, Sept. 7, 1970; children: Gretchen Marie, Nicholas Todd. BSBA, Ohio State U., 1967. CPA, Wis., Ohio. Sr. acct. Peat Marwick Mitchell and Co., Columbus, Ohio, 1967-75; dir. internal auditing Armco Ins. Group, Inc., Milw., 1975-82; chief fin. officer Universal Reins. Corp., Milw., 1982-85, Milw. Mut. Ins. Co., 1985—; bd. dirs. Milw. Fin. Corp., 1986—, Milw. Equity Svcs., 1987—. Treas. Camp Five Found., Laona, 1986. Served to sgt. U.S. Army, 1968-70, Korea. Mem. AICPA, Wis. Soc. CPAs (chmn. ins. com. 1985-87), Fin. Execs. Inst. Roman Catholic. Office: Milw Mut Ins Co 803 W Michigan St Milwaukee WI 53233

WEITZEL, WILLIAM CONRAD, JR., lawyer, oil company executive; b. Washington, Feb. 6, 1935; s. William Conrad and Pauline Lillian (Keeton) W.; m. Loretta LeVeck, Mar. 10, 1978; children: William Conrad III, Richard S., Sarah L. AB, Harvard U., 1956, LLB, 1959; postgrad., MIT, 1974. Bar: D.C. 1961. Law clk., chief judge U.S. Cts. Md., Balt., 1959-60; asst. U.S. atty., Washington, 1961-66; atty. Texaco, Inc., White Plains, N.Y., 1966-73; assoc. gen. counsel Texaco, Inc., 1973-76, gen. counsel, 1977-82, v.p., gen. counsel, 1982-84, sr. v.p., gen. counsel, 1984—; Pres. Texaco Philanthropic Found., Inc. Mem. internat. adv. bd. The Transnational Lawyer. Vice chmn. adv. bd. Southwestern Legal Found.; mem. adv. bd. Parker Sch. Fgn. and Comparative Law at Columbia U.; gen. counsel commn. of bus. coun. N.Y. State. Served with USN, 1960-61. Mem. ABA, Conn. Bar Assn., D.C. Bar Assn., Assn. Gen. Counsel (v.p., bd. dirs.), Am. Law Inst., Westchester-Fairfield Corp. Counsel Assn. (pres. 1981, chmn., chief legal officers com. 1982—), Am. Petroleum Inst. (gen. com. on law, chmn. 1983-84). Republican. Episcopalian. Clubs: Country (Darien, Conn.), Harvard (Fairfield County) (pres. 1987—). Home: 1 Gracie Ln Darien CT 06820 Office: Texaco Inc 2000 Westchester Ave White Plains NY 10650

WEITZENHOFFER, AARON MAX, JR., art gallery director; b. Oklahoma City, Oct. 30, 1939; s. Aaron Max and Clara Irene (Rosenthal) W. BFA, U. Okla., 1963. Co. mgr. La Jolla (Calif.) Playhouse, 1963-64; dir. David B. Findlay Gallery, N.Y., 1965-69; pres. Gimpel-Weitzenhoffer Gallery, N.Y.C., 1965-69; dir. Seminole Mfg. Co., Columbus, Miss.; adj. prof. drama U. Okla. Chief pub. relations Okla. Health Dept., 1964-65. Trustee Am. Acad. Dramatic Arts; chmn. Circle Repertory Co.; bd. dirs. New Dramatists. Recipient Tony award, 1978, Disting. Service Citation U. Okla., 1988. Mem. The Players, Art Dealers Assn., Am. League Theatres and Producers, Century Assn., Delta Kappa Epsilon (trustee found.). Republican. Home: 70 E 77th St New York NY 10021 Office: 724 Fifth Ave New York NY 10019

WEITZER, BERNARD, telecommunications executive; b. Bronx, N.Y., Sept. 22, 1929; s. Morris R. and Eva (Kurtz) W.; m. Anne DeHaven Jones, Nov. 5, 1982. BS, CCNY, 1950; MS, NYU, 1951, postgrad., 1951-54. Mgr., asst. v.p. systems engring and analysis Western Union Telegraph Co., Upper Saddle River, N.J., 1966-71, v.p. engring. and computer systems, 1976-85, sr. v.p. ops., 1985-88; exec. v.p., gen. mgr. Western Union Teleprocessing Industries, Inc., Mahwah, N.J., 1971-76; Dir. U.S. Telecommunications Tng. Inst.; mem. adv. com. TV communications U.S. Info. Agy. Served to lt. U.S. Army, 1954-57. Mem. Chaines des Rotisseurs, Internat. Wine Food Soc. Home: 6 Horizon Rd Fort Lee NJ 07024 Office: Western Union One Lake St Upper Saddle River NJ 07458

WEJCHERT, ANDRZEJ, architect; b. Gdansk, Poland, May 21, 1937; arrived in Ireland, 1964; s. Tadeusz and Irena (Moigis) W.; m. Danuta Kornaus, Nov. 16, 1965; children: Agnieszka, Michael. Degree in engring. architecture, Warsaw (Poland) Poly., 1961. Architect Design Office of Pub. Bldgs., Warsaw, 1959-64, Risterucci Agence, Paris, 1964; prin. A. Wejchert-Architect, Dublin, Ireland, 1964-74; ptnr. A&D Wejchert Architects, Dublin, 1974—; assessor European Archtl. Heritage Yr., Ireland, 1976-88; external examiner Sch. Architecture, U. Coll., Dublin, 1982-85, assessor student residencies U. Dublin Competition, 1988. Architect bldgs. including, U. Coll. Dublin, Tech. Parks, Limerick, Ireland and Dublin, Town Ctr., Blanchardstown, Ireland., Gen. Hosp. Naas, 1987-89. Recipient 1st pl. award for design of New U., 1964, diploma Europa Nostra, 1982, 1st pl. award Nat. Trust Ireland, 1984, 1st award Competition Govt. Bldgs., 1989; archtl. works named Bldg. of Yr. Plan Archtl. Mag., 1980, 84, 87. Fellow Royal Inst. Architects Ireland (registered, council 1976—, gold medal 1977, commendation 1985, High Commendation 1989); mem. Royal Inst. Brit. Architects. Office: 10 Lad Ln, Dublin 2, Ireland

WELBER, DAVID ALAN, accountant; b. York, Pa., Oct. 14, 1949; s. Harry and Julia Welber. BS in Acctg., York Coll., 1975. CPA, Pa.; cert. fin. planner. Acct. Einhorn, Butler, Gingerich & Co., York, 1974-82; ptnr. Bergdoll & Martin, York, 1984-86; prin. David A. Welber, CPA, York, 1982-84, 86—. Mem. council Colony Park Homeowners Assn., York, 1982-84; bd. dirs. Exchange Club Ctr. for Prevention of Child Abuse, Harrisburg, Pa., 1986—, Rehab. and Indsl. Tng. Ctr., York, 1987—; co-chmn. Ohev Sholom Bd. Edn., York, 1987—. Mem. AICPA (Edn. award 1973), Fin. Planners, Internat. Assn. Fin. Planning. Republican. Jewish. Club: Exchange of York (treas. 1984—). Office: David A. Welber CPA 1 Marketway W York PA 17401

WELBER, PHILIP HAROLD, retired retail executive, real estate company executive, business consultant; b. Columbus, Ohio, Mar. 7, 1913; s. Will and Sadie (Weiss) W.; m. Molly Waruck, Jan. 1, 1939; children: Susan Welber Youdovin, Michael, Barbara Welber Berebitsky. BA in Econs., Ohio State U., 1936. Journalist South Bend (Ind.) Tribune, 1933-36; buyer Robertson's Dept. Store, South Bend, 1937-40, div. mdse. mgr., 1940-46, exec. v.p., 1946-52, pres., chief exec. officer, 1952-77; pres. Bessina Realty Corp., South Bend, 1952-88; bus. cons. to retail stores, South Bend, 1977-88. Pres. South Bend Downtown Council, 1958-68; bd. dirs. Michiana council Boy Scouts Am., 1960-80; mem. South Bend Bd. Edn., 1962-64. Recipient Brotherhood award NCCJ, 1955, Past Pres.'s award Temple Beth-El, 1987, numerous others. Mem. Photog. Soc. Am., Elks. Office: 211 W Washington Ste 1806 South Bend IN 46601

WELCH, BETTY LEONORA, accountant; b. Missoula, Mont., July 18, 1961; d. George Oliver and Betty June (Dolton) W. BBA, U. Mont., 1983. CPA, Mont. Staff acct. Ellis & Assocs., Boise, Idaho, 1984; acct. Glacier Electric Coop., Cut Bank, Mont., 1984-86, office mgr., 1986—; income tax cons. Mem. AICPA, Beta Gamma Sigma. Democrat. Roman Catholic. Avocations: skiing, sewing, reading, hunting. Office: Glacier Electric Coop Inc 410 E Main St Cut Bank MT 59427

WELCH, JAMES MILTON, archaeologist; b. Tampa, Aug. 16, 1957; s. Milton Keith Welch and Emma Myrtle (Hewlett) Rivers; m. Sunday Angel Giambrone, Aug. 4, 1985. AA, U. S.Fla., 1976, BA, 1978, MA, 1983. Mem. archaeol. crew U. S.Fla., Tampa, 1977-78, U. Miss., Greenwood, 1978, State of Fla., Tampa, 1981; archaeol. technician Bur. Land Mgmt. U.S. Dept. Interior, Boise, Idaho, 1979-80; mem. archaeol. crew Piper Archaeol. Research Inc., St. Petersburg, Fla., 1981; archaeologist, project dir. dept. anthropology U. S. Fla., St. Petersburg, 1981-83; staff archaeologist Archaeol. Cons. Inc., Worland, Wyo., 1983-84; prin. investigator, owner Frontier Archaeology, Worland, 1984—. Contbr. articles to profl. jours. Bd. dirs. Wyo. Council Humanities, 1985—, sec. 1988—; mem. citizen adv. council Worland Dist. Bur. Land Mgmt., 1988—. Mem. Soc. Profl. Archaeologists, Wyo. Assn. Profl. Archaeologists, Soc. Am. Archaeology, Am. Anthropol. Assn., Plains Anthropol. Conf. Methodist. Home: 1521 Howell Ave Worland WY 82401 Office: Frontier Archaeology PO Box 1315 Worland WY 82401

WELCH, JOHN FRANCIS, JR., electrical manufacturing company executive; b. Peabody, Mass., Nov. 19, 1935; s. John Francis and Grace (Andrews) W.; children—Katherine, John, Anne, Mark. B.S. in Chem. Engring, U. Mass., 1957; M.S., U. Ill., 1958, Ph.D., 1960. With Gen. Electric Co., Fairfield, Conn., 1960—, v.p., 1972, v.p., group exec. components and materials group, 1973-77, sr. v.p., sector exec., consumer products and services sector, 1977-79, vice chmn., exec. officer, 1979-81, chmn., chief exec. officer, 1981—; also dir. Gen. Electric Fin. Services. Patentee in field. Mem. Nat. Acad. Engring. (chmn.), Fed. Res. Bd. (dir.), Bus. Coun. (vice chmn.), Bus. Roundtable. Office: GE 3135 Easton Turnpike Fairfield CT 06431

WELCH, JUNE SHEILA, petroleum company executive; b. Jacksonville, Fla., June 9, 1939; d. Robert Paul and Carrie (Drawdy) W.; divorced, 1970; children: Stacy Lorraine Harker, Lisa Jane Harker, Carrie Bess McGonigle. BA, Calif. State U., Long Beach, 1960; JD, Western State U., 1974. Tchr. various pub. schs., So. Calif., 1961-71; ednl. cons. Western State U., Fullerton, Calif., 1972-74; account exec. Mass. Mut. Life Ins., Long Beach, 1975-77; sole practice Santa Ana, Calif., 1978-81; pres. Calista Petroleum Co., Paramount, Calif., 1982—; corp. counsel Bear Welding, Inc., Long Beach. Mem. U.S. Senate Inner Circle, Calif. Reps. Mem. Nat. Liquid Petroleum Gas Assn. (state law and regulations com.), Western Liquid Gas Assn. (ins. com.), Los Angeles County Bar Assn., Orange County Bar Assn., Calif. Women Lawyers. Office: Calista Petroleum Co 6510 Alondra Blvd Paramount CA 90723

WELCH, L. DEAN, manufacturing executive; b. Emmett, Idaho, July 24, 1928; s. Roy W. and Luella (Bader) W.; m. Elizabeth Gay, Apr. 27, 1958; 1 child, Caroline Gay. BS, U. Idaho, 1950. Sales rep. Idaho Power Co., 1950-52; purchasing supr. Boeing Airplane Co., 1952-57; mgr. purchasing HITCO subs. Armco Inc., 1957-63, v.p. materials, 1963-66; v.p., gen. mgr. HITCO Def. Products Div., 1966-72, group v.p., 1972-79; v.p. stainless, advanced materials div. Armco Inc., 1979-80, pres. stainless steel div., 1980-81; pres., chief operating officer Ladish Co. Inc., Cudahy, Wis., 1981-85, pres., chief exec. officer, 1985—, also bd. dirs.; bd. dirs. First Wis. Trust Co., Milw. Mem. adv. com. U. Wis.-Whitewater, U. Wis.-Milw.; mem. corp. com. Milw. Sch. Engring. Mem. Soc. for Advancement of Materials and Process Engring., Am. Def. Preparedness Assn., Am. Security Council (nat. adv. bd.), Beta Gamma Sigma (hon.). Office: Ladish Co Inc 5481 S Packard Ave Cudahy WI 53110

WELCH, LOUIE, corporate consultant, former trade organization executive, former mayor; b. Lockney, Tex., Dec. 9, 1918; s. Gilford E. and Nora (Shackelford) W.; m. Iola Faye Cure, Dec. 17, 1940; children: Guy Lynn, Gary Dale, Louie Gilford, Shannon Austin, Tina La Joy. B.A. magna cum laude, Abilene Christian U., 1940, LL.D. (hon.), 1981; H.H.D. (hon.), Okla. Christian U., 1982; LL.D. (hon.), Pepperdine U., 1981, Lubbock Christian Coll, 1983. Councilman at large Houston, 1950-52, 56-62; mayor of Houston 1964-73, mayor emeritus, 1974—; pres. Houston C. of C., 1974-85; cons. 1985—; bd. dirs. 1st Tex. Savs. Assn., Gibraltar Savs. Assn., Kanaly Trust Co. Pres. Tex. Mcpl. League, 1959-60, U.S. Conf. of Mayors, 1972-73; trustee Abilene Christian U.; chmn. Tex. Water Devel. Bd., 1987; bd. dirs. Park Plaza Hosp. Mem. Tex. Mayors and Councilmens Assn. (past pres.), Nat. League Cities (past v.p.) Am. C. of C. Execs. (dir.), Houston C. of C. (pres. 1974-85). Clubs: Cen. Houston (exec. com. 1987), Heritage (Bd. of govs. 1987). Home: 9658 Longmont Houston TX 77063 Office: 1200 Smith Suite 3060 Houston TX 77002

WELCH, R. DEWEY, b. South Bend, Ind., Feb. 27, 1928; s. Ralfred Michael and M. Roine (Smith) Welch; m. Phyllis Ann Hiatt, Oct. 25, 1952; children—Susan Hiatt, Douglas. BS in Mktg., Ind. U., 1952. With Barger Packaging Corp., Elkhart, Ind., 1952—, sales mgr., 1957-60, v.p. mktg., 1961-70, exec. v.p., 1963-71, pres., 1972-84, chmn., chief exec. officer, 1985—; dir., mem. exec. com. First Nat. Bank Elkhart (Ameritrust), 1974—; dir., chmn. audit com. Riblet Products Corp., Elkhart, 1978—. Chmn. Elkhart County United Way, 1977, Elkhart Rep. Com., 1984; nat. chmn. Ind. U. Ann. Giving Campaign, 1979, 80; bd. dirs. Ind. U. Found., 1986. Sgt. U.S. Army, 1946-48, PTO. Recipient Disting. Svc. award Elkhart Jaycees, 1960, Distinguished Owner-Mgr. award Ind. U., 1978, E.M. Morris award Ind. U. at So. Bend, 1978. Mem. Elkhart Exch. Club (pres. 1957), Elkhart Better Bus. Bur. (pres. 1960), Ind. U. Nat. Alumni Assn. (v.p. 1984-86, pres. 1986-87, nat. chmn. ann. campaign 1979-80), Nat. Paperbox and Packaging Assn. (dir. 1976, 80), Paperboard Packaging Coun. (mem. adv. bd. 1978—), Sigma Nu, Exch. Club, Elcona Country Club (Elkhart). Republican. Avocations: golf, fishing, sailing. Home: 1610 East Lake Dr W Elkhart IN 46514 Office: Barger Packaging Corp 1511 W Lusher Ave Elkhart IN 46515

WELCH, RONALD J., actuary; b. Luling, Tex., June 26, 1945; s. Billie C. and Irene (Anton) W.; m. Leslie Ann Herman, Oct. 9, 1971; children: Kelley, Stephen. BBA, U. Tex., 1966; MS, Northeastern U., 1968. V.p., actuary Am. Nat. Ins. Co., Galveston, Tex., 1975-80, sr. v.p., actuary, 1980-86, sr. v.p., chief actuary, 1986—; bd. dirs. Standard Life & Accident Ins. Co., Oklahoma City, Am. Nat. Property & Casualty Ins., Springfield, Mo., Am. Nat. Ins. Co. of Tex., Galveston, Commonwealth Life and Accident Ins. Co., St. Louis. Fellow Soc. of Actuaries; mem. Am. Acad. Actuaries. Office: Am Nat Ins Co 1 Moody Pla Galveston TX 77550

WELCH, STEWART HENRY, III, financial advisor; b. Birmingham, Ala., June 29, 1951; s. Stewart Henry and Sally (Baker) W.; m. Kathie M. Welch, Sept. 20, 1980. BS, U. Ala., 1973. Cert. fin. planner; chartered fin. cons. Rep. Conn. Mut. Life Co., Birmingham, 1973-84; founder, owner, mgr. Welch Fin. Advisors, Birmingham, 1984—. Mem. Internat. Assn. Fin. Planning (pres. Ala. 1988-89), Internat. Assn. Cert. Fin. Planners, Registry Fin. Practitioners, Estate Planning Coun. Birmingham, Kiwanis. Presbyterian. Office: 200 S 28th St Birmingham AL 35233

WELCH, WALTER ANDREW, JR., lawyer; b. Dec. 13; s. Walter Andrew and Myrtle Marie (Kunzmann) W. J.D. Pepperdine U., 1980, U.S. Dept. Justice Legal Edn. Inst., 1985. Bar: Calif., N.J., U.S. Customs and Patent Appeals, U.S. Tax Ct., U.S. Ct. Mil. Appeals, U.S. Claims Ct., U.S. Ct. Appeals (3d, 4th, 5th and 9th cirs.), U.S. Dist. Ct. (so. and cen. dists.) Calif., U.S. Dist. Ct. N.J.; lic. comml. pilot. Sole practice, Los Angeles and Washington, 1981—; real estate broker, Calif., 1981—, Va. 1984—; vis. asst. prof. aviation law So. Ill. U., 1986—. Contbr. articles to legal revs. Grantee and fellow Pepperdine U. Sch. Law, 1978-80. Mem. AIAA, Lawyer-Pilot's Bar Assn., Assn. Naval Aviation, Marine Corps Aviation Assn., Fed. Bar Assn., Assn. Trial Lawyers Am., ABA, Internat Legal Soc., Calif. State Bar (del. conv. 1981—). Office: PO Box 99698 San Diego CA 92109

WELGE, DONALD EDWARD, food manufacturing executive; b. St. Louis, July 11, 1935; s. William H. and Rudelle (Fritze) W.; m. Mary Alice Childers, Aug. 4, 1962; children: Robert, Tom. B.S., La. State U., 1957. With Gilster-Mary Lee Corp., Chester, Ill., 1957—, pres., gen. mgr., 1965—; dir. Buena Vista Bank of Chester. Former chmn. St. John's Luth. Bd. Edn. 1st lt. Transp. Corp, U.S. Army, 1958-63. Named So. Ill. Bus. Leader of Yr. So. Ill. U., 1988. Mem. Perryville C. of C. (pres. 1989—), Alpha Zeta, Phi Kappa Phi. Republican. Lutheran. Home: 5 Knollwood Dr Chester IL 62233 Office: Gilster Mary Lee Co 1037 State St Chester IL 62233

WELIKSON, JEFFREY ALAN, lawyer; b. Bklyn., Jan. 8, 1957; s. Bennet Joseph and Cynthia Ann Welikson; m. Laura Sanders, Aug. 19, 1979; children: Gregory Andrew, Joshua Stuart. BS, U. Pa., 1976, MBA, 1977; JD, Harvard U., 1980. CPA, N.Y.; bar: N.Y. 1981. Assoc. Shearman & Sterling, N.Y.C., 1980-83; staff counsel Reliance Group Holdings Inc., N.Y.C., 1983-84; dir. legal dept., 1984-85, asst. v.p., corp. counsel, 1985-88, v.p., asst. gen. counsel, 1988—. Contbg. editor Harvard U. Internat. Law Jour., 1979-80. Mem. ABA, N.Y. State Bar Assn., Am. Inst. CPAs. Office: Reliance Group Holdings Inc Park Ave Plaza New York NY 10055

WELIN, WALTER, financial advisor; b. Lund, Sweden, Sept. 20, 1908; s. Lars and Adele (Hellegren) W.; m. Ulla Olsson, Nov. 25, 1950; 1 child, Lars. Grad. Econs. and Fin., U. Lund, MA in Polit. Sci. 1943, grad. law sch. 1945. Dir. dept. The Royal Swedish Patent Office, Stockholm, 1948-74; fin. advisor/cons. in pvt. practice, Lund. Club: St. Knut Guild. Mem. N.Y. Acad. Scis., Nat. Geographic Soc. Address: Siriusgatan 25 S-223, 57 Lund Sweden

WELLBROCK-REEVES, MARYLOU, financial planner; b. Summit, N.J., Dec. 19, 1959; d. Richard Otto and Helen (Drennen) W.; m. Richard Harold, Jan. 13, 1985; 1 child, Rachael Elizabeth. BS in Commerce, Rider Coll., 1981. Cert. fin. planning, 1987. Fin. planner E.F. Hutton and Co., Inc., N.Y.C., 1981-83, asst. v.p., 1984-86; acct. exec. San Diego Securities, Inc., 1983-84; mgr., asst. v.p. fin. planning dept. Summit Bancorp., 1986-89; pres. Thomas Mack Assocs., 1989—. Adv. council No. N.J. Fedn. of Planning Ofls., 1987; councilwoman Rockaway Twp., 1988—; mem. Rockaway Rep. Com. Mem. Internat. Assn. Fin. Planners, Inst. of Cert. Fin. Planners. Republican. Roman Catholic. Home and Office: 32 Hibernia Rd Rockaway NJ 07866

WELLER, ANDREW M., steel company executive. Gen. mgr., v.p., treas. Bethlehem (Pa.) Steel Corp. Office: Bethlehem Steel Corp 8th & Eaton Aves Bethlehem PA 18016

WELLER, ROBERT NORMAN, motel executive; b. Harrisburg, Pa., Feb. 1, 1939; s. Charles Walter and Martha Ann (MacPherson) W.; m. Nancy M. Wood, June 21, 1975; children—Wendi Elizabeth, Terrie Lynn, Nikki Ann. B.S., Cornell U., 1969. Mgr. Hall's Motor Transit Co., Harrisburg, Pa., 1961-65; market research analyst Carrolls Devel. Corp., Syracuse, N.Y., 1970-72; asst. to pres. Econo-Travel Motor Hotel Corp., Norfolk, Va., 1972-74; dir. franchise sales Econo-Travel Motor Hotel Corp., 1975, pres., dir., 1976-84; pres., dir. Econo-Travel Devel. Corp., Norfolk, 1977-84; pres. Internat. Data Bank Ltd., 1985-86; pres., dir. Econo Lodges of Am., 1986—. Served in USMC, 1957-60. Mem. Am. Mgmt. Assn. Home: 3027 Lynndale Road Virginia Beach VA 23452 Office: Econo Lodges of Am Inc 6135 Park Rd Suite 200 Charlotte NC 28210

WELLFORD, TEN EYCK THOMPSON, stockbroker, research analyst; b. Richmond, Va., Oct. 23, 1952; s. McDonald and Margaret (Thompson) W.; m. Eleanor Lee Smith, June 24, 1978; children: Mary Carter, Ten Eyck Jr. BA, U. Va., 1976; MS, Va. Commonwealth U., 1981, MBA, 1981. V.p. Branch, Cabell & Co., Richmond, 1981—. Office: Branch Cabell & Co 919 E Main St 17th Floor Richmond VA 23219

WELLING, W. LAMBERT, investment banker; b. N.Y.C., Oct. 25, 1932; s. Charles Hulbert and Mary Goethe (Lambert) W.; m. Louise Alison Partridge, Apr. 15, 1961; children: Andrew, David. BA, Middlebury Coll., 1954; MBA, Columbia U., 1958. From salesperson to corp. venture mgr. Scott Paper Co., Phila., 1958-72; v.p. Federal Street Capital Corp., Boston, 1972-80; ptnr. Pace Cons. Group, Wellesley, Mass., 1980-83; mng. dir. Ulin Morton Bradley & Welling, Boston, 1984—. Chmn. warrant com. Town of

Dover, Mass., 1976-80; sr. warden St. Dunstan's Episc. Ch., Dover, 1975-78. Mem. Inst. Mgmt. Cons., Assn. Corp. Growth. Episcopalian. Home: 9 Sherbrooke Dr Dover MA 02030 Office: Ulin Morton Bradley & Welling 75 Federal St Boston MA 02110

WELLINGTON, ROBERT HALL, manufacturing company executive; b. Atlanta, July 4, 1922; s. Robert H. and Ernestine V. (Vossbrinck) W.; m. Marjorie Jarchow, Nov. 15, 1947; children: Charles R., Robert H., Christian J., Jeanne L. B.S., Northwestern Tech. Inst., 1943; M.S. in Bus. Adminstrn, MBA, U. Chgo., 1958. With Griffin Wheel Co., 1946-61; v.p. parent co. AMSTED Industries Inc., Chgo., 1961-74, exec. v.p., 1974-80, pres., chief exec. officer, 1981-88, chmn. bd., chief exec. officer, 1988—, also dir.; bd. dirs. L.E. Myers Co., Chgo., DeSoto Inc., Chgo., Centel, Money Market Assets, Research Fund, Inc., Prudential Intermediate Income Fund, Inc. Served to lt. USN, 1943-46. Clubs: Chicago, Chgo. Athletic, Economic, Mid-America, Comml. Office: Amsted Industries Inc 205 N Michigan Ave Chicago IL 60601

WELLMAN, BARCLAY ORMES, furniture company executive; b. Jamestown, N.Y., May 13, 1936; s. Albert Austin and Leona (Greenlund) W.; m. Diane Taylor, July 2, 1960; children: Barclay Ormes Jr., Taylor A., Alexandra C. BA, Dartmouth Coll., 1959; grad., U.S. Army War Coll., 1982. Interior designer Wellman Bros., Inc., Jamestown, 1963-64, treas., 1964—, pres., 1978—. Trustee Lakeview Cemetery Assn., Jamestown, 1978—; Sheldon Found., Jamestown, 1981—, Emma Willard Sch. Brig. gen. USAR. Mem. Am. Soc. Interior Designers (v.p. 1972-74), Am. Appraisers Assn., Am. Legion, Res. Officers Assn., Sr. Army Res. Comdrs. Assn., Sportsmens Club, Moon Brook Country Club, Delta Kappa Epsilon. Republican. Presbyterian. Home: 1235 Prendergast Ave Jamestown NY 14701 Office: Wellman Bros Inc 130 S Main St Jamestown NY 14701

WELLMAN, W. ARVID, window manufacturing executive; b. 1918. With Andersen Corp., Bayport, Minn., 1937—, pres., from 1975, now chmn. bd., chief exec. officer, dir. Office: Andersen Corp Foot N 5th Ave Bayport MN 55003

WELLNITZ, CAROL LEE, accountant, consultant; b. Elwood, Ind., Sept. 8, 1947; d. Donald Eugene and Lois Mabel (Uetz) Kincaid; m. Craig O. Wellnitz, Jan. 23, 1988. BS, Purdue U., 1968; postgrad., Butler U., 1974, Nash Community Coll., 1987; MBA, Campbell U., 1989. Cert. mgmt. acct. Adminstrv. asst. Ind. Bell Tel., Indpls., 1968-69; acctg. supr. Herff Jones Co., Indpls., 1970-74; acctg. mgr. Burger Chef Systems, Inc., Indpls., 1974-82; asst. controller Hardee's Food Systems, Inc., Rocky Mount, N.C., 1983-88; pres. Carol Craig Assocs., Indpls., 1987—; v.p., controller Ind. Account Mgmt., Indpls., 1988—; cons., v.p. Cyborg Users Assn., Chgo., 1985-87. Contbr. articles to profl. jours. Bd. dirs. Jr. Achievement, Rocky Mount, 1986-87; chmn. Girl Scouts U.S., RAF Alconbury, UK, 1969-70; fundraiser Resources Youth, Rocky Mount, 1985. Mem. Inst. Mgmt. Acctg., Nat. Assn. Female Execs. Republican. Methodist. Club: Northgreen Ladies Golf Assn. (treas. 1985-86). Office: Carol Craig Assocs PO Box 44162 Indianapolis IN 46204

WELLS, ARTHUR STANTON, manufacturing company executive; b. Kingsport, Tenn., Jan. 8, 1931; s. Arthur Stanton and Blanche Welch (Duncan) W.; m. Ellen N. Blackburn, June 15, 1957; children: Arthur S., Thomas B., Emily B., Richard R. B.S., Yale U., 1953; M.B.A., Harvard U., 1957. Fin. analyst Eastman Kodak Co., Kingsport, Tenn., 1957-65; mgr. profit analysis Xerox Corp., Rochester, N.Y., 1966-68; asst. treas. Xerox Corp., Stamford, Conn., 1969-76, treas., 1976-79; v.p. fin. Barnes Group Inc., Bristol, Conn., 1979-86, exec. v.p. fin., 1987—; assoc. dir. Conn. Bank & Trust Co., Hartford. Trustee, treas. Wilton (Conn.) Library Assn., 1972-78; bd. dirs. New Eng. Opera Assn., 1980-83; trustee Conn. Pub. Expenditure Council Inc., mem. exec. com. Served with AUS, 1953-55. Mem. Fin. Execs. Inst. Democrat. Home: 101 Spectacle Ln Wilton CT 06897 Office: Barnes Group Inc 123 Main St Bristol CT 06010

WELLS, CHARLES WILLIAM, utility executive; b. Springfield, Ill., June 25, 1934; s. William Ward and Maxine Deloris (Harris) W.; m. Lois Vasconcelles, Mar. 5, 1954; children: David, Susan, Amy. Student, Springfield Jr. Coll., 1952-54; B.S. in Elec. Engring., U. Ill., 1956; M.B.A., 1977. With Ill. Power Co., 1958—, v.p., 1972-76, exec. v.p., 1976—, also dir. Served with USN, 1956-58. President of Decatur, Decatur Racquet. Home: 3 Westmoreland Pl Decatur IL 62521 Office: Ill Power Co 500 S 27th St Decatur IL 62525

WELLS, DALE KENT, treasurer; b. Three Rivers, Mich., Oct. 23, 1930; s. William Franklin and Mabel Florence (Keonneker) W.; m. bonnie Lee Peterson, Feb. 14, 1958; children: Jeanne Marie, Steven Lee, William Gregory. BA, Mich. State U., 1957, MBA, 1959. Auditor U.S. GAO, Dallas, 1960-64, Buick Motor div. Gen. Motors Corp., Flint, Mich., 1964-65; sec.-treas. W.F. Wells & Sons, Inc., Three Rivers, Mich., 1965—; also bd. dirs. W.F. Wells, Inc. Moderator First Bapt. Ch., Kalamazoo, 1988. Sgt. USAF, 1950-54. Mem. Classic Car Club Am. Mus. (bd. dirs. 1988, pres. 1989—), Kalamazoo Antique Auto Club (pres. 1974), Three Rivers Antique Auto Club (pres. 1969, 86). Home: 7906 S 10th St Kalamazoo MI 49009 Office: WF Wells & Sons Inc 16645 Heimbach Rd Three Rivers MI 49093

WELLS, DAMON, JR., investment company executive; b. Houston, May 20, 1937; s. Damon and Margaret Corinne (Howze) W.; BA magna cum laude, Yale U., 1958; BA, Oxford U., 1964, MA, 1968; PhD, Rice U., 1968. Owner, chief exec. officer Damon Wells Interests, Houston, 1958—. Bd. dirs. Child Guidance Center of Houston, 1970-73, Jefferson Davis Assn., 1973-81; trustee Christ Ch. Cathedral Endowment Fund, 1970-73, 84-88, chmn., 1987-88, Kinkaid Sch., 1972-86, Kinkaid Sch. Endowment Fund, 1981-86; hon. friend of Somerville Coll., Oxford U., 1988—; mem. Sr. Common Room, Pembroke Coll., Oxford U., 1972—; trustee Capt Allen retreat of Episc. Diocese of Tex., 1976-78; founding bd. dirs. Brit. Inst. U.S., 1979-80; mem. pres.' council Tex. A&M U., 1983—. Fellow Jonathan Edwards Coll., Yale U., 1982—; hon. fellow Pembroke Coll., Oxford U., 1984—. Mem. English-Speaking Union (nat. dir. 1970-72, v.p. Houston br. 1966-73), Council Fgn. Affairs, Phi Beta Kappa, Pi Sigma Alpha. Episcopalian. Clubs: Coronado, Houston Country, Houston; Yale (N.Y.C.); United Oxford and Cambridge U. (London); Cosmos (Washington). Author: Stephen Douglas: The Last Years, 1857-1861, 1971. Home: 5555 Del Monte #2404 Houston TX 77056 Office: River Oaks Bank Bldg Suite 806 2001 Kirby Dr Houston TX 77019

WELLS, DONNA FRANCES, distribution company executive; b. Lima, Ohio, Dec. 19, 1948; d. Arthur Robert and Frances Lucille (Knudtson) W.; m. Darrell Donald Erickson, Nov. 26, 1980. Cert., Parks Bus. Sch., 1972; student, Sheridan Coll., 1984—. Dir. purchasing Wolff Distbg., Gillette, Wyo., 1973—. Mem. Nat. Assn. Purchasing Mgmt., Nat. Assn. of Female Execs., Gillette Racing Assn. (aux. v.p. 1986—), VFW Aux., Am. Legion Aux. Home: 105 Sequoia Gillette WY 82716

WELLS, ELLEN MOORE, health care administrator; b. Crites, W.Va., Sept. 21, 1944; d. Albert and Esclene (Muncy) Moore; children: Scott D., Jon T. AA in Nursing, U. Charleston, 1971; BS in Nursing, Marshall U., 1977; MEd, U. Louisville, 1980; postgrad., Ind. Perdue U., 1980-85. Staff nurse Grant Hosp. and Riverside Hosp., Columbus, Ohio, 1971-73; asst. dir. nursing Charleston Area (W.va.) Med. Ctr., 1974-75; asst. exec. dir. Charterton Hosp., LaGrange, Ky., 1976-77, HealthCare of Louisville, 1977-80; asst. exec. dir. patient svcs. and ambulatory care Humana Hosp.-U. Louisville, 1980-84; exec. dir., plan administr. Humana Health Plan of Ohio, Columbus, 1984-86; exec. v.p., chief operating officer Mt. Carmel Health Horizons, Columbus, 1986—. Contbr. articles to profl. jour. Recipient Nurse of the Yr. award Ky. ambulatory Care Adminstrs., Louisville, 1984. Mem. Am. Acad. Med. Adminstrs., Am. Coll. Health Care Execs., Am. Nurses Assn., Nat. League for Nursing, Ky. Acad. Ambulatory Care Adminstrn. Episcopalian. Home: 7944 Hightree Dr Westerville OH 43081

WELLS, FRANK G., lawyer, film studio executive; b. Mar. 4, 1932. BA summa cum laude, Pomona Coll., 1953; MA in Law, Oxford (Eng.) U., 1955; LLB, Stanford U., 1959. Former vice chmn. Warner Bros. Inc.; ptnr.

Gang Tyre & Brown, 1962-69; pres., chief operating officer Walt Disney Co., Burbank, Calif., 1984—. Co-author: Seven Summits. Bd. trustees Pomona Coll., Nat. History Mus., Sundance Inst.; bd. overseers for RAND/UCLA Ctr. Study of Soviet Behavior; mem. svcs. policy adv. com. U.S. Trade Regulation. 1st lt. U.S. Army, 1955-57. Rhodes scholar, 1955. Mem. ABA, State Bar Calif., L.A. County Bar Assn., Explorer's Club, Phi Beta Kappa. Office: The Walt Disney Co 500 S Buena Vista St Burbank CA 91521

WELLS, HARRY KENNADY, spice and food processing company executive; b. Balt., Sept. 4, 1922; s. Clifton Kennady and Ruth Jones (Coale) W.; m. Lois Luttrell, Sept. 8, 1946; children: Katherine Anne Wells Witbeck, Robert Grayson, David Kennady. BS in Mech. Engring., U. Md., 1943. With McCormick & Co., Inc., Balt., 1946—; v.p., gen. mgr. Schilling div. McCormick & Co., Inc., San Francisco, 1966-68; v.p. McCormick & Co., Inc., 1968-69, pres., 1969-79, chmn. bd., chief exec. officer, 1977-87, chmn. bd., 1987-88, also bd. dirs.; bd. dirs. McCormick de Mexico (S.A.), Mexico City, McCormick Properties, Inc., Hunt Valley, Balt. Gas & Electric Co., Md. Nat. Bank, Balt., Md. Nat. Corp., Balt., PHH Group, Inc., Hunt Valley, Loyola Fed. Savs. & Loan Assn., Balt., Armstrong World Industries, Inc., Lancaster, Pa., Fidelity & Deposit Cos. Md., Balt. Past mem. San Francisco Safety Council; v.p. Hillsborough (Calif.) Bd. Edn., 1965, pres., 1966; mem. Md. sponsoring com. Radio Free Europe Fund, Balt.; bd. dirs. Mid-Atlantic Legal Found., Phila.; former mem. nat. adv. council Salvation Army, N.Y.C.; former dir. United Fund Central Md., Balt.; past trustee, mem. exec. com. Community Chest Balt. Area; former trustee McDonogh (Md.) Sch.; trustee Nutrition Found., N.Y.C., Food and Drug Law Inst., Washington. Served to lt. USN, 1943-46. Named Outstanding Engring. Alumnus U. Md. Sch. Engring., 1976. Mem. Grocery Mfrs. Am. (dir.), NAM (former chmn., dir.), Alpha Tau Omega. Methodist. Clubs: Baltimore Country (Balt.), Center (Balt.), Maryland (Balt.); Towson; Hunt Valley Golf (Md.); Stone Harbor Yacht. (N.J.), Annapolis Yacht (Md.). Lodges: Masons; KT; Shriners. Office: McCormick & Co Inc 11350 McCormick Rd Hunt Valley MD 21031

WELLS, JOEL REAVES, JR., bank holding company executive; b. Troy, Ala., Nov. 14, 1928; s. Joel Reaves and Julia (Talley) W.; m. Betty Stratton, June 27, 1953; children: Linda, Martha, Joel. B.S.B.A., U. Fla., 1950, J.D., 1951. Bar: Fla. Ptnr. Maguire, Voorhis & Wells, Orlando, Fla., 1956-75; pres. Major Realty Co., Orlando, 1972-75; exec. v.p. Sun Banks, Inc., Orlando, 1975-76, pres., 1976—; chief exec. officer, 1982—; chmn. Sun Banks of Fla., Inc., Orlando, from 1982; now also pres., dir. SunTrust Banks, Inc., Atlanta; bd. dirs. parent co. Sun Bank, N.A., Coca-Cola Enterprises, Inc., Atlanta, Columbian Mut. Life Ins. Co., Binghamton, N.Y. Mem. Fla. Council of 100, from 1975; pres. Central Fla. Devel. Com., 1965; chmn. Mcpl. Planning Bd., Orlando, 1962, 63; pres. United Appeal Orange County, 1960; trustee Berry Coll., Rome, Ga. Recipient Disting. Service award Orlando Jaycees, 1960. Mem. Orlando C. of C. (pres. 1970), Atlanta C. of C. (bd. dirs.). Methodist. Clubs: Rotary (pres. 1966-67), Univ., Citrus, Country (Orlando). Office: SunTrust Banks Inc PO Box 4418 Atlanta GA 30302 also: Sun Banks Inc 200 S Orange Ave Orlando FL 32801

WELLS, JOHN ANDREW, retail executive; b. Ft. Smith, Ark., Apr. 11, 1926; s. Aubrey J. and Bertie Lee (Stout) W.; m. Ila Marie Degen, Aug. 21, 1944; children: Alice Jane Wells Randall, John A. Jr. BSBA, U. Ark., 1949. Sect. mgr. J.C. Penney, Ft. Smith, 1949-54; sect. mgr. J.C. Penney, Oklahoma City, 1954-57, store mgr., 1963-65; sales, mdse. mgr. J.C. Penney, San Antonio, 1957-59, store mgr., 1959-63; dist. mgr. J.C. Penney, Dallas, 1965-68, sr. v.p. real estate and constrn svcs., 1988—; dist. mgr. J.C. Penney, Atlanta, 1968-69, regional v.p., 1978-86; dist. mgr. J.C. Penney, New Orleans, 1969-71, Tampa, Fla., 1972; coord. full line dept. J.C. Penney, N.Y.C., 1972-73, mgr. retail mktg., 1974-75, dir. treasury stores and supermarkets, 1976-77, sr. v.p. dir. mktg., 1986-87, sr. v.p. real estate and constrn. svcs., 1987; sr. v.p. real estate and constrn. svcs. J.C. Penney, Dallas, 1988—. Served with USN, 1944-46, PTO. Mem. Atlanta Athletic Club, Gleneagles Club. Republican. Methodist. Office: JC Penney Co Inc 14841 N Dallas Pkwy Dallas TX 75240

WELLS, JOHN NELSON, financial analyst; b. Columbus, Ohio, Sept. 11, 1962; s. Nelson Wells and Gladys Louise (Simpkins) Cox; m. Connie Lynn Ricketts, June 21, 1986. BA, Capital U., 1985. CPA, Ohio. Staff acct. Arthur Andersen & Co., Columbus, 1985-88; fin. analyst Nat. Continental Ins., Beachwood, Ohio, 1988—. Mem. AICPA, Ohio Soc. CPAs, Nat. Assn. Accts., Franklin County Big Bros./Big Sisters. Methodist. Home: 372 Richmond Rd Richmond Heights OH 44143 Office: Nat Continental Ins 3401 Enterprise Pkwy Beachwood OH 44122

WELLS, JOSEPH M(ERTON), retired energy executive; b. East Chicago, Ind., Jan. 14, 1922; s. Samuel Ralph and Helen Beatrice (Ketner) W.; m. Eileen Agnes Ponsonby, Sept. 1, 1972; 1 child, R. Dodge. S.B. cum laude, Harvard U., 1943, LL.B., 1952. Bar: Ill. 1953. Assoc., then ptnr. Ross & Hardies, Chgo., 1952-64; sec. Peoples Gas Light and Coke Co., Chgo., 1963-67, v.p., 1966-69; v.p. Peoples Energy Corp., Chgo., 1969-72; v.p., gen. counsel Peoples Gas Light and Coke Co., Chgo., 1972-81; v.p., gen. counsel MidCon Corp., Lombard, Ill., 1981-84, vice chmn., 1984-89; v.p. Occidental Petroleum Corp., Los Angeles, 1986-89. Bd. dirs. Council Community Services Met., Chgo., 1966-77, pres., 1970-72. Capt. U.S. Army 1943-49. Mem. ABA, Chgo. Bar Assn., Fed. Energy Bar Assn. Clubs: University (Chgo.), Econ. (Chgo.); The DuPage (Oakbrook Terrace, Ill.). Office: MidCon Corp 701 E 22d St Lombard IL 60148

WELLS, PATRICIA BENNETT, business administration educator; b. Park River, N.D., Mar. 25, 1935; d. Benjamin Beekman Bennett and Alice Catherine (Peerboom) Bennett Breckinridge; A.A., Allan Hancock Coll., Santa Maria, Calif., 1964; B.S. magna cum laude, Coll. Great Falls, 1966; M.S., U. N.D., 1967, Ph.D., 1971; children—Bruce Bennett, Barbara Lea Ragland. Fiscal acct. USIA, Washington, 1954-56; public acct., Bremerton, Wash., 1956; statistician U.S. Navy, Bremerton, 1957-59; med. services accounts officer U.S. Air Force, Vandenberg AFB, Calif., 1962-64; instr. bus. adminstrn. Western New Eng. Coll., 1967-69; vis. prof. econs. Chapman Coll., 1970; vis. prof. U. So. Calif. systems Griffith AFB, N.Y., 1971-72; assoc. prof., dir. adminstrn. mgmt. program Va. State U., 1973-74; assoc. prof. bus. adminstrn. Oreg. State U., Corvallis, 1974-81, prof. mgmt., 1982—, univ. curriculum coordinator, 1984-86, dir. adminstrv. mgmt. program, 1974-81, pres. Faculty Senate, 1981; cons. process tech. devel. Digital Equipment Corp., 1982. Pres., chmn. bd. dirs. Adminstrv. Orgnl. Services, Inc., Corvallis, 1976-83, Dynamic Achievement, Inc., 1983—; bd. dirs. Oreg. State U. Bookstores, Inc., 1987—. Cert. adminstrv. mgr. Pres. TYEE Mobil Home Park, Inc. Fellow Am. Bus. Communication (mem. internat. bd. 1980-83, v.p. Northwest 1981, 2d v.p. 1982-83, 1st v.p. 1983-84, pres. 1984-85); mem. Am. Bus. Women's Assn. (chpt. v.p. 1979, pres. 1980, named Top Businesswoman in Nation 1980, Bus. Assoc. Yr. 1986), Assn. Info. Systems Profls., Adminstrv. Mgmt. Soc., AAUP (chpt. sec. 1973, chpt. bd. dirs. 1982, 84-897), pres. Oreg. conf. 1983-85), Am. Vocat. Assn. (nominating com. 1976), Associated Oreg. Faculties, Nat. Bus. Edn. Assn., Nat. Assn. Tchr. Edn. for Bus. Office Edn. (pres. 1976-77, chmn. public relations com. 1978-81), Corvallis Area C. of C. (v.p. chamber devel. 1987-88, pres. 1988—, Pres.' award 1986), Sigma Kappa. Roman Catholic. Lodge: Rotary. Contbr. numerous articles to profl. jours. Office: Oreg State U Coll Bus 418C Bexell Corvallis OR 97331

WELLS, PETER SCOVILLE, marketing executive; b. N.Y.C., Apr. 25, 1938; s. Jonathan Godfrey and Eleanore Shannon (Scoville) W.; student U. Va., 1956-58, Columbia U., 1959-61; m. Patricia Ann Trent, Dec. 8, 1973; 1 son by previous marriage, Peter Scoville. Asst. to controller Laird & Co., N.Y.C., 1961-63; asst. to purchaser charge ops. Goldman Sachs, N.Y.C., 1963-64; mgr. new bus. dept. B.J. Herkimer Co., N.Y.C., 1964-67; divisional policy and procedures adminstr. Paine, Webber, Jackson & Curtis, Inc., N.Y.C., 1967-70, asst. to exec. cashier, 1970-73, asst. v.p., mgr. employment services, adminstr. equal employment opportunity, 1973-80; personnel officer, exec. recruiter N.Y. Stock Exchange, 1980-86; mgr. employment N.Y. Stock Exchange, sr. v.p. Wesley Brown & Bartle, 1986-87; sr. v.p., dir. Alliance Mktg., Inc., 1987; ptnr. Richards & Wells, 1988—. Cons. human affairs Gracie Sq. Hosp. Served with AUS, 1958. Mem. SAR, Phi Kappa Psi. Home: 449 E 78th St New York NY 10021 Office: 20 E 46th St Rm 903 New York NY 10017

WELLS, RICHARD A., electronics company executive; b. Houston, June 9, 1943; s. Odell A. and Murrie B. (Scallorn) W.; m. Sue Ellen Juel, Aug. 23, 1964; children: Anne Elizabeth, Robert Martin. BA, U. Tex., 1964; MS, U. Ill., 1969. Flight contr. IBM/NASA, Houston, 1964-67; mem. faculty U. Ill., Urbana, 1967-70; with Gould Inc., Boston, 1970-72, Cleve., 1972-77; founder, pres., chief exec. officer KMW Systems, Austin, Tex., 1977—. Contbr. articles to profl. jours. Trustee Laguna Gloria Art Found., Austin, 1984—; mem. Austin Econ. Devel. Commn., 1987, Technology Industry Legis. Task Force, 1986—. Mem. Nat. Computer Graphics Assn., Assn. of Computing Machinery, Austin C. of C. (bd. dirs. 1988—), Mensa. Clubs: Lost Creek, Hills, Lakeway (Austin). Office: KMW Systems Corp 100 Shepherd Mountain Pla Austin TX 78730

WELLS, RICHARD H., hotel company executive; b. Stillwater, Okla., June 24, 1940; s. James R. and Edna Ruth (McKnight) W.; children: Shanley Renne, Richard Carlyle, Amy Luru. B.S. in Gen. Bus., Okla. State U., 1964. Sr. fin. analyst Conoco, Houston, 1964-69; v.p. planning Union Planters Nat. Bank, Memphis, 1969-75; v.p. fin. planning Inn devel. Holiday Inns, Memphis, 1975-78, v.p. corp. adminstrn., 1979-80; sr. v.p. planning-adminstrn. Harrah's, Reno, 1980-86; v.p. Bally's Casino Hotels, Reno, 1986—. Mem. Rno Downtown Redevel. Com., 1982-83. Served with USAR, 1958-61. Mem. Reno C. of C. (dir. 1983), Fin. Exec.s Inst. (pres. 1977-78). Home: PO Box 3781 Reno NV 89504

WELLS, ROGER, architect, land planner; b. Bournemouth, Dorset, Eng., June 6, 1941; came to U.S., 1947; s. James Sidney and Cecil (Dundas Mouat) W.; m. Sandra Joy Bradford, June 15, 1963; children: Heather G., Andrew B., Sara S. BS in Plant Scis., Rutgers U., 1963; MArch with honors, U. Pa., 1966, M of Land Architecture, 1976. Registered architect and profl. planner, N.J. Prin. Rahenkamp Sachs Wells Inc., Phila., 1964-79; pres. Roger Wells Inc., Haddonfield, N.J., 1979—; tchr. architecture Drexel U., Phila., 1970-72, Rutgers U., New Brunswick, N.J, 1972, U. Pa., Phila., 1974-87; lectr. in field. Contbr. articles to profl. jours. Trustee Haddonfield Devel. Co. 1969-70; profl. advisor Camden County Parks Commn., 1971; mem. Haddonfield Zoning Bd., 1981—, chmn. 1988. Recipient State Merit award Pa.-Del. Soc. Landscape Architects, 1979; named Alumni of Yr., Rutgers U., 1979. mem. Am. Soc. Landscape Architects (Nat. Merit award 1972, 74, Nat. Honor award 1986), N.J. Soc. Landscape Architects (pres. 1985-87, State Merit award 1985-86), Am. Inst. Cert. Planners, Am. Planning Assn. Club: S.O.V. (Phila.) (sec. 1984—). Office: 132 Haddon Ave Haddonfield NJ 08033

WELLS, RONA LEE, consumer products company executive; b. Beaumont, Tex., Aug. 23, 1950; d. Ray Peveto and Frances (Manning) Reed; m. Harry Hankins Wells, Mar. 22, 1975. BS in Systems Engrng, So. Meth. U., 1972. Registered profl. engr., Tex. With initial mgmt. devel. program Southwestern Bell Corp., Houston, 1972-73, engr. and inventory coord., 1973-74, sr. engr. supr., 1974-75, engrng. project supr., 1975-77, dist. supr. maj. project, 1977-79, dist. supr. materials, 1979; mgr. field svcs. CNA Fin. Corp., Chgo., 1979-80, mgr., asst. to v.p., 1980, area mgr. support svcs., 1980-82, area mgr. acctg. svcs., 1982; dir. bldg. and office mgmt. Kimberly-Clark, Neenah, Wis., 1982-85; ops. specialist Kimberly-Clark, New Milford, Conn., 1985-86, acting supt., 1985, project leader, 1985-88, ops. mgr., 1988—. Mem. Nat. Def. Exec. Res., Washington, 1979—; bd. dirs. Faulkner County United Way, 1989—. Named one of Outstanding Young Women of Am., 1988. Mem. Inst. Indsl. Engrs. (sr.), Soc. Women Engrs. (sr.), NSPE, NAFE, Sigma Tau. Home: 60 Richland Hills Conway AR 72032 Office: Kimberly-Clark Corp 480 Exchange Conway AR 72032

WELLS, WILLIAM STEVEN, marketing communications consultant, syndicated cartoonist; b. Detroit, Aug. 19, 1945; s. Ronald and Eleanor (Vancea) W.; m. Mary Rudolph, Nov. 27, 1969; children: Adam, David. AB, Hamilton Coll., 1967. Journalist New Haven Register, Providence Jour., Detroit Free Press, 1968-75; exec. asst. to Mich. Gov. William Milliken, Lansing, 1975-76; account exec. Fleishman-Hillard, Inc., St. Louis, 1976-78; v.p., mgr. Doremus & Co., Mpls., 1978-80; sr. v.p., mng. dir. Hill & Knowlton, Inc., Mpls., 1980-84; pres. Wells and Co., 1984-87; chmn., chief exec. officer Wells and Miller, Mpls., 1988—; co-author syndicated bus. cartoon strip Executive Suite, United Features Syndicate. Contbr. articles to profl. jours. Served with USNR, 1968-69. Mem. Nat. Investor Relations Inst., Issues Mgmt. Assn. Republican. Clubs: Mpls., Edina Country, Minn. Squash Raquets Assn. Office: Wells and Miller 250 Thresher Square W 700 S Third St Minneapolis MN 55415

WELNA, MICHAEL JEROME, video company owner; b. Mpls., Jan. 12, 1958; s. Jerome Lawrence and Margaret Jeanne (Sauber) W. Student, U. Minn., 1983. Mgr. Pizza Hut, St. Paul, 1983-84, Ground Round Restaurant, Mpls., 1984; mgr. internat. ops. Video Update, Inc., St. Paul, 1984-85; gen. mgr. Video Update, Inc., Kuala Lumpur, Malaysia, 1986; owner Video Update, Inc., Edina, Minn., 1988—, Mpls., 1988—; gen. mgr. Eksum Trebor, Ltd., Mpls., 1986—; owner Welnel, Inc. dba Video Update, Plymouth, Minn., 1988—; productivity cons. Directorate Pub. Rds., Oslo, 1982; mem. energy conservation research team No. States Power Co., Mpls., 1982. Sponsor Children Internat., Bangkok, 1986—. Mem. Internat. Assn. of Students in Econs. and Commerce. Democrat. Roman Catholic. Home: 412 5th St NE Waseca MN 56093 Office: 5055 France Ave S Minneapolis MN 55410

WELS, RICHARD HOFFMAN, lawyer; b. N.Y.C., May 3, 1913; s. Isidor and Belle (Hoffman) W.; m. Marquerite Samet, Dec. 12, 1954; children: Susan, Amy. A.B., Cornell, 1933; LL.B., Harvard U., 1936; postgrad., U. Ariz., 1944. Bar: N.Y. 1936. Spl. asst. dist. atty. N.Y. Co., 1936-37; assoc. Handel & Panuch, N.Y.C., 1937-38; mem. legal staff, asst. to chmn. SEC, Washington, 1938-42; spl. asst. atty. gen. U.S. and spl. asst. U.S. atty., 1941-42; spl. counsel Com. Naval Affairs, U.S. Ho. of Reps., 1943, Sea-Air Commn., Nat. Fedn. Am. Shipping, 1946; trustee, sec. William Alanson White Inst. Psychiatry, N.Y.C., 1946—; vice. chmn., dir. Am. Parents Com.; mem. Moss & Wels, 1946-57, Moss, Wels & Marcus, 1957-68, Sulzberger, Wels & Marcus, 1968-72, Moss, Wels & Marcus, 1972-78, Sperry, Weinberg, Wels, Waldman & Rubenstein, 1979-84; ptnr. Wels & Zerin, 1985—; gen. counsel Bowling Proprs. Assn. Am., 1956-67, N.Y. State Bowling Proprs. Assn., Am. Acad. Psychoanalysis; commr. Interprofl. Comn. on Marriage and Div.; lectr. Practising Law Inst.; dir. H-R Television, Inc., Belgrave Capital Corp., Broadcast Data Base, Inc., Belgrave Securities Corp.; chmn. bd. govs. Islands Research Found.; bd. govs., chmn., trustee Daytop Village, Inc.; chmn. bd. trustees Bleuler Psychotherapy Center; trustee N.Y. State Sch. Psychiatry, Margaret Chase Smith Library, Skowhegan, Maine. Co-author: Sexual Behavior and the Law; bd. editors Family Law Quar.; contbr. articles to profl. jours. Vice chmn. Am. Jewish Com., now mem. nat. exec. bd. Served from ensign to lt. USNR, 1942-46; mem. staff Under Sec. Forrestal, 1943-44; in 1944-46, P.T.O. Mem. ABA (fin. officer, mem. council Am. family law sect.), N.Y. State Bar Assn. (chmn. family law sect.), N.Y. City Bar Assn., Am. Acad. Matrimonial Lawyers (gov.), Am. Legion, Naval Order U.S., Mil. Order World Wars, Fed. Bar Assn., Res. Officers Assn., Assn. I.C.C. Practitioners, Fed. Communications Bar Assn., Pi Lambda Phi, Sphinx Head. Clubs: Harmonie (gov.), Harvard, Cornell (N.Y.C.); Nat. Lawyers (Washington); Sunningdale Country (Scarsdale, N.Y.), Statler (Ithaca, N.Y.). Home: 480 Park Ave New York NY 10022 Office: Wels & Zerin 55 E 59th St New York NY 10022

WELSH, JUDSON BOOTH, banker; b. Rochester, N.Y., Oct. 22, 1945; s. Frederic Sager and Helen (Groves) W. BA in Econs., St. Lawrence U., 1964-67; M in Internat. Mgmt., Thunderbird Grad. Sch. Internat. Mgmt., 1972-73. Statistician, Eastman Kodak, Ltd., London, 1966; ter. rep. Eastman Kodak Co., Rochester, 1970-73; asst. v.p. Chem. Bank Internat., 1973-77, founder Chem. Bank Rep. Office, regional rep. W. Africa, Abidjan, Ivory Coast, 1977-79; asst. v.p. 1st Nat. Bank of Boston, 1980-86; founderBoston Bank Cameroon, 1979-81; fin. cons., gen. mgr. Flightways, 1982-83 ; asst. v.p. Africa div., Fidelity Bank Phila., London, 1986—; dir. Buildis S.A., Geneva; founder Buildis, Sarl, Abidjan; fin. cons. Banque Nationale d'Epargne et du Credit, Abidjan, 1984-85; leader seminars for W. African nations; advisor West Africa chpt. Internat. Exec. Service Corps. Served to lt. USN, 1967-70, Vietnam. Decorated D.S.M. (Vietnam). Mem. Am. Mgmt. Assn., Airplane Owners and Pilots Assn. Acad. Polit. Sci., Table Round Abidjan (charter). Author internat. credit seminar. Home: 31 Fitzjames Ave, London W14, England Office: Fidelity Bank Phila/Africa div, 1 Bishopsgate, London EC2 N3AB, England

WELSH, NOEL RICHARD, financial planning executive; b. Cleve., Dec. 25, 1938; s. George Dallas and Kathryn Marie (Needham) W.; m. Maureen Frances O'Brien, Aug. 13, 1960 (div. May 1980); children: Sharon Marie, Laura Noelle, David Edward. Cert. fin. planner. Mgr. for annuity cos. Ohio and Tex., 1965-70; resident mgr. Anchor Nat. Fin. Services Inc., Houston, 1970—; prin. Welsh Capital Planning Inc., Houston, 1970—. Pres. bd. dirs. Unity Ch. of Christianity, Houston, 1985-87. Served to capt. USAF, 1959-65. Mem. Inst. Cert. Fin. Planners, Houston Chpt. Internat. Assn. for Fin. Planning (bd. mem. and officer 1985—). Republican. Home: 1616 Prairie Mark Houston TX 77077 Office: Welsh Capital Planning Inc 10333 Richmond Suite 660 Houston TX 77042

WELTER, WILLIAM MICHAEL, marketing and advertising executive; b. Evanston, Ill., Nov. 18, 1946; s. Roy Michael and Frances (DeShields) W.; m. Pamela Bassett, June 11, 1971; children: Barclay, Robert Michael. BS, Mo. Valley Coll., 1966. Account exec. Leo Burnett Co., Inc., Chgo., 1966-74; v.p., account supr. Needham Harper Worldwide, Chgo., 1974-80; v.p. mktg. Wendy's Internat., Inc., Dublin, Ohio, 1981, sr. v.p. mktg., 1981-84, exec. v.p., 1984-87; owner, chief exec. officer Haunty & Welter Mktg./Advt. Cons. Co., Worthington, Ohio, 1987—. Founder Santa's Silent Helpers, Columbus, Ohio, 1985. Mem. Ad Fedn. Columbus, Scioto Country Club, Muirfield Country Club, Lakes Golf and Country Club, The Lakes Golf and Country Club. Home: 4311 Woodhall Rd Columbus OH 43220 Office: Haunty & Welter 7700 Rivers Edge Dr Worthington OH 43235

WELTON, KATHLEEN ANN, editor, publisher; b. Santa Monica, Calif., Apr. 10, 1956; d. Gregory Clifford and Ruth Marlene (Coggan) W. BA, Stanford U., 1978. Sales rep. D. Van Nostrand, San Francisco, 1978-79, sales supr., 1979-80; bus. editor D. Van Nostrand, N.Y.C., 1980-81, Praeger Pubs., N.Y.C., 1981-82; sr. editor Dow Jones-Irwin Inc., Homewood, Ill., 1982-87; exec. editor Longman Group USA, Chgo., 1987—. Recipient Stanford Assocs. Outstanding Achievement award, 1982. Republican. Club: Stanford of Ill. Home: 6007 N Sheridan Rd Chicago IL 60660 Office: Longman Fin Svcs Inst 520 N Dearborn Chicago IL 60610

WELTON, ROBERT BREEN, aircraft manufacturing company executive; b. Waterbury, Conn., Mar. 21, 1938; s. Robert Smithwick and Marian (Munson) W.; m. Mary E. Hardt, Jan. 7, 1961; children: Lori, Cheryl, Kathryn. Student, Bentley Sch. Acctg. and Fin., Waltham, Mass., 1957; BS, Quinnipiac Coll., 1961. CPA, Conn. With Simon Co., Madison, Ga. and Watertown, Conn., 1961-73; sr. v.p., treas. Hangar One, Inc., Atlanta, 1973-84, Beech Holdings, Inc. (subs. Beech Aircraft Corp.), Wichita, Kans., 1984—; asst. controller comml. mktg. Beech Aircraft Corp., Wichita, 1987—. Mem. Nat. Assn. Accts. (v.p. local chpt. 1970). Republican. Roman Catholic. Lodge: Rotary. Office: Beech Aircraft Corp 9709 E Central PO Box 85 Wichita KS 67201

WELTY, WILLIAM JOHN, transportation executive, accountant; b. Dixon, Ill., Nov. 16, 1945; m. Judy L. Welty; children: Kelly, Bryce. BS in Acctg., No. Ill. U. CPA, Ill. Sr. auditor Coopers & Lybrand, Rockford, Ill., 1969-72; plant controller Walton Products Co., Atlantic, Iowa, 1972-73; mfg. group controller Caron Internat., Inc., Rochelle, Ill., 1973-77; asst. controller U.S. Reduction Co., E. Chgo., Ind., 1977-79; corp. controller Allied Van Lines, Inc., Broadview, Ill., 1979-82, v.p. fin., chief fin. officer, 1982—; Mem. tax adv. panel Am. Movers Conf. Vol. YMCA-sponsored basketball. With USNG. Mem. AICPA, Ill. Soc. CPA's, Am. Trucking Assn. (household goods dir. Nat. Acctg. & Fin. Council). Office: Allied Van Lines Inc 2120 S 25th Ave Broadview IL 60153

WEN, TIEN KUANG, real estate executive; b. Meihsien, China, Feb. 11, 1924; M.A., Columbia U., 1950, LLD Marquis Found., 1988; m. Chong Chook Yew, Dec. 24, 1946; children—Ming Kang, Sui Han, Chiu Chi, Hsia Min. Sec., Chinese C. of C., Chinese Mining Assn., 1952-55; Chinese mgr. Banque de L'Indochine, Kuala Lumpur, 1958-71; chmn. Selangor Properties Ltd., Kuala Lumpur, 1963—, Chong Chook Yew Sdn. Bhd., TK Wen & Co. Sdn. Bhd., and Bungsar Hill Holdings Sdn. Bhd.; mng. dir. Pusat Bandar Damansara Sdn. Bhd., Damansara Devel. Sdn. Bhd. Chmn., Malayan Public Library Assn., 1957—, others; CD World U. Conf., 1984, hon. chmn. Tung Shin Hosp., justice of peace. Decorated D.P.M.P., Sultan of Perak, 1966; P.S.M., King, 1984. Mem. Basketball Assn. (hon.chmn.), Table Tennis Assn. (hon. chmn.), Kayin Assn., (hon. chmn.), Kwantung Assn. (gov. com.). Home: 33A Jalan Balau, Damansara Heights, Kuala Lumpur Malaysia Office: 6A Jalan Batai, Damansara Heights, Kuala Lumpur Malaysia

WENCKUS, JAMES R., insurance executive; b. Chgo., Feb. 28, 1941; m. Patricia A. Renner; children: Jeffry, Jacey. BA, Miami U., Oxford, Ohio, 1963; postgrad., Aurora Coll., 1964. CPCU. Tchr. Aurora (Ill.) Pub. Schls., 1964-67; underwriting supr. Farmers Ins., Aurora, 1967-72; underwriting mgr. Prudential Prop. & Casualty, Oakbrook, Ill., 1972-75; sales mgr. Farmers Ins., Dupage County, Ill., 1975-77, Phoenix, Ariz., 1977-82; v.p. mktg. Mid-Am. Preferred, North Kansas City, Mo., 1982-84; with Country Cos., Bloomington, Ill., 1984-85, v.p. agy., 1985—. Mem. Soc. CPCUs, Nat. Assn. Life Underwriters. Club: Toastmasters. Office: Country Cos 1701 Towanda Ave Bloomington IL 61701

WENDEBORN, RICHARD DONALD, manufacturing company executive; b. Winnipeg, Man., Can.; came to U.S., 1976; s. Curtis and Rose (Lysecki) W.; m. Dorothy Ann Munn, Aug. 24, 1957; children: Margaret Gayle, Beverly Jane, Stephen Richard, Peter Donald, Ann Elizabeth. Diploma, Colo. Sch. Mines, 1952; grad., Advanced Mgmt. Program, Harvard, 1975. With Canadian Ingersoll-Rand Co., Montreal, 1952—; gen. mgr., v.p., dir. Canadian Ingersoll-Rand Co., 1968, pres., 1969-74, chmn. bd., 1976—; exec. v.p. Ingersoll-Rand Co., Woodcliff Lake, N.J., 1976—; bd. dirs. IR Can., IR Holdings-U.K., Calif. Pellet Mill; mem. Can. Govt. Oil and Gas Tech. Exchange Program with USSR, 1972—, Minerals and Metals Mission to Peoples Republic China, 1972—. Mem. Resource Fund Colo. Sch. Mines. Recipient Disting. Achievement medal Colo. Sch. Mines, 1973. Mem. Machinery and Equipment Mfrs. Assn. Can. (dir. 1974—, past chmn.), Tau Beta Pi. Home: 34 Grist Mill Ln Upper Saddle River NJ 07458 Office: Ingersoll-Rand Co 200 Chestnut Ridge Rd Woodcliff Lake NJ 07675

WENDEL, FAYE F., coin equipment manufacturing executive; b. Newark, Sept. 16, 1928; d. John Thomas and Sara Rose (Agliozzo) Fiorenza; m. Daniel C. Wendel, Nov. 26, 1949; children—Catherine C., Daniel C. III, Wayne J. Sec., P. Ballantine & Sons, Newark, 1946-49; head hostess, asst. to mgr. Bambergers-Carriage House Restaurant, 1971-74; sec. Peter Wendel & Sons, Inc., Irvington, N.J., 1961-78; sec. Wendel Industries, Inc., Union, N.J., 1978-80, pres., 1980—; pres. D.C. Wendel Corp., 1982—. Tchrs. aide St. Ann Sch.; asst. treas. Ladies Aux. St. Rose of Lima Ch., 1963. Mem. Short Hills Assn., Twig Group of Overlook Hosp., Rotary Assn., Am. Soc. Profl. and Exec. Women. Clubs: Republican, Short Hills Racquet. Home: 33 Quaker Rd Short Hills NJ 07078 Office: 1012 Greeley Ave N Union NJ 07083

WENDELBOE, JOHN H., investment banker; b. Warren, Pa., Apr. 20, 1941; s. N. Plue and Elisabeth (Eaton) W.; m. Susan Toettcher, Mar. 14, 1970; 1 child, Adam H.T. BA in Econs., Coll. of Wooster, 1963; MBA, U. Mich., 1967. Asst. cashier Citibank, N.Y.C., 1967-70; chief operating officer Datacraft Corp., Ft. Lauderdale, Fla., 1970-71; sr. v.p. J. Henry Schroder Bank & Trust, N.Y.C., 1971-82; pres. Baring Bros. Inc., N.Y.C., 1982—; bd. dirs. Landauer Assocs., N.Y.C., P.C. Leasing Co., South Norwalk, Conn. Mem. Brit.-Am. C. of C. (bd. dirs. 1978—). Office: Baring Bros Inc 450 Park Ave New York NY 10022

WENDT, EDWARD GEORGE, JR., insurance company executive; b. Yonkers, N.Y., Apr. 20, 1928; student Roanoke Coll., 1946-47; A.B., U. Mich., 1949; m. Teresa C. Maziarz; children—Sally, Suzanne, Jason, Edward George III, Joseph Alexander, Colin Anthony. With N.Y. Life Ins. Co., N.Y.C., 1949—, asst. actuary, 1956-59, asst. v.p., 1959-63, actuary, 1963-66, 2d v.p., actuary, 1966-72, v.p., group actuary, 1972-77, sr. v.p., 1977—, vice chmn., chief exec. officer corp. med. mgmt.; exec. v.p. Sanus Corp. Health Systems. Chartered Life Underwriter. Fellow Soc. Actuaries. Home: 200 E 66th St New York NY 10021 Office: NY Life Ins Co 51 Madison Ave New York NY 10010

WENDT, ELIZABETH WARCZAK, insurance company executive; b. Chgo., Aug. 27, 1931; d. John George and Elizabeth Marion (Jankowski) Warczak; m. John Edward Wendt, Oct. 31, 1953 (div.); children: John Alan, Brian Arthur, James Michael. Student Loyola U., Chgo., 1951-52; BSBA, St. Mary-of-the-Woods Coll., 1980; postgrad. Chgo. Kent Coll. Law, 1981-82. Asst. to actuary Globe Life Ins. Co., Chgo., 1970-74; asst. compliance officer Globe Life/Ryan Ins. Group, Chgo., 1974-86; mgr. credit product devel., 1986—; mem. FLMI Soc. Chgo., 1983—; co. rep. Consumer Credit Ins. Assn., Chgo., 1983—; co. rep., mem. Handout Com. Life & Health Compliance Assn., 1979—. Election judge, 1984—. Mem. United Farm Workers Support Com., Chgo. Fellow Life Mgmt. Inst.; mem. Inst. Distaff Execs. Assn., Nat. Assn. Ins. Women (dir. Chgo. chpt. 1981-82). Democrat. Roman Catholic. Home: 7341 Canterbury Pl Downers Grove IL 60516

WENDT, GARY CARL, finance company executive; b. Portage, Wis., Mar. 13, 1942; s. Walter Carl and Dorothy Mae (Neesam) W.; m. Lorna Joyce Jorgenson, July 31, 1965; 1 dau., Sarah Rachel. B.S. in Civil Engring., U. Wis., 1965; M.B.A., Harvard U., 1967. V.p. La. Co. Inc., Houston, 1967-71, Diversified Advisor, Miami, 1971-75; v.p. Gen. Electric Credit Corp., Stamford, Conn., 1976-84, exec. v.p., dir., 1984-86; pres., chief exec. officer Gen. Electric Capital Corp. (formerly Gen. Electric Credit Corp.), Stamford, Conn., 1986—; pres. Gen. Electric Fin. Services, 1986—; bd. dirs. Kidder Peabody Group, Polaris Aircraft, Inc., Trafalger Developers, Miami, 1976-81, Astrodomain Corp., Houston, 1976-78, Puritan Ins. Co., Providence, 1981—; chmn. bd. Aquisition Funding Corp., Stamford, Conn., 1981—. Bd. dirs. Southwestern Conn. Comml. and Indsl. Orgn., 1986—; chmn. Stanford United Way Campaign, 1986; councilman St. John's Luth. Ch., Stamford, 1977—. Mem. Am. Assn. Lessors (planning com. 1981—), Tau Beta Pi, Phi Kappa Phi, Chi Epsilon, Delta Epsilon. Lutheran. Club: Landmark (Stamford, Conn.). Office: GE Capital Corp 570 Lexington Ave New York NY 10022 *

WENDT, GREGORY ALLEN, banker; b. Sunbury, Pa., Feb. 15, 1963; s. John David and Carol Elizabeth (Jorstad) W. AAS, Williamsport Area Community Coll., 1983; BS cum laude, Millersville U., 1985. Staff trainee No. Cen. Bank, Williamsport, Pa., 1985-86; loan officer I No. Cen. Bank, Lewisburg, Pa., 1986-87; asst. community office mgr. No. Cen. Bank, Montoursville, Pa., 1987—. Recipient Bus. Mgmt. Faculty award Williamsport Area Community Coll., 1983. Mem. Am. Bankers Assn. Republican. Methodist. Lodge: Rotary (dir. 1988—). Home: 1710 Rear Four Mile Dr Williamsport PA 17701 Office: No Cen Bank 450 Broad St Montoursville PA 17754

WENDT, HENRY, III, pharmaceutical company executive; b. Neptune City, N.J., July 19, 1933; s. Henry II and Rachel L. (Wood) W.; m. Holly Peterson, June 23, 1956; children: Henry IV, Laura. AB, Princeton U., 1955. With Smith, Kline & French Labs, Phila., 1955-70, v.p. mktg., gen. mgr., 1970-71; pres., chief operating officer Smith Kline Corp., Phila., 1971-76, also bd. dirs.; chief exec. officer SmithKline Beckman Corp., Phila., 1982-87, pres., 1982, chmn., 1987—; bd. dirs. ARCO; dir. Asia-Pacific ops. Louis A. Allen Assn., 1967-70; chmn. U.S. -Japan Bus. Council. Contbr. articles to profl. jours. Bd. dirs. Phila. Contributionship; trustee Phila. Mus. Art; mem. adv. council dept. East Asian studies Princeton U. Mem. The Bus. Roundtable, ARCO (bd. dirs.). Club: Phila. Merion Cricket. Office: SmithKline Beckman Corp 1 Franklin Pla Philadelphia PA 19101

WENDT, THOMAS GENE, controller; b. Watertown, Wis., May 14, 1951; s. Walter Harry and Gladys Florence (Munzel) W. BBA, U. Wis., Whitewater, 1973. CPA, Wis. Auditor Coopers & Lybrand, Milw., 1973-75; supr. Conley, McDonald, Sprague & Co., Milw., 1975-80; dir. fin. E. Cen./Select Sires, Waupun, Wis., 1981—, also rec. sec., bd. dirs.; bd. dirs. Moravian Homes Inc., Mueller Apartments Inc. Bd. dirs. Marquardt Meml. Manor, Inc., Watertown, Wis., 1985—, sec. and treas. bd. dirs., 1986—; bd. dirs. Marquardt Found., 1988—, forward campaihn chmn., 1988; pres. bd. trustees Watertown Moravian Ch., 1981-84; adv. del. Western Dist. Synod, Wis., 1982, 86. Mem. Am. Inst. CPA's, Wis. Inst. CPA's, Milw. Art Mus. Office: E Central/Select Sires PO Box 191 Waupun WI 53963

WENDZEL, ALTON CHARLES, fruit and produce grower, processor and shipper; b. Watervliet, Mich., July 30, 1930; s. Robert G. and Pauline (Roekle) W.; m. Mildred Janke, Aug. 14, 1954; children—Gregory (dec.), Bradley, Jill Anne. Fruit and produce grower, Watervliet, 1950-60; owner Greg Orchards Farm, Watervliet, 1962—; pres. Greg Orchards & Produce, Inc., Millburg, Mich., 1979—; pres. Coloma Frozen Foods, Inc. (Mich.), 1978—; dir. Peoples State Bank, St. Joseph, Mich. Mem. Internat. Apple Inst. (exec. bd., v.p., pres. 1982, chmn. bd. 1984), United Fresh Fruit and Vegetable Assn., Canners and Freezers Assn., Farm Bur., Mich. Agrl. Coop. Mktg. Assn. Mich. State Hort. Soc. (v.p., bd. dirs. 1988, pres. 1989). Republican. Lutheran. Club: Lions. Office: Greg Orchards Produce Inc 4949 N Branch Rd Benton Harbor MI 49022

WENK, DENNIS CHARLES, insurance company executive; b. Evergreen Park, Ill., Apr. 6, 1952; s. Charles Martin and Barbara Jean (Timmons) W.; m. Manette Jean McReynolds, May 14, 1978; children: Marissa Ann, Natalie Mary. Student Coe Coll., 1970-72; A.A. in Bus. and data processing, Moraine Valley Community Coll., 1974; B.S. in Computer Sci., No. Ill. U., 1977, M.B.A. in Fin. and Acctg., 1985. Cert. systems profl.; cert. data processor; cert. info. systems auditor. Programmer, analyst Allied Mills, Inc., Chgo., 1977-78; sr. cons. Consumer Systems, Oakbrook, Ill., 1978-79; acct. mgr. C.B.M., Schaumburg, Ill., 1979-80; EDP audit cons. Beatrice Cos., Chgo., 1980-82; mgr. data ctr. Zurich-Am. Inst. Co., Schaumburg, Ill., 1982-86; v.p. info. processing Heller Fin., Chgo., 1986—; pres., chief exec. officer Disaster Avoidance and Recovery Services, Inc., Arlington Heights, Ill., 1988—. Author: Management Accounting for MIS; contbr. articles to profl. jours. Mem. Assn. Computing Machinery, Computer Measurement Group. Avocations: tennis, racketball, volleyball, golf, skiing. Home: 201 Bryant Ave Glen Ellyn IL 60137

WENNERHOLM, ROY, JR., manufacturing executive; b. 1931. BSEE, San Jose State Coll., 1959; postgrad., UCLA, 1962. With N.Am. Aviation, 1962-66; chief engring. United Aircraft Corp., 1966-69; with Litton Industries, 1969-72; pres. Wheelabrator-Frye Inc., 1973; with Joy Mfg. Co., 1973-79; pres., chief operating officer Ecolaire Inc., 1979-85, chmn. bd. dirs., 1985-87; chmn., pres. Joy Techs. Inc., Pitts., 1987—, chief exec. officer, also dir. With USAF, 1951-54. Office: Joy Mfg Co Coal Machinery Group 120 Liberty St Franklin PA 16323 *

WENTZ, HOWARD BECK, JR., manufacturing company executive; b. Pitts., Jan. 10, 1930; s. Howard and Emmy Lou W.; m. Judith Ann Blough, June, 1958; children: Howard, Roger, Elizabeth. B.S.E., Princeton U., 1952; M.B.A., Harvard U., 1957. Mfg. exec. TRW Corp., 1957-60; assoc. Robert Heller and Assocs., Cleve., 1960-63; exec. v.p. Paterson-Leitch Co., Cleve., 1963-69; pres. Duff-Norton subs. Amstar Corp., Charlotte, N.C., 1969-72; corp. v.p. parent co. Duff-Norton subs. Amstar Corp., N.Y.C., 1972-79; exec. v.p. Duff-Norton subs. Amstar Corp., 1979-81; chief operating officer Amstar Corp., 1979-81, pres., 1981—, chief exec. officer, 1982—, chmn., 1983—, also bd. dirs.; dir. Am. European Reins. Co., Skandia Corp., Hudson Ins. Corp., Colgate-Palmolive Co., Crompton & Knowles Corp. Served with USN, 1952-55. Office: Amstar Corp 1251 Avenue of the Americas New York NY 10020 *

WENTZ, THEODORE EMORY, heavy equipment manufacturing company executive; b. Pitts., Aug. 10, 1931; s. Welker Wallace and Kathryn Ebberts) W.; B.A. cum laude, Amhest Coll., 1953; B.S. magna cum laude, U. Buffalo, 1958, M.B.A., 1960; m. Eleanor Frances Donald, July 23, 1955; 1 child, Donald Richard. Asso. cons. Touche Ross & Co., San Francisco, 1960-65; div. controller Varian Assos., Palo Alto, Calif., 1965-69; dir. fin. Symbolic Control, Inc., San Mateo, Calif., 1969-70; controller Clementina Ltd., San Francisco, 1971-73; dir. fin. Probe Systems, Inc., Sunnyvale, Calif., 1973-76; v.p. fin. Viking Industries, Inc., Chatsworth, Calif., 1976-78; chief fin. officer Calavar Corp., Santa Fe Springs, Calif., 1979-80; v.p. fin. Web Press Corp., Seattle. Served with USNR, 1953-55. C.P.A., Calif. Mem. Calif. Soc. C.P.A.s, Calif. C.P.A. Found. Edn. and Research. Home and Office: 20850 NE 26th Pl Redmond WA 98053

WERBIN, STANLEY RUSSELL, music store owner; b. Bklyn., May 9, 1947; s. Joseph and Lillian (Behrman) W.; m. Sandra Lee Dykins, Sept. 12, 1987. BA in Biology, Queens Coll.-CUNY, 1969; MS in Biol. Chemistry, U. Mich., 1971. Co-owner Elderly Instruments Inc., East Lansing, Mich., 1972-75; sec., treas. Elderly Instruments Inc., Lansing and East Lansing, 1975-85, pres., 1985—. Mem. adv. bd. Guitar Player mag. Mem. Nat. Assn. Music Merchants. Office: Elderly Instruments Inc PO Box 14210 1100 N Washington Lansing MI 48901

WERCHOLUK, RICHARD ROBERT, insurance agency executive; b. Passaic, N.J., Nov. 30, 1954; s. Jerry and Marilyn (Zomack) W.; m. Louella Mae Shampang, July 25, 1981; 1 child, Amanda Lynn. Student, Broome Community Coll., Binghamton, N.Y., 1972-74, U. Md., Keflavik, Iceland, 1978-79, U. Hawaii, 1979-80, U. State N.Y., Albany, 1987-88. Charter pilot, instr. Fly Hawaii, Honolulu, 1977-79; chef Friars Inn, Binghamton, 1979-80; sales mgr. Empire Healthcare, Binghamton, 1980-81; large accounts exec. Sentry Ins., Albany, N.Y., 1981-84; mgr. assoc. accounts A.W. Lawrence & Co., Albany, 1984-85; sr. account exec. Jardine Ins. Brokers, Schenectady, N.Y., 1985-86; dir. sales Mang. Assocs., Albany, 1986-87; pres. S.A. Casale, Inc., Albany, 1987—. Contbr. articles to profl. jours. Served as sgt. USAF, 1972-77. Mem. Assn. Wall and Ceiling Industries Internat., N.Y. Restaurant Assn., Nat. Asbestos Council, Albany Life Underwriters, Profl. Ins. Agts., Ins. Mktg. Services Assn., N.Y. Ins. Wholesalers Assn., Mass. Mktg. Inst., Albany C. of C. (membership com. 1987—). Home: 32 Cheshire Pl Niskayuna NY 12309 Office: SA Casale Inc 1913 Central Ave Albany NY 12205

WERLE, MICHAEL JOSEPH, technology company executive; b. Washington, Apr. 13, 1940; s. Francis Bernard and Evelyn Mae (Case) W.; m. Patricia Marie Murray, Sept. 7, 1962; children: Kevin C., Keith M., Christina M. BSE, Va. Poly. Inst., 1963, MSE, 1965, PhD, 1968. Research engr. U.S. Naval Ordinance Lab., Silver Spring, Md., 1963-68; asst. prof. engring. Va. Poly. Inst. and State U., Blacksburg, 1968-71; assoc. prof. engring. U. Cin., 1971-75, prof. engring., 1975-77; mgr. United Techs. Research Ctr., East Hartford, Conn., 1977-87; dir. tech. acqusition United Techs. Corp., Hartford, Conn., 1988—. Contbr. articles to profl. jours.; patentee in field. Fellow AIAA (assoc.); mem. ASME, Tau Beta Pi, Omicron Delta Kappa, Phi Kappa Phi. Roman Catholic. Home: 4 Porter Dr West Hartford CT 06117 Office: United Techs Corp 1 Financial Plaza Hartford CT 06101

WERNER, DEBORAH SUE, automobile manufacturing company executive; b. Anderson, Ind., Nov. 9, 1955; d. William Ernest and Loretta Joyce (Stakel) W. BSBA, Cen. Mich. U., 1977; postgrad., Cornell U., 1987. Trainee Detroit Diesel Allison div. GM, Romulus, Mich., 1976-77; apprentice coord. Detroit Diesel Allison div. GM, Romulus, 1978-80; EEO rep. salary personnel rep. Detroit Diesel Allison div. GM, Detroit, 1980-82; area hire coord., ednl. cons. Consol. Personnel Ctrs., Detroit, 1982-84; staff asst. indsl. rels. staff Corp. Hdqrs., Detroit, 1984-86; work group mgr., labor rels. rep. Buick-Oldsmobile-Cadillac group GM, Lake Orion, Mich., 1984-86; orgnl. devel. cons. Chevrolet-Pontiac of Can. group GM, North Tarrytown, N.Y., 1984-86, supr. human resource devel., 1986—; guest prof. Marist Coll., Poughkeepsie, N.Y., 1988. Mem. continuing edn. adv. com. Marymount Coll. N.Y. State Grantee, 1987. Mem. Am. Soc. Tng. and Devel., EEO Forum Greater Detroit, Evadne, Alpha Kappa Psi. Republican. Methodist. Home: 107 Danbury Rd Apt 3 Ridgefield CT 06877 Office: GM CPC Group 199 Beekman Ave North Tarrytown NY 10591

WERNER, ELAINE CLAIRE, retail company executive; b. Cleve., July 20, 1951; d. Russell Howard and Martha Jane (Flatt) W. BA in Bus. and Retailing, Miami U., Oxford, Ohio, 1973. Merchandising trainee Marshall Field & Co., Skokie, Ill. and Chgo., 1970-72; merchandiser Abraham & Straus, Bklyn., 1973-75; mgr., merchandiser Emotional Outlet, Inc., N.Y.C., 1975—, chief operating officer, 1985-88; asst. store mgr. in merchandising Bonwit Teller, N.Y.C., 1988—; mem. faculty dept. continuing edn. Parsons Sch. Design, N.Y.C., 1988—. Vol. Bella Abzug campaigns, Geraldine Ferraro campaign; speaker, vol., fundraiser, lobbyist Nat. Abortion Rights Action League, N.Y.C., 1981—. Scholar Nat. Tea Co., 1969, PTO, 1969, Alpha Phi, 1973. Mem. Am. Women's Econ. Devel. Orgn. for Women in Bus. (seminar conf. participant 1984—), NOW (bd. dirs. N.Y.C. chpt.), Nat. Honor Soc. Home: 360 E 55th St New York NY 10022 Office: Bonwit Teller Trump Tower 4 E 57th St New York NY 10022

WERNER, JOANNE LOUCILLE, financial executive; b. Midland, Mich., Jan. 20, 1940; d. Ewald George and Martha (Yuchlal) W. AAS, Ea. Nazarene Coll., Quincy, Mass., 1972; BAS, Boston U., 1977; MBA, Suffolk U., Boston, 1979. Prog. asst. Dept. Def., Washington, 1966-68, budget analyst, 1968-70; budget analyst Dept. of Navy, Washington, 1970-72; budget analyst Gen. Svcs. Adminstrn., Boston, 1972-77, sr. budget analyst, 1977-79; sr. fin. mgmt. specialist HUD, Boston, 1979—. Editor newsletter Baystatement, 1980-81. With USNR. Sioux Falls Coll. grantee, 1959; named Sailor of Yr. USNR, 1985. Mem. Am. Soc. Women Accts. (bd. dirs. 1986-88). Democrat. Home: 1449 Quincy Shore Dr Quincy MA 02169 Office: US Dept HUD Office Pub Housing 10 Causeway St Boston MA 02222

WERNER, KENNETH PHILIP, banker; b. Bay Shore, N.Y., May 23, 1957; s. Gustave Sigurd and Sally (Ragonesi) W.; m. Deborah Ann Nakasian, June 14, 1986; 1 child, Michael Philip. BS in Chemistry, Bucknell U., 1979; MBA in Mktg., SUNY, Albany, 1981. Ops. research analyst Ameritrust Co., Cleve., 1981-83, ops. officer, 1983-87, automatic teller machine mgr., 1987—. Mem. Beta Gamma Sigma. Home: 7942 Gallowae Ct Mentor OH 44060 Office: Ameritrust Co 900 Euclid Ave T 26 Cleveland OH 44115

WERNER, R(ICHARD) BUDD, business executive; b. Lorain, Ohio, Aug. 27, 1931; s. Paul Henry and Bessie Marie (Budd) W.; m. Janet Sue Kelsey, Aug. 28, 1932; children: Richard Budd, David Kelsey, Mary Paula. B.S. in Commerce, Ohio U., 1953. C.P.A. Sr. auditor Arthur Andersen & Co., Cleve., 1955-59; various fin. positions Glidden Co., Cleve., 1959-65; v.p., asst. treas. Harshaw div. Kewanee Oil Co., Cleve., 1965-72; v.p. finance, treas. Weatherhead Co., Cleve., 1973-77, Hauserman, Inc., Cleve., 1977-81; v.p. fin., chief fin. officer SPX Corp., Muskegon, Mich., 1981—; v.p. fin. Sealed Power Corp., Muskegon; trustee, chmn. fin. com. Sisters of Mercy Health Corp. Mem. Lakewood (Ohio) City Council, 1972-73. Served as lt. Q.M.C. U.S. Army, 1953-55. Mem. Fin. Execs. Inst., Mich. Soc. C.P.A.s. Clubs: Century, Muskegon Yacht, Muskegon Country, Spring Lake Country, Chgo. Athletic Assn. Home: Spring Lake MI 49456 Office: Sealed Power Corp 100 Terrace Plaza Muskegon MI 49443

WERNER, ROBERT ALLEN, finance company executive; b. Columbus, Ohio, June 17, 1946; s. Donald Edward and Dorothy (Cramer) W.; m. Sharon Ann Walters, Sept. 9, 1967; children: Jennifer Noel, Adam Kyle. BS, Ohio State U., 1968. CPA, Ohio. Auditor Peat, Marwick, Mitchell & Co., Columbus, 1968-69, 71-76; v.p. fin. Landmark, Inc., Columbus, 1976-85, Countrymark Inc. (merger with Landmark, 1985), Columbus, 1985—; bd. dirs. Landmark Inc., Columbus, 1985—, Silver Grove Fleeting, Silver Grove, Ky. Served to 1st lt. U.S. Army, 1969-71. Mem. Am. Inst. CPA's, Ohio Soc. CPA's, Nat. Soc. Accts. for Coops., Nat. Council Farmer Coops. Republican. Lutheran. Office: Countrymark Inc 4565 Columbus Pike Delaware OH 43015

WERNER, STUART LLOYD, business executive; b. N.Y.C., June 2, 1932; s. Leroy Louis and Frances Werner; B.Arch., Rensselaer Poly. Inst., 1954; children—Joan Leslie, Susan Lyn, Richard Wayne. Partner in charge architecture Werner-Dyer & Assos., Washington, 1959-68; v.p. Rentex Corp., Phila., 1968-70; pres. Werner & Assos., Inc., Washington, 1970-81; v.p. spl. projects ARA Services, Inc.; v.p. ARA, 1981-83; chmn. STN Computer Services, Inc., Falls Church, Va., 1983—; pres. Werner & Monk, Inc., 1984-87; mem. indsl. engring. terminology U.S. Standards Inst. Bd. dirs. Watergate South, Opera Soc., Friends of the Corcoran Gallery, Washington. Served with AUS, 1955-57. Mem. AIA, Am. Inst. Indsl. Engrs., Marinette Yacht Club, Masons,Tau Beta Pi. Republican. Contbr. articles to tech. jours. Home: 700 New Hampshire Ave NW Washington DC 20037 Office: STN Inc 5113 Leesburg Pike Falls Church VA 22041

WERNER, TERRY JOHN, insurance company executive; b. Huron, S.D., Feb. 24, 1949; s. Otto Walter and Catherine (Murphy) W.; m. Joan Marie Henmiller, Mar. 18, 1978; children: Katarina, Kristin. BA in Polit. Sci., Huron Coll., 1973; postgrad., U. Mont., 1974-78. Grizzly bear biologist State of Mont., Missoula, 1974-78; tchr. biology Columbia Falls (Mont.) Pub. Schs., 1978-80; gen. ins. agt. KC, Columbia Falls, 1980—. Mem. Northwestern Mont. Assn. Life Underwriters (bd. dirs. 1987-88), Nat. Assn. Fraternal Ins. Counselors, Gen. Agts. Mgrs. Conf. Democrat. Roman Catholic. Home: PO Box 1725 Columbia Falls MT 59912 Office: KC PO Box 1700 Columbia Falls MT 59912

WERRIES, E. DEAN, food distribution company executive; b. Tescott, Kans., May 8, 1929; s. John William and Sophie E. Werries; m. Marjean Sparling, May 18, 1962. B.S., U. Kans., 1952. With Fleming Foods Co., Topeka, 1955-81, exec. v.p., 1973-76; exec. v.p. Eastern ops. Fleming Foods Co., Phila., 1976-78; pres. Fleming Foods Co., Oklahoma City, 1978-81; pres., chief operating officer Fleming Cos., Inc., Oklahoma City, 1981-88, also dir.; pres., chief exec. officer Fleming Cos., Inc., 1988—. Served with U.S. Army, 1952-54, Korea. Mem. Nat. Am. Wholesale Grocers Assn. (bd. dirs. 1979—), Food Mktg. Inst. (bd. dirs. 1984—), Ind. Grocers Alliance (bd. dirs. 1984—). Republican. Presbyterian. Office: Fleming Cos Inc 6301 Waterford Blvd Oklahoma City OK 73118

WERTH, F. WILLIAM, manufacturing executive; b. Milw., Nov. 8, 1936; s. Francis Charles and Bernice Garnett (Luderus) W.; m. Mary Jo Hilgendorf, June 21, 1958 (div. 1971); children: Kathy J., Kelly J., Karen J., Kristin J.; m. Jolene Kay Stafford, Mar. 2, 1977. Grad. high sch., Milw. Apprentice L & W Tool, Milw., 1950-58; foreman Reed City (Mich.) Tool & Die Corp., 1958-69, pres., 1969-77, chief exec. officer, prin., 1977—. Mem. U.S. C. of C. Republican. Roman Catholic. Office: Reed City Tool & Die Corp 603 E Church St Reed City MI 49677

WERTHEIM, ROBERT HALLEY, national security consultant; b. Carlsbad, N.Mex., Nov. 9, 1922; s. Joseph and Emma (Vorenberg) W.; m. Barbara Louise Selig, Dec. 26, 1946; children: Joseph Howard, David Andrew. Student, N.Mex. Mil. Inst., 1940-42; B.S., U.S. Naval Acad., 1945; M.S. in Physics, M.I.T., 1954; postgrad., Harvard U., 1969. Commd. ensign U.S. Navy, 1945, advanced through grades to rear adm., 1972; assigned Spl. Projects Office, Washington, 1956-61, Naval Ordnance Test Sta., China Lake, 1961-62, Office Sec. Def., Washington, 1962-65; head Missile br. Strategic Systems Project Office, Washington, 1965-67; dep. tech. dir. Missile br. Strategic Systems Project Office, 1967-68, tech. dir., 1968-77, dir., 1977-80; sr. v.p. Lockheed Corp., 1981-88; cons. nat. def. 1988—; mem. Charles Stark Draper Lab., Inc.; mem. sci. adv. groups Def. Nuclear Agy., Def. Advanced Research Projects Agy. and Joint Strategic Target Planning Staff, Nat. Security Adv. Group, Los Alamos Nat. Lab., House Armed Svcs. Com. Def. Sci. Bd., Nat. Rsch. Coun. Decorated Legion of Merit, D.S.M. with cluster, Navy Commendation medal, Joint Service Commendation medal; recipient Rear Adm. William S. Parsons award Navy League U.S., 1971. Fellow AIAA; hon. mem. Am. Soc. Naval Engrs. (Gold Medal award 1972), Nat. Acad. Engring., U.S. Naval Inst., Nat. Acad. of Scis. (com. on internat. security and arms control), Army-Navy Country Club, Bernardo Heights Country Club, Cosmos, Masons, Sigma Xi, Tau Beta Pi. Home: 17705 Devereux Rd San Diego CA 92128 also: Sci Applications Internat Corp 10260 Campus Point Dr San Diego CA 92121

WERTHEIMER, THOMAS, film executive; b. N.Y.C., 1938. BA, Princeton U., 1960; LLB, Columbia U., 1963. V.p. bus. affairs subs. ABC, 1964-72; with MCA, Inc., Universal City, Calif., 1972—, v.p. Universal TV div., corp. v.p., 1974-83, exec. v.p., 1983—, also bd. dirs. Office: MCA Inc 100 Universal City Plaza Universal City CA 91608

WESCOTT, STEPHEN WALTER, financial planning company executive; b. Montclair, N.J., May 17, 1953; s. Ronald William and Janet Louise (Wardle) W.; m. Beverly Ann Carlson, May 29, 1976; children: Keith, Michelle. Cert. fin. planner. Salesman Fly Faire, Inc., Ft. Lee, N.J., 1973-76; sales mgr. Prudential Ins. Co., Clifton, N.J., 1976-79; ptnr., planner Changebridge Group, Inc., Montville, N.J., 1979-86; regional mgr. Fin. Network, Mountain Lake, N.J., 1986-87; dir. planning Du Frane Fin. Svcs., Morristown, N.J., 1987—; instr. Nat. Inst. Am., 1986—. With USNR, 1972-73. Mem. Internat. Assn. Fin. Planners, Inst. Cert. Fin. Planners (v.p. edn. 1987-88, pres. 1988—), Registry Fin. Planning Practitioners. Republican. Methodist. Home: RD 10 Box 10394 Kemah Lake Rd Newton NJ 07860 Office: Du Frane Fin Svcs 4 Headquarters Pla Morristown NJ 07960

WESENBERG, JOHN HERMAN, association executive; b. Davenport, Iowa, Jan. 16, 1927; s. Herman B. and Nell (Watterson) W.; m. Alice Jane McMahill, Sept. 10, 1949; children: Anne, John, Sue, James. Student, Iowa State U., 1944-45, 47, Amherst Coll., 1946; B.A., U. Iowa, 1951, M.A., 1952; postgrad., Northwestern U., 1952-55, Mich. State U., 1956-67. Research asso. Bur. Bus. and Econ. Research, U. Iowa, 1949-52; asst. mgr. Danville (Ill.) C. of C., 1952-54; exec. v.p. Belleville (Ill.) C. of C., 1954-57; sec. Retail Mchts. and Central Dist. Bur., Des Moines, 1957-62; exec. v.p. Greater Des Moines C. of C., 1963-80; sec. Greater Des Moines Com., 1963-80; sr. exec. v.p. Greater Albuquerque C. of C., 1980-82, Met. Tulsa C. of C., 1982—; trustee Employee Stock Ownership Plan, Internat. Bank, Washington, 1977-80, 83-84; lectr. Inst. Orgn. Mgmt., Mich. State U., 1959-67, 69-70, U. Colo., 1970, 75, 78, 79, 81, 85, 87, Syracuse U., 1971, U. Santa Clara, Calif., 1972, 74-75; lectr. Tex. Christian U., 1971, 73, U. Del., 1973-76, 80, 82, U. Ga., 1973, 82, 86, U. Notre Dame, 1975, 81, So. Meth. U., 1975-76, 81, 84, 85, 87, Mills Coll., 1976, San Jose Coll., 1981, U. Okla., 1984, 86, 88, 89. Co-chmn. Des Moines Mail Users Council, 1963-68; sec.-treas. Des Moines Housing Corp., Baseball, Inc., 1963-80; sec. Des Moines Devel. Corp., Des Moines Industries, Inc., 1963-80, Community Improvement, Inc., 1968-80, Greater Des Moines Community Found., 1968-80; treas. Greater Des Moines Shippers Assn., 1971-80; trustee Fringe Benefits, Inc., Washington, 1969-82; mem. exec. com. Iowa Council on Econ. Edn., 1978-80; mem. planning com. Grand View Coll., 1976-80; mem. adv. council, region VIII SBA, 1973-80; Mem. bd. regents Inst. Orgn. Mgmt., Mich. State U., 1962-67, chmn., 1965-66; bd. regents U. Colo., 1977-80, So. Meth. U., 1980-81; vice chmn. nat. bd. regents Inst. for Orgn. Mgmt., 1978-79, chmn., 1979-80; trustee U. Albuquerque, 1980-82. Served with USAAF, 1944-46. Mem. Am. C. of C. Execs. (dir. 1965-73, 84—, pres. 1971-72), C. of C. U.S. (dir. 1979-81), Iowa C. of C. Execs. (dir. 1960-66, pres. 1964), Okla. C. of C. Execs. (dir. 1983-86, pres. 1986), Am. Retail Execs. Assn. (dir. 1961-63), Ill. Mfrs. Assn. (exec. com. So. div. 1955-57), St. Louis Indsl. Council (v.p. 1957), Okla. C. of C. and Industry (mem. exec. com., bd. dirs. 1986) Industries for Tulsa (sec. 1986—), Am. Arbitration Assn., Nat. Assn. Housing and Redevel. Ofcls., Internat. Downtown Exec. Assn., Iowa Bd. Internat. Edn., Mountain States Assn. (v.p. 1980-81), Beta Theta Pi (gen. sec. 1974-80, trustee 1974-80). Club: Des Moines. Home: 6718 E 65th Pl Tulsa OK 74133 Office: Met Tulsa C of C 616 S Boston Tulsa OK 74119

WESSE, DAVID JOSEPH, university official; b. Chgo., May 5, 1951; s. Herman Theodore and Lorraine Joan (Holland) W.; m. Deborah Lynn Smith, Oct. 11, 1975; children: Jason David, Eric Joseph. AA, Thornton Coll., 1971; postgrad., Purdue U., 1971-72; BS, Ill. State U., 1973; MS, Loyola U., 1983. Adminstrv. mgr. Donnelley Directory Corp., Chgo., 1974-76, Loyola U., Chgo., 1976-79, Joint Commn. on Accreditation Hosps., Chgo., 1979-81; adminstrv. dir., asst. sec. Northwestern U., Evanston, Ill., 1981—. Pres., bd. dirs. Riverdale Library Dist., 1975, Riverdale Youth Commn., 1975. Recipient Service Recognition award Riverdale Library Dist., 1975. Mem. Adminstrv. Mgmt. Soc. (bd. dirs. Chgo. chpt. 1983-88, pres. 1986-87, mem. bd. regents 1986-88), Nat. Assn. Coll. and Univ. Bus. Officers (com. mem. 1986-87, 89-90), Lambda Epsilon. Lutheran. Home: 207 S Washington St Wheaton IL 60187 Office: Northwestern U 633 Clark St Evanston IL 60208

WESSEL, JEFFREY HALL, bank executive; b. Duluth, Minn., Apr. 25, 1942; s. Leo R. and Mabel (Hall) W.; m. Susan E. Parker, July 22, 1967; children—Katherine M., Brandon J. B.A., U. Minn., 1964, J.D., 1967. With The Northern Trust Co., Chgo.; now exec. v.p., head corp. fin. services; dir. No. Trust Futures Corp.; chmn. No. Investment Mgmt. Co. Club: Valley Lo (bd. dirs.). Home: 777 Sunset Ridge Northfield IL 60093 Office: No Trust Co 50 S LaSalle St Chicago IL 60675

WESSEL, PETER A., real estate executive; b. Syracuse, N.Y., Dec. 16, 1954. BA, St. Lawrence U., Canton, N.Y., 1977; JD, Georgetown U., 1981. Bar: D.C. 1982. Assoc. Stephen C. Glassman, P.C., Washington, 1980-81; fin. planner CIGNA Corp., McLean, Va., 1982; assoc. Warner & Stackpole, Washington, 1983; project mgr. Prudential Bache Securities Co., N.Y.C., 1984-85; gen. mgr. Prudential Property Co., Newark, 1986—. Mem. D.C. Bar. Office: Prudential Property Co Prudential Plaza Suite 2500 1050 17th St Denver CO 80265

WESSELINK, DAVID DUWAYNE, finance company executive; b. Webster City, Iowa, Sept. 5, 1942; s. William David and Lavina C. (Haahr) W.; m. Linda R. DeWitt, Dec. 27, 1971; children: Catherine, Bill. BA in Bus., Cen. Coll., 1964; MBA, Mich. State U., 1970. Tchr. Peace Corps, Turkey, 1964-66, Karabuk Koleji, Turkey, 1967-68, Robert Koleji, Turkey, 1969-70; research analyst Household Fin. Corp., Chgo., 1971-73, asst. dir. research, 1973-77; asst. treasurer Household Fin. Corp., Prospect Heights, Ill., 1977, v.p., dir. research, 1977-82, group v.p., chief fin. officer, 1982-86, sr. v.p., chief fin. officer, 1986—, v.p., treas., 1988—. Dir. Am. Cancer Soc., Northbrook, Ill., 1988—, Glenkirk Found., Northbrook, 1988—. Mem. The Econ. Club Chgo., Fin. Execs. Inst., Nat. Leadership Com.-Cen. Challenge at Cen. Coll. Office: Household Internat Inc 2700 Sanders Rd Prospect Heights IL 60070

WESSELS, ALFRED JOSEPH, JR., health care service executive, alderman; b. St. Louis, Sept. 5, 1946; s. Alfred Joseph and Florence (Kellerman) W.; m. Gloria Ann Bewen, Dec. 26, 1969; children: Jason N., Benjamin F., Sara M., Carrie E. BSBA, St. Louis U., 1971, MA in Urban Affairs, 1974. Personnel officer St. Louis City Hosp., 1974-77, asst. adminstr., 1977-79, assoc. adminstr., 1979-82; dir. adminstr. King Khalid U. Hosp., Riyadh, Saudi Arabia, 1982-84; exec. dir. St. Louis Peregrine Soc., 1984—; alderman 13th ward City of St. Louis, 1985—; bd. dirs. Human Devel. Corp. Met. St. Louis. Adv. bd. Bevo-Long Community Sch., St. Louis, 1985—; active Mo. Mcpl. League, 1985—. Served with U.S. Army, 1966-68, Vietnam. Mem. St. Louis Ambassadors, St. Louis U. Alumni Council. Democrat. Roman Catholic. Home: 3955 Dover Pl Saint Louis MO 63116 Office: St Louis Peregrine Soc 2343 Hampton Ave Saint Louis MO 63139

WESSLING, GREGORY JAY, retail executive; b. Chgo., Dec. 11, 1951; s. Robert J. and Doris (Tosch) W.; m. Mary Anne Richmond, Nov. 16, 1974; children: Douglas A., James R., Robert E. BBA, U. N.C., 1974; postgrad., Wake Forest U. Sch. Bus., 1974-76, MBA, 1987. Store mgr. Lowe's Co., Inc., Winston-Salem, N.C., 1973-76; mktg. mgr. Lowe's Co., Inc., North Wilkesboro, N.C., 1976—, dir. merchandising, 1978-80, v.p. merchandising, 1980—; bd. dirs. DJR Corp., Winston-Salem. Mem. Home Ctr. Leadership Council. Republican. Presbyterian. Office: Lowe's Cos Inc PO Box 1111 North Wilkesboro NC 28656-0001

WESSLING, JEFFREY NEAL, service executive, treasurer, accountant; b. Louisville, Sept. 14, 1958; s. John T. and Norma L. (Kempf) W. BA, Bellarmine Coll., 1980. CPA, Ky. Acct. Coopers & Lybrand, Louisville, 1980-81; asst. controller Great Fin. Fed. Savs. and Loan, Louisville, 1982-84; v.p., treas. Kentucky Fried Chicken Nat. Advt. Group Inc., Louisville, 1985—. Fundraiser Am. Heart Assn., Louisville, 1987—. Mem. Ky. Soc. CPA's, Am. Inst. CPA's. Republican. Roman Catholic.

WESSNER, KENNETH THOMAS, management services executive; b. Sinking Springs, Pa., May 1, 1922; s. Thomas Benjamin and Carrie Eva (Whitmoyer) W.; m. Norma Elaine Cook, Jan. 25, 1945; children—Barbara Wessner Anderson, David Kenneth. BS, Wheaton (Ill.) Coll., 1947; HHD (hon.), King's Coll., 1988. Dist. mgr., then mgr. sales promotion Club Aluminum Products Co., 1947-54; with Servicemaster Industries Inc., Downers Grove, Ill., 1954—; v.p. Servicemaster Industries Inc., Downers Grove, 1961, exec. v.p., 1972-75, chief operating officer, 1972-74, pres., 1973-81, chief exec. officer, 1975-83, chmn. bd., 1981—, bd. dirs.; pres., chief operating officer Servicemaster Hosp. Corp. Div., Downers Grove, 1962-72; bd. dirs. Bell Fed. Savs. and Loan Assn., Chgo., Health Providers Ins. Co. Chmn. bd. trustees Wheaton (Ill.) Coll.; mem. adv. coun. grad. sch. bus. U. Chgo.; trustee Chgo. Sunday Evening Club, Health Rsch. and Ednl. Trust, Prison Fellowship Ministries. With USAAF, 1943-46. Recipient Outstanding Chief Exec. Officer in Svcs. Industry award Fin. World mag., 1980, Top Chief Exec. Officer in Indsl. Svcs. Industry award Wall St. Transcript, 1979-83; named Profl. and Bus. Leader of Yr., Religious Heritage Am., 1981. Mem. Am. Mgmt. Assn., Am. Hosp. Assn., Beta Gamma Sigma. Clubs: Chgo. Golf (Wheaton); Econs. (Chgo.); Imperial Golf, Naples Yacht (Fla.). Home: 2355 Gulf Shore Blvd N Naples FL 33940 Office: The ServiceMaster Co 2300 Warrenville Rd Downers Grove IL 60515

WEST, ALFRED PAUL, JR., financial services executive; b. Brooksville, Fla., Dec. 7, 1942; s. Alfred Paul Sr. and Jane (Coogler) W.; m. Loralee Smith, June 16, 1964; children: Angela Paige, Alfred Paul III, Andrew Palmer. B in Aerospace Engring., Ga. Inst. Tech., 1964; MBA, U. Pa., 1967, postgrad., 1967-68. Chmn., chief exec. officer SEI Corp., Wayne, Pa., 1968—, pres., 1978—. Bd. dirs. All-Star Forum, Phila., 1983—; bd. dirs. grad. exec. bd. Wharton Sch. of Bus., 1983—; bd. dirs. World Affairs Council, Phila., 1985—. Republican. Presbyterian. Office: SEI Corp 680 E Swedesford Rd Wayne PA 19087

WEST, CAROLYN JO, land development company executive, financial consultant; b. Paducah, Ky., July 4, 1935; d. Joe Ed and Leona (Burks) Holly; m. William B. West, Sept. 28, 1957 (dec.); 1 dau., Holly Lynn Pierce. B.S., Pepperdine U., 1957; postgrad., Calif. State U.-Fullerton, 1965-67. Bookkeeper Quality Produce Co., Santa Ana, Calif., 1957-69; asst. mgr., controller Savi Devel. Corp., Orange, Calif., 1969-75; treas., controller So. Pacific Constrn. Co., Garden Grove, Calif., 1975-77; asst. controller, chief acct. Dunn Properties Corp., Santa Ana, 1977-79; v.p., treas., controller, chief fin. officer Saddleback Assocs. Inc., Santa Ana, 1979—; cons. Nantell Investments, Fountain Valley, Calif., 1977—; cons., chief fin. officer Gilmer Properties, Orange, 1980—, Churchill Comml. Brokerage Inc., 1987—; cons. investors, land developers., 1977—. Founder Helping Hands, Hillview Acres Children's Home, pres. 1963-67; leader trainer Girl Scouts U.S.A., Orange County, Calif., 1967-70; fund raiser, Orange County Democratic Com., 1968; speaker So. Calif. Women's Ch. Confs.; tchr. Bible classes, Ch. of Christ, Santa Ana and Garden Grove. Recipient outstanding service awards Girl Scouts U.S.A., 1969, Hillview Acres Children's Home, 1971. Mem. Delta Chi Omega (pres. 1954-55). Home: 8763 Rogue River Fountain Valley CA 92708 Office: Saddleback Assocs Inc PO Box 17899 Irvine CA 92713

WEST, EDWARD ALAN, graphics communications executive; b. Los Angeles, Dec. 25, 1928; s. Albert Reginald and Gladys Delia (White) W.; m. Sonya Lee Smith, Jan. 2, 1983; children: Troy A., Tamara L. A.A., Fullerton Coll., 1966; student, Cerrotos Coll., 1957, UCLA, 1967. Circulation mgr. Huntington Park (Calif.) Signal Newspaper, 1946-52; newspaper web pressman Long Beach (Calif.) Press Telegram, 1955-62; gravure web pressman Gravure West, Los Angeles, 1966-67; sales engr. Halm Jet Press, Glen Head, N.Y., 1968-70; salesman Polychrome Corp., Glen Head, 1970-74; supr. reprographics Fluor Engring & Construction, Irvine, Calif., 1974-81; dir. reprographics Fluor Arabia, Dhahran, Saudi Arabia, 1981-85, Press Telegram, Long Beach, 1986—. Author: How to Paste up For Graphic Reproduction, 1967. Editor The Blue & Gold Legion of Honor unit El Bekal Temple, 1989—. Served as sgt. USMC, 1952-55. Decorated three battle stars, Korea. Mem. Newspaper Web Pressman's Union #285 (bd. dirs. 1966—), In-Plant Printing Assn. (cert. graphics communications mgr. 1977, editor newsletter 1977—, pres. Orange County chpt. 1979—; Internat. Mem. of Yr. 1980), VFW. Presbyterian. Lodges: Mason, Shriners (v.p. South Coast club). Home: 198 Monarch Bay South Laguana CA 92677 Office: 604 Pine Long Beach CA 90844

WEST, ERNEST PATRICK, JR., water and wastewater utility executive; b. Chattanooga, Apr. 30, 1925; s. Ernest Patrick and Martha Permelia (Jones); m. Minnie Lou Stipe, Sept. 11, 1948; children: James Michael, Patricia Lynne, Sylvia Marie. B in Indsl. Engring., Ga. Inst. Tech., 1950. Registered profl. engr. Gas engr., supt. various agys. in Southeast, 1950-68; supt. gas dept. City of Cartersville, Ga., 1968-69; supt. water and sewer City of Bartow, Fla., 1969-73; mgr. sewer and water Orange County, Orlando, Fla., 1973-77, pub. utilities dir., 1977-79; exec. dir. So. Seminole and No. Orange

County Wastewater Transmission Authority, Maitland, Fla., 1979—. Served with USN, 1943-46, PTO. Mem. NSPE, Fla. Engring. Soc., Water Pollution Control Fedn. Baptist. Home: 3008 Greenmount Rd Orlando FL 32806 Office: South Seminole and North Orange County Wastewater Transmissi 410 Lake Howell Rd PO Box 1837 Maitland FL 32751

WEST, HERBERT BUELL, foundation executive; b. Birmingham, Apr. 19, 1916; s. Edward Hamilton and Clarine (Buell) W.; AB, Birmingham-So. Coll., 1936; m. Maria Selden McDonald, Nov. 29, 1946; children: Maria Newill, Herbert Buell, William McDonald, Maria Selden, Jane Hamilton. Writer, v.p., account supr. Batten, Barton, Durstine & Osborn, Inc., N.Y.C., 1936-66; dir., mem. distbn. com. N.Y. Community Trust, N.Y.C., 1967—; pres., dir. Community Funds, Inc., 1967—, James Found., Inc., 1968—, Fairfield County Coop. Found., 1984—. Pres., chmn. bd. Am. br. Internat. Social Service, 1966-72, v.p., 1972-83, bd. dirs., 1972—; trustee United Community Funds and Council Am., 1968-71, Fay Sch., Southborough, Mass., 1970-80; trustee NYU Med. Center, 1973—, mem. exec. com., 1979-84; chmn. bd. trustees, chmn. exec. com. The Found. Center, 1975-81; warden St. Luke's Episcopal Ch., Darien, Conn., 1976-79; chmn. joint com. United Way/Community Found. Cooperation, 1987—, com. mem. Greater N.Y. Fund/United Way, 1976-81; bd. dirs. Welfare Research, Inc., 1972—, chmn. bd. dirs., 1978-84; bd. dirs., mem. exec. com. Nat. Charities Info. Bur., Inc., 1978—; bd. dirs. Council on Founds., 1980-87, vice chmn., 1984-87; bd. dirs. Am. Council Nationalities Service, 1983—; pres. A Better Chance in Darien (Conn.), 1980-83, bd. dirs., 1983-85. Maj. Adjutant Gen. Corps, AUS, 1941-46. Decorated Legion Merit. Mem. N.Y. Regional Assn. of Grantmakers (v.p., dir. 1979-82), Interphil (London). Episcopalian (mem. nat. exec. council 1961-68). Clubs: Century Association, University. Home: 28 Driftway Ln Darien CT 06820 Office: NY Community Trust 415 Madison Ave New York NY 10017

WEST, J. ROBINSON, petroleum company executive, former government official; b. Bryn Mawr, Pa., Sept. 16, 1946; m. Eileen Shields, May 1982; 2 daus., Lily Eileen, Kate Cristy. B.A., U. N.C., 1968; J.D., Temple U., 1973. Mem. staff White House, Washington, 1974-76; asst. to Sec. of Def. Dept. Def., Washington, 1976, dep. asst. sec. for internat. econ. affairs, 1976-77; v.p., 1st v.p. Blyth, Eastman, Dillon and Co., 1977-80; mem. Reagan Transition Team, 1980-81; asst. sec. Dept. Interior, Washington, 1981-83, pvt. cons., 1983-84; pres., chief exec. officer Petroleum Fin. Co., 1984—; bd. dirs. Filtration Scis. Corp., Trans Alaska Pipeline, Liability Fund. Bd. dirs. Fr.-Am. Found.; mem. Chief of Naval Ops. Exec. Panel; pres. Wyeth Endowment for Am. Art. Mem. Internat. Inst. Strategic Studies. Home: 1524 28th St NW Washington DC 20007 Office: Petroleum Fin Co Ltd Suite 700 1140 Connecticut Ave Washington DC 20036

WEST, JACQUELINE BROWN, marketing and management consultant; b. Oylons, France, Jan. 7, 1955; (parents Am. citizens); d. M.L. and Juanita (Hines) Brown; m. William C. West, Jr., Dec. 19, 1981; 1 child, Zaria Iman. BA, Howard U., 1977; MBA, Rutgers U., 1980. Congl. intern U.S. Congress, Washington, 1976; asst. mgr. Household Fin. Corp., Alexandria, Va., 1977-78; pvt. cons. 1978-79; asst. bus. mgr. TRW, Redondo Beach, Calif., 1980-85; cost mgr. TRW, Redondo Beach, 1987—; pres. Jacqueline B. West and Assocs., L.A., 1985—; cons. Chase Manhattan Bank, N.Y.C., 1978-79, Small Bus. Devel. Ctr., Newark, 1978-79, Minority Small Bus. Investment Co., Newark, 1978-79, Ceysef-Summerscope, Hollywood, Calif., 1984-86, Orchid Pub. Rels., Hollywood, 1985-86, Lee Bailey Prodns., North Hollywood, Calif., 1986-87; bd. dirs., treas. All That Dance Co., Inglewood, Calif., 1987-88. Contbr. articles to profl. jours. Mem. D.C. Bd. Elections and Ethics, 1975-77, L.A. council Girl Scouts U.S., 1985. Mem. Am. Mktg. Assn., Econs. and Fin. Affiliates (v.p. programs 1986-87), Howard U. Alumni Assn., Rutgers Black MBA Assn., Howard U. Club (fin. sec. 1988). Home: 3941 Buckingham Rd Los Angeles CA 90008 Office: TRW One Space Park Redondo Beach CA 90278

WEST, JAMES (WALLEED S. AL-FADHLY), retail executive; b. L.A., Aug. 28, 1953; s. Walid Sherif Al-Fadly and Engelina Van Asperen. BFA, Calif. Inst. Arts, 1974. Font editor Autologic, Inc., Nebury Park, Calif., 1974-75; art dir. William E. Wilson, Palos Verdes, Calif., 1975-77; music dir., program dir. Sta. KJCK, KJCK-FM, Junction City, Kans., 1977-79; dir. adminstrn. Leading Jewelers, L.A., 1979—; dir. advt. Mayfair Music Hall, Santa Monica, Calif., 1980-82,; cons. Radiographic Systems, Santa Fe Springs, Calif., 1980-81, Video Depot., Burbank, Calif., 1981-84; recruiter Calif. Inst. Arts, Valencia, 1972-76; guest lectr. Kansas State U., Manhattan, 1977-78. Author: How to Publish A High School Underground Newspaper, 1970; editor, art dir. Ragazine, 1972; producer films including Home Movie, 1971, Nightrider, 1975 (Chris plaque 1975, Gold Cindy award Film Producers Am. 1975, John Peckham award V.I. Film Festival 1975, finalist Chgo. Internat. Film Festival 1975). Campaign mgr. Siamis for City Coun., 1969. Scholar State of Calif., 1970-74, Calif. Inst. Arts, 1970-71. Mem. Advt. Prodn. Assn., Rosicrucian. Republican. Home: PO Box 66302 Los Angeles CA 90066 Office: 3424 S Centinela Ave Los Angeles CA 90066

WEST, JAMES TILGHMAN, insurance company executive; b. Santa Rosa, Calif., Jan. 10, 1951; s. Edward Goldsborough and Mary Alice (Lindebloom) W.; m. Sylvia Marie Lundberg, Feb. 2, 1976; 1 child, Brandon Tilghman. Student, U. Ariz., 1969-71, Calif. State Coll., 1971-72. CLU. Agt. Mut. Benefit Life Ins. Co., Santa Rosa, 1975-82; ptnr. Burpee, Colvin, West & Rogers, Santa Rosa, 1982-86; pres. Advanced Benefits, Santa Rosa, 1986—. Mem. Am. Soc. CLU's (bd. dirs. 1981-82), Nat. Assn. Life Underwriters (bd. dirs. 1978-80), Internat. Found. Employee Benefit Plans, Redwood Empire Estate Planning Coun. (bd. dirs. 1985-87). Republican. Episcopalian. Office: Advanced Benefits 141 Stony Circle Ste 220 Santa Rosa CA 95401

WEST, JOHN CARL, lawyer, former ambassador; b. Camden, S.C., Aug. 27, 1922; s. Shelton J. and Mattie (Ratterree) W.; A.B., The Citadel, 1942; LL.B. magna cum laude, U. S.C., 1948; m. Lois Rhame, Aug. 29, 1948; children: John Carl, Douglas Allen, Shelton Anne. Bar: S.C. 1947. Ptnr. West, Holland, Furman & Cooper, Camden, 1947-70, West, Cooper, Bowen, Beard & Smoot, Camden, 1975-77; mem. S.C. Senate, 1954-66; lt. gov. State of S.C., 1966-70, gov., 1971-75; ambassador to Kingdom of Saudi Arabia, 1977-81; individual practice law, Hilton Head Island, S.C., 1981—; disting. prof. Middle East studies U. S.C., 1981—; dir. Donaldson, Lufkin & Jenrette, Whittaker Corp., Circle S Industries, Inc.; of counsel McNair Law Firm, Hilton Head Island, S.C., 1988—. Trustee Presbyn. Coll., So. Center Internat. Studies. Served to maj. AUS, 1942-46. Decorated Army Commendation medal; comdr. Order of Merit (W. Ger.). Mem. Phi Beta Kappa. Democrat. Presbyterian (elder). Address: PO Drawer 13 Hilton Head Island SC 29938

WEST, JOHN DUNHAM, retired manufacturing company executive; b. Chgo., May 24, 1906; s. Charles C. and Julia B. (Dunham) W.; m. Ruth Cronk St. John, June 28, 1932. Student, Beloit Coll., 1924-25, D.Sc. (hon.), 1980; M.E., Cornell U., 1932; LHD (hon.), Lakeland Coll., 1987. Pres. Manitowoc Co., Inc., Wis., 1957-81; chief exec. officer Manitowoc Co., Inc., 1981-86, chmn. bd. dirs., 1981-87; dir. emeritus Manitowoc Savs. Bank, Employers Ins. of Wausau, Wis. Recipient Disting. Service citation U. Wis. Coll. Engring., Madison, 1982. Mem. Soc. Advancement Mgmt. (Profl. Mgr. citation 1959). Home: 915 Memorial Dr Manitowoc WI 54220 Office: Manitowoc Co Inc PO Box 66 500 S 16th St Manitowoc WI 54220

WEST, RICHARD CHARLES, construction company executive; b. Tampa, Fla., June 13, 1945; s. Walter Graham and Helen (Springer) W.; m. Pamela Edds, June 18, 1966; 1 child, Chandra Lorene. B in Bldg. Constrn., U. Fla., 1968. Project mgr. Porfiri Constrn., Miami, Fla., 1970-71, Preston H. Haskell Co., Jacksonville, Fla., 1971-74; sr. project mgr. Ira H. Hardin Co., Atlanta, 1974-81; with McDevitt & Street Co., 1981-85, 86-88; sr. project mgr. Atlanta, 1981-83; v.p. ops. Dallas, 1983, Charlotte, N.C., 1983; sr. v.p., div. mgr. Richmond, Va., 1984-85, Atlanta, 1986-88; exec. v.p. A.R. Weeks & Assocs., Atlanta, 1985-86; sr. mgr. Forest City Comml. Co., Inc., Cleve., 1988—. Vol. worker Woodruff Arts Ctr.-Arts Alliance, Atlanta, 1982-86, team capt., 1987. Served to 1st lt. U.S. Army, 1968-70. Mem. Pi Kappa Alpha. Republican. Clubs: Atlanta Athletic. Home: 3810 Loch Highland Pkwy Roswell GA 30075 Office: Forest City Comml Constrn Co 10800 Brookpark Rd Cleveland OH 44130

WEST, ROBERT C., engineering company executive; b. Keytesville, Mo., 1920; BCE, Ga. Inst. Tech., 1949; married. With Sverdrup Corp., St. Louis, 1953—, chief engr., 1967-68, v.p., 1968-69, exec. v.p., 1969-73, chief operating officer, 1973-75, pres., chief exec. officer, 1975-77, chmn. bd., pres., 1977-82, chmn. bd., 1982-88, chmn. emeritus, 1988; bd. dirs. Centerre Bank, St. Louis, Angelica Corp; mem. adv. com. Export-Import Bank U.S. Bd. dirs. St. Louis Region Commerce and Growth Assn., Laclede Sch. Law, Ranken Tech. Inst.; chmn. bd. Webster U., 1982-87; emeritus bd. dirs. Mo. Goodwill Industries; bd. dirs. St. Louis Area council Boy Scouts Am., now pres. North Cen. Region Nat. Exec. Bd.; mem. nat. adv. bd. Ga. Inst. Tech. Recipient Engr. of Yr. award, 1976, Herbert Hoover medal, 1985; Achievement award medal Engrs. Club St. Louis, 1977; Mo. Honor award for disting. service in engring., 1981; Silver Beaver award Boy Scouts Am., 1985. Registered profl. engr. Fellow Am. Cons. Engrs. Council, ASCE (Profl. Recognition award 1981); mem. Mo. Corp. for Sci. and Tech. (chmn. bd. dirs.). Office: Sverdrup Corp 801 N 11th St Saint Louis MO 63101

WEST, ROBERT H., manufacturing company executive; b. 1938. A.B., Princeton U., 1960. V.p. First Nat. Bank of Kansas City, 1962-68; asst. treas. Butler Mfg. Co., Inc., Kansas City, Mo., 1968-70, controller bldg. div., 1970-73, corp. v.p., controller bldgs. div., 1973-74, sr. v.p. adminstrn., 1974-76, exec. v.p., 1976-78, pres., chief operating officer, 1978-86, chmn., chief exec. officer, 1986—, also dir.; bd. dirs. Kansas City Power & Light Co., Nat. Assn. Mfrs., Santa Fe So. Pacific Corp., Commerce Bancshares Inc. Bd. dirs. St. Lukes Hosp. Served to 1st lt. U.S. Army, 1960-62. Office: Butler Mfg Co Inc BMA Tower Penn Valley Park Kansas City MO 64108

WEST, ROBERT LEWIS, financial planner; b. Springfield, Ohio, Aug. 18, 1951; s. Robert Leslie and Julia Belle (Early) W.; m. Helen Marie Isreal, July 24, 1982. Student Ohio State U., 1969-70, Wright State U., 1971-73; grad. Coll. for Fin. Planning, 1982. Cert. fin. planner. Ind. ins. broker and agt., 1973-79; founder Green & West Agy., Columbus, Ohio, from 1977; area sales mgr. Fireman's Fund Am. Life, San Rafael, Calif., from 1979; founder, owner West R L Fin. Planning, Columbus, from 1980; founder, owner Capital Research Services, from 1983; now investment broker, cert. planner, v.p. investments Dean Witter Reynolds Inc., Dayton, Ohio; adj. faculty Coll. Fin. Planning, Denver; cons. in field. Organizer, pres. Children's Christian Research Found. Mem. Internat. Assn. Registered Fin. Planners (bd. govs. 1986), Inst. Cert. Fin. Planners. Republican. Lutheran. Home: 2141 Old Vienna Dr Dayton OH 45459 Office: One First National Pla Ste 1120 Dayton OH 45402

WEST, ROBERT VAN OSDELL, JR., petroleum executive; b. Kansas City, Mo., Apr. 29, 1921; s. Robert Van Osdell and Jacqueline (Quistgaard) W.; divorced; children: Robert Van Osdell, III, Kathryn Anne, Suzanne Small, Patricia Lynn; m. Helen L. Boecking, 1978. BS, U. Tex., 1942, MS, 1943, PhD, 1949. Registered profl engr., Tex. Petroleum engr. Slick Urschel Oil Co., 1949-56; pres. Slick Secondary Recovery Corp., 1956-59; v.p. Texstar Corp., 1959; pres. Texstar Petroleum Co. subs. Texstar Corp., 1959-64; founder Tesoro Petroleum Corp., San Antonio, 1964, chmn. bd. dirs., chief exec. officer, 1971-88, chmn. bd., 1988—; bd. dirs. Continental Telecom Inc., Frost Nat. Bank, ; engring. found. adv. council U. Tex.; adv. council, trustee St. Mary's U. Sch. Bus. Trustee Tex. Research and Tech. Found. San Antonio; past trustee San Antonio City Public Service Bd.; trustee S.W. Research Inst.; bd. dirs. Ford's Theatre, Washington; past chmn. San Antonio Econ. Devel. Found.; dir. World Affairs Council, San Antonio; chmn. bd. dirs. Tiwanaku Archaeol. Found., Bolivia.; chmn. exec. com. Caribbean/Central Am. Action, Washington; chmn. gen. campaign United Way of San Antonio and Bexar County, 1986, vice chmn. bd. trustees, 1988—; chmn. pub. sector campaign subcom. United Way of Am., 1988—. Named Disting. Grad., U. Tex. Coll. Engring., 1973; recipient People of Vision award Nat. Soc. Prevention of Blindness, 1982, Internat. Citizens award World Affairs Council, 1986, Good Scout award Boy Scouts Am., 1987. Mem. Am. Petroleum Inst. (bd. dirs.), Ind. Petroleum Assn. Am., Tex. Ind. Producers and Royalty Owners Assn., Mid-Continent Oil and Gas Assn. (bd. dirs.), 25 Year Club Petroleum Industry, Assn. Pvt. Enterprise Edn. (Herman W. Lay Meml. award 1986), Am.'s Soc., Nat. Petroleum Council, Sigma Chi (Signifigant Sig award 1979). Episcopalian. Club: All-Am. Wildcatters. Office: Tesoro Petroleum Corp 8700 Tesoro Dr San Antonio TX 78286

WEST, ROGER SEIKER, III, securities executive; b. Exmore, Va., Mar. 23, 1949; s. Roger Seiker Jr. and Midred (Shockley) W.; m. Terry Haynie, Aug. 15, 1981. Student, Gulf Coast Coll., Panama City, Fla., 1968-69. Pres. Peninsula Home Improvement, Exmore, 1970-80; chmn., chief exec. officer Brokers Securities, Inc., Norfolk, Va., 1980—, also bd. dirs. Named Small Bus. Adminstrn. Man of Yr., 1976. Mem. Regional Investment Brokers Syndicate (bd. dirs. regional), Va. Traders Assn. Republican. Methodist. Lodge: Moose. Home: 4636 Boxford Rd Virginia Beach VA 23456 Office: Brokers Securities Inc 6161 Kempsville Cir Norfolk VA 23456

WEST, STEPHEN OWEN, food products executive; b. Atlanta, Mar. 27, 1946; s. Hoyt Owen and Dorris (Long) W.; m. Judy Maynard. BSEE, Ga. Inst. Tech., 1969; MBA in Finance, Ga. State U., 1974, MPA, 1977. Assoc. engr. Ga. Power Co., Atlanta, 1972-74; credit rep. Atlantic Steel Co., Atlanta, 1974-76, fin. analyst, 1976-79, asst. treas., 1979-80; dir. fin. analysis Gold Kist, Inc., Atlanta, 1980-83, treas., 1983—. Vol. Atlanta United Way, 1984-86. Lt. j.g. USN 1969-72. Mem. Nat. Soc. Accts. for Coops. (chapt. pres. 1988—), Atlanta C. of C. Office: Gold Kist Inc 244 Perimeter Ctr Pkwy NE Atlanta GA 30346

WEST, TERENCE DOUGLAS, furniture company design executive; b. Twin Falls, Idaho, Sept. 12, 1948; s. Clark Ernest and Elsie Erma (Kulm) W. BS, San Jose State U., 1971. Indsl. designer Clement Labs., Palo Alto, Calif., 1970-74, U.S. Govt., Washington, 1974-78; dir. design Steelcase, Inc., Grand Rapids, Mich., 1978—; guest lectr. San Jose State U., 1988, Lehigh U., 1988; guest lectr. Art Ctr. Coll. Design, Pasadena, Calif., 1989; design jurist Women's Archtl. League Portland (Oreg.), Oreg. Sch. Design, Portland chpt. AIA, 1979. Com. mem. San Jose Urban Coalition, 1971-72; Fulbright Fellowship on Design and Design Edn. in Great Britain. Contbr.: Behaviour and Information Technology, 1987; also articles to profl. jours., patentee sensor seating. Mem. Archtl. League of N.Y., Nat. Trust for Hist. Preservation, Inst. Bus. Designers, Am. Soc. Interior Designers Industry Found. Interior Edn. and Research, Indsl. Designers Soc. Am., Design Mgmt. Inst. Democrat. Lutheran. Home: 9655 Ravine Ridge SE Caledonia MI 49316 Office: Steelcase Inc PO Box 1967 Grand Rapids MI 49501

WEST, THOMAS LOWELL, JR., insurance company executive; b. Cedar Bluff, Va., June 7, 1937; s. Thomas Lowell and Kathleen (Bowling) W.; m. Katharine Thompson, Feb. 13, 1960; children: Thomas Lowell III, John Gardner, Katharine Covington. BS in Indsl. Engring., U. Tenn., 1959. CLU, 1967; chartered fin. cons., 1987. Asst. supr. Aetna Life Ins. Co., Memphis, 1960-62, supr., 1962-67, asst. gen. agt., 1967-69; gen. agt. Aetna Life Ins. Co., Jackson, Miss., 1969-80; regional v.p. Aetna Life & Casualty, Hartford, Conn., 1980-85; v.p. Aetna Life Ins. and Annuity Co., Hartford, 1985-88, sr. v.p. exec. com. and investment com., 1988—, also bd. dirs.; v.p. Aetna Fin. Services, Hartford, 1986-87; pres., bd. dirs. Structured Benefits, Inc., Hartford, 1985—, Systemized Benefits Adminstrn., Inc., SBFI, 1988. Named to Hall of Fame, Jackson Assn. Life Underwriters, 1977. Mem. Am. Soc. CLU's and ChFC, Am. Soc. Pension Actuaries (assoc.), Assn. for Advanced Life Underwriters (assoc.), Nat. Assn. Life Underwriters, Internat. Assn. Fin. Planners. Republican. Presbyterian. Home: 53 Mountain Brook Rd West Hartford CT 06117 Office: Aetna Life & Casualty Co 151 Farmington Ave Hartford CT 06156

WEST, WILLIAM LEWIS, business owner, investor; b. Vidor, Tex., Mar. 10, 1944; s. Wiley Lewis and Evelyn (Smith) W.; m. Sherrie Alice Westmoreland, Nov. 15, 1986; 1 child, Dane Donaldson. BBA, U. Tex., 1966, MBA, 1967. Sr. fin. analyst Continental Oil Co., Houston, 1967-78; pvt. mgmt. cons. Westlan Assocs., Inc., 1978-84; owner Westland Assocs. (Fantastic Sam's), Houston, 1984—. Active Young Reps., Austin, Tex., 1967. 1st lt. U.S. Atmy, 1968-70, Vietnam. Decorated Bronze Star. Mem. Am. Mgmt. Soc., Phi Kappa Phi, Beta Gamma Sigma, Sigma Iota Epsilon, Pine Forest Country Club. Office: Fantastic Sam's 7346 Antoine Houston TX 77088

WESTBAY, HARRY H., government relations consultant; b. London, Aug. 11, 1930; came to U.S., 1932; s. Harry Herron Jr. and Helen Margaret (Andrus) W.; m. Margaret Mary Clifford, Feb. 17, 1973; children: Cynthia, Peter. BA, Amherst Coll., 1952. Various positions Procter & Gamble Co., Cin., 1955-66; adminstrv. asst. U.S. Ho. Reps., Washington, 1967-68; exec. asst. Rep. Nat. Com., Washington, 1969-70; prin. Westbay Assocs., Washington, 1971-72; mgr. fed. govt. affairs St. Regis Paper Co., Washington, 1973-84; mgr. internat. policy dept. U.S. C. of C., Washington, 1985-87; pvt. practice Alexandria, Va., 1987—. Pres. Terrace Park PTA, Cin., 1963-65. Capt. USMC 1953-55, Korea. Mem. Mount Vernon Hockey Club (Alexandria) (pres. 1986-87). Office: 1800 Diagonal Rd Alexandria VA 22314

WESTBROOK, KENNETH KIRK, hospital administrator; b. Long Beach, Calif., May 25, 1950; s. Woodrow Wilson and Phyllis E. (Kirk) W.; m. Linda Diane Kuhn, June 19, 1976; children: Bryan, Sandra, Rochelle. AA in Econs., Cerritos Coll., 1972; AS in Respiratory Therapy, Rio Hondo Coll., 1975; BBA, U. Redlands, 1982, MA in Mgmt., 1986, MBA, 1989. Asst. dir. pulmonary svcs. La Mirada (Calif.) Med. Ctr., 1974-75, Rio Hondo Hosp., Downey, Calif., 1975-80; dir. cardiopulmonary svcs. Los Altos Hosp., Long Beach, 1980-82, South Bay Hosp., Redondo Beach, Calif., 1982-84; adminstrv. dir. support svcs. Robert F. Kennedy Med. Ctr., Hawthorne, Calif., 1984-87; assoc. adminstr. Charter Suburban Hosp., Paramount, 1988—; educator El Camino Coll., Torrance, Calif., 1985-87. Editor: The Respiratory Practitioner, 1985—; contbr. articles to profl. jours. Named one of Outstanding Young Men in Am., 1985. Mem. Am. Coll. Health Care Execs., Health Care Execs. So. Calif., Calif. Soc. for Respiratory Care, Am. Assn. for Respiratory Care, Nat. Bd. for Respiratory Care. Lodge: Rotary. Office: Charter Med Corp 577 Mulberry St Macon GA 31201

WESTBROOK, PAUL, financial adviser, retirement specialist; b. Milw., Dec. 4, 1939; s. John and Anna Westbrook; m. Doris Westbrook, June 29, 1968; 1 child, Ashley. BS, U. Wis., 1963; MS, George Washington U., Ft. Monroe, Va., 1966. Cert. fin. planner. Adminstr. Allied Chem., N.Y.C., 1967-70, Avon Products, Suffern, N.Y., 1970-73, Am. Express, N.Y.C., 1973-77; nat. dir. fin. and retirement planning Buck Cons., Inc., N.Y.C., 1977-87; pres. Westbrook Fin. Advisers, Inc., Watchung, N.J., 1987—; speaker nat. and local planning orgn. confs. Mem. Internat. Assn. Fin. Planning (bd. dirs. N.Y.C. chpt. 1986), Inst. Cert. Fin. Planners. Home and Office: 225 Ridge Rd Watchung NJ 07060

WESTERFIELD, PUTNEY, business executive; b. New Haven, Feb. 9, 1930; s. Ray Bert and Mary Beatrice (Putney) W.; m. Anne Montgomery, Apr. 17, 1954; children: Bradford, Geoffrey, Clare. Grad., Choate Sch., 1942-47; B.A., Yale, 1951. Co-founder, v.p. Careers, Inc., N.Y.C., 1950-52; mgr. S.E. Asia Swen Publs., Inc., Manila, Philippines, 1952; mem. joint adv. commn. Korea, 1953-54; polit. officer Am. embassy, Saigon, Vietnam, 1955-57; asst. to pub. Time mag., N.Y.C., 1957-59, asst. circulation dir., 1959-61; circulation dir. Time mag., 1961-66, asst. pub., 1966-68; asst. pub. Life mag., N.Y.C., 1968; pub. Fortune mag., N.Y.C., 1969-73; pres. Chase World Info. Corp., N.Y.C., 1973-75; v.p. Boyden Assocs. Internat., San Francisco, 1976-80, sr. v.p., western mgr., 1980-84; pres., chief exec. officer Boyden Assocs. Internat., N.Y.C. and San Francisco, 1984—. Bd. dirs. Urban League, N.Y.C., 1969-71, Children's Village, 1968-71, Mediterranean Sch. Found., 1969-71, Nat. Boys Club, 1970-73, U.S.-S. Africa Leaders Exchange Program, 1971—, Bus. Council for Internat. Understanding, 1974-76, Yale-China Assn., 1975-78; trustee Choate Sch., Wallingford, Conn., 1967-76, Westover Sch., Middlebury, Conn., 1975-79, Watch Hill Chapel Soc., 1963-77, Assn. Yale Alumni, 1972-75, 80-83. Clubs: Links, Yale, Union League (N.Y.C.); Burlingame Country (Hillsborough, Calif.); Pacific Union, Bohemian (San Francisco); California (Los Angeles); Round Hill (Greenwich, Conn.). Home: 360 Robinwood Ln Hillsborough CA 94010 Office: Boyden Assocs Internat One Maritime Plaza Suite 1760 San Francisco CA 94111 also: Boyden Internat Inc 260 Madison Ave New York NY 10016

WESTERMAN, GEORGE W., utilities executive; b. Glenside, Pa., Feb. 11, 1939; s. George W. and Rosa (Hudson) W.; m. Ethel Westerman, May 7, 1977; children: Kim, Steve, Joyce, Cathy. BS in Bus. Adminstrn., Drexel U., 1962. Asst. wage and salary adminstr. Standard Press Steel Co., Jenkintown, Pa., 1962-66; adminstr. asst. personnel Oxford Paper Co., Rumford, Maine, 1966-68; asst. mgr. employee relations UGI Corp., King of Prussia, Pa., 1968-69, mgr. employee relations, 1969-71, mgr. adminstrv. services, 1971-73, v.p. adminstrv. services, 1973-80, v.p. adminstrn., 1980-85, sr. v.p. adminstrn., 1985—. Republican. Lutheran. Office: UGI Corp 460 N Gulph Rd King of Prussia PA 19406

WESTERMAN, WILLIAM LESLIE, packaging company executive; b. Bklyn., July 22, 1931; s. Leslie Conrad and Lucille Gertrude (Hildebrand) W.; m. Rosemary Grace Handlon; children: Leslie, John, Julie, Phillip, Ann. BA, Lehigh U., 1953, BS, 1954; MS, State U. Iowa, 1958; MBA, NYU, 1981. Indsl. engr. U.S. Dept. Def., Rock Island, Ill., 1956-58; pres. Rapid Electrotype Co., N.Y.C., 1958-64; v.p. RKO Gen., N.Y.C., 1964-72; pres. Cellu-Craft Inc., New Hyde Park, N.Y., 1973—. Co-author: Principles and Design of Production Control Systems, 1958. Served with U.S. Army, 1954-56. Named Disting. Alumni, Lehigh U., 1983. Mem. Flexible Packaging Assn. (bd. dirs., chmn. 1984-85, Flexographic Packager of Yr. 1988), Flexographic Tech. Assn. (bd. dirs. 1982-83), Found. Flexographic Tech. Assn. (chmn. 1982-83). Office: Cellu-Craft Inc 4242 31st St N Saint Petersburg FL 33714

WESTERVELT, ROBERT MOORE, physics educator; b. Phila., Oct. 9, 1949; s. Robert Moore and Marie Louise (Jefferson) W. BS in Physics with honors, Calif. Inst. Tech., 1971; PhD in Physics, U. Calif., Berkeley, 1977; AM (hon.), Harvard U., 1986. Prof. physics and applied physics Harvard U., Cambridge, Mass., 1979-84, assoc. prof. physics and applied physics, 1984-86, prof. physics, Gordon McKay prof. applied physics, 1986—; co-chmn. Gordon Conf. on Condensed Matter Physics, 1988; bd. editors Physica D-Nonlinear Phenomena, 1986—. Recipient Ross N. Tucker Meml. award Intel Corp., 1977; Chancellor's fellow U. Calif. Berkeley, 1971. Mem. Am. Physical Soc., Office of Naval Rsch Options Rev. Panel. Office: Harvard U Div Applied Scis Cambridge MA 02138

WESTFALL, RICHARD MERRILL, chemist, research administrator; b. Denver, Dec. 17, 1956; s. Robert Raymond and Madelyn Evastine (Cornwell) W. Student, U. Colo., 1976-80. Mem. lab. staff NOAA, Boulder, Colo., 1978-79, Solar Energy Rsch. Inst., Golden, Colo., 1979-80; dir. rsch. Galactic Products, Denver, 1981-82; pres., dir. rsch. CEL Systems Corp., Arvada, Colo. and Schertz, Tex., 1982—; process chemist, optical detector fabrication engr. Tex. Med. Instruments, Schertz, 1986-87; dir. rsch., chief exec. officer Galactic Mining Industries, Denver, 1988-89; founder, exec. dir. Galactic Ednl. Devel. Inst., Denver, 1989—. Inventor electrolytic growth tin and other metals, and process, 1980-82; patentee in field. Mem. AIAA, Air Force Assn. Home: 4838 Stuart St Denver CO 80212

WESTGARD, ROLF ERIK, real estate corporation executive, marketing consultant; b. Cumberland, Md., Feb. 15, 1930; s. Rolf Westgard and Gudrun Palmstrom; m. Nolinda Joanne Wells, July 27, 1957; children: Erik, Lisa, Richard, Karen. BA, U. Mich., 1951; MBA, Stanford U., 1957. V.p. 3M Co., St. Paul, 1964-85, cons., 1985—; pres. Inland Hills Co., Lakeland, Minn., 1979—; cons. Energy Conversion Devices, Troy, Mich., 1988, Am. Mgmt. Systems, Rosslyn, Va., 1988. Contbr. articles to profl. jours. Trustee Metro State U., St. Paul, 1982-87, Big Bros./Big sisters, St. Paul, 1985—. Mem. Assn. for Info. and Image Mgmt., North Oaks Club, Santa Rosa Country Club. Office: Inland Hills Co 55 Lakeland Shores Rd Lakeland MN 55043

WESTON, EDWARD, art dealer, consultant; b. N.Y.C., Feb. 25, 1925; s. Joseph and Mona (Gould) W.; m. Ann Jean Weston, May 4, 1974; children: Jon Marc, Cari Alyn Rene. News editor Sta. WMCA, N.Y.C., 1940-41; announcer news dept. Sta. WSAV, Savannah, Ga., 1941-43; newscaster, disc jockey Sta. WNOX, Knoxville, Tenn., 1943-45; program dir. Sta. WXLH, Okinawa, Japan, 1945-47; newscaster, announcer Sta. WAVZ, New Haven, 1947-48; program dir. Sta. WCCC, Hartford, Conn., 1948-49; asst. gen. mgr. Sta. WCPO AM-FM-TV, Cin., 1949-59; pres., gen. mgr. Sta. WZIP, Cin., 1959-61; pres. Weston Entertainment, Northridge, Calif., 1961—; chmn. bd. Fulton J. Sheen Communications; pres. Inspirational Programs, Inc., 1983—, Weston Editions, 1970—, Marilyn Monroe Editions, 1975—. Producer TV/

video cassettes Life Is Worth Living; PBS TV series How to Paint with Elke Sommer, 1984. Founder Cin. Summer Playhouse, 1950. Served with U.S. Army, 1945-46. Recipient Outstanding News Coverage award Variety mag., 1949, Outstanding Sta. Ops. award Variety mag., 1950, Best Programming award Nat. Assn. Radio TV Broadcasters, 1951. Home: 10511 Andora Ave Chatsworth CA 91311 Office: Weston Entertainment 19355 Business Ctr Dr Northridge CA 91324

WESTON, JOSH S., data processing company executive; b. 1928; married. B.S., CCNY, 1950; M.A., U. New Zealand, 1951. Exec. v.p. Popular Services, Inc., 1955-70; v.p. planning adminstrn. Automatic Data Processing, Inc., Roseland, N.J., 1970-75, exec. v.p., 1975-77, pres. from 1977, chief exec. officer, 1982—, former chief operating officer, now also chmn.; dir. Popular Services, Inc., Supermarkets General Corp., Pub. Service Electric & Gas Co. Office: ADP Inc 1 Automatic Data Processing Blvd Roseland NJ 07068 *

WESTON, M. MORAN, II, educator, real estate developer, banker; b. Tarboro, N.C., Sept. 10, 1910; s. Milton Moran and Catharine C. (Perry) W.; m. June 27, 1946; children: Karann Christine, Gregory. BA, Columbia U., 1930, PhD, 1954, STD (hon.), 1968; DD (hon.), Va. Theol. Sch., 1964; DHL (hon.), Fordham U., 1988. Bus. mgr. St. Philips Episcopal Ch., N.Y.C., 1948-51; exec. sec. Christian Citizenship Nat. Council, Episcopal Ch., N.Y.C., 1951-57; rector, chief executive officer St. Philips Ch. and Community Svc. Council, N.Y.C., 1957-82; sr. prof. SUNY, Albany, 1959-77, prof. emeritus, 1977—; pvt. housing developer 1982—; vis. prof. U. Ife, Ile-Ife, Nigeria, 1977; chmn. bd. Carver Fed. Savs. Bank, N.Y.C., 1980—; bd. mem., founder, Carver Fed. Bank, N.Y.C., 1948—; trustee Columbia U., 1969-81, trustee emeritus, 1981—; trustee St. Augustine Coll., Raleigh, N.C., 1970—, Mt. Sinai Hosp. Med. Sch. and Ctr., N.Y.C., 1971—; trustee emeritus, Columbia U., 1981—; pres. 6 housing corps. Author: Social Policy, 1964. Trustee NAACP Legal Def. Fund, N.Y.C., 1965—, Fgn. Policy Assn., N.Y.C., 1980-89, Phelps Stokes Fund, N.Y.C., 1970-80. Recipient St. Augustine's Cros., Archbishop of Canterbury, London, England, 1981, Excellence award Columbia Grad. Alumni Assn., N.Y.C., 1982, Humanitarian award N.Y. Urban League, N.Y.C., 1982, Humanitarian award N.Y. YMCA, N.Y.C, 1982. Mem. Housing for People (founder, pres. 1980—), Nat. Assn. for Affordable Housing, (founder, pres. 1987—), Sigma Pi Phi (pres. Zeta chpt. 1983-86). Club: Lotos (N.Y.C.). Lodge: Elks (Hon. Supreme Exalted Ruler 1946-50). Home: 253 Blvd E New Rochelle NY 10801 Office: Carver Fed Savs Bank 75 West 125 St New York NY 10801

WESTON, ROBERT, financial planner; b. Newark, Sept. 10, 1924; s. Irving George and Regina (Luxner) W.; m. Cynthia Joy Weber, June 20, 1948; children: Steven, James, Bonnie, Beth, Susan. BS in Edn., Montclair State U., 1949; MA in Edn., Seton Hall U., 1951. Cert. fin. planner, registered investment advisor. V.p.-in-charge of sales Hugh Johnson & Co., Eatontown, N.J., 1967-77; registered rep. Advest, Eatontown, 1977-78, Ind. Fin. Planners Corp., Eatontown, 1978-79, Anchor Nat. Fin. Svcs., Eatontown, 1979—; pres. Robert Weston & Co., Eatontown, 1979—; bd. dirs. Ocean Ind. Bank, Ocean Twp., N.J. Mem. West Long Br. (N.J.) Bd. Edn., 1957-68, pres. 1967; bd. dirs. West Long Branch Planning Bd., 1985-88. With USAAF, 1943-45. Mem. Internat. Assn. Fin. Planning, Inst. Cert. Fin. Planners, Lions. Republican. Jewish. Office: Robert Weston & Co 125 Wyckoff Rd Eatontown NJ 07724

WESTON, ROGER LANCE, banker; b. Waukegan, Ill., Mar. 2, 1943; s. Arthur Walter and Vivian Dawn (Thompson) W.; m. Kathleen Plotzke, Sept. 15, 1979; children: Cynthia Page, Kent Andrew, Arthur Eladio, Rebecca Dawn, Alice Sinclair, Elliott Churchill, Evan Walter. BS, MacMurray Coll., 1965; MBA, Washington U., St. Louis, 1967. Investment adviser Harris Trust & Savs. Bank, Chgo., 1967-69; sr. investment counselor Security Suprs., Chgo., 1969-70; exec. v.p., treas., chief fin. officer Telemed Corp., Hoffman Estates, Ill., 1971-79; vice chmn. Bank Lincolnwood, Ill., 1979-85; pres., chief exec. officer GSC Enterprises, Lincolnwood, 1979-85, EVCO, Inc., Itasca, Ill., 1985-87; vice chmn., chief exec. officer Evanston (Ill.) Bank, 1985-88; chmn. bd. dirs., pres., chief exec. officer GreatBanc, Inc., Itasca, 1986—. Mem. Barrington Hills (Ill.) Zoning Bd. Appeals, 1987, com. Asian art Art Inst. Chgo., 1987. Mem. Washington U. Eliot Soc. (chmn. membership com. 1986—), Univ. Club. Republican. Presbyterian. Home: 77 Spring Creek Rd Barrington Hills IL 60010 Office: GreatBanc Inc One Pierce Pl Ste 700 W Itasca IL 60143

WESTON, ROY FRANCIS, environmental consultant; b. Reedsburg, Wis., June 25, 1911; s. Charles Frederick and Hattie (Jensen) W.; m. Madeleen Elizabeth Kellner, Dec. 31, 1934; children—Susan Weston Thompson, Katherine Weston. B.C.E., U. Wis., 1933; M.C.E., NYU, 1939. Registered profl. engr., 18 states; diplomate Am. Acad. Environ. Engrs. (pres. 1973-74). Jr. hwy. engr. Wis. Hwy. Dept., 1934-36; dist. engr. Wis. Dept. Health, 1936-37; san. engring. research fellow NYU, N.Y.C., 1937-39; san. engr. Atlantic Refining Co., Phila., 1939-55; pres., chmn. bd. Roy F. Weston, Inc., West Chester, Pa., 1955—; environ. cons. Contbr. numerous articles on environ. control to profl. publs. vis. com. dept. civil and urban engring. U. Pa., Phila., also Ctr. for Marine and Environ. Studies, Lehigh U.; mem. Pa. Gov.'s Energy Council; mem. indsl. and profl. adv. com. Pa. State U. Recipient Disting. Service citation U. Wis., 1975, George Washington medal Phila. Engrs., 1973. Fellow ASCE, Am. Pub. Health Assn.; mem. Nat. Soc. Profl. Engrs. (Engr. of Yr. award 1973), Pa. Soc. Profl. Engrs. (Engr. of Yr. award 1970), Nat. Acad. Engring., Water Pollution Control Fedn. (Arthur Sidney Bedell award 1959, Indsl. Wastes medal 1950), Am. Inst. Chem. Engrs., Am. Chem. Soc., Air Pollution Control Assn., Cons. Engrs. Council, Water Resources Assn., Delaware River Assn. (pres. 1976-77). Clubs: Overbrook Golf, Phila. Engrs. Office: Roy F Weston Inc Weston Way West Chester PA 19380

WESTON, WILLARD GALEN, diversified holdings executive; b. Eng., Oct. 29, 1940; s. W. Garfield Weston and Reta L. Howard; m. Hilary Frayne, 1966; 2 children. LLD honoris causa, U. Western Ont. Pres., chmn. bd. Wittington Investments Ltd. (parent co. of other Weston cos.) and George Weston Ltd.; chmn. bd. dirs. Holt Renfrew & Co. Ltd., Loblaw Cos. Ltd., Weston Foods Ltd., Weston Resources Ltd., Brown Thomas Group Ltd. (Ireland); vice chmn. bd. dirs. Fortnum & Mason plc (U.K.); bd. dirs. George Weston Holdings Ltd. (U.K.), Associated British Foods plc (U.K.), Can. Imperial Bank of Commerce. Pres. The W. Garfield Weston Found., The Weston Can. Found.; bd. dirs. Lester B. Pearson Coll. Pacific, United World Colls., Operation Raleigh, Can.; life mem. Royal Ont. Mus., Art Gallery Ont. Mem. Badminton and Racquet Club, York Club, Toronto Club, Guards Polo Club, Lyford Cay Club. Office: George Weston Ltd, 22 St Clair Ave E, Suite 2001, Toronto, ON Canada M4T 2S3

WESTRAN, ROY ALVIN, insurance company executive; b. Taft, Oreg., Apr. 30, 1925; s. Carl A. and Mae E. (Barnhart) W.; m. Dawn M. Oeschger, Oct. 18, 1952; children: Denise, Thomas, Michael, Dawna. B.B.A., Golden Gate Coll., 1955, M.B.A., 1957. Mem. sales staff C.A. Westran Agy., Taft, 1946-49; underwriter Fireman's Fund Group, San Francisco, 1949-52; ins. mgr. Kaiser Aluminum Chem. Co., Oakland, 1952-66; pres., dir. Citizens Ins. Co., Howell, Mich., 1967—; chmn. bd. 1st Nat. Bank, Howell; pres. Am. Select Ins. Co., Columbus, Ohio, 1967-85, dir., 1967—; pres. Beacon Ins. Co. Am., Westerville, Ohio, 1967-85, dir., 1967—; pres., dir. Citizens' Man, Inc.; v.p., dir. Hanover Ins. Co., Massachusetts Bay Ins. Co.; bd. dirs. Oakland Kaiser Fed. Credit Union, 1957-60, Calif. Compensation Fire Co. Mem. ins. adv. council Salvation Army, San Francisco, 1957-60; chmn. drive United Way, Livingston County, 1980; bd. dirs., mem. exec. com. Portage Trails council Boy Scouts Am., 1970-72; trustee, mem. exec. com. Child and Family Services Mich., 1972-75; past bd. dirs. McPherson Health Ctr., Howell; bd. dirs. Cleary Coll., 1984-85; mem. adv. council Olivet Coll., 1984—. Served with U.S. Army, 1943-46. Mem. Ins. Inst. Am., Mich. C. of C. (past dir.), Am. Soc. Ins. Mgmt. (past pres.), Soc. CPCU's (nat. pres. 1968-69), Traffic Safety Assn. Detroit (trustee 1967—), Traffic Safety for Mich. Assn. Office: Citizens Ins Co Am 645 W Grand River Howell MI 48834

WESTRICK, STEVEN J., insurance agent; b. Ft. Wayne, Ind., Apr. 6, 1961; s. David Arthur and Joan Evelyn (Ashby) W.; m. Kimberly Sue Hurley, Oct. 24, 1981; children: Daniel C., Benjamin M. Grad., Bishop Luers High Sch., Ft. Wayne, 1979. With maintenance dept. Westrix Corp., Ft. Wayne, 1976-81; laborer Wilbert Vault, Ft. Wayne, 1981-83; mgr. circulation dept. Ft. Wayne Newspaper, 1983-84; sales mgr. Combined Ins., Ft. Wayne, 1984-86; sales agt. Allstate Ins., Ft. Wayne, 1986—. Active Kiwanis Internat., 1987—; cons. Jr. Achievement, Ft. Wayne, 1988—. Republican. Roman Catholic. Office: Allstate Ins Co 9161 Lima Rd Fort Wayne IN 46818

WETMORE, JOHN BIERCE, accountant, small business owner; b. Canton, Ohio, Mar. 13, 1951; s. Calvin B. and Joan E. (Schatlman) W.; m. M. Kathleen Smith, July 6, 1974; children: Ann, Katie, John Jr. BSBA, Xavier U., 1973, MBA, 1974. CPA, Ohio. Staff acct. Wetmore & Co., Inc., North Canton, Ohio, 1974-80, v.p., 1980-87, pres., 1988—; data processing mgr. Computer Systems Assocs., North Canton, 1979-88; owner The Cupboard, North Canton, 1981-88; mng. ptnr. D&J Enterprises, North Canton, 1981-88; pres. Heartland Devel., Inc., North Canton, 1986—; cons. Profit Sharing Com., Wooster, Ohio, 1983—, Belle Fontaine, Ohio, 1985—; Investment Com., Triffin, Ohio, 1985—. Chmn. audit com. St. Peter's Ch., also mem. fin. com. Recipient Cert. Merit Canton Jaycees, 1983. Mem. Am. Inst. CPA's, Ohio Soc. CPA's, Personal Fin. Planners, Canton C. of C., Canton Jaycess (Cert. Merit 1983). Republican. Roman Catholic. Home: 402 25th St NW Canton OH 44709 Office: Wetmore & Co Inc 5233 Stoneham Rd North Canton OH 44720

WETRICH, JAMES GLEASON, health science facility adminstrator; b. Fontana, Calif., Jan. 18, 1957; s. Raymond Mortimer and Mary (Wallace) W.; m. Nancy Whitenack, Sept. 17, 1983; children: Richard Marcus, Matthew Wallace. BS, U. S.C., 1979; MPH, Tulane U., 1982. Adminstrv. resident Alton Ochsner Med. Found., New Orleans, 1981-82, asst. to hosp. dir., 1982; v.p. Met. Hosp. Council New Orleans, 1982-84; cons. Pitts Mgmt. Assocs., Atlanta, 1984-86, v.p., 1986-87; dir. bus. devel. Univ. Hosp. Consortium, Chgo., 1987-89; mgr. corp. strategic planning Abbott Labs., Abbott Park, Ill., 1989—. Mem. med. com. Internat. Summer Spl. Olympics, Baton Rouge, 1983. Mem. Am. Coll. Healthcare Execs., Healthcare Fin. Mgmt. Assn. (adv.), Chgo. Health Execs. Forum, New Orleans Health Forum (v.p. 1983-84), Tulane Alumni in Health Systems Mgmt. (v.p. 1983-84, pres. 1984-85), Tulane Alumni Assn. (bd. dirs. 1984-89), Tulane Med. Alumni Assn. (bd. dirs. 1983—). Republican. Roman Catholic. Office: Abbott Labs 1 Abbott Park Rd Abbott Park IL 60064

WETTERAU, THEODORE C., diversified food wholesaler; b. St. Louis, Nov. 13, 1927; s. Theodore C. and Edna (Ehrlich) W.; m. Helen Elizabeth Killion, Feb. 20, 1954; children: T. Conrad, Mark Stephen, Elizabeth Killion. BA, Westminster Coll., Fulton, Mo., 1952, LLD (hon.), 1977, LHD (hon.), Westminster Coll. With Wetterau, Inc., Hazelwood, Mo., 1952—, v.p. mktg., 1960-63, exec. v.p., 1963-70, pres., from 1970, chief exec. officer, 1970—, chmn., 1974—, also bd. dirs.; bd. dirs. Centerre Bank of St. Louis, Godfrey Co., Waukesha, Wis. Bd. dirs. Mark Twain Inst., Boy Scouts Am., St. Louis Symphony Soc., Operation Rearch (all St. Louis); trustee Westminster Coll.; chmn., adv. bd. St. Louis Salvation Army; mem. Pres.'s Council of Community Assn. Schs. for the Arts, St. Louis; ex officio trustee Food Industry Crusade Against Hunger, hon. chmn., 1988. Served with U.S. Army, 1946-47, Korea. Named Man of Month, Progressive Grocer mag., 1966, Sales Exec. of Yr., Sales and Mktg. Execs. St. Louis, 1977; recipient Aggus Disting. Pub. Service award, 1980, Nat. Disting. Service award Am. Jewish Com., 1980, Bus. and Profl. award Religious Heritage of Am., 1980, Golden Plate award, 1974. Mem. Nat. Wholesale Grocers Assn. (gov., past chmn. bd.), Ind. Grocers Alliance (past chmn., bd. dirs.), Food Mktg. Inst. (bd. dirs.), U.S. C. of C. (bd. dirs., mem. food agr. com.), Knights of Round Table, Knights of the Cauliflower Ear. Clubs: Univ., Old Warson Country, St. Louis. Office: Wetterau Inc 8920 Pershall Rd Hazelwood MO 63042

WETTIG, MARILYN PELLEY, real estate executive; b. Hampton, Iowa, July 10, 1937; d. Harold Edward and Mildred Mary (Lange) Danner; m. Dolan El Ray Pelley, Sept. 4, 1955 (div. 1985); m. Carl Louelle Wettig, Oct. 10, 1987; children: Lori, Tami, Pami. Lic. realtor, Kans. Interior decorator Interiors of Distinction, Derby, Kans., 1970-76; bookkeeper Egan Constrn. Co., Derby, 1975-77; realtor Egan Realty, Derby, 1977-79, English Realty, Derby, 1979-84, Plaza Del Sol Realty, Derby, 1984—. Mem. Nat. Assn. Realtors, Kans. Assn. Realtors, Wichita Met. Bd. Realtors (bd. dirs. 1983-84, Pres.'s Club award 1981-88), Am. Bus. Women's Assn., Derby C. of C., Sighma Chi Upsilon. Republican. Episcopalian. Home: 1415 Wagonwhell Ct Derby KS 67037

WETZEL, EDWARD THOMAS, publishing company executive; b. Indpls., Apr. 16, 1937; s. Edward George and Sarah Catherine Wetzel; divorced; children: Raymond, Cynthia. BA, Bethany (W.Va.) Coll., 1959; MBA, U. Mass., Amherst, 1963. Market research analyst Gen. Electric Co., Pittsfield, Mass., 1960-63; editor, spl. projects dir., asst. v.p. DMS, Inc., Greenwich, Conn., 1964-70; pres. Industry News Service, Inc., Wilton, Conn., 1970—, Wilton Vol. Ambulance Corps, 1976-81, 83-87; bd. dirs. Southwestern Conn. EMS Council. Served to 2d lt. USAFR, 1959-65. Recipient Disting. Citizen award Town of Wilton, 1986. Mem. Internat. Platform Assn. Lodge: Kiwanis (v.p., bd. dirs. Wilton chpt.). Editor and pub. various def. industry publs. and info. services. Home: 701 Ridgefield Rd Wilton CT 06897 Office: Industry News Svc Inc PO Box 457 Wilton CT 06897

WETZLER, MONTE EDWIN, lawyer; b. N.Y.C., May 7, 1936; s. Alvin and Sally (Epstein) W.; m. Sally Jane Elsas, Dec. 19, 1963; 1 son, Andrew Elsas. A.B., Brown U., 1957; LL.B., U. Va., 1960; LL.M. in Taxation, NYU, 1966. Bar: N.Y. 1960, Calif. 1979. Assoc. Regan Goldfarb Heller Wetzler & Quinn, N.Y.C., 1960-66, ptnr., 1966-73, mng. ptnr., 1973-81; sr. v.p., gen. counsel Damson Oil Corp., N.Y.C., 1981-82, exec. v.p., chief fin. officer, 1982-86; pres. B&D Equities Inc., 1986-88; ptnr. Breed, Abbott & Morgan, N.Y.C., 1988—; bd. dirs. Gensler & Schwab, N.Y.C. Editor: Selected Problems in Securities Law, 1972. Counsel, N.Y. State Senate Com. on Housing, N.Y.C. Recipient Service award Practicing Law Inst., N.Y.C., 1973. Mem. ABA, N.Y. State Bar Assn., Bar Assn. City N.Y., Am. Mgmt. Assn., Harmonie Club (gov. 1983-84, 86-88), Cedar Point Tacht CLub, Phi Delta Phi, Order of Coif. Republican. Jewish. Home: 829 Park Ave New York NY 10021 Office: Breed Abbott & Morgan 153 E 53d St New York NY 10022

WEXLER, ERIK GOLDSCHMIDT, communications company executive; b. N.Y.C., May 12, 1963; s. Joel Lewis Goldschmidt and Joyce Ann (Riech) Wexler. AA, U. Hartford, 1983, BA, 1985, MBA, 1987. V.p. Jameron, Inc., N.Y.C., 1983-86; pres. Wexler and Assocs., Inc., Farmington, Conn., 1985-87; pres., chmn. Venture Mktg., Inc., Farmington, Conn., 1985-88; devel. officer U. Hartford, West Hartford, Conn., 1985-87, cons., 1987-88; pres., chief exec. officer Media Corp. of Am., Inc., Avon, Conn., 1987—, chmn. bd., 1987—; pres. Wexler & Assocs., Inc., Farmington, Conn., 1985-87; pres., chmn Venture Mktg., Inc., Farmington, 1985-88; pres., chief exec. officer Media Corp. Am., Inc., Avon, Conn., 1987-88, also chmn. bd. dirs. Regent U. Hartford, West Hartford, 1986-87; fin. dir. Labriola for Gov. 1987, Bridgeport, Conn. Mem. Tau Kappa Epsilon. Republican. Jewish. Home: 64 Avonwood Rd Apt C-18 Avon CT 06001 Office: U Hartford Office of Devel 200 Bloomfield Ave West Hartford CT 06117

WEXNER, LESLIE HERBERT, retail apparel chain executive; b. Dayton, Ohio, 1937. BS with honors, Ohio State U., 1959, HHD (hon.), 1986; LLD (hon.), Hofstra U., 1987. Founder, pres., chmn. bd. The Limited, Inc., fashion chain, Columbus, 1963—; dir., mem. exec. com. Banc One Corp., Sotheby's Holdings Inc.; mem. bus. adminstrn. adv. council Ohio State U. Bd. dirs. Columbus Urban League, 1982-84, Hebrew Immigrant Aid Soc., N.Y.C., 1982—; trustee Columbus Symphony Orch.; co-chmn. Internat. United Jewish Appeal Com.; nat. vice chmn. United Jewish Appeal; bd. dirs., mem. exec. com. Am. Jewish Joint Distbn. Com., Inc.; trustee Columbus Jewish Fedn., 1972, Capitol South Community Urban Redevel. Corp., Columbus Mus. Art; chmn. Columbus Capital Corp. for Civic Improvement. Named Man of Yr. Am. Mktg. Assn., 1974. Mem. Young Presidents Orgn., Sigma Alpha Mu. Club: B'nai B'rith. Office: The Limited Inc 2 Limited Pkwy Box 16000 Columbus OH 43216

WEYAND, CARLTON DAVIS, composer, music publisher, designer; b. Buffalo, Feb. 19, 1916; s. William George and Mary E. (Davis) W.; m. Annemarie M. Nos, July 19, 1947. Student Millard Fillmore Coll., 1937, Syracuse U., 1939, Bryant Stratton, 1973. Singer-entertainer stage/radio, 1924-40; barge capt., Erie Canal, N.Y., 1936, 39; contractor Weyand Bldg., Buffalo, 1947-54; self-employed designer, Buffalo, 1954-67; pub. Weyand Music, Depew, N.Y., 1967—; musician-piano arranger, Depew, 1967—; owner Da-Car Recording Co., 1967—. Composer, pub. Moon Over the River, 1940, My Old Hometown, 1942, The 80's Song Folio, 1977, Grey Mood Tonight, 1978, Song for Freedom, 1978, Piano Classics Collection, 1988; composer Bicentennial Suite, 1787—, collection piano classics and preludes, 1988; pub. A Father for Christmas, 1983 (Hazel Adair, Werner Janssen), 1984, To Seal Our Love (Werner Janssen, Lockerbie), 1984; composer, publisher Yesterday, A Love Ago, 1980, Change of Heart, 1980, Now I Know, 1980, Empty Sea, 1980; collaborator, pub. Thanks, Mr. Handel (Werner Janssen, W. Brandin), 1988; performed as singer at Maxine Theatre, 1930, Marble Arch Theatre, London, 1944; presented The Man Who Came to Dinner, Erlanger Theatre and Buffalo TV, 1950; performed under psuedonym Tex Davis, 1936. Sec., Pan Am. Club, Buffalo, 1951; charter officer Blvd. Players, Inc. Served with USAF, 1941-47; ETO. Recipient Electric Motor Control award Niagara Mohawk Power Corp., Buffalo, 1964. Fellow AIA, Archaeol. Inst. Am. (editorial bd.); mem. ASCAP, Nat. Acad. Popular Music, N.Y.C., 1987, Am. Biog. Inst. (research bd. advisors, (hon.) 1987), Nat. Music Pubs. Assn., AGAG, NMPA, Planetary Soc. (charter mem), Internat. Platform Assn., Songwriter's Guild. Republican. Lutheran. Club: Frohsinn Singing Soc. (Buffalo) (tenor 1948-54). Avocations: oil-painting, sketch drawing, Roman history. Home: 297 Rehm Rd Depew NY 14043

WEYENBERG, DONALD RICHARD, chemist; b. Glenvil, Nebr., July 11, 1930; s. Clyde H. and Elva I. (Hlavaty) W.; m. Barbara Ann Oppenheim, Dec. 26, 1955; children: Ann Louise, Thomas Richard. B.S. in Chemistry, U. Nebr., 1951; Ph.D., Pa. State U., 1958; P.M.D. Program, Harvard U., 1968. Research chemist Dow Corning Corp., Midland, Mich., 1951-65, research mgr., 1965-68, dir. corp. devel., 1968-69, dir. silicone research, 1969-71, bus. mgr., 1971-76, dir. research, 1976-79, v.p. research and devel., 1979-86, sr. v.p. research and devel., 1987—; bd. dirs. Dow Corning. Bd. editors: Organometallics Jour., 1980—; contbr. articles to sci. jours., chpts. to books; patentee silicone materials. Bd. visitors Memphis State U., 1981—; mem. indsl. bd. advisors U. Nebr., 1988. Named Alumni fellow Pa. State U., 1988. Mem. Am. Chem. Soc. (chmn. Midland sect. 1967 Outstanding Achievement in Promotion Chem. Scis. award Midland sect.), Indsl. Research Inst., N.Y. Acad. Scis., Sigma Xi. Lodge: Rotary. Home: 4601 Arbor Dr Midland MI 48640 Office: Dow Corning Corp 2200 W Salzburg Rd Box 994 Midland MI 48686

WEYERHAEUSER, GEORGE HUNT, forest products company executive; b. Seattle, July 8, 1926; s. John Philip and Helen (Walker) W.; m. Wendy Wagner, July 10, 1948; children: Virginia Lee, George Hunt, Susan W., Phyllis A., David M., Merrill W. BS with honors in Indsl. Engring., Yale U., 1949. With Weyerhaeuser Co., Tacoma, 1949—, successively mill foreman, br. mgr., 1949-56, v.p., 1957-62, exec. v.p., 1962-66, pres., 1966-88, chmn., chief exec. officer, 1988—, chmn., 1988—; bd. dirs. Boeing Co., SAFECO Corp., Chevron Copr.; mem. adv. bd. sch. of bus. adminstrn. U. Wash., the Bus. Council, Bus. Roundtable, Wash. State Bus. Roundtable. Office: Weyerhaeuser Co Tacoma WA 98477

WEYGAND, LAWRENCE RAY, insurance company executive; b. South Haven, Mich., Jan. 5, 1940; s. Ray and Lorraine (Berkins) W.; B.A., Drake U., 1962, postgrad., 1962-63; m. Paula West, May 2, 1987; 1 son, Chad C. Comml. multi-peril ins. underwriter Aetna Casualty & Surety Co., Mpls., also Indpls., 1964-66, Safeco Ins. Co., Denver, 1966-69; pres., chmn. bd. Weygand & Co., ins. agts., brokers and consultants, Denver, 1969—; pres. Homeowners Ins. Agy., Inc., Scottsdale, Ariz., Homeowners Ins., Inc., Denver, Weygand & Co. of Ariz., Inc., Scottsdale, Transatlantic Underwriters, Inc.; owner U.S. Insurors, Inc., Ariz. Dealers Ins. Services, Inc., Colo. Dealers Ins. Services, Inc., Denver, Storage Pak Ins., Inc.; owner, pres. gen. agy. serving Colo., Ariz., Nev., Utah and N.Mex.; asst. to Gov. State of Iowa, 1961-62. Mem. bus. community adv. council Regis Coll., Denver, 1976—. Mem. Ind. Ins. Agts. Colo. (chmn. fair and ethical practice com.), Ind. Ins. Agts. Am., Profl. Ins. Agts. Colo., Profl. Ins. Agts. Am., Alpha Tau Omega. Republican. Congregationalist. Club: Denver Athletic. Office: 1250 S Parker Rd Denver CO 80231

WEYGAND, LEROY CHARLES, trade association administrator; b. Webster Park, Ill., May 17, 1926; s. Xaver William and Marie Caroline (Hoffert) W.; BA in Sociology cum laude, U. Md., 1964; m. Helen V. Bishop, Aug. 28, 1977; children: Linda M. Weygand Vance (dec.), Leroy Charles, Cynthia R., Janine P. Enlisted in U.S. Army, 1944, commd. 2d lt., 1950, advanced through grades to lt. col., 1966; service in Korea, 1950; chief phys. security U.S. Army, 1965-70; ret., 1970; pres. Weygand Security Cons. Srvcs., Anaheim, Calif., 1970—, W & W Devel. Corp., 1979—; security dir. Jefferies Banknote Co., 1972-78; exec. dir Kern County Taxpayers Assn., 1986—; dir. Mind Psi-Biotics, Inc. Bd. dirs. Nat. Assn. Control Narcotics and Dangerous Drugs. Decorated Legion of Merit. Mem. Am. Soc. Indsl. Security. Contbr. articles profl. jours. Patentee office equipment locking device. Home: 19880 Comanche Pl PO Box 140 Tehachapi CA 93581 Office: Kern County Taxpayers Assn 1415 18th St Ste 407 Bakersfield CA 93301

WEYHER, HARRY FREDERICK, III, grain company executive; b. N.Y.C., Mar. 9, 1956; s. Harry F. and Barbara (McCusker) W.; m. Anda Gailitis, July 7, 1984; 1 child, Harry F. IV. BA, Middlebury Coll., 1977. Treas. Bunge Corp., N.Y.C., 1977—. Mem. Racquet & Tennis Club. Home: 279 Westport Rd Wilton CT 06897 Office: Bunge Corp 1 Chase Manhattan Plaza New York NY 10005

WEYLER, WALTER EUGEN, manufacturing company executive; b. Berwyn, Ill., Sept. 21, 1939; s. Eugen J. and Else E. (Deeg) W.; m. Nancy Prudence Haines; children—Walter Eugen, Peter C., Amy H. B.E.E., Mich. State U., 1961; M.B.A., Harvard U., 1963. Mktg. mgr. integrated circuit product line Tex. Instruments Corp., Dallas, 1963-68; mfg. mgr. semicondr. div. ITT, West Palm Beach, Fla., 1968-74; various positions Gen. Electric Co., Waterford, N.Y., 1974-82; v.p., gen. mgr. mobile communications Gen. Electric Co., Lynchburg, Va., 1982-85; pres., chief operating officer Graco, Inc., Mpls., 1985—. Trustee Minn. Orch., Mpls., 1985. Mem. Mpls. C. of C. (trustee 1987). Clubs: Interlachen (Mpls.), Minneapolis. Home: 7715 Stonewood Ct Edina MN 55435 Office: Graco Inc 4050 Olson Memorial Hwy Minneapolis MN 55440

WHALEY, CHARLES HENRY, IV, communications company executive; b. Elmhurst, N.Y., Jan. 15, 1958; s. Charles Henry III and Edna Mae (Squire) W.; m. Jeanette Marie Smith, Sept. 26, 1987. AAS in Electrical Tech., Queensborough Community Coll., Bayside, N.Y., 1979. Testing engr. GTE/Telenet, Mount Laurel, N.J., 1979-81; field service engr. Gen. Dynamics Communications Co., St. Louis, 1981-82; ops. engr. United Techs. Communications Co., Pine Brook, N.J., 1982-84; sr. ops. engr. United Techs. Communications Co., N.Y.C., 1984-85, ops. supr., 1985-86; project mgr. Telex Computer Products, N.Y.C., 1986; pres. Pertel Communications Corp., Queens Village, N.Y., 1986—. Democrat. Presbyterian. Office: Pertel Communications Corp 220-24 Jamaica Ave Queens Village NY 11428 also: Pertel Communications Corp 5 National Dr Windsor Locks CT 06096

WHALEY, PEGGY ELAINE (ELLIS), advertising executive; b. Cleve., Tenn., Nov. 30, 1939; d. Edward Darrell and Pauline (Earley), E.; m. Leo J. Whaley, Mar. 29, 1957; children: Sherri, Angela, Traci. Student, Cleve. Coll., 1964-65, Dayton Coll., 1970-72. Office mgr., corp. officer So. Gen. Products Inc., Ringgold, Ga., 1967-73; office mgr. Joe Goodson CPA, Dalton, Ga., 1974-78; comptroller Profl. C&C, Inc., Dalton, 1980-83; editor, assoc. pub. S.E. Floor Covering mag., Dalton, 1983; prin. Whaley & Assocs., Dalton, 1983—; pub., editor Peggy Whaley News Report Internat., Dalton, 1982-85. Co-editor: Today and Tomorrow Became Yesterday, 1986; contbr. numerous articles to newspapes, mags. Sec., v.p. Whitfield County Reps., Dalton, 1968-80; mem. adv. bd. SBA. Mem. World Trade Coun., Creative Arts Guild Writers Group, N.Y. Bus. Press Editors Inc., Nat. Assn. Accts., Nat. Assn. Floor Covering Women (nat. dir. 1984—), Dalton C. of C., Dalton Regional Library Bd. (chmn. 1980-86), Dalton-Whitfield Regional Libr. Found. (bd. mem. 1986—), Pilot Club, LWV (publicity chmn. 1976-81), Toastmasters Internat. (v.p. 1982). Republican. Baptist. Home: 5433 Red Clay Rd Cohutta GA 30710 Office: Whaley & Assocs PO Box 205 Dalton GA 30722

WHARTON, CLIFTON REGINALD, JR., insurance company executive, former academic administrator; b. Boston, Sept. 13, 1926; m. Dolores Duncan, 1950; children: Clifton, Bruce. BA, Harvard U., 1947; MA, Johns Hopkins U., 1948, LLD (hon.), 1970; MA, U. Chgo., 1956, PhD in Econs., 1958; LLD (hon.), U. Mich., 1970, Wayne State U., 1970, Cen. Mich. U., 1970, Oakland U., 1971, Georgetown U., 1976, CCNY, 1978, Albany Law Sch., 1980, Wright State U., 1979, Duke U., 1981, Amherst Coll., 1983, U. Ill., 1984; LHD (hon.), Columbia U., 1978, Brandeis U., 1981, NYU, 1981, U. Conn., 1983, U. Mass., Boston, 1985, U. Vt., 1987, Tuskegee U., 1987, Tufts U., 1988; LittD (hon.), N.C. Agrl. and Tech. State U., 1986, So. Ill. U., 1987, George Mason U., 1988. Exec. trainee Am. Internat. Assn. Econ. and Social Devel., 1948-49, program analyst, 1949-51, head reports and analysis, 1951-53; rsch. asst. econs. U. Chgo., 1953-56, rsch. assoc., 1956-57; exec. assoc. Agrl. Devel. Coun., 1957-58, assoc., 1958-64, dir. Am. univs. rsch., 1964-67, v.p., 1967-69; pres. Mich. State U., 1970-78; chancellor SUNY System, 1978-87; chmn., chief exec. officer Tchrs. Ins. & Annuity Assn. Coll. Retirement Equities Fund, N.Y.C., 1987—; vis. prof. U. Malaya, Singapore, 1958-64, Stanford U., 1964-65; mem. Presdl. Task Force Agr. in Vietnam, 1966; adv. panel on East Asia and Pacific State Dept., 1966-69; mem. Presdl. mission to Latin Am., 1969, Presdl. Com. on World Hunger, 1978-80, Nat. Coun. on Fgn. Lang. and Internat. Studies, 1980-81; chmn. bd. internat. food and agrl. devel. AID, State Dept., 1976-83; co-chmn. Commn. on Security and Econ. Assistance, Dept. State, 1983; dir. Ford Motor Co., 1973—, Equitable Life Assurance Soc., 1969-82, PBS, 1970-73, Time Inc., 1982—, Fed. Res. Bank N.Y., dep. chmn., 1982-86, Burroughs Corp., 1973-77, Federated Dept. Stores, 1985-88. Co-author: Patterns for Lifelong Learning, 1973; editor: Subsistence Agriculture and Economic Development, 1969; contbr. articles to profl. jours. Trustee Rockefeller Found., 1970-87, chmn., 1982-87; trustee Asia Soc., 1967-77, Overseas Devel. Coun., 1969—, Carnegie Found., 1970-79, Agrl. Devel. Counc., 1973-80, Aspen Inst. Humanistic Studies, 1980—, Com. Econ. Devel., 1980—, Counc. Fin. Aid to Edn., 1983-86, Counc. Fgn. Relations, 1983—, Fgn. Policy Assn., 1983-87, MIT Corp., 1984-86, Acad. Ednl. Devel., 1985-86. Mem. Am. Agrl. Econs. Assn., Am. Econs. Assn., Assn. Asian Studies, Nat. Acad. Edn., Bus.-Higher Edn. Forum (com. for econ. devel.), Trilateral Commn., Internat. Assn. Agrl. Econs. Club: Univ. (N.Y.C.). Office: TIAA-CREF 730 3rd Ave New York NY 10017

WHEATCROFT, JOHN DAVID, real estate corporation officer; b. Kirksville, Mo., Oct. 9, 1948; s. George Richard and Anita (Lyon) W. BA, U. Tex., 1971, postgrad., 1988—. Investment broker Coldwell Banker Comml. Real Estate, Dallas, 1983-85; asst. v.p. MRealty Corp., Dallas, 1985-87; v.p. Republic of Tex. Properties, Dallas, 1987—; instr. comml. real estate U. Tex., 1985-87. Mem. Urban Land Inst. (assoc.). Episcopalian. Office: Republic of Tex Properties 325 N Saint Paul Ste 910 Tower II Dallas TX 75201

WHEATLEY, ARTHUR EDWIN, JR., insurance company executive; b. Chester, Pa., Jan. 19, 1943; s. Arthur E. Sr. and Kathryn (Scott) W.; m. Linda Susan Ponsitory, July 31, 1973; children: Scott Arthur, Ryan Barry. BA in Econs., Davis & Elkins Coll., 1965. Assoc. in risk mgmt. Conn. Claims; supr. Liberty Mut. Ins. Co., Atlanta, Charlotte, N.C. and East Orange, N.Y., 1971-74; ins. coordinator Becton-Dickinson & Co., Rutherford, N.J., 1974-78; mgr. property and liability ins Scovill, Inc., Waterbury, Conn., 1978-85; v.p., dir. risk mgmt. The Pittston Co., Greenwich, Conn., 1985—. With USAF, 1967-71. Mem. Risk and Ins. Mgmt. Soc., Woodbury-Bethew Youth Soccer (bd. dirs. 1987—, Woodbury, Conn.). Office: The Pittston Co One Pickwick Plaza Greenwich CT 06836

WHEATLEY, ROBERT RAY, III, marketing executive; b. Amarillo, Tex., Sept. 24, 1934; s. Robert Ray Jr. and Lila Amanda (Townsend) W.; m. Judy Lee Bevington, 1965; 1 child, Robert Todd; m. Nora Jean Madden, July 26, 1972; 1 child, James Ray. BS, West Tex. U., 1956; MBA, Calif. Coast U., 1985, PhD, 1988. Sr. contract adminstr. Martin Marietta, Denver, 1968-76; owner, operator John Deere Dealership, Broomfield, Colo., 1976-80; engring. analyst Rockwell Internat., Houston, 1980-84; mktg. mgr. ICC Space Systems, Houston, 1984-85; v.p. bus. devel. Presearch, Inc., Houston, 1985-88; dir. NASA mkgt. QuesTech Rsch. Corp., McLean, Va., 1988; mgr. Houston ops. Axiom Corp., Webster, Tex., 1988—. Capt. U.S. Army 1956-60. Mem. Am. Mktg. Assn., Am. Legion, Elks. Lutheran. Home: 704 Balmoral Ct Friendswood TX 77546

WHEATON, JOHN SOUTHWORTH, distribution company executive; b. Balt., Dec. 26, 1928; s. Ezra Almon and Ruth Adelaide (Otis) W.; m. Joy Lorraine Thuressen, Dec. 16, 1950; children: Sandra, Jason, Christopher. B.A., Stanford U., 1951; M.B.A., Columbia U., 1953. Mgr. fin. TRW, Inc., Redondo Beach, Calif., 1956-60; v.p. ops. Bissett-Berman Corp., Santa Monica, Calif., 1960-71; v.p. ops. control Foremost-McKesson, Inc., San Francisco, 1971-74; v.p. planning and analysis McKesson Corp., San Francisco, 1974-86, exec. v.p. adminstrn., 1986—; bd. dirs. Armor All, Irvine, Calif., Pharm. Card Systems, Scottsdale, Ariz. Served to lt. USNR, 1953-56. Club: Olympic. Office: McKesson Corp One Post St San Francisco CA 94104

WHEELER, BETTY ELLER, foundation administrator; b. Elkin, N.C., Feb. 21, 1938; d. Wade Edward and Dempsie (Smith) Eller; m. Stanley B. Wheeler, May 29, 1959 (div. June 1981); children: Mark Edward, Jonathan Burke. BA in Sociology, Tex. Tech U., 1958, postgrad., 1958-59. Elem. sch. tchr., Slaton, Tex., 1959-60; dist. dir. Camp Fire Girls, Lubbock, Tex., 1960-63; child welfare worker Lubbock (Tex.) City-County Child Welfare, 1964-67; officer Lubbock County (Tex.) Juvenile Probation, 1967-68; vol. staff Nat. Camp Fire Girls, Tex. and N.Mex., 1975-76; cons. social services Milam's Children's Tng. Cen., Lubbock, 1975-76; asst. exec. dir. Lubbock Day Care Assn., 1972-77; cons. fund raising Easter Seal Soc., Lubbock, 1978; dir. Christian Edn. St. Paul's Epis. Ch., Lubbock, 1971-83; interim dir. All Saints Epis. Sch., Lubbock, 1980-81; exec. dir. YWCA Lubbock, 1981—; bd. dirs. Tex. Coalition Juvenile Justice 1986—; adv. council Cultural Affairs Council 1985—, Teen Connection 1987-88. Bd. dirs. Lubbock Heritage Soc. 1985—; delegate St. Dem. Conv., Austin 1986; chmn. Elec. Utility Bd. 1982, City-County Health Bd., Citizens Com. for Lubbock County Juvenile Detention Ctr., South Plains Youth Council, Dupre and Parsons Elem. Schs. PTA Bds., Tex. Tech Arts and Scis. Adv. Council, United Way, Lubbock Symphony Guild; del. 1970 Gov.'s Conference on Children and Youth; vol. Salvation Army Soup Kitchen; polit. campaign worker Dem. Party; participant in numerous other civic activities. Named one of Outstanding Young Women Am., Lubbock Bus. and Profl. Women's Club, 1968, Lubbock's Woman of the Yr., Altrusa Club, 1968. Mem. Nat. Assn. YWCA Execs., United Way Exec. Dirs. Assn. (past chmn.), South Plains Chpt. Nat. Soc. Prevention Child Abuse (bd. dirs.), Interagency Action Council, Exec. Forum., Jr. League (community v.p. 1978-79, exec. com. 2 yrs., bd. dirs. 4 yrs., sustaining advisor 2 yrs.), Delta Delta Delta (mem. adv. council). Home: 3310 55th St Lubbock TX 79413 Office: YWCA 3101 35th St Lubbock TX 79413

WHEELER, DAVID WAYNE, accountant; b. Charlottesville, Va., June 1, 1952; s. Daniel Gordon and Marion Elaine (Booth) W. BS in Acctg., Va. Poly. Inst. and State U., 1975. CPA, Va. Staff acct. Robert M. Musselman, Charlottesville, Va., 1971-76; pvt. practice acctg. Charlottesville, Va., 1976-77; sec., treas. Wheeler & Hancher Ltd., Charlottesville, Va., 1977-79; pres. David W. Wheeler Ltd., Charlottesville, Va., 1980—. Contbr. articles to profl. jours. Treas., bd. dirs. East Rivanna Vol. Fire Dept., Albemarle County, Va., 1983—; bd. dirs. Literacy Vols. of Am., Charlottesville, Albemarle, 1988—. Mem. Va. Soc. CPA's, Am. Inst. CPA's (taxation div.). Baptist. Home: Wedgewood Rt 1 Box 152-C Keswick VA 22947 Office: 400 Court Sq Charlottesville VA 22901

WHEELER, ELTON SAMUEL, financial executive; b. Salinas, Calif., Oct. 25, 1943; s. Luther Elton and Naomi E. (Beatty) W.; BS, Calif. State U., 1966; m. Patricia Lynne McCleary, Sept. 2, 1967; children—Pamela Kathleen, Leslie Elizabeth-Anne, Deborah Suzanne, Jonathan Samuel. Acct., Coopers & Lybrand, Oakland, Calif., 1967-70; controller Adams Properties, Inc., San Francisco, 1970-71, treas., 1972-75, v.p., chief fin. officer, 1976-77; v.p., chief fin. officer Adams Capital Mgmt. Co., San Francisco, 1977-79, pres., chief exec. officer, 1979-87; pres., chief exec. officer, dir. Calif. Real Estate Investment Trust, 1980-88; dir. Franklin Select Real Estate Income Trust, 1989—. Served with USMCR, 1966-72. CPA, Calif. Mem. Nat. Assn. Real Estate Investment Trusts, Inc. (sec., bd. govs.), Am. Inst. CPAs, Calif. Soc. CPAs. Club: Olympic. Office: PO Box 567 Columbia CA 95310

WHEELER, JIMMY W., director of economic studies; b. Kansas City, Mo., Mar. 14, 1948; s. J. W. and Thaina May (Brown) W.; m. Susan Charles Campbell, Aug. 15, 1973. BA, U. Mo., 1971; MA, Rutgers U., 1975. Research asst. U. Mo., Kansas City, 1972-73; teaching asst. Rutgers U., New Brunswick, N.J., 1973-75, inst., 1975-76; asst. prof. Fla. Internat. U., 1976-77; profl. staff Hudson Inst., Croton-on-Hudson, N.Y., 1977-79, sr. profl., 1979-82, dep. dir. econ. studies, 1982-84; dir. econ. studies Hudson Inst., Indpls., 1984—. Co-author: Japanese Industrial Development Policies in the 1980s, 1982, The Competion: Dealing with Japan, 1985, Western European Adjustment to Structural Economic Problems, 1987, Beyond Recrimination: Perspective on the US-Taiwan Trade, 1987. Bd. dirs. Ind. Export & Internat. Bus. Project (Indpls.), 1985-86, Japan-Am. Soc. Ind. Mem. Am. Econ. Assn., Soc. Policy Modeling, World Future Soc., Council on Fgn. Relations (Ind. com.), Am. Assn. Chinese Studies. Office: Hudson Inst 5395 Emerson Way Indianapolis IN 46226

WHEELER, JOHN ERNEST, JR., oil company executive; b. Leonardtown, Md., Nov. 28, 1952; s. John Ernest and Margaret Louise (Johnson) W.; m. Catherine Maria McConville, Oct. 21, 1978; 1 child, Justin. BA in Acctg., Loyola Coll., Balt., 1974, MBA in Fin., 1985. CPA, Md. Staff acct. Ernst & Whinney, Balt., 1974-76; auditor Crown Cen. Petroleum, Balt., 1976-77, sr. auditor, 1977-78, acctg. mgr., 1978-79, div. controller, 1979-81, controller, 1981-84, v.p., controller, 1984—. Treas. Crown Cen. Polit. Action Com., 1985—; bd. dirs. Easter Seals of Md., 1989—. Mem. AICPA, Md. Assn. CPA's, Fin. Execs. Inst., KC. Roman Catholic. Office: Crown Cen Petroleum Corp One N Charles St Box 1168 Baltimore MD 21201

WHEELER, KATHERINE N., urban planner; b. St. Louis, June 28, 1939; d. Hiram and Emily (Lewis) Norcross; m. W. Mark Wheeler III, Jan. 2, 1965; children: Tim, Andrew, Geoffrey, Beth. BA in History, Boston U., 1962; MA in English Lit., Portland (Oreg.) State U., 1970, MA in Urban Planning, 1978. Pvt. practice tour operator Portland, 1985—. Contbr. Scribe, 1986—, Pdx Bus. Jour., 1987—. Mem. Portland Oreg. Visitors Assn., City of Portland Club, Racquet Club, Athletic Club. Democrat. Episcopalian. Clubs: City of Portland, Racquet, Athletic, Multnowah. Home and Office: 745 NW Culpepper Terr Portland OR 97210

WHEELER, LARRY RICHARD, accountant; b. Greybull, Wyo., Nov. 30, 1940; s. Richard F. and Olive B. (Fredrickson) W.; m. Marjorie A. Frady, Dec. 20, 1961; m. Patricia C. Marturano, Dec. 3, 1977; children: Anthony, Richard, Teresa, Kara. BS, U. Wyo., 1965. CPA, Colo. Staff acct. H. Greger CPA, Ft. Collins, Colo., 1965-66, sr. acct. Lester Draney & Wickham, Colorado Springs, Colo., 1966-67; acct., controller/treas., J.D. Adams Co., Colorado Springs, 1967-74; ptnr. Wheeler Pierce & Hurd, Inc., Colorado Springs, 1974-80; gen. mgr., v.p. Schneebeck's, Inc., Colorado Springs, 1980-81; prin. L.R. Wheeler & Co., P.C., Colorado Springs, 1981—; dir. Schneebeck's Industries, Williams Printing, Inc. Mem. U.S. Taekwond Union; bd. dirs. Domestic Violence Prevention Ctr. Paul Stock Found. grantee, 1962. Mem. Internat. Assn. Fin. Planners, Am. Inst. CPA's, Nat. Contract Mgmt. Assn., Colo. Soc. CPA's. Club: Colorado Springs Country. Office: 317 E San Rafael Colorado Springs CO 80903

WHEELER, PAUL JAMES, real estate executive; b. Mpls., Jan. 8, 1953; s. Philip James and Phyllis Lavonne (Holmquist) W.; m. Marianne Marie Stanton, June 3, 1978; children: Allison, Nathan, Kathryn. BA in Econs., DePauw U., 1975; MBA in Mgmt., Northwestern U., 1977. CPA, Ill. Acct. Deloitte, Haskins & Sells, Chgo., 1976-79; v.p. fin. Quinlan & Tyson, Inc., Evanston, Ill., 1979-82; sr. v.p. The Inland Group, Inc., Oakbrook, Ill., 1982—; bd. dirs. Am. Nat. Downers Grove, Inland Am. Ins. Co., Inland Securities Corp., Oak Brook, Ill. Mem. Ill. Soc. CPA's, Real Estate Securities and Syndication Inst., Internat. Assn. Fin. Planning, Investment Ptnrship. Assn. Republican. Presbyterian. Home: 255 Ridgeway Ln Libertyville IL 60048 Office: Inland Real Estate Corp 2901 Butterfield Rd Oak Brook IL 60521

WHEELER, RICHARD WARREN, banker; b. Boston, Feb. 8, 1929; s. Wilfrid and Sybil Constance (Leckenby) W.; m. Betty Ann Owens, Sept. 9, 1950; children: Emily, Susan Knight, Thomas Adams, Alice Owens, Sarah Bennett. B.A., Williams Coll., 1952; P.M.D., Harvard Bus. Sch., 1962. With Citibank, N.A., 1952-82; assigned to Citibank, N.A., Hongkong, Manila and Tokyo, 1953-69; v.p. Citibank, N.A., 1967-69; sr. v.p. Citibank, N.A., N.Y.C., 1969-82; head internat. relations unit Citibank, N.A., 1977-82; exec. v.p. Asia Soc., 1982-84; pres. Asia Internat. Bank, 1984-85; sr. v.p., gen. mgr. Bank of the Philippine Islands, N.Y.C., 1985—. Bd. dirs., v.p. Am. Australian Assn.; organizing dir. Nat. Council U.S.-China Trade; bd. dirs.; chmn. exec. com. Presiding Bishop's Fund for World Relief; mem. spl. refugee adv. panel Dept. State; chmn. adv. council Harvard Center for Study World Religions; mem. adv. bd. Georgetown Center for Contemporary Arab Studies, 1977-79, Harvard U. Center for East Asian Studies, Center for Strategic and Internat. Studies, 1970-80; v.p. exec. council Harvard Bus. Sch., 1971-75; chmn. bus. and industry adv. council to OECD com. on capital markets and capital movements; mem. exec. com. Asean-U.S. Bus. Council, Sudan-U.S. Bus. Council, India-U.S. Bus. Council, U.S.-Korea Econ. Council; dir. v.p., treas. Philippine Am. C. of C.; trustee Cambridge Sch., Weston, Mass. Served with AUS, 1946-47. Mem. Japan Soc. (chmn. exec. com., dir.), Nat. Planning Assn. (trustee, treas.), Nat. Fgn. Trade Coun. (dir., exec. com.), Internat. C. of C. (vice chmn., trustee U.S. coun.), U.S. Assn. for Internat. Migration (bd. dirs., treas., exec. com.), Coun. on Fgn. Rels., Univ. Club, Bronxville Field Club, Hodegaya Golf Club, Tokyo Lawn Tennis Club. Episcopalian. Home: 181 Boulder Trail Bronxville NY 10708 Office: 805 3d Ave 28th Floor New York NY 10022

WHEELER, ROBERT CHANNING, JR., health maintenance organization executive; b. Evanston, Ill., Mar. 4, 1952; s. Robert Channing Wheeler and Mary M. (Whitmire) Brown; m. Elizabeth Joan Mellor, June 1, 1951; children: Joy Carolyn, Anne Miriam. BA, BS, Stanford U., 1977, MA, 1978; MBA, UCLA, 1983. Program assoc. Community Cancer Control L.A., 1979-80; dir. prevention UCLA Cancer Ctr., Westood, 1980-83; sr. staff mgr. FHP Inc., Fountain Valley, Calif., 1983-84; dir. provider rels. Maxicare Health Plans, L.A., 1984-85, v.p., exec. dir., 1985-86, regional v.p., 1987—; bd. dirs. Maxicare Calif. Corp., L.A., Gen. Med. Health Plan, Orange, Calif. Author: Preventing Lung Cancer in Los Angeles, 1983. Bd. dirs. Ladera Heights Community Hosp., L.A., 1987-88. Republican. Episcopalian. Office: Maxicare Health Plans 5200 W Century Blvd Los Angeles CA 90045

WHEELER, THOMAS BEARDSLEY, insurance company executive; b. Buffalo, Aug. 2, 1936; s. William Henry and Ruth (Matthews) W.; m. Anne Tuck Robertson, Nov. 15, 1961; children—Elizabeth Comstock, Wendy Bennett. B.A., Yale U., 1958. C.L.U. Sales rep. IBM, White Plains, N.Y., 1961-62; sales rep., asst. gen. agt. Mass. Mut. Life Ins. Co., Boston, 1962, gen. agt., 1972-83; exec. v.p. Mass. Mut. Life Ins. Co., Springfield, 1983-86, pres., 1987—; bd. dirs. Bank of Boston Corp. Co-author: Managing Sales Professionals, 1984. Trustee Springfield Coll., 1985—, Am. Coll., Bryn Mawr, Pa., 1987—, Baystate Health Systems, Inc., Springfield, 1983—, Springfield Orch. Assn., Basketball Hall of Fame, Springfield. Served to lt. USNR, 1958-60, Mediterranean, Atlantic, Pacific. Mem. Yale Univ. Devel. Bd., Springfield Life Underswriter's Assn., Am. Soc. C.L.U.s (Pioneer Valley chpt., pres. Boston chpt. 1980-81), Boston Life Underswriter's Assn. (pres. 1972-73), Mass. Assn. Life Underwriters (pres. 1976-77), Million Dollar Round Table. Republican. Clubs: Yale of N.Y., Colony (Springfield), Longmeadow Country, Boca Grande, Chapoquoit Yacht (sec. 1973-75); The Links (N.Y.C.). Office: Mass Mut Life Ins Co 1295 State St Springfield MA 01111

WHEELER, WILLIAM BRYAN, III, systems company executive; b. Kissimmee, Fla., June 21, 1940; s. William Bryan and Olive Mae (Criner) W.; m. Mary Sue Lewis, Dec. 29, 1961 (div. Jan. 1987); children: Alicia Nanette, Bryan; m. Vickie Lynn Von Tempske, Mar. 20, 1988. Student U. Fla., 1958-59, U. Md., 1967-68; B.L.A., U. Ga., 1975; Ph.D., Bangor Inst., 1978. Meteorol. supr. Pan Am. World Airways, 1962-63; asst. engr. Fla. Road Dept., Orlando, 1963-64; tech. supr. Xerox Corp., 1964-65; sr. field engr. Fed. Electric Corp., Rome, 1965-66; systems engr. Bendix Corp., 1966-70; devel. dir. East Coast Stainless Steel, Lanham, Md., 1970-71; regional planner Middle Flint Planning and Devel. Commn., Ellaville, Ga., 1975-78; planning dir. Northeast Ga. Area Planning and Devel. Commn., Athens, 1978-81; dist. mgr. CASA Data Systems, Athens, 1981-82; v.p. Select Systems, Inc., Atlanta, 1982-86; network mgr. Universal Data, Atlanta, 1987—. Vice pres. Sumter County Bicentennial Beautification Com., 1976-77. Author: (Pseudonym Rhuddlwm Gawr) The Quest--The Discovery of the Cauldron of Immortality, The Way Part II of The Quest, Celtic Crystal Magick, vol. 1. Served with USMC, 1958-61. Mem. Am. Soc. Landscape Architects, Am. Soc. Med. Computing and Electronics, Am. Planning Assocs. Democrat.

WHELAN, JOHN WILLIAM, stockbroker; b. Pitts., Mar. 3, 1955; s. James Samuel and Catherine Ann (Gallagher) W. BA in Econs., Washington & Jefferson Coll., 1977; MBA in Fin., U. Pitts., 1981. Cert. fin. planner. Fin. cons. Merrill, Lynch, Pierce, Fenner & Smith, New Kensington, Pa., 1982-86; assoc. mgr. Prudential-Bache Securities, Fox Chapel, Pa., 1986-89, Pitts., 1989—. Columnist, Your Money, 1987-89. Mem. Inst. Chartered Fin. Analysts, Inst. Cert. Fin. Planners. Roman Catholic. Home: 824 Fairways Dr Oakmont PA 15139 Office: Prudential Bache Securities 2700 USX Tower Pittsburgh PA 15219

WHELEHAN, DAVID D., insurance company executive; b. Garden City, N.J., Dec. 13, 1942; s. J. Donald and Florence (Seitz) W.; m. JoAnn Sproviere, Dec. 17, 1966; children: T. Scott, Brian. BA, Holy Cross Coll., 1964; JD, George Washington U., 1967. CLU; chartered fin. cons. Atty. Conn. Mut. Life Ins. Co., Hartford, 1967-70, asst. counsel, 1970-73, dir., 1973-77; gen. agt. Conn. Mut. Life Ins. Co., Woodbury, N.Y., 1977-85; exec. v.p. Conn. Mut. Life Ins. Co., Hartford, Conn., 1985-88; pres. CM Transnational SA, Luxembourg, 1988-89, CM Alliance Internat. Ltd., 1989—. Chmn. Old State House Assoc., Hartford, 1988—. Mem. L.I. Assn. Gen. Agts. and Mgrs. (pres. 1983), Nassau CLU Assn. (pres. 1982). Office: 140 Garden St Hartford CT 06154

WHELESS, LARRY, corporate professional; b. High Point, N.C., Mar. 19, 1939; s. Walter Hermon and Johnsie Lee (Moffit) W.; m. Sylvia A. Smith, Aug. 22, 1965; children: Todd, Heather. BS in Acctg., High Point Coll., 1961. CPA, N.C. Acct. Seidman, High Point, 1961-65; acct. Ricca Nelson & Gant, Durham, N.C., 1965-69, ptnr., 1969-71; treas. Black Industries, Durham, 1971—. Office: Black Industries Inc 2816 N Roxboro St Durham NC 27704

WHIDDEN, ROBERT LEE, JR., health care consultant; b. Beverly, Mass., Oct. 10, 1943; s. Robert Lee and Phyllis Alma (Patch) W.; A.B. in English, Harvard U., 1965; m. Lois Ann Lapeza, Mar. 4, 1972. Dir. indsl. relations Nat. Radio Co., Melrose, Mass., 1965-70; div. dir. Lowell (Mass.) Gen. Hosp., 1970-75; asst. adminstr. Union Hosp., Lynn, Mass., 1975-85; pres. Surgi/1 div., 1984-86, R.L. Whidden and Co., Andover, Mass., 1986—; Query, 1986—; prin. cons. Charlton Meml. Hosp., Fall River, Mass., 1987—; pres. Thinc., Andover, 1988—; hosp. rep. delegated rev. com. Eastern Mass. Profl. Standards Rev. Orgn., bd. dirs., 1984—; ex-officio mem. Integrated Data Demonstration Grant Com. Blue Cross Mass., 1982—; cons. quality assurance. Bd. dirs. Lowell Area Continuing Edn. Ctr., Nat. Found. Environ. Control, 1971, Hospice of North Shore, Inc.; bd. dirs., chmn. Northshore Manpower Coalition; mem. corp. edn. adv. bd. North Shore Community Coll., 1981—; mem. North Shore Econ. Council, 1981—; dir. clin. planning AtlantiCare Med. Ctr., Inc., Lynn, Mass., 1985-86; pres. R.L. Whidden & Co. healthcare cons., 1986—; pres. TH Inc, Andover, Mass., 1986—; mem. Mass. Health Data Adv. Council; mem. nominating com. Eastern Mass. PSRO, mem. pvt. ins. rev. com., mem. ambulatory surgery com. Nat. Merit scholar, 1960-61. Mem. Mass. Hosp. Assn. (mem. program rev. com. 1982—, chmn. mgmt. com. 1984—, mem. facilities and service com. class of 1987), New Eng. Hosp. Assembly, Am. Soc. Law and Medicine, Health Care Mgmt. Assn., Am. Mgmt. Assn., Phi Beta Kappa. Episcopalian. Clubs: Myopia Polo (patron), Willows and Cedardale Racquet, Hasty Pudding, Andover Tennis. Inventor quality assurance methodology known as "Physician Focussed Concurrent Monitoring". Home: 3 Spruce Circle Andover MA 01810 Office: RL Whidden 3 Spruce Ln Andover MA 01810-4020

WHILDEN, WALTER BURLESON, investment executive; b. Dallas, Dec. 22, 1938; s. Willis Cameron and Georgiabel (Burleson) W.; m. Jennie Finocchiaro, May 4, 1963; children: Charles B., David W., Jennifer L. BBA, U. Okla., 1961; MBA, Drexel U., 1964. Chartered fin. analyst; cert. fin. planner. Asst. v.p. Provident Nat. Bank, Phila., 1963-72, Farmers Bank of Del., Wilmington, 1972-77; dir. rsch., v.p. Valley Forge Investment Mgmt. Co., Pa., 1977; v.p. Merc.-Safe Deposit & Trust Co., Balt., 1977—; adj. faculty Coll. for Fin. Planning, Balt., 1984, 86-88; adv. com. mem. for investment course, Denver, 1985., advanced Portfolio Mgmt. Course, Denver, 1986; panelist Coll. Fin. Planning Annual Conf., Denver, 1989. Creator audio tape Bond Portfolio Management, 1989. Treas., Third Bapt. Ch., Phila., 1964-65; trustee Faith Bapt. Ch., Brookhaven, Pa., 1967-76; elder Fellowship Chapel, Jarrettsville, Md., 1983-84. Capt. U.S. Army, 1961-68. Mem. Fin. Analysts Fedn., Inst. Cert. Fin. Planners, Omicron Delta Kappa, Phi Eta Sigma, Delta Sigma Pi, Delta Upsilon. Republican. Avocations: woodworking, fishing, gardening, model building. Office: Mercantile Safe Deposit & Trust Co 2 Hopkins Pla Baltimore MD 21201

WHIPPLE, GEORGE STEPHENSON, architect; b. Evanston, Ill., Sept. 21, 1950; s. Taggart and Katharine (Brewster) W.; m. Lydia Buckley, May 30, 1981; children: Katherine Elizabeth, John Taggart. B.A., Harvard U., 1974; student Boston Architectural Ctr., 1975-76. Vice-pres., Call Us Inc., Edgartown, Mass., 1970-74; pres. Cattle Creek Assocs., Carbondale, Colo., 1976—, Earthworks Constrn., Carbondale, 1978-87; pres., Whipple and Brewster Corp., Aspen, 1988—. Chmn., Redstone Hist. Preservation Commn., Colo. Mem. Pitkin County Planning and Zoning Commn., 1989—. Mem. Rocky Mountain Harvard Club. Office: 121 S Galena Ste 203 Aspen CO 81611

WHIPPLE, KENNETH, automotive company executive; b. 1934. BS, MIT, 1958. With Ford Motor Co., Dearborn, Mich., 1958—, systems mgr. Ford Credit, 1966-69, mgr. mgmt. svcs. dept. fin. staff, 1969-71, systems analysis mgr. fin. staff, 1971-74, asst. contr. internat. fin. staff, 1974-75, v.p. fin. Ford Credit, 1975-77, exec. v.p. Ford Credit, 1977-80, pres. Ford Credit, 1980-84, v.p. corp. strategy analysis, 1984-86, v.p., 1986-88; chmn. Ford of Europe Inc. Ford Motor Co., 1986-88; exec. v.p., pres. Ford Fin. Svcs. Group, Dearborn, 1988—. Office: Ford Motor Co American Rd Dearborn MI 48121

WHISNAND, ROY VAN ARSDEL, management consultant; b. Providence, Jan. 26, 1944; s. Roy V. and Jane Ann (Morris) W.; m. Campbell Baker, June 11, 1966; children: Tyler, Carter. AB, Brown U., 1966; MBA, U. Va., 1968. V.p. Stone and Webster Inc., N.Y.C., 1972-86, exec. v.p., 1986-87; pres. Stone and Webster Mgmt. Cons. Inc., N.Y.C., 1984-86; ptnr. Combined Capital Mgmt., N.Y.C., 1987—; bd. dirs. NUI Corp., Bridgewater, N.J. Mem. N.Y. Soc. Security Analysts. Office: Combined Capital Mgmt 1 Penn Pla New York NY 10119

WHISTLER, ROY LESTER, chemist, educator, industrialist; b. Morgantown, W.Va., Mar. 21, 1912; s. Park H. and Cloe (Martin) W.; m. Leila Ann Barbara Kaufman, Sept. 6, 1935; 1 child, William Harris. B.S., Heidelberg Coll., 1934, D.Sc. (hon.), 1957; M.S., Ohio State U., 1935; Ph.D., Iowa State Coll., 1938; D.Litt. (hon.), St. Thomas Inst., 1982; D.Agr., Purdue U., 1985. Instr. chemistry Iowa State Coll., 1935-38; research fellow Bur. Standards, 1938-40; chemist, later sect. leader No. Regional Research Lab., Dept. Agr., 1940-46; prof. biochemistry Purdue U., 1946-76, Hillenbrand distinguished prof., asst. dept. head, 1974-82; Hillenbrand disting. prof. emeritus Purdue U., Lafayette, Ind., 1982—; chmn. Inst. Agrl. Utilization Research, 1961-75; vis. lectr. U. Witwatersrand, 1961, 65, 77, 85, Czechoslovakia and Hungary, 1968, 85, Japan, 1969, Taiwan, 1970, Argentina, 1971, New Zealand, Australia, 1967, 74; vis. lectr. Acad. Sci., France, 1975, Vladivostock Acad. Sci., 1976, Brazil, 1977, Egypt, 1979; lectr. Bradley Polytech. Inst., 1941-42, People's Repulic China, 1985; adv. Whistler Ctr. for Carbohydrate Chemistry; indsl. cons. Dir. USAir, Pfanstiehl Lab., Inc., Sperti Drug Products, Greenwich Pharm. Inc.; mem. NRC sub-com. nomenclature biochemistry; pres. Lafayette (Ind.) Applied Chemistry. Author: Polysaccharide Chemistry, 1953, Industrial Gums, 1959, 2d rev.

edit., 1976, 3d rev. edit., 1987; rev. edit.: Methods of Carbohydrate Chemistry, series, 1962—; co-author: Guar, 1979; also numerous sci. papers.; Editor: Starch-Chemistry and Technology, 2 vols., 1965, 67, rev. edit., 1984; editor: Jour. Carbohydrate Research, 1960—, Starchs Chemistry and Technology, 1985 ; bd. advisers: Advances in Carbohydrate Chemistry, 1950—, Organic Preparations and Procedures Internat., 1970—, Jour. Carbo-Nucleosides-Nucleotides, 1973-77, die Starke, Starch, 1979—; contbr. 500 articles to profl. jours. Recipient Sigma Xi Research award Purdue U., 1953; named one of ten outstanding starch chemists Chgo. sect. Am. Chem. Soc., 1948; recipient Hudson award Am. Chem. Soc., 1960, Anselme Payen award, 1967, Starch award Japanese, 1967, Carl Lucas Alsburg award, 1970; German Saare medal, 1974; Thomas Burr Osborne award, 1974; Spencer award Am. Chem. Soc., 1975; Disting. Service award Am. Chem. Soc., 1983, Roy L. Whistler internat. award in carbohydrates named in his honor, Whistler Ctr. for Carbohydrate Research, Purdue U., named in his honor. Fellow AAAS, Am. Chem. Soc. (chmn. Purdue sect. 1949-50, carbohydrate div. 1951, cellular div. 1962, nat. councilor 1953—, bd. dirs. 5th dist. 1955-58, chmn. com. edn. and students, chmn. sub-com. polysaccharide nomenclature, symposium dedicated in his honor 1979, hon. fellow award cellulose div. 1983), Am. Inst. Chemistry (pres. 1982-83), Am. Assn. Cereal Chemists (pres. 1978), Internat. Carbohydrate Union (pres. 1972-74); mem. Lafayette Applied Chemistry (pres. 1970—), Argentine Chem. Soc. (life), Sigma Xi (pres. Purdue sect. 1957-59, nat. exec. com. 1958-62, hon. life mem. 1983—), Phi Lambda Upsilon. Lodge: Rotary (pres. 1966).

WHITACRE, EDWARD E., JR., telecommunications executive; b. Ennis, Tex., Nov. 4, 1941; m. Linda Lawrence, Aug. 8, 1964; children: Jessica Lynn, Jennifer Rae. BS in Indsl. Engring., Tex. Tech U., 1964. Asst. v.p. engring. and network services Southwestern Bell Telephone Co., Dallas, 1977-78, dir. network distbn. services, 1979-80, v.p. centralized services, 1980-82; gen. mgr. customer services Southwestern Bell Telephone Co., San Antonio, 1978-79; v.p. Kans. Southwestern Bell Telephone Co., Topeka, 1982-84, pres. Kans. div., 1984-85; group pres. Southwestern Bell Corp., St. Louis, 1985-86, v.p. revenues and pub. affairs, vice-chmn., chief fin. officer, 1986-88, pres., chief operating officer, 1988—; v.p. revenues and pub. affairs, vice-chmn., chief operating officer Southwestern Bell Telephone Co., 1986-88, pres., chief operating officer, 1988—; bd. dirs. Mercantile Bancorp., Inc., St. Louis, Mercantile Bank, Anheuser-Busch Cos., Inc., 1988—. Bd. dirs. St. Louis area council Boy Scouts Am., 1986—, Tex. Tech Univ. and Health Scis. Research Found., Lubbock, 1986—; pres. coun. Tex. Tech Univ., 1989—; bd. dirs. St. Louis Art Mus. Served to 1st lt. U.S. Army, 1966, res., 1967-72. Mem. U.S. Telephone Assn. (bd. dirs. 1986-88), Old Warson Country Club, The St. Louis Club, Mo. Athletic Club, The Bogey Club, Golf Club Okla. Office: Southwestern Bell Corp 1 Bell Ctr Suite 4212 Saint Louis MO 63101

WHITAKER, GILBERT RILEY, JR., business economist, university dean; b. Oklahoma City, Oct. 8, 1931; s. Gilbert Riley and Melodese (Kilpatrick) W.; m. Ruth Pauline Tonn, Dec. 18, 1953; children: Kathleen, David Edward, Thomas Gilbert. B.A., Rice U., 1953; postgrad., So. Methodist U., 1956-57; M.S. in Econs., U. Wis., Madison, 1958, Ph.D. in Econs. (Ford Found. dissertation fellow), 1961. Instr., Northwestern U. Sch. Bus., 1960-61, asst. prof. bus. econs., 1961-64, asso. prof., 1964-66, research asso. Transp. Center, 1962-66; asso. prof. Washington U., St. Louis, 1966-67; prof. Washington U., 1967-76, adj. prof. econs., 1968-76, asso. dean Sch. Bus. Adminstrn., 1969-76; dean, prof. bus. econs. M.J. Neeley Sch. Bus., Tex. Christian U., 1976-79; dean, prof. Sch. Bus. Adminstrn., U. Mich., 1979—; dir. Am. Assembly of Collegiate Schs. of Bus., 1984—, dir. Washington campus, 1980—, chmn. 1985-88, v.p., pres. elect, 1988—; bd. dirs. Lincoln Nat. Corp., Johnson Controls, Inc., Comerica, Inc., Comerica Bank, Detroit, Structural Dynamics Research Corp.; sr. economist banking and currency com. U.S. Ho. of Reps., 1964; trustee Grad. Mgmt. Admissions Council, 1972-75, chmn., 1974-75. Author: (with Marshall Colberg and Dascomb Forbush) books including Business Economics, 6th edit., 1981, (with Roger Chisholm) Forecasting Methods, 1971. Served with USN, 1953-56. Mem. Am. Econ. Assn., Am. Fin. Assn., Nat. Assn. Bus. Economists, Ft. Worth Boat Club. Home: 2360 Londonderry Ann Arbor MI 48104 Office: U Mich Sch Bus Adminstrn Ann Arbor MI 48109

WHITE, AUGUSTUS AARON, III, orthopaedic surgeon, marketing consultant; b. Memphis, June 4, 1936; s. Augustus Aaron and Vivian (Dandridge) W. AB cum laude, Brown U., 1957; MD, Stanford U., 1961; D of Med Sci, Karolinska Inst., Sweden, 1969; Advanced Mgmt. Program, Harvard U., 1984; DHL (hon.), U. New Haven, 1987. Diplomate Nat. Bd. Examiners, Am. Bd. Orthopaedic Surgery. Intern U. Mich. Hosp., Ann Arbor, 1961-62; asst. resident in gen. surgery Presbyn. Med. Center, San Francisco, 1962-63; asst. resident in orthopaedic surgery Yale Med. Center, New Haven, 1963-65; sr. instr., resident orthopaedic surgery Yale Med. Center, 1965-66; asst. prof. orthopaedic surgery Yale Med. Sch., 1969-72, assoc. prof., 1972-76, prof., 1977-78, dir. biomech. research dept. orthopedics, 1978—; prof. orthopedic surgery Harvard Med. Sch., 1978—; orthopedic surgeon-in-chief Beth Israel Hosp., Boston, 1978—; sr. assoc. orthopedic surgery Children's Hosp. Med. Ctr., Boston, 1979—; assoc. in orthopedic surgery Brigham & Women's Hosp., Boston, 1980—; cons. div. surgery Sidney Farber Cancer Inst., Boston, 1980—; mktg. cons. Swimex Corp.; researcher biocmechanics lab. Beth Israel Hosp.; cons. orthopaedic surgery West Haven (Conn.) VA Hosp., 1970—, Hill Health Center, New Haven, 1970—; chief orthopedic surgery Conn. Health Care Plan, 1976-78; mem. adv. council Nat. Inst. Arthritis, Metabolism and Digestive Disease, NIH, 1979-82; mem. admissions com. Yale Med. Sch., 1970-72; presenter, moderator Symposium on Cervical Myelopathy, San Francisco, 1987; chmn. grant rev. com. NIH, 1985. Author: monograph Analysis of the Mechanics of the Thoracic Spine in Man, Leprosy, The Foot and The Orthopaedic Surgeon at Am. Acad. Orthopaedic Surgeons, 1970; book Clinical Biomechanics of the Spine, 1978; Symposium on Idiopathic Low Back Pain, 1982, Your Aching Back-A Doctor's Guide to Relief, 1983; contbr. articles to profl. jours., chpts. to sci. books. Trustee Brown U., Providence, 1971-76, bd. fellows, 1981—; trustee Northfield Mt. Hermon Sch., Northfield, Mass., 1976-81; chmn. corp. com. on minority affairs Brown U., Providence, 1981-86; mem. The Partnership, Boston, 1984—. Served to capt. AUS, 1966-68. Decorated Bronze Star medal; named 1 of 10 Outstanding Young Men U.S. Jr. C. of C., 1969, Exceptional Black Scientist of Year CIBA-GEIGY Corp., 1982; recipient Martin Luther King, Jr. Med. Achievement award, 1972, Kappa Delta award, nat. prize for outstanding research in orthopaedics field, 1975; nat. award for spinal research Eastern Orthopaedic Assn., 1980; Disting. Service award Northfield Mt. Hermon Sch. Alumni Assn., 1983; William Rogers award Associated Alumni Brown U., 1984; Outstanding Achievement award Delta Upsilon, 1986; Am.-Brit.-Canadian Travelling fellow Am. Orhopedic Assn., 1975. Fellow Am. Acad. Orthopaedic Surgeons, Scoliosis Research Soc.; mem. Orthopaedic Research Soc., Cervical Spine Research Soc., Internat. Soc. for Study Lumbar Spine, Internat. Soc. Orthopaedic Surgery and Traumatology, Nat. Med. Assn., Cervical Spine Research Soc. (pres. 1988), Scoliosis Research Soc., Sigma Xi, Sigma Pi Phi. Club: Harvard (Boston).

WHITE, CHARLES NEIL, personnel executive; b. Meadowbrook, N.Y., Aug. 16, 1953; s. Lawrence and Ann (Kaufman) W.; m. Clara Anne Schroer, Aug. 17, 1974; 1 child, Laurel Hope. AA, Nassau Community Coll., Garden City, N.Y., 1973; BA, Slippery Rock U., 1975; postgrad., U. Pitts., 1979-80. Program supr. Cath. Social Service, Butler, Pa., 1977-80; personnel specialist Turtle Creek Valley MH/MR, Inc., Braddock, Pa., 1980-82, Allegheny Co. Health Dept., Pitts., 1982—; cons. in field. Contbr. articles to profl. jours. Tchr. ARC, Butler, Pa., 1980—. Hofstra U. Acad. Hons. scholar, 1974; N.Y. State Regents scholar, 1972. Mem. Am. Soc. Personnel Adminstrn., Pitts. Personnel Assn., Internat. Personnel Mgmt. Assn. Democrat. Jewish. Office: Allegheny County Health Dept 3333 Forbes Ave Pittsburgh PA 15213

WHITE, CLARA JO, graphoanalyst; b. County Cherokee, Tex., June 26, 1927; d. William and Elmira (Johnson) Walker; m. Jeff Davis White, May 5, 1950; children: Anita, Jackie, Mona Lisa, Jeris, Gina. Cert., Ft. Worth Bus. Coll., 1947; AA, Riverside City Coll., 1986; cert. mgmt. and supervisory devel., U. Calif., Riverside, 1986. Cert. Graphoanalyst 1977; cert. master graphoanalyst 1979; cert. mus. docent tng., 1977. Owner, pres. White Handwriting Analysis Service, Riverside, Calif., 1982—; lectr., cons. Graphoanalysis, Riverside, 1977—; presenter in field. Asst. editor (commemorative book) Reflections, 1986. Mem. YWCA, Riverside, com. Riverside Mental Health Assn., 1981—, U.S. Olympic Com., 1984; v.p. Heritage House Mus., Riverside, 1981—, co-pres., 1985-86, pres. 1986-87; historian Riverside Juvenile Hall Aux., 1984—, pres., 1987—; vol. teacher's aide County of Riverside Juvenile Ct. Schs., 1979—; mem. Riverside Mus. Assocs., bd. dirs., 1985-87, vol. 1985-88, aux. historian 1984—, pres., 1987-88; mem. Met. Mus. Assocs., 1960—. Recipient Cert. of Merit Riverside County Probation Dept., F.H. Butterfield Sch., 1980, Golden Poet award, 1987; named Vol. of Yr. Riverside City Coll., 1982; named to Hall of Fame Riverside Juvenile Hall Aux., 1984. Mem. Internat. Graphoanalysis Soc. (life, cert. master graphoanalyst; 2d and 1st v.p., pres. So. Calif. chpt., pres. excellence award 1982, 83, 84), Internat. Graphoanalysis Soc. (cert. of merit 1981, pres. citation of merit 1988), U.S. Olympic Soc., Nat. Assn. Female Execs., Smithsonian Inst. (assoc.), Riverside C. of C., The Research Council of Scripps Clinic and Research Found. Club: Women's Networking (Riverside). Home and Office: 7965 Helena Ave Riverside CA 92504

WHITE, CYNTHIA CAROL, sales executive; b. Ft. Worth, Oct. 16, 1943; d. Charlie Bounds and Bernice Vera (Nunley) Rhoads; m. Franklin Earl Owen, Oct. 20, 1961 (div. Jan. 1987); children: Jeffrey Wayne, Valeria Ann, Carol Darlena, Pamela Kay; m. John Edward White, Jan. 1, 1988. Cert. Keypuncher, Comml. Coll., 1963; student, Tarrant County Jr. Coll., 1974-77; BBA in Mgmt., U. Tex., Arlington, 1981. Keypunch operator Can-Tex. Industries, Mineral-Wells, 1966-67; sec. Electro-Midland Corp., Mineral-Wells, 1967-68; exec. sec. to v.p. sales Pangburn Co., Inc., Ft. Worth, 1972-78; bookkeeper, sec. CB Svc., Ft. Worth, 1978-82; sales coord. Square D Co., Ft. Worth, 1982—. Mem. NAFE. Baptist. Home: 125 Plaza Blvd #1031 Hurst TX 76053 Office: Square D Co 5208 Airport Freeway Ste 110 Fort Worth TX 76117

WHITE, DENZIL WILMOT, petroleum equipment company executive; b. East Palestine, OH, June 10, 1916; s. Frank and Ethel (Akenhead) W.; m. Louise E. Stump, Aug. 18, 1940; children: Robert D., Richard K. BS in Edn., Kent State U., 1939; diploma Applied Sci., Case Sch., 1942. Instr. East Palestine Pub. Schs., 1939-41; field engr. Shell Oil Co., Cleve., 1941-46; div. engr. Amco. Corp., Cleve., 1946-50; mgr. pump and filter div. Telco, Inc., Cleve., 1950-61; mfg. agt. Denny White & Co., Cleve., 1961-65, pres., 1965-81, corp. cons., 1981—. Mem. Am. Soc. Petroleum Ops. Engrs., Cleve. Engring. Soc., Instrument Soc. Am. Republican. Lutheran.

WHITE, DON WILLIAM, bank executive; b. Santa Rita, N.Mex., June 27, 1942; s. Thomas Melvin and Barbara (Smith) W.; m. Jacqueline Diane Bufkin, June 12, 1965; children: Don William Jr., David Wayne. BBA, Western N.Mex. U., 1974, MBA, 1977. Field acct. Stearns Roger Corp., Denver, 1967-70; controller, adminstrv. mgr. USNR Mining and Minerals Inc., Silver City, N.Mex., 1970-72; devel. specialist County of Grant, Silver City, 1973-77; divisional controller Molycorp. Inc., Taos, N.Mex., 1977-78; mgr. project adminstrn. Kennecott Minerals Co., Hurley, N.Mex., 1978-83; sr. v.p. Sunwest Bank Grant County, Silver City, N.Mex., 1983-84, exec. v.p., 1984-85, pres., chief exec. officer, 1985—. Bd. dirs. Silver City/Grant County Econ. Devel., 1983—; councilman Town Silver City, 1977; chmn. Dems. for Senator Pete Domenici, 1986. Named Outstanding Vol., Silver City/Grant County Econ. Devel., 1987, FFA, 1985. Mem. Am. Bankers Assn., N.Mex. Bankers Assn., Bank Adminstrn. Inst., Assn. Commerce and Industry, N.Mex. Mining Assn. (assoc.). Lodge: Rotary. Office: Sunwest Bank Grant County 1203 N Hudson PO Box 1449 Silver City NM 88062

WHITE, DONALD LOUIS, financial services executive; b. Detroit, May 15, 1934; s. Henry E. and Katharine (Plavljanich) W.; m. Marilyn Elizabeth May 20, 1960; children: Brian Keith, Maureen Elizabeth. Grad. high sch., Detroit. Agt., dist. mgr. Equitable Life Assurance Soc., Detroit, 1969-76; pres. Donald L. White & Assocs., Inc., St. Clair Shores, Mich., 1977—; bd. dirs. Millennium Svc. Corp., West Bloomfield, Mich., 1987—. Mem. Grosse Pointe (Mich.) Crisis Club, Internat. Assn. Fin. Planners, Kiwanis (pres. local club 1968, 88). Office: Donald L White & Assocs Inc 22777 Harper Ave Ste 206 Saint Clair Shores MI 48080

WHITE, EDWARD ALLEN, electronics company executive; b. Cambridge, Jan. 1, 1928; s. Joseph and Bessie (Allen) W.; m. Joan Dixon, Dec. 22, 1949 (div. Aug. 1978); children—Dixon Richard, Leslie Ann White Lollar; m. Nancy Rhoads, Oct. 6, 1979. B.S., Tufts U., 1947. Chmn., chief exec. officer Bowmar Instrument Corp., Acton, Mass., 1951—, White Technology Inc., Phoenix, 1980-86; pres. Ariz. Digital Corp., Phoenix, 1975—; chmn., chief exec. officer AHI, Inc., Ft. Wayne, Ind., 1970-88; mem. World Bus. Council, Huntington, N.Y., 1978—. Patentee in field. Bd. dirs. Gov.'s Council Children, Youth and Families, Phoenix, 1982-84, Planned Parenthood Fedn. Am., 1984-88; pres., bd. dirs. Planned Parenthood Central and No. Ariz., 1984-88; trustee Internat House, N.Y.C., 1973-75, Tufts U., 1973-83. Mem. Tau Beta Pi. Clubs: River, Racquet & Tennis (N.Y.C.), Paradise Valley Country. Home: 5780 Echo Canyon Circle Phoenix AZ 85018 Office: Bowmar Instrument Corp 5050 N 40th St Phoenix AZ 85018

WHITE, FRANK WALTON, manufacturing executive; b. Kansas City, Mo., Nov. 22, 1926; s. Frank Owen and Edith Mayo (Brown) W.; m. Ann McVay, Apr. 9, 1955; children: Deborah Ann White Hetherington, Jennifer Mayo, Rebecca Bruce. AB, Washington U., St. Louis, 1950; MBA, Auburn U., 1976. With sales and prodn. dept. Brown-White-Lowell Press, Kansas City, Mo., 1950-59; gen. mgr. printing Honolulu Star-Bulletin, 1959-67; stockbroker Schwabacher & Co., Honolulu, 1967-70; v.p. resident mgr. Litton Industries Carlisle Div., Honolulu, 1970-76; v.p. adminstrn. Litton Industries Graphics Div., Los Angeles, 1976-77; div. dir. personnel Ingersoll-Rand Co., Woodcliff Lake, N.J., 1977-88; personnel cons. Hamilton-Ryker Co., Mayfield, Ky., 1988—; adj. prof. bus. murray (Ky.) State U., 1988—. Served to col. USAFR, 1944-80. Decorated Legion of Merit. Mem. Am. Soc. Personnel Adminstrs., Outriggger Cane Club, Mayfield Country Club, Daedalians, Rotary (pres. Mayfield club 1988-89), Phi Delta Theta (alumni pres. Honolulu chpt. 1973-74). Republican. Baptist. Clubs: Outrigger Canoe; Mayfield (Ky.) Country. Lodges: Daedalians, Rotary (pres. Mayfield club 1988—). Office: Hamilton-Ryker Co PO Box 366 Mayfield KY 42066

WHITE, GARY JENE, manufacturing company executive; b. Denver, Sept. 30, 1954; s. Roy George and Dela Ree (Kellner) W.; m. Suzanne Elizabeth Graham, Aug. 3, 1979; children: Aaron Timothy, Nathanael Paul. BS, U. Colo., 1976. Mgr. data processing Kissinger Petroleums Corp., Englewood, Colo., 1976-81; mgr. systems and devel. Worldwide Energy Corp., Denver, 1981-83, mgr. data processing, 1983-86; mgr. data processing Dixie Products Bus. div. James River Corp., Lexington, Ky., 1987—. Elder Evang. Presbyn. Ch. of Am. Mem. Data Procesing Mgmt. Assn., Hewlett Packard Internat Users Group, Hewlett Packard Supergroup. Republican. Office: Dixie Products Bus div James River Corp Harbison Rd Lexington KY 40511

WHITE, GERALD ANDREW, chemical company executive; b. L.I., N.Y., Aug. 2, 1934; s. Charles Eugene and Grace Mary (Trojan) W.; m. Mary Alice Turvey, June 8, 1957; children—Kevin, Patricia, Timothy, Megan. B.Ch.E., Villanova U., 1957; cert. advanced mgmt. program, Harvard Bus. Sch., 1975. Staff engr. Air Products and Chems., Inc., Allentown, Pa., 1962-65, mgr. systems devel., 1965-66, group controller, 1969-72, corp. controller, 1974-76, v.p. planning, 1977-82, v.p. fin., 1982—. Pres. United Way in Lehigh County, 1981; bd. dirs. Pa. Council on Econ. Edn., 1981; trustee, treas. Allentown Art Mus., 1984; trustee, com. chmn. on bd. affairs Allentown Coll. St. Francis de Sales, Center Valley, 1983. Served to lt. USN, 1957-62. Recipient J. Stanley Morehouse Meml. award Villanova U. Coll. Engring., 1983. Mem. Am. Inst. Chem. Engrs., Fin. Execs. Inst. (pres. northeastern Pa. chpt. 1974-75), Tau Beta Pi. Home: Rte 1 Box 51 Center Valley PA 18034

WHITE, HAROLD EDGAR, publisher, editor; b. Bangalore, India, Nov. 11, 1913; s. Harold Edgar and Fannie Alice (Fowler) W.; m. Eva Mathilda Anderson, July 23, 1937. BA, North Central Coll., 1935, LLD, 1977. Owner, editor, pub. Naperville (Ill.) Sun, 1936—; owner, pub. Lisle Twp. (Ill.) Sun, 1947—, Bolingbrook (Ill.) Sun, 1982—, Romeoville (Ill.) Sun, 1982—, Fox Valley (Ill.) Sun, 1984—; chief exec. officer Sun Printing Co., Naperville; pres., chmn. bd. Sun Cos. of Naperville; sec.-treas. Naper Aero Club Airport, Inc., 1956-82. Chmn. S.E. Fox Valley Emergency Med. Services Council, 1974-81. Mem. DuPage County Pubs. Assn. (pres. 1983-86), Ill. Press Assn., Nat. Editorial Assn., Suburban Aviation Assn., Am. Bonzana Soc., Naperville C. of C., Sigma Delta Chi. Club: Cress Creek Country. Lodges: Moose, Lions. Home: 9S 281 Aero Dr PO Box 133 Naperville IL 60566 Office: 9 W Jackson PO Box 269 Naperville IL 60566

WHITE, HAROLD R., insurance and health care inforamtion company executive; b. Bklyn., Jan. 16, 1936; s. Harold George and Margurite (Huot) W.; m. Dolores Angelina Iannuzzi, Jan. 23, 1965; children: Michael A., Denise M. AAS, Staten Island (N.Y.) Community Coll., 1961; BBA, The Coll. of Ins., N.Y.C., 1969. Sales agent Am. Mut. Ins., N.Y.C., 1961-62; mktg. adminstrv. asst. The Hartford Group, N.Y.C., 1962-70; asst. sec. The Hartford Group, Hartford, Conn., 1971-88; sales engr. Insco System Corp., Neptune, N.J., 1970-71; sr. account exec. Health Info. Systems, Inc., W. Hartford, Conn., 1988—. Treas. Andover, Hebron, and Marlborough Youth Services, Hebron, Ct., 1984—; pres. Marlborough (Conn.) Assn. for Sr. Housing, 1985—; mem. bd. fin. Town of Marlborough, 1984, mem. bd. selectmen, 1985. Served as airman 1st class USAF, 1954-58. Republican. Home: 56 Kellogg Rd Marlborough CT 06447 Office: Health Info Systems Inc 922 New Britain Ave West Hartford CT 06110

WHITE, JAMES ROBERT, state agency administrator; b. Clovis, N.Mex., Sept. 2, 1947; s. Alvin Clifton and Doris Lucille (Henrichsen) W.; m. Joan Elizabeth Cox, May 30, 1970; 1 child, Amanda Lyn. BBA, Eastern N.Mex. U., 1970, MBA, 1976. Tax auditor N.Mex. Taxation & Revenue Dept., Roswell, N.Mex., 1970-76; collection and enforcement mgr. N.Mex. Taxation & Revenue Dept., Las Cruces, 1976-78, dist. bur. chief, 1978-80; dist. bur. chief N.Mex. Taxation & Revenue Dept., Albuquerque, 1980-82; dir. revenue div. N.Mex. Taxation & Revenue Dept., Santa Fe, 1982-86, dir. audit and compliance div., 1986-87, dir. taxpayer info., 1987—; part-time lectr. U.Mex., Albuquerque, 1987-88, mem. adminstrv. bd., 1986-87. Co-chmn. adminstrv. council Covenant United Meth. Ch., Albuquerque, 1982, council on ministries, 1983, fin. sec. 1984, chmn. adminstrv. bd., 1986. Named one of Outstanding Young Men Am., U.S. Jaycees, 1981; recipient Exemplary Performance Incentive award N.Mex. Tax and Revenue Dept., 1982. Mem. Nat. Assn. Tax Adminstrs., Nat. Tax Assn.-Tax Inst. Am., Multi-state tax Commn., Western States Assn. Tax Adminstrs., United Meth. Men (v.p. 1986-88, dist. pres. 1989—). Democrat. Methodist. Lodge: Sertoma (sec. Roswell chpt. 1973). Home: 8408 San Francisco NE Albuquerque NM 87109 Office: N Mex Tax & Revenue Dept PO Box 630 Santa Fe NM 87509-0630

WHITE, JAMES SPRATT, IV, textiles executive, lawyer; b. Rock Hill, S.C., June 23, 1941; s. James Spratt III and Grace (Huggin) W.; m. Sandra Hagler, July 27, 1963; children: James Spratt V, Walter McElhaney, Samuel Crawford. AB in History, Wofford Coll., 1963; JD, U. S.C., 1968. Bar: S.C. 1968. Atty. Whaley, McCutchen & Blanton, Columbia, S.C., 1968-71; atty. Springs Industries, Inc., Fort Mill, S.C., 1971-81, gen. atty., 1981-83, sr. v.p. human resources, sec., 1983-88, sr. v.p., sec., gen. counsel, 1988—. Chmn. Fort Mill Sch. Bd., 1985—. Office: Springs Industries Inc 205 N White St Fort Mill SC 29715

WHITE, JEFF V., administrative services company executive; b. Mobjack, Va., Jan. 8, 1925; s. Leonard S. and Gracie F. (Drisgill) W.; m. Rosalyn White, Dec. 29, 1946; children: Robert, Lynne. With Equifax, Inc., Atlanta, 1942—; successively asst. v.p., v.p., v.p. and ops. mgr., exec. v.p., pres. Credit Bur. Inc. affiliate Equifax, Inc., Atlanta, 1962-74; v.p. Equifax, Inc., Atlanta, 1976-77, group v.p., 1977-79, exec. v.p., 1979-81, pres., 1981-87, chief exec. officer, 1983—, vice chmn., 1987-88, chmn., chief exec. officer, 1988—, also bd. dirs.; bd. dirs. affiliated cos. 1st Nat. Bank Atlanta, 1st Atlanta Corp., Cen. Atlanta Progress; mem. adv. council Coll. Bus. Adminstrn. Ga. State U., INROADS/Atlanta. Mem. adv. council United Way of Metro Atlanta; mem. bd. visitors Emory U. Served to lt. U.S. Army, 1943-46. Mem. Can. Am. Soc. Southeast U.S. Office: Equifax Inc 1600 Peachtree St NW Atlanta GA 30302

WHITE, JOHN FRANCIS, retired education administrator; b. Waukegan, Ill., Oct. 11, 1917; s. Edward Sydney and Lilah M. (McCormick) W.; m. Joan Glasow, May 15, 1943; children: Susan White Morris, Michael S., Christopher S. AB, Lawrence U., 1941; AM, U. Chgo., 1944; LHD (hon.), Lawrence U., 1961; LLD (hon.), Cornell Coll., 1964, Hamilton Coll., 1966; LittD (hon.), Temple U., 1968. Admissions counsellor Lawrence U., Appleton, Wis., 1941-44; dir. admissions Ill. Inst. Tech., Chgo., 1944-45, asst. dean students, 1945-46, dean students, 1946-48, dean and dir. devel. program, 1948-50; v.p. Western Res. U., Cleve., 1950-55; gen. mgr. Sta. WQED-TV, Pitts., 1955-58; pres. Nat. Ednl. TV, N.Y.C., 1958-69, Cooper Union, N.Y.C., 1969-80; pres. emeritus Cooper Union, 1980—; cons. The Aspen Inst., 1980-88; bd. dirs. Orange & Rockland Utilities, Inc., Pearl River, N.Y., Shearson, Lehman, Hutton Asset Mgmt., N.Y.C., Viacom Internat., Inc. Trustee Cathedral St. John the Divine, N.Y.C., 1978-88; vestryman Trinity Parish, 1979-86. Mem. Univ. Club, Tuxedo Club (gov., chmn. 1970-78). Episcopalian. Home: 97 Turtle Dr Sarasota FL 34236

WHITE, JOHN FRANK, manufacturing company executive; b. Chgo., Oct. 29, 1950; s. Frank Anton White and Muriel (Henerata) White Clausen; m. Linda Susan Kaste, Aug. 5, 1972; children: Erick, Gregory. BS, No. Ill. U., 1972, MS, 1978. Supr. human resources A.B. Dick, Chgo., 1972-77; mgr. compensation benefits Sun Electric Corp., Crystal Lake, Ill., 1978-79; dir. human resources Union Spl. Corp., Chgo., 1979-85; v.p. human resources Montgomery Elevator Co., Moline, Ill., 1985—; assoc. prof. Roosevelt U., Chgo., 1982-83, Northwestern U., Evanston, Ill., 1983-85. Asst. com. chmn. Boy Scouts Am., Moline, 1988. Mem. Am. Soc. Pers. Adminstrs. (regional dir. 1986—), Soc. Pers. Adminstrs. Greater Chgo. (bd. dirs. 1979-83), Exch. Club. Republican. Home: 3418 54th St Moline IL 61265 Office: Montgomery Elevator Co One Montgomery Ct Moline IL 61265

WHITE, KATHERINE PATRICIA, lawyer; b. N.Y.C., Feb. 1, 1948; d. Edward Christopher and Catherine Elizabeth (Walsh) W. BA in English, Molloy Coll., 1969; JD, St. John's U., 1971. Bar: N.Y. 1972, U.S. Dist. Ct. (ea. and so. dists.) N.Y., 1973, U.S. Supreme Ct. 1976. Atty. Western Electric Co., Inc., N.Y.C., 1971-79, AT&T Co., Inc., N.Y.C., 1979-83, AT&T Communications, Inc., N.Y.C., 1984—; adj. prof. law N.Y. Law Sch., N.Y.C., 1987-88, Fordham U. Sch. of Law, 1988—. Vol. Sloan Kettering Inst., 1973, North Shore U. Hosp., 1975, various fed., state and local polit. campaigns; judge N.Y. State Bicentennial Writing Competition, N.Y.C., 1977-78; chmn. Com. to Elect Supreme Ct. Judge, N.Y.C., 1982. Mem. Am. Corp. Counsel Assn., N.Y. State Bar Assn. (bus. and banking law com. real estate law sect., corp. counsel sect.), Assn. of Bar of City of N.Y. (adminstrv. law com. 1982-85, young lawyers com. 1976-79, judge nat. moot ct. competition 1979—), Cath. Lawyers Guild for Diocese of Rockville Ctr. (pres. 1980-81), St. John's U. Sch. Law Alumni Assn. (pres. L.I. chpt. 1986-88), Women's Nat. Republican Club (bd. govs. 1988—). Clubs: Metropolitan, Wharton Bus. Sch. N.Y. (N.Y.C.). Home: 5 Starlight Ct Babylon NY 11704 Office: AT&T Communications Inc 32 Ave of the Americas New York NY 10013

WHITE, LARRY LEE, electronics executive; b. Iowa City, Aug. 5, 1937; s. Walter Henry and Dorothy (Stutzman) W.; m. Barbara Jean Leonard, Aug. 30, 1959; children: Kari Kay, Tobin Lee. B.A., Hastings (Nebr.) Coll., 1960; postgrad. in law, LaSalle Extension U., 1969. Asst. mgr. credit dept. Inland div. Security First Nat. Bank, Riverside, Calif., 1960-62; mem. pres.'s staff Bourns, Inc., Riverside, 1962-67; spl. asst. to pres. Bourns, Inc., 1967-68, corp. sec., 1968—, v.p. adminstrn., 1970-79, sr. v.p. fin. and adminstrn., corp. sec., 1979-86, exec. v.p. fin. and adminstrn., corp. sec., 1986-87, exec. v.p., chief fin. officer and corp. sec., 1987-88, pres., exec. v.p., chief fin. officer, sec., 1988—; bd. dirs. Ohmic, S.A. Precision Monolithics, Inc., Bourns Electronics (Ireland) Inc., Bourns Instruments Inc., Wendover Investments Inc., Bourns Asia Pacific Inc., Bourns Asia Pacific Pte. Ltd., Bourns Puerto Rico Inc., Bourns de Mexico, Componentes de la Mesa, Bourns Electronics (Taiwan) Ltd., Bourns Internat. Svcs., Inc., Bourns Networks, Inc., Bourns Sensors/Controls, Inc. Trustee Bourns Found., Riverside Community Found., 1986; pres. bd. trustees Riverside City Library, 1965; chmn. adv. bd. Riverside Salvation Army, 1966; pres. Riverside Civic League, 1966, Riverside Jr. C. of C., 1964; pres. bd. trustees Calvary Presbyterian Ch., Riverside, 1972; bd. dirs. Riverside United Way, 1975, Riverside Community Hosp. Corp., 1987—; chmn. Riverside Youth Basketball Assn., 1976-77; pres., trustee U. Redlands, 1983-87; pres. Riverside County Swim Conf., 1977-79; pres. Community Health Corp., dir.; elder Calvary Presbyn. Ch., 1980-81. Named Outstanding Local Pres., Calif.

Jaycees, 1964; recipient Riverside Disting. Service award, 1965. Republican. Club: Victoria.

WHITE, MARGIT TRISKA, financial planner; b. Greenport, N.Y., June 4, 1932; d. Joseph A. and Esther M. (Olstad) Triska; m. Robert Lamar Cannon (div. 1971); children: Catherine Margit, Sandra Leigh, Robert Milchrist II. BA, Duke U., 1954. Cert. fin. planner. Adminstr. Washington Opportunities for Women, 1971-80; account exec. Merrill Lynch, Bethesda, Md., 1980-82; account exec., fin. planner Prudential Bache Securities, Washington, 1982—. Mem. Internat. Assn. Fin. Planners, Inst. Cert. Fin. Planners, Women in Housing and Fin., Zeta Tau Alpha. Presbyterian. Office: Prudential Bache Securities 1130 Connecticut Ave Washington DC 20036

WHITE, NORMAN OAKLEY, air pollution control systems company executive; b. Detroit, Apr. 8, 1921; s. Harold M. and Doris Ann (Hatch) W.; B.S., Tri-State U., 1943; m. Betty Ann Brand, June 25, 1943; children—William, Diane, Steven, Barbara. Engr., Curtiss Wright, Patterson, N.J., 1943-44; engr. Kelsey Hayes Wheel, Detroit, 1946-50; engr. sales H. M. White Inc., Detroit, 1950-62, pres., 1962—; chmn. bd. White Environ. Inc.; dir. Clean Air Tech. Inc. Mem. exec. com., trustee Tri-State U. Served with USMCR, 1944-46. Mem. Sheet Metal Air Conditioning Nat. Assn., Econ. Club Detroit. Republican. Methodist. Clubs: Orchard Lake Country, Ocean Reef, Detroit Athletic. Patentee air pollution equipment. Home: 3660 Franklin Rd Bloomfield Hills MI 48013 Office: 12855 Burt Rd Detroit MI 48223

WHITE, PETER VINCENT, manufacturing executive; b. N.Y.C, July 11, 1940; s. Peter Vincent and Rita Katherine (Terry) W.; m. Carol Jean Burke, Oct. 1, 1966; children: Justin M., Kristin K. Grad., NYU, 1963; MBA, St. John's U., 1971; postgrad., Dartmouth Coll., 1978. CPA, N.Y. Supr. Arthur Andersen & Co., N.Y.C., 1963-67; mgr. consolidation acctg. Gulf & Western Industries Inc., N.Y.C., 1967-71; mgr. corp. acctg. Wheelabrator-Frye Inc., N.Y.C., 1971-73; dir. acctg. Anaconda Am. Brass Co., N.Y.C., 1973-76; asst. corp. controller Anaconda Co., N.Y.C., 1976-78; controller Arco Metals, N.Y.C., 1978-81; v.p., controller Cabot Corp.-Cabot Beryl Co., Reading, Pa., 1981-82; v.p. fin., controller Cabot Products, Indpls., 1982-86; v.p. fin., treas. Charter Power Systems Inc., Plymouth Meeting, Pa., 1986—; pres. VarTeck Inc., Houston, 1984-86; bd. dirs. BCMS, France, Cabot Alloys, Eng. and Switzerland, DBCJ, Fed. Republic Germany, S.A. Marvin, Brazil, Industria Nacobe Ltd., Mex., Martec Ltd., Mex., Anaconda Can. Ltd., Maga-Flex Ltd., Eng. Mem. Southbury Sch. Bd., 1974, com. sch. negating, 1974, com. sch. bldg., 1975; chmn. budget United Fund, 1975. Mem. AICPA, Nat. Assn. Accts., Fin. Execs. Inst., Controllers Coun. Bus. and Tax Planning Bd., Pa. Young Reps., Elks, KC. Roman Catholic. Home: 2059 Spring Valley Rd Lansdale PA 19446

WHITE, RALPH PAUL, textile company executive; b. Watertown, Mass., Aug. 1, 1926; s. Irving William and Margaret Sarah (McGowan) W.; m. Shirley Irene Christie, Nov. 22, 1947; children: Karin Ann, Eric John. BS in Indsl. Engring., Columbia U., 1951; postgrad., Yale U., 1958-59. Instr. engring. mechanics U. Conn., Torrington, 1956-57; mgr. data processing. B.F. Goodrich Co., Shelton, Conn., 1958-61; ptnr., mgmt. cons. Bavier, Bulger & Goodyear, New Haven, 1961-66; v.p. Davidson Rubber Co., Dover, N.H., 1966-69; pres. Davidson Rubber Co., Dover, 1969-80; group v.p. parent co. Ex-Cell-O, Troy, Mich., 1980-83; pres. Troy (N.H.) Mills Inc., 1983-86, chief exec. officer, 1983—, chmn., 1987—, also bd. dirs.; bd. dirs. J.A. Wright Co., Keene, N.H., J.D. Cahill Co., Hampton, N.H., IPC Co., Bristol, N.H. Mem. N.H. Indsl. Devel. Authority, 1972-80, 85—; bd. visitors Whittemore Sch. Bus. U. N.H., Durham., 1984—. Mem. Am. Inst. Indsl. Engrs., Soc. Automotive Engrs., N.H. Bus. and Industry Assn. (bd. dirs. 1970-80, pres. 1972-73, vice chmn. 1984—), Abenaqui Country Club, Keene Country Club, Detroit Athletic Club. Democrat. Roman Catholic. Home: 22 Old Common Peterborough NH 03458 Office: Troy Mills Inc 18 Monadnock St Troy NH 03465

WHITE, RANDALL WAYNE, educational development executive; b. Keystone, Okla., Jan. 11, 1942; s. Wiley and Helen (Ottinger) W.; m. Carol L. Thompson, Feb. 1, 1964; children: Craig M., Todd R. BS, Okla. State U., 1963. Acctg. mgr. Mapco, Tulsa, 1963-69; controller CCI Corp., Tulsa, 1969-71, PepsiCo., Tulsa, 1971-74; pres. Arctic Express, Tulsa, 1975-80; chief fin. officer NICOR Drilling, Tulsa, 1980-83; pres. Ednl. Devel. Corp., Tulsa, 1983—; bd. dirs. Okla. Osteopathic Hosp. Tulsa, 1987—, Original Chili Bowl, Inc., 1986—. Mem. Shadow Mountain Racquet Club, Kiwanis (bd. dirs. Tulsa club 1988). Republican. Methodist. Home: 10385 S 76th E Ave Tulsa OK 74133 Office: Ednl Devel Corp 10302 E 55 Pl Tulsa OK 74147

WHITE, REBECCA ANNE, pharmaceutical company manager; b. Erie, Pa., Aug. 16, 1949; d. Francis Edward and Anne Frances (Schwartz) W.; children: Matthew John, Anne Catherine. BS, Gannon U., 1979; MA, Cleve. State U., 1988. Ter. mgr. Hoffmann-LaRoche, Inc., Nutley, N.J., 1979—; counselor St. Vincent Health Ctr., Erie, 1978-79. Named Scholastic All Am. Achiever, 1988. Mem. Phi Alpha Theta, Pi Gamma Mu.

WHITE, REID, venture capital management consultant; b. Lexington, Va., Apr. 14, 1935; s. Reid and Alice Marion (Miller) W.; B.A., Yale U., 1957; m. M. Laird Trowbridge, Feb. 29, 1964; children—Emilie Trowbridge, Gillian Cahill. Asst. cashier 1st Nat. City Bank (now Citicorp), N.Y.C., 1957-63; v.p. Bank Calif., NA, San Francisco, 1963-67; gen. ptnr. Shields & Co., N.Y.C., 1967-74; pres. Quidnet group venture capital cos., Princeton, 1974—; dir. Monikers, Inc., Winston-Salem, J.P. Industries Inc., Ann Arbor, Chemos Corp., Newark, Pierson Industris, Inc., Palmer, Mass. Trustee Princeton Youth Fund, 1975-85 , pres., 1981-83; trustee McCarter Theatre, Princeton, 1978-87, Chamber Symphony of Princeton, 1987—, Westminster Choir Coll., Princeton, 1989—; mem. Yale Devel. Bd., 1989—. Served as 1st lt. U.S. Army, 1958. Mem. Nat. Assn. Small Bus. Investment Cos. Clubs: Yale of N.Y.C., Pretty Brook Tennis. Office: One Palmer Sq Suite 425 Princeton NJ 08542

WHITE, RICHARD EDMUND, marketing executive; b. Reading, Pa., June 8, 1944; s. Carl Marshall and Miriam Elizabeth (Curry) W.; m. Kristen Margaret Lloyd, June 17, 1967; children: Ross, Peter, Andrew. BS in Econs., U. Pa., 1967; MBA with distinction, U. Mich., 1968. Gen. mgr. mktg. H. J. Heinz Co., Pitts., 1970-81; dir. mktg. Seven Up Co., St. Louis, 1981-83; v.p. mktg. & sales Herr Foods, Inc., Nottingham, Pa., 1984—. Chmn. finance Sewickley Borough Coun., Pa., 1977-81; pres. So. Chester CountyDevel. Foundn. , Jennersville, Pa., 1988—; personnel chmn., bd. gov. So. Chestern County Med. Ctr., Jennersville, 1988—; program chmn., bd. mgrs., So. Chester City YMCA, West Grove, Pa., 1988—; campaign chmn. Avon Grove United Way, 1988. Republican. Presbyterian. Home: 425 Ewing Rd West Grove PA 19390 Office: Herr Foods Inc PO Box 300 Nottingham PA 19362

WHITE, ROBERT E., banker; b. Miami, Fla., June 24, 1943; s. David Ward and Agnes (Lamb) W.; m. Deborah G. Clark, Jan. 30, 1965; children: Christine, Keary, Robert Jr. BS, Fla. State U., 1965. From mgmt. trainee to br. mgr. Marine Midland Bank, N.Y.C., 1966-71; with S.E. Bank, N.A., Miami, Fla., 1971—, sr. corp. v.p., 1985—. Bd. dirs. Doctor's Hosp., Coral Gables, Fla., 1988—; trustee Fla. Ind. Coll. Fund, Lakeland, 1986—, Ctr. Fine Arts, Miami, 1988. 1st lt. USCGR, 1964-69. Mem. Riviera Club (Coral Gables, bd. dirs. 1987—), Bath Club, Miami Club. Office: SE Bank NA One Southeast Fin Ctr Miami FL 33131

WHITE, ROBERT JAMES, financial executive; b. Darby, Pa., Oct. 7, 1958; s. Robert Clarence and Dorothy (Mackey) W.; m. Patricia Anne Pearse, Sept. 22, 1984; 1 child, Meaghan Theresa. BS in Acctg., Pa. State U., 1981. CPA, Pa. Staff auditor Stockton Bates and Co., Phila., 1980-83; sr. internal auditor Johnson Matthey Investments, Inc., Malvern, Pa., 1983-84; controller pigments dept. Johnson Matthey Investments, Inc., Irvington, N.J., 1984-85; controller colours and printing div. Johnson Matthey Investments, Inc., West Chester, Pa., 1985-88; ptnr. Source Fin., Wilmington, Del., 1988—; pvt. practice tax cons., Oxford, Pa., 1987—. Mem. Nat. Assn. Accts., Controller's Council, Pa. Inst. CPAs, Am. Inst. CPAs, Delta Sigma Phi. Republican. Methodist. Home: 1101 Hayesville-Cream Rd Oxford PA 19363 Office: Source Fin Mfrs Hanover Pla 1201 Market St Ste 1701 Wilmington DE 19801

WHITE, ROBERT JAMES, food company executive; b. Chgo., July 7, 1928; s. William James and Catherine Ethnea (Briscoe) W.; m. Marjorie Mary Trainor, Oct. 1, 1955; children—Moira B., Lisa A., Daniel R., Timothy V., Brian T. B.C.E., Marquette U., 1951; M.B.A., U. Chgo., 1959. Cons., Booz Allen & Hamilton, Chgo., 1960-66; new products mgr. Gen. Mills, Inc., Mpls., 1966-69, mktg. dir. Golden Valley div., 1969-70, mgr. venture devel., 1970-76; dir. planning and devel. ConAgra, Inc., Omaha, 1976, v.p. planning and devel., 1976—. Served as lt. (j.g.) USN, 1951-54, Pacific. Mem. Assn. for Corp. Growth, Coun. Planning Execs. Conf. Bd., Inc. Roman Catholic. Office: Con Agra Inc One Central Park Plaza Omaha NE 68102

WHITE, ROBERT MILES FORD, life insurance company executive; b. Lufkin, Tex., June 9, 1928; s. Sullivan Miles and Faye Clark (Scurlock) F.; m. Mary Ruth Wathen, Nov. 10, 1946; children: Martha, Robert, Benedict, Mary, Jesse, Margaret, Maureen, Thomas. BA, Stephen F. Austin State U., 1948; BBA, St. Mary's U., San Antonio, 1955; MS in Fin. Services, Am. Coll., Bryn Mawr, Pa., 1981, MS in Mgmt., 1986. CLU. Tchr. Douglas (Tex.) Pub. Schs., 1946-47, Houston Pub. Schs., 1948-51; office mgr. Heat Control Insulation Co., San Antonio, 1951-53; acct. S.W. Acceptance Co., San Antonio, 1953-55; sec.-treas. Howell Corp., San Antonio, 1955-64; agt. New Eng. Mut. Life Ins. Co., San Antonio, 1964-71; br. mgr. Occidental Life Ins. Co. of Calif., San Antonio, 1971-84; gen. agt. Transam. Occidental Life Ins. Co., 1984—. Mem. citizens liaison com. San Antonio Ind. Sch. Dist., 1972-78, EEO Council, 1974-80. Mem. San Antonio Estate Planners Council, S.W. Pension Conf., Nat., Tex., San Antonio assns. life underwriters, Am. Soc. CLU's., Internat. Assn. Fin. Planners, Gen. Agts. and Mgrs. Assn., Am. Risk and Ins. Assn., Internat. Platform Assn., Tex. Hist. Soc., East Tex. Hist. Soc., San Antonio, S.E. Tex. Geneal. Soc., S.E. Tex. Hist. Soc., Sons of Republic of Tex., SAR, Kappa Pi Sigma. Republican. Roman Catholic. Home: 701 Sunshine Dr E San Antonio TX 78228 Office: 7461 Callaghan Rd Suite 307 San Antonio TX 78229

WHITE, ROBERT OSGOOD, banker; b. Boston, Dec. 13, 1922; s. Joseph Lyman and Mary (Chapin) W.; m. Barbara O'Donovan, Sept. 18, 1948; children—Peter Markley, David Chapin, Thomas Whitney, Robert Osgood Jr. Grad. Phillips Acad., Andover, Mass., 1941; B.A., Yale U., 1944; grad. advanced mgmt. program Harvard U., 1969. With Chemical Bank, N.Y.C., 1946-87, now sr. v.p.; dir. Am. Dist. Telegraph, N.Y.C., Sunley Holdings Am., Orlando, Fla., BAnk of Darien (Conn.), Hometown Bank Corp. Chmn. bd. N.Y. Heart Assn.; bd. dirs. United Way N.Y.C.; fin. chmn. Darien Republican Com. (Conn.). Served to capt. USMC, 1942-46, 51-52, PTO, CBI. Episcopalian. Club: Wee Burn Country (Darien) (bd. dirs. 1980—), Mill Reef Club (Antigua). Office: Chem Bank 277 Park Ave New York NY 10172

WHITE, ROBERT SCOTT, infosystems executive; b. Angola, Ind., Feb. 19, 1951; s. Robert S. White and Iona B. (Huntington) Crain; m. Danette J. DeMara, July 1, 1972; children: Graham T., Adam D., Elise M. BBA, Tri-State U., 1973; MBA, Kent State U., 1988. Computer programmer The Timken Co., Canton, Ohio, 1973-76, sr. software programmer, 1977-82, supr. systems analysts, 1982-83, mgr. internat. systems, 1983-84, mgr. data and telecom, 1985-86, gen. mgr. info. systems, 1986—. Active Canton City Oversight Com., 1985. Mem. Internat. Communications Assn. Office: The Timken Co 1835 Dueber Ave SW Canton OH 44706

WHITE, RONALD LEON, merchant banking executive; b. West York, Pa., July 14, 1930; s. Clarence William and Grace Elizabeth (Gingerich) W.; m. Estheranne Wieder, July 31, 1951; children—Bradford William, Clifford Allen, Erick David. B.S. in Econs, U. Pa., 1952, M.B.A., 1957. Cost analysis supr. Air Products & Chem. Corp., Allentown, Pa., 1957-60; cost control mgr. Mack Trucks, Inc., Allentown, 1960-64; mgmt. cons. Peat, Marwick, Mitchell & Co., Phila., 1964-66; mgr. profit planning Monroe, The Calculator Co. (div. Litton Industries), Orange, N.J., 1966-67, controller, 1967-68; v.p. fin. Bus. Systems Group of Litton Industries, Beverly Hills, Calif., 1968-70; pres. Royal Typewriter Co. div., Hartford, Conn., 1970-73; exec. v.p., chief operating officer, treas. Tenna Corp., Cleve., 1973-75, pres., dir., 1975-77; v.p. fin. Arby's Inc., Youngstown, Ohio, 1978-79; exec. v.p., dir. Roxbury Am., Inc., 1979-81; v.p. fin., treas. Royal Crown Cos., Inc., Atlanta and Miami Beach, Fla., 1981-86, TDS Healthcare Systems Corp., Atlanta, 1987-88; v.p. Corp. Fin. Assocs., Atlanta, 1988—; instr. acctg. Wharton Sch. U. Pa., 1952-53, instr. industry, 1953-54. Served to lt. USNR, 1954-57. Mem. Am. Mgmt. Assn., Nat. Assn. Accountants, Nat. Assn. Corp. Dirs., Fin. Execs. Inst., Acacia. Mem. United Ch. Christ (deacon). Lodges: Masons, Rotary. Home: 2362 Kingsgate Ct Dunwoody GA 30338 Office: Corp Fin Assocs 6600 Peachtree Dunwoody Rd 300 Embassy Row Ste 670 Atlanta GA 30328

WHITE, R(UFUS) ELTON, manufacturing company executive; b. Gary, W.Va., May 29, 1942; s. John K. and Mae Virginia (Hawks) W.; m. Gordon Ann McConkey, June 8, 1965; children: David Allen, Patricia Ruth. B.S.B.A., Berea Coll., 1965; M.B.A., U. Ky., 1967. With NCR Corp., 1967—; asst. v.p. treasury ops. NCR Corp., Dayton, Ohio, 1975; v.p. adminstrn. and personnel NCR Corp., 1975-80; v.p. NCR Corp., Middle East/Africa region, 1980-85; v.p. product mktg. and strategic planning NCR Corp., 1985-87, exec. v.p., 1987; exec. v.p. U.S. Data Processing Group, 1988—. Trustee Cen. Presbyn. Ch., Dayton, Dayton Opera, 1982-83, 85-86, Berea Coll., 1987. Mem. Fin. Execs. Inst., Am. Mgmt. Assn. (trustee), Dayton C. of C. Home: 6642 Imperial Woods Rd Dayton OH 45459 Office: NCR Corp 1700 S Patterson Blvd Dayton OH 45479

WHITE, SAMUEL, finance company executive; b. Malden, Mass., Mar. 29, 1924; s. Harry and F. (Gutman) W.; m. Fay Lillian Richardson, May 7, 1941; children: Christopher, Robert, Sharon. MBA, Harvard U., 1950. Corp. v.p. Liggett Group, N.Y.C., 1951-80; chmn. WHW Holding Co., Washington, 1981—, T.D. Co., N.Y.C., 1982-86, Heller-White Inc., Greenwich, Conn., 1986—; bd. dirs. Lightoller, Jersey City, N.J., Trans-capital Corp. Bd. dirs. Stamford Hosp. Found., 1985. Named Man of Yr. Fedn. Cath. Charities, Fedn. Protestant Hilanthropies, Fedn. Jewish Philanthropies. Jewish. Clubs: Darien (Conn.) Country, Friars (N.Y.C.), Rockefeller Luncheon.

WHITE, STEVE MICHAEL, accountant; b. South Bend, Ind., Dec. 10, 1959; s. Jeremiah and Millie (Scruggs) W. BS, Ind. U., 1982. CPA, Ind. Fiscal officer City of South Bend, 1984-87, auditor, 1987—; instr. acctg. Ivy Tech., South Bend, 1986-87. Home: 1606 Johnson St South Bend IN 46628 Office: City of South Bend 227 W Jefferson Blvd South Bend IN 46601

WHITE, STEVEN JAMES, electronics manufacturing company executive; b. Bryn Mawr, Pa., Aug. 31, 1951; s. Aubrey and Kate (Nicol) W. Student Stevens Inst. tech., 1969-73; BSEE, U. Wash., 1983; postgrad. MIT, 1988—. Design engr. Sundstrand Corp., Redmond, Wash., 1973-75; sr. design engr., 1977-79; project engr. resource Control, Redmond, 1975-77; chmn., chief exec. officer Tech. Arts Corp., Seattle, 1979—; pres., dir. Fibre Graphics Corp, 1986—; pres. Tech. Arts, Seattle, cons. 1977-83. Patentee white scanner 3D measurement, high resolution measurement, colorgraphics digitizing. Mem. IEEE, Tau Beta Pi. Office: Tech Arts Corp 15660 NE 36th St Suite 200 Redmond WA 98052

WHITE, THOMAS LEE, JR., data processing executive; b. Waco, Tex., Apr. 15, 1944; s. Thomas Lee and Myrtle Faye (Walden) W.; m. Susan McKinney, Feb. 15, 1965 (div. 1970); 1 child, Thomas Lee III. BBA, U. Tex., 1966, MBA, 1970. Systems analyst Tex. Hwy. Dept., Austin, 1966-72, FritoLay, Dallas, 1972-74; with sales dept. Service Bur. Corp., Dallas, also Tulsa, 1974-77; western div. mgr. CompuServe, Dallas, 1977-82; v.p. Lloyd Bush and Assocs., Dallas, 1982-83; pres. ACC, Inc., Dallas, 1983—, Dimension Software Systems, Inc., Dallas, 1984—. Office: Dimension Software System Inc 1717 Walnut Hill Ln Suite 104 Irving TX 75038

WHITE, THOMAS STUART, JR., financial analyst; b. San Diego, Sept. 7, 1943; s. Thomas Stuart and June Waters (Kiser) W.; m. Carol Sue Unger, Nov. 30, 1969 (div. 1985); children: Candice, Thomas III; m. Stathy Manos, May 2, 1987; children: Viki, Katherine, Nicholas. BA, Duke U., 1965. Trainee Goldman Sachs, N.Y.C., 1966-67; security sales Goldman Sachs, Chgo., 1967-70; with mgmt. Lehman Bros., Chgo., 1970-74; gen., ptnr. Thomas White & Assocs., Chgo., 1974-77; portfolio mgr. Blyth Eastman Dillon, Chgo., 1977-79, Morgan Stanley, Chgo., 1979-83; chief investment officer The Chgo. Group, 1983—. Sgt. USMCR, 1965-71. Republican. Greek Orthodox. Home: 1448 N Lake Shore Dr Chicago IL 60610 Office: Morgan Stanley 440 La Salle St Chicago IL 60605

WHITE, TODD RANDALL, accountant; b. Columbus, Ohio, Feb. 18, 1962; s. Carl Kenneth and Sarah Ann (Hetrick) W.; m. Lisa Marie Hill, June 1, 1985. Student, Capital U., 1980-81; BSBA, Ohio State U., 1984; MBA, U. Wis., 1986. CPA. Asst. controller Worthington Industries, Columbus, 1981-83; teaching asst. U. Wis., 1984-86; sr. acct. Price Waterhouse, Cin., 1986—. Exec. advisor Jr. Achievement Greater Cin., 1987—; active in Ptnr. in Edn., 1987—. Mem. Am. Inst. CPA's, Ohio Soc. CPA's, Cin. C. of C. Republican. Home: 8437 Brandon Hill Ct Cincinnati OH 45244 Office: Price Waterhouse 1900 Central Trust Ctr Cincinnati OH 45202

WHITE, TOM WILLIAM, strategic planning and marketing executive; b. Decatur, Ill., Nov. 3, 1941; s. George William and Dorene Louise (Murphy) W.; m. Jane Colette Aylward, Apr. 18, 1987; children: Douglas, Gregory. BS in Bus., Ea. Ill. U., 1964; MBA, So. Ill. U., 1965. Supr. prodn. planning U.S. Steel Corp., Joliet, Ill., 1965-68; mgr. mktg. research and planning Nordberg Mfg. Co., Milw., 1968-70; dir. cons. svcs. Rexnord Inc., Milw., 1970-86; dir. strategic planning Rexnord Inc., Brookfield, Wis., 1986-87; pres. White & Assocs., Greenfield, Wis., 1987—; vis. lectr. So. Ill. U., Carbondale, Ea. Ill. U., Charleston, U. Wis., Milw. Contbr. articles to profl. jours. Mem. Am. Mktg. Assn., Planning Forum, Soc. Advancement Mgmt. (hon.). Methodist. Home and Office: 5349 Somerset Ln S Greenfield WI 53221

WHITE, TOM WILLINGHAM, business executive; b. McAllen, Tex., Feb. 16, 1943; s. Louis Thomas and Leota Faye (Grimm) W.; m. Lauryn G. Longwell, Mar. 8, 1968; children: Brad Edward, Parker Thomas, Landan Allen. BBA, U. Tex., 1965. Acct. Haskins & Sells, CPA's, Houston, 1965-67, Paul Veale, CPA, McAllen, Tex., 1967-68; pvt. practice acctg., Corpus Christi, Tex., 1969-79; officer, co-owner Andrews Distbg. Co., Inc., Corpus Christi, 1976—; pres., co-owner Miller of Dallas, Inc., 1980—, Miller Brands, Inc., Denver, 1986—. Mem. chancellor's coun. U. Tex. System. Mem. Am. Inst. CPA's, Tex. Soc. CPA's, Wholesale Beer Distbrs. Tex., Nat. Beer Wholesalers Assn., Dallas Citizens Council, Young Pres.'s Orgn., U. Tex. Ex-Students Assn., Dallas C. of C. Clubs: Corpus Christi Yacht, Dallas Verandah, Aerobics Activity Ctr., Crescent. Home: 5026 Middlegate Dallas TX 75229 Office: 2730 Irving Blvd PO Box 57208 Dallas TX 75207

WHITE, WILLIS SHERIDAN, JR., utilities executive; b. nr. Portsmouth, Va., Dec. 17, 1926; s. Willis Sheridan and Carrie (Culpepper) W.; m. LaVerne Behrends, Oct. 8, 1949; children: Willis Sheridan III, Marguerite Louise White Spangler, Cynthia Diane. B.S., Va. Poly. Inst., 1948; M.S., Mass. Inst. Tech., 1958. With Am. Electric Power Co. System, 1948—; asst. engr. Am. Electric Power Service Corp., N.Y.C., 1948-52, asst. to pres., 1952-54, office mgr., 1954-57, adminstrv. asst. to operating v.p., 1958-61; div. mgr. Am. Electric Power Service Corp. (Appalachian Power Co.), Lynchburg, Va., 1962-66; asst. gen. mgr. Am. Electric Power Service Corp. (Appalachian Power Co.), Roanoke, Va., 1966-67, asst. v.p., 1967-69, v.p., 1969, exec. v.p., dir., 1969-73; sr. exec. v.p. ops., dir. Am. Electric Power Service Corp., N.Y.C., 1973-75, vice chmn. ops., dir., 1975—, chmn., chief exec. officer; formerly pres. Cen. Ohio Coal Co., until 1988, chmn., chief exec. officer, 1988—, also bd. dirs.; dir. Am. Electric Power Co., N.Y.C., 1972—, chmn. bd., chief exec. officer, 1976—; chmn., dir. AEP Energy Services, Inc., AEP Generating Co., Appalachian Power Co., Roanoke, Va., Columbus So. Power Co., Ind. Mich. Power Co., Ky. Power Co., Kingsport Power Co., Mich. Power Co., Ohio Power Co., Wheeling Power Co.; pres., dir. Ohio Valley Electric Corp., Ind.-Ky. Electric Corp., 1977—, Beech Bottom Power Co., Blackhawk Coal Co., Cedar Coal Co., Cardinal Operating Co., Castlegate Coal Co., Cedar Coal Co., Central Appalachian Coal Co., Central Coal Co., Central Ohio Coal Co., Central Operating Co., Franklin Real Estate Co., Ind. Franklin Realty Co., Central Operating Co., Colomet, Inc., Franklin Real Estate Co., Kanawha Valley Power Co., Mich. Gas Exploration Co., Ind. Franklin Realty, Price River Coal Co., Simco, Inc., So. Appalachian Coal Co., So. Ohio Coal Co., Twin Br. R.R. Co., W.Va. Power Co., Wheeling Electric Co., Windsor Power House Coal Co.; pres. Internat. Conf. on Large High Voltage Elec. Systems (CIGRE). Trustee, Battelle Meml. Inst.; bd. visitors Va. Poly. Inst. and State U. Served with USNR, 1945-46. Sloan fellow, 1957-58. Mem. IEEE, Nat. Coal Assn. (dir.), Nat. Coal Council (bd. dirs.), Assn. Edison Illuminating Cos. (exec. com.), NAM (dir.), Nat. Acad. Engring., Eta Kappa Nu. Methodist. Office: Appalachian Power Co 40 Franklin Rd Roanoke VA 24022 also: Battelle Meml Inst 505 King Ave Columbus OH 43201 *

WHITEHEAD, BARBARA ELAINE, insurance executive; b. Miami, Fla., Nov. 25, 1947; d. James Edward and Bettie Louise (Whilden) Buck; divorced; 1 child, Kelly Allison. BS, SUNY, Albany, 1986. CPCU. Asst. v.p., mktg. dir. Almours-Carswell, Inc., Jacksonville, Fla., 1982—. Mem. Soc. CPCUs, Sales and Mktg. Execs., Ind. Ins. Agts. Am., Jacksonville C. of C. Republican. Episcopalian. Home: 7701 Baymeadows Circle W Unit 1084 Jacksonville FL 32256 Office: Almours-Carswell Inc 1650 Prudential Dr Ste 304 Jacksonville FL 32207

WHITEHEAD, CARL FRANCIS, engineering and construction company executive; b. N.Y.C., July 8, 1927; s. Carl Vail and Mabella (Budgick) W.; m. Vivian Helen Mathias, May 3, 1952. B.C.E., Rensselaer Poly. Inst., 1951. registered profl. engr. 19 states. Engineer Ebasco Services, Inc., N.Y.C., 1951-68, project mgr., 1968-76, v.p., 1976-78, sr. v.p., 1978-82, group v.p., 1982-87, sr. v.p., gen. mgr., 1988—; dir. Ebasco Services, Inc., Ebanal S.A. de C.V., Ebasco B.V., Ebasco Cayman Ltd., Ebasco Corp., Ebasco Engring. & Constrn. Corp., Ebasco Industries Inc., Ebasco Italia S.r.l., Ebasco Services Internat., Inc., Ebasco Services Singapore Pte. Ltd., Ebasco-CTCI Corp.; dir., pres. Ebasco Internat. Corp., Ebasco Overseas Corp.; v.p. Ebasco Services of Can. Ltd. Contbr. articles to profl. jours. Mem. Harbor Control Com., Lloyd Harbor, N.Y., 1982—. Served with U.S. Army, 1945-46. Fellow ASCE; mem. U.S. Com. on Large Dams, Chi Epsilon. Republican. Roman Catholic. Club: Lloyd Harbor Yacht. Home: 1 Fiddlers Green Lloyd Harbor NY 11743 Office: Ebasco Svcs Inc 2 World Trade Center New York NY 10048

WHITEHEAD, JOHN W., lawyer, organization administrator; b. Pulaski, Tenn., July 14, 1946; s. John M. and Alatha (Wiser) W.; m. Virginia Carolyn Nichols, Aug. 26, 1967; children: Jayson Reau, Jonathan Mathew, Elisabeth Anne, Joel Christofer, Joshua Benjamen. BA, U. Ark., 1969, JD, 1974. Bar: Ark. 1974, U.S. Dist. Ct. (ea. and we. dists.) Ark. 1974, U.S. Supreme Ct. 1977, U.S. Ct. Appeals (9th cir.) 1980, Va. 1981, U.S. Ct. Appeals (7th cir.) 1981. Spl. counsel Christian Legal Soc., Oak Park, Ill., 1977-78; assoc. Gibbs & Craze, Cleve., 1978-79; sole practice law Manassas, Va., 1979-82; pres. The Rutherford Inst., Manassas, Va., 1982—, also bd. dirs.; frequent lectr. colls., law schs.; past adj. prof. O.W. Coburn Sch. Law. Author: The Separation Illusion, 1977, Schools on Fire, 1980, The New Tyranny, 1982, The Second American Revolution, 1982, The Stealing of America, 1983, The Freedom of Religious Expression in Public High Schools, 1983, The End of Man, 1986, An American Dream, 1987, several others; contbr. numerous articles to profl. jours.; contbr. numerous chpts. to books. Served to 1st lt. U.S. Army, 1969-71. Named Christian Leader of Yr. Christian World Affairs Conf., Washington, 1986. Mem. ABA, Ark. Bar Assn., Va. Bar Assn. Office: The Rutherford Inst 9411 Battle St Manassas VA 22110

WHITEHILL, CLIFFORD LANE, lawyer; b. Houston, Apr. 14, 1931; s. Clifford H. and Catalina Borega (Yarza) W.; m. Daisy Mae Woodruff, Apr. 18, 1959; children: Clifford Scott, Alicia Anne, Stephen Lane. BA, Rice U., 1954; LLB, U. Tex., 1957; LLM, Harvard U., 1958. Bar: Tex. 1957, Minn. 1962. Assoc. Childress, Port and Crady, Houston, 1957-59; auditor Haskins and Sells, 1959; asst. gen. counsel Tex. Butadiene and Chem. Co., N.Y.C., 1959-62; with Gen. Mills, Inc., Mpls., 1962—, sr. v.p., gen. counsel, 1981—, sec., 1983—. Chmn. Chanhassen Housing and Redevel. Authority; mem. dean's coun. Hamline U. Sch. Law; mem. adv. com. Nat. Chamber Litigation Ctr.; trustee Food and Drug Law Inst., Meridian House Internat.; assoc.

bd. dirs. Minn. Opera; bd. dirs. Minn.-Uruguay Ptnrs. Am., Nat. Hispanic Scholarship Fund, Fund Legal Aid Soc.; mem. coun. Better Bus. Bur. Mem. ABA, Minn. Bar Assn., Tex. Bar Assn., Am. Arbitration Assn. (bd. dirs.), Grocery Mfrs. Assn. Am. (legal steering com.), Nat. Assn. Mfrs. (bd. dirs., state dir.), UN Assn. U.S., Bus. Roundtable (chmn. com.), Harvard Club, Lafayette Club. Republican. Roman Catholic. Office: Gen Mills Inc 1 General Mills Blvd Minneapolis MN 55426

WHITEHORNE, ROBERT ALVIN, business educator; b. Portsmouth, Va., June 20, 1925; s. Stanford Laferty and Ruth (Speight) W.; B.E.E., Va. Poly. Inst., 1948, M.E.E., 1951; m. Margaret Kirby, Sept. 6, 1946; children—Lynn Whitehorne Sacco, Robert Alvin, Cynthia Leigh Moore. Engr., IBM Corp., Poughkeepsie, N.Y., 1950-54, lab. adminstr., Kingston, N.Y., 1954-56, dir. employee relations, Armonk, N.Y., 1956-72, resident mgr. Mid-Hudson Valley, Poughkeepsie, 1972-74; v.p.-personnel and orgn. planning Sperry & Hutchinson Co., N.Y.C., 1976-79; exec. v.p. Michelin Tire Corp., Grenville, S.C., 1974-76; dir. CODESCO, Inc., SPAN-America, Inc.; mem. faculty Coll. Bus. Adminstrn., U. S.C., Columbia, 1979-85; mem. faculty Coll. William and Mary, 1985—. Former trustee U. S.C. Bus. Partnership Found.; mem. plans for progress com. Pres.'s Commn. on Equal Employment Activity, 1963-68. Served with USMCR, 1944-46. Methodist. Club: Kingsmill. Home: 216 Fairfax Way Williamsburg VA 23185-6546 Office: Coll William and Mary Sch Bus Adminstrn Williamsburg VA 23187

WHITEHOUSE, BRUCE ALAN, meeting planner; b. Bloomfield, N.J., Sept. 22, 1932; s. William Harold and Anna Marion (Axford) W.; m. Virginia Shirley Earle, May 7, 1955; children: Bruce Alan II, James William, Daniel Earle, Deirdre Anne, Laura Lynn. Student, Fairleigh-Dickinson U., 1962-68. Mgr. retail store Essex Lawn Mower Co., Inc., East Orange, N.J., 1954-56; mgr. br. warehouse Elmco Distbrs., Inc., Bethpage, N.Y., 1956-59, mgr. customer service, 1961-64; sales rep H.D. Hudson Mfg. Co., Inc., Chgo., 1961-64; with Bailey-Whelan Corp., West Orange, N.J., 1964-66; plant mgr. King Container Corp., Rockaway, N.J., 1966-70; road mgr. Rogers Transfer, Great. Meadows, N.J., 1970-73; inventory specialist Johnson Scale Co., West Caldwell, N.J., 1973-81; pres. SPG Sales, Lafayette, N.J., 1981-86; mktg. services dir. Lion Tech., Inc., Lafayette, 1986-88, adminstrv. mgr., 1988-89, asst. to the pres., 1989—; pres. Episcopal Fed. Credit Union, Newark, 1981-82. Trustee Sparta (N.J.) Pub. Library, 1986—, Health Village Retirement Community, 1989; mem. Diocesan council of Newark, 1973-81, Eagles Nest Camp Bd., Newark, 1980-87, deputy to Provinical Synod, 1989—. Served with U.S. Army, 1951-54. Clubs: Country Theater (Branchville, N.J.) (treas. 1970-73), Cornerstone Playhouse. Lodge: Rotary (Paul Harris fellow 1987). Home: 16 Lewis Ln Sparta NJ 07871 Office: Lion Group PO Drawer 700 Lafayette NJ 07848

WHITEHOUSE, JACK PENDLETON, public relations executive; b. Los Angeles, Aug. 18, 1924; s. Marvin and Lola Katherine (Gerber) W.; m. Phyllis Jeanne Stockhausen, Mar. 6, 1964 (div. 1983); 1 child, Mark Philip. Student, The Principia Coll., 1942-43, UCLA, 1945-49. Editor Los Angeles Ind. Pub. Co., 1946-48; writer UCLA Office Pub. Info., 1948-51; mng. editor Yuma (Ariz.) Daily Sun, 1951-53; assoc. editor Desert Mag., 1953-54; owner Whitehouse & Assocs., Los Angeles, 1954-55; dir. West Coast press relations Shell Oil Co., Los Angeles, 1955-56; pub. relations dir. Welton Becket & Assocs., Los Angeles, 1956-58; owner, pres. Whitehouse Assocs. Inc., Los Angeles, 1958—, Internat. Pub. Relations Co. Ltd., Los Angeles, 1959—; exec. dir. Japan Steel Info. Ctr., Los Angeles, 1966—; frequent guest lectr. to colls., univs. Author: International Public Relations, 1978. Mem. Los Angeles World Affairs Council; advisor Japanese Philharmonic Soc., 1975—. With AC, U.S. Army, 1943-45. Mem. Pub. Relations Soc. Am., Japan-Am. Soc. (exec. council 1968—), Fgn. Trade Assn. (bd. dirs. 1978-80), Japan-Calif. Assn., Greater Los Angeles Press Club. Office: Internat Pub Relations Ltd 523 W 6th Los Angeles CA 90014

WHITE-HUNT, KEITH, industrial development executive; b. Rowlands Gill, Eng., Sept. 6, 1950; s. Thomas William and Louisa (Robson) W-H.; m. Brenda Liddle, Jan. 1, 1970; children: Keith Brendan, John Roland, Daniel Thomas, Brooke Arran, Edward James. BA in Econ. Studies with honors, U. Exeter, United Kingdom, 1973; MS in Indsl. Mgmt., U. Bradford, Eng., 1975; cert. in edn., U. Leeds, 1976; DSc in Bus. Econs., U. Lodz, Poland, 1982; postgrad., Cornell U., 1986, Stanford U., 1987. Registered cons. in info. tech., registered cons. in export sales. Asst. prof. U. Bradford, 1973-77; assoc. prof. U. Sokoto, Nigeria, 1977-78, U. Stirling, Scotland, 1978-80; v.p. corp. devel. Lithgows Ltd., Scotland, 1980-83; deputy chief exec.. & pres. N. Am. Yorkshire & Humberside Deve. Assn., Eng., 1983—; vis. prof. U. R.I., 1980—, Tech. U. of Lodz, 1980—, U. of Lodz, 1985—; bd. dirs. White-Hunt Industries Ltd., Eng. contbr. numerous articles to profl. jours. Recipient David Forsyth award U. Leeds, 1976, Amicus Poloniae award for Contbn. to Coop. Acad. Research in Poland, 1981. Fellow British Inst. Mgmt., Inst. Sales and Mktg. Mgmt., Inst. Petroleum, Internat. Inst. Social Econs., Chartered Inst. Mktg.; mem. Inst. Info. Scientists, Inst. of Wastes Mgmt. Lodge: Rotary. Home: 141 Pepper Ct Los Altos CA 94022 also: 102 Valley Dr, Ben Rhydding, Ilkley, West Yorkshire LS29 8PA, England Office: Yorkshire & Humberside Devel 435 Tasso St Ste 140 Palo Alto CA 94301 also: Yorkshire & Humberside, Westgate House, 100 Wellington St, Leeds, West Yorkshire LS1 4LT, England

WHITEHURST, WILLIAM WILFRED, JR., management consultant; b. Balt., Mar. 4, 1937; s. William Wilfred and Elizabeth (Hogg) W.; B.A., Princeton, 1958; M.S., Carnegie Inst. Tech., 1963; m. Linda Joan Potter, July 1, 1961; children—Catherine Elizabeth, William Wilfred, III. Mathematician Nat. Security Agy., Fort George G. Meade, Md., 1961-63; mgmt. cons. McKinsey & Co., Inc., Washington, 1963-66; partner L.E. Peabody & Assos., Washington, 1966-69, exec. v.p., dir. L.E. Peabody & Assos., Inc., Lanham, Md., 1969-82, pres., dir., 1983-86, pres. W.W. Whitehurst & Assoc., Inc., Cockeysville, Md., 1986—. Served to lt. USNR, 1958-61. Mem. Operations Research Soc. Am., Inst. Mgmt. Scis., Washington Soc. Investment Analysts. Episcopalian. Clubs: University, Princeton (Washington); Princeton (N.J.) Quadrangle. Home and Office: 12421 Happy Hollow Rd Cockeysville MD 21030

WHITELEY, BENJAMIN ROBERT, insurance company executive; b. Des Moines, July 13, 1929; s. Hiram Everett and Martha Jane (Walker) W.; m. Elaine Marie Yunker, June 14, 1953; children—Stephen Robert, Benjamin Walker. B.S., Oreg. State U., 1951; M.S., U. Mich., 1952; postgrad. advanced mgmt. program, Harvard U. Clk. group dept. Standard Ins. Co., Portland, Oreg., 1956-69, asst. actuary group dept. then asst. actuary acturial dept., 1959-63, asst. v.p., asst. actuary, 1963-64, asst. v.p., assoc. actuary, 1964-70, v.p. group ins. adminstrn., 1970-72, v.p. group ins. div., 1972-80, exec. v.p. group ins., 1980-81, exec. v.p., 1981-83, pres., 1983—, also bd. dirs.; bd. dirs. Gunderson, Inc., Portland, U.S. Bank of Oreg. Past pres. Columbia Pacific council Boy Scouts Am.; chmn. bd., trustee Pacific U., Forest Grove, Oreg.; bd. dirs. St. Vincent Med. Found., Portland, Oreg. Served to 1st lt. USAF, 1952-55. Recipient Silver Beaver award Boy Scouts Am., 1983. Fellow Soc. Actuaries; mem. Am. Acad. Actuaries (bd. dirs. 1984-86), Am. Council of Life Ins. (bd. dirs. 1986), Internat. Congress Actuaries, Portland C. of C. (bd. dirs.). Republican. Methodist. Clubs: Arlington, Waverley Country, Multnomah Athletic (Portland, Oreg.). Home: 3740 SW Jerald Ct Portland OR 97221 Office: Standard Ins Co 1100 SW 6th Ave Portland OR 97204

WHITEMAN, H(ORACE) CLIFTON, banker; b. Visalia, Calif., July 23, 1925; s. Horace Clifton and Henrietta Emma (Stewart) W.; m. Shirley Deyo, Nov. 28, 1953 (div. Apr. 1977); children: Susan Elizabeth, Pamela Stewart Ritz, Elizabeth Lyle Braun; m. Joan Coffin, June 6, 1977. BA, Dartmouth Coll., 1950, MBA, 1951. V.p. Morgan Guaranty Trust Co., N.Y.C., 1951-68; sr. v.p., chief fin. officer Investors Diversified Services, Inc., Mpls., 1968-76; pres., trustee The Bowery Savs. Bank, N.Y.C., 1976-78; sr. v.p. The Irving Trust Co., N.Y.C., 1978-82; exec. v.p. The Bank of Tokyo Trust Co., N.Y.C., 1982—; sr. dep. gen. mgr. The Bank of Tokyo, Ltd., N.Y.C. Republican. Presbyterian. Clubs: The Links, Down Town (N.Y.C.), Piping Rock (Locust Valley, N.Y.). Home: 136 E 64th St New York NY 10021 Office: The Bank of Tokyo Trust Co 100 Broadway New York NY 10005

WHITEMAN, JOSEPH DAVID, lawyer, fluid power components company executive; b. Sioux Falls, S.D., Sept. 12, 1933; s. Samuel D. and Margaret (Wallace) W.; m. Mary Kelly, Dec. 29, 1962; children: Anne Margaret, Mary Ellen, Joseph David, Sarah Kelly, Jane. B.A., U. Mich., 1955, J.D., 1960. Bar: D.C. 1960, Ohio 1976. Assoc. Cox, Langford, Stoddard & Cutler, Washington, 1959-64; sec., gen. counsel Studebaker group Studebaker Worthington, Inc., N.Y.C., 1964-71; asst. gen. counsel. United Telecommunications, Inc., Kansas City, Mo., 1971-74; v.p., gen. counsel, sec. Weatherhead Co., Cleve., 1974-77, Parker Hannifin Corp., Cleve., 1977—. Served as lt. USNR, 1955-57. Mem. ABA, Beta Theta Pi, Phi Delta Phi. Republican. Roman Catholic. Home: 23349 Shaker Blvd Shaker Heights OH 44122 Office: Parker Hannifin Crop 17325 Euclid Ave Cleveland OH 44112

WHITFIELD, DAVID LEWIS, architect; b. Vincennes, Ind., Mar. 17, 1937; s. Joseph Lewis and Verna Irene (Allen) W.; m. Rosalie Ann Boyer, Nov. 19, 1960; children: Mark, Scott, Kathleen, Patrick. Student, Vincennes U., 1955-56, U. Ill., 1956-60; BArch, Washington U., St. Louis, 1964. Registered profl. architect, Mo., Ill., Ind., Ga., N.C., Va., W.Va., Md., D.C. Architect L.W. Routt & Assocs., Vincennes, 1958, J.H. Kolbrook, Louisville, 1959; v.p. Bank Bldg. Corp., St. Louis, 1960-84; pres. DLW Inc., Chesterfield, Mo., 1984—. Served with U.S. Army, 1960-64. Mem. AIA (com. mem. 1980—), Chesterfield C. of C., Mo. Coun. Architects, Comprehensive Plan Commn. City of Chesterfield. Office: DLW Inc 14266 Dinsmoor Dr Chesterfield MO 63017-2910

WHITFIELD, DENNIS E., government official; b. Albany, Ga., July 9, 1948; married. B.A., U. Ga., 1971. Dir. voter registration program Republican Nat. Com., regional political dir. for the Southeast, dir. edn. and trng., dir. political affairs; chief of staff to U.S. trade rep. Dept. Labor; dep. sec. Dept. Labor, Washington, 1985—. Office: Labor Dept 200 Constitution Ave NW Rm S2018 Washington DC 20210 *

WHITLEY, PEGGY CALDWELL, business executive; b. Cleveland, Tex., Aug. 21, 1945; d. Homer S. and Dorothy Jane (Bailes) Gilbert; m. Bob L. Caldwell, Apr. 12, 1967; children—Brian Lee, Brandon Lee; m. Donald Lynn Whitley, Jan. 21, 1984. Vice pres., dir. Agri-Sul, Inc., Mineola, Tex., 1969-78; v.p., dir. Agri-Sul Canada, Ltd., Calgary, Alta., 1974-78; owner Hickory Hut, Mineola, Tex., 1973-75; regulatory analyst Tex. Eastern Transmission Corp., Houston, 1978-84; owner Resource Mgmt. Dynamics, Humble, Tex., 1981-85; mgr. agrl. systems Gulf Markets Internat., Manama, Bahrain, 1984-85, mgr. fin. and adminstrn., water service div., 1986—. Mem. Am. Entrepreneurs Assn., Exec. Female, Am. Mgmt. Assn. Republican. Baptist. Home: PO Box 520 Coldsprings TX 77331 Office: PO Box 2709, Manama Bahrain

WHITLINGER, GENE P., finance company executive; b. Pitts., 1933. Grad., Duquesne U., 1959. V.p. ops. western U.S. GMAC, Detroit. Office: GMAC 3044 W Grand Blvd Detroit MI 48202 *

WHITLOCK, MARK DOUGLAS, engineer; b. Hillsboro, Ill., Apr. 20, 1953; s. Jacob Oscar and Maxine (Young) W.; m. Karen Nelson, July 9, 1977; children: Douglas N., Geoffrey A. BA, Greenville Coll., 1975; BS in Civil Engring., U. Ill., 1977. Registered profl. engr., Ill. Gen. mgr. Structural Rubber Products Co., Springfield, Ill., 1977—. Pres. Light and Life Men Central Ill., 1988; chmn. advancement com. Springfield Boy Scouts Am., 1985-87. Mem. Ill. Soc. Profl. Engrs. (v.p. Capital chpt. 1988—, named Young Engr. of Yr. 1988), Cen. Ill. Rubber Group, Joints and Bearings Rsch. Council, Am. Chem. Soc. (mem. rubber div.), Rotary. Home: 5 Boulder Point Springfield IL 62702 Office: Structural Rubber Products PO Box 2439 Springfield IL 62705

WHITMAN, CARL EDWARD, shipbuilding company executive, lawyer; b. Doylestown, Ohio, Jan. 4, 1930; s. P. Carl and Marget L. W.; m. Helen L., Sept. 12, 1953; 1 son, Kurt. LL.B., Ohio State U., 1954. Bar: Ohio, Ill., Wis., Va. Treas., tax counsel Packaging Corp. Am., Chgo., 1967-74; sr. v.p., gen. counsel J.I. Case Co., Racine, Wis., 1974-83, Newport News Shipbldg., Va., 1983—. Office: Newport News Shipbldg & Dry Dock Co 4101 Washington Ave Newport News VA 23607

WHITMAN, MARTIN J., investment banker; b. N.Y.C., Sept. 30, 1924; s. Irving and Dora (Cukier) W.; B.S. magna cum laude, Syracuse U., 1949; M.A., New Sch. for Social Research, 1956; postgrad. Princeton U., 1949-50; m. Lois M. Quick, Mar. 10, 1956; children—James Q., Barbara E., Thomas I. Research analyst, buyer Shearson Hammill & Co., N.Y.C., 1950-56; analyst William Rosenwald Co., N.Y.C., 1956-58; head research Ladenburg, Thalmann & Co., N.Y.C., 1958-60; gen. partner Gerstley Sunstein & Co., Phila., 1960-67; v.p., dir. Blair & Co., Inc., N.Y.C., 1967-68; pres. M.J. Whitman & Co. (now Inc.), N.Y.C., 1969—; pres., chief exec. officer Equity Strategies Fund, Inc., 1984—; mng. dir. Whitman Heffernan Rhein & Co., Inc., 1987—; dir. KCP Holding Co., 1987—; former dir. Mathematica Inc., Princeton, N.J.; former vice-chmn. GNMR, Inc., N.Y.C.; adj. prof. fin. Yale U., New Haven, 1972-83; cons. disclosure study SEC, 1968; cons. Pres.'s Commn. on Accident at Three Mile Island, 1979. Bd. dirs. Ctr. for Humanities, 1987—. Served with USNR, 1942-46. Chartered fin. analyst. Mem. N.Y. Soc. Security Analysts, Phila. Econ. Soc. Jewish. Author: (with M. Shubik) The Aggressive Conservative Investor, 1979; contbr. numerous articles to profl. publs., also booklets. Home: 285 Central Park W New York NY 10024

WHITMARSH, THEODORE FRANCIS, lawyer, investor; b. Englewood, N.J., Sept. 25, 1918; s. Karl Russell and Catherine (Clarke) W.; A.B., Harvard U., 1942; LL.B., Fordham U., 1950; m. Mary Louise Ward, Feb. 19, 1944; children—Linda L., Carol P., Dorothy S. Bar: N.Y. 1950. Asst. sec., dir. Frances H. Leggett & Co., 1950-52, v.p., sec., dir., 1955-59; sec., dir. Thames & Hudson Pub. Co., N.Y.C., 1952-53; v.p., gen. mgr., asst. sec., dir. Hogan-Faximile Corp., 1959-64, pres., dir. Hogan Faximile Corp. of Can. Ltd., 1962-64, 103 E. 75th St. Apts., Inc., 1957-70, Audley Clarke Co., 1968-88 . Served with AUS, 1942-46. Mem. Am., N.Y. State bar assns., Assn. Bar City N.Y., Huguenot Soc. Am. (pres., dir. 1975-78). Clubs: Pilgrims, River, Union, Church (N.Y.C.); Piping Rock. Home: 183 Linden Ln Glen Head NY 11545 Office: 260 Fifth Ave New York NY 10001

WHITMER, GILBERT NORMAN, lawyer; b. Glendive, Mont., May 22, 1942; s. Edgar L. and Josephine (Grabowski) W. BS in Mktg., U. Colo., 1965, JD, 1971. Bar: Colo. Supreme Ct., 1972, U.S. Dist. Ct., 1972, U.S. Supreme Ct., 1984. Legal staff asst. to presiding judge Colo. Dist. Ct., Boulder, 1970-72; trial lawyer Bernard & Moreland P.C., Boulder, 1972-76; instr. paralegal studies Arapahoe Community Coll., Boulder, 1976-77; gen. counsel Nat. Farmers Union Property and Casualty Co., Denver, 1977—. Mem. ABA, Am. Corp. Counsel Assn., Colo. Bar Assn., Denver Bar Assn., Colo. Assn. Corp. Counsel (bd. dirs.). Republican. Home: 1499 S Lima St Aurora CO 80012 Office: Nat Farmers Union Property & Casualty Co 10065 E Harvard Ave Denver CO 80251

WHITMER, JOSEPH MORTON, benefits consulting firm executive; b. Sacramento, Apr. 29, 1942; s. Carlos Raymond and Elizabeth Ellen (McDonald) W.; m. Judith Leigh Johnson, Aug. 11, 1963 (dec. Jan. 1985); children: Karen L., Brian D.; m. Paula Ann Thurman, Mar. 29, 1986; 1 stepchild, Julie Anne. BS in Acctg., U. Ky., 1964, JD, 1967. Ptnr. Veal & Whitmer, Nicholasville, Ky., 1967-68; v.p., sec., gen. counsel and dir. Consol. Mgmt. Services, Eagles Nat. Life Ins. Co., First Mut. Ins. Co., First. Mut. Life Ins. Co., Lexington, Ky., 1970-75; sole practice Lexington, Ky., 1975—; v.p., dir. Profl. Adminstrs. Ltd., Lexington, Ky., 1968-86, pres. chief exec. officer, 1987—. Mem. bd. overseers Duke U. Comprehensive Cancer Ctr., Durham, N.C., 1987—, co-chair Melanoma Consortium, 1987. Named one of Outstanding Young Men Am., 1975. Mem. ABA, Ky. Bar Assn., Fayette County Bar Assn., Internat. Found. Employee Benefit Plans, Soc. Profl. Benefit Adminstrs. Democrat. Methodist. Office: Profl Adminstrs Ltd-Pension and Group Cons Inc. 1141 Red Mile Rd Lexington KY 40504

WHITMORE, GEORGE MERLE, JR., management consultant executive; b. Tarrytown, N.Y., Jan. 1, 1928; s. George Merle and Elizabeth Helen (Knodel) W.; m. Priscilla Elizabeth Norman, Mar. 30, 1963; children: Elizabeth Lawrence, George Norman, Stephen Bradford. BE, Yale U., 1949; MBA, Harvard U., 1951. Test engr. Gen. Electric Co., Bridgeport, Conn., Erie, Pa., 1949; research asso. Harvard Bus. Sch., Boston, 1951-52; asso. Cresap, McCormick Paget Inc., N.Y.C., 1954-59, prin., 1959-61, partner, 1961-69, v.p., dir., 1969-79, mng. dir., chief exec. officer, 1979-81; mng. dir. Ayers, Whitmore & Co., Inc., N.Y.C., 1981-88, Ayers, Whitmore div. A.T. Kearney, Inc., N.Y.C., 1988—. chmn. bd. Classified Fin. Corp., San Francisco, Philo Smith & Co., Inc., Stamford, Conn.; bd. dirs. RTI, Inc., Rockaway, N.J. Trustee, former bd. pres. Hackley Sch., Tarrytown, N.Y., Salisbury (Conn.) Sch. Served with USAF, 1952-53. Mem. Inst. Mgmt. Cons. (founding mem.), Newcomen Soc., Tau Beta Pi. Presbyterian. Clubs: Stanwich (former dir.) (Greenwich); Yale (N.Y.C.). Home: 4 Cedarwood Dr Greenwich CT 06830 Office: AT Kearney Ayers Whitmore Div 875 3d Ave New York NY 10022

WHITMORE, KAY REX, photographic company executive; b. Salt Lake City, July 24, 1932; s. Rex Grange and Ferrol Terry (Smith) W.; m. Yvonne Schofield, June 6, 1956; children: Richard, Kimberly, Michele, Cynthia, Suzanne, Scott. Student, U. Utah, 1950-53, B.S., 1957; M.S., M.I.T., 1975. With Eastman Kodak Co., Rochester, N.Y., 1957—, engr. film mfg., 1957-67; with factory start-up Eastman Kodak Co., Guadalajara, Mex., 1967-71; various mgmt. positions film mfg. Eastman Kodak Co., Rochester, 1971-74, asst. v.p., gen. mgr. Latin Am. Region, 1975-79, v.p., asst. gen. mgr. U.S. and Can. Photog. Div., 1979-80, exec. v.p. and gen. mgr., 1981-83, pres., 1983—, also dir.; bd. dirs. The Chase Manhattan Corp., Chase Lincoln First Bank, Bus. Council State of N.Y.; chmn. Indsl. Mgmt. Council. Bd. dirs. Nat. Council for Minorities in Engring.; trustee U. Rochester. Served with U.S. Army, 1953-55. Mem. Rochester C. of C. (bd. dirs.), Am. Soc. Quality Control. Mormon. Office: Eastman Kodak Co 343 State St Rochester NY 14650

WHITMORE, RUFUS WARD, JR, training executive. s. Rufus W. Sr. and Bernice (McJimpson) W.; m. Patricia Virginia Bevekly, June 1969; 1 child, Bryan L. BS in Social Sci., U. Ark., 1966; postgrad., Fairfield U., 1974, NYU, 1980, Springfield Coll., 1984, Dartmouth Coll., 1988. Dir. program Chgo. Commons Assn., 1967-68; coord. child care Chgo. Community Urban Opportunity, 1968-70; dir. group and community svc. Hall Neighborhood House, Bridgeport, Conn., 1970-73; exec. dir. Southfield Community Orgn. Inc., Stamford, Conn., 1973-86, Opportunity Industrialization Ctr. of R.I., Providence, 1986—. Vol. Vista, 1966-67; trustee, exec. com. Providence Pub. Library, 1986—, R.I. Group Health Assn., Providence, 1987—, Butler Hosp., Providence, 1987—; trustee NCCJ, 1986—. Recipient Community Svc. awards Stamford NAACP, State of Conn. Legis., Conn. Head Start Parent Assn. Mem. C. of C., Rotary, Turks Head Club, Brownson County Club (bd. dirs. 1986), Kappa Alpha Psi. Republican. Baptist. Home: 3300 Park Ave Bridgeport CT 06606 Office: OIC of RI 1 Hilton St Providence RI 02905

WHITNEY, EDWARD BONNER, investment banker; b. Glen Cove, N.Y., June 6, 1945; s. Edward Farley and Millicent Bonner (Bowring) W.; m. Martha Congleton Howell, Aug. 17, 1974; children—William Howell, John Howell. B.A., Harvard U., 1966, M.B.A., 1969. Systems engr. IBM, Cambridge, Mass., 1966-67; assoc. Dillon, Read & Co. Inc., N.Y.C., 1969-74, v.p., 1975-79, sr. v.p., 1980-83, mng. dir., 1984—, also bd. dirs. Mem. Securities Industry Assn. (corporate fin. com. 1983—). Club: Heights Casino (Bklyn.). Office: Dillon Read & Co Inc 535 Madison Ave New York NY 10022

WHITNEY, JAMES BANNER, accountant, food products executive; b. Rome, Ga., Dec. 26, 1952; s. James Neel and Sara (Banner) W.; m. Rebecca Erck, Sept. 11, 1976; children: Amanda, Neil, Andrew. BBA, West Ga. Coll., 1974; M in Acctg., U. Ga., 1976. CPA, N.C. Acct. A.M. Pullen & Co., Winston-Salem, N.C., 1976-81, Daniel, McKee & Co., Winston-Salem, 1981; v.p. fin. Royal Cake Co., Inc., Winston-Salem, 1982-87, chief exec. officer, 1987—. Mem. AICPA, Cookie and Snack Bakers Assn. Office: Royal Cake Co Inc 315 Cassell St Winston-Salem NC 27107

WHITNEY, RALPH ROYAL, JR., financial executive; b. Phila., Dec. 10, 1934; s. Ralph Royal and Florence Elizabeth (Whitney) W.; m. Fay Wadsworth, Apr. 4, 1959; children: Lynn Marie, Paula Sue, Brian Ralph. BA, U. Rochester, 1957, MBA, 1972. Spl. agt. Prudential Ins. Co., Rochester, N.Y., 1958-59; div. mgr. Prudential Ins. Co., Rochester, 1959-63; gen. agt. Nat. Life Vt., Syracuse, 1963-64; controller Wadsworth Mfg. Assocs. Inc., Syracuse, 1964-65, v.p., 1965-68, pres., 1968-71; pres. Warren Components Corp., Warren, Pa., 1968—; pres., mng. prin. ptnr. Hammond Kennedy Whitney & Co., N.Y.C., 1972—; chmn. IFR Systems Inc.; chmn., chief exec. officer Holbrook Patterson Inc., Grobot File Co. Am.; bd. dirs. Excel Industries Corp., Regency Electronics Inc. Mfg. Co., Baldwin Tech. Corp., Unistrut Corp. of Am., Selas Corp. Am., D.M. Mossberg & Son Inc. Episcopalian. Clubs: N.Y. Yacht, Lotus (N.Y.C.); Century (Syracuse), Merion Cricket. Home: 100 Grays Ln #108 Haverford PA 19041

WHITNEY, RONALD DUNN, real estate development executive, university official, lawyer; b. Chgo., Apr. 26, 1954; s. Robert E. and Joan (Prendergast) W.; m. Carol Coleman, May 26, 1979; children: Natalie Campbell, Celia Coleman. BA, George Washington U., 1976; JD, Del. Law Sch., 1982. Claims rep. Hartford Ins. Co., Wilmington, Del., 1975-79, Am. Mut. Ins. Co., Bryn Mawr, Pa., 1979-81; legal asst. Pickett, Jones Elliott Kristol & Schnee, Wilmington, 1981-83; sr. claims examiner Colonial Ins. Co. Calif., Wilmington, 1983-84; dir. real estate and risk mgmt. Drexel U., Phila., 1985—; pres., bd. dirs. Acad. Properties, Inc., Phila., 1986—. Mem. vestry St. John's Episcopal Ch., Wilmington, 1987—. Mem. Nat. Assn. Corp. Real Estate Ofcls., Univ. Risk Mgrs. Assn. (editor 1988—), Assn. Univ. Real Estate Ofcls. Home: 707 Nottingham Rd Wilmington DE 19805 Office: Acad Properties Inc 3318 Cherry St Philadelphia PA 19104

WHITNEY, WILLIAM GORDON, investment management company executive; b. Rochester, N.Y., Oct. 12, 1922; s. William and Marguerite (Gordon) W.; B.S. in Adminstrv. Engring., Cornell U., 1943; M.B.A. with distinction, Harvard U., 1951; m. Margaret M. Deis, Mar. 16, 1971; children—Carol Joy, Lance A., Valerie A., Fredericka A., William A. Field engr. Norma Hoffman Bearings Corp., Stanford, Conn., 1946-49; cons. McKinsey & Co., N.Y.C., 1951-54; v.p. Am. Airlines, Inc., N.Y.C., 1954-62; gen. mgr. Martin Marietta Corp., Balt., 1963-68; pres. Whitney & Co., Inc., Rochester, 1969—; chmn. Whitney Holdings Ltd., N.Y.C., 1984—. Served as aviation engring. officer USN, 1944-46. Mem. Delta Upsilon. Office: Whitney Co Inc 2507 Browncroft Blvd Rochester NY 14625

WHITSETT, JOHN FREDERICK, brass foundry executive; b. Los Angeles, Sept. 25, 1940; s. William Paul Jr. and Mary Elizabeth (Atkinson) W.; divorced; children: Jeffrey, Peter, Lisa Troeger; m. Kirsten Holst, Oct. 15, 1978; 1 child, John Kristian. BA, Occidental Coll., 1962. Research assoc. Econs. Research Assocs., Los Angeles, 1966-69; asst. to pres. Guy F. Atkinson Co., San Francisco, 1969-71; owner, operator Stone Boat Yard, Alameda, Calif., 1972-76, Standard Brass Foundry, Oakland, Calif., 1974—; mem. adv. bd. Fin. Ctr. Bank, San Francisco, 1983—; bd. dirs. Guy F. Atkinson Co. Mem. adv. bd. Rowell Ranch Rodeo, Haywood, Calif., 1986—; bd. dirs. Neighborhood Pool, Orinda, Calif., 1987—. Served to lt. USN, 1962-66, Vietnam. Republican. Office: Standard Brass Foundry 2220 Livingston St Suite 208 Oakland CA 94606

WHITTAKER, SAM EDWIN, investment banking executive; b. 1937; s. Chester George and Violet Ruth (Bohman) W.; m. Barbara Stewart Lindsay, (div. 1985); children: Lindsay Bohman, Ashley Phillips. BA in Econs., Vanderbilt U., 1960; postgrad., NYU, 1963-64, U. North Fla., 1973-74. Sales trainee Halsey, Stuart & Co., Inc., N.Y.C., 1962-64; investment advisor Intervest, Inc., N.Y.C., 1964-65; account exec. Walston & Co., Inc. (formerly Hayden Stone, Inc.), Jacksonville, Fla., 1965-73; investment exec. Shearson, Hayden Stone, Inc., Jacksonville and Delray Beach, Fla., 1973-78; pres. U.S. Mfg. Corp., Ft. Lauderdale, Fla., 1978-81; realtor assoc. Keyes Co. Realtors, Delray Beach, 1981-82; with S.E. Whittaker Real Estate, Delray Beach, 1982-84; exec. v.p., chief exec. officer Trizak Fin. Group, Inc., Delray Beach, 1984-86; pres. Southeast Atlantic Capital Corp., Delray Peach, Fla., 1987—. Mem. Keyes Million Dollar Round Table Pres. Com., Nat. Assn. Security Dealers, Fin. Analysts Soc. of Jacksonville, Hayden Stone Pres. Council. Office: SE Atlantic Capital Corp 3701 S Flagler Dr West Palm Beach FL 33405

WHITTELSEY, HENRY NEWTON, telecommunications company executive; b. Chgo., Sept. 8, 1942; s. Souther and Harriet (Nelson) W.; m. Frances Cerra, Sept. 12, 1971; children: Christopher Cerra, Eric Cerra. Student, Boston U., 1961-62, Jackson State U., 1962-63, Boston U., 1962-63. Gen. mgr. Tropical Hardwoods, Inc., Peru and Honduras, 1964-67; gen. mgr., asst. H. Newton Whittelsey, Inc., Vallejo Naval Sta. Yard, Calif., 1967-68; nat. accounts sales mgr. Am. Photocopy Equipment Co., N.Y.C., 1968-72; pres., chief exec. officer Whitcom div. Executone Metro Inc., So. Hauppauge, N.Y., 1972—; adv. com. telecommunications curriculum N.Y. Inst. Tech., 1985—. Contbr. articles to newspapers and trade jours. Fund raiser Inter-Media Art Ctr., Huntington, N.Y., 1983—, L.I. YMCA; trustee Heckscher Mus., Huntington, 1985; active Bay Hills Property Owners Assn. Recipient Pres.' Club award, Am. Photocopy Equipment Co., 1970-71, Field Goal Club award, Executone, Inc., 1973, 78, 79, 84, 85, 86, 87. Mem. N.Y. State Telecommunications Assn. (treas. 1984-86, v.p. 1986-88, pres. 1988), N. Am. Telecommunications Assn. (bd. dirs.), Assocs. for Commerce and Industry (bd. dirs. 1983—), L.I. Exec. Network (bd. dirs.), L.I. Assn., Hauppauge Indsl. Assn., Mayflower Soc. Republican. Episcopalian. Home: 50 Summit Dr Huntington Bay LI NY 11743 Office: Whitcom 2990 Expressway Dr S South Hauppauge NY 11722-1477

WHITTIER, CHARLES TAYLOR, JR., investment company executive; b. Cedar Falls, Iowa, Nov. 29, 1941; s. Charles Taylor and Sara Jane (Leckrone) W.; student Montgomery Jr. Coll., 1959-62; B.S., Morehead U., 1964; M.B.A., Temple U., 1968; postgrad. U. Okla., 1971-77; m. Wendi Lynn Walker, June 18, 1978; children—Megan Rose, Courtney Lynn. Cost analyst Philco-Ford Corp., Ft. Washington, Pa., 1967, programs adminstr., 1967-69, sr. salary adminstr., 1969-70, mgr. indsl. relations for U.S. and Third Country nations, Saigon, Vietnam, 1970, Southeast Asia liaison, Phila., 1971; pres. Internat. Enterprises, Norman, Okla., 1971-76, Transnational Corp., Norman, 1977—, v.p., treas. mining co., 1977-81; pres. CTEC Inc., 1979—, Transnational Energy Corp., 1983—, Whittier Fin. Corp., 1979—.past cons. to Okla. Aeronautical Commn.; past cons and acting pres. Aviation FBO Co. Past mem. Internat. Assn. Students in Econs. and Commerce (bd. advisers; mem. nat. com.). Mem. Internat. Assn. for Fin. Planning, AAUP, Aircraft Owners and Pilots Assn., Oklahoma City Internat. Trade Club, Licensing Execs. Soc., World Mariculture Soc., Colo. Mining Assn. Mem. Christian Ch. (Disciples of Christ). Co-editor: The Conduct of Bus. Overseas: An Okla. Perspective, 1974. Home: 2226 Lindenwood Ln Norman OK 73071 Office: PO Box 5969 Norman OK 73070

WHITTINGTON, (CHARLES) AVEN, cotton company executive; b. Greenwood, Miss., Dec. 10, 1917; s. Will M. Whittington; m. Hortense Spann Griffin; children: Mrs. James C. Sumner Jr., Charles Aven Jr., George G. Griffin Jr., Mrs. Coleman L. Bailey. BA in Econs., Princeton U., 1939. Farmer; chmn. bd. Staple Cotton Coop. Assn.; chmn. Staplcotn, Greenwood, Miss., also bd. dirs.; chmn. bd. Yazoo Valley-Minter City Oil Mill Inc., Farmer's Supply Coop.; chmn. Farm Credit Banks New Orleans, 1981, past bd. dirs.; bd. dirs. Delta Purchasing Fedn., Bank of Commerce; mem. Cotton Bd., past chmn.; chmn. bd. Nat. Cotton Council. Deacon First Bapt. Ch.; trustee Miss. Coll; past pres. Delta Council, Delta area council Boy Scouts Am., Greenwood Little Theatre, Miss. Assn. Conservation Commrs., Miss. Heart Assn. Lodge: Kiwanis (past pres. Greenwood club). Home: 911 Myrtle St Greenwood MS 38930 Office: Staplcotn 214 W Market St Box 547 Greenwood MS 38930 also: Rt 3 Box 65 Greenwood MS 38930

WHITTINGTON, ROBERT WALLACE, corporate professional; b. Birmingham, Ala., Sept. 25, 1967; s. Dorsey and Frances (Kohn) W.; m. Karen Smith, Dec. 10, 1967 (div. 1984). BS, Auburn U., 1955; BA, U. Miami, Fla., 1956; MS, Cornell U., 1958. Chief exec. officer Travel Ctrs., Inc., Chgo.; pres. Svc. Ctrs., Inc., Sarasota, Fla., 1970-88. Served to lt. U.S. Intelligence, 1960-62, Korea. Mem. Fla. Hort. Soc., Am. Landscape Assn., Fly Fisherman Assn., Can. Salmonoid Assn., Fla. Turf Assn., Am. Soc. Travel Agts. (bd. dirs. 1961-63). Home and Office: 6609 Peacock Rd Sarasota FL 34242

WHITTINGTON, VERLE GLENN, petroleum company executive; b. Fairfield, Iowa, Dec. 2, 1929; s. Harold William and Grace Marie (Wilson) W.; m. Pauline Curran, Oct. 31, 1952; children: Kathleen Ann, James Edd, Mark Steven, Carol Lynn, John Joseph, Michael Aaron. B.A., Parsons Coll., Fairfield, 1952; J.D., U. Iowa, 1955. With Shell Oil Co., 1955—; mgr. non-exempt employee relations and indsl. safety Shell Oil Co., N.Y.C., 1968-70; mgr. indsl. relations, employee relations orgn. Shell Oil Co., Houston, 1970-73; treas. Shell Oil Co., 1973-75, v.p. employee relations, 1975—; chmn. Conf. Bd.'s Human Resource Mgmt. Com.; bd. dirs. R&F Coal Co., Turris Coal Co., Triton Coal Co., Marrowbone Coal Co., Wolf Creek Coal Co., Shell Mining Co., Shipyard River Coal Terminal Co., Scallop Corp., Pike County Coal Co.; chmn. trustees Shell Pension Fund, Provident Fund. Bd. dirs., Jr. Achievement SE Tex.; mem. Houston Loaned Exec. Com.; sec./treas. Exec. Service Core Houston; trustee Nat. Ctr. Occupational Readjustment. Mem. ABA (trustee), Iowa Bar Assn., Houston Bar Assn., Labor Policy Assn. (chmn. exec. com., dir.), Unemployed Benefits Assn. (bd. dirs.), Bus. Roundtable (exec. com. and employee relations com.), Petroleum Club Houston. Roman Catholic. Club: Elk. Club: River Plantation Country (Conroe). Home: 101 Biloxi Ct Conroe TX 77302 Office: Shell Oil Co One Shell Plaza PO Box 2463 Houston TX 77001

WHITWAM, DAVID RAY, appliance manufacturing company executive; b. Stanley, Wis., Jan. 30, 1942; s. Donald R. and Lorraine (Stoye) W.; m. Barbara Lynne Peterson, Apr. 13, 1963; children: Mark, Laura, Thomas. B.S., U. Wis., 1967. Gen. mgr. sales So. Calif. div. Whirlpool Corp., Los Angeles, 1975-77; mdse. mgr. ranges Benton Harbor, Mich., 1977-79, dir. builder mktg., 1979-80, v.p. builder mktg., 1980-83, v.p. whirlpool sales, 1983-85, vice chmn., chief mktg. officer, 1985-87, chmn., pres., chief exec. officer, 1987—, also bd. dirs.; bd. dirs. Combustion Engring. Inc., Stamford, Conn. Pres. bd. dirs. The Soup Kitchen, Benton Harbor, 1980—; mem. Nat. Council Housing Industry, Washington. Served to capt. U.S. Army, 1968-68. Fellow Aspen Inst. Republican. Lutheran. Club: Point O'Woods (Benton Harbor). Office: Whirlpool Corp 2000 US 33 N Benton Harbor MI 49022 *

WHORF, DAVID FAXON, insurance representative; b. Boston, Sept. 11, 1928; s. Clarence P. and Dora (Homer) W.; m. Mary Evelyn Harmer; children: Steven Cutler, Catherine A., Deborah Lazell. BA cum laude, Amherst (Mass.) Coll., 1950. CLU. Case officer CIA, Washington, 1950-53; mgmt. trainee Union Mut. Life, Portland, Maine, 1955-57, field supr., 1958-60, agt., 1963-84; asst. mgr. Union Mut. Home Office Agy., Portland, Maine, 1960-63; registered rep., agt. Integrated Resources Equity Corp., Maccabees Mut., others., Portland, 1984—. Mem. Rep. Town Com., Falmouth, Maine, 1970-84; mem. adv. bd. Salvation Army, Portland, 1976—. With U.S. Army, 1953-55. Mem. Am. Soc. CLUs, Maine Assn. Life Underwriters (pres. 1966-67, nat. committeeman 1981—), Nat. Assn. Life Underwriters (trustee 1976-80), Maine Estate Planning Council (bd. dirs. 1980-83), Maine Life Underwriters (treas. polit. action com. 1987-88), Chesuncook Property Assn., Owners/Leasers Assn.(treas. Chesuncook chpt. 1985-86, pres. 1983-85). Republican. Home: 4 Tanya Ln Falmouth ME 04105 Office: Planned Fin Services 482 Congress St Portland ME 04101

WHORTON, BILL M., financial planner; b. Petersburg, Tex., July 2, 1933; s. Walter Mack and Alba Kateria (Germany) W.; children: Stephen E., Suzanne, Michael D.; m. Isla JoEllen Dutton Caudle, Mar. 7, 1976. Student, Tex. Tech. U., 1951-53. Cert. fin. planner. V.p. Lubbock (Tex.) Nat. Bank, 1950-81; fin. planner Pennington Bass Cos., Lubbock, 1981—. Mem. Internat. Assn. Fin. Planners (treas., chpt. dir. 1987-88), Inst. Cert. Fin. Planners (cert.). Republican. Mem. Ch. of Christ. Home: 3104 79th St Lubbock TX 79423 Office: Pennington Bass Cos 1001 Main St Suite 100 Lubbock TX 79401

WIBBELSMAN, ROBERT JOHN, financial investment executive; b. Eau Claire, Wis., Mar. 27, 1939; s. Clemence Joseph and Adele (Dilger) W.; m. Martha Ann Warren, Jan. 27, 1962; children: Robert J. Jr., Warren Mahlon; m. Nancy Casto Benson, Feb. 9, 1984. AB, Johns Hopkins U., 1961. Asst. syndicate mgr. Auchincloss, Parker, Redpath, N.Y.C., 1964-67; br. mgr. Wood, Struthers, and Winthrop, Los Angeles, 1967-70; v.p. trading William O'Neil and Co., Los Angeles, 1970-74; v.p. mgmt., stockbroker Cantor Fitzgerald and Co., Beverly Hills, Calif., 1974-84, Kayne Anderson and Co., Los Angeles, 1984—; Contbr. articles on mktg. to various publs. and mags., 1980—. Com. mem. Johns Hopkins Alumni Council. Served to 2d lt. U.S. Army, 1961-67. Mem. Bond Club Los Angeles, N.Y. Futures Exchange. Episcopalian. Club: Maryland (Balt.). Home: 518 N Saltair Ave Los Angeles CA 90049 Office: Kayne Anderson and Co 1800 Ave of Stars Los Angeles CA 90067

WIBLE, JAMES ORAM, plastics company executive; b. Pitts., June 30, 1949; s. Lewis Alfred and Wilda (Boa) W.; m. Norma Joan Klaus, Sept. 20, 1975; children: Judson F., Jerald L., Leslie K. BA, Allegheny Coll., 1971; MBA, Xavier U., 1974. Sales rep. Pitts. Paint & Glass Industries, Cin., 1971-72, Detroit, 1973-75; pres. Am. Colors, Inc., Sandusky, Ohio, 1975—. Pres. Montessori Parents Assn., Huron, Ohio, 1986, bd. dirs., 1986—, Montessori Child Enrichment Ctr., 1986—; pres. bd. trustees 1st Presbyn. Ch. Sandusky, 1981. Mem. Soc. Plastics Industry, Fiberglass Fabrication Assn., Plum Brook Country (Sandusky) Club, Lonque Vue Club (Verona, Pa.). Republican. Clubs: Plum Brook Country (Sandusky); Longue Vue (Verona, Pa.). Home: 2509 Fairway Ln Sandusky OH 44870 Office: Am Colors Inc 1321 1st St Sandusky OH 44870

WICHLENSKI, JOHN JOSEPH, manufacturing executive; b. St. Louis, Nov. 27, 1943; s. John L. and Helen A. (Dempski) W.; m. Doylene Marie Schulte, Aug. 27, 1966; children: Jill, John Joseph Jr., Jane. BS in Indsl. Engring., St. Louis U., 1965; MS in Engring., Washington U., St. Louis, 1968. Acctg. supr. S.W. Bell Telephone Co., St. Louis, 1965-66; indsl. engr. Olin Corp., East Alton, Ill., 1966-71, mgr. scheduling, 1971-73, mgr. mfg. methods, 1973-75, dir. engring., 1975-83, dir. ammunition ops., 1983-86; v.p. ops. Engineered Air Systems, Inc., St. Louis, 1986—; instr. Washington U., St. Louis, 1969-81. Bd. dirs. Mississippi Valley chpt. Jr. Achievement, 1987—. Fellow Washington U., 1967-68. Mem. Am. Def. Preparedness Assn., St. Louis U. Alumni Council, Forest Lake Club (St. Louis). Roman Catholic. Home: 14225 Dinsmoor Chesterfield MO 63017 Office: Engineered Air Systems Inc 1270 N Price Rd Saint Louis MO 63132

WICK, BARBARA DIEBOLD, insurance executive; b. Durham, N.C., July 22, 1942; d. William Diebold and Janet (Hart) Sylvester; m. Thomas Ashton Wick, June 15, 1964; children: Cynthia Anne, Kevin William, Kristine Elaine. BA in Zoology, Swarthmore Coll., 1964; MAT, U. Chgo., 1966; A.R.M., Ins. Sch. Chgo., 1988. V.p. Condominium Ins. Specialists Am., Inc., Arlington Heights, Ill., 1981—; exec. v.p. Community Assn. Risk Mgmt. and Ins. Cons., Inc. (CARMIC), Arlington Heights, 1986—; instr. ins. Harper Coll., Palatine, Ill., 1984—. Contbr. articles to profl. jours. Mem. N.W. Mcpl. Conf., 1978—; election judge Cook County, 1976-83; pres. Village of Northfield, 1985—, trustee, 1977-85, zoning commr., 1976-78; trustee Community Assns. Inst., 1983—, pres. Rsch. Found., 1984-86, chmn. pub. policy com., 1986—, pub. ofcls. com., 1988—, on numerous other coms.; pres. Northfield Community Nursery Sch.; v.p. Winnetka-Northfield Family Svcs.; chmn. PTA-Northfield Art Fest. Mem. Phi Beta Kappa. Democrat. Home: 2044 Middlefork Rd Northfield IL 60093 Office: CARMIC 3930 Ventura Suite 450 Arlington Heights IL 60004

WICK, ROBERT L., JR., physician, airline executive; b. Pitts., Oct. 3, 1930; s. Robert L. and Helen Elizabeth (Gollings) W.; married; children: Robert D., Susan E., Douglas M. BS, Va. Mil. Inst., 1951, Carnegie Mellon U., 1955; MD, U. Pitts, 1959; MS, Ohio State U., 1962. Diplomate Am. Bd. Preventive Medicine. Intern South Side Hosp., Pitts., 1959-60; resident physician Ohio State U., 1960-62; chief aerostandards br. FAA, Washington, 1963-65; project engr. Airesearch Corp., L.A., 1965-67; prof. Ohio State U., Columbus, 1967-77; corp. med. dir. Am. Airlines, Dallas-Ft. Worth, 1977—; vice chmn. med. panel Air Transport Assn., Washington, 1983-88, chmn., 1988—; chmn. med. adv. com. Internat. Air Transport Assn., Geneva, 1987-88. Contbr. articles to profl. jours. Mem. President's Com. on Employment of Handicapped, 1982—. U.S. Army, 1951-53, Korea, 1966-67, Vietnam; maj. gen. USAR., 1986—, dep. surgeon gen. Lovelace Found. fellow, 1962-63; holder 3 aviation world speed records. Fellow Aerospace Med. Assn. (Tamisea award 1975); mem. Civil Aviation Med. Assn. (pres. 1974-75), Flying Physicians Assn. (pres. 1976-77), Internat. Acad. Aviation and Space Medicine (academician), Airlines Med. Dirs. Assn. (pres. 1986-87). Home: 1006 Loch Lomond Dr Arlington TX 76012 Office: Am Airlines Inc PO Box 619617 MD 4100 Dallas-Ft Worth Airport TX 75261

WICKE, JOHN MICHAEL, insurance executive, accountant; b. Camp Mackall, N.C., June 5, 1945; s. Emil John and Sara (Stancil) W.; B.S. in Econs. and Acctg., St. Peter's Coll., Jersey City, 1967, EDP cert., 1974; M.B.A., Monmouth Coll., 1980; CPA, N.Y., N.J. m. Virginia Ann McGovern, Aug. 5, 1967; children—Elizabeth, Michael. Asst. to v.p. customer relations Gimbel Bros. N.Y.C., 1970-72; acct. Irving Trust Co., N.Y.C., 1972-73; fin. planning mgr. Prudential Ins. Co., Newark, 1973-79; adminstrv. assoc. to exec. v.p. Blue Cross, N.Y.C., 1980-82; controller Ashford Holding Co., N.Y.C., 1982-84; v.p. mgmt. services Blue Cross Blue Shield, N.Y.C., 1984-88; chief fin. officer, treas. Am. Med. Ins. Co., 1988—. Trustee, Matawan-Aberdeen (N.J.) Library, 1980; mem. Aberdeen Twp. Council, 1978-81, mayor, 1980, chmn. Planning Bd., 1976-78. Served to capt., field arty. U.S. Army, 1967-70; Vietnam. Decorated Bronze Star (3), Air medal (3), others; named to St. Peter's Coll. Athletic Hall of Fame. Mem. Am. Inst. CPA's, N.J. Conf. Mayors. Roman Catholic (lector 1975-82). Home: 27 Colonial Dr Matawan NJ 07747 Office: 622 3d Ave New York NY 10017

WICKHAM, JEANNE ANN, accountant; b. Montour Falls, N.Y., Feb. 22, 1953; d. Richard Sheldon and Annella Jane (Robinson) W. BS, Cornell U., 1975; MS, Syracuse U., 1976; MBA, Babson Coll., 1981. Tchr. biology, chemistry Alfred Almond Cen. Sch., Almond, N.Y., 1976-77; fin. research asst. Andrea Szmyt, Cambridge, Mass., 1981-83; acct. Boston Gas Co., 1983-84, Eaton Fin. Corp., Framingham, Mass., 1986-87; pvt. practice acctg. Granbury, Tex., 1987—. Mem. Inst. Cert. Mgmt. Accts., Am. Mgmt. Assn., Nat. Assn. Accts. (Ft. Worth chpt.), Pi Lambda Theta (nat. treas. 1986—), Alpha Sigma. Home and Office: 352 Cherokee Dr Pecan Plantation Granbury TX 76048

WICKI, DIETER, banker; b. Escholzmatt, Switzerland, June 11, 1931; s. Michael H.H. and Anna L. Wicki; m. Inge V. Schroth, May 26, 1958; 1 child, Norbert. Dr Rer Pol in Polit. Econs., U. Berne, Switzerland, 1958. Ptnr., owner Dr. D. Wicki Group Cos., Zurich, Switzerland, 1962-80; dir. Capital Adv. Ltd., Zurich, 1980-81; v.p., dir. McLeod Young Weir Internat. Ltd., London, 1981-88, fin. cons., 1989—; ind. investment cons. Zurich, 1989—. Author: Der Finanzausgleich zwischen Staat und Gemeinden im Kanton Bern, 1958, Neue Chancen fuer Gewinne mit Zinspapieren, 1981, Kanadische Goldminenaktien, 1984; editor News Flash weekly letter, Goldminenaktien, 1982-86, Corporate Canada Monthly Bulletin, 1989—. Mem. Can. Securities Inst. (rep.). Office: Bellerivestrasse 65, CH-8008 Zurich Switzerland

WICKISER, SUSAN CHAREST, financial planner; b. Anchorage, Oct. 29, 1946; d. Darrell Charest and Dorlis Elaine (Evans) Charest Patton; m. Jimmy Wayne Wickiser, Dec. 20, 1975; children: Barry E. Marshall, Brad D. Marshall. BA in Edn., Ariz. State U., 1968; MA in Mgmt., Webster Coll., 1978. Tchr. Gilbert (Ariz.) High Sch., 1968-69, United Sch. Dist. #402, Augusta, Kans., 1979-82; fin. planner IDS Fin. Svcs., Wichita, Kans., 1982—; instr. Butler County Community Coll., Andover, Kans., 1987—; Kans. del. to White House Conf. on Small Bus., 1986. Fund dr. chair Four Winds Girl Scout Coun. U.S.A., 1987; lay leader United Meth. Ch., Augusta, 1987—. Mem. Inst. Cert. Fin. Planners (mem. nat. com. 1985-86), Nat. Assn. Women Bus. Owners (bd. dirs. 1984—), Andover C. of C. (bd. dirs. 1986-88), Wichita Soc. Inst. Cert. Fin. Planners (pres. 1984—), AAUW. Republican. Home: Rt 5 Box 735 Augusta KS 67010

WICKS, HARRY OLIVER, III, mechanical engineer; b. Wyandotte, Mich., Jan. 2, 1931; s. Harry O. Jr. and Dorothy Ellsworth (Worthman) W.; m. Barbara Lois Clark, June 11, 1955 (dec.); 1 stepson, Kenneth M. Burrows. Student, Rensselaer Poly. Inst., Troy, N.Y., 1948-51; BS, SUNY, Buffalo, 1967. Cert. tchr., N.Y. Design engr. Ford Motor Co., Buffalo, 1963-70; chief engr. Acme Hwy. Products Co., Buffalo, 1970-72; pres. Harwick Design, Inc., Hamburg, N.Y., 1975—; mgr. engring. Curtiss-Wright Corp., Buffalo, 1978-79; chief engr. Railmaster System, Inc., Hamburg, 1983-87; cons. Roadrailer, Chicago Heights, Ill., 1987—. Patentee in field. Mem. dist. com. Erie County (N.Y.) Dem. Com., 1963-83. Served with U.S. Army, 1952-54. Mem. Hamburg C. of C. Methodist. Lodges: Masons (32 degree), Shriners. Home: 5386 Scranton Rd Hamburg NY 14075

WIDDER, CHARLES JOSEPH, insurance company executive; b. N.Y.C., Mar. 6, 1941; m. Margaret M. Gaffney, Mar. 19, 1966; children: Kathryn Ann, Margaret M., Charles J. BBA in Acctg., Iona Coll., 1964; MBA in Profl. Mgmt., Pace Coll., 1971. Sr. v.p., controller North Am. Reins. Corp., N.Y.C., 1971-86; exec. v.p., chief fin. officer U.S. Internat. Reins. Co., N.Y.C., 1986—, also bd. dirs.; bd. dirs. The Home Re Syndicate, Inc., City Syndicate Mgrs., Inc., U.S. Internat. Reinsurance Services (H.K.) Ltd. Mem. Reins. Assn. Am. (tech. com.), Soc. Ins. Accts. (past pres.). Home: 19 Innes Rd East Brunswick NJ 08816 Office: US Internat Reins Co 59 Maiden Ln 2d Floor New York NY 10038

WIDDER, KENNETH JON, pathologist, educator; b. Chgo., Jan. 14, 1953; s. Alan A. and Edith Widder. BS, Carleton Coll., 1974; MD, Northwestern U., Evanston, Ill., 1979. Intern Duke U., Durham, N.C., 1979-80, resident in pathology, 1980-81; asst. clin. prof. pathology U. Calif., San Diego, 1981-84, assoc. clin. prof., 1984—; chmn., chief exec. officer Molecular Biosystems, Inc., San Diego, 1981—; cons. Eli Lilly & Co., Indpls., 1978-83; mem. adv. com. Congl. Sci. and Tech. Com., Washington, 1986—. Editor: Methods in Enzymology: Drug and Enzyme Targeting, 1985; patentee in field. Recipient Wiley J. Forbus award N.C. Sco. Pathology, 1981. Mem. AAAS, Am. Soc. Clin. Pathologists, Sigma Xi. Office: Molecular Biosystems Inc 10030 Barnes Canyon Rd San Diego CA 92121-2722

WIDDRINGTON, PETER NIGEL TINLING, brewery, food company executive; b. Toronto, Ont., Can., June 2, 1930; s. Gerard and Margery (MacDonald) W.; m. Betty Ann Lawrence, Oct. 12, 1956; children: Lucinda Ann, Andrea Stacy. B.A. with honors, Queen's U., Kingston, Ont., 1953; M.B.A., Harvard, 1955. Salesman Labatt's Co., London, Ont., 1955-57; asst. regional mgr. So. Ont. region Labatt's Ont. Breweries Ltd., 1957-58, regional mgr., 1958-61; gen. mgr. Kiewel & Pelissiers, Winnipeg, 1961-62, Labatt's Man. Breweries Ltd., Winnipeg, Man., 1962-65, Labatt's B.C. Breweries Ltd., Vancouver, B.C., 1965-68; pres. Lucky Breweries Inc., San Francisco, 1968-71; v.p. corp. devel. John Labatt Ltd., 1971-73, sr. v.p., 1973, pres., chief exec. officer, 1973-87, chmn., chief exec. officer, 1987—; bd. dirs. BP Can. Ltd., Toronto Blue Jays Baseball Club, Brascan Ltd., John Labatt Ltd., Can. Imperial Bank of Commerce, Ellis-Don Ltd., Laidlaw Transp. Ltd., Grocery Mfrs. Am., Hayes-Dana Inc. Bd. dirs. The Fraser Inst., Vancouver; bd. govs. Olympic Trust Fund of Can. Home: Doncaster Ave, London, ON Canada N6G 2A1 Office: John Labatt Ltd, 451 Ridout St N, London, ON Canada N6A 5L3

WIEDEMANN, JOSEPH ROBERT, insurance company executive; b. Chgo.; s. Joseph Matthew and Ann Elizabeth (Zittman) W.; m. Ree McClure, Dec. 26, 1950; children: Sue Wiedemann Evans, Patti Wiedemann Podziomek, Jane Wiedemann Candela, Mary Wiedemann Darling, Julie Wiedemann Gotsch, Joseph, Thomas. BBA, Loyola U., Chgo., 1950. Sr. v.p. CNA Ins. Co., Chgo., 1952-77; v.p. Frank B. Hall Co., N.Y.C., 1977-79; pres., dir. Union Indemnity Ins. Co., N.Y.C., 1977-79, BCS Fin. Corp., Chgo., 1979-83; pres. C.V. Starr & Co., San Francisco, 1983-84, Lexington Ins. Co., Boston, 1985-87, Landmark Ins. Co., Los Angeles, 1986-87; v.p. Am. Internat. Group, 1986—; pres. Am. Home Assurance Co., N.Y., 1987—. City parking commr. Reading, Pa., 1970-73. Served to sgt. U.S. Army, 1950-52, Korea. Republican. Roman Catholic. Clubs: Thorngate Country (Deerfield, Ill.); World Trade (San Francisco); Andover Country (Mass.). Home: 250 South End Ave #14B New York NY 10280 Office: Am Home Assurance Co 70 Pine St 6th Fl New York NY 10270

WIEDER, DOUGLAS MARX, textile company executive, computer consultant; b. Cleve., Mar. 9, 1952; s. Ira James and Judith Ruth (Marx) W.; m. Arlene Sandra Smason, Oct. 9, 1977; 1 child, Nori Beth. BA, Tulane U., 1974, MBA, 1976. CPA, Ohio. Campus sales rep. Eastern Airlines, New Orleans, 1974-76; acct. Mill Distbrs., Cleve., 1976-78, sec., treas., 1978—; acct. A.H. Ganger & Co., CPA's, Cleve., 1984—. Charter mem. Cleve. Hist. Warehouse Dist., 1983; mem. Greater Cleve. Growth Assn., 1982, Playhouse Sq. Assn., 1983; mem., dir. Miles Ahead, Inc., 1988—. Lodge: Rotary (bd. dirs., treas. 1988—). Office: Mill Distbrs Inc 18370 S Miles Industrial Pkwy Cleveland OH 44128

WIELAND, R. RICHARD, II, pharmaceutical company executive; b. Portsmouth, Ohio, Dec. 25, 1944; s. R. Richard and Helen (McClure) W.; m. Ann Newton, June 20, 1970; children: Lauren, Melissa. BA, Monmouth Coll., 1968; MBA, Washington U., St. Louis, 1970. Fin. mgr. Procter & Gamble, Cin., 1970-78; chief fin. officer Acoustiflex Co., Chgo., 1978-80; v.p. controller Oak Tech., Chgo., 1980-84; sr. v.p. fin., chief fin. officer Lyphomed Inc., Chgo., 1984—. Bd. dirs. sr. citizens program, Cin., 1976-78, Monmouth (Ill.) Coll. Alumni Group, 1982—; fund raiser United Appeal, Chgo. Mem. Fin. Ex. Inst., Nat. Investor Relations Inst., N.Am. Fin. Planning Assn. Republican. Presbyterian. Home: 10 Ambrose Ln Barrington IL 60010 Office: LyphoMed Inc 10401 W Touhy Ave Rosemont IL 60018

WIELAND, ROBERT RICHARD, lawyer, manufacturing executive; b. Columbus, Ohio, Jan. 30, 1937; s. Robert Milton and Evelyn Marion (Turner) W.; m. Sara J. Gerhart, Dec. 17, 1966; 1 child, Christopher David. BA, Ohio State U., Columbus, 1958, JD, 1960. Bar: Ohio 1960, Ill. 1966. Atty. Ohio Bell Telephone Co., Cleve., 1960-65, United Air Lines, Inc., Chgo., 1965-67; asst. gen. counsel, asst. sec. Youngstown Sheet and Tube Co., Ohio, 1967-73, Mead Corp., Dayton, Ohio, 1974-76; v.p., gen. counsel, sec. Huffy Corp., Dayton, 1976—; dir., officer H.C.A., Inc., YLC Enterprises, Inc., Gerico, Inc., Snugli, Inc., Memline Corp., Washington Inventory Svc.; sec. Huffy Found., Inc.; mng. dir. Huffy Internat. Finance N.V.; dir. Takata-Gerico Corp. Trustee Byron R. Lewis Edn. Fund, 1976-80; pres. Miami Valley council Boy Scouts Am., 1987-89; trustee Dayton Art Inst., 1987—; v.p. Friends of Aullwood, 1981-84; trustee Miami Valley Sch., 1985-86; bd. visitors Dayton Sch. Law, 1987—. Served with USAF, 1961-62. Mem. ABA, Ohio Bar Assn., Dayton Bar Assn., Am. Arbitration Assn. (arbitration panel), Am. Soc. Corp. Secs. (v.p. S.W. Ohio chpt. 1986-87, pres. 1987-88), Sigma Pi (pres. 1972-74). Office: Huffy Corp 7701 Byers Rd Miamisburg OH 45342

WIELAND, WILLIAM DEAN, health care consulting executive; b. Peoria, Ill., Feb. 15, 1948; s. George William and Virginia Lee (Delicath) W.; m. Joyce Lumia; 1 child, William Michael. BBA, Bradley U., 1971. Asst. adminstr. Galesburg (Ill.) Cottage Hosp., 1974-75; v.p. Anton & Damian, Iowa City, 1976-77; mgr. Clifton, Gunderson & Co., Peoria, 1977-80; v.p. OHMS Health Mgmt. Services, Columbus, 1980-84; dir., cons. VHA Cons. Services, Tampa, Fla., 1984-88; div. mgr. Voluntary Hosps. Am. Inc., Tampa, Fla., 1988—; cons. Vol. Hosps. Am. Cons. Service, Tampa, 1984-88, OHMS Health Mgmt Services, Columbus, 1980-84; small bus. cons. Clifton, Gunderson & Co, 1977-80. Mem. Hosp. Mgmt. Systems Soc., Healthcare Fin. Mgmt. Assn., Soc. for Hosp. Planning & Mktg., Inst. Indsl. Engrs. Club: American Business (Peoria) (bd. dirs. 1978-80). Office: 3030 N Rocky Point Dr W Ste 750 Tampa FL 33607

WIELECH, DENNIS DAVID, telecommunications company executive, financial consultant; b. Balt., Oct. 2, 1936; s. George Vitold Wielech and Sylvia Earlene (LaGue) Wielech Braithwaite; m. Victoria Teresa Grzymala, Sept. 8, 1962; children—Kathryn Denise, D. David. Student Balt. City Coll., 1952-55, Johns Hopkins U., 1964-67; cert. fin. planner Coll. for Fin. Planning, Denver, 1972. C.L.U. Fin. cons. Dennis D. Wielech & Assocs., Balt., 1966-82; v.p., dir. internat. mktg. Internat. Mobile Machines Corp., Phila., 1982-86; chmn. bd. Omnilink Internat. Corp., Glen Burnie, Md., 1986-87; pres. and chief exec. officer Advanced Superconductor Techs., Inc., Balt., 1987—. bd. dirs. MIT Enterprise Forum of Washington, D.C.-Balt., Inc. Mem. Am. Soc. C.L.U.s (pres. Balt. chpt. 1974-75), Nat. Assn. Corp. Dirs. (founding-Metro Washington, D.C.-Balt. chpt.), Balt. Assn. Fin. Planners (pres. 1970-75), Md. Assn. Life Underwriters (pres. 1977), Md. Assn. Health Underwriters (pres. 1976, Man of Yr. 1976). Roman Catholic. Home: Guilford House 4001 Greenway Baltimore MD 21218 Office: Omnilink Internat Corp 7310 Ritchie Hwy Suite 601 Glen Burnie ND 21061

WIELGUS, CHARLES JOSEPH, information services company executive; b. Hadley, Mass., Jan. 2, 1923; s. Joseph John and Anna Mary (Armata) W.; m. Irene Helen Graham, Jan. 1, 1949; children: Charles, Paul, Martha Jane. B.S. summa cum laude in Bus. Adminstrn, Bryant Coll., 1947, D.S. in Bus. Adminstrn. (hon.), 1977. With Bigelow-Sanford Carpet Co., Enfield, Conn. and N.Y.C., 1947-56; with Reuben H. Donnelley Corp. (subs. Dun & Bradstreet Corp.), Chicago and N.Y.C., 1956-71; v.p. personnel Dun & Bradstreet, Inc. (subs.), 1971-73; v.p. personnel Dun & Bradstreet Corp., 1973-76, sr. v.p. human resources, 1976-82, exec. v.p. human resources and communications, 1983—; adj. faculty New Sch. Social Research, 1977—, mem. adv. com. Masters program in human resources, 1977—; mem. adv. council on mgmt. edn. N.Y.C. C. of C., 1975-80; mem. bus. edn. adv. com. N.Y.C. Bd. Edn., 1977—; dir. Nat. Ctr. Career Life Planning, 1986—; mem. adv. council on human resources mgmt. Nat. Conf. Bd., 1987—. Bd. dirs. United Cerebral Palsy Assn. Westchester, 1966-75; trustee Operation Hope, Inc., 1966-75, active local and state Republican orgns., 1965-75. Served in USAF, 1943-46. Mem. Nat. Alliance Bus. (dir., steering com.). Clubs: Univ, Larchmont Shore. Home: 151 Rockingstone Ave Larchmont NY 10538 Office: The Dun & Bradstreet Corp 299 Park Ave New York NY 10017

WIEN, STUART LEWIS, retired supermarket chain executive; b. Milw., Sept. 11, 1923; s. Julius and Mildred (Rosenberg) W.; m. Charlotte Jean Milgram, June 4, 1949; children: Steven, John, William, Thomas.; m. Sheila B. Davis, July 25, 1982; stepchildren: Andrew, Stephen, Laurence, Geoffrey. B.S., UCLA, 1947. Chmn. bd. Milgram Food Stores, Inc., Kansas City, Mo., 1979-84; bd. dirs. UMB Funds. Trustee Menorah Med. Ctr.; hon. fellow Truman Library; bd. regents Rockhurst Coll.; bd. dirs. Greater Kansas City chpt. ARC. Served with USNR, 1944-46. Clubs: Oakwood Country, Jewish Chautauqua Soc. Lodges: Rotary, B'nai B'rith.

WIENER, HARRY, pharmaceutical company executive, physician; b. Vienna, Austria, Oct. 29, 1924; s. Joseph and Beile W.; m. Charlotte Baran, May 1, 1982. B.S., Bklyn. Coll., 1945; M.D., L.I.U., 1949. With Pfizer Inc., N.Y.C., 1958—, dir. profl. info., 1958—. Served with M.C., AUS, 1953-55; Korea. Author: Generic Drugs--Safety and Effectiveness, 1973, Schizophrenia and Anti-Schizophrenia, 1977, Findings in Computed Tomography, 1979. Mem. AMA, N.Y. Acad. Medicine, Am. Med. Writers Assn. Developer Wiener numbers for calculation of phys. properties of hydrocarbons, 1947, proposer theory of human pheromones, 1966, genetics-environment symmetry in schizophrenia, 1976. Home: 429 E 52d St New York NY 10022 Office: 235 E 42d St New York NY 10017

WIENER, MARK ALAN, financial executive; b. Poughkeepsie, N.Y., Oct. 31, 1961; s. Stanley Joseph and Evelynne (Krichman) W.; m. Nancy Ellen Zetley, Sept. 7, 1986. BA in Internat. Law, So. Meth. U., Dallas, 1983; MBA in Fin., Seton Hall U., 1988. Analyst cash mgmt. Booz Allen & Hamilton, Inc., Florham Park, N.J., 1983-85; treasury analyst GAF Corp., Wayne, N.J., 1985-86; cash mgr. Young & Rubicam Co., N.Y.C., 1986-88, mgr. fin., 1988; treas. Z Mgmt., Inc., Milw., 1989—; pres. Mark Alan Cons., Milw., 1988—. Mem. Nat. Corp. Cash Mgrs. Assn., Wis. Cash Mgrs. Assn. Jewish. Home: 641 Evergreen Ct Bayside WI 53217 Office: Z Mgmt Inc 8870 N Port Washington Rd Milwaukee WI 53217

WIENER, ROBERT CHARLES, food company executive; b. San Salvador, El Salvador, June 8, 1952; came to U.S., 1966; BS, Syracuse U., 1974; MBA, NYU, 1977. Fin. analyst Eli Lilly & Co., Indpls., 1977-78; mktg. planning mgr. Am. Standard, San Paulo, Brazil, 1978-79; gen. mgr. Integral Yoga Natural Foods, N.Y.C., 1980-82; owner, pres. Food from Friends, Arlington, Va., 1983-84; pres., gen. mgr. Integral Yoga Natural Foods (formerly Blue Mountain Natural Foods), Charlottesville, Va., 1983—. Home: Rt 1 Box 172 Buckingham VA 23921 Office: Blue Mountain Natural Market 923 Preston Ave Charlottesville VA 22901

WIER, PATRICIA ANN, publishing executive; b. Coal Hill, Ark., Nov. 10, 1937; d. Horace L. and Bridget B. (McMahon) Norton; m. Richard A. Wier, Feb. 24, 1962; 1 dau., Rebecca Ann. B.A., U. Mo., Kansas City, 1964; M.B.A., U. Chgo., 1978. Computer programmer AT&T, 1960-62; lead programmer City of Kansas City, Mo., 1963-65; with Playboy Enterprises, Chgo., 1965-71; mgr. systems and programming Playboy Enterprises, 1971; with Ency. Brit., Inc., Chgo., 1971—; v.p. mgmt. services Ency. Brit. USA, 1975-83, exec. v.p. adminstrn., 1983-84; v.p. planning and devel. Ency. Brit., Inc., 1985, pres. Compton's Learning Co. div., 1985; pres. Ency. Brit. (USA), 1986—; exec. v.p. Ency. Brit., Inc., 1986—; mem. council U. Chgo. Grad. Sch. Bus., Northwestern U. Assocs.; chmn. Compton's Learning Co., 1987—. Mem. fin. Coun. Archdiocese of Chgo., Coun. of Grad. Sch. of Bus. U. of Chgo. Mem. Direct Selling Assn. (bd. dirs. 1984—, chmn. 1987—), Women's Council U. Mo. Kansas City (hon. life), Com. 200, The Chgo. Network. Roman Catholic. Office: Ency Britannica Inc 310 S Michigan Ave Chicago IL 60604

WIERSMA, DANIEL MARK, development company executive; b. Grand Rapids, Mich., Nov. 17, 1961; s. Robert Sidney and Betty Lou (Woudenberg) W.; m. Nancy Anne DeVries, Sept. 17, 1983. BS in Fin., Ferris State U., 1983. Mem. instl. sales staff Paine Webber Inc., Chgo., 1983-88; v.p. fin. Hartland Devel. Corp., Grand Rapids, Mich., 1988—. Office: Hartland Devel Corp 500 Riverfront Plaza Bldg 55 Campau St NW Grand Rapids MI 49503

WIESCHENBERG, KLAUS, chemical company executive; b. Hannover, Ger., Mar. 2, 1932; came to U.S., 1959; s. Heinz and Ruth (Wilke) W.; Abitur, Hermann Billung Gymnasium, Celle, Ger., 1951; B.A., Fairleigh Dickinson U., Madison, N.J., 1974, M.B.A., 1977; m. Nona Bodareva, June 7, 1958; children—Michael, Axel, Natasha. Export/import corr. Deutsche Bank, Hannover, 1953; export corr. Hoechst AG, Frankfurt, Germany, 1954-55; various mktg. positions Am. Hoechst Corp., 1956-68, various fin. positions, 1969-78; v.p. planning corp. div., Somerville, N.J., 1978-85; v.p. Office of Pres. and Corp. Devel., 1985-87; v.p. corp. devel. Hoechst Celanese Corp., 1987—. Past pres. Toastmasters Internat., Charlotte, N.C., 1962. Mem. Comml. Devel. Assn. (chmn. membership com. 1984-86), Am. Mgmt. Assn., Planning Forum (v.p. N.Y. Met. chpt. 1986—). Republican. Eastern Orthodox. Home: 494 Steel Gap Rd Bridgewater NJ 08807 Office: Route 202 206 N Somerville NJ 08876

WIESE, DANIEL EDWARD, marketing and communications researcher; b. Cedar Rapids, Iowa, June 16, 1936; s. Erwin Edward and Bernice Virginia (Cristy) W.; m. Mary Virginia Smith, Nov. 3, 1958 (div. 1982); children: Anne, John, Amy; m. JoBeth Kuehl, Aug. 6, 1982; children: Jamie, Jill, Eric. BS, Iowa State U., 1958. Research assoc. Meredith Pub. Co., Des Moines, 1961-65; research dir. Popular Sci. Pub. Co., N.Y.C., 1965-66; assoc. research dir. Reader Digest Assn., N.Y.C., 1966-67; research dir. Successful Farming div. Meredith Corp., Des Moines, 1967-77; mgr. Agtrack div. Chilton Research Services, Radnor, Pa., 1977-80; v.p., dir. research services Creswell, Munsell, Fultz & Zirbel Inc., Cedar Rapids, 1980-1986; pres. Dan Wiese Market & Research Direction, Cedar Rapids, 1986—. Mem. editorial adv. bd. Agrimarketing mag., 1989. Bd. dirs. Plymouth Congl. Nursery Sch., Des Moines, 1975; mktg. com. Cedar Rapids Symphony, 1984; mem. adv. bd. Cedar Rapids Better Bus. Bur., Area Mktg. Task Force. Capt. U.S. Army, 1959. Mem. Nat. Agri-Mktg. Assn. (chmn. mktg. research com. 1982-83), Advt. Fedn. of Cedar Rapids (1st v.p. 1988—, bd. dirs. 1987—), Am. Mktg. Assn.,Cedar Rapids C. of C. Home: 1381 39th St Pl Marion IA 52302 Office: Dan Wiese Market & Rsch Direction 425 2d St SE Box 604 Ste 610 Marion IA 52302

WIESE, TERRY EUGENE, sales and marketing executive; b. East St. Louis, Ill., Apr. 2, 1948; s. Herman and Opal F. (Terry) W.; m. Janet T. Kimmel, Apr. 1988; stepchildren: Meghan R. Kimmel, Kristen M. Kimmel. B.S. in Engring., U.S. Mil. Acad., 1973. Commd. 2d lt. U.S. Army, 1973, advanced through grades to capt., resigned, 1978; sales rep. McDonnell Douglas Automation Co., St. Louis, 1978-80; br./dist. mgr. United Computing Systems, St. Louis, 1980-81; mgr. affiliate sales Uninet, Inc., Kansas City, Mo., 1981-82, dir. hdqrs. sales, 1982-83, dir. central area sales, Lenexa, Kans., 1983-84, dir. nat. accounts/central area sales, 1984, dir. field engring., 1984; dir. nat. accounts MCI Telecommunications, Washington, 1984-86; v.p. mktg. Instnl. Communications Co., McLean, Va., 1986—; v.p. market devel. No. Telecom Co., Richardson, Tex., 1987—, v.p. networks mktg., 1988—; telecommunications cons. United Way, 1982—. Author: ARTEPS for Nuclear Units, 1977; Lance Nuclear Missile ARTEP, 1978; Honest John Rocket ARTEP, 1978; ARTEP for Division/Brigade Elements, 1978. Pres. Aid Assn. for Lutherans, Collinsville, Ill., 1978-80; chmn. stewardship/budget com. Good Shepard Luth. Ch., Collinsville, 1979-81; chmn. United Way campaign, 1982-84. Mem. Am. Assn. Cost Engrs., Regional Commerce and Growth Assn. Republican. Home: 3305 Terry Dr Plano TX 75023 Office: No Telecom Palisades II 2435 North Central Expwy Richardson TX 75080

WIESLER, JAMES BALLARD, retired banker; b. San Diego, July 25, 1927; s. Harry J. and Della B. (Ballard) W.; m. Mary Jane Hall, Oct. 3, 1953; children: Tom, Ann, Larry. B.S., U. Colo., 1949; postgrad., Stonier Sch. Banking, Rutgers U., 1962, Advanced Mgmt. Program, Harvard U., 1973. With Bank of Am., NT & SA, 1949-87; v.p., mgr. main office San Jose, Calif., 1964-69, regional v.p. Cen. Coast adminstrn., 1969-74; sr. v.p., head No. European Area office Frankfurt, Fed. Republic of Germany, 1974-78; exec. v.p., head Asia div. Tokyo, 1978-81; exec. v.p., head N.Am. div. Los Angeles, 1981-82; vice chmn., head retail banking San Francisco, 1982-87; ret. 1987; bd. dirs. Visa USA, Visa Internat.; bd. dirs., chmn. Bank Adminstrn. Inst. Pres. Santa Clara County Unit Fund, 1969, 70, San Jose C. of C., 1968; fin. chmn. Santa Clara County Republicans, 1967-74; dir. San Diego Armed Svcs. YMCA, Sci. Application Internat., Inc.; hon. consul-gen. for Japan. With USNR, 1945-46. Mem. San Diego Zool. Soc. (dir.). Presbyterian. Clubs: Bohemian, Burlingame Country, Los Angeles Country; San Diego Country. Home: 605 San Fernando St San Diego CA 92106 Office: Bank of Am Nat Trust & Savs 450 B St San Diego CA 92101

WIESNER, JOHN JOSEPH, retail chain store executive; b. Kansas City, Mo., Mar. 31, 1938; s. Vincent A. and Jane Ann (Hagerty) W.; m. Georgiana Schild, Oct. 17, 1961; children—Susan, John V., Gretchen. B.S. in Bus. Adminstrn., Rockhurst Coll., 1960. Vice pres., controller Fisher Foods, Cleve., 1970-77; asst. corp. controller Richardson Vicks, N.Y.C., 1960-70; sr. exec. v.p. Pamida, Inc., Omaha, 1977-85, vice chmn., chief exec. officer, 1985-87; pres. , chief exec. officer C.R. Anthony Co., Oklahoma City, 1987—. Bd. dirs. Omaha Girls' Club, 1983—, Omaha Area Council on Alcohol and Drug Abuse, 1983—; bd. dirs. Fontenelle Forest, Omaha, chmn., 1983, 84; mem. bd. regents Rockhurst Coll., Kansas City, Mo. Named Bus. Assoc. of Yr., Am. Bus. Women's Assn., 1983. Mem. Nat. Assn. Accts. Republican. Roman Catholic. Clubs: Omaha, Field (Omaha).

WIESNER, SHARON MARIE, investment banker, oil production executive; b. Omaha, July 16, 1938; d. Ralph Remmington and Evelyn Adeline (Morris) Von Bremer; m. Virgil James Wiesner, Apr. 4, 1959 (div. 1982); children—Scott James, Lydia Marie, Michelle Elizabeth. B.A., Creighton U., 1959; M.A., U. Nebr.-Omaha, 1964, postgrad., 1979-82. Owner, v.p. Wiesner Distbg. Co. Inc., Lincoln, Nebr., 1966-72, Wiesner Tire Co. Inc., Omaha, 1972-75; v.p. Fin. Inc., Omaha, 1975-82; with fin., sales oil Am. Internat. Sales Corp., Dallas, 1982-83; pres. Joint Capital Resources, Dallas, 1983—;del. Richland Coll. Oil Industry Seminar, 1987, Dresser-Atlas Oil Logging Seminar. Editor: Born Rich: A Historical Book of Omaha, 1978. Author: Slanting News, 1959; Critical Study of Iago's Motivation, 1964. Vice pres. Assistance League Omaha, 1973-78; fund raiser Opera Omaha; v.p. women's bd. Omaha Community Playhouse; v.p. Lincoln Symphony Guild, 1966-71; bd. dirs. Omaha Jr. Theatre, 1975-79. Named Outstanding Young Woman Jr. C. of C., Norfolk, Nebr., 1964; recipient Valuable Service awards Lincoln Gen. Hosp., Omaha Community Playhouse. Mem. AAUW, Omaha Writers Group, The Quill, Landmarks Inc., Nat. Beer Wholesalers, Logging and Geol. Inst., Omaha Symphony Guild (v.p. 1973-78), Omaha C. of C., Lincoln C. of C., Brownville Hist. Soc., Brownville Fine Arts Assn., Nebr. Kennel Club, Dalmatian Club Am., Minn.-St. Paul Dalmatian Club, Blue Ribbon Dog Breeders, Beta Sigma Phi, Omicron Delta Kappa, Phi Delta Gamma, Theta Phi Alpha (pres. 1958-59). Club: Womens (v.p. 1966-70). Avocations: painting; music; art; writing. Office: Joint Capital Resources PO Box 12518 Dallas TX 75225

WIEWEL, ROGER NORTH, forest products company executive; b. Bronxville, N.Y., Apr. 26, 1927; s. Walter Hoelling and Marie North (Ryley) W.; m. Kay Hammarstrom, Oct. 5, 1975; children: Andrew Lockhart, Roger North, Eric Lockhart, Evelyn. B.S. in Mech. Engring., Carnegie Inst. Tech., 1950; M.B.A., Harvard U., 1952. In prodn. and sales Weyerhaeuser, 1952-61; dist. sales mgr. Stora Kopparberg Corp., N.Y.C., 1961-64; v.p. paper/paperboard sales S.W. Forest Industries, Phoenix, 1964-66; sr. v.p. mktg. group MacMillan Bloedel Ltd., Vancouver, B.C., Can., 1966-89; sr. v.p. product devel. MacMillan Bloedel Ltd., Vancouver, 1989—; bd. dirs. MB (S.E. Asia) Ltd., Powell River-Alberni Sales Corp., Vancouver Island Stevedoring, MacMillan Bloedel Pty. Ltd., MacMillan Bloedel Inc., Export Sales Co. Ltd. Served with U.S. Navy, 1945-48. Mem. B.C. Forestry Assn. Republican. Home: 870 Wildwood Ln, West Vancouver, BC Canada V7S 2H6 Office: MacMillan Bloedel Ltd, 1075 W Georgia St, Vancouver, BC Canada V6E 3R9

WIGGER, G. EUGENE, service executive; b. Union City, Ind., July 17, 1944; s. Marvelle Phillip and Mary Ethel (Roth) W.; m. M. Diane Bisciotti, Apr. 6, 1979. BS, Ball State U., 1967; MS, Ind. U., 1968. Dir. catering Washington (D.C.) Hilton Hotel, 1969-75, Hyatt Regency Nashville, 1975-76; dir. food and beverage Opryland Hotel, Nashville, 1976-77; dir. catering Hyatt Regency on Capital Hill, Washington, 1977-78; owner, pres. Creative Culinary Concepts, Ltd., Washington, 1978; dir. catering Sheraton Washington Hotel, Washington, 1978-81; corp. dir. food and beverage Arltec Sheraton Group, Washington, 1981-83; corp. dir. catering Diplomat Resort and Country Clubs, Hollywood, Fla., 1983-84; dir. catering Marriott's Harbor Beach Resort, Ft. Lauderdale, Fla., 1984—. Author: (books) Catering To Your Every Whim, 1989, Themes, Dreams and Schemes, 1989. 1st lt. USAF, 1964-68. Mem. Nat. Assn. Catering Execs. (nat. 1st v.p. 1977-79), Chaine des Rotisseurs (maitre de table), Internat. Spl. Events Soc. (founder). Lodge: Masons. Office: Marriott's Harbor Beach Resort 3030 Holiday Dr Fort Lauderdale FL 33316

WIGGINS, DEWAYNE LEE, financial executive; b. Stillwater, Okla., Jan. 6, 1949; s. Lloyd Lee Wiggins and Joyce Yvonne (Blair) Saunders; m. Susan Sochinski, Sept. 9, 1978. BS in Acctg., Okla. State U., 1972; MBA, Ind. U., 1984. Pilot Braniff Internat., Dallas, 1977-82; investment analyst Duff & Phelps, Inc., Chgo., 1984-86; portfolio mgr. Centerre Trust Co., St. Louis, 1986-88; pres. Lindbergh Capital Mgmt., Inc., St. Louis, 1988—. Contbr. rsch. papers to profl. publs. Mem. Regional Commerce and Growth Assn., St. Louis, 1988—; corp. contact and recruiter United Way, St. Louis, 1988—. Capt. USAF, 1972-76. Mem. Ind. U. Alumni Assn., Beta Gamma Sigma. Republican. Roman Catholic. Office: Lindbergh Capital Mgmt Inc 111 W Port Plaza Ste 600 Saint Louis MO 63146

WIGGINS, LARRY WAYNE, commercial banker; b. Millen, Ga., Nov. 18, 1950; s. Brantley Lee and Ruth (Hadden) W.; m. Jackie Alain Webster, Aug. 10, 1973; children: Amanda Jill, Lauren Maureen. AS in Polit. Sci., Middle Ga. Coll., 1970; BS in History/Edn., Ga. So. Coll., 1973. Auditor, field rep. Ford Motor Credit Corp., Augusta, Ga., 1973-74; mgr. credit First Augusta Bank & Trust, 1974-77, credit officer, 1977-81; v.p., sec. Bank of Columbia County, Harlem, Ga., 1982-89; corp. credit mgr. thermal Ceramics, Augusta, 1989—. Charter mem. Leadership Columbia Co., Martinez, Ga., 1987—; vice chmn. Columbia County Dem. exec. com., 1985-86, 88-90. Mem. Am. Inst. Banking (pres. 1979-80), Bank Adminstrn. Inst., Robert Morris Assocs., Nat. Assn. credit Mgrs. Methodist. Lodge: Rotary (chpt. pres. 1985-86, dist. treas. 1985-86). Home: 4509 Glennwood Dr Evans GA 30809 Office: Thermal Ceramics 2102 Old Savannah Rd Augusta GA 30906

WIGGINS, NANCY BOWEN, real estate broker; b. Richmond, Va., Oct. 9, 1948; d. William Roy and Mary Virginia (Colson) Bowen; m. Samuel Spence Saunders, Aug. 16, 1969 (div. 1977); m. Edwin Lindsey Wiggins, Jr., Apr. 16, 1983; children: Neal Bowen, Mark Edwin. AA, St. Mary's Coll., Raleigh, N.C., 1968; postgrad., Trinity U., 1968-69; BA, U.S. Internat. U., San Diego, 1970; MA, U. Tex., Arlington, 1975; postgrad., Tulane U., 1976-77. Bank teller Bank of Am., San Diego, 1971-72; lectr. U. Tex., Arlington, 1974-76; instr. Johnson C. Smith U., Charlotte, N.C., 1977-78; human services planner Centralina Council of Govt., Charlotte, 1978-80; mkt. research analyst First Union Nat. Bank, Charlotte, 1980-81; mkt. rep. Burroughs Corp., Charlotte, 1981-83; ptnr. market researcher George Selden & Assocs., Charlotte, 1983-84; pres., broker Bowen Wiggins Co., Charlotte, 1984—; instr. U. N.C., Charlotte, 1984-85, 87—; bdb. dirs. Roy Bowen, Inc., Frogmore, S.C; prin. The Medusa Group. Contbr. articles to profl. jours. Vice chmn. United Cerebral Palsy Council, Charlotte, 1984; chmn., bd. dirs. Carriage House Condominium Assn., Charlotte, 1980-82; mem. Mayor's Budget Adv. Com., Charlotte, 1980-81, Mecklenburg Dem. Women's Club, Charlotte Women's Polit. Caucus, YMCA. Mem. Nat. Assn. Real Estate Appraisers, N.C. Assn. Appraisers (bd. dirs.), So. Polit. Sci. Assn., Charlotte Apt. Assn., Pi Sigma Alpha, Charlotte Sales Exec. Club. Democrat. Episcopalian. Clubs: South Park Execs., YMCA. Home: 6425 Felton Ct Charlotte NC 28226 Office: 2915 Providence Rd Charlotte NC 28211

WIGGINS, PAGE, marketing representative; b. N.Y.C., Apr. 24, 1962; s. Paul Gray and Marybeth (Page) W.; m. Mary Beth Riggs, Sept. 12, 1987. BS, Wabash Coll., 1984. Mktg. trainee IBM, Evansville, Ind., 1984-85, mktg. rep., 1985-86, account mktg. rep., 1986—. Tchr. Jr. Achievement, Evansville; reader Regional Aid, Evansville. Mem. Am. Chem. Soc. (cert.). Republican. Club: Oak Meadow Country (Evansville).

WIGGINS, WALTON WRAY, publisher; b. Roswell, N.Mex., May 13, 1924; s. Miles Burgess and Mona Cecil (Brown) W.; grad. Motion Picture Cameraman Sch., Astoria, N.Y., 1945; m. Roynel Fitzgerald, Apr. 30, 1963; children—Walton Wray, Kimberly Douglas, Lisa Renee. Free-lance photojournalist for nat. mags., 1948-60; dir. public relations Ruidoso Racing Assn., Ruidoso Downs, N.Mex., 1960-69, v.p., 1967-68; founder, pub. Speedhorse Publs., Roswell, N.Mex. and Norman, Okla., 1969-78; owner/operator Wiggins Galleries Fine Art, 1978—; pres. Quarter Racing World, 1970-78, Am. Horse Publs., Washington, 1978; del. leader People to People, Internat. Served with U.S. Army, 1943-46. Recipient Detroit Art Dirs. award, 1955, Greatest Contbr. award Quarter Racing Owners Am., 1974. Mem. Overseas Press Club, Am. Soc. Mag. Photographers, Am. Horse Publs. Republican. Author: The Great American Speedhorse, 1978; Cockleburs and Cowchips, 1975; Alfred Morang-A Neglected Master, 1979; Ernest Berke-Paintings and Sculptures of the Old West, 1980; Juan Dell-The First Lady of Western Bronze, 1981; Go Man Go-The Legendary Speedhorse, 1982; The Transcendental Art of Emil Bisttram, 1988. Office: 526 Canyon Rd Santa Fe NM 87501

WIGGINS-WALCOTT, GWENDOLYN ANN, financial systems executive, consultant; b. Bklyn., May 25; d. Francis and Ann Lee (Jackson) Wiggins; 1 child, Gabrielle Ann. BA, CUNY; MBA, L.I. U., 1976. Staff acct. Mitchell and Titus, CPAs, N.Y.C., 1976-77; chief acct. Nat. Commn. on Observance of Internat. Women's Yr., N.Y.C., 1977-78; controller Port Royal Communications, 1978-79; internal auditor Port Authority of N.Y. and N.J., 1979-81, mgr.-in-tng., 1981-83, mgr. fin. systems, 1983—; prin. G.A. Wiggins & Assocs., Bklyn., 1977—. Co-chmn. bd. dirs. Ch. Ushers Assn. of Bklyn. and L.I., 1979-81; mem. Community Planning Bd., Bklyn., 1982-84. Thomas A. Ellis Oratorical scholar, 1968. Mem. Nat. Assn. Black Accts. (regional v.p. 1982-84, pres. N.Y. chpt. 1978-80, nat. dir. 1980-82), Nat. Assn. Accts. (assoc. dir. 1982-84), Fin. Women's Assn., Coun. Concerned Black Execs. (bd. dirs. 1981-88). Democrat. Baptist. Club: Toastmasters (N.Y.C.). Home: 325 Clinton Ave Suite 8B Brooklyn NY 11205

WIGHT, GEORGE, civil engineer, bank executive; b. Joliet, Ill., June 7, 1928; s. Raulin B. and Rose G. (Dowers) W.; m. Cathie Lee Faurie; children: Jan, George Jr. BCE, Iowa State U., 1952; postgrad., Keller Grad. Sch. Mgmt., 1978-81. Registered profl. engr., Ill. Pres. Wight Cons., Barrington, Ill., 1954—, Tempo, Inc., Orlando, Fla., 1985—; chmn. Community Bank Galesburg, Ill., 1988—; bd. dirs. Bank of Ill., Villa Park and Normal; mem. Ill. State Water Resources Commn., 1982-85; chmn. Midwest Coll. Engring., Lombard, Ill., 1984-86. Elected bd. mem. Sch. Dist. 118, Wauconda, Ill., 1975-78; mem. Pub. Arts Adv. Commn., Ill., 1979-81; mem. leadership coun. 48th Ward Aldermsn's Office, Chgo., 1987-88. With USN, 1946-48. Fellow ASCE; mem. NSPE, Am. Planning Assn., Am. Water Works Assn. (award Ill. sect. 1979). Home: 6007 N Sheridan Rd Chicago IL 60660 Office: Wight Cons 127 S Northwest Hwy Barrington IL 60010

WIGLEY, WILLARD ROBERT, JR., stockbroker; b. Waco, Tex., May 7, 1919; s. Willard Robert and Florence (Patten) W.; m. Jerry McDonald, July 20, 1946; children: Sherry Susanne, Karen Grace, Florence Elisa. AB, Princeton U., 1942. Supr. Clint W. Murchison, 1945-47; with E.F. Hutton & Co., Inc., Dallas, 1947-88, ptnr., 1953, regional v.p., 1962—, vice chmn., 1967-86, vice chmn. emeritus, 1986—; with Shearson Lehman Hutton, Dallas, 1988—, emeritus, 1986-88, vice chmn. emeritus, 1988—; bd. dirs. Caribbean Marine Bag 'N Baggage, Garvon, Inc.; chmn. bd. dirs. N.Am. Cattle Co., 1974-77; bd. govs. N.Y. Stock Exchange, 1966-69. Served with USAAF, 1942-45. Mem. Phi Beta Kappa. Episcopalian. Clubs: Brook Hollow Golf, Dallas Petroleum. Home: 5528 Meaders Ln Dallas TX 75229 Office: Shearson Lehman Hutton 500 N Akard Ste 3900 Dallas TX 75201

WIGMORE, BARRIE ATHERTON, investment banker; b. Moose Jaw, Sask., Can., Apr. 11, 1941; came to U.S., 1970; s. Fred Henry and Pauline Elizabeth (Atherton) W.; m. Deedee Dawson, Aug. 24, 1964. B. Edn., U. Sask., Can., 1962, B.A., 1963; M.A., U. Oreg., 1964; B.A., Oxford U., Eng., 1966, M.A., 1971. Investment banker A.E. Ames & Co. Ltd., Toronto, Ont., Can., 1966-70; investment banker Goldman, Sachs & Co., N.Y.C., 1970—. Author: The Crash and Its Aftermath, A History of U.S. Securities Markets 1929-33, 1985. Democrat. Clubs: River, Downtown Assn. Home: 1 W 72d St New York NY 10023 Office: Goldman Sachs & Co 85 Broad St New York NY 10004

WIGSTEN, PAUL BRADLEY, JR., computer and financial consultant; b. Elmira, N.Y., June 27, 1947; s. Paul B. and Josephine N. (Lyman) W.; m. Joan Van Pelt, June 6, 1953 (div. 1974); children: Tracy A., Kelly L. BS, Cornell U., 1969; MBA, Syracuse U., 1986. Cert. info. systems auditor. Mgmt. training GTE Sylvania, Camillus and Batavia, N.Y., 1969-72; data systems supr. GTE Sylvania, Smithfield, N.C., 1972-74; sr. auditor GTE Service Corp., Syracuse, N.Y., 1974-77; bus. systems analyst GTE Products Corp., Stamford, Conn., 1977-79; systems planning mgr. GTE Service Corp., Stamford, 1979-80; project mgr. Philips ECG, Inc., Seneca Falls, N.Y., 1980-83; mgr. internal control Philips ECG, Inc., 1983-84, gen. mgr., 1984-86; mgr. new bus. Amperex Electronic Corp., Slatersville, R.I., 1987-88; dir. fin. and info. systems Consol. Electronics Industries Corp., Stamford, Conn., 1989—. Trustee, treas. Mynderse Library, Seneca Falls, 1982-87; v.p. Community Ctr., Seneca Falls, 1982-87; commr. Seneca Falls Parks & Recreation Commn. Served with USAR, 1970-76. Mem. Nat. Assn. Accts., EDP Auditors Assn. Republican. Roman Catholic. Office: Consol Electronics Industries Corp 1 Landmark Sq Stamford CT 06901

WIKE, D. ELAINE, business executive; b. Ridgecrest, Calif., Sept. 26, 1954; d. Robert G. and Jimmie Mae (Sallee) Field; student U. Houston, 1975-77; m. Mike Wike, Oct. 14, 1978; children—Mike II, Angelina Elaine, William V., Danielle Elizabeth. Legal sec. Morgan, Lewis & Bockius, Washington, 1977-78; legal asst. Alfred C. Schlosser & Co., Houston, 1972-77, 78-81, Jerry Sadler, atty., Houston, 1982-83; founder, owner DEW Profl. & Bus. Services, Houston, 1979—; office mgr. Law Offices Mike Wike, Houston, 1983—. Treas., Wilhelm Schole Parents Orgn., 1981-82; vol. campaign worker, (Ron Paul for Congress and Reagan for Pres.), 1975, 76; mem. Republican Presdl. Task Force. Mem. Young Ams. for Freedom, Nat. Notary Assn., Nat. Assn. Female Execs., Am. Soc., Notaries. Republican. Mem. Christian Ch. Office: 2421 S Wayside Dr Houston TX 77023

WIKSTEN, BARRY FRANK, communications executive; b. Seattle, June 23, 1935; s. Frank Alfred and Alice Gertrude (Ensor) W.; m. Madeleine Schmeil, Nov. 23, 1979; children: Karen Anne, Eric Marshal, Kurt Edward. BA, Miami U., Oxford, Ohio, 1960; MA, Fletcher Sch. Law and Diplomacy, 1961. Dir. econ. programs U.S. Council, Internat. C. of C., N.Y.C., 1962-63; with TWA, N.Y.C., 1964-79, dir. fin. relations, 1972, v.p. pub. affairs, 1973, v.p. pub. relations, 1974-75, sr. v.p. pub. affairs, mem. airline policy bd., 1976-79; v.p. corp. adminstrn. Trans World Corp., 1979-82, also sec. corp. policy com., mem. consumer affairs com. and corp. compensation com.; sr. v.p. communications CIGNA Corp., Phila., 1982-84, sr. v.p. pub. affairs, 1984—. Served with USMC, 1954-57. Mem. Pub. Affairs Research Council (mem. conf. bd.), Am. Council Life Ins. (pub. relations program com.), Ins. Info. Inst. (spl. communications oversight com.), World

Affairs Council Phila. (bd. dirs.). Clubs: Union League (N.Y.); The Athenaeum. Office: Cigna Corp One Logan Sq Philadelphia PA 19103

WILBOURN, GORDON GENE, investment banker; b. Little Rock, Feb. 8, 1933; s. Walter Blann and Maude (Moore) W.; m. Meredith Ann Miller, June 19, 1955; children: Gordon, Melanie. BA, Hendrix Coll., 1954; MS in Edn., U. Cen. Ark., 1957. Coach, instr. Clinton (Ark.) Sch. Dist., 1954-55, Little Rock Sch. Dist., 1955-56; coach, instr., adminstr. Hendrix Coll., Conway, Ark., 1956-70; mgr. investment banking Stephens, Inc., Little Rock, 1971—. Bd. dirs. Florence Crittenton Home for Girls, Little Rock, 1982-88, Bapt. Health Found. Bd., Little Rock, 1987—. With USNR, 1951-55. Mem. Nat. Assn. Security Dealers, Ark. Assn. Security Dealers, Pub. Securities Assn. Methodist. Office: Stephens Inc 114 E Capitol Little Rock AR 72201

WILCH, KATHLEEN ANNE, financial planner; b. N.Y.C., Nov. 10, 1950; d. Louis Lawrence and Elizabeth A. (Kali) Caffo; m. Larry D. Wilch, Jan. 23, 1971; children: Leslie A., Kerry Lynne, Adam Louis. BGS, E. Tex. State U., 1982. Cert. fin. planner. Ind. fin. planner Findlay, Ohio, 1976-79, Texarkana, Tex., 1979—; fin. planner, stockbroker specializing in custom pension plans and retirement planning Affiliated Securities, Texarkana, 1988—. Active Rep. Women's Club, Texarkana; officer Texarkanan Soccer Assn. 1986—. Mem. Internat. Assn. Fin. Planners (chair spl. task force on worker's compensation), Texarkana C. of C., Nat. Assn. Chs. on the Rock. Home: 6006 Shadyside Texarkana TX 75503 Office: Affiliated Securities 615 Olive St Texarkana TX 75501

WILCOCK, JAMES WILLIAM, private corporation executive, retired capital equipment manufacturing company executive; b. Dayton, Ohio, Sept. 2, 1917; s. Lewis Floyd and Blanche Irene (Conner) W.; m. Catherine Crosby, July 19, 1941; 1 child, Tod C. B.S., U. Mich., 1938; postgrad., Ohio Wesleyan U., 1938-41. With 3M Co., 1948-52, Oliver Iron and Steel Co., 1952-56; mktg. mgr., then mgr. Sturtevant div. Westinghouse Elec. Corp., 1956-62; pvt. cons. 1962-65; with Joy Mfg. Co., Pitts., 1965—, sr. v.p., 1967, pres., chief exec. officer, 1967-76, chmn. bd., chief exec. officer, 1976-82, ret., 1982, chmn. exec. com., 1982-87; chmn., pres. Pace Industries, Inc., 1984-88, corp. cons., 1989—; dir. POGO Producing Co., H.H. Robertson Co., Mellon-Stuart Co., Copperweld Corp., Michael Baker Corp., Harris Corp., L.B. Foster Co.; adj. prof. U. Pitts. Served as officer AUS, 1942-46. Republican. Episcopalian. Clubs: Duquesne, Allegheny Country, John's Island. Office: 3355 Oxford Ctr Pittsburgh PA 15219

WILCOX, CHERYL ANN, financial executive; b. Warren, Ohio, Dec. 24, 1948; d. Austin William and Anne Marie (Palo) Davis; m. Robert H.L. Wilcox, June 10, 1972 (dec. 1980). AA in Bus., Youngstown U., 1972. Acct., Can. Dental Assn., Ottawa, Ont., 1977-78, Acctg. and Bus. Cons., Ft. Lauderdale, Fla., 1979-80; compt. Cosby's Inc., Delray Beach, Fla., 1980-81; mortgage officer Spanish River Resort, Delray Beach, 1981-83; compt. Marine Reins., Miami Beach, Fla., 1983-85, Marine R. Corp., Miami, 1985—, also bd. dirs.; sec.-treas. M.R. Cows Inc., 1984-88; corp. sec. Northdale Pla., Inc., Miami, 1985—; corp. sec. WOW Travel, 1988—. Bd. dirs. Big Bros./Big Sis. Broward, Ft. Lauderdale, 1985—. Recipient Arion award Nat. Honor Soc., 1966, A-Rate award Ohio Solo Vocal Competition State of Ohio, 1966. Mem. NAFE., Women's Exec. Assn. Club: Foundlings (Miami). Avocation: scuba diving. Office: Marine R Corp 11077 Biscayne Blvd Miami FL 33161

WILCOX, DAVID BERTELL, food manufacturing executive; b. Liberty, Mo., May 18, 1930; s. David B. and Mary G. (Banks) W.; m. Betsy Ross, Aug. 15, 1955 (dec. Nov. 1985); children: Mary Lou, Juliet, Ruth. BS in Econs. with high honors, U. Ill., 1956. Cert. Am. Inst. Banking. Dist. rep. Union Carbide Corp., various locations western U.S., 1956-61; gen. trainee First Nat. Bank, Memphis, 1961-62, first trainee asst. to exec. v.p., 1962-63, lending officer, 1963-64, mgr. mcpl. services dept., 1964-65; controller, asst. sec. treas. Mitchum Co./Graham and Warren, Inc., Paris, Tenn., 1965-67; sec., treas., controller Mitchum Co./Graham and Warren, Inc., 1967-71; v.p. adminstrn. Mitchum Co., 1971-72; v.p. fin. and adminstrn. and sec. treas. Jim Adams Corp., Paris, 1973-75; sec. P&L Systems, Inc., Paris, 1975-76; pres. Pagliacci, Inc., Paris, 1972-79, Allegro Fine Foods, Inc., Paris, 1978—; cons. to govt. on small bus., export mktg., indsl. devel., fin., indsl. and employee relations, 1972—. Mem. Paris Planning Commn., 1973-75, Paris City Commn., 1971-83, Henry County Vocat. Agrl. Adv. Com., 1985—, Henry County Ct. Budget Com., Fiscal Study Commn., Airport Commn.; bd. dirs. Pub. Utilities, 1975-83, Puryear Commn. Devl. Assn.; pres. Tenn. Export Devel. Assn., 1983-86; chmn. Henry County Indsl. Devel. Com., 1984-88, Am. Indsl. Mgmt. Evaluation Team USDA, 1985, Henry County Plant Mgmt. Assn.; leader Bedford Forrest dist. Boy Scouts Am. Served as hosp. corpsman 2nd class USN, 1948-52. Named Hon. Chpt. Farmer Future Farmers Am., 1971, Hon. State Farmer, 1985. Mem. Greater Paris C. of C. (dir., treas., mem. exec. com. mem.). Home: 307 Jackson St Paris TN 38242 Office: Allegro Fine Foods Inc PO Box 1262 Paris TN 38242

WILCOX, DAVID ERIC, consultant; b. Cortland, N.Y., Sept. 4, 1939; s. James A. and Lucille (Fiske) C.; B.S. in Elec. Engring., U. Buffalo, 1961; postgrad. Syracuse U., 1965, Marist Coll.; M.S., U. Bridgeport, 1977; Ed.D. candidate Rutgers U.; m. Phyllipa Ann Wilcox, Jan. 23, 1977; children—Terri L., Cindy A., Jana L. Research engring. mgr. input/output devices Rome (N.Y.) Air Devel. Center, 1966-70; dir. sales Mercon Inc., Winsooki, Vt., 1970-73, dir., 1972—; pres. Wilcox Tng. Systems, Newburgh, N.Y., 1973—; prin. Exec. Effectiveness, Inc., N.Y.C.; instr. Dale Carnegie courses. Pres. N.Y. State Jaycees, 1972-73, chmn. bd., 1973-74; dir. U.S. Jaycees, 1970-71; bd. dirs., v.p. N.Y. State Spl. Olympics, 1972-73; bd. dirs. Family Counseling Service, Inc. Served to lt. USAF, 1961-65. Registered profl. engr., N.Y. Mem. Soc. Info. Display, IEEE, N.Y., State Soc. Profl. Engrs., Internat. Transactional Analysis Assn., Internat. Platform Assn. Methodist. Author: Information System Sciences, 1965; also articles. Patentee in field. Home: 511 River Rd Newburgh NY 12550 Office: Rock Cut Rd Newburgh NY 12550 also: 30 W 60th St New York NY

WILCOX, EVERETT HAMMOCK, JR., lawyer; b. Clearwater, Fla., Apr. 25, 1944; s. Everett Hammock Sr. and Alice (Wilson) W.; m. Janet Elaine Springman, June 7, 1967; children: Alexis Shields, Merrill Morrow. BA, Duke U., 1966; MA, U. Fla., 1969, JD with honors, 1971. Bar: Fla. 1972, D.C. 1972, Ga. 1980. Law clk. to judge U.S. Ct. Appeals (5th cir.), Jacksonville, Fla., 1971-72; assoc. Alston & Bird (formerly Alston, Miller & Gaines), Washington, 1972-78, ptnr., 1978; ptnr. Alston & Bird (formerly Alston, Miller & Gaines), Atlanta, 1979—; speaker various orgns. and schs. Exec. editor U. Fla. Law Rev., 1971. Mem. econ. devel. adv. bd. Fulton County, Atlanta, 1986-88; asst. counsel campaign Carter for Pres., 1976; co-counsel Va. Carter Campaign, 1976; chmn. trade devel. com. Cobb Internat. Ctr., Atlanta, 1982-85, mem. steering com., 1982-86; vice-chmn., chmn. exec. com. Southeastern regional adv. bd. Inst. of Internat. Edn., 1985-89; mem. gov.'s mission to Far East, del. Japan/U.S. S.E. Assn.; sec. World Tech. Ctr., 1983-86, trustee, 1983-87. Fellow Soc. Internat. Bus. Fellows (mem. selection com. 1983-85, bd. dirs. 1985-86, v.p. 1986-87, counsel 1987-88, v.p. program com. 1988—); mem. ABA (sect. on internat. law), Internat. Bar Assn. (sect. on bus. law), D.C. Bar Assn., Fla. State Bar Assn., Ga. Bar Assn., Atlanta Bar Assn., Swiss-Am. C. of C., Order of Coif. Office: Alston & Bird One Atlantic Ctr 1201 W Peachtree St Atlanta GA 30309-3424

WILCOX, JAMES LYMAN, real estate developer; b. Columbus, Ohio, Nov. 5, 1938; s. Frank Lyman and Florence (Felton) W.; children: Alicia, Joe. BA, Ohio State U., 1960, JD, 1962; MBA, Harvard U., 1966. Bar: Ohio 1962. Spl. agt. FBI, Portland, Oreg., 1962-64; owner J.L. Wilcox & Co. and Countrytyme Inc., Columbus, Ohio, 1966—. Contbg. author: The Computer Utility, 1966. Mem. Columbus Bd. Realtors, Soc. Ex-FBI Agts., Harvard Bus. Sch. Alumni Assn., Chgo. Farmers Club, Columbus Farmers Club (founder 1981). Home: 1358 Bayshore Dr Columbus OH 43204 Office: Countrytyme Inc 3980 Broadway Grove City OH 43123

WILCZAK, WAYNE EDWARD, banker; b. Chgo., May 13, 1948; s. Edward Frank and Dorothy (Goslawski) W.; m. Judy Bernadette Modelski, Aug. 25, 1973. BS, U. Ill., Chgo., 1970; MBA, Rosary Coll., 1979. With Continental Ill. Nat. Bank, Chgo., 1972-81; ops. auditor No. Ill. Gas Co., Aurora, 1981; officer The Fuji Bank Ltd., Chgo., 1981-83; v.p. Pathway Fin., Matteson, Ill., 1983-85; sr. v.p. Pathway Fin., Matteson, 1985—; bd. dirs. Coconut Bay Resorts, Ft. Lauderdale, Fla. Ofcl. Ill. High Sch. Athletic Assn. Mem. Robert Morris Assn. (sr. assn. rep. 1983—). Office: Pathway Fin 20821 S Cicero Ave Matteson IL 60443

WILD, HEIDI KARIN, oil company executive; b. Detroit, July 28, 1948; d. Lauren Daggett and Eleanor Stephanie (Churchman) Wild; m. Francis Michael Robinson, Oct. 2, 1982. BS, Western Mich. U., 1971; MBA, U. Hawaii, 1985. Tchr. secondary edn. St. Clair Sch. System, St. Clair Shores, Mich., 1971-74; personnel asst. Union Camp Corp., Kalamazoo, 1974-76; receptionist, typist Pacific Resources Inc., Honolulu, 1976-77, sec., 1977-78, adminstrv. asst., 1978, mktg. and supply analyst, 1978-80, coord. light product supply and exch., 1980-81, mgr. product supply, 1981-83, dir. product supply, 1983-85, gen. mgr. light products, 1985, gen. mgr. supply and distbn. 1985-86, mgr. petroleum coordination, 1986-87, acting v.p. supply and distbn., 1987-88, gen. mgr. Hawaii supply, 1988—; bd. dirs. PRI Fed. Credit Union. Mem. adv. bd. Coll. Bus. U. Hawaii. Mem. U. Hawaii MBA Alumni Group (pres. bd. dirs. 1988—), Hawaii Soc. Corp. Planners, Navy League, U. Hawaii Alumni Assn. (1st v.p., bd. dirs. 1988—), Western Mich. U. Alumni Assn., Sierra Club, Beta Gamma Sigma. Clubs: Petroleum (L.A.); Plaza, PRI Golf. Avocations: golf, travel. Office: Pacific Resources Inc 733 Bishop St Honolulu HI 96813

WILD, STEPHEN KENT, insurance marketing company executive; b. Omaha, Nov. 18, 1948; s. Roger Charles and Marguerite Mae W.; m. Cheryl Katherine Sparano, June 5, 1971; children—Deric Justin, Drew Ian. Student Ottawa U., 1967-68, U. Nebr.-Omaha, 1968-71. Internal auditor Kirkpatrick, Pettis, Smith and Polian, Omaha, 1971-75; fin. planner First Fin. Planning Group, Omaha, 1975-80; mng. gen. agt. E.F. Hutton Life Ins. Co., Omaha, 1980-81; chmn. bd. Fin. Dynamics, Omaha, 1981—, Securities Am., Inc., 1984—; life ins. cons. Mem. Nat. Assn. Life Underwriters, Internat. Assn. Fin. Planners. Baptist. Home: 16561 Nina Circle Omaha NE 68130 Office: 7100 W Center Rd Suite 500 Omaha NE 68106-2798

WILDASIN, GEORGE LEE, real estate corporation officer; b. Muscatine, Iowa, Apr. 12, 1946; s. Levi John and Mildren Bernice (Johnson) W. BA, Tex. Christian U., 1968; MBA, La. State U., 1973; postgrad., U. Tulsa, 1973-74. Sr. mortgage loan analyst Lincoln Nat. Life Ins., Co., Ft. Wayne, Ind., 1974-77; asst. v.p. DRG Fin. Corp., Houston, 1977-80; v.p. Broadway Nat. Bank, San Antonio, 1980-81, Tex. Bank, San Antonio, 1982-83; sr. v.p. Tesoro Fin. Group Inc., San Antonio, 1983-85; pres. Blue Star Properties, Inc., San Antonio, 1985—; cons. Alamo Savs. Assn. Tex., San Antonio, 1985-86. Mem. Nat. Assn. Realtors (cert. comml. investment), Tex. Assn. Realtors, San Antonio Bd. Realtors, San Antonio Mortgage Bankers Assn. Republican. Presbyterian. Home: 10915 Whisper Hollow San Antonio TX 78230 Office: 326 Cave Ln San Antonio TX 78209

WILDE, PAUL CECIL, accountant; b. Ft. Dodge, Iowa, Dec. 25, 1950; s. Cecil Francis and Laura Clara (Buhner) W.; m. Beverly Jeane Smith, Sept. 2, 1972; children: Adam Spencer, Emily Ellen. BBA, U. Northern Iowa, 1973; BA in Acctg., Buena Vista Coll., 1982. Bookeeper Ellsworth Freight Lines, Eagle Grove, Iowa, 1973-82; acct. Boone Valley Coop., Eagle Grove, 1982-84; dir. acctg. Umthun Trucking Co., Eagle Grove, 1984—. United Methodist. Lodge: Masons. Home: 216 S Lincoln Eagle Grove IA 50533 Office: Umthun Trucking Co 911 S Jackson Eagle Grove IA 50533

WILDE, WILSON, insurance company executive; b. Hartford, Conn., Sept. 24, 1927; s. Philip Alden and Alice Augusta (Wilson) W.; m. Joanne Gerta Menzel, June 19, 1953; children—Stephen W., David W., Elisabeth L., Richard A. Student, Swarthmore Coll., 1945-46; BA, Williams Coll., 1949. Sales agt. Conn. Gen. Life Ins. Co., Hartford, 1949-53; with Hartford Steam Boiler Inspection & Ins. Co., 1953—, exec. v.p., 1970-71, pres., chief exec. officer, 1971—, also dir.; dir. Boiler Inspection & Ins. Co. Can., Toronto, Ont., Can., Shawmut Nat. Corp., Radian Corp., Emhart Corp., Shawmut Nat. Corp., GenRad Corp., Phoenix Mut. Life Ins. Co., Phoenix Re Corp. Corporator Inst. Living, Hartford; corporator St. Francis Hosp., Hartford, Mt. Sinai Hosp.; hon. bd. dirs. Hartford Stage Co., 1973—, Jr. Achievement, Old State House Assn., 1976—; trustee Loomis-Chaffee Sch., 1974—, chmn. bd., 1988—. Served with USNR, 1945-47, 51-53. Mem. Am. Ins. Assn. (dir.), Ins. Assn. Conn. (dir.). Club: Hartford (pres. 1974). Office: Hartford Steam Boiler One State St 12th Fl Hartford CT 06102

WILDEBUSH, JOSEPH FREDERICK, economist; b. Bklyn., July 18, 1910; s. Harry Frederick and Elizabeth (Stolzenberg) W.; A.B., Columbia, 1931, postgrad Law Sch., 1932; LL.B., Bklyn. Law Sch., 1934, J.D., 1967; m. Martha Janssens, July 18, 1935; children—Diane Elaine (Mrs. Solon Finkelstein), Joan Marilyn (Mrs. Bobby Sanford Berry); m. Edith Sorensen, May 30, 1964. Admitted to N.Y. State bar, 1934, Fed. bar, 1935; practice law, N.Y.C., 1934-41; labor relations dir. Botany Mills, Passaic, N.J., 1945-48; exec. v.p. Silk and Rayon Printers and Dyers Assn. Am., Inc., Paterson, N.J., 1948-70; exec. v.p. Textile Printers and Dyers Labor Relations Inst., Paterson, 1954-70; mem. panel labor arbitrators Fed. Mediation and Conciliation Service, N.Y. State Mediation Bd., N.J. State Mediation Bd., N.J. Pub. Employment Relations Commn., Am. Arbitration Assn.; co-adj. faculty Rutgers U., 1948—; lectr. Pres. Pascack Valley Hosp., Westwood, N.J., 1950-64, chmn. bd., 1964-67, chmn. emeritus, 1967—; pres. Group Health Ins. N.J., 1962-65, chmn. bd., 1965-80; dir. Group Health Ins. N.Y., 1950—. Served as maj. Engrs. Corps, AUS, 1941-43. Mem. N.Y. County Lawyers Assn., Am. Acad. Polit. and Social Sci., Indsl. Relations Research Assn., Ret. Officers Assn., Nat. Geog. Soc. Lutheran. Contbr. articles profl. jours. Home and Office: 37 James Terr Pompton Lakes NJ 07442

WILDER, CHARLES, insurance company executive; b. N.Y.C., Apr. 4, 1949; s. Nathan and Melanie (Beittel) W.; M. Denise Hope Daley, Mar. 17, 1973; children: Rachel Lauren, Adam David. BA in Math., CUNY, 1971; postgrad., CCNY, 1972-75. Fin. analyst Equitable Life Assurance Soc., N.Y.C., 1972-78, mgr., 1978-82, 1978-82, asst. v.p., 1982-85, v.p., 1985-87; sr. v.p. pension fin. mgmt. group Equitable Life Assurance Soc., Secaucus, N.J., 1987—.

WILDER, CHARLES WILLOUGHBY, lawyer; b. Newton, Mass., Jan. 27, 1929; s. Philip Sawyer and Elisabeth (Clark) W.; m. Elinor Gardner Dean, Nov. 2, 1957; children: Michael, Stephen, Elisabeth. BA, Bowdoin Coll., 1950; LLB, Columbia U., 1957. Bar: N.Y. 1958. Assoc. White & Case, N.Y.C., 1957-58; law clk. to judge U.S. Ct. Appeals (2d cir.), N.Y.C., 1958-59; atty. Gen. Electric Co., 1959-67; from counsel to v.p., dep. gen. counsel, sec. Tex. Gulf Sulphur Co. (name changed to Texasgulf Inc. 1973), N.Y.C. and Stamford, Conn., 1967—; v.p., dep. gen. counsel, sec. Elf Aquitaine, Inc., Stamford, 1983—. Served to lt. (j.g.) USNR, 1951-54. Mem. ABA, N.Y. State Bar Assn., Assn. of Bar of City of N.Y., Westchester-Fairfield Corp. Counsel Assn. Democrat. Office: Elf Aquitaine Inc High Ridge Park PO Box 10037 Stamford CT 06904-2037

WILDERMUTH, CHARLES EDWARD, accountant; b. Portsmouth, Ohio, Aug. 15, 1955; s. Theodore Carl Wildermuth and Laura Etta (Miller) Cornwell. BS, Ohio U., 1977, BBA, 1978, MBA, 1979. CPA, Ohio, Fla. Acct. Arthur Andersen & Co., Cin., 1979-81, Coopers & Lybrand, West Palm Beach, Fla., 1981-84; dir. fin. Gunster, Yoakley, Criser & Stewart, West Palm Beach, 1984—. Mem. econ. study com. City of West Palm Beach, 1984; mem. Palm Beach County Sports Authority, 1987—; treas. South Fla. Sci. Mus., West Palm Beach, 1983-86. Ohio U. scholar, 1978. Mem. Am. Inst. CPAs, Fla. Inst. CPAs, Assn. Legal Adminstr., ABA (assoc.), Executive Club, Yacht Club (West Palm Beach). Methodist. Home: 4200 12th St #415 West Palm Beach FL 33409 Office: Gunster Yoakley Criser & Stewart 777 S Flagler Dr Ste 500 West Palm Beach FL 33401

WILDHACK, WILLIAM AUGUST, JR., lawyer; b. Takoma Park, Md., Nov. 28, 1935; s. William August and Martha Elizabeth (Parks) W.; m. Martha Moore Allston, Aug. 1, 1959; children: William A. III, Elizabeth L. B.S., Miami U., Oxford, Ohio, 1957; J.D., George Washington U., 1963. Bar: Va. 1963, D.C. 1965, Md. 1983, U.S. Supreme Ct. 1967. Agt. IRS, No. Va., 1957-65; assoc. Morris, Pearce, Gardner & Beitel, Washington, 1965-69; sole practice Washington, 1969; v.p., corp. counsel B.F. Saul Co. and affiliates, Chevy Chase, Md., 1969-87, Chevy Chase Savs. Bank, F.S.B. and affiliates, 1987—; sr. v.p. B.F. Saul Real Estate Investment Trust, Chevy Chase, 1972-87. Mem. Arlington Tenant Landlord Commn., 1976—; pres. Am. Cancer Soc., Arlington unit, 1970-71. Mem. Am. Soc. Corp. Secs., ABA, Md. Bar Assn., D.C. Bar, Va. Bar, Arlington County Bar Assn., D.C. Assn. Realtors, Phi Alpha Delta. Presbyterian. Office: Chevy Chase Savs Bank FSB 8401 Connecticut Ave Chevy Chase MD 20815

WILDING, DIANE, general manager, marketing executive, computer system engineer; b. Chicago Heights, Ill., Nov. 7, 1942; d. Michael Edward and Katherine Surian; m. Manfred Georg Wilding, May 7, 1975 (div. 1980). BSBA in Acctg. magna cum laude, No. Ill. U., 1963; postgrad., U. Chgo., 1972-74; Cert. German Lang., Goethe Inst., Rothenburg, Fed. Republic Germany, 1984. Lic. cosmetologist. Systems engr. IBM Corp., Chgo., 1963-68; data processing mgr. Am. Res. Corp., Chgo., 1969-72; system rsch. and devel. project mgr. Continental Bank, Chgo., 1972-75; fin. industry mktg. rep. IBM Can., Ltd., Toronto, Ont., 1976-79; mktg. exec. regional telecommunications Control Data Corp., Atlanta, 1980-84; gen. mgr. The Plant Plant, Atlanta, 1985—; pioneer installer on-line Automatic Teller Machines. Author: The Canadian Payment System: An International Perspective, 1977. Mem. Chgo. Coun. on Fgn. Rels.; bd. dirs. Easter House Adoption Agy., Chgo., 1974-76. Mem. Internat. Brass Soc., Goethe Inst., Mensa. Clubs: Ponte Verde (Fla.); Royal Ont. Yacht, Libertyville Racquet. Home: PO Box 95189 Atlanta GA 30347

WILDNAUER, RICHARD HARRY, pharmaceutical company executive; b. New Kensington, Pa., Feb. 14, 1940; s. Richard Michael and Rosemary Elizabeth (Moore) W.; BS in Chemistry, St. Vincent Coll., 1962; PhD in Biochemistry, W.Va. U., 1966; postgrad. (NSF fellow) U. Kans., 1967; MBA in Mgmt., Rider Coll., 1974; m. Sharon Ann Novick, Jan. 22, 1966; 1 dau., Tara Lynne. NIH trainee W.Va. U., 1963-66; sr. research assoc. in skin biology, exploratory research div. Johnson and Johnson Domestic Operating Co., New Brunswick, N.J., 1975, assoc. mgr. tech. planning, exploratory research div., 1975-77; sr. project coordinator, new products, pharm. div. McNeil Labs., Ft. Washington, Pa., 1977-79; dir. new product devel. Janssen Pharmaceutica Inc., New Brunswick, N.J., 1979-82, v.p. research and devel., 1982-88; v.p. tech. and bus. devel., Johnson & Johnson, New Brunswick, N.J., 1988—. Trustee, bd. dirs. United Way Cen. N.J., 1988—. Mem. N.Y. Acad. Scis., Soc. for Investigative Dermatology, Am. Mgmt. Assn., Med. Mycology Soc., Am. Acad. Dermatology, Pharm. Advt. Club, Sigma Xi. Roman Catholic. Contbr. articles to profl. jours. Home: 6 Pilgrim Run East Brunswick NJ 08816 Office: Johnson & Johnson One Johnson & Johnson Plaza New Brunswick NJ 08933

WILES, BETTY JANE, accountant; b. Scott County, Ark., Dec. 21, 1940; d. Edd and Nellie Margaret (Richey) Staggs; m. Ralph A. Wiles, July 18, 1959; children: Ralph A. Jr., Penny Margaret. BBA magna cum laude, Henderson State Coll., 1983. CPA, Ark. Sec. Royalty Holding Co., Oklahoma City, 1959-65, Rector & Eubanks, Mena, Ark., 1966-69; paralegal Shaw & Shaw Attys., Mena, Ark., 1969-83; pvt. practice acctg. Mena, Ark., 1984—. Cons. advisory bd. Mena High Sch., 1985-86, St. John Library, Rich Mountain Community Coll., 1987—, Rich Mountain Community Coll. Service Adv. com., 1988—. Mem. AAUW, Ark. Soc. CPA's. Baptist. Club: Mena Lioness. Home: PO Box 522 Mena AR 71953 Office: 311 DeQueen St Mena AR 71953

WILEY, SCOTT TAYLOR, investment banker; b. Teaneck, N.J., Nov. 26, 1949; s. Eugene Taylor and Elinor Starr (Sullivan) W.; A.B. with honors in Econs., Dartmouth Coll., 1971; M.B.A., U. Chgo., 1973; m. Joy Gwenn McArthur, June 24, 1972; children—Peter, Glen. Vice pres. Morgan Guaranty Trust Co. of N.Y., N.Y.C., 1973-81; pres. Copeland, Wickersham, Wiley & Co., N.Y.C., 1981—. bd. dirs. Premier Bank, N.Am., Vanderbilt Petroleum, Inc., Gulf Exploration Cons., Inc., Excaliber Resources, Inc., Bear Creek Corp.; dir. Premier Bank, N.A. Dallas Gas & Electric Inc. Mem. juvenile conf. com. Borough of Oradell (N.J.), 1975-79, mem. planning bd., 1979—. Mem. Nat. Assn. Petroleum Investment Analysts (dir. 1978—, treas. 1979, sec. 1980, pres. 1982), N.Y. Soc. Security Analysts, N.Y. Oil Analysts Group, Tex. Mid-Continent Oil and Gas Assn., Fin. Analysts Fedn. Clubs: Dartmouth of No. N.J. (trustee 1975-78, 81—, sec. 1976-78, 81); Dartmouth of N.Y. Home: 653 Center St Oradell NJ 07649 Office: 52 Vanderbilt St New York NY 10017

WILEY, WILLIAM BRADFORD, publisher; b. Orange, N.J., Nov. 17, 1910; s. William Carroll and Isabel (LeCato) W.; m. Esther T. Booth, Jan. 4, 1936; children: William Bradford II, Peter Booth, Deborah Elizabeth Wiley. A.B., Colgate U., 1932, LL.D. (hon.), 1966. With John Wiley & Sons, Inc., N.Y.C., 1932—; sec., v.p. and sec., exec. v.p., treas. John Wiley & Sons, Inc., 1938-56, pres., 1956-71, chmn., 1971—, dir., 1942—; chmn., dir. John Wiley & Sons, Can., John Wiley & Sons Ltd., London, Jacaranda-Wiley, Ltd., Brisbane; dir. Wiley Eastern Ltd., India; mem. mgmt. bd. MIT Press. Trustee emeritus Colgate U., Drew U. Cordier fellow Columbia U. Episcopalian. Clubs: Met. Opera, Players (N.Y.C.); Sakonnet Golf (R.I.), Sakonnet Yacht (R.I.); Baltusrol (N.J.) Golf. Home: 57 Prospect Hill Ave Summit NJ 07901 Office: Bailey's Ledge Little Compton RI 02837 also: John Wiley & Sons Inc 605 3rd Ave New York NY 10158

WILHITE, CLAYTON EDWARD, advertising executive; b. Saginaw, Mich., Aug. 9, 1945; s. Clayton Robson and Ruth Margaret (Westendorf) W.; m. Ann Denise Douglass, June 27, 1970. B.A. in Polit. Sci., U. Mich., 1967, M.B.A., 1969. Account exec., account supr. Foote, Cone & Belding, Chgo. and Sydney, Australia, 1969-75; v.p., account supr. McCann-Erickson, N.Y.C., 1975-77; exec. v.p., dir. Ammirati & Puris Inc., N.Y.C., 1977-83; mktg. dir. Young & Rubicam Ltd., London, 1983-85; chief exec., mng. dir. D'Arcy, Masius, Benton & Bowles (formerly D'Arcy, MacManus, Masius, Inc.), St. Louis, 1985—, pres., 1988—; bd. dirs. DMB&B Inc. Mem. Exec. Campaign 1976 In-House Advt. Agy. for Pres. Ford Re-election Com., Washington; bd. dirs. Lindenwood Coll., St. Louis Symphony, Boy Scout Council, Civic Entrepreneurs Orgn., Young Pres. Orgn., Repertory Theatre of St. Louis, Arts and Edn. Council of St. Louis. Mem. Phi Beta Kappa. Republican. Lutheran. Clubs: River (N.Y.C.); Racquet, Advt., Media (St. Louis); Mo. Athletic, Noonday. Office: D'Arcy Masius Benton & Bowles Inc 1 Memorial Dr Saint Louis MO 63102

WILHITE, COLBERT ROLAND, chemical and oil company executive; b. Mangum, Okla., Sept. 29, 1931; s. Clarence Calvin and Margaret (Baker) W.; m. Carol Jenkins, Mar. 22, 1958; 1 child, Lisa Gayle. B.A. in Bus. Adminstrn., U. Okla., 1957, M.B.A., 1958. Various positions pipeline dept. Conoco, Inc., Ponca City, Okla., 1958-68, mgr. transp. dept., 1968-72; mgr. Western Hemisphere planning Conoco, Inc., Houston, 1972-73; mgr. investor relations Conoco, Inc., Stamford, Conn., 1973-77; v.p. external affairs Conoco, Inc., Houston and Wilmington, Del., 1977-86; v.p. state affairs E.I. DuPont de Nemours and Co., Wilmington, 1987—. Mem. adminstrv. bd. Aldersgate United Methodist Ch., Wilmington, 1985—; bd. dirs. Keep Am. Beautiful, N.Y.C., Students in Free Enterprise, Bolivar, Mo.; adv. coun. State Legis. Leaders Found., Council of State Govts.' Corp. Assn. Group. With USN, 1951-55, PTO. Mem. Am. Petroleum Inst. (chmn. gen. com. state relations 1985-86), Chem. Mfrs. Assn. (state affairs com.). Club: University (Washington). Office: E I du Pont de Nemours & Co External Affairs Dept 1007 Market St Wilmington DE 19898

WILINSKI, EDWIN ALFRED, construction company executive; b. N.Y.C., Mar. 15, 1938; s. Edwin Alfred and Kathryn (Rinko) W.; m. Diane Mary Symkowski, May 5, 1962; children: Eric, Karin, Adrienne, Suzanne, Laura. B.S., Ga. Inst. Tech., 1959; J.D., Bklyn. Law Sch., 1970. Agt. IRS, N.Y.C., 1959-66; with Fischbach & Moore, Inc., N.Y.C., 1967—, sec., 1970—, v.p., 1978-80; exec. v.p. adminstrn. Fischbach Corp., N.Y.C., 1980—; dir. Fischbach Corp., 1981—. Served with AUS, 1961-62. Home: Massapequa NY 11758 Office: Fischbach Corp 485 Lexington Ave New York NY 10017

WILKEN, PAUL WILLIAM, optometrist; b. Sandusky, Ohio, Nov. 14, 1951; s. Carl Anthony and Mary Ellen (Gentry) W.; m. Linda Irene Nierstheimer, Sept. 1, 1973; children: Jennifer, Carl, Michelle, Benjamin. BS, Ohio State U., 1973, OD, 1977. Optometrist John Wasylik, Sandusky, 1977-79; owner, v.p. John E. Wellman OD, Inc., Celina and St. Marys, Ohio, 1979—, Wellman, Wilken & Assocs., Wapakoneta, Ohio, 1983—, Piqua, Ohio, 1984—, Lima, Ohio, 1985—, Van Wert, Ohio, 1985. Author: (newspaper column) Vision Care, 1980-81. Mem. Sch. Curriculum Council, Celina, 1982-84, 1987—; speaker, cons. Mercer County Council on Aging,

Mercer County Diabetic Support Group, Celina, 1980—, Joint Twp. Dist. Meml. Hosp. Diabetic Support Group, 1986—, Van Wert County Diabetic Support Group, 1987—. Mem. Am. Optometric Assn., Ohio Optometric Assn., N.W. Ohio Optometric Assn., Ohio State U. Alumni Assn. (life), Epsilon Psi Epsilon (Pledge of Yr. award 1975). Republican. Roman Catholic. Lodge: Rotary (sec. 1979-84, pres. 1985-86, govs. rep.1988-89). Avocations: flying, motivational speaking. Home: 616 N Main St Celina OH 45822 Office: Wellman Wilken 119 W Summit St Celina OH 45822

WILKERSON, MARJORIE JOANN MADAR, insurance company executive; b. Spokane, Wash., Dec. 2, 1930; d. Joseph Robert and Margaret Muriel (McKee) Madar; m. Billy E. Wilkerson, Jan. 9, 1953; 1 child, Wesley James McEarl. Student U. Puget Sound, 1948; B.A., UCLA, 1949; postgrad. So. Meth. U., 1958. Mgmt. to agt. Travelers Ins. Cos., Houston and Dallas, 1952-63; sr. account agt. Allstate Ins. Cos., Tacoma, 1966—; cons in field; lectr. various colls. and univs. Author: Sex and Society, 1976. Editor publ. Chiropractic Edn., also newsletter. Pres., co-founder Pierce County Women's Polit. Caucus, Tacoma; editor: (newsletter) Millionaire Life Ins. Agts., Caucus State of Wash., Seattle; lobbiest Caucus and prior for ERA, Olympia, Wash.; citizen lobbiest Worker Right to Know, Olympia, 1984-85; spokesperson Community effort to protect zoning, Gig Harbor, Wash., 1980-84; bd. dirs., sec. Beaumont Art Mus., Tex., 1954-57; pres. Walnut Hill League, N. Dallas, 1957-65; established first Girl Scout Program in Beaumont Girl Scouts U.S., 1955; mem. citizen lobby for higher standards of air quality. Grantee activist to study Washington Commn. for Humanities, 1974-75. Office: 15 Oregon Ste 304 Tacoma WA 98409

WILKERSON, WILLIAM HOLTON, banker; b. Greenville, N.C., Feb. 16, 1947; s. Edwin Cisco and Agnes Holton (Gaskins) W.; m. Ellen Logan Tomskey, Oct. 27, 1973; 1 child, William Holton Jr. AB in Econs., U. N.C., 1970. Asst. v.p. First Union Nat. Bank, Greensboro, N.C., 1972-77; v.p. Peoples Bank & Trust Co., Rocky Mount, N.C., 1977-79; sr. v.p. Hibernia Nat. Bank, New Orleans, 1979-86; exec. v.p. Peoples Bank and Trust Co., 1987—. Bd. advisor Jr. League, New Orleans, 1986; bd. dirs. Trinity Episc. Sch., New Orleans, 1986, Community Ministries Inc., Rocky Mount, 1988—. Mem. Robert Morris Assoc., New Orleans C. of C., Boston Club, New Orleans Country Club, Benvenue Country Club, Kiwanis, Omicron Delta Epsilon, Chi Beta Phi, Phi Sigma Phi. Republican. Avocations: golf, tennis. Home: 336 Iron Horse Rd Rocky Mount NC 27804

WILKES, HAYNES MILLER, insurance executive; b. Johnson City, Tenn., Apr. 2, 1949; s. Clem Cabell and Dorothy Jane (Miller) W.; m. Bonnie Jean Osborne, Aug. 10, 1973; children: Haynes Miller Jr., Joseph Osborne. BS, East Tenn. State U., 1971; postgrad., Memphis State U., 1987. Lic. ins. broker, real estate broker, Tenn. Account exec. STa. WJHL-TV, Johnson City, 1971-72; sales rep. CSX Transp., Inc., Balt., 1972-79; v.p. First Tenn. Bank, Johnson City, 1979-87; ins. broker Duke Ingram Ins. Agy., Johnson City, 1987—. Bd. dirs. Johnson City Eye & Ear Hosp., 1984—, Quillen-Dishner Coll. Medicine, Johnson City, 1985—; fin. chmn. Johnson City United Way, 1986. Episcopalian. Club: Johnson City Country (bd. dirs. 1984-87). Lodge: Rotary. Home: 805 N Mountain View Cir Johnson City TN 37601 Office: Haynes Miller Wilkes 805 N Mountain View Cir Johnson City TN 37601

WILKINS, JERRY LYNN, lawyer, clergyman; b. Big Spring, Tex., June 1, 1936; s. Claude F. and Grace L. (Jones) W.; children by previous marriage: Gregory, Tammy, Scott, Brett; m. Valerie Ann Nuanez, Aug. 1, 1986. BA, Baylor U., 1958, LLB, 1960. Bar: Tex. 1960, U.S. Dist. Ct. (no. dist.) Tex. 1960, U.S. Ct. Appeals (5th cir.); ordained to ministry, 1977. Pvt. practice, Dallas, 1960—; capt. Air Am., Vietnam, 1967-68, Joint Church Aid, Biafra, 1969-70, TransInternat. Airlines, Oakland, Calif., 1977-79; gen. counsel First Tex. Petroleum, Dallas, 1982; owner Wooltex, Inc., Dallas, 1983—; owner, dir., legal counsel Intermountain Gas Inc., Dallas, 1983-84; founder, dir. Comanche Peak Reclamation Inc. bd. dirs. Engineered Roof Cons., Continental Tex. Corp., Arlington, Landlord Rsch. Inc., Acklin Pain Rsch. Inst., Inc., Irving, Tex., Silver Leaf Metals Internat. Inc., Silver Leaf Mining Inc., Tex. Recycling Industries, Inc.; founder, chmn. bd. dirs. Tex. Reclamation Industries, Inc.; bd. dirs., v.p. for legal affairs, underwriter Lloyds U.S. Inc.; bd. dirs., co-founder R.O.A.S., Inc., Maritime Internat., Inc., Maritime Oil Recovery, Inc., Moriah Oil Recovery Barges, Inc., Megas Homes Internat., Urex Internat.; mem. legal counsel, bd. dirs. U.S. Fiduciary Co. Inc., U.S. Fiduciary Trust Co. Inc.; cons. in field. Author: Gods Prosperity, 1980; So You Think You Have Prayed, 1980, Gods Hand in my Life, America, The Land of Sheep for Slaughter, I.R.S., America's Gestapo; Editor numerous books; contbr. articles to profl. jours. Bd. dirs., pres. Beasley For Children Found. Inc., Dallas, 1978—; mem. Republican Presdl. Task Force, Washington, 1984—; bd. dirs., pilot Wings for Christians, Dallas, 1976—, Wings for Christ, Waco, Tex., 1976—. Recipient Cert. of Appreciation Parachute Club of Am., 1966; cert. of record holder for high altitude sky diving State of Tex., 1966, 67; Cert. of Achievement, Tex. State Guard, 1968. Mem. ABA, Nat. Lawyers Assn., Plaintiff Trial Lawyers Assn., Internat. Platform Assn., Tex. Trial Attys. Assn., Assn. Trial Lawyers Am., Quiet Birdmen, Tex. Outdoor Writers Assn., NRA, Tex. Rifle Assn., Parachute Assn. Am., P51 Mustang Pilots Assn., Phi Alpha Delta, U.S. Senatorial Club, U.S. Parachute Club (Monterey, Calif.). Avocations: shooting, hunting, fishing, flying, sports. Achievements: atty. (2 Tex. landmark cases) securing custody of female child for stepfather against natural parents, securing outside jail work program for convicted man, others. Office: PO Box 59462 Dallas TX 75229

WILKINS, WILLIAM S., insurance company executive; b. Wyandotte, Mich., Aug. 30, 1942; m. Karen Wilkins, June 14, 1969. A.S. in Engring., Henry Ford Coll., 1966; degree in bus. adminstrn. Wayne State U., 1970; exec. program Stanford U., 1986. Programmer, Uniroyal, Inc., Allen Park, Mich., 1966-70; v.p. D.P. Alexander Hamilton Life, Farmington, Mich., 1970-80, John Alden Life, Miami, Fla., 1980—, sr. v.p., chief info. officer, bd. dirs., pres., chief exec. officer John Alden Systems Co; exec. v.p. Continental Life & Accident, Boise, 1982-85. Office: John Alden Fin Corp 7300 Corp Ctr Dr Miami FL 33120

WILKINSON, DANIEL FRANCIS, investment counselor; b. Charleston, Ill., Aug. 28, 1940; s. Leonard Quay and Grace Eloise (Whitlock) W.; m. Candace Lee Hughes, Sept. 21, 1971; children: Scott Lee, Todd Curtis, Kyle Cushing, Melissa Bowquay. BS, U. Indpls., 1963; postgrad., N.Y. Inst. Fin., 1981. Cert. fin. planner. Supt. sales Coll./Univ. Corp., Indpls., 1963-70; dir. equity sales Hamilton Funding Corp., Farmington, Mich., 1970-73; v.p. Pioneer Group, Boston, 1973—; pres. Wilkinson Fin. Corp., Phoenix, 1981—; guest lectr. Ariz. State U., Tempe, 1981—; mem. adv. com. Ariz. Securities Div., Phoenix, 1984—. With U.S. Army, 1965-67. Named to Internat. Assocs., Fin. Svc. Corp., Atlanta, 1981, 82, 83, 84. Mem. Inst. Cert. Fin. Planners (regional chmn. 1987-88), Internat. Assn. Fin. Planning (pres. 1980, Mem. of Yr. 1980). Republican. Unitarian. Home: 5539 E Sanna St Paradise Valley AZ 85253 Office: Wilkinson Fin Corp 6991 E Camelback Rd #D 212 Scottsdale AZ 85251

WILKINSON, DAVID ANTHONY, finance company executive; b. London, Dec. 2, 1951; came to U.S., 1977; s. Clifford A. and B. Margaret (Boult) W.; m. Marianne C. Heilmann, Jan. 2, 1982; children: Charles, James. BS in Biol. Scis. with honors, U. East Anglia, 1973; MS in Econs., U. London, 1977. Mgmt. trainee Unilever Ltd., London and Gloucester, Eng., 1973-75; cons. Boston Cons. Group, Boston and London, 1977-82; asst. to pres. City Investing Co., N.Y.C., 1982-85; v.p. Home Group Inc., N.Y.C., 1985—; bd. dirs. Hoover Group, Roswell, Ga., Am. Techs. Inc., Bloomfield Hills, Mich. Mem. Explorers Club, Greenwich Country Club, Lansdowne Club. Home: Piping Brook E Middle Patent Rd Bedford NY 10506 Office: Home Group Inc 59 Maiden Ln 27th Floor New York NY 10038

WILKINSON, DONALD LLOYD, treasurer, lawyer, accountant; b. Jasper, Tex., June 26, 1937; s. Charlie Mack and Francis Juanita (Brannon) W.; m. Carolyn Copeland, July 31, 1965; children: Wendy LaFaun, Matthew Monroe. BBA in Acctg., Lamar U., 1959; JD, South Tex. Coll., 1975. Bookkeeper Henry Kory, Beaumont, Tex., 1957-58; field agt. IRS, Corpus Christi, Tex., 1959-60, Houston, 1962-71; asst. sec., treas. Gulf Ports Crating Co., Houston, 1971-82; controller Champion Mfg., Houston, 1982; asst. controller Superior Derrick & Subs., Houston, 1982-83; pvt. practice acctg. Houston, 1982-83; treas., v.p. Morris Export & Subs., Houston, 1983—. With U.S. Army, 1960-62, ETO. Mem. ABA, Tex. Bar Assn., Export Packers Assn. (treas., pres., v.p. 1975-78).

WILKINSON, EUGENE PARKS, nuclear engineer; b. Long Beach, Calif., Aug. 10, 1918; s. Dennis William and Daisy Amelia (Parks) W.; m. Janice Edith Thuli, Mar. 28, 1942; children: Dennis Eugene, Stephen James, Marian Lynn, Rodney David. AB in Chemistry, San Diego State U., 1938. Instr. chemistry San Diego State U., 1938-39; commd. ensign U.S. Navy, 1940, advanced through grades to vice adm., 1970; served various locations including 1st comdg. officer USS Nautilus (1st nuclear-powered submarine), 1953-57; 1st comdg. officer USS Long Beach, 1959-63, 1st nuclear-powered surface ship; ret. 1974; exec. v.p. Data Design Labs., Cucamonga, Calif., 1977-80; pres., chief exec. officer Inst. Nuclear Power Ops., Atlanta, 1980-84, pres. emeritus, 1984—; bd. dirs. Commonwealth Edison Co., Chgo., Data Design Labs., Advanced Resource Devel. Corp., Columbia, Md., Mgmt. Analysis Co., San Diego, chmn. bd. Decorated Legion of Merit, Silver Star, D.S.M. with three oak leaf clusters, others, Order Sacred Treasure Japan; recipient George Westinghouse Gold medal ASME, 1983, Oliver Townsend medal Atomic Indsl. Forum, 1984. Mem. Am. Soc. Naval Engrs., Am. Nuclear Soc., Navy League, Submarine League (bd. dirs. 1985—), Rotary. Home: 1449 Crest Rd Del Mar CA 92014

WILL, JAMES FREDRICK, steel company executive; b. Pitts., Oct. 12, 1938; s. Fred F. and Mary Agnes (Ganter) W.; m. Mary Ellen Bowser, Dec. 19, 1964; children: Mary Beth, Kerry Ann. BSEE, Pa. State U., 1961; MBA, Duquesne U., 1972. Works mgr. Kaiser Steel Corp., Fontana, Calif., 1976-78, v.p. ops., 1978-80, v.p. planning, 1980-81, exec. v.p., 1981, pres., 1981-82; exec. v.p., pres. indsl. group Cyclops Corp., Pitts, 1982-86; pres., chief operating officer Cyclops Corp., Pitts., 1986-88, pres., chief exec. officer, 1989—. Mem. AIME, Assn. Iron and Steel Engrs. Home: 1521 Candlewood Dr Pittsburgh PA 15241 Office: Cyclops Corp 650 Washington Rd Pittsburgh PA 15228

WILL, THOMAS JOSEPH, engineering services executive; b. Evansville, Ind., June 20, 1939; s. Paul Henry and Margaret Frances (Clark) W.; m. Colleen R. Toohey, Sept. 27, 1958; children: Thomas J. II, Cheryl A. Will, Deborah L. Will Valenti, Paul Henry II. BSEE, U. N.Mex., 1965; MSEE, U.S. Naval Post Grad. Sch., Monterey, Calif., 1973, MS in Mgmt., 1974. Commd. ensign USN, 1965, advanced through grades to lt. comdr., 1973, ret., 1978; exec. v.p. Analysis & Tech., Inc., North Stonington, Conn., 1978—. Scoutmaster Boy Scouts Am., Fed. Republic Germany, 1969-71, asst. scoutmaster, Prundale, Calif., 1971-74; coach Babe Ruth Little League, Waterford, Conn., 1975-82. Mem. Navy League, Navy Submarine League, Am. Def. Preparedness Assn., Armed Forces Communications Engring. Assn. Republican. Office: Analysis & Tech Inc Rte 2 Box 220 Technology Park North Stonington CT 06359

WILLARD, H(ARRISON) ROBERT, electrical engineer; b. Seattle, May 31, 1933; s. Harrison Eugene and Florence Linea (Chelquist) W.; B.S.E.E., U. Wash., 1955, M.S.E.E., 1957, Ph.D., 1971. Staff asso. Boeing Sci. Research Labs., Seattle, 1959-64; research asso. U. Wash., 1968-72, sr. engr. and research prof. applied physics lab., 1972-81; sr. engr. Boeing Aerospace Co., Seattle, 1981-84; dir. instrumentation and engring. MetriCor Inc. (previously Tech. Dynamics, Inc.), 1984—. Served with AUS, 1957-59. Lic. profl. engr., Wash. Mem. IEEE, Am. Geophys. Union, Phi Beta Kappa, Sigma Xi, Tau Beta Pi. Contbr. articles to tech. jours. Patentee in field. Office: 18800 142d Ave NE Ste 4 Woodinville WA 98072

WILLARD, JOHN GERARD, consultant, author, lecturer; b. Pitts., Nov. 20, 1952; s. Cornelius Merle and May E. (Hinds) W.; BA in Journalism, Duquesne U., Pitts., 1974; m. Lorraine L. Franze, Sept. 2, 1978; children: Mary Elizabeth, Kristen Anne, Lisa Lorraine, Jessica Kathleen. Producer, dir. air talent Sta. WDUQ-FM, Pitts., 1971-73; master control tech. dir. Sta. KDKA-TV, Pitts., 1973; cons. communications Better Bus. Bur., Pitts., 1974; asst. account exec. Marc & Co., Advt., Pitts., 1975; adminstr. employee benefit adminstrn. Rockwell Internat. Corp., Pitts., 1975-80, adminstr. relocation and corp. personnel procedures, 1980-81, mgr. corp. policy, 1981-82; pres. John G. Willard Cons., 1982—. Contbr. articles in field. Mem. Am. Mensa Ltd., Internat. Platform Assn., Smithsonian Nat. Instn., Nat. Rifle Assn. (markmanship instr.), Stage 62, Kappa Tau Alpha, Alpha Tau Omega. Office: 360 Middlegate Dr Bethel Park PA 15102

WILLARD, ROBERT STEPHEN, marketing executive; b. N.Y.C., Sept. 9, 1944; s. Robert Sherman and Elizabeth A. (McGuire) W.; m. Carolyn Ruth Crouse, May 30, 1970; children: Kathryn Leslie, Christopher Patrick, Matthew Simon. BS, Georgetown U., 1966, MSA, 1979. Assoc. exec. dir. Georgetown U. Alumni Assn., Washington, 1970-76; asst. spl. projects U.S. Rep. Jim Attox, Washington, 1977; dir. Data Processing Mgmt. Assn., Washington, 1977-78; v.p. govt. relations Info. Industry Assn., Washington, 1978-85; dir. govt. markets Mead Data Cen., Inc., Dayton, Ohio, 1985—; organizer Info. Policy Discussion Group, Washington, 1978-84; chmn. Capitol Hill Hi-Tech Expo, Washington, 1985. Mng. editor: Understanding U.S. Information Policy, 1982. Treas. Adv. Neighborhood Commn., D.C., 1976-77. Capt. U.S. Army, 1966-70. Mem. Am. Soc. Info. Sci., ALA, Assn. Am. Lobbyists. Democrat. Home: 9250 Clyo Rd Spring Valley OH 45370 Office: Mead Data Cen Inc PO Box 933 Dayton OH 45401

WILLAX, PAUL ANTHONY, bank executive, economist, journalist; b. Buffalo, May 26, 1939; s. Oscar W. and Celia G. (Kubanek) W.; children: Jennifer Lee, Jonathan Paul. BS, Canisius Coll., Buffalo, 1961, LHD (hon.), 1986; MBA, SUNY, Buffalo, 1967. Instr. econs. SUNY, Buffalo, 1961-62, adj. prof., 1986—; economist, dir. research and edn. Buffalo Area C. of C., 1962-67; exec. dir. N.Y. State Joint Legis. Com., Albany, 1968-69; chmn. bd., chief exec. officer Empire of Am. FSA, Buffalo, 1967—, also bd. dirs.; exec. dir. Ctr. for Entrepreneurial Leadership, Buffalo, 1986—; chmn. bd. Kazoo Co., Inc., Eden, N.Y., 1972-85, Ecol. Dynamics Corp.; pres. Oscar Willax & Son, Inc., Willax Dry Goods, Inc.; pres., bd. dirs. Electromedia Techs., Inc.; mem. adv. bd. New Eng. Life Ins. Co., 1987—; bd. dirs. Millard Fillmore Hosps., Adam, Meldrum & Anderson Co.; adj. lectr., 1969-83. Author: An Economic Analysis of New York State: Its Metropolitan Areas, 1973, Aspects of Venture Feasibility Analyses, 1973, Service Planning for the Retail Marketplace, 1976, Preparing for the New Role of the Militia, 1977, Liability Management in Perspective, 1978, Preparing for the 1980's, 1980, A Survivor's Guide to Coping with the Future, 1981; editor: Bus. Briefs, 1962-67, Update, 1970-75, Bankers' Markets, 1977-78; producer radio and TV series, 1962—; host TV series Minding Everybody's Business, 1981—; columnist Buffalo Evening News, 1974-76, Am. Banker, 1976—. Econ. counsel N.Y. State Constnl. Conv., 1967; chmn. fin. com., mem. exec. com. Erie County Rep. Com., 1979—; mem. Gov.'s Council on State Priorities, 1982. Served as brig. gen. N.Y. N.G., 1957—. Recipient Outstanding Service award Buffalo Area C. of C., 1969, Disting. Alumni award Canisius Coll., Service and Leadership award Savs. Instns. Mktg. Soc. Am., 1976, Americanism award Freedoms Found., 1964, 76. Mem. Am. Econ. Assn., Am. Acad. Polit. and Social Sci., Am. Mktg. Assn., Young Pres.'s Orgn. Roman Catholic. Office: Empire of America FSA One Empire Tower Buffalo NY 14202

WILLBANKS, ROGER PAUL, publishing and book distributing company executive; b. Denver, Nov. 25, 1934; s. Edward James and Ada Gladys (Davis) W.; m. Beverly Rae Masters, June 16, 1957; children—Wendy Lee, Roger Craig. B.S., U. Denver, 1957, M.B.A., 1965. Economist, bus. writer, bus. forecaster Mountain States Telephone Co., Denver, 1959-66; dir. pub. relations Denver Bd. Water Commrs., 1967-70; pres. Royal Publs. Inc., Denver, 1971—, Nutri-Books Corp., Denver, 1971—, Inter-Sports Book and Video, 1986—. Editor Denver Water News, 1967-70, Mountain States Bus., 1962-66. Mem. Gov. of Colo.'s Revenue Forecasting Com., 1963-66. Served with U.S. Army, 1957-58. Recipient pub. relations award Am. Water Works Assn., 1970. Mem. Am. Booksellers Assn., Nat. Nutritional Foods Assn., Pub. Relations Soc. Am. (charter mem. health sect.), Denver C. of C., SAR. Republican. Lutheran. Clubs: Columbine Country, Denver Press, Auburn Cord Duesenberg, Rolls Royce Owners, Classic Car of Am., Denver U. Century (Denver). Address: Royal Publs Inc PO Box 5793 Denver CO 80217

WILLCOX, FREDERICK PRESTON, inventor; b. Los Angeles, Aug. 1, 1910; s. Frederick William and Kate Lillian (Preston) W.; m. Velma Rose Gander, 1935; 1 dau., Ann Louise. Grad. high sch. Self-employed research and devel. engr. and cons., 1939-51; govt. cons., 1949-50, 61-65; tech. v.p. Fairchild Camera & Instrument Corp., 1951-60; inventor, researcher, developer, New Canaan, Conn., 1960—. Holder over 90 patents in photog., graphic arts and data communications equipment, high speed teleprinters and typewriters; photography work exhibited Smithsonian Gallery. Served to maj. U.S. Army, 1940-45. Recipient Sherman Fairchild Photogrammetric award Am. Soc. Photogrammetry, 1951. Fellow AAAS; mem. Am. Soc. Photogrammetry and Remote Sensing, Soc. Photog. Scientists and Engrs., ASME, AIAA, Optical Soc. Am., Am. Def. Preparedness Assn. Episcopalian. Avocations: machine sculpture, photography. Home and Office: 565 Oenoke Ridge New Canaan CT 06840

WILLES, MARK HINCKLEY, food industry executive; b. Salt Lake City, July 16, 1941; s. Joseph Simmons and Ruth (Hinckley) W.; m. Laura Fayone, June 7, 1961; children: Wendy Anne, Susan Kay, Keith Mark, Stephen Joseph, Matthew Bryant. AB, Columbia U., 1963, PhD, 1967. Mem. staff banking and currency com. Ho. of Reps., Washington, 1966-67; asst. prof. fin. U. Pa., Pitts., 1967-69; economist Fed. Res. Bank, Phila., 1967, sr. economist, 1969-70, dir. research, 1970-71, v.p., dir. research, 1971, 1st v.p., 1971-77; pres. Fed. Res. Bank of Mpls., 1977-80; exec. v.p., chief fin. officer Gen. Mills, Inc., Mpls., 1980-85, pres., 1985—. Office: Gen Mills Inc 1 General Mills Blvd Minneapolis MN 55426

WILLETT, ROSLYN LEONORE, public relations executive, food service consultant; b. N.Y.C., Oct. 18, 1924; d. Edward and Celia (Stickler) S.; m. Edward Willett (seperated); 1 child, Jonathan Stanley. BA, Hunter Coll., N.Y.C., 1944; postgrad., Columbia U., 1944, CUNY, 1947-48, NYU, 1947-48, 52. Dietitian YWCA, N.Y.C., 1944; tech. and patents libr. Stein Hall & Co., N.Y.C., 1944-46, food technologist tech. svcs. and devel. dept., 1946-48; editor McGraw-Hill, Inc., N.Y.C., 1949-50, Harcourt Brace Jovanovich, Inc., N.Y.C., 1950-54; pub. rels. writer Farley Manning Assocs., N.Y.C., 1954-58; cons. pub. rels. and food svc. Roslyn Willett Assocs., Inc., N.Y.C., 1959—; adj. prof. Hunter Coll., 1955-56, Polytech. Univ., N.Y., 1981-82; lectr. in field. Author: The Woman Executive in Woman in Sexist Society, 1971. chmn. Woman's Polit. Caucus, Inc., N.Y., N.J., Conn., 1971-73; v.p. Mid Hudson Arts and Sci. Ctr., Poughkeepsie, N.Y.; bd. dirs. Small Bus. Task Force Assn. for Small Bus. and Professions, 1981-85, Regional Adv. Coun. Fed. Small Bus. Adminstrn., 1976-78, Rhinebeck Chamber Music Soc., 1985-86. Mem. Pub. Rels. Soc. Am. (accredited), Food Svc. Cons. Soc. Internat., N.Y. Acad. Scis., Inst. Food Technologists, Paris Club. Home: Hunn's Lake Rd Stanfordville NY 12581 Office: 441 West End Ave New York NY 10024

WILLEY, DONALD EDWARD, construction company executive, industrial engineer; b. Solley, Md., May 6, 1938; s. Neal Frederick and Anna Christina (Haslip) W.; m. Glenda Gail Russell, Jan. 8, 1959 (div. 1968); children: Donald Russell, Lori Lee; m. Cynthia Margaret Bull, June 14, 1970. BS in Indsl. Engring., Calif. West U., 1983; MS in Engring, Calif. Coast U., 1986. Sales rep. Cambridge Fin. Corp., Balt., 1960-62; owner Willey Bros. Constrn. Co., Balt., 1962-64; ironworker Local #16, Balt., 1964-77; v.p. Emarco Corp., Balt., 1977-83, v.p., corp. sec., dir. engring., 1983—; pres. Container Depot Inds., Balt., 1985—; ptnr. Real Estate Equipment & Machinery Assocs.; bd. dirs. Emarco Container Corp; pres. Internat. Cylinders Co. Mem. U.S. Congl. Adv. Bd., Washington, 1984—, NSC, Alexandria, Va. Served to sgt. USMC, 1956-60. Mem. Soc. Am. Mil. Engrs., Am. Soc. Mech. Engrs., Am. Welding Soc., Engring. Soc. Balto (bd. dirs., mem. com. 1984—), Nat. Rifle Assn. (life). Democrat. Roman Catholic. Club: Chartwell Golf and Country (Severna Park, Md.). Lodge: Masons. Home: 206 Oak Dr Pasadena MD 21122 Office: Emarco Corp 8211 Fischer Rd Baltimore MD 21222

WILLEY, JAMES PETERSON, management consultant; b. Logan, Utah, May 9, 1950; s. Lynn Robison and Marie (Peterson) W.; m. Marci Ann Movitz, Mar. 11, 1971; children: April, James Scott, Michelle, Jeffrey David. BS, Utah State U., 1972; MBA, Fla. Inst. Tech, 1980. Commd. U.S. Army, 1972, advanced through grades to maj.; comdr. hdqrs. and Main Co. U.S. Army, Ft. Hood, Tex., 1974-76; comdr. 48th Maint. Co. U.S. Army, Baumholder, Fed. Republic Germany, 1976-77; sec., gen. staff U.S. Army, Heidelberg, Fed. Republic Germany, 1977-79; resigned U.S. Army, 1983; asst. prof. N.C. State U., Raleigh, 1979-83; pres. MLV Inc., Raleigh, N.C., 1983-84; v.p. fin. Evergreen Mgmt. Corp., Southern Pines, N.C., 1984-88; v.p., gen. mgr. Distbn. Services, Inc., Atlanta, 1988—; cons. Miller/Zell Inc., Atlanta, 1985-88, Adcom, Inc., Detroit, 1988—, Ship Am. Freight Exeditors, Detroit, 1988—, Mail Am., Ft. Lauderdale; chief fin. officer JHC Enterprises Inc., Southern Pines, Car-Ten, Inc., Memphis, Fluid Services, Inc., Louisville. Chmn. Southern Pines Boy Scout Com., Raleigh Boy Scout Com. Named Top Developer Jiffy Lube Internat. Inc., 1984, 85. Mem. Am. Mgmt. Assn., Am. Equipment Lessors, Pi Sigma Alpha (v.p. 1971-72), Delta Sigma Phi (faculty advisor 1980-83), . Sandhills (N.C.) C. of C. (corp. rep.). Republican. Mormon. Home: 3591 Morishop Cove Marietta GA 30064

WILLEY, MYRTLE DENNEY, steel company executive; b. Jacksonville, Ill., July 7, 1918; d. Benjamin Harrison and Lora Edna (Burke) Denney; student Brown's Bus. Coll., 1935-36; m. George A. Corbett, Sept. 25, 1945 (div. 1964); 1 son, Michael Denney Corbett; m. Leland B. Willey, Sept. 14, 1972. Fashions buyer Emporium, Jacksonville, 1936-40; photographer Olin Mills Studio, Chattanooga, 1941-45; floor mgr. W.T. Grant Co., Jacksonville, 1945-50; with Peoples Water & Gas Co., Miami Beach, Fla., 1950-56; with T.W. Dick Co., Gardiner, Maine, 1956—, exec. v.p., 1968-76, pres., treas., gen. mgr., 1976—, owner, 1984—. corporator Gardiner Savs. Inst., 1974—. Chmn. fin. com., treas., exec. bd. Gardiner Gen. Hosp., 1975-80; treas. Gardiner Gen. Hosp. Women's Bd. Aux., 1973-80; budget com., dir. United Way, Augusta, Maine, 1975-81; pres. Kennebec Valley United Way, 1979-80; bd. dirs. Kennebec Valley Med. Ctr., 1980—, pres. Aux., 1980-82, 83—; mem. nat. women's bd. Northwood Inst., Midland, Mich., 1985—; patron Forum A, U. Maine, Augusta, 1974—, Portland (Maine) Symphony Orch., 1976—. Recipient Disting. Woman's medal Northwood Inst., 1985; appointed to Maine Commn. for Women Gov. John R. McKernan, 1988—, vice-chmn. Gov.'s Bus. Adv. Coun. Gov. McKernan, 1988—. Mem. Augusta Music Jazz Soc. (v.p. 1976—), Maine Good Roads Assn., Assn. Gen. Contractors, Small Bus. Assns. New Eng., Women Constrn. Owners and Execs. (v.p. 1984), Maine Soc. Entrepreneurs, Nat. Assn. Women in Constrn. (pres. chpt., mem. liaison com. 1982—), Maine State C. of C. (dir. 1979-82), Kennebec Valley C. of C. (dir. 1981—), Maine Better Transp. Assn. (v.p. 1983-85). Republican. Episcopalian. Club: Zonta (pres. 1981-83, Dist. I treas. 1982-86, lt. gov. 1987-88, gov. 1988—). Home: 2 Ash St Hallowell ME 04347 Office: 1 Summer St PO Box 60 Gardiner ME 04345

WILLIAMS, ARTHUR, III, financial analyst; b. Paterson, N.J.; s. Arthur and Eleanor (Schmitt) W.; m. Sandra C. Castaldo; children: Arthur IV, Melinda S., Thomas N. BA, Dartmouth Coll., 1963, MBA with distinction, 1964. Chartered fin. analyst. Dir. retirement plan investments McKinsey & Co., N.Y.C.; bd. dirs. Kemmerer Bottling Group, Joliet, Ill. Author: Managing Your Investment Manager. Dir. United Way Campaign, Summit, N.J., 1985. Mem. Inst. for Quantative Rsch. in Fin. (dir. 1982—), Fedn. Securities Analysts, Dartmouth Alumni Club (pres. 1972-84). Home: 8 Sunset Dr Summit NJ 07901 Office: McKinsey & Co 55 E 52nd St New York NY 10022

WILLIAMS, ASHTON STEELE, financial consultant, business broker; b. Abington, Pa., Sept. 14, 1960; s. Frank Barbar Williams and Alice Randle (Steele) Semke; m. Amy Delone, Nov. 17, 1984. Student, Roanoke Coll., 1979-80. Equity and options broker Janney Montgomery Scott, Phila., 1982-87; ptnr., pres. Wings Fin. Assn. Ltd., Phila., 1986-89; pres. ASW Enterprises Inc., Chadds Ford, Pa., 1989—. Active Gulph Mills (Pa.) Civic Assn., 1985—. Mem. Aircraft Owners and Pilots Assn. Republican. Episcopalian. Home: 370 Balligomingo Rd Gulph Mills PA 19428

WILLIAMS, BARRY LAWSON, real estate executive; b. N.Y.C., July 21, 1944; s. Otis Lenzy and Ilza Louise (Berry) W.; m. Adrienne Maria Foster, May 24, 1977; children: Barry C., Jaime, Andrew. AB, Harvard U., 1966, JD, 1971, MBA, 1971. Bar: Calif. 1975. Sr. cons. McKinsey & Co., San Francisco, 1971-78; mng. prin. Bechtel Investments Inc., San Francisco, 1979-87; pres. Williams Pacific Ventures Inc., Redwood City, Calif., 1987—; ptnr. WDG-Ventures, CAC, Redwood City, 1987—; pres. C.N. Flagg Inc., Meriden, Conn., 1988—; bd. dirs. Am. Pres. Co., Oakland, Calif., 1984—,

Northwestern Life Ins. Co., Milw., 1987—; chmn. bd. Pacific Presbyn. Med. Ctr., San Francisco, 1980—. Republican. Episcopalian. Office: Williams Pacific Ventures Inc 3 Lagoon Dr Suite 250 Redwood City CA 94065

WILLIAMS, CAROLYN ELIZABETH, manufacturing executive; b. Los Angeles, Jan. 24, 1943; d. George Kissam and Mary Eloise (Chamberlain) W.; m. Richard Terrill White, Apr. 9, 1972; children: Sarah Anne, William Daniel. BS, Ga. Inst. Tech., 1969; MM, Northwestern U., 1988. Saleswoman Ea. Airlines, Atlanta, Montreal (Can.) and Seattle, 1964-69; job analyst Allied Products Corp., Atlanta, 1969-70; mgr. Allied Products Corp., Frankfort, Mich., 1970-71; planning analyst, sr. planning analyst Allied Products Corp., Chgo., 1972-74, dir. planning, 1974-76, staff v.p. planning, 1976-79, v.p. planning and bus. research, 1979-86, v.p. corp. devel., chief planning officer, 1986—. Leader Girl Scouts U.S., Highland Park, Ill.; Sunday sch. tchr. Highland Park Presbyn. Ch. Office: Allied Products Corp 10 S Riverside Plaza Chicago IL 60606

WILLIAMS, CHARLES DAVID, oil and steel company executive; b. Mineola, Tex., July 16, 1935; s. Floyd L. and Audie N. (Hall) W.; m. Shirley R. Dodd, Jan. 31, 1954; children; Jan, Charles D. Jr. BS in Petroleum Engring., Tex. A&M U., 1957, MS in Petroleum Engring., 1959; MBA in Fin., So. Meth. U., 1971. Asst. to exec. v.p. Atlantic Richfield Co., N.Y.C., 1971-72; dir. planning Atlantic Richfield Co., Dallas, 1972-76; mgr. investor relations Atlantic Richfield Co., L.A., 1976-79; v.p. investor affairs Tex. Oil and Gas Corp., Dallas, 1979-86; v.p. investor relations USX Corp., Pitts., 1986—. Mem. Soc. Petroleum Engrs., N.Y. Soc. Security Analysts, Petroleum Investor Relations Assn., Sigma Xi, Beta Gamma Sigma. Republican. Baptist. Office: USX Corp 600 Grant St Pittsburgh PA 15230

WILLIAMS, CHARLES DUDLEY, engineering company executive; b. Uvalda, Ga., Oct. 19, 1933; s. Joel Dudley and Mary Louise (poore) W.; m. Janelle Foskey, Nov. 13, 1956; children: Jennifer, Roger Judd. BS in Civil Engring., Ga. Inst. Tech., 1961. Jr. engr. Brown Engring. Co., Huntsville, Ala., 1963-64; project structural engr. Concrete Materials Ga., Forest Park, Ga., 1964-66; project mgr. Gilbert/Commonwealth, Reading, Pa., 1966-71, Reading and Jackson, Mich., 1972-75; sr. project mgr. Gilbert/Commonwealth, Jackson, 1975-79, dir. projects, 1979-84; v.p., gen. mgr. power Gilbert/Commonwealth, Reading, Pa., 1984-86, pres., 1986—; project mgr. Hardaway Contracting Co., Columbus, Ga., 1971-72. Mem. ASCE. Republican. Methodist. Office: Gilbert/Commonwealth Inc PO Box 1498 Reading PA 19603

WILLIAMS, CHARLES LEE, corporate professional; b. Detroit, Jan. 27, 1947; s. Robert Henry III and Helen Mary (Stiefel) W.; m. Jewel Elizabeth Davis, June 19, 1971; children: Rachel, David, Jennifer, Nathan. BS, Wayne State U., 1968; MA, Chapman Coll., 1973; diploma, Air Command & Staff Coll., 1981. Cert. master navigator, 1984. Combat crew mem. Pacific Air Forces USAF, South East Asia, 1969-71; instr. navigator tng. sch. USAF, Mather, Calif., 1971-74; flight commdr. officer tng. sch. USAF, Lackland, Tex., 1974-77; group exec. officer, flight examiner 34th tactical airlift tng. group USAF, Little Rock, 1977-80; chief contr. 21st air force ops. ctr. USAF, McGuire, N.J., 1981-84; regional v.p. A.L. Williams Corp., Mount Holly, N.J., 1984-87; sr. v.p. A.L. Williams Corp., Moorestown, N.J., 1987—. Decorated Disting. Flying Cross, three Vietnam Air medals, Vietnamese Cross of Gallantry; Named Inst. of Yr., 1976. Republican. Assembly of God. Home: 11 Wendover Ct Mount Laurel NJ 08054 Office: A L Williams Corp 110 Marter Ave Ste 206 Moorestown NJ 08057

WILLIAMS, CHARLOTTE (BUNNY) BELL, sales and marketing executive; b. Houston, Mar. 29, 1944; d. Curtis Blucher and Annie Mae (Jacobs) Bell; m. Edward Arthur Williams, Oct. 24, 1980. Student, Tex. Christian U., 1962-63; BA, U. Tex., Dallas, 1977. Realtor James M. Brown Realtors, Tex., 1979-80; realtor, broker Hank Dickerson Realtors, Dallas, 1980-81, Merrill Lynch Realty, Plano, 1981-83; dir. mktg. KPT Inc., Dallas, 1984-88; pres. Re: Source, Dallas, 1988-89, The Direct Source Inc., Dallas, 1989—; speaker in field. Contbr. articles to profl. and popular jours. Patron Susan G. Komen Found., Dallas, 1987—; sponsor Dallas Women's Found., 1986—, 500 Inc., Dallas, 1987—; active Women's Found. Dallas, 1986—; co-chmn. Rolex/Corrigan's Cup Polo Ball, Dallas, 1989. Recipient Disting. Sales award Sales and Mktg. Execs., 1986, 87. Mem. AAUW, North Dallas Fin. Forum, Am. Soc. Profl. and Exec. Women, Data Processing Mgmt. Assn. (bd. dirs. 1980-88), Women in Direct Response, Direct Mktg. Assn. North Tex. (sec. 1988—), U.S. Polo Assn., Greater Dallas C. of C. Republican. Methodist. Home and Office: The Direct Source Inc 6508 Duffield Dr Dallas TX 75248-1314

WILLIAMS, DAVE HARRELL, investment executive; b. Beaumont, Tex., Oct. 5, 1932; s. George Davis and Mary (Hardin) W.; m. Reba White, Mar. 15, 1975. B.S. in Chem. Engring, U. Tex., 1956; M.B.A. (Baker scholar, Teagle fellow), Harvard U., 1961. Chartered fin. analyst. Chem. engr. Exxon Corp., Baton Rouge, 1959; security analyst deVegh & Co., N.Y.C., 1961-64; dir. research Waddell & Reed, Kansas City, Mo., 1964-67; exec. v.p. Mitchell Hutchins, Inc., N.Y.C., 1967-77; chmn. bd. Alliance Capital Mgmt. Corp., N.Y.C., 1977—; bd. dirs. Harvard Mgmt. Co. Contbr.: articles to Fin. Analysts Jour. Mem. mus. bd. Nat. Acad. Design; trustee Coll. Retirement Equities Fund. Served with USNR, 1956-59. Mem. Bond Club N.Y., Econ. Club N.Y., Fin. Analysts Fedn. (past officer, dir.), N.Y. Soc. Security Analysts (past pres.). Presbyterian. Clubs: Knickerbocker, Down Town Assn, Century Assn. Office: Alliance Capital Mgmt Corp 1345 Avenue of the Americas New York NY 10105

WILLIAMS, DAVID PERRY, manufacturing company executive; b. Detroit, Nov. 16, 1934; s. M.S. Perry and Virginia (Hayes) W.; m. Jill Schneider, July 27, 1972; children: Tracy, Perry, David, William, Nell. B.A., Mich. State U., 1956, M.B.A., 1964. V.p. sales Automotive div. Kelsey Hayes Co., Romulus, Mich., 1958-71; v.p., mgr. automotive product line ITT, N.Y.C., 1971-76; v.p., dir. Budd Co., Troy, Mich., 1976-79, sr. v.p. ops., dir., 1979-80, sr. v.p., chief ops. officer, 1980-86, pres., chief operating officer, dir., 1986—; chmn. Consortium for Human Devel., Troy, Mich., 1982—. Served to 1st lt. USAF, 1956-58. Mem. Soc. Automotive Engrs., Engring. Soc. Detroit, Soc. Mfg. Engrs., Nat. Assn. Mfrs. (bd. dirs. 1988—), PGA Nat. Club, Beta Gamma Sigma. Republican. Episcopalian. Clubs: Bloomfield Hills Country, Country of Detroit, Yondotega, Detroit Athletic; Royal and Ancient Golf Club of St. Andrews (Scotland). Home: 333 Lincoln St Grosse Pointe MI 48230 Office: The Budd Co 3155 Big Beaver Rd Box 2601 Troy MI 48084

WILLIAMS, DAVID SAMUEL, insurance company executive; b. Purcell, Okla., Oct. 16, 1926; s. David Skelton and Mattie Carolyn (Kimberlin) W.; m. Gloria Jean Trudgeon, Jan. 14, 1951; children: Mellanie K., David R., Gary B., Kimberly R. BA, U. Okla., 1950; LLB, LaSalle Extension U., 1968. With U.S. Fidelity & Guaranty Cos., various locations, 1952-74; asst. mgr. U.S. Fidelity & Guaranty Cos., Albuquerque, 1963-66; mgr. U.S. Fidelity & Guaranty Cos., San Jose, Calif., 1966-74; v.p. Eldorado Ins. Co., Palo Alto, Calif., 1974-77, exec. v.p., chief operating officer, 1977-78; v.p. Eldorado Mgmt. Co., Palo Alto, Calif., 1973-78, chief operating officer, exec. v.p., 1978; mng. dir. Eldorado Service Corp., 1974-76, exec. v.p., 1976-78; ptnr. William Ranch Co., 1977—, William Pecan Co., 1977—; owner David S. Williams and Assocs., 1988—; chmn. bd., pres. Homeland Gen. Corp., Homeland Ins. Co. and Homeland Indsl. Corp., San Jose, Calif., 1978—; pres. Homeland Mgmt. Corp. (Cayman) Ltd., 1980, Homeland Internat. (Bermuda) Ltd., 1982—; chmn. bd. On Line Ins. Systems, Inc., 1982—; underwriting mem. Lloyds of London, 1979—; adv. bd. Pacific Valley Bank, 1975—; tchr. Albuquerque U., 1957-58, N.Mex. U., 1958-59, bd. dirs. Fin. Guardian Group, Inc., Kansas City, Mo. Mem. indsl. panel Stanford Research Inst., 1968; mgmt. cons. County Santa Clara Edn. Dept., 1968-73; mem. Calif. adv. com. Ins. Services Office; bd. dirs. ins. council City of Hope, Los Angeles; committeeman pioneer council Boy Scouts Am., 1968. Served to maj. AC U.S. Army, 1944-46, 50-52. Recipient Outstanding Fieldman's award for N.Mex., N.Mex. Insurors Assn., 1959. Mem. Cen. Coast Fieldmen's Assn., Assn. Calif. Ins. Cos. (dir.), Sigma Alpha Epsilon. Lutheran. Clubs: San Jose Athletic, Rotary (pres. 1974); Univ. San Jose, British-Am., Center., San Francisco Comml. Home: 14198 Juniper Ln Saratoga CA 95070 Office: Homeland Internat Inc Palo Alto CA

WILLIAMS, DOLORES LOUISE, telecommunications executive; b. Rockford, Ill., Apr. 20, 1937; d. Arthur F. and Erma Lee (Johnson) Warner; divorced; 1 child, Leona Marie Williams Pierce. BE, Ottawa (Kans.) U., 1959. Cert. tchr., Kans., Tenn. Tchr., acting principal Navajo Indian Reservation, N.Mex. and Ariz., 1959-62; service rep. Ill. Bell., Rockford, 1972-74; sr. service rep. Michigan Bell, Jackson, 1964-67; sr. service rep. South Central Bell, Memphis, 1967-70, unit supr. bus. office, 1974-81; asst. sales mgr. AT&T and South Central Bell, Nashville and Memphis, 1981—; asst. dir. HWPC Child Care Tng. Program, Memphis, 1970-71; dir. Shelby County Headstart, Memphis, 1971-73. Recipient Outstanding Service award Warren Headstart Ctr., Memphis, 1973, Bell System Eagle award, 1981. Mem. Am. Mgmt. Assn., NAACP, NSV Urban League, Robertson Assn. Jehovah's Witness. Home: 500 Michele Dr Antioch TN 37013

WILLIAMS, DONALD CLINTON, management consultant; b. St. Louis, Feb. 27, 1929; s. R. Arthur and Deborah (Catlin) W.; B.A., Hamilton Coll., 1951; M.B.A., Harvard U., 1953; m. Suzanne Talbot, Aug. 10, 1957; children—Donald Clinton, Bradford H., Bruce T. Sales rep. U.S. Steel Corp., Detroit, 1957-62; gen. mgr. Mich. div. Interstate United Corp., Detroit, 1962-65; with Heidrick & Struggles, Inc., 1965-78, sr. v.p., mgr. Midwest, dir., Chgo., 1973-78; pres. Donald Williams Assocs., Inc., Chgo., 1978—; dir. Cavendish Investing Ltd. Mem. adv. bd. Outward Bound, 1982—. Served with USNR, 1953-56. Mem. Alpha Delta Phi. Clubs: Paradise Valley Country, Glen View; Chicago, Economic, Harvard Bus. Sch. (Chgo. and Phoenix). Home: 8717 N 69th St Paradise Valley AZ 85253 Office: 303 W Madison Ste 1900 Chicago IL 60606

WILLIAMS, DORIS TERRY, institution director; b. Middleburg, N.C., Oct. 26, 1951; d. Robert and Lucy (Hargrove) Terry; m. Thomas Williams, Aug. 29, 1981 (div. 1986); children: Adriel Lemuel, Ariel LaShawn. BA, Duke U., 1972; MEd, N.C. State U., 1976, PhD in Edn., 1983. Pub. relations N.C. Blue Cross/Blue Shield, 1972; tech. writer pub. relations Floyd B. McKissick Enterprises, Soul City, N.C., 1972-73; instr., counselor Vance-Granville Community Coll., Henderson, N.C., 1973-75, dir. adult basic edn., 1975-82, counselor, 1982-84; instr. Shaw U., Raleigh, N.C., 1978-83; assoc. dir. N.C. Health Manpower Devel. Co., Chapel Hill, N.C., 1984-87; dir. N.C. Ctr. for the Study Of Black History, N.C. Cen. U., Durham, 1987—, prin., Pen & Press Inc., 1987—; co-owner Pen & Press United and Ednl. Cons. Contbr., editor Oracles of Truth, 1983—; cons. in field. Sec. bd. dirs. Sound and Print United Sta. WVSP, 1973—; mem. N.C. Black Women's Polit. Congress, Warren County, 1985, Warren County Bd. edn., 1988; chairperson Warren County Polit. Action Com. Subcom. on Edn.; bd. dirs. N.C. Ctr. Literacy Devel., Creative Learning Ctr.; mem. N.C. Black Leadership Caucus, adv. bd. Sta. WSHA-FM; sec. Vance County Task Force on Domestic Violence, Vance County Task Force on Delinquency Prevention; mem. Warren County (N.C.) Bd. Edn. Mem. Nat. Minority Health Affairs Assn., Nat. Assn. Female Execs., Am. Assn. Adult and Continuing Edn. Democrat. Mem. Apostolic Ch. Avocations: writing, travel, reading, acting. Home: PO Box 465 Manson NC 27553 Office: Pen & Press United 304-D Hillsboro St Oxford NC 27565 other: NC Cen U Ctr for Study Black History 521 Nelson St Durham NC 27707

WILLIAMS, DOUGLAS, management consultant; b. Newburgh, N.Y., Oct. 13, 1912; s. Everett Frank and Marjorie Tuthill W.; m. Esther Grant, Sept. 23, 1939; children: Penelope Williams Winters, Grant. AB, Cornell U., 1934; MBA, Harvard U., 1936. With Air Reduction Co., 1936-37, Am. Inst. Pub. Opinion, 1938, Elmo Roper Co., 1939-40; assoc. dir. Nat. Opinion Research Ctr., U. Denver, 1940-42; pres. Douglas Williams Assos., Carefree, Ariz. and N.Y.C., 1948—. Pres. Community Chest, Larchmont, N.Y., 1959; bd. mgrs. West Side YMCA, N.Y.C., 1957-60; mem. nat. adv. bd. Heard Mus.; mem. Ariz. State U. Council of 100, Ariz. State U. Council of Emeritus Advisers, Foothills Com. Adv. Council. Served to lt. col. U.S. Army, 1942-45. Republican. Episcopalian. Clubs: Larchmont Yacht, Desert Mountain, Garden of the Gods, Harvard, Union League, Cornell, Winged Foot Golf, Desert Forest Golf, Ariz. Home: 7612 E Horizon Dr PO Box 941 Carefree AZ 85377 Office: Exec Ctr PO Box 941 Carefree AZ 85377

WILLIAMS, DOYLE Z., administrator, educator; b. Shreveport, La., Dec. 18, 1939; s. Nuell O. and Lurline (Isbell) W.; m. Maynette Derr, Aug. 20, 1967; children: Zane Derr, Elizabeth Marie. B.S., Northwestern State U., 1960; M.S. in Acctg., La. State U., 1962, Ph.D., 1965. C.P.A., La., Tex. Mgr. spl. edn. projects Am. Inst. C.P.A.'s, N.Y.C., 1967-69; assoc. prof. Tex. Tech. U., Lubbock, 1969-71, prof. acctg., 1972-73, coordinator, prof. area acctg., 1973-78; prof. acctg. U. So. Calif., L.A., 1978—, dean Sch. Acctg., 1986-88; vis. prof. U. Hawaii, Honolulu, 1971-72. Author over 30 jour. articles and books. Named Mem. Yr. Nat. Assn. Accts., 1967; named Outstanding Acctg. Educator Beta Alpha Psi, 1982, Disting. mem. faculty Calif. C.P.A. Found., 1983. Mem. Am. Acctg. Assn. (dir. edn. 1973-75, pres. 1984-85), AICPA (council 1983-89, v.p. 1987-88, bd. dirs. 1987-89), Fedn. Schs. Accountancy (pres. 1982), Adminstrs. Acctg. Programs (pres. 1977-78). Lodge: Rotary. Home: 3867 Tiffany Ct Torrance CA 90905 Office: U of So Calif Sch Bus Adminstrn University Park Los Angeles CA 90089

WILLIAMS, EARLE CARTER, professional services company executive; b. Selma, Ala., Oct. 15, 1929; s. Henry Earle and Nora Elizabeth (Carter) W.; m. June Esther Anson, Sept. 7, 1951; children: Gayle Marie, Carol Patrice, Sharon Elaine. B.E.E., Auburn U., 1951; postgrad., U. N.Mex., 1959-62. Registered profl. engr., N.Mex. Utilities design engr. Standard Oil Co. Ind., Whiting, 1954-56; mem. tech. staff Sandia Corp., Albuquerque, 1956-62; sr. engr. BDM Internat., Inc., El Paso, Tex., 1962-64; spl. projects dir. BDM Internat., Inc., 1964-66, dir. ops., 1966-68; v.p., gen. mgr. BDM Internat., Inc., Vienna, Va., 1968-72; pres., chief exec. officer BDM Internat., Inc., Vienna and McLean, Va., 1972—; also dir. BDM Internat., Inc.; mem. Naval Research Adv. Com., 1984—, chmn. 1986—; mem. Am. Bus. Conf., 1982-88, dir., 1985-88; bd. dirs. Greater Washington Bd. Trade, 1985-86. Exec. com., steering com. El Paso Community Coll., 1968-69, trustee, 1969-70; commr. Fairfax County Econ. Devel. Authority, 1976-80, chmn., 1978-80; mem. Va. State Bd. for Community Colls., 1980-87; bd. dirs. Cen. Va. Ednl. TV Corp., 1978-87; chmn. George Mason Inst. Indsl. Policy Bd., 1982—; bd. dirs. Wolf Trap Found., 1984—, vice chmn., 1985-87, chmn. 1988—; trustee Va. Found. for Ind. Colls., 1984-87; dir. The Atlantic Council of the U.S., 1987—. With AUS, 1951-53. Mem. Profl. Services Council (dir. 1974—, pres. 1976-79), Am. Mgmt. Assn., Armed Forces Communications and Electronics Assn. (dir. 1978-82, 86-87, internat. v.p. 1979-82, 84-85, chmn. 1988—, Dist. Service award 1987), NSPE, Pres. Assn., Am. Def. Preparedness Assn. (dir. 1984—, vice chmn. 1985-87), Fairfax County C. of C. (dir. 1976-86), Eta Kappa Nu. Presbyterian. Clubs: City, (Washington), Metropolitan (Washington). Office: BDM Internat Inc 7915 Jones Branch Dr McLean VA 22102

WILLIAMS, EDSON POE, retired automotive company executive; b. Mpls., July 31, 1923; s. Homer A. and Florence C. Williams; m. Irene Mae Streed, June 16, 1950; children: Thomas, Louise, Steven, Linnea, Elisa. B.S.M.E. cum laude, U. Minn., 1950. Spl. purpose machinery operator 1946-50; mfg. mgr., project engr. Crestliner div. Bigelow Sanford Inc., 1950-53, v.p., mgr. mfg. and engring., 1953-58, pres., 1958-63; with Ford Motor Co., 1963-87, mgr. customer svc. div., 1973; gen. mgr. Ford Motor Co. (Ford Mexico), 1973-75; pres. Ford Motor Co. (Ford Mid-East & Africa), 1975-82, Ford Motor Co. (Ford Asia-Pacific Inc.), 1979-87; v.p. Ford Motor Co., 1975-82, v.p.-gen. mgr. N.Am. truck ops., 1982-86, v.p. Ford Diversified Products ops., 1986-87. Served with USAAF, 1942-46. Mem. Fairlane Club, Collier Athletic Club. Home: 32808 Outland Trail Birmingham MI 48010 also: 606 21st Ave S Naples FL 33940 Office: Am Rd Rm 423 Dearborn MI 48121

WILLIAMS, EDWARD DAVID, data processing executive; b. Scranton, Pa., June 20, 1932; s. David Thomas and Mabel (Sims) W.; B.B.A., Hofstra U., 1960; postgrad. in Bus. Adminstrn., Fairleigh Dickenson U., 1979; m. Natalie Imnadze, Oct. 18, 1952; children—Denise, Claudia. Cons., Cresap, McCormick and Paget, N.Y.C., 1964-65; sr. mgmt. cons. Union Carbide Corp., N.Y.C., 1965-67; asst. controller data processing Western Union, N.Y.C., 1967-69; v.p. mgmt. info. systems ABC, Hackensack, N.J., 1970-86; v.p., chief info. officer Blue Cross Blue Shield of N.J., Newark, 1986—. Served with U.S. Army, 1948-52. Decorated Silver Star with oak leaf cluster, Bronze Star with V, Purple Heart with 2 oak leaf clusters. Mem. adv. bd. YMCA. Mem. Soc. Mgmt. Info. Systems, N.J. C. of C., Profit Oriented Systems Planning Bd. (bd. dirs.). Republican. Club: Masons. Speaker in field. Office: Blue Cross & Blue Shield NJ 12 Vreeland Rd Florham Park NJ 07932

WILLIAMS, EDWARD EARL, JR., educator, financial executive; b. Houston, Aug. 21, 1945; s. Edward Earl and Doris Jewel (Jones) W.; m. Susan M. Warren, June 28, 1983; children—Laura Michelle, David Brian. B.S. (Benjamin Franklin scholar, Jesse Jones scholar), U. Pa., 1966; Ph.D. (Tex. Savs. and Loan League fellow, NDEA fellow), U. Tex., 1968. Asst. prof. econs. Rutgers U., New Brunswick, N.J., 1968-70; asso. prof. fin. McGill U., Montreal, Que., Can., 1970-73; v.p., economist Service Corp. Internat., Houston, 1973-77; prof. adminstrv. sci. Rice U., Houston, 1978-82, Henry Gardiner Symonds prof., 1982—; chmn. bd. Service Tech. Internat., Inc., Houston, 1976—; chmn. bd., pres. Tex. Capital Investment Advisers, 1979—; chmn. bd. First Tex. Venture Capital Corp., 1983—; dir. Equus Capital Corp., Yellow Cab Service Corp., Video Rental of Pa. Inc., Associated Bldg. Services Co.; investment com. Service Corp. Internat. Mem. Fin. Mgmt. Assn., Internat. Platform Assn., Beta Gamma Sigma, Alpha Kappa Psi. Author: An Integrated Analysis for Managerial Finance, 1970; Investment Analysis, 1974; Business Planning for the Entrepreneur, 1983; contbr. articles to profl. jours. Home: 12903 Forest Meadow Dr Cypress TX 77429 Office: Rice U Jesse H Jones Grad Sch Adminstrn Houston TX 77001

WILLIAMS, FRANK ROWLANDS, III, food service management executive; b. Buffalo, Sept. 14, 1942; s. Frank Rowlands Jr. and Sydney Jean (Davies) W.; m. Florence Ann Farrell, July 20, 1963; children: Frank R. IV, John F., Kimberley. AAS, Erie Community Coll., 1962; BS, SUNY, Buffalo, 1970. Mgr. Service Systems Corp., Buffalo, 1968-70, dir. ops., 1970-72, regional dir., 1972-74, nat. sch. dir., 1974-77, adminstrv. dir., 1977-79; regional v.p. Service Systems Corp., Pasadena, Calif., 1979-84; corp. v.p. Service Systems Corp., Buffalo, 1984-87; regional v.p. Marriott Corp., Buffalo, 1987—; mem. food mgmt. program bd. Villa Maria Coll., Buffalo, 1974-79, food systems mgmt. bd. Buffalo State U., 1975-81. Bd. dirs. Grand Island Christian Sch., Grand Island, N.Y., 1978-79; trustee Bible Presbyn. Ch., Grand Island, 1976—, elder, 1987-88, supt. Sunday sch., 1988. Mem. N.Y. State Restaurant Assn., Nat. Restaurant Assn. Home: 111 Dolphin Dr Grand Island NY 14072 Office: Marriott Corp PO Box 352 Buffalo NY 14240

WILLIAMS, GARY ALAN, management consultant; b. Houston, May 24, 1950; s. Jesse W. and Bertha M. (Collins) W.; m. Valerie A. Newman, Aug. 25, 1973; children: Jordan P., Jacqueline Blair. BBA, U. Tex., 1972. Mktg. rep. IBM, Houston, 1973-75, project leader, 1975-78; mktg. mgr. IBM, Dallas, 1978-80; mgr. Coopers & Lybrand, Dallas, 1980-82, dir., 1982-84, ptnr., 1984—; council U. Tex. Info. Systems Adv. Council, Austin, Tex., 1985—. Bd. dirs. U.S.A. Film Festival, Dallas, 1988. Democrat. Methodist. Office: Coopers & Lybrand 1999 Bryan St Ste 3000 Dallas TX 75201

WILLIAMS, GENA KAY, automotive dealership executive; b. Fairfax, Va., Apr. 12, 1963; d. Leon Ellis and Vena Pearl (Hicks) W. BS, U. Ariz., 1981; postgrad. Hofstra U., 1983; student in Archtl. Drafting, ITT Tech. Inst., Sacramento, 1988—. Cert. mgmt acctg., internal auditor. Controller TGI Friday's, Tuscon, Ariz., Westbury, N.Y., 1980-83; auto dealer, bus. mgr. Williams, Inc., Hampton, Va., 1983—. ROTC scholar U. Ariz., Tucson, 1979. Mem. Peninsula Assn. Credit Execs., Internat. Freelance Photography Assn., Nat. Assn. Accts., Nat. Assn. Female Execs., Am. Mgmt. Assn., Peninsula Women's Network, Intertel, Triple Nine Soc., Mensa. Republican. Presbyterian. Lodge: Rosicrucians, Martinist. Avocations: photography, skiing, violin, languages.

WILLIAMS, GORDON BRETNELL, construction company executive; b. Phila., Apr. 3, 1929; s. Thomas W. and Helen (Berryman) W.; m. Susan M. Cunningham, June 20, 1953; children: Lucy Chase, Marcus Bretnell. B.S., Yale, 1951. Registered profl. engr., Mich., Ohio, Tex. Chief indsl. engr. Chrysler Corp., Detroit, 1954-57; pres., dir. Cunningham-Limp Co., Birmingham, Mich., 1957-76; v.p.-mktg. H.K. Ferguson Co., Cleve., 1976-78; pres. H.K. Ferguson Co., 1979-85, vice chmn., 1986—. Bd. dirs. St. Vincent Charity Hosp. and Health Center, Cleve. Served as ensign, ordnance USNR, 1952-54. Mem. Phi Gamma Delta. Clubs: Union (Cleve.); Yale of Ohio. Home: 12700 Lake Ave Lakewood OH 44107 Office: HK Ferguson Co One Erieview Pla Cleveland OH 44114

WILLIAMS, HARRY JOHN, JR., accountant; b. Marion, Ill., Mar. 10, 1924; s. Harry John and Helita (Durham) W.; BBA, Tulane U., 1948; m. Joanne Elizabeth Schwartz, Nov. 1, 1947 (dec. Jan. 29, 1985); children: Kathleen W. Thompson, Marianne W. Antoine, Barbara W. Moose, Harry John III; m. Mary Elizabeth Spencer, July 3, 1985. With Peat, Marwick, Mitchell and Co., St. Louis, 1948-53; pvt. practice acctg., New Orleans, 1953-76; mng. partner Harry Williams and Co., New Orleans, 1976-81; pres. Harry Williams Co. (a profl. corp.), 1981-88; ptnr. J. Earl Pedelahore & Co., New Orleans, 1988—; lectr. Tulane U., 1953-56; co-founder Asso. Regional Acctg. Firms, chmn., 1969-71; speaker profl. seminars and meetings. Served with USNR, 1943-46. Mem. AICPA, La. Soc. CPAs (pres. New Orleans chpt. 1964-65, parliamentarian 1971-72, dir. 1964-65, 71-72, mem. trial bd. 1972-76, chmn. 1972-73, chmn. numerous coms.), New Orleans Estate Planning Council (treas. 1970-71), New Orleans Bd. Trade (dir. 1984—, chmn. fin. com. 1987-88), Chamber New Orleans and River Region, Econ. Devel. Council, Com. of 50, Pi Kappa Alpha. Clubs: Pickwick, So. Yacht, World Trade Center of New Orleans (dir. 1975—, pres. 1984). Roman Catholic. Democrat. Editor: La. C.P.A., 1961-62; contbr. articles to profl. jours. Home: 6824 Vicksburg St New Orleans LA 70124 Office: J Earl Pedelahore & Co 203 Carondelet St Suite 630 New Orleans LA 70130

WILLIAMS, HENRY RUDOLPH, b. Wilmington, N.C., Oct. 23, 1919; s. Henry R. and Virginia L. (Hewlett) W.; B.C.S., Benjamin Franlin U., 1949; M.B.A., George Washington U., 1952; m. Elsie Virginia Gray, Apr. 25, 1942; children—Cheryl A., Deborah L. With Hamilton Nat. Bank, Washington, 1937-42, IRS, 1945-52, ICC, Washington, 1952-67, Office of Sec., U.S. Dept. Transp., Washington, 1967-69, U.S. Fed. R.R. Adminstrn., Washington, 1969-74; sr. fin. analyst U.S. Ry. Assn., Washington, 1974-75, ret. 1988; asst. to v.p.-fin. Mo.-Kans.-Tex. R.R. Co., Denison, Tex., 1975, successively asst. v.p.-fin., asst. v.p. and comptroller; dir. Okla.-Kans.-Tex. R.R. Co. Served in U.S. Army, 1942-45, 61-62. Recipient Achievement award U.S. Dept. Transp., Sec.'s award meritorious achievement. Mem. R.R. Ins. Mgmt. Assn., Assn. Am. R.R.s, Denison C. of C. Republican. Baptist. Club: Denison Rod and Gun Country. Home: 2600 Brookhaven Circle Denison TX 75020 Office: 104 E Main St Denison TX 75020

WILLIAMS, HOOPER ANDERSON, JR., university administrator, consultant; b. Nashville, Aug. 13, 1918; s. Hooper Anderson Sr. and Ivy Day (Stone) W.; m. Mary Ellen Johnston, July 13, 1942 (div. 1952); 1 child, Penelope Nancy; m. Patricia Mary Densham, Dec. 30, 1975. BE, Vanderbilt U., 1940; MS in Indsl. Engring., Ill. Inst. Tech., 1950; PhD in Engring., Stanford U., 1973. Design engr. Differential Steel Car Co., Findlay, Ohio, 1940-41; asst. prof. Ill. Inst. Tech., Chgo., 1946-51; plant supt. Squire Dingee Co., Chgo., 1951-53; chief plant engr. Magnaflux Corp., Chgo., 1953-57; cons. Cresap McCormack &Paget, Chgo., 1957-61; gen. mgr. Chgo. Miniature Lamp, 1961-65; prof. engring., dir. indsl. mgmt. program sch. engring. San Jose (Calif.) State U., 1965-87, prof. emeritus, 1987—; cons. Williams Assocs., San Jose, 1965—. Author: Network Analysis of Housing Industry, 1971. Col. USMC, 1941-46, PTO, Res. 1937-78. Decorated Bronze Star medal. Mem. SAR. Home: 2150 Violet Way Campbell CA 95008 Office: San Jose U Sch Engring Washington Sq San Jose CA 95192

WILLIAMS, HOWARD W., coal company executive; b. Somerset, Ohio, Dec. 26, 1926; m. Jacqueline Williams; children: Mark, Scott, Sally, Stacy. AA, Meredith Bus. Coll., 1948. Office clk. Ludowici-Celandon Co., New Lexington, Ohio, 1949-51; warehouse clk. Sunnyhill Coal Co. (acquired by Peabody Coal Co. in 1959), New Lexington, 1951-61; pumper Sunnyhill mine div. Peabody Coal Co., New Lexington, 1961-63, electrician Sunnyhill mine div., 1963, 3d shift pit foreman Sunnyhill mine div., 1963-64, asst. supt., drilling and shooting foreman Sunnyhill mine div., 1964-65; supt. Simco Surface mine div. Peabody Coal Co., Coshocton, Ohio, 1965-69, gen. supt. surface mines Ohio and Ala. Simco Surface mine div., 1969-70; gen.

supt. Ky. Surface mines Peabody Coal Co., Madisonville, 1970-71; dir. south surface div. Peabody Coal Co., Evansville, Ind., 1971-73; v.p. western surface group Peabody Coal Co., St. Louis, 1973-78, group v.p. surface ops Cen. and Western Regions, 1978-79; v.p. Peabody Coal Co., Evansville, 1979-85, pres. Ind. div., 1979-80; pres. Ea. div. Peabody Coal Co., Henderson, Ky., 1980-85, pres., 1985—, also bd. dirs. Bd. dirs. Community Meth. Hosp., Henderson, Henderson United Way. Served with USN, 1945-46. Mem. Nat. Coal Assn. (bd. dirs.), Bituminous Coal Operators Assn. 9bd. dirs.), Ind. Coal Mining INst. (past pres.), Ohio Mining and Reclamation Assn. (bd. dirs.), King Coal Club, Henderson C. of C. (bd. dirs.). Office: Peabody Coal Co 1951 Barrett Ct Box 1990 Henderson KY 42420-1990

WILLIAMS, HUGH ALEXANDER, JR., mechanical engineer, consultant; b. Spencer, N.C., Aug. 18, 1926; s. Hugh Alexander and Mattie Blanche (Megginson) W.; BS in Mech. Engring., N.C. State U., 1948, MS in Diesel Engring. (Norfolk So. R.R. fellow), 1950; postgrad. Ill. Benedictine Coll. Inst. Mgmt., 1980; m. Ruth Ann Gray, Feb. 21, 1950; children: David Gray, Martha Blanche Williams Heidengren. Jr. engr.-field service engr. Baldwin-Lima Hamilton Corp., Hamilton, Ohio, 1950-52, project engr., 1953-55; project engr. Electro-Motive div. Gen. Motors Corp., La Grange, Ill., 1955-58, sr. project engr., 1958-63, supr. product devel. engine design sect., 1963-86, staff engr., advanced mech. tech., 1986-87. Trustee Downers Grove (Ill.) San. Dist., 1965—, pres., 1974—; pres. Ill. Assn. San. Dists., 1976-77, bd. dirs., 1977—; mem. statewide policy adv. com. Ill. EPA, 1977-79; mem. DuPage County Intergovtl. Task Force Com., 1988—; elder 1st Presbyn. Ch., Downers Grove. Served with USAAC, 1945. Registered profl. engr., Ill. Fellow ASME (Diesel and Gas Engine Power Div. Speaker awards 1968, 84, Div. citation 1977, Internal Combustion Engine award 1987, exec. com. Internal Combustion Engine div. 1981-87, 88—, chmn. 1985-86, sec. 1988—); mem. Soc. Automotive Engrs., ASME (chmn. Soichiro Honda medal com. 1987—), Lions, Masons (32 degree). Republican. Editor: So. Engr., 1947-48; contbr. articles to profl. jours. Patentee in field. Home: 1119 Blanchard St Downers Grove IL 60516

WILLIAMS, JAMES B., banker; b. Sewanee, Tenn., Mar. 21, 1933; s. Eugene G. and Ellen (Bryan) W.; m. Betty G. Williams, July 11, 1980; children—Ellen, Elizabeth, Bryan. A.B., Emory U., 1955. Pres. Peachtree Bank & Trust Co., Chamblee, Ga., 1962-64; chmn. bd. 1st Nat. Bank & Trust Co., Augusta, Ga., 1971-73; vice chmn. Trust Co. of Ga., Atlanta, 1977-81; pres. Trust Co. of Ga., 1981-89; vice chmn. SunTrust Banks, Inc., Atlanta, 1985—; pres. SunBanks, Inc., Orlando, Fla., 1986-89; bd. dirs. The Coca-Cola Co., Genuine Parts Co., Rollins Inc., Georgia-Pacific Corp., RPC Energy Services, Inc. (all Atlanta), Columbia Pictures Entertainment, Inc., N.Y., Sonat Inc., Birmingham. Trustee Emory U., Westminster Schs., Robert W. Woodruff Health Scis. Ctr. Served to lt. USAF, 1955-57. Mem. Am. Bankers Assn., Res. City Bankers Assn. Presbyterian. Clubs: Piedmont Driving (Atlanta), Capital City (Atlanta), Commerce (Atlanta). Office: SunTrust Banks PO Box 4418 Atlanta GA 30302 also: Sun Banks Inc 200 S Orange Ave Orlando FL 32801

WILLIAMS, JAMES B., tire company executive; b. Toronto, Ont., Can., Oct. 16, 1945; s. Norman James and Marie (McBride) W.; m. Kathleen Mary Fitzgerald, May 10, 1969; children: Jason Lawrence, Laura Marie. BA, U. Toronto, Ont., Can., 1967; MBA, U. Toronto, 1969. V.p. fin. and adminstrn., chief fin. officer Dominion Stores Ltd., Toronto, 1969-85; exec. v.p. fin. and adminstrn., chief fin. officer Gt. Atlantic & Pacific Tea Co. Can. Inc., Toronto, 1985-86; exec. v.p. fin. and adminstrn., chief fin. officer Can. Tire Corp. Ltd., Toronto, 1986, exec. v.p. mktg., real estate, constrn. and distbn., 1986—. Office: Can Tire Corp Ltd, 2180 Yonge St, Toronto, ON Canada M4P 2V8

WILLIAMS, JAMES DUNMORE, manufacturing company executive; b. Erie, Pa., July 8, 1941; s. Warren Dee Williams and Meredythe Lucille (Duncombe) Schaefer; m. Janet Isabelle Chartley, July 13, 1963 (div. 1978); children: Jason Lewis, Jeffrey Francis; m. Dawn Rae Talerico, May 5, 1979. Student, Gannon U., 1963-72, Pa. State U., 1973-74. Various mgmt. positions in info. systems, prodn., materials, mfg. Gen. Electric Co., Erie, 1962-79; with Smith Meter Inc., A Moorco Internat. Co., Erie and Houston, 1979—; ops. mgr. Smith Meter Inc., A Moorco Internat. Co., Erie, 1982-86; ops. mgr. multi-ops. Smith Meter Inc., A Moorco Internat. Co., Erie and Houston, 1986—. Cons. Opportunities Industrialization Ctr., Erie, 1965-68; vice-maj. fund drive YMCA, Erie, 1971-73; active Erie United Way, 1972—. Served with U.S. Army, 1959-60. Mem. Am. Prodn. and Inventory Control Soc., Am. Mgmt. Assn., Erie Maennerchor. Republican. Roman Catholic. Home: 608 Nagle Rd Erie PA 16511 Office: Smith Meter Inc 1813 McClelland Ave Erie PA 16510

WILLIAMS, JAMES KELLEY, diversified resources company executive; b. Bentonia, Miss., Mar. 29, 1934; s. James C. and Katheryn (Kelley) W.; m. Jean Pittman, June 16, 1956; children: James Kelley, George P., Clifford C. B.S. in Chem. Engring, Ga. Inst. Tech., 1956; M.B.A., Harvard U., 1962. Mgr. corp. planning and devel. First Miss. Corp., Jackson, 1967-69, v.p., 1969-71, pres., chief exec. officer, 1971-88, chmn., pres., chief exec. officer, 1988—; mem. adv. council Degussa Corp.; dir. Deposit Guaranty Corp., Deposit Guaranty Nat. Bank. Bd. dirs. Miss. Econ. Council, Com. for Econ. Devel., Washington, Bus. & Industry Polit. Edn. Com.; trustee Piney Wood Country Life Sch.; deacon Northminster Baptist Ch.; trustee Miss. Found. Ind. Colls.; chmn. Inst. for Tech. Devel. for Miss.; mem. exec. com. Jackson Internat. Trade Com. Served with USAF, 1957-60. Mem. Fertilizer Inst., Newcomen Soc., Mfg. Chemists Assn., Agribus. Promotion Council, World Bus. Council. Clubs: Jackson Country, River Hills, Hundred of Jackson. Office: First Miss Corp 700 North St Box 1249 Jackson MS 39202-3095

WILLIAMS, JAMES LEONARD, hospital adminstrator; b. Bethlehem, Pa., July 3, 1953; s. David Robert and Margalene (Starks) W.; m. Maria Rafaela Viera-Ortiz, June 19, 1982. BS, Slippery Rock U., 1975; MS, Georgetown U., 1981; M Hosp. Mgmt., Yale U., 1984. Investment advisor Commonwealth Investments, Dallas, 1981-82; blood donor recruiter Wadley Inst. Medicine, Dallas, 1982; adminstrv. specialist Humana Hosp.-Med. City, Dallas, 1984-85, asst. exec. dir., 1985-88; assoc. exec. dir. Humana Hosp., San Antonio, 1988—; instr. Tae Kwon Do, Dallas Coll., 1984-88. Bd. dirs. Dallas chpt. Am. Heart Assn., 1987-88. Maj. USMC, 1975-81, SE Asia, now USMCR. Mem. Am. Coll. Healthcare Execs., Health Care Fin. Mgmt. Assn., Am. Assn. Med. Adminstr., Marine Corp Assn., Force Recon Assn., N. Dallas C. of C., Dallas C. of C. Republican. Roman Catholic. Home: PO Box 29501 San Antonio TX 78229-0501

WILLIAMS, JAMES ROBERT, insurance agent; b. Eagletown, Okla., Sept. 24, 1929; s. Ollie Hamilton and Bathsheba Ruth (Petty) W.; m. Betty Ruth Harland, Apr. 17, 1949 (div. 1977); children: Judy, Stephen, Nancy; m. Anna Sue Dodd, Dec. 17, 1977; children: Donna Chapman, Deborah Teller. Student, Sonoma State U., 1965—. Ins. agt. State Farm Ins. Co., Corning, Calif., 1960, Burney, Calif., 1960-61, Susanville, Calif., 1961—. Active Assemblies of God Ch., Santa Cruz, Calif., Susanville Sch. Bd. 1965-72, Susanville PTA, 1965—; dist. comdr. Royal Ranger Boys Group, 1964-65. Democrat. Lodges: Masons, Shriners, Rotary (pres. 1972, Paul Harris fellow 1986). Home: PO Box 818 Susanville CA 96130 Office: State Farm Ins 115 N Mesa St Susanville CA 96130

WILLIAMS, JEFFREY LEE, credit union association executive; b. Ft. Worth, Oct. 30, 1958; s. Gary Lee and Barbara Ann (Womack) W.; m. Holly Holcomb, Dec. 2, 1978; children: Candice Gabrielle, Crysti Leigh. BS in Econs., Tex. A&M U., 1982. Owner, chief exec. officer Williams Maintenance Svcs., College Station, Tex., 1978-81; assoc. analyst Continental Pipeline Co., Inc., Lake Charles, La., 1982-83; adminstrv. coordinator Conoco, Inc., Atlanta, 1984-86; contr., asst. treas. Ga. Credit Union Affiliates, Atlanta, 1986-87, v.p., 1987—; asst. treas. Ga. Credit Union League and Affiliate, Atlanta, 1986—, Ga. Cen. Credit Union, Atlanta, 1986—, Credit Union Svc. Corp., Atlanta, 1987—. Author, editor: Introduction to Oil Pipeline Industry, 1984. Outreach leader First Bapt. Ch., Lake Charles, La., 1983, Sunday Sch. tchr., Snellville, Ga., 1987. Mem. Am. Credit Union League Execs., Ga. Ind. Automobile Dealers Assn. Republican. Baptist. Home: 4172 Summer Pl Snellville GA 30278 Office: Ga Credit Union Affiliates 2400 Pleasant Hill Rd Duluth GA 30136

WILLIAMS, JEROME DENEAN, educator; b. Phila., Jan. 11, 1947; s. Jerome Jay and Gloria Elizabeth (Dixon) W.; m. Lillian Regina Harrison, June 21, 1969; children: Denean, Derek, Daniel, Dante, Dachia. BA, U. Pa., 1969; MS, Union Coll., 1975; PhD, U. Colo., 1986. Publicist Gen. Electric Co., Phila., 1969-70; copywriter Gen. Electric Co., Schnectady, N.Y., 1970-71, sr. publicist, 1971-75, supr., 1975-78; mgr. pub. info. Solar Energy Research Inst., Golder, Colo., 1978-80; v.p. Sierra Services, Arvada, Colo., 1980-87; asst. prof. Pa. State U., University Park, 1987—. Mem. Acad. Mktg. Sci., Am. Acad. Advt., Am. Mktg. Assn., Am. Psychol. Assn., Assn. for Consumer Research. Jehovah's Witness. Home: 101 Norle St State College PA 16801 Office: Pa State U 707C Bus Adminstrn Bldg University Park PA 16802

WILLIAMS, JERRY O., graphics equipment and service company executive; b. Indianapolis; married; 2 children. BA, DePauw U., 1961; BS, Purdue U., 1964; MS, U. Pa., 1967. V.p. corp. planning Alusuisse Am Inc.; mgr. Gen. Electric Co., Fairfield, Conn.; v.p. corp. planning AM Internat., Chgo., 1981-82, pres. Bruning div., 1982-85; pres., chief operating officer AM Internat., 1985-88, also bd. dirs., to 1988; bd. dirs. U.S. West, Colo. Office: 100 S Wacker Dr Ste 1111 Chicago IL 60606 *

WILLIAMS, JIMMY NELSON, JR., lighting management company executive; b. Mobile, Ala., May 8, 1959; s. Jimmy Nelson and Betty Jean (Lane) W.; m. Rebecca Irene Buzbee, Sept. 24, 1977 (div. 1980); 1 child, Dawn Kae; m. Margaret Parke, July 9, 1983. Grad. high sch., Fairhope, Ala. Mgr. dairy Delchamps, Fairhope, 1977-78; lighting technician Flourescent Maintenance Svc., Brooksville, Fla., 1978-81, gen. mgr., 1982-84, pres., 1984—. Mem. Hernando County C. of C., Internat. Assn. Lighting Mgmt. Cos. (v.p. 1987—). Home: 29399 Soult Rd Brooksville FL 34601 Office: Fluorescent Maintenance Svc Inc 6238 Spring Lake Hwy Brooksville FL 34605

WILLIAMS, JOEL JAY, company treasurer; b. Houston, Nov. 30, 1948; m. Shirley Nash, Sept. 3, 1970 (div. 1979); 1 child, Joel Jay, Jr.; m. Jo Ann Kelly, Dec. 30, 1981; children: Jaynaia, Jay Shaun. AA, Laney Coll., 1972; BA in History, U.S. Internat. U., San Diego, 1974. Asst. mgr. Household Fin., Houston, 1974-76; acct. Tex. So. U., Houston, 1976-78; longshoreman Internat. Longshoreman Assn., Houston, 1980—; sec., treas. Harbor Eight Stevedores Inc., Houston, 1986—. Democrat. Baptist. Office: Harbor Eight Stevedores Inc 10202 I-01 East #204 Houston TX 77029

WILLIAMS, JOHN, automotive executive; b. Ripley, Miss., June 9, 1936; s. John C. and Annie (Huddleston) W.; m. Bonnie Abbott, Apr. 12, 1958; children: Donald, Bonita Williams Prosser. Student, Memphis State U., 1974, N.W. Miss. Jr. Coll., 1975. Mgr. parts Oakley-Keese, Memphis, 1973-78, Kirk Ford, Grenada, Miss., 1978-80, Ben Garner Ford, Starkville, Miss., 1980-82; store mgr. Auto Shack, Columbus, Miss., 1982-84; mgr. parts Friendly Ford Inc., Springfield, Mo., 1984—. Served with U.S. Army, 1955-58, Korea. Mem. Am. Mgmt. Assn., Ford Parts Mgrs. Club (pres. 1979). Republican. Baptist. Home: 2542 S Delaware Springfield MO 65804 Office: Friendly Ford Inc 3241 S Glenstone Springfield MO 65804

WILLIAMS, JOHN DALE, business and marketing consultant; b. Carrollton, Mo., Oct. 13, 1943; s. Dale C. and Mary (Weinhold) W.; m. Lana L. Elgin, Mar. 22, 1962 (div. 1971); 1 child, Jeffrey D. BA, U. Mo., 1970, MA, 1976. Disc jockey, newswriter Sta. KAOL-FM, Carrollton, 1959-61; quality assurance engr. Gen. Dynamics/Astronautics, San Diego, 1962-64; prodn. controller solar div. Internat. Harvester Co., San Diego, 1965-67; polit. cons. Mayor Charles B. Wheeler, Kansas City, Mo., 1970-71; clinic dir. Greater Kansas City Mental Health Clinic, 1971-81, Kansas City Drug Abuse Program, 1981-84; bus. and mktg. cons., 1984—; cons. Jackson County Legislature, Kansas City, 1981-87; controller, gen. mgr., Kansas City Ctr., 1985—; programs, systems cons., Softhaus Ltd., 1986—; co-owner Big Niangua Ranch, 1987—; dir. Jackson County Mental Health Levy Bd., Kansas City, 1982-83. Bd. dirs. Com. for County Progress, Kansas City, 1982—; mem. Kansas City Jazz Commn., 1982-87; pres. Com. of Ind. Young Dems., 1971-73; v.p. Jackson County Dem. Alliance, 1978-79; Dem. committeeman, Kansas City, 1979-81. Mem. Phi Kappa Phi, Phi Alpha Theta. Office: Kansas City Ctr 917 McGee St Kansas City MO 64106

WILLIAMS, JOHN E., III, finance corporation executive; b. Yeadin, Pa., Jan. 19, 1936; s. John E. Jr. and Marjorie M. (Hartzell) W.; m. Bonnie Jean Lushbaugh, Nov. 10, 1961; children: John E. IV, David E. Student, Princeton U.; BA, Dickinson Coll., 1959. V.p. First Pa. Bank, N.Am., Phila., 1973-78; pres. Commoloco Inc., San Juan, P.R., 1979-81; sr. v.p. Mfr. Hanover Consumer Services, Huntingdon Valley, Pa., 1982-84, exec. v.p., 1984—. Republican. Episcopalian. Office: Mfrs Hanover Consumer Svcs 3103 Philmont Ave Huntingdon Valley PA 19006

WILLIAMS, JOHN IRVING, JR., business executive; b. N.Y.C., Jan. 7, 1954; s. John Irving Sr. and Ruth Lolita (Johnson) W.; m. Diane Blanchet Pierce, June 14, 1986; children: Miguel, Ashley. BA, Amherst Coll., 1975; JD, MBA, Harvard U., 1979. Bar: Mass. 1979, N.Y. 1980. Cons. Bain and Co., Boston, 1978-83; v.p. mktg. Softbridge Microsystems Corp., Cambridge, Mass., 1983-85; v.p., group head Chem. Bank, N.Y.C., 1985-87; v.p. practice devel. Gartner Group Consulting, Stamford, Conn., 1987-88; sr. v.p. strategic planning and bus. devel. Am. Express Travel Related Svcs. Co., Inc., 1988—. Trustee Amherst Coll., Mass., 1984—; dir. Beechmont Neighborhood Assn., New Rochelle, N.Y., 1987—, pres., 1988—; mem. Kent Sch. Alumni Council, Conn., 1976-80. Home: 10 Pryer Pl New Rochelle NY 10804 Office: Am Express Travel Related Svcs Co Inc American Express Tower World Financial Center New York NY 10285

WILLIAMS, JOHN JAMES, JR., architect; b. Denver, July 13, 1949; s. John James and Virginia Lee (Thompson) W.; m. Mary Serene Morck, July 29, 1972. BArch, U. Colo., 1974. Registered architect, Colo. Project architect Gensler Assoc. Architects, Denver, 1976, Heinzman Assoc. Architects, Boulder, Colo., 1977, EZTH Architects, Boulder, 1978-79; prin. Knudson/Williams PC, Boulder, 1980-82, Faber, Williams & Brown, Boulder, 1982-86, John Williams & Assocs., Boulder, 1986—; panel chmn. U. Colo. World Affairs Conf.; vis. faculty U. Colo. Sch. Architecture and Planning, Coll. Environtl. Design. Author (with others) State of Colorado architect licensing law, 1986. Commr. Downtown Boulder Mall Commn., 1985-88; bd. dirs. U. Colo. Fairway Club, 1986-88. Recipient Teaching Honorarium, U. Colo. Coll. Architecture and Planning, 1977, 78, 79, 80, 88, Excellence in Design and Planning award City of Boulder, 1981, 82, Citation for Excellence, WOOD Inc., 1982, Disting. Profl. Service award Coll. Environ. Design U. Colo., 1988. Mem. Nat. Council Architect Registration Bd., AIA, (sec., bd. dirs. Colo. North chpt. 1985-86, 88, sec. 1987, 88, ednl. fund Fisher I traveling scholar 1988), Architects and Planners of Boulder (v.p. 1982), Nat. Golf Found. (sponsor), Am. Philatelic Soc., Kappa Sigma (chpt. pres. 1970). Home: 3345 16th ST Boulder CO 80302 Office: John Williams & Assocs 1137 Pearl St Suite 206 Boulder CO 80302

WILLIAMS, JOSEPH DALTON, pharmaceutical company executive; b. Washington, Pa., Aug. 15, 1926; s. Joseph Dalton and Jane (Day) W.; m. Mildred E. Bellaire, June 28, 1973; children: Terri, Daniel. B.Sc. in Pharmacy, U. Nebr., 1950, D.Pharmacy (hon.), 1978; D.H.L., Albany Coll. Pharmacy, Union U., 1980, Rutgers U., 1987, Long Island U., 1988; D.Sc. (hon.), Phila. Coll. Pharmacy and Sci., Long Island U., 1988. Pres. Parke-Davis Co., Detroit, 1973-76; pres. pharm. group Warner-Lambert Co., Morris Plains, N.J., 1976-77; pres. Internat. Group, 1977-79; pres., dir. Warner-Lambert Corp., 1979-80, pres., chief operating officer, 1980-84, chief exec. officer, 1985, chmn., 1985—; bd. dirs. AT&T, J.C. Penney & Co., Exxon Corp. Bd. dirs. People to People Health Found.; trustee Columbia U. Served with USNR, 1943-46. Mem. Am. Pharm. Assn., N.J. Pharm. Assn. Clubs: Links (N.Y.C.); Pine Valley (N.J.) Golf; Baltusrol Golf (Springfield, N.J.); Mid Ocean (Bermuda). Office: Warner-Lambert Co 201 Tabor Rd Morris Plains NJ 07950

WILLIAMS, JOSEPH HILL, diversified industry executive; b. Tulsa, June 2, 1933; s. David Rogerson and Martha Reynolds (Hill) W.; m. Joseph Hill Jr., Peter B., James C.; m. Terese T. Ross, May 7, 1977; stepchildren: Margot Kunkel, Jennifer Ross. Diploma, St. Paul's Sch., 1952; B.A., Yale U., 1956, M.A. (hon.), 1977; postgrad., Sch. Pipeline Tech. U. Tex., 1960. Field employee div. domestic constrn. Williams Cos., Tulsa, 1958-60, project coordinator div. engring., 1960-61; project supt. Iran, 1961-62, asst. resident mgr., 1962-64; project mgr. 1964-65, resident mgr., 1965-67; exec. v.p. Tulsa, 1968—, pres., chief operating officer, 1971-78, chmn., chief exec. officer, 1979—; bd. dirs. Am. Express Co. Bd. dirs. Industries for Tulsa; fellow, trustee Yale Corp. Served with AUS, 1956-58. Mem. Am. Petroleum Inst. (dir.), Council on Fgn. Relations, Nat. Petroleum Council, Conf. Bd., Okla. C. of C., Met. Tulsa C. of C. (dir., past chmn.). Episcopalian. Clubs: Southern Hills Country, Tulsa; Springdale Hall (Camden, S.C.); Augusta (Ga.); Nat. Golf; Links (N.Y.); Grandfather Golf and Country (Linville, N.C.). Office: Williams Cos Inc 1 Williams Ctr PO Box 2400 Tulsa OK 74102

WILLIAMS, LARRY E., oil company executive; b. Chickasha, Okla., July 11, 1936; s. J. Emmett and Zella M. (Venrick) W.; m. Xan Z. Hart, Sept. 7, 1957; children—Jesslyn, Jon. BS in Mech. Engring., U. N.Mex., 1958, MS in Mech. Engring., 1959. Various positions Cities Svc. Co., 1959-74; v.p. Cities Svc. Co., Tulsa, 1974-83; pres., chief exec. officer Nat. Coop. Refinery Assn., McPherson, Kans., 1983—; bd. dir. McPherson Bank and Trust Co., Jayhawk Pipeline Co., Wichita, Kans., Osage Pipeline Co., Denver, Kaw Pipeline Co., Denver, Petroleum Resources Co., Cushing, Okla., Farmers Alliance Mut. Ins. Co., McPherson; pres., bd. dir. Clear Creek, Inc., McPherson, 1983—. Bd. dirs. United Way, McPherson, 1983—. Mem. Nat. Petroleum Refiners Assn. (bd. dirs.), Am. Ind. Refiners Assn., Am. Petroleum Inst., Nat. Coun. Farmer Coops. (bd. dirs., energy policy com.), Coop. League U.S.A., Am. Petroleum Inst. Clubs: Country (McPherson), Petroleum (Wichita). Office: Nat Coop Refinery Assn PO Box 1404 2000 S Main St McPherson KS 67460

WILLIAMS, LARRY RITCHIE, analytic services company executive, educator; b. Concord, N.C., Aug. 31, 1935; s. Robert Lewis and Louise (Black) W.; m. Betty Lou Whitt, June 5, 1957; children: Elizabeth Louise Williams Thomas, Larry Ritchie Jr. BA, U. N.C., 1957; MS in Systems Mgmt., U. So. Calif., 1971; postgrad., U. Calif., Berkeley, 1971-72. Commd. 2d lt. USMC, 1957, advanced through grades to col., 1979, served various locations worldwide including Vietnam, Norway, Beirut., ret., 1984; assoc. prof. U. So. Calif., L.A., 1984-88; sr. systems analyst Decisions and Designs, Inc., McLean, Va., 1985-86; assoc. prof. U. Denver, 1988; founder, pres. Heimat Corp., Hamilton, Va., 1987—; program mgr. Light Armored Vehicle Directorate, Quantico, Va., 1981-82. Contbr. articles to profl. publs. Decorated Bronze Star, Legion of Merit, Order of Cedars (Lebanon). Mem. Marine Exec. Assn., Mil. Ops. Rsch. Soc., Assn. Eagle Scouts, Phi Kappa Phi. Episcopalian. Home: Rt 1 Box 208 Hamilton VA 22068 Office: Heimat Corp PO Box 402 Hamilton VA 22068

WILLIAMS, LAWRENCE WALTER, hospital administrator; b. Wilmington, Del., Aug. 25, 1951; s. Lawrence Wilmer and Laura Helen (Treleaven) W. BA, U. Del., 1973; M in Pub. Adminstrn., SUNY, Albany, 1974. Cert. mental health adminstr. Staff devel. specialist Wilton (N.Y.) Devel. Ctr., 1974-76; asst. bus. officer J.N. Adam Devel. Ctr., Perrysburg, N.Y., 1976-78; assoc. budget analyst MR/DD, Albany, 1978-79, chief budget analyst, 1979-81; bus. officer Letchworth Village Devel. Ctr., Theills, N.Y., 1981-85; dep. dir. adminstrn. I Sagamore Children's Psychiat. Ctr., Melville, N.Y., 1985—; lectr. SUNY, Albany, 1979-81; instructor N.Y. State Dept. Civil Service, Albany, 1981, N.Y. State Office of State Comptroller, Albany, 1982. Chmn. United Fund Campaign, Perrysburg, 1977. Mem. Assn. Mental Health Adminstrs. (dep. gov. 1985-86, program chmn. 1982, pres. N.Y. State chpt. 1985-86, nat. com. on state chpts. 1986-88, 89—), Am. Coll. Healthcare Execs., N.Y. State Assn. Facility Dirs. Methodist. Home: 9 Nevinwood Pl Huntington NY 11743 Office: Sagamore Children's Psychiat Ctr 197 Half Hollow Rd Melville NY 11747

WILLIAMS, LOUIS BOOTH, college president emeritus; b. Paris, Tex., Oct. 15, 1916; s. William Louis and Maggie Jo (Booth) W.; AA, Paris (Tex.) Jr. Coll., 1935; BBA, U. Tex., 1951; MBA, E. Tex. State U., 1961; LLD (hon.), Tex. Wesleyan U., 1976; m. Mary Lou Newman, Oct. 15, 1938; children: Joanne Williams Click, Louis Booth. Profl. local C. of C. exec., Austin, Navasota and Paris, Tex., 1938-44; mgr. Bireley's Beverages, Denison, Tex., 1946-49; asst. to pres. Paris Jr. Coll., 1949-52; personnel mgr. Paris Works, Babcock & Wilcox Co., 1952-67; pres. Paris Jr. Coll., 1968-83, pres. emeritus, 1983—; dir. Liberty Nat. Bank, Paris, McCuistion Regional Med. Ctr., vice chmn. Served with USNR, lt. comdr. ret. Recipient Silver Beaver award Boy Scouts Am., 1956; Paul Harris fellow Rotary Internat., 1974. Mem. Am. Assn. Community Jr. Colls., Tex. Assn. Colls. and Univs. (pres. 1981), Assn. Tex. Jr. Colls. (pres. 1976), Theta Kappa Omega, Delta Sigma Pi, Phi Theta Kappa (hon.). Democrat. Methodist. Lodge: Rotary (dist. gov. 1985-86). Author: The Organization, Administration and Functions of a Local Chamber of Commerce, 1937. Home: 3170 Laurel Ln Paris TX 75460 Office: Paris Jr Coll Clarksville St Paris TX 75460

WILLIAMS, MELVIN THOMAS, JR., business consultant; b. N.Y.C., Nov. 24, 1942; s. Melvin Thomas Williams and Ruby (Slader) Brown; m. Diane Cephas, May 3, 1975 (div. 1987); children: Keith Gregory, Todd Elliott. BS, Central State U., Wilberforce, Ohio, 1964; MS, Columbia U., 1976. Staff acctg. comptroller's dept. IBEC, N.Y.C., 1966-68, fin. analyst treas. dept., 1968-70; exec. v.p. housing constrn. subs. IBEC, S.C. and Va., 1970-73; mgr. ops. devel. and analysis, corp. hdqrs. staff IBEC, N.Y.C., 1973-75; mgr. internat. div. Patient Care Publ., Inc., Darien, Conn., 1975-79; v.p., dir. Patient Care Publ., Inc., Darien, 1979-80; pres. Patient Care Internat., Inc., Darien, 1980-82; chmn. Delphi Cons. Group, Inc., White Plains, N.Y., 1982—; bd. dir. Jonston Internat. Pub. Co., N.Y.C. 1st lt. U.S. Army, 1964-66. Mem. 100 Black Men, Omega Psi Phi. Republican. Office: Delphi Cons Group Inc 5 Corp Pk Dr Ste 311 White Plains NY 10604

WILLIAMS, MICHAEL THOMAS, architect, real estate developer; b. Oak Park, Ill., June 4, 1940; s. Harry Letcher and Ruth Elizabeth (Huelster) W.; m. Barbara Jo McLaren, Aug. 10, 1963; children: Donald Stuart, Joanna Hope. BArch with honors, U. Ill., 1963; MArch, U. Pa., 1964. Archtl. designer Shaw-Metz, Chgo., 1963-66; project designer Metz, Train, Olson, Youngren, Chgo., 1966; coordinator design dept. Graham, Anderson, Probst & White, Chgo., 1966-73; sr. project designer Welton Becket & Assocs., Chgo., 1973-74; ptnr. Williams/Pollock/Assocs, Wheaton, Ill., 1974—; prin., pres. W/P/A Devel., Ltd., Wheaton, 1978—; prin., sec., treas. Williams/Pollock/Assocs Ltd., Wheaton, 1985—; mng. ptnr. The Meister Group, Wheaton, 1986—; bd. dirs. Unibanctrust/Hawthorne Bank, Wheaton, Marianjoy Rehab. Hosp., Weaton. Chmn. Cosley Found., Wheaton, 1986—; mem. sch. bd. local sch. dist., Wheaton, 1978-79; mem. Zoning Code Rev. Commn., Carol Stream, Ill., 1984-85, Wheaton Plan Commn., 1970-78, Wheaton Bldg. Commn., 1978. Mem. AIA, Sigma Chi Corp. (dir. Kappa Kappa sect., 1985—), Sigma Chi (v.p., treas. 1962-63), Lions. Office: Williams Pollock Assocs Ltd 210 N Hale St Wheaton IL 60187

WILLIAMS, MILFORD BERRY, accountant; b. Gastonia, N.C., June 19, 1942; s. Wallace Morgan and Zelda (Crain) W.; m. Barbara Ann Bailey, Dec. 30, 1972; 1 child, Brian Lee. BBA, Ga. State U., 1973; MBA, Winthrop Coll., 1976. CPA, N.C. Sr. clk. J.A. Jones Constrn. Co., Norcross, Ga., 1970-71; cost acct. Western Electric Co., Norcross, 1971-73; acct. City of Rock Hill, S.C., 1973-82, Collis & Wilson, CPA's, Gastonia, 1982-84; prin., owner Milford Barry Williams, CPA, Belmont, N.C., 1984—. Mem. Rep. Nat. Com., 1982-88. With U.S. Army, 1964-67, Vietnam. Fellow N.C. Assn.CPA's, Am. Legion (sec., treas. Ft. Oglethorpe, Ga. 1968-71). Baptist. Home: 1511 Easy St Belmont NC 28012 Office: 103 E 3rd St Gastonia NC 28054

WILLIAMS, NOEL D., JR., electrical contractor; b. San Francisco, Jan. 14, 1950; s. N. Douglas Sr. and Thais (Thurston) W.; m. Dana Francis Kari, Dec. 15, 1971 (div. 1975); children: Stacie, Kari. Student, U. Utah, 1967-69; AAS in Elec., Utah Tech Coll., 1978. With Rocky Mountain Trane, Salt Lake City, 1972-78; elec. supr. Rocky Mountain Mech. & Elec., Salt Lake City, 1978-86; v.p. Rocky Mountain Elec., Salt Lake City, 1986-87, prodn. mgr., 1987—. Chmn. State Elec. Bd., Salt Lake City to date, prog. adv. com. Salt Lake Community Coll., 1985—. Mem. Internat. Assn. Elec. Inspectors, Nat. Fire Protection Assn., Internat. Conf. Bldg. Officials, Internat. Assn. Electrical Inspectors (cert.). Office: Rocky Mountain Elec 3412 S West Temple Salt Lake City UT 84115

WILLIAMS, PAUL H., textile executive; b. Clarksdale, Miss., Jan. 4, 1938; s. Henry Wall and Thelma G. (McKeithen) W.; m. Judy Kelly, Mar. 14, 1959; children: Kathy, Kelly. B in Chem. Engr., Ga. Inst. Tech., 1960. With R & D dept. Celanese Fibers Co., Charlotte, N.C., 1960-64; with Fibers Industries Inc., Greenville, S.C. and Salisbury, N.C., 1964-73; mfg. tech. dir. Fibers Industries Inc., Charlotte, 1973-76, mfg. dir. then v.p. mfg., 1976-81; v.p. mktg. tech. Celanese Fibers Mktg. Co., Charlotte, 1981-82; dir. textiles, tech. Celanese Textile Fibers, Charlotte, 1982-86; exec. v.p. Celanese Can. Inc., Montreal, 1986-87, exec. v.p., pres. textile group, 1987-88, pres., pres. textile group, 1988—; mem. can. adv. bd. Allendale Ins. Co.; mem. nat. adv. bd. chem. engr. Ga. Tech.; bd. dirs. Monterey Textiles, Inc., Can. Textiles Inst. Past trustee Textile Rsch. Inst.; past dir. N.C. State U. Engring. Found.; past bd. dirs. Jr. Achievement, Charlotte. Office: Hoechst Celanese Corp 1211 Ave of the Americas New York NY 10036 Office: Celanese Can Inc, 800 Dorchester Blvd W, Box 617, Montreal, PQ Canada H3C 3K8

WILLIAMS, PHILLIP ADGER, insurance company executive; b. Greensboro, N.C., Mar. 31, 1928; s. John Wesley and Lila Lee (Darnell) W.; m. Joan Jeanette Morel, Oct. 26, 1958; children: Paige Leigh, Gail Darnell, Christopher Steven. Student, Guilford Coll., 1946; BA, U. N.C., 1951. V.p. The Travelers Ins. Co., Hartford, Conn., 1967-72; v.p. and actuary The Travelers Corp., Hartford, 1972-84; sr. v.p. and actuary The Travelers Corp., The Travelers Ins. Co. and subs., Hartford, 1984—; pres. Constn. Plaza Corp., Hartford, 1970-71, pres. Tabco, Inc., Hartford, 1971-76; bd. dirs. Constn. State Ins. Co., Hartford. Editor: Automobile Insurance Ratemaking, 1961. Mem. exec. bd. gov.'s com. on services and expenditures, Hartford, 1971. Served as sgt. U.S. Army, 1946-48. Mem. (fellow) Casualty Actuarial Soc. (pres. 1977-78, bd. dirs. 1972-80), (charter mem.) Am. Acad. Actuaries (pres. 1982-83, bd. dirs. 1975-85), Actuarial Standards Bd. Republican. Congregationalist. Club: Hartford. Home: 127 Robin Rd Glastonbury CT 06033 Office: The Travelers Corp 1 Tower Sq Hartford CT 06183

WILLIAMS, R. OWEN, investment banker; b. Balt., Apr. 14, 1952; s. H. Richard and Gloria C. (Connell) W. AB, Dartmouth Coll., 1974; MA, Cambridge U., Eng., 1976. Mktg. profl. Salomon Bros., Inc., N.Y.C., 1977-78, L.A., 1978-79, San Francisco, 1979-86; sales mgmt. com. Salomon Bros., Inc., Tokyo, 1986-87; product sales mgr., nat. sales mgr. gov. dept. Salomon Bros., Inc., N.Y.C., 1987—. Producer: (film) Secret War, 1987. Home: 52 E 72d New York NY 10021 Office: Salomon Bros 1 New York Pla New York NY 10004

WILLIAMS, RALPH WATSON, JR., retired securities company executive; b. Atlanta, July 2, 1933; s. Ralph Watson and Minnie Covington (Hicks) W.; m. Nancy Jo Morgan, Mar. 19, 1955; children: Ralph Watson III, Nancy Jane, John Martin Hicks. Student, Davidson Coll., 1951; B.B.A., U. Ga., 1955. Trainee banking Trust Co. Ga., Atlanta, 1955; mcpl. sales staff Courts & Co., Atlanta, 1955-57; v.p., salesman securities First Southeastern Corp., Atlanta, 1957-60; br. mgr. Francis I. duPont & Co., 1960-69; spl. partner duPont Glore Forgan Inc., N.Y.C., 1969-70; gen. partner Glore Forgan Inc., 1970, exec. v.p., 1971—, sr. v.p., 1972—; also dir.; sr. v.p., dir., mem. exec. com. duPont-Walston Inc., 1973-74; sr. v.p. E.F. Hutton & Co. Inc., 1974-81; exec. v.p. Shearson Lehman Hutton Inc., Atlanta, 1981-89. Mem. Nat. Assn. Security Dealers (chmn. dist. com. 7), Benedicts Atlanta, Phi Delta Theta. Methodist. Clubs: Commerce (Atlanta), Capital City (Atlanta), Piedmont Driving (Atlanta). Home: 4740 Millbrook Dr NW Atlanta GA 30327

WILLIAMS, RICHARD DONALD, wholesale food company executive; b. Audubon, Iowa, Feb. 19, 1926; s. Walter Edward and Olga M. (Christensen) W.; m. Carol Francis, June 17, 1950; children: Gayle, Todd, Scott. B.A., Ohio Wesleyan U., 1948; M.B.A., Northwestern U., 1949. Dir. indsl. and public relations Gardner div. Diamond Nat. Corp., Middletown, Ohio, 1949-61; with Fleming Cos., Inc., 1961—; v.p. personnel Fleming Cos., Inc., Oklahoma City, 1972-76; sr. v.p. human resources Fleming Cos., Inc., 1976-80, exec. v.p. human resources, 1980—. Pres. Jr. Achievement, Topeka, Kans., 1972; v.p. Last Frontier council Boy Scouts Am., Oklahoma City, 1980; campaign chmn. United Way Greater Oklahoma City, 1980, v.p., 1981—, pres., 1985-87; bd. dirs. Communities Council Central Okla., Oklahoma City chpt. ARC, Support Ctr. Okla. , Better Bus. Bur., Okla. City Beautiful. Served with USN, 1944-46. Mem. Am. Soc. Personnel Adminstrn., Soc. Advancement Mgmt., Am. Mgmt. Assn., Phi Gamma Delta. Clubs: Quail Creek Country (Oklahoma City), Petroleum (Oklahoma City); Baille 'd Oklahoma, La Chaine des Rotisseurs. Office: Fleming Cos Inc 6301 Waterford Blvd Oklahoma City OK 73126

WILLIAMS, RICHARD JAMES, food service executive; b. Goliad, Tex., Aug. 19, 1942; s. L. D. and Freida Irene (Watkins) W.; m. Shirley Ann Mihalik, July 11, 1967; children: Kenneth F., Dawn L. AA, Santa Ana Jr. Coll. (Calif.), 1965. Area mgr. Jack in the Box Restaurant, San Diego, 1972-80; v.p. ops. Franchise Dirs., Inc., Bradley, Ill., 1980-81; area supr. Pizza Hut of Am., Inc., Lombard, Ill., 1981-83; regional dir. of food svc. Montgomery Ward Co., Chgo., 1983-84, v.p. ops. Golden Bear Restaurants, Mt. Prospect, Ill., 1983-84; franchise area dir. Wendy's Internat., Oakbrook Terrace, Ill., 1984-85; regional mgr. franchise ops. Godfather's Pizza, Inc., 1985—. Author: Anthology of American High School Poetry, 1959. Served with USMC, 1960-72. Decorated Silver Star, Bronze Star. Republican. Mem. Chs. of Christ. Home: 221 Wianno Ln Schaumburg IL 60194 Office: Godfather's Pizza Inc 9140 W Dodge Rd Omaha NE 68114

WILLIAMS, ROBERT LYLE, retail furnishings company executive; b. Nowata, Okla., June 22, 1942; s. Clifford Lyle and Eula Mae (Barnes) W.; m. Lorene Linnet Dillahunty, June 12, 1965; 1 child, Eleanor Lynn. B.S., Okla. State U., 1964; M.B.A., Baylor U., 1965. Acctg. supr. Southwestern Bell Telephone Co., Houston, 1965-66; fin. exec. Ford Motor Co., Dearborn, Mich., 1969-80; treas. Ford Brazil, Sao Paulo, 1976-79, Agrico Chem. Co., Tulsa, 1980-82; v.p., chief fin. officer Texas City Refining, Inc., Tex., 1983-88; sr. v.p. Furnishings 2000, Inc., San Diego, 1988—; chmn. Galveston County Taxpayers Research Council, 1987—. Served to lt. USN, 1966-69. Republican. Presbyterian. Office: Furnishings 2000 Inc 11230 Sorrento Valley Rd San Diego CA 92121

WILLIAMS, ROBERT MANN, venture capitalist; b. Mineloa, N.Y., Apr. 10, 1940; s. Henry diVillers and Emma (Mann) W.; m. Virginia Lea, June 29, 1963; children: Robert, Kathryn, Eleanor. BA, Bucknell U., 1962; MBA, U. Bridgeport, 1971; Cert. Advanced Mgmt. Program, Harvard U., 1973. Acct. Tambrands, N.Y.C., 1964-69; asst. treas., asst. to pres. CIT Fin. Corp., N.Y.C., 1969-77; v.p. Assocs. Corp. N.Am., Dallas, 1977-79; chmn. RFE Mgmt. Corp., New Canaan, Conn., 1979—, also bd. dirs.; bd. dirs. Tambrands Inc., and other pvt. cos. Served to 1st lt. U.S. Army, 1962-64. Republican. Office: RFE Mgmt Corp 36 Grove St New Canaan CT 06840

WILLIAMS, ROBERT STEWART, entertainment company executive; b. Uniontown, Pa., Sept. 10, 1944; s. Jack Christopher and Ann Gertrude Williams; m. Deborah Robertson, Sept. 11, 1975. children: John Chistopher, Justin Scott, Whitney Bridget. Student St. John's Sch., Uniontown, Pa. Pres. Republic Personnel Service, Inc., Virginia Beach, Va., 1966-68, Nat. Personnel Services, Inc., Virginia Beach, 1966-69; chmn. bd., chief exec. officer Wil-Var Enterprises, Virginia Beach, 1969-75; pres., chief operating officer Spotlite Entertainment Enterprises, Ltd., N.Y.C., 1975—; pres., chmn. bd. and chief exec. officer Wilholl Communications, Inc., 1980—; chmn. bd., founding mem. P.C. Worldwide, 1982—. Named Theatrical Producer of Yr., 1980; recipient Performance Readers Poll award; named Producer of Yr., Neptune Internat., 1975-76. Republican. Roman Catholic. Home: 184 Laurel Hill Rd Mount Lakes NJ 07046 Office: Spotlite Enterprises Ltd 221 W 57th St New York NY 10019

WILLIAMS, RONALD DAVID, electronics materials executive; b. Marshall, Ark., Mar. 15, 1944; s. Noble Kentucky and Elizabeth (Karns) W.; m. Beth L. Williams, Nov. 1977; children: Stephanie Noble, Keith Michael. BA, Columbia U., 1966, BS, 1967, MBA, 1973. Process engr. DuPont, Deepwater, N.J., 1966; design engr. Combustion Engring. Co., Hartford, 1971; cons. Arthur Andersen & Co., N.Y.C., 1973-76; corp. planner Amax Inc., Greenwich, Conn., 1976-77, group planning adminstr., 1978-80, mgr. corp. planning and analysis, 1980-84, dir. fin. analysis, 1984-86; project mgr. Olin Corp., Stamford, Conn., 1977-78; mgr. ops planning, analysis Savin Corp., Stamford, 1986-88; dir. fin., Bandgap Tech. Corp., Broomfield, Colo., 1988—. Served with USN, 1967-70: Vietnam. NASA traineeship, 1971; S.W. Mudd scholar, 1971. Mem. AAAS, Am. Chem. Soc., Fgn. Policy Assn., Am. Mgmt. Assn. Democrat. Club: Appalachian Mountain, Stamford Running, Boulder Road Runners. Home: 7361 S Meadow Ct Boulder CO 80301 Office: Bandgap Tech Corp 891 A Interlocken Pkwy Broomfield CO 80020

WILLIAMS, RONALD DAVID, manufacturing company executive; b. Stephenville, Tex., Jan. 18, 1946; s. James David and Mildred Lois (Beidleman) W.; m. Malinda Carol McCombs, Feb. 19, 1972; 1 child, Stephanie Jane. BBA, U. Tex., 1968; MBA, North Tex. State U., 1969. Adminstrv. mgr. DYNA Systems Inc., Irving, Tex., 1969-74; dir. sales personnel, dist. sales mgr., nat. sales mgr., v.p. sales, v.p. mktg. Keystone Valve USA, Houston, 1975-86; internat. product coordinator Keystone Internat. Inc., Houston, 1986-88; pres. Keystone Valve Mex., 1988—; instituted overseas div. DYNA Systems Inc., Birmingham, Eng., 1974; developed middle east ops., Keystone Valve, Arab Gulf countries, 1981-84. Vol. Irving (Tex.) Police, 1971-73; deacon, Bammel Rd. Ch. of Christ, Houston, 1983—. Mem. Valve Mfrs. Assn., Nat. Assn. Mfrs., Prestonwood Forest Club. Republican. Home: 14522 Ravenhurst Houston TX 77070 Office: Keystone Internat Inc 9600 W Gulf Bank Dr Houston TX 77040

WILLIAMS, RONALD JOHN, electrical engineer, educator; b. Blue Ash, Ohio, Dec. 14, 1927; s. John Wolfe and Ethel Virginia (Scheve) W.; B.S., Okla. A&M Coll., 1949; M.S., Okla. State U., 1963; Ph.D., Tex. A&M U., 1969; m. Patricia Whelan, Aug. 10, 1946; children: Carolyn Virginia (Mrs. Dan Roy Byrne), Eamonn Timothy. Asst. dean applied scis. Del Mar Coll., Corpus Christi, Tex., 1969-71, chmn. engring. tech., 1967-70, prof. engring. tech., 1968—; prof. emeritus, 1988; vis. prof. engring. tech. Tex. A&M U., 1971-72; dir. engring. tech. programs U. Ala., 1985-87; participant World Conf. on Edn. in Applied Engring. and Engring. Tech., Cologne, W.Ger., 1984, Internat. Conf. on Small Computers, Macau, 1985; pres. Scheve Inc.; cons. in field. NSF-Sci. Faculty fellow, 1964-65; named tchr. of year Tex. Jr. Coll., 1969, Piper prof., 1984; AEC trainee, 1965. Fellow Accreditation Bd. for Engring. and Tech.; mem. IEEE (Centennial Medal 1984), Nat., Tex. (pres. Nueces chpt. 1983-84, chmn. state ethics com. 1984-85) Socs. Profl. Engrs., ACM, Am. Nuclear Soc., N.Y. Acad. Scis., ASME, ASCE, AIAA, ISA, AIME, ASEE, ASSE, IIE, SAME, Soc. Mfg. Engrs., Sigma Xi, Eta Kappa Nu, Tau Beta Pi, Tau Alpha Pi. Democrat. Roman Catholic. Home: PO Box 6027 Corpus Christi TX 78466

WILLIAMS, RONALD OSCAR, systems engineer; b. Denver, May 10, 1940; s. Oscar H. and Evelyn (Johnson) W. BS in Applied Math., U. Colo. Coll. Engring., 1964, postgrad. U. Colo., U. Denver, George Washington U. Computer programmer Apollo Systems dept., missile and space div. Gen. Electric Co., Kennedy Space Ctr., Fla., 1965-67, Manned Spacecraft Ctr., Houston, 1967-68; computer programmer U. Colo., Boulder, 1968-73; computer programmer analyst def. systems div. System Devel. Corp. for NORAD, Colorado Springs, 1974-75; engr. def. systems and command-and-info. systems Martin Marietta Aerospace, Denver, 1976-80; systems engr. space and communications group, def. info. systems div. Hughes Aircraft Co., Aurora, Colo., 1980—. Vol. fireman Clear Lake City (Tex.) Fire Dept., 1968; officer Boulder Emergency Squad, 1969-76, rescue squadman, 1969-76, liaison to cadets, 1971, personnel officer, 1971-76, exec. bd., 1971-76, award of merit, 1971, 72, emergency med. technician 1973—; spl. police officer Boulder Police Dept., 1970-75; spl. dep. sheriff Boulder County Sheriff's Dept., 1970-71; nat. adv. bd. Am. Security Coun., 1979—, Coalition of Peace through Strength, 1979—; mem. Rep. Nat. Com., Nat. Rep. Senatorial Com. Served with USMCR, 1958-66. Decorated Organized Res. medal; recipient Cost Improvement Program award Hughes Aircraft Co., 1982, Systems Improvement award, 1982, Top Cost Improvement Program award, 1983. Mem. AAAS, Math. Assn. Am., Am. Math. Soc., Soc. Indsl. and Applied Math., AIAA, Armed Forces Communications and Electronics Assn., Assn. Old Crows, Am. Def. Preparedness Assn., Marine Corps Assn., Air Force Assn., Nat. Geog. Soc., Smithsonian Instn. (assoc.), Met. Opera Guild, Colo. Hist. Soc., Hist. Denver, Inc., Historic Boulder, Inc., Denver Art Mus., Denver Botanic Gardens, Denver Mus. Natural History, Denver Zool. Found., Inc., Am. Mensa Ltd., Denver Mile Hi Mensa, Hour of Power Eagles Club. Lutheran. Home: 7504 W Quarto Ave Littleton CO 80123-4332 Office: Hughes Aircraft Co Bldg S-75 MS CHL 16800 E Centretech Pkwy Aurora CO 80011

WILLIAMS, SMITH JAMES, JR., association executive; b. Balt., Aug. 22, 1945; s. Smith James Sr. and Margie N. Williams. Mgr., tng. dir. Am. Assn. Congress of Mgmt., 1988—; tng. coach staff at conf. Home and Office: 1428 N Fulton Baltimore MD 21217

WILLIAMS, SUSAN EILEEN, urban planner; b. Chgo., Dec. 13, 1952; d. Joseph Andrew and Alice (Regnier) W.; 1 child, Ryan Joseph. AA in Polit. Sci., Coll. of Desert, Palm Desert, Calif., 1971; BA in Polit. Sci., U. Calif., Riverside, 1973; M of Pub. Adminstrn., Consortium Calif. State Colls. and Univs., 1982. Planning trainee City of Indio, Calif., 1975-79, assoc. planner, 1979-80, prin. planner, 1980—, prin. planner redevel. agy., 1983—. Mem. Am. Planning Assn., Assn. Environ Profls., Ill. Geneal. Soc., Geneal. Club Am. Roman Catholic. Office: City of Indio 100 Civic Center Mall PO Drawer 1788 Indio CA 92202

WILLIAMS, THEODORE EARLE, diversified manufacturing company executive; b. Cleve., May 9, 1920; s. Stanley S. and Blanche (Albaum) W.; m. Rita Cohen, Aug. 28, 1952; children—Lezlie, Richard Atlas, Shelley, William Atlas, Wayne, Marsha, Patti. Student, Wayne U., 1937-38; BS in Engring, U. Mich., 1942, postgrad. in bus. adminstrn, 1942. Pres. Wayne Products Co., Detroit, 1942-43, Los Angeles, 1947-49; pres. Williams Metal Products Co., Inglewood, Calif., 1950-69; chmn. bd., pres., chief exec. officer Bell Industries, Los Angeles, 1970—; instr. U. Mich., 1942. Patentee in field. Served to 1st lt. AUS, 1943-46. Recipient Humanitarian award City of Los Angeles, 1977. Mem. Am. Soc. Mfg. Engrs. Democrat. Home: 435 N Layton Way Los Angeles CA 90049 Office: Bell Industries Inc 11812 San Vicente Blvd Los Angeles CA 90049

WILLIAMS, THEODORE SPECHT, JR., stockbroker; b. N.Y.C., Feb. 10, 1962; s. Theodore Specht and Sara (Comfort) W.; m. Stacia Jean Allen, Apr. 12, 1986. BA in Bus. Adminstrn., Rollins Coll., 1985. Real estate salesman Cheval Polo and Golf Club, Tampa, Fla., 1985-86; stockbroker Adler Coleman & Co., N.Y.C., 1986—; mem. N.Y. Stock Exchange, 1988—. Mem. Kappa Alpha. Republican. Presbyterian. Home: 101 W 79th St Apt 50 New York NY 10024 Office: Adler Coleman & Co 20 Broad St New York NY 10000

WILLIAMS, THERESA GAY, savings and loan company official; b. Dyersburg, Tenn., June 6, 1962; d. Herman Raye Williams and Betty Ann (Harris) Cooper. BS in Edn., Memphis State U., 1984, MS in Edn., 1984. Lic. real estate and mortgage broker, Fla. Mortgage loan processor Drew Mortgage/Investors Residential Co., Melbourne, Fla., 1985-86; comml. mortgage broker Indicom, Inc., Melbourne, 1986-87; residential mortgage solicitor Mortgage Svcs. Am., Cocoa, Fla., 1987; account exec. 1st Citizens Fed. Savs. & Loan Assn., Melbourne, 1987—; bd. dirs. Spl. Spotlight Theatre. Dir. Miss Memphis State Pageant, 1982-83. Mem. Home Builders and Ctrs. Assn. (pub. affairs com. 1988—, mortgage fin. com. 1988—, vice chmn. orientation com. 1988—, chmn. Fla. Children's Home 1988—, Assoc. of Month award 1988), South Brevard Profl. Network, NAFE, Greater Brevard C. of C., Mortar Bd, Kappa Delta Pi, Tau Alpha Pi. Home: PO Box 360383 Melbourne FL 32936-0383 Office: 1st Citizens Fed Savs & Loan Assn 1699 Sarno Rd Ste 18-19 Melbourne FL 32935

WILLIAMS, THOM ALBERT, insurance company executive; b. St. Louis, Dec. 31, 1941; s. Thom Reid and Martha Ann (Ruth) W.; m. Susan Melissa Raemdonck, Nov. 26, 1966(div. Feb. 1980); children: Thom Raemdonck, Kenneth Reid; m. Mary Virginia Thomas, March 4, 1981; children; Priety Thomas, Glee Morrissey. BBA, Washington U., St. Louis, 1962; postgrad., U. Pa., 1962-63. Assoc. trader Norris Grain Co., St. Louis, 1960; mgr. Crane Co., St. Louis and Chgo., 1961-62; dir. U.W. Mid Am. & V.W. Ins. Co., St. Louis, 1963-67; ptnr. Hodge & Williams Ins. Brokers, St. Louis, 1965-70; chmn. Williams Group Co., St. Louis, 1969-78; v.p. Marsh and McLennan, St. Louis, 1969-78; ptnr. Downtown Ford, St Louis, 1970-72; chmn., chief exec. officer Bryant Group Cos., St Louis, 1978—, Brytal Ltd., St Louis, 1987—; bd. dirs. EHL Ins. Group, St. Louis; exec. v.p., bd. dirs. Taylor Thomas Co., 1988—. Mem. Am. Assn. Ins. Mgmt. Cos.; pres. Assn. of Am. Mgmt.; Arts and Edn. Coun., St. Louis, St. Louis Symphony Soc., St. Louis Zoo Assn., Mo. Athletic Club. Office: Brytal Ltd 901 N Spoede Saint Louis MO 63146

WILLIAMS, TIMOTHY JON, inventor, publisher; b. Guthrie, Okla., July 26, 1961; s. Johnny William and Joyce Ann (Irick) W. Grad. high sch., Guthrie. Owner, mgr. Cobre Foundries, Guthrie, 1978-79; founder, owner T. Williams Enterprises, Guthrie, 1983—, Willow Publs., Guthrie, 1987—. Mem. Okla. Inventors Congress, Invention Devel. Soc. Republican. Methodist. Home and Office: Rt 6 Box 751 Guthrie OK 73044

WILLIAMS, TIMOTHY WAYNE, mortgage company executive; b. Knoxville, Tenn., Oct. 3, 1955; s. Ladonuel and Ouida Faye (Welch) W.; m. Judy Katherine Mize, Dec. 6, 1974; children: Timothy Wayne II, Jennifer Kay. Student, Draughon's Jr. Coll., 1974; BS in Acctg., U. Tenn., 1987. Acctg. clk. Clayton Homes Inc., Knoxville, 1974-76; loan officer Vanderbilt Mortgage, Knoxville, 1976-81, v.p. VMF, gen. mgr., 1981-85, v.p. CMH, gen. mgr., 1985—; mem. exec. com. Knoxville Retail Mchts. Credit Assn., 1987—, bd. dirs. Mem. Manufactured Housing Fin. Assn. Republican. Baptist. Office: Clayton Homes Inc PO Box 15169 Knoxville TN 37901

WILLIAMS, VELMA ELAINE, insurance executive; b. Coldspring, Tex., Sept. 13, 1950; d. Frank Sr. and Mary Jane (Jackson) Phlegm; m. Richard Henry Williams Jr., Aug. 14, 1970 (div. June 1982); children: Keta Dawn, Verlynn Elaine. BS in Criminology, Sam Houston State U., 1974. Asst. dir. Williams and Sons Mortuary, Huntsville, Tex., 1970-75; underwriter Allstate Ins. Co., Houston, 1975-78, Am. Gen. Ins. Co., Houston, 1978-81, Bayly, Martin & Foy Ins. Agy., Houston, 1981-82; prin., owner V.E. Phlegm Agy., Houston, 1982—. Writer, marketer commls., short plays, skits for children. Mem. Pine Village North Civic Club, Houston. Mem. Nat. Ins. Women's Assn., Nat. Female Execs. Assn., Nat. Ind. Agts. Assn., United Negro Coll. Fund, Rainbow Coalition Assn. Democrat. Lodge: Heroine of Jericho.

WILLIAMS, VERONICA ANN, management information systems marketing manager; b. Washington, Feb. 8, 1956; d. Vernon and Shirley Ann (Felton) W. BA, Brandeis U., 1977; MBA, Northwestern U., 1979. Systems mktg. rep. Control Data Corp., Chgo., 1979-81, mktg. rep., 1981-82; staff mgr. AT&T, Basking Ridge, N.J., 1982-84; nat. account exec. AT&T, N.Y.C., 1984-86; mgr. bus. planning AT&T, Berkeley Heights, N.J., 1986-87; product mgr. AT&T, Morristown, N.J., 1987-88; dist. mgr. Unisoft Corp., N.Y.C., 1988-89; acct. mgr. Lotus Devel. Corp., N.Y.C., 1989—; pres. Absolute Computer Techs., Inc., N.Y.C, 1989—. Mem. South Orange Planning Bd., 1985-87, South Orange Citizens Budget Adv. Com., 1983—. Mem. Nat. Black MBA Assn. (fin. chmn. Chgo. br. 1979-81, Performance award 1981). Home: 541 Scotland Rd South Orange NJ 07079 Office: Absolute Computer Techs PO Box 978 South Orange NJ 07079

WILLIAMS, WALTER BAKER, mortgage banker; b. Seattle, May 12, 1921; s. William Walter and Anna Leland (Baker) W.; m. Marie Davis Wilson, July 6, 1945; children: Kathryn Williams-Mullins, Marcia Frances Williams Swanson, Bruce Wilson, Wendy Susan. BA, U. Wash., 1943; JD, Harvard U., 1948. With Bogle & Gates, Seattle, 1948-63, ptnr., 1960-63; pres. Continental Inc., Seattle, 1963—; bd. dirs. United Graphics Inc., Seattle, 1973-86, Fed. Nat. Mortgage Assn., 1976-77. Rep. Wash. State Ho. of Reps., Olympia, 1961-63; sen. Wash. State Senate, Olympia, 1963-71; chmn. Econ. Devel. Council of Puget Sound, Seattle, 1981-82; pres. Japan-Am. Soc. of Seattle, 1971-72; chmn. Woodland Park Zoo Commn., Seattle, 1984-85. Served to capt. USMC, 1942-46, PTO. Recipient Brotherhood Citation, NCCJ, Seattle, 1980. Mem. Mortgage Bankers Assn. of Am. (pres. 1973-74), Wash. Mortgage Bankers Assn., Fed. Home Loan Mortgage Corp. Adv. Com., Wash. Savs. League (bd. dirs.). Republican. Congregationalist. Club: Rainier (pres. 1987-88) (Seattle). Lodge: Rotary (pres. local club 1984-85).

WILLIAMS, WALTER BERNARD, manufacturing company executive; b. Bklyn., May 1, 1942; s. Walter Bernard and Veronica Helen (Rodnite) W.; A.S., SUNY, Stony Brook, 1973; student Sem. Immaculate Conception, 1976-80; m. Jean Elizabeth Kempski, Aug. 18, 1962; children—Walter, Thomas, Peter, Katherine, Daniel. Systems mgr., Potter Instrument Co., Inc., Plainview, N.Y., 1962-70; mgmt. cons., N.Y.C., 1970-73; dir. mgmt. info. services MDS Bucode, Bohemia, N.Y., 1973-75; materials cons. Grumman Data Systems, Bethpage, N.Y., 1975-77; v.p. ILC Data Device Corp., Bohemia, 1977—; mem. adv. com. to pres., chmn. disaster planning com. Rapid Am. Co., N.Y.C., 1977-87, mem. guide Inc. and Guide Top Computer Exec. Group, 1985—; assoc. pastor Roman Cath. Parish of the Resurrection, Farmingville, N.Y., 1988—. Co-author Mission of the Church in the Roman Catholic Diocese of Rockville Centre, 1981. Mem. Bishop's Task Force to Determine Diocesan Priorities, 1978-81; moderator adult edn. dept. St. Margaret of Scotland Parish, Selden, N.Y., 1970-88; pres. ILCE Fed. Credit Union, 1979-83, dir., 1981-83; mem. fin. com. Diocese of Rockville Centre, 1981-88, mem. adv. bd. on permanent deaconate, 1983—, mem. diocesan religious studies faculty, 1982—, chmn. com. on curriculum devel., continuing edn. for permanent deacons, 1983—. Recipient Pius X medal, 1979; ordained deacon Roman Catholic Ch., 1979. Mem. Data Processing Mgmt. Assn., Soc. Mgmt. Info. Systems, Am. Prodn. and Inventory Control Soc., Mid-lantic COPICS Users Assn. (chmn. requirements com. 1981-85), Guide Internat., Inc. (Top Computer Exec. Group). Office: 105 Wilbur Pl Bohemia NY 11716

WILLIAMS, WALTER FRED, steel company executive; b. Upland, Pa., Feb. 7, 1929; s. Walter James and Florence (Stott) W.; m. Joan B. Carey, Aug. 26, 1950; children—Jeffrey F., Richard C., Douglas E. B.Civil Engring. summa cum laude, U. Del., 1951; postgrad., Harvard, 1969; D (hon.), Allentown Coll., 1983. With Bethlehem Steel Corp., Pa., 1951—, asst. chief engr. on staff v.p. operations, 1965-66, chief engr. constrn., 1966-67, chief engr. projects group engring. dept., then mgr. engring. in charge projects, design and constrn., 1967-68, asst. to v.p. engring., 1968, asst. v.p. shipbldg., 1968-70, v.p. shipbldg., 1970-75, v.p. steel operations, 1975-77, sr. v.p. steel operations, 1978-80, pres., chief operating officer, 1980-85, chmn., chief exec. officer, 1986—, also dir. Served to 1st lt. U.S. Army, 1951-53. Mem. Am. Iron and Steel Inst. (bd. dirs.), Nat. Assn. Mfrs. (bd. dirs.), Bus. Roundtable, Internat. Iron and Steel Inst. (bd. dirs.), Conf. Bd., Bus. Coun. Methodist. Clubs: Saucon Valley Country (Bethlehem). Home: Saucon Valley Rd 4 Bethlehem PA 18015 Office: Bethlehem Steel Corp 8th & Eaton Aves Bethlehem PA 18016

WILLIAMS, WALTER W., molded rubber and plastic products manufacturing company executive. With GE, 1956-87, v.p., gen. mgr. housewares and audio products div., 1979-83; chmn., pres. Gen. Electric Info. Svcs. Co., 1983-86; sr. v.p. mktg. and sales GE, 1986-87; now pres., chief operating officer Rubbermaid Inc., 1986—, also bd. dirs. Office: Rubbermaid Inc 1147 Akron Rd Wooster OH 44691 •

WILLIAMS, WENDY KAY, accountant; b. Columbus, Ohio, Sept. 23, 1963; d. Robert C. and Sally Ruth (Bisantz) W. BA, Wittenberg U., 1985. CPA, Ohio. Sr. auditor Ernst and Whinney, Columbus, 1985-88; fiscal dir. Quincy (Mass.) Community Action Programs, Inc., 1988—. Co-chmn., vol. adv. com. Franklin County Children Services, 1987; vol. Big Brothers and Big Sisters, 1986—; mem. Columbus Jaycees, 1985-88, bd. dirs., 1988. Mem. Ohio Soc. CPAs. Office: Quincy Community Action Programs Inc 1509 Hancock St Quincy MA 02169

WILLIAMS, WILLARD GORDON, accountant; b. Pearisburg, Va., June 5, 1948; s. Aubrey M. and JoAnn Williams; m. Brenda Rolen, April 12, 1969; 1 child, Travis. AA, Nat. Bus. Coll., 1969; BA, Upper Iowa U., 1974; MBA, James Madison U., 1989. Controller VPI Facilities Inc., Blacksburg, Va., 1970-79; controller/treas. Massapowax Sand & Gravel Corp., Fredericksburg, Va., 1979-82, RMC Inc., Harrisonburg, Va., 1982—. Named One of Outstanding Young Men Am., 1979. Mem. Nat. Assn. Accts. (v.p. 1982-88, pres. 1988-89). Lodges: Kiwanis, Lions. Office: RMC Inc 1030 S High St Harrisonburg VA 22801

WILLIAMS, WILLIAM HENRY, II, newspaper publishing executive; b. Birmingham, Ala., Oct. 21, 1931; s. Calvin Thomas and Lillian Elizabeth (Levey) W.; m. Lewis Mozelle Hensley, Feb. 28, 1959; 1 child, William Henry III. Student, Baylor U., 1952-55. Printer Waco (Tex.) Tribune-Herald, 1950-59; internat. rep. Internat. Typog. Union, Colorado Springs, Colo., 1960-68; editor, gen. mgr. Colorado Springs Free Press, 1969-70; dir. labor relations The Morning Telegraph, N.Y.C., 1970-72; gen. mgr. Daily Racing Form, Hightstown, N.J., 1972—; mem. adv. council journalsim dept. Baylor U., Waco, 1970-72. Chmn. Freehold (N.J.) Area Hosp., Inc., 1982-83, Cen. N.J. Health Affiliates, Freehold, 1987-88; vice chmn. Ctr. for Aging, Inc., Freehold, 1985—; dep. mayor Freehold Twp. Com., 1987; com.man Twp., 1987—, mayor, 1989—; chmn. Mayor's Task Force Substance Abuse. Served as sgt. U.S. Army, 1950-56. Named an Hon. Trustee Freehold Area Hosp., 1985—. Mem. Am. Newspaper Pubs. Assn., Newspaper Personnel Relations Assn., N.J. Press Assn., NCCJ (Brotherhood award 1986). Republican. Lutheran. Club: Exchange (Hightstown) (charter pres.). Lodges: Masons (32 degree), Shriners, Optimists (charter mem. Freehold chpt.). Home: 45 Kettle Creek Rd Freehold NJ 07728 Office: Daily Racing Form Inc 10 Lake Dr Hightstown NJ 08520

WILLIAMS, WINTON HUGH, civil engineer; b. Tampa, Fla., Feb. 14, 1920; s. Herbert DeMain and Alice (Grant) W.; grad. Adj Gens. Sch., Gainesville, Fla., 1943; student U. Tampa, 1948; grad. Transp. Sch., Ft. Eustis, Va., 1949; B.C.E., U. Fla., 1959; grad. Command and Gen. Staff Coll., Ft. Levenworth, Kans., 1964, Engrs. Sch., Ft. Belvoir, 1965, Indsl. Coll. Armed Forces, Washington, 1966, Logistics Mgmt. Center, Ft. Lee, Va., 1972; m. Elizabeth Walser Seelye, Dec. 18, 1949; children—Jan, Dick, Bill, Ann. Constrn. engr. air fields C.E., U.S. Army, McCoy AFB, Fla., 1959-61, Homestead AFB, Miami, Fla., 1961-62; civil engr. C.E., Jacksonville (Fla.) Dist. Office, 1962-64, chief master planning and layout sect., mil. br., engring. div., 1964-70; chief master planning and real estate div. Hdqrs. U.S. Army So. Command, Ft. Amador, C.Z., 1970-75, spl. asst. planning and mil. constrn. programming Marine Corps Air Bases Eastern Area, Marine Corps Air Sta., Cherry Point, N.C., 1975-82; cons. engr., Morehead City, N.C., 1982—. Mem. Morehead City Planning Bd., 1982—; active Boy Scouts, C.Z.; mem. nat. council U. Tampa. Served with AUS, World War II, Korean War; ETO, Korea; col. Res. Decorated Breast Order of Yun Hi (Republic of China); presdl. citation, Meritorious Service medal (Republic of Korea); eagle scout with gold palm; registered profl. engr., Fla., N.C., C.Z. Fellow ASCE; mem. Res. Officers Assn. (life, v.p. C.Am. and S.Am.), Nat. Soc. Profl. Engrs., Profl. Engrs. N.C., Am. Soc. Photogrammetry, Prestressed Concrete Inst. (profl.), Soc. Am. Mil. Engrs. (engr.), Nat. Eagle Scout Assn., Nat. Rifle Assn. Am., Am. Legion (life), Order Arrow, Theta Chi. Presbyterian. Lion. Clubs: Fort Clayton Riding (pres.), Fort Clayton Golf, Gamboa Golf and Country, Balboa Gun, Am. Bowling Congress. Home and Office: 4408 Coral Point Dr Morehead City NC 28557

WILLIAMSON, BARBARA DIANE, lawyer, consultant; b. Riverside, N.J., July 24, 1950; d. Frederick Raymond and Dorothy (Jessup) Ott; m. Luis Williamson, May 4, 1973. BFA, William Paterson Coll., 1972; lic. vocat. nurse, Yakima Valley Community Coll., 1981; BS in Nursing with honors, Seattle U., 1983; MS in Community Health Nursing with honors, U. Wash., 1984; JD, U. Puget Sound, 1988. Bar: N.J. 1988; cert. hazardous control mgr. Art tchr. Delran (N.J.) Twp. Schs., 1972-78; recreational coordinator Delran (N.J.) Twp. Summer Schs., 1973-76; RN Yakima (Wash.) Valley Meml. Hosp., 1980-85; occupational health cons., researcher Evergreen Legal Services, Granger, Wash., 1986; environ. analyst Westinghouse Hanford Co., Richland, Wash., 1987; atty. Westinghouse Co., Richland, 1988—; cons. Occupational and Envirn. Cons. Svcs., 1988; occupational health and safety mgmt. researcher U. Hosp., Seattle, 1983-84; pesticide educator Evergreen Legal Services, Granger, Wash., 1986; smoking policy cons. U. Puget Sound Law Sch., Tacoma, 1986-87; researcher, legal assoc. Dept. of Ecology Wash. State Atty. Gen., Lacey, 1987. Grantee U. Puget Sound, 1986, Alaskan-Northwest Synod of Presbyn. Chs., 1986. Mem. ABA, Wash. Assn. Occupational Health Nurses, Wash. State Pub. Health Assn. (legis. com. 1984), N.W. Occupational Health Nurses Assn. (mem. nominating com. 1984), Am. Pub. Health Assn., Am. Assn. of Occupational Health Nurses, Phi Delta Phi, Alpha Sigma Nu, Sigma Theta Tau. Home: 1900 Stevens Dr Box 626 Richland WA 99352 Office: Westinghouse Co. B3-06 1100 Jadwin Ave Richland WA 99352

WILLIAMSON, DAVID LEE, financial planner; b. Pitts., Sept. 4, 1949; s. Edgar Lee Williamson and Hazel Adele (Stewart) Stratton; m. Sandra Jean Perlman, Aug. 25, 1974; children: Leah, Megan. BA in Psychology, Pa. State U., 1971; MA in Psychology, Calif. State U., Fresno, 1980; cert., Coll. for Fin. Planning, Denver, 1987. Adult instr. Fresno Unified Sch. Dist., 1974-84, instr. fin. planning, 1986—; fin. planner Waddell & Reed, Inc., Fresno, 1984-85, Fin. Adv. Assocs., Inc., Fresno, 1985—. Mem. Internat. Assn. for Fin. Planning, Inst. Cert. Fin. Planners. Office: Fin Adv Assocs Inc 2650 W Shaw St Ste 103 Fresno CA 93711

WILLIAMSON, EDWARD B., III, financial executive; b. Wichita, Kans., Jan. 20, 1947; s. Edward B. and Helen (Poindexter) W.; m. Georganna L. Hobson, Aug. 11, 1977; 1 child, Adam Edward. B in Bus., U. Md., 1971. Dir., comptroller Associated Labs., Wichita, 1971-74; dir., pres., chief exec. officer Sci. Labs., Denver, 1974-85, Vitro Diagnostics, Denver, 1986—, Securities, USA, Englewood, Colo., 1987—, CEA Lab., Inc., Lakewood, Colo., 1987—; dir., v.p., sec. Adam Zachary, Lakewood, 1987—, Charmara, Littleton, Colo., 1987—, Mendell/Denver, Denver, 1987—, Aero Magnetics, Inc., Englewood, Colo., 1988—. Served with USMC, 1967-71. Office: Securities USA 5325 S Valentia Way Ste 100 Englewood CO 80111

WILLIAMSON, ERNEST LAVONE, petroleum company executive; b. Perryton, Tex., Sept. 10, 1924; s. Ernest and Mabel Robert (Donnell) W.; m. Gertrude Florence Watkins, Dec. 2, 1950; children: Richard Dean, Judith Watkins, Mary Nan, David Ernest. BSEE, U. Okla., 1950; student, Hill's Bus. Coll., 1943. Sales and service rep. Hughes Tool Co., 1950-52; with land dept. Phillips Petroleum Co., 1952-54; with La. Land & Exploration Co., New Orleans, 1954—, exec. v.p., 1967-74, pres., 1974-84, chief operating officer, 1982-83, chief exec. officer, 1984-88, chmn., 1985-88, also dir.; bd. dirs. Hibernia Nat. Bank, New Orleans, Halliburton Co. Mem. adv. bd. Salvation Army, 1971—; bd. govs. Tulane U. Med. Ctr.; bd. visitors U. Okla.; bd. dirs. World Trade Ctr., New Orleans Jr. Achievement. Served with U.S. Army, 1943-46, PTO. Mem. Am. Assn. Petroleum Landmen, Ind. Petroleum Assn. Am., Mid-Continent Oil and Gas Assn. (chmn. 1980-81), Am. Petroleum Inst., Nat. Assn. Mfrs. (bd. dirs.), New Orleans and the River Region C. of C. (bd. dirs.), Nat. Petroleum Council, Natural Gas Supply Assn. (past chmn.), Metairie Country Club, Plimsol Club, Petroleum Club, Internat. House, Tchefuncta Country Club. Presbyterian. Office: La Land & Exploration Co 909 Poydras St PO Box 60350 New Orleans LA 70160

WILLIAMSON, FLETCHER PHILLIPS, real estate broker; b. Cambridge, Md., Dec. 16, 1923; s. William Fletcher and Florence M. (Phillips) W.; student U. Md., 1941, 42; m. Betty June (Stoker), Apr. 6, 1943; 1 son, Jeffrey Phillips; m. 2d, Helen M. Stumberg, Aug. 28, 1972. Test engr. Engring. Lab., Glen Martin Co., 1942-43; salesman Corkran Ice Cream Co., Cambridge, 1946-50; real estate broker, 1950—; chmn. bd. Williamson Real Estate, Dorchester Corp., 1963-72; bd. dirs. WCEM, Inc., 1966-75; vice chmn. bd., dir. Nat. Bank of Cambridge, 1979—; dir. Cam-Storage Inc., Dorchester Indsl. Devel. Corp., Delmarva Bank Data Processing Ctr.; co-receiver White & Nelson, Inc. Bd. dirs. Delmarva council Boy Scouts Am.; past pres. Cambridge Hosp., United Fund of Dorchester County; bd. dirs. Del. Mus. Natural History, Dorchester County Pub. Library; bd. dirs., v.p. Game Conservation Internat. Served as ordnance tech. intelligence engr. AUS, 1943-46; ETO. Mem. Md. Real Estate Assn. (gov. 1956-66), Outdoor Writers Assn., Nat. Rifle Assn., Nat. Def. Preparedness Assn., Cambridge Dorchester C. of C. (dir. 1955—), Power Squadron (comdr. 1954-56), Dorchester County Bd. Realtors (pres.), Explorers Club, Soc. of S. Pole. Methodist. Clubs: Rolling Rock, Shikar Safari, Anglers, Chesapeake Bay Yacht, Camp Fire, Md., Georgetown. Lodges: Masons, Shriners.

WILLIAMSON, GILBERT PEMBERTON, JR., computer company executive; b. Danville, Calif., Apr. 26, 1937; m. Joyce Caroline (Schaefer), Aug. 28, 1960; children: Jennifer Mary, Heidi Elizabeth. AA in Elec. Engring., Diablo Valley Coll., 1957; BS in Indsl. Mgmt., San Jose State U., 1960. V.p. NCR Corp., Dayton, Ohio, 1974-86, exec. v.p., 1987-88, pres., 1988—.

WILLIAMSON, JOHN THOMAS, minerals company executive; b. Atlanta, Oct. 1, 1925; s. Walter Berry and Clare (Mathews) W.; m. Ava Gene Shealy, June 11, 1949; children: John Thomas, Ava Clare, Robin E., Leila Ann. Student, N. Ga. Coll., 1942-43; BS in Indsl. Engring., Ga. Inst. Tech., 1949. Registered profl. engr., Ga. Chief engr. Thiele Kaolin Co., Sandersville, Ga., 1949-57; assoc. W.C. Davis and Assocs., Atlanta and Tallahassee, 1957-60; chief engr. So. Clays, Inc., Gordon, Ga., 1960-63; asst. gen. mgr. Freeport Kaolin Co., N.Y.C., 1972-77, v.p., gen. mgr., 1977-78, pres., 1978-85; cons., gen. mgr. Gordon ops. Engelhard Corp., N.J., 1985-86; pres. IMPEX Corp., Milledgeville, Ga., 1987—; bd. dirs. Freeport Export Corp., Freeport Overseas Sales Co. Patentee on processing kaolins; contbr. articles to profl. jours. Mem. adv. bd. Ga. Coll., 1979-82, found. bd., 1983—, vice chmn. found. bd., 1988-89; mem. nat. adv. bd. Ga. Tech. Inst., 1979-85, adv. bd. sch. mgmt. U. Ga., 1979-80. With USNR, 1943-46. Mem. TAPPI, China Clay Producers, Ga. State Mining Assn., Ga. Soc. Profl. Engrs., Ga. Bus. and Industry Assn. (bd. dirs. 1978-83), Bus. Coun. Ga. (bd. dirs. 1983-88), Ga. C. of C., Lions. Baptist. Home: 1810 Tanglewood Rd Milledgeville GA 31061 Office: IMPEX Corp PO Box 1028 Milledgeville GA 31061 Also: IMPEX Corp 157 Darien Hwy Brunswick GA 31520

WILLIAMSON, ROBERT CHARLES, marketing executive; b. West Chester, Pa., Jan. 3, 1925; s. Herman Gideon and Grace (Faddis) W.; m. Frances Yvonne Ishmael, Apr. 10, 1945 (div. July 1969); children: Robert C. Jr., Edward H., Richard F., Kathryn G.; m. Mary Elizabeth Bogle, Oct. 1, 1983. BS, Naval Sci. Sch., Monterey, Calif., 1959; postgrad. in Internat. Relations, Naval War Coll., Newport, R.I., 1960. Commd. ensign, designated naval aviator USN, 1944, advanced through grades to comdr., 1963, ret., 1966; gen. mgr. Springfield (Va.) Assocs., 1966-69; v.p. CCC Corp., Rosslyn, Va., 1969-70; pres. WILCO Assocs., Mt. Vernon, Va., 1970-73; dir. mktg. Documail Systems, Lenexa, Kans., 1973-80; N.Am. mktg. mgr. Leigh Instruments, Waterloo, Ont., Can., 1981-83; v.p. Tabs Assocs., Abingdon, Md., 1983-87; pres. WILLMAR Assocs. Internat., Brandon, Fla., 1987—. Mem. Nat. Assn. Presort Mailers (exec. dir. 1984—), Ret. Officers' Assn., Assn. Former Intelligence Officers, Assn. Naval Aviation. Club: Army and Navy. Home and Office: 3906 Butternut Ct Brandon FL 33511

WILLIAMSON, ROBERT WEBSTER, brokerage house executive; b. Springfield, Ill., Dec. 10, 1942; s. Robert W. and Catherine (Jackson) W.; m. M. Eleanor Brushwood, June 23, 1984; children: R. Todd, Elizabeth, Thomas. BS, Northwestern U., 1965, JD, 1968. Bar: Ill. 1968. V.p. internat. Continental Ill. Nat. Bank, Chgo., 1967-73; mgr. corp. fin. Continental Ill. Ltd., London, 1973-77; sr. v.p. Merrill Lynch and Co., London, Hong Kong, N.Y.C., 1977—. Mem. Chgo. Bar Assn., Hong Kong Jockey Club. Office: Merrill Lynch & Co Inc World Financial Ctr New York NY 10080-0746

WILLIAMSON, VIKKI LYN, finance executive; b. Huntington, W.Va., June 30, 1956; d. Ernest E. and Wanda C. (Cole) W. BA in Secondary Edn., English, Temple U., 1978; postgrad. in Acctg. and Fin., U. Cin., 1984—. CPA, Ohio; cert. tchr., Tenn., Ohio. Tchr. Springfield Christian Acad., Tenn., 1978-79; acctg. asst. Children's Hosp. Med. Ctr., Cin., 1979-84; asst. dir. fin. svcs. U. Cin. Med. Ctr., 1984-85, dir. fin. svcs., 1985-88, dir. fin. and adminstrn., 1988—; instr. Miami U., Oxford, Ohio, 1984—; bd. dirs. Contemporary Dance Theatre, 1987—. Mem. Healthcare Fin. Mgmt. Assn., Am. Assn. Blood Banks, Ohio Assn. Blood Banks (fin. com. mem. 1986—), Assn. Women Adminstrs. (fin. com. mem. 1987—), U. Cin. Assn. Mid-Level Adminstrs. (bd. dirs. 1987—), Am. Inst. CPA's, Alpha Epsilon Theta, Beta Gamma Sigma, Delta Mu Delta. Office: U Cin Med Ctr Hoxworth Blood Ctr 3231 Burnet Ave ML #55 Cincinnati OH 45267

WILLIG, BILLY WINSTON, metal processing executive; b. Temple, Tex., Mar. 11, 1929; s. Bruno William and Mary Sophia (Barth) W.; m. Lanelle Clyde Brooks, Sept. 11, 1951; children: Bruce Wayne, Jana Lynn. BS in Mech. Engring., U. Tex., 1951. Pres. Western Iron Works, San Angelo, Tex., 1950—; Bd. dirs. San Angelo Industries, Inc., pres. 1975-80; pres., bd. dirs. West Tex. Indsl. Devel. Corp., 1980—. Mem. Nat. Council Boy Scouts Am., pres. Area IV 1980-83; v.p. S. Cen. Region, 1984-87; nat. rep. Boy Scouts Am., 1986—; mem. adv. bd. Salvation Army, 1979—, chmn. 1984; v.p. Dist. VI Area PTA, 1983-85, sec. 1986-87; v.p. West Tex. C. of C., 1984-85; mem. Hwy. 87 Improvement com., 1983—, pres., 1983-88; bd. dirs. YMCA, 1977—, pres. 1980-82, exec. com. 1983—; chmn., bd. dirs. city council adv. com. San Angelo Pub. Housing Authority, 1985—, chmn. 1988—; chmn. Concho Valley Pvt. Industry Council, 1982—; trustee San Angelo Ind. Sch. Dist., 1966-84; trustee Tex. Assn. Sch. Bds., 1975-84, sec.-treas. 1982-83, bd. dirs. Tex. Sch. Services Found., 1982-84, chmn. Unemployment Compensation Trust, 1982-84. Recipient Silver Antelope award Boy Scouts Am., 1988. With U.S. Army Corp Engrs., 1952-54. Recipient Silver Beaver award Boy Scouts Am., 1976; named Ex-Student of Yr., Angelo State U., 1984. Mem. Am. Foundrymen's Soc., Tex. Assn. Pvt. Industry Councils (bd. dirs. 1984—, treas. 1987, v.p. 1989), Concho Valley Pvt. Industry Council (chmn. 1984), San Angelo Mfrs. Assn. (pres. 1981—), Angelo State U. Ex-Students Assn. (bd. dirs. 1983-87, v.p. 1985-86, pres. 1986-87), San Angelo C. of C. (pres. 1978, mil. affairs. com. 1984—, chmn. hwy. com. 1986—, Citizen of Yr. 1979). Presbyterian. Club: Concho Yacht (commodore 1969). Lodges: Rotary. (pres. 1980), Masons. Home: 1618 Shafter San Angelo TX 76901 Office: Western Iron Works Inc 21 E State St San Angelo TX 76903

WILLIG, LESLIE AUGUST, photography equipment manufacturing company executive; b. Ft. Wayne, Ind., Jan. 29, 1926; s. August Aloysius and Laura Elizabeth Willig; children: Constance J. Willig Hansen, Diana K. Willig Brummer, Larry A., Rosanne M. WIllig Johnson, Laura L. BS, Purdue U., 1947; MA, U. Louisville, 1951; PhD, U. Iowa, 1956. Asst. dean of men U. Iowa, Iowa City, 1954-56; asst. dir., assoc. prof. Purdue U., Ft. Wayne, 1956-60; exec. v.p. Tri-State U., Angola, Ind., 1960-70; v.p., bd. dirs. Bankers Investment Corp., Ft. Wayne, 1966-75; chmn. bd. dirs., chief exec. officer, pres. Photo Control Corp., Mpls., 1974—; bus. broker and cons. mgmt., Ft. Wayne, 1970—; sec., bd. dirs. North Snow Bay, Inc. Chmn. Internat. Sci. Fair Council, 1967; co-founder, bd. dirs. Sci. Edn. Found. Ind., 1963—, chmn., 1986-88. Served to capt. USNR, 1944-47, 51-53. Recipient Disting. Pub. Service award Navy Dept., 1973. Mem. Am. Psychol. Assn., Midwest Psychol. Assn., Naval Res. Assn. (nat. pres. 1971-73, Merit award 1974). Roman Catholic. Club: Summit (Ft. Wayne). Home: Rural Rt 1 Box 778 Fremont IN 46737 Office: Photo Control Corp 4800 Quebec Ave N Minneapolis MN 55428 also: 812 Commerce Bldg Fort Wayne IN 46802

WILLIS, CHARLES RALPH, accountant; b. Toledo, Nov. 13, 1947; s. Huston and Wilhelmina (Spencer) W.; m. Sharlon Lynn Bunts, Nov. 27, 1967; children: Nickelle Renee, Concha Lynn. BBA in Fin., U. Toledo, 1979. Cost clk. Doehler Jarvis div. N.L. Industries, Toledo, 1970, quality control statistician, 1970-72, supr. inventory control, 1972-74, supr. cost acctg., 1974-77, sr. internal auditor, 1977-78, mgr. div. stores and purchase, 1978-80; contbr. Sunshine Children's Home, Maumee, Ohio, 1980-81; v.p. adminstrn. United Way Greater Toledo, 1981—; fin. planner Toledo, 1984—. Mem. alumni Toledo Scape, 1980—; bd. dirs. Cordelia Martin Health Ctr., Toledo, 1983—, Family Life Edn. Coun., Toledo, 1984—. Decorated Bronze Star. Mem. Bldg. Owners and Mgrs. Assn., Toledo, 1983. Office: United Way Greater Toledo 1 Stranahan Sq Toledo OH 43604

WILLIS, DENNIS DARYL, consulting engineer; b. Norton, Va., Apr. 29, 1948; s. Virgil Hyman and Reva Mae (Hubbard) W., m. Elizabeth Jewell Short, June 15, 1967; children: Kristi, Kimberly. BSCE, Va. Poly. Inst. and State U., 1970; postgrad., Pa. State U., Colo. Sch. Mines, Harvard U., 1975, 76, 78-79. Registered profl. engr., Ky., Va., W.Va., Tenn. Project engr. Island Creek Coal Co., Keen Mountain, Va., 1970-73; design engr. Wiley & Wilson, Inc., Lynchburg, Va., 1973-74; v.p. head mining div. Thompson & Litton, Inc., Wise, Va., 1974-80, pres., 1980-85; pres. Willis, Skeen & Assocs., Norton, 1985—; pres. Highland Land & Mineral Co., Inc., Wise, 1978-85, Willis Enterprises, Norton, 1980—, Corpotal, Inc., Wise, 1982-85; instr. Coal Overview course, 1979-80. Contbr. articles to profl. jours. Mem., deacon, Norton Christian Ch.; mem. treas., Norton Indsl. Devel. Auth.; dir. Community Home Care; past mem. Norton City Sch. Bd. Named one of Outstanding Young Men of Am., U.S. Jaycees, 1984; recipient Airman award Dept. Aviation, 1985, Cert. Recognition award Va. Dept. Aviation 1985. Mem. ASCE, NSPE, Am. Cons. Engrs. Council (chmn. nat. mining com., govtl. affairs steering com.), Va. Cons. Engrs. Council (past v.p. Western div., Design Excellence award 1979), Soc. Mining Engrs., Profl. Engrs. Pvt. Practice, Assn. Mining and Reclamation Profls. (founder), Va. Mining and Reclamation Assn. (bd. dirs. 1976—), Jaycees (sec. 1974-75). Mem. Christian Ch. Lodge: Lions. Home: 513 Chestnut St Norton VA 24273 Office: Willis Skeen & Assocs 310-A Kentucky Ave Norton VA 24273

WILLIS, GEORGE EDMUND, chemical processing and electrical manufacturing executive; b. Newmarket, Ont., Can., July 16, 1920; came to U.S., 1925; s. George Clarence and Marion Romer (Gillespie) W.; m. Dorothy Anne Rice, June 7, 1943; children: Dorothy Anne, Jacqueline Pamela, Marion Jean, George Patterson Rice, James Edmund, Lorna Isabel; m. Rolande Germaine deLipowski Hastings, July 23, 1983; stepchildren: Julian Martin, Marianne Frances. BS in Chem Engring. cum laude, Mich. State U., 1942; MBA, Harvard U., 1947; DHL (hon.), Lake Erie Coll., 1984. Engr. Lincoln Electric Co., Cleve., 1947-51, supt., 1951-59, v.p., 1959-69, exec. v.p., 1969-72, pres., 1972-87, chief exec. officer, 1987—, also chmn. bd.; bd. dirs. Lincoln Big Three, Inc., Baton Rouge, Big Three Lincoln Alaska, Inc., Anchorage, Big Three Lincoln (U.K.) Ltd., Ross-Shire Scotland, Lincoln Electric Co. (Europe) S.A., Grand-Quevilly, France, Lincoln Electric Co. Can., Ltd., Toronto, Ont., Lincoln Electric Co. (Australia) Pty., Ltd. Chmn. bd. trustees, treas. Camp Ho Mita Koda; bd. govs. Geauga County YMCA; bd. trustees Lake Erie Coll.; trustee, exec. com. Cleve. Council World Affairs, active Cleve. Com. Fgn. Relations. Served to maj. AUS, 1942-46, ETO. Decorated Bronze Star with oak leaf cluster. Mem. Am. Welding Soc., Wire Assn., Greater Cleve. Growth Assn., Cleve. Engring. Soc., Elec. Mfrs. Club, Alpha Chi Sigma, Tau Beta Pi, Phi Kappa Phi. Clubs: Fifty, Harvard Bus. Sch. (Cleve.); Chagrin Valley Hunt, St. Christopher's-by-the-River, The Hangar. Home: 11661 Sperry Rd Chesterland OH 44026 Office: Lincoln Electric Co 22801 St Clair Ave Cleveland OH 44117

WILLIS, GLENN HARRY, oil company executive; b. Magnolia, Ark., Apr. 18, 1922; s. Bernard Barnwell and Mary Irene (Thornton) W.; m. Louise McKinney, May 11, 1948; children: Stephen, Susan, Mary Lynn, Glenda. Oil buyer Standard Oil of Ind., New Orleans, 1950-55; oil buyer Clark Oil & Refining Corp., Dallas, 1955-56, v.p. crude oil supply and transp. dept., 1966-76; v.p., dir. Intercontinental Petroleum Corp., Inc., Dallas, 1976-77; pres., dir. Dorchester Petroleum Co., Dallas, 1977—, Dorchester Refining Co., Dallas, 1977—, Dorchester Pipeline Co., Dallas, 1977—, Dorchester Gas Corp., Dallas, 1977—; pres., chmn. bd. Dor-Texan Petroleum, Inc., 1981-86; exec. v.p. Clark Maritime, Inc.; pres. Am. Shield Refining Co., 1987—; bd. dirs. Southcap Pipeline Co., Chgo. Pipeline Co., Clark Pipeline Co., Arabian Shield Devel. Co. Active precinct worker Dem. party, 1956—. Served with AUS, 1940-45. Decorated Combat Infantryman's badge. Mem. Am. Inst. Mining Engrs. Clubs: Petroleum of Dallas, Dallas Athletic, Austin (Tex.). Home: 11084 Erhard Dr Dallas TX 75228 Office: 12700 Park Cental Dr Suite 415 Dallas TX 75251

WILLIS, HAROLD WENDT, SR., real estate developer; b. Marion, Ala., Oct. 7, 1927; s. Robert James and Della (Wendt) W.; student Loma Linda U., 1960, various courses San Bernardino Valley Coll.; m. Patsy Gay Bacon, Aug. 2, 1947 (div. Jan. 1975); children: Harold Wendt II, Timothy Gay, April Ann, Brian Tad, Suzanne Gail; m. Vernette Jacobson Osborne, Mar. 30, 1980 (div. 1984); m. Ofelia Alvarez, Sept. 23, 1984; children: Ryran Robert, Samantha Ofelia. Ptnr., Victoria Guernsey, San Bernardino, Calif., 1950-63, co-pres., 1963-74, pres., 1974—; owner Quik-Save, 1966—, K-Mart Shopping Ctr., San Bernardino, 1969—; pres. Energy Delivery Systems, Food and Fuel, Inc. San Bernardino City water commr., 1965—. Bd. councillors Loma Linda (Calif.) U., 1968-85, pres., 1971-74. Served as officer U.S. Mcht. Marine, 1945-46. Recipient Silver medal in 3000 meter steeplechase Sr. Olympics, U. So. Calif., 1979, 81, 82, 83; lic. pvt. pilot. Mem. Calif. Dairy Industries Assn. (pres. 1963, 64), Liga Internat. (2d v.p. 1978, pres. 1982, 83). Seventh-day Adventist (deacon 1950-67). Office: PO Box 5607 San Bernardino CA 92412

WILLIS, JOHN PATRICK, chemist; b. Albany, N.Y., Mar. 10, 1947; s. John James and Mary Catherine (Varden) W.; B.S., Iona Coll., 1969; M.S., SUNY, Oswego, 1974; Ph.D., U. Conn., 1977; m. Tientje Jane Dirzuweit, July 22, 1972. Assoc. prodn. chemist Winthrop Labs., Rensselaer, N.Y., 1970-72; rsch. chemist Uniroyal, Inc., Middlebury, Conn., 1977-79; postdoctoral researcher U. Minn., Mpls., 1979-80; mgr. chem. rsch. Nova Biomed. Corp., Newton, Mass., 1980-83; founder, chmn. Ilex Corp., Marlboro, Mass., 1983-87; med. cons., 1987-88; founder T.J. Assocs., Biomed. Cons., 1987—; v.p., chief operating officer Sharon Drive Corp., Westlake, Ohio, 1988—. U. Conn. Rsch. Found. fellow, 1976. Mem. adv. bd. Clin Lab. Practice, Mass. Dept. Pub. Health, 1986-87, 128 Entrepreneurs' Ctr., Waltham, Mass., 1986-88, tech. adv. coun. Edison Beiotech. Ctr., Cleve., 1988—. Fellow Am. Inst. Chemists; mem. Am. Chem. Soc., Electrochem. Soc., Am. Assn. Clin. Chemistry, N.Y. Acad. Scis., Sigma XI, Phi Kappa Phi, Phi Lambda Upsilon. Democrat. Roman Catholic. Rsch. in bioelectrochemistry and organic electrochemistry; patentee in field.

WILLIS, MCDONALD, educational administrator; b. Atlanta, Dec. 18, 1937; s. William Paul and Essilee (McDonald) W.; m. Pamela Noel Williams, Sept. 9, 1961; children—Pamela Candace, Rachael Anne. BA, Oglethorpe U., 1959; postgrad Ga. State U., 1963-66, West Ga. Coll., 1968-71. Cert. fund raising exec. Nat. Soc. Fund Raising Execs. Mgmt. officer trainee Trust Co. Ga., Atlanta, 1963-66; dir. alumni affairs West Ga. Coll., Carrollton, 1966-70; headmaster Rutledge Acad., Ga., 1970-71, Oak Mountain Acad., Carrollton, 1971-73; mortgage loan officer Days Inns Am., Atlanta, 1973-74; v.p. devel. Reinhardt Coll., Waleska, Ga., 1974—; bd. dirs. Citizens Bank, Ball Ground, Ga. Lt. (j.g.) USNR, 1959-63. Mem. Coun. Advancement and Suport Edn., Nat. Soc. Fund Raising Execs. Democrat. Baptist. Avocations: racquetball, tennis, golf, reading, music. Office: Reinhardt Coll PO Box 98 Waleska GA 30183

WILLIS, RAYMOND LLOYD, manufacturing executive; b. Graham, Ky., Jan. 12, 1936; s. William R. and Margaret O. (Vinson) W.; m. Virginia B. Witherspoon, June 12, 1965 (div. Mar. 1978). AB, Western Ky. U., 1959, MA, 1962. Account exec. CIGNA, N.Y.C., 1965-72; cons. Peat, Marwick, Mitchell Co., N.Y.C., 1972-76; corp. dir. United Technologies Corp., Hartford, Conn., 1976—; chmn. bd. dirs. UTC Pension Trust, Ltd., London, 1982—; bd. dirs. Assn. Pvt. Pension and Welfare Plans, Washington, 1978—; trustee Retirement System for Savs. Banks, N.Y.C., 1983—, Employee Benefits Research Inst., Washington, 1980—. Republican. Presbyterian. Home: 180 Fern St West Hartford CT 06119 Office: United Technologies Corp #1 Financial Plaza Hartford CT 06101

WILLIS, STANLEY EARL, II, retired psychiatrist, municipal government official; b. Hoisington, Kans., July 9, 1923; s. Stanley Earl and Leota Pearl (Brewer) W.; m. Edith Clark Blair, June 23, 1945 (dec.); 1 child: Alan Matson. BA, Stanford U., 1944; MD, McGill U., 1948; JD, U. San Diego, 1968. Diplomate Am. Bd. Psychiatry and Neurology. Commd. lt. USN, 1948, advanced through grades to comdr.; pres. Park Manor Hotel, Inc., San Diego, 1978-80; mng. ptnr. Willis & Willis, San Diego, 1980—, The Centre Assocs.; pres. Gentry Farm Enterprises, Inc., 1988-89; commr. civil service City of San Diego, 1986—; pvt. practice psychiatry, San Diego, 1957. Author: Understanding and Counseling Male Homosexual, 1967; co-author: New Dimensions in Psychosomatic Medicine; contbr. articles profl. jours. Bd. dirs. San Diego Civic Light Opera Assn., 1959-61; pres. La Jolla (Calif.) Stage Co., 1983-85. Fellow Am. Psychiat. Assn. (life), Am. Psychoanalytic Physicians; mem. AMA, Calif. Med. Assn., San Diego Yacht Club. Republican. Episcopalian. Home: 7161 Encelia Dr La Jolla CA 92037

WILLIS, WILLIAM HAROLD, JR., management consultant, executive search specialist; b. Harrisburg, Pa., Dec. 19, 1927; s. William Harold and Elizabeth Tilford (Keferstein) W.; BA, Yale U., 1949; m. Pauline Sabin Smith, Oct. 15, 1955; children: Wendell Willis Livingston, Christopher, Gregory. Mktg. mgr. Owens-Corning Fiberglas Corp., N.Y.C., 1956-62; div. mgr. AMF, Inc., Greenwich, Conn., 1962-65; ptnr. Devine, Baldwin & Willis, N.Y.C., 1965-70; pres. William H. Willis, Inc., N.Y.C., 1970—. Bd. dirs. Girls Clubs Am., Inc., N.Y.C., 1962-80, treas., chmn. fin. com., 1961-76, chmn. devel. com., 1976-77; expdn. leader Am. Mus. Nat. History

Davison-Willis Expdn. to Madagascar; vestryman St. Barnabas Episcopal Ch., Greenwich, Conn., 1978-81; bd. dirs. Greenwich Hosp. Corp.; human resources com. YMCA of Greater N.Y.; del. People to People Citizen Amb. Program, del. traveling to Peoples Republic of China. With U.S. Army, 1950-52. Mem. Assn. Exec. Search Cons. (dir. 1979-82). Republican. Clubs: Yale, Racquet and Tennis (N.Y.C.). Home: 55 Zaccheus Mead Ln Greenwich CT 06831-3716 Office: 164 Mason St Greenwich CT 06830

WILLIS, WILLIAM HENRY, marketing executive; b. Canton, Ohio, Mar. 15, 1951; s. William Lincoln and Gwendolyn Ann (Wasem) W.; m. Rebecca Ann Klinker, June 16, 1973; children: Kristen Ann, Patrick Michael, Susan Kathleen. BSBA, Ohio State U., 1973; M of Mgmt., Northwestern U., 1974. Assoc. product mgr. H.J. Heinz Co., Pitts., 1974-76; product mgr. Pillsbury Co., Mpls., 1976-77, mktg. mgr., 1977-79, group mktg. mgr., 1979-81; dir. bus. planning Pepsico, Inc., Purchase, N.Y., 1981-82, dir. mktg., 1982-85; exec. v.p. mktg. Ogden Allied Svcs. Corp., N.Y.C., 1985-87, exec. v.p. indsl. svcs., 1987—. Exec. fundraiser Minn. Orch. Guaranty Fund, Mpls., 1979; United Way chmn. Pillsbury Co., Mpls., 1980. Named Advertiser of Yr. Aviation mag., 1986. Mem. New Canaan (Conn.) Field Club. Republican. Roman Catholic. Office: Ogden Allied Svcs Corp 2 Pennsylvania Pla 25th Fl New York NY 10121

WILLISCROFT, THOMAS FRANCIS, manufacturing executive; b. Ashby-De-La-Zouch, England, Nov. 23, 1923; arrived in Can., 1947; came to U.S., 1957; s. Harry Heward and Elizabeth Katharine (Dent) W.; m. Dawn Gay Ostrander, Aug. 15, 1964; 1 child, Shelley Katharine. Bs in Engring., London U., 1947. Cert. profl. engr., Ont., Can. Instr. U. Toronto, Ont., 1947-49; design engr. Kimberly Clark Corp., Terrace Bay, Ont., 1949-57; lubrication engr. Kimberly Clark Corp., Coosa River, Ala., 1957-58; chief maintenance engr. Kimberly Clark Corp., Munising, Mich., 1958-67; plant engr. Menasha Corp., North Bend, Oreg., 1967-71, gen. mgr., 1971-82; gen. mgr. container div. Weyerhaeuser Co., North Bend, 1981—. Chmn. City Planning Commn., City of Munising, 1966-67. Mem. Rotary.

WILLISON, BRUCE GRAY, banker; b. Riverside, Calif., Oct. 16, 1948; s. Walter G. and Dorothy (Phillips) W.; m. Gretchen A. Illig; children: Patrick, Bruce G., Kristen, Jeffery, Geoffrey, Lea. B.A. in econs., UCLA, 1970; M.B.A., U. So. Calif., 1973. With Bank of Am., Los Angeles, 1973-79; dir. mktg. First Interstate Bancorp, Los Angeles, 1982-83; exec. v.p. world banking group First Interstate Bank, Los Angeles, 1983-85; pres., chief exec. officer First Interstate Bank, 1985-86; chmn., chief exec. officer First Interstate Bank Oreg., Portland, 1986—. Served to lt. USN, 1970-72. Home: Portland OR Office: First Interstate Bank Oreg 1300 SW 5th Ave Portland OR 97201

WILLMAN, JOHN NORMAN, management consultant; b. St. Joseph, Mo., Jan. 19, 1915; s. John N. and Frances (Potter) W.; m. Victoria King, May 9, 1941; 1 dau., Victoria. Student, St. Benedict's Coll., 1936; B.A., St. Louis U., 1979. With Am. Hosp. Supply Corp., 1940-59, v.p., 1954-59; with Brunswick Corp., St. Louis, 1959-68; v.p. Brunswick Corp., 1961-68, pres. Health and Sci. div., 1961-68; v.p. Sherwood Med. Industries, Inc., St. Louis, 1961-67; pres. Sherwood Med. Industries, Inc., 1967-72, vice chmn. bd., 1972-73, also dir.; pres., chief exec. officer, dir. IPCO Corp., White Plains, N.Y., 1973-78; mgmt. cons. 1978—. Clubs: Old Warson Country (St. Louis), St. Louis (St. Louis), Noonday (St. Louis). Home: 530 N Spoede Rd Creve Coeur MO 63141

WILLMANN, CAMILLA CLAUDIA, tax preparation company executive; b. Greenville, Ill., Jan. 27, 1916; d. Charles Harrison and Dorcas Camilla (Foulon) McLean; m. Frederick E. Willmann, Jan. 27, 1945; children—Charles L., Mary S., William E., Max Louie. Owner, mgr. H & R Block, Greenville. Treas. Bond County Health Improvement; sec. Utlaut Hosp. Aux.; charter mem. Bond County Extension, U. Ill.; mem., Sponsor Illini Midstate Tumblers; sponsor women's slowpitch softball team. Recipient various awards H & R Block. Enrolled agt. IRS, U.S. Treasury Dept. Mem. Greenville C. of C., Bond County Bus. and Profl. Club (charter; treas., chmn. fin. com.), Greenville Retailers Assn. Republican. Roman Catholic. Home: Rt 2 Box 231 Pocahontas IL 62275 Office: 9153 S 3d St Greenville IL 62246

WILLMOTT, PETER SHERMAN, retail executive; b. Glens Falls, N.Y., June 1, 1937. B.A., Williams Coll., 1959; M.B.A., Harvard U., 1961. Sr. fin. analyst Am. Airlines, N.Y.C., 1961-63; mgr. cons. Booz, Allen & Hamilton, N.Y.C., 1964-66; treas. Continental Baking Co., Rye, N.Y., 1966-69, v.p., 1969-74; sr. v.p. fin. Fed. Express Corp., Memphis, 1974-77, exec. v.p. fin. and adminstrn., 1977-80, pres., chief operating officer, 1980-83, now bd. dirs.; pres., chief exec. officer Carson Pirie Scott & Co., Chgo., 1983—, chmn., 1984—, also bd. dirs. Office: Carson Pirie Scott & Co 36 S Wabash Ave Chicago IL 60603

WILLOUGHBY, RODNEY ERWIN, oil company executive; b. Dallas, July 24, 1925; s. Charles V. and Juanita (Jones) W.; m. Marie J. Johnston, Feb. 27, 1954; five children. B.B.A., Tulane U., 1945; M.B.A., Harvard U., 1947. Mem. dean's staff Harvard Bus. Sch., 1947-48; with ECA, Paris, France, 1948-49; petroleum attache Am. embassy, London, Eng., 1949-52; concession mgr. Gulf Oil Corp., N.Y.C., 1952-55; mem. fgn. staff Standard Oil Co. Calif., San Francisco, 1955-65; pres. Refineria Conchan Chevron, Peru, 1965-69, Chevron Oil Co. Latin Am., 1969-71; v.p., treas. Chevron Corp. (formerly Standard Oil Co.), Calif., San Francisco, 1971-84; v.p. fgn. Chevron Corp. (formerly Standard Oil Co.), 1984—; dir. Caltex Corp. Trustee U. San Francisco, Fine Arts Mus. San Francisco. Served to lt. (j.g.) USNR, 1943-46. Clubs: Pacific Union, Burlingame Country. Office: Chevron Corp 225 Bush St San Francisco CA 94104

WILLOUR, DAVID ROGER, banker; b. Wooster, Ohio, Feb. 28, 1939; s. Paul and Anabel (Clouse) W.; m. Judith Ann Fulcomer, Sept. 8, 1962; children: Geoffrey Thomas Lee, Douglas Dean. AB, Coll. Wooster, 1961; MBA, U. Pa., 1964; diploma Nat. Grad. Trust Sch., 1972. Corp. trust adminstr. Cen. Nat. Bank, Cleve., 1964-69; trust officer, then asst. v.p. Equibank N.A., Pitts., 1969-74; asst. v.p. Mellon Bank, N.A., Pitts., 1974-78, v.p., 1978-84, head trust employee benefit adminstrv. div., 1980, head new trust product devel. div., 1982, head trust mktg. and new ventures, 1983-84; v.p., head instnl. and employee benefits dept. Conn. Bank and Trust Co., Hartford, 1984-86, mng. v.p., head instnl. div., 1986-88, sr. v.p., 1988—; also lectr. civic groups, bus. assns. profl. confs. Contbr. articles to profl. jours. Vestryman, sec., chmn. fin. com. Fox Chapel (Pa.) Episc. Ch., 1974-78; chmn. membership com., mem. search com. St. John's Ch., West Hartford, 1988; active Pitts. Campaign for Wooster Coll. Mem. Am. Bankers Assn., Wharton Grad. Sch. Alumni Assn., Stock Transfer Assn. Cleve., Stock Transfer Assn. Pitts., Estate Planning Coun. Pitts., Greater Pitts. Employee Benefit Coun. (vice chmn. 1977-82), Corp. Fiduciaries Assn. Western Pa., Estate and Bus. Planning Coun. of Hartford, Conn., Assn. MBA Execs., Cleve. Athletic Club, Rotary, University Club, 514 Club, Hartford Club. Republican. Home: 44 Brenway Dr West Hartford CT 06117 Office: Conn Bank and Trust Co One Constitution Plaza Hartford CT 06115

WILLS, AUDREY ELIZABETH, bank executive; b. Phila., Mar. 28, 1930; d. Theodore A. and Mary C. (Dixon) W. AA, Villanova, 1966. Operations officer First Pa. Bank, Phila., 1961-66, asst. v.p., div. head, 1966-74, v.p., 1974-85, divisional v.p., 1985—; bd. dirs. Del. Valley Bank Methods Assn., Phila.; cons. Fraud Control Bureau, PHila., 1970—, Hurst Assocs., Springfield, Pa., 1986—, L & L Custom Catering Inc., Frederick, Pa., 1980—. Author: Loss Prevention Awareness, 1979; author and exec. producer of film: Tell it to the Judge, 1986; contbr. articles to various publications; editor: Prevention Awareness newsletter. Mem. Phila. Art Mus. Assn., 1975—; mem. New Hanover Civic Assn., (township, Pa.), 1975-81; mem. Greater Phila. Cultural Alliance, 1976—; mem. Smithsonian Assocs., Washington, 1980—; mem. Paradise (environmental) Watchdogs, Frederick, Pa., 1987; mem. Phila. Clearing House Fraud Commn. (past chmn.); chair women's achievement forum Phila. YWCA, 1988, bd. trustees, 1989. Recipient Cert. of Appreciation Dept. Defense USAF Guard and Reserve, 1985, Cert. achievement Women's Forum YWCA of Phila., 1987. Mem. Pa. Bankers Assn., Am. Mgt. Assn., Am. Inst. of Banking, Bank Adminstrn. Inst., Del. Valley Fin. and Security Officer's Assn. Club: Cen. Perklomen Bus. and Profl. Women. Home: Renninger Rd Frederick PA 19435 Office: First Pa Bank 3020 Market Philadelphia PA 19101

WILLSON, JULIE, financial planner; b. Stockton, Calif., Jan. 30, 1958. BA, U. Calif., Irvine, 1979. Supr. tng. dept., br. investment officer Am. Savs. and Loan Assn., Whittier, Calif., 1979-83; fin. cons. Shearson Am. Express, Orange, Calif., 1983-84; investment services officer Discount Investments Am. (now Griffin Fin. Services), Long Beach, Calif., 1984-86; account exec. Morgan, Olmstead, Kennedy and Gardner, Newport Beach, Calif., 1986; fin. planner Christopher Weil and Co., Inc., Newport Beach, 1986-88; fin. cons. Empire Nat. Securities Inc., Irvine and Laguna Hills, Calif., 1988—; presenter seminars, Long Beach, Newport Beach, 1984—. Contbr. articles on personal fin. to local newspapers. Mem. Inst. Cert. Fin. Planners (cert.), Internat. Assn. Fin. Planners, Bus. and Profl. Women (Young Careerist award 1988), Nat. Assn. Female Execs. Office: Empire of Am 5325 University Dr Irvine CA 92715

WILMANSKI, DIANE CAROL, data processing auditor; b. Phila., Oct. 15, 1954; d. Walter John and Doris Lillian (lewis) W. BA, La Salle U., 1976. Programmer Provident Nat. Bank, Phila., 1976-80; sr. EDP auditor Fed. Res. Bank, Phila., 1980-84, Johnson and Johnson, New Brunswick, N.J., 1984-87; audit supr. Squibb Corp., Princeton, N.J., 1987—; guest speaker various firms Bank Adminstrn. Inst. Mem. EDP Auditors' Assn. (speaker), Computer Security Inst., Alpha Epsilon. Democrat. Roman Catholic. Home: 7120 Algon Ave Philadelphia PA 19111 Office: PO Box 4000 Princeton NJ 08543-4000

WILSON, ALEXANDER MURRAY, retired mining company executive; b. Tulare, Calif., May 17, 1922; s. Alexander Murray and Grace (Creech) W.; m. Beverlee Elayne Forsblad, Jan. 4, 1948; children—Shelley, Kristin, Alexis. B.S. in Metall. Engring., U. Calif., Berkeley, 1948. With Bradley Mining Co., Stibnite, Idaho, 1948-51, Molybdenum Corp. Am., Nipton, Calif., 1951-54; with Utah Internat. Inc., San Francisco, 1954-87, pres., 1971-79, chief exec. officer, 1978-87, chmn. bd. dirs., 1979-87; mem. Kaiser Aluminum Retirement com., Internat. Adv. Bd., SRI; bd. dirs. The Clarkson Co., Fireman's Fund Corp. Bd. dirs. Smith-Kettlewell Eye Research Inst. Served with AUS, 1944-46. Mem. Mining and Metall Soc. Am., Soc. Mining Engrs. Office: 550 California St San Francisco CA 94104

WILSON, ALLAN BYRON, interactive graphics company executive; b. Jackson, Miss., Aug. 19, 1948; s. Allen Bernice Wilson and Mary Pickering (Levereault) W.; m. Ines Ghinato, May 19, 1975; 1 child, Lucas Ghinato. B.S., Rice U., 1970, M.S. in Elec. Engring., 1971. Systems adminstr. Max Planck Institut für Kohlenforschung, Mülheim Ruhr, Fed. Republic Germany, 1971; systems programmer Digital Equipment Corp., Maynard, Mass., 1972-74, mktg. specialist, 1974-75, mktg. mgr., 1976-79; internat. ops. dir. Intergraph Corp., Huntsville, Ala., 1980-82, v.p. corp. and internat. ops., 1982-83, exec. v.p., 1983—. Contbr. articles to profl. jours. Mem. Assn. for Computing Machinery, IEEE. Home: 576 Rainbow Dr Madison AL 35758 Office: Intergraph Corp One Madison Industrial Park Huntsville AL 35807

WILSON, BETTY MAY, finance company executive; b. Moberly, Mo., Mar. 13, 1947; d. Arthur Bunyon and Martha Elizabeth (Denham) Stephens; m. Ralph Felix Martin, Aug. 22, 1970 (div. May 1982); m. Gerald Robert Wilson Sr., Mar. 3, 1984; stepchildren: Gerald Robert Jr., Heather Lynn, Jeffrey Michael. BS in Acctg. and Bus. Adminstrn., Colo. State U., 1969. CPA, Mo. Tax mgr. Arthur Andersen and Co., St. Louis, 1969-75; v.p., asst. sec., dir. taxes ITT Fin. Corp., St. Louis, 1975—; sr. v.p., bd. dirs. Lyndon Ins. Co., St. Louis, 1977—, ITT Lyndon Life Ins. Co., ITT Lyndon Property Ins. Co., St. Louis, 1977—. Mem. AICPA, Mo. Soc. CPA's, Am. Fin. Services Assn. (chmn. tax com. 1987-88), Tax Execs. Inst. Inc. (bd. dirs. St. Louis chpt., past sec., past. pres.), Mo. Girls Racing Assn. (pres. 1977-82). Baptist. Office: ITT Fin Corp 12555 Manchester Rd Saint Louis MO 63131

WILSON, BEVERLY JEAN, educational administrator; b. Detroit, Apr. 14, 1937; d. Gordon Charles and Dorothy Margaret (Fowler) Anderson; m. David Charles Wilson, Sept. 2, 1961; 1 child, Timothy Reardon. BA in Edn., U. Mich., 1959; postgrad., Mich. State U., 1961; MA in Edn., Fitchburg (Mass.) State U., 1981. Tchr. St. Clair Shores (Mich.) Sch. Dist., 1959-63, various pub. schs., Calif., Colo., N.Y., 1963-65, Dept. Def., Italy and Fed. Republic Germany, 1966-78; asst. v.p. Merchants Nat. Bank, Leominster, Mass., 1979-85; adminstrv. asst. to sr. v.p. Mass. Higher Edn. Assistance Corp., Boston, 1985-87, dir. lender and sch. relations, 1987—; mem. grad. council Fitchburg State Coll., 1979-81. Author: Computers Made Easy, 1981; contbr. articles to profl. jours. Mem. budget com. United Way, Leominster/Fitchburg, 1983-86. Edn. Policy Program fellow Inst. Ednl. Leadership, 1987. Mem. Mass. Assn. Fin. Aid Adminstrs., Eastern Assn. Fin. Aid Adminstrs., Nat. Assn. Fin. Aid Adminstrs., Nat. Assn. Banking Women (1st v.p. 1986-87), Internat. Officers' Wives Club (pres. 1969-71). Democrat. Lutheran. Office: Mass Higher Edn Assist Corp 330 Stuart St Boston MA 02116

WILSON, BRENDA RICHARDSON, bank executive; b. Huntsville, Tex., Dec. 23, 1953; d. Douglas Dorril Richardson and Georgia Pauline (Johnson) Tyson; m. Stephen Fredrick Wilson, Dec. 20, 1975; 1 child, Grant Edward. BS, Tex. A&M U., 1976, MS, 1979; grad., Southwestern Grad. Sch. Banking, 1986. V.p. Frost Bank, San Antonio, 1979-82; sr. v.p. First Victoria (Tex.) Nat. Bank, 1982—; instr. sch. banking Tex. Tech U., Lubbock, 1984-86. Bd. dirs. City of Port Lavaca (Tex.) Parks Bd., Calhoun County Libr., Port Lavaca, Crisis Hotline, Inc., Calhoun County, Victoria Adult Literacy Coun., Women's Crisis Ctr., Victoria; v.p. Friends of Calhoun County Library. Mem. Bank Mktg. Assn. (product adv. bd.), Phi Kappa Phi, Gamma Sigma Delta. Methodist. Home: 1015 N Hwy 35 Bypass Port Lavaca TX 77979 Office: First Victoria Nat Bank PO Box 1338 Victoria TX 77902

WILSON, BRUCE B., telecommunications executive; b. Buffalo, June 19, 1944; s. Charles V. Jr. and Ruth (Byer) W.; m. Roberta M. Patton, May 20, 1967; 1 child, Douglas. BS in Econs., U. Pa., 1967; MBA, U. Denver, 1973. Treasury mgr. Mountain States Tel.&Tel., Denver, 1972-77, asst. treas., 1978-83, treas., 1983-85; supr. pension fund AT&T, N.Y.C., 1977-78; exec. dir., asst. treas. US West, Inc., Englewood, Colo., 1985—; v.p. US West Capital Funding, Englewood, 1986—. Bd. dirs. Colo. Youth Symphony Orchs., Denver, 1986—. Served to capt. USMC, 1967-71, Vietnam. Mem. Fin. Analysts Fedn. (chartered), Fin. Exec. Inst., Denver Soc. Security Analysts. Clubs: Metropolitan (Englewood); Ranch Golf and Country (Westminster, Colo.). Home: 1411 E Cornell Pl Englewood CO 80110 Office: US West Inc 7800 E Orchard Rd Englewood CO 80111

WILSON, BRUCE BRIGHTON, transportation executive; b. Boston, Feb. 6, 1936; s. Robert Lee and Jane (Schlotterer) W.; m. Elizabeth Ann MacFarland, Dec. 31, 1958; children: Mabeth, Mary, Bruce Robert, Caroline Daly. A.B., Princeton U., 1958; LL.B., U. Pa., 1961. Bar: Pa. 1962. Assoc. Montgomery, McCracken, Walker & Rhoads, Phila., 1962-69; atty. U.S. Dept. Justice, Washington, 1969-79; dep. asst. atty. gen. antitrust div. U.S. Dept. Justice, 1971-76; spl. counsel Consol. Rail Corp., Phila., 1979-81, gen. counsel litigation and antitrust, 1981-82, v.p., gen. counsel, 1982-84, v.p. law, 1984-87, sr. v.p. law, 1987—; dir. Trailer Train Co., Chgo., 1980-82, Penn Car Leasing, Wynnewood, Pa., 1983. Fellow Salzburg Seminar in Am. Studies (Austria), 1965; fellow Felz Inst. State and Local Govt., 1967. Mem. ABA, Phila. Bar Assn. Club: Corinthian Yacht. Home: 224 Chamounix Rd Saint Davids PA 19087 Office: Consol Rail Corp 6 Penn Center Plaza Philadelphia PA 19103

WILSON, BRUCE E., insurance company executive; b. Providence, July 5, 1935; s. Richard A. and Marin B. (Waterman) W.; m. Virginia T. Leek, Feb. 18, 1956; children: Bruce Jr., James B., Suzanne L. BS in Acctg., U. R.I., 1957. CLU. Adminstr. Travelers Ins. Co., Hartford, Conn., 1958-65; adminstr. employee benefits The Foxboro (Mass.) Co., 1965-69, mgr. corp. risk ins., 1969—; instr. Bristol Community Coll., Fall River, Mass., 1983—. Contbr. articles to profl. jours. Mem. fin. sch. planning com. Town of Wrentham, Mass., 1967-73, earth removal com., 1965-70. Capt. USAR, 1957-65. Fellow Mass. Risk Ins. Soc. (past pres., bd. dirs. 1979-85), Risk Mgmt. Coun., Machinery and Allied Products Inst., Lions (past pres., bd. dirs. Wrentham chpt. 1980-85). Republican. Home: 46 Lakeside Ave PO Box 898 Wrentham MA 02093 Office: The Foxboro Co 33 Commercial St B52-IL Foxboro MA 02035

WILSON, CARL ARTHUR, real estate broker; b. Manhasset, N.Y., Sept. 29, 1947; s. Archie and Florence (Hefner) W.; m. Mary Elizabeth Coppes; children: Melissa Starr, Clay Alan. Student UCLA, 1966-68, 70-71. Tournament bridge dir. North Hollywood (Calif.) Bridge Club, 1967-68, 70-71; computer operator IBM, L.A., 1967-68, 70-71; bus. devel. mgr. Walker & Lee Real Estate, Anaheim, Calif., 1972-76; v.p. sales and mktg. The Estes Co., Phoenix, 1976-82, Continental Homes Inc., 1982-84; pres. Roadrunner Homes Corp., Phoenix, 1984-86, Lexington Homes, Inc., 1986, Barrington Homes, 1986—; adv. dir. Liberty Bank. Mem. Glendale (Ariz.) Citizens Bond Coun., 1986-87, Ariz. Housing Study Commn., 1988, Valley Leadership, 1988—; pres.'s coun. Am. Grad. Sch. Internat. Mgmt., 1985—; vice-chmn. Glendale Planning and Zoning Commn., 1986—, chmn., 1987—; mem. bd. trustees Valley of Sun United Way, 1987—, chmn. com. Community Problem Solving and Fund Distbn., 1988—. Mem. Nat. Assn. Homebuilders (bd. dirs. 1985—), Cen. Ariz. Homebuilders Assn. (adv. com. 1979-82, treas. 1986, sec. 1987, v.p. 1987-89, pres. 1989—, bd. dirs. 1985—); mem. bd. adjustments City of Glendale, 1976-81, chmn., 1980-81, mem. bond coun., 1981—; planning and zoning commr. City of Glendale, 1981—; mem. real estate edn. adv. coun. State Bd. Community Coll., 1981—; precinct committeeman, dep. registrar, 1980-81. With U.S. Army, 1968-70. Mem. Glendale C. of C. (dir. 1980-83), Sales and Mktg. Coun. (chmn. edn. com. 1980, chmn. coun. 1981—, Mame grand award 1981). Home: PO Box 10141 Phoenix AZ 85064

WILSON, CARL WELDON, JR., construction company executive, civil engineer; b. Norfolk, Va., Sept. 4, 1933; s. Carl Weldon and Janie Marie (Ludford) W.; m. Jean Roberts, Feb. 13, 1960; children: Lisa Ann, Carl Weldon III. BCE, Tex. A&M U., 1954. Registered profl. engr., Tex. Engr. Magnolia Petroleum Co., Morgan City, La., 1954-55, Brown & Root, Houston, 1957-60; project mgr. Claude Everett Constrn. Co., Houston, 1960-62; pres. Falcon Constrn. Co., Houston, 1962-63; pres., owner Wilson Engring. and Constrn. Co., Houston, 1963-68; v.p. Divcon, Inc., Houston, 1968-71, Wilson Industries, Inc., Houston, 1971-81; pres., prin. owner BS&B Engring. Co., Inc., Houston, 1981—; chmn. Task Internat., Inc., Houston, 1986—. Served to 1st lt. U.S. Army, 1955-57. Republican. Episcopalian. Home: 750 Bison Houston TX 77079 Office: BS&B Engring Co Inc 7324 Southwest Freeway Houston TX 77074

WILSON, CHARLES H(ARRISON), retired air force officer, financial planner, human resource development professional; b. Chgo., Sept. 6, 1941; s. Charles E. and Lorraine F. (Parker) W.; m. Shirley Ann Porter, Feb. 11, 1968; children: Audrey M., Angela M., Andrew M. BS, So. Ill. U., 1964; BA, U. Md., 1976; MA, Webster U., 1979. Commd. 2d lt. USAF, 1964, advanced through grades to lt. col., 1981; pers. dir. air force logistics command USAF, Wright-Patterson AFB, Ohio, 1980-83; dir. DEF logistics agy. USAF, Washington, 1983-86; ret. USAF, 1984; exec. dir. exec. leadership program Dept. Def., Washington, 1976—; adj. prof. Park Coll., St. Louis, 1977-80; mcpl. cons. City of Dayton, Ohio, 1980. Patentee microwave oven carousel. Bd. dirs., v.p. Credit Union. Fellow D.C. Life Under Writers Tng. Coun.; mem. Classification and Compensation Soc., Am. Soc. Tng. and Devel., Internat. Pers. Mgmt. Assn. (human rights commn.), Omega Psi Phi, Toastmasters. Democrat. Methodist. Home: 5911 Edsall St Alexandria VA 22304

WILSON, CHARLES JOHN, dentist, health care company executive; b. Detroit, Oct. 9, 1930; s. Carl John Wilson and Marion Ellen (Leathers) Moran. BA, Albion Coll., 1952; DDS, Northwestern U., 1956; MS, Marquette U., 1961. Diplomate Am. Bd. Quality Assurance and Utilization Rev. Physicians. Pvt. practice dentistry Milw., 1958-67, 78—; pres. Bio-Research Assocs., Inc., 1965-87, chmn., 1987—; bd. dirs. U. Nat. Bank, Milw., Casper Environ., Inc., Milw.; assoc. clin. prof. U. Wis., Milw., 1983—; dir. Dental Network Am., Oakbrook Terr., Ill., 1985—. Capt. U.S. Army, 1956-58. Fellow Internat. Assn. for Dental Research, AAAS, Internat. Coll. Dentists; mem. ADA, Wis. Acad. Arts, Scis. and Letters, Fedn. Dentaire Internationale, Am. Acad. Dental Group Practice (pres.-elect). Republican. Unitarian. Home: 2640 N Terrace Ave Milwaukee WI 53211 Office: Northpoint Dental Group Ltd 2315 N Lake Dr Milwaukee WI 53211

WILSON, CHARLES THOMAS, textile executive, consultant, venture capitalist; b. Memphis, Feb. 8, 1941; s. Charles Lewis and Mary Frances (Parks) W.; m. Alice Elaine Ford, June 20, 1964; children: Elaine, Mary Jane. BS in Commerce, U. Ky., 1963. Dir. corp. acctg. Celanese Corp., N.Y.C., 1977-78; owner, cons. Strategic Planning Services, Charlotte, N.C., 1974—; controller Fiber Industries, Inc., Charlotte, 1974-76, dir. planning, 1979-81; dir. bus. devel. Celanese Fibers, Charlotte, 1981-82, v.p., gen. mgr. Hoechst Celanese Separations Products div., 1983-87; chmn. Rosegate Internat., Matthews, N.C., 1987—; v.p. Textile Corp. of Am., 1987-88. Trustee Wingate (N.C.) Coll., 1986; chmn. Wingate Coll., 1989; deacon, tchr. Candlewyck Bapt. Ch., Charlotte, 1986. Recipient Wall St. Jour. award, 1963. Mem. Nat. Assn. Accts. Democrat. Baptist.

WILSON, DELANO DEE, manufacturing executive, consultant; b. Great Falls, Mont., Apr. 15, 1934; s. William McKinley and Alvina Henrietta (Beck) W.; m. Marilyn Ann Harant, Nov. 14, 1959; children: Robin David, Leslie Ann Wilson Ginac, Christian William. BSEE, Mont. State U., 1959. Analytical engr. GE, Schenectady, N.Y., 1960-64, sr. engr., 1964-69, mgr. alternating current studies, 1969-72; mgr. engring. projects GE, Phila., 1972-74; prin. engr. Power Techs., Inc., Schenectady, 1974-82; v.p., prin. engr. Power Techs., Inc.-Tech. Assessment Group, Schenectady, 1980-85; pres., chief exec. officer Power Tech. Internat., Inc., Schenectady, 1986—; expert witness, cons., Internat. Conf. on High Voltage Systems, Paris, 1974-86, U.S. rep., 1986—. Author, co-author 5 books; contbr. numerous tech. papers to profl. jours.; patentee in field (2). Bd. dirs. Ellis Hosp., Schenectady, 1987—, Schenectady County YMCA, 1989—. With U.S. Army, 1954-56. Fellow IEEE (Disting. Service award 1988, mem. trans. and dist. com., exec. bd. Power Engring. Soc. 1988—); mem. Am. Nat. Standards Inst. (vice chmn. 1978—), Nat. Fed. Indsl. Bus., Schenectady C. of C. Club: Mohawk. Lodge: Rotary. Office: Power Techs Inc 1482 Erie Blvd PO Box 1058 Schenectady NY 12301

WILSON, DON M., financial executive; b. Benton Harbor, Mich., Feb. 1, 1948; s. Norman Clifford and Ruth Bernice (Oxley) W.; m. Jeaneen Jo Holm Burgess, June 8, 1970 (div. 1986); children: Todd, Trina; m. Jean Kay Shiner Kaye; stepchildren: Ryan, Emily, Katie. BSBA, Walla Walla Coll., 1970. Unit mgr. White Meml. Med. Ctr., L.A., 1970-71, patient bus. mgr., 1971-74; asst. adminstr., chief fin. officer Longmont (Colo.) United Hosp., Longmont, 1974-87; adminstrv. dir. Computer Interface Corp., Denver, 1987; fin. analyst Sacred Heart Corp., Denver, 1987-88, chief fin. officer, 1988—. Mem. Medicaid task force State of Colo. Mem. Hosp. Fin. Mgmt. Assn. (treas. Colo. chpt. 1977, mem. reimbursement task force 1988), Colo. Hosp. Assn. (mem. acuity/charges task force), Vol. Hosp. Assn. (mem. joint audit task force). Home: 2300 Horseshoe Circle Longmont CO 80501 Office: Sacred Heart Corp 2861 W 52d Ave Denver CO 80221

WILSON, DON MATTHEW, III, corporate banking executive; b. Ravenna, Ohio, Jan. 24, 1948; s. Don Matthew and Helen Jane (Strimple) W.; m. Lynn Suzanne Byron, Oct. 13, 1984. A.B. cum laude, Harvard U., Cambridge, Mass., 1970; M.B.A., Dartmouth Coll., Hanover, N.H., 1973. Mng. dir. Chem. Bank, N.Y.C., 1973—. Republican. Congregationalist Clubs: Harvard (N.Y.C.); Rockaway Hunting (L.I.). Office: Chem Bank 277 Park Ave New York NY 10172

WILSON, EDDIE LEON, financial service manager; b. Vashti, Tex., May 8, 1940; s. Jessey Thomas and Dollie Annly (Watson) W.; m. Karen Marie Brown, Apr. 8, 1981. AA in Aero. Operation, Coll. San Mateo, 1968; cert., Coll. Fin. Planning, Denver, 1984. Asst. credit mgr. Gen. Electric Co., Burlingame, Calif., 1969-80; registered rep. Waddell and Reed, San Jose, Calif., 1980-85; div. mgr. Waddell and Reed, San Jose, 1985-87, Sacramento, 1988—. Served with USAF, 1962-66. Mem. Internat. Assoc. Fin. Planners, Inst. Cert. Fin. Planners. Republican. Baptist. Office: Waddell and Reed 100 Howe Ave #155 N Sacramento CA 95825

WILSON, EDGAR BYRON, business executive; b. Albany, N.Y., May 13, 1931; s. Harold Edgar and Marie Elizabeth (Brush) W.; m. Mary Beth Weilbacher, Aug. 2, 1956. BA, St. Lawrence U., 1953; MBA, Harvard U., 1955. Mkt. dir. Richardson-Vicks, Inc., N.Y.C., Paris, Manila, 1957-64; chief exec. officer Japan Kimberly-Clark Corp., Neenah, Wis., 1964-68, France, 1968-71; v.p. internat. div. Pillsbury Co., Mpls., 1971-76; exec. v.p. Shaklee Corp., San Francisco, 1976-79; pres., chief exec. officer Almay Cosmetics, Inc., N.Y.C., 1979-84, Hathaway Group of Warnaco, N.Y.C., 1984-86; chmn. Global Brands, Inc., N.Y.C., 1986—; chmn., chief exec. officer Sero Co., Branford, Conn., Mortin Jonap, Ltd., Hauppauge, N.Y.; bd. dirs. William Schneider, Inc., Miami. Trustee St. Lawrence U., Canton, N.Y., 1986—, San Francisco Ballet, 1978; devel. dir. Cen. Park Conservancy, N.Y.C., 1983—. With USAR, 1955-57. Mem. Eastward Ho Club (gov. 1986—). Republican. Home: 39 E 79th St New York NY 10021 Office: Global Brands Inc 1090 Avenue of the Americas New York NY 10104

WILSON, GARY LEE, entertainment company executive; b. Alliance, Ohio, Jan. 16, 1940; s. Elvin John and Fern Helen (Donaldson) W.; m. Susan Browne Moody, Aug. 11, 1962; children: Derek, Christopher. B.A., Duke U., 1962; M.B.A., Wharton Sch., U. Pa., 1963. Vice pres. fin., dir. Trans-Philippines Investment Co., Manila, 1964-70; exec. v.p., dir. Checchi & Co., Washington, 1971-73; exec. v.p. fin. Marriott Corp., Washington, 1973-85; exec. v.p., dir. The Walt Disney Co., Burbank, Calif., 1985—; elected bd. dirs. Northwestern Airline, 1987. Office: The Walt Disney Co 500 S Buena Vista St Burbank CA 91521

WILSON, GERALD EVERETTE, financial executive; b. Houston, Nov. 2, 1953; s. Clifford Dennis and Naomi Betty (Falls) W.; m. Marsherria Ervin, Aug. 14, 1978; 1 child, Gerrad Everette. BA in Econs., Stanford U., 1976, MA in Econs., 1976; MS in Acctg., U. Houston, 1978. CPA, Tex.; cert. fin. planner. Mem. staff Arthur Young & Co., Houston, 1976-80, mgr., 1980-84, prin., 1984-86; founder, pres., chmn. bd. dirs. Wilson Fin. Group, Inc., Houston, 1986—; bd. dirs. Cedar Crest Funeral Home Inc., Dallas, Thompson Funeral Home Inc., Sacramento, So. Funeral Home Inc., Memphis, Whitehaven Chapel Inc., Memphis, Mainland Funeral Home, LaMarque, Tex., Morris-Bates Funeral Home, Ft. Worth, Paradise Funeral Home, Houston, Carl Barnes Funeral Home, Inc., Houston. Bd. dirs. Stanford U. Athletic Bd., Palo Alto, Calif., 1985—, Leadership Houston, 1985-87, Houston Proud, 1988; chmn. sec. Steering Com. Harris County Parks, Tex., 1986—; mem. adv. bd. Houston Ind. Sch. Dist., 1986—. Named Outstanding Young Houstonian Houston Jaycees, 1985, Outstanding Young Texan Tex. Jaycees, 1985, Outstanding Black Houstonian Riverside Hosp., 1986. Mem. Am. Inst. CPA's, Tex. Soc. CPA's, Inst. Fin. Planning, Houston C. of C., Katy C. of C. Democrat. Baptist. Office: Cowperwood Ctr 15415 Katy Freeway Suite 515 Houston TX 77094

WILSON, GRAHAM ALASTAIR, accountant; b. London, Nov. 24, 1949; s. Douglas A. and Nina A. (Masters) W.; Carol A. Buckles, June 9, 1973; children: Adriane, Geoffrey, Ryan. BS in Acctg., Ill. State U., 1972. CPA. Audit mgr. Arthur Andersen & Co., Chgo., Tulsa, 1972-79; chief. fin. officer Braden Steel Corp., Tulsa, 1979-88, Econotherm Energy Systems Corp., Tulsa, 1984-88; v.p. fin. and adminstrn. Lowrance Electronics, Inc., Tulsa, 1988—. Mem. Leadership Tulsa, 1981; treas. Bethany Luth. Ch., 1982-83, Tulsa Bus. Health Group, 1983. Mem. Fin. Execs. Inst., Am. Inst. CPA's, Okla. Soc. CPA's. Republican. Lutheran. Office: Lowrance Electronics Inc 12000 East Skelly Dr Tulsa OK 74128

WILSON, HARRY B., public relations company executive; b. St. Louis, May 17, 1917; s. H. Burgoyne and Margaret (Drew) W.; m. Helen Cain, July 27, 1940 (dec. Oct. 1983); children: Margaret Wilson Pennington, Harry B., Andrew B., Daniel B., Josephine Wilson Havlak, Julie Wilson Sakellariadis, Ellen; m. Mary Virginia Peisch, Apr. 7, 1984. Ph.B., St. Louis U., 1938. Mng. editor Sedalia (Mo.) Capital, 1939-40; reporter Kansas City Star; also state capital bur. chief St. Louis Globe-Democrat, 1940-42, polit. writer, columnist, 1946-52; corr. Business Week mag., 1948-52; with Fleishman-Hillard Inc., St. Louis, 1953; sr. ptnr. Fleishman-Hillard Inc., 1964-70, pres., 1970-74, chmn. bd., 1974-88, sr. ptnr., 1988—. Bd. dirs. St. Louis Symphony Soc.; mem. St. Louis Zool. Park Commn. Served with USNR, 1942-46. Home: 5240 Westminster Pl Saint Louis MO 63108 Office: Fleishman Hillard Inc 200 N Broadway Saint Louis MO 63102

WILSON, HENRY DONALD, information industry executive; b. New Rochelle, N.Y., Nov. 21, 1923; s. Andrew and Edith (Rose) W.; m. Mary Louise Baron, Dec. 8, 1951; children: Edith Ramaley Bice Chandler, Anne Baron. BA, Yale U., 1944; LLB, Columbia U., 1948. Bar: N.Y. 1949. Assoc. Sullivan & Cromwell, N.Y.C., 1946; dir. United World Federalists, Inc., N.Y.C., Cleve., Hartford, Conn., 1950-55; assoc. Paul, Weiss, Rifkind, Wharton & Garrison, N.Y.C., 1955-59; dir. U.S. Peace Corps., Ethiopia, 1964-66; sr. cons. Arthur D. Little, Inc., N.Y.C., 1960-69; pres. R.W. Devel. Corp., N.Y.C., 1970-73; organizer, pres. Mead Data Cen., Inc., N.Y.C., 1970-71, vice chmn. bd., 1972-73; ptnr. Wall, Wilson & Graff, Inc., White Plains, N.Y., 1973-77, The Devel. Corp., White Plains, 1978-79; pvt. practice cons. White Plains, 1980; ptnr. Lessac Research, White Plains, 1969—, H. Donald Wilson, Inc. (named changed to Wilson & McLane Inc. 1985), Rye, N.Y., 1981—; lectr. NYU Alternate Media Ctr, 1981-82, Iona Coll. Hagan Sch. Bus., 1985-86. Contbr. articles to profl. jours. Mem. organizing com, bd. dirs., exec. chmn. New Directions, Washington, 1974-78, White Plains Dem. (treas. city com. 1959-60); chmn. bd. World Federalists Assn., Washington, 1973-76. Llt. (j.g.) USN, 1944-46, PTO. Mem. Com. Venture Group, Info. Industry Assn. (chmn. new bus. com. 1985-86, chmn. ind. res. com 1987—). Home: 20 Vermont Ave White Plains NY 10606 Office: Wilson & McLane Inc 350 Theodore Fernd Ave Rye NY 10580

WILSON, IAN HOLROYDE, management consultant, futurist; b. Harrow, England, June 16, 1925; came to U.S., 1954; s. William Brash and Dorothy (Holroyde) W.; m. Page Tuttle Hedden, Mar. 17, 1951 (div. Dec. 1983); children: Rebecca, Dorothy, Ellen, Holly, Alexandra. MA, Oxford U., 1948. Orgn. cons. Imperial Chem. Industries, London, 1948-54; various staff exec. positions in strategic planning, mgmt. devel. Gen. Electric Co., Fairfield, Conn., 1954-80; sr. cons. to maj. U.S. and internat. cos. SRI Internat., Menlo Park, Calif., 1980—; exec. in residence Va. Commonwealth U., Richmond, 1976. Author: Planning for Major Change, 1976; (with others) Business Environment of the 70's, 1970; mem. editorial bd. Planning Rev., Oxford, Ohio, 1973-81; Am. editor Long Range Planning Jour., London, 1981—. Chmn. Citizen's Long Range Ednl. Goals Com., Westport, Conn., 1967-70; mem. strategic process com. United Way of Am., Alexandria, Va., 1985—. Served to capt. Brit. Army, 1943-45, ETO. Mem. AAAS, Planning Forum, World Future Soc. Unitarian. Home: 165 Alpine Terr San Francisco CA 94117 Office: SRI Internat 333 Ravenswood Ave Menlo Park CA 94025

WILSON, J. ROBERT, utility company executive; b. Meade, Kans., Dec. 3, 1927; s. Robert J. and Bess O. (Osborne) W.; m. Marguerite Jean Reiter, Nov. 27, 1960; 1 son, John Ramsey. B.A., Kans. U., 1950, LL.B., 1953. Bar: Kans. 1953, Nebr. 1961, Colo. 1981. Practiced in Meade, 1954-57; county atty. Meade County, Kans., 1954, 56; city atty. Meade, 1954-57; asst. gen. counsel Kans. Corp. Commn., 1957-59, gen. counsel, 1959-61, mem., 1961; atty. KN Energy, Inc., 1961-75, personnel dir., 1964-67, v.p., treas., 1968-75, exec. v.p., 1975-78, pres., chief operating officer, 1978-82, pres., chief exec. officer, 1982-85, chmn., pres., chief exec. officer, 1985-88, chmn., 1988—. With USNR, 1945-46. Mem. Phi Kappa Sigma. Democrat. Home: 1725 Foothills Dr S Golden CO 80401 Office: KN Energy Inc 12055 W 2d Pl Lakewood CO 80228

WILSON, JAMES DACUS, SR., sales executive; b. Greenville, S.C., Feb. 16, 1947; s. Haudie Dacus and Mary Ellen (Mundy) W.; m. Christine Elizabeth McClellan; children: James D. Jr., Samuel Scott, Mindy Ellen, Michael Shane, Christie Lee. Student, Gordon Jr. Coll., 1967, Greenville Tech. Coll., 1969. Sales, asst. mgr. H.B. Owsley & Son, Inc., Greer, S.C., 1970-78; mgr., co-owner King Printing Co., Greenville, 1978-81; sr. cost estimator Jeffrey Mfg. Co., Greenville, 1981-82; v.p. sales Rainsville (Ala.) Ch. Pew Mfg. Co., 1982—; owner Wilson's Ch. Interiors. Served with USN, 1967. Named Eagle Scout Boy Scouts Am., Greenville, 1960. Mem. Internat. Platform Assn., Order of De Molay, Moose. Republican. Baptist. Home: Rt 3 Box 412 Fyffe AL 35971 Office: Rainsville Ch Pew Mfg Co 434 Main St E Rainsville AL 35986

WILSON, JAMES JOHN, construction and real estate executive; b. N.Y.C., Apr. 18, 1933; s. Daniel J. and Mary (O'Donnell) W.; B.C.E., Manhattan Coll., 1955; m. Barbara A. Wilson, July 27, 1957; children—Kevin John, Elizabeth Ann, Thomas Brian, Mary Patricia, James Michael, Brian Joseph. Pres., chmn. Interstate Gen. Corp., Hato Rey, P.R., 1965—; pres., chmn. Wilson Securities Corp.; chmn. Interstate Land Devel. Corp., Inc., Interstate St. Charles, Inc.; adv. council Banco Popular de P.R., 1968-70. Pres., Buck Hill Falls Community Assn.; bd. dirs. Hill Sch. Recipient Alumni award for outstanding businessman Manhattan Coll., 1969. Mem. New Communities Council, Urban Land Inst., Am. Arbitration Assn., Va. Thoroughbred Assn., No. Va. Angus Assn., Soc. Am. Mil. Engrs. (pres. 1958), Nat. Assn. Home Builders (pres. P.R. chpt. 1963, dir. 1962-65), Young Pres. Orgn. (pres. Caribbean chpt. 1968-69), Manhattan Coll. Alumni Assn., World Bus. Council, Chief Execs. Orgn. Clubs: Caparra Country; N.Y. Athletic (N.Y.C.); University (Washington). Middleburg (Va.) Tennis; Banker's of P.R. Home: Dresden Farm Box 392 Middleburg VA 22117 also: Buck Hills PA 18323 Office: 222 Smallwood Village Ctr Saint Charles MD 20601 also: Box 3908 San Juan PR 00936

WILSON, JAMES LAWRENCE, chemical company executive; b. Rosedale, Miss., Mar. 2, 1936; s. James Lawrence and Mary Margaret (Klingman) W.; m. Barbara Louise Burroughs, Aug. 30, 1958; children: Lawrence Burroughs, Alexander Elliott. B.Mech. Engring., Vanderbilt U., 1958; M.B.A., Harvard, 1963. Vice pres. Nyala Properties, Inc., Phila., 1963-65; staff assoc. Rohm & Haas Co., Phila., 1965-67; exec. asst. to pres. Rohm & Haas Co., 1971-72, treas., 1972-74; regional dir. Rohm & Haas Co., Europe, 1974-77; group v.p. Rohm & Haas Co., 1977-86, vice-chmn., 1986-88, chmn., 1988—; treas. Warren-Teed Pharms., Inc., Columbus, Ohio, 1967-68, v.p., 1969; pres. Consol. Biomed. Labs., Inc., Dublin, Ohio, 1970-71; dir. Rohm and Haas Co., Balt., Shipley Co., Inc., Vanguard Group Investment Cos. Co-author: Creative Collective Bargaining, 1964. Bd. mgrs. St. Christopher's Hosp. for Children, 1978-80; chmn. bd. dirs. Warminster Gen. Hosp., 1980-87; bd. dirs., mem. exec. com. United Hosps. Inc., 1980— ; mem. Engring. Council of Vanderbilt U., 1980-84, pres., 1985-86; bd. govs. Eastern div. Pa. Economy League, 1977-88, chmn., 1983; trustee Vanderbilt U., 1987—, Culver Ednl. Found., 1988—. Mem. Vanderbilt U. Alumni Assn. (dir. 1981-86). Office: Rohm & Haas Co Independence Mall W Philadelphia PA 19105

WILSON, JAMES RICALTON, data processing executive; b. Washington, Oct. 18, 1959; s. George Cadman and Joan (Gibbons) W.; m. Carolyn Anne Beckman, Sept. 21, 1985. BA, Bucknell U., 1981; postgrad., George Washington U. Computer specialist Compucare-Baxter/Travenol, McLean, Va., 1982-84; prin. investigator DOCUnet, NASA, Washington, 1984-86; prin. Applied Expertise, Arlington, Va., 1984—; mem. sr. tech. staff Gen. Scis. Corp., Laurel, Md., 1985—, Office of Comml. Programs and Office of Space Sci. NASA, Washington, 1985—; sr. cons. Info. Systems and Networks Corp., Bethesda, Md., 1986—. Campaign treas. Andrews for State Del., McLean, 1984-85; mem. exec. com. Pa. Common Cause, 1978-81; mem. Arlingtonians for a Better County, 1987-88. Mem. Data Processing Mgmt. Assn., Assn. Computing Machinery, Space Policy Inst., AAAS. Presbyterian. Office: Applied Expertise 2002 N Kenmore Arlington VA 22207

WILSON, JAMES WILLIAM, lawyer; b. Spartanburg, S.C., June 19, 1928; s. James William and Ruth (Greenwaldt) W.; m. Elizabeth Clair Pickett, May 23, 1952; children: Susan Alexandra Wilson Albright, James William. Student, Tulane U., 1945-46; B.A., U. Tex., Austin, 1950, LL.B., 1951. Bar: Tex. bar 1951. Practiced in Austin, 1951-79; partner McGinnis, Lochridge & Kilgore (and predecessors), 1960-76; counsel Stubbeman, McRae, Sealy, Laughlin & Browder, 1976-79; sr. v.p. and gen. counsel Brown & Root, Inc., Houston, 1980—, also dir.; asst. atty. gen., 1957-58; counsel Senate Democratic Policy Com.; legis. asst. to senate majority leader Lyndon B. Johnson, 1959-60; lectr. U. Tex. Law Sch., 1962-63; dir. Continental Air Lines, Tex. Air Corp., Ea. Airlines, Inc., Highlands Ins. Co. Served from ensign to lt. (j.g.) USNR, 1952-55. Fellow Tex. Bar Found.; mem. ABA, Tex. Bar Assn., Harris County Bar Assn., Am. Law Inst., Order of Coif, Phi Beta Kappa. Home: 3218 Reba Dr Houston TX 77019 Office: Brown & Root Inc PO Box 3 4100 Clinton Dr Houston TX 77001

WILSON, JOHN EDWARD, JR., corporate financial executive; b. Plattsburgh, N.Y., Feb. 29, 1956; s. John Edward and Patricia (Garvey) W. AAS in Bus. Mgmt., Clinton Community Coll., 1976; BS in Mgmt., Clarkson Coll., 1978, MBA, 1979. Prof. fin. Clarkson Coll., Potsdam, N.Y., 1979-80; product acct. Alcoa, Massena, N.Y., 1980-82; credit rep., sr. credit rep. Alcoa, L.A., 1982-84; treas., fin. analyst Alcoa, Pitts., 1984—. Mem. Jaycees (treas. Massena chpt. 1981-82). Roman Catholic. Home: 909 River Oaks Dr Pittsburgh PA 15215 Office: Alcoa 1501 Alcoa Bldg Pittsburgh PA 15219

WILSON, JOHN OLIVER, economist, educator, banker; b. St. James, Mo., May 22, 1938; s. John Riffie and Jacquetta Ruth (Linck) W.; B.A. in Math., Northwestern U., 1960; Ph.D. in Econs., U. Mich., 1967; m. Beclee Newcomer, Jan. 28, 1961; children—Beth Anne, Benjamin Duncan. Asst. prof. Yale U., 1967-70; asst. dir. Office Econ. Opportunity, Washington, 1969-71; asst. sec. HEW, 1972; dir. North Star Research Inst., Mpls., 1972-74; with Bank of Am., San Francisco 1975—, chief economist, 1982—; prof. Grad. Sch. Pub. Policy U. Calif., Berkeley, 1979—. Bd. visitors Joint Center for Urban Studies, Harvard U.-M.I.T. Served with U.S. Navy, 1960-63. Ford Found. fellow, 1966-67. Mem. Am. Econ. Assn., Western Econ. Assn., Nat. Assn. Bus. Economists. Democrat. Presbyterian. Author: After Affluence, Economics to Meet Human Needs 1980, Middle Class Crisis: The American and Japanese Exprience, 1983, The Power Economy, Building An Economy That Works, 1985; contbr. articles to profl. jours. Office: PO Box 37000 San Francisco CA 94137

WILSON, KENNETH ALAN, sports broadcasting executive; b. Seattle, Dec. 30, 1958; s. Campbell Thomas and Priscilla Joan (Buck) W.; m. Carylyn Caspersen, Aug. 11, 1984. Student, Columbia Basin Community Coll., Pasco, Wash., 1977-78; BS, Cornell U., 1982. Account exec. Sta. KNDO-TV, Yakima, Wash., 1982, Sta. KATU-TV, Portland, Oreg., 1982-86; broadcast sales mgr. Portland Trailblazers Assn., 1986—. Asst. coach Portland Youth Football, 1985-88. Republican. Home: 10360 SW Hawthorne Ln Portland OR 97225 Office: Portland Trailblazers 700 NE Multnomah Portland OR 97232

WILSON, LAWRENCE GRAHAM, III, binational center executive; b. Mobile, Ala., June 6, 1944; came to Ecuador, 1969; s. Lawrence Graham and Mary Blanche (Williams) W.; m. Lesvia Irene Lima, Oct. 8, 1969 (div.); children—Wendy, Vanessa, Stephanie, Nicole. B.S. in Biology, Troy State U., 1966; Med. Technologist, Providence Hosp., Mobile, Ala., 1972. Tchr. biology Am. Sch. of Guayaquil, Ecuador, 1969-71; owner, mgr. Bioanalytical Lab., Guayaquil, 1973-76; owner, gen. mgr. Wilson Co. Ltd., Guayaquil, 1976-86; dir. Ecuadorean U.S. Cultural Ctr., Guayaquil, 1982—. Bd. dirs. Fulbright Commn., Guayaquil, 1975-83; a founder, bd. dirs. Interamerican Acad., Guayaquil, 1978, "Por Cristo" Med. Charity, 1984—; pres. bd. Am. Sch. of Guayaquil, 1984—. Served with USN, 1966-68. Mem. Am. Soc. Clin. Pathologists (assoc. mem.; registered med. technologist), Am. C. of C. (pres. 1982-83). Roman Catholic. Club: Nautico (Guayaquil). Avocations: metal detecting, fishing, coin collecting. Office: PO Box 5717, Guayaquil Ecuador

WILSON, LEONARD M., food products executive; b. 1926. BA, Dartmouth Coll., 1946; MS, Columbia Coll., 1951. Economist Shell Oil Co., 1953-55, GM, Detroit, 1955-60, E.I. duPont de Memours, Wilmington, Del., 1960-63; sr. v.p., economist United Fruit Co., 1963-71; ind. cons. 1971-76; pres. Agribus. Assocs., 1976-83; exec. v.p. HP Hoods Inc., 1983-86, pres., 1986—. With USN, 1944-46. Office: HP Hood Inc 500 Rutherford Ave Boston MA 02129

WILSON, LEWIS LANSING, insurance executive; b. Cobleskill, N.Y., Jan. 26, 1932; s. Clarence A. and Ordella (Walker) W.; m. Barbara Jane Kathan, June 7, 1952; children: Susan W. Coleman, Joan, Peter L. Grad. high sch., Cobleskill, 1950. Cert. profl. ins. agt., 1988, CIC, 1988. Mgr. claims Sterling Ins. Co., Cobleskill, 1950-57; ins. agt. State Farm Ins. Co., Cobleskill, 1957-59; pres. Lewis L. Wilson, Inc., Cobleskill, 1959—; Owner Wilson Telephone Exchange, Cobleskill, 1978-86, Wilson Security, Inc., Cobleskill, 1981-86; rep. N.Y. Map Program, 1985-88. Town chmn. Cobleskill Rep. Party, 1978-83; chmn. Schoharie County Rep. Com., N.Y., 1983—, Cobleskill SUNY Found. Fund Drive; commr. Schoharie County Bd. Elections, 1983—; pres. Cobleskill Cen. Sch., Community Hosp. Schoharie County, Cobleskill. Mem. Profl. Ins. Agts. (pres. 1989, bd. dirs. 1984—, v.p. 1987—, 1st v.p. 1988—, Ins. Agt. of Yr. 1986), N.Y. Ind. Ins. Agts. (regional v.p.), N.Y. Life Underwriters. Republican. Methodist. Lodges: Rotary (pres. Cobleskill chpt., gov. dist. 719 1982, Paul Harris fellow 1985-86), Elks (exalted ruler, hon. founder nat. found. 1980). Home: 31 Grandview Dr Cobleskill NY 12043 Office: PO Box 39 Cobleskill NY 12043

WILSON, MALCOLM, banker, lawyer, former governor N.Y. State; b. N.Y.C., Feb. 26, 1914; s. Charles H. and Agnes (Egan) W.; m. Katharine McCloskey, Sept. 6, 1941 (dec. Jan. 1980); children: Kathy, Anne. BA, Fordham U., 1933, LLB, 1936, LLD, 1959; LLD, Siena Coll., 1959, Pace Coll., 1959, St. Bonaventure Coll., 1960, SUNY, 1978, Bklyn. Law Sch., 1962, Canisius Coll., 1963, Le Moyne Coll., 1964, St. John Fisher Coll., 1964, Manhattan Coll., 1964, Columbia U., 1974; LHD, Alfred U., 1961. Bar: N.Y. 1936. Sole practice White Plains; ptnr. Kent, Hazzard, Jaeger, Wilson, Freeman & Greer, White Plains, N.Y., 1946-77, of counsel, 1986—; chmn. bd., chief exec. officer Manhattan Savs. Bank, N.Y.C., 1977-86; mem. N.Y. State Assembly from 1st Westchester Dist., 1939-58; lt. gov. State of N.Y., 1959-73, gov., 1974; bd. dirs. Shearson Lehman Hutton,Inc., Colin Service Systems, Inc. Bd. dirs. Catholic Youth Orgn., Archdiocese N.Y., Farmers Mus., N.Y. State Hist. Assn.; trustee NCCJ. Served with USNR, 1943-45. Recipient John Peter Zenger award N.Y. State Soc. Newspaper Editors, 1957. Mem. ABA, N.Y. State Bar Assn., Westchester County Bar Assn., Ancient Order Hibernians, Soc. Friendly Sons St. Patrick, N.Y. Farm Bur. Lodge: K.C. Home: 24 Windsor Rd Scarsdale NY 10583 Office: 199 Main St White Plains NY 10601

WILSON, MARTEL DEOVARN, JR., recreational resort executive; b. Stockton, Calif., Dec. 21, 1936; s. Martel D. Sr. and Elizabeth (Grieve) W.; m. Noel Wilson (div. 1978); 1 child, Elisabeth Noelle; m. Margaret M. Mullane, Aug. 2, 1980. BSMI, U. Colo., 1959; MBA, Cornell U., 1961. Mgr. budget and standards Riegel Paper Co., Milford, N.J., 1962-66; v.p., controller S-K-I Ltd., Killington, Vt., 1966-88, v.p., chief fin. officer, 1988—; bd. dirs. Chittenden Corp., Burlington, Vt., Bldg. Material Distbrs. Inc., Galt, Calif. Bd. dirs. Rutland (Vt.) Regional Med. Ctr., 1979-84, pres. 1982-84, mem. investment adv. com., 1987—; trustee Coll. of St. Joseph, Rutland, 1980-81; chmn. bd. dirs. Comprehensive Health Resources Inc., Rutland, 1984-86. Mem. Rutland Region C. of C. (bd. dirs. 1975-79, pres. 1977-78), Rotary (pres. Killington 1976). Office: S-K-I Ltd Killington Rd Killington VT 05751

WILSON, MICHAEL JOSEPH, newspaper executive; b. Houston, June 11, 1953; s. Joseph Henry and Mary Beth (Kelley) W.; m. Lynne Freeman, June 24, 1978; children: Stephanie Elizabeth, Amanda Leigh. BJ, U. Tex., 1975. Sales rep. Dow Jones, Houston, 1977-79, Wall Street Jour. subs. Dow Jones, N.Y.C., 1980-83; internat. advt. dir. Wall Street Jour. subs. Dow Jones & Co., N.Y.C., 1983-86, mktg. dir. for spl. reports, 1986-87; dir. advt. Asian Wall St. Jour., Hong Kong, Hong Kong, 1987—. Mem. Internat. Advt. Assn., Nat. Investor Relations Inst., Am. C. of C. in Hong Kong, Hong Kong Pubs. Soc. Office: Asian Wall Street Jour, GPO Box 9825, Hong Kong Hong Kong

WILSON, PAT LEIGHTON, insurance company executive, communications executive; b. Falfurrias, Tex., May 21, 1939; s. Buel Woodrow and Joyce Etoy (Moore) W.; m. Esther Epstein, Oct. 11, 1958; children: Angela Monette, Mark Patton, Lisa Renée. Student, Baylor U., 1957-58; BBA, St. Mary's U., San Antonio, 1966. CPA, Tex. Staff acct. Lewis & Montag, San Antonio, 1964-69; tax specialist Deloite Haskins & Sells, San Antonio, 1969-73; chief fin. officer Alamo Title Co., San Antonio, 1973—, also bd. dirs.; chief fin. officer Alamo Title Ins. Co. Tex., San Antonio, 1973—, also bd. dirs.; pres. Mission Communications, Inc., San Antonio, 1988—; bd. dirs. Century Land Title Co., Houston, Summit Bank, San Antonio. Mem. AICPA (mem. council), Tex. Soc. CPA's (bd. dirs. 1983—, v.p. 1986-87), San Antonio Soc. CPA's (pres. 1983-84), Tex. Land Title Assn. (bd. dirs. 1985-86), North Tex. C. of C., Greater San Antonio C. of C. (adv. dir. 1983-84). Mem. Christian Ch. Clubs: Dominion, Los Compadres (San Antonio). Avocations: reading, golf. Office: Alamo Title Ins Co Tex 613 NW Loop 410 Suite 100 San Antonio TX 78216

WILSON, PAUL ABERNATHY, financial and logistics executive; b. Perth Amboy, N.J., Apr. 2, 1948; s. Harold Paul and Mary (Abernathy) W.; m. Mildred Frances Bedwell, Jan. 30, 1971; children: Kathryn Erin, Jonathan Paul. BS, U.S. Naval Acad., 1970; grad., Navy Supply Corps Sch., 1972; MBA in Fin. Mgmt., George Washington U., 1976. Lic. investment broker. Commd. ensign USN, 1970, advanced through grades to lt. comdr., 1986; mgr. Nashville distbn. ctr. Matco Tools, Nashville, 1986—; math. and mgmt. educator Roger Williams Coll., Bristol, R.I., 1976-78. Recipient various service awards. Mem. Lions. Home: 440 Meadowlark Ln La Vergne TN 37086

WILSON, PAUL HOLLIDAY, JR., lawyer; b. Schenectady, N.Y., Sept. 4, 1942; s. Paul H. and Sarah Elizabeth (MacLean) W.; m. Elaine Hawley Griffin, May 30, 1964; children: Hollace, Paul, Kirsten, Katherine. AB, Brown U., 1964; LLB, MBA, Columbia U., 1967. Bar: N.Y. 1967, U.S. Dist. Ct. (so. dist.) 1968. Law clk. U.S. Dist. Ct. (so. dist.) N.Y., N.Y.C., 1967-68; assoc. Debevoise & Plimpton, N.Y.C., 1968-75, ptnr., 1976—, fin. ptnr., 1980-88. Vice-chmn., trustee St. Michael's Montessori Sch., N.Y.C., 1977-79, chmn. bd. trustees, 1979-81. Mem. ABA, Assn. Bar City N.Y. (mem. commn. on securities regulations 1985-88). Club: Vineyard Haven Yacht (Mass.)(vice-commodore 1985, commodore 1986-87). Office: Debevoise & Plimpton 875 Third Ave New York NY 10022

WILSON, RICHARD DALE, executive training, consulting company; b. L.A., July 22, 1933; s. Wayne Merle and June Lillian (Buys) W.; m. Nancy Irene Colby, 1974; children: Christopher, Jennifer, Janie, Matthew, Dixie, Tracey, Mark, Mysti, Tiffany. BA, San Jose Coll., 1964; LLB, Blackstone Law Sch., 1974; postgrad., Harvard U., 1987, Kennedy Western U., 1988. TV news anchor, overseas correspondent, investigative reporter numerous TV stas., 1964-75; legis. services dir. Utah State Legis., Salt Lake City, 1976; pres. Nat. Inst. for Tng. and Consulting, Salt Lake City, 1977—; sr. cons. The Co. Cons., 1981—; pres. Nat. Inst. for Sales Tng. and Cons. Authors: Handwriting 12 Keys to Every Personality, 1968, How to Avoid Malpractice in Real Estate Brokerage, 1979, 10 Basic Habits Superstar Salesperson , 1986, 10 Critical Steps to Building a Profitable Sales Organization, 1987, 10 Basic Habits of a Superstar Sales Manager, 1989; editor, pub. The Co. Cons. Newsletter, 1985—; contbr. articles to profl. jours. Media planner Rep. Conv., N.D., 1972; organizer Rep. Conv., Calif., 1964; del. Utah State Conv., 1976. Sgt. USMC, 195-57, Korea. Recipient Gavel award ABA, 1973; named Regional Dir. Yr. Westworld Services, Inc., 1981. Mem. Soc. Profl. Cons., Am. Handwriting Analysis Found., Nat. Assn. Realtors, Realtors Nat. Mktg. Inst. Mormon. Home: 1460 South 100 E Orem UT 84058 Office: Nat Inst Sales Tng Inc 2696 N University Ave #270 Provo UT 84604

WILSON, ROBERT SIDNEY, banker; b. Philipsburg, Pa., May 2, 1947; s. Sidney Milford and Dorothy Hazel (Edelblute) W.; m. Ann Marie Mills, Dec. 19, 1969; children: Matthew, Amanda, Courtney. BBA in Mktg., U. Akron, 1974. Mgmt. trainee Cen. Trust Co. Northeastern Ohio, Canton, 1974-76; mng. officer Cen. Trust Co., Canton, 1976-79; asst. cashier 1st Nat. Bank Cin., 1979-81, asst. v.p., 1981-82, regional v.p., 1982-85; regional v.p. Citibank Ariz. (formerly United Bank Ariz.), Phoenix, 1985—. Fin. chmn., bd. dirs. Tempe (Ariz.) YMCA, 1986-88; bd. dirs. Tempe chpt. Am. Cancer Soc., 1986-87; mem. East Valley Ptnrship., Tempe, 1986—; vice chmn. Tempe campaign United Way, 1988—; found. bd. mem. St. Luke's Hosp., Tempe; bd. mem. Valley of the Sun United Way, 1989—. Mem. Robert Morris & Assocs. (regional assoc.), Am. Inst. Banking, Tempe C. of C. (bd. dirs., vice chmn., Svcs. award 1987), Am. Electronics Assn. Republican. Lodge: Rotary. Office: Citibank 64 E Broadway Tempe AZ 85282

WILSON, ROBIN MARIE, financial analyst; b. Newton, Mass., Aug. 16, 1962; d. Robert H. and Dolores T. (Gargaro) W. BS, Boston Coll., 1984; postgrad., Babson Coll., 1985—. Telemktg. rep. ADP, Waltham, Mass., 1984-85; assoc. program analyst Raytheon Co., Wayland, Mass., 1985-87;

program analyst Raytheon Co., Marlboro, Mass., 1987-88; program analyst Raytheon Co., Wayland, Mass., 1988-89, sr. program analyst, 1989—. Admissions vol. Boston Coll. Alumni Assn., 1985—. Mem. Sudbury/Wayland Mgmt. Club, Raytheon Mgmt. Club. Home: 59 Eaton Rd Framingham MA 01701 Office: Raytheon Co 430 Boston Post Rd Wayland MA 01778

WILSON, SCOTT EDWARDS, venture capitalist; b. Ann Arbor, Mich., Apr. 20, 1954; s. William Sleight and Marit Williams (Andersen) W.; m. Jane Elizabeth Brock, July 30, 1983. AB, Bowdoin Coll., 1975; MBA, Dartmouth Coll., 1980. Math tchr., coach Worcester (Mass.) Acad., 1975-78; asst. v.p. Bank of Boston, 1980-84; v.p. Boston Fin. Group, 1984-86, 3i Capital Corp., Boston, 1986—. Office: 3i Capital Corp 99 High St Suite 1530 Boston MA 02110

WILSON, TERRENCE RAYMOND, manufacturing executive; b. St. Louis, July 1, 1943; s. Raymond Lemuel and Eula Ellen (Sutton) W.; student Drury Coll., 1961-62, St. Louis Jr. Coll., 1962-64, Mo. U., 1965-67; m. Judy Marie Coleman, May 23, 1964; children—John Scott, Dustin Martin. Program control planning adminstr. McDonnell Aircraft, St. Louis, 1962-65, 67; mgmt. control mgr. Vitro Labs., Silver Spring, Md., 1966; mgr. customer service Teledyne Wis. Motor, Milw., 1968-69, dir. ops., 1970-71, dir. mktg., 1972-73; gen. mgr. Teledyne Still-Man, Cookeville, Tenn., 1973-74, pres. multiplant div., 1975-78, group exec. Teledyne, Inc., 1979-84; pres. Teledyne Indsl. Engines, 1984-87; pres. Morgan Corp., Morgantown, Pa., 1987—. Bd. dirs. Tenn. Tech. U. Coll. Bus. Found. Mem. Nat. Mgmt. Assn., Am. Mgmt. Assn., Sales and Mktg. Execs., Mfrs. Assn. Berks County (bd. dirs.), Beta Gamma Sigma. Roman Catholic. Lodge: K.C. Home: 308 Logan Ave Wyomissing PA 19610 Office: One Morgan Way Morgantown PA 19543

WILSON, TERRY L., investment banker; b. Bloomington, Ind., June 1, 1962; s. Stephen M. and Rita K. (Walters) W. Student, U. Chgo., 1980-81, U. London, 1985; BA, Skidmore Coll., 1987; postgrad., U. South Sch. Theol., 1986—. Sr. paralegal Law Offices Rudolph W. Savich, Bloomington, 1983-84; with internat. dept. Conn. Bank and Trust Factors, N.Y.C., 1985-86; with fin. dept. Paine Webber, N.Y.C., 1986-87; sole cons. investment banker N.Y.C., 1987—; con. Merrill Lynch, N.Y.C., 1986; lectr. Internat. Ctr., 1986—; clin. pastoral edn., chaplain St. Luke's Hosp. Ctr., Columbia U., N.Y.C., 1987-88. Author: Lenten Meditations, 1987, (co-author) In Residence, 1981; contbr. articles to profl. jours. Youth campaign coordinator, U.S. Rep. Lee H. Hamilton, Washington, 1982; co-convener, organizer Nat. Voter Registration Conf. at Harvard U., Cambridge, Mass., 1984; pres., Ind. Pub. Interest Research Groups and Insts., Bloomington, 1983-84; precinct com. mem., state conv. judge, Ind. Dem. Party, Indpls., 1984; mem. Episc. Diocese of N.Y. Inst. of Theol., 1987-88, AIDS Mininstry Food Pantry St. Luke-in-the-Fields, 1987—; stewardship com., parish life com., St. Mark's Ch. in-the-Bowery, N.Y.C., 1985—; treas., ESEI Cult. Found., N.Y.C., 1987-88, v.p., 1988—, Korean Music Inst. of N.Y., 1985—, Cath.-Episc. Lower East Side Anti-Displacement Project, 1986-88; parish coordinator Project Domicile, Partnership for th eHomeless, 1986—; bd. dirs. Citizen's Action Coalition of Ind., 1982-84. Named Advent Preacher Cathedral Ch. of St. John the Divine, 1987. Fellow Carnigie Council on Ethics and Internat. Affairs; mem. Nat. Soc. Pub. Accts. (elected del. to nat. conv. 1987), Am. Mgmt. Assn., Nat. Tax Assn. (com. mem.), Nat. Assn. Bus. Economists, N.Y. Banker's Group, Waseda U. Alumni Assn. of N.Y.C., English Speaking Peoples Union, N.Y. Br. Audobon Soc., Archtl. League of N.Y., Muncpl. Art Soc., Asia Soc., Am. Film Inst. in N.Y., Alpha Kappa Psi. Clubs: English Speaking Union, Asia Soc., N.Y. Soc. Library, Mercantile Library, Chgo., Princeton, Williams. Home: 221 E 5th Ave New York NY 10003 Office: 6 Cooper St New York NY 10276

WILSON, THOMAS C., engineering consultant; b. Portsmouth, Ohio, July 3, 1953; s. Thomas W. and Ruth E. (Vodak) W.; m. Joan C. Wilson, Aug. 19, 1972; children: Scott, Jeff, Brian, Adam. BSCE, Iowa State U., 1975; MBA, U. Nebr., 1987. Assoc. systems engr. InterNorth, Omaha, 1975-82, systems engr., 1977-82, sr. systems engr., 1980-82; sr. project engr. Peoples Natural Gas, Council Bluffs, Iowa, 1982-85; dir. EnerGroup, Inc., Omaha, 1985-86, mgr., 1986—. Contbr. articles to profl. jours. Pres. Millard Star Soccer Assn., Omaha, 1984. Mem. ASCE. Democrat. Mem. United Ch. Home: 10311 Y St Omaha NE 68127 Office: EnerGroup Inc 1815 Capitol Ave Omaha NE 68102

WILSON, THORNTON ARNOLD, retired aerospace company executive; b. Sikeston, Mo., Feb. 8, 1921; s. Thornton Arnold and Daffodil (Allen) W.; m. Grace Miller, Aug. 5, 1944; children: Thornton Arnold III, Daniel Allen, Sarah Louise Wilson Anderson. Student, Jefferson City (Mo.) Jr. Coll., 1938-40; B.S., Iowa State Coll., 1943; M.S., Calif. Inst. Tech., 1948; M.S. Sloan fellow, MIT, 1952-53. With Boeing Co., Seattle, 1943—, asst. chief tech. staff, project engrng. mgr., 1957-58, v.p., mgr. Minuteman br. aerospace div., 1962-64, v.p. ops. and planning, 1964-66, exec. v.p., dir., 1966-68, pres., 1968—, chief exec. officer, 1969-86, chmn. bd., 1972-88, chmn. emeritus, 1988—; dir. PACCAR, Inc., Weyerhaeuser Co., USX Corp., Hewlett Packard, Inc. Bd. govs. Iowa State U. Found.; trustee Seattle U.; mem. corp. MIT, Nat. Acad. Engrng. Fellow Am. Inst. Aeronautics and Astronautics. Office: The Boeing Co PO Box 3707 Seattle WA 98124

WILSON, TIMOTHY ALLEN, electronics company executive; b. Syracuse, N.Y., July 2, 1948; s. James and Gloria (Rohadfox) W.; m. Carrie E. Pettiford, Sept. 19, 1970; children: Chanelle T., Derek S.J. BBA in Mgmt., Clark U., 1985; MS in Applied Mgmt., Lesley Coll., 1987. Programmer, analyst Digital Equipment Corp., Maynard, Mass., 1978; sr. programmer, analyst Digital Equipment Corp., Marlboro, Mass., 1978-81, programming supr., 1981-83, systems and program mgr., 1983-84; info. services conf. Digital Equipment Corp., Westminster, Mass., 1984-85; bus. cons. mgr. Digital Equipment Corp., Northboro, Mass., 1985-87; mgr. user services Digital Equipment Corp., Maynard, Mass., 1987-88, mgr. computer services ea. Mass., 1988—. Advisor Jr. Achievement, Northboro, 1984-86. Office: Digital Equipment Corp 129 Parker St Maynard MA 01754

WILSON, VALENTINE L., packaging company executive; b. Phila., Nov. 30, 1925; s. Valentine and Madeline (Winternitz) W.; m. Judith Pleet, Dec. 28, 1950; children: Val P., Andrew N., Victoria Goodman. Student, Temple U. Past pres. S. Walter Packaging Corp., Phila., now chief exec. officer, chmn. bd. dirs. Past v.p. Northeast Phila. C. of C. Mem. Am. Lung Assn., Willowcrest Bamburger. Club: Philmont Country (Huntingdon Valley, Pa.) (pres. 1982-84). Office: S Walter Packaging Corp 87 Commerce Dr Telford PA 18969 also: 12001 Ventura Pl Studio City CA 91604

WILSON, WILLIAM EDWARD, electronics executive; b. Carlsbad, N. Mex., Feb. 3, 1940; s. William Page and Frances (Foster) W.; m. Carolyn Carter Whiting, June 8, 1963; children: Kristin, Carter. BEE, Cornell U., 1963; MSEE, Syracuse U., 1969; MBA, U. N.Mex., 1975. Tech. staff Sandia Labs., Albuquerque, 1969-74; bus. devel. mgr. Rockwell Internat., Newport Beach, Calif., 1974-75; bus. dir. Rockwell Internat., Dallas, 1975-79; v.p. engrng. Amplica, Inc., Newbury Park, Calif., 1979-84; pres. Amplica, Inc. subs. Comsat Gen. Corp., Newbury Park, Calif., 1984-88; pres., chief exec. officer, chmn. bd. dirs. Pacific R & D Inc., Glendale, Calif., 1988—. Served to 1st lt. USAF, 1964-67. Mem. IEEE. Republican. Home: 1662 Hawksway Ct Westlake Village CA 91361 Office: Pacific R&D Inc 1612 W Glenoaks Blvd Glendale CA 91201

WILSON, WILLIAM R., land planner; b. Indpls., July 24, 1954; s. Robert Morris and Lois Eleanor (Jenkins) W. Land planner Adair & Brady, Inc., West Palm Beach, Fla., 1974-87; prin. Wilson Enterprises, Lake Worth, Fla., 1987—. Pres. Fla. Ednl. Found., Inc., Hollywood, 1986—. Mem. Am. Inst. Cert. Planners, Am. Planning Assn., Palm Beach County Planning Congress. Office: Wilson Enterprises PO Box 508 Lake Worth FL 33460

WILTSE, DORR NORMAN, insurance executive; b. Caro, Mich., Sept. 20, 1911; s. Norman Anson and Evie Markham (McCartney) W.; student Eastern Mich. U., 1931-33; teaching cert. Central Mich. U., 1933-37; m. Gladys May Garner, Nov. 11, 1932; children: Dorr Norman, Saire Christina. Tchr., Tuscola County (Mich.) Public Schs., 1931-42; br. mgr. Mich. Mut. Ins. Co., Caro, 1942-75; city assessor, Caro, 1964—, also casualty ins. cons., Caro, 1975-79. Vice pres. Caro Devel. Corp., 1975-79, pres., 1983—; adv. bd. DeMolay Found. of Mich., 1965-67; founder, pres. Watrousville-Caro Area Hist. Soc., 1972-75, 78; pres. Caro Hist. Commn., 1975-79; chmn. bd. Caro Community Hosp. Endowment Found., 1982—; chmn. Caro Bicentennial Commn., 1975-76; mem. Com. to Elect Pres. Gerald R. Ford, 1975-76; mem. Indianfields-Caro-Almer Planning Commn., 1972-79; co-chmn. Mich. Sesquicentennial for Tuscola County, 1986-87. Named Citizen of Yr. Caro C. of C., 1975, Patriotic Citizen VFW, 1988. Mem. Mich. Assessors Assn., Caro Masonic Bldg. Assn., Inc. (pres. 1974-79), Nat. Trust Hist. Preservation, Nat. Hist. Soc., Hist. Soc. Mich., Huguenot Soc. Mich., Saginaw Geneal. Soc., Mich. Archaeol. Soc. Democrat. Presbyterian (elder). Clubs: Caro Lions (pres. 1946), Mich. Mut. Quarter Century, Masons (past master), Shriners. Author: The First Hundred Years, 1978; The Hidden Years of the Master, 1976; The Wiltse Saga, 1980; A Look in Your Own Backyard, 1983. Home: 708 W Sherman St Box 143 Caro MI 48723 Office: 247 S State St Caro MI 48723

WIMBERLY, BEADIE RENEAU (LEIGH), financial services executive; b. Fouke, Ark., Apr. 18, 1937; d. Woodrow Wilson and Grace B. (Winkley) Reneau; m. Benjamin Leon Price, 1954 (div. 1955); m. Elbert William Wimberly, Dec. 16, 1956; children—Stephanie Elaine Wimberly Davis, Jeffrey Scott, Lael Wimberly Carter Alston. Student William & Mary Coll., 1964-65, U. Md.-Ludwigsburg/Stuttgart, 1966-68, Northwestern State U. La., 1973-75, Cornell U., 1979, Leonard Sch., 1983. Cert. ins. agt.; registered gen. securities rep. SEC, registered investment adviser SEC. Internat. trainer of trainers North Atlantic council Girl Scouts, Fed. Republic Germany, 1965-69, 76-78; inventory master The Myers Co., Inc., El Paso, Tex., 1970; abstract asst. Vernon Abstract Co., Inc., Leesville, La., 1970-71; sec. to chief utilities and pollution control Dept. Army, U.S. Civil Service, Ft. Polk, La., 1971-72, asst. to post safety officer, 1972-73, adminstr. tech. Adj. Gen.'s Office, 1973-75, sr. library technician post libraries, 1975, personnel staffing specialist, Stuttgart, Fed. Republic Germany, 1976-79, voucher examiner Fin. and Acctg. Office, Ft. Polk, 1980-81; chief exec. officer Fin. Strategies, Inc., Leesville, La., 1981—, stockbroker, corp. exec., 1983—, mktg. exec., 1983—; labor cons. AFL/CIO, Ft. Polk, 1981—; br. office mgr. Anchor Nat. Fin. Services Inc.; dir., treas. Wimberly Enterprises, Inc. Bd. dirs. Calcasieu Parish council Boy Scouts Am., 1982-83, active, 1988—; treas. Vernon Parish Hist./Geneal. Soc., 1986-87; pres. Vernon Parish Helpline/Lifeline, 1985; charter mem. Nat. Mus. of Women in the Arts; mem. Vernon Parish Arts Council; mem. La. Supreme Ct. Task Force on Women in the Cts. of La. Mem. Pilot Internat., Internat. Assn. Fin. Planners, Nat. Assn. Govt. Employees (v.p. Ft. Polk chpt. 1980-81), Internat. Platform Assn., C. of C., Assn. U.S. Army, Am. Assn. Fin. Profls., Nat. Women's Polit. Caucus, Am. Soc. Mil. Comptrollers, LWV-La. (state bd. dirs. 1986-87, treas. Leesville chpt. 1982-87), NOW (Ruston-Grambling chpt.). Republican. Baptist. Club: Toastmasters (named Competent Toastmaster, 1979). Lodge: Rotary (bd. mem.-at-large Leesville club 1988—). Office: Fin Strategies Inc 302 N 5th St Leesville LA 71446

WIMBERLY, PATRICIA ANN, electronics product management executive; b. Lafayette, La., Dec. 8, 1951; d. George Allen and Verna (Comeaux) W.; divorced; children: T. Scott Guilbeaux II, Amanda L. Guilbeaux. BS, U SW La., 1974. Programmer Blue Cross La., Baton Rouge, 1974-77; programmer analyst Blue Cross/Blue Shield, Denver, 1977-79; systems engr. Electronic Data Systems Fed., Denver, 1979-80; programmer/analyst Info. Handling Systems, Englewood, Colo., 1980-81, sr. mgr. electronic products dept., 1981-84, asst. dir. electronic products, 1984-86, dir. optical pub., 1986-88; dir. Electronic Products, 1988—. Democrat. Roman Catholic. Office: Info Handling Svcs 15 Inverness Way E Englewood CO 80150

WIMMER, JAY STEPHEN, real estate developer, entrepreneur; b. Slaton, Tex., Sept. 28, 1954; s. Anton Andrew and Valeria (Heinrich) W.; m. Peggy Lee Hemphill, Nov. 9, 1985; 1 child: Brook Marshall. BBA in Acctg., Angelo State U., 1976. CPA, Tex. With audit dept. Arthur Andersen & Co., Dallas, 1976-79; entrepreneur Dallas and Rockwall, Tex., 1979—; pres., bd. dirs. Carpetmasters Inc., Garland, Tex.; bd. dirs. Greater Edn. Inc., Dallas. Republican. Roman Catholic. Home: 4133 Grasmere Lower Dallas TX 75205 Office: Carpetmasters Inc 11413 LBJ Freeway Garland TX 75041

WINAHRADSKY, MICHAEL FRANCIS, drug company executive; b. Syracuse, N.Y., Oct. 21, 1948; s. Frank F. and Genelle M. (Charmley) W.; m. Linda L. Peters, Oct. 10, 1981; children: Kevin M., Kari M. Distbn. ctr. supr. Fay's Drug Co. Inc., Liverpool, N.Y., 1967-76, distbn. ctr. mgr., 1976-81, asst. v.p. distbn., 1981-82, v.p. distbn., 1982—; guest speaker Syracuse (N.Y.) U., 1984. Participant cen. N.Y. chpt. Cystic Fibrosis Bowl for Breath, 1987-88. Mem. Warehouse Edn. and Research Council, Nat. Fire Protection Assn., Boat Owners Assn. of U.S. Lodge: Moose. Home: 1677 Channelside Trail Baldwinsville NY 13027 Office: Fay's Drug Co Inc 7245 Henry Clay Blvd Liverpool NY 13088

WINBIGLER, LEON FRANCIS, retail executive; b. Brookfield, Mo., 1926. Grad., U. Mo., 1948. Pres. Root Dry Goods Co., 1954-55, MacDougall Southwick Co., 1955-62, Lion Dry Goods Co., 1962-74; v.p. Mercantile Stores Co., Inc., Wilmington, Del., 1968-74, now chmn., chief exec. officer, also bd. dirs. Office: Merc Stores Co Inc 1100 N Market St Wilmington DE 19801

WINCHELL, WILLIAM OLIN, mechanical engineer, educator, lawyer; b. Rochester, N.Y., Dec. 31, 1933; s. Leslie Olin and Hazel Agnes (Apker) W.; m. Doris Jane Martenson, Jan. 19, 1957; children: Jason, Darrell, Kirk. BME, GMI Engring. and Mgmt. Inst., 1956; MSc, Ohio State U., 1970; MBA, U. Detroit, 1976; JD, Detroit Coll. Law, 1980. Bar: Mich. 1981, U.S. Dist. Ct. (ea. dist.) Mich. 1981, U.S. Ct. Appeals (6th cir.) 1982, U.S. Supreme Ct. 1985, N.Y. 1988; registered profl. engr., Mich., N.Y. Cons. Gen. Motors Corp., Detroit and Warren, Mich. and Lockport, N.Y., 1951-87; sole practice Royal Oak, Mich., 1981-88; assoc. prof., chmn. dept. indsl. engring. and mech. Alfred (N.Y.) U., 1987—. Mem. Royal Oak Long Range Planning Commn., 1980. Served to lt. commdr. USNR, 1956-76. Burton fellow Detroit Coll. Law, 1978. Fellow Am. Soc. Quality Control (v.p. 1985-89); mem. ABA, Mich. Bar Assn., Soc. Mfg. Engrs., Inst. Indsl. Engrs., Am. soc. Engring Educators, Tau Beta Pi, Beta Gamma Sigma. Roman Catholic. Club: North Star Sail. Office: Alfred U Sch Engring Div Indsl and Mech Engring Alfred NY 14802

WINCHESTER, ELIZABETH YOUNG, interior designer, consultant, space planner; b. Elgin, Ill., Dec. 7, 1934; m. Charles A. Winchester; 1 child, Susan. BA, Northwestern U., 1957; cert., N.Y. Sch. Interior Design, 1974; student Grad. Sch. Design, Harvard U., 1976. Exec. in fashion, cosmetics, design, promotion various orgns., N.Y.C., 1957-73; prin. Winchester Design, N.Y.C., 1974—. Mem. The Fashion Group, Inc., The Archtl. League. Club: Apawamis (Rye, N.Y.). Home and Office: Winchester Design 400 E 55th St New York NY 10022

WINDELS, PAUL, JR., lawyer; b. Bklyn., Nov. 13, 1921; s. Paul and Louise E. (Gross) W.; m. Patricia Ripley, Sept. 10, 1955; children: Paul III, Mary H., James H.R., Patrick D. AB, Princeton U., 1943; LLB, Harvard U., 1948. Bar: N.Y. 1949. Spl asst. counsel N.Y. State Crime Commn., 1951; asst. U.S. atty. Ea. Dist. N.Y., 1953-56; N.Y. regional adminstr. SEC, 1956-61, also spl. asst, U.S. atty. for prosecution securities frauds, 1956-58; lectr. law Am. Inst. Banking, 1950-57; ptnr. Windels, Marx, Davies & Ives and predecessor firms, 1961-88, of counsel, 1988—. Author: Our Securities Markets-Some SEC Problems and Techniques, 1962. Trustee, pres. Bklyn. Law Sch.; trustee, past pres. Fed. Bar Coun.; trustee, treas. French Inst./Alliance Française; chmn. French-Am. Monument Found.; mem. adv. bd. NYU Inst. French Studies, SUNY marine scis. lab.; mem. Woods Hole Oceanographic Inst. Capt. F.A. AUS, 1943-46, ETO; maj. arty. Res. Recipient Flemming award for fed. svc.; decorated chevalier Order French Acad. Palms; officer Nat. Order Merit France. Fellow Am. Bar Found.; mem. ABA, N.Y. State Bar Assn., Assn. of Bar of City of N.Y., Assn. N.Y. County Lawyers Assn. Republican. Presbyterian. Office: Windels Marx Davies & Ives 156 W 56th St New York NY 10019

WINDHAM, EFFORD HUBERT, educational adminstrator; b. Lamar, S.C., May 8, 1941; s. Edmond H. and Birdie (Freeman) W.; m. Phyllis White, June 29, 1968; children: Tara Ann, Kimberly Dawn. BBA, U.S.C., 1964, MEd, 1984; postgrad., Nova U. V.p. bus. affairs Florence (S.C.)-Darlington Tech. Coll., 1967—. Office: Florence-Darlington Tech Coll Drawer 8000 Florence SC 29501

WINDHORST, DELMAR EUGENE, corporate officer; b. Kansas City, MO, Nov. 23, 1930; s. Martin Henry and Dorothy Evelyn (Yandell) W.; m. Anna Helena Scharf, Apr. 15, 1950; children: Kenneth Allan, Franklin Eugene, David Eric. Grad. high sch., Rockport, Mo. Driller Adcock Pipe & Supply, San Antonio, 1961-63; mgr. warehouse Maverick Clarke, San Antonio, 1963-67; clk. MKT R.R., San Antonio, 1967-74; corp. officer Windy's Water Works Inc. subs. Delanco Inc., San Antonio, 1974—; cons. Delanco Inc., San Antonio, 1982—. Patentee in field. Served with USAF, 1948-54, U.S. Army, 1957-61. Mem. Nat. Fedn. Ind. Bus. (action leader). Republican. Lutheran. Home: Rt 30 Box 822 San Antonio TX 78221

WINE, WILLIAM PHILIP, financial executive, consultant; b. Montreal, Can., June 26, 1944; came to U.S., 1987; s. Abraham Jonah and Rose (Gural) W.; m. Sandra Frema Shuster, Apr. 4, 1967. Degree in Acctg., McGill U., 1967. V.p. fin. Superex Can. Ltd., Toronto, Ont., 1967-82; fin. cons. Leonard, Wine, Waldman & Assocs., Toronto, 1984-85; investment broker various, Toronto, 1982-87, Raymond James & Assocs., Lighthouse Point, Fla., 1987-88; cons. Property Tax Cons. Service, Boca Raton, Fla., 1988; fin. cons. Shearson Lehman Hutton, Pompano Beach, 1988—. Office: 1601 NE 23rd St Pompano Beach FL 33061

WINEBERG, JONATHAN MARTIN, communications executive; b. Akron, May 4, 1955; s. Martin Francis and Mary (Yakus) W.; m. Melissa Abigail Edmonson, July 9, 1983. BSEE, U. Akron, 1978; postgrad., Johns Hopkins U., 1984-85. Communication engr. Tex. Internat. Airlines, Houston, 1978-79, sr. communication engr., 1979-80; sr. systems analyst Trans-World Airlines, Kansas City, Mo., 1980-81; communications specialist Occidental Petroleum, Houston, 1981-82; dir. message services Aero. Radio, Annapolis, Md., 1982-85, sr. dir. data services, 1985-86; dep. dir. data automation svcs. Internat. Air Transport Assn., 1986—. Mem. IEEE. Republican. Lutheran. Office: 26 Chemin de Joinville, PO Box 160, CH 1216 Geneva Switzerland

WINES, DAVID JOEL, investment banker, options executive; b. Harvey, Ill., May 13, 1944; s. Joseph John and Agnes Virginia (Cienkus) W.; m. Terry Lynn Panici, Dec. 15, 1962; children: Wendy Lynn, David Joel II. Diploma in Transp. and Traffic Mgmt., Coll. Advanced Traffic and Transp., Chgo., 1968. Pres., chief exec. officer Dater Inc., Cable, Wis., 1976-80; owner restaurant and lounge Manteno, Ill., 1980-85; v.p. investments Lehman Bros., Chgo., 1985—. Active Jaycees, Flossmoor, Ill., 1984. Lodge: Moose. Home: 615 Oak St Peotone IL 60468 Office: Lehman Bros 190 S LaSalle St Chicago IL 60603

WINETT, SAMUEL JOSEPH, manufacturing company executive; b. Chgo., June 15, 1934; s. Maurice and Ruby (Caplan) W.; m. Susan Carol Finkel, Apr. 24, 1957; children: Bradley, William, James. BS in Acctg., U. Ill., 1956; MBA, U. Chgo., 1970. CPA, Ill. Staff auditor Arthur Young & Co., Chgo., 1958-63; with Outboard Marine Corp., Waukegan, Ill., 1963—, asst. controller, 1974-78, controller ops., 1978-86, v.p. fin., 1986—. Served as 1st lt. U.S. Army, 1956-58. Mem. Am. Inst. CPA's, Ill. CPA Soc., Fin. Execs. Inst. Home: 3128 Maple Leaf Dr Glenview IL 60025 Office: Outboard Marine Corp 100 Sea Horse Dr Waukegan IL 60085

WING, JAMES ERWIN, investment advisor; b. Grand Rapids, Mich., Sept. 21, 1958; s. Ray Erwin and Helen May (Dennis) W.; m. Dana Mason, Oct. 13, 1984. B.S., Babson Coll., 1980. Owner McNally-Wing Co., Wellesley, Mass., 1976-80; investment advisor E.F. Hutton, Chestnut Hill, Mass., 1980-85; investment adviser, v.p. Drexel Burnham Lambert, Boston, 1985—. Republican. Home: 585A Gray St Westwood MA 02090 Office: Drexel Burnham Lambert 1 Federal St 34th Floor Boston MA 02110

WING, JOHN BRIAN, energy executive; b. Potsdam, N.Y., July 20, 1946; s. Ivan F. and Martha (Virta) W.; m. Karen Jean Milanese, Aug. 29, 1970; children Christina, Brian Patrick. BS, U.S. Mil. Acad., West Point, N.Y., 1968; MBA, Harvard U., 1980. Commd. 2d lt. U.S. Army, 1968, advanced through grades to capt., 1970, served as aviation unit commdr., 1971-73, resigned, 1973; project mgr. N.Y. Power Authority, N.Y.C., 1974-78; sr. v.p., gen. mgr. Fla. Hydrocarbons Co., Winter Park, 1980-82; gen. mgr. Gen. Electric Co., Schenectady, N.Y., 1983-85; sr. v.p. Houston Natural Gas, 1985-86; ind. devel. and investor Houston, 1986-87; chmn., chief exec. officer Enron Cogeneration Co., Houston, 1987-88, The Wing Group, Inc., Daytona Beach, Fla., 1988—; vice-chmn., bd. dirs. Embry-Riddle Aero. U., Daytona Beach, 1988; owner, bd. dirs. Boston Beer Co.; chmn., owner John B. Wing Interests, Inc.; owner River Capital; active energy commn. State of TEx., 1987-88.. Mem. Gov.'s Com. on Tex. Energy Resources, Austin, 1986, Tex. House Com. on Energy, Austin, 1988. Baker scholar Harvard U., 1980. Home: 6 S Brokenfern Dr Woodlands TX 77380 Office: The Wing Group Inc 3 Riverway Ste 950 Houston TX 77056

WINGARD, PAUL L., data processing executive; b. Greenville, Ala., Dec. 25, 1952; s. Paul Ray and Betty Ruth (Horn) W. BSEE, Auburn U., Ala., 1976. Elec. engr. H. Hale Vickrey & Assocs., Inc., Mobile, Ala., 1976-80; computer salesman Cado Sys. of Mobile, Inc., 1980-83; pres. Distributive Network Sys., Inc., 1983—. Chmn. America's Jr. Miss, Mobile, 1984-88. Republican. Mem. Reorganized Ch. of Jesus of Latter Day Saints. Office: Distributive Network Systems Inc PO Box 851178 Mobile AL 36685-1178

WINGATE, EDWIN HENRY, retail company executive; b. Lincoln, Nebr., Aug. 29, 1932; s. James Roy and Andrena Blanch (Carlson) Wingate Lausen; m. Mary Quinlan, June 12, 1955; children—Jennifer, Laurel. B.S., Kans. State U., 1954; M.B.A., U. Calif., Berkeley, 1959. Vice pres. personnel Continental Airlines, Los Angeles, 1963-69; v.p., gen. mgr. Toro Co., Mpls., 1969-74; sr. v.p. personnel & orgnl. planning Pillsbury Co., Mpls., 1974-78; sr. v.p. adminstrn. Shaklee Corp., San Francisco, 1978-80; sr. v.p. personnel Dayton Hudson Corp., Mpls., 1980—; bd. dirs. Linbeck Corp., Houston, The Iams Co., Dayton, Ohio. Bd. dirs. Am. Inst. Mng. Diversity, Inc., 1986—, Skaggs Inst., Brigham Young U., Provo, Utah, 1986-89, TCOIC, Mpls. Capt. USAF, 1954-57. Republican. Presbyterian. Home: 12509 Briarwood Terr Minnetonka MN 55343 Office: Dayton-Hudson Corp 777 Nicollet Mall Minneapolis MN 55402

WINGER, DENNIS LAWRENCE, medical products company executive; b. Niagara Falls, N.Y., Nov. 24, 1947; s. James W. and Millicent Rose (McCabe) W.; m. Barbara Lee Waldman, May 19, 1984. BA, Siena Coll., 1969; MBA, Columbia U., 1974. Various fin. positions Continental Can Co., N.Y.C., 1974-77; v.p. fin. Continental Can Brazil, Sao Paulo, 1977-80; gen. mgr. Latin Am. ops. Continental Can Internat., Stamford, Conn., 1980-81, gen. mgr. fin., 1981-82; v.p. Cooper Devel. Co., Palo Alto, Calif., 1982-87, controller, 1982-83, treas., 1983-87; v.p., chief fin. officer Cooper Cos. Inc., Palo Alto, 1987—. Home: 2828 Jackson St San Francisco CA 94115 Office: The Cooper Cos Inc 3145 Porter Dr Palo Alto CA 94304

WINIKOFF, ROBERT LEE, lawyer; b. N.Y.C., May 17, 1946; s. Abraham and Anne (Brawer) W.; m. Enid L. Rabinowitz, July 13, 1969; children: Meredith, Brian, Deborah. BA, Ithaca Coll., 1968; JD, William & Mary Coll. of Law, 1973. Bar: N.Y. 1974, U.S. Dist. Ct. (ea. and so. dists.) N.Y. 1974, U.S. Tax Ct. 1974, U.S. Ct. Appeals (2d cir.) 1974. Assoc. Dewey, Ballantine, Bushby, Palmer & Wood, N.Y.C., 1973-76, Goldman Cooperman & Levitt, N.Y.C., 1977-79. Comments editor William & Mary Law Rev., 1972-73. Mem. ABA, N.Y. State Bar Assn., Assn. of Bar of City of N.Y., Omicron Delta Kappa. Democrat. Jewish. Home: 4 Hemptor Rd New City NY 10956 Office: Cooperman Levitt & Winikoff PC 800 3d Ave New York NY 10022

WINK, ALAN NEAL, financial executive; b. Newark, Jan. 30, 1957; s. Jack and Freida (Lapidus) W.; m. Donna Susan Schrob, Oct. 2, 1983; children: Jason, Daniel. BA, Rutgers U., 1979, MBA, 1987. Staff acct. Price Waterhouse, Morristown, N.J., 1979-80; auditor ops. Gulf Western R.R., N.Y.C., 1980-81; sr. auditor Warner Communications, N.Y.C., 1981-85; dir. fin. analysis The Home Group, N.Y.C., 1985—; cons. Hoffman LaRoche, 1985-87, Merrill Lynch, 1985-87, Rutgers U., 1985-87. Office: The Home Group 59 Maiden Ln New York NY 10038

WINKELSTERN, PHILIP NORMAN, financial executive; b. N.Y.C., Aug. 1, 1930; s. Philip and Lydia Mae (Kaiser) W.; m. Bette Louise Grugett, June

15, 1956; children: Philip J., Kristen N. B.A., Mich. State U., 1956. Fin. analyst Gen. Electric, Schenectady, 1956-61; div. controller Ford Motor Co., Dearborn, Mich., 1961-75; sr. v.p. Comml. Inertech, Youngstown, Ohio, 1975—; dir. Comml. Inertech, 1984—, McDonald Steel Co. Chmn. Better Bus. Bur., Youngstown, 1977; trustee Western Res. Care Assn., Cin., 1987—. Served with USMC, 1951-53. Mem. Fin. Execs. Inst., Am. Mgmt. Assn., Machinery and Allied Products Inst., C. of C. Office: Comml Inertech 1775 Logan Ave Youngstown OH 44501

WINKIN, JUSTIN PHILIP, engineering executive; b. Englewood, N.J., July 14, 1922; s. John Quirin and Cora (Senner) W.; widowed; children: Justin, John, Susan. BSME, Rensselaer Polytech. Inst., 1944; postgrad., NYU, 1951-53. Registered profl. engr., N.J. Student engr. Babcock & Wilcox, N.Y.C., 1946-47, field service engr., 1947-50, staff engr., 1950-58; ops. engr. Jersey Cen. Power and Light, Morristown, N.J., 1958-63; staff engr., dir., v.p. engring. Foster Wheeler Energy Corp., Livingston, N.J., 1963-77, sr. v.p., 1979-82; v.p., cons. Foster Wheeler Energy Corp., Clinton, N.J., 1987—; pres. Foster Wheeler Ltd., St. Catherines, Can., 1979-82, also bd. dirs., 1972-87; v.p., group exec. Foster Wheeler Corp., Livingston, 1982-87; bd. dirs. Generadores De Vapor, S.A., Madrid, Spain, Belco Pollution Corp., Livingston, Foster Wheeler Energy Applications, Livingston. Contbr. articles to profl. jours; patentee in field. Mem. Radburn Assn., Fair Lawn, N.J., 1950—; pres. Radburn Theater, Fair Lawn, 1975-77. Served to lt. USN, 1944-46, PTO. Fellow ASME. Republican. Presbyterian. Home: 19-12 Radburn Rd Fairlawn NJ 07410 Office: Foster Wheeler Corp Perryville Corp Park PO Box 4000 Clinton NJ 08809

WINKLER, WILLIAM RICHARD, accountant; b. Darby, Pa., Oct. 30, 1947; s. William Charles and Dorothy Rosanna (Huebner) W.; m. Susan Patricia Morris, Dec. 27, 1969; children: Valerie Meta, Caroline Dorothy. BS, Drexel U., 1970. CPA, Pa. Staff acct. Deloitte Haskins & Sells, Phila., 1969-74; sr. acct. Deloitte Haskins & Sells, Chattanooga, 1974-76; mgr. corp. acctg. Philips Industries, Inc., Dayton, Ohio, 1977-87, dir. corp. acctg., 1988—; acct. Philips Industries Inc., Dayton, 1981—. Campaign floor capt. United Way, Dayton, Ohio, 1979-80; pres. Nutt Rd. Estates Homeowners Assn., Centerville, Ohio, 1985, 86; coach Soccer Assn. for Youth, Centerville, 1986—. Mem. Am. Inst. CPA's, Pa. Inst. CPA's (proctor exam 1973). Lutheran. Office: Philips Industries Inc 4801 Springfield St Dayton OH 45431

WINN, DAVID B., insurance company executive; b. Savannah, Ga., Apr. 10, 1937; s. James Bailey and Willie (Baker) W.; m. Carol Anne Havird, Dec. 22, 1957; children: Kathryn Novander, David B. Jr., James H. BS in Indsl. Mgmt., Ga. Tech. Inst., 1959; MBA in Bus. Adminstrn., Ga. State Coll., 1965. Ins. trainee Allstate Ins. Co., Atlanta, 1960-65, underwriting div. supr., 1965-66, mgmt. trainee, 1966, zone underwriter, 1966-67; underwriting div. mgr. Tex., 1967-68; field underwriting rev. mgr. Northbrook, Ill., 1968-69; underwriting mgr. Denver, 1969-72, Seattle, 1972-76; zone underwriting mgr. Bannockburn, Ill., 1976-77; asst. regional mgr. N.J., 1977-78; regional v.p. Barrington, Ill., 1978-81, Mich., 1981-82; pres. Can., 1982-84; v.p. corp. strategic planning Northbrook, Ill., 1984-85, field exec., v.p. cen. terr., 1985-86, territorial v.p., ea. terr., 1986-88, group v.p., 1988—. Served to capt. U.S. Army, 1959-60. Republican. Episcopalian. Office: Allstate Ins Co Allstate Pla Northbrook IL 60062

WINN, HERSCHEL CLYDE, retail electronics company executive; b. Hill County, Tex., Dec. 14, 1931; s. Herschel C. and Alta Fay; m. Dorothy Carolyn Martin, June 24, 1961; children—Celia Carol, Macey Sheryl. B.A., U. Tex., Austin, 1958, LL.B., 1960. Bar: Tex. bar 1960. Atty. Tex. Hwy. Dept., 1960-61; trial atty. Internat. Service Ins. Co., 1961-63; judge Johnson County, Tex., 1963-68; with Tandy Corp., 1968—, v.p., 1976-79, sec., 1975—, sr. v.p., 1979—. Bd. dirs. Better Bus. Bur. Tarrant County, 1971-87; dir. Van Cliburn Piano Competition, 1984—; bd. dirs. Downtown Ft. Worth, Inc., 1985—, Youth Orch. Greater Ft. Worth, 1984-87, Family Service, Inc., 1984—, Ft. Worth Conv. and Visitors Bur., 1986—. Served with AUS, 1953-55. Mem. Am. Bar Assn., State Bar Tex., Tarrant County Bar Assn. (pres. corp. counsel sect. 1980-81). Methodist. Office: Tandy Corp 1800 One Tandy Ctr Fort Worth TX 76102

WINN, STEWART DOWSE, JR., engineer, construction management consultant; b. Newcastle-Upon-Tyne, Eng., Apr. 8, 1936; s. Stewart Dowse and Frances (Faust) W.; m. Elizabeth Dial Gray, Feb. 2, 1963; 1 child, Michael Stewart. BS in Indsl. Engring., Ga. Inst. Tech., 1958, MS in Indsl. Engring., 1963. Registered profl. engr., Tex., Calif., Ala. Engr. Brown Engring. Co., Cape Canaveral, Fla., 1963-64, Dow Chem. Co., Cape Canaveral, Fla., 1964-66; sr. engr. Tex. Instruments, Dallas, 1966-68; owner Winn & Assocs., Dallas, 1968-76; control mgr. Wash. Pub. Power Supply System, Olympia, 1976-83; v.p. O'Brien-Kreitzberg & Assocs., Merchantville, N.J., 1983—. Lt. USN, 1958-63. Mem. Am. Inst. Indsl. Engrs. (pres. Dallas chpt. 1967-68), Am. Soc. Cost Engrs., Project Mgmt. Inst., Nat. Soc. Profl. Engrs., St. George's Club. Republican. Presbyterian. Home: 3 Oak Terr Merchantville NJ 08109 Office: O'Brien Kreitzberg & Assocs 4350 Haddonfield Rd Ste 300 Pennsauken NJ 08109

WINOGRAD, AUDREY LESSER, advertising executive; b. N.Y.C., Oct. 6, 1933; d. Jack J. and Theresa Lorraine (Elkind) Lesser; m. Melvin H. Winograd, Apr. 29, 1956; 1 child, Hope Elise. Student, U. Conn., 1950-53. Asst. advt. mgr. T. Baumritter Co., Inc., N.Y.C., 1953-54; asst. dir. pub. relations and creative merchandising Kirby, Block & Co., Inc., N.Y.C., 1954-56; div. mdse. mgr., dir. advt. and sales promotion Winograd's Dept. Store, Inc., Point Pleasant, N.J., 1956-73, v.p., 1960-73, exec. v.p., 1973-86; pres. AMW Assocs., Ocean Twp., N.J., 1976—. Editor bus. newsletters. Bd. dirs. Temple Beth Am, Lakewood, N.J., 1970-72. Mem. Jersey Pub. Relations & Advt. Assn. (pres. 1982-83), Monmouth Ocean Devel. Council, Monmouth County Bus. Assn. (pres. 1988—, bd. dirs. 1985—), Retail Advt. Conf., N.J. Assn. Women Bus. Owners, Soc. Prevention Cruelty to Animals, Am. Soc. Prevention Cruelty to Animals, Humane Soc., Friends of Animals, Animal Protection Inst. Office: AMW Assocs 10 Pine Ln Ocean NJ 07712

WINSLOW, EDWARD JOHN, financial planning company executive; b. Miami, Fla., Sept. 26, 1954; s. Edward J. and Elva Jean (Zalf) W.; m. Deborah Dale Price, Dec. 27, 1975. AA, Miami Dade Jr. Coll., 1973; BBA, Fla. Internat. U., 1975. Asst. treas. Am. Bankers Ins. Group, Miami, 1977-80; fin. mgr. Digital Equipment Corp., Colorado Springs, Colo., 1981; pres. Personal Fin. Planning, Inc., Colorado Springs., 1982-83, bd. dirs., 1982—; pres. First Am. Fin. Coop., Colorado Springs, 1984—; CPA, Colo.; chartered fin. cons. Mem. Am. Inst. CPA's, Inst. Cert. Fin. Planners. Home: 1011 Sun Dr Colorado Springs CO 80906 Office: 1st Am Fin Coop 410 N 21st St Ste 203 Colorado Springs CO 80904

WINSLOW, FRANCES EDWARDS, city official; b. Phila., Sept. 12, 1948; d. Harry Donaldson and Anna Louise (McColgan) E.; m. David Allen Winslow, June 6, 1970; children: Frances Lavinia, David Allen Jr. BA, Drew U., 1969, MA, 1971; M Urban Planning, NYU, 1974, PhD, 1978. Adminstrv. asst. Borough of Florham Park, N.J., 1970-73; instr. Kean Coll., Union, N.J., 1973-75; adminstrv. asst. Irvine (Calif.) Police Dept., 1984-86; coord. emergency svcs. City of Irvine, 1986—. Contbr. articles to profl. publs. V.p. San Diego Chaplains Wives, 1976-79; treas. Girl Scouts U.S.A., Yokohama, Japan, 1980-81. Recipient Vol. Svc. award Navy Relief Soc., Camp Pendleton, Calif., 1984; Lasker Found. fellow, 1972. Mem. Nat. Assn. Police Planners (sec. Orange County 1984-85, v.p. 1985-86), Am. Soc. for Pub. Adminstrn. (program com. Orange County 1987—), Acad. Criminal Justice Sci. (publ. com. 1987—), Internat. City Mgrs. Assn. (assoc.), Creekers Club (Irvine, pres. 1986), Officer Wives Club (Camp Pendleton, pres. 1983-84, treas. 1982-83), Yokohama Internat. Women's Club (v.p. 1980-81). Republican. Methodist. Home: 19 Soaring Hawk Irvine CA 92714 Office: City of Irvine 1 Civic Ctr Dr Irvine CA 92714

WINSTON, MICHAEL G., director organizational development; b. Bklyn., Jan. 23, 1951; s. Ralph and Irene (Sochrin) W.; BA cum laude, Ohio U., 1972; MA, U. Notre Dame, 1975; PhD, U. Ill., 1977; postgrad. exec. program, Stanford U., U. Pa.; m. Margaret M. Sumption, Sept. 28, 1980; 1 child, Chelsie Blair. Instr. psychology U. Ill., 1975-77; cons. psychologist Mgmt., Health and Devel. Corp., Los Angeles, 1977-78, sr. psychologist, 1978, v.p. orgnl. devel., 1978-79; v.p. orgn. devel. Creative Mgmt. Systems, Encino, Calif., 1980-81; dir. orgn. devel. Lockheed Corp., Burbank, Calif., 1981-85; dir. human resources devel., McDonnell-Douglas Corp., Huntington Beach, Calif., 1985-87, sr. dir. orgn. devel., 1987-88; dir. orgn. devel. Motorola, Inc., Rolling Meadows, Ill., 1988—. Adj. prof. Grad. Sch. Bus. and Mgmt., Pepperdine U., 1981, Golden Gate U., San Francisco, 1982, U. San Francisco, 1982, U. Calif., Irvine, 1986; keynote speaker World Acad. Mgmt. Conf., The Hague, Netherlands, 1987, SW Productivity Conf., 1987, Am. Productivity Conf., 1987, 88. Mem. exec. devel. com. Advanced Tech. Industries Adv. Council, Calif. Inst. Tech.; mem. exec. devel. adv. council, U. Calif. Mem. Am. Psychol. Assn., Calif. Psychol. Assn., Am. Mgmt. Assn., Human Resources Planning Soc. (keynote speaker annual conv. 1985), Am. Soc. Tng. and Devel., Phi Kappa Phi, Kappa Delta Pi, Phi Delta Kappa.

WINTER, HENRI LEONARD-MAURICE, accountant; b. Vevey, Switzerland, Dec. 21, 1943; came to U.S., 1953, naturalized, 1959; s. Adolphe and Czypa (Kalisher) W.; B.A., N.Y. Inst. Tech., 1969; M.B.A., St. Johns U., 1973; m. Sari Spilky, May 19, 1964; 2 children. With Marshall Granger & Co., Mamaroneck, N.Y., 1968-79, partner, 1977-79; v.p. fin., chief fin. officer Carl Zeiss, Inc., N.Y.C., 1979-81, asst. treas., 1979-81; ptnr. C.P.A. firm, Mamaroneck, 1981-85, mng. ptnr., 1985—. C.P.A., N.Y. Mem. Am. Inst. C.P.A.s, N.Y. State Soc. C.P.A.s., Nat. Conf. C.P.A. Practitioners. Editor acctg./tax publ. 1974—. Office: 1600 Harrison Ave Mamaroneck NY 10543

WINTER, JOHN ALEXANDER, realtor, real estate appraiser; b. Cin., July 2, 1935; s. George Edward and Mary Alma (McAuliffe) W. B.S., Georgetown U., 1957. Ptnr. Winter & Winter, Cleve., 1957-76; residential salesman Moreland Hills Co., Chagrin Falls, Ohio, 1976-77; residential appraiser Kiebler, Smith & Co., Chardon, Ohio, 1977—; founder, pres. Cert. Appraisal Svc. Co., Shaker Heights, Ohio, 1985—; v.p., dir. The Gas Pipe Co., Chagrin Falls, 1973—. Contbr. articles to profl. jours. Pres. New Eng. Soc. of Cleve. and Western Res., 1976-77, 83-84, Shaker Heights Republican Club, 1977-84; v.p., trustee Shaker Hist. Soc., 1985—. Recipient Service award Pres. Ronald Reagan, 1984, New Eng. Heritage award New Eng. Soc., 1984. Mem. Cleve. Independance Day Assn. (v.p., trustee 1957—, Treharne award 1984), Am. Assn. Cert. Appraisers, Ohio Assn. Realtors, Nat. Assn. Realtors (Ben Franklin award 1983), Cathedral Latin Alumni Assn. (trustee 1965—, v.p.). Roman Catholic. Clubs: Georgetown (pres. 1966-67); Cleve. of Washington (trustee 1984—). Avocations: tennis, sailing, coin collecting. Home: 19271 Shaker Blvd Shaker Heights OH 44122 Office: Cert Appraisal Svc Co 19271 Shaker Blvd Shaker Heights OH 44122

WINTER, JOHN CALVIN, III, insurance company executive; b. Williamsport, Pa., Nov. 7, 1948; s. John C. II and Margaret (Stiber) W.; m. Suzanne Gorman Fenders, July 9, 1986; children: Derek, Shane, John. BA, St. Olaf Coll., 1970. Actuarial asst. Equitable Life Assurance, N.Y.C., 1970-71; dir. actuarial services Continental Am. Life Ins. Co., Wilmington, Del., 1972-75; sr. lectr. MARA Inst. Tech., Shah Alam, Malaysia, 1975-76; 2d v.p. product devel. Sun Life Group, Atlanta, 1976-80; v.p. product devel. John Alden Ins. Cos., Miami, Fla., 1980-82, v.p., chief actuary, 1982-84, sr. v.p. fin. and corp. services, 1984—; sr. v.p., chief fin. officer, also bd. dirs. John Alden Fin. Corp., Miami, 1987—. Mem. Soc. Actuaries, Am. Acad. Actuaries. Republican. Office: John Alden Fin Corp 7300 Corporate Center Dr Miami FL 33126-1208

WINTER, PETER MARTYN, marketing professional; b. Lower Hutt, Wellington, New Zealand, Sept. 19, 1949; came to U.S., 1981; s. Thomas Patric and Sheilah Maureen (Tracy) Middleton. BA, Victoria U., Wellington, 1970; MA with honors, Victoria U., 1972. Producer, writer BBC, London, 1977-81; exec. editor Keycom Electronic Pub., Chgo., 1982-83; pres. Digital Applications Internat., Inc., 1983-85, Online Internat. Inc., London and N.Y.C., 1986-87; v.p. mktg. Newspaper Advt. Bur., N.Y.C., 1987—; bd. dirs. emeritus Third Millenium Inc., N.Y.C. Author: Commonsense Videotex, 1985; inventor. Mem. Info. Industry Assn. Democrat. Home: 160 Fremd Ave A1 Rye NY 10580 Office: Newspaper Advt Bur 1180 Avenue of the Americas New York NY 10036

WINTER, RICHARD LAWRENCE, financial and health care consulting company executive; b. St. Louis, Dec. 17, 1945; s. Melvin Lawrence and Kathleen Jane (O'Leary) W.; B.S. in Math., St. Louis U., 1967, M.S. in Math. (fellow), 1969; M.B.A., U. Mo., St. Louis, 1976; m. Pauline Alma Pardee, Nov. 10, 1984; 1 child, George Bradford; children from previous marriage—Leigh Ellen, Jessica Marie. Research analyst Mo. Pacific R.R., St. Louis, 1971-73; dir. fin. relations Linclay Corp., St. Louis, 1973-74; asst. v.p. 1st Nat. Bank in St. Louis (name now Centerre Bank, N.A.), 1974-79; v.p. fin. UDE Corp., St. Louis, 1979-81; pres. Health Care Investments, Ltd., St. Louis, 1981—, Fin. & Investment Cons., Ltd., St. Louis, 1981; lectr. math. U. Mo.-St. Louis, 1972-74, St. Louis U., 1982—. Active various fund raising activities including St. Louis Symphony, Jr. Achievement, United Way St. Louis, Arts and Edn. Fund, St. Louis, 1974-79. Served with U.S. Army, 1969-71. Mem. Pi Mu Epsilon. Roman Catholic. Club: Mo. Athletic (St. Louis). Home: 1321 Green Tree Ln Saint Louis MO 63122 Office: PO Box 11586 Saint Louis MO 63105

WINTERER, PHILIP STEELE, lawyer; b. San Francisco, July 8, 1931; s. Steele Leland and Esther (Hardy) W.; m. Patricia Dowling, June 15, 1955; children: Edward J., Amey C. B.A., Amherst Coll., 1953; LL.B., Harvard U., 1956. Bar: N.Y. 1957, Republic of Korea 1958. Assoc. Debevoise & Plimpton, N.Y.C., 1956-65, ptnr., 1966—; dir. Am. Savs. Bank, FSB, 1972—. Contbr. articles to profl. publs. Pres. Am. Italy Soc.; chmn. emeritus Sch. Am. Ballet, Inc.; chmn. exec. com. Phipps Houses. Recipient Amherst Coll. medal for Eminent Service, 1980. Mem. Coun. Fgn. Rels., Am. Law Inst., Assn. of Bar of City of N.Y., N.Y. State Bar Assn., ABA, Nat. Assn. Bond Attys., Citizens Housing and Planning Coun. N.Y., N.Y. Sci. Policy Assn., N.Y. Acad. Scis., Tax Forum, Phi Beta Kappa Assocs. Home: 1165 5th Ave New York NY 10029 Office: Debevoise & Plimpton 875 3d Ave New York NY 10022

WINTERER, WILLIAM G., hotel executive; b. St. Louis, July 7, 1934; s. Herbert O. and Dorothy (Sprengnether) W.; B.A., U. Fla., 1956; M.B.A., Harvard U., 1962; m. Victoria Thompson, Sept. 2, 1967; children—William, Andrew, Britton, Mark. Mgr. corporate fin. dept., partner Goodbody & Co., 1966-69; pres. Fla. Capital Corp., Greenwich, Conn., 1969-72; owner Griswold Inn, Essex, Conn., 1972—, Town Farms Inn, Middletown, Conn., 1978-85, Dock N' Dine at Saybrook Point, Old Saybrook, Conn., 1981-86; bd. dirs. Zimmer Corp., Bostwick Invest Co., Fla. Capital Corp., Bostwick Invest Co.,; chmn. audit com. Custom Marine, Inc., 1986—; mem. adv. bd. United Bank and Trust. Life trustee, founding pres. Conn. River Found. at Steamboat Dock; trustee Ivoryton Playhouse Found., 1979-82; corporator Middlesex Hosp.; commissioner Conn. Hist. Commn., 1979-82; bd. dirs. Gov.'s Vacation Travel Council, 1976-79, chmn., bd. trustees Conn. River Mus. at Steamboat Dock. Served with USCG Res. Mem. Conn. Restaurant Assn. (dir. 1973-77). Republican. Roman Catholic. Clubs: N.Y. Yacht, Seawanhaka Corinthian Yacht, Essex Yacht (bd. govs.), Pettipaug Yacht, Ocean Cruising; Harvard, Williams (N.Y.C.); Hartford; Old Lyme Beach; English Speaking Union, St. George's Soc. Home: Turtle Bay Essex CT 06426

WINTERS, CHERYL LOUISE, sales executive; b. Niagara Falls, N.Y., Apr. 25, 1947; d. William Joseph and Virginia Louise (Greene) W. AAS, Adirondack Community Coll., 1975. RN. RN critical care St. Clare's Hosp., Schenectady, N.Y., 1975-79; RN ICU Glenns Falls (N.Y.) Hosp., 1979-80; sales and svc. rep. Clin. Data, Inc., Brookline, Mass., 1980-82; dir. regional devel. Med-Care Convalescent Supply Co., Inc., Rhinebeck, N.Y., 1982-85; sales mgr. ea. ops. Vortec Health Care, Cin., 1985-86; diagnostic sales rep., tng. assoc. MallincKrodt, Inc., St. Louis, 1986—. Mem. Am. Cancer Soc., Saratoga Springs, N.Y., 1985; del. to People's Republic China for People to People Internat., 1988. Mem. Nat. Assn. Female Execs., Am. Mgmt. Assn., NE Radiology Adminstrs., Soc. Radiological Technologists (capital dist.), Soc. Nuclear Medicine (capital dist.). Republican. Home: 37 Jaipur Ln Saratoga Springs NY 12866 Office: Mallinckrodt Inc 675 McDonnel Blvd Saint Louis MO 63134

WINTERS, ROBERT CUSHING, insurance company executive; b. Hartford, Conn., Dec. 8, 1931; s. George Warren and Hazel Keith (Cushing) W.; m. Patricia Ann Martini, Feb. 10, 1962; children: Sally, Beth. B.A., Yale U., 1953; M.B.A., Boston U., 1963. With Prudential Ins. Co. Am., 1953—, v.p. actuary, 1969-75, sr. v.p. Cen. Atlantic home office, 1975-78, exec. v.p., Newark, 1978-84, vice chmn., 1984-86, chmn., chief exec. officer, 1987—. Served with AUS, 1954-56. Fellow Soc. Actuaries; mem. Am. Acad. Actuaries (past pres.), Regional Plan Assn. (dir.), Partnership for N.J., N.J. C. of C. (dir.), Greater Newark C. of C. (chmn. bd. 1985-87), Am. Council Life Ins. (bd. dirs.), Bus. Council, Bus. Roundtable, Sigma Xi. Office: The Prudential Ins Co Am 745 Broad St Prudential Plaza Newark NJ 07101

WINTERS, THOMAS BERNARR, mechanical engineer, campground director; b. Ironton, Ohio, Sept. 18, 1931; s. Raymond Franklin and Adryenne Beryl (Lynd) W.; m. Dolores Jean Leis, Aug. 30, 1953. Attended Franklin U. With Westinghouse Electric Co., Columbus, Ohio, 1956-69; with Westreco, Marysville, Ohio, 1969—, design engr., 1969—; pres., chief exec. officer Winters Recreational Area, Raymond, Ohio, 1981—, also bd. dirs. Patentee icemaker, water delivery, defrost timer, others. Served with USNR, 1949-59. Methodist. Office: 20267 SR 347 Raymond OH 43067

WIPPERN, RONALD FRANK, financial and corporate consultant; b. Huntington, W.Va., June 28, 1933; s. Virgil V. and Lucille (Hotzfield) W.; m. Jill Kathleen Nelson, June 20, 1982; children: Christopher, Mitchell, Stacy, Joscelyn. BS, U. Colo., 1955, MBA, 1961; PhD, Stanford U., 1964; MA (hon.), Yale U., 1979. Asst. prof. U. Minn., Mpls., 1964-66; assoc. dean, assoc. prof. Dartmouth Coll., Hanover, N.H., 1966-71; prof. IMEDE Mgmt. Devel. Inst., Lausanne, Switzerland, 1971-73; assoc. prof. Harvard U. Bus. Sch., Boston, 1973-76; prof. Yale U., New Haven, 1976-87; pres. Ronald F. Wippern, Inc., New Caanan, Conn., 1987—; bd. dirs. Super D Corp., N.Y.C., Big V Holdings, Inc., N.Y.C.; cons. McKinsey & Co., Inc., N.Y.C., 1973—, 1st Boston Corp., N.Y.C., 1986—, Bankers Trust Co., N.Y.C., 1985—, Toronto Dominino Bank, 1988—. Author: Shipping Investments, 1975, Cases in Modern Financial Management, 1980; contbr. numerous articles in profl. jours. Expert witness U.S. Ho. of Reps., 1975; cons. Ford Found., N.Y.C. and Latin Am., 1967-71. Served to lt. USN, 1956-59. Ford Found. fellow, 1961-64. Mem. Am. Econ. Assn., Am. Fin. Assn. Democrat. Office: 815 Silvermine Rd New Canaan CT 06840

WIRE, WILLIAM SHIDAKER, II, apparel and footwear executive; b. Cin., Jan. 5, 1932; s. William Shidaker and Gladys (Buckmaster) W.; m. Alice Dumas Jones, Aug. 31, 1957; children: Alice Wire Freeman, Deborah Wire Suber. Student, U. of South, 1950; AB, U. Ala., 1954, JD, 1956; LLM, NYU, 1957. Bar: Ala. 1956. Atty. Hamilton, Denniston, Butler & Riddick, Mobile, 1959-60; with Talladega Ins. Agy., Ala., 1961-62; with Genesco, Inc., Nashville, 1962—, now chmn., chief exec. officer; dir. Genesco, Inc., First Am. Nat. Bank Nashville. Trustee, Leadership Nashville Found.; bd. dirs. In Roads-Nashville, Inc. Served with USAF, 1957-59. Mem. Fin. Execs. Inst., Kappa Alpha. Presbyterian. Clubs: Belle Meade Country (Nashville); Cumberland; Shoal Creek (Ala.). Home: 6119 Stonehaven Dr Nashville TN 37215 Office: Genesco Inc Genesco Park Nashville TN 37202

WIRSCHING, CHARLES PHILIPP, JR., brokerage house executive, investment executive; b. Chgo., Oct. 26, 1935; s. Charles Philipp and Mamie Ethel (York) W.; m. Beverly Ann Bryan, May 28, 1966. BA, U. N.C., 1957. Sales rep. Adams-Millis Corp., Chgo., 1963-67; ptnr. Schwartz-Wirsching, Chgo., 1968-70; sec., dir. Edwin H. Mann, Inc., Chgo., 1971-74; stockbroker Paine Webber, Inc., Chgo., 1975-85, account v.p., 1986—. Republican. Episcopalian. Home: 434 Clinton Pl River Forest IL 60305 Office: Paine Webber Inc 55 W Monroe Chicago IL 60603

WIRTH, ERIC JOHN, banker; b. Astoria, N.Y., Nov. 19, 1929; s. John Frederick and Frida (Dollinger) W. BS, NYU, 1951. Credit investigator Bankers Trust Co., N.Y.C., 1954-56, credit analyst, 1956-64, asst. treas., 1964-68, asst. v.p., 1968-72, v.p., 1972-82; gen. credit auditor, sr. v.p. Bankers Trust N.Y. Corp., N.Y.C., 1982—. 1st lt. U.S. Army, 1951-53. Mem. Robert Morris Assocs., Douglaston Club. Republican. Methodist. Home: 47-34 244th St Douglaston NY 11362 Office: Bankers Trust Co 280 Park Ave New York NY 10017

WIRTSCHAFTER, IRENE NEROVE, tax consultant, past realtor; b. Elgin, Ill., Aug. 5; d. David A. and Ethel G. Nerove; B.C.S., Columbus U., 1942; enrolled agt. IRS; m. Burton Wirtschafter, June 2, 1945 (dec. 1966). Commd. ensign Supply Corps, U.S. Navy, 1944, advanced through ranks to capt., 1956; comdg. officer Res. Supply Unit, 1974-75; ret., 1976; agt. office internat. ops. IRS, 1967-75, internat. banking specialist, now pvt. practice tax cons., Washington; ; sr. intern program U.S. Senate, 1981; mem. Sec. of Navy's Adv. Com. Ret. Personnel, 1984-86, VA Adv. Com. for Women Vets., 1987—. Past troop leader Girl Scouts U.S.A.; lt. col. and mission pilot CAP; comml. instrument pilot; founder Sr. Action Com. Brevard County, 1981; chmn. College Park Airport Johnny Horizon Day, 1975; mem. Patuck Air Force Base Retiree Adv. Coun.; Navy liason officer Commander's Retiree Coun. Patrick Air Force Base, 1985—; elected dir. Space Coast Philharmonic, 1986; bd. dirs. Cocoa Beach Citizens League, 1987; co-chmn. Internat. Women's Yr. Take Off Dinner, Washington, 1976; mem. Nat. Com. Internat. Forest of Friendship, Atchison, Kans.; 1st v.p. Friends of Cocoa Beach Library, 1987-88, pres. 1988—; mem. Cocoa Beach Bus. Improvement Council (Fla.); elected rep. Silver Haired Legislature, Fla., 1985—. Named hon. citizen of Winnipeg (Can.), 1966, Atchison, New Orleans, 1988; Ky. col., La. col. Mem. Naval Res. Assn. (nat. treas. 1975-77, nat. adv. com. 1985—), Ninety Nines (past chpt. and sect. officer; 99 Achievement awards), AAUW (officer, achievement award), Naval Order U.S. (treas. nat. capitol commandry), Assn. Naval Aviation (nat. trustee), Assn. Enrolled Agts., Cocoa Beach Area C. of C., MBR (military affairs com., Cocoa Beach code enforcement bd., sr. adv. com. Cape Canaveral Hosp.), Internat. Platform Assn., Silver Wings (bd. dirs.), Tailhook Assn. First female Supply Corps officer to be assigned sea duty, 1956. Home: 1825 Minutemen Causeway Cocoa Beach FL 32931

WISE, ALLEN FLOYD, insurance executive; b. Wichita, Kans., Aug. 20, 1942; s. Woodrow and Constance (Weber) W.; m. Hanna Jo Dunlap, June 6, 1964; children: Marc, Brian. BA in Econs., Wichita State U., 1964. Regional mgr. Travelers Ins., Hartford, Conn., 1964-78; sr. v.p. Union Fidelity Life, Phila., 1978-85; exec. v.p. U.S. Health Care, Phila., 1985-88, pres., 1988-89; pres. Corp. Health Adminstrs., Moorestown, N.J., 1989—; bd. dirs. Mo. Blue Cross, St. Louis. Home: 2841 Furlong Rd Doylestown PA 18901 Office: US Healthcare Inc 980 Jolly Rd Box 1109 Blue Bell PA 19422

WISE, CHARLES WILLIAM, III, insurance company executive; b. York, Pa., Oct. 7, 1951; s. Charles William Jr. and Charlotte (Mundis) W.; m. Holly Sue Smith, Dec. 7, 1974; 1 child, Heather Britta. BBA, Indiana U. of Pa., 1973; grad. Emerging Execs. Program, Pa. State U., 1982, grad. Fin. Concepts for Gen. Mgmt., 1988. CPA, Pa. Staff, sr. incharge acct. Miller and Co. CPAs, York, 1973-77; supr. fin. and operational audit Pa. Blue Shield, Camp Hill, Pa., 1977-79, mgr. fin. and operational audit, 1979-86, mgr. systems audit, 1982-86, mgr. acct. svc.-sales support, 1984-86, dir. corp. audit, 1986—; bd. dirs. Glo Investment Co., Mt. Wolf, Pa., Wolfy and Co., Orlando, Fla. Contbr. articles to profl. jours. Trustee J.W. Thompson Trust, York. Mem. AICPA, Pa. Inst. CPAs, Ins. Internal Audit Group. Republican. Methodist. Home: 515 Alton Ln York PA 17402 Office: Pa Blue Shield 1800 Center St Camp Hill PA 17011

WISE, GARY LAMAR, electrical engineering and mathematics educator, researcher, investment researcher; b. Texas City, Tex., July 29, 1945; s. Calder Lamar and Ruby Lavon (Strom) W.; m. Mary Estella Warren, Dec. 28, 1974; 1 child, Tanna Estella. BA summa cum laude, Rice U., 1971; MSE, Princeton U., 1973, MA 1973, PhD, 1974. Postdoctoral research assoc. Princeton U., N.J., 1974; asst. prof. Tex. Tech U., Lubbock, 1975-76; asst. prof. U. Tex., Austin, 1976-80, assoc. prof., 1980-84, prof. elec. and computer engring. and math., 1984—; tech. reviewer Army Research Office, Durham, N.C., 1976, Air Force Office Sci. Research, Washington, 1980, 83—, Harper and Row Pubs., N.Y.C., 1982-83, NSF, 1984, 87, Springer-Verley Pubs., N.Y.C., 1987-88, John Wiley and Sons Pubs., N.Y.C., 1988—; cons. Baylor Coll. Medicine, Houston, 1972; mem. control group League City Nat. Bank, 1978-82; speaker at numerous tech. confs. Contbr. chpts., numerous articles to profl. publs. Recipient award for outstanding contbns. to Coll. Engring., U. Tex. Engring. Found., 1979, 81; Air Force Office Sci. research grantee, 1976—; research contracts E-Systems, Inc., 1983-85; Carroll D. Simmons Centennial teaching fellow U. Tex., Austin, 1982-84. Mem. IEEE, Soc. Indsl. and Applied Math., Am. Math. Soc., Inst. Math. Stats.,

Math. Assn. Am., Eta Kappa Nu, Phi Beta Kappa, Tau Beta Pi. Methodist. Home: 8 Muir Ln Austin TX 78746 Office: U Tex Dept Elec & Computer Engring Austin TX 78712

WISE, HARRY H., securities industry executive; b. Cambridge, Mass., Oct. 1, 1938; s. Robert and Ethel (Pastan) W.; m. Dorothy Kalins, Feb. 11, 1968 (div. 1970); m. Katherine Erlandson, June 12, 1983. BA, Harvard U., 1960, MBA, 1966; postgrad., Yale U., 1960-61. Assoc. McKinsey & Co. Inc., N.Y.C., 1966-68; v.p. Carl Marks & Co. Inc., N.Y.C., 1968-72, Source Capital, Inc., Los Angeles, 1972-74; mgr. pvt. investments Citibank N.A., N.Y.C., 1974-76; exec. v.p. Am. Capital Ptnrs., N.Y.C., 1976-81; pres. Madison Equity Capital Corp., N.Y.C., 1981—; chmn. HW Assocs., Inc., N.Y.C., 1981—; bd. dirs. Empire Ins. Group, N.Y.C., First Charter Life Ins. Co.; exec. com. Unicorn Ventures, Inc., N.Y.C., 1982-84. Author HW Petroleum Newsletter, 1986—. V.p., bd. dirs. Associated Camps, Inc., N.Y.C., 1982—; bd. dirs. Associated YM & YWHA's Greater N.Y., N.Y.C., 1982—; commencement marshal, aide Harvard U., Cambridge, Mass., 1984-85. Served to capt. USAFR, 1961-64. Mem. Nat. Assn. Corp. Dirs., Harvard U. Alumni Assn. (mem. com. 1981—), Econ. Round Table San Francisco. Jewish. Clubs: Harvard of N.Y. (admissions com.), Harvard Bus. Sch. of Greater N.Y. (exec. v.p., bd. dirs. 1975-83, Achievement award 1972, 82); East Hampton (N.Y.) Tennis; Harvard of Boston. Home: Daniels Ln Sagaponack NY 11962 Office: HW Assocs Inc 505 Park Ave 20th Foor New York NY 10022

WISE, RICHARD EVANS, corporate training director; b. Lancaster, Pa., Sept. 24, 1947; s. William Edmund and Dorothy Christelle (Evans) W.; m. Kathrine Suzanne Keller, Jan. 2, 1971; 1 child, Thomas Edmund. BS, West Chester (Pa.) U., 1970; MEd, Pa. State U., 1976, PhD, 1980. Project adminstrn. mgr. Hartford Ins. Group, 1977-80; v.p., tng. mgr. Conn. Nat. Bank, 1980-83; corp. tng. and devel. dir. Travelers Corp., Hartford, 1983—; cons. R.E. Wise and Assocs., Hartford, 1982—; adj. prof. Hartford Grad. Ctr.; pres. Am. Inst. Banking; editorial bd. mem. Internat. Jour. of Instrnl. Media. Contbr. articles to various profl. jours.; designer Travelers Management Development Continuum, 1984-86. Mem. Hartford Mgmt. Devel. Adv. Bd., Greater Hartford Arts Council. Named Outstanding Alumnus Pa. State U., 1987; Chapter of Excellence Am. Inst. of Banking, 1983. Mem. Assn. for Ednl. Communications and Tech. (cert. of Merit, 1986, Outstanding Practice award, 1983), Am. Soc. for Tng. and Devel., Phi Delta Kappa. Democrat. Methodist. Lodge: Masons. Home: 8 Cobblestone Way Windsor CT 06095 Office: Travelers Corp One Tower Square Hartford CT 06183

WISE, ROBERT LESTER, utilities executive; b. Curwensville, Pa., Oct. 4, 1943; s. Robert Lester Wise and Kathryn Elizabeth (Riddle) Husak; m. Sandra Lee Leonard, June 12, 1965; 1 child: Robert L. III. BSME, Lafayette Coll., 1965. Registered profl. engr., Pa. Cadet engr., jr. engr. Pa. Electric Co., Johnstown, 1965-68, stat. supr. prodn., sta. supt. ops., 1968-71, sta. supt., mgr. generating stas., 1971-79, asst. v.p. ops., v.p. ops., 1979-82, v.p. generation engring. and support, 1982-83, v.p. ops., 1984-86, pres., chief operating officer, dir., 1986—; bd. dirs. GPU Service Corp., 1986—, GPU Nuclear Corp., Parsippany, N.J., 1986—, Pa. Electric Co., Johnstown, 1986—. Bd. dirs. U.S. Nat. Bank & U.S. Bancorp, Johnstown, 1987, Johnstown Area Econ. Devel. Corp., 1987, Johnstown Indsl. Park, Indsl. Devel. Corp., 1987, Penn's Woods Council, Boy Scouts Am., 1980, Johnstown Symphony Orch., 1988; mem. exec. com. Greater Johnstown Com., 1987, Pa. Electric Assn., Harrisburg, 1987, Cambria-Somerset Labor Mgmt. Com., 1987, exec. adv. com. Johnstown Bus. Council on Health Care, 1987,U.S. Dept. Energy Innovative Control Tech. adv. panel, Washington, 1987;. Republican. Club: Sunnehanna Country. Office: Pa Electric Co 1001 Broad St Johnstown PA 15905

WISE, WILLIAM ALLAN, oil company executive, lawyer; b. Davenport, Iowa, July 10, 1945; s. A. Walter and Mary Virginia (Kuhl) W.; m. Marie Figge, Sept. 27, 1969; children—Vivian Marie, Genevieve Marie, Mary Elizabeth. B.A., Vanderbilt U.; J.D., U. Colo. Bar: Colo. Prin. counsel El Paso Natural Gas, Tex., 1970-80, sr. v.p. mktg., 1985-87, exec. v.p. mktg., 1987—; asst. gen. counsel in Houston The El Paso Co., 1980-82, v.p., gen. counsel, 1983, sr. v.p., gen. counsel and sec., 1983-85; dir. The El Paso Co., Tex., El Paso Natural Gas, Tex.; mem. natural gas adv. bd. NYMEX; mem. mgmt. com. Mojave Pipeline Co. Contbr. articles to profl. jours. Bd. dirs. YMCA, El Paso, 1983; adv. bd. Natural Resources Law Ctr., U. Colo. Mem. ABA (legal com.), Interstate Natural Gas Assn. Am. (gas requirements com.). Republican. Roman Catholic. Clubs: Forest, El Paso Country, George Town. Home: 5605 Westside Dr El Paso TX 79932 Office: El Paso Natural Gas Co 304 Texas St El Paso TX 79901

WISEKAL, FRANK W(ILLIAM), sales and services company executive; b. N.Y.C., Dec. 23, 1934; s. William W. and Anna (Sledge) W.; m. Norma Governale, Jan. 7, 1955; children: Susan, Richard, John, Lee Ann. B.A. in Indsl. Mgmt., C.W. Post Coll., 1968; grad. mgmt. devel. program, Harvard U., 1972. Bus. mgr. Grumman Aerospace Co., Bethpage, N.Y., 1958-70, dir. contracts, 1970-74; v.p. Grumman Am., Savannah, Ga., 1974-78; sr. v.p., treas. Gulfstream Am. Corp., Savannah, Ga., 1978-79, exec. v.p., 1979-80; sr. v.p., chief fin. officer Falcon Jet Corp., Teterboro, N.J., 1980-83, pres., chief exec. officer, 1983—. Served with USN, 1954-57. Roman Catholic. Home: 809 Trailing Ridge Rd Franklin Lakes NJ 07417 Office: Falcon Jet Corp Teterboro Airport Teterboro NJ 07608

WISHART, RONALD SINCLAIR, chemical company executive; b. Bklyn., Mar. 1, 1925; s. Ronald Sinclair and Elizabeth Lathrop (Phillips) W.; m. Betty B. Burnup, Sept. 14, 1951 (dec. Dec. 1973); children—Michael Sinclair, James Ronald; m. Eleanor Dorothy Parrish Dooley, Jan. 11, 1975; step children—Donna Dooley Gaunitz, Arthur D. Dooley. BSChemE, Rensselaer Poly. Inst., 1948. Engr., chemist Linde air div. Union Carbide Corp., Tonawanda, N.Y., 1948-51; sales rep. Chgo., Cleve., 1951-56; region mgr. Chgo., 1956-57; product mgr., mktg. mgr. Silicones div. N.Y.C., 1957-64, gen. mgr., pres., 1964-66, pres. devel. and coating materials divs., 1966-71, corp. dir. energy and transp. policy, 1972-82, v.p. fed. govt. regulations, 1983-85; v.p. pub. affairs Danbury, Conn., 1985—; chief of staff to chmn. of corp. Union Carbide, N.Y.C., 1984—; mem. adv. council Gas Research Inst., Energy Modeling Ctr., Stanford U., 1979-83, Environ. and Energy Policy Ctr., John F. Kennedy Sch. Pub. Policy, Harvard U., 1980-87; chmn. exec. dir. Electricity Consumers Resource Council, Washington, 1976-79. Author: The Marketing Factor, 1966; contbr. chpts. to books and articles to profl. jours.; patentee silicones formulas. Vol. Am. Field Service, Burma, 1944-45; elder White Plains Presbyn. Ch., N.Y.; trustee, bd. dirs. St. Christopher's Jenni Clarkson Home, 1968—; trustee Westchester Putnam council Boy Scouts Am., White Plains, N.Y., 1985—. Mem. Am. Mgmt. Assn. (v.p. 1966-69), Chem. Mfrs. Assn. (chmn. energy com. 1974-78), Nat. Petroleum Refiners Assn. (v.p. 1972-76, issues com. chmn. 1985—), Internat. Fedn. Ind. Energy Users (chmn. 1978), Am. Chem. Soc., Soc. Chem. Industry, NAM (energy com.), U.S. C. of C. (energy com.), Whipporwill Country Club, Capitol Hill Club, Univ. Club, Washington Golf and Country Club, Met. Club. Republican. Presbyterian. Home: 26 Frog Rock Rd Armonk NY 10504 Office: Union Carbide Corp 39 Old Ridgebury Rd Danbury CT 06817

WISHNER, STEVEN R., retail executive; b. N.Y.C., Mar. 21, 1950; s. Jerome and Florence (Wanger) W.; m. Lauri Ruth Berkson, June 5, 1977; children: Andrew R., Sara M. BA, Colgate U., 1972; MBA, Cornell U., 1976. 2nd v.p. Chase Manhattan Bank, N.Y.C., 1976-78; functional v.p. Chase Manhattan Bank, 1978; dir. fin. svcs. Gen. Instrument Corp., Clifton, N.J., 1978-79; asst. to treas. Gen. Instrument Corp., 1979-81; dir. fin. svcs. Viacom Internat. Inc., N.Y.C., 1981-82; asst. treas. Viacom Internat. Inc., 1982-86; v.p., treas. Zayre Corp., Framingham, Mass., 1987—; bd. dirs. Leonard Morse Occupational Health Svcs., Inc., Natick, Mass. Mem. Fin. Execs. Inst., Nat. Assn. Corp. Treas., Nat. Investor Rels. Inst., Nat. Retail Mchts. Assn., Cornell U. Alumni Assn. (co-chmn. admissions com., alumni exec. coun. 1987—), Masons. Home: 92 Fox Run Rd Sudbury MA 01776 Office: Zayre Corp 770 Cochituate Rd Framingham MA 01701

WISHNICK, WILLIAM, chemical company executive; b. Bklyn., Nov. 9, 1924; s. Robert I. and Freda M. (Frankel) W.; m. Dion Imerman, June 16, 1949 (div. 1969); children: Elizabeth Anne (dec.), Gina I., Amy Jo, Kendall Freda; m. Lisa Fluet, July 12, 1975. Student, Carnegie Inst. Tech., 1942, 45-47; B.B.A., U. Tex., 1949. With Witco Chem. Co., Inc., N.Y.C., 1949—; v.p. Witco Chem. Co., Inc., 1954-56, treas., 1956—, exec. v.p., 1957-64, chmn. bd., 1964—, chief exec. officer, 1971—, also dir.; pres., dir. Witco Chem. Co., Can., Ltd., 1958-62, vice chmn. bd., 1962-64, chmn. bd., 1964—; pres. Sonneborn Chem. & Refining Corp.; dir. Witco Chem. Co. Ltd., Eng., Golden Bear Oil Co., Los Angeles, Witco Chem. (France) S.A.R.L. Trustee Mt. Sinai Hosp., N.Y.C.; Carnegie Mellon U. Fellow Poly. Inst. N.Y. Mem. Am. Chem. Soc., Am. Petroleum Inst., Salesmen's Assn. Am. Chem. Industry., Tau Delta Phi. Republican. Clubs: Chemists (past trustee, jr. v.p.); Harmonie (N.Y.C.); Standard (Chgo.). Office: Witco Corp 520 Madison Ave New York NY 10022 *

WISNIEWSKI, RICHARD JOHN, insurance company executive; b. Erie, Pa., Mar. 30, 1950; s. Richard J. and Dorothy M. (Gorney) W.; m. Judith M. Koper, July 17, 1971; children: Michael, Julie. Student, Gannon U., 1970. Adjuster Erie (Pa.) Ins. Group, 1970-75, claim supr., 1975-80, asst. v.p., 1983-88, v.p., 1988—; bd. dirs. Erie Ind. House; mem. com. Ins. Fedn. Pa., 1978—. Bd. dirs. Independence House, 1987-88; mem. Pa. Genetic Disease Adv. Council, 1981-84. Mem. Erie Claims Assn. (pres., bd. govs. 1975—), Pa. Claims Assn. (bd. govs. 1970—). Democrat. Roman Catholic. Office: Erie Ins Group 100 Erie Ins Pl Erie PA 16530

WISSMAN, JACK PAUL, financial executive; b. Sidney, Ohio, Apr. 9, 1952; s. Paul Kenneth and Alice Carol (Schmidt) W.; m. Elizabeth Ann Duffell, Aug. 21, 1984; children: Danielle, Jack Paul, Jr. BSBA, Bowling Green U., 1974. CPA, Fla. Successively audit staff mem., audit sr., audit mgr. Arthur Andersen & Co., Tampa, Fla., 1974-81; v.p. fin. and adminstrn. Lamalie Assocs., Inc., Tampa, 1981—. Mem. AICPA, Fla. Inst. CPAs., Carrollwood Village Country Club (Tampa). Office: Lamalie Assocs Inc 13920 N Dale Mabry PO Box 273260 Bldg 3 Tampa FL 33688-3260

WIST, ABUND OTTOKAR, biomedical engineer, radiation physicist, educator; b. Vienna, Austria, May 23, 1926; s. Engelbert Johannes and Augusta Barbara (Ungewitter) W.; m. Suzanne Gregson Smiley, Nov. 30, 1963; children: John Joseph, Abund Charles. BS, Tech U. Graz, 1947; MEd, U. Vienna, 1950, PhD, 1951. Research and devel. engr. Hornyphon AG, Vienna, 1952-54, Siemens & Halske AG, Munich, Germany, 1954-58; dir. research and devel. Brinkman Instruments Co., Westbury, N.Y., 1958-64; sr. scientist Fisher Sci. Inc., Pitts., 1964-69; mem. faculty U. Pitts., 1970-73; asst. prof. computer sci. Va. Commonwealth U., 1973-76, asst. prof. biophysics, 1976-82, asst. prof. physiology and biophysics, 1982-84, asst. prof. radiology, 1984—, founder, gen. chmn. Symposium Computer Applications in Med. Care, Washington, 1977-79, grad. faculty, 1988—. Author: Electronic Design of Microprocessor Based Instrumentation and Control Systems, 1986; contbr. numerous articles and chpts. to profl. jours. and books; patentee in electronic and lab. instrumentation. NASA/Am. Soc. Engring. Edn. faculty fellow, summer 1975; U.S. biomed. engring. del. People's Republic China, 1987. Mem. IEEE (sr.), ASTM, Am. Chem. Soc., N.Y. Acad. Scis., AAAS, Richmond Computer Club (founder, pres. 1977-79), Biomed. Engring. Soc., Am. Assn. Physics in Medicine. Roman Catholic. Home: 9304 Farmington Dr Richmond VA 23229 Office: 1101 E Marshall St PO Box 72 Richmond VA 23298

WIST, G(EORGE) RICHARD, financial planner; b. Sewickley, Pa., June 27, 1945; s. George Richard and Elanor Hallie (Portor) W.; m. Sandra Jane Williams, Apr. 8, 1972; children: Kriston Tanner, Kenton Richard. BS, Clarion State U., 1969. Cert. fin. planner. Tchr. sci. Peters Twp. Sch. Dist., Pitts., 1969-70; asst. mgr. Nemacolin Inn., Farmington, Pa., 1970-72; pres., owner Smoky Mountain River Expeditions, Hot Springs, N.C., 1972-82; engr., project mgr. S&W Constrn. Co., Salt Lake City, 1980-83; account exec. E.F. Hutton, Provo, Utah, 1983-87; v.p. investments Gt. Western Fin. Securities, Palm Beach Gardens, Fla., 1987—. Mem. Eastern Profl. River Outfitters Assn. (pres., sec., founder 1976-80), Internat. Assn. Fin. Planners, Lions (pres. 1986-87). Republican. Home: 4422 Daffodil Circle S Palm Beach Gardens FL 33410 Office: Gt Western Fin Securities 4470 Northlake Blvd Palm Beach Gardens FL 33410

WISWELL, ALFRED IRVIN, electronics executive; b. Boston, Mass., May 13, 1935; s. Irvin Alfred and Ellen Marie (Hart) W.; m. Barbara Christina Marcello, July 1, 1967. AB cum laude, Suffolk U., 1965; MBA, Loyola U., Chgo., 1974. Research asst. Harvard U., Cambridge, Mass., 1964-65; mktg. mgr. Perin Products, Randolph, Mass., 1966-69; sales and mktg. mgr. Northwestern Golf Co., Chgo., 1970-74; v.p. sales TCS Corp., Providence, 1974-76; group product mgr. Sheldahl, Inc., East Providence, 1976-78; v.p. Am. Bus. Cons., Clinton, N.J., 1978-81; gen. mgr. Wells Fargo Alarm Services, Providence, 1982—; pres. A.I. Wiswell and Assoc. Mgmt. Cons., Pawtucket, R.I., 1974; adj. prof. StonehillColl., N. Easton, Mass., 1981; lectr. various colls. Author: Professional Salesmanship, 1979, Distribution Development, 1980, Contact Marking Specialist, 1981, Excel in Management, 1984. Exec. com. Greater Boston Young Democrats, Boston, 1960. Served to capt. AUS, 1953-57. Mem. Am. Mktg. Assn., Am. Soc. of Indsl. Security. Roman Catholic. Club: Westport Yacht (Mass.). Home: 90 Anawan Rd Pawtucket RI 02861 Office: Wells Fargo Alarm Svcs 333 Smith St Providence RI 02908

WISWELL, EMILY MARY HULL, real estate broker; b. Port Angeles, Wash., Sept. 21, 1918; d. Jay Tenneson and Emily Anne (Edwards) H.; m. Andrew M. Wiswell, Oct. 24, 1947; children: Andrew M. Jr., Harry Stevens II, Hank Fenderson. Student, U. Wash., 1935-37, El Capitan Coll. of Theatre, L.A., 1937-39, Aiken Tech. Coll., 1980, 81, 87, 88; AB, U. S.C., Aiken, 1988; MS, Realtors Inst., 1983. Cert. real estate broker and real estate appraiser. With Buchanan & Co., L.A., 1938-42, Davis & Bevin, L.A., 1942-44, Dancer Fitzgerald & Sample, N.Y.C., 1944-47; rep. fashion sales and costumes Doncaster, Aiken and Bronxville, N.Y., 1967-71, 73-76; owner, broker-in-charge Mary Wiswell GRI Properties, Ltd., Aiken, 1984—; dealer Lincoln Home Logs. Actress (stage): Sleep No More, 1945, Soldier's Wife, 1946, Find the Woman, 1946, (film) Swamp Woman, 1942, radio and TV, 1944-47. Tchr. Sunday sch., Reformed Ch., Bronxville, 1951-71, chair Royal Crown Ball, 1953, chair bridge party for blind children's fund, 1954; chair, founder Lawrence Hosp. Women's Aux. Patients Svc., Bronxville, 1958; asst. town meetings, Westchester County, N.Y., 1958; den mother, scout leader Boy Scouts Am., 1959-67; sec. Rose Hill Art Ctr., Aiken, 1975-76; chair harness race Am. Cancer Soc., Aiken, 1976—; mem. Aiken Art Coun., 1984—. Named Eagle Scout Mother Boy Scouts Am., Bronxville, 1970. Mem. Nat. Assn. Realtors, S.C. Bd. Realtors, Aiken Bd. Realtors, Augusta/North Augusta Bd. Realtors, Panhellenic Assn., Internat. Orgn. Real Estate Appraisers, Aiken Tennis Club (leader), Houndslake Country Club, Woodside Plantation Club. Republican. Episcopalian. Home: 40 Lundee Ct Aiken SC 29801 Office: 327 Park Ave SW Aiken SC 29801

WIT, HAROLD MAURICE, investment banker, lawyer, investor; b. Boston, Sept. 6, 1928; s. Maurice and Martha (Bassist) W.; divorced; children: David Edmund, Hannah Edna. A.B. magna cum laude, Harvard, 1949; J.D. (editor law jour.), Yale, 1954. Bar: N.Y. 1954. Assoc. Cravath, Swaine & Moore, N.Y.C., 1954-58; asst. sec. One William St. Fund, Inc., N.Y.C., 1958-59; v.p., sec. One William St. Fund, Inc., 1959-60; assoc. Allen & Co., 1960-70; assoc Allen & Co., Inc., 1965—, v.p., 1965-70, exec. v.p., 1970—, mng. dir., mem. exec. com.; dir., mem. exec. com. Toys-R-Us, Inc.; dir. chmn. exec. com. div. Allegheny & Western Energy Corp.; bd. dirs. Champion Road Machinery Ltd. Co-founder Group for South Fork; mem. Panel on Future of Govt. in N.Y., 1979-80. Served with Mass. N.G., 1947-50; lt. (j.g.) USNR, 1951-53. Mem. VFW, Am. Legion, Phi Beta Kappa, Phi Delta Phi. Clubs: University (N.Y.C.), Harvard (N.Y.C.); Harvard (Boston). Home: 160 E 65th St New York NY 10021 also: Cross Hwy East Hampton NY 11937 Office: Allen & Co Inc 711 Fifth Ave New York NY 10022

WITCHER, DANIEL DOUGHERTY, pharmaceutical company executive; b. Atlanta, May 17, 1924; s. Julius Gordon and Myrtice Eleanor (Daniel) W.; divorced; children: Beth S., Daniel Dougherty Jr., J. Wright, Benjamin G.; m. Betty Lou Middaugh, Oct. 30, 1982. Student, Mercer U., 1946-47, Am. Grad. Sch. Internat. Mgmt., 1949-50. Regional dir. Sterling Drug Co., Rio de Janeiro and Sao Paulo, Brazil, 1951-56; gen. mgr. Mead Johnson & Co., Sao Paulo, 1956-60; area mgr. Upjohn Internat., Inc., Sao Paulo, 1960-64; v.p. Upjohn Internat., Inc., Kalamazoo, 1964-70, group v.p., 1970-73; pres., gen. mgr. Upjohn Internat., 1973-86; v.p. Upjohn Co., 1973-86, sr. v.p., bd., 1986—, asst. to pres., 1988—, chmn., 1982-87; trustee Am. Grad. Sch. Internat. Mgmt., 1981—. With USNR, 1943-46. Mem. Pharm. Mfrs. Assn. (chmn. internat. sect. 1981-82, 85-86). Republican. Episcopalian. Office: The Upjohn Co 7000 Portage Rd Kalamazoo MI 49001

WITHERS, ALTON MERRILL, financial executive; b. San Antonio, Nov. 17, 1926; s. Walter Weyland Withers and Norma L. (Smith) Stendebach; m. Marion Ruth Guthrie, Apr. 20, 1947; children: Alton M. Jr., Deborah R. Withers Flannery. BA in Acctg., Tex. A&M U., 1949. Controller Sears Roebuck and Co., 1949-57; staff acct. Sears Roebuck and Co., Chgo., 1957-59; comptroller Sears Roebuck S.A., Sao Paolo, Brazil, 1959-63; group controller Sears Roebuck and Co., Denver, 1964-66; catalog order controller Sears Roebuck and Co., Phila., 1966-68, regional controller, 1968-76; v.p. Spiegel Inc., Oak Brook, Ill., 1976-84; sr. v.p., chief fin. officer Spiegel Inc., Oak Brook, 1985—; pres. acceptance corp. Spiegel Inc., 1988—; bd. dirs. Oak Brook Bank, First Oak Brook Bancshares, Eddie Bauer, Inc., Honeybee, Inc. Served as corp. USAF, 1945-47. Republican. Baptist. Clubs: DuPage (Oak Brook Terr., Ill.); Monroe (Chgo.). Lodge: Masons. Office: Spiegel Inc Regency Towers 1515 W 22nd St Oak Brook IL 60522

WITHERS, W. RUSSELL, JR., broadcasting executive; b. Cape Girardeau, Mo., Dec. 10, 1936; s. Waldo Russell Sr. and Dorothy Ruth (Harrelson) W.; m. Kathy J. Withers; 1 dau., Dana Ruth; 1 stepchild, Anthony White. BA, S.E. Mo. State U., 1958. Disc jockey Sta. KGMO Radio, Cape Girardeau, 1955-58; account exec. Sta. WGGH Radio, Marion, Ill., 1961-62; v.p. LIN Broadcasting Corp., Nashville, 1962-69; exec. v.p., dir. Laser Link Corp., Woodbury, N.Y., 1970-72; owner Withers Broadcasting of Hawaii, 1975-79, Withers Broadcasting of Minn., 1974-79, Withers Broadcasting Cos., Iowa, 1981—, Mood Music Ill., Mt. Vernon, 1973—, Mood Music, Inc., Cape Girardeau, 1972—, Royal Hawaiian Radio Co., Inc., others; owner various radio and TV stas. including KREX-TV, Grand Junction, Colo., KREY-TV, Montrose, Colo., KREG-TV, Glenwood Springs, Colo., KREZ-TV, Durango, Colo.; majority owner Page Ins. Cos.; chmn. bd., chief exec. officer Withers Beverage Corp., Mobile, Ala., 1973-79; chmn. adv. bd. Mut. Network; dir. Theatrevision, Inc., Turneffe Island Lodge, Ltd., Belize, C.Am., Sta. WDTV, Clarksburg, W.Va., Sta. WMIX/AM-FM, Mt. Vernon, Ill., Stas. KGMO/KAPE, Cape Girardeau; owner Page Ins. and Real Estate Cos. Mem. Mt. Vernon Tourism and Conv. Bur. Bd.; chmn. Mt. Vernon Airport Authority. With U.S. Army, 1957-58. Mem. Mt. Vernon C. of C. (bd. dirs.), Nat. Assn. Broadcasters, Ill. Broadcasters Assn., Sigma Chi. Christian Scientist. Clubs: Stadium, Mo. Athletic (St. Louis). Lodge: Elks. Home: 1 Sleepy Hollow Mount Vernon IL 62864 Office: PO Box 1508 Mount Vernon IL 62864

WITHERSPOON, WILLIAM, investment economist; b. St. Louis, Nov. 21, 1909; s. William Conner and Mary Louise (Houston) W.; student Washington U. Evening Sch., 1928-47; m. Margaret Telford Johanson, June 25, 1938; children—James Tomlin, Jane Witherspoon Peltz, Elizabeth Witherspoon Vodra. Research dept. A. G. Edwards & Sons, 1928-31; pres. Witherspoon Investment Co., 1931-34; head research dept. Newhard Cook & Co., 1934-43; chief price analysis St. Louis Ordnance Dist., 1943-45; head research dept. Newhard Cook & Co., 1945-53; owner Witherspoon Investment Counsel, 1953-64; ltd. partner Newhard Cook & Co., economist, investment analyst, 1965-68; v.p. research Stifel, Nicolaus & Co., 1968-81; lectr. on investments Washington U., 1948-67. Mem. Clayton Bd. of Edn., 1955-68, treas., 1956-68, pres., 1966-67; mem. Clayton Park and Recreation Commn., 1959-60; trustee Ednl. TV, KETC, 1963-64; mem. investment com. Gen. Assembly Mission Bd. Presbyterian Ch. U.S., Atlanta, 1976-79, mem. permanent com. ordination exams, 1979-85. Served as civilian Ordnance Dept., AUS, 1943-45. Chartered fin. analyst. Mem. St. Louis Soc. Fin. Analysts (pres. 1949-50). Club: Mo. Athletic (St. Louis). Home: 6401 Ellenwood Clayton MO 63105-2228

WITHUHN, WILLIAM LAWRENCE, museum administrator and curator, railroad economics consultant; b. Portland, Oreg., Aug. 12, 1941; s. Vernon Lawrence and Ruth Eleanor (Ferguson) W.; B.A., U. Calif.-Berkeley, 1963; M.B.A. with distinction, Cornell U., 1977, M.A., 1980, postgrad., 1980-82; m. Gail Joy Hartman, Nov. 22, 1964; children—James, Thomas, Harold. Commd. regular 2d lt. U.S. Air Force, 1963, advanced through grades to capt., 1967; indsl. engr., asst. dir. manpower and orgn., Travis AFB, Calif., 1964-65; global, polar, tactical, and instr. navigator worldwide, 1965-72; spl. ops. navigator, Vietnam, 1969-70; select lead navigator Mil. Airlift Command, 1970-72; ret., 1972; intern, then staff asst. U.S. Ho. of Reps., 1973-74; v.p. Va. & Md. R.R. Co., Cape Charles, Va., 1977-81; v.p. Md. & Del. R.R., Federalsburg, Md., 1977-81; sr. v.p. Ont. Midland R.R., Ont. Central R.R., Sodus, N.Y., 1979-83; v.p. Rail Mgmt. Services, Inc., Syracuse, N.Y., 1979-83, RSA Leasing Co., Syracuse, 1980-83; exec. v.p. Am. Coal Enterprises, Inc., Akron, Ohio, 1980-82; v.p., gen. mgr. Allegheny So. Ry., Martinsburg, Pa., 1982-83; adminstr. dept. history of sci. and tech. Nat. Museum Am. History, Smithsonian Instn., Washington, 1983—, supervising curator div. transp., 1983—, dep. chmn. dept. sci. and tech., 1984—; dir. Rail Mgmt. Services, Inc., Syracuse, N.Y., The Waring Group, Inc., transp. cons., Salisbury, Md.; cons. Pa. Hist. and Mus. Commn., 1982—. Decorated D.F.C. with cluster, Bronze Star, Air Medal with 11 clusters. De Karman fellow, 1979-80; Smithsonian fellow, 1980-81. Mem. Am. Inst. Indsl. Engrs., AAAS, History of Sci. Soc., Am. Hist. Assn., Soc. for History of Tech., Ry. and Locomotive Hist. Soc. (pres.), Am. Shortline R.R. Assn., Internat. Assn. Ry. Oper. Officers (formerly Ry. Fuel and Oper. Officers Assn.), Theta Chi. Club: Cornell (Washington). Contbr. articles to profl. jours. Home: 6311 Barr's Ln Lanham MD 20706 Office: Nat Mus Am History Smithsonian Instn Room 5010 Washington DC 20560

WITT, HELEN MERCER, government official, lawyer; b. Atlantic City, July 13, 1933; m. Edward A. Witt; 5 children. B.A., Dickinson Coll., 1955; J.D., U. Pitts., 1969. Mem. law firms Cleland, Hurtt & Witt, and Witt & Witt, 1970-74; asst. to chmn. U.S. Steel Corp./United Steelworkers Am. Bd. Arbitration, 1975-82, mem. Nat. Mediation Bd., 1983-88, chmn., 1984, 87; chmn. Iron Ore Industry Bd. Arbitration, 1989—; pvt. practice artibration, 1989—. Office: Nat Mediation Bd 1425 K St NW Washington DC 20572

WITT, RICHARD ALLEN, insurance company executive; b. Milw., Nov. 29, 1951; s. Thomas Edward and Arleene Harriet (Fabrykowski) W.; m. Pamela J. Swenson, July 17, 1987. BS in Bus. Adminstrn. summa cum laude, Creighton U., 1974. Chartered fin. analyst. Jr. securities analyst United Benefit Life Ins., Omaha, 1974-76, securities analyst, 1976-78, sr. securities analyst, 1978, asst. v.p., 1978-83; second v.p. Mut. of Omaha Ins. Co., Omaha, 1983-86, v.p., 1986-88, sr. v.p., 1988—. Fellow Fin. Analysts Fedn., Omaha-Lincoln Soc. Fin. Analysts (treas. 1982-83, sec. 1983-84, v.p. 1984-85, pres. 1985-86); mem. Inst. Chartered Fin. Analysts (grader 1986—). Office: Mut of Omaha 3301 Dodge St Omaha NE 68175

WITT, ROBERT CHARLES, finance educator; b. Tyndall, S.D., Aug. 24, 1941; s. Emmanuel M. and Hilda Veronica (Link) W.; m. Laura Gutierrez, May 21, 1974; 1 child, Kristina Monique. BA cum laude, BS with honors, U. S.D., 1964; MS in Actuarial Sci., U. Wis., 1966; MA in Econs., U. Pa., 1968, PhD in Bus. and Applied Econs., 1972. CLU. Teaching asst. U. Wis., Madison, 1965; instr. econs. Augustana Coll., Sioux Falls, S.D., 1965-66; instr. bus. stats. Temple U., Phila., 1969-70; prof. fin. U. Tex., Austin, 1970—, CBA Found. prof., 1980-82, Blades prof., 1982-86, Gus Wortham chaired prof., 1984—, also chmn. fin. dept., 1984-88; vis. prof. fin. U. B.C., Vancouver, Can., 1979; advisor U.S. Senate Subcom. on Antitrust and Monopoly, 1969-70, Ill. Ins. Laws Study Commn., 1975-78, Tex. Legis., 1973—, Atty. Gen.'s Office, State of Tex., 1984, Ins. Info. Inst., 1982-86, Tex. Legis., 1973—. Assoc. editor Jour. Risk and Ins., 1976-86, Benefits Quarterly, 1985—; contbg. editor Ins. Abstracts and Revs., 1982—; mem. rsch. and pub. adv. bd., referee Jour. Ins. Issues and Practices, 1977—; contbr. articles to profl. jours. Bd. govs. Internat. Ins. Soc., 1981—, chmn. rsch. roundtable, 1984—; mem. adminstrv. bd. S.S. Huebner Found. for Ins. Edn., Wharton Sch. U. Pa., 1983-87; chmn. doctoral dissertation awards com. State Farm Cos. Found., 1989—. Rsch. grantee Heubner Found. law found. U. Tex.q, Ill. Legis., Grad. Sch. Bus. U. Tex., Tex. Atty. Gen., various yrs. since 1976. Mem. Am. Risk and Ins. Assn. (pres., bd. dirs. 1980-87, Outstanding Feature Article award 1974, 76, 85, 86), S.S. Huebner Found. (adminstrv. bd. 1987—), Am. Fin. Assn., Am. Econ. Assn., Fin. Mgmt. Assn., Risk Theory Seminar (chmn. 1977), Fin. Execs. Inst. Office: U Tex Dept Fin CBA 6-222 Austin TX 78712

WITTELS, HOWARD BERNARD, health care company executive; b. Mpls., Jan. 25, 1950; s. Joseph and Anne (Tokman) W. BA, U. Minn., 1973, MS, 1977. Utilization rev. evaluation specialist Found. for Health Care Evaluation, Mpls., 1978-79; dir. clin. research Med Gen., Inc., Mpls., 1979-80; mgr. clin. programs St. Jude Med., St. Paul, 1980-81; mgr. regulatory affairs and profl. services 3M Co., St. Paul, 1981-85; dir. regulatory affairs Dacomed Corp., Mpls., 1985-86; v.p. regulatory affairs Schneider (USA), Inc., Mpls., 1986—; pres. Bio Statistical Assocs. Cons., Mpls., 1980-88. Mem. Phi Beta Kappa. Jewish. Home: 1563 Oakways Wayzata MN 55391 Office: Schneider USA Inc 2905 Northwest Blvd Minneapolis MN 55441

WITTENBERG, JON ALBERT, accountant; b. Valparaiso, Ind., Mar. 22, 1939; s. Fred E. and Elizabeth (DeWaal) W.; m. Joann S. Zachwieja, May 13, 1967; children: Brad, Glen, Pam. BS, Ind. U., 1961. CPA, Ill. Auditor Ernst & Whinney, Chgo., 1961-66; fin. analyst Amoco Chems., Chgo., 1966-69; controller Nat. Van Lines, Broadview, Ill., 1969-76, Consolidated Millimerey, Chgo., 1976—. Mem. Am. Inst. CPA's, Ill. Soc. CPA's, Nat. Assn. Accts. Home: 1297 W New Britton Dr Hoffman Estates IL 60195 Office: Consol Millinery Co 18 S Michigan Ave Ste 605 Chicago IL 60611

WITTER, DEAN, III, computer executive; b. N.Y.C., May 27, 1947; s. Dean and Faith (Atkins) W.; m. Rebekah Ann Ferran, June 14, 1969; children: Allison C., Brooks A. BA, Harvard U., 1969; MBA, Stanford U., 1973. Lease underwriter Matrix Leasing Internat., San Francisco, 1973-74, U.S. Leasing Internat., San Francisco, 1974-76; lease mgr. Amdahl Corp., Sunnyvale, Calif., 1976-78, dir. leasing, 1978-81, controller U.S. ops., 1981-83, treas., 1983-89, v.p., 1985-89; bd. dirs. Zack Electronics, San Francisco. Trustee Dean Witter Found., San Francisco, 1981—, Sorensen Found., San Francisco, 1988—; bd. dirs. Mission Hospice Inc. of San Mateo County. Served with U.S. Army, 1969-71. Mem. Fin. Execs. Inst., Nat. Assn. Corp. Treas., Treas. Club of San Francisco, Phi Beta Kappa. Republican.

WITTFOHT, HANS HEINRICH HERMANN, construction consultant; b. Wittingen, Germany, Nov. 26, 1924; s. Johann and Anna (Kleineberg) W.; Dipl.-Ing., Tech. Hochschule Karlsruhe, 1951, Dr.-Ing., 1963; Dr.-Ing. E.h., Tech. U. Stuttgart, 1979; m. Irma Redmann, July 29, 1950; children—Dörte, Jens. With Polensky & Zöllner Gesellschaft mbH & Co., Frankfurt am Main, Fed. Republic Germany, 1951—, dept. dir., 1959-68, mng. dir., 1968—, ptnr., 1970—, pres., 1980-87; pres. German Concrete Assn., 1985—; lectr., nat. and internat. congresses. Served with tank, arty. corps. German Army, 1942-45. Decorated Iron Cross I; recipient nat. Ehrenzeichen des VDI, 1977; internat. medal FIP, 1978; with Emil-Mörsch Denkmünze des Deutschen Beton-Vereins, 1981; Golden medaille Gustave Magnel, 1984, Silver medal Ville de Paris, 1987, Kerensky medal, 1988; hon. fellow The Inst. pf Structural Engrs., 1986; also awards for bridge constrn. in nat., internat. competitions. Mem. German Concrete Soc. (chmn.), German Soc. Engrs. (bd. dirs.), Research Assn. Underground Transp. Facilities (bd. dirs.), Internat. Assn. Bridge and Structural Engring. (v.p. tech. com.), Fédération Internationale de la Précontrainte (hon. pres., mem. presidium). Author: Kreisfoermig gekruemmte Träger, 1964; Triumph der Spannweiten, 1972; Building Bridges, 1984; contbr. numerous articles to profl. lit. Patentee in field of bridge bldg. Home: 20 Am Kiekeberg, 2000 Hamburg 55 D, Federal Republic Germany Office: 61 Bahnhofstrasse, 6200 Wiesbaden 1, Federal Republic of Germany

WITTIG, RAYMOND SHAFFER, lawyer; b. Allentown, Pa., Dec. 13, 1944; s. Raymond Baety and Alice (Shaffer) W.; m. Beth Glover, June 21, 1975; children—Meaghan G., Allison G. B.A., Pa. State U., 1966, M.Ed., 1968; J.D., Dickinson Sch. Law, 1974. Bar: Pa. 1974, D.C. Ct. Apls. 1978. Research psychologist Intext Corp., Scranton, Pa., 1968; minority counsel, procurement subcom. and gen. oversight subcom. Small Bus. Com., U.S. Ho. of Reps., Washington, 1975-76, 77-78, counsel full Ho. Small Bus. Com. 1979-84; sole practice, Washington, 1984-88. Served to capt. U.S. Army, 1969-71. Mem. Nat. Fedn. Ind. Bus., U.S. C. of C. (small bus. council), Nat. Order Barristers. Club: Capitol Hill. Home: 4618 Holly Ridge Rd Rockville MD 20853

WITTLINE, HELMUT J., controller; b. Cleve., Mar. 19, 1958; s. Leo and Berta (Steine) W.; m. Lori Ann Mikols, Feb. 10, 1979; children: Joseph H., Eric J., Andrea L. BBA, Cleve. State U., 1983. CPA, Ohio. Acctg. clk. Cleve. Twist Drill, 1980-81, cost acct., 1982-83, mgr. inventory control, 1984-86; sr. cost analyst Durkee Famous Foods, Cleve., 1985-87; mgr. cost acctg. Rotek, Inc., Aurora, Ohio, 1987-88, controller, 1988—. Designer cycle counting system. Mem. AICPA. Republican. Roman Catholic. Home: 4120 Clague Rd North Olmsted OH 44070

WITTMAN, RONALD EDGAR, small business owner; b. Camden, N.J., July 27, 1944; s. Edgar Walter and Ruth Christine (Townsend) W.; children by previous marriage: Ronald E. Jr., Scott M., Ryan J.; m. Ann Zensen Cleeland, Sept. 11, 1987. BS, Long Island U., 1966, MS, 1968. Chief indsl. engr. Am. Standard Corp., Carteret, N.J., 1968-72; owner, mgr., chief exec. officer J. Wittman & Sons Inc., Moorestown, N.J., 1972—, Wittman Heating & Air Conditioning Inc., Dayton, N.J., 1981—, Wittman Mech. Corp., Sterling, Va., 1986—. Served with USNR, 1966-69. Mem. Soc. Am. Mil. Engrs. Home: 1 Hartzel Ct Mount Laurel NJ 08054 Office: J Wittman & Sons Inc 1253 N Church St Moorestown NJ 08057

WITTNER, LOREN ANTONOW, public relations executive, lawyer; b. N.Y.C., May 2, 1938; s. Henry Warren and Miriam Margo (Antonow) W.; m. Judith Ginsberg, June 21, 1959 (div. Sept. 1972); children: Jennifer Leslie, Elizabeth Anne; m. Dianna Marks, Apr. 2, 1975. AB, Columbia U., 1958; JD, Harvard U., 1961. Bar: N.Y. 1961, Ill. 1966. Assoc. O'Dwyer & Bernstien, N.Y.C., 1961-62, Emil & Kobrin, N.Y.C., 1962-66; assoc. Antonow & Fink, Chgo., 1966-70, ptnr., 1970-77; rep. of Sec. U.S. Dept. Commerce, Chgo. and Washington, 1977-81; exec. v.p. Daniel J. Edelman, Inc., Chgo., 1981—; chmn. Midwest region Fed. Regional Council, 1978-79. Served with USAR, 1961-65. Mem. ABA. Club: Union League (Chgo.).

WITTWER, WILLI, banker; b. Romanshorn, Switzerland, July 20, 1944; parents: Ernst and Ida (Schlaepfer) W. Degree in banking, Switzerland. With Swiss Bank Corp., Bischofszell, Switzerland, 1960-63; trainee Swiss Bank Corp., Lausanne, 1963-66, N.Y.C., 1966-69; various officer positions Swiss Bank Corp., Basel, Switzerland, 1969-78; deputy head internat. corp. bus. Swiss Bank Corp., Zurich, Switzerland, 1978-80; sr. v.p. Swiss Bank Corp., N.Y.C., 1981, exec. v.p., 1982—, chief exec. officer. Bd. dirs. Internat. Ctr. N.Y., N.Y.C. Mem. Inst. Internat. Banks, Am. Inst. Banking, Swiss Soc. N.Y., Downtown Assn. Club: Racquet and Tennis (N.Y.C.). Office: Swiss Bank Corp 4 World Trade Ctr New York NY 10048

WITTY, ROBERT WILKS, insurance services company executive; b. Vicksburg, Miss., Apr. 20, 1941; s. N.W. and Jennie (Barber) W.; m. Sally Van Tilborg, Jan 26, 1964; children: Deborah, Theresa, Robin. BBA, U. Miss., 1964; LLB, LaSalle U., 1968; postgrad., Ga. State U., 1981. With Crawford & Co., 1964—; adjuster Lima, Ohio, 1964-66, Findlay, Ohio, 1966-68; sr. adjuster N,Y,C,, 1969-72; supr. br. New Orleans, 1972-76; asst. field supr. home address Atlanta, 1976-78, asst. v.p., 1978-80, v.p., 1980-81; regional v.p., regional ops. mgr. Northeast region, Montvale, N.J., 1981-85; pres., chief operating officer Am. Internat. Adjustment Co. (subs. A.I.G.), 1985-86; pres., chief exec. officer Am. Internat. Health & Rehab. C. (subs. AIAC), 1986—, also bd. dirs.; bd. dirs. Am. Internat. Adjustment Co., Am. Internat. Recoveries, Inc. Recipient Outstanding Contbn. award East Orange City Council, 1987, Support award East Orange Womens Club, 1987. Mem. Atlanta Claims Assn., Profl. Ins. Agts. of N.Y., Profl. Ins. Agts. of Northeast, Loss Exec. Council. Presbyterian. Home: 6 Davis Ct Martinsville NJ 08836 Office: 50 Clinton St East Orange NJ 07019

WIWI, ROBERT PAUL, gas and electric company executive; b. Cin., Oct. 24, 1941; m. Sharon Mary Morrison. B.S.E.E., U. Cin., 1964; M.B.A., Xavier U., 1969. V.p. elec. ops. Cin. Gas & Electric Co., 1976-87, sr. v.p. customer and corp. services, 1987—. Named Disting. Alumni, U. Cin., 1984. Mem. IEEE, Assn. Edison Illuminating Cos., Edison Electric Inst., East Cen. Area Reliability Coordinating Council. Office: Cin Gas & Electric Co 139 E 4th St Cincinnati OH 45202

WOBST, FRANK GEORG, banker; b. Dresden, Germany, Nov. 14, 1933; came to U.S., 1958, naturalized, 1963; s. Robert Georg and Marianne (Salewsky) W.; m. Joan Shuey Firkins, Aug. 24, 1957; children: Franck Georg, Ingrid, Andrea. Student, U. Erlangen, 1952-54, U. Goettingen, 1954-58, Rutgers U., 1964. With Fidelity American Bankshares, Inc., Lynchburg, Va., 1958-74, exec. v.p., dir., 1974-85; chmn., chief exec. officer, dir. Huntington Nat. Bank, 1974-85, chmn. exec. com., 1986—; chief exec. officer dir. Huntington Bancshares, Inc., 1974—. Mem. Greater Columbus C. of C., Am. Inst. Banking, Assn. Res. City Bankers, Robert Morris Assos., Newcomen Soc. Club: Scioto Country. Home: 129 N Columbia Ave Columbus OH 43209 Office: Huntington Bancshares Inc 41 S High St PO Box 1558 Columbus OH 43287

WOEHRLE, JEFF WILLIAM, wholesale bait supply company owner; b. East Stroudsburg, Pa., Dec. 12, 1959; s. William Thomas and Marjorie C. (Smith) W. Grad. high sch., Swiftwater, Pa.; diploma, Conn. Sch. Broadcasting and Communications, Stratford, 1982. Pres. Woehrle's Wholesale, Mt. Pocono, Pa., 1975—; pres., chmn. Tiab Communications, Mt. Pocono, 1985—. Mem. Pocono Mts. C. of C. (pub. relations com.). Republican. Home: 444 Park Ave Mount Pocono PA 18344-1308 Office: Rt 940 Mount Pocono PA 18344

WOGSLAND, JAMES WILLARD, heavy machinery manufacturing executive; b. Devils Lake, N.D., Apr. 17, 1931; s. Melvin LeRoy and Mable Bertina (Paulson) W.; m. Marlene Claudia Clark, June 1957; children: Karen Lynn, Steven James. BA in Econs., U. Minn., 1957. Various positions fin. dept. Caterpillar Tractor Co., Peoria, Ill., 1957-64, treas., 1976-81; mgr. fin. Caterpillar Overseas S.A., Geneva, 1965-70, sec.-treas., 1970-76; dir.-pres. Caterpillar Brasil S.A., São Paulo, 1981-87; exec. v.p. Caterpillar, Inc., Peoria, 1987—, also bd. dirs.; bd. dirs. Comml. Nat. Bank, Peoria, Protection Mut. Ins. Co., Park Ridge, Ill. Mem. adv. bd. St. Francis Hosp., Peoria, 1987—; bd. dirs. Peoria Area Community Found., 1986—; trustee Eureka Coll., 1987—. Served as sgt. USAF, 1951-55. Republican. Presbyterian. Club: Mt. Hawley Country (Peoria). Home: 6203 Jamestown Rd Peoria IL 61615 Office: Caterpillar Inc 100 NE Adams St Peoria IL 61629

WOHLER, MARYBETH H., controller; b. Framingham, Mass., July 14, 1961; d. Charles F. and Cecelia (Hynek) W. BA in Acctg., U. Lowell, 1983. Acct. Microamerica, Inc., Marlborough, Mass., 1984-87; controller IMC Systems Group, Inc., Waltham, Mass., 1987—. Mem. Nat. Assn. Female Execs., Small Bus. Assn. New Eng. Office: IMC Systems Group Inc Reservoir Pl 1601 Trapelo Rd Waltham MA 02154

WOHLMUT, THOMAS ARTHUR, communications exec.; b. Perth, Australia, Feb. 19, 1953; came to U.S., 1957, naturalized, 1963; s. Arthur John and Georgina Elfreida (Pipek) W.; B.A. cum laude, UCLA, 1975; m. Debra Lynn Hansen, Aug. 1, 1979 1 child, Katherine Emily. TV prodn. asst. (All in the Family, Mary Tyler Moore Show, Carol Burnett Show, Emmy Awards Show), CBS, Hollywood, Calif., 1971-74; video disc producer I/0 Metrics Corp., Calif., 1975-77; dir., writer Innovative Media Inc., Menlo Park, Calif., 1977-78; pres. Wohlmut Media Services, Sunnyvale, 1978—; cons. Bechtel Power Corp., Sunset Mag., Xerox-Diablo Systems, Pacific Gas & Electric Co., Elec. Power Research Inst., Advanced Micro Devices, Amdahl Corp., IBM-Rolm; lectr. in field. Recipient Bronze Anvil award Pub. Rels. Soc. Am., 1988, Cindy award Assn. Visual Communicators, 1988. Mem. Internat. TV Assn. (past. pres. San Francisco chpt., v.p. for Alaska, Wash., Idaho, Oreg., Utah, Nev., No. Calif., Joyce Nelson award 1987), Soc. Visual Communicators, Internat. Interactive Communications Soc. (founder, 1st pres.), Am. Soc. Tng. and Devel., Am. Film Inst. Office: 2600 Central Ave Suite L Union City CA 94587

WOHLUST, RONALD E., insurance company executive; b. Racine, Wis., Apr. 12, 1937; s. Elmer and Lillian H. (Krumroy) W.; m. Beverly Ann Metzuk, May 30, 1959; children: Eric R., Alison C. Student, U. Wis., Milw., 1955-58, U. Va., 1983. CPCU. Claim adjuster Mut. Svc. Casualty St. Paul, Milw., 1959-60, U.S. Fedelity & Guaranty Co., Milw., 1960-67; successively bond claim examiner, asst. supt. bond claim, asst. sec., asst. v.p. U.S. Fedelity & Guaranty Co., Balt., 1967-84, v.p., 1984—, also bd. dirs. Mem. Am. Ins. Assn. (claim exec. council 1984—), Soc. of CPCU, Ins. Inst. Am. (assoc. mgmt. adv. com., assoc. in claim adv. com.), Ins. Crime Prevention Inst. (bd. govs. 1988—). Home: 1805 Leadburn Rd Towson MD 21204 Office: US Fidelity & Guaranty Co 100 Light St PO Box 1138 Baltimore MD 21203

WOIT, ERIK PETER, corporate executive, lawyer; b. Riga, Latvia, Mar. 10, 1931; s. Walter E. and Sigrid (Radzins) W.; m. Bonnie Jean Ford, June 16, 1953; children: Peter Gordon, Steven Ford. A.B., Allegheny Coll., 1953; J.D., Harvard U., 1956. Bar: N.Y. 1959. Asso. firm Mudge, Stern, Baldwin & Todd, N.Y.C., 1956-57, 60-62; asst. sec., internat. counsel Richardson-Merrell, Inc., 1962-71; sec., gen. counsel Amerace Corp., N.Y.C., 1971-73, v.p., group exec., 1973-74, pres. ESNA div., 1974-77, sr. v.p. adminstrn., 1977-83; sr. v.p. Orient Express Hotels, Inc., N.Y.C., 1983—; chmn. Sea Containers Am. Inc., 1984—; sr. v.p. Sea Containers Ltd., 1987—. Served to capt. USMCR, 1957-60. Mem. Assn. Bar City N.Y., Am. Bar Assn., Sigma Alpha Epsilon. Clubs: Harvard, Sky (N.Y.C.). Home: 559 West Rd New Canaan CT 06840 Office: 1155 Ave of the Americas New York NY 10036

WOJCIK, CASS, decorative supply company executive, former city official; b. Rochester, N.Y., Dec. 3, 1920; s. Emil M. and Casimira C. (Krawiecz) W.; student Lawrence Inst. Tech., 1941-43, Yale U., 1943-44, U.S. Sch. for European Personnel, Czechoslovakia, 1945; m. Lilliam Leocadia Lendzion, Sept. 25, 1948; 1 son, Robert Cass. Owner, Nat. Florists Supply Co., Detroit, 1948—, Nat. Decorative, Detroit, 1950—; co-owner Creation Center, Detroit, 1955-60; cons.-contractor hort.-bot. design auto show displays, TV producers, designers and decorators. Mem. Regional Planning and Evaluation Council, 1969—; city-wide mem. Detroit Bd. Edn., 1970-75; commr. Detroit Public Schs. Employees Retirement Commn., until 1975; mem. Area Occupational Ednl. Commn., Ednl. Task Force; chmn., grand marshal Ann. Gen. Pulaski Day Parade, Detroit, 1970, 71; mem. Friends of Belle Isle; mem. Nat. Arboretum Adv. Council, U.S. Dept. Agr., 1982-83; mem. pastoral council Archidiocese of Detroit, 1983-86, 88—; v.p. student affairs Barna Inst., Ft. Lauderdale, Fla.; vice chmn. 13th Congl. Dist. Rep. Party Mich., 1987—; elected to 1988 electoral coll. Served with U.S. Army, 1944-46. Decorated Bronze Star; recipient citation Polish-Am. Congress, 1971. Mem. S.E. Mich. Council Govts., Mich., Nat. sch. bd. assns., Big Cities Sch. Bd. Com., Nat. Council Great Cities Schs., Mcpl. Finance Officers Assn. U.S., Nat. Council Tchr. Retirement, Central Citizens Com. Detroit, Internat. Platform Assn., Mich. Heritage Council, Nat. Geog. Soc. Roman Catholic. Club: Polish Century (Detroit). Home: 451 Lodge Dr Detroit MI 48214

WOLANIN, SOPHIE MAE, tutor, lecturer, civic worker; b. Alton, Ill., June 11, 1915; d. Stephen and Mary (Fijalka) W. Student Pa. State Coll., 1943-44; cert. secretarial sci. U. S.C., 1946, BSBA cum laude, 1948; PhD (hon.), Colo. State Christian Coll., 1972. Clk., stenographer, sec. Mercer County (Pa.) Tax Collector's Office, Sharon, 1932-34; receptionist, social sec., nurse-technician to doctor, N.Y.C., 1934-37; coil winder, assembler Westinghouse Electric Corp., Sharon, 1937-39, duplicator operator, typist, stenographer, 1939-44, confidential sec., Pitts., 1949-54; exec. sec., charter mem. Westinghouse Credit Corp., Pitts., 1954-72, hdqrs. sr. sec., 1972-80, reporter WCC News, 1967-68, asst. editor, 1968-71, asso. editor, 1971-76; student office sec. to dean U. S.C. Sch. Commerce, 1944-46, instr. math., bus. adminstrn., secretarial sci., 1946-48. Publicity and pub. relations chmn., corr. sec. South Oakland Rehab. Council, 1967-69; U. S.C. official del. Univ. Pitts. 200th Anniversary Bicentennial Convocation, 1986; mem. nat. adv. bd. Am. Security Council; mem. Friends Winston Churchill Meml. and Library, Westminster Coll., Fulton, Mo.; active U. S.C. Ednl. Found. Fellow; charter mem. Rep. Presdl. Task Force, trustee; sustaining mem. Rep. Nat. Com.; permanent mem. Nat. Rep. Senatorial Com.; patron Inst. Community Service (life), U. S.C. Alumni Assn. (Pa. state fund chmn. 1967-68, pres. council 1972-76, ofcl. del. rep. inauguration Bethany Coll. pres. 1973); mem. Allegheny County Scholarship Assn. (life), Allegheny County League Women voters, AAUW (life), Internat. Fedn. U. Women, N.E. Historic Geneal. Soc. mem. (life), Hypatian Lit. Soc. (hon.), Acad. Polit. Sci. (Columbia) (life), Bus. and Profl. Women's Club Pitts. (bd. dirs. 1963-80, editor Bull. 1963-65, treas. 1965-66, historian 1969-70, pub. relations 1971-76, Woman of Year 1972), Met. Opera Guild, Nat. Arbor Day Found., Kosciuszko Found. (assoc.), World Literary Acad., Missionary Assn. Mary Immaculate Nat. Shrine of Our Lady of Snows; charter mem. Nat. Mus. Women in Arts, Statue Liberty Ellis Island Found. Inc., Shenago Conservancy (life); supporting mem. Nat. Woman's Hall of Fame; recipient numerous prizes Allegheny County Fair, 1951-56; citation Congl. Record, 1969; medal of Merit, Pres. Reagan, 1982; others. Fellow Internat. Inst. Community Service (founder), Internat. Biog. Assn., mem. World Inst. Achievement (rep.), Am. Biog. Inst. Rsch. Assn. (life patron, nat. advisor), Liturgical Conf. N. Am. (life), Westinghouse Vet. Employees Assn., Nat. Soc. Lit. and Arts, Early Am. Soc., Am. Acad. Social and Polit. Sci., Societe Commemorative de Femmes Celebres, Nat. Trust Historic Preservation, Am. Counselors Soc. (life), Am. Mus. Natural History (asso.), Nat. Hist. Soc. (founding mem.), Anglo-Am. Hist. Soc. (charter), Nat. Assn. Exec. Secs., Internat. Platform Assn., Smithsonian Assos., Asso. Nat. Archives, Nat., Pa., Fed. bus. and profl. women's clubs, Mercer County Hist. Soc. (life), Am. Bible Soc., Polish Am. Numismatic Assn., Polonus Philatelic Soc., UN Assn. U.S., Polish Inst. Arts and Scis. Am. Inc. (assoc.), N.Y. Acad. Scis. (assoc.), Am. Council Polish Cultural Clubs Inc. Roman Catholic (mem. St. Paul Cathedral Altar Soc., patron organ recitals). Clubs: Jonathan Maxcy of U. S.C. (charter); Univ. Catholic of Pitts.; Key of Pa., Fedn. Bus. and Profl. Women (hon.); Coll. (hon.) (Sharon). Contbr. articles to newspapers. Home: 5223 Smith-Stewart Rd SE Girard OH 44420

WOLCOTT, EUGENE AARON, corporate professional; b. Fountain City, Wis., Sept. 23, 1923; s. Clair Chester and Murriel Alice (Irmscher) W.; m. Nannie John Knipp, June 11, 1944; 1 child, Nancy Eileen Wolcott McCreary. AA, Henderson County Jr. Coll., Athens, Tex., 1960; student, So. Meth. U., 1965-70, U. Tex., 1971-76. Flight instr. Brit. Royal Air Force and USAF, Terrell, Tex., 1941-46; supr. cost analysis Ford Motor Co., Dallas, 1947-70; controller Sterling Packing & Gasket Co., Houston, 1970; v.p., controller Texstar Plastics, Grand Prairie, Tex., 1970-78; v.p., treas., controller Texstar Plastics, Grand Prairie, 1978—. Former mayor City of Terrell, Tex., 1955-57; chmn. Dem. Precinct of Terrell, 1965-89; advisor Arlington Ind. Sch. Dist. Vocat. Office Edn. Program, 1982—. Named Citizen of Yr. Ford Motor Co., Dallas, 1959-60. Mem. Nat. Assn. Accts. (bd. dirs. 1965-69). Republican. Methodist. Club: Terrell Aviation (pres. 1958-59). Home: 2702 Ashbury Dr Arlington TX 76105 Office: Texstar Inc 802 Avenue J East Grand Prairie TX 75050

WOLCOTT, JOHN WINTHROP, III, business executive; b. Balt., Dec. 3, 1924; s. John Winthrop, Jr. and Dorothy C. (Fraser) W.; m. Elizabeth Thelin Hooper, Apr. 24, 1948 (div. 1985); children: John Winthrop IV, Elizabeth T., Katherine C.; m. Karen E. Jones, Oct. 1, 1985. B.Indsl. Engring., Gen. Motors Inst., 1951. Registered profl. engr., Ohio. With Gen. Motors Corp., 1946-53, Weatherhead Co., Cleve., 1957-60; v.p. H.K. Porter Co., Inc., Pitts., 1960-64; pres. Ametek, Inc., N.Y.C., 1964-66; v.p. Am. Machine & Foundry Co., 1966-77, group exec. process equipment group, 1967-70; exec. v.p. ops. AMF, Inc., 1970-77; pres., chief exec. officer, dir. Transway Internat. Corp., N.Y.C., 1978-86, chmn. bd., 1982-86; adv. bd. Lepercq, de Neuflize & Co., Inc., N.Y.C., 1986—. Served with USCGR, 1943-46. Mem. Soc. Automotive Engrs., Soc. Colonial Wars. Episcopalian. Clubs: Mt. Kisco Country Maryland (Balt.); Brook (N.Y.C.). Home: 14 Wolf Hill Rd Chappaqua NY 10514 Office: Lepercq de Neuflize & Co Inc 345 Park Ave New York NY 10154

WOLCOTT, ROBERT WILSON, JR., business executive; b. Phila., Nov. 20, 1926; s. Robert Wilson and Alice (Huston) W.; m. Margaret Hoopes, June 24, 1949; children—Allyn M., Anne H. BSCE, Princeton U. Vice pres., gen. mgr. Internat. Mill Service div. IU Internat. Corp., Phila., 1963-65, pres., 1965-70; group v.p. IU Internat. Corp., Phila., 1970-82, exec. v.p., 1982-88; cons. Phila., 1988—; bd. dirs. Echo Bay Mines Ltd., Edmonton, Alta., Envirosafe Services Inc., King of Prussia, Pa. Bd. dirs. The Church Farm Sch., Exton, Pa., 1981—, Zool. Soc. Phila., 1983—; trustee The Free Library of Phila., 1986—. Mem. Am. Iron & Steel Inst., AIME. Clubs: Merion Cricket (Haverford, Pa.); Gulph Mills Golf (King of Prussia, Pa.); Phila., Union League (Phila.). Home: 236 Atlee Rd Wayne PA 19087 Office: 1818 Market St 34th Floor Philadelphia PA 19103

WOLD, JOHN SCHILLER, geologist, former congressman; b. East Orange, N.J., Aug. 31, 1916; s. Peter Irving and Mary (Helff) W.; m. Jane Adele Pearson, Sept. 28, 1946; children: Peter Irving, Priscilla Adele, John Pearson. A.B., St. Andrews U., Scotland and Union Coll., Schenectady, 1938; M.S., Cornell U., 1939. Dir. Fedn. Rocky Mountain States, 1966-68; v.p. Rocky Mountain Oil and Gas Assn., 1967, 68; mem. Wyo. Ho. of Reps., 1957-59; Republican candidate for U.S. Senate, 1964, 70; mem. 91st Congress at large from, Wyo.; pres. BTU, Inc., J & P Corp., Wold Nuclear Co., Wold Mineral Exploration Co., Casper, Wyo.; founding pres. Wyo. Heritage Found., Central Wyo. Ski Corp.; chmn. Natural Gas Pipeline Authority; chmn. Wyo. Nat. Gas Pipeline Authority, 1987—; bd. dirs. Plains Petroleum Co., Coca Mines, Inc. Contbr. articles to profl. jours. Chmn. Wyo. Rep. Com., 1960-64, Western State Rep. Chmns. Assn., 1963-64; mem. exec. com. Rep. Nat. Com., 1962-64; chmn. Wyo. Rep. State Fin. Com.; Active Little League Baseball, Boy Scouts Am., United Fund, YMCA, Boys Clubs Am.; pres. Wyo. Heritage Soc.; former pres. bd. trustees Casper Coll.; trustee Union Coll. Served to lt. USNR, World War II. Named Wyo. Man of Yr. AP-UPI, 1968; Wyo. Mineral Man of Yr., 1979. Mem. Wyo. Geol. Assn. (hon. life, pres. 1956), Am. Assn. Petroleum Geologists, Ind. Petroleum Assn. Am., AAAS, Wyo. Mining Assn., Sigma Xi, Alpha Delta Phi. Episcopalian (past vestryman, warden). Home: 1231 W 30th Casper WY 82601 Office: Mineral Resource Ctr Ste 200 Casper WY 82604

WOLDERLING, JOHANNES ALEX, manufacturing executive; b. Surabaya, Indonesia, Mar. 29, 1927; came to The Netherlands, 1946; s. Hendrik Carel Wolderling and Sophia Schwarz; widowed; children: Helen Margot, Ester Gabrielle. Grad., Tech. Coll., Rotterdam, The Netherlands, 1948; Student, Tech. U., Delft, 1950-53; BSME, U. Economics, Rotterdam, 1960-62. Engr. Royal Dutch Blast Furnaces and Steel Mills, IJmuiden, The Netherlands, 1948-53; engr. Amsterdam Rubber and Palm Oil Plantation Co., Sumatra, Indonesia, 1953-58, Royal Dutch Blast Furnaces and Steel Mills, IJmuiden, 1958-62; tech. prod. mgr. Bruynzeel lumber Co., Suriname, S. Am., 1962-66; orgn./ systems engr. Fokker Aircraft Co., Schiphol, The Netherlands, 1966-69; sales engr. civil aircraft Fokker Aircraft Co., Schiphol, 1969-73, area mgr. civil aircraft, 1973-79; sales dir. civil aircraft Fokker Aircraft Co., Amsterdam, The Netherlands, 1979-87; advisor Fokker Aircraft Co., Amsterdam, 1987—; mem. supervisory bd. Aviona Internat., Antwerp, 1988—.

WOLF, CLARENCE, JR., stock broker; b. Phila., May 11, 1908; s. Clarence and Nan (Hogan) W.; m. Alma C. Backhus, Sept. 11, 1942. Student, Pa. Mil. Prep. Sch., Chester, Pa., 1921; grad., Swarthmore (Pa.) Prep. Sch., 1923. Bar: Phila.-Balt. Stock Exchange 1937. Founder French-Wolf Paint Products Corp., Phila., 1926; pres. French-Wolf Paint Products Corp., until 1943; asso. Reynolds Securities, Inc. (now Dean Witter Reynolds Inc.), 1944-86; spl. rep. Reynolds Securities, Inc. (now Dean Witter Reynolds Inc.), Miami Beach, Fla., 1946-86; v.p. investments Reynolds Securities, Inc. (now Dean Witter Reynolds Inc.), 1944-86, E.F. Hutton, 1987—; registered investment advisor Miami, 1986—; dir. Superior Zinc Co., 1938-44, Hercules Cement Co., 1937-57, Rand Broadcasting Co. (owners radio and television stas., also hotels), 1946-68, Amcord, Inc., 1958-79 (formerly Am. Cement Corp.), vice chmn., mem. exec. com., 1970-79; pres. Even Letters Corp. Author: $even Letter$ - An Investment Primer, 1980, $even Letters$ Investment Guidebook, 1988. Pres. Normandy Isles Improvement Assn., Miami Beach, 1952-53; mem. Presidents Council Miami Beach, 1952—. Mem. Alumnus Assn. Pa. Mil. Coll. (dir. Fla. chpt. 1961-64). Clubs: Jockey (Miami, Fla.); Com. of 100. Home: Jockey Club 11111 Biscayne Blvd Apt 858 Miami FL 33161 Office: 1101 Brickell Ave BIV Tower Suite 800 Miami FL 33131

WOLF, DALE JOSEPH, utilities company executive; b. Hays, Kans., Aug. 21, 1939; s. Henry and Irene Elizabeth (Basgall) W.; m. Patricia Ann Ceule, May 28, 1966; children: Suzanne, Sara. BS in Bus. Adminstrn., Ft. Hays State U., 1961; MBA in Fin., U. Mo., 1970. Various acctg. and fin. positions Mo. Pub. Service Co., Kansas City, Mo., 1962-77, treas., 1977-84, v.p., treas., 1984-85; v.p. fin. UtiliCorp United, Inc., Kansas City, 1985—. Mem. Fin. Execs. Inst., Corp. Fin. Inst. Republican. Roman Catholic. Lodge:

Kiwanis (pres. 1977-78). Office: UtiliCorp United Inc 911 Main Kansas City MO 64105

WOLF, DON ALLEN, hardware wholesaler executive; b. Allen County, Ind., June 18, 1929; s. Ellis Adolphus and Bessie Ruth (Fortman) W.; m. Virginia Ann Lunz, Oct. 8, 1949; children—Rebecca, Donna, Richard, Lisa. Student exec. course, Ind. U., 1969. With Hardware Wholesalers Inc., Fort Wayne, Ind., 1947—; purchasing mgr. Hardware Wholesalers Inc., 1957—, v.p., gen. mgr., 1967-80, pres., 1980—; dir. Lyal Electric Co., Fort Wayne Nat. Bank. Pres., bd. dirs. Big Brothers, Fort Wayne, 1973-74; nat. pres. Big Brothers Soc. Am., 1977-80; bd. dirs. Russell Mueller Research Found., 1970—. Mem. Nat. Wholesale Hardware Assn. (dir. 1977—, pres. 1984-85, named Hardware Wholesaler of Year 1973, 85), Ind. State C. of C. (dir.), Fort Wayne C. of C. (dir. 1973-74, 78). Republican. Lutheran. Office: Hardware Wholesalers Inc PO Box 868 Fort Wayne IN 46801 also: 6502 Nelson Rd Fort Wayne IN 46803

WOLF, HANS ABRAHAM, pharmaceutical company executive; b. Frankfurt, Fed. Republic Germany, June 27, 1928; came to U.S., 1936, naturalized, 1944; s. Franz Benjamin and Ilse (Nathan) W.; m. Elizabeth J. Bassett, Aug. 2, 1958; children: Heidi Elizabeth, Rebecca Anne, Deborah Wolf Streeter, Andrew Robert. AB magna cum laude, Harvard U., 1949, MBA, 1955; PhB, Oxford U., 1951. Math instr. Tutoring Sch., 1946-47; statis. research Nat. Bur. Econ. Research, N.Y.C., 1948-49; researcher Georgetown U., 1951-52; confidential aide Office Dir. Mut. Security, Washington, 1952; analyst Ford Motor div. Ford Motor Co., Dearborn, Mich., summer 1954; foreman prodn. M&C Nuclear Inc., Attleboro, Mass., 1955-57; asst. supt. prodn. Metals & Controls Corp., Attleboro, 1957-59, mgr. product dept., 1959-62, controller, 1962-67; asst. v.p., controller materials and services group Tex. Instruments Inc., Dallas, 1967-69, treas., v.p., 1969-75; v.p. fin., chief fin. officer Syntex Corp., Palo Alto, Calif., 1975-78, exec. v.p., 1978-86, vice chmn., chief adminstrv. officer, 1986—, also bd. dirs.; also bd. dirs. Clean Sites Inc., Palo Alto, Calif.; bd. dirs. Beta Phase Corp., Clean Sites, Inc., Alexandria, Va. Author: Motivation Research—A New Aid to Understanding Your Markets, 1955. Mem. Norton (Mass.) Sch. Bd., 1959-62, chmn., 1961-62; pres., bd. dirs. Urban League Greater Dallas, 1971-74; bd. dirs. Dallas Health Planning Council, mem. community adv. com., 1973-75; bd. dirs., pres. Children's Health Council of the Mid Peninsula; cubmaster Boy Scouts Am., 1976-78; elder United Ch. Christ, 1970-73, vice chmn. gen. bd., 1970-71, moderator, 1978-80; trustee Pacific Sch. Religion, 1986—, World Affairs Council San Francisco, 1986—. Served with USAF, 1952-53. Mem. Am. Mgmt. Assn. (planning council fin. div. 1970-76), Phi Beta Kappa. Office: Syntex Corp 3401 Hillview Ave Palo Alto CA 94304

WOLF, JAMES ANTHONY, insurance company executive; b. Washington, May 10, 1945; s. Arthur William and Marie Antoinette (Dalton) Wolf; m. Sheila Marie Regan, June 27, 1968; children: Jayne Ann, Elizabeth. BS in Fin. cum laude, Boston Coll., 1967. Mktg. rep. IBM, Newark, N.J., 1967-68, Boston, 1970-78; mktg. mgr. IBM, N.Y.C., 1978-81; 2nd v.p. Tchrs. Ins. & Annuity Assn., N.Y.C., 1981-82, v.p., 1982-85, sr. v.p., 1985—. Served to sgt. U.S. Army, 1968-70, Vietnam. Mem. Am. Mgmt. Assn. Republican. Roman Catholic. Home: 233 Ridge Common Fairfield CT 06430 Office: Tchrs Ins & Annuity Assn Am 730 3rd Ave New York NY 10017

WOLF, JOHN STEVEN, commercial development project manager; b. Portsmouth, Ohio, Sept. 4, 1947; s. John Andrew and Betty Lee Wolf; A.S. in Civil Engring. Tech., Ohio Coll. Applied Sci., 1967; B.S. in Civil Engring., Ohio U., 1975. Project engr. Columbus & So. Ohio Electric Co., 1974-75; staff project engr. Goodyear Atomic Corp., Piketon, Ohio, 1975-78; constrn. mgr., project engr. Am. Electric Power Service Corp., Lancaster, Ohio, 1978-83; project mgr. F. and P. Mgrs., Inc., Columbus, Ohio, 1983-85, Target Constrn. Co., Columbus, 1985—; participant Am. Mgmt. Assn. Seminar on Planning, Scheduling and Controlling Tech. Projects. Served with U.S. Army, 1968-69; Vietnam. Decorated Army Commendation medal (2); registered profl. engr., Ohio. Mem. Nat. Soc. Profl. Engrs., Ohio Soc. Profl. Engrs. Methodist. Club: Masons, Scottish Rite, Shriners. Home: 3000 Potawamie Dr London OH 43140 Office: Target Constrn Co 4150 Tuller Rd Ste 236 Dublin OH 43017

WOLF, MARTIN HOWARD, environmental company executive; b. Bklyn., Nov. 9, 1948; s. Harold and Rose (Linksman) W.; m. Marcia Anne Laidig, Nov. 23, 1971 (dec. 1986); children: Benjamin Laidig, Alexana Laidig. BS in Chemistry, Worcester Polytech., 1971; MS in Chemistry, Yeshiva U., 1974. Sr. chemist CIBA-Geigy Corp., Greensboro, N.C., 1969-76; applications chemist Spectra Physics, Inc., Piscataway, N.J., 1976-77; mgr. Thermo Electron Corp., Waltham, Mass., 1977-80; mgr. Cambridge Analytical Assoc., Boston, 1980-81, v.p., 1981-82, pres., 1982—, also dir. Contbr. over 20 articles to profl. jours. Mem. N.Y. Acad. Sci., AAAS, Am. Chem. Soc., Am. Mgmt. Assn. (pres.). Home: 646 Boston Post Rd Weston MA 02193 Office: Cambridge Analytical Assocs 1106 Commonwealth Ave Boston MA 02215

WOLF, MARY ZIETLOW, manufacturing company executive; b. New London, Wis., Feb. 26, 1950; d. Gordon Leo and Melane Mary (Simonis) Z.; student U. Wis., Stevens Point, 1968-70, part time, 1977-80; m. Rodney A. Wolf, 1980; children—Dirk, Wayne. Adminstrv. asst. K.F. Kellogg, Northfield, Ill., 1970-74; prodn. mgr. M.R. Ceramics, Inc., Iola, Wis., 1974-77; plant mgr. Weber Tackle Co., Stevens Point, Wis., 1977-81; v.p. Rodmar Co., Amherst Junction, Wis., 1981-85, Rodmar Mfg. Inc., Nelsonville, Wis., 1985—; mgr. Rodmar Acctg. and Tax Services, 1984—; Mem. Tomorrow River Fine Arts Council, sec., 1985—; mem. Tomorrow River PTO, 1987—, v.p. 1987, pres. 1988. Mem. Nat. Assn. Female Execs., Nat. Assn. Tax Practitioners. Roman Catholic. Home: 8946 Loberg Rd Amherst Junction WI 54407 Office: PO Box 68 3000 Hwy 161 Nelsonville WI 54458

WOLF, MAURICE, lawyer; b. London, Eng., Oct. 15, 1931; came to U.S., 1947; s. D.I. and Esther (de Miranda) W.; m. Yolanda Pazmino, May 4, 1963; children: J. David, Monica Maria. Cert., Universidad Nacional Autonoma de Mexico, Mexico City, 1957; BA with honors, UCLA, 1959; LLB, Columbia U., 1962. Bar: N.Y. 1962, D.C. 1964, U.S. Supreme Ct. 1980. Atty., advisor Office Satellite Communications, FCC, Washington, 1962-66, counsel, 1966-72; sr. counsel Inter-Am. Devel. Bank, Washington, 1972-77; sr. ptnr. Wolf, Arnold & Cardoso P.C., Washington, 1977—. Contbr. articles to profl. jours.; co-author Doing Business With The International Development Agencies in Washington, 1983. Pres. Riverside Civic Assn., Fairfax, Ct., 1969-70, 77-80, v.p. 1976-77; co-chmn. Mt. Vernon council, Fairfax, 1969-70. Harlan Fiske Stone scholar, Columbia U., 1962. Mem. N.Y. Bar Assn., D.C. Bar Assn. (chmn. internat. investment fin. subcom. 1978), Am. Soc. Internat. Law, Inter-Am. Bar Assn., Fed. Bar Assn., Columbia Soc. Internat. Law (pres. 1961-62), Am. Mgmt. Assn., Internat. Nat. Dem. Club, Williams Club. Home: 8354 Wagon Wheel Rd Alexandria VA 22309 Office: Wolf Arnold & Cardoso PC 350 K St Washington DC 20007

WOLF, ROBERT HOWARD, advertising executive, marketing consultant; b. N.Y.C., Feb. 11, 1942; s. Charles and Dorothy (Goldstein) W.; m. Rebecca Helene Beck, Feb. 26, 1978; children—Jessica Leigh, Caroline Beth. B.A., Long Island U., 1964; M.B.A., Adelphi U., 1967. Mktg. mgr. Lever Bros, N.Y.C., 1967-70; mgmt. supr Wells, Rich, Greene, N.Y.C., 1971-77, sr. v.p., mng. dir., 1978-81; sr. v.p., gen. mgr. Kenyon & Eckhardt, Los Angeles, 1981-83; exec. v.p., gen. mgr. Chiat/Day Advt., N.Y.C., 1983-87, pres., chief exec. officer, vice chmn., 1987—, bd. dirs. Mem. N.Y. Advt. Club, Los Angeles Advt. Club. Club: Riviera Tennis (Los Angeles); Tennisport Tennis (N.Y.C.). Home: 9817 Hythe Ct Beverly Hills CA 90210 Office: Chiat/Day Advt 320 Hampton Dr Venice CA 90291

WOLF, ROSE BARRY, tax consultant, educator; b. Colchester, Conn., Apr. 27, 1921; d. Samuel David and Lena Sylvia (Hoffman) Barry; grad. in acctg. Pace Inst., 1946; m. Lester Wolf, Sept. 28, 1947 (dec.); children—Beverly Sheila, Perry Stewart. Office mgr. HY & D. Agar Realty, Inc., Bklyn., 1946-47, Joseph Love, Inc., N.Y.C., 1947-48; real estate accountant, tax accountant Benjamin Passilia, N.Y.C., 1948-67; acct. Val Stream Volkswagen, Valley Stream, N.Y., 1967-67; sr. tax acct. Columbia Pictures Industries, Inc., N.Y.C., 1968-73; comptroller Matthews, Inc., Beverly Hills, Calif., 1973-74, Alexander & Friends., Inc., El Segundo, Calif., 1974-76; tax cons., pres. Group Services Internat., Tarzana, Calif., 1976—; treas. Travel Group Inc., Anaheim, Calif.; employment sec.-treas. Midway Energy Inc., Tarzana, 1978; citizens adv. com. Valley Coll. Accredited in accountancy; enrolled to practice before IRS. Mem. Nat. Soc. Pub. Accts., Am. Soc. Profl. Accts. (pres. 1985-86), Am. Soc. Women Accts. (corr. sec., pres. 1986—), Nat. Assn. Enrolled Agts. (chmn. Yellow Pages advt. Los Angeles chpt.), Am. Bus. Women's Assn. (treas.). Democrat. Clubs: B'nai B'rith, Seaford Dramatic. Columnist, Weekend mag., San Fernando Valley. Office: 6442 Coldwater Canyon Blvd Ste 105 North Hollywood CA 91606

WOLF, STEPHEN M., airline executive; b. Oakland, Calif., Aug. 7, 1941. BS, San Francisco State U., 1965. Various positions Am. Airlines, Los Angeles, 1965-79, v.p. western div., 1979-81; sr. v.p. mktg. Pan Am. World Airlines, N.Y.C., 1981-82; pres., chief operating officer Continental Airlines, Houston, 1982-83; pres. Republic Airlines, Mpls., 1984-85, pres., chief exec. officer, 1985-86; chmn., pres., chief exec. officer Tiger Internat., Los Angeles, 1986-87; pres., chief exec. officer United Airlines Inc., Chgo., 1987—; chmn., pres., chief exec. officer Allegis Corp. (now UAL Corp.), 1987—; bd. dirs. Payless Cashways Inc. Mem. Air Transp. Assn. (bd. dirs. 1985—), Mpls. C. of C. Clubs: Union League, Wings (N.Y.); Mpls. Office: United Airlines Inc PO Box 66100 Chicago IL 60666 *

WOLF, STEVEN PETER, oil company executive; b. Waseca, Minn., May 18, 1945; m. Elizabeth Wagner. BA in Mktg., U. Minn., 1970, MS, 1972. Various positions Exxon Corp., 1972-81; mgr. compensation Kerr-McGee Corp., Oklahoma City, 1981-82; dir. human resources Kerr-McGee Corp., 1982-84, dir. bus. devel., 1984-85, v.p. adminstrn., 1985-87, sr. v.p., 1987—. Pres., bd. dirs. Big Bros./Big Sisters, Oklahoma City, 1984—; mem. exec. com. Am. Heart Assn., Oklahoma City, 1985-87. Club: Whitehall (bd. dirs. 1985-87). Office: Kerr-McGee Corp 123 Robert S Kerr Ave Oklahoma City OK 73125

WOLF, TIMOTHY VAN DE WINT, food products company executive; b. Apr. 27, 1953; s. Charles and Theresa Wolf; m. Mary Therese Merritt. BA in Econs. cum laude, Harvard U., 1974; MBA, U. Chgo., 1976. Fin. analyst to sr. fin. analyst Tennant Co., Mpls., 1976-79; mgr. mktg. planning and analysis Electrolux div. Consolidated Food Corp., Stamford, Conn., 1979-80; mgr. bus. planning Pepsi USA, Purchase, N.Y., 1980-81, mgr. bus. devel. and competitive analysis, 1981-82, dir. bus. planning fountain beverage div., 1982-84; sr. dir. bus. planning Taco Bell Corp., Irvine, Calif., 1984-86, v.p., controller, 1986—; bd. dirs. Irvine Med. Ctr. Harvard Coll. scholar, Cambridge, Mass. Clubs: Harvard of So. Calif., U. Calif. Chancellor's (Irvine). Home: 18 Rustling Wind St Irvine CA 92715 Office: Taco Bell Co 17901 Von Karman St Irvine CA 92714

WOLFE, EDWARD HARVEY, venture capital company executive; b. Balt., July 10, 1945; s. Meyer and Florence (Merin) W.; m. Elizabeth Ann Loesser (div. Oct. 1982); 1 child, Eric M. BS in Acctg., U. Md., 1967; MBA, SUNY, Albany, 1972. Controller Larry Hogan Assocs., Washington, 1965-67; cons. acctg. systems IBM, N.Y.C., 1967-71; pres. Prescription Svcs., Inc. div. ARA, Houston, 1971-72, Wolfe Resources Internat., Houston, 1973-83, Telcom Engring., Inc., St. Louis, 1983-86; pres., mng. ptnr. Multicom Svcs., Inc., Houston, 1986—; bd. dirs. Gold Acorn Capital Corp., Houston; cons. Houston Internat. Teleport, Spectradayne, Inc., Dallas, Telesat Can., Ottawa, Ont. Author: Program for International Market Penetration, 1983. Lobbyist various orgns., Austin, Tex., 1975—. With U.S. Army, 1968-69. Mem. MIT Enterprise Forum Tex., Univ. Club. Republican. Jewish. Office: Multicom Svcs Inc 2409 Bering Dr Ste 7 Houston TX 77057

WOLFE, ESTEMORE ALVIS, insurance company executive; b. Crystal Springs, Miss., Dec. 29, 1919; s. Henry and Vinia (Crump) W. BS, Jackson State Coll., 1947; postgrad. Fla. Meml. Coll., 1948-49, NYU, 1952-53; MEd, Wayne State U., 1951; MA, Purdue U., 1953; DEd, Boston U., 1958; LHD (hon.), Wilberforce U., 1959; LittD (hon.), Creighton U., 1961; LHD (hon.), Syracuse U., 1963; postgrad. Purdue U., 1964. Dir. med. technicians Detroit Tb Sanitorium, 1947-48; ednl. cons., mass media specialist Detroit Bd. Edn., 1948—; v.p., sec. Wright Mut. Ins. Co., Detroit, 1955—; v.p., sales dir. promotions Elramco Enterprises, Inc., Albany, N.Y., 1983—; mem. internat. adv. Hamilton Funding Corp.; dir. Ind. Prodns. Corp., also chmn. nat. edn. com. for educators; lectr., guest prof. Gt. Lakes Coll., Assumption Coll. (Can.), Wayne U., 1953-56, Jackson State Coll., Bethany Coll., U. Detroit, Wis. State U., Stevens Point, So. U. (La.); pres. nat. bd. Kids Kollege Jackson State U., 1987; writer column Detroit Times; cons. to pres. P. Lenud & Co. Mem. White House Conf. of Children and Youth, 1960; mem. Council on Aging, 1965-66; campaign chmn. devel. fund drive Jackson State Coll. 1970-71, trustee Devel. Found., 1984—; organizer, pres. Detroit chpt. Friends of AMISTAD, 1972, nat. v.p., 1972-73, nat. pres. and bd. dirs., 1973—; chmn. bd. trustees Detroit Met. Symphony Orch.; trustee Nat. Negro Archives Mus., Washington, Mich. council Arts, Scis. and Letters, Bethany (W.Va.) Coll., Meth. ch. Served with AUS, 1942-46. Recipient Nat. Human Relations award Clark U., 1969, citation Am. Airlines in recognition of contbns. to devel. air transp. and nat. air power, 1969, Presdl. citation for performance beyond call of duty, 1945, citation and plaque outstanding service and leadership City of Detroit, 1973, Achievement award Jackson State U. Alumni Assn., also Centennial medallion, also trophy Southeastern Mich. alumni chpt., 1984, plaque Kiwanis Clubs, 1978, Am. Heritage Found. award, 1980, key to City, Omaha; Estemore A. Wolfe Daymayoral proclaimation and key to City Cin., 1988; Pres.emeritus endowed scholarship award Nat. Friends of AMISTAD; numerous other plaques and citations for leadership in bus., civic orgns., edn. devel., CASE TWO award Council for Advancement and Support for Higher Edn., 1979, plaque U. Detroit, 1979, 2d Century award Jackson State U., 1979, Spirit of Detroit award Detroit City Council, 1980, Key to City of New Orleans, 1980, Outstanding Alumnus award Boston U., 1981, life membership plaque Friends of Amistad, 1981, Nat. Leadership award Friends of Amistad, 1986, plaque for hist. achievements Am. Heritage Found., 1984, Pearl Cross of Distinction, Central United Meth. Ch., Detroit, Freedom Bowl award Miller Brewing Co., 1985, cert. of Merit Mich. Senate, 1986, 15 more awards, 1984-86; Estemore A. Wolfe Day proclaimed in Davenport, Iowa, 1980; named hon. staff col. Gov. Miss., 1977. Mem. NAACP, Nat. Soc. Visual Edn., Nat. Geog. Soc., Am. Acad. Social and Polit. Sci., Nat. Ins. Assn., Detroit Fedn. Tchrs., Detroit Assn. Radio and TV, Detroit Assn. Film Tchrs., Internat. Platform Assn., Detroit Schoolmen's Club, Detroit Roundtable, Nat. Congress Parents and Tchrs., Orgn. Alumni Assn. Wayne State U. (pres.), Nat. Alumni Assn. Jackson State U. (pres. 1976—, regional dir.). Democrat. Lodge: Kiwanis (Lafayette Park pres. 1983, World Service plaque 1985, Disting. Club Pres. plaque 1985, Exemplary Service award 1985). Office: 2995 E Grand Blvd Detroit MI 48202

WOLFE, GARY JOHNSON, financial executive; b. Wilmington, N.C., Sept. 13, 1937; s. Vivian Earcelle (Johnson) W.; m. Carolyn Wilson; children: Kimberly L., Steven G. AA, Wilmington Coll., 1957; BS, U. N.C., 1959. CPA, N.C., S.C, Ga. Acct. A.M. Pullen & Co., Danville, Va., 1959-62; with Cherry, Bekaert & Holland, Charlotte, N.C., 1962—; ptnr. Cherry, Bekaert & Holland, Charlotte, 1967—; ptnr. in charge Cherry, Bekaert & Holland, Beaufort, N.C., 1967-70; ptnr. in charge Cherry, Bekaert & Holland, Atlanta, 1970-78, mem. exec. com., 1973—, ptnr. regional ops., 1974-78; mng. ptnr., chief exec. officer Cherry, Bekaert & Holland, Charlotte, 1978—; exec. bd. dirs. Summit Internat., Inc. Contbr. articles to jours. and chpts. to books. Mem. AICPA (adv. com. Group B), N.C. Assn. CPAs, S.C. Assn. CPAs, Ga. Soc. CPAs, Nat. Assn. Accts., Civitan Club, Exchange Club, Rotary. Office: Cherry Bekaert & Holland 3100 One First Union Ctr Charlotte NC 28202-6006

WOLFE, JAMES RONALD, lawyer; b. Pitts., Dec. 10, 1932; s. James Thaddeus and Helen Matilda (Corey) W.; m. Anne Lisbeth Dahle Eriksen, May 28, 1960; children: Ronald, Christopher, Geoffrey. B.A. summa cum laude, Duquesne U., 1954; LL.B. cum laude, NYU, 1959. Bar: N.Y. 1959. Assoc. Simpson Thacher & Bartlett, N.Y.C., 1959-69, ptnr., 1969—. Coeditor: West's McKinney's Forms, Uniform Commercial Code, 1965. Served to 1st lt. U.S. Army, 1955-57. Mem. ABA, N.Y. State Bar Assn., Assn. Bar City N.Y., Am. Judicature Soc., N.Y. Law Inst., Internat. Platform Assn. Republican. Roman Catholic. Home: 641 King St Chappaqua NY 10514 Office: Simpson Thacher & Bartlett 425 Lexington Ave New York NY 10017

WOLFE, JOHN ALLEN, geologist, consultant; b. Riverton, Iowa, June 3, 1920; s. Asa Allen and Alice (Thomas) W.; Geol. Engr., EM, Colo. Sch. Mines, 1947, MS, 1954; PhD, Columbia Pacific U., 1983; m. Adelfa Guamos, 1972; children: James Perry, Cynthia Wolfe Burke. Dir. exploration Ideal Cement Co., Denver, 1948-65; geol. cons., Philippines, Latin Am., 1965-68; pres. Mineral Resources Cons., Houston, 1968-72; ptnr. Schoenike, Wolfe & Assocs., Houston, 1970-75; pres. Taysan Copper, Inc., Manila, 1973—; v.p. Kenmare Minerals Inc., Manila, 1988—, also bd. dirs.; profl. lectr. Nat. Inst. Geol. Scis., U. Philippines, 1984—; lectr., cons. in field; mem. Colo. Mining Industry Devel. Bd., 1963-65. Fellow Geol. Soc. Am.; mem. AAAS, Am. Mining Congress (gov. 1963-65), Colo. Mining Assn. (pres. 1963), Am. Inst. Mining Engrs., Geol. Soc. Philippines (founding), Am. Geophys. Union, Assn. Geologists for Internat. Devel., Soc. Econ. Geologists, Am. Inst. Profl. Geologists. Republican. Author: Mineral Resources, a World Review, 1984. Contbr. articles to profl. jours. Home: care Taysan Copper Inc, MCCPO Box 1868, Makati Philippines Office: 6363 Richmond Ave Ste 210 Houston TX 77057

WOLFE, JOHN WALTON, investment banker; b. Columbus, Ohio, Sept. 4, 1928; s. Edgar T. and Alice (Alcorn) W.; m. Norina Vannucci, July 20, 1978; children by previous marriage—Ann M., Robert F., Victoria G., Douglas B. Student, Miami U., Oxford, Ohio, 1946-47. With Ohio Nat. Bank of Columbus, 1948-57; v.p. BancOhio Corp. (bank holding co.), Columbus, 1957-74, also dir.; chmn. bd. Ohio Co., Columbus, 1974—, also dir.; chmn. bd. Dispatch Printing Co., 1975—; chmn. Shepherd Hill Corp.; dir. RadiOhio Inc., AgLands, Brodhead Garrett Co., WBNS-TV Inc., VideoIndiana Inc., Ohio Equities Inc., Trylor-Woodcraft Inc. Trustee More Bus. for Columbus Inc.; pres. Wolfe Assos. Inc., charitable found., Columbus; sec.-treas. Columbus Capital Corp. for Civic Improvements; pres. Ohio Cancer Found.; chmn. Coalition for Cost Effective Health Services. Mem. Nat. Assn. Security Dealers. Clubs: Athletic of Columbus, Buckeye Lake Yacht, Columbus, Columbus Country, Columbus Maennerchor, Muirfield Village Golf, Nat. Press, Press of Columbus. Lodges: Masons, Shriners. Office: The Ohio Co 155 E Broad St Columbus OH 43215

WOLFE, KENNETH L., food products manufacturing company executive; b. 1939; married. B.A., Yale U., 1961; M.B.A., U. Pa., 1967. With Bankers Trust Corp., 1961-62; with Hershey Foods Corp., Pa., 1968—, asst. treas., 1968-70, budget dir., 1970-76, treas., 1976-80, v.p. fin. adminstrn. Hershey Chocolate Co., from 1980, v.p., chief fin. officer, 1981-84, sr. v.p., chief fin. officer, 1984-85, pres., chief operating officer, 1985—, also dir. Office: Hershey Foods Corp 100 Mansion Rd E PO Box 814 Hershey PA 17033 *

WOLFE, RAPHAEL DAVID, business executive; b. Toronto, Ont., Can., Aug. 3, 1917; s. Maurice and Tillie (Manovitz) W.; m. Rose Senderowitz; children—Jonathan, Elizabeth. B.A., U. Toronto, 1939; PhD (hon.), U. Haifa, Israel, 1988. Chmn., chief exec. officer Oshawa Group Ltd., Toronto, 1958—; pres. Can. Jewish News; hon. bd. dirs. Bank of Nova Scotia; bd. dirs. Confedn. Life Ins. Co., Food Mktg. Inst. Trustee Toronto Gen. Hosp. Found.; bd. govs. Mt. Sinai Hosp.; hon. pres., bd. dirs. Can. Friends Haita U.; bd. dirs. Can. Coun. Christins and Jews, Baycrest Ctr. for Geriatric Care, Coun. for Can. Unity. Served with RCAF, 1943-46. Decorated Order of Can., 1980—; recipient Human Rels. award Can. Coun. Christians and Jews, 1968; Ben Sadowski Award of Merit, 1975; named Can. Retailer of Yr., 1987. Mem. Can.-Israel C. of C. and Industry (hon. chmn.). Clubs: Montefiore, Oakdale, Primrose. Office: 302 The East Mall, Islington, ON Canada M9B 6B8

WOLFE, THEODORE JOSEPH, food company executive; b. Columbus, Ohio, Oct. 15, 1935; s. Luby Raymond and Mary Francis (Dooley) W.; m. Nancy Elin Kupper, Oct. 9, 1937. AB, U. Notre Dame, 1957; MS, Columbia U., 1958. Asst. brand mgr. Procter & Gamble Co., Cin., 1961-64, brand mgr., 1964-67; product mgr. Welch Foods, Inc., Westfield, N.Y., 1967, group product mgr., 1967-68, mgr. mktg., 1968-69, dir. mktg., 1969, v.p. mktg., 1969-77, sr. v.p. sales and mktg., 1977-79; exec. v.p. Welch Foods, Inc., Concord, Mass., 1979—, also bd. dirs. Chmn. United Appeal, Mt. Washington, Ohio, 1964. Served with U.S. Army, 1958-59. Mem. Internat. Jelly and Preserve Assn. (bd. dirs. 1980—, pres. 1982-84), Concord Grape Assn. (pres. 1978-80). Republican. Roman Catholic. Club: Nashawtuc Country (Concord).

WOLFENSON, AZI U., electrical, mechanical and industrial engineer, consultant; b. Rumania, Aug. 1, 1933; came to Peru, 1937; s. Samuel G. and Polea S. (Ulanowski) W.; m. Rebeca Sterental, Jan. 10, 1983; 1 child, Michael Ben; children by previous marriage—Ida, Jeannette, Ruth, Moises, Alex. Mech., Elec. Engr., Universidad Nacional de Ingenieria, Peru, 1955; M.Sc. in Indsl. Engring., U. Mich., 1966; Indsl. Engr., U. Nacional de Ingenieria, Peru, 1967; Ph.D. in Engring. Mgmt., Pacific Western U., 1983, Ph.D. in Engring. Energy, Century U., 1985, D in Philosophy of Engring. (hon.) World U. Roundtable, Ariz., 1987. Power engr. Peruvian Trading Co., 1956-57; gen. mgr. AMSA Ingenieros S.A., 1957-60; prof. Universidad Nacional de Ingenieria, Peru, 1956-72, dean mech. and elec. engring., 1964-66, dean indsl. engring., 1967-72; dir. SWSA Automotive Parts, Peru, 1954-77; project mgr. Nat. Fin. Corp., Cofide, 1971-73; Peruvian dir. Corporacion Andina de Fomento, CAF, 1971-73; rep. in Peru, CAF, 1973-74; pres. DESPRO cons. firm, 1973-76; exec. pres. Electroperu, 1976-80; cons. engr., 1964—; dir. Tech. Transference Studies, 1971-72. Mem. Superior Council Electricity, 1964-66; metal mech. expert for andean group, 1970-71; Nat. council Foreing Investment and Tech. Transfer, 1972-73; mem. Consultive Council Ministry Economy and Fin., 1973-74; pres. Peruvian Jewish Community, 1966-70, Peruvian Hebrew Sch., 1976-78; promoter, co-founder, gen. mgr. La Republica Newspaper, Peru, 1981; pres. PROA project promotion AG, Switzerland, 1982—; cofounder El Popular, 1983, El Nacional newspapers, 1985. Recipient awards Order Merit for Disting. Services, Peru, 1980, Disting. by City Council of Huancayo, 1980, Trujillo, 1978, Huaral, 1979, Piura, 1980, Disting. Contbn. award City of Lima, 1970, 71, Disting. Contbn. to Elec. Devel. in Peru, 1979; others; named 1979 Exec., Gente mag., recognition Israel Govt., 1967, Disting. Comision Integracion Electrica Regional, CIER, medal, 1984. Fellow Inst. Prodn. Engrs., Brit. Inst. Mgmt.; mem. Colegio Ingenieros Peru, Instituto Peruano de Ingenieros Mecanicos (pres. 1965-66, v.p. 1967, dir. 1969, 70, 76), Asociacion Electrotechnica del Peru, ASME, AIIE (sr.), MTM Assn., Am. Soc. Engring. Edn., Am. Inst. Mgmt. Sci., AAAS, Assn. Mgmt. Sci. (dir. 1968), Asociacion Peruana Avance Ciencia, Inst. Adminstrv. Mgmt., British Inst. Mgmt., Am. Nuclear Soc. (vice chmn. Swiss sect. 1988), Alumni Assn. of the Mich., Pacific Western and Century U., United Writers Assn., Swiss Soc. Writers, others. Author: Work Communications, 1966, Programmed Learning, 1966, Production Planning and Control, 1968, Transfer of Technology, 1971, National Electrical Development, 1977, Energy and Development, 1979, El Gran Desafio, 1981, Hacia una politica economica alternativa, 1982, The Power of Communications: The Media, 1987. Contbr. articles to newspapers and jours. Clubs: Club der 200, FCL, Hebraica. Home: Haldenstrasse 24, 6006 Lucerne Switzerland

WOLFF, BRIAN RICHARD, metal manufacturing company executive; b. L.A., Dec. 11, 1955; s. Arthur Richard and Dorothy Virginia (Johnson) W.; m. Sue Patricia Sargent, Oct. 1, 1983; children: Ashley Rachael, Taryn Nicole. BSBA, Calif. State U., Chico, 1980. Sales rep. Federated Metals Corp./ASARCO, Long Beach, Calif., 1980-82, dist. sales mgr., 1983-84; sales mgr. Copper Alloys Corp., Beverly Hills, Calif., 1982-83; dir. mktg. Federarted-Fry Metals/Cookson, Long Beach, Industry and Paramount, Calif., 1984-87; regional sales mgr. Colonial Metals Co., L.A., 1987—; cons. tech. sales GSP Metals & Chems. Co., 1987; cons. sales Calif. Metal Exch., L.A., 1987—. Mem. citizens adv. com. on bus. Calif. Legis., 1983. Mem. Non Ferrous Founders Soc., Am. Foundrymen Soc., Am. Electroplaters Soc., Metal Finishers Soc., Calif. Cir. Assn. Republican. Presbyterian. Office: Colonial Metals Co 1960 E 48th St Los Angeles CA 90058

WOLFF, IVAN LAWRENCE, venture capitalist; b. Bklyn., Oct. 9, 1944; s. Zachary Henry and Gertrude (Abramowitz) W.; m. Susan R. Joseph, June 18, 1967; 1 child, Adam Gregory. B.A., Cornell U., 1966; M.B.A. with distinction, Harvard U., 1968. Cert. fin. analyst. Mktg. mgr. Hughes Aircraft Co., Culver City, Calif., 1968-74; mktg. mgr. M-A Com, Burlington, Mass., 1974-76; div. mgr. customer strategy AT&T, Basking Ridge, N.J., 1976-81; v.p., securities analyst Donaldson, Lufkin, & Jenrette, N.Y.C., 1981-84; sr. v.p., prin. Rothschild, Inc. (Rothschild Venture), N.Y.C., 1984-87, mng. dir., 1987—; dir. Doelz Networks, Inc., Irvine, Calif., Shared Communications Services, N.Y.C., Telenova, Inc., Los Gatos, Calif., Ironics,

Inc., Ithaca, N.Y., Integrated Network, Bridgewater, N.J., Applitek, Inc., Wakefield, Mass., Mosaic Systems, Troy, Mich. Pres. Cornell Alumni Class, Ithaca, 1981, v.p., 1986—; bd. dirs. Smugglers' Notch Condominium Assn., Jeffersonville, Vt., 1982-85. Mem. Inst. Cert. Fin. Analysts. Republican. Office: Rothschild Inc 1 Rockefeller Pla New York NY 10020

WOLFF, ROBERT CHARLES, real estate executive; b. Oak Park, Ill., Oct. 3, 1952; s. Louis Julius and LaVerne (Nerud) W.; m. Debra Lee Chiamonte, May 20, 1977 (div. 1982); 1 child, Dustin; m. Karen Joy Johnston, May 21, 1988. Student, U. Md., 1971-73, Met. State Coll., Denver, 1975. Lic. real estate broker, Colo.; cert. residential specialist. Real estate sales rep., mgr. Moore & Co., Ft. Collins, Colo., 1975-82; broker assoc., ptnr. The Group Inc., Ft. Collins, 1982-87; prin. Bob Wolff Real Estate Co., Ft. Collins, 1987—; speaker in field. Contbr. articles to profl. jours. Treas. Larimer County Jr. Achievement, 1981-82, bd. dirs.; mem. mktg. adv. com. Light and Power Utility, City of Ft. Colllins. Named Outstanding Young Man Am., 1986; recipient Disting. Guest Lectr. award, Temple U., 1987. Mem. Realtors Nat. Mktg. Inst. (sr. instr. 1980—, numerous coms.), Ft. Collins Bd. Realtors (numerous coms., Realtor Yr. award 1982), Colo. Assn. Realtors (numerous coms.), Nat. Assn. Realtors (numerous coms.). Republican. Roman Catholic. Home: 1318 Calabasas Ct Fort Collins CO 80525 Office: Bob Wolff Real Estate 375 E Horsetooth Shores 6 Ste 201 Fort Collins CO 80525

WOLFORD, ROY, JR., publishing executive; b. Majestic, Ky., Sept. 6, 1946; s. Roy Sr. and Edith (Daugherty) W.; m. Judy Karen Wunder, June 19, 1969; children: Christopher Paul, Alexander Dean. Student, Eastern Ky. U., 1967. Auditor Dispatch Printing Co., Columbus, Ohio, 1969-79; bus. mgr. Ohio Mag., Inc., Columbus, Ohio, 1979—. Bd. dirs. YMCA, Columbus, 1984—. Served with U.S. Army, 1967-69, Vietnam. Mem. Audit Bur. Circulations, City-Regional Mag. Assn., Regional Pub. Assn., Mag. Pub. Assn. Republican. Presbyterian. Home: 1379 Birchwood Dr Columbus OH 43228 Office: Ohio Mag Inc 40 S Third St Columbus OH 43215

WOLFRAM, STEPHEN, physicist, computer company executive; b. London, Aug. 29, 1959; came to U.S., 1978; Degree, Eton Coll., 1976, Oxford U., 1978; PhD in Theoretical Physics, Calif. Inst. Tech., 1979. With Calif. Inst. Tech., Pasadena, 1979-82, Inst. for Advanced Study, Princeton, N.J., 1983-86; prof. physics, math, computer sci. U. Ill., Champaign, 1986—; pres., chief exec. office Wolfram Rsch. Inc., Champaign, 1987—. Author: Mathematica, 1988, Theory and Applications of Cellular Automata, 1986; editor jour. Complex Systems, 1987—. Fellow MacArthur Found., 1981. Office: Wolfram Rsch Inc PO Box 6059 Champaign IL 61826

WOLFSON, CONRAD, journalist; b. N.Y.C., Feb. 12, 1924; s. Harry Charles and Lillie (Grossman) W.; m. Eva Goldman, Sept. 9, 1951; children: Shoshanah Gertrude, Helen Anne. Bus. reporter N.Y. Times, 1947-48; reporter Harrisburg (Pa.) Evening News, 1950-51, The Jersey Jour., Jersey City, 1955-61; editor LI Star Jour., 1961-67, The Jersey Jour., Jersey City, 1967—. Mem. Am. Newspaper Guild, N.Y. Press Club, New Jersey Press Club. Democrat. Jewish. Office: The Jersey Jour 30 Journal Sq Jersey City NJ 07306

WOLFSON, DENNIS MEYER, real estate investor and broker; b. Jacksonville, Fla., Apr. 22, 1941; s. Samuel William W.; m. Arlene Weissman, June 29, 1967. BBA, U. Ga., 1963. Asst. v.p. Indsl. Fin. Corp., Boston, 1964-67; v.p. real estate Universal Marion Corp., Jacksonville, 1967-70; v.p. to sr. v.p. Daylight Industries, Inc., Jacksonville, 1970-87, also bd. dirs.; owner, mgr. Dennis M. Wolfson Real Estate, Jacksonville, 1987—; Trustee Wolfson Family Found., Inc., Jacksonville. Trustee Joslin Diabetes Ctr., Boston, Jacksonville Jewish Community Alliance. Mem. Am. Numismatic Assn., Am. Numismatic Soc., Sawgrass County Club. Republican. Office: 2853 Dawn Rd Jacksonville FL 32207

WOLFSON, GARY MAREMONT, executive search company executive; b. Chgo., June 27, 1950; s. J. Theodore and Natalie B. (Brandwein) W.; m. Linda Mark, Nov. 5, 1978; children: Jeffrey Mark, Kevin Mathew. BBA, U. Denver, 1972. Dir. mktg. Bus. Builders Internat., Chgo., 1973-78; v.p. Sales and Mgmt. Search, Chgo., 1978-80; pres. The Search Group, Inc., Northfield, Ill., 1980-87; dir. exec. search Blackman, Kallick & Bartelstein, Northfield, 1987—; cons., bd. dirs. Career Link Corp., Chgo., 1982-83. Vice chmn. jr. bd. Michael Reese Hosp., Chgo., 1976-77; chmn. jr. bd. Highland Park (Ill.) Hosp., 1986—. Mem. Nat. Assn. Personnel Cons. Republican. Office: Black Kallick Bartlestein 300 S Riverside Plaza Suite 660 Chicago IL 60606

WOLFSON, NEAL GERALD, investment company executive; b. Boston, May 4, 1960; s. S. Kenneth and Elinor Miriam (Godes) W. BA, Boston U., 1983. Campaign field coord., press sec. to Rep. Edward Markey, U.S. Ho. of Reps., Bostn, 1984-86; domestic polity advisor U.S. Ho. of Reps., Washington, 1986; v.p. Internat. Bus. Group, Boston, 1987—; pub. rels. cons. Promo Internat., Cambridge, Mass., 1987; co-founder Internat.a Trading House Dubai, United Arab Emirates. Avocations: writing, boating, travel. Office: Internat Bus Group 124 Mt Auburn St Cambridge MA 02138

WOLFUS, DANIEL EDWARD, savings and loan executive; b. Buenos Aires, Mar. 3, 1946; came to U.S., 1957; naturalized, 1962; s. Jack and Joanne Ida (Shapiro) W.; m. Christine Mary Marshall, Aug. 27, 1967; children: Staphanie Melissa, Devoney Elizabeth. BA, UCLA, 1967, MBA, 1969. Research analyst Econ. Research Assocs., Los Angeles, 1968-69; corp. fin. assoc. E.F. Hutton & Co., Inc., Los Angeles, 1969-71, asst. v.p., 1971-73, v.p., 1974-78, 1st v.p., 1979-81, sr. v.p., 1981-82; chmn. bd., pres. Hancock Savs. and Loan Assn., Los Angeles, 1982—; bd. dirs. Calif. League Savs. Instns.; vice chmn. Yosemite Fund; trustee Yosemite Assn. Bd. mgrs. Wilshire YMCA. Home: 423 S Las Palmas St Los Angeles CA 90020 Office: 3550 Wilshire Blvd Los Angeles CA 90010

WOLINSKY, DAVID, metal processing company executive. Exec. v.p. Metall. Inc., N.Y.C. Office: Metall Inc 25 E 39th St New York NY 10016 *

WOLITARSKY, JAMES WILLIAM, securities industry executive; b. Tarrytown, N.Y., Feb. 19, 1946; s. Edward and Beulah (Kemmet) W.; m. Margaret Ann Gaffney, Sept. 5, 1970; children: James Jr., Matthew. BA, Franklin & Marshall Coll., 1968; MBA, NYU, 1973. Auditor Hertz, Herson & Co., N.Y.C., 1970-73; comml. loan officer The Phila. Nat. Bank, 1973-76; chief fin. officer Almo Electronics Corp., Phila., 1976-80; dir. budget and control Paine Webber Inc., N.Y.C., 1981-82, dir. mktg. adminstrn., 1982-83, dir. mut. funds and asset mgmt., 1983-84; sr. v.p., dir. product mgmt. Phila. Nat. Bank, 1984-86; exec. v.p., chief fin. officer The Moseley Holding Corp., N.Y.C., 1986-87; pres., chief exec. officer Moseley Securities Corp., N.Y.C., 1987-88; exec. v.p. Gruntal Fin. Corp., N.Y.C., 1988—. Served to sgt. U.S. Army, 1966-70, Vietnam. Decorated Bronze Star, Vietnam Cross of Gallantry. Mem. Securities Industry Assn. Episcopalian. Club: Phila. Racquet. Home: 978 Ivycroft Rd Wayne PA 19087 Office: Gruntal Fin Corp 14 Wall St New York NY 10005

WOLK, ALAN SCOTT, chemical company executive; b. Phila., Mar. 20, 1957; s. Arthur Isadore and Doris Winifred (Moonshine) W.; m. Roni Susan Resnick, Nov. 11, 1979; 1 child, Jordan Lee. Student, LaSalle U., 1974-76; BBA, Temple U., 1978, MBA, 1979. Fin. analyst E.I. DuPont De Nemours and Co., Wilmington, Del., 1979-80, tax analyst, 1980-81, tax analyst-studies, 1981-83, supr. fed. tax, 1983-85; dir. refined products acctg. Conoco, Inc. subs. E.I. DuPont De Nemours and Co., Ponca City, Okla., 1985-87; sr. fin. cons. internat. fin. E.I. DuPont De Nemours and Co., Wilmington, Del., 1987-88, mgr. bus. and fin. analysis med. products dept., 1988—; instr. fin. Wilmington Coll., 1981-85. V.p. Beacon Hill Condominium Assn., Wilmington, 1981-83, Temple Emanuel, Ponca City, 1986.

WOLK, YALE M., health care executive; b. Mpls., Apr. 11, 1945; s. Arnold D. and Marcia (Moorvitz) W.; m. Roberta Lynn Goldman, Mar. 4, 1967; children: Sonya, Erin. BA, Mich. State U., 1966; MHA, U. Minn., 1971. Adminstrv. asst. Dekalb Gen. Hosp., Smithville, Tenn., 1971-73; asst. adminstr. Saginaw Osteo. Hosp., Mich., 1973; asst. adminstr. Community Hosp. Ottawa, Ill., 1973-74, chief exec. officer, pres., 1974-89, N. Cen. Svc. Corp., Ottawa, 1984-89 ; dir. Community Hosp. Ottawa, N. Cen. Svc. Corp.; chief exec. officer, Thorek Hosp. and Med. Ctr., Chgo., 1989—. mem. coun. on pub. rels. Ill. Hosp. Assn., Naperville, 1984-89 . Advisor: A Guide to Stategic Planning for Hospitals, 1979. Bd. dirs., sec., treas. Camp Fire Coun., Ottawa, 1980-83; bd. dirs. LaSalle County Coun. on Alcoholism, Ottawa, 1982-89 ; task force mem. LaSalle County State Atty., Ottawa, 1984. 1st lt. U.S. Army, 1967-69. Named Outstanding Young Person Ottawa Jaycees, 1979. Mem. Am. Coll. Healthcare Execs., Minn. Program Alumni Assn., C. of C. (bd. dirs. 1984-89). Rotary. Avocations: handball, racketball, golf, cycling. Office: Thorek Hosp and Med Ctr 850 W Irving Park Rd Chicago IL 60613

WOLKOWSKI, LESZEK AUGUST, marketing specialist; b. Wilno, Poland, Jan. 14, 1941; s. John and Halina Teresa (Wankowicz) W.; m. Barbara M. Szlachcic, Mar. 22, 1968 (div.); 1 child, Grazyna Grace; m. 2d, Rosita Perez, June 16, 1981 (div.); m. 3d, Anna Krol, June 10, 1982 (div.); 1 child, Leszek August; m. 4th, Grace Baginski, July 3, 1986 (div.). Baccalaureate, Lycee Polonais de Paris, 1961; student, Cen. Sch. Econs., Warsaw, Poland, 1961-62, U. Warsaw, 1962-65, U. Paris, 1965-67; BA with honors, U. Ill., 1969; MA, Loyola U., Chgo., 1975; PhD in Comparative Internat. Edn. and Psychology, Loyola U., 1979. Instr. modern langs. Loyola U., Chgo., 1969-71; tchr. Notre Dame High Sch., Niles, Ill., 1971-76; instr. Skokie (Ill.) Coll., 1971-79; tchr. modern langs. and debate Adlai Stevenson High Sch., Lincolnshire, Ill., 1976-78; instr. English Roper IBG Corp., Wheeling, Ill., 1977-78; ins. agt. Mass. Life Ins. Co., Chgo., 1978; real estate broker Gen. Devel. Corp., Chgo., 1978; dist. mktg. dir. U.S. C. of C., Oak Brook, Ill., 1979—; dir. Poland-Austria Program, 1975, German Exchange Program, 1977. Producer Am. debut of singer Waldemar Kocon, Chgo., 1984. Recipient awards for effective mktg., 1980, 81, 82, Million Dollar Mktg. award, 1987. Mem. Polish-Am. Educators Assn., Loyola U. Chgo. Alumni Assn., Phi Delta Kappa. Office: US C of C 2000 Spring Rd Ste 600 Oak Brook IL 60521

WOLLARD, LESLIE ANN, accountant; b. Flint, Mich., Sept. 2, 1946; d. Therold Benjamin and Joyce Ellen (Clemens) Miller; m. Gary Lee Wollard, 1975; children: Christopher James, Adam Benjamin. AB, Mott Community Coll., 1967; BBA, U. Mich., 1986. Staff acct. Millhouse & Holaly, CPA's, Flint, 1967-70; acct. office mgr. T.S. Jenkins Advt., Flint, 1970-73; v.p., mgr. media Dallas C. Dort Advt., Flint, 1973-75; staff acct. Rachor & Pyper, CPA's, Flint, 1975-76; contr., office mgr. Cen. Mich. Petroleum, Flint, 1976-83, Flint Ceiling & Partition, 1983-84; contr., mgr. Kerton Indsl. Ctr., Holly, Mich., 1984-86; contr., adminstrv. supr. Genesee Psychiat. Ctr., Flint, 1986-87; contr. Pomco Assocs., Palmetto, Fla., 1987—. Recipient Wall St. Jour. award, 1987, U. Mich. Bus. Club award, 1987. Mem. U. Mich. Alumni, Manatee County Assn. for the Learning Disabled, Palma Sola Bay Yacht Club (Bradenton, Fla.).

WOLLENBERG, RICHARD PETER, paper manufacturing company executive; b. Juneau, Alaska, Aug. 1, 1915; s. Harry L. and Gertrude (Arnstein) W.; m. Leone Bonney, Dec. 22, 1940; children: Kenneth Roger, David Arthur, Keith Kermit, Richard Harry, Carol Lynne. BS in Mech. Engring, U. Calif.-Berkeley, 1936; MBA, Harvard U., 1938; grad., Army Indsl. Coll., 1941; D in Pub. Affairs (hon.), U. Puget Sound, 1977. Prodn. control Bethlehem Ship, Quincy, Mass., 1938-39; with Longview (Wash.) Fibre Co., 1939—, safety engr., asst. chief engr., chief engr., mgr. container operations, 1951-57, v.p., 1953-57, v.p. ops., 1957-60, exec. v.p., 1960-69, pres., 1969-78, pres., chief exec. officer, 1978-85, pres., chief exec. officer, chmn. bd., 1985—, also bd. dirs.; mem. Wash. State Council for Postsecondary Edn., 1969-79, chmn., 1970-73; mem. western adv. bd. Allendale Ins. Bassoonist SW Washington Symphony. Chmn. bd. trustees Reed Coll., Portland. Served to lt. col. USAAF, 1941-45. Mem. NAM (bd. dirs. 1981-86), Pacific Assn. Pulp and Paper Mfrs. (pres. 1982—), Inst. Paper Chemistry (trustee), Wash. State Roundtable. Home: 1632 Kessler Blvd Longview WA 98632 Office: Longview Fibre Co PO Box 606 Longview WA 98632

WOLLERT, GERALD DALE, food company executive; b. LaPorte, Ind., Jan. 21, 1935; s. Delmar Everette and Esther Mae W.; m. Carol Jean Burchby, Jan. 26, 1957; children—Karen Lynn, Edwin Del. B.S., Purdue U., 1957. With Gen. Foods Corp., 1959—; dir. consumer affairs Gen. Foods Corp., White Plains, N.Y., 1973-74; mng. dir. Cottee Foods div. Gen. Foods Corp., Sydney, Australia, 1974-76; gen. mgr. Mexico div. Gen. Foods Corp., Mexico City, 1978-79; pres. Asia/Pacific ops. Gen. Foods Corp., Honolulu, corp. v.p. worldwide coffee and internat. div., 1979—; dir. Gen. Foods cos., Japan, Peoples Republic China, Korea, India, Taiwan, Singapore, Philippines. Webelos leader Boy Scouts Am., Mexico City, 1978-79; co. gen. chmn. United Fund campaign, Battle Creek, Mich., 1964-65, White Plains, N.Y., 1972-73. Served with U.S. Army, 1958. Mem. Asian-U.S. Bus. Council. Club: Oahu (Hawaii) Country. Office: Gen Foods Corp 615 Piikoi St Honolulu HI 96814

WOLPER, MARSHALL, financial consultant; b. Chgo., Nov. 19, 1922; s. Harry B. and Bessie (Steiner) W.; m. Thelma R. Freedman, April 15, 1957 (div. Oct. 1968); m. Jacqueline N. Miller, Sept. 19, 1969 (div. Jan. 1976); m. Lucee I. G. Lee, Mar. 20, 1985; stepchildren—Robert Insinga, Cyndi Insinga Wolper. B.A. in Polit. Sci. and Econs., U. Ill., 1942. Chartered fin. cons. With Kent Products, Chgo., 1946; pres. Marshall Industries, Chgo., 1947-52; with Equitable Life Assurance Soc., 1953—, nat. honor agt., 1966, nat. sales cons., 1967—; sr. partner Wolper & Katz, 1958—; partner Wolper and Katz Thoroughbred Racing Stable, 1977-82; instr. life underwriting and pensions U. Miami, 1959—; pres. Marshall Wolper Co., 1963—; chmn. bd. M.W. Computer Systems, Inc., 1971-80; pres. Marshall Wolper Pension Sers. Inc., 1978-80, Wolper, Ross & Co., 1980—; lectr. life ins., employee benefit plans, pensions, estate planning to various univs. and spl. meetings; pres. Greater Miami Tax Inst., 1963, Estate Planning Council Greater Miami, 1969-70; faculty Practicing Law Inst., 1967—; mem. adv. com., lectr. Inst. on Estate Planning. Author: Medical Entities Taxed as Corporations, 1961, Tax and Business Aspects of Professional Corporations and Associations, 1968; contbr. articles to profl. jours. Bd. dirs. Dade County chpt. ARC, Profl. Selling Inst. Served to 1st lt. AUS, World War II, ETO. Decorated Bronze Star, Purple Heart; recipient Paragon award Equitable Life Assurance Soc., 1972; C.L.U. Mem. Am. Soc. C.L.U.s (pres. Miami chpt. 1963, inst. faculty 1963-65, dir. 1966-67, regional v.p. 1968), The Am. Coll. (joint com. on continuing edn. 1965—), Nat. Assn. Life Underwriters (lectr. 1963, 66, 81), Million Dollar Round Table (life mem., speaker 1962-81, exec. com. 1974-78, pres. 1977), Assn. Advanced Life Underwriting (lectr. 1966, pres. 1972), Am. Soc. Pension Actuaries (dir.), Nat. Assn. Pension Consultants and Adminstrs. (treas.). Home: 714 W DiLido Dr Miami Beach FL 33139 Office: 1570 Madruga Ave Coral Gables FL 33146 also: 555 Madison Ave New York NY 10022

WOLSON, CRAIG ALAN, lawyer; b. Toledo, Feb. 20, 1949; s. Max A. and Elaine B. (Cohn) W.; m. Janis Nan Braun, July 30, 1972 (div. Mar. 1986); m. Ellen Carol Schulgasser, Oct. 26, 1986. BA, U. Mich., 1971, JD, 1974. Bar: N.Y. 1975, U.S. Dist. Ct. (so. and ea. dists.) N.Y. 1975, U.S. Ct. Appeals (2d cir.) 1975, U.S. Supreme Ct. 1978. Assoc. Shearman & Sterling, N.Y.C., 1974-81; v.p., asst. gen. counsel Thomson McKinnon Securities Inc., N.Y.C., 1981-85; v.p., sec., gen. counsel J.D. Mattus Co., Inc., Greenwich, Conn., 1985-88; also bd. dirs. J.D. Mattus Co., Inc., Greenwich; v.p., asst. gen. counsel Chem. Bank, N.Y.C., 1988—; dep. clk. Lucas County Courthouse, Toledo, 1968-69, 71-72. Articles and adminstrv. editor U. Mich. Law Rev., 1973-74. Mem. ABA, N.Y. State Bar Assn., Assn. of Bar of City of N.Y., Westchester-Fairfield Corp. Coun. Assn., Phi Beta Kappa, Phi Eta Sigma, Pi Sigma Alpha. Home: 13 Dingletown Rd Greenwich CT 06830 Office: Chem Bank 380 Madison Ave New York NY 10017

WOLTER, DUANE ROLAND, retail executive; b. Milw., July 18, 1948; s. Roland Arthur and Haroldean (Tegge) W.; m. Gail M. Kieckhefer (div. 1980); m. Margaret Shelton, June 27, 1981; children: Sean Zachary, Megan Meinhart. BS in Bus. Adminstrn., Marquette U., 1971. CPA. Staff auditor Arthur Andersen and Co., Milw., 1971-72, sr. auditor, 1972-74, audit mgr., 1974-76; dir. acctg. May Dept. Stores Inc., St. Louis, 1976-78, dir. planning Venture Stores div., 1978-79; v.p., corp. controller H.J. Wilson Co. Inc., Baton Rouge, 1979-84; v.p. fin. Home Depot Inc., Atlanta, 1984-86; sr. v.p., chief fin. officer McCrory Stores, York, Pa., 1986-87; exec. v.p., chief fin. officer Ames Dept. Stores Inc., Hartford, Conn., 1987—; adv. bd. dirs. Conn. Nat. Bank, Hartford, 1987—. Sgt. USAR, 1966-72. Mem. Am. Inst. CPA's, Fin. Execs. Inst., Wis. Soc. CPA's, Conn. Soc. CPA's. Roman Catholic. Office: Ames Dept Stores Inc 2418 Main St Rocky Hill CT 06067

WOMACK, RICHARD MARVIN, manufacturing company executive; b. New Orleans, Jan. 21, 1936; s. David Ray and Amoret Donelson (Gates) W.; m. Eva Robuck, June 8, 1957; children: Ray (dec.), Mike, Deanna. B.S. in Engring., U. Tex.- U.-Austin, 1957, M.B.A., 1959. Mgr. bar soap and household cleaning products div. Procter & Gamble Co., Cin., 1978-79, v.p. U.S. mfg., 1980-81, v.p. engring., 1982-84, v.p. purchases, 1985-86, v.p. purchases and quality, 1987—. Bd. dirs. Jr. Achievement, Inc., Denver, 1979—; bd. dirs. Jobs for Cin. Grads., 1982—, Nat. Minority Supply Devel. Council, 1986—. Recipient Neil H. McElroy award Community Chest of Greater Cin., 1983. Episcopalian. Club: Queen City (Cin.). Office: Procter & Gamble Co One Procter & Gamble Plaza Cincinnati OH 45202

WONG, ANDREW HEI-MING, manufacturing and laboratory manager; b. Hong Kong, Mar. 24, 1950; came to U.S., 1971.; s. Alex Wen-An and Shirley S. (Chen) Huang; m. Florence Nip, June 1, 1973; children: Wesley S., Jennifer S. BS in Chemistry, McGill U., 1971; MS in Phys. Chemistry, U. Calif., Berkeley, 1974, MSChemE, 1974; MBA, Coll. St. Thomas, St. Paul, 1980. With 3M Co., St. Paul, 1974—, lab mgr. indsl. optics div., 1986—, mfg. mgr. indsl. optics div., 1987-89, bus. unit mgr. optical systems, 1989—. Inventor in field. J.W. McConnel scholar, 1969-71, Nat. Research Council Scholar, 1971. Home: 7885 Somerset Ct Woodbury MN 55125 Office: 3M Co 3M Ctr 235 2D 15 Saint Paul MN 55144

WONG, BENJAMIN WINGNIN, finance executive; b. Hong Kong, June 20, 1949; came to U.S., 1970; s. Ding Lun and Ling Sik (Lui) W.; m. Cecilia Y. Wong, Mar. 22, 1974; children: Vivian, Christopher. BS with high honors, U. Wis., Stevens Point, 1973; MBA with distinction, Northwestern U., 1974. Fin. analyst Chemed Corp., Cin., 1974-76, mgr. fgn. exchange, 1976-78, asst. treas., 1978-87; chmn., pres. New Asia Bank, Chgo., 1987—. Recipient Disting. Scholar award Northwestern U., 1974. Mem. Assn. MBA Execs. Club: Bankers. Home: 1232 Redcliffe Woodridge IL 60517 Office: New Asia Bank 222 W Cermak Chicago IL 60616

WONG, CHIN WAH, quantity surveyor; b. Singapore, Mar. 4, 1954; s. Joon Kai and Jee Lan (Kam) W.; m. Edna Teo Beng Kuan, Oct. 28, 1986. BS in Bldg. with honors, U. Singapore, 1979. Contracts officer Jurong Town Corp., Singapore, 1979-85, exec. contracts officer, 1985—; quantity surveyor Mass Rapid Transit Corp., Singapore, 1985-88. Served to lt. arty. Singapore Armed Forces, 1972-75. Mem. Singapore Inst. Surveyors and Valuers (Gold Medal 1979). Club: Jurong Country. Home: 10 Lakepoint Dr, Apt #12-49, Singapore 2264, Singapore Office: Jurong Town Corp, Singapore Singapore

WONG, DESMOND C., corporate finance director; b. Oct. 4, 1950; s. W.S. Wong and Y.M. Law. BS with distinction, Ind. U., 1973; MBA, Harvard U., 1977. CPA, Ill. Staff auditor Peat, Marwick, Mitchell & Co., Chgo., 1973-75, audit supr., 1977-79, sr. cons., 1980-81, mgmt. cons. mgr., 1981-82; mgr. corp. fin. Sears, Roebuck & Co., Chgo., 1983-84, dir. corp. fin., 1985-86, corp. dir. fin., 1986—; bd. dirs. Sears Investment Mgmt. Co., Chgo. Mem. treasury dept. task force Pres.'s pvt. sector Survey on Cost Control, Washington, 1982; pres. Harvard Bus. Sch. Club, Chgo., 1984-85; bd. dirs. Mid Am. chpt. ARC, Chgo., 1985—, treas., 1988, Ind. U. Alumni Club, 1986—. Mem. AICPA, Ill. Soc. CPA's, Ind. U. Alumni Assn. (exec. coun. 1982-85), Harvard Bus. Sch. Assn. (alumni coun. 1988—), Ind. U. Sch. Bus. Alumni Assn. (bd. dirs. bus. 1986—), Beta Gamma Sigma, Phi Eta Sigma, Beta Alpha Psi, Delta Sigma Pi, Blue Key, Met. Club, Harvard Club. Office: Sears Roebuck & Co Sears Tower BSC 34-36 Chicago IL 60684

WONG, JAMES BOK, economist, engineer, technologist; b. Canton, China, Dec. 9, 1922; came to U.S., 1938, naturalized, 1962; s. Gen Ham and Chen (Yee) W.; m. Wai Ping Lim, Aug. 3, 1946; children: John, Jane Doris, Julia Ann. BS in Agr., U. Md., 1949, BS in Chem. Engring., 1950; MS, U. Ill., 1951, PhD, 1954. Research asst. U. Ill., Champaign-Urbana, 1950-53; chem. engr. Standard Oil of Ind., Whiting, 1953-55; process design engr., research engr. Shell Devel. Co., Emeryville, Calif., 1955-61; sr. planning engr., prin. planning engr. Chem. Plastics Group, Dart Industries, Inc. (formerly Rexall Drug & Chem. Co.), Los Angeles, 1961-66, supr. planning and econs., 1966-67, mgr. long range planning and econs., 1967, chief economist, 1967-72, dir. econs. and ops. analysis, 1972-78, dir. internat. techs., 1978-81; pres. James B. Wong Assocs., Los Angeles, 1981—; chmn. bd. dirs. United Pacific Bank, 1988—; tech. cons. various corps. Contbr. articles to profl. jours. Bd. dirs., pres. Chinese Am. Citizens Alliance Found.; mem. Asian Am. Edn. Commn., 1971-81. Served with USAAF, 1943-46. Recipient Los Angeles Outstanding Vol. Service award, 1977. Mem. Am. Inst. Chem. Engrs., Am. Chem. Soc., VFW (vice comdr. 1959), Commodores (named to exec. order 1982), Sigma Xi, Tau Beta Pi, Phi Kappa Phi, Pi Mu Epsilon, Phi Lambda Upsilon, Phi Eta Sigma. Home: 2460 Venus Dr Los Angeles CA 90046

WONG, KENT CHI, contract administrator; b. N.Y.C., Jan. 31, 1959; s. Hem Gat and Rosemary (Lee) W.; m. Bessie Lau, Sept. 6, 1986. BSBA in Fin. and Mktg., Boston U., 1981. Contract asst. Raytheon Co., Lexington, Mass., 1981-83; contract specialist Raytheon Co., Andover, Mass., 1983-85; contract adminstr. Gen. Electric Co., Lynn, Mass., 1985; sr. contract adminstr. Gen. Electric Co., 1985-86, Raytheon Co., Bedford, Mass., 1986-87; prodn. group mgr. Raytheon Co., Andover, 1988. Recipient of Air Def. award (hon.), U.S. Army (1987), Artillery Soldier, Artillery Ctr. & Sch. Office: Raytheon Co 350 Lowell St AN2-D04 Andover MA 01810

WONG, THOMAS C., JR., bank executive; b. Canton, People's Republic China, Apr. 4, 1948; came to U.S., 1963; s. Thomas C. and Tue-yeen W.; m. Karen Lee Champlin, Aug. 19, 1973; children: Erika, Laura. BA, U. Redlands, 1973; M in Internat. Mgmt., Am. Grad. Sch. Internat. Mgmt., 1973. Asst. v.p. N.C. Nat. Bank, Charlotte, 1974-78; chief fin. officer The Slosman Corp., Ashville, N.C., 1978-79; asst. v.p. Hamilton Bank, Lancaster, Pa., 1979-81; v.p. and mgr. internat. div. Dominion Bank Shares Corp., Roanoke, Va., 1981—; mem. Va. Dist. Export Council, 1988—. Mem. Internat. Trade Assn. Western Va. (pres. 1988—). Office: Dominion Bankshares Corp 213 S Jefferson St Roanoke VA 24040

WOO, VERNON YING-TSAI, lawyer, real estate developer; b. Honolulu, Aug. 7, 1942; s. William Shu-Bin and Hilda Woo; m. Arlene Gay Ischar, Feb. 14, 1971; children: Christopher Shu-Bin, Lia Gay. BA, U. Hawaii, 1964, MA, 1966; JD, Harvard U., 1969. Pres. Woo Kessner Duca & Maki, Honolulu, 1972-87; pvt. practice law Honolulu, 1987—; judge per diem Honolulu Dist. Ct., 1978-84. Bd. dirs. Boys and Girls Club of Honolulu, 1985—, pres. 1989; counsel Hawaii Med. Assn., 1988—. Mem. ABA, Hawaii Bar Assn., Honolulu Bd. Realtors, Waikiki Yacht Club (judge advocate 1987—), Pacific Club. Home: 2070 Kalawahine Pl Honolulu HI 96822 Office: 1019 Waimanu St Ste 205 Honolulu HI 96814

WOOD, CHARLES EUGENE, manufacturing company executive; b. Rockford, Ohio, May 9, 1936; s. Carl E. and Viola M. (Beldon) W.; m. Marlene L. Senger, July 18, 1954; hcildren: Sandy, Tom, Jim, Steve. BS, Findlay Coll., 1959; MBA in Mgmt., Bowling Green State U., 1985. Systems analyst Coopers Tire & Rubber Co., Findlay, 1959-64; systems and audit mgr. Coopers Tire & Rubber Co., 1964-66, systems mgr., 1966-69, dir. data processing, 1969-84, v.p. info. systems, 1984—. Mem. Assn. for System Mgmt., Computer Mgmt. Assn. (pres. 1979-80, bd. dirs. 1980-81), Hancock Inventors Club (Findlay, pres.), United States Power Squadron (Fostoria, Ohio, treas.), Elks. Home: 2016 Washington Ave Findlay OH 45840 Office: Cooper Tires & Rubber Co Lima and Western Aves Findlay OH 45840

WOOD, DONALD W., chemical company executive; b. Toledo, June 14, 1925; s. Eldred K. and Alma L. (Rutchow) W.; m. Karin M. Von Owstein, Jan. 22, 1966; children: Gregory, Claudia, Nicola, Julia. PhD, U. Ill., 1952. V.p. Exxon Chems. Europe, Brussels, 1963-72, Exxon Chem. USA, Houston, 1972-78; pres. Oxirane Corp., London, 1978-81; sr. v.p. Arco Chems. Co., Phila., 1981-87; pres. Arco Chem. Asia-Pacific, Hong Kong, 1988—; bd. dirs. Arco Chems. Co., Inroads of Phila. Bd. dirs. Netherlands-Am. Amity Trust, Washington, 1985-88, Pa. Opera Theater, Phila., 1984—, Phila. World Affairs Council, 1983—. Sgt. U.S. Army, 1943-46, ETO. Mem. Phila. Union League, Merion (Pa.) Cricket Club. Home: 500 Hillbrook Rd Bryn

Mawr PA 19010 Office: Arco Chem Co 3801 W Chester Pike Newtown Square PA 19073

WOOD, FREDERICK S., manufacturing company executive; b. 1928. BS, U. Dayton, 1952; postgrad., U.S. Naval Acad., 1970. Internat bus. advisor U.S. Govt., 1961-78; with Gen. Dynamics Corp., St. Louis, 1978—, now exec. v.p. Office: Gen Dynamics Corp Pierre Laclede Ctr Saint Louis MO 63105-1861 *

WOOD, GOERGE MARK, JR., investment banker; b. Montgomery, Ala., Sept. 6, 1925; s. George Mark and Mattie (Pegues) W.; m. Barnett Branson, Apr. 4, 1951 (div. 1968); 1 child, Meri Wood Moody; m. Marguerite McDaniel Wood, June 23, 1979; stepchildren: Arthur G. Powell III, Frances Elizabeth Powell, Marguerite M. Powell. Student, Auburn U., 1942, U. Ill., 1942-43; BS, U. Tex., 1947; postgrad., U. Ala., 1947. Chmn., chief exec. officer George M. Wood & Co., Inc., Montgomery, Ala., 1947—. Served to lt. U.S. Navy, 1950-51; Korea. Mem. Nat. Securities Traders Assn., Nat. Assn. Securities Dealers (vice chmn. dist. 5 1988—), Kiwanis (past pres.). Republican. Episcopalian. Clubs: Montgomery Country, Pioneers of Montgomery. Home: 3425 Thomas Ave Montgomery AL 36111 Office: George M Wood & Co Inc 210 Commerce St Montgomery AL 36104

WOOD, JAMES, supermarket executive; b. Newcastle-upon-Tyne, Eng., Jan. 19, 1930; came to U.S., 1974; s. Edward and Catherine Wilhelmina (Parker) W.; m. Colleen Margaret Taylor, Aug. 14, 1954; children: Julie, Sarah. Grad., Loughborough Coll., Leicestershire, England. Chief food chain Newport Coop. Soc., S. Wales, U.K., 1959-62, Grays Food Coop. Soc., Eng., 1962-66; dir., joint dep. mng. dir. charge retailing Cavenham, Ttd., Hayes, Eng., 1966-80; pres. Grand Union Co., Elmwood Park, N.J., 1973-79; chief exec. officer, dir. Grand Union Co., from 1973, chmn. bd., 1979-80; chmn. bd., chief exec. officer, pres. Gt. Atlantic & Pacific Tea Co., Inc., 1980—; bd. dirs. Irma Fabrikerne A/S, Denmark, Schering-Plough Corp. Bd. govs. James Madison Coll., Harrisonburg, Va. Served with Brit. Army, 1948-50. Mem. Food Mktg. Inst. (bd. dirs.). Roman Catholic. Office: Gt Atlantic & Pacific Tea Co 2 Paragon Dr Montvale NJ 07645

WOOD, JAYNEE SMITH, real estate developer; b. Beaumont, Tex., July 26, 1954; d. John Sterling and Mildred (Sumerow) Smith; m. Samuel Eugene Wood, Apr. 5, 1980; children—Samantha, Stephanie, Amanda, Samuel Smith, Baker Sterling. BSBA Okla. State U., 1976. Lic. engr. N.C. Territory rep. Armstrong World Industries, Raleigh, N.C., 1976-80; owner, developer J.S. Wood Broker Assoc., Raleigh, 1980—; v.p. Sam Wood Assocs., Inc., Raleigh, 1981—, dir., sec., 1981—; ptnr. SAJA Assocs., Raleigh, 1982—; owner, cons. Splty. Products, Raleigh, 1983—; co-founder, owner Carolina Specialty Products, Inc. Contbr. articles and designs to profl. jours. Vice pres. Breakfast Club Constrn., Raleigh, 1983-85; mem. various coms. United Methodist Ch., Raleigh, 1984-85, Bayleaf Bapt. Ch., Raleigh, spl. com. United Way, Raleigh, 1985. Recipient sales awards and Outstanding Achievement award Integrated Ceiling Systems, 1985. Mem. Illumination Engrs. Soc. Republican. Baptist. Avocations: golf; boating; tennis; skiing. Home: PO Box 31506 Raleigh NC 27622 Office: Sam Wood Assocs Inc 8909 Midway Rd W PO Box 31506 Raleigh NC 27612

WOOD, JOHN DENISON, utility company executive; b. Calgary, Alta., Can., Sept. 28, 1931; s. Ernest William and Ellen Gartshore (Pender) W.; m. Christena Isabel; 1 dau., Donna M. BSCE, U. B.C., 1953; MSCE, Stanford U., 1954, PhDCE and Engring. Mechs., 1956. Research asst. in civil engring. and engring. mechs. Stanford U., Palo Alto, Calif., 1953-56; assoc. mgr. dynamics dept. Engring. Mechs. Lab. Space Tech. Labs., Inc., Redondo Beach, Calif., 1956-63; pres., dir. Mechs. Research, Inc., El Segundo, Calif., 1963-66; sr. v.p. engring. and research ATCO Ind., Ltd., Calgary, Alta., 1966-68, sr. v.p. eastern region, 1968-75, sr. v.p. planning, 1975-77; pres., chief exec. officer ATCO Industries N.A., Ltd., Calgary, Alta., 1977-82, ATCOR Resources Ltd., Calgary, 1982-84; pres., chief operating officer Can. Utilities Ltd., Edmonton, Alta., 1984-88; pres., chief exec. officer Can. Utilities, Ltd., Edmonton, Alta., 1988—, also bd. dirs.; bd. dirs. ATCO Ltd., Can. Utilities, Ltd., ATCOR Ltd., ATCO Enterprises Ltd., Frontec Logistics Corp., BioTechnica Internat., Inc., Vencap Equities Alta. Ltd.; chmn. bd., chief exec. officer Can. Western Nat. Gas Co. Ltd., Northwestern Utilities Ltd., Alta. Power Ltd., Northland Utilities Enterprises Ltd. Co-author: Ballistic Missile and Space Vehicle Systems, 1961. Mem. pres.'s club adv. com. U. Alta; mem. Jr. Achievement of Can. Athlone fellow. Mem. Engring. Inst. of Can., Sci. Research Soc. Am., Assn. Profl. Engrs. Alta., Sigma Xi, Tau Beta Pi. Baptist. Clubs: Glencoe, Earl Grey, Calgary Petroleum, Mayfair Golf and Country. Office: Canadian Utilities Ltd, 10035 105th St, Edmonton, AB Canada T5J 2V6 also: Can Western Natural Gas Co Ltd, 909-11 Ave S W, Calgary, AB Canada T2R 1L8

WOOD, JOHN FREDERICK, JR., banker; b. Stamford, Conn., June 6, 1947; s. John Frederick and Kathryn (Lord) W.; m. Terrie Eaton Egert, July 12, 1975; children: Lindsey Eaton. BA in History, Rollins Coll., 1969, MBA in Fin., 1974. V.p. Union Trust Co., Stamford, 1974-79; sr. v.p. Conn. Nat. Bank, Hartford, 1979—. V.p. fin. Literacy Vols. Am., Stamford, 1988; trustee Land Trust, Darien, Conn., 1987—. With U.S. Army, 1969-72. Mem. Wee Burn Country Club, Tokeneke Club, Landmark Athletic Club. Republican. Episcopalian. Home: 124 Leroy Ave Darien CT 06820 Office: Conn Nat Bank 777 Main St Hartford CT 06103

WOOD, L. ROBERT, insurance executive. V.p. N.E. employee rels. Aetna Life and Casualty Co., Hartford, Conn. Office: Aetna Life & Casualty Co 151 Farmington Ave K344 Hartford CT 06156 *

WOOD, LARRY (MARY LAIRD), journalist, author, university educator, public relations executive; b. Sandpoint, Idaho; d. Edward Hayes and Alice (McNeel) Small; children: Mary, Marcia, Barry. BA magna cum laude, U. Wash., 1938, MA with highest honors, 1940; postgrad., Stanford U., 1941-42, U. Calif., Berkeley, 1946-47; cert. in photography, U. Calif., Berkeley, 1971; postgrad. journalism, U. Wis., 1971-72, U. Minn., 1971-72, U. Ga., 1972-73; postgrad. in art, architecture and marine biology, U. Calif., Santa Cruz, 1974-76, Stanford Hopkins Marine Sta., Santa Cruz, 1977-80. Feature writer and columnist 1939—; prof. pub. relations, journalism and investigative reporting, San Diego State U., 1974, 75; disting. vis. prof. journalism San Jose State U., 1976; assoc. prof. journalism Calif. State U., Hayward, 1978; prof. sci. and environ. journalism U. Calif. Berkeley Extension grad. div., 1979—; press del. Am. Geophysical Union Internat. Conf., 1988. Contbr. over 3,000 articles on real estate, architecture, edn., oceanography, science, environment, bus. and travel for newspapers, nat. mags., popular sci. mags., nat. and internat. newspaper syndicates, inflight mags., city mags., travel and architecture mags. including Oakland Tribune, Seattle Times, San Francisco Chronicle, Parade, San Jose Mercury News, Christian Sci. Monitor, MonitoRadio, Sports Illus., Mechanix Illus., Popular Mechanics, Parents, House Beautiful, Oceans, Sea Frontiers, PSA Mag., AAA Westways, AAA Motorland, Hawaiian Airlines in Paradise, Linguapress, Travel & Leisure, Family Handyman, Chevron USA. Significant works include home and garden columnist and editor, 5-part series Pacific Coast Ports, 5-part series Railroads of the West, San Francisco Cultural Scene, Endangered Species, Megamouth New Species of Shark, Columbia Alaska's Receding Glacier (selected as top sci. article in U.S., 1987), Calif. Underwater Parks, Ebey's Landing Nat. Hist. Preserve, Los Angeles Youth Gangs, Hist. Carousels. Co-author over 20 books including: McGraw-Hill English for Social Living, 1944, Fawcett Boating Books, 1956-66; co-author: Fodor's San Francisco, Fodor's California, 1989, Charles Merrill Focus on Life Science, Focus on Physical Science, 1983, 87; 8 works selected for use by Woltors-Nordoff-Longman English Language Texts, 1988; reviewer for Charles Merrill texts, 1983-84; book reviewer for Professional Communicator, 1987—. Nat. chmn. travel writing contest for U.S. univ. journalism students Assn. for Edn. in Journalism/Soc. Am. Travel Writers, 1979-83; judge writing contest for Nat. Assn. Real Estate Editors, 1982-84; mem. adv. bd. KRON/TV, 1986—. Numerous awards, honors, citations, speaking engagements including induction into Broadway Hall of Fame, Seattle, 1984, citations for environ. writing from Nat. Park Service, U.S. Forest Service, Bur. Land Mgmt., Oakland Mus. Assn., Oakland C. of C.; co-recipient Nat. Headliner award for Best Sunday Newspaper Mag. Mem. Pub. Relations Soc. Am. (charter mem. travel, tourism and edn. div.), Nat. Sch. Pub. Relations Assn., Environ. Cons. N.Am., Assn. Edn. in Journalism (exec. bd. nat. mag. div. 1978, panel chmn. 1979, 80), Women in Communications (nat. bd. officer 1975-77), Soc. Profl. Journalists (nat. bd. for hist. sites 1980—), Nat. Press Photographers Assn., Nat. Assn. Sci. Writers, Calif. Writers Club (officer 1967, 72), Am. Assn. Med. Writers, Am. Film Inst., Am. Heritage Found. (citation 1986, 87, 88), Soc. Am. Travel Writers, Internat. Oceanographic Found., Oceanic Soc., Calif. Acad. Environ. News Writers, U. Wash. Alumni (life, charter mem. ocean scis. alumni), U. Calif.-Berkeley Alumni (life), Stanford Alumni, Mortar Board Alumnae Assn., Phi Beta Kappa, Theta Sigma Phi. Home: 6161 Castle Dr Oakland CA 94611

WOOD, NEIL RODERICK, real estate development company executive; b. Winnipeg, Man., Can., Aug. 22, 1931; s. Reginald and Pearl (Beake) W.; m. Jean Mitchell Hume, Aug. 10, 1957; children: Barbara, David, John, Brian. B.Com., U. Man., 1952; M.B.A., Harvard U., 1955. Asst. mgr. Ont. real estate investment office Gt. West Life Assurance Co., 1955-59; with Cadillac Fairview Corp. Ltd. (and predecessor), Willowdale, Ont., 1959-61, 63-81; exec. v.p. Cadillac Fairview Corp. Ltd. (and predecessor), 1968-71, pres., 1971-81, vice chmn., 1980-81; pres. N.R. Wood Devel. Co. Ltd., 1982—; exec. v.p., dir. Campeau Corp., 1985-86; pres., chief exec. officer Markborough Properties Inc., Toronto, Ont., Can., 1986—; past pres., trustee Internat. Council Shopping Centers; bd. dirs. Hudson's Bay Co., Can. Inst. Pub. Real Estate Cos.; bd. govs. Olympic Trust. Mem. Urban Land Inst., Met. Toronto Bd. Trade, Toronto Club, Rosedale Golf Club, Lambton Golf Club, Granite Club, Beaumaris Club, Lost Tree Club, Loxahatchee Golf Club, Beacon Hall Club. Home: 17 Whitney Ave, Toronto, ON Canada M4W 2A7 Office: Markborough Properties Inc, 1 Dundas W, Toronto, ON Canada M5G 2T2

WOOD, NICHOLAS BURGWIN, warehouse developer; b. N.Y.C., July 8, 1931; s. Richardson King and Mildred Burgwin W.; B.A., Cornell U., 1952; m. Sanko Kamiyama, May 8, 1954 (div.); children—Olivia Midori, Francesca Ayame, John Kamiyama; m. Jane Sperry Anderson, Dec. 5, 1982. With various firms engaged in redevel. of downtown areas, New Haven and Bridgeport, Conn., Buffalo, 1957-68; pres. Nicholas Wood & Assocs., Inc., nat. warehouse and office developer, Bridgeport, 1968—; guest lectr. Harvard U., Yale U., CCNY. Del., White House Conf. on Small Bus., 1980. Served with 1st Radio Broadcast and Leaflet Group, 1953-54. Recipient 1st prize sculpture Yomiyuri Ind. Exhibit, 1954; 1st prize painting Bridgeport Arts Council Exhibit, 1983. Mem. Warehousing Edn. and Research Council (founding mem.), Nat. Council Phys. Distbn. Mgmt. Democrat. Author: The Family Firm in Japan, 1963, Different Dimensions, 1989, 2' Almost Never Equals 4, 1989; contbr. articles to bus. jours; creator new form of operating lease financing using tax exempt bonds, management software program. Office: Nicholas Wood & Assocs Inc 243-A Front St New Haven CT 06513

WOOD, QUENTIN EUGENE, oil company executive; b. Mechanicsburg, Pa., Mar. 5, 1923; s. Lloyd Paul and Greta (Myers) W.; m. Louise Lowe, Apr. 14, 1958. B.S., Pa. State U., 1948. Petroleum engr. Quaker State Oil Refining Corp., Parkersburg, W.Va., 1948-52; chief engr. Quaker State Oil Refining Corp., Bradford, Pa., 1952-55; mgr. prodn. Quaker State Oil Refining Corp., 1955-68; v.p. prodn. Quaker State Oil Refining Corp., Oil City, Pa., 1968-70; exec. v.p. Quaker State Oil Refining Corp., Oil City, 1970-73, pres., chief ops. officer, 1973-75; pres., chief exec. officer Quaker State Oil Refining Corp., 1975-82, chmn., chief executive officer, 1982-88, chmn. bd., 1988—; dir. Mellon Bank Corp., Pa. Mfrs. Ins. Co.; chmn. industry tech. adv. com. U.S. Bur. Mines, 1960-70, Penn Grade Tech. Advisory Com., 1955-69, Pa. Oil and Gas Conservation Commn., 1961-71. Pres. bd. trustees Pa. State U. Served to 1st lt. USAAF, 1943-46. Mem. Am. Inst. Metall. Engrs., Pa. Grade Crude Oil Assn. (dir.), Pa. Oil Producers Assn. (past pres., dir. Bradford dist.), Am. Petroleum Inst. (dir.), Nat. Petroleum Refiners Assn. Home: 5 Crestview Dr Oil City PA 16301 Office: Quaker State Corp 255 Elm St Oil City PA 16301

WOOD, RICHARD CARSON, marketing professional; b. N.Y.C., Oct. 17, 1946; s. Carson R. and Eleanor Louise (Sartain) W.; m. Virginia Ruth Hyde. BA, Ky. Wesleyan Coll., 1968. Sales rep. Formica Corp., Wayne, N.J., 1968-73; cons. mktg. methods McGraw Hill Constrn. Info. Systems, N.Y.C., 1973-80; mgr. architecture and nat. sales, mltg. dir. Laticrete Internat., Inc., Bethany, Conn., 1980—; mktg. cons. C.E. Kaiser Co., Houston, 1983-85. Author numerous articles in field. Mem. Constrn. Specifications Inst., Am. Wall and Ceiling Inst., Assn. Tile Terazzo and Marble Contractors and Affiliates, U.S. Power Squad Club. Home: 91 Quarry Hill Cheshire CT 06410 Office: Laticrete Internat Inc One Laticrete Pk N Bethany CT 06525

WOOD, RICHARD DONALD, pharmaceutical company executive; b. Brazil, Ind., Oct. 22, 1926; s. Howard T. and Dorothy F. (Norfolk) W.; B.S., Purdue U., 1948, LL.D., 1973; M.B.A., U. Pa., 1950; D.Sc., Butler U., 1974; LL.D., DePauw U., 1972, Phila. Coll. Pharmacy and Sci., 1975, Ind. State U., 1978; m. Billie Lou Carpenter, Dec. 29, 1951; children—Catherine Ann Wood Lawson, Marjorie Elizabeth. Gen. mgr. ops. in Argentina, Eli Lilly & Co., 1961, dir. ops., Mex. and Central Am., 1962-70, pres. Eli Lilly Internat. Corp., 1970-72, now dir.; pres. Eli Lilly & Co., Indpls., 1972-73, pres., chmn. bd., chief exec. officer, dir., 1973—, also dir.; dir. Chem. N.Y. Corp., Amoco Corp., Dow Jones & Co. Bd. dirs. Lilly Endowment, Inc.; trustee Indpls. Mus. of Art, DePauw U., Am. Enterprise Inst. for Public Policy Research, Com. Econ. Devel.; bd. dirs. U.S.-USSR Trade and Econ. Council; mem. President's Export Council. Mem. Council on Fgn. Relations, Bus. Roundtable, The Conf. Bd. Presbyterian. Clubs: Links (N.Y.C.); Meridian Hills Country, Woodstock (Indpls.). Office: Eli Lilly & Co Lilly Corporate Ctr Indianapolis IN 46285

WOOD, ROBERT CHARLES, lawyer, financial consultant; b. Chgo., Apr. 8, 1956; s. Roy Edward and Mildred Lucille (Jones) W.; m. Jenny Jo Briggs, Oct. 1984; children: Jaqueline Jones, Reagan Keith. BA in History, BBA in Real Estate, So. Meth. U., 1979, JD, 1982. Bar: Tex. 1983. Appraiser McClellan-Massey, Dallas, 1977-79; researcher, acquisitions officer Amstar Fin. Corp., Dallas, 1979-80; prin. Robert Wood Cons., Dallas, 1981—; cons. plan mktg. cos., 1983-84; pvt. practice law, Dallas, 1983-84; gen. counsel Diversified Benefits, Inc., Dallas, 1985-86; nat. accounts mgr. Lomas & Nettleton Real Estate Group, Dallas, 1987-88; sr. pension cons. Eppler, Guerin & Turner, 1988—. Mem. So. Meth. U. Law Rev., 1981-82; contbr. articles to profl. pubnls. Bd. dirs. Am. Cancer Soc., Dallas unit, 1982-87, mem. spl. events com., 1986-87, crusade com., 1987-88. Mem. Tex. Bar Assn., Phila. Bar Assn., Phi Gamma Delta. Avocations: tennis, bicycling. Home: 3304 Leahy St Dallas TX 75229 Office: 1445 Ross Ave #2300 Dallas TX 75202

WOOD, ROBERT KENNETH, management consultant; b. Phila., June 4, 1940; s. Robert Benson and Marion Borie (Schaffer) W.; m. Patricia Anne Knowles, June 19, 1965; children: Karen Elizabeth, Julie Knowles, Leslie Anne. BME, Cornell U., 1963; MPA, Princeton U., 1966, MS in Engring., 1966. Asst. project engr. AEC, Washington, 1967-68; assoc. Planning Rsch. Corp., Washington, 1968-70; sr. assoc. Planning Rsch. Corp., McLean, Va., 1970-72, Systan, Inc., Washington, 1972-76; project mgr. Logistics Mgmt. Inst., Bethesda, Md., 1976-79, program dir., 1979-85, v.p., 1985—. Capt. U.S. Army, 1965-67, Vietnam. Mem. Nat. Assn. Bus. Economists, Nat. Contract Mgmt. Assn. Office: Logistics Mgmt Inst 6400 Goldsboro Rd Bethesda MD 20817

WOOD, TIMOTHY MCDONALD, diversified manufacturing company executive, controller; b. Sioux City, Iowa, Dec. 3, 1947; s. John Wallace and Nancy Patricia (McDonald) W.; m. Rebecca Jeanne Ryan, July 18, 1970; children: Kelly Rebecca, Ashley Ryan. BS in Acctg., U. S.D., 1969; grad. advanced mgmt. program, Harvard U., 1983. CPA. Mem. audit staff and mgmt. Peat, Marwick, Mitchell & Co., Chgo., 1971-72; projects mgr. Borg-Warner Corp., Chgo., 1977-79; v.p., controller Automotive Parts div. Borg-Warner Corp., Franklin Pk., Ill., 1979-80; asst. controller Borg-Warner Corp., Chgo., 1980-85, v.p., controller, 1985—. V.p., bd. dirs. Nat. Kidney Found. Ill., 1985—. Served to 1st lt. U.S. Army, 1970-71. Mem. Ill. Soc. CPA's. Am. Mgmt. Assn., Fin. Execs. Inst., Machinery & Allied Products Inst. (fin. council). Clubs: Chgo. Athletic, Harvard (Chgo.). Home: 6733 LeRoy Lincolnwood IL 60646 Office: Borg-Warner Corp 200 S Michigan Ave Chicago IL 60604

WOOD, WILLIAM MCBRAYER, lawyer; b. Greenville, S.C., Jan. 27, 1942; s. Oliver Gillan and Grace (McBrayer) W.; m. Nancy Cooper, Feb. 17, 1973; children: Margaret, Walter, Lewis. BS in Acctg., U. S.C., 1964, JD cum laude, 1972; LLM in Estate Planning (scholar), U. Miami, 1980. Bar: S.C. 1972, Fla. 1979, D.C. 1973, U.S. Tax Ct. 1972, U.S. Ct. Claims 1972, U.S. Supreme Ct. 1977. Intern ct. of claims sect., tax div. U.S. Dept. Justice, 1971; law clk. to chief judge U.S. Ct. Claims, Washington, 1972-74; ptnr. firm Edwards Wood, Duggan & Reese, Greer and Greenville, 1974-78; asst. prof. law Cumberland Law Sch., Samford U., Birmingham, Ala., 1978-79; faculty Nat. Inst. Trial Advocacy: N.E. Regional Inst., Hofstra U., 1979, 83-88, Fla. Regional Inst., 1989—, teaching team 5th intensive trial techniques course, 1983; ptnr. firm Shutts & Bowen, Miami, 1980-85; sole practice, Miami, 1985—. Contbg. editor: The Lawyers PC; Fla. editor: Drafting Wills and Trust Agreements; substantive com. editor ABA: The Tax Lawyer, 1983—; Pres. Piedmont Heritage Fund., Inc. 1975-78; del. State Rep. Grassroots Conv., 1985, Presdl. II Conv., 1987; exec. committeeman Dade County Republicans, 1988—. Served with USAF, 1965-69, Vietnam. Decorated Air Force Commendation medal; recipient Am. Jurisprudence award in real propery and tax I, 1971; winner Grand prize So. Living Mag. travel photo contest, 1969. Mem. ABA (taxation sect.), S.C. Bar Assn., Fla. Bar Assn., D.C. Bar Assn., Greer C. of C. (pres. 1977, Outstanding leadership award 1976), Greater Greenville C. of C. (dir. 1977), Order Wig and Robe, Estate Planning Council South Fla., Omicron Delta Kappa. Episcopalian. Club: Bankers (bd. govs. 1989—). Lodge: Masons, Rotary. Office: One Biscayne Tower Suite 1616 Miami FL 33131-1310

WOOD, WILLIAM RANSOM, former university president, city official, corporate executive; b. nr. Jacksonville, Ill., Feb. 3, 1907; s. William James and Elizabeth (Ransom) W.; m. Margaret Osborne, 1930 (dec. 1942); 1 son, William Osborne (dec. 1978); m. Dorothy Jane Irving, Mar. 18, 1944; children: Mark Irving, Karen Jane Parrish. A.B., Ill. Coll., 1927, LL.D., 1960; M.A., U. Iowa, 1936, Ph.D., 1939. Tchr., coach pubs. schs. Mich., Iowa, Ill., 1928-46; asst. Supt. Evanston Twp. Schs., Ill., 1948-50; specialist jr. colls. and lower divs. U.S. Office Edn., 1950-53; program planning officer (U.S. Office Edn.), 1953; dean statewide devel. higher edn. U. Nev., 1954-55, acting chmn. dept. English, 1955-56, acad. v.p., 1955-60, acting pres., 1958-60; pres. U. Alaska, 1960-73; mayor Fairbanks, Alaska, 1978-80; pres. Pacific Alaska Assocs., Ltd.; exec. v.p. Fairbanks Indsl. Devel. Corp., Festival Fairbanks '84; mem. staff study needs and resources higher edn. FAO, Libya, 1955; mem. study group off-duty ednl. program armed forces in Europe, U.S. Dept. Def., 1955; del. Am. Assembly Fgn. Relations, 1957-58; chmn. Nev. com. Fulbright scholarships, 1957-58; mem. chancellor's panel SUNY; mem. sci. group traveling to Antarctica, New Zealand, Australia. Editor: Looking Ahead, 1953, From Here On, 1954, All Around the Land, 1954, Youth and The World, 1955, To Be an American, 1957; author, editor: On Your Own, 1953; co-editor: Short Stories as You Like Them, 1940, Youth Thinks it Through, 1941, Just for Sport, 1943, Fact and Opinion, 1945, Short Short Stories, 1951, Study of Financing of Higher Education in Asia, 1968; poet: Not From Stone, 1983. Chmn. Alaska Am. Cancer Soc.; v.p. Alaska council Boy Scouts Am.; mem. bd. Rampart Dam adv. com.; mem. Gen. Med. Scis. Nat. Adv. Council, Alaska Higher Edn. Facilities Commn., 1967, Alaska Small Bus. Adv. Council, 1968, Satellite Communications Task Force; spl. asst. to mayor for trade and devel., Fairbanks North Star borough, 1984—; chmn. Greater Fairbanks Community Hosp. Found.; mem. White House Fellows Selection Panel, Nat. Adv. Council on Edn. Professions Devel.; chmn. Alaska Heart Assn.; mem. Alaskan Command Civilian Adv. Bd., 1962—; bd. dirs. U. Alaska Found., exec. dir. Fest. Fairbanks '84, 1981—. Served to lt. USNR, 1943-46; capt. USNR, ret. 1968. Recipient Outstanding Alaskan award, 1984, Alaskan of Yr. award, 1985, Centennial award Alexis de Tocqueville Soc., 1987. Fellow Arctic Inst. N. Am.; mem. Am. Geog. Soc., Assn. Higher Edn. (exec. com.), Nat. Univ. Extension Assn., N.W. Assn. Secondary and Higher Schs., Western Assn. Colls., Navy League, AAAS, Assn. Applied Solar Energy (adv. council 1959), Am. Assn. Land-grant Colls. and State Univs., Internat. Assn. Univ. Presidents (exec. com.). Methodist. Clubs: Explorers, Fairbanks Petroleum, Washington Athletic. Lodge: Rotary (gov. dist. 503 1985-86). Office: Pacific Alaska Assocs Ltd 665 10th Ave Fairbanks AK 99701

WOOD, WILLIS BOWNE, JR., utility holding company executive; b. Kansas City, Mo., Sept. 15, 1934; s. Willis Bowne Sr. and Mina (Henderson) W.; m. Dixie Gravel, Aug. 31, 1955; children: Bradley, William, Josh. BS in Petroleum Engring., U. Tulsa, 1957; grad. advanced mgmt. program, Harvard U., 1983. Various positions So. Calif. Gas Co., Los Angeles, 1960-74, v.p. then sr. v.p., 1975-80, exec. v.p., 1983-84; pres., chief exec. officer Pacific Lighting Gas Supply Co., Los Angeles, 1981-83; exec. v.p. Pacific Lighting Corp. (name changed to Pacific Enterprises), Los Angeles, 1984—. Trustee Harvey Mudd Coll., Claremont, Calif., Calif. Med. Ctr., Los Angeles, S.W. Mus. Los Angeles. Mem. Soc. Petroleum Engrs., Am. Gas Assn., Pacific Coast Gas Assn., Pacific Energy Assn. Republican. Presbyterian. Clubs: Calif. (L.A.), Center (Orange County), City Club on Bunker Hill. Office: Pacific Enterprises 810 S Grand Ave Los Angeles CA 90017

WOODALL, WILLIAM LEON, insurance executive; b. Kirby, Ark., July 29, 1923; s. Ocie Doan and Hazel Cornelia (Paslay) W.; m. Patricia Ann Reese, Sept. 30, 1950; children: Michael Reese, David William, Stacy Ann. BS, Miami U., Oxford, Ohio, 1947. CPCU. Home office underwriter Ohio Casualty Group Ins. Cos., Hamilton, 1947-52, underwriter Mpls. br. office, 1952-53, field rep., Des Moines, 1953-54, underwriter Detroit br. office, 1962-64, mgr. Indpls. br. office, 1964-68, company v.p., Hamilton, 1968-77, sr. v.p., 1977-84, exec. v.p., sec., 1984-88, pres., chief oper. officer, 1988—, also bd. dirs.; ptnr. Cady Ins. Agy., Burlington, Iowa, 1954-62. Republican. Methodist. Lodge: Elks. Home: 116 Craig Dr Hamilton OH 45013 Office: Ohio Casualty Corp 136N 3rd St Hamilton OH 45025

WOODARD, DOROTHY MARIE, insurance broker; b. Houston, Feb. 7, 1932; d. Gerald Edgar and Bessie Katherine (Crain) Floeck; student N.Mex. State U., 1950; m. Jack W. Woodard; June 19, 1950 (dec.); m. Norman W. Libby, July 19, 1982. Partner, Western Oil Co., Tucumcari, N.Mex., 1950—; owner, mgr. Woodard & Co., Las Cruces, N.Mex., 1959-67; agt., dist. mgr. United Nations Ins. Co., Denver, 1966-74; agt. Western Nat. Life Ins. Co., Amarillo, Tex., 1976—. Exec. dir. Tucumcari Indsl. Commn., 1979—; dir. Bravo Dome Study Com., 1979—; owner Libby Cattle Co., Libby Ranch Co.; regional bd. dirs. N.Mex., Eastern Plains Council Govts., 1979—. Mem. Tucumcari C. of C. Club: Mesa Country. Home: PO Box 823 Tucumcari NM 88401

WOODARD, LEE EDWIN, lawyer; b. Syracuse, N.Y., Mar. 8, 1955; s. Eugene Harvey and Eugenia (Firestone) W.; m. Patricia Lynn Morris, June 25, 1983. BA, Hobart Coll., 1977; JD, Vt. Law Sch., 1982. Bar: N.Y. 1983, U.S. Dist. Ct. (no. dist.) N.Y. 1983. Assoc. Selbach Law Offices, Syracuse, 1982-83; ptnr. Baum & Woodard, Syracuse, 1983—; adj. prof. Cazenovia (N.Y.) Coll., 1988—; bankruptcy trustee U.S. Dist. Ct. (no. dist) N.Y., 1987—. Mem. Madison County Bar Assn., Onondaga County Bar Ass. Republican. Episcopalian. Club: Manlius (N.Y.) Rod & Gun. Office: Baum & Woodard 224 Harrison St Suite 316 Syracuse NY 13202

WOODBRIDGE, HENRY SEWALL, management consultant; b. N.Y.C., Sept. 20, 1906; s. George and Harriet (Manley) W.; m. Dorothy Steese White, Jan. 8, 1928 (dec. May 1981); children: Henry Sewall, Anne Sidney (Mrs. William Pickford), Victoria (Mrs. Richard G. Hall). Student, Harvard U., 1923-26. With Stone & Webster, Inc., 1926-27; gen. mgr., dir. Raymond Whitcomb, Inc., 1927-40; bus. mgr., asst. to pub. Boston Evening Transcript, 1940-41; former v.p. Am. Optical Co., Southbridge, Mass.; dir. Am. Optical Co., 1941-77; pres. Todd-AO Corp., N.Y.C., 1954-58; fin. and mgmt. cons. 1958—; chmn. bd. True Temper Corp., 1960-66, pres., 1964-65; cons. Editoria Guias LTB SA, Rio de Janeiro and São Paulo, Brazil, 1966-83, Barwick Industries, 1967—, Internat. Horizons, Inc., 1975-85, Learning Techs., Inc., 1985—; pres., mng. dir. Hillwood Corp., 1966-84; also dir.; dir. Hambro Am. Bank & Trust Co., Vesper, Inc., Union Labor Life Ins. Co. Chmn., Sch. Bldg. Com. Pomfret (Conn.), 1943-47, 58-60; mem. Fin. Com. Brookline (Mass.), 1936-39; chmn. Fire, Safety, Pub. Welfare Sub-Com., 1938-39; mem. Conn. Devel. Commn., 1948-55; industry rep. Nat. War Labor Bd., 1942-45; mem. safety equipment adv. com. WPB, 1942-46; trustee Old Sturbridge Village, 1941—, chmn., 1965-66; trustee Middlesex Sch., Day-Kimball Hosp. Mem. Indsl. Relations Research Assn., New Eng. Soc. N.Y. (pres. 1962-65), Soc. Cincinnati in State of N.H. Episcopalian. Clubs: Harvard U., Union (N.Y.C.); Harvard U., Tavern (Boston); Harvard U.

Faculty (Cambridge, Mass.); Met., Cosmos (Washington). Home: Drumlin-Ho Pomfret CT 06258 Office: PO Box 156 Pomfret CT 06258

WOODBURY, THOMAS BOWRING, II, insurance company executive, lawyer; b. Salt Lake City, Sept. 15, 1937; s. Thomas Bowring and Beulah B. Woodbury; m. Kathleen Thompson, June 15, 1965; children—Leslie, Thomas, Todd, Matthew, Ashley. A.B. cum laude, Brigham Young U., 1962; J.D., U. Utah, 1966; postgrad. Oxford U. (Eng.), 1961, U. London, 1959-60. Bar: Utah, 1966, N.Y. 1974, Pa. 1982. Assoc. McKay & Burton, Salt Lake City, 1966-72; assoc. gen. counsel Am. Re-Ins. Co., N.Y.C., 1972-78; sr. v.p., gen. counsel Ins. Co. of N.Am., Phila., 1978-82; exec. v.p., gen. counsel, sec. Home Ins. Co., N.Y.C., 1982-87; sr. v.p., gen. counsel Comml. Union Ins. Co., Boston, 1987—. Mem. N.Y. State Bar Assn., Pa. Bar Assn., Utah Bar Assn., Assn. Bar City N.Y. n. Republican. Mormon. Office: Comml Union Ins Co One Beacon St Boston MA 02108

WOODFIELD, DENIS BUCHANAN, health care company executive; b. N.Y.C., Oct. 23, 1933; s. William Frederick and Margery Brunton (Hoyt) W.; m. Rosemary Humphries, Feb. 16, 1963; children: Katherine, Nicholas, Elizabeth. BA, Harvard U., 1954; PhD, Oxford U., 1962. Trainee Chase Manhattan Bank, N.Y.C., 1962-65; analyst Gen. Electric, N.Y.C., 1965-68; banking dir. Pan Am. World Airways, N.Y.C., 1968-74; dir. treasury services Johnson & Johnson, New Brunswick, N.J., 1974—; bd. dirs. Middlesex Assurance Co., Hamilton, Bermuda, 1975—, Tarpon Ins. Co., Hamilton, 1975—, Monmouth Co., Hamilton, 1975—. Author: Surreptitious Printing in England 1550-1640, 1973, English Armorial Bookbindings, 1958. Trustee Princeton Pub. Library, 1978—; bd. dirs. Am. Friends of Oxford Union Soc. Served as cpl. U.S. Army, 1954-57, ETO. Named hon. mem. Sr. Common Room, Lincoln Coll., Oxford U., 1978. Mem. Manorial Soc. Gt. Britain (U.S. chmn. 1981—). Episcopalian. Clubs: Grolier (N.Y.C.), Am. Yacht (Rye, N.Y.); Nassau (Princeton, N.J.). Home: 883 Lawrenceville Rd Princeton NJ 08540 Office: Johnson & Johnson One Johnson & Johnson Plaza New Brunswick NJ 08933

WOODFORD, DUANE HUGH, electrical equipment manufacturing company executive, electrical engineer; b. Dunseith, N.D., Jan. 1, 1939; s. Harold George and Edna Evelyn (Lagerquist) W.; m. Grace Carol Vandal, July 18, 1962; children—Robert Kent, Kim Ann. B.S. in Elec. Engring., U. N.D., 1961; student Western Electric grad. engring. tng. program, 1962; Mini M.B.A., Coll. St. Thomas, 1977, postgrad., 1978. Sr. sales engr. Electric Machinery Steam Turbine Motor and Generator div. Dresser-Rand Co., Hartford, Conn., 1969-76, product mktg. mgr., Mpls., 1976-79, mgr. parts and service, 1979-80, commercial ops. mgr., 1980-83, gen. mgr., 1983-87, v.p., gen. mgr., 1987—; power engr. Western Electric, Chgo., 1961-63; application engr. Electric Machinery, Steam Turbine, Motor and Generator div. Dresser-Rand Co., Mpls., 1963-65, sales engr., N.Y.C., Pitts., 1965-68. Scoutmaster Boy Scouts U.S., Aurora, Ill., 1962-63; coach, Babe Ruth Baseball, Plymouth, Minn., 1978-80; treas. PTA, Wayzata (Minn.) Sch. Dist. 284, 1978-79; . Served with USMC, 1960-66. Mem. ASME (sec. gas turbine div. electric utility com. 1972-74), TAPPI. Republican. Methodist. Home: 1630 Shadyview Ln Plymouth MN 55447 Office: Electric Machinery Steam Turbine Dresser-Rand Co 800 Central Ave Minneapolis MN 55413

WOODGER, WALTER JAMES, JR., management consultant; b. N.Y.C., Aug. 29, 1913; s. Walter James and Annie (Keast) W.; A.B., Bowdoin Coll., 1935; LL.B., Fordham U., 1939; m. Valerie McCormick, June 23, 1979. With internat. dept. J.P. Morgan & Co., N.Y.C., 1935-49; asst. mgr. London office Chase Manhattan Bank, 1949-55; treas. Warren Petroleum Internat. Corp. subs. Gulf Oil Corp. and mgr. gas and gas liquids Gulf Eastern Co., London, 1955-65; exec. v.p. Boyden Indsl. Services, Inc., N.Y.C., 1965-72; pres. Woodger Assos., Inc., N.Y.C., 1972—. Served to capt. Judge Adv. Gen. Corps, U.S. Army, 1943-47; ETO. Decorated Reconnaissance Franç aise. Mem. Am. Bar Assn., N.Y. Bar, Judge Adv. Gen.'s Assn., Clubs: Williams (N.Y.C.), Am. (London), Palm-Aire Country (Sarasota), Tournament Players (Sarasota), BirdKey Yacht (Sarasota).

WOODHALL, JOHN ALEXANDER, JR., construction company executive; b. Peoria, Ill., Oct. 10, 1929; s. John Alexander and Marion Ellen (Solstad) W.; B.B.A., U. Minn., 1952; m. Donna Irene Simmons, Aug. 21, 1948; children—John Alexander, Susan, Cheryl, Douglas, Robert. Project supt. Central States Constrn. Co., Willmar, Minn., 1953-57, v.p., project mgr., 1957-60; v.p., area mgr. Allied Enterprises, Willmar, 1960-69; exec. v.p. Central Allied Enterprises, Inc., Canton, Ohio, 1969-74, chmn., chief exec. officer, 1974—. Vice chmn. Minn. Gov.'s Occupational Safety Health Adv. Council; bd. dirs., chmn. Minn. Safety Council, chmn., 1983; pres. W. Central Safety Council, 1979; bd. dirs. Nat. Safety Coun., 1984—, v.p., 1987-89, vice chmn., 1989—; dist. commr. Viking coun. Boy Scouts Am., 1969-71. Mem. Am. Mgmt. Assn., Am. Arbitration Assn., Associated Gen. Contractors Am. (dir.), Associated Gen. Contractors Minn. (pres. 1977), Pres.'s Assn. Lutheran. Clubs: Kiwanis (Willmar); Masons, Shriners, Mpls. Athletic. Home: 3201 Croydon Dr NW Canton OH 44718 also: 4 Belleview Blvd Apt 404 Belleair FL 34616 Office: Cen Allied Enterprises PO Box 80449 Canton OH 44708-0449 also: PO Box 80449 Canton OH 44708

WOODHOUSE, JOHN FREDERICK, food distribution company executive; b. Wilmington, Del., Nov. 30, 1930; s. John Crawford and Anna (Houth) W.; m. Marilyn Ruth Morrow, June 18, 1955; children: John Crawford II, Marjorie Ann Woodhouse Purdy. BA, Wesleyan U., 1953; MBA, Harvard U., 1955. Bus. devel. officer Can. Imperial Bank of Commerce, Toronto, Ont., 1955-59; various fin. positions Ford Motor Co., Dearborn, Mich., 1959-64, Cooper Industries, Inc., Mount Vernon, Ohio, 1964-67; treas., Houston, 1967-69; treas. Crescent-Niagara Corp., Buffalo, 1968-69; exec. v.p., chief fin. officer Sysco Corp., Houston, 1969-71, pres., chief operating officer, 1972-83, pres., chief exec. officer, 1983-85, chief exec. officer, chmn. bd., 1985—, also bd. dirs., mem. exec. com.; bd. dirs. NCNB, Tex., NCR Corp. Chmn. Mich. 16th dist. Rep. Club, 1962-64; treas. Cooper Industries Found., 1967-69; trustee Wesleyan U. 1976—, vice-chmn. trustee, 1986—; ruling elder Presbyn. ch. Mem. Houston Soc. Fin. Analysts, Fin. Execs. Inst., Harvard Bus. Sch. Club (bd. dirs.), Sigma Chi. Office: Sysco Corp 1390 Enclave Pkwy Houston TX 77077-2027

WOODLAND, GORDON CARTER, yacht manufacturing executive; b. Aberdeen, Wash., Oct. 29, 1924; s. Earle Clement and Marian Alma (Carter) W.; student U. Oreg., 1942, Tex. A&M U., 1943, Princeton U., 1945, U. Willamette, 1945, U. Colo., 1946; A.B., U. Wash., 1949; Cour Pratique, U. de Grenoble (France), 1950, Centre Univ. de Meditterraneen, 1950; m. Joanne Katherine Bouse, May 7, 1955; children—Michael Sean, Leslie Denise, Kristyn Ann, Kimberly Diane. Self employed in logging, Aberdeen, 1946-50; mgr. C. of C., Anacortes, Wash., 1951-54; mgr. sales and promotion Skagit Plastics, La Conner, Wash., 1955-60; west coast mgr. Traveler Boat div. Stanray Corp., Chgo., 1961-62, field sales mgr., 1962-63, gen. sales mgr., 1963-64, v.p. sales, 1964-66; gen. sales mgr. Pearson Yachts div. Grumman Allied Industries, Inc., Portsmouth, R.I., 1966-74, asst. gen. mgr., dir. mktg., 1974-76, gen. mgr., 1976—; cons. seminars Am. Mgmt. Assn.; speaker seminars Sales Execs. Clubs N.Y., Chgo. Pres. Pheasant Hill Assn., Portsmouth, 1976; mem. local sch. bd. adv. com., 1971, Title I Reading Inst., Portsmouth Sch. Dist.; bd. dirs. Seaport '76, 1976—; campaign chmn. Wash. Gov. Arthur B. Langlie for U.S. Senate, 1956; bd. dirs. Newport County Local Devel. Corp.; mem. R.I. Gov.'s Adv. Com. Strategic Devel., Nat. Adv. Com. U.S. Trade Negotiations. Served with USN, 1941-45, to lt. comdr. USNR, 1948-72; comdr. R.I. Naval Militia. Recipient certificate of appreciation Am. Sail Tng. Assn., 1976, 82, commendation Sales Execs. Club N.Y., 1965, Plankowner's cert. Seaport '76, 1978; notary pub., R.I. Mem. Nat. Assn. Engine and Boat Mfrs., Boating Industry Assn. (dir.), Boat Mfrs. Assn. (dir.), Nat. Marine Mfrs. Assn. (dir., sec., fin., memberships, shows coms.), Am. Sail Tng. Assn. (dir.), Boat Mfrs. Assn. (chmn., sec.-treas.), R.I. Marine Trade Assn. (dir.), R.I. Assn. for Sail (dir.), Narragansett Bay Yachting Assn., C. of C. Newport County (dir.), Naval Res. Assn., Nat. Athletic Scholastic Soc., U. Wash. Alumni Assn., Sigma Nu. Republican. Roman Catholic. Clubs: Twenty Hundred (commodore); R.I. Commodores; Turtle; Barrington (R.I.) Yacht. Home and Office: 5163 N A1A #617 Ocean Harbour FL 34949

WOODLEY, THOMAS FRED, investment banker; b. San Antonio, Jan. 7, 1952; s. Fred and Charlotte (Ehlers) W. BBA, U. Tex., 1974, M in Profl. Acctg., 1975. CPA, Tex.; registered investment advisor, securities broker Nat. Assn. Securities Dealers; lic. real estate broker. Tax acct. Ernst & Whinney, San Antonio, 1975-76; tax acct. T.F. Woodley & Co., San Antonio, 1976-80, investment banker, 1980-83; investment banker San Antonio Venture Group, 1984—; prof. acctg. Trinity U., San Antonio, 1979-80. Mem. Tex. Soc. CPA's (editorial bd. 1986-87), Assn. for Corp. Growth. Office: San Antonio Venture Group 4600 Broadway San Antonio TX 78209

WOODMANSEE, GLENN EDWARD, employee relations executive; b. Feb. 8, 1936; s. Glenn E. and Elaine (Turnquist) Harty; m. Sharon E. Horne, Sept. 5, 1959; chidlren: Lynn Ann, Thomas Edward. Student, Coe Coll., 1954-55; BS, Ariz. State U., 1960. Assoc. group mem. Prudential Ins. Co., Seattle, 1960-64; regional mgr. Blue Cross, N.Y.C., 1964-72; mgr. employee benefits McDermott Inc./Babcock & Wilcox, New Orleans, 1972-82; dir. employee relations Tidewater Inc., New Orleans, 1982—. Bd. dirs. CPC Hosp., New Orleans, 1988—; pres. Manalapan Rep. Club, Englishtown, N.J., 1977; county committeeman N.J. Rep. Party, Englishtown, 1970-77. Served to cpl. U.S. Army, 1955-57. Recipient N.Y.C. Marathon medal N.Y.C. Track Club, 1987. Mem. Am. Soc. Personnel Assocs., Bus. Coalit. Health (treas. 1986-88, pres. 1988—), Tng. & Devel. Assn. Am., Risk Ins. Mgmt. Soc. Republican. Presbyterian. Club: New Orleans Athletic, South Shore Yacht. Home: 3510 Mimosa Ct New Orleans LA 70131 Office: Tidewater Inc 1440 Canal St New Orleans LA 70112

WOOD PRINCE, WILLIAM NORMAN, investments and real estate developer; b. Tulsa, Oct. 25, 1942; s. William Henry and Eleanor (Edwards) W.P.; m. Jonna Rosamond Leanard, Nov.7, 1967 (div. 1983); children: Scott Clarkson, Patrick Bernard. BA, Vanderbilt U., 1964. Account exec. Needham Harper & Steers, Chgo., 1965-68; brand mgr. Armour-Dial, Chgo., 1968-70; account supr. J. Walter Thompson, Chgo., 1970-75; sr. v.p. D'Arcy, Masius, Wynn Williams, Chgo., 1975-77; chmn. F.H. Prince & Co., Chgo., 1977—; bd. dirs. Blvd. Bancorp., Chgo.; advisor Arral Pacific Equity Trust, Hong Kong, 1987—. Trustee Ill. Inst. Technology, Chgo., 1982-86, St. George's Sch., Newport, R.I., 1983—; aux bd. Art Inst. Chgo., 1974—. Mem. Racquet (gov. 1081-87), Chgo. Club, Racquet and Tennis Club. Republican. Episcopalian. Office: FH Prince & Co 10 S Wacker Dr #2575 Chicago IL 60606

WOODRUFF, BRENDA BISHOP, association administrator, law librarian; b. Palestine, Tex., July 10, 1945; d. William Perry and Leta Faye (Fitzgerald) Bishop; div., 1985; 1 child, Marya. BS, East Tex. State U., 1965, MLS, 1966. Lab. technician Poisonous Plant Lab. of USDA, Logan, Utah, 1967-71; cataloger Austin (Tex.) Pub. Library, 1971-74, Univ. Library, Cambridge, Eng., 1974-76; instr. library sci. dept. U. Okla., Norman, 1977; dir. Wood County Law Library, Bowling Green, Ohio, 1977-81; dir., law librarian Toledo Law Assn., 1981—; cons. Defiance (Ohio) County Law Library, 1982. Mem. editorial bd. Banks Baldwin Pub. Co., Cleve., 1987—; indexer: (book) Genetics and Biology of Drosophila, 1975-79. Mem. Am. Assn. Law Librs., Ohio Libr. Assn., Ohio Regional Assn. Law Librs. (sec. 1982-84, treas. 1985-87, v.p., pres. elect 1989—), LWV (sec. 1981-83). Democrat. Methodist. Office: Toledo Law Assn Lucas County Courthouse Toledo OH 43624

WOODRUM, ROBERT LEE, public relations executive; b. Merkel, Tex., Mar. 3, 1945; s. Bill and Norma (Shea) W.; m. Linda Mary Larkin, July 20, 1968; children: Jennifer, Michael. B.A., Calif. State U., 1967; postgrad., U. Okla., 1974. Press sec. U.S. Senate, Washington, 1977-78; dir. pub. affairs U.S. Office Personnel Mgmt., Washington, 1979-80; pres. Corp. Communications, Washington, 1980-82; v.p. Norton Simon Inc., N.Y.C., 1982-83; with Nat. Football League, N.Y.C., 1983-84; exec. dir. Ritz Paris Hemingway Award; pres. Ritz Paris Internat., 1984-86; sr. v.p. The Home Group, Inc., 1986—. Advisor USIA, Washington, 1980; advisor ARC, 1983, White House Vets. Com., 1979-80. Served to lt. comdr. USN, 1968-77. Decorated Navy Achievement medal 2. Club: New York Athletic. Home: 120 Long Neck Point Rd Darien CT 06820 Office: 59 Maiden Ln New York NY 10038

WOODS, BARRY ALAN, lawyer; b. N.Y.C., Nov. 21, 1942; s. Harry E. and Lillian (Breath) W.; m. Elsie Payene, Dec. 1980; children: Meredith Rose, Pamela Brett, B. Morgan. BS, N.Y. U., 1965, LLM in Taxation, 1969; JD, Bklyn. Law Sch., 1968. Bar: N.Y. 1968, U.S. Tax Ct. 1969, P.R. 1970, U.S. Dist. Ct. P.R. 1971; Ptnr. firm Baker & Woods, Santurce, P.R., 1970-76; mng. partner Woods & Woods, Hato Rey, P.R., 1976-81, Woods Rosenbaum Luckeroth & Perez-Gonzalez, 1981—; spl. cons. Tax Mgmt., Inc.; mem. Bur. Nat. Affairs, Adv. Bd. Internat. Taxation. Mem. Am. Soc. Internat. Law, Am. Bar Assn., Colegio de Abogados de P.R. Clubs: Caribe Hilton Swimming and Tennis, Pan Am. Gun, Bankers of P.R., NYU, Rum Rock Tennis. Author: United States Business Operations in Puerto Rico; Repatriation of Puerto Rico Source Earnings-Implication of Proposed Section 936; other publs. in field. Office: PO Box 1292 Hato Rey PR 00919

WOODS, DAVID WAYNE, electrical engineer; b. Aguadilla, P.R., Aug. 3, 1957; s. Weston Floy and Willie Ruth (Smith) W.; m. Shelia Denice Skaggs, Oct. 17, 1981; children: Jennifer Leigh, Sara Denise. BSEE, U. Ark., 1981. Asst. engr. Ark. Power and Light Co., Blytheville, 1981-83, assoc. engr., 1983-85, engr. I-planning, 1985-86, engr., I-design supr., 1986—. Career orientation speaker Boy Scouts Am., 1986—, dist. explorer chmn., 1989; bd. dirs. Ark. Power and Light Community Vols., Blytheville, 1988, v.p. bd. dirs., 1989; vol. Am. Cancer Soc., Blytheville, 1987. Mem. Ark. Soc. Profl. Engrs. Baptist. Office: Ark Power and Light 405 W Park Blytheville AR 72315

WOODS, HOWARD JAMES, JR., civil engineer; b. Elizabeth, N.J., Oct. 11, 1955; s. Howard James and Catherine (Hurring) W.; m. Patricia Edelin Wilson, Sept. 25, 1982. BCE cum laude, Villanova U., 1977, MCE, 1985. Registered profl. engr. N.Y., N.J., Pa., Md., N.Mex. Environ. engr. EPA, Phila., 1977-81; project engr. Johnson, Mirmiran & Thompson, Silver Spring, Md., 1981-83; dir. engring. eastern div. Am. Water Works Service Co., Haddon Heights, N.J., 1983-85, mgr. ops. eastern div., 1985-86, dir. planning, 1986-88, ea. regional mgr. engring., 1988—. Named one of Oustanding Young Men Am., Jaycees, 1984, Outstanding Civil Engring. Alumnus, Grad. Sch. Villanova U., 1986; recipient John J. Gallen award Villanova U. Coll. of Engring. Tech. Achievement award. Mem. ASCE, Nat. Soc. Profl. Engrs. (water policy issue expert 1983—), Nat. Water Well Assn., Am. Water Works Assn., Cousteau Soc., People for Am. Way, Am. Mgmt. Assn., Tau Beta Pi Assn. Democrat. Roman Catholic. Club: Villanova (Phila.). Home: 51 Warren St Beverly NJ 08010 Office: Am Water Works Service Co 500 Grove St Haddon Heights NJ 08035

WOODS, JAMES DUDLEY, manufacturing company executive; b. Falmouth, Ky., July 24, 1931; s. Alva L. and Mabel L. (Miller) W.; m. Darlene Mae Petersen, Nov. 8, 1962; children: Linda, Debbie, Jeffrey, Jamie. AA, Long Beach City Coll., 1958; BA, Calif. State U.-Fullerton, 1967, postgrad., 1968-70. Mgr. planning and control Baker Internat. Corp., Los Angeles, 1965-68, v.p. fin. and adminstrn. Baker div., 1968-73, corp. v.p., group fin. officer, 1973-76, corp. v.p., 1977, past exec. v.p.; pres., chief exec. officer Baker Internat. Corp., Houston; also dir. Baker Internat. Corp.; pres. Baker Packers, Houston, 1976-77, Baker Oil Tools, Orange, Calif., 1977-87; now chmn., pres., chief exec. officer Baker Hughes Inc., Houston. Served with USAF, 1951-55. Republican. Lutheran. Office: Baker Hughes Inc 3900 Essex Ln Houston TX 77027 *

WOODS, JOHN WITHERSPOON, banker; b. Evanston, Ill., Aug. 18, 1931; s. J. Albert and Cornelia (Witherspoon) W.; m. Loti Moultrie Chisolm, Sept. 5, 1953; children: Loti, Cindy, Corrie. BA, U. of South, 1954. With Chem. Bank, N.Y.C., 1954-69; v.p., head Chem. Bank (So. div.), 1965-69; chmn., chief exec. officer Am South Bancorp., 1972—, Am South Bank N.A., 1983—; dir. Protective Life Ins. Co., Birmingham, Ala., Power Co. Birmingham. Trustee So. Research Inst., Birmingham, Tuskegee Inst.; bd. dirs. Community Chest-United Way Jefferson County, past pres.; past chmn. working com. of 35 Gov.'s Ednl. Reform Commn.; bd. dirs. Ala. Inst. Deaf and Blind Found.; co.-chmn, bd. dirs. Ala. Mgmt. Improvement Program, Inc. 1st lt. USAF, 1955-57. Named to Ala. Acad. Honor. Mem. Birmingham Area C. of C. (pres. 1978, dir., exec. com.), Assn. Res. City Bankers, Assn. Bank Holding Cos. (bd. dirs.). Office: AmSouth Bancorp 1900 5th Ave N Ste 1400 PO Box 11007 Birmingham AL 35203

WOODS, LAWRENCE MILTON, airline company executive; b. Manderson, Wyo., Apr. 14, 1932; s. Ben Ray and Katherine (Youngman) W.; m. Joan Frances Van Patten, June 10, 1952; 1 dau., Laurie. B.Sc. with honors, U. Wyo., 1953; M.A., N.Y. U., 1973, Ph.D., 1975; LL.D., Wagner Coll., 1973. Bar: Mont. 1957; C.P.A., Colo., Mont. Accountant firm Peat, Marwick, Mitchell & Co. (C.P.A.'s), Billings, Mont., 1953; supervisory auditor Army Audit Agy., Denver, 1954-56; accountant Mobil Producing Co., Billings, Mont., 1956-59; planning analyst Socony Mobil Oil Co., N.Y.C., 1959-63; planning mgr. Socony Mobil Oil Co., 1963-65; v.p. North Am. div. Mobil Oil Corp., N.Y.C., 1966-67; gen. mgr. planning and econs. North Am. div. Mobil Oil Corp., 1967-69, v.p., 1969-77, exec. v.p., 1977-85, also dir.; pres., chief exec. officer, dir. Centennial Airlines, Inc., 1985—; bd. dirs. Handy & Harman, The Aid Assn. for Lutherans Mutual Funds. Author: Accounting for Capital, Construction and Maintenance Expenditures, 1967, The Wyoming Country Before Statehood, 1971, Sometimes the Books Froze, 1985, Moreton Frewen's Western Adventures, 1986; co-author: Takeover, 1980; contbr.: Accountants' Encyclopedia, 1962. Bd. dirs. Atlantic Council U.S., U. Wyo. Research Corp. Served with AUS, 1953-55. Mem. ABA, Mont. Bar Assn., Am. Inst. CPA's. Republican. Lutheran. Club: Pinnacle (N.Y.C.). Office: Centennial Airlines Inc PO Box 1860 Worland WY 82001

WOODS, MARCUS EUGENE, electric utility company executive, lawyer; b. Huntington, Ind., June 11, 1930; s. Harry Milton and Birtha Marie (Becker) W.; m. Jean Ann Vickers, Nov. 27, 1965; children: Marcus Eugene, Patrick Douglas, Edith Marie. B.B.A., Marquette U., 1952; J.D., Ind. U., 1960. Bar: Ind., U.S. Dist. Ct. (so. dist.) Ind. 1960, U.S. Ct. Appeals (7th cir.) 1963. Dep. atty. gen. State of Ind., Indpls., 1960-65; atty. Indpls. Power & Light Co., 1965-67, asst. sec., 1967-73, sec., gen. counsel, 1973—, v.p., 1980—; sec., gen. counsel IPALCO Enterprises, Inc., 1983—; dir. Property and Land Co., Inc., Indpls. Served with USAF, 1952-56. Mem. Ind. State Bar Assn., Indpls. Bar Assn., Edison Electric Inst. (legal com.), Am. Soc. Corp. Secs. Republican. Roman Catholic. Clubs: Athletic; Columbia (Indpls.). Home: 59 Carnaby Dr Brownsburg IN 46112 Office: Indpls Power & Light Co 25 Monument Circle Indianapolis IN 46204

WOODS, RANDALL J., manufacturing company official; b. Chgo., June 4, 1948; m. Carol Ann Kresse, Dec. 28, 1969; children: Paul, Carrie. AB, Princeton U., 1970; MBA, U. Chgo., 1975. Fin. mgr. ins. and benefits FMC Corp., Chgo., 1976-77, asst. dir. internat. fin., 1978, dir. risk mgmt., 1983-88, dir. risk mgmt and benefits adminstr., 1988—; v.p. Pentagon Pattern & Engring. Co., Chgo., 1979-83; bd. dirs. Corp. Officers and Dirs. Assurance Co., Bermuda. Mem. Risk and Ins. Mgmt. Soc. Office: FMC Corp 200 E Randolph Dr Chicago IL 60601

WOODS, REGINALD FOSTER, insurance company executive; b. Charleston, W.Va., Sept. 25, 1939; s. Reginald Foster and Jean Lee (Hill) W.; m. Katharine Terry Norden, May 11, 1963; children: Eric Arthur, Elizabeth Terry, Tracy Lee. BME, Cornell U., 1961, MBA., 1963. Mktg. specialist Gen. Electric Co., N.Y.C., 1963-64; dir. flight equipment and facilities planning Eastern Airlines, N.Y.C., 1964-70; v.p. planning Butler Internat., Inc., Montvale, N.J., 1970, sr. v.p. fin., 1971-80, exec. v.p., 1980-86, pres., 1986-87; pres. N.J. Life Ins. Co., Paramus, N.J., 1987—; dir. Benedetto, Gartland& Co., Paramus, N.J., 1988—. Clubs: Ridgewood Country, Wings. Office: NJ Life Ins Co East 15 Midland Ave Paramus NJ 07653-0981

WOODS, ROBERT EMMETT, commercial bank executive; b. Bklyn., Oct. 6, 1946; s. John Francis and Catherine M. (Ryan) W.; m. Patricia Helen Sloan, Sept. 8, 1973; children: Jennifer M., Kevin J. BBA, St. Francis Coll., Bklyn., 1973; MBA, Fordham U., 1976. Credit analyst Morgan Guaranty Trust Co., N.Y.C., 1973-77; asst. v.p., dep. mgr. banking Bayerische Vereinsbank, N.Y.C., 1977-81; v.p. group head Amsterdam Rotterdam Bank, N.Y.C., 1981-84; v.p., regional mgr. Berliner Handels und Frankfurter Bank, N.Y.C., 1984-89; v.p. Kyowa Bank, Ltd., N.Y.C., 1989—. Gen. mgr. Old Bridge (N.J.) Wings Hockey Club, 1987—. Served with U.S. Army, 1968-71. Am. Gas Assn. (mem. bankers adv. council 1982—). Roman Catholic. Home: 46 Ivanhoe Dr Manlapan NJ 07726 Office: Kyowa Bank Ltd One World Trade Ctr Ste 4673 New York NY 10048

WOODS, ROBERT LAWRENCE, insurance company executive, consultant; b. Los Angeles, May 17, 1911; s. Walter A. and Alice (Strang) W.; A.B., U. Calif. at Los Angeles, 1933; C.L.U., Am. Coll. Life Underwriters, 1937; m. Dorothy Welbourn, Oct. 10, 1942; children—Robert Lawrence, Susan Welbourn Woods Barker. With Los Angeles agy. of Mass. Mut. Life Ins. Co., 1934—, asst. gen. agt., 1938-46, assoc. gen. agt., 1946-49, gen. agt. in partnership, 1949-57, sole gen. agt., 1957-73. Fund raising chmn. Los Angeles chpt. ARC, 1961, dir., 1960-63. Trustee Am. Coll., 1958-61, 71-79. Served to lt. col., inf., AUS, 1941-46. Recipient John Newton Russell award Nat. Assn. Life Underwriters, 1971, Will G. Farrell award Los Angeles Life Ins. Assns., 1974; named to Mgmt. Hall of Fame, Nat. Gen. Agts. and Mgrs. Conf., 1974. Mem. Am. Soc. C.L.U.'s (pres. Los Angeles 1953-54, nat. pres. 1959-60), Mass. Mut. Gen. Agts. Assn. (pres. 1959-60), Gen. Agts. and Mgrs. Assn. (pres. Los Angeles 1957-58, nat. pres. 1967-68), Phi Gamma Delta. Home: 720 N Oakhurst Dr Beverly Hills CA 90210 Office: 4401 Wilshire Blvd Los Angeles CA 90010

WOODS, SANDRA KAY, brewing company real estate executive; b. Loveland, Colo., Oct. 11, 1944; d. Ivan H. and Florence L. (Betz) Harris; m. Gary A. Woods, June 11, 1967; children: Stephanie Michelle, Michael Harris. BA, U. Colo., 1966, MA, 1967. Personnel mgmt. specialist CSC, Denver, 1967; asst. to regional dir. HEW, Denver, 1968-69; urban renewal rep. HUD, Denver, 1970-73, dir. program analysis, 1974-75, asst. regional dir. community planning and devel., 1976-77, regional dir. fair housing, 1978-79; mgr. ea. facility project Adolph Coors Co., Golden Colo., 1980, dir. real estate, 1981, v.p. corp. real estate, 1982—; pres. Industries for Jefferson County (Colo.), 1985. Mem. Exec. Exchange, The White House, 1980; bd. dirs. Golden Local Devel. Corp. (Colo.), 1981-82; fundraising dir. Coll. Arts and Scis., U. Colo., Boulder, 1982-89, U. Colo. Found.; mem. exec. bd. NCCJ, Denver, 1982—; v.p. Women in Bus., Inc., Denver, 1982-83; mem. steering com. 1984 Yr. for All Denver Women, 1983-84. Named one of Outstanding Young Women Am., U.S. Jaycees, 1974, 78, Fifty Women to Watch, Businessweek, 1987, Woman of Achievement YWCA, 1988. Mem. Indsl. Devel. Resources Council (bd. dirs. 1986—), Am. Mgmt. Assn., Denver C. of C. (bd. dirs. 1988—, Disting. Young Exec. award 1974, mem. Leadership Denver, 1976-77), Colo. Women's Forum, Nat. Assn. Office and Indsl. Park Developers (sec. 1988, treas. 1989), Phi Beta Kappa, Beta Kappa, Pi Alpha Alpha. Republican. Presbyterian. Club: PEO (Loveland, Colo.). Office: Adolph Coors Co Real Estate 807 Golden CO 80401

WOODS, WIFRED RUFUS, editor, publisher; b. Wenatchee, Wash., Sept. 30, 1919; s. Rufus and Mary (Greenslit) W.; m. Kathleen K. Kingman, Dec. 1, 1951; children: Kara Woods Hunnicutt, Rufus G., Gretchen K. BA, U. Wash., 1947. Printer Wenatchee World, 1937-78, stereotyper, pressman, 1940-41, reporter, photographer, 1947-50, editor, pub., 1950—; bd. dirs. Cen. Wash. Bank, Wenatchee, Wenatchee Mountain, Inc. Mem. Wash. State Centennial Commn., Olympia, Wash., 1983. Recipient Nat. Voluntary Service award Nat. Park and Recreation Assn., Washington, 1983. Mem. Am. Forestry Assn. (bd. dirs. 1970—, past pres.). Club. Wash. Athletic. Home: 1107 Orchard Ave Wenatchee WA 98801 Office: Wenatchee World 14 N Mission Wenatchee WA 98801

WOODSIDE, WILLIAM STEWART, service company executive; b. Columbus, Ohio, Jan. 31, 1922; s. William Stewart and Frances (Moorman) W. B.S. in Bus. Adminstrn, Lehigh U., 1947; M.A. in Econs, Harvard, 1950. With Am. Can Co., 1950—; asst. to v.p., gen. mgr. Am. Can Co. (Dixie Cup div.), Easton, Pa., 1962-64; adminstrv. asst. to chmn. bd. Am. Can Co. (Dixie Cup div.), 1964-66, v.p., 1966-69, sr. v.p. packaging, 1969-74, exec. v.p. operations, 1974-75, pres., chief operating officer, 1975-80, pres., chief exec. officer, 1980-87, chmn. exec. com., 1980-87, chief exec. officer, 1980-86, chmn. exec. com., 1987-88; chmn. Sky Chefs, Inc., 1987—. Office: Primerica Corp 9 W 57th St New York NY 10019

WOODSMALL, JAMES VERNON, lawyer; b. Kansas City, Mo., July 23, 1950; s. James Robert and Catherine Marie (Ames) W.; m. kathleen Patricia, July 6, 1974; children: Megan, Andrea. BA, Northwestern U., 1975, JD,

1978. Bar: Ind., Mich., U.S. Supreme Ct. Ptnr. Warrick, Weaver & Boyn, Elkhart, Ind., 1978—; bd. dirs. McDowell Enterprises, Inc., Elkhart. Pres. Am. Lung Assn. No. Cen. Ind., South Bend, 1984-85; chmn. Elkhart Chamber Gen. Legis. Subcom., 1985—. Mem. Ind. Bar Assn., Mich. Bar Assn., ABA, Elkhart County Bar Assn., Elkhart City Bar Assn., Kiwanis (bd. dirs. 1981—, pres. 1987-88), Elks. Republican. Home: 23425 Greenleaf Elkhart IN 46514 Office: Warrick Weaver & Boyn 121 W Franklin St Ste 400 Elkhart IN 46516

WOODSON, STEPHEN WILLIAM, collection agency executive; b. Kansas City, Mo., May 31, 1950; s. William Albert and Patricia Marguerite (May) W.; A.A., Maple Woods Community Coll., 1977. Asst. mgr. Pub. Fin., San Pedro, Calif., 1973-74; asst. to v.p. MOAMCO, Mpls., 1974-75; pres. Met. Collection Services, Inc., North Kansas City, Mo., 1975-81, Regional Collection Services, 1981-84; collection cons. Blue Valley Fed. Savs. & Loan, 1975-86; pres. Transam. Collection Services, 1986—. Active Big Bros. and Sisters, Kansas City, Mo., 1977—; counselor Mo. Dept. Probation and Parole; pres. Job Readiness, Inc., 1983-86; mem. citizens adv. bd. Kansas City Alliance Bus. Task Force. Served with USN, 1967-70. Recipient Whitehall Found. Scholastic award, 1968. Mem. Internat. Traders Assn., Am. Collectors Assn., Northland C. of C. Democrat. Lutheran. Office: PO Box 34687 Kansas City MO 64116

WOODWARD, ALBERT BRUCE, JR., radio broadcaster, investment advisor, arbitrator, expert witness; b. Los Angeles, May 25, 1941; s. Albert Bruce and Virginia Hannah (Lacey) W.; m. Marilyn Ann Werner, June 23, 1962; children: Albert Bruce III, William Garth, Michelle Ann. Student, U. So. Calif., 1960-62; BS in Polit. Sci., U. Nebr., Omaha, 1974; MA in Internat. Mgmt., Monterey (Calif.) Inst. Internat. Studies, 1976. Cert. fin. planner. Pres. Tex. Internat. Cons. Inc., Dallas, 1965-79; div. mgr. Waddell & Reed Inc., Kansas City, Kans., 1979-83; chmn. Woodward Fin. Group Inc., Denver, 1983—; bd. dirs. Associated Planners Securities Corp., Los Angeles; mem. securities commr. adv. com. State of Colo., 1988—. Author: How To Be A Financial Planner, 1980; editor Planning & Computing 1979-86; host (radio program) The Money Corner, KNUS Radio, Denver, 1986-88, Bus. Radio Network, 1988-89. Chmn. parents div. Kent Denver Fund, 1985-87. Served to maj. U.S. Army, 1962-65, Vietnam. Decorated D.F.C., Bronze Star with 4 bronze oak leaf clusters, Purple Heart with 2 bronze oak leaf clusters. Mem. Inst. Cert. Fin. Planners (ethics com. 1986-87), Internat. Assn. for Fin. Planning (local pres. 1984-85, local chmn. bd. dirs. 1985-86), Internat. Bd. Standards and Practice Cert. Fin. Planners, Am. Arbitration Assn., Registry Fin. Planning Practitioners, Am. Legion. Republican. Episcopalian. Clubs: Denver Athletic, Denver Metropolitan. Lodges: Masons, Shriners, Elks. Home: 3561 S Dawson St Aurora CO 80014 Office: The Woodward Fin Group Inc 300 S Jackson Suite 500 Denver CO 80209

WOODWARD, M. CABELL, JR., corporation financial executive; b. Pitts., Jan. 29, 1929; s. M. Cabell and Anne (Cary) W.; m. Helen Boushee, July 24, 1954; children: Margaret Beale, Anne Cary. B.A., Princeton U., 1951; M.B.A., NYU, 1962. Asst. v.p. The Hanover Bank, N.Y.C., 1954-61; asst. treas. Continental Baking Co., Rye, N.Y., 1961-62; treas. Continental Baking Co., 1962-66, v.p. fin., dir., 1966-69; exec. v.p. ITT Continental Baking Co., Rye, 1969; pres. ITT Continental Baking Co., 1969, chief exec. officer, 1971-78; exec. v.p., chief fin. officer ITT Corp., N.Y.C., 1978-85; vice chmn., chief fin. officer ITT Corp., 1985—, dir., 1980—; dir. Melville Corp., Capital Cities/ABC, Inc. Served to capt. USMCR, 1951-53. Republican. Episcopalian. Office: ITT Corp 320 Park Ave New York NY 10022

WOODWARD, ROBERT J., JR., insurance executive; b. 1941; married. BA, Capital U., 1964, JD, 1971. With Nationwide Gen. Ins. Co., Columbus, 1964—, v.p., 1975—; v.p. Nationwide Life Ins. Co., Columbus, Nationwide Mut. Ins. Co., Columbus, Nationwide Mut. Fire Ins. Co., Columbus. Office: Nationwide Mut Ins Co One Nationwide Plaza Columbus OH 43216 *

WOODWARD, ROBERT SIMPSON, IV, economics educator; b. Easton, Pa., May 7, 1943; s. Robert Simpson and Esther Evans (Thomas) W.; B.A., Haverford Coll., 1965; Ph.D., Washington U., St. Louis, 1972; m. Mary P. Hutton, Feb. 15, 1969; children—Christopher Thomas, Rebecca Marie. Brookings Econ. Policy fellow HEW, Washington, 1975-76; asst. prof. U. Western Ont. (Can.), London, 1972-77; asst. prof. Sch. Medicine, Washington U., St. Louis, 1978-86, assoc. prof., 1986—; pres. Writing Assessment Software, Inc., 1987— . Mem. adv. council Mo. Kidney Program, 1980-86, vice-chmn., 1983, chmn. 1984-85; coop. mem. Haverford Coll., 1968—. NDEA fellow, 1968-71; Kellogg Nat. fellow, 1981-84. Mem. Am. Econs. Assn., Am. Statis. Assn. Contbr. articles to profl. jours. Home: 7050 Westmoreland St University City MO 63130 Office: 4547 Clayton Ave Saint Louis MO 63110

WOODWARD, WILLIAM J. D., retail executive. s. Charles N. W. Exec. v.p., chief oper. officer Woodward's Ltd., Vancouver, B.C., Can. Office: Woodwards Ltd, 101 W Hastings St, Vancouver, BC Canada V6B 4G1 *

WOODWARD, WILLIAM LEE, savings and loan company executive; b. Lexington, Ky., Jan. 12, 1926; s. Joel Henry and Ophelia Martha (Wallace) W.; A.B., U. Ky., 1950, M.A., 1952; m. Dorothy J. Dekle, Dec. 31, 1949; children—Pamela, William Lee, Martha. Tchr., Lafayette High Sch., 1950-52; asst. prin. Ft. Benning (Ga.) Children's Schs., 1952-53; asst. mgr. Lexington (Ky.) Fed. Savs. & Loan Assn., 1953-54, exec. v.p., 1954-73, pres., 1973—; bd. dirs. Savs. & Loan Data Corp., Cin. Pres., Lexington Deaf Oral Sch., 1968; trustee Midway (Ky.) Coll., 1968-80; treas. Bluegrass Found., 1967—; dir. Ky. Housing Corp., 1979-80. Served with USN, 1944-46. Mem. Ky. Savs. and Loan League (pres. 1969). Mem. Christian Ch. Clubs: Rotary, Lafayette. Office: 2020 Nicholasville Rd Lexington KY 40503

WOODWELL, DONALD RICHARD, computer executive; b. Drexel Hill, Pa., Feb. 21, 1941; s. Horace Davis and Margaret Ellen (Steele) W.; m. Doris Kathryn Hibbs, July 18, 1964; children: Donna Lynn, Douglas Richard. BS in Indsl. Engring., Pa. State U., 1962; MS in Systems Mgmt., U. So. Calif., 1967. Salesman IBM, Washington, Phila., 1968-75; sales staff IBM, Valley Forge, Pa., 1975-77; mktg. mgr. IBM, Phila., 1977-80; sr. forecaster IBM, Atlanta, 1980-82; mgr. bus. planning IBM, Princeton, N.J., 1982-84; mgr. mktg. program IBM, Piscataway, N.J., 1986-88; sr. engr. IBM, Raleigh, N.C., 1988—; pres. D&D Royalties, Inc., Belle Mead, N.J., 1984—; adj. prof. CCNY, 1987-88. Author: Automate Financial Port, 1983, 2d edit., 1986, Getting the Most from Your Home Computer, 1983, Using Dow Jones Info Systems, 1984, Managing PC Workstations, 1984. Pres. Montgomery Baseball League, Belle Mead, 1985; chmn. Montgomery United Meth. Ch., 1986. Capt. USAF, 1962-68. Republican. Office: IBM Corp Miami Blvd & Alexander Rd Research Triangle Park NC 27709

WOODWORTH, GERALD DEWAYNE, insurance agent; b. Quincy, Ill., Dec. 4, 1944; s. Alva E. and Rose (Jackson) W.; m. Irene Mae Walbring, Dec. 5, 1964; children: Kip, Lisa, Trena, Alisha. Student, Quincy Inst. Tech., Ga. State U. Die maker Olin Chem. Co., Kankakee, Ill., 1965-75; ins. agt. Gulf Life Ins. Co., Griffin, Ga., 1975-78, Woodworth & Assocs., Jonesboro, Ga., 1978—. Mem. Profl. Ins. Agts. Baptist. Home: 8531 N shore Dr Jonesboro GA 30236 Office: Woodworth & Assocs 696 Morrow Ind Blvd Suite C-9 Jonesboro GA 30236

WOODY, CAROL CLAYMAN, data processing executive; b. Bristol, Va., May 20, 1949; d. George Neal and Ida Mae (Nelms) Clayman; B.S. in Math., Coll. William and Mary, Williamsburg, Va., 1971; M.B.A. with distinction (IBM Corp. fellow 1978, Stephen Bufton Meml. Ednl. Found. grantee, 1978-79), Babcock Sch., Wake Forest U., 1979; m. Robert William Woody, Aug. 19, 1972. Programmer trainee GSA, 1971-72; systems engr. Citizens Fidelity Bank & Trust Co., Louisville, 1972-75; programmer/analyst-tng. coordinator Blue Bell, Inc., Greensboro, N.C., 1975-79; supr. programming and tech. services J.E. Baker Co., York, Pa., 1979-82, fin. design supr. bus. systems Lycoming div. AVCO, Stratford, Conn., 1982-83; project mgr. Yale U., 1984—; co-owner Sign of the Sycamore, antiques; mem. Data Processing Standards Bd., 1977, CICS/VS Adv. Council, 1975; speaker Nat. Fuse Conf., 1989. Mem. Am. Bus. Woman's Assn. (chpt. v.p. 1978-79; Merit award 1978), Nat. Assn. Female Execs., Delta Omicron (alumni pres. 1973-75, regional chmn. 1979-82). Republican. Presbyterian. Author various manuals. Home: PO Box 1450 Guilford CT 06437 Office: 155 Whitney Ave New Haven CT 06510

WOOLARD, EDGAR SMITH, JR., chemical company executive; b. Washington, N.C., Apr. 15, 1934; s. Edgar Smith and Mamie Rowena (Boone) W.; m. Peggy Lou Harrell, June 9, 1956; children: Barbara Annette, Lynda Denise. BS, N.C. State U., 1956. Gen. mgr. textile fibers E.I. du Pont de Nemours & Co Inc., Wilmington, Del., 1978-81, v.p. textile fibers, 1981-83, exec. v.p., 1983-85, vice chmn., 1985-87, pres., chief operating officer, 1987-89, chmn., 1989—, also bd. dirs.; bd. dirs. N.C. Textile Found., Raleigh, Citicorp., IBM Corp. Bd. dirs. Young Men's Christian Assn., Wilmington, 1977—; trustee Med. Ctr. Del., 1985—, N.C. State U. and Winterthur Mus. Served to lt. U.S. Army, 1957. Lodges: Rotary, Masons. Office: E I Du Pont de Nemours & Co 1007 Market St Wilmington DE 19898

WOOLDREDGE, WILLIAM DUNBAR, independent oil and gas company executive; b. Salem, Mass., Oct. 27, 1937; s. John and Louise (Sigourney) W.; m. Johanna Marie; children: John, Rebecca Wistar. B.A., Colby Coll., 1961; M.B.A., Harvard, 1964. Staff assoc. Sun Oil Co., Phila., 1964-67; treas. Ins. Co. N.Am., Phila., 1967-72; treas. B.F. Goodrich Co., Akron, Ohio, 1972-84, sr. v.p., 1978-79, exec. v.p., chief fin. officer, mem. mgmt. com., 1979-84; chief fin. officer, exec. v.p., dir. Belden & Blake Corp., North Canton, Ohio, 1984—; sr. v.p., chief fin. officer, dir. Belden & Blake Oil Prodn., Inc., 1984—; bd. dirs. Belden and Blake Internat, Ltd., Hamilton, Bermuda, Transohio Savs. Bank, Cleve., Freeway Corp., Cleve. Bd. dirs. Salvation Army, Akron Roundtable; chmn. bd. trustees Children's Hosp. Med. Center, Akron.; trustee Colby Coll. With U.S. Army, 1956-58. Mem. Fin. Execs. Inst. Episcopalian. Club: Country of Hudson. Home: 7330 Valley View Dr Hudson OH 44236 Office: 7555 Freedom NW North Canton OH 44720

WOOLF, RONALD ALAN, data processing executive; b. Lubbock, Tex., May 18, 1862; s. Alfred Monroe and Frances Ann (Kimberling) W. BS in Computer Sci., North Tex. State U., 1988. Sr. computing technician Bell Helicopter Textron, Ft. Worth, 1984—. Coach Arlington Boys Club, 1986-88. Republican. Baptist. Clubs: Bell Helicopter Golf League (Ft. Worth) (v.p. 1987-89), N.T.C.C. (Denton) (treas. 1988-89). Home: 6813 Quail Run Watauga TX 76148 Office: Bell Helicopter Textron PO Box 482 Dept 87 Fort Worth TX 76101

WOOLF, STEVEN MICHAEL, artistic director; b. Milw., Dec. 23, 1946; s. Raleigh and Lenore (Shurman) W. BA in Theatre, U. Wis., 1968, MFA, 1971. Prodn. stage mgr. The Juilliard Sch. Drama, N.Y.C., 1973-75; project producer Musical Theatre Lab., N.Y.C., 1974-75; prodn. stage mgr. Barter Theatre, Abingdon, Va., 1976-79, Stagewest, Springfield, Mass., 1976-79; prodn. mgr. Repertory Theatre of St. Louis, 1980-83, acting artistic dir., mng. dir., 1983-85, mng. dir., 1985-86, artistic dir., 1986—; adj. faculty Webster U., St. Louis, 1982—; mem. nat. negotiating coms. League of Resident Theatres, N.Y.C., 1986—; on-site evaluator Nat. Endowment for the Arts, 1985. Dir. (plays) A Life in the Theatre, 1982, The Crucible, 1986, Company, 1987, The Voice of the Prairie, 1988, The Boys Next Door, 1989. Mem. ad hoc coms. for funding Mo. Arts Coun., St. Louis, 1988; chair citizen rev. panel Regional Arts Commn., St. Louis, 1986. Mem. Soc. of Stage Dirs. and Choreographers, Actors Equity Assn. Office: Repertory Theatre of St Louis 130 Edgar Rd Saint Louis MO 63119

WOOLFORD, WILLIAM ALLEN, small business owner; b. Balt., Nov. 7, 1919; s. William Allen and Jeane (Hurst) W.; m. Mary Jo Ryan, Feb. 21, 1959; children:Jean M. Aitken, Julie A. Bates, Lisa J. Cramer. BSCE, Colo A&M Coll., 1951. Reg. profl. engr., 16 states. Staff appraiser Justin H. Haynes & Co., Denver, 1951-53; chief engr. Denver Wood Products Co., Denver, 1960-65; v.p. mktg. Ken R. White Co., Denver, 1967-72, Tech. Svc. Co., Denver, 1972-75, DMJM Phillips Reister, Denver, 1975-77; pres. Woolford Co., Aurora, Colo., 1953—. 1st lt. U.S. Army, 1940-46. Fellow ASCE; mem. Nat. Acad. Forensic Engrs. (diplomate), Am. Inst. Real Estate Appraisers, Am. Soc. Appraisers, Internat. Right of Way Assn.,University, Heather Ridge. Home: 13961 E Marina Dr Apt 409 Aurora CO 80014 Office: William Woolford & Assocs 12200 E Iliff Ave Ste 100 Aurora CO 80014

WOOLLEY, DONALD EUGENE, banker; b. Worcester, Mass., Sept. 11, 1922; s. Vern Clark and Emma (Walker) W.; BA, George Washington U., 1947, postgrad., 1947-48; MBA, NYU, 1952; m. Mollie Barker, Jan. 12, 1968; children: Susan L., Melissa W., Jonathan A. Econ. analyst, Chase Manhattan Bank, N.Y.C., 1948-55; economist, then v.p., Bankers Trust Co., N.Y.C., 1955-72, v.p., head econs. dept., 1972-78, sr. v.p., chief economist, 1978-84; econ. cons., Westdeutsche Landesbank, 1984—. Trustee N.Y. Council on Econ. Edn. Served with U.S. Navy, 1943-46. Mem. U.S. C. of C., Am. Bankers Assn., N.Y. Commerce and Industry Assn., Nat. Assn. Bus. Economists (former mem. council), N.Y. Assn. Bus. Economists (past pres.), Am. Statis. Assn., Am. Fin. Assn., Forecasters Club. Republican. Editor: Bankers Trust Co., biannual publ., 1972-84, Credit and Capital Markets. Home: 2000 Linwood Ave Apt 14N Fort Lee NJ 07024 Office: Westdeutsche Landesbank 450 Park Ave New York NY 10022

WOOLSEY, SUZANNE HALEY, management consultant; b. San Francisco, Dec. 27, 1941; d. William Harrison and Beryl (Wilkerson) Haley; m. Robert James Woolsey, Aug. 15, 1965; children: Robert, Daniel, Benjamin. BA, Stanford U., 1963; MA, Harvard U., 1965, PhD, 1970. Psychology trainee Veterans Hosp., West Haven, Conn. and Washington, 1966-68; assoc. prof. Fed. City Coll., Washington, 1968-70; dir. policy analysis for social service and human devel. Sec. of HEW, Washington, 1970-75; research program dir. The Urban Inst., Washington, 1975-77; assoc. dir. Office of Mgmt. and Budget, Washington, 1977-80; ptnr. Coopers & Lybrand, Washington, 1980—; nat. adv. bd. Pvt. Sector Council, Washington; bd. dirs. Nat. Rehab. Hosp., Washington; vis. com. Duke U. Pub. Policy Inst., Durham, N.C.; mem. humanities and sci. council Stanford U., 1983-87. Mem. long range planning com. Norwood Sch., Bethesda, Md., 1988; chmn. pastoral nominating com. of Chevy Chase Presbyn. Ch., Washington, 1986. Recipient Tribute to Women in Internat. Industry Nat. YMCA, 1981. Mem. Nat. Acad. Scis. (coms. 1980—), Ctr. for Excellence in Govt., Tchrs. Ins. Annuity Fund (policyholder's nominating com. chair 1987-88). Office: Coopers & Lybrand 1800 M St NW Washington DC 20036

WOOSNAM, RICHARD EDWARD, venture capitalist, lawyer; b. Anderson, Ind., June 27, 1942; s. Richard Wendell and Ruth (Cleveland) W.; m. Susan L. Mangel, Aug. 21, 1965; children: Cynthia S., Elizabeth C. BS, Ind. U., 1964, JD, 1967, MBA, 1968. Bar: Ind. 1967, U.S. Dist. Ct. (so. dist.) Ind. 1967. Instr. bus. law Ind. U., Bloomington, 1966-68; assoc. Ferguson, Ferguson & Lloyd, Bloomington, 1967-68; dep. prosecutor Monroe County (Ind.), Bloomington, 1967-68; tax acct. Price Waterhouse, Phila., 1968-69; v.p., treas. Innovest Group, Inc., Phila., 1969-82, chmn., pres., 1983—, also dir.; guest lectr. Wharton Sch. Bus., U. Pa., Ind. U., Bloomington, 1975—; bd. dirs. Capital Mgmt. Corp., Modern Video Prodns., Inc., Skyworks, Inc., Pearce Perrone & Co., Inc.; adv. council Nat. Entrepreneurship Found. Mem. ABA, Ind. Bar Assn., World Affairs Council. Republican. Methodist. Club: Union League of Phila. Home: 429 Leopard Rd Berwyn PA 19312 Office: 1700 Market St Suite 1228 Philadelphia PA 19103

WOOTTEN, HUBERT EUGENE, III, financial analyst; b. Gallatin, Tenn., May 26, 1949; s. Hubert Eugene and Rebecca Anne (Higgison) W.; m. Mary Elizabeth MacNary, Oct. 10, 1948; children: Kimberly Campbell, Tammy Ponce, Virginia, Rebecca. BS, Mid. Tenn. State U., 1971. Cert. fin. planner. Environmentalist Met. Nashville Health Dept., 1971-75; distbn. mgr. Nova, Inc., Nashville, 1973-75; gen. mgr. Port Royal Inn, Hilton Head Island, S.C., 1975-79; dir. mgr. Jefferson Standard Life Ins. Co., Nashville, 1979-82; fin. planner Nat. Planning Svcs., Inc., Nashville, 1982—. Named Man of Yr., Nashville Gen. Agts. and Mgrs. Assn., 1986. Mem. Donelson-Hermitage C. of C., Donelson-Hermitage Exchange Club (pres.-elect 1988). Office: Nat Fin Planning Svcs Inc 1800 Church St Ste 300 Nashville TN 37138

WOOTTON, MACK EDWARD, food products company executive; b. Lafayette, Ind., Sept. 4, 1937; s. Ralph Edward and Thelma Athel (McCarty) W.; m. Linda Nell Spence, June 19, 1960; children: Jeffrey David, Kella Linn. AB, Ind. U., 1959. Employment supr. Cen. Soya Co. Inc., Ft. Wayne, Ind., 1964-65, tng. dir., 1965-66, product control mgr., 1971-73, corp. compensation dir., 1973-77, dir. personnel services, 1977-83, dir. sales chemurgy div., 1983-84, gen. mgr. chemurgy div., 1984-85, v.p. adminstrn., corp. sec., 1985—; plant personnel mgr. Cen. Soya Co. Inc., Chattanooga, 1966-71. Mem. allocations com. United Way, Ft. Wayne; mem. adv. com. Ind. Vocat. Tech. Coll., Ft. Wayne, 1978-85; trustee Parkview Meml. Hosp., Ft. Wayne; bd. dirs. McMillen Health Ctr., Ft. Wayne. Served to capt. USAF, 1959-64. Mem. Am. Mgmt. Assn. (human resources council 1986—), Ind. C. of C. (personnel and labor relations com. 1978-83). Republican. Methodist. Home: 6017 Monarch Dr Fort Wayne IN 46815 Office: Cen Soya Co Inc PO Box 1400 Fort Wayne IN 46801

WORENKLEIN, JACOB J., lawyer; b. N.Y.C., Oct. 1, 1948; s. Abraham and Cela (Zyskind) W.; m. Marion Knopf, June 27, 1967; children: David, Daniel, Laura. BA, Columbia U., 1969; MBA, JD, NYU, 1973. Bar: N.Y. 1974. Assoc. Milbank, Tweed, Hadley & McCloy, N.Y.C., 1973-81, ptnr., 1982—, also firm exec. com., 1984-86, chmn. firm planning com., 1988—; chmn. Utility Leasing Conf., 1988. Contbr. articles to profl. jours. Pres. Old Broadway Synagogue, N.Y.C., 1978—; trustee Fedn. Jewish Philanthropies, N.Y.C., 1984-86; bd. of overseers, United Jewish Appeal-Fedn. Jewish Philanthropies, 1987—, chmn. lawyers' div. major gifts, 1989—. Mem. ABA (electricity and utility financing com.), N.Y. State Bar Assn. (sec. action unit toward more effective legislature 1975), Assn. of Bar of City of N.Y., Fed. Energy Bar Assn., Down Town Assn., Phi Beta Kappa. Office: Milbank Tweed Hadley & McCloy 1 Chase Manhattan Pla New York NY 10005

WORKMAN, CHARLES CLEVELAND, JR., management consultant; b. Lineville, Ala., Apr. 14, 1913; s. Charles Cleveland and Emma Franklin (Jones) W.; B.S., Auburn U., 1934; m. Jane Lucille Pinaire, Aug. 19, 1944 (dec.); 1 dau., Janet Susan Workman Baltzer; m. Bessie Kate Bradford, Mar. 23, 1968 (dec.); m. Shelby Gause Freeman, June 28, 1985. Trainee, Consol. Millinery Co. of Chgo., 1934-35, br. mgr., Miami, Fla. also Allentown, Pa., 1935-36; asst. dept. mgr. Stewart Dry Goods Co., Louisville, 1937; with IBM Corp., 1937-70, sales rep., Louisville, 1937-40, br mgr., Shreveport, La., 1946-49, Houston, 1950-54, mgr. Southeast dist., Atlanta, 1955-62, dir. mktg. Fed. Systems div., Washington, 1963, mgr. aerospace and dist. br., Atlanta, 1964-70; pres. Mgmt. Services, Inc., Atlanta, 1971-74; So. regional mgr. TLW Corp., Atlanta, 1974-76; mgmt. cons., Atlanta, 1977—; gen. ptnr. Midtown Investment Properties, Etowah Investment Properties, Dawson Investment Opportunity. Bd. dirs. Goodwill Industries, 1960-73, pres., 1972-73; various offices ARC, 1937-71, United Way, 1937-71; mem. U.S. Congressional Adv. Bd., Am. Security Council, 1980—. Served to lt. col. AUS, 1940-45. Mem. SAR, Nat. Assn. Accts., Nat. Sales Execs. Club. Republican. Presbyterian (deacon). Clubs: Kiwanis Internat., Cherokee Town and Country. Address: 9790 Huntcliff Trace Atlanta GA 30350

WORKMAN, ELIOT WAYNE, insurance executive; b. N.Y.C., July 10, 1939; s. Nathan Mark and Molly (Jacobs) W.; m. Bonnie Naila, 1969 (dec. 1981); children: Joseph, Cindy, Ailene, Karen, Amy, Steven; m. Catherine A. Thisted, Feb. 11, 1985. BA in Fin., Calif. Western U., 1974, MBA in Mktg., 1974. With Am. Tool Products Co., 1973-76; v.p. sales and mktg. Western Financial Svcs., 1976-79; owner, pres. Eliot Workman Ins. Agy., L.A., 1970-80, Simi Valley, Calif., 1981—; cons. in field. Lt. comdr. USN, 1957-64. Home and Office: 1507 N Rogue St Placentia CA 92670

WORKMAN, LAURAL ANN, retail association executive; b. Monrovia, Calif., Feb. 13, 1960; d. Albert Robert and Laura Louise (Benton) W. BMus, U. Oreg., 1983. Acctg. clk. Renfield Importers, N.Y.C., 1981-82; adminstrv. asst. Internat. Council Shopping Ctrs., N.Y.C., 1983-84, meetings mgr., 1984-85, western meetings dir., San Francisco, 1986—. Co-author: Guide to ICSC Idea Exchanges, 1985. Mem. NOW, Nat. Assn. Female Execs., Phi Beta (pres. 1981-82). Democrat. Avocations: classical musician, tennis, travel, swimming. Home: 5401 Diamond Heights Blvd Apt 4 San Francisco CA 94131 Office: Internat Council Shopping Ctrs 353 Sacramento St Suite 400 San Francisco CA 94111

WORLEY, GRACE MARIE, financial planner; b. Indpls., Aug. 10, 1949; d. Donald H. and M. Helen (Niehoff) Struck; m. Scott E. Worley, July 13, 1971 (div. 1977); 1 child, Heather; m. Thomas J. Mouzakis, June 1, 1986; 1 child, Maria L. BA, Ind. U., 1971; MBA, Ind. U., Indpl., 1988. Cert. fin. planner. Mgr. pub. affairs Allstate Ins. Co., Indpls., 1973-85; fin. planner Creative Fin. Planning, Indpls., 1985, Fin. Strategies Group, Indpls., 1986, Worley Mouzakis Adv. Inc., Indpls., 1986—; adj. instr. Ind. U., Indpls., 1986—, Coll. Fin. Planning, Denver, 1988—. Pres. Big Sisters Greater Indpls., 1980-81. Mem. Internat. Assn. Fin. Planning (treas. Ind. chpt. 1987), Inst. Cert. Fin. Planners (v.p. Ind. chpt. 1988—), Network of Women in Bus. Exec. Club (founding, chmn. 1987, Bus. Woman of Yr. 1987). Office: Worley Mouzakis Adv Inc 8515 Cedar Pl Dr #103B Indianapolis IN 46240

WORMINGTON, DANNY MARK, lending company executive; b. Hobbs, N.Mex., Jan. 10, 1965; s. Jimmie Howard and Mary Helen (Bounous) W. AS in Computer Sci., Okla. Jr. Coll., Tulsa, 1987. Br. mgr. Am. Lenders Service Co., Little Rock, 1987-88, Tulsa, 1988—. Republican. Methodist. Office: Am Lenders Svc Co PO Box 470746 Tulsa OK 74147

WORREL, CHARLES JOSEPH, real estate company executive; b. Austin, Tex., Aug. 15, 1946; s. Eva May (Kinzbach) Worrel; m. Sandra Hughes, Apr. 1983 (div.); children: Chad, Daniel, Ethan. BA, U. Tex., 1969. Pres. Onion Creek Reconstrn. Co., San Antonio, 1974-82; land specialist Coldwell-Banker Comml. Real Estate Co., San Antonio, 1983-86; regional dir. acquisitions Century Investments Co., Houston and Nashville, 1986-87; acquisitions, research officer Landmark Capital Corp., Nashville, 1987—. Mem. Austin Writers League. Home: PO Box 150424 Nashville TN 37215 Office: Landmark Capital Corp 222 3d Ave N Suite 420 Nashville TN 37201

WORSHAM, JAMES E., aircraft company executive. B.S., Vanderbilt U., 1948; M.S., U. Ark., 1950. Engring. designer engine devel. programs Gen. Electric Co., 1951-71, gen. mgr. Evendale mil. advanced engines dept., 1971-73, v.p., gen. mgr. mil. engine projects div. aircraft engring. bus. group, 1973-76, v.p., gen. mgr. airline programs div., 1976-78, v.p., gen. mgr. comml. engine programs div., 1978-79, v.p., gen. mgr. comml. engine ops., 1979-81, v.p., gen. mgr. market devel. ops. aircraft engine bus. group, 1981-82; exec. v.p. Douglas Aircraft Co., Long Beach, Calif., 1982, pres., 1982-87, 88-89; corp. v.p. aerospace group exec. McDonnell Douglas Corp., St. Louis, 1987-88; chmn., GPA, Pacific and Asia Guinness Peat Aviation, Shannon, Ireland, 1989—. Office: Guinness Peat Aviation, GPA House, Shannon Ireland other: McDonnell Douglas Corp PO Box 516 Saint Louis MO 63166 *

WORTELL, BRENTON RICHARD, manufacturing company executive; b. Chgo., Aug. 9, 1955; s. Marvin Richard and Esther Ruth (Gerber) W.; m. Kathryn Gould, Apr. 15, 1984; children: Rachel, Rebecca. BS, De Paul U., 1979; cert. in advanced mgmt., U. Chgo., 1980. Sales engr. Triton Industries, Inc., Chgo., 1979-81, plant ops. mgr., 1981-84; v.p. Bell & Thorn, Inc., Chgo., 1984-89; pres. Triton Industries & Bell & Thorn, Inc., Chgo., 1989—. Mem. Soc. Mfg. Engrs. (sr.), Mfg. Mgrs. Assn. (sr.), Am. Soc. for Quality Control (sr.), Commonwealth Assn. (bd. dirs. 1986—), Precision Metalforming Assn. (chmn. worldclass selling conf. 1988, pres. 1988—), Phi Alpha Theta. Republican. Jewish. Office: Bell & Thorn Mfg Inc 4259 S Western Ave Chicago IL 60609

WORTH, JAMES GALLAGHER, engineer, chemist; b. Phila., Sept. 20, 1922; s. Wilmon W. and Elsie (Gallagher) W.; Assoc. Sci., Rochester Inst. Tech., 1949; B.S., U. Miami, 1949-51; postgrad. U. So. Calif., 1961—; m. Esther Alberta Cring, Sept. 11, 1943 (dec. 1981); children—Nancy Jeanne, Constance Anne, James Gallagher; m. Barbara Marie Demarest, Mar. 22, 1985. Chem. technician Internat. Paper Co., 1942-43, Eastman Kodak Co., 1946-49; pres., founder, engr.-chemist Applied Research Labs. Fla., Inc., Hialeah, 1949-84, chmn. bd., 1956-84; pres., chmn. bd. Ra-Chem Lab., Inc., Hialeah, 1964-66; Worth Engring., Inc., Hialeah, 1984—. Served to maj. USAAF, 1943-46; with USAFR, 1946-82. Registered profl. engr., Calif., Fla. Fellow Am. Inst. Chemists; mem. Am. Chem. Soc., Am. Soc. Testing Materials, Am. Metals Soc., Nat. Soc. Profl. Engrs., Fla. Engring. Soc., Nat.

Fire Protection Assn. Democrat. Methodist. Mason. Home: 751 Oriole Ave Miami Springs FL 33166 Office: 650 Palm Ave Hialeah FL 33010

WORTHEN, JOHN A., insurance executive. From v.p. to sr. v.p. John Hancock Mut. Life Ins. Co. Office: John Hancock Mut Life Ins Co PO Box 111 Boston MA 02117 *

WORTHINGTON, O. DOUGLAS, insurance company executive; b. Angola, Ind., Aug. 11, 1949; s. Olin Earl and Emily Irene (Groshon) W.; m. Marsha Ann Sheets, June 6, 1970; children: Amy Michelle, Joel Douglas. BS, Ball State U., 1971. CPA, Ind. Audit supr. Ernst & Whinney, Ft. Wayne, Ind., 1971-78; v.p. finance Thunderbird Products Corp., Decatur, Ind., 1979-81; asst. v.p. Lincoln Nat. Pension Ins. Co., Ft. Wayne, 1981-85, 2d v.p., 1985—; v.p. Lincoln Nat. Investment Mgmt. Co., Ft. Wayne, 1986—; treas. controlle Lincoln Nat. Direct Placement Fund, Inc., Ft. Wayne, 1987—, Lincoln Nat. Convertible Securities Fund, Inc., Ft. Wayne, 1987—. Mem. com. United Way Allen County, Ft. Wayne; bd. dirs.SCAN, Inc., Ft. Wayne, 1985—; participant leadership Ft. Wayne, 1988—; pres. North Ind. Conf. Found., Marion, Ind., 1988—. Mem. AICPA, Am. Life Office Mgmt. Assn., Ind. Assn. CPA's, Nat. Assn. Accts. (com. chmn. 1982). Methodist. Home: 2827 Buckhurst Run Fort Wayne IN 46815 Office: Lincoln Nat Investment Mgmt Co 1300 S Clinton St Fort Wayne IN 46801

WORTHY, K(ENNETH) MARTIN, lawyer; b. Dawson, Ga., Sept. 24, 1920; s. Kenneth Spencer and Jeffrie Pruett (Martin) W.; m. Eleanor Vreeland Blewett, Feb. 15, 1947 (dec. July 1981); children: Jeffrie Martin, William Blewett; m. Katherine Teasley Jackson, June 17, 1983. Student, The Citadel, 1937-39; B.Ph., Emory U., 1941, J.D. with honors, 1947; MBA cum laude, Harvard U., 1943. Bar: Ga. 1947, D.C. 1948. Assoc. mem. firm Hopkins, Sutter, Hamel & Park (formerly Hamel & Park), Washington, 1948-52; partner Hopkins, Sutter, Hamel & Park (formerly Hamel & Park), 1952-69, 72—; chief counsel IRS, 1969-72; also asst. gen. counsel Treasury Dept., 1969-72; dir. Beneficial Corp., 1977—; mem. Nat. Council Organized Crime, 1970-72; cons. Justice Dept., 1972-74. Author: (with John M. Appleman) Basic Estate Planning, 1957; contbr. articles to profl. jours. Del. Montgomery County Civic Fedn., 1951-61, D.C. Area Health and Welfare Coun., 1960-61; mem. Emory Law Sch. Coun., 1976—; trustee Chelsea Sch., 1981—; trustee St. John's Coll., Annapolis, Md. and Santa Fe, 1987—. Served to capt. AUS, 1943-46, 51-52. Recipient Treasury Exceptional Service award and medal, 1972, IRS Commrs. award, 1972. Fellow Aspen Inst., Am. Bar Found., Am. Coll. Tax Counsel (bd. regents 1980-88, vice chmn. 1983-85, chmn. 1985-87); mem. Ga. Bar Assn., D.C. Bar Assn., Fed. Bar Assn. (nat. council 1969-72, 77-79), ABA (council taxation sect. 1965-68, vice chmn. 1968-69, 72-73, chmn. 1973-74; Ho. of Dels. 1983—; chmn. audit com. 1985—, del. Nat. Conf. Lawyers and C.P.A.s 1981-87), Am. Law Inst., Nat. Tax Assn., Phi Delta Theta, Phi Delta Phi, Omicron Delta Kappa. Episcopalian (chmn. dept. finance Washington Diocese 1969-70). Clubs: Chevy Chase, Metropolitan, National Lawyers, City Tavern (Washington); Harvard (N.Y.C.); James River Country (Newport News, Va.). Home: 5305 Portsmouth Rd Bethesda MD 20816 Office: Hopkins Sutter Hamel & Park 888 16th St NW Washington DC 20006

WOSNITZKY, CATHY GARNER, sales executive, performer; b. Houston, Oct. 2, 1957; d. Charles Richard Garner Sr. and Audrey Lucille (Shadwell) Bain; m. Daniel Glenn Wosnitzky, Feb. 5, 1977; children: Aaron Matthew, Brandon Alastair. Student, Wharton County Jr. Coll., 1979-81, Houston Community Coll., 1979-81. Sales mgr. Tupperware U.S.A., Houston, 1979-81; sales supr. Criterion Telephone, Houston, 1983-84; systems cons. Modcom of Huston, 1984; owner, performer Cat Boxe Theatre, Houston, 1984—; sales mgr. TMC Am., Inc., Houston, 1985-86; ter. mgr. Millicom, Inc., Houston, 1987; sales mgr. Telecom Inc., Houston, 1987—. Author: (play) The Princess, The Dragon and The Wicked Stepmother, 1984, Snow White and the Four Dwarves, 1985. Mem. Nat. Assn. Female Execs., Career Saleswomen's Assn., Am. Soc. Bus. and Profl. Women, Fedn. Houston Profl. Women, SW Communications Assn. Mormon. Club: The Gallifreyan Consulate (Houston) (treas. 1983-86).

WOTTON, BRIAN EDWARD, accountant; b. Newark, Jan. 6, 1959; s. Stewart Davis and Jean Winifred (Gunnerson) W.; m. Tonimarie Vicino, July 18, 1981. BS in Acctg. cum laude, Ft. Lauderdale Coll., 1983. CPA, N.J. Cost acct. Brunner & Lay Inc., Ft. Lauderdale, Fla., 1981-82; sr. acct. Curchin & Co., CPA's, Red Bank, N.J., 1982-85, Grossman Weinberg & Assocs., CPAs, Neptune, N.J., 1985-87, Concurrent Computer Corp., Tinton Falls, N.J., 1987—. Republican. Presbyterian. Office: Concurrent Computer Corp 106 Apple St Tinton Falls NJ

WRAGG, LAISHLEY PALMER, JR., lawyer; b. Pitts., Oct. 11, 1933; s. Laishley Palmer and Irma Grace (Hill) W.; m. Marilyn Jean Smith, Apr. 26, 1957; children: Laishley P., Peter M.B. BBA, U. Mich., 1955; LLB cum laude, Harvard U., 1960; diploma in comparative legal studies Trinity Hall Coll., Cambridge U. (Eng.), 1961. Bar: N.Y. 1962, U.S. Supreme Ct. 1974, Conseil Juridique, France 1977. Assoc. Cravath, Swaine & Moore, N.Y.C., 1961-62, 1965-69, Paris, 1963-65; assoc. Curtis, Mallet-Prevost, Colt & Mosle, N.Y.C., 1969-70, ptnr., 1970—. Mem. U.S. Dept. State ad hoc com. on large constrn. projects; U.S. del. to 15th-20th sessions of UNCITRAL. Served to lt. USN, 1955-57. Mem. Assn. of Bar of City of N.Y., U. S. Council of Internat. C. of C. (com. on restrictive bus. practices), Inter-Am. Bar Assn., French Am. C. of C., France Am. Soc. (N.Y.C.). Republican. Presbyterian. Clubs: Am. Yacht (Rye, N.Y.); Hawks (Cambridge, Eng.), Ekwanok County (Manchester, Vt.); Automobile de France (Paris); Harvard of N.Y., Duquesne (Pitts.). Contbr. articles on law to profl. jours. Home: 123 E 75th St New York NY 10021 Office: Curtis Mallet-Prevost Colt & Mosle 101 Park Ave New York NY 10178

WRAPP, HENRY EDWARD, business administration educator; b. Paragould, Ark., Mar. 26, 1917; s. Alba Henry and Mildred (Dennis) W.; m. Marguerite Amy Hill, Aug. 19, 1950; children—Jennifer, Gregory, Stephen, Amy, Katherine. B.C.S., U. Notre Dame, 1938; M.B.A., Harvard U., 1948, D.C.S., 1951. With E.I. duPont deNemours & Co., Inc., 1939-43; prof. Harvard U., 1955-62; prof. bus. policy U. Chgo., 1963-83, assoc. dean, 1965-70; faculty St. Vincent De Paul Sem., Boynton Beach, Fla., 1983—. Served to lt. USNR, 1943-46. Clubs: Delray Dunes Country (Boynton Beach, Fla.). Home: 4738 S Lake Dr Boynton Beach FL 33436

WRAY, ANDREW MADISON, III, financial planner; b. Memphis, Nov. 23, 1945; s. Andrew Madison Jr. and Aline (Moran) W.; children: Andrew Madison IV, LeeAnne. BBA, Memphis State U., 1967; Cert., Coll. for Fin. Planning, Denver, 1985. Account rep. Weede & Co., N.Y.C., 1975-76; pres., owner Universal Security System, Memphis, 1976-79; agt. Thomas Wellford & Son, Memphis, 1979-81; spl. agt. Banker's Life, Memphis, 1981-84; prin. Wray, Fugitt & Howard Asset Mgmt. Inc., Memphis, 1984—; mem. adj. faculty Coll. for Fin. Planning, 1986-87; mem. part-time faculty Memphis State U., 1987-89. Mem. Memphis Symphony, Dixon Gallery. Mem. Internat. Assn. for Fin. Planners (treas. Memphis chpt. 1987—, v.p. membership 1988, bd. dirs. 1987-89), Registry Fin. Planning Practitioners, Inst. Cert. Fin. Planners (cert.), Life Underwriters Assn., Red Apple Club (Eden Isle, Ark.), Summit (Memphis). Roman Catholic. Office: Wray Fugitt & Howard Asset Mgmt 755 Crossover Ln Ste 131 Memphis TN 38117

WRAY, WILLIAM KEELEY, real estate executive; b. Plattsburg, N.Y., Nov. 14, 1958; s. Robert Oakley and Rosanne Frances (Keeley) W.; m. Nancy Joan Heiss, Nov. 14, 1981; children: Keeley, Katharine, William Jr. BS, U.S. Mil. Acad., 1980; MSCE, Stanford U., 1981. Registered profl. engr., Va. Commd. 2d lt. U.S. Army, 1980, advanced through grades to capt., 1984, resigned, 1986; mgr. investment rsch. DIHC Mgmt. Corp., Atlanta, 1986-89; exec. v.p. GDR Properties, Providence, 1989—. Fellow NSF, 1980. Republican. Roman Catholic. Home: PO Box 372 East Greenwich RI 02818 Office: GDR Properties 260 W Exchange Ctr Providence RI 02903

WRIGHT, ARTHUR MCINTOSH, lawyer, industrial products company executive; b. El Dorado, Kans., Dec. 9, 1930; s. Ray Arthur and Anna (McIntosh) W.; A.B., Grinnell Coll., 1952; LL.B., Harvard, 1958; m. Mary Alice Smaltz, June 23, 1956; children: David A., Steven E., Carolyn E. Bar: Mo. 1959, Ill. 1964. Assoc. Swanson, Midgley, Jones, Blackmar & Eager, Kansas City, Mo., 1958-64; corp. atty. Baxter Labs., Inc., Morton Grove, Ill., 1964-67; v.p., sec., counsel N.Am. Car Corp., Chgo., 1968-71; sec., corp. counsel Ceco Corp., Chgo., 1971-77; v.p., gen. counsel, sec. Ill. Tool Works Inc., Chgo., 1977—. Mem. New Trier Twp. High Schs. Bd. Edn., 1977-85, pres., 1983-85; bd. advisors Chgo. Vol. Legal Services Found., 1982—, chmn., 1984-86. Served with U.S. Army, 1953-55. Mem. ABA, Ill. Bar Assn., Chgo. Bar Assn. (chmn. corp. law depts. com. 1981-82), Am. Judicature Soc., Am. Soc. Corp. Secs., Sigma Delta Chi. Presbyterian. Office: Ill Tool Works Inc 8501 W Higgins Rd Chicago IL 60631

WRIGHT, CHERYL ANNE, purchasing executive, computer operations assistant; b. Sanford, Fla., June 22, 1966; d. Ralph Edward and Linda Cheryl (Williams) W. Student, Seminole community Coll., 1984—. Computer operator Coxcreen, Inc., Sanford, Fla., 1985-86, First Fed. Seminole, Sanford, 1986, Harris/Lanier, Altamonte Springs, Fla., 1987-89, Kazeck & Assocs., Altamonte Springs, 1986; purchasing asst. computer operator The Babcock Co., Inc., Winter Park, Fla., 1987—. Republican. Roman Catholic. Home: 204 Bennett St Winter Springs FL 32708 Office: The Babcock Co 1555 Howell Branch Rd Winter Springs FL 32789

WRIGHT, DANA JACE, real estate executive; b. Cleve., Apr. 20, 1952; d. William James and Murl Jean (White) Ewing; m. David Alan Samball, June 22, 1968 (div. Apr. 1971); 1 child, David; m. David M. Wright, July 11, 1981; children: William James, Karen Marie. Assoc. in Nursing, Valencia Community Coll., 1973, AA, 1973; BS in Respiratory Therapy, U. Cen. Fla., 1975; MEd, Auburn U., 1979; D in Nursing, Case Western Res. U., 1982. RN, Fla., Ohio, N.Y., Ga.; cert. emergency med. technician; cert. and registered respiratory therapist; lic. real estate agt., N.Y. Nursing asst. Holiday Hosp., Orlando, Fla., 1970-71, staff nurse critical care unit, intensive care unit, 1973; pvt. duty nurse Med. Personnel Pool, Orlando, 1973-74; nurse critical care burn team Upjohn, Inc., Augusta, Ga., 1976-77; ednl. dir. dept. respiratory therapy U. Hosp., Augusta, 1975-76; mem. staff respiratory therapy VA Hosp., Augusta, 1976-77; clin. instr. respiratory therapy Med. Coll. Ga., Augusta, 1976-77, Columbus Coll., 1977-78; ednl. dir. respiratory therapy Med. Ctr. Hosp., Columbus, 1977-79; staff nurse, relief supr. Kelly Health Care, Beachwood, Ohio, 1979-81; staff nurse Med. Staff, Inc., Cleve., 1981-83; dir. nursing The Arcade, Cleve., 1983; pres. Wright Properties, Buffalo, 1987—; mem. nursing resources panel North Ohio Lung Assn., 1981-82. Treas. Ch. Women's Assn., Snyder, N.Y., 1985—; mem. membership task force UCC Ch.,snyder, 1988, mem. child care bd., 1986—, Profl. Parent Network, Buffalo, 1987—. Mem. Am. Nurse's Assn., Am. Assn. Nurses Practicing Independently (assoc.), Nat. Student Nurses Assn., AAUW. Mem. Buffalo Investors Group, Western N.Y. Real Estate Investors, Property Mgrs. Group., Ask Women, Greater Buffalo Bd. Realtors. Republican. Home and Office: 49 Colony Ct Snyder NY 14226

WRIGHT, DOUGLAS CHANDLER, JR., paper company executive; b. Montclair, N.J., Dec. 13, 1934; s. Douglas Chandler and Helen G. (Henning) W.; m. Sarah Lee Roman, Dec. 30, 1961; children—Douglas Chandler, Gregory Rawson. B.A., Yale U., 1957; M.B.A., Harvard U., 1965. Systems analyst N.J. Bell Telephone Co., 1957-59, McGraw-Hill Pub. Co., N.Y.C., 1959-60; mgr. systems Ednl. Testing Service, Princeton, N.J., 1960-63; sr. v.p., chief fin. officer Hammermill Paper Co., Erie, Pa., 1965-87; v.p., chief fin. officer Great Northern Nekoosa, Norwalk, Conn., 1987—; mem. adv. bd. Arkwright Ins. Co., Conn. Nat. Bank. Mem. Fin. Execs. Inst., Am. Paper Inst. (chmn. fin. com.). Home: 2 Haskell Ln Darien CT 06820 Office: Gt No Nekoosa Corp 401 Merritt 7 PO Box 5120 Norwalk CT 06856-5120

WRIGHT, FELIX E., manufacturing company executive; b. 1935; married. Student, East Tex. State U., 1958. With Leggett & Platt, Inc., Carthage, Mo., 1959—, sr. v.p., from 1976, chief operating officer, exec. v.p., 1979, now pres., chief operating officer, 1985—. Office: Leggett & Platt Inc 1 Leggett Rd Carthage MO 64836 *

WRIGHT, GEORGE CULLEN, electronics company executive; b. Anderson, S.C., June 28, 1923; s. Benjamin Norman and Essie Floride (Cole) W.; m. Kathleen Ashe, Oct. 19, 1947; children: Carol Ann (Mrs. John C. Marquardt), George Cullen, Florenda Jean, William Norman. BS, Clemson U., 1948. Asst. supt. Duke Power Co., 1949-56; city mgr. Gaffney, S.C., 1956-60; v.p. mktg. Hubbard & Co.,, Chgo., 1960-65; dir. Methode Electronics, Inc., Rolling Meadows, Ill., 1956—; v.p., dir. Anchor Coupling Co., Inc., Libertyville, Ill., 1973—; pres., dir. Exec. Extension & Ventures, Inc., Barrington, Ill., 1976—, White Marlin Marine, Inc., Anderson, S.C., 1976—, Piedmont Corp., 1986—. Patentee in field. Pres. Barrington East Ass., 1968-70. Served with AUS, 1942-45. Mem. AIEE Electron Industry Assn., Am. Mgmt. Assn. Lodges: Rotary, Sertoma (pres. 1963-65). Home: 224 Jolly Rd Townville SC 29689

WRIGHT, HELEN KENNEDY, editor, librarian; b. Indpls., Sept. 23, 1927; d. William Henry and Ida Louise (Crosby) Kennedy; m. Samuel A. Wright, Sept. 5, 1970; 1 child, Carl F. Prince II (dec.). BA, Butler U., 1945, MS, 1950; MS, Columbia U., 1952. Reference librarian N.Y. Pub. Library, N.Y.C., 1952-53, Bklyn. Pub. Library, 1953-54; cataloger U. Utah, 1954-57; librarian Chgo. Pub. Library; asst. dir. pub. dept. ALA, Chgo., 1958-62, editor Reference Books Bull., 1962-85; asst. dir. for new product planning, pub. services, 1985—; managing editor ALA Yearbook, 1988—. Contbr. to Ency. of Careers, Ency. of Library and Info. Sci., New Book of Knowledge Ency., Bulletin of Bibliography, New Golden Book Encyclopedia. Mem. Phi Kappa Phi, Kappa Delta Pi, Sigma Gamma Rho. Roman Catholic. Home: 1138 W 111th St Chicago IL 60643 Office: ALA 50 E Huron Chicago IL 60611

WRIGHT, HOWARD LEWIS, accounting firm executive; b. Detroit, Mar. 31, 1934; s. Asa Howard and Edrie (Albin) W.; m. Audrey Plummer, Apr. 2, 1955; children: Kevin, Lawrence, Sharon. BA, Mich. State U., 1955, MA, 1956. CPA, Mich., D.C. Staff mgr. Arthur Andersen & Co., Detroit, 1956-67, ptnr., 1967-74; ptnr. Arthur Andersen & Co., Washington, 1974—. Author: (with others) Federal Income Taxation of Banks and Financial Institutions, 1981, A Guide to Bank Taxation; editor Viewpoint Washington newsletter. Pres. Epilepsy Found. Nat. Capital Area, Washington, 1980-82. Fellow Am. Inst. CPA's. Republican. Mem. United Ch. of Christ. Clubs: University (Washington); Westwood Country (Vienna, Va.). Office: Arthur Andersen & Co 1666 K St NW Washington DC 20006

WRIGHT, JAMES CHALMERS, III, accountant; b. San Jose, Calif., Dec. 10, 1959; s. Benjamin Bakewell and Mary (Meals) W.; m. Susan Wright, Feb. 22, 1986 (div. 1988). BS in Acctg., Menlo (Calif.) Sch. Bus., 1982; MS in Acctg., Golden Gate U., 1988. Staff accountant Wayne Bennett, San Francisco, 1982-83; staff auditor Peat Marwick Mitchell, Newport Beach, Calif., 1983-84; dir. internat. audit Santa Margarita Co., San Juan Capistrano, Calif., 1984-86, sr. fin. analyst, 1986-88, dir. fin. acctg., 1988—. Bank of Am. grantee, 1981. Mem. AICPA. Home: 16 El Vaquero Rancho Santa Margarita CA 92688 Office: Santa Margarita Co 28811 Ortega Hwy San Juan Capistrano CA 92675

WRIGHT, JAMES WELLINGTON, JR., insurance executive; b. Trenton, N.J., Aug. 10, 1949; s. James Wellington Sr. and Eleanor Marie (Hammond) W.; m. Deborah Elaine Brown, Oct. 20, 1973; children: Heather Nicole, Melinda Leigh. BS, Glassboro (N.J.) Coll., 1979. Adjuster Kemper Ins., Tampa, Fla., 1974-76; asst. v.p. Jersey Internat. Admiral Ins., Cherry Hill, N.J., 1976-85; mgr. ops. MacDuff Underwriters, Daytona Beach, Fla., 1985-88; v.p. underwriting investors Ins. Co. Am., Laurence Harbor, N.J., 1988—. Mem. Jaycees (bd. dirs., v.p. Tampa chpt. 1973-76, sec., pres. Collingswood, N.J. chpt. 1979-85). Republican. Presbyterian. Office: Investors Ins Co Am 100 Metro Park South Laurence Harbor NJ 07733

WRIGHT, JERRY RAYMOND, oil company executive; b. Princeton, Ind., Mar. 29, 1935; s. Ottis L. and Dorothy Mae (McCandless) W.; children: Stephanie, Diane, William; m. Barbara Kay Waggoner, June 2, 1962. BS in Petroleum Engring., N.Mex. Sch. Mines, 1963. Petroleum engr., various positions Cities Service Co./Occidental Petroleum Corp., Okla., Tex., N.Y., 1963-83; v.p. joint ventures Occidental Petroleum Corp., London, 1983-86; chief operating officer Can. Occidental Petroleum Ltd., Calgary, Alt., 1986—. Sgt. USMC, 1953-57, Korea. Office: Can Occidental Petroleum Ltd, 1500 635 8th Ave SW, Calgary, AB Canada T2P 3Z1

WRIGHT, JOHN KING, corporate lawyer; b. Birmingham, Ala., Sept. 28, 1947; s. Leslie Stephen and Lolla Catherine (Wurtele) W.; m. Elizabeth Faye Ezell, Aug. 14, 1971; children: Catherine Susan, Elizabeth Anne. AB, Samford U., 1969; JD, Cumberland Sch. Law, Birmingham, 1972. Bar: Ala.; CLU. Law clerk Ala. Supreme Ct., Montgomery, 1972-73; corp. atty. Protective Life Ins. Co., Birmingham, 1973-81; asst. v.p., corp. atty. Protective Life Corp., Birmingham, 1981-85, 2d v.p., 1985-87, v.p., 1988—. Pres. Jefferson-Shelby Lung Assn., Birmingham, 1983-85; treas. Am. Lung Assn. Ala., 1985—. Served to capt. Ala. Air N.G., 1969-78. Mem. Ala. Bar Assn., Birmingham Bar Assn., Am. Corp. Counsel Assn., Am. Council Life Ins. (legal sect.), Life Office Mgmt. Assn., FLMI. Republican. Baptist. Lodge: Rotary (pres. Vestavia Hills club 1980-81). Home: 2725 Vestavia Forest Pl Birmingham AL 35216 Office: Protective Life Corp PO Box 2606 Birmingham AL 35202

WRIGHT, JOHN PARDEE, investment company executive; b. Hong Kong, May 9, 1957; s. William Bigelow and Polly (Pardee) W.; m. Mary Porter, Nov. 24, 1979; children: Heather Marie, Justin Pardee. Cert., L'Institut De Sci. Politique, Paris, 1978; BA, Middlebury (Vt.) Coll., 1979; MBA, Amos Tuck Sch., 1984. Fin. trainee Gen. Mills, Inc., Mpls., 1979-80, asst. mgr., 1980-81, mgr., 1981-82; fin. analyst Keefe, Bruyette & Woods, Inc., Hartford, Conn., 1984-86, v.p., 1986—; tchr. New Eng. Sch. of Banking, Williamstown, Mass., 1987—. Treas. local chpt. Phillips Exeter Acad., Hartford, 1987—; off campus interviewer Middlebury Coll., Simsbury, Conn., 1981-86. Republican. Congregationalist.

WRIGHT, JOHN ROBERT (JACK), horticulturist; b. Twin Falls, Idaho, July 13, 1940; s. Loyd Kenneth and Bessie Margaret (Roberts) W.; m. F. Elaine Jacobs, Aug. 2, 1959; children—Douglas Wayne, David Scott, Teresa Lynn. Mgr., Kimberly Nurseries, Inc., Twin Falls, 1967—, pres., prin., 1978—; founder, pres. Bonanza Investment Group, Twin Falls, 1974—, Smith & Wright Investment Group, Twin Falls, 1978—; founder J.R. Wright Investment Group, 1981; ptnr. Liberty Enterprises Investment Group. Scoutmaster, Snake River Cub Scout council Boy Scouts Am., 1970-74; mem. City Council, 1984, pres. 1985-86, 87-88; acting mayor City of Kimberly, 1986, police commr. City of Kimberly, 1986-88, City Library Bd., 1985, Park and Recreation Bd., 1985, Planning and Zoning Commn., 1984-85. Served with AUS, 1962. Mem. Twin Falls C. of C., Idaho Tree and Nursery Assn., Nat. Assn. Watch and Clock Collectors, Assn. Gen. Contractors. Republican. Christian. Club: Masons (32 deg.). Home: 824 N Main St Kimberly ID 83341 Office: Route 3 Twin Falls ID 83301

WRIGHT, LINDA JEAN, banker; b. Chgo., Dec. 14, 1949; d. Eugene P. and Rosemary Margaret (Kiley) Kemph; student Loretto Heights Coll., 1967-69, U. Ill.-Urbana, 1970-71; m. Kelly W. Wright, Jr., Feb. 1979 (div. 1984); m. Samuel Neuwirth Klewans, Aug. 28, 1986. Asst. to v.p. Busey 1st Nat. Bank, Urbana, 1969-72; spa mgr., supr. sales tng. Venus and Apollo Health Club, San Antonio, 1973-76; owner Plant Shop, San Antonio, 1976-77; with Enterprise Bank, Falls Church, Va., 1977-84, comml. lending officer, 1978-84, sr. v.p., 1979-84, corp. sec. of bd. dirs., 1980-84; pres., chief exec. officer Fairfax Savs. Bank, 1984-87; pres., chief exec. officer Bankstar, N.A. (formerly Bank 2000 of Reston, N.A.), 1988— Apptd. pub. official State of Va. Chmn. exec. com. Fairfax-Falls Ch. United Way, United Way Capital Area, Washington, 1984-85; Fairfax County Spl. Task Force, 1986; mem. Fairfax Com. of 100, 1987; mem., bd. dirs. Hospice No. Va., Arlington, 1985-86, chmn. No. Va. Local Devel. Corp., Va. Small Bus. Fin. Authority, Richmond, 1984—; mem. operating bd. Fairfax Hosp., 1987—; pres. No. Va. Transp. Alliance, 1987—. Mem. Fairfax County C. of C. (dir., v.p., pres. 1987—), Nat. Assn. Bank Women (chmn. No. Va. group 1980-81). Roman Catholic. Club: Fairfax Hunt. Avocations: aviation, fox hunting.

WRIGHT, MARGARET TAYLOR, marketing consultant; b. Wilmington, N.C., Nov. 8, 1949; d. Thomas Henry and Margaret (Taylor) W. BA, U. N.C., 1972; MBA, Wake Forest U., 1978. Child advocacy specialist Child Advocacy Council Dept. Human Resources, Raleigh, N.C., 1973-74; region dir. N.C. Office for Children Dept. Human Resources, Winston-Salem, 1974-76; product mgr. food div. Am. Home Products, N.Y.C., 1978-80; account exec. Ted Bates Advt., N.Y.C., 1981; product mgr. C.F. Mueller div. McKesson, Inc., Jersey City, 1981-83; mgr. new products Popsicle div. Sara Lee Corp., Englewood, N.J., 1983-86; pres. Wright Mktg. Blueprint, N.Y.C., 1987—. Co-author: (pamphlets) Children--Helping Them Grow, 1973. Youth coord. Jim Holshouser Gubernatorial Campaign, New Hanover County, N.C., 1972; mem. Jr. League, N.Y. and N.C., 1972-84. Mem. Am. Mktg. Assn. (exec.), Princeton Club. Republican. Episcopalian. Office: Wright Mktg Blueprint 59 E 54th St Ste 72 New York NY 10022

WRIGHT, MICHAEL WILLIAM, wholesale food company executive; b. Mpls., June 13, 1938; s. Thomas W. and Winifred M. Wright; m. Susan Marie Guzy. B.A., U. Minn., 1961, J.D. with honors, 1963. Ptnr. Dorsey & Whitney, Mpls., 1966-77; sr. v.p. Super Valu Stores, Inc., Mpls., 1977-78, pres., chief operating officer, 1978—, chief exec. officer, 1981—, chmn., 1982—; bd. dirs., chmn. Fed. Res. Bank, Mpls.; bd. dirs. Deluxe Corp., Mpls., Honeywell, Inc., The Musicland Group, Internat. Assn. Chain Stores, Food Mktg. Inst., Nat. Am. Wholesale Grocers Assn.; chmn. Minn. Bus. Partnership. 1st lt. U.S. Army, 1964-66. Office: Super Valu Stores Inc 11840 Valley View Rd PO Box 990 Minneapolis MN 55440

WRIGHT, MICHAEL WILLIAM, management consultant; b. Stockton, Calif., Oct. 10, 1946; m. Rebecca Wright; children: Maurine, Matthew, Anne. Mgr. div. Pure & Simple Natural Foods, San Jose, Calif., 1970-72; plant supr. Idaho Potato Foods, Idaho Falls, 1972-74; cons. small bus. Trim-Line div. 3M Corp., Billings, Mont., 1975-80; gen. mgr. Kurz Instruments, Monterey, Calif., 1980-83; v.p. mktg. and adminstrn. Integrated Air Systems, Smith Industries, Child's Hill, Eng., 1983-86; chief operating officer Tri Dim Filter Corp., Hawthorne, N.J., 1986-88; pres., mgmt. cons. Michael W. Wrights & Assocs., Sacramento, 1988—; speaker in field. Contbr. articles to profl. jours.; inventor isokinetic sample system. dir. ctr. contamination control U. Ariz., Tucson, 1984-86. Mem. IEEE, Inst. Environ. Scis., Am. Mgmt. Assn. Office: Michael W Wright & Assocs 3400 Watt Ave Ste 203 Sacramento CA 95821

WRIGHT, NADINE ANOHIN, data processing executive; b. Harbin, Hailongjiang, Peoples Rep. China, Sept. 30, 1945; came to U.S., 1960; d. Feofan Firsovitch and Tamara Viacheslavovna (Firsova) Anohin; m. Harry Franklin Wright, Nov. 22, 1978; children: Adrian Christopher, Devon Brhett. AA, City Coll. San Francisco, 1966; diplomas in French and internat. econs., U. Strasbourg, France, 1967, 69; BA, San Francisco State U., 1972, MBA, 1976. Programmer, auditor electronic and data processing Bechtel Corp., San Francisco, 1973-76; specialist electronic data processing Levi Strauss and Co., Frankfurt, Brussels, 1976-78; chief analyst/tech. advisor Calif. State Automobile Assn., San Francisco, 1978-79; supr. electronic data processing audit Crocker Bank, San Francisco, 1979-80, Ampex Corp., Redwood City, Calif., 1980-81; sr. staff analyst, sr. electronic data processing auditor Safeway Stores Corp., Oakland, Calif., 1981-86; cons. Breuners Inc., San Ramon, Calif., 1987—, Bay Area Remodeling and Construction, San Francisco, 1987—; systems engr. IBM Corp., San Francisco 1972-73. Chmn. Community Chest VFW, San Francisco, 1965. Mem. Inst. Internal Auditors (bd. dirs. 1987—, chmn. electronic data processing audit 1983-84), Nat. Assn. Accts. (scholarship com. 1982-83), Electronic Data Processing Auditor Assn. Democrat.

WRIGHT, PAUL E., manufacturing company executive; b. 1931; married. BS, Calif. Poly. State U., 1958; MS, U. Pa., 1960; postgrad., Harvard U., 1976. With RCA, 1958-86, successively dir. advanced tech. labs., gen. mgr. astro-electronics, v.p. gen. mgr. aerospace and def., sr. v.p. corp. planning and devel.; pres., chief operating officer Fairchild Industries Inc., Chantilly, Va., 1986-88, also bd. dirs., 1988; chmn., pres. Chrysler Tech., Washington, 1988—. Served with USAF, 1950-54. Office: Chrysler Technologies 1100 Connecticut Ave NW Ste 730 Washington DC 20036

WRIGHT, PAUL KENNETH, real estate development executive; b. Akron, Ohio, Mar. 2, 1919; s. Paul F. and Gladys Nevada (Rasey) W.; m. Lura

Frances Brown, Feb. 5, 1943 (div. Feb. 1987); children: Victor, Sharon, David, Rebecca, Robert, James. Student, U. Akron, 1939, U. Ga., 1963-65, U. Okla., 1966-69, U. Evansville, 1984. Sales rep. Graybar Electric Co., Evansville, Ind., 1947-52; ind. sales rep., Evansville, 1953-60; dir. econ. devel. Louisville C. of C., 1961-65; dir. indsl. devel. Evansville C. of C., 1966-67; exec. v.p. Henderson (Ky.) C. of C., 1968-69; v.p. Nat. City Bank, Evansville, 1970-83; pres. So. Ind. Bank, Newburgh, 1984; exec. dir. Warrick County Local Devel. Corp., Boonville, Ind., 1985—; sec. Evansville Indsl. Found., 1967-68. Sec., treas. Kentuckiana World Commerce Coun., Louisville, 1964-66; bd. dirs. Mental Health Assn., Evansville, 1975-83, Goodwill Industries, Evansville, 1975-83. Mem. Ind. Area Devel. Coun., Ind. Assn. for Econ. Devel. Office: Warrick County Local Devel Corp 301 W Main St Boonville IN 47601

WRIGHT, RICHARD DONALD, financial executive; b. Chester, Pa., Mar. 18, 1936; s. Richard H. and Anita C. (Howery) W.; BBA, Pa. State U., 1963; m. Joan Cooke, Oct. 24, 1959; children—Richard, Paul, Susan. Trainee, corp. fin. mgmt., internal auditor, corp. staff auditor RCA, Cherry Hill, N.J., 1963-66; with Smith Kline French Labs. div. Smith Kline Beckman Corp., Phila., 1966-83, mgr. budget, 1966-69, mgr. planning and control, 1969-70, mgr. fin. ops., 1970-72, controller mfg. ops., 1972-73, dir. fin. planning, 1973-74, controller pharm. ops., U.S., 1974-79; v.p., dir. Franklin Town Corp., pres. F.T. Mgmt. Corp. affiliate Smith Kline Corp., 1979-83, controller, 1983-85, v.p., dir., 1985-88, v.p., dir. chief fin. officer, 1988—; with Henkels and McCoy Inc., 1983—, Blue Bell, Pa. . Mem. Fin. Execs. Inst. (cert.), Planning Execs. Inst., Ocean County Bd. Realtors, Nat. Assn. Accts., Sigma Tau Gamma. Lectr. in field. Home: 104 Shadow Lake Dr Vincentown NJ 08088

WRIGHT, RICHARD G., optical company executive; b. Syracuse, N.Y., Mar. 11, 1934; s. Herbert G. and Marguerite (Wood) W.; m. Barbara Ann Lutzy, Aug. 18, 1954; children: Linda, Richard Jr., Pamela, Michelle, Craig. Student, Colgate U., 1953-54; BS, Syracuse U., 1957. Dir. mktg. soft contact lens div. Am. Optical Co., Southbridge, Mass., 1976-79, gen. mgr. soft contact lens div., 1979-81; exec. v.p. Barnes-Hind div. Revlon, Inc., N.Y.C., 1981-83, pres., 1983-85; pres. Revlon Vision Care Internat., N.Y.C., 1985-86; pres., chief operating officer Foster-Grant Corp., Leominster, Mass., 1986—. Home: 15 Revere Dr Ridgefield CT 06877 Office: Foster-Grant Corp 1 Foster Grant Plaza Leominster MA 01453

WRIGHT, RICHARD JOHN, business executive; b. Bklyn., June 17, 1951; s. David Francis and Mary Catherine (Hehir) W.; m. Linda Marie Green, May 24, 1975; children: Sean, Bridget. B.S. in Physics with honors, Bates Coll., 1973; M.B.A., Rutgers U., 1974. C.P.A. Mgr. Coopers & Lybrand, N.Y.C., 1975-81; chief fin. officer Drexel Burnham Lambert, N.Y.C., 1981—; bd. dirs., mem. exec. com., treas. Drexel Burnham Lambert Group Inc., chief fin. officer, asst. treas. Drexel Burnham Lambert Govt. Securities, Inc. Mem. Fin. Exec. Inst., AICPA, N.Y. State Soc. CPAs, Securities Industry Assn. (tax policy com.). Office: Drexel Burnham Lambert Inc 60 Broad St New York NY 10004

WRIGHT, RICHARD LEE, engineer; b. Wichita, Kans., Dec. 4, 1949; s. Junior Lee and Mary Jane (Pray) W.; m. Randi L. Fell, Sept. 12, 1969 (div. 1971); 1 child, Mark Erin; m. Beverly Ann Moore, Mar. 2, 1973; children: Richelle LeAnn, Rita Linn. Diploma, Fairview High Sch., Boulder, Colo., 1968. Drafting engr. Beech Aircraft, Boulder, 1968-69, with aircraft assembly dept., 1973-74, design engr., 1974, with Level I & II Q.C. dept., 1975-77; with Level III Q.C. dept. Wichita Brass & Aluminum Foundry, 1977-82; Level III NDT engr. Ind. Gear Works Systems Inc., Indpls., 1982—. Active Am. Legion, Oaklandon, Ind., 1986—. Served as sgt. U.S. Army, 1969-71. Mem. Am. Soc. Non-Destructive Testing, Am. Soc. Quality Control, U.S. Chess Fedn., Freelance Photographers Assn. Republican. Baptist. Home: 6276 Eastgate Oaklandon IN 46236 Office: IGW Systems Inc 9000 Precision Dr Indianapolis IN 46236

WRIGHT, TERRY RICHMOND, quality control engineer; b. Shelby, N.C., July 8, 1957; s. Douglas Richmond and Lillie Mae (Goines) W.; m. Linda Gail Owens, Oct. 13, 1979; 1 child, Tara Lynn. BBA in Acctg. with high honors, Cleve. Coll., 1983; postgrad., Gardner Webb Coll. Project coordinator Steadman Corp., Gastonia, N.C., 1977-79; quality control technician Timken Co., Iron Station, N.C., 1979-84, process control supr., 1984—. Mem. Alpha Chi, Alpha Beta Phi. Republican. Baptist. Home: Rt 2 Box 273B Maiden NC 28650 Office: Timken Co 1 Timken Pl Iron Station NC 28080

WRIGHT, THOMAS JAMES, chemical company executive; b. Livingston, Mont., June 13, 1932; s. William James and Mary Doreen (Smyth) W.; m. Sandra Gray Church, Jan. 29, 1962; children: James Bland, Jacqueline Doreen. BS in Metall. Engring., Mont. Sch. Mines, 1959. With minerals research lab. N.C. State U., Ashville, 1959-64; project engr. Texasgulf, Inc., Aurora, N.C., 1964-65, process engr., 1965-67, mill supt., 1967-71, acid plant supt., 1971-73, asst. gen. mgr., 1975-78; gen. mgr. Texasgulf Chems. Co., Aurora, 1978-79; sr. v.p. prodn. Texasgulf Chems. Co., Raleigh, N.C., 1979-81, pres., 1981—; plant mgr. Agrico Chem. Co., South Pierce, Fla., 1973-75; bd. dirs. Texasgulf, Inc., Stamford, Conn., Elf Aquitaine, Inc., Stamford, Compania Exploradora Del Istmo, Mexico City. Served with U.S Army, 1954-56. Mem. Am. Mining Congress, N.C. Engring. Found. (past bd. dirs.), Sulphur Inst. (bd. dirs.), Phosphate Chem. Export Assn. (bd. dirs.), Potash and Phosphate Inst. (past bd. dirs.), Internat. Fertilizer Assn., N.C Water Resources Research Inst., Farm Care U.S.A., Raleigh C. of C. Roman Catholic. Clubs: North Ridge Country, MacGregor Downs Country, Capital City (Raleigh). Office: Texasgulf Chem Co PO Box 30321 Raleigh NC 27622-0321

WRIGHT, THOMAS WILLIAM, automotive parts company executive; b. Pineland, Tex., Aug. 13, 1941; s. Stonewall Obed Wright and Mary Lois (Williams) Barkley; m. Judy Ann Andrews, Nov. 29, 1968; children: Thomas Wesley, Daniel Scott. BA, U. Tex., 1964; MS, Tex. Christian U., 1968; MBA, U. Dallas, 1976. CPA, Tex.; cert. in data processing. Computer programmer Gen. Dynamics, Ft. Worth, 1964-68; dir. data processing Gen. Automotive Parts Corp., Dallas, 1968-82, v.p. data processing, 1982-84; mgr. acctg. and data processing Genuine Parts Co., Dallas, 1984-85; v.p., treas. Genuine Parts Co., Atlanta, 1985—. Instr. Jr. Achievement Atlanta, 1987. Mem. Am. Inst. CPA's.

WRIGHT, VERNON ORVILLE, communications and computer executive; b. Mound City, Kans., Sept. 9, 1920; s. Albert and Pearle (Mitchell) W.; m. Judith Ann Sharp, Dec., 15, 1988. BA, U. Kans., 1942. With IBM Corp., 1950-71, group dir. systems and tech. div., Harrison, N.Y., 1970-71; pres. systems devel. div. RCA, Marlboro, Mass., 1971-73; v.p. bus. devel. group Xerox Corp., El Segundo, Calif., 1973-75; pres. MCI Communications Corp., Washington, 1975-85, vice chmn., 1985—, chief exec. officer, 1987—, also dir. Comdr. USN, 1942-50. Republican. Episcopalian. Office: MCI Communications Corp 1133 19th St NW Washington DC 20036

WRIGHT, WILLIAM BIGELOW, financial executive; b. Rutland, Vt., Dec. 21, 1924; s. Earl Smith and Christine (Bigelow) W.; m. Polly Pardee, Aug. 27, 1949; children: Christine, Henry, John, Lucy. AB, Princeton U., 1950. With Chubb & Son, N.Y.C., 1950-53; various positions Am. Internat. Group, 1953-57; asst. to the pres. Johnson & Higgins, Caracas, Venezuela, 1957-63; pres. Marble Fin. Corp., Rutland, 1968-83, chmn. bd., 1983—; bd. dirs. Bunbury Co., Princeton, N.J. V.p., treas. Windham Found., Grafton, Vt.; sch. commr. City of Rutland, 1966-75; chmn. Vt. Blue Cross and Blue Shield, 1980-83; treas., bd. dirs. Northeast chpt. 10th Mountain Div. Assn., 1987—; trustee, treas. Green Mountain Coll., Poultney, Vt. With U.S. Army, 1943-46. Mem. Ivy Club, Princeton Club N.Y.C. Republican. Congregationalist. Home: Mendon VT 05701 Office: Marble Bank PO Box 978 Rutland VT 05701

WRIGHTSON, JOHN CHAFFE, marketing consultant; b. Elizabeth, N.J., May 27, 1923; s. George Dawson and Sadie (Chaffe) W.; m. Mary Reneham, May 16, 1952; children: Margaret, Elizabeth. Grad., Hotchkiss Sch., 1941; student, Yale U., 1941-43. Salesman Cluett, Peabody & Co., N.Y.C., 1946-48, Burlington Mills Corp., N.Y.C., 1948-54; sales mgr. Southerland Knitting Mills, N.Y.C., 1954-58; pres. Heritage Quilts, Inc., N.Y.C., 1958-66, chmn., 1966-82, chief exec. officer, 1958-82, ret., 1982; cons. Internat. Exec. Service Corps., Stamford, Conn., 1985—; bd. dirs. Am. Maize-Products Co., Stamford. Inventor snug sack quilting garment. 1st lt. USAF, 1942-46, PTO. Recipient service award Internat. Exec. Service Corps, 1986. Republican. Roman Catholic. Home: PO Box 95 Watkins Hill Rd Walpole NH 03608 Office: Am Maize-Products Co 250 Harbor Dr Stamford CT 06904

WRIGLEY, WILLIAM, corporation executive; b. Chgo., Jan. 21, 1933; s. Philip Knight and Helen Blanche (Atwater) W.; m. Alison Hunter, June 1, 1957 (div. 1969); children: Alison Elizabeth, Philip Knight, William.; m. Julie Burns, Nov. 28, 1981. Grad., Deerfield Acad., 1950; B.A., Yale, 1954. With Wm. Wrigley Jr. Co., Chgo., 1956—, v.p., 1960-61, pres., chief exec. officer, 1961—; dir. Wm. Wrigley Jr. Co., 1960—, Wrigley Philippines, Inc., Wrigley Co., Ltd. (U.K.), Wrigley Co. (N.Z.), Ltd., Wrigley Co. Pty., Ltd. (Australia), The Wrigley Co. (H.K.) Ltd. (Hong Kong), Wrigley Co. (E. Africa) Ltd. (Kenya), Wrigley Co. (P.N.G.) Pty. Ltd., Wrigley & Co. Ltd., Japan; chmn. William Wrigley Jr. Co. Found.; mem. audit com. Grocery Mfrs. Am., Inc.; dir., mem. com. non-mgmt. dirs., mem. nominating com. Texaco Inc.; dir., mem. compensation com. Nat. Blvd. Bank of Chgo.; dir. Am. Home Products Corp.; dir., mem. exec. com., chmn., chief exec. officer Santa Catalina Island Co. Bd. dirs. Wrigley Meml. Garden Found.; bd. dirs., mem. personnel com. Northwestern Meml. Hosp.; benefactor, mem. Santa Catalina Island Conservancy; mem. adv. bd. Center for Sports Medicine, Northwestern U. Med. Sch., 1976—; trustee Chgo. Latin Sch. Found., 1975—; dir. Geneva Lake Water Safety Com., 1966—, mem. exec. com., 1968—. Served from ensign to lt. (j.g.) USNR, 1954-56; now lt. comdr. Res. Mem. Navy League U.S., Chgo. Hist. Soc., Field Mus., Wolf's Head Soc., U. So. Calif. Oceanographic Assos., Catalina Island Museum Soc., Delta Kappa Epsilon. Clubs: Saddle and Cycle, Racquet, Chicago Yacht, Tavern (Chgo.), Commercial (Chgo.); Catalina Island Yacht, Calif., Catalina Island Gun; Los Angeles Yacht, Lake Geneva (Wis.) Country, Lake Geneva Yacht; The Brook (N.Y.C.). Office: Wm Wrigley Jr Co 410 N Michigan Ave Chicago IL 60611

WRISTON, KATHRYN DINEEN, lawyer, corporate executive; b. Syracuse, N.Y.; d. Robert Emmet and Carolyn (Bareham) Dineen; m. Walter B. Wriston, Mar. 14, 1968; 1 stepchild. Student, U. Geneva, 1958-59; BA cum laude, Smith Coll., 1960; LLB, U. Mich., 1963. Bar: N.Y.1964, U.S. Ct. Appeals (2nd cir.) 1964, U.S. Supreme Ct. 1968. Assoc. Shearman & Sterling, N.Y.C., 1963-68; bd. dirs. Warner Computer Systems Inc., Sante Fe So. Pacific Corp., Chgo. Chmn. Pres.'s Com. White House Fellows, 1982-83; mem. vis. com. U. Mich. Law Sch., 1973-75; bd. overseers Rand Inst. for Civil Justice, 1985—; vice chair Fordham U., Bronx, N.Y., 1980-81, trustee, 1971-77, 78-81; trustee Northwestern Mut. Life Ins. Co., Milw., 1986—; trustee Practising Law Inst., 1975—, v.p., 1985—. Fellow Am. Bar Found.; mem. ABA, AICPA (bd. dirs. 1986—), Nat. Assn. Accts., Am. Arbitration Assn. (bd. dirs. 1982—), Fin. Women's Assn. N.Y., N.Y. County Lawyers Assn. (legal aid com. 1973-76), N.Y. State Bar Assn., Assn. of Bar of City of N.Y.

WROBEL, ROBERT FRANKLIN, lawyer; b. Chgo., Dec. 24, 1944; s. Frank and Julia (Szili) W.; m. Patricia L. Nixon, Aug. 11, 1968; children: Jeffrey, Stephen. B.S. in Fin., U. Ill.-Urbana, 1967, J.D., 1970. Bar: Mo. 1970, Kans. 1973. Atty. Stinson, Mag & Fizzell, Kansas City, Mo., 1970-73; sr. v.p., gen. counsel, chief adminstrv. officer The Marley Co., Mission Woods, Kans., 1973—, also bd. dirs. Bd. dirs. Kansas City Ballet Assn., 1984-88. Office: Marley Co 1900 Shawnee Mission Pkwy Mission Woods KS 66205

WRUBLE, BRIAN FREDERICK, insurance company executive; b. Kalamazoo, Apr. 18, 1943; s. Milton and Rose Muriel (Nathanson) W.; m. Susan Roberta Shifrin, June 23, 1968 (div. Oct. 1984); children—Amy Carolyn, Jordon Todd; m. Kathleen Wilson Bratton, Apr. 20, 1985. B.E.E., Cornell U., 1965, M.E.E., 1966; M.B.A. with distinction, NYU, 1976. Field engr. Sperry Corp., Lake Success, N.Y., 1966-69; v.p. Alliance One Instl. Services, Inc., N.Y.C., 1970-76; pres. Undershaft Corp., N.Y.C., 1974-88; v.p. H. C. Wainwright and Co., Inc., N.Y.C., 1976-77, Wainwright Securities, Inc., N.Y.C., 1977; v.p., co-mgr. fundamental equities research Smith Barney, Harris Upham & Co., N.Y.C., 1977-79; exec. v.p. chief fin. ops. Equitable Life Assurance Soc. U.S., N.Y.C., 1979—; chmn., pres., chief exec. officer Equitable Capital Mgmt. Corp., N.Y.C., 1985—; chmn., pres. Equitable Realty Assets Corp., Atlanta, 1983—; v.p., dir. TELMARI, Inc., N.Y.C., 1982-83, Equitable Variable Life Ins. Co., 1987—; chmn. Equico Capital Corp., N.Y.C., 1984—, chief exec. officer Equitable Gen. of Okla., Oklahoma City, 1985-86; bd. dirs. Advanced System Applications Inc., 1985-87, Frye Copysystems Inc., N.Y.C.; trustee Equitable Retirement Plans, N.Y.C., 1980-86. Author: The Pollution Revolution, 1971. Vice chmn. Boys Choir of Harlem, N.Y.C., 1984—. Mem. IEEE, Fin. Analysts Fedn., N.Y. Soc. Security Analysts, Inst. Chartered Fin. Analysts (chartered fin. analyst, assoc. editor CFA Digest 1983—). Republican. Jewish. Office: Equitable Capital Mgmt Corp 1285 Ave of Americas New York NY 10019

WU, ALBERT KING, real estate executive, small business owner; b. Macao, Oct. 8, 1949; came to U.S., 1968; s. N. Bower and Joyce (Hsu) W. AA, De Anza Coll., 1970; BS, San Jose State U., 1973; LLB, Peninsula Law Sch., 1986. Pres. Wu Realty Corp., Santa Clara, Calif., 1977—, Am Wurth Capital, Inc., Santa Clara, 1984—. Mem. Internat. Counc. Shopping Ctrs., Nat. Assn. Realtors, Calif. Assn. Realtors. Home: PO Box 3286 San Jose CA 95156

WU, ANTHONY BING, aerospace engineer; b. Houston, Aug. 14, 1950; s. M. Bing and Mary (Chin) W.; 1 child, Danielle. BME, U. Houston, 1974, MME, 1977, M in Indsl. Engring., 1980, PhD in Bus. and Engring., 1983. Registered profl. engr., Calif., Tex. Aerospace engr. Johnson Space Ctr. NASA, Houston, 1974-77, tech. mgr. space shuttle program, 1977-81, mem. exec. staff, 1981-84, with exec. devel. program, 1985, mem. exec. staff, space flight and space sta., 1985-88; budget examiner aeronautics, space sta., nat. space coun. Exec. Office of Pres. Office Mgmt. and Budget, Washington, 1989—. Mem. Tau Beta Pi, Pi Tau Sigma, Alpha Pi Mu. Office: Office Mgmt and Budget Exec Office Pres 725 17th St NW Washington DC 20503

WU, JONATHAN CHARNGHAU, accountant, consultant; b. Chungli, Republic of China, Feb. 12, 1953; came to U.S., 1980; s. Fupei and Lianmei (Liu) W.; m. Liming Han, Mar. 25, 1979. BS, Fujen U., Taipei, Republic of China, 1975; M in Mgmt., Northwestern U., 1982; MA, U. Ill., Chgo., 1985. CPA, Tex. Asst. to v.p. Shus Found., Taipei, 1977-78; ptnr. Bianko Co., Taipei, 1978-80; adj. lectr. Roosevelt U., Chgo., 1983-84; sr. fin. systems analyst Tex. Dept. Community Affairs, Austin, 1984-86, asst. dir. acctg. system, 1986-87, dir. data services, 1987; chief fin. officer Full Employment Council, Kansas City, Mo., 1987—; acctg. and tax systems cons., Austin, 1984—. Author, editor: Job Tng. Ptnrship. Act Fin. Mgmt. Manual, 1986, Food Science, 1978; also articles. Served to 2d lt. Chinese Air Force, 1975-77. Mem. Am. Inst. CPA's, Tex. Soc. CPA's, Inst. Mgmt. Accts. (cert.), Inst. Internal Auditors (cert.), Northwestern Mgmt. Assn. Home: 9410 NW 60th Parkville MO 64152 Office: Full Employment Council 1740 Paseo Kansas City MO 64108

WU, LI-PEI, banker; b. Changhwa, Taiwan, Sept. 9, 1934; came to U.S., 1968; s. Yin-Su and Chiao-Mei (Hsiao) W.; m. Jenny S. Lai, Mar. 24, 1963; children: George T., Eugene Y. BA, Nat. Taiwan U., 1957; MBA, Kans. State U., Ft. Kays, 1969; Comml. Banking Exec. Program, Columbia U., 1974. Staff acct., asst. controller, asst. v.p., v.p. Nat. Bank Alaska, Anchorage, 1969-73, v.p. controller, 1973-76, sr. v.p. chief fin. officer, 1976-78; chmn. exec. com. Alaska Nat. Bank of the North, Anchorage, 1978-79, chief adminstrv. officer, 1979-80, pres., 1980-81; pres., chief exec. officer Gen. Bank, Los Angeles, 1982-84, chmn., pres, chief exec. officer, 1984—; fin. cons. alaska '84, 1981-82, Western Airlines, Los Angeles, 1981-82, Microsci. Internat. Corp., San Jose, Calif., 1986-87; bd. dirs. Simons, Li & Assocs., Ft. Collins, Colo. Mem. Rep. Senatorial Inner Circle, Washington. Mem. Taiwanese Am. Citizens League (life mem.). Office: Gen Bank 201 S Figueroa St Los Angeles CA 90012

WU, NORMAN NASH, bond portfolio manager; b. Cambridge, Mass., Jan. 17, 1955; s. Stephen S. and Grace W. Wu. BA, U. Rochester, 1977; MBA with high honors, Boston U., 1979. Chartered fin. analyst. Investment analyst John Hancock Mut. Life Ins. Co., Boston, 1977-81; bond analyst Fidelity Mgmt. and Research, Boston, 1981-82; bond portfolio mgr. State St. Bank and Trust Co., Boston, 1982-87, State St. Research and Mgmt. Co., Boston, 1987—; pres., real estate mgmt. Newton-Webster Assocs., Newton, Mass., 1980-86. Recipient Paderewski award Nat. Piano Auditions Guild, 1973. Mem. Fin. Analysts Fedn., Boston Soc. Security Analysts, Bond Analyst Soc. Boston (pres. 1986-89). Episcopalian. Office: State St Rsch and Mgmt Co One Financial Ctr Ste 3800 Boston MA 02101

WU, RAYMOND CHUNG L., infosystems executive; b. Taipei, Taiwan, June 18, 1951; s. Jong K. and Sue-Ying (Ho.) W.; m. Ingrid Chen, May 18, 1976; children: Charlotte, Edmond. BS in Indsl. Engring., Nat. Chen-Kung U., Taiwan, 1972; MBA, Tenn. State U., 1977. Asst. mgr. Formosa Plastic Group, Taipei, 1974-76; mgr. prodn. control FMC Co., San Jose, Calif., 1978-85; materials mgr. corp. mgmt. info. systems Solectron Corp., San Jose, 1985-87, dir. corp. info. systems, 1987—; owner Kingstile Indsl. Corp., San Jose, 1979; bd. dirs. Eveready Indsl. Corp., San Jose. Fellow Asian Mgmt. League; mem. Am. Prodn. and Inventory Control Soc. (cert.), Systems Mgmt. Assn., Am. Purchasing Assn., Taiwanese-Am. C. of C. (dir.), Asian-Am. Mfg. Assn. Office: Solectron Corp 2001 Fortune Dr San Jose CA 95131

WU, TSE CHENG, research chemist; b. Hong Kong, Aug. 21, 1923; s. Shau Chuan and Shui (Chan) W.; BS, Yenching U., 1946; MS, U. Ill., 1948; PhD, Iowa State U., 1952; m. Janet Ling, June 14, 1963; children: Alan, Anna, Bernard. Came to U.S., 1947, naturalized, 1962. Prodn. chemist, Yungli Industries, Tangku, China, 1946-47; rsch. asso. Iowa State U., Ames, 1952-53; rsch. chemist duPont Co., Waynesboro, Va., 1953-60; rsch. GE, Waterford, N.Y., 1960-71; sr. rsch. chemist Abcor, Inc., Wilmington, Mass., 1971-77; rsch.assoc. Allied-Signal, Inc., Morristown, N.J., 1977-88; cons., 1989—. Mem. Troy Arts Guild, 1968-71, Morris County Art Assn., 1981—. Recipient Gold medallion award for inventions GE, 1967; Allied Corp. patent award, 1983. Eastman Kodak Rsch. fellow, 1951-52. Mem. Am. Chem. Soc., Sigma Xi, Phi Kappa Phi, Phi Lambda Upsilon, Alpha Chi Sigma. Contbr. profl. jours. Patentee in polymer chemistry and organosilicon chemistry. Home: 14-E Dorado Dr Morristown NJ 07960

WUEST, GEORGE ELMER, corporate treasurer; b. Louisville, Aug. 30, 1915; s. Walter R. and Kathern (Erbele) W.; m. Clara Evelyn Huffman, Apr. 15, 1942; children: Elmer Glenn, Ruth Evelyn. BME, U. Louisville, 1937, BL, 1941. V.p. Wuest Bros. Inc., Louisville, 1947-84, pres., treas., 1984—. Served with U.S. Army, 1945-46. Office: Wuest Bros Inc 936 Hill St Louisville KY 40208

WULFF, ROBERT KING, utility executive; b. Bklyn., Nov. 14, 1938; s. John F. and Marjorie (King) W.; m. Sarah Bender, June 8, 1975; children: Theodore J.B., Pablo Yglesias. AB, Colgate U., 1960; LLB, Harvard U., 1968. Bar: Mass. 1969. Atty. New Eng. Power Svc. Co., Westborough, 1968-75, clk., 1973, asst. gen. counsel, 1975-81, sec., 1978, corp. counsel, 1982—; sec. Narragansett Energy Resources Co., Providence, 1987—; clk. NEES Energy, Inc., Marlboro, Mass. Bd. dirs. Tent City Corp., Boston; deacon Old South Congl. Ch., Boston. Served to lt. USNR, 1962-66. Mem. ABA, Boston Bar Assn., North Hatley Club (Que., Can.). Republican. Home: 27 Gray St Boston MA 02116 Office: New Eng Power Svc Co 25 Research Dr Westborough MA 01582

WULIGER, ERNEST M., mattress and bedding manufacturing company executive; b. Cleve., Dec. 10, 1920; married. Student, U. Chgo. Chmn., chief exec. officer, dir. Ohio Mattress Co., Cleve., 1938—; with Ohio-Sealy Mattress Mfg. Co., Cleve., 1938—, exec. v.p., sec., 1953-62, exec. v.p., gen. mgr., 1962-63, pres., chief operating officer, treas., 1963-82, chmn., dir., chief exec. officer, 1982—. Office: Ohio Mattress Co 1300 E 9th St Cleveland OH 44114 *

WULKER, LAURENCE JOSEPH, investment executive, educator; b. Cin., Apr. 6, 1945; s. Joseph Laurence and Dorothea Clare (Link) W. BS, Xavier U., Cin., 1967, MA, 1971; cert. fin. planner, Coll. Fin. Planner, 1985. Instr. Lloyd High Sch., Erlanger, Ky., 1967-68, Elder High Sch., Cin., 1968-73, Peoples High Sch., Cin., 1973-74, Regina High Sch., Cin. Tech. U., Cin., 1974-75; stockbroker Harrison-Bache, Cin., 1976-78; investment exec., fin. planner Paine Webber, Cin., 1978—; instr. U. Cin., 1981—, Nat. Inst. Fin., South Plainfield, N.J., 1986—; speaker at numerous seminars 1984—; systems operator Investor Forum, Compuserve, 1985-86. Author: (column) Japanese-Am. League Newsletter, 1985—; contbr. articles to Cin. Enquirer, Cin. Post, Cin. Bus. Courier. Active in many civic activites. Fulbright scholar Dept. Health, Edn. and Welfare, 1972; named 1 of best 200 Stockbrokers Country Money mag., 1987. Mem. Internat. Assn. Fin. Planning (past pres. Cin. chpt. 1985-86), Miami Valley Soc. Inst. Cert. Fin. Planning, Stock & Bond Club, Cin. C. of C. (active in numerous coms.), Updowntowners, Japenese-Am. League. Roman Catholic. Home: 566 Purcell Ave Cincinnati OH 45205 Office: Paine Webber 425 Walnut St Ste 2400 Cincinnati OH 45202

WURDEMAN, LEW EDWARD, data processing corporation consultant; b. Colorado Springs, Colo., Oct. 31, 1949; s. Robert Martin and Shirley Gladys (Reetz) W. Student U. Tex., El Paso, 1967-69, U. Minn., 1969-72. Adminstr. Control Data Corp., Bloomington, Minn., 1969-81, product specialist, 1981-83, systems mgr., 1983-84, cons., 1984—. Republican. Lutheran. Clubs: German Shepherd Dog of Mpls., German Shepherd Dog of Am. Avocations: dog breeding, training, computers, photography. Home: 5827 210th St W Farmington MN 55024-9617 Office: Control Data Corp PO Box 1305 BLCW1X Minneapolis MN 55440

WURR, PETER REINHARD, management and marketing consultant; b. Neumuenster, Germany, June 23, 1943; s. Alwin and Erna Johanna (Milahn) W.; m. Sonja-Petra Czybulka, Aug. 3, 1984; children: Peter Philipp, Julia Katharine. BA, U. Cologne, 1964; postgrad. in psychology, U. Goettingern, 1964-65, U. Freiburg, 1964-65. Apprentice Dresdner Bank AG, Cologne, Fed. Republic Germany, 1960-62; sales rep. Remington-Rand Univac GmbH, Frankfurt, Bonn, Fed. Republic Germany, 1966-68; br. mgr. Mohawk Data Scis. GmbH, Hanover, Fed. Republic Germany, 1969-72; gen. mgr. CIT-Transac GmbH, Frankfurt, 1975-77; founder, pres. PRW-Unternehmensberatung GmbH, Koerdorf/Taunus, Fed. Republic Germany, 1978—. Co-author: Yearbook Office Automation, 1985, 86, Marketing for Computers and New Media, 1985, Dictionary of Computer Sciences, 1987; author: Men Who Wrote Computer History; editor Office Mgmt., 1982—; corr. Datamation mag., 1985; editor-in-chief IT-Market, 1987—. Mem. ADI, Assn. German EDP Users (bd. dirs. 1970-72, 82-85), German Journalists Assn., German-Am. C. of C., Assn. Computer Sci. (hon. press officer Artificial Intelligence sect. 1988—). Home and Office: Neuwagenmuehle, 5429 Koerdorf-Taunus Federal Republic of Germany

WURSTER, THOMAS STEPHEN, consultant; b. Cin., Oct. 18, 1952; s. Warren Louis and Jean Mildred (Yolton) W.; B.A., Cornell U., 1974; M.B.A., U. Chgo., 1978; Ph.D., Yale U., 1978. Cons., Boston Cons. Group, 1978-82, mgr., 1982-86, v.p., bd. dirs., 1986—. instr. John E. Anderson Grad. Sch. Bus. UCLA, 1986—. Home: 2776 Carmar Dr Los Angeles CA 90046 Office: Boston Cons Group 333 S Grand Ave Los Angeles CA 90071

WURTELE, CHRISTOPHER ANGUS, paint and coatings company executive; b. Mpls., Aug. 25, 1934; s. Valentine and Charlotte (Lindley) W.; m. Heather Campbell (div. Feb. 1977); children—Christopher, Andrew, Heidi; m. Margaret Von Blon, Aug. 21, 1977. BA, Yale U., 1956; MBA, Stanford U., 1961. Vice pres. Minn. Paints, Inc. (merged with Valspar Corp 1970), Mpls., 1962-65, exec. v.p., 1965, pres., chief exec. officer, 1965-70; pres., chief exec. officer The Valspar Corp., Mpls., 1970-73, chmn., chief exec. officer, 1973—; dir. Gen. Mills Inc.; dir. Donaldson Co., Mpls. Found., Northwestern Nat. Life Ins. Co., Bd. dirs. Walker Art Ctr. Served with USN, 1956-59. Mem. Am. Bus. Conf., Mpls. Club, Nat. Paint & Coatings Assn. (bd. dirs.). Episcopalian. Home: 2409 E Lake of the Isles Pkwy Minneapolis MN 55405 Office: Valspar Corp 1101 Third St S Minneapolis MN 55415

WURTS, WILLIAM WHITNEY, financial consulting company executive; b. Paterson, N.J., Apr. 14, 1937; s. John Halsey and LaVonne (Whitney) W.; m. Oct. 12, 1962; children: Anne, Patricia, John, Elizabeth. BA, Yale U., 1959. Mgmt. trainee Wells Fargo Bank, San Francisco, 1961-62; from acct.

exec. to sr. v.p. Merrill Lynch Capital Markets, Seattle, 1962-85; founder Wurts, Johnson & Co. Investment & Performance Cons., 1986—. Mem. precinct com. Bellevue, Wash. Reps., 1964-66. Served with U.S. Army, 1960-62. Mem. Western Pension Conf. (pres. 1976-77), Seattle C. of C., Yale Alumni Assn. Western Wash. (pres. 1970-71). Republican. Episcopalian. Clubs: Broadmore Golf, Wash. Athletic (Seattle). Lodge: Rotary. Office: Wurts Johnson & Co 111 Third Ave Ste 1200 Seattle WA 98101

WURTZEL, ALAN LEON, retail company executive; b. Mount Vernon, N.Y., Sept. 23, 1933; s. Samuel S. and Ruth (Mann) W.; m. Irene C. Rosenberg, Oct. 9, 1988; children from previous marriage: Judith Halle, Daniel Henry, Sharon Lee. A.B., Oberlin Coll., 1955; postgrad., London Sch. Econ., 1955-56; LL.B. cum laude, Yale, 1959. Bar: Conn. 1959, D.C. 1960, Va. 1968. Law clk. Chief Judge David L. Bazelon, U.S. Ct. Appeals, D.C., 1959-60; assoc. Fried, Frank, Harris, Shriver & Kampelman, Washington, 1960-65; legisl. asst. to Senator Joseph Tydings, 1965-66; with Cir. City Stores, Inc. (formerly Wards Co., Inc.), Richmond, 1966—, v.p., 1968-70, pres., 1970-83, chief exec. officer, 1973-86, chmn., 1983—; pres. NATM Buying Corp., 1978-86; pres. Operation Independence, 1987-88. Bd. dirs. Office Dept., Inc., Boca Raton, Fla., Tribeer Corp., N.Y.C.; pres Jewish Community Fedn. Richmond, 1984-86; vice rector, bd. visitors Va. Commonwealth U. Mem. Phi Beta Kappa. Home: 1747 Corcoran St NW Washington DC 20009 Office: Cir City Stores Inc 2040 Thalbro St Richmond VA 23230

WYAND, ROBERT RICE, II, investment company executive; b. Hagerstown, Md., Jan. 6, 1938; s. Robert Rice and Ruth (Knadler) W.; divorced; children: Robert Rice III, Abigail; m. Anne Lewis Robison, Mar. 9, 1989. BA in Econs., Franklin & Marshall Coll., Lancaster, Pa., 1959; MA in Econs., Pa. State U., 1961. Fin. economist, bd. govs. Fed. Res. System, Washington, 1962-64; asst. to pres. Fed. Res. Bank Atlanta, 1964-68; economist, securities analyst Montag & Caldwell, Atlanta, 1968-70, prin., 1978-84; economist Abbey Internat. Corp., Atlanta, 1970-71; economist, investment mgr. Ga. Internat. Corp., Atlanta, 1971-73; First v.p. Schroder, Naess & Thomas, Atlanta and Washington, 1973-78; portfolio mgr. Fidelity Mgmt. and Rsch. Investment Mgmt. Svc., Boston, 1978; prin. Seawell, Wyand, Murray & Stewart, Inc., Boston, 1984-87; pres. Strategic Portfolio Mgmt., Inc., Boston, 1987—; also bd. dirs. Strategic Portfolio Mgmt., Inc.; chmn. bd. dirs. Summa Capital Corp, Atlanta; bd. dirs. various entrepreneurial cos., Atlanta; lectr. Ga. Inst. Tech., Atlanta, 1988—. Contbr. articles to profl. publs. Served to 1st lt. U.S. Army, 1961. Fellow Fin. Analysts Fedn.; mem. Atlanta Soc. Fin. Analysts. Club: Beech Aero (Atlanta). Methodist. Office: Summa Capital Corp 1200 Ashwood Pkwy Ste 350 Atlanta GA 30338

WYANT, JOSEPH ANDREW, cablevision company executive, photographer; b. Weston, W.Va., Jan. 23, 1949; s. John Frederick and Evelyn Isabel (Mount) W. BA in Geography, W.Va. U., 1971; postgrad. Ohio State U., 1975—. CCTV prodn. coordinator Columbus (Ohio) State Inst., 1972-77; mgr. Ponderosa System, Inc., Lancaster, Ohio, 1978; media specialist Cleveland Heights-University Heights (Ohio) Bd. Edn., 1979-81; dir. programming Viacom Cablevision, Cleve., 1981-84, dir. mktg. Viacom Cablevision, Dayton, Ohio, 1984-89; gen. mgr. TKR Cable, Warwick, N.Y., 1989—; freelance photographer, Cleve., 1979—; speaker in field. Author: Viacom Is..., 1983; contbr. photog. studies to profl. publs. Mem. dist. communications com. United Meth. Ch., Cleve., 1982-83; cons. lay pub. relations adv. com. Cleveland Heights-University Heights Bd. Edn., 1983; mem. citizens adv. com. Kettering Bd. Edn., 1985. Recipient cert. of Honor Radio-TV Council Greater Cleve., Inc., 1982; cited by Ohio Senate for Outstanding Contbn. to Community Relations, 1984. Mem. Ohio Cable TV Assn. (cablecasting com. 1982-84), Dayton Advt. Club (bd. dirs. 1988-89), Nat. Fedn. Local Cable Programmers, Cable TV Adminstrn. and Mktg. Soc. Office: care TKR Cable 19 South St Warwick NY 10990

WYATT, CARY COZEAN, engineer, industrial company executive; b. Hutchinson, Kans., June 24, 1942; s. Carl Everett and Mary Lucille (Cozean) W.; m. Constance Ann Hall, Mar. 5, 1966; children: Christopher William, Casey Carlson. BS in Indsl. Engring., Kans. State U., Manhattan, 1965; MBA, U. Tulsa, 1973. Engr. Standard Oil Calif., El Segundo, 1965-66, McDonnell-Douglas Corp., St. Louis, 1966-68; prodn. mgr. Nelson Electronic div. Gen. Signal, Tulsa, 1968-73; v.p. mfg. Black Sivals & Bryson-Safety Systems, Tulsa, 1973-78; pres., chief exec. officer Cherokee Nation Industries, Inc., Stilwell, Okla., 1978—, also bd. dirs.; bd. dirs. Cherokee Nation Industries, Inc., Stilwell, Transport Devel. Corp., Tahlequah, Okla., Comml. Bank & Trust, Muskogee, Okla. Vice-chmn. Northeastern State U. Ednl. Found., Tahlequah, Okla., 1984—; trustee Bacone Coll., Muskogee, 1985—; founder scholarship program Cherokee Nation Industries, 1985; mem. Gov.'s Corp. Exec. of Okla. Team, Oklahoma City, 1988—. Mem. Am. Inst. Indsl. Engring. (pres. 1972-73), Okla. Acad. State Goals, Sigma Phi Epsilon, Sigma Iota Epsilon, Beta Gamma Sigma. Republican. Presbyterian. Lodge: Kiwanis (bd. dirs. Stilwell chpt. 1985—). Office: Cherokee Nation Industries Inc PO Box 860 Hwy 51 W Stilwell OK 74960

WYATT, M. MILDRED, public relations and advertising consultant; b. Gary, Ind., Aug. 11, 1922; d. Mark E. and Stella (Wuletich) Wajagich; A.B., Ind. U., 1946. Reporter, Logansport (Ind.) Pharos-Tribune, 1946-52; supr. press relations Ill. Inst. Tech. and Armour Research Found., Chgo., 1953-58; assoc. editor Electrical/Electronic Procurement Mag., Chgo., 1958-59; mng. editor Indsl. Research Mag., Beverly Shores, Ind., 1960-61; account exec. Donald Young Assocs., Chgo., 1961-63, Fulton-Morrissey Co., Chgo., 1963-65; account supr. Griswold-Eshelman, Chgo., 1965-68; v.p. pub. relations K&A Advt., Chgo., 1968-69; pres. Wyatt Communications, Inc., Chgo., 1969—; mem. steering com., chmn. communications Nat. Computer Conf. (chmn. special activities 1987), 1981, chmn. ofcl. activities, 1987. Bd. dirs. NCCJ, Chgo., 1975-85, mem. exec. com., 1980-85; bd. dirs. Met. Chgo. YWCA, 1970; mem. Loop Center Com., 1963-75. Mem. Pub. Relations Soc. Am. (v.p. 1982-83, treas., 1980-82), Women in Communications (pres. Chgo. chpt. 1970-71), Women's Advt. Club Chgo. (v.p. 1969, 74). Office: Wyatt Communications Inc 320 N Michigan Ave Chicago IL 60601

WYATT, OSCAR SHERMAN, JR., energy company executive; b. Beaumont, Tex., July 11, 1924; s. Oscar Sherman Sr. and Eva (Coday) W.; m. Lynn Wyatt; children: Carl, Steven, Douglas, Oscar Sherman III, Brad. BS in Mech. Engring., Tex. Agrl. and Mech. Coll., 1949. With Kerr-McGee Co., 1949; with Reed Roller Bit Co., 1949-51; ptnr. Wymore Oil Co., 1951-55; founder Coastal Corp., Corpus Christi, Tex., 1955; now chmn., chief exec. officer. Coastal Corp., Houston. Served with USAAF, World War II. Home: 1620 River Oaks Blvd Houston TX 77019 Office: Coastal Corp 9 Greenway Pla E Houston TX 77046

WYCOFF, ROBERT E., petroleum company executive; b. Tulsa, 1930; married. B.S.M.E., Stanford U., 1952, M.S.M.E., 1953. With Atlantic Richfield Co., Los Angeles, 1953—, various engring. and mgmt. positions, 1957-70, mgr. western region Internat. div., 1971-73, v.p., resident mgr. Alaska region N.Am. Producing div., 1973-74, corp. planning v.p., 1974-77, sr. v.p. planning and fin., 1977-80, exec. v.p., 1980-84, chief corp. officer, 1984, vice chmn., 1985, pres., chief operating officer, 1986—, also dir. Mem. ASME, Am. Petroleum Inst. Office: Atlantic Richfield Co 515 S Flower St Los Angeles CA 90071

WYMAN, AUDREY JANE, comptroller; b. Glasgow, Scotland, Mar. 23, 1955; came to U.S., 1960; d. Kenneth Albert and Jane Hewitt (McGuire) W. BS in Acctg. cum laude, Fairleigh Dickinson U., Teaneck, N.J., 1976; MBA in Acctg., Fairleigh Dickinson U., Rutherford, N.J., 1988. Asst. to pres. Apex Trucking Co. Inc., Secaucus, N.J., 1974-76; sr. acct. Irwin D. Marks & Co. CPA's, Hackensack, N.J., 1976-77, Wallin, Simon, Black & Co. CPAs, N.Y.C., 1977-80; sr. internal auditor Warner-Lambert Inc., Morris Plains, N.J., 1980-82; comptroller Charles Klatskin Co. Inc., Teterboro, N.J., 1982—. N.J. State scholar, 1972-76; faculty scholar Fairleigh Dickinson U., 1972-76. Mem. Soc. Advancement of Women's Music (treas.). Roman Catholic.

WYMAN, HERBERT JACK, marketing executive; b. San Francisco, Aug. 27, 1921; s. Herbert Wayne and Ruth B. (Jacobs) Wyman; m. Barbara Rose Voorsanger, Apr. 28, 1951 (div. Nov. 1979); children: Gareth, John, Joann; m. Elaine Johnson Snay, Jan. 3. 1980. Student, San Mateo City Coll., 1939-40; AA, San Francisco City Coll., 1941; student, San Francisco State Coll., 1942-43. Account exec., prodn. mgr. Kirschner & Co., San Francisco, 1946-50; pres., founder Wyman Co., San Francisco, 1950-83; pres., founder Wyman Communications Inc., Scottsdale, Ariz., 1988-89, Larkspur, Calif., 1989—. Contbr. articles to religious and bus. jours. Bd. trustees Ross (Calif.) Sch. Dist., 1969-71. Served with U.S. Navy, 1943-46, Atlantic. Mem. Am. Assn. Advt. Agys. (chmn. No. Calif. council 1965—). Republican.

WYMAN, MORTON, greeting card company executive; b. Cleve., 1922; (married). Grad., Cleve. State U., 1960. With Am. Greetings Corp., 1940—, v.p. plant ops. and purchasing, 1960-68, group v.p., 1968-69, exec. v.p., 1969—. Office: Am Greetings Corp 10500 American Rd Cleveland OH 44144

WYMER, ROBERT ERNEST, metals company executive; b. Marlinton, W.Va., Feb. 9, 1947; s. Elmer and Blanche Margaret (Harper) W.; m. Holly Elizabeth Cline, Dec. 28, 1968; children: Robert Ernest Jr., Jill Allison. AS, W.Va. Inst. Tech., 1968, BS, 1986. Dir. recreation area W.Va. Dept. Natural Resources, Charleston, 1965-67; insp. hwy. constrn. W.Va. Dept. Hys., Elkins, 1968; supr. shift prodn. Union Carbide Corp., Alloy, W.Va., 1969-73, indsl. engr., 1973-74, mgr. mobile equipment dept., 1974-79; asst. plant mgr., supt. mines and calcite Acme Limestone Co., Ft. Springs, W.Va., 1979-81; supr. maintenance Elkem Metals Co., Alloy, 1981-83, master mechanic, 1984-87, mgr. maintenance project, 1987-88, mgr. maintenance and engring., 1988%. Coach Montgomery (W.Va.) Little Rockets Midget Football, 1976-77;; pres. Pratt Vol. Fire Dept., Inc., 1977—; scout leader Boy Scouts Am., Handley, W.Va., 1978. Republican. Roman Catholic. Offic: Elkem Metals Co PO Box 613 Alloy WV 25002-0613

WYNN, CLAUDE THEODORE, business administration educator, college dean; b. Newark, Sept. 9, 1935; s. Claude Lester Wynn and Marie Bertha (Seymour) W.; m. Darlene Joan Galle, Nov. 20, 1955; children: Claude Anthony, Lori Christene, Stacy Marie. BBA, Wichita State U., 1962, MBA, 1963; PhD, U. Kans., 1975. Instr. mktg. Northeastern U., Boston, 1964-65; asst. prof. mktg. Wichita (Kans.) State U., 1965-71; assoc. prof. bus. adminstrn. Weber State Coll., Ogden, Utah, 1971-75, dir. rsch. ctr., 1973-75, chmn. bus. dept., 1982-87, dean Sch. Bus. and Econs., 1987—; pres., rsch. dir. Cen. States Rsch. and Tng., Inc., Wichita, 1967-70; vis. prof. U. Utah, Frankfurt, Fed. Republic Germany and Athens, Greece, 1976-77. Contbr. articles to profl. jours. Mem. Am. Mktg. Assn., Blue Key, Alpha Kappa Psi. Office: Weber State Coll Sch Bus and Econs Ogden UT 84408-3802

WYNN, KARLA WRAY, agricultural products company executive; b. Idaho Falls, Idaho, Oct. 1, 1943; d. William and Elma (McCowin) Lott; m. Russell D. Wynn, June 7, 1963; children: Joseph, Jeffrey, Andrea. Student, Idaho State Coll., 1961-62, Coll. Holy Names, 1962-63, Providence Coll. Nursing, 1962-63, Idaho State U., 1984-89. Co-owner R.D. Wynn Farms, Am. Falls, Idaho, 1963—, office mgr., 1975-84; co-owner Redi-Gro Fertilizer Co., Am. Falls, 1970—, office mgr., 1980-84; pres. Lakeside Farms, Inc., Am. Falls, 1975—. Watercolor paintings and ceramics exhibited at various statewide art shows. Lutheran. Office: Redi Gro Fertilizer Co Box 202 American Falls ID 83211

WYNNE, ARTHUR VINCENT, JR., press clipping bureau executive; b. Orange, N.J., Oct. 4, 1933; s. Arthur Vincent and Majorie E. (Stout) W.; B.A., U. Mich., 1955; M.B.A., U. Chgo., 1962; m. Patricia Ann Walters, Sept. 24, 1960 (div. Jan. 1982); children: Arthur Vincent III, Bradley Allen, Cathy; m. Sandra Anne Gerow, Apr. 21, 1982. With Burrelle's Press Clipping Service, 1955—, midwest sales mgr., 1958-60, nat. sales mgr., N.Y.C., 1960-75, partner, 1961-88; pres. Internationale Fedn. Press Clipping Bureaux, Paris, 1965-70, New Eng. Newsclips, Framingham, Mass., 1970—; bd. dirs. Hudson City Savs. Bank, Paramus, N.J. chmn., past pres. N.Am. Conf. Press Clipping Services, N.Y.C. Pres. Republican Club, Livingston, 1966; councilman Livingston, N.J., 1967-71; mayor Livingston, 1968; trustee Newark Acad. Served to 1st lt. USAAF, 1956-58. Named Livingston Young Man of Year, 1966; recipient Disting. Service award Publicity Club N.Y., 1964. Mem. Public Relations Soc. Am., Employers Assn. N.J. (pres. 1976-78), Livingston Jaycees, N.J. Press Assn. Sigma Chi. Presbyterian. Club: Publicity of New York. Avocations: flying, skiing, tennis. Home: 90 Carriage House Rd Bernardsville NJ 07924

WYNNE, BAYARD EDMUND, management consultant; b. Pitts., Sept. 6, 1930; s. Bayard Edmund and Gertrude (Starr) W.; m. Evelyn F. Wolff, Sept. 19, 1953 (div. 1980); children: Andrew Jerome, Daniel Bayard, Teresa Starr. BSCE, Carnegie-Mellon U., 1953, BS in Indsl. Mgmt., 1955, MS in Indsl. Adminstrn., 1956; PhD in Mgmt. Info. Systems, U. Minn., 1972. Registered profl. engr., Washington, Minn. Asst. corp. controller Weyerhaeuser Co., Tacoma, Wash., 1962-67; v.p. Super Valu Stores, Inc., Hopkins, Minn., 1967-70; lectr. U. Wis., Milw., 1972-76; prin., mgr. Arthur Andersen & Co., Chgo., 1976-86; mng. ptnr. Wynne Affiliates; bd. dirs. Houston-Starr Co., Pitts.; prof. ops. and systems mgmt., dir. inst. research Ind. U.; adj. prof. several instns., 1962-76. Contbr. articles to profl. jours. Bd. dirs. Local Sch. Systems, Mpls., 1968-72. Fellow Soc. Prodn. and Industry Control; founder Mgmt. Sci. Roundtable; mem. Tech. Assn. of Pulp and Paper Industry (former pres.), Inst. of Mgmt. Scis., Coll. Practice of Mgmt. Sci. (jour. editor), Inst. Indsl. Engrs. (sr.), Soc. Info. Mgmt., Triple Nine Soc., Beta Gamma Sigma. Republican. Clubs: University, East Bank (Chgo.). Home: 2238 E Cape Cod Dr Bloomington IN 47401 Office: Ind Univ Sch Bus 10th & Fee Ln Bloomington IN 47405

WYNNE, JOHN BENEDICT, banker; b. Stamford, Conn., June 19, 1930; s. Edward Victor and Helen Theresa (Collins) W.; m. Sally Lila Mazzeo, Jan. 26, 1957; children: John Benedict, Stephen D., Lila T., Jean M., Anthony E. BA, Trinity Coll., 1952; JD, NYU, 1957; cert., Grad. Sch. Bus. Harvard U., 1969. Bar: N.Y. 1959, Conn. 1957. Atty. Fed. Res. Bank of N.Y., N.Y.C., 1957-63; sr. v.p., sec. bd. Chem. Bank, N.Y.C., 1963—. Chmn. Leukemia Soc. Am.; past pres. Asthma and Allergy Soc. Am. Served to 1st lt. USAF, 1952-54. Mem. ABA, Bar Assn. City of N.Y., Conn. Bar Assn., N.Y. State Bar Assn. Home: 1 Nedley Ln Greenwich CT 06831 Office: Chem Banking Corp 277 Park Ave New York NY 10172

WYNNYCKYJ, LEO GEORGE, management consultant; b. Jabloniw, Ukraine, Feb. 21, 1931; s. Julian and Jaroslawa (Satursky) W.; came to Can., 1948, naturalized, 1955; B in Commerce, Concordia U., Can., 1953, B.A. in Econs., 1955; M.B.A., U. Western Ont. (Can.), 1957; PhD, Pacific Western U., 1985. Fin. analyst CIL, Montreal, Que., 1957-60; fin. planning mgr. Structural Steel div., chief acct. Canron, Montreal, 1960-65; mfg. analysis mgr. Massey Ferguson Co., Toronto, Ont., 1965-66; functional dir. Touche Ross, Mgmt. Cons., Toronto, 1966-67; partner, pres. RMC Resources Mgmt. Cons. Ltd., Toronto, 1968-76; exec. dir. Strait of Canso Devel. Office, Halifax, N.S., 1976-77; pres. LGW Bus. Cons. Ltd., Ottawa, Ont., 1977—. Served to maj., arty. Can. Army Militia, 1952-64. Cert. mgmt. acct. Fellow Soc. Mgmt. Accts. Can.; mem. Soc. Mgmt. Accts. Ont. (pres. 1973-74), Royal Can. Mil. Inst. Office: 1371 Chattaway Ave, Ottawa, ON Canada K1H 7S2

WYSER-PRATTE, GUY PATRICK, securities trader; b. Vichy, France, June 21, 1940; came to U.S., 1947; s. Eugene John and Margaret (Pratte) W-P.; m. Heather McNulty, Mar. 29, 1969 (div. 1981); children—Joelle, Danielle; m. Vivien Augusta Green, Sept. 28, 1984. B.A. in History, U. Rochester, 1962; M.B.A., NYU, 1970. Arbitrage analyst Wyser-Pratte & Co., N.Y.C., 1966-67; asst. mgr. arbitrage dept. Bache & Co., N.Y.C., 1967-71; mgr. arbitrage dept. Prudential-Bache Securities, N.Y.C., 1971—, exec. v.p., dir., 1976—. Author monographs Risk Arbitage, Risk Arbitage II. Bd. dirs. Internat. Rescue Com. Served to capt. USMC, 1962-66. Republican. Roman Catholic. Clubs: Metropolitan (gov.), Doubles (N.Y.C.). Home: 510 Park Ave New York NY 10021 Office: Prudential Bache Securities 199 Water St New York NY 10292

WYSOCKI, ROBERT ADAM, telecommunications company executive; b. Syracuse, N.Y., Apr. 29, 1945; s. Adam Joseph and June Pauline (Guenthner) W.; m. Mary Tapogna, Feb. 9, 1969; children: Christopher R., Lauren M. BS, U.S. Mil. Acad., 1967; MBA, Pace U., 1984. Mgr. treasury N.Y. Telephone, Albany, 1973-76; corp. cash mgr. N.Y. Telephone, N.Y.C., 1977-80, mgr. pension fund, 1980-81, mgr. long-term fin., 1981-82; investment dir. pension fund NYNEX Corp., N.Y.C., 1983-87, dir. investor rels., 1988—. Dir. West Point Soc. of N.Y., 1978. Capt. Signal Corps U.S. Army, 1967-71. Mem. Nat. Investor Relations Inst., Investment Tech. Assn., Urban Land Inst., Fin. Analyst Fedn., N.Y. Soc. Security Analysts. Republican. Roman Catholic. Home: 16 Cherokee Dr Brookfield Center CT 06805 Office: NYNEX Corp 335 Madison Ave Room 2104 New York NY 10017

WYSONG, RANDY LEE, medical and nutritional products executive, researcher,; b. Midland, Mich., May 21, 1943; s. Donald Vernon and Elizabeth Jeannette (Hagley) W.; m. Betty Jo Jablonski, Feb. 4, 1964 (div. 1979); children: Stephen, Carrie, Tyler, Leah, Deidre; m. Julie Jean Gillis, Apr. 24, 1981; children: Lucas, Logan. Assoc., Delta Coll., 1963; BS, Mich. State U., 1965, DVM, 1968. Gen. practice vet. medicine Colo. and Mich., 1968-85; prin., researcher Wysong Med. Corp., Midland, 1979—; prof. Lansing (Mich.) Coll., 1972-75. Author: The Creation-Evolution Controversy, 1975; health and nutrition newsletter; inventor in field. Recipient Entrepreneur of Yr. award Saginaw Valley State Coll., 1986. Mem. AVMA, Nat. Health Fedn., Am. Assn. Cereal Chemists, Inst. Food Tech., Union concerned Scientists, Am. Holistic Med. Assn., World Wildlife Fund, Amnesty Internat., The Nature Conservancy, AAAS. Home: 2210 El Rancho Midland MI 48640 Office: Wysong Med Corp 1880 N Eastman Midland MI 48640

XAFA, ARISTÉA, finance company executive; b. Geneva, Oct. 8, 1950; d. Ilias Nicholas and Mary Constantine (Macrea) X. Diploma in languages, U. Geneva, 1972, MS in Econs., 1973; MS in Fin., MIT, 1975. Asst. fin. mgr. Omran Techlar, Tehran, Iran, 1975-78; v.p. fin. REDEC, Jeddah, Saudi Arabia and London, 1978-80; advisor to pres. Onassis Group, 1981; v.p. fin. Global Investments, Boston, 1981-84; fin. cons. Quantum Corp., Boston, 1984—; v.p. Union Bank of Switzerland, Zurich, 1988—; cons. Global Monetary Project, Washington, 1983—; v.p. fin. MIT Alumni Club, Boston, 1985-87; mem. alumni coun. MIT. Office: Union Bank Switzerland, 45 Bahnhofstrasse, Zurich Switzerland

XANTHOPOULOS, DIOMEDES, jeweler; b. Athens, Greece, May 2, 1926; s. Constantin and Elly (Stavrianos) X.; m. Angelique Papagianopoulos, Oct. 2, 1955; children: Maria-Elly, Celia. Degree in Econs., Univ. Econ. and Comml. Studies, Athens, 1947. Jeweler in family enterprises Athens, 1953—. Contbr. articles to econ. jours. Served as res. officer Royal Hellenique Navy, 1947-53. Decorated Silver Cross; recipient Medal of Resistance During German Occupation World War II, 1983. Clubs: Golf of Athens, Cercle d'Athenes. Lodges: Masons (32 degree), Rotary (past pres.). Home: 4 Voukourestiou St, 105 64 Athens Greece Office: Xanthopoulos Jeweler, 4 Voukourestiou St, 105 64 Athens Greece

YABLONSKY, DENNIS, data processing executive; b. Pitts., June 5, 1952; s. John and Jean (Santina) Y.; m. Veronica Mulvey; children: Kristen, Katherine. BS in Indsl. Mgmt., U. Cin., 1975. Mem. staff Cincom, Cin., 1976-81, mgr. worldwide sales, 1981-82, v.p. mktg., 1983-84, pres., chief operating officer, 1985-87; pres., chief exec. officer Carnegie Group Inc., Pitts., 1987—. Bd. dirs. Citizens for Community Values, Cin. Mem. Pitts. High Tech. Coun. Republican. Roman Catholic. Office: Carnegie Group Inc 5 PPG Pl Pittsburgh PA 15222

YACKIRA, MICHAEL WILLIAM, communications company executive; b. N.Y.C., Aug. 14, 1951; s. Alan Israel and Lillian (Landau) Y.; m. Roberta Guido, July 24, 1977; children: Steven, Andrew. BS in Acctg., CCNY, 1972. Sr. acct. Arthur Andersen, N.Y.C., 1972-75; v.p. St. Joe Petroleum, Houston, 1975-83; mgr. fin. analysis U.S. Industries, Stamford, Conn., 1983-84; dir. bus. analysis and research GTE Svc. Corp., Stamford, 1984-85, dir. bus. devel. and analysis, 1985-86, asst. controller budget planning and analysis, 1986-87; v.p. fin. and revenues GTE Fla., Tampa, 1987-88; v.p. fin. and info. mgmt. GTE Info. Svcs., Tampa, 1988—. Mem. sch. accountancy adv. council U. S.Fla.; bd. dirs., chmn. program com. Fin. Exec. Inst. Mem. Fla. Mcht. Assn. (bd. dirs., fin. com.). Office: GTE Info Svcs 101 Kennedy Blvd PO Box 2924 Tampa FL 33601-2924

YAEGER, BILLIE PATRICIA, advertising sales executive; b. Boston, Mar. 17, 1949; d. Harold Stern and Marie Frances (Levenson) Y. Student, Logos Bible Coll. Office mgr., NE rep. Ticketron, Inc., Boston, 1968-73; owner, mgr. Performance King, Natick, Mass., 1973-74, House of Portraits, Lakeland, Fla., 1974-75; employment counselor Snelling & Snelling, Lakeland, 1975-77; advt. sales account exec. The Ledger/N.Y. Times, Lakeland, 1977—. Recipient Chmn. of Bd. award N.Y. Times, 1984-85, 10 Yr. Service award The Ledger/N.Y. Times, 1987, 88, Commendation award Fla. Dept. Law Enforcement, 1986; named Salesperson of Yr. The Ledger, 1987. Mem. Nat. Assn. Female Execs. Republican. Avocations: photography, writing, waterskiing.

YAEGER, DOUGLAS HARRISON, gas company executive; b. St. Louis, Mar. 3, 1949; s. Walter Earl and Mary Eloise (Drinkwater) Y.; m. Lynn Mary Halloran, June 24, 1951; children: Lauren Harrison, Drew Halloran. BS, Miami U., Oxford, Ohio, 1971; MBA, St. Louis U., 1976. Sales asst. Miss. River Transmission Corp., St. Louis, 1974-75, coordinator mktg. and regulatory supply, 1975-78, coordinator mktg. and supply, 1978, mgr. mktg. and supply coordination, 1978-81, asst. v.p. mktg., 1981-82, v.p. mktg., 1982-86, sr. v.p. mktg., 1986-88; exec. v.p. Miss. River Transmission Corp., 1988—. Mem. Am. Gas Assn., So. Gas Assn., Interstate Natural Gas Assn., Assn. Corp. Growth, Sunset Country, Media, Strathalbyn Farm. Office: Miss River Transmission Corp 9900 Clayton Rd Saint Louis MO 63124

YAGER, JOHN WARREN, lawyer, banker; b. Toledo, Sept. 16, 1920; s. Joseph A. and Edna Gertrude (Pratt) Y.; m. Dorothy W. Merki, July 25, 1942; children: Julie M., John M. AB, U. Mich., 1942, JD, 1948. Bar: Ohio 1948. Sole practice Toledo, 1948-64; trust officer Toledo Trust Co., 1964-69; v.p., trust officer First Nat. Bank, Toledo, 1969—; sec. First Ohio Bancshares, Inc., 1980-85. Pres. Toledo Met. Park Dist., 1971-85, Neighborhood Health Assn., 1974-75, councilman, Toledo, 1955-57, 60-61, mayor, 1958-59; bd. dirs. Toledo-Lucas County Library, 1968-70, Riverside Hosp., Downtown Toledo Assn.; past pres. Toledo Legal Aid Soc., Toledo Council Chs., Toledo Mcpl. League, Econ. Opportunity Planning Assn., Toledo, Com. on Relations with Toledo, Spain. Served to maj. USMC, 1942-46, 50-52. Decorated Bronze Star; named one of 10 Outstanding Young Men in Toledo, 1952, 54, 55. Mem. Ohio Bar Assn., Toledo Bar Assn., Toledo Estate Planning Council, Delta Tau Delta. Club: Belmont Country (Toledo). Home: 29301 Bates Rd Perrysburg OH 43551-3808 Office: First Nat Bank Toledo 606 Madison Ave Toledo OH 43604

YAGODA, DAVID VITAL, real estate investor and consultant; b. N.Y.C., Sept. 12, 1927; s. Meyer and Sarah (Freilich) Y.; student Yeshiva Coll., 1945-47, CCNY, 1947-48; LL.B., Bklyn. Law Sch., 1950; m. Grace S. Udell, Nov. 23, 1967; children—Janet L., Barbara A. Exec., Premier Toy Corp., N.Y.C., 1950-67; pres. Meysar Realty Corp., N.Y.C., 1967—, David Yagoda, Inc., N.Y.C., 1980—; v.p. MYM Realty Corp., N.Y.C., 1970—; partner, chief exec. officer Four Star Holding, N.Y.C., 1978—. Trustee, Gt. Neck (N.Y.) Synagogue, 1969—, pres., 1975-77; trustee Boys Town of Jersualem, 1986—, Yeshiva U., 1987—; vice chmn. bd. trustees Stern Coll. for Women, 1987—; mem. Gt. Neck Democratic Com., 1972-81; pres. Gt. Neck Dem. Club, 1980-84 trustee North Shore Hebrew Acad., 1976—. Mem. Real Estate Bd. N.Y. Club: B'nai B'rith. Home: 150 E 69th St New York NY 10021 Office: 1501 Broadway New York NY 10036

YAMADA, NOBUYUKI CHRIS, real estate company executive; b. Tokyo, Oct. 8, 1953; came to U.S., 1987; s. Hiroshige and Sayoko (Kawazoe) Y.; m. Masumi Margaret Ma-eda, Nov. 20, 1981; 1 child, Tatsuya. BA, Tokyo U. Fgn. Studies, 1976; MBA, Ind. U., 1978. With Mitsui Real Estate Sales Co., Ltd., Tokyo, 1983—; sr. v.p. Mitsui Real Estate Sales U.S.A. Co., Los Angeles, 1987—. Office: Mitsui Real Estate Sales 800 Wilshire Blvd Ste 1550 Los Angeles CA 90017

YAMAGUCHI, TAMOTSU, bank executive; b. Hokkaido, Japan, Oct. 11, 1930; came to U.S., 1986; s. Chuji and Nami (Inouye) Y.; married; children: Takashi, Masako. BS in Econs., U. Tokyo, 1953. With Bank of Tokyo,

1953-63; dept. mgr. fgn. exchange and funds ops. Bank of Tokyo, Dusseldorf, Fed. Rep. Germany, 1963-66, London, 1966-70; acting gen. mgr. Bank of Tokyo, Tokyo, 1970-79; pres., dir. Bank of Tokyo, Sao Paulo, Brazil, 1979-82; gen. mgr., bd. dirs. Bank of Tokyo Ltd., Tokyo, 1982-84, mng. dir.Asian Regions, 1984-86, resident mng. dir., 1986-87; resident sr. mng. dir. Bank of Tokyo Ltd., New York, 1987—; chmn. bd. Bank Tokyo Trust Co., New York, 1986—; bd. dirs. Bank Tokyo Can., Toronto, Ont.; chmn. bd. Union Bank, L.A. Served with Japanese Navy, 1945. Mem. Japanese C. of C. N.Y. (bd. dirs. 1986—), Japanese Am. Assn. N.Y. (bd. dirs. 1987—), The Nippon Club Inc. (bd. dirs. 1986—), Japan Naval Soc., Asia Soc. (trustee 1987—), Japan Soc. (bd. dirs. 1987—). Club: Nippon (N.Y.C.). Office: Bank of Tokyo Trust Co 100 Broadway New York NY 10005

YAMAKAWA, DAVID KIYOSHI, JR., lawyer; b. San Francisco, Jan. 25, 1936; s. David Kiyoshi and Shizu (Negishi) Y. BS, U. Calif.-Berkeley, 1958, JD, 1963. Bar: Calif. 1964, U.S. Supreme Ct. 1970. Prin. Law Offices of David K. Yamakawa Jr., San Francisco, 1964—; bd. dirs. Mt. Zion Ventures Inc. Dep. dir. Community Action Agy., San Francisco, 1968-69; dir. City Demonstration Agy., San Francisco, 1969-70; mem. adv. coun. Calif. Senate Subcom. on the Disabled, 1982-83; chmn. community residential treatment system adv. com. Calif. Dept. Mental Health, 1980-85, San Francisco Human Rights Commn., 1977-80; pres. Legal Assistance to the Elderly, 1981-83 ; 2d v.p. Nat. Conf. Social Welfare, 1983—; v.p. Region IX, Nat. Mental Health Assn., 1981-83; vice-chmn. Mt. Zion Hosp. and Med. Ctr., 1986-88 ; bd. dirs. United Neighborhood Ctrs. of Am., 1977-83, ARC Bay Area, 1988—; chmn. bd. trustees United Way Bay area, 1983-85; chief fin. officer Assisi Nature Coun./USA, 1987—; v.p. Friends of Legal Assistance to the Elderly, 1984—; vice chmn. Friends of the San Francisco Human Rights Commn., 1985—; bd. dirs. Ind. Sector, 1986—, Keep Librs. Alive, 1986—, La Madre de los Pobres, 1982—, Nat. Concilio Am., 1987—, Friends of the Arts, 1987—; pres. Coun. Internat. Programs, San Francisco, 1987—. Recipient John S. Williams Outstanding Planning and Agy. Rels. vol. award United Way of the Bay Area, 1980, Mortimer Fleishhacker Jr. Outstanding Vol. award United Way, 1985, Spl. Recognition award Legal Assistance to the Elderly, 1983, Commendation award Bd. Suprs. City and County of San Francisco, 1983, cert. Honor, 1985, San Francisco Found. award, 1985; David Yamakawa Day proclaimed in San Francisco, 1985. Mem. ABA (Liberty Bell award 1986), Internat. Inst. San Francisco (bd. dirs. 1989—). Office: 582 Market St Ste 410 San Francisco CA 94104

YAMMINE, RIAD NASSIF, oil company executive; b. Hammana, Lebanon, Apr. 12, 1934; s. Nassib Nassif and Emilie (Daou) Y.; came to U.S., 1952, naturalized, 1963; m. Beverly Ann Hosack, Sept. 14, 1954; children: Kathleen Yammine Griffiths, Cynthia Yammine Rotman, Michael. BS in Petroleum Engring., Pa. State U., 1956; postgrad. Advanced Mgmt. Program, Harvard U., 1977. Registered profl. engr., Ohio. Engr. Trans-Arabian Pipe Line Co., Saudi Arabia, 1956-61; with Marathon Pipe Line Co., 1961-75, mgr. Western div., Casper, Wyo., 1971-74, mgr. Eastern div., Martinsville, Ill., 1974-75; mktg. ops. div. mgr. Marathon Oil Co., 1975-83; pres. Marathon Pipeline Co., 1983-84; v.p. supply and transp. Marathon Petroleum Co., 1984-88, dir., 1984—; pres. EMRO Mktg. Co., 1988—; also officer, bd. dirs. various subs. Patentee in field. Mem. ch. council, chmn. finance com. First Luth. Ch., Findlay; past trustee, Fisk U. Mem. ASME, Am. Petroleum Inst. Republican. Club: Findlay Country. Home: 624 Winterhaven Dr Findlay OH 45840 Office: 539 S Main St Findlay OH 45840

YANAGIHARA, JOHN HIDEKI, insurance, investment company executive; b. Honolulu, July 8, 1953; s. Masuo and Tomoyo (Kimura) Y.; m. Rae Hisayo Tanaka, Mar. 25, 1978. Student, U. Hawaii, 1971-75. CLU, chartered fin. cons. Agt. Conn. Gen. Life Ins. Co., Honolulu, 1979-80, Conn. Mut. Life Ins. Co., Honolulu, 1981-86; dir. investment CM Alliance, Honolulu, 1986—, advanced sales dir., 1987—; ptnr. Benefit Planning Resources, Honolulu, 1983—. Contbr. numerous articles to fin. publs. Mem. Nat. Assn. Life Underwriters, East Honolulu Assn. Life Underwriters (bd. dirs., treas. 1988—), Honolulu Soc. CLU's and Chartered Fin. Cons. (estate planning coun.), Million Dollar Round Table, Small Bus. Hawaii (bd. dirs. 1986—), Pacific Club, Oahu Country Club, Rotary. Home: 111 Olaa Pl Honolulu HI 96817 Office: CM Alliance 1600 Kapiolani Blvd Ste 1130 Honolulu HI 96814-3898

YANCEY, DAVID PRICE, software development company executive; b. Charlottesville, Va., Nov. 26, 1949; s. Scott Garris and Jen Lea (Guthrie) Y.; m. Kathleen Ann Blake, Aug. 4, 1973; children: Genevieve Ann, Matthew Price. BS in Indsl. Engring., Va. Poly. Inst. and State U., 1972, ME in Systems Engring., 1977; PhD, Purdue U., 1981. Engring. aide Corning Glass Works, Greencastle, Pa., 1972-74; indsl. engr. Mack Trucks, Inc., Hagerstown, Md., 1974-76; sr. systems cons. Pritsker & Assocs., Inc., West Lafayette, Ind., 1981-82, bd. dirs., 1982-86, v.p. software devel., 1986—. Contbr. articles to profl. jours. Mem. Soc. for Computer Simulation, Inst. for Mgmt. Sci., Toastmasters Club (pres. 1988—). Office: Pritsker & Assocs Inc 1305 Cumberland Ave West Lafayette IN 47906

YANCEY, ORSON PIERRE, consulting software engineer; b. Syracuse, N.Y., Oct. 6, 1955; s. Gerald and Lena (Lyndaker) Y. BS in Engring. and Computer Sci., Cornell U., 1979; postgrad., Boston U. CAM devel. engr. Gen. Electric Co., Lynn, Mass., 1980-83; software engr. New England Telephone, Boston, 1984; project engr., software quality assurance BYTEX/IBM Corp., Southborough, Mass., 1984-85; systems architect XRE Corp./Albany Med. Ctr., Littleton, Mass., 1985; with Genrad Corp., West Concord, Mass., 1985; prin. software engr. Wang Labs., Lowell, Mass., 1986; UNIX internals engr. Interactive Systems Corp., Boston, 1986; project software engr. Polaroid Co., Cambridge, Mass., 1986-87; prin. UNIX software engr. SYMMETRIX, Inc., Ipswich, Mass., 1987; network software engr. BBN Communications Corp., Cambridge, 1987-88; sr. software engr BBN Advanced Computers, Cambridge, 1988; software engr. Siemens Med. Electronics, Danvers, Mass., 1988; architect MCI/IBM Corp., Milford, Conn., 1988—. Mem. Nat. Sci. Found. Network, 1988—. Mem. Triangle Frat Club. Home and Office: 217 Harvard St Unit 1R Cambridge MA 02139 also: care Samuel P Yancey RD 1 Croghan NY 13327

YANCEY, ROBERT EARL, JR., oil company executive; b. Ashland, Ky., June 16, 1945; s. Robert E. Sr. and Estelline (Tackett) Y.; m. Nina McGee, June 16, 1962; children: Rob, Yvonne, Elizabeth. BS in Chem. Engring., Cornell U., 1967. Supt. Catlettsburg (Ky.) Refinery, 1976-79; exec. asst. Ashland (Ky.) Petroleum Co., 1979-80, group v.p., 1980-81, sr. v.p., 1981-86, pres., 1986—; sr. v.p., group operating officer Ashland Oil Inc., 1988—. Republican. Home: 504 Amanda Furnace Dr Ashland KY 41101 Office: Ashland Petroleum Co PO Box 391 Ashland Dr Ashland KY 41114

YANDOLI, JOSEPH VICTOR, gas company executive; b. Jersey City, May 29, 1930; s. Cosimo J. and Marianne (Saporito) Y.; m. Josephine Yandoli, Apr. 18, 1953 (dec. June 1980); children: Nadine Yandoli Diaz, Dianne, Donna Yandoli Amalfitano, Marianne. BS, Rutgers U., 1959; postgrad., Dartmouth Coll., 1967-69. With Columbia Gas Systems Svc. Corp., 1949-68; acct. Columbia Gas Systems Svc. Corp., N.Y.C., 1958-63, sr. analyst, 1968-70; mgr. credit Pitts. Gas. Co., N.Y.C., 1970; dir. credit Pitts. Gas. Co., Wilmington, Del., 1970-73; dir. ins. Pitts. Gas. Co., Wilmington, 1973-84; asst. treas. risk mgmt. Columbia Gas System Svc. Corp., Wilmington, 1984—; credit mgr. CPA, Pitts. Bd. dirs. Tri-Village Jaycees, Columbus,1965. Mem. Am. Gas Assn. (chmn. risk com. 1987-88, plaque for leadership 1988), Risk Ins. Mgrs. Soc. (chmn. utility and drilling sessions New Orleans 1985, plaque for excellence 1985), Delmarva Risk Study Group (chmn. 1983), Phila. Ins. Soc., Pipeline Ins. Mgrs. (chmn. 1986), Assoc. Electric and Gas Ins. Svc. (underwriting com. 1983), Energy Ins. Mut. (adv. com. 1988). Republican. Roman Catholic. Office: Columbia Gas System Svc Corp 20 Monchanin Rd Wilmington DE 19807

YANKER, ROBERT HENRY, diversified operations executive; b. Pitts., Oct. 9, 1932; s. Henry Christian and Anna Kathryn (Babilon) Y.; m. Mary Margaret Crawley, Sept. 1, 1956; children: Mary Anne, Robert H., Rodney S., Randall S., Holly M. BS in Indsl. Mgmt., Duquesne U., 1954, MBA, 1960. Cert. mfg. engr. Systems mgr. Elec. Mfr., Pitts., 1960-68; plant mgr. Constrn. Machinery, Aurora, Ill., 1969-79; v.p. ops. Rail Car Mfr., Chgo., 1980-83; exec. v.p. Safety Tng. Orgn., Hobart, Ind., 1984; chief ops. officer Leaded Crystal Mfr., Grapeville, Pa., 1985, Frozen Food Mfr., Florence, Ky., 1986, Machine Tool Mfr., Springfield, Vt., 1987, Ceramics Co., Newell, W.Va., 1988—; bd. dirs. Roofing Materials Mfr., Cons. Firm. Alderman, City of Aurora, bd. dirs. Ill. United Way, 1976. Served to 1st lt. U.S. Army, 1954-56. Roman Catholic. Club: Fox Valley Indsl. (pres. 1974-75) Lodge: Moose.

YANNOPOULOS, MARINOS, banker; b. Athens, Greece, Aug. 7, 1953; s. Stamatios and Emilia (Gerolymbou) Y.; m. Evagelia Nikolopoulou, Dec. 9, 1978; children: Maria-Eleni, Alexia, Andreas. Student, Athens Coll., 1972; BA in Econs., Deree-Pierce Coll., Athens, 1975; MA, U. Sussex, Eng., 1976; MBA, Manchester (Eng.) Bus. Sch., 1978. Lead auditor Esso Europe Inc., Rome, 1978-80; treas. Esso Greece, Athens, 1980-83; dealer money mkt. Chase Manhatan Bank, N.Y.C., 1983-84, dealer fgn. exchange, 1984-86; country mgr. treasury Chase Manhatan Bank, Milano, Italy, 1986—. Mem. Assn. Tesorieri Inst. Creditizie, Forex Club Italiano, Borsa de Milano. Christian Orthodox. Club: Athens Tennis. Office: Chase Manhattan Bank, Piazza Meda 1, 20121 Milan Italy

YANOWITZ, JOEL, investment company executive; b. Cleve., Jan. 5, 1955; s. Bennett and Donna (Karon) V. Student, Thomas Jefferson Coll., 1974-75, Empire State Coll., 1981-82, Columbia U., 1985-86. Asst. mgr. Erewhon, Inc., Boston, 1975-77; pres. Relationship Ednl. Corp., Waltham, Mass., 1977-82; dir. cons. services Innovation Assocs. Inc., Framingham, Mass., 1982—; ptnr. Fourys Investment Partnership, Cleve., 1985—; bd. dirs. African Food and Peace Found., Wellesley, Mass. Mem. Am. Soc. for Tng. and Devel. Office: Innovation Assocs Inc PO Box 2008 Framingham MA 01701

YAO, HILDA MARIA HSIANG, banker; b. Honolulu, Sept. 11, 1956; d. Hsin-Nung and Dorothy Wen (Wu) Y. BA cum laude, U. Pacific, 1975; MA, U. Wis., 1976. Ops. analyst Visa Internat., San Mateo, Calif., 1977-80; sr. product mgr. Bank of Am., San Francisco, 1980-81, asst. v.p., strategic planner Calif. electronic banking div., 1981-84, v.p., div. strategic planner U.S. wholesale svcs. world banking div., 1984-85, v.p., head dealer corp. svcs., 1985—. Bd. dirs. alumni sect. U. Pacific, Stockton, Calif., 1984-85; treas. pres.'s jr. adv.coun. Bank of Am., 1982-83. U. Wis. fellow, 1975-76, alumni fellow U. Pacific, 1983. Mem. Nat. Vehicle Leasing Assn. (treas. 1988—), World Affairs Counc., Calif. Acad. Scis., Commonwealth Club Calif., Bank Am. Club. Home: PO Box 590297 San Francisco CA 94159 Office: Bank of Am World Hdqrs 555 California St San Francisco CA 94104

YAP, KIE-HAN, engineering executive; b. Yogyakarta, Java, Indonesia, Sept. 16, 1925; s. Hong-Tjoen and Souw-Lien (Tan) Y.; m. Kiauw-Lan The, Mar. 7, 1954; children—Tjay-Hok, Tjay-Yong. Ir, Tech. U. Delft, Netherlands, 1953. Dir., Research Inst. Mgmt. Sci., U. Delft, 1955-61; dir., founder CBO Mgmt. and Tech. Systems Ctr., Rotterdam, Netherlands, 1961—; lectr. various univs., Western Europe and U.S., 1961—. advisor internat. orgns., 1961—. Contbr. articles to profl. jours. Mem. Royal Inst. Engrs. Netherlands. Home: Hoyledesingel 14, Rotterdam 3054 EK, The Netherlands

YARBROUGH, DIANE FULLER, accountant; b. Columbia, S.C., Nov. 6, 1961; d. Herman Randolph Fuller and Fern (Brigman) Cooper; m. Michael Wayne Yarbrough, June 23, 1979; 1 child: Matthew Fuller. BS in Bus. Adminstrn., Winthrop Coll., 1983, MBA, 1986. CPA, S.C. Staff acct. Moore, Pierce & Harrell CPAs, Rock Hill, S.C., 1981-84, Charles E. Boggs, CPA, Lancaster, S.C., 1986-88; pvt. practice Great Falls, S.C., 1988—. Sunday Sch. tchr., 1981—, chmn. Christian edn., 1987-88, Circle 4, Women of the Ch., 1987-88, Great Falls (S.C.) Presbyn. Ch. Mem. AICPA, S.C. Assn. CPAs. Republican. Home and Office: 100 Edgewood Ave Great Falls SC 29055

YARMOLINSKY, ADAM, lawyer, educator; b. N.Y.C., Nov. 17, 1922; s. Avrahm and Babette (Deutsch) Y.; m. Harriet Leslie Rypins, Mar. 24, 1945 (div. 1981); children: Sarah Franklin, Tobias, Benjamin Levi, Matthew Jonas; m. Jane C. Vonnegut, Oct. 20, 1984 (dec. Dec. 1986). A.B., Harvard U., 1943; LL.B., Yale U., 1948. Law clk. to Judge C.E. Clark U.S. Ct. Appeals (2d cir.), 1948-49; assoc. Root, Ballantine, Harlan, Bushby & Palmer, N.Y.C., 1949-50; law clk. to Justice Stanley Reed U.S. Supreme Ct., 1950-51; assoc. Cleary, Gottlieb, Friendly & Ball, Washington, 1951-55; dir. Washington office Fund for the Republic, Inc., 1955-56, sec., 1956-57; pub. affairs editor Doubleday & Co., Inc., 1957-59; cons. pvt. founds. 1959-61, spl. asst. sec. of def., 1961-64; dep. dir. Pres.'s Anti-Poverty Task Force, 1964; chief U.S. Emergency Relief Mission to Dominican Republic, 1965; prin. dep. asst. sec. def. for internat. security affairs 1965-66; prof. law Harvard U., 1966-72; mem. inst. politics John F. Kennedy Sch. Govt., 1966-72; chief exec. officer Welfare Island Devel. Corp., 1971-72; Ralph Waldo Emerson univ. prof. U. Mass., 1972-79, on leave, 1977-79; counselor ACDA, 1977-79; of counsel Kominers, Fort, Schlefer & Boyer, Washington, 1979—; prof. policy scis. grad. program U. Md. Balt. County, Balt., 1985—; acting provost U. Md. Balt. County, Catonsville, 1986-87, provost, 1987—; lectr. Am. U. Law Sch., 1951-56, Yale U. Law Sch., 1958-59; adj. prof. Georgetown U. Law Ctr., 1984-85; cons. Office Tech. Assessment, 1974-77; Mem. gov.'s adv. council Mass. Comprehensive Health Planning Agy., 1972-76; nat. adv. com. Inst. for Research on Poverty, 1972-77; mem. adv. council inter-univ. seminar on Armed Forces and Soc.; mem. governing council U. Wyo. Faculty Seminar;. Author: Recognition of Excellence, 1960, The Military Establishment, 1971, Paradoxes of Power, 1983; also articles in periodicals.; Editor: Case Studies in Personnel Security, 1955, Race and Schooling In the City, 1980; Spl. corr.: The Economist, London, 1956-60. Trustee Bennington Coll., 1984—, chmn. bd. dirs. 1986-88, Robert F. Kennedy Meml., Vera Inst. Justice, New Directions Ednl. Fund, 1979-82, Ind. Sector, 1980-84; trustee govt. rels. com. Ctr. for Nat. Policy, 1984—, chmn., 1989—; bd. dirs. Com. for Nat. Security, chmn. bd., 1986—, Am. Sch. of Tangier, Ocean Research and Edn. Soc., 1980-85. With USAAF, 1943-46. Recipient Distinguished Pub. Service medal Dept. Def., 1966. Fellow Am. Acad. Arts and Scis.; mem. ABA, Assn. Bar City N.Y., (chmn. com. sci. and law 1984-87), Am. Law Inst., Hudson Inst., Internat. Inst. Strategic Studies, Inst. Medicine of Nat. Acad. Scis. (council 1970-77, com. on human rights 1978—), Council Fgn. Relations. Clubs: Coffee House, Century Assn. (N.Y.C.); Federal City (Washington). Office: Univ Md Office of Provost Baltimore County Baltimore MD 21228

YARRIGLE, CHARLENE SANDRA SHUEY, real estate executive and investment counselor; b. Redlands, Calif., July 25, 1940; d. Troy Frank and Anna (Miskew) Shuey; m. Robert Charles Yarrigle, Oct. 16, 1965 (div. July 1985); children: Stephanie Ann, Steven Charles. AA, San Bernardino (Calif.) Coll., 1965; student, Ariz. State U., 1965-66; BS, Northern Mich. U., 1976, postgrad., 1976-77. Clk. Bungalow Grocery, Redlands, 1957-59; operator Pacific Telephone Co., San Bernardino, 1958-61; service rep. So. Calif. Gas, San Bernardino, 1961-66; tchr. bus. Gwinn (Mich.) High Sch., 1976-78; realtor, investment counselor Century 21 Curragh Downs, Fair Oaks, Calif., 1978—; tchr. Project 100,000, Sheppard AFB, Wichita Falls, Tex., 1966-70. Mem. steering com., adv. bd. Sacramento (Calif.) Bd. Realtors, 1981—; vol. Easter Seal Soc., ARC San Bernardino, 1968-72. Mem. Nat. Assn. Realtors, Calif. Assn. Realtors, Nat. Assn. Female Execs., Sierra Club, Eagles. Republican. Office: Century 21 Curragh Downs 4401 Hazel Ave Suite 115 Fair Oaks CA 95628

YASCHIK, HENRY, land development and business investment executive; b. Tucuman, Argentina, Dec. 3, 1910; s. Nathan and Elka Y.; m. Sylvia Vlosky, Feb. 11, 1940; children: Anne Yaschik Silverman, Marsha Yaschik Kronick, Bonnie Yaschik Friedman. Grad. high sch., Charleston, S.C. Prin. Yaschik Enterprises, Charleston, 1936—; pres. Henry Yaschik Ins. Agy., Charleston, 1937-85, Yaschik Devel. Co., Inc., Charleston, 1955—, Charleston Capital Corp., 1961—. Pres. Hebrew Benevolent Soc., 1954-55, Israel Bond Dr., 1959; bd. dirs. Jewish Social Svc., 1959—, Charleston Opera Co., 1974—, Yaschik Fund for Jewish Studies, 1986—; v.p. Jewish Children Svcs., Atlanta, 1975—; treas. Jewish Community Housing, Inc., Sherman House, 1982—. With USNGR, 1944-45. Mem. Trident C. of C. (ednl. com. 1961-64), NASBIC (bd. govs. 1966), ADL (bd. dirs. so. region 1952), Masons, B'nai B'rith (pres. Charleston chpt. 1946, bd. dirs. dist. 5 1952-53). Home: 28 Devereaux Ave Charleston SC 29403 Office: PO Box 328 Charleston SC 29402 also: 111 Church St Charleston SC 29401

YASNYI, ALLAN DAVID, television production company executive; b. New Orleans, June 22, 1942; s. Ben Z. and Bertha R. (Michalove) Y.; B.B.A., Tulane U., 1964; m. Lesley E. Behrman, Dec. 8, 1968; children—Benjamin Charles, Evelyn Judith. Free-lance exec. producer, producer, writer, actor and designer for TV, motion picture and theatre, 1961-73; producer, performer The Second City; dir. fin. and adminstrn. Quinn Martin Prodns., Hollywood, Calif., 1973-76, v.p. fin., 1976-77, exec. v.p. fin. and corp. planning, 1977; vice chmn., chief exec. officer QM Prodns., Beverly Hills, Calif., 1977-78, chmn. bd., chief exec. officer, 1978-80; pres., chief exec. officer The Synapse Communications Group, Inc., 1981—; chmn. bd. dirs. Found. of Global Broadcasting. Trustee Hollywood Arts Council; exec. v.p., trustee Hollywood Hist. Trust; bd. dirs. Internat. Ctr. for Intergative Studies. Served with U.S. Army, 1964-66. Mem. Acad. TV Arts and Scis., Am. Advt. Fedn., Am. Mgmt. Assn., Hollywood Radio and TV Soc., Hollywood C. of C. (dir., vice-chmn.), Screen Actors Guild. Office: 3343 Laurel Canyon Blvd Studio City CA 91604

YATES, ELTON G., petroleum industry executive; b. Slidell, La., July 31, 1935; s. Elton O. and Leona E. (Sollberger) Y.; m. Jo Ellen Levy, Apr. 11, 1955; children—Sherlyn, Michele, Steven. B.S. in Petroleum Engring, La. State U., 1957. Petroleum engr. Texaco Inc., various locations, 1957-68; dist. engr. Texaco Inc., Corpus Christi, Tex., 1968-70; div. devel. engr. Texaco Inc., Houston, 1970-71; coordinator joint ops. Texaco Inc., N.Y.C., 1971-75; pres., gen. mgr. Texaco Iran, London, 1975-77; asst. gen. mgr. producing Eastern Hemisphere Texaco Inc., N.Y.C., 1977-78; gen. mgr. producing Harrison, N.Y., 1978-79, corp. v.p., dept. head producing, 1979-82; div. pres. Texaco Oil Trading and Supply, 1981-82; pres. Texaco Middle East/Far East, 1982-84, Texaco Latin Am./West Africa, 1984-87; corp. sr. v.p. Texaco Inc., White Plains, N.Y., 1987—; bd. dirs. Arabian Am. Oil Co., also numerous Texaco Inc. co. subs. Mem. Soc. Petroleum Engrs. of AIME, Phi Epsilon Tau. Methodist. Clubs: Country of Darien (Conn.); Pinehurst (N.C.). Office: Texaco Inc 2000 Westchester Ave White Plains NY 10650

YATES, GENE ALLAN, JR., financial executive; b. Jackson, Miss., May 11, 1959; s. Gene A. and Christine (Bourgeois) Y.; m. Kendall Schull, Dec. 31, 1986. BBA, So. Meth. U., 1981. Registered rep. Eppler, Guerin & Turner, Dallas, 1982-84; v.p., dir. Southwest Securities Inc., Dallas, 1984-86; adviser Cigna Fin. Services, Jackson, 1986—. Mem. Nat. Assn. Securities Dealers, N.Y. Stock Exchange, Inst. Cert. Fin. Planning. Episcopalian. Club: River Hills Tennis (Jackson). Office: Cigna Fin Svcs 440 Trustmark Bldg Jackson MS 39201

YATES, JERE EUGENE, business educator, management consultant; b. Memphis, Apr. 4, 1941; s. Emmett Eugene and Naomi Christine (Whitfield) Y.; m. Carolyn Kay Hall, June 8, 1962; children: Camille, Kevin, Brian. BA, Harding U., 1963, MTh, MA, 1966; PhD, Boston U., 1968. Instr. Harding U., Searcy, Ark., 1967-69; prof. bus. Pepperdine U., Malibu, Calif., 1969—; cons. Hughes Aircraft Co., Los Angeles, 1973—, Allied-Signal Corp., N. Hollywood, Calif., 1985—. Author: Managing Stress, 1979 (membership book award, 1979); contbr. articles to profl. jours. Mem. Acad. Mgmt., AAUP. Republican. Mem. Ch. of Christ. Clubs: N. Ranch Country (Westlake, Calif.), Westlake Tennis and Swim. Office: Pepperdine Univ Malibu CA 90265

YAWORSKY, GEORGE MYROSLAW, physicist, technical and management consultant; b. Aug. 4, 1940; s. Myroslaw and Mary (Yaworsky) Y.; m. Zenia Maria Smishkewych, Sept. 9, 1972; 1 dau., Maria Diana. B.S. in Physics, Rensselaer Poly. Inst., 1962, M.B.A., 1977, Ph.D. in Physics, 1979; M.S. in Physics, Carnegie-Mellon U., 1964. Physicist Republic Steel Research Ctr., Independence, Ohio, 1966-68; tech. and mgmt. cons. in ops. research, mktg. analyses, computer modeling, sci. programming and other areas to state govt., pvt. cos., 1972-81; internat. tech. assessment and analysis cons. EG&G, Inc., Rockville, Md., 1981-82; program dir.-computer integrated mfg. Eagle Research Group, Arlington, Va., 1982-83; prin. investigator high volume mfg. Sci. Applications, Inc., McLean, Va., 1983-84; cons. computer integrated mfg., materials sci., tech. transfer and mgmt., 1984—; mem. U.S. del. to Coordinating Com. for Multilateral Export Controls, Paris, 1982. Contbr. articles to profl. jours. Recipient Physics Teaching award Rensselaer Poly. Inst., 1971; John Huntington scholar; Rensselaer Alumni scholar. Mem. N.Y. Acad. Scis., Robotics Internat. of Soc. Mfg. Engrs. (sr.), Computer and Automated Systems Assn. of Soc. Mfg. Engrs. (sr., chmn. Greater Washington chpt. 1985—), Am. Phys. Soc., Am. Assn. Physics Tchrs., Am. Prodn. and Inventory Control Soc., AAAS, Rensselaer Alumni Assn., Am. Assn. for Artificial Intelligence, Robotic Industries Assn., Internat. Platform Assn., Sigma Xi. Office: 2000 S Eads St Arlington VA 22202

YAXLEY, MARY EVENSON, financial planner; b. Fairbury, Ill., Mar. 7, 1954; d. Francis Michael and Loretta Agnus (Jordan) Bridgett; m. Thomas Edward Yaxley, June 7, 1986. BS with highest honors, U. Ill., 1976. CPA, Ill.; cert. fin. planner. Staff acct. Filbey Summers & Co., Champaign, Ill., 1976-80; ptnr. Filbey Summers & Co., Champaign, 1980-82, McGladrey Hendrickson & Pullen, Champaign, 1982-84; v.p. fin. planning Cozad Fin. Planning Corp., Champaign, 1985—. Mem. Am. Inst. CPA's (Elijah Watt Sells award 1976), Estate Planning Council (pres. 1985-86), Internat. Assn. Fin. Planners (treas. 1985-87), Ill. Soc. CPA's, Central Ill. Women CPA's (v.p. 1988-89), Exec. Club Champaign County (pres. 1986-87), Illini Quarterback Club (pres. 1987-88). Office: Cozad Fin Planning Corp 2500 Galen Dr Champaign IL 61821

YEAGER, CHARLES V., financial executive; b. Lafayette, Ind., Sept. 23, 1939; s. Randall G. and Gladys (Stauffer) Y.; m. Dixie D. Yeager, June 25, 1961 (div. 1975); children: Laura, Jerry, Steve; m. Judith Huff, Sept. 13, 1975; children: Tonda, Todd, Benjamin. BA, Hanover Coll., 1961; MS in Fin., Am. Coll., 1977. Cert. fin. planner. Field rep. Aetna Life & Casualty Co., Cleve., 1961-63; sales rep. C.V. Yeager & Assoc., Warsaw, Ind., 1963-80; fin. planner Yeager-Swanson Fin. Corp., Warsaw, 1981-84; pres. fin. planning div. SYM Fin. Corp., Warsaw, 1985—. Coach Kosciusko County Soccer League, Warsaw, 1983—, Warsaw Little League, 1974-81; founder, bd. dirs. Kosciusko County Pee Wee Football, Warsaw, 1985—; pres. parents cabinet Taylor U., 1985—; chmn. Christian Businessmen's Com., 1982. Recipient Disting. Service award Warsaw Jaycees, 1968. Mem. Inst. Cert. Fin. Planners. Republican. Baptist. Office: SYM Fin Corp PO Box 1236 Warsaw IN 46580

YEAGER, DAVID LEROY, utility company executive; b. Youngstown, Ohio, Feb. 12, 1935; s. LeRoy and Marjorie (Ballington) Y.; m. Margaret Scott; children: David, Karen Fetterhoff, Ellen. BEME, Youngstown State U., 1959. Superintendent of electric and steam sales Ohio Edison Co., Youngstown, 1968-70; dir. comml. indsl. mktg. Ohio Edison Co., Akron, Ohio, 1971-76, project coordination mgr., 1976-78, asst. to exec. v.p., 1978-79, asst. to pres., 1980-85, v.p., 1985—. Active Summit County Unit Am. Cancer Soc., Akron, v.p. 1979-81, pres. 1981-83, bd. dirs. 1972—. Mem. ASME, NSPE, ASHRAE, Cascade Club, Harvard Bus. Sch. Club. Office: Ohio Edison Co 76 S Main St Akron OH 44308

YEAGER, GEORGE MICHAEL, investment counsel; b. Pelham Manor, Sept. 5, 1934; s. Harold Caldwell and Marybelle Alden (Glos) Y.; m. Barbara Gow, July 7, 1962; children: Scott Alden, Kathryn Gow. AB, Dartmouth Coll., 1956, MBA, 1957. Adminstrv. asst. Fed. Res. Bank N.Y., 1957-59; v.p. Yeager & Anderson, Inc., N.Y.C., 1959-60; pres. Yeager, Wood & Marshall, Inc., N.Y.C., 1960—. Mem. Investment Counsel Assn. Am. (gov.), Fin. Analysts Fedn., N.Y. Soc. Security Analysts, Am. Pension Conf., Univ. Club, Econ. Club, Bronxville Field Club, Mill Reef Club, Siwanoy Country Club. Republican. Home: 2 Elm Rock Rd Bronxville NY 10708 Office: 630 Fifth Ave Ste 2910 New York NY 10111

YEAGER, PAUL DAVID, holding company executive; b. Galveston, Tex., June 10, 1938; s. Charles B. and Mary (Clinch) Y.; m. Toni Lee Valestrino, Nov. 9, 1968; children: Patricia, Anne. BS, Pepperdine U., 1969; MBA, Calif. State U., Fullerton, 1974. Sr. fin. analyst mgr. Hughes Tool Co., Los Angeles, 1959-69; mgr., fin. analyst ITT Cannon Electronics, Los Angeles, 1969-74; comptroller, asst. comptroller O.M. Scott & Sons, W. Atlee Burpee, Marysville, Ohio, 1974-80; v.p. fin. O.M. Scott & Sons, Marysville, 1986—; v.p. fin. Lawn Garden Group Internat. Telephone & Telegraph, Marysville, 1980-86; v.p. fin. CDS Holding Corp., Marysville, 1986—; cons. in field; tchr. Ohio State U., Columbus, 1985. With USN, 1955-59. Mem. Fin. Exec. Inst., Inst. Mgmt. Acctg., Am. Inst. CPA's, Nat. Assn. Accts. Democrat.

Roman Catholic. Home: 17910 Timber Ln Rd Marysville OH 43040 Office: O M Scott & Sons 14111 Scottslawn Rd Marysville OH 43041

YEARLEY, DOUGLAS CAIN, mining and manufacturing company executive; b. Oak Park, Ill., Jan. 7, 1936; s. Bernard Cain and Mary Kenny (Howard) Y.; m. Elizabeth Anne Dunbar, Feb. 8, 1958; children: Sandra, Douglas Jr., Peter, Andrew. BMetE, Cornell U., 1958; postgrad., Harvard U., 1968. Engr. welding Gen. Dynamics, Groton, Conn., 1958-60; dir. research, project engr. Phelps Dodge Copper Products, Elizabeth, N.J., 1960-68; mgr. ops. Phelps Dodge Internat. Co., N.Y.C., 1968-71; v.p. ops. Phelps Dodge Tube Co., L.A., 1971-73; exec. v.p. Phelps Dodge Cable and Wire Co., Yonkers, N.Y., 1973-75; pres. Phelps Dodge Brass Co., Lyndhurst, N.J., 1975-79, Phelps Dodge Sales Co., N.Y.C., 1979-82; v.p. mktg. Phelps Dodge Corp., N.Y.C., 1979-82, sr. v.p., 1982-87, exec. v.p., 1987-89, chmn., chief exec. officer, 1989—, also bd. dirs.; bd. dirs. Valley Nat. Bank, Valley Nat. Corp., Phoenix. Mem. Nat. Elect. Mfrs. Assn. (bd. dirs. 1983—), Internat. Copper Rsch. Assn. (bd. dirs. 1987—), Copper Devel. Assn. (chmn. 1989—), Nat. Assn. Mfrs. (bd. dirs. 1988—), Sky Club (N.Y.C.), Echo Lake Country Club (Westfield, N.J.), Nat. Assn. Mfrs., Mansion Club. Republican. Congregationalist. Home: 8201 Via del Lago Scottsdale AZ 85258 Office: Phelps Dodge Corp 2600 N Central Ave Phoenix AZ 85004-3014

YEE, PHILLIP KOON HIN, engineer; b. Honolulu, Feb. 19, 1916; s. Sheong and Shee (Leong) Y.; m. Maybelle W.Y. Lee, May 6, 1939; children—Curtis Q.H., Gary Q.L., Stephen Q.S. B.S. in Civil Engring., U. Hawaii, 1938. Registered profl. engr., Hawaii. Sports cartoonist Honolulu Star-Bull., 1934-45; planning draftsman Territorial Planning Bd., Honolulu, 1938-39; civil engr. U.S. Engrs. Office, Honolulu, 1940-41, head water supply sect., 1941-45; asst. supt. Suburban Water System, City and County Honolulu, 1945-60; engr. P. Yee & Assocs. Inc., Honolulu, 1960—; pres. Ala Moana Investment Corp., Honolulu, 1960-65, Intercontinental Corp., Honolulu, 1965-70; dir. Phillip K.H. Yee & Assocs., Honolulu. Mem. Cons. Engrs. Council Trade Mission IV, S.E. Asia, 1968; mem., citizen ambassador People to People waste water mgmt. delegation People's Republic of China, 1983. Recipient Cert. of Appreciation, U.S. Dept. Commerce, Washington, 1968. Mem. Cons. Engrs. Council, Am. Security Council, U.S. Congl. Adv. Bd. (state advisor). Astarian, Ashtar Command, Am. Biog. Inst. Rsch. Assn. (dep. gov. 1988, Medal of Honor 1985, World Biog. Hall of Fame Hist. Preserve Am. 1986). Club: Engring. Assocs. (Honolulu). Home: 1885 Paula Dr Honolulu HI 96816 Office: Phillip KH Yee & Assocs Inc 243 Liliuokalani Ave Honolulu HI 96815

YEE, RAYMOND W., oil company executive; b. July 10, 1952; married; children: Christina, Carisa, Raymond. BS in Chem. Engring., Northeastern U., Boston, 1975; M. in Engring., MBA, Dartmouth Coll., 1977. Acquisitions mgr. Standard Oil Chem. Co., Cleve., 1981-82, mgr. strategic analysis, 1982-84, mgr. control dept., 1984-85, mgr. devel., 1985-87; mgr. econ. evaluation and corp. devel. BP Am., Inc. (formerly Standard Oil Co.), Cleve., 1987—. Mem. Comml. Devel. Assn., Planning Forum, Am. Inst. Chem. Engrs. Home: 10195 Deer Run Brecksville OH 44141 Office: BP Am Inc 200 Public Sq 39-D Cleveland OH 44114-2375

YELENSKY, SANDRA GAIL, financial planner; b. Mt. Clemens, Mich., June 6, 1948; d. Ben and Jean (Harrison) Lax; children: Kollin, Erica. BA, Wayne State U., 1970, MLS, 1971. Cert. fin. planner. Librarian Farmington Hills (Mich.) Pub. Library, 1972-77, Southfield (Mich.) Pub. Library, 1978-81; pvt. practice fin. planning Birmingham, Mich., 1981—. Mem. Founders Soc. Detroit Inst. Arts, 1983—. Mem. Internat. Assn. Fin. Planners, Inst. Cert. Fin. Planners. Clubs: Econ., Women's Econ. (Detroit). Office: 30150 Telegraph #245 Birmingham MI 48010

YELSEY, NEIL DAVID, investor; b. Roslyn, N.Y., May 21, 1958; s. Benjamin and Anne (Astrachan) Y.; m. Beth Ester Freedman, Sept. 7, 1987. BS, Swarthmore Coll., 1980. Programmer, analyst Salomon Bros., Inc., N.Y.C., 1981-82, stock analyst telecommunication svcs., 1983-84, sr. stock analyst telecommunication svcs., 1985-86, v.p., equity trading strategist, 1987—. Mem. N.Y. Soc. Security Analysts, Fin. Fedn. Analysts. Office: Salomon Bros Inc One New York Pla New York NY 10004

YELVINGTON, JAMES CLAUDE, III, insurance executive, real estate broker; b. Athens, Tex., Mar. 26, 1957; s. Bill J. and Beverly Anne (England) Y. Student, Lon Morris Coll., 1975-76, U. Tex., 1981; BA, SW Tex. State U., 1986. Agt. real estate Meisler Realty Group, Austin, Tex., 1982-83; owner, broker Austin Exec. Apartments, Austin, 1983-87; ins. exec. Allstate Ins. Co., Austin, 1987—. Union liason Glen Jones for Congress, Jacksonville, Tex., 1976. Mem. Austin Bd. Realtors, K.A. Alumni. Democrat. Episcopalian. Lodge: Mason. Home: 1003 Austin Highlands Blvd Austin TX 78745 Office: The Advantage Co 1900 E Oltorf Ste 110 Austin TX 78741

YEN, DAVID WEI-LUEN, computer engineer; b. Chang-hwa, Republic of China, Sept. 24, 1951; came to U.S., 1975.; s. Te-Maw and Shoon-hwa (Luh) Y.; m. Grace Shau-Ling Jen, Jan. 9, 1977; children: Irene, Christine. BS, Nat. Taiwan U., 1973; MS, U. Ill., 1977, PhD, 1980. Sr. mem. tech. staff ESL/TRW, Sunnyvale, Calif., 1980-82; mem. research staff IBM, San Jose, Calif., 1982-84; dir. hardware devel. Cydrome, Inc., Milpitas, Calif., 1984—. Mem. IEEE (sec. computer standards com. 1983-84), Eta Kappa Nu, Phi Kappa Phi. Office: Cydrome Inc 1589 Centre Pointe Dr Milpitas CA 95035

YERKES, RAY L., financial executive; b. Kansas City, Mo., Sept. 26, 1940; s. Lewis and Lois (Hammond) Y.; m. Karn D. Weadick, May 1, 1981; children: Rod, Robyn, Rhonda, Amy. BS in Acctg., Oklahoma City U., 1963. V.p., br. mgr. Paine Webber, Inc., Sun City, Ariz., 1984-88; v.p. assoc. br. mgr. Thompson McKinnon Assocs., Scottsdale, Ariz., 1988—; exec. v.p. Great Mo. Life, Springfield, 1970-75; dir. Imperial Inc. Life, Atlanta, 1975-80; lectr. in field. Home: 4401 E Acoma Dr Phoenix AZ 85032 Office: Thompson McKinnon Assocs 7150 E Camelback Ste 160 Scottsdale AZ 85251

YERMAN, ROBERT NEIL, accountant; b. N.Y.C., Jan. 16, 1940; s. Nat W. and Tina (Barotz) Y.; m. Judith Linn, Apr. 15, 1962 (div. Dec. 1969); children: Gregory Marc, Gary Jay.; m. Anne V. DeLue, May 21, 1972; children: Brant Matthew Peace, Lesley Elizabeth Hope. Student, Alfred U., 1956-58; BA, CUNY, 1960; postgrad., Fairleigh Dickinson U., 1962-67. Ptnr. J. Linn & Co., CPA's, N.J., 1963-69, Office Insp. Gen. HUD, Washington, 1975-76, Touche Ross & Co., Washington, 1977—; ptnr. in charge of client svcs. Touche Ross & Co. Middle Atlantic Group, Washington. Contbr. articles to profl. jours. Trustee, treas. Arena Stage; bd. dirs. Jr. Achievement; friend Capital Childrens' Mus., Washington Opera, Leadership Washington. Mem. AICPA, N.Y. State Soc. CPA's (former chmn. internat. ops. com.), D.C. Inst. CPA's, Pres.'s Exec. Exchange Alumni Assn., Leadership Washington, Desiree Club, Nat. Press Club, Masons. Home: 9100 Falls Rd Potomac MD 20854 Office: 1900 M St NW Washington DC 20036

YEUTTER, CLAYTON KEITH, U.S. secretary of agriculture; b. Eustis, Nebr., Dec. 10, 1930; s. Reinhold F. and Laura P. Y.; m. Lillian Jeanne Vierk; children—Brad, Gregg, Kim, Van. B.S., U. Nebr., 1952, J.D., 1963, Ph.D. in Agrl. Econs., 1966. Rancher Nebr., 1957-75; mem. faculty dept. agrl. econs. U. Nebr., Lincoln, 1960-66, dir. Mission in Columbia, 1968-70; exec. asst. Gov. Nebr., 1966-68; adminstr. Consumer & Mktg. Service U.S. Dept. Agr., Washington, 1970-71, asst. sec., 1973-74; regional dir. Com. for Reelection of Pres., 1972; asst. sec. agr. for internat. affairs and commodity programs U.S. Dept. Agr., Washington, 1974-75; dep. spl. trade rep. Exec. Office of Pres., Washington, 1975-77, U.S. trade rep., 1985-89; sr. ptnr. Nelson, Harding, Yeutter & Leonard, Lincoln, Nebr., 1977-78; pres., chief exec. officer Chgo. Mercantile Exchange, 1978-85; sec. U.S. dept. agr., 1989—. Contbr. numerous articles to profl. jours. trustee Garrett-Evangelical Theol. Sem., Evanston, Ill.; bd. dirs. Chgo. Council on Fgn. Relations; bd. visitors Sch. Bus. Adminstrn. Georgetown U.; trustee, mem. exec. com. Farm Found., Oak Brook, Ill. Served with USAF, 1952-57. Recipient Israel prime Minister's medal; Disting. Service award Am. Soc. Agrl. Cons., 1978; Agrl. Achievement award Knights of Ak-Sar-Ben, 1978; Chgo. Farmers Disting. Service to Agr. award. Mem. Nebr. Bar Assn. Republican. Methodist.

YEWAISIS, JOSEPH STEPHEN, finance company executive; b. Newark, Jan. 12, 1939; s. Joseph S. and Julia Amelia (Baltutis) Y.; m. Nancy Kernan, Sept. 11, 1965; children: Colleen, Joseph, Maureen. BS in Acctg., St. Peter's Coll., Jersey City, 1961. CPA, N.J. Acct. Peat, Marwick, Mitchell & Co., Newark, 1961-69; exec. v.p. Yorkwood Savs. and Loan Assn., Maplewood, N.J., 1969-72; pres., chmn. bd. dirs. First Savs. Bank, SLA, 1972—; pres., bd. dirs. Savers Fin. Corp.; bd. dirs. Fed. Home Loan Bank of N.Y., 1986—. Mem. banking adv. bd. State of N.J., 1981-86; vice-chmn., dir. Raritan Bay Health Svcs. Corp., Perth Amboy; chmn. spl. events Middlesex County unit Am. Cancer Soc., 982—; trustee United Way Cen. Jersey, 1978—; bd. dirs. Raritan Bay Area YMCA, 1973, Raritan Bay Med. Ctr., 1975—, Evergreen Community Corp., 1983-87. Mem. U.S. League of Savs. Assns. (legis. com., bd. dirs. 1986—), N.J. Savs. League (chmn. 1984-85), Perth Amboy C. of C. (treas. 1979-80), Am. Inst. CPA's, N.J. Soc. CPA's, Mortgage Bankers Assn. Clubs: Colonial Country, Plainfield (N.J.) Country; 200 Club (pres. 1988—) (Middlesex County) (treas. 1980-88, pres. 1988—). Lodges: Kiwanis, Lions. Office: 339 State St Perth Amboy NJ 08862

YIANNOPOULOS, ATHANASSIOS NICHOLAS, legal educator; b. Thessaloniki, Greece, Mar. 13, 1928; came to U.S., 1953, naturalized, 1963; s. Nicholas A. and Areti T. (Alvanos) Y.; m. Mirta Valdes, May 9, 1982; children—Maria, Nicholas, Alexander, Philip. LL.B., U. Thessaloniki, 1950; M.C.L., U. Chgo., 1954; LL.M. (Walter Perry Johnson fellow in law), U. Calif., Berkeley, 1955, J.S.D., 1956; J.D., U. Cologne, W. Ger., 1961. Bar: Greece 1958. Mem. faculty La. State U., Baton Rouge, 1958-79; W.R. Irby prof. law Tulane U. Law Sch., New Orleans, 1979—; in charge revision La. Civil Code, Law Inst., 1962—. Author: Civil Law Property, 2d edit, 1980, Personal Servitudes, 3d edit, 1989, Predial Servitudes, 1983; (with T. Schoenbaum) Admiralty and Maritime Law, 1984; editor: Louisiana Civil Code, annually 1980—; contbr.: articles to various periodicals Ency. Brit. Pres. Baton Rouge Symphony Assn., 1972-73; bd. dirs. Music Soc., 1961-79. Served to 2d lt. Greek Army, 1950-53. Mem. Order of Phoenix, Am. Acad. Fgn. Law, Phi Alpha Delta. Mem. Greek Orthodox Ch. Club: Baton Rouge City. Office: Tulane U Sch Law New Orleans LA 70118

YINGLING, ADRIENNE E(LIZABETH), communications company executive; b. Hershey, Pa., June 10, 1959; d. Richard Terry Yingling and Dolores Jean (Ott) Brown. BA in Acctg., N.C. State U., 1989. Lic. real estate assoc., N.C. Asst. mgr. Fast Fare, Raleigh, 1979-80; statis. analyst S.P.A.R., Elmsford, N.Y., 1980-81; relocation dir., sales assoc. Realty World, Cary, N.C., 1981-83; product mgr. Southeastern Electronics, Raleigh, 1983-84; results acct. No. Telecom, Research Triangle Park, N.C., 1984-88. Mem. Nat. Assn. Female Execs., Nat. Assn. Accts., N.C. State U. Acctg. Soc., Ayn Rand Inst., Phi Kappa Phi, Omicron Delta Epsilon. Avocations: photography, painting, reading, aerobics, dance. Home and Office: 111 Hidden Oaks Dr #1D Cary NC 27513

YINGLING, BARRY EUGENE, emergency health service executive; b. Hanover, Pa., Dec. 28, 1951; s. Richard Bruce and Jacquelin Louise (Myers) Y. Student, York Coll. of Pa., 1969-76, Pa. State U., 1982-84. Dir. planning and devel. Emergency Health Svcs. Fedn., Camp Hill, Pa., 1980-81; pres., chief exec. officer Emergency Health Svcs. Fedn., Lemoyne, Pa., 1981—, 1985—; chmn. Health Resources Planning and Devel., Harrisburg, Pa., 1978-87; bd. dirs. York County (Pa.) Emergency Med. Svcs. Inst.; trustee Lebanon Valley (Pa.) Gen. Hosp., 1984-88. Contbr. articles to profl. jours. Treas. Pa. Health Planning Assn., 1985—; chmn. local bd. SSS, York, Pa., 1972-76. Recipient vol. recognition award City of York, 1980. Mem. Soc. Non-profit Orgns., Titanic Hist. Soc., Cen. Pa. Health Planning and Mktg. Assn., Internat. Soc. of Pres. Non-profit Orgns., MENSA. Republican. Episcopalian. Home: 7 S Keesey St York PA 17402 Office: Emergency Health Svcs Fedn 105 Old York Rd New Cumberland PA 17070

YLVISAKER, WILLIAM TOWNEND, manufacturing executive; b. St. Paul, Feb. 25, 1924; s. Lauritz S. and Winifred Jean (Townend) Y.; m. Jane Penelope Mitchell, May 11, 1972; 1 son, Jon Alastair; children by previous marriage: Laurie Ellen, Elizabeth Maren, Amy Townend. Grad., Lawrenceville Sch., 1943; B.S., Yale U., 1948. Security analyst Bank N.Y., 1948-49; gen. mgr. Lake Forest Motor Sales, Ill., 1949-52; v.p., gen. mgr. Pheoll Mfg. Co., Chgo., 1952-58; pres. Parker-Kalon div. Gen. Am. Transp. Corp., Clifton, N.J., 1958-61; group v.p., dir. Gen. Am. Transp. Corp., Chgo., 1961-67; chmn., chief exec. officer Gould Inc., 1967-86, chmn. exec. com., 1986; pres. Corp. Focus, Inc., 1987—, Penske Tank Co., 1987—; chmn. Mercury Metals, 1987—; pres., chief exec. officer Datron Inc., 1988—; bd. dirs. Penske Corp., Red Bank, N.J., RTE Corp., Brookfield, Wis., GNB Inc., Mendota Heights, Minn. Bd. dirs. United Republican Fund Ill.; council Grad. Sch. Bus., U. Chgo.; trustee Lawrenceville (N.J.) Sch., Rush-Presbyn.-St. Luke's Med. Sch., Solomon R. Guggenheim Found.; bd. govs. U.S. Polo Assn. Served as ensign USNR, 1943-45. Mem. Conf. Bd., U.S. Polo Assn. (gov.), Northwestern U. Assos. Clubs: Links (N.Y.C.); Barrington Hills Country; Racquet (N.Y.C.), Chicago (Chgo.); Palm Beach Polo and Country (West Palm Beach, Fla.); Bath and Tennis (Palm Beach); Meadow (Rolling Meadows, Ill.). Office: Datron Inc 2300 N Barrington Rd Hoffman Estates IL 60195

YOCHEM, BARBARA JUNE, sales executive, shooting coach, lecturer; b. Knox, Ind., Aug. 22, 1945; d. Harley Albert and Rosie (King) Runyan; m. Donald A. Yochem (div. 1979); 1 child, Morgan Lee; m. Don Heard, Dec. 12, 1987. Grad. high school, Knox, Ind., 1963. Sales rep. Hunter Woodworks, Carson, Calif., 1979-84, sales mgr., 1984-87; sales rep. Comml. Lumber and Pallet, Industry, Calif., 1987—; owner By By Prodns., Glendora, Calif., 1976—. Contbr. articles to profl. jours. Recipient U.S. Bronze medal U.S. Olympic Com., 1976, World Bronze Medal U.S. Olympic Com., 1980. Office: By By Prodns PO Box 1676 Glendora CA 91740

YOCHMOWITZ, MICHAEL GEORGE, biostatistician, computer educator, consultant; b. Bklyn., Apr. 27, 1948; s. David and Charlotte Dorothy (Haber) Y.; m. Yolanda Maria Pearson, Apr. 1, 1978; 1 child, Samuel Alexander. BA cum laude, , Union Coll., 1970, BS cum laude, 1970; MA, U. Rochester, 1972; MPH, U. Mich., 1973, PhD, 1974. Chief sci. analyst function U.S. Air Force Sch. Aerospace Medicine, Brooks AFB, Tex., 1974-79, chief hazard evaluation function, 1979-85, chief statis. analysis function, 1986-87; instr. math. San Antonio Coll., 1977-85, dir. Computer Learning Ctr., 1983—, pres. Computer & Stats. Inc., 1986—; cons. dept. oncology Health Sci. Ctr., San Antonio, 1979-80; abstractor Exec. Scis. Inst., Whippany, N.J., 1979-85. Contbr. articles to profl. jours. and Ency. Statis. Scis. V.p. Council for Internat. Relations, San Antonio, 1985-86; computer contbr. San Antonio Exec., Real Estate Newsline, San Antonio; bd. dirs. One Elm Place, San Antonio. Grantee NSF, 1970-72; USPHS trainee, 1972-73; UpJohn Gen. fellow, 1973-74. Served to capt. USAF, 1974-79. Mem. Am. Statis. Assn., Biometric Soc., Data Processing Mgrs. Assn., San Antonio N. Side C. of C., Alamo City C. of C., Sigma Xi. Jewish. Avocations: model railroading, reading, gardening, travel, volleyball. Home: 19919 Encino Royale San Antonio TX 78259 Office: Computer Learning Ctr 11107 Wurzbach Rd #301 San Antonio TX 78230

YOCKEY, ANTHONY SCOTT, financial placement agent, consultant, compute softwar consultant; b. Fremont, Ohio, Mar. 14, 1956; s. Layton E. and Carol S. Yockey; m. Penny L. Rife, Aug. 25, 1979; children: Kathleen S., Angela D., Cassandra L. Student, U. Toledo, 1974-75, Davis Jr. Coll., Toledo, 1980-81. Pres. Anthony S. Yockey Enterprises Inc., Toledo, 1977—; owner, mgr. Nat. Fin. Corp., Toledo, 1979-82, Progressive Pub. Group, Toledo, 1984-88, Trans-Continental Services, Toledo, 1985-87; pres., chief exec. officer Yockey, Jordan & Yockey, Inc., Toledo, 1987—, v.p. Comprehensive Fin. Services div., 1987—, v.p. Comprehensive Fin. Group, 1987. Republican. Methodist. Home: 610 Colburn St Toledo OH 43609-3304 Office: Yockey Jordan & Yockey PO Box 4095 Toledo OH 43609

YODER, PATRICIA DOHERTY, public relations executive; b. Pitts., Oct. 30, 1939; d. John Addison and Camella Grace (Conti) Doherty; children—Shari Lynn, Wendy Ann. BA, Duquesne U., 1961. Press sec. U.S. Ho. of Reps., 1965-69; pub. affairs dir. Citizens Cable Communications Inc., Ft. Wayne, Ind., 1973-74; dir. office of pub. info. City of Ft. Wayne, 1975-76; asst. mgr. pub. and corp. communications Mellon Bank N.A., Pitts., 1977-79; v.p. pub. affairs Am. Waterways Operators Inc., Washington, 1980-83; sr. v.p., gen. mgr. Hill and Knowlton Inc., Pitts., 1983-87, exec. v.p., dir. internat. banking, 1989—; sr. v.p. corp. and pub. affairs, PNC Fin. Corp, Pitts., 1987-89. Trustee The Ellis Sch., Pitts., Shadyside Hosp., Pitts., Human Resources Rsch. Orgn., Arlington, Va.; bd. dirs. Children's Mus., Pitts.; bd. dirs., exec. com., Civic Light Opera. Mem. Pitts. Field Club, Duquesne Club, Pitts. Athletic Assn. Roman Catholic. Home: 6112 Kentucky Ave Pittsburgh PA 15206 Office: 3 Gateway Ctr Pittsburgh PA 15222

YOFFE, MORRIS, health care company executive; b. Mt. Carmel, Pa., Aug. 8, 1929; s. Max and Sarah (Wishkin) Y.; BS, Drexel U., 1953; postgrad. Nova U., Ft. Lauderdale, Fla., 1987—. CPA, Pa.; lic. nursing home adminstr.; m. Chickee Esther Faith Margulis, June 25, 1955; children—Seth Michael, Eve Nicole, Josh Aron and Lori Jo (twins). Sr. acct. Adler Faunce & Leonard, CPA's, Phila., 1956-58; individual practice acctg., Phila., 1958-63; pres. dir. Corp. Planners, Inc., Laverock, Pa., 1962-82; sr. ptnr. Yoffe, Herman & Co., CPA's, Phila., 1963-70; founder, dir., pres., chief exec. officer Am. Med Affiliates, Inc., Ft. Washington, Pa., 1968-83, Anon Anew, Inc., Boca Raton, Fla., 1983—, Anon Anew at Tampa, Inc., 1987—; gen. ptnr. Highland Office Ctr. Assocs., Ft. Washington, Pa., 1983—; adj. prof. Drexel U., 1978-86. Mem. Cheltenham Twp. (Pa.) Citizens Adv. Bd., 1974-82, chmn., 1981-82; bd. dirs. Met. Hosp., Phila., 1974-86, Solomon Schechter Day Sch., Wynnewood, Pa., 1975—; bd. dirs. Citizens Crime Commn., Phila., 1978-82, Beth Sholom Synagogue, Elkins Park, Pa., 1977—, v.p., 1982-83, treas., 1983-84, pres.,1984-86, Anti-Defamation League, Nat. commr., 1984—, bd. dirs. Palm Beach Chpt., 1986—; bd. dirs. Temple Beth-El, Boca Raton, Fla., 1987—, Jewish Family Svc., 1987—, Israel Bonds Orgn., 1987—. Recipient Alumni Achievement award, 1988, State of Israel Health Care Svcs. Tribute award, 1978. Fellow Am. Coll. Nursing Home Adminstrs.; mem. Am., Pa. Insts. CPA's, Blue Key, Penna Soc., Met. Phila. Anti-Defamation League (vice chmn. 1977-81, chmn. 1982-84), Anti-Defamation League Soc. Fellows (nat. vice chmn. 1978—), Boca Raton C. of C. (econ. devel. com.), Drexel U. Astra Club. Home: 19657 Oakbrook Ct Boca Raton FL 33434 Office: 2600 NW Fifth Ave Boca Raton FL 33431

YOFFE, STUART ALAN, lawyer, insurance company executive; b. Everett, Mass., June 23, 1936; m. Jane Anne DeLeone, June 30, 1962; children: Jonathan, Justin. BS in Engring., U.S. Coast Guard Acad., 1958; JD, Columbia U., 1965; LLM, Boston U., 1970. Bar: Mass., 1966. Commd. ensign USCG, 1958, advanced through ranks to lt., resigned, 1962, served to capt. res.; retired USCGR, 1985; v.p. and counsel John Hancock Mut. Life Ins. Co., Boston, 1986—; mem. adv. council Hartford Inst. Ins. Taxation. Trustee Boston Ballet Co., 1970—, Jackson Homestead, Newton Mass., 1988—; bd. dirs. Fund for the Arts in Newton, 1983—. Recipient Pub. Action for the Arts award, 1980, spl. commendations for vol. service to arts U.S. Dept. Transp., 1984. Mem. Assn. Life Ins. Counsels, Am. Council Life Ins. (legal section. com.). Home: 123 Langley Rd Newton MA 02159 Office: John Hancock Mut Life Ins Co PO Box 111 Boston MA 02117

YOHE, ROBERT L., chemical company executive; b. N.Y.C., May 11, 1936; s. Robert C. and Berdene (Walker) Y. BSChemE, Lafayette Coll., 1958; MBA, Harvard U., 1964. With sales product mgmt. Hooker Chem. Corp., Niagara Falls, N.Y., 1964-68; pres. Chinook Mobilodge, Inc., Yakima, Wash., 1968-71, Environ. Svcs., Inc., Midland Park, N.J., 1971-72; dir. indsl. systems Hooker Chem. Corp., Niagara Falls, 1972-76, v.p., gen. mgr. Durez div., 1976-79, v.p., gen. mgr. environ. safety & health, 1980-81; gen. mgr. indsl. chems. Uniroyal Inc., Oxford, Conn., 1981-83; v.p. mergers, acquisitions Olin Corp., Stamford, Conn., 1983-85, pres. chems. group, 1985—; corp. EVP Olin Corp., Stamford, 1987—; bd. dirs. Chlorine Inst., Washington, Tri-Star Sports Inc., Middletown, Conn.; advisors sch. mgmt. SUNY, Buffalo, 1979-80, De Graff Meml. Hosp., No. Tonawanda, N.Y., 1979. Bd. dirs. United Way, No. Tonawanda, 1978-79; mem. Nat. Lafayette Coun., Easton, Pa., 1987-88. Lt. USN, 1959-72. Mem. Amb's. Round Table (forum world affairs 1988—), Conn. Golf Club, Highfield Country Club (Middlebury, Conn.), Harvard Club N.Y. Office: Olin Corp 120 Long Ridge Rd Stamford CT 06904

YOKELY, RONALD EUGENE, mechanical engineer, research corporation executive; b. High Point, N.C., Feb. 7, 1942; s. Clarence Eugene and Grayce (Waddy) Y.; B.S. in Mech. Engring., N.C. State U., Raleigh, 1963; m. E. Joanne Williams, July 6, 1963; children—Rhonda Lynette, Rene Michelle. Test engr. McDonnell Aircraft Corp., St. Louis, 1963-67; sect. mgr. simulation products div. Singer Co., Houston, 1967-73; engring. mgr. Aeronutronic Ford Corp., Houston, 1973-76; sr. v.p. Onyx Corp., Bethesda, Md., 1976-78; pres., treas. Acumenics Research & Tech., Inc. subs. Hadron, Inc., Fairfax., Va., 1978—; corp. v.p. Hadron, Inc., Fairfax, 1983—; cons. FAA, 1975-76. Registered profl. engr., Tex. Mem. AIAA, IEEE, Nat. Soc. Profl. Engrs., AAAS, , Omega Psi Phi. Episcopalian. Co-author: Microcomputers—A Technology Forecast and Assessment to the Year 2000, 1980, Japanese transl., 1981. Home: 10894 Lake Windermere Dr Great Falls VA 22066 Office: 9990 Lee Hwy Fairfax VA 22030

YOKOGAWA, KIYOSHI, engineer, researcher; b. Saiki, Ohita, Japan, Sept. 28, 1946; arrived in Kure, 1974; s. Suekichi and Hatsuko (Suzuki) Y.; m. Masako Hirokaga, Apr. 29, 1972; children: Jun, Chisaki. BS in Engring., Kyoto U., 1969, MS in Engring., 1971; D in Engring., Hokkaido U., 1985. Registered profl. engr. Asst. prof. The Iron and Steel Tech. Coll., Amagasaki, Hyogo, Japan, 1971-74; researcher Govt. Indsl. Research Inst. Chugoku, Ministry of Internat. Trade and Industry, Kure, Hiroshima, 1974-80; sr. researcher Govt. Indsl. Research Inst. Chugoku, MITI, Kure, Hiroshima, 1980—; cons. Nat. Space Devel. Agy. Japan, Tokyo, 1986—. Contbr. articles to profl. jours.; patentee in field. Mem. The Japan Inst. Metals (Metallographic Photograph prize 1976), The Iron and Steel Inst. Japan. Home: Agachuo 5-10-40-101, Kure, Hiroshima 737, Japan Office: Govt Indsl Rsch Inst Chugoku, MITI, Hiro-Suehiro 2-2-2, 737-01 Kure, Hiroshima Japan

YON, EUGENE T., management consultant; b. Mt. Hope, W.Va., Dec. 29, 1936; s. Gildo and Odilla Y.; m. Rosemary Rovito, Aug. 20, 1960; children: Steven, Kevin. BEE, U. Cin., 1960; MSEE, Case Inst. Tech., 1962, PhD, 1965. Staff scientist Avco Corp. Electronics Div., Cin., 1965-67; asst. prof. engring. Case Western Reserve U., Cleve., 1967-69, assoc. prof., 1969-72, 1972-74; v.p. Booz-Allen & Hamilton, Cleve., 1974-84, N.Y.C., 1988—; v.p. Combustion Engring., Stamford, Conn., 1984-85, pres. sect., 1985-88. Contbr. articles to profl. jours.; patentee in field. Ford Found. fellow, 1960-64. Mem. IEEE, Sigma Xi, Eta Nappa Nu, Tau Beta Pi. Home: 316 Green Oak Sweetwater Oaks Longwood FL 32779 Office: Booz Allen & Hamilton 101 Park Ave New York NY 10178

YONTZ, KENNETH FREDRIC, medical and chemical company executive; b. Sandusky, Ohio, July 21, 1944; s. Kenneth Willard and Dorothy (Kromer) Y.; m. Jean Ann Marshall, July 21, 1962 (div. Aug. 1982); children: Terri, Christine, Michael, Jennifer; m. Karen Glojek, July 7, 1984. BSBA, Bowling Green State U., 1971; MBA, Eastern Mich. U., 1979. Fin. planning mgr. Ford Motor Co., Rawsonville, Mich., 1970-74; fin. mgr. Chemetron Corp., Chgo., 1974-76, pres. fire systems div., 1976-80; pres. electronics div. Allen Bradley Co., Milw., 1980-83, group. pres. electronics, 1983-85, exec. v.p., 1985-86; chmn. bd., pres., chief exec. officer Sybron Corp., Milw., 1986—, also bd. dirs.; Bd. dirs. Sybron Corp., Milw., Aerovox Inc., New Bedford, Mass. Mem. Westmore Country Club, PGA West, Milw. AthleticClub, University Club, Montclair Golf Club. Episcopalian. Office: Sybron Corp 411 E Wisconsin Ave Milwaukee WI 53122

YOOS, ROBERT CALVIN, JR., banking executive; b. Huntington, N.Y., Feb. 27, 1950; s. Robert C. and Eileen M. (Bates) Y.; m. Irena M. Libutti, June 13, 1971; children: Robert C. III, Sean T. BA in English, St. Francis Coll., Loretto, Pa., 1972. Trader Sumitomo Bank Ltd., N.Y.C., 1972-79; v.p., treas. Mutibanco Comermex N.Y. Agy., N.Y.C., 1979—. Office: Multibanco Comermex NY Agy 1 Exchange Pla New York NY 10006

YOPP, JOHANNA FUTCHS, medical office administrator; b. Wilmington, N.C., Sept. 6, 1938; d. Richard and Louise (Friedman) Futchs; m. James D. Yopp Jr., Dec. 26, 1959; children: Beverly, Lynn, James III, Sara Katherine. BA, U. N.C., Greensboro, 1960. Tchr. New Hanover County Schs., Wilmington, N.C., 1960-62, Winston-Salem (N.C.) Forsyth County Schs., 1962-68; mgr. James D. Yopp Jr. MD, Winston-Salem, 1971—. Vol. Winston-Salem/Forsyth County Schs., Winston-Salem Optimist Soccer Club, 1970-73; leader Girl Scouts U.S., Winston-Salem, 1970-73; pres. Mt. Tabor High Sch. PTA, WInston-Salem, 1986-87, 87-88; mem. Forsyth-Stokes Med.

Aux., Bowman Gray Med. Ctr. Aux. (Winston-Salem), Winston Salem and Forsyth County PTA Coun.; Greensboro centennial planning bd. U. N.C. Mem. NAFE, Am. Mgmt. Assn. Republican. Lutheran. Home: 3410 Thoresby Ct Winston-Salem NC 27104 Office: 602 Forsyth Med Pk Winston-Salem NC 27103

YORK, ANDREW GREEN, III, modeling school administrator; b. Waterbury, Conn., Nov. 7, 1950; s. Andrew Green and Dorothy (Stevens) Y.; m. Permelia Carol Hardesty, Apr. 20, 1982; 1 child, Autumn Gabrielle. BS, Bently Coll., 1973; MBA, Suffolk U., 1975. Sales rep. Barbizon Sch., West Hartford, Conn., 1976-79; mktg. dir. Barbizon Sch., Rochester, N.Y., 1979-80; pres. Barbizon Sch., Tulsa, 1980—; cons. York & Assocs., West Hartford, 1977-79. Contbr. articles to profl. jours. Chmn. Rep. Town Com., Torrington, Conn., 1979. With U.S. Army, 1970-76. Office: Model Am Inc 5401 S Sheridan St Ste 101 Tulsa OK 74145

YORK, DOUGLAS ARTHUR, manufacturing, construction company executive; b. Centralia, Ill., June 5, 1940; s. Harry Bernice and Violet Alvera (Johnstone) Y.; student San Diego State Jr. Coll., 1957; m. Linda Kay McIntosh, Sept. 13, 1958; children—Deborah Ann, Darren Anthony. With Meredith & Simpson Constrn. Co./DBA Pressure Cool Co., Indio, Calif., 1958—, v.p., 1968—, sec., gen. mgr., 1976-82, pres., 1982—. Commr., Riverside County Parks; mem. Bldg. and Housing Appeals Bd. City of Indio, City of Coachella, Calif.; bd. dirs. Coachella Valley wild Bird Ctr. Mem. ASHRAE, Calif. Assn. Park and Recreation Commrs. and Bd. Mems., Internat. Conf. Bldg. Officials. Republican. Office: 83-801 Ave 45 Indio CA 92201

YORK, JOHN C(HRISTOPHER), lawyer, investment banker; b. Evansville, Ind., Apr. 27, 1946; s. James Edward and Madge (Wease) Y.; m. Judith Anne Carmack, Aug. 24, 1968; children—George Edward Carmack, Charlotte Bayley, Alice Mercer. BA, Vanderbilt U., 1968; JD, Harvard U., 1971. Bar: Ill. 1971, U.S. Dist. Ct. (no. dist.) Ill. 1971. Assoc. firm Mayer Brown & Platt, Chgo., 1971-74; sr. v.p., sec., prin. JMB Realty Corp., Chgo., 1974-84; pres. Robert E. Lend Co. Inc., 1984—, Packard Properties Inc., 1984—; counsel Bell, Boyd & Lloyd, Chgo., 1986—; bd. dirs. McKeever Electric Supply Co., Columbus, Ohio. Bd. dirs. Landmarks Preservation Coun. of Ill., 1972—, Streeterville Corp., 1986-87, Washington Sq. Health Found., 1985—, Henrotin Hosp., 1976—; mem. vestry St. Chrysostom's Ch., 1980—. Mem. ABA, Chgo. Bar Assn., Lambda Alpha Internat., Chgo. Club, Casino Club, Racquet Club, Saddle and Cycle Club. Republican. Episcopalian. Home: 1242 Lake Shore Dr Chicago IL 60610 Office: Robert E Lend Co Inc One N La Salle St Chicago IL 60602

YORKE, MARIANNE, lawyer; b. Ridley Park, Pa., Nov. 4, 1948; d. Joseph George and Catherine Veronica (Friel) Y. BA, West Chester U., 1970; JD, Temple U., 1980; MS, U. Pa., 1987. Bar: Pa. 1981. Real estate mgr. CIGNA Service Co., Phila., 1981-85, asst. dir., Phila., 1985—; cons., 1981-82; real estate atty. Garfinkel & Volpicelli, Phila., 1980-81; prin., mng. ptnr. Yorke/Eisenman, Real Estate, Phila., 1976-88, prin., mng. ptnr. Yorke/Mac Lachlin Real Estate, Phila, 1989—; lectr. Women in the Arts, 1982—. Contbr. articles to profl. jours. Solicitor Pa. Ballet, Phila., 1983—, United Way, Phila., 1983—; mem. steering com. U. Pa., 1986—, dir. alumni assn., 1987—; mem. adv. com. for econ. devel. Luth. Settlement House Adv.; bd. dirs. Hamilton Townhouse Assn., 1989, chmn. ins. com., 1989—. Recipient Performance Recognition award for Excellence in Negotiations, 1987, 88. Mem. ABA (forum on constrn.), Pa. Bar Assn. (condominium and zoning coms.), Phila. Bar Assn., Phila. Women Real Estate Attys., Nat. Assn. Corp. Real Estate Execs. (comml. coun.), Internat. Atty's Roundtable, Women's Law Caucus, German Soc., Phi Alpha Delta. Republican. Roman Catholic. Home: 1910 Nectarine St Philadelphia PA 19130 Office: CIGNA Svc Co Real Estate Dept 1600 Arch St 17T Philadelphia PA 19103

YOSKOWITZ, IRVING BENJAMIN, manufacturing company executive, lawyer; b. Bklyn., Dec. 2, 1945; s. Rubin and Jennie Y.; m. Carol L. Magil, Feb. 11, 1973; children: Stephen M., Robert J. BBA, CCNY, 1966; JD, Harvard U., 1969; postgrad., London Sch. Econs., 1971-72. Bar: D.C., N.Y., Conn. Programmer IBM, East Fishkill, N.Y., 1966; systems analyst Office Sec. Def., Washington, 1969-71; asso. firm Arnold & Porter, Washington, 1972-73; atty. IBM, 1973-79; regional counsel IBM, Bethesda, Md., to 1979; dep. gen. counsel United Technologies Corp., Hartford, Conn., 1979-81; v.p. and gen. counsel United Technologies Corp., 1981-86; sr. v.p., gen. counsel United Techs. Corp., 1986—. Mem. editorial bd. Harvard U. Law Rev., 1968-69. Trustee Mt. Sinai Hosp., 1984. With U.S. Army, 1969-71. Knox fellow, 1971-72. Mem. ABA, Am. Corp. Counsel Assn. (bd. dirs. 1982-85), Assn. Gen. Counsels. Office: United Techs Corp United Techs Blvd Hartford CT 06101

YOST, LYLE EDGAR, farm equipment manufacturing company executive; b. Hesston, Kans., Mar. 5, 1913; s. Joseph and Alma (Hensley) Y.; m. Erma Martin, July 31, 1938; children: Byron, Winston, Susan, Cameron. B.S. B.A, Goshen Coll., 1937; postgrad., U. Ind., 1940. With St. Joseph Valley Bank, Elkhart, Ind., 1938-41; tchr. Wakarusa (Ind.) High Sch., 1942-45; founder Hesston Corp., Kans., 1947, pres., 1949-83; now chmn. bd. Hesston Corp.; dir. Bank IV, Hesston State Bank. Bd. dirs., past pres. Farm and Indsl. Equipment Inst.; mem. Gov.'s Com. for Partners for Progress Kans.-Paraguay, State Rural Devel. Adv. Council; chmn. com. establishing creamery in Uruguay, 1967; mem. State Dept. cultural del. to USSR, 1967; chmn. pres.'s adv. council Hesston Coll. (Kans.); Bd. dirs. Mennonite Econ. Devel. Assos.; chmn. Prince of Peace Chapel, Aspen Colo.; trustee Wichita State U. Endowment Assn., Wesley Med. Endowment Found. Named Farmarketing Man of Year Nat. Agrl. Advt. and Marketing Assn., 1969; Kansan of Achievement in Bus., 1972; Kansan of Year, 1974. Mem. Alpha Kappa Psi. Home: 1200 Ridge Rd Hesston KS 67062 Office: Hesston Corp 420 W Lincoln Blvd Hesston KS 67062

YOST, WILLIAM ARTHUR, III, lawyer; b. Greensburg, Pa., Apr. 7, 1935; s. William Arthur Jr. and Virginia (Penny) Y.; m. Katherine Luedke, Apr. 20, 1963; children: Virginia, Alexander. AB, Haverford Coll., 1957; LLB, Yale U., 1960. Bar: Wis. 1960, Tex 1984. Assoc. Erbstoeszer, Cleary & Zabel, Milw., 1960-61; atty. Allis-Chalmers Co., Milw., 1961-68, Pabst Brewing Co., Milw., 1968-70, Ft. Howard Paper Co., Green Bay, Wis., 1970-72; corp. counsel, sec., v.p. adminstrn. Will Ross Inc., Milw., 1972-78; pres. Yost, Krombach & Schmitt, S.C., Cedarburg, Wis., 1978-83; sr. v.p. legal and sec. Pearle Inc., Dallas, 1983—, also bd. dirs. Mem. ABA, Internat. Bar Assn., Tex. Bar Assn., Wis. Bar Assn., Dallas Bar Assn., Am. Corp. Counsel Assn., Yale Club, Town Club, T-Bar Racquet Club. Republican. Episcopalian. Office: Pearle Inc 2534 Royal Ln Dallas TX 75229

YOUELL, MARY LOUISE, writer, commercial; b. Spencer, Iowa, Aug. 12, 1957; d. Eugene Wallace Jr. and Jane Belle (Hammett) Y. BA in French, Spanish, Wheaton Coll., 1979; AAS in Advt., Communications., Fashion Inst. Tech., N.Y.C, 1985. Auditor Bank Shares, Inc., Mpls., 1980-82; asst. to mktg. dir. Good Food Mag. (Triangle Communications Inc.), N.Y.C, 1985-87; copywriter PaineWebber Inc., N.Y.C, 1987—; chief fin. officer, pres. Bank Svc. Dept. Inc., Manson, Iowa, 1975—. Mem. St. Bartholomew's Community Club. Office: PaineWebber Inc 1285 Ave of the Americas New York NY 10019

YOUNG, A. THOMAS, electronics and missiles company executive; b. Nassawadox, Va., Apr. 19, 1938; s. William Thomas and Margaret (Colonna) Y.; m. Page Carter Hayden, June 24, 1961; children: Anne Blair, Thomas Carter. BMechE, B in Aero. Engring., U. Va., 1961; M in Mgmt., MIT, 1972. Designer Newport News (Va.) Shipbldg. & Drycock Co., 1961; with NASA, 1961-82; various positions Langley Research Ctr., Hampton, Va., 1961-69; staff mem. and mission dir. Viking Project Hampton, 1969-76; dir. Hdqrs. Planetary Program Washington, 1976-79; dep. dir. Ames Research Ctr., Moffett Field, Calif., 1979-80; dir. Goddard Space Flight Ctr., Greenbelt, Md., 1980-82; with Martin Marietta Corp., 1982—; v.p. research Bethesda, Md., 1982-83; v.p., gen. mgr. Balt. Aerospace, 1983-84, pres., 1984-85; exec. v.p., then. pres. Orlando (Fla.) Aerospace, 1985-87; pres. Electronics & Missiles Group, Orlando, 1987—; bd. dirs. Sun Bank, Orlando; chmn. Gov.'s Space Commn., Tallahassee, Fla., 1987-88. Prin. Ctr. for Excellence in Govt., Washington, 1987; trustee U. Cen. Fla., 1987—; mem. Orange County (Fla.) Sch. Bd. Found., 1987—. Sloan fellow MIT, 1971-72; decorated DSM Viking Project NASA, 1977; recipient Outstanding Leadership medal Voyager Program NASA, 1980, Meritorious Exec. Presdl. Rank award Pres. Jimmy Carter, 1980, Disting. Exec. award Pres. Ronald Reagan, 1981. Fellow AIAA, Am. Astronautical Soc. Republican. Methodist. Office: Martin Marietta Corp Electronics & Missiles Group PO Box 555837 MP 100 Orlando FL 32855-5837 also: Martin Marietta Corp 6801 Rockledge Dr Bethesda MD 20817

YOUNG, AUSTIN PRENTISS, III, auditor; b. Houston, Nov. 11, 1940; s. Austin P. Jr. and Grace Mary (Barbato) Crenshaw; m. Jacklyn Joy Goodroe (div. Oct. 1983); m. Susan Critenden Roach, Apr. 13, 1985; children: Lisa Lee Jilek, Adam Edward Young, Kathryn Bennet Bailey, Charles William Bailey III. BBA, U. Tex., 1962. CPA, Tex., N.Y. With profl. staff Peat Marwick Main & Co., Houston, 1962-74, ptnr., 1977-86; ptnr. Peat Marwick Main & Co., N.Y.C., 1974-77; chief fin. officer Sun Resorts Ltd., N.A., St. Maarten, 1986-87; sr. v.p. gen. auditor Am. Gen. Corp., Houston, 1987-88, exec. v.p., chief fin. officer, 1988—. Served to capt. Q.M. U.S. Army, 1962-70. Mem. Zool. Soc. Houston (v.p. 1978-86, bd. dirs. 1988—), Escape Ctr., Inc. (bd. dirs. 1988—), Exchange Club (pres. 1984-85). Office: Am Gen Corp 2929 Allen Pkwy Houston TX 77019

YOUNG, B. J. BOND, national/international marketing executive; b. Dowagiac, Mich., Mar. 26, 1948; d. Charles W. and Agnes Mary Ann (Hampel) Sarabyn; m. Alexander Young, Oct. 9, 1982. Student, Northwood Inst. Pvt. practice mktg. communications N.Y.C., Chgo., Washington, 1967-78; ptnr. Bond & Polos Communications Cons., Chgo., 1974-78; advt. mgr. H. Wilson Co. div. Ebsco, South Holland, Ill., 1978-81, dir. mktg., 1981-84; pres., owner On Target Solutions, Ft. Lauderdale, Fla., 1984—. Active fed. and state polit. campaign mgmt. Recipient various profl. awards. Mem. Internat. Platform Assn. Home: 619 Orton Ave #601 Fort Lauderdale FL 33304

YOUNG, BARNEY THORNTON, lawyer; b. Chillicothe, Tex., Aug. 10, 1934; s. Bayne and Helen Irene (Thornton) Y.; m. Sarah Elizabeth Taylor, Aug. 31, 1957; children: Jay Thornton, Sarah Elizabeth, Serena Taylor. B.A., Yale U., 1955; LL.B., U. Tex., 1958. Bar: Tex. 1958. Assoc. Thompson, Knight, Wright & Simmons, Dallas, 1958-65; ptnr. Rain, Harrell, Emery, Young & Doke, Dallas, 1965-87; mem. firm Locke Purnell Rain Harrell (A Profl. Corp.), 1987—; dir. Horchow Mail Order, Inc., Jones-Blair Co. Mem. adv. council Dallas Community Chest Trust Fund, Inc., 1964-66; bd. dirs. Mental Health Assn. Dallas County, Inc., 1969-72; trustee Hockaday Sch., Dallas, 1971-77, Dallas Zoolog. Soc., 1986—; trustee Lamplighter Sch., Dallas, 1976—, chmn. bd. trustees, 1983-86; trustee St. Mark's Sch., Dallas, 1970—, pres., 1976-78; trustee The Found. for the Callier Ctr. and Communication Disorders, 1988—, Friends of the Ctr. for Human Nutrition, 1988—; bd. dirs. Trammell Crow Family Found., 1984-87; mem. Yale Devel. Bd., 1984—. Fellow Tex. Bar Found.; mem. Am., Tex., Dallas bar assns., Am. Judicature Soc., Order of Coif, Phi Beta Kappa, Pi Sigma Alpha, Phi Gamma Delta, Phi Delta Phi. Clubs: Dallas, Dallas Country, Dallas County Republican Men's (bd. dirs. 1977-79), Petroleum (Dallas); Yale (Dallas, N.Y.C.). Home: 6901 Turtle Creek Blvd Dallas TX 75205 Office: Locke Purnell Rain Harrell Suite 2200 2200 Ross Ave Dallas TX 75201-6776

YOUNG, CAROL ANNE, financial planner; b. Ames, Iowa, Apr. 4, 1951; m. Harold Young, Jan. 19, 1985. BA, Simpson Coll., 1972. Cert. fin. planner. Asst. planner Iowa Crime Commn., Des Moines, 1973-75; systems analyst Adapt Inc., Des Moines, 1975-77; dir. Ea. Iowa Area Crime Commn., Cedar Rapids, 1977-81; registered rep. All Am. Mgmt. Corp., West Des Moines, 1981—; owner, pres. Assoc. Fin. Planners Inc., West Des Moines, 1983—. Pres. bd. dirs. Area Substance Abuse Coun., Cedar Rapids, 1979-80; mem. Jr. League Des Moines, 1981-88; chmn. State Foster Care Rev. Bd., Des Moines, 1984—; pres. bd. dirs. Family Counseling Ctr., Des Moines, 1985-86. Mem. Internat. Assn. Fin. Planning (pres. Cen. Iowa chpt. 1989—), Inst. Cert. Fin. Planners, Am. Bus. Women's Assn. (pres. 1987—, Woman of Yr. 1985). Office: Assoc Fin Planners Inc 1233 8th St West Des Moines IA 50265

YOUNG, CHARLES NEWTON, insurance executive; b. Kansas City, Mo., Aug. 27, 1944; s. George Newton and Bernice (Edwards) Y.; m. Linda Harmon (div. 1981); children: Scott, Jason; m. Florence Morris, Mar. 17, 1982; children: Amber Morris, Sean Morris. BA in Econs., Park Coll., Parkville, Mo., 1968. CLU, RHU. Acct. Trans World Airlines, Kansas City, 1967-69; gen. mgr. N.Y. Life Ins. Co., Aurora, Ill., 1969-80; sr. dir. Blue Cross and Blue Shield Assn., Chgo., 1980-83; v.p. Blue Cross and Blue Shield of Okla., Tulsa, 1983-86; dist. mgr. Blue Cross and Blue Shield of Tenn., Nashville, 1986—. Reserve officer Hendersonville (Tenn.) Police Dept., 1987—; bd. dirs. Downtown tulsa YMCA, 1984-86. Served with Mo. Air NG, 1966-72. Mem. Chartered Life Underwriters (Nashville chpt.), Nashville C. of C. Republican. Episcopalian. Home: 104 Ridge Ct S Hendersonville TN 37075 Office: Blue Cross and Blue Shield of Tenn PO Box 22269 Nashville TN 37202

YOUNG, ERIC ALAN, public holding company executive; b. N.Y.C., Jan. 23, 1958; s. Richard George and Joan Sheri (Pomeranz) Y. BA, Lawrence U., 1980; MBA, Vanderbilt U., 1982. Acct. Arthur Andersen & Co., Ft. Worth, 1982-86; contr., asst. sec. TeleCom Corp., Dallas, 1986—. Mem. Assn. for Corp. Growth, AICPA, Tex. Soc. CPAs. Office: TeleCom Corp 1545 W Mockingbird Ln Ste 7000 Dallas TX 75235

YOUNG, ERIKA ROSEMARY, mining equipment company executive, real estate corporation executive; b. Denver, Dec. 19, 1958; d. Michael and Rosemary (Route) Jelen; m. Paul Mark Young, May 24, 1977. Asst. cashier Jefferson County Pub. Schs., Lakewood, Colo., 1976-78; mgr. Golden (Colo.) Food Store Ptnrship., 1978-80; v.p., ops. mgr. Jelen and Son, Inc., Golden, 1980—; owner, broker E.L.M. Realty and Devel., Inc, Golden. Editor newsletter Fairmount Improvement Assn., Jefferson County, Colo., 1980. Precinct com. chairwoman Jefferson County Reps., 1982—. Mem. Ivory Club, 100 Club (Jefferson County). Roman Catholic. Office: Jelen and Son Inc 14000 W 44th Ave Golden CO 80403 also: ELM Realty and Devel Inc Golden CO 80403

YOUNG, EVERETT CLAIR, industrial designer; b. Bondville, Ill., Sept. 21, 1922; s. George Henry and Iva Belle (Mitchell) Y.; children by previous marriage: Jerry, Kerry, Jan, Sandra, Cindy, Rennie, Glen. BA in Indsl. Design, U. Ill., 1947; MA in Vocational Edn., No. Ariz. U., 1985. Indsl. designer New Metal Crafts, Chgo., 1947-50, Van Esso Inc., Chgo., 1950-52, Phil R. Hinkley, Cleve., 1953-54; design cons. Young Enterprises, Cleve., 1955-65; free-lance designer U. Ill and Ariz. State U., 1966-78; dir. research Intergalactic, Inc., Flagstaff, Ariz., 1983—, pres., researcher, 1983—. Author: History's Greatest Epochal Lie, 1977; inventor, patentee heat shields and housing structures used in Gemini and Apollo spacecraft; other patents in field. Served with USAAF. Recipient Spirit of Arizona award Ariz. State. Senate, 1985. Home and Office: 855 N Dobson #2060 Chandler AZ 85224-6902

YOUNG, FRANK NOLAN, JR., commercial building contracting company executive; b. Tacoma, Wash., Feb. 26, 1941; s. Frank N. and Antoinette (Mahncke) Y.; m. Susan E. Bayley, Aug. 13, 1965; children—Sandra Susanne, Frank Nolan. B.A. in Bus. and Fin., U. Wash., 1963. Vice pres. Strand Inc., Bellevue, Wash., 1966-73; pres., treas., chief exec. officer, dir. Gall Landau Young Constrn. Co. Inc., Bellevue, 1973—; v.p., sec., dir. Cascade Structures, Kirkland, Wash., 1972—. Mem. Assoc. Gen. Contractors (pres. Seattle 1985, trustee 1968—, nat. dir.). Republican. Episcopalian. Clubs: Rainier, Lakes, TAS Ski Found. (pres. 1983-84), Overlake Golf and Country; Seattle Yacht. Lodges: Elks, Masons, Shriners, Royal Order Jesters (impresario 1983—). Home: 5005 E Mercer Way Mercer Island WA 98040 Office: Gall Landau Young PO Box 6728 Bellevue WA 98008

YOUNG, FRED RICHARD, military electronics manufacturing executive; b. Jonesboro, Ill., Jan. 6, 1937; s. Ivory and Amy E. (Mays) Y.; m. Bonnie M. Forester Young, Apr. 7, 1955 (div. Feb. 1978); children: Fred J., Daniel W. (dec.); m. Tillie Ann Chapa, Mar. 24, 1979; children: Marci A., Sean R. BS in Econs., Rollins Coll., 1968; MS in Bus. Fin., Cen. Mich. U., 1977. Enlisted USAF, 1954, advanced through grades to capt., 1969, ret., 1979, successively mil. procurement officer, chief tng., contract law negotiator; pres. ins. corp. USAF, Salt Lake City, Los Angeles, Chgo., San Francisco, Detroit, Cleve., 1979-87; dir. govt. contracts Westronix, Inc., Salt Lake City, 1985—; v.p. contracts Astech Inc., Murray, Utah, 1989—, also bd. dirs.; seminar lectr. Med. Malpractice Inst., Salt Lake City, 1986-87. Contbr. articles to profl. jours. Mem. Ind. Ins. Agts. Am., Rotary (com. chmn. Salt Lake City, Paul Harris fellow 1986). Office: Westronix Inc 6952 South 185 West Salt Lake City UT 84047 also: Astech Inc 5248 Pinemont Murray UT 84123

YOUNG, GARY LYNN, corporation executive. BS, U. Ill., 1969; MBA, U. Chgo., 1975. With sales and mktg. dept. Continental Can. Co., Norwalk, Conn., 1969-86; dir. new bus. devel. Container Systems div. Continental Can Co., West Chicago, ILL., 1986-87; gen. mgr. Qualiplus USA, Oak Brook, Ill., 1987-88; v.p. sales Heuft USA, Downers Grove, Ill., 1988—. Home: 655 Chesterfield Ave Naperville IL 60540 Office: Heuft USA 2512 Wisconsin Ave Downers Grove IL 60515

YOUNG, GERRY ARNETT, financial planning director; b. Kansas City, Mo., Feb. 11, 1942; s. Harry Hugh Young and Frieda Anne (Faltermeier) Hill; m. Joyce Holden Mackenzie, May 10, 1969; children: Stacey, Douglas. BS in Chem. Engring., Oreg. State U., 1964, MBA in Fin., 1971. Analyst, So. Pacific Transp., San Francisco, 1971-73; mgr. fin. planning So. Pacific Communications, Burlingame, Calif., 1973-78; comptroller, chief fin. officer Telecomm Systems, Eugene, Oreg., 1978-79; owner Fin. Strategies NW, Eugene, 1979-86; v.p. fin., chief fin. officer Bus. Info. Ctr., 1981-83; dir. planning and corp. devel. Allnet Communications, 1986—; dir. E & D/Editing & Design, 1982-86. Co-author: Computer Assisted Business Plans, 1986; contbr. articles to profl. jours. Lt. USN, 1964-69, Vietnam; to capt. Res., 1985—. Mem. U.S. Naval Inst., Navy League U.S. (pres. Eugene 1982-86), Lane Leaders Assn. (pres. 1984-85), Beta Gamma Sigma, Pi Kappa Pi. Republican. Roman Catholic. Avocations: golf, history, basketball. Home: 4727 Driftwood Dr Milford MI 48042 Office: Allnet Communications Scvs 30300 Telegraph Rd Birmingham MI 48010

YOUNG, J. ANTHONY, motion picture company executive. Student, Edinburgh U. With Arthur Andersen & Co., Glasgow, Scotland; v.p. fin. EMI Films, Inc.; with P.A. Mgmt. Cons., Ltd., EMI Med. Ltd., London; with Lorimar Prodns., Inc., Culver City, Calif., from 1979, past sr. v.p. fin.; former exec. v.p., chief fin. officer Lorimar Telepictures Corp., Culver City; pres. MCA Enterprises Internat. MCA Inc., Universal City, Calif., 1988—. Office: MCA Inc 100 Universal City Pla Bldg 124 Universal City CA 91608 *

YOUNG, JAY ALAN, clothing manufacturing company; b. Atlantic, Iowa, May 3, 1943; s. Harvey Amos and Florence (Piper) Y.; m. Beth Rosenfield, July 17, 1976; children: Megan Anne, Daren Jon. BBA, U. Iowa, 1966. V.p. mktg., advt. Salvatori Corp., Altanta, 1963-75; treas. Pants & Duds, Ltd., Englewood, Colo., 1972-84; v.p., nat. mgr. Levis Belts, Chgo., 1985—; owner, mgr. Rocky Mtn. Apparel Sales, Littleton, Colo., 1975—; gen. ptnr. Tonahutu Ridge Devel. Group, Littleton, 1981—. Home: 7900 W Layton Ave Apt 848 Littleton CO 80123 Office: PO Box 809 Grand Lake CO 80447

YOUNG, JOAN CRAWFORD, advertising executive; b. Hobbs, N.Mex., July 30, 1931; d. William Bill and Ora Maydelle (Boone) Crawford; m. Herchelle B. Young, Nov. 23, 1971 (div.). B.A., Hardin Simmons U., 1952; postgrad. Tex. Tech. U., 1953-54. Reporter, Lubbock (Tex.) Avalanche-Jour., 1952-54; promotion dir. KCBD-TV, Lubbock, 1954-62; account exec. Ward Hicks Advt., Albuquerque, 1962-70; v.p. Mellekas & Assocs., Advt., Albuquerque, 1970-78; pres. J. Young Advt., Albuquerque, 1978—. Bd. dirs. N.Mex. Symphony Orch., 1970-73, United Way of Greater Albuquerque, 1985—. Recipient Silver medal N.Mex. Advt. Fedn., 1977. Mem. N.Mex. Advt. Fedn. (dir. 1975-76), Am. Advt. Fedn., Greater Albuquerque C. of C. (dir. 1984). Republican. Author: (with Louise Allen and Audre Lipscomb) Radio and TV Continuity Writing, 1962. Home: 3425 Avenida Charada NW Albuquerque NM 87107 Also: 303 Roma NW Albuquerque NM 87102

YOUNG, JOEY ALLEN, corporate executive; b. Ruston, La., Oct. 26, 1958; s. Charles William and Jean (Jennings) Y.; m. Lori Jean Matney, Aug. 11, 1984; children: Andrew Bailey, Christopher Jordan. Cert. in elec. engring., Quachita Vocat. Tech., 1982; postgrad., La. Tech. U., 1982-83, U. Houston, 1983-85. Electrician Trio Elec. Co., Monroe, La., 1977-82, estimator, 1985-86; activities dir. YMCA, Alexandria, La., 1982; missionary YMCA, Ft. Necessity, La., summer 1982; youth intern West Meml. Bapt. Ch., Houston, 1983, student pastor, 1983-85, v.p., 1986—. Dir. mission Rapides Bapt. Assn., Alexandria, 1982; coordinator youth La. Bapt. Conv., 1983; leader bible study Buckner Bapt. Haven, Houston, 1985. Named One of Outstanding Young Men in Am., 1985. Republican. Home: 702 Glenmar Monroe LA 71201 Office: Trio Elec Co Inc 4217 Sterlington Hwy Monroe LA 71211

YOUNG, JOHN ALAN, electronics company executive; b. Nampa, Idaho, Apr. 24, 1932; s. Lloyd Arthur and Karen Eliza (Miller) Y.; m. Rosemary Murray, Aug. 1, 1954; children: Gregory, Peter, Diana. B.S. in Elec. Engring, Oreg. State U., 1953; M.B.A., Stanford U., 1958. Various mktg. and finance positions Hewlett Packard Co. Inc., Palo Alto, Calif., 1958-63, gen. mgr. microwave div., 1963-68, v.p. electronic products group, 1968-74, exec. v.p., 1974-77, chief oper. officer, 1977-84, pres., 1977—, chief exec. officer, 1978—, also bd. dirs.; bd. dirs. Wells Fargo Bank, Wells Fargo Co., Chevron Corp. Chmn. ann. fund Stanford, 1966-73, nat. chmn. corp. gifts, 1973-77; Bd. dirs. Mid-Peninsula Urban Coal., 1971-80, co-chmn., 1975-80; mem. adv. council Grad. Sch. Bus., Stanford U., 1967-73, 75-80, univ. trustee, 1977-87, chmn. Pres.'s Commn. Indsl. Competitiveness, 1983-85; chmn. Nat. Jr. Achievement, 1983—. Served with USAF, 1954-56. Mem. Am. Electronics Assn. (founder, chmn. council on competitiveness, 1986), Policy Com. Bus. Roundtable, Bus. Council, Pacific Union Club, Palo Alto Club.

YOUNG, LINDA KATHLEEN, health science association executive; b. Fowler, Kans., Apr. 30, 1954; d. Ralph Edward and Ruth Evelyn (Cornelson) Y.; m. Andre Fountain. BS in Nursing, Cen. State U., Edmond, Okla., 1976. RN. Staff nurse med./surg. and coronary care unit Presbyn. Hosp., Oklahoma City, 1976-79; mgr. nursing Hillcrest Osteo. Hosp., Oklahoma City, 1979-80; staff nurse, mgr. Oklahoma U. Teaching Hosp., Oklahoma City, 1981-82; pres. New Life Programs, Oklahoma City, 1981-88, Nursing Entrepreneurs, Ltd., Oklahoma City, 1988—; mgr. Internat. Health Supply, Oklahoma City, 1988—; coordinator lactation cons. program, State of Okla., 1981—, new life car seat rental program at various hosps., 1983—; cons., speaker Success Co., Oklahoma City, 1984—; owner Rainbows Overhead Graphic Media, Oklahoma City, 1984. Founder Praxis Coll., Oklahoma City, 1988. Named Mentor of Yr., Okla. Metroplex Childbirth Network, Oklahoma City, 1984. Mem. Am. Nurses Assn., Internat. Childbirth Edn. Assn., Internat. Lactation Cons. Assn., Nurse Assocs. Am. Coll. Obs. and Gyns. Office: Nursing Entrepreneurs Ltd PO Box 75393 Oklahoma City OK 75507

YOUNG, LUCILE W., insurance executive; b. Valdosta, Ga., May 15, 1949; d. John V. and Allyene (Long) Wynne; m. John R. Young, June 23, 1972; children: John Sadler, Katherine McIntyre. BBA, U. Ga., 1971; M in Ins., Ga. State U., 1979. CPCU. Agt. Frank B. Hall & Co., Atlanta, 1971-73, asst. mgr. mass mktg., 1974-76, v.p., mgr. mass mktg., 1977-89, pres. Hartsfield div., 1989—. Named one of Outstanding Young Women Am., 1978. Mem. Ga. Soc. CPCU's, Profl. Ins. Agts., Assn. U.S. Army, Beta Gamma Sigma, Alpha Omicron Pi (2d v.p., 1970-71). Office: Frank B Hall & Co Georgia Inc 1005 Virginia Ave Ste 300 Atlanta GA 30354

YOUNG, PETER HOLDEN, JR., wholesale food company executive; b. L.A., Jan. 26, 1932; s. Peter Holden and Marian (Hockensmith) Y.; m. LUanna Gregson, Aug. 26, 1953; children: VAlerie, Wendy, Peter, Gregson. Student, Stanford U., 1950; BA, Occidental Coll., 1953. Mgr. trainee Young's Market Co., L.A., 1953-55, liquor salesman, 1955-57, sales mgr. meat div., 1957, mgr. splty. foods, 1958-85, pres. splty. foods., 1985—; advisor to gen. trade publs. Mem. Nat. Assn. for Splty. Food Trade (hon. show chmn. 1983, show mgr. Anaheim, Calif. 1984). Republican.

YOUNG, PETER RICHARD, manufacturing company executive; b. Newcastle, Eng., Dec. 25, 1944; s. Kenneth Henry and Marian Heather (Phillips) Y.; m. Avrial Eugenie Young, Nov. 30, 1973; children: Desia G., Roxzan I.,

Phillippa N., Kyle R. BSc, U. Bristol, 1966, PhD, 1969. Mgr. overseas investment Fisons Ltd., London, 1970-74, gen. mgr., Toronto, 1974-79, v.p. fin., Bedford, Mass., 1979—; chmn. Haake Buchler Instruments Inc., Saddle Brook, N.J., 1981—. Fellow Inst. Cost and Mgmt. Accts.; mem. Can. Inst. Chemists, Brit. Inst. Mgmt., Royal Inst. Chemistry. Anglican. Clubs: Oriental (London); Harare (Zimbabwe); Nat. (Toronto). Home: 53 Tarbell Spring Rd Concord MA 01742 Office: 2 Preston Ct Bedford MA 01730

YOUNG, ROBERT A., III, freight systems executive; b. Ft. Smith, Ark., Sept. 23, 1940; s. Robert A. and Vivian (Curtis) Y.; m. Mary Carleton McRae; children—Tracy, Christy, Robert A. IV, Stephen. BA in Econs., Washington and Lee U., 1963. Supr. terminal ops. Ark. Best Freight, Ft. Smith, 1964-65; pres. Data-Tronics Inc, Ft. Smith, 1965-67; sr. v.p. Nat. Bank of Commerce, Dallas, 1967-70; v.p. fin. Ark. Best Corp., Ft. Smith, 1970-73, exec. v.p., 1973, pres., chief operating officer, 1973-88, chief exec. officer, 1988—; pres. ABF Freight Systems, Inc., Ft. Smith, 1979—; dir. First Nat. Bank, Ft. Smith. Pres. United Way, Ft. Smith, 1981; past chmn. bd. dirs. Sparks Regional Med. Ctr., Ft. Smith, 1985; chmn. bd. trustees Ark. Coll.; bd. dirs. ATA Found., Inc. Served with USAF, 1963. Recipient Silver Beaver award Boy Scouts Am. Mem. Am. Trucking Assn. (vice chmn.), Ark. State C. of C. (v.p., bd. dirs.), Phi Delta Theta. Presbyterian. Home: PO Box 48 Fort Smith AR 72902 Office: ABF Freight Systems Inc 301 S 11th St Fort Smith AR 72901

YOUNG, ROBERT C., banker; b. N.Y.C., Mar. 15, 1960; s. Robert J. and Gloria L. (Sandhop) Y.; m. Amy S. Trapp. BS cum laude, NYU, 1982, MBA, 1985. Asst. v.p. Chem. Bank, N.Y.C., 1982-86; project mgr. GE Credit Corp., Stamford, Conn., 1986-87; asst. v.p. Merrill Lynch Capital Mkts., N.Y.C., 1987—. Republican. Avocations: golf, swimming, skiing. Home: 330 E 39th St Apt 18P New York NY 10016 Office: Merrill Lynch Capital Mkts 250 Vesey St New York NY 10281

YOUNG, ROBERT LERTON, insurance brokerage company executive; b. Columbus, Ohio, Feb. 21, 1936; s. Robert Lerton and Ada Beatrice (Aderholt) Y.; m. Caroline Page Dickey, May 10, 1980. Student, U. Ill., 1953-55, Ohio State U., 1958-60. Mgr. actuarial dept. Gates McDonald & Co., Columbus, 1959-66; dist. mgr. Gates McDonald & Co., Oakland, Calif., 1966-70; v.p., founder Nat. Compensation Services, Inc., Pleasant Hill, Calif., 1970-71; v.p. Fred S. James & Co., Inc., Pleasant Hill and San Francisco, 1971—; v.p. Fred S. James & Co., Inc., Chgo., 1976—, pres. Claims Mgmt. Services div., 1985; cons. Los Angeles County Self Ins. Program; mem. adv. com. Calif. Dept. Indsl. Relations; tchr. Calif. Extension, 1970; lectr. Am. Mgmt. Assn. Contbr. articles in field to profl. jours. Mem. Pleasant Hill Youth Commn. Served with U.S. Army, 1955-58. Recipient Service award Chartered Property and Casualty Underwriters, 1971, 75. Mem. Ins. Inst. Am. (risk mgmt. diploma), Am. Soc. Safety Engrs. (indsl. safety diploma), Nat. Council Self-Insurers, Internat. Assn. Indsl. Accident Bds. and Commns., Calif., Ariz., Wash., Pa., Mass., Ga., Fla. self-insurers assns. Club: Metropolitan (Chgo.). Office: Fred S James & Co 230 W Monroe St Chicago IL 60606

YOUNG, ROBYN JEAN, financial planner, accountant, securities and insurance agent; b. Havre, Mont., Aug. 18, 1954; d. Robert D. and Pat (Craine) Morrison; m. Chris R. Young, Mar. 22, 1974; children: Kelsen E., Kristen N. BS in Bus. Adminstrn. and Acctg., U. Mont., 1978. CPA, Mont.; cert. fin. planner; registered rep. securities and ins. agt. Staff acct. Galusha, Higgins & Galusha, CPA's, Havre, Mont., 1981-83; instr. No. Mont. Coll., Havre, 1984; controller Havre Med. Clinic, 1985-86; fin. planner Rincover Fin. Services, Havre, 1987—. Mem. adv. council Regional Youth Adv. Council, Havre, 1987—. Mem. AICPA, Inst. Cert. Fin. Planners, Internat. Assn. Fin. Planners, Soroptimist (pres. 1988). Office: 747 W 9th St Havre MT 59501

YOUNG, ROGER AUSTIN, natural gas distribution company executive; b. Boston, Feb. 2, 1946; s. Robert Harris McCarter and Gloria Bond (Tenney) Y.; m. Linda Furste, Sept. 6, 1975; children: Catherine Simms, Geoffrey Furste. B.A., Princeton U., 1968. Systems analyst Orange and Rockland Utilities, Inc., Spring Valley, N.Y., 1968-72; asst. v.p. Bay State Gas Co., Boston, 1972-75, v.p., 1975-80; exec. v.p. Bay State Gas Co., Canton, Mass., 1980-81; pres. Bay State Gas Co., Canton, 1981—. Bd. dirs. New Eng. Council. Mem. Am. Gas Assn. (bd. dirs.), New Eng. Gas Assn. (chmn. 1984-85), Newcomen Soc., Asssociated Gas Distbrs. (exec. com.). Congregationalist. Clubs: The Country (Brookline, Mass.); Colonial (Princeton, N.J.). Home: 68 Old Orchard Rd Sherborn MA 01770 Office: Bay State Gas Co 120 Royall St Canton MA 02021

YOUNG, SHIRLEY JEAN, small business owner; b. Galveston, Tex., Mar. 18, 1944; d. Rufus H. and Ena I. (Carter) Y. Diploma in computers, basic programming, Halix Inst., 1988. Histologic technician, med. sec. St. Mary's Hosp., Galveston, 1963-66; clk.-typist Am. Oil Co., Texas City, 1967-68, Am. Nat. Ins. Co., Galveston, 1969-75; med. sec. U. Tex. Med. Br., Galveston, 1975-83; owner WORDS ETC (Software Design), Galveston, 1983—; cons. Art From The Heart, Livingston, Tex., 1984—. Author: Winning Words, 1987; contbr. articles to bus. publs. Mem. Nat. Fedn. for Decency, 1984—. Mem. NAFE, Am. Soc. Profl. and Exec. Women, Computer Entrepreneur Assn. Am., Am. Soc. Clin. Pathologists (assoc.), 700 Club, 1000 Club. Baptist. Home: 8020 Steward Rd Galveston TX 77551 Office: WORDS ETC 2705 61st St Ste B #308 Galveston TX 77551-1838

YOUNG, THOMAS J., mortgage company executive; b. Midland, S.D., June 12, 1949; s. R.H. and Gwen (Jones) Y.; divorced 1976; children: Susan, Mike, Mark (twins); m. Joyce Young, Aug. 25, 1979. BS in Bus. Adm., St. Joseph Coll., Phila., 1972; postgrad., John Marshall Law Sch., Atlanta, 1977-78. Br. mgr. Borg Warner Acceptance Corp., Cocoa, Fla., 1973-77; regional credit mgr. Comml. Credit Equipment Corp., Atlanta, 1977-79; div. credit mgr. GEICO, Atlanta, 1979-82; account exec. Bank Am., Atlanta, 1982-83; regional V.P. Security Pacific Nat. Bank, Atlanta, 1983-86; v.p. Consol. Capital Co., Atlanta, 1986-88; pres., chief exec. officer Tha Wall St. Mortage Co., Atlanta, 1988—; bd. dirs. TJY & Assoc., The Crogan Corp. (chmn.) Lawrenceville, Ga.; cons. Small Bus. Assn., Atlanta; faculty speaker at Ga. Tech. Bd. dirs., v.p. Pop Warner Youth Football Assn., Doraville, Ga., 1977-79; chmn. Sch. Adv. Com. Lawrenceville, 1985; commr. Lawrenceville Housing Authority, 1986—; high sch. football referee. Recipient Task Force award Rep. Party, Washington, 1985. Mem. Am. Arbitration Assn., Mortgage Banker Assn., Crittendon Research Group (natl. speaker). Baptist. Home: 147 Mediterranean Ln Lawrenceville GA 30245

YOUNG, VERA MILLER, portfolio manager; b. Galveston, Tex., Nov. 11, 1927; d. Thomas Morgan and Vera (Shaw) Miller; m. William Jackson Standley, Feb. 17, 1949 (dec. 1973); children: Weldon, Yvonne Standley Huffhines, Mansel; m. William Jackson Young, July 3, 1975 (dec. 1979). AB, Galveston Coll., 1972. Analyst Am. Nat. Ins. Co., Galveston, 1972-74, securities analyst, 1974-78, sr. securities analyst, 1978-83, asst. v.p., 1984-86, 87—; v.p., portfolio mgr. Securities Mgmt. & Svcs. Co. and subs., Galveston, 1987—. Office: Am Nat Ins Co 1 Moody Pla Galveston TX 77550

YOUNG, WILLIAM TERRY, financial planner; b. Rockford, Ill., June 13, 1948; s. Lee and Dorothy A. (Rowley) Y.; m. Mary Peck, Aug. 3, 1983; children: Jason D. Conety, Jonathon B. Conety. Student, Coll. Fin. Planning, Denver, 1984-87; BS in Computer Sci., Franklin Pierce Coll., 1985. Cert. Fin. Planner. Prin. William T. Young, Fin. Planner, Keene, N.H., 1983—; pres. Plus Philanthorpic Strategies, Plus Coll. Fin. Planning, Plus Retirement Planning, Keene, 1987—; tchr. Keene Community Edn. program, 1984—. Contbr. articles to newspapers. Mem. Inst. Cert. Fin. Planners, Keene C. of C. (chmn. edn. com.). Lodge: Lions. Office: Fin Planner PO Box 1117 Keene NH 03431

YOUNG, WILLIAM VICTOR, banker; b. Albany, Calif., Apr. 25, 1937; s. Victor Albert and Nina Barbara (McNamara) Y.; B.A., San Jose State U., 1959; M.A., U. Oreg., 1966; postgrad. Grad. Sch. Credit and Fin. Mgmt., London U., 1978; A.M.P., Harvard U., 1983; m. Genevieve Murphy, Sept. 22, 1962; children—William Mark, Michael Patrick, Sarah Elizabeth. With Bank of America, 1966—, v.p., mgr., Rotterdam, Netherlands, 1973-76, regional v.p. Central Am./Caribbean Area, Guatemala City, Guatemala, 1976-78, sr. v.p. Central Europe Area, Frankfurt, W. Ger., 1978-81, exec. v.p. Latin Am./Caribbean div., Caracas, Venezuela, 1981-86, exec. v.p., internat. div., San Francisco, 1986—, Europe, Middle East, Africa divs., Lodnon, 1988; mem. mgmt. adv. council Bank of Am. N.T. and S.A.; mem. world banking div. exec. council Bank of Am.; dep. chmn. European Brazilian Bank Ltd., London. Served to 1st lt. U.S. Army, 1959-61. Mem. Council of Ams., Brazil-U.S. Bus. Council, Argentine-U.S. Bus. Council, Venezuelan-Am. C. of C., Found. for Mgmt. Edn. in Central Am. Home: PO Box 37000 San Francisco CA 94137 Office: Bank of Am Nat Trust & Savs Assn 555 California St San Francisco CA 94104

YOUNGBLOOD, GARY CECIL, natural gas company executive; b. Birmingham, Ala., Oct. 30, 1943; s. Horace Cecil and Iva Juliet (Wood) Y.; m. Cheryl Diane Black, Jan. 25, 1964; children: Kristin Diane, Gary Bradley, Mark Alan. BS, Ala. Coll., 1965. Utility analyst U.S. Steel Corp., Fairfield, Ala., 1966-69; mgmt. trainee Ala. Gas Corp., Leeds, 1969-70; leakage supr. Ala. Gas Corp., Birmingham, 1970-71, asst. supt. adminstrn., 1971-72; local mgr. Ala. Gas Corp., Marion, Ala., 1972-75; dist. mgr. Ala. Gas Corp., Anniston, Ala., 1975-82; exec. staff asst. Ala. Gas Corp., Birmingham, 1982-84, dist. mgr., 1984-85, v.p. Birmingham ops., 1985—; bd. dirs. Minority Enterprise Small Bus. Investment Co., Birmingham. Bd. govs. Ala. Ind. Colls., 1986—; bd. dirs. Met. YMCA, Birmingham, 1986—, Summerfest, Birmingham, 1987—, Met. Arts Coun., Birmingham, 1987—; mem. alumni coun. Leadership Birmingham, 1986—. Recipient Redge Bearden Svc. award Marion Jaycees, 1973, Disting. Scouter award Choccolocco coun. Boy Scouts Am., 1982, appreciation award United Way Cen. Ala., 1987; named Outstanding Young Mem Am., 1974. Mem. Am. Gas Assn., So. Gas Assn., Ala. Natural Gas Assn. (bd. dirs. 1983—, pres. 1988—), Birmingham Area C. of C., Rotary (bd. dirs. Anniston 1981-82, Birmingham 1987-88). Methodist. Office: Ala Gas Corp 2100 6th Ave Birmingham AL 35203

YOUNGDAHL, RUSSELL C(HARLES), utility company executive; b. Galesburg, Ill., Mar. 26, 1924; s. Carl Harry and Nellie J. (Ericson) Y.; m. Mary Louise Anderson, Nov. 10, 1945; children: Karen Youngdahl Pawlick, Ann Youngdahl Smith, Russell C., Kathryn Youngdahl Stauss. B.S.E.E., U. Mich., 1946; M.B.A., MIT, 1963. With Consumers Power Co., Jackson, Mich., 1946-83, exec. v.p. energy supply, 1974-81, exec. v.p. corp. planning, 1981-83; pres. RAM, 1983—; pres., chief oper. officer L.I. Lighting Co., Hicksville, N.Y., 1987-89. Trustee Alma Coll., 1972—; elder 1st Presbyn. Ch., Jackson. Served to lt. USN, 1942-45, PTO. Named Disting. Alumnus U. Mich., 1974; Sloan fellow, 1962-63. Fellow IEEE (pres. chpt. 1960-61); mem. Mich. Electric Assn. (pres.). Club: Jackson Country (pres. 1976).

YOUNGER, ANITA BETH, entrepreneur; b. Niceville, Fla., June 26, 1964; d. Charles Douglas and Margaret Anna (McElhaney) Y. BSBA, U. Tulsa, 1986. Stockholder, pres. dir. Grand Trine, Inc., Tulsa, 1986—; stockholder, initiator, promoter Strategic Internat., Inc., Denver, 1987—; incorporator Select Petroleum, Inc., Tulsa, 1988; sec., dir. BDS Investments, Inc., Tulsa, 1986-87, Success Drilling, Inc., Tulsa, 1986-87, Venture Holding Co., Tulsa, 1986-87; cons. G.S. Limited Partnership, Denver, 1986, computer cons. The Worthmore Group, Inc., Tulsa, 1988. Mem. NAFE, Kappa Delta. Republican. Home: 4752 S Harvard #85 Tulsa OK 74135

YOUNGERS, MARION ANTHONY, service company executive; b. Hospers, Iowa, July 6, 1930; s. Peter Louis and Susanna (Robinet) Y.; m. Peggy Van Patten, June 12, 1954; children: Nicholas, Sidney, Michelle, Jeffrey, Lisa. BS, U. Iowa, 1953; JD, U. Mich., 1959. Tax atty. Reynolds Metals Co., Richmond, Va., 1959-67; mgr. income taxes Control Data Corp., Mpls., 1967-68; v.p. taxes, gen. counsel Rexnord, Inc., Milw., 1969-87; v.p., gen. counsel Valuation Rsch. Corp., Milw., 1988—. Co-editor: (handbook) Political Action Committee Handbook, 1981. V.p., bd. dirs. Wis. Pub. Expenditure Found., Madison, 1982—; chmn. tax com. Wis. Mfrs. and Commerce, Madison, 1976—; various tax coms. Wis. Dept. Revenue, Office of Gov. Wis., various civic orgns. 1st lt. USAF, 1953-55. Mem. ABA, Internat. Fiscal Assn., Tax Exec. Inst. (pres. local chpt. 1974-75, nat. dir. 1976-78). Home: 19110 Timberline Dr Waukesha WI 53186 Office: Valuation Research Corp 411 E Wisconsin Ave Milwaukee WI 53202

YOUNK, JAMES L., treasurer; b. Green Bay, Wis., May 11, 1942; s. Roy J. and Val C. (Krielkamp) Y.; m. Kathleen A. Rick, June 24, 1987; children: Kirk, Ann, Mark, David, Justin. BS in Acctg., St. Norbert Coll., W. DePere, Wis., 1964. Acct. Am. Can, Neenah, Wis., 1964-67; staff acct. Realist, Inc., Menomonee Falls, Wis., 1967-70, controller, 1970-87, treas., 1987—. Served to 2nd lt. USAR, 1967-74. Fellow Nat. Assn. of Accts. (bd. dirs. 1972). Home: 264 Green Valley Pl West Bend WI 53095 Office: Realist Inc PO Box 67 Menomonee Falls WI 53051

YOUNT, GEORGE STUART, paper company executive; b. Los Angeles, Mar. 4, 1949; s. Stanley George and Agnes (Pratt) Y.; m. Geraldine Marie Silvio, July 18, 1970; children: Trisha Marie, Christopher George. Grad. student, Harvard U., 1983-86. Mgmt. trainee Fortifiber Corp., L.A., 1969-71, asst. to v.p. ops., 1971-75, adminstrv. v.p., treas., sec., 1975-85, exec. v.p., sec., chief fin. officer, 1985—; treas., bd. dirs. Stanwall Corp., L.A.; past pres. Hollister Ranch Cattle Coop., Gaviota, Calif.; bd. dirs. Consol. Media Corp., Pasadena, Calif. Team leader L.A. United Way, 1981-86; mem. Drug Abuse Resistance Edn. Com., 1986—; bd. dirs. Big Bros. of Greater Los Angeles, 1984-87. Mem. Am. Paper Inst., Nat. Assn. Corp. Dirs., Harvard Bus. Club So. Calif. Clubs: Jonathan (Los Angeles); San Marino City (Calif.); Harvard Bus. Sch. So. Calif. Lodge: Rotary. Home: 684 Winston Ave San Marino CA 91108 Office: Fortifiber Corp 4489 Bandini Los Angeles CA 90023-4777

YOUNT, THOMAS LEO, electronics company executive; b. Birmingham, Ala., Mar. 23, 1928; s. Thomas and Hazel Lee (Felts) Y.; B Engring., Vanderbilt U., 1952; m. Jane Wilkerson, Sept. 5, 1953; children—Lee Yount, Margaret Yount Polen, Pamela White. Asst. to v.p. purchasing Westinghouse Electric Corp., Pitts., 1952-56; gen. mgr. Internat. Electronic Industries, Nashville, 1956-61; chmn., chief exec. officer ORTEC, Inc., Oak Ridge, 1961-71; sr. v.p. EG&G Inc., Wellesley, Mass., 1971-83; commr. employment security State of Tenn., 1983-84; venture capital and mgmt. cons., 1984-88; bd. dir., chmn. exec. compensation com., chmn. investment com., mem. exec. com. Sovran Bank East; bd. dir. First Cumberland Bank. Trustee, mem. exec. com. Oak Ridge Hosp. of Methodist Ch.; mem. com. of visitors Vanderbilt U. Engring. Schs.; mem. adv. coun. coll. bus. U. Tenn.; mem. Tenn. Indsl. and Agrl. Devel. Com., 1981-85; mem. alumni bd. Vanderbilt U.; co-chmn. Tenn. Tech. Corridor Task Force, 1982; elder First Presbyn. Ch.; dir., exec. com. Bill Wilkerson Hdqrs. and Spl. Ctr., Martha O'Bryan Bd. With USN, 1946-48. Named Jaycee Young Man of Yr., 1963. Mem. C. of C. Oak Ridge, Soc. Internat. Bus. Fellows, Tau Beta Pi, Omicron Delta Kappa, Beta Gamma Sigma. Club: Belle Meade Country, University. Lodge: Rotary (sr. active Nashville club, hon. mem. Oak Ridge).

YOUTAN, NORMAN, accounting executive; b. Los Angeles, Jan. 19, 1938; s. Joseph Stanley and Millie (Weisenfeld) Y.; m. Esther Bertha Schapira, Nov. 30, 1968; children: Caryn, Michael. BS, UCLA, 1960. CPA. Acct. Youtan, Cohen & Mann, Los Angeles, 1961-65; mgr., v.p. CCM Computax, El Segundo, Calif., 1965-78; gen. mgr. TACS div. Itel, Los Angeles, 1978-79; pres. TACS div. CSC (formerly div. Itel), Los Angeles, 1979—. Served with USAF, 1960-66. Mem. Am. Inst. CPA's, Calif. CPA Soc. Democrat. Jewish. Home: 19223 Berclair Ln Tarzana CA 91356 Office: CSC TACS Div 4515 Eagle Rock Blvd Los Angeles CA 90041 *

YU, AITING TOBEY, engineering executive; b. Chekiang, China, Jan. 6, 1921; came to U.S., 1945, naturalized, 1955; s. H.K. and A. (Chow) Y.; m. Natalie Kwok, Nov. 10, 1951; children: Pamela, Leonard T. BS, Nat. Cen. U., Chungking, China, 1943; SM, MIT, 1946; PhD, Lehigh U., 1949; MBA, Columbia U., 1972. Registered profl. engr., N.Y., N.J., Ala., Wis., Minn., Fla. Asst. prof. engring. NYU, 1949-51; design engr. Hewitt-Robins Inc. div. Litton Industries, 1951-54, chief design engr., 1955-58, engring. mgr., 1958-59; dir. systems engring. Hewitt-Robins Inc. div. Litton Industries, Totowa, N.J., 1967-68, v.p. ops., 1968-71; tech. dir. West S.Am. Overseas Corp., N.Y.C., 1959-67; prin. A.T. Yu Cons. Engrs., 1971-72; pres., chmn. Orba Corp., Mountain Lakes, N.J., 1972—. Contbr. articles to profl. jours.; patentee in field. Mem. AIME (chmn. minerals processing div., SME pres. 1986), NSPE, ASCE, Soc. Naval Architects and Marine Engrs., Nat. Acad. Forensic Engrs., Sigma Xi. Home: 3284 Masters Dr Clearwater FL 34621 Office: Orba Corp 49 Old Bloomfield Ave Mountain Lakes NJ 07046

YUDA, LAWRENCE FRANK, manufacturing executive; b. Cleve., Sept. 18, 1939; s. Frank James and Helen Marie (Balik) Y.; m. Sandra Lee Card, Feb. 14, 1959; children: Lawrence Jr., Lois, Tracie. BME, Fenn Coll., 1964. Draftsman Hertner Electric, Cleve., 1957-63; machine designer E.T.C. Inc., Cleve., 1963-68, supr. research and devel., 1968-74; founder, pres. Compact Air Products Inc., Cleve., 1974-79, Westminster, S.C., 1979—. Patentee in field. Named Businessman of Yr. Westminster C. of C., 1987. Mem. Nat. Assn. Mfrs., Soc. Mfg. Engrs., Robotic Industries Assn. Office: Compact Air Products Inc Hwy 123 PO Box 499 Westminster SC 29693

YUN, CHUL KOO, financial planning company executive; b. Seoul, Mar. 13, 1939; came to U.S., 1966; m. Insun Haw, Mar. 19, 1966; children: Charles T., Andrea S. BA, Seoul Nat. U., 1962; MBA, U. Ky., 1967; PhD, U. Mich., 1973. Cert. fin. planner. Mkt. analyst Gen. Motors Corp., Detroit, 1973-76, adminstr. internat. mktg., 1976-83, mgr. strategic study, gen. purchasing activities, 1983-87, commodity mgr. ferrous materials, purchasing activities, 1983-87; pres. C.K. Fin. Planning Svcs., Bloomfield Hills, MIch., 1987—. Served to lt. Korean Navy, 1963-66. Mem. Acad. Internat. Bus., Internat. Assn. for Fin. Planning, Inst. for Cert. Fin. Planners, Beta Gamma Sigma. Office: 5269 Fairmont Hill Ct Bloomfield Hills MI 48013

YUN, PETER SUBUENG, economics educator; b. Yong-Wol, Korea, June 7, 1936; s. Sea Young and Soon Oak (Kim) Y.; m. Sandy J. Forsythe, June 21, 1970; children: Amy Rebecca, Peter Jung. B.A., U. Ga., 1966, Ph.D., 1975; M.A., U. Okla., 1968. Asst. prof. econs. Clinch Valley Coll., Wise, Va., 1974-79, assoc. prof., 1979-86, prof., 1986—; chmn. bus. div., 1979-86. Pres., Universal Bus. Services, Wise, 1981—; dir. Va. Gov.'s Sch for the gifted Clinch Valley Coll., 1987—. Invest-in-America grantee, 1979, 80; recipient Outstanding Alumni award Emmanuel Coll., 1984. Mem. Am. Econ. Assn., So. Econ. Assn. Home: PO Box 2620 Wise VA 24293 Office: Clinch Valley Coll PO Box 16 Wise VA 24293

YURKO, ALLEN MICHAEL, finance company executive; b. Montreal, Que., Can., Sept. 25, 1951; came to U.S., 1959; s. Mike and Catherine (Ewanishan) Y.; m. Gayle Marie Skelley, Aug. 23, 1986 (div. Dec. 1987). BA in Bus. and Econs., Lehigh U., 1973; MBA, Baldwin-Wallace Coll., 1981. Acctg. mgr. Eaton Corp., Phila., 1973-77, asst. controller, 1977-78; group controller Cleve., 1982-83; div. controller Joy Mfg. Co., Franklin, Pa., 1978-82; chief fin. officer Mueller Holdings Corp., Annapolis, Md., 1983-89, also bd. dirs.; v.p. fin., chief fin. officer Siebe, Inc. Robert Shaw Controls Co., Richmond, Va., 1989—. Mem. Nat. Assn. Accts. (pres. local chpt. 1980-81), Am. Mgmt. Assn., Chartwell Country Club (Severna Park, Md.), Pleasure Cove Yacht Club. Republican. Presbyterian. Office: Mueller Holdings Corp 175 Admiral Cochrane Dr Annapolis MD 21401

YURTOGLU, KEMAL ALPAGO, mining engineer; b. Elazig, Turkey, Dec. 1, 1951; s. Fazil and Naciye (Ergin) Y.; m. Nesrin Kahraman; children: Ahu, Kaan. BS with high honors, Middle East Tech. U., Ankada, Turkey, 1976; MS with honors, Black Sea U., Trabzon, Turkey, 1987. Registered profl. mining and geology engr. Shift engr. Mortas Colemanite Mine, Buras, Turkey, 1974-76; underground prodn. engr. ETAS Zinc Mine, Izmir, Turkey; product mgr. ETAS Lead-Zinc Mine, Giresun, Turkey, 1979-86, gen. mgr., 1986—; tech. controller Phelps Dodge-Cayeli Project, Rize, Turkey. Served with Turkish Army, 1982. Mem. Chamber Mining Engrs., Rotary(Giresun chpt.). Club: Giresunspor. Home: Sahilyolu 1/4 Tirebolu, Giresun Turkey Office: ETAS Madencilik Ltd, Koprubasi Madeni Tirebolu, Giresun Turkey

YUTHASASTRKOSOL, CHARIN, real estate corporation officer, family business owner; b. Bangkok, Dec. 30, 1930; came to U.S., 1954; d. Luang Prasertwithirut and Jaruke (Boontham) B.; m. Prapakorn Yuthasastrkosol, Feb. 23, 1953. A, Strayer Coll., 1959. Dir. pub. realtions Twining Corp., Balt., 1979—; chmn. bd., chief exec. officer Yuthasart-Kosol, Inc., Havertown, Pa. Over 170 ballroom dancing awards, 1978—. Mem. Temple U. Assn. Ret. Profls. (faculty), Phila.-Del. Valley Restaurant Assn. (dir.), Bus. and Profl. Women Assn. Bangkok Thailand (life). Home: 2507 Darby Rd Havertown PA 19083 Office: Twining Corp 4004 Greenway Baltimore MD 21218

ZABAN, ERWIN, diversified manufacturing company executive; b. Atlanta, Aug. 17, 1921; s. Mandle and Sara Unis (Feidelson) Z.; m. Judy Zaban; children: Carol Zaban Cooper, Laura Zaban Dinerman, Sara Kay Franco. Officer Zep Mfg. Co., 1942-62; exec. v.p. Nat. Service Industries, Atlanta, 1962-66, pres., 1966-79, chief exec. officer, 1972-87, chmn., 1975, also dir.; bd. dir. Nat. Bank of Atlanta, Engraph, Inc., First Wachovia Corp.; elected mem. bd. visitors Berry Coll. Bd. dirs. Atlanta Symphony Orch., 1982, Jewish Home for the Aged, 1985; trustee Atlanta Hist. Soc., 1985. Named Man of Yr. B'nai B'rith, 1977, Father of Yr. Father's Day Council, 1982; recipient Disting. Service award Atlanta Urban League, 1979, Human Relations award Anti-Defamation League, 1981. Clubs: Progressive, Standard. Office: Nat Svs Industries Inc 1180 Peachtree St NE Atlanta GA 30309 *

ZABROSKE, JAMES GEORGE, financial executive; b. Chgo., June 21, 1958; s. Elmer Albert and LaVerne Marie (Claussen) Z. BS in Polit. Sci., Ariz. State U., 1981; postgrad., Northwestern U. Credit account mgr. Montgomery Ward Co., Chgo., 1982-84, sr. credit mgr., 1984-87; nat. collection mgr. World Book Fin., Inc., Chgo., 1987—. Mem. Chgo. Art Inst., Chgo. Lyric Opera. Republican. Home: 394 Graceland #12 Des Plaines IL 60016 Office: World Book Fin Inc Merchandise Mart Pla Chicago IL 60054

ZACCAGNI, RICHARD FRANKLIN, construction company executive; b. Springfield, Ill., Jan. 4, 1934; s. John Nonnie and Josephine Catherine (Bunker) Z.; m. Barbara Ann Konkal, Aug. 18, 1956; children: Andrea M. Wyer, Richard J., Gregory R., Patrice M. Student law, U. Detroit, 1952, 56. Rep. sales Burroughs Corp., Detroit, 1956-57, Campbell Soup Co., Detroit and Toledo, 1957-59; chief exec. officer Crystal Aluminum Products Co., Toledo, 1959-61; regional mgr. Airco/Hilite Co., Addison, Ill. and Toledo, 1961-66; owner, chief exec. officer ZMC, Inc., Addison, 1966—; trustee pension and welfare Sheet Metal Union, Carol Stream, Ill., 1986—; treas., bd. dirs. Cen. Credit Union, Bellwood, Ill., 1986—. Patentee in field. Served with USCG, 1953-55. Mem. Nat. Sheet Metal and Air Conditioning Contractors Assn., No. Ill. Sheet Metal Contractors Assn., Nat. Homebuilders Assn., No. Ill. Homebuilders Assn., Greater Chgo. Homebuilders Assn., Ill. Mfrs. Assn. Republican. Roman Catholic. Home: 3729 Venard Downers Grove IL 60515

ZACCONE, SUZANNE MARIA, sales executive; b. Chgo., Oct. 23, 1957; d. Dominic Robert and Lorretta F. (Urban) Z. Grad. high sch., Downers Grove, Ill. Sales sec. Brookeridge Realty, Downers Grove, 1975-76; sales cons. Kafka Estates Inc., Downers Grove, 1975-76; adminstrv. asst. Chem. Dist., Inc., Oak Brook, Ill., 1976-77; sales rep., mgr. Anographics Corp., Burr Ridge, Ill., 1977-85; pres., owner Graphic Solutions, Inc., Downers Grove, 1985—. Recipient Supplier Mem. award Internat. Bottled Water Assn., 1987-88; named Supplier of Yr. Gen. Binding Corp., 1988. Mem. Women in Mgmt., Nat. Assn. Female Execs., Sales and Mktg. Execs. of Chgo., Women Entrepreneurs of DuPage County (budget chmn.). Avocations: reading, sailing, cooking, needlepoint, scuba diving. Office: Graphic Solutions Inc 150 Shore Dr Burr Ridge IL 60521

ZACH, DAVID MICHAEL, futurist, public speaker; b. Monroe, Wis., Aug. 15, 1957; s. Robert Gladwin and Margaret (Sanders) Z. BA in Polit. Sci., U. Wis., 1979; MS in Future Studies, U. Houston, 1981. Forecasting analyst Johnson Controls, Milw., 1980-82; adj. prof. Sch. Edn. U. Wis., Milw., 1982-85; trend analyst Northwestern Mut. Life Ins. Co., Milw., 1984-87; owner, mgr. Innovative Futures, Milw., 1987—; adj. prof. Carthage Coll;, Kenosha, Wis., 1988—. Pub. newsletter Directions, 1987—. Mem. Future Milw., 1984; chmn. edn. com., bd. dirs. Goals for Greater Milw. 2000, 1980-83; mem. sch. mgmt. coun. Kosciuszko Sch., 1987—. Mem. Nat. Speakers Assn., Wis. Profl. Speakers Assn., Kiwanis. Office: Innovative Futures PO Box 11077 Milwaukee WI 53202

ZACH, W. CHRISTIAN, banker; b. Vienna, Austria, May 17, 1946; came to U.S., 1965; s. Franz and Anny Z.; m. Diane Zach, June 17, 1978; 1 child, Anne-Marie. BS in Fin., Calif. State U., Sacramento, 1976; MBA, Golden Gate U., 1980. Vis. prof. Kepler Universität, Linz, Austria, 1981—; adj. prof. Golden Gate U., 1980—; pres. Sierra Resources, Rancho Cordova, Calif., 1982-83, also bd. dirs.; pres. Mercantile Bank, Sacramento, 1984—, also bd. dirs. Served with U.S. Army, 1966-68, USAFR, 1973-82. Mem. Fin. Mgmt. Honor Soc., Vietnam Vets. Leadership Program. Address: Mercantile Bank 455 Capitol Mall Sacramento CA 95814

ZACHARIAH, BOBBY VERGHESE, beverage company executive; b. India, June 23, 1942; came to U.S., 1971; s. A.V. and Mary (Verghese) Z.; m. Liby Ann Thomas, Sept. 14, 1969; children: Vinoo, Anita. BS in Elec. Engring., Birla Inst. Tech. and Sci., Pilani, India, 1966; MBA, Lynchburg Coll., 1976. Grad. trainee, project engr. Tata Iron and Steel Co., Jamshedpur, India, 1966-73; buyer, sr. buyer Nuclear Power Generation Co. Babcock & Wilcox, Lynchburg, Va., 1973-78; mgr. purchasing Bailey Controls div. Babcock & Wilcox, Wickliffe, Ohio, 1978-80; mgr. purchasing Adolph Coors Co., Golden, Colo., 1980-81, dir. purchasing, 1981, dir. project materials and contracts, 1981-88, dir. plant materials, 1988—. Chmn. Pvt. Industry Council Jefferson County (Colo.), 1986—; mem. Jefferson County Corrections Bd., 1986—; mem. vestry St. James Episc. Ch., Wheat Ridge, Colo., 1985—. Mem. Nat. Assn. Purchasing Mgmt. (cert. purchasing mgr.), Am. Prodn. and Inventory Control Soc. (cert. in prodn. and inventory mgmt.), Nat. Contracts Mgmt. Assn. Republican. Home: 2961 Kendrick St Golden CO 80401 Office: Adolph Coors Co 12th and Ford Golden CO 80401

ZACHARIAS, JAMES, sales representative; b. Dunkirk, N.Y.; s. Casper and Catherine Elizabeth (McKeon) Z.; m. Kathryn Ann Wuersile, June 25, 1960; children; Catherine, Ann Marie, Rosemary, Paul, Christopher, Stephen. BBA, St. Bonaventure U., 1955. Records supr. Cease Commissary Systems, Dunkirk, 1955-56; sales rep. CT Corp. Systems, Buffalo, Cleve., 1959-63, ADT Protection, Cleve., Cin., 1964-76; sales rep., sr. sales rep. Honeywell Protection, Cin., 1976—. With U.S. Army, 1956-58. Mem. Am. Soc. Indsl. Security, So. Ohio Indsl. Fire Protection Assn. Office: Honeywell Protection Svcs Div 1131 Race St Cincinnati OH 45210

ZACHARIAS, RITA TIMMONS, realtor; b. Dagsboro, Del., Jan. 31, 1934; d. William Edgar and Ethel Mae (Burton) Timmons; m. Jerrold Matthew Zacharias, Aug. 14, 1954; children: Jerrold Matthew, Dana Timmons, David Stuart. BA, U. Del., 1955. Realtor Rucker Enterprises and Realtors, Arlington, Va., 1976—. Mem. Dulin United Meth. Women, past pres. Mem. Million Dollar Sales Club (multiple listing svc. com. 1987—). Democrat. Home: 2333 N Oak St Falls Church VA 22046 Office: Rucker Enterprises and Realtors 1403 N Courthouse Rd Arlington VA 22201

ZACHARIAS, THOMAS ELLING, real estate developer; b. Morristwon, N.J., Feb. 19, 1954; s. John Elling and Muriel (Eckes) Z.; m. Clelia LeBoutillier, June 22, 1985; children: Clelia Delafield, John Livingston. BArch and Urban Planning, Princeton U., 1976; M in Pub. and Pvt. Mgmt., Yale U., 1979. Project dir. N.Y. State Urban Devel. Corp., N.Y.C., 1979-81; assoc. Corp. Property Investors, N.Y.C., 1981-83, asst. v.p., 1983-86, v.p., 1986—. Chmn. Mus. Modern Art Adv. Svc., N.Y.C., 1981-87; mem. steering com. Whitney Mus. Lobby Gallery Assocs., N.Y.C., 1985—; bd. dirs. Creative Time, N.Y.C., 1982-88, Nat. Acad. Design, 1988—. Fgn. Study grantee McConnel Found., London, 1975. Mem. Nat. Acad. Design (bd. dirs. 1988—), Internat. Counc. Shopping Ctrs., Yale Club, Meadow Club. Home: 1255 Fifth Ave New York NY 10029 Other: 65 Post Crossing Southampton NY 11968 Office: Corp Property Investors 305 E 47th St New York NY 10017

ZACHARY, LOUIS GEORGE, manufacturer, chemical consultant; b. Cambridge, Mass., Aug. 14, 1927; s. George E. and Angelike (Hantsis) Zacharakis; A.B. in Chemistry, Harvard U., 1950; M.B.A., Columbia U., 1951; m. Lillie Vletas, Apr. 20, 1955; children—Leslie A., Louis George. Prodn. supr. Dewey & Almy Co., Acton, Mass., 1951-52; salesman chem. div. Union Camp Corp., Wayne, N.J., 1952-59, sales mgr. chem. div., 1959-62, gen. mgr. chem. ops., 1962-66, gen. mgr. chem. div., 1970-78, v.p., 1974-78; v.p. Drake Mgmt Co., N.Y.C., 1966-70; sr. v.p. GAF Corp., N.Y.C., 1978-82, mem. office of chmn., 1981-82; cons., 1983-84; chmn., chief exec. officer Universal Die Casting, Inc., Saline, Mich., 1984—. Mem. vis. com. chem. engring. dept. Johns Hopkins U., Balt., 1981-83. Served with USN, 1945-46. Mem. Chem. Mfrs. Assn. (dir. 1979-83), Synthetic Organic Chem. Mfrs. Assn., Soc. Chem. Industry. Clubs: Baltusrol Golf; Harvard (N.Y.C.). Co-editor: Tall Oil and Its Uses, 1965. other: 3485 Narrow Gauge Way Ann Arbor MI 48105-2576

ZACHARY, RONALD F., retail executive; b. Los Angeles, Aug. 18, 1938; s. Raymond and Anne Marie (Klimo) Z.; m. Yvonne Marie MacKinnon, Aug. 29, 1959; children—Matthew, Deanna. B.S., U. San Francisco, 1963. Mgr. pub. relations Safeway Stores, Inc., Washington, 1970-71, mgr. employee pub. relations, 1971-74; mgr. personnel systems Safeway Stores, Inc., Oakland, Calif., 1974-78, mgr. personnel services, 1978-79, v.p., 1979-86, exec. officer, sr. v.p. human resources, 1986—; dir. Heals HMO, Emeryville, Calif. Trustee Alta Bates Hosp. Served with U.S. Army, 1957-63. Mem. Am. Mgmt. Assn., Nat. Assn. Employers on Health Care Alternatives (chmn. 1985-86), San Francisco Bus. Group on Health (vice chmn. 1982—). Republican. Roman Catholic. Club: Oakland Athletic. Office: Safeway Stores Inc 201 4th St Oakland CA 94660

ZACHMANN, WILLIAM FRANCIS, computer/communications industry market research company executive; b. Cleve., Oct. 19, 1942; s. Kurt Wilhelm and Jean (O'Konski) Z.; BA, Harvard U., 1966; m. Elizabeth Ann Loftus, June 7, 1980. Programmer/analyst Cambridge Computer Assocs. (Mass.), 1967-69; systems research officer First Nat. Bank Boston, 1969-74; dir. research Forum Corp., Boston, 1974-75; coordinator personnel adminstrn. Harvard U., Cambridge, 1976-77; mgr. tech. support CallData Systems, Boston, 1977-79; v.p. tech. assessment Internat. Data Corp., Framingham, Mass., 1979-83; v.p. corp. research Internat. Data Corp., Framingham, Mass., 1983-87, sr. v.p., 1987-88; pres. Canopus Research, Duxbury, Mass., 1988—. Mem. City Mgrs. Adv. Com. on Cable TV, Cambridge, 1979-83. Mem. IEEE., Assn. for Computing Machinery, Harvard (Boston), Harvard Faculty (Cambridge). Author: Keys to Application Development Productivity, 1981; contbg. editor Computer Industry Report, 1982-88, Communications and Distributed Resources Report, 1983-87 , PC World mag., 1987-88; columnist On Communications mag., 1984-86, Software News mag., 1984-86, Computerworld mag., 1986-88, Infoworld mag., 1987-88, Micromarketworld mag., 1985-87, PC Mag., 1988—, PC Week mag., 1988—, MacUser mag., 1988—. Home: 160 Standish St PO Box 1540 Duxbury MA 02331 Office: Canopus Rsch PO Box 2805 Duxbury MA 02331

ZACKS, HYMAN JOSEPH, lawyer, accountant; b. Bklyn., Mar. 22, 1938; s. Archie and Fannie (Jablonski) Z.; m. Sulamita Weingort, Feb. 21, 1970 (div. June 1984); children: Michelle, Steven, Michael; m. Valerie Ann Nemeth, Oct. 28, 1984. BSBA, U. Denver, 1959; JD, NYU, 1963, LLM in Taxation, 1966. Bar: N.Y. State 1967, U.S. Tax Ct. 1967, U.S. Supreme Ct. 1970; CPA, Calif., N.Mex., Tex. Tax mgr. Oppenheim, Appel & Dixon, N.Y.C., 1970-72; ptnr. Levitz, Zacks & Ciceric, Inc., San Diego, 1972—; instr. acctg. U. Calif., San Diego, 1975-80, 81, Calif. Continuing Edn. of Bar, 1982. With U.S. Army, 1963. Mem. Am. Inst. CPA's, Calif. Soc. CPA's, Am. Assn. Atty-CPA's. Office: Levitz Zacks & Ciceric Inc 701 B St 4th fl San Diego CA 92101

ZAFERIOU, PAUL JOHN, retail owner; b. Bronx, N.Y., Apr. 9, 1934; s. John A. and Julia A. (Gorgey) Z.; m. Phyllis K. Stephanou, July 12, 1959; children: Julie, Stephanie, Diane. AAS in Hort., Cornell U., 1954; AAS in Acctg., Westchester Community Coll., 1970; BA in Mgmt., Pace U., 1974; postgrad., NYU, 1986—. Lic. real estate broker, N.Y. Chmn. bd. Colony Flower Shop Inc., White Plains, N.Y., 1957—; pres. Viz-A-Viz Inc., White Plains, 1973—; v.p. White Plains Wholesale Inc., 1986—; pres. Nycomn. Trustee Greek Orthodox Ch. of Savior, Rye, N.Y. 1965-71; pres. Good Counsel Acad. Fathers Club, White Plains, 1977-79, United Way, White Plains, 1980-81, dist. chmn. Boy Scouts of Am., Westchester County, 1981-82, bd. dirs. Cen. Westchester YMCA, White Plains, 1985—, Rep. City Com. White Plains, 1983—, U.S. Selective Svc., 1984—; mem. White Plains Vol. Fire Dept., Keep White Plains Clean Com., 1981, Citizens Budget Rev. Com. exec. com. White Plains Rep. Com. 1983—, campaign mgr., 1981-85, dist. leader, 1981—; mem. adv. bd. Salvation Army. Served with U.S. Army, 1955-57. Recipient award for bus. ethics Westchester County C. of C. Mem. White Plains C. of C. (founder retail coun. 1967, chmn. civic and beautification com 1963), Univ. Club (pres. 1980-81), N.Y. Teleflora Internat. (bd. dirs. 1986—), Lions Club Internat., Sigma Alpha Epsilon. Republican. Lodges: Rotary (bd. dirs. 1985—), Masons. Home: 17 Richbell Rd White Plains NY 10605 Office: 55 Church St White Plains NY 10601

ZAGAR, LAWRENCE THOMAS, financial executive; b. Aliquippa, Pa., Apr. 17, 1921; s. Anthony and Mary (Padavich) Z.; B.S., St. Vincent Coll., Latrobe, Pa., 1944, postgrad. Southwestern U., Los Angeles, 1953, UCLA, 1955-60; Ph.D. (hon.), 1974; m. Sylvia Louise Puskarich, May 11, 1946; 1 son, Terence Richard. Controller, Cath. Youth Orgn., Archidocese of Los Angeles, 1947-51; cost acct. Solar Mfg. Corp., 1953; cost acct. Ducommun Metals & Supply Co., Los Angeles, 1954-56, mgr. profit improvement dept., 1957-60, project control mgr., 1958-60, corp. budget mgr., 1960-62; mgr. fin. planning and controls Riverside Cement Co., Los Angeles, 1962-63; v.p. fin. Medallion Printers & Lithographers, Los Angeles, 1963-64, also dir.; asst. sec.-treas., controller Pacific Western Industries, Inc., Los Angeles, 1965-66, asst. sec., 1966-67; sec.-treas. Simi Valley Rock Products, Inc., 1965-70, Glenn E. Walker Corp., Walnut, Calif., 1965-67, Mountain Rock Products, Upland, Calif., 1965-67; pres. Furnishings Complete, Los Angeles, 1967-69; chief adminstrv. officer Jules Strongbow Enterprises, Inc., Los Angeles, 1968-70; v.p. Fin. Communications Clearing House, Los Angeles, 1970-71, pres., 1971-85, pres. emeritus, 1985—, also dir.; mem. U.S. Senatorial Bus. Adv. Bd., 1980-84, 87—; Joint Presdl./Congl. Steering Com., 1980-84; spl. adv. U.S. Congressional Adv. Bd., 1984-87. Mem. Calif. Athletic Commn.; mem. So. Calif. Golden Gloves Com., 1948-68; bd. dirs. Boxers and Wrestlers Fund, Inc.; bd. govs., chmn. fin. com. Vols. of Am., Los Angeles, 1978—; mem. pres.'s council Calif. State Poly. U., 1980—. Served from pvt. to 1st lt. USMC, 1942-46, comdg. officer, 1951-53, maj., 1954. Recipient Letterman of Distinction award St. Vincent Coll., 1984. Mem. St. Vincent Alumni Assn. Republican. Roman Catholic. Author articles in field. Home: 4360 W 4th St Los Angeles CA 90020 Office: 3691 Bandini Blvd Los Angeles CA 90023

ZAHARY, ROBERT GENE, accounting educator; b. West Frankfort, Ill., Sept. 30, 1942; s. Joe and Iona Madge (Culley) Z. BS, Oreg. State U., 1965; MBA, U. So. Calif., 1972, PhD, 1982; BA, Calif. State U., Los Angeles, 1975. CPA, Calif. Mng. ptnr. Pasadena (Calif.) Vinyl Products, 1967-69; acct. Lee Sheridan & Co., Los Angeles, 1969-70; assoc. prof. biology Calif. State U., Los Angeles, 1982-84, asst. prof. acctg., 1984-87, assoc. prof., 1987—, assoc. v.p. ops., 1988—; coordinator Orgn. Tropical Studies, San Jose, Costa Rica, 1983. Editor: Tropical Biology: An Ecological Approach, 1985; contbr. articles to profl. jours. Grantee Lerner Grey Fund for Marine Research, Theodore Roosevelt Meml. Fund for Wildlife Research, Janss Found., ARC. Fellow So. Calif. Acad. Scis. (treas. 1983-84, v.p. 1985-87, pres. 1987-89, bd. dirs. 1980—); mem. AICPA, Calif. State Soc. CPAs, Sigma Xi (grantee). Home: 1480 N Mentor Pasadena CA 91104 Office: Calif State U 5151 State Univ Dr Los Angeles CA 90032

ZAHM, ROCK L., corporate executive, electronics instructor; b. Huntington, Ind., Jan. 6, 1961; s. Eldon L. and Patricia M. (Hiser) Z.; m. Tanya Ann Harter, Jan. 26, 1985. AS in Elec. Engring., ITT Tech. Inst., 1981. Registered profl. engr., Ind. Foreman Ft. Wayne (Ind.) Irrigation Svc., 1977-86; electronic engr. govt. and indsl. Magnavox, Ft. Wayne, 1981-86; instr. electronics Ft. Wayne Community Schs., 1986—; pres. Zahm Industries Inc., Ft. Wayne, 1986—; engr. Sta. WMEE/WQHK, Ft. Wayne, 1986—; chief instr. Specialty Vehicle Inst. Am., Costa Mesa, Calif., 1985—. Democrat. Roman Catholic. Office: Preferred Irrigation 408 Ross St Fort Wayne IN 46802-1011

ZAISER, SALLY SOLEMMA VANN, retail book company executive; b. Birmingham, Ala., Jan. 18, 1917; d. Carl Waldo and Einnan (Herndon) Vann; student Birmingham-So. Coll., 1933-36, Akron Coll. Bus., 1937; m. Foster E. Zaiser, Nov. 11, 1939. Acct., A. Simionato, San Francisco, 1958-65; head acctg. dept. Richard T. Clarke Co., San Francisco, 1966; acct. John Howell-Books, San Francisco, 1967-72, sec., treas., 1972-83, 84-85, dir., 1982-85; sec. Great Eastern Mines, Inc., Albuquerque, 1969-81, dir., 1980-85. Braille transcriber for ARC, Kansas City, Mo. 1941-45; vol. worker ARC Hosp. Program, São Paulo, Brazil, 1952. Mem. Book Club Calif., Calif. Hist. Soc., Soc. Lit. and Arts, Gleeson Library Assocs. (dir. 1984-87, editor GLA newsletter 1984-87), Nat. Notary Assn., Capital Hill Club, Theta Upsilon. Republican. Episcopalian. Home: 355 Serrano Dr Apt 4-C San Francisco CA 94132

ZAJAC, SCOTT ALLEN, banker; b. Chgo., Aug. 6, 1960; s. Richard Anthony and Nora Edith (James) Z.; m. Jan Annette Parker, Oct. 19, 1960. BS in Pub. Adminstrn., U. Mo., 1983; MBA in Fin., St. Louis U., 1986. Cert. Cash Mgr. Corp cash mgr. Citicorp Mortgage, Inc., St. Louis, 1986-1988, staff v.p. sr. cash, bond analyst, 1988--; cons. Realty Exchange Inc., St. Louis, 1987--. Mem. Sigma Phi Epsilon (alumni officer 1987), Nat. Corp Cash Mgmt. Assn., Mo. Realtors Assn., Nat. Assn. Realtors. Republican. Roman Catholic. Home: 1030 N Harrison Kirkwood MO 63122 Office: Citicorp Mortgage Inc 15851 Clayton Rd Saint Louis MO 63011

ZAJONC, GUY MATTHEW, lawyer, venture management company executive; b. Beverly, Mass., June 15, 1952; s. Fred Henery and Margaret Harlow (Shelton) Z.; m. Susan Jarratt, July 14, 1974; children: Austen Adams, Taylor Jarratt. BS in Bus., So. Ill. U., 1974; JD, Gonzaga U., 1977. Bar: Wash. 1977, U.S. Dist. Ct. (ea. dist.) Wash. 1978. Ptnr. Zajonc & Jolicoeur, Spokane, Wash., 1978-88; sec.-treas., gen. counsel Buffalo Inc., Spokane, 1984-88; pres. Quest Venture Mgmt. Inc., Spokane, 1987—, Q.M. Venture Group Ltd., Spokane, 1987-88; mng. ptnr. Quest Venture Ptnrs., L.P., Spokane, 1988—. Mem. region I adv. bd. Wash. Dept. Social and Health Services, 1982. Nat. Collegiate Athletics Assn. scholar, 1970--74. Mem. Wash. State Bar Assn., Spokane Bar Assn. Office: S 528 Lincoln St Spokane WA 99204

ZAK, LEONARD EUGENE, lawyer; b. Chgo., Mar. 22, 1929; s. Eugene Albert and Rose (Grezegorski) Z.; m. Bonnie Haberer; children: Peter Sperry, David Grinnell, Megan Merritt, Ursula Kinnerly. BA, Carleton Coll., 1951; JD, Northwestern U., 1954. Bar: Ill. 1954. Assoc. McBride & Baker, Chgo., 1956-65; ptnr. McBride & Baker, 1965-80; v.p., gen. counsel Harza Engring. Co., Chgo., 1980—; bd. dirs. Stenning Industries, Inc., Chgo., Profl. Soc. Ins. Svc., Inc., Chgo., Alpha Grove, Inc., Chgo. Bd. dirs. Mark Morton Meml. Fund, Chgo.; spl. asst. to U.S. Atty. Gen., Chgo., Washington, 1967-68. With U.S. Army, 1954-56. Mem. ABA, Chgo. Bar Assn., Ill. Bar Assn., Tower Club (Chgo.). Republican. Episcopalian. Home: 2738 Woodbine Evanston IL 60201 Office: Harza Engring Co 150 S Wacker Dr Chicago IL 60606

ZAK, SUZANNE, securities analyst; b. Passaic, N.J., Dec. 16, 1959; d. Edward and Teresa (Marchinak) Z. BA, Princeton U., 1982; MBA, Rutgers U., 1983. Chartered fin. analyst. Analyst Axe-Houghton Mgmt., Tarrytown, N.Y., 1983-85; v.p. J & W Seligman and Co., N.Y.C., 1985—. Mem. N.Y. Soc. of Securities Analysts, Fin. Analysts Fedn. Roman Catholic. Club: Princeton (N.Y.C.). Home: 94 Daniel Ave Rutherford NJ 07070 Office: J & W Seligman and Co One Bankers Trust Plaza New York NY 10006

ZAKI, OMAR S., hospitality company executive, physician; b. Lahore, Pakistan, Apr. 15, 1945; came to U.S., 1967; s. Mohammed A. and Bashir N. Zaki; m. Anne Louise Ross, July 23, 1977; children: Alexander, Sarah, Jason. MD, Harvard U., 1973. Diplomate Am. Bd. Internal Medicine. Resident Lenox Hill Hosp., N.Y.C., 1962; intern Beth Israel Med. Ctr., N.Y.C., 1967; resident Peter Bent Brigham Hosp., Boston, 1973; practice medicine specializing in internal medicine Falls Church, Va., 1976—; pres. Va. Investment Group Inc., Falls Church, Va., 1980—, Va. Hospitality Assocs., Inc., Falls Church, Va., 1982—; chmn. bd. dirs. Franklin's Printing and Publishing Co., Rockville, Md. Mem. Am. Hotel and Motel Assn., Fairfax County C. of C. Club: Harvard. Office: Va Hospitality Assocs Inc 7700 Lessburg Pike Falls Church VA 22043

ZAKIN, JONATHAN NEWELL, computer industry executive; b. Suffern, N.Y., Aug. 18, 1949; s. Paul Peter and Shirley Ruth (Friedman) Z.; m. Esther Karlinsky, Jan. 1972 (div. Aug. 1976); m. Andrea Elisabeth Schutze, June 9, 1984; children: Carl Hartwig, Hans Christopher. BS in Mgmt., NYU, 1971; MBA, Harvard U., 1976. Mgr. fin. planning Prudential Lines Inc., N.Y.C., 1971-74, asst. to pres., 1976-77; assoc. J. Henry Schroder Corp., N.Y.C., 1977-78; gen. mgr. Brisk & Kindle Ltd., London, 1978-80; pres. Cosma Internat., Brussels, 1980-84; v.p. sales and mktg. Winterhalter, Inc., Ann Arbor, Mich., 1984-86; exec. v.p. mktg. and sales U.S. Robotics, Inc., Skokie, Ill., 1987—. Mem. Monroe Club, Harvard Club. Home: 1546 Green Bay Rd Highland Park IL 60035 Office: US Robotics 8100 N McCormick Ave Skokie IL 60076

ZALAZNICK, DAVID WAYNE, investment banker, investor; b. N.Y.C., Apr. 16, 1954; s. Louis H. and Ruth F. Zalaznick; BA, Cornell U., 1976; MBA, Columbia U., 1978; m. Barbara Milstein, June 3, 1979. Assoc. in investment banking Merrill Lynch White Weld Capital Markets Group, 1978-80; v.p. Carl Marks & Co. Inc., 1980-82; ptnr. Jordan Co., N.Y.C., 1982—; mng. ptnr. Jordan/Zalaznick, Capital Co., 1985—; pres. Jordan/Zalaznick Realty Ventures, 1986—; pres. Jordan/Zalaznick Advisors, Inc., 1986—; bd. dirs. Carmike Cinemas Inc., House of Ronnie Inc., Allied Wholesale Inc., Marisa Christina Inc., Jones Mfg. Co. Inc., Jordan Industries, Inc., Eastern Home Products, Inc., Paco Holdings Inc., Cape Craftsmen, Inc., Indsl. Sales Co., Inc., Gator Holdings, Inc., Seagull Lighting Products, Inc., Am. Safety Razor, Inc. Office: 315 Park Ave S New York NY 10010

ZALECKI, PAUL HENRY, lawyer, automotive executive; b. Toledo, Oct. 14, 1931; s. Walter D. and Hattie S. (Oniszko) Z.; m. Mary Louise Sakowski, Sept. 29, 1956; 1 child, Karen Ann. A.B. magna cum laude, U. Notre Dame, 1953; LL.B. magna cum laude, Harvard U., 1956. Bar: Mich. 1957, Ohio 1960. Atty. Kaiser Jeep Corp., Toledo, 1961-66; atty. Gen. Motors Corp., Detroit, 1966—, v.p., sec. Served with U.S. Army, 1956-58. Mem. ABA, Ohio and Mich. Bar Assns. Republican. Roman Catholic. Clubs: Bloomfield Hills Country, Renaissance (Detroit), Inverness (Toledo). Home: 1371 Cedar Bend Dr Bloomfield Hills MI 48013

ZALOKAR, ROBERT FRANK, truck manufacturing company executive; b. Cleve., May 6, 1931; s. Frank and Mary Z.; m. Donna J. Blaskevica, Aug. 22, 1953; children: Laura, Debbie, Patrice, Barbara, Lisa, Robert. BS in Mech. Engring., Gen. Motors Inst., 1953; postgrad., Harvard U., 1980. Registered profl. engr., Md. Supr. diesel engine div. GM, Cleve., 1953-59; research engr. Mack Trucks, Inc., Allentown, Pa., 1959-60, mgr. applied mech. sect., 1960-65, exec. engr. research, 1965-66, mgr. research dept., 1966-69, mgr. devel. and test ctr., 1969-71, chief engr. vehicle devel. lab., 1971-77, dir. product devel., 1977-78, v.p. product devel., 1978-82, sr. v.p. product and engring., 1982-84, exec. v.p. product and engring., 1984—; Trustee GMI Engring. and Mgmt. Inst., Flint, Mich., 1986—. Mem. Soc. Automotive Engrs. Roman Catholic. Office: Mack Trucks Inc 2100 Mack Blvd Box M Allentown PA 18105

ZAMPELAS, MICHAEL HERODOTOU, accountant; b. Nicosia, Cyprus, Mar. 19, 1937; s. Herodotos and Maria (Michael) Z.; m. Loukia Rodhitou, Sept. 8, 1958; children—Koula, Maria, Irene. F.C.A., Inst. Chartered Accts. in Eng. and Wales, 1960-65. Sr., Maiden Penny Quick & Co., London, 1960-66; mgr. Price Waterhouse, Nicosia, 1966-68; ptnr. Ioannou, Zampelas & Co., 1968-70; chmn., mng. ptnr. Coopers & Lybrand/Ioannou, Zampelas & Co., 1970—. Loan commr. Govt. of Cyprus, Nicosia, 1982-88 ; chmn. bd. dirs. Cyprus Forest Industries Ltd., 1983—, Cyprus Ports Authority, 1986-88. Author: Cyprus-The Way for Businessmen and Investors, 1984, 2d edit., 1987; co-author Developing Cyprus into a Financial and Commercial Centre, 1987. Fellow Inst. Chartered Accts. in Eng. and Wales; mem. Inst. C.P.A. of Cyprus (pres. 1978-80), Cyprus-Am. Assn., Cyprus-Austrian Assn., Inst. Dirs. London. Christian Orthodox. Club: London-Am. Lodges: Rotary, Lions, Masons. Office: Coopers & Lybrand/Ioannou Zampelas & Co, 3 Themistocle, 3 Themistocles Dervis St, POB 1612, Nicosia Cyprus

ZAMPIELLO, RICHARD SIDNEY, metals and trading company executive; b. New Haven, May 7, 1933; s. Sidney Nickolas and Louise Z.; B.A., Trinity Coll., 1955; M.B.A., U. Bridgeport, 1961; m. Helen Shirley Palsa, Oct. 10, 1961; 1 son, Geoffrey Richard. With Westinghouse Elec. Corp., Pitts., 1955-64; exec. v.p. Ullrich Copper Corp., subs. Foster Wheeler, Kenilworth, N.J., 1964-71; sr. v.p. Gerald Metals, Inc., Stamford, Conn., 1971-85; group v.p. Diversified Industries Corp., St. Louis, 1985—; pres. Plume and Atwood Brass Mill div. Diversified Industries Corp., Thomaston, Conn., 1985—. Mem. ASME, Soc. Mfg. Engrs., AIME. Clubs: Yale, Mining (N.Y.C.); Lake Waramug Country (Washington, Conn.), Washington Country. Home: Woodbury Rd Washington CT 06793 Office: 235 E Main St Thomaston CT 06787 also: Diversified Industries Inc 101 S Hanley Rd Clayton MO 63105

ZANOT, CRAIG ALLEN, lawyer; b. Wyandotte, Mich., Nov. 15, 1955; s. Thomas and Faye Blanch (Sperry) Z. AB with distinction, U. Mich., 1977; JD cum laude, Ind. U., 1980. Bar: Ind. 1980, U.S. Dist. Ct. (so. dist.) Ind. 1980, U.S. Dist. Ct. (no. dist.) Ind. 1981, U.S. Ct. Appeals (6th cir.) 1985, U.S. Dist. Ct. (ea. dist.) Mich. 1987. Law clk. to presiding justice Allen County Superior Ct, Ft. Wayne, 1980-81; ptnr. Davidson, Breen & Doud P.C., Saginaw, Mich., 1981—. Mem. ABA, Mich. Bar Assn., Ind. Bar Assn., Saginaw County Bar Assn. Roman Catholic. Home: 2085 Marlou Ct Saginaw MI 48603 Office: Davidson Breen & Doud PC 1121 N Michigan Ave Saginaw MI 48602

ZARB, FRANK GUSTAVE, investment company executive; b. N.Y.C., Feb. 17, 1935; s. Gustave and Rosemary (Antinora) Z.; m. Patricia Koster, Mar. 31, 1957; children: Krista Ann, Frank, Jr. B.B.A., Hofstra U., 1957, M.B.A., 1962, L.H.D., 1975. Trainee Cities Service Oil Co., N.Y.C., 1957-62; gen. partner Goodbody & Co., N.Y.C., 1962-69; exec. v.p. CBWL-Hayden Stone, Inc. (investment banking), N.Y.C., 1969-71; asst. sec. U.S. Dept. Labor, Washington, 1971-72; exec. v.p. Hayden Stone, Inc., N.Y.C., 1972-73; assoc. dir. Office of Mgmt. and Budget, Washington, 1973-74; asst. to Pres., U.S., 1974-77; adminstr. Fed. Energy Adminstrn., Washington, 1974-77; adv. U.S. Congress and State of Alaska, 1977-78; gen. ptnr. Lazard Freres & Co., N.Y.C., 1977—; director Securities Investor Protection Corp, Washington, 1988—; dir. Energy Fund, Hay Systems, Inc., Lazard Asia Ltd., Comml. Credit Co. Author: The Stockmarket Handbook, 1969, Handbook of Financial Markets, The Municipal Bond Handbook. Bd. dirs. Nat. Council for U.S.-China Trade, Council for U.S. and Italy; trustee Gerald R. Ford Found.; chmn. bd. trustees Hofstra U., 1986-87. Recipient Disting. Scholar award Hofstra U., 1974. Mem. Am. Soc. Pub. Adminstrn. (hon. life), Council Fgn. Relations, Securities Investor Protection Corp. Office: Lazard Freres & Co One Rockefeller Plaza New York NY 10020

ZAREMBO, THEODORE ANDREW, real estate appraiser; b. Mineola, N.Y., Dec. 31, 1946; s. Theodore and Mary (Krawiec) Z.; m. Catherine Skahill, Aug. 7, 1977; children: Jordan, Brendan, Garret. BA, Adelphi U., 1971. Real estate appraiser Joseph J. Balke & Assoc., Woodbury, N.Y., 1974-77; asst. v.p. Chem. Bank, N.Y.C., 1977-83; v.p., mgr. Coldwell Banker Comml. Group, N.Y.C., 1983-88, 1st. v.p. ea. div., mgr. adv. svcs., 1988—. Sgt. U.S. Army, 1971-73. Mem. Am. Inst. Real Estate Appraisers (N.Y. chmn. admissions 1987-88, admissions com. 1983-86, asst. chief examiner bd. examiners 1985-88, bd. dirs. 1988—). Roman Catholic. Home: 21 Chestnut St Garden City NY 11501 Office: Coldwell Banker Adv Svcs 437 Madison Ave New York NY 10022

ZARWAN, JOHN, infosystems specialists; b. N.Y.C., May 25, 1949; s. Saul David and Shirley (Frolick) Z.; m. Sandra Horne, June 21, 1973; children: Elijah Joseph, Aaron Frederick. AB, Stanford U., 1970, MA, Yale U., 1972, M of Philosophy, 1973, PhD, 1977. Asst. prof. Coll. Charleston (S.C.), 1976-79; hon. fellow dept. agrl. econs. U. Wis., Madison, 1978-79; assoc. Pims Assocs. Strategic Planning Inst., Cambridge, Mass., 1979-81; v.p. Pims Assocs. Strategic Planning Inst., Cambridge, 1981-84; mgr. bus. devel. Compugraphic Corp., Wilmington, Mass., 1984-85; sr. product mgr. Compugraphic Corp., Wilmington, 1985-86, mgr. market planning, 1986; dir. planning NEC Info. Systems, Boxboro, Mass., 1986—; speaker in field. Contbr. articles to profl. jours. Named Outstanding Young American, 1977. Mem. Am. Econs. Assn., Am. Agrl. Econs. Assn., Am. Hist. Assn., Nat.

Print Equipment & Supplies Assn. (market research com. 1985-86), Assn. African Studies, Phi Beta Kappa (Stanford U.). Office: NECIS 1414 Massachusetts Ave Boxboro MA 01719

ZAWODNY, ALBERT MICHAEL, manufacturing company executive; b. Balt., Nov. 15, 1927; s. Vincent Paul and Frances Marie (Bialek) Z.; m. Ellen Virginia Derr, June 26, 1948. BS in Acctg., U. Balt., 1954. CPA, Md. Mgr. EDP Holabird Signal Depot, Balt., 1947-51; sr. acct. Deloitte, Haskins & Sells, Balt., 1951-56; asst. controller J. Schoeneman, Inc., Balt., 1957-63; treas. Head Ski Co., Balt., 1963-70; exec. v.p. Lion Bros. Co., Inc., Balt., 1970-82; v.p., treas. Worcester Mfg. Co., Balt., 1983—. Mem. Am. Inst. CPA's, Md. Assn. CPA's, Fin. Execs. Inst. Office: Worcester Mfg Co 111 W Timonium Rd Timonium MD 21093

ZDOBYLAK, ANDREW MARTIN, corporate executive, homebuilder; b. Gary, Ind., May 9, 1951; s. John Edward and Frances (Jagoda) Z.; m. Karen Ann Bringol, Oct. 7, 1980; children: Amy Frances, John Claymille. Student, U.S. Mil. Acad., 1970-72; BA, Rutgers U., 1975. Project mgr. Gen. Homes, 1976-79; project mgr. Gemcraft Homes, Inc., San Antonio, 1979-80, div. mgr., 1980-82, v.p., 1982, pres., 1983-88, sr. v.p., 1983, 88—. Mem. Greater Houston Builders Assn. (trustee 1988—), San Antonio Builders Assn. Republican. Roman Catholic. Home: 4704 Mimosa Circle Richmond TX 77469

ZECCA, ANTHONY RAYMOND, steel manufacturing company executive; b. Phila., Nov. 14, 1946; s. Anthony and Rose Francis (Dipietrandonio) Z.; m. Lynda Louise Stripling, June 22, 1968; children: Melanie, Karen. BS in Metall. Engring., Drexel U., 1968, MS in Materials Engring., 1970, PhD, 1973. Rschr. Armco, Inc., Middletown, Ohio, 1973-77; asst. mgr. taxes Armco, Inc., Middletown, 1977-81; mgr. oilfield equipment Armco, Inc., Houston, 1981-85; mgr. fin. analysis Armco, Inc., Parsippany, N.J., 1986—; cons. Am. Productivity Ctr., Houston, 1985-86. Author: Powder Metallurgy Processing, 1978; contbr. articles to tech. jours. Mem. Franklin City (Ohio) Planning Commn., 1975-78, Warren County (Ohio) Planning Commn., 1976-78, vice chmn. 1978. Mem. AAAS, Am. Soc. for Metals, AIME, Assn. for Corp. Growth, Smoke Rise Club, Tau Beta Pi, Alpha Sigma Mu, Sigma Pi Sigma. Republican. Roman Catholic. Home: 115-40 Undercliff Rd Kinnelon NJ 07405 Office: Armco Inc 300 Interpace Pkwy Parsippany NJ 07054

ZEEMAN, JOHN R., air transportation company executive; b. 1937; married. Student, Northwestern U. With Gen. Electric Co., 1960-64; account exec. N.W. Ayer & Son, 1964-67, Leo Burnett Co., 1967-71; dir. advt. United Airlines, Inc., Chgo., 1971-74, v.p. mktg. Western div., 1974-76, v.p. passenger mktg., 1976-81, from sr. v.p. mktg., sr. v.p. Cen. div. to exec. v.p. mktg., planning, 1981-89; mng. dir., chief exec. officer Galileo. Office: Galileo Distbn Systems, Galileo House, Windmill Hill Bus Pk, Swindon SN5 9NX White Hall Way, England also: United Air Lines Inc PO Box 66100 Chicago IL 60666 *

ZEGEER, MOSES SCOTT, lawyer; b. Weirton, W.Va., Sept. 20, 1960; s. Moses Zegeer and Ellinora Veronica (Starr) Cagna. BS, W.Va. U., 1982; JD, George Washington U., 1985. Bar: Pa. 1985, W.Va. 1985, D.C. 1985. Atty. Ernst and Whinney, Pitts., 1985-88, Strassburger McKenna Gutnick and Potter, Pitts., 1988—. Trustee scholar George Washington U., 1982. Mem. ABA, W.Va. Bar Assn., Pa. Bar Assn., D.C. Bar Assn. Democrat. Roman Catholic. Office: Strassburger McKenna et al 322 Blvd of the Allies Ste 700 Pittsburgh PA 15222

ZEH, GEOFFREY N., labor union administrator; b. Hackensack, N.J., Jan. 24, 1943; m. Chryssa Zografos; children: Jason, Justin. BA, Rutgers U., 1965; JD, George Washington U., 1969. Assoc. Mulholland & Hickey, Washington, 1970-75; dir. research Brotherhood Maintenance Way Employes, Detroit, 1975-82, sec., treas., 1982-86, pres., 1986—. Editor: Brotherhood Maintenance Way Employes Jour., 1986—. Mem. ABA, Mich. Bar Assn., D.C. Bar Assn., Assn. Interstate Commerce Commn. Practitioners, Ry. Labor Execs. Assn. (vice chmn. 1986—), AFL&CIO (exec. counsel Mich., 1987—). Office: Brotherhood Maintenance Way Employes 12050 Woodward Ave Detroit MI 48203-3596

ZEHFUSS, LAWRENCE THOMAS, hardware supply company executive; b. Pitts., Feb. 2, 1938. BSBA, Duquesne U., 1960. C.P.A., Pa. Accountant, analyst H.J. Heinz Co., Pitts., 1960-61; public acct. P.A. Love & Co., Pitts., 1961-65; fin. mgr. Am. Hardware Supply Co., Butler, Pa., 1965-70, v.p. fin., treas., 1970-79, chief exec. officer, from 1979, pres., 1979—; dir. corp., bank; speaker for industry assns. Vice chmn. Butler Meml. Hosp. Mem. Pres.'s Assn. Office: Am Hardware Supply Co PO Box 1510 Butler PA 16001 *

ZEHR, NORMAN ROBERT, association administrator; b. Niagara Falls, N.Y., May 19, 1930; s. George Andrew and Ina Kate (Morrell) Z.; Engr. of Mines, Colo. Sch. Mines, 1952, M.S., 1956; m. Janet Hutchinson, Apr. 24, 1976; children—Jeannette Ann, Leslie. Sales trainee Ingersoll-Rand Co., N.Y.C., 1955-56, sales engr., Lima, Peru, 1956-64, regional mgr. mining and constrn. sales, Lima, Peru and N.Y.C., 1964-68, gen. sales mgr. Latin Am., N.Y.C., 1968-69, gen. mgr. Latin Am. ops., N.Y.C., 1969-71, v.p. Ingersoll Rand Internat., Woodcliff Lake, N.J., 1971-72, pres., 1972-83, , v.p. Ingersoll-Rand Co., 1975-83; exec. dir. Colo. Sch. Mines Alumni Assn., 1984—. Served with AUS, 1952-54. Recipient Colo. Sch. Mines Disting. Achievement medal, 1977. Mem. AIME, Scabbard and Blade, Nat. Soc. Pershing Rifles, Mining and Metall. Soc. Am., Sigma Nu. Club: Mining. Office: Colo Sch Mines Twin Towers Golden CO 80401

ZEIDMAN, SYLVAN ARNOLD, airline company revenue accountant; b. Elizabeth, N.J., Jan. 28, 1947; s. Sam and Sara (Smolensky) Z. AA, Union Coll., Cranford, N.J., 1967; BA, Rutgers U., 1969; postgrad., Baruch Coll., 1983-84. Mgr. shipping dept. Seymour's Inc., N.Y.C., 1972-79; mgr. Deffaa Travel Bur., 1979-83; v.p. Southwest Tours, Bklyn., 1980-84; auditor acctg./rev. account dept. Tower Air, Inc., Jamaica, N.Y., 1983—. Contbr. The Jewish Travel Guide, 1983-84. Mem. Rep. Nat. Com.; active Presdl. Trust, Presdl. Fund; mem. (charter) Citizens Against Govt. Waste, Citizen Com. for Right to Keep and Bear Arms (citizen of yr. 1987). Named Citizen of Yr., Citizen Com. For the Right to Keep and Bear Arms, 1987. Mem. Rutgers U. Alumni Assn. Home: 701 Empire Blvd 5B (R-57) Brooklyn NY 11213

ZEIEN, ALFRED M., consumer products company executive; b. N.Y.C., Feb. 25, 1930; s. Alphonse and Betty (Barthelemy) Z.; m. Joyce Valerie Lawrence, Dec. 26, 1952; children—Scott, Grey, Claudia. B.S., Webb Inst.; M.B.A. postgrad., Harvard U. Group v.p. Gillette Co., Boston, 1973-74, sr. v.p., 1978-81, vice chmn., 1981—; div. gen. mgr. Braun AG, Frankfurt, Federal Republic of Germany, 1974-76, chmn. bd., 1976-78; bd. dirs. Polaroid Corp., Cambridge, Mass., Repligen Corp., Cambridge, Square D Co., Palatine, Ill. trustee Univ. Hosp., Boston, 1983—. Home: 185 Old Pickard Rd Concord MA 01742 Office: Gillette Co Prudential Tower Bldg Boston MA 02199

ZELL, SAMUEL, transportation leasing company executive; b. Chgo., Sept. 28, 1941; married. BA, U. Mich., 1963, JD, 1966. With Yates Holleb and Michelson, 1966-68; pres. Equity Fin. and Mgmt. Co., 1968—; chmn., pres. Great Am. Mgmt. and Investment Inc., 1981—; chmn., chief exec. officer Itel Corp., 1985—, also bd. dirs. Office: Gt Am Mgmt & Investment Inc 2 N Riverside Pla 6th Fl Chicago IL 60606 *

ZELMAN, MARTIN IRA, financial executive; b. Paterson, N.J., May 19, 1952; s. David and Toby (Torens) Z.; m. Deborah Miliman, Dec. 20, 1975; children: Matthew, Daniel, Benjamin, Elizabeth. BA in Math., UCLA, 1974, MBA in Ops. Rsch., 1976. Sr. fin. analyst TRW Energy Products Group, Los Angeles, 1976-79, mgr. fin. planning, 1979-81; plant controller Fasteners div. TRW, Mountainside, N.J., 1981-84; fin. mgr. Fasteners div. TRW, Cambridge, Mass., 1984-85, dir. fin., 1985—. Fin. sec. Temple Israel, Sharon, Mass., 1987—. Mem. Nat. Assn. Accts., Am. Philatelic Soc., Fin. Exec. Inst. Republican. Jewish. Office: Fasterners Div TRW 265 3d St Cambridge MA 02142

ZEMAITIS, ALGIRDAS JONAS ALEXIS, international organization official; b. Salniskiai Manor, Lithuania, Mar 9, 1933; came to U.S., 1949, naturalized, 1954; s. Vincentas Petras and Bronislava (Rusecki-Ruseckas) Z. Prince de Druck; m. Vanda Jadvyga Kibort-Kybartas, Apr. 5, 1956; children: Alexis-Pius-Kestutis, Maria-Birute, Rita-Vilia, Paulus-Algirdas, Julia-Dalia.; grad. student U. Bonn, Fed. Republic Germany, 1954-56, BA (hon.) Balliol Coll., Oxford (Eng.) U., 1959, MA, 1964; v.p. Union-Chretienne-Democrate d'Europe Cen. S/J, Paris, 1955-59; asst. to pres., sr. economist Borg-Warner Internat. Corp., Chgo., 1959-61; dir. gen. Market Facts ROC Internat., Chgo., 1962-63; internat. economist Sears, Roebuck & Co., Chgo., 1963-66; sr. internat. trade officer AID, U.S. Dept. of State., Washington, 1966-68; economist FAO, UN, Rome, 1968-75, country project officer, 1975-83, dep. rep. in the Sudan, Khartoum, 1983-86. Contbr. articles to profl. jours. Chmn., Bonn Komite Litauisches Welt Gemeinschaft, Bonn, 1954-56; del. Internat. Christian Democratic Movement, Europe and Latin Am., 1955-66. Served with AUS, 1952-54. Decorated Papal Knight Grand Officer, Equestrian Order Holy Sepulchre of Jerusalem. Mem. various profl. and acad. socs. Home: Collegio Lituano, 20 Via Casalmonferrato, 00182 Rome Italy Office: FAO, 00100 Rome Italy

ZEMKE, (E.) JOSEPH, computer company executive. Chief operating officer Auto-Trol Tech., Denver, 1981-84; chief operating officer Amdahl Corp., Sunnyvale, Calif., 1985—, pres., 1987—. Office: Amdahl Corp 1250 E Arques Ave Sunnyvale CA 94086 *

ZEMKO, CHARLES EDWARD, small business owner; b. New London, Conn., Mar. 11, 1949; s. Andrew Augustus and Wilma Jean (Muray) Z.; m. Virginia Mary Vesgilio, July 4, 1970 (div. May 1974); 1 child, Anthony; m. Patricia Elizabeth Conway, Sept. 3, 1982; children: David Bennett, Sarah. AS, Mohegan Community Coll., 1974; student, U. Hartford, 1974-76. Engr. in tng. State of Conn., Norwich, 1969-72; survey part chief Hub Corp., Colchester, Conn., 1972-73, Archenback Realty Co., Essex, Conn., 1973-74; model maker Gen. Dynamics Electric Boat, Groton, Conn., 1974; self employed in furniture repair Salem, Conn., 1974-76, cons., 1976-88; pres. OZ Enterprises, Inc., Colchester, Conn., 1988—. Chmn. Salem Dem. Town Com., 1980-88, Salem Zoning Bd Appeals, 1983-87, Salem Econ. Devel. Com., 1985-87; selectman Salem Bd Selectmen, Salem, 1987-89. Roman Catholic. Home: 228 Hartford Rd Salem CT 06415 Office: PO Box 2111 228 Hartford Rd Salem CT 06415-0320

ZENDLE, HOWARD MARK, software development researcher; b. Binghamton, N.Y., June 8, 1949; s. Abraham and Evelyn (Hershowitz) Z. BA in Physics summa cum laude, SUNY-Binghamton, 1972, MA, in Physics, 1976; MS, in elec. engring. Syracuse U., 1987. With IBM, Owego, N.Y., 1974—, staff programmer, 1978-83, mgr. microprocessor applications software, 1979-81, mgr. tactical avionics software, 1981-82, adv. programmer, 1983-86, sr. programmer, 1986—. Sec., Men's Club Beth David Synagogue, Binghamton, 1984-85, v.p., 1986-88; bd. dirs. Jewish Community Ctr., Binghamton, 1983-86. Recipient Informal awards IBM, 1975, 78, 81, 83. Mem. Assn. for Computing Machinery, IEEE. Republican. Club: Central Electric Railfan's Assn., Phi Beta Kappa, Sigma Pi Sigma. Lodge: Masons. Avocations: railfanning, research into history of industrial development in America.

ZEPKA, RODGER, sales executive; b. Trenton, N.J., Apr. 13, 1957; s. Joseph and Jeannette (Rogers) Z.; m. Pamela G. Sims, Feb. 15, 1987. BS in Commerce, Rider Coll., 1980. Rental rep. Hertz Corp., Trenton, 1977-79, sales rep., 1980-82; major account mgr. ITT USTS, Cleve., 1982-83, Washington, 1983-84; sr. major account mgr. ITT USTS, Edison, N.J., 1984-85; regional sales mgr. ITT USTS, N.Y.C., 1986—. Rep. committeeman 66th dist. Edison Twp. Office: ITT USTS 67 Broad St New York NY 10004

ZEPLOWITZ, LEE BEN, finance company executive; b. Buffalo, Dec. 16, 1957; s. Herbert M. and Helen A. (Sterzelbach) Z.; m. Karen Weizer, July 11, 1982; 1 child, Julie. AAS, SUNY, Delhi, 1978; cert. archeology, Tel Aviv U., 1979; BS, Temple U., 1982. CPA, Pa.; lic. gen. securities rep., lic. life and health ins. agt. Sr. audit acct. Morris J. Cohen & Co. CPA's, Phila., 1982-84; sr. tax acct. Goldenberg/Rosenthal CPA's, Phila., 1984-86; fin. planner Wescott Fin. Planning Group, Phila., 1986-87; fin. planner, investment adv. Leupold Fin. Planning Assn., Cherry Hill, N.J., 1987—; seminar speaker in field. VIP blood donor ARC, 1976—; mem. dist. fin. com. Boy Scouts Am., Camden (N.J.) County, 1988; solicitor United Jewish Appeal, Phila., 1982—. Mem. AICPA, Pa. Inst. CPA's, Internat. Assn. for Fin. Planning, Inst. Cert. Fin. Planners, Cherry Hill C. of C., South Jersey C. of C., Phila.-Israel C. of C. (bd. dirs.), South Jersey C. of C., Beta Alpha Psi. Jewish. Home: 1 E Wilmot Ave Havertown PA 19083 Office: Leupold Fin Planning Assn Inc 1902 Fairfax Ave Cherry Hill NJ 08003

ZERFOSS, LESTER FRANK, management consultant, educator; b. Mountaintop, Pa., Nov. 2, 1903; s. Clinton and Mabel (Wilcox) Z.; B.A. cum laude, Pa. State U., 1926, M.Ed., 1934, Ed.D., 1958; m. Harriet Mildred Cary, Dec. 21, 1928 (dec. Dec. 1978); children—Patricia Ann (Mrs. Thomas Sibben), Clinton Cary, Robert Williamson; m. Irma J. Allen, July 12, 1980. Coll. tchr., pub. sch. adminstr., Pa., 1928-41; supr. design, devel. Gen. Motors Inst., 1942-46; head supervisory devel. Detroit Edison Co., 1946-52; corporate tng. dir. Am. Enka Corp. (N.C.), 1952-59, dir. indsl. relations, mgmt. services, 1959-66, mgmt. cons. tech., mgmt. devel., 1966-73; prof. psychology, dir. mgmt. devel. programs U. N.C. at Asheville, 1966-74, prof. mgmt. and developmental psychology, chmn. dept. mgmt., 1974-76 emeritus prof. mgmt., 1976—; pres. L.F. Zerfoss Assos., Inc., Mgmt. Consultants, 1976—; cons. on mgmt. devel. State of N.C. Mem. N.C. Personnel Bd., 1966-72, Southeastern Regional Manpower Adv. Com., 1966-71, N.C. Community Coll. Adv. Council, 1966—. Trustee, exec. bd., chmn. instructional com. Brevard Coll.; trustee Mountain Manpower Corp. Recipient Disting. Prof. award U. N.C., 1976. Mem. Am. Mgmt. Assn. (lectr. mgmt. devel. pres.'s assn.), Nat. Soc. Advancement Mgmt. (profl. mgr. citation 1962), Am. Soc. Tng. and Devel., Phi Delta Kappa (Disting. Service award 1982), Kappa Phi Kappa, Iota Alpha Delta, Kappa Delta Pi, Delta Sigma Phi. Contbg. author Training and Development Handbook, 1967, Management Handbook for Plant Engineers, 1978, Psychology in Action, 1978; author: Developing Professional Personnel in Business, Industry and Government, 1968, (with Irma Zerfoss) All God's Children Got Wings, 1988; contbr. to Personnel Administration in the Collegium, 1982; contbr. articles to profl. jours. Home and Office: PO Box 386 Liberty SC 29657

ZERQUERA-FISCHER, CYNTHIA, computer professional; b. Coral Gables, Fla., Sept. 19, 1959; d. Roberto Emilio Zerquera and Dorothy Arline (Owen) Rogers; m. Thomas Gerard Fischer; Apr. 6, 1985. A in Physician Assistance, Sawyer U., 1979; student, Northeastern U. Physician's asst. R.I. Hosp., Providence, 1979-83; mental health asst. Commonwealth of Mass., Framingham, 1983-84; adminstrv. asst. MicroAm., Inc., Framingham, 1984-85, ops. mgr., 1985-87; mgmt. info. systems trainer MicroAm., Inc., Marlboro, Mass., 1987-88; mgm.t info. systems tng. mgr. MicraAmerica, Marlboro, Mass., 1988—. Bd. dirs. R.I. State Council on the Arts, Providence, 1978; pres. Young Adult Ministry Southeastern Conf. United Methodist Ch., Framingham, 1986-87; adv. Commn. on Edn. Wesley United Methodist Ch., Framingham, 1983-87, youth ministry First United Meth. Ch., Milford, Mass., 1987—. Mem. Nat. Assn. Female Execs. Home: 339 Purchase St Milford MA 01757

ZERWECK, RICHARD, JR., computer company executive, offical; b. Jersey City, Dec. 2, 1932; s. Richard and Louise Caroline (Kranz) Z.; A.A., Drake Coll., 1957; m. Edith B. Schmidt, June 13, 1953; children—Duane Robert, Keith Ross. Data processing operator Chubb & Sons Underwriters, 1951-53, W.Va. Pulp & Paper, 1955-59; mgr. data processing ops. Sterling Movies, N.Y.C., 1959-62, Halcon Internat., N.Y.C., 1962-72, Stone & Webster, N.Y.C., 1972-73; mgr. computer services-scheduling applications Brown & Root, Houston, 1973-84; founder Micro Computing Plus, Inc., 1982—, pres., 1984—; cons. project mgmt. Served with USN, 1953-55. Mem. Data Processing Mgmt. Assn., Project Mgmt. Inst., K & H User Assn. (pres. 1981-82). Republican. Clubs: Masons, Shriners, KT. Home: 20019 Ricewood Way Katy TX 77449

ZIAMA, ALLEN, computer software engineer; b. Monrovia, Liberia, Feb. 15, 1953; came to U.S., 1974; s. Francis and Kiabeh-Korlu (Suppo) Z.; m. Yvonne Johnson, Dec. 1978 (div. 1981). BS in Math., U. Liberia, Monrovia, 1973; MS in Computer Sci., Ohio State U., 1976. Tech. analyst Burroughs Corp., Detroit, 1976-78, project mgr., 1979-81, mgr. systems engring., 1981-83; system tech. analyst Borroughs S.A., France, 1978-79; v.p. Omni Systems Inc., Southfield, Mich., 1983-86; pres. Alpha Technologies Corp., Troy, Mich., 1986-87; pres., owner Xytec Corp., Southfield, 1987—. Mem. Assn. of Computing Machinery. Office: Xytec Corp 15565 Northland Dr Ste 602 W Southfield MI 48075

ZICK, LEONARD OTTO, accountant, manufacturing executive, financial consultant; b. St. Joseph, Mich., Jan. 16, 1905; s. Otto J. and Hannah (Heyn) Z.; student Western State U., Kalamazoo; m. Anna Essig, June 27, 1925 (dec. May 1976); children—Rowene (Mrs. A. C. Neidow), Arlene (Mrs. Thomas Anton), Constance Mae (Mrs. Hilary Snell), Shirley Ann (Mrs. John Vander Ley) (dec.); m. 2d, Genevieve Evans, Nov. 3, 1977. Sr. ptnr. firm Zick, Campbell & Rose Accts., South Bend, Ind., 1928-48; sec.-treas. C. M. Hall Lamp Co., Detroit, 1948-51, pres. 1951-54, chmn. bd., 1954-56; pres., treas., dir. Allen Electric & Equipment Co. (now Allen Group, Inc.), Kalamazoo, 1954-57, pres., treas., dir. The Lithibar Co., Holland, Mich., 1957-61; fin. v.p., treas., dir. Crampton Mfg. Co., 1961-63; mgr. corp. fin. dept. Manley, Bennett, McDonald & Co., Detroit, 1963-68; mgr. Leonard O. Zick & Assocs., Holland, 1968-88; former dir. Eberhard's Foods, Inc., Grand Rapids. Former mem. Mich. Republican Central Com.; trustee YMCA Found., Clearwater, Fla. Mem. Nat. Assn. Accts. (past nat. v.p., dir.), Mich. Self Insurers Assn. (past pres.), Fin. Execs. Inst., Stuart Cameron McLeod Soc. (past pres.), Peninsular Club, Holland Country Club, Union League, Macawtawa Yacht Club, East Bay Country Club, Rotary (Paul Harris fellow). Lutheran. Home: 1609 F-225 Country Club Dr Largo FL 34641-2245 also: 99 W 11th St Holland MI 49423

ZICKER, ROBERT GEORGE, data processing executive; b. Orange, N.J., Oct. 23, 1943; s. Frank John and Helen Margaret (Plum) Z.; m. Patricia Sue Osburn, June 1967 (div. Jan. 1974); m. Barbara Carlene Pierce, Oct. 25, 1975; children: Michelle Lee, Timothy Robert. Student, Capitol Engring. Engr. field Mobile/Microwave Div. RCA, Newark, N.J., 1961-66; mgr. systems engring. Mobilphone Service, Tulsa, 1970-73, Little Rock, 1973-75; cons. telecommunications Adaptive Engring., St. Charles, Mo., 1975-77; v.p. engring. devel. Commterm Inc., Billerica, Mass., 1977-86; cons. telecommunications BBL Industries, Atlanta, 1986—; pres. Voice Message Desk Systems, San Diego, 1986—. Inventor in field. Served in USAF, 1966-70. Home: Rt 1 Box 129 Heber Springs AR 72543 Office: Voice Message Desk Systems 2550 5th Ave Suite 124 San Diego CA 92103

ZIEBARTH, KARL REX, railroad executive, consultant; b. Reading, Pa., May 25, 1938; s. Robert Kurt and Leah Evelyn (DuBor) Z.; m. Gisela Hermine Hader, Nov. 13, 1970; children: Viktoria, Alexander, Elena. B.A., Yale U., 1959. Security analyst Bank of N.Y., 1960-63; 2d v.p. Hayden, Stone, Inc., N.Y.C., 1963-70; asst. v.p. Dominick and Dominick, N.Y.C., 1970-71; v.p., sec., treas. Mo.-Kans.-Tex. R.R. Co., Dallas, 1970-78; exec. v.p. fin. Mo.-Kans.-Tex. R.R. Co., 1979-88, also dir.; dir. Trailer Train, 1971-78, Texas City Terminal Ry., Galveston, Houston & Henderson R.R. Co., Electra Communications Corp., N.Mex. Fed. Savs. & Loan. Trustee Phila. Soc., 1975-78, Dallas Ballet Assn., 1981-86, Am. Econ. Found., 1989—. Capt. USAR, 1960-69. Clubs: Racquet (Chgo.); Petroleum (Dallas); Reform (London); Yale (N.Y.C.). Office: 3626 N Hall St Ste 405 Dallas TX 75219

ZIEGEL, BARI ANN, marketing professional; b. N.Y.C., Nov. 25, 1959; d. Leonard and Norma (Nemeth) Z.; m. Steven M. Rosman, Sept. 8, 1984; 1 childm Michael Sima Ziegel. BBA, Hofstra U., 1980. Ops., sales rep. Unitours, Inc., N.Y.C., 1980-82; adminstrv. asst. Bozell and Jacobs, Inc., N.Y.C., 1982-83, Parfums Stern, Inc., N.Y.C., 1983-85; mgmt. assoc. Citicorp Indsl. Credit, Inc., Harrison, N.Y., 1985-87; mktg. officer Citicorp Indsl. Credit, Inc., Rye, N.Y., 1987-88; mgr. area AT&T Credit Corp., Valhalla, N.Y., 1988—. Mem. Nat. Assn. Female Execs. Jewish. Office: AT&T Credit Corp 100 Summit Lake Dr 2d fl Valhalla NY 10595

ZIEGELE, WILLIAM JOHN, appliance manufacturing company executive; b. Peoria, Ill., Aug. 13, 1940; s. William and Louise (Steiner) Z.; m. Marilyn Jeanette Otte, Mar. 29, 1970; children: Scott David, Michael Brian, Sarah Jane. BSBA, Valparaiso U., 1963; MBA, Butler U., 1975. Sr. acct. Ernst & Whinney, Indpls., 1963-67; gen. mgr., cost acct. Jenn Air Corp. div. Jenn Industries Inc., Indpls., 1967-71; controller Jenn Industries Inc., Indpls., 1971-75, treas., controller, 1975-80; chief fin. officer, v.p. fin. Jenn Air Corp. Jenn Industries Inc. subs. Carrier Corp., Indpls., 1980-82; treas. Jenn Industries Inc. subs. Maytag Corp., Indpls., 1982-88; v.p., controller Jenn Air Co. div. Maytag Corp., Indpls., 1982—; also bd. dirs. Jenn Industries Inc., Indpls. vice-chmn. agy. rev. com. United Way, Indpls., 1982—; fin. chmn. Metro Health Maintenance Orgn., Indpls., 1980-85; active Boy Scouts Am., Indpls., 1981—; treas., mem. exec. com. Luth. Child and Family Services, Indpls., 1975-82. With U.S. Army, 1963-69. Recipient Richard G. Rowland award Indpls. Jaycees, 1968-69. Mem. Fin. Execs. Inst., Hillcrest Country Club. Republican. Lutheran. Home: 6269 Harbridge Rd Indianapolis IN 46220 Office: Jenn Air Co 3035 N Shadeland Ave Indianapolis IN 46226

ZIEGLER, ARTHUR B., banker; b. N.Y.C., May 27, 1930; s. Albert B. and Edith Elizabeth (Yorden) Z.; m. Barbara A. Bronner, Jan. 6, 1951. Student, Syracuse U. Coll., 1947-49, Banker Sch., 1954, Northwestern U., 1958-59; grad. program mgmt. devel., Harvard U., 1961. Asst. advt. mgr. Am. Stores Co., 1947-52; with Marine Midland Banks, Inc., Buffalo, 1952—; asst. v.p. Marine Midland Banks, Inc., 1959-63, v.p., 1963-69, sr. v.p. in adminstrn., 1969-73, exec. v.p., 1973-80, sr. exec. v.p., 1980-85, with office of chmn., 1986—, mem. mgmt. com., 1975-80, mem. sr. policy com., 1980-88; chmn. Marine Midland Bank (Del.) N.A., Wilmington, 1988—; vice-chmn. Mastercard Internat., 1985-86, chmn., 1987—; bd. dirs. Eurocard Internat., Brussels. Chmn. bd. regents Canisius Coll., Buffalo, 1986-88. Mem. Bank Mktg. Assn. (nat. pres. 1978-79, bd. dir.), Pub. Rels. Soc. Am. (chpt. pres. 1967-68). Presbyn. Clubs: Buffalo; Orchard Park Country (Orchard Park); City Midday, Sky (N.Y.C.). Home: Stonehenge Farms Orchard Park NY 14127 Office: Marine Midland Banks Inc Marine Midland Ctr Buffalo NY 14203

ZIEGLER, JAMES RUSSELL, computer consultant; b. Warren, Pa., Oct. 10, 1922; s. LeRoy Curtis and Daisy (Gesin) Z.; BS in Elec. Engring., Pa. State U., 1943, MA in Math., 1948; m. Maxine Evelyn Hogue, Feb. 10, 1952 (dec. Nov. 1968); children—Evalinde Aurelia, Charlotte Elaine, Curtis Wayman, Bruce Allan; m. Florence M. Bowler, 1969 (div. 1975); 1 child, Scott. UHF wave guide rsch. Norden Corp., N.Y.C., 1943-44; instr. math. Pa. State Coll., 1946-48; instr. math. U. Calif. at L.A., 1948-54, rsch. asso., statistician tchrs. characteristics study sponsored by Am. Coun. on Edn., 1951-54; mgr. programming svcs. electronic computers Nat. Cash Register Co., Hawthorne, Calif., 1954-68; pres. Turn-Key Computer Applications, 1968-75; dir. So. Fed. Savs. & Loan Assn., L.A., 1968-69; adv. dir. Coast Fed. Savs. & Loan Assn., L.A., 1969-74; sr. cons. analyst NCR Co., San Diego, 1975-78, San Diego Cash Register Co., 1978-80; computer cons. Yemen Arab Rep. Nat. Water and Sewerage Authority, 1980-87; tech. cons. Office Naval Rsch. Study; data processing cons. psychol. rsch. projects U. So. Calif., also U. Utah. With USMCR, 1944-46; PTO. Mem. Tau Beta Pi, Sigma Tau, Eta Kappa Nu. Republican. Methodist. Mason. Author: Time Sharing Data Processing Systems, 1967; also numerous articles. Home: 1050 Pinecrest Ave Escondido CA 92025

ZIEGLER, WILLIAM, III, diversified industry executive; b. N.Y.C., June 26, 1928; s. William and Helen (Murphy) Z.; m. Jane Elizabeth Troy, Feb. 22, 1952; children: Melissa Jane, William Troy, Peter Martin, Cynthia Curtis, Helen Matilda, Karl Huttig. B.A., Harvard U., 1950; M.B.A., Columbia U., 1962. Vice pres. GIH Corp., N.Y.C., 1959-64, pres., 1964—, dir., 1955—; dir. Am. Maize Products Co., N.Y.C., 1958—; now also chmn. bd., chmn. exec. com., chief exec. officer; pres., dir. Park Ave. Operating Co., Inc., 1958—; chmn., chief exec. officer Am. Fructose Corp., Jno. H. Swisher & Son, Inc., Lloyd Lumber div. Am. Maize Products Co. Bd. dirs. Foresight, Inc., New Haven; pres. E. Matilda Ziegler Found. for Blind; sec. Matilda Ziegler Pub. Co. for Blind; mem. nat. adv. council Hampshire Coll.; Trustee, bd. dirs. Darien Community YMCA; bd. dirs. Project Orbis, Inc., Maritime Ctr. at Norwalk; trustee Lavelle Sch. for Blind. Served from ensign to lt. comdr. USNR, 1952-54. Mem. Southwestern Area Commerce and Industry Assn. Conn. (dir.). Clubs: N.Y. Yacht, Noroton (Conn.) Yacht. Home: 161 Long Neck Point Rd Darien CT 06820 Office: Am Maize Products Co 250 Harbor Dr Stamford CT 06904-2128

ZIELINSKI, PAUL EDMUND, mechanical engineer; b. Toledo, Nov. 4, 1944; s. Edmund Frank and Helen Evelyn (Szmania) Z.; m. Mary Szalkowski, Feb. 7, 1969; children: Bobbi Cher, Robin Jane. BS in Mech. Engring., U. Toledo, 1968, MBA in Fin., 1982. Furnace engr. Owens-Ill., Toledo, 1971-76, corp. safety engr., 1976-78; mgr. process engring. Lily Tulip Inc., Augusta, Ga., 1978-86; v.p., gen. mgr. Team Engring., Augusta, 1986-88; mgr.-engr. Marathon Engrs./Architects/Planners, Augusta, 1988—. Patentee in field. Mem. gov. com. Aquinas High Sch., 1988. Maj. U.S. Army, 1969, Vietnam. Mem. Augusta C. of C., Am. Inst. Plant Engrs., ASME, Res. Officers Assn. Republican. Roman Catholic. Home: 2938 Foxhall Circle Augusta GA 30907

ZIFFREN, LESTER, international public relations consultant; b. Rock Island, Ill., Apr. 30, 1906; s. Davis J. and Rose Ziffren; m. Edythe Wurtzel, May 21, 1937 (dec. 1977); 1 dau. B.J., U. Mo., 1927. Various positions UPI, 1927-37; writer, prodn. exec. 20th Century Fox Studios, Beverly Hills, Calif., 1937-42; dir. Office of Coordinator Inter-Am. Affairs, Santiago, Chile, 1942-45; 1st sec., pub. affairs officer USIA, Am. Embassy, Bogota, Colombia, Santiago, Chile, 1951-54; dir. pub. relations Braden Copper Co. subs. Kennecott Copper Corp., Chile, 1954-60; dir. pub. relations, advt. Kennecott Copper Corp., N.Y., 1961-71; internat. pub. relations cons., N.Y., 1971—; cons. Kennecott, Peabody Coal Co., Minerec Corp., Cerro Corp. Decorated comdr. Order Merit, Bernardo O'Higgins, Republic of Chile, 1946. Mem. Am. Fgn. Service Assn., Americas Found. (v.p., treas. 1985—), Pub. Relations Soc. Am., Diplomatic and Ret. Officers, Soc. Silurians, Bolivarian Soc. U.S. (treas., v.p.), Pan Am. Soc. U.S. (treas.), N.Am.-Chilean C. of C. (exec. dir.). Clubs: Dacor Inc., Nat. Press, Army, Navy (Washington); Overseas Press (N.Y.C.). Home and Office: 220 E 81st St New York NY 10028

ZILBERBERG, NAHUM NORBERT, publishing and communications executive; b. Manheim, Germany, Feb. 13, 1925; s. Mendel Max and Pasia Paula (Morgenstern) Z.; came to U.S., 1957, naturalized, 1961; grad. Sem. for Art Tchrs., Tel Aviv, 1952; BFA, Yale U., 1960, MFA, 1961; m. Rita Orechovsky, 1946 (div.); children: Oded, Doron; m. Barbara Cahn, 1968 (div.); children: Jedediah, Noah. Print shop apprentice, 1936; master of trade, lectr. on printing, 1940; prof. Sem. for Art Tchrs., Tel Aviv, also tchr. arts and crafts in elementary and high sch., 1952-57; teaching fellow Yale U., New Haven, 1958-61; designer Macmillan Pub. Co., Inc., 1963; asst. designer, Harcourt Brace & World (name changed to Harcourt Brace Jovanovich, Inc.), 1964-72, v.p. Center for Study of Instrn. div., San Francisco, 1972-73, pres. Harcourt Brace Jovanovich Films div., San Francisco, 1973-80; founder, pres. NZ Videodisc Prodns., Mill Valley, Calif., 1980—; founder, pres., chmn. bd. Silver Mountain Pubs., Mill Valley, 1986—; founder You're Publishing, Inc., Mill Valley, 1987—; adj. prof. edn. tech. San Francisco State U. Served with Israel Def. Forces, 1948-5. Recipient film and audio-visual awards including: Grand award Internat. Film and TV Festival N.Y., 1976, 80, Gold awards 1977, 78, 79, 80; Cindy award Info. Film Producers Am., 1976, Gold Camera award U.S. Indsl. Film Festival, 1977, Gold Camera award for videodisc U.S. Indsl. Film Festival, 1979, Gold Hugo award Chgo. Internat. Film Festival, 1980, Gold awards, 1977, 78; Gold award 10th Ann. Festival of Ams., 1977; Disting. Tech. Service awards Soc. Tech. Communication, 1979; Gold award Houston Internat. Film Festival, 1979; grand award Film Council Greater Columbus, 1981. Mem. Bookbuilders West, Am. Inst. Graphic Arts, Calif. Humanities Assn., Assn. Ednl. Communications and Tech. (study com. on videodisc). Address: 412 Corte Madera Town Ctr Corte Madera CA 94925

ZILINSKAS, MATTHEW JEROME, manufacturing company executive; b. Chgo., Sept. 20, 1947; s. Matthew Joseph Zilinskas and Clora Elizabeth (Wright) Jones; m. Carol Diane Parlee, June 7, 1969; children: Catherine Beth, Michael Jerome. BS, U.S. Mil. Acad., 1969; MBA, Harvard U., 1973. Commd. 2d lt. U.S. Army, 1969, advanced through grades to capt., resigned, 1977; sr. fin. analyst Nestle, White Plains, N.Y., 1977-79; asst. mgr. fin. planning Kennecott Copper Standard Oil, Stamford, Conn., 1979-80; div. controller Carborundum Standard Oil, Niagara Falls, N.Y., 1980-84; dir. fin. analysis Dorr Oliver Standard Oil, Stamford, Conn., 1984-87; controller Dorr-Oliver, Stamford, 1987; chief fin. officer Farrel Corp., Ansonia, Conn., 1987-89; controller Kearney-Nat., Inc., White Plains, N.Y., 1989—. Served to capt. U.S. Army, 1969-77. Home: 49 Webster Rd Ridgefield CT 06877

ZILKHA, DANIEL ABDULLA, management executive; b. Cairo, Oct. 1, 1942; came to U.S., 1961, naturalized, 1978; s. Abdulla Khedoury and Zmira (Many) Z.; m. Frances Porteous Rogers, Dec. 15, 1970; children: Leonora, Nathaniel, Rebecca, Zmira. BSE, Princeton U., 1964; MBA, Harvard U., 1969. Founding ptnr. Soditic, S.A., Geneva, 1970-79; chmn. Auction Holdings Inc., N.Y.C., 1979-85; pub. Art Auction mag., N.Y.C., 1979-84; ptnr. Tribal Assets Mgmt., Portland, Maine, 1983—. Trustee Internat. Found. for Art Research, 1981—, Portland Mus. Art, 1983—, Portland Sch. Art, 1983-88, Prouts Neck (Maine) Assn., 1983—, Waynflete Sch., Portland, 1983—; vice chmn. internat. bus. com. Met. Mus. Art, N.Y.C., 1982-87. Clubs: Knickerbocker (N.Y.C.); Cumberland (Portland); Somerset (Boston); Prouts Neck Country.

ZILKHA, EZRA KHEDOURI, banker; b. Baghdad, Iraq, July 31, 1925; came to U.S., 1941, naturalized, 1950; s. Khedouri A. and Louise (Bashi) Z.; m. Cecile Iny, Feb. 6, 1950; children: Elias Donald, Donna Zilkha Krisel, Bettina Louise. Grad., Hill Sch., Pottstown, Pa., 1943; AB, Wesleyan U., Middletown, Conn., 1947; LLD (hon.), Wesleyan U., 1987. Pres. Zilkha & Sons, Inc., N.Y.C., 1956—; bd. dirs. Chgo. Milw. Corp., Chgo., Newhall Land & Farming, Calif., CIGNA Corp., Phila., Cambridge Assocs., Boston, Mchts. Grain & Transp., N.Y.C.; bd. dirs., chmn. bd. Union Holdings, Inc., Kans. Trustee Internat. Center for Disabled, N.Y.C., French Inst., N.Y.C., Brookings Inst., Washington; trustee emeritus Wesleyan U.; former trustee Spence Sch., N.Y.C. Decorated chevalier Légion d'Honneur, officier Ordre National du Merite (France). Mem. Council Fgn. Relations. Clubs: Racquet and Tennis (N.Y.C.), Knickerbocker (N.Y.C.); Meadow (Southampton, N.Y.); Travellers (Paris), Polo (Paris). Office: Zilkha and Sons 30 Rockefeller Pla New York NY 10112

ZIMCOSKY, TIMOTHY EDWARD, financial planner; b. Detroit, Mar. 18, 1954; s. Edward Vincent and Anne Delores (Glamp) Z.; m. Linda Kay Pilgrim, June 25, 1977; children: Zachary Taylor, Andrew Tyler. BS, Ferris State U., 1976; MBA, Oakland U., 1979. Cert. fin. planner. Safety engr. Ford Motor Co., Dearborn, Mich., 1976-80; registered rep. Pa. Securities Co., Southfield, Mich., 1981-82; fin. planner Audrey Pearl CFP, Inc., Southfield, 1981-82; tng. dir. Mut. Svc. Corp., Detroit, 1982-84; owner, fin. planner Tezco Fin. Svcs., Birmingham, Mich., 1984—. Contbr. articles to mags. Mem. Nat. Rep. Senatorial Com., Washington, Rep. Presdl. Task Force. Mem. Internat. Assn. Fin. Planning, Inst. Cert. Fin. Planners. Roman Catholic. Home: 5662 Belmont Circle West Bloomfield MI 48322 Office: Tezco Fin Svcs 31000 Telegraph 100 Birmingham MI 48010

ZIMMER, ALAN MARK, retail jewelry chain executive; b. Wilmington, N.C., Jan. 18, 1959; s. William Rudell and Roberta (Goldfarb) Z. BBA, U. Ga., 1980; MBA, Tulane U., 1982. Exec. v.p. Reeds Jewelers, Wilmington, 1981-85, pres., chief exec. officer, 1985—. Mem. Merchandise Discussion Group, Internat. Council Shopping Ctrs., B'nai B'rith. Office: Reeds Jewelers Inc 2525 S 17th St Wilmington NC 28403

ZIMMER, SHARON MAURA, lawyer; b. N.Y.C., May 23, 1949; d. Louis K. and Lillian R. (Rosenberg) Z.; m. Robert H. Mayer, Jan. 23, 1983; 1 child, Gregory Loren. BA, Bryn Mawr Coll., 1970; JD, U. Pa., 1973; LLM in Taxation, NYU, 1976. Bar: N.Y. 1974. Assoc. Hofheimer Gartlir and Gross, N.Y.C., 1973-79; ptnr. Hofheimer, Gartlir, Gottlieb and Gross, N.Y.C., 1979—. Mem. ABA, N.Y. State Bar Assn., N.Y.C. Bar Assn. Office: Hofheimer Gartlir & Gross 633 3d Ave New York NY 10017

ZIMMERMAN, BILL J., oil company executive, lawyer; b. Coffeyville, Kans., Aug. 13, 1932; s. Ralph R. and Nellie E. (Brown) Z.; m. Marianne Belt, Nov. 21, 1953 (div. 1980); children—Kurt R., Julie M., Jennifer L.; m. Patsy Cantrell, Dec. 8, 1980. B.B.A., Southern Meth. U., 1954; J.D., Denver U., 1964. Bar: Colo. 1964, Calif. 1967, N.Y. 1969, Tex. 1973, Okla. 1978. Acct., sr. gas agent, atty., regional atty. Shell Oil Co., 1958-76; sr. group counsel NL Industries, Inc., Houston, 1976-77; assoc. gen. counsel Kerr-McGee Corp., Okla. City, 1977-80; v.p., gen. counsel Superior Oil Co., Houston, 1980-83, Union Pacific Resources Co., Fort Worth, 1983—. Mem. Nat. Republican Party, Tarrant County Rep. Com., Tex. Served to sgt. U.S. Army, 1955-57. Mem. ABA, Am. Corp. Counsel Assn. (dir. 1983—), Am. Petroleum Inst., Ind. Petroleum Assn. Am., Fort Worth C. of C. Republican. Methodist. Clubs: Petroleum, Shady Oaks Country (Fort Worth). Home: 908 Roaring Springs Rd Fort Worth TX 76114 Office: Union Pacific Resources Co PO Box 7 Mail Sta 4007 Fort Worth TX 76101

ZIMMERMAN, BRYANT KABLE, lawyer; b. Mt. Morris, Ill., Nov. 19, 1922; s. Milo D. and Hazel G. (Kable) Z.; m. Harriet Bong, Jan. 20, 1946; children: Paula Zimmerman Veloski, Keith, Craig. A.B., Augustana Coll., 1946; student, Washington U., St. Louis, 1942-43; LL.B., Harvard U., 1948. Bar: Calif. 1949. Assoc. counsel McCutchen, Doyle, Brown & Enersen, San Francisco, 1949-63; v.p., gen. counsel FrancoWestern Oil Co., Bakersfield, Calif., 1963-65; sr. v.p., sec., chief legal officer, dir. Guy F. Atkinson Co., South San Francisco, Calif., 1965-88; of counsel Pettit & Martin, San Francisco, 1988—. Bd. dirs., v.p. Republican Alliance, 1965-74; bd. dirs., sec. Atkinson Found., 1967-88; trustee Willamette U., 1978—; chmn. Nat. Constrn. Employer's Council, 1985-86; bd. dirs. Calif. Taxpayers Assn., 1986-88, Californians for Compensation Reform, 1984-88; chmn. Council on Multiemployer Pension Security, 1983-86. Served with USAAF, 1942-46. Mem. Nat. Constructors Assn. (dir. 1980-81, chmn. 1983). Methodist. Home: 75 Del Monte Dr Hillsborough CA 94010 Office: Pettit & Martin 101 California St San Francisco CA 94111

ZIMMERMAN, FRANK RAYWORTH, communications executive; b. Ypsilanti, Mich., Aug. 22, 1931; s. Frank B. and Hazel (Rayworth) Z.; m. Barbara Faye Marie Kellogg, June 30, 1951; children: Deborah, Paul, Judith, John. BS, Ea. Mich. U., 1955. Mgr. traffic Mich. Bell Tel. Co., Detroit, 1955-74, gen. mgr. operator svcs., 1974-76, asst. v.p. revenues, 1976-78, v.p. pub. rels./revenues, 1978-83, exec. v.p., chief operating officer, 1983; sr. v.p. corp. affairs Ameritech, Chgo., 1983-87; pres., chief exec. officer Ill. Bell Tel. Co., Chgo., 1987—, also bd. dirs.; co-chair, bd. dirs. NCCJ, Chgo. and No. Ill. region, 1985—, also bd. dirs.; bd. dirs. Dearborn Park Corp., Chgo., 1987—; prin. Chgo. United, 1987—. Mem. bus. adv. coun. Chgo. Urban League, 1987—, Northwestern U. Assocs., Chgo., 1988—, Corp. Mgmt. Assistance Program, 1988—. Chgo. Cen. Area Com., 1988—; mem. fin. rsch. and adv. coun. City of Chgo., 1987—; chmn. Gen. Bus. Group., United Way/Crusade of Mercy Campaign, 1989; mem. Chgo. Com., 1987—; trustee Ill. Inst. Tech., 1987—; mem. Met. Chgo. Info. Ctr. Project Policy Com., 1987—, The Chgo. Com., 1987—, Northwestern U. Assocs., Chgo., 1988—; mem. Econ. Devel. Commn. of Chgo. Strategic Planning Com., 1988—; mem. governing bd. Ill. Coun. on Econ. Edn., 1988—; mem. exec. bd., mem. commissioning com. USS Abraham Lincoln, 1988—; trustee Ravinia Festival Assn., Chgo., 1988—, Shedd Aquarium, Chgo., 1988—. Recipient Bronze award Jr. Achievement, Detroit, 1982, Silver award, 1983, Disting. Alumnus award Ea. Mich. U., 1986. Republican. Methodist. Clubs: The Chgo., The Econ. Chgo., The Comml. Avocations: swimming, boating. Office: Ill Bell Tel Co 225 W Randolph St Chicago IL 60606

ZIMMERMAN, JAMES M., retail company executive; b. 1944. Chmn. Rich's Dept. Store div. Federated Dept. Stores, 1984-88; pres., chief operating officer Federated and Allied Dept. Stores, Cin., 1988—. Office: Federated & Allied Dept Stores 7 W 7th St Cincinnati OH 45202 also: Allied Stores Corp 1114 Avenue of the Americas New York NY 10036 *

ZIMMERMAN, JEAN, lawyer; b. Berkeley, Calif., Dec. 3, 1947; d. Donald Scheel Zimmerman and Phebe Jean (Reed) Doan; m. Gilson Berryman Gray III, Nov. 25, 1982; children: Charles Donald Buffum, Catherine Elisabeth Phebe (twins); stepchildren: Alison Travis, Laura Rebecca, Gilson Berryman. BSBA, U. Md., 1970; JD, Emory U., 1975. Bar: Ga. 1975, D.C. 1976, N.Y. 1980. Asst. mgr. investments FNMA, Washington, D.C., 1970-73; assoc. counsel Fuqua Industries Inc., Atlanta, 1976-79; assoc. Sage Gray Todd & Sims, N.Y.C., 1979-84; assoc. counsel J. Henry Schroder Bank & Trust Co., N.Y.C., 1984-85, asst. gen. counsel, 1985-86; assoc. gen. counsel, 1987, assoc. gen. counsel, IBJ Schroder Bank & Trust Co., N.Y.C., 1987—, asst. sec., 1988—; Founder, officer ERA Ga., Atlanta, 1977-79; bd. dirs. Ct. Apptd. Spl. Advs., 1988—. Mem. ABA, N.Y. State Bar Assn., Ga. Assn. Women Lawyers (bd. dirs. 1977-79), LWV, DAR, Democrat. Office: IBJ Schroder Bank & Trust Co One State St New York NY 10004

ZIMMERMAN, JOHN G., financial executive; b. Detroit, July 30, 1940; s. John Edward and Ruth (Schmelzer) Z.; m. Carol Lee Valleau, Sept. 9, 1961; children: Julie, Jennifer. BSBA, Wayne State U., 1963; MBA, Case Western Res., 1968. Trainee various fin. positions Fed.-Mogul Corp., Detroit and Southfield, Mich., 1961-65; plant controller Fed.-Mogul Corp., Mentor, Ohio, 1965-68; div. controller Fed.-Mogul Corp., Southfield, 1968-70, mgr. indsl. engring. planning systems, 1970-71; mgr. spl. projects Questor Corp., Toledo, 1971-72, mgr. treasury adminstrn., 1972-73, asst. treas., 1973-78, treas., 1978-83; treas. Champion Spark Plug Co., Toledo, 1983—; cons. Leroy (N.Y.) Industries,1982-83. Mem. Fin. Execs. Inst. (sec. 1982-83, 1st v.p.1983-84, pres. 1984-85). Home: 4922 Eastwick Dr Toledo OH 43614 Office: Champion Spark Plug Co 900 Upton Ave Toledo OH 43661

ZIMMERMAN, MORTIMER FRED, financial executive; b. Bklyn., July 17, 1922; s. Isaac and Esther (Goodman) Z.; m. Annette Furman, Oct. 19, 1947; children: John Mitchell, Robert Peter. B.B.A., CCNY, 1947; postgrad., N.Y. U., 1964-67. C.P.A., N.Y. Controller L. Grossman Sons, Inc., Mass., 1958—; treas. ABC Consol. Corp., L.I. City, N.Y., Berlo Vending Co., Confection Cabinet Corp., ABC Gladieux Corp., 1963—; v.p. finance Nytronics, Inc., 1968-70; v.p.-treas., chief financial officer Russ Togs, Inc., N.Y.C., 1970—; lectr. Am. Mgmt. Assn., N.Y.C.; mem. mid-Manhattan adv. bd. Mfrs. Hanover Trust Co. Served with AUS, 1943-45. Mem. Financial Execs. Inst., Am. Inst. CPA's. Jewish (past pres. temple). Home: 5 Vista Dr Great Neck NY 11021 Office: Russ Togs Inc 27-11 49th Ave Long Island City NY 11101

ZIMMERMAN, RICHARD ANSON, food company executive; b. Lebanon, Pa., Apr. 5, 1932; s. Richard Paul and Kathryn Clare (Wilhelm) Z.; m. Nancy J. Cramer, Dec. 27, 1952; children: Linda Joan, Janet Lee. B.A. in Commerce, Pa. State U., 1953. Asst. sec. Harrisburg (Pa.) Nat. Bank, 1956-58; with Hershey Foods Corp., Pa., 1958—; asst. to pres. Hershey Foods Corp., 1965-71, v.p., 1971-76, pres., chief operating officer, 1976-84, pres., 1984-85, chief exec. officer, 1984—, chmn., 1985—; dir. Hershey Trust Co., Irving Bank Corp. & Irving Trust Co., Pa. Bus. Roundtable (chmn.). Served as lt. U.S. Navy, 1953-56. Recipient Alumni fellow award Pa. State U., 1978, Disting. Alumni award Pa. State U., 1987, N.C.C.J. Nat. Brotherhood award, 1988. Mem. Grocery Mfrs. Am. (bd. dirs.), Pa. C. of C. (dir.), Alumni Assn. Pa. State U. (pres. 1982-83), Phi Kappa Psi. Methodist. Clubs: Carlton, Masons, Rotary (pres. Hershey club 1973-74), Hershey Country. Office: Hershey Foods Corp 100 Mansion Rd E PO Box 810 Hershey PA 17033 *

ZIMMERMAN, ROBERT EARL, lawyer; b. Kansas City, Mo., Feb. 11, 1928; s. Julius Joseph and Kathryn Bernadine (Highcock) Z.; A.A., Kansas City (Mo.) Jr. Coll., 1947; LL.B., U. Kansas City, 1950; m. Pauline Ann Stephens, Sept. 16, 1950; children—Elaine, David, Mark, Carol. Admitted to Mo. bar, 1950; assoc. firm Madden & Burke, Kansas City, Mo., 1950-51, 53-60; exec. v.p. Stephens Industries, Inc., Kansas City, 1957-63; with Kansas City So. Industries, Inc., 1964—, successively, atty., gen. atty., asst. gen. counsel, gen. counsel, v.p. and gen. counsel, v.p. law, 1964-82, sr. v.p. law, 1982—; dir. Kansas City So. Ry. Co., La. and Ark. Ry. Co. Served with USMC, 1944-45, with USAF, 1951-53. Mem. ABA, Mo. Bar, Am. Judicature Soc., Kansas City Bar Assn., Lawyers Assn. of Kansas City, Assn. ICC Practitioners. Roman Catholic. Clubs: Hallbrook Farms, Kansas City, Leawood Country, K.C. Office: Kansas City So Industries 114 W 11th St Kansas City MO 64105

ZIMMERMAN, RUSSELL RICHARD, aerospace engineer; b. Pitts., Oct. 12, 1942; s. Elwood Booth and Lois Hileman (Shultz) Z. BS, Rochester Inst. Tech., 1965. Engr. Data Corp., Dayton, 1965-67; mgr. precision lab. Data Corp., Manned Spacecraft Ctr., Tex., 1967-71; mgr. photographic engring. Mead Tech. Labs., Dayton, 1971-76, div. dir. imaging scis., 1976-78, v.p. imaging systems, 1978-81; v.p., gen. mgr. MTL Systems, Inc., Dayton, 1981-87, pres., chief exec. officer, 1987—, also bd. dirs.; cons. NASA, Houston, 1967-75, USAF, Dayton, 1971—; trustee Engring and Sci. Found. of Dayton, 1987—. Contbr. various tech. papers and articles to profl. jour. Founder, chmn. bd. of trustees AIDS Found. Dayton, Inc., 1988—; exec. order of Ohio Commodore gubernatorial appointment 1988. Mem. Soc. Photographic Scis. and Engrs., Am. Soc Photogrammetry and Remote Sensing. Assn. Ohio Commodores (gov. appt.), Engring. Club. Methodist. Home: 415 N Park Pl Yellow Springs OH 45387

ZIMMERMAN, WILLIAM EDWIN, newspaper editor and publisher; b. Bklyn., Feb. 2, 1941; s. George and Ruth (Edelbaum) Z.; m. Teodorina Bello, Dec. 13, 1969; 1 child, Carlota Pastora. BA, Queens Coll., 1962. Pres. Guarionex Press, Ltd., N.Y.C., 1979—; various positions with Am. Banker, N.Y.C., 1962-82, editor, 1982-89; editor-in-chief Banking Week, 1986-89; dep. editor., sr. v.p. Sunday Bus. sect., The N.Y. Times, 1989—. Author: How to Tape Instant Oral Biographies, 1979; A Book of Questions to Keep Thoughts and Feelings, 1984, and Make Beliefs, 1987. Mem. Am. Oral History Assn., N.Y. Fin. Writers Assn., Am. Soc. Bus. Writers, Overseas Press Club, Deadline Club, Am. Soc. Bus. Press Editors, Dowtown Athletic Club, N.Y. Athletic Club, Sigma Delta Chi. Democrat. Jewish. Office: New York Times 229 W 43rd St New York NY 10036

ZIMMERMANN, ROBERT LAURENCE, marketing professional; b. Mpls., Jan. 1, 1932; s. Lawrence and Bertha Mabel (Foss) Z. BA, U. Minn., 1954, MA, 1965, PhD, 1970. Asst. prof. psychology U. Winnepeg, Man., Can., 1968-69; research assoc. psychiatry research unit U. Minn., Mpls., 1969-75; sr. scientist biometrics lab. George Washington U., Washington, 1975-76; pvt. cons. research design and data analysis Mpls., 1976-84; sr. research mgr. Maritz Market Research, Mpls., 1984—; clin. asst. prof. psychiatry dept. U. Minn., Mpls., 1976—; external rev. officerFDA, Washington, 1974-77. Contbr. numerous articles to profl. jours. Fellow NIMH, 1958, 61, 69-71; merit fellow State of Minn. Mem. AAAS, Am. Psychol. Assn. Democrat. Home: 1920 S First St #1104 Minneapolis MN 55454 Office: Maritz Market Research Inc 6800 France Ave S Minneapolis MN 55435

ZINBARG, EDWARD DONALD, insurance company executive; b. N.Y.C., Oct. 24, 1934; s. Harry and Esther (Cohen) Z.; m. Barbara Scheffres, Dec. 20, 1956; children—Elizabeth, Allison. B.B.A. magna cum laude, CuNY, 1954; M.B.A., U. Pa., 1955; Ph.D., NYU, 1959. Adj. prof. fin. CUNY, N.Y.C., 1958-73; with Prudential Ins. Co. Am., Newark, 1960—, chief economist, 1967-70, research dir. common stock, 1970-74, corp. fin. dept., 1974-78, sr. v.p. asset mgmt. dept., 1978-88, exec. v.p., 1988—. Author: (with J.B. Cohen and A. Zeikel) Investment Analysis and Portfolio Management, 5th edit., 1987, Guide to Intelligent Investing, 1978. Mem. investment com. United Way of Essex and West Hudson, N.J., 1972—; trustee Trenton (N.J.) State Coll., 1978—, Oheb Shalom Congregation, South Orange, N.J., 1976—. Mem. N.Y. Soc. Security Analysts, Am. Fin. Assn. Home: 5 Hardwell Rd Short Hills NJ 07078 Office: The Prudential Ins Co of Am Prudential Plaza Newark NJ 07101

ZINBERG, ALLAN, medical company executive; b. Bronx, Mar. 22, 1942; s. Louis and Claire (Tannenbaum) Z.; m. Barbara Sieger, Aug. 13, 1966; children: Jennifer, Felice, Andrew. MS, L.I. U., 1973; MBA, Iona Coll., 1975. With Strasenburgh Labs., N.Y.C., 1966-68; advt. mgr. Am. Heart Assn., N.Y.C., 1968-75; pres. CDI Med. Services, Bloomfield, Conn., 1975—; bd. dirs. Anderson Group, Inc., Bloomfield, Magic Years, Inc., Wilkes Barre, Pa., Seratronics Inc., Concord, Calif.; adv. bd. Merrill Lynch Mng. Ptnrs., N.Y.C., 1985—. Contbr. articles to profl. jours. Mem. exhibits com. Am. Heart Assn. Mem. Am. Soc. Ultrasound, Soc. Magnetic Resources in Imaging, N.Am. Soc. Pacing and Electrophysiology. Home: 19 Woodhaven Dr Simsbury CT 06070 Office: CDI Med Services Inc 1280 Blue Hills Ave Bloomfield CT 06002

ZINMAN, JACQUES, former insurance agency executive; b. Phila., Nov. 7, 1922; B.S., U. Va., 1943; postgrad. U. Pa., 1945-46. Chmn., The Zinman Group, Ins. Agy., 1950-82. Mem. exec. com. Pa. state Republican fin. com.; mem. Presdl. Electoral Coll. from Pa., 1972; bd. dirs. Pop Warner Nat. Football League. Served to ensign USNR, 1943-44. Recipient Outstanding Young Man Phila. award Jewish Nat. Fund, 1961. Mem. Ins. Soc. Phila., Variety Club, Theta Delta Chi. Lodge: Masons. Contbr. articles to profl. jours. Office: Lakes Agy of Fla 629 E Atlantic Blvd Pompano Beach FL 33060

ZINN, DONALD J., management consultant; b. Nyack, N.Y., July 7, 1954; s. Gilbert A. and Lilian Zinn; m. Linda Curtis, Aug. 28, 1977; children: Jason, Daniel. BS, Cornell U., 1976; MBA, NYU, 1982. Auditor Deloitte Haskins & Sells, N.Y.C., 1976; mktg. rep. Control Data, N.Y.C., 1976-78; account exec. Chase Econometrics, N.Y.C., 1978-79; treas. Mgmt. Dynamics, N.Y.C., 1980-82; v.p. Mgmt. Dynamics, Elmsford, N.Y., 1982-84; pres. Mgmt. Dynamics, Tarrytown, N.Y., 1985—. Contbr. articles to profl. publs. Named one of Small Bus. Person of Yr. U.S. SBA, 1989. Mem. Assn. Data Processing Service Orgns. (bd. dirs. 1987—). Home: 3 Elena Dr Peekskill NY 10566 Office: Mgmt Dynamics 555 White Plains Rd Tarrytown NY 10591

ZIPERSKI, JAMES RICHARD, lawyer, trucking company executive; b. Milw., May 27, 1932; s. George Felix and Louise (Medema) Z.; m. Patricia Jean Hoag, June 28, 1958; children—Jean Marie, David Carrington, James Patrick. B.S., Marquette U., 1953, J.D., 1957. Bar: Wis. 1957, U.S. Supreme Ct., 1967, U.S. Ct. Appeals, 1978. Resident counsel Schwerman Trucking Co., Milw., 1957—, sec., 1962—, exec. v.p. corp., 1977-80, exec. v.p., 1980-86; exec. v.p., corp. and sec. Evergreen Holding Corp. (parent co. Schwerman Trucking Co.), Milw., 1987—, also bd. dirs.; dir. Gt. Am. Savs. & Loan Assn. Served with AUS, 1953-55. Mem. Transp. Lawyers Assn., Westmoor Country Club, Kiwanis, Alpha Kappa Psi, Phi Delta Phi. Home: 2110 Swan Blvd Wauwatosa WI 53226 Office: Evergreen Holding Corp 629 S 29th St PO Box 736 Milwaukee WI 53201-0736

ZIPP, ANNE WORSHAM, management consultant; b. Ft. Worth, June 26, 1961; d. Arthur Neil and Hope (Worsham) Z. BA, Vanderbilt U., 1983; MBA, Harvard U., 1986. Research assoc. TCS Mgmt. Group, Nashville, 1983-84; personnel planning intern IBM Corp., Armonk, N.Y., 1985-86; mgmt. cons. Touche Ross, Atlanta, 1986—. Trustee Diamond Jubilee Found. Alpha Omicron Pi; mem. Atlanta Symphony Assocs., 1986—, Am. Cancer Soc., Atlanta. Republican. Presbyterian. Home: 3024 C Spring Hill Rd Smyrna GA 30080 Office: Touche Ross 225 Peachtree St NE Ste 1400 Atlanta GA 30043

ZIPP, BRIAN ROGER, securities industry executive; b. Cleve., Nov. 20, 1953; s. Jack David and Eleanor (Marks) Z. BA cum laude, Tulane U., 1975; MS, Columbia U., 1977; MBA, Harvard U., 1982. Registered securities trader and options principal. Sr. economist US Treasury Dept., Washington, 1977-80; exec. v.p. Shearson Lehman Hutton, N.Y.C., 1982—, sr. v.p. and mgr., 1986—; v.p. Lehman Bros., N.Y.C., 1984-86; bd. dirs. Participants Trust Co. Casework vol. Big Bros. of Am., Washington, 1978-80; vol. United Way, N.Y.C., 1986—. Columbia U. Internat. scholar 1975-77. Mem. Pub. Securities Assn. (exec. bd. 1988), Harvard Club, Mentor Harbor Yacht Club, Omicron Delta Kappa, Kappa Delta Kappa. Home: 301 W 57th St New York NY 10019 Office: Shearson Lehman Hutton Inc 200 Vesey St 9th fl New York NY 10285

ZITO, JAMES ANTHONY, railroad company executive; b. Oak Park, Ill., Feb. 5, 1931; s. Bruno and Concetta (Kalasardo) Z.; m. Mary B. De Stasio, July 9, 1983; children: Antony, Antonia. Student, Elmhurst Coll., 1956-57, Stanford U., 1981. Sr. v.p. ops. Chgo. & North Western Transp. Co., 1976—, also bd. dirs.; bd. dirs. Kansas City (Mo.) Terminal Ry. Club: St. Charles (Ill.) Country. Home: 1655 Persimmon Dr Saint Charles IL 60174 Office: Chgo & North Western Transp Co One North Western Ctr 165 N Canal St Chicago IL 60606

ZNEIMER, STEPHAN, accountant; b. N.Y.C., June 10, 1917; s. Edward and Gertrude (Segale) Z.; BBA, CCNY, 1938; m. Selma June Kohn, June 15, 1941; children—Richard Edward, Carole Ann. Acct. Bernard Citron, CPA, N.Y.C., 1938-42; pvt. practice acctg.,N.Y.C., 1942-46, Wilkes-Barre, Pa., 1946-80; with Baron, Strassman and Zneimer CPA's, 1980—. Life trustee Temple Israel of Wilkes-Barre; mem. community relations com. Jewish Fedn. Greater Wilkes-Barre; del. Pa. Jewish Coalition. Mem. Am., Pa. (mem. com.

on legislation, com. fed. taxation, estate planning com.), insts. C.P.A.s, N.Y. State Soc. C.P.A.s, Alumni Soc. CCNY. Jewish. Mason (Shriner). Home: 133 White Birch Ln Dallas PA 18612 Office: 39 Public Sq Wilkes-Barre PA 18701

ZOCCHI, LOUIS JOSEPH, game company executive; b. Chgo., Feb. 16, 1935; s. Louis Alexander and Martha (Adams) Z.; m. Elissa Lorelei Scott, June 8, 1959 (Sept. 1976); children: David, Suzanne, LaRee, Lisa; m. Sharon Annette Olson, May 25, 1985; 1 child, Heidi Olson. Cert. air traffic controller, 1955, air traffic control instr., 1964. Commd. USAF, 1954, advanced through grades to tech. sgt.; air traffic controller USAF, Offut AFB, Nebr., 1954, Lincoln AFB, Nebr., 1955-59, Misawa AFB, Japan, 1959-63, Holloman AFB, N.Mex., 1963-64; air traff control instr. USAF, Keesler AFB, Miss., 1964-70; air traffic controller USAF, Mather AFB, Calif., 1970-71, Kimpo AFB, Korea, 1971-72, George AFB, Calif., 1972-73; air traffic instr. USAF, Biloxi, Miss., 1973-75; ret. USAF, 1975; owner Zocchi Distributors, Victorville, Calif., 1972—; pres. Gamescience, Inc., Cedarhurst, N.Y., 1974—; cruise dir. Europa Star cruise ship, 1988. Designer (games) Battle of Britain, 1968, Star Fleet Battle Manual, 1977 (Gamesday award 1981), Basic and Advanced Fighter Combat, 1980 (H.G. Wells award 1981); inventor Zocchihedron 100 sided dice, 1985. Recipient Hobbyist award Metro Detroit Gamers, 1979, Spl. Service award Strategists Club award, 1982, Charles Roberts Adventure Gaming Hall of Fame award, 1987. Mem. Game Mfrs. Assn. (chmn. membership com. 1978-84, v.p. 1978-84, bd. dirs. 1985), Internat. Brotherhood Magicians, Hobby Industry Assn. (pres. gaming div. 1981), Gulf Coast Jazz Soc., Soc. Am. Magicians (pres.). Home: 7604 Newton Dr North Biloxi MS 39501 Office: Gamescience Inc 1512 30th Ave Gulfport MS 39501

ZOCH, DONALD RAYMOND, investment advisor; b. Teaneck, N.J.; s. Bernard Peter and Dorothy C. Zoch; m. Kathleen Price, Dec. 18, 1982. BA, Cath. U. Am., Washington, 1976. Cert. fin. planner. Chief exec. officer Zoch & Zoch Assocs., Inc., Fairfield, N.J., 1976—, Zoch & Zoch Fin. Group, Inc., Fairfield, 1976—. Mem. Inst. Cert. Fin. Planners, Registry Fin. Planning Practitioners, Internat. Assn. Fin. Planning. Office: Zoch & Zoch Assocs Inc 710 Rt 46 E Suite 100 Fairfield NJ 07006

ZOFFER, H. JEROME, educator, university dean; b. Pitts., July 23, 1930; s. William and Sarah Leah (Fisher) Z.; m. Maye Rattner, July 19, 1959; children: Gayle Risa, William Michael. B.B.A., U. Pitts., 1952, M.A., 1953, Ph.D., 1956; C.P.C.U., Am. Inst., Phila., 1954. Sales and mgmt. cons. 1952-60; instr. Sch. Bus. Adminstrn., U. Pitts., 1953-56, asst. prof., 1956-59; assoc. prof. Sch. Bus. Adminstrn., U. Pitts. (Joseph M. Katz Grad. Sch. Bus.), 1959-66; prof. Sch. Bus. Adminstrn., U. Pitts. (Grad. Sch. Bus.), 1966—, chmn. dept. real estate and ins., 1958-60, dir. spl. studies, 1960-62, asst. dean for acad. affairs, 1962-65, assoc. dean for adminstrn., 1965-68, dean Grad. Sch. Bus., 1968—; dir. Red Bull Inns of Am., Inc. 1978-86, Penn. Traffic Co., 1977-87, Oliver Realty Co., 1980-87; Ford Found. fellow in applied math. U. Pa., Phila., 1961-62; mem. visitation com. Am. Assembly Collegiate Schs. of Bus., 1972—, mem. standards com., 1974-78, mem. exec. com., 1975-87, chmn. accreditation research com., 1974-84, v.p. bd. dirs., 1984-85, pres., 1985-86; chmn. Middle States Evaluation Accrediting Teams, 1967—. Author: The History of Automobile Liability Insurance Rating: 1900-1958, 1959; also monographs.; contbr. articles to profl. jours. Bd. dirs., v.p. Leadership Inst. for Community Devel., 1968-73, Allegheny chpt. Epilepsy Found. Am., 1971-77; bd. dirs. Pitts. Dist. Export Council, 1974-77; bd. govs. Internat. Ins. Seminars, Inc., 1968-77; mem. festival bd. Three Rivers Arts Festival, 1988—; mem. steering com. Leadership Pitts., 1986—; bd. dirs. Student Cons. Project, U. Pitts., 1970—, Consortium for Cooperation and Competitiveness, 1986—, Moral Force in the Workplace, 1986—. Named Man of Yr. in Edn., Vectors Pitts., 1986. Mem. Am. Econ. Assn., AAUP, Soc. C.P.C.U., Soc. for Psychol. Study Social Issues, Inst. Mgmt. Scis., Middle Atlantic Assn. Colls. Bus. Adminstrn. (pres. 1972-73), Am. Assn. Univ. Adminstrs. (exec. com. 1971-79, pres. 1975-77, dir. 1980-83, pres. found. 1983—), Omicron Delta Gamma, Beta Gamma Sigma (pres. Beta chpt. 1964-68). Club: University (bd. dirs. 1988—). Home: 5620 Aylesboro Ave Pittsburgh PA 15217 Office: U Pitts Katz Grad Sch of Bus Pittsburgh PA 15260

ZOLLER, GEORGE GUY, financial executive; b. Phila., July 4, 1951; s. Karl F. and Elizabeth M. (Caputo) Z.; m. JoAnn T. Connaghan, June 9, 1972; children: Kristen A., Erika M., Mark A. BS in Acctg. and Mgmt., Drexel U., 1974. CPA. Staff acct. Price Waterhouse, 1974-75, ITE/Imperial, Springhouse, Pa., 1975-76; chief fin. officer, corp. controller Aydin Corp., Fort Washington, Pa., 1976-80; corp. controller Decision Data Computer Corp., Horsham, Pa., 1980-82; chief fin. officer, v.p. fin. Infotron Systems, Cherry Hill, N.J., 1982-84; chief fin. officer, v.p. fin. and adminstrn. Rabbit Software, Malvern, Pa., 1985—. Mem. AICPA, Pa. Inst. CPAs. Office: Rabbit Software Corp 7 Great Valley Pkwy Malvern PA 19355

ZOLLER, RICHARD BERNARD, transportation company financial executive; b. Stillwater, Minn., May 3, 1929; s. Bernard Fredrick Z. and Vivian Montrose (Paul) Palmquist; m. Olive Leane Nilsen, July 12, 1952; children: Eric Thorstein, Kristin Elise. BS, U. Minn., 1953, PhD, 1958. Chartered fin. analyst; registered investment advisor. Dir. econ. research Peavey Co., Mpls., 1958-62; economist Armour & Co., Chgo., 1962-66, mgr. capital appropriation, 1966-68; dir. investments Armour & Co. and Greyhound Corp., Chgo., 1968-79; v.p. investments Greyhound Corp., Phoenix, 1979—. Author research publs. in agrl. econs., 1955-58. Bd. dirs. Phoenix Symphony Assn. Exec. Com., 1986; bd. dirs. Handicap Village of Ariz., Phoenix, 1975-84; chmn. Ariz. Gov.'s Employment Security Adv. Council, 1980, Ariz. Retirement System Investment Adv. Council, 1987—. With U.S. Army, 1951-52, Korea. Mem. Phoenix Soc. Fin. Analysts (pres. 1985). Office: Greyhound Corp 1914 Greyhound Tower Phoenix AZ 85077

ZOMORRODIAN, ASGHAR, educator; b. Shiraz, Fars, Iran, Dec. 12, 1941; came to U.S., 1974; s. Ali Akbar and Khadijeh Z.; m. Fatemeh Malek, Mar. 20, 1966. BA, Shiraz U., Iran, 1963; MS, Tehran U., Iran, 1968; MPA, U. So. Calif., Los Angeles, 1976; PhD (hon.), U. So. Calif., 1978. Dep. dir. Agrl. Bank, Tehran, 1963-65; div. dir. Civil Service Commn., Tehran, 1965-73, mem. bd., 1979-80; vice chancellor State Mgmt. Ctr., Tehran, 1977-79, prof., chancellor, 1980-83; prof. Univ. of Mgmt., Tehran, 1983-84, U. So. Calif., 1984-87; prof. dept. mgmt. U. Denver, 1987—; dep. dir. indsl. relations Khuzestan Devel. Project, Ahwaz, Iran, 1963-64. Author: Indigenous of a Management Theory, 1987, Innovative Organization Model, 1986, Management Techniques, Planning and Control, 1978. Faculty rep. U. Mgmt., Tehran, 1982-83; employee union rep. Civil Service, Tehran, 1981-82; chmn. student assn. Shiraz U., 1959-60. UN fellow, 1979; Iran ministry of Sci. fellow, 1974; CENTO fellow, 1971; RCD fellow, Pakistan, 1968. Mem. Project Mgmt. Inst., Am. Assn. Tng. and Devel., Am. Mgmt. Assn., Assn. Profs. and Scholars Iranian Heritage (dir. 1976-78),l Mgmt. Acad. Iran (chmn. 1979-83). Clubs: Pars, AAA. Home: 2809 Montrose Ave #7 Glendale CA 91214 Office: U So Calif Los Angeles CA 90089-0021 also: U Denver Denver CO 80208

ZONDERVAN, PETER JOHN (PAT ZONDERVAN), publisher, religious organization executive; b. Paterson, N.J., Apr. 2, 1909; s. Louis and Nellie Petronella (Eerdmans) Z.; m. Mary Swier, May 21, 1934; children: Robert Lee, Patricia Lucille, William J., Mary Beth. Student. pub. schs., Grandville, Mich.; D.Litt. (hon.), John Brown U., 1969; Litt.D., Lee Coll., 1972; LL.D., Campbellsville Coll., Ky., 1985; L.H.D. (hon.), Taylor U, Upland, Ind., 1985. Co-founder Zondervan Pub. House, Grandville, Mich., 1931, Grand Rapids, Mich., 1932—; co-founder Zondervan Corp., Grand Rapids, 1955—; pres. Grand Rapids Camp of Gideons, 1938-41, chaplain, 1944-46, pres., 1947-48; pres. internat. trustee, 1950-52; v.p. Gideons Internat., 1952-55, pres., 1956-59, treas., 1972-75, chaplain, 1975-78; Bd. dirs. Christian Nationals Evangelism Commn., San Jose, Calif.; bd. dirs. Winona Lake Christian Assembly, Ind., 1937—, sec., 1961—; b. dir. Maranatha Bible and Missionary Conf., Muskegon, Mich., 1961; organizer, 1st chmn. Christian Businessmen's Com., Grand Rapids, 1942; chmn. com. for city-wide Evangelistic meeting, 1946. Honored with declaration of P.J. Zondervan Day in Grand Rapids, Dec. 1973. Mem. Internat. Platform Assn. Clubs: Lotus (Grand Rapids) (pres. 1949, 65-67); Peninsular of Grand Rapids, Blythefield Country and Golf; Boca Golf (Boca Raton, Fla.). Office: Zondervan Corp 1415 Lake Dr SE Grand Rapids MI 49506

ZOOG, JOHN ERIC, manufacturing company executive; b. Sea Isle City, N.J., Oct. 31, 1948; s. Alois Harry and Margaret Mary (Keating) Z.; m. Irene S. Iwachiw, Sept. 15, 1973; children: Christopher, Keri. BS in Indsl. Engring., Rutgers U., 1971. Indsl. engr. Colgate-Palmolive Co., Jersey City, 1971-73; supr. compensation data Colgate-Palmolive Co., N.Y.C., 1973-75, mgr. benefit plan devel., 1975-77; employee relations mgr. Colgate-Palmolive Co., Kansas City, 1977-80; internat. benefits mgr. Colgate-Palmolive Co., N.Y.C., 1980-82, asst. dir. internat. benefit plans, 1982-84, dir. benefit plans, 1984—; mem. membership group Fgn. Benefits Study Group, 1987—. Coach, Plainsboro-Cranbury Little League, N.J., 1986, West Windsor PBA Basketball League, N.J., 1986—. Served with USNG, 1971-77. Mem. Nat. Assn. Mfrs. (mem. employee benefits com. 1985—), Am. Pension Conf., Council Employee Benefits. Roman Catholic. Office: Colgate-Palmolive Co 300 Park Ave New York NY 10022

ZORN, ERIC STUART, retail department store chain executive; b. Newark, Oct. 2, 1948; s. Arthur and Evelyn (Bernstein) Z.; m. Lois Karen Green, Nov. 29, 1979. Student, Fairleigh Dickinson Coll., Wayne, N.J., Upsala Coll., East Orange, N.J. Cash ops. supr. Vornado Inc., Garfield, N.J., 1966-69; corp. auditor Mangel Stores Corp., N.Y.C., 1969-70; sr. v.p. Jamesway Corp., Secaucus, N.J., 1970—; pres. Omnia Protective Services Inc., Ft. Lee, N.J., 1979—, 1530 Owners Corp. (coop. bldg.), Ft. Lee. Mem. Internat. Mass Retailing Inst. (chmn. loss prevention group 1979-82), N.J. Retail Mchts. Assn. (2d vice chmn.), Internat. Soc. Stress Analysts, Soc. Strategic Planning. Republican. Jewish. Home: 1530 Palisade Ave Fort Lee NJ 07024 Office: Jamesway Corp 40 Hartz Way Secaucus NJ 07094

ZOSS, ABRAHAM OSCAR, chemical company executive; b. South Bend, Ind., Feb. 17, 1917; s. Harry and Fannie (Friedman) Z.; B.S. in Chem. Engring., U. Notre Dame, 1938, M.S., 1939, Ph.D., 1941; m. Betty Jane Hurwich, Dec. 24, 1939; children—Roger, Joel, Hope Zoss Schladen; m. 2d, Magda Szanto, May 26, 1978. With Gen. Aniline & Film Corp., Easton, Pa., 1941-47, tech. mgr., Linden, N.J., 1947-55, plant mgr., 1955-57; mgr. mfg. adminstrn., chem. div. Minn. Mining & Mfg. Co., St. Paul, 1957-58, prodn. mgr. chem. div., 1958-60; v.p. Photek Inc., West Kingston, R.I., 1960-62; asst. corp. tech. dir. Celanese Corp., N.Y.C., 1962-65, corp. tech. dir., 1965-66, corp. dir. comml. devel., 1966-69; v.p. corp. devel. Tenneco Chems., Inc., N.Y.C., 1969-71, Universal Oil Products Co., Des Plaines, Ill., 1971-72; group v.p. Engelhard Industries div. Engelhard Minerals & Chem. Corp., Murray Hill, N.J., 1972-74, v.p. bus. devel., 1974-77; v.p. corp. devel. CPS Chem. Co., Inc., Old Bridge, N.J., 1977, dir., v.p., chief adminstrv. officer, 1978-84; pres. Bus. Devel. Internat., Verona, N.J., 1984—; mem. field info. agy. Office Tech. Service, Commerce Dept., Europe, 1946; teaching asst. U. Notre Dame, 1939-41. Mem. Met. Mus. Art, N.Y.C., Mus. Modern Art, N.Y.C. Recipient Centennial Sci. award U. Notre Dame, 1965; cert. profl. chemist Am. Inst. Chemists. Fellow Am. Inst. Chemists, AAAS; mem. Am. Chem. Soc., Am. Inst. Chem. Engring., N.Y. Acad. Scis., Comml. Devel Assn., Soc. Chem. Industry. Club: Chemists (N.Y.C.). Contbr. articles to profl. publs. Patentee in field. Office: Claridge House One Suite 502 Verona NJ 07044

ZOTTOLI, DANNY, data processing executive; b. Yonkers, N.Y., Nov. 15, 1946; s. Danny Anthony and Anna Theresa (Jakubik) Z.; m. Mary Elizabeth Eich, Nov. 6, 1971; children: Michael, Deborah. BBA in Mktg. summa cum laude, Iona Coll., 1968, MBA in Fin., 1971. Fin. analyst George S. Sharp, Inc., N.Y.C., 1968-69; dir. systems GRC Data Corp., Inc., N.Y.C., 1969-82; dir. mgmt. info. systems Prudential Lines, Inc., N.Y.C., 1982-83; gen. mgr. BFC Marine Svcs., Bklyn., 1983-84; v.p. info. svcs. Moody's Investors Svc. div. Dun & Bradstreet, N.Y.C., 1984—; cons. Zottoli Assocs., Tuckahoe, N.Y., 1983-84; lectr. Iona Coll., New Rochelle, N.Y., 1968-69. Sgt. USMCR, 1971-76. Iona Coll. fellow, 1970. Mem. Info. Industry Assn., Data Processing Mgmt. Assn., Am. Soc. Info. Scis. Republican. Roman Catholic. Office: Moody's Investors Svc 99 Church St New York NY 10007

ZRAKET, CHARLES ANTHONY, systems research and engineering company executive; b. Lawrence, Mass., Jan. 9, 1924; s. Habib and Martha (Beshara) Z.; m. Shirley Ann Camus, Oct. 13, 1961; children: David C., Suzanne M., Elizabeth A., Caroline A. BEE, Northeastern U., Boston, 1951; SMEE, MIT, 1953; PhD in Engring. (hon.), Northeastern U., 1988, DEng (hon.), 1988. Mem. research staff digital computer lab., group leader MIT, 1951-53, group leader digital computer lab., Lincoln Lab., 1953-58; tech. dir., then sr. v.p. MITRE Corp., Bedford, Mass. and McLean, Va., 1958-78, exec. v.p., chief oper. officer, 1978-86, pres., chief exec. officer, 1986—, also trustee; trustee bd. overseers Ctr. Naval Analyses, 1984—; bd. dirs. Bank of Boston. Contbr. articles to Science, Daedalus, IEEE jours.; editor: Managing Nuclear Operations. Trustee Hudson Inst.; chmn. Gov. Mass. Adv. Com. Info. Systems, 1978—; mem. Northeastern U. Corp. Council. Served with AUS, 1943-46. Decorated Bronze Star, Purple Heart with oak leaf cluster, Combat Inf. badge; named Disting. Corp. Leader, MIT, 1985, Outstanding alumni, Northeastern U., 1985. Fellow IEEE, AIAA, AAAS; mem. Council on Fgn. Relations, N.Y. Acad. Scis., Sigma Xi, Tau Beta Pi, Eta Kappa Nu. Home: 71 Sylvan Ln Weston MA 02193 Office: MITRE Corp Burlington Rd Bedford MA 01730

ZSCHAU, JULIUS JAMES, lawyer; b. Peoria, Ill., Apr. 1, 1940; s. Raymond Johann Ernst and Rosamond Lillian (Malicoat) Z.; m. Leila Joan Krueger, Aug. 7, 1971; children—Kristen Elisabeth, Kimberly Erna, Kira Jamie, Karla Johanna. B.S., U. Ill., Champaign, 1964, J.D., 1966; LL.M., John Marshall Law Sch., 1978. Bar: Ill. 1966, Fla. 1975. Atty., Ill. Central Gulf R.R. Co., Chgo., 1966-68; assoc. Coin & Sheerin, Chgo., 1968-70, Snyder, Clarke, Dalziel, Holmquist & Johnson, Waukegan, Ill., 1970-72; csl. Ill. Center Corp., Chgo., 1972-74; v.p., gen. csl., sec. Am. Agronomics Corp., Tampa, Fla., 1974-76; pres. Sorota & Zschau, Clearwater, Fla., 1976—; bd. dirs. Attys. Title Ins. Fund, Inc.; dir. Pinellas Review, Inc., Attys. Title Services, Inc.; chmn. com. on land trusts, exec. com. real property sect., vice chair grievance com. Fla. Bar, chair leadership conf. 1987. Bd. dirs. Attys. Title Ins. Fund.; mem. Pinellas County Exec. Com.; mem. Tampa Regional Planning Coun. Served to capt. USNR, 1962—. Mem. ABA (chmn. condominium newsletter com., chair com. on purchase and sale of residential realty), Ill. Bar Assn., Chgo. Bar Assn., Clearwater Bar Assn. (past pres.), Fla. Council Bar Assn. (pres., past chmn. vol. bar liaison com.), Fla. Coun. of Bar Pres. (pres.), Clearwater C. of C. (bd. govs., exec. com.). Republican. Lutheran. Clubs: Harborview, Countryside Country (Clearwater, Fla.); Masons, Scottish Rite, Shriners. Editor Res Ipsa Loquitur, 1982-84. Home: 1910 Saddlehill Rd N Dunedin FL 34698

ZUBAN, ANATOLY TONY, securities trader; b. Jersey City, July 24, 1952; s. Gregory and Nina (Grinenko) Z. BS, U. Calif., Irvine, 1974. Claims rep. Farmer's Ins., Anaheim, Calif., 1976-77; med. sales rep. William H. Rorer, Inc., Ft. Washington, Pa., 1977-78; profl. med. rep. Abbott Labs., North Chicago, Ill., 1978-80, 81-85; regional mktg. rep. Beckman Instruments, Irvine, 1980-81; regional sales mgr. Ohaus Scale Corp., Florham Park, N.J., 1985-86; nat. OEM sales engr. Greco Systems, El Cajon, Calif., 1986-87; fin. cons. Shearson, Lehman, Hutton, Rancho Sante Fe, Calif., 1987-89; account exec. Prudential-Bache Securities, Carlsbad, Calif., 1989—. Mem. Kiwanis. Republican. Ukranian Orthodox. Home: 3930 Cmto Del Mar Surf San Diego CA 92130 Office: Prudential-Bache Securities 701 Palomar Airport Rd Ste 100 Carlsbad CA 92009

ZUBRZYCKI, CHARLES R., advertising executive; b. Camden, N.J., Feb. 21, 1950; s. Charles and Anna (Sakewitz) Z. BA, U. Notre Dame, 1972; MA, U. Calif., Berkeley, 1979; MBA, U. Chgo., 1981. Fin. analyst Amoco Corp., Chgo., 1981-82; sr. auditor Amoco Corp., Denver, 1982-86; bus. analyst Quaker Oats Com., Chgo., 1986-87; acct. planner Wyse Advt., Cleve., 1987—. Contbr.: (book) Alcohol and Human Memory, 1977; contbr. articles to psychol. jour., 1973. NSF grantee, U. Notre Dame, 1971. Democrat. Roman Catholic. Home: 2781 Hampshire #201 Cleveland Heights OH 44106 Office: Wyse Advt 24 Public Sq Cleveland OH 44113

ZUCCARO, ROBERT S., controller; b. Oceanside, N.Y., Jan. 22, 1957; s. Joseph John Sr. and Georgia (Christy) Z.; m. Mary C. Moreno, June 21, 1980 (dec. 1983); m. Michele A. Baldasare, Aug. 10, 1985; 1 child, Marie Elaina. BS in Acctg., C.W. Post Coll., 1979. CPA, N.Y. Supr., mgr. Ernst & Whinney, Melville, N.Y., 1979-83; supr. fin. reporting Shearson Lehman Bros., N.Y.C., 1983-84; corp. contr., asst. sec. Lumex, Inc., Bayshore, N.Y., 1984—; bd. dirs. Medmarc, Burlington, Vt. Mem. Am. Inst. CPA's, N.Y. Soc. CPA's. Roman Catholic. Lodge: KC. Office: Lumex Inc 100 Spence St Bay Shore NY 11706-2290

ZUCKER, LEONARD CHARLES, trucking executive, rabbi; b. Bronx, June 13, 1933; s. Ralph Gilbert and Elsie (Himmelstein) Z.; m. Elaine Trachtman, Dec. 25, 1955; children: Anne, Esther Lynne, Rhea Miriam, Ronald Gary. BA, Yeshiva U., 1951; postgrad. Acad. Advanced Traffic, 1955. Ordained rabbi, 1957. With Charlton Bros. Transp. Co., Inc., Phila., 1953-58; sales mgr. Phila.-Pitts., Carriers, Phila., 1958-61; dist. sales rep. Preston Trucking Co., Inc., 1961-65; v.p. Drake Motor Lines Inc., Cherry Hill, N.J., 1965-76; exec. v.p., chief operating officer Pinto Trucking Service, Inc., Phila., 1976-83, pres., 1984-86; pres. L. Zucker Assocs., 1986—. Author: Why Be a Transportation Specialist, 1971, Safety Guide for the Motor Carrier, 1973. Bd. dirs. Motor Transport Labor Relations, Phila., 1973-76; rabbi Congregation B'nai Tikvah, Turnersville, N.J., 1975—. Served with U.S. Army, 1953-55. Mem. Assn. ICC Practitioners, Transp. Law Practitioners U.S., Delta Nu Alpha. Democrat. Jewish. Clubs: Air Cargo, Nat. Fedn. Men's, Fifth Wheel, Traffic and Transp. Home: 321 Brookline Ave Cherry Hill NJ 08002 Office: 602 E Front St Essington PA 19029

ZUCKERMAN, FREDERICK WILLIAM, automotive company executive; b. N.Y.C., May 4, 1934; s. Harry and Anne David (Wiener) Z.; m. Donna Lee Towne, Jan. 31, 1957 (div. 1967); children: Lee Ann, Susan Bain; m. Jeanne M. Smith, July 8, 1988. B.S., Ohio State U., 1955; M.B.A., Columbia U., 1958; D.B.A. (hon.), Avila Coll., 1983. Various fin. mgmt. positions Ford Motor Co., Dearborn, Mich., 1959-67; various fin. mgmt. positions IBM Corp., Armonk, N.Y., 1967-79; asst. corp. controller Chrysler Corp., Detroit, 1979-81, gen. asst. corp. controller, 1981, v.p., treas., 1981—; chmn. Automotive Fin. Services, Inc.; dir. Chrysler Fin. Corp., Troy, Mich., 1981—, Chrysler Realty Corp., Detroit, 1983—; dir. System Industries, Milpitas, Calif.; dir. law enforcement Assistance Found., N.Y.C. Served to lt. U.S. Army, 1956-65. Mem. Nat. Bankers Assn. (corp. adv. group), Nat. Assn. Corp. Treas., Fin. Execs. Inst., Soc. of Internat. Treas. London, Columbia Grad. Sch. Bus. Alumni Assn. (pres. 1976-77), Atrium Club (N.Y.C.). Home: 605 Park Ave New York NY 10021 Office: Chrysler Corp 12000 Chrysler Dr Highland Park MI 48288

ZUCKERMAN, MARTIN HARVEY, personnel director; b. N.Y.C., Feb. 20, 1942; s. Merwin and Helen (Weinstein) Z.; m. Joyce S. Harris, July 26, 1969; children: Lyle, Evan. BA, NYU, 1963; JD, St. John's U., 1965; LLM, NYU, 1966. Bar: N.Y. 1966. Field atty. Nat. Labor Relations Bd., N.Y.C., 1966-70; sr. atty. Simpson, Thatcher & Bartlett, N.Y.C., 1970-80; v.p. compensation and benefits Mfrs. Hanover Trust Co., N.Y.C., 1980-1983, sr. v.p., asst. personnel dir., 1984-86, exec. v.p., personnel dir., 1986—. Bd. trustees, Drs. Hosp., 1984—, Beth Isreal Hosp., 1987—; treas. Puerto Rican Legal Def. Fund, mem. exec, com., 1985—. Served with U.S. Army, 1967-69. Mem. N.Y. State Bar Assn., N.Y. County Lawyers Assn. Office: Mfrs Hanover Corp 320 Park Ave 23rd Fl New York NY 10022

ZUCKERMAN, MITCHELL, art auction firm executive, lawyer; b. N.Y.C., Apr. 13, 1946; s. Morton and Minna (Miller) Z.; m. Joanne Zuckerman, May 21, 1973; children—Robert, Suzanne. B.A., U. Rochester, 1968; M.A., Harvard U., 1971; J.D., Columbia U., 1974. Assoc. Weil Gotshal & Manges, N.Y.C., 1974-79; sr. v.p., dir. Sotheby's Inc., N.Y.C., 1979-88; sr. v.p. corp. devel. Sotheby's Holdings, Inc., 1986—; pres. Sotheby's Fin. Services Inc., N.Y.C., 1988—. Office: Sotheby's Holdings Inc 1334 York Ave New York NY 10021

ZUEGEL, HERBERT HENRY, infosystems executive; b. Oak Park, Ill., June 23, 1930; s. Herbert H. and Margaret (Gebhardt) Z.; m. Barbara L. Burgis, Aug. 21, 1954; children: Nancy, Carol. BS, Millikin U., 1952. Various positions Ill. Bell Telephone Co., Chgo., 1952-83; dir. budgets and systems Ameritech Corp., Chgo., 1983-85; dir. mgmt. info. systems Wm. Wrigley Jr. Co., Chgo., 1986—; speaker Nat. Computer Conf., Chgo., 1987, Nat. Communications Conf., Chgo., 1987, U. Chgo. Grad. Sch., 1986—, Ill. Inst. Tech. Grad. Sch., 1988. Mem. adv. bd. U. Ill. Chgo., 1989—, Blue Ribbon Task Force, Cook County, Ill., 1978, Bd. Edn., Park Ridge, Ill., 1972-74; active Art Inst. Chgo., Lincoln Pk. Zoo Soc., Chgo. Architecture Found., Chgo. Hist. Soc., Chgo. Hort. Soc., Grocery Mfrs. Am. Sgt. U.S. Army, 1952, Korea. Named Outstanding Alumnus Millikin U., Decatur, Ill., 1965. Mem. Soc. Info. Mgmt. Methodist. Office: William Wrigley Jr Co 410 N Michigan Ave 14th Floor Chicago IL 60611

ZUEHLKE, WILLIAM HENRY, financial consultant, former life insurance company executive; b. Appleton, Wis., Apr. 19, 1915; s. William H. and Ina (Babcock) Z.; Ph.B., Lawrence U., 1936; m. Muriel Mae Heidemann, May 2, 1953. Trading and syndicate mgr. Harris, Hall & Co., investment bankers, Chgo., N.Y., 1936-46; sr. v.p., dir. investments Aid Assn. for Lutherans, Appleton, Wis., 1946-77; dir. emeritus First Nat. Bank of Appleton, Post Corp., Appleton. Trustee, Lawrence U., Valparaiso U., State of Wis. Investment Bd., 1975-77; bd. adjustment Santa Cruz County; bd. dirs. Tunnel Springs Ranch Corp. Served to lt. comdr. USNR, 1941-46. Paul Harris fellow. Mem. Chartered Fin. Analysts, Fraternal Investment Assn., Soc. Tympanuchus Cupido Pinnatus, Ariz. Nature Conservancy, Primieria Alta Hist. Soc., Heard Mus., Tucson Mus. Art, Ariz.-Sonora Desert Mus., Los Charros del Desierto (Tucson), Sigma Phi Epsilon. Republican. Lutheran. Clubs: Rotary, Old Pueblo (Tucson). Home: Tunnel Springs Ranch Sonoita AZ 85637 Office: PO Box 326 Sonoita AZ 85637

ZUG, JAMES WHARTON, accountant; b. Bryn Mawr, Pa., July 22, 1940; s. Harry and Anne (Mayer) Z.; m. Debora Collier, Dec. 28, 1963; children—Laura Anne, Wendy C., James Wharton Jr. B.A., Princeton U., 1962; M.B.A., Harvard Bus. Sch., 1964. Ptnr., Coopers & Lybrand, Frankfurt, Ger., 1973-75, Phila., 1975-77, Pitts., 1978-82, Phila., 1982-86, mng. ptnr., Balt., 1986—. Bd. dirs. Balt. Symphony Orch., 1986—, Acad. of Fin. 1986—, Ch. Farm Sch., Frazier Pa., 1976—, German Soc. of Pa., 1982-84. Recipient Sells C.P.A. Exam award, Am. Inst. C.P.A.s, 1966. Mem. Am. Inst. C.P.A.s, Pa. Soc. C.P.A.'s, Md. Assn. CPA's, Merion Cricket Club (dir. 1976-78). Office: Coopers & Lybrand Redwood Tower 217 Redwood St Baltimore MD 21202

ZURAWSKI, VINCENT RICHARD, JR., biotechnology company executive, research scientist; b. Irvington, N.J., June 10, 1946; s. Vincent Richard and Norma Mary (Alliston) Z.; m. Mary R. Stanziola, Aug. 18, 1968; children—Daniel Vincent, John Alliston. B.A., Montclair State Coll., 1968; Ph.D., Purdue U., 1973. Postdoctoral research fellow chemistry dept. Purdue U., West Lafayette, Ind., 1974; research fellow dept. medicine Harvard Med. Sch., Boston, 1975-78, instr. dept. medicine, 1978-79; research fellow dept. medicine Mass. Gen. Hosp., Boston, 1975-79; co-founder, v.p., tech. dir. Centocor, Inc., Malvern, Pa., 1979-82, sr. v.p., tech. dir., 1982-83, exec. v.p., tech. dir., 1983-86, corporate sec., 1981-86, sr. v.p. tech. affairs, Harvard Med. Sch., Boston, 1986-87, sr. v.p., chief scientific officer, 1987—; lectr. Harvard Med. Sch., 1985—. Contbr. articles to profl. jours. and chpts. to books; patentee in field; pioneer in clin. applications of monoclonal antibodies; frequent lectr. on topic. With USAR, 1969-79. NIH postdoctoral fellow, 1976-78; Med. Found. research fellow, 1978-79; NIH grantee, 1985, 87. Mem. AAAS, Am. Chem. Soc., Am. Soc. Microbiology, Am. Assn. Lab. Animal Sci., Am. Soc. Biol. Chemists, Am. Assn. Immunologists, Tissue Culture Assn., Soc. Nuclear Medicine. Office: Centocor Inc 244 Great Valley Pkwy Malvern PA 19355

ZURCHER, MARVIN, manufacturing company executive; b. Monroe, Ind., Apr. 16, 1938; s. Chris F. and Martha (Ebnit) Z.; m. Evelyn H. Griffiths, Nov. 14, 1958; children: Gregory, Cary. Student, Ind. U., Purdue U. Mgr. Custom Quality Upholstery, Berne, Ind., 1954—, Zurcher Hunting Equipment Co., Berne, 1981—; prodn. foreman Berne Furniture Co., 1968-85; editor Nat. Bowhunting mag., Berne, 1985—; freelance outdoor writer, photographer. Author: Rotated Dies Explained, Hunting the Black Bear, Hunting the Whitetail Deer, Trapping the Red Fox, fiction romance novel Walk Through This Life With Me; contbr. articles to hunting mags. Mem. NRA (life). Democrat. Avocations: hunting, outdoor activities, reading, photography. Home: 412 Wabash St Berne IN 46711

ZUREK, RONALD STEPHEN, sales executive; b. East Chicago, Ind., Apr. 6, 1957; s. Stanley John and Joann Beverly (Dernulc) Z.; m. Patricia G. Harris, July 18, 1981; children; Ryan, Heather. BA, Purdue U., 1987. Dist. sales mgr. Ferderated-Fry Metals, Altoona, Pa., 1979-84, Complete-Reading Elec. Co., Hillside, Ill., 1984-86; regional sales mgr. Hi-Grade Alloy Corp., East Hazel Crest, Ill., 1986-88; mktg. mgr. Hi-Grade Alloy Corp, East Hazel Crest, Ill., 1988; mgr. Midwest region Vitronics Corp., Newmarket, N.H., 1989—. Active Trade Winds Rehab. Orgn., Gary, Ind., 1987—. Mem. Am. Mktg. Assn., Surface Mount Tech. Assn., Purdue U. Mktg. Assn. (dir. advt. and promotion 1981-82, pres. 1982-84).

ZUR LOYE, DIETER, chemical company executive; b. Berlin, Sept. 26, 1928; came to U.S., 1975; s. Otto and Gertrud (Laux) zur L.; m. Hella Elisabeth Troeger, July 20, 1957; children: Axel Otto, Hans-Conrad, Karen Elisabeth. MBA, U. Frankfurt, Fed. Republic Germany, 1952; grad., Advanced Mgmt. Program Harvard U., 1970. With Hoechst Aktiengesellschaft, Frankfurt-Main, Fed. Republic Germany, 1955-75, mktg. dir. plastics exports, 1967-70, dir. corp. planning and coordination, 1970-75; group v.p. fin. and acctg. Am. Hoechst Corp., Somerville, N.J., 1975-78, exec. v.p., 1978-80, sr. exec. v.p., 1980-83, chief fin. officer, 1975-80, chief operating officer, 1980-83, pres., chief exec. officer, 1983-87; pres., bd. dirs. Hoechst Corp. (formerly Hoechst Capital Corp.), Somerville, 1975—; vice chmn. Hoechst Celanese Corp., Somerville, 1987, chmn., 1987—; vice pres., bd. dirs. Messer Griesheim Industries, Inc., Valley Forge, Pa.; bd. dirs. Hoechst-Roussel Pharms., Inc., Newark, First Fidelity Bank (formerly Fidelity Union Bank); trustee Found. of U. of Medicine and Dentistry of N.J. Presbyterian. Clubs: Roxiticus Golf, Deutscher Verein, Univ. Office: Hoechst Celanese Corp Rte 202-206 N Somerville NJ 08876

ZWICK, CHARLES JOHN, banker; b. Plantsville, Conn., July 17, 1926; s. Louis Christian and Mabel (Rich) Z.; m. Joan Wallace Cameron, June 21, 1952; children: Robert Louis, Janet Ellen. B.S. in Agrl. Econs, U. Conn., 1950, M.S., 1951; Ph.D. in Econs, Harvard U., 1954. Instr. U. Conn., 1951, Harvard, 1954-56; head logistics dept. RAND Corp., 1956-63, mem. research council, 1963-65; asst. dir. U.S. Bur. Budget, 1965-68, dir., 1968-69; pres. S.E. Banking Corp., Miami, from 1969, now also chief exec. officer, also bd. dirs., chmn., 1982—; chmn., chief exec. officer SE Bank N.A.; bd. dirs. Manville Corp., S.E. Mortgage Co., So. Bell Tel. & Tel. Co., Mastercard Internat., Inc.; trustee Aerospace Corp.; mem. panel econ. advisers Congl. Budget Office. Mem. council Internat. Exec. Service Corps; chmn. Carnegie Endowment for Internat. Peace, Rand Corp., U. Miami, Brookings Instn.; chmn. Pres.'s Commn. on Mil. Compensation; chmn. Fla. State Comprehensive Plan Com. Served with AUS, 1946-47. Mem. Conf. Bd., Econ. Soc. So. Fla., Fla. Council of 100, Greater Miami C. of C., Assn. Res. City Bankers, Phi Beta Kappa. Home: 4210 Santa Maria St Coral Gables FL 33146 Office: SE Banking Corp 1 SE Financial Ctr Miami FL 33131

ZWICK, JACK, accounting company executive; b. Montreal, Que., Can., Jan. 29, 1936; s. David and Leah (Rachael) Z.; m. Shifra Nulman, Aug. 2, 1964; children: Marc, Hildee, Michael. BA, Wayne State U., 1958. CPA, Mich., N.Y. Acct. Adler & Havelik, Detroit, 1958-59; sr. acct. Hyman Beale & Co., Detroit, 1959-61, Jonick, Robbins, Greene & Sosnoff, N.Y.C., 1961-68; supr. mgr., ptnr. Laventhol & Horwath, Southfield, Mich., 1969—; mng. ptnr. Detroit office Laventhol & Horwath. Contbr. articles to profl. jours. Pres. Young Israel Southfield, 1978; mem. nat. bd. Jewish Nat. Fund, past. pres. Detroit region; past v.p. Akiva Hebrew Day Sch.; mem. zoning commn. City of Southfield; trustee Jewish Fedn. Apts. Mem. Am. Inst. CPA's, Mich. Assn. CPA's, Am. Israel C. of C. and Industry Mich. (pres. 1986). Democrat. Jewish. Office: Laventhol & Horwath 3000 Town Ctr Ste 3200 Southfield MI 48075-1358

ZWIGARD, BRUCE ALBERT, brokerage house executive; b. Newark, Apr. 10, 1948; s. Albert Henry and Doris Emily (Sigmund) Z.; m. Eva Crescencia Lan, June 24, 1973; children: Brian Albert, Bradley William. BA, Rider Coll., 1971; MBA, Fla. Internat. U., 1976. Tchr. physics Wardlaw Sch., Plainfield, N.J., 1971-72; tchr. physics Dade County Schs., Miami, Fla., 1972-77, tchr. gifted, 1977-79; registered rep. Investacorp Inc., Miami Lakes, Fla., 1979-80, v.p., 1980-81, pres., chmn. bd. dirs., 1981—. Office: Investacorp Inc 15450 New Barn Rd Miami Lakes FL 33014

ZYLSTRA, CHARLES DAVID, financial analyst; b. Washington, May 14, 1963; s. Roger E. Zylstra and Shirley A. (Albritton) Zylstra Hope. BS, Va. Commonwealth U., 1986. Real estate broker Hope Realty, Leesburg, Va., 1986-88; fin. analyst Perpetual Real Estate Services, McLean, Va., 1988—; bd. dirs. Zylstra Communications Corp., Yankton, S.D. Mem. Nat. Assn. Realtors, Loudon County Bd. Realtors (Million Dollar Sales Club 1986), Grad. Realtors Inst. Republican. Episcopalian. Office: Perpetual Real Estate Svcs 1750 Old Meadow Rd McLean VA 22102

ZYLSTRA, STANLEY JAMES, farmer, food company executive; b. Hull, Iowa, Dec. 18, 1943; s. Jerald S. and Dora (Te Slaa) Z.; m. Ruth Eileen Van Batavia, Jan. 3, 1964; children: Rachel Ann, Carl Dean. BA, Northwestern Coll., 1965; MA, Univ. S.D., 1969. Math tchr., counselor Boyden-Hull Sch., 1965-73; farmer Hull, 1970—; dir. Land O'Lakes, Mpls., 1985—, chmn. bd. dirs., 1988—. Mem. Kiwanis (pres. 1974-75). Republican. Mem. Reformed Church in America. Home: RR 1 Box 200 Hull IA 51239 Office: Land O'Lakes Inc 4001 Lexington Ave N Arden Hills MN 55126 *